The
Ultimate
MOVIE
THESAURUS

★ *Christopher Case* ★

A Henry Holt Reference Book

Henry Holt and Company ★ New York

A Henry Holt Reference Book
Henry Holt and Company, Inc.
Publishers since 1866
115 West 18th Street
New York, New York 10011

Henry Holt ® is a registered
trademark of Henry Holt and Company, Inc.

Copyright © 1996 by Christopher Case
All rights reserved.
Published in Canada by Fitzhenry & Whiteside Ltd.,
195 Allstate Parkway, Markham, Ontario L3R 4T8.

Library of Congress Cataloging-in-Publication Data
Case, Christopher.
The ultimate movie thesaurus / Christopher Case.—1st ed.
      p.   cm.—(A Henry Holt reference book)
1. Motion pictures—Catalogs.   2. Motion pictures—Plots,
themes, etc.—Dictionaries.   I. Title.   II. Series.
PN1998.C323   1996   96-36427
016.79143'75—dc20   CIP

ISBN 0-8050-3496-X

Henry Holt books are available for special promotions
and premiums. For details contact: Director, Special Markets.

First Edition—1996

Designed by Betty Lew

Printed in the United States of America.
All first editions are printed on acid-free paper. ∞

1 3 5 7 9 10 8 6 4 2

Contents

Acknowledgments

Special thanks to Brendan Korb for his undying—if sometimes erratic—typing help, my mother, Janice Scott Williams, for her emergency financial help, my grandmother Virginia Case for letting me finish it all in her living room, and George Lowe for Cuff to Cuff.

Thanks to the people at Henry Holt who were so avid about this project from the start: Laurent Stanevich in the beginning, but most of all Paula Kakalecik, who put up with delays and numerous computer disasters. Thanks also to the people at Claris Works, particularly Steve Sullivan, who spent several hours walking me through the use of their Filemaker Pro 2.1 database program, without which this book would not have been finished. (Unfortunately, I didn't know that until I was too deep into it.) With their help I was able to figure out a way to reformat the data to make it all work, avoiding yet another disaster.

Foreword

This project initially began because as a film student, movie studio underling, and an avid film buff all of my life, I was having too much trouble finding films for academic, professional, and reference purposes, as well as interesting titles for personal entertainment. This was mostly due to the decline in recent years of the quality of new films in general; but having had many classes in film history and appreciation, and being known for having memorized the entire history of Oscar nominations at age twelve (which is how I first became exposed to a standard of films to seek out), I was still having trouble accessing titles, particularly the "oldies but goodies." I was certain that I hadn't seen everything worth seeing. However, since completing *The Movie Thesaurus*, I feel that I have seen much of what is worth seeing—5,639 films in this book at last count. That may seem incredible, or just plain stupid, but I used to get paid to do it.

Since attending New York University's Tisch School of the Arts Dramatic Writing Program and Columbia University's Graduate Film Division, and having worked in numerous Hollywood development-office and script-reading positions, I've added to my film buff status a more professional perspective. Consequently, this book should be particularly interesting to anyone interested in making movies as well as in simply enjoying viewing them. Inside you will find both academic (e.g., Film Noir) and Hollywood terms (e.g., Fish out of Water Stories, Buddy Films). I wish I'd had such an extensive resource when I was writing all those college papers.

The categories section of the book started as a project of mine when I began as an intern at Vestron Pictures. I was given free rein to read the coverage, or critiques, of several thousand scripts they had accumulated since the company's beginnings. In my naive optimism, I at once found it hard to accept that there's "nothing new under the sun," but I quickly discovered the extent to which most scripts had been "influenced" by others. Call it "intertextualism" or "homage," or "retreads" as I do in this book, but it's the new combination of elements, most of which we've already seen somewhere else, that can still make a great film today. One of the ways you can use *The Movie Thesaurus* is to see more easily the derivative nature of much of today's Hollywood "product." Hopefully, filmmakers will find it a source of inspiration and guidance rather than a new tool to help them manufacture more remakes.

I still have about 200 films I'm dying to see, if I can ever find them. In the meantime, I'm hoping that *The Movie Thesaurus* will help you find the movies you've been wanting to see—and especially the ones you didn't know you were looking for.

How to Use This Book

To find a movie similar to one you like:

a) Look up the title, and the "similar titles" line below the synopsis, credits, and categories will lead you directly to other choices, or

b) Find subjects and themes that appeal to you about the title you like, and reference those in the second part of the book, "Category Entries."

To find a film about a particular subject, such as Screwball Comedy, New Orleans, or Shelley Winters Drowns:

Search the Category Entries for these themes. There will be a list of films under these headings plus several related categories which may lead to a more specific, similar aspect, such as Starting Over, Death, or Redemption, that you might be interested in.

To find a film of a particular genre or sub-genre:

Do the same. For example, if you are in the mood for a ROMANCE, but a more light-hearted one, look up Romantic Comedy to lead you to a list of such films. You can then skim the list and begin getting ideas, or find at least one title you already are familiar with, find it in the Title Entries, and check the list of SIMILAR FILMS, which should give you several ideas. Maybe you don't want just any romance, but one like *The Way We Were*, and, by looking that title up, you see that the aspect you most identify with is "Romance-Girl Wants Boy" or "Wallflowers and Hunks."

SAMPLE ENTRY

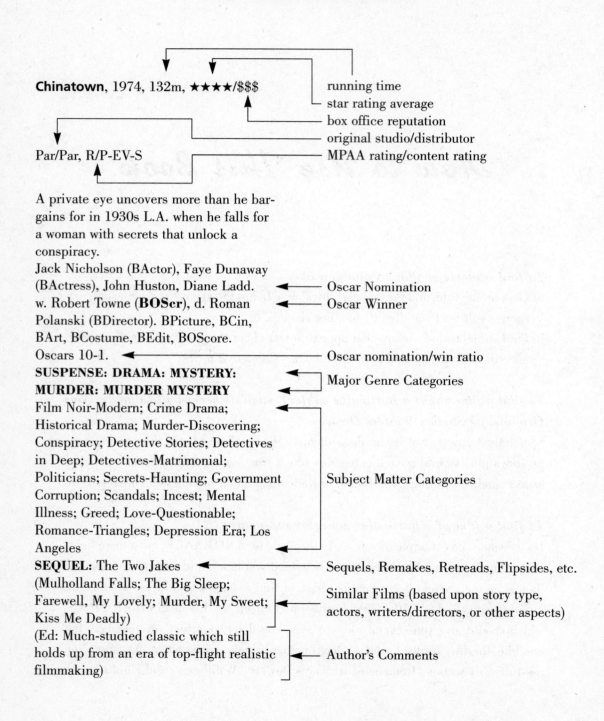

Chinatown, 1974, 132m, ★★★★/$$$ — running time
— star rating average
— box office reputation
— original studio/distributor
Par/Par, R/P-EV-S — MPAA rating/content rating

A private eye uncovers more than he bargains for in 1930s L.A. when he falls for a woman with secrets that unlock a conspiracy.
Jack Nicholson (BActor), Faye Dunaway (BActress), John Huston, Diane Ladd. ◄— Oscar Nomination
w. Robert Towne (**BOScr**), d. Roman ◄— Oscar Winner
Polanski (BDirector). BPicture, BCin, BArt, BCostume, BEdit, BOScore.
Oscars 10-1. ◄— Oscar nomination/win ratio
SUSPENSE: DRAMA: MYSTERY: ◄
MURDER: MURDER MYSTERY ◄— Major Genre Categories
Film Noir-Modern; Crime Drama; Historical Drama; Murder-Discovering; Conspiracy; Detective Stories; Detectives in Deep; Detectives-Matrimonial; Politicians; Secrets-Haunting; Government Corruption; Scandals; Incest; Mental Illness; Greed; Love-Questionable; Romance-Triangles; Depression Era; Los Angeles ◄— Subject Matter Categories
SEQUEL: The Two Jakes ◄— Sequels, Remakes, Retreads, Flipsides, etc.
(Mulholland Falls; The Big Sleep; Farewell, My Lovely; Murder, My Sweet; Kiss Me Deadly) ◄— Similar Films (based upon story type, actors, writers/directors, or other aspects)
(Ed: Much-studied classic which still holds up from an era of top-flight realistic filmmaking) ◄— Author's Comments

KEYS

CRITICAL STAR RATINGS:

(denoting the consensus quality of a film)

★★★★   A great film of either current or future classic status.

★★★½   A near-great film which enjoyed critical success if not also popular.

★★★   A good film which not everyone may like but which is worth seeing.

★★½   A fair-to-good film that contains some flaws and may not be worth seeing.

★★   Poor to fair with major flaws.

★ or ★½   Very poor.

BOX OFFICE RATINGS:

(These approximate and relative ratings are based on the figures in the appendix Box Office Hits by Year. Limited release and "art house" films are compared on a different scale from that used for major studio releases. The ratings are relative to the periods in which the film was released. For instance, if *What's Up, Doc?* were released today with the same number of tickets sold at current prices as were sold in 1972 at $2.50 per ticket, the gross would be close to $200 million, or approaching *Mrs. Doubtfire*'s 1993 status.)

NOTE: These ratings do not take into consideration video sales, but if the film was originally a TV movie, the symbol # corresponds to the $.

$$$$$ A blockbuster hit of the highest level (*Gone With the Wind, Jurassic Park,* etc.)

$$$$$ A blockbuster (currently a $100 million gross or $50 million rental)

$$$$ A big hit but not a mass hit (currently a $60 million gross)

$$$ A moderate hit (currently a $30 million gross)

$$ Not a hit, but a fair amount of tickets sold (currently $20 million gross or less for art films)

$ A flop or totally ignored by moviegoers (usually currently less than $10 million gross or under $2 million for an art film)

> is a dividing marker which usually means that categories or synopses following it apply to multiple titles or remakes of the same title, such as the three versions of *The Lodger.*

CREDITS:

w. writer (screenplay)

d. director

Adaptations: these designations often follow the w. for the screenwriters. If the original work's title is different, it is listed in *italics*.

N-adap   Novel adaptation from the original work by . . .

P-adap   Play adaptation from the original work by . . .

S-adap   Screenplay adaptation, from a previous film written by . . .

SS-adap   Short story adaptation from the original work by . . .

TV-adap   Television play adaptation from the original work by . . .

NF-adap   Adapted from a nonfiction source.

MPAA RATINGS:

G

PG

PG-13

R

NC-17

X

NR (Not Rated)

VR is a straight-to-video release for which there was most likely no theatrical release at all.

LR is a limited release film, for which a low box office rating should be taken into consideration.

CONTENT RATINGS:

S   Sexual Content

P   Profanity

V   Violence

B&G   Blood & Gore

FN   Female Nudity

FFN   Female Frontal Nudity

MN   Male Nudity

MFN   Male Frontal Nudity

(E preceding any of the above denotes "E"xtreme use of this content.)

OSCARS/ACADEMY AWARDS:

(listed on nominated and winning films at end of entry): Any entry in **bold** (i.e., **BPicture**) denotes that the nomination was also the award winner. B&W (i.e., BB&WCin): means Black & White, for previous years when certain technical arts awards were given in both color and B&W categories.

BPicture	Best Picture
BActress	Best Actress
BActor	Best Actor
BSActress	Best Supporting Actress
BSActor	Best Supporting Actor
BDirector	Best Director
BOScr	Best Original Screenplay
BOStory	Best Original Story (in years when it was given, pre-1958)
BAScr	Best Adapted Screenplay
BScr	Best Screenplay (in years where adapted or original was not designated)
BOScore	Best Original Score
BMScore	Best Musical Score
BDScore	Best Dramatic Score
BMCScore	Best Musical Comedy Score
BCin	Best Cinematography
BEdit	Best Film Editing
BSound	Best Sound
BSFX	Best Special (Visual) Effects
BSEdit	Best Sound (Effects) Editing
BArt	Best Art Direction/Set Decoration
BCostume	Best Costume Design
BDoc	Best Documentary Feature
BFLFilm	Best Foreign Language Film
B&W	black & white
C	color (for the pre-1967 years when many categories had two winners, color and black & white)

STUDIO & VIDEO DISTRIBUTOR ACRONYMS:

ABC	ABC Entertainment/Circle Films
ACA/Academy	Academy Entertainment
ALL/Allied	Allied Artists
AP-PBS	American Playhouse
Applause	Applause Video
Atlantic	Atlantic Video
Barr	Barr Films
BV/Buena Vista	Buena Vista/Disney
CAN/Cannon	Cannon Pictures
CBS-Fox	CBS-Fox or Fox Video in the 90s
Cine	Cinevista
CIG	Cinema Guild
Col	Columbia Pictures
Col-Tri	Columbia-Tri-Star Video
CRC	Criterion
Crown	Crown Pictures/Video
CVC/Conn	Connoisseur Video Company
DIS/Disney	Walt Disney Co.
EMB/Embassy	Embassy (previously Avco-Embassy)
EMI	Thorn-EMI or HBO Video (later)
FCT/Facets	Facets Video Catalogue
Fries	Fries Video
FXL	Fox-Lorber Video
FXV/Fox or 20th	Fox Video/20th Century-Fox
Goldwyn	Goldwyn Co. or Samuel Goldwyn
HBO	HBO Pictures or Video
Hemdale	Hemdale Pictures/Video
Hwd/Hollywood	Hollywood Pictures (Disney)
ITC	ITC Films
IVE	International Video
JHV	Jim Henson Video (Disney)
LAA	Lum & Abner Associates
Lorimar	Lorimar Video (Karl-Lorimar or WB)
Live	Live Entertainment or Video
LTY/Light	Lightyear Entertainment

Miramax	Miramax Films (Disney)
MCA-U	Universal/MCA-U Video
MCEG	MCEG Films/Video
MED/Media	Media Video
MGM-UA	MGM-UA, UAC, etc.
MPI	MPI Video
NL/New Line	New Line Cinema Video (Columbia)
Nos	Nostalgia Video
NW/New World	New World Video
NYF	New Yorker Video
ORI/Orion	Orion Pictures Video
Par	Paramount Video
PBS	PBS Video
Polygram	Polygram Pictures or Video
Prism	Prism Video
REP/Republic	Republic Video
RKO	RKO Video (before 1951 are Turner)
SUE/Sultan	Sultan Entertainment
SVS/Sony	Sony Video (Columbia)
Time-Life	Time-Life Video
Touch/Touchstone	Touchstone (Disney)
Tri/Tri-Star	Tri-Star
Trimark	Trimark Pictures
Triboro	Triboro Entertainment
Turner	Turner Pictures
TWE	Trans-World Entertainment
UAC	UA Classics (now MGM-UA)
Vestron	Vestron Pictures or Video
VMK/Vidmark	Vidmark
VTR	Video Treasures Catalogue
Voyager	Voyager Company Video/Laserdiscs
War/WB	Warner Brothers
WOV	Worldvision Video
XVC/Xenon	Xenon Video

A

Aaron Loves Angela, 1975, 98m, ★★1/2/$, Col/NA, PG. Black version of Romeo & Juliet set in Harlem. Kevin Hooks, Irene Cara. P-adap. William Shakespeare, d. Gordon Parks.
DRAMA: MELODRAMA: ROMANCE: Young People; Black Casts; Lover Family Dislikes; Romance-Mismatched; Revisionist Films; Shakespeare; Black Screenwriters; Black Directors
REMAKE OF: Romeo & Juliet (Romeo & Juliet; Jason's Lyric; Ode to Billy Joe; Romeo & Juliet)
Aaron Slick from Punkin Crick, 1952, 95m, ★★★/$$$, Par/NA, AMC. A country bumpkin girl is tricked into giving up her farm in order to get enough money to go to the city, but a nice farmer is wise to the con. Dinah Shore, Alan Young, Robert Merrill. w. Claude Binyon, P-adap. W. B. Hare, d. Binyon.
MUSICALS: COMEDY: Musical Comedy; **ROMANCE:** Musical Romance; Romantic; Comedy; City vs. Country; Con Artists; Simple Minds; Farm Life; Small-Town Life; Turning the Tables; Country People; Hidden Gems
(Ed: A very colorful extravaganza you wouldn't expect from the outset, with rather witty lyrics)
Abandoned, 1949, 79m, ★★/$, U/NA. A reporter (Dennis O'Keefe) helps a girl

(Gale Storm) find a baby and winds up in the black market. w. Irwin Gielgud, d. Joseph Newman.
DRAMA: SUSPENSE: Crime Drama; Social Drama; Babies-Stealing/Selling; Journalists; Saving Someone; Abandoned People; Forgotten Films

ABBOTT & COSTELLO SERIES

Abbott & Costello Go to Mars, 1953, 77m, ★★/$$, U/MCA-U. w. John Grant, D.D. Beauchamp, d. Charles LaMont.
COMEDY: Comedy-Slapstick; Comedians; **SCI-FI:** Outer Space Movies; Fools-Bumbling
Abbott & Costello in Hollywood, 1945, 83m, ★★1/2/$$$, MGM/MGM-UA, w. Nat Perrin, Lou Breslow, d. Sylvan Simon.
COMEDY: Comedy-Slapstick; Comedians; Fools-Bumbling; Hollywood Life
Abbott & Costello in the Foreign Legion, 1950, 80m, ★★/$$, U/MCA-U. w. John Grant, Leonard Stern, Martin Ragaway, d. Charles Lamont.
COMEDY: Comedy-Slapstick; Comedians; Fools-Bumbling; Foreign Legion
Abbott & Costello Lost in Alaska, 1952, 76m, ★★/$$, U/NA. w. Martin Ragaway, Leonard Stern, d. Jean Yarbrough.

COMEDY: Comedy-Slapstick; Comedians; Fools-Bumbling; Alaska
Abbott & Costello Meet Captain Kidd, 1952, 70m, ★★/$$, WB/Nos, VCI. w. Howard Dimsdale, John Grant, d. Charles Lamont.
COMEDY: Comedy-Slapstick; Comedians; Fools-Bumbling; Pirates
Abbott & Costello Meet Dr. Jekyll & Mr. Hyde, 1953, 77m, ★★1/2/$$, U/MCA-U. w. John Grant, Lee Loeb, d. Charles Lamont.
COMEDY: HORROR: SUSPENSE: Horror Comedy; Comic Thriller; Comedy-Slapstick; Fools-Bumbling
Abbott & Costello Meet Frankenstein, 1948, 83m, ★★★/$$$, UI/MCA-U. w. Robert Lees, Frederick Rinaldo, John Grant, d. Charles Barton.
COMEDY: HORROR: SUSPENSE: Horror Comedy; Comic Thriller; Comedy-Slapstick; Fools-Bumbling
Abbott & Costello Meet the Invisible Man, 1951, 82m, ★★1/2/$$, UI/MCA-U. w. Robert Lees, Frederick Rinaldo, John Grant, d. Charles Lamont.
COMEDY: SUSPENSE: Comic Thriller; Comedy-Slapstick; Fools-Bumbling; Invisibility
Abbott & Costello Meet the Keystone Cops, 1955, 79m, ★★1/2/$$,

UI/MCA-U. w. John Grant, d. Charles Lamont.
COMEDY: Comedy-Slapstick; Comedians; Fools-Bumbling; Police Comedy

Abbott & Costello Meet the Killer: Boris Karloff, 1949, 84m, ★★/$$$, UI/MCA-U, w. Hugh Wedlock, Howard Schneider, John Grant, d. Charles Barton.
COMEDY: HORROR: SUSPENSE: Horror Comedy; Comic Thriller; Comedy-Slapstick; Fools-Bumbling

Abbott & Costello Meet the Mummy, 1955, 79m, ★★1/2/$$, UI/MCA-U, Facets. Pretty much self-explanatory. w. John Grant, d. Charles Lamont.
COMEDY: HORROR: SUSPENSE: Horror Comedy; Comic Thriller; Comedy-Slapstick; Fools-Bumbling; Mummies

The Abdication, 1974, 103m, ★★1/2/$, WB/NA. The story of Queen Christina of Sweden's quest for religious understanding with Catholicism in Rome, where she falls in love with a Cardinal. Liv Ullman, Peter Finch, Cyril Cusack, Michael Dunn. w. P-adap. Ruth Wolff, d. Anthony Harvey.
DRAMA: Historical Drama; Costume Drama; **ROMANCE:** Romantic Drama; Queens; Priests; Cardinals; Rome; Sweden; Religion; Female Protagonists; Female Screenwriters
(Queen Christina)

The Abductors, 1957, 80m, ★★1/2/$$, 20th/Monarch. Several thieves in the 1870s steal Lincoln's body from its tomb and try to ransom it. Victor McLaglen, George Macready. w. Ray Wander, d. Andrew MacLaglen.
ACTION: DRAMA: Kidnappings; Hide the Dead Body; Lincoln-Abraham
(The Doctor and the Devils; Frankenstein Stories)

Abe Lincoln in Illinois, 1939, 110m, ★★★1/2/$$$, RKO/Media, RKO, Turner. The young days of the small-town lawyer who made it to Washington. Raymond Massey. w. Grover Jones, P-adap. Robert Sherwood, d. John Cromwell.
DRAMA: Biographies; Historical Drama; 1800s; Presidents; Politicians; Rise to Power; Famous People-Young; Midwestern Life; Lincoln-Abraham
(Young Mr. Lincoln; Abraham Lincoln)
(Ed: Widely considered to be the quintessential Lincoln film)

Abel, 1985, 96m, ★★1/2/$, First Floor/NA. When his mother kicks him out, a young man who's still living at home past thirty finds a new place to live-with his father's girlfriend. Alex Van Warmerdam. w. d. Alex Von Warmerdam.
DRAMA: COMEDY DRAMA: Black Comedy; Romance-Triangles; Family Drama; Young Men; Virgins; Mistresses; Fathers and Sons; Starting Over; Writer-Directors
(Getting It Right; The Game Is Over; Damage)

Abie's Irish Rose, 1946, 96m, ★★★/$$, UA-Bing Crosby/NA. An Irish girl marries a Jewish boy and families feud. Joanne Dru, Richard Norris. w. P-adap. Ann Nichols, d. Edward Sutherland.
DRAMA: MELODRAMA: Feuds; Lover Family Dislikes; Romance-Mismatched; Jewish People
(Ed: Based on one of the longest running plays in history)

Abilene Town, 1946, 89m, ★★1/2/$$, UA/Nos. A moral marshal (Randolph Scott) goes after some cattle rustlers. Rhonda Fleming, Lloyd Bridges, Edgar Buchanan. w. Harold Schumate, d. Edwin Marin.
WESTERN: DRAMA: Police Stories; Cattle Rustlers; Texas; Man vs. Man

The Abominable Dr. Phibes, 1971, 94m, ★★★/$$$, AIP/Vestron, Live, R/V-S-B&G. A deranged man (Vincent Price) whose wife died in surgery seeks to kill everyone involved, including the surgeon (Joseph Cotten), who must perform the same risky procedure on his own son as part of Phibe's plan. w. James Whitton, William Goldstein, d. Robert Fuest.
HORROR: SUSPENSE: Horror Comedy; Black Comedy; Camp; **MURDER:** Serial Killers; Revenge; Revenge on Doctors; Avenging Death of Someone; Deaths One by One; Psycho Killers; Evil Men; British; 1920s
SEQUEL: Dr. Phibes Rises Again
(Theater of Blood; Comedy of Terrors; Who's Killing the Great Chefs of Europe?)

The Abominable Snowman, 1957, 85m, ★★1/2/$$, Warner/NA. Explorers make it to the top of a mountain, but there's an ominous, unseen creature waiting for them. Christopher Lee, Forrest Tucker. w. TV-adap. Nigel Kneale, d. Val Guest.
HORROR: SUSPENSE: TRAGEDY: Monsters; Monsters-Legends; Mountain Climbing; Himalayas; Snow Settings; Deaths-One by One
(The Thing [1951]; Bigfoot; Yeti)

About Face, 1952, 94m, ★★/$$, WB/NA. The rise of a small-time gangster. Eddie Bracken, Gordon Macrae, Joel Grey, Dick Wesson. w. Peter Milne, d. Roy del Ruth.
DRAMA: Crime Drama; **ACTION:** Mob Stories; Power-Rise to
REMAKE OF Brother Rat.
(Murder Inc.; Pretty Boy Floyd; Kiss of Death [1947])

About Last Night, 1986, 113m, ★★★1/2/$$$, Tri/RCA-Col, R/P-S-FN-MRN. Two 20-somethings aren't sure they're in love or whether they want to live together but have plenty of input from friends. Rob Lowe, Demi Moore, Jim Belushi, Elizabeth Perkins. w. Tim Kazurinsky, Denise DeClue, P-adap. David Mamet, d. Edward Zwick.
DRAMA: COMEDY DRAMA: ROMANCE: Romantic Comedy; Settling Down; Newlyweds; Marriage-Impending; Romance-Choosing the Right Person; Wisecracking Sidekicks; Bratpack Movies; Yuppies; 20-Somethings; 1980s; Chicago; Hidden Gems; Female Screenwriters
(St. Elmo's Fire; Sleepless in Seattle; He Said, She Said; Barefoot in the Park; Period of Adjustment)

About Mrs. Leslie, 1954, 104m, ★★★/$$, Par/NA. A retired singer (Shirley Booth) has one last big affair with a rich man who dies and leaves her enough money to begin again with a boardinghouse full of eccentric people. Robert Ryan, Alex Nicol. w. Ketty Frings, Hal Kanter, d. Daniel Mann.
DRAMA: ROMANCE: MELODRAMA: Romantic Drama; Character Studies; Spinsters; Singers; Inheritance at Stake; Starting Over; Boardinghouses; Quiet Little Films; Female Protagonists; Female Screenwriters
(According to Mrs. Hoyle; The L-Shaped Room; The Matchmaker; Hot Spell; Come Back Little Sheba; The Balcony)

Above and Beyond, 1952, 122m, ★★1/2/$$$, MGM/MGM-UA. The story of the man who pushed the button to drop the first atomic bomb. Paul Tibbets. Robert Taylor, Eleanor Parker, James Whitmore, Larry Keating. w. Melvin Frank, Norman Panama, SS-adap. Bernie Lay, d. Frank & Panama.
DRAMA: War Movies; Biographies; Bombs-Atomic; World War II Movies; Historical; Drama

(Fat Man and Little Boy; Day One; Enola Gay)

Above Suspicion, 1943, 90m, ★★★/$$, MGM/MGM-UA. An American couple in Europe (Fred MacMurray, Joan Crawford) is asked to spy against the Nazis and winds up in a chaotic, silly mess. Conrad Veidt, Basil Rathbone, Reginald Owen. w. Keith Winter, Melville Baker, Pat Coleman, N-adap. Helen MacInnes, d. Richard Thorpe.
COMEDY: COMEDY DRAMA: MYSTERY: Comic Mystery; Spy Films; Spies; Spoofs-Spy; Americans Abroad; Nazi Stories; Germans as Enemy; Partners-Married
(A Night to Remember; The Thin Man SERIES)

Above the Law, 1989, 99m, ★★1/2/$$, WB/WB, R/P-S-EV. Martial arts expert tracks down a drug lord sponsored by the CIA and involved with the mob. Steven Seagal. w. Steven Presfield, Ronald Schusett, Andrew Davis, Steven Seagal, d. Davis.
ACTION: Martial Arts; Mob Stories; Crime Drama; Vigilantes; CIA Agents; Drugs
(Hard to Kill; Under Siege; Clear and Present Danger; License to Kill)

Above the Rim, 1994, 96m, ★★1/2/$$, PG-13/P. A young black man in the ghetto must decide between the local world of drugs and violence and his potential college basketball career, both of which he's introduced to on the neighborhood courts. Duane Martin, Tupac Shakur, Leon, Marlon Wayans, Tonya Pinkins. w. Jeff Pollack, Barry Michael Cooper, d. Jeff Pollack.
DRAMA: Sports Movies; Inner-City Life; Black Casts; Black Men; Drugs-Dealing; Decisions-Big; Basketball; Social Climbing; Dreams
(Juice; Hoop Dreams; White Men Can't Jump; Fast Break; Laurel Avenue)

Above Us the Waves, 1956, 92m, ★★1/2/$$, Rank/Republic. A British submarine sneaks through fjords in Norway to attack German ships there. John Mills, John Gregson, Donald Sinden. w. Robin Estridge, d. Ralph Thomas.
DRAMA: ACTION: Action Drama; Underwater Adventure; War Movies; World War II Movies; Submarines; British Films; Germans as Enemy

Abraham Lincoln, 1930, 97m, ★★1/2/NA, UA/Nos. Early years and rise of the log-cabin President. Walter

Huston, Una Merkel, Edgar Dearing. w. Steven Vincent Benet, Garrit Lloyd, d. D. W. Griffith.
DRAMA: Biographies; Historical Drama; Episodic Stories; Presidents; Lincoln-Abraham; Rise to Power
(Young Mr. Lincoln; Abe Lincoln in Illinois)

Abroad with Two Yanks, 1944, 80m, ★★1/2/$$, Edward Small/Live. Two sailors on shore leave chase the women wherever they land in the Pacific, but love may catch up with them. Dennis O'Keefe, William Bendix, Helen Walker, John Abbott. w. Charles Rodgers, Wilkie Mahoney, Ted Sills, d. Allen Dwan.
COMEDY: ROMANCE: Romantic Comedy; Sailors; War at Sea; World War II Era; Shore Leave
(On the Town; Shore Leave; Follow the Fleet; Two Sailors and a Girl)

Abschied von Gestern, 1966, 90m, ★★1/2/$, Kairosfilm/NA. A Jewish girl in the 1960s escapes from East Berlin to the West, but once over the wall becomes so lonely and disillusioned that she returns. w. d. Alexander Kluge.
DRAMA: SATIRE: Escape Adventures; Escape from Iron Curtain; Young Women; Female Protagonists; Illusions Destroyed; German Films; Communists; Berlin; Writer-Directors

Absence of Malice, 1981, 116m, ★★★1/2/$$$, Columbia/RCA-Col, PG/P-S. A reporter (Sally Field) wreaks havoc in possible criminal's (Paul Newman, BActor) life with publicity, so he begins to exact revenge using romance as a weapon. Melinda Dillon (BSActress). w. Kurt Ludetke (BAScr), d. Sydney Pollack. Oscars: 3-0.
DRAMA: ROMANCE: Ethics; Journalists; Journalist as Detective; Rumors; Love-Questionable; Ostracism; Love-Unprofessional; Double Crossing; Clever Plots & Endings; Accused Unjustly?; Suicidal Tendencies; Female Protagonists
REMAKE/RETREAD: Heart of Justice.
(Heart of Justice; The Verdict; Jagged Edge; The Ploughman's Lunch; The Sweet Smell of Success)

The Absent-Minded Professor (B&W), 1961, 97m, ★★★1/2/$$$$, Disney/Disney, G. Eccentric inventor makes his Model-T fly with flubber, the bouncy wonder-fuel. Fred MacMurray, Tommy Kirk, Keenan Wynn, Nancy

Olson, Ed Wynn. w. Bill Walsh, d. Robert Stevenson. BB&WCin. Oscars: 1-0.
CHILDREN'S: FAMILY: Fantasy; Comedy-Disneyesque; Inventors; Eccentric People; SCI-FI: Futuristic Films; Elixirs/Dream Cures; Basketball; Blockbusters
SEQUEL: Son of Flubber
(Son of Flubber; Honey, I Shrunk the Kids; Honey, I Blew Up the Kid; Follow Me, Boys)

Absolute Beginners 1986, 107m, ★★★/$$, OrionC/Orion, PG-13/S. Teens in the dawn of the rock era in London. Various musical stars. David Bowie, Ray Davies, Sade. w. Richard Burridge, Christopher Wicking, Don McPherson, N-adap. Colin MacInnes, d. Julien Temple.
MUSICALS: Music Movies; ROMANCE: Biographies; Musicians; Singers; Music; Video Style; 1950s England; Teenage Movies; Rebels; British Films; Beatnik Era
(Backbeat; I Wanna Hold Your Hand; The Cool Ones; Help; Mrs. Brown)

Absolute Quiet, 1936, 71m, ★★1/2/$$, MGM/NA. A millionaire invites investors to his ranch and they begin dying before the deal is done. Lionel Atwil, Louis Hayward, Raymond Walburn, J. Carrol Naish. w. Harry Clork, d. George Seitz.
MURDER MYSTERY: MURDER: MYSTERY: Mystery-Whodunits; Murders-One by One; Murder-Invitation to
(And Then There Were None; The Last of Sheila; Castle in the Desert; The Most Dangerous Game; Remember Last Night?; The House on Haunted Hill)

Absolution (Murder by Confession), 1981, 105m, Bulldog/TWE, Facets. A weak-willed priest running a boarding school is coerced into murder by a malicious student. Richard Burton, Dominc Guard, Dai Bradley, Billy Connolly, Andrew Keir. w. Anthony Schaffer, d. Anthony Page.
DRAMA: SUSPENSE: MURDER: Murder-Coerced into; Priests; Boarding Schools; Men and Boys; Malicious Menaces; Evil Men; Clever Plots & Endings; Blackmail
(Night of the Iguana; Term of Trial; These Three; The Children's Hour)

The Abyss, 1989, 140m, ★★1/2/$$$, 20th/CBS-Fox, PG-13/P. An attempt at rescuing nuclear submarine leads to discovery of sci-fi underwater life. Mary Elizabeth Mastrantonio, Ed Harris, Michael Biehn. w. d. James Cameron.

BCin, BArt, BSound, **BSFX**, BSEditing.
ADVENTURE: Underwater Adventure;
SCI-FI: Fantasy; Spectacles; Special
Effects; Submarines; Marriage on the
Rocks; Monsters-Underwater; Big
Budget; Major Flops; Writer-Directors
GENRE GLUT, 1989: Leviathan, Deep
Star Six.
(Fantastic Voyage; Leviathan; Deep Star
Six; Sea Quest [TV Series])
Accatone, 1961, 120m, ★★★/$$, Cino
del Duca-Arco/Water. A street pimp is
pursued by the police after a series of
problems. Franco Citti, Franca Pasut.
w. d. Peir Palo Pasolini.
DRAMA: Art Films; Prostitutes-Low
Class; Pimps; Fugitives from the Law;
Italian Films; Streetlife; Writer-Directors
(Satyricon; Saint Jack; Street Smart;
Fortune and Men's Eyes; American
Gigolo; Mama Rosa)
Accent on Love, 1941, 61m,
★★¹/₂/$$, 20th/NA. A real estate execu-
tive quits his job to become a tenants'
rights activist. George Montgomery, Osa
Massen, J. Carrol Naish. w. John Larkin,
SS-adap. Dalton Trumbo, d. Ray
McCarey.
COMEDY DRAMA: DRAMA: ROMANCE:
Message Films; Fighting for Rights;
Rebels; Politicians
Accent on Youth, 1935, 77m,
★★★/$$$, Par/NA. A playwright finds
his secretary has a thing for him, but will
it interfere with the work? Herbert
Marshall, Sylvia Sidney, Philip Reed. w.
Herbert Fields, Claude Binyon, P-adap.
Samson Raphaelson, d. Wesley Ruggles.
COMEDY: ROMANCE: Romantic
Comedy; Love-Infatuations; Writers;
Secretaries; Romance with Boss
REMAKES: Mr. Music; But Not for Me.
(Wife vs. Secretary; My Dear Secretary;
This Happy Feeling; More than a
Secretary)
Accident, 1967, 105m, ★★★/$$,
London Ind./Prism. When a student dies
in a car wreck, a man who was his tutor
recalls the events leading up to the acci-
dent, including a country holiday. Dirk
Bogarde, Stanley Baker, Michael York,
Jacqueline Sassard, Vivien Merchant. w.
Harold Pinter, N-adap. Nicholas Mosley,
d. Joseph Losey.
DRAMA: TRAGEDY: Art Films; Avant-
Garde; Flashbacks; Deaths-Accidental;
Death-Mourning a; Students and
Teachers; British Films

(Betrayal; The Homecoming [1973];
Wetherby; Providence)
(Ed: One of Pinter's more accessible
works [though based on another writer's
novel], yet not as interesting or complex
as, say, *Betrayal*)
The Accidental Tourist, 1988, 121m,
★★★¹/₂/$$$, WB/WB, PG/S. Eccentric
travel writer (William Hurt) and
estranged wife (Kathleen Turner) reunite
after their son has died, just as the
writer's met a goofy dog trainer (Geena
Davis, **BSActress**) and may have fallen
in love again. Bill Pullman, Amy Wright.
w. Frank Galati, (BAdapScr), N-adap.
Anne Tyler, d. Lawrence Kasdan.
BPicture. Oscars: 4-1.
DRAMA: ROMANCE: COMEDY DRAMA:
Romantic Drama; Romance-Mismatched;
Mid-life Crisis; Death-Dealing with;
Redemption; Starting Over; Children-
Parting with; Widowers; Writers;
Eccentric People; Baltimore
(Alice Doesn't Live Here Anymore;
Breathing Lessons)
According to Mrs. Hoyle, 1951, 60m,
★★¹/₂/$, Monogram/NA. A retired
schoolteacher (Spring Byington) in a
boardinghouse suspects naughty goings-
on downstairs. w. W. Scott Darwin,
Barney Gerard, d. Jean Yarbrough.
COMEDY: COMEDY DRAMA: Comic
Mystery; Thieves; Detectives-Amateur;
Boardinghouses; Spinsters; Teachers
(About Mrs. Leslie; The Balcony; The
Man Upstairs; The L-Shaped Room; It All
Came True; A Kiss in the Dark)
Accused, 1936, 85m, ★★/$$, Criterion-
UA/Henwood. A dancer in Paris is killed
and his wife is the prime suspect, but
who will a detective believe? Douglas
Fairbanks, Jr., Dolores DelRio, Googie
Withers. w. Zoe Akiens, George Barraud,
Harold French, d. Thornton Freeland.
MYSTERY: COMEDY: Comic Mystery;
MURDER: MURDER MYSTERY:
Accused Unjustly?; Romance with
Suspect; Dancers; Paris; Female
Screenwriters
The Accused, 1948, 101m, ★★★/$$,
Par/Par AMC. A student rapes a teacher,
and when he comes back for more she
has to decide what to do. Loretta Young,
Robert Cummings, Wendell Corey, Sam
Jaffe, Douglas Dick. w. Ketti Frings, d.
William Dieterle.
**DRAMA: MURDER: MURDER MYS-
TERY: MYSTERY: SUSPENSE:** Detective

Stories; Detectives-Police; Psychologists;
Mystery-Whodunits; Social Drama;
Rape/Rapists; Revenge on Rapist;
Murderers-Female; Professors; Teachers
and Students; Murder in Self Defense;
Women in Jeopardy; Good Premise
Unfulfilled; Coulda Been Good; Ahead of
its Time; Female Screenwriters
(The Accused [1988]; Outrage [1956];
Rider on the Rain; Extremities)
(Ed: Douglas Dick would probably have
to change his name today, as he played
the rapist)
The Accused, 1988, 110m, ★★★/$$$,
Par/Par, R/P-S-EV-FFN. Woman who's
been raped gets a prosecutor who presses
charges against those men who cheered it
on. Jodie Foster (**BActress**), Kelly
McGillis. w. Tom Topor, d. Johnathan
Kaplan. Oscars: 1-1.
DRAMA: Courtroom Drama;
Rape/Rapists; Fighting the System;
Revenge; Women's Rights; Ordinary
People; Working Class; Female Protag-
onists
(Last Exit to Brooklyn; Cry Rape; Nuts;
The Accused [1948]; Trial; A Passage
to India)
Accused of Murder, 1956, 74m, ★★/$,
Rep/NA. The mistress of a sleazy lawyer
becomes the chief suspect when he is
murdered. Vera Ralston, David Brian,
Sidney Blackmer, Lee Van Cleef. w. Bob
Williams, W.R. Burnett, N-adap Burnett
(*Vanity Row*), d. Joe Kane.
**MURDER: MYSTERY: MURDER MYS-
TERY:** Romance with Boss; Accused
Unjustly?; Framed?; Lawyers; Corruption;
Mistresses
Ace Eli and Rodger of the Skies,
1973, 92m, ★★/$, 20th/NA. A father-
and-son aerial stunt team makes it way
across the countryside in the 1920s. Cliff
Robertson, Pamela Franklin, Eric Shea,
Rosemary Murphy, Bernadette Peters,
Alice Ghostley. w. Claudia Salter, Steven
Spielberg, d. John Erman.
**DRAMA: MELODRAMA: FAMILY: CHIL-
DREN'S:** Fathers and Sons; Airplanes;
Air Daredevils; World War I Era; 1920s;
Midwestern Life; Female Screenwriters
(The Great Waldo Pepper; The Gypsy
Moths; Those Magnificent Men in Their
Flying Machines; Cotton Candy)
Ace High, 1969, 123m, ★★/$$, Par/Par,
Facets, R/EV. A wild-west outlaw gets
another chance to redeem himself.
Terence Hill, Eli Wallach, Brock Peters,

Bud Spencer, Kevin McCarthy. w. d. Guiseppe Colizzi
WESTERNS: Westerns-Spaghetti; Redemption; Death-Impending; Starting Over; Thieves; Writer-Directors

Ace in the Hole (The Big Carnival), 1953, 112m, ★★★★/$, Par/NA (AMC). A reporter (Kirk Douglas) sick of New Mexico can't wait to get out and when a man gets stuck in hole in cave, he stages a fake rescue attempt to milk the story and put the man's life at risk. w. Billy Wilder, IAL Diamond (BOScr), d. Billy Wilder. Oscars: 1-0.
DRAMA: SATIRE: Black Comedy; Rescue Drama; Crisis Situations; Trapped in a Hole; Buried Alive; Journalists; Saving Someone; Corruption; Ethics; Greed; New Mexico; Overlooked; Underrated; Forgotten Films; Flops-Major; Hidden Gems
(Nothing Sacred; Absence of Malice; The Well; Garden of Evil; Baby Jessica)

Ace of Aces, 1933, 76m, ★★/$$, RKO/Turner. An artist refuses to enlist for World War I but then reconsiders and finds himself a hero, but with more regrets than had he stayed at home. Richard Dix, Elizabeth Allan, Theodore Newton, Ralph Bellamy. w. John Saunders, H.W. Hannemann, SS-adap. Saunders (*Bird of Prey*), d. J. Walter Rubin.
DRAMA: War Movies; Cowards; Artists; World War I Movies
(Dawn Patrol; The Last Flight; Hail the Conquering Hero; Americana)

Aces High, 1977, 104m, ★★/$, EMI/NA, PG. In the British Air Force during World War I, certain practices lead to unnecessary deaths of young flyers. Malcolm McDowell, Christopher Plummer, Simon Ward, Peter Firth, John Gielgud, Trevor Howard, Ray Milland. w. Howard Barker, d. Jack Gold.
DRAMA: War Movies; World War I Movies; Death-Impending; Soldiers; Scandals; British Films; All-Star Casts
REMAKE OF: Journey's End
(Journey's End; Gallipoli; Memphis Belle; Friendly Fire)

Aces, Iron Eagle 3, 1992, 98m, ★★/(VR), Tri-Star/Col-Tri, PG-13/V-P. This time, the flying Colonel heads to South America to do battle with a drug cartel, without the aid of his young sidekick from the others. Louis Gossett, Jr., Rachel McLish, Paul Freeman, Horst Buchholz, Christopher Cazenove, Fred Dalton Thompson. d. John Glen.
ACTION: Pilots-Military; Escape Drama; Drugs-Dealing; South America; Black Men
SEQUEL TO: Iron Eagle and Iron Eagle 2

Ace Ventura, Pet Detective, 1993, 87m, ★★★/$$$$, WB/WB, PG-13/S-P-MRN. A goofy pet retriever is called in on a dolphin snatching which may be his last case-if he doesn't kill himself first just by everyday living or die from kissing what turns out to be a man. Jim Carrey, Courtney Cox, Sean Young, Dan Marino. w. Jim Bernstein, Tom Shadyac, Jim Carrey, d. Shadyac.
COMEDY: Comedy-Slapstick; Cartoonlike Movies; Chase Movies; Kidnappings; Animals in Jeopardy; Spoofs-Detective; Detective Stories; Football; Sharks; Dolphins; Pet Stories; Eccentric People; Fools-Bumbling; Men as Women; Transsexuals; Miami; Sleeper Hits
(Pink Panther SERIES; The Late Show; The Black Marble; Dumb and Dumber; The Mask)
SEQUEL: Ace Ventura-When Nature Calls
(Ed: A real-life pet detective in Miami, Alfredo Perez was the apparent inspiration for this)

Ace Ventura: When Nature Calls, 1995, 105m, ★★★/$$$$, WB/WB, PG-13/P-S. When Ace loses a client's pet in a mishap, he goes to Africa and beyond on a soul-searching trip, into wilds even more junglelike than his own mind. Jim Carrey, Ian McNeice, Simon Callow. w. d. Steve Oedekerk.
COMEDY: Comedy-Slapstick; Spoofs; Animal Stories; Detective Stories; Africa; Blockbusters; Writer-Directors
SEQUEL TO: Ace Ventura, Pet Detective.
(Dumb and Dumber; The Mask)

Across 110th Street, 1972, 102m, ★★1/2/$$, UA/MGM-UA, Fox, R/EV. A police detective puts himself on the line tracking down black thieves who stole from the Mob. w. Luther Davis, N-adap. Wally Ferris, d. Barry Scheer.
ACTION: Crime Drama; Revenge; Mob Stories; Police Stories; Detectives-Police; Thieves; Black vs. White; Race Relations
(Assault on Precinct 13; New Jack City; Fort Apache the Bronx; They Call Me Mr. Tibbs; Shaft SERIES)

Across the Bridge, 1957, 103m, ★★★/$, Ind/LCA. An English thief hides out in Mexico and winds up assuming the identity of a man he kills there, but it may not keep Scotland Yard off the trail. Rod Steiger, David Knight, Marla Landi. N-adap. Graham Greene, d. Ken Annakin.
SUSPENSE: Fugitives from the Law; Thieves; Hiding Out; Mexico; British Films; Identities-Assumed; Forgotten Films; Coulda Been Great
(The Fugitive [1947]; Second Chance)

Across the Pacific, 1942, 97m, ★★★/$$, WB/MGM-UA. A man is coaxed into spying for pro-Japanese sympathizers in Hawaii-just before Pearl Harbor changed everything. Humphrey Bogart, Mary Astor, Sydney Greenstreet, Sen Yung, Richard Loo, Charles Halton. w. Richard MacCauley, Serial-adap. Robert Carson, d. John Huston.
DRAMA: Action Drama; Spy Films; Spies; World War II Movies; Pearl Harbor; Japan as Enemy; Traitors
(All Through the Night; The Adventures of Tartu)

Across the Wide Missouri, 1951, 78m, ★★1/2/$$, MGM/MGM-UA. A fur trapper marries an Indian girl and learns to live in her community in the early 1800s. Clark Gable, Richardo Montalban, John Hodiak, Adolphe Menjou, J. Carrol Naish, Howard Keel (Narrator). w. Talbot Jennings, d. William Wellman.
WESTERN: DRAMA: ROMANCE: Romance-Interracial; Race Relations; Indians-American; Narrated Films
(Dances with Wolves; A Man Called Horse)

Action for Slander, 1938, 83m, ★★1/2/$$, London Films/VY. A man defends his honor when caught cheating at a game of cards in stuffy old England. Clive Brook, Ann Todd. w. Ian Dalrymple, Miles Malleson, N-adap. Mary Borden, d. Tim Whelan.
DRAMA: MELODRAMA: Liars; Con Artists; Defending Oneself; Gambling; Ethics

Action in Arabia, 1944, 72m, ★★/$$, RKO/Turner. An American journalist (George Sanders) is caught in a skirmish between Nazis and French soldiers in the Middle East. Gene Lockhart, Virginia Bruce, H.B. Warner. w. Philip McDonald, Herbert Bieberman, d. Leonid Moguy.
DRAMA: ACTION: Action Drama; War Movies; Journalists; Middle East; Nazi Stories; Arab People; Germans as Enemy

Action in the North Atlantic, 1943, 127m, ★★1/2/$$$, WB/MGM-UA. Ships heading with supplies and men for battle in Russia are attacked en route by German submarines. Humphrey Bogart, Raymond Massey, Alan Hale, Ruth Gordon, Sam Levene. w. John Lawson, story Guy Gilpatrick (BOStory), d. Lloyd Bacon. Oscars: 1-0.

DRAMA: ACTION: Action Drama; War Movies; Adventure at Sea; War at Sea; Journies; Russia; Germans as Enemy; World War II Movies; Submarines

Action Jackson, 1988, 93m, ★★/$$, Lorimar/WB, R/S-V. A black cop (Carl Weathers) is framed for murder while investigating the deaths of union workers. Craig T. Nelson, Vanity. w. Robert Renau, d. Craig Baxley.

ACTION: Detective Stories; Detectives-Police; Crime Drama; Black Men; Framed?; Accused Unjustly?; Blaxploitation; Unions

Act of Love, 1954, 104m, ★★½/$$$, UA/NA. An American soldier falls in love with a French girl during World War II, but when times become tense and he is sent away, she sinks into deep despair. Kirk Douglas, Dany Robin, Barbara Laage, Robert Strauss, Brigitte Bardot. w. Irwin Shaw, N-adap. Alfred Hayes (*The Girl on the Cia Flaminia*), d. Anatole Litvak.

ROMANCE: DRAMA: MELODRAMA: Soldiers; Americans Abroad; Suicidal Tendencies; Paris; World War II Movies; Romance-Doomed; Depression
(A Farewell to Arms; One Hour with You; Arch of Triumph)

An Act of Murder (*Live Today for Tomorrow*), 1948, 91m, ★★½/$, U/NA. A judge assists his wife in suicide when she becomes deathly sick and then faces the law he enforces. Fredric March, Florence Eldridge, Edmond O'Brien, Geraldine Brooks. w. Michael Blankford, Robert Thoeren, N-adap. Ernst Lothar (*The Mills of God*), d. Michael Gordon.

DRAMA: Social Drama; ROMANCE: MURDER: Accused Unjustly?; Death-Dealing with Euthanasia; Judges; Message Films; Ahead of Its Time
(Right of Way; The Bramble Bush; Whose Life Is It Anyway?)

Act of the Heart, 1970, 103m, ★★/$, U/NA. A girl from the Canadian country (Genevieve Bujold) goes to the big city, falls in love with a monk (Donald Sutherland), and must deal with his unavailability. w. d. Paul Almond.

ROMANCE: DRAMA: Romantic Drama; Romance with Clergy; Romance-Doomed;

Young Women; Priests; Female Protagonists; City vs. Country; Canadian Films; Writer-Directors
(The Runner Stumbles; The Thorn Birds; The Sea Wife; Camila [1984])

Act of Violence, 1949, 82m, ★★★/$$, MGM/NA. A soldier wanting vengeance on a fellow POW who gave up information has to decide how far to go. Van Helfin, Robert Ryan, Janet Leigh, Mary Astor. w. Robert Richards, SS-adap. Collier Young, d. Fred Zinneman.

DRAMA: MELODRAMA: Revenge; POWs; Men in Conflict; Post-World War II Era; Cowards

Act One, 1963, 110m, ★★/$$, WB/NA. Biography of writer Moss Hart and his rise out of Brooklyn to Broadway. George Hamilton, George Segal, Jason Robards, Jack Klugman, Sam Levene, Eli Wallach. w. d. Dore Schary, NF-adap. Moss Hart.

DRAMA: Biographies; Autobiographical Stories; Writers Fame-Rise to; Coulda Been Good; Flops-Major
(Youngblood Hawke; Enter Laughing; Funny Girl; Career; King of the Hill; The Actress [1953])

Actors and Sin, 1952, 82m, ★★½/$, UA/Col, HEG. First part: Father of a failed actress who's committed suicide makes her death looks like a murder to finally bring her attention, and Second Part: A nine-year-old girl writes a romantic script for a movie, but doesn't want anyone to know her age so she can masquerade. Edward G. Robinson, Marsha Hunt, Dan O'Herlihy, Eddie Albert, Jenny Hecht. w. d. Ben Hecht.

DRAMA: SATIRE: COMEDY DRAMA: Black Comedy; Hollywood Life; Multiple Stories; Secrets-Keeping; Girlhood; Actresses; Fame-Rise to; Female Protagonists; Forgotten Films; Cult Films; Writer-Directors
(Power, Passion, Murder; Dead of Night; The Bad and the Beautiful; The Big Knife)

An Actor's Revenge, 1963, 114m, ★★★/$, Studio Daie/New Yorker. An actors runs across the man who ruined his family financially and begins murdering to even the score. w. Daisuke Ito, N-adap. Otokichi Mikami, d. Kon Ichikawa.

DRAMA: TRAGEDY: Murders-One by One; Actors; Revenge; Class Conflicts; Japanese Films
(Theater of Blood; The Bad Sleep Well; Who's Killing the Great Chefs of

Europe?; The Abominable Dr. Phibes; Comedy of Terrors)

The Actress, 1928, 90m, ★★½/$$, MGM/NA. A famous actress in the late 1800s marries a rich man who loves her work, but can she grow to love him? Norma Shearer, Ralph Forbes. w. Albert Lewin, Richard Schayer, P-adap. Arthur Pinero, d. Sidney Franklin.

DRAMA: ROMANCE: MELODRAMA: Actresses; Marrying Up; Social Climbing
(Blonde Venus; Darling; East Lynne; Anna Christie)

The Actress, 1953, 91m, ★★★/$$, MGM/MGM-UA. The story of young actress Ruth Gordon's rise to stardom on stage, particularly with her father's help (Spencer Tracy). Jean Simmons, Teresa Wright, Mary Wickes, Anthony Perkins. w. Ruth Gordon, P-adap. Gordon (*Years Ago*), d. George Cukor.

DRAMA: COMEDY DRAMA: MELO-DRAMA: Coming of Age; Fame-Rise to; Actresses; Fathers & Daughters; Feisty Females; Female Protagonists; Female Screenwriters
(Morning Glory; Stagestruck; Act One)

Ada, 1961, 109m, ★★/$, MGM/NA. A prostitute (Susan Hayward) marries an aspiring politician and then must help him when her past comes back to haunt him. Dean Martin, Ralph Meeker, Martin Balsam, Wilfrid Hyde-White. w. Arthur Sheekman, William Driskill, N-adap. Wirt Williams (*Ada Dallas*), d. Daniel Mann.

MELODRAMA: DRAMA: Soap Operas; Power-Rise; Past-Haunted by; Romance with Prostitutes; Prostitutes-High Class; Marrying Up; Social Climbing; Politicians; Scandals; Blackmail
(Blaze; Anna Christie; Love; I Thank a Fool; This Property is Condemned; The Angel Wore Red)

Adalen 31, 1969, 115m, ★★★/$, Svensk/NA. A strike at a paper factory wind up in a major conflict in an otherwise peaceful country. Peter Schildt. w. d. Bo Wiederberg.

DRAMA: Social Drama; Unions; Strikes; Political Films; Swedish Films; Writer-Directors
(Matewan; Strike; Blue Collar; Last Exit to Brooklyn; The Angry Silence)

Adam, 1984, 100m, ★★★/$$$$, NBC/NBC, NA. A couple (Jobeth Williams, Daniel J. Travanti) searches for their missing son, a fight which raised

< skip>
</ skip>
awareness to child theft. w. Allan Leight, d. Michael Tuchner.

DRAMA: Social Drama; Missing Persons; Missing Children; Quests; Children-Parting with; Murderers-Child; Molestation-Child; True Stories; Kidnappings; TV Movies

SEQUEL: Adam: His Song Continues. (Without a Trace; Missing; Into Thin Air; The Vanishing)

Adam and Eva, 1923, 83m, ★★½/$$$, Par/NA. A rich girl deals with her father's newfound poverty by finding a new love. Marion Davies, T. Roy Barnes. w. Luther Reed, P-adap. Guy Bolton, George Middleton, d. Robert G. Vignola.

DRAMA: MELODRAMA: ROMANCE: Riches to Rags; Rich People; Young Women

Adam and Evelyne, 1949, 92m, ★★½/$$, Rank/NA. When a wealthy man's best friend dies, he winds up adopting the friend's daughter-and falling for her, too. Stewart Granger, Jean Simmons, Helen Cherry, Wilfrid Hyde White. w. Noel Langley, Leslie Storm, George Barraud, Nicholas Phipps, d. Harold French.

COMEDY: DRAMA: ROMANCE: Romantic Comedy; Children-Adopted; Young Women; Romance-Older Men/Younger Women; Children-Inherited; Fathers & Daughters
(Daddy Longlegs; Mad About Music; Blame It on Rio)
(Ed: Pretty risque for the day-and done more than once then)

Adam at 6 A.M., 1970, 100m, ★★/$$, NG/Fox, R/S-P-MRN. An idealistic but weary young college professor leaves California for a regular job in rural Missouri where he meets girls while skinny-dipping and tries to fit in. Michael Douglas, Lee Prucell, Joe Don Baker, Grayson Hall, Louise Latham, Meg Foster. w. Stefan Karpf, Eleanor Karpf, d. Robert Scheerer.

DRAMA: COMEDY DRAMA: ROMANCE: Nature-Back to; Fish out of Water Stories; Professors; Young Men; Rural Life; City vs. Country; Female Screenwriters; Midwestern Life

Adam Had Four Sons, 1941, 81m, ★★½/$$$, Col/Col. A governess comes to take care of a man and his sons and winds up with more than a job. Ingrid Bergman, Warner Baxter, Susan Hayward, Fay Wray, Richard Denning. w. Michael

Blankford, William Hurlbut, N-adap. Charles Bonner (*Legacy*), d. Gregory Ratoff.

DRAMA: MELODRAMA: Family Drama; **ROMANCE:** Romance-Older Men/Younger Women; Babysitters; Widowers; Fathers & Sons; Mothers-Surrogate/Adopted
(The Sound of Music; The King and I; Anna and the King of Siam; Edward My Son; The Bells of St. Mary's)

Adam's Rib, 1922, Silent, 86m, ★★★/$$$, Par/NA. When her mother begins an affair with a European count, a girl decides to make a play for the man to prevent her parents' marriage from destruction. Milton Sills, Elliot Dexter, Anna Nilsson. w. Jeanie McPherson, d. Cecil B. DeMille.

MELODRAMA: Soap Opera; Romance with Married Person; Mothers & Daughters; Romance with Relative's Lover; Female Screenwriters

Adam's Rib, 1950, 101m, (B&W), ★★★★/$$$$, MGM/MGM-UA. D.A. (Spencer Tracy) winds up prosecuting a woman who shot at her cheating husband, only his lawyer wife (Katharine Hepburn) decides to defend this woman. Sparks fly in and out of the courtroom as their marital struggles mirror those of their clients in the courtroom. Judy Holliday, Tom Ewell, David Wayne. w. Garson Kanin, Ruth Gordon (BOScr), d. George Cukor. Oscars: 1-0.

COMEDY: SATIRE: Marriage Comedy; Cheating Men; Battle of the Sexes; Courtroom Drama; Trials; Crimes of Passion; Romantic Comedy; Romance-Bickering; Romance-Married Couples; Marriage on the Rocks; Lawyers; Female Screenwriters; Tracy & Hepburn
(Woman of the Year; Pat and Mike; Desk Set; Legal Eagles; Hard Hat and Legs; Guess Who's Coming to Dinner)

The Addams Family, 1991, 102m, ★★★/$$$$$, Orion-Par/Par, PG-13/P. The morbid and bizarre but always humorous family finds it fortune at stake when Uncle Fester reappears-but is it really Fester? Raul Julia, Anjelica Huston, Christopher Lloyd, Christina Ricci, Dan Hedaya, Elizabeth Wilson, Dana Ivey, Jimmy Workman. w. Caroline and Larry Thompson, d. Barry Sonnenfeld.

COMEDY: HORROR: Horror-Comedy; Black Comedy; Comedy-Morbid;

Halloween; Impostors; Inheritances at Stake; Houses-Creepy; Blockbusters; Comic Characters; Female Screenwriters; TV Series Movies

SEQUEL: Addams Family Values

Addams Family Values, 1993, 93m, ★★★/$$$, Par/Par, PG-13/P. This time a conniving seductress is out to marry and rob Uncle Fester while the kids are sent off to cheerful camp for rich kids where they intend to sabotage the Thanksgiving show. Raul Julia, Anjelica Huston, Christopher Lloyd, Christina Ricci, Jimmy Workman, Joan Cusack. w. Paul Rudnick, d. Barry Sonnenfeld.

COMEDY: HORROR: Horror-Comedy; Black Comedy; Comedy-Morbid; Halloween; Inheritances at Stake; Houses-Creepy; Comic Characters; Dangerous Women; Marrying Up; Camps; Putting on a Show; Snobs vs. Slobs; TV Series Movies
(Munsters Go Home; The Abominable Dr. Phibes; Haunted Honeymoon; Young Frankenstein)

The Adjuster, 1992, 102m, ★★★/$, Orion/Orion, R/S-FN-MN. An insurance adjuster gets way too involved with his clients, emotionally and sexually. Elias Koteas, Arsinee Khanjian. w. d. Atom Egoyan.

DRAMA: Erotic Drama; Art Films; Psychological Drama; Bisexuality; Gay Men; Insurance Scams; Multiple Stories; Character Studies; Canadian Films; Writer-Directors
(Speaking Parts; Exotica; Law of Desire; Drowning by Numbers)

Adventure for Two (*The Demi-Paradise*), 1943, 114m, ★★★/$$, Two Cities/NA. A Russian comes to England to observe life and finds some interesting oddities there. Laurence Olivier, Penelope Ward, Margaret Rutherford, Leslie Henson. w. Anatole de Grunwald, d. Anthony Asquith.

DRAMA: COMEDY DRAMA: Fish out of Water Stories; Russians; Social Satire; Hidden Gems; Forgotten Films
(Moscow on the Hudson; Coming to America; Crocodile Dundee; Ninotchka)

Adventure in Washington, 1941, 84m, ★★/$, Col./NA. A congressional page is selling secrets to Wall Street about bills in the Senate, so Senators try to figure out how to handle it. w. Lewis Foster, Arthur Caesar, d. Alfred Green.

DRAMA: Spies; Scandals; Politicians; Washington D.C.; Congressmen/Senators; Wall Street

Adventure Island, 1947, 66m, ★½/$, Par/SNC. Several not-so-bright people wind up on a desert island inhabited only by a crazy man. Paul Kelly, Rory Calhoun, Rhonda Fleming. w. Maxwell Shane, N-adap. Robert Louis Stevenson (*Ebb Tide*), d. Peter Stewart (Sam Newfield).

HORROR: SCI-FI ADVENTURE: Islands Scientists-Mad

REMAKE OF: Ebb Tide
(Mysterious Island; Ebb Tide; The Island of Dr. Moreau; The Most Dangerous Game)

The Adventurers, 1970, 171m, ★★/$$$, Par-Avco/Par, R/S-V-FN. A young man who has left his Central American roots for the jetset life in Europe returns for vengeance on the man who killed his mother, meanwhile Candice Bergen, Bekim Fehmiu, Alan Badel, Olivia deHavilland, Leigh Taylor-Young, Fernando Ray, Ernest Borgnine. w. Michael Hastings, Lewis Gilbert, N-adap. Harold Robbins, d. Gilbert.

MELODRAMA: Erotic Drama; Fashion World; Sexy Women; Sexy Men; Central America; Revenge; Rape/Rapists; Rich People; Jetsetters; 1970s; Unintentionally Funny; Forgotten Films; Flops-Major; Curiosities
(Bloodline; Myra Breckinridge; The Carpetbaggers)
(Ed: Made money but lies in the turkey hall of fame for bizarrities)

Adventures in Babysitting, 1987, 99m, ★★½/$$$, Touchstone/Touchstone, PG. When the kids goes wild on a big city adventure, the babysitter tries to rein them in before mom and dad get back. Elizabeth Shue, Penelope Ann Miller, Maia Brewton, Keith Coogan, Anthony Rapp, Calvin Levels. w. David Simkins, d. Christopher Columbus.

COMEDY: Action Comedy; Comedy of Errors; Chase Movies; One Day Stories; Parents Are Gone; Parents Are Gone from Chicago; Race Against Time; Suburban Kids Babysitters; Teenagers; Young Women; Female Protagonists
(Risky Business; Ferris Bueller's Day Off; Don't Tell Mom the Babysitter's Dead; Home Alone; Uncle Buck; Mrs. Doubtfire)

The Adventures of Arsene Lupin, 1956, 103m, ★★★/$$, Lambor/NA. The legendary French jewel thief makes another round of heists, managing to outwit the Kaiser even. Robert Lamoreaux. w. Jacque Becker, Albert Simonen, SS-adap. Maurice LeBlanc, d. Becker.

DRAMA: Crime Drama; Capers; Jewel Thieves; Heist Stories; French Films; 1900s
(Arsene Lupin Returns; To Catch a Thief)

The Adventures of Baron Munchausen, 1943, 134m, ★★★/$, UFA/NA. The modern Baron Munchausen tells fabulous stories of his famous ancestor and it gradually becomes clear that the man he's referring to is in fact himself, granted immortality by a magician. Hans Albers, Wilhelm Bendow, Michael Bohnen, Marina Von Ditmar. w. Berthold Burger (Erich Kastner), d. Josef von Blaky.

ADVENTURE: CHILDREN'S: FAMILY: Storytellers; Elderly Men; Immortality; Multiple Stories; Magic; Episodic Stories
REMAKE: 1987 version

The Adventures of Baron Munchausen, 1987, 125m, ★★★/$, Col/RCA-Col, PG. The 18th-century baron tells wild, bizarre tales to his grandson and they're lived out with great detail and adventure. John Neville, Uma Thurman, Robin Williams, Eric Idle. w. Charles McKeown, Terry Gilliam, N-adap. Rudolph Erich Raspe, d. Terry Gilliam.

ADVENTURE: Fantasy; **CHILDREN'S:** Storytellers; **SCI-FI:** Eccentric People; Grandfathers-Fascinating; Costume Drama; Spectacles; Death-Personified; Production Design-Outstanding; Balloons; Episodic Stories; Flops-Major
(Time Bandits; Brazil; The Princess Bride)

The Adventures of Barry McKenzie, 1972, 114m, ★★★/$$, Col/NA. The actor who plays Dame Edna plays a very different character-a rakish Australian on the loose in England searching for women while wreaking havoc. w. Barry Humphries, Bruce Beresford, d. Beresford.

COMEDY: Comedy of Errors; Playboys; Fools-Bumbling; Fish out of Water Stories; Forgotten Films; Underrated
(Alvin Purple; Alvin Rides Again; Crocodile Dundee)

The Adventures of Buckaroo Banzai Across the 8th Dimension, 1984, 103m, ★★★/$, Orion/Orion, Vestron, R/P-V. A superhero brain surgeon and rock star fights an evil nemesis escaped from the asylum, with an odd assortment of characters caught in the middle. John Lithgow, Peter Weller, Ellen Barkin, Jeff Goldblum. w. d. W. D. Richter.

SCI-FI: Black Comedy; Fantasy; Cult Films; Mad Scientists; Eccentric People; Special Effects; Cartoonlike Movies; Writer-Directors; Flops-Major
(Robocop SERIES; Ricochet; A Clockwork Orange; Big Trouble in Little China)
(Ed: A big-budget turkey on its initial release, it picked up major midnight movie business)

The Adventures of Bullwhip Griffin, 1967, 110m, ★★★/$$, Disney/Disney, G. Two snotty, upper-crusty types and their butler head to the wild west and wind-up being able to take better acre of themselves than you might think. Roddy McDowell, Karl Malden, Suzanne Pleshette, Harry Guardino, Bryan Russell, Hermione Baddely, Cecil Kellaway. w. Lowell Hawley, N-adap. Sid Fleishman (*By the Great Horn Spoon*), d. James Nielson.

COMEDY: WESTERN: Western Comedy; Spoofs-Westerns; Fish out of Water Stories; Snobs vs. Slobs; Nerds vs. Macho Men; Servants; Heroes-Unlikely
(Fancy Pants; The Pale Face; The Ruggles of Red Gap; The Shakiest Gun in the West)

The Adventures of Captain Fabian, 1951, 100m, ★★/$, Rep/NA. A captain (Errol Flynn) returns to New Orleans to seek revenge on the rich family who ruined his father. w. Errol Flynn, N-adap. Robert Shannon (*Fabulous Ann Medlock*), d. William Marshall.

ADVENTURE: MELODRAMA: Costume Drama; Revenge; Rich vs. Poor; Rich People-Decadent; New Orleans; 1800s
(The Adventures of Don Juan; Flame of New Orleans)

Adventures of Casanova, 1948, 83m, ★★½/$, Eagle-Lion/NA. The great lover and leader returns to old Sicily to help overthrow the King of Naples while helping the folks out on the way. Arturo de Cordova, Lucille Brenner. w. Crane Wilbur, Walter Bullock, Ken deWolf, d. Roberto Gavaldon.

ADVENTURE: DRAMA: Costume Drama; Historical Drama; Legends; Turning the Tables; Italy; British Films

(Casanova [1976]; Casanova '70; The Adventures of Don Juan; The Affairs of Cellini)

The Adventures of Don Juan, 1948, 110m, ★★★/$$$$, WB/MGM-UA. The great lover has to change his ways in order to save the real love of his life-his Queen. Errol Flynn, Viveca Lindfors, Alan Hale, Ann Rutherford, Romney Brent, Raymond Burr. w. George Oppenheimer, Harry Kurnitz, d. Vincent Sherman.

ADVENTURE: ROMANCE: MELO-DRAMA: Costume Drama; Sexy Men; Romance-Choosing the Right Person; Swashbucklers; Queens; Saving Someone; 1600s; Spain
(The Adventures of Casanova; The Affairs of Cellini; Don Juan; The Gambler)

The Adventures of Eliza Frazer, 1976, 114m, ★★★/$, New World/New World, USA, R/S-P-MRN. In old Australia, a shipwrecked British couple have randy adventures while trying to stay out of trouble. Susannah York, Trevor Howard, Leon Lissek. d. Tim Burstall.

COMEDY: FARCE: Erotic Comedy; Shipwrecked; Australia; Fugitives; British Films
(The Bawdy Adventures of Tom Jones; Joseph Andrews; Tom Jones)
(Ed: Has its moments and general fun-if you like bawdy farces that aren't too swift)

The Adventures of Ford Fairlane, 1990, 96m, ★★1/2/$, 20th/Fox, R/EP-S-V. A crass detective in Hollywood tries to solve the murder of a DJ while running across assorted baddies in the record business. w. Daniel Waters, James Cappe, David Arnott, SS-adap. Rex Wiener, d. Renny Harlin.

ACTION: MYSTERY: MURDER: MUR-DER MYSTERY: Detective Stories; Hollywood Life; Singers; Radio Life; Comedians
(Brainsmasher: A Love Story; Hudson Hawk)

The Adventures of Gerard, 1970, 91m, ★★1/2/$, UA/NA. Spies and farce during the time of Napoleon with love on the line. Peter McEnery, Claudia Cardinale, Eli Wallach, Jack Hawkins. w. Hal Craig, SS-adap. Arthur Conan Doyle, d. Jerzy Skolimowski.

COMEDY DRAMA: FARCE: ROMANCE: Romantic Comedy; Costume Drama; Spies; Spoofs-Spy; 1800s; Napoleon

The Adventures of Hajji Baba, 1954, 94m, AA/NA. An ordinary man in olda Arabia is able to help a princess escape from the bad guys by happenstance. John Derek, Elaine Stewart, Thomas Gomez. w. Richard Collins, d. Don Weiss.

ADVENTURE: ROMANCE: Arab People; Fairy Tales; Legends

The Adventures of Huckleberry Finn, 1960, 107m, ★★★/$$$, MGM/MGM-UA. Tony Randall, Eddie Hodges, Patty McCormack, Neville Brand, Judy Canova. w. James Lee, d. Michael Curtiz.

The Adventures of Huckleberry Finn, 1985, 125m, ★★★/$$, PBS-AP/MCA-U. Sada Thompson, Lillian Gish, Jim Dale, Richard Kiley, Geraldine Page, Butterfly McQueen, Barnard Hughes, Frederic Forrest. d. Peter Hunt.

TV MOVIES: ADVENTURE: Boyhood; 1800s Journeys; Friendships-Interracial; Black Men; Classic Literary Adaptations; American Myth; All-Star Casts
(Huckleberry Finn; Tom Sawyer; The Adventures of Tom Sawyer; Tom and Huck; Pudd'nhead Wilson)

The Adventures of Marco Polo, 1938, 100m, ★★1/2/$$$, Goldwyn-UA/Goldwyn. The famous explorer heads to China and finds, among other treasures to bring back, a beautiful young woman. Gary Cooper, Sigrid Gurie, Basil Rathbone, Alan Hale. w. Robert Sherwood, d. Archie Mayo.

ADVENTURE: Costume Drama; Historical Drama; ROMANCE: Explorers; Asia; China; Journies
(The Good Earth; Marco Polo [TV Mini-Series]; The Black Rose; Dragon Seed)

The Adventures of Milo and Otis, 1989, 76m, ★★1/2/$$ (America) $$$$$$ (Japan), Virgin-Col/Col, G. A Japanese dog leaves his farm to chase after his kitten friend who's floated off downstream. Dudley Moore (narrator). w. Mark Saltzman, Masanori Hata, d. Hata.

CHILDREN'S: FAMILY: Cartoons; Animal Stories; Rescue Drama; Chase Movies; Animals-Talking; Japanese Films; Journies
(The Incredible Journey; Homeward Bound)
(Ed: One of the most popular films in Japanese history)

The Adventures of Reinette and Mirabelle, 1989, 95m, ★★★/$, Ind/New Yorker. A country girl and a Parisian

sophisticated lady share an apartment and have a series of adventures, romantic and otherwise, which each woman, because of her background, sees and experiences in quite a different manner. Joelle Miquel, Jessica Forde, Philippe Laudenbach, Marie Riviere, Beatrice Romand. w. d. Eric Rohmer.

DRAMA: COMEDY DRAMA: Country vs. City; Paris; Friendships-Intergenerational; Character Studies; Writer-Directors; French Films; Hidden Gems
(Entre Nous; One Sings, the Other Doesn't; Therese and Isabelle; Peppermint Soda; Summer)

The Adventures of Robin Hood, (1938/Color) 102m, ★★★★/$$$$, WB/WB. Sherwood forest vigilante steals from rich to give to the poor in lush technicolor. Errol Flynn, Olivia DeHavilland, Basil Rathbone. w. Seton Miller, Norman Reilly Raine, d. Michael Curtiz, William Keighley.

ADVENTURE: Comic Adventure; British; Medieval Times; Classics; Fighting the System; Rich vs. Poor; Robin Hood Stories
(REMAKES: Robin Hood: Prince of Thieves; Robin Hood [animated])
(Captain Blood; The Story of Robin Hood and his Merry Men; The Flame and the Arrow)

The Adventures of Robinson Crusoe, 1952, 90m, ★★★1/2/$$$, 20th/NA. The famous classic story of a sailor on a desert island learning to live by himself until a friend arrives. Dan O'Herlihy (BActor), Jaime Fernandez. w. Luis Bunuel, Philip Roll, N-adap. Daniel Defoe, d. Bunuel.

DRAMA: ADVENTURE: Survival Drama; Lonely People; Character Studies; Stranded; Shipwrecked; Stranded on an Island; Man vs. Nature; Friendships-Male
REMAKES: Crusoe; Lt. Robinson Caruso; Man Friday

The Adventures of Sadie, 1955, 83m, ★★★/$$, 20th/Fox. A beautiful young lady is stranded on a desert island with three fellows and the chase begins. Joan Collins, George Cole, Kenneth More, Robertson Hare, Hermione Gingold. w. d. Noel Langley, N-adap. Norman Lindsay, *The Cautious Amorist*.

COMEDY: Romantic Comedy; Stranded; Islands; Stranded on an Island; Shipwrecked; Sexy Women; Men Fighting Over Women; Romance-Triangles; Hidden Gems

(Too Many Husbands; The Admirable Crichton; The Sea Wife; Castaway)

The Adventures of Sherlock Holmes, 1939, 83m, ★★★½/$$$$, RKO/Turner. The evil Dr. Moriarty shows up to thwart Holmes while trying to steal the crown jewels from the palace in first of series. Basil Rathbone, Nigel Bruce, Ida Lupino. w. Edwin Blum, William Drake, d. Alfred Werker.

MYSTERY: Detective Stories; British Films; 1900s; Villains-Classic; Sherlock Holmes; Jewel Thieves; Mindgames
SEQUELS: the rest of the Sherlock Holmes SERIES, this being the first
(The Seven-Percent Solution; Young Sherlock Holmes; They Might Be Giants)

The Adventures of Sherlock Holmes' Smarter Brother, 1975, 91m, ★★½/$$, 20th/CBS-Fox, PG. Sherlock's heretofore unknown brother manages to solve a case despite being a bumbling idiot. Gene Wilder, Marty Feldman, Madeline Kahn, Leo McKern, Dom DeLuise, Roy Kinnear. w. d. Gene Wilder.

COMEDY: Spoofs; Comic Mystery; **MYSTERY:** Comedy-Slapstick; Sherlock Holmes; Fools-Bumbling; Writer-Directors; Actor Directors
(The Secret Life of Sherlock Holmes; They Might Be Giants; Start the Revolution Without Me; Without a Clue)

The Adventures of Tartu, 1943, 103m, ★★½/$$, MGM/HHT. A British spy infiltrates Nazi camps to get to a poison gas factory and destroy it. Robert Donat, Valerie Hobson, Glynis Johns. w. Howard Rogers, John Lee Mahin, Miles Malleson, d. Harold Bucquet.

ACTION: Spy Films; Spies; World War II Stories Movies; Nazi Stories; Germans as Enemy; British Films

The Adventures of Tom Sawyer, (1938), 77m, ★★★★/$$$$, Selznick-UA/Fox. The classic tale of the lying, mischievous brat everyone comes to love but no one believes when he says he knows who committed a murder. Tommy Kelly, Walter Brennan. w. John Weaver, d. Norman Taurog. BArt. Oscars: 1-0.

COMEDY DRAMA: ADVENTURE: MURDER: Trail of a Killer; Indians-American; Boyhood; 1800s; Classics-Literary Adaptations; Children-Brats; Rebels; Liars; Unbelieved
REMAKES: Tom Sawyer (1973)
(The Adventures of Huckleberry Finn; Tom and Huck)

The Adventures of the Wilderness Family, 1975, 100m, ★★½/$$$, PIE/NA. A city family moves to a lake in the mountains and makes friends with goofy hermits and animals. Robert Logan. w. d. Stuart Raffil.

FAMILY: CHILDREN'S: COMEDY DRAMA: MELODRAMA: Family Comedy; Nature-Back to; City vs. Country; Sleeper Hits; Writer-Directors
(Packing It In; Grizzly Adams)

The Adventuress (*I See a Dark Stranger*), 1945, 112m, ★★★/$$$, Ind-British/NA. An Irish girl, who's also an IRA member and despises the English, decides to spy for the Germans during World War II, but upon meeting a British soldier may reconsider. Deborah Kerr, Trevor Howard, Raymond, Huntley, Norman Shelley. w. Frank Launder, Sidney Gilliat, Wolfgang Wilhelm, d. Launder.

DRAMA: MELODRAMA: Spy Films; Spies; **ROMANCE:** World War II Stories; Spies-Female; Ireland; England; IRA; Female Protagonists; Germans as Enemy; British Films
(Odd Man Out; Joan of Paris)

Advise and Consent, 1962, 139m, ★★★/$$$, Univ/MCA-U, WB. Power struggles over liberal senator nominated to cabinet position. Henry Fonda, Charles Laughton, Walter Pidgeon, Gene Tierney. w. Gore Vidal, d. Otto Preminger.

DRAMA: Political Drama; Power Struggles; Politicians; Washington D.C.; Presidents; Corruption; Ethics
(The Best Man; State of the Union; The Last Hurrah)

The Advocate, 1994, 101m, ★★★/$, Miramax/Miramax, R/ES-P-V-FFN-MFN. When a pig is accused of murder in middle-ages England, a sort of traveling public defender must use what little reason there is in the day to figure out who really did it, in what turns out to be a conspiracy of sorts. Colin Firth, Nicol Williamson, Amina Annabi, Lysette Anthony, Jim Carter, Michael Gough, Ian Holm, Donald Pleasence. w. d. Leslie Megahey.

COMEDY: Black Comedy; Historical Drama; **SATIRE: MURDER: MYSTERY: MURDER MYSTERY:** Erotic Comedy; Detectives Stories; Animal Stories; Gypsies; Conspiracy; Dream Sequences; Cults; Middle Ages; Coulda Been Great; British Films; Hidden Gems

(The Canterbury Tales [1971]; The Name of the Rose; Stealing Heaven; The Star Chamber)
(Ed: Portrays the virtues of keeping less-than-bright people in the constraints of religion; though the mystery may not be thrilling, the advocate's adventures are)

Affair in Trinidad, 1952, 98m, ★★½/$$$, Col/RCA-Col. The husband of a singer in a tropical port is killed by mobsters, so when his brother arrives to investigate, she helps him track down the killers-and possibly love as well. Rita Hayworth, Glenn Ford. w. Oscar Saul, James Gunn, d. Vincent Sherman.

SUSPENSE: MURDER: Mob Stories; Trail of a Killer; **ROMANCE:** Brothers; Avenging Death of a Loved One; Islands
(Gilda; Cover Girl; Miss Sadie Thompson; The Mighty Quinn)

An Affair to Remember, 1956, 115m, ★★★/$$$$, Universal/CBS-Fox. Couple falls in love aboard a ship, soon to part before tragedy may or may not bring them back together. Cary Grant, Deborah Kerr. w. Delmer Daves, Leo McCarey, S-adap. McCarey, d. Leo McCarey.

DRAMA: MELODRAMA: ROMANCE: Tearjerkers; Romance-Reluctant; Ships-Cruise; Disabled People; Romance on Vacation; Empire State Building; Blockbusters
REMAKE OF: Love Affair (1939);
REMAKE: Love Affair (1994); **HOMAGE:** Sleepless in Seattle
(Love Affair; Sleepless in Seattle; The Other Side of the Mountain; One Night of Love; The Big Street)

The Affairs of Annabel, 1938, 68m, ★★½/$$, RKO/Turner. An actress (Lucille Ball) is conned by her agent (Jack Oakie) into several Method-acting real-life situations to get a job, including going to jail. w. Bert Granet, Paul Yawitz, d. Lew Landers.

COMEDY: SATIRE: Hollywood Life; Hollywood Satire; Actresses; Disguises; Comedy of Errors
SEQUEL: Annabel Takes a Tour
(Annabel Takes a Tour; Best Foot Forward; Easy Living; Fuller Brush Girl)

The Affairs of Cellini, 1934, 90m, ★★★/$$$, 20th/NA. An Italian nobleman gets around from bedroom to bedroom. Fredric March, Constance Bennett, Frank Morgan (BSActor), Fay Wray, Louis Calhern. w. Bess Meredyth, P-adap.

Edwin Mayer, The Firebrand, d. Gregory LaCava. BCin, BArt. Oscars: 3-0.

COMEDY: FARCE: ROMANCE: Romantic Comedy; Screwball Comedy; Costume; Drama; Playboys; Italians; 1500s; Forgotten Films; Faded Hits; Female Screenwriters
(The Adventures of Casanova; The Adventures of Don Juan; The Gambler)

The Affairs of Dobie Gillis, 1956, 74m, ★★1/2/$$, MGM/MGM-UA. The klutzy, dateless teen's first foray into film, before the famous series. Bobby Van, Debbie Reynolds, Bob Fosse. w. Max Schulman, d. Don Weis.

COMEDY: ROMANCE: Romantic Comedy; High School Life; Teenagers; Teenage Movies; Coming of Age; Narrated Films; Nerds; 1950s
SEQUEL: TV Series (1950s)

The Affairs of Susan, 1945, 110m, ★★1/2/$$$, Par/NA. Susan is loved and recalled by four different men she's had in her life. Joan Fontaine, George Brent, Walter Abel, Don Defore, Dennis O'Keefe. w. Richard Flournoy, Laszlo Gorog, T. Monroe, d. William Seiter.

COMEDY DRAMA: DRAMA: ROMANCE: Character Studies; Flashbacks; Memories; Multiple Stories; Young Women
(What a Way to Go; Woman Times Seven; A Letter to Three Wives)

Afraid of the Dark, 1992, 91m, ★★★/$ (LR), Sovereign/Col, PG-13/V. A vision-impaired little boy has premonitions about a slasher on the loose and is particularly worried about his totally blind mother. James Fox, Paul Gann, Fanny Ardant, Clare Holman. w. d. Mark Peploe.

SUSPENSE: HORROR: Serial Killers; Women in Jeopardy; Children in Jeopardy; Child Protagonists; Mothers & Sons; Blind People; Writer-Directors
(The Lady in White; Wait Until Dark; Fallen Idol; Cameron's Closet; Jennifer 8; Blink)

The African Queen, 1951, 105m, ★★★★/$$$$, Romulus-UA/Fox. A hardened drinking man and an uptight missionary join forces to fight the Germans in the middle of Africa, only to be sunk in love. Humphrey Bogart (**BActor**), Katharine Hepburn (**BActress**), Robert Morley. w. James Agee (**BAScr**), adap. CS Forster, d. John Huston (**BDir**). Oscars: 4-1.

DRAMA: COMEDY DRAMA: ADVENTURE: ROMANCE: Romantic Adventure; Romance-Opposites Attract; Underdog Stories; Battle of the Sexes; Tough Guys & Religious Women; Spinsters; Missionaries; Alcoholics; Africa; World War I Stories; Jungle Life; Nazi Stories; Heroes-Unlikely; River Trauma

REMAKE/RETREAD: Rooster Cogburn (Rooster Cogburn; Heaven Knows, Mr. Allison; Angel and the Badman; The Rainmaker; Mogambo)

Africa Screams, 1949, 79m, ★★1/2/$$, UA/Congress. Abbott and Costello bungle a safari in the jungle. w. Earl Baldwin, d. Charles Barton.

COMEDY: Comedy-Slapstick; **CHILDREN:** Africa; Jungles; Safaris; Fools-Bumbling; Abbott & Costello SERIES

Africa, Texas Style, 1967, 106m, ★★1/2/$, Par/Republic. A British Kenyan trying to start a safari ranch hires two Texas cowpokes to help him out. w. Andy White, d. Andrew Marton.

ADVENTURE: COMEDY DRAMA: Africa; Safaris; Fish out of Water Stories; British Films
(Daktari; Born Free; Clarence, the Cross-Eyed Lion)

After Dark, My Sweet, 1990, 105m, ★★★1/2/$$, Avenue/Live, R/P-V-S-MRN. Slow-witted boxer (Jason Patric) is caught up in conspiracy to kidnap rich child but may wind up fallguy by falling in love. Rachel Ward, Bruce Dern. w. Bob Redlin, N-adap. Jim Thompson, d. James Foley.

DRAMA: SUSPENSE: Film Noir-Modern; Erotic Thriller; Love-Questionable; Kidnappings; Simple Minds; Romance-Triangles; Framed?; Double Crossings; Jim Thompson-eqsue; Boxing; Hidden Gems; Ind Films
(The Grifters; Seance on a Wet Afternoon; Family Plot; Delusion; Coup de Torchon; Killer Inside Me)

After Hours, 1985, 97m, ★★★1/2/$$, Geffen-WB/WB, R/P-V-S-FN. Nightmare journey for lonely guy (Griffin Dunne) trying to find girl, but when he's mistaken as a criminal, he's persecuted and chased wrongly by vigilantes. Teri Garr, Rosanna Arquette, Catherine O'Hara, Linda Fiorentino, Will Patton. w. Joseph Minion, d. Martin Scorsese.

Black Comedy; **COMEDY:** Chase Movies; Nightmares; Nightmare Journies; Mistaken Identity; Murphy's Law Stories; Accused Unjustly?; Fugitives; One-Day Stories; Elusive Women; Lonely People; Surrealism; New York Life; Artists; Paranoia; All-Star Casts; Hidden Gems (The Cabinet of Dr. Caligari; Groundhog Day; Mirage)

After Office Hours, 1935, 75m, ★★★/$$$, MGM/NA. A newspaper reporter (Clark Gable) and the gossip columnist (Constance Bennett) team up to solve a murder. Billie Burke, Henry Travers. w. Herman J. Mankiewicz, d. Robert Z. Leonard.

COMEDY: Screwball Comedy; **MYSTERY: MURDER: MURDER MYSTERY:** Comic Mystery; Journalists; Detectives-Amateur (Adventure in Manhattan; The Mad Miss Manton)

After the Fox, 1966, 103m, ★★★1/2/$$, Mirisch-UA/Fox. Criminal posing as director (Peter Sellers) uses faded American star (Victor Mature) to stage cover for big heist but is thwarted by a real director coming in. Vittorio DeSica, Britt Ekland. w. Neil Simon, d. Vittorio deSica.

COMEDY: Action Comedy; Heist Stories; Fugitives; Fugitives from the Mob; Fugitives From the Law; Prison Escapes; Italy; Crossing the Line; Multiple Performances; Disguises; Making Movies; Films Within Films
(The Mouse That Roared; I'm All Right; Jack; The Party; The Bobo)

After the Rehearsal, 1985, 72m, ★★★/$, Embassy/Col, PG-13. Relationships of a theater director and his actresses. Lena Olin, Ingrid Thulin, Erland Josephson. w. d. Ingmar Bergman.

DRAMA: MELODRAMA: Theater Life; Bergmanesque; Swedish Films; Directors; Actors; Actresses; Writer-Directors

After the Shock, 1990, 92m, ★★1/2/$$$, Par/Par. Story of the 1989 San Francisco earthquake told from several points of view. Yaphet Khotto, Rue McClanahan, Jack Scalia. w. d. Gary Sherman.

DRAMA: Disaster Stories; Earthquakes; Multiple Stories; True Stories; Writer-Directors; TV Movies
(Quake; The Big One; Earthquake)

Against a Crooked Sky, 1975, 89m, ★★★/$$, Ind/Live, Vestron. When the sister of a boy has been kidnapped, he sets out with an old codger into the wild west to find her. Richard Boone, Stewart Petersen, Geoffrey Land. w. Douglas G. Stewart, Eleanor Lamb, d. Earl Bellamy.

WESTERN: FAMILY: CHILDREN'S: ADVENTURE: Missing Persons;

Kidnappings; Indians-American; Men and Boys
(The Searchers; In Search of the Castaways)
(Ed: Better for children)

Against All Flags, 1952, 83m, ★★¹/₂/$$, U/MCA-U. A British scoundrel of the seas (Errol Flynn) pirates Spanish ships during war time to help his king. Maureen O'Hara, Anthony Quinn, Mildred Natwick. w. Aeneas Mackenzie, Joseph Hoffman, d. George Sherman.
ADVENTURE: Swashbucklers; Costume Drama; Adventure at Sea; Pirates; 1600s
REMAKE: The King's Pirate
(The King's Pirate; The Adventures of Captain Fabian; The Adventures of Captain Kidd; That Forsyte Woman)

Against All Odds, 1984, 128m, ★★★/$$$, Columbia/RCA-Col, R/P-V-S-FN-MRN. Man hired by sleaze to locate his wife falls for her when he does, but may incur the wrath of his supposed friend. Jeff Bridges, James Woods, Rachel Ward. w. Eric Hughes, d. Taylor Hackford.
DRAMA: ROMANCE: Film Noir-Modern; Romance-Triangles; Dangerous Men; Love-Questionable; Fugitives from the Mob; Affairs-Clandestine; Double Crossings; Cuckolded; Jealousy; Mexico; Los Angeles
REMAKE OF: Out of the Past
(Out of the Past; Road House; After Dark, My Sweet; Mad Dog & Glory; Revenge)
(Ed: Not much class, but the tension's still there)

Against the Wind, 1948, 96m, ★★★/$$, Ealing/Nos. Civilians are trained to be saboteurs during the war in London, but one has defiant sentiments. Simne Signoret, Robert Beatty, Jack Warner. w. TEB Clarke, Micheal Pertwee, d. Charles Crichton.
DRAMA: War Movies; World War II Movies; Sabotage; Spies; Undercover; Traitors; British Films

Agatha, 1979, 98m, ★★★/$$, WB/WB, PG. Agatha Christie disappeared for several days in 1926 and a reporter tracks her down in this version of what may have really happened. Vanessa Redgrave, Dustin Hoffman. w. Alvin Sargent, N-adap. Kathleen Tynan, d. Michael Apted.
DRAMA: True Stories; Hypothetical Stories; True or Not?; Missing Persons; Writers British; 1920s
(The Disappearance of Aimee)

L'Age d'Or, See L
Age Isn't Everything, 1991, 91m, ★¹/₂/(VR), Vestron/Vestron, PG-13/P. A college student becomes an old man on the inside while maintaining his youthful facade. Jonathan Silverman, Robert Prosky, Rita Moreno, Paul Sorvino. w. d. Douglas Katz.
COMEDY: Role Reversal; Body Switching; Aging; Elderly People; Young Men; Writer-Directors
(18 Again; Prelude to a Kiss; Like Father Like Son; Vice Versa; Big)

The Agency, 1981, 96m, ★★/$, New World/New World, PG. An ad agency tries subliminal advertising, but the idea should have been used on this film to give it something . . . anything. Robert Mitchum, Lee Majors, Valerie Perrine, Saul Rubinek. w. d. George Kaczender.
COMEDY: COMEDY DRAMA: SATIRE: Advertising World; Unintentionally Funny; Writer-Directors

Age of Consent, 1969, 103m, ★★★/$, Col/RCA-Col, R/S. On a small island off of Australia, an artist decides that the granddaughter of his drunkard neighbor is what he needs to pass the time. James Mason, Helen Mirren. w. Peter Yeldham, N-adap. Norman Lindsay, d. Michael Powell.
DRAMA: Romance-Reluctant; Romance-Older Men/Younger Women; Artists; Islands; Australia; British Films; Forgotten Films; Overlooked
(Lolita; Night of the Iguana)

The Age of Innocence, 1934, 71m, ★★¹/₂/$, RKO/Turner. Irene Dunne, John Boles, Lionel Atwill. w. Sarah Mason, Victor Heerman, d. Philip Moeller. Female Screenwriters

The Age of Innocence, 1993, 137m, ★★★¹/₂/$$, Col/Col-Tri, PG. Daniel Day Lewis, Michelle Pfeiffer, Winona Ryder (BSActress), Joanne Woodward (narrator), MaryBeth Hurt, Miriam Margolyes, Geraldine Chaplin. w. Jay Cocks, Martin Scorsese (BAScr), N-adap. Edith Wharton, d. Scorsese. BArt, **BCostume**. Oscars: 4-1.
>High society in 1870s New York is examined through a romantic triangle and the conventions and conformist rules of the day both binding and confusing it.
DRAMA: MELODRAMA: Social Drama; ROMANCE: Romantic Drama; Romance-Triangles; Romance-Choosing the Right

Person; Romance-Forbidden; Love-Questionable; Costume; Drama; Conformism; Social Climbing; Marriage Impending; Engagements-Breaking; Marriages-Forced; Divorce; Cousins; 1800s; New York Life; Narrated Films
(The French Lieutenant's Woman; The Bostonians; The Europeans; Howards End; Portrait of a Lady; The Piano; Sense and Sensibility)
(Ed: [1993] More visual than the similar Merchant-Ivory films, but without the charm and energy somehow. It seems too staid and unnatural with its narration and discussions often neglecting character development, though it may get better on second viewing)

Agnes of God, 1985, 97m, ★★★/$$$, Columbia/RCA-Col, PG/S. A nun is accused of aborting or killing her baby, but she claims to be a virgin, and a psychiatrist (Jane Fonda) has to figure out whether she's been raped somehow or if this is a miracle. Meg Tilly (BSActress), Anne Bancroft (BActress). w. P-adap. John Pielmeier, d. Norman Jewison. BOScore. Oscars: 3-0.
DRAMA: MYSTERY: Religion; Babies-Having; Abortion Dilemmas; Fantasy; What if . . . Stories; Accused Unjustly; Psychologists; Psychologist as Detective; Nuns; Virgins; Female Protagonists

The Agony and the Ecstasy, 1965, 140m, ★★★/$$$, 20th/CBS-Fox. The pope persuades Michelangelo to give up sculpting long enough to paint the Sistine Chapel, and the rest is history. Charlton Heston, Rex Harrison, Diane Cilento, Harry Andrews. w. Philip Dunne, N-adap. Irving Stone, d. Carol Reed.
DRAMA: MELODRAMA: Historical Drama; Costume Drama; Artists; Artists-Famous; Popes; Ancient Times; Biographies; True Stories; Rome
(The Leopard; The Cardinal; Shoes of the Fisherman; Lust for Life)

Aguirre, the Wrath of God, 1972, 90m, ★★★/$ (LR), New Yorker/New Yorker. In the 1500s, a Spanish leader takes a group of men down a dangerous tropical river by raft on a quest and soon loses his mind and perhaps their lives. Klaus Kinski, Ruy Guerra. w. d. Werner Herzog.
DRAMA: ADVENTURE: Art Films; German Films; 1500s; Leaders-Tyrant; Mental Illness; Obsessions; Writer-Directors
(Fitzcarraldo)

Ah, Wilderness, 1935, 101m, ★★★/$$$, MGM/MGM-UA. A family in an all-American small town at the turn of the century experiences several rather inconsequential but interesting changes and crises. Wallace Beery, Lionel Barrymore, Eric Linden, Spring Byington, Mickey Rooney, Aline MacMahon, Bonita Granville. w. Albert Hackett, Frances Goodrich, P-adap. Euegene O'Neill, d. Clarence Brown.

COMEDY DRAMA: DRAMA: MELO-DRAMA: FAMILY: Family Drama; Small-Town Life; 1900s; Female Screenwriters
MUSICAL REMAKE: Summer Holiday
(You Can't Take It with You; Life with Father; Andy Hardy SERIES; Summer Holiday; Mother Carey's Chickens)

Ain't Misbehavin', 1955, 82m, ★★1/2/$$, U/NA. A young redheaded woman (Piper Laurie) marries a million-aire and must learn the graces of good living, having been a dancer before. Rory Calhoun, Reginald Gardiner, Jack Carson, Barbara Britton, Mamie Van Doren. w. Ed Buzzell, Philip Rapp, Devery Freeman, d. Buzzell.

COMEDY: ROMANCE: Romantic Comedy; Romance-Older Men/Younger Women; Social Climbing; Marrying Up; Svengalis; Dancers; Snobs vs. Slobs
(Pygmalion; My Fair Lady; Educating Rita; Pretty Woman)

Air America, 1990, 112m, ★★/$$, Carolco-Tri-Star/Live, PG-13/P-V. CIA agent-pilot (Mel Gibson) and his side-kick (Robert Downey, Jr.) fly comic mis-sions over Laos. Nancy Travis, Ken Jenkins, David Marshall Grant. w. John Eskow, Richard Rush, NF-adap. Christopher Robbins, d. Roger Spottiswoode.

ACTION: COMEDY: Action Comedy; Airplanes; Pilots-Military; Vietnam; Asia; CIA Agents; Undercover
(Lethal Weapon SERIES; The Firebirds; Into the Sun)

Air Force, 1943, 124m, ★★1/2/$$$$, WB/WB. War heroes abound as a ship makes its way through air and sea battles across the Pacific. John Garfield, Gig Young, Arthur Kennedy, Harry Carey. w. Dudley Nichols (BOScr), d. Howard Hawks. BEdit, BCin. Oscars: 3-1.

ACTION: War Movies; War Battles; Pilots-Military; War at Sea; Pearl Harbor; Conservative; Value Films; Feelgood Films

(The Fighting Seabees; Action in the North Atlantic; Flying Leathernecks)

Airheads, 1994, 94m, ★★/$, 20th/Fox, R/P-S. Three stupid headbangers take over a radio station to get their band's demo tape played and become celebrities in the process. Brendan Fraser, Steve Buscemi, Adam Sandler, Chris Farley, Michael McKean, Judd Nelson, Joe Mantegna, Ernie Hudson, Michael Richards, Amy Locane, Nina Siezmasko. w. Rich Wilkes, d. Michael Lehmann.

COMEDY: SATIRE: Rock Stars; Musicians; Simple Minds; Young Men; Hostage Situations; Radio Life; Flops-Major
(Pump Up the Volume; Kings and Desperate Men; This Is Spinal Tap; SFW)

Airplane!, 1980, 86m, ★★★★/$$$$, Par/Par, PG/P. Spoof of air disaster films with visual gags galore. Robert Hays, Julie Hagerty, Lloyd Bridges, Leslie Nielsen. w. d. Jim Abrahams, Jerry Zucker, David Zucker.

COMEDY: Spoofs; Gag Comedy; Disaster Movies; Romantic Comedy; Airplanes; Airplane Crashes
SEQUEL: Airplane 2, the Sequel

Airplane 2, the Sequel, 1982, 85m, ★★★/$$$, Par/Par, PG. Sequel to spoof, but not by original creators. Robert Hays, Julie Hagerty, William Shatner, Leslie Nielsen. w. d. Ken Finkleman.

COMEDY: Spoofs; Gag Comedy; Disaster Movies; Romantic Comedy; Redemption; Airplanes

SEQUEL TO: Airplane!
(Hot Shots; The Naked Gun SERIES; Blazing Saddles; Young Frankenstein; High Anxiety; Airport SERIES; The Big Bus; Kentucky Fried Movie)

Airport, 1970, 137m, ★★★/$$$$, Universal/MCA-U, PG. Crisis builds as flight to Europe has a bomber onboard and the microcosmic slice of life stories of those in the air and on the ground. Burt Lancaster, Dean Martin, Helen Hayes (**BSActress**), Jacqueline Bisset, Maureen Stapleton (BSActress). w. George Seaton (BAScr), N-adap. Arthur Hailey, d. George Seaton. BPicture, BDirector, BEdit, BCin, BArt, BOScore Oscars: 9-1.

DRAMA: SUSPENSE: Disaster Movie; Bombs; Airplanes; Elderly Women; Terrorists; Psycho-Killers; Multiple Stories; Ensemble Films; All-Star Cast; Crisis Situations; Blockbusters

SEQUELS: Airport 1975/1977/1979;
SPOOFS: Airplane!
(Ed: If only they'd had good security back then, then no bomb and no movie)

Airport 1975, 1974, 106m, ★★★/$$$, Universal/MCA-U, PG. Small plane hits cockpit of 747 just as it's approaching the Rockies. Karen Black, Charlton Heston, Helen Reddy, Gloria Swanson. w. Doningalls, d. Jack Smight.

DRAMA: SUSPENSE: Disaster Movies; Airplanes; Nuns; Crisis Situations; Female Protagonists; All-Star Casts
SEQUEL TO: Airport

Airport 1977, 1977, 113m, ★★★/$$$, Universal/MCA-U, PG. This time, billion-aire Jimmy Stewart is shipping paintings in a plane with an all-star cast aboard when art thieves ditch the plane in the process of trying to steal the works. Jack Lemmon, Lee Grant, Olivia de Havilland, Joseph Cotten, Brenda Vaccaro. w. Michael Scheff, David Spector, d. Jerry Jameson.

DRAMA: SUSPENSE: Disaster Movies; Heist Stories; Airplanes; Airplane Crashes; Female Protagonists; All-Star Cast; Crisis Situations; Underwater Adventure; Art Thieves
SEQUEL TO: Airport and Airport 1975
(Raise the Titanic)

Airport '79, The Concorde (*The Concorde, Airport 79*), 1979, 113, ★★/$, U/MCA-U, PG/V The fastest plane in the world, en route from Washington to Paris, is beset by problems causing all hell to break loose among the passengers. Alain Delon, Susan Blakely, Robert Wagner, Sylvia Kristel, George Kennedy, Eddie Albert, Bibi Andersson, John Davidson, Martha Raye, Cicely Tyson, Mercedes McCambridge. w. Eric Roth, d. David Lowell.

SUSPENSE: DRAMA: Disaster Stories; Airplanes; Russians; Cold War Era; Hostage Situations; Terrorists; All-Star Casts; Unintentionally Funny; Flops-Major
(The Towering Inferno; The Poseidon Adventure; The High and the Mighty; Passenger 57)

Akira Kurosawa's Dreams, 1990, 120m, ★★★/$$, WB/WB, PG. A fable-like film with history lessons and allegor-ical stories about the deteriorating environment and other lofty subjects. Akira Terao, Martin Scorsese, Mitsuko Beisho. w. d. Kurosawa.

DRAMA: Fantasy; Allegorical Stories; Dreams; Environmental Dilemmas; Japanese Films; Writer-Directors (Rhapsody in August; Koyaanisqatsi; Powannisqatsi)

The Air Up There, 1994, 94m, ★★1/2/$$, Polygram-U/Polygram, PG-13/P. A white basketball scout goes to Africa to find new court stars among the tribes. Kevin Bacon. w. Max Apple, d. Paul Michael Glazer.

COMEDY: Sports Movies; Basketball; Africa; Fish out of Water Stories; White Among Blacks; Americans Abroad (Cool Runnings; Fast Break; The Scout)

Aladdin, 1992, 90m, ★★★1/2/$$$$, Disney/Disney, G. A little boy finds a magic lamp with a genie (Robin Williams) and winds up with a princess and a magic carpet to see "a whole new world." w. d. John Musker, Ron Clements, Ted Elliott, Terry Rossio. BOScore, **BOSong.**
Oscars: 2-1.

MUSICAL: Cartoons; **ADVENTURE ACTION:** Boyhood; Genies; Love-First; Middle East; Arab People; Child Protagonists (Ali Baba and the Forty Thieves; The Thief of Baghdad; The Return of Jafar)

The Alamo, 1960, 161m, ★★★/$$$$, 20th/CBS-Fox, V. Texans battle the Mexican army for freedom at the legendary landmark. John Wayne, Richard Widmark, Laurence Harvey, Chill Wills (BSActor), Frankie Avalon. w. James Edward Grant, d. John Wayne. BPicture, BCCin, BOSong, BOScore, BEdit. Oscars: 6-0.

WESTERNS: War Battles; War Movies; Historical Drama; True Stories; Alamo Stories; Epics; Cast of Thousands; All-Star Casts; Texas; Big Budgets; Best Picture Nominees (How the West Was Won; The Last Command; Lone Star of Gold)

Alamo Bay, 1985, 98m, ★★1/2/$, Tri-Star/RCA-Col, PG-13. Texas fishermen have trouble getting along with Vietnamese refugees who tred on territory and undercut their prices. Ed Harris, Amy Madigan. w. Alice Arlen d. Louis Malle.

DRAMA: Social Drama; Class Conflicts; Fish out of Water Stories; Immigrants; Race Relations; Southerns; Texas; Asian Americans; Quiet Little Films; Ordinary People Stories; Female Screenwriters

Alan and Naomi, 1992, 95m, ★★★/VR, Col/Col, PG. A Brooklyn boy during World War II makes friends with a girl just coming out of a tragic existence during the holocaust and learning to live in America. Lukas Haas, Vanessa Zaoul, Michael Gross, Kevin Connolly, Zohra Lampert. w. Jordan Horowitz, d. Sterling Van Wagenen.

DRAMA: ROMANCE: World War II-Post Era; New York Life; Friendships Between Sexes; Boys; Girls; Love-First; Hidden Gems; Coulda Been Great (My Antonia; Swing Kids; Sophie's Choice)

Albuquerque, 1948, 89m, Par/NA. The nephew of the town despot goes against him to help a small wagon line stay going. Randolph Scott, Barbara Britton, George Gabby Hayes, Lon Chaney Jr. w. Gene Lewis, Clarence Young, N-adap Luke Short, d. Ray Enright.

WESTERN: Western-City Titles; Mortgage Drama; Rebels; Evil Men; Fighting for Rights

Al Capone, 1959, 105m, ★★★/$$, AA/Fox. The rise and ironic fall of Chicago's biggest mobster from prohibition days to jail. Rod Steiger, Nehemiah Persoff, Martin Balsam, Fay Spain. w. Marvin Wald, Henry Greenberg, d. Richard Wilson.

DRAMA: Crime Drama; Mob Stories; Mob Wars; Biographies; Criminal Biographies; True Stories; Chicago; Docudrama; Episodic Stories; Rise and Fall Stories (Capone, 1974; The Untouchables; The Scarface Mob; Scarface [1932])

The Alchemist, 1981, 84m, ★1/2/$, Ind/Vestron, Live, R/V-S. A beautiful woman is able to cure a man of a curse put on him which she may have overcome, too. Robert Ginty, Lucinda Dooling. w. Alan Adler, d. Charles Band.

HORROR: Fantasy; Cures/Elixirs

Alex and the Gypsy, 1976, 99m, ★★/$, 20th/CBS-Fox, R/P-S. A man sick of his seedy life as a bail bondsman (Jack Lemmon) has his midlife crisis with a gypsy-type girl he runs into (Genevieve Bujold). James Woods. w. Lawrence Marcus, N-adap. Stanley Elkin, The Bailbondsman, d. John Korty.

COMEDY DRAMA: ROMANCE: MELO-DRAMA: Midlife Crisis; Romance-Older Men/Younger Women; Ordinary People Stories; Starting Over; Gypsies; Flops-Major (Avanti!; The April Fools; King of the Gypsies)

Alex in Wonderland, 1971, 109m, ★★★1/2/$$, UA/MGM-UA, R/P-S. A movie director (Donald Sutherland) who's had a great success with his first film goes on a quest for a second hit, leading him to some soul-searching in early-70s Hollywood. Ellen Burstyn. w. Paul Mazursky, Larry Tucker, d. Paul Mazursky.

DRAMA: COMEDY DRAMA: SATIRE: Hollywood Life; Making Movies; Directors; Autobiographical; 1970s (8½; Play It as It Lays; The Pickle; Stardust Memories; The Last Tycoon; Movers and Shakers; The Day of the Locust)

Alexander Nevsky, 1938, 107m, ★★★★/$$, Mosfilm/VY. In the middle ages, the prince of Russia defeats Germans invading from the south in great battle sequences. Nicolai Chersakov. w. Pyotr Pavelnko, Sergei Eisenstein, d. Eisenstein.

DRAMA: War Movies; Epics; Historical Drama; Princes; War Battles; Russian Films; Russia; Germans as Enemy; Cast of Thousands; Film History

Alexander's Ragtime Band, 1938, 106m (B&W), ★★★/$$$$, 20th/CBS-Fox. A songwriting team has many problems due to loving the same woman over several decades. Tyrone Power, Alice Faye, Don Ameche, Ethel Merman, Jack Haley, Jean Hersholt, John Carradine. w. Kathryn Scola, Lamar Trotti (BOStory), d. Henry King. BPicture, BArt, BEdit, BScore. Oscars: 5-1.

MELODRAMA: ROMANCE: MUSICAL: Musical Romance; Theater Life; Romance-Triangles; Men Fighting Over Women; Musicians; Episodic Stories; Big Band Era; Female Screenwriters (Rhapsody in Blue; My Gal Sal; Three Little Words)

Alexander the Great, 1955, 135m, ★★1/2/$$$, MGM/MGM-UA. The rise of the great leader of the Middle East in ancient times but who tragically died at the same age as Jesus. Richard Burton, Fredric March, Claire Bloom, Harry Andrews, Peter Cushing, Danielle Darrieux. d. Robert Rossen.

DRAMA: Historical Drama; Royalty; Kings; Biographies; Middle East; Ancient Times (The Man Who Would Be King; The Robe)

Alexander, the Other Side of Dawn, 1977, 100m, NBC/Movies Unltd. A teenager (Leigh McCloskey) hops a bus to Hollywood and winds up a prostitute to survive, but does pretty well. w. d. John Erman.

DRAMA: Prostitutes-Male; Camp; Gay Men; Bisexuality; Hollywood Life; Curiosities
(Midnight Cowboy; Dawn: Portrait of a Runaway)

Alfie, 1966, 114m, ★★★★/$$$$, Par/Par, PG/S. Ladies' man (Michael Caine, BActor) tells his own story as he goes through his string of "birds" trying to decide whether or not to find true love. Shelley Winters, Vivien Merchant (BSActress). w. Lewis Gilbert, P-adap. Bill Naughton, d. Gilbert (BOScr, BDir); BPicture, BOSong. Oscars: 6-0.

COMEDY-DRAMA: Character Studies; Episodic Stories; Settling Down; Playboys; Single Men; Abortion Dilemmas; Romance-Older Women/Younger Men; Sexism; Mod Era; Crossing the Line; Narrated Films; British Films
SEQUEL: Alfie, Darling; **RETREAD:** The Rachel Papers
(The Rachel Papers; Darling; Shampoo; Twenty-One; Shirley Valentine [same team]; Alfie, Darling)

Alfredo, Alfredo, 1973, 97m, ★★/$, Par/Par, PG. A nerd in Italy marries a beautiful woman and then finds it's more than he bargained for. Dustin Hoffman, Stefania Sandrelli, Carla Gravina. d. Pietro Germi.

COMEDY: COMEDY DRAMA: Marriage Comedy; Newlyweds; Young Men; Italian Films; Italy; Fish out of Water Stories; Nerds; Forgotten Films

Algiers, 1938, 95m, ★★★/$$$, UA/Nos, Congress. A master thief falls in love and this hampers his business. Charles Boyer (BActor), Hedy Lamarr, Gene Lockhart (BSActor), Alan Hale. w. John Lawson, James M. Cain, d. John Cromwell. BCin. Oscars: 3-0.

DRAMA: ROMANCE: Romantic Drama; Romance-Reluctant; Sexy Women; Thieves; Playboys; Settling Down; Africa
REMAKE: Casbah
(Casablanca; Casbah; Morocco; To Catch a Thief)

Ali Baba and the Forty Thieves, 1944, 87m, U/MCA-U. From the tales of the Arabian Nights, servant Ali has to buy a new wife for his master's harem and winds up finding a thieves' cave full of stolen treasures. What to do? Fernandel, Samia Gamel. w. Jacques becker, Marc Maurette, Maurice Griffe, d. Becker.

ADVENTURE: COMEDY DRAMA: Thieves; Treasure Hunts; Arab People; Legends; Servants
(Aladdin; The Thief of Bagdad; The Arabian Nights)

Ali Baba Goes to Town, 1937, 81m, ★★½/$$, 20th/NA. A bum falls off the back of a train going through Hollywood and wakes up on the set of an Arabian Nights movie and guess what he thinks. Eddie Cantor, Tony Martin, John Carradine. w. Harry Tugend, Jack Yellen, d. David Butler.

COMEDY: MUSICAL: MUSICAL COMEDY: Comedy-Slapstick; Amnesia; Mistaken Identities; Misunderstandings; Hollywood Life; Homeless People; What if . . . Stories

Alice, 1990, 95m, ★★★½/$$, Orion/Orion, PG/S. Rich bored housewife (Mia Farrow) gets a magic invisibility potion and finds out what's really going on behind her back as a man (Joe Mantegna) pursues her for an affair-due to the love potion she also found. William Hurt, Cybill Shepherd, Keye Luke. w. d. Woody Allen, (BOScr). Oscars: 1-0.

COMEDY: Screwball Comedy; Fantasy; Romance-Clandestine Affairs; Shy People; Cheating Women; Invisible People; Potions; Magic; Muses; Revenge on Cheaters; Upper Class; New York Life; Life Transitions; Midlife Crisis
(Husbands and Wives; The Women; Manhattan Murder Mystery; The Purple Rose of Cairo)

Alice Adams (B&W), 1935, 99m, ★★★★/$$$, RKO/Turner. A young girl (Katharine Hepburn, BActress) hoping to marry well in the 20s soon finds out some of the realities of love and life. Fred MacMurray. w. Dorothy Yost, Mortimer Offner, Jane Murfin, N-adap. Booth Tarkington, d. George Stevens. BPicture. Oscars: 2-0.

DRAMA: MELODRAMA: ROMANCE: Coming of Age; Love-First; Character Studies; Class Conflicts; Social Climbing; Snobs; Young Women; Female Protagonists; Wallflowers & Hunks; Best Picture Nominees; Female Screenwriters
(Member of the Wedding; The Heart Is a Lonely Hunter; Sabrina; Morning Glory; Seventeen)

Alice Doesn't Live Here Anymore, 1974, 113m, ★★★★/$$$, WB/WB, PG/P-S. Housewife (Ellen Burstyn, **BActress**) is widowed and takes her son

on the road to find a job singing, but winds up waiting tables instead, however does find a boyfriend, too. Diane Ladd (BSActress), Kris Kristofferson, Jodie Foster. w. Robert Getchell (BOScr), d. Martin Scorsese (BDirector). Oscars: 4-1.

COMEDY DRAMA: DRAMA: Women's Films; Starting Over; Widows; Dreams; Mothers Alone; Making a Living; Working Class; Mid-Life Crisis; Eccentric People; Musicians; Southwestern Life
(Diary of a Mad Housewife; Up the Sandbox; The Accidental Tourist; The Rain People)

Alice in the Cities, 1974, 110m, ★★½/$$, Ind/Facets, R. A German writer visiting America winds up taking a girl back to Germany much to his dismay, though she turns out to be endearing. Rudiger Vogler. w. d. Wim Wenders.

DRAMA: COMEDY DRAMA: Men and Girls; Children-Inherited; Writers; German Films; Germans; Writer-Directors
(Sundays and Cybele; Paper Moon; Little Miss Marker)

Alice in Wonderland, 1951, 75m, ★★★★/$$$$, Disney/Disney, G. The Lewis Carroll adventure through the looking glass is Disneyfied in excellent, flawless form. d. Clyde Geronimi, Hamilton Luske, Wilfred Jackson. BOSong, BOScore. Oscars: 2-0.

CHILDREN'S: FAMILY: Fairy Tales; Cartoons; Wallflowers; Princes; Wallflowers & Hunks; Race Against Time; Rabbits; Stepmothers; Kingdoms
(Cinderella; Peter Pan)

Alice's Restaurant, 1969, 111m, ★★★/$$$, UA/CBS-Fox, PG/S-P. Hippies hang out avoiding the draft and commune at a New England restaurant where they wind-up running afoul of local garbage ordinances. Arlo Guthrie, James Broderick. w. Venable Herndon, d. Arthur Penn (BDirector). Oscars: 1-0.

COMEDY DRAMA: Anti-Establishment Films; Fighting the System; Hippies; Ethics; Accused-Unjustly; Vietnam Era; Coming of Age; Alternative Lifestyles
(I Love You; Alice B. Toklas; The Baby Maker; Easy Rider; Woodstock; Generation; Joe)

Alice, Sweet Alice, 1976, 96m, ★★½/$, Ind/Republic, R/EV-B&G. A little girl may have killed her parents and sister (Brooke Shields) in clever and bizarre ways. d. Alfred Sole.

SUSPENSE: HORROR: MYSTERY: MUR-DER MYSTERY: Murderers-Child; Serial Killers; Parent vs. Child; Child Protagonists; Female Protagonists; Clever Plots & Endings
(The Bad Seed; The Little Girl Who Lives Down the Lane)

Alien, 1979, 116m, ★★★/$$$$, #1 1979, 20th/Fox, R/EV-B&G. A terrible monster/parasite is aboard a mining ship in outer space who likes to impregnate humans before killing them. Sigourney Weaver, Tom Skerritt, Yaphet Khotto, John Hurt, Veronica Cartwright, Harry Dean Stanton, Ian Holm. w. Dan O'Banion, Walter Hill, d. Ridley Scott. **BSFX,** BEditing, BSound, BArt, BCinema; Oscars: 5-1.
HORROR: SUSPENSE: SCI-FI: Monsters; Outer Space Movies; Rogue Plot; Aliens-Outer Space-Evil; Androids; Heroines; Murders-One by One; Human Eaters; Stalkers; Kill the Beast; Female Protagonists
SEQUELS: Aliens; Alien 3
(Jaws; The Thing; Outland)

Alien Nation, 1988, 89m, 20th/CBS-Fox, ★★1/2/$$, PG-13/V. Aliens from outer space have to get along with the humans in futuristic L.A. and what amounts to racial tensions are the result. James Caan, Mandy Patinkin. w. Rockne S. O'Bannon, d. Graham Baker.
DRAMA: Crime Drama; **SCI-FI:** Futuristic Films; Aliens-Outer Space, Good; Allegorical Stories; Race Relations; Conspiracy; Police-Corruption
SEQUEL: TV Series spinoff, 1989.

Aliens, 135m, 1986, ★★★1/2/$$$$, 20th/CBS-Fox, R/EV-B&G-EP. Sigourney Weaver (BActress) comes back to life from hypersleep only to find herself on another ship where not one but a colony of aliens is devouring the humans. A mixture of the original and the military group from "The Thing" unite to do battle. Michael Biehn, Paul Reiser. w. d. James Cameron (BAScr). **BSound, BSound Edit,** BEditing, BCinema, **BSFX,** Oscars: 7-3.
HORROR: SUSPENSE: SCI-FI: Monsters; Outer Space Movies; Rogue Plots; Aliens-Outer Space-Evil; Murders-One by One; Human Eaters; Soldiers; Androids; Unbelieved; Corporation as Enemy; Stalkers; Kill the Beast; Heroines; Female Protagonists; Writer-Directors
SEQUEL TO: Alien; **SEQUEL:** Alien 3

REMAKES/RETREADS: The Thing; Them. (The Thing; Jaws; Them)
(Ed: On one hand, a thoroughly original and independent sequel to the original, but on the other hand, borrowing bits and pieces from The Thing, Them, and other 50s Sci-Fi-ers. The sum total is an excellent film, regardless)

Alien 3, 1992, 115m, ★★1/2/$$$, 20th/Fox, R/EV-B&G-EP. This time, Ripley (Sigourney Weaver) is sent to a prison colony in space where at least one acid-dripping critter happens to be lurking again. Will she make it this time? Charles Dutton, Charles Dance. w. David Giler, Walter Hill, Larry Ferguson, Vincent Ward, d. David Fincher.
HORROR: SUSPENSE: SCI-FI: Monsters; Outer Space Movies; Rogue Plots; Aliens-Outer Space-Evil; Prison Drama; Murders-One by One; Female Protagonists; Human Eaters; A Female Among Males; Rape/Rapists; Unbelieved; Heroines
SEQUEL TO: Alien; Aliens
(Outland; Seven)

Alive, 1993, 124m, ★★★/$$$, Hollywood/Hollywood, PG-13/EV. A planeload of Argentine rugby players crash lands on top of an Andes mountain and must survive without food for weeks. Ethan Hawke, Vincent Spano, Josh Hamilton. w. John Patrick Shanley, NF-adap. Piers Paul Read, d. Frank Marshall.
DRAMA: TRAGEDY: True Stories; Survival Drama; Rescue Drama; Cannibalism; Stranded; Airplane Crashes; Disaster Movies; Mountain Climbing; Ensemble Films; Ensembles-Male; South America
REMAKE OF: Survive! (1976)
(Survive!; The Donner Party; Five Came Back; K2; The Snows of Kilimanjaro; The Sands of the Kalahari; The Flight of the Phoenix)

Alive and Kicking, 1958, 94m, ★★★/$, E-L/NA. Three little old ladies escape from a rest home to live together on an island near Ireland. Estelle Winwood, Sybil Thorndike, Kathleen Harrison, Stanley Holloway, Joyce Carey. w. Denis Cannan, d. Cyril Frankel.
COMEDY DRAMA: DRAMA: Elderly Women; Escape Adventures; British Films; Ireland; Islands
(Going in Style; Fried Green Tomatoes; Strangers in Good Company)

All About Eve (B&W), 1950, 138m, ★★★★/$$$$, 20th/Fox. Young protege actress (Anne Baxter, BActress) tries to upstage her veteran mentor (Bette Davis, BActress) on-stage and off through clever means, becoming the monster she wants to subsume. Celeste Holm (BSActress), Thelma Ritter (BSActress), Gary Merrill (BSActor), George Sanders (**BSActor**). w. d. Joseph Mankiewicz (**BDirector, BScr**). **BPicture,** BEdit, BB&WCin, BB&WArt, **BSound,** BOScore, **BB&W Costume.** Oscars: 14-6, all-time nomination record
DRAMA: MELODRAMA: Understudies/Proteges; Feuds; Women in Conflict; Actresses; Mean Women; Evil Women; Feisty Females; Theater Life; Revenge; Liars; Mid-Life Crisis; Jealousy; Female Protagonists; Stories Which Begin Again; Writer-Directors
(Valley of the Dolls; Anna; 42nd Street; The Turning Point)

The All-American Boy, 1974, 118m, ★★1/2/$, WB/WB-NA, R/EV-S-FN-MN. A young boxer (Jon Voight) makes it up the regional ranks quickly, trying to maintain a relationship along the way. Anne Archer, Carol Androsky. w. d. Charles Eastman.
DRAMA: ROMANCE: Romance-Reluctant; Love-First; Character Studies; Boxing; Sports Movies; Fame-Rise to; Young Men; Dreams; Writer-Directors
(Stay Hungry; Homeboy; Raging Bull)

The All-American Murder, 1991, 94m, ★★/$, Prism/Prism, R/V-P. A college student is accused of murder and has a day to find out who really did it. Charlie Schlatter, Christopher Walken, Josie Bisset, Joanna Cassidy, Richard Kind. w. Barry Sandler, d. Anson Williams.
SUSPENSE: MYSTERY: MURDER: MUR-DER MYSTERY: College Life; Race Against Time; One Day Stories; Accused Unjustly?; Framed?

Allan Quatermain and the Lost City of Gold, 1986, 99m, ★★/$$, Cannon/MGM-UA, PG. Adventurer Quatermain goes on a quest for his missing brother who's gone on a quest for a missing white tribe in Africa. Richard Chamberlain, Sharon Stone, James Earl Jones. w. Gene Quintano, d. Gary Nelson.
ADVENTURE: COMEDY: Comic Adventure; Missing Persons; Quests; Africa; Unintentionally Funny

REMAKE OF: King Solmon's Treasure; **SEQUEL** to King Solomon's Mines (1985)

All Creatures Great and Small, 1974, 92m, ★★★/$$, EMI/Fox. A veterinarian travels the English countryside helping man and animal alike. Anthony Hopkins, Simon Ward, Lisa Harrow, Freddie Jones. w. Hugh Whitemore, N-adap. James Herriot, d. Claude Whatham.
COMEDY DRAMA: MELODRAMA: Feel-Good Films; **FAMILY:** Old-Fashioned Recent Films; Veterinarians; Animal Stories; Doctors; England; Rural Life; British Films
SEQUELS: It Shouldn't Happen to a Vet; All Things Bright and Beautiful
(Dr. Dolittle; The Three Lives of Thomasina)

All Dogs Go to Heaven, 1989, 84m, ★★★/$$$, UA/MGM-UA, G. A dog who was killed by a Mob hit dog comes back to get his revenge. Voices of Burt Reynolds, Dom DeLuise, Vic Tayback, Loni Anderson, Charles Nelson Reilly. w. David Weiss, d. Don Bluth.
CHILDREN'S: Cartoons; **FAMILY:** Heaven; Angels; Dead-Back from the; Mob Stories; Animal Stories; Animals in Jeopardy; Revenge; Hitmen
(Heaven Can Wait; The Heavenly Kid; Oliver & Co.; Lady & the Tramp)
SEQUEL: 1996

Allegro Non Troppo, 1976, 75m, ★★★/$ (LR), BMG/BMG. Animated interpretations of great symphonies in homage to Disney. w. d. Bruno Bozzetto.
Fantasy; Cartoons; Musicians; Music Video Style
(Fantasia; Aria)

All Fall Down, 1962, 111m, ★★★/$$, MGM/MGM-UA. When a drifter comes home to stay with his family, his affair with an older woman causes tensions that could lead to murder. Brandon de Wilde, Warren Beatty, Angela Lansbury, Eva Marie Saint, Constance Ford. w. William Inge, d. John Frankenheimer.
DRAMA: TRAGEDY: Family Drama; **MURDER:** Crimes of Passion; Drifters; Young Men-Angry; Small-Town Life; Romance-Older Women/Younger Men; Brothers; Coming of Age; Illusions Destroyed; Midwestern Life
(Hud; Picnic; The Dark at the Top of the Stairs; Splendor in the Grass)

Alligator, 1980, 94m, ★★★/$, Ind/Live, R/V-P. Giant alligator emerges to wreak havoc on a city years after it's flushed as

a pet down the toilet. Robert Forster, Michael Gazzo, Dean Jagger. w. John Sayles, Lewis Teague.
HORROR: Horror Comedy; Spoofs; Animal Monsters; Black Comedy; Kill the Beast; Murders-One by One; Alligators; Ind Films

Alligator II: The Mutation, 1991, 92m, ★★/$, Col/Col, R/V-P. This time, toxic waste has made the alligator from the sewers bigger than ever. Joseph Bologna, Dee Wallace Stone, Steve Railsback. w. Curt Allen, d. Jon Hess.
HORROR: Horror Comedy; Spoofs; Animal Monsters; Black Comedy; Kill the Beast; Murders-One by One; Alligators
SEQUEL TO: Alligator
(Piranha; Killer Fish; Tentacles)

An Alligator Named Daisy, 1955, 88m, ★★¹/₂/$$, Rank/NA. A songwriter is beset with a pet alligator that likes to hide in pianos and wreck his romances. Donald Sindon, Diana Dors, Stanley Holloway, Margaret Rutherford. w. Jack Davies, N-adap Charles Terrot, d. J. Lee-Thompson.
COMEDY: COMEDY DRAMA: Comedy of Errors; Animal Stories; Fish out of Water Stories; Pet Stories; Alligators; British Films
(Troublesome Pets; Clarence the Cross-Eyed Lion; Turner and Hooch; The Ugly Dachshund; Beethoven)

The Alligator People, 1959, 74m, ★★/$$, 20th/NA. A vaccination turns recipients into alligators like those it was derived from. George Macready, Beverly Garland. w. Orville Hampton, d. Roy del Ruth.
HORROR: SCI-FI: Humans into Animals; Animal Monsters; Unintentionally Funny; Alligators
(Sssss)

All in a Night's Work, 1961, 94m, ★★★/$$, UA/MGM-UA. Secretary gets mink coat through misunderstanding with her boss while on vacation that implicates her as being less than virtuous. Shirley MacLaine, Dean Martin. w. Edmund Beloin, Maurice Richlin, Sidney Sheldon, d. Joseph Anthony.
COMEDY: Romantic Comedy; Office Comedy; Misunderstandings; Female Protagonists; Secretaries; Romance with the Boss
(Easy Living; That Touch of Mink; The Solid Gold Cadillac)

All I Want for Christmas, 1991, 92m, ★★/$$, Par/Par, G. Two kids want their parents to get back together for Christmas and set out to get their wish. Ethan Randall, Harley Jane Kozak, James Sheridan, Lauren Bacall. w. Thom Eberhardt, Richard Allan Kramer, d. Richard Lieberman
COMEDY DRAMA: MELODRAMA: Christmas; Divorce; Child Protagonists; Reunions
(The Parent Trap; One Magic Christmas)

All My Sons, 1949, 122m, ★★★¹/₂/$$, U/MCA-U. Man tries to deal with death of his son in a war plane he may have manufactured faulty parts for. Burt Lancaster, Edward G. Robinson. w. Chester Erskine, P-adap. Arthur Miller, d. Irving Reis.

All My Sons, 1986, 122m, AP-PBS-TV/MCA-U, ★★★/$$, Aidan Quinn, James Whitmore, Joan Allen. P-adap. Arthur Miller, d. John Power.
DRAMA: TRAGEDY: Social Drama; Family Drama; World War II Era; Murder-Debate to Confess; Fathers & Sons; Ethics; Corruption; TV Movies; Sabotage
(Death of a Salesman)

The Allnighter, 1987, 94m, ★¹/₂/$, U/MCA-U, R/P-S-FN. A trio of college girls party their way out of senior year. Susanna Hoffs, John Cusack, Michael Ontkean, Pam Grier. w. MI Kessler, Tamara Hoffs, d. Hoffs.
COMEDY: Party Movies; College Life; Young Women; Teenage Movies; Female Protagonists; Female Directors
(Private School; The Pleasure Seekers)

All Night Long, 1961, 95m, ★★¹/₂/$, Rank/NA. A musician attempts killing his wife in the belief she's cheating on him-a rumor started as a lie by a rival. Patrick McGoohan, Richard Attenborough, Betsy Blair. w. Nel King, Peter Achilles, d. Basil Dearden.
DRAMA: TRAGEDY: Jealousy; Cheating Women; Musicians; Revisionist Films
REMAKE/UPDATING: Othello
(Othello; Unfaithfully Yours)

All Night Long, 1981, 88m, ★★★¹/₂/$$, Universal/MCA-U, R/P-S. Executive demoted to all-night store falls for the older mistress of his young son. Gene Hackman, Barbra Streisand, Kevin Dobson, Dennis Quaid. w. W.D. Richter, d. Jean-Claude Tramont.
COMEDY DRAMA: Romantic Comedy; Comedy-Light; Romance-Older

Women/Younger Men; Romance with Relative's Lover; Romance-Forbidden; Working Class; Cheating Women; Country Singers; Bimbos; Simple Minds; Risking it All; Ordinary People Stories; Hidden Gems; Underrated
(Petulia; Middle-Age Crazy; Twice in a Lifetime)

All of Me, 1984, 93m, ★★★/$$$, Universal/MCA-U, PG. A goofy lawyer (Steve Martin, BActor, NYFC) becomes half-possessed by cranky, rich, dying heiress (Lily Tomlin) who wanted to be reincarnated, only not into him. The question is how to get her out of his system. Victoria Tenant, Dana Elcar. w. Phil Alden Robinson, d. Carl Reiner.
COMEDY: Romantic Comedy; Body Switching; Screwball Comedy; Old-Fashioned Recent Films; Role Reversals; Rich People; Mean Women; Romance-Mismatched; Reincarnation; Magic; Con Artists; Inheritances at Stake; Multiple Performances; Multiple Personalities; Lawyers
(Heart Condition; Switch)
(Ed: Why aren't Carl Reiner's other films this good? Could it be the script that made the difference?)

All Quiet on the Western Front, 1930, 130m, ★★★★/$$$$, Universal/MCA-U. German soldier sees through the glory of war to its evils. Lew Ayres. w. Lewis Milestone, Maxwell Anderson, George Abbott (BScr), N-adap. E. M. Remarque, d. Lewis Milestone (**BDirector**).
BPicture, BCin. Oscars: 4-2.
DRAMA: World War I Movies; War Movies; War Battles; Ethics; Coming of Age; Young Men; Death-Dealing with
REMAKE: TV (1979)
(Grand Illusion; The Red Badge of Courage; Wings)

All That Heaven Allows, 1955, 89m, ★★½/$$$, U/MCA-U. A wealthy, sophisticated woman (Jane Wyman) falls in love with her simple-minded gardener (Rock Hudson) no matter what the neighbors think. w. Peg Fenwick, d. Douglas Sirk.
ROMANCE: MELODRAMA: Tearjerkers; Romance-Mismatched; Romance-Older Women/Younger Men; Class Conflicts; Romance-Lover Family Dislikes; Mentally Disabled; Simple Minds; Female Screenwriters
REMAKE: Ali-Fear Eats the Soul
(Tim; Being There; Magnificent Obsession [1954])

All That Jazz, 1979, 123m, ★★★½/$$$, 20th-Columbia/CBS-Fox, R/P-S-FN. A director of musicals' life begins coming apart as he anticipates death after a heart attack. Roy Scheider (BActor), Anne Reinking, Jessica Lange. w. d. Bob Fosse (BOScr, Director). BPicture, BCin, **BArt**, BEdit, BAScore, BCostume. Oscars: 9-4.
MUSICAL: DRAMA: Musical Drama; Autobiographical Stories; Theater Life; Death-Impending; Death-Dealing With; Death-Personified; Angels; Flashbacks
(Cabaret; Sweet Charity; Faded Hits)

All That Money Can Buy (*The Devil and Daniel Webster*), 1941, 106m, ★★★★/$$$, RKO/Turner. A farmer tries to sell his soul to the devil but before he has to give it up, he gets a trial and a very good lawyer. Walter Huston (BActor), James Craig, Anne Shirley, Edward Arnold, Jane Darwell, Gene Lockhart. w. Dan Totheroh, SS-adap. Stephen Vincent Benet, d. William Dieterle. **BOScore**. Oscars: 2-1.
DRAMA: COMEDY DRAMA: SATIRE: Selling One's Soul; Farm Life; 1800s; Courtroom Drama; Lawyers; Satan; Hidden Gems; Faded Hits
(Angel on My Shoulder; Dr. Faustus; Faust; Mister Frost; The Devil and Max Devlin)

All the Fine Young Cannibals, 1960, 112m, ★★★/$$, MGM/NA. The story of musician Chet Baker (Robert Wagner) is loosely told and elaborated upon as the young, ambitious, glamourous clique he lived with is melodramatized in technicolor. Natalie Wood, George Hamilton, Susan Kohner, Pearl Bailey. w. Robert Thom, N-adap. Rosamond Marshall, *The Bixby Girls*, d. Michael Anderson.
DRAMA: MELODRAMA: Biographies; Biographies Fictional; Romance-Triangles; Brothers & Sisters; Incest; Musicians; Beautiful People; Camp
(Home from the Hill; The Subterraneans; The Beat Generation; Let's Get Lost)
(Ed: Much-maligned for its clichés, it's a glossy, sometimes campy, good ole soap opera)

All the Brothers Were Valiant, 1953, 101m, ★★½/$$, MGM/MGM-UA. Brothers fight and squabble on a whaling ship until they have to work together to survive. Stewart Granger, Robert Taylor, Ann Blyth, Kenan Wynn, James Whitmore, Lewis Stone. w. Harry Brown, N-adap. Ben Ames Williams, d. Richard Thorpe.
DRAMA: MELODRAMA: Men in Conflict; Sibling Rivalry; Brothers; Ships; Adventure at Sea; Fishermen; 1800s

All the King's Men (B&W), 1949, 109m, ★★★★/$$$, Columbia/RCA-Col. Southern politician (based on Huey P. Long) is out of control with pork barrel politics and greed as his power grows. Broderick Crawford (**BActor**), John Ireland (BSActor), Mercedes McCambridge (**BSActress**). w. Robert Rossen (**BAScr**), N-adap. Robert Penn Warren, d. Robert Rossen (BDirector). **BPicture, BEdit**. Oscars: 7-5.
DRAMA: Political Drama; Biographies-Fictional; Southerns; Louisiana; Corruption; Power-Rise to Politicians; Ethic; Pulitzer Prize Adaptations
(The King Fish; A Face in the Crowd; Citizen Kane; Blaze; The Last Hurrah)

All The Marbles, 1980, 113m, ★★/$$, MGM/MGM-UA, PG/P-S. A man running a women's wrestling team hopes of going to the bigtime in Vegas. Peter Falk, Vicki Frederick, Laurene Landon, Burt Young. w. Mel Frohman, d. Robert Aldrich.
COMEDY: COMEDY DRAMA: Sports Movies; Role Reversals; Wrestling; Working Class; Underdog Stories

All the Mornings of the World (Tous Les Matins du Monde), 1992, 115m, ★★★/$$$, Orion/Orion, R/S-FN-MRN. The court composer for Louis XIV recalls his strict master and his ill-fated attempt at seducing his teacher's daughter. Gerard Depardieu, Jean-Pierre Marielle, Anne Brochet, Guillaume Depardieu, Caroline Sihol, Carole Richert, Violaine Lacroix, Nadege Teron. w. Pascal Quignard, Alain Corenau, N-adap. Pascal Quignard, d. Alain Corneau.
DRAMA: ROMANCE: Romantic Drama; Romance-Doomed; Episodic Stories; Historical Drama; Memories; Music Composers; Kings; Royalty; Narrated Films; French Films
(Impromptu; Amadeus; Farinelli)

All the President's Men, 1976, 138m, ★★★★/$$$$, #3 1976, WB/WB, PG. Rookie reporters uncover the scandal of the century when the Watergate burglary is botched and they get inside information. Robert Redford, Dustin Hoffman, Jason Robards (**BSActor**), Jane Alexander (BSActress). w. William Goldman (**BAScr**), NF-adap. Bob

Woodward, Carl Bernstein, d. Alan Pakula (BDirector). BPicture, BArt, BEdit. Oscars: 7-4.

MYSTERY: DRAMA: Political Drama; Political Thriller; Detective Stories; Journalists as Detectives; Journalists; Corruption; Washington D.C.; Conspiracy; Ethics; Buddy Films; Blockbusters
(The Parallax View; Quiz Show)

All the Right Moves, 1983, 91m, ★★1/2/$$, 20th/CBS-Fox, PG/P-S. Football player in mining town hopes to get out of town on a scholarship despite trouble with the coach. Tom Cruise, Craig T. Nelson. w. Michael Kane, d. Michael Chapman.

DRAMA: Sports Movies; Football; Working Class; Underdog Stories; Dreams; Coming of Age; Poor People; Small-Town Life; American Dream; Mining Towns
(Rudy; Risky Business; Breaking Away)

All the Vermeers in New York, 1992m, 87m, ★★★/$, AP-Goldwyn/ Goldwyn. A Wall Streeter eases tensions looking at paintings, particularly Vermeers in the Metropolitan Museum, where he meets a beautiful French actress. Their romance parallels the corruption and delusions of New York itself, as illusory as the paintings. Stephen Lack, Emmanuelle Chaulet, Grace Phillips, Katherine Bean. w. d. Jon Jost.

DRAMA: ROMANCE: Romantic Drama; Art Films; Artists; Museums; New York Life; Writer-Directors
(Naked in New York; New York Stories; Slaves of New York)

All the Way Home, 1963, 103m, ★★★1/2/$$, Par/NA. When a patriarch of a Southern family is killed, the mother has to scrape by with the kids by whatever means necessary. Robert Preston, Jean Simmons, Aline MacMahon, Pat Hingle, Michael Kearney. w. Philip Reisman, P-adap. Tad Mosel, N-adap. James Agee, *A Death in the Family*, d. Alex Segal.

DRAMA: TRAGEDY: MELODRAMA: Southerns; Family Drama; Mothers-Struggling; Widows; Death-Dealing with; Biographies-Fictional; Autobiographical Stories; Ordinary People Stories; Quiet Little Films; Coulda Been Great; Writers; Pulitzer Prize Adaptations
(Places in the Heart; The Glass Menagerie; A Woman of Independent Means)
(Ed: Could have been a classic, but the style is a bit too staid all the way around)

All the Way Up, 1970, 97m, ★★/$$, EMI/NA, PG. A father makes it up the ladder any way he can in England, stepping on whomever's in the way-until his son moves in to compete with him. Warren Mitchell, Pat Heywood, Elaine Taylor. w. Philip Mackie, P-adap. David Turner, *Semi-Detached*, d. James MacTaggart.

DRAMA: COMEDY DRAMA: Black Comedy; **FARCE: SATIRE:** Social Climbing; Fathers & Sons; Men in Conflict; Generation Gaps; Social Drama; Social Satire; Betrayals; Mindgames
(Wall Street; The Man in the Grey Flannel Suit; Patterns; The Garment Jungle; Executive Suite)

All the Young Men, 1960, 87m, ★★/$$, Col/RCA-Col. A black man is in charge of mostly white men in the Korean War and racial tensions add to that of the fighting. Sidney Poitier, Alan Ladd, James Darren, Mort Sahl. w. d. Hal Bartlett.

DRAMA: Social Drama; War Movies; War Battles; Korean War; Black vs. White; Black Among Whites; Race Relations; Bigots; Soldiers; Writer-Directors
(Mark of the Hawk; Master Harold and the Boys; The Defiant Ones)

All This and Heaven, Too, 1940, 143m, ★★★/$$$$, WB/WB. A French aristocrat (Charles Boyer) develops a passion for his governess and then plots to murder his wife so she won't divorce or scandalize him. Bette Davis, Barbara O'Neil, Virginia Weidler, Jeffrey Lynn. w. Casey Robinson, N-adap Rachel Field, d. Anatole Litvak.

DRAMA: SUSPENSE: MURDER: ROMANCE: MELODRAMA: Cheating Men; Murder of Spouse; Rich People; Rich People-Decadent; Romance-Triangles; Babysitters
(Gaslight; Leave Her to Heaven)

All This and World War II, 1976, 88m, ★★1/2/$ 20th/CBS-Fox. Newreel footage of the war together with film clips and songs of the era. w. d. Susan Winslow. Documentary; Filmumentaries; World War II Movies; World War II Era; Nostalgia

All Through the Night, 1942, 107m, ★★★/$$$, WB/MGM-UA. The mob takes on Nazi spies and American traitors in wartime New York. Humphrey Bogart, Conrad Veidt, Peter Lorre, Judith Anderson, Jackie Gleason, William Demarest, Phil Silvers. w. Leonard Spiegelgass, Edwin Gilbert, d. Vincent Sherman.

COMEDY DRAMA: Action Comedy; Crime Drama; Mob Stories; Mob Wars; Spies; Nazi Stories; World War II Era; Fugitives from the Mob; Traitors (Saboteur; The Rocketeer; Across the Pacific)

All You Need Is Cash (*The Rutles*), 1978, 70m, ★★★/$$, Ind/Music Video Dist. A parody of rockumentaries tracing the rise of the fab four group The Rutles, as opposed to the Beatles, starring Monty Pythoners. Eric Idle, Neil Innes, Gilda Radner, Dan Aykroyd, John Belushi, George Harrison, Paul Simon, Mick Jagger. w. d. Eric Idle, Gary Weis.

COMEDY: Spoofs; Spoofs-Documentary; Rockumentaries; Musicians; Biographies; Biographies-Fictional; British Films; Cult Films; Monty Pythoners
(This Is Spinal Tap; Fear of a Black Hat)

Almost a Man, 1978, 51m, ★★★/$$, PBS/Karl-Lorimar. Coming of age story about a young black migrant farm worker in the Depression. LeVar Burton, Madge Sinclair, Robert Dogui. SS-adap. Richard Wright.

DRAMA: Black Casts; Black Men; Coming of Age; Farm Life; Depression Era; Classic Literary Adaptations; TV Movies
(Sounder; Nothing But a Man; Roots)

Almost an Angel, 1990, 95m, ★★/$$, Par/Par, PG. A thief somehow makes it heaven and comes back as an angel to set things straight. Paul Hogan, Elias Koteas, Linda Koslowski, Doreen Lang. w. Hogan, d. John Cornell.

COMEDY: Comedy-Light; Dead-Back from the; Thieves; Heaven; Angels; Coulda Been Good; Good Premise Unfulfilled
(Heaven Can Wait; The Heavenly Kid; Crocodile Dundee)

Almost Angels, 1962, 93m, ★★★/$$, Disney/Disney. A boy makes it into the Vienna boys' choir and sings his little high-pitched heart out. Vincent Winter, Peter Weck. w. Vernon Harris, R. A. Stemmle, d. Steven Previn.

DRAMA: MELODRAMA: FAMILY: CHILDREN'S: Singers; Vienna; Boyhood
(Farinelli; The Miracle of the White Stallions)

An Almost Perfect Affair, 1979, 93m, ★★1/2/$, Par/Par, R/S. A film producer

(Keith Carradine) goes to the Cannes film festival and romances the wife of an Italian producer there (Monica Vitti). w. Walter Bernstein, Don Peterson, d. Michael Ritchie.

ROMANCE: DRAMA: Romantic Drama; Erotic Drama; Riviera Life; Americans Abroad; Romance on Vacation; Romance-Triangles; Hollywood Life; Italians
(A Man in Love; Quartet)

Almost Pregnant, 1991, 90m, ★★1/2/$$, Ind/Col, R/ES-FN. A sexy young woman wants to get pregnant so desperately, but her husband is sterile, so they decide to try out all of his friends for the position of surrogate father. Tanya Roberts, Kevin Conway, Joan Severance, Dom DeLuise. w. Fred Stroppel, d. Michael DeLuise.

COMEDY: Marriage Comedy; Sex Comedy; Erotic Comedy; Babies-Having; Surrogate-Fathers; Sexual Problems; Coulda Been Good; TV Movies; Ind Films
(Ed: A 60s sex comedy gone trashy cable)

Almost You, 1984, 96m, ★★1/2/$, 20th/Fox, R/S. When a yuppie couples' life is altered by a car wreck, the wife's injuries require a nurse, which leads to even more problems. Brooke Adams, Griffin Dunne, Josh Mostel, Karen Young, Laura Dean, Dana Delaney, Spalding Gray. w. Johnathan Elias, d. Adam Brooks.

COMEDY DRAMA: Marriage Comedy; **ROMANCE:** Romantic Comedy; New York Life; Yuppies
(Love Matters; The Promise)

Aloha, Bobby and Rose, 1975, 85m, ★★1/2/$$$, WB/WB, R/S-V. An ordinary working guy (Paul LeMat) is an innocent bystander caught up with criminals and winds up headed for Mexico with his girlfriend. Dianne Hull, Robert Carradine. w. d. Floyd Mutrux.

ACTION: Action Drama; Crime Drama; **MURDER:** Road Movies; Outlaw Road Movies; Fugitives; Fugitives from the Law; Fugitives form the Mob; Crossing the Border; Los Angeles; Ordinary People vs. Criminals; Ordinary People Stories; Ordinary Person Turned Criminal; Writer-Directors
(They Live by Night; True Romance; Badlands; Bonnie and Clyde)

Aloha Summer, 1988, 98m, ★1/2/$, WB/WB. A teenager spends the summer in Hawaii and comes of age with some politically correct lessons thrown in.

Chris Makepeace, Tia Carrere, Yuji Okumoto. w. Mike Greco, d. Timmy Lee Wallace.

DRAMA: Teenage Movies; Teenagers; Summer Vacation; Hawaii; Coming of Age; Love-First
(California Dreaming; North End; My Bodyguard)

Alone in the Dark, 1982, 92m, ★★/$, NL/NL, R/P-EV. Mental patients break out of the asylum and wreak havoc. Jack Palance, Martin Landau, Dwight Schultz, Donald Pleasance. w. d. Jack Sholder.

HORROR: Asylums; Psycho Killers; Stalkers; Mental Illness; Prison Escapes; Serial Killers; Writer-Directors; Blackouts
(Asylum; Halloween)

Along Came Jones, 1945, 90m, ★★1/2/$$, UA/MGM-UA. Two cowboys are unwitting bystanders to murder and wind-up being accused themselves. Gary Cooper, William Demarest, Loretta Young, Dan Duryea, Russel Simpson. w. Nunnally Johnson, N-adap. Alan LeMay, d. Stuart Heisler.

WESTERN: COMEDY DRAMA: MURDER: Fugitives from the Law; Accused Unjustly?; Framed?; Cowboys; Mistaken Identities

Along the Great Divide, 1951, 88m, ★★1/2/$$, WB/WB. A marshal wants to find the real murderer in a case and prevents the hanging of the wrong man before finding him. Kirk Douglas, Virginia Mayo, Walter Brennan, John Agar. w. Walter Doniger, Lewis Meltzer, d. Raoul Walsh.

WESTERN: DRAMA: MURDER: MURDER MYSTERY: Accused Unjustly?; Detectives-Police; Saving Someone
(The Ox-Bow Incident)

The Alphabet Murders, 1966, 90m, ★★/$, MGM/MGM-UA. The great Poirot is on another case where the killer has decided to go in alphabetical order. Tony Randall, Robert Morley, Anita Ekberg, Maurice Denham. w. David Pursall, Jack Sedden, N-adap. Agatha Christie (*The ABC Murders*), d. Frank Tashlin.

MYSTERY: MURDER: MURDER MYSTERY: COMEDY: Comic Mystery; Mystery-Whodunits; Agatha Christie; Detective Stories; Clever Plots & Endings; Coulda Been Great; Flops-Major
(And Then There Were None; Ten Little Indians; Death on the Nile; Murder on the Orient Express; Evil Under the Sun)

(Ed: Tony Randall's miscasting plus the muddling of a sharp plot with comic asides spelled disaster)

Alphaville, 1965, 100m, ★★★/$$, CinemaV/Nos, Sinister. A secret agent from the present travels into outer space to an alternate universe in the future and instead of finding a colleague finds a cold, harsh world. Eddie Constantine, Anna Karina, Akim Tamiroff, Howard Vernon. w. d. Jean-Luc Godard.

DRAMA: SATIRE: MYSTERY: SCI-FI: Fantasy; Futuristic Films; Art Films; Avant-Garde Films; Missing Persons; Computers; Oppression; Alienation; French Films; French New Wave Films; Outer Space Movies; Writer-Directors
(Fahrenheit 451; Journey to the Far Side of the Sun)

Alpine Fire, 1987, 117m, ★★1/2/$, Vestron/Vestron, R/S-FN-MN. A sister and her deaf brother are all alone on a Swiss farm and begin a relationship in the barn. Thomas Nock, Johnanna Lier. w. d. N-adap. Fredi Murer.

DRAMA: ROMANCE: Romance-Forbidden; Incest; Brothers and Sisters; Deaf People; French Films; Art Films; Alps; Writer-Directors; Ind Films
(Beau Pere; All the Fine Young Cannibals; Luna; Les Enfants Terribles; Murmur of the Heart)
(Ed: The title is just a bit inappropriately lurid considering the subject matter)

Alsino and the Condor, 1982, 89m, ★★★/$$, Ind/Facets. During the Nicaraguan regime of Somoza, a young boy dreams about flying above all of the problems like a condor. Dean Stockwell, Alan Esquivel. d. Miguel Littin.

DRAMA: Fantasy; Allegorical Stories; Social Drama; War Stories; Central America; Boys; Dreams; Fantasies
(The Boy Who Could Fly; El Norte)

Altered States, 1980, 102m, ★★★/$$$, WB/WB, R/P-S-V-FN-MN. Scientist gets involved with sensory deprivation chambers and halucinogenics, resulting in some bad trips taking him right to his soul and possibly death. William Hurt, Blair Brown, Charles Haid. w. N-adap. Paddy Chayefsky (Sidney Aaron), d. Ken Russell. BSound, BOScore.

DRAMA: SCI-FI: Psychological Drama; Hypothetical Stories; Scientists; Professors; Experiments; Drugs; Heaven; Hell; Marriage on the Rocks; Boston

(The Fly; Brainstorm [1983]; The Time Machine)

Alvarez Kelly, 1966, 116m, ★★1/2/$$, Col/RCA-Col. A cattle rancher winds up caught between two sides of the Civil War closing in. William Holden, Richard Widmark, Janice Rule, Patrick O'Neal. w. Franklin Coen, d. Edward Dmytryk.
DRAMA: WESTERN: Civil War Era; Cattle Ranchers; Texas
(Red River; Bad Company)

Alvin Purple, 1973, 97m, ★★1/2/$$$, AIP/New World, R/S-P-FN-MRN. A young man who is somehow irresistible to well-endowed women keeps losing jobs until he becomes a window-washer at a convent. Graeme Blundell, Abigail, Lynette Curran. w. Alan Hopgood, d. Tim Burstall.
COMEDY: Erotic Comedy; FARCE: Sexy Men; Sexy Women; Nuns; Teenage Movies; Promscuity; Australian Films
SEQUEL: Alvin Rides Again
(Alvin Rides Again; The Bawdy Adventures of Tom Jones; Alfie, Darling)

Alvin Rides Again, 1974, 89m, ★★/$$, AIP/New World, R/S-P-FFN-MRN. Alvin's up to it again. Graeme Blundell, Alan Finney, Abigail. w. Alan Hopgood, d. David Bilcock, Robin Copping.
COMEDY: Erotic Comedy; FARCE: Sexy Men; Sexy Women; Teenage Movies; Promscuity; Australian Films
SEQUEL TO: Alvin Purple
(Ed: Not as good as the first, which wasn't so good. Title's intent is dissimilar to *Herbie Rides Again*)

Always, 1989, 121m, ★★★/$$, Universal/MCA-U, PG/S. A firefighter pilot is encouraged by a dead pilot's ghost into being with the ghost's ex-girlfriend. Richard Dreyfuss, Holly Hunter, Audrey Hepburn, Brad Johnson. w. Jerry Belson, Diane Thomas, d. Steven Spielberg.
ROMANCE: DRAMA: Romantic Drama; Pilots; Heaven; Angels; Ghosts; Death-Dealing with; Female Screenwriters
REMAKE OF: A Guy Named Joe
(Ghost; Blithe Spirit; Kiss Me Goodbye; Truly Madly Deeply)

Always Goodbye, 1938, 75m, ★★/$$$, 20th/NA. An unwed mother gives her baby up for adoption but then later wants it back and has to deal with the consequences. Barbara Stanwyck, Herbert Marshall, Ian Hunter, Cesar Romero, LynnBari. w. Kathryn Scola, Edith Skouras, d. Sidney Lanfield.

DRAMA: MELODRAMA: Social Drama; Tearjerkers; Mothers-Uwed; Children-Adopted; Babies-Having; Depression Era; Poor People; Female Screenwriters
REMAKE OF: Gallant Lady
(Losing Isaiah; White Banners; Gallant Lady; Bad Girl; To Find a Man; Back Roads)

Always in My Heart, 1942, 92m, ★★★/$$, WB/WB. A man gets out of prison to return home and find his daughter grown and about ready to marry. Walter Huston, Kay Francis, Gloria Warren, Una O'Connor. w. Adele Commandini, P-adap. Dorothy Bennett, Irving White (*Fly Away Home*), d. Joe Graham.
DRAMA: MELODRAMA: Fathers & Daughters; Reunions; Ex-Convicts; Episodic Stories; Female Screenwriters

Always Leave Them Laughing, 1949, 116m, ★★/$$, WB/WB. A vaudevillian comic puts everything into his career, even as it's fading. Milton Berle, Bert Lahr, Virginia Mayo, Ruth Roman, Alan Hale. w. Jack Rose, Mel Shavelson, d. Roy del Ruth.
DRAMA: MELODRAMA: Character Studies; Comedians Vaudeville
(The Entertainer; The Comic; Tribute)

Always Together, 1948, 78m, ★★★/$$, WB/WB. A millionaire leaves his money to a shop girl (Joyce Reynolds) but when he doesn't die, he has many problems as a result. Robert Hutton, Cecil Kellaway, Humphrey Bogart, Errol Flynn. w. Henry & Phoebe Ephron, IAL Diamond, d. Fred DeCordova.
COMEDY: Screwball Comedy; Inheritances at Stake; ROMANCE: Romantic Comedy; Death-Impending; Underrated; Overlooked; Forgotten Films; All-Star Cameos; Female Screenwriters

Amadeus, 1984, 158m, ★★★★/$$$, Orion/Orion, R/S. The legend of the music prodigy Mozart's relationship with the tyrannical and jealous rival Salieri (F. Murray Abraham, **BActor**) and the role he may have played in the young genius' (Tom Hulce, **BActor**) premature death. Jeffrey Jones, Elizabeth Berridge. w. P-adap, Peter Schaffer (**BAScr**), d. Milos Forman (**BDirector**). **BPicture, BCinema, BArt**, BEditing, **BCostume, B Sound.** Oscars: 10-8.
DRAMA: Biographies; Understudies/Proteges; Feuds; Men in Conflict; Friendships-Male; Jealousy; Musicians;

Music Composers; Vienna; Operas; Production Design-Outstanding (Impromptu; All the Mornings in the World; Farinelli; Valmont; Dangerous Liaisons)

Amarcord, 1974, 127m, ★★★1/2/$$$, Par/Par, R/S. The story of director Federico Fellini's small hometown in Italy and the people he knew there growing up. Magali Noel, Bruno Zamin. w. d. Federico Fellini (BOScr, BDirector). BFFilm. Oscars: 3-1.
DRAMA: MELODRAMA: Art Film; Coming of Age; Small-Town Life; Interwoven Stories; Multiple Stories; Writer-Directors
(La Strada; Intervista; Cinema Paradiso; My Sweet Little Village)

The Amateur, 1982, 112m, ★★1/2/$, 20th/Fox, R/V-P. A CIA computer expert travels into intrigue and danger when his girlfriend is killed and he wants to find the culprit. John Savage, Christopher Plummer, Marthe Keller, Arthur Hill, Ed Lauter. d. Charles Jarrott.
SUSPENSE: ACTION: Action Drama; Central America; MURDER: MYSTERY: MURDER MYSTERY: CIA Agents; Detective Stories; Detectives-Amateurs; Surveillance

Amateur Night at the Dixie Bar and Grill, 1979, 100m, ★★★/$$$, CBS/NA. It's talent night at a Southern honkytonk and several people are hinging dreams on it. Candy Clark, Don Johnson, Dennis Quaid, Henry Gibson, Victor French. w. d. Joel Schumacher
COMEDY DRAMA: COMEDY: Dreams; Country Music; Southerns; Contests; Ordinary People Stories; Writer-Directors; TV Movies
(Nashville; Honky Tonk Freeway)

The Amazing Dr. Clitterhouse, 1938, 87m, ★★★1/2/$$, WB/WB. A sociologist joins the mob to learn about its ways from the inside but becomes hooked on the money and power. Humphrey Bogart, Edward G. Robinson, Claire Trevor, Donald Crisp. w. John Huston, John Wexley, P-adap. Barre Lyndon, d. Anatole Litvak.
DRAMA: Crime Drama; Mob Stories; Ordinary People Turned Criminal; Character Studies; Gambling; Professors; Sociologists
(Bullets or Ballots; Kansas City Confidential; They Live by Night; Shoeshine; I Stole a Million)

Amazing Grace and Chuck, 1987, 115m, ★★/$, Tri-Star/RCA-Col PG. A little boy writes a letter to Amazing Grace, a famous basketball player, and soon everyone's talking about nuclear disarmament. Jamie Lee Curtis, Gregory Peck, Alex English, William Petersen, Joshua Zuehike. w. David Field, d. Mike Newell.
DRAMA: MELODRAMA: Social Drama; Feelgood Films; Nuclear Energy; Bombs-Atomic; Boys and Men; Message Films; Basketball

The Amazing Howard Hughes, 1977, 119m, ★★★/$$$, CBS/MGM-UA, Facets. Biopic of the eccentric millionaire magnate from his opulent beginnings through his Hollywood escapades and up to his reclusive end. Tommy Lee Jones.
DRAMA: Biographies; True Stories; Rich People; Lonely People; Eccentric People; Hollywood Life; Hollywood Biographies; TV Movies
(Melvin and Howard)

The Amazing Mr. Blunden, 1972, 100m, ★★★/$, Hemdale-EMI/Media, G. Children move into a nice old man's old mansion with their mother and soon they're seeing children ghosts who take them back in time to live out the tragedy that trapped their spirits. Diana Dors, Laurence Naismith, James Villiers, w. d. Lionel Jeffries.
CHILDREN'S: FAMILY: DRAMA: Ghost Stories; Houses-Creepy; Time Travel; Child Protagonists; England; British Films; Writer-Directors
(The Turn of the Screw; The Nightcomers; The Haunting)

Amazing Stories, 1985, 70m, ★★★/$$$$, U/MCA-U, G. Several episodes involving the fantastic and macabre from Steven Spielberg. A failed TV pilot. Kevin Costner, Casey Sziemasko, Kiefer Sutherland, Danny DeVito, Rhea Perlman. d. Steven Spielberg, DeVito.
SCI-FI: ACTION: ADVENTURE: Fantasy; Multiple Stories; TV Movies

Amazon, 1990, 88m, ★★1/2/$, Ind/Live. A fugitive hides out in the Amazon with a gold miner while a pretty young woman comes in and tries to get them to help to save the rainforest. Robert Davi, Rae Dawn Chong, Kari Vaananen. d. Mika Kaurismaki.
ACTION: DRAMA: Action Drama; Environmental Dilemmas; Jungles; Fugitives from the Law; Redemption; Brazil; Rainforests
(At Play in the Fields of the Lord; The Burning Season; FernGully)

Amazon Women on the Moon, 1987, 85m, ★★★/(VR) $$, U/MCA-U, R/P-FN. A parody of 50s sci-fi low-budget epics is interspersed with other low-budget spoof skits. Rosanna Arquette, Michelle Pfeiffer, Ralph Bellamy, Carrie Fisher, Griffin Dunne, Steve Guttenberg. w. Michael Barrie, Jim Mulholland, d. Joe Dante, Carl Gottlieb, Peter Horton, John Landis, Robert K. Weiss.
COMEDY: Spoofs; SCI-FI: Comedy-Skit; Comedy-Slapstick
(Kentucky Fried Movie; Cat Women on the Moon; The Groove Tube)

The Ambassador, 1984, 97m, ★★/$, Cannon/MGM-UA, PG. A diplomat in Israel is constantly under fire by Arabs while his wife is secretly in bed with one of their leaders. Robert Mitchum, Ellen Burstyn, Rock Hudson, Donald Pleasance. w. Max Jack, N-adap. Elmore Leonard (52 Pick-Up), d. J. Lee Thompson.
DRAMA: SUSPENSE: Spies; Cheating Women; Diplomats; Middle East; Americans Abroad; Romance-Triangles; Kidnappings; Arab People; Jewish People; Israel
(Assassination)
(Ed: The story may be lifted from 52 Pick-Up, but the style and suspense aren't)

Amber Waves, 1982, 98m, ★★★/$$$, ABC/Time-Life. A farmer and his model-actor son clash on the farm when the son returns home. Dennis Weaver, Kurt Russell, Mare Winningham. d. Joseph Sargent.
DRAMA: Family Drama; Fathers & Sons; Farm Life; City vs. Country; Models; Actors; Rural Life; TV Movies

The Ambulance, 1990, 95m, ★★★/$, Vestron/Col, R/V-S-B&G. A comic artist unwittingly uncovers a plot to sell body parts via a mysterious ambulance which spirits away into the night after setting up diabetics for the fall. Eric Roberts, James Earl Jones, Megan Gallagher, Richard Bright, Janine Turner, Eric Braeden, Red Buttons. w. d. Larry Cohen.
SUSPENSE: MYSTERY: HORROR: Black Comedy; Medical Thriller; Missing Persons; Journalists; Body Parts; Writer-Directors; Hidden Gems; Underrated
(Coma; The Donor)

The Ambushers, 1967, 102m, ★★/$$, Col/Col. A flying saucer the government is testing disappears, so Matt Helm, suave, womanizing, secret agent goes into action. Dean Martin, Senta Berger, Janice Rule, James Gregory. w. Herbert Baker, d. Henry Levin.
ACTION: Action Comedy; Spoofs; Spoofs-Spy; Secret Agents; UFOs
(The Wrecking Crew)

America, 1924, 122m, ★★★/$$$$, UA/NA. Slice of Life of the Revolutionary War. Neil Hamilton, Carol Dempster, Lionel Barrymore. w. John Pell, d. D.W. Griffith.
DRAMA: Epics; War Movies; War Battles; Slice of Life; Multiple Stories; Revolutionary War; Silent Films
(Birth of a Nation; Revolution)

America, America, 1963, 177m, ★★★/$$, WB/WB. A Greek man living in Turkey at the turn of the century dreams of coming to America to see the statue of liberty. Stathis Giallelis, Frank Wolff, Harry Davis. w. d. Elia Kazan (BOScr, BDirector). BPicture. Oscars: 3-0.
DRAMA: Epics; Family Sagas; Immigrants; American Dream; Dreams; Faded Hits; 1900s; Mediterranean; Forgotten Films; Writer-Directors; Autobiographical Stories

Americana, 1973/1981, 90m, ★★1/2/$, Vestron/Vestron, R/V-P. A Vietnam vet returns to his small midwestern town and tries to build a merry go round, but the locals object. David Carradine, Barbara Hershey, Bruce Carradine, John Barrymore, Jr. w. Richard Carr, d. David Carradine.
DRAMA: Veterans-Vietnam; Small-Town Life; Coulda Been Good; Dreams
REMAKE/RETREAD: Ikiru.

American Anthem, 1986, 100m, ★1/2/$$, WB/WB, PG-13/S. Love and politics on the gymnastics mat. Janet Jackson-Gretsky, Mitch Gaylord, Michelle Phillips. d. Albert Magnoli.
ACTION: ROMANCE: Sports Movies; Unintentionally Funny; Camp; Olympics
(Gymkata; Diving In)

An American Dream, 1966, 103m, ★★1/2/$$, WB/WB, R/S-FFN. A TV anchorman plots to kill his alcoholic wife and winds up pursued by the mob, putting his life on the line to save another woman. Stuart Whitman, Janet Leigh, Eleanor Parker, J.D. Cannon, Lloyd Nolan, Murray Hamilton. w.

Mann Rubin, N-adap. Norman Mailer, d. Robert Gist.

DRAMA: TRAGEDY: SATIRE: Mob Stories; Murder-Debate to Confess; Guilty; Conscience; Murder of Spouse; TV Life; Saving Someone

American Dreamer, 1984, 97m, ★★/$$ ABC-20th/CBS-Fox, PG. An ordinary housewife (JoBeth Williams) gets caught-up in a new life in Europe when she slips and falls and thinks she's her favorite romance novelist. Tom Conti. d. Rick Rosner.

COMEDY: FARCE: Screwball Comedy; Comedy-Slapstick; Amnesia; Romance; Novelists; Paris; Female Protagonists; Ordinary People in Extraordinary Situations; Housewives
(Romancing the Stone; Desperately Seeking Susan; They Might Be Giants)
(Ed: Shades of old screwball, most of which works, but ultimately, it's too over the top, and coming on the heels of *Romancing the Stone* didn't help)

American Flyers, 1985, 114m, ★★1/2/$$, WB/WB, PG-13/P-MRN. Two brothers (Kevin Costner, David Grant) go on a cross-country bike race as one hides a disease from the other. w. Steve Tesich, d. John Badham.

DRAMA: MELODRAMA: Road Movies; Tearjerkers; Disease Movies; Bicycles; Road Movies; Death-Dealing with; Death-Impending; Friendships-Male; Buddy Films; Brothers
(Breaking Away; Dominick & Eugene)

The American Friend, 1977, 127m, ★★★/$, Ind/Facets, R/V-P. An innocent German is forced into killing a gangster when he thinks he's dying. Bruno Ganz, Dennis Hopper. w. Wim Wenders, N-adap. Patricia Highsmith (*Ripley's Game*), d. Wim Wenders.

DRAMA: SUSPENSE: Mob Stories; **MURDER:** Murder-Coerced; Hitmen; Ordinary People in Extraordinary Situations; Fugitives; Fugitives from the Mob; Innocent Bystanders; Death-Impending, False

American Friends, 1991, 95m, ★★1/2/$, Virgin/Vidmark, Fox, PG-13. A British professor falls in love with younger American woman even though he needs to be unmarried to handle the job he's been waiting for. Michael Palin, Trini Alvarado, Connie Booth, Alfred Molina. w. Palin, Tristam Powell, d. Powell.

COMEDY: ROMANCE: Romantic Comedy; Romance-Reluctant; Romance-Older Men/Younger Women; Settling Down; Nerds; Professors; British Films; Americans Abroad; Idiot Plots
(Angel Face; The Secret Partner)

American Gigolo, 1980, 117m, ★★★1/2/$$$, Par/Par, R/P-S-V-FFN-MFN. Professional ladies' man turns the wrong trick and winds up framed for murder while falling in love with a senator's wife. Richard Gere, Lauren Hutton. w. d. Paul Schrader.

MYSTERY: MURDER MYSTERY: Erotic Drama; Film Noir-Modern; Romance-Clandestine; Framed?; Saving One's Self; Prostitutes-Male; Sexy Men; Los Angeles; Beverly Hills; Writer-Directors
(Light Sleeper)

American Gothic, 1988, 90m, ★1/2/$, Vidmark/Vidmark, R/EV-B&G. A family that stays together by murdering together gets some visitors on their island. w. Burt Wetanson, Michael Vines, d. John Hough.

HORROR: Serial Killers; Black Comedy; Islands; Houses-Creepy
(Motel Hell; Tales from the Crypt)

American Graffiti, 1973, 110m, ★★★★/$$$$, Lucasfilm-Universal/MCA-U, PG/P-S. The antics of seniors on the last night of summer cruising in their small California town before having to face adulthood. Ron Howard, Richard Dreyfuss, Cindy Williams, Harrison Ford, Paul LeMat, Candy Clark (BSActress). w. Walter Huyck & Gloria Katz, George Lucas (BOScr), d. Lucas (BDirector). BPicture. Oscar: 5-0.

COMEDY: COMEDY DRAMA: Coming of Age; Ensemble Films; Teenage Movies; Small-Town Life; Life Transitions; 1950s; California; All-Star Casts; Autobiographical Stories; Blockbusters; Nostalgia; Ind Films

SEQUEL: More American Graffiti
(Diner; Mischief; The Last Valentino)

American Heart, 1994, 114m, ★★★/$, Ind/Live, R/P-S. An ex-con comes out of prison and is reunited with his teenage son, but re-starting a family in the seedier side of town isn't so easy and life isn't helped by the con's unwillingness to change. Jeff Bridges, Edward Furlong, Lucinda Jenney, Tracey Kapisky. w. Peter Silverman, d. Martin Bell.

DRAMA: Family Drama; Social Drama; Fathers & Sons; Homeless People; Ex-Convicts

American Hot Wax, 1978, 91m, ★★1/2/$$$, Par/Par, R/P. A DJ recalls the early days of rock 'n roll and record-making. Rim McIntire, Fran Drescher, Jay Leno, Laraine Newman, Chuck Berry, Jerry Lee Lewis. w. John Kaye, d. Floyd Mutrux.

COMEDY DRAMA: Rockumentary; Docudrama; Teenage Movies; Radio Singers; Musicians; 1950s; Flashbacks; Nostalgia; Memories
(FM; Rock Around the Clock)

An American in Paris, 1951, 113m, ★★★★/$$$, MGM/MGM-UA. Artist (Gene Kelly) goes to Paris to paint and meets a dancer with whom he dances his fantasies away. Leslie Caron. w. Alan Jay Lerner (BOScr), d. Vincente Minnelli (BDirector). **BPicture, BOScore, BCArt, BCCin, BCCostume, BEdit.** Oscars: 8-6.

MUSICAL: DRAMA: Musical Drama; **MELODRAMA:** Musical-Romance; **ROMANCE:** Romantic Drama; Fantasy; Dance Movies; Dancers; Ballet; Surrealism; Paris; Painters; Production Design-Outstanding
(Gigi; Lili; Anchors Aweigh; Moulin Rouge; Singin' in the Rain)

American Me, 1992, 125m, ★★★/$, Tri/Col-Tri, R/EP-EV-S. A gritty, unyielding look at Hispanic gangs in prison and one man who tries to cope once he's out (Edward James Olmos). William Forsythe, Pepe Serna, Danny de la Paz. w. Floyd Mutrux, Desmond Nakano, d. Olmos.

DRAMA: TRAGEDY: Prison Drama; Gangs-Latin; Latin People; Starting Over; Film Noir-Modern
(Ma Familia)

American Ninja, 1985, 90m, ★★/$$$, Cannon/MGM-UA, R/EV-P. Two ex-servicemen trained in martial arts go after gunrunners in the Phillipines. Michael Dudikoff, Steve James. w. Paul deMieleche, Avi Kleinberger, Gideon Amir, d. Sam Firstenberg.

ACTION: Arms Dealers; Martial Arts

American Ninja 2, The Confrontation, 1987, 90m, ★★/$$, Cannon/Media, R/EV-P. Martial artists take on a drug lord who's turning Marine he kidnaps into zombies. Michael Dudikoff, Steve James. w. Gary Conway, James Booth, d. Sam Firstenberg.

ACTION: Martial Arts; Zombies; Kidnappings; Rescue Adventure

American Ninja 3, Blood Hunt, 1989, 90m, ★1/2/$$, Cannon/MGM-UA, R/EV. A martial arts hero is infected with a deadly virus by men who killed his father, so he must go after those who did before it's too late for revenge.
REMAKE/RETREAD: DOA, 1949/1988.
ACTION: Avenging Death of Loved One; Race Against Time; Martial Arts

An American Romance, 1944, 151m, ★★1/2/$$$, MGM/MGM-UA. An immigrant becomes an industrial magnate at the expense of his marriage and family life. Brian Donlevy, Ann Richards, John Qualen. w. Herbert Dalmas, William Ludwig, d. King Vidor.
DRAMA: Social Drama; Rise to Power; Rags to Riches; Immigrants; American Dream; Dreams
(Edward, My Son; From the Terrace)
(Ed: Not much of a romance)

An American Tail, 1986, 81m, ★★★/$$$, Amblin-Universal/MCA-U, G. An immigrant mouse named Fievel's adventures after reaching Ellis Island. Voices of Christopher Plummer, Madeline Kahn, Dom DeLuise, Cathianne Blore. w. Judy Freudberg, Tony Geiss, d. Don Bluth.
CHILDREN'S: FAMILY: Cartoons; Musical-Animated; Music Movies; Immigrants; American Dream; Animal Stories; Animals-Talking; Rodents

An American Tail 2: Fievel Goes West, 1991, 75m, ★★★/$$, Amblin-U/MCA-U, G. Fievel the mouse goes west at the insistence of a con artist cat. Voices of James Stewart, Philip Glasser, Dom DeLuise, Amy Irving, John Cleese, Jon Lovitz. w. Flint Dille, Charles Swensen, d. Phil Nibblelink.
CHILDREN'S: FAMILY: WESTERNS: Western Comedy; Cartoons; Musical-Animated; Music Movies; Con Artists; Fish out of Water Stories; Immigrants; American Dream; Animal Stories; Animals-Talking; Rodents
(Ed: Mice are usually more leery of cats)

The American President, 1995, 115m, ★★★1/2/$$$, CR-Col/Col, PG-13/S. The single president takes a girlfriend, but many of the same old things happen as with anyone-forgetting dates, forgetting to call. . . . Michael Douglas, Annette Bening, Martin Sheen, Michael J. Fox, Richard Dreyfuss, Anna Deveare Smith, David Paymer, Shawna Waldron, Samantha Mathis. w. Aaron Sorkin

(BOScr), d. Rob Reiner. BCMScore. Oscars: 2-0.
COMEDY: COMEDY DRAMA: ROMANCE: Romantic Comedy; Presidents; Dating Scene; Old-Fashioned Recent Films; Starting Over; Female Protagonists
(Dave; Kisses for My President; Wall Street)

An American Werewolf in London, 1981, 97m, ★★★/$$, Universal/MCA-U,-R/P-EV-B&G-MRN. Two American backpackers (David Naughton, Griffin Dunne) out on the English moors are attacked by werewolf. One lives but becomes a wolf occasionally and must hide. Jenny Agutter. w. d. John Landis.
HORROR: Black Comedy; Morbid Comedy; Horror Comedy; Comedy & Violence; Werewolves; Fugitives; Humans into Animals; Secrets-Keeping; England; Writer-Directors
(Wolf; Innocent Blood; The Howling; The Wolfman)
(Ed: Inconsistent, but the black humor has developed a following)

The Americanization of Emily, 1964, 117m, ★★★1/2/$$, MGM/MGM-UA, PG/S. Soldier is attempt to make him the first man to hit the shores of Normandy while having and affair with Englishwoman who is a virgin. Julie Andrews, James Garner. w. Paddy Chayefsky (BOScr), d. Delbert Mann. Oscars: 1-0.
DRAMA: ROMANCE: MELODRAMA: Virgins; World War II Era; Soldiers; Young Women; Pregnancy Problems; England; Americans Abroad
(The Moon Is Blue; Yanks)

Americathon, 1979, 85m, ★★/$, WB/WB, PG/P. Nearing the year 2000, with the deficit having driven the country into bankruptcy, a telethon is held to save the day. Peter Riegert, John Ritter, Nancy Morgan, Harvey Korman, Fred Willard, Meatloaf, Elvis Costello, Howard Hesseman, Jay Leno, Chief Dan George. w. Monica Johnson, d. Neal Israel.
COMEDY: SATIRE: Spoofs; TV Life; Coulda Been Good; Futuristic Films

The Amityville Horror, 1979, 117m, ★★1/2/$$$$, #5 1979, AIP-Filmways/WB, R/P-V. A family moves into a quaint house on the coast and is besieged with bizarre happenings which may have resulted from murders on the

premises. James Brolin, Margot Kidder. w. Sandor Stern, NF-adap. Jay Anson, d. Stuart Rosenberg.
HORROR: SUSPENSE: Haunted Houses; Satanism; Occult; Possessions; Supernatural; True Stories; True or Not?; Ghosts; Blockbusters; Faded Hits; Sleeper Hits
(The Exorcist; Poltergeist; The Entity)
(Ed: Scarier if you're a kid; seems more intelligent, too)

The Amityville Horror 2, The Possession, 1982, 110m, ★★/$$$, DEG/Sultan, R. The story of how the house in Amityville got possessed as a psychotic young man kills several people in it and the people who move into it after realize it's possessed. w. Tommy Lee Wallace, d. Damien Damiani.
HORROR: SUSPENSE: Possessions; Satanism; True Stories; True or Not?; Haunted Houses; Murders-Mass
PREQUEL TO: The Amityville Horror

Amityville 4, 1989, 95m, ★★/$$$, Vidmark/Vidmark. The spirits have been transported to a California suburb and it's time for an exorcism again. Patty Duke, Jane Wyatt, Norman Lloyd, Brandy Gold. d. Sandor Stern.

Amityville, a New Generation, 1993, 92m, ★★/$, Rep/Rep, R/EV-B&G. A mirror leads to a haunting and dreams of a murder. Ross Patridge, Julia Nickson-Soul, David Naughton, Richard Roundtree. w. Chris DeFaria, Antonio Toro, d. John Murlowski.

The Amityville Curse, 1990, 91m, ★1/2/$, Rep/Rep, R/EV-B&G. Another unwitting (to put it mildly) family moves into the infamous house. Kim Coates, Dawna Wightman, Helen Hughes, Jan Rubes. d. Tom Barry.

Amityville 1992: It's About Time, 1992, 95m, ★★1/2/VR, Chanticleer/Republic, R/EV-B&G. Well-appointed but nonsensical continuation of the haunted house opus, only this time the house is in a California suburb and the spirit has apparently been transported in a clock which disturbs time causing much horrific confusion, and a bit of suspense. Stephen Macht, Shawn Weatherly. d. Tony Randel.
HORROR: SUSPENSE: Haunted Houses; Suburbia; Parent vs. Child; Time Travel; Illusions/Hallucinations; Possessions; TV Movies
SEQUEL in Amityville SERIES

(Ed: Some good scares and interesting ideas, but not worth most viewers' time)

The Amorous Adventures of Moll Flanders, 1965, 125m, ★★★/$$, Par/Par. A naughty, promiscuous servant girl sleeps her way everywhere anytime. Kim Novak, Richard Johnson, George Sanders, Lili Palmer, Angela Lansbury, Leo McKern, Vittorio DeSica, Daniel Massey. w. Dennis Cannan, Roland Kibbee, N-adap. Daniel Defoe, d. Terence Young.

COMEDY: Erotic Comedy; **FARCE:**
ROMANCE: Romantic Comedy; Sexy Women; Promiscuity; Forgotten Films; Underrated; All-Star Casts
(The Adventures of Eliza Frazer; Fanny Hill; Tom Jones; Joseph Andrews)
(Ed: Much of the energy of Tom Jones and a similar story, but without the twisting, revelatory plot)

Amos and Andrew, 1993, 96m, ★★¹/₂/$, Col/Col, PG-13/P-V. When a black playwright settles on a mostly white island, he's thought to be a crook just because of his color, but the locals employ a real crook to try and cover up their misfires. Nicolas Cage, Samuel Jackson, Michael Lerner, Margaret Colin, Giancarlo Esposito, Dabney Coleman, Bob Balaban, Brad Dourif. w. d. E. Max Frye.

COMEDY: SATIRE: Black Men; Black vs. White Paranoia; Islands; Small-Town Life; Writers; Thieves; Race Relations; Coulda Been Good; Good Premise Unfulfilled; Writer-Directors

Amsterdamned, 1988, 113m, ★★¹/₂/$$, Vestron/Vestron, R/EV. A police detective investigates prostitute murders in the canals of the Dutch city which may be done by some rather unorthodox methods. Huub Stapel, Monique VandeVen. w. d. Dick Maas.

ACTION: SUSPENSE: MURDER: MURDER MYSTERY: Detective Stories; Chase Movies; Chases-Boats; Trail of a Killer; Murders of Prostitutes; Prostitutes-Low Class; Writer-Directors
(Ed: Not all that bad, though the trailer did get unintended laughs)

Amy, 1981, 100m, ★★¹/₂/$, Disney/Disney, G. A young woman leaves her husband to teach at a school for the deaf and blind in the early 1900s. Jenny Agutter, Barry Newman, Kathleen Nolan, Nannette Fabray. d. Vincent McEveety.

DRAMA: MELODRAMA: Teachers; Deaf People; Blind People; Coming of Age; Young Women; 1900s; Old Fashioned Recent Films; Female Protagonists
(The Miracle Worker; My Brilliant Career)

Anastasia, 1956, ★★★¹/₂/$$$$, 20th/CBS-Fox. A woman appears after the Russian Revolution claiming to be the lost daughter of the Czar Nicholas and is used in a political game. Ingrid Bergman (**BActress**), Helen Hayes, Yul Brynner. w. Arthur Laurents, P-adap. Marcel Maurette, d. Anatole Litvak. BScore. Oscars: 2-1.

DRAMA: MYSTERY: Missing Persons; Amnesia; Russians; Time Sleepers; Impostors; Female Protagonists; Incredible but Mostly True
REMAKE: TV (1984)

Anastasia, 1984, 190m, ★★★/$$$, NBC/PBS. An updating with more accurate details of the mysterious claims of the woman who may or may not be heir to the Russian empire which was deposed with the Revolution. Amy Irving, Olivia de Havilland, Jan Niklas, Edward Fox, Susan Lucci, Elke Sommer, Claire Bloom, Rex Harrison, Omar Sharif. w. Jim Goldman, d. Marvin Chomsky.

DRAMA: Historical Drama; True or Not?; True Stories; Royalty; Princesses; Amnesia; Time Sleepers; 1920s; Impostors; Female Protagonists; TV Movies; Mini-Series; Incredible but Mostly True

Anatomy of a Murder, 1959, 161m, ★★★★/$$$$, Universal/MCA-U. Lawyer (Jimmy Stewart, BActor) defends soldier for murdering the man who raped his wife. Lee Remick (BSActress), Ben Gazzara, George C. Scott (BSActor), Arthur O'Connell (BSActor), Eve Arden, Kathryn Grant. w. Wendell Mayes (BAScr), N-adap. Robert Traver, d. Otto Preminger (BDirector). BPicture, BAScr, BB&WCin, BEdit. Oscars: 9-0.

DRAMA: Courtroom Drama; **MYSTERY:**
MURDER MYSTERY: Lawyers; Rape/Rapists; Small-Town Scandal
(To Kill a Mockingbird; Fatal Vision)

Anchors Aweigh, 1945, 140m, ★★★/$$$$$, MGM/MGM-UA. Two singing and dancing sailors meet up with a boy who'd like to join the navy and a dancing mouse. Gene Kelly, Frank Sinatra, Kathryn Grayson, Dean Stockwell. w. Isobel Lennart, d. George Sidney.

Animation-Partial; Cartoons; Sailers; Animals-Talking; Boyhood; Rodents; Female Screenwriters
(On the Town; An American in Paris)
(Ed: Notable as one of the first experiments with live action and animation)

And Baby Makes Six, 1979, 104m, ★★★/$$$$, NBC/NA. A woman with five children (Colleen Dewhurst) finds out in her 40s she's pregnant again. w. Shelly List, d. Waris Hussein.

DRAMA: MELODRAMA: Midlife Crisis; Babies-Having; Babies-Having, Late in Life; Starting Over; Female Protagonists; Female Screenwriters; TV Movies
(The Tenth Month; Prudence and the Pill)

The Anderson Tapes, 1972, 98m, ★★¹/₂/$$, Columbia/RCA-Col, R. Thieves rob apartments in a well-planned heist over the holidays. Sean Connery, Dyan Cannon, Martin Balsam, Ralph Meeker, Christopher Walken. w. Frank Pierson, N-adap. Lawrence Sanders, d. Sidney Lumet.

DRAMA: COMEDY DRAMA: Capers; Heist Stories; Thieves; Blackmail; Surveillance; Ex-convicts
(The Hot Rock; The Real McCoy)

And God Created Woman, 1957, 92m, ★★★/$$$$, Ind/Vestron, S-FN. A beautiful French girl becomes a nymphomaniac on the beach. Brigitte Bardot, Curt Jurgens, Jean-Luis Tritignant, Christian Marquand. w. Roger Vadim, Raoul Levy, d. Vadim.

DRAMA: Erotic Drama; **COMEDY**
DRAMA: Promiscuity; Coming of Age; Sexy Women; Riviera Life; French Films; Ind Films

And God Created Woman, 1988, 100m, ★★/$, Vestron/Vestron, R/P-S-V-FFN-MRN. A sexy woman (Rebecca DeMornay) gets married so she can get paroled from prison and being a singer, if her past doesn't catch up to her. w. R.J. Stewart, d. Roger Vadim.

DRAMA: ROMANCE: Erotic Drama; Fugitives from the Law; Sexy Women; Ex-Convicts; Criminals-Female; Singers; Dreams
(Ed: It has only the title and the director in common with the original)

And Justice for All, 1979, 117m, ★★★/$$$, Columbia/RCA-Col, R/P-S. Lawyer (Al Pacino, BActor) defends bad judge on charges he murdered a prostitute. John Forsythe, Christine Lahti. w.

Barry Levinson, Valerie Curtin (BOScr), d. Norman Jewison. Oscars: 2-0.

DRAMA: SATIRE: Black Comedy; Social Drama; Courtroom Drama; Rape/Rapists; Corruption; Rebels; Fighting the System; Lawyers; Judges
(Network; Article 99; Scent of a Woman; City Hall)
(Ed: In some ways, it's a blow-hard of a movie, but the energy of Pacino redeems it)

And Now for Something Completely Different, 1972, 89m, ★★★/$$$, Col/RCA-Col, R/P-S. The first of the Monty Python films is a series of skits from the show mostly for the American market. w. Graham Chapman, John Cleese, Terry Gilliam, Terry Jones, Eric Idle, Michael Palin, d. Ian MacNaughton.
COMEDY: Comedy-Skit; Comedy-Slapstick; Bathroom Humor; British Films; Comedians
(The Life of Brian; The Meaning of Life; John Cleese on How to Irritate People)

And Now the Screaming Starts, 1973, 91m, ★★¹/₂/$$, AIP/Media, R/V-S. A new bride moves with her husband into an old country home where a ghost proceeds to drive her insane. Peter Cushing, Stephanie Beacham, Herbert Lom, Patrick Magee, Ian Ogilvy. w. Roger Marshall, N-adap. David Case (Fengriffen), d. Roy Ward Baker.
HORROR: SUSPENSE: Ghost Stories; Newlyweds; Houses-Creepy; Women in Jeopardy; Dangerous Men; Dangerous Spouse; Insane-Plot to Drive
(Rebecca; The Amityville Horror; The Turn of the Screw; The Nightcomers)

And Now, Tomorrow, 1944, 86m, ★★/$$$, Par/NA. A well-heeled young woman's charm turns sour when she goes deaf and her beau leaves her and she has to settle for her ear doctor. Loretta Young, Alan Ladd, Susan Hayward, Beulah Bondi, Cecil Kellaway, Barry Sullivan. w. Frank Partos, Raymond Chandler, N-adap. Rachel Field, d. Irving Pichel.
DRAMA: MELODRAMA: Tearjerkers; **TRAGEDY:** Starting Over; Disease Stories; Deaf People; Romance with Doctor
(Dark Victory; Bright Victory; Magnificent Obsession)

And Now, My Love, 1975, 121m, ★★★/$$, Columbia/RCA-Col, R/S-FN. Wealthy woman meets naughty younger

man for an unusual fling. Marthe Keller. w. d. Claude LeLouche.

DRAMA: COMEDY DRAMA: ROMANCE: Romantic Drama; Erotic Drama; French Films; Romance-Mismatched; Romance-Older Men/Younger Women; Rich People; Rich People-Decadent; Female Protagonists; Writer-Directors
(Ash Wednesday; Damage; Bobby Deerfield; That Obscure Object of Desire)

And the Ship Sails On, 1984, 138m, ★★¹/₂/$, Col/Col, R. A ship in the World War I era carries a group of eccentric to bizarre passengers, one of whom's mission it is to scatter the ashes of a deceased opera diva. w. Federico Fellini, Tonino Guerra, d. Fellini.
DRAMA: Art Films; Avant-Garde; Surrealism; Ships; Fantasy; Eccentric People; Italian Films
(City of Women; Ginger and Fred)

And Then There Were None (Ten Little Indians), 1945, 98m, ★★★¹/₂/$$$, UA/Nos, VCI. Ten people are invited to a mansion on an island and the murders begin. Walter Huston, Barry Fitsgerald, Louis Hayward, Roland Young, Richard Haydn, Judith Anderson, Mischa Auer. w. Dudley Nichols, N-adap. Agatha Christie, d. Rene Clair.
MYSTERY: MURDER: MURDER MYSTERY: Mystery-Whodunit; Black Comedy; Comic Mystery; Murders-One by One; Murder-Invitation to; Agatha Christie
(Ten Little Indians; The Alphabet Murders; The Last of Sheila)
(Ed: Infamous for being called Ten Little Niggers in England)

Andre's Mother, 1990, 90m, ★★★/$$$, AP-PBS/Goldwyn, NR/S. The stern, cold mother of a man dying of AIDS has to face the facts at the insistence of his lover. Sada Thompson, Richard Thomas, Sylvia Sidney. w. Terence McNally. Emmy winner for script.
DRAMA: Mothers & Sons; Lover Family Dislikes; AIDS Stories; Stern Women; Gay Men; Homophobia; Death-Dealing with; TV Movies; Hidden Gems
(Summer Wishes; Winter Dreams; An Early Frost)
(Ed: Powerful, but if you see Summer Wishes, there are some major similarities)

Androcles and the Lion, 1955, 96m, ★★★/$$, RKO/Turner. The fable of the slave who, after taking a thorn from a lion's paw when he's thrown into the ring

to be eaten, the lion suddenly doesn't have an appetite. Alan Young, Jean Simmons, Robert Newton, Victor Mature, Maurice Evans, Elsa Lanchester, Gene Lockhart. w. Chester Erskine, P-adap. George Bernard Shaw, d. Erskine.
COMEDY DRAMA: Legends; Animals-Smart; Rome; Ancient Times

The Andromeda Strain, 1971, 130m, ★★★¹/₂/$$$$, Universal/MCA-U, PG. A terrible mutant virus has landed from outer space from the desert and will soon kill all human life if not stopped. Arthur Hill, James Olson. w., N-adap. Michael Crichton, d. Robert Wise.
SUSPENSE: SCI-FI: Medical Thriller; Race Against Time; Epidemics; Disease Stories; Aliens-Outer Space-Evil; Scientists; Experiments; Desert Life; Paranoia; Rogue Plots; Hidden Gems
(Outbreak; Warning Sign; The Cassandra Crossing; The Blob; Liquid Sky; The Stand)

And You Thought Your Parents Were Weird, 1991, 92m, ★★/$, Vidmark/Vidmark, PG. Two whizkids invent a robot to keep them company, but things so don't work as smoothly as planned. Marcia Strassman, Joshua Miller, Edan Gross, John Quade, Sam Behrens. w. Tony Cookson, d. Cookson.
COMEDY: SCI-FI: CHILDREN'S: FAMILY: Boys; Computers; Robots

Andy Warhol's Bad, 1977, 100m, ★★★/$, Ind/Sultan, Par. A woman who has an electrolysis company also runs a hitwoman company where people can hires females to bump off pets and children. Perry King, Carroll Baker, Susan Tyrell, Stefania Cassini. d. Jed Johnson.
COMEDY: SATIRE: Spoofs; Black Comedy; Murder-Comic Attempts; Hitwomen; Animals in Jeopardy; Children in Jeopardy; Cult Films; Ind Films
(Desperate Living; Female Trouble)

Andy Warhol's Dracula, 1974, 106m, ★★★/$$, Ind/Gem. A stud woos the women for Dracula from the garden of a big mansion. Udo Kier, Joe Dallesandro, Vittorio DeSica, Roman Polanski. w. d. Paul Morissey.
HORROR: Horror Comedy; Erotic Drama; Erotic Comedy; Sexy Men; Cult Films; Vampires; Spoofs-Vampire; Writer-Directors; Ind Films

Andy Warhol's Flesh, 1968, 105m, ★★¹/₂/$, Vaughn-Par/Par, R/ES-MFN-FFN. A male prostitute in New York floats from one client to another and has trouble connecting with people outside of "work" as well. Joe Dallesandro, Geraldine Smith, Patti D'Arbanville, Candy Darling, Jackie Curtis. w. d. Paul Morrissey.

DRAMA: Erotic Drama; Art Films; Avant-Garde Films; Documentary Style; Prostitutes-Male; Prostitutes-Low Class; Greenwich Village; Cult Films; Writer-Directors; Ind Films

Andy Warhol's Frankenstein, 1974, 95m, ★★1/2/$$, Ind/Par, Lebell. A spoof on the classic story with Dr. Frankie as a necrophiliac with the donors for his monsters. Udio Kier, Monique van Vooren, Joe Dallesandro. w. d. Paul Morissey.

HORROR: Spoofs-Horror; Dead-Back from the; Frankenstein; Body Parts; **MURDER:** Writer-Directors; 3-D Movies; Ind Films

Andy Warhol's Heat, 1972, 100m, ★★1/2/$, Score/Par, R/ES-FN-MN. A television star on the skids moves into a fleabag L.A. hotel and takes up with a former screen bombshell past her prime. Joe Dallesandro, Sylvia Miles, Andrea Feldman. w. d. Paul Morrissey, John Hallowell.

DRAMA: Documentary Style; Actors; Midlife Crisis; Bimbos; Hollywood Satire; Hollywood Life; Nervous Breakdowns; Erotic Drama; Riches to Rags; TV Life; Cult Films; Ind Films
(Sunset Boulevard)

Angel, 1984, 92m, ★★/$$, NW/NW, R/S-P. A girl who's a good student by day and hooker by night deal with a killer on the streets while turning tricks and meeting eccentric local streetpeople. Donna Wilkes, Cliff Gorman, Rory Calhoun, Susan Tyrrell, Dick Shawn, Elaine Giftos. w. Robert Vincent O'Neil, Joe Cala, d. O'Neil.

DRAMA: ACTION: MURDER: CrimeDrama; Trail of a Killer; Detectives-Amateur; Dual Lives; Prostitutes-Low Class; Prostitutes-Child; Teenagers; Runaways; Homeless People; Eccentric People

SEQUEL: Avenging Angel
(Crimes of Passion)

Angel and the Badman, 1947, 100m, ★★1/2/$$$, Republic/Republic. A Quaker girl tries to convert an outlaw to her way of life, but is he just playing along for love? John Wayne, Gail Russell, Harry Carey, Bruce Cabot. w.d. James Edward Grant.

DRAMA: MELODRAMA: ROMANCE: WESTERN: Romance-Reluctant; Romance-Opposites Attract; Tough Guys & Religious Women; Religion; 1800s
(Rooster Cogburn; Heaven Knows; Mr. Allison; The African Queen; Two Mules for Sister Sara)

An Angel at My Table, 1990, 160m, ★★★/$, Col/Col, PG. The life of a poet supposedly suffering from schizophrenia, Janet Frame. Kerry Fox, Alexia Keogh. w. Laura Jones, NF-adap. Janet Frame, d. Jane Campion.

DRAMA: Character Studies; Disease Stories; Mental Illness; Shy People; Nerds; Writers; Poets; New Zealand; Female Screenwriters; Female Directors; Female Protagonists; Ind Films
(Frances; Stevie; Beautiful Dreamers; The Piano; Sweetie; Heavenly Creatures)

Angel Baby, 1961, 97m, ★★1/2/$, MGM/NA. When a mute girl learns to speak after supposedly being cured by a preacher, she has a crisis of faith when she catches him sinning. George Hamilton, Salome Jens, Mercedes McCambridge, Joan Blondell, Henry Jones, Burt Reynolds. N-adap. Elsie Barber, Jenny Angel, d. Paul Wendkos, Hubert Cornfield.

MELODRAMA: Mute People; Preachers; Religion; Redemption; Cures/Solutions-Search for Forgotten Films; Curiosities

Angel Face, 1952, 91m, ★★1/2/$$, RKO/Turner. An insane girl begins killing her family by coercing the family driver to help, but when she tries to off him, the gig may be up. Jean Simmons, Robert Mitchum, Herbert Marshall, Barbara O'Neil. w. Frank Nugent, Oscar Millard, d. Otto Preminger.

MURDER: DRAMA: TRAGEDY: Murderers-Female; Murders-One by One; Suicidal Tendencies; Mental Illness; Murder-Persuaded to
(Pretty Poison; The Bad Seed; Violette)

Angel Heart, 1987, 112m, ★★1/2/$$, Tri-Star/Live, R-NC-17/ES-V-B&G. A detective travels to New Orleans to solve a case and soon finds himself dealing with devil and voodoo, without any control over himself. Mickey Rourke, Robert De Niro, Lisa Bonet, Charlotte Rampling. w. d. Alan Parker, N-adap. William Hjortsberg (*Falling Angel*)

SUSPENSE: MURDER: MYSTERY: MURDER MYSTERY: Romance-Interracial; Satan; Occult; New Orleans; Suspecting

Oneself; Film Noir-Modern; Southerns; Southerns-Foreign Directors of
(Detour; Black Angel; Shattered)

Angel in My Pocket, 1968, 95m, ★★1/2/$$, U/NA. A preacher adjusts to a new small town with his family with the help of a friend. Andy Griffith, Jerry Van Dyke, Kay Medford, Lee Meriweather, Gary Collins, Margaret Hamilton, Edgar Buchanan, Henry Jones. w. Jim Fritsell, Everett Greenbaum, d. Alan Rafkin.

COMEDY DRAMA: MELODRAMA: FAMILY: Family Comedy; Preachers/Ministers; Small-Town Life; New in Town; Angels
(Follow Me, Boys; Cold Turkey)

Angel on My Shoulder, 1946, 101m, ★★★/$$$, UA/Nos. The devil promises a mobster he can have his soul back if he returns to Earth in the body of a judge who's tough and makes him soft on criminals. Paul Muni, Claude Rains, Anne Baxter. w. Harry Segall, Roland Kibbee, d. Archie Mayo.

COMEDY DRAMA: Fantasy; Selling One's Soul; Satan; Dead-Back from the; Judges; Good vs. Evil; Mob Stories; Reincarnation; Ethics; Corruption; Government Corruption; Hidden Gems
(All That Money Can Buy; Heaven Can Wait; Here Comes Mr. Jordan)

Angels and Insects, 1995, ★★★/$, AP-Goldwyn/Goldwyn, R/S-MFN. An explorer just back from a shipwrecked journey to study Darwin's theories in the wild is taken in by a wealthy Darwin supporter. He falls for a young lady there and finds himself in a sexual-political battle which mirrors the survival of the fittest in the wild. Mark Rylance, Kristen Scott Thomas, Patsy Kensit, Jeremy Kemp, Douglas Henshall. w. Belinda Haas, Philip Haas, d. Philip Haas, N-adap. Morpho Eugenia.

DRAMA: Erotic Drama; Social Drama; England; Allegorical Stories; Rich People-Decadent; Female Screenwriters
(The Comfort of Strangers; The Draughtsman's Contract)

Angels in the Outfield, 1951, 102m, ★★★/$$$, MGM/MGM-UA. Paul Douglas, Janet Leigh, Keenan Wynn, Donna Corcoran, Lewis Stone, Spring Byington, Ellen Corby. w. Dorothy Kingsley, George Wells, d. Clarence Brown.
Female Screenwriters

Angels in the Outfield, 1994, 101m, ★★1/2/$$$, Touchstone/Touchstone, PG.

Danny Glover, Tony Danza, Christopher Lloyd, Brenda Fricker, Ben Johnson. w. Holly Goldberg Sloan, d. William Dear. Angels swoop down and help out an ailing baseball team.
COMEDY: Fantasy; Sports Movies; Angels; Baseball; Men and Boys; Comebacks; Ensembles-Male
(Field of Dreams)
The Angel Wore Red, 1960, 105m, ★★/$, MGM/MGM-UA. A priest and a hooker wind up in each other's arms in the middle of the Spanish Civil War. Ava Gardner, Dirk Bogarde, Joseph Cotten, Vittorio de Sica. w.d. Nunnally Johnson.
DRAMA: MELODRAMA: ROMANCE: Romance-Mismatched; Good vs. Evil; Romance-Opposites Attract; Romance with a Prostitute; Religious Men & Sexy Women; Romance with Clergy; War Movies; Priest; Prostitutes-High Class; Spain; Spanish Civil War; Writer-Directors
(For Whom the Bell Tolls; Arise, My Love; The Naked Maja; Miss Sadie Thompson; Crimes of Passion; Anna Christie)
Angela, 1977, 100m, ★★/$, Ind/Sultan. An older woman and younger man fall in love only to find they are related. Sophia Loren, Steve Railsback, John Huston. w.d. Boris Sagal.
DRAMA: ROMANCE: TRAGEDY: Mothers & Sons; Love-Forbidden; Romance-Intergenerational; Incest; Oedipal Stories; Female Protagonists
(Oedipus Rex; The Grifters; Spanking the Monkey; The Miracle [1990])
(Ed: A seemingly presposterous idea that has survived centuries, but not this movie)
Angelina, 1947, 98m, ★★1/2/$, Luxora/NA. An ordinary Italian housewife becomes an activist in the reconstruction after the war. Anna Magnani, Franco Zeffirelli. w. Suso Cecchi D'Amico, Piero Tellini, Luigi Zampa, d. Zampa.
DRAMA: MELODRAMA: Political Drama; Housewives; Politicians-Female; Feisty Females; Female Protagonists; World War II-Post Era; Italian Films
(Open City; Paisan)
Angelo, My Love, 1984, 91m, ★★★/$ (LR), Col/Col, PG-13/P. True story, fictionalized, of a child hustler Robert Duvall (who plays himself) found in Manhattan, a gypsy boy named Angelo (Angelo Evans) who fascinated him

enough with his streetwise, cocky ways that he made a film about him. w.d. Robert Duvall.
DRAMA: Docudrama; Biographies-Fictional; Streetlife; Con Artists; Free Spirits; Fathers & Sons; Men and Boys; Gypsies; Fathers-Surrogate; Writer-Directors; Actor Directors
(Gloria; King of the Gypsies; Convicts)
Angels with Dirty Faces, 1938, 97m, ★★★1/2/$$$$, WB/WB. Boyhood friends grow apart when one becomes a gangster and the other becomes a preacher. James Cagney (BActor), Humphrey Bogart, Ann Sheridan, Pat O'Brien, The Deadend Kids. w. (story) Roland Brown (BOStory), (script) John Wexley, Warren Duff, d. Michael Curtiz (BDirector). Oscars: 3-0.
DRAMA: Crime Drama; Inner City Life; Friendships-Lifetime; Mob Stories; Warner Gangster Era; Feuds; 1930s Episodic Stories
(True Confessions; Once Upon a Time in America; Manhattan Melodrama; The Devil Is a Sissy)
Angie, 1994, 108m, ★★/$, 20th/Fox, R/P-S-FN. A young Italian woman in New York finds herself at a crisis point when she becomes pregnant and decides to leave her working-class boyfriend for an uptown Irish lawyer who may not want another man's child-and then goes searching for her mentally ill mother in Texas. Geena Davis, Aida Turturro, Stephen Rea, Philip Bosco, Jenny O'Hara. w. Todd Graff, N-adap. Aura Wing, d. Martha Coolidge.
MELODRAMA: COMEDY DRAMA: ROMANCE: Young Women; Single Women; Mothers Alone; Marriage-Impending; Mothers & Daughters; Babies-Having; Family Comedy; Family Drama; New York Life; Italians; Narrated Films; Female Protagonists; Coulda Been Great
(True Love; Moonstruck)
(Ed: Davis is so-so to miscast, especially in comparison to her more ethnic co-stars; plus, the heelish nature of Rea's character and the fiancé border on gratuitous male-bashing. Madonna fought for and lost the part and would have been more suited, if not necessarily better)
The Angry Silence, 1960, 94m, ★★★/$$, B-L/NA. A factory worker who won't join an unofficial strike is dealt with by his co-workers which gives the communists in the area a reason to campaign harder. Richard Attenborough, Michael

Craig, Pier Angeli, Laurence Naismith. w. Bryan Forbes, Michael Craig, Richard Gregson (BOScr), d. Guy Green.
DRAMA: Social Drama; Unions; Strikes; Men in Conflict; Class Conflicts; Factory Life; Working Class; Ordinary People Stories; British Films
(I'm Alright; Jack; Norma Rae; Matewan)
Angus, 1995, 91m, ★★★/$, Hollywood/Hollywood, PG. The travails of an overweight boy coming of age, a refreshing twist, except that his name is burden enough. Charlie Talbert, George C. Scott, Rita Moreno, Kathy Bates, Chris Owen, Lawrence Pressman, Ariana Richards, Anna Thompson. w. Jill Gordon, d. Patrick Read Johnson.
DRAMA: CHILDREN'S: Coming of Age; Teenagers; Weight Problems; Looksism; Boyhood; Female Screenwriters; Child Protagonists
(Georgy Girl; Babycakes; Marty)
Animal Behavior, 1989, 79m, ★★/$, Ind/HBO, R/S-P. A romance traingle develops between an animal researcher and a music professor and a friend. Karen Allen, Armand Assante, Holly Hunter, Josh Mostel, Richard Libertini. w. Susan Rice, d. Jenny Bowen.
DRAMA: ROMANCE: Romantic Drama; Eccentric People; Romance-Triangles; Coulda Been Good; Animal Stories; Professors
Animal Crackers, 1930, 98m, ★★★★/$$$$, Par/Par. The Marx Brothers crash a posh party and chaos results, especially when a painting turns up missing. Groucho Marx, Marx Brothers. w. Morrie Ryskind, P-adap. Ryskind, George F. Kaufman, d. Victor Heerman.
COMEDY: FARCE: Gag Comedy; Screwball Comedy; Party Movies; Snobs vs. Slobs; Snobs; Upper Class; Art Thieves
(Cocoanuts; Duck Soup; Brain Donors)
Animal Farm, 1955, 75m, ★★★/$$, Ind/VY. Animals take over their farm from the owner and do things themselves, but find it's not so easy, and that classes still persist. w.d. John Halas, Joy Batchelor, N-adap. George Orwell.
DRAMA: Cartoons; **CHILDREN'S:** Social Drama; **SATIRE:** Class Conflicts; Allegorical Stories; Farm Life; Animals-Talking; Animal Stories
The Animal Kingdom, 1932, 95m, ★★★/$$$, RKO/Turner. A book publisher thinks of every possible good reason there would be for having a mistress

and why his wife shouldn't care, but of course, she does. Leslie Howard, Ann Harding, Myrna Loy, Neil Hamilton. w. Horace Jackson, P-adap. Philip Barry, d. Edward Griffith.
COMEDY DRAMA: ROMANCE: Screwball Comedy; Comedy of Manners; Romantic Comedy; Romance-Triangles; Cheating Men; Writers; Mistresses
REMAKE: One More Tomorrow.
(One More Tomorrow; Wife vs. Secretary; Any Wednesday)
Animal House, see National Lampoon's Animal House.
Ann Vickers, 1933, 72m, ★★★/$$$, RKO/Turner. A rebellious feminist-type gets put in her place by life in general and settles for a judge who's got no integrity but can get her what she's decided she wants. Irene Dunne, Walter Huston, Conrad Nagel, Bruce Cabot, Edna May Oliver. w. Jane Murfin, N-adap. Sinclair Lewis, d. John Cromwell.
DRAMA: MELODRAMA: Social Drama; Marrying Up; Social Climbing; Women's Rights; Feisty Females; Corruption; Judges; Female Protagonists; Female Screenwriters
(A Woman Rebels; Bad Girl; Ada; Blonde Venus)
Anna, 1988, 101m, ★★★/$$, Vestron/ Vestron, R/S. A Czech actress (Sally Kirkland, BActress) comes to America to continue work as a star but is soon eclipsed by a beautiful young model (Paulina Porizkova) she's mentored. w. Agnieska Holland, d. Yurek Bogayevicz. Oscars: 1-0.
DRAMA: MELODRAMA: Tearjerkers; Understudies/Proteges; Rivalries; Actresses; Eastern Europeans; Immigrants; Dreams; Female Protagonists; Hidden Gems; Czech People/Films; Ind Films
(All About Eve; Valley of the Dolls; The Turning Point)
(Ed: Kirkland really comes through on this one, but watch out for most of her others)
Anna and the King of Siam, 1946, 128m, ★★★/$$$$, 20th/CBS-Fox. The basis for *The King and I* musical, a governess arrives to take care of the many, many children of a king who could use a spanking. Irene Dunne, Rex Harrison, Linda Darnell, Gale Sondergaard (BSActress), Lee J. Cobb. w. Talbot Jennings, Sally Benson (BScr), N-adap.

Margaret Landon, d. John Cromwell. **BCin,** BOScore. Oscars: 4-1.
DRAMA: COMEDY DRAMA: ROMANCE: Romance-Mismatched; Romance-Reluctant; Spinsters; Teachers; Babysitters; Playboys; Kings; Asia; Female Screenwriters; Female Protagonists
REMAKE: The King and I
(The King and I; The Sound of Music; The Ghost and Mrs. Muir; Blithe Spirit; Adam Had Four Sons)
Anna Christie, 1930, 90m, ★★★★/$$$, MGM/MGM-UA. Past of a former hooker comes back to haunt her when she falls for a sailor. Greta Garbo, Charles Bickford. w. Frances Marion, P-adap. Eugene O'Neill, d. Clarence Brown.
ROMANCE: MELODRAMA: TRAGEDY: DRAMA: Prostitutes-High Class; Secrets-Haunting; Past-Haunted by; Female Screenwriters; Female Protagonists; Classic Tragedy
(Cinderella Liberty; Miss Sadie Thompson; The Angel Wore Red; Love; Romance)
Anna Karenina, 1935, 95m, ★★★★/ $$$, MGM/MGM-UA. A woman in old Russia falls for a man but she's already married and tragedy is the result. Greta Garbo. w. Clemence Dane, Salka Viertel, N-adap. Tolstoi, d. Clarence Brown.
Anna Karenina, 1948, 139m, ★★½/ $$, London/Goodtimes. A woman in old Russia falls for a man but she's already married and tragedy is the result. Vivien Leigh, Kieron Moore, Ralph Richardson. w. Jean Anouilh, Guy Morgan, Julian Duvivier, d. Duvivier.
Anna Karenina, 1985, CBS/Vestron, ★★★/$$$. A woman in old Russia falls for a man but she's already married and tragedy is the result. Jacqueline Bisset, Christopher Reeve. d. Simon Langton. TV Movies
(Ed: Bisset is good and the story still has its impact, if not as glossy a production)
>TRAGEDY: DRAMA: MELODRAMA: Tearjerkers; Romance-Doomed; Romance-Forbidden; Infidelity; Russians; Romance-Triangles; Female Protagonists; Classic Tragedy
REMAKE OF: Love
(The Awakening/Grand Isle; Love; Hedda; A Doll's House; Romance)
Anne and Muriel, 1971, 108m, ★★★/$$, Ind/NA. A French writer falls in love with not one but two British

women who are sisters, and has to choose. Jean Pierre Leaud, Kika Markham, Stacey Tendeter, Sylvia Marriott. w. Francois Truffaut, Jean Gruault, N-adap. Henri-Pierre Roche, d. Truffaut.
ROMANCE: DRAMA: Romantic Drama; Erotic Drama; Romance-Triangles; Writers; Romance-Choosing Right Person; Sisters; French Films
(Love on the Run; Therese and Isabelle)
Anne of the Thousand Days, 1969, 145m, ★★★½/$$$, Universal/MCA-U, PG. Henry VIII (Richard Burton, BActor) and wife Anne Boleyn (Genevieve Bujold, BActress) have a child but Henry isn't satisfied and decides to get rid of her as he had his other wives. Anthony Quayle (BSActor). w. John Hale, Bridget Boland (BAScr), P-adap. Maxwell Anderson, d. Charles Jarrott. BPicture, BCin, BArt, BOScore, **BCostume,** BSound; Oscars: 10-1.
DRAMA: TRAGEDY: Historical Drama; Costume Drama; Marriage Drama; Evil Men; Mean Men; Abused Women; Death-Impending; Elizabethan Era; King Henry VIII; Classic Tragedy; Faded Hits
(Mary, Queen of Scots; Mary of Scotland; The Private Lives of Elizabeth & Essex; The Virgin Queen; Elizabeth R.)
L'Annee Dernier a Marienbad, see Last Year at Marienbad
Annie, 1982, 128m, ★★½/$$$$, Rastar-Columbia/RCA-Col, G. Classic tale of the orphan and the billionaire, Daddy Warbuck (Albert Finney), who adopts her, despite her evil orphanage mistress (Carol Burnett). w. Carol Sobieski, P-adap. Martin Charnin, Thomas Meehan, Charles Strouse, d. John Huston.
MUSICAL: Musical Comedy; Orphans; Evil Women; Rich People; Upper Class; Cartoon Heros; Fathers Alone; Female Protagonists; Girlhood; Child Protagonists; Depression Era; Coulda Been Great
Annie Get Your Gun, 1950, 107m, ★★★/$$$, MGM/MGM-UA. A sharp-shooting girl from the mountains joins a traveling gun show and falls in love with the owner via song. Betty Hutton, Howard Keel, Edward Arnold, J. Carrol Naish, Louis Calhern. w. Sidney Sheldon, P-adap. Herbert and Dorothy Fields, d. George Sidney.
MUSICAL: COMEDY: MUSICAL COMEDY: WESTERNS: Western Comedy;

ROMANCE: Romantic Comedy; Feisty Females; Female Protagonists; Rodeos; Hillbillies; Fish out of Water Stories; Coming of Age Heroines
(Annie Oakley; Calamity Jane; Buffalo Bill & the Indians; Buffalo Girls)

Annie Hall, 1977, 94m, ★★★★/$$$$, UA/MGM-UA, R/P-S. Romance of two neurotic New Yorkers turns poignant and insightful in brilliant character studies. Woody Allen (BActor), Diane Keaton (**BActress**). w. Woody Allen, Marshall Brickman (**BOScr**), d. Allen (**BDirector**). BPicture.
Oscars: 5-4.
COMEDY: Romantic Comedy; Character Studies; Autobiographical Stories; Romance-Mismatched; Episodic Stories; Neurotic People; New York vs. Los Angeles; Nerds & Babes; Nerds; Interviews; Smart vs. Dumb; Therapy; Writers; Narrated Films; New York Life
(Manhattan; Play it Again, Sam; Manhattan Murder Mystery; Hannah and Her Sisters)

Annie Oakley, 1935, 88m, ★★/$$$, RKO/Turner. A sharpshooting girl from the mountains joins a traveling gun show and falls in love with the owner. Barbara Stanwyck, Preston Foster, Melvyn Douglas. w. Joel Sayre, John Twist, d. George Stevens.
COMEDY: COMEDY DRAMA:
ROMANCE: Romantic Comedy; Feisty Females; **WESTERNS:** Western Comedy; Coming of Age; Female Protagonists; Rodeos
(Annie Get Your Gun; Calamity Jane; Buffalo Bill & the Indians; Buffalo Girls)

The Anniversary, 1968, 95m, ★★1/2/$, WB/NA, R/B&G-V. An angry, blinded widow will not let her sons grow up to leave the nest and keeps them coming back to pay respects for their father she hated and may have killed. Bette Davis, Jack Hedley, James Cossins, Elaine Taylor. w. Jimmy Sangster, P-adap. Bill MacIlwraight, d. Roy Ward Baker.
HORROR: SUSPENSE: DRAMA: Black Comedy; Evil Women; Blind People; Mama's Boys

Another Country, 1984, 90m, ★★★/$$, Orion/Orion, R/S-MRN. Two boarding school friends become lovers before becoming spies. Rupert Everett, Colin Firth, Cary Elwes. w. Julian Mitchell, P-adap. Julian Mitchell, d. Marek Kanievska.

DRAMA: ROMANCE: Coming of Age; Double Lives; Homoeroticism; Gay Men; Spies; Boarding Schools; Boys' School; British; 1920s; Beautiful People; Flashbacks; Traitors; Scenery-Outstanding
(Maurice; A Separate Peace; Dead Poets Society)
(Ed: A very beautiful film that has little to do with spying and more to do with living a double life)

Another 48 Hours, 1990, 95m, ★★/$$$$, Par/Par, R/EP-EV-S. The story remakes itself as the cop (Nick Nolte) gets the convict (Eddie Murphy) out of prison for another drug-busting, criminal-catching spree. w. John Fasano, Jeb Stuart, Larry Gross, Fred Braughton, d. Walter Hill.
ACTION: COMEDY: Action Comedy; Detectives-Police; Buddy Cops; Buddy Films; Drugs-Dealing; Black & White Together
(48 Hours; Beverly Hills Cop SERIES; Lethal Weapon SERIES)
(Ed: Although the original was at the beginning of a trend, this seems like a retread of not only itself but the *Lethal Weapon* series)

Another Stakeout, 1994, 108m, ★★1/2/$, Touchstone/Touchstone, PG-13/P-V-S. Sequel to the buddy cop *Stakeout* with the two sparring buddies playing father-son with a female cop as mom on an undercover case involving the mob. Richard Dreyfuss, Emilio Estevez, Rosie O'Donnell, Cathy Moriarty, Madeleine Stowe, John Ruubinstein, Marcia Strassman, Dennis Farina. w. Jim Kouf, d. John Badham.
COMEDY: Comic Thriller; Police Comedy; Police Stories; Undercover; Detectives-Police; Battle of the Sexes; Buddy Cops; Mob Stories; Female Law Officers; Coulda Been Good
SEQUEL TO: Stakeout (1987)
(Stakeout; Cops and Robbersons)

Another Thin Man, 1939, 105m, ★★★/$$$$, MGM/MGM-UA. William Powell and Myrna Loy in the third of the series, marking the birth of Nick and Nora's first son. w. Frances Goodrich, Albert Hackett, N-adap. Dashiel Hammett, d. W.S. Van Dyke.
COMEDY: ROMANCE: Romantic Comedy; **MYSTERY:** Comic Mystery; **MURDER MYSTERY:** Mystery-Whodunit; Detective Stories; Detective Couples; Partners-Married; Female Screenwriters

(The Thin Man; After the Thin Man; A Night to Remember)
(Ed: Not as good as the first, but the charm and Mr. Stewart are there)

Another Time, Another Place, 1958, 98m, ★★/$$, Par/Par. An American woman writer in England during the war has an affair with a married British soldier, but can they outlast the war? Lana Turner, Barry Sullivan, Glynis Johns, Sean Connery. w. Stanley Mann, N-adap. Leonore Coffee, d. Lewis Allen.
ROMANCE: MELODRAMA: Tearjerkers; Americans Abroad; World War II Era; England; Writers; Romance with Married Person; Cheated Upon Meet
(Indiscretion of an American Wife; Yanks; Hanover Street)

Another Woman, 1988, 84m, ★★★★/$$, Orion/Orion, R/S. An intelligent, strong, but cold woman professor (Gena Rowlands) looks inside herself when she overhears the counseling sessions of a very trouble woman she then wants to help. Mia Farrow, Gene Hackman, Sandy Dennis, Martha Plimpton. w. d. Woody Allen.
DRAMA: Character Studies; Stern Wome; Crossing the Line; Bergmanesque; Monologues-Interior; Professors; Narrated Films; Female Protagonists; Underrated; Psychologists; Therapy; Eavesdropping; Hidden Gems; Writer-Directors
(Wild Strawberries; Diary of a Mad Housewife; Interiors; Autumn Sonata; Gloria; A Woman Under the Influence)
(Ed: Underrated character study may become an Allen masterpiece, especially for Rowland's performance)

Another You, 1991, 98m, ★1/2/$$, Tristar/Col-Tri, PG-13/P-V. A con artist takes a constant liar under his wing to manipulate his talents to criminal use, but the plans go awry. Gene Wilder, Richard Pryor, Mercedes Ruehl, Vanessa Williams, Stephen Lang, Kevin Pollak. d. Maurice Phillips.
COMEDY: Criminals-Stupid; Buddy Films; Liars; Con Artists; Good Premise Unfulfilled
(Stir Crazy; See No Evil, Hear No Evil)

Anthony Adverse, 1936, 141m, ★★★1/2/$$$$, WB/WB. A young man tours 1840s America and runs into Abraham Lincoln and man other soon-to-be-famous people. Frederich March, Olivia de Havilland, Edmund Gwenn, Claude Rains, Gale Sondergaard

(BSActress). w. Sheridan Gibney, N-adap. Hervey Allen, d. Mervyn LeRoy. BPicture, BADirector, **BScore, BCin, BEdit.** Oscars: 6-4.
DRAMA: COMEDY DRAMA: ADVENTURE: Historical Drama; Road Movie; Abraham Lincoln; 1800s; Famous People When Young; Episodic Stories; Faded Hits (Young Mr. Lincoln, Abe Lincoln in Illinois; Johnny Appleseed [Disney cartoon short])

A Nous la Liberte, 1931, 87m, ★★★/$, Ind/Nos. Two old friends remember their days as bums. One becomes an industrial leader, and the other a loner who studies nature. Henri Marchand, Raymond Cordy, Rolla France, Paul Olivier, Jacques Shelly, Andre Michaud. w. d. Rene Clair.
DRAMA: Memories; Episodic Stories; Homeless People; Social Climbing; Depression Era; Dreams; Writer-Directors; French Films

Antonia and Jane, 1991, 75m, ★★★/$$, Par/Par, R/S-P. A satire on two women's long friendship, which is constantly in conflict as both are so very different. Imelda Staunton, Saskia Reeves, Patricia Leventon, Alfred Hoffman. w. Marcy Kahan, d. Beeban Kidron.
DRAMA: COMEDY DRAMA: SATIRE: Women in Conflict; Friendships-Female; Friendships-Lifetime; Episodic Stories; Female Screenwriters; Female Protagonists
(Entre Nous; Beaches; The Turning Point)

Ants, 1977, 100m, ★★/$$$, ABC/Live, Vestron. A resort becomes prey for the little varmints, and this is no picnic. Suzanne Somers, Robert Foxworth, Myrna Loy, Lynda Day George, Bernie Casey, Barry Van Dyke. d. Robert Scheerer.
HORROR: Insects; Monsters-Animal; Camp; Deaths-One by One; Unintentionally Funny; TV Movies (Empire of the Ants; Frogs; Kingdom of the Spiders; Arachnophobia; The Swarm)

Antonia's Line, 1995, 110m, ★★★/$$, First Look/NA, R/S. The lives of several fairly radical and humorous Dutch women, flashing back from present-day to the postwar era, and explaining how they do without men. Willeke van Ammelrooy, Els Dottermans, Jan Decleir. w. d. Marleen Gorris. **BFLFilm.** Oscars: 1-1.
COMEDY DRAMA: Family Drama; Women's Films; Ensemble Films; Ensembles-Female; Flashbacks

Any Wednesday, 1966, 109m, ★★★/$$$, Par/Par, PG/S. Young woman winds up mistress to rich, older executive only to find the apartment he pays for being occupied by another, younger executive with whom she has to double-date with her older one and his wife. Jane Fonda, Dean Jones, Jason Robards. w. Julius J. Epstein, Philip C. Epstein, P-adap. Muriel Resnick, d. Robert Ellis Miller.
COMEDY: Romantic Comedy; **FARCE:** Romance-Clandestine; Mistresses; Secrets-Keeping; Cheating Men; Blackouts; Affair Lairs; Romance-Triangles; Executives; Roommates (Sunday in New York; The Moon Is Blue; The Apartment; Period of Adjustment)

Any Which Way You Can, 1980, 116m, ★★/$$$$, WB/WB, PG/P-EV. Clint hits the road in his truck with his orangutan, ready to fistfight a bunch of rednecks. Sondra Locke, Anne Ramsay, Glen Campbell. w. S. Sherman, d. Buddy Van Horn.
COMEDY: ACTION: Action Comedy; Road Movies; Chase Movies; Rednecks; Country People; Primates; Animals-Smart; Gamblers; Fugitives from the Mob; Boxers; Macho Men; Kidnappings
SEQUEL TO: Every Which Way But Loose (Every Which Way But Loose; Convoy)

Apache Uprising, 1965, 90m, ★★1/2/$$, Par/Par. Stagecoach passengers survive an Indian attack at a station. Rory Calhoun, Corinne Calvet, John Russell, Lon Chaney Jr., DeForest Kelley. w. Harry Sanford, Max Lamb, d. R. G. Springsteen.
WESTERNS: Indians-American, Conflict with; **TRAGEDY:** Journies; Nightmare Journies; Wagon Trains
(Fort Apache; Wagonmaster; Indian Fighter; Stagecoach)

The Apartment (B&W), 1960, 125m, Mirisch-UA/CBS-Fox, MGM-UA, ★★★★/$$$$. Young insurance executive (Jack Lemmon, BActor) loans his pad out for executive flings on the side and soon is climbing the ladder only to find the girl (Shirley MacLaine, BActress) he loves may be unattainable after all. Fred MacMurray, Jack Kruschen (BSActor). w. Billy Wilder, IAL Diamond (**BOScr**), d. Billy Wilder (**BDirector**). **BPicture**, BB&WCin, **BB&W Art**, BSound, **BEdit.** Oscars: 10-5.
COMEDY DRAMA: DRAMA: Office Comedy; Business Life; Affair Lairs;

Young Men; American Dream; Life Transitions; Ethics; Social Climbing; Conformism; Lonely People; Elusive Women; Mistresses; Bosses-Bad; Nosy Neighbors; Suicidal Tendencies; Apartment Buildings; New York Life (How to Succeed in Business Without Really Trying; The Man in the Grey Flannel Suit; Any Wednesday; The Secret of My Success)
(Ed: The perfect comedy drama)

Apartment Zero, 1989, 114m, ★★★1/2/$$, Academy/Academy, R/S-P-EV-B&G-MRN. A nervous young man (Colin Firth) rents his extra room out to a very dubious American (Hart Bochner) who could be a mercenary serial bisexual killer. w. Martin Donovan, David Koepp, d. Martin Donovan.
SUSPENSE: MYSTERY: MURDER MYSTERY: Rogue Plots; Serial Killers; Roommates; Roommates from Hell; Lonely People; Neurotic People; Homo-eroticism; Accused-Unjustly?; Bisexuality; Hitchcockian; Sexy Men; Apartment Buildings; Neighbors-Troublesome; Ostracism; Mercenaries; South America; Argentina; Movie Theaters; Underrated; Hidden Gems; Cult Films; Ind Films
(Single White Female; The Tenant; Pacific Heights; The Official Story; Kiss of the Spider Woman)

The Ape, 1943, 62m, ★★/$, Monogram/Nos. A mad scientist kills an ape and runs around in its skin, stalking humans for their spinal fluid, which is supposed to cure polio. Boris Karloff, Maris Wrixon, Gertrude Hoffman, Henry Hall. w. Curt Siodmak, Richard Carroll, P-adap. Adam Shirk, d. William Nigh.
HORROR: SUSPENSE: Scientists-Mad; Primates; Cures/Elixirs; Humans into Animals

Apocalypse Now, 1979, 153m, ★★★1/2/$$$$, Zoetrope-UA/MGM-UA, R/EV. Vietnam soldiers journey up a dark, dangerous river to find another soldier (Marlon Brando) who has created a bizarre kingdom for himself. Martin Sheen, Robert Duvall (BSActor). w. d. Francis Ford Coppola (BDirector), N-adap. Joseph Conrad. BPicture, **BCinema**, BEdit, **BSound.** Oscars: 6-2.
ADVENTURE: Epics; Vietnam War; War Movie; Kingdoms; Evil Men; Corruption; Jungle Life; Men in Conflict
REMAKE OF: Heart of Darkness

(Heart of Darkness; Farewell to the King; The Deer Hunter; Platoon)

The Appaloosa, 1966, 98m, ★★1/2/$$, Universal/MCA-U, PG/S. A cowboy's dream of starting a stud farm with his prize horse is disrupted by locals who think he's molested their girl. Marlon Brando, Anjanette Comer, John Saxon, Frank Silvera w. James Bridges, Roland Kibbee, N-adap. Robert MacLeod, d. Sidney J. Furie.

WESTERNS: Westerns-Neo; DRAMA: Social Drama; Molestation-Child; Cowboys; Small-Town Scandals; Accused Unjustly?; Ahead of its Time; Curiosities; Horses

(The Mark; Lolita)

The Apple Dumpling Gang, 1975, 100m, ★★★/$$$$ Disney/Disney, G. Three kids get rich on gold and get caught up in a robbery attempt with goofy bank robbers (Bill Bixby, Susan Clark, Don Knotts, Tim Conway). d. Norman Tokar.

CHILDREN'S: COMEDY: WESTERNS: Western-Comedy; Bank Robberies; Criminals-Stupid; Disney Comedy; Orphans

SEQUEL: The Apple Dumpling Gang Rides Again

The Apple Dumpling Gang Rides Again, 1979, 88m, ★★1/2/$$$, Disney/Disney, G. Two bumbling bank robbers trying to go straight get mixed up with a sheriff, the cavalry, Indians and another outlaw gang. Bill Bixby, Susan Clark, David Wayne, Don Knotts, Tim Conway, Slim Pickens. w. Don Tait, N-adap, w. Jack M. Bickham, d. Norman Tokar.

CHILDREN'S: COMEDY: WESTERNS: Western-Comedy; Bank Robberies; Criminals-Stupid; Disney Comedy; Orphans

SEQUEL TO: The Apple Dumpling Gang (Hot Lead and Cold Feet; The Shakiest Gun in the West)

The Applegates, 1990, 90m, ★★1/2/$, Ind/Media, Fox, PG-13/P-S-B&G. A seemingly normal family in the suburbs is really a family of giant mutant insects who can transform themselves into humans. They're from the Amazon and they've come to America to avenge nuclear power. Ed Begley, Jr., Stockard Channing, Dabney Coleman, Cami Cooper, Bobby Jacoby, Savannah Smith Boucher. w. Michael Lehmann, Redbeard Simmons, d. Lehmann.

COMEDY: SATIRE: SCI-FI: Fantasy; Disguises; Impostors; Monsters-Mutant; Insects; American Dream; Suburban Life; Coulda Been Good

(The Coneheads; Heathers)

Appointment for Love, 1941, 89m, ★★1/2/$, Universal/NA. A playwright and a doctor agree to marry for purely practical purposes. Charles Boyer, Margaret Sullivan, Eugene Pallette, Rita Johnson. w. Bruce Manning, Felix Jackson, d. William A. Seiter.

ROMANCE: Romance-Reluctant; Marriage of Convenience; Marriages-Fake; Writers; Doctors

(Without Love; This Thing Called Love; The Lady Is Willing)

Appointment in Honduras, 1953, 79m, ★★/$$, RKO/Turner. Four criminals and three "civilians" escape through the jungle during a revolution. Glenn Ford, Ann Sheridan, Zachary Scott. w. Karen de Wolf, d. Jacques Tourneur.

ACTION: ADVENTURE: Escape Adventure; Central America; Jungles; Political Unrest; Female Screenwriters

Appointment with Death, 1988, 91m, ★★★/$, Cannon/WB, PG. Hercule Poirot solves murders in 1930s Palestine. Peter Ustinov, Lauren Bacall, Carrie Fisher, John Gielgud, Piper Laurie. w. Anthony Shaffer, Peter Buckman, Michael Winner, N-adap, w. Agatha Christie, d. Michael Winner.

MYSTERY: MURDER: MURDER MYSTERY: Mystery-Whodunit; All-Star Cast; Middle East; Agatha Christie

(Death on the Nile; Evil Under the Sun; Murder on the Orient Express)

Appointment with Venus, see Island Rescue

Apollo 13, 1995, U/MCA-U. True story of the space mission to the moon which seemed to go fine until malfunction almost doomed its crew. Tom Hanks, Kevin Bacon, Bill Paxton, Gary Sinise, Ed Harris, Kathleen Quinlan. d. Ron Howard.

DRAMA: SUSPENSE: Survival Drama; Astronauts; Outer Space Movies; Historical Drama; Ensemble Films; Ensembles-Male; 1970s

(Marooned; Capricorn One; Space)

The April Fools, 1969, 95m, ★★★/$$$ NG/CBS-Fox, R/S. A married man (Jack Lemmon) in the mod art world begins again with a sexy French girl (Catherine Deneuve) but may get himself into trou-

ble. Charles Boyer, Myrna Loy, Harvey Korman, Melinda Dillon, Sally Kellerman. d. Stuart Rosenberg.

COMEDY DRAMA: ROMANCE: Romantic Comedy; Midlife Crisis; Starting Over; Romance-Older Men/Young Women; Romance-Mismatched; Romance-Brief; Beautiful People; Mod Era; 1960s London; Sexy Women; Time Capsules; Hidden Gems; Forgotten Films

(Avanti!; Alex and the Gypsy; Middle-Age Crazy)

April Fool's Day, 1986, 90m, ★★/$$, Par/Par, R/EV-S-B&G. A rich girl invites several college friends to her home in the wilderness, where they begin dropping like the pesky flies on the lake-or do they? Deborah Foreman, Jay Baker, Griffin O'Neal, Pat Barlow. w. Danilo Bach, d. Fred Walton.

HORROR: COMEDY: Horro Comedy; Murders-One by One; Hoaxes; Murder-Invitation to; Teen Horror Flicks of 80s; Teenage Movies; Teenagers

(Friday the 13th SERIES; And Then There Were None; Ten Little Indians)

April in Paris, 1952, 100m, ★★1/2/$$$, WB/WB. A chorus girl gets her big break in Paris. Doris Day, Ray Bolger, Claude Dauphin. w. Jack Rose, Melville Shavelson, d. David Butler.

MUSICAL: COMEDY: Musical Comedy; ROMANCE: Dancers; Actresses; Paris; Fame-Rise to

Arabesque, 1966, 105m, ★★1/2/$$$, UniversalMCA-U, PG/V. A professor is kidnapped and forced into deciphering a message leading to Middle East intrigue and a beautiful, possibly double-crossing femme fatale. Gregory Peck, Sophia Loren. d. Stanley Donen.

SUSPENSE: Comic Thriller; ACTION: Action Comedy; Spy Films; Spies; Chase Movie; Dangerous Women; Double Crossings; Scientists; Kidnappings; Mindgames; Puzzles to Solve; Hitchcockian; Arab People

(Charade; North by Northwest; Mirage)

(Ed: Fun, but rather silly; certainly below Hitchcock; then again, ahead of its time with style of silly comedy mixed with thrills)

Arachnophobia, 1990, ★★★/$$$$, Hollywood/Hollywood, PG-13/V-B&G. Spiders from South America terrorize a small town in California-lots of spiders, but fear not, there are exterminators, unless they're exterminated themselves first. John Goodman, Jeff Daniels, Harley Jane Kozak, Julian Sands, Stuart Pankin, Henry Jones. w. Wesley Strick, Don Jakoby, d. Frank Marshall.

HORROR: Horror Comedy; Black Comedy; Deaths-One by One; Insects; Monsters-Animal Phobias; Spiders (Kingdom of Spiders; Ants; Empire of the Ants; The Swarm)

Arch of Triumph, 1948, 120m, ★★★/$$, Selznick/CBS-Fox. Ingrid Bergman is in love with an Austrian refugee who may be on the opposite side of the war in France. Charles Boyer, Charles Laughton. N-adap. Erich Maria Marquez, d. Lewis Milestone.

DRAMA: ROMANCE: Romantic Drama; Love-Questionable; World War II-Resistance; Traitors; Paris (Casablanca; Joan of Paris; The Adventuress)

Are Husbands Necessary?, 1942, 79m, ★★¹/₂/$$, Par/NA. A quarrelling couple decide to adopt but it may not solve their problems. Ray Milland, Betty Field, Patricia Morrison, Eugene Pallette, Richard Haydn. w. Tess Slesinger, Frank Davis, N-adap, w. Isabel Scott Rorick, *Mr. and Mrs. Cugat*, d. Norman Taurog.

MELODRAMA: DRAMA: COMEDY DRAMA: Children-Adopted; Marriage Drama; Mothers Alone

Are You Being Served?, 1977, 95m, ★★★/NA, EMI/NA. The sales staff of a clothing store goes on a trip to the Costa Plonka. John Inman, Frank Thornton, Mollie Sugden, Trevor Bannister. w. Jeremy Lloyd, David Croft, d. Bob Kellett.

COMEDY: FARCE: Screwball Comedy; British Films; TV Series Movies; Department Stores (No Sex Please, We're British; Fawlty Towers)

Aren't We All?, 1932, 67m, ★★★/$$, Par/NA. A "society lady" is unfaithful to her husband, which leads to all kinds of complications. Gertrude Lawrence, Hugh Wakefield, Owen Nares, Harold Huth. w. Basil Mason, Gilbert Wakefield, P-adap, w. Frederick Lonsdale, d. Harry Lachman, Rudolf Maté.

COMEDY DRAMA: SATIRE: Social Satire; Comedy of Manners; Cheating Women; Rich People; British Films; England (Private Lives; The Twentieth Century; Joy of Living)

Aria, 1988, 90m, ★★★/$, Academy/Academy, R/S-FN-MN. A series of music videos of opera arias, from realistic to surrealistic. d's. Robert Altman, Bruce Beresford, Bill Bryden, Nicholas Roeg, Jean-Luc Godard, Ken Russell, Franc Roddam, Charles Sturridge, Julien Temple.

DRAMA: Anthology; Music Video Style; Music Movies; Revisionist Films

Arise, My Love, 1940, 113m, ★★¹/₂/$$, Par/NA. American journalists struggle with politics, life, and love in Europe during the Spanish Civil War. Claudette Colbert, Ray Milland, Walter Abel. w. Charles Brackett, Billy Wilder, d. Mitchell Liesen.

DRAMA: MELODRAMA: ROMANCE: Romantic Drama; Journalists; Americans Abroad; Political Unrest; Spanish Civil War (For Whom the Bell Tolls; The Angel Wore Red)

The Aristocats, 1970, 78m, ★★★★/$$$$, Disney/NA, G. An evil butler deliberately "loses" two cats for fear they will inherit his mistress' wealth. The neighborhood animals band together to restore them to their family. Voices of Phil Harris, Eva Gabor, Sterling Holloway, Scatman Crothers. w. Larry Clemmons and others, d. Wolfgang Reitherman.

CHILDREN'S: FAMILY: MUSICAL: Musical-Animated; Cartoons; Animated; Cats; Paris; Chase Movies; Inheritances at Stake (101 Dalmations; Lady & the Tramp; The Rescuers)

Arizona, 1940, 125m, ★★¹/₂/$$$, Col/Col. A traveling Missouri cowboy teams up with an Arizona spitfire to combat villians who attack her wagon trains. Jean Arthur, William Holden, Warren William Paul Harvey. w. Claude Binyon, d. Wesley Ruggles.

WESTERN: Western Comedy; **ROMANCE:** Romantic Comedy; Wagon Trains; Free Spirits; Feisty Females; Forgotten Films (The African Queen; Rooster Cogburn)

The Arkansas Traveler, 1938, 85m, ★★★/$$, Par/NA. A benevolent stranger helps a small-town widow keep her newspaper alive. Bob Burns, Fay Bainter, Jean Parker. w. Viola Brothers Shore, George Sessions Perry, SS-adap. Jack Cunningham, d. Alfred Santell.

COMEDY: COMEDY DRAMA: Mortgage Drama; Newspapers; Comedians; Comedy-Character; Southerns; Widows; Female Screenwriters

Armed and Dangerous, 1986, 88m, ★★/$, Col/RCA-Col, PG/P. A former lawyer and ex-cop uncover corruption as bumbling security guards. John Candy, Eugene Levy, Robert Loggia. w. Harold Ramis, Peter Torokvei, Brian Grazer, Harold Ramis, James Keach, d. Mark L. Lester.

COMEDY: Comedy of Errors; Police Comedy; Corruption; Police Corruption; Fools-Bumbling (Berserk!; Police Academy SERIES)

Armed Response, 1986, 95m, ★★/$, Cinetel/Cinetel, R/S-EV. A Japanese gangster hires a private eye to recover a rare jade antique. David Carradine, Lee Van Cleef. w. T. L. Lankford, d. Fred Olen Ray.

ACTION: Mob Stories; Japanese Mob; Detective Stories; Martial Arts (The Challenge; American Ninja)

Armored Command, 1961, 99m, ★★/$, Allied Artists/Fox. During World War II, a beautiful Nazi spy infiltrates American ranks. Howard Keel, Tina Louise, Burt Reynolds. w. Ron W. Alcorn, d. Byron Haskin.

DRAMA: Spy Films; Spies; Spies-Female; Nazi Stories; World War II Stories; Forgotten Films

The Army in the Shadows, 1969, 143m, ★★¹/₂/$, Films Corona-Fono Roma/NA. Traitors infiltrate resistance fighters in Lyon during World War II. Lino Ventura, Simone Signoret, Jean-Pierre Cassel. w. d. Jean-Pierre Melville, N-adap. Joseph Kessel.

DRAMA: Spy Films; Spies; World War II-Resistance; World War II Stories; Traitors; French Films

Army of Darkness, 1993, 81m, ★★/$$, U/MCA-U, R/EV-B&G-S. A time traveler in medieval England finds himself besieged by undead soldiers in this sci-fi outing, as he runs to save himself and get back to present day. Bruce Campbell, Embeth Davidtz. d. Sam Raimi.

HORROR: ACTION: Horror Comedy; Black Comedy; Camelot Stories; Time Travel; Zombies (The Evil Dead; Evil Dead 2; Darkman)

Arnold, 1973, 100m, ★★¹/₂/$$, Avco/Live. Cassettes left after death by a wealthy, evil man with a very large, very creepy house with a personality of its own thwart the greed of his would-be inheritors. Stella Stevens, Roddy McDowell, Elsa Lanchester, Farley Granger, Victor Buono. w. Jameson Brewer, John Fenton Murray, d. Georg Fenady.

HORROR: Black Comedy; Deaths-One by One; Inheritances at Stake (The Legacy)

Around the World in 80 Days, 1956, 178m, ★★★ 1/2/$$$$$, UA/MGM-UA, G. After a bet, a wealthy Brit goes around the world in a balloon, among other things, in a race with many interesting globe-hopping stopovers. David Niven, Shirley MacLaine, Cantinflas, Buster Keaton. w. James Poe, S.J. Perelman, John Farrow (BAScr), N-adap. Jules Verne, d. Michael Anderson (BDirector). **BPicture, BCCinema,** BCArt, BCCostume, **BEditing, BOScore.** Oscars: 8-5.

ADVENTURE: Comic Adventure; Spectacles; Epics; Race Against Time; Balloons; World Travel; Journies; International Cast; All-Star Casts; Scenery-Outstanding

REMAKE: TV (1989)

(The Great Race; Those Magnificent Men in Their Flying Machines; Great Expectations)

Around the World Under the Sea, 1966, 110m, ★★/$$, MGM/MGM-UA, G. A state-of-the-art sub travels the underwater world repairing sensors to give early warning of volcanoes. Lloyd Bridges, Shirley Eaton, Brian Kelly, Keenan Wynn. w. Arthur Weiss, Art Arthur, d. Andrew Marton.

ADVENTURE: Underwater Adventure; Volcanoes; Submarines; World Travel (Voyage to the Bottom of the Sea)

The Arousers, 1970, 126m, ★★ 1/2/$$, Ind/Sultan, R/S-V-B&G. A psychotic good-looking young man tries to have sex with many women, but all are inappropriate, so he kills them-until one puts a stop to it, because, of course, the movie had to end. Tab Hunter, Naydyne Turney, Roberta Collins, Angel Fox. d. Curtis Hanson.

HORROR: SUSPENSE: MURDER: Murders-One by One; Murders of Women; Serial Killers; Spoofs-Horror; Sexy Men; 1970s; Cult Films; Curiosities (Ed: Hanson went on to Hitchcock retreads, then *The Hand that Rocks the Cradle* and *The River Wild*)

The Arrangement, 1969, 120m, ★★ 1/2/$$, WB/WB, R/P-S. An old man

reflects on his empty life, though he was a successful advertising man with a beautiful young woman in his life. Kirk Douglas, Faye Dunaway, Deborah Kerr, Richard Boone, Hume Cronyn. wd. Elia Kazan, N-adap, w. Elia Kazan.

DRAMA: MELODRAMA: Biographies-Fictional; Midlife Crisis; Elderly Men; Romance-Older Men/Younger Women; Advertising World (Edward, My Son; Patterns; Death of a Salesman)

Arriverderci, Baby! (*Drop Dead, Darling*), 1966, 100m, ★★ 1/2/$, WB/Par. A widow killer meets a gold digger and they try to outsmart each other in the kill department. Tony Curtis, Rosanna Schiaffino, Lionel Jeffries, Zsa Zsa Gabor. w. d. Ken Hughes, SS-adap. Richard Deming, (*The Careful Man*).

COMEDY: MURDER: Murder of Spouse; Murder Attempts-Comic; Golddiggers; Turning the Tables; Mindgames; Murderers-Black Widow; Coulda Been Good

REMAKE/RETREAD: Divorce, Italian Style (Divorce, Italian Style; How to Murder Your Wife; Prizzi's Honor; Dirty Rotten Scoundrels) (Ed: The humor is on the silly side, rather than the dark)

Arrowsmith, 1931, 99m, ★★★/$$$, Goldwyn-UA/Goldwyn. Country doctor goes to Caribbean to study plants for cures to diseases. Ronald Colman, Helen Hayes, Myrna Loy. w. Sidney Howard, N-adap. Sinclair Lewis, d. John Ford. BPicture, BArt, BCin, BScr. Oscars: 4-0.

DRAMA: ADVENTURE: Social Drama; Medical Drama; Cures/Solutions-Search for; Doctors; Ethics; Greed; Caribbean (The Story of Dr. Wassel; Not as a Stranger; Dodsworth)

Arsenal, 1929, 99m, (Silent) ★★★/NA, Vufku/Nos. The 1914 Russian war is made worse by labor strikes. S. Svashenko, A. Buchma, M. Nademsky. w. d. Alexander Dovzhenko.

DRAMA: War Stories; Russian Revolution; Strikes; Russian Films; Writer-Directors; Silent Films (Strike; The Battleship Potemkin)

Arsene Lupin, 1932, 75m, ★★★/$$, MGM/NA. A "gentleman thief" of Paris is almost caught stealing the Mona Lisa. John Barrymore, Lionel Barrymore, Karen

Morley. w. Carey Wilson, Lenore Coffee, Bayard Veiller, d. Jack Conway.

COMEDY DRAMA: Comedy-Light; Art Thieves; Heist Stories

Arsene Lupin Returns, 1938, 81m, ★★ 1/2/$$, MGM/NA. The gentleman thief, reformed now, helps detectives track down a notorious colleague in crime. Melvyn Douglas, Warren William, Virginia Bruce, John Halliday. w. James Kevin McGuiness, Howard Emmett Rogers, George Harmon Coxe, d. George Fitzmaurice.

COMEDY DRAMA: Comedy-Light; Art Thieves; Heist Stories; Ex-Convicts; Detective Stories (To Catch a Thief, The Pink Panther)

Arsenic and Old Lace (B&W), 1944, 118m, ★★★★/$$, WB/CBS-Fox. A dashing bachelor theater critic comes home to announce marriage to old aunts who raised him, only to find they have a very strange hobby in the basement. Cary Grant, Josephine Hull, Raymond Massey, Peter Lorre, Priscilla Lane. w., P-adap. Joseph Kesselring, d. Frank Capra.

FARCE: COMEDY: Black Comedy; Comedy-Morbid; Murders-One by One; Hide the Dead Body; Murderers-Nice; Elderly Women; Secrets-Keeping; Playboys; Hidden Gems (Ladies in Retirement; The Trouble with Harry; You Can't Take It with You) (Ed: Though some snobs prefer the play version, it's still brilliant)

Arthur, 1981, 97m, ★★★★/$$$$$, Orion-WB/WB, PG/P-S. A rich, overgrown brat (Dudley Moore, BActor) who loves the bottle and the broads falls for a common shoplifter (Liza Minnelli), much to the consternation of his jilted rich girlfriend (Jill Eikenberry) and sarcastic butler (John Gielgud, **BSActor**). Geraldine Fitzgerald. w. d. Steve Gordon (BOScr). **BOSong.** Oscars: 4-2.

COMEDY: ROMANCE: Romantic Comedy; Screwball Comedy; Romance-Choosing the Right Person; Inheritances At Stake; Rich People; Rich vs. Poor; Romance-Class Conflicts; Lover; Family Dislikes; Pickpockets; Alcoholism; Blockbusters; Old-Fashioned Recent Films; Sleeper Hits

SEQUEL: Arthur 2: On the Rocks

Arthur 2, On the Rocks, 1989, 113m, ★★/$, Orion/Orion, PG-13/P-S. Arthur is now married to his favorite shoplifter but rough times are ahead without that big inheritance. Dudley Moore, Liza Minnelli. d. Bud Yorkin.

COMEDY: ROMANCE: Romantic Comedy; Marriage Comedy; Poor People; Riches to Rags; Alcoholics
(Ed: Rough times are ahead for the audience, too)

Article 99, 1992, 100m, ★★1/2/$$, Orion/Orion, R/P-V-S. At a V.A. hospital, doctors have to break the rules to serve their patients, often in ways that make one wonder who should be the patients. Ray Liotta, Keifer Sutherland, Forest Whitaker. w. Ron Cutler, d. Howard Deutsch.

DRAMA: COMEDY DRAMA: SATIRE: Social Drama; Social Satire; Veterans; Hospitals; Doctors; Anti-establishment Films; Government as Enemy
(The Hospital; Brittania Hospital; And Justice for All; Network; Born on the Fourth of July)
(Ed: Has its moments and did have great potential, but not *Network* or *Dog Day Afternoon* is this; again, if it had been made in the 70s with a more austere sensibility, who knows?)

Artists and Models, 1937, 97m, ★★★/$$, Par/NA. An advertising executive on an account for a silverware company needs a model-and a girlfriend. Jack Benny, Ida Lupino, Richard Arlen, Gail Patrick. w. Walter de Leon, Francis Martin, d. Raoul Walsh.

COMEDY: ROMANCE: Romantic Comedy; Romance-Unprofessional; Advertising World; Models; Artists; Comedians

Artists and Models, 1955, 109m, ★★★/$$$, Par/Par. The dreams of a hapless geek are used by his friend in comic strips. Foreign agents and CIA officials get interested and all hell breaks loose. Dean Martin, Jerry Lewis, Shirley MacLaine, Dorothy Malone, Eva Gabor, Anita Ekberg. w. Frank Tashlin, Don McGuire, d. Frank Tashlin.

COMEDY: Music Movies; Comedy-Slapstick; Comedy of Errors; Models; Artists; Dancers; Comic Heroes; Nerds; Nerds & Babes; Martin & Lewis
(The Caddy; My Friend Irma; Pardners; Scared Stiff; How to Murder Your Wife)

Artists and Models Abroad, 1938, 90m, ★★1/2/$$, Par/NA. A Texas millionaire helps a troupe of models stranded in Paris. Jack Benny, Joan Bennett, Mary Boland. w. Howard Lindsay, Russell

Crouse, Ken Englund, d. Mitchell Leisen.

COMEDY: ROMANCE: Romantic Comedy; Stranded; Models; Paris; Oil People; Comedians

The Art of Love, 1965, 99m, ★★1/2/$$, Universal/MCA-U. An unsuccessful artist fakes his suicide and as a result, his work becomes extremely chic. James Garner, Dick Van Dyke, Angie Dickinson, Elke Sommer, Ethel Merman, Pierre Olaf. w. Carl Reiner, d. Norman Jewison.

COMEDY: SATIRE: ROMANCE: Romantic Comedy; Artists; Con Artists; Death-Faked; Suicidal Tendencies
(Ed: He should have gotten himself murdered and collected the insurance, too)

Ashanti: Land of No Mercy, 1979, 117m, ★★/$, Col/TWE, PG. The wife of a W.H.O. official is kidnapped by slave traders in West Africa. Michael Caine, Omar Sharif, Peter Ustinov, Rex Harrison. w. Stephen Geller, N-adap. Alberto Vasquez-Figueroa, *Ebano*, d. Richard Fleischer.

DRAMA: SUSPENSE: Kidnappings; Slavery-White; Africa
(The Wilby Conspiracy; Black Rain [1989]; The Wind and the Lion)

Ash Wednesday, 1974, 99m, ★★1/2/$, Sagittarius-Par/Par, R/S-MRN. A woman has a facelift and heads to the Alps for fun in bed while calling her ailing husband at home. Elizabeth Taylor, Henry Fonda, Helmut Berger. w. Jean Claude Tramont, d. Larry Peerce.

DRAMA: MELODRAMA: ROMANCE: Romantic Drama; Character Studies; Midlife Crisis; Alienation; Cosmetic Surgery; Depression; Female Protagonists; Americans Abroad; Prostitutes-Male; Sexy Men; Coulda Been Good; Alps
(And Now My Love; The Driver's Seat)

Ashes and Diamonds, 1958, 96m, ★★★/$$, Film Polski/Sultan. A soldier continues killing after the war is over, unable to stop the obsession. Zbigniew Cybulski, Ewa Krzyzazanowska. w. d. Andrzej Wajda, N-adap. Jerzy Andrzejewski.

DRAMA: MURDER: Serial Killers; Soldiers; Obsessions; World War II-Postwar Era; Polish Films; Europeans-Eastern; Writer-Directors

Ask Any Girl, 1959, 98m, ★★★/$$, MGM/MGM-UA. A receptionist in New York City goes after married executives and gets into trouble. David Niven,

Shirley MacLaine, Jim Backus. w. George Wells, N-adap. Winifred Wolfe, d. Charles Walters.

COMEDY: ROMANCE: Romantic Comedy; Sex Comedy; Romance with Married Person; Business Life; Secretaries; Executives
(All in a Night's Work; That Touch of Mink)

Aspen Extreme, 1993, 128m, ★★1/2/$, Hollywood/Hollywood, PG-13/S-P-MN. A hunky ski instructor in guess where longs to break out of the constraints of being a gigolo and become a writer in this semi-autobiographic tale of heroism on the slopes and on the sheets. Paul Gross, Peter Berg, Finola Hughes, Teri Polo, Martin Kemp, Nicolette Scorsese. w. d. Patrick Hasburgh.

DRAMA: MELODRAMA: Sports Movies; Skiing; Romantic Drama; Young Men; Friendships-Male; Sexy Men; Prostitutes-Male; Writers; Autobiographical Stories; Writer-Directors
(Downhill Racer, American Gigolo)
(Ed: So serious and glossy, it's laughable)

The Asphalt Jungle (B&W), 1950, 112m, ★★★★/$$$, MGM/MGM-UA. A gangster gets out of prison to reunite gang for one more heist, but it may be everyone's last. Sterling Hayden, Sam Jaffe (BSActor), Marilyn Monroe, Jean Hagen. w. Ben Maddow, John Huston (BScr), N-adap. W.R. Burnett, d. John Huston (BDirector). BB&WCin. Oscars: 4-0.

DRAMA: TRAGEDY: Crime Drama; Film Noir; Heist Stories; Mob Stories; Reunions; Hiding Out; Fugitives From the Law; One Last Time; Ex-Convicts

REMAKES: The Badlanders; Cairo; Cool Breeze
(The Killing; Reservoir Dogs; Pulp Fiction; Cairo; The Badlanders; Cool Breeze; Rififi)

The Asphyx, 1973, 99m, ★★/$, Ind/Media, VCI. A Victorian man aims to rid his body of the spirit of death, thereby becoming immortal. Robert Stephens, Robert Powell, Jane Lapotaire. w. Brian Comport, d. Peter Newbrook.

HORROR: SCI-FI: Fantasy; Reincarnation; Immortality; Victorian Era; Dead-Back from the

The Assassin, 1961, 105m, ★★1/2/$, Titanus-Vides-SGC/NA. A successful antique dealer is accused of murder. Marcello Mastroianni, Salvo Randone, Micheline Presle. w. Elio Petri and others, d. Elio Petri.

DRAMA: MURDER: Accused Unjustly?; Framed; Italian Films; Assassination Plots (Divorce, Italian Style)

Assassination, 1987, 88m, ★★/$, Ind/NA. Headquarters arranges for spy to be killed, so he has to go on the lam. Ian Hendry, Edward Judd, Frank Windsor. w. Michael Sloan, d. Peter Crane.
SUSPENSE: Spy Films; Assassination Plots; Presidents; Hitmen; Spies; Fugitives from the Law; Conspiracy

The Assassination Bureau, 1969, 110m, ★★★/$$, Par/Par. A lady writer (Diana Rigg) falls into a ring of hitmen and terrorist-types in turn of the century England and Italy when she falls in love with a primary leader. Oliver Reed, Telly Savalas, Beryl Reid, Clive Revill, Curt Jurgens. w. Michael Relph, Wolf Mankowitz, d. Basil Dearden.
COMEDY: FARCE: Black Comedy;
ROMANCE: Romantic Comedy; Comedy-Slapstick; Terrorists; Assassination Plots; Italy; Venice; Journalists; Female Protagonists; Undercover; Forgotten Films; Overlooked at Release; Hidden Gems
(A Flea in Her Ear; Hotel Paradiso)

The Assassination of Trotsky, 1972, 103m, ★★¹/₂/$, DEG/Republic. Russian former leader Trotsky is in exile in a small village in Mexico when a killer comes to pay a call. Richard Burton, Alain Delon, Romy Schneider, Valentina Cortese. w. Nicholas Mosley, Masolino D'Amico, d. Joseph Losey.
DRAMA: Biographies; True Stories; Historical Drama; Spies; Assassinations; Leaders; Hiding Out; Mexico; Russians; Communists

Assassins, 1995, 130m, ★★★/$$$, WB/WB, R/EV-P. A world-class hitman has some competition who's knocking off his assignments before he can. So he goes after the other predator-but is the predator after him, and what about the woman in between? Sylvester Stallone, Antonio Banderas, Julianne Moore. w. Andy Wachowski, Larry Wachowski, d. Richard Donner.
ACTION: SUSPENSE: Cat-and-Mouse Stories; Hitmen; Hitwomen; Spain; Computer Terror; Men in Conflict; Assassinations
(The Specialist; Nighthawks)
(Ed: Yet another good premise that carries better than one would think for Stallone, but it's muddled in its-get this-

complexity. Wasn't Julianne Moore in everything in '95?)

The Assault, 1987, 149m, ★★★¹/₂/$$ (LR), Cannon/MGM-UA, R/V-S. A boy who's family is taken away in the Nazi occupation of Holland, but who survives the war himself, years later meets several of the people who witnessed a terrible Nazi murder one night on their street. w. Gerard Soeteman, N-adap. Harry Mulisch, d. Fons Rademaker. **BFFilm.** Oscars: 1-0.
DRAMA: MELODRAMA: TRAGEDY: Nazi Stories; World War II Era; Child Protagonists; Episodic Stories
(The Nasty Girl; The Diary of Anne Frank; Europa, Europa; Max and Helen; Schindler's List)

Assault on Precinct 13, 1976, 90m, ★★★/$, 20th/Media. A police station is attacked by a gang for the retribution of one of its members. Austin Stoker, Darwin Joston, Laurie Zimmer. w. d. John Carpenter.
ACTION: Crime Drama; Police Stories; Inner City Life; Revenge; Police vs. Mob; Writer-Directors; Cult Films
(Across 110th Street; Fort Apache, the Bronx; Attica)

The Assisi Underground, 1985, 178m, ★★/$, Cannon/MGM-UA, PG/V. Monks hide Jews during World War II. Ben Cross, James Mason, Maximilian Schell. w. d. N-adap. Giuseppe Ramati.
DRAMA: ADVENTURE: War Movies; World War II Movies; Jewish People; Jews-Saving; Priests; Monks; Hiding Out; Anti-semitism; Nazi Stories; Concentration Camps
(The White Rose; The Shop on Main Street; The Golem; Bittere Ernte)
(Ed: A noble and important story is bogged down with ciphers and stereotypes for characters)

The Associate, 1982, 93m, ★★¹/₂/$, Triumph/Embassy, Sultan, R/S-P. A financial consultant can't even keep his own finances in order, so he invents a scheme of having a fictitious partner to correct things, which works until someone finds out. Michel Serrault, Claudine Auger, Catherine Alric. w. Jean Claude Carriere, d. Rene Gaineville.
COMEDY: COMEDY DRAMA: Con Artists; Impostors; Identities-Assumed; Executives; Office Comedy; French Films
(The Front)

As Summers Die, 1986, 100m, ★★¹/₂/$$, Ind/Cinergi. A Southern lawyer fights the Klan to support a black family in crisis. Scott Glenn, Jamie Lee Curtis, Penny Fuller, Bette Davis, Beah Richards. N-adap. Winston Groom, d. Jean Claude Tramont.
DRAMA: Race Relations; Southerns; Courtroom Drama; Black vs. White Lawyers; Lawyers as Detectives; Ku Klux Klan; TV Movies
(To Kill a Mockingbird; The Phenix City Story; I'll Fly Away; Mississippi Burning)
(Ed: Well-intentioned but lacking in bite. From the writer of Forrest Gump)

Asylum (House of Crazies), 1972, 92m, ★★¹/₂/$$, AIP/Media, R/V-S. Four horror stories of insanity are linked together by interdependent. Peter Cushing, Barbara Parkins, Patrick Magee, Charlotte Rampling, Britt Ekland, Herbert Lom, Robert Powell. w. Robert Bloch, d. Roy Ward Baker.
HORROR: Asylums; Mental Illness; Multiple Stories; British; Committed-Wrongly; Insane-Plot to Drive; Clever Plots & Endings; All-Star Casts
(Tales from the Crypt; Torture Garden; Alone in the Dark)

As You Like It, 1936, 96m, ★★★/$$, 20th/NA. The travails of an exiled king rise and fall in the mythical Forest of Arden. Elisabeth Bergner, Laurence Olivier, Sophie Stewart. w. J. M. Barrie, Robert Cullen, P-adap. w. William Shakespeare, d. Paul Czinner.

As You Like It, 1992, 117m, ★★★/$, Sands Films/NA. Orlando falls in love with the banished and disguised Rosalind in the Forest of Arden. James Fox, Emma Croft, Cyril Cusack. Play-William Shakespeare, d. Christine Edzard.
Female Directors
COMEDY: COMEDY DRAMA: Kings Royalty; Middle Ages; Hiding Out; Shakespeare; Classic Play Adaptations

At Close Range, 1986, 115m, ★★★/$, Orion/Orion, R/P-S-EV. A criminal father (Christopher Walken) drags his redneck sons into the fray with him, resulting in murder. Sean Penn, Mary Stuart Masterson. w. Nicholas Kazan, d. James Foley.
DRAMA: Social Drama; **MURDER:** Crime Drama; Murder-Learning to; True Stories; Southerns; Ethics; Fathers & Sons;

Rednecks; Family Drama; Forgotten Films; Coulda Been Great
(In Cold Blood; Badlands; Bloody Mama; White Heat; Southern Comfort; Bad Boys)

Athena, 1954, 96m, ★★¹/₂/$$, MGM/MGM-UA. Two sisters raised as health fanatics meet men who try to corrupt them. Debbie Reynolds, Jane Powell, Edmond Purdom, Vic Damone, Louis Calhern, Linda Christian, Virginia Gibson. w. William Ludwig, Leonard Spigelgass, William Ludwig, d. Richard Thorpe.
COMEDY: ROMANCE: Romantic Comedy; Sisters Romance-Bickering; Romance-Opposites Attract; Corruption; Virgins

At Long Last Love, 1975, 114m, ★★/$, 20th/CBS-Fox, PG. A musical comedy star (Cybill Shepherd) and a millionaire (Burt Reynolds) cross paths, falling in love and haphazardly working their way through what was supposed to be an Astaire-Rogers remake. Eileen Brennan, Madeline Kahn, John Hillerman, Mildred Natwick. w. d. Peter Bogdanovich.
MUSICAL: ROMANCE: MUSICAL ROMANCE: 1930s; Actresses; Rich People; Flops-Major; Nostalgia
(Ed: Another of Bogdanovich's forays into genre pieces, but not as bad as what has been said, nor is Cybill, or Burt-if you consider it as an experiment, which failed)

At Play in the Fields of the Lord, 1991, 186m, Orion/Orion, R/P-V-MN. Missionaries from America invade the Amazon and do battle with each other while trying to save the souls of natives who are losing their land and way of life. Tom Berenger, Kathy Bates, Aidan Quinn, John Lithgow, Daryl Hannah, Tom Waits. w. Jean-Claude Carriere, Hector Babenco, N-adap. Peter Mathiessen, d. Babenco.
DRAMA: ADVENTURE: Social Drama; Marriage on the Rocks; Amazon River; South America; Rainforests; Brazil; Missionaries; Religion; Obsessions; Nature-Back to; Flops-Major
(The Emerald Forest; Medicine Man; Amazon; The Mission)

At the Circus, 1939, 87m, MGM/MGM-UA, ★★★/$$$. The Marx Brothers go to the big top and wreak havoc while trying to save the circus. Groucho Marx, Marx Brothers. w. Irving Brecher, d. Ed Buzzell.

COMEDY: FARCE: Screwball Comedy; Gag Comedy; Circuses; Marx Brothers; Mortgage Drama
(Marx Brothers SERIES; Brain Donors; Big Top Pee Wee)

At the Earth's Core, 1976, 90m, ★★¹/₂/$$, AIP/WB. Scientists in Victorian England burrow with giant drill into a land of dinosaurs. Peter Cushing, Doug McClure. w. Milton Subotsky, N-adap. E. R. Burroughs, d. Kevin Connor.
ADVENTURE: SCI-FI: Fantasy; Dinosaurs; Earth-Center of; Time Travel
(Journey to the Center of the Earth; Time After Time; The Land That Time Forgot)

L'Atalante, see L.

Atlantic City, 1981, 104m, ★★★★/$$, Par/Par, R/P-S-FFN. An old gambler (Burt Lancaster, BActor) wants one last chance to make it and in the process meets up with his young, beautiful neighbor (Susan Sarandon, BActress) who may or may not make it a complete getaway. w. John Guare (BOScr), d. Louis Malle (BDirector). BPicture. Oscars: 5-0.
DRAMA: ROMANCE: Romance-Older Men/Younger Women; Character Studies; Starting Over; Redemption; Rejuvenation; Drugs-Dealing; Gambling; Fugitives from the Mob; Old vs. Young; Atlantic City; Quiet Little Films; Hidden Gems
(Breezy; La Belle Noiseuse; That Obscure Object of Desire; Fedora; Pretty Baby)
(Ed: Barely released, it has taken on classic stature over the years)

The Atomic City, 1952, 85m, ★★★/$$, Par/Par. The son of an atomic scientist is kidnapped and the ransom is secrets-unless the FBI and the scientist can find him first. Gene Barry, Lydia Clarke. w. Sidney Boehm (BOScr), d. Jerry Hopper. Oscars: 1-0.
SUSPENSE: ACTION: Kidnappings; Bombs-Atomic; Fathers & Sons; Saving Someone; Searches; Scientists; Race Against Time

The Atomic Kid, 1954, 86m, ★★/$, Republic/Republic. A gold prospector (Mickey Rooney) is contaminated by uranium but turns out to be immune (?!), which helps him thwart the communists. w. Benedict Freeman, John Murray, Blake Edwards. d. Leslie Martinson.
COMEDY: Fantasy; Bombs-Atomic; Radiation Poisoning; Spies; Communists; Cold War Error; Gold Mining
(Ed: So that's what's with Mickey)

Attack, 1956, 104m, ★★/$, UA/NA. A weak-willed leader takes a platoon into combat in Belgium during the height of World War II. Jack Palance, Eddie Albert, Lee Marvin, Buddy Ebsen, Richard Jaeckel. w. James Poe, P-adap. Norman Brooks (The Fragile Fox), d. Robert Aldrich.
ACTION: Action Drama; War Stories; World War II Movies; Cowards
(The Red Badge of Courage; Battle of the Bulge)

Attack of the 50-Foot Woman, 1958, 72m, ★★¹/₂/$$, AA/Fox. A woman is captured by a spaceship and turned into a mutant. Allison Hayes, William Hudson. w. Mark Hanna, d. Nathan Hertz.

Attack of the 50-Foot Woman, 1993, 95m, ★★¹/₂/$$, HBO/HBO, PG. Daryl Hannah, Daniel Baldwin.
SCI-FI: Sci-Fi, 1950s; Fantasy; DRAMA: Aliens-Outer Space, Bad; Giants; Female Protagonists; Unintentionally Funny; Monsters-Mutants; (1993) Allegorical Stories; Ind Films (1958)
(The Incredible Shrinking Woman; The 30-Foot Bride of Candy Rock)
(Ed: The second is more serious and supposedly allegorical, but the first is more entertaining)

Attack of the Killer Tomatoes, 1980, 87m, ★★★/$$$, Ind/Media, PG. Giant rolling tomatoes wreak and roll havoc onto a town's inhabitants. David Miller, George Wilson. w. Costa Dillon, Steve Peace, John DeBello, d. DeBello.
COMEDY: SCI-FI: Spoofs; Spoofs-Horror; HORROR: Black Comedy; Deaths-One by One; Monsters; Monsters-Mutants; Camp; Objects with Personalities
SEQUEL: Return of the Killer Tomatoes.
(The Blob)

The Attic, 1980, 92m, ★★¹/₂/$, Ind/Fox, R. A spinster spends her time in the attic of her father's house to get away from him, but is still always under his control. Carrie Snodgress, Ray Milland, Rosemary Murphy, Ruth Cox. d. George Edwards.
SUSPENSE: DRAMA: Psychological Drama; Spinsters; Lonely People; Stern Men; Fathers & Daughters; Hiding Out; Coulda Been Great; Ind Films
(Diary of a Mad Housewife; That Cold Day in the Park; Rachel, Rachel)

The Attic: The Hiding of Anne Frank, 1988, 95m, ★★★/$$$, AT&T-CBS/Cabin Fever. The story of the Dutch woman who hid Anne Frank's family and her own fears of being caught if the family was found. Mary Steenburgen, Pauul Scofield, Huub Stapel, Eleanor Bron, Miriam Karlin, Lisa Jacobs. w. William Hanley, NF-adap. Miep Gies, *Anne Frank Remembered*, d. John Erman. Emmy nominee.

DRAMA: Historical Drama; True Stories; Behind the Scenes; Revisionist Films; Hiding Out; Fugitives-Harboring; Nazi Stories; World War II Stories; Female Protagonists; Autobiographical Stories; Girls; TV Movies
(The Diary of Anne Frank; The Shop on Main Street; The Assissi Underground; The Hiding Place)

Attica, 1980, 97m, ★★★/$$$, CBS/Sultan, V. Docudrama overview of the prison uprising. George Grizzard, Charles Durning, Anthony Zerbe, Roger E. Mosley. w. d. Marvin Chomsky.

Attica, 1994, 100m, ★★★/$$, HBO/HBO, R/V-EP-MN. A young prison guard faces the great prison uprising. Kyle McLachlan, Samuel Jackson.

DRAMA: TRAGEDY: Prison Drama; Political Unrest; Riots; True Stories; Black Men; Black vs. White; TV Movies
(Assault on Precinct 13; Cool Hand Luke; Ghosts of the Civil Dead; The Big House; American Me)

Au Revoir, les Enfants, 1987, 103m, ★★★¹/2/$$$, OrionC/Orion, PG. A French boy is friends with a Jewish boy and watches as the death camp round-ups begin in World War II. Gaspard Manesse, Raphael Fejto. w. d. Louis Malle (BOScr, BFFilm). Oscars: 2-0.

DRAMA: Social Drama; World War II Stories; War at Home; World War II Stories; Memories; Nazi Stories; Anti-Semitism; Jewish People Boyhood; Autobiographical Stories; Children-Parting with/Losing; Narrated Films; French Films; Writer-Directors
(Europa, Europa; Sophie's Choice; Schindler's List; The White Rose)

Audrey Rose, 1977, 113m, ★★¹/2/$, UA/MGM-UA, R/V. A girl has nightmares of a fire and her mother finds she's the reincarnation of a girl who died in one. Marsha Mason, Anthony Hopkins. w. N-adap. Frank deFelitta, d. Robert Wise.

SUSPENSE: MELODRAMA: HORROR: Reincarnation; Nightmares; Mothers & Daughters; Possessions; Fires; Coulda Been Good

(The Search for Bridey Murphy; The Exorcist; The Memories of Eva Ryker)

Auntie Lee's Meat Pies, 1992, 100m, ★★/VR, Ind./Col, R/ES-V-B&G-FN. Auntie's pie business is helped by her four nieces selling them (all played by Playboy bunnies), but no one knows the yummy ingredients are the hunks they lured to bed and death. Karen Black, Pat Morita, Pat Paulsen, Huntz Hall, Michael Berryman, David Parry. d. Joseph Robertson.

COMEDY: Black Comedy; **MURDER:** Murders-One by One; Sexy Women; Bimbos; Erotic Comedy; Spoofs; Cannibalism; Ind Films
(Sweeney Todd; Demon Barber of Fleet Street; Arsenic and Old Lace)

Auntie Mame, 1958, 160m, ★★★★/$$$$$, WB/WB. The all-time model for free spirits and feisty females, rich Auntie Mame (Rosalind Russell, BActress) finds her spirit temporarily dimmed by the Depression and, ironically, by her eccentric and cockamamy friends and relations. Peggy Cass (BSActress). Forest Tucker, Coral Browne. N-adap. Dennis Tucker, d. Morton daCosta. BPicture, BCin, BCArt, BEdit. Oscars: 6-0.

COMEDY: Feisty Females; Charismatic People; Episodic Stories; Riches to Rags; Raising Children Alone; Alternative Lifestyles; Snobs Roaring 20s; Female Protagonists; Rich People; Alternative Lifestyles; Novel and Play Adapations

MUSICAL REMAKE: Mame
(Mame; Gypsy; The Women; Take a Letter, Darling; The Madwoman of Chaillot)

Australia, 1989, 124m, ★★¹/2/$, Ind/NA. A businessman comes back to Belgium from Australia to handle family problems and meets a woman with whom he begins an affair. Jeremy Irons, Fanny Ardant. w. Jean Gruault, Jacques Audiard, Jean-Jacques Andrien, d. Andrien.

DRAMA: ROMANCE: MELODRAMA: Family Drama; Romance with Married Person; Midlife Crisis; Australia; French Films
(Damage; The Last Days of Chez Nous)

Author! Author!, 1982, 110m, ★★¹/2/$$, 20th/CBS-Fox, PG/P. Playwright's wife leaves him with her kids from previous marriages and he must cope while working on a new play. Al Pacino, Tuesday Weld, Dyan Cannon. w. Israel Horowitz, d. Arthur Hiller.

MELODRAMA: COMEDY DRAMA: Divorce; Starting Over; Fathers Alone; Writers; Theater Life; Mothers Who Leave; Parents vs. Children
(Kramer vs. Kramer, See You in the Morning)

The Autobiography of Miss Jane Pittman, 1974, 110m, ★★★¹/2/$$$$, CBS/Prism. Cicely Tyson's landmark performance of the 100-year-old woman who lived from the days of slavery to the 70s. Michael Murphy. w. Tracy Keenan Wynn, N-adap. Ernest Gaines. d. John Korty. Winner of 9 Emmys.

DRAMA: MELODRAMA: Black Women; Autobiographical Stories; Biographies-Fictional; Social Drama; Historical Drama; Episodic Stories; Character Studies; Tearjerkers; Slavery; Elderly Women; Civil War Era; Race Relations; Southerns; Narrated Films; Interviews; Female Protagonists; TV Movies
(A Woman Called Moses; Sounder; Driving Miss Daisy)
(Ed: Clunky in the TV-movie form with each act including another encapsulation of racism, but the water fountain scene is timeless, as is Tyson's performance)

Autobus, 1991, 98m, ★★★/$, Canal Plus/NA, PG-13/V-S. A young man hijacks a schoolbus to get to his girlfriend and changes lives other than his own in the process. Yvan Attal, Kristin Scott-Thomas. w. d. Eric Rochant.

DRAMA: TRAGEDY: ROMANCE: Hostages; Kidnappings; Hijackings; Young Men-Angry; Young Men; Depression; Mental Illness; Writer-Directors
(The Kidnapping at Chowchilla [TV Movie])

Autumn Leaves, 1956, 108m, ★★¹/2/$$, Col/RCA-Col. A mentally ill, good-looking young man (Cliff Robertson) marries an older woman (Joan Crawford) and proceeds to let his disturbances rub off on more than himself. Lorne Greene, Vera Miles. w. Jack Jevne, Lewis Meltzer, Robert Blees, d. Robert Aldrich.

ROMANCE: DRAMA: SUSPENSE: Murder-Attempted; Romance-Older Women/Younger Men; Dangerous Men; Dangerous Spouses; Bigamy; Mental Illness; Psycho Killers; Women in Jeopardy
(Betty Blue; A Kiss Before Dying)

Autumn Sonata, 1978, 97m, ★★★½/ $$, Svensk-Embassy/Fox, PG. Famous pianist returns to daughter after years apart and confronts their estranged relationship. Ingrid Bergman (BActress), Liv Ullmann. w. d. Ingmar Bergman.
DRAMA: Reunions; Swedish Films; Mothers Who Leave; Mothers & Daughters; Pianists; Stern People; Writer-Directors; Bergmanesque (Face to Face; Cries and Whispers; Persona; Interiors; Another Woman; Terms of Endearment)
(Ed: Basically, only for Bergman fans, Ingmar or Ingrid)
Avalanche, 1978, 91m, ★★/$, NW/NW, PG. Mia Farrow, Rock Hudson, and Robert Forster wait for the snow to fall. w. Claude Pola, Corey Allen, d. Corey Allen.
Disaster Movies; **MELODRAMA:** Skiing; Snow Settings; Mountain Settings; Rescue Drama
Avalanche Express, 1979, 88m, ★★½/$, 20th-Lorimar/WB, P-V. International spies all wind-up on the same train across Europe for various intrigue-oriented and sometimes humorous reasons. Robert Shaw, Lee Marvin, Linda Evans, Maximilian Schell, Mike Connors. w. Abraham Polonsky, N-adap. Colin Forbes, d. Mark Robson.
ACTION: ADVENTURE: Spy Films; Spies; International Casts; Good Premise Unfulfilled; Overlooked at Release (The Train; Murder on the Orient Express; The Cassandra Crossing)
Avalon, 1990, 128m, ★★★/$$, Tri/Col-Tri, PG. A family saga of immigrants making the American dream come true in Baltimore, centering on the post-war years, until tragedy sets them back. Armin Mueller-Stahl, Aidan Quinn, Elizabeth Perkins, Joan Plowright. w. d. Barry Levinson (BOScr). Oscars: 1-0.
DRAMA: FAMILY: Family Stories; **MELO-DRAMA: TRAGEDY:** Episodic Stories; Autobiographical Stories; Comebacks; Immigrants; American Dream; Fires; Baltimore; TV Life; Writer-Directors

(Tin Men; Diner; Tucker; America, America)
Avanti!, 1972, 144m, ★★½/$$, UA/MCA-U, PG/S. A man (Jack Lemmon) goes to an Italian resort to get the body of his father who's died-but he runs into the mistress who was there when it happened (Juliet Mills) and who he may fall for, too. Clive Revill. w. Billy Wilder, IAL Diamond, P-adap. Samuel Taylor, d. Wilder.
COMEDY: COMEDY DRAMA:
ROMANCE: Romantic Comedy; Romance with Relative's Lover; Midlife Crisis; Romance-Older Men/Younger Women; Italy; Americans Abroad; Funerals; Forgotten Films; Hidden Gems (The April Fools; Alex and the Gypsy; Wild Is the Wind)
The Avenging Conscience, 1914, 78m, ★★★/$$$, Mutual/Voyager. A murderer hears the beating heart of his victim through a wall. w. d. D. W. Griffith, SS-adap. Edgar Allen Poe ("The Tell-Tale Heart").
HORROR: MURDER: Guilty Conscience; Secrets-Haunted by; Insane-Plot to Drive; Haunted Houses (Fall of the House of Usher; The Tell-Tale Heart; Woman Screaming)
The Aviator, 1985, 104m, ★★/$, MGM-UA/MGM-UA, PG. A pilot and a spoiled rich girl combat the elements when he crash lands in the Sierras. Christopher Reeve, Rosanna Arquette, Jack Warden, Sam Wanamaker. w. Marc Norman, N-adap, w. David Connell, d. George Miller.
COMEDY DRAMA: MELODRAMA:
ROMANCE: Romantic Comedy; Romance-Bickering; Romance-Class Conflicts; Fish out of Water Stories; Airplanes; Airplane Crashes; Pilots-Military Stranded; Coulda Been Good (Swept Away; High Road to China)
L'Avventura, see **L**.
The Awakening, 1980, 102m, ★★/$$, Orion/WB, PG/V. An archaeologist (Charlton Heston) believes an ancient Egyptian spirit may have possessed his daughter. Stephanie Zimbalist, Susannah

York, Jill Townsend. w. Allan Scott, Chris Bryant, Clive Exton, N-adap. Bram Stoker, *Jewel of the Seven Stars,* d. Mike Newell.
SUSPENSE: HORROR: SCI-FI:
Mummies; Egypt; Possessions; Fathers & Daughters; Archaeologists (Sphinx; Dr. Phibes Rises Again; The Mummy's Hand; The Mummy's Shroud)
Awakenings, 1990, 121m, ★★★/$$$, 20th/CBS-Fox, PG. A meek scientist discovers what may be a cure for patients who have been catatonic for decades, but will it be permanent? Robin Williams, Robert De Niro (BActor), Julie Kavner. w. Steve Zaillian (BAScr), NF-adap. Oliver Sacks, d. Penny Marshall. BPicture. Oscars: 3-0.
DRAMA: MELODRAMA: True Stories; Docudrama; Tearjerkers; Asylums; Cures-Search for; Medical Detectives; Medical Drama; Scientists; Doctors; Mental Illness; Time Sleepers; Childlike People; Simple Minds; Female Directors (Lorenzo's Oil; Son-Rise: Miracle of Love; Rain Man; Birdy)
(Ed: A bit too manipulative and clichéd, but nonetheless effective)
The Awful Truth (B&W), 1937, 92m, Columbia/RCA-Col, ★★★★/$$$. A husband who's divorcing his wife wreaks havoc on her new relationship, until she gets even. Cary Grant, Irene Dunne (BActress), Ralph Bellamy (BSActor). w. Robert Riskind (BScr), d. Leo McCarey (**BDirector**). BPicture, BEdit. Oscars: 6-1.
COMEDY: Screwball Comedy; Romantic Comedy; Romance-Married Couple; Marriage Comedy; Divorce; Marriage on the Rocks; Revenge; Custody Battles; Dogs; Hidden Gems
MUSICAL REMAKE: Let's Do it Again. (The Philadelphia Story; Hard Promises; Love Crazy; War of the Roses; My Favorite Wife; Send Me No Flowers; Irreconcilable Differences)
(Ed: A classic marriage comedy, though the pacing is more like a play than contemporary screwball comedies)

Films by Title

B

Babar, The Movie, 1989, 79m, ★★★/$$, Canada-Ind./Family Home Ent., G. Babar, now elephant king of French Africa, recounts his life as a youngster. Based on the classic children's books. w. Peter Sauder, J. D. Smith, John DeKlein, Raymond, Jaffelice, Alan Bunce, N-adap. Jean de Brunhoff, Laurent de Brunhoff, d. Bunce.
CHILDREN'S: FAMILY: Cartoons; Fantasy; Africa; Boyhood; Elephants; Animals-Talking; Animal Stories
Babbitt, 1934, 74m, ★★½/$$, WB/WB. A businessman leads a frustrating life in a small Minnesota town in the early 1900s. Guy Kibbee, Aline MacMahon, Alan Hale. w. Mary McCall, N-adap. Sinclair Lewis, d. William Keighley.
DRAMA: Social Drama; Message Films; Midlife Crisis; Business Life; Stern Men; Ordinary People Stories; Midwestern Life; Small-Town Life; 1900s Corruption; Classic Literary Adaptations; Female Screenwriters
(East of Eden; Arrowsmith; Dodsworth)
Babe, 1995, 93m, ★★★★/$$$, U/MCA-U, G. An orphaned talking pig named Babe is taken in by a farmer and consequently by his sheepdog, which is when the pig decides he wants to be a sheepdog and uses his polite requests to herd the cantankerous sheep instead of bark-ing, thereby saving his own hide. James Cromwell (BSActor). w. Chris Noonan and George Miller (BAScr), d. Chris Noonan (BDirector). BPicture, **BVFX, BArt,** BEdit. Oscars: 7-1.
COMEDY: Allegorical Films; **CHILDREN'S: FAMILY:** Fairy Tales; Farm Life; Animal Stories; Political Satire; Dogs; Animals Talking; Australian Films; Sleeper Hits
(Gordy; Animal Farm)
The Babe, 1992, 115m, ★★½/$$, U/MCA-U, PG-13/S. A more in-depth, warts-and-all tale of the great baseball player with more humor than, say, *The Natural,* but not the lyricism or character. John Goodman, Kelly McGillis, Trini Alvarado, Bruce Boxleitner, Peter Donat. w. John Fusco, d. Arthur Hiller.
DRAMA: Biographies; Baseball; Sports Movies; 1900s; Marriage on the Rocks
(The Natural; Eight Men Out; The Babe Ruth Story; Pride of the Yankees)
The Babe Ruth Story, 1948, 107m, ★★½/$$$, AA/Fox. Superficial tale of the great baseball player. William Bendix, Claire Trevor, Charles Bickford. w. Bob Considine, George Callahan, d. Roy del Ruth.
DRAMA: Biographies; Sports Movies; Fame-Rise to; Baseball
(The Babe; The Lou Gehrig Story; Pride of the Yankees)

Babes in Arms, 1939, 96m, ★★★/$$$$, MGM/MGM-UA. The first of the Andy Hardy series where the kids of retired vaudeville stars revive the form in a barn. Mickey Rooney (BActor), Judy Garland, Charles Winninger. w. Jack McGowan, Kay Van Riper, P-adap. Rodgers & Hart, d. Busby Berkeley. BOScore. Oscars: 2-0.
MUSICAL: COMEDY: MUSICAL COMEDY: ROMANCE: Romantic Comedy; Vaudeville; Theater Life; Teenagers; Small-Town Life; Andy Hardy SERIES
SEQUELS: Babes on Broadway; Andy Hardy SERIES
Babes in Toyland, 1934, 77m, ★★★/$$, MGM/MGM-UA, Turner. Stan Laurel, Oliver Hardy. w. Nick Grinde, Frank Butler, P-adap. Glen MacDonough, d. Gus Meins.
REMAKE: 1961
Babes in Toyland, 1961, 105m, ★★½/$$$, Disney/Disney. Annette Funicello, Tommy Sands, Ray Bolger, Tommy Kirk, Ed Wynn. w. Ward Kimball, Joe Rinaldi, Lowell Hawley, d. Jack Donohue. BOScore. Oscars: 1-0. Santa's elves make a mistake and crank out some giant wooden soldiers that happen to come in handy when an evil anti-Christmas villain shows up.
MUSICAL: MUSICAL COMEDY: CHILDREN'S: FAMILY: Fantasy; Christmas;

Santa Claus; Good vs. Evil; Fairy Tales; Little People
(Santa Claus; The Wonderful World of the Brothers Grimm; Tom Thumb; Beach Party)

Babes on Broadway, 1941, 118m, ★★1/2/$$$$, MGM/MGM-UA. Andy Hardy & Co. head to Broadway with a show and struggle to make it. Mickey Rooney, Judy Garland, Virginia Weidler, Fay Bainter. w. Fred Finklehoffe, Elaine Ryan, d. Busby Berkeley. BOSong: "How About You?" Oscars: 1-0.
MUSICAL: COMEDY: MUSICAL COMEDY: ROMANCE: Romantic Comedy; Vaudeville; Theater Life; Teenagers; Small-Town Life

Babette Goes to War, 1959, 103m, ★★1/2/$$, Ind/NA. A beautiful French girl (Brigitte Bardot) is sent as a spy during the war to foil the Nazi's plan to invade England. w. Raoul Levy, Gerard Oury, d. Christian Jacque.
COMEDY: FARCE: War Movies; Spoofs-Spies; Spy Films; Spies; Military Comedy; French Films; Sexy Women; World War II Movies
(Mata Hari, Joan of Paris; And God Created Woman)

Babette's Feast, 1987, 102m, ★★★1/2/$$, OrionC/Orion, PG. Spinsters in Norway house hire a French cook named Babette who changes their lives via her wonderful food and demeanor. Stephane Audran, Bibi Andersson. w. Gabriel Axel, SS-adap. Isak Dinesen, d. Bille August. **BFLFilm.** Oscars: 1-1.
DRAMA: Ordinary People Stories; Spinsters; Lonely People; Ensemble Films; Dinner Parties; Lyrical Films; Quiet Little Films; Danish Films; Scandinavia; International Casts; Female Protagonists; Hidden Gems; Cult Films
(The House of the Spirits; Pelle the Conqueror; Like Water for Chocolate; Antonia's Line)

The Baby and the Battleship, 1956, 96m, ★★★/$, B-L/Nos, Valencia. Two British sailors (John Mills, Richard Attenborough) find an Italian baby while docked and decide to keep it as long as possible. Bryan Forbes, Lisa Gastoni, Lionel Jeffries. w. Jay Lewis, Gilbert Hackforth-Jones, Bryan Forbes, d. Jay Lewis.
COMEDY: FARCE: Ships; Babies; Men and Babies; Missing Persons; Sailors British Films; Italians

(Three Men and a Baby; Three Men and a Cradle; The Three Godfathers)

Baby Blue Marine, 1976, 90m, ★★1/2/$$, Col/Col, R/S-P. A marine who disappointed himself and commanders returns home and decides to make himself into a hero despite the situation. Jan Michael Vincent, Glynnis O'Connor, Katherine Helmond, Richard Gere. w. Standford Whitmore, d. John Hancock.
DRAMA: SATIRE: ROMANCE: Con Artists; Soldiers; Liars; Small-Town Life; World War II Era-Post
REMAKES/RETREADS: Hail the Conquering Hero
(Streamers; Tribes; Hail the Conquering Hero)

Baby Boom, 1987, 110m, ★★★1/2/$$$, MGM-UA/MGM-UA, PG. Executive (Diane Keaton) finds she's inherited a baby but doesn't have the time to do anything with it, until some adjustments are made. w. Nancy Meyers, Charles Shyer, d. Charles Shyer.
COMEDY: Screwball Comedy; Family Comedy; Career Women; Mothers Alone; Children-Adopted; City vs. Country; Babies-Inheriting; Nature-Back to; Women Raising Children Alone; Inheritances at Stake; House Havoc; Women's Rights; Veterinarians; Underrated; Old-Fashioned Recent Films; Hidden Gems
COMEDY REMAKE OF: Kramer vs. Kramer
(Bachelor Mother; Mr. Blandings Builds His Dream House; Kramer vs. Kramer; Annie Hall)
(Ed: A smart, thorough script with some big laughs, though we've seen a few before; Keaton is great. Proves they can make 'em like they used to)

Babycakes, 1989, 94m, ★★1/2/$$, CBS/Turner. A chubby girl finds a hunky boyfriend, but will it last? Ricki Lake, Craig Sheffer, Paul Benedict, Betty Buckley, John Karlen. d. Paul Schneider.
COMEDY DRAMA: MELODRAMA: ROMANCE: Romantic Comedy; Wallflowers & Hunks; Dreams; Weight Problems; Funerals; Romance-Mismatched; TV Movies
REMAKE OF: Sugarbaby
(Sugarbaby; Before and After; The Sterile Cuckoo; Circle of Friends)

Baby Doll (B&W), 1956, 114m, ★★★1/2/$$$, WB/WB, S. The owner of a decadent plantation tries to keep his

teenage wife from mixing with unsavory men from town, but she's a bit too coquette-ish. Karl Malden, Carroll Baker (BActress). w. P-adap. Tennessee Williams (BScr), 27 Wagonloads of Cotton, d. Elia Kazan. Oscars: 2-0.
DRAMA: MELODRAMA: Southerns; Plantation Life; Cheating Women; Romance-Triangles; Lovers-Unsatisfied; Jealousy; Romance-Older Men/Younger Women; Marriage of Convenience; Cuckolded; Sexy Women; Sexual Kinkiness; Young Women Mississippi; Female Protagonists; Tennessee Williams-esque; Hidden Gems
(Lolita; The Fugitive Kind; The Rose Tattoo)
(Ed: Primarily appealing to Williams' and Southern fans-and those of sex kittens. Condemned by the Catholic church upon release)

Baby Face, 1933, 70m, ★★★/$$$, WB/WB. A shop girl works and kisses her way up the ladder. Barbara Stanwyck, George Brent, John Wayne. w. Gene Markey, Kathryn Scola, Mark Canfield, d. Alfred E. Green.
DRAMA: MELODRAMA: ROMANCE: Sexy Women; Ordinary People Stories; Promiscuity; Women's Films; Forgotten Films; Female Screenwriters

Baby, It's You, 1983, 105m, ★★★/$$, Par/Par, R/S-P. A girl goes to college and tries to maintain a romance with her dreamer Italian boyfriend from back home in New Jersey though she's moving up. Rosanna Arquette, Vincent Spano. w. d. John Sayles.
COMEDY DRAMA: ROMANCE: Romantic Comedy; Coming of Age; Romance-Mismatched; Romance-Class-Crossed; Teenagers; College Life; Life Transitions; Love-First; Virgins; Class Conflicts; Dreams; Lover Family Dislikes; Coulda Been Great; Dream Girls; Writer-Directors; Ind Films
(Dirty Dancing; China Girl; Desperately Seeking Susan)
(Ed: Thoughtful and charming, though slight on plot)

The Baby Maker, 1970, 109m, ★★★/$$$, NG/WB, R/S-FN. A barren couple hires a surrogate mother in this story before its time. Barbara Hershey. w. d. James Bridges.
DRAMA: MELODRAMA: Marriage on the Rocks; **ROMANCE:** Romance-Triangles; Mothers-Surrogate;

Alternative Lifestyles; Babies-Having; Custody Battles; Hippies; Free Spirits; 1970s; Female Protagonists; Ahead of Its Time; Writer-Directors
(Baby M; Generation; Bob and Ted and Carol and Alice)
(Ed: Some may think it's dated, but it's a great time capsule)

Baby's Day Out, 1994, 98m, ★★¹/₂/$, 20th/Fox, PG. A baby gets loose and eludes everyone, including several detectives and cops, and goes on incredible adventures. Joe Mantegna, Adam Worton, Jacob Worton, Lara Flynn Boyle, Joe Pantoliano, Fred Dalton Thompson, John Neville. w. John Hughes, d. Patrick Read Johnson.
COMEDY: Chase Stories; Babies; Police Comedy; Chicago; Flops-Major; Good Premise Unfulfilled
(Honey, I Blew Up the Kids)

Baby, Secret of the Lost Legend, 1985, 92m, ★★/$, Touchstone/Disney, G. Young scientist couple stumble upon a lost baby dinosaur and try to protect it. Sean Young, William Katt. w. Clifford Green, Ellen Green, d. B.W.L. Norton.
ADVENTURE: Comic Adventure; CHILDREN'S: Dinosaurs; Disney Africa; Scientists; Explorers
(At the Earth's Core; King Kong; Jurassic Park)

The Babysitter, 1980, 96m, ★★★/$$$, ABC-Ind/NA. A family hires a nanny who turns out to have a psycho past as she tries to destroy the family for the love of the husband, downing those who get in her way. Stephanie Zimbalist, Patty Duke, William Shatner, Quinn Cummings, John Houseman. d. Peter Medak.
SUSPENSE: Psycho-Killers; Babysitters; Babysitters-Evil; Murderers-Female; Obsessions; Camp; Hidden Gems; TV Movies
REMAKE/RETREAD: The Hand That Rocks the Cradle
(The Hand That Rocks the Cradle; The Guardian; The Babysitter [1969])
(Ed: Zimbalist is cold as the killer, and the rest of the cast fine as the unwitting victims, though the dialogue and plot could have been more substantial)

The Babysitters Club, 1995, 100m, ★★¹/₂/$, Col/Col, PG. Seven teenage girls pool their resources like an agency so that each can cover for the other if one has a date and doesn't want to baby-sit,

and this is the story of some of their amorous adventures during one summer. Ellen Burstyn, Bruce Davison, Schuyler Fisk, Larisa Oleynik, Zelda Harris. w. Dalene Young, N-adap. Ann M. Martin, d. Melanie Mayron.
COMEDY: Baby-sitters; Suburban Life; High School Life; Coming of Age; Ensemble Films; Ensembles-Female; Girlhood; Female Screenwriters; Female Protagonists; Female Directors
(Now and Then)

Baby, Take a Bow, 1934, 76m, ★★★/$$$, 20th/Fox. A gangster on the mend's little girl helps him out of a jam Shirley Temple, James Dunn, Claire Trevor. w. Philip Klein, E. E. Paramore, d. Harry Lachman.
COMEDY: MELODRAMA: COMEDY DRAMA: Men and Girls; Fathers & Daughters; Thieves; Accused Unjustly; Child Protagonists
(Little Miss Marker; Sorrowful Jones; Paper Moon)
(Ed: Shirley's first big feature, before the musical hits)

Baby, the Rain Must Fall, 1965, 100m, ★★★/$$, Columbia/RCA-Col. An ex-con (Steve McQueen) goes home to his ex-wife, and his boredom leads him to pursue a singing career on the honkytonk circuit. Lee Remick. w. P-adap. Horton Foote (*The Traveling Lady*), d. Robert Mulligan.
DRAMA: Starting Over; Ordinary People; Dreams; Singers; Country Music; Texas; Rednecks; Ex-convicts
(Tender Mercies; The Cincinnati Kid)
(Ed: Without the poetic style of Foote's later *Mercies*, it's a fascinating character and class study)

The Bachelor, 1993, 105m, ★★★/$, Tri-Star/Col-Tri, PG-13/P-S. A family tragedy transforms a lonely doctor's life as he tries to find true love and lust in a world repressing it. Keith Carradine, Miranda Richardson, Max Von Sydow, Kristin Scott Thomas. w. Robert Faenza, Ennio de Concini, Hugh Fleetwood, d. Faenza.
DRAMA: Character Studies; Life Transitions; Doctors; Single Men; TRAGEDY: Death-Dealing with; Repression; Hidden Gems; Ind Films
(Petulia)

The Bachelor and the Bobby-Soxer, 1947, 95m, ★★★¹/₂/$$$$, RKO/Turner. A playboy artist (Cary Grant) has a fatal attraction in the young sister (Shirley

Temple) of the judge (Myrna Loy) he's frequently in the court of for his escapades and is basically sentenced to date the girl. w. Sidney Sheldon (**BOStory**, BOScr), d. Mervyn LeRoy. Oscars: 2-1.
COMEDY: ROMANCE: Romantic Comedy; Situation Comedy; Infatuations; Playboys; Romance-Older Men/Younger Women; Judges; Matchmakers; Men and Girls; Hidden Gems; Blockbusters
(I'd Rather Be Rich; Three Smart Girls; Daddy Longlegs; Mad About Music)
(Ed: A good ole romantic comedy, though it's fairly kinky if you think about it)

Bachelor in Paradise, 1961, 109m, ★★¹/₂/$$, MGM/MGM-UA. An advice columnist joins the suburban California country club set to learn more about love in real life and encounters several entanglements. Bob Hope Lana Turner, Janis Paige, Don Porter, Paula Prentiss, Jim Hutton, Agnes Moorehead. w. Valentine Davies, Hal Kanter, d. Jack Arnold. BOSong. Oscars: 1-0.
COMEDY: SATIRE: FARCE: Suburban Life; Rich People; Writers Multiple Stories; 1960s
(The Chapman Report; Serial; Laura Lansing Slept Here; [TK])

Bachelor Mother, 1939, 81m, ★★★/$$$$, RKO/Turner. Ginger Rogers rescues abandoned baby and may or may not need the help of a few good men. w. Norman Krasna, d. Garson Kanin.
COMEDY DRAMA: MELODRAMA: Mothers Alone; Orphans; Children-Abandoned; Babies-Finding; Abandoned People; Mothers-Adopted; Female Protagonists
REMAKE: Bundle of Joy
(Baby Boom; Three Men and a Baby/Three Men and a Cradle; The Three Godfathers; Bundle of Joy)

Bachelor Party, 1957, 93m, ★★★★/$$, UA/Fox, S. Several accountants throw a party for a fellow worker but soon realize their own despair while trying to join in on what should be his happiness. Don Murray, E.G. Marshall, Jack Warden, Carolyn Jones (BSActress). w. TV/P-adap. Paddy Chayefsky, d. Delbert Mann. Oscars: 1-0.
DRAMA: Character Studies; Social Drama; Pre-life Crisis; Young Men; Ensemble Films; Ensembles-Male; New York Life; 1950; Ordinary People Stories; Sexy Women; Party Movies; Marriage on

the Rocks; Ahead of Its Time; Hidden Gems
(The Men's Club; That Championship Season; Thursday's Game; 12 Angry Men; Watch It)
(Ed: One of the few insightful films on male group behavior)

Bachelor Party, 1984, 106m, ★★/$$$, 20th/CBS-Fox, R, S-P-FFN. Chaos and debauchery before the wedding. Tom Hanks. w. Neal Israel, Pat Proft, Bob Israel, d. Neal Israel.
COMEDY: Party Movies; Lover Family Dislikes; Young Men; Rebels; Free Spirits; Wild People; Bathroom Humor; College Life; Fraternity Life
(Animal House; Foolin' Around; Splash)

Backbeat, 1994, 100m, ★★★/$$, Gramercy/MCA-U, PG-13/S-P. The early days of the Beatles' rise are documented as one young member, Stu Sutcliff, decides to follow a girl and splits from the greatest group of all time. Stephen Dorff, Sheryl Lee, Ian Hart, Gary Bakewell. w. Michael Thomas, Stephen Ward, Iain Softley, d. Softley.
COMEDY DRAMA: DRAMA: Biographies; Musicians; Rock Stars; Famous People When Young; Romance-Triangles; Men Fighting Over Women; England; 1960s; Mod Era
(I Wanna Hold Your Hand; Absolute Beginners; All You Need Is Cash; Help; A Hard Day's Night; Let It Be)

Back from the Dead, 1957, 78m, ★★/$, 20th/NA. A woman on her honeymoon becomes possessed by the spirit of his first wife who died. Peggie Castle, Marsha Hunt, Arthur Franz. w. N-adap. Catherine Turney, d. Charles Warren.
SUSPENSE: HORROR: Dead-Back from the; Possessions; Ghosts; Newlyweds; Houses-Creepy

Back Roads, 1981, 94m, ★★★/$$, CBS/WB, PG, S. A hooker (Sally Field) and a drifter (Tommy Lee Jones) ride the busses through the south while she searches for her lost child, possibly finding love instead. w. Gary DeVore, d. Martin Ritt.
DRAMA: ROMANCE: Romance with Prostitute; Southerns; Road Movies; Mothers Who Leave; Drifters; Prostitutes-Low Class; Overlooked at Release; Old-Fashioned Recent Films; Quiet Little Films; Sally Field Goes Southern
(It Happened One Night; Heartaches; Norma Rae)

(Ed: A quirky, "small" film which flopped as a follow-up to *Norma Rae,* but it has its old-fashioned moments)

Back Street, 1932, 93m, ★★★/$$$, U/NA. Irene Dunne, John Boles, Zasu Pitts. w. Gladys Lehmann, Lynn Starling, N-adap. Fannie Hurst, d. John Stahl.

Back Street, 1941, 89m, ★★1/2/$$$, U/NA. Margaret Sullavan, Charles Boyer, Richard Carlson. w. Bruce Manning, Felix Jackson, d. Robert Stevenson. BOScore. Oscars: 1-0.

Back Street, 1961, 107m, ★★1/2/$$, U/MCA-U. Susan Hayward, John Gavin, Vera Miles. w. Eleanore Griffin, William Ludwig, d. David Miller.
A mistress puts up with her married man for half of her adult life and suddenly ponders changing the situation.
MELODRAMA: ROMANCE: DRAMA: Romance with Married Person; Mistresses; Single Women; Episodic Stories; Romance-Triangles; Life Transitions; Decisions-Big
(Ada; A Life of Her Own; The Dark at the Top of the Stairs; Any Wednesday)

Back to Bataan, 1945, 97m, ★★1/2/$$$, RKO/Turner. When the crucial post of Bataan is cut off in World War II, a colonel rallies the boys round the flag and stands tall as an attack nears. John Wayne (of course), Anthony Quinn, Beulah Bondi, Lawrence Tierney. w. Ben Barzman, Richard Landau, d. Edward Dmytryk.
DRAMA: Action Drama; War Movies; War Battles; World War II Era; Ensembles-Male; South Pacific Islands
(Bataan)

Back to School, 1986, 94m, ★★★/$$$, Orion/Orion, PG-13/P-S. A wealthy man (Rodney Dangerfield) decides he wants to go back to college with his son (Keith Gordon) to finish the degree he never had, and the result is calamity, chaos, and parties. Sally Kellerman. w. Steve Kampmann, Harold Ramis, Peter Torokvei, Will Porter, d. Alan Metter.
COMEDY: Party Movies; Comedians; Fathers & Sons; College Life; Midlife Crisis; Older Men/Young Women; Starting Over; Back to School; Sleeper Hits
(Ed: A party movie for young and old. A big surprise hit)

Back to the Beach, 1987, 92m, ★★1/2/$$, Par/Par, PG. Frankie and Annette return to the sun and sand with their own kids partying with songs old and

new. Frankie Avalon, Annette Funicello, Connie Stevens, Jerry Mathers, Bob Denver, Barbara Billingsley, Tony Dow, Paul Reubens, Edd Byrnes, Don Adams. d. Lyndall Hobbs.
COMEDY: Nostalgia; Beach Movies; MUSICALS: Musical Comedy; Party Movies; Coulda Been Great
(Beach Blanket Bingo; Grease; Beach Party)

Back to the Future, 1985, 116m, ★★★★/$$$$$, Universal/MCA-U, PG/V. A teenage boy (Michael J. Fox) travels back in time to when his parents met and may foul up their romance. Christopher Lloyd, Crispin Glover, Lea Thompson. w. Bob Gale, Robert Zemeckis (BOScr), d. Robert Zemeckis. BSound, BOSong. Oscars: 3-0.
COMEDY: SCI-FI: ACTION: Romantic Comedy; Action Comedy; Fantasy; Time Travel; Time Machines; Fish out of Water Stories; Parents vs. Children; Teenagers; Scientists; Oedipal Stories; 1950s; Blockbusters
SEQUELS: Back to the Future 2, 3
(Ed: A future classic, though the sequels pale by comparison)

Back to the Future 2, 1989, 116m, ★★1/2/$$$$, U/MCA-U, PG. This time Fox and Lloyd discover the present has been changed in the future and must set it straight-or something like that. Michael J. Fox, Christopher Lloyd, Lea Thompson, Charles Fleischer. w. Bob Gale, Robert Zemeckis, d. Zemeckis.
ACTION: SCI-FI: Fantasy; Action Comedy; Time Travel; Time Machines; Teenagers; Futuristic Films; Scientists
(Ed: Pretty confusing and not particularly entertaining; special effects are good, though)

Back to the Future 3, 1990, ★★★/$$$, U/MCA-U, PG. This time they go back to the wild west and run into a teacher (Mary Steenburgen) whom the scientist falls for but may not be able to stay with, as their traveling days may be over. Michael J. Fox, Lea Thompson, Elizabeth Shue, Richard Dysart. w. Bob Gale, Robert Zemeckis, d. Zemeckis.
COMEDY: ACTION: Action Comedy; Fantasy; SCI-FI: ROMANCE: Romantic Comedy; WESTERN: Western Comedy; Time Travel; Time Machines; Scientists; Trains
(Peggy Sue Got Married; The Time Machine)

Backdraft, 1991, 136m, ★★½/$$$, I-U/MCA-U, R/S-P-V. Two firemen brothers discover an arsonist within their own ranks and track him down while fighting his gigantic fires. Kurt Russell, William Baldwin, Robert De Niro, Donald Sutherland, Jennifer Jason Leigh, Scott Glenn, Rebecca DeMornay. w. Gregory Widen, d. Ron Howard.
DRAMA: ACTION: Action Drama; Fires; Fires-Arsonists; Detective Stories; Detectives-Amateur; Corruption; Rescue Dramas; Chicago; Trail of a Killer
(The Hellfighters; In Old Chicago; City of Hope; The Towering Inferno)
(Ed: Apparently the detective story and blaze effects were reason enough for a feature film, but the story is slight and the family drama thrown in becomes distracting rather than enhancing)
Backfire, 1987, 91m, ★★/$$, Virgin/Vidmark, R. A Vietnam vet's nightmares may be the clues to a murder. Karen Allen, Keith Carradine, Jeff Fahey, Dean Paul Martin. w. Larry Brand, Rebecca Reynolds, d. Gilbert Cates.
SUSPENSE: MYSTERY: MURDER: MURDER MYSTERY: Vietnam Veterans; Nightmares; Flashbacks
Backtrack, 1988, 102m, ★★½/(VR), Vestron/Vestron, Live, R/S-P-V. An artist witnesses a murder and then must change her identity to evade a hitman who may be out to kill her, but also seems to be infatuated with her. Jodie Foster, Dennis Hopper, Dean Stockwell, Vincent Price, John Turturro. d. Dennis Hopper.
SUSPENSE: Chase Stories; Hitmen; Fugitives from the Mob; Fugitives from a Murderer; Witness to Murder; Kidnappers-Sympathizing with; Artists; Women in Jeopardy; Dangerous Men; Identities-Assumed; Good Premise Unfulfilled
Bad, see Andy Warhol's Bad
The Bad and the Beautiful (B&W), 1952, 118m, ★★★½/$$$, MGM/MGM-UA. A young producer and the people he steps on on the way up the ladder look back in anger. Kirk Douglas (BActor), Gloria Grahame (**BSActress**), Lana Turner. w. Charles Schnee (**BOStory, BOScr**), d. Vincente Minnelli.
BB&WCin, BB&WArt. Oscars: 6-5.
DRAMA: MELODRAMA: SATIRE: Film Noir; Hollywood Life; Evil Men; Power-Rise to Corruption; Mindgames; Revenge; Greed Funerals; Flashbacks; Episodic

Stories; Narrated Films
(Citizen Kane; Two Weeks in Another Town; The Barefoot Contessa)
(Ed: A hard-edged soap opera, reminiscent of Citizen Kane [only in its story], though its ambitions are far less)
Bad Boys, 1983, 123m, ★★★/$$, Universal/MCA-U, R/. Juvenile prison drama pits tough gang members against king of the brat packers. Sean Penn, Esai Morales, Ally Sheedy. w. Ron DiLello, d. Rick Rosenthal.
DRAMA: ROMANCE: Teenagers; Teenage Movies; Prison Drama; Bratpack Movies; Juvenile Delinquents; Coming of Age; Gangs-Street; Chicago; Film Noir-Modern
(Dead Man Walking; At Close Range; Boystown; Angels with Dirty Faces)
(Ed: More enlightening than entertaining)
Bad Boys, 1995, 126m, ★★/$$$, Col/Col, R/EP-S-FN. When $100 million of heroin is stolen from a police station, two black police detectives have to reclaim it with the help of a shady seductress who may set them off track. Martin Lawrence, Will Smith, Tea Leoni, Tcheky Karyo, Joe Pantoliano, Theresa Randle, Marg Helgenberger, Nestor Serrano, Julio Oscar Mechoso, Saverio Guerra, Anna Thomson, Kevin Corrigan, Michael Imperioli. w. Michael Barrie, Jim Mulholland, Doug Richardson, d. Michael Bay
ACTION: Action Comedy; Buddy Cops; Police Stories; Police Comedy; Drugs-Dealing; Black Men; Miami
(Lethal Weapon 3; Drop Zone; 48 Hours)
Bad Company, 1972, 93m, ★★/$$, Par/Par, R/V-P. Jeff Bridges and Barry Brown are AWOL heading to the wild west during the Civil War while making pit stops for robberies. w. Robert Benton, David Newman, d. Robert Benton.
DRAMA: ADVENTURE: WESTERNS: Road Movies; Outlaw Road Movies; Civil War; Soldiers; Fugitives; Fugitives from the Law; Dangerous Men; Underrated; Forgotten Films
(Ed: Mostly forgotten but worth finding, especially for Bridges fans)
Bad Company, 1995, 108m, ★★½/$, Touchstone/Touchstone, R/EP-EV-S. A black man and white woman, both ex-CIA agents working for an independent "hit firm" where no job is too reprehensible for these professional spies and killers. But soon they fall in lust for each other and also for taking over their com-

pany. Which lust is greater? Ellen Barkin, Laurence Fishburne, Frank Langella, Spalding Gray, Michael Beach, Gia Carides, David Ogden Stiers. w. Ross Thomas, d. Damian Harris
SUSPENSE: DRAMA: Crime Drama; Erotic Thriller; Film Noir-Modern; CIA Agents; Hitmen; Hitwomen; Black & White Together; Romance-Interracial; Power Struggles; Battle of the Sexes; Overlooked at Release; Coulda Been Great
Bad Day at Black Rock, 1955, 81m, ★★★½/$$$, MGM/MGM-UA, G/V. A conspiratorial man enters a desert town to solve a mystery and major conflict results. Spencer Tracy (BActor), Lee Marvin, Robert Ryan, Dean Jagger, Walter Brennan, Ernest Borgnine. w. Millard Kaufman, SS-adap. Howard Breslin (Bad Time at Hondo), d. John Sturges (BDirector). BScr. Oscars: 3-0.
MYSTERY: MURDER MYSTERY: WESTERNS: Westerns-Modern; SUSPENSE: Conformism; Small-Town Life; Dangerous Men; Corruption; Desert Life; New in Town; Hidden Gems
(Ed: Tracy's performance is as good as it gets)
Bad Dreams, 1988, 84m, ★★/$, 20th/Fox, R/EV-B&G-S. When a young woman whose cult committed suicide awakes from the coma she slipped into instead of dying, she is stalked by a cult member zombie who wants to make certain she follows the others in death. Bruce Abbott, Jennifer Rubin, Richard Lynch, Harris Yulin, Susan Ruttan. w. Andrew Fleming, Steven DeSouza, d. Fleming.
HORROR: SUSPENSE: Women in Jeopardy; Cults; Suicidal Tendencies; Nightmares; Zombies; Hospitals; Asylums; Ind Films
(Nightmare on Elm Street SERIES)
Badge 373, 1973, 116m, ★★½/$, Par/Par, R/EV. A cop (Robert Duvall) is driven to vigilante steps when his partner is killed and he's suspended after a suspect dies under suspicious circumstances. w. Pete Hamill, d. Howard Koch.
DRAMA: Crime Drama; Detective Stories; Detectives-Police; Vigilante Police; Police Stories; Revenge; Forgotten Films; Overlooked
(Death Wish; The French Connection; The Laughing Policeman; The Blue Knight)

Bad Girl, 1931, 90m, ★★★/$$$, 20th/NA. Two teenagers have to get married and find the real world of domestic life more troublesome than the street life they lead. Sally Eilers, James Dunn. w. Edwin Burke (**BScr**), N-adap. Vina Delmar, d. Frank Borsage (**BDirector**). BPicture. Oscars: 3-2.

DRAMA: ROMANCE: Social Drama; Message Films; Ordinary People Stories; Young People; Newlyweds; Teenagers; Mothers-Unwed; Depression Era
(Born Bad; Ann Vickers; They Live by Night

Bad Girls, see **Les Biches**

Bad Influence, 1990, 99m, ★★1/2/$$, TriumphCol/RCA-Col, R/P-V-S-FN. A yuppie (James Spader) and his rich girlfriend are thwarted by his new pal (Rob Lowe) who systematically sets out to destroy his life. Lisa Zane, Christian Clemenson. w. David Koepp, d. Curtis Hanson.

SUSPENSE: Framed?; Videotape Scandals; Videotape Scandals w/ James Spader; Dangerous Men; Mindgames; Friends as Enemies; Double Crossings; Upper Class; Yuppies; Turning the Tables (Strangers on a Train; Apartment Zero; Single White Female; Storyville)
(Ed: Ultimately silly due to the third act, but worth a look, especially for the irony of Lowe's videotaping-shot soon after his own scandal-and Spader in yet another videotape story)

The Bad Lieutenant, 1992, 96m, ★★★/$$, Aries/Live, R/EP-EV-FN-MFN. An extremely jaded cop (Harvey Keitel) investigates the rape of a nun and confronts his own demons while sinking to levels lower than the scum he busts. w. Zoe Lund, Abel Ferrara, d. Ferrara.

DRAMA: MURDER: MURDER MYSTERY: Detective Stories; Detectives-Police; Social Drama; Corruption; Evil Men; Police Corruption; Nuns; Rape/Rapists; Obsessions; Promiscuity; Drugs-Addiction; Drugs-Dealing; Ind Films; Female Screenwriters
(Dangerous Game; Taxi Driver; Reservoir Dogs)

Badlands, 1974, 94m, ★★★1/2/$$, Par/Par, R/V-S. True story of juvenile sociopath Charles Starkweather (Martin Sheen) and the young girl (Sissy Spacek) he picks up for a midwestern murder spree. w. d. Terence Malick.

DRAMA: ROMANCE: Road Movies; Outlaw Road Movies; Fugitives from Law; Fugitives; True Stories; Crime Drama; Murder Sprees; Criminal Couples; Midwesterns; Juvenile Deliquents; Mass Murderers; Writer-Directors

REMADE/RETOLD (TV): Murder in the Heartland
(Murder in the Heartland; Bonnie and Clyde; Gun Crazy; Kalifornia)
(Ed: Not as much fun as *Bonnie and Clyde*, but more naturalistic and "artsy")

Bad Man's River, 1972, 89m, ★★/$$, Ind/NA, R/V. Several wild west outlaws take on the job of blowing up a munitions arsenal in Mexico with some chaotic complications. Lee Van Cleef, James Mason, Gina Lollobrigida. w. Philip Yordan, Eugenio Martin, d. Martin.

WESTERN: Westerns-Spaghetti; **ACTION:** Action Comedy; Western Comedy; Heist Stories; Mexico

The Bad News Bears, 1976, 102m, ★★★/$$$$, Par/Par, PG/EP. A coach (Walter Matthau) who'd rather be somewhere else and a ragtag team of mall rats find themselves winning for once when a girl (Tatum O'Neal) joins the team w. Bill Lancaster, d. Michael Ritchie.

COMEDY: CHILDREN'S: Children-Brats; Sports Movies; Battle of the Sexes; Female Among Males; Bathroom Humor; Baseball; 1970s Ensemble Films; Ensembles-Male; Ensembles-Children

SEQUELS: The Bad News Bears in Breaking Training; The Bad News Bears Go to Japan.

RETREAD: Ladybugs
(Ed: A good kid's movie adults may like, though the language was originally shocking)

The Bad News Bears in Breaking Training, 1977, 100m, ★★/$$$, Par/Par, PG/EP. After losing their coach and star female player, the Bears must find a new one before going to Little League nationals. William Devane, Jimmy Baio. w. Paul Brickman, d. Michael Pressman.

COMEDY: CHILDREN'S: Baseball; Ensembles-Children; Ensembles-Male; Sports Movies; Ensemble Films; Bathroom Humor
(Ed: What's the point without the two main stars?)

The Bad News Bears Go to Japan, 1978, 91m, ★★/$$, Par/Par, PG/EP. The

original writer is back without even the replacement stars. Tony Curtis. w. Bill Lancaster, d. John Berry.

COMEDY: CHILDREN'S: Baseball; Sports Movies; Bathroom Humor; Boyhood; Ensembles-Male; Ensembles-Children; Ensemble Films
>(The Sandlot; Mr. Baseball; Ladybugs; The Big Green; The Mighty Ducks)

The Bad Seed, 1956, 129m, ★★★1/2/$$$$, 20th/CBS-Fox. When a monstrous brat decides she should have won a grade school award, the real winner suddenly dies, and so do some of the neighbors who are onto the killer's identity. Nancy Kelly (BActress), Patty McCormack (BSActress), Eileen Heckart (BSActress). w. John Lee Mahin, P-adap. Maxwell Anderson, d. Mervyn LeRoy.

The Bad Seed, 1986, 100m, ★★★/$$$, ABC/ABC. Blair Brown, Lynn Redgrave, Keith Carradine. d. Paul Wendkos. TV Movies

DRAMA: SUSPENSE: MURDER: TRAGEDY: Evil Children; Children-Brats; Serial Killers; Murderers-Nice; Murders-One by One; Mothers-Alone; Jealousy; Suicidal Tendencies; Female Protagonists

REMAKE (TV): The Bad Seed
(The Little Girl Who Lives Down the Lane; Alice, Sweet, Alice; The Good Son)
(Ed: Good remake, but not much different. Only *Little Girl* compares to this original child murderess)

The Bad Sleep Well, 1960, 152m, ★★★1/2/$$, Col/Col. Corruption and power struggles in a Japanese business. Toshiro Mifune. w. Akria Kurosawa, Hideo Oguni, Eijiro Kusaka, Ryuzo Kikushima, Shinobu Hashimoto, N-adap. Ed McBain, d. Akira Kurosawa.

DRAMA: Social Drama; Corruption; Conformism; Business Life; Executives; Japanese Films
(Executive Suite; Patterns; Rising Sun)

Bad Timing: A Sensual Obsession, 1980, 123m, ★★1/2/$, Northal/NW, R/ES-FN-MN. An American woman recently divorced has an affair with psychologist in modern day Vienna leading to much bizarre behavior and sex. Theresa Russell, Art Garfunkel, Harvey Keitel, Denholm Elliott. w. Yale Udoff, d. Nicolas Roeg.

DRAMA: Erotic Drama; **MELODRAMA:** Vienna; Romance with Psychologist; Sexy Women; Surrealism; Art Films; Ind Films

(The Man Who Fell to Earth; Eureka; Cold Heaven)

Bagdad Cafe, 1988, 91m, ★★★¹/₂/$$, Island/Island, Live, PG. A German tourist (Marianne Sagebrecht) is abandoned in the desert and finds work with an eccentric black woman (CCH Pounder) who runs a cafe and motel. Jack Palance. w. d. Percy Adlon. BOSong ("I Am Calling You"). Oscars: 1-0.
COMEDY DRAMA: Black Comedy; Comedy-Light; Starting Over; Fish out of Water Stories; Abandoned People; Restaurant Settings; Desert Life; Small-Town Life; Germans; Vacations; Female Protagonists; Art Films; Writer-Directors; Ind Films
(Rosalie Goes Shopping; Sugarbaby)
(Ed: The humor is more accessible than one would expect from such an "art film")

Le Bal, see L

Balalaika, 1939, 102m, ★★★/$$, MGM/MGM-UA. Russians in exile in Paris live their lives with music after the Revolution-but before the next war came along. Nelson Eddy, Ilona Massey, Charlie Ruggles, Frank Morgan. w. Jacques Deval, Leon Gordon, P-adap. Eric Maschwitz, d. Reinhold Schunzel.
MUSICAL: MUSICAL COMEDY: Paris; Russians; Musicals-Operettas
(Ninotchka; Anastasia; The Sun Also Rises; The Moderns)

La Balance, see L

The Balcony, 1963, 86m, ★★★/$, WR/Mystic Fire, Ingram. A madam (Shelley Winters) and the girls of a brothel continue on during wartime as though all were normal. Shelley Winters, Peter Falk, Lee Grant, Ruby Dee, Leonard Nimoy. w. Ben Maddow, P-adap. Jean Genet, d. Joseph Strick.
DRAMA: MELODRAMA: Prostitutes-Low Class; Futuristic Films; Art Films; Allegorical Stories; Avant-Garde; Ensemble Films; Forgotten Films
(A House Is Not a Home; Personal Services; The L-Shaped Room; Cabaret; According to Mrs. Hoyle)

Ball of Fire (B&W), 1941, 111m, ★★★¹/₂/$$$$, Goldwyn-UA/Goldwyn. A stripper-mob girl (Barbara Stanwyck, BActress) is interviewed by a nerdy professor (Gary Cooper) for a book on slang, so when she needs a place to hide, she turns to his institute. w. Billy Wilder, Charles Brackett, Thomas Monroe

(BOStory), d. Howard Hawks. BOScore. Oscars: 3-0.
COMEDY: Romantic Comedy; Romance-Opposites Attract; Hiding Out; Fugitives from the Mob; Mob Comedy; Smart vs. Dumb; Extroverted vs. Introverted; Strippers; Professors; Nerds; Mob Girls; Free Spirits; Wild People; Shy People
MUSICAL REMAKE: A Song Is Born.
(The Lady Eve; Sister Act; The Owl and the Pussycat; Hiding Out; Snow White & the Seven Dwarfs)
(Ed: A wonderful romantic comedy, though the romance is reluctant and strained)

Ballad of a Soldier, 1959, 89m, ★★★/$$, Mosfilm/Nos. A soldier in Russia takes a leave before returning to the battle front and facing death. Vladimir Ivashev. w. Valentin Yoshov, Girgori Chukrai, d. Chukrai.
DRAMA: MELODRAMA: Tearjerkers; Death-Impending; Soldiers; War Movies; War Battles
(Gallipoli; War and Peace; Dr. Zhivago)

The Ballad of Cable Hogue, 1970, 121m, ★★¹/₂/$$, WB/WB, R/EV. A gold-miner finds a fortune and then is robbed, so he plots his bloody revenge. Jason Robards, David Warner, Strother Martin, Slim Pickens. w. John Crawford, Edward Penney, d. Sam Peckinpah.
WESTERN: DRAMA: Revenge; Westerns-Revenge; Double Crossing; Greed; Gold Mining
(Bring Me the Head of Alfredo Garcia; The Treasure of the Sierra Madre; Chato's Land)

The Ballad of Josie, 1967, 102m, ★★/$$, U/MCA-U. Doris Day is a widow in the old west who starts over as a sheep farmer and must live in a man's world. Peter Graves, George Kennedy, Audrey Christie. w. Harold Swanton, d. Andrew V. MacLaglen.
COMEDY DRAMA: WESTERN: Western Comedy; Women's Films; Female Protagonists; Mothers Alone; Female Among Males; Widows; Starting Over; Farm Life

The Ballad of the Sad Cafe, 1991, 101m, ★★¹/₂/$ (LR), MI-Col/Col-Tri, Sony, PG-13/S-V. When a man is released from prison, he returns to his shrewish tomboy wife who runs a country store and seeks revenge. w. Michael Hirst, P-adap. Edward Albee, N-adap. Carson McCullers, d. Simon Callow.

DRAMA: MELODRAMA: TRAGEDY: Tomboys; Weddings; Southerns; Depression Era; Gothic Style; Virgins; Revenge
(Ed: Nice to look at, hard to understand. Only for fans of Redgrave or the book, or maybe not)

Balto, 1995, 74m, ★★/$$, U/MCA-UA, G. The story of a sled dog who delivers medicine to a remote town in the Northwest wilderness, based on a true story. Voices: Kevin Bacon, Bob Hoskins, Bridget Fonda, Jim Cummings, Phil Collins. w. Cliff Ruby, Elana Lesser, David Steven Cohen, and Roger S. H. Schulman, SS-adap. Ruby and Ms. Lesser, d. Simon Wells.
Cartoons; CHILDREN'S: Dogs; Rescue Drama; True Stories
(Iron Will; Call of the Wild)

Bambi, 1942, 69m, ★★★★/$$$$$, Disney/Disney, G. A fawn whose mother is killed seeks refuge with wilderness animals. w. d. David Hand. BOScore, BOSong. Oscars: 2-0.
CHILDREN'S: Cartoons; MELODRAMA: Disney; Wilderness Life; Animals-Talking; Orphans; Tearjerkers; Rabbits
(Ed: A classic, of course)

Bananas, 1971, 82m, ★★★/$$$, UA/MGM-UA, PG. A New York nerd (Woody Allen) winds up involved in a Central American coup through a series of misadventures. Louise Lasser, Howard Cosell. w. d. Woody Allen.
COMEDY: SATIRE: Political Comedy; Spoofs; Comedy of Errors; Misunderstandings; Fish Out of Water Stories; Central America; Political Unrest; Writer-Directors
(The In-Laws; Take the Money and Run; Sleeper)
(Ed: Allen at his silly best)

Band of Angels, 1957, 127m, ★★/$$, WB/WB. After the civil war, a slave owner (Clark Gable) takes on a mistress (Yvonne DeCarlo) who finds out some secrets about herself and the owner. Sidney Poitier, Efrem Zimbalist. w. John Twist, Ivan Goff, Ben Roberts, N-adap. Robert Penn Warren, d. Raoul Walsh.
MELODRAMA: DRAMA: TRAGEDY: Secrets-Haunting; Race Relations; Interracial Romance; Interracial People; Slavery; Civil War Era; Southerns; Coulda Been Good
(Gone With the Wind; Mandingo; Showboat)
(Ed: Glamorous but slow and disjointed)

The Band Wagon, 1953, 112m, ★★★1/2/$$$, MGM/MGM-UA. A movie star whose career is down goes to Broadway to do musical written by his friends. Fred Astaire, Cyd Charisse, Nanette Fabray. w. Betty Comden, Adolph Green, d. Vincente Minnelli.
MUSICALS: COMEDY: MUSICAL COMEDY: Actors; Theater Life; Redemption; Comebacks; Dancers; Female Screenwriters (Babes on Broadway; Silk Stockings; The Barkleys of Broadway; On the Town)
(Ed: A good team effort movie full of optimism and fun, whose silliness isn't obvious due to the pace)

Bandolero, 1968, 106m, ★★1/2/$$$, 20th/CBS-Fox. Two brothers on the lam take beautiful woman hostage for protection on their way to Mexico. James Stewart, Dean Martin, Racquel Welch. w. James Lee Barrett, d. Andrew McLaglen.
WESTERN: ADVENTURE: ACTION: Chase Movies; Road Movies; Hostages; Kidnappings; Fugitives from the Law; Fugitives; Mexico; Crossing the Border; Rape/Rapists; Women In Jeopardy; Faded Hits; Forgotten Films
(Ed: Originally a hit, it's been forgotten, but worth it for diehards of westerns or the stars)

Bang the Drum Slowly, 1973, 97m, ★★★/$$$, Par/Par, PG. Baseball buddies help each other when one begins dying of cancer. Robert De Niro, Michael Moriarty, Vincent Gardenia (BSActor). w., N/TV-adap. Mark Harris, d. John Hancock. Oscars: 1-0.
DRAMA: MELODRAMA: Disease Stories; Tearjerkers; Crying in Baseball; Dying Young; Friendships-Male; Friendships-Great; Baseball; Sports Movies
REMAKE OF (TV): Bang the Drum Slowly (1956)
(Brian's Song; Love Story; The Lou Gehrig Story)
(Ed: Not up to De Niro's later films, but an interesting look at male friendship and baseball)

Banjo on My Knee, 1936, 95m, ★★★/$$$, 20th/NA. Newlyweds have trouble when the groom gets into a fight. Barbara Stanwyck, Joel McCrea, Buddy Ebsen, Walter Brennan. w. Nunnally Johnson, N-adap. Harry Hamilton, d. John Cromwell.
DRAMA: COMEDY DRAMA: ROMANCE: Newlyweds; Marriage on the Rocks; Gambling; Mississippi; Southerns

The Bank Dick, 1940, 74m, ★★★1/2/$$$, U/MCA-U. A shiftless fellow (W.C. Fields) finds himself in a series of chaotic, coincidental situations including stopping a bank robbery, being made a bank guard, and inheriting a gold mine. w. W.C. Fields (Mahatma Kane Jeeves), d. Eddie Cline.
COMEDY: FARCE: Comedy of Errors; Bank Robberies; Fools-Bumbling; Comedy-Character
(The Dentist; International House)

The Bank Shot, 1974, 83m, ★★1/2/$$, UA/NA, PG. A bank robber doesn't rob the money, he steals the whole bank, and so begins the chase. George C. Scott, Joanna Cassidy, Sorrell Booke. w. Wendell Mayes, N-adap. Donald Westlake, d. Gower Champion.
COMEDY DRAMA: Chase Movies; FARCE: Heist Stories; Bank Robberies; Good Premise; Unfulfilled; Coulda Been Great
(The Flim Flam Man; Thunderbolt and Lightfoot; Slither; A Man, a Woman, and a Bank)

Banning, 1967, 102m, ★★1/2/$$, U/MCA-U, PG. A golf pro's liaisons with several women at a posh California country club get a little chancy. Robert Wagner, Anjanette Comer, Jill St. John, James Farentino, Gene Hackman. w. James Lee, d. Ron Winston. BOSong. Oscars: 1-0.
DRAMA: ROMANCE: Romantic Drama; Sexy Men; Playboys; Country Club Life; Rich People; Promiscuity; 1960s; Golf
(Shampoo; Doctors' Wives; Kaleidoscope; American Gigolo)

Barabbas, 1962, 144m, ★★1/2/$$, Col-DEG/RCA-Col. The Biblical figure who is pardoned instead of Jesus Christ must deal with this as he does time instead in mines and becomes a warring Christian. Anthony Quinn, Vittorio Gassman, Ernest Borgnine, Jack Palance, Arthur Kennedy. w. Christopher Fry, Nigel Balchin, Deigo Fabri, Ivo Perille, N-adap. Par Lagervist, d. Richard Fleischer.
DRAMA: ADVENTURE: Biblical Stories; Epics; Cast of Thousands; Ancient Times
(The Robe; Spartacus; The Shoes of the Fisherman)

Barbarella, 1968, 98m, ★★★/$$$$, Par/Par, R/ES-FN. Adventuress (Jane Fonda) goes from one outlandish planetary fantasy situation to another, encountering such characters as the original

Duran Duran. John Phillip Law. w. Terry Southern, N-adap. Jean-Claude Forest, d. Roger Vadim.
COMEDY: ADVENTURE: Fantasy; Comic Adventure; Psychedelic Era; Outer Space; Movies; Bimbos; Sexy Women; Sexy Men; Anti-Establishment Films; Female Protagonists
(Candy; Galaxina; Flesh Gordon)
(Ed: For camp and Fonda fans; good, bizarre, slightly dirty fun)

The Barbarian and the Geisha, 1958, 105m, ★★1/2/$$, UA/Fox. A diplomat in the 19th century (John Wayne) goes to Japan to open trade and deal with the customs of the women. Eiko Ando, Sam Jaffe. w. Charles Grayson, d. John Huston.
DRAMA: Historical Drama; ROMANCE: Romantic Drama; Diplomats; Japan; Romance-Interracial; Flops-Major
(My Geisha; The Countess from Hong Kong; Blood Alley; The Conqueror)
(Ed: Pretty much overblown)

Barbarosa, 1982, 90m, ★★1/2/$, Universal/MCA-U, PG. An older outlaw teaches a farmboy how to make it on the frontier of old Texas. Willie Nelson, Gary Busey. w. William Witliff, d. Fred Schepisi.
WESTERN: DRAMA: Friendships-Intergenerational; Friendships-Male; Understudies/Proteges; Coming of Age Overlooked; Coulda Been Good
(The Mechanic; Convicts; Honeysuckle Rose)
(Ed: An interesting story, but not very entertaining unless you love Nelson)

The Barbary Coast, 1935, 90m, ★★★/$$$, Goldwyn-UA/Goldwyn. A chanteuse in old Frisco deals with the advances of her saloon boss amid the locals. Miriam Hopkins, Edward G. Robinson, Walter Brennan, Joel McCrea. w. Ben Hecht, Charles MacArthur, d. Howard Hawks.
COMEDY DRAMA: ROMANCE: MELODRAMA: Singers; West-Old; Bosses-Bad; Sexual Harassment; San Francisco; 1800s; Female Protagonists
(San Francisco; The Flame of the Barbary Coast)
(Ed: An oddity in tone for the era, but interesting)

Barcelona, 1994, 101m, ★★★/$$, Fine Line/Fine Line, PG-13/P-S. Two American friends, one a yuppie, the other a naval officer, try to meet women in the

Spanish city while avoiding terrorists and being mistaken for CIA agents, all amid pretentious conversation and anti-Americanism. Taylor Nichols, Chris Eigeman, Tushka Bergen, Mira Sorvino, Pep Munne, Hellena Schmied, Nuria Badia, Thomas Gibson, Jack Gilpin. w. d. Whit Stillman.

COMEDY DRAMA: Art Films; Buddy Films; Friendships-Male; Americans Abroad; Americans as Enemy; Intellectuals; Sailors; Quiet Little Films; Spain; Violence-Sudden; Yuppies; Writer-Directors
(Metropolitan; My Dinner with Andre)
(Ed: Only for fans of *Metropolitan*. Too dry to be very funny, with only moments of real inspiration and not much emotion to care about the characters by)

The Barefoot Contessa, 1954, 128m, ★★★/$$$, UA/MGM-UA, Fox. A movie director (Humphrey Bogart) promotes a dancer (Ava Gardner) actress with the help of a press agent (Edmund O'Brien, **BSActor**) who's suspicious of the situation. w. d. Joseph L. Mankiewicz (BOScr). Oscars: 2-1.
DRAMA: SATIRE: Hollywood Life; Making Movies; Actresses; Directors; Love-Questionable; Disguises; Rise to Fame
(Mistress; The Sweet Smell of Success; The Bad and the Beautiful; The Countess from Hong Kong)
(Ed: A fun, insightful look at Hollywood)

The Barefoot Executive, 1971, 95m, ★★1/2/$$$, Disney/Disney, G. TV network mail boy uses the special powers of a chimp to help him rise to power when he finds the chimp has the same taste as Mr. & Mrs. Average Viewer. Kurt Russell, John Ritter. w. Joseph McEveety, d. Robert Butler.
COMEDY: CHILDREN'S: Fantasy; Animals-Smart; Primates; Power-Rise; Power-Rise to, of Idiot; Business Life; TV Life; Hollywood Life; Faded Hits
(Monkey Trouble; The Computer Wore Tennis Shoes; Ed)
(Ed: Decent children's fare, unusually savvy and satirical for Disney; originally a hit)

Barefoot in the Park, 1967, 105m, ★★★1/2/$$$$, Par/Par. A newlywed couple try to save money by roughing it in tiny rooftop apartment in New York with many problems. Jane Fonda, Robert Redford, Mildred Natwick (BSActress), Charles Boyer. w. P-adap. Neil Simon, d. Gene Saks.
COMEDY: Romantic Comedy; Newlyweds; Making a Living; Lawyers; Housewives; Female Protagonists; New York Life; 1960s
(Period of Adjustment; About Last Night; Mr. and Mrs. Smith; Made for Each Other; Sunday in the Park; The Electric Horseman)
(Ed: Probably the best of the newlywed comedies)

Barfly, 1987, 99m, ★★★/$$, Cannon/MGM-UA, R/P-S. An alcoholic poet (Mickey Rourke) meets up with a down-and-out mystery woman (Faye Dunaway), and they drink together while falling in love, despite a literary agent (Alice Krige) who wants more than his poetry. w., N-adap. Charles Bukowski, d. Barbet Schroeder.
DRAMA: Biographies; Autobiographical; Alcoholics; Skid Row; Hollywood; Poor People; Depression; Love-Reluctant; Romance-Triangles; Jealousy; Quiet Little Films; Ind Films
(Days of Wine and Roses; The Lost Weekend; Leaving Las Vegas)
(Ed: Can be depressing in its bleakness, but creates a fascinating underworld)

Bar Girls, 1995, 95m, ★★/$, Ind/NA, R/ES-P-FN. The cliches of the lives of lesbians barhopping in L.A. are much like those of heterosexuals, but not necessarily very entertaining, either. Nancy Allison Wolfe, Liza D'Agostino, Justine Slater, Paula Sorge, Camila Griggs, Michael Harris, Pam Raines w. P-adap. Lauran Hoffman, d. Marita Giovanni.
DRAMA: Ensemble Films; Lesbians; Nightclubs; Los Angeles; Female Protagonists; Female Screenwriters; Female Directors; Gay & Lesbian Films
(Go Fish; Lianna; Desert Hearts)

The Barkleys of Broadway, 1949, 109m, ★★1/2/$$, MGM/MGM-UA. Two musical comedy stars (Fred Astaire, Ginger Rogers) bicker their way into a break-up and then try a comeback as she becomes a big dramatic actress. Billie Burke. w. Adolph Green, Betty Comden, d. Charles Walters.
MUSICAL: MUSICAL COMEDY: ROMANCE: Romantic Comedy; Romance-Bickering; Theater Life; Dancers; Comebacks; Actresses; Astaire & Rogers; Female Protagonists; Female Screenwriters

(A Star Is Born; The Band Wagon; The Guardsman)

Barnacle Bill, 1941, 90m, ★★1/2/$$, MGM/MGM-UA, Turner. A fisherman on the docks (Wallace Beery) romances a crusty woman (Marjorie Main) in the hopes of getting money for his business. Virginia Weidler. w. Jack Jevne, Hugo Butler, d. Richard Thorpe.
COMEDY: ROMANCE: Romantic Comedy; Ordinary People Stories; Poor People; Fishermen; Romance-Middle-Aged
(Min and Bill; Tugboat Annie)

Barnacle Bill (*All at Sea*), 1957, 87m, ★★1/2/$$, Ealing/NA. A sailor whose family has ridden the seas for generations gets seasick too much, so he goes ashore at a resort to try and make it with the eccentric locals. Alec Guinness, Irene Browne, George Rose, Lionel Jeffries. w. TEB Clarke, d. Charles Frend.
COMEDY: Comedy-Light; Comedy of Errors; Nerds; Ships; Resorts; Eccentric People; Small-Town Life; British Films

The Barretts of Wimpole Street, 1934, 109m, ★★/$$$$, MGM/MGM-UA. Norma Shearer, Fredric March, Charles Laughton, Maureen Sullivan. w. Ernst Vajda, Claudine West, Donald Ogden Stewart, P-adap. Rudolph Besier, d. Sidney Franklin.

The Barretts of Wimpole Street, 1956, 105m, ★★1/2/$$, MGM/MGM-UA. Jennifer Jones, Bill Travers, John Gielgud, Virginia McKenna. w. John Dighton, d. Sidney Franklin.
Famous poet Robert Browning is pursued by disabled Elizabeth Barrett, despite her restrictive father and soon a classic romance blossoms, but not without troubles.
DRAMA: MELODRAMA: Romance-Lover Family Dislikes; Costume Drama; Historical Drama; True Stories; Writers Poets; Disabled People; 1800s
(The Heiress; The Belle of Amherst [play])

Barry Lyndon, 1975, 183m, ★★★/$$$, WB/WB, PG. An Irish drifter winds his way through restoration period Britian with many adventures. Ryan O'Neal, Marisa Berenson. w. Stanley Kubrick, N-adap. William Makepeace Thackeray, d. Stanley Kubrick (BDirector). BPicture, **BCinema**, BEdit, **BCost, BArt, BAScore**. Oscars: 7-4.
DRAMA: Road Movies; Costume Drama; Historical Drama; Drifters; Multiple

Stories; Romance-Class Conflicts; Episodic Stories; 1700s; England; Lyrical Films; Outstanding Production Design; Outstanding Scenery

(Tom Jones; The Return of Martin Guerre; Vanity Fair; Becky Sharp; The Age of Innocence [1993])

(Ed: More beautiful than entertaining)

Bartleby, 1970, 79m, ★★★/$, Col/White Star, G. A bizarre young clerk named Bartleby says "I'd prefer not to" to too much in life and eventually withers, much to the consternation of his boss. Paul Scofield, John McEnery. w. Anthony Friedmann, Rodney Carr-Smith, SS-adap. Herman Melville, d. Friedmann.

DRAMA: Allegorical Stories; Depression; Mental Illness; Surrealism; 1800s; British Films; Classic Literary Adaptations

Barton Fink, 1991, 121m, ★★★/$$, 20th/Fox, R. A New York writer comes to Hollywood in the Depression and stays in a hotel full of strange happenings. John Turturro, John Goodman, Michael Lerner. w. Joel & Ethan Coen, d. Joel Coen.

DRAMA: SATIRE: Art Film; Surrealism; Hollywood Life; Writers; Eccentric People; Neighbors-Troublesome; Fires; 1930s; Coulda Been Great

(The Last Tycoon; Miller's Crossing; The Hudsucker Proxy; Fargo)

(Ed: For fans of weird films that seem incompletely realized)

Based on an Untrue Story, 1993, 90m, ★★★/$$ (VR), 20th-TV/Fox. A perfume maker (Morgan Fairchild) loses her sense of smell and goes on a chaotic journey to find her real parents for an olfactory nerve transplant, on the way finding family members beset with every tragedy to ever hit tabloid TV. Dyan Cannon, Harvey Korman, Ricki Lake, Victoria Jackson, Michael St. Gerard.

COMEDY: Spoofs; **FARCE:** Complicated Plots; Clever Plots & Endings; TV Movies; Docudrama; Hidden Gems; Overlooked; Impostors; Family/Heritage-Search for; Disease Movies

(Ed: Fairchild is great as the senseless heroine with Dyan Cannon not who she thought she was and a cast of zany family members and serial killers. Featuring the theme song, "The Girl Is Clueless." Not quite up to John Waters' best, but very good for TV)

Les Bas-Fonds, see **L**

Basic Instinct, 1992, 128m, ★★★/ $$$$$, Carolco-Tri/LIVE, R/EP-EV-ES-FFN-MN. An icepick murderess may actually be a bisexual authoress-millionairess who has lured the cop on the case into her web. Michael Douglas, Sharon Stone, George Dzunda, Jeanne Tripplehorn, Leilani Sarelle. w. Joe Eszterhas, d. Paul Verhoeven. BOScore, BEdit. Oscars: 2-0.

SUSPENSE: MYSTERY: MURDER: MURDER MYSTERY: Detective Stories; Detectives in Deep; Trail of a Killer; Serial Killers; Murderers-Female; Romance with Suspect; Enemies-Sleeping with; Bisexuality; Lesbians; San Francisco

REMAKE/RETREAD: Vertigo

(Vertigo; Black Widow [1987]; Jagged Edge; Mirage [1994]; Sliver; Diabolique [1996])

(Ed: If Kim Novak had been a killer and Hitchcock had no finesse, this might be *Vertigo* done 90s style, unfortunately)

Basket Case, 1982, 89m, ★★/$, Ind/Media, R/EV-B&G. Two Siamese twins seek revenge on the doctor who separated them. w. d. Frank Henelotter.

Basket Case 2, 1990, 89m, ★★/$$, Ind/Image, R/B&G. This time, the twins find a community of freaks like themselves. w. d. Frank Henenlotter.

Basket Case 3, 1992, 90m, ★★/$$, Ind/MCA-U, R/V-B&G. One of the Siamese twins has children and must protect them. w. Frank Henenlotter, Robert Martin, d. Henenlotter.

HORROR: Revenge; Twins; Independent Films; Revenge on Doctors; Disabled People; Monsters-Human

The Bat, 1959, 78m, ★★½/$$, AA/Nos. A mystery writer (Agnes Moorehead) rents an old house and soon she and her guests are besieged by a psychotic man (Vincent Price) looking for money he hid there. w. d. Crane Wilbur, P-adap. Mary Roberts.

The Bat Whispers, 1930, 82m, ★★★/$$, UA/Nos. Earlier version of *The Bat.* Chester Morris, Una Merkel. w. d. Roland West, P-adap. Mary Roberts.

HORROR: SUSPENSE: Malicious Menaces; Houses-Creepy; Writers; Treasure Hunts

REMAKE OF: The Bat (1926), The Bat Whispers (1930)

Bataan, 1943, 114m, ★★½/$$$$, MGM/MGM-UA. A platoon of soldiers in the Pacific guard a bridge against the Japanese and soon face reality. Robert Taylor, George Murphy, Thomas Mitchell, Lloyd Nolan, Desi Arnaz. w. Robert Andrews, d. Tay Garnett.

DRAMA: War Movies; War Battles; Deaths-One by One; Soldiers; World War II Movies

REMAKE/RETREAD: The Lost Patrol (Back to Bataan)

Bathing Beauty, 1944, 101m, ★★★/$$$, MGM/MGM-UA. A successful songwriter wants to retire early but his greedy music publisher decides to convince his swimming fiancee that he needs more songs to sell. Esther Williams, Red Skelton, Basil Rathbone, Keenan Wynn. w. Dorothy Kingsley, Allen Boretz, Frank Waldman, d. George Sidney.

MUSICAL: ROMANCE: Musical Romance; Swimming; Songwriters; Singers; Mindgames; Female Screenwriters

(Neptune's Daughter; The Duchess of Idaho)

Batman, the Movie, 1966, 105m, ★★★/$$, 20th/CBS-Fox. Spinoff of the TV series with camp and children's edge where all of the main four villains join forces against Batman. Adam West, Burt Ward, Cesar Romero, Frank Gorshin, Burgess Meredith, Lee Meriwether. w. Lorenzo Semple Jr., d. Leslie Martinson.

ACTION: COMEDY: Action Comedy; Camp; Comic Heroes; Cartoonlike Films; Good vs. Evil; TV Series Movies; Villains-Classic; Submarines

Batman, 1989, 126m, ★★★/$$$$$, WB/WB, PG-13/V. The caped crusader (Michael Keaton), sans Robin, takes on the Joker (Jack Nicholson) while romancing and saving Vicki Vale (Kim Basinger). w. Warren Skaaren, Sam Hamm, d. Tim Burton. BCin, **BArt, BSound,** BSEdit, BVFX. Oscars: 5-2.

ACTION: ADVENTURE: Film Noir-Modern; Villains-Classic; Comic Heroes; Damsel in Distress; Revenge; Rule the World-Plot to; Fighting Evil; Blockbusters

SEQUELS: Batman Returns; Batman Forever

(Ed: Long on atmosphere, short on original story. Nicholson's worth it)

Batman Forever, 1995, 121m, ★★★/ $$$$$, WB/WB, PG/V. When the Riddler is thrown out of his lab, he goes on an experimental rampage from which only Batman with his new circus-refugee sidekick, Robin, can save Gotham City. Val Kilmer, Tommy Lee Jones, Jim Carrey, Nicole Kidman, Chris O'Donnell, Drew

Barrymore. w. Lee Batchler, Janet Scott Batchler, Akiva Goldsman, Comic-adap. Bob Kane, d. Joel Schumacher. BArt, BSound. Oscars: 2-0.

ACTION: ADVENTURE: Comic Heroes; Men and Boys; Buddy Films; Circus Life; Scientists-Mad; Blockbusters; Female Screenwriters

Batman Returns, 1992, 121m, ★★★/$$$$, WB/WB. PG-13/V. The caped crusader (Michael Keaton) takes on the two-faced Catwoman (Michelle Pfeiffer), the Penguin (Danny DeVito) in a plot to change the weather and rule the world. w. Sam Hamm, Daniel Waters, d. Tim Burton. BVFX, BMakeup, BArt. Oscars: 3-0.

ACTION: ADVENTURE: Cartoon Heroes; Feisty Females; Dangerous Women; Fighting Evil; Villains-Classic; Rule the World-Plot to; Blockbusters

SEQUEL TO: Batman

SEQUEL: Batman Forever

(Ed: Michelle and the art direction save it from being an overblown misfire)

(Superman; Dick Tracy)

Battement de Coeur, 1940, 100m, ★★★/$$, Ind/NA. A poor girl in the Paris slums joins a school for pickpockets but winds up picking up the diplomat she picks the pocket of. Danielle Darrieux, Andre Luguet. w. Jean Villeme, Max Colphet, Michel Duran, d. Henri Decoin.

COMEDY: ROMANCE: Romantic Comedy; Romance-Opposites Attract; Thieves; Con Artists; Pickpockets; Diplomats; Paris

REMADE AS: Heartbeat (1941)

(Heartbeat; Pygmalion; Children of Paradise)

batteries not included, 1987, 107m, ★★★/$$$, Universal/MCA-U, PG. Tenants in a condemned building in New York are assisted in saving their home by tiny UFOs. Jessica Tandy, Hume Cronyn, Elizabeth Pena, Dennis Boutsikaris. w. Matthew Robbins, Brad Bird, Brent Maddock, S.S. Wilson, Mick Garris, d. Matthew Robinson.

CHILDREN'S: FAMILY: SCI-FI: Fantasy; Mortgage Drama; Elderly People; Friendships-Interracial; New York Life; Poor People; UFOs; Alien Lifeforms; Special Effects; Coulda Been Great

(Ed: Not quite *Cocoon*, but okay, especially with Tandy and Cronyn)

Battle Cry, 1955, 149m, ★★/$$$, WB/WB. A boot camp for Marines includes several romances before combat. Van Heflin, Aldo Ray, Tab Hunter, Dorothy Malone, Raymond Massey, Nancy Olson, Anne Francis. w. N-adap. Leon Uris, d. Raoul Walsh.

DRAMA: MELODRAMA: ROMANCE: War Movies; World War II Movies; War Battles; Multiple Stories; Interwoven Stories; Soldiers

Battle for the Planet of the Apes, 1973, 92m, ★★1/2/$$, 20th/CBS-Fox, PG/V. A prequel to the four before it, telling of the nuclear holocaust which led to apes taking over. Roddy McDowell, Claude Akins, John Huston, Paul Williams. w. John William Corrington, Joyce Hooper Corrington, d. J. Lee Thompson.

ADVENTURE: ACTION: SCI-FI: War Movies; War Battles; Primates; Apocalyptic Stories

PREQUEL TO: Planet of the Apes SERIES

(Ed: Only for *Apes* series fans)

Battle Hymn, 1957, 108m, ★★/$$, U/MCA-U. An American missionary founds an orphanage in Korea during the war. Rock Hudson, Dan Duryea, Martha Hyer. w. Charles Grayson, Vincent Evans, d. Douglas Sirk.

DRAMA: Biographies; True Stories; Missionaries; Ministers/Preachers; Korean War; Orphans

(Keys to the Kingdom; Inn of the Sixth Happiness; Hornet's Nest; A Farewell to Arms [1957])

Battle of Algiers, 1965, 123m, ★★★/$$, AA/Ingram. A convict mercenary joins terrorists in their war against the French colonial government in North Africa. Brahim Haggiag, Jean Martin. w. Franco Solinas (BOScr), d. Gillo Pontecorvo (BDirector). BFLFilm Oscars: 3-0.

DRAMA: ACTION: War Movies; War Battles; Terrorists; Political Unrest; Africa; Ex-Convicts; Italian Films

(Z; The Dogs of War; Soldier of Orange)

Battle of Britain, 1969, 132m, ★★★/$$, UA/CBS-Fox. A slice of life of England on the nights the German aerial attacks of World War II began. Laurence Olivier, Robert Shaw, Michael Caine, Christopher Plummer, Kenneth More, Susannah York, Michael Redgrave, Edward Fox, Trevor Howard, Ralph Richardson. w. James Kennaway, Wilfrid Greatorex, d. Guy Hamilton.

DRAMA: ACTION: World War II Movies; Pilots-Military; War Battles; Germans as Enemy; Multiple Stories; Interwoven Stories; Slice of Life Stories; England; British Films; All-Star Casts; Cast of Thousands

(Suppose They Threw a War and Nobody Came?; A Bridge Too Far; All This and World War II; Hope and Glory)

(Ed: Notable for its stellar cast)

Battle of the Neretva, 1969, 106m, ★★★/$, Ind/Republic. The Yugoslavian resistance of Italian and German invasions is detailed. Yul Brynner, Curt Jurgens, Orson Welles, Franco Nero. w. Ugo Pirro, d. Veljko Bulajic. BFLFilm Oscars: 1-0.

ACTION: DRAMA: Action Drama; War Movies; World War II Movies; War Battles; Germans as Enemy; Europeans-Eastern

The Battle of the Bulge, 1965, 141m, ★★★/$$$, WB/WB. The famous battle is detailed as the Americans have trouble at Ardennes due to a particularly clever German leader. Henry Fonda, Robert Shaw, Robert Ryan, Telly Savalas, Dana Andrews, Charles Bronson. w. Philip Yordan, Milton Sperling, John Melson, d. Ken Annakin.

ACTION: DRAMA: Action Drama; War Stories; War Battles; Germans as Enemy; World War II Movies; All-Star Casts; Ensemble Films; Ensembles-Male; Battle of the Bulge

(Battleground; A Bridge Too Far)

The Battle of the Sexes, 1960, 88m, ★★★/$$, ABF/Moore. A woman efficiency expert streamlines a textile mill in Scotland and an accountant sets out to undo her good work which may cost more than if she'd never come. Peter Sellers, Constance Cummings, Robert Morley. w. Monja Danieschewsky, SS-adap. James Thurber, *The Catbird Seat*, d. Charles Crichton.

COMEDY: SATIRE: COMEDY DRAMA: Black Comedy; Mindgames; Revenge; Battle of the Sexes; Working Class; Scotland; Hidden Gems

(The Efficiency Expert; I'm Allright, Jack; Desk Set)

Battleground, 1949, 118m, ★★★/$$$$, MGM/MGM-UA. The first major telling of the Battle of the Bulge with an all-star cast. Van Heflin, James Whitmore (BSActor), John Hodiak, Ricardo Montalban, Marshall Thompson. w.

Robert Pirosh (**BOScr**), d. William Wellman (BDirector). BPicture, **BCCin,** BEdit. Oscars: 6-2.

ACTION: DRAMA: Action Drama; War Movies; War Battles; World War II Movies; Ensemble Films; Ensembles-Male; All-Star Casts; Battle of the Bulge (The Battle of the Bulge; A Bridge Too Far)

The Battleship Potemkin, 1925, 75m (Silent/also sound), ★★★★/NA, Ind/Republic, Nos. The classic silent film, the famous Odessa steps scene which has been imitated often, centered around a Russian coup in 1905. w. d. Sergei Eisenstein.

DRAMA: TRAGEDY: Political Unrest Russians; Russian Films; Writer-Directors; Film History (Arsenal; Strike; Ballad of a Soldier) (Ed: Where the train station scene from *The Untouchables* came from)

The Bawdy Adventures of Tom Jones, 1976, 94m, ★★1/2/$$, U/MCA-U, R/S. A musical version of the classic story of the randy young dandy and his wayward ways. Nicky Henson, Trevor Howard, Terry-Thomas, Georgia Brown, Joan Collins. w. Jeremy Lloyd, P-adap. Don McPherson, N-adap. Henry Fielding, d. Cliff Owen.

COMEDY: MUSICAL: MUSICAL COMEDY: FARCE: Misunderstandings; Mistaken Identities; Children-Long Lost; Sexy Men; Young Men; Promiscuity; England; 1700s; British Films

REMAKE OF: Tom Jones (Joseph Andrews; The Adventures of Eliza Frazer; Alvin Purple; Alvin Rides Again)

Baxter!, 1972, 100m, ★★1/2/$, 20th-EMI/NA. An American boy in London witnesses the death of a friend and then must undergo speech therapy. Patricia Neal, Scott Jacoby, Britt Ekland, Lynn Carlin. w. Reginald Rose, d. Lionel Jeffries.

DRAMA: MELODRAMA: TRAGEDY: Mentally Disabled; Mute People; Boys; Women and Boys; Disabled People; Psychologists; Americans Abroad; England; British Films; Female Protagonists

Baxter, 1990, 82m, ★★★/$$, Ind/Fox-Lorber, PG-13. A dog goes from one master to the next and the audience gets his perspective on the whole thing through interior monologues as he rebels and tries

to live the way he wants to. Lise Delamere, Jean Mercure, Jacques Spiesser, Catherine Ferran. w. Jerome Bolvin, Jacques Audlard, d. Bolvin.

COMEDY DRAMA: Pet Stories; Dogs; Animals-Talking; **SATIRE:** Black Comedy; Hand Me Down Stories; Coming of Age; French Films; Curiosities (Look Who's Talking Now; Babe) (Ed: The animal movie for the more sardonic)

The Bay Boy, 1984, 107m, ★★/$, HBO-Orion/Orion, PG. A Canadian teenager doubts his choice to become a priest. Kiefer Sutherland, Liv Ullman, Peter Donat. w. d. Daniel Petrie.

DRAMA: MELODRAMA: Teenagers; Coming of Age; Young Men; Priests; Canadian Films; Small-Town Life; Depression Era; 1930s; Writer-Directors

Beach Blanket Bingo, 1965, 96m, ★★★/$$, AIP/NA. Wild shenanigans on the beach in one of the best of the series, centering all around a kidnapping. Frankie Avalon, Annette Funicello, Linda Evans, Don Rickles, Buster Keaton, Paul Lynde, Harvey Lembeck. w. Sher Townsend, Leo Townsend, d. William Asher.

COMEDY: MUSICALS: Musical Comedy; Beach Movies; Camp; Teenagers; Teenage Movies; Kidnappings; Skydiving (Beach Party; Back to the Beach; The Happening)

Beach Party, 1963, 104m, ★★★/$$$, AIP/New World. A anthropology writer (Bob Cummings) goes to the beach to study mating habits of the youngsters and runs into Annette and Frankie & Co. Annette Funicello, Frankie Avalon, Dorothy Malone, Vincent Price, Morey Amsterdam w. Lou Rusoff, d. William Asher.

COMEDY: SATIRE: Music Movies; Beach Movies; Teenage Movies; Teenagers; Writers; Camp; Cult Films (Beach Blanket Bingo; The Ghost in the Invisible Bikini; Back to the Beach; Muscle Beach Party)

Beaches, 1988, 123m, ★★1/2/$$$, Touchstone/Touchstone, PG/S-P. Two women (Bette Midler, Barbara Hershey) become friends as children and follow each other's lives for years. w. Mary Agnes Donoghue, N-adap. Iris Rainer Dart. d. Garry Marshall.

DRAMA: MELODRAMA: Disease Stories; Tearjerkers; Death-Dealing with;

Friendships-Female; Friendships-Lifetime; Episodic Stories; Singers; Feuds; Jealousy; Womens' Films; Girlhood; Female Protagonists; Female Screenwriters (The Turning Point; Stella; Terms of Endearment; Entre Nous; Antonia and Jane; Love Story [1970]; For the Boys) (Ed: A superficial tearjerker that wants to be *The Turning Point* and *Terms of Endearment* all in one; star chemistry works, but that's about it)

The Bear, 1988, 90m, ★★★/$$$, Tri/Col-Tri, PG/V. A little orphan bear tries to make it on his own in the Canadian wilderness. w. Gerard Brach, N-adap. Ja mes Curwood, d. Jean-Jacques Annaud.

DRAMA: CHILDREN'S: FAMILY: Animals-Smart; Nature-Back to; Canadian Films; Animal Movies (The Incredible Journey; Homeward Bound; The Bears and I)

The Bears and I, 1974, 89m, ★★★/$$$, Disney/Disney. A new park ranger (Patrick Wayne) takes on three bear cubs as pals. Chief Dan George, Michael Ansara. w. John Whedon, N-adap. Robert Franklin Leslie, d. Bernard McEveety.

COMEDY DRAMA: CHILDREN'S: FAMILY: Animal Stories; Pet Stories; Nature-Back to

The Beast Must Die, 1974, 93m, ★★1/2/$$, Ind/NA. A millionaire holds a hunting game party to kill a werewolf on the loose, but the guests may be the prey. Peter Cushing, Calvin Lockhart. w. Michael Winder, James Blish, d. Paul Annett.

HORROR: SUSPENSE: MYSTERY: MURDER: Mystery-Whodunit?; Murders-One by One; Werewolves; Mindgames (The Most Deadly Game; Ten Little Indians)

Beast of the City, 1932, 80m, ★★1/2/$$, MGM/NA. A police captain sets out on a vendetta against a mobster. Walter Huston, Jean Harlow, Wallace Ford, Jean Hersholt. w. John Lee Mahin, W.R. Burnett, d. Charles Brabin.

DRAMA: Crime Drama; Mob Stories; Revenge; Police-Vigilante; Police vs. Mob; Policemen

The Beastmaster, 1982, 118m, ★★/$$, MGM-UA/MGM-UA, PG/V. A young man of royal birth is stolen as a child by a witch and winds up in the wilds raised by a martial arts expert to trains him to be a warrior. Marc Singer, Tanya Roberts, Rip Torn, John Amos. w. Don Coscarelli, Paul Pepperman, N-adap. Andre Norton, d. Don Coscarelli.

ACTION: Martial Arts; Sword & Sorcery; Medieval Times; Magic; Good vs. Evil; Animals-Talking

The Beastmaster 2, 1991, 107m, ★★/VR, Republic/Republic, V. A continuation of the original with more emphasis on the magical animals the sorcerer speaks to and time travel. Marc Singer, Sarah Douglas, Wings Hauser, Kari Wuhrer. w. R. J. Robertson, Jim Wynorski, Sylvio Tabet, Ken Hauser, Doug Miles, d. Tabet.

ACTION: Martial Arts; Sword & Sorcery; Medieval Times; Magic; Good vs. Evil; Time Travel; Animals-Talking
(Yor; Hercules [TV Series])

The Beat, 1988, 101m, ★★/$, Vestron/Vestron, R/V-P. A new kid enters a world of hip and rather benign street gangs in an inner city neverland who unbelievably are tamed by poetry and rap. John Savage, Kara Glover, Paul Dillon. w. d. Paul Mones.

DRAMA: Poets; Writers; Inner City Life; Gangs-Street; Curiosities; Writer-Directors
(Kids; Fame)

The Beat Generation (*This Rebel Age*), 1959, 95m, ★★★/$$, Ind/NA. A group of beatniks are invaded by a rapist on a rampage. Ray Danton, Steve Cochran, Fay Spain, Mamie Van Doren, Jackie Coogan. w. Richard Matheson, Lewis Meltzer, d. Charles Haas.

DRAMA: MELODRAMA: Beatnik Era; Rape/Rapists; Cult Films; Forgotten Films; 1950s; Ind Films
(The Subterraneans; The Arousers)

Beat Street, 1984, 106m, ★★/$, Orion/Orion. A black breakdance version of Saturday Night Fever, et. al. Guy Davis, Rae Dawn Chong, Saundra Santiago. w. Andy Davis, David Gilbert, Paul Golding, d. Stan Latham

COMEDY DRAMA: Teenage Movies; Teenagers; Dance Movies; Music Movies
(Breakin'; Breakin' 2; Krush Groove)

Beat the Devil, 1954, 89m, ★★★/$, UA/CBS-Fox. A potpourri of eccentrics with great lines to say travel on a rickety boat to North Africa to go after land with uranium, an ironic treasure. Humphrey Bogart, Jennifer Jones, Gina Lollobrigida, Peter Lorre, Robert Morley, Edward Underblown. w. Truman Capote, John Huston, N-adap. James Helvick (Claude Cockburn), d. Huston.

COMEDY DRAMA: DRAMA: Black Comedy; Eccentric People; Journies; Ships; Africa; Quests; Ensemble Films; Cult Films; Flops-Major
(Ship of Fools; The Barefoot Contessa)
(Ed: Originally a flop, a quirky film for Huston and Bogart fans)

Beau Brummell, 1924, 92/104m, ★★¹/2/$$$, WB/Nos. John Barrymore, Mary Astor. w. Dorothy Farnum, d. Harry Beaumont.

Beau Brummell, 1954, 111m, ★★★/$$$, MGM/MGM-UA. Stewart Granger, Elizabeth Taylor, Peter Ustinov, Robert Morley, Rosemary Harris. w. Karl Tunberg, P-adap. Clyde Fitch, d. Curtis Bernhardt.

A debonair man rises in society by becoming friends with the Prince of Wales in 16th-century England, but when the friendship fails due to his arrogance, so does his life.

DRAMA: MELODRAMA: Historical Drama; Costume Drama; **ROMANCE:** Romantic Drama; Friendships-Male; Friends with Royalty; Playboys; Sexy Men; Romance-Triangles; Princes; 1600s; England; Royalty
(Becket; The Lion in Winter; The Virgin Queen; Elizabeth & Essex)

Beau Geste, 1926, 120m, ★★★/$$$$, Par/NA. Ronald Colman, Neil Hamilton, Noah Beery, William Powell, Victor McLaglen. w. Paul Scholfield, N-adap. P.C. Wren, d. Herbert Brenon.
SEQUEL: Beau Ideal (1931)

Beau Geste, 1939, 114m, ★★★/$$$$, Par/MCA-U. Gary Cooper, Ray Milland, Robert Preston, Brian Donlevy (BSActor), J. Carrol Naish, Donald O'Connor, Broderick Crawford. w. Robert Carson, d. William Wellman. BArt. Oscars: 2-0.

Beau Geste, 1966, 105m, ★★¹/2/$$, U/MCA-U. Telly Savalas, Guy Stockwell, Doug McClure, Leslie Nielsen. w. d. Douglas Heyes. (The ending is changed and the production more B and violent.)

Three British brothers decide to join the foreign legion and go to battle in the Middle East where their grit is put to the ultimate test.

DRAMA: MELODRAMA: TRAGEDY: War Movies; War Battles; Brothers; Friendships-Male; Foreign Legion; Arab People; England; Middle East; World War I Era; 1900s; Classic Tragedy

SEQUEL: Beau Ideal; **REMAKE:** The Last Remake of Beau Geste (1977) (Gallipoli; The Four Feathers; Lawrence of Arabia; The Last Remake of Beau Geste)

Beau Ideal, 1931, 75m, ★★¹/2/$$, RKO/NA. Sequel to silent original, it tells the story of surviving brother and his involvement in yet another Middle Eastern war. Lester Vail, Loretta Young. w. Paul Scholfield, N-adap. P. C. Wren, d. Herbert Brenson.

DRAMA: War Movies; War Battles; England; Middle East; Arab People; Foreign Legion
SEQUEL TO: Beau Geste (1926)

Beau James, 1957, 107m, ★★/$$, Par/NA. Biography of the flashy and somewhat infamous mayor of New York during the 20s, Jimmy Walker. Bob Hope, Paul Douglas, Vera Miles, Alexis Smith, Darren McGavin, Jack Benny, George Jessel, Jimmy Durante, Walter Winchell. w. Jack Rose, Melville Shavelson, NF-adap. Gene Fowler, d. Shavelson.

DRAMA: MELODRAMA: COMEDY DRAMA: Biographies; Leaders; Politicians; Corruption; Political Corruptions; 1920s-Roaring
(Ed: A flop due primarily to Hope's miscasting and/or overbearing comedic baggage)

Le Beau Marriage, see L

Beau Pere, 1981, 125m, ★★★/$$, Col/Media, R/S. A young man falls for his gorgeous teenage stepdaughter and tries to fight off the urge for incest. Patrick Dewaere, Nathalie Baye, Ariel Besse. w. d. Bertrand Blier.

DRAMA: SATIRE: Erotic Drama; Family Drama; Fathers & Daughters; Stepfathers; Incest; Romance-Forbidden; Girls; Men and Girls; Coulda Been Great; Hidden Gems; Writer-Directors
(Betty Blue; Lolita; Blame It on Rio)

The Beautiful Blonde from Bashful Bend, 1949, 77m, ★★¹/2/$, 20th/CBS-Fox. A kooky saloon dancer (Betty Grable) accidentally shoots the town sheriff and goes into hiding as a schoolteacher, until her past catches up. Cesar Romero, Sterling Holloway. w. d. Preston Sturges.

COMEDY: Screwball Comedy; **WESTERNS:** Western Comedy; Free Spirits; Fugitives from the Law; Dual Lives; Accidents; Female Protagonists; Flops-Major; Forgotten Films; Writer-Directors

(Paleface; The Miracle of Morgan's Creek)
(Ed: A forgotten but colorful misfire from Sturges)

Beautiful Dreamers, 1990, 105m, ★★1/2/$, Hemdale/Hemdale, R. Walt Whitman's time in a Canadian mental asylum is helped by a friendship with a doctor. Colm Feore, Rip Torn. w. d. John Kent Harrison.
DRAMA: MELODRAMA: Biographies; True Stories; Gay Men; Asylums; Mental Illness; Friendships-Male; Friendships-Great; Writers; Poets; Canadian Films; Writer-Directors
(Angel at My Table)

Beauty and the Beast, 1946, 92m, ★★★/$$, Goldwyn/Goldwyn. Jean Cocteau's macabre and mystical version of the famous fable romance. w. d. Jean Cocteau.
DRAMA: HORROR: ROMANCE: Cult Films; French Films; Art Films; Writer-Directors; Ind Films
(Orpheus; Blood of a Poet; Carrington)

Beauty and the Beast, 1991, 85m, ★★★★/$$$$$, Disney/Disney, G. A prince who's been turned into a lion-like beast lives in a castle alone until a beautiful girl steps in and love blossoms despite his looks. Paige O'Hara, Robby Benson, Angela Lansbury. w. Linda Woolverton, d. Gary Trousdale, Kirk Wise. BPicture, BSound, BOSong "Be Our Guest," **BOSong** "Beauty and the Beast," BOSong "Belle," **BOScore**. Oscars: 6-2.
ROMANCE: Cartoons; **CHILDREN'S: FAMILY:** Fairy Tales; Fantasy; **MUSICALS:** Musical Fantasy; Castles; Kingdoms; Female Screenwriters; Blockbusters; Sleeper Hits
(The Little Mermaid; Aladdin; Pocahontas)
(Ed: Only cartoon ever nominated for Best Picture; opened up the musical cartoon with the incredible background action seeming so much like live action)

Beauty for the Asking, 1939, 68m, ★★1/2/$, RKO/Turner. Lucy invents a best selling skin cream and is financed by her husband's ex-wife, leading to minor complications. Lucille Ball, Patric Knowles, Donald Woods, Frieda Inescort. d. B.P. Fineman.
COMEDY DRAMA: MELODRAMA: Marriage Comedy; Marriage Drama;

Romance-Triangles; Ex-Spouse Trouble; Inventors; Female Protagonists

Bebe's Kids, 1992, 74m, ★★★/$, Par/Par, PG. A black Romeo takes a girl out of the theme park and she brings along four rambuncious kids who have more fun by themselves than on the rides. Voices of Vanessa Bell Calloway, Faizon Love, Tone Loc, Nell Carter. w. Reginald Hudlin, d. Bruce Smith.
Cartoons; FAMILY: CARTOON: Black Men; Black Women; Black Casts; Brats-Children; Free Spirits; Curiosities

Because of You, 1952, 95m, ★★1/2/$$, U/MCA-U. A woman just out of prison remarries but keeps her secret a past until she's involved in another crime which may end everything. Loretta Young, Jeff Chandler, Frances Dee. w. Ketti Frings, d. Joseph Pevney.
DRAMA: MELODRAMA: Tearjerkers; Starting Over; Criminals-Female; Marriage on the Rocks; Past-Haunted by the; Female Protagonists; Female Screenwriters; Women in Prison
(I Want to Live!; Blonde Venus; Ada; Caged Fear)

Because You're Mine, 1952, 103m, ★★1/2/$$, MGM/MGM-UA. An opera singer goes off to war. Mario Lanza, James Whitmore, Doretta Morrow, Dean Miller. d. Alexander Hall.
MUSICALS: Opera; Opera Singers; War Stories; Soldiers; Forgotten Films
(The Student Prince)

Becket, 1964, 148m, ★★★1/2/$$$, Par/Par. King Henry II's conflicts with the archbishop of Canterbury and the unusual friendship that develops. Richard Burton (BActor), Peter O'Toole (BActor), John Gielgud (BSActor). w. Edward Anhalt (**BAScr**), P-adap. James Goldman, d. Peter Glenville (BDirector). BPicture, BCCin, BCArt, BCCostume, BOScore, BEdit, BSound. Oscars: 12-1.
DRAMA: Historical Drama; Costume Drama; Friendships-Great; Friendships-Male; Friendships with Royalty; Medieval Times; Kings; Homo-eroticism; Power Struggles; Popes
(The Lion in Winter; Beau Brummell; Richard III)

Becky Sharp, 1935, 83m, ★★★/$$, RKO/Turner. A precocious girl climbs the social ladder in old England and becomes one of the aristocracy, though her origins remain part of her. Miram Hopkins (BActress), Cedric Hardwicke, Frances

Dee, Billie Burke. w. Francis Faragoh, P-adap. Landon Mitchell, N-adap. William Makepeace Thackeray, Vanity Fair, d. Rouben Mamoulian.
DRAMA: COMEDY DRAMA: Costume Drama; Social Drama; Social Climbing; Young Women; Female Protagonists; Feisty Females England; Classic Literary Adaptations
(Alice Adams; Vanity Fair; Little Women)
(Ed: The first major color film, recently restored yet still dated)

Becoming Colette, 1992, 97m, ★★1/2/$, Academy/Academy, R/S-FN-MN. Story of the famous writer Colette who became famous writing about many of her own sexual escapades. Mathilda May, Virginia Madsen, Klaus Maria Brandauer, Paul Rhys. w. Ruth Graham, d. Danny Huston.
COMEDY DRAMA: Erotic Drama; Memories; Sexy Women; Writers; Autobiographical Stories; Biographies; Paris; Female Protgaonists; Female Screenwriters
(Henry and June; Chanel Solitaire)

Bed and Board, 1970, 97m, ★★★/$$, Col/RCA-Col, R/S. The fourth in five films about the boy of the original *400 Blows* growing up and dealing with adulthood and marriage. Jean-Pierre Leaud, Claude Jade. w. Francois Truffaut, Claude de Givray, Bernard Revon, d. Truffaut.
DRAMA: MELODRAMA: Life Transitions; Pre-Life Crisis; Cheating Men; Romance with Married Person; Marriage Drama; Newlyweds; French Films
SEQUEL TO: The 400 Blows, part of the Atoine Doinel series
(Love on the Run; Stolen Kisses; The 400 Blows)

Bedazzled, 1967, 107m, ★★★/$$$, 20th/CBS-Fox. A working class cook is saved from suicide by a Faustian type who offers him seven wishes for his soul, including one for a woman (Raquel Welch). Dudley Moore, Peter Cook. w. Peter Cook, d. Stanley Donen.
COMEDY: Spoofs; Satan; Elusive Women; Dreams; Suicidal Tendencies; Cult Films; British Films
(All That Money Can Buy; 30 Is a Dangerous Age; Cynthia; The End; Hunk)

The Bedford Incident, 1965, 102m, ★★★/$$$, Col/RCA-Col. An American ship chases a menacing Russian submarine through the Arctic and winds up firing an atomic weapon. Richard Widmark,

Sidney Poiteir, James MacArthur, Martin Balsam, Donl Sutherland. w. James Poe, N-adap. Mark Rascovitch, d. James B. Harris.

ACTION: SUSPENSE: THRILLER: DRAMA: Military Movies; War Movies; Chase Movies; Ships; Arctic; Submarines; Bombs-Atomic
(The Hunt for Red October; Gray Lady Down; Fail Safe; Crimson Tide)

Bedknobs and Broomsticks, 1971, 117m, Disney/Disney, G, ★★★/$$$$. Lady (Angela Lansbury) helps children and the British war effort through her witchery, meeting animated animals while flying on her four-poster bed. BOSScore, BOSong, **BSFX**. Oscars: 3-1.

CHILDREN'S: ADVENTURE: MUSICALS: Musical Fantasy; Animation-Partial; Fantasy; Cartoon; Magic; Animals-Talking; Witches; World War II Era; British; Disney
(Mary Poppins; Mr. Limpet)

Bedlam, 1946, 79m, ★★★/$$, RKO/Turner. An asylum reformer winds up being committed herself. Boris Karloff, Anna Lee. w. Val Lewton, d. Mark Robson.

HORROR: Social Drama; Film Noir; Asylums; Committed-Wrongly; Insanity; 1800s; England; Nightmares; Forgotten Films; Cult Films; Hidden Gems; Ind Films
(Asylum; Committed; The Snakepit; Frances; Will There Really be a Morning?; Dream Lover [1994])
(Ed: A fascinating, forgotten B-movie)

Bedroom Eyes, 1986, 90m, ★★/VR, Ind/Fox, R/S-FN-MN. A yuppie voyeur is accused of the murder of the woman he spies on. Kenneth Gilman, Dayle Haddon, Chstrine Cattall. d. William Fruet.

SUSPENSE: Erotic Thriler; **MURDER:** Voyeurs; Accused Unjustly; Framed?; Yuppies

Bedroom Eyes 2, 1989, 85m, ★★/VR, Ind/Vidmark, R/ES-V-MN-FN. When he discovers his wife is cheating, a yuppie wants her dead, but when she turns up just that, did he do it? Wings Hauser, Kathy Shower, Linda Blair. d. Chuck Vincent.

SUSPENSE: Erotic Thriller; **MURDER:** Murder of Spourse; Suspecting Oneself; Murder-Clearing Oneself

The Bedroom Window, 1987, 112m, DEG-Lorimar/WB, R, ★★¹/2/$$. A yuppie (Steve Guttenberg) is accused of mur-

der when he covers for his lover, who is also his boss's wife. Isabelle Huppert, Elizabeth McGovern. w. d. Curtis Hanson.

SUSPENSE: THRILLER: MURDER: MURDER MYSTERY: Framed?; Accused Unjustly; Romance-Unprofessional; Romance-Clandestine; Romance with Boss's Lover; Impostors; Liars; Rape/Rapists; Murder-Clearing Oneself; Saving Oneself; Saving Someone; Mistresses; Hitchcockian; Romance-Triangles; Mindgames; Double Crossings; Writer-Directors
(Rear Window)
(Ed: Some interesting takes on a familiar plot, but terrible dialogue and preposterous situations drag it down)

Bedtime for Bonzo, 1951, 83m, ★★¹/2/$$, U/MCA-U. A college professor (Ronald Reagan) runs an experiment raising a chimp as a human baby. Diana Lynn, Walter Slezak. w. Val Burton, Lou Breslow, d. Fred de Cordova.

COMEDY: COMEDY DRAMA: Experiments; Animals-Smart; Primates; Psychologists; Professors; Cult Films; Unintentionally Funny
SEQUEL: Bonzo Goes to College
(Monkey Business; Monkey Trouble)
(Ed: Only for those interested in the Reagan novelty)

A Bedtime Story, 1933, 89, ★★★/$$, Par/NA. A very socially active Frenchman's life is interrupted when he winds up with an abandoned baby. Maurice Chevalier, Helen Twelvetrees. w. Ben Glazer, N-adap. Roy Horniman (*Bellamy the Magnificent*), d. Norman Taurog.

COMEDY: COMEDY DRAMA: MELODRAMA: Men and Babies; Playboys; Settling Down; Babies-Orphaned; Abandoned People

Bedtime Story, 1941, 85m, ★★★/$$$, Col/NA. An actress married to a playwright decides she wants to take a breather just when he's written a great play for her. Loretta Young, Frederic March, Robert Benchley, Eve Arden. w. Horace Jackson, Grant Garrett, Richard Flournoy, d. Alexander Hall.

COMEDY: ROMANCE: Romantic Comedy; Screwball Comedy; Marriage Comedy; Writers; Actresses
(Lily in Love; Chapter Two)

Bedtime Story, 1964, 99m, ★★★/$$$, U/MCA-U. Two playboy shysters head to

the Riviera to bilk women out of money, jewels, whatever-until they meet their match. Marlon Brando, David Nivens, Shirley Jones, Dody Goodman. w. Stanley Shapiro, Paul Henning, d. Ralph Levy.

COMEDY: Romantic Comedy; Playboys; Con Artists; Riviera Life; Turning the Tables

REMAKE: Dirty Rotten Scoundrels
(Dirty Rotten Scoundrels; Love Is a Ball; Dumb and Dumber)
(Ed: The remake is funnier in some ways, though sillier in others, but Brando in a comedy is interesting)

The Beekeeper, 1986, 122m, ★★¹/2/$, Ind/NA. A schoolteacher retired in Greece picks up a hitchhiker and finds himself at the nadir of his life. Marcello Mastroiainni. w. Theodorus Angelopoulos, Dimitris Nollas, d. Angelopoulos.

DRAMA: Character Studies; **MELODRAMA ROMANCE:** Romance-Older Men/Younger Women; Greece; Teachers; Overlooked

Beer, 1985, 82m, ★★/$, Orion/Orion, PG-13. An ad executive creates a media sensation in the way she promotes a new brand of beer centering around macho jerks. Loretta Swit, Rip Torn, Kenneth Mars, David Alan Grier. w. Allan Weissbecker, d. Patrick Kelly.

COMEDY: SATIRE: Advertising World; Macho Men; Class Conflicts
(Whoops; Apocalypse! [1986]; The Agency)

Beethoven, 1992, 89m, ★★★/$$$$, UY/MCA-U, PG/P. When a family gets a St. Bernard, they don't bargain for the messes, chaos, and the kidnappers or animal experimenters after it. Charles Grodin, Bonnie Hunt, Dean Jones, Oliver Platt, Stanley Tucci, David Duchovny. w. John Hughes, Amy Holden, d. Brian Levant.

Beethoven's 2nd, 1993, 93m, ★★/$$$, U/MCA-U, PG/P. The big St. Bernard has pups and the same old messes problems with kidnappers again. Charles Grodin, Bonnie Hunt, Debi Mazar, Christopher Penn. w. Len Blum, d. Rod Daniel.

COMEDY: FAMILY: CHILDREN'S: Family Comedy; Pet Stories; Nuisances; Dogs; Kidnappings
(Turner and Hooch; K-9; Digby)

Beetlejuice, 1988, 92m, ★★★/$$$$$, WB/WB, PG/P. A dead couple haunt the bizarre people who move into their dream house, with the aid of a very strange

spirit. Geena Davis, Alec Baldwin, Michael Keaton, Catherine O'Hara, Winona Ryder. w. Caroline Thompson, Tim Burton d. Tim Burton.
COMEDY: Fantasy; Morbid Comedy; Cartoonlike Films; Afterlife; Haunted Houses; Ghosts; Eccentric People; Newlyweds; Female Screenwriters; Female Protagonists
(Topper; Blithe Spirit; Kiss Me Goodbye; Ghost)
(Ed: Starts off charming, becoming morbid and bizarre, but always great to look at)
Before Sunrise, 1995, 101m, ★★★/$, Col/Col, R/S-P. A young American couple meets on a train to Vienna and talks and romances their way to Paris, but not much else, and in this realistic romance, that's just fine. Ethan Hawke, Julie Delpy, Andrea Eckert, Hanno Poschl, Karl Bruckschwaiger, Tex Rubinowitz, Erni Mangold, Dominik Castell. w. Richard Linklater, Kim Krizand, d. Richard Linklater.
DRAMA: ROMANCE: Romantic Drama; Austria/Vienna; Vacations-European; Romance on Vacation; 20-Somethings; Trains; Quiet Little Films; Hidden Gems; Old-Fashioned Recent Films
(Brief Encounter; Love with the Proper Stranger; Dazed and Confused; Slacker; Rome Adventure)
The Beguiled, 1971, 109m, ★★★1/2/$$$, WB/WB, PG. A Confederate soldier (Clint Eastwood) whose leg is wounded is rescued by a bizarre mistress (Geraldine Page) of a remote girls' school who has no plans of letting him go. w. John B. Sherry, Grimes Grice, N-adap. Thomas Cullinan, d. Don Siegel.
DRAMA: HORROR: SUSPENSE: Southerns; Nightmares; Gothic Soldiers; Abused Men Trapped; Men and Girls; Girls' School; Evil Women; Civil War Era; Forgotten Films; Hidden Gems
(Misery; The Collector; Hush, Hush, Sweet Charlotte; Whatever Happened to Baby Jane?)
(Ed: A great one for Southern gothic and Eastwood fans)
Behave Yourself, 1951, 81m, ★★★/$$, RKO/Nos. A young man and his bimbo wife are chased by criminals after unwittingly witnessing a robbery. Shelley Winters, Farley Granger. w. d. George Beck.
COMEDY: Action Comedy; Chase Movies; Witnesses; Innocent Bystanders;

Fugitives from the Mob; Dogs; Bimbos; Newlyweds; Ahead of its Time; Hidden Gems; Writer-Directors
(A Slight Case of Murder; A Night to Remember, The Thin Man SERIES; After Office Hours)
(Ed: Ahead of its time with its fugitive comedy plot)
Behold a Pale Horse, 1964, 118m, ★★1/2/$$, Col/Goodtimes. A Spanish rebel returns from exile to assassinate a corrupt police official. Gregory Peck, Omar Sharif, Anthony Quinn, Mildred Dunnock, w. J. P. Miller, N-adap. Emeric Pressburger, Killing a Mouse on Sunday, d. Fred Zinneman.
DRAMA: WESTERN: Westerns-Spaghetti; Good vs. Evil; Comebacks; Power Struggles; Assassinations; Rebels; Evil Men; Spain; Spanish Civil War
Being at Home with Claude, 1992, 86m, ★★★/$, Academy/Academy, Facets, R/S-V-MN. A young male prostitute is suspected of the murder of his lover and a cop wants to get to the bottom of why he may have done it. Roy Dupuis, Jacques Godin. w. Jean Boudin, d. Johanne Boisvert.
DRAMA: Erotic Drama; **MURDER: MYSTERY: MURDER MYSTERY:** Detective Stories; Detectives-Police; Prostitutes-Male; Gay Men; Murders of Homosexuals; French Films
(L'Homme Blesse; American Gigolo)
Being Human, 1994, 125m, ★★/$, 20th/Fox, PG-13/V-P. A man goes through the centuries learning all sorts of supposed lessons about humanity in the different reincarnations he experiences. Robin Williams, John Turturro, Vincent D'Onfrio, Lorriane Bracco, Hector Elizondo, William H. Macy, Lindsay Crouse. w. d. Bill Forsyth.
COMEDY: COMEDY DRAMA: SATIRE: Episodic Stories; Time Travel; Flops-Major; Life Lessons; Character Studies; Multiple Performances; Historical Drama
DRAMATIC FLIPSIDE: to Bill & Ted's Excellent Adventure
(Bill and Ted's Excellent Adventure; Woman Times Seven)
(Ed: Well-intentioned and should have been a tour de force for Williams)
Being There, 1979, 124m, ★★★★/$$$, Lorimar-UA/CBS-Fox, PG. A childlike gardener (Peter Sellers, BActor) for a wealthy man is cast out on the street when the man dies, only to be bumped

into by the mistress (Shirley MacLaine) of a dying billionaire (Melvyn Douglas, BSActor) who takes his simple views on the state of the world as profound and makes him famous. w. adap. Jerzy Kosinski, d. Hal Ashby. Oscars: 2-1.
DRAMA: COMEDY DRAMA: SATIRE: Fish out of Water Stories; Social Drama; Noble Savages; Black Comedy; Simple Minds; Politicians; Fools; Fame-Rise to; Rich People; Death-Impending; Mistresses; Washington D.C.; Power-Rise to; Power-Rise to, of Idiot
(A Face in the Crowd; The Party; The Hudsucker Proxy)
(Ed: Certain to be a classic)
The Believers, 1987, 114m, ★★1/2/$$, Orion/Orion, R/V-S. A man finds himself caught up in a cult practicing Santa Ria voodoo rituals leading to murder. Martin Sheen, Helen Shaver, Jimmy Smits. w. Mark Frost, N-adap. Nicholas Conde (*The Religion*), d. John Schlesinger.
SUSPENSE: HORROR: Cults; Occult Satanism; Evil People; Curses; Supernatural; Good Premise Unfulfilled; Coulda Been Good
(The Guyana Tragedy; Split Image; Ticket to Heaven; The Seventh Victim)
Belizaire the Cajun, 1986, 103m, ★★1/2/$, Ind/Fox, PG. Romance in the swamps of South Louisiana between the whites and the Acadians, namely a faith healer and a married woman. Armand Assante, Gail Youngs, Will Patton, Stephen McHattie, Robert Duvall. w. d. Glen Pitre.
DRAMA: ROMANCE: Romantic Drama; Southerns; 1800s Religion; Preachers; Romance with Married Person; Swamp Life; Cajuns
(Gal Young'un; Louisiana; Shy People; Mandingo)
Bell, Book, and Candle, 1958, 103m, ★★★/$$$, Columbia/RCA-Col. A beautiful and chic New York witch (Kim Novak) casts a love spell on her handsome next-door neighbor (James Stewart) that may spell love as long as she can keep her witchery secret. w. Daniel Taradash, P-adap. John Van Druten, d. Richard Quine.
COMEDY DRAMA: Romantic Comedy; Witches; Occult; Magic; Potions; New York Life; Beautiful People; 1950s
(I Married a Witch; Bewitched [TV Series]; Vertigo)
(Ed: A beautiful look at 50s New York and Novak)

Belle Epoque, 1994, 125m, ★★★¹/₂/$$, Sony/Sony, R/S-FN. A young soldier escaping the Spanish Civil War meets up with an old man who lets him stay in his home which is soon to be visited by his four gorgeous, wanton daughters. w. Rafael Azcona, d. Fernando Trueba. BFLFilm. Oscars: 1-1.
COMEDY DRAMA: ROMANCE: Romantic Comedy; Erotic Comedy; Male Among Females; Young Men; Young Women Soldiers; Spain; Spanish Civil War; Spanish Films; Elusive Men; Lesbians
(Tom Jones; The Graduate)

Il Bell Antonio, see I

The Bellboy, 1960, 72m, ★★★/$$, Par/Par. Jerry Lewis wreaks havoc on a Miami hotel and manages never to speak while doing it. Milton Berle. w. d. Jerry Lewis.
COMEDY: FARCE: Comedy of Errors; Farce-Bedroom; Slapstick Comedy; Character Comedy; Faded Hits; Forgotten Films; Writer-Directors; Actor Directors
(The Nutty Professor; The Disorderly Orderly; The Errand Boy, Blame It on the Bellboy)
(Ed: The French are right about most of Lewis' work, as time continues to prove, and this one is one of his best)

La Belle Americain, see L

Belle du Jour, 1967, 100m, ★★★¹/₂/$$, Cinema V/Connoisseur. A housewife finds a second life in a Parisian whore-house. Catherine Deneuve, Jean Sorel, Michel Piccoli. w. Luis Bunuel, Jean-Claude Carriere, N-adap. Joseph Kessel, d. Luis Bunuel.
DRAMA: Prostitutes-High Class; Dual Lives; Secrets; Housewives; French Films; Doctors; Female Protagonists
(The Young Girls of Rochefort; Repulsion; Les Biches; Diary of a Chambermaid; Crimes of Passion)

La Belle et la Bete, see L
La Belle Noiseuse, see L

The Belle of New York, 1952, 82m, ★★¹/₂/$$, MGM/MGM-UA. A playboy in the gay 90s dances and falls for a girl working for the Salvation Army. Fred Astaire, Vera-Ellen, Marjorie Main, Keenan Wynn, Alice Pearce. w. Robert O'Brien, Irving Elinson, d. Charles Walters.
MUSICAL: ROMANCE: Musical Romance; Romance-Older Men/Younger Women; Playboys; 1890s
(Guys and Dolls; The Band Wagon)

Belle of the Yukon, 1945, 84m, ★★¹/₂/$$, U-I/MCA-U. A dancehall singer-dancer (Gypsy Rose Lee) and a few tough guys wind-up in a bank robbery plot. Randolph Scott, Dinah Shore, Bob Burns. w. James Grant, d. William Seiter.
MUSICAL: COMEDY: Musical Comedy; Heist Stories; Bank Robberies; **WESTERNS:** Western Comedy; Dancers; Female Protagonists
(The Spoilers)

The Belles of St. Trinians, 1955, 90m, ★★★/$$$, London/Hemdale. A naughty girls' school has gone out of control (for the 50s, anyway) and it's not only the girls who are playing around. Began a long series. w. Frank Launder, Sidney Gilliatt, Val Valentine, SS-adap. Ronald Searle, d. Launder.
COMEDY: Screwball Comedy; **FARCE:** Girls Schools; Con Artists; Teenagers; Girlhood; British Films; Female Protagonists
SEQUELS: Blue Murder at St. Trinians, The Pure Hell of St. Trinians, The Great St. Trinians Train Robbery
(Ed: Rather tame but often witty)

Bellisima, 1951, 112m, ★★★/$, Ind/Cinema Guild. A stage mother tries to get her daughter into the movies. Anna Magnani, Walter Chiari. w. Suso Cecchi d'Amico, Francesco Rosi, Luschino Visconti, Cesare Zavatitini, d. Visconti.
DRAMA: MELODRAMA: Mothers & Daughters; Movie Making; Italy; Italian Films; Stagemothers; Mothers-Troublesome; Actresses; Girlhood; Female Protagonists
(Sophia Loren: Her Own Story; Gypsy; Angela; Mama Rosa)

The Bell Jar, 1978, 107m, ★★★/$$, Avco-Embassy/Embassy, Vestron, R/S-MRN. A young woman (Marilyn Hasset) leaves her mentally ill mother (Julie Harris) to go to college but has trouble adjusting. w. Marjorie Kellogg, N-adap. Sylvia Plath, d. Larry Peerce.
DRAMA: Coming of Age; Love-First; Life Transitions; Depression; Pre-life Crisis; Mental Illness; College Life; Virgins Suicidal Tendencies; Suicidal Tendencies of Young People; Alienation; Young Women; Female Protagonists; 1950s Female Screenwriters
(The Heart Is a Lonely Hunter; I Never Promised You a Rose Garden; Alice Adams)

(Ed: Plath fans may be disappointed, but it's still a realistic look at a young woman's alienation)

Bellman and True, 1988, 112m, ★★★/$, Handmade/MGM-UA, Vestron, R/V. An older computer hacker helps a young, naive crook with his heist. Bernard Hill, Derek Newark, Kieran O'Brien. w. Desmond Lowder, Richard Loncraine, Michael Wearing, N-adap. Lowder, d. Loncraine.
DRAMA: Crime Drama; Heist Stories; Thieves; Teachers and Students; Computers; British Films
(Breaking In; Hackers)

Bells Are Ringing, 1960, 127m, ★★★/$$$, MGM/MGM-UA. An answering service operator/gossip (Judy Holliday) is pursued by a playboy (Dean Martin) who only knows her voice. w. P-adap. Betty Comden, Adolph Green, Jules Styne, d. Vincente Minnelli. BAScore. Oscars: 1-0.
COMEDY: MUSICALS: Musical Comedy; Romantic Comedy; Romance-Mismatched; Gossip/Rumors; Playboys; Single Women; Telephone Problems; Dentists; Female Protagonists; Female Screenwriters
(Pillow Talk; The Solid Gold Cadillac; Born Yesterday)

The Bells of St. Mary's, 1945, 126m, ★★★/$$$$$, RKO/Turner. Nun (Ingrid Bergman, BActress) tries to save church and orphanage from being demolished. Bing Crosby (BActor), Henry Travers. w. Dudley Nichols, d. Leo McCarey (BDirector). BPicture, BEdit, BOSong, BScore. Oscars: 7-0.
MELODRAMA: Mortgage Drama; Tearjerker; Nuns; Priests; Orphans; Blockbusters
SEQUEL TO: Going My Way
(Going My Way; Blossoms in the Dust; Adam Had Four Sons)
(Ed: Melodrama and Mortgage Drama in quaint marriage)

Belly of an Architect, 1987, 118m, ★★★/$$, Cinecom/Cinecom, R/S-FN-MRN. An American designing a museum in Rome (Brian Dennehy) has trouble with his marriage realizing his visions, and finds he is sick, bringing him to a crisis point. Chloe Webb. w. d. Peter Greenaway.
DRAMA: Character Studies; Midlife Crisis; Psychological Drama; Nervous Breakdowns; Artists; Marriage on the Rocks; Rome; Suicidal Tendencies;

Death-Impending; Americans Abroad; Writer-Directors
(Drowning by Numbers; Death in Venice)
(Ed: The kind of character study usually reserved for or only allowed to be about women where process overrules progress in the telling of the story)

Beloved Infidel, 1959, 123m, ★★★/$$, 20th/CBS-Fox. The rocky love story of columnist Sheilah Graham and novelist F. Scott Fitzgerald. Deborah Kerr, Gregory Peck, Eddie Albert. w. Sy Bartlett, NF-adap. Sheilah Graham, Gerold Frank, d. Henry King.

DRAMA: MELODRAMA: ROMANCE: Autobiographical Stories; Romantic Drama; Romance-Doomed; Biographies; True Stories; Alcoholism; Writers; Hollywood Life; Hollywood Biographies; 1940s Female Protagonists
(Tender Is the Night; When a Man Loves a Woman)
(Ed: Its lack of insight is further overwhelmed with too much melodrama)

Ben, 1972, 94m, ★★½/$$$, Par/Par, R/V-B&G. A demented young man trains rats who like to kill. Lee Harcourt Montgomery, Arthur O'Connell, Rosemary Murphy, Meredith Baxter. w. Gilbert Ralston, d. Phil Karlson. BOSong. Oscars: 1-1.

HORROR: Monsters-Animal; Psycho Killers; Nerds; Rodents
SEQUEL TO: Willard
(Ed: Michael Jackson sings the title love song to a rodent)

Ben Hur, 1959, 217m, ★★★½/$$$$, MGM/MGM-UA. Two friends who are now enemies fight it out in a chariot race amid religious conflict. Charlton Heston (**BActor**), Stephen Boyd, Hugh Griffith (**BSActor**). w. Karl Tunberg (**BAScr**), d. William Wyler (**BDirector**). **BPicture, BCinema, BEdit, BCost, BArt, BSound, BSFX.** Oscars: 12-11, all-time record wins.

DRAMA: ACTION: ADVENTURE: Epics; Historical Drama; Biblical Stories; Friendship-Male; Rivalries; Horse Racing; Men in Conflict; Ancient Times; Cast of Thousands; Blockbusters; Jesus Christ; Production Design-Outstanding
REMAKE OF: Ben Hur (1926)
(Spartacus; The Ten Commandments; The Agony and the Ecstasy)

Ben-Hur: A Tale of Christ, 1925, 148m, ★★★½/$$$$, MGM/MGM-UA. This story emphasizes the plight of the

Jews under the Romans more. w. Bess Meredyth, Carey Wilson, N-adap. Lew Wallace, d. Fred Niblo.

DRAMA: ACTION: ADVENTURE: Epics; Historical Drama; Biblical Stories; Friendship-Male; Rivalries; Racing Jewish People; Casts of Thousands; Blockbusters; Spectacles; Female Screenwriters; Silent Films; Jesus Christ; Production Design-Outstanding
REMAKE: 1959

Bend of the River, 1952, 91m, ★★½/$$$, U/MCA-U. A wagon trains manages to get to Oregon avoiding the Indians, but comes up against a local nemesis. James Stewart, Arthur Kennedy, Rock Hudson, Julie Adams, Stepin Fetchit. w. Borden Chase, N-adap. William Gulick, Bend of the Snake, d. Anthony Mann.

WESTERNS: Men in Conflict; Good vs. Evil; Journies; Pioneers; Wagon Trains

Beneath the Planet of the Apes, 1970, 95m, ★★★/$$$, 20th/CBS-Fox, PG/. James Franciscus is another astronaut who searches for other humans amid the apes and finds them where they hid during the nuclear holocaust, under the surface. Charlton Heston, Linda Harrison, Kim Hunter, Maurice Evans, Victor Buono. w. Paul Dehn, Mort Abrahams, d. Ted Post.

ADVENTURE: SCI-FI: Fantasy; **ROMANCE:** Astronauts; Futuristic Films; Primates; Humans into Animals; Animals-Talking; End of the World Stories; Disabled People; Cult Films
SEQUEL TO: Planet of the Apes;
SEQUELS: Escape from the Planet of the Apes; Battle for the Planet of the Apes; Conquest of the Planet of the Apes
(Ed: One of the better sequels, proving they didn't really need Heston, just a plot)

Beneath the 12 Mile Reef, 1953, 102m, ★★/$$, 20th/CBS-Fox. Sponge divers off of the Florida coast fall in love while avoiding angry octopi. Robert Wagner, Terry Moore, Gilbert Roland, Peter Graves, J. Carrol Naish, Richard Boone. w. A. I. Bezzerides, d. Robert Webb. BCCin. Oscars: 1-0.

ACTION: MELODRAMA: Underwater Adventure; Divers; Florida; Octopi-Angry

Benji, 1974, 87m, ★★★/$$$$$, Mulberry/Vestron, G. Two kidnapped children are rescued by a loveable mutt. Edgar Buchanan. w. d. Joe Camp.

CHILDREN'S: ADVENTURE: MELO-DRAMA: Kidnappings; Rescue Adventure; Chase Movies; Animal Stories; Dogs; Sleeper Hits; Blockbusters; Writer-Directors
SEQUELS: Oh, Heavenly Dog; Benji the Hunted (Ed: A huge surprise hit, though only for kids)

Benji the Hunted, 1987, 88m, ★★½/$$, Mulberry-Disney/Disney, G. Benji returns and is shipwrecked, this time helping other animals as he makes his way home being followed. w. d. Joe Camp.

CHILDREN'S: ADVENTURE: Chase Movies; Rescue Adventure; Shipwrecked; Journies; Animal Stories; Dogs
PREQUELS: Benji; Oh, Heavenly Dog
(The Incredible Journey; Homeward Bound; Yellow Dog)

The Benny Goodman Story, 1955, 116m, ★★½/$$$, U/MCA-U. Biopic of the Jewish Chicago clarinet player's rise to fame in the 30s. Steve Allen, Donna Reed, Berta Gertsen, Harry James. w. d. Valentine Davies.

DRAMA: MELODRAMA: Biographies; Musicians; Big Band Era; Jewish People; Writer-Directors
(The Fabulous Dorseys; The Glenn Miller Story)

Berkeley Square, 1933, 87m, ★★★/$$, 20th/NA. A man owns a house which has special powers as a time machine, sending him back a century as a previous owner. Leslie Howard (**BActor**), Heather Angel, Valerie Taylor. w. Sonya Levien, John Balderston, P-adap. Balderston, d. Frank Lloyd.

MELODRAMA: ROMANCE: Fantasy; **SCI-FI:** Time Travel; Magic; Reincarnation
REMAKE: The House on the Square
(The Time Machine; The Two Worlds of Jenny Logan, Time After Time)

Berlin Alexanderplatz, 1983, 931m, ★★★/$$, UAC/MGM-UA, R/S-P. The lives of an apartment complex in Berlin are chronicled in this mini-series originally shown in theaters in U.S., a different episode each night. d. Rainer Werner Fassbinder.

DRAMA: MELODRAMA: Art Films; Interwoven Stories; Ordinary People Stories; Germany; German Films; Mini-Series; Berlin

Berlin Express, 1948, 86m, ★★½/$$, RKO/Turner. A German on a train to

Berlin is under heavy guard which may yet be penetrated. Merle Oberon, Robert Ryan, Paul Lukas. w. Harold Medford, d. Jacques Tourneur.

SUSPENSE: Spy Films; Spies; Germany; World War II Era; Nazi Stories; Trains; Berlin
(Night Train to Munich; Avalanche Express; The Train)

Berserk!, 1967, 96m, ★★/$, Col./RCA-Col. Circus mistress Joan Crawford tries to conceal a series of murders under her big top. Diana Dors, Ty Hardin, Judy Geeson, Michael Gough. w. Herman Cohen, Aben Kandel, d. Jim O'Connolly.

HORROR: SUSPENSE: Circus Life; Murders-One by One; Camp; Cult Films; B-Movies; Female Protagonists

Bert Rigby, You're a Fool!, 1989, 94m, ★★/$, Lorimar-WB/WB, PG. A British miner goes to Hollywood and tries to make it big in musicals. Robert Lindsay, Anne Bancroft, Corbin Bersen, Robbie Coltrane, Bruno Kirby, Liz Smith. w. d. Carl Reiner.

COMEDY: Musical Comedy; Dancers; FARCE: Hollywood Life; Writer-Directors
(Ed: A bizarre attempt to use Lindsay's talents after a Broadway triumph)

Best Boy, 1979, 111m, ★★★1/2/$ (LR), Ind/NA. Documentary story of a mentally disabled man 52 years old but with the mentality of a child, whose family finds him very endearing as they relate how they've coped with and been affected by him w. d. Ira Wohl.

Documentaries; MELODRAMA: Docudrama; Mentally Disabled; Tearjerkers; Childlike; People; Writer-Directors; Ind Films
(Rain Man; Bill)

Best Defense, 1984, 94m, ★1/2/$$, Par/Par, PG. As a tank goes out of control in battle, we flashback to the goofy designer and the problems leading up to the fiasco. Dudley Moore, Eddie Murphy (bit part), Kate Capshaw, George Dzundza, Helen Shaver. w. Gloria Katz, Willard Huyck, N-adap. Robert Grossbach, *Easy and Hard Ways Out*, d. Huyck.

COMEDY: FARCE: Military Comedy; Comedy of Errors; Middle East; Fools-Bumbling; Flops-Major; Arms Dealers; Female Screenwriters
(Deal of the Century; Tank)
(Ed: From the writers of *Howard the Duck*. This was adapted from a book. Was

it bad to begin with, or did it just get worse in the translation?)

Best Foot Forward, 1943, 95m, ★★1/2/$$, MGM/MGM-UA. An actress (Lucille Ball) hoping to get some press goes to a ball at a military college full of young men. William Gaxton, Virginia Weidler, Harry James, June Allyson, Gloria deHaven. w. Irving Brecher, Fred Finklehoffe, P-adap. Cecil Holmes, d. Edward Buzzell.

MUSICAL: COMEDY: ROMANCE: Musical Comedy; Romantic Comedy; Actresses; Boys Schools; Military Comedy; Infatuations
(Affairs of Annabel; Thousands Cheer)

Best Friends, 1982, 108m, ★★★/$$$, WB/WB, PG/S-P. Screenwriters fall in love and go home to their parents when they decide to get married, but will they re-write the ending? Burt Reynolds, Goldie Hawn. w. Barry Levinson, Valerie Curtin, d. Barry Levinson.

COMEDY DRAMA: Romantic Comedy; Marriage-Impending; Marriage Comedy; Writers; Screenwriters; Friends in Love; Elderly People; Hollywood Life; Partners-Married; In-Laws; Female Screenwriters (Starting Over; Up Close and Personal; Broadcast News)
(Ed: Very middle-of-the-road, but charming)

The Best Intentions, 1992, 181m, ★★★/$$, Svensk-Academy/Academy, PG-13. A Swedish priest decides to marry a nurse but must first overcome some roadblocks, even though the marriage may not be worth it. Samuel Froler, Pernilla August, Max von Sydow. w. Ingmar Bergman, d. Bille August.

DRAMA: MELODRAMA: Character Studies; Romance-Lover; Family Dislikes; Romance-Doomed?; Newlyweds; Decisions-Big; Marriage-Impending; Priests; Swedish Films; 1900s
(Ed: 1992 Cannes Festival: Best Film, Best Actress)

The Best Little Girl in the World, 1981, 96m, ★★★/$$$$, ABC/NA. Parents try to deal with their daughter's anorexia. Jennifer Jason Leigh, Eva Marie Saint, Charles Durning, Melanie Mayron, Viveca Lindfors, Ally Sheedy, Lisa Pelikan, Jason Miller. d. Sam O'Steen.

DRAMA: Weight Problems; Young Women; Girls; High School Life;

Character Studies; Family Drama; Parents vs. Children; TV Movies
(Kate's Secret)

The Best Little Whorehouse in Texas, 1982, 114m, ★★1/2/$$$$$, Universal/MCA-U, R/S-FFN-MRN. A sheriff tries to close down a whorehouse but the madame sings her way into his britches. Burt Reynolds, Dolly Parton, Charles Durning (BSActor). w. P-adap. Larry L. King, Peter Masterson, d. Colin Higgins. BOSong. Oscars: 2-0.

COMEDY: MUSICAL: Musical Comedy; Country Music; Prostitutes-High Class; Southerns; Texas; Politicians; Corruption; Big Budget; Blockbusters; Coulda Been Great
(Rhinestone; WW & the Dixie Dancekings)
(Ed: On several levels it may be a mess, but Dolly still makes it worthwhile-it was a huge grosser)

The Best Man, 1964, 102m, ★★★1/2/$$$, UA/MGM-UA. Two presidential candidates get some advice from a former president who's dying and must face the reality of their ambition. Henry Fonda, Cliff Robertson, Lee Tracy, Edie Adams, Kevin McCarthy, Margaret Leighton, Ann Sothern, Mahalia Jackson. w. P-adap. Gore Vidal, d. Franklin J. Schaffner.

DRAMA: Political Drama; Politicians; Washington D.C.; Death-Impending; Teachers and Students; Presidents
(Advice and Consent; Running Mates; The Candidate; Power)

The Best of Everything, 1959, 121m, ★★1/2/$$, 20th/NA. The social lives of young women follow them to work at a sophisticated women's magazine run by a tough cookie. Joan Crawford, Hope Lange, Stephen Boyd, Louis Jourdan, Brian Aherne, Suzy Parker, Martha Hyer, Diane Baker, Robert Evans. w. Edith Sommer, Mann Rubin, N-adap. Rona Jaffe, d. Jean Negulesco.

MELODRAMA: ROMANCE: Women's Films; Writers Publishing World; Young Women; New York Life; Social Climbing; 1950s Soap Operas; Female Screenwriters; Female Protagonists
(A Life of Her Own; Peyton Place; Return to Peyton Place)

Best of the Best, 1989, 95m, ★★/$$, Ind/Col, R/EV. American tae kwon do experts go up against a team of Koreans.

Eric Roberts, James Earl Jones, Sally Kirkland, John Dye. w. Paul Levine, Phillip Rhee, d. Bob Radler.
ACTION: Underdog Stories; Martial Arts; Sports Movies; Korea
(The Challenge; Kickboxer **SERIES:** Bloodsport)

The Best of Times, 1986, 105m, ★★/$$, U/MCA-U, PG-13/S-P. Old teammates who lost a big game in high school get a chance to relive the experience and win this time. Robin Williams, Kurt Russell. w. Ron Shelton, d. Roger Spottiswoode.
COMEDY: Sports Movies; Reunions-Class; Men Proving Themselves; Underdog Stories; Football; Midlife Crisis; Ensembles-Male
(That Championship Season; The Men's Club)

Best Seller, 1987, 110m, ★★1/2/$$, Hemdale/Hemdale, R/EV-P. A retired hitman (James Woods) hires a retired cop/crime novelist to write his story; however, certain people don't want it told. Brian Dennehy, Victoria Tennant. w. Larry Cohen, d. John Flynn.
SUSPENSE: THRILLER: CrimeDrama; Hit Men; Writers Secrets-Keeping; Coulda Been Good
(Ed: Fairly clever and original, though ultimately disappointing)

The Best Years of Our Lives (B&W), 1946, 170m, ★★★★/$$$$, RKO/Turner. World War II vets come home to a life that's different and difficult to deal with. Frederick March (**BActor**), Dana Andrews, Myrna Loy, Harold Russell (**BSActor**). w. Robert Sherwood (**BScr**), N-adap. MacKinlay Kantor, Glory for Me. d. William Wyler (**BDirector**).
BPicture, BScore, BEdit. Oscars: 7-7.
DRAMA: MELODRAMA: Social Drama; Soldiers; World War II Era; Reunions; Life Transitions; Marriages-Impending; Multiple Stories; Slice of Life; Class Conflicts; Blockbusters
REMAKE: Returning Home (TV series, 1977)
(Since You Went Away; The Men; Mrs. Miniver; Coming Home; Born on the Fourth of July)
(Ed: Almost a mini-series with its many characters; far more realistic and mature than most films of its day)

Betrayal, 1983, 95m, 20th/CBS-Fox, ★★★1/2/$$. A man (Jeremy Irons) has an unusual affair with the wife (Patricia Hodge) of his friend (Ben Kingsley), told in an unusual way. w. P-adap. Harold Pinter (BAScr), d. David Jones. Oscars: 1-0.
DRAMA: ROMANCE: Psychological Drama; Art Films; Romance-Triangles; Romance with Friend's Lover; Infidelity; Affairs-Clandestine; Betrayals; Cuckolded; Avant-Garde; Flashbacks
(Sunday, Bloody Sunday; The Homecoming)
(Ed: Must like British drama, Irons, Kingsley, and/or Pinter; if you do, it's great)

Betrayed, 1954, 108m, ★★1/2/$$, MGM/MGM-UA. A Dutch spy collaborates with a World War II Resistance leader who may be a traitor. Clark Gable, Victor Mature, Lana Turner, Louis Calhern, Wilfird Hyde White. w. Ronald Millar, George Froeschel, d. Gottfried Reinhardt.
DRAMA: Spies MELODRAMA: World War II Movies; Traitors; World War II-Resistance; Betrayals

Betrayed, 1989, 129m, ★★★/$$, UA/MGM-UA, R/EP-EV-S. An FBI agent (Debra Winger) goes undercover on a farm in Iowa to find out whether a farmer (Tom Berenger) was responsible for a Jewish DJ's death and is forced to join his white supremacy group as well as his bed. w. Joe Esztherhas, d. Costa-Gavras.
SUSPENSE: Political Drama; MYSTERY: MURDER MYSTERY: Assassination Plots; FBI Agents; Female Law Officers; Detectives in Deep; Undercover; Bigots; Love-Dangerous; Love-Questionable; Dangerous Men; Female Protagonists; Anti-Semitism; Jewish People; Ku Klux Klan; Betrayals; White Supremacists; Farm Life; Midwestern; Coulda Been Great
(Jagged Edge; Black Widow; The Thomas Crown Affair)
(Ed: A dramatic misfire with good intentions, degenerating into a spy soap)

The Betsy, 1978, 125m, ★★/$$, AA/Fox, R/S. Power struggles at a car corporation and the obsession over the model called Betsy. Laurence Olivier, Katharine Ross, Robert Duvall, Tommy Lee Jones, Jane Alexander, Lesley-Anne Down, Edward Herrmann. w. William Bast, Walter Bernstein, N-adap. Harold Robbins, d. Daniel Petrie.

DRAMA: MELODRAMA: Erotic Drama; Car Racing; Corporate Life; Rich People; Obsessions; Power Struggles; All-Star Casts
(Ed: It's amazing the cast they got for this)

Betsy's Wedding, 1990, 94m, ★★1/2/$, Touchstone/Touchstone, PG. A wedding costs so much, the father of the bride has to go to extreme measures to pay it off. Alan Alda, Molly Ringwald, Madeline Kahn, Anthony LaPaglia, Joe Pesci, Catherine O'Hara, Joey Bishop, Nicolas Coster. w. d. Alan Alda.
COMEDY: Weddings; Family Comedy; Ensemble Films; Making a Living; Fathers & Daughters; Fathers-Struggling; Coulda Been Good; Writer-Directors
(The In-Laws; A Wedding; Father of the Bride)

Better Late Than Never, 1983, 87m, ★★1/2/$, 20th/Fox, PG. Elderly bachelors (David Niven, Art Carney) are told via tape after an old flame dies that her daughter was really one of theirs, too-but whose? And there's money at stake depending on whom the young girl warms up to. Maggie Smith, Kimberly Partridge, Catherine Hicks. w. d. Bryan Forbes.
COMEDY: Comedy-Light; Inheritances at Stake; Fathers & Daughters; Elderly Men; Father-Who's the; Riviera Life; Playboys; Con Artists; Girls; British; Writer-Directors
(Bueno Sera; Mrs. Campbell; Lily in Love)
(Ed: Nice-looking; okay if you like the stars)

Better Off Dead, 1985, 97m, ★★★/$, 20th/Fox, PG-13/EP-S-V. A teenager who's lost his girlfriend decides to kill himself, but in failing to do so, decides then to go after her new boyfriend. John Cusack, Curtis Armstrong, Dian Franklin, Kim Darby, David Ogden Stiers, Taylor Negron. w. d. Steve Holland.
COMEDY: Black Comedy; Suicidal Tendencies; Young Men; High School Life; Revenge; Murder-Comic Attempts; Teenagers; Teenage Movies; Underrated; Hidden Gems; Cult Films; Writer-Directors
(The End; Say Anything; How I Got into College)

Betty Blue, 1986, 106m, ★★★/$$, 20th/CBS-Fox, R/ES-V-FFN-MFN. A young man falls in love with a wild girl with a fiery edge that nearly kills them both. w. d. Jean-Jacques Benieix, N-adap. Phillippe Dijan. BFFilm. Oscars: 1-0.

DRAMA: ROMANCE: TRAGEDY: Romantic Drama; Erotic Drama; Mental Illness; Saving Someone; Episodic Stories; French Films; Fires; Fires-Arsonists; Suicidal Tendencies; Coulda Been Great
(Bitter Moon; When a Man Loves a Woman)
(Ed: For fans of French Films or erotic drama. Very sexual and tense)

Between Friends, 1983, 105m, ★★★/$$$, HBO/Vestron, PG. Two divorcees find solace in friendship with each other. Carol Burnett, Elizabeth Taylor. d. Lou Antonio.

COMEDY: COMEDY DRAMA: Friendships-Female; Divorce; Midlife Crisis; TV Movies

Between the Lines, 1977, 101m, ★★★/$, Midwest Films/Vestron, PG. All-star cast works on an alternative paper in Boston and fights to save it while covering myriad stories. John Heard, Jeff Goldblum, Lindsay Crouse, Jill Eikenberry, Bruno Kirby, Stephen Collins, Michael J. Pollard. w. Fred Barron, d. Joan Micklin Silver.

DRAMA: Ensemble Films; Newspapers; Boston; Female Directors; Mortgage Drama; Alternative Lifestyles; Coulda Been Great; Overlooked at Release; Forgotten Films; Ind Films
(The Paper)

Between Two Women, 1986, 105m, ★★★1/2/$$$, ABC/King. When a woman marries a man, his cantankerous mother insinuates her way into their lives, until her illness brings the two women together. Farrah Fawcett, Colleen Dewhurst, Michael Nouri. d. Jon Avnet.

DRAMA: MELODRAMA: Character Studies; Stern Women; Death-Dealing with; Marriage Drama; Friendships-Female; Friendships-Intergenerational; In-Laws-Troublesome; Mothers-Troublesome; TV Movies; Hidden Gems; Flashbacks; Narrated Films
(Terms of Endearment; The Turning Point)
(Ed: An excellent TV movie worthy of the acclaim independent and "art" films usually receive)

The Beverly Hillbillies, 1993, 93m, ★★1/2/$$$, 20th/Fox, PG. A compendium of cliches of the series as the Clampetts go from the Ozarks to land of swimming pools and palm trees, whereupon Jed is beset by a golddigger and Granny is kidnapped. Jim Varney, Lily Tomlin, Cloris Leachman, Lea Thompson, Erika Eleniak, Dabney Coleman, Rob Schneider. w. Larry Konner, Mark Rosenthal, Jim Fisher, Jim Staahl, d. Penelope Spheeris.

COMEDY: Screwball Comedy; Fish out of Water Stories; Hillbillies; City vs. Country; Inheritances at Stake; Con Artists; Kidnappings; Beverly Hills; Rich People; Rags to Riches; Coulda Been Great; Female Directors; TV Series Movies
(Ma and Pa Kettle SERIES; Lum n Abner SERIES; The Brady Bunch Movie)
(Ed: The performances are the only real elements making it worth a look, particularly Leachman's)

Beverly Hills Cop, 1984, 124m, ★★★/$$$$$, Par/Par, PG-13/P-V. A Detroit black cop (Eddie Murphy) is transferred to Beverly Hills and uses humorous methods to catch the bad guys. Judge Reinhold, Bronson Pinchot, Ronnie Cox. w. Daniel Petrie, Jr. (BOScr), d. Martin Brest. Oscars: 1-0.

COMEDY: ACTION: Action Comedy; Fish Out of Water; Black Men; Cops-Vigilante; Practical Jokers; Beverly Hills; Snobs vs. Slobs; Blockbusters
SEQUEL: Beverly Hills Cop 2
(Ed: A good action comedy, bouyed by Murphy, though not as funny as the grosses might lead one to believe)

Beverly Hills Cop 2, 1987, 103m, Par/Par, PG-13, ★★/$$$$. Axel Foley (Eddie Murphy) is at it again in this more violent and active action comedy about a black cop in a white world. Judge Reinhold, JurgenProchnow, Brigitte Nielsen, Dean Stockwell, Ronnie Cox, Allen Garfield. w. Larry Ferguson, Warren Skaaren, David Giler, Dennis Klein, d. Tony Scott.

COMEDY: ACTION: Action Comedy; Fish Out of Water; Black Men; Cops-Vigilante; Practical Jokers; Beverly Hills; Snobs vs. Slobs; Blockbusters
(Ed: More over the top than the first, but lacking the spontaneity and the comedy-after all, it is a sequel)

Beverly Hills Cop 3, 1994, 109m, ★★/$$, Par/Par, R/EP-V. Murphy goes undercover in a Disneyland-like amusement park and the guns begin firing. Eddie Murphy, Judge Reinhold, Hector Elizondo, Stephen McHattie, Bronson Pinchot. w. Steven deSouza, d. John Landis.

COMEDY: ACTION: Action Comedy; Amusement Parks; Black Men; Police Comedy; Undercover; Drugs-Dealing; Flops-Major
(48 Hours; Another 48 Hours; Bad Boys; Drop Zone)

Beverly Hills Madam, 1986, 100m, ★★★1/2/$$$, NBC/Orion, PG/S. Faye Dunaway plays a rich madam who's losing control of her business and finds herself alone, too. Robin Givens, Melody Anderson, Donna Dixon. d. Harvey Hart.

DRAMA: MELODRAMA: Life Transitions; Prostitutes-High Class; Beverly Hills; Stern Men; Career Women; Madams; Female Protagonists; TV Movies
(Mayflower Madam)

Beware, My Lovely, 1952, 77m, ★★1/2/$$, RKO/Turner. A woman (Ida Lupino) takes on a handyman (Robert Ryan) who may be a psychotic. w. P-adap. Mel Dinelli, *The Man*, d. Harry Horner.

DRAMA: MELODRAMA: SUSPENSE: Mental Illness; Drifters; Women in Jeopardy; Female Protagonists; Servants

Beware! The Blob!, 1971, 88m, ★★1/2/$, Col/NA. A small town is devoured when a blob lands and starts creeping about. Robert Walker, Gwynne Gilford, Carol Lynley, Burgess Meredith, Larry Hagman, Shelly Berman. w. Jack Woods, Anthony Harris, d. Larry Hagman.

HORROR: SCI-FI: Spoofs; Spoofs-Horror; Monsters; Aliens-Outer Space-Evil; Human Eaters; Deaths-One by One
SEQUEL TO: The Blob (1958)
(The Blob [1988]; Return of the Blob)
(Ed: Bad but fun)

Beyond a Reasonable Doubt, 1956, 80m, ★★★/$$, RKO/Turner. A writer decides to fake evidence in a murder case in which he's the main suspect so that it will be discovered and the case dismissed, but it may backfire and lead to doubts he really did commit the murder. Dana Andrews, Joan Fontaine, Sidney Blackmer. w. Douglas Morrow, d. Fritz Lang.

SUSPENSE: MURDER: MURDER MYSTERY: THRILLER: Framed?; Accused

Unjustly; Clever Plots & Endings; Coulda Been Great; Forgotten Films; Underrated

Beyond the Forest, 1949, 96m, ★★½/$$, WB/WB. A woman bored in a small Illinois town goes to Chicago to have an affair, then commits murder and must deal with it. Bette Davis, Joseph Cotten, Ruth Roman. w. Lenore Coffee, N-adap. Stuart Engstrand, d. King Vidor.

MELODRAMA: TRAGEDY: DRAMA: MURDER: Romance-Triangles; Romance with Married Person; Revenge; Suicidal Tendencies; Life Transitions; Female Screenwriters; Camp; Forgotten Films; Female Protagonists

(The Letter; Dangerous; Hush, Hush, Sweet Charlotte)

(Ed: Contains the classic line "What a dump," but little else other than a preposterous yet somehow fascinating plot)

Beyond the Limit, 1983, 103m, ★★/$, Par/Par, R/P-S-FN-MRN. A doctor in South America (Richard Gere) has an affair with a diplomat's (Michael Caine) wife in the midst of a revolution brewing. Bob Hoskins. w. Christopher Hampton, N-adap. Graham Greene, (The Honorary Consul), d. John MacKenzie.

DRAMA: Political Drama; ROMANCE: Romantic Drama; Diplomats; Americans Abroad; Doctors; Romance-Triangles; Cheating Women; Romance with Friend's Lover; Romance with Married Person; Romance-Dangerous; South America; Latin People; Flops-Major; Forgotten Films

(Under the Volcano; Power)

(Ed: Unfortunately, very boring)

Beyond the Poseidon Adventure, 1979, 114m, ★½/$$, 20th/CBS-Fox, PG/V. Rescue workers try to find the loot in the capsized cruise liner from the original film Michael Caine, Sally Field, Telly Savalas, Karl Malden, Shirley Jones, Shirley Knight, Peter Boyle, Jack Warden, Slim Pickens, w. Elson Gidding, d. Irwin Allen.

MELODRAMA: Treasure Hunts; Disaster Movies; Rescue Drama; Shipwrecked; Ships; All-Star Casts

(Ed: Awful)

Beyond the Valley of the Dolls, 1970, 109m, ★★★½/$$, 20th/Fox, R/S-P-FN. An unauthorized sequel/spoof to Valley of the Dolls in which three cool chicks come to Hollywood to make it big with their band and find themselves in

the midst of more decadence than they dreamed, leading to sex and tragedy. Parallels in plot and timing to the Tate-LaBianca murders (esp. since Sharon Tate was in the original Dolls) led many to dismiss this camp classic at the time as being in bad taste, but it's more timely even now. w. Roger Ebert, d. Russ Meyers.

COMEDY: SATIRE: Black Comedy; Erotic Comedy; Spoof; TRAGEDY: Party Movies; Camp; Cult Films; Hollywood Life; Singers; Musicians; Beautiful People; Mod Era; Orgies; 1960s; Overlooked at Release; Underrated; Time Capsules

UNOFFICIAL SEQUEL TO: Valley of the Dolls

(Myra Breckinridge; Candy; Barbarella; Faster Pussycat; Kill! Kill!; Helter Skelter)

(Ed: A camp classic, time capsule of the dawn of the sexual revolution)

Beyond Therapy, 1987, 93m, ★★½/$, NW/NW, R/S-P. A man (Jeff Goldblum) in a relationship with a man (Christopher Guest) decides to meet a woman (Julie Hagerty) through the personals and chaos results. w. Robert Altman, Christopher Durang, P-adap. Durang, d. Altman.

COMEDY: FARCE: Romantic Comedy; Screwball Comedy; Black Comedy; Therapy; Psychologists; Bisexuality; Gay Men; Cheating Men; Romance-Triangles; Personal Ads; Misunderstandings; Alternative Lifestyles

(Ready to Wear; Sunday; Bloody, Sunday; X, Y & Zee)

(Ed: Only worth it for the performances, as confusing and offensive as they may be. Jackson and Conti are excellent)

Beyond This Place, see Web of Evidence

B.F.'s Daughter, 1948, 106m, ★★★/$$$, MGM/MGM-UA. A feisty, ambitious woman (Barbara Stanwyck) pushes her scholarly husband to prominence and wealth only to find an inheritance may be hers. Van Heflin, Charles Coburn, Keenan Wynn, Spring Byington. w. Luther Davis, N-adap. John P. Marquand, d. Robert Z. Leonard. BB&W Costume. Oscars: 1-0.

DRAMA: ROMANCE: Romantic Drama; Fame-Rise to; Professors; Writers Inheritances at Stake; Children-Adopted; Children-Long Lost; Woman Behind the

Man; Feisty Females; Women's Films; Female Protagonists

REMAKE/RETREAD: Peg's Paper

(Peg's Paper; Harriet Craig; Ada)

Bhowani Junction, 1956, 110m, ★★½/$$, MGM/MGM-UA. The loves and problems of a British-Indian young woman (Ava Gardner) as the Brits begin to lose power in India. Stewart Grager, Francis Matthews, Bill Travers. w. Sonya Levine, Ivan Moffat, N-adap. John Masters, d. Goerge Cukor.

DRAMA: MELODRAMA: ROMANCE: Epics; Young Women Romance-Interracial; India; Female Screenwriters; Female Protagonists

(Flame Over India; Elephant Walk; A Passage to India)

The Bible, 1966, 174m, ★★★/$$$$, 20th/Fox, PG/V-FN-MN. Bits and pieces of parables and legends from the Old Testament, beginning with Adam and Eve-truly nude in 1966. Michael Parks, Ulla Bergryd, Richard Harris, John Huston, Stephen Boyd, Ava Gardner, George C. Scott, Peter O'Toole. w. Christopher Fry, d. John Huston. BOScore. Oscars: 1-0.

DRAMA: Epics; Episodic Stories; Multiple Stories; Biblical Stories; Middle East; Ancient Times; All-Star Casts

(The Greatest Story Ever Told; The Robe)

Biches, Les, see Bad Girls

The Bicycle Thief, 1949, 90m, ★★★★/$$, Ind/Nos. A man fighting for work in postwar Italy has the bicycle he needs for his work stolen, and searches throughout his town for it, enduring the pain of how much such a seemingly easily replaceable thing means. Lamberto Maggiorani, Enzo Staiola. w. Cesare Zavattini (BOScr), d. Vittorio deSica. BFLFilm. Oscars: 2-1.

DRAMA: MELODRAMA: TRAGEDY: Social Drama; Ordinary People Stories; Poor People; Tearjerkers; Quiet Little Films; Art Films; Classic Films; Italian Films; Bicycles; Italy; World War II-Post Era; Chase Movies; Film History

SPOOF: The Icicle Thief

(Shoeshine; Bitter Rice; Open City)

(Ed: This classic is a must-see, and since there's little dialogue the fact that it's foreign shouldn't matter much to those who don't like subtitles)

Big, 1988, 102m, ★★★½/$$$$, 20th/CBS-Fox, PG. A boy wishes he were

grown up and it happens overnight, so he finds a job and romance at a toy company. Tom Hanks (BActor), Elizabeth Perkins, Mercedes Ruehl, Robert Loggia. w. Gary Ross, Anne Spielberg (BOScr), d. Penny Marshall. Oscars: 2-0.
COMEDY: Romantic Comedy; Fantasy; What if . . . Stories; Fish out of Water; Role Reversal; Body Switching; Time Travel; Childlike People; Simple Minds; Female Directors; Female Screenwriters (Vice Versa; Like Father; Like Son; Regarding Henry; Forrest Gump; 18 Again)
(Ed: The best of the role-reversal movies)
Big Bad Mama, 1974, 87m, ★★1/2/$$, AIP/New World, R/V-P-B&G. Bad Mama (Angie Dickinson) goes on a family-style crime spree after being widowed. William Shatner, Tom Skerritt, Susan Sennett. w. William Norton, Frances Doel, d. Steve Carver.
ACTION: Action Drama; Crime Drama; Chase Movies; Bank Robberies; Depression era; Widows; Mothers-Troublesome; Camp; Female Protagonists; Female Screenwriters (Bonnie and Clyde; Bloody Mama; Thelma and Louise)
(Ed: Campy action, but more dumb than hip)
The Big Blue, 1988, 118m, ★★1/2/$$, WEG-Col/Col, PG-13/S. Two French deep-sea divers adventure about and rescue a dolphin with a woman between them. Rosanna Arquette, Jean-Marc Barr, Jean Reno. w. Luc Besson, Robert Garland, Marilyn Godlin, Jacques Mayol, Marc Perrier, d. Besson.
DRAMA: MELODRAMA: Fantasy; Underwater Adventure; Adventure at Sea; Animal Rights; Dolphins; Romance-Triangles; French Films; Americans Abroad
The Big Bounce, 1969, 102m, ★★/$, WB/NA. An ex-con ex-GI falls back into trouble while working at a California motel. Ryan O'Neal, Leigh Taylor Young, Van Heflin, Lee Grant. w. Robert Dozier, N-adap. Elmore Leonard, d. Alex March.
DRAMA: Rebels; Soldiers; Starting Over; Young Men; Young Men-Angry
(Ed: Looks a lot like a TV movie, and it's hard to see who it was aimed at-young rebels or flag-waving old fogies)
The Big Brawl, 1980, 95m, ★★1/2/$, WB/WB, R/EV. A Chinese man in Chicago goes up against the local mob.

Jackie Chan, Jose Ferrer, Mako. w. d. Robert Clouse.
ACTION: Action Comedy; Martial Arts; Chinese People; Mob Stories; Ordinary People vs. Criminals
The Big Broadcast, 1932, 78m, ★★★/$$$$, Par/NA. A big show with stars pitching in saves a radio station from the brink. Bing Crosby, Kate Smith, George Burns, Gracie Allen, Cab Calloway, The Mills Brothers. w. George Marion, N-adap. William Manley, Wild Waves, d. Frank Tuttle.
MUSICAL: Dance Movies; Dancers; Radio Life; Depression era; Mortgage Drama; All-Star Casts; Ensemble Films
The Big Broadcast of 1936, 1935, 97m, ★★★/$$$, Par/NA. A sex-starved kooky countess kidnaps the suave star of a radio soap opera and gets a surprise. Jack Oakie, George Burns, Gracie Allen, Bing Crosby, Ethel Merman, Amos 'n Andy, Mary Boland, Charles Ruggles. w. Walter de Leon, Francis Martin, Ralph Spence, d. Norman Taurog.
MUSICALS: COMEDY: Dance Movies; Radio Life; Royalty; Kidnappings; Fatal Attractions; All-Star Casts; Ensemble Films
(The King of Comedy; Heartbreak Hotel)
The Big Broadcast of 1937, 1936, 100m, ★★1/2/$$, Par/NA. Advertisers give a radio station manager a "run for his money." Jack Benny, George Burns, Gracie Allen, Bob Burns, Martha Raye, Ray Milland, Benny Goodman and his Orchestra. w. Erwin Gelsey, Arthur Kober, Barry Travers, Walter de Leon, Francis Martin, d. Mitchell Leisen.
COMEDY: MUSICALS: Radio Life; All-Star Casts; Ensemble Films
The Big Broadcast of 1938, 1937, 90m, ★★1/2/$$$, Par/NA. A practical joker causes all sorts of trouble for his twin brother, a steamboat owner. W. C. Fields, Bob Hope, Martha Raye, Dorothy Lamour, Shirley Ross, Leif Erickson, Shep Fields and his Rippling Rhythm Orchestra. w. Walter de Leon, Francis Martin, Ken Englund, Frederick Hazlitt Brennan, d. Mitchell Leisen. **BOSong** ("Thanks for the Memories"). Oscars: 1-1.
MUSICALS: COMEDY: Ensemble Films; Practical Jokes; Twins; Brothers; All-Star Casts
The Big Bus, 1976, 88m, ★★★/$, Par/Par, PG/P. A giant atomic-powered bus travels cross country leading to major

swerves on the curves chaos with an all-star cast. Stockard Channing, Joseph Bologna, John Beck, Ned Beatty, Ruth Gordon, Sally Kellerman, Lynn Redgrave, Richard Mulligan, Larry Hagman, Bob Dishy, Rene Auberjonois, Jose Ferrer, Harold Gould. w. Fred Freeman, Larry Cohen, d. James Frawley.
COMEDY: FARCE: Spoofs; Disaster Movies; Comedy of Errors; Buses; Road Movies; Overlooked at Release; Ahead of its Time; Coulda Been Great (Airplane!; Airplane II; Naked Gun SERIES)
(Ed: Ahead of its time by a few years, not all there, but worth checking out)
Big Business, 1988, 97m, ★★★/$$$, Touchstone/Touchstone, PG/P. Two sets of twins are switched at birth, and forty years later the two sets of mismatched sisters finally bump into each other with confusing, revelatory results. Bette Midler, Lily Tomlin, Fred Ward. w. Dori Pierson, Marc Rubel, d. Jim Abrahams.
FARCE: COMEDY: Mistaken Identities; Business Life; Misunderstandings; Twins; Sisters; Rich Bitches; Snobs vs. Slobs; Country Folk; Teams-Mismatched; Coulda Been Great; Gay Men; Female Protagonists; Female Screenwriters (The Boys from Syracuse; Outrageous Fortune; Ruthless People; All of Me; Start the Revolution Without Me; The Corsican Brothers)
(Ed: A good farce, though often not in control. Midler and Tomlin make it worthwhile)
The Big Chill, 1983, 123m, ★★★1/2/$$$$, Columbia/RCA-Col, R/S-P-FN. College friends reunite when another dies at the home of two who have married. Kevin Kline, Glenn Close (BSActress), William Hurt, Jeff Goldblum, Tom Berenger, Meg Tilly, Mary Kay Place. w. Meg and Lawrence Kasdan (BOScr), d. Lawrence Kasdan. BPicture. Oscars: 3-0.
DRAMA: COMEDY DRAMA: MELODRAMA: Ensemble Films; Midlife Crisis; Reunions-Class; Friendships; Suicidal Tendencies; Funerals; Yuppies; Mothers Alone; College Life; South Carolina (Return of the Secaucus Seven; St. Elmo's Fire; Indian Summer; Parallel Lives)
(Ed: Derivative, but with original characters and good humor. Quintessential baby-boomer material)

The Big Clock (B&W), 1948, 105m, ★★★¹/₂/$$, RKO/Turner. A man (Ray Milland) is framed for murder due to circumstantial evidence, taking the heat for someone higher up, and only has so long to find enough evidence to clear himself. Charles Laughton. w. John Latimer, N-adap. Kenneth Fearing, d. John Farrow.
SUSPENSE: Film Noir; **MURDER**: Conspiracy; Accused Unjustly; Framed?; Fugitives; Race Against Time; Bosses-Bad
REMAKE: No Way Out
(No Way Out [1987]; The Fugitive [1993]; Three Days of the Condor)
(Ed: A good thriller, but the remake is actually better, though completely different)
The Big Combo, 1955, 87m, ★★★/$$, RKO/Prism. A mob girl helps a cop to infiltrate the mob and snare some bad guys, but not before enduring a little torture. Cornel Wilde, Richard Conte, Jean Wallace, Earl Holliman, Lee Van Cleef. w. Philip Yordan, d. Joseph E. Lewis.
SUSPENSE: Crime Drama; Mob Stories; Mob Girls; Undercover; Women in Jeopardy; Torture; Film Noir; Coulda Been Great
(Marked Woman; Mary Burns; Fugitive)
The Big Country, 1958, 166m, ★★★¹/₂/$$$, UA/MGM-UA. A modern western where two families fight over water rights on the range, in a veiled allegory to the cold war. Gregory Peck, Jean Simmons, Burl Ives (**BSActor**), Charlton Heston, Carroll Baker, Charles Bickford, Chuck Connors. w. James R. Webb, Sy Bartlett, Robert Wilder, N-adap. Donald Hamilton, d. William Wyler. BOScore. Oscars: 2-1.
WESTERN: DRAMA: Family Drama; Epics; Feuds; Power Struggles; Romance-Lover; Family Dislikes; Allegorical Stories
(The Lolly-Madonna War; The Long, Hot Summer; Duel in the Sun; Cat on a Hot Tin Roof)
Big Deal on Madonna Street, 1958, 105m, ★★★/$$$, Lux-Vides-Cinecittà-Ind/Connoisseur. A group of bumbling thieves spends more time in jail than out, and when they're out, their plans are always ill-conceived, as when they drill through the wall of a bank, only to find they're in the wrong room once through. Vittorio Gassman, Renato Salvatori, Toto, Marcello Mastroianni. w. Age Scarpelli,

Suso Cecchi d'Amico, Mario Monicelli, d. Mario Monicelli.
COMEDY: Comedy-Light; Heist Stories; Ensemble Films; Comedy of Errors; Criminals-Stupid; Fools-Bumbling; Thieves; Bank Robberies; Italian Films
REMAKE: Crackers
(Crackers; The Hot Rock; Disorganized Crime)
The Big Easy, 1987, 108m, ★★★¹/₂/$$$, 20th/Fox, R/S-V-MRN. A local New Orleans detective (Dennis Quaid) and a D.A. sent in (Ellen Barkin) spar while solving a murder, finding themselves entangled in more than conspiracy. Campbell Scott, Ned Beatty. w. Daniel Petrie, Jr., d. Jim McBride.
MYSTERY: MURDER MYSTERY: ROMANCE: SUSPENSE: THRILLER: COMEDY DRAMA: Comic Thriller; Crime Drama; Detective Stories; Detective Couples; Police Corruption; Romance-Bickering; Conspiracy; Romance-Reluctant; Detective Couples; New Orleans
(Undercover Blues; Sea of Love; Adam's Rib; Tightrope)
(Ed: A good thriller with atmosphere, romance, good characters, and a plot that doesn't peter out)
The Big Fisherman, 1959, 166m, ★★★/$$, Centurion-MGM/NA. A biblical story about King Herod's stepdaughter and her plans to assassinate him. Howard Keel, Alexander Scourby, Susan Kohner, John Saxon, Herbert Lom, Ray Stricklin, Beulah Bondi. w. Howard Estabrook, Rowland V. Lee, N-adap. Lloyd C. Douglas, (from the Bible), d. Frank Borzage.
DRAMA: MELODRAMA: Biblical Stories; Epics; Historical Drama; Ancient Times; Middle East; Assassination Plots; Fathers & Daughters
The Big Fix, 1978, 108m, ★★¹/₂/$$, Universal/MCA-U. An industrial inspector uncovers government corruption while toodling around with his kid in a VW convertible. Richard Dreyfuss, Susan Anspach, Bonnie Bedelia, John Lithgow. w. Roger L. Simon, N-adap, d. Jeremy Paul Kagan.
MYSTERY: COMEDY DRAMA: Comic Mystery; Detective Stories; Detectives-Private; Detectives-Amateur; Fathers & Sons; Corruption; Government Corruption
(Ed: A disappointing follow-up for Dreyfuss to *The Goodbye Girl*)

Big Foot, 1971, 76m, ★/$$, Ind/NA, PG/V. Big Foot attacks a motorcycle gang and takes off with one of their chicks. John Carradine. w. Richard Slater, J. White, d. Richard Slater.
HORROR: ACTION: Camp Kidnappings; Animal Monsters; Legends
(The Legend of Boggy Creek, Harry and the Hendersons; The Abominable Snowman)
Big Girls Don't Cry . . . They Get Even, 1992, 104m, ★★¹/₂/$, NewLine/Col, PG. A girl from a "broken home" runs away, finding the alternative even less appetizing. Griffin Dunne, Dan Futterman, Patricia Kalember, Ben Savage. w. Frank Mugavero, SS-adap. Mark Goddard, Melissa Goddard, d. Joan Micklin Silver.
COMEDY: COMEDY DRAMA: Girlhood; Eccentric People; Coming of Age; Teenagers; Family Comedy; Vacations
The Big Green, 1995, 100m, ★★¹/₂/$$, Disney/Disney, PG. A young coach leads a goofy bunch of kids to a soccer tournament while we learn a little about their problems at home. Steve Guttenberg, Olivia d'Abo, Jay O. Sanders. w. d. Holly Goldberg Sloan.
COMEDY: CHILDREN'S: Sports Movies; Underdog Stories; Ensembles-Children; Soccer; Writer-Directors; Female Directors; Female Screenwriters
(The Mighty Ducks; The Bad News Bears)
The Big Heat, 1953, 90m, ★★¹/₂/$$, Col/Col. A bomb intended for a police detective kills his wife instead, so he begins a man hunt. Glenn Ford, Gloria Grahame, Alexander Scourby, Lee Marvin. w. Sydney Boehm, N-adap. William P. McGivern, d. Fritz Lang.
DRAMA: SUSPENSE: MELODRAMA: Crime Drama; Film Noir; Revenge; Death-Accidental; Bombs; Police Stories; Detectives-Police
(Death Wish; Badge 373)
The Big House, 1930, 88m, ★★★/$$$, MGM/MGM-UA. The prison-break movie which established the genre. Chester Morris, Wallace Beery, Robert Montgomery, Lewis Stone, Leila Hyams. w. Frances Marion, d. George Hill.
ACTION: DRAMA: Action Drama; Prison Drama; Prison Escape
(Escape from Alcatraz; Attica)
Big Jake, 1971, 110m, ★★¹/₂/$$, Cinema Center/Fox. When his grandson is kidnapped, an aging cattle rancher

takes actions to rescue the boy. John Wayne, Richard Boone, Maureen O'Hara, Bobby Vinton, Bruce Cabot, Harry Carey Jr. w. Harry Julian Fink, R. M. Fink, d. George Sherman.

WESTERNS: Kidnappings; Searches; Grandfathers; Fathers & Sons
(The Searchers; The Sons of Katie Elder)

The Big Knife, 1955, 111m, B&W, ★★★1/2/$$, UA/Facets. A Hollywood actor (Jack Palance) is blackmailed into staying with his contract to continue on as a pretty boy amid Hollywood debauchery. w. d. Robert Aldrich, P-adap. Clifford Odets.

SUSPENSE: Film Noir; Hollywood Life; Hollywood Satire; Blackmail; Actors Double Crossings; Betrayals; All-Star Casts; Hidden Gems; Forgotten Films; Cult Films
(The Bad and the Beautiful; Barton Fink; Two Weeks in Another Town; Kiss Me Deadly)

The Big Lift, 1950, 119m, ★★/$, 20th/Nos. Two soldiers involved in the Berlin airlift argue over whether it will work or not while racing against time. Montgomery Clift, Paul Douglas, Cornell Borchers. w. d. George Seaton.

DRAMA: War Stories; World War II Stories; Rescue Drama; Race Against Time; Berlin; Germans as Enemy; Forgotten Films; Writer-Directors

The Big Man, 1990, 116m, ★★1/2/$, Palace-Miramax/HBO, R/EV-S. A man becomes an amateur boxer after losing his job as a miner. Liam Neeson, Joanne Whalley-Kilmer, Billy Connolly, Ian Bannen. w. Don MacPherson, N-adap. William McIlvanney, d. David Leland.

DRAMA: Sports Movies; Boxing; Men in Conflict; Working Class; Poor People; Mining Towns; British Films

Big Man on Campus, 1989, 102m, ★1/2/VR, Vestron/Vestron, PG. Quasimodo is the Hunchback of UCLA in modern day and in love with a student with bad guys after her. Tom Skerritt, Corey Parker, Allan Katz, Cindy Williams, Jessica Harper. d. Jeremy Paul Kagan.

COMEDY: Revisionist Films; Nerds; Nerds & Babes; Women in Jeopardy; Heroes-Unlikely; College Life; Good Premise Unfulfilled

RETREAD OF: The Hunchback of Notre Dame
(Ed: Cute title, stupid, bad-looking movie)

The Big Mouth, 1967, 107m, ★★★/$$, Col/Col. A dying gangster has a double in a nervous bank teller who gets involved in a plot involving stolen diamonds. Jerry Lewis, Harold J. Stone, Susan Day, Buddy Lester, Del Moore. w. Jerry Lewis, Bill Richmond, d. Jerry Lewis.

COMEDY: Comedy-Slapstick; Heist Stories; Jewel Thieves; Innocent Bystanders; Informers; Fools-Bumbling; Criminals-Stupid
(Johnny Stecchino; The Pink Panther)

The Big One, The Great Los Angeles Earthquake, 1991, 105m, ★★1/2/$$$$, NBC/Vidmark. Seismologist and mom decides predictions of a quake are real, but not enough people listen when an unexpected fault gives way, sending all those who didn't heed the warning to their just demise. Joanna Kerns, Ed Begley, Jr. d. Larry Ellkann.

DRAMA: Disaster Stories; Survival Drama; Earthquakers; Los Angeles; Female Protagonists; Multiple Stories; TV Movies
(Earthquake; Quake)
(Ed: The special effects are good for a TV movie, and the story is okay)

The Big Picture, 1989, 99m, ★★1/2/$, Col/RCA-Col, PG-13/P-S. A midwestern boy wins a student-Oscar-like award from an AFI-like school in L.A., subsequently getting courted and chewed up by the Hollywood machine. Kevin Bacon, Emily Longstreth, J. T. Walsh, Jennifer Jason Leigh, Martin Short, Michael McKean. w. Michael Varhol, Christopher Guest, Michael McKean, d. Christopher Guest.

SATIRE: COMEDY: COMEDY DRAMA: Moviemaking; Hollywood Life; Hollywood Satire; Young Men; Directors; Film Students; Ethics; Coulda Been Great; Ind Films
(Mistress; Movers and Shakers)

Big Red, 1962, 89m, ★★★/$$, Disney/Disney. A dog is saved by an orphan boy as a puppy and when full grown, saves the boy. Walter Pidgeon, Gilles Payant, Emile Genest. w. Louis Pelletier, d. Norman Tokar.

DRAMA: CHILDREN'S: FAMILY: MELODRAMA: Pet Stories; Boyhood; Boy and His Dog; Dogs; Saving Someone
(Lassie Come Home; Old Yeller; Savage Same; Dog of Flanders; Fluke; Yellow Dog)

The Big Red One, 1980, 113m, ★★★/$$$, Orion/WB, R/.EV. A stern sergeant

(Lee Marvin) drives his young soldiers into battle in World War II Europe, regardless of whether they're ready for it or not. Mark Hammill. w. d. Samuel Fuller.

DRAMA: Action Drama; War Movies; War Battles; World War II Stories; Stern Men; Leaders-Tyrants; Soldiers; Young Men; Writer-Directors
(Patton; The Dirty Dozen; A Bridge Too Far)

The Big Sky, 1952, 122m, ★★1/2/$$, RKO/Turner. Two Kentucky cowboys on a trek through Missouri are deterred by Indian attacks. Kirk Douglas, Arthur Hunnicutt, Elizabeth Threatt, Dewey Martin, Buddy Baer. w. Dudley Nichols, N-adap. A. B. Gurthrie Jr., d. Howard Hawks.

WESTERNS: Journies; West-Old; Cowboys; Indians-American
(Across the Wide Missouri; Daniel Boone)

The Big Sleep, 1946, 114m, ★★★★/$$$$, WB/MGM-UA. Detective Philip Marlowe (Humphrey Bogart) helps out a wealthy woman and finds himself involved in a dark conspiracy of murder where things are resolved so easily or clearly. w. William Faulkner, Jules Furthman, Leigh Brackett, N-adap. Raymond Chandler, d. Howard Hawks.
(The Maltese Falcon; Chinatown; To Have and Have Not; Key Largo)

The Big Sleep, 1977, 99m, ★★1/2/$, Col/Col, PG/V. A remake of the 1946 film, set in London. Robert Mitchum, Sarah Miles, Richard Boone, Candy Clark, Edward Fox, Joan Collins, James Stewart, Oliver Reed. w. d. Michael Winner. N-adap. Raymond Chandler.

MYSTERY: MURDER: MURDER MYSTERY: Film Noir; Detective Stories; Detectives in Deep; Detectives-Private; Missing Persons; Protecting Someone; Los Angeles; 1940s

COMEDY REMAKES/SPOOFS: The Cheap Detective; Who's Harry Crumb?
(Harper; Farewell, My Lovely; The Maltese Falcon)
(Ed: Oft-imitated, and though the plot may be hard to follow for some, stick with it)

The Big Steal, 1949, 72m, ★★/$$, RKO/Media. When the payroll at an army base turns up missing, an officer is blamed, and he must pursue the real culprit to Mexico. Robert Mitchum, Jane Greer, William Bendix, Ramon Novarro.

w. Gerald Drayson Adams, Geoffrey Homes, SS-adap. Richard Wormser, *The Road to Carmichael's*, d. Don Seigel.

ACTION: MYSTERY: SUSPENSE: Chase Movies; Framed?; Accused Unjustly; Film Noir; Crossing the Border; Soldiers; Fugitives from the Law
(Second Chance; Out of the Past; Blowing Wild)
(Ed: Reteams Mitchum and Greer from *Out of the Past*, but that's about it)

The Big Store, 1941, 80m, ★★★/$$, MGM/MGM-UA. A department store hires an odd detective to curb their theft problems, but winds up with bigger problems than that. Groucho Marx, Chico Marx, Harpo Marx, Margaret Dumont, Douglas Dumbrille. w. Sid Kuller, Hal Fimberg, Ray Golden, d. Charles Reisner.

COMEDY: Comedy of Errors; Comedy-Slapstick; Department Stores; Marx Brothers; Fools-Bumbling
(At the Circus; Room Service; Animal Crackers)

The Big Street, 1942, 88m, ★★½/$$, RKO/Turner. A lowly waiter falls for a wheelchair-bound singer and sacrifices everything for her, receiving nothing in return. Classic tale of co-dependency. Henry Fonda, Lucille Ball, Eugene Pallette, Virginia Weidler, Agnes Moorehead, Ozzie Nelson and his Orchestra, Ray Collins. w. Leonard Spigelgass, SS-adap. Damon Runyan, *Little Pinks*, d. Irving Reis.

DRAMA: MELODRAMA: ROMANCE: Love-Unrequited; Tearjerkers; Disabled People; Stern Women; Singers
(Love Affair; An Affair to Remember; The Other Side of the Mountain)
(Ed: Low rent for Fonda on the heels of *The Grapes of Wrath*. Shades of *Love Affair* with a big difference-the daring of Fonda's character to be weak)

The Big Town, 1987, 110m, ★★★/$, Col/RCA-Col,. A poor hustler (Matt Dillon) makes his way in the gambling world meeting people, good and bad alike. w. Robert Pool, d. Ben Bolt.

DRAMA: MELODRAMA: ROMANCE: Romance-Triangles; Good vs. Evil; Gambling; Power-Rise to; Great Art Direction; 1950s Chicago; Overlooked; Flops-Major; Revisionist Films
(Fever Pitch; The Hustler; Rumblefish)
(Ed: A great-looking, if not immensely entertaining, film that echoes the gangster films of the 30s in an updated fashion)

The Big Trail, 1930, 110m, ★★½/$$, 20th/Fox. The Oregon trail poses harsh obstacles for a wagon train struggling westward. John Wayne, Marguerite Churchill, El Brendel, Tully Marshall, Tyrone Power, Ward Bond, Helen Parrish. w. Jack Peabody, Marie Boyle, Florence Postal, d. Raoul Walsh.

WESTERNS: Wagon Trains; West-Old; Ensemble Films; Female Screenwriters
(Stagecoach; Across the Great Divide)

The Big Trees, 1952, 89m, ★★/$, WB/Nos. The California redwoods seem to be doomed with the conniving plans of a corrupt lumberman. Then a group of Quakers teaches him respect for the trees, and he mends his ways. Kirk Douglas, Eve Miller, Patrice Wymore, Edgar Buchanan, John Archer, Alan Hale Jr. w. John Twist, James R. Webb, d. Felix Feist.

DRAMA: MELODRAMA: Message Films; Religion; Ethics; Environmental Dilemmas; Forgotten Films
REMAKE OF: Valley of the Giants

Big Trouble in Little China, 1986, 99m, ★★½/$$, 20th/CBS-Fox, R/EV-S. A San Francisco truck driver matches wits with a Chinese magician and travels into another dimension. Kurt Russell, Kim Cattrall, Dennis Dun, James Hong, Victor Wong, Kate Burton. w. W. D. Richter, Gary Goldman, David Z. Weinstein, d. John Carpenter.

SCI FI: Fantasy; **ACTION:** Martial Arts; Truck Drivers; San Francisco; Cult Films
(The Shadow; The Adventures of Buckaroo Banzai Across the 8th Dimension)

Big Wednesday, 1978, 120m, WB/WB. Three surfers get back together after the Vietnam war. Jan-Michael Vincent, William Katt, Gary Busey, Darrell Fetty. w. John Milius, Dennis Aaberg, d. John Milius.

DRAMA: Teenage Movies; Reunions; Young Men; Friendships-Male; Surfers; Beach Movies; California; Sports Movies; Vietnam Era; Vietnam Veterans

The Bigamist, 1956, 97m, ★★½/$$, Royal-Filmel-Alba/Nos. A traveling salesman is wrongly accused of bigamy and taken to court. Marcello Mastroianni, Vittorio de Sica, Franca Valeri, Giovanna Ralli. w. Sergio Amidei, Age Scarpelli, Franco Rosi, Elio Talarico, d. Luciano Emmer.

COMEDY DRAMA: Bigamy; Accused Unjustly; Salesmen; Italy; Italian Films; Trials
(Divorce, Italian Style; Micki and Maude)

The Biggest Bundle of Them All, 1967, 110m, ★★½/$$, MGM/NA. A group of gangsters drag their old comrade out of "retirement" to involve him in the heist of five million dollars worth of platinum. Raquel Welch, Robert Wagner, Vittorio de Sica, Edward G. Robinson, Godfrey Cambridge. w. Josef Shaftel, Sy Salkowitz, d. Ken Annakin.

ACTION: Action Comedy; CrimeDrama; Heist Stories; Mob Stories; One Last Time; Female Among Males; Sexy Women; Ensemble Films; Ensembles-Male; Reunions
(Silver Bears; The Hot Rock; The Italian Job)

Biggles, 1986, 92m, ★★/$, Yellowbill-Tambarle-Ind./New World. A modern New York yuppie time travels back to 1917 to help out a daredevil pilot in his feats. Neil Dickson, Alex Hyde-White, Peter Cushing, Fiona Hutchinson, Marcus Gilbert. w. John Groves, Kent Walwin, (characters created by Captain W. E. Johns), d. John Hough.

ADVENTURE: SCI-FI: Time Travel; Pilots-Airplane; Pilots-Daredevil; Yuppies; World War I Era; 1980s

Bikini Beach, 1964, 100m, ★★½/$$$, AIP/Sultan. A developer wants to build a retirement community on a California beach populated by swingin' babes and dudes, who don't like the idea of giving up their surf turf. Frankie Avalon, Annette Funicello, Martha Hyer, Don Rickles, Harvey Lembeck, Keenan Wynn, Boris Karloff. w. William Asher, Leo Townsend, Robert Diller, d. William Asher.

COMEDY: Beach Movies; Teenage Movies; Teenagers; Corporation as Enemy; Mortgage; Drama; Save the Land
(Beach Party; Beach Blanket Bingo; Back to the Beach)

Bilitis, 1977, 95m, ★★/$, Ind/Media. A virgin at a girls' schools finds sex very interesting. Patti D'Arbanville, Mona Kristensen. d. David Hamilton.

COMEDY: Erotic Comedy; Sex Comedy; Girls' Schools; Teenagers; Teenage Movies; Curiosities; Girls; Young Women; Virgins Coming of Age; Ind Films
(Little Darlings; Private School; Screwball Academy)

Bill, 1981, 97m, ★★★/$$$$, CBS/Media. A retarded man tries to live outside of the institution with the help of a young man.

Mickey Rooney, Dennis Quaid. d. Anthony Page.

Bill: On His Own, 1983, 100m, ★★★/$$$$, CBS/Live. More of Bill's life in the real world dealing with his mental disability. Mickey Rooney, Helen Hunt, Teresa Wright, Dennis Quaid. d. Anthony Page.

DRAMA: COMEDY DRAMA: MELO-DRAMA: Tearjerkers; Eccentric People; Mentally Disabled; Friendships-Intergenerational; Making a Living; TV Movies

Bill and Ted's Bogus Journey, 1991, 93m, ★★/$$, Orion/Orion, Nelson, PG-13/P-S. Killed by their android doubles, Bill and Ted must trick Death at various games (in a parody of *The Seventh Seal*) to return to life and have further adventures. (Originally titled *Bill and Ted Go to Hell*.) Alex Winter, Keanu Reeves, Jeff Miller, David Carrera, George Carlin. w. Ed Solomon, Chris Matheson, d. Pete Hewitt.

COMEDY: ADVENTURE: Comic Adventure; SATIRE: Teenagers; Teenage Movies; Time Travel; Journies; Suburban Life; Androids; Hell; Death-Personified; Simple Minds; Surfers

SEQUEL TO: Bill and Ted's Excellent Adventure

Bill and Ted's Excellent Adventure, 1989, 90m, ★★★/$$$, Orion/Nelson, PG-13/P-S. Two braindead high school chums go back through time to do their history paper the easy way-by meeting the figures they're supposed to study. d. Stephen Herek.

COMEDY: ADVENTURE: Comic Adventure; SATIRE: Teenagers; Teenage Movies; Suburban Life; California; Time Travel; Journies; Surfers; Simple Minds; Sleeper Hits

SEQUEL: Bill and Ted's Bogus Journey. (Fast Times at Ridgemont High; Being Human)

A Bill of Divorcement, 1932, 69m, ★★★/$$$, RKO/Fox, Turner. John Barrymore, Katharine Hepburn, Billie Burke, David Manners, Paul Cavanagh. w. Howard Estabrook, Harry Wagstaff Gribble, P-adap. Clemence Dane, d. George Cukor.

A Bill of Divorcement, 1940, 69m, RKO/NA. A remake of above, with few changes. Adolphe Menjou, Maureen O'Hara, Patric Knowles, Herbert Marshall, C. Aubrey Smith, Dame May

Whitty. w. Dalton Trumbo, d. John Farrow.

>A middle-aged man, having spent several years in a mental institution, comes home to find his family has changed radically in his absence.

DRAMA: MELODRAMA: Marriage on the Rocks; Divorce; Reunions; Mental Illness; Asylums; Time Sleepers

Billie, 1965, 87m, ★★1/2/$, UA/MGM-UA. A teenage girl gets into trouble with boys because she beats them at sports, though perhaps not at love. Patty Duke, Jim Backus, Jane Greer, Warren Berlinger, Billy de Wolfe, Charles Lane, Dick Sargent. w. Ronald Alexander, P-adap. *Time Out for Ginger*, d. Don Weis.

COMEDY DRAMA: Coming of Age; Girlhood; Tomboys; Sports Movies; Female Among Males; Running; Suburban Life

(Me, Natalie; Just One of the Guys; Tammy SERIES; Gidget SERIES)

The Billion Dollar Brain, 1967, 111m, ★★/$, UA/NA. A former secret agent named Harry Palmer agrees to transport mysterious cargo to Finland, unwittingly becoming part of a conspiracy by a madman to take over the world. Michael Caine, Oscar Homolka, François Dorléac, Karl Malden, Ed Begley. w. John McGrath, N-adap. Len Deighton, d. Ken Russell.

Spy Films; Spies; Secret Agents; British Films; Conspiracy; Rule the World-Plots to Computers

(The Ipcress File; Funeral in Berlin; Get Carter)

(Ed: Ken Russell's visuals are fascinating, though not conventional for the genre)

Billy Bathgate, 1991, 106m, ★★1/2/$, Touchstone/Touchstone, R/EV-P-FFN. A young man's apprenticeship into the New York in the 1920s leads him to an unusual friendship with mobster Dutch Schultz (Dustin Hoffman). Loren Dean, Nicole Kidman, Bruce Willis, Steve Buscemi. w. Tom Stoppard, N-adap. E. L. Doctorow, d. Robert Benton.

DRAMA: Crime Drama; Mob Stories; Mob Wars; Character Studies; Criminal Biographies; Proteges; Men and Boys; Romance-Triangles; Romance-Older Women/Younger Men; Coming of Age; Jewish People; New York Life; 1920s; 1930s; Depression Era; Flops-Major (Once Upon a Time in America; The Godfather SERIES; Mobsters; Ragtime)

(Ed: Great period detail, but not much of a story when it comes to dramatic detail)

Billy Budd, 1962, 112m, ★★★/$$, Allied/Fox. A young, wild youthful sailor finally can't bear the yoke of oppression any longer and kills his oppressive captain, then stands trial. Peter Ustinov, Robert Ryan, Terence Stamp, Melvyn Douglas, Paul Rogers. w. Peter Ustinov, Robert Rossen, N-adap. Herman Melville, d. Peter Ustinov.

DRAMA: TRAGEDY: MURDER: Courtroom Drama; Trials; Historical Drama; Courts Martial; Ships; Young Men; Sailors; Leaders-Tyrant; Evil Men; Violence-Sudden

(The Bounty; Mutiny on the Bounty)

Billy Galvin, 1986, 94m, ★★1/2/$, American Playhouse/Vestron, PG. In a working-class family in Boston, tensions arise between a father and son. Karl Malden, Lenny Von Dohlen, Joyce Van Patten, Toni Kalem, Paul Guilfoyle. w. d. John Gray.

DRAMA: Character Studies; Fathers & Sons; Men in Conflict; Working Class; Ordinary People Stories; Boston; Writer-Directors; TV Movies

Billy Jack, 1971, 114m, ★★1/2/$$$$, WB/WB, PG/V. Legendary anti-establishment hero Jack (Tom Laughlin) this time helps out the American Indians in a vigilante stance. w. d. Tom Laughlin.

DRAMA: ACTION: Action Drama; Social Drama; Anti-establishment Films; Vigilantes; Corruption; Indians; Martial Arts; Blockbusters; Sleeper Hits; Faded Hits; Writer-Directors

SEQUEL TO: Born Losers

(Born Losers; The Legend of Billy Jean)

(Ed: Interesting because of the period)

Billy Liar, 1963, 98m, ★★★/$$, Vic Films/EMI, HBO. In a small northern English town, an employee of the undertaker has a Walter-Mitty-like fantasy life. Tom Courtenay, Julie Christie, Wilfred Pickles, Mona Washbourne, Ethel Griffies. w. Keith Waterhouse, Willis Hall, P-adap/N-adap. Keith Waterhouse (inspired by Thurber's Walter Mitty), d. John Schlesinger.

COMEDY DRAMA: Fantasy; Comedy-Morbid; Fantasies; Young Men; Liars; Funerals; Coming of Age; Novel & Play Adaptations; Rural Life; Small-Town Life; British Films; England

(The Secret Life of Walter Mitty; The

Chicken Chronicles; The Loneliness of the Long Distance Runner)

Billy Madison, 1995, 88m, U/MCA-U, PG-13/P-S. A bratty son has to prove he can take over the family corporation and makes a bet he can hammer through first through the twelfth grades again-at lightning speed, however. Adam Sandler, Bradley Whitford, Joshua Mostel, Bridgette Wilson, Norm MacDonald, Darren McGavin, Mark Beltzman, Larry Hankin, Theresa Merritt. w. Tim Herlihy, Adam Sandler, d. Tamra Davis.
COMEDY: Back to School; School Life; Comedy-Character; Inheritances at Stake; Fathers & Sons; Men Proving Themselves; Men and Boys; Aging-Reverse; Saturday Night Live Movies; Bets
(Tommy Boy; Happy Gilmore)

Billy Rose's Jumbo, 1962, 125m, ★★★/$$$, MGM/MGM-UA. Life in a musical circus. Doris Day, Martha Raye, Jimmy Durante, Stephen Boyd, Dean Jagger. w. Sidney Sheldon, d. Charles Walters.
MUSICALS: FAMILY: COMEDY: Musical Comedy; Circus Life; MELODRAMA: Elephants; Animal Stories
(The Greatest Show on Earth; Trapeze; Heller in Pink Tights)

Billy the Kid, 1941, 95m, ★★★/$$$, MGM/MGM-UA. Pat Garrett, the famous western sheriff, hunts down Billy, as the Kid stays one step ahead. Johnny Mack Brown, Wallace Beery, Kay Johnson, Karl Dane, Roscoe Ates. w. Wanda Tuchock, Laurence Stallings. Charles MacArthur, d. King Vidor.
WESTERN: Manhunts; Chase Movies; Men in Conflict; Fugitives from the Law; Female Screenwriters
(Pat Garrett and Billy the Kid; Gore Vidal's Billy the Kid)

Billy the Kid vs. Dracula, 1965, 89m, Circle-Embassy/Sultan, Nos. Dracula pursues Billy the Kid's fiancee. Chuck Courtney, John Carradine, Melinda Plowman, Virginia Christine, Harry Carrey Jr. w. Carl K. Hittleman, d. William Beaudine.
WESTERNS: Western Comedy; Spoofs-Western; Spoofs-Vampire

Biloxi Blues, 1988, 106m, ★★★/$$$, U/MCA-U, PG-13/P-S. Story of a young New Yorker (Matthew Broderick) in the army down south and the many lessons he learns along the way dealing with, among others, a frustrating drill sergeant

and his first hooker. Christopher Walken, Park Overall, Barry Miller. w. P-adap. Neil Simon, d. Mike Nichols.
COMEDY: COMEDY DRAMA: Coming of Age; Autobiographical Stories; Young Men; North vs. South; Fish out of Water Stories; Soldiers; Military Comedy; Military Stories; Stern Men; North vs. South
SEQUEL TO: Brighton Beach Memoirs; SEQUEL: Broadway Bound (Brighton Beach Memoirs; Broadway Bound; Mister Roberts; An Officer and a Gentleman)
(Ed: A more dramatic Neil Simon well worth a look, even if the military angle is a turn-off)

The Bingo Long Traveling All-Stars and Motor Kings, 1976, 110m, ★★¹/₂/$$, MGM/MCA-U. An all-black baseball team in the 1940s has the usual sports ups and downs, which are compounded by the racism they encounter. Billy Dee Williams, James Earl Jones, Richard Pryor, Rico Dawson. w. Hal Barwood, Matthew Robbins, N-adap. William Brashler, d. John Badham.
COMEDY DRAMA: DRAMA: Sports Movies; Baseball; Black Casts; Black Men; Ensemble Films; Ensembles-Male; Road Movies; Race Relations; Black vs. White; Ahead of its Time
(The Jackie Robinson Story)

Birch Interval, 1977, 104m, ★★¹/₂/$, Ind/Media. A young city girl learns about life when she goes off to the country to live with Amish relatives. Eddie Albert, Rip Torn, Susan McClung, Ann Wedgeworth, Bill Lucking. w. Joanna Crawford, N-adap. d. Delbert Mann.
DRAMA: City vs. Country; Amish People; Girls; Rural Life; Farm Life; Cults; Female Screenwriters; Ind Films
(Friendly Persuasion; Witness)

Bird, 1988, 161m, ★★★/$$, WB/WB. The life story of Charlie Parker, the brilliant jazz saxophonist, focusing on the deterioration of his personal life, due primarily to his drug dependence. Forest Whitaker. w. Joel Oliansky, d. Clint Eastwood. BSound. Oscars: 1-1.
DRAMA: Character Studies; Black Men; Biographies; Musicians; Music Dies; Quiet Little Films; Jazz Life; Music Movies; 1940s; Actor-Directors
(Round Midnight; Lady Sings the Blues; Mo' Better Blues)
(Ed: Very slow and languid, but well worth it)

Bird of Paradise, 1932, 80m, ★★★/$$$, RKO/Nos. Joel McCrea, John Halliday, Dolores del Rio, Skeets Gallagher. w. Wells Root, d. King Vidor.

Bird of Paradise, 1951, 100m, ★★¹/₂/$$, 20th/NA. A sea adventurer meets a beautiful girl on a South Sea island, eventually marrying her, much to the dismay of her family. Louis Jourdan, Jeff Chandler, Debra Paget, Everett Sloane, Jack Elam. w. d. Delmer Daves.
ROMANCE: ADVENTURE: DRAMA: Romantic Drama; Lover Family Dislikes; Romance-Interracial; Sailors; South Pacific; Islands
(Hurricane; The Adventures of Sadie)

Bird on a Wire, 1990, 110m, ★★/$$$$, WB/WB, PG-13/P-S-V-MRN. A witness relocation fugitive (Mel Gibson) incognito as a hairdresser runs into his old flame (Goldie Hawn) and tries to hide out with her despite each showing their derriere ostentatiously and often. Joan Severance, Bill Duke, Stephen Tobolowsky, David Carradine. w. Louis Venosta, David Seltzer, Eric Lerne, d. John Badham.
COMEDY: Action Comedy; Romantic Comedy; Love Reunited; Murder Witness; Fugitives; Fugitives from the Mob; Fugitives from the Law; Veterinarians
(Flashback; Protocol; Air America; Hanky Panky)
(Ed: Ridiculous retread shenanigans children will find more enjoyable, although all the butt shots [literally here] aren't very appropriate for them)

The Bird with the Crystal Plumage, 1969, 98m, ★★¹/₂/$$, Argento-Ind/VCI. A suspected murderer encounters his next "victim," who turns out to be a psychopath himself. Suzy Kendall, Tony Musante. w. d. Dario Argento.
SUSPENSE: THRILLER: MURDER: MURDER MYSTERY: Serial Killers; Trail of a Killer; Accused Unjustly; Framed?; Birds; Saving Oneself; Italy; Italian Films; Forgotten Films; Writer-Directors

The Birdman of Alcatraz, 1962, 148m, ★★★/$$$, UA/CBS-Fox. A prisoner, serving a life sentence for murder on the famed island raises birds and has a gentle nature despite his past. Burt Lancaster (BActor), Karl Malden, Thelma Ritter (BSActress), Edmond O'Brien, Betty Field, Telly Savalas (BSActor). w. Guy Trosper, NF-adap. Thomas E. Gaddis, d. John Frankenheimer. BB&WCin. Oscars: 4-0.

DRAMA: MELODRAMA: Character Studies; Prison Drama; Murderers-Nice; Biographies; True Stories; San Francisco; Mothers & Sons; Birds
(The Shawshank Redemption; Elmer Gantry)

The Birds, 1963, 120m, ★★★¹/2/$$$$, Univ/MCA-U, PG/V, B&G. Nature runs amok when birds attack the citizens of a California island. Tippi Hedren, Rod Taylor, Suzanne Pleshette, Jessica Tandy. w. Evan Hunter, SS-adap. Daphne DuMaurier, d. Alfred Hitchcock.

The Birds II, 1994, 100m, ★★¹/2/$$, Showtime/MCA-U. Return to the attacking birds and trying to figure out what happened the first time. Brad Johnson.

HORROR: SUSPENSE: Psychological Thriller; Animal Monsters; Rogue Plots; Man vs. Nature; Human Eaters; Women in Jeopardy; Children in Jeopardy; California; Islands; Hitchcockian
(Ed: The first big one of the animal monster movies with many subtextual implications)

Birdy, 1984, 120m, ★★★¹/2/$$, Col/Col, R/EV-P-MRN. The strange friendship of two young men who went to Vietnam and are now haunted by the horrors, one of whom has become catatonic. Matthew Modine, Nicolas Cage. w. Sandy Kroopf, Jack Behr, N-adap. William Wharton, d. Alan Parker.

DRAMA: MELODRAMA: War Stories; Soldiers; Friendships-Great; Friendships-Male; Young Men; Mental Illness; Nervous Breakdowns; Flashbacks; Vietnam War; Past-Haunted by the Fantasies; Illusions; Nightmares; Lyrical Films; Philadelphia; Birds; Coma
(Full Metal Jacket; Rain Man; A Midnight Clear; Awakenings)
(Ed: Beautiful, lyrical film of male friendship and the nightmares of war)

Birth of a Nation, 1915, 159m, ★★★/ $$$$$, Griffith/Republic. The famous epic of the Civil War, in which the Ku Klux Klan are the heroes. Henry B. Walthall, Mae Marsh, Miriam Cooper, Lillian Gish, Raoul Walsh, Donald Crisp. w. D. W. Griffith, Frank E. Woods, N-adap. Thomas Dixon Jr., *The Clansmen*, d. D. W. Griffith.

DRAMA: Epics; War Stories; Historical Drama; War Battles; Civil War Era; Race Relations; Ku Klux Klan; Blockbusters; Film History; Silent Films
(Intolerance; America; The Klansman)

The Birth of the Blues, 1941, 85m, ★★¹/2/$$, Par/NA. A New Orleans jazz band has its ups and downs. Bing Crosby, Mary Martin, Brian Donlevy, Jack Teagarden, Eddie Rochester Anderson, Carolyn Lee. w. Harry Tugend, Walter de Leon, d. Victor Schertzinger.

DRAMA: MELODRAMA: Musicians; Singers; New Orleans; Jazz Life

The Biscuit Eater, 1940, 82m, ★★★/$$, Par/NA. Two friends, one white and one black, teach a junkyard dog to hunt. Billy Lee. d. Stuart Heisler, SS-adap. James Street.

The Biscuit Eater, 1972, 90m, ★★¹/2/$$, Disney/Disney. Remake of above. Johnny Whittaker, Earl Holliman, Lew Ayres. d. Vincent McEveety, SS-adap. James Street.

DRAMA: MELODRAMA FAMILY: CHILDREN'S: Dogs; Boy and His Dog; Pet Stories; Boyhood; Friendships-Male; Friendships-Interracial; Black vs. White; Race Relations; Southerns
(Savage Sam; Old Yeller; Where the Red Fern Grows; Napoleon and Samantha; Far From Home)

The Bishop's Wife, 1947, 108m, ★★★/$$$, Goldwyn-RKO/Goldwyn. An angel (Cary Grant) comes down to earth to help a bishop regain his sense of priorities. Cary Grant, Loretta Young, David Niven, Monty Woolley, James Gleason, Gladys Cooper, Elsa Lanchester. w. Robert E. Sherwood, Leonardo Bercovici, N-adap. Robert Nathan, d. Henry Koster (BDirector). BPicture, BEdit, **BSound,** BScore. Oscars: 5-1.

COMEDY DRAMA: MELODRAMA: Fantasy; Marriage; Comedy; Preachers/Ministers; Religion; Angels; Life Transitions; Christmas; Taxi Drivers
REMAKE: The Preacher's Wife (1996)
(It's a Wonderful Life; Angel on My Shoulder; Here Comes Mr. Jordan; Heaven Can Wait)

The Bitch, 1979, 94m, ★★/$$, Brent Walker-EMI/EMI, R/S-P-FFN-MRN. A gangster moll in London has an affair with the wrong man. Joan Collins, Kenneth Haigh, Michael Coby, Ian Hendry, Carolyn Seymour, Sue Lloyd, Mark Burns. w. d. Gerry O'Hara, SS-adap. Jackie Collins.

MELODRAMA: Erotic Drama; Mob Stories; Hitmen; Mob Girls; London; Sexy Men; Sexy Women; Romance-Dangerous; Fugitives from the Mob

(The Stud; Lucky/Chances; The World Is Full of Married Men)

The Bitch (*La Garce*), 1984, 100m, ★★★/$, Sara Films-FR3-Ind/NA. A cop convicted of rape, upon finishing his sentence, gets work as a private eye and finds himself on a case involving the woman he raped. Isabelle Huppert, Richard Berry, Vittorio Mezzogiomo, Jean Benguigui, Jean-Claude Legay, Jean-Pierre Moulin, Clement Harrari. w. Pierre Fabre, Laurent Heynemann, Christine Pascal, A. M. Delocque Fourcaud, d. Christine Pascal.

DRAMA: Police Stories; Ex-Convicts; Rape/Rapists; Turning the Tables; Secrets-Haunted by; Guilty Conscience
(The Woolgatherer [play]; Extremities)

Bite the Bullet, 1975, 131m, ★★★/$$$, Col/RCA-Col, PG/P-V. A 700-mile horse race forms the backdrop for this tale of male comradery and competition. Gene Hackman, Candice Bergen, James Coburn, Ben Johnson, Ian Bannen, Jan-Michael Vincent, Paul Stewart. w. d. Richard Brooks.

ADVENTURE: WESTERNS: Road Movies; Chase Movies; Horses/Horse Racing; Contests/Competitions; Cowboys; Female Among Males; Desert Settings; Writer-Directors
(The Wind and the Lion; The Professionals)

Bittere Ernte (*Angry Harvest*), 1985, 102m, ★★★/$, Filmkunst/Facets, Ingram. A Jewish woman, hiding from the Nazis, finds refuge in a country house occupied by a shy farmer. Armin Muller-Stahl, Elisabeth Trissenaar, Kathe Jeanicke, Hans Beerhenke. w. Paul Hengge, Agnieszka Holland, d. Agnieszka Holland.

DRAMA: Escape Drama; World War II Stories; Nazi Stories; Jews-Saving; Jewish People; Farm Life; Female Protagonists; Germany; German Films; Germans as Enemy; Female Screenwriters; Female Directors
(The Attic; The Shop on Main Street; A Love in Germany)

Bitter Moon, 1994, 139m, ★★★¹/2/$, CanalTriumph/Col-Tri, R/S-P-FFN-MRN. A crippled American writer on board a European ocean liner tells an English couple the strange story of his life, focusing on his darkly sadomasochistic relationship with his beautiful French wife. Peter Coyote,

Emmaunuelle Seigner, Hugh Grant, Kristin Scott-Thomas, Victor Banerjee, Sophie Patel, Stockard Channing. w. Roman Polanski, Gérard Brach, John Brownjohn, N-adap. Pascal Bruckner, d. Roman Polanski.

DRAMA: Psychological Drama; Art Films; Marriage Drama; Marriage on the Rocks; Abused Women; Swapping Partners; Corruption; Evil Men; Writers; Disabled People; Ships; International Casts; New Year's Eve; Narrated Films; Hidden Gems; Underrated

(Betty Blue; The Comfort of Strangers; Who's Afraid of Virginia Woolf?; Sirens)

Bitter Rice (*Riso Amaro*), 1949, 108m, ★★★/$$, Lux Films/Facets. A thief running from the law seeks refuge with a buxom country girl in the rice fields of Italy. Only this country girl isn't so simple-she's got his number and tries to steal his loot. Silvana Mangano, Raf Vallone, Doris Dowling, Vittorio Gassman. w. Carlo Lizzani, Carlo Musso, Gianni Puccini, Corrado Alvaro, Ivo Perillo, Giuseppe de Santis, d. Giuseppe de Santis. BOStory. Oscars: 1-0.

DRAMA: Fugitives from the Law; Thieves; Hiding Out; Turning the Tables; Double Crossing; Mindgames; Neo-Realistic Films; Italian Films; Italy

(Scene of the Crime; Obsessione; Paisan)

Bitter Sweet, 1933, ★★★/$$, UA/Nos. Anna Neagle, Fernand Gravet, Miles Mander. w. Lydia Hayward, Herbert Wilcox, Monckton Hoffe, P-adap. Noel Coward, d. Herbert Wilcox.

Female Screenwriters

Bitter Sweet, 1940, 94m, ★★★/$$$, MGM/MGM-UA. A gambler in 1875 Vienna seeks revenge on a concert violinist who stole his girlfriend. Jeanette Macdonald, Nelson Eddy, George Sanders, Felix Bressart, Ian Hunter, Fay Holden, Curt Bois. w. Lesser Samuels, P-adap. Noel Coward, d. W. S. Van Dyke II. BCCin, BArt. Oscars: 2-0.

ROMANCE: Music Movies; **MUSICAL:** Musical Romance; **MELODRAMA:** Romantic Drama; **TRAGEDY:** Romance-Doomed; Musicians; Gamblers; Vienna; 1870s

The Bitter Tears of Petra Von Kant, 1972, 124m, ★★★/$$, Col/Col, Karl, R/S-FN. A model finds lesbian love in the fashion world, but soon jealousies complicate what seemed to be bliss. Margit Carstensen, Irm Hermann, Hanna Schygulla. w. d. Rainer Werner Fassbinder.

DRAMA: ROMANCE: Romantic Drama; Lesbians; Fashion World; Jealousy; Romance-Triangles; Bisexuality; Alternative Lifestyles; Ahead of its Time; Forgotten Films; Hidden Gems; German Films; Female Protagonists; Writer-Directors

(Fox and His Friends; The Marriage of Maria Braun; Veronika Voss; Lianna; Bar Girls)

Bittersweet Love, 1976, 92m, ★½/$, Ind/Sultan. After they are married, two young lovers find out that they have the same father. Lana Turner, Robert Alda, Celeste Holm, Robert Lansing. w. Adrian Morrall, D. A. Kellogg. d. David Miller.

MELODRAMA: TRAGEDY: ROMANCE: Incest; Children-Long Lost; Misunderstandings; Romance-Doomed; Camp; Forgotten Films; Unintentionally Funny

(Angela; Oedipus Rex)

(Ed: Uh-oh. Bittersweet doesn't quite cut it)

Black and White in Color, 1976, 90m, ★★★/$$, Lorimar-WB/WB. Comfortable colonialists in French West Africa at the turn of the century must rise to the occasion when war breaks out. Jean Carnet, Jacques Dufilho, Catherine Rouvel, Jacques Spiesser, Dora Doll. w. Georges Conchon, Jean-Jacques Annaud, d. Jean-Jacques Annaud. BFLFilm. Oscars: 1-1.

SATIRE: COMEDY DRAMA: Black Comedy; Political Unrest; Ensemble Films; Imperialist Problems; War Stories; French Films; Sleeper Hits; Race Relations; Black vs. White; Africa; Sleeper Hits

Black Angel, 1946, 80m, ★★★/$$, U-I/MCA-U. An alcoholic prone to blackouts searches for his wife's murderer and makes a shocking discovery. Dan Duryea, Peter Lorre, Broderick Crawford, June Vincent, Wallace Ford. w. Roy Chanslor, N-adap. William Irish, d. Roy William Neal.

MURDER: MURDER MYSTERY: MYSTERY: Fugitives from the Law; Murder of Spouse; Trail of a Killer; Suspecting Oneself; Abused Men; Alcoholics; Film Noir; Coulda Been Great

(The Morning After; Angel Heart; Detour)

The Black Arrow, 1948, 76m, ★★½/$$, Col-Disney/Disney. A medieval knight seeks to avenge his father's death. Louis Hayward, Janet Blair, George Macready, Edgar Buchanan, Paul Cavanagh. w. Richard Schayer, David P. Sheppard, Thomas Seller, N-adap. R. L. Stevenson, d. George Douglas.

DRAMA: ADVENTURE: Medieval Times; Historical Drama; Costume Drama; Revenge; Avenging Death of Someone

Blackbeard, The Pirate, 1952, 99m, ★★½/$$, RKO/Turner. A pirate-hunter, Sir Henry Morgan, is sent to the Caribbean in the 1600s to "deal with" the rogue pirate Blackbeard. Robert Newton, Linda Darnell, Keith Andes, William Bendix, Torin Thatcher. w. Alan le May, d. Raoul Walsh.

ADVENTURE: Costume Drama; Pirates; Chase Movies; Bounty Hunters; Caribbean; Ships; 1600s

Blackbeard's Ghost, 1967, 107m, ★★★/$$$, Disney/Disney, G. Old ladies who own a hotel formerly frequented by Blackbeard are helped by his ghost when they hit on hard times. Peter Ustinov, Dean Jones, Suzanne Pleshette, Elsa Lanchester, Richard Deacon. w. Bill Walsh, Don Da Gradi, d. Robert Stevenson.

COMEDY: FAMILY: CHILDREN'S: Fantasy; Spoofs; Ghosts; Comedy-Disney; Elderly Women; Hotels

(The Brass Bottle; Ghost; Blithe Spirit; Gus)

(Ed: Though it starts off charmingly enough, it soon degenerates into lame slapstick at a track meet, of all things)

Black Beauty, 1946, 74m, 20th/Media. A young girl in Victorian England searches for her runaway colt. Mona Freeman, Richard Denning, Evelyn Ankers, J. M Kerrigan, Terry Kilburn. w. Lillie Hayward, Agnes Christie Johnston, N-adap. Anna Sewell, d. Max Nosseck.

Black Beauty, 1971, 106m, Par/Par, G. Remake of above, this time involving a young boy's search for his horse, who passes from one cruel owner to the next. Mark Lester, Walter Slezak, Peter Lee Lawrence, Maria Rohm. w. Wolf Mankowitz, N-adap. Anna Sewell, d. James Hill.

Black Beauty, 1994, 95m, ★★★/$, Par/Par, G. The journeys of a horse and its several owners and the boy who loves her most. Andrew Knott, Sean Bean, David Thewlis, Peter Cook, Peter

Davison. w. d. Caroline Thompson, N-adap. Anna Sewell.

Female Directors; Female Screenwriters

DRAMA: FAMILY: CHILDREN: MELO-DRAMA: Tearjerkers; Horses; Pet Stories; Hand-Me-Down Stories; British Films; Child Protagonists

(My Friend Flicka; National Velvet; Seabiscuit)

The Blackboard Jungle, 1955, 101m, ★★★1/2/$$$$, MGM/MGM-UA. A teacher tames his class of hoodlums. Set against the backdrop of early rock n' roll. Introduced the hit song "Rock Around the Clock." Glenn Ford, Anne Francis, Louis Calhern, Margaret Hayes, John Hoyt, Richard Kiley, Sidney Poitier, Vic Morrow. w. d. Richard Brooks, N-adap. Evan Hunter.

DRAMA: Social Drama; Inner City Life; Teachers; Teachers & Students; Teachers-Inner City; Rebels; Juvenile Delinquents; Race Relations; 1950s; Ahead of its Time; Sleeper Hits

(Lean on Me; To Sir with Love; Teachers; Up the Down Staircase; Dangerous Minds)

Black Caesar, 1973, 96m, ★★/$, Filmways-Ind/Orion, R/EV-P-S. A black gangster tries to wrestle control of Harlem operations from the Mafia. Fred Williamson, D'Urville Martin, Julius W. Harris, Gloria Hendry, Art Lund, Val Avery, Minnie Gentry. w. d. Larry Cohen.

ACTION: Crime Drama; Black Casts; Mob Stories; Black Men; Blaxploitation Era; Good; Premise Unfulfilled; Revisionist Films; Writer-Directors

REMAKE/RETREAD: Little Caesar;

SEQUEL: Hell up in Harlem

(Little Caesar; Shaft; Superfly; Across 110th Street)

(Ed: Interesting but missed the mark)

The Black Cat, 1934, 65m, ★★★/$$$, Universal/Media, MCA-U. A devil-worshipping Austrian architect is summoned to the castle of a compatriot doctor, who secretly plots a bizarre "revenge" upon the architect for betraying their country in World War I. Boris Karloff, Bela Lugosi, David Manners, Jacqueline Wells, Egon Brecher. w. Peter Ruric, d. Edgar G. Ulmer.

HORROR: Satanism; Occult Castles; Revenge; Forgotten Films; Cats; Lonely People

(Cat People; Dracula)

The Black Cauldron, 1985, 80m, ★★1/2/$$, Disney/Disney, PG/V. A

swashbuckling hero must fight witches, magic swords and animated skeletons to achieve his goal. voices of Freddie Jones, Nigel Hawthorne, John Hurt, John Huston, John Byner, Arthur Malet. w. David Jonas, Vance Gerry, Ted Berman, Richard Rich, Al Wilson, Roy Morita, Peter Young, Art Stevens, Joe Hale, N-adap. Lloyd Alexander, *The Chronicles of Prydain*, d. Ted Berman, Richard Rich.

CHILDREN'S: FAMILY: ACTION: ADVENTURE: Cartoons; Fantasy; Witches; Magic; Sword & Sorcery; Medieval Times; Flops-Major

(Dragonslayer; The Sword in the Stone)

Black Christmas (*Silent Night, Evil Night*), 1974, 100m, ★★/$, EMI/WB, R/V. College girls are stalked by Santa. Olivia Hussey, Keir Dullea, Margot Kidder, Andre Martin, John Saxon. w. Roy Moore, d. Robert Clark.

HORROR: Stalkers; Serial Killers; Murderers-Nice; Santa; Christmas; Ahead of its Time

(Silent Night; Deadly Night SERIES)

Black Fury, 1935, 92m, ★★★/$$, WB/Fox. Corruption and unsafe practices at a coal mining operation are uncovered by a miner, prompting his political awakening. Paul Muni, Karen Morley, William Gargan, Barton MacLane, John Qualen, J. Carrol Naish. w. Abem Finkel, Carl Erickson, P-adap. Harry R. Irving, *Bohunk*, d. Michael Curtiz.

DRAMA: Social Drama; Political Drama; Corruption; Corporation as Enemy; Mining Towns; Whistleblowers; Ordinary People Stories

Black God, White Devil, 1964, 110m, ★★★/$, New Cinema/Festival Films. A fanatic who preaches a philosophy of suffering and violence attracts peasant followers, doomed by their ignorance. Yona Magalhaes, Geraldo Del Rey, Othon Bastos, Maurico Do Valle, Lidio Silva. w. d. Glauber Rocha.

HORROR: Cults; Con Artists; Religious Zealots; Charismatic People

The Black Hand, 1949, 92m, ★★1/2/$, MGM/NA. An Italian boy in turn-of-the-century New York seeks the murderers of his father, leading him to the Mafia. Gene Kelly, J. Carrol Naish, Teresa Celli, Marc Lawrence, Frank Puglia, Barry Kelley. w. Luther Davis, d. Richard Thorpe.

DRAMA: SUSPENSE: Mob Stories; Crime Drama; Witness to Murder; Witness to

Murder-Child; Film Noir; Child Protagonists; Italians; Forgotten Films; Curiosities

The Black Hole, 1979, 97m, ★★/$$$$, Disney/Disney, PG/V. The black hole doubles for the octopus in this veiled remake of *20,000 Leagues Under the Sea* with cute robots a la *Star Wars*, too. Maximilian Schell, Anthony Perkins, Roddy McDowell. w. Jeb Rosebrook, Gerry Day, d. Gary Nelson. BCin. Oscars: 1-0.

ACTION: SCI-FI: Fantasy; ADVENTURE: Evil Men; Power Struggles; Outer Space; Futuristic Films; Robots

REMAKE/RETREAD OF: 20,000 Leagues Under the Sea; Star Wars

(Ed: 20,000 leagues in the hole)

Black Legion, 1937, 83m, ★★★/$$, WB/WB, MGM-UA. The Ku Klux Klan lures a factory worker into their fold but he may yet turn on them. Humphrey Bogart, Erin O'Brien Moore, Dick Foran, Ann Sheridan, Robert Barrat. w. Robert Lord, Abem Finkel, William Wister Haines (BOStory), d. Archie Mayo. Oscars: 1-0.

DRAMA: Social Drama; Crime Drama; Ku Klux Klan; Bigots; Race Relations; Whistleblowers; Ethics; Conformism; Ahead of its Time

(Storm Warning; The Klansman; Mississippi Burning)

Blackmail, 1929, 78m, ★★★/$$, BIP-Ind/Republic, Nos. The investigation of a murder leads a Scotland Yard inspector to his girlfriend as the prime suspect. He conceals this fact from his superiors and is blackmailed. Anny Ondra, Sara Allgood, John Longden, Charles Paton, Donald Calthrop, Cyril Ritchard. w. Alfred Hitchcock, Benn W. Levy, Charles Bennett, P-adap. Charles Bennett, d. Alfred Hitchcock.

SUSPENSE: MURDER: MURDER MYSTERY: Detective Stories; Murderer-Debate to Reveal; Protecting Someone; Blackmail; Secrets-Keeping; Enemies-Sleeping with; British Films; Hitchcockian

Blackmail, 1939, 81m, ★★1/2/$$, MGM/MGM-UA. A man wrongly convicted is pursued by a blackmailer immediately upon his release from prison. Edward G. Robinson, Ruth Hussey, Gene Lockhart, Esther Dale. w. David Hertz, William Ludwig, d. H. C. Potter.

DRAMA: Crime Drama; Framed?; Accused Unjustly; Blackmail; Ex-Convicts

Blackmailed, 1950, 85m, ★★½/$, GFD/NA. A blackmailer gets a dose of his own medicine, when his dupes conspire to murder him. Dirk Bogarde, Mai Zetterling, Fay Compton, Robert Flemyng, Harold Huth. w. Hugh Mills, Roger Vadim, N-adap. Elizabeth Meyers, *Mrs. Christopher*, d. Marc Allégret.

DRAMA: SUSPENSE: MURDER: Murder-Attempted; Conspiracy; Blackmail; Turning the Tables; Dose of Own Medicine-Given

(Mr. Klein; Flesh and the Devil)

The Black Marble, 1980, 113m, ★★★/$$, Avco-Embassy/Sultan, New Line, PG/P-S. A police detective (Robert Foxwroth) and his kooky woman partner (Paula Prentiss) go searching for a kidnapped dog and wind up in deep doo-dah. Harry Dean Stanton, Barbara Babcock. w. N-adap. Joseph Wambaugh, d. Harold Becker.

COMEDY DRAMA: MYSTERY: MURDER: MURDER MYSTERY: Crime Drama; Black Comedy; Murders of Children; Detective Stories; Detectives-Police; Chase Movie; Kidnappings; Animals in Jeopardy

(The Late Show; Ace Ventura, Pet Detective; The Choir Boys; The Onion Field)

Black Moon Rising, 1985, 100m, ★★/$$, Thorn EMI-New World/New World, R/V-S. A super-spy hired by the U.S. is pursued for valuable evidence he hides in the back of his high-tech car. Tommy Lee Jones, Linda Hamilton, Robert Vaughn, Richard Jaeckel, Keenan Wynn. w. John Carpenter, Desmond Nakano, William Gray, d. Harley Cokliss.

ACTION: Chase Movies; Chases-Car; Spy Films; Spies; Secret Agents; Fugitives from the Law

Black Narcissus, 1947, 99m, ★★★★/$$, Archer-U/MCA-U, Voyager. The story of a British nun (Deborah Kerr) dealing with the harsh environment of the convent she runs in the Himalayas and its tragic effects on the nuns there with her and the man she secretly loves. w. d. Michael Powell, Emeric Pressburger, N-adap. Rumer Godden. BCCin, BCArt. Oscars: 2-2.

DRAMA: TRAGEDY: Flashbacks; Spinsters; Lonely People; Sexuality; Nuns; Life Transitions; Religion; Death of a Child; Himalayas; Lyrical Films; Scenery-Outstanding; Outstanding-Production Design; Hidden Gems

(Agnes of God; The Nun's Story; Heaven Knows, Mr. Allison; The Inn of Sixth Happiness)

(Ed: One of the most beautiful films ever made)

The Black Orchid, 1958, 96m, ★★★/$, Par/Par. An Italian New York woman is upset when her widowed father plans to marry a gangster's widow. Sophia Loren, Anthony Quinn, Ina Balin, Jimmy Baird, Mark Richman. w. Joseph Stefano, d. Martin Ritt.

DRAMA: MELODRAMA: ROMANCE: Romance-Middle-Aged; Lover Family Dislikes; Fathers & Daughters; Mob Stories; Italians

Black Orpheus, 1958, 106m, ★★★/$$, Dispatfilm-Gemma-Tupan/Fox. A black streetcar operator in Rio accidently kills his girlfriend, then journeys to the underworld to be with her in the afterlife. Breno Mello, Marpessa Dawn, Ademar da Silva, Lourdes de Oliviera. w. Vinitius de Moraes, d. Marcel Camus. BFLFilm. Oscars: 1-1.

DRAMA: ROMANCE: TRAGEDY: MURDER: Death-Accidental; Guilty Conscience; Hiding Out; Allegorical Stories; South America; Black Men; Black Casts; Latin People; International Casts; Brazil

The Black Pirate, 1926, 76m, ★★★/$$$$, (B&W, Silent), Douglas Fairbanks-UA/VY, Republic. A swash-buckling adventure in which a sailor avenges his father's death at the hands of a band of pirates. Douglas Fairbanks, Billie Dove, Donald Crisp, Sam de Grasse. w. Douglas Fairbanks, Jack Cunningham, d. Albert Parker.

ADVENTURE: ACTION: Pirates; Swashbucklers; Blockbusters

(The Black Swan; The Crimson Pirate)

Black Rain, 1988, 123m, ★★★/$, Imamura Productions-Hayashibara-Tohokushinsha/Fox-Lorber. After the bomb, a Hiroshima family struggles with life in the ruins and the ravages of radiation sickness. Yoshiko Tanaka, Kazuo Kitamura, Etsuko Ichihara, Shoichi Ozawa, Norihei Miki. w. Toshiro Ishido, Shohei Imamura, N-adap. Masuji Ibuse, d. Shohei Imamura.

DRAMA: Family Stories; Survival Drama; Historical Drama; **TRAGEDY:** Bombs-Atomic; Radiation Poisoning; World War II Era-Post; Japanese Films; Japan

(The Day After; Hiroshima, Mon Amour)

Black Rain, 1989, 126m, ★★½/$$$, Par/Par, R/EV-P-S-FN. An American police detective (Michael Douglas) and his partner (Andy Garcia) go to Japan to solve a murder and suddenly are up against the Yakuza, the Japanese mob, and get in deeper than ever imagined. w. Craig Bolotin, Warren Lewis, d. Ridley Scott.

ACTION: Action Drama; Police Stories; **MYSTERY: MURDER MYSTERY:** Mob Stories; Mob-Asian; Police vs. Mob; Detective Stories; Detectives-Police; Japan Slavery; Prostitutes-High Class; Americans Abroad

(Rising Sun; The Yakuza; Blade Runner)

(Ed: Style over substance)

Black Rainbow, 1989, 103m, ★★/$, Ind/Fox, Media. A fortune teller foresees many violent deaths, including that of her father. Rosanna Arquette, Jason Robards, Tom Hulce, Mark Joy, Ron Rosenthal. w. d. Mike Hodges.

DRAMA: THRILLER: MURDER: Psychological Thriller; Fortune Tellers; Saving Oneself; Psychics; Fathers & Daughters; Writer-Directors

(Eyes of the Laura Mars; The Clairvoyant; The Medusa Touch; Fear)

The Black Robe, 1990, 105m, ★★★/$ (LR), Goldwyn/Goldwyn, R/V-FN-MN. European explorers encounter Indians along the Canadian trail in a very realistic adventure. w. Brian Moore, N-adap, d. Bruce Beresford.

DRAMA: ADVENTURE: WESTERNS: Historical Drama; Westerns-Neo Explorers; West-Old; Indians-American; 1600s Canada; Revisionist Films

(Burke and Wills; Mountains of the Moon)

(Ed: Almost too realistic)

The Black Room, 1935, 75m, ★★½/$$, Col/Goodtimes. A virtuous leader's power is usurped by his evil twin brother, who holds him captive. Boris Karloff, Marian Marsh, Katherine de Mille, Thurston Hall. w. Henry Myers (from the writings of Arthur Strawn), d. Roy William Neill.

HORROR: Power Struggles; Men in Conflict; Evil Men; Twins; Brothers

The Black Rose, 1950, 120m, ★★★/$$, 20th/NA. A 13th-century English scholar has many adventures and is knighted for scientific discoveries he makes searching through Mongolia. Tyrone Power, Orson Welles, Cecile Aubry, Jack Hawkins, Finlay Currie, Michael Rennie. w. Talbot

Jennings, N-adap. Thomas B. Costain, d. Henry Hathaway.

ADVENTURE: DRAMA: Journies; Explorers; Epics; Historical Drama; Costume; Drama; Middle Ages; Monks
(The Adventures of Marco Polo; The Razor's Edge)

Black Sabbath, 1963, 99m, ★★/$, AIP/HBO. Three horror stories introduced by Boris Karloff. Jacqueline Pierreux, Michele Mercier, Boris Karloff, Mark Damon. w. Anton Chekhov, Howard Snyder, Leo Tolstoy, d. Mario Bava.

HORROR: Multiple Stories; Trilogies; Occult; Classic Literary Adaptations
(The Fall of the House of Usher; Histoires Extraordinaires; Comedy of Terrors)

The Black Sleep, 1956, 81m, ★★/$, UA/NA. In the 1800s, a brain surgeon experiments on people who turn into freaks and eventually come after him. Basil Rathbone, Bela Lugosi, Lon Chaney Jr., John Carradine, Akim Tamiroff, Tor Johnson. w. John C. Higgins, d. Reginald Le Borg.

HORROR: Scientists-Mad; Experiments; Humans into Animals; Human Monsters; Turning the Tables; Zombies

The Black Stallion, 1979, 118m, ★★★/$$$, Z-UA/MGM-UA, G. The classic tale of a boy and his horse who saved him from drowning and the dream to turn him into a champion. Mickey Rooney, Teri Garr, Kelly Reno. w. Melissa Mathison, William Witliff, J. Rosenberg, N-adap. Walter Farley, d. Carol Ballard.

DRAMA: MELODRAMA: CHILDREN'S: FAMILY: Horses/Horse Racing; Pet Stories; Animals in Jeopardy; Lyrical Films; Child Protagonists; Scenery-Outstanding; Female Screenwriters

SEQUEL: The Black Stallion Returns.
(National Velvet; Black Beauty; My Friend Flicka; Seabiscuit)
(Ed: Beautiful and charming, though somewhat inconsistent)

The Black Stallion Returns, 1983, 103m, ★★½/$$, MGM-UA-Zoetrope/Fox, G. A sequel in which the boy, now a teenager, must search through Morocco to get his horse back. Kelly Reno, Ferdy Mayne, Woody Strode, Vincent Spano, Allen Goorwitz. w. Richard Kletter, Jerome Kass, N-adap. Walter Farley, d. Robert Dalva.

DRAMA: MELODRAMA: CHILDREN'S: FAMILY: Horses/Horse Racing; Pet Stories; Animals in Jeopardy; Searches; Kidnappings; Africa; Great Cinematography; Lyrical Films; Child Protagonists

SEQUEL TO: The Black Stallion
(National Velvet; Black Beauty; My Friend Flicka; Seabiscuit)
(Ed: Not as good as the first)

Black Sunday, 1960, 83m, ★★★/$$, Galatra-Jolly/Sinister Video. An attractive witch, put to death, comes back to torment her killers. Barbara Steele, John Richardson, Ivo Garrani. w. d. Mario Bava, SS-adap. Gogol.

HORROR: COMEDY DRAMA: MURDER: Black Comedy; Comedy-Morbid; Dead-Back from the; Witches; Revenge; Italian Films

Black Sunday, 1977, 143m, ★★★/$$$, Par/Par, R/V-P. Terrorists comandeer a blimp in order to spray bullets into the super bowl game audience. Bruce Dern, Robert Shaw, Marthe Keller. w. Ernest Lehman, Kenneth Ross, Ivan Moffat, N-adap. Thomas Harris, d. John Frankenheimer.

SUSPENSE: Race Against Time; Terrorists; Crisis Situations; Blackmail; Snipers; Mass Murderers; Football
(Two Minute Warning; Nighthawks)
(Ed: Good suspenser, though very exploitative and obvious in many ways)

The Black Swan, 1942, 85m, ★★★/$$$, 20th/NA. A former pirate is made governor of Jamaica and hires his old pirate friends to help him rid the place of looters. Tyrone Power, Maureen O'Hara, Laird Cregar, Thomas Mitchell, George Sanders, Anthony Quinn. w. Ben Hecht, Seton I. Miller, N-adap. Rafael Sabatini, d. Henry King.

DRAMA: ACTION: Action Drama; Pirates; Swashbucklers; Costume Drama; Caribbean; Islands Politicians
(Captain Kidd; The Adventures of Captain Fabian; The Crimson Pirate)

Black Widow, 1954, 95m, ★★½/$$, 20th/NA. A young up-and-coming Broadway starlet is murdered and her producer is the prime suspect. Ginger Rogers, Van Heflin, George Raft, Gene Tierney, Peggy Ann Garner, Reginald Gardner. w. d. Nunally Johnson, N-adap. Patrick Quentin, *Fatal Woman*.

MURDER: MYSTERY: MURDER MYSTERY: Mystery-Whodunits; Actresses; Theater Life

(Rehearsal for Murder; Stage Fright; The Velvet Touch)

Black Widow, 1987, 103m, ★★★½/$$$, 20th/CBS-Fox, R/S-FN. An FBI agent (Debra Winger) follows a hunch that a series of deaths of rich men are murders and are related to one woman (Theresa Russell) she then begins pursuing-in more ways than one. w. Ron Bass, d. Bob Rafelson

SUSPENSE: MURDER: MYSTERY: MURDER MYSTERY: Psychological Thriller; Cat and Mouse Stories; Detective Stories; Detectives in Deep; Serial Killers; Trail of a Killer; Female Law Officers; Murderers-Female; Men in Jeopardy; Undercover; Disguises; Mindgames; FBI Agents; Female Protagonists; Homoeroticism; Lesbians; Romance-Dangerous; Romance-Unprofessional; Hawaii; Underrated
(Betrayed; Silence of the Lambs; Shadow of a Doubt; The Lady in Question)
(Ed: Despite Russell's erratic performance-particularly her bad Southern accent-it's good to great, depending on how worried you are about the men, who are treated as disposably as murdered women in similar movies, or whether you're into the lesbian cat-and-mouse tension)

The Black Windmill, 1974, 106m, ★★½/$$, Universal/MCA-U. There's no one to turn to as a secret service agent's son is kidnapped by spies. Michael Caine, Janet Suzman, Joseph O'Conor, Donald Pleasance. w. Leigh Vance, N-adap. Clive Egleton (*Seven Days to a Killing*), d. Don Seigel.

SUSPENSE: Chase Movies; Spies; Kidnappings; Fathers & Sons; Secret Agents; Searches
(Ashanti: Land of No Mercy; Puzzle of a Downfall Child; Frantic)

Blacula, 1972, 92m, ★★½/$$, AIP/Orion, R/V-S-B&G. In Transylvania, the original Dracula makes a vampire out of an African prince. His body is subsequently brought back to life in modern-day Los Angeles. William Marshall, Vonetta McGee, Denise Nicholas, Gordon Pinsent, Charles Macaulay. w. Joan Torres, Raymond Koenig, d. William Crain.

HORROR: Horror Comedy; Vampires; Spoofs-Vampire; Dead-Back from; Black Casts; Black Men; Camp Revisionist Films; Africans; Blaxploitation Era; Female Screenwriters; Black Directors

Blade Runner, 1982, 125m, ★★★¹/₂/$$$, WB/WB, R/V-S. A cop (Harrison Ford) in the dark future world of L.A. androids and rampant crime takes on a seemingly unstoppable villain (Rutger Hauer). Sean Young, Darryl Hannah, Joanna Cassidy. w. David Peoples, Hampton Fancher, N-adap. Philip K. Dick (*Do Androids Dream of Electric Sheep?*), d. Ridley Scott.
ACTION: MYSTERY: Chase Movies; Film Noir-Modern; **SCI-FI:** Bounty Hunters; Manhunts; Futuristic Films; Los Angeles; Villains-Classic; Androids; Outstanding Production Design
(Black Rain; Johnny Mnemonic)
(Ed: Not for mile-a-minute action fans, and only watch the director's cut)
Blame It on Rio, 1984, 90m, ★★¹/₂/$$$, 20th/Vestron, Live, R/S-FFN. Two men take their daughters to Rio for a vacation and one (Michael Caine) winds up having an affair with the other's daughter. w. Larry Gelbart, Charlie Peters, S-adap. Claude Berri (*Un Moment d'Egarement*), d. Stanley Donen.
COMEDY: Romantic Comedy; Romance-Older Men/Younger Women; Vacation Romance; Romance with Friend's Relative; Men and Girls; Virgins; Coming of Age; Friends as Enemies; Friendships-Male; South America; Foreign Film Remakes
REMAKE OF: Un Moment d'Egarement (Lolita; Age of Consent; Baby Doll; Beau Pere)
(Ed: Leave it to the French to make the original of this-and a comedy at that)
Blame It on the Bellboy, 1992, 78m, ★★★¹/₂/$$, Touchstone/Touchstone, PG/P-S. The lives of a corporate stooge, a real estate agent, and a hitman become entwined as the bellboy at their Venetian hotel mixes up the names Orton, Lorton, and Horton. Dudley Moore, Bryan Brown, Richard Griffiths, Andreas Katsulas, Patsy Kensit, Bronson Pinchot. w. d. Mark Herman.
COMEDY: FARCE: Screwball Comedy; Farce-Bedroom; Chase Movies; Mob Comedy; Hitmen; Misunderstandings; Mix-Ups; Hotels; Venice; International Casts; Underrated; Hidden Gems; Writer-Directors
(Hotel Paradiso; Once Upon a Crime; What's Up, Doc?)
(Ed: May be silly to some, but the sheer frenetic nature and pay-offs are very well worth it, especially for fans of farce)

Blame It on the Night, 1984, 85m, ★★/$, Tri-Star/CBS-Fox. A 13-year-old boy is reunited with the rock-star father who abandoned him for the road. Nick Mancuso, Byron Thames, Leslie Ackerman, Dick Bakalyan. w. Len Jenkin, d. Gene Taft.
DRAMA: MELODRAMA: Fathers & Sons; Reunions; Boyhood; Orphans; Teenagers; Singers; Musicians; Abandoned People
Blank Check, 1994, 93m, ★★¹/₂/$$$, Disney/Disney, G. When a kid gets a check from a mobster, he cashes it for a million and then has to go on the lam. Brian Bonsall, Miguel Ferrer, Michael Lerner, Ric Ducommon, Tone Loc, Karen Duffy. w. Colby Carr, Blake Snyder, d. Rupert Wainwright.
COMEDY: CHILDREN'S: What if.. Stories; Mob Stories; Mob Comedy; Children in Jeopardy; Sleeper Hits; Disney Comedy
(Hiding Out; Sister Act; Money for Nothing)
(Ed: Preposterous, but so what? A little more adult and dangerous than the old Disney stuff, but with the old whimsy)
Blankman, 1994, 92m, ★¹/₂/$, Col/Col, PG-13/P-V. An amateur superhero tries to fight crime in the ghetto if he can stay out of trouble himself. Damon Wayans, Robin Givens, David Alan Grier, Jason Alexander, Jon Polito. w. Damon Wayans, J. F. Lawton, d. Mike Binder.
COMEDY: Spoofs; Heroes-Comic; Black Men; Inner City Life; Flops-Major
(Meteor Man; Hero at Large; Major Payne)
Blaze, 1989, 108m, ★★★/$$, Touchstone/Touchstone, R/S-FN. The affair governor Earl Long (Paul Newman) of Louisiana had with stripper Blaze Starr (Lolita Davidovich), leading to his downfall. w. d. Ron Shelton, NF-adap. Blaze Starr.
DRAMA: COMEDY DRAMA: Biographies; True Stories; Romance-Clandestine; Romance with Married Person; Romance with Prostitute; Politicians; Scandals; Southerns; Corruption; Strippers; Overlooked at Release; Writer-Directors
(All the King's Men; The King Fish; Bull Durham)
Blazing Saddles, 1974, 90m, ★★★/$$$$$, WB/WB, R/P. A black man (Cleavon Little) is made sheriff of an old-west town run primarily by Jews (Mel

Brooks, Harvey Korman), and chaos erupts among the townspeople. Madeline Kahn (BSActress). w. Andrew Bergman, Norman Steinberg, Mel Brooks, Richard Pryor, Alan Unger, d. Mel Brooks. BOSong. Oscars: 2-0.
COMEDY: WESTERN: Spoofs; Spoofs-Western; Western Comedy; Fish Out of Water; Bathroom Humor; Cowboys; Black Men; Jewish People; Race Relations; Black Among Whites; Blockbusters (Young Frankenstein; High Anxiety; Beverly Hills Cop; Citand slickers)
(Ed: Dated but still has its moments)
Bleak Moments, 1971, 110m, ★★★/$, Autumn-Memorial-BFI/NA. Scenes from the boring and lonely lives of the inhabitants of a south London suburb. Anne Raitt, Sarah Stephenson, Eric Allan, Mike Bradwell. w. d. Mike Leigh.
DRAMA: Docudrama; Ordinary People Stories; Art Films; Multiple Stories; Suburban Life; England; British Films; Writer-Directors
(High Hopes; 28 Up)
Bless the Beasts and the Children, 1971, 110m, ★★¹/₂/$$, Col/RCA-Col, G. A group of young boys try to save a herd of buffalo from slaughter. Bill Mumy, Barry Robins, Miles Chapin, Jesse White, Ken Swofford. w. Mac Benoff, N-adap. Glendon Swarthout, d. Stanley Kramer. BOSong. Oscars: 1-0.
DRAMA: MELODRAMA: FAMILY: CHILDREN'S: Tearjerkers; Teenage Movies; Teenagers; Boyhood; Cowboys; Animal Rights; Saving Someone
Blessed Event, 1932, 84m, ★★★/$$, WB/MGM-UA. A motormouth gossip columnist mouths off once too often and finds himself in deep trouble he can't necessarily talk his way out of. Lee Tracy, Ned Sparks, Mary Brian, Dick Powell, Ruth Donnelly, w. Howard Green, P-adap. Manuel Seff, Forest Wilson, d. Roy del Ruth.
COMEDY: Screwball Comedy; Situation Comedy; Journalists; Gossips/Rumors; Time Capsules; New York Life; 1930s
Blessing, 1995, 100m, ★★★/$, Ind/NA, PG. Life on a Wisconsin for a young woman and her temperamental parents is chronicled as she dreams about California and meeting the right fellow. Melora Griffis, Carlin Glynn, Guy Griffis, Clovis Siemon, Gareth Williams, Randy Sue Latimer, Tom Carey, Frank Taylor. w. d. Paul Zehrer.

COMEDY DRAMA: Family Drama; Character Studies; Girls; Young Women; Fathers & Daughters; Farm Life; Dreams; Writer-Directors; Ind Films

Blind Ambition, 1982, 95m, ★★½/$$$, CBS/Time-Life. The life special counsel to Nixon, John Dean and his wife Mo during the Watergate crisis. Martin Sheen, Rip Torn, Theresa Russell.

DRAMA: Presidents; Scandals; True Stories; Biographies; Marriage Drama; Romance-Older Men/Younger Women; Marriage on the Rocks; Washington D.C.; TV Movies

(All the President's Men; Born Again; Nixon)

Blind Date, 1987, 95m, ★★½/$$$, Tri-Star/RCA-Col, PG-13/P. A gorgeous woman (Kim Basinger), who turns out to be a klutzy date from hell for her eager suitor (Bruce Willis), destroys his life but may actually love him-while her psychotic ex tracks them down. John Larroquette, William Daniels, Phil Hartman. w. d. Blake Edwards.

COMEDY: Comedy of Errors; Romantic Comedy; **FARCE:** Chase Movies; Dating Scene; Comedy-Slapstick; Jealousy; Romance-Triangles; One Day Stories; Writer-Directors

(Skin Deep; Fatal Instinct; Switch)

(Ed: This movie is literally all over the place, but might be fun for diehard slapstick fans)

Blindfold: Acts of Obsession: 1994, 93m, ★★/(VR), Ind/Avenue. A young woman seeing a psychiatrist decides to therapeutically explore her sexual fantasies, but it leads to murder. Shannen Doherty, Michael Woods, Judd Nelson, Kristian Alfonso. w. d. Lawrence Simeone.

SUSPENSE: Erotic Thriller; Psychologists; Hypnosis; Fantasies; Sexual Problems; **MURDER:** Nightmares; Good Premise Unfulfilled; Writer-Directors

(Dream Lover [1986]; Whispers in the Dark)

Blind Fury, 1989, 86m, ★★★/$, Col/Col, R/EV. A martial arts expert, blinded in an accident, takes on a drug cartel. Rutger Hauer, Terrance O'Quinn, Brandon Call, Noble Willingham, Lisa Blount, Nick Cassavetes. w. Charles Robert Carner, screenplay-adap. Tyozo Kasahara, d. Phillip Noyce.

ACTION: COMEDY: Action Comedy; Spoofs; Black Comedy; Blind People; Martial Arts; Good Premise Unfulfilled; Coulda Been Great; Overlooked at Release; Curiosities

REMAKE/RETREAD: Blind Justice (1994)

Blind Husbands, 1919, 98m, ★★★/$$$ (B&W, Silent), Universal/Voyager, Goodtimes. A rich American is cuckolded when an Austrian officer dallies with his wife in the Alps. Erich Von Stroheim, Sam de Grasse, Gibson Gowland, Francella Billington. w. d. Erich Von Stroheim.

DRAMA: ROMANCE: Romantic Drama; Romance-Triangles; Rich People; Americans Abroad; Austria Alps; Writer-Directors; Silent Films

Blind Side, 1993, 92m, ★★½/$$, HBO/HBO, R/V-P-S. When a couple has a hit-and-run accident in Mexico, their victim follows them home to American to try and blackmail them and rape the wife. Rutger Hauer, Ron Silver, Rebecca DeMornay. d. Geoff Murphy.

SUSPENSE: Malicious Menaces; Revenge; Death-Accidental; Rape/Rapists; Kill the Beast; Accidents; Dead-Back from the; Mexico; Yuppies; TV Movies

(Unlawful Entry; Consenting Adults)

(Ed: Okay, but run-of-the-mill for the genre)

Blind Spot, 1993, 99m, ★★½/$$, Republic/Republic, PG-13/S-P. A family drama about a mother and daughter and destruction of their lives through drugs. Joanne Woodward, Laura Linney, Fritz Weaver, Reed Diamond. w. Nina Sheingold, d. Michael Uno.

DRAMA: Drugs-Addictions; Mothers & Daughters; Family Drama; TV Movies

Blink, 1994, 106m, ★★★/$$, Col/Col, R/S-P-V. A cornea transplant has visions with her new eyes, but only a day after she's witnessed something. So when she sees the man who kills her neighbor, how long will it be until he figures out he meant to kill her instead-and will the cop in love with her stop him? Madeleine Stowe, Aidan Quinn, Laurie Metcalf, James Remar. w. Dana Stevens, d. Michael Apted.

SUSPENSE: Psychological Thriller; Women in Jeopardy; Organ Donors; Organ Donor Murder; **MURDER: MYS-TERY: MURDER MYSTERY:** Witness to Murder; Blind People; Serial Killers; Detectives-Police; Romance-Unprofessional; Female Screenwriters; Female Protagonists; Good Premise Unfulfilled

(Wait Until Dark; Jennifer 8; Hear No Evil; Criminal Law; The Donor)

(Ed: Good idea with nice touches, but full of plotholes and makes Chicago look very ugly)

Bliss, 1985, 93m, ★★½/$, New World/ New World, PG. A heart attack prompts an advertising executive to reassess his life. In doing so, he finds that his wife and children are monsters that he can't abide, so he leaves them to "follow his bliss." Barry Otto, Lynette Curran, Helen Jones, Miles Buchanan, Gia Carides, Tim Robertson, Jeff Truman, Bryan Marshall. w. Ray Lawrence, Peter Carey, N-adap. Peter Carey, d. Ray Lawrence.

DRAMA: Family Stories; Marriage on the Rocks; Death-Dealing with; Redemption; Near-Death Experience; Midlife Crisis; Life Transitions; Starting Over; Advertising World; Australian Films; Quiet Little Films

(All That Jazz; Heart Condition)

The Bliss of Mrs. Blossom, 1968, 93m, ★★★/$$, Par/Par, S. In swinging London, a housewife keeps her lover in the attic. Hilarity ensues from his near-collisions with her husband. Richard Attenborough, Shirley MacLaine, James Booth, Freddie Jones, Patricia Routledge. w. Alec Coppel, Denis Norden, d. Joe McGrath.

COMEDY: Romantic Comedy; Romance-Triangles; Cheating Women; Hiding Out; Overlooked at Release; Hidden Gems; Good Premise Unfulfilled; Female Protagonists; England; Americans Abroad

(Ed: A quirky curiosity, especially good for MacLaine fans)

Blithe Spirit, 1946, 96m, ★★★★/$$$, 20th/Fox, Lebell Video. A man (Rex Harrison) who's remarried now has the rapier wit of a ghost haunting him now that he's remarried-the ghost of his ex-wife. Kay Hammond, Constance Cummings, Margaret Rutherford, Hugh Wakefield, Joyce Carey, Jacqueline Clark. w. Noel Coward, David Lean, Anthony Havelock-Allan, Ronald Neame, P-adap. Noel Coward, d. David Lean. **BSFX.** Oscars: 1-1.

COMEDY: Comedy of Manners; Fantasy; Screwball Comedy; Romantic Comedy; Romance-Triangles; Wives-Troublesome; Ghosts; Roommates from Hell; Fortunetellers; What If Stories; British Films

(Kiss Me Goodbye; Ghost; The Ghost & Mrs. Muir; Topper; The Scoundrel; Truly, Madly, Deeply)

(Ed: Many stick to the stage version as the best, but the look here is certainly great. Lean also had *Brief Encounter* the same year)

The Blob, 1958, 86m, ★★★1/2/$$$, Par/Par, G. A UFO drops off something that keeps growing and eating Steve McQueen's little town. Steve McQueen, Aneta Corseaut, Olin Howlin, Earl Rowe. w. Theodore Simonson, Kate Phillips, d. Irwin S. Yeaworth Jr.

HORROR: SUSPENSE: Rogue Plots; Human Eaters; Deaths-One by One; Teenagers; Small-Town Life; Paranoia; 1950s Movie Theaters; Female Screenwriters

SEQUELS/REMAKES: Beware of the Blob, The Blob (1988)

(Ed: One of the best teen sci-fi horror flicks, especially worth it for the early McQueen)

The Blob, 1988, 92m, ★★/$, Tri-Star/Col-Tri, PG-13/V-P. Update of the 50s classic. Kevin Dillon, Shawnee Smith, Donovan Leitch, Jeffrey DeMunn, Candy Clark, Joe Seneca. w. Chuck Russell, Frank Darabout, d. Chuck Russell.

HORROR: SUSPENSE: Rogue Plots; Human Eaters; Deaths-One by One; Teenagers; Small-Town Life; Paranoia

REMAKE OF: The Blob (1958)

(Ed: The special effects may be better, but that's about it)

Blockade, 1938, 84m, ★★1/2/$, Walter Wanger-UA/NA. A pacifist farmer is called to arms during the Spanish Civil War. Henry Fonda, Madeleine Carroll, Leo Carrillo, John Halliday, Vladimir Sokoloff, Reginald Denny. w. John Howard Lawson, d. William Dieterle.

DRAMA: War Stories; Soldiers; Farm Life; Spanish Civil War; Spain; Peaceful People

(Friendly Persuasion; For Whom the Bell Tolls)

Blonde Venus, 1932, 97m, ★★★/$$$$, Par/Par. An English research chemist has a lot on his hands when he marries a sexy German lounge singer who strays far from home. Marlene Dietrich, Herbert Marshall, Cary Grant, Dickie Moore. w. Jules Furthman, S. K. Lauren, d. Joseph Von Sternberg.

DRAMA: MELODRAMA: ROMANCE: Romantic Drama; Tearjerkers; Marriage

Drama; Cheating Women; Midlife Crisis; Singers; Journies; Ahead of its Time; Women Who Leave; Runaways; Housewives; Romance; Love

(Blue Angel; Anna Christie)

Blondie, 1938, 68m, ★★1/2/$$$, Col/Movies Unltd. Based on the popular comic strip, this story of a harried suburban family man and his ditzy blond wife had some well-observed domestic comedy mixed in with the usual stereotypes of the period. Arthur Lake, Penny Singleton, Larry Simms, Daisy the Dog, Jonathan Hale, Gene Lockhart. w. Richard Flournoy, comic strip-adap. Chick Young, d. Frank R. Strayer.

COMEDY: Screwball Comedy; Domestic Life; Comic Heroes; Suburban Life; Wives-Troublesome; Simple Minds; Young Men

SEQUELS: some two dozen short films, then two TV series in the 50s and 60s

Blood Alley, 1955, 115m, ★★1/2/$$$, WB/WB. An American sailor unjustly imprisoned in China escapes with the help of sympathetic Chinese, whom he in turn escorts to Hong Kong. John Wayne, Lauren Bacall, Paul Fix, Joy Kim, Anita Ekberg. w. N-adap. A. S. Fleischmann, d. William Wellman.

DRAMA: MELODRAMA: Escape Drama; Prison Escapes; Prison Drama; Accused Unjustly; POWs: Sailors; China; Hong Kong

(The Barbarian and the Geisha; The Conqueror)

Blood and Black Lace, 1964, 90m, ★★/$, Emmepi-Ind/Media. In a fashion designer's studio, women turn up murdered in gruesome ways. Cameron Mitchell, Thomas Reiner, Mary Arden. w. Marcel Fondato, Giuseppe Barilla, Mario Bava, d. Mario Bava.

HORROR: SUSPENSE: MURDER: Murders-One by One; Murders of Women; Serial Killers; Trail of a Killer; Fashion World; Camp; Unintentionally Funny; Forgotten Films; Ind Films

(Peeping Tom; Lady Beware; The Eyes of Laura Mars)

Blood and Concrete, 1990, 96m, ★★★/VR, IRS/Col, R/EP-S-EV-FRN. A con-man (Billy Zane) is on the lam from drug dealers wanting a sex wonder-drug after a scumbag he tried to steal from turns up dead and he winds up running into a suicidal woman (Jennifer Beals) who's a nymphomaniac when she's not

trying to off herself or ex-boyfriends. Darren McGavin, James LeGros. w. Richard LaBrie, Jeffrey Reiner, d. Reiner.

COMEDY: ACTION: Action Comedy; Black Comedy; Film Noir-Modern; Eccentric; People; Promiscuity; Sexy Women; Sexy Men; Drugs-Dealing; Homosexual Murderers; Gay Men; Los Angeles; L.A. 90s; Indies Overlooked; Underrated; Coulda Been Great; Coincidences; Ind Films

(Quick; Floundering; Inside Monkey Zetterland)

(Ed: Great cutting-edge humor, situations and characters the word quirky doesn't begin to do justice to, though it's an acquired taste. Jennifer Beals may not have been able to flashdance, but she can sing)

Blood and Sand, 1922, 80m (Silent, B&W), Par/Republic, Nos. A Spanish noblewoman is pursued and finally won over by a lowly matador. Rudolph Valentino, Nita Naldi, Lila Lee Walter Long. w. June Mathis, N-adap. Vicente Blasco Ibanez, d. Fred Niblo.

Female Screenwriters

Blood and Sand, 1941, 123m, 20th/Fox. Remake of above. Tyrone Power, Rita Hayworth, Linda Darnell, Nazimova, Anthony Quinn, John Carradine, Monty Banks. w. Jo Swerling, N-adap. Vicente Blasco Ibanez, d. Rouben Mamoulian.

ROMANCE: DRAMA: MELODRAMA: Romantic Drama; Latin People; Bullfighting; Lyrical Films; Spain

Bloodbath at the House of Death, 1983, 92m, EMI-Wildwood/Genesis, R/B&G-V. Scientists try to quantify the goings-on at a haunted house. Kenny Everett, Pamela Stephenson, Vincent Price, Gareth Hunt, Don Warrington, John Fortune. w. Ray Cameron, Barry Cryer, d. Ray Cameron.

HORROR: Haunted Houses; Supernatural Danger; Scientists; Ghosts; British Films; England

(Poltergeist; The Haunting; The Green Man)

Blood Beach, 1980, 90m, ★★/$, Ind/Media, R/V-B&G. Swimmers are disappearing mysteriously when it is discovered that a monster lurks below the sand waiting to suck them down. David Huffman, Marianna Hill, Jon Saxon, Otis Young, Burt Young. w. Jeffrey Bloom, SS-adap. Jeffrey Bloom, Steven Nalevansky, d. Jeffrey Bloom.

HORROR: Horror Comedy; Spoofs; Deaths-One by One; Beach Movies; Camp

SPOOF OF: Jaws

Blood Beast Terror, 1969, 81m, ★★/$, Tigon/Monterey, R. A scientist in Victorian England creates half-human/half-moth creatures who kill and wreak havoc generally. Robert Flemyng, Peter Cushing, Wanda Ventham, Vanessa Howard. w. Peter Bryan, d. Vernon Sewell.

HORROR: Scientists-Mad; Experiments; Humans into Animals; Animal Monsters; Murders-One by One; British Films

Bloodbrothers, 1978, 116m, ★★★/$$, Par/Par, R/V-P. The tensions build up to the boiling point in an Italian-American family in New York when one of the sons decides to leave the family business. Paul Sorvino, Tony Lo Bianco, Richard Gere, Lelia Goldoni. w. Walter Newman, N-adap. Richard Price, d. Robert Mulligan.

DRAMA: Family Stories; Family Drama; Brothers; Italians; New York Life
(Family Business [1986]; Harry and Son)

Blood Feud, 1979, 112m, ★★1/2/$$, UA/Fox, R/S-V. An Italian socialist and a petty thief seek the affections of the same Sicilian woman against the backdrop of the rise of fascism in Italy. Sophia Loren, Marcello Mastroianni, Giancarlo Giannini, Mario Scarpetta. w. d. Lina Wertmuller.

DRAMA: MELODRAMA: ROMANCE: Romance-Triangles; Feisty Females; Female Screenwriters; Female Directors; Writer-Directors
(Marriage, Italian Style; A Special Day)

Blood from the Mummy's Tomb, 1971, 94m, ★★★/$$, Hammer-MGM/NA. Members of a British expedition team to Egypt are killed one by one by the daughter of their leader, who is possessed by the spirit of the mummified Egyptian princess they brought back to England with them. Andrew Keir, Valerie Leon, James Villiers, Hugh Burden, Rosalie Crutchley, Aubrey Morris, David Markham. w. Christopher Wicking, N-adap. Bram Stoker, (*Jewel of the Seven Stars*), d. Seth Holt, Michael Carreras.

HORROR: MURDER: Deaths-One by One; Murderers-Female; Egypt; Archaeologists; Serial Killers; Mummies; Possessions; British Films; Overlooked at Release; Underrated

(The Awakening; The Mummy; The Mummy's Hand; Curse of the Mummy)

Bloodfist, 1989, 85m, ★1/2/$$, Concorde/MGM-UA, R/EV-P. A kick-boxer plans to beat his brother's killers. Don "The Dragon" Wilson, Joe Marie Avellana, Michael Shaner. w. Robert King, d. Terence H. Winkless.
Female Screenwriters

Bloodfist II, 1990, 88m, ★1/2/$$, Concorde/MGM-UA, R/EV-P. To complete a rescue, a kickboxer must infiltrate an island fortress. Don "The Dragon" Wilson, Rina Reyes, Joe Marie Avellana, Robert Marius. w. Catherine Cyran, d. Andy Blumenthal.
Female Screenwriters

Bloodfist III, 1992, 88m, ★1/2/$, Concorde/New Horizons, R/EV-P. A kick-boxer, imprisoned for a crime he didn't commit, defends his friend against other inmates. Don "The Dragon" Wilson, Richard Roundtree, Gregory McKinney, Rick Dean. w. Allison Burnett, Charles Mattera, d. Oley Sassone.

ACTION: Sports Movies; Men in Conflict; Martial Arts; Female Screen-writers

Bloodhounds of Broadway, 1952, 90m, ★★★/$$, 20th/NA. A soft-hearted gangster helps an orphan girl "put on a show" using her dogs; it becomes a hit. Mitzi Gaynor, Scott Brady, Mitzi Green, Marguerite Chapman, Michael O'Sheaw. w. Sy Gomberg, SS-adap. Damon Runyan, d. Harmon Jones.

COMEDY DRAMA: MELODRAMA: Multiple Stories; Mob Stories; Streetlife; Ordinary People Stories; New Year's Eve; New York Life; All-Star Casts

Bloodhounds of Broadway, 1989, 101m, ★★1/2/$ (LR), AP-PBS/Col, PG. A series of Damon Runyan stories involving gangsters, dames, and other low-lifes, all coming together on New Year's Eve, 1928. Josef Sommer, Madonna, Tony Azito, Jennifer Grey, Tony Longo, Rutger Hauer, Matt Dillon, Julie Hagerty, Randy Quaid, William Burroughs. w. d. Howard Brookner, SS-adap. Damon Runyan
TV Movies

COMEDY DRAMA: MELODRAMA: Multiple Stories; Mob Stories; Streetlife; Ordinary People Stories; New Year's Eve; New York Life; All-Star Casts
(Guys and Dolls; Little Miss Marker; Sorrowful Jones)
(Ed: The 1989 version is more true to the

stories and far more expansive, though not as entertaining)

Bloodline, 1979, 117m, ★★/$$$, Par/Par, R/P-S-FN. Audrey Hepburn must find out who murdered her father, a pharmaceutical tycoon, before they murder *her*. Audrey Hepburn, Ben Gazzara, James Mason, Claudia Mori, Omar Sharif, Irene Papas, Romy Shneider. w. Laird Koenig, N-adap. Sidney Sheldon, d. Terence Young.

MELODRAMA: MYSTERY: MURDER: Women in Jeopardy; Murder-Attempted; Fathers & Daughters; Avenging Death of a Loved One; Fashion World; Pornography World; Rich People-Decadent
(The Naked Face; Scruples; Mistral's Daughter; Rage of Angels)

Blood of a Poet, 1931, 58m, ★★★/$$, Vicomte de Noailles/Voyager, Hollywood Home. A poet has visions while, above him, a chimney falls off the roof. Lee Miller, Enrique Rivero, Pauline Carton, Feral Benga, Barbette. w. d. Jean Cocteau.

DRAMA: Poets; Writers; Illusions; Art Films; Avant Garde; Surrealism; Hidden Gems; Writer-Directors; Film History
(Beauty and the Beast [1946]; Orpheus)

Blood on Satan's Claw, 1970, 93m, ★★1/2/$$, Tigon-Chilton/MGM-UA. A devil's claw artifact is found by children in a 17th-century English village, leading to supernatural chaos. Patrick Wymark, Linda Hayden, Barry Andrews, Tamara Ustinov. w. Robert Wynne-Simmons, d. Piers Haggard.

HORROR: Satanism; Possessions; 1600s; England; Child Protagonists

Blood on the Moon, 1948, 88m, ★★1/2/$$, RKO/Media, Turner. A cowboy is betrayed by the man who he thought was his best friend, but who in fact is an evil cattle rustler. Robert Mitchum, Barbara Bel Geddes, Robert Preston, Walter Brennan. w. Lillie Hayward, N-adap. Luke Short, d. Robert Wise.

WESTERNS: Cowboys; Cattle Rustlers; Friends as Enemies; Betrayals; Female Screenwriters
(The Violent Men; Forty Guns; Abilene Town)

Blood on the Sun, 1945, 98m, ★★★/$$$, Cagney-UA/Nos. An American editor in Tokyo reveals a Japanese plot for world domination long before World War II. James Cagney,

Sylvia Sidney, Wallace Ford, Rosemary de Camp. w. Lester Cole, d. Frank Lloyd. **BB&WArt.** Oscars: 1-1.

DRAMA: SUSPENSE: Detective Stories; Americans Abroad; Journalists; Conspiracy; Rule the World-Plot to; Japanese as Enemy

Blood Relatives, 1977, 100m, ★★/$, Cinevideo-Filmel/Cin Int'l, R/V. A young girl accuses her brother of murdering their cousin. Donald Sutherland, Stephane Audran, Micheline Lanctot, Aude Landry, Lisa Langlois, Donald Pleasence, David Hemmings. w. Claude Chabrol, Sydney Banks, N-adap. Ed McBain, d. Claude Chabrol.

SUSPENSE: Psychological Thriller; **MYSTERY: MURDER: MURDER MYSTERY:** Murderers-Child; Accused Unjustly; Framed?; Brothers & Sisters; Cousins; International Casts; French Films

Blood Simple, 1984, 97m, ★★★½/$$$, Circle/MCA-U, R/EV-P-S. A couple (Frances McDormand, John Getz) are having an affair behind her husband's back and when they decide to kill him, he may not stay dead. M. Emmet Walsh. w. Joel and Ethan Coen, d. Joel Coen.

SUSPENSE: THRILLER: MURDER: Black Comedy; Comedy-Morbid; Hide the Dead Body; Dead-Back from the; Buried Alive; Romance with Married Person; Romance-Triangles; Cheating Women; Jealousy; Sleeper Hits; Cult Films; Texas; Hidden Gems
(Diabolique; The Trouble with Harry; Buried Alive; Barton Fink; Miller's Crossing; Fargo)
(Ed: A truly innovative black comic thriller, though it loses its punch after the first go-round)

Bloodsport, 1987, 92m, ★★/$$, Cannon/WB. An American kickboxing and martial arts expert enters a secret competition in Hong Kong, where he gets his kicks. Jean Claude Van Damme, Donald Gibb, Leah Ayres, Forest Whitaker. w. Sheldon Lettich, Christopher Crosby, Mel Friedman, d. Newt Arnold.

ACTION: Sports Movies; Martial Arts; Contest/Competitions; Hong Kong
(Bloodfist SERIES; Kickboxer SERIES; The Challenge)

Bloody Mama, 1970, 90m, ★★★/$$, AIP/Vestron, Live. During the Depression, a gang consisting of Kate

Barker and her four sons wreak havoc on the countryside until they reach their bitter end. Shelley Winters, Pat Hingle, Don Stroud, Diane Varsi, Bruce Dern, Robert De Niro. w. Robert Thom, d. Roger Corman.

ACTION: Crime Drama; **TRAGEDY:** Crime Sprees; Mothers & Sons; Criminal Biographies; Criminal Mothers; Southerns; Depression Era; Female Protagonists; Arkansas
(Big Bad Mama; White Heat; Bonnie and Clyde; Boxcar Bertha)

Blossoms in the Dust, 1941, 99m, ★★★/$$$$, MGM/MGM-UA. A woman whose child and husband die starts an orphanage. Greer Garson (BActress), Walter Pidgeon, Felix Bressart, Marsha Hunt, Fay Holden. w. Anita Loos (based on the life of Edna Gladney), d. Mervyn Le Roy. BPicture, **BCArt,** BCCin. Oscars: 4-1.

MELODRAMA: Tearjerkers; True Stories; Biographies; Orphans; Social Drama; Female Protagonists; Female Screenwriters
(The Bells of St. Mary's; Mrs. Miniver; Pollyanna; Jane Eyre; Boys Town)
(Ed: Once again, Garson is impossibly sweet and benevolent, but it works for those who want an old-fashioned weepy)

Blow Out, 1981, 107m, ★★½/$$, FWA-Orion/WB, R/V-P-S. A sound technician (John Travolta) just happens to have taped a piece of conversation revealing the murder of a politician. Nancy Allen, John Lithgow. w. d. Brian DePalma.

SUSPENSE: MURDER MYSTERY: MYSTERY: Murder-Discovering; Witness to Murder; Conspiracy; Politicians; Surveillance

REMAKE/RETREAD OF: Blow Up; The Conversation
(Blow Up; The Conversation; The Parallax View; Body Double; Dressed to Kill)
(Ed: Very derivative but worth a look for some, in fact, some are obsessed with it)

Blow Up, 1966, 111m, ★★★★/$$$$, MGM/MGM-UA, R/S-FN. A hip, mod photographer (David Hemmings) in London may have photographed clues to a murder, but will he figure them out before he's driven insane? Vanessa Redgrave, Sarah Miles. w. Tonino Guerra, Michelangelo Antonioni, d. Antonioni.

MYSTERY: MURDER MYSTERY: Art Films; Avant Garde; Detectives-Amateur; Murder-Discovering; Mod Era; Photographers; Beautiful People; 1960s British Films; Hidden Gems; Film History; Cult Films

REMAKE/RETREAD: Blow Out
(The Conversation; Blow Out; L'Avventura; Zabriskie Point; Peeping Tom; The Idol; Darling; Morgan!)

Blowing Wild, 1953, 88m, ★★½/$$, WB/Republic. Against the backdrop of Mexican oil fields, a love triangle develops between a driller and the mentally unstable wife of an old friend. Gary Cooper, Barbara Stanwyck, Anthony Quinn, Ruth Roman, Ward Bond. w. Philip Yordan, d. Hugo Fregonese.

DRAMA: MELODRAMA: ROMANCE: Romance with Friend's Lover; Romance-Triangles; Mental Illness; Oil People; Mexico
(Bordertown; Out of the Past; The Furies)

Blown Away, 1994, 121m, ★★★/$$, MGM/MGM-UA, R/EV-P. An IRA bomb expert is after a former fellow terrorist who's now a renegade bomber. Jeff Bridges, Tommy Lee Jones, Suzy Amis, Lloyd Bridges, Forest Whitaker. w. Joe Battner, John Rice, d. Stephen Hopkins.

ACTION: SUSPENSE: Action Drama; Bombs; IRA; Terrorists; Chase Stories; Manhunts; Flops-Major; Coulda Been Great
(Nighthawks; Patriot Games)
(Ed: Goes over some tired territory in a more intelligent, though less entertaining way)

Blue, 1994, 76m, ★★½/$, Ind/New Yorker. The last days of experimental director Derek Jarman are chronicled against a blue screen by narration only. Derek Jarman. w. d. Jarman.

DRAMA: Art Films; Avant-Garde Films; Autobiographical Stories; Biographies; Directors; British Films; Writer-Directors
(The Garden; Edward II)

The Blue Angel, 1930, 103m, ★★★★/$$$$, 20th/Nos, Fox. A middle-aged professor (Emil Jannings) becomes obsessed with a singer (Marlene Dietrich) who could care less. w. Robert Liebmann, Karl Zuckmayer, Karl Vollmoeler, N-adap. Heinrich Mann (*Professor Unrath*), d. Josef Von Sternberg.

The Blue Angel, 1959, 107m, ★★/$, 20th/NA. A remake of above, with a more "realistic" tone. Curt Jurgens, May Britt,

Theodore Bikel, John Banner. w. Nigel Balchin, N-adap. Heinrich Mann, (*Professor Unrath*), d. Edward Dmytryk.

DRAMA: MELODRAMA: ROMANCE: Romantic Drama; Romance-Boy Wants Girls; Obsessions; Singers; Extroverts vs. Introverts
(Manpower; Blonde Venus; Ball of Fire; Death in Venice; Exotica)

The Blue Bird, (Color) 1940, 88m, ★★★/$$$, 20th/Fox. A little girl (Shirley Temple) searches for a mythical bird which will bring untold happiness. Spring Byington, w. Ernest Pascal, P-adap. Maurice Maeterlinck, d. Walter Lang.

CHILDREN'S: Fantasy; Journeys; Birds; Cats; Heaven; Child Protagonists; Female Protagonists

REMAKE OF: 1918 version

REMAKE: 1976

The Blue Bird, 1976, 99m, ★★¹/₂/$ (LR), 20th/NA. Remake. Patsy Kensit, Jane Fonda, Elizabeth Taylor, Todd Lookinland, Ava Gardner, Cicely Tyson, Will Geer. w. Hugh Whitemore, Alfred Hayes, P-adap. Maurice Maeterlinck, d. George Cukor.

CHILDREN'S: Fantasy; Journeys; Birds; Cats; Heaven; Child Protagonists; Female Protagonists; All-Star Casts

REMAKE OF: 1940 version
(The Wizard of Oz; The Wiz; The Magic Flute)

Blue Chips, 1994, 108m, ★★¹/₂/$, Par/Par, PG-13/P-S. A coach in his first losing season has to choose between the collegiate powers pushing him to buy players and his own integrity. Nick Nolte, Mary McDonnell, Shaquille O'Neal, Alfre Woodard, Ed O'Neill, J. T. Walsh, Larry Bird, Bobby Knight. w. Ron Shelton, d. William Friedkin.

DRAMA: Sports Movies; Coaches; Basketball; White Among Blacks; Black Men; Midlife Crisis; Ethics; Corruption
(Hoosiers; Slap Shot; The Program; Celtic Pride)

Blue City, 1986, 83m, ★¹/₂/$, Par/Par, R/P-V-S. A fellow returns to his Southern small town and tries to avenge his father's murder, becoming a vigilante to do so. Judd Nelson, Ally Sheedy, Paul Winfield, Anita Morris, David Caruso, Julie Carmen. w. Walter Hill, Lukas Heller, d. Michelle Manning.

DRAMA: Crime Drama; Revenge; Vigilantes; Southerns; Small-Town Life; Unintentionally Funny; Bratpack Movies

Blue Collar, 1978, 114m, ★★★¹/₂/$ (LR), U/MCA-U, R/EP-S. The lives of several factory workers in Detroit are chronicled as their lives change and deteriorate on the assembly line until one worker (Richard Pryor) gets the idea to rob the factory safe. Richard Pryor, Harvey Keitel, Yaphet Khotto, Ed Begley Jr. w. Paul Schrader, Leonard Schrader, d. Paul Schrader.

DRAMA: Social Drama; Ensemble Films; Heist Stories; Revenge; Worker vs. Boss; Unions; Ordinary People Stories; Factory Workers; Fighting for Rights; Friendships-Interracial; Strikes
Overlooked at Release; Hidden Gem
(On the Waterfront; Matewan; Norma Rae; Straight Time; Silkwood)

The Blue Dahlia, 1946, 99m, ★★★/$$$, Par/Par. A soldier returns from World War II to find his unfaithful wife murdered and himself the prime suspect. Alan Ladd, Veronica Lake, William Bendix, Howard da Silva, Doris Dowling. w. Raymond Chandler, d. George Marshall.

MYSTERY: MURDER: MURDER MYSTERY: SUSPENSE: Soldiers; Cheating Women; Suspecting Oneself; Saving Oneself; Film Noir; Accused Unjustly; Framed? Fugitives from the Law
(The Glass Key; This Gun for Hire; The Black Angel)

Blue Denim, 1959, 89m, ★★★/$$$, 20th/NA. A young unmarried girl considers an abortion, but her boyfriend may do right by her if coerced. Carol Lynley, Brandon de Wilde, Macdonald Carey. w. Edith Sommer, Philip Dunne, P-adap. James Leo Herlihy, William Noble, d. Philip Dunne.

DRAMA: MELODRAMA: Abortion Dilemmas; Teenagers; Teenage Movies; Marriages-Forced; Faded Hits; Forgotten Films; Ahead of Its Time
(To Find a Man; Peyton Place; Return to Peyton Place; Love with a Proper Stranger) (Ed: Scandalous in its day)

Blue Hawaii, 1961, 101m, ★★¹/₂/$$$$, UA/CBS-Fox. Elvis plays a G.I. on leave in Honolulu, with the requisite romance and music following. Elvis Presley, Joan Blackman, Nancy Walters, Roland Winters, Angela Lansbury. w. Hal Kanter, d. Norman Taurog.

COMEDY DRAMA: ROMANCE: Teenagers; Teenage Movies; Music Movies; Singers; Hawaii; Soldiers

Blue Ice, 1992, 105m, ★★¹/₂/$$, HBO/HBO, R/P-S. A nightclub owner's secret past as a spy comes out when a routine request from his mistress leads him into international intrigue. Michael Caine, Sean Young, Ian Holm, Bobby Short, Patricia Hayes, Bob Hoskins. w. Ron Hutchinson, N-adap. Ted Allbeury, d. Russell Mulcahy.

SUSPENSE: MURDER: Conspiracy; Heist Stories; Secret Agents; Romance-Older Men/Younger Women; Mistresses; Missing Persons; Arms Dealers; Unintentionally Funny
(Half Moon Street; Green Ice)

Blue Iguana, 1988, 88m, ★★¹/₂/$, Par/Par, R/S-V. A private eye goes south of the border, but his naivete gets him into more trouble than it's worth to solve the case of a imbezzler. Dylan McDermott, Jessica Harper, James Russo, Dean Stockwell, Pamela Goley, Tovah Feldshuh. w. d. John Lafia.

COMEDY: Spoofs-Detective; Detective Stories; Detectives-Private; Central America; Chase Stories; Bank Robberies; Thieves; Coulda Been Good

Blue in the Face, 1995, 90m, ★★★/$, Miramax/Miramax, R/P-S. The characters who inhabit the New York City neighborhood in and around a cigar store drift past. Harvey Keitel, Lou Reed, Roseanne, Jim Jarmusch, Lily Tomlin, Michael J. Fox, Mel Gorham, Mira Sorvino, Madonna, RuPaul. w. Wayne Wang and Paul Auster, d. Wayne Wang, Paul Auster.

COMEDY: COMEDY DRAMA: Streetlife; Inner-City Life; Homeless People; Ordinary People Stories; Improvisational Films; New York Life

SEQUEL TO: Smoke
(Smoke; Bloodhounds on Broadway; Five Corners)

The Blue Lagoon, 1948, 103m, ★★★/$$, U/NA. More tame and romantic earlier version of shipwrecked youthful love. Jean Simmons, Donald Houston, Noel Purcell, Cyril Cusack. w. Frank Launder, John Baines, Michael Hogan, N-adap. H. de vere Stacpole, d. Launder.

The Blue Lagoon, 1980, 102m, ★★/$$$$, Col/RCA-Col, R/S-FN-MN. Tale of two children stranded on a desert isle and how they grow up and discover love but not clothes. Brooke Shields, Christopher Atkins, Leo McKern,

William Daniels. w. Douglas Day Stewart, d. Randal Kleiser. BCin. Oscars: 1-0.
DRAMA: ROMANCE: Stranded; Stranded on an Island; Islands; Coming of Age; Love-Firsts; Young People; Sexuality; South Pacific
REMAKE OF: 1948 version; **SEQUEL:** Return to the Blue Lagoon
(Hurricane; Paradise; Summer Lovers)
(Ed: Only interesting to those of an age usually not allowed to see it)
The Blue Lamp, 1949, 84m, ★★/$$, Ealing/Facets. A young police trainee is shocked when his mentor is killed in a shootout, but he apprehends the killer and brings him to justice. Jack Warner, Jimmy Hanley, Dirk Bogarde, Meredith Edwards, Patrick Doogan, Peggy Evans. w. T.E.B. Clarke, d. Basil Dearden.
DRAMA: Crime Drama; **MURDER:** Police Stories; Death-Dealing with; Trail of a Killer; Detectives-Police; Avenging Death of Loved One; Friendships-Male; Mentors
The Blue Max, 1966, 156m, ★★/$$$, 20th/Fox. A fighter pilot in World War I steals the wife of his commanding officer. George Peppard, James Mason, Ursula Andress, Jeremy Kemp. w. David Pursall, Jack Seddon, Gerald Hanley, N-adap. Jack Hunter, d. John Guillermin.
ACTION: War Stories; Romance-Triangles; Cheating Women; Traitors; Betrayals; Evil Men; Young Men; Revenge; Pilots-Military; World War I Era
Blue Monkey, 1987, 97m, ★ 1/2/$, Col/Col, R/V-P-S. An alien-infected plant impregnates a man with its seeds, then the man becomes a plant monster. Steve Railsback, Susan Anspach, Joe Flaherty. d. William Fuest.
SCI-FI: HORROR: Aliens-Outer Space, Evil; Babies-Men Having; Monsters-Human; Parasites; Plants
(Day of the Triffids; Invasion of the Body Snatchers)
The Blues Brothers, 1980, 113m, ★★★/$$$$, Universal/MCA-U, R/P-V-S. The white soul singers of *Saturday Night Live* fame race through and wreck Chicago while performing in between car chases and multitudinous crashes. Dan Ackroyd, John Belushi, Aretha Franklin, James Brown, Ray Charles, John Candy. w. John Landis, Dan Aykroyd, d. John Landis.
COMEDY: ACTION: Action Comedy; Chase Movies; **FARCE:** Comedy of Errors; Fugitives from Law; Fugitives; Car Chases; Car Wrecks; SNL Movies; Saturday Night Live Movies; Comedy-Skit; Singers; Brothers; Musicians; Chicago
(Neighbors; Into the Night; 1941)
(Ed: Car chase and wreck fanatics take note)
Blues in the Night, 1941, 88m, ★★ 1/2/$$, WB/WB. The romantic and musical adventures of a travelling jazz band. Priscilla Lane, Richard Whorf, Lloyd Nolan, Betty Field, Elia Kazan, Wallace Ford. w. Robert Rossen, P-adap. Edwin Gilbert (*Hot Nocturne*), Anatole Litvak. BOSong. Oscars: 1-0.
MELODRAMA: Musicians; Music Band Life; Ensemble Films; Jazz Life; Road Movies
Blue Sky, 1991/1994, 101m, ★★★/$, Orion/Orion, R/S-P-FN. A manic depressive wife of an Army nuclear testing engineer is coming apart at the seams with the restrictive nature of their life. But when her husband is framed in the Blue Sky project by a man she had an affair with, it's up to her to pull herself together to get him cleared. Jessica Lange (BActress), Tommy Lee Jones, Amy Locane, Powers Boothe, Chris O'Donnell. w. Rama Laurie Stagner, Arlene Sarner, Jerry Leichtling, d. Tony Richardson. Oscars: 1-1.
DRAMA: Character Studies; Marriage Drama; Mothers & Daughters; Sexy Women; Mental Illness; Cheating Women; Military Stories; Nuclear Energy; Committed-Wrongly; Bombs-Atomic; Conspiracy; Ethics; Coulda Been Great; 1960s Nostalgia; Jessica Lange Goes Southern; Hidden Gems; Overlooked at Release; Female Protagonists; Female Screenwriters
(Sweet Dreams; Diary of a Mad Housewife)
(Ed: Although it wraps up too neatly and happily, Lange's enchanting, detailed performance and the world the film creates makes this well worth seeing. It's unfortunate they didn't stick to a simpler, more profound character study. Originally produced in 1991, it was shelved due to Orion's bankruptcy and released after director Richardson's death)
Blue Steel, 1988, 102m, ★★ 1/2/$$, Vestron/Vestron, R/EV-P-S. A woman cop (Jamie Lee Curtis) is stalked by a killer she's tracking (Ron Silver). w. Kathryn Bigelow, Eric Red, d. Kathryn Bigelow.
SUSPENSE: MURDER: Serial Killers; Trail of a Killer; Stalkers; Psycho Killers; Female Law Officers; Women in Jeopardy; Female Protagonists; Female Directors; Camp; Unintentionally Funny; Female Screenwriters
(Silence of the Lambs; Black Widow)
Blue Thunder, 1983, 110m, ★★ 1/2/$$$$, Col/RCA-Col, R/V-P-FN. A Vietnam veteran has flashbacks when working as a cop in a special high-tech Los Angeles helicopter crew. Roy Scheider, Warren Oates, Candy Clark, Daniel Stern, Malcolm McDowell. w. Dan O'Bannon, Don Jakoby, d. John Badham.
ACTION: Action Drama; **SUSPENSE:** Crime Drama; Chase Movies; Police Stories; Pilots; Vietnam Veterans; Los Angeles; Voyeurs; Mental Illness; Nervous Breakdowns; Faded Hits
The Blue Veil, 1951, 114m, ★★ 1/2/$$$, RKO/Turner. A pediatric nurse descends into poverty, only to be lifted up by her former patients. Jane Wyman (BActress), Charles Laughton, Richard Carlson, Joan Blondell, Agnes Moorehead (BSActress), Cyril Cusack, Natalie Wood. w. Norman Corwin, S-adap. François Campaux (*Le Voile Bleu*), d. Curtis Bernhardt. Oscars: 2-0.
MELODRAMA: DRAMA: Tearjerkers; Saving Someone; Depression; Riches to Rags Nurses; Female Protagonists
(All That Heaven Allows; Magnificent Obsession; Lady for a Day; Pocketful of Miracles; The Snake Pit; Not as a Stranger)
Blue Velvet, 1986, 120m, ★★★ 1/2/$, DEG/Lorimar-WB, R/EP-EV-S-FFN-MRN. A youngman (Kyle MacLachlan) home to see his sick father finds a human ear in a field and soon finds himself being drawn in by the underworld of his little town. Laura Dern, Isabella Rosellini, Dennis Hopper, Dean Stockwell. w. d. David Lynch (BDirector). Oscars: 1-0.
MYSTERY: MURDER MYSTERY: Art Films; Comic Thriller; Black Comedy; Comedy-Morbid; Film Noir-Modern; Murder-Discovering; Small-Town life; Underworld; Southerns; Corruption; American Myth; Romance-Forbidden; Romance-Dangerous; Romance-Triangles; Romance-Older Women/Younger Men; Abused Women; Detectives-Amateur; Jealousy; Writer-Directors; Cult Films; Sleeper Hits
(Wild at Heart; Twin Peaks [TV Series])

(Ed: So controversial, it's a must-see, but not for the squeamish. May take few viewings to get a feel for it. Didn't find a sizeable audience until video)

Blue Water, White Death, 1971/75, 99m, ★★★/$$$, Ind/NA. Documentary of great white shark hunters, re-released in the wake of Jaws. w. d. Peter Gimbel.
Documentary; Sharks; Animal Monsters; Ind Films
(Jaws; The Sharkhunters; Shark!)

Blume in Love, 1973, 117m, ★★★1/2/$$, WB/WB, R/S. A divorce lawyer (George Segal) is found cheating and soon finds himself getting divorced, though he wants his wife (Susan Anspach) back from the hippie musician (Kris Kristofferson) she's found. Shelley Winters. w. d. Paul Mazursky.
DRAMA: COMEDY DRAMA: Marriage Drama; Marriage on the Rocks; Romance-Boy Wants Girl; Romance-Triangles; Romance with Married Person; Cheating Men; Divorce; Lawyers; Romance-Reunited; Los Angeles; 1970s; Writer-Directors
(Alex in Wonderland; Divorce Wars: A Love Story; The Marrying Man; Bob&Carol&Ted&Alice; Loving)

Boardwalk, 1979, 100m, ★★★/$, ITC/NA Crime in Coney Island plagues an old couple who've lived there all their lives, until, finally, they take matters into their own hands. Ruth Gordon, Lee Strasberg, Janet Leigh, Joe Silver, Eddie Barth. w. Stephen Verona, Leigh Chapman, d. Stephen Verona.
DRAMA: Crime Drama; Elderly People; Turning the Tables; Revenge; Ordinary People vs. Criminals; New York Life
(The Goodbye People; Fighting Back)

The Boat, see Das Boot.

The Boatniks, 1970, 99m, ★★★/$$$, Disney/Disney, G. A klutzy Coast Guard officer can't do anything right until he bumbles into, and thwarts, a band of jewel thieves. Phil Silvers, Robert Morse, Stefanie Powers, Norman Fell, Wally Cox, Don Ameche, Joey Forman. w. Arthur Julian, d. Norman Tokar.
COMEDY: FAMILY: CHILDREN'S: Fools-Bumbling; Heroes-Unlikely; Comedy-Disney; Criminals-Stupid; Jewel Thieves; Boats
(Ensign Pulver; Herbie Rides Again; Blackbeard's Ghost; That Darn Cat)

Bob&Carol&Ted&Alice, 1969, 105m, ★★★1/2/$$$$, Columbia/RCA-Col, Goodtimes, R/ES-FN-MRN. Two hip couples in L.A. decide to be really hip and swap partners for a lark after awareness retreats-but can they handle it? Natalie Wood, Elliott Gould (BSActor), Dyan Cannon (BSActress), Robert Culp. w. d. Paul Mazursky. Oscars: 2-0.
COMEDY DRAMA: SATIRE: Marriage Comedy; Marriage Drama; Marriage on the Rocks; Romance with Married Person; Cheating Men; Cheating Women; Swapping Partners; Alternative Lifestyles; Beautiful People; Jetsetters; Mod Era; 1960s; Los Angeles; Sexual Revolution; Time Capsules; Female Protagonists
(The April Fools; Blume in Love; Alex in Wonderland; The Last Married Couple in America)
(Ed: Another time capsule of the dawn of the sexual revolution; still fairly shocking)

Bob le Flambeur, 1955, 102m, ★★★1/2/$$$, Ind/Tri-Col. A bored gambler (Roger Duchesne) decides to rob his favorite casino. Isabel Corey. w. d. Jean-Pierre Melville.
DRAMA: Crime Drama; Heist Stories; Gambling; French Films; French New Wave Films; Playboys; Writer-Directors
(The Killing; Dollars; Silver Bears; The Hot Rock; Killing Zoe; Rififi)

Bob Roberts, 1992, 104m, ★★★/$$, Touchstone/Touchstone, PG. A pseudo-documentary about a suave and smarmy young politician who poses as a populist but really is a wheeler-dealer investor. Tim Robbins, Giancarlo Esposito, Alan Rickman, Ray Wise, Gore Vidal, Susan Sarandon, John Cusack, Bob Balaban. w. d. Tim Robbins.
SATIRE: COMEDY: COMEDY DRAMA: Politicians; Political Satire; Documentary Style; Biographies-Fictional; Power-Rise to; Con Artists
(The Candidate; A Face in the Crowd)

Bobby Deerfield, 1977, 124m, ★★1/2/$$, FA-WB/WB, PG/S. A race car driver (Al Pacino) falls in love with a woman (Marthe Keller) while in Europe, but she has a fatal disease. w. Alvin Sargent, N-adap. Erich Maria Remarquez (*Heaven Has No Favourites*), d. Sydney Pollack.
DRAMA: MELODRAMA: ROMANCE: Romantic Drama; Tearjerkers; Disease Stories; Dying Young; Car Racing; Americans Abroad; Flops-Major
(And Now, My Love; Love Story; Author! Author!)

(Ed: Only for real Pacino and romance fans)

The Bobo, 1967, 105m, ★★/$, WB/WB. A singing matador (Peter Sellers) attempts to serenade a Spanish (really Swedish) young lady (Britt Ekland), despite her thwarting him w. P-adap. David R. Schwarz, N-adap. Burt Cole (*Olimpia*), d. Robert Parrish.
COMEDY: FARCE: ROMANCE: Romantic Comedy; Romance-Boy Wants Girl; Comedy; Slapstick; Race Against Time; Bets; Misunderstandings; Singers; Spain
(After the Fox; The Party)

Bocaccio '70, 1962, 165m, ★★★/$$, Embassy/Facets. A three-part comedy about sex and marriage with three different directors in which, first, a shy man wins a night with a beautiful woman, then a bored housewife becomes a mistress, and, finally, a pin-up girl pops off the wall much to men's delight. Sophia Loren, Anita Ekberg, Romy Schneider. w. Federico Fellini, Tullio Pinelli, Ennio Flaiano, Suso Cecchi D'Amici, Luchino Visconti, Cesare Zavattini, d. Vittorio De Sica, Federico Fellini, Luchino Vischonti.
COMEDY: COMEDY DRAMA: ROMANCE: Romance-Mismatched; Multiple Stories; Trilogies; Prostitutes; Nerds; Extroverted vs. Introverted; Sexy Women; Surrealism; Italian Films; Art Films
(Yesterday, Today, & Tomorrow; The Umbrellas of Cherbourg; The Yellow Rolls Royce; Divorce, Italian Style; Marriage, Italian Style)

Bodies, Rest & Motion, 1993, 94m, ★★1/2/$, FineLine/NewLine, R/P-S-FN-MRN. Slow-moving 20-somethings in the Arizona desert make slow love and then move on. Bridget Fonda, Eric Stoltz, Phoebe Cates, Tim Roth. w. Roger Hedden, d. Michael Steinberg.
DRAMA: ROMANCE: Romantic Drama; 20-Somethings; Romance-Choosing Right Person; Quiet Little Films; Single Women; Ordinary People Stories; Southwestern Life; Alienation; Life Transitions; Female Protagonists
(Singles; Reality Bites; Naked in New York; Sleep with Me)
(Ed: You'll probably be bored out of your gourd, if you're not asleep first-unless you're nuts about Bridget, who's good, but that's not enough here)

Body and Soul, 1947, 104m, ★★★/$$$, Republic/Republic. A young boxer cheats

his way to the top. John Garfield (BActor), Lilli Palmer, Hazel Brooks, Anne Revere, William Conrad. w. Abraham Polonsky (BOScr), d. Robert Rossen. **BEdit.** Oscars: 3-1.
DRAMA: MELODRAMA: Sports Movies; Boxing; Cheating Men; Liars; Con Artists; Fame-Rise to; Stagelike Films; Lyrical Films; Film Noir
(Requiem for a Heavyweight; Champion; Somebody Up There Likes Me; Force of Evil)
Body and Soul, 1981, 100m, ★★/$$, Cannon/MGM-UA, R/V-S. A boxer goes for the big money to finance his kid sister's operation. Leon Isaac Kennedy, Jayne Kennedy, Muhammed Ali, Peter Lawford. w. Leon Isaac Kennedy, S-adap. Abraham Polonsky, d. George Bowers.
MELODRAMA: ACTION: Sports Movies; Boxing; Tearjerkers; Saving Someone; Sisters; Disease Movies
(Ed: Boxing is the only thing in common with the original; action melodramas are rare)
Body Bags, 1993, 95m, ★★★/$$, Republic/Republic, R/EV-B&G. Three stories involve a baseball player with an eye donation with visions of its own from the previous owner, a man who'll do anything to cure his baldness, and woman in jeopardy in the middle of nowhere. Robert Carradine, Stacy Keach, David Warner, Deborah Harry, Sheena Easton, Twiggy, John Agar, Mark Hamill, Alex Datcher. w. Billy Brown, Dan Angel, d. Tobe Hooper, John Carpenter.
HORROR: SCI-FI: Body Parts; Multiple Stories; Women in Jeopardy; Body Parts; Blind People; Paranoia; TV Movies; Mini-Series
(Creepshow; Tales from the Darkside; Tales from the Crypt; Trilogy of Terror)
Body Double, 1984, 109m, ★★1/2/$, Col/RCA-Col, R/P-EV-B&G-S-FN. An actor (Craig Wasson) spies on a woman and sees her murdered with a power drill, which involves him in a conspiracy with a porno star (Melanie Griffith). w. Robert Averch, Brian DePalma, d. DePalma.
SUSPENSE: THRILLER: MURDER MYS-TERY: MYSTERY: Framed?; Saving Yourself Blood and Gore; Pornography World; Conspiracy; Voyeurs; Phobias; Bimbos; Dual Lives
REMAKE/RETREAD OF: Rear Window, Vertigo

(Blow Out; Dressed to Kill; Raising Cain; Vertigo; Rear Window)
(Ed: A very grotesque thriller that's not so thrilling and at times absolutely ridiculous, but to DePalma fans, it apparently doesn't matter much)
The Bodyguard, 1992, 129m, ★★1/2/ $$$$$, WB/WB, R/S-P. A singer, receiving threats on her life hires a former CIA agent to be her bodyguard. They, of course, fall in love. Whitney Houston, Kevin Costner, Gary Kemp, Ralph Waite, Bill Cobbs. w. Lawrence Kasdan, d. Mick Jackson. BOSong. Oscars: 2-0.
ROMANCE: MELODRAMA: SUSPENSE: Music Movies; Murder-Attempted; Conspiracy; Protecting Someone; Bodyguards; Romance with Protector; Romance-Reluctant; Romance-Bickering; Feisty Females Betrayals; Sisters Singers; Actresses; Blockbusters
(A Star Is Born [1976]; Someone to Watch Over Me)
(Ed: Preposterous, especially since the stars seem to have little chemistry together, with Whitney being the greater, if more annoying, presence, but the writing, primarily the plot, carries it across somehow)
Body Heat, 1981, 113m, ★★★1/2/$$, Ladd-WB/WB, R/P-S-FN-MN. A small-town lawyer (William Hurt) is seduced completely by a woman (Kathleen Turner) wanting to get rid of her husband, but perhaps, also her newfound lover. Richard Crenna. w. d. Lawrence Kasdan.
SUSPENSE: MURDER: MYSTERY: MURDER MYSTERY: Erotic Thriller; ROMANCE: Film; Noir-Modern; Mindgames; Double Crossings; Dangerous Women; Love-Questionable; Romance-Triangles; Romance with Married Person; Clever Plots & Endings; Inheritances at Stake; Lookalikes; Southerns; Lawyers; Writer-Directors
(Double Indemnity; Out of the Past; Basic Instinct; Fatal Instinct; The Postman Always Rings Twice)
(Ed: Reminiscent of *Double Indemnity*, yes, but it starts and ends with a fresh take and far more eroticism)
The Body in the Library, 1987, 155m, ★★1/2/$, BBC/Fox. Miss Marple takes her sweet, doughtery time to find the killer of the body among the books in this Agatha Christie opus from England. Joan

Hickson. w. N-adap. Agatha Christie, d. Silvio Narizzano.
MYSTERY: MURDER: MURDER MYS-TERY: Agatha Christie; Detective Stories; Detectives-Female; TV Movies
(Ed: Hickson plays Miss Marple as a very droll, slow sleuth, as opposed to Angela Lansbury's spry take in *The Mirror Crack'd*)
Body of Evidence, 1992, 99m, ★★/$, DEG-MGM/MGM-UA, R/P-ES-FN-MRN. A woman is accused of killing her wealthy, elderly husband with too much intense sex. In order to make a more solid case, she demonstrates this on her attorney. Madonna, Willem DaFoe, Joe Mantegna, Anne Archer, Julianne Moore, Jurgen Prochnow, Frank Langella. w. Brad Mirman, d. Uli Edel.
SUSPENSE: THRILLER: MURDER: MYSTERY: MURDER MYSTERY: Courtroom Drama; Erotic Thriller; Dangerous Women; Romance with Lawyer; Romance-Unprofessional; Accused Unjustly; Sexy Women; Bimbos; Unintentionally Funny
(Dangerous Game; Basic Instinct; Death by Sex; Liquid Sky)
(Ed: Sad. Poor Madonna, or better yet, poor Willem)
The Body Snatcher, 1945, 77m, ★★★1/2/$$, RKO/Turner. A mad doctor (Boris Karloff) has an assistant who steals the body parts he needs for his experiments, but what will happen when he can't find anymore that are already dead? Bela Lugosi. w. Philip MacDonald, Val Lewton, SS-adap. Robert Louis Stevenson, d. Robert Wise.
HORROR: SUSPENSE: MURDER: Serial Killers; Murders-One by One; Body Parts; Scientists-Mad; Frankenstein Stories; Film Noir
(The Doctor and the Devils; Frankenstein)
Body Snatchers, 1993, 87m, ★★★/$ (LR), WB/WB, R/V-P-B&G-FFN. A girl with her EPA surveyor father is staying at a military base when the pods start coming and taking over. Gabrielle Anwar, Terry Kinney, Meg Tilley, Forest Whitaker, Lee Ermey. w. Stuart Gordon, Dennis Paoli, Nicholas St. John, d. Abel Ferrara.
HORROR: SCI-FI: Aliens-Outer Space; Evil; Paranoia; Toxic Waste; Environmental Dilemmas; Government as Enemy; Military Stories; Parasites; Mental Illness; Murders-One by One;

Fugitives; Small-Town Life; Conformism; Young Women; Allegorical Stories; Revisionist Films; Narrated Films; Female Protagonists
REMAKE OF: Invasion of the Body Snatchers
(Invasion of the Body Snatchers; Prophecy; Impulse)
(Ed: Completely rethought but not better)
Body Slam, 1987, 89m, ★★/$, Hemdale/Sultan. A down-and-out talent agent accidently invents "Rock n' Wrestling," a craze which really takes off. Dirk Benedict, Tanya Roberts, Roddy Piper, Lou Albano, Charles Nelson Reilly. w. Shel Lytton, Steve Burkow, d. Hal Needham.
ACTION: Music Movies; Sports Movies; Curiosities; Wrestling
(Take Down; All the Marbles)
Boeing-Boeing, 1965, 102m, ★★1/2/$$, Par/Par. A womanizer uses bachelor pad as landing pad for international babes and confusion results. Tony Curtis, Jerry Lewis, Dany Saval, Thelma Ritter. w. Edward Anhalt, P-adap. Marc Camoletti, d. John Rich.
COMEDY: FARCE: Sex Comedy; Comedy-Slapstick; Misunderstandings; Playboys; Affair Lairs; Pilots-Airplane; Americans Abroad; Paris; Stagelike Films
(Ladies' Man [1961]; Three on a Couch; Pillow Talk; Don't Make Waves)
Boiling Point, 1993, 93m, ★★1/2/$$, WB/WB, R/EV-P-S. A federal agent trying to solve his partner's murder returns to his home town at the same time an ex-con gets out of the clink and has to make amends with the mob, with both of their paths soon to collide. Wesley Snipes, Dennis Hopper, Lolita Davidovich, Valerie Perrine, Tony LoBianco, Seymour Cassel, Dan Hedaya. w. d. James Harris.
DRAMA: Crime Drama; Mob Stories; Police vs. Mob; Police vs. Criminal; Detective Stories; FBI Agents; **MURDER:** Chase Stories; Cat and Mouse Stories; Men Fighting Over Women; Film Noir-Modern; Coulda Been Good; Writer-Directors
(Ed: More of a crime drama than a thriller)
The Bold and the Brave, 1956, 87m, ★★★/$$, RKO/Turner. An American batallion of various types of soldier with varying degrees head into battle in the Italian campaign of 1944. Wendell Corey,

Mickey Rooney, Nicole Maurey, Don Taylor. w. Robert Lewin, d. Lewis Foster.
ACTION: DRAMA: Action Drama; War Stories; World War II Stories; Soldiers; Italy; Korean War
(The Bridges at Toko-Ri; To Hell and Back)
Bolero, 1934, 85m, ★★★/$$$, Par/NA. A dancer in New York travels to Europe and leaves his cares behind, becoming an international club-hopper much to the chagrin of his girlfriend. George Raft, Carole Lombard, Sally Rand, Ray Milland. w. Carey Wilson, Kubec Glasmon, Ruth Ridenour, Horace Jackson, d. Wesley Ruggles.
DRAMA: MELODRAMA: Dancers; Dance Movies; Nightclub Life; Playboys; Americans Abroad; Female Screenwriters
Bolero, 1984, 105m, ★/$$, Cannon/Vestron, R/P-S-FFN-MN. Bo Derek tries to solve an impotency problem with her beau by learning the maneuvers of a bullfighter-or is it the fact she's nude most of the time that does the trick? George Kennedy. w. d. John Derek.
MELODRAMA: Erotic Drama; Sexual Problems; Unintentionally Funny; Camp; Major Flops; Writer-Directors
(10; A Change of Seasons; Ghosts Can't Do It)
(Ed: Only for diehard Bo fans)
Bombay Talkie, 1970, 105m, ★★1/2/$, MI-Ind/Sultan, Ingram. An American woman vacationing in Bombay falls for two Indian filmakers. Jennifer Kendal, Sashi Kapoor, Zia Mohyeddin. w. Ruth Prawer Jhabvala, James Ivory, d. James Ivory.
DRAMA: MELODRAMA: ROMANCE: Romance-Triangles; Directors; Movie Making; Indian People; British Films; Female Screenwriters
(Shakespeare Wallah; Heat and Dust)
Bombshell, 1933, 91m, ★★★1/2/$$$$, MGM/MGM-UA. A starlet puts in for an image overhaul which leads to more than a few complications for her entourage. Jean Harlow, Lee Tracy, Frank Morgan. w. Jules Furthman, John Lee Mahin, P-adap. Caroline Francke, Mack Crane, d. Victor Fleming.
COMEDY: Screwball Comedy; **FARCE:** Bimbos; Sexy Women; Actresses; Starting Over; Hollywood Life; 1930s; Hidden Gems; Forgotten Films
(Red Dust; Saratoga; Libeled Lady)
Bonfire of the Vanities, 1990, 117m, ★★/$, WB/WB, PG-13/P. A businessman

(Tom Hanks) is having an affair with a bimbo (Melanie Griffith) when they accidentally run over a black man, and a massive scandal erupts. Bruce Willis, Alan King, Kim Cattrall, Saul Rubinek, Morgan Freeman, F. Murray Abraham. w. Michael Cristofer, N-adap. Tom Wolfe, d. Brian DePalma.
COMEDY: Black Comedy; **SATIRE:** Romance with Married Person; Romance-Clandestine; Romance-Triangles; Scandals; Yuppies; New York Life; Corruption; Accidents; Greed; Wall Street; Losing it All; Novel Adapations; Flops-Major; Coulda Been Great; 1980s
(Wall Street; Pursuit of Happiness)
(Ed: Only worth seeing in the sense of wanting to see a train wreck. It alienates with its cartoonish ways the very audience it could have captured who'd read the book)
Bonjour, Tristesse, 1958, 94m, ★★★/$$$, Col/Col. A beautiful young woman (Jean Seberg) is having a romance with a rebellious young Frenchman while her father (David Niven) is seeing a woman (Deborah Kerr) who wants to rein her in. w. N-adap. Francoise Sagan, d. Otto Preminger.
DRAMA: MELODRAMA: ROMANCE: Young Women; Fathers & Daughters; Coming of Age; Stepmothers; Lover Family Dislikes; Love-Firsts; Riviera Life; Vacations; Vacation Romance; Female Protagonists; Female Screenwriters
(A Summer Place)
(Ed: Glossy, entertaining soaper)
Bonnie and Clyde, 1967, 122m, ★★★★/$$$$$, WB/WB, R/EV-S-FN. A would-be playboy (Warren Beatty, BActor) and a waitress (Faye Dunaway, BActress) meet up in Depression-era Texas and decide to rob some banks. The rest is history. Gene Hackman (BSActor), Estelle Parsons (**BSActress**), Michael J. Pollard (BSActor), Gene Wilder. w. Robert Benton, David Newman (BOScr), d. Arthur Penn (BDirector). BPicture, **BCinema.** Oscars: 9-2.
DRAMA: TRAGEDY: Crime Drama; **COMEDY DRAMA: ACTION:** Action Drama; Action Comedy; Black Comedy; Chase Movies; Road Movies; Comedy & Violence; Outlaw Road Movies; Criminal Biographies; Criminal Couples; Fugitives From the Law; Crime Sprees; Bank Robberies; Depression Era; True Stories;

Romance-Troubled; Sleeper Hits; Anti-Establishment Films; Blockbusters (Badlands; The Getaway; Gun Crazy; Murder in the Heartland; Thelma and Louise; True Romance; Natural Born Killers)

(Ed: Very controversial in its time, it's been imitated many times since with its on-the-run plot and mixture of violence and humor. Major, established critics panned it upon its release, then some actually retracted reviews once it had struck a youthful chord in the anti-establishment late 60s)

Bonnie Prince Charlie, 1948, 140m, ★★★/$$, BL-London/Nos. An epic about the Stuarts of Scotland and their return from banishment, bidding to rule once again. David Nivens, Margaret Leighton, Jack Hawkins, Judy Campbell. w. Clemence Dane, d. Anthony Kimmins.

DRAMA: ADVENTURE: Epics; Historical Drama; Costume Drama; Royalty; Family; Saga; Scotland; British Films
(Mary, Queen of Scots; Mary of Scotland)

Bonnie Scotland, 1935, 80m, ★★/$$$, MGM/MGM-UA. Two Americans travel to Scotland to claim their inheritance, only to find that it doesn't exist. They then decide to join the army and end up in India. Stan Laurel, Oliver Hardy, James Finlayson, Daphne Pollard. w. Frank Butler, Jeff Moffitt, d. James Horne.

COMEDY: Inheritances at Stake; Fools-Bumbling; Fish out of Water Stories; India; Scotland
(Abbott & Costello in the Foreign Legion; Gunga Din)

Bon Voyage!, 1962, 130m, ★★1/2/$$$, Disney/Disney, G. An all-American family headed by Fred MacMurray goes on vacation in Europe. Jane Wyman. w. Bill Walsh, N-adap. Marrijane and Joseph Hayes, d. James Nielsen.

FAMILY: COMEDY DRAMA: Family Stories; Family Comedy; Americans Abroad; Vacations; Vacations-European; Conservative Value Films; Comedy-Disney

COMIC FLIPSIDE: National Lampoon's European Vacation.
(A Light in the Piazza; Three Coins in the Fountain; Follow Me, Boys!)

La Bonne Soupe, see L

Les Bonnes Femmes, see L

Bon Voyage, Charlie Brown, 1980, 76m, ★★★/$$, NG/Par, G. The Peanuts gang become exchange students in Europe in this feature-length cartoon. w.

Charles Schulz, d. Bill Melendez.
Cartoons; **CHILDREN'S: FAMILY:** School Life; Vacations-European; **MELODRAMA:** (You're a Good Man, Charlie Brown)

Book of Love, 1990, 87m, ★★1/2/$$$, Touchstone/Touchstone, PG/P-S. The reminiscences of a writer about when he was 16 and had a crush on a girl. Chris Young, Keith Coogan, Aeryk Egan, Danny Nucci. w. William Kotzwinkle, N-adap. (*Jack in the Box*), d. Robert Shaye.

COMEDY: ROMANCE: Romance-Boy Wants Girl; Coming of Age Memories; Writers; Teenagers; Teenage Movies
(Can't Buy Me Love; Mischief)

Boom!, 1969, 113m, ★★1/2/$, U/NA. A wealthy, beautiful woman owns an island, but the man she chooses to share it with after all of her others have died may have more than romance in mind. Elizabeth Taylor, Richard Burton, Noel Coward, Michael Dunn, Joanna Shimkus. w. Tennessee Williams, *The Milk Train Doesn't Stop Here Anymore*, d. Joseph Losey.

DRAMA: MELODRAMA: ROMANCE: Romance-Doomed; Death-Impending; Rich People; Poets; Drifters; Islands Riviera Life; Volcanoes; Hidden Gems; Flops-Major; Tennessee Williams-esque; Female Protagonists
(The Roman Spring of Mrs. Stone; Suddenly Last Summer)
(Ed: Worth seeing as a curiosity, though Williams loved it)

Boom Town, 1940, 116m, ★★1/2/$$, MGM/MGM-UA. Two friends strike oil and deal with the women between them. Clark Gable, Spencer Tracy, Claudette Colbert, Hedy Lamarr, Frank Morgan, Lionel Atwill, Chill Wills. w. John Lee Mahin, SS-adap. James Edward Grant, d. Jack Conway.

COMEDY DRAMA: DRAMA: ROMANCE: Romance-Triangles; Oil People; Friendships-Male; Faded Hits
(Honky Tonk; San Francisco)

Boomerang, 1947, 88m, ★★★1/2/$$, 20th/NA. A church official in a small town is shot. The DA prevents an innocent scapegoat from being convicted, but can he find the real culprit? Dana Andrews, Jane Wyatt, Lee J. Cobb, Cara Williams, Arthur Kennedy, Robert Keith, Ed Begley. w. Richard Murphy (BOScr), d. Elia Kazan. Oscars: 1-0.

DRAMA: SUSPENSE: MURDER: MYSTERY: MURDER MYSTERY: True

Stories; Docudrama; Courtroom Drama; Accused Unjustly; Saving Someone; Detective Stories; Lawyers as Detectives; Ethics; Forgotten Films; Hidden Gems

Boomerang, 1992, 117m, ★★★/$$$, Par/Par, R/P-S-FN. A cosmetics executive has an unsuccessful affair with his female boss who treats him like a woman, on his road to true love. Eddie Murphy, Robin Givens, Halle Berry, David Alan Grier, Martin Lawrence, Grace Jones, Eartha Kitt, Melvin Van Peebles. w. Barry W. Blaustein, David Sheffield, d. Reginald Hudlin.

COMEDY: COMEDY DRAMA: ROMANCE: Romantic Comedy; Black Casts; Black Men; Black Women; Role Reversals; Battle of the Sexes; Turning the Tables; Executives; Business Life; Underrated; Black Screenwriters; Black Directors
(Strictly Business; The Distinguished Gentleman)

The Boost, 1988, 95m, ★★★/$, Hemdale/Vestron, R/P-S. A yuppie couple (James Woods, Sean Young) can't deal with their cocaine habit and everything else all at once. w. Daryl Ponicsan, d. Harold Becker.

DRAMA: ROMANCE: Marriage Drama; Marriage on the Rocks; Drugs-Addictions; Obsessions; Coulda Been Great
(Clean and Sober; Torchlight)

Bopha!, 1993, 121m, ★★★/$$, Par/Par, PG-13/V. A father and son's conflict leads to greatness amid the antiapartheid movement's peak in South Africa, but it also leads to tragedy. Danny Glover, Maynard Eziashi, Alfre Woodard, Malcolm McDowell, Robin Smith, Marius Weyers. w. Brian Bird, John Wienick, P-adap. Percy Mitwa, d. Morgan Freeman.

DRAMA: TRAGEDY: Social Drama; South Africa; Black Casts; Black Men; Black Women; Fathers & Sons; Apartheid; TV Movies
(Mandela; Cry Freedom; A World Apart; A Dry White Season)

The Border, 1982, 107m, ★★1/2/$, Universal/MCA-U, R/P-S. A Texas cop (Jack Nicholson) becomes corrupt and takes bribes from illegal aliens, until he falls for a Mexican woman with children. Valerie Perrine, Warren Oates, Harvey Keitel. w. Deric Washburn, Walon Green, David Freeman, d. Tony Richardson.

DRAMA: ROMANCE: Midlife Crisis; Marriage on the Rocks; Corruption;

Corruption-Police; Greed; Romance-Interracial; Crossing the Border; Texas

Borderline, 1980, 105m, ★★/$$, ITC/Fox, R/EV-P. A patrolman on the Mexico border hunts down illegals and corrupt smugglers. Charles Bronson, Bruno Kirby, Karmin Murcelo, Ed Harris. w. Steve Kline, Jerrold Freedman, d. Jerrold Freedman.

ACTION: Police Stories; Bounty Hunters; Aliens-Illegal; Mexico; Texas; Crossing the Border

Bordertown, 1934, 80m, ★★½/$$, WB/NA. In the north of Mexico, a small-town lawyer has an affair with a businessman's wife. Paul Muni, Bette Davis, Margaret Lindsay, Eugene Pallette, Hobart Cavanaugh. w. Laird Doyle, Wallace Smith, N-adap. Carroll Graham, d. Archie Mayo.

DRAMA: MELODRAMA: Romance with Married Person; Romance with Lawyer; Romance-Triangles; Cuckolded; Crossing the Border; Texas; Mexico

REMAKE/RETREAD: Blowing Wild (Blowing Wild; Out of the Past)

Boris & Natasha, 1992, 88m, ★½/$, MCEG-Academy/New Line, PG/V. The kooky, creepy Russian spies from the *Rocky and Bullwinkle* cartoons come to life as they try to keep from blowing themselves up on their missions to destroy, et al. Sally Kellerman, Davis Thomas, Paxton Whitehead, Andrea Martin, Alex Rocco. d. Charles Martin Smith.

COMEDY: Spoofs-Spy; Spies; Terrorists; Cartoonlike Films; Russians

Born Again, 1978, 110m, ★★/$, Avco/Sultan, G. The true story of a Watergate conspirator, Charles Colson, who "saw the light" in prison. Dean Jones, Anne Francis, Jay Robinson, Dana Andrews. w. Walter Block, d. Irving Rapper.

DRAMA: MELODRAMA: Religion; Watergate; Political Drama; Redemption; Conservative; Value Films; True Stories; Autobiographical Stories
(Blind Ambition; Nixon)

Born Free, 1966, 96m, ★★★/$$$, Columbia/RCA-Col, G. A wife of a British game warden in Kenya (Virginia McKenna) raises and tames a wild lion amid beautiful music. w. Gerald L. C. Copley, N-adap. Joy Adamson, d. James Hill. BOSong, BOScore. Oscars: 2-2.

DRAMA: MELODRAMA: ADVENTURE: Africa; Animals in Jeopardy; Animal Rights; Animal Stories; Sleeper Hits; Faded Hits; Safaris; Female Protagonists

SEQUELS: Living Free, Born Free (TV Series)
(Gorillas in the Mist; Daktari; Hatari)

Born in East L.A., 1987, 84m, ★★★/$$, U/MCA-U, R/P-S. A legal Hispanic man (Cheech Marin) gets deported to Mexico with a bunch of illegal aliens. Daniel Stern, Paul Rodriguez. w. d. Cheech Marin.

COMEDY: SATIRE: Mistaken Identities; Misunderstandings; Immigrants; Comedians; Character Comedy; Kidnappings; Accused Unjustly; Prison Comedy; Los Angeles; Mexico; Latin People; Writer-Directors; Actor Directors
(Up in Smoke; Nice Dreams; Shrimp on the Barbie)

Born Losers, 1967, 112m, ★★½/$$$$, AIP/Live, Vestron, R/V-P. The first of the Billy Jack films in which several teens accuse a motorcycle gang of raping them. Tom Laughlin, Jane Russell, Jeremy Slate, Elizabeth James. w. d. Laughlin.

DRAMA: MELODRAMA: ACTION: Rape/Rapists; Motorcycles; Vigilantes; Hippies; Teenagers; Teenage Movies; Anti-Establishment Films; 1960s Rebels; Accused Unjustly; Framed?; Actor Directors; Writer-Directors; Ind Films

SEQUEL: Billy Jack
(Billy Jack; The Wild Angels; The Wild One)

Born on the Fourth of July, 1989, 150m, ★★★★/$$$, Universal/MCA-U, R/EP-EV-S. A Vietnam vet (Tom Cruise, BActor) comes home to more horrors than what he endured in war after being disabled in battle. Kyra Sedgwick, Willem Dafoe. w. Ron Kovic, Oliver Stone (BAScr), NF-adap. Ron Kovic, d. Oliver Stone (**BDirector**). BPicture, BCin, BEditing, **BSound**, BOScore. Oscars: 8-2.

DRAMA: Social Drama; Vietnam War; Vietnam Era; True Stories; Autobiographical Stories; Veterans; Anti-Establishment Films; Disabled People
(Coming Home; Platoon; The Best Years of Our Lives; Heaven and Earth; Nixon)
(Ed: Powerful description of being pro-Vietnam war and then antiwar, although a bit too long)

Born to Be Bad, 1934, 70m, ★★½/$$$, 20th/NA. When her illegitimate son is taken from her, a "bad girl" tries to win the affections of the man who adopted him. Loretta Young, Cary Grant, Jackie Kelk, Henry Travers, Harry Green. w. Ralph Graves, d. Lowell Sherman.

DRAMA: MELODRAMA: ROMANCE: Children-Adopted; Mothers-Unwed; Children-Long Lost; Criminals-Female

Born to Be Bad, 1950, 70m, ★★½/$$, RKO/Turner. Another "bad girl" film in which the "heroine" sleeps her way to the top, losing her "one true love," a poor novelist who couldn't help her up the ladder. Joan Fontaine, Robert Ryan, Zachary Scott, Mel Ferrer. w. Edith Sommer, N-adap. Anne Parish (*All Kneeling*), d. Nicholas Ray.

DRAMA: MELODRAMA: Power-Rise to; Female Protagonists; Feisty Females; Evil Women; Dangerous Women; Love-Questionable; Romance-Unrequited; Female Screenwriters
(Darling; Bad Girl; Backstreet; Ada)

Born to Be Wild, 1994, 91m, ★★/$, WB/WB, PG. A rebellious adolescent boy falls for a gorilla named Katie and saves her from evil experimenting types by taking her to Canada. Will Horneff, Helen Shaver, John C. McGinley, Peter Boyle, Tom Wilson, Titus Welliver, Jean Marie Barnwell. w. John Bunzel, Paul Young, d. John Gray.

CHILDREN'S: Animal Stories; Animal Rights; Primates; Escape Adventure; Child Protagonists
(Monkey Trouble; Ed; Bedtime for Bonzo)
(Ed: Played by a man in a fakey suit, even the kids were laughing at this, not necessarily with it)

Born to Dance, 1936, 105m, ★★★/$$$, MGM/MGM-UA. Sailors on shore leave in New York seek out romance. Eleanor Powell, James Stewart, Virginia Bruce, Una Merkel, Sid Silvers, Reginald Gardner, Buddy Ebsen. w. Jack McGowan, Sid Silvers, B. G. De Sylva, d. Roy del Ruth.

MUSICALS: Dance Movies; Dancers; **ROMANCE:** Romantic Comedy; Sailors; Shore Leave
(On the Town; 100 Men and a Girl)

Born to Kill, 1947, 92m, ★★★½/$$, RKO/Turner. A man (Lawrence Tierney) marries a rich woman but soon wants her sister instead. Claire Trevor. w. Eve Greene, Richard Macauley, d. Robert Wise.

SUSPENSE: MURDER: Film Noir; Romance-Triangles; Jealous; Romance-

Clandestine; Cult Films; Overlooked; Female Screenwriters; Hidden Gems

Born Yesterday (B&W), 1950, 103m, ★★★★/$$$$, Columbia/RCA-Col. The bimbo mistress (Judy Holliday, **BActress**) of a corrupt politician is assigned a tutor (William Holden) so she'll stop embarassing him but she may yet surprise him. w. Albert Mannheimer, P-adap. Garson Kanin (**BAScr**), d. George Cukor. BPicture.

Born Yesterday, 1993, 102m, ★★/$$, Hollywood/Hollywood, PG-13/P-V-S. Remake of above, but nowhere near the finesse. Melanie Griffith, Don Johnson, John Goodman. w. Douglas McGrath, S-adap. Garson Kanin, d. Luis Mandoki. Unintentionally Funny; Revisionist Films; Flops-Major

COMEDY: COMEDY DRAMA:
ROMANCE: Romantic Comedy; Romance with Teacher; Underdog Stories; Smart vs. Dumb; Simple Minds; Bimbos; Women Fighting the System; One Woman Among Men; Mistresses; Politicians; Teachers & Students; Turning the Tables; Female Protagonists
(Pygmalion; Educating Rita; The Solid Gold Cadillac; Working Girl)
(Ed: The first one is a classic, the second is an over-the-top mess)

The Borrower, 1989, 88m, ★★/$, Cannon/WB. An extraterrestrial with a chronic head-explosion problem must "borrow" heads from unfortunate strangers he selects at random-only he doesn't give them back. Rae Dawn Chong, Don Gordon, Antonio Fargas, Tom Towles. w. Mason Nage, Richard Fire, d. John McNaughton.
HORROR: SCI-FI: Black Comedy; Horror Comedy; Aliens-Outer Space, Evil; Murders-One by One; Unintentionally Funny; Camp; Exploding Heads; Ind Films
(X-tro; Scanners; The Hidden)

The Borrowers, 1993, 199m, ★★★/$$, BBC/Turner, G. Tiny people live under the floor in a British house and have little tiny adventures. Ian Holm, Penelope Wilson, Rebecca Callard. d. John Henderson, N-adap. May Norton.
CHILDREN'S: FAMILY: Cartoonlike Films; Fantasy; Little People; Shrinking People; British Films; TV Movies

The Boss, 1956, 89m, ★★★/$, UA/NA. In the wake of World War I, a corrupt politician takes advantage of the depressed economy to rule a town with an iron fist. John Payne, William Bishop, Gloria McGhee, Doe Avedon, Joe Flynn. w. Ben L. Parry, d. Byron Haskin.
DRAMA: MELODRAMA: Crime Drama; Political Drama; World War II-Post Era; Politicians; Corruption; Government as Enemy; Ordinary People Turned Criminal

The Boston Strangler, 1968, 120m, ★★★/$$$, 20th/Fox, PG/V-S. A serial killer (Tony Curtis) is followed until caught by a detective (Henry Fonda) intent on figuring him out. George Kennedy. w. Edward Anhalt, NF-adap. Gerold Frank, d. Richard Fleischer.
DRAMA: SUSPENSE: MYSTERY: MURDER MYSTERY: Detective Stories; Detectives-Police; Trail of a Killer; Serial Killers; Women in Jeopardy; Multiple Personalities; Rape/Rapists; Mental Illness; Ahead of Its Time
(The Silence of the Lambs; Manhunter; No Way to Treat a Lady)

The Bostonians, 1984, 120m, ★★★/$$, Almi/Almi, Vestron, Live, PG. A middle-aged feminist (Vanessa Redgrave, **BActress**) in 1800s Boston gets a protege (Madeleine Potter) who is more attractive and persuasive, and though the feminist is attracted to her, she is also jealous of the attentions paid this girl by a Southern gentleman (Christopher Reeve). w. Ruth Prawer Jhabvala, N-adap. Henry James, d. James Ivory.
DRAMA: Social Drama; **ROMANCE:** Costume Drama; Homo-eroticism; Lesbians; Proteges/Understudies; Teachers and Students; Ethics; 1800s-Late; Boston; Classic; Literary Adaptations
(The Age of Innocence; A Room with a View; Howards End; The Portrait of a Lady; Maurice; Sense and Sensibility)
(Ed: Not quite up to the level of *A Room with a View* or *Howards End,* but Redgrave's performance is very memorable)

Botany Bay, 1952, 94m, ★★1/2/$$, Par/Barr Films. A young man on a convict ship in the late 1700s is in love with the same woman as the ship's captain is. James Mason, Alan Ladd, Patricia Medina, Murray Matheson. w. Johnathan Latimer, N-adap. Charles Nordhoff, James Hall, d. John Farrow.
DRAMA: ROMANCE: TRAGEDY: Romance-Triangles; Men in Conflict; Accused Unjustly; Ships; Young Men; Early America; 1700s

Bottoms Up, 1934, 85m, ★★1/2/$$, 20th/NA. Out-of-work actors in Hollywood are engaged by their agent in a money-making scheme that requires them to pose as British dignitaries. Spencer Tracy, Pat Paterson, John Boles, Sid Silvers, Thelma Todd, Robert Emmett O'Connor. w. B. G. De Sylva, David Butler, Sid Silvers, d. David Butler.
MUSICAL: Music Movies; **COMEDY DRAMA:** Con Artists; Impostors; Disguises; Making a Living; Unemployment; Actors; Hollywood Life

Boudu Saved from Drowning, 1932, 87m, ★★★1/2/$$, Michael Simon-Jean Gehret-Ind/Interama. A bourgeois French family lives to regret having saved a tramp from his own suicide attempt. Michael Simon, Charles Grandval, Marcelle Hainia, Séverine Lerczinska. w. d. Jean Renoir, P-adap. René Fauchois.
COMEDY DRAMA: COMEDY: Homeless People; Rich vs. Poor; Rich People; French Films; Hidden Gems
REMAKE: Down and Out in Beverly Hills

Bound and Gagged, a Love Story, 1993, 96m, ★1/2/$, Ind/Trimark, R/S-FN. A young woman kidnaps her sexy friend as a lure to get a rock-star type and winds up on a wild chase. Elizabeth Saltarelli, Karen Black, Ginger Lynn Allen, Chris Denton. w. d. Daniel Appleby.
COMEDY: Erotic Comedy; Sexy Women; Kidnappings; Dating Scene; Chase Stories; Good Premise; Unfulfilled; Writer-Directors

Bound for Glory, 1976, 147m, ★★★1/2/$$, UA/MGM-UA, R. Biography of folksinger Woody Guthrie (David Carradine) as he travels during the Depression. Melinda Dillon, Ronny Cox, Randy Quaid. w. Robert Getchell (**BAScr**), NF-adap. Woody Guthrie, d. Hal Ashby. BPicture, **BCin**, **BAScore.** Oscars: 4-2.
DRAMA: Biographies; Autobiographical Stories; Depression Era; Road Movies; Fame-Rise to; Musicians; Music Composers; Singers; Country Music; Folk Singers; Dreams; Forgotten Films; Hidden Gems; Quiet Little Films; Faded Hits
(Wasn't That a Time; Tender Mercies; Baby, the Rain Must Fall; Sweet Dreams; Coal Miner's Daughter; Alice's Restaurant; Who Is Harry Kellerman and Why Is He Saying These Terrible Things About Me?)

The Bounty, 1984, 130m, ★★★/$$, Orion/Orion, PG-13/V-S-FFN. Remake of *Mutiny on the Bounty* where sailor Fletcher Christian (Mel Gibson) leads a ship against a tyrannical captain (Anthony Hopkins). Laurence Olivier. w. Robert Bolt, d. Roger Donaldson.
DRAMA: ADVENTURE: Power Struggles; Leaders-Tyrant; Adventure at Sea; Classics; Islands; Court Martial; Revisionist Films
REMAKE OF: Mutiny on the Bounty (1935, 1962)
(Mutiny on the Bounty; Billy Budd)
(Ed: Perhaps not as glossy and exciting as the first, or as musical as the second, but probably the most realistic and still worth the time)
The Bounty Hunters, 1989, 91m, ★★/$, AIP/New World, R/V. A man (Robert Ginty) goes on a rampage to avenge a friend's death. d. Robert Ginty.
ACTION: Action Drama; Revenge; Avenging Death of Loved One; Trail of a Killer; Ind Film
(Death Wish; Midnight Run)
A Bout de Souffle, see **Breathless**
Bowery at Midnight, 1943, 63m, ★★1/2/$$, Monogram/Nos. A manager of a mission has an evil double life at night. Bela Lugosi, John Archer, Wanda McKay. w. Gerald Schitzer, d. Wallace Fox.
HORROR: Crime Drama; **MURDER:** Double Lives
(Dark Eyes of London)
The Bourne Identity, 1988, 195m, ★★★/$$$$, ABC-WB/WB, V. A man wakes up and can't remember his true identity, but the clues are leading to either that of a CIA Agent or a terrorist, and when he kidnaps a woman to help him in his race against time, she falls in love regardless. Richard Chamberlain, Jaclyn Smith, Denholm Elliott, Anthony Quayle, Donald Moffatt, Yorgo Voyagis. w. Carol Sobieski, N-adap. Robert Ludlum, d. Roger Young.
SUSPENSE: Spy Films; Spies; Chase Stories; Amnesia; CIA Agents; Terrorists;
MYSTERY: Conspiracy; Race Against Time; TV Movies; Mini-Series
(Three Days of the Condor; Total Recall)
Boxcar Bertha, 1972, 97m, ★★/$$$, AIP/Vestron, Live, R/V-S-FN-MN. A poor-white-trash version of *Bonnie and Clyde,* only there's more sex this time and the robbers ride the rails. Barbara Hershey, David Carradine. w. Joyce &

John Corrington, d. Martin Scorsese.
DRAMA: Road Movies; Crime Drama; **ROMANCE:** Criminal Couples; Crime Sprees; Heist Stories; Southerns; Thieves; Trains; Hillbillies; Arkansas; Female Protagonists; Female Screenwriters (Bonnie and Clyde; Badlands; Murder in the Heartland; Gun Crazy; Bloody Mama)
Boxing Helena, 1993, ★★/$, Orion/Orion, R/EV-ES-FN-MN. A surgeon falls in love with a young woman and, supposedly in order to save her life, amputates her limbs so that she's completely dependent upon him, when he couldn't even get a date previously. Julian Sands, Sherilyn Fenn, Bill Paxton, Art Garfunkel, Nicolette Scorsese. w. d. Jennifer Lynch.
DRAMA: Erotic Drama; Message Films; Art Films; Avant-Garde Films; Abused Women; Allegorical Stories; Doctors; Stalkers; Female Screenwriters; Female Directors; Writer-Directors; Female Protagonists; Coulda Been Good; Flops-Major; Ind Films
(Ed: For all of the attention of the court battle against Kim Basinger, who withdrew from the project after a verbal agreement, there wasn't much worth fighting about)
The Bowery, 1933, 92m, ★★1/2/$$$, 20th/NA. A gang war erupts in turn-of-the-century New York when a gangland figure jumps off the Brooklyn Bridge on a dare. Wallace Beery, George Raft, Pert Kelton, Jackie Cooper, Fay Wray, Herman Bing. w. Howard Estabrook, James Gleason, d. Raoul Walsh.
DRAMA: Crime Drama; Mob Stories; Mob Wars; Gangs-Street; Accidents; Bets; New York Life; 1900s
A Boy and His Dog, 1975, 87m, ★★★/$$, Ind./Media, R/P-V-S-FN. A young man (Don Johnson) and his dog with ESP roam a post-apocalyptic world in search of food, shelter and women until he joins a cult. w. L. Q. Jones, N-adap. Harlan Ellison, d. L. Q. Jones.
SCI-FI: DRAMA: Black Comedy; Fantasy; Futuristic Films; Apocalyptic Films; Pet Stories; Animals-Talking; Boy and His Dog; Dogs; Robots; Telepathy; Young Men; Cults; Cult Films; Clever Plots & Endings; Sleeper Hits
(The Omega Man; Mad Max SERIES)
Boy, Did I Get a Wrong Number!, 1966, 99m, ★★1/2/$$$, UA/MGM-UA, PG/S. A real estate man (Bob Hope) in

Oregon winds up hiding a fugitive movie star (Elke Sommer) who fled wearing only bubbles from her movie set bath. Phyllis Diller. w. Burt Styler, Alber E. Lewin, George Kennett, d. George Marshall.
COMEDY: Fugitives; Misunderstandings; Missing Persons; Hiding Out; Actresses; Hollywood Life; City vs. Country; Fish out of Water Stories; Sexy Women; Babes & Nerds
(Ball of Fire; A Song Is Born)
(Ed: The best part is seeing Elke running out in bubbles)
The Boy Friend, 1971, 135m, ★★★/$$, MGM/MGM-UA, PG. A send-up of Busby Berkeley-type musicals from the 20s and 30s with an American-British cast: Twiggy, Tommy Tune, Christopher Gable, Glenda Jackson. w. Ken Russell, P-adap. Sandy Wilson, d. Ken Russell.
MUSICAL: Musical Comedy; Musical Drama; **SATIRE: COMEDY DRAMA:** Spoofs; Hollywood Life; Hollywood Satire; 1920s; Outstanding Production Design
(Thoroughly Modern Millie; Pennies from Heaven)
(Ed: Not particularly entertaining, but fascinating for the cast and the production design)
Boyfriends and Girlfriends (*My Girlfriend's Boyfriend*), 1989, 102m, ★★★/$$, Orion/Orion, PG/S. Relationship troubles among the suburbanite youngsters of France. Emmanuelle Chaulet, Sophie Renoir, Anne-Laure Meury. w. d. Eric Rohmer.
COMEDY DRAMA: ROMANCE: Romantic Drama; Young People 20-somethings; Ensemble Films; Ensembles-Young People; Swapping Partners; Romance-Triangles; Slice of Life Stories; Suburban Life; French Films; Writer-Directors
(Summer; Pauline at the Beach; Full Moon in Paris; Reality Bites; St. Elmo's Fire)
(Ed: The alternate title was better; French bratpack angst and oblivion)
Boy on a Dolphin, 1957, 111m, ★★★/$, 20th/NA, AMC. An archaeological artifact is discovered by a beautiful Greek woman while swimming. It becomes a "pearl of great price" as men, motivated by greed, lust, or scientific curiosity, search it and *her* out. Alan Ladd, Sophia Loren, Clifton Webb, Laurence Naismith, Alexis Minotis, Jorge Mistral. w. Ivan Moffat, Dwight

Taylor, N-adap. David Divine, d. Jean Negulesco.

MELODRAMA: COMEDY DRAMA: Archaeologists Finding Valuables; Art Thieves; Fugitives from the Mob; Sexy Women; Dolphins; Greece; Mediterranean; Hidden Gems; Coulda Been Great; Quiet Little Films; Forgotten Films

The Boy Who Could Fly, 1986, 114m, ★★★/$$, Lorimar/WB, PG. A young boy (Jay Underwood) dreams about flying away from his troubled life. Fred Savage, Bonnie Bedelia, Louise Fletcher, Lucy Deakins, Mindy Cohn. w. d. Nick Castle.

CHILDREN'S: FAMILY: DRAMA: MELODRAMA: Fantasy; Dreams; Boyhood; Coming of Age; Flying People; Hiding Out; Old-Fashioned Recent Films; Writer-Directors; Disneyesque
(Radio Flyer; Alsino and the Condor)
(Ed: An old-fashionable fable)

The Boy Who Had Everything, 1984, 94m, ★★¹/2/$, NA. In the middle of the Vietnam War, an Australian college student has an identity crisis. Jason Connery, Diane Cilento, Laura Williams, Lewis Fitzgerald. w. d. Stephen Wallace.

DRAMA: Pre-life Crisis; Anti-Establishment Films; Rebels; Young Men; College Life; Fraternity Life; Vietnam War Era; Australian Films; Writer-Directors

The Boy with Green Hair, 1948, 82m, ★★★/$$$, MGM/MGM-UA-Turner. An orphaned boy (Dean Stockwell) in World War II is an outcast because of the color of his hair. w. Ben Barzman, Alfred Lewis Levitt, SS-adap. Betsy Beaton, d. Joseph Losey.

DRAMA: MELODRAMA: Orphans; Misfits; Ostracism; Boyhood; World War II Era; Allegorical Stories; Time Capsules
(Ed: A color capsule of the 40s, plus you get to see a tyke named Dean Stockwell. A good idea to have worked into *Quantum Leap*)

The Boys from Brazil, 1978, 123m, ★★★/$$$, 20th/CBS-Fox, R, V-B&G. Joseph Mengele (Gregory Peck) is still hiding in Brazil and a Nazi-hunter (Laurence Olivier, BActor) has uncovered his plot to reproduce little Hitlers from DNA. w. Heywood Gould, adap. Ira Levin, d. Franklin J. Schaffner. BOScore. Oscars: 2-0.

SUSPENSE: MYSTERY: MURDER: Chase Movies; **SCI-FI:** Murders-One by

One; Race Against Time; Nazi Stories; Hitler; Vigilantes; Trail of a Killer; Evil Men; Rule the World-Plot to; Biographies-Fictional; Experiments; Children-Adopted; Mad Scientists; South America; What if . . . Stories
(Little Nikita; Marathon Man; Jurassic Park; Nazi Hunter: The Beate Klarsfeld Story)
(Ed: A far-fetched idea [hopefully] made plausible and the most exciting chase ever involving two elderly men)

The Boys from Syracuse, 1940, 74m, ★★¹/2/$$, Universal/NA. In ancient Greece, identical twins switched at birth have opposing fates. Allan Jones, Joe Penner, Charles Butterworth, Rosemary Lane, Laurence Hervey, Martha Raye. w. Leonard Spigelgass, Charles Grayson, Paul Gerard Smith, P-adap. George Abbott (from William Shakespeare, *The Comedy of Errors*), d. Edward A. Sutherland.

COMEDY DRAMA: COMEDY: Comedy of Manners; Comedy of Errors; **MUSICALS:** Music Movies; Twins; Body Switching; Mix-Ups; Misunderstandings; Revisionist Films; Classic Literary Adaptations
(Big Business; Start the Revolution Without Me; The Corsican Brothers; The Comedy of Errors)

The Boys in Company C, 1977, 127m, ★★¹/2/$$$, Col/Col, R/P. A tyrannical drill sergeant puts his new recruits through hell before going to Vietnam. Stan Shaw, Andrew Stevens, Craig Wasson. w. Rick Natkin, Sidney J. Furie, d. Sidney J. Furie.

DRAMA: TRAGEDY: Evil Men; Military Stories; Stern Men; Soldiers; Vietnam Era; Vietnam; Forgotten Films; Coulda Been Good
(Full Metal Jacket; An Officer and a Gentleman; Baby Blue Marine; Streamers; Tribes)

The Boys in the Band, 1970, 119m, ★★★/$$, 20th/CBS-FOX, R/P-S. The hit play about several gay men in the late 60s from diverse backgrounds who get together for a birthday party with a beautiful young man as the main present, leading to confrontations. Lawrence Luckinbill, Leonard Frey, Kenneth Nelson, Cliff Gorman, Robert LeTourneaux, Peter White. w. P-adap. Mort Crowley, d. William Friedkin.

DRAMA: COMEDY DRAMA: MELODRAMA: Ensemble Films; Ensembles-

Male; Friendships-Male; Gay Men; Bisexuality; Secrets-Keeping; Double Lives; 1960s; Stagelike Films; Ahead of its Time
(Longtime Companion; Some of My Best Friends Are . . . ; Parting Glances)
(Ed: A bit dated, but still resonant. Amazing Friedkin went from this to *The French Connection*)

The Boys Next Door, 1985, 90m, ★★¹/2/$, New World/New World, R/P-S. Two preppie teenagers (Maxwell Caulfield, Charlie Sheen) decide to go on a crime spree before they turn 18 and become adults. w. Glen Morgan, James Wong, d. Penelope Spheeris.

ACTION: Crime Drama; Road Movies; Outlaw Road Movies; Chase Movies; Car Chases; Thieves; Buddy Films; Juvenile Delinquents; Rebels; Criminal Couples; Female Directors
(Dangerous Curves; Repo Man; The Chase [1994])

Boys' Night Out, 1962, 115m, ★★★/$$$, MGM/MGM-UA. One woman services three married men in her friend's "bachelor pad," or is she up to something far less suspicious? James Garner, Kim Novak, Tony Randall, Howard Duff, Howard Morris, Oscar Homolka, Patti Page. w. Ira Wallach, d. Michael Gordon.

COMEDY: COMEDY DRAMA: ROMANCE: Romantic Comedy; Sex Comedy; **FARCE:** Misunderstandings; Female Among Males; Sociologists; Experiments; Affair Lairs; Female Protagonists
(The Chapman Report; Bachelor in Paradise; Doctors' Wives; The Pad and How to Use It; Sex and the Single Girl)

Boys on the Side, 1995, 115m, ★★★/$$$, WB/WB, R/P-S. A black nightclub singer and a white yuppie get together through the classifieds to travel cross-country in this female road movie. They pick up a wild friend of the singer's and head for San Diego, sharing secrets and heading toward a few climactic revelations. Whoopi Goldberg, Mary-Louise Parker, Drew Barrymore, James McConaughey, James Remar, Billy Wirth, Anita Gillette, Estelle Parsons. w. Don Roos, d. Herbert Ross.

COMEDY DRAMA: MELODRAMA: Buddy Films-Female; Road Movies; Road to California; Trials; AIDS Stories; Singers; Yuppies; Sexy Women;

Ensembles-Female; Women's Films (Leaving Normal; Thelma and Louise; Breaking All the Rules; Terms of Endearment; Dying Young)

Boys Town, 1938, 96m, ★★★1/2/$$$$, MGM/MGM-UA. Father Flannagan (Spencer Tracy, **BActor**) takes on one incorrigible youngster (Mickey Rooney) while dealing with his dream of a large orphanage in Nebraska. w. John Meehan, Dore Schary (BScr), SS-adap. Eleanore Griffin, Schary (**BOStory**), d. Norman Taurog (BDirector). BPicture. Oscars: 5-2.
DRAMA: MELODRAMA: Orphans; Fathers-Surrogate; Fathers & Sons; Men and Boys; Priests; Boyhood; Juvenile Delinquents; Reformers; Rebels
SEQUEL: Men of Boys Town
(Going My Way; The Bells of St. Mary's; The Devil Is a Sissy; Bad Boys [1983]; Captains Courageous)

Boyz N the Hood, 1991, 112m, ★★★1/2/$$$$, Col/Col-Tri, R/EV-S-EP. A young black man in the South Central section of L. A. tries to live decently amid the human degradation and violence of his neighborhood streets. Ice Cube, Cuba Gooding Jr., Morris Chestnut, Larry Fishburne, Nia Long, Tyra Ferrell. w. d. John Singleton (BOScr, BDirector). Oscars: 2-0.
DRAMA: TRAGEDY: Crime Drama; Family Drama; Black Casts; Black Men; Young Men; Fathers & Sons; Los Angeles; Gangs-Black; Marriage on the Rocks; Black Directors; Black Screenwriters; Writer-Directors
(Menace II Society; South Central; Laurel Avenue; Deep Cover)

Braddock, see **Missing in Action 3**
The Brady Bunch Movie, 1995, 95m, ★★★/$$$$, Par/Par, PG/P-S. The Brady clan is alive and well and living in the 90s but still in the 70s, so to speak, as the world has changed for the worse all around them, yet they continue on their merrily oblivious way. Shelley Long, Gary Cole, Christopher Daniel Barnes, Christine Taylor, Paul Sutera, Jennifer Elise Cox, Jesse Lee, Jean Smart, Michael McKean, Barry Williams, Olivia Hack, RuPaul, Ann B. Davis, Eric Nies, Davy Jones, Mickey Dolenz, Peter Tork, Florence Henderson. w. Laurice Elehwany, Rick Copp, Bonnie Turner, Terry Turner, d. Betty Thomas.
COMEDY: SATIRE: Spoofs; Suburban Life; Comedy-Gag; Family Comedy;

Ensemble Films; TV Series Movies; Mortgage Drama; Siblings; Fish out of Water Stories; Lesbians; Time Capsules; 1990s; 1970s
SEQUEL: The Brady Bunch Movie 2
(The Beverly Hillbillies)

The Brain (*Le Cerveau*), 1969, 115m, ★★/$, Par/Par. An eclectic band of the world's master criminals try to rob NATO. David Niven, Jean-Paul Belmondo, Bourvil, Eli Wallach, Silvia Monti. w. Gérard Oury, Marcel Julian, Daniele Thompson, d. Gérard Oury.
COMEDY: Heist Stories; Capers; British Films
(Ed: They shoulda used one on this)

Brain Damage, 1988, 94m, ★1/2/$, Ind/Par, R/V-S-B&G. A teenager is menaced by a parasitic being on drugs. Rick Herbst, Jennifer Lowry, Theo Barnes, Vicki Darnell. w. d. Frank Henenlotter.
HORROR: Aliens-Outer Space, Evil; Drugs; Teenagers; Parasites; Good Premise; Unfulfilled; Writer-Directors

Brain Donors, 1992, 79m, ★★★/$, Par/Par, PG-13/S-P. A Marx Brothers–like band of morons devises a scheme to rid a wealthy widow of her money. John Turturro, Bob Nelson, Mel Smith, Nancy Marchand. w. Pat Proft, d. Dennis Dugan.
COMEDY: FARCE: Con Artists; Comedy-Slapstick; Fools-Bumbling; Revisionist Films; Inheritances at Stake; Coulda Been Great
(Marx Brothers SERIES; The Lady Killers; Naked Gun SERIES; Barton Fink)
(Ed: The trailer looked great, but unfortunately, the movie was much longer. Although for fans of this, it's passable)

The Brain Eaters, 1958, 60m, ★★/$, AIP/Nos. In a small town with a low special-effects budget, people start acting strange, though they "look just as normal as you and me." Edwin Nelson, Alan Frost, Jack Hill, Joanna Lee, Jody Fair, Leonard Nimoy. w. Gordon Urquart, d. Bruno Vesota.
HORROR: SCI-FI: Sci-Fi-1950s; Paranoia; Lookalikes; Human-Eaters
(Invasion of the Body Snatchers; It Came from Outer Space; I Married a Monster from Outer Space)

Brainscan, 1994, 95m, ★★/$, Ind/Live, R/V-P. A teenage computer whiz goes into the virtual reality territory and finds not only fantasies, but murder as well. Edward Furlong, Frank Langella. w.

Andrew Kevin Walker, d. John Flynn.
ACTION: SUSPENSE: MURDER: Virtual Reality; Video Games; Computers; Teenagers; Teenage Movies; Coulda Been Good
(The Lawnmower Man; Total Recall; Virtual Reality)

Brain Smasher: A Love Story, 1993, 88m, ★/$, Vidmark/Vidmark, PG-13/P-V. Ninjas are after a club bouncer and his bimbo girlfriend. Andrew Dice Clay, Teri Hatcher. d. Albert Pyun.
ACTION: COMEDY: Action Comedy; Chase Stories; Fugitives from the Mob; Martial Arts
(The Adventures of Ford Fairlane)

Brainstorm, 1965, 110m, ★★1/2/$, WB/NA. A woman jumps off a bridge and is saved from drowning by a stranger. They gradually fall in love, and he murders her husband, after which she throws him a curve. Jeffrey Hunter, Anne Francis, Dana Andrews, Viveca Lindfors, Stacy Harris. w. Mann Rubin, d. William Conrad.
SUSPENSE: THRILLER: MELODRAMA: MURDER: ROMANCE: Murder-Invitation to; Romance-Triangles; Saving Someone; Coulda Been Good; Forgotten Films; Mental Illness; Double Crossing
(Ed: After an interesting start, it falls apart into melodrama)

Brainstorm, 1983, 106m, ★★★/$, MGM/MGM-UA, PG. A new means of telepathy is discovered by scientists, but the government is lurking nearby. Christopher Walken, Natalie Wood, Cliff Robertson, Louise Fletcher. w. Robert Stitzel, Philip Frank Messina, Bruce Joel Rubin, d. Douglas Trumbull.
DRAMA: SCI-FI: MELODRAMA: Telepathy; Experiments; Scientists; Computers; Government Corruption; Government as Enemy; Illusions/Hallucinations; Virtual Reality
(Altered States; Johnny Mnemonic)

The Bramble Bush, 1960, 104m, ★★1/2/$$, WB/WB. When a doctor goes to his hometown to help a dying friend, he falls for the friend's wife, and when euthanasia comes into question, it may be seen as murder. Richard Burton, Barbara Rush, Tom Drake, Jack Carson, Angie Dickinson, James Dunn, Henry Jones, Frank Conroy. w. Philip Yordan, d. Daniel Petrie.
SUSPENSE: MURDER: Accused Unjustly; Framed?; Murder-Clearing

Oneself; Euthanasia; Doctors; Forgotten Films
(Right of Way; Whose Life Is It Anyway?)

Bram Stoker's Count Dracula, 1970, 98m, ★★¹/₂/$, Hemdale/NA, R/V-B&G. A faithful, if boring, adaptation of the novel, in which an English real estate agent goes stark raving mad after being bitten by a Transylvanian count who seeks his counsel in finding a cool London pad. Christopher Lee, Herbert Lom, Klaus Kinski, Frederick Williams, Maria Rohm, Soledad Miranda, Jack Taylor. w. Peter Welbeck (Harry Alan Towers), Carlo Fadda, Milo C. Cuccia, Dietmar Behnke, N-adap. Bram Stoker, d. Jess (Jesús) Franco.
HORROR: SUSPENSE: MURDER: Human Monsters; Vampires; Murders-One by One; Classic Literary Adaptations; Revisionist Films; 1970s England; British Films
(Bram Stoker's Dracula [1992], Dracula 1972 A.D.)

Bram Stoker's Dracula, 1992, 128m, ★★★/$$$$, Col/Col-Tri, R/S-EV-B&G. Going back to the classic story, Dracula has a thing for a lovely Victorian lady who looks like his wife who died centuries before-before he sold his soul and became so hideous-and he uses her beau to get her, but will he be able to keep her with all of the other evil she knows he's brought? Winona Ryder, Gary Oldman, Keanu Reeves, Anthony Hopkins. w. Jim Hart, N-adap. Bram Stoker, d. Francis Ford Coppola. **BMakeup, BCostume,** BSoundFX, BArt. Oscars: 4-3.
HORROR: SUSPENSE: ROMANCE: Romantic Drama; MURDER: Murders-One by One; Vampires; Selling One's Soul; England; Victorian Era; Revisionist Films; Classic Literary Adaptations
(Vampire LISTINGS: Dracula [1979]; Bram Stoker's Dracula [1970])

Brannigan, 1975, 111m, ★★¹/₂/$$, UA/MGM-UA, PG/V. A Chicago cop follows an American gangster to London. John Wayne, Richard Attenborough, Judy Geeson, Mel Ferrer, James Booth. w. Christopher Trumbo, Michael Butler, William P. McGivern, William Norton, d. Douglas Hickox.
ACTION: Crime Drama; Police Stories; Detective Stories; Chase Movies; Detectives-Police; Americans Abroad; Fish out of Water Stories; Coulda Been Good; England

The Brasher Doubloon, 1947, 72m, ★★¹/₂/$, 20th/NA. A Philip Marlowe story in which the famed hardboiled detective searches for the thief of a rare coin. George Montgomery, Nancy Guild, Florence Bates, Conrad Janis, Fritz Kortner. w. Dorothy Bennett, N-adap. Raymond Chandler (*The High Window*), d. John Brahm.
MYSTERY: Conspiracy; Detective Stories; Detectives-Private; Thieves; 1940s Female Screenwriters
(The Big Sleep; The Lady in the Lake; Farewell, My Lovely; Marlowe)

Brass Target, 1978, 111m, ★★¹/₂/$$, MGM/MGM-UA, R/V-P. The proposed story of General Patton's possible murder at the hands of gold thieves. Sophia Loren, George Kennedy, Max Von Sydow, John Cassavetes, Patrick McGoohan, Robert Vaughn, Ed Bishop, Bruce Davison, Edward Herrmann. w. Alvin Boretz, N-adap. Frederick Nolan (*The Algonquin Project*), d. John Hough.
ACTION: DRAMA: Conspiracy; MURDER: True or Not?; Assassination Plots; Heist Stories; Coulda Been Good

Braveheart, 1995, 170m, ★★★/$$$, Par/Par, R/EV-P-S-MRN. The apocryphal tale of the liberator of Scotland in the Middle Ages, told with old-fashioned swashbuckling style and equally archaic notions and biases. Mel Gibson, Sophie Marceau, Patrick McGoohan, Catherine McCormack, James Robinson, Brendan Gleeson. w. Randall Wallace (BOScr), d. Mel Gibson (**BDirector**). **BPicture, BCin,** BEdit, BArt, BSound, BCostume, BCDScore, **BSoundEdit, BMakeup.** Oscars: 10-5.
ADVENTURE: ACTION: War Stories; Middle Ages; Scotland Epics; Historical Drama; Rebels; Kings; Gay Men; Homophobia; Sleeper Hits
(Rob Roy; The Last Valley; Edward II)
(Ed: Out of nowhere, in a very bad year for standout films, this emerged at the Oscar nominations after winning virtually nothing else previously. It didn't even do very well at the box office in its original release)

Brazil, 1985, 131m, ★★★¹/₂/$$, Universal/MCA-U, R/P-V. A worker in a maze of futuristic bureaucracies (Jonathan Pryce) is mistaken for a terrorist amid the chaos of his dark society. Robert De Niro, Katherine Helmond, Bob Hoskins, Michael Palin. w. Tom Stoppard,

Terry Gilliam, Charles McKeown (BOScr), d. Terry Gilliam. BArt. Oscars: 2-0.
COMEDY DRAMA: FARCE: SATIRE: Black Comedy; Social Satire; Comedy of Errors; Ordinary People in Extraordinary Situations; Futuristic Films; Man vs. Society; Oppression; Bombs; Terrorists; Faded Hits; Cult Films; Outstanding Production Design
(Time Bandits; The Adventures of Baron Munchausen; The President's Analyst; 1984; Modern Times; Winter Kills; Twelve Monkeys)

Bread and Chocolate, 1973, 112m, ★★★/$$, Ind/NA. An immigrant waiter in Switzerland just can't win. His life falls apart as he's accused of murder and exposing himself at the same time. Nino Manfredi, Anna Karina, Johnny Dorelli, Paulo Turco. w. Franco Brusati, Iaia Fiastri, Nino Manfredi, d. Franco Brusati.
COMEDY: Comedy of Errors; FARCE: Misunderstandings; Identities-Mistaken; Accused Unjustly; Framed?; Waiters; Italians; Italian Films

Breaker Morant, 1980, 107m, ★★★¹/₂/$$$, NW/NW, R/P-V. Several soldiers are court-martialed under dubious circumstances during the Boer War. Edward Woodward, Bryan Brown, Jack Thompson. w. Johnathan Hardy, Bruce Beresford, David Stevens (BAScr), P-adap. Kenneth Ross, d. Bruce Beresford. Oscars: 1-0.
DRAMA: Courtroom Drama; Accused Unjustly; War Stories; Military Movies; Soldiers; Power Struggles; Courts Martial; World War I Era; Australian Films
(A Few Good Men; The Caine Mutiny Court Martial; Gallipoli)

Breakfast at Tiffany's, 1961, 114m, ★★★★/$$$$, Par/Par, NR/S. A country girl (Audrey Hepburn, BActress) gone sophisticate makes her living as a pseudo-mistress who's immune to love until a gigolo/writer (George Peppard) moves in upstairs and teaches her a few things. w. George Axelrod (BAScr), N-adap. Truman Capote, d. Blake Edwards (BDirector). **BOSong, BScore.** Oscars: 5-2.
COMEDY-DRAMA: COMEDY: ROMANCE: Romantic Comedy; SATIRE: Settling Down; Love-Reluctant; Playgirls; Prostitutes-High Class; Prostitutes-Male; Romance with Prostitute; Mistresses; Social Climbing; Free Spirits; Beautiful People; New York Life; Jetsetters; Dreams

(Funny Face; Paris When It Sizzles; How to Steal a Million; Hands Across the Table)

The Breakfast Club, 1985, 95m, ★★★¹/₂/$$$$, Universal/MCA-U, PG-13/P-S. Several teenagers are sentenced to Saturday detention together and true feelings and music videos emerge while they're locked up. Molly Ringwald, Judd Nelson, Emilio Estevez, Ally Sheedy, Anthony Hall. w. d. John Hughes.

DRAMA: COMEDY DRAMA: Teenage Movies; Bratpack Movies; High School Life; Class Conflicts; Suburban Life; Ensemble Films; Ensembles-Young People; Stagelike Films; Underrated; Time Capsules; Writer-Directors

(Pretty in Pink; Permanent Record; St. Elmo's Fire; Sixteen Candles; Dazed and Confused)

(Ed: The writing could be more in-depth and the characters a little less extreme, but it's still quite realistic and dramatic)

Breakfast for Two, 1937, 65m, ★★★/$$, RKO/NA. A wealthy woman marries for love but trains her hubby to be a good little breadwinner, too. Barbara Stanwyck, Herbert Marshall, Donald Meek, Glenda Farrell, Eric Blore, Etienne Girardot. w. Charles Kaufman, Paul Yawitz, Viola Brothers Shore, d. Alfred Santell.

COMEDY: FARCE: Screwball Comedy; Marriage Comedy; Woman Behind the Man; Playboys; Settling Down; Heiresses; Oil People; Texas; Hidden Gems; Forgotten Films

(Harriet Craig; Born to Be Bad)

Breakheart Pass, 1975, 94m, ★★¹/₂/$$, UA/MGM-UA, R/V. Murder and intrigue take place aboard a train heading through the rockies in the late 1800s. Charles Bronson, Ben Johnson, Richard Crenna, Jill Ireland, Charles Durning, Archie Moore, Ed Lauter. w. Alistair MacLean, N-adap., d. Tom Gries.

WESTERN: ACTION: MYSTERY: MURDER: MURDER MYSTERY: Trains; Trail of a Killer; Heist Stories; Could Been Good; Good Premise Unfulfilled

(Murder on the Orient Express; Avalanche Express)

Breakin', 1984, 87m, ★★/$$$, Cannon/MGM-UA, PG/P. A new dance style is introduced by street kids in New York. Lucinda Dickey, Adolfo "Shabba-Doo" Quinones, Michael "Boogaloo-Shrimp" Chambers, Ben Lokey, Tracey

"Ice T" Marrow. w. Charles Parker, Allen DeBevoise, Gerald Scaife, d. Joel Silberg.

Breakin' 2: Electric Boogaloo, 1984, 94m, ★★/$$, Cannon/MGM-UA, PG/P. Kids put on a show to raise money for a local center. w. Jan Ventura, Julie Reichert, d. Sam Firstenberg.

COMEDY: Music Movies; Dance Movies; Dancers; Inner City Life; Black Casts; Putting on a Show

(Krush Groove; Beat Street)

Breaking Away, 1979, 100m, ★★★¹/₂/$$$$, 20th/CBS-Fox, PG/P. Four guys from the wrong side of town enter a bicycle race to beat the right side of town even though their future may not be any brighter afterward. Dennis Quaid, Dennis Christopher, Daniel Stern, Barbara Barrie (BSActress), Paul Dooley. w. Steve Tesich (BOScr), d. Peter Yates (BDirector). BPicture, BAScore. Oscars: 5-1.

COMEDY DRAMA: Underdog Stories; Sports Movies; Ensemble Films; Bicycling; Teenagers; Young Men; Ensembles-Male; Snobs vs. Slobs; Class Conflicts; Coming of Age; Life Transitions; Friendships-Male; Midwestern Life; Sleeper Hits

(Quicksilver; American Flyers; Rocky; Rudy)

Breaking Glass, 1980, 104m, ★★¹/₂/$, GTO-Par/Par, R/S-P. A punk band flirts with small-time fame, and its singer cracks up. Hazel O'Connor, Phil Daniels, Jon Finch, Jonathan Pryce. w. d. Brian Gibson.

DRAMA: Music Movies; 1980s; Time Capsules; Rock Stars; Nervous Breakdowns; Singers; Musicians; British Films; Cult Films; Writer-Directors

(Sid and Nancy; Quadrophenia; Tommy)

Breaking In, 1989, 91m, ★★★/$$, Goldwyn/Goldwyn, PG-13/P. A veteran burglar (Burt Reynolds) takes on a student (Casey Siemaszko) and tries to make a comeback. Sheila Kelley, Stephen Tobolowsky. w. John Sayles, d. Bill Forsyth.

COMEDY DRAMA: Comedy-Light; Understudies/Proteges; Teachers and Students; Thieves; Comebacks; Midlife Crisis

(Bellman and True; The Mechanic)

Breakout, 1975, 96m, ★★¹/₂/$$$, Col/Col, R/V-P. A rescue artist climbs a mammoth stone face to get to a man in a prison atop it. Charles Bronson, Robert Duvall, John Huston, Randy Quaid, Jill Ireland, Sheree North. w. N-adap.

Howard B. Kreitsek, Frank Kowalski (Ten Second Jailbreak), d. Tom Gries.

ACTION: Rescue Drama; Prison Escapes; Escape Adventure; Saving Someone; Mexico; Mountain Climbing; Accused Unjustly

(The Eiger Sanction; Cliffhanger; For Your Eyes Only)

The Breaking Point, 1950, 97m, ★★¹/₂/$, WB/NA. A sailor allows smugglers to use his boat until they go too far by murdering his friend. John Garfield, Patricia Neal, Phyllis Thaxter, Juano Hernandez, Wallace Ford, Edmon Ryan. w. Ranald MacDougall, N-adap. Ernest Hemingway (To Have and Have Not), d. Michael Curtiz.

DRAMA: MURDER: Sailors; Florida; Avenging Death of a Loved One; Friendships-Male

(To Have and Have Not; Key Largo; and The Gun Runners, all based on Hemingway's To Have and Have Not)

Breaking the Rules, 1992, 100m, ★★/$, HBO/HBO, PG-13/S-P. Three young buddies go on the road to pursue their dreams while one is really dying of that dreaded movie disease. Jason Bateman, Johnathan Silverman, C. Thomas Howell, Kent Bateman, Annie Potts. w. Paul Shapiro, d. Neal Israel.

COMEDY: COMEDY DRAMA: Road Movies; Road Movies-Three Guys; Camping; Dreams; Disease Stories; Young Men; Coming of Age; Teenagers; Teenage Movies

(Calendar Girl; Coupe de Ville; Fandango; Staying Together; Teen Wolf Too)

(Ed: The tearjerker element would apparently appeal to maudlin, fanzine-crazed teenyboppers, but the male bonding stuff?)

Breaking the Sound Barrier (The Sound Barrier), 1952, 118m, ★★★¹/₂/$$, London Films-UA/NA. In his race to break the sound barrier before the Americans, a British aircraft tycoon sacrifices almost everything, including the safety of his pilots. Ralph Richardson, Nigel Patrick, Ann Todd, John Justin, Denholm Elliott. w. Terence Rattigan, d. David Lean.

DRAMA: Pilots-Military; Military Stories; Ethics; Race Against Time; Quests; Dreams; British Films; Forgotten Films; Hidden Gems

(The Right Stuff; The Memphis Belle)

(Ed: Richardson won several awards, including the New York Film Critics')

Breaking Up Is Hard to Do, 1979, 96m, ★★/$$$, ABC/Vidmark. Several divorced men take a beach house together and try to avoid nervous breakdowns by playing volleyball and girlwatching. Billy Crystal, Jeff Conaway, Tony Musante, Bonnie Franklin, Ted Bessell, David Ogden Stiers, Trish Stewart. d. Lou Antonio.
DRAMA: COMEDY DRAMA: Ensembles-Male; Beach Movies; Single Men; Divorce; TV Movies
(Hard Bodies; The Men's Club; That Championship Season)

Break of Hearts, 1935, 78m, ★★★/$$, RKO/Turner. A young female composer (Katharine Hepburn) deals with her marriage to an older conductor (Charles Boyer). w. Sarah Y. Mason, Victor Heerman, Anthony Veiller, d. Philip Moeller.
DRAMA: MELODRAMA: ROMANCE: Marriage Drama; Marriage on the Rocks; Romance-Older Men/Younger Women; Musicians; Female Protagonists; Female Screenwriters
(Intermezzo; Quality Street; The Little Minister; The Competition; Unfaithfully Yours)

A Breath of Scandal, 1960, 98m, ★★1/2/$, Par/Par. A European noblewoman takes up with an American capitalist to the consternation of her family and the European Community in general. Sophia Loren, Maurice Chevalier, John Gavin, Angela Lansbury, Milly Vitale. w. Walter Bernstein, P-adap. Ferenc Molnar (*Olimpia*), d. Michael Curtiz.
DRAMA: ROMANCE: Romantic Drama; Costume Drama; Historical Drama; Lover; Family Dislikes; Scandals; Royalty; Romance-Class Conflicts
REMAKE OF: His Glorious Night (MGM, 1929)
(Lady L.; The Millionairess)

Breathless (*A Bout de Souffle*), 1959, 90m, ★★★/$$$, Ind/Nos. A cop killer on the lam spends large amounts of time philosophizing about French and American culture while hiding out in his American girlfriend's Parisian apartment in this key work of the French New Wave. Jean-Paul Belmondo, Jean Seberg, Daniel Boulanger, Jean-Pierre Melville, Jean-Luc Goddard. w. Jean-Luc Goddard, SS-adap. François Truffaut, d. Jean-Luc Goddard.
DRAMA: Art Films; Avant Garde; Erotic Drama; ROMANCE: Outlaw Road Movies; Criminal Couples; Fugitives; Fugitives from the Law; Cop Killers; Las Vegas; Sexy Men; Sexy Women; Clever Plots & Endings; French Films; French New Wave Films

Breathless, 1983, 100m, ★★1/2/$, Orion/Orion, R, P-S-FFN-MFN. A remake of the cop killer on the run story reset from France to Vegas with the fugitive (Richard Gere) running and hiding with a French girl (Valerie Kaprisky) instead of an American one. w. Jim McBride, LM Kit Carson, d. McBride.
DRAMA: Erotic Drama; ROMANCE: Fugitives; Fugitives from Law; Cop Killers; Las Vegas; Sexy Men; Sexy Women; Clever Plots and Endings; Crossing the Border
REMAKE OF: Breathless (1959)
(American Gigolo; Wild at Heart)
(Ed: Whether you like this depends entirely upon how much you like Gere)

A Breed Apart, 1984, 95m, ★1/2/$, Hemdale/Hemdale, PG. A would-be bald eagle poacher is thwarted by a zealous environmentalist. Rutger Hauer, Powers Boothe, Kathleen Turner, Donald Pleasence. w. Paul Wheeler, d. Philippe Mora.
DRAMA: Environmental Dilemmas; Animal Rights; Mountain Climbing; Flops-Major
(Ed: Boring and pointless. Sad for all involved)

Breezy, 1973, 107m, ★★/$, Universal/MCA-U, PG/S. A bright-eyed hippy chick breathes life into an older man. William Holden, Kay Lenz, Roger C. Carmel, Marj Dusay, Joan Hotchkis. w. Jo Heims, d. Clint Eastwood.
ROMANCE: DRAMA: Romantic Drama; Romance-Older Men/Younger Women; Free Spirits; Midlife Crisis; Hippies; Flops-Major; Coulda Been Good
(Love in the Afternoon; Atlantic City; Petulia)

Brenda Starr, 1986/1991, 94m, ★★/$, Col/Col, PG. Crack reporter, the demure Brenda, heads to South America to save the world from a mad scientist in this comic adaptation. Brooke Shields, Timothy Dalton, Tony Peck, Diana Scarwid, Jeffrey Tambor. w. James Buchanan, d. Robert Ellis Miller.
COMEDY DRAMA: Comic Heroes; Detective Stories; Detectives-Female; Journalists as Detective; Female Protagonists; Rule the World-Plot to; Flops-Major
(Ed: Looks good, but looks are deceiving)

Brewster McCloud, 1970, 101m, ★★★/$, MGM/MGM-UA, PG. A young man (Bud Cort) hides up inside the Houston Astrodome wanting to fly like a bird to the suffering of his girlfriend (Shelley Duvall) while an angel watches over him (Sally Kellerman). Michael Murphy, Stacy Keach. w. Doran Cannon, d. Robert Altman.
COMEDY: COMEDY DRAMA: Black Comedy; Comedy-Light; Fantasy; Mental Illness; Dreams; Angels; Flying People; Eccentric People; Cult Films
(MASH; Harold and Maude)

Brewster's Millions, 1935, 84m, ★★★/$$$, British and Dominion/NA. As a test of his playboy credentials, a British heir must spend a million pounds in two months in order to receive the rest of his inheritance. Jack Buchanan, Lili Damita, Nancy O'Neil, Amy Veness, Sebastian Shaw. w. Arthur Wimperis, Paul Gangelin, Douglas Furber, Clifford Grey, Donovan Pedelty, Wolfgang Wilhelm, P-adap. George Barr McCutcheon, d. Thornton Freeland.
REMAKE OF: 1916 and 1921 silent versions

Brewster's Millions, 1945, 79m, ★★/$$, Edward Small-UA/Media. A remake of above film, in an American setting. Dennis O'Keefe, Eddie "Rochester" Anderson, Helen Walker, Thurston Hall. w. Sig Herzig, Charles Rogers, d. Allan Dwan.

Brewster's Millions, 1985, 97m, ★★/$$$, Universal/MCA-U, PG/P. Man (Richard Pryor) inherits millions from a long-lost relative, but there's a stipulation in the will-he's supposed to have to buy so many things, he'll be so sick of having so much money, he won't want it. John Candy, Lonette McKee, Hume Cronyn. w. Hershel Weingrod, Timothy Harris, Walter Hill, N-adap. George McCutcheon, d. Walter Hill.
COMEDY: Comedy-Situation; Race Against Time; Rich People; Inheritances at Stake; Heirs; Bets; Greed
REMAKE OF: 1945 version, six other adaptations
(Easy Money; Arthur; Arthur 2, On the Rocks)

Brian's Song, 1970, 73m, ★★★/$$$$$, ABC/Col, G. An all-time ratings champ, a black football star, Gayle Sayers, (Billy Dee Williams), has a white football buddy, Brian Piccolo (James Caan), who's dying of cancer. d. Buzz Kulik.

DRAMA: MELODRAMA: Tearjerkers; Disease Stories; Death-Dealing with; Friendships-Male; Sports Movies; Football; True Stories; Blockbusters; TV Movies; Crying in Football
(Bang the Drum Slowly; Love Story)
The Bride, 1985, 113m, ★★/$, 20th/ CBS-Fox, R/S. A revised version of the *Bride of Frankenstein* with Sting as the doctor and Jennifer Beals as the bride. w. Lloyd Fonvielle, d. Franc Roddam.
DRAMA: ROMANCE: HORROR: Mad Scientists; Flops-Major; Revisionist Films
REMAKE OF: The Bride of Frankenstein
The Bride Came C.O.D., 1941, 92m, ★★★/$$$, WB/MGM-UA. A pilot in need of money plans to take an unwitting heiress to a group of kidnappers with whom he will share the ransom they'll ask. Unfortunately, his plane crashes in the desert on the way, and he's stuck with her trying to survive. Bette Davis, James Cagney, Harry Davenport, Stuart Erwin, Eugene Pallette. w. Julius J. Espstein, Philip Epstein, d. William Davenport.
COMEDY: Comedy of Errors; Romance-Reluctant; Romance-Bickering; Kidnappings; Heiresses; Pilots-Airplane; Airplane Crashes; Desert Settings; Feisty Females; Stranded; Stranded on an Island; Survival Drama
(Swept Away; Castaway)
The Bride Is Much Too Beautiful, 1958, 90m, ★★★/$$$, Ind/Nos. A farm girl (Brigitte Bardot) from France is brought to Paris for the bright lights of the fashion runways and romance with a man (Louis Jourdan). d. Fred Surin.
DRAMA: MELODRAMA: ROMANCE: Dreams; Fashion World; French Films; City vs. Country; Fame-Rise to
(Babette Goes to War; And God Created Woman; Mahogany; A New Kind of Love)
Bride of Frankenstein, 1935, 75m, ★★★1/2/$$$, Universal/MCA-U. A black-comic re-framing of the Frankenstein tale, in which the doctor must make a mate for his creation. Boris Karloff, Colin Clive, Elsa Lanchester, Ernest Thesiger, Valerie Hobson, E. E. Clive, Dwight Frye. w. John L. Balderston, William Hurlbut, d. James Whale.
HORROR: Black Comedy; **ROMANCE: SATIRE:** Monsters-Manmade; Matchmakers; Frankenstein; Hidden Gems
(The Bride; Re-Animator 2)

Bride of the Gorilla, 1951, 76m, ★★/$, Ind/Nos. An island woman injects a rubber plantation owner with a serum that brings out the beast in him. Barbara Payton, Lon Chaney Jr., Raymond Burr, Tom Conway, Paul Cavanagh. w. d. Curt Siodmak.
HORROR: Human Monsters; Cures/Elixirs; Scientists-Mad; Experiments; Poisons; Uninentionally Funny; Writer-Directors
Bride of the Monster, 1955, 69m, ★★/$, Edward D. Wood/Nos. A mad scientist invents an atomic ray that enhances the strength of whatever gets in its way. Unfortunately, he aims it at an octopus, who gets really mad about it. Bela Lugosi, Tor Johnson, Tony McCoy, Loretta King.
HORROR: Scientists-Mad; Experiments; Monsters-Mutant; Octopi-Angry; Unintentionally Funny
The Bride Walks Out, 1936, 81m, ★★1/2/$$, RKO/Turner. A woman gets tired of having to scrimp and save on her husband's paltry wages. Besides, she has her own career. Barbara Stanwyck, Gene Raymond, Robert Young, Helen Broderick, Hattie McDaniel. w. P. J. Wolfson, Philip G. Epstein, d. Leigh Jason.
COMEDY: MELODRAMA: Making a Living; Marriage Comedy; Marriage on the Rocks; Female Protagonists; Ahead of Its Time
(B.F.'s Daughter; Breakfast for Two)
The Bride Wore Black, 1968, 107m, ★★★/$$, UA/MGM-UA, PG/S-V. A woman whose fiancé was killed by a group of co-conspirators kills them off one by one. Jeanne Moreau, Jean-Claude Brialy, Michel Bouquet, Charles Denner. w. François Truffaut, Jean-Louis Richard, N-adap. William Irish, d. François Truffaut.
DRAMA: SUSPENSE: MYSTERY: Detective Stories; Murders-One by One; Murderers-Female; Widows; Murderers-Black Widow; Character Studies; Trail of a Killer; Female Protagonists; Hitchcockian; Time Capsules; 1960s; French Films
(Ed: Lovely to look at, but rather slow)
The Bride Wore Red, 1937, 103m, ★★★/$$, MGM/MGM-UA. A chorus girl gets thrown into high society when she's brought to a count's resort and pursued by two rich men. Joan Crawford, Robert

Young, Franchot Tone, Billie Burke. w. Tess Slesinger, Bradbury Foote, P-adap. Ferenc Molnar (*The Girl from Trieste*), d. Dorothy Arzner.
DRAMA: ROMANCE: Music Movies; Dancers; Romance-Triangles; Social Climbing; Resorts; Female Screenwriters; Female Directors
Brides of Dracula, 1960, 85m, ★★★/$$, U-Hammer/MCA-U. One of Dracula's followers, Baron Meinster, is locked in his room by his suspicious mother. Unfortunately, a servant lets him out to wreak havoc at a boarding school for girls. David Peel, Peter Cushing, Freda Jackson, Martita Hunt, Yvonne Monlaur, Andrée Melly. w. Jimmy Sangster, Peter Bryan, Edward Percy, d. Terence Fisher.
HORROR: Vampires; Murders-One by One; Boarding Schools; Murders of Females
Brideshead Revisited, 1982, 540m, ★★★/$$$, BBC-PBS/PBS, Facets, BBC. An architectural painter in Edwardian era England finds himself caught in the spell of a very wealthy family, and particularly their enigmatic son, Sebastian, his great friend with a stuffed bear named Aloysius. Jeremy Irons, Anthony Andrews, Diana Quick, Laurence Olivier, John Gielgud, Stephane Audran, Calie Bloon, Mona Washbourne. N-adap. Evelyn Waugh, d. Charles Sturridge, Michael Lindsay-Hogg.
DRAMA: ROMANCE: Romantic Drama; Friendships-Great; Friendships-Male; Artists; Homo-Eroticism; Edwardian Era; Costume Drama; Rich People; Rich vs. Poor; Sleeper Hits; Cult Films; British Films; Mini-Series
(Maurice; The French Lieutenant's Woman)
The Bridge, 1991, 99m, ★★1/2/$, Moonlight-British Screen-Film Four/NA, R/S. A young English artist vacationing on the Continent meets a married woman and has an affair. Saskia Reeves, David O'Hara, Joss Ackland, Anthony Higgins, Rosemary Harris. w. Adrian Hodges, d. Sydney MacCartney.
DRAMA: ROMANCE: Romantic Drama; Romance-Older Women/Younger Men; Romance with Married Person; Vacation Romance; Vacations; Young Men
The Bridge of San Luis Rey, 1944, 85m, ★★★1/2/$$, UA/New World. A flimsy bridge in Peru collapses with five

people on it, sending them plunging to their deaths. In flashbacks, we learn why they all happened to be on that bridge at that unfortunate time. Lynn Bari, Francis Lederer, Nazimova, Louis Calhern, Akim Tamiroff, Donald Woods. w. Howard Estabrook, N-adap. Thornton Wilder, d. Rowland V. Lee.

DRAMA: TRAGEDY: Ensemble Films; Disaster Stories; Historical Drama; True or Not; Character Studies; Flashbacks; South America; Hidden Gems
(Friday the Thirteenth [1933])

The Bridge on the River Kwai, 1957, 161m, ★★★★/$$$$, Columbia/RCA-Col, NR/V. British POWS in World War II Asia build a bridge for the Japanese while their free fellow soldiers are on their way to destroy it before it's put to use. Alec Guiness (**BActor**), William Holden, Sessue Hayakawa (**BSActor**), Jack Hawkins. w. Robert Bolt (**BAScr**), N-adap. Pierre Boulle, d. David Lean (**BDirector**). **BPicture, BCin, BEdit, BScore.** Oscars: 8-7.

DRAMA: Epics; War Movies; **ADVEN-TURE:** Friendship-Male; POWs; World War II Stories; Sabotage; Asia; British Films; Japanese as Enemy; Special Teams-Military; Best Picture Winners
(Stalag 17; The Deer Hunter; The Mission)

A Bridge Too Far, 1977, 175m, ★★½/$$$, UA/MGM-UA, R/P-V. Allied forces try to cut off the Germans on their march through Holland, but the mission is doomed, though full of stars: James Caan, Michael Caine, Robert Redford, Sean Connery, Laurence Olivier, Liv Ullman, Edward Fox, Dirk Bogarde, Gene Hackman. w. William Goldman, d. Richard Attenborough.

DRAMA: War Movies; Epics; World War II Era; Ensemble Films; Misunderstandings; All-Star Casts; International Casts; Big Budgets; Major Flops; Battle of the Bulge
(The Battle of the Bulge; Battleground)

The Bridges at Toko-Ri, 1955, 103m, ★★★/$$$, Par/Par, NR/V. A civilian lawyer who's now a pilot in the Korean War has opposition to his mission but has to continue on anyway. William Holden, Grace Kelly, Frederic March, Mickey Rooney. w. Valentine Davies, N-adap. James Michener, d. Mark Robson. **BSFX.** Oscars: 1-1.

DRAMA: ROMANCE: War Stories; Korean War; Anti-establishment Films;

Lawyers; Peaceful People; Patriotism; Pilots-Military; Military Stories
(The Bold and the Brave; To Hell and Back)

Brief Encounter, 1946, 85m, ★★★★/$$$, Rank-U/Par. A couple of commuters in the British countryside (Celia Johnson, **BActress**; Trevor Howard) meet regularly and soon develop a restrained romance, though each is already involved. w. David Lean, David Havelock (**BAScr**), P-adap. Noel Coward, d. David Lean (**BDirector**). Oscars: 3-0.

REMAKE: Brief Encounter (1974)

Brief Encounter, 1974, 103m, ★★½/$$, U/NA. Sophia Loren, Richard Burton. P-adap. Noel Coward, d. Alan Bridges.

>ROMANCE: DRAMA: Romantic Drama; Affairs-Clandestine; Narrated Films; Female Protagonists; Trains; Suburban Life
(Falling in Love; And Now, My Love; An Affair to Remember; Love Affair)

A Brief History of Time, 1992, 85m, ★★★½/$$, PBS/Par. The theories of time and history of scientist Stephen Hawking, narrated by the ailing man himself. Stephen Hawking. w. Hawking, d. Errol Morris.

Documentaries; Historical Drama; Scientists; Narrated Films; Hidden Gems

Brigadoon, 1954, 108m, ★★★½/$$$$, MGM/MGM-UA. Two Americans on vacation in Scotland discover a singing and dancing village which is possibly only a mirage. Gene Kelly, Van Johnson, Cyd Charisse. w. P-adap. Lerner & Loewe, d. Vincente Minnelli.

MUSICAL: ADVENTURE: Musical Fantasy; **FAMILY:** Fantasy; Time Travel; **ROMANCE:** Scotland; Illusions/Hallucinations; Americans Abroad; Vacations
(Finian's Rainbow; The Luck of the Irish)

Bright Angel, 1991, 94m, ★★½/$$, HBO/HBO, R/V-S. A young man and woman meet up on the way to their home-town, with one trying to find his long-lost mother, and the other, an ex-con, trying to get her brother out of jail by whatever means necessary. Dermot Mulroney, Lili Taylor, Sam Shepard, Valerie Perrine, Burt Young, Bill Pullman, Mary Kay Plave, Delroy Lindo, Kevin Tighe. w. Richard Ford, d. Michael Fields.

DRAMA: Saving Someone; **ROMANCE:** Vigilantes; Children-Longlost; Orphans; Brothers; Prison Escapes

Bright Eyes, 1934, 90m, ★★★/$$$$, 20th/Fox. Shirley Temple sings and dances her way through a custody battle she's at the center of. James Dunn, Jane Withers. d. David Butler.

MUSICALS: MELODRAMA: Musical Drama; Divorce; Custody Battles; Girlhood; Child Protagonists

Bright Lights, Big City, 1988, 110m, ★★½/$$, 20th/CBS-Fox, R/P-S. Yuppie (Michael J. Fox) has breakdown when his wife leaves him, and he tells you all about it. Swoosie Kurtz. w. N-adap. Jay McInerney, d. James Bridges.

DRAMA: SATIRE: Character Studies; Yuppies; Bratpack Movies; New York Life; Beautiful People; Fashion World; Pre-Life Crisis; Narrated Films; Nervous Breakdowns; Young Men; Alienation
(Less Than Zero; Slaves of New York; The Secret of My Success)

Bright Road, 1953, 69m, ★★½/$, MGM/NA. In a southern black school in the fifties, a troubled boy finally gains acceptance when he rids the place of bees. Dorothy Dandridge, Harry Belafonte, Robert Horton, Philip Hepburn. w. Emmet Lavery, d. Gerald Mayer.

DRAMA: Black Casts; Southerns; Ostracism; Boyhood; Ahead of Its Time; Forgotten Films
(Carmen Jones; A Hero Ain't Nothin' but a Sandwich; Cornbread Ernie and Me)
(Ed: An odd premise, perhaps forgotten for a reason)

Bright Victory, 1951, 97m, ★★★/$$$, Universal/NA. A soldier, blinded by a mortar shell in World War II, has to deal with his new handicap after the war. Arthur Kennedy (**BActor**), Peggy Dow, Julie Adams, James Edwards, Will Geer, Jim Backus. w. Robert Buckner, N-adap. Baynard Kendrick, d. Mark Robson. **BSound.** Oscars 2-0.

MELODRAMA: Character Studies; Comebacks; Disabled People; Disabled but Nominated; Blind People; Soldiers; Veterans; Forgotten Films
(Dark Victory; The Best Years of Our Lives; On Wings of Eagles)

Brighton Beach Memoirs, 1985, ★★★/$$, Universal/MCA-U, PG. Neil Simon's memoirs of growing up in Brooklyn with many relatives battling for the bathroom, leading the hero to talk to the camera. Johnathan Silverman, Blythe Danner, Judith Ivey, Jason Alexander. w. P-adap. Neil Simon, d. Herbert Ross.

COMEDY: FAMILY: Family Stories; Coming of Age; Autobiographical Stories; Boyhood; Jewish People; New York Life; 1940s; Coulda Been Great; Crossing the Line; Narrated Films

TRILOGY SEQUELS: Biloxi Blues; Broadway Bound.

(Radio Days; Brooklyn Bridge [TV Series])

Brighton Rock, 1947, 92m, ★★★/$$, Associated British-Charter Films/ Horizon. A young girl in a British seaside town naively falls for a young gangster, who marries her only to secure his alibi in a murder case. Richard Attenborough, Hermione Baddeley, Harcourt Williams, Carol Marsh. w. Graham Greene, Terence Rattigan, N-adap. Graham Greene, d. John Boulting.

DRAMA: SUSPENSE: MURDER: Crime Drama; Mob Stories; Romance-Dangerous; Enemy-Sleeping with the; Love-Questionable; Women in Jeopardy; British Films

(Shadow of a Doubt; Deceived; Rebecca)

Brighty of the Grand Canyon, 1967, 89m, ★★/$$, Ind/Karol. A mule and the men who ride her (Joseph Cotten) through the canyon. d. Norman Foster.

CHILDREN'S: FAMILY: ADVENTURE: Animal Stories; Desert Settings; Elderly Men; Men and Girls

(Ed: Poor Joseph Cotten)

Brimstone and Treacle, 1983, 99m, ★★★1/2/$$, UAC/MGM-UA, R, P-S-FFN-MRN. A strange young man (Sting) enters a home where a middle-aged couple have a beautiful daughter on life-support, and he begins to have his way with everything. Denholm Elliott. w. Dennis Potter, d. Richard Loncraine.

DRAMA: Psychological Drama; Black Comedy; Comedy-Morbid; Art Films; Malicious; Menaces; Drifters; Death-Dealing with; Disabled People; Mindgames; Dangerous Men; Eccentric People; Wild People; Young Men; Comas; British Films; Underrated; Hidden Gems; Cult Films

(Entertaining Mr. Sloane; The Bride; Quadrophenia)

(Ed: Due to Sting's other films, and the film's similarity to *Mr. Sloane,* it's been unduly ignored)

Bring Me the Head of Alfredo Garcia, 1974, 112m, ★★★/$$$, UA/ MGM-UA, R/P-EV-B&G. A piano player in the wild west gets caught up in a Mexican gang of lowlifes, leading to vio-

lence and vengeance. Warren Oates, Gig Young, Kris Kristofferson. w. Guy Dawson, Sam Peckinpah, d. Peckinpah.

DRAMA: WESTERN: ACTION: Bounty Hunters; Violence-Sudden; Road Movies; Rewards at Stake; Blood and Gore; Revenge

(The Wild Bunch; The Ballad of Cable Hogue; Chato's Land)

Bring on the Night, 1985, 97m, ★★1/2/$$$, UAC/MGM-UA. Sting's rock-umentary detailing the formation of his first band after The Police for his first solo album with music videos. Rockumentary; Concert Film; Autobiographical Stories; Music Videos; Rock Stars

Bringing Up Baby (B&W/C), 1937, 97m, ★★★★/$$, RKO/Turner. A nerdy professor (Cary Grant) needs a grant from a museum and a madcap heiress (Katharine Hepburn) related to the donor is getting in the way by avoiding him then changing her mind and following him to find a dinosaur bone. w. Dudley Nichols, SS-adap. Hagar Wilde, d. Howard Hawks.

COMEDY: FARCE: Screwball Comedy; Race Against Time; Romance-Opposites Attract; Romance-Girl Wants Boy; Romance-Reluctant; Class Conflicts; Accident Prone; Treasure Hunts; Archaeologists; Nerdy Professors; Nuisances; Heiresses-Madcap; Upper Class; Class Conflicts; Mistaken Identities; Misunderstandings; Mix-Ups; One-Day Stories; 1930s; Ahead of its Time; Cult Films

(What's Up, Doc?; My Man Godfrey; Holiday; Sylvia Scarlett)

(Ed: Not a hit at first, but soon picked up steam in revival houses and on TV. A much-imitated classic that is the epitome of the screwball comedy and the bicker-ing romance)

Brink of Life, 1958, 84m, ★★★/$$, Svensk-Embassy/Voyager. Three Swedish women (Bibi Andersson, Ingrid Thulin, Eva Dahlbeck) are examined in a mater-nity ward before their births. w. d. Ingmar Bergman.

DRAMA: MELODRAMA: Art Films; Swedish Films; Babies-Having; Women's Films; Female Protagonists; Writer-Directors; Bergmanesque

The Brinks Job, 1978, 103m, ★★★/$$$, Universal/MCA-U, PG/P. The true story of the robbery of a Brinks armored car

office by a bunch of misfits on the brink of screwing it up. Peter Falk, Peter Boyle, Warren Oates. w. Walon Green, NF-adap. Noel Behn (*The Big Stick-Up at Brinks*), d. William Friedkin.

COMEDY DRAMA: Action Comedy; Heist Stories; Capers; Comedy of Errors; Ensemble Films; Thieves; Criminals-Stupid; True Stories; Hidden Gems (Silver Bears; The Italian Job; The Lavender Hill Mob; The Great Train Robbery; Whiffs)

Brittania Hospital, 1982, 112m, ★★1/2/$$, EMI-Universal/EMI-HBO, R/S-MFN-B&G. Pure and total chaos at a British hospital where a body transplant experiment goes haywire, a strike is impending, an expose is being filmed, and the Queen is on the way. d. Lindsay Anderson.

COMEDY: SATIRE: FARCE: Black Comedy; Morbid Comedy; Hospitals; Body Parts; Misunderstandings; Switch-Ups; Strikes

SEQUEL TO: If . . . and O Lucky Man! (The Hospital; If; O Lucky Man!; Article 99)

Broadcast News, 1987, 132m, ★★★1/2/$$$$, 20th/Fox, R/P-S-MRN. A female TV producer (Holly Hunter, BActress) has a best friend (Albert Brooks, BSActor) who loves her, but she may love the dopey anchorman (William Hurt, BActor) instead. w. d. James L. Brooks (BOScr, BDirector). BPicture, BEdit. Oscars: 7-0.

COMEDY: ROMANCE: Romantic Comedy; **COMEDY DRAMA: SATIRE:** Romance-Mismatched; Midlife Crisis; Romance-Triangles; Jealousy; Romance-Follow Your Heart; Friends in Love; Smart vs. Dumb; Extroverted vs. Intro-verted; Neurotic People; Single Women; Career Women; TV Life; Journalists; Washington D.C.; Female Protagonists (The Mary Tyler Moore Show [TV Series]; Switching Channels; His Girl Friday; Up Close and Personal)

Broadway Bill, 1934, 104m, ★★/$$, Col/NA. An underdog wins the Derby, making a rich man of his humble, easy-going trainer. Warner Baxter, Myrna Loy, Walter Connolly, Helen Vinson, Douglass Dumbrille, Paul Harvey, Ward Bond. w. Robert Riskin, SS-adap. Mark Hellinger, d. Frank Capra.

COMEDY DRAMA: Rags to Riches; Horse Racing; Bets; Underdog Stories

Broadway Bound, 1991, 94m, ★★★/ $$$, ABC Productions/ABC, NR. An autobiographical story of a two brothers in a lower-class New York neighborhood who dream of escaping from their family tensions and writing for Broadway. Anne Bancroft, Hume Cronyn, Corey Parker, Jonathan Silverman. w. P-adap. Neil Simon, d. Paul Bogart.
DRAMA: MELODRAMA: COMEDY
DRAMA: Coming of Age; Pre-Life Crisis; Family Stories; Autobiographical Stories; Mothers and Sons; Mothers-Troublesome; Mothers-Struggling; Jewish People; Writers; 1940s; TV Movies
Trilogy: Brighton Beach Memoirs; Biloxi Blues.
(Lost in Yonkers; Radio Days; Enter Laughing)
(Ed: More dramatic than the previous two in the trilogy, and though more insightful, less entertaining)
Broadway Danny Rose (B&W), 1984, 84m, ★★★★/$$$, Orion/Orion, PG/P. A two-bit talent agent (Woody Allen) finds himself mistaken for the boyfriend of a mobster's girl (Mia Farrow). w. d. Woody Allen (BOScr, BDirector). Oscars: 2-0.
COMEDY: Chase Movies; Action Comedy; Capers; Fugitives from the Mob; Fugitives from a Murderer; Identities-Mistaken; Romance-Reluctant; Romance-Mismatched; Mob Girls; Mob Comedy; New York Life; Fortunetellers; Ventriloquists; Hidden Gems
(Manhattan Murder Mystery; Zelig; The Purple Rose of Cairo; Into the Night; Sister Act; Something Wild; Mr. Saturday Night; Forget Paris)
(Ed: Great performances from Allen, but especially Farrow. Entertaining for even those who don't get Woody's usual humor)
Broadway Melody, 1929, 110m, ★★★/ $$$$, MGM/MGM-UA. Of historical interest as the first ever fully singing movie musical. The origin of the cliche in which a chorus girl gets her big break when the star can't perform. Charles King, Anita Page, Bessie Love, Jed Prouty, Kenneth Thompson, Eddie Kane. w. James Gleason, Norman Houston, Edmond Goulding, d. Harry Beaumont.
MUSICALS: Fame-Rise to; Understudies; Theater Life; Dancers; Singers
(Forty-Second Street; All About Eve)
Broadway Melody of 1936, 1935, 103m, ★★★/$$$, MGM/MGM-UA. A snitty columnist butts heads with a

dogged Broadway producer. Jack Benny, Robert Taylor, Una Merkel, Eleanor Powell, June Knight, Vilma and Buddy Ebsen. w. Jack McGowan, Sid Silvers, Harry Conn, SS-adap. Moss Hart, d. Roy del Ruth.
Broadway Melody of 1938, 1937, 110m, MGM/MGM-UA. The show almost doesn't go on, due to tensions backstage. Eleanor Powell, George Murphy, Sophie Tucker, Judy Garland, Robert Taylor, Buddy Ebsen, Sid Silvers, d. Roy del Ruth.
Broadway Melody of 1940, 1939, 102m, MGM/MGM-UA. The struggle of a dancing couple to see their names in lights against the background of other power struggles on Broadway. Fred Astaire, Eleanor Powell, George Murphy, Douglas Macphail, Frank Morgan. w. Leon Gordon, George Oppenheimer, SS-adap. Jack McGowan, Dore Schary, d. Norman Taurog.
MUSICALS: Theater Life; Singers; Dancers; Actors; Actresses; Ensemble Films; All-Star Casts; Putting on a Show
Broken Arrow, 1950, 92m, ★★1/2/$$$, 20th Fox. Apache warriors and the white settlers in their area learn to live together with the help of a humane Army scout. James Stewart, Jeff Chandler, Debra Paget, Basil Ruysdael, Will Geer. w. Michael Blankfort, N-adap. Elliot Arnold, d. Delmer Daves.
WESTERNS: Indians-American; Indians-American, Conflict with; Pioneers
Broken Blossoms, 1919, 95m, (B&W, Silent), ★★★1/2/$$$$, UA/Nos. A cruel father in a Chinese slum of London kills his daughter, and in turn is killed by her lover, who then kills himself. Lillian Gish, Donald Crisp, Richard Berthelmess. wd. D. W. Griffith, SS-adap. Thomas Burke (*The Chink and the Child* from *Limehouse Nights*).
DRAMA: MELODRAMA: TRAGEDY: MURDER: Chinese People; London; Fathers & Daughters; Murders of Children; Suicidal Tendencies
Broken Lance, 1954, 96m, ★★★/$$$, 20th/Fox. An iron-fisted cattle rancher drives his sons away with his stern, unbending ways. Spencer Tracy, Richard Widmark, Robert Wagner, Jean Peters, Katy Jurado, Earl Holliman, E. G. Marshall. w. Richard Murphy, SS-adap. Philip Yordan, d. Edward Dmytryk.
WESTERN: DRAMA: Cattle Ranchers;

Fathers & Sons; Stern Men; Faded Hits (Edward, My Son; The Mountain; Hud)
Broken Noses, 1987, 77m, (B&W), ★★★/$, Mainline-Kira Films/Mainline, NR. A beautifully shot, abstract documentary about an Olympic boxer and the young boys he trains. Andy Minsker, The Mount Scott Boxing Team. d. Bruce Weber. Documentaries; Art Films; Sports Movies; Boxing; Boyhood; Men and Boys; Homoeroticism; Coming of Age
(Ed: More about the rituals of masculinity and male bonding than about the sport itself)
A Bronx Tale, 1993, 120m, ★★★/$$, 20th-Savoy/20th, R/V. The story of a boy growing up under the mob in his neighborhood in the Bronx during the 60s and the relationship he develops with a leader (Chazz Palminteri) after he witnesses a murder he committed and doesn't turn him in-which leads him into much trouble when he falls for a black girl. Robert De Niro, Lillo Brancato, Chazz Palmintieri, Frank Capra, Taral Hicks, Joe Pesci. w. P-adap. Chazz Palmintieri, d. Robert De Niro.
DRAMA: TRAGEDY: Coming of Age; Autobiographical Stories; Mob Movies; Fathers & Sons; Men and Boys; Friendships-Male; Friendships-Great; Proteges; New York Life; Race Relations; Black vs. White; Episodic Stories; Italians; 1960s; Narrated Films; Actor; Directors
(Mean Streets; GoodFellas; Five Corners)
(Ed: The climax is a bit too coincidental, but the story's genuine nature carries it along, though its ethics may seem out of place)
The Brood, 1979, 90m, Avco-Embassy/ Embassy, R, P-V-B&G, ★★★/$$$. A therapist experiments with ways for passive patients to express their anger outwardly and the result is blood and gore via a woman whose children kill every time she gets mad. Samantha Eggar, Art Hindle, Oliver Reed. w. d. David Cronenberg.
HORROR: SUSPENSE: SCI-FI: MURDER: Child Murderers; Mothers & Children; Experiments; Scientists-Mad; Psychics; Writer-Directors; Cult Films
(Scanners; Videodrome; The Class of Miss MacMichael)
The Brother from Another Planet, 1984, 109m, Island/CBS-Fox, R, ★★★/ $$$. An alien (Joe Morton) lands in

Harlem and happens to be black, so he fits right in, except for the fact that he's a mute, has three toes, and can "mind-meld" with video machines. Tom Wright, Caroline Aaron, Randy Sue Carter. w. d. John Sayles.

COMEDY: Black Comedy; **SATIRE: COMEDY DRAMA:** Black Protagonists; Black Men; Aliens-Outer Space, Good; Fish out of Water Stories; Bounty Hunters; New York Life; Writer-Directors

(Brother John; Splash; Coming to America)

Brother John, 1972, 94m, ★★★/$$, Col/Col, PG. A black man appears claiming to Jesus returned, but nobody believes him. Meanwhile, he checks out the racial situation. Sidney Poitier, Will Geer, Paul Winfield. d. James Goldstone.

COMEDY DRAMA: SATIRE: Black Men; Black Casts; Angels; Southerns; Race Relations; Jesus Christ; Revisionist Films; Unions; Working Class

(The Brother from Another Planet; The Prophecy)

Brother Rat, 1938, 89m, ★★¹/2/$$, WB/NA. Young officers in training at a military academy pull pranks and get their come-uppance. Wayne Morris, Eddie Albert, Ronald Reagan, Priscilla Lane, Jane Bryan, Jane Wyman. w. Richard Macaulay, Jerry Wald, P-adap. Fred Finklehoffe, John Monks, d. William Keighley.

COMEDY: Military Comedy; Military Schools; Forgotten Films; Practical Jokers

Brother Sun, Sister Moon, 1973, 121m, ★★★/$$, Par/Par, R/S-V-MRN. A historical drama of the life Francis of Assisi. Graham Faulkner, Judi Bowker, Alec Guinness, Leigh Lawson, Valentina Cortese. w. d. Franco Zeffirelli.

DRAMA: Biographies; Historical Drama; Costume Drama; Middle Ages; Young Men; Writer-Directors

(Romeo and Juliet; The Devils; Queen Margot)

The Brotherhood, 1968, 98m, ★★¹/2/$$, Par/Par. Two brothers in the Mafia struggle to get to the top, fueled by their sibling rivalry and mutual ambition. Kirk Douglas, Alex Cord, Luther Adler, Irene Papas, Susan Strasberg. w. Lewis John Carlino, d. Martin Ritt.

DRAMA: Crime Drama; Mob Stories; Brothers; Italians; Rivalries; Friends as Enemies

(Once Upon a Time in America; Manhattan Melodrama; Mean Streets; GoodFellas)

Brotherhood of Satan, 1971, 92m, ★★/$, Col/Goodtimes, R/V. Paganism takes hold in a small town, and weird things start happening. Strother Martin, L. Q. Jones, Charles Bateman, Anna Capri. w. William Welch, d. Bernard McEveety.

HORROR: Satanism; Ordinary People Turned Criminal; Small-Town Life

The Brothers, 1947, 98m, ★★¹/2/$, Triton/NA. In a turn-of-the-Century fishing village in the British Isles, a parentless young woman disrupts the lives of a staid fishing family. Patricia Roc, Maxwell Reed, Duncan Macrae, Will Fyffe, Finlay Currie. w. Muriel and Sydney Box, N-adap. L. A. G. Strong, d. David Macdonald.

DRAMA: Orphans; Nuisances; Small-Town Life; Fishermen; British Films; Brothers

The Brothers Karamazov, 1958, 146m, ★★★/$$$, MGM/MGM-UA. A father and his three sons come to blows as their changing lives collide in a changing 19th-century Russia. Yul Brynner, Lee J. Cobb (BSActor), Richard Basehart, William Shatner. w. Richard Brooks, N-adap. Theodor Dostoyevsky, d. Richard Brooks. Oscars: 1-0.

DRAMA: TRAGEDY: Epics; Life Transitions; Classics; Fathers & Sons; Russian; Brothers

(Doctor Zhivago; Taras Bulba)

The Brothers McMullen, 1995, 97m, ★★★/$$, 20th/Fox, R/S-P. The story of a suburban Irish family of mostly brothers who find themselves in their 20s and, although a bit confused, still a family. Edward Burns, Shari Albert, Maxine Bahns, Catharine Bolz, Peter Johansen. w. d. Edward Burns.

DRAMA: COMEDY DRAMA: Family Drama; Brothers; 20-Somethings; Ind Films; Young Men; Actor-Directors; Writer-Directors

(Kicking and Screaming; True Love)

(Ed: Nice, but hardly enlightening or extraordinary, except for the shoestring budget on which it was made)

The Browning Version, 1951, 90m, ★★★/$$, GFD/Home Vision. A teacher at an English boarding school, upon retiring, discovers that he's widely hated. He decides to atone for his life with one last act of kindness. Michael Redgrave, Jean

Kent, Nigel Patrick, Wilfrid Hyde White. w. P-adap Terence Rattigan, d. Anthony Asquith.

DRAMA: MELODRAMA: Teachers; Boarding Schools; Retirement; Starting Over; Midlife Crisis; Stern Men; Mean Men; Redemption; Hidden Gems

REMAKE: 1995

(Term of Trial; Goodbye, Mr. Chips; Monsieur Hire)

Brubaker, 1980, 119m, ★★★/$$$, 20th/CBS-Fox, R, P-V-S. A new prison warden (Robert Redford) goes in as a prisoner to see what needs to be reformed and undercovers dead bodies instead. Yaphet Khotto. w. W. D. Richter, d. Stuart Rosenberg.

DRAMA: MYSTERY: MURDER: MURDER MYSTERY: Murders-Mass; Social Drama; Prison Drama; Political Drama; True Stories; Disguises; Undercover; Corruption; Fighting the System; Reformers; Rape-Male

RETREAD: Death Warrant

(Cool Hand Luke; The Shawshank Redemption; Ghosts of the Civil Dead)

(Ed: Loosely based on incidents at a prison farm in Arkansas, though set in a different state)

The Buccaneer, 1938, 125m, ★★★/$$$, Par/Par. Andrew Jackson enlists the aid of pirate Jean Lafitte in the War of 1812. Fredric March, Franciska Gaal, Akim Tamiroff, Margot Grahame, Walter Brennan, Beulah Bondi, Anthony Quinn, Montagu Love. w. Jeanie Pacpherson, Edwin Justus Mayer, Harold Lamb, C. Gardner Sullivan, d. Cecil B. de Mille. BCin. Oscars: 1-0.

The Buccaneer, 1958, 121m, Par/Par, ★★★/$$$. Future President Andrew Jackson (Charlton Heston) teams up with the famed pirate Jean Lafitte (Yul Brynner) in order to fight the British in the war of 1812. w. Jesse L. Lasky Jr., Bernice Mosk (from the earlier screenplay), d. Anthony Quinn.

REMAKE OF: 1938 version

ADVENTURE: ACTION: Adventure at Sea; War Stories; War Battles; War of 1812; Epics; Costume Drama; Historical Drama; Presidents; Power Struggles; Pirates; Swashbucklers; Enemies Unite; Actor Directors

(Ed: Though this remake is less entertaining, the visuals are often incredible)

Buck and the Preacher, 1971, 103m, ★★★/$$, Col/Col, PG. A racial-themed western in which runaway slaves are chased by Klansmen and aided by outlaw wagon-train riders. Sidney Poitier, Harry Belafonte, Ruby Dee, Cameron Mitchell, Denny Miller, Nita Talbot, John Kelly. w. Ernest Kinoy, d. Sidney Poitier.

WESTERN: ACTION: COMEDY DRAMA: Black Casts; Slavery; Chase Movies; Bounty Hunters; Race Relations; Black vs. White; Revisionist Films; Actor Directors; Black Directors
(The Skin Trade; Posse)

Buck Privates, 1941, 84m, ★★★/$$$$, Universal/MCA-U. A fish-out-of-water tale in which two bumbling idiots mistakenly join the army. Bud Abbott, Lou Costello, Lee Bowman, Alan Curtis, Jane Frazee, The Andrews Sisters, Shemp Howard. w. Arthur T. Horman, d. Arthur Lubin.

COMEDY: Military Comedy; Misunderstandings; Comedy of Errors; Fools-Bumbling; Abbott & Costello; Fish out of Water Stories; Soldiers
(Private Benjamin; In the Army Now; Bonnie Scotland)

Buckaroo Banzai, see Adventures of . . .

Buddy Buddy, 1981, 96m, ★★★/$, MGM/MGM-UA, R/P. A hitman (Walter Matthau) and a fellow wanting to commit suicide (Jack Lemmon) share a hotel room and get on each other's nerves. w. Billy Wilder, IAL Diamond, P-adap. Francis Veber, d. Wilder.

COMEDY: Black Comedy; Morbid Comedy; Suicidal Tendences; Roommates from Hell; Buddy Films; Coulda Been Great

REMAKE OF: A Pain in the A—
(The Odd Couple; The Front Page; Grumpy Old Men; Les Comperes; La Chevre)

The Buddy Holly Story, 1978, 113m, Columbia/RCA-Col, PG, ★★★1/2/$$$. The life story and sudden end to the life of pop star Buddy Holly (Gary Busey, BActor). d. Steve Rash. BAScore. Oscars: 2-0.

DRAMA: TRAGEDY: Biographies; Music Movies; True Stories; Singers; Music Dies; Airplane Crashes; Musicians; 1950s
(La Bamba; Sweet Dreams; Elvis)

The Buddy System, 1983, 110m, ★★1/2/$, 20th/Key, PG-S-P. A woman (Susan Sarandon) sending her son to a school in another district meets-thanks to her son-a father (Richard Dreyfuss) of

another child and starts a carpool romance despite the fact that he's got someone. d. Glenn Jordan.

COMEDY DRAMA: ROMANCE: Romantic Comedy; Romance-Reluctant; Matchmakers; Starting Over; Fathers Alone; Mothers Alone; Mothers & Sons; Female Protagonists; Forgotten Films
(Ed: Cute, but you'll expect more from the talent)

Buddy's Song, 1990, 106m, ★★/$, Vidmark/Vidmark. An aging rocker manages his son's band, and the two clash over artistic and professional issues. Roger Daltrey, Chesney Hawkes, Sharon Duce, Paul McKenzie. w. N-adap. Nigel Hinton, d. Claude Whatham.

DRAMA: Music Movies; Musicians; Fathers & Sons; British Films

Buffalo Bill, 1944, 89m, ★★★/$$$, 20th/Fox. An old-fashioned biopic about William "Buffalo Bill" Cody, the real cowboy turned traveling showman. Joel McCrea, Maureen O'Hara, Linda Darnell, Edgar Buchanan, Anthony Quinn. w. Aeneas Mackenzie, Clements Ripley, Cecile Kramer, d. William Wellman.

DRAMA: WESTERN: Biographies; Rodeos; Indians-American

Buffalo Bill and the Indians, or Sitting Bull's History Lesson, 1976, 118m, ★★★/$, DEG-Par/Par, PG/V. During a break in his roadshow tour, William Cody philosophizes about his mythos and American culture. w. Alan Rudolph, Robert Altman, P-adap. Arthur Kopit (The Indians), d. Robert Altman.

DRAMA: WESTERN: Character Studies; Biographies; Historical Drama; Art Films; Flops-Major; Revisionist Films; Indians-American; Rodeos
(Buffalo Girls; Buffet Froid; The Life and Times of Judge Roy Bean)

Buffet Froid, 1979, 93m, ★★★/$$, Sara Films-Antenna 2/Interama. A cop and two new friends discover over a meal that they share a love of murdering people. Gérard Depardieu, Bernard Blier, Jean Carmet Geneviève Page. w. d. Bernard Blier.

DRAMA: SUSPENSE: MURDER: Murderers-Nice; Black Comedy; Ordinary People; Turned Criminal; Police Stories; Writer-Directors; French Films
(Going Places; Strangers on a Train; Bad Influence)

Buffy, the Vampire Slayer, 1992, 98m, ★★/$$, 20th/Fox, PG-13/V-B&G-S.

A cheerleader becomes a vampire killer when a mysterious stranger tells her of a new onslaught of the bloodsuckers in her suburban playground. Kristy Swanson, Rutger Hauer, Donald Sutherland, Luke Perry, Paul Reubens, Randall Batinkoff, Candy Clark, Natasha Gregson, Michele Abrams. w. Joss Whedon, d. Fran Rubel Kazul.

HORROR: Horror Comedy; Spoofs-Vampire; Female Protagonists; Teenagers; Coulda Been Good; Female Directors
(Innocent Blood)

Bug, 1975, 100m, ★1/2/$, Par/Par, R/V. An earthquake unleashes giant insects from the core of the earth. w. William Castle, Thomas Page, N-adap. Thomas Page (The Hephaestus Plague), d. Jeannot Szwarc.

HORROR: SCI-FI: Monsters-Mutant; Earthquakes; Insects
(Ants; Frogs; Arachnophobia)

Bugsy, 1991, 137m, ★★★1/2/$$$, Tri-Star/Col-Tri, R/S-P-EV. Gangster Bugsy Siegel (Warren Beatty, BActor) goes to Hollywood to become a star and instead finds an actress (Annette Bening), with whom he starts Las Vegas instead. Harvey Keitel (BSActor), Ben Kingsley (BSActor). w. James Foley (BOScr), d. Barry Levinson (BDirector). BPicture, **BCinema, BArt,** BEdit, BCost. Oscars: 10-2.

DRAMA: Biographies; **MURDER:** Crime Drama; Mob Stories; Mob Wars; Hitmen; True Stories; Evil Men; Evil Women; Love-Questionable; Criminal Biographies; Dreams; Las Vegas; Hollywood Biographies; Hollywood Life; Eccentric People
(The Godfather; The George Raft Story; Capone; The Untouchables; Bonnie and Clyde)

Bugsy Malone, 1976, 93m, ★★★/$$, Par/Par, G. An all-child cast sings and dances and shoots their way through this spoof of 30s gangster movies. Jodie Foster, Scott Baio. w. d. Alan Parker.

MUSICAL: DRAMA: Musical Drama; Spoofs; **CHILDREN'S:** Crime Drama; Mob Stories; Film Noir-Modern; Child Protagonists; Children-Little Adults; Cult Films; Writer-Directors
(Pennies from Heaven)

Bull Durham, 1988, 107m, ★★★1/2/ $$$$, Orion/Orion, R, P-S-FFN-MRN. A minor league baseball player (Kevin Costner) meets up with a colorful woman

(Susan Sarandon) who sleeps with a different player each season to train him in her "method." Tim Robbins. w. d. Ron Shelton (BOScr). Oscars: 1-0.

COMEDY: ROMANCE: Romantic Comedy; Erotic Comedy; Romance-Triangles; Baseball; Sports Movies; Redemption; Midlife Crisis; Eccentric People; Free Spirits; Single Women; Southerns; Sexy Women; Sexy Men; Proteges/Understudies
(Major League; Blaze)

Bulldog Drummond, (SERIES), 1929, 90m, NA, Goldwyn/NA. An ex-GI "adventurer for hire" accepts an assignment to rescue a girl's uncle from an evil faux "nursing home." Ronald Colman, Joan Bennett, Claud Allister, Lilyan Tashman, Montagu Love, Lawrence Grant.

Bulldog Drummond at Bay, 1937, 78m, (BIP/ABPC). Drummond breaks up a ring of spies posing as a peace-promoting organization. John Lodge, Dorothy Mackaill, Victor Jory, Claude Allister, Richard Bird. w. Patrick Kirwan, James Parrish, N-adap. N. A. (Sapper), d. Norman Lee.

Bulldog Drummond Strikes Back, 1934, 83m, (UA/20th). Is Mr. Drummond settling down? It seems so, as he gets married. But before he even gets to his honymoon, he's summoned on another adventure. Ronald Colman, Loretta Young, C. Aubrey Smith, Charles Butterworth, Una Merkel. w. Nunnally Johnson, d. Roy del Ruth. **SERIES:** from 1922 to 1970, sporadically.

MYSTERY: Detective Stories; Playboys; Saving Someone; Detectives-Private; England

A Bullet for the General, 1966, 126m, ★★/$, MCM-Col/Col. A group of mercenaries, planning to assassinate a Mexican coup leader, are joined by an American "gun-for-hire." Gian-Maria Volontè, Klaus Kinski, Martine Beswick, Lou Castel, Jaime Fernandez. w. Salvatore Laurani, Franco Solinas, d. Damiano Damiani.

ACTION: DRAMA: Political Drama; Political Unrest; Assassinations Hitmen; Mercenaries; Mexico

Bullets or Ballots, 1936, 81m, ★★★/ $$$, WB/WB. An undercover cop infiltrates the ranks of the mob in order to break it up, but may betray not only friends but his own conscience-if he's not caught first. Edward G. Robinson, Joan Blondell, Humphrey Bogart, Barton MacLane. w. Seton I. Miller, d. William Keighley.

DRAMA: Crime Drama; Mob Stories; Undercover; Spies; Police Stories; Detective Stories; Detectives-Police; Betrayals; Gambling; Friends as Enemies; Warner Gangster Era
(The Amazing Dr. Clitterhouse)

Bullets Over Broadway, 1994, 94m, ★★★/$$, Miramax/Miramax-Touchstone, PG-13/S. A writer is brought to Broadway for his big break on stage and winds up tangling with a cast of eccentric divas and nuts, and eventually even the mob. John Cusack, Dianne Wiest (**BSActress**), Chazz Palmintieri (BSActor), Jennifer Tilly (BSActress), Tracey Ullman. w. Woody Allen, Douglas McGrath (BOScr), d. Woody Allen (BDirector). BCostume, BArt. Oscars: 7-1.

COMEDY: FARCE: Screwball Comedy; Theater Life; Putting on a Show; Writers; Actors; Actresses; Mob Comedy; 1920s; Eccentric People; Ensemble Films; Writer-Directors; Old-Fashioned Recent Films
(The Purple Rose of Cairo; Radio Days; Broadway Danny Rose; The Freshman)

The Bullfighter and the Lady, 1951, 125m, ★★1/2/$$$, Republic-John Wayne/Republic. An American in Mexico takes bullfighting lessons and accidentally gets his mentor killed. Robert Stack, Gilbert Roland, Joy Page, Katy Jurado, Virginia Grey. w. James Edward Grant, d. Budd Boetticher.

DRAMA: ACTION: ROMANCE: TRAGEDY: Accidents; Bullfighting; Betrayals; Friendships-Male; Mexico

The Bullfighters, 1945, 61m, ★★★/$$, 20th/Fox. A case of mistaken identity occurs when a dimestore flatfoot in Mexico is taken for a matador. Stan Laurel, Oliver Hardy, Richard Lane, Margo Woode, Carol Andrews. w. Scott Darling, d. Mel St. Clair.

COMEDY: FARCE: Identities-Mistaken; Misunderstandings; Bullfighting; Mexico; Laurel & Hardy

Bullitt, 1968, 119m, ★★★1/2/$$$$, WB/WB, R/V-S. A detective (Steve McQueen) uncovers corruption and murder in a race against time to clear his name. Robert Vaughan, Jacqueline Bisset. w. Alan Trustman, d. Peter Yates. BEditing, BSound. Oscars: 2-1.

ACTION: DRAMA: MYSTERY: MURDER MYSTERY: Crime Drama; Detective Stories; Chase Movies; Cops-Vigilante; Detectives-Police; Detectives in Deep; Framed?; Accused Unjustly; Saving Oneself; Police Stories; Police Corruption; Trail of a Killer; San Francisco; Car Chases; San Francisco Chases
(The Thomas Crown Affair; The French Connection; Dirty Harry; The Fugitive; 48 Hours)
(Ed: It's too slow by today's standards but has more details of character and plot that make it more interesting)

Bullseye!, 1990, 92m, ★★/$, Castle Premier-21st Century/Col. Two crooks, masquerading as nuclear scientists, nearly blow up the planet. Michael Caine, Roger Moore, Sally Kirkland, Deborah Barrymore. w. Leslie Bricusse, Laurence Marks, Maurice Gran, SS-adap. Leslie Bricusse, Michael Winner, Nick Mead, d. Michael Winner.

COMEDY: Black Comedy; Con Artists; Scientists; Nuclear Energy; Bombs-Atomic; Lookalikes; Coulda Been Good; British Films

Bullshot, 1983, 85m, ★★1/2/$, Handmade/Hemdale. A "spoof" on the Bulldog Drummond series, in which "Bullshot Crummond" does battle with the evil Count Otto von Bruno. Alan Shearman, Diz White, Ron House, Frances Tomelty, Michael Aldridge. w. Ron House, Diz White, Alan Shearman, d. Dick Clement.

COMEDY: Spoofs; Spoofs-Detectives; Detective Stories; British Films

Bundle of Joy, 1956, 98m, ★★★/$$$, RKO/VCI. When she finds an baby left on her doorstep, a single girl has trouble convincing people it's not hers. Debbie Reynolds, Eddie Fisher, Adolphe Menjou, Tommy Noonan, Nita Talbot, Una Merkel, Robert H. Harris. w. Norman Krasna, Arthur Sheekman, Robert Carson, d. Norman Taurog.

MUSICALS: MELODRAMA: Musical Drama; **ROMANCE:** Tearjerkers; Mothers-Surrogate; Children-Adopted; Mothers Alone; Misunderstandings; Scandals; Mothers-Unwed; Babies-Having Babies-Abandoned

MUSICAL REMAKE OF: Bachelor Mother.
(Bachelor Mother; Baby Boom; My Six Loves)

Bunny Lake Is Missing, 1965, 107m, ★★★/$$, Col/RCA-Col, PG. An unwed American woman living in London gets separated from her daughter. When she seeks help to find her, she can't convince anyone that her daughter actually exists. Laurence Olivier, Carol Lynley, Keir Dullea, Noel Coward, Martita Hunt, Finlay Currie. d. Otto Preminger.

DRAMA: MYSTERY: SUSPENSE: Psychological Drama; Detective Stories; Missing Persons; Missing Children; Unbelieved; Mental Illness; Brothers & Sisters; Girls; Mothers Alone; Americans Abroad; England; Underrated; Coulda Been Great; Mod Era; England; Time Capsules

(Without a Trace; Missing; So Long at the Fair)

(Ed: The dark, macabre nature of the film gives it a unique feel, this despite a plot twist that's been copied quite a bit but is hard to swallow)

Bunny O'Hare, 1971, 92m, ★★1/2/$$, AIP/New World. Bette Davis and Ernest Borgnine embarass themselves as an aging couple dressed who maraude around the country on motorcycles dressed as hippies robbing banks. Bette Davis, Ernest Borgnine, Jack Cassidy, Joan Delaney, Jay Robinson, John Astin. w. Stanley Z. Cherry, Coslough Johnson, d. Gerd Oswald.

COMEDY DRAMA: ACTION: Action Comedy; Black Comedy; Elderly People; Comedy & Violence; Criminal Couples; Spoofs; Bank Robberies; Camp

(Bonnie and Clyde; Skidoo; Harold and Maude)

Buona Sera, Mrs. Campbell, 1968, 113m, ★★★/$$, UA/MGM-UA. A group of World War II veterans have a twenty-year reunion in the Italian village they liberated. Three of them discover they've been paying child support to the same local woman. w. Melvin Frank, Denis Norden, Sheldon Keller, d. Melvin Frank.

COMEDY: COMEDY DRAMA: Mothers-Unwed; Children-Long Lost; Veterans; Italy; Italians; Americans Abroad; Reunions; Father-Who's the

REMAKE/RETREAD: Mediteranneo?

(Three Men and a Little Lady; Better Late than Never)

(Ed: Has some very good moments)

The Burbs, 1989, 103m, ★★/$$$, Universal/MCA-U, PG-13/P. A man (Tom Hanks) moves into the suburbs and soon finds he has very strange neighbors. Carrie Fisher, Corey Feldman. w. Dana Olsen, d. Joe Dante.

COMEDY: HORROR: Horror Comedy; Black Comedy; Neighbors-Troublesome; Suburban Life; Special Effects; Comedy & Violence; Cartoonlike Movies

(Neighbors; Tales from the Crypt)

Bureau of Missing Persons, 1933, 75m, ★★★/$$, WB/MGM-UA. A detective in charge of this police division must deal with a strange woman with a past and various other stories in his professional life which intermingle with her personal side. Bette Davis, Lewis Stone, Pat O'Brien. d. Roy Del Ruth.

DRAMA: Crime Drama; Missing Persons; Police Stories; Detectives-Police; Forgotten Films

Burden of Dreams, 1982, 94m, NW/NW, NR, ★★★/$ (LR). A documentary on the troubled making of the epic *Fitzcarraldo* in the Amazon. w. d. Les Blank.

Documentary; Making Movies; Filmumentary; Obsessions; South America; Amazon River

(Heart of Darkness; Fitzcarraldo; Aguirre, the Wrath of God)

Burglar, 1987, 98m, ★★★/$$, WB/WB, R/EP-S-MRN. A clever burglar (Whoopi Goldberg) is framed for murder and has to disguise herself to clear her name. Bobcat Goldthwait, Lesley Ann Warren. w. Hugh Wilson, Joseph Loeb, Martin Weisman, N-adap., d. Wilson.

COMEDY: MYSTERY: Comic Mystery; **MURDER MYSTERY:** Framed?; Saving Oneself; Feisty Females; Thieves; Con Artists; Disguises; Female Protagonists

(Jumpin' Jack Flash; Kiss Shot)

The Burglars, 1971, 105m, ★★1/2/$$, Col/NA. A cop is after three burglars-to bring them to justice, or to steal their loot? Omar Shariff, Jean-Paul Belmondo, Dyan Cannon, Renato Salvatori. w. Vahe Katcha, Henri Verneuil, N-adap. David Goodis (The Burglar), d. Henri Verneuil.

COMEDY DRAMA: Heist Stories; Con Artists; Thieves; Detective Stories; Police Stories; Corruption-Police; Good Premise Unfulfilled; Coulda Been Great

(The Anderson Tapes; The Thomas Crown Affair)

Buried Alive, 1990, 93m, ★★★/$$, U/MCA-U, PG-13/S-V. A woman and her lover poison her husband, but he doesn't die so easily. Tim Matheson, Jennifer Jason Liegh, William Atherton, Hoyt Axton. w. Mark Carducci, d. Frank Darabont.

SUSPENSE: MURDER: Poisons; Cheating Women; Murder of Spouse; Buried Alive; Dead-back from the; Murder-Comic Attempts; TV Movies (Blood Simple; Diabolique)

(Ed: Has some very good moments)

Burke and Wills, 1986, 120m, ★★★/$$, New Line/New Line, PG-13. An adventure of the explorers who were the first to make it all the way across Australia. Jack Thompson, Nigel Havers, Greta Scacchi. d. Graeme Clifford.

ADVENTURE: DRAMA: Historical Drama; Costume Drama; Epics; Journies; Explorers; Australian Films

(Mountains on the Moon; The Black Robe)

The Burmese Harp, 1956, 116m, ★★★1/2/$$, Ind/Conoisseur. A Japanese soldier, thinking the war is still on, hides out in the Burmese jungle and buries his comrades. Shoji Yasui, Rentaro Mikuni, Tatsuya Mihashi. w. Natto Wada, N-adap. Michio Takeyama, d. Kon Ichikawa. BFLFilm. Oscars: 1-0.

DRAMA: World War II-Post Era; Jungles; Mental Illness; Misunderstandings; Japanese Films

(Hell in the Pacific)

Burn! (*Queimada*), 1969, 112m, ★★★/$, MGM/MGM-UA, Voyager, PG. A diplomat finds himself in the middle of political tensions when the British try to control a Caribbean island without regard to the locals' needs. Marlon Brando. d. Gillo Pontecorvo.

DRAMA: Political Drama; Political Unrest; Diplomats; Caribbean; Americans Abroad; Italian Films; Imperialist Problems

(The Year of Living Dangerously; The Ugly American; The Comedians)

The Burning, 1982, 90m, ★1/2/$, Ind/NA, R/V-B&G. At a summer camp, vengeance is attained through murder. Holly Hunter, Jason Alexander, Brian Matthews, Leah Ayres. d. Tony Mayhem.

HORROR: MURDER: Revenge; Camping; Camp; Forgotten Films; Curiosities

The Burning Bed, 1984, 104m, ★★★1/2/$$$$$, NBC/CBS-Fox, NR/V. A beaten housewife (Farrah Fawcett, BActress Emmy nom.) fights back with fire and has to defend herself further in court. Paul LeMat, Richard Masur. w. Rose Goldenburg, NF-adap. Faith McNulty, d. Robert Greenwald. Multiple Emmy nominee.

DRAMA: Social Drama; Courtroom Drama; Abused Women; True Stories; Women Against the System; Fires; Flashbacks; Narrated Films; Blockbusters; Female Protagonists; Female Screenwriters (Extremities; Murder by Reason of Insanity; Dolores Claiborne)
(Ed: One the best TV movies ever made, a breakthrough for Fawcett and a must-see)
The Burning Season, 1994, 100m, ★★★1/2/$$$, HBO/HBO. A man struggles against big business and local greed to save a rain forest, but he's beset with many problems in the process. Raul Julia, Edward James Olmos, Sonia Braga, Esai Morales, Jose Perez. d. John Frankenheimer. Multiple Golden Globe winner.
DRAMA: Social Drama; Rebels; Fighting the System; Message Films; Rainforests; South America; Latin People; TV Movies; Brazil
(At Play in the Fields of the Lord; Amazon; Medicine Man; Bye Bye Brazil)
Burning Secret, 1988, 107m, Vestron/ Vestron, ★★★/$, PG. An American woman (Faye Dunaway) falls for a mysterious aristocrat (Klaus Maria Brandauer) in turn of the century Vienna and a secret crops up, which complicates matters. w. d. Andrew Birkin, SS-adap. Stefan Sweig.
DRAMA: ROMANCE: Love-Reluctant; Mothers & Sons; Secrets-Haunting; Austria/Vienna
REMAKE OF: Brennendes Geheimnis (German, 1933).
Burnt Offerings, 1976, 115m, ★★1/2/ $$$, UA/MGM-UA, PG/V-B&G. The old mansion down south a family is staying in is possessed by evil spirits. Oliver Reed, Karen Black, Bette Davis. d. Dan Curtis.
HORROR: SUSPENSE: Satanism; Possessions; Haunted Houses; Southern Gothic; Houses-Creepy
(The Sentinel; Harvest Home; The Amityville Horror SERIES; Sister, Sister)
Bus Stop, 1956, 96m, ★★★1/2/$$$, 20th/Fox. A singer (Marilyn Monroe) stops off at a bus stop and cafe where a country boy (Don Murray) pursues her amids the local customers waiting for the bus. Hope Lange. w. George Axelrod, P-adap. William Inge, d. Joshua Logan.
DRAMA: MELODRAMA: COMEDY DRAMA: ROMANCE: Romance-Boy Wants Girl; Ordinary People Stories; Dreams; Free Spirits; Singers; Busses; Sexy Women

(Alice Doesn't Live Here Anymore; Picnic)
(Ed: Probably Monroe's best performance)
The Bushido Blade, 1979, 104m, ★★/$, Ind/NA. In 1854, when a Shogun warrior's sword is stolen, a U.S.-Japanese treaty is threatened. Richard Boone, Frank Converse, Toshiro Mifune, Laura Gemser, James Earl Jones, Mako. w. William Overgard, d. Tom Katani.
DRAMA: Historical Drama; War Stories; Political Drama; Political Unrest; Thieves; Searches; Diplomats; Americans Abroad; Japan
Bushwhacked, 1995, 90m, ★★/$, 20th/20th, PG-13/S-P. A man accused of murder hides out as a scout leader and winds up with the scouts on a camp-out, which gives our fugitive a way to also become a fish out of water in the wilderness. Daniel Stern, Jon Polito, Brad Sullivan, Ann Dowd, Anthony Heald. w. John Jordan, Danny Byers, Tommy Swerdlow, Michael Goldberg, d. Greg Beeman.
COMEDY: Fugitives from the Law; Hiding Out; Boy Scouts; Fish out of Water Stories
(Hiding Out; The Wrong Guys; Meatballs; Ernest Goes to Camp)
Business as Usual, 1988, 89m, ★★★/$, WB/WB, PG. A sexual harassment suit in England is filed and dealt with in a court not used to such things. Glenda Jackson, Cathy Tyson. w. d. Lezli-Ann Barrett.
DRAMA: Social Drama; Courtroom Drama; Trials; Accused Unjustly?; Lawyers; Hairdressers; Sexual Harassment; Business Life; Scandals; Women Fighting the System; British Films; Overlooked at Release; Female Protagonists; Female Screenwriters; Female Directors; Writer-Directors (Disclosure; 9 to 5; The Accused [1988]; Oleanna)
Buster, 1988, 94m, ★★★/$$, Handmade-Hemdale/HBO, R/P-V-S. The true story of a bank robber (Phil Collins) and his wife (Julie Walters) as he plans a robbery and getaway-and it just may work out. w. Colin Schindler, d. David Green.
DRAMA: COMEDY DRAMA: ROMANCE: Criminal Couples; Heist Stories; Thieves; Bank Robberies; Marriage Drama; Marriage on the Rocks; True Stories; True or Not?
(Murph the Surf; Whiffs)

Buster and Billie, 1974, 100m, ★★★/$$ Col/RCA-Col, R, P-S-MFN-FFN. A young man in the 1940s South (Jan Michael Vincent) falls for a slow country girl (Joan Goodfellow) who his family and friends don't approve of. Pamela Sue Martin. w. Ron Turbeville, d. Daniel Petrie.
DRAMA: ROMANCE: Romance-Reluctant; Romance-Doomed; Romance-Follow Your Heart; Coming of Age; Southerns; Young Men; Lover Family Dislikes; Love-First; Wallflowers & Hunks
(Ode to Billy Joe; Ramblin' Rose)
Bustin' Loose, 1980, 94m, ★★1/2/$$, Universal/MCA-U, PG/P. An ex-con (Richard Pryor) winds up as a summer camp bus driver and has to deal with the unruly kids. Cicely Tyson. d. Oz Scott.
COMEDY: COMEDY DRAMA: ROMANCE: Road Movies; Children-Brats; Black Men; Black Women; Black Casts
The Busy Body, 1966, 102m, ★★1/2/$$, Castle-Par/NA. When it's discovered that a gangster was buried in a suit with a million dollars in the lining, a mad rush to exhume him begins. Robert Ryan, Sid Caesar, Arlene Golonka, Anne Baxter, Kay Medford, Charles McGraw. w. Ben Starr, N-adap. Donald E. Westlake, d. William Castle.
HORROR: Race Against Time; Rewards at Stake; Treasure Hunt; Funerals; Coulda Been Good
Butch and Sundance, The Early Days, 1979, 110m, ★★1/2/$$, 20th/CBS-Fox, PG/V. The story of how the famous criminal duo got together and became so famous. Tom Berenger, William Katt. w. Allan Burns, S-adap. William Goldman, d. Richard Lester.
WESTERN: DRAMA: Road Movies; Famous People When Young; Buddy Films; Thieves; Heist Stories
PREQUEL TO: Butch Cassidy and the Sundance Kid
Butch Cassidy and the Sundance Kid, 1969, 110m, ★★★1/2/$$$$$, 20th/CBS-Fox, PG/V-S. Two outlaws (Robert Redford, Paul Newman) head to South America to avoid prosecution, continuing to rob to survive. Katharine Ross. w. William Goldman (**BOScr**), d. George Roy Hill (BDirector). BPicture, **BCin**, BEditing, **BOSong**, **BOScore**. Oscars: 7-4.
WESTERNS: ACTION: ADVENTURE: COMEDY DRAMA: Action Comedy;

Western Comedy; Comic Adventure; Heist Stories; Chase Movies; Road Movies; Outlaw Road Movies; Buddy Films; Criminal Biographies; Partners in Crime; Fugitives from the Law; Romance-Triangle; South America; Sexy Men; Blockbusters

PREQUEL: Butch and Sundance: The Early Days

(The Sting; Young Guns)

The Butcher's Wife, 1991, 107m, ★★¹/₂/$$, Par/Par, PG-13/P-S. A young woman from North Carolina with psychic powers (Demi Moore) moves into Greenwich Village with a butcher (George Dzundza) she happened to meet back home. In her new home she begins affecting the lives of neighbors in odd ways until one of them falls for her (Jeff Daniels). Mary Steenburgen, Margaret Colin, Frances McDormand. d. Terry Hughes.

COMEDY DRAMA: ROMANCE: Fantasy; Telepathy; Psychics; Fish out Water Stories; Romance-Boy Wants Girl; Romance with Psychologist; Strangers in Town; Eccentric People; City vs. Country; Magic; Realism; Magic; New York Life; Soap Opera Shows; Coulda Been Good

(Princess Caraboo; Splash)

Butterfield 8, 1960, 108m, ★★★/$$$$, MGM/MGM-UA, NR/S. A high-class prostitute (Elizabeth Taylor, **BActress**) wants the love of a wealthy marred man (Laurence Harvey) but can't get him to leave his wife (Dina Merrill). w. Charles Schnee, John Michael Hayes, N-adap. John O'Hara, d. Daniel Mann. Oscars: 1-1.

DRAMA: ROMANCE: TRAGEDY: Prostitutes-High Class; Rich vs. Poor; Romance-Doomed; Romance-Unrequited; Alienation; Suicidal Tendencies; Telephone Numbers; Female Protagonists

(Sessions; Klute; Sweet Charity; Nights of Cabria)

Butterflies Are Free, 1972, 109m, ★★★¹/₂/$$$, Columbia/RCA-Col, PG, S. A blind young man (Edward Albert) falls in love with a free-wheeling hippie actress (Goldie Hawn) despite the protests of his snobby mother (Eileen Heckart, **BSActress**). w. Leonard Gershe, d. Milton Katzelas. BCinema, BSound. Oscars: 3-1.

COMEDY: COMEDY DRAMA: ROMANCE: Romantic Comedy; Blind People; Mothers and Sons; Anti-Establishment Films; Free Spirits; Hippies; San Francisco

(The Landlord; Cactus Flower; There's a Girl in My Soup)

Butterfly, 1981, 107m, ★¹/₂/$$, Ind/Vestron, Live. In Depression-era Arizona, a teenage sexpot reunites with the father who abandoned her, has sex with him, and starts a murder spree. N-adap. James M. Cain, d. Matt Cimber.

MELODRAMA: SUSPENSE: MURDER: Film Noir-Modern; Erotic Drama; Incest; Sexy Women; Promiscuity; Crime Sprees; Murderers-Female; Depression Era; Desert Settings; Unintentionally Funny; Forgotten Films

(The Lonely Lady)

By Love Possessed, 1961, 115m, ★★¹/₂/$$, UA-Mirisch-Seven Arts/MGM-UA. A romantic entanglement soap opera involving the upper-crust of Massachusetts. Lana Turner, Efrem Zimbalist Jr., Jason Robards Jr., Barbara Bel Geddes, George Hamilton, Everette Sloane. w. John Dennis, N-adap. James Gould Cozzens, d. John Sturges.

MELODRAMA: ROMANCE: Soap Opera; Ensemble Films; Betrayals; Romance-Triangles; Secrets-Haunting; New England; Boston; Rich People

(Peyton Place; From the Terrace)

(Ed: An upperclass, citified Peyton Place)

By the Light of the Silvery Moon, 1953, 101m, ★★¹/₂/$$$, WB/WB. At the end of World War I, a veteran returns to his small town, to find things much changed, including the affections of his girlfriend. Doris Day, Gordon Macrae, Leon Ames, Rosemary de Camp, Mary Wickes.

MUSICAL: ROMANCE: Musical Drama; **MELODRAMA:** Soldiers; World War I Era; Reunions

Bye Bye Birdie, 1963, 112m, ★★★/$$$, Col/RCA-Col. A pop star modeled after Elvis has been drafted. Before he goes overseas, he'll have a farewell TV show that pulls out all the stops and has the suburban teenybop-pers obsessed while a songwriter tries to sell a song to him. Janet Leigh, Dick Van Dyke, Maureen Stapleton, Ann-Margaret, Bobby Rydell, Ed Sullivan, Paul Lynde, Robert Paige. w. Irving Brecher, P-adap. Michael Stewart, d. George Sidney.

MUSICAL: COMEDY: Musical Comedy; **SATIRE:** Singers; Teen Idols; Hunks; Musicians; Suburban Life; Teenagers; Teenage Movies

(Grease; Damn Yankees)

(Ed: An atrocious song starts it off, but it gets better)

Bye Bye Braverman, 1968, 92m, ★★¹/₂/$, WB/NA, PG/S. After a funeral, a group of Jewish New Yorkers get smashed and reflect on their lives. George Segal, Jack Warden, Joseph Wiseman, Sorrell Booke, Jessica Walter, Phyllis Newman, Zohra Lampert, Alan King, Godfrey Cambridge. w. Herbert Sargent, N-adap. Wallace Markfield (*To an Early Grave*), d. Sidney Lumet.

COMEDY: COMEDY DRAMA: Comedy-Morbid; Funerals; Ensemble Films; Ensembles-Male; Reunions; Underrated; Forgotten Films

(The Big Chill; The Men's Club; Loving; The Bachelor Party [1957])

Bye Bye Brazil, 1979, 115m, ★★¹/₂/$$, Ind/Fox-Lorber. Gypsy singers tour the Brazilian countryside, witnessing the dramatic changes to the rainforest and surroundings. Jose Wilker, Betty Faria. d. Carlos Diegues.

DRAMA: South America Jungle Life; Environmental Dilemmas; Fantasy; Art Films; Gypsies; Brazil

(Pixote; At Play in the Fields of the Lord; The Burning Season)

Bye Bye Love, 1995, 99m, ★★¹/₂/$$, 20th/Fox, PG-13/S-P. Three divorced dads with partial custody of their children try to start new lives. Matthew Modine, Randy Quaid, Paul Reiser, Janeane Garafolo. d. Sam Weisman.

COMEDY: Romantic Comedy; Romance-Bickering; Ensembles-Male; Family Comedy; Dating Scene; Starting Over; Song Title Movies; Young Men

(Breaking Up Is Hard to Do; Starting Over; Watch It)

C

Cabaret, 1972, 119m, ★★★★/$$$$, Allied-ABC/CBS-Fox, PG/S. A showgirl (Liza Minnelli, **BActress**) meets a young man (Michael York) during the rise of Hitler in Berlin and thinks she's finally in love despite the warning signs. Joel Grey (**BSActor**). w. Jay Presson Allen (**BAScr**), N-adap. Christopher Isherwood, P-adap. d. Bob Fosse (**BDirector**). BPicture, **BCinema**, BEditing, **BSound, BCostume, BArt, BAScore**, Oscars: 10-8.
DRAMA: MUSICAL: Musical Drama; Music Movies; ROMANCE: Romance-Triangles; Alternative Lifestyles; Bisexuality; Homoeroticism; Actresses; Singers; Berlin; Germans; World War II Era; Nazi Stories; Theater Life; Female Protagonists; Wallflowers; Wallflowers & Hunks
MUSICAL REMAKE OF: I Am a Camera
(I Am a Camera; The Sheltering Sky; Something for Everyone; All That Jazz)
Cabin Boy, 1994, 80m, ★★½/$, Touchstone/Touchstone, PG-13/P-S. A naive young man becomes a cabin boy among a crew of burly sailors and has numerous, wacky misadventures. Chris Elliott, Ann Magnuson, Russ Tamblyn, Ritch Brinkley, James Gammon, Brian Doyle-Murray, Ricki Lake, David Letterman. w. d. Adam Resnick.

COMEDY: Fantasy; Adventure at Sea; Fools-Bumbling; Coulda Been Great; Writer-Directors
(Ed: Not Jerry Lewis, not Jim Carrey, and not much else besides a few good gags, unfortunately. A general rule-beware of movies that are this short)
The Cabinet of Dr. Caligari, 1919, 69m (B&W, Silent), ★★★★/$$, Ind/Republic. A sideshow hypnotist tricks a sleepwalker into murder and may himself be insane-if the whole story is really happening. w. Carl Mayer, Hans Janowitz, d. Robert Wiene.
HORROR: SUSPENSE: MURDER: Sleepwalkers; Hypnotism; Houses-Creepy; Asylums; Mental Illness; Nightmares; Fantasies; Illusions/Hallucinations; Scientists-Mad
The Cabinet of Caligari, 1962, 104m, ★★/$$, 20th/NA. A woman's car breaks down and then falls into a nightmare at the house she knocks on the door of for help-where the evil Caligari lives, but is it really happening? Glynis Johns, Dan O'Herlihy. w. Robert Bloch, d. Roger Kay.
HORROR: SUSPENSE: Women in Jeopardy; Kidnappings; Houses-Creepy; Stranded; Revisionist Films; Psychologists; Mental Illness; Nightmares; Fantasies; Illusions/Hallucinations; Scientists-Mad

(Ed: Little to do with the original classic except the nightmare gimmick)
The Cabin in the Cotton, 1932, 77m, ★★½/$$, WB/MGM-UA. A white sharecropper incurs the wrath of a southern belle. Richard Bathelmess, Bette Davis, Dorothy Jordan, David Landau. w. Paul Green, N-adap Harry Knoll, d. Michael Curtiz.
MELODRAMA: ROMANCE: Romance-Class Conflict; Revenge; Evil Women; Plantations; Southerns; Rich vs. Poor; Sisters
(Jezebel; The Little Foxes; Queen Bee)
Cabin in the Sky, 1943, 100m, ★★★½/$$$, MGM/MGM-UA-Turner. A man deals with good and evil on his way to the cabin in the sky, singing with a black cast all the way. Eddie Anderson, Lena Horne, Ethel Waters, Louis Armstrong. w. Joseph Shrank, P-adap. Lynn Root, d. Vincente Minnelli.
MUSICALS: Fantasy; Musical Fantasy; Good vs. Evil; Heaven; Black Men; Black Women; Black Casts; Satan; Hidden Gems
(Green Pastures; Stormy Weather; Cabiria, see Nights of Cabiria)
Cactus, 1986, 95m, ★★★/$, Ind/Lorimar, NR. A young woman (Isabelle Huppert) goes to Australia for a vacation and she loses an eye in an accident. In her recovery, she meets a blind man and falls in

love, learning far more about life from this new point of view. Robert Menzies, Norman Kaye. w. Paul Cox, Norman Kaye, Bob Ellis, d. Paul Cox.

DRAMA: ROMANCE: Ordinary People Stories; Medical Recovery; Blind People; Vacation; Vacation Romance; Australian Films; Ind Films; Female Protagonists
(A Woman's Tale)

Cactus Flower, 1969, 103m, ★★★/$$$, Col/RCA-Col, PG/S. In a plot to confuse his young girlfriend (Goldie Hawn, **BSActress**), an older dentist (Walter Matthau) gets his uptight secretary (Ingrid Bergman) to pretend to be his wife, a ploy which may wreck old relationships and build new ones. Jack Weston, Rick Lenz, Vito Scotti. w. IAL Diamond, P-adap. Abe Burrows, French P-adap. Pierre Barillet, Jean Pierre Gredy, d. Gene Saks. Oscars: 1-1.

COMEDY: COMEDY DRAMA: ROMANCE: Romantic Comedy; FARCE: Romance-Older; Men/Younger Women; Romance-Reluctant; Marriages-Fake; Dentists; Secretaries; Impostors; Cheating Men
(There's A Girl in My Soup; Butterflies Are Free)

Caddie, 1976, 107m, ★★¹/2/$, Ind/NA. A woman tired of her husband's philandering takes her kids and tends bar to make a living. Helen Moore, Jack Thompson. w. Joan Long, AB-adap. Caddie, d. Donald Crombie.

DRAMA: MELODRAMA: Character Studies; Ordinary People Stories; Mothers-Struggling; Mothers Alone; Australian Films; Autobiographical Stories; Female Protagonists; Female Screenwriters
(Alice Doesn't Live Here Anymore)

The Caddy, 1953, 95m, ★★¹/2/$$$, Par/Par. Semi-autobiographical skits about a comedy act (Martin & Lewis) and their beginnings. Dean Martin, Jerry Lewis, Donna Reed, Barbara Bates. w. Edmund Hartmann, Danny Arnold, d. Norman Taurog. BOSong, "That's Amore." Oscars: 1-0.

COMEDY: Comedy-Skits; Memories; Flashbacks; Comedians; Fame-Rise to; Autobiographical Stories; Friendships-Male
(My Friend Irma; Hollywood or Bust; Scared Stiff)

Caddyshack, 1980, 90m, ★★★/$$$$, Orion-WB/WB, R/P-S. A suburban

teenager (Michael O'Keefe) takes a summer job at the snobby country club and finds himself in the middle of burrowing groundhogs and slapstick on the greens. Bill Murray, Chevy Chase, Ted Knight, Rodney Dangerfield. w. Brian Doyle-Murray, Harold Ramis, Douglas Kenney, d. Harold Ramis.

COMEDY: FARCE: Party Movies; Comedy-Slapstick; Bathroom Humor; Snobs vs. Slobs; Teenagers; Rich People; Country Club Life; Golf
SEQUEL: Caddyshack 2
(Meatballs; Back to School)

Caddyshack 2, 1988, 98m, ★¹/2/$$, Orion/Orion, PG, P-S,. A sequel to the original, but the cast is completely different, except for a few cameos (Dan Aykroyd, Chevy Chase) wasted. Jackie Mason, Dyan Cannon, Robert Stack, Paul Bartel. w., d. Alan Arkush.

COMEDY: Party Movies; Slapstick; Bathroom Humor; Rich People; Snobs vs. Slobs; Golf

Cadillac Man, 1990, 97m, ★★¹/2/$$, Orion/Orion, R, P-V. A car salesman (Robin Williams) whose life is falling apart finds himself taken hostage by a crazy man (Tim Robbins) and has to get himself together. Pamela Reed, Fran Drescher. w. Ken Friedman, d. Roger Donaldson.

COMEDY DRAMA: Black Comedy; Hostage Situations; Tragi-Comedy; Midlife Crisis; Marriage on the Rocks; Con Artists; Suburban Life; Sudden Violence; Jealousy; Psycho Killers; Murderers-Mass; Good Premises Unfulfilled; Coulda Been Good
(Used Cars; Dog Day Afternoon)

Cadence, 1990, 97m, ★★/$, Ind/Republic, R/P. A racist sergeant sends a black soldier to the stockade, resulting in conflicts among his troops. Charlie Sheen, Martin Sheen, F. Murray Abraham, Larry Fishburne. w. Dennis Schyrack, Martin Sheen, N-adap. Gordon Weaver, d. Martin Sheen.

DRAMA: Military Stories; Soldiers; Race Relations; Bigots; Black vs. White; Black Men; Men in Conflict; Actor-Directors; Ind Films
(Tribes; Baby Blue Marine; An Officer and a Gentleman)

Caesar and Cleopatra, 1946, 134m, ★★★/$$, B-L/NA. Caesar (Claude Rains) takes a queen in Egypt with comical results (Vivien Leigh) in this adaptation

of the Shaw play. w. P-adap. George Bernard Shaw, d. Gabriel Pascal.

COMEDY DRAMA: ROMANCE: Epics; Costume Drama; Historical Drama; Leaders; Queens; Royalty; Power Struggles; Ancient Times; Biographies; Egypt; Middle East; Forgotten Films (Cleopatra, 1934, 1963; Julius Caesar [1953])

Cafe Metropole, 1937, 84m, ★★★/$$$, 20th/NA. An American heiress is seduced by a man she thinks is Russian royalty but who is really a bankrupt American. Loretta Young, Adolphe Menjou, Tyrone Power, Charles Winninger, Gregory Ratoff. w. Jacques Duval, d. Edward Griffith.

COMEDY: ROMANCE: Romantic Comedy; Romance on Vacation; Impostors; Con Artists; Fortune Hunters; Paris; Americans Abroad; Stagelike Films; Forgotten Films
(Bedtime Story; Dirty Rotten Scoundrels)

Cafe Romeo, 1991, 93m, ★★/VR, CBC-Republic/Republic, R/P-S. The lives of several people who hang out at an Italian area cafe, centering around a young waitress trying to decide whether to get married or not. Catherine Mary Stewart, Johnathan Crombie. d. Rex Bromfield.

DRAMA: Ensemble Films; Restaurant Settings; Family Drama; Coming of Age; Marriage-Impending; Engagements-Breaking; Canadian Films

Cafe Society, 1939, 83m, ★★¹/2/$$, Par/NA. Tired of a tabloid reporter, a socialite marries him in the hope of fooling and embarassing him ultimately, but she may only fool herself. Madeleine Carroll, Fred MacMurray, Shirley Ross. w. Virginia Van Upp, d. Edward Griffith.

COMEDY: ROMANCE: Romantic Comedy; Marriage Comedy; Marriages-Fake; Romance-Reluctant; Nuisances; Turning the Tables; Journalists; Rich People; Romance-Class Conflict; Female Screenwriters; Female Protagonists
(Libeled Lady; The Philadelphia Story)
Cage Aux Folles I, II, III, see L for La Cage Aux Folles

Caged, 1950, 96m, ★★★/$$$, Par/NA. A young woman (Eleanor Parker, BActress) is sent to prison and becomes as bad as what she was presumed to be when she went in. Agnes Moorehead, Ellen Corby, Jane Darwell, Hope Emerson (BSActress). w. Virginia

Kellogg, Bernard Schoenfeld (BOScr), d. John Cromwell. Oscars: 3-0.

DRAMA: MELODRAMA: Prison Drama; Women in Prison; Ensemble Films; Ensembles-Female; Women's Films Alienation; Accused Unjustly; Fighting the System; Female Protagonists; Female Screenwriters

REMAKE: House of Women
(I Want to Live; Caged Heat)

Caged Fear, 1992, 94m, ★½/$, New Line/New Line, R/V-P-S-FN. When a young newlywed couple has a spat and winds up in a shootout, the young bride is jailed and it's up to hubby to get her out. David Keith, Deborah May, Ray Sharkey, Loretta Devine, Karen Black. w. d. Bobby Houston.

ACTION: Action Drama; Prison Drama; Prison Escape; Newlyweds; Marriage on the Rocks; Women in Prison

Caged Heat, 1974, 83m, ★★/$$, AIP/ New World, R/P-V-S-FN. When an innocent woman goes to jail, the tough cookies there harden her up but soon, they change their ways preparing to live on the outside again. Juanita Brown, Erica Gavin, Barbara Steele. w. d. Jonathan Demme.

ACTION: Prison Drama; Women in Prison; Accused Unjustly; Camp; Writer-Directors
(Jackson County Jail; Caged; Caged Fear)

Cage of Gold, 1950, 83m, ★★½/$$, Ealing/NA. A young woman's first husband returns after disappearing and then is suddenly murdered. Jean Simmons, David Farrar, James Donald, Herbert Lom. w. Jack Whittingham, d. Basil Dearden.

SUSPENSE: MURDER: MYSTERY: MURDER MYSTERY: Women in Jeopardy; Missing Persons; Young Women; British Films; Forgotten Films; Good Premise Unfulfilled

Cahill: United States Marshal, 1973, 103m, ★★½/$$$, WB/WB, PG/V. A stern old lawman investigating a robbery begins to suspect that his own unruly sons may be involved. John Wayne, George Kennedy, Gary Grimes, Neville Brand, Jackie Coogan. w. Harry Julian Fink, Rita Fink, d. Andrew V. MacLaglen.

WESTERN: MYSTERY: DRAMA: MELO-DRAMA: Bank Robberies; Detective Stories; Detectives-Police; Fathers & Sons; Stern Men; Parents vs. Children; Marshals; Suspecting Oneself; Ethics

Cain and Mabel, 1936, 90m, ★★★/ $$$, WB/NA. A boxer has got it bad for a showgirl, but the feelings may not always be mutual for either, resulting in sparring out of the ring. Clark Gable, Marion Davies, Allen Jenkins, Ruth Donnelly, Roscoe Karns. w. Laird Doyle, H. C. Witwer, d. Lloyd Bacon.

COMEDY: ROMANCE: Romantic Comedy; Sports Movies; Boxing; Romance with Boxer; Romance-Reluctant
(Designing Woman; The Main Event)

The Caine Mutiny, 1954, 125m, ★★★½/$$$$, Col/RCA-Col. When the cantankerous captain of a destroyer panics during a hurricane tensions boil over among the other officers, leading to insubordination. Humphrey Bogart, Jose Ferrer, Van Johnson, Fred MacMurray, Robert Francis, E. G. Marshall, Lee Marvin, Claude Akins. w. Stanley Roberts, N-adap Herman Wouk, d. Edward Dmytryk.

DRAMA: Courtroom Drama; Trials; Military Movies; Ensemble Films; Ensembles-Male; Ethics; Power Struggles; Stern Men; Mental Illness; Sailors; Ships; Courts Martial; Novel and Play Adaptations; Pulitzer Prize Adaptations

REMAKE: The Caine Mutiny Court Martial (TV, 1988)
(Mutiny on the Bounty; A Few Good Men; Breaker Morant)

The Caine Mutiny Court Martial, 1988, 100m, ★★★/$$$, CBS/Vidmark. A remake of the classic story of Captain Queeg and the power struggles on board his ship which led to the courtroom. Jeff Daniels, Peter Gallagher, Eric Bogosian, Michael Murphy, Brad Davis, Kevin J. O'Connor, Dan Jenkins. N-adap. Herman Wouk, d. Robert Altman.

DRAMA: Courtroom Drama; Trials; Military Movies; Ensemble Films; Ensembles-Male; Ethics; Power Struggles; Stern Men; Mental Illness; Sailors; Ships; Courts Martial; Novel and Play Adaptations; Pulitzer Prize Adaptations; TV Movies

REMAKE OF: 1954 version

Cairo, 1942, 101m, ★★★/$$, MGM/ MGM-UA. A journalist in Egypt during the War meets an American actress and mistakenly believes she's a spy-but may believe he's in love soon. Jeannette McDonald, Robert Young, Ethel Waters, Reginald Owen, Lional Atwil. w. John McClain, d. W.S. Van Dyke.

COMEDY: ROMANCE: Romantic Comedy; Spies; Misunderstandings; Identities-Mistaken; World War II Era; Egypt; Actresses; Journalists

Cairo, 1963, 91m, ★★/$, MGM/NA. A band of ex-cons reunite for one last heist at the Cairo Museum but it may not be so easy to pull off. George Sanders, Richard Johnson. w. Joanne Court, d. Wold Rilla.

DRAMA: Crime Drama; Heist Stories; Jewel Thieves; Reunions; One Last Time; Female Screenwriters

REMAKE OF: The Asphalt Jungle

Cal, 1984, 102m, ★★★/$$, Goldcrest-Goldwyn/WB, PG/S. A Catholic man in Ireland falls in love with the widow of a man he had a hand in killing, then must deal with his conscience. Helen Mirren, John Lynch. w. N-adap. Bernard MacLaverty, d. Pat O'Connor.

DRAMA: ROMANCE: MURDER: Secrets-Keeping; Guilty Conscience; Murder-Debate to Reveal Killer; Ireland; Irish Films

Calamity Jane, 1953, 101m, ★★★/$$$, WB/WB. Goofy singing wild west cow gal Jane finds love with Wild Bill Hickok while helping out a traveling show with a few songs. Doris Day, Howard Keel. w. James O'Hanlon, d. David Butler.

BOSong, "Secret Love," BMScore. Oscars: 2-1.

MUSICAL: COMEDY: Musical Comedy; **ROMANCE:** Musical Romance; Tomboys; Accident Prone; Female Protagonists
(Buffalo Girls; Annie Oakley)

Calcutta, 1947, 83m, ★★/$$, Par/NA. Two military pilots track down the killer of a friend in the shadier side of India. Alan Ladd, Gail Russell, William Bendix. w. Seton Miller, d. John Farrow.

DRAMA: MURDER: Trail of a Killer; Avenging Death of Loved One; Friendship-Male; Pilots-Military; World War II Era; India; Good Premise Unfulfilled

Calendar Girl, 1993, 85m, ★★½/$, Col/Col, PG-13/P-S-MRN. Three young men take a road trip in a convertible (where has that been done before?) to California to try and meet Marilyn Monroe, and so on . . . Jason Priestly, Gabriel Olds, Jerry O'Connell, Joe Pantoliano, Stephen Tobolowsky, Chubby Checker. w. Paul Shapiro, d. John Whitesell.

COMEDY: COMEDY DRAMA:
Infatuations; Young Men; Teenagers; Teenage Movies; Actresses; Fans-Crazed; Stalkers; Road Movies-Guys in Convertibles; Road Movies; Road to California; Beach Movies; Nudists; 1950s Nostalgia
(Coupe de Ville; Breaking the Rules; Heartbreak Hotel; Coldblooded)
(Ed: Not so bad as these things go, and Priestley is surprisingly good)

California Dreaming, 1979, 93m, ★★1/2/$, AIP/Vestron, PG/S-P. A young guy heads to the beaches and tries to fit in. Dennis Christopher, Glynnis O'Connor, John Calvin, Tanya Roberts, Seymour Cassel. d. John Hancock.
COMEDY DRAMA: Coming of Age; Beach Movies; Young Men; Teenagers; Teenage Movies; 1970s
(Ed: A more sensitive beach movie)

California Split, 1974, 108m, ★★★/$$, 20th/NA, R, P-S. Two gamblers (Donald Sutherland, Elliott Gould) team up after they're robbed by the man they beat at poker to go against the system, meeting many interesting characters along the way. w. Joseph Walsh, d. Robert Altman.
COMEDY: COMEDY DRAMA: Black Comedy; Gambling; Bets; Ordinary People Storie; Friendships-Male; Buddy Films; Prostitutes-Low Class; Prostitutes with Heart of Gold
(M*A*S*H; S*P*Y*S)

California Suite, 1978, 103m, ★★★1/2/$$$, Columbia/RCA-Col, PG/P-S. Four stories all involving relationships in crisis from infidelity to divorce to pure chaos intertwine around the Beverly Hills Hotel. Jane Fonda, Walter Matthau, Bill Cosby, Richard Pryor, Maggie Smith (**BSActress**), Michael Caine, Elaine May, Alan Alda. w. Neil Simon (BOScr), d. Herbert Ross. BArt. Oscars: 3-1.
COMEDY: COMEDY DRAMA: Marriage Comedy; **FARCE:** Multiple Stories; Interwoven Stories; Marriage on the Rocks; Actresses; Black People; Misunderstandings; Hotels; Beverly Hills; New York vs. LA; Oscars
(Plaza Suite; Annie Hall; London Suite)

Caligula, 1980, 156m, ★/$$, Penthouse/Penthouse, Vestron, X/P-EV-S-MFN-FFN. An X-rated look at the debauchery and excess of the sadistic emperor of Ancient Rome (Malcolm MacDowell) with an all-star cameo cast. Peter O'Toole,

John Gielgud. w. Bob Guccione, Gore Vidal, d. Bob Guccione.
DRAMA: Erotic Drama; Leaders-Tyrant; Alternative Lifestyles; Orgies; Flops-Major; Cult Films
(Aphrodite)

Call Me, 1988, 98m, ★★/$, Vestron/Vestron, R/S-P-V. A sexy obscene phone caller gets a woman going until she sees the caller murder someone and realizes she could be next. Patricia Charbonneau, Patti D'Arbanville, Sam Freed, Boyd Gaines. d. Sallace Mitchell.
SUSPENSE: MURDER: Witness to Murder; Telephone Terror; Voyeurs; Erotic Thriller
(Ed: Passable)

Call Me Bwana, 1963, 103m, ★★1/2/$$, UA/MGM-UA. A white man poses as an African tribesman on a mission for NASA to recover a space probe that landed in the jungle. Bob Hope, Anita Ekberg, Edie Adams, Lionel Jeffries. w. Nate Monaster, Johanna Harwood, d. Gordon Douglas.
COMEDY: COMEDY DRAMA: Comic Adventure; Astronauts; White Among Blacks; White as Black; Disguises; Impostors; Jungle Life; Africa; Curiosities
(Soul Man; True Identity)
(Ed: Politically incorrect by today's standard, pretty silly by any standard)

Call Me Genius, (The Rebel), 1960, 105m, ★★★/$, Associated British/NA. A British suburbanite businessman gives up his staid life and leaves his friends and family to go to Paris to become an artist. Tony Hancock, George Sanders, Paul Massie, Margit Saad, Gregoire Aslan, Dennis Price, Irene Handl, Oliver Reed, John Wood. w. Alan Simpson, Ray Galton, d. Robert Day.
DRAMA: COMEDY DRAMA: Character Studies; Midlife Crisis; Artists; Paris; Dreams; Starting Over; Hidden Gems

Call Me Madam, 1953, 117m, ★★★1/2/$$$, 20th/Fox. A Washington socialite gets appointed to the foreign service in fictitious Lichtenberg and ruffles some feathers while singing her way through the festivities. Ethel Merman, Donald O'Connor, George Sanders, Vera-Ellen. w. Arthur Sheekman, P-adap Howard Lindsay, Russel Crouse, d. Walter Lang.
BMScore. Oscars: 1-1.
MUSICALS: SATIRE: COMEDY: Musical Comedy; Political Satire; Fish out of Water Stories; Feisty Females;

Ambassadors; Politicians-Female; Female Among Males; Washington D.C.; Kingdoms; Female Protagonists
(There's No Business Like Show Business)

Call Me Mister, 1951, 95m, ★★/$, 20th/NA. A dancing couple tour the orient after the war. Betty Grable, Dan Dailey, Danny Thomas, Dale Robertson, Richard Boone. w. Albert E. Lewin, Burt Styler, d. Lloyd Bacon.
MUSICALS: ROMANCE: Musical Romance; Military Comedy; Dancers; Dance Movies; World War II-Post Era Soldiers; Partners-Married

Calling Northside 777, 1948, 111m, ★★★/$$, 20th/Fox. A story from the Chicago police blotter about a reporter who helps a poor woman clear her son of murder charges. James Stewart, Lee J. Cobb, Helen Walker, Kazia Orzazewski, d. Jerome Cady, Jay Dratler, d. Henry Hathaway.
DRAMA: SUSPENSE: MURDER: Crime Drama; Police Stories; Detective Stories; Saving Someone; Accused Unjustly; Journalist as Detective; Journalists; Chicago; Time Capsules; Telephone Numbers
(The Wrong Man; Just Cause; The FBI Story)

Call of the Wild, 1935, 81m, ★★1/2/$$, 20th/NA. After her husband dies, a young woman is all alone in the harsh north country, until she meets an adventuring prospector with a unique. Clark Gable, Loretta Young, Jack Oakie, Reginald Owen. w. Gene Fowler, Leonard Praskins, N-adap. Jack London, d. William Wellman.
ADVENTURE: DRAMA: MELODRAMA: WESTERNS: ROMANCE: Romance-Reluctant; West-Old; Pioneers; Drifters; Widows; Starting Over; Pet Stories; Dogs; Alaska; Snow Settings; Forgotten Films; Classic Literary Adaptations
(Silence of the North; Belle of the Yukon)

Call of the Wild, 1972, 100m, ★★1/2/$, 20th/MPI. In the goldrush days, a wild dog befriends a miner and helps him out of tough spots. Charlton Heston, Michele Mercier, Raimund Harmstorf. w. Harry Alan Trowers, Wyn Wells, Peter Yeldman, d. Ken Annakin.
ADVENTURE: DRAMA: MELODRAMA: WESTERNS: ROMANCE: Romance-Reluctant; West-Old; Pioneers; Drifters; Widows; Starting Over; Pet Stories; Dogs;

Alaska Snow Settings; Forgotten Films; Classic Literary Adaptations
(Silence of the North; The Journey of Natty Gann; Iron Will)

Callaway Went Thataway, 1951, 81m, ★★★/$, MGM/NA A washed up old cowboy star descends into a drunken stupor as his old films regain popularity, and someone has to stand in for him at public appearances. Dorothy McGuire, Fred MacMurray, Howard Keel, Jesse White. w. d. Melvin Frank, Norman Panama.

COMEDY: WESTERNS: Western Comedy; Actors; Alcoholics; Impostors-Actors; Cowboys; Comebacks; Good Premise Unfulfilled
(My Favorite Year)

Calling Bulldog Drummond, 1951, 80m, ★★1/2/$$, MGM/NA. A band of crooks is terrorizing the town until Drummond comes to save the day. Walter Pidgeon, Margaret Leighton, Robert Beatty, David Tomlinson, Peggy Evans, Charles Victor. w. Howard Emmett Rogers, Gerard Fairlie, Arthur Wimperis, d. Victor Saville.

Crime Drama; **MYSTERY:** Detective Stories; Thieves; Small-town Life
(Bulldog Drummond; Bullshot)

Calling Dr. Gillespie, 1942, 84m, ★★1/2/$$, MGM/NA. A former patient of Dr. Gillespie's apparently dissatisfied with his service breaks into the hospital to exact revenge. Lionel Barrymore, Philip Dorn, Phil Brown, Donna Reed, Nat Pendleton, Mary Nash, Donna Reed. w. Kubee Glassmon, Willis Goldbeck, Harry Ruskin, d. Harold S. Bucquet.

DRAMA: MELODRAMA: Doctors; Hospitals; Revenge; Revenge on Doctors

Calling Dr. Kildare, 1939, 86m, ★★★/$$$MGM/MGM-UA. The young doctor seeks the advice of his mentor, Dr. Gillespie, when he gets implicated in a murder. Lew Ayres, Lionel Barrymore, Lana Turner, Nat Pendleton. w. Harry Ruskin, Willis Goldbeck, d. Harold S. Bucquet.

DRAMA: MELODRAMA: MURDER: Accused Unjustly; Saving Someone; Doctors; Hospitals; Mentors/Proteges

Camelot, 1967, 178m, ★★★1/2/$$$, WB-7 Arts/WB. A musical version of the tales of King Arthur and the knights of the round table. Richard Harris, Vanessa Redgrave, David Hemmings, Lionel Jeffries, Laurence Naismith. w. Alan Jay Lerner, N-adap. T. H. White (*The Once and Future King*), d. Joshua Logan. **BCCin, BCArt,** BSound, **BAScore, BCCostume.** Oscars: 5-3.

MUSICALS: DRAMA: Musical Drama; **ROMANCE:** Power Struggles; Camelot Stories; Medieval Times; England; Legends; Fairy Tales; Magic; British Films; Coulda Been Great
(First Knight; The Sword in the Stone)
(Ed: President Kennedy's favorite stage musical becomes a good but not great movie)

The Cameraman, 1928, 78m, ★★★1/2/$$, MGM/MGM-UA. A cameraman gets a job with the newsreels in order to win over a movie star he's obsessed with. Buster Keaton, Marceline Day, Harry Gribbon, Harold Goodwin. w. Clyde Bruckman, Lex Lipton, Richard Schayer, d. Edward Sedgewick.

COMEDY: Comedy-Slapstick; Silent Film Era; Hollywood Life; Hollywood Satire; Fans-Obsessed; Infatuations; Actresses; Photographers

Cameron's Closet, 1987, 86m, ★★/$, Medusa-Ind./Col, PG-13/V. A psychiatrist subjects his son to experiments in telekenesis and the naughty boy grows a skulking homunculus in his closet. Cotter Smith, Mel Harris, Scott Curtis, Chuck McCann. w. SS-adap. Gary Brandner. d. Armand Mastroianni.

SUSPENSE: HORROR: Scientists; Experiments; Possessions; Monsters; Supernatural; Dangers; Boys; Dchild Protagonists; Unbelieved
(The Lady in White; Poltergeist; Afraid of the Dark)

Camila, 1984, 105m, ★★★/$, Col/Col, Sultan. In the 1800s an upper-crust family is scandalized when their headstrong daughter has an affair with a priest. Susu Pecoraro, Imanol Arias, Hector Alterio, Carlos Munoz. w. Maria Luisa Bemberg, Beda Docampo Feijoo, Juan Bautista Stagnaro, d. Maria Luisa Bemberg.

MELODRAMA: ROMANCE: Romance with Priest; Romance-Unprofessional; Romance-Older Men/Younger Women; Scandals; Small-Town Scandals; Lover Family Dislikes; Rich vs. Poor; Religion; Priests; Female Screenwriters; Female Directors

Camilla, 1995, 104m, ★★★/VR, PG/FRN. A young woman on the road to Canada meets up with an elderly woman running away from home and her bother-some son, leading to a meeting of the minds between two diverse women. Jessica Tandy, Bridget Fonda, Graham Green, Hume Cronyn, Howie Mandel, Elias Koteas. w. Paul Quarrington, d. Deepa Mehta.

DRAMA: MELODRAMA: Character Studies; Road Movies; Friendships-Intergenerational; Friendships-Female; Young Women; Elderly Women; Female Protagonists; Hidden Gems
(Fried Green Tomatoes; The Trip to Bountiful)

Camille, 1936, 108m, ★★★1/2/$$$$, MGM/MGM-UA. A woman (Greta Garbo, BActress) falls ill with consumption while trying to gain the love of the one man she truly wants (Robert Taylor). Lionel Barrymore. w. Frances Marion, James Hilton, Zoe Akins, N-adap. Alexandre Dumas, d. George Cukor. Oscars: 1-0.

MELODRAMA: ROMANCE: DRAMA: Romantic Drama; **TRAGEDY:** Romance-Girl Wants Boy; Tearjerkers; Prostitutes-High Class; Disease Stories; Love-Reluctant; Costume Drama; 1800s; Female Protagonists; Female Screenwriters

REMAKE OF: 3 silent versions; **REMAKE:** 1985, TV
(Anna Karenina; Love Story; Love; Romance)

Camille Claudel, 1988, 149m, ★★★/$$$, Orion/Orion, R/S-FFN. The artist and model (Isabelle Adjani, BActress) for sculptor Rodin (Gerard Depardieu) eventually breaks free and creates her own works. w. Bruno Nuyutten, Marilyn Goldin, NF-adap. Reine-Marie Paris, d. Bruno Nyutten. BFLFilm. Oscars: 2-0.

DRAMA: ROMANCE: Romantic Drama; Costume Drama; Biographies; Artists; Artists-Famous; Romance-Reluctant; Life Transitions; Female Protagonists; Female Screenwriters
(Belle Noizeuse; The Story of Adele H; Queen Margot)

Campus Man, 1987, 94m, ★★/$, Par/Par, PG-13/S-P. When a college student's beefcake calendar threatens his friend/model's athletic amateur standing, he must make a difficult decision-beefcake cash or friendship. John Dye, Steve Lyon, Morgan Fairchild, Miles O'Keefe, Kim Delaney. d. Ron Casden.

MELODRAMA: Hunks; 1980s; Ethics; Friendships-Male; College Life; Camp; Unintentionally Funny; Time Capsules

Canadian Bacon, 1995, 90m, ★★1/2/$$, WB/WB, PG-13/P-V. A spoof of the possibility of a border war between the U.S. and Canada, based on a misunderstanding which ignites patriotism to ridiculous extents on both sides. Alan Alda, John Candy, Kevin Pollack, Rhea Perlman, Rip Torn, Bill Nunn, Steven Wright. w. d. Michael Moore.
COMEDY: FARCE: Misunderstandings; Military Comedy; Writer-Directors; Canada
(Wagons East!; The Russians Are Coming, the Russians Are Coming)
(Ed: Candy's last and the director of *Roger & Me*'s first feature)
Can-Can, 1960, 131m, ★★★/$$$, 20th/CBS-Fox. In the Paris of Lautrec, a cabaret dancer is arrested for doing the can-can. Frank Sinatra, Shirley MacLaine, Maurice Chevalier, Louis Jourdan, Juliet Prowse. w. Dorothy Kingsley, Charles Lederer, d. Walter Lang. BMScore. BCCostume. Oscars: 2-0.
MUSICALS: COMEDY: Musical Comedy; ROMANCE: Dance Movies; Dancers; Courtroom Drama; Trials; Paris; Gay 90s; Female Screenwriters
(Fanny; Irma La Douce)
Can Hieronymus Merkin Ever Forget Mercy Humppe and Find True Happiness?, 1969, 117m, ★★/$, U/NA. An aging performer assembles a pyramid of memorabilia on the beach and camps out. Anthony Newley, Joan Collins, George Jessel, Milton Berle, Bruce Forsyth. w. Herman Raucher, Anthony Newley, d. Anthony Newley.
COMEDY DRAMA: Comedians; Beach Movies; Nervous Breakdowns; Eccentric People; Flops-Major
Cancel My Reservation, 1972, 99m, ★★/$, Naho Enterprises-Col/Col. A talk show host goes to his ranch for a little R&R and gets involved in a murder plot. Bob Hope, Eva Marie Saint, Anne Archer, Ralph Bellamy, Forrest Tucker. w. Arthur Marx, Robert Fisher, N-adap. Louis L'Amour (The Broken Gunn), d. Paul Bogart.
COMEDY: MURDER: MYSTERY: MURDER: MYSTERY: Comic Mystery; Vacations; Talk Shows; TV Life
(Ed: Bob Hope's last and not his best)
The Candidate, 1972, 109m, ★★★★/$$$, 20th/CBS-Fox, PG. Robert Redford plays a glad-handing young politician being groomed by a team of experts for

the senate, but he may have gotten into more than he bargained for. Peter Boyle, Melvyn Douglas, Allen Garfield, Karen Carlson, Quinn Redeker. w. Jeremy Lerner (**BOScr**), d. Michael Ritchie. Oscars: 1-1.
DRAMA: COMEDY DRAMA: SATIRE: Political Campaigns; Politicians; Political Drama; Power-Rise to; Ethics; Young Men; California
(Power; Tanner '88; All the King's Men; The Seduction of Joe Tynan)
Candide, 1960, 90m, ★★1/2/$, Pathe/NA. A modern retelling of the famous story of the eternal optimist who ignores the horrors of the world. This time he's exposed to the Nazis and South American wars. Jean-Pierre Cassel, Daliah Lavi, Pierre Brasseur, Nadia Gray. w. d. Norbert Carbonneaux, N-adap. Voltaire.
DRAMA: SATIRE: Art Films; Avant-Garde Films; Drifters; Nazi Stories; South America; Political Unrest; Revisionist Films; French Films; Classic Literary Adaptations
Candleshoe, 1977, 101m, ★★1/2/$$, Disney/Disney, G. Kidnappers claim to have the daughter of an upper crusty British family, but they're just bluffing, and the butler knows it. David Niven, Helen Hayes, Jodie Foster, Leo McKern, Vivian Pickels. w. David Swift, Rosemary Anne Sisson, N-adap. Michael Innes (Christmas at Candleshoe), d. Norman Tokar.
COMEDY: Comedy-Disney; Americans Abroad; Kidnappings; Impostors; Rich People; Inheritances at Stake; Child Protagonists; Women and Girls; Female Protagonists; Coulda Been Good
(Freaky Friday; Caroline?)
Candy, 1968, 115m, ★★★/$$, UA/MGM-UA. A young, naive nymphet goes on a journey around the world, running from the clutches of lecherous and lascivious men. Ewa Aulin, Richard Burton, Marlon Brando, James Coburn, Walter Matthau, John Huston, Elsa Martinelli, Ringo Starr. w. Buck Henry, N-adap. Terry Southern, d. Christian Marquand.
COMEDY DRAMA: COMEDY: SATIRE: Erotic Comedy; ADVENTURE: Comic Adventure; Sexy Women; Simple Minds; Bimbos; Sexual Harassment; Eccentric People; Young Women; All-Star Cast; All-Star Cameos; Hidden Gems; Female

Protagonists; Camp; Cult Films; Underrated
(Barbarella; The Magic Christian)
Candyman, 1992, 93m, ★★★/$$$, Universal/MCA-U, R, P-EV-B&G. A social worker (Virginia Madsen) investigates a legendary ghost in the notorious Cabrini Green projects in Chicago, only to have the ghost commit murders she may be blamed for. w. Bernard Rose, N-adap. Clive Barker, d. Bernard Rose.
HORROR: SUSPENSE: MURDER: Framed?; Accused Unjustly; Sociologists; Asylums; Black Men; Black Women; Inner City Life; Ghosts; Legends; Nightmares; Illusions/Hallucinations; White Among Blacks; Chicago; Female Protagonists
Candyman: Farewell to the Flesh, 1995, 99m, ★★/$$, Gramercy-U/MCA-U, R/EV-B&G-P. The Candyman legend continues as the vengeful slave continues to haunt a housing project, only now it's off to New Orleans for Mardi Gras and more terror and hallucinations. Tony Todd, Kelly Rowan, Timothy Carhart, Veronica Cartwright, Joshua Gibran Mayweather, Fay Hauser, William O'Leary. w. Rand Ravich, Mark Kruger, N-adap. Clive Barker, d. Bill Condon.
HORROR: Ghosts; Illusions/Hallucinations; Murders-One by One; New Orleans; Black Men
(Hellraiser SERIES; In the Mouth of Madness; The Dark Half)
Candy Mountain, 1987, 92m, ★★/$, Oasis/Republic. An aspiring rock musician searches for the guru of the guitar. Kevin J. O'Connor, Harris Yulin, Tom Waits, Roberts Blossom, Joe Strummer. w. Rudy Wurlitzer, d. Robert Frank, Rudy Wurlitzer.
COMEDY DRAMA: ADVENTURE: Road Movies; Searches; Musicians; Curiosities; Canadian Films
Cannery Row, 1982, 120m, ★★★/$, MGM/MGM-UA, R/S. A marine biologist in the 40s lives in a slummy waterfront community full of eccentric layabouts. Nick Nolte, Debra Winger, Audra Lindley, Frank McRae, M. Emmet Walsh, John Huston, w. d. David S. Ward, N-adap. John Steinbeck.
COMEDY DRAMA: ROMANCE: Ordinary People Stories; Working Class; Fishermen; Factory Life; Coulda Been Great; Classic Literary Adaptations;

1940s Flops-Major; Underrated; Overlooked at Release
(Of Mice and Men; Tortilla Flat; The Grapes of Wrath)
(Ed: More famous for the casting then un-casting of Raquel Welch and the pro-tracted legal battle as a result)

The Cannonball Run, 1981, 95m, ★★/$$$$, Universal/MCA-U, PG/P. A caravan of hot-rods travel the country in a race to California, driven by various and sundry macho men, kooks, and bimbos. Burt Reynolds, Farrah Fawcett, Dom DeLuise, Dean Martin, Sammy Davis Jr., w. Brock Yates, d. Hal Needham.
ACTION: CHILDREN'S: Action Comedy; Chase Movies; Race Against Time; Car Racing; Road Movies; All-Star Casts; All-Star Cameos; Rat Pack Movies
SEQUEL: The Cannonball Run 2
(Smokey and the Bandit; The Great Race; Cherry 2000; Gumball Rally)

The Cannonball Run 2, 1984, 108m, ★/$$, U/MCA-U, PG/P. A sequel where the minimalistic story is the same, but most of the names of the guilty have changed. Burt Reynolds, Shirley McLaine, Dean Martin, Sammy Davis, Jr., Marilu Henner, Frank Sinatra. w. Hal Needham, Albert S. Ruddy, Harvey Miller, d. Needham.
ACTION: CHILDREN'S: Action Comedy; Chase Movies; Race Against Time; Car Races; Road Movies; All-Start Casts; All-Star Cameos; Rat Pack Movies
SEQUEL TO: The Cannonball Run
(Ed: Actually worse than the first, but that's no shock)

Can She Bake a Cherry Pie?, 1983, 90m, ★★★/$$, Jaglom-Rainbow/Par, PG/S. A woman whose husband recently left starts over again with a neurotic hypochondriac on the road to a quirky romance. Karen Black, Michael Jaglom, Michael Margotta, Frances Fisher. w. d. Henry Jaglom.
COMEDY: ROMANCE: Romantic Comedy; Neurotic People; Eccentric People; Starting Over; Single Women; Single Men; Hypochondriacs; New York Life; Cult Films; Writer-Directors
(Little Murders, Sitting Ducks; Always)

Can't Buy Me Love, 1987, 94m, ★★1/2/$$$, Touchstone/Touchstone, PG-13/S. A rich but timid nerd pays a cheer-leader to be his escort at high school to improve his popularity, winding up with more than just a simple solution. Patrick Dempsey, Amanda Peterson, Courtney Gains, Seth Green. w. Michael Swerdlick, d. James Foley.
COMEDY: Hired Dates; Teenagers; Teenage Movies; High School Life; Nerds; Nerds & Babes; Sleeper Hits; Song Title Movies
(Book of Love; Some Girls; Happy Together)

Can't Stop the Music, 1980, 105m, ★1/2/$$, EMI/Republic, PG. The famous disco group in the fictitious story of their rise. The Village People, Valerie Perrine, Paul Sand, Bruce Jenner, Tammy Grimes. w. Bronte Woodward, Allan Carr, d. Nancy Walker.
MUSICALS: Music Movies; Rock Stars; Musicians; Fame-Rise to; Musicals-Disco Era; Disco Era; Flops-Major; Curiosities; Camp

A Canterbury Tale, 1944, 124m, ★★1/2/$$, Rank/Hemdale. In England a government official gets exposed in a scandal. Eric Portman, Sheila Sim, John Sweet, Dennis Price, Esmond Knight, Charles Hawtrey, Hay Petrie. w. d. Michael Powell, Emeric Pressburger.
MELODRAMA: Political Drama; Corruption; Politicians; Political Corruption; World War II Era; Scandals; British Films; Writer-Directors
(Scandal)

The Canterbury Tales, 1971, 109m, ★★★/$$$, UA/Water Bearer, R/P-S-FN-MFN. On a pilgrimage, a group of medieval peasants pass the time by telling each other stories of bizarre and often humorous and bawdy happenings of their day. Pier Paolo Pasolini, Hugh Griffith, Laura Betti, Tom Baker. w. d. Pier Paolo Pasolini, SS-adap. Chaucer.
COMEDY DRAMA: Erotic Comedy; Multiple Stories; Medieval Times; Italy; England; Italian Films; Art Films; Sleeper Hits; Writer-Directors

The Canterville Ghost, 1944, 95m, ★★★/$$$, MGM/Public. A girl in wartime England happens to have a cas-tle with a ghost which the local GIs find rather interesting when trying to date her. Charles Laughton, Margaret O'Brien, Robert Young. w. Edwin Blum, d. Jules Dassin.
COMEDY DRAMA: ROMANCE: Ghosts; Nusiances; Soldiers; World War II Era; Castles; England
(Casper; Haunted Honeymoon; Scared Stiff)

Canyon Passage, 1946, 99m, ★★/$$, U/NA. The pioneering men and women who built the West are shown in their struggles to tame the wild and wooly land and lay the tracks of the continental rail-road. Dana Andrews, Patricia Roc, Hoagy Carmichael, Brian Donlevy. w. Ernest Pascal, William Fosche, d. Jacques Tourneur.
WESTERNS: MELODRAMA: Quests; Pioneers; West-Old; Trains

Cape Fear, 1962, 105m, ★★★/$$, U/MCA-U. A criminal (Robert Mitchum) comes back after prison to haunt the prosecutor (Gregory Peck) who sent him there and his family (Polly Bergen). w. James R. Webb, N-adap. John D. McDonald, *The Executioners*, d. J. Lee Thompson.

Cape Fear, 1991, 128, ★★★/$$$$, Universal/MCA-U, R, P-V-S-FFN. Remake of above, emphasizing the stalker and horror aspects of the psycho-killer and women being in jeopardy more often. Robert De Niro (BActor), Nick Nolte, Jessica Lange, Juliette Lewis (BSActress). w. Wesley Strick, S-adap. James R. Webb, d. Martin Scorsese. Oscars: 2-0.
Jessica Lange Goes Southern
SUSPENSE: Psychological Thriller; Murderers; Rogue Plots; Revenge; Convict's Revenge; Criminal Pursues Good Guy's Family; Innocence Lost; Ethics; Psycho-Killers; Stalkers; Rape/Rapists; Southerns; Protecting Someone; Rednecks; Lawyers; Men and Girls; North Carolina
REMAKE OF: Cape Fear (1961)
(Fatal Attraction; Night of the Hunter)
(Ed: Not Scorsese's best but his biggest hit)

Capone, 1975, 101m, ★★/$, 20th/NA, R/V-P-FN. The big-time Chicago gang-ster muscles his way to the top of the crime heap. Ben Gazzara, Sylvester Stallone, Susan Blakely, Harry Guardino, John Cassavetes. w. Howard Browne, d. Steve Carver.
ACTION: Crime Drama; Criminal Biographies; Capone; Chicago; Mob Stories; Biographies

Caprice, 1967, 98m, ★★1/2/$$, 20th/NA. A woman working for a cosmet-ics giant uncovers a web of intrigue when she looks into her boss's mysterious death. Doris Day, Richard Harris, Edward Mulhare, Ray Walston, Jack

Kruschen, Lilia Skala. w. Jay Jayson, Frank Tashlin, d. Frank Tashlin.

COMEDY: FARCE: MURDER: Spoofs-Spy; Spies-Industrial; Conspiracy; Detective Stories; Spoofs-Detectives; Detectives-Amateur; Detectives-Female; Riviera Life; Spies-Female; Female Protagonists
(The Glass Bottom Boat)
(Ed: Good for Doris fans who will watch her in anything, but this is from her period of decline)

Capricorn One, 1978, 128m, ★★1/2/$$, UA/CBS-Fox, PG/P. A conspiracy at NASA is uncovered when a driven reporter finds that a multimillion-dollar probe to Mars was completely fabricated. Elliot Gould, James Brolin, Brenda Vaccaro, Sam Waterston, O. J. Simpson, Hal Holbrook,. Telly Savalas, Karen Black. w. d. Peter Hyams.

DRAMA: SUSPENSE: Conspiracy; Political Drama; Astronauts; Hoaxes; Political Corruption; Good Premise; Unfulfilled; What if . . . Stories; Writer-Directors

Captain America, 1989, 97m, ★★/$, 21st Century/Col, PG. The comic book superhero is unfrozen and does battle against the Red Skull. Matt Salinger, Ronny Cox, Ned Beatty, Darren McGavin, Michael Nouri, Melinda Dillon. w. Stephen Tolkin, d. Albert Pyun.

ACTION: ADVENTURE: Heroes-Superhuman; Comic Heroes; Good vs. Evil; Time Sleepers; Frozen People; Rule the World-Plot to

Captain Blood, 1935, 99m, ★★★/$$$$, WB/WB. In England a young doctor is wrongly accused of helping anti-government rebels and he escapes to become a pirate in the Caribbean. Errol Flynn, Olivia de Havilland, Basil Rathbone, Lionel Atwill. w. Casey Robinson, N-adap. Rafael Sabatini, d. Michael Curtiz.

ADVENTURE: ACTION: Adventure at Sea; Fugitives from the Law; Accused Unjustly; Doctors; Anarchists; Rebels; Traitors; Escape Adventure; Pirates Caribbean; Swashbucklers
(The Crimson Pirate; Mutiny on the Bounty; The Adventures of Captain Fabian; Captain Kidd; Treasure Island)
(Ed: Errol's breakthrough role)

Captain Carey, USA, 1950, 83m, ★★1/2/$$$, Par/NA. During World War II, an informer among an American platoon in Italy betrays them to their ene-

mies. When the war is over, one of the members of the platoon returns to Italy to exact justice. Alan Ladd, Francis Lederer, Wanda Hendrix, Joseph Calleia, Angela Clarke, Frank Puglia. w. Robert Thoeren, N-adap. Martha Albrand (*Dishonored*), d. Mitchell Leisen.
BOSong. Oscars: 1-0.

DRAMA: War Stories; Informers; Revenge; Traitors; War Stories; World War II Stories; Italy
(Ed: Most notable for the song "Mona Lisa")

Captain Horatio Hornblower, 1951, 117m, ★★1/2/$$, WB/WB. An English sailor in the 1800s is victorious in battles with the Spanish and French and also in winning the heart of his lady love. Gregory Peck, Virginia Mayo, Robert Beatty, James Robertson Justice. w. Ivan Goff, Ben Roberts, Aeneas Mackenzie, N-adap. C. S. Forester, d. Raoul Walsh.

ADVENTURE: Adventure at Sea; War at Sea; Pirates; **ROMANCE:** Men Fighting Over Women; Leaders-Military; Spain; 1800s

Captain Kidd, 1945, 89m, ★★1/2/$$, UA/Nos. A pirate tricks the King into ordering his ships into a trap, but he gets foiled in the end. Charles Laughton, Randolph Scott, Barbara Britton, Reginald Owen, John Carradine. w. Norman Reilly Raine, d. Rowland V. Lee.

ADVENTURE: Adventure at Sea; Pirates; Swashbucklers; Ships; War Stories; War at Sea; Kings; Double Crossings
(Mutiny on the Bounty; Captain Blood)

Captain Newman, M.D., 1963, 126m, ★★★/$$$, U/MCA-U. A psychiatrist sees into the sometimes chaotic and ironic lives of the soldiers on his base. Gregory Peck, Tony Curtis, Angie Dickinson, Eddie Albert, Bobby Darin, James Gregory, Dick Sargent. w. Richard L. Breen, Phoebe and Henry Ephron, N-adap. Leo Rosten.

COMEDY: COMEDY DRAMA: Psychologists; Ensemble Films; Ensembles-Male; Female Among Males; Military Comedy; Soldiers

Captain Ron, 1992, 93m, ★★★/$$$, Touchstone/Disney, PG-13/P-S. An ordinary family from Chicago (Martin Short, Mary Kay Place) buy Clark Gable's old yacht and take off to the Caribbean under the guidance of the cool, sexy, bumbling Captain Ron (Kurt Russell) and chaos begins. d. Thom Eberhardt.

COMEDY: Family Stories; Family Comedy; Vacations-Family; Caribbean; Sexy Men; Sailing; Extrovert vs. Introvert; Nuisances
(Ed: Not as bad as you might think)

Captains Courageous, 1937, 116m, ★★★★/$$$$, MGM/MGM-UA. A lonely, sensitive, rich boy falls overboard a cruise liner and is saved by rough and rugged sailors. He gradually develops a father-son type relationship with a particular Portuguese sailor who takes a special liking to him. Spencer Tracy (**BActor**), Lionel Barrymore, Freddie Bartholomew, Mickey Rooney. w. John Lee Mahin, Marc Connelly, Dale Van Every, N-adap. Rudyard Kipling, d. Victor Fleming. BPicture, BScr, BEdit. Oscars: 4-1.

COMEDY DRAMA: ADVENTURE: CHILDREN'S: FAMILY: Tearjerkers; Fathers-Surrogate; Rescue Adventure; Adventure at Sea; Fishermen; Men and Boys; Boys; Children in Jeopardy; Runaways; Orphans; Rich Kids; Rich vs. Poor; Coming of Age
TV Remake, 1977 with Karl Malden.
(The Old Man and the Sea; Boys Town)

Captains of the Clouds, 1942, 113m, ★★1/2/$$$, WB/NA. A big air battle proves the mettle of a Canadian fighter pilot who had previously shown a cavalier attitude. James Cagney, Dennis Morgan, Brenda Marshall, George Tobias, Alan Hale, Reginald Denny, Paul Cavanagh. w. Arthur T. Horman, Richard Macaulay, Norman Reilly Raine, d. Michael Curtiz.

ACTION: War Stories; Pilots-Military; World War II Stories; Men Proving Themselves; Forgotten Films

The Captive Heart, 1946, 108m, ★★★/$$, Ealing/Nos. The hemmed-in lives and small daily heartbreaks of inhabitants of a German P.O.W. camp. Michael Redgrave, Jack Warner, Basil Radford, Mervyn Johns. w. Angus Macphail, Guy Morgan, d. Basil Dearden.

DRAMA: TRAGEDY: POWs; Prison Drama; Nazi Stories; Soldiers; Letters; Germans as Enemy; British Films; Germany; Hidden Gems
(Stalag 17; Night Train to Munich)

The Car, 1977, 98m, ★★/$$, U/MCA-U, PG/V. In a small desert town, an unmanned vehicle starts running people over. James Brolin, Kathleen Lloyd, John Marley, R. G. Armstrong, John Rubenstein. w. Dennis Shyrack, Michael Butler, Lane Slate, d. Elliot Silverstein.

HORROR: SUSPENSE: ACTION: Car Chases; Objects with Personalities; Desert Settings; Murders-One by One; Rogue Plots; Kill the Beast; Camp; Unintentionally Funny
(Christine; Duel; Jaws; Tremors)
(Ed: As ridiculous as it may seem, it does have its moments of terror)
Caravans, 1978, 123m, ★★1/2/$$, U/NA. The daughter of an American politician marries an Iranian and leaves him to join a Bedouin caravan. When her father hears of her situation, he sends a young foreign officer out to find her. Anthony Quinn, Michael Sarrazin, Jennifer O'Neill, Christopher Lee, Joseph Cotten, Barry Sullivan. w. Nancy Voyles Crawford, Thomas A. MacMahon, Lorraine Williams, N-adap. James A. Michener, d. James Fargo.
ADVENTURE: ROMANCE: Middle East; Desert Settings; Journeys; Missing Persons; Americans Abroad; Fathers & Daughters
(The Wind and the Lion; Far Pavilions)
Carbon Copy, 1981, 92m, ★★1/2/$$, Hemdale/Col, Sultan. A conservative businessman has a son he's never seen. When they finally meet, he's shocked to learn that his son is black. George Segal, Susan Saint James, Jack Warden, Dick Martin, Denzel Washington. w. Stanley Shapiro, d. Michael Schultz.
COMEDY: SATIRE: Race Relations; Children-Long Lost; Romance-Interracial; Bigots; Class Conflicts; Fathers & Sons; Curiosities; Good Premise Unfulfilled; Coulda Been Good
(Soul Man; Call Me Bwana; A Family Thing)
The Cardinal, 1963, 175m, ★★★/$$, WB/WB. A priest moves up in the Church struggling against oppression wherever he sees it. Tom Tryon, Carol Lynley, Dorothy Gish, Maggie Macnamara, John Huston, Robert Morse, Burgess Meredith, John Saxon, Romy Schneider. w. Peter Sauder, d. Arna Selznick.
DRAMA: Priests Power-Rise; Biographies-Fictional; Young Men; Epics; Religion; Popes/Cardinals; Forgotten Films; Hidden Gems; Coulda Been Great
(Monsignor; The Shoes of the Fisherman)
Cardinal Richelieu, 1935, 83m, ★★1/2/$$, 20th/NA. A historical costume drama of the courtisan and Svengali behind Louis XIII. George Arliss, Maureen O'Sullivan, Edward Arnold, Cesar Romero. w. Maude

Howell, Cameron Rogers, W. P. Lipscomb, d. Rowland V. Lee.
DRAMA: MELODRAMA: Costume Drama; **ROMANCE:** Romantic Drama; Historical Drama; Prostitutes-High Class; Kings; Priests; Svengalis; Female Screenwriters
The Care Bears Adventure in Wonderland, 1987, 75m, ★★/$$, 20th/Fox. The Care Bears follow Alice through the lookinglass. Voices of Colin Fox, Bob Dermer, Eva Almos, Dan Hennessy. w. Susi Snooks, John DeKlein, SS-adap. Peter Sauder.
ADVENTURE: CHILDREN'S: Cartoon; Animal Stories; Revisionist Films; Fairy Tales
The Care Bears Movie, 1985, 75m, ★★1/2/$$$, Nelvana/Live, Vestron, G. The Care Bears combat a nemesis and prevail. Voices of Mickey Rooney, Georgia Engel, Harry Dean Stanton. w. Peter Sauder, d. Arna Selznick.
CHILDREN'S: FAMILY: Cartoons; Animal Stories; Good vs. Evil
Career, 1959, 105m, ★★★/$$$, Par/Par. A Broadway star's rise from Midwestern obscurity, dealing with alcoholism and other actorly traumas. Dean Martin, Tony Franciosa, Shirley MacLaine, Carolyn Jones, Donna Douglas. d. Joseph Anthony.
DRAMA: Actors; Theater Life; Fame-Rise to; Dreams; Woman Behind the Man; Ratpack Movies; Alcoholism; Illusions Destroyed; Faded Hits
(All the Fine Young Cannibals; Youngblood Hawke; A Hatful of Rain)
Career Opportunities, 1991, 85m, ★★1/2/$, U/MCA-U, PG. A young man (Frank Whaley) keeps getting fired from minimum wage jobs because of his rich fantasy life-until he winds up as night clean-up boy at a Target and meets the most beautiful girl in town (Jennifer Connelly). Dermott Mulroney, John Candy. w. John Hughes, d. Bryan Gordon.
COMEDY: CHILDREN'S: Romantic Comedy; Romance-Boy Wants Girl; Unemployment; Young Men; Pre-Life Crisis; Working Class; Fantasies; Free Spirits; Midwestern Life; Old-Fashioned Recent Films
(Ed: A low-rent Ferris Bueller; Whaley can be annoying, but film is charming at times, esp. Connelly; interesting cameos)
Carefree, 1938, 80m, ★★★/$$, RKO/Turner. A woman is undecided about

whether to marry her boyfriend, so he sends her to a hypnotist. Fred Astaire, Ginger Rogers, Ralph Bellamy, Hattie McDaniel, Franklin Pangborn. w. Allan Scott, Ernest Pagano, d. Mark Sandrich.
COMEDY: ROMANCE: Romantic Comedy; Screwball Comedy; Hypnotism; Psychologists; Marriage-Impending; Engagements-Breaking; Marriage Comedy; Misunderstandings; Astaire & Rogers; Good Premise Unfulfilled; Coulda Been Great; Hidden Gems
(It Had to Be You; On Approval; Holiday)
(Ed: Not quite what it easily could have been)
Careful, He Might Hear You, 1985, 116m, ★★★1/2/$$, 20th/Fox, PG. A boy is torn between rival family factions after his mother's death, just before his father returns to the picture. Nicholas Gledhill, Wendy Hughes, Robyn Nevin, John Hargreaves. w. d. Carl Schultz, N-adap. Sumner Locke Elliott.
DRAMA: Character Studies; Boyhood; Family Drama; Fathers & Sons; Mothers & Sons; Custody Battles; Australian Films; Hidden Gems; Depression Era; Child Protagonists
(The Long Day Closes; Hope and Glory; The Other)
The Caretaker (The Guest), 1964, 105m, ★★★/$$, Ind/NA. A hobo moves in on two brothers and changes their lives. Alan Bates, Robert Shaw, Donald Pleasence. w. Harold Pinter, d. Clive Donner.
DRAMA: SATIRE: Art Films; Incest; Avant-Garde; Social Satire; Social Drama; Family Drama; Homeless People; Reformers; Friendships-Male; Brothers; Stagelike Films; British Films
(The Homecoming; Accident; Fool for Love; Entertaining Mr. Sloane)
The Caretakers, 1963, 97m, ★★★/$$, UA/CBS-Fox. A state mental hospital's patients and staff are profiled. Polly Bergen, Robert Stack, Joan Crawford, Diane McBain, Janis Paige, Robert Vaughn, Herbert Marshall, Constance Ford. w. Henry F. Greenberg, N-adap. Daniel Telfer, d. Hall Bartlett.
DRAMA: Mental Illness; Asylums; Psychologists; Multiple Stories; Biographies-Fictional; Hospitals
(Committed; Bedlam; The Interns)
The Carey Treatment, 1972, 101m, ★★1/2/$$, MGM/NA. An investigation into the death of an abortion patient throws a doctor in harm's way. James

Coburn, Jennifer O'Neill, Skye Aubrey, Pat Hingle. w. James P. Bonner, N-adap. Jeffrey Hudson (*A Case of Need*), d. Blake Edwards.

DRAMA: Social Drama; Abortion Dilemmas; Detective Stories; Doctors; Guilty Conscience; Medical Detectives; Forgotten Films; Curiosities
(Criminal Law; Daddy's Gone A-Hunting)

Car 54, Where Are You?, 1990/1994, ★★/$, Orion/Orion, PG-13/P-V. Goofy cops bungle around with a witness protection situation in this remake of the 60s series. David Johansen, Fran Drescher, Rosie O'Donnell, John McGinley, Nipsey Russell, Al Lewis, Daniel Baldwin, Jeremy Piven. w. Ebbe Roe Smith, Erik Tarloff, d. Bill Fishman.

COMEDY: TV Series Movies; Police Comedy; Spoofs; Fools-Bumbling; Coulda Been Good

Carlito's Way, 1993, 145m, ★★★/$$$, U/MCA-U, R/EV-EP-FFN-MRN. A drug-dealing con artist having just gotten out of jail after 5 years in 1976 wants one last go-round before getting out and starting over legit in Florida. Al Pacino, Penelope Ann Miller, Sean Penn, John Leguizamo. w. David Koepp, N-adap. Edwin Torres, d. Brian DePalma.

DRAMA: Mob Stories; Mob Wars; Crime Drama; **ROMANCE:** Romance-Older Men/Younger Women; One Last Time; Redemption; Race Against Time; Dancers; Nightclubs; Drugs-Dealing; Inner City Life; Latin People; Convicts' Revenge; 1970s Narrated Films
(Straight Time; The Friends of Eddie Coyle)

Carmen, First Name (by Jean-Luc Godard), see **F** for **First Name Carmen**.

Carmen, 1983, 95m, ★★/$$, Ind/Media, R/S. The story of Carmen is again brought to the screen as a modern dance film with erotic lovers entangled across the floor. Antonio Gades, Laura Del Sol. w. Carlos Saura, Gades, d. Saura.

DRAMA: ROMANCE: Music Movies; Dance Movies; Spanish Films

Carmen (Opera), 1984, 152m, ★★★¹/₂/$$(LR), Col/Col, PG. A more faithful adaptation of the opera starring opera greats Julia Migenes-Johnson and Placido Domingo. w. M-adap. Bizet, d. Francesco.

DRAMA: ROMANCE: Opera; Musical Dramas; Opera Singers; Spain
(La Traviata; Yes, Giorgio)

Carmen Jones, 1954, 105m, ★★★¹/₂/$$$, 20th/Lebell. An updating of the Carmen legend with a black cast in which a blue collar girl marries a soldier and pays a heavy price for infidelity. Dorothy Dandridge, Harry Belafonte, Pearl Bailey. w. Harry Kleiner, d. Otto Preminger.

DRAMA: ROMANCE: MUSICALS: Musical Romance; Revisionist Films; Black Casts; Black Women; Black Men; Military Stories; Soldiers; Romance-Class Conflicts; Opera; Hidden Gems; Cult Films
(Stormy Weather; Bright Road)

Carnal Knowledge, 1971, 96m, ★★★¹/₂/$$$, Embassy/Embassy, R/P-S. Two men's (Jack Nicholson, Art Garfunkel) changes over a period of years marked by sexual experiences. Candice Bergen, Ann-Margret (BSActress). w. N-adap. Jules Feiffer, d. Mike Nichols. Oscars: 1-0.

DRAMA: Episodic Stories; Coming of Age; Friendships-Male; Sexuality; Life Transitions; College Life; Business Life; Executives; Men Proving Themselves; 1970s
(The Men's Club; The Bachelor Party)

Car 99, 1935, 70m, ★★/$, Par/NA. A rookie state trooper bungles an important arrest and makes ammends by bringing in bank robbers. Fred MacMurray, Ann Sheridan, Guy Standing. w. Karll Detzer, C. Gardner Sullivan, d. Charles Barton.

DRAMA: Crime Drama; Police Stories; Bank Robberies; Men Proving Themselves

Carnival of Souls, 1962, 80m, ★★★/$$, Ind/Nos, V. A woman has a car crash during a fling with two fellows and is subsequently haunted by her organ (which she plays at church). w. John Clifford, d. Harold Harvey.

HORROR: Gothic Style; Cult Films; Midwestern Life; Female Protagonists; Curiosities
(Night of the Living Dead; Dementia 13)

Carny, 1980, 105m, ★★/$, Lorimar-UA/WB, R/S-P. A travelling carnival gets shaken up by three strange people who seem to have a strange relationship. Gary Busey, Jodie Foster, Robbie Robertson, Meg Foster, Elisha Cook Jr. w. Thomas Baum, d. Robert Kaylor.

DRAMA: ROMANCE: Eccentric People; Working Class; Rednecks; Circus Life;

Romance-Triangles; Curiosities; Coulda Been Good

Carousel, 1957, 128m, ★★★/$$, 20th/CBS-Fox. A petty thief gets killed during a failed robbery. Fifteen years later when his family is struggling, his ghost comes back to help them out. Gordon Macrae, Shirley Jones, Cameron Mitchell, Gene Lockhart. w. Phoebe and Henry Ephron, P-adap. Ferenc Molnar (*Liliom*), d. Henry King.

MUSICALS: DRAMA: Musical Drama; Ghosts; Dead-Back from the; Thieves; **MURDER:** Family Drama; Hidden Gems; Faded Hits

The Carpetbaggers, 1964, 150m, ★★★/$$$$$, Par/Par. A young heir takes control of his father's airplane factory and makes it profitable. With his newfound money he decides to make pictures in Hollywood. George Peppard, Carroll Baker, Alan Ladd, Martin Balsam, Bob Cummings, Leif Erickson. w. John Michael Hayes, N-adap. Harold Robbins, d. Edward Dmytryk.

MELODRAMA: ROMANCE: Romantic Drama; Family Drama; Power-Rise to; Pilots-Airplane; Heirs; Sexy Men; Hollywood Life; Directors; Movie Making; 1920s; 1930s; Depression Era; Biographies-Fictional; Faded Hits; Blockbusters
(Bugsy; The Story of Howard Hughes)
(Ed: Veiled story of Howard Hughes, but hardly noticeable)

Carrie (*Sister Carrie*), 1952, 122m, ★★★/$$$, Par/Par. A simple farm girl goes to Chicago at the turn of the century and falls in love with a rich restaurant manager who goes broke funding her attempts at a stage career. Laurence Olivier, Jennifer Jones, Miriam Hopkins, Eddie Albert. w. Ruth and Augustus Goetz, N-adap. Theodore Dreiser, d. William Wyler.

DRAMA: ROMANCE: Romantic Drama; Romance-Class Conflicts; Social Drama; Cousins; Farm Life; City vs. Country; Marrying Up; Actresses; Risking it All; 1900s; Midwestern Life; Chicago; Hidden Gems
(Ethan Frome; The Age of Innocence; The Heiress; Beyond the Forest)

Carrie, 1976, 116m, ★★★¹/₂/$$$, UA/MGM-UA, R, P-V-B&G-FFN. A teenage girl (Sissy Spacek, BActress) becomes the class joke thanks to her repressive religious zealot mother (Piper

Laurie, BSActress) and the mean girls at school who like to play mindgames; but Carrie has more than the ability to play games with her mind. Nancy Allen, Amy Irving, William Katt. w. Larry Cohen, N-adap. Stephen King, d. Brian DePalma. Oscars: 2-0.

HORROR: SUSPENSE: SCI-FI: Revenge; Coming of Age Psychics; Supernatural Danger; Possessions; Wallflowers; Women in Conflict; Beauty Queens; Abused Children; Practical Jokers; Beauty Pageants; High School Life; Teenage Movies; Teenagers; Evil Women; Religious Zealots; Female Protagonists; Sleeper Hits; Stephen King
(The Fury; The Shining)

Carrington, 1995, 123m, ★★★¹/₂/$$, Gramercy/MCA-U, R/S-FN-MN. The tomboy/lesbian painter falls for the eccentric male writer Lytton Strachey in this true story of a doomed but pleasant romance between two bisexual/gay people, which is strained by their other love interests in the country. Emma Thompson, Jonathan Pryce, Steven Waddington, Samuel West, Rufus Sewell. NF-adap. Lytton Strachey, Michael Holroyd, w. d. Christopher Hampton.

DRAMA: ROMANCE: Writers; Painters; Bisexuality; Gay Men; Lesbians; Alternative Lifestyles; Biographies; British Films
(Another Country)

The Cars That Ate Paris, 1974, 91m, ★★¹/₂/$, Ind/Col. Strange goings on in a remote Australian town where car parts at the junkyard take on lives of their own. Terry Camillieri, Kevin Miles. w. d. Peter Weir.

COMEDY DRAMA: Black Comedy; **HORROR:** Horror Comedy; Curiosities; Australian Films; Car Wrecks; Cult Films

Car Wash, 1976, 97m, ★★★/$$$, Par/Par, R/P-S. A series of crazy people stop by a sudsery in L.A., not that the employees are any more sane, but they dance their way around and through it all. Franklin Ajaye, George Carlin, Irwin Corey, Richard Pryor, Bill Duke. w. Joel Schumacher, d. Michael Schultz.

COMEDY: Music Movies; Comedy-Skit; One Day Stories; Working Class; Comedians; Black Casts; Eccentric People; Camp; Blaxploitation Era; Cult Films; Musicals-Disco Era; Disco Era; 1970s

(D.C. Cab; Amateur Night at the Dixie Bar and Grill)

Casablanca (B&W), 1943, 102m, ★★★★/$$$$, WB/CBS-Fox. A man (Humphrey Bogart, BActor) falls for a young woman (Ingrid Bergman) while in North Africa during World War II, but love may be fleeting. Claude Rains (BSActor), Paul Henreid, Sydney Greenstreet, Peter Lorre, Conrad Veidt. w. Julius Epstein, Philip Epstein, Howard Koch (BScr), P-adap. Murray Bennett, Joan Allen, *Everybody Comes to Rick's*, d. Michael Curtiz (**BDirector**). **BPicture**, BScore, BEdit, BB&WCin. Oscars: 8-3.

ROMANCE: MELODRAMA: DRAMA: Romantic Drama; Film Noir; World War II Stories; Romance-Doomed; Romance-Triangles; Romance-Older Men/Younger Women; Escape Drama; Morocco; Sleeper Hits
(Havana; Play It Again, Sam; Algiers; Arch of Triumph)
(Ed: A surprise hit at the time, this is one classic that actually did get the accolades it deserved at the time of its release)

Casanova (Fellini's Casanova), 1976, 163m, ★★★/$$, 20th/Fox, R/S. A surrealistic look at the fabled 18th-century philanderer. The characters he beds down are Fellini's idea of central casting. Donald Sutherland, Tina Aumont, Cicely Browne, Carmen Scarpitta. w. Federico Fellini, Barnadino Zapponi, d. Federico Fellini.

COMEDY DRAMA: ROMANCE: Romantic Drama; Erotic Drama; **SATIRE:** Playboys; Sexy Men; Sexy Women; Cheating Men; Legends; Promiscuity; Biographies; Italy; Italian Films; 1700s; Hidden Gems
(Casanova '70; City of Women; Bocaccio '70)

Casanova Brown, 1944, 99m, ★★¹/₂/$$, U/MGM-UA. A couple have just divorced when the husband discovers that the wife is pregnant. Gary Cooper, Teresa Wright, Frank Morgan, Anita Louise, Patricia Collinge, w. Nunnally Johnson, P-adap. Floyd Dell, Thomas Mitchell (*Bachelor Father*), d. Sam Wood.

MELODRAMA: Marriage Drama; **ROMANCE:** Babies-Having Divorce; Romance-On Again/Off Again; Forgotten Films

REMAKE OF: Little Accident
(Penny Serenade; Made for Each Other)

Casanova's Big Night, 1954, 86m, ★★¹/₂/$$, Par/Par. A tailor's apprentice

gets his big break when Casanova, on the lamb from creditors, asks him to "stand in." Bob Hope, Joan Fontaine, Basil Rathbone, Vincent Price, Audrey Dalton, Hugh Marlowe, John Carradine, Lon Chaney Jr. w. Hal Kanter, Edmund Hartmann, d. Norman Z. McLeod.

COMEDY: Impostors; Actors; Fugitives; Fugitives from the Mob; Innocent Bystanders; Chase Stories

Casanova '70, 1965, 113m, ★★★/$$, 20th/Fox, S. A revised, futuristic (for 1965) look at the great lover and his ladies through a satiric perspective. Virna Lisi. w. Tonino Guerra, d. Mario Monicelli.

DRAMA: SATIRE: COMEDY DRAMA: Futuristic Films; Playboys; Sexy Men; Sexy Women; Promiscuity; Revisionist Films; Italian Films; Art Films
(Casanova; Bocaccio '70; Alphaville)

A Case for Murder, 1993, 94m, ★★¹/₂/$, U/MCA-U, R/S-P-V. A top young lawyer is on a roll until a friend is murdered and the wife is the suspect. But when a woman lawyer is teamed with him for the case, she begins to suspect some conflicts with the case which may unravel some secrets. Peter Berg, Jennifer Grey, Belinda Bauer. w. Duncan Gibbins, Pablo Fenjves, d. Duncan Gibbins.

SUSPENSE: MURDER: MYSTERY: MURDER MYSTERY: Lawyers; Accused Unjustly; Good Premise Unfulfilled

Casey's Shadow, 1978, 117m, ★★¹/₂/$$, Rastar-Col/RCA-Col, G. A French Louisiana family breeds a racehorse in New Mexico and wins the big race. Walter Matthau, Alexis Smith, Robert Webber, Murray Hamilton. w. Carol Sobieski, SS-adap. John McPhee (*Ruidoso*), d. Martin Ritt.

COMEDY DRAMA: FAMILY: CHILDREN'S: MELODRAMA: Men and Girls; Horses; Competitions; Southwestern Life; Cajuns
(The Black Stallion; National Velvet)

Cash McCall, 1960, 102m, ★★¹/₂/$$, WB/WB. A star stock trader starts to lose his knack when he falls in love. James Garner, Natalie Wood, Nina Foch, Dean Jagger, E. G. Marshall, Henry Jones, Otto Kruger. w. Lenore Coffee, Marion Hargrove, N-adap. Cameron Hawley, d. Joseph Pevney.

COMEDY DRAMA: ROMANCE: Romantic Comedy; Settling Down; Life

Transitions; Playboys; 1960s Business Life; Stock Brokers; Young Men; Forgotten Films; Coulda Been Great; Female Screenwriters

(The Art of Love; Move Over, Darling; The Thrill of it All)

Casino, 1995, 170m, ★★★/$$$, U/MCA-U, R/EP-V-S. The chronicle of several mafia-type casino men, and a few of their women, from the 60s to the decline of the mob's power in Vegas in the 80s. Robert De Niro, Sharon Stone (BActress), Joe Pesci, James Woods, Don Rickles, Alan King, Kevin Pollak, L. Q. Jones, Jerry Vale, Steve Allen, Jayne Meadows, Frankie Avalon. w. Nicholas Pileggi, Martin Scorsese, NF-adap. Nicholas Pileggi, d. Martin Scorsese. Oscars: 1-0.

DRAMA: Crime Drama; Epics; Ensemble Films; Las Vegas Gamblers; Mob Stories; Marriage on the Rocks; Prostitutes-High Class; Episodic Stories; 1960s; 1970s; 1980s

(Good Fellas; Bugsy; Basic Instinct)

(Ed: A major disappointment for many, but not a flop)

Casino Royale, 1967, 130m, ★★★/$$$$, UA/MGM-UA, PG. An international conglomerate of master criminals called SMERSH tries to take over the world and James Bond is called into action. w. Wolf Mankowitz, John Law, Michael Sayers, N-adap. Ian Fleming, d. John Huston.

COMEDY: ADVENTURE: ACTION: Action Comedy; Spoofs; Spoofs-Spy; Spy Films; Secret Agents; All-Star Casts; Ensemble Films; Curiosities; James Bond

Casper, 1995, 96m, ★★★/$$$$, U/MCA-U, G. A girl and her father move into a huge, Gothic mansion where a cute little ghost befriends her. But at the same time, there are bad ghosts who abuse Casper, the friendly ghost, and an evil couple who are planning to get to the bottom of a treasure somewhere in the house. Christina Ricci, Bill Pullman, Cathy Moriarty, Eric Idle. w. Sherri Stoner & Deanna Oliver, d. Brad Silberling.

CHILDREN'S: Fantasy; Ghosts; Treasure Hunts; Mean Women; Fathers & Daughters; Supernatural Danger; Haunted Houses; Female Protagonists; Female Screenwriters; Child Protagonists; Animation-Partial

(Ghostbusters)

Casque d'Or (Golden Marie), 1952, 96m, ★★★1/2/$$, Speva/NA. An Apache is brought to turn-of-the-century Paris and falls in love with a woman of the slums. Unfortunately, it all ends tragically. Simone Signoret, Serge Reggiani, Claude Dauphin. w. Jacques Becker, Jacques Companeez, d. Jacques Becker.

DRAMA: TRAGEDY: MELODRAMA: ROMANCE: Romantic Drama; Fish out of Water Stories; Paris; Indians-American; Romance-Interracial; Forgotten Films; Hidden Gems; French Films

Cass Timberlane, 1947, 119m, ★★★/$$$, MGM/MGM-UA. A bawdy street girl marries a stuffy judge, and they each have a hard time getting used to each other. Spencer Tracy, Lana Turner, Zachary Scott, Mary Astor, Albert Dekker. w. Donald Ogden Stewart, N-adap. Sinclair Lewis, d. George Sidney.

COMEDY DRAMA: Marriage Comedy; Judges; Stern Men; Feisty Females; Extroverted vs. Introverted; Romance-Bickering; Romance-Class Conflicts; Coulda Been Good

The Cassandra Crossing, 1976, 129m, ★★★/$$$, Avco/CBS-Fox, PG/S-V. A terrorist onboard a train threatens to unleash a fatal plague on the passengers. Sophia Loren, Richard Harris, Ava Gardner, Burt Lancaster, Martin Sheen, Lee Strasberg, John Phillip Law, O. J. Simpson. w. Tom Makiewicz, Robert Katz, George Pan Cosmatos, d. George Pan Cosmatos.

SUSPENSE: Disaster Stories; Ensemble Films; Race Against Time; Stranded; Epidemics; Disease Stories; Trains; Detective Stories; Terrorists; Disguised as Priest; All-Star Casts; International Casts

(Under Siege 2; Outbreak)

(Ed: Remarkably good considering how these international all-star things usually go)

Cast a Dark Shadow, 1955, 82m, ★★1/2/$$, Frobisher/Facets. A retired barmaid takes up with a man and later learns he murdered his former wife. Dirk Bogarde, Margaret Lockwood, Kay Walsh, Kathleen Harrison, Robert Flemyng, Mona Washbourne. w. John Cresswell, P-adap. Janet Green (*Murder Mistaken*), d. Lewis Gilbert.

DRAMA: ROMANCE: Romance-Dangerous; Dangerous Men; **MURDER:** Murder of Spouse; Mental Illness; Marriage on the Rocks

(Rebecca; Deceived; The Secret Beyond the Door)

Cast a Giant Shadow, 1966, 142m, ★★1/2/$$, UA/MGM-UA. A veteran tired of civilian life as a lawyer volunteers for the Israeli army and fights the Palestinians. Kirk Douglas, Angie Dickinson, Senta Berger, Luther Adler, Stathis Giallelis, Chaim Topol, John Wayne, Frank Sinatra, Yul Brynner, Jeremy Kemp. w. Melville Shavelson, NF-adap. Ted Berkman, d. Melville Shavelson.

DRAMA: ACTION: Action Drama; Military Stories; War Stories; Israel; Middle East; Jewish People; Anti-Semitism; Veterans

Castaway, 1987, 118m, ★★1/2/$, Cannon/WB, R/S-FFN-MRN. A man puts in a personal ad for a "rent-a-wife" to take with him to a tropical isle. He's happy when a beautiful London woman answers, but she didn't realize sex was to be part of the package. Oliver Reed, Amanda Donohue, Georgina Hale. w. Allan Scott, NF-adap. Lucy Irvine, d. Nicolas Roeg.

DRAMA: Erotic Drama; Islands Stranded; Stranded on an Island; **ROMANCE:** Romantic Drama; Battle of the Sexes; Hired Dates; Prostitute-Ordinary People Turned; Personal Ads; Art Films; British Films

(Swept Away; Heaven Knows, Mr. Allison)

(Ed: More realistic than funny)

The Castaway Cowboy, 1974, 91m, ★★★/$$$, Disney/Disney, G. In the late 1800s, a sailor from out West winds up in Hawaii and helps a failing potato farmer start raising cattle. James Garner, Vera Miles, Robert Culp, Eric Shea, Elizabeth Smith. w. Don Tait, d. Vincent McEveety.

ADVENTURE: COMEDY: CHILDREN'S: FAMILY: Disney Comedy; Comic Adventure; Pacific Islands; Hawaii; Farm Life; Sailors; Drifters; 1800s; Hidden Gems

Castle in the Desert, 1942, 62m, ★★★/$$, 20th/Fox. An erratic millionaire builds a mansion in the desert and his houseguests start disappearing mysteriously. Charlie Chan comes on the scene to investigate. Sidney Toler, Arleen Whelan, Richard Derr, Douglass Dumbrille, Henry Daniell, Steve Geray, w. John Larkin, d. Harry Lachman.

MYSTERY: MURDER: MURDER MYSTERY: Rich People; Murder-Invitation to; Murders-One by One; Houses-Creepy; Detective Stories; Mystery-Whodunit?; Charlie Chan

Castle Keep, 1969, 107m, ★★½/$$, Col/NA. A 10th-century castle full of valuable artifacts is occupied and defended to the death by American soldiers. Or are they already dead? Burt Lancaster, Peter Falk, Jean Pierre Aumont, Patrick O'Neal, Al Freeman Jr., Tony Bill, Bruce Dern. w. Daniel Taradash, David Rayfiel, N-adap. William Eastlake.
SUSPENSE: SCI-FI: HORROR: Castles; Soldiers; Middle Ages; Illusions/Hallucinations; Ghosts; Curiosities (The Keep; The Train)
Castle of Doom (Vampyr), 1932, 83m, ★★★/$$, Tobis/Nos. A traveler staying at a country inn dreams that he's surrounded by vampires and may actually be. Julian West, Sybille Shmitz, Maurice Schutz. w. Christen Jul, Carl Dreyer, SS-adap. Sheridan Le Fanu (*Carmilla*), d. Carl Dreyer.
HORROR: Vampires; Nightmares; Saving Oneself; Illusions/Hallucinations (Nosferatu; The Dark Old House; Dracula)
Casual Sex?, 1987, 97m, ★★/$$, U/MCA-U, R/S-P. Two young women go to a health resort to find love and only find more of the same it seems. Leah Thompson, Victoria Jackson, Stephen Shellen, Mary Gross, Peter Dvorsky, Andrew Dice Clay. w. P-adap. Wendy Goldman, Judy Toll, d. Genevieve Robert.
COMEDY: ROMANCE: Sex Comedy; Battle of the Sexes; Sexuality; Promiscuity; Romance-Choosing the Right Person; Female Protagonists; Single Women; Young Women; Jerks; Female Directors; Female Screenwriters
Casualties of War, 1989, 113m, ★★½/$$, Col/RCA-Col, R/EV-EP. Story of Vietnam soldiers' rape and murder of a Vietnamese girl and the soldier who couldn't keep his silence (Michael J. Fox). Sean Penn, John Leguizamo. w. David Rabe, NF-adap. Daniel Lang, d. Brian De Palma.
DRAMA: War Movies; Vietnam War; Vietnam Vets; True Stories; Rape/Rapists; Past-Haunted by the; Flashbacks (Streamers; Platoon; Conduct Unbecoming; Town Without Pity)
Cat and Mouse, 1958, 79m, ★★★/$, Eros/NA. A criminal hid his stash before being executed for murder. Afterward, his former accomplices harass his daughter looking for the loot. Lee Patterson, Ann Sears, Hilton Edwards, Victor Maddern,

George Rose, Roddy McMillan. w. d. Paul Rotha, N-adap. Michael Halliday.
DRAMA: Crime Drama; **COMEDY DRAMA:** Ex-Convicts; Executions; Treasure Hunts; Capers; Cat and Mouse; Inheritances at Stake; Finding the Loot; Hidden Gems
(Gaslight [1939]; There Was a Crooked Man)
The Cat and the Canary, 1927, 84m, ★★★/$$$, B&W, silent, U/Nos, VY. A wealthy eccentric old woman dies and, when her family gathers to read the will, comes back to haunt some of its more greedy members. Creighton Hall, Laura La Plante, Forrest Stanley, Tully Marshall, Gertrude Astor. w. Alfred Cohn, Robert F. Hill, P-adap. John Willard, d. Paul Leni.
REMAKES: 1939, 1979; **SPOOF:** The Old Dark House
The Cat and the Canary, 1939, 72m, ★★★½/$$$, Par/NA. A hilarious remake that introduced Bob Hope to the world in top form. Bob Hope, Paulette Goddard, Gale Sondergaard, Douglass Montgomery, John Beal, George Zucco, Nydia Westman, Elizabeth Patterson. w. Walter de Leon, Lynn Starling, P-adap. John Willard, d. Elliot Nugent.
REMAKE OF: 1927 version; **REMAKE:** 1979 version (British)
The Cat and the Canary, 1979, 98m, Col/Col, PG/S. A remake of above with a British cast. Not as much fun. Honor Blackman, Michael Callan, Edward Fos, Wendy Hiller, Beatrix Lehmann, Olivia Hussey, Wilfrid Hyde-White. w. d. Radley Metzger, P-adap. John Willard.
COMEDY: COMEDY DRAMA: FARCE: Ensemble Films; Inheritances at Stake; Finding the Loot; Eccentric People; Rich People; Family Comedy; Feuds
Cat Ballou, 1965, 96m, ★★★½/$$$$, Columbia/RCA-Col. When her father is threatened by a gunfighter, young and pretty Cat Ballou hires a drunk with a twin to protect him. But when everything goes awry, she has to do the protecting herself. Jane Fonda, Lee Marvin (**BActor**), Michael Callan, Dwayne Hickman, Nat King Cole, John Marley, Reginald Denny. w. Walter Newman, Frank Pierson (**BAScr**), N-adap. Roy Chanslor, d. Eliot Silverstein. BOSong, BOScore, BEdit. Oscars: 5-1.
COMEDY: WESTERNS: Western Comedy; Spoofs-Western; Comedy-

Slapstick; Fools-Bumbling; Hitmen; Gunfighters; Fathers & Daughters; Alcoholics; Protecting Someone; Twins; Lookalikes; Criminals-Female; Ordinary People Turned Criminal; Female Protagonists; Sleeper
(Blazing Saddles; Arthur; McClintock!)
Cat Chaser, 1989, 90m, ★★½/VR, Vestron/Vestron, R/S-V. A woman married to a fugitive from the Dominican Republic is visited by an old boyfriend interested in the loot her Latino lover has hidden. Peter Weller, Kelly McGillis, Charles Durning, Frederic Forrest, Juan Fernandez. w. James Borelli, Elmore Leonard, N-adap. Elmore Leonard, d. Abel Ferrara.
SUSPENSE: MYSTERY: Fugitives from the Law; Caribbean; Dangerous Men; Treasure Hunts; Finding the Loot; Coulda Been Good
Catch Me a Spy, 1971, 94m, ★★/$, Rank/Prism. A British spy in Russia falls for the wife of a Russian spy and sets up an elaborate double-crossing scheme. Kirk Douglas, Trevor Howard, Tom Courtenay, Marlene Jobert, Bernard Blier. w. Dick Clement, Ian La Frenais, N-adap. George Marten, Tibor Meray, d. Dick Clement.
SUSPENSE: DRAMA: Spy Films; Spies; KGB Agents; Russia; Russians as Enemy; Double Crossing; Romance with Married Person; Cheating Women; British Films (Russia House; The Looking Glass War)
Catch 22, 1970, 121m, ★★★/$$$$, Par/Par, R/P-S. An army man (Alan Arkin) tries desperately to get out of the insanity of World War II in the Mediterranean and the insanity of his commanders by claiming he's insane, only, of course, he can't be insane if he claims to be. Alan Arkin, Jon Voight, Jack Gilford, Martin Sheen, Buck Henry, Art Garfunkel, Charles Grodin, Richard Benjamin, Martin Balsam, Anthony Perkins, Orson Welles, Bob Newhart. w. Buck Henry, N-adap. Joseph Heller, d. Mike Nichols.
DRAMA: COMEDY DRAMA: Black Comedy; Military Movies; War Movies; Soldiers; Mental Illness; Young Men; Fantasies; Anti-Establishment Films; Vietnam Era; All-Star Casts; Suicidal Tendencies; Cult Films
(Mediterraneo; M*A*S*H)
The Catered Affair, 1956, 93m, ★★★/$$, MGM/MGM-UA. A cabbie's

daughter is engaged and his wife wants a grand wedding, which he's too embarrassed to admit he can't afford. Bette Davis, Ernest Borgnine, Debbie Reynolds, Barry Fitzgerald, Rod Taylor, Robert Simon. w. Gore Vidal, (Teleplay)-adap. Paddy Chayevsky, d. Richard Brooks.
DRAMA: MELODRAMA: ROMANCE: Family Drama; Romance-Class Conflicts; Working Class; Weddings; Wives-Troublesome; Marriage-Impending; Taxi Drivers
(Marty; The Bachelor Party)
Catherine the Great, 1934, 93m, ★★★/$$, London-Korda/Sultan, Voyager. The rise of the Queen of Russia and her descent into madness with the prince she married. Elisabeth Bergner, Douglas Fairbanks Jr., Flora Robson, Gerald du Maurier, Irene Vanbrugh, Griffith Jones, Joan Garner. w. Lajos Biro, Arthur Wimperis, Marjoerie Deans, P-adap. Melchior Lengyle, Lajos Biro (*Czarina*), d. Paul Czinner.
DRAMA: Costume Drama; Historical Drama; Queens; Leaders-Female; Russia; Mental Illness; Biographies; Royalty; Female Protagonists
(Great Catherine; Young Catherine; Rasputin)
Cat on a Hot Tin Roof, 1958, 108m, ★★★★/$$$$, MGM/MGM-UA. A young man (Paul Newman, BActor) drowns memories of the past with liquor while his wife (Elizabeth Taylor, BActress) tries to hold things together while under pressure herself. Burl Ives, Judith Anderson. w. Richard Brooks, James Poe (BAScr), P-adap. Tennessee Williams, d. Richard Brooks (BDirector). BPicture, BCCin. Oscars: 6-0.
Cat on a Hot Tin Roof, 1984, 122m, ★★★1/2/$$, PBS/Vestron, PG/S. Jessica Lange, Tommy Lee Jones, Kim Stanley, and Rip Torn in a more faithful staging of the classic play. d. Jack Hofsiss.
DRAMA: MELODRAMA: Marriage Drama; Marriage on the Rocks; Character Studies; Secrets-Consuming; Past-Haunted by the; Nervous Breakdowns; Alcoholics; Sexual Problems; Childless Women; Newlyweds; In-Laws–Troublesome; Plantation Life; Southerns; Pulitzer Prize Adaptations; Tennessee Williamsesque
(The Long, Hot Summer; The Hot Spell; Baby Doll; A Streetcar Named Desire)

Cat People, 1942, 73m, ★★★1/2/$$$, RKO/Turner. A young woman believes a curse has been placed on her that will turn her into a black panther, and soon she is haunted by the cries of one. w. De Witt Bodeen, d. Jacques Tourneur.
HORROR: SUSPENSE: Film Noir; Humans into Animals; Human Eaters; Hauntings; Women in Jeopardy; Hidden Gems
REMAKE: Cat People (1983)
Cat People, 1983, 118m, ★★★/$$, Univ/MCA-U, R/P-EV-B&G-S-FN. A gory, erotic remake of the classic horror film with more detail, but not as much atmosphere, elaborating on bestiality and incest themes. Nastassja Kinski, Malcolm McDowell, John Heard, Annette O'Toole, Ed Begley, Jr. w. Alan Ormsby, d. Paul Schrader.
HORROR: SUSPENSE: Erotic Thriller; Erotic Drama; Human Eaters; Humans into Animals; Monsters-Human; Incest; New Orleans; Rogue Plots; Kill the Beast; Men in Jeopardy
REMAKE OF: Cat People (1942)
Cat's Eye, 1985, 93m, ★★1/2/$$, DEG-20th/Fox, PG-13/V-B&G. A trio of horror stories, all involving evil cats. Drew Barrymore, James Woods, Alan King, Kenneth McMillan, Robert Hays, Candy Clark. w. Stephen King, d. Lewis Teague.
HORROR: SUSPENSE: Animal Stories; Monsters-Animal; Cats; Pet Stories; Trilogies; Multiple Stories
Cattle Annie and Little Britches, 1979, 98m, ★★★/$, Hemdale-UA/NA. Two young women go out West to make their livelihoods ropin' cattle with the help of an old cowpoke. Burt Lancaster, John Savage, Rod Steiger, Diane Lane, Amanda Plummer, Scott Glenn. w. N-adap. Robert Ward, d. Lamont Johnson.
WESTERNS: Westerns-Neo; Men and Girls; Girls; Young Women Rodeos; Cattle People; Female Among Males; Hidden Gems
(Annie Oakley; Annie Get Your Gun!; Bad Girls)
Cattle Queen of Montana, 1954, 88m, ★★/$, RKO/Turner. When her father dies, a woman must learn to do as he did and defend her newly inherited ranch from rustlers. Barbara Stanwyck, Ronald Reagan, Gene Evans, Lance Fuller, Anthony Caruso. w. Robert Blees, Howard Estabrook, d. Allan Dwan.

WESTERNS: DRAMA: Fathers & Daughters; Female Among Males; Feisty Females; Cattle Herded by Barbara Stanwyck; Cattle People; Cattle Rustlers; Female Protagonists; Montana Cattle Problems
(The Furies; Montana; Blowing Wild)
Cat Women of the Moon, 1953, 63m, ★★/$, Three Dimensional Pictures/Rhino. Astronauts land on the moon and find out that the title is not false advertising. Sonny Tufts, Victor Jory, Marie Windsor. w. Roy Hamilton, d. Arthur Hilton.
SCI-FI: Outer Space Movies; Humans into Animals; Cats; Cult Films; Sexy Women; Bimbos; Camp; Unintentionally Funny; 3-D Movies
Caught, 1949, 88m, ★★★/$$, MGM/MGM-UA, Republic. A millionaire abuses his wife and she leaves him for another man. She soon finds out she's pregnant with his child, however, and must decide what to do-a perilous situation. James Mason, Barbara Bel Geddes, Robert Ryan, Natalie Schaefer, Curt Bois. w. Arthur Laurents, N-adap. Libbie Block, d. Max Ophuls.
SUSPENSE: Film Noir; Dangerous Spouse; Dangerous Men; Abused Women; Marriage on the Rocks; Rich People; Marrying Up; Babies-Having; Cheating Women; Romance-Triangles; Coulda Been Great; Hitchcockian
(Deceived; Suspicion; Casanova Brown)
(Ed: Apparently the millionaire is based loosely on Howard Hughes)
Caught in the Act, 1993, 93m, ★★1/2/$$, U/MCA-U, PG-13/S-V. An unemployed actor is lured into a web of deceit and murder when an actress seduces him and disappears. Gregory Harrison, Leslie Hope, Patricia Clarkson, Kevin Tighe. w. Ken Hixon, d. Debroah Reinisch.
SUSPENSE: Conspiracy; Framed?; Actors; **MURDER: MYSTERY: MURDER MYSTERY:** Murder-Clearing Oneself
Caught in the Draft, 1941, 82m, ★★★/$$$, Par/MCA-U. A Hollywood actor and professional coward tries his darndest but can't avoid being drafted. Bob Hope, Lynne Overman, Dorothy Lamour, Irving Bacon, Eddie Bracken. w. Harry Tugend, d. David Butler.
COMEDY: Military Comedy; Soldiers; Actors; World War II Era; Cowards; Comedy of Errors; Faded Hits

(In the Army Now; Bonnie Scotland)
(Ed: Good title, but not a standout, except for Hope fans)

Cause for Alarm, 1951, 74m, ★★¹/₂/$, MGM/MGM-UA, Nos. A woman is being framed for murder and must intercept a package of false evidence that may clinch the case against her. Loretta Young, Barry Sullivan, Bruce Cowling, Irving Bacon. w. Mel Dinelli, Tom Lewis, d. Tay Garnet.
SUSPENSE: Accused Unjustly; Framed?;
MURDER: MYSTERY: MURDER MYS-TERY: Murder-Clearing Oneself; Letters; Conspiracy; Coulda Been Good; Female Protagonists
(The Accused; The File on Thelma Jordan)

Cavalcade, 1932, 109m, ★★★/$$$, 20th/Fox. In turn-of-the-century England, a family struggles with losing its sons in both the Boer War and World War I. Clive Brook, Diana Wynyard (BActress), Ursula Jeans, Herbert Mundin, Una O'Connor, Irene Brown. w. Reginald Berkeley, P-adap. Noel Coward, d. Frank Lloyd (**BDirector**). BPicture, BArt. Oscars: 4-3.
DRAMA: MELODRAMA: Family Drama; Sagas; Epics; 1900s England; Faded Hits; War at Home; Forgotten Films; Hidden Gems
(This Happy Breed; Random Harvest)

Caveman, 1981, 92m, ★★/$$, UA/ MGM-UA, PG/S-P. A prehistoric man deals with cantankerous cavewomen and farting dinosaurs. Ringo Starr, Dennis Quaid, Jack Gildord, Barbara Bach, Avery Schreiber. w. Rudy de Luca, Carl Gottlieb, d. Carl Gottlieb.
COMEDY: Spoofs; Prehistoric Times; Cavemen; Sex Comedy; Erotic Comedy; Bathroom Humor; Dinosaurs; Coulda Been Great
(One Million Years, B.C.; Quest for Fire)
(Ed: Has its moments, but not enough)

CB4: The Movie, 1993, 83m, ★★/$$, U/MCA-U, R/EP-V-S. Two "gangsta rap-pers" rap their way out of jail and into politics. Chris Rock, Allen Payne, Phil Hartman, Chris Elliott. w. Chris Rock, Nelson George, Robert Locash, d. Tamra Davis.
COMEDY: Spoofs; Black Casts; Prison Drama (Comedy); Gangs-Black; Black Men; Power-Rise to, of Idiot
(Fear of a Black Hat; Houseguest; House Party)

Ceiling Zero, 1935, 95m, ★★¹/₂/$$, WB/MGM-UA. An airline pilot has adventures on the ground and in the air. James Cagney, Pat O'Brien, June Travis, Stuart Erwin, Henry Wadsworth. w. P-adap. Frank Wead, d. Howard Hawks.
DRAMA: ACTION: Action Drama; Pilots-Airline; Faded Hits; Forgotten Films

Celia, 1988, 103m, ★★★/$, BCB/NA. In suburban Australia, a young girl who is very close to her grandmother retreats into a fantasy world when she dies. Rebecca Smart, Nicholas Eadie, Victoria Longley, Mary-Anne Fahey. w. d. Ann Turner.
DRAMA: Coming of Age; Illusions/Hallucinations; Death-Dealing with; Grandmothers-Fascinating Dreams; Fantasies; Girls; Australian Films; Female Protagonists; Female Screen-writers; Female Directors; Child Protag-onists; Coulda Been Great; Hidden Gems; Writer-Directors
(Dream Child; Rachel, Rachel; Desert Bloom; A Woman's Tale)

The Cemetery Club, 1993, 114m, ★★★/$$, Touchstone/Touchstone, PG/P-S. Three widows, who happen to be Jewish, try to start over on the dating scene while still visiting their husbands' graves regu-larly. Ellen Burstyn, Olympia Dukakis, Diane Ladd, Danny Aiello, Lainie Kazan, Christina Ricci, Bernie Casey. w. P-adap. Ivan Menchell, d. Bill Duke.
COMEDY: COMEDY DRAMA: Friendships-Female; Widows; Death-Dealing with; Starting Over; Dating Scene; Romance-Middle Aged; Elderly Women; Jewish People; Black Directors; Female Protagonists
(Steel Magnolias; Moonstruck; The Golden Girls TV SERIES)

Centennial Summer, 1946, 102m, ★★★/$$, 20th/NA. A family all go to Philadelphia's Great Exposition of 1876 to find their separate pleasures at the fair. Jeanne Crain, Cornel Wilde, Linda Darnell, William Eythe, Walter Brennan, Constance Bennett, Dorothy Gish. w. Michael Kanin, N-adap. Albert E. Idell, d. Otto Preminger.
COMEDY DRAMA: Family Comedy; FamilyDrama; Vacations; 1800s; Multiple Stories; ROMANCE: Nostalgia; Time Capsules
(State Fair; Margie)

Central Park, 1932, 57m, ★★★/$, WB/NA. Tales of the inhabitants and passersby of the famed New York park. Richard Barhelmess, Sally Eilers, Tom Brown, Glenda Farrell, Harold Huber. w. Rian James, James Seymour, SS-adap. Jack Moffit (*Hawk's Mate*), d. William Wellman.
DRAMA: Documentary Style; Homeless People; New York Life; Slice-of-Life Stories; Multiple Stories; Time Capsules; Curiosities

A Certain Smile, 1958, 105m, ★★★/$$, 20th/NA. A young girl falls in foolish puppy love with her playboy uncle, and he must gently bring her down. Christine Carere, Rossano Brazzi, Joan Fontaine, Bradford Dillman, Eduard Franz, Kathryn Givney, Steve Geray. w. Frances Goodrich, Albert Hackett, d. Jean Negulesco.
COMEDY: COMEDY DRAMA: ROMANCE: Romantic Comedy; Infatuations; Romance-Older Men/Younger Women; Romance with Relative; Girls; Men and Girls; Female Screenwriters; Female Protagonists
(The Bachelor and the Bobbysoxer; The Member of the Wedding; Mad About Music; Daddy Longlegs)

C'est la Vie, 1990, 96m, ★★★/$, Ind-Electric/NA. Two sisters spy their mother flirting with a younger man when the fam-ily's on summer vacation at the beach. By the time vacation's over, mommy wants to file for divorce. Nathalie Baye, Richard Berry, Zabou, Jean-Pierre Bacri. w. Diane Kurys, Alain Le Henry, d. Diane Kurys.
DRAMA: Family Drama; ROMANCE: Romantic Drama; Cheating Women; Marriage on the Rocks; Beach Movies; Vacations; Vacation Romance; Vacations-Family; Sisters Mothers & Daughters; Divorce; French Films; Art Films; Quiet Little Films; Female Screenwriters; Female Directors; Female Protagonists

Chained, 1934, 77m, ★★¹/₂/$$$, MGM/MGM-UA. A woman who is nor-mally a faithful wife lets her hair down and has an affair on a sea journey. Joan Crawford, Clark Gable, Otto Kruger, Stuart Erwin, Una O'Connor, Akim Tamiroff. w. John Lee Mahin, d. Clarence Brown.
ROMANCE: Vacations; Vacation Romance; Ships; Cheating Women; Romance with Married Person; Forgotten Films

The Chairman (*The Most Dangerous Man in the World*), 1969, 99m, ★★/$, 20th/NA. A literal walking time-bomb goes to Red China on a mission. Gregory Peck, Anne Heywood, Arthur Hill,

Conrad Yama. w. Ben Maddow, N-adap. Richard Kennedy.

SUSPENSE: SCI-FI: Spy Films; Spies; Secret Agents; Cold War Era; Communists; Suicidal Tendencies; China; Exploding Heads; Coulda Been Great (Johnny Mnemonic; The Manchurian Candidate)

The Chalk Garden, 1964, 106m, ★★★/$$, U/MCA-U. A governess takes on the job of managing a rich elderly woman's rebellious grandaughter, but it's more than just a babysitting job. Edith Evans (BSActress), Deborah Kerr, Hayley Mills, John Mills, Felix Aylmer, Elizabeth Sellars, w. John Michael Hayes, N-adap. Enid Bagnold, d. Ronald Neame. Oscars: 1-0.

DRAMA: CHILDREN'S: FAMILY: Girls; Babysitters; Rebels; Women and Girls; Illusions Destroyed; England; Hidden Gems
(Pollyanna; Clara's Heart; The King and I)
(Ed: A beautiful film with a neverland atmosphere to escape into)

The Challenge, 1982, 112m, ★★/$$, CBS-WB/WB, R/V-P. An American boxer goes to Japan to compete and unwittingly gets involved in a local feud between two brothers. Scott Glenn, Toshiro Mifune, Conna Kei Benz, Atsuo Nakamura. w. Richard Maxwell, John Sayles, d. John Frankenheimer.

ACTION: Boxing; Sports Movies; Martial Arts; Japan; Feuds; Brothers; Americans Abroad; Competitions; Underdog Stories

The Champ, 1931, 87m, ★★★½/ $$$$$, MGM/MGM-UA. A down-and-out boxer (Wallace Beery, **BActor**), is caught in a custody battle for his little boy (Jackie Cooper) as he's trying to fight his way back in the ring. Irene Rich. w. Leonard Praskins, Frances Marion (**BOStory**), d. King Vidor (BDirector). BPicture. Oscars: 4-2.

MELODRAMA: DRAMA: Tearjerkers; Fathers and Sons; Custody Battles; Divorces; Children-Parting with; Sports Movies; Boxing; Children-Little Adults; Boys; Men and Boys

REMAKE: The Champ (1979)
(Kramer vs. Kramer; Rocky V)

The Champ, 1979, 121m, ★★/$$$, MGM/MGM-UA, PG/V. The remake of the classy tearjerker set in the same time period, with Jon Voight, Ricky Schroeder and Faye Dunaway. w. Walter Newman, d. Franco Zeffirelli.

MELODRAMA: DRAMA: Tearjerkers; Fathers and Sons; Custody Battles; Divorces; Children-Parting with; Sports Movies; Boxing; Children-Little Adults; Boys; Men and Boys

REMAKE OF: The Champ (1931)
(Kramer vs. Kramer; Rocky V)

Champagne for Caesar, 1950, 99m, ★★★/$$, Cardinal-UA/VCI. A bookish brain determines to get back at a soap company by winning the quiz show they sponsor. Ronald Colman, Vincent Price, Celeste Holm, Barbara Britton, Art Linkletter. w. Hans Jacoby, Fred Brady, d. Richard Whorf.

COMEDY: SATIRE: TV Life; Game Shows; 1950s; Revenge; Nerds; Turning the Tables; Corporation as Enemy; Birds; Hidden Gems
(Quiz Show; Sitting Pretty; A Double Life)

Champion, 1949, 99m, ★★★/$$$, Stanley Kramer-UA/Republic. A prize-fighter makes an alliance with the mob in order to facilitate his rise. In the process he loses his friends and family-and possibly everything. Kirk Douglas, Arthur Kennedy, Marilyn Maxwell, Paul Stewart, Ruth Roman, Lola Albright. w. Carl Foreman, SS-adap. Ring Lardner, d. Mark Robson.

ACTION: DRAMA: TRAGEDY: Action Drama; Sports Movies; Mob Stories; Fame-Rise to; Boxing; Risking It All; Sleeper Hits; Hidden Gems; Faded Hits (Raging Bull; The Killers; Requiem for a Heavyweight)
(Ed: Douglas' big breakthrough after B-pictures)

Champions, 1983, 115m, ★★½/$$, Avco/Sultan, PG. The true story of a dying jockey and his broken-down horse who win one last race before going on to greener pastures. John Hurt, Edward Woodward, Ben Johnson, Jan Francis, Peter Barkworth. w. Evan Jones, NF-adap. Bob Champion, Jonathan Powell, d. John Irvin.

MELODRAMA: Sports Movies; Horses; Disease Stories; True Stories; British Films
(Phar Lap; Bang the Drum Slowly; Brian's Song)

Chan Is Missing, 1982, 80m, ★★★/$, Wang-Ind/New Yorker, PG. Two Chinese cab drivers in San Francisco's Chinatown search halfheartedly for a man who has stolen their money. But the title may refer more to the fact that Charlie Chan is missing from this film: i.e., that this is an unstereotypical Chinese detective film.

Wood Moy, Marc Hayashi, Lauren Chew, Peter Wang, George Woo. w. Isaac Cronin, Wayne Wang, Terrel Steltzer, d. Wayne Wang.

COMEDY: COMEDY DRAMA: Chinese People; Asian-Americans; Taxi Drivers; Missing Persons; Detective Stories; Detectives-Amateur; Art Films; Hidden Gems
(Eat a Bowl of Tea; Life Is Cheap . . .)

Chances Are, 1989, 108m, ★★★/$$, Tri-Star/RCA-Col, PG-13/S. A widow (Cybill Shepherd) has a new love (Ryan O'Neal), but so does her daughter (Mary Stuart Masterson) in a young man (Robert Downey, Jr.), who turns out to be the reincarnation of the widow's husband and the daughter's father. w. Perry & Randy Howze, d. Emile Ardolino.

COMEDY: FARCE: Romantic Comedy; Screwball Comedy; Romance-Reunited; Dead-Back from the; Incest; Romance with Relative; Reincarnation; Old-Fashioned Recent Films
(Heaven Can Wait; Blithe Spirit; Kiss Me Goodbye)

Chandler, 1971, 88m, ★★/$, MGM/NA. An attempt to recreate a forties-style detective film in the "realistic," cynical seventies results in a story about a private dick who loses his job and in desperation agrees to guard a government witness. Warren Oates. w. John Secret Young, d. Paul Magwood.

MYSTERY: SUSPENSE: Film Noir-Modern; Detective Stories; Detectives-Private; Bodyguards; Witnesses-Protecting; Unemployment; Revisionist Films
(Marlowe; The Long Goodbye)

A Change of Habit, 1969, 93m, ★★½/$$, U/MCA-U, G. A nun in street clothes helps a young, hip doctor deal with life in the ghetto hospital where he works. Elvis Presley, Mary Tyler Moore, Barbara McNair. d. William Graham.

COMEDY DRAMA: MELODRAMA: ROMANCE: Nuns; Social Workers; Doctors; Inner-City Life
(Ed: Nice but boring)

A Change of Seasons, 1980, 102m, ★★/$$, 20th/CBS-Fox, R/S-FN. A crusty old professor has a mid-life crisis and takes a mistress. His wife finds creative ways to pay him back. Shirley MacLaine, Bo Derek, Anthony Hopkins, Michael Brandon. w. Erich Segal, Ronni Kern, Fred Segal, d. Richard Lang.

COMEDY: Sexy Comedy; Cheating Men; Sexy Women; Midlife Crisis; Turning the Tables; Revenge; Revenge on Cheaters; Marriage on the Rocks; Bimbos
(Ten; Loving Couples; A Month by the Lake)

The Changeling, 1980, 102m, AFD/Vestron, ★★★/$$$, R. When his wife dies, a professor moves into a house which appears to be haunted by the ghost of a child who was murdered there years before. George C. Scott, Melvyn Douglas, Trish Van Devere, Jean Marsh, Barry Morse. w. William Gray, Diana Maddox, d. Peter Medak.

HORROR: SUSPENSE: Ghosts; Possessions; Supernatural Dangers; Haunted Houses; Murders of Children; Faded Hits
(The Haunting; The Amityville Horror)

Chantilly Lace, 1993, 102m, ★★1/2/$$, Col/Col, R/P-S. Several career women meet at one of their group's resort home and compare notes. Jill Eikenberry, Helen Slater, Ally Sheedy, Lindsay Crouse, Jobeth Williams, Martha Plimpton, Talia Shire. w. d. Linda Yellen, Rosanne Erhlich.

COMEDY DRAMA: DRAMA: Ensembles-Female; Ensemble Films; Vacations; Career Women; Female Screenwriters; Female Directors; Female Protagonists; Women's Films; TV Movies; Improvisational Films
(Moonlight and Valentino; Waiting to Exhale)

Chaplin, 1992, 145m, ★★/$$, U/MCA-U, PG-13/S. A biopic of the great silent film artist, focusing on his offscreen dalliances as well as on-screen achievements. Scandal takes the fore in the latter part, which deals with his exile from America. Robert Downey Jr. (BActor), Dan Aykroyd, Geraldine Chaplin, Kevin Dunn, Anthony Hopkins, Kevin Kline, Diane Lane, Penelope Ann Miller, Paul Rhys, Marisa Tomei, James Woods. w. William Boyd, Bryan Forbes, William Goldman, Diana Hawkins, NF-adap. Charles Chaplin (*My AutoBiographies*), David Robinson (*Charlie Chaplin-His Life and Art*), d. Richard Attenborough. BArt, BOScore. Oscars: 3-0.

DRAMA: Biographies; Historical Drama; Hollywood Life; Hollywood Biographies; Hollywood Satire; Fame-Rise to; Silent Film Era; 1900s; All-Star Casts; Epics;

Old-Fashioned Recent Films; Autobiographical Stories
(Modern Times; Monsieur Verdoux)

The Chapman Report, 1962, 125m, ★★★/$$$, WB/NA, S. A take on the Kinsey Report, in which a doctor does sexual research in the suburbs. Shelley Winters, Claire Bloom, Glynis Johns, Efrem Zimbalist Jr., Jane Fonda, Ray Danton, Ty Hardin, Andrew Duggan. w. Wyatt Cooper, Don M. Mankiewicz, N-adap. Irving Wallace, d. George Cukor.

DRAMA: COMEDY DRAMA: SATIRE: Suburban Life; Multiple Stories; Psychologists; Sociologists; Sexual Problems; Sexuality; Promiscuity; Interviews; Doctors; Ahead of Its Time; Repression; 1960s Repression; Marriage Drama; Hidden Gems; Time Capsules
(Doctor's Wives, Boys' Night Out)
(Ed: Interesting and daring for its time, though dated by any standard today)

Chapter Two, 1979, 124m, ★★★/$$$, Col/RCA-Col, PG/S. A writer (James Caan) and his actress wife (Marsha Mason) try to reconcile a crumbling relationship. Valerie Harper, Joe Bologna. w. P-adap. Neil Simon, d. Robert Moore.

DRAMA: COMEDY DRAMA: MELODRAMA: ROMANCE: Romantic Comedy; Romantic Drama; Autobiographical Stories; Episodic Stories; Marriage Drama; Marriage on the Rocks; Divorce; Dating Scene; Starting Over; Writers; Actresses; Wisecracking Sidekicks
(Starting Over; Lily in Love; Only When I Laugh)

Charade, 1952, 83m, ★★1/2/$, Portland-Ind/Nos. A young woman sketches the man who just murdered her friend, unbeknownst to her, and two other stories of macabre intrigue. James Mason, Pamela Mason, Scott Forbes, Paul Cavanagh, Bruce Lester. w. James and Pamela Mason, d. Roy Kellino.

SUSPENSE: MURDER: MYSTERY: MURDER MYSTERY: Multiple Stories; Trilogies
(Dead of Night; Night Gallery SERIES)

Charade, 1963, 113m, ★★★/$$$$, Universal/MCA-U. A woman (Audrey Hepburn) whose husband has died finds he was a criminal when a suave man (Cary Grant) appears saying he's an investigator looking for loot. James Coburn, Walter Matthau. w. Peter Stone, d. Stanley Donen. BOSong. Oscars: 1-0.

SUSPENSE: MURDER: MYSTERY: MURDER MYSTERY: Comic Mystery; Comic Thriller; Murder of Spouse; **ROMANCE:** Romantic Comedy; Treasure Hunt; Thieves; Love-Questionable; Dangerous Men; Secret Agents; Beautiful People; Mindgames; Undercover; Hitchcockian
(To Catch a Thief; Arabesque; How to Steal a Million)
(Ed: Pure fun, if a bit silly at times and without the genuinely harrowing moments Hitchcock would have been able to create within the comical atmosphere)

Charge of the Light Brigade, 1936, 115m, ★★★1/2/$$$$, WB/MGM-UA, Fox. The British ignite a battle the Surat Khan to even a score with much bravery and the ever present "stiff upper lip" when 'tis their glory to die in battle. Errol Flynn, Olivia de Havilland, Patric Knowles, Donald Crisp, C. Aubrey Smith, David Niven, Nigel Bruce, C. Henry Gordon, Spring Byington. w. Michel Jacoby, Rowland Leigh, d. Michael Curtiz, with Jack Sullivan (**BAss't Director**). BOScore. Oscars: 2-1.

Charge of the Light Brigade, 1968, 141m, ★★1/2/$, UA/MGM-UA. A remake with mod stylings from the hip sixties. Trevor Howard, John Gielgud, David Hemmings, Vanessa Redgrave, Jill Bennett, Harry Andrews, Peter Bowles. w. Charles Wood, d. Tony Richardson.

ADVENTURE: ACTION: DRAMA: Action Drama; Power Struggles; Asia; Imperialist Problems; War Stories; War Battles; Epics; Soldiers; England; British Films
(Gunga Din; Lives of a Bengal Lancer; The Four Feathers)

Charing Cross Road, see E for **84 Charing Cross Road**

Chariots of Fire, 1981, 124m, ★★★★/$$$$, Ladd-WB/WB, PG. A Christian and a Jew race against each other until a race is held on the sabbath and conviction overcomes competition. Ian Charleson, Ben Cross, Ian Holm (**BSActor**), Nigel Havers, Alice Krige, w. Colin Welland (**BOScr**), d. Hugh Hudson (**BDirector**), **BPicture, BOScore, BCostume, BArt.** Oscars: 7-4.

DRAMA: MELODRAMA: Religious Films; Costume Drama; Ethics; Sports Movies; Running; Conservative Value Films; Jewish People; Old-Fashioned Recent Films; British Films; 1920s; Sleeper Hits; Quiet Little Films; True Stories

(Friendly Persuasion; Brideshead Revisited; Howard's End)

Charley and the Angel, 1974, 92m, ★★¹/₂/$$, Disney/Disney, G. In the 30s, a clerk at a sporting goods store narrowly escapes death on a routine basis, until his guardian angel finally gets fed up. Fred MacMurray, Cloris Leachman, Harry Morgan, Kurt Russell, Kathleen Cody, Edward Andrews, Barbara Nichols. w. Roswell Rogers, N-adap. Will Stanton, *The Golden Evenings of Summer*, d. Vincent McEveety.
COMEDY DRAMA: Fantasy; Angels; Comedy-Disney; FAMILY: Family Comedy; Depression Era, Old-Fashioned Recent Films
(Angel on My Shoulder; Angel in My Pocket)

Charley's Aunt, 1941, 81m, ★★★/$$$, 20th/Facets, Grapevine. An Oxford student helps out his friend in a pinch by posing as his aunt and all sorts of farcical situations ensue. Jack Benny, Kay Francis, James Ellison, Anne Baxter, Laid Cregar, Edmund Gwenn, Reginald Owen, Richard Haydn. w. George Seaton, P-adap. Brandon Thomas, d. Archie Mayo.
COMEDY: FARCE: Impostors; Men as Women; College Life; England; Coulda Been Great; Hidden Gems
(La Cage Aux Folles; Tootsie; Mrs. Doubtfire)

Charley Varrick, 1973, 111m, ★★★¹/₂/ $$, Universal/MCA-U, R/P-S-V. An ex-con (Walter Matthau) has devised a big heist of mob money being laundered at a small bank that's easy prey. Andrew Prine, Joe Don Baker. w. Howard Rodman, Dean Risener, N-adap. John Reese, *The Looters*, d. Don Siegel.
ACTION: Heist Stories; Chase Movies; Fugitives; Fugitives From the Mob; Ex-Convicts; Bank Robberies; Police Corruption; One Last Time; Double-Crossings; Clever Plots & Endings; Escape Adventure; Crossing the Border; Southwestern Life; Overlooked at Release; Underrated; Hidden Gems
(The Pursuit of D.B. Cooper; The Friends of Eddie Coyle)

Charlie Bubbles, 1968, 91m, ★★★¹/₂/ $$, U/NA, PG. A novelist loses the drive and inspiration that led to his fortune and fame, so he decides to give them up and return to his working-class roots. But alas,

he finds you can't go home again. Albert Finney, Billie Whitelaw, Liza Minnelli, Colin Blakely, Timothy Garland, Diana Coupland, Alan Lake. w. Shelagh Delaney, d. Albert Finney.
DRAMA: KITCHEN SINK DRAMA; COMEDY DRAMA: Young Men; Rich vs. Poor; Class Conflicts; Working Class; Riches to Rags; Writers; Midlife Crisis; Balloons; British Films; 1960s; Hidden Gems

Charlie Chan and the Curse of the Dragon Queen, 1980, 95m, ★★/$, American Cinema/Media, PG. A curse on Charlie Chan's family takes several generations to be fully realized. Peter Ustinov, Angie Dickinson, Richard Hatch, Brian Keith, Roddy McDowell. w. Stan Burns, David Axelrod, d. Clive Donner.
COMEDY: MYSTERY: Comic Mystery; Curses; Mystery-Whodunit; Murders-One by One; Coulda Been Good

Charlotte's Web, 1973, 85m, ★★★¹/₂/ $$$, Par/Par, G. A spider convinces barnyard animals of their farmer's not-so-altruistic intentions, despite their good faith. Voices of Debbie Reynolds, Henry Gibson, Paul Lynde, Martha Scott, Agnes Moorehead. w. Earl Hamner Jr., N-adap. E.B. White, d. Charles A. Nichols, Iwao Takamoto.
CHILDREN'S: FAMILY: Cartoons; Tearjerkers; Animal Stories; Death-Dealing with; Farm Life; Insects; Charismatic People; Spiders; Hidden Gems; Faded Hits
(Babe; Stuart Little; Animal Farm)
(Ed: A great story that can't go wrong, especially with bright kids)

Charly, 1968, 103m, ★★★/$$$, ABC-Cinerama/Fox, PG/S. A retarded man (Cliff Robertson, **BActor**) is turned into a savant scholar through psychological experiments and falls in love with his mentor (Claire Bloom), but what will he do as the effects wear off? Lilia Skala, Leon Janney. w. Stirling Siliphant, N-adap. Daniel Keyes, *Flowers for Algernon*, d. Ralph Nelson. Oscars: 1-1.
DRAMA: ROMANCE: Underdog Stories; Mentally Disabled; Simple Minds; Teachers; Teachers & Students; Romance with Student; Reformers; Coming of Age; Childlike People; Sleeper Hits; Disabled but Nominated
(Rain Man; A Dangerous Woman; Stanley and Iris)

The Charmer, 1989, 312m, ★★★/$$, BBC/Signet, PG. A con-man playboy stops at nothing in late-30s England to get what he wants, even if it means murder. Nigel Havers, Rosemary Leach, Bernard Hepton. w. Allan Prior, d. Alan Gibson.
SUSPENSE: MURDER: Playboys; Sexy Men; 1930s; British Films; TV Movies

Charming Sinners, 1929, 85m (B&W, Silent), ★★¹/₂/$$, Ind/NA. A woman (Ruth Chatterton) whose husband is cheating romances a former boyfriend to make him jealous. William Powell, Clive Brook, Mary Nolan, Florence Eldridge. w. Doris Anderson, d. Robert Milton.
MELODRAMA: Romance-Triangles; Jealousy; Cheating Men; Cheating Women; Romance with Married Person; Revenge; Revenge on Cheater; Turning the Tables; Romance-Reunited

The Chase, 1947, 84m, ★★¹/₂/$$, Nero Pictures/Nos. A shell-shocked veteran forgets that he's married, gets involved with criminals, and later falls in love with his wife. Robert Cummings, Michele Morgan, Peter Lorre, Steve Cochran, Lloyd Corrigan, Jack Holt. w. Philip Yordan, N-adap. Cornell Woolrich, d. Arthur Ripley.
SUSPENSE: ACTION: Action Drama; Amnesia; Veterans; World War II-Post Era; Ordinary People Turned Criminal; Chase Stories
(Mister Buddwing)

The Chase, 1966, 135m, ★★★/$$. A prison break fugitive (Robert Redford) affects his small hometown as he seeks refuge nearby. Marlon Brando, Jane Fonda, Angie Dickinson, Robert Duvall, Janice Rule, E. G. Marshall, Miriam Hopkins. w. Lillian Hellman, N-adap. Horton Foote, d. Arthur Penn.
DRAMA: MELODRAMA: Chase Movies; Prison Escapes; Fugitives from the Law; Small-Town Scandal; Ensemble Films; Southerns; Texas; All-Star Casts; Coulda Been Great
(Hurry Sundown; The Fugitive)

The Chase, 1994, 87m, ★★¹/₂/$, 20th/Fox, PG-13/S-P-V. A carjacker gets more than he bargained for when he steals the car of an heiress and the heiress herself-who has an unrelenting father. Charlie Sheen, Kristy Swanson, Josh Mostel, Ray Wise, Henry Rollins. w.d. Adam Rifkin.

ACTION: COMEDY: Action Comedy; Road Movies; Road Movies-Transporting Girls; Chase Stories; Car Chases; Heiresses; Thieves; Stern Men; Fathers & Daughters; Kidnapper-Sympathizing with; Writer-Directors
(Three for the Road)

Chase a Crooked Shadow, 1958, 87m, ★★★/$$, NA. A woman (Anne Baxter) is shocked when her supposedly dead brother shows up to claim his part of an inheritance. Richard Todd, Herbert Lom. w. David Osborn, Charles Sinclair, d. Michael Anderson.

SUSPENSE: DRAMA: Hitchcockian; Dead-Back from the; Inheritances at Stake; Brothers & Sisters; Children-Long-lost; Good Premise Unfulfilled; Coulda Been Great

The Chastity Belt, 1967, 110m, ★★/$, WB/NA. A newlywed in the 12th century has to go off to the Crusades, so he locks his wife in a chastity belt. She eventually gets fed up and tracks him down on the battlefields. Tony Curtis, Monica Vitti, Hugh Griffith, John Richardson, Nino Castelnuovo. w. Luigi Magni, Larry Gelbart, d. Pasquale Festa Campanile.

COMEDY: FARCE: Sex Comedy; Middle Ages; Marriage Comedy; Repression; Revisionist Films; Italian Films; Coulda Been Good

Chato's Land, 1972, 110m, ★★½/$$, UA/MGM-UA. An Indian (Charles Bronson) is chased by a posse for murder of a marshal. Jill Ireland, Jack Palance, Richard Basehart, James Whitmore. w. Gerald Wilson, d. Michael Winner.

WESTERN: MURDER: Chase Movies; Fugitives from the Law; Indians-American; Bounty Hunters; Marshals; Police Stories
(Bring Me the Head of Alfredo Garcia)

Chattahoochee, 1989, 97m, ★★★/$, Hemdale/Vestron, A man (Gary Oldman) cracks up and begins shooting from his house. When he's sent to an institution, he details the injustices. Frances McDormand, Pamela Reed, Dennis Hopper. w. James Hickey, d. Mick Jackson.

DRAMA: Social Drama; Government Corruption; Fighting the System; Asylums; Prison Drama; Nervous Breakdowns; Mental Illness; Quiet Little Films
(Brubaker; The Snake Pit)

Chattanooga Choo Choo, 1984, 102m, ★★/$$, April Fools/HBO, PG. A man restores a train for one last run in order to collect an inheritance. George Kennedy, Barbara Eden. w. d. Bruce Bilson

COMEDY: ADVENTURE: Comic Adventure; Trains; Journies; One Last Time; Inheritances at Stake

Chatterbox, 1943, 76m, ★★/$$, Republic/NA. A talkative country gal tries to make it in the "theahtuh." Anne Shirley, Phillips Holmes, Edward Ellis, Erik Rhodes, Margaret Hamilton, Granville Bates. w. Sam Mintz, P-adap. David Carb, d. George Nichols Jr.

COMEDY: COMEDY DRAMA: Actresses; Fame-Rise to; Dreams; Theater Life
(Morning Glory; Stagestruck)

Che!, 1969, 96m, ★/$, Ind/NA. The unintentionally funny story of Latin revolutionary Che Guevara. Omar Sharif, Jack Palance, Robert Loggia. w. Michael Wilson, Sy Bartlett, d. Richard Fleischer.

DRAMA: Biographies; Latin People; Terrorists; Political Unrest; Cuba; South America; Camp; Major Flops

The Cheap Detective, 1978, 92m, ★★★/$$$$. A detective (Peter Falk) resembling a mish-mash of 40s movie detectives takes on a convoluted case involving every stereotype and cliche of film noir. Ann-Margret, Eileen Brennan, Stockard Channing, James Coco, Louise Fletcher, Marsha Mason, Madeline Kahn. w. Neil Simon, d. Robert Moore

COMEDY: Spoofs; Film Noir-Modern; Camp; Detective Stories; Spoofs-Detective; Comedy of Errors; All-Star Casts; Ensemble Films; Fools-Bumbling
SPOOF OF: The Big Sleep.
(Pink Panther SERIES; Murder by Death; Who's Harry Crumb?; The Black Bird)

Cheaper by the Dozen, 1950, 85m, ★★★/$$, 20th/NA. An efficiency expert organizes his family of twelve children. Clifton Webb, Myrna Loy, Jeanne Crain, Edgar Buchanan, Barbara Bates, Betty Lynn. w. Lamar Trotti, NF-adap. Frank B. Gilbreth Jr., Ernestine Gilbreth Carey, d. Walter Lang.

COMEDY: COMEDY DRAMA: Family Comedy; Eccentric People; Stern Men; Efficiency Experts; Fathers-Troublesome; Parents vs. Children
(Sitting Pretty; Mr. Belvedere SERIES)

Cheaper to Keep Her, 1980, 92m, ★/$$, Ind/Media, PG. A P.I. tracks down deadbeat husbands who won't pay alimony. Mac Davis, Tovah Feldshuh, Jack Gilford, Rose Marie. w. Herschel Wingrod, Timothy Harris, d. Ken Annakin.

COMEDY: Detectives-Matrimonial; Detective Stories; Good Premise Unfulfilled; Custody Battles; Divorce

Checking Out, 1989, 96m, ★★/$ (VR), Vestron/Vestron, PG. A young man's friend dies and he quickly becomes a health-freak paranoid hypochondriac and drives his family nuts. Jeff Daniels, Melanie Mayron, Ann Magnuson. w. Joe Esterhas, d. David Leland.

COMEDY: Black Comedy; Hypochondriacs; Death-Impending; Paranoia; Family Comedy; Midlife Crisis; Marriage on the Rocks; Good Premise Unfulfilled
(Send Me No Flowers; Short Time; Living It Up)

The Check Is in the Mail, 1986, 91m, ★★/$, Ind/NA. A man decides to create the ultimate do-everything do-it-yourself house. Brian Dennehy, Anne Archer. w. d. Joan Darling.

COMEDY: Computers; Comedy-Situation; Curiosities; Forgotten Films; Female Screenwriters; Female Directors

Cheech and Chong: Still Smokin', 1983, 92m, ★★/$, Par/Par, R/P-S. Two pothead buddies attend a Burt Reynolds–Dolly Parton film festival in Amsterdam. w. Thomas Chong, Cheech Marin, d. Thomas Chong.

COMEDY: Drugs-Addictions; Latin People; Comedians; Buddy Films; Bathroom Humor

Cheech & Chong's Next Movie, 1980, 99m, ★★/$$$, U/MCA-U, R/EP-S. The further adventures of the pothead Bing and Bob. Cheech Marin, Thomas Chong, Evelyn Guerrero, Betty Kennedy. w. Cheech Marin, Thomas Chong, d. Thomas Chong.

COMEDY: Drugs-Addictions; Latin People; Comedians; Buddy Films; Bathroom Humor

Cheech & Chong's Nice Dreams, 1981, 89m, ★★/$$, Col/RCA-Col, R/P-S. Cheech and Chong sell pot from an ice cream truck. Cheech Marin, Thomas Chong. w. Cheech Marin, Thomas Chong, d. Thomas Chong.

COMEDY: Drugs-Addictions; Latin People; Comedians; Buddy Films; Bathroom Humor

Cheech & Chong's The Corsican Brothers, 1984, 90m, ★/$, Ind/Live,

R/P-S. During the French Revolution, two goofy dopes swash their buckles. Cheech Marin, Thomas Chong, Roy Dotrice, Shelby Fiddis, Rikki Marin, Rae Dawn Chong, Robbi Chong. w. Cheech Marin, Thomas Chong, d. Thomas Chong.

COMEDY: Drugs-Addictions; Latin People; Comedians; Buddy Films; Brothers; Bathroom Humor; French Revolution

(Born in East L.A.; Shrimp on the Barbie)

Cheers for Miss Bishop, 1941, 95m, ★★★/$$, RKO/Nos. The life of a consummate small-town schoolteacher is chronicled. Martha Scott, Edmund Gwenn, Sterling Holloway. w. Adelaide Heilbron, N-adap. Bess Streeter Aldrich, d. Tay Garnett.

MELODRAMA: Biographies-Fictional; Teachers; Charismatic People; Small-Town Life; Female Protagonists; Hidden Gems; Time Capsules

(The Corn Is Green; The Prime of Miss Jean Brodie)

Cherry 2000, 1988, 93m, ★★/$, Orion/Orion, PG-13/S-P. A man in futuristic world who loves a female robot goes on a journey for parts for her and runs into a real woman. Melanie Griffith, David Andrews, Ben Johnson, Tim Thomerson. d. Steve deJarnatt.

ACTION: COMEDY: Action Comedy; Road Movies; Futuristic Films; Apocalyptic Stories; Robots; Androids; ROMANCE: Romantic Comedy; Journies; Car Racing

(Heartbeeps; Mad Max SERIES; Gumball Rally)

Cheyenne Autumn, 1964, 145m, ★★★/$$$, WB/WB. Cheyenne Indians are returned to their original land after being relocated by the government. Richard Widmark, James Stewart, Arthur Kennedy, Carroll Baker, Edward G. Robinson, Dolores Del Rio, Sal Mineo, Karl Malden, Ricardo Montalban, John Carradine, George O'Brien. w. James R. Webb, N-adap. Mari Sandoz, d. John Ford.

DRAMA: WESTERNS: Cavalry; Native Americans; Indians-American; Westerns-Neo; Journies; Reunions; Government as Enemy; Ahead of Its Time

The Cheyenne Social Club, 1970, 103m, ★★★/$$$, NG-WB/WB, PG/S. After a long journey, an upstanding man finds he's inherited what turns out to be a whorehouse in the old west. James Stewart, Henry Fonda, Shirley Jones. w. James Lee Barrett, d. Gene Kelly.

WESTERN: Western Comedy; COMEDY: Prostitutes-Low Class; Pimps; Madams; Inheritances at Stake; Heirs; Hidden Gems

(McClintock!; McCabe and Mrs. Miller)

Chicago Joe and the Showgirl, 1990, 103m, ★★½/$, Hemdale/Live, R/S-V. A soldier in England during the war (Kiefer Sutherland) hooks up with a psychotic dancer (Emily Lloyd) who pushes him into committing crimes leading to murder. Patsy Kensit. w. David Yallop, d. Bernard Rose.

DRAMA: MURDER: Evil Women; Soldiers; World War II Era; Americans Abroad; Criminal Couples; True Stories; Murder-Coerced to

(Gun Crazy; Bonnie & Clyde)

The Chicken Chronicles, 1977, 94m, ★★/$, Avco/Col, PG/S. A high school senior (Steve Guttenberg) wants to sleep with the class beauty before he graduates. Phil Silvers, Ed Lauter, Meredith Baer, Lisa Reeves. w. Paul Diamond, d. Francis Simon

COMEDY: Teenage Movies; Coming of Age; Sexuality; High School Life; Virgins; Young Men; Curiosities

(Can't Buy Me Love)

Chiefs, 1983, 200m, ★★★/$$$$, CBS/New World. When a South Carolina town experiences serial killings of young men, the town powers-that-be try to hush it all up, but one man soon uncovers the crimes and scandal. Charlton Heston, Paul Sorvino, Keith Carradine, Brad Davis, Billy Dee Williams, Wayne Rogers, Stephen Collins, Tess Harper, Victoria Tennant. d. Jerry London.

DRAMA: True Stories; Serial Killers; Murders of Homosexuals; Southerns; Detective Stories; Detectives-Police; TV Movies; Miniseries

(The John Wayne Gacy Story; The Atlanta Child Murders)

La Chienne, see L for La

A Child Is Waiting, 1963, 102m, ★★★/$$, UA/MGM-UA. An educator (Burt Lancaster) tries to treat retarded children at a boarding school with the help of an eccentric woman who takes a shine to one particular boy. Judy Garland, Gena Rowlands, Bruce Ritchey, Steven Hill, Paul Stewart, Lawrence Tierney. w. Abby Mann, d. John Cassavetes.

DRAMA: Mentally Disabled; Teachers; Teachers & Students; Women and Boys; Boys; Spinsters; Eccentric People; Infatuations; Mothers-Surrogate; Boarding Schools; Hidden Gems; Curiosities

(Baxter [1972]; David and Lisa)

The Children, 1980, 89m, ★★/$$, Northal/Vestron, R/V-B&G. After a busload of children are contaminated with radiation, they scorch anyone they hug. Martin Shaker, Gale Garnett, Gil Rogers. d. Max Kalmanowicz.

HORROR: Evil Children; Nuclear Energy; Monsters-Mutant; Fires; Curiosities

(Children of the Corn; Village of the Damned; Children of the Damned)

The Children, 1990, 115m, ★★½/$, New World/New World, R. A Brazilian engineer returns home from a trip to find he's inherited a brood of rug rats, disrupting his wedding plans. Ben Kingsley, Kim Novak, Siri Neal, Geraldine Chaplin, Joe Don Baker, Rupert Graves. w. Timberlake Wertenbaker, N-adap. Edith Wharton, d. Tony Palmer.

DRAMA: COMEDY DRAMA: Marriage-Impending; Engagements-Breaking; Children-Brats; Parents vs. Children; Children-Inherited; Overlooked at Release

REMAKE OF: The Marriage Playground

The Childhood of Maxim Gorky, 1938–40, (3 Parts: 101m, 98m, 104m), Mosfilm/NA. The famous Russian writer's early life is chronicled, from growing up in the country to working on a ship and eventually going to university and becoming a writer. Alexei Lyarsky, Y. Valbert, M. Troyanovski, Valeria Massalitinova. w. Mark Donskoi, I. Grudzev, d. Mark Donskoi.

DRAMA: Biographies; Writers; Russians; Russia; Episodic Stories; Fame-Rise to; Russian Films

Children of a Lesser God, 1986, 116m, ★★★½/$$$, Par/Par, R/S-FN. A teacher of the deaf (William Hurt, BActor) falls in love with a rebellious student (Marlee Matlin, BActress), and stormy romance results. Piper Laurie (BSActress), Philip Bosco. w. Hesper Anderson, Mark Medoff, P-adap. Mark Medoff (BAScr), d. Randa Haines. BPicture. Oscars: 5-1.

ROMANCE: DRAMA: Romantic Drama; Romance-Troubled; Deaf People; Mute People; College Life; Misunderstandings; Teachers; Teachers & Students; Romance with Student; Disabled but Nominated; Female Directors; Female Screenwriters (A Patch of Blue; Voices)

Children of Hiroshima, 1952, 97m, ★★★/$, Kendai/NA. In Japan seven years after the war a schoolteacher returns to Hiroshima in a harrowing homecoming. Nobuko Otowa, Chikako Hoshawa, Niwa Saito. w. d. Keneto Shindo, N-adap. Arata Osada.
DRAMA: Docudrama; Documentary Style; Bombs-Atomic; Japanese People; Japan; Japanese Films; Teachers; Reunions

Children of the Corn, 1984, 93m, ★★/$$, New World/New World, R/V-B&G. A couple are driving down a deserted country road at night and accidentally run over a boy in the road. When they examine the body, they discover he was already dead at the hands of a weird cult, which they get caught up in. Peter Horton, Linda Hamilton, R. G. Armstrong, John Franklin. w. George Goldsmith, SS-adap. Stephen King, d. Fritz Kiersch.
HORROR: Accidents; Cults; Murders of Children; Conspiracy
(Blindside; Endangered Species)

Children of Paradise, 1945, 195m, ★★★★/$$, Ind/Voyager, Criterion. An actor in Old Paris finds a beautiful but elusive woman, but love for them is also elusive as they journey through the theater world there and the social changes of the day. Jean-Louis Barrault, Arletty, Pierre Brasseur, Maria Casares. w. Jacques Prevert, d. Marcel Carne.
DRAMA: ROMANCE: Romantic Drama; Fantasy; Social Drama; Theater Life; Actors; Actresses; Art Films; French Films; 1800s; Hidden Gems; Film History

Children of the Damned, 1964, 90m, ★★1/2/$$, MGM/MGM-UA. Six British wonderkids are brought to the UN but are later discovered to be the spawn of aliens. Ian Hendry, Alan Badel, Barbara Ferris, Alfred Burke, Sheila Allen, Ralph Michael, Martin Miller. w. John Briley, d. Anton M. Leader.
HORROR: SUSPENSE: SCI-FI: Aliens-Outer Space, Evil; UFOs; Monsters-Children; Evil Children; Cult Films; British Films
SEQUEL TO: Village of the Damned
(Village of the Damned; The Children; Children of the Corn)

The Children's Hour (B&W), 1961, 109m, ★★★1/2/$$$, UA/MGM-UA, S. Two women (Audrey Hepburn, Shirley MacLaine) run a girls' school until a lying, vindictive student begins rumors they're lesbians which could be founded. Fay Bainter (BSActress). w. P-adap. Lillian Hellman, d. William Wyler. BB&WCin. Oscars: 2-0.
DRAMA: TRAGEDY: Secrets-Consuming; Homophobia; Lesbians; Rumors; Suicidal Tendencies; Suicidal Tendencies of Homosexuals; Revenge; Children-Brats; Girls' School; Friendships-Female; Spinsters; Ahead of its Time; Ostracism; Female Screenwriters; Female Protagonists
(These Three/REMAKE OF: These Three; Tea and Sympathy; Lianna; Victim; The Prime of Miss Jean Brodie; The Browning Version)
(Ed: Obtuse but still daring)

Child's Play, 1972, 100m, ★★★/$, Par/NA. In a boys' Catholic boarding school one of the teachers is harassed in creative ways by another who may be truly evil. James Mason, Robert Preston, Beau Bridges, Ronald Weyland. w. Leon Prochnik, P-adap. Robert Marasco, d. Sidney Lumet.
HORROR: SCI-FI: Supernatural Danger; Malicious Menaces; Boarding Schools; Boys' Schools; Teachers; Teachers & Students; Evil Men; Curiosities
(The Browning Version; If . . .)

Child's Play, 1988, 87m, ★★1/2/$$$$, MGM/MGM-UA, R/P-EV-B&G. A child's toy has been possessed by the evil spirit of a killer, and the boy's mother (Catherine Hicks) has to deal with the bloody consequences. Chris Sarandon, Brad Dourif, Dinah Manoff. w. Don Mancini, John Lafia, Tom Holland, d. Holland.

Child's Play 2, 1990, 84m, ★★/$$$, MGM/MGM-UA, R/P-EV-B&G. More of the same, only not as good by any means. Jenny Agutter, Alex Vincent, Gerrit Graham, Brad Dourif, Grace Zabriskie. w. Don Mancini, d. John Lafia.

Child's Play 3, 1991, 90m, ★1/2/$$, Universal/MCA-U, R/V-B&G. Here we go again, only worse. Justin Whalin, Perrey Reeves, Andrew Robinson, Brad Dourif. w. Don Mancini, d. Jack Bender.
HORROR: SUSPENSE: Horror Comedy; Black Comedy; Comedy-Morbid; Monsters-Toys; Possessions; Mothers-Struggling; Children in Jeopardy; Women in Jeopardy; Murders-One by One; Rogue Plots; Kill the Beast; Dead-Back from the; Sleeper Hits
REMAKE/RETREAD OF: Trilogy of Terror, The Bad Seed
(Trilogy in Terror; The Bad Seed)
(Ed: Take the maniac doll from *Trilogy in Terror* and the plot of *The Bad Seed*, only the child's doll is the evil one this time, and this is what you get. Despite the derivations, it works because of the original character of the toy.)

Chilly Scenes of Winter (Head Over Heels), 1980, 97m, ★★★/$, UA/MGM-UA. A government employee remembers his longstanding but inconsistent affair with an eccentric woman. John Heard, Mary Beth Hurt, Peter Riegert, Kenneth McMillan, Gloria Grahame. w.d. Joan Micklin Silver, N-adap. Ann Beattie.
DRAMA: ROMANCE: Romantic Drama; Eccentric People; Romance-Doomed; Romance with Married Person; Cheating Men; Cult Films; Female Screenwriters; Female Directors

Chimes at Midnight (Falstaff), 1966, 115m, ★★★/$$, Ind/Facets. Orson Welles' long overlooked version of *Falstaff*, Shakespeare's famous play of friendship and betrayal. Prince Hal hangs out with a motley crew as a lad, including the fat, boistrous Falstaff. But when Hal becomes king, he turns a cold shoulder toward him. Orson Welles, Keith Baxter, John Gielgud, Margaret Rutherford, Jeanne Moreau, Fernando Rey. w. d. Orson Welles.
DRAMA: TRAGEDY: Shakespeare; Revisionist Films; Betrayal; Friends as Enemies; Kings; Double Crossings; Friendships-Male; Friends with a King; Writer-Directors

China, 1943, 79m, ★★/$$$, Par/NA. An American businessman in China becomes a mercenary and single-handedly holds back the Chinese army. Alan Ladd, Loretta Young, William Bendix, Philip Ahn, Iris Wong, Sen Yung, Richard Loo. w. Frank Butler, N-adap. Reginald Forbes (*The Fourth Brother*), d. John Farrow.
ACTION: War Stories; Patriotic Films; Americans Abroad; China; Chinese People; Mercenaries; Arms Dealers; Forgotten Films

China Beach, 1988, 95m, ★★★/$$, WB/WB, PG/V-S. The pilot for the series about Vietnam nurses during the war. Major Emmy winner. Dana Delaney,

Chloe Webb, Robert Picardo, Nan Woods, Michael Boatman, Marg Helgenberger, Tim Ryan, Brian Wimmer. w. John Sacret Young, d. Rob Holcomb.

DRAMA: Ensemble Films; Ensembles-Female; Vietnam War; Women at War; Nurses; TV Movies; Feisty Females; Female Protagonists

China Clipper, 1936, 85m, ★★¹/2/$$$, WB/NA. A pilot is obsessed with making a link to China with his early commercial airline. Meanwhile, at home, his wife is feeling lonely. . . . Pat O'Brien, Beverly Roberts, Ross Alexander, Humphrey Bogart, Marie Wilson. w. Frank 'Spig' Wead, d. Ray Enright.

ADVENTURE: Pilots-Military; Explorers; Dreams; World Travel; Marriage on the Rocks

China Girl, 1942, 95m, ★★/$$, 20th/NA. A journalist working for the newsreels in China meets a local girl and falls in love. Gene Tierney, George Montgomery, Lynn Bari, Victor McLaglen, Alan Baxter, Sig Rumann. w. Ben Hecht, d. Henry Hathaway.

ROMANCE: MELODRAMA: Journalists; Americans Abroad; Romance-Interracial; Photographers; China; Chinese People

China Girl, 1987, 88m, ★★¹/2/$$, Vestron/Vestron, PG-13/S-V. A modern-day Mafioso Romeo meets a girl with connections to Chinatown gangs in New York. James Russo, Richard Panebianco, Sari Chang, David Caruso, Russell Wong, Joey Chin, James Hong. w. Nicholas St. John, d. Abel Ferrara.

ROMANCE: ACTION: Crime Drama; Romance-Doomed; Romance-Interracial; Chinese People; Asian-Americans; Gangs-Asian; Mob Stories; Romance-Dangerous; Italians; Coulda Been Good

China Moon, 1991/1994, 99m, ★★¹/2/$, Orion/Orion, R/V-S-P. In a small town in Florida, a wealthy woman has an affair with a cop to get away from her abusive and cheating husband. However, when the husband dies, the cop may be in deeper than he ever thought he could be-and then some. Ed Harris, Madeleine Stowe, Charles Dance, Benicio del Toro, w. Roy Carlson, d. John Bailey.

SUSPENSE: MURDER: Murder of Spouse; Cheating Women; Romance-Dangerous; Murderers-Female; Police Stories; Framed?; Double-Crossings; Dangerous Women; Romance-Triangles; Clever Plots & Endings; Coulda Been Good

REMAKE/RETREAD: Body Heat (Body Heat; Double Indemnity) (Ed: A few interesting twists, but with the settings and some of the scenes right out of Body Heat, the plotholes seem to grow)

China Seas, 1935, 90m, ★★★/$$$, MGM/MGM-UA. A pirate ship attacks a cruise ship filled with vacationing socialites just as a typhoon is brewing out at sea. Clark Gable, Jean Harlow, Wallace Beery, Rosalind Russell, Lewis Stone. w. Jules Furthman, James Kevin McGuinness, N-adap. Crosbie Garstin, d. Tay Garnett.

DRAMA: ACTION: Action Drama; Disaster Stories; Ships; Hijackings; Pirates Asia; Pacific Ocean (Hurricane; Ship of Fools; Grand Hotel)

The China Syndrome, 1979, 123m, ★★★★/$$$$, 20th/CBS-Fox, PG/P. A reporter (Jane Fonda) uncovers problems at a nuclear reactor which may lead to disaster. Jack Lemmon (BActor), Michael Douglas. w. Mike Gray, T.S. Cook, James Bridges (BOScr), d. James Bridges. BArt. Oscars: 4-0.

DRAMA: SUSPENSE: Political Drama; Social Drama; Message Films; Disaster Movies; Conspiracy; Nuclear Power; Journalists; Journalists as Detectives; Detective Stories; Corruption; Corporate Corruption; Fighting The System; Government as Enemy; Female Among Males; Female Protagonists (Silkwood; Rage; Acceptable Risks) (Ed: Release timed perfectly with the Three-Mile Island disaster. The film with no score)

Chinatown, 1974, 132m, ★★★★/$$$, Par/Par, R/P-EV-S. A private eye uncovers more than he bargains for in 1930s LA when he falls for a woman with secrets unlocking a conspiracy. Jack Nicholson (BActor), Faye Dunaway (BActress), John Huston, Diane Ladd; w. Robert Towne (**BOScr**), d. Roman Polanski (BDirector). BPicture, BCin, BArt, BCos, BEditing, BOScore; Oscars 10-1.

SUSPENSE: DRAMA: MYSTERY: MURDER: MURDER MYSTERY: Film Noir-Modern; Crime Drama; Historical Drama; Murder-Discovering; Conspiracy; Detective Stories; Detectives in Deep; Detectives-Matrimonial; Politicians; Secrets-Haunting; Government Corruption; Scandals; Incest; Mental Illness; Greed; Love-Questionable; Romance-Triangles; Depression Era; Los Angeles

SEQUEL: The Two Jakes (The Big Sleep; Farewell, My Lovely; Murder, My Sweet; Kiss Me Deadly) (Ed: Much-studied classic that still holds up, from an era of top-flight, realistic filmmaking)

Chisum, 1970, 111m, ★★¹/2/$$$, WB/WB, PG/V. A cattle rancher gets rustled but is helped out by, among others, Pat Garrett and Billy the Kid. John Wayne, Ben Johnson, Forrest Tucker. w. Andrew J. Fenady, d. Andrew V. McLaglen.

WESTERNS: Cattle Ranchers; Cattle Rustlers; West-Old; Turning the Tables; Revenge

Chitty Chitty Bang Bang, 1968, ★★★¹/2/$$$, UA/MGM-UA, G. An inventor (Dick Van Dyke) follows his children with his crazy contraptions when they're kidnapped and taken to a bizarre kingdom. w. Roald Dahl, Ken Hughes, d. Ken Hughes. BOSong. Oscars: 1-0.

MUSICAL: COMEDY: CHILDREN'S: FAMILY: Musical Comedy; **ADVENTURE:** Fantasy; Inventors; Eccentric People; Kidnappings; Kingdoms; Widowers; Fathers Alone; Balloons; Cult Films (Willy Wonka & The Chocolate Factory; Mary Poppins)

Chloe in the Afternoon (L'Amour l'Apres Midi), 1972, 97m, ★★★¹/2/$$$, Ind/Cinematheque, R/S. A man has fantasies of getting back together with an old flame. When it actually happens, it merely serves to make him appreciate his wife more. Bernard Verley, Zouzou, Francoise Verley, Daniel Ceccaldi. w. d. Eric Rohmer.

ROMANCE: DRAMA: Romantic Drama; Romance-Reunited; Romance-Class Conflict; Fantasies; Cheating Men; Romance with Married Person; Infatuations; Obsessions; Cult Films; Hidden Gems; French Films; Writer-Directors (My Night at Maud's; Claire's Knee)

Chocolat, 1988, 105m, ★★★/$$, Orion/Orion, R/S. A French woman from a West African colonial plantation family recalls her childhood and through hindsight realizes the tragedy of racism. Isaach De Bankole, Giula Boschi, Francois Cluzet, Jean-Claude Adelin. w. Claire Denis, Jean-Pol Fargeau, d. Claire Denis.

DRAMA: Memories; Imperialist Problems; Africa; Race Relations;

Romance-Interracial; Bigots; French Films; Black vs. White

The Chocolate Soldier, 1941, 102m, ★★1/2/$$$, MGM/MGM-UA. A backstage romance develops between members of an opera company. Nelson Eddy, Rise Stevens, Nigel Bruce, Florence Bates, Nydia Westman. w. Keith Winter, Leonard Lee, d. Roy del Ruth.

MELODRAMA: MUSICALS: Musical Romance ROMANCE: Theater Life; Opera; Musicals-Operettas
(The Firefly; Bittersweet)

The Chocolate War, 1988, 103m, ★★1/2/$ (VR), MCEG/Virgin, PG. A student and the headmaster of his school get into verbal war over the selling of candy in this power struggle of old and young and coming of age. John Glover, Ian Mitchell Smith, Jenny Wright, Wally Ward, Bud Cort, Adam Baldwin. w. d. Keith Gordon, N-adap. Robert Cormier.

DRAMA: Coming of Age; Ethics; Competitions; Boys Schools; Boys; Teenagers; Teachers & Students
(If . . . ; A Separate Peace; Taps; A Midnight Clear)

Choice of Arms, 1981, 117m, ★★★/$$, Media/Media, PG-13/V-S. A mobster hides out in rural France with his younger wife, but soon a menace decides to cause some trouble centering around their past. Gerard Depardieu, Catherine Deneuve, Yves Montand. w. d. Alain Corneau.

DRAMA: SUSPENSE: Mob Stories; Hiding Out; Small-Town Life; Past-Haunted by the; French Films; Hidden Gems; Coulda Been Great; Writer-Directors
(Scene of the Crime)

The Choirboys, 1977, 119m, ★★1/2/$$, Lorimar/MCA-U, R/EP-V. The beat cops in the urban jungle are worse than any of the degenerates they pick up. Charles Durning, Lou Gossett Jr., Perry King, Stephen Macht, Tim McIntyre, Randy Quaid, Blair Brown. w. Christopher Knopf, N-adap. Joseph Wambaugh, d. Robert Aldrich.

DRAMA: ACTION: Police Stories; Inner City Life; Ensemble Films; Ensembles-Male; Female Among Males; Law Officers-Female; 1970s; Time Capsules
(The Black Marble; The Blue Knight; Super Cops)

CHOMPS, 1979, 89m, ★★/$, 89m, AIP/Vestron, PG. A man invents a robot dog, which he sells as a security system (CHOMPS stands for Canine Home Protection System). Wesley Eure, Jim Backus, Valerie Bertinelli, Red Buttons, Hermione Baddeley, d. Don Chaffey.

CHILDREN'S: FAMILY: Pet Stories; Dogs; Robots; Thieves

Choose Me, 1984, 106m, ★★★/$$, Island-Alive/Charter, PG/S. A dangerous mystery man seduces a lonely radio therapist. She doesn't know that right before they met, the mysterious lover had just been released from a mental hospital. Genevieve Bujold, Keith Carradine, Lesley Ann Warren, Rae Dawn Chong, w. d. Alan Rudolph.

DRAMA: ROMANCE: Romantic Drama; Talk Shows; Radio Life; Psychologists; Dangerous Men; Romance-Dangerous; Mental Illness; Asylums; Fatal Attractions; Quiet Little Films; Cult Films; Writer-Directors; Female Protagonists

A Chorus Line, 1985, 117m, ★★1/2/$$, Universal/MCA-U, PG-13/P-S. The lives of the various members of a stage musical are chronicled; based on the longest running Broadway show in history. Michael Douglas, Audrey Landers, Alyson Reed. w. Arnold Schulman, P-adap. Michael Bennett, Marvin Hamlisch, d. Richard Attenborough. BEdit. Oscars: 1-0.

DRAMA: MUSICAL: MUSICAL DRAMA: Music Movies; Multiple Stories; Ensemble Films; Dancers; Dance Movies; Theater Life; Behind the Scenes; Flashbacks; Monologues-Interior; Crossing the Line; Young Men; Young Women; Actors; Actresses; Stagelike Films; Pulitzer Prize Adaptations; Flops-Major; Forgotten Films; Actor Directors
(Ed: This is a good film, but paled in comparison to the stage version as the reception was a good-sized thud for all the expectations.)

A Chorus of Disapproval, 1988, 100m, ★★1/2/$, Hemdale/Hemdale, PG/S. A local play production company in a small suburb is joined by a suave stranger, and he's immediately set upon by a gaggle of altos and sopranos. Anthony Hopkins, Jeremy Irons, Richard Briers, Gareth Hunt, Patsy Kensit, Prunella Scales. w. Michael Winner, Alan Ayckbourn, P-adap. Alan Ayckbourn, d. Michael Winner.

COMEDY: COMEDY DRAMA: Comedy-Light; Small-town Life; New in Town; Sexy Men; Women Fighting Over Men; Theater Life; Ordinary People Stories; Eccentric People; Coulda Been Good; British Films; Overlooked at Release

The Chosen, 1981, 108m, ★★★/$$, The Chosen Film Company/Embassy, NA, PG. A feud between Zionists and Hassidic Jews erupts in New York and a young man questions his family's traditions because of it. Maximilian Schell, Rod Steiger, Robby Benson, Barry Miller, Hildy Brooks. w. Edwin Gordon, N-adap. Chaim Potok, d. Jeremy Paul Kagan.

DRAMA: FAMILY: Jewish People; Religion; Coming of Age; Young Men; Feuds
(Yentl; Fiddler on the Roof)

Christ Stopped at Eboli, 1979, 155m, ★★★1/2/$, Vides Cinematografica/Col, PG. A doctor in Italy is exiled to a remote village in 1935 because he stands against the prevailing political winds of the time. Gian Maria Volonte, Alain Cuny, Paolo Bonacelli, Lea Massari, Irene Papas, Francois Simon. w. Francesco Rosi, Tonino Guerra, Raffaele La Capria, NF-adap. Carlo Levi, d. Francesco Rosi.

DRAMA: Political Unrest; Hiding Out; Rebels; Doctors; Italians; Italy; Oppression; Hidden Gems

Christiane F., 1981, 124m, ★★★1/2/$$$, 20th/Media, R/P-S. The story of a young girl (Natja Brunkhorst) who goes from a normal life in Germany to life on the streets as a drug addicted prostitute, before she's of high-school age. w. Herman Weigel, d. Ulrich Edel.

DRAMA: Social Drama; Drugs-Addictions; Girlhood; Teenagers; Prostitutes-Low Class; Prostitutes-Child; Inner City Life; True Stories; Germany; German Films
(Vagabond; Dawn: Portrait of a Runaway)

Christine, 1983, 110m, ★★1/2/$$$, Universal/MCA-U, R/P-V. A teenager (Keith Gordon) renovates a car to impress a girl, but the car is possessed and soon he is, too. John Stockwell, Alexandra Paul, Robert Prosky, Harry Dean Stanton. w. Bill Phillips, N-adap. Stephen King, d. John Carpenter.

HORROR: SUSPENSE: Rogue Plots; Murders/Deaths-One by One; Romance-Boy Wants Girl; Man vs. Machine; Monsters-Machines; Objects with Personalities; Occult; Possessions; Jealousy; Revenge; Young Men; Stephen King
(Maximum Overdrive; Cujo; The Car)

A Christmas Carol, 1938, 69m, ★★★1/2/$$$, MGM/MGM-UA. Scrooge, the miser, says "bah humbug" to Christmas and treats his employee badly until one Christmas eve he's visited by four spirits who take him to his past, present, and future and sober him up. Reginald Owen, Gene Lockhart, Kathleen Lockhart, Terry Kilburn, Leo G. Carroll, Lynne Carver. w. Hugo Butler, N-adap. Charles Dickens, d. Edwin L. Marin.
DRAMA: Fantasy; Ghosts; Christmas; Stern Men; Evil Men; Redemption; Nightmares; Death-Impending; Turning the Tables; Message Films
SPOOF: Scrooged.
(Scrooge; It's a Wonderful Life)
A Christmas Carol, see also **Scrooge, Scrooged, A Muppet Christmas Carol**
Christmas Holiday, 1944, 93m, ★★1/2/$$, U/MCA-U. A cabaret singer rues the day she unwittingly married a murderer, but now must shield him from the law out of loyalty. Deanna Durbin, Gene Kelly, Dean Harens, Gladys George, Richard Whorf, Gale Sondergaard. w. Herman J. Mankiewicz, N-adap. Somerset Maugham, d. Robert Siodmak.
DRAMA: MURDER: Marriage on the Rocks; Dangerous Men; Dangerous Spouses; Singers; Hiding Out; Fugitives-Harboring; Christmas; Curiosities
(Ed: Sweetheart Durbin's foray into drama with a perky title but not much box office)
Christmas in Connecticut, 1945, 101m, ★★★/$$, MGM/MGM-UA. A housekeeping columnist doesn't practice what she preaches and has to learn everything she writes about or risk exposure for the holidays. Barbara Stanwyck, Reginald Gardiner, Sydney Greenstreet, Dennis Morgan. d. Peter Godfrey.
Hidden Gems
Christmas in Connecticut, 1992, 93m, ★★/$$$, Turner/Turner, G. A remake of the above with a few modern updates and twists, but not as good. Dyan Cannon, Kris Kristofferson, Tony Curtis, Richard Roundtree. d. Arnold Schwarzenegger.
Actor Directors
COMEDY: COMEDY DRAMA: Christmas; Journalists; Impostors; Race Against Time; Housewives; Family Comedy; Career Women
(Woman of the Year)
Christmas in July, 1940, 67m, ★★★1/2/$$$, Par/Par. A poor couple in

love enter a contest and win a big prize, changing their lives forever, but not all for the better. Dick Powell, Ellen Drew, Ernest Truex, Al Bridge, Raymond Walburn, William Demarest. w. d. Preston Sturges.
COMEDY: COMEDY DRAMA: SATIRE: Social Satire; Lotteries; Life Transitions; Rags to Riches; Poor People; Hidden Gems; Writer-Directors
(Sullivan's Travels; The Great McGinty; Melvin and Howard)
Christmas Lilies of the Field, 1984, 96m, ★★1/2/$$$, MPI/MPI. The black soldier returns in this sequel to see the nuns and the mission he helped build and winds up building an orphanage. Billy Dee Williams, Maria Schell, Fay Hauser. w. d. Ralph Nelson.
MELODRAMA: Black Men; Nuns; Orphans; Desert Settings; Christmas; Black Among Whites; TV Movies
SEQUEL TO: Lilies of the Field.
(The Bells of St. Mary's)
Christopher Columbus, 1949, 104m, ★★1/2/$$, Ind/LCA. Columbus goes to Queen Isabella and asks for her patronage to embark on a voyage around the world, defying the contemporary theory that the world was flat. Fredric March, Florence Eldridge, Francis L. Sullivan, Linden Travers. w. Muriel and Sydney Box, Cyril Roberts, d. Davi MacDonald.
Christopher Columbus: The Discovery, 1992, 121m, 120m, ★★/$$, WB/WB, PG. A somewhat revisionist view of the famous explorer which acknowledges the fact that he pillaged and disrespected native populations when he arrived in the New World. Marlon Brando, Tom Selleck, George Corraface, Rachel Ward, Robert Davi, Catherine Zeta Jones, Oliver Cotton, Benicio Del Torro, Matthieu Carriere, Nigel Terry. w. John Briley, Cary Bates, Mario Puzo, d. John Glen.
ADVENTURE: Historical Drama; Explorers; Adventure at Sea; Kings; Queens; Caribbean; Central America
(1492: Conquest of Paradise)
Christopher Strong, 1933, 72m, ★★★/$$, RKO/Turner. A female pilot, loosely based on Amelia Earhart, detests the idea of married life so much that she contemplates suicide when she becomes pregnant by the married man with whom she's carrying on an affair. Katharine Hepburn, Colin Clive, Billie Burke,

Helen Chandler, Ralph Forbes, Irene Browne, Jack La Rue. w. Zoe Akins, N-adap. Gilbert Frankau, d. Dorothy Arzner.
DRAMA: MELODRAMA: TRAGEDY: Romance with Married Person; Babies-Having; Mothers-Unwed; Pilots-Airline; Feisty Females; Suicidal Tendencies; Forgotten Films; Curiosities; Ahead of its Time; Biographies-Fictional; Female Protagonists; Female Screenwriters
(Amelia Earhart; Flight for Freedom)
Chronicle of a Death Foretold, 1987, 110m, ★★1/2/$, Virgin/NA. A doctor's best friend died mysteriously in his youth. Twenty-seven years later, he goes back to his hometown and unravels the mystery. Rupert Everett, Ornella Muti, Gian Maria Volonte, Irene Papas, Lucia Bose, Anthony Delon, Alain Cluny. w. Francesco Rosi, Tonino Guerra, N-adap. Gabriel Garcia Marquez, d. Francesco Rosi.
DRAMA: MYSTERY: MURDER: Friendships-Male; Doctors; Good Premise Unfulfilled
The Chronicles of Narnia, 1989, 180m, ★★1/2/$$, PBS-BBC/Facets, PBS. Children go into a fantasy world of talking animals and allegorical moral situations to navigate. Barbara Kellerman, Jeffery Perry, Sophie Cook. N-adap. C.S. Lewis, d. Alex Kirby.
CHILDREN'S: FAMILY: Fantasy; Allegorical Stories; Animals-Talking; TV Movies
Chuck Berry: Hail Hail Rock n Roll, see **Hail, Hail, Rock n Roll**
Chu Chu and the Philly Flash, 1981, 100m, ★★1/2/$, 20th/Fox, PG. A drunken former baseball star meets up with a Carmen Miranda street performer when they both claim they lost the same briefcase-but it really belongs to the mob. Carol Burnett, Alan Arkin, Jack Warden, Danny Aiello, Adam Arkin, Ruth Buzzi. w. Barbara Dana, d. David Lowell Rich.
COMEDY: Con Artists; Inner City Life; Finding Money; Alcoholics; Mob Stories; Mob Comedy; San Francisco; Coulda Been Great; Female Screenwriters
(Ed: The performances are there, but the script and direction isn't)
C.H.U.D., 1984, 90m, ★★/$, Ind/Vestron, Sultan, R/V-B&G. Creepy things-Cannibalistic Humanoid Underground Dwellers-live in the sewers of New York and like to drag people down to their level. John Heard, Daniel Stern,

Christopher Curry, Kim Griest, John Goodman. d. Douglas Cheek.

C.H.U.D.2, Bud the Chud, 1989, 84m, ★/$, Vestron/Vestron, R/V-B&G. Teens get into the action this time around and try to figure out how to kill the beasties. Brian Robbins, Bill Calvert, Gerrit Graham, Bianca Jagger, Robert Vaughan. d. David Irving.

HORROR: Monsters; Cannibalism; Curiosities

Cimarron, 1930, 130m, ★★★/$$$, RKO/Turner. An Oklahoma man stakes his claim in the days of homesteading. He struggles to get a ranch going and raise a family from 1890 to 1915. Richard Dix, Irene Dunne, Estelle Taylor, Nance O'Neil, William Collier Jr., Roscoe Ates, George E. Stone, Stanley Fields, Edna May Oliver. w. Howard Estabrook, N-adap. Edna Ferber, d. Wesley Ruggles.

Cimarron, 1960, 147m, ★★/$, MGM/MGM-UA. A dull remake of above. Glenn Ford, Maria Schell, Anne Baxter, Lili Darvas, Russ Tamblyn, Henry Morgan, David Opatoshu, Charles McGraw, Aline MacMahon, Edgar Buchanan, Arthur O'Connell, Mercedes McCambridge, Vic Morrow, Robert Keith, Mary Wickes, Royal Dano, Vladimir Sokoloff. w. Arnold Schulman, d. Anthony Mann.

Flops-Major

DRAMA: Family Drama; Cattle Ranchers; Southwestern Life; 1900s
(Giant; So Big)

The Cincinnati Kid, 1965, 113m, ★★¹/₂/$$$, MGM/MGM-UA, PG. A huge stud-poker game in New Orleans attracts all the gambling big shots, but none so big as the Cincinnati Kid with few more tricks up his sleeve than cards. Steve McQueen, Edward G. Robinson, Karl Malden, Ann-Margret, Tuesday Weld, Joan Blondell, Rip Torn, Jack Weston, Cab Calloway, Jeff Corey. w. Ring Lardner Jr., Terry Southern, N-adap. Richard Jessup, d. Norman Jewison.

DRAMA: COMEDY DRAMA: Gambling; Games; New Orleans; Playboys; Faded Hits; Forgotten Films
(Kaleidoscope; Bullitt; The Gambler)

Cinderella, 1950, 75m, ★★★★/$$$$, Disney/Disney, G. A beautiful girl is kept at home by her evil and ugly stepsisters, but her fairy godmother grants her one night at a ball, where she enchants a prince and loses a glass slipper. Voices of Illene Woods, William Phipps, Eleanor Audley, Rhoda Williams, Lucille Bliss, Verna Felton. (Supervisor) Ben Sharpsteen, d. Wilfred Jackson, Hamilton Luske, Clyde Geronimi.

Cartoons; ROMANCE: Princes; Rags to Riches; Fantasy; Fairy Tales; Cinderella; Stories; Parents vs. Children; Evil Women; Women in Conflict; Rodents
(Alice in Wonderland; Peter Pan)

Cinderella Jones, 1946, 89m, ★★★/$$, WB/NA. A brainy nerd gets lucky when a bombshell pretends to be in love with him and they marry. He later learns that she married him for an inheritance. Joan Leslie, Robert Alda, S. Z. Sakall, Edward Everett Horton, Julie Bishop, William Prince, Charles Dingle, Ruth Donnelly, Elisha Cook Jr., Hobart Cavanaugh, Chester Clute. w. Charles Hoffman, Philip Wylie, d. Busby Berkeley.

COMEDY: MUSICAL: Musical Comedy; Marriage-Fake; Inheritances at Stake; Nerds; Nerds & Babes

Cinderella Liberty, 1973, 117m, ★★★/$$$, 20th/Fox, R/S-P. A sailor sees the humanity in a prostitute he meets while on shore leave and a rocky romance develops in the slums. James Caan Marsha Mason (BActress), Eli Wallach, Kirk Calloway, Allyn Ann McLerie. w. N-adap. Darryl Ponicsan, d. Mark Rydell. BOSong. Oscars: 2-0.

DRAMA: ROMANCE: Romantic Drama; Romance-Reluctant; Romance with Prostitute; Prostitutes-Low Class; Sailors; Shore Leave; Inner City Life; Poor People
(Romance; The Goodbye Girl)

Cinderella, 1960, 91m, ★★¹/₂/$$, Par/Par. A male version of the Cinderella story-Lewis style. Jerry Lewis, Ed Wynn, Judith Anderson, Anna Maria Alberghetti, Henry Silva, Robert Hutton, Count Basie. w. d. Frank Tashlin.

COMEDY: MUSICALS: Musical Comedy; Comedy-Slapstick; Fools-Bumbling; Cinderella Stories; Revisionist Films; Role Reversal; Fairy Tales; Men as Women

Cinema Paradiso, 1989, 122m, ★★★¹/₂/$$$$, Miramax/Miramax-HBO, PG. A director looks back on influential experiences of his childhood in a small Italian coastal town, especially working as a projectionist's assistant at the local cinema. Antoelli Attli, Enzo Cannavale, Isa Danieli, Leo Gullotta, Marco Leonardi, Pupella Maggio, Agnese Nano, Leopoldo Trieste, Salvatore Cascio, Jacques Perrin, Philippe Noiret. w. d. Giuseppe Tornatore.

DRAMA: Coming of Age; Memories; Boyhood; Movie Theaters; Directors; Autobiographical Stories; World War II-Post Era; Italy; Small-town Life; Italian Films; Writer-Directors; Sleeper Hits
(Everybody's Fine; The Last Picture Show)

Circle of Friends, 1995, 107m, ★★★/$$, Savoy/HBO, PG-13/S. Wallflower wants the school hunk, but wallflower's best friend wants him, too. Will her charm overwhelm him? Chris O'Donnell, Minnie Driver, Geraldine O'Rawe, Saffron Burrows, Colin Firth, Alan Cumming. w. Andrew Davies, N-adap. Maeve Binchy, d. Pat O'Connor.

COMEDY DRAMA: ROMANCE: Romantic Drama; Coming of Age; Romance-Triangles; Boarding Schools; Girls; Women Fighting Over Men; Wallflowers; Wallflowers & Hunks; Ireland; Irish Films; 1950s; Hidden Gems; Female Protagonists
(Georgy Girl; The Sterile Cuckoo; Rich in Love; Widow's Peak)

Circle of Power, 1983, 103m, ★★¹/₂/$, Media/Media, R/S-FN. A psychologist into rather alternative methods tries to cure businessmen of whatever problems they may have blocking their potential, running from alcoholism to gayness. Yvette Mimieux, John Considine, Terence Knox, Cindy Pickett. w. d. Bobby Roth.

DRAMA: Psychological Drama; Psychologists; Cures/Solutions-Search for; Curiosities; Writer-Directors

Circle of Two, 1980, 105m, ★★/$, Ind/Vestron, PG. A teenage girl falls in love with a sixty-year-old artist, and a melodramatic relationship develops. Richard Burton, Tatum O'Neal, Nuala Fitzgerald, Kate Reid, Robin Gammell, Patricia Collins. w. Thomas Hedley, N-adap. Marie Terese Baird (A Lesson in Love), d. Jules Dassin.

MELODRAMA: ROMANCE: Romance-Older Men/Younger Women; Men and Girls; Canadian Films; Curiosities; Unintentionally Funny
(Sudie and Simpson; Sundays and Cybele)

The Cisco Kid, 1994, 96m, ★★/$$, Turner/Turner. Cisco helps rebels win the freedom of old Mexico and becomes a hero in the villages. Jimmy Smits, Cheech

Marin, Sadie Frost. w. Michael Kane, Luis Valdez. d. Valdez.

ACTION: DRAMA: Action Drama; **WESTERNS:** Mexico; Latin People; Political Unrest; Revisionist Films; TV Movies
(Old Gringo; Viva Zapata)

Cisco Pike, 1971, 94m, ★★/$$, Col/RCA-Col. A rock singer in L.A. is set up in a drug bust by a narcotics cop. Kris Kristofferson, Gene Hackman, Karen Black, Harry Dean Stanton. w. d. Bill L. Norton.

DRAMA: Crime Drama; Police Stories; Drugs-Dealing; Rock Stars; Framed?; Writer-Directors; Anti-Establishment Films; Forgotten Films
(Alex in Wonderland; Blume in Love; Tequila Sunrise)

The Citadel, 1938, 113m, ★★★/$$$, MGM/MGM-UA. A young idealistic doctor in England works in mining areas, but the stress gets to be too much and he soon heads off to a cushy suburban practice. Robert Donat (BActor), Rosalind Russell, Ralph Richardson, Emlyn Williams, Penelope Dudley Ward, Francis L. Sullivan, Rex Harrison. w. Elizabeth Hill, Ian Dalrymple, Emlyn Williams, Frank Wead, N-adap. A. J. Cronin, d. King Vidor (BDirector). BPicture, BScr. Oscars: 4-0.

DRAMA: Doctors; Class Conflicts; City vs. Country; Mining Towns; England; British Films; Female Screenwriters
(Arrowsmith; Doc Hollywood; City of Joy)

Citizen Kane, 1941, 119m, ★★★★/$$, RKO/Turner. The rise of a newspaper media mogul from meager beginnings to his lonely castle, as told by those left in the wake of his life. Orson Welles (BActor), Joseph Cotten, Dorothy Comingore, Everett Sloane, Ray Collins, Paul Stewart, Ruth Warrick, Erskine Sanford, Agnes Moorehead, Harry Shannon, George Coulouris, William Alland, Fortunio Bonanova. w. Herman J. Mankiewicz, Orson Welles (**BOScr**), d. Orson Welles (BDirector). BPicture, BB&WCin, BB&WArt, BSound, BEdit, BScore. Oscars: 9-1.

DRAMA: Biographies-Fictional; Biographies; Power-Rise to; Social Drama; Political Drama; Politicians; Rich People; Evil Men; Stern Men; Episodic Stories; Art Films; Film History
(There are no similar films)

Citizen Cohn, 1992, 112m, ★★★/$$$, HBO/HBO, R/P-S. Biography of the infamous partner to McCarthy during the red scare of the 50s, Roy Cohn, a homophobic but actually closeted lawyer who died of AIDS, tracing his rise to power and swift fall. James Woods, Joe Don Baker, Joseph Bologna, Ed Flanders, Frederic Forrest, Lee Grant, Pat Hingle. w. David Franzoni, d. Frank Pierson.

DRAMA: Biographies; Evil Men; Stern Men; McCarthy Era; Bigots; Hypocrisy; Gay Men; Homophobia; AIDS Stories; TV Movies
(Angels in America)

The City and the Dogs, 1985, 135m, ★★1/2/$, Ind/NA. A cadet and an honest officer expose corruption and brutality at a military academy. Pablo Serra, Gustavo Bueno, Luis Alvarez, Jan Manuel Ochva, Eduardo Adrianzen. w. Jose Watanbe, N-adap. Mario Vargas Llosa, d. Francisco J. Lombardi.

DRAMA: Military Schools; Soldiers; Corruption; Ethics; Latin People; Spanish Films

City Boy, 1993, 120m, ★★★/$, G. In the 1900s, a boy makes his way from industrial Chicago to the great Pacific Northwest and is torn between becoming a lumberjack or saving the forests. Christian Campbell, James Brolin, Sarah Chalke. w. d. John Kent Harrison.

DRAMA: ADVENTURE: FAMILY: Boys; Coming of Age; Chicago; City vs. Country

City for Conquest, 1940, 106m, ★★1/2/$$, WB/WB. Two very different brothers from a working-class New York neighborhood help each other out. One, a composer, switches from popular to classical music while his brother, a truck driver and amateur boxer, becomes blinded in a fight. James Cagney, Ann Sheridan, Frank Craven, Donald Crisp, Arthur Kennedy, Frank McHugh, George Tobias, Anthony Quinn, Jerome Cowan, Lee Patrick, Blanche Yurka, Thurston Hall. w. John Wexley, N-adap. Aben Kandel, d. Anatole Litvak.

MELODRAMA: Brothers; Episodic Stories; Working Class; Music Composers; Boxing; Blind People; Tearjerkers; Forgotten Films
(True Confessions; Angels with Dirty Faces)

City in Fear, 1980, 135m, ★★★/$$$, CBS/Live, PG/S-V. A psycho killer is on the loose in the big city and a journalist gets a tip that puts him in contact with the killer-but so close, and yet so far. David Janssen, Mickey Rourke, Robert Vaughan, Susan Sullivan, William Daniels, Perry King, William Prince. d. Alan Smithee (Jud Taylor).

SUSPENSE: Manhunts; Trail of a Killer; Serial Killers; Journalist as Detective; Murders-One by One

City Lights, 1931, 87m, ★★★★/$$$, UA/Fox. The "Little Tramp" falls in love with a blind flower girl and pretends to be a millionaire to impress her. Charles Chaplin, Virginia Cherrill, Florence Lee, Harry Myers. w. d. Charles Chaplin.

COMEDY: Comedy-Slapstick; **MELO-DRAMA: ROMANCE:** Romantic Comedy; Comedy-Character; Rich People; Impostors; Blind People; Writer-Directors; Film History
(Modern Times; Chaplin)

City of Hope, 1991, 130m, ★★★/$, Col/Col, R/P-S-V. In Hudson City, New Jersey, the city is run by corrupt politicians and everyone from local bar owners to contractors get special favors if they scratch the right backs. Fires, beatings, and other urban chaos are the result. Vincent Spano, Joe Morton, Tony Lo Bianco, Barbara Williams, Stephen Mendillo, Chris Cooper, Charlie Yanko, John Sayles, Gloria Foster, Tom Wright. w. d. John Sayles.

DRAMA: Social Drama; Social Satire; Hospitals; Fires; Corruption; Government Corruption; Ethics; Political Drama; Politicians; Family Drama; Multiple Stories; Interwoven Stories; Coulda Been Great; Underrated; Hidden Gems; Writer-Directors
(City Hall; The Hospital)

City of Joy, 1992, 135m, ★★1/2/$, WB/WB, PG. An American doctor at a free clinic in Calcutta gets swept up in a local struggle against gangsters taking over poor sections of the city. Patrick Swayze, Pauline Collins, Om Puri, Shabana Azmi, Art Malik, Ayesha Dharker, Santu Chowdhury, Imran Badsah Khan. w. Mark Medoff, NF-adap. Dominic LaPierre, d. Roland Joffé.

MELODRAMA: ADVENTURE: Doctors; Saintly People; India; Mob Stores; Ordinary People vs. Criminals; Reformers; Flops-Major
(The Citadel; The Mission)

City of the Dead, see **Horror Hotel**

City of Women, 1981, 140m, ★★★/$$, R/S-FN. Fellini's fantasy vision of just that, a city of women, with slides, roller coasters, and orgies of women involving the semi-autobiographical hero. w. Federico Fellini, Bernardino Zapponi, d. Federico Fellini.

DRAMA: Fantasy; Erotic Drama; Dreams; Fantasies; Art Films; Avant-Garde Films; Elusive Women; Orgies

(8½; La Dolce Vita; And the Ship Sails On)

City Slickers, 1991, 114m, ★★★/$$$$$, Castle-Col/New Line, PG-13/P. Three nerdy New Yorkers (Billy Crystal, Bruno Kirby, Daniel Stern) go on a cattle-rustling vacation to live out childhood dreams, misled by Westerns. Jack Palance (**BSActor**), Helen Slater. w. Lowell Ganz, Babaoo Mandel, d. Ron Underwood. Oscars: 1-1.

COMEDY: COMEDY DRAMA: Fish out of Water Stories; Western Comedy; Western-Modern; City vs. Country; Rural Life; Stern Men; Cattle Rustlers; Cattle People; Nerds; Camping; Nerd vs. Macho; Jewish People; Men Proving Themselves; Bullfighting; Female Among Males

SEQUEL: City Slickers 2

(Fancy Pants; Funny Farm; Running Scared)

(Ed: In many ways, a one-joke comedy, but it's fleshed-out enough to work)

City Slickers 2: The Legend of Curly's Gold, 1994, 116m, ★★/$$, CR-Col/Col, PG-13/P-V. The city dudes return to the ranch and look for gold up against old Curly's evil twin, who's after it, too. Billy Crystal, Daniel Stern, Jon Lovitz, Patricia Wettig, Taylor Vince, David Paymer, Josh Mostel. w. Billy Crystal, Bablaoo Mandel, Lowell Ganz, d. Paul Welland.

COMEDY: Western Comedy; Fish out Water Stories; Treasure Hunts; Stern Men; Twins; Jewish People; City vs. Country; Camping; Flops-Major

City Streets, 1931, 86m, ★★★/$$$, Par/NA. A gangster's daughter takes the fall for her man, but he gets her out. Now she's exposed to her rivals. Sylvia Sidney, Gary Cooper, Paul Lukas, Guy Kibbee, William Boyd. w. Max Marcin, Oliver Garrett, Dashiel Hammett, SS-adap. Ernest Booth, *Ladies of the Mob*, d. Rouben Mamoulian.

ACTION: Action Drama; Crime Drama; Mob Stories; Mob Girls; Women in Jeopardy; Power Struggles; Mob Wars; Hidden Gems

(Street Scene; Dead End)

Claire's Knee, 1970, 106m, ★★★/$$$, Ind/Media, R/S. One man's obsession about wanting to touch the knee of a woman named Claire-really, and how it affects his life. Jean-Claude Brialy, Aurora Cornu, Beatrice Romand, Laurence de Monaghan, Michele Montel, Gerard Falconetti, Fabrice Luchini. w. d. Eric Rohmer.

DRAMA: ROMANCE: Romance-Boy Wants Girl; Ordinary People Stories; Obsessions; Elusive Women; Art Films; French Films; Writer-Directors

(My Night at Maud's; Pauline at the Beach; That Obscure Object of Desire; Chloe in the Afternoon)

The Clairvoyant, 1934, 80m, ★★½/$$, RKO/NA. A charlatan claims to have predictive powers and is surprised and frightened when he finds out that he actually does. Claude Rains, Fay Wray, Jane Baxter, Mary Jane, Athole Stewart, Ben Field, Felix Aylmer, Donald Calthrop. w. Charles Burnett, Bryan Edgar Wallace, Robert Edmunds, N-adap. Ernst Lothar, d. Maurice Elvey.

SUSPENSE: Psychological Drama; Psychics; Future-Seeing the; Forgotten Films; Curiosities

(The Medusa Touch; Eyes of Laura Mars)

Clambake, 1967, 98m, ★★/$$, MGM/MGM-UA. The son of an oil tycoon decides to leave his father's stuffy life to party on the beach. Elvis Presley, Shelley Fabares, Bill Bixby, James Gregory. w. Arthur Browne Jr., d. Arthur H. Nadel.

MUSICALS: ROMANCE: Musical Romance; Beach Movies; Rock Stars; Oil People; Rebels

The Clan of the Cave Bear, 1986, 100m, ★★½/$$, PG-13/V-S. Hairy prehistoric Neanderthals chase a blonde bombshell in their midst. Daryl Hannah, Pamela Reed, James Remar, Thomas G. Waites. w. John Sayles, N-adap. Jean M. Auel, d. Michael Chapman.

DRAMA: ADVENTURE: Chase Stories; Women in Jeopardy; Prehistoric Times; Sexy Women; Cave People; Coming of Age

(Quest for Fire; One Million B.C.)

(Ed: The novel was a huge bestseller, but this sold only a week's worth of tickets)

Clara's Heart, 1988, 108m, ★★½/$$, PG. The wise and witty ways of a black Jamaican nanny (Whoopi Goldberg) and her little white boy charge (Neil Patrick Harris). w. Mark Medoff, d. Robert Mulligan.

MELODRAMA: COMEDY DRAMA: FAMILY: Babysitters; Black Women; Women & Boys; Mentors

(Corrina, Corrina; For Love of Ivy; The Chalk Garden)

(Ed: Charming but cliched and somewhat defiant of political correctness)

Clarence, the Cross-Eyed Lion, 1965, 98m, ★★★/$$$, MGM/MGM-UA, G. Animal preservationists in Africa deal with a pet lion. Marshall Thompson, Betsy Drake, Richard Haydn. w. Alan Calliou, Marshall Thompson, Art Arthur, d. Andrew Marton.

CHILDREN'S: FAMILY: Animal Stories; Animal Rights; Pet Stories; Africa; Veterinarians; Pet Stories; TV Pilot Movies

SEQUEL: Daktari TV Series.

(Daktari; Born Free; An Alligator Named Daisy)

(Ed: Originally in theaters, it became the TV Series soon after)

Clash by Night, 1952, 105m, ★★½/$, RKO/Turner. A girl who left her little fishing community for the big city returns in mysterious circumstances and stirs up old jealousies. Barbara Stanwyck, Paul Douglas, Robert Ryan, Marilyn Monroe, J. Carrol Naish. w. Alfred Hayes, P-adap. Clifford Odets, d. Fritz Lang.

DRAMA: MELODRAMA: Reunions; MYSTERY: Jealousy; Men Fighting Over Women; Forgotten Films

Clash of the Titans, 1981, 118m, ★★★/$$$, MGM/MGM-UA, PG/V. Perseus (Harry Hamlin) fights the evil Greek Gods in order to marry the girl of his dreams (Judi Bowker), but he must first get her away from a monstrous beast who owns her. Laurence Olivier, Maggie Smith, Burgess Meredith, Ursula Andress, Sian Phillips. w. Beverley Cross, d. Desmond Davis.

ACTION: ADVENTURE: Animation-Stop; Monsters-Mythology; Mythology; Monsters-Animal; Greece; Ancient Times; Quests; Marriage-Impending; Women in Jeopardy; Saving Someone; Fighting Evil; Female Screenwriters; Sleeper Hits

(The Golden Voyage of Sinbad)

Class, 1983, 98m, ★★½/$$$, Orion/Orion, R/S-FN. A prep-school student

(Andrew McCarthy) is seduced by the mother (Jacqueline Bisset) of his roommate (Rob Lowe), and numerous complications arise. Cliff Robertson, Stuart Margolin, John Cusack. w. Jim Kouf, David Greenwalt, d. Lewis John Carlino.

COMEDY DRAMA; ROMANCE:
Romantic Comedy; Erotic Comedy; Romance-Older Women/Younger Men; Romance-Clandestine; Virgins; Coming of Age; Romance with Friend's Parent; Bratpack Movies
(The Grasshopper; Summer of '42)

Class Action, 1990, 109m, ★★★/$$, 20th/Fox, PG/P-S. A young woman lawyer finds herself up against her father, who's also a lawyer, when she handles a case involving a car model that explodes on impact. Mary Elizabeth Mastrantonio, Gene Hackman, Colin Friels, Joanna Merlin, Larry Fishburne, Donald Moffat, Jan Rubes. w. Carolyn Shelby, Christopher Ames, Samantha Shad, d. Michael Apted.

SUSPENSE: DRAMA: Courtroom Drama; Legal Thriller; Trials; Conspiracy; Corporate Corruption; Lawyers; Fathers & Daughters; Detective Stories; Lawyers as Detectives; Parents vs. Children; Accidents; Female Screenwriters; Female Protagonists
(Music Box; Jagged Edge; The January Man)
(Ed: The Pinto Story? Actually, the car is called the Meridien. Not much better than most TV movies of the same type except in the way the case is developed)

Class Act, 1992, 98m, ★★/$, WB/WB. Two buddies in high school, one a nerd and one a loser, trade places. Christopher Reid, Christopher Martin, Karyn Parsons, Alysia Rogers, Meschach Taylor, Doug E. Doug. w. John Semper, Cynthia Friedlob, Michael Swerdlick, Wayne Rice, Richard Brenne, d. Randall Miller.

COMEDY: Identities-Assumed; Nerds; Body Switching; Role Reversal; High School Life; Black Men
(Trading Places; Making the Grade)

Class of '84, 1981, 98m, ★★★/$$, Ind/Vestron, R/EV-EP-S. A new teacher at an inner-city school discovers the students are more than just your average juvenile delinquents. Perry King, Merrie Ross, Timothy Van Patten, Roddy McDowall. w. Mark Lester, John Saxton, Tom Holland, d. Mark Lester.

ACTION: HORROR: Crime Drama; Juvenile Delinquents; Rebels; Young Men-Angry; Criminals-Female; High School Life; Teachers; Teachers & Students; Fish out of Water Stories; Inner City Life; Cult Films; Overlooked at Release; Blood & Gore
SEQUEL: Class of 1999.
(Blackboard Jungle; Dangerous Minds)

Class of '44, 1973, 95m, ★★★/$$, WB/WB, R/S-P. The boy from *Summer of '42* grows up and goes to college during the war, still dealing with sexual problems and new experiences, of course. Gary Grimes, Jerry Houser, William Atherton, Sam Bottoms, Deborah Winters. w. Herman Raucher, d. Paul Bogart.

MELODRAMA: COMEDY DRAMA:
Coming of Age; College Life; Teenagers; Teenage Movies; Nostalgia; World War II Era; Young Men; 1940s
SEQUEL TO: Summer of '42
(Carnal Knowledge; American Graffiti)

The Class of Miss MacMichael, 1978, 90m, ★★1/2/$, Brut-Embassy/NA. A British schoolteacher goes slumming and runs into trouble. Glenda Jackson, Oliver Reed, Michael Murphy, Rosalind Cash. w. Judd Bernard, N-adap. Sandy Hutson, d. Silvio Narizzano.

DRAMA: Social Drama; Teachers; Teachers & Students; Inner-City Life; British Films; Female Protagonists
(Up the Down Staircase; Dangerous Minds; Cutting Class)

Class of 1999, 1990, 98m, ★★/$, Vestron/Vestron, R/V-B&G. Robotic forces take over the most corrupt and unruly high school in the future. Bradley Gregg, Stacy Keach, Malcolm McDowell, Traci Lin, John Ryan, Pam Grier. w. C. Courtney Joyner, Mark Lester, d. Mark Lester.

ACTION: HORROR: Crime Drama; Futuristic Films; Juvenile Delinquents; Androids; Rebels; Young Men-Angry; Criminals-Female; High School Life; Teachers; Teachers & Students; Fish out of Water Stories; Inner-City Life; Cult Films; Blood & Gore
SEQUEL TO: Class of '84
Class Reunion, see National Lampoon's Class Reunion

Claudelle Inglish, 1961, 99m, ★★1/2/$$, WB/NA. A sexy young thing spurns a rich fellow for the more animalistic charms of other young men with less dough. Diane McBain, Arthur Kennedy,

Constance Ford, Chad Everett, Claude Akins, Will Hutchins. w. Leonard Freeman, N-adap. Erskine Caldwell, d. Gordon Douglas.

MELODRAMA: ROMANCE: Southerns; Sexy Women; Promiscuity; Marrying Up; Romance-Choosing the Right Person; Romance-Reluctant; Free Spirits; Coulda Been Good; Hidden Gems; Camp; Tennessee Williamsesque
(Picnic; This Property Is Condemned; Baby Doll)

Claudia, 1943, 92m, ★★★/$$, 20th/NA. A naive young woman with an older husband learns the ropes. Dorothy McGuire, Robert Young, Ina Claire, Reginald Gardiner. w. Morrie Ryskind, N-adap. P-adap. Rose Franken, d. Edmund Goulding.

MELODRAMA: ROMANCE: Marriage Drama; **COMEDY DRAMA:** Pre-Life Crisis; Young Women; Newlyweds; Romance-Older Men/Younger Women; Womens' Films; Female Protagonists

Claudine, 1974, 92m, ★★★/$$$, 20th/NA, PG. A black mother (Diahann Carroll, BActress) tries to hold her family together and have a life of her own by building a relationship with a respectable man (James Earl Jones) her gaggle of children may destroy. w. Tina & Lester Pine, d. John Berry. Oscars: 1-0.

DRAMA: COMEDY DRAMA: ROMANCE: Mothers-Struggling; Black Women; Black Casts; Black Men; Working Class; Ordinary People Stories; Families-Large; Parents vs. Children; Female Protagonists; Female Screenwriters; Black Screenwriters; Black Directors
(Crooklyn; Alice Doesn't Live Here Anymore; Used People; Hollow Image [TV Movie])

Clean Slate, 1994, 107m, ★★/$, MGM/MGM-UA, PG. A P.I. with a blind dog has amnesia and is unable to remember the murder he witnessed, but the killer may be after him anyway. Dana Carvey, Valeria Golino, James Earl Jones, Kevin Pollak, Michael Murphy. w. Robert King, d. Mick Jackson.

COMEDY: Detective Stories; Detectives-Private; Dogs; Amnesia; Witness to Murder; **MURDER:** Fugitive from a Murderer; Comedy-Slapstick

Clean and Sober, 1988, 124m, ★★★/$$, WB/WB, PG-13/S-P. A yuppie out of control on drugs and booze goes to a detox center and battles changing.

Michael Keaton, Kathy Baker, Morgan Freeman, Tate Donovan, M. Emmet Walsh. w. Tod Carroll, d. Glenn Gordon Caron.

MELODRAMA: Social Drama; Drugs-Addictions; Alcoholics; Greed; Yuppies; Redemption; Starting Over; Midlife Crisis (The Mark; The Boost; Torchlight; Leaving Las Vegas)

Clear and Present Danger, 1994, 130m, ★★★/$$$$, Par/Par, PG-13/V. CIA operative Jack Ryan is thrown into a plot against South American drug lords when a politician is murdered and he unravels a connection from the President to drugs. Harrison Ford, Anne Archer, James Earl Jones, Willem Dafoe, Ann Magnuson. w. Steven Zaillian, Donald Stewart, N-adap. Tom Clancy, d. Philip Noyce.

ACTION: SUSPENSE: Political Thriller; Chase Stories; CIA Agents; Spy Films; Spies; South America; Conspiracy; Double Crossings; Drugs-Dealing

SEQUEL TO: Patriot Games (Patriot Games; The Hunt for Red October)

(Ed: Not as good as *Patriot Games*, but still good)

Cleopatra, 1934, 100m, ★★★/$$$, Par/Par, NR/S-FN. The early sound version with enough sexuality that the Hayes censorship office cracked down right after its release. Focusing on the great Egyptian queen's fondness for Roman Mark Antony. Claudette Colbert, Henry Wilcoxon, Warren William, Gertrude Michael, Joseph Schildkraut, Ian Keith, C. Aubrey Smith, Leonard Mudie, Irving Pichel. w. Waldemar Young, Vincent Lawrence, d. Cecil B. de Mille. BPicture, **BCin**, BEdit. Oscars: 3-1.

ROMANCE: DRAMA: Romantic Drama; Epics; Ancient Times; Romans; Egypt; Queens; Leaders-Military; Production Design-Outstanding

(Sign of the Cross; Cleopatra [1963])

Cleopatra, 1963, 246m, ★★★/$$$$, 20th/Fox. A more expansive telling of the story of the Queen's rise and then her involvement with Caesar and Mark Antony, leading to tragedy. Elizabeth Taylor, Rex Harrison (BActor), Richard Burton, Pamela Brown, Hume Cronyn, Martin Landau, Roddy McDowall. w. Joseph L. Mankiewicz, Ranald MacDougall, Sidney Buchanan, d. Joseph L. Mankiewicz. BPicture, **BBCin,**

BCArt, BSound, BEdit, BOScore, **BCCostume.** Oscars: 8-3.

ROMANCE: DRAMA: Romantic Drama; Epics; Ancient Times; Romans; Egypt; Queens; Leaders-Military; Production Design-Outstanding; Flops-Major; Blockbusters

(The Robe; SHE; Elizabeth and Essex)

(Ed: For some it's a bore, but the sheer spectacle is enough to pass the time. It does take quite a time, and though recorded as a flop because of its incredible cost, it was a major hit in terms of ticket sales)

Cleopatra Jones, 1973, 80m, ★★1/2/$$, WB/WB, R/P-S-V. A black CIA agent goes undercover literally and figuratively to stop drug dealers. Tamara Dobson, Shelley Winters, Bernie Casey, Brenda Sykes. w. Max Julien, Sheldon Keller, d. Jack Starrett.

ACTION: Spy Films; CIA Agents; Law Officers-Female; Spies-Female; Black Women; Drugs-Dealing; Undercover; Blaxploitation Era; Cult Films; Curiosities; Female Protagonists

SEQUEL: Cleopatra Jones and the Casino of Gold

Cleopatra Jones and the Casino of Gold, 1975, 96m, ★★/$$, WB/WB, R/P-S-V. The black female CIA operative heads to Hong Kong and infiltrates martial-arts thugs dealing drugs. Tamara Dobson, Stella Stevens, Normal Fell. w. William Tennant, d. Chuck Bail.

ACTION: Spy Films; CIA Agents; Law Officers-Female; Spies-Female; Black Women; Drugs-Dealing; Undercover; Asia; Hong Kong; Blaxploitation Era; Cult Films; Curiosities; Female Protagonists

SEQUEL TO: Cleopatra Jones

The Client, 1994, 120m, ★★★/$$$$$, Col/Col, PG-13/P-V. When a boy and his little brother witness a gangster trying to commit suicide and come upon information about the murder of a senator from Louisiana, they become media celebrities, and the older one needs a lawyer to defend him in court and hide him from the mobsters wanting revenge. Susan Sarandon, Tommy Lee Jones, Brad Renfro, Mary Louise Parker, Anthony LaPaglia, Ossie Davis, J.T. Walsh, Anthony Edwards, Will Patton, Anthony Heald. w. Robert Getchell, Akiva Goldsman, d. Joel Schumacher.

SUSPENSE: MELODRAMA: Children in Jeopardy; Witness to Murder; Chase

Stories; Hiding Out; Boys; Women and Boys; Child Protagonists; Mothers-Surrogate; Innocent Bystanders; Mob Stories; Lawyers; Lawyers as Detectives; Legal Thriller; Race Against Time (Witness; The Pelican Brief; The Firm)

(Ed: Could have been better, much better, with the two best Grisham characters yet [not saying too much], and fine performances, however, surrounded with complete cardboard stereotypes)

Cliffhanger, 1993, 106m, ★★★/$$$$, Carolco-Tri/Col-Tri, R/EV-P. Terrorists hijacking a shipment of $100 million crash-land in a Rocky Mountain rescue zone and then must kidnap expert rescue mountain climbers in order to locate their lost cases of money in the snow. Sylvester Stallone, Janine Turner, John Lithgow, Ralph Waite, w. Michael France, Sylvester Stallone, d. Renny Harlin.

ACTION: ADVENTURE: Treasure Hunts; Double Crossings; Terrorists; Heist Movies; Rescue Drama; Hijackings; Snow Settings; Skiing; Airplane Crashes; Mountain Climbing; Kidnappings; Redemption; Escalating Plots

SPOOF: Ace Ventura: When Nature Calls.

(Die Hard; Die Hard 2; The Eiger Sanction; K2)

(Ed: "Die Hard on the Mountain." Excellent action feature whose implausibilities are quickly forgotten due to the pace. I would've held onto that money in the avalanche, though)

Cloak and Dagger, 1946, 106m, ★★1/2/$$, USP/Republic. A scientist goes behind the iron curtain on a mission to get to a kidnapped scientist held by the Nazis. Gary Cooper, Lilli Palmer, Robert Alda, Valdimir Sokoloff. w. Albert Maltz, Ring Lardner Jr., d. Fritz Lang.

ADVENTURE: Spy Films; Spies; CIA Agents; Iron Curtain-Behind the; Scientists; Kidnappings; World War II Stories; Nazi Stories; Coulda Been Good; Forgotten Films

Cloak and Dagger, 1984, 101m, ★★★/$$, Universal/MCA-U, PG/V. A kid (Henry Thomas) comes upon top secret information via a video game wanted by spies. Dabney Coleman, Michael Murphy, Christina Nigra, John McIntire. d. Richard Franklin.

SUSPENSE: MYSTERY: CHILDREN'S: FAMILY: Spy Films; Spies; Chase Movies;

Child Protagonists; Unbelieved; Elderly People; Underrated; Hidden Gems

The Clock, 1945, 91m, ★★★¹/₂/$$$, MGM/MGM-UA. After a girl singer meets a GI in Grand Central Station, they're on the road to marriage within a day. Judy Garland, Robert Walker, James Gleason, Lucille Gleason, Keenan Wynn, Marshall Thompson. w. Robert Nathan, Joseph Schrank, SS-adap. Paul and Pauline Gallico, d. Vincente Minnelli.

ROMANCE: MELODRAMA: Romantic Drama; World War II Era; Soldiers; New York Life; Time Capsules; Big Band Era; Singers

(New York, New York; Waterloo Bridge; Hanover Street)

Clockers, 1995, 109m, ★★★/$$, U/MCA-U, R/EP-EV. A young, inner-city black boy is ordered by the drug dealer he assists to off a fast-food worker who didn't do right. But when the kid's straight-arrow brother confesses, the white cop on the case smells a rat. Harvey Keitel, John Turturro, Delroy Lindo, Mekki Phifer, Isaiah Washington, Keith David, Pee Wee Love, Regina Taylor. w. Richard Price & Spike Lee, N-adap. Richard Price, d. Spike Lee.

ACTION: SUSPENSE: MYSTERY: MURDER: MURDER MYSTERY: Detective Stories; Detectives-Police; White Among Blacks; Inner-City Life; Drugs-Dealing; Black Men; Black Directors; Black Screenwriters

(Homicide; Sea of Love; Deep Cover)

Clockwise, 1986, 96m, ★★★/$, EMI-U/EMI-HBO, PG. A provincial English school's headmaster tries to get to a professional conference in London but has a hell of a time getting there, due to a bad confluence of circumstances. John Cleese, Alison Steadman, Penelope Wilton, Stephen Moore. w. Michael Frayn, d. Christopher Morahan.

COMEDY: FARCE: Race Against Time; Murphy's Law Stories; Comedy of Errors; Teachers; British Films; Hidden Gems; Coulda Been Great; Monty Pythoners

(Fawlty Towers SERIES; A Fish Called Wanda)

(Ed: A little too dry and British to work well as the great entertainment the talents involved could have brought)

A Clockwork Orange, 1971, 136m, ★★★★/$$$$, WB/WB, X-R/P-S-FFN-MFN. A rebellious young man (Malcolm McDowell) and his team of thugs wreak havoc on innocent people in the decayed future. w. Stanley Kubrick (BAScr), N-adap. Anthony Burgess, d. Kubrick (BDirector). BPicture, BEdit. Oscars: 4-0.

DRAMA: Psychological Drama; Futuristic Films; SCI-FI: SATIRE: Social Satire; Juvenile Delinquents; Wild People; Dangerous Men; Young Men; Brainwashing; Rebels; Anti-establishment Films; British Films; Ahead of Its Time; Time Capsules

(Bladerunner; Class of 1984; Class of 1999)

Close Encounters of the Third Kind, 1977, 135m, ★★★★/$$$$$, Columbia/RCA-Col, PG. A man (Richard Dreyfuss) is encountered by a UFO and feels drawn on a pilgrimage to where they will meet again. Melinda Dillon (BSActress), Teri Garr, Francois Truffaut. w. d. Steven Spielberg (BDirector). BCin, BEdit, BSound, BSFX, BArt, BOScore. Oscars: 8-1.

ADVENTURE: SCI-FI: FAMILY: Fantasy; Epics; UFOs; Aliens-Outer Space, Good; Journies; Quests; Dreams; Blockbusters

(Communion; A Fire in the Sky)

(Ed: There is much dispute about Spielberg's writing credit with claims other writers had much to do with it)

Closely Watched Trains, 1966, 89m, ★★★¹/₂/$$, Czech-Ind/Fox-Lorber. A railway guard during the war in Czechoslovakia falls in love with a woman and hopes to lose his virginity. But she leads him on, and into intrigue which may not pay off. Vaclav Nekcar, Jitka Bendova, Vladimir Valenta, Josef Somr. w. d. Jiri Menzel, N-adap. Bohumil Hrabal. BFLFilm. Oscars: 1-1.

COMEDY DRAMA: SUSPENSE: War Stories; World War II Stories; Spies; Spy Films; Virgins; Coming of Age; Young Men; Ordinary Person Turned Criminal; Trains; Czech Films; Europeans-Eastern

Close My Eyes, 1991, 108m, ★★¹/₂/$, Academy/Academy, R/S. A brother and sister who have been separated most of their lives, meet again and wind up in a romance-but do they know what they're doing? Alan Rickman, Saskia Reeves, Clive Owen, Karl Johnson. w.d. Stephen Poliakoff.

DRAMA: Art Films; MELODRAMA: ROMANCE: Incest; Brothers & Sisters; Children-Long Lost; Reunions; Romance-Doomed; British Films; Writer-Directors

The Closer, 1991, 87m, ★★¹/₂/$, Academy/Academy, R/P-V. A middle-aged salesman has a crisis as his job has taken over his life for so long, he doesn't know who he is. Danny Aiello, Michael Pare, Joe Cortese, Justine Bateman, Diane Baker, James Karen. w. Robert Keats, Louis LaRusso, d. Dimitri Logothetis.

DRAMA: Social Drama; Character Studies; Working Class; Ordinary People Stories; Men's Films; Salesmen; Midlife Crisis; Coulda Been Good; Good Premise Unfulfilled

(Death of a Salesman; Save the Tiger; Glengarry Glen Ross; 29th Street)

Closet Land, 1991, 93m, ★★/$, I-Universal/MCA-U. A kindergarten teacher (Madeleine Stowe) is interrogated by a ruthless government official (Alan Rickman) for subversive activities. w. d. Rhada Bharadwaj.

DRAMA: SCI-FI: Futuristic Films; Surrealism; Torture; Oppression; Stagelike Films; Writer-Directors; Female Screenwriters; Female Directors; Coulda Been Good

(Fahrenheit 451)

(Ed: Totally unfilmic and unrelenting. Fascinating to a point, interminable after)

Close to Eden, 1991, 120m, ★★★/$, Ind/Par, PG. A Russian truck driver crashes into a ditch and is taken in by a Mongolian shepherd while he recovers. Bayaertu Badema, Vlodomir Gostukhin, Babuskha. w. Nikita Mikhalkov, Roustam Ibraguimbekov, d. Nikita Mikhalkov. BFLFilm. Oscars: 1-0.

DRAMA: Rescue Drama; Saintly People; Allegorical Stories; Art Films; Russians; Truck Drivers; Russian Films

The Clown, 1952, 91m, ★★¹/₂/$$, MGM/MGM-UA. A clown star who's washed-up has a kid encouraging him to try a comeback. Red Skelton, Jane Greer, Tim Considine. w. Martin Rackin, d. Robert Z. Leonard.

MELODRAMA: Circus Life; COMEDY DRAMA: Tearjerkers; Comebacks; Alcoholics; Men and Boys; Fathers & Sons; Starting Over

(Shakes, the Clown; The Champ; The Comic)

Club Paradise, 1986, 96m, ★★/$$, WB/WB, PG-13/S-P-FN. Shenanigans at an island resort, centering around Robin Williams, who is running a ramshackle resort. Andrea Martin, Rick Moranis,

Peter O'Toole, Twiggy, Adolph Caesar, Eugene Levy, Joanna Cassidy. w. Harold Ramis, Brain Doyle-Murray, Ed Roboto, Tom Leopold, Chris Miller, David Standish, d. Harold Ramis.

COMEDY: FARCE: Comedy of Errors; Vacations; Resorts; Ensemble Films; Coulda Been Good

(The Last Resort; Exit to Eden)

(Ed: Pretty putrid)

Clue, 1985, 96m, ★★/$, Par/Par, PG. The game characters come to life in a drawing-room comedy mystery with alternate endings. Madeline Kahn, Eileen Brennan, Martin Mull, Tim Curry, Christopher Lloyd, Michael McKean, Lesley Ann Warren. w. d. Johnathan Lynn.

COMEDY: MYSTERY: MURDER: MURDER MYSTERY: Comic Mystery; Mystery-Whodunits; Ensemble Films; Writer-Directors

(Murder By Death; The Cheap Detective)

Clueless, 1995, 97m, ★★★/$$$$, Par/Par, PG-13/S. When a rich girl named Cher who lives in Beverly Hills and lives with her widowed father decides to move toward losing her virginity, she encounters some interesting friends, a gay studmuffin, a jerk, and . . . her stepbrother. Will she survive the insanity of her own kooky world or wind up facing the harshness of reality? Not in this movie. Alicia Silverstone, Stacey Dash, Brittany Murphy, Paul Rudd, Donald Faison, Breckin Meyer, Jeremy Sisto, Justin Walker, Elisa Donovan, Dan Hedaya, Wallace Shawn, Twink Caplan. w. d. Amy Heckerling, N-adap. *Emma*, Jane Austen.

COMEDY: SATIRE: Beverly Hills; Rich People; Girlhood; Coming of Age; Los Angeles; Romance with Relative; High School Life; Simple Minds; Sleepers; Female Protagonists; Female Screenwriters; Female Directors

(Heathers; Square Pegs [TV Series]; Foxes; Troop Beverly Hills; Fast Times at Ridgemont High)

(Ed: The Austen connection makes this a refreshing twist, though it bears little resemblance to reality, except in a Disney world where teen sex is all the rage, though the clothing fits Disney. The most profitable film of the summer of 1995-$53 million gross on $12 million expenses)

Cluny Brown, 1946, 100m, ★★★/$$, 20th/NA, AMC. A young woman goes to work for England and has a romance with a war refugee in this comedy of manners. Jennifer Jones, Charles Boyer, Richard Haydn, Una O'Connor, Peter Lawford, Helen Walker, Reginald Gardiner, Reginald Owen. w. Samuel Hoffentein, Elizabeth Reinhardt, N-adap Margery Sharp, d. Ernst Lubitsch.

COMEDY DRAMA: Comedy of Manners; **ROMANCE:** Romantic Comedy; Comedy-Light; **SATIRE:** Romance-Reluctant; World War II Era; England; Hidden Gems

(The Shop Around the Corner; To Be or Not to Be)

(Ed: Lubitsch's last major film)

Coach, 1978, 100m, ★★/$$, Media/Media, R/P-MRN. A woman coach (Cathy Lee Crosby) takes over a boys' basketball team and encounters obstinance-plus hunky romance. Michael Blehn. w. d. Bud Townsend.

DRAMA: ROMANCE: Romance-Older Women/Younger Men; Romance with Teacher; Underdog Stories; Female Among Males; Fish out of Water Stories; Writer-Directors; Female Protagonists

Coal Miner's Daughter, 1980, 124m, ★★★★/$$$$, Universa/MCA-U, PG/S. The little girl from Kentucky, Loretta Lynn (Sissy Spacek, **BActress**) makes it up the ranks to country music stardom despite troubles. Beverly D'Angelo, Tommy Lee Jones. w. Tom Rickman (BAScr), d. Michael Apted (BDirector). BPicture, BEdit, BArt, BCin. Oscars: 7-1.

DRAMA: Biographies; Singers; Career Women; Country Life; Country Music; Working Class; Rags to Riches; Fame-Rise to; Nervous Breakdowns; Drugs-Addictions; Southerns; British Directors of Southerns; Sleeper Hits; Female Protagonists

(Sweet Dreams; The Rosemary Clooney Story; Stand By Your Man; What's Love Got to Do With It?)

(Ed: What seemed like it could have been a routine TV movie or worse has become a minor classic; became a grass-roots smash with things like Loretta Lynn's Crisco oil cross-promotions)

Cobb, 1994, 130m, ★★★/$, WB/WB, R/EP-V. Baseball legend Ty Cobb recounts his sanitized life story to a writer helping him with his autobiography, *My Life in Baseball*. But the true story of Cobb is nowhere in the pages of that book as this writer character based on the real author, Al Stump, uncovers the truth of Cobb's father's murder, Cobb as rapist, woman beater, and possibly killer, and certainly as a psychotic liar who's heroic public image was exactly opposite to what colleagues thought of him. Tommy Lee Jones, Robert Wuhl, Lolita Davidovich, Lou Myers, J. Kenneth Campbell, Eloy Casados, Rhoda Griffis, Paula Rudy. w. d. Ron Shelton, NF-adap. Al Stump

DRAMA: Biographies; Writers-Autobiographical Stories; Behind the Scenes; Baseball; Flashbacks; Abused Women; Heroes-False; Evil Men; Secrets-Keeping; Overlooked at Release; Flops-Major; Coulda Been Great

(The Babe; The Natural; The Great Santini)

Cobra, 1986, 87m, ★★/$$$, Cannon-WB/WB, PG-13/EV-P. A crazed LA cop goes after a serial killer leading to a motorcycle chase. . . . Sylvester Stallone, Brigitte Nielsen, Reni Santoni, Andrew Robinson. w. Stallone, N-adap. Paula Gosling, Fair Game, d. George Pan Cosmatos.

ACTION: Police Stories; Trail of a Killer; Detective Stories; Detectives-Police; Chase Movies; Serial Killers; Psycho Killers

(Nighthawks; Dirty Harry; Lock Up)

The Coca-Cola Kid, 1985, 94m, ★★½/$$, Cinecom/Cinecom, R/S-FFN. An American goes to deal with a Coke franchise problem in Australia and meets a sexy woman who complicates his easy plans. Eric Roberts, Greta Scacchi, Bill Kerr. w. Frank Moorhouse, d. Dusan Makavejev.

COMEDY DRAMA: ROMANCE: Executives; Americans Abroad; Australia; Corporation as Enemy; Mothers & Daughters; Aborigines

(Local Hero; The Efficiency Expert)

Cocktail, 1988, 103m, ★★/$$$$, Touchstone/Touchstone, PG-13/S-P. A frat boy (Tom Cruise) goes to the islands to tend bar and meet women (Elisabeth Shue). w. N-adap. Heywood Gould, d. Roger Donaldson.

DRAMA: COMEDY DRAMA: ROMANCE: Young Men; Romance-Boy Wants Girl; Romance-Bickering; Caribbean; Vacations; Vacation Romance; Teenage Movies

(Top Gun; Private Resort)

(Ed: The only good thing out of this was marginal-the Beach Boys comeback, "Kokomo")

The Cocoanuts, 1929, 96m, ★★★/$$$, Par/MCA-U. A hotel manager tries to get in on a real estate scheme in the Florida swamps. The Marx Brothers, Margaret Dumont, Oscar Shaw. w. George S. Kaufman, Morrie Ryskind, d. Robert Florey, Joseph Shantley.
COMEDY: FARCE: Ensemble Films; Con Artists; Hotels
(Animal Crackers; Duck Soup)
(Ed: Dated, literally, by its early technical inferiority, but still worth it)

Cocoon, 1985, 117m, ★★★/$$$$, 20th/CBS-Fox, PG/S. Pods from outer space land in a swimming pool at a retirement community and a young man stumbles into their plot to take over and re-colonize on Earth, leading to the discovery of their rejuvenating water. Steve Guttenberg, Don Ameche (**BSActor**), Jessica Tandy, Hume Cronyn, Brian Dennehy, Tawny Welch, Wilford Brimley, Maureen Stapleton, Jack Gilford, Gwen Verdon. w. Tom Benedek, N-adap. David Sapirstein, d. Ron Howard. BSFX. Oscars: 2-1.
SCI-FI: COMEDY DRAMA: ROMANCE: Romantic Comedy; Fantasy; What If . . . Stories; Elderly People; Romance-Elderly; Sexy Women; Aliens-Outer Space, Good; Retirement; Redemption; Aging-Reverse; Rejuvenation; Florida
(batteries not included; Death Becomes Her)
(Ed: Cute but not much more)

Cocoon, The Return, 1988, 116m, ★★/$$, 20th/CBS-Fox, PG. After going into outer space, the eldsters return to rescue more pods in the pool needing new life. Steve Guttenberg, Don Ameche, Jessica Tandy, Hume Cronyn, Brian Dennehy, Tawny Welch, Wilford Brimley, Maureen Stapleton, Jack Gilford, Gwen Verdon. w. Stephen McPherson, Elizabeth Bradley, d. Daniel Petrie.
SCI-FI: COMEDY DRAMA: ROMANCE: Romantic Comedy; Fantasy; What If . . . Stories; Elderly People; Romance-Elderly; Sexy Women; Aliens-Outer Space, Good; Retirement; Redemption; Rejuvenation; Florida

Code Name: Emerald, 1985, 95m, ★★1/2/(VR), NBC-MGM/Fox. A spy goes behind enemy lines to Paris to ensure that an American POW doesn't spill the plans for the D-Day invasion. Ed Harris, Max von Sydow, Horst Buchholz, Helmut Berger. w. Ronald Bass, N-adap. Bass, The Emerald Illusion, d. Johnathan Sanger.

SUSPENSE: Spy Films; Spies; Secret Agents; World War II Stories; POWs; D-Day; Paris

Code of Silence, 1985, 100m, ★★1/2/$$, Orion/Orion, R/P-V. A drug raid in Chicago starts mob war between the cops and different drug dealers. Chuck Norris, Henry Silva, Bert Remsen. w. Michael Butler, Dennis Shryack, Mike Gray, d. Andy Davis.
ACTION: Crime Drama; Police Stories; Mob Stories; Mob Wars; Drugs-Dealing; Police vs. Mob; Chicago

Cohen and Tate, 1988, 86m, ★★1/2/$, Nelson/Nelson, PG-13/V-P. After a boy witness a hit, two mobster hitmen kidnap him but have trouble doing away with him. Roy Scheider, Adam Baldwin, Harley Cross. w.d. Eric Red.
SUSPENSE: ACTION: Crime Drama; Kidnappings; Mob Stories; Hitmen; Witness to Murder; Witness to Murder-Child; Children in Jeopardy; Good Premise Unfulfilled; Coulda Been Great; Writer-Directors
(The Window; Witness)

Cold Feet, 1989, 94m, ★★1/2/$, Live/Live, R/S-P. Eccentric criminals stash jewels into a racehorse's stomach in Montana, a heist which leads to an unusual romance. Keith Carradine, Sally Kirkland, Tom Waits, Rip Torn, Kathleen York, Bill Pullman. w. Thomas McGuane, Jim Harrison, N-adap. McGuane, d. Robert Dornheim.
COMEDY: Black Comedy; ROMANCE: Romantic Comedy; Heist Stories; Jewel Thieves; Eccentric People; Coulda Been Good
(Rancho DeLuxe)

Cold Heaven, 1992, 103m, ★★/$, Hemdale/Hemdale, R/P-S-V. A woman's husband aparently dies while on vacation, but when he apparently reappears, she has strange visions and ideas resulting from it. Theresa Russell, Mark Harmon, James Russo, Talia Shire, Will Patton, w. Alan Scott, N-adap. Brian Moore, d. Nicolas Roeg.
DRAMA: Psychological Drama; Art Films; Dead-Back from the; MYSTERY: Ghosts; Illusions/Hallucinations
(Sweet Bird of Youth [1989]; Whore)

Cold Sassy Tree, 1989, 95m, ★★★1/2/$$$, Turner/Turner. Amid the life already going on there, a beautiful old maid (Faye Dunaway) moves to a small southern town to take care of and

marry an elderly widower (Richard Widmark), much to the consternation of the early-1900s locals. w. Joan Tewksbury, N-adap. Olive Ann Burns, d. Joan Tewksbury.
DRAMA: ROMANCE: Romantic Drama; Spinsters; Widowers; Love-Questionable; Marriages-Convenience; Romance-Older Men/Younger Women; Secrets-Keeping; Ostracism; Elderly Women; Grandfathers; Boys; Coming of Age; Gossip; Small-town Life; Southerns; Narrated Films; Under-rated; Hidden Gems; Female Screen-writers; Female Directors; Writer-Directors
(Wildflower; Sudie and Simpson)
(Ed: Proves Dunaway still has it with the right script and director)

Cold Sweat, 1993, 93m, ★★/$, Par/Par, R/P-V-S. A hitman is haunted by a victim, so he decides to get out of the business, but a seductress may change that. Ben Cross, Shannon Tweed, Adam Baldwin, Dave Thomas. w. Richard Beattie, d. Gail Harvey.
SUSPENSE: Erotic Thriller; Hitmen; Ghosts; Past-Haunted by the; Nightmares; Mob Stories; Starting Over; Convict Goes Straight; Female Directors

Cold Turkey, 1970, 99m, ★★★/$$$, UA/MGM-UA, G. A small town in Iowa will win money if everyone can stop smoking. Dick van Dyke, Carl Reiner, Jean Stapleton, Bob Newhart, Vincent Gardenia. w. Norman Lear, N-adap. Margaret and Neil Rau (*I'm Giving Them Up for Good*), d. Norman Lear.
COMEDY: FARCE: Race Against Time; Competitions; Drugs-Addictions; Bets; Midwestern Life; Small-town Life
(The Russians Are Coming . . .)

The Collector, 1965, 119m, ★★★1/2 $$$, Columbia/RCA-Col, S. A lonely young man (Terence Stamp) kidnaps a beautiful young artist (Samantha Eggar, BActress) and keeps her like he catches and keeps butterflies, but she won't be as submissive. w. Stanley Mann, John Kohn (BAScr), N-adap. John Fowles, d. W. Wyler (BDirector). Oscars: 3-0.
DRAMA: ROMANCE: TRAGEDY: Character Studies; Hostage Situations; Kidnappings; Romance-Unrequited; Infatuations; Obsessions; Mental Illness; Lonely People; British Films; Mod Era; Hidden Gems
(Misery; The Beguiled)

(Ed: The first of such stories, the novel is a classic, and though the film isn't quite up to that level, it still resonates)

Colonel Redl, 1985, 114m, ★★★/$$, Ind/Ingram, Facets. A man rises to power as a military leader in the Hungarian army but soon becomes undone and winds up a spy on a suicide mission. Klaus Maria Brandauer, Hans Christian Blech, Armin Mueller Stahl. w. Istvan Szabo, Peter Dobai, d. Istvan Szabo, BFLFilm. Oscars: 1-0.

DRAMA: TRAGEDY: Biographies-Fictional; Character Studies; Leaders-Military; Spies; Europeans-Eastern; Iron Curtain-Behind the; Suicidal Tendencies

Colorado Territory, 1949, 93m, ★★1/2/$$, WB/WB. A bank robber trying to go straight after escaping from prison makes the mistake of trying to pull one last job on which to retire. It ends up being his last job, period. Joel McCrea, Virginia Mayo, Dorothy Malone, Henry Hull, John Archer, James Mitchell, Morris Ankrum, Basil Ruysdael, Frank Puglia. w. John Twist, Edmund H. North, d. Raoul Walsh.

WESTERNS: TRAGEDY: Prison Escape; Convict Goes Straight; One Last Time; Bank Robberies; Heist Stories

Color Me Dead, 1969, 97m, ★★1/2/$, ITC/Republic. Low budget remake of *D.O.A.* in which a man discovers he's been slowly poisoned. With little time to live, he has to find his killer if no antidote can be found first. Tom Tryon, Carolyn Jones, Rick Jason. w. Russel Rouse, Clarence Greene, d. Eddie Travis.

SUSPENSE: MURDER: Poisons; Race Against Time; MYSTERY: MURDER MYSTERY: Chase Movies; Saving Oneself; Death-Impending

REMAKE/RETREAD OF: D.O.A.

The Color of Money, 1986, 119m, ★★★/$$$, Touchstone/Touchstone, R/S-P. A pool hustler (Paul Newman, **BActor**) makes his comeback while teaching a new kid (Tom Cruise) the ropes with pool and women. Mary Elizabeth Mastrantonio (BSActress), Helen Shaver, John Turturro. w. Richard Price, S-adap. Walter Tevis, d. Martin Scorsese. BCin, BArt, BSound. Oscars: 5-1.

DRAMA: Character Studies; Redemption; Comebacks; Friendships-Male; Pool; Teachers; Teachers & Students; Mentors/Proteges; Con Artists

SEQUEL TO: The Hustler

(The Hustler; The Mechanic; The Baltimore Bullet; Nobody's Fool)

Color of Night, 1994, 118m, ★★1/2/$$, Touchstone/Touchstone, R/ES-EV-FN-MN. A psychologist is murdered, so a friendly colleague decides the culprit is one of his group therapy clients and takes over the sessions to solve the case. Bruce Willis, Jane March, Scott Bakula, Lance Henriksen, Kevin J. O'Connor, Ruben Blades, Lesley Ann Warren. w. Matthew Chapman, Billy Ray, Richard Rush, d. Rush.

SUSPENSE: Erotic Thriller; Psychological Thriller; Psychologists; Psychologists as Detective; MURDER: Sexy Women; Good Premise Unfulfilled

(Whispers in the Dark; Dream Lover)

The Color Purple, 1985, 150m, ★★★1/2/$$$$$, WB/WB, PG/P-S. A black woman (Whoopi Goldberg, BActress) rebells against her abusive husband and finds solace with other women. Oprah Winfrey (BSActress), Danny Glover, Margaret Avery (BSActress). w. Menno Meyjes (BAScr), N-adap. Alice Walker, d. Steve Spielberg. BPicture, BCinema, BArt, BCostume, BOScore, BOSong, BEdit. Oscars: 11-0, tie for all-time loser with *The Turning Point*.

DRAMA: COMEDY DRAMA: Character Studies; Ensemble Films; Ensembles-Female; Women Fighting the System; Single Women; Black Casts; Black Women; Women's Rights; Abused Women; Epistolaries; Episodic Stories; Southerns; 1900s Georgia; Pulitzer Prize Adaptations; Old-Fashioned Recent Films; Blockbusters

Colors, 1988, 120m, ★★1/2/$$$, Orion/Orion, R/EP-V. A veteran cop and a rookie try to stop gang wars in L.A. Robert Duvall, Sean Penn, Maria Conchita Alonzo, Randy Brooks, Damon Wayans. w. Michael Schiffer, d. Dennis Hopper.

DRAMA: ACTION: Action Drama; Police Stories; Crime Drama; Mob Wars; Gangs-Black; Gangs-Latin; Gangs-Street; Los Angeles; Partners-Mismatched; Mentors/Proteges; Sleeper Hits; Faded Hits

Coma, 1978, 113m, ★★★1/2/$$$, MGM/MGM-UA, PG/S. A woman doctor (Genevieve Bujold) discovers a secret body-parts cartel, which her boyfriend (Michael Douglas) may be a part of. Elizabeth Ashley, Rip Torn. N-adap. Robin Cook, w. d. Michael Crichton.

SUSPENSE: MURDER: MYSTERY: MURDER MYSTERY: Medical Thrillers; Conspiracy; Murder-Discovering; Romance-Dangerous; Women in Jeopardy; Organ Donor Murders; Organ Donors; Body Parts; Unbelieved; Undercover; Doctors; Detective Stories; Medical Detectives; Detectives-Amateur; Detectives-Female; Comas Hospitals; Female Protagonists

(Virus [TV Movie]; Blink)

The Comancheros, 1961, 108m, ★★1/2/$$$, 20th/CBS-Fox. When a Texas Ranger and his prisoner travel through the coutnry and find a camp of men arming themselves for rebellion, they reconcile to clean things up. John Wayne, Stuart Whitman, Nehemiah Persoff, Lee Marvin, Ina Balin, Bruce Cabot. w. James Edward Grant, Clair Hauffaker, d. Michael Curtiz.

WESTERNS: ACTION: Police Stories; Enemies Unite; Journies; War Battles; Anarchists; Arms Dealers

Combination Platter, 1993, 84m, ★★1/2/$, Ind/NA. An Asian immigrant gets a job at a Queens Chinese restaurant and tries to fit in with the Americans. Jeff Lau, Colleen O'Brien, Lester Chan. w. Tony Chan, Edwin Baker, d. Chan.

COMEDY DRAMA: Fish out of Water Stories; Immigrants; Chinese People; Asian-Americans; New York Life

(Dim Sum; The Wedding Banquet)

Come and Get It, 1936, 99m, ★★★/$$$, Goldwyn-UA/Goldwyn. A rich man in the Midwest timberlands has several affairs and many friends over the years in his adventures. Edward Arnold, Frances Farmer, Walter Brennan (BSActor) Andrea Leeds. w. Jules Furthman, Jane Murfin, N-adap. Edna Ferber, d. Howard Hawks, William Wyler. BEdit. Oscars: 2-1.

COMEDY DRAMA: Biographies-Fictional; Power-Rise to; ROMANCE: Young Men; Elderly Men; Rich People; Midwestern Life; 1800s Early America; Female Screenwriters

(The Toast of New York)

Come Back Charleston Blue, 1972, 101m, ★★1/2/$$, WB/WB, R/P-S-V-MRN. Two police detectives team up in Harlem to track down a mobster thought to be dead but who seems to be up to his old tricks again. Godfrey Cambridge, Raymond St. Jacques, Peter deAnda, Jonelle Allen. w. Bontsche Scweig, Peggy

Elliott, N-adap. Chester Himes, d. Mark Warren.

COMEDY DRAMA: MYSTERY: Crime Drama; Detective Stories; Detectives-Police; Detectives-Private; Police Stories; Black Casts; Blacks vs. Whites; New York Life; Inner City Life; Female Screenwriters; Blaxploitation Era
(Cotton Comes to Harlem; Black Caesar; Watermelonman)

Come Back, Little Sheba (B&W), 1952, 99m, ★★★¹/₂/$$$, Par/Par. A woman (Shirley Booth, **BActress**) must nurse her alcoholic doctor husband (Burt Lancaster) and deal with demons from the past while her daughter moves on. Terry Moore (BSActress). Richard Jaeckel. w. Ketti Frings, P-adap. William Inge, d. Daniel Mann. Oscars: 3-1.

DRAMA: MELODRAMA ROMANCE: Past-Haunted by the; Alcoholism; Romance-Older Women/Younger Men; Lonely People; Doctors; Midwestern Life; Small-town Life; Midlife Crisis; Female Protagonists; Female Screenwriters; Tennessee Williams-esque
(The Rose Tattoo; Cat on a Hot Tin Roof; About Mrs. Leslie; Hazel [TV Series])
(Ed: Lancaster's playing of a much older man throws things off a bit, but also gives Booth more time to shine)

Come Back to the Five and Dime, Jimmy Dean, Jimmy Dean, 1983, 110m, ★★★/$, Ind/Sultan, PG/S. Three waitresses have a party in their diner and remember back to when James Dean died and their delusions about him. Karen Black, Sandy Dennis, Cher, Sudie Bond, Kathy Bates. w. P-adap Ed Graczyk, d. Robert Altman.

DRAMA: COMEDY DRAMA: Character Studies; Ensemble Films; Ensembles-Female; Memories; Fans-Crazed; James Dean Fans; Waitresses; Obsessions; Texas; Restaurant Settings; Reunions; Transsexuals; Southerns; Stage Filmings; Stagelike Films
(9-30-55; Silkwood; Frankie and Johnny)

Come Blow Your Horn, 1963, 112m, ★★★/$$$, Par/Par. A boy travels to New York to see his hot-shot brother and becomes jealous of his success. Frank Sinatra, Tony Bill, Lee J. Cobb, Molly Picon, Jill St. John, Barbara Rush, Dan Blocker. w. Norman Lear, P-adap. Neil Simon, d. Bud Yorkin.

COMEDY: COMEDY DRAMA: Brothers; Fish out of Water Stories; Extrovert vs.

Introvert; City vs. Country; New York Life; Playboys
(Goodbye, Charlie; I Ought to Be in Pictures; Only When I Laugh)

Come See the Paradise, 1990, 133m, ★★¹/₂/$, 20th/CBS-Fox, PG-13/S. When the Japanese internment camps are started after the Pearl Harbor attack, a Japanese woman married to an American man is taken from him. Dennis Quaid, Tamlyn Tomita. w. d. Alan Parker.

DRAMA: MELODRAMA ROMANCE: Marriage Drama; Concentration Camps; Prison Drama; Pearl Harbor; Japanese as Enemy; Japanese People; Romance-Interracial; World War II Stories; Writer-Directors
(Heaven and Earth; A Thousand Pieces of Gold)

Come September, 1961, 112m, ★★¹/₂/$$$, U/NA. A rich American man away from his home in Italy finds out upon his return that his naughty mistress there has turned the villa into a hotel and has found a beau. Rock Hudson, Gina Lollobrigida, Sandra Dee, Bobby Darin, Walter Slezak, Brenda deBanzie, Joel Grey. w. Stanley Shapiro, Maurice Richlin, d. Robert Mulligan.

COMEDY: ROMANCE: Romantic Comedy; Sex Comedy; Romance-Triangles; Romance-On Again/Off Again; FARCE: Affair Lairs; Hotels; Mistresses; Cheating Women; Rich People; Italy; Americans Abroad
(Any Wednesday; Strange Bedfellows)

Come to the Stable, 1949, 94m, ★★★/$$$, 20th/NA. Two French nuns warm up a small town dead set against their building a new hospital. Loretta Young (BActress), Celeste Holm (BSActress), Hugh Marlowe, Elsa Lanchester (BSActress), Thomas Gomez. w. Oscar Millard, Sally Benson, Clare Boothe Luce (BOStory), d. Henry Koster. BB&WCin, BB&WArt, BOScore, BOSong. Oscars: 8-0.

COMEDY DRAMA: Tearjerkers; American Myth; Capra-esque; Nuns; Hospitals; Small-town Life; Faded Hits; Forgotten Films; Hidden Gems
(The Bells of St. Mary's; The Singing Nun)
(Ed: One of the most Oscar-nominated, most overlooked and underplayed films ever)

The Comedians, 1967, 160m, ★★★/$, MGM/MGM-UA, PG. A group of people

are caught under the Haitain coup of Papa Doc in the 60s and have to figure out how to set aside their own problems in order to get out. Richard Burton, Elizabeth Taylor, Alec Guinness, Peter Ustinov, Lillian Gish, Paul Ford, Roscoe Lee Browne, Cicely Tyson, James Earl Jones. w. N-adap. Graham Greene, d. Peter Glenville.

COMEDY DRAMA: SATIRE: Political Drama; Political Satire; Ensemble Films; Multiple Stories; Slice of Life Stories; Political Unrest; Leaders-Tyrant; Islands Caribbean; Hidden Gems; Curiosities
(The Ugly American; Burn!; The Honorary Consul; The V.I.P.s)

The Comedy of Terrors, 1963, 88m, ★★★/$$, AIP/Movies Unltd. Two competing funeral home directors decide to accelerate the deaths of prospective clients in order stake their claim in the estates sooner. Vincent Price, Peter Lorre, Boris Karloff, Basil Rathbone, Joe E. Brown. w. Richard Matheson, d. Jacques Tourneur.

HORROR: Black Comedy; Comedy-Morbid; Funerals; Morgues; Murders-One by One; **MURDER:** Forgotten Films; Hidden Gems
(Theater of Blood; The Loved One; Greedy)
(Ed: Actually, the title is just a bit better than the film)

Comes a Horseman, 1978, 188m, ★★★/$$, UA/CBS-Fox, PG/S. A cattle king of Montana is out to take the land from individuals fighting to keep their lives and property in a time passing. Jane Fonda, James Caan, Jason Robards, George Grizzard, Richard Farnsworth (BSActor), Jim Davis. w. Dennis Clark, d. Alan J. Pakula.

DRAMA: WESTERNS: ROMANCE: Cowboys; Cattle Ranchers; Save the Farm; Mortgage Drama; Montana Cattle Problems

Comfort and Joy, 1984, 106m, ★★¹/₂/$$, U/MCA-U, PG. When two ice cream companies in Scotland get into a feud, a radio DJ is caught in the middle. Bill Paterson, Eleanor David, Alex Norton. w.d. Bill Forsyth.

COMEDY: FARCE: COMEDY DRAMA: Feuds; Comedy-Slapstick; Radio Life; Scotland
(Consuming Passions; Local Hero)

The Comfort of Strangers, 1991, 99m, ★★★/$, Skouras/Par, R/S-P-V-

B&G-FFN-MN. A British couple (Rupert Everett, Natasha Richardson) stay in the Venice villa of a very strange and dangerous couple (Christopher Walken, Helen Mirren). w. Harold Pinter, N-adap. Ian McEwan, d. Paul Schrader.

DRAMA: MURDER: TRAGEDY: Art Films; Avant-Garde Films; Surrealism; Dangerous Men; Rich People-Decadent; Beautiful People; Venice; Evil Men; Mental Illness; Violence-Sudden

(The Cook, The Thief, His Wife & Her Lover; The Hunger; Light Sleeper)

The Comic, 1969, 95m, ★★1/2/$, Col/Col. The rise and fall of a comedian from silent film days, apparently based mostly upon Buster Keaton. Dick Van Dyke, Mickey Rooney, Cornel Wilde, Carl Reiner, Michele Lee. w. Carl Reiner, Aaron Rubin, d. Carl Reiner.

COMEDY DRAMA: DRAMA: Biographies-Fictional; **TRAGEDY:** Hollywood Life; Comedians; Silent Film Era; Flops-Major; Coulda Been Great; Underrated; Forgotten Films

(The Clown; Chaplin)

Comin' at Ya!, 1981, 101m, ★★/$$, Filmways/Orion, Vestron, PG. Originally shot in 3-D, but without this gimmick, it's a pretty formulaic Western revenge saga of a man who goes after the outlaws who kidnapped his fiancée. Tony Anthony, Gene Quintano, Victoria Abril, Ricardo Palacios. w. Wolf Lowenthal, Lloyd Battista, Gene Quintano, Tony Petitto, d. Ferdinando Baldi.

WESTERNS: ACTION: Three-D Movies; Revenge; Western-Revenge; Kidnappings

Coming Home, 1978, 127m, ★★★★/$$$, UA/MGM-UA, R/P-S-FN-MRN. A woman (Jane Fonda, **BActress**) whose husband is away in Vietnam (Bruce Dern, BSActor) has an affair with a veteran paraplegic (Jon Voight, **BActor**) until the husband comes home and finds out. Penelope Milford (BSActress). w. Waldo Salt, Nancy Dowd, Robert Jones (**BOScr**). d. Hal Ashby (BDirector). BPicture, BEditing. Oscars: 8-3.

DRAMA: MELODRAMA: ROMANCE: TRAGEDY: Romance-Clandestine; Romantic Drama; Cheating Women; Jealousy; Romance-Triangles; Disabled People; Disabled but Nominated; Suicidal Tendencies; Veterans; War at Home; Vietnam Era

(The Best Years of Our Lives; The Deerhunter; Welcome Home)

Coming to America, 1988, 116m, ★★★/$$$$$, Par/Par, PG-13/S-P. A king of a fictitious African kingdom comes to America to find a queen and winds up working in a McDonald's, among other things. Eddie Murphy, Arsenio Hall, John Amos, James Earl Jones, Madge Sinclair, Shari Headley. w. David Sheffield, Barry Blaustein, Eddie Murphy, Art Buchwald, d. John Landis.

COMEDY: Fish out of Water Stories; Black Men; Black Casts; Multiple Performances; Kings; Queens; Royalty; Africans; Africa; Kingdoms; Black as White; Fairy Tales; Blockbusters

(Beverly Hills Cop SERIES; The Golden Child; The Mouse That Roared)

(Ed: The writing credits were the subject of a famous court case in which Buchwald sued for original story credit and in the process revealed the shifty accounting practices of the studio which claimed the film grossed over $120 million but never made a profit)

Command Decision, 1949, 111m, ★★1/2/$$, MGM/MGM-UA. A look at World War II from the strategist's perspective in their war rooms, rather than the usual front-line infantryman's point of view. Clark Gable, Walter Pidgeon, Van Johnson, Brian Donlevy, John Hodiak, Charles Bickford, Edward Arnold, Richard Quine, Cameron Mitchell, Ray Collins, John McIntire. w. William R. Laidlaw, George Froeschel, P-adap. William Wister Haines, d. Sam Wood.

ACTION: Action Drama; War Stories; World War II Stories; Power Struggles; Behind the Scenes

(MacArthur; Fail Safe; Battleground)

Commando, 1985, 88m, ★★1/2/$$$, 20th/CBS-Fox, PG-13/V. A special squadron is sent to a banana republic to rid the country of a ruthless dictator. Arnold Schwarzenegger, Rae Dawn Chong, Dan Hedaya, Vernon Wells, David Patrick Kelly. w. Steven de Souza, d. Mark L. Lester.

ACTION: ADVENTURE: Special Teams-Military; Central America; Latin People; Leaders-Tyrant

(The Terminator; Raw Deal)

The Commies Are Coming, the Commies Are Coming, 1956, 60m, ★★★/$, RHI. A documentary at the height of the Cold War Era where Jack Webb narrates what would happen if the Reds came marching ashore. Jack Webb,

Andrew Duggan, Robert Conrad. d. George Waggner.

Documentaries; Camp; Unintentionally Funny; Cold War Era; McCarthy Era; What If . . . Stories; Russians as Enemy

(Atomic Cafe; Reefer Madness; Heavy Petting)

The Commitments, 1991, 118m, ★★★/$$, 20th/Fox, PG-13/P-S. A group of kids in Dublin form a soul band, reasoning that "the Irish are the Blacks of Europe." They have many backstage squabbles and romances, and are sometimes set upon by their overly ambitious young manager. Robert Arkins, Michael Aherne, Angeline Ball, Maria Doyle, Dave Finnegan, Bronagh Gallagher, Felim Gormley, Glen Hansard, Dick Massey, Andrew Strong. w. Dick Clement, Ian La Frenais, Marc Abraham, N-adap. Roddy Doyle, d. Alan Parker.

COMEDY DRAMA: Music Movies; Ensemble Films; Musicians; Power Struggles; Behind the Scenes; Rock Stars; Fame-Rise to; Irish People; Ireland; Irish Films

(The Snapper; Sammie and Rosie Get Laid)

Communion, 1989, 101m, ★★/$, Vestron/Vestron, PG-13/V. Billed as a "true story" of the author's abduction by aliens who turn out to be friendly beings merely wanting to communicate. Christopher Walken, Lindsay Crouse, Joel Carlson, Frances Sternhagen, Andreas Katsulas. w. NF-adap. Whitley Strieber, d. Philippe Mora.

SCI-FI: DRAMA: Aliens-Outer Space, Evil; True or Not?; Autobiographical Stories; Writers; Flops-Major; Curiosities

(Close Encounters)

Company Business, 1991, 104m, ★★/$, MGM/MGM-UA, R/V-P-S. A CIA Agent is assigned to swap a Russian double agent who's been working for America with a U-2 pilot in Berlin. But it turns out there are others and other motives involved in the deal and the agent finds that he himself is at risk. Gene Hackman, Mikhail Barysnikov, Terry O'Quinn. w.d. Nicholas Meyer.

ACTION: Spy Films; Spies; Chase Stories; Conspiracy; Russians as Enemy; Berlin; Coulda Been Good; Writer-Directors

(The Package; The Spy Who Came in from the Cold; The Russia House; White Nights)

(Ed: The story is too muddled and seems like one long chase for no particular reason. The fact a lot of other spy films end up this way is still no excuse, and the comic tone spoils the danger that should be there)

Company Limited, 1971, 112m, ★★★/$, Ind/NA. In Calcutta, an American-educated Indian businessman uses unscrupulous methods to increase sales. Sharmila Tagore, Barun Chanda, Parumita Chowdhury. w. d. Satyajit Ray, N-adap. Shankar (*Seemabaddha*).
DRAMA: Corruption; Ethics; Salesmen; India; Indian Films

The Company of Strangers, see **Strangers in Good Company**

The Company of Wolves, 1984, 95m, ★★1/2/$$, ITC/EMI-HBO, PG/V. A young woman has highly charged, sexual and horrific dreams of wolves which seemingly come true. Angela Lansbury, David Warner, Graham Crowden, Brian Glover, Sarah Patterson, Micha Bergese, Stephen Rea. w. Angela Carter, Neil Jordan, SS-adap. Angela Carter, d. Neil Jordan.
HORROR: SUSPENSE: Psychological Drama; Psychological Thriller; Nightmares; Monsters-Animal Surrealism; Curiosities; British Films
(Ed: A definitely unique-looking film, but not exactly an entertaining suspenser)

The Competition, 1980, 129m, ★★1/2/$$$, Rastar-Col/RCA-Col, PG/S. A former prodigy (Richard Dreyfuss) determines to return triumphant in a piano competition in San Fransisco. This has the effect of also pitting him against his lover (Lee Remick). Amy Irving, Sam Wanamaker, Joseph Calli. w. d. Joel Oliansky. BOScore, BSound. Oscars: 2-0.
MELODRAMA: ROMANCE: Pianists; Music Composers; Competitions; Battle of the Sexes; Understudies; Teachers and Students; Writer-Directors
(Mr. Holland's Opus; Voices)

Compulsion, 1959, 103m, ★★★1/2/$$, 20th/NA. A dramatic exploration of the infamous Leopold and Loeb case, about the homosexual University of Chicago students in the 1920s, inspired by Dostoyevski's *Crime and Punishment* to commit the "perfect crime," who pick a young man at random and murder him without motivation. Dean Stockwell, Bradford Dillman, Orson Welles, Diane Varsi, E. G. Marshall, Martin Milner, Richard Anderson, Robert Simon. w.

Richard Murphy, P-adap. Meyer Levin, d. Richard Fleischer.
DRAMA: Psychological Drama; Courtroom Drama; **MURDER:** Murders of Children; Perfect Crimes; Psycho Killers; Murderers-Homosexual; Gay Men; Scandals; True Stories; 1920s Chicago; Rich People; Rich-Decadent
(Swoon; Rope; In Cold Blood)

Compromising Positions, 1985, 99m, ★★★1/2/$$$, Par/Par, R/S-P. A Long Island housewife (Susan Sarandon) gets too curious about the death of her philandering dentist (Joe Mantegna) and uncovers the covers of her bedroom community. Edward Herrmann, Judith Ivey, Joan Allen. w. N-adap. Susan Isaacs, d. Frank Perry.
MYSTERY: MURDER MYSTERY: Comic Mystery; **SATIRE:** Black Comedy; Comedy-Morbid; Ensemble Films; Suburban Life; Detective Stories; Detectives-Amateur; Journalists as Detectives; Ordinary People Stories; Housewives; Husbands-Troublesome; Dentists; Underrated; Hidden Gems
(Dear Inspector; Confidentially Yours)
(Ed: A brilliant, light satire on suburbia, though the mystery is tertiary)

The Computer Wore Tennis Shoes, 1970, 90m, ★★1/2/$$$, Disney/Disney, G. A mediocre college student gets shocked by a computer and has its database transfered into his brain. Kurt Russell, Cesar Romero, Joe Flynn, William Schallert, Alan Hewitt. w. Joseph L. McEveety, d. Robert Butler.
COMEDY: Computers; Geniuses; College Life; Comedy-Disney
(The Barefoot Executive)

Comrades, 1987, 180m, ★★★/$, Ind/NA. In the 1830s in England, farm workers who protest harsh conditions and low wages are convicted of criminal activity and deported to the Australian penal colony. Robin Soans, William Gammara, Stephen Bateman, Philip Davis, Jeremy Flyn, Keith Allen, Alex Norton, Michael Clark, Arthur Dignam, James Fox, Freddie Jones, Vanessa Redgrave, Imelda Stauton. w. d. Bill Douglas.
DRAMA: Historical Drama; Strikes; Prison Drama; Farm Life; England; Australia; Corruption; British Films; TV Movies

The Comrades of Summer, 1992, 90m, ★★1/2/$$, HBO/HBO, PG-13/P-S. A baseball coach can only find a job in Russia, and cultures clash when he heads

to Moscow. Joe Mantegna, Natalia Negoda, Mark Rolston, Eric Allen Kramer, Michael Lerner, w. Robert Rodat, d. Tommy Lee Wallace.
COMEDY DRAMA: Sports Movies; Baseball; Russians; Russia Coaches; Americans Abroad; Fish out of Water Stories; TV Movies

Conagher, 1991, 94m, ★★1/2/$$, Turner/Turner. A cowboy defies settling down with a widow, finally love gets him out of the saddle. Sam Elliott, Katharine Ross, Barry Corbin, Bick Taylor, Daniel Quinn. d. Reynaldo Villalobos.
WESTERNS: ROMANCE: Cowboys; Widows; Love at Last; Romance-Middle-Aged; TV Movies
(The Sacketts; The Shadow Riders)

Conan, the Barbarian, 1981, 129m, ★★★/$$$$, DEG-U/MCA-U, R/EV-S-FN. In the days of sword-and-sorcery, a pumped-up young barbarian seeks to avenge the murder of his parents. Arnold Schwarzenegger, James Earl Jones, Max Von Sydow, Sandahl Bergman, Ben Davidson, Mako, Gerry Lopez. w. John Milius, Oliver Stone, from a character created by Robert E. Howard, d. John Milius.
ACTION: MURDER: Murder of Parents; Ancient Times; Middle Ages; Sword & Sorcery; Revenge; Orphans
SEQUEL: Conan, the Destroyer
(Conan the Destroyer; Red Sonja; The Last Valley)
(Ed: Quite complex and artful for an action picture that was Mr. Universe's first big hit)

Conan, the Destroyer, 1984, 101m, ★★1/2/$$$, DEG-U/MCA-U, R/EV-S. In the Dark Ages, a queen who rules her territory with an iron fist blackmails Conan into undertaking a dangerous quest by promising to revive his first love. Arnold Schwarzenegger, Grace Jones, Wilt Chamberlain, Mako, Tracey Walter, Sarah Douglas. w. Stanley Mann, d. Richard Fleischer.
ACTION: Blackmail; Dead-Back from the; Evil Women; Queens; Ancient Times; Middle Ages; Sword & Sorcery
SEQUEL: Conan, the Destroyer
(Conan, the Barbarian; Red Sonja; The Last Valley)

The Concorde, see **Airport '79, The Concorde**

Condorman, 1981, 90m, ★★/$, Disney/Disney, PG/V. A comic-book artist starts having delusions that he is his character, but finds being a superhero isn't all its cracked up to be. Michael Crawford, Oliver Reed, Barbara Carrera, James Hampton, Jean-Pierre Kalfon. w. Marc Sturdivant, Glen Caron, Mickey Rose, N-adap. Robert Sheckley (The Game of X), d. Charles Jarott.

COMEDY: Comic Heroes; Dreams; Fantasies; Artists; Flying People; Heroes-Superhuman

(Hero at Large; Delirious)

Conduct Unbecoming, 1975, 107m, ★★1/2/$, British Lion/CRV. Among the British troops in India in the 1890s, a young inductee is accused of raping a local woman and must find the real culprit to exonerate himself. Michael York, Stacy Keach, Trevor Howard, Christopher Plummer, Richard Attenborough, Susannah York, James Faulkner. w. Robert Enders, P-adap. Barry England, d. Michael Anderson.

DRAMA: Rape/Rapists; Accused Unjustly; Murder-Clearing Oneself; India; 1890s; Imperialist Problems; Coulda Been Good

(A Passage to India; To Kill a Mockingbird; An Innocent Man; The Wrong Man)

Coneheads, 1993, 85m, ★★1/2/$$, Par/Par, PG-13/P-S. When conical French family who consumes mass quantities settles in the burbs, problems arise when their people come back for them and daughter Connie starts dating. Dan Aykroyd, Jane Curtin, Laraine Newman, Jason Alexander, Michelle Burke, Chris Farley, Michael McKean, Phil Hartman, Chris Rock, David Spade, Dave Thomas, Julia Sweeney. w. Dan Aykroyd, Tom Davis, Bonnie Turner, d. Steven Barron.

COMEDY: Comedy-Character; Comedy-Skit; Saturday Night Live Movies; Aliens-Outer Space; Good Suburbia; Fish out of Water Stories; Eccentric People; Cartoonlike Movies; Coulda Been Great

(The Applegates; Third Rock from the Sun TV Series)

(Ed: Should have been and would be, if you could understand more of it. Some great jokes and a good theme song, if you listen closely)

The Confession, 1970, 160m, ★★★/$, Ind/NA. A minister is imprisoned and forced to confess to anti-communist activities when Prague is taken over by the Russians in 1951. Yves Montand, Simone Signoret, Gabriele Ferzetti, Michel Vitold. w. Jorge Semprun, NF-adap. Lise and Artur London, d. Costa-Gavras.

DRAMA: Political Drama; Preachers/Ministers; Accused Unjustly; Communists; Iron Curtain-Behind the; Russians as Enemy; Political Unrest

Confessions of a Hit Man, 1994, 93m, ★★1/2/$, Hemdale/Hemdale, R/V-P-S. Young hunk steals money from his mafia don uncle and has to pay for it by starting over. James Remar, Micahel Wright, Emily Longstreth. w. Tony Cincirpini, Larry Leahy, d. Leahy.

SUSPENSE: ACTION: Crime Drama; Thieves; Mob Stories; Hitmen

Confessions of a Nazi Spy, 1939, 110m, ★★★/$$$, WB/NA. Nazis working underground in the U.S. are rooted out and nailed to the wall by FBI agents who doggedly pursue them. Edward G. Robinson, Paul Lukas, George Sanders, Francis Lederer, Henry O'Neill, Lya Lys, James Stephenson, Sig Rumann, Dorothy Tree, Joe Sawyer. w. Milton Krims, John Wexley, NF-adap. Leon G. Turrou, d. Anatole Litvak.

DRAMA: Crime Drama; Nazi Stories; FBI Agents; Spies; World War II Era; Forgotten Films

Confessions of a Window Cleaner, 1974, 90m, ★★/$$, Col/NA, R/S-FN-MRN. A window cleaner has liaisons with the lonely women he spies on through the windows he cleans-until they're found out and more than glass breaks. Robin Askwith, Anthony Booth, Sheila White, Dandy Nicholls, Bill Maynard, Linda Hayden, John Le Masurier, Joan Hickson, Richard Wattis, Katya Wyeth, Sam Kydd.

COMEDY: Erotic Comedy; Voyeurs; Playboys; Romance with Married Person; Bimbos

(Alvin Purple; Alvin Rides Again)

Confidential Agent, 1945, 122m, ★★1/2/$$, WB/NA. An agent from Spain under the Franco regime comes to England for a liaison with an unscrupulous arms dealer and ends up falling in love with his daughter. Charles Boyer, Lauren Bacall, Katina Paxinou, Peter Lorre, Victor Francen, George Coulouris, Wanda Hendrix, George Zucco, Miles Mander. w. Robert Buckner, d. Herman Shumlin.

DRAMA: Spies; Arms Dealers; **ROMANCE:** Romantic Drama; Spain; England; World War II Era; Forgotten Films

(Algiers; Arch of Triumph)

Confidential Report, see Mr. Arkadin

Confidentially Yours, 1984, 110m, B&W, ★★★/$$, 20th/CBS-Fox, PG/S. When a man is framed for murder, his loving secretary tries to find the real killer with her intuition. Fanny Ardant, Jean Louis Trintignant. w. Suzanne Schiffman, N-adap. The Long Saturday Night, Charles Williams, d. Francois Truffaut.

SUSPENSE: MYSTERY: MURDER: MURDER MYSTERY: Framed?; Accused Unjustly; Secretaries; Detective Stories; Detectives-Female; Detectives-Amateur; Female Protagonists; Female Screenwriters; Hitchockian

(Dear Inspector; Compromising Positions)

(Ed: More mystery than suspense, but well worth it for mystery, Truffaut, or French film fans)

Conflict of Interest, 1992, 88m, ★1/2/$, HBO/HBO, R/P-V-S. A new cop is menaced by a thug who sets his son up for murder, kills his wife, and then kidnaps the son's girlfriend-and manages never to get caught, until the inevitable confrontation. Judd Nelson, Christopher McDonald, Alyssa Milano. w. Gregory Miller, Michael Angell, d. Gary Davis.

ACTION: SUSPENSE: Stalkers; Malicious Menaces; Psycho-Killers; Framed?; **MURDER:** Murder-Clearing Oneself; Kidnappings; Unintentionally Funny

(Relentless SERIES; From the Hip)

The Conformist, 1971, 105m, ★★★★/$$, Par/Par, R/P-S-V. A timid man just wants to fit in; unfortunately for him, he's in Italy in 1938, and "fitting in" means aligning yourself with the fascists. When he becomes an informer, he finds he can't deal with the pressure. Jean-Louis Trintignant, Stefania Sandrelli, Gastone Moschin, Enzo Taroscio, Dominique Sanda, Pierre Clementi. w. d. Bernardo Bertolucci.

DRAMA: Psychological Drama; Ethics; Corruption; World War II Stories; Conformism; Nerds; 1930s; Nazi Stories; Oppression; Liars; Betrayals; Art Films; Writer-Directors

Congo, 1995, 107m, ★★★/$$$$, Par/Par, PG-13/EV-P. When a search party goes to central Africa looking for a perfect diamond to run a satellite system, the people back in America watch them get slaughtered by unseen, horrible creatures. So off they go into the jungle to find what's left of the party, if only the diamond, and eventually encounter the beasts themselves. Dylan Walsh, Laura Linney, Ernie Hudson, Tim Curry, Grant Heslov, Joe Don Baker, Lorene Noh, Misty Rosas, Mary Ellen Trainor. w. John Patrick Shanley, N-adap. Michael Crichton, d. Frank Marshall.

ADVENTURE: Comic Adventure; Disneyesque; Africa; Jewel Thieves; Treasure Hunts; Jungles; Primates (Stanley and Livingstone; King Solomon's Mines)

(Ed: Good for a Disney high-tech adventure; bad for a monster thriller which it was advertised as. The ad campaign was praised when it obviously fooled much of the audience coming in)

A Connecticut Yankee, 1931, 96m, ★★★/$$$, 20th/Fox. A modern man returns to the days of King Arthur and his knights and shows them the folly of their ways. Will Rogers, Maureen O'Sullivan, Myrna Loy, Frank Albertson, William Farnum. w. William Conselman, SS-adap. Mark Twain (*A Connecticut Yankee in King Arthur's Court*), d. David Butler.

COMEDY: Fantasy; Time Travel; Camelot Stories; Fish out of Water Stories; Hidden Gems; Faded Hits

A Connecticut Yankee in King Arthur's Court, 1949, 106m, ★★★/$$$, Par/MCA-U. A musical version of the famous Twain fable. Bing Crosby, Rhonda Fleming, William Bendix, Cedric Hardwicke, Murvyn Vye. w. Edmund Beloin, d. Tay Garnett.

MUSICAL: COMEDY: Musical Comedy; Musical Fantasy; Fantasy; Time Travel; Camelot Stories; Fish out of Water Stories

REMAKE: A Kid in King Arthur's Court (Brigadoon)

The Conqueror, 1955, 112m, ★★/$, Hughes/MCA-U. A very Hollywood-ized biopic of the legendary Mongolian warrior Genghis Khan and his conquest of the majority of the known world in the late 12th century. John Wayne, Susan Hayward, Pedro Armendariz, John Hoyt, William Conrad, Agnes Moorehead, Thomas Gomez, Ted de Corsia, Lee Van Cleef. w. Oscar Millard, d. Dick Powell.

DRAMA: Historical Drama; Spectacles; Biographies; Ancient Times; Asia; China; Flops-Major; Camp; Curiosities;

Unintentionally Funny; Actor Directors (Genghis Khan; Blood Alley; Shogun) (Ed: Notorious for several of the cast members, particularly Moorehead, Wayne, and director Powell, dying of cancer years after the shoot was first made on radiation contaminated land in Nevada. Dirt from there was even placed on the back lot for further shooting)

Conquest, 1937, 115m, ★★★/$$, MGM/MGM-UA. All of Napoleon's military conquests meant nothing compared to his conquest of a beautiful woman named Josephine. Greta Garbo, Charles Boyer, Reginald Owen, Alan Marshall, Henry Stephenson, Dame May Whitty, Leif Erickson. w. Samuel Hoffenstein, Salka Viertel, S. N. Behrman, from a Polish play dramatized by Helen Jerome, d. Clarence Brown.

DRAMA: ROMANCE: Romantic Drama; Historical Drama; Napoleon; Female Screenwriters; Forgotten Films

RETELLING: Desiree (Desiree; Waterloo)

Conquest of the Planet of the Apes, 1972, 85m, ★★1/2/$$, 20th/CBS-Fox, PG/V. In the 1990s America, apes from the future are used as slaves, but they revolt, and the cycle continues. Roddy McDowall, Don Murray, Ricardo Montalban, Natalie Trundy, Hari Rhodes, Severn Darden. w. Paul Dehn, d. J. Lee Thompson.

ACTION: SCI-FI: Fantasy; Primates; Futuristic Films; Political Unrest; Slavery; War Stories

SEQUEL TO: Battle for the Planet of the Apes (Planet of the Apes SERIES)

Conrack, 1974, 106m, ★★★1/2/$$, 20th/Fox, G. An all-black school in South Carolina has a period of adjustment when a white teacher comes into their midst; but the white superintendent doesn't like his inspirational teaching methods. Jon Voight, Paul Winfield, Hume Cronyn, Madge Sinclair, Tina Andrews. w. Irving Ravetch, Harriet Frank Jr., N-adap. Pat Conroy (*The Water Is Wide*), d. Martin Ritt.

DRAMA: MELODRAMA: Teachers; Teachers & Students; Charismatic People; Southerns; Swamp Life; Black Casts; White Among Blacks; Young Men; Race Relations; Rebels; Free Spirits; Hidden Gems (Stand and Deliver; The Prince of Tides; Blackboard Jungle; Dangerous Minds)

Consenting Adult, 1985, 100m, ABC-TV/USA, ★★★/$$$$. A mother (Marlo Thomas) suspects her son may be gay as he discovers this himself. Martin Sheen, Barry Tubb. w. John McGreevey, d. Gilbert Cates.

DRAMA: Coming of Age; **ROMANCE:** Mothers and Sons; Gay Men; Homophobia; Secrets-Consuming; Sexuality; Death-Dealing with; Episodic Stories; Alternative Lifestyles; Female Protagonists (Andre's Mother; An Early Frost; Summer Wishes, Winter Dreams)

Consenting Adults, 1992, 99m, ★★1/2/$$, Hollywood/Hollywood, R/P-V-B&G-S-FFN-MRN. A yuppie couple (Kevin Kline, Mary Elizabeth Mastrantonio) get new neighbors (Kevin Spacey, Rebecca Miller) with swapping and swindling on their minds. w. Matthew Chapman, d. Alan J. Pakula.

SUSPENSE: MURDER MYSTERY: MYSTERY: Psychological Thriller; Framed?; Friends as Enemies; Marriage Drama; Alternative Lifestyles; Swapping Partners; Saving Oneself; Murder of Spouse; Neighbors-Troublesome; Con Artists; Insurance Scams; Disguises; Dual Lives; Suburban Life; Coulda Been Great

Conspirator, 1949, 85m, ★★★/$$, MGM/MGM-UA. A young woman finds out her new husband is actually a communist and has to decide what to do-before the husband kills her to keep her quiet. Robert Taylor, Elizabeth Taylor, Robert Flemyng, Honor Blackman. w. Sally Benson, Gerard Fairlie, d. Victor Saville.

MELODRAMA: SUSPENSE: Dangerous Spouses; Enemy-Sleeping with; Communists; McCarthy Era; Cold War Era; Murder of Spouse; Dangerous Men; Newlyweds; Traitors; Good Premise Unfulfilled; Female Protagonists; Female Screenwriters; Forgotten Films (Keeper of the Flame; Saboteur [1932]; The Stranger)

The Constant Husband, 1955, 88m, ★★★/$, BL-London/NA. A man loses his memory and gradually realizes that he's married to multiple women. Rex Harrison, Kay Kendall, Margaret Leighton, Cecil Parker, Nicole Maurey, George Cole, Raymond Huntley, Michael Hordern. w. Sidney Gilliat, Val Valentine, d. Sidney Gilliat.

COMEDY: FARCE: Marriage Comedy; Amnesia; Bigamy; British Films

(Micki and Maude; Unfaithfully Yours; The Honey Pot)

The Constant Nymph, 1933, 98m, ★★1/2/$$, WB/NA. A musician and composer leaves his wealthy wife for his student, who has a weak heart. Brian Aherne, Victoria Hopper, Lyn Harding, Mary Clare, Jane Baxter. w. Margaret Kennedy, Basil Dean, from their play based on her novel. d. Basil Dean.

The Constant Nymph, 1943, 112m, ★★★/$$, WB/NA. A remake of above with a bigger budget. Charles Boyer, Joan Fontaine (BActress), Alexis Smith, Brenda Marshall, Charles Coburn, Dame May Whitty, Peter Lorre, Joyce Reynolds, Jean Muir, Edward Ciannelli, Montagu Love, Andre Charlot. w. Kathryn Scola, d. Edmund Goulding. Oscars: 1-0.

MELODRAMA: ROMANCE: Romantic Drama; Cheating Men; Marriage on the Rocks; Romance with Teacher; Pianists; Music Composers; Disease Stories; Tearjerkers; Faded Hits; Female Screenwriters; Female Protagonists (Frenchman's Creek; Forever Amber; Suspicion)

Consuming Passions, 1988, 100m, ★★1/2/$, Goldwyn/Goldwyn, R/S-B&G. A confectioner gains profits by adding ground-up human remains to his chocolates. Vanessa Redgrave, Jonathan Pryce, Prunella Scales, Freddie Jones. w. Michael Palin, d. Giles Foster.

COMEDY: Black Comedy; Comedy-Morbid; Cannibalism; Cannibalism-Funny (The Cook, The Thief, His Wife and Her Lover; Sweeney Todd; Fried Green Tomatoes; Eating Raoul; Comfort and Joy)

Continental Divide, 1981, 103m, ★★★/$$, U/MCA-U, PG/S. A big-city newspaper columnist is in love with a biologist studying the bald eagle and agrees reluctantly to follow her into the wilderness, which he can't stand. John Belushi, Blair Brown, Allen Goorwitz, Carlin Glynn. w. Lawrence Kasdan, d. Michael Small.

COMEDY: ROMANCE: Romantic Comedy; Romance-Bickering; Romance-Reluctant; Nature-Back to; Fish out of Water Stories; Hiding Out; Journalists; Battle of the Sexes; Mountain People; City vs. Country; Underrated; Hidden Gems; Forgotten Films; Coulda Been Great; Old-Fashioned Recent Films (The Electric Horseman; The Neighbors) (Ed: May be Belushi's best work)

The Conversation, 1974, 113m, ★★★★/$$, Par/Par, R/P-S. A wiretapper (Gene Hackman) may have heard clues to a murder and has to decide what to do about it. Teri Garr, Frederic Forrest, Cindy Williams. w. d. Francis Ford Coppola (BOScr). BPicture, BSound. Oscars: 3-0.

DRAMA: MYSTERY: MURDER MYSTERY: Murder-Discovering; Psychological Drama; Ethics; Voyeurs; Surveillance; Nervous Breakdowns; Murder-Debate to Reveal Killer; Alienation; Midlife Crisis; Ethics; Decisions-Big; Hidden Gems (Blow Up; Blow Out; Rear Window)

Conversation Piece, 1974, 121m, ★★1/2/$, Ind/NA. When an aging bachelor professor rents his upper-floor apartment to a countess and her nubile daughters, he comes face to face with his latent, unfulfilled desires and impending death. Burt Lancaster, Helmut Berger, Claudia Marsani, Silvana Mangano. w. Luchino Visconti, Suso Cecchi d'Amico, Enrico Mediolі, d. Luchino Visconti.

DRAMA: ROMANCE: Romantic Drama; Character Studies; Elderly Men; Lonely People; Death-Impending; Professors; Italy; Italian Films

Convicts, 1990, 95m, ★★★/VR, FilmDallas/NA, PG/V. An old man and a boy travel the South on the lam around the turn of the century. Robert Duvall, Lukas Haas, Carlin Glynn. w. Horton Foote, d. Peter Masterson.

DRAMA: Friendships-Intergeneration; Friendships-Male; Men and Boys; Fugitives from the Law; Southerns; Hidden Gems (Stars Fell on Henrietta; Breaking In) (Ed: Unreleased but occasionally on cable)

Convoy, 1978, 110m, ★★/$$$, UA/Fox, PG. A truck driver becomes a local hero on his route for defying "smokey" the cop who tries to trap him. Kris Kristofferson, Ali MacGraw, Ernest Borgnine, Burt Young, Madge Sinclair. w. B. W. L. Norton, based on the song by C. W. McCall, d. Sam Peckinpah.

ACTION: Truck Drivers; Road Movies; Fugitives from the Law; Police Comedy; 1970s Camp; Time Capsules (Smokey and the Bandit; High Ballin')

Coogan's Bluff, 1967, 94m, ★★★/$$$, U/MCA-U, PG/V. A killer escapes prison in New York and ends up in Arizona, where he's escorted back by a local sheriff who finds life in the big city interesting. Clint Eastwood, Lee J. Cobb, Susan Clark, Don Stroud, Tisha Sterling, Betty Field, Tom Tully. w. Herman Miller, Dean Riesner, Howard Rodman, d. Don Siegel.

ACTION: Action Drama; Crime Drama; Police Stories; Fish out of Water Stories; Trail of a Killer; Fugitives from the Law; Southwestern Life; New York Life (The Cowboy Way; Crocodile Dundee) (Ed: Basis for McCloud TV series)

The Cook, the Thief, His Wife, and Her Lover, 1989, 124m, ★★1/2/$$$, Miramax/Miramax, R/P-S-B&G-FN-MN. A brutish lout who runs a restaurant is cheated on by his wife in another room and he exacts a violent and grim revenge. Very stylized, with each room of the restaurant emphasizing a different color; as the characters move from one realm to another, the color of their clothes changes as well. Richard Bohringer, Helen Mirren, Michael Gambon, Alan Howard, Tim Roth, Ciaran Hinds, Gary Olsen, Ewan Stewart, Ron Cook, Liz Smith. w. d. Peter Greenaway.

COMEDY DRAMA: Black Comedy; Comedy-Morbid; Cannibalism; Double Crossings; Cheating Men; Cheating Women; Romance-Triangles; Alternative Lifestyles; British Films; Sleeper Hits; Writer-Directors; Art Films (Consuming Passions; Eating Raoul; Sweeney Todd; A Zed and Two Noughts; Drowning by Numbers; The Comfort of Strangers)

Cookie, 1989, 93m, ★★1/2/$, Lorimar-WB/WB, PG-13/P-S. "Like father, like daughter" is the rule, even when it comes to gangsters as kooky Cookie comes of age. Peter Falk, Dianne Wiest, Emily Lloyd, Michael V. Gazzo, Brenda Vaccaro, Adrian Pasdar, Jerry Lewis, Ricki Lake. w. Nora Ephron, Alice Arlen, d. Susan Seidelman.

COMEDY: COMEDY DRAMA: Mob Stories; Mob Comedy; Mob Girls; Good Premise; Unfulfilled; Free Spirits; Feisty Females; Old-Fashioned Recent Films; Female Screenwriters; Female Directors; Female Protagonists (My Blue Heaven [1990]; Wish You Were Here)

Cool Hand Luke, 1967, 126m, ★★★1/2/$$$$, WB/WB, R/P-V-S. A convict serving a two-year sentence in a labor camp becomes a hero by bucking authority, but his planned escape may not go as

planned. Paul Newman (BActor), George Kennedy (**BSActor**), Jo Van Fleet, J. D. Cannon, Lou Antonio, Robert Drivas, Strother Martin, Clifton James. w. Donn Pearce, Frank R. Pierson, N-adap. Donn Pearce, d. Stuart Rosenberg. Oscars: 2-1.
DRAMA: Prison Drama; Rebels; Southerns; Prison Escapes; Social Drama; Faded Hits; Young Men; Ensemble Films; Ensembles-Male; Torture
(Chattahoochee; The Shawshank Redemption; Jackson County Jail; Brubaker)
(Ed: Famous for the line, "What we have here is a failure to communicate")
The Cool Ones, 1967, 96m, ★★¹/₂/$, WB/WB. A pop singer comes out of semi-retirement to stage a comeback. Roddy McDowall, Debbie Watson, Robert Coote, Phil Harris, Nita Talbot. w. Joyce Geller, d. Gene Nelson.
COMEDY: Mod Era; 1960s; Time Capsules; Rock Stars; Singers; Teenagers; Teen Idols; Comebacks; Female Screenwriters
(Lord Love a Duck; The Idol)
Cool Runnings, 1993, 98m, ★★★/$$$$, Touchstone/Touchstone, PG. Several black Jamaicans and their overweight, jolly American coach (John Candy) try to make it into the 1988 winter Olympics as a bobsled team, but much calamity besets their struggle. John Candy, Leon, Doug E. Doug, Marco Branbilla, Malik Yoba. w. Tommy Swerdlow, Lynn Seifert, Michael Goldberg, d. Jon Turteltaub.
COMEDY: True Stories; Fish out of Water Stories; Comedy of Errors; Underdog Stories; Black Casts; Black Men; White Among Blacks; Coaches; Caribbean; Snow Settings; Olympics; Sleeper Hits
Cool World, 1992, 102m, ★★¹/₂/$$, Par/Par, PG-13/P-S. A cartoonist creates an alternate reality called Cool World and he and his characters, including cartoon gangsters and a gorgeous blond bombshell, flit in and out of reality. Kim Basinger, Gabriel Byrne, Brad Pitt, Michele Abrams, Deirdre O'Connell, Janni Brenn-Lowen. w. Michael Grais, Mark Victor, d. Ralph Bakhi.
SCI-FI: Fantasy; Cartoons; Animation-Partial; Bimbos; Sexy Women; Writers; Artists; Virtual Reality; Mob Comedy; Mob Girls; Coulda Been Good; Curiosities; Flops-Major
(Heavy Metal; Fritz the Cat; Who Framed Roger Rabbit)

Cooperstown, 1993, 100m, ★★¹/₂/$$, Turner/Turner, PG. A former baseball player is haunted by a play he made that lost the World Series chances for his team and his chance at the hall of fame in Cooperstown-and blames an old pal who just died. The pal's ghost returns to haunt him, but also tempts him to look back at all the old memories. Alan Arkin, Graham Greene, Hope Lange, Josh Charles, Ed Begley Jr., Ann Wedgeworth, Paul Dooley, Joanna Miles, Charles Haid. w. Lee Blessing, d. Haid.
MELODRAMA: DRAMA: Past-haunted by the; Friendships-Male; Baseball; One Last Time; Ghosts; Memories; Actor Directors; TV Movies
(Kiss Me Goodbye; Field of Dreams)
Cop, 1987, 110m, ★★¹/₂/$, Atlantic/Atlantic, R/EP-EV-S-FN-B&G. A cop's obsessive search for a serial killer destroys his personal life, causing his wife to leave him. James Woods, Lesley Ann Warren, Charles Durning, Charles Haid, Raymond J. Barry, Randi Brooks, Steven Lambert, Christopher Wynne, Jan McGill. w. d. James B. Harris, N-adap. James Ellroy (*Blood on the Moon*).
ACTION: Crime Drama; Police Stories; Trail of a Killer; Serial Killers; Obsessions; Malicious Menaces; Nervous Breakdowns; Corruption; Police Corruption; Police Brutality
(The Bad Lieutenant; Dead Certain; Best Seller)
Cop and a Half, 1993, 87m, ★¹/₂/$, U/MCA-U, PG. After a black boy witnesses a murder and the cops need him to finger the killer, the kid blackmails the cops into letting him join the force for a while before he'll fess up. Burt Reynolds, Norman Golden, Ray Sharkey, Ruby Dee, Holland Taylor. w. Arne Olsen, d. Henry Winkler.
COMEDY: Black Among Whites; Boys; Men and Boys; Police Comedy; Witness to Murder; Blackmail; Murder-Debate to Reveal Killer; Actor Directors
COMIC FLIPSIDE OF: Witness
(Rent-a-Cop; The Lemon Drop Kid)
Cop au Vin, 1984, 110m, ★★★/$, Ind/NA. A group of murders in the French provinces incites an investigation that exposes the pettiness of the locals as well as the murder plot. Jean Poiret, Stephane Audran, Michel Bouquet, Jean Topart, Lucas Blevaux, Pauline Lafont,

Caroline Cellier. w. Dominique Roulet, Claude Chabrol, N-adap. Dominique Roulet (*Un Mort En Trop*), d. Claude Chabrol.
DRAMA: Crime Drama; **MYSTERY: MURDER: MURDER MYSTERY:** Serial Killers; Detective Stories; Detectives-Police; French Films
(Choice of Arms; Scene of the Crime; Flesh of the Orchid)
Copacabana, 1947, 91m, ★★¹/₂/$$, UA/NA. An agent, in a pinch, has to make one act into two. He gets into trouble when "both" acts are booked on the same night. Groucho Marx, Carmen Miranda, Steve Cochran, Gloria Jean, Andy Russell. w. Laslo Vadnay, Allen Boretz, Howard Harris, d. Alfred E. Green.
COMEDY: Nightclubs; Mix-Ups; Misunderstandings; Putting on a Show; **FARCE:** Forgotten Films; Marx Brothers
Cops and Robbersons, 1994, 93m, ★★★/$, Tri/Col-Tri, PG-13/P-S-MN. The boring lives of a suburban family headed by a man obsessed with cop shows are jump-started when the cops set up a stakeout and have the run of their house to spy on a mobster living incognito next door, but chaos and slapstick is all they initially find. Chevy Chase, Jack Palance, Dianne Wiest, Robert Davis. w. Bernie Somers, d. Michael Ritchie.
COMEDY: Comedy-Slapstick; Comedy-Light; Police Comedy; Suburban Life; Family Comedy; Police vs. Mob; Neighbors-Troublesome; Underrated; Coulda Been Great
(Stakeout; Another Stakeout)
(Ed: It has some major problems, but if it had been French, the critics would have loved it)
Coquette, 1929, 75m, ★★★/$$$$, UA/MGM-UA. A beautiful Southern belle flirts with all the men in town. Mary Pickford (**BActress**), Johnny Mack Brown, Matt Moore, William Janney. w. John Grey, Allen McNeil, Sam Taylor, P-adap. George Abbott, Anne Preston, d. Sam Taylor. Oscars: 1-1.
COMEDY: ROMANCE: Romantic Comedy; Free Spirits; Southerns; Faded Hits
The Corn Is Green, 1945, 118m, ★★★/$$, WB/MGM-UA. In the late 1800s an idealistic Welsh woman starts a school in a mining community and has her first success when one of her pupils

gets a scholarship to Oxford. Bette Davis, John Dall, Nigel Bruce, Joan Lorring, Rhys Williams, Rosalind Ivan, Mildred Dunnock, Arthur Shields. w. Casey Robinson, Frank Cavett, P-adap. *(Emlyn Williams)*, d. Irving Rapper.

The Corn Is Green, 1979, 100m, ★★★¹/₂/$$$$, CBS/NA. More realistic, sumptuous updating with Hepburn in command on a bicycle. Katharine Hepburn (BActress, Emmy nomination). d. Anthony Harvey.

DRAMA: Character Studies; Teachers; Teachers and Students; Mining Towns; England; Hidden Gems; Wales
(The Prime of Miss Jean Brodie; Madame Sousatzka)

Cornered, 1945, 102m, ★★★/$$, RKO/Turner. A Quebequois pilot in World War II searches for the traitor who got his wife killed. Dick Powell, Micheline Cheirel, Walter Slezak, Morris Carnovsky. w. John Paxton, John Wexley, d. Edward Dmytryk.

DRAMA: Avenging Death of Someone; World War II Stories; Pilots-Military; Murder of Spouse; Trail of a Killer; Manhunts; Traitors; Forgotten Films; Film Noir
(Murder, My Sweet; Death Wish)

Corrina, Corrina, 1994, 113m, ★★★/$$, New Line/New Line, PG. An intelligent black woman takes a job as a housekeeper to a white man and his motherless daughter, resulting in romance and an interesting family, since it's set in the 50s. Whoopi Goldberg, Ray Liotta, Tina Majorino, Don Ameche, Anita Baker. w. d. Jessie Nelson.

COMEDY DRAMA: ROMANCE: Family Comedy; Romance-Interracial; Romance with Servant; Widowers; Girls; Fathers & Daughters; Fathers Alone; Suburban Life; 1950s; Writer-Directors; Black Women; Female Protagonists
(Clara's Heart; For Love of Ivy; The Long Walk Home; Houseboat)

The Corsican Brothers, 1942, 111m, ★★★/$$$, UA/Live. Siamese twins are successfully separated but remain psychologically inseparable as they have swashbuckling adventures together. Douglas Fairbanks Jr., Akim Tamiroff, Ruth Warrick, J. Carrol Naish, H. B. Warner, Henry Wilcoxon. w. George Bruce, Howard Estabrook, d. Gregory Ratoff.

ADVENTURE: ACTION: Action Comedy; Swashbucklers; Costume Drama; Twins;

Brothers; Classic Literary Adaptations; Faded Hits

SEQUEL: Bandits of Corsica; **REMAKES:** 1984 TV versions, Cheech and Chong as The Corsican Brothers.

Corvette Summer, 1979, 104m, ★★★/$$, MGM/MGM-UA, PG/S. A student in L.A. has his Corvette stolen and searches for it. Mark Hamill, Annie Potts, Eugene Roche, Kim Milford, Richard McKenzie. w. Hal Barwood, Matthew Robbins, d. Matthew Robbins.

COMEDY DRAMA: Teenagers; Teenage Movies; **ROMANCE:** Romantic Comedy; 1970s; Thieves
(California Dreaming; Flatbed Annie and Sweetiepie)

The Cotton Club, 1984, 127m, ★★¹/₂/$$, Orion/Orion, R/P-V-S. From the famous Harlem nightclub, a trumpeter with the mafia rises to movie stardom as a mob war ensues. Richard Gere, Diane Lane, Gregory Hines, Fred Gwynne, Bob Hoskins, Lonette McKee, Nicolas Cage. w. Francis Ford Coppola, William Kennedy, Mario Puzo, d. Coppola.

DRAMA: MELODRAMA ROMANCE: Romantic Drama; **MUSICALS:** Music Movies; Black Men; Black Women; Nightclubs; Ensemble Films; Musicians; Fame-Rise to; Mob Stories; Mob Wars; Mob Girls; Coulda Been Great; Flops-Major; Production Design-Outstanding
(Public Eye; The Godfather SERIES)
(Ed: Also famous for the "Cotton Club Murder" case associated with the production, which at one time implicated producer Robert Evans, who went broke after this flopped)

Cotton Comes to Harlem, 1970, 97m, ★★★/$$$, UA/Fox, R/P-S. When a black preacher starts a scam to get people to pay to go back to Africa, two police detectives find themselves in the strange world of Harlem after him. Godfrey Cambridge, Raymond St. Jacques, Calvin Lockhart, Redd Foxx. N-adap. Chester Himes, d. Ossie Davis.

COMEDY: ACTION: Action Comedy; **MYSTERY:** Comic Mystery; Police Stories; Police Comedy; Black Men; Black and White Together; Buddy Cops; Buddy Films; Hidden Gems; Faded Hits; Preachers; Con Artists; Black Directors; Actor Directors

SEQUEL: Come Back Charleston Blue

The Couch Trip, 1988, 98m, ★★/$$, Orion/Orion, PG-13/P-S. A mental

patient escapes and pretends to be radio psychologist who's actually on vacation, but his advice soon becomes suspect. Dan Aykroyd, Walter Matthau, Charles Grodin, Donna Dixon, Mary Gross, Arye Gross, David Clennon. w. Will Alda, Steven Kampmann, d. Michael Ritchie.

COMEDY: Identities-Assumed; Radio Life; Psychologists; Mental Illness; Impostors; Good Premise Unfulfilled
(Three on a Couch; Straight Talk)

Countdown, 1968, 102m, ★★¹/₂/$, WB/WB. Early Robert Altman story about the early astronauts and the toll the space program took on them psychologically, with the men themselves and their families. James Caan, Robert Duvall, Michael Murphy, Ted Knight, Joanna Moore, Robert Altman. d. Robert Altman.

DRAMA: Psychological Drama; Family Drama; Astronauts; Nervous Breakdowns; Forgotten Films; Curiosities
(The Right Stuff; Apollo 13; Space)
(Ed: Much more introspective than *Apollo 13*, without the gloss)

The Count of Monte Cristo, 1934, 114m, ★★★¹/₂/$$$, UA/Media. Robert Donat, Louis Calhern, Sidney Blackmer. d. Rowland Lee.

The Count of Monte Cristo, 1974, 104m, ★★★/$$$, CBS/Live, V. Richard Chamberlain, Kate Nelligan, Donald Pleasence, Trevor Howard, Tony Curtis, Louis Jourdan. d. David Greene.
The classic story where the wrongly accused count searches for and finds a great treasure told about to him by a prison inmate which he uses to exact revenge against the royals who set him up.

ADVENTURE: Prison Drama; Escape Drama; Revenge; Royalty; Framed?; Accused Unjustly; Finding the Loot; Treasure Hunts; 1700s; Evil Men

Count Yorga, Vampire, 1970, 90m, ★★¹/₂/$$, AIP/NA. A vampire is at work in LA, sucking up to the Hollywood set. Robert Quarry, Roger Perry, Micahel Murphy. d. Bob Kelljan.

HORROR: Vampires; Revisionist Films; Los Angeles; 1970s
(Count Dracula; A.D. 1972; Get Shorty)

A Countess from Hong Kong, 1967, 120m, ★★/$, UA/NA. A supposed countess stows away in the room of a diplomat on a ship and romance begins, sort of.

Sophia Loren, Marlon Brando, Charlie Chaplin. w. d. Chaplin.

COMEDY: ROMANCE: Romantic Comedy; Ships; Diplomats; Coulda Been Great; Flops-Major; Royalty; Impostors; Writer-Directors
(Limelight; City Lights; Monsieur Verdoux)

Country, 1984, 109m, ★★★/$$,
Touchstone/Touchstone, PG. A strong farm woman tries to hold her family together after bankruptcy and a tornado stare them down. Jessica Lange (BActress), Sam Shepard, Wilford Brimley, Matt Clark. w. Bill Witliff, d. Richard Pearce. Oscars: 1-0.

DRAMA: MELODRAMA: Family Drama; Social Drama; Farm Life; Mortgage Drama; Save the Farm; Ordinary People Stories; Feisty Females; Mothers-Struggling; Tornadoes; Female Protagonists; Quiet Little Films
(The River; Places in the Heart; Miles from Home; Tender Mercies; Friendly Fire)
(Ed: Nice, quiet, and naturalistic)

The Country Girl, 1954, 104m,
★★★1/2/$$$, Par/Par. An alcoholic actor tries to make a comeback with his stern wife pushing him along, but it may not be meant to be. Bing Crosby (BActor), Grace Kelly (**BActress**), William Holden, Gene Reynolds. w. d. George Seaton (BDirector, BAScr), P-adap. Clifford Odets. BPicture, BB&WCin, BB&WArt. Oscars: 7-1.

DRAMA: Alcoholics; Actors Comebacks; Woman Behind the Man; Stern Women; Theater Life; Behind the Scenes; Character Studies; Marriage Drama; Stagelike Films

REMAKE: 1982 version with Faye Dunaway, TV stage taping
(Leaving Las Vegas; Harriet Craig; Career)

Country Life, 1995, 107m, ★★★/$,
Miramax/Miramax, PG-13/S-P. In this veiled, revisionist remake of *Uncle Vanya* (the second for the year), a man and his niece run a sheep farm in Australia when the niece's father pops up with a new wife and announces he wants to sell his interest in the farm. A family crisis ensues and loyalties are put to the test, even as disloyalties are exposed. Sam Neill, Greta Scacchi, John Hargreaves, Kerry Fox, Michael Blakemore, Googie Withers, Maurie Fields, Robyn Cruze, Ron Blanchard. w. d. Michael Blakemore.

DRAMA: Family Drama; Fathers & Daughters; Children-Long Lost; Power Struggles; Revisionist Films; Australia; Save the Farm
(Vanya on 42nd Street; The Three Sisters; The Cherry Orchard)

Coup de Torchon, 1981, 128m,
★★★/$$, UAC/Fox, R. A sheriff in an African French colonial town has many problems and may just go to extremes to get rid of them. Philip Noiret, Isabelle Huppert, Guy Marchand, Stephane Audran. w.d. Bertrand Tavernier, N-adap. Jim Thompson, *Pop. 1280*. BFLFilm. Oscars: 1-0.

SUSPENSE: Crime Drama; Police Stories; Police Corruption; Small-Town Life; Africa; Imperialist Problems; French Films; Jim Thompson-esque; **MURDER:** Ethics; Pimps
(After Dark My Sweet; White Mischief)

Coupe de Ville, 1990, 97m, ★★1/2/$$,
U/MCA-U, PG-13/P-S. Three Joes head off in a Caddy convertible to Florida and so on . . . Patrick Dempsey, Daniel Stern, Arye Gross, Joe Bologna, Alan Arkin, Annabeth Gish. w. Mike Binder, d. Joe Roth.

MELODRAMA: COMEDY DRAMA: Road Movies; Road Movies-Guys in Convertibles; Friendships-Male; Ensembles-Male
(Breaking the Rules; Calendar Girl; Fandango)
(Ed: A good supporting cast can't save this from looking and sound like every other dopey film of its kind)

The Court Jester, 1955, 101m, ★★★1/2/$$$, Par/Par. A court jester and some rebels tell the king of their kingdom to get off the throne. Danny Kaye, Glynis Johns, Basil Rathbone, Angela Lansbury, Mildred Natwick, John Carradine. w. d. Norman Panama.

MUSICALS: COMEDY: Musical Comedy; Swashbucklers; Kings; Kingdoms; Comedians; Fools-Bumbling; Faded Hits; Hidden Gems; Writer-Directors
(Wonder Man; A Connecticut Yankee in King Arthur's Court)

The Court Martial of Jackie Robinson, 1990, 94m, ★★★/$$,
Turner/Turner. The story of the great black athlete's refusal to take a back seat on a bus while in the army which led to an arrest and trial. Andrew Braugher, Ruby Dee, Daniel Stern, Stan Shaw, Paul Dooley, Bruce Dern. d. Larry Pearce.

DRAMA: Biographies; True Stories; Black Men; Race Relations; Southerns; Soldiers; Black Soldiers; Courtroom Drama; Rebels; Oppression; Military Stories
(The Long Walk Home; The Medgar Evers Story; The Ernest Green Story)

Courtship, 1987, 84m, ★★★1/2/$,
PBS/WB. A well-to-do Texas small-town girl causes a bit of scandal by eloping with a traveling salesman. Hallie Foote, William Converse-Roberts, Amanda Plummer, Rochelle Oliver. w. P-adap. Horton Foote, d. Howard Cummings.

MELODRAMA: DRAMA: Small-town Life; Texas; Southerns; Ordinary People Stories; Marriage-Elopement; Dating Scene; **ROMANCE:** Romantic Comedy; Scandals; Hidden Gems; TV Movies
(St. Valentine's Day; 1918; The Trip to Bountiful)

The Courtship of Eddie's Father,
1962, 117m, ★★★/$$$, MGM/MGM-UA. A widower with a Chinese maid and small son tries to find a new wife, but he has to pass the tests of his son. Glenn Ford, Ron Howard, Shirley Jones, Stella Stevens Dina Merrill, Jerry Van Dyke. w. John Gay, N-adap. Mark Toby, d. Vincente Minnelli.

COMEDY: COMEDY DRAMA:
ROMANCE: Romantic Comedy; Family Comedy; Fathers & Sons; Boys; Servants; Chinese People; Widowers; Starting Over; Dating Scene
(A Hole in the Head; Bachelor Father TV SERIES; Sleepless in Seattle)
(Ed: Spawned the even more successful TV series with Bill Bixby)

Cousin, Cousine, 1976, 95m,
★★★1/2/$$$, Gaumont-Northal/Fox, R/P-S-FN-MRN. Distant cousins, a man and a woman, fall in love over a period of time meeting at family functions from weddings to funerals-despite the fact they're cheating. Marie Christine Barrault (BActress), Victor Larous, Marie France Pisier. w. Jean Charles Tachella, Danielle Thompson (BOScr), d. Tachella. BFLFilm. Oscars: 3-0.

COMEDY DRAMA: ROMANCE:
Romantic Drama; Romantic Comedy; Family Comedy; Romance with Relative; Cheating Men; Cheating Women; Romance-Forbidden; Cousins; French Films; Sleeper Hits; Hidden Gems; Female Screenwriters; Female Protagonists
REMAKE: Cousins
(Four Weddings and a Funeral)

Cousins, 1989, 113m, ★★★/$$, Par/Par, PG-13/S-P. A remake of the French version with a more melodramatic and lush Hollywood feel and a shift of focus in favor of the male lead, though still with the European Rossellini for effect. Isabella Rossellini, Ted Danson, Sean Young, William Petersen. w. Stephen Metcalfe, d. Joel Schumacher.
COMEDY DRAMA: MELODRAMA: ROMANCE: Romantic Drama; Romantic Comedy; Family Comedy; Romance with Relative; Cheating Men; Cheating Women; Romance-Forbidden; Cousins; French Films; Sleeper Hits; Hidden Gems; Foreign Film Remakes
REMAKE OF: Cousine, Cousin.

Cover Girl, 1944, 107m, ★★★/$$$$, Col/RCA-Col. Sultry Hayworth has to decide whether to become a big-time model or follow romance with a club owner. The question is ignored as to why she can't have both. Rita Hayworth, Gene Kelly, Phil Silvers. d. Charles Vidor. BCCin, BCArt, BSound, **BMScore,** BOSong (Long Ago and Far Away). Oscars: 5-1.
MUSICALS: MELODRAMA: ROMANCE: Musical Romance; Models; Decisions-Big; Dance Movies; Sexy Women; Hidden Gems
(Gilda; Funny Face)

The Cowboy and the Lady, 1938, 91m, ★★★/$$$, Goldwyn/Goldwyn. While her father is running for President, a madcap heiress finds a cowboy at a rodeo to amuse her and soon marry her, but Daddy doesn't approve. Gary Cooper, Merle Oberon, Walter Brennan, Fuzzy Knight. d. H.C. Potter. **BSound,** BOScore, BOSong. Oscars: 3-1.
COMEDY: ROMANCE: Romantic Comedy; Screwball Comedy; Romance-Class Conflicts; Lover Family Dislikes; Presidents; Political Campaigns; Heiresses-Madcap; Hidden Gems
(It Happened One Night; That Uncertain Feeling; The Prizefighter and the Lady; The Main Event; Never a Dull Moment [1950])

The Cowboys, 1972, 128m, ★★1/2/$$$, WB/WB, G. A crusty cattle rancher is forced into using a group of juvenile delinquents on a massive cattle drive, but before they rope in the cows, he has to rope them in. John Wayne, Roscoe Lee Browne, A. Martinez, Bruce Dern, Slim Picken, Colleen Dewhurst, Robert

Carradine. w. Harriet Frank, Irving Ravetch, d. Mark Rydell.
WESTERNS: Western Comedy; Men and Boys; Cattle Ranchers; Juvenile Delinquents; Female Screenwriters
(Bless the Beasts and the Children; Trouble Along the Way; McClintock!; Three Godfathers)

The Cowboy Way, 1994, 128m, ★★/$$, WB/WB, PG-13/P-S-MRN. Two cowpokes go to the Big Apple to avenge a friend's death and team up with a black New York cop who wants to be a cowboy like they supposedly are. The result is a Crocodile Dundee-fish-out-of-water retread. Woody Harrelson, Kiefer Sutherland, Dylan McDermott, Ernie Hudson, Marg Helgenberger. w. Bill Witliff, Rob Thompson, d. Gregg Champion.
COMEDY: Fish out of Water Stories; Western Comedy; Avenging Death of Someone; City vs. Country; New York Life; Flops-Major
(Harley Davidson and the Marlboro Man; Crocodile Dundee; Coogan's Bluff; White Men Can't Jump)

Crackers, 1984, 92m, ★★/$, U/MCA-U, PG/P-S. Several bumbling safecracking thieves try a heist, but bumble it up. Robert Duvall, Sean Penn, Jack Warden, Christine Baranski, Wallace Shawn. d. Louis Malle.
COMEDY: COMEDY DRAMA: Heist Stories; Criminals-Stupid; Ensemble Films; Coulda Been Good; Flops-Major; Foreign Film Remakes; Forgotten Films
REMAKE OF: Big Deal on Madonna Street
(Disorganized Crime; Trouble in Paradise; The Dion Brothers; Quick Change)

Cracking Up, 1995, 90m, ★★★/$, Ind/NA, R/S-P. A crack-using hipster in the East Village of New York City stops at nothing in his ruthless pursuit of women, a showbiz career, and . . . crack. Matt Mitler, Carolyn McDermott, Sherry Anderson, John Augustine. w. Matt Mitler, Theodore P. Lorusso, d. Matt Mitler
DRAMA: Art Films; SATIRE: Character Studies; Drugs-Addictions; Actors New York Life; Losing it All; Playboys; Actor Directors; Writer-Directors

The Crash of Silence (Mandy), 1952, 93m, ★★★/$$, Ealing/NA. The story of a deaf girl and how she gets treatment at a

school in England. Jack Hawkins, Mandy Miller, Terence Morgan, Phillis Calvert. w. Nigel Balchin, Jack Whittingham, N-adap. Hilda Lewis, *This Day Is Ours*, d. Alexander Mackendrick.
DRAMA: MELODRAMA: Deaf People; Docudrama; Documentary Style; Girlhood; Child Protagonists; British Films
(The Miracle Worker; A Child Is Waiting; Baxter! [1972])

Crazy People, 1987, 109m, 91m, ★★/$$, Par/Par, PG-13/S-P. An advertising executive cracks up when he becomes honest and wants to level with the consumers. But his bosses think he's ready for the asylum. Dudley Moore, Paul Reiser, Daryl Hannah, Mercedes Ruehl. w. Mitch Markowitz, d. Tony Bill.
COMEDY: Advertising World; Asylums; Nervous Breakdowns; Liars; Ethics; Mental Illness; Psychologists; Turning the Tables; Good Premise Unfulfilled
(How to Get Ahead in Advertising; The Dream Team; Putney Swope; The Agency)
(Ed: Reminds one of a British Ealing comedy from the 50s, but only in the premise, because after that, except for some chuckles with the ads, it's all downhill. The use of "crazy" in the title set off protests by mental health advocates)

The Creature from the Black Lagoon, 1954, 79m, ★★★/$$$, U/MCA-U. Scientists investigating life on the Amazon find some life that likes to take others back with it to the deep. Richard Carlson, Julie Adams, Richard Denning. w. Arthur Rosa, d. Jack Arnold.
HORROR: Monsters-Animal; 3-D Movies; Amazon River; Rogue Plots; Murders-One by One; Sleeper Hits

Creepshow, 1982, 120m, ★★1/2/$$$, Laurel-WB/WB, PG/P-V-B&G. Several tales from Stephen King, among others, involving the usually creepy tales of death and insanity, and in particular, some roaches. Hal Holbrook, Adrienne Barbeau, Viveca Lindfors, E.G. Marshall, Leslie Nielsen. w. Stephen King, d. George Romero.

Creepshow 2, 1987, 89m, ★★/$, Laurel-New World/New World, R/EV-B&G. More of the same, based upon Stephen King short stories. w. George Romero, d. Michael Gornick.
HORROR: Multiple Stories; Horror Comedy; Black Comedy; Monsters-

Human; Buried Alive; Insects; Stephen King
(Tales from the Darkside: The Movie; Trilogy in Terror; Tales from the Hood)

Cries and Whispers, 1973, 91m, ★★★1/2/$$$, Embassy/Embassy, WB. The inner stories of three sisters, one of whom is dying while the others care for her, and their maid. Soon they all feel as though they are dying. Liv Ullman, Harriet Andersson, Ingrid Thulin, Kary Sylway. w.d. Ingmar Bergman (BDirector, BOScr). BPicture, **BCin**, BCostume. Oscars: 5-1.
DRAMA: Art Films; Lonely People; Death-Dealing with; Character Studies; Alienation; Sisters; Swedish Films; Writer-Directors; Hidden Gems
(Persona; Autumn Sonata; Face to Face)

Crime and Punishment, 1935, 88m, ★★★/$$, Col/Col. A man in Russia who believes he's committed the perfect murder and robbery is soon whittled down by his own guilty conscience. Peter Lorre, Edward Arnold, Miriam Marsh. S.K. Lauren, Joseph Anthony, d. Joseph Von Sternberg.

Crime and Punishment, 1935, 110m, ★★★1/2/$, Ind/Facets. The much more faithful and acclaimed French version of the classic. Harry Baur, Pierre Blacher. w. Marcel Ayme, Chenal, Christian Stengel, d. Chenal.
French Films
DRAMA: MURDER: Thieves; Guilty Conscience; Police Stories; Cat and Mouse Stories; Psychological Drama; Russia
(Crimes and Misdemeanors)

Crimes and Misdemeanors, 1989, 104m, ★★★1/2/$$$, Orion/Orion, PG-13/P. A doctor (Martin Landau, BSActor) who needs to get rid of his mistress (Anjelica Huston) is paralleled with a man (Woody Allen) who's considering cheating on his wife. Mia Farrow, Alan Alda, w.d. Woody Allen (BOScr). Oscars: 2-0.
DRAMA: Character Studies; **COMEDY DRAMA: MURDER:** Redemption; Infidelity; Ethics; Parallel Stories; Murder-Debate to Confess; Murder of Lover/Spouse; Guilty Conscience; Hitmen; Doctors; Mistresses; Writer-Directors
(Crime and Punishment; Another Woman)

Crimes of Passion, 1984, 102m, ★★★/$$, New World/New World, X-R/ES-EP-V-FFN-MN, A hooker by night/fashion designer by day (Kathleen

Turner, NYFC: BActress) meets up with a suburban husband (John Laughlin) and a priest (Anthony Perkins) wanting to change her but falling apart themselves. Annie Potts. w. Barry Sandler. d. Ken Russell
DRAMA: COMEDY DRAMA: Black Comedy; **SATIRE:** Prostitutes-Low Class; Dual Lives; Multiple Personalities; Multiple Performances; Disguises; Suburban Life; Missionaries
(Miss Sadie Thompson; Rain; Nights of Cabria; Body Heat)

Crimes of the Heart, 1986, 114m, ★★★★/$$$, DEG/Lorimar-WB, PG/S. Three sisters (Diane Keaton, Jessica Lange, Sissy Spacek [BActress]) are reunited by the illness of their grandfather and one's attempted murder of her husband, but one, in particular, can't face up to it all. Tess Harper (BSActress). w. adap. Beth Henley (BAScr), d. Bruce Beresford. Oscars: 3-0.
COMEDY DRAMA: Tragi-Comedy; Comedy-Morbid; Black Comedy; Ensemble Films; Ensembles-Female; Sisters; Suicidal Tendencies; Southerns; Female Protagonists; British Directors of Southerns; Mississippi; Pulitzer Prize Adaptations; Jessica Lange Goes Southern; Underrated; Hidden Gems
(Miss Firecracker; Steel Magnolias; Rich in Love; The End; Better Off Dead)
(Ed: A gem of a movie which has some laugh-out-loud lines, including a situation with a cat under a sheet and a suicide attempt)

Criminal Law, 1989, 110m, ★★★/$$, Hemdale/Hemdale, R/P-S-V. A lawyer (Gary Oldman) is defending a possible murderer (Kevin Bacon) who taunts him with the idea he may be guilty. Tess Harper. w. Mark Kasdan, d. Martin Campbell.
SUSPENSE: MURDER MYSTERY: MYSTERY: Psychological Thriller; Mystery-Howdunit; Courtroom Drama; Murder-Debate to Reveal Killer; Abortion Dilemmas; Serial Killers; Psycho Killers; Kill the Beast; Rape/Rapists; Lawyers; Lawyers as Detectives; Lawyer vs. Client; Coulda Been Great
(Jagged Edge; Primal Fear; Guilty as Sin)
(Ed: A bit over the top, but works if you buy the motive)

Criss Cross, 1947, 98m, ★★★/$$, U/MCA-U. An armored-car guard gets drawn into a heist by his ex, but gets in

far deeper than expected. Burt Lancaster, Yvonne deCarlo, Tony Curtis. w. Daniel Fuchs, d. Robert Siodmak.
Crime Drama; **SUSPENSE:** Heist Stories; Bank Robberies; Double Crossings; Blackmail; Film Noir; Hidden Gems
(The Killers; The Killing; Gun Crazy; They Live By Night; Thieves Like Us; Body Heat; Double Indemnity)

Criss Cross, 1992, 100m, ★★★/$, WB/WB, PG/S-P. A single mother (Goldie Hawn) strips to make ends meet in 1969 Key West, but her son, who's her main reason for making the extra money, doesn't approve. James Gammon, David Arnott, Keith Carradine, Arliss Howard, Steve Buscemi. w. N-adap. Scott Sommer, d. Chris Menges.
DRAMA: MELODRAMA: Slice of Life Stories; Ordinary People Stories; Mothers-Struggling; Strippers; Mothers & Sons; 1960s; Vietnam Era; Vietnam Vets; Narrated Films; Florida Keys; Coulda Been Great; Time Capsules
(Alice Doesn't Live Here Anymore; Men Don't Leave; The Sugarland Express; A World Apart)
(Ed: Not much entertainment value or insight, but interesting slice of life)

Critical Condition, 1986, 100m, ★★/$$, Par/Par, PG-13/P-S. During a blackout a man winds up filling the shoes of a doctor in a hospital but doesn't have a clue as to what he's doing. Richard Pryor, Joe Mantegna, Rachel Ticotin, Ruben Blades. d. Michael Apted.
COMEDY: Impostors; Identities-Assumed; Blackouts; Hospitals; Doctors; Black Men
(The Great Impostor; Moving)
(Ed: Particularly embarassing, considering the director)

Crocodile Dundee, 1986, 102m, ★★★1/2/$$$$$, Par/Par, PG/P. A wild-west free spirit (Paul Hogan) from down under is brought to New York by a reporter and amid his misadventures in the city as a noble savage, he falls in love. w. Paul Hogan, Ken Shadie (BOScr), d. Peter Faiman. Oscars: 1-0.
COMEDY: ADVENTURE: Comic Adventure; Fish out of Water Stories; **ROMANCE:** Romantic Comedy; Saving Someone; Protecting Someone; Australia; Australian Films; New York Life; Sleeper Hits; Blockbusters
SEQUEL: Crocodile Dundee 2 (1988)
(Tarzan's New York Adventure; Moscow

on the Hudson; The Cowboy Way; Coogan's Bluff)

Cromwell, 1970, 139m, ★★★/$$, Col/Col, PG. The battle between King Charles and Oliver Cromwell, who sought to free the serfs of England in the British Civil War. Richard Harris, Alec Guinness, Robert Morley, Timothy Dalton, Patrick Magee. w. d. Ken Hughes.

DRAMA: Historical Drama; Power Struggles; Kings; Oppression; Slavery; Costume Drama; British Films; England; Writer-Directors

(A Man For All Seasons; Becket)

Crooklyn, 1994, 112m, ★★★/$$, U/MCA-U, PG-13/P-S. A black family in Brooklyn, much like a poorer version of Lee's own, struggles to stay together and grow up during the 70s. Alfre Woodard, Delroy Lindo, Zelda Harris, David Patrick Kelly. w. Joie Lee, Cinque Lee, d. Spike Lee.

DRAMA: Family Drama; Sibling; 1970s; Autobiographical Stories; Musicians; Mothers-Struggling; Black Casts/Films; Black Women; Black Men; Female Screenwriters; Black Screenwriters

(Mo' Better Blues; Claudine; The River Niger)

Cross Creek, 1983, 122m, ★★★★/$, EMI-U/EMI-HBO, PG. The writer of *The Yearling* (Mary Steenburgen) moves to Florida to get closer to nature and characters, finding a beautiful paradise. Alfre Woodard (BSActress), Rip Torn (BSActor), Joanna Glass, Dana Hill. w. Dalene Young, NF-adap. Marjorie Kinnans Rawlings, d. Martin Ritt. BOScore, BCostume; Oscars: 4-0.

DRAMA: Character Studies; Biographies; Autobiographical Stories; Fish out of Water Stories; Writers Romance-Reluctant; True Stories; Southerns; Nature-Back to; Country Life; Florida; Swamp Life; Female Protagonists; Female Screenwriters

(The Yearling; Marvin and Howard; One Magic Christmas)

Cross My Heart, 1988, 91m, ★★1/2/$, U/MCA-U, PG-13/S-P. Two single young people try to date, but will their personal lives get in the way? Martin Short, Annette O'Toole, Paul Reiser. d. Armyan Bernstein.

COMEDY: Comedy-Light; ROMANCE: Romantic Comedy; Romance-Reluctant; Dating Scene; Young People; Stagelike Films

Crossfire, 1947, 86m, ★★★1/2/$$, RKO/Turner. Three soldiers are suspected of murdering a Jewish man in a hotel after the war and an unusual investigation and conspiracy unravel. Robert Young, Robert Mitchum, Robert Ryan (BSActor), Gloria Grahame (BSActress). w. N-adap. Richard Brooks (*The Brick Foxhole*) (BOScr), d. Edward Dmytryk (BDirector). BPicture. Oscars: 5-0.

DRAMA: MURDER: MURDER MYSTERY: MYSTERY: Soldiers; World War II-Post Era; Hotels; Anti-Semitism; Jewish People; Film Noir; Sleeper Hits; Ahead of its Time; Forgotten Films; Faded Hits; Hidden Gems

(Gentleman's Agreement; The Detective [1968]; A Few Good Men; Anatomy of a Murder)

(Ed: Originally supposedly written about homosexuality by then soon-to-be writer/director Richard Brooks who later handled *Cat on a Hot Tin Roof*'s transition to the screen)

Crossing Delancey, 1988, 97m, ★★★/$$, WB/WB, PG-13/S-P. A nice Jewish girl has everyone looking for a husband for her. Will she go after the sexier guy or the nerdier pickle salesman? Amy Irving, Peter Riegert, Jeroen Krabbe, Sylvia Miles, Reizi Bozyk. w. Suzzy Roche, Susan Sandler, d. Joan Micklin Silver.

COMEDY: ROMANCE: Romantic Comedy; Comedy-Light; Single Women; Jewish People; Matchmakers; Elderly Women; Romance-Choosing the Right Person; New York Life; Female Protagonists; Female Screenwriters; Female Directors; Women's Films

(Chilly Scenes of Winter)

The Crossing Guard, 1995, 117m, ★★★/$, Ind R/P-S. A man whose daughter was killed by a drunk driver intends to kill the driver now that he's out of prison, but which man has suffered the most during those intervening years? Jack Nicholson, David Morse, Anjelica Huston, Robin Wright, Piper Laurie, Richard Bradford, John Savage, Priscilla Barnes, Kari Wuhrer, Leo Penn. w. d. Sean Penn.

DRAMA: Alcoholics; Avenging Death of Someone; Men in Conflict; Fathers; Writer-Directors

(The Woolgatherer [play]; The Indian Runner; Death Wish)

Crossroads, 1986, 96, ★★/$, Col/RCA-Col, PG/P-S. A white kid wanting to play the blues breaks an old black blues star out of a nursing home and takes him on a tour down south, finding music and a few dangers along the way. Ralph Macchio, Joe Seneca, Jami Gertz, Joe Morton. w. John Fusco, d. Walter Hill.

COMEDY DRAMA: Road Movies; Men and Boys; Black & White Together; Musicians; Satan; Thieves

The Crow, 1994, 100m, ★★1/2/$$$, New Line/New Line, R/V-P-S. After he is murdered, a young man comes back as a superhero of the dark to avenge his death and protect his girlfriend. Brandon Lee, Ernie Hudson, Michael Wincott, David Patrick Kelly. w. Davis Schow, John Shirley, d. Alex Proyas.

ACTION: Comic Heroes; Avenging Death of Someone; Revenge; Dead-Back from the; Ghosts

(Rapid Fire)

(Ed: Notable as the film on which Lee was killed by a real bullet in a prop gun)

The Crowd, 1928, 98m, ★★★★/$$, MGM/MGM-UA. The classic film of a working man and his family trying to make a living among the masses, oppressed by the wealthy they work for. James Murray. d. King Vidor.

DRAMA: Alienation; Making a Living; Class Conflicts; Social Drama; Business Life; 1920s; Time Capsules; Hidden Gems; Film History; Silent Films

(Modern Times; The Cameraman)

Cruising, 1980, 106m, ★★★/$$$, Lorimar-UA/Fox, R/ES-V-MN. A police detective goes a step too far in his investigation of serial killings of gay men in New York. Al Pacino, David Dukes, Karen Allen, Powers Boothe. w. d. William Friedkin.

DRAMA: MURDER: Detective Stories; Detectives-Police; Undercover; Homophobia; Men in Jeopardy; Serial Killers; Murders of Homosexuals; Gay Men; 1970s; Ahead of its Time; Coulda Been Great; Writer-Directors

(The Detective [1968]; Tightrope)

(Ed: Controversy over the film sparked box-office but overshadowed the film's better points)

The Crush, 1993, 89m, ★★/$$, WB/WB, R/P-S-V. A psycho rich girl wants the young writer who lives in the guest house-alive, preferably, but if not, then dead. Cary Elwes, Alicia Silverstone, Jennifer Rubin. w.d. Alan Shapiro.

SUSPENSE: Psychological Thriller; Psycho Killers; Infatuations; Fatal Attractions; Romance-Older Men/Younger Women; Murderers-Female; Rich People; Writers
(The Temp; Fatal Attraction; Play Misty for Me)

Crusoe, 1988, 94m, ★★★/$, Island/Island, PG-13. Retelling of the classic shipwrecked man alone on the Pacific island tale. Aidan Quinn, w. Walon Green, Christopher Logue, N-adap. Daniel Defoe, d. Caleb deschanel.

DRAMA: ADVENTURE: Stranded on an Island; Island; Shipwrecked; Lonely People; Revisionist Films
(The Adventures of Robinson Crusoe, Man Friday)

Cry Baby, 1990, 85m, ★★★/$, U/MCA-U, PG/P. A teen rock star sets 1950s Baltimore aflutter as a stern female high school principal tries to silence him and keep him away from her daughter. Johnny Depp, Amy Locane, Polly Bergen, Susan Tyrrell, Traci Lords, Ricki Lake, Iggy Pop, Troy Donahue. w.d. John Waters.

COMEDY: MUSICAL: Musical Comedy; Spoofs-Musical; Rock Stars; Romantic Comedy; Stern Women; Lover Family Dislikes; Juvenile Delinquents; Baltimore; 1950s; Writer-Directors
(Hairspray; Serial Mom; Bye Bye Birdie)

Cry Freedom, 1987, 158m, ★★1/2/$$, U/MCA-U, PG. The story of South African civil rights leader Steven Biko through the eyes of the journalist he befriended. Kevin Kline, Denzel Washington (BSActor), Penelope Wilton, Zales Mokae. w. John Briley, d. Richard Attenborough.

DRAMA: Social Drama; Race Relations; Saintly People; South Africa; Apartheid; Journalists; Black Men
(Mandela; Bophal; Gandhi; A Dry White Season; A World Apart; Cry the Beloved)
(Ed: From the team who brought us *Gandhi*. Its piety overwhelms anything it has going for it)

The Crying Game, 1992, 112m, ★★★1/2/$$$$, Miramax/Miramax, R/P-S-V-MFN. When a man escapes the IRA and travels to England to apologize to the girlfriend of a man he was responsible for killing, he doesn't realize what he's getting into, and his past is catching up with him. Stephen Rea (BActor), Jaye Davidson (BSActor), Miranda Richardson, Forest Whitaker. w. Neil Jordan (**BOScr**),

D. Jordan (BDirector). BPicture, BEditing. Oscars: 6-1.

SUSPENSE: DRAMA: ROMANCE: Romance-Doomed; Romance-Mismatched; Hairdressers; IRA; Ireland; Men as Women; Clever Plots & Endings; Sleeper Hits; British Films
(The Last Seduction; M. Butterfly)

Cuba, 1979, 122m, ★★1/2/$, UA/Fox, R/S-V-P. A mercenary soldier during the Castro revolution finds a steamy romance amid the gunfire and cigar smoke. Sean Connery, Brooke Adams, Jack Weston, Denholm Elliott, Chris Sarandon, Hector Elizondo. w. Charles Wood, d. Richard Lester.

DRAMA: ROMANCE: Romantic Drama; War Stories; Caribbean; Communists; Forgotten Films
(Havana; Casablanca)

Cujo, 1983, 91m, ★★/$$$, ITC-WB/WB, R/EV-B&G. The Satanic, rabid dog of Stephen King's bestseller wreaks havoc on a mother and son stranded in the middle of nowhere. Dee Wallace, Daniel Hugh-Kelly, Ed Lauter, Christopher Stone. w. N-adap. Stephen King, d. Lewis Teague.

HORROR: Monsters-Animal; Mothers & Sons; Possessions; Possessed Animals; Dogs; Animal Stories; Stephen King
(Devil Dog; Hound of Hell; Silver Bullet; Christine)

A Cry in the Dark, 1988, 121m, ★★★1/2/$$, Cannon-WB/WB, PG. A woman in Australia (Meryl Streep, BActress) loses her baby while camping in the desert, claiming a dingo dog took it, but is accused and tried for murder. A true story. Sam Neill. w. Robert Caswell, Fred Schepisi, NF-adap. John Bryson, Evil Angels, d. Fred Schepisi. Oscars: 1-0.

DRAMA: Courtroom Drama; **MYSTERY: MURDER MYSTERY:** Accused Unjustly; Bigots; Religion; Rumors; Missing Persons; Missing Children; Ordinary People Stories; Human Eaters; True Stories; Australia
Earlier version: Who Killed Baby Azaria?
(Before and After; An Innocent Man)

The Cure, 1995, 105m, ★★1/2/$$, U/MCA-U, PG. When the neighborhood bully manages uncharacteristically to make friends with the ostracized kid in the down the street who has AIDS, he also becomes inspired to find that of the title. Brad Renfro, Anabella Sciorra,

Diana Scarwid, Bruce Davidson. d. Peter Horton.

MELODRAMA: CHILDREN'S: FAMILY: Disease Storiesp; AIDS Stories; Cures-Search for; Boys; Children-Brats
(Brian's Song; Something for Joey; Philadelphia; Lorenzo's Oil)

Curly Sue, 1991, 101m, ★★1/2/$$$, WB/WB, PG. A little girl and her con artist father come to a turning point when a woman lawyer falls in love with at least the girl. John Belushi, Kelly Lynch, Allison Portman, John Getz, Fred D. Thompson. w. d. John Hughes.

COMEDY: CHILDREN'S: FAMILY: MELODRAMA: Tearjerkers; Women and Girls; Fathers & Daughters; Lawyers; Old-Fashioned Recent Films; Writer-Directors
(Bright Eyes; Paper Moon; Little Miss Marker; Cookie)

The Curse of the Cat People, 1944, 79m, ★★1/2/$, RKO/Turner, Media. A girl follows the visions she has of her dead mother, a victim of the curse, who may pass it along. Simone Simon, Kent Smith, Jane Randolph. d. Robert Wise.

HORROR: SUSPENSE: Possessions; Ghosts; Girls; Cats; Curses
SEQUEL TO: The Cat People
(Cat People [1942]; Cat People [1982])
(Ed: Toned-down from the original and not really a sequel, anyway)

Curse of the Pink Panther, 1983, 110m, ★1/2/$, MGM-UA/MGM-UA, PG. Another post-Sellers sequel using footage from earlier efforts with him, as a detective tries to find the bumbling inspector. Ted Wass, Robert Wagner, David Niven, Joanna Lumley, Herbert Lom. w.d. Blake Edwards.

COMEDY: FARCE: Slapstick; Detective Stories; Fools-Bumbling; Writer-Directors; Compilation Films
(The Trail of the Pink Panther; The Pink Panther SERIES)

Curse of the Werewolf, 1960, 92m, ★★1/2/$$, Hammer-U/MCA-U. A more artistic, inventive take on the legend, set in 1800s England. Oliver Reed, Clifford Evans. d. Terence Fisher.

HORROR: Werewolves; Revisionist Films; Humans into Animals; 1800s
(Werewolf of London)

Cutter and Bone (Cutter's Way), 1981, 109m, ★★1/2/$, UA/MGM-UA, R/P-S. A disabled Vietnam vet and a hustler pal discover a murder but find it difficult to justify doing anything about it. Jeff

Bridges, Lisa Eichhorn, John Heard, Ann Dusenberry. d. Ivan Passer.

DRAMA: MYSTERY: MURDER: MURDER MYSTERY: Art Films; Cult Films; Disabled People; Veterans-Vietnam; Ethics; Con Artists
(River's Edge)

Cutthroat Island, 1995, 123m, ★★1/2/$$, MGM/MGM-UA, PG-13/P-V-S. When the daughter of a pirate who has a third of a treasure map tattooed on his scalp goes on the seas to find it, she meets up with a young man who helps her find love and her way, if not the treasure. Geena Davis, Matthew Modine, Frank Langella, Maury Chaykin, Stan Shaw, Paul Dillon. w. Robert King, Marc Norman, d. Renny Harlin.

ACTION: ADVENTURE: Pirates; Female in Male Domain; Chase Stories; Treasure Hunts; 1700s; Female Protagonists; Flops-Major
(The Adventures of Eliza Fraser; Pirates; Captain Blood)

The Cutting Edge, 1992, 110m, ★★1/2/$$, MGM/MGM-UA, PG/S-P. A figure skating prima donna has to get along with her womanizing hockey partner when she needs a replacement in time for the Olympics. Sparks fly on ice. Moira Kelly, D.B. Sweeney, Roy Dotrice, Terry O'Quinn. w. Tony Gilroy, d. Paul Michael Glaser.

COMEDY: ROMANCE: Romantic Comedy; Romance-Bickering; Romance-Opposites Attract; Skating; Hockey; Olympics; Mean Women; Macho Men; Sports Movies; Coulda Been Great; Good Premise Unfulfilled
(Pat and Mike; A Touch of Class)

Cyborg, 1989, 85m, ★★/$$, Cannon/MGM-UA, R/EV-P. In a post-apocalyptic world, an android protects the good people from the bad. Jean Claude Van Damme, Deborah richter. w. Kitty, Chalmer, d. Albert Pyun.

ACTION: Apocalyptic Stories; Androids; Protecting Someone; Female Screenwriters
(Universal Soldier; The Terminator)

Cyrano de Bergerac, 1950, 112m, ★★★/$$$, UA/Nos. Jose Ferrer (**BActor**), Mala Powers, William Prince, Elena Verdugo. w. Carl Foreman, d. Michael Gordon. Oscars: 1-1.

Cyrano de Bergerac, 1990, 138m, ★★★★/$$$, Orion/Orion, PG. Gerard Depardieu (BActor), Jacques Weber, Anne brochet. w. Jean-Claude Carriere, Jean-Paul Rappeneau, d. Rappaneau. **BCostume**, BArt, **BFLFilm**, BMakeup. Oscars: 5-1.
The classic French story of the large-nosed man who thought the beautiful Roxanne wouldn't love him because of his appearance, but helps his friend to romance her by writing his lines and letters to her. It works, but not for the right man.
French Films

COMEDY DRAMA: ROMANCE: Romantic Drama; **MELODRAMA:** Love-Unrequited; Infatuations; Romance-Boy Wants Girl; Tearjerkers; Impostors; Liars; Letters; Looksism; Classic Play Adaptations

COMIC REMAKE: Roxanne
(Roxanne; The Shop Around the Corner; I Sent a Letter to My Love; The Truth About Cats and Dogs)

D

Da, 1988, 102m, ★★★/$, FilmDallas-Premier/NA, PG. A middle-aged American playwright of Irish descent returns home for his father's funeral and finds emotions and memories stirred in himself that he had hardly remembered by talking to his father's ghost. Barnard Hughes, Martin Sheen, William Hickey, Doreen Hepburn. w. P-adap. Hugh Leonard, d. Matt Clark.
DRAMA: Character Studies; Fathers & Sons; Ghosts; Death-Dealing with; Funerals; Irish People; Ireland
(Dad; I Never Sang for My Father)
Dad, 1989, 118m, ★★½/$$, Universal/MCA-U, PG. A middle-aged man with a troubled relationship with his father gets to know him better, ironically, when he learns that his dad is dying. Jack Lemmon, Ted Danson, Olympia Dukakis, Kathy Baker, Kevin Spacey, Ethan Hawke. w. d. Gary David Goldberg, N-adap. William Wharton.
COMEDY DRAMA: MELODRAMA: Tearjerkers; Fathers & Sons; Death-Impending; Grandfathers-Fascinating; Family Drama; Life Transitions
(Da; Grumpy Old Men; Kotch)
Daddy Longlegs, 1955, 126m, ★★★/$$$, 20th/CBS-Fox. A girl who is an orphan has a mystery man who funds her life and who she falls in love with. Fred Astaire, Leslie Caron, Fred Clark,

Thelma Ritter, Terry Moore, Larry Keating. w. Phoebe & Henry Ephron, d. Jean Negulesco. BMScore, BOSong, "Something's Gotta Give." Oscars: 2-0.
MUSICALS: ROMANCE: COMEDY DRAMA: Musical Romance; Dance Movies; Romance-Older Men/Younger Women; Infatuations; Orphans; Benefactors; Rich People; Rich vs. Poor; Female Screenwriters
Daddy Nostaglia (*These Foolish Things*), 1990, 106m, ★★★/$, Ind/Facets. A young woman writer goes home to take care of her father who's bedridden. Dirk Bogarde, Jane Birkin, Emmanuelle Bataille. w. Colo Tavernier O'Hagan, d. Bertrand Tavernier.
DRAMA: Character Studies; Reunions; Nurses; Writers; Fathers & Daughters; Disabled People; Quiet Little Films; French Films; Hidden Gems
(Tatie Danielle; Death in Venice)
Daddy's Dyin' (Who's Got the Will?), 1990, 101m, ★★★/$, UA/MGM-UA, PG-13/P-S. When an old man on the Texas prairie is on his deathbed, his four children and their spouses and lovers descend upon the old home to find his will and get what's coming to them. But family ties and tensions complicate the hunt. Tess Harper, Beau Bridges, Beverly D'Angelo, Judge Reinhold, Molly McClure, Patrika Darbo, Amy Wright,

Keith Carradine. w. P-adap. Del Shores, d. Jack Fisk.
COMEDY: COMEDY DRAMA: Ensemble Films; Family Comedy; Inheritances at Stake; Siblings; Death-Impending; Southerns; Texas; Rednecks; Singers; Hippies; Stern Women; Hidden Gems (Greedy; Crimes of the Heart; Stars and Bars)
(Ed: Some great moments with a great cast, particularly Darbo and McClure in plum parts)
Daddy's Gone A-Hunting, 1969, 108m, ★★★/$, WB/WB, R/S-P. A woman gets pregnant with a man who turns out to be a psychopath, and she decides to have an abortion. After they part ways, he returns years later to exact his revenge. Carol White, Paul Burke, Scott Hylands, Andrew King. w. Larry Cohen, Lorenzo Semple, d. Mark Robson.
SUSPENSE: Psychological Drama; Malicious Menaces; Stalkers; Romance Reunited; Past-Haunted by the; Fatal Attractions; Psycho Killers; Kill the Beast; Forgotten Films; Underrated; Hidden Gems; Ahead of Its Time
(The Hand That Rocks the Cradle; The Tie That Binds; Pretty Poison)
Daisy Kenyon, 1947, 99m, ★★½/$$, 20th/NA. A middle-aged woman in the fashion business deals with two men at the same time. Joan Crawford, Henry Fonda,

Dana Andrews, Ruth Warrick, PeggyAnn Garner. w. David Hertz, N-adap Elizabeth Janeway, d. Otto Preminger.

MELODRAMA: ROMANCE: Romance-Triangles; Romance-Choosing the Right Person; Fashion World; Career Women; Womens' Films
(Back Street; Humoresque; Mannequin; The Best of Everything)

Daisy Miller, 1974, 92m, ★★★/$, Par/Par, PG. A rich girl touring Europe meets a young man in Italy, but the love isn't meant to last. Cybill Shepherd, Barry Brown, Cloris Leachman, Mildred Natwick, Eileen Brennan, James MacMurtry. w. Frederic Raphael, SS-adap. Henry James, d. Peter Bogdanovich.

COMEDY DRAMA: Comedy of Manners; **MELODRAMA: ROMANCE: TRAGEDY:** Disease Stories; Death-Impending; Romance-Doomed; Victorian Era; Americans Abroad; Young Women
(Portrait of a Lady; A Room with a View; The Bostonians)

Dallas, 1950, 94m, ★★½/$$, WB/WB. A man makes up for his being a colonel in the Confederacy by taming the town of Dallas. Gary Cooper, Ruth Roman, Raymond Massey, Steve Cochran, Leif Erickson. w. John Twist, d. Stuart Heisler.

WESTERNS: Civil War Era; Police Stories; Redemption; Starting Over; Texas

Damage, 1992, 112m, ★★★½/$$, New Line/New Line, R/P-ES-FFN-MFN. A foreign minister (Jeremy Irons) begins an affair with his son's (Rupert Graves) girlfriend (Juliette Binoche) without his wife (Miranda Richardson, BSActress) knowing until they go one step too far. w. David Hare, adap. Josephine Hart, d. Louis Malle. Oscars: 1-0.

DRAMA: Romantic Drama; Erotic Drama; **TRAGEDY:** Affairs-Doomed; Infidelity; Obsessions; Violence-Sudden; Romance-Triangles; Love with Relative's Lover; London; Paris Diplomats; Upper Class; Jealous Wives; Romance-Intergenerational; British
(The Game Is Over; The Comfort of Strangers; Blue)

The Dam Busters, 1954, 125m, ★★★/$$, Ealing/HomeVision. Dams are blown up in the war effort with new technology. Michael Redgrave, Richard Todd, Casil Sydney. w. R.C. Sheriff, NF-adap. Guy Gibson, Paul Brickhill, d. Michael Anderson.

ACTION: War Stories; World War II Stories; War Battles; Germans as Enemy; Bombs

Damn Yankees, 1958, 110m, ★★★/$$$$, WB/WB. A baseball team on the skids gets an offer from the devil which could turn things around-or not. Gwen Verdon, Tab Hunter, Ray Walston, Russ Brown, Shannon Bolin. w. MP-adap. George Abbott, N-adap. Douglas Wallop, d. Abbott, Stanley Donen.

MUSICALS: COMEDY: Musical Comedy; Fantasy; Sports Movies; Baseball; Selling One's Soul; Underdog Stories; Satan; Sexy Women; Dangerous Women
(Bye Bye Birdie; Major League)
(Ed: Huge hit on Broadway, the film wasn't so big with critics but had big box-office)

The Damned, 1969, 164m, ★★★/$$, WB/WB, R/S-P. A wealthy German industrial family begins to splinter under pressure from the Nazis. Dirk Bogarde, Ingrid Thulin, Helmut Berger. w. Nicola Badalucco, Enrico Medioli, Luchino Visconti (BOScr), d. Visconti. Oscars: 1-0.

DRAMA: TRAGEDY: Family Drama; World War II Era; Nazi Stories; Germany; Rich People; International Casts
(The Garden of the Finzi-Continis; Au Revoir les Enfants)

A Damsel in Distress, 1937, 101m, ★★★/$$, RKO/Turner. A dancer goes to England and falls for a royal dame there. Fred Astaire, Joan Fontaine, George Burns, Gracie Allen, Reginald Gardiner. w. P. G. Wodehouse, S.K. Lauren, Ernest Pagano, d. George Stevens.

MUSICALS: ROMANCE: Dance Movies; Dancers; Musical Romance; Americans Abroad; Romance-Class Conflict
(Ed: Astaire without Rogers and a little less than normal)

Dance Macabre, 1991, 97m, ★½/$, Col/Col, R/V-B&G. A man with split personalities falls for a woman who looks just like his dead lover. Robert Englund, Michelle Zeitlin. w. d. Greydon Clark.

HORROR: SUSPENSE: Lookalikes; Obsessions; **MURDER:** Psycho-Killers; Multiple Personalities; Writer-Directors
(Dr. Jekyll & Mr. Hyde; Vertigo; Mirage [1994])

Dance with a Stranger, 1985, 101m, ★★★/$$, Goldwyn/Goldwyn, R/S-P-V. A woman with a past loves a man so much she decides she'll kill him to keep him from someone else. Miranda Richardson,

Rupert Everett, Ian Holm. w. Shelagh Delaney, d. Mike Newell.

DRAMA: ROMANCE: Fatal Attractions; **MURDER:** Biographies; Crimes of Passion; True Stories; Murderers-Female; Romance-Dangerous; Dangerous Women; Evil Women; Executions
(I Want to Live; Chicago Joe and the Showgirl; Leave Her to Heaven)

Dancers, 1987, 99m, ★★½/$, Cannon/Cannon, PG/S. A ballet gets rejuvenated when a new ballerina joins the company and the lead dancer falls in love with her. Mikhail Baryshnikov, Allessandra Ferri, Leslie Browne. w. Sara Kernochan, d. Herbert Ross.

MELODRAMA: ROMANCE: Dance Movies; Dancers; Ballet; Behind the Scenes; Female Screenwriters
(White Nights; The Turning Point)

Dances with Wolves, 1990, 180m, ★★★/$$$$$, Orion/Orion, PG/S-MRN. A U.S. Cavalry officer learns to live with a tribe of Indians amid a lot of great scenery. Kevin Costner (BActor), Mary McDonnell (BSActress), Graham Greene (BSActor), Robert Pastorelli, Charles Rocket, Rodney Grant. w. N-adap. Michael Blake (BAScr), d. Kevin Costner (**BDirector**). **BPicture**, **BOScore, BCin, BArt, BSound, BEdit**, BCostume. Oscars: 12-7.

WESTERNS: DRAMA: ADVENTURE: Indians-Raised by; Westerns-Neo Epics; Cavalry; Lyrical Films; Revisionist Films; Blockbusters; Sleeper Hits
(A Man Called Horse; Little Big Man; Legends of the Fall)

Dancing Co-Ed, 1939, 90m, ★★½/$$$, MGM/MGM-UA. Schwab's soda counter girl Lana Turner dances while she goes to school and becomes a star. Lana Turner, Richard Carlson, Artie Shaw, Monty Woolley. w. Albert Mannheimer, Albert Treynor, d. Sylvan Simon.

MUSICALS: Dance Movies; Fame-Rise to; Hollywood Live; American Myth
(Presenting Lily Mars; Gilda; Our Dancing Daughters)

Dancing in the Dark, 1949, 92m, ★★½/$$, 20th/NA. When a movie star from the silent days becomes a talent scout, he winds up finding his daughter. William Powell, Adolphe Menjou, Mark Stevens, Betsy Drake, Hope Emerson. w. Mary McCall, P-adap. George S. Kaufman, Howard Deitz, Arthur Schwartz, *The Band Wagon*, d. Irving Reis.

MELODRAMA: COMEDY DRAMA:
Music Movies; Hollywood Life; Actors;
Comebacks; Children-Long Lost; Incest;
Fathers and Daughters
(Angela; The Miracle [1990]; Soapdish)

Dancing Lady, 1933, 94m, ★★★/$$$,
MGM/MGM-UA. A dancer has two men
in her life, her long-supporting manager
and an exciting playboy. Joan Crawford,
Clark Gable, Fred Astaire, Franchot
Tone, May Robson, Nelson Eddy. w.
Allen Rivkin, P.J. Wolfson, N-adap.
James Bellah, d. Robert Z. Leonard.
ROMANCE: MELODRAMA: Romance-
Choosing the Right Person; Romance-
Triangles; Playboys; Dancers
(Our Dancing Daughters; Humoresque)

A Dandy in Aspic, 1968, 107m,
★★1/2/$, Col/Col. Problems arise when a
double agent receives orders to pull a hit-
on himself. Laurence Harvey, Tom
Courtenay, Lionel Stander, Mia Farrow,
Harry Andrews, Peter Cook. w. N-adap.
Derek Marlowe, d. Anthony Mann.
SUSPENSE: Psychological Drama; Spy
Films; Spies; Secret Agents; Good
Premise Unfulfilled; Hitmen; Cold War
Era
(The Spy Who Came in from the Cold;
Prizzi's Honor; The Manchurian
Candidate)

Dangerous, 1935, 78m, ★★★/$$$,
WB/WB. An actress hits bottom with her
drinking and tries to pull herself together.
Bette Davis (**BActress**), Franchot Tone,
Margaret Lindsay. w. Laird Doyle, d.
Alfred E. Green. Oscars: 1-0.
DRAMA: Character Studies; Alcoholics;
Nervous Breakdowns; Actresses;
Comebacks; Redemption; Starting Over
(Smash-Up, the Story of a Woman; The
Morning After; Jezebel)

Dangerous Crossing, 1953, 75m,
★★★/$$, 20th/NA. A woman's husband
disappears after they've boarded a cruise
liner for Europe. No one believes he even
existed until it's too late. Jeanne Craine,
Michael Rennie, Carl Betz. w. Leo
Townsend, John Carr, d. Joseph Newman.
SUSPENSE: Missing Persons; Women in
Jeopardy; Missing Person Thriller;
Murder of Spouse; Ships; Searches;
Unbelieved
REMAKE: TV (1992)
(The Lady Vanishes; The Vanishing)

Dangerous Curves, 1988, 93m, ★★/$,
Vestron/Vestron, PG/S-V. When two
friends drive a sports car cross-country,

their mischief gets them into trouble.
Robert Stack, Tate Donovan, Danielle von
Zertmaeck, Robert Klein, Elizabeth
Ashley, Leslie Nielsen. w. d. David
Lewis.
ACTION: SUSPENSE: Chase Stories; Car
Chases; Road Movies; Road Movies-
Transporting Girls; Teenagers; Teenage
Movies; Writer-Directors
(No Man's Land; Fandango; Coupe de
Ville)

Dangerous Game, 1993, 107m, ★★/$,
Aries/MGM-UA, R/EP-V-S-FN. The story
of a renegade film director with a turbu-
lent marriage takes his frustrations out on
the movie set, particularly on the main
actress. Madonna, Harvey Keitel, James
Russo, Nancy Ferrara. w. Nicholas St.
John, d. Abel Ferrara.
DRAMA: Psychological Drama; Movie
Making; Directors; Actresses; Abused
Women; Art Films; Coulda Been Good;
Marriage Drama; Ind Films
(Living in Oblivion; The Bad Lieutenant;
Faces; Husbands)

Dangerous Liaisons, 1960, see Les
Liaisons Dangereuses
Dangerous Liaisons, 1988, 130m,
★★★★/$$$, Lorimar-WB/WB, R/S-FFN.
A devious lady (Glenn Close, BActress)
and her old lover (John Malkovich) make
bets as to whether he can seduce a virgin
(Uma Thurman) and wife (Michelle
Pfeiffer, BSActress) with much at stake.
Swoosie Kurtz, Mildred Natwick. w. P-
adap. Christopher Hampton (BAScr), N-
adap. Cholderclos deLaclos, d. Stephen
Frears. BPicture, BCin, **BArt**, **BCost**,
BAScore. Oscars: 8-3.
DRAMA: TRAGEDY: MELODRAMA:
Costume Drama; Mindgames; Power
Struggles; Double Crossings; Betrayals;
Bets; Love-Questionable; Romance-
Triangles; Dangerous Women; Dangerous
Men; Revenge; Past-Haunted by the;
Epistolaries; Letters; Novel and Play
Adaptations; 1700s; Classic Literary
Adaptations; Classic Tragedy; Production
Design-Outstanding
REMAKE OF: Les Liaisons Dangereuses
(1960)
OTHER VERSION: Valmont, 1989
(The Draughtsman's Contract; Restoration)

Dangerous Minds, 1995, 94m,
★★1/2/$$$$, Hollywood/Hollywood, R/P-
S-V. A white female ex-Marine goes to
teach at an inner-city school which is
predominantly black and finds the educa-

tional process may be her own challenge
first before she can have an impact on
the students. Michelle Pfeiffer, George
Dzundza, Courtney B. Vance, Robin
Bartlett, Beatrice Winde, John Neville,
Lorraine Toussaint, Renoly Santiago,
Wade Dominguez, Asia Minor, Bruklin
Harris. w. Ronald Bass, NF-adap. My
Posse Don't Do Homework, LouAnne
Johnson, d. John Smith.
DRAMA: Social Drama; High School Life;
Teachers & Students; Teachers-Inner
City; Inner-City Life; White Among
Blacks; Black Casts; True Stories;
Juvenile Delinquents; Female
Protagonists; Sleepers
(Blackboard Jungle; Up the Down
Staircase; The Beat; To Sir With Love;
The White Shadow TV SERIES)
(Ed: Brought to the screen with Pfeiffer's
starpower; Andy Garcia, who played the
love interest, was completely cut from the
film-hence the short running time)

Dangerous Moves, 1985, 100m,
★★★/$, Spectrafilm/Lorimar-WB. An
international chess game is the setting for
a miniature cold war allegory with a cur-
rent Russian and a former one. Michel
Piccoli, Leslie Caron, Liv Ullman,
Alexandre Arbait. w. d. Richard Dembo.
BFLFilm. Oscars: 1-1.
DRAMA: Men in Conflict; Allegorical
Stories; Competitions; Games;
Mindgames; Cold War Era; French Films
(Ed: Actually a Swiss film but mostly in
French)

Dangerous When Wet, 1953, 95m,
★★★/$$$, MGM/MGM-UA. A family of
swimmers from Arkansas wins the
English Channel under sponsorship.
Esther Williams, Charlotte Greenwood,
William Demarest, Fernando Lamas, Jack
Carson. w. Dorothy Kingsley, d. Charles
Walters.
COMEDY: MUSICALS: Family Comedy;
Fish out of Water Stories; Swimming;
Arkansas; England; Americans Abroad;
Female Screenwriters
(The Duchess of Idaho; Neptune's
Daughter)

A Dangerous Woman, 1993, 101m,
★★★/$, Gramercy-U/MCA-U, R/V-S-
MRN. A mentally disabled young woman
living with her glamorous aunt on an
orange plantation has her life changed by
a sexy drifter who seduces her. But when
a friend's jerk boyfriend steals money and
blames it the woman, she then becomes

"dangerous" in standing up for herself. Debra Winger, Barbara Hershey, Gabriel Byrne, David Straithairn, John Terry, Chloe Webb, Jan Hooks, Paul Dooley, Laurie Metcalf. w. Naomi Foner, d. Stephen Gyllenhaal.

DRAMA: TRAGEDY: Character Studies; ROMANCE: Romance-Doomed; Virgins; Mentally Disabled; Romance with Relative's Lover; Drifters; Thieves; Liars; Accused Unjustly; Single Women; Narrated Films; Female Protagonists; Female Screenwriters
(David and Lisa; Charly; Rain Man; A Patch of Blue)

Daniel, 1983, 129m, ★★/$, Par/Par, R/P-S-V. A young man (Timothy Hutton) deals with his parents' lives as possible communists. Lindsay Crouse, Ed Asner, Ellen Barkin. w. Michael Weller, N-adap. E.L. Doctorow, d. Sidney Lumet.

DRAMA: Biographies-Fictional; Political Drama; Political Activists; Accused Unjustly; McCarthy Era; Communists; Parents-Troublesome; Parents vs. children; Saving Someone; Spies; Cold War Era; Oppression; Betrayals; Dual Lives
(The Front; The Way We Were; Guilty by Suspicion)

Dante's Inferno: The Life of Dante Gabriel Rossetti, 1969, 90m, ★★1/2/$, Ind/Ingram, R/P-S. Biopic of the famed Victorian-era painter who was anything but Victorian. Oliver Reed. w. d. Ken Russell.

DRAMA: Erotic Drama; Painters; Artists-Famous; Biographies; Forgotten Films; Writer-Directors

Danton, 1982, 136m, ★★1/2/$, Triumph-Col/RCA-Col, R/MN. Thinkers of the French Enlightenment work toward a new philosophy for France through letters as change takes place elsewhere. Gerard Depardieu, Wojciech Pszoniak. w. Jean-Claude Carriere, P-adap. Stanislav Przynyszewska, *The Danton Affair*, d. Andrej Wajda.

DRAMA: Political Unrest; Political Drama; Art Films; Historical Drama; Friendships-Male; French Revolution; 1700s; Polish Films; French Films; International Casts; Letters
(A Tale of Two Cities; Man of Iron)

Darby O'Gill and the Little People, 1959, 90m, ★★★/$$$, Disney/Disney, G. When an Irishman falls down a well he meets up with little people with special powers that change his life. Albert Sharpe, Sean Connery, Jimmy O'Dea, Estelle Winwood. w. Lawrence Watkin, SS-adap. H. T. Kavanagh, d. Robert Stevenson.

CHILDREN'S: FAMILY: Fantasy; Magic; Little People; Disney Comedy; Irish People; Leprechauns
(The Gnome Mobile)

The Dark Angel, 1935, 105m, ★★★/$$$, Goldwyn-UA/Goldwyn. After a soldier is blinded in battle, he tries to marry off his girlfriend to another man who can see while keeping his problem a secret. Merle Oberon, Fredric March, Herbert Marshall, Janet Beecher. w. Lillian Hellman, Mordcount Shairp, d. Sidney Franklin.

MELODRAMA: ROMANCE: Tearjerkers; Blind People; Disease Stories; Finding New Mate for Spouse; Secrets-Keeping; World War I Stories; Female Screenwriters
(Bright Victory; Dark Victory)

The Dark Angel, 1991, 150m, ★★★/$, BBC/Fox, PG/V. A young woman inherits a fortune from her creepy uncle Silas who apparently haunts the family digs in England, leading to conflict among family members and creepy goings-on. Peter O'Toole, Beatie Edney, Jane Lapotaire, Tim Woodward. d. Peter Hammond.

DRAMA: COMEDY DRAMA: Inheritances at Stake; Heiress; England; Houses-Creepy; TV Movies
(The Green Man; The Ruling Class)

The Dark at the Top of the Stairs, 1960, 124m, ★★★1/2/$$$, WB/WB. A boy learns about his father's affair and his sister's coming of age in his 1920s Kansas town. Robert Preston, Dorothy McGuire, Shirley Knight (BSActress), Angela Lansbury, Eve Arden, Frank Overton. w. Harriet Frank, Irving Ravetch, P-adap. William Inge, d. Delbert Mann. Oscars: 1-0.

DRAMA: MELODRAMA: Family Drama; Coming of Age; Boyhood; Brothers & Sisters; Cheating Men; Marriage on the Rocks; Romance with Married Person; Mistresses; Small-town Life; Midwestern Life; Tennessee Williamsesque
(A Fall Down; Come Back Little Sheba)

Dark Command, 1940, 92m, ★★1/2/$$$, Republic/Republic. Civil War strife outbreaks in vigilante groups in 1860 Kansas. John Wayne, Claire Trevor, Walter Pidgeon, Gabby Hayes, Marjorie Main. w. Grover Jones, Lionel Houser, Hugh Herbert, N-adap. W.R. Burnett, d. Raoul Walsh.

WESTERNS: Men in Conflict; Civil War Era; Vigilantes; Midwestern Life; Political Unrest; Political Activists
(The Last Command; Alvarez Kelly)

The Dark Corner, 1946, 98m, ★★★/$$, 20th/Fox. A PI thinks he's being stalked by an enemy who turns up dead, leading him to wonder who's really after him. Mark Stevens, Clifton Webb, Lucille Ball, Kurt Krueger, William Bendix. w. Jay Dratler, Bernard Schoenfeld, Leo Rosten, d. Henry Hathaway.

MYSTERY: MURDER: MURDER MYSTERY: Detective Stories; Detectives in Deep; Malicious Menaces; Stalkers; Film Noir; Forgotten Films
(Murder, My Sweet)

The Dark Crystal, 1982, 94m, ★★★/$$$, ITC-AFD-U/NA. On a planet of bizarre muppets, two child muppets search for a piece of the mysterious crystal that rules their kingdom. w. David Odell, d. Jim Henson, Frank Oz.

CHILDREN'S: Fantasy; SCI-FI: Magic; Outer Space Movies; Treasure Hunts; Searches; Good vs. Evil Puppets; Muppets; Sleeper Hits; Forgotten Films; Hidden Gems
(Labyrinth)
(Ed: Too slow and dark for most children, but teens may like it)

The Dark Half, 1990/1993, 122m, ★★★/$$, Orion/Orion, R/EV-B&G. Stephen King's tale about a writer not unlike himself who writes under a psuedonym whom he decides to stage a death for. But when foes of the fictitious man begin dying, the writer has a real problem coming up with a suitable ending. Timothy Hutton, Amy Madigan, Michael Rooker, Julie Harris, Rutanya Alda. w. d. George Romero, N-adap. Stephen King.

HORROR: SUSPENSE: MURDER: Murders-One by One; Twins; Evil Men; Revenge; Parasites; Writers; Stalkers; Framed?; Accused Unjustly; Blackmail; Impostors; Identities-Assumed; Stephen King
(Brotherly Love; In the Mouth of Madness)
(Ed: Not half bad)

Darkman, 1990, 91m, ★★★/$$$, U/MCA-U, R/EV-S. A scientist terribly deformed in an experiment becomes a hunchback hero trying to discover who's out to get him and his lover. Liam Neeson, Frances McDormand, Colin Friels, Larry Drake. w. Chuck Pfarrer, Sam Raimi, Ivan Raimi, Daniel Goldin, Joshua Goldin, d. Sam Raimi.

ACTION: HORROR: SCI-FI: Conspiracy; Dead-Back from the; Saving Someone; Saving One's Self; Heroes-Unlikely; Scientists; Experiments; Accidents; Disguises; Disabled People
(Army of Darkness)

The Dark Mirror (B&W), 1947, 85m, ★★★1/2/$$$$, WB/WB. Twin sisters (Olivia de Havilland, BActress) vie for the attentions of the same man (Don Ameche), who is a psychiatrist and who believes one to be a murderer. w. Vladimir Pozner (BOScr), d. Robert Siodmak. Oscars: 1-0.

SUSPENSE: MYSTERY: MURDER MYSTERY: Film Noir; Psychological Drama; Psychologists; Romance with Psychologist; Twins; Split Personalities; Insanity; Mindgames; Role Reversals; Clever Plots & Endings
REMAKE: TV (1984)
(Dead Ringers; Never Talk to Strangers)

Dark Obsession, 1990, 97m, ★★1/2/$, PSM/PSM, R/S-FN-MN. A couple likes to live out their sexual fantasies, but when a car accident happens, nervous breakdowns are the result. Gabriel Byrne, Amanda Donohoe, Michael Hordern, Judy Parfitt, Sadie Frost. w. Tim Rose Price, d. Nick Broomfield.

DRAMA: Erotic Drama; Psychological Drama; True Stories; Sexual Kinkiness; Alternative Lifestyles; Promiscuity; Sexy Men; Sexy Women; Nervous Breakdowns
(The Rapture; Love Matters)

Dark of the Sun (The Mercenaries), 1968, 100m, ★★1/2/$, MGM/MGM-UA. A mercenary soldier is assigned to procur and then transport a train of diamonds. Rod Taylor, Jim Brown, Yvette Mimieux, Kenneth More. w. Quentin Werthy, Adrian Spies, d. Jack Cardiff.

ADVENTURE: ACTION: Heist Movies; Mercenaries; Africa; Jewel Thieves; Journies; Good Premise Unfulfilled; Coulda Been Good

Dark Passage, 1947, 106m, ★★★1/2/$$$, WB/WB. A convict (Humphrey Bogart) accused of murdering his wife escapes prison and is harbored by a young woman (Lauren Bacall) who followed his trial and believes he's innocent, but will he have time, with the help of a new face, to find the real murderer? Agnes Moorehead. w.d. Delmer Daves, N-adap. David Goodis.

DRAMA: MYSTERY: Crime Drama; **MURDER:** Film Noir; Ex-Convicts; Prison Escapes; Identities-Assumed; Fugitives from the Law; Accused Unjustly; Cosmetic Surgery; Monologues-Interior
REMAKE/RETREAD: Johnny Handsome
(The Fugitive; The Lady in the Lake)

The Dark Past, 1948, 75m, ★★★/$, Col/Col. A doctor's home is broken into by thieves, who soon are made to wish by the doc that they hadn't. William Holden, Lee J. Cobb, Nina Foch, Adele Jergens. w. Philip MacDonald, Marvin Wald, Oscar Saul, d. Rudolph Mate.

SUSPENSE: Crime Drama; Thieves; Hostage Situations; Ordinary Person vs. Criminals; Turning the Tables; Psychiatrists
REMAKE: Blind Alley
(The Desperate Hours; The Small Voice)

Dark Star, 1974, 83m, ★★★/$, Ind/VCI. An outer space mission is affected by claustrophobia and an alien creature on board. Brian Narelle, Dre Pahich, Dan O'Bannon. w. John Carpenter, Dan O'Bannon, d. Carpenter.

SCI-FI: Outer Space Movies; Black Comedy; Aliens-Outer Space, Evil; Paranoia; Sleeper Hits
(Alien; Star Wars; Silent Running)

Dark Victory, 1939, 105m, ★★★1/2/$$$$, WB/WB, MGM-UA. A rich woman who lives life to fullest goes blind from a brain tumor and faces death with a lover. Bette Davis (BActress), George Brent, Humphrey Bogart, Ronald Reagan, Geraldine Fitzgerald, Henry Travers. w. Casey Robinson, P-adap. George Brewer, Bertram Bloch, d. Edmund Goulding.

MELODRAMA: TRAGEDY: Tearjerkers; Disease Stories; **ROMANCE:** Death-Impending; Blind People; Rich People; Lonely People; Romance with Doctor; Blockbusters
REMAKE: Stolen Hours
(Magnificent Obsession; A Patch of Blue; Bright Victory)

Dark Waters, 1944, 93m, ★★1/2/$, Ind/Sultan. A woman returns to her hometown in the swamps of Louisiana after her parents' deaths drive her to a breakdown, but of course, someone is out to make her crazy by causing her tragedies. Merle Oberon, Franchot Tone, Thomas Mitchell, Fay Bainter, Elisha Cook Jr, John Qualen. d. Andre de Toth.

DRAMA: SUSPENSE: Psychological Drama; Psychological Thriller; Insane-Plot to Drive; Nervous Breakdowns; Death-Dealing with; Women in Jeopardy; Forgotten Films

Dark Wind, 1991, 111m, ★★1/2/$, Carolco/Live. An Indian police officer checks into some drug murders on his reservation to thwart the FBI. Lou Diamond Phillips, Gary Framer, Fred Ward, John Karlen. w. Neil Jiminez, Eric Bergren, Mark Horowitz, N-adap. Tony Hillerman, d. Errol Morris.

MYSTERY: MURDER: MURDER MYSTERY: Detective Stories; Detectives-Police; Police Stories; Drugs-Dealing; Indians-American; Desert Settings; Coulda Been Good
(Thunderheart; Powwow Highway; Incident at Oglala)

Darling (B&W), 1965, 127m, ★★★★/$$$, Embassy/Embassy, Col, NR/S. A young British woman (Julie Christie, BActress) makes her climb to fame as a model by using men (Dirk Bogarde, Laurence Harvey). w. Frederic Raphael (BOScr), d. John Schlesinger (BDirector). BPicture, BCostB&W, BArtB&W. Oscars: 6-3.

DRAMA: Character Studies; Biographies-Fictional; Fame-Rise to; Love-Questionable; Fashion World; Actresses; Models; Betrayals; Beautiful People; Mod Era; Lonely People; Fairy Tales; Marrying Up; Princesses; Episodic Stories; British Films; Sleeper Hits; Hidden Gems
(Alfie; Twenty-One; Petulia)

Darling Lili, 1970, 136m, ★★★/$, Par/Par, G. A German spy-singer in World War I has an American soldier on her tail for love, not necessarily war. Julie Andrews, Rock Hudson, Jeremy Kemp, Lance Percival. w. Blake Edwards, William Peter Blatty, d. Edwards.

COMEDY: ROMANCE: Romantic Comedy; **FARCE: MUSICALS:** Music Movies; World War I Stories; Spies; Misunderstandings; Soldiers; Actresses; Singers; Dual Lives; Coulda Been Great
(Star!; The Tamarind Seed)

D.A.R.Y.L., 1985, 99m, ★★/$, Col/RCA-Col, G. A robot runs into trouble when it develops emotions. Mary Beth Hurt, Michael McKean, Kathryn Walker, Colleen Camp. w. David Ambrose, Allan Scott, Jeffrey Ellis, d. Simon Wincer.

COMEDY DRAMA: SCI-FI: Androids; **CHILDREN'S: FAMILY:** Boyhood; Man vs. Machine; Coulda Been Good (Mac and Me; Bladerunner)

Das Boot, 1982, 150m, ★★★¹/₂/$$$, Col/Col, R/P-V. A German U-boat's tensions under the seas during battle in World War II, facing almost certain death. Jurgen Prochnow, Herbert Gronemeyer, Klaus Wenneman. w. d. Wolfgang Petersen (BDirector, BAScr). **BFLFilm.** Oscars: 3-1.

DRAMA: TRAGEDY: Psychological Drama; Submarines; Military Stories; World War II Stories; Adventure at Sea; Americans as Enemy; Germans; German Films (Crimson Tide; Gray Lady Down; The Hunt for Red October)

Date with an Angel, 1987, 114m, ★★/$$, Tri-Star/HBO, PG/S. An ordinary hunky guy fishes an angel out of his backyard pool and is so overwhelmed with her beauty and, of course, serenity, that he decides to ditch his rich girlfriend. Michael Knight, Emmanuelle Beart, Phoebe Cates, David Dukes, Bibi Besch, Albert Macklin. d. Tom McLoughlin.

COMEDY: ROMANCE: Romantic Comedy; Angels; Engagements-Breaking Romance-Choosing Right Person; Old-Fashioned Recent Films (Splash) (Ed: Miss Beart is perfect, at least in looks. In ripping off *Splash*, the least they could have done was not have her fished out, too)

A Date with Judy, 1948, 113m, ★★¹/₂/$$, MGM/MGM-UA. A teenage girl thinks her older friend is having an affair, but it's really much more innocent. Wallace Beery, Jane Powell, Elizabeth Taylor, Carmen Miranda, Xavier Cugat, Robert Stack. w. Dorothy Cooper, Dorothy Kingsley, d. Richard Thorpe.

MUSICALS: COMEDY: Musical Comedy; **ROMANCE:** Misunderstandings; Friendships-Female; Small-town Life; Time Capsules; Female Protagonists; Female Screenwriters (The Bachelor and the Bobbysoxer; My Friend Irma)

Dave, 1993, 110m, ★★★¹/₂/$$$, WB/WB, PG-13/S. A lookalike (Kevin Kline) is hired to double for the President, but when the real commander in chief goes into a coma, he must pretend to be

him, even trying to fool the estranged first lady (Sigourney Weaver). Frank Langella, Faith Prince. w. Gary Ross (BOScr), d. Ivan Reitman. Oscars: 1-0.

COMEDY: SATIRE: ROMANCE: Romantic Comedy; Social Satire; Fish out of Water Stories; Capra-esque; Impostors; Identities-Assumed; Presidents; Politicians' Wives; Lookalikes; Royalty-Sudden; Washington D.C.; Sleeper Hits

RETREAD OF: The Prisoner of Zenda (The Prisoner of Zenda; Tootsie; The Man in the Iron Mask; The American President)

David and Bathsheba, 1951, 116m, ★★¹/₂/$$$$$, 20th/CBS-Fox. King David wants a woman and decides to have lied in order to keep her. Gregory Peck, Susan Hayward, Robertson Justice, Raymond Massey, Jayne Meadows, Kieron Moore. w. Philip Dunne (BScr), d. Henry King. BCCin, BOScore, BCArt. Oscars: 4-0.

DRAMA: ROMANCE: Biblical Stories; Ancient Times; Romance with Married Person; Jealousy; Crimes of Passion; Cheating Women; Kings; Blockbusters (King David; Solomon and Sheba)

David and Lisa (B&W), 1962, 94m, ★★★★/$$, NR, WR/RCA-Col. Unique romance of two mentally ill and disabled young people (Keir Dullea, Janet Margolin) who meet in a boarding school. They must overcome their parents and the psychologists to give each other a chance. w. Eleanor Perry (BAScr), N-adap. Theodore Isaac Rubin, d. Frank Perry (BDirector). Oscars: 2-0.

DRAMA: ROMANCE: Romantic Drama; Love-First; Coming of Age; Mentally Disabled; Mental Illness; Psychologists; Boarding Schools; Eccentric People; Cult Films; Hidden Gems; Female Screenwriters (Benny and Joon; Sundays and Cybele; A Patch of Blue)

David Copperfield, 1935, 132m, ★★★★/$$$$, MGM/MGM-UA. Story of the young orphan abused by his stepfather, whose aunt helps him grow up to become a successful writer and get married to the girl of his dreams. Freddie Bartholemew, Frank Lawton, W. C. Fields, Roland Young, Edna May Oliver, Maureen O'Sullivan, Basil Rathbone, Lionel Barrymore, Elsa Lanchester, Arthur Treacher. w. Hugh Walpole, Howard Estabrook, N-adap. Charles

Dickens, d. George Cukor. BPicture, BEdit. Oscars: 2-0.

DRAMA: MELODRAMA: Biographies-Fictional; **ROMANCE:** Boyhood; Orphans; Abused Children; Writers; All-Star Casts; Episodic Stories; 1800s

Davy Crockett, 1955, 93m, ★★★/$$$$, Disney/Disney. Stories of the famous pioneer fighter who trailblazed Tennessee and Kentucky and then made it to the battle of the Alamo. Fess Parker, Buddy Ebsen. w. Tom Blackburn, d. Norman Foster.

WESTERN: ADVENTURE: Pioneers; Early America; 1800s

SEQUEL: Davy Crockett and the River Pirates, 1950s TV SERIES

Dawn of the Dead, 1979, 127m, ★★★/$$$, Laurel-Ind/Republic, R/EV-B&G. Zombies awake one night and take over the countryside. David Emge, Ken Foree. w. d. George Romero.

HORROR: Zombies; Murders-One by One; Cult Films; Writer-Directors

SEQUEL TO: Night of the Living Dead.

SEQUEL: Day of the Dead.

The Dawn Patrol, 1938, 103m, ★★★/$$$, WB/MGM-UA, Fox. Flyers in World War I France prepare to go into battle. Errol Flynn, Basil Rathbone, David Niven, Melville Cooper, Donald Crisp, Barry Fitzgerald. w. Seton Miller, Dan Totheroh, d. Edmund Goulding.

ACTION: War Stories; World War I Stories; Pilots-Military; Death-Impending

A Day at the Races, 1937, 109m, ★★★★/$$$, MGM/MGM-UA. The Marx brothers bet on the horses and help out a rich girl. Groucho Marx, the Marx Brothers, Maureen O'Sullivan. w. Robert Pirosh, George Seaton, George Oppenheimer, d. Sam Wood.

COMEDY: Comedy-Skit; Comedy-Slapstick; Horse Racing; Ensemble Films (Animal Crackers; Duck Soup; The Big Store)

The Day After, 1983, 126m, ★★★/$$$$$, ABC/Sultan, PG/V. An atomic strike hits America and the effects of the survivors of Kansas City are explored. Jason Robards, Jobeth Williams, John Lithgow, Steve Guttenberg. w. d. Nicholas Meyer.

DRAMA: Message Films; Apocalyptic Stories; Bombs-Atomic; Ensemble Films; Cold War Era; Writer-Directors; TV Movies; Blockbusters (Testament; Amerika)

Daybreak, 1993, 100m, ★★★/$$, HBO/HBO, R/V-P-S-FN-MN. In an apocalyptic future world riddled with AIDS, a young rebellious white woman risks everything for the love of an infected black man. Moira Kelly, Cuba Gooding Jr., Martha Plimpton, Omar Epps, John Savage. w.d. Stephen Tolkin.
DRAMA: SCI-FI: Futuristic Films; AIDS Stories; Apocalyptic Stories; Epidemics; Prison Drama; Romance-Interracial; Romance-Forbidden; Inner City Life; New York Life; Poor People; Writer-Directors
(The Omega Man; A Boy and His Dog)
Day for Night, 1973, 120m, ★★★★/$$$, WB/WB, PG/S-P. Francois Truffaut's autobiographical story of the making of a film starring Jacqueline Bisset and Jean-Pierre Leaud. Valentina Cortese (BSActress). w. Suzanne Schiffman, Francois Truffaut (BOScr), d. Francois Truffaut (BDirector). **BFLFilm** (1973). Oscars: 4-1.
COMEDY DRAMA: SATIRE: Movies within Movies; Moviemaking; Directors; Autobiographical Stories; Actresses; Documentary Style; French Films; Narrated Films; Female Screenwriters
(The French Lieutenant's Woman; 8½; Stardust Memories)
A Day in the Death of Joe Egg, 1971, 106m, ★★★/$, Col/Col. A schoolteacher and his wife have a hyperactive daughter who complicates their already struggling lives. Alan Bates, Janet Suzman, Peter Bowles, Joan Hickson. w. P-adap. Peter Nichols, d. Peter Medak.
COMEDY DRAMA: Family Drama; Character Studies; Mentally Disabled; Teachers; Forgotten Films; Hidden Gems
(Baxter!; Son-Rise; Miracle of Love)
A Day in October, 1992, 96m, ★★1/2/$, Academy/Fox, PG-13/V-S. A Jewish woman rescues a resistance fighter in Denmark who's warning of the Nazis and their true intentions. D. B. Sweeney, Kelly Wolf, Tovah Feldshuh, Daniel Benzali. w. Damian Slattery, d. Kenneth Madsen.
DRAMA: World War II Stories; Jewish People; Saving Someone; Rescue Drama; Escape Drama; Nazi Stories; Germans as Enemy
Day of the Dead, 1985, 102m, ★★1/2/$, Laurel/Republic, R/EV-B&G. The Zombies have taken over, and a scientist is trying to make them more

human-like so the humans can co-exist, but it may not work. Lori Cardille, Terry Alexander. w.d. George Romero.
HORROR: Zombies; Scientists; Reformers; Cult Films
The Day of the Dolphin, 1973, ★★★/$, Avco-Embassy/Col-New Line, PG. A scientist working with dolphins and their radar abilities discovers a plot to use them to deliver a bomb to a boat carrying the President. George C. Scott, Trish Van Dever, Paul Sorvino, Fritz Weaver. w. Buck Henry, N-adap. Robert Merle, d. Mike Nichols. BSound, BOScore. Oscars: 2-0.
SUSPENSE: MYSTERY: Conspiracy; Animal Stories; Presidents; Assassinations; Dolphins; Scientists; Experiments; Underrated; Forgotten Films
(Ed: An oddity from every angle, but interesting)
Day of the Jackal, 1973, 142m, ★★★1/2/$$$, Universal/MCA-U, R/S-V. An assassin (Edward Fox) plots to shoot the president of France by using disguises to get to him. w. Kenneth Ross, N-adap. Frederick Forsyth, d. Fred Zinneman. BEditing. Oscars: 1-0.
SUSPENSE: Spy Films; Spies; Detective Stories; Assassinations; Chase Movies; Disguises; Serial Killers; Murders-One by One; Rogue Plots; Fugitives from the Law; Race Against Time
(In the Line of Fire; The Man Who Knew Too Much)
The Day of the Locust, 1975, 143m, ★★★/$$, Par/Par, R/S-V. A young man entering Hollywood life finds much mental illness and alcoholism among the has-beens and wanna-bes, which leads to tragedy for one. Donald Sutherland, William Atherton, Karen Black, Burgess Meredith (BSActor), Geraldine Page, Richard Dysart. w. Waldo Salt, N-adap. Nathanael West, d. John Schlesinger. BCin. Oscars: 2-0.
DRAMA: TRAGEDY: SATIRE: Character Studies; Hollywood Life; Depression Era; Nervous Breakdowns; Alcoholics; Classic Literary Adaptations; Hidden Gems; Quiet Little Films
(The Last Tycoon; Chinatown)
The Day of the Triffids, 1962, 95m, ★★1/2/$$, Ind/Media, Prism. A meteor shower blinds people and causes plants to mutate and become people-eaters. Howard Keel, Nicole Maurey, Kieron

Moore, Alexander Knox. w. Philip Yordan, N-adap. John Wyndham, d. Steve Sekely.
SCI-FI: HORROR: Plants; Monsters-Mutant; Meteors; Apocalyptic Stories; Paranoia; Cult Films; Camp
(Them)
Day of Wrath, 1943, 105m, ★★★1/2/$, Ind/Nos. A woman burned in old Germany for witchcraft curses the preacher who condemned her, leading to death and treachery for him and his descendants. Thorkild Rose, Lisbeth Movin. w. Carl Dreyer, Poul Knudsen, Mogens Skot-Hansen, P-adap. Hans Wier Jansen, d. Carl Dreyer.
DRAMA: TRAGEDY: Revenge; Witchcraft; Executions; Curses; Episodic Stories; German Films; 1700s
(The Crucible; Saint Joan)
Day One, 1989, 141m, ★★★/$$$, ABC/World Vision. Slice of life about the race to finish the first atomic bomb with the Manhattan Project. Brian Dennehy, David Straithairn, Michael Tucker, Hume Cronyn, Richard Dysart, Barnard Hughes, Hal Holbrook, David Ogden Stiers. w. David Rintel, d. Joseph Sargent.
DRAMA: Historical Drama; Bombs-Atomic; Scientists; True Stories; World War II Stories; Race Against Time; TV Movies
(Fat Man and Little Boy; The Enola Gay)
The Day the Earth Caught Fire, 1961, 99m, ★★★/$$, BL/Republic. Atomic tests cause the earth to whirl off its axis closer to the sun. Edward Judd, Janet Munro, Leo McKern. w. Wolf Mankowitz, Val Guest, d. Guest.
SCI-FI: Sci-Fi-1950s; Apocalyptic Stories; Fires; Bombs-Atomic; British Films; Forgotten Films
(War of the Worlds; Invaders from Mars)
The Day the Earth Stood Still, 1951, 92m, ★★★1/2/$$$, Par/Par. When a flying saucer lands at the Washington Monument, the alien visitor takes human form and escapes into the public to find top scientists to warn them about imminent apocalypse if Earth doesn't change its violent ways. He stays in a boardinghouse where he befriends a boy and his mother, who's the only one who can save him. Michael Rennie, Patricia Neal, Hugh Marlowe, Sam Jaffe, Billy Gray, Frances Bavier. d. Robert Wise.

SCI-FI: Sci-Fi-1950s; Message Films; Apocalyptic Stories; Cold War Era; UFOs; Aliens-Outer Space, Good; Robots; Washington D.C.; Blackouts; Allegorical Stories; Cult Films

The Day the Fish Came Out, 1967, 109m, ★★1/2/$, 20th/NA. A Greek isle is contaminated by nuclear waste and a band of eccentric, mod, futuristic people converge to investigate and be victimized by the happening. Candice Bergen, Tom Courtenay, Sam Wanamaker, Colin Blakely, Ian Ogilvy. w. d. Michael Cacoyannis.

COMEDY DRAMA: SATIRE: Spoofs; Art Films; Avant-Garde Films; Toxic Waste; Nuclear Energy; Bombs-Atomic; Futuristic Films; Mod Era; Greece; Islands; Curiosities; Writer-Directors

Days of Heaven, 1978, 95m, ★★★1/2/$, Par/Par, R/S-P. Two lovers pretend to be brother and sister and leave Chicago for the plains of Texas to start over with the woman's younger tomboy sister, but life isn't so easy once there. Richard Gere, Brooke Adams, Sam Shepard, Linda Manz. w. d. Terence Malick. **BCin**, BOScore, BEdit, BCostume. 4-1.

DRAMA: ROMANCE: Romance-Triangles; Ordinary People Stories; Farm Life; Brothers & Sisters; Runaways; Tomboys; Slice of Life Stories; Quiet Little Films; Narrated Films; Scenery-Outstanding; Writer-Directors

Days of Thunder, 1990, 107m, ★★/$$$, Par/Par, PG-13/S-P. A young race car driver pulls out all the stops to beat an old pro and win the girl. Tom Cruise, Nicole Kidman, Robert Duvall, Randy Quaid, Cary Elwes, Fred Dalton Thompson. w. Robert Towne, Tom Cruise, d. Tony Scott.

ACTION: Action Drama; Underdog Stories; Sports Movies; Car Racing; Generation Gap; Young Men; Men Proving Themselves
(Le Mans; Grand Prix; Far and Away)
(Ed: Days of Blunder)

Days of Wine and Roses, 1958, 89m, ★★★/$$$, CBS/MGM, RHI. Playhouse 90 original story about a couple destroyed by alcoholism. Cliff Robertson, Piper Laurie. d. John Frankenheimer.

Days of Wine and Roses, 1962, ★★★1/2/$$, WB/WB. A couple of married alcoholics battle it out and try to recover but may not make it. Jack Lemmon

(BActor), Lee Remick (BActress), Jack Klugman, Charles Bickford, Alan Hewitt, Jack Albertson. w. J.P. Miller, d. Blake Edwards. **BOSong.** Oscars: 3-1.

DRAMA: COMEDY DRAMA: TRAGEDY: Marriage Drama; Social Drama; Message Films; Alcoholics; Midlife Crisis; Redemption
(Leaving Las Vegas; The Lost Weekend; Smash-Up; The Story of a Woman; Dangerous; The Morning After)

Dazed and Confused, 1993, 117m, ★★★/$$, Gramercy-U/MCA-U, R/EP-S-V. The last day of school for a bunch of alienated potheads in a small Southern town in 1975 is chronicled all through the night as they cross each other's paths and manage to stay alive. Jason London. w. d. Richard Linklater.

COMEDY DRAMA: COMEDY: SATIRE: High School Life; Drugs; 1970s; Cult Films; Small-town Life; Suburban Life; Southerns; Slice of Life; Ordinary People Stories; Teenagers; Teenage Movies; Coming of Age; Quiet Little Films; Party Movies; One Day Stories; Writer-Directors
(American Graffiti; Slacker; Before Sunrise)

D.C. Cab, 1984, 100m, ★★★/$$, U/MCA-U, RKO, R/P-S. A slice of life about freewheeling cabbies in Washington D.C. and their campy adventures. Mr. T, Adam Baldwin, Leif Erickson, Irene Cara, Anne DeSalvo, Jill Schoelen, Marsha Warfield, Gary Busey. w. Joel Schumacher, Topper Carew, d. Schumacher.

COMEDY: Action Comedy; Kidnappings; Taxi Drivers; Detectives-Amateur; Heroes-Unlikely; Camp; Cult Films; Writer-Directors
(Amateur Night at the Dixie Bar and Grill; Car Wash)

The Dead, 1987, 83m, ★★★/$, Vestron/Vestron, PG. A get-together for Irish friends in old Ireland becomes a reflection on the past for all. Anjelica Huston, Donal McCann, Dan O'Herlihy. w. Tony Huston (BAScr), N-adap. James Joyce, Dubliners, d. John Huston. BCostume. Oscars: 2-0.

DRAMA: COMEDY DRAMA: Costume Drama; Memories; Ordinary People Stories; Sisters; Spinsters; Dinner Parties; Ireland
(Babette's Feast; Ulysses; Portrait of the Artist as a Young Man)
(Ed: John Huston's last)

Dead Again, 1991, 131m, ★★★1/2/$$$, Par/Par, R/V-P. A detective (Kenneth Branagh) rescues a woman who can't remember who she is (Emma Thompson) and discovers they may have been doomed lovers in another life. Derek Jacobi, Andy Garcia, Robin Williams. w. Scott Frank, d. Kenneth Branagh.

SUSPENSE: ROMANCE: MYSTERY: MURDER MYSTERY: Film Noir-Modern; Reincarnation; Amnesia; Romance-Reunited; Saving Someone; Parallel Stories; Secrets-Haunting; Hitchcockian; 1940s; Los Angeles
(Spellbound; The Reincarnation of Peter Proud; The Big Sleep; Peter's Friends)

Dead Ahead, the Exxon Valdez Disaster, 1993, 90m, ★★1/2/$$, HBO/Imperial. The title says it all. Rip Torn, Christopher Lloyd, Michael Murphy, David Morse, John Heard, Bob Gunton, Mark Metcalf. w. Michael Baker, d. Paul Seed.

DRAMA: True Stories; Docudrama; Accidents; Oil People
(Barbarians at the Gate; Free Willy 2)
(Ed: Pretty slow, fairly clunky, and not too enlightening-we know it happened and how doesn't necessarily matter)

Dead Alive, 1993, 97m, ★★1/2/$, Vidmark/Vidmark, R/EV-B&G-S. A monkey in New Zealand bites a kid's mother, who then turns into a crazed monster. Timothy Blame, Elizabeth Moody. w.d. Peter Jackson.

HORROR: SCI-FI: Monsters-Animal; Primates; New Zealand; Writer-Directors

Dead Bang, 1989, 103m, ★★1/2/$, WB/WB, R/EV-P-S. A vigilante cop from LA (Don Johnson) goes on the trail of a cop-killer, leading him deep into a white supremacist ring. Tim Reid, Penelope Ann Miller. d. John Frankenheimer.

ACTION: Detective Stories; Detectives-Police; Police-Vigilante; Chase Movies; Rebels; Bigots; Ku Klux Klan; Murderers of Police; Unintentionally funny; Camp
(Betrayed; Guilty as Sin)

Dead Boyz Can't Fly, 1993, 92m, ★★/$$, VCI/VCI, R/EP-S-EV. Inner-city revenge as project dwellers go on a burglary spree to express their dissatisfaction with the establishment's exploitation of their neighborhood. Delia Sheppard, Mark McCulley, Sheila Kennedy, Ruth Collins, Brad Friedman. d. Howard Winters.

ACTION: Action Drama; Revenge; Inner-City Life; Black Casts; Thieves
(Juice; Zebrahead; The DROP Squad)

Dead End, 1937, ★★★¹/2/$$$, Goldwyn-UA/Goldwyn. A rich people's apartment complex towers over the Bowery district in New York where an assortment of street kids are met by a couple. Joel McCrea, Sylvia Sidney, Humphrey Bogart, Wendy Barrie, Marjorie Main, Claire Trevor (BSActress), Ward Bond, The Dead End Kids. w. Lillian Hellman, P-adap. Sidney Kingsley, d. William Wyler. BPicture, BCin, BArt. Oscars: 4-0.

DRAMA: MELODRAMA: TRAGEDY: Multiple Stories; Slice of Lice Stories; Rich vs. Poor; Mob Stories; Street Life; Inner-City Life; Homeless People
(Street Scene)

Deadfall, 1968, 120m, ★★¹/2/$, 20th/NA, PG/S. A planned heist goes afoul when one of two partners falls for the other's wife, who's unfulfilled since her husband is gay. Michael Caine, Eric Portman, Nanette Newman, Giovanna Ralli. w. d. Bryan Forbes.

DRAMA: Heist Stories; **ROMANCE:** Romantic Drama; Romance-Triangles; Jewel Thieves; Bisexuality; Gay Men; Forgotten Films; Coulda Been Good; Ahead of Its Time; Writer-Directors
(The Italian Job; Silver Bears)

Deadfall, 1993, 99m, ★★¹/2/$, Vidmark/Vidmark, R/P-S-V. Father and son con artists' scam goes awry when dad is killed by junior, leading to many dangerous secrets of dad's being exposed. James Coburn, Michael Biehn, Nicolas Cage, Sarah Trigger, Charlie Sheen, Peter Fonda. w. David Peoples, d. Christopher Coppola.

SUSPENSE: MURDER: Father & Sons; Murder of Parent; Secrets; Con Artists

Dead Heat, 1988, 86m, ★★/$, New World/New World, PG-13/P-V. A cop is brought back to life as a zombie to help his partner find his killer. Joe Piscopo, Treat Williams, Lindsay Frost, Darren McGavin, Vincent Price. w. Craig Black, d. Mark Goldblatt.

ACTION: Action Comedy; Police Comedy; Dead-Back from the; Zombies; **MURDER:** Murder of Police; Trail of a Killer
(Ghost; Heart Condition)

Dead Heat on a Merry Go Round, 1967, 108m, ★★¹/2/$$, Col/Col. A convict decides to get back in the business

and skip out on his parole officer to pull a heist at the airport. James Coburn, Aldo Ray, Camilla Sparv, Rose Marie, Robert Webber. w. d. Bernard Girard.

ACTION: Heist Stories; Ex-Convicts; Race Against Time; Airports; Bank Robberies; Playboys; Forgotten Films; Writer-Directors
(Harry in Your Pocket; Thunderbolt and Lightfoot; The President's Analyst)

Dead in the Water, 1991, 90m, ★★¹/2/$, U/MCA-U, PG-13/P-S. A lawyer and his mistress plot to murder his greedy wife, but when the wrong person is murdered, it appears he's been framed. Bryan Brown, Anne DeSalvo, Teri Hatcher, Veronica Cartwright. w. Eleanor Gaver, Robert Seidenberg, d. Bill Condon.

SUSPENSE: MURDER: Framed?; Accused Unjustly; Accidents; Double Crossings; Mix-Ups; Cheating Men; Murder of Spouse; Good Premise Unfulfilled; Female Screenwriters

Deadlier Than the Male, 1966, 101m, ★★★/$$, UA/NA. Two nasty female spies wreak havoc in the Riviera as Bulldog Drummond searches for them in connection with some assassinations. Elke Sommer, Richard Johnson, Nigel Green, Sylva Koscina, Suzanne Leigh. w. Jimmy Sangster, David Osborn, Liz Charles-Williams, d. Ralph Thomas.

ACTION: Action Comedy; Detective Stories; Secret Agents; Spies-Female; Spy Films; Spies; Assassinations; Riviera Life; Camp; Curiosities; Female Screenwriters
(Fathom; Never Say Never Again)

Deadline USA, 1952, 87m, ★★¹/2/$$, 20th/NA. A newspaper goes up against the mob and risks the consequences. Humphrey Bogart, Kim Hunter, Ethel Barrymore, Ed Begley, Jim Backus. w. d. Richard Brooks.

DRAMA: Crime Drama; Mob Stories; Newspapers; Ethics; Journalists; Journalists as Detectives; Writer-Directors

Deadlock, 1991, 103m, ★★¹/2/$, VTR/Media, R/P-S-V. In the future, a man and woman escape from prison with collars that will explode if they get more than 100 yards apart from each other. Mimi Rogers, Rutger Hauer, Joan Chen, James Remar, Stephen Tobolowsky. d. Lewis Teague.

SCI-FI: ACTION: Prison Escapes; Chase Stories; Race Against Time; TV Movies;

Cuff to Cuff; Exploding Heads
(D.O.A. [1988]; Scanners; Speed)

The Deadly Affair, 1966, 106m, ★★★/$$, Col/NA. When a man at an embassy apparently commits suicide, a cohort begins digging and uncovers a conspiracy. James Mason, Simone Signoret, Harry Andrews, Maximillian Schell, Max Adrian, Lynn Redgrave. w. Paul Dehn, N-adap. John Le Carré, *Call for the Dead*, d. Sidney Lumet.

DRAMA: Spy Films; Spies; Conspiracy; **MURDER: MYSTERY: MURDER MYSTERY:** Detective Stories; Avenging Death of Someone; Suicidal Tendencies; Diplomats; Forgotten Films; Hidden Gems
(The Spy Who Came in From the Cold; The Looking Glass War)
(Ed: Not the most entertaining-it is Le Carré, but intriguing, as the genre should be)

Deadly Currents, 1993, 93m, ★★/$, Col/Col, R/P-V. A CIA agent on a Caribbean island unravels some old secrets of a bar owner there, leading to a situation neither bargains for. George C. Scott, William Petersen, Julie Carmen, Alexei Sayle, Trish Van Devere, Philip Anglim. w. James Buchanan, d. Carl Schultz.

SUSPENSE: Detective Stories; CIA Agents; Elderly Men; Secrets; Past-Haunted by the; Coulda Been Good
(Ed: Deadly dull, but looks good)

Deadly Friend, 1986, 99m, ★★¹/2/$, WB/WB, R/V-B&G. A genius nerd makes a girl who's been assaulted into a robot so she can exact revenge on her assailant. Matthew Laborteaux, Kristy Swanson, Anne Twomey. w. Bruce Joel Rubin, N-adap. Diana Hentsell, d. Wes Craven.

HORROR: SUSPENSE: Androids; Dead-Back from the; Revenge; Rape/Rapists; Revenge on Rapists; Geniuses; Teenagers; Coulda Been Good

Deadly Matrimony, 1992, 130m, ★★¹/2/$$$, NBC/Live. A playboy lawyer kills his wife, but a Chicago cop is hot on his trail and has to fight mob connections to the police to catch the guy. Brian Dennehy, Treat Williams, Embeth Davidtz, Susan Ruttan, Lisa Eilbacher, Terry Kinney.

SUSPENSE: MURDER: Murder of Spouse; Mob Stories; Police Stories; Detectives-Police; Trail of a Killer; Chicago; TV Movies

The Deadly Trap, 1971, 100m, ★★1/2/$, U/MCA-U, Facets. A chic couple in Paris have their children kidnapped and go crazy trying to find them. Faye Dunaway, Frank Langella, Barbara Parkins. w. Sidney Buchman, Eleanor Perry, N-adap. Arthur Cavanagh, *The Children Are Gone*, d. Rene Clement.
SUSPENSE: MYSTERY: Art Films; Kidnappings; Searches; Missing Children; Missing Person Thriller; Paris; Time Capsules; Coulda Been Great; Female Screenwriters
(Don't Look Now; Seance on a Wet Afternoon)
(Ed: Too much ambiance, too little suspense)
Dead Man Walking, 1995, 122m, ★★★1/2/$$$, Gramercy/MCA-U, R/P. The debate about capital punishment is raised once more in this story of a nun who counsels an inmate on Death Row, finding a unique relationship in her efforts with him as he is about to be executed. Susan Sarandon (**BActress**), Sean Penn (BActor), Robert Prosky, Raymond J. Barry, R. Lee Ermey, Celia Weston, Lois Smith, Scott Wilson, Roberta Maxwell, Margo Martindale. w. d. Tim Robbins (BAScr, BDirector), NF-adap. Sister Helen Prejean. BOSong. Oscars: 5-1.
DRAMA: Tragedy; Nuns; Friendships Between Sexes; Executions; Prison Drama; Saving Someone; Religion; Louisiana; True Stories; Female Protagonists
(Someone Has to Shoot the Picture; Mrs. Soffel; I Want to Live!)
Dead Men Don't Wear Plaid (B&W), 1982, 89m, ★★★/$$$, Universal/MCA-U, PG. A detective (Steve Martin) meets a dame with a secret (Rachel Ward) and unravels the mystery with help of old film clips. w. Carl Reiner, George Gipe, Steve Martin, d. Carl Reiner.
COMEDY: MYSTERY: MURDER MYSTERY: Comic Mystery; Film Noir; Spoofs; Detectives in Deep; Dangerous Women; Multiple Stories; All-Star Cast; Film Compilations
(Airplane; The Black Bird)
Dead of Night, 1945, 104m, ★★★1/2/$$, Ealing/EMI-HBO. A man has a series of nightmares belonging to other people, involving ghosts and other terrifying things and leading to murder. Mervyn Johns, Roland Culver, Sally Ann Howes, Mary Merrall. w. John Baines,

Angus MacPhail, SS-adap. Baines, MacPhail, H. G. Wells, E. F. Benson, d. Cavalcanti, Charles Crichton, Robert Hamer, Basil Dearden.
HORROR: SUSPENSE: Multiple Stories; Psychological Thriller; Interwoven Stories; Nightmares; Ghosts; MURDER: Mental Illness; Insane-Plot to Drive; Buses; Ventriloquists
(Brighton Rock; The Uninvited; Trilogy in Terror; Magic)
(Ed: Chilling but not very frightening by today's standards)
Dead of Night, 1977, 76m, ★★1/2/$$, ABC/Live. A trilogy of terror and the supernatural including vampires and reincarnation. Joan Hackett, Patrick Macnee, Anjanette Comer. w. Richard Matheson, d. Dan Curtis.
HORROR: SCI-FI: Vampires; Reincarnation; Dead-Back from the; Multiple Stories; TV Movies
(Salem's Lot; Trilogy in Terror)
Dead of Winter, 1987, 103m, ★★★/$, MGM/MGM-UA, R/V. An actress (Mary Steenburgen) is lured into a trap by a supposed director and friend but instead finds murder. Roddy McDowell, Josef Sommer. w. Marc Schmuger, Mark Malone, d. Arthur Penn.
SUSPENSE: MURDER: Conspiracy; Mindgames; Stranded; Lookalikes; Insane-Plot to Make; Actresses; Snow Settings; Old-Fashioned Recent Films; Underrated; Multiple Performances
(Dead Ringer; The Shining; Die! Die! My Darling)
(Ed: A campy chiller with a few very good moments)
Dead On, 1993, 87m, ★★/$, Orion/Orion, R/P-S-V. Two lovers decide to off not one's spouse but both of their spouses. But, as always, things backfire. Matt McCoy, Shari Shattuck, Tracy Scoggins, David Aykroyd, Thomas Wagner. d. Ralph Hemecker.
SUSPENSE: MURDER: Murder of Spouse; Murder-Exchanging; Cheating Men; Cheating Women; Double Crossings
(Body Heat; Diabolique)
Dead Poet's Society, 1989, 135m, ★★★1/2/$$$$$, Touchstone/Touchstone, PG. Several different boys come to terms with various problems with the aid of an inspirational teacher (Robin Williams, BActor). But it ends in tragedy. w. Thom Schulman (**BOScr**), d. Peter Weir (BDirector). BPicture. Oscars: 4-1.

DRAMA: COMEDY:
DRAMA: TRAGEDY: Inspirational; Coming of Age Dreams; Suicidal Tendencies; Suicidal Tendencies of Young People; Teachers; Secrets-Keeping; Teachers & Students; Boarding Schools; Boys' School; Friendships-Male; Fraternity Life; Sleeper Hits; Blockbusters
(Seize the Day; A Separate Peace; Tea and Sympathy; The Devil's Playground; Spanking the Monkey)
(Ed: A little too maudlin but still effective)
The Dead Pool, 1988, 91m, ★★/$$$, WB/WB, R/P-S-V. Dirty Harry has a series of murders linked by a list of famous people that a group bet on as to when they will die-and they're on target. Clint Eastwood, Patricia Clarkson, Liam Neeson, Evan Kim, David Hunt, Jim Carrey. w. Steve Sharon, Durk Pearson, Sandy Shaw, d. Buddy Van Horn.
ACTION: Police Stories; MURDER: MYSTERY: MURDER MYSTERY: Detective-Stories; Detectives-Police; Trail of a Killer; Serial Killers; Murders-One by One; San Francisco; Unintentionally Funny; Camp
(Sudden Impact; Ditry Harry SERIES)
(Ed: Full of cliches and tongue-in-cheek, this is the comic Dirty Harry-or is it just that bad? Especially the exploding little remote control car)
Dead Presidents, 1995, 122m, ★★1/2/$$, Hollywood/Hollywood, R/EP-S-B&G-EV. A black Vietnam vet who saw incredible war horrors comes home and gets involved with a gang of thieves after his job ends. They intend to rob the Federal Reserve of the worn-out money it's planning to shred, hence the title (referring to the presidents on the money). Larenz Tate, Keith David, Chris Tucker, Freddy Rodriguez, Rose Jackson, Martin Sheen. w. Michael Henry Brown, Allen & Albert Hughes, d. The Hughes Brothers.
DRAMA: ACTION: Heist Stories; Bank Robberies; Veterans-Vietnam; Black Men; Black Soldiers; Black Screenwriters; Black Directors; Directed by Brothers
(The Revolutionary; Panthers; Katherine)
Dead Reckoning, 1947, 100m, ★★1/2/$$, Col/RCA-Col. When a veteran and his pal are on the way to Washington to receive medals, one disappears and the

other discovers a conspiracy behind it. Humphrey Bogart, Lizabeth Scott, Morris Carnovsky, Charles Cane, Wallace Ford. w. Oliver Garrett, Steve Fisher, d. John Cromwell.

MYSTERY: Missing Persons; Conspiracy; Film Noir; Friendships-Male; Veterans; Dangerous Women; Washington D.C.

Dead Ringer, 1964, 116m, ★★★/$$, WB/WB. A twin kills her sister and takes over her life to live in a highrise and exact her revenge. Bette Davis, Karl Malden, Peter Lawford, Philip Carey, Jean Hagen, Estelle Winwood. w. Albert Beich, Oscar Millard, d. Paul Henried.

SUSPENSE: MURDER: Identities-Assumed; Revenge; Jealousy; Twins; Sisters; Cult Films; Camp; Multiple Performances

(Dead Ringers; The Dark Mirror; Dead of Winter)

Dead Ringers, 1988, 115m, ★★★/$$, 20th/CBS-Fox, R/P-V-S-MN. Two gynecologists are brothers and also twins and like making things confusing for a woman they love while they compete and try to destroy each other. Jeremy Irons (BActor, NYFC), Genevieve Bujold. w. David Cronenberg, Norman Snider, N-adap. Barry Wood, d. Cronenberg.

HORROR: DRAMA: SUSPENSE: TRAGEDY: Psychological Thriller; Psychological Drama; Romance-Triangles; Twins; Twins-Evil; Brothers; Doctors; Jealousy; Mindgames; Homoeroticism; Men Fighting Over Women

(Jack's Back; Dark Mirror; Never Talk to Strangers)

The Dead Zone, 1983, 103m, ★★★/$$, Lorimar-DEG-Par/Par, R/P-S-V. A man discovers the ability to see the future and believes something happening with the President will precipitate the end of the world. Christopher Walken, Brooke Adams, Tom Skerritt, Herbert Lom, Anthony Zerbe, Colleen Dewhurst. w. Jeffrey Boam, N-adap. Stephen King, d. David Cronenberg.

HORROR: SUSPENSE: Psychological Thriller; Psychics; Seeing the Future; Apocalyptic Stories; Presidents; Evil Men; Accidents; Comas; Cult Films

(The Medusa Touch; The Stand)

Deal of the Century, 1983, 99m, ★★1/2/$$, WB/WB, PG/P. A shady and goofy arms dealer sells defective equipment which may truly backfire on him and his colleagues. Chevy Chase,

Sigourney Weaver, Gregory Hines, Richard Libertini, Wallace Shawn. w. Paul Brickman, d. William Friedkin.

COMEDY: Arms Dealers; Military Comedy; Central America; Accidents; Salesmen

(Best Defense)

Dear America: Letters Home from Vietnam, 1988, 84m, ★★★1/2/$$, Ind/HBO, PG/P. Documentary tracing letters from soldiers in Vietnam to loved ones back home, read by an all-star cast. d. Bill Couturie.

Documentaries; True Stories; Vietnam War; Veterans-Vietnam; Epistolaries; Soldiers; All-Star Casts; Hidden Gems

(Platoon; Coming Home)

Dear Heart, 1964, 114m, ★★★/$$, WB/WB. Two middle-aged people at a convention fall for each other, but the spinsterish woman may be let down once again. Geraldine Page, Glenn Ford, Angela Lansbury, Michael Anderson Jr., Barbara Nichols, Alice Pearce, Neva Patterson. w. Tad Mosel, d. Delbert Mann. BOSong. Oscars: 1-0.

DRAMA: ROMANCE: MELODRAMA: Tearjerkers; Romance-Middle-Aged; Spinsters; Lonely People; Forgotten Films; Hidden Gems

(Summertime; Summer and Smoke; Rachel, Rachel)

Dear Inspector, 1977, 105m, ★★★/$, Ind/NA. A woman detective is on the trail of a killer with the help of her boyfriend, but may have bit off more than she can chew. Annie Girardot, Phillipe Noiret, Catherine Alric. w. Michel Audiard, Phillipe deBroca, N-adap. JeanPaul Rouland, Claude Olivier, d. de Broca.

MYSTERY: Detective Stories; **MURDER: MURDER MYSTERY:** Trail of a Killer; Comic Mystery; Comic Thriller; Romantic Comedy; Detectives-Female; Detective Couples; Hidden Gems; Female Protagonists

(Compromising Positions; Confidentially Yours)

Dear John, 1964, 111m, ★★★/$, Ind/NA. An unwed mother has a romance with a man of the seas in a small Swedish town. Jarl Kulle, Christina Scholin. w. d. Lars Lindgren, N-adap. Olle Lansburg.

ROMANCE: DRAMA: Romantic Drama; Mothers-Unwed; Flashbacks; Swedish Films; Quiet Little Films

Dear Ruth, 1947, 95m, ★★★/$$, Par/NA, AMC. A girl writes love letters to a soldier she has a crush on using her older sister's pictures, which causes quite a problem when he returns. William Holden, Joan Caulfield, Mona Freeman, Edward Arnold. w. Arthur Sheekman, P-adap. Norman Krasna, d. William Russell.

COMEDY: ROMANCE: Romantic Comedy; Impostors; Epistolaries; Misunderstandings; Episodic Stories; Sisters; Soldiers; Hidden Gems

(The Truth About Cats and Dogs; Cyrano de Bergerac)

Death and the Maiden, 1994, 103m, ★★1/2/$, Fine Line/New Line, R/P-S-V. In a vague, South American, fascistic country (take your pick), the wife of a political official who was raped and tortured thinks her husband's friend is the one who did her the most damage while held in captivity blindfolded. She was once supposedly wrong in accusing a man of being one of the culprits, but she's certain this time. She ties him up and beats him until he'll confess, but is she correct and do two wrongs make a right? Sigourney Weaver, Ben Kingsley, Stuart Wilson. w. P-adap. Ariel Dorfman, d. Roman Polanski.

DRAMA: SUSPENSE: Psychological Drama; Psychological Thriller; Hostage Situations; Torture; Past-Haunted by the; Rape/Rapists; Revenge on Rapist; Turning the Tables; Accused Unjustly; Oppression; South America; Flops-Major; Stagelike Films

(Extremities; The House of the Spirits; Kiss of the Spider Woman)

(Ed: This major stage hit died on the screen, stagebound, rather cliche, and fogbound)

Death Becomes Her, 1992, 107m, ★★★1/2/$$$$, Universal/MCA-U, R/P-V. Two feuding women, a wealthy actress (Meryl Streep) and an old friend (Goldie Hawn), steal a man back and forth (Bruce Willis) while battling wrinkles until a mysterious woman (Isabella Rossellini) gives them an elixir of youth with calamitous consequences. Ian Ogilvy. w. David Koepp, d. Robert Zemeckis. **BSFX.** Oscars: 1-1.

COMEDY: Black Comedy; Morbid Comedy; Fantasy; **SCIFI:** Cartoonlike Movies; Romance-Triangles; Revenge; Women in Conflict; Women Fighting

over Men; Friendships-Female; Mean Women; Cures/Elixirs; Aging; Aging-Reverse; Rejuvenation; Cosmetic Surgery; Beverly Hills; Actresses; Female Protagonists
(Rich and Famous; Old Acquaintance; The Turning Point; She-Devil; The Mirror Crack'd)
(Ed: Some very good moments make up for a perhaps not entirely satisfying climax, but if you like bitchfights, this is the creme de la creme)

Death in Brunswick, 1990, 109m, ★★¹/₂/$, Ind/NA. A man accidentally kills a co-worker and asks a friend to help him get rid of the body, which may not be so easy. Sam Neill, Zoe Carides, John Clarke. w. John Ruane, Boyd Oxlade, N-adap. Oxlade, d. Ruane.
MURDER: Black Comedy; Death-Accidental; Hide the Dead Body; Australian Films; Overlooked at Release; Underrated; Hidden Gems
(Over Her Dead Body; The Trouble with Harry)

Death in Venice, 1969, 124m, ★★★¹/₂/$$, WB/WB, PG. A man (Dirk Bogarde) has come to Venice for his last days and finds himself enchanted with a young blond boy. w. Nicola Badalucco, Luchino Vischonti, N-adap. Thomas Mann, d. Luchino Visconti.
DRAMA: Character Studies; Death-Impending; Elderly Men; Obsessions; Infatuations; Gay Men; Homoeroticism; Italian Films; Venice; Classic Literary Adaptations; Men and Boys; 1900s; Lyrical Films
(Lolita; The Damned; Victim)

Death of a Gunfighter, 1969, 100m, ★★¹/₂/$, U/MCA-U. A marshal in a small western town won't give up the post and has to deal with anarchy. Richard Widmark, Lena Horne, John Saxon, Carroll O'Connor. w. Joseph Calvelli, d. Robert Totten.
WESTERNS: Duels; Men in Conflict; Anarchists; Forgotten Films; Marshals; Police Stories

Death of a Salesman, (B&W), 1950, 112m, ★★★★/$$, Col/RCA-Col. A salesman (Fredric March, BActor), finding he's unable to continue supporting his family, faces a major crisis, affecting his sons who want to be different. Kevin McCarthy (BSActor), Mildred Dunnock (BSActress), Cameron Mitchell. w. P-adap. Arthur Miller,

d. Lazlo Benedek. BB&WCin, BScore. Oscars: 5-0.

Death of a Salesman, 1985, 150m, ★★★★/$$$$, CBS-/Lorimar-WB. Dustin Hoffman, John Malkovich, Kate Reid, Stephen Lang. w. P-adap. Arthur Miller, d. Volker Schlondorff.
DRAMA: TRAGEDY: Social Drama; Midlife Crisis; Depression; Alienation; Class Conflicts; Making a Living; Fathers and Sons; Fathers-Struggling; Brothers; Ordinary People Stories; Pulitzer Prize Adaptations; Classic Literary Adaptations
(The Man in the Grey Flannel Suit; I Never Sang for My Father; All My Sons; Patterns; Imaginary Crimes)

Death on the Nile, 1978, 140m, ★★★/$$, EMI-U/MCA-U, PG/V. Poirot goes on a cruise with a bunch of upper-crusty Brits who have a secret resulting in murder. Peter Ustinov, Bette Davis, Mia Farrow, David Niven, Maggie Smith, Angela Lansbury, Jack Warden, Olivia Hussey, Jane Birkin, Simon MacCorkindale. w. Anthony Shaffer, N-adap. Agatha Christie, d. John Guillermin. **BCostume.** Oscars: 1-1.
MYSTERY: MURDER: MURDER MYSTERY: Mystery-Whodunits; Detective Stories; Ensemble Films; Ships; Heiresses; All-Star Casts; Middle East; Agatha Christie
(Murder on the Orient Express; Evil Under the Sun; Appointment with Death)

Death Race 2000, 1975, 79m, ★★¹/₂/$$, New World/New World, R/V-S. In the future, whoever kills the most with their vehicles wins. David Carradine, Sylvester Stallone, Mary Woronov. w. Robert Thom, Charles Griffith, Ib Melchior, d. Paul Bartel.
ACTION: SCI-FI: Futuristic Films; Motorcycles; Car Racing; Car Wrecks
(Rollerball; Gumball Rally; Cherry 2000)

Death Takes a Holiday, 1934, 78m, ★★★/$$, Par/NA. A prince who is Death comes to earth to find out why everyone is so afraid of him and settles with a wealthy family to possibly find love. Fredric March, Evelyn Venable, Gail Patrick, Katherine Alexander. w. Maxwell Anderson, Gladys Lehmann, Walter Ferris, P-adap. Maxwell Anderson, Alberto Casella, d. Mitchell Liesen.
COMEDY DRAMA: SATIRE: Fantasy; Death-Dealing with; Romantic Comedy;

Rich People; Death-Personified; Female Screenwriters
(The Witches of Eastwick)

Deathtrap, 1982, 112m, ★★★¹/₂/$$$, WB/WB, V-S. An older, washed-up playwright (Michael Caine) would like to steal the play of a younger admirer (Christopher Reeve) but his wife (Dyan Cannon) objects, leading to a intricate, fascinating tangled web. Irene Worth. w. Jay Presson Allen, P-adap. Ira Levin, d. Sidney Lumet.
SUSPENSE: MURDER: Murder of Spouse; Mindgames; Double Crossings; Clever Plots & Endings; Complicated Plots; Cat and Mouse; Dead-Back from the; Psychics; Writers; Gay Men; Bisexuality; Homosexual Secrets; Jealousy; Female Screenwriters
(Sleuth; Diabolique; Let's Scare Jessica to Death; Blood Simple)
(Ed: One of the all-time great mindgame thrillers living up to the tension of the play)

Death Warrant, 1990, 111m, ★★/$$, MGM/MGM-UA, PG-13/EV-P. A cop goes undercover in a prison to solve a series of murders. Jean Claude VanDamme, Robert Guillaume, Cynthis Gibb. d. Deran Serafian.
ACTION: MURDER: MYSTERY: MURDER MYSTERY: Detective Stories; Detectives-Police; Martial Arts; Prison Drama; Undercover
REMAKE/RETREAD OF: Brubaker.

Death Watch, 1980, 126m, ★★★/$, Ind/Sultan, R/P-S. In the terrible future, a dying woman's last days are secretly taped by Big Brother via a man in her life with a camera that's been installed in his forehead. Romy Schneider (who did die soon after), Harvey Keitel, Harry Dean Stanton, Max Von Sydow. w. Bertrand Tavernier, David Rayfiel, d. Tavernier.
DRAMA: SCI-FI: Futuristic Films; Death-Impending; Voyeurs; Romance-Dangerous; Oppression; French Films; Hidden Gems
(A Simple Story)

Death Wish, 1974, 94m, ★★★/$$$$, Universal/MCA-U, R/P-S-V. When a man's (Charles Bronson) wife and daughter are raped and killed, he goes on a vengeance hunt for who did it. Hope Lange. w. Wendell Mayes, d. Michael Winner.
DRAMA: ACTION: Social Drama; Vigilantes; Avenging the Death of Someone; Revenge; Rape/Rapists;

Revenge on Rapist; Death-Dealing With; Ordinary People Stories; New York Life; Sleeper Hits

Death Wish 2, 1981, 95m, ★★/$$$, Cannon/Cannon-WB, R/EV-P-S. More rapes and murders to avenge. Charles Bronson, Jill Ireland, Vincent Gardenia, J. D. Cannon, Anthony Franciosa. w. David Engelbach, d. Michael Winner. (Ed: A parody of the first)

Death Wish 3, 1985, 90m, ★★/$$, Cannon/MGM-UA, R/EV-P. This time, a gang gets the treatment for terrorizing Bronson's apartment building. Charles Bronson, Deborah Raffin, Martin Balsam. w. Michael Edmonds, d. Michael Winner. Gangs-Street

Death Wish 4, 1987, 99m, ★/$, Cannon/Media, R/EV-P. Drug dealers in LA get it this time. Charles Bronson, Kay Lenz. w. Gail Morgan Hickman, d. J. Lee-Thompson. Female Screenwriters

Death Wish 5, 1994, 95m, ★/$, Vidmark/Vidmark, R/EV-P-B&G. Charles Bronson, Lesley Anne Down, Michael Parks. w.d. Allan Goldstein.

ACTION: Revenge; Avenging Death of Someone; Rape/Rapists; Inner City Life; Vigilantes

Deceived, 1992, 117m, ★★1/2/$$, Touchstone/Touchstone, R/V-S. A woman suspects her art dealer husband of having an affair, then finds out it's more than that. Goldie Hawn, John Heard. w. Mary Agnes Donoghue, Derek Saunders, d. Damian Harris.

SUSPENSE: MYSTERY: Dangerous Spouse; Love-Questionable; Dangerous Men; Art Thieves; Deaths-Faked; Women in Jeopardy; Bigamy; Museums; Female Screenwriters; Female Protagonists (Suspicion; Undercurrent; Sleeping with the Enemy; Never Talk to Strangers) (Ed: A good-looking film with far too many coincidences and plot holes to make the oblivious then suspicious Goldie character empathetic)

The Deceivers, 1988, 112m, ★★1/2/$, MI-WB/WB, PG. A Brit in India goes undercover in a secret society of assassins in the early 1800s. Pierce Brosnan, Saeed Jeffrey. w. Michael Hirst, N-adap. John Masters, d. Nicholas Meyer.

DRAMA: ADVENTURE: Assassinations; Hitmen; Secret Agents; Undercover; India; British Films; 1800s; Overlooked at Release; Coulda Been Good

Deception, 1946, 112m, ★★★/$$, WB/WB. A woman who had an affair with a cellist has found another man when he returns to claim her. Bette Davis, Claude Rains, Paul Henreid, John Abbott. w. John Collier, P-adap. Louis Verneuil, *Monsieur Lamberthier*, d. Irving Rapper.

MELODRAMA: ROMANCE: Romance-Triangles; Tearjerkers; Engagements-Breaking; Musicians; Jealousy; Men Fighting over Women; Cuckolded

REMAKE OF: Jealousy (1929) (The Great Lie; Now, Voyager)

Deception, 1992, 90m, ★★/$, Live/Live, PG-13/S-P. A woman whose husband is presumed dead sets out to find him and instead finds romance and intrigue at the end of the tale with the man who may hold the key to whether the husband is alive or not. Andie MacDowell, Liam Neeson, Jack Thompson, Jeffy Corey. w. Robert Dillon, Michael Thomas, d. Graeme Clifford.

SUSPENSE: ROMANCE: Romantic Drama; **MYSTERY:** Missing Persons; Female Protagonists (Cold Heaven; Under Suspicion)

Decline of the American Empire, 1986, 101m, ★★★/$$, U/MCA-U, R/S. Several middle-aged French-Canadians discuss their positions in life while trying to work-out and think-out to keep young. Dorothee Berryman, Pierre Curzi, Louise Portal, Remy Girard. w. d. Denys Arcand.

DRAMA: COMEDY DRAMA: Ensemble Films; Marriage Drama; Midlife Crisis; Quiet Little Films (The Big Chill; Metropolitan)

The Decline of Western Civilization, 1981, 100m, ★★★/$$, Media/Media, R/P-S. Documentary about the L.A. punk rock scenes of the early 80s. w.d. Penelope Spheeris.

The Decline of Western Civilization 2: The Metal Years, 1988, 90m, ★★1/2/$$, Col/Col, R/EP-S. Documentary on the L.A. music scene of the late 80s, centering around the heavy metal glamour bands. w. d. Penelope Spheeris. Rockumentaries; Documentaries; Rock Stars; Musicians; Los Angeles; 1980s; Young People; Female Directors; Female Screenwriters; Cult Films

The Deep, 1977, 124m, ★★/$$$, Col/RCA-Col, PG/S. Treasure hunters are beset by sabotagers wanting the loot. Jacqueline Bisset, Nick Nolte, Robert Shaw, Louis Gossett, Eli Wallach. w.

Peter Benchley, Tracy Keenan Wynn, N-adap. Benchley, d. Peter Yates.

ACTION: ADVENTURE: Underwater Adventure; Treasure Hunts; Sabotage; Sexy Women (Ed: Got a huge push being the follow-up from the writer of *Jaws*, but with only circling sharks and a bomb blast or two and nothing else, *The Deep* sunk and stunk)

The Deep Blue Sea, 1955, 99m, ★★1/2/$$, 20th/NA. A married woman's lover dumps her and drives her over the edge. Vivien Leigh, Kenneth More, Eric Portman, Emlyn Williams, Arthur Hill. w. P-adap. Terrence Rattigan, d. Anatole Litvak.

MELODRAMA: ROMANCE: Romance-Doomed; Romance with Married Person; Cheating Women; Midlife Crisis; Suicidal Tendencies; Female Protagonists; Women's Films (The Roman Spring of Mrs. Stone)

Deep Cover, 1991, 112m, ★★★1/2/$$ (LR), Fine Line/New Line, R/EP-EV. A black cop (Larry Fishburne) goes undercover as a drug dealer to infiltrate the street trade in L.A., but partnered with a yuppie dealer with big dreams (Jeff Goldblum), he may stray and go deeper than he ever thought. w. Michael Tolkin, Henry Bean, d. Bill Duke.

DRAMA: Crime Drama; Police Stories; Police Corruption; Social Drama; Drugs-Dealing; Detective Stories; Detectives-Undercover; Detectives in Deep; Film Noir-Modern; Murder-Learning to; Government as Enemy; Elixirs/Dream Drugs; Corruption; Ethics; Enemies-Sympathizing with; Black Men; Narrated Films; Black Directors; Underrated; Hidden Gems (Serpico; Prince of the City; Bad Company) (Ed: Not as hard-hitting and realistic as it might have been in the early 70s, but still remarkable)

Deepstar Six, 1989, 100m, ★★/$, Trimark/Trimark, PG-13/P-S. A monster from the bottom of the sea harasses a drilling crew. Taurean Blacque, Nancy Everhard, Greg Evigan, Miguel Ferrer, Matt McCoy, Nia Peeples, Cindy Pickett. w. Lewis Abernathy, Geoff Miller, d. Sean Cunningham.

HORROR: SUSPENSE: Underwater Adventure; Monsters-Underwater; Murders-One by One (1989 Genre Glut: The Abyss; Leviathan)

162

(Ed: The worst of the '89 underwater monsters)

The Deer Hunter, 1978, 182m, ★★★★/$$$$, EMI-U/MCA-U, R/EV-P. Several friends (Robert De Niro [BActor], Christopher Walken [**BSActor**], John Cazale, John Savage) go on a hunting trip which mirrors their subsequent drafting to Vietnam, leaving their small-town life behind to face the horror of war and life after. Meryl Streep (BSActress). w. (story) Michael Cimino, Quinn Redeker, Louis Garfinkle, (script) Derek Washburn (BOScr), d. Michael Cimino (**BDirector**). BPicture, BCin, **BEdit**, **BSound**. Oscars: 9-5.

DRAMA: War Stories; Epics; Vietnam War; Journeys; Friendships-Male; Ordinary People Stories; Hunters; Working Class; Suicidal Tendencies; Missing Persons; POWs; Torture; Mining Towns; Small-town Life; Weddings; Pennsylvania; Faded Hits
(Coming Home; Apocalypse Now; Platoon; Hamburger Hill; The Hanoi Hilton)

Defending Your Life, 1991, 111m, ★★★½/$$$, WB/WB, PG/S. A man (Albert Brooks) is killed and winds up defending his life while falling in love with a woman (Meryl Streep) with whom he may or may not get to spend eternity. Rip Torn, Lee Grant, Buck Henry. w. d. Albert Brooks.

COMEDY: ROMANCE: Romantic Comedy; Romance-Boy Wants Girl; Angels; Heaven; Religion; Redemption; Reincarnation; Religion; Old-Fashioned Recent Films; Underrated; Writer-Directors
(Heaven Can Wait [1943, 1978]; Here Comes Mr. Jordan; Lost in America; Modern Love)

Defense of the Realm, 1985, 96m, ★★½/$, Enigma/Col, PG. A newspaper reporter gets involved with a story involving a British MP and a Russian. Gabriel Byrne, Greta Scacchi, Denholm Elliott, Ian Bannen, Bill Paterson, Martin Stellman, d. David Drury.

DRAMA: Political Drama; Journalists; Journalists as Detectives; Mindgames; Conspiracy
(The Ploughman's Lunch; The Whistleblower)

Defenseless, 1991, 104m, ★★★/$$, New Visions/Vista, R/P-V-B&G-S-FN-MRN. A woman lawyer defends a friend of hers for the murder of her husband-

who was also the lawyer's secret lover, only problem is, she found the body first and may be implicated extensively herself. Barbara Hershey, Mary Beth Hurt, Sam Shepard, J.T. Walsh, Sheree North, Kellie Overby, Jeff Burkhart, d. Martin Campbell.

SUSPENSE: MURDER: MYSTERY: MURDER MYSTERY: Romance-Triangle; Romance with Friend's Lover; Romance-Clandestine; Secrets-Haunting; Incest; Pornography World; Framed?; Accused Unjustly; Reunions; Friendship-Female; Murderers-Female; Female Protagonists
(Ladykiller; Silent Fall)

The Defiant Ones, 1958, 96m, ★★★/$$$$, UA/MGM-UA. Two escaped convicts, one black and one white, are chained together still as they run and have to learn to tolerate each other. Sidney Poitier (BActor), Tony Curtis (BActor), Theodore Bikel (BSActor), Charles McGraw, Lon Chaney, Jr., Cara Williams (BSActress). w. Nathan Douglas, Harold Jacob Smith (**BOScr**), d. Stanley Kramer (BDirector). BPicture, BEdit, **BB&WCin**. Oscars: 9-2.

DRAMA: ACTION: Chase Movies; Escape Adventure; Prison Escape; Race Relations; Black vs. White; Men in Conflict; Southerns; Mississippi; Ahead of its Time; Time Capsules; Cuff to Cuff
(I Am a Fugutive of a Chain Gang; In the Heat of the Night)

The Deliberate Stranger, 1986, 188m, ★★★/$$$$, NBC-WB/WB, V. True story of the infamous good-looking lawyer serial killer Ted Bundy, who killed over two dozen women across the country, eluding police with his charm and status. Mark Harmon, Frederic Forrest, M. Emmet Walsh, John Ashton, Bonnie Bartlett, Glynnis O'Connor, Ben Masters, George Grizzard. d. Marvin Chomsky.

DRAMA: Docudrama; True Stories; Serial Killers; Murderers-Nice; Murders of Women; Trail of a Killer; Playboys; Lawyers; Episodic Stories; TV Movies; Miniseries
(Henry: Portrait of a Serial Killer)

A Delicate Balance, 1975, 134m, ★★★/$, American Film Theater/NA, PG. A family dominated by a grandmother matriarch comes to blows at a reunion. Katharine Hepburn, Paul Scofield, Joseph Cotten, Lee Remick, Kate Reid, Betsy Blair. w. P-adap. Edward Albee, d. Tony Richardson.

DRAMA: Character Studies; Family Drama; Ensemble Films; Elderly Women; Midlife Crisis; Stern Women; Stern Men; Reunions; Aging; Death-Impending; Stagelike Films; Pulitzer Prize Adaptations; Stage Filmings
(The Gathering; Who's Afraid of Virginia Woolf?)

The Delicate Delinquent, 1956, 101m, ★★½/$$, Par/Par. A goofy kid decides to become a policeman and leave the strets behind, but were they more unsafe before or after? Jerry Lewis, Darren McGavin, Martha Hyer. w. d. Don McGuire.

COMEDY: Comedy-Character; Fools-Bumbling; Police Stories; Police Comedy; Juvenile Delinquents; Mentors; Writer-Directors
(Cinderfella; The Errand Boy; The Bell Boy)

Delicatessen, 1990, 99m, ★★★/$, Ind/Par, R/V-B&G. In a futuristic world, a butcher in an apartment building sells people as food and blackmails those who don't want to be the next for dinner-until a band of vegetarians strikes out. Dominqiue Pinon, Marie-Laure Dougnac, Jean Clude Dreyfus. w. d. Jean-Pierre Jeunet, Marc Caro.

HORROR: SATIRE: Art Films; Horror Comedy; Black Comedy; Cannibalism; Futuristic World; Blackmail; Surrealism; Curiosities
(The City of Lost Children; The Cook, The Thief, His Wife, and Her Lover; Sweeney Todd; Consuming Passions)

Delinquent, 1995, 84m, ★★★/$, Ind/NA, R/P-V-S. Two Irish brothers start over in New York after the death of their mother, and things go smoothly for the young men-for a while. But when the younger brother runs off, murder is what he finds. Desmond Devenish, Shawn Batten, Jeff Paul, Marisa Townshend, Ian Eaton. w. d. Peter Hall.

DRAMA: Coming of Age MURDER: Juvenile Deliquents; Young Men-Angry; Rebels; Writer-Directors; Independent Films; Ireland

Delirious, 1991, 96m, ★★½/$, MGM/MGM-UA, PG/P-S. A soap opera writer (John Candy) wakes up inside the fictitious town he writes about, but can he write himself out of what becomes both a dream and a nightmare? Mariel Hemingway, Emma Samms, Raymond Burr, Charles Rocket, Renee Taylor,

Robert Wagner, Jerry Orbach. d. Tom Mankiewicz.

COMEDY: Writers; Soap Operas; TV Life; Fantasies; Amnesia; Accident Prone; Romance-Older Men/Younger Women; Soap Opera Shows; Good Premise Unfulfilled
(Groundhog Day; In the Mouth of Madness)
(Ed: Candy is excellent, but the script is lacking)

Deliverance, 1972, 109m, ★★★1/2/ $$$$, WB/WB, R/P-S. Four men (Burt Reynolds, Jon Voight [BActor], Ned Beatty, Ronny Cox) go on a rafting trip through deepest Appalachia only to be besieged by nightmare rednecks. w. NF-adap. John Dickey, d. John Boorman (BDirector). BPicture. Oscars: 3-0.

DRAMA: HORROR: ADVENTURE: SUSPENSE: Friendships-Male; Saving Oneself; Nature-Back to; Vacations; Vacations-Nightmare; Rape/Rapists; Rape-Male; Hunters; Georgia; Rednecks; Hillbillies; River Trauma; Sleeper Hits; Cult Films
(The Most Deadly Game; Southern Comfort)

Delta Force, 1986, 129m, ★★/$$$, Cannon/MGM-UA, R/EV-P. Action-exploitation replay of the TWA hijacking in the Middle East and the SWAT team who saves them. Chuck Norris, Lee Marvin, Martin Balsam, Joey Bishop, Shelley Winters, Robert Forster, Lainie Kazan, George Kennedy, Hanna Schuygulla, Susan Strasberg. w. James Bruner, Menahem Golan, d. Golan.

ACTION: Hijackings; Hostage Situations; Airplanes; Secret Agents; Special Teams; Middle East

Delta Force 2, 1990, 111m, ★★/$, Cannon/MGM-UA, R/EV-P. This time a drug kingpin in South America is the target of the teams' assignment. Chuck Norris, Billy Drago, Richard Jaeckel. w. Lee Reynolds, d. Aaron Norris.

ACTION: Secret Agents; Special Teams-Military; South America; Drugs-Dealings

Delta Heat, 1992, 91m, ★★1/2/$, Academy/Academy, R/EV-P-S. When a new drug goes on the street market of L.A., a cop travels to New Orleans to do battle with the thugs who deal it and who've killed his partner. Anthony Edwards, Lance Henriksen, Betsy Russell, Rod Masterson. d. Michael Rischa.

ACTION: Crime Drama; Police Stories; Murder of Police; Avenging Death of Someone; Drugs-Dealing; New Orleans
(One False Move)

Dementia 13, 1963, 81m, ★★1/2/$, AIP/Nos, V-B&G. An Irish noble family is attacked in its estate by a vicious axe murderer. Luana Anders, William Campbell, Bart Patton, Mary Mitchell. w. d. Francis Ford Coppola.

HORROR: Serial Killers; Castles; Houses-Creepy; Ireland; Cult Films

The Demi-Paradise, see **Adventure for Two**

Demolition Man, 1993, 115m, ★★1/2/$$$, WB/WB, R/EV-P-S. In the future, two overly violent fellows, one a criminal (Wesley Snipes) and one a cop (Sylvester Stallone), are defrosted from their freezer punishment into a utopian society where their conflict becomes entertainment. Sandra Bullock, Nigel Hawthorne. w. Daniel Waters, Robert Reneau, Peter Lenkov, d. Marco Brambilla.

ACTION: Men in Conflict; Futuristic Films; **SCI-FI:** Frozen People; Time Sleepers; Ex-Convicts; Utopia; Police Stories; Chase Stories
(Rollerball; Total Recall; Judge Dredd)

Demon Knight (*Tales from the Crypt Presents*), 1995, 120m, ★★1/2/$$, U/MCA-U, R/EV-B&G-S-FFN. An emissary of Satan follows an emissary of God around, trying to gain control of a key to the universe containing the blood of Christ. The result is gorrific. Billy Zane, William Sadler, Jada Pinkett, Brenda Bakke, CCH Pounder, Dick Miller, Thomas Haden Church, John Schuck, Gary Farmer, Charles Fleischerd. w. Ethan Reiff, Cyrus Voris, Mark Bishop, d. Ernest Dickerson.

HORROR: Black Comedy; Horror Comedy; Good vs. Evil; Satan; Jesus Christ; Power Struggles; Chase Stories; Black Directors
(Tales from the Hood; Tales from the Crypt)

Demon Seed, 1977, 95m, ★★1/2/$, MGM/MGM-UA, R/S-V. A computer takes over for its inventor and incubates a child with his wife, locking everyone else out of the house and basically raping her. Julie Christie, Fritz Weaver, Gerrit Graham, Berry Kroeger, Lisa Lu. w. Robert Jaffe, Roger O. Hirson, N-adap. Dean R. Koontz, d. Donald Cammell.

SCI-FI: HORROR: Women in Jeopardy; Rape/Rapists; Babies-Having; Scientists; Experiments; Man vs. Machine; Computers; Computer Terror; Ahead of Its Time; Good Premise Unfulfilled
(Ed: What was laughed at at the time seems less and less preposterous as technology increases)

Dennis the Menace, 1993, 96m, ★★★/$$$$, WB/WB, PG. Cute but mischievous Dennis torments crochety old Mr. Wilson and winds up with a pirate named Switchblade Sam after him, but, of course, he comes out smiling. Mason Gamble, Walter Matthau, Christopher Lloyd, Joan Plowright, Leah Thompson, Billie Bird, Paul Winfield. w. John Hughes, d. Nick Castle.

COMEDY: CHILDREN'S: FAMILY: Boys; Children-Brats; Men and Boys; Grandfathers; Nuisances; Pirates; Sleeper Hits

Dersu Uzala, 1975, 140m, ★★★/$$, Mosfilm-Toho/Sultan. A friendship develops slowly between two hard-bitten men, a Mongolian hunter and a Russian surveyor, initially wary of each other. Maxim Munzuk, Juri Solomine. w. Yuri Nagibin, Akira Kurosawa, d. Akira Kurosawa.
BFLFilm. Oscars: 1-1.

DRAMA: Character Studies; Art Films; Friendships-Male; Rivalries; International Casts; Japanese Films; China; Russia

Desert Bloom, 1986, 104m, ★★★/$ (LR), AP-Col/RCA-Col, PG/S-V. A girl tries to hide away as her family problems are exacerbated when her stepfather comes on to his sister-in-law. Meanwhile, nuclear testing nearby in the desert has everyone worried. Annabeth Gish, Jon Voight, JoBeth Williams, Ellen Barkin, Allen Garfield. w. d. Eugene Corr.

DRAMA: Character Studies; Coming of Age; Family Drama; Slice of Life Stories; Quiet Little Films; Girlhood; Teenagers; Desert Settings; Las Vegas; Bombs-Atomic; 1950s; Overlooked at Release; Forgotten Films; Writer-Directors
(Blue Sky; Mystic Pizza; Ruby in Paradise)
(Ed: Pretentious little slice of life with some conflict but no real drama, yet one of the better things American Playhouse has been involved with)

The Desert Fox, 1951, 88m, ★★★/$$$, 20th/Fox. A historical drama chronicling Rommel's first unsuccessful campaign in

North Africa and his triumphant return. James Mason, Jessica Tandy, Cedric Hardwicke, Luther Adler, Everett Sloane, Leo G. Carroll, George Macready. w. Nunnally Johnson, NF-adap. Desmond Young (*Rommel*), d. Henry Hathaway.
ADVENTURE: DRAMA: War Stories; **ACTION:** Action Drama; World War II Stories; Desert Settings; Military Leaders; Historical Drama; Biographies; Africa
SEQUEL: The Desert Rats.
(Raid on Rommel; The Desert Rats)
Desert Fury, 1947, 96m, ★★1/2/$$, Par/NA. Against the backdrop of the Arizona desert, a melodrama plays out in which a woman falls for a "bad man" who may in fact be a murderer. Lizabeth Scott, Wendell Corey, Burt Lancaster, Mary Astor. w. Robert Rossen, N-adap. Ramona Stewart (*Desert Town*), d. Lewis Allen.
SUSPENSE: MYSTERY: MURDER: MELODRAMA: Dangerous Men; Romance-Dangerous; Desert Settings; Dangerous Spouses; Enemy-Sleeping with the
Desert Hearts, 1985, 91m, ★★★/$$, Goldwyn/Goldwyn, R/S-P-FFN. A woman who travels to Reno in the fifties to get a divorce finds herself in a colony of lesbians and dabbles a bit in it herself. Helen Shaver, Patricia Charbonneau, Audra Lindley. w. Natalie Cooper, N-adap. Jane Rule (*Desert of the Heart*), d. Donna Deitch.
COMEDY DRAMA: ROMANCE: Lesbians; Gay Awakenings; Alternative Lifestyle; Homoeroticism; Life Transitions; Divorce; Female Protagonists; Female Screenwriters; Female Directors
(Lianna; Bar Girls; The Women)
Desert Law, 1990, 155m, ★★/$ (VR), Ind/NA, R/P-S-V. A ten-year-old boy, the son of an Arab nobleman and his New York businesswoman wife, is kidnapped by a Middle Eastern group of which he is to be the leader. His mother hires an ex-CIA agent to get him back. Rutger Hauer, Carol Alt, Omar Sharif, Elliott Gould, Kabir Bedi. w. Adriano Bolzoni, Sergio Donati, Luigi Montefiori, d. Duccio Tessari.
ACTION: Kidnappings; Children in Jeopardy; CIA Agents; Mothers & Sons; Arab People; Coulda Been Good
(The Wind and the Lion; Target)
The Desert Rats, 1953, 88m, ★★1/2/$$, 20th/Fox. Further adventures of Rommel, after *The Desert Fox*, in which he defeats

an Australian division in Tobruk. James Mason, Richard Burton, Robert Newton, Robert Douglas. w. Richard Murphy, d. Robert Wise.
ADVENTURE: DRAMA: War Stories; **ACTION:** Action Drama; World War II Stories; Desert Settings; Military Leaders; Historical Drama; Biographies
SEQUEL TO: The Desert Fox
Desert Victory, 1943, 60m, ★★1/2/$$, British Ministry of Information/NA. A documentary about British troops under the command of General Montgomery fighting the Nazis in Tripoli. d. David MacDonald.
Documentaries; World War II Stories; British Films; Soldiers; Time Capsules; Desert Settings
Design for Living, 1933, 88m, ★★1/2/$$, Par/NA, AMC, A&E. A woman and the two men who love her decide to live together-all three of them. Gary Cooper, Fredric March, Miriam Hopkins, Edward Everett Horton, Franklin Pangborn. w. Ben Hecht, P-adap. Noel Coward, d. Ernst Lubitsch.
COMEDY DRAMA: ROMANCE: Romance-Triangles; Ménage à Trois; Romantic Comedy; Men Fighting Over Women; Americans Abroad; Stagelike Films; Coulda Been Great
(Willie and Phil; A Small Circle of Friends; Threesome; The Shop Around the Corner)
(Ed: A misfire all around due to the fact the script was changed drastically from the play and it was miscast; very slow-moving, too)
Designing Woman, 1957, 118m, ★★★/$$$$, MGM/MGM-UA. A fashion designer (Lauren Bacall) and a sportswriter (Gregory Peck) wind up in a mess when his life and boxing conflict with their new marriage. w. George Wells (**BOScr**), d. Vincente Minnelli. Oscars: 1-1.
COMEDY: ROMANCE: Romantic Comedy; Romance-Opposites Attract; Romance-Bickering; Sports Movies; Boxing; Fashion World; Ahead of Its Time; Hidden Gems; Faded Hits
(Woman of the Year; Pat and Mike; The Main Event; The Prizefighter and the Lady)
(Ed: Had a pacing and energy and silliness that didn't become the main staple of romantic comedies until the late 70s)
Desire, 1936, 89m, ★★★/$$, Par/NA. A beautiful Spanish jewel thief ignites the passion of an American businessman

abroad. Marlene Dietrich, Gary Cooper, John Halliday, William Frawley, Akim Tamiroff, Alan Mowbray. w. Edwin Justus Mayer, Waldemar Young, Samuel Hoffenstein, from a German film (*Die schonen Tage von Aranjuez*), P-adap. Hans Szekely, R. A. Stemmle, d. Frank Borzage.
ROMANCE: DRAMA: MELODRAMA: Thieves; Jewel Thieves; Criminals-Female; Vacations; Vacation Romance; Americans Abroad; Spain; Forgotten Films; Female Protagonists
(To Catch a Thief; The Blue Angel)
Desire and Hell at Sunset Motel, 1991, ★★/VR, Ind/Fox, PG-13/V-S. When a wife follows her husband on a sales trip to Disneyland and begins having an affair, hubby puts a PI on her, leading to murder. Sherilyn Fenn, Whip Hubley, David Hewlett, David Johansen, Paul Bartel. w. d. Allen Castle.
SUSPENSE: Erotic Thriller; **MURDER:** Cheating Women; Hitmen; Murder of Spouse; Detectives-Matrimonial; Vacations; Salesmen; Jim Thompson-esque; Coulda Been Good; Writer-Directors
(Two-Moon Junction; Kiss and Tell)
Desire Me, 1947, 91m, ★★/$, MGM/NA. A mysterious stranger brings news from the war to a Norman woman that her husband died in a concentration camp. She ends up falling in love with him, but then her husband returns. Greer Garson, Robert Mitchum, Richard Hart, George Zucco. w. Marguerite Roberts, Zoe Atkins, Casey Robinson, N-adap. Leonard Frank, d. George Cukor, Mervyn Le Roy, Jack Conway.
DRAMA: MELODRAMA: Marriage Drama; Romance Reunited; World War II Stories; Romance-Dangerous; Concentration Camps; Dead-Back from the; Flops-Major; Good Premise Unfulfilled
(The Return of Martin Guerre; Sommersby)
(Ed: Three directors, one after the other, does not a classic film usually make)
Desire Under the Elms, 1958, 111m, ★★1/2/$$, Par/Par. The son of a widowed New England farmer doesn't take it well when dad brings home a sexy bombshell to marry. Sophia Loren, Burl Ives, Anthony Perkins, Frank Overton, Pernell Roberts. w. Irwin Shaw, P-adap. Eugene O'Neill, d. Delbert Mann.

DRAMA: ROMANCE: Family Drama; Fathers & Sons; Stepmothers; Life Transitions; Sexy Women; Coming of Age; Classic Literary Adaptations; Coulda Been Great
(Long Day's Journey into Night; Strange Interlude)

Desiree, 1954, 110m, ★★½/$$, 20th/Fox. The augmented history of Napoleon's affair with Desiree, and Josephine's reaction to it. Jean Simmons, Marlon Brando, Merle Oberon, Michael Rennie. w. Daniel Taradash, N-adap. AnneMarie Selinko, d. Henry Koster. BCArt, BCCostume. Oscars: 2-0.

MELODRAMA: ROMANCE: Romance-Triangles; Cheating Men; Costume Drama; Historical Drama; Biographies; Leaders-Tyrant; Military Leaders; Napoleon; Woman Behind the Man; 1800s; Female Protagonists
(Ed: Worth it to see Brando out of place in a costume drama)

Desk Set, 1957, 103m, ★★★½/$$$, 20th/Fox. When a computer is set to put people out of work, a network corporate researcher (Katharine Hepburn) isn't sure what to think of the computer specialist (Spencer Tracy) who may steal her job- and her heart. Gig Young. w. Henry & Phoebe Ephron, P-adap. William Marchant, d. Walter Lang.

COMEDY: SATIRE: ROMANCE: Romantic Comedy; Comedy-Light; Corporate Life; Man vs. Machine; Computers; Business Life; Romance-Reluctant; Romance-Triangles; Romance-Middle-Aged; Romance-Opposites Attract; Librarians; Female Screenwriters; Female Protagonists; Tracy & Hepburn
(Adam's Rib; Pat and Mike; Guess Who's Coming to Dinner)

Despair, 1978, 119m, ★★★/$, Ind/Karl-Lorimar. A Russian immigrant in the Weimar-era Berlin finds life there alienating. His recurring violent fantasies begin to play themselves out in reality. Dirk Bogarde, Andrea Ferreol, Volker Spengler, Klaus Lowitsch. w. Tom Stoppard, N-adap. Vladimir Nabokov, d. Rainer Werner Fassbinder.

DRAMA: Character Studies; Fantasies; Nightmares; **TRAGEDY:** Mental Illness; Fish out of Water Stories; Alienation; Depression; Immigrants; Russians; German Films; Art Films; Berlin
(Moonlighting [1982])

Desperate Characters, 1971, 106m, ★★★/$, ITC-Par/Par, PG. On the east side of Manhattan, a group of friends deals with the daily trials of modern urban life. Shirley MacLaine, Gerald S. O'Loughlin, Kenneth Mars, Sada Thompson. w. d. Frank D. Gilroy, N-adap. Paula Fox.

DRAMA: Slice of Life Stories; Ensemble Films; Marriage Drama; Depression; Alienation; Inner City Life; New York Life; Urban Life; Suburban Life; Time Capsules; Hidden Gems; Coulda Been Great
(City for Conquest; Used People)

The Desperate Hours, 1955, 112m, ★★★/$$, Par/Par. A suburban family has their house taken over by three escaped convicts but eventually outsmarts them. Fredric March, Humphrey Bogart, Martha Scott, Arthur Kennedy, Gig Young, Dewey Martin, Mary Murphy. w. P&N-adap. Joseph Hayes, d. William Wyler.

DRAMA: SUSPENSE: Crime Drama; Hostage Situations; Ordinary Person vs. Criminal; Race Against Time; One-Day Stories; Prison Escapes; Suburban Life; Novel and Play Adaptations

Desperate Hours, 1990, 105m, ★★/$, DEG-MGM/MGM-UA, R/V-S-P-FFN. A desperate remake, with a few good performances and moments. Mickey Rourke, Anthony Hopkins, Mimi Rogers, Lindsay Crouse, Kelly Lynch. w. Lawrence Konner, Mark Rosenthal, Joseph Hayes, P&N-adap. Joseph Hayes, d. Michael Cimino.

DRAMA: SUSPENSE: Crime Drama; Hostage Situations; Ordinary Person vs. Criminal; Race Against Time; One-Day Stories; Prison Escapes; Suburban Life; Unintentionally Funny; Coulda Been Good; Novel and Play Adaptations
(Dog Day Afternoon; Cadillac Man)
(Ed: Good moments in the house, and though not sublime, it turns ridiculous in the chase sequence)

Desperate Journey, 1942, 109m, ★★★/$$$, WB/WB. A group of G.I.s fight their way out of a German POW camp. Errol Flynn, Alan Hale, Ronald Reagan, Nancy Coleman. w. Arthur Horman, d. Raoul Walsh.

DRAMA: ACTION: Action Drama; World War II Stories; Ensemble Films; Ensembles-Male; POWs; Survival Drama; Prison Drama; Prison Escapes; Journies; Germans as Enemy
(Stalag 17; The Great Escape; Victory)

Desperate Living, 1977, 95m, ★★★/$$, New Line/New Line, R/S-P. A suburban woman's frustration leads her to murder her husband and escape to Mortville, a community of degenerate lesbians, to live a more interesting if not satisfying life. Mink Stole, Susan Lowe, Edith Massey, Mary Vivian Pearce, Jean Hill. w. d. John Waters.

SATIRE: COMEDY: Black Comedy; Comedy-Morbid; **MURDER:** Murder of Spouse; Psycho Killers; Murderers-Nice; Neurotic People; Housewives; Suburban Life; Lesbians; Alternative Lifestyles; Cult Films; Camp; Hidden Gems; Coulda Been Great; Writer-Directors
(Serial Mom; Female Trouble; Polyester)

Desperately Seeking Susan, 1985, 104m, ★★★/$$$, Orion/Orion, PG-13/S-P. A young housewife from New Jersey (Rosanna Arquette) goes to Manhattan for an adventure and winds up getting amnesia and assuming the identity of a free-wheeling party girl (Madonna), until they meet up, that is. Aidan Quinn, Mark Blum, Steven Wright, Laurie Metcalf, Robert Joy. w. Leora Barish, d. Susan Seidelman.

COMEDY DRAMA: COMEDY: FARCE: Screwball Comedy; Amnesia; Mistaken Identities; Impostors; Dual Lives; Housewives; Free Spirits; Sexy Women; Playgirls; Greenwich Village; Beautiful People; Personal Ads; Movie Theaters; Female Protagonists; Female Screenwriters; Female Directors; Coulda Been Great
(Smithereens; Dangerous Game; She-Devil)

Destination Tokyo, 1943, 135m, ★★★/$$$, WB/MGM-UA. A submarine on a mission to bomb Tokyo harbor runs into trouble and tension. Cary Grant, John Garfield, Alan Hale, John Ridgely, Dane Clark, Warner Anderson, William Prince, Robert Hutton, John Forsythe. w. Delmer Daves, Albert Maltz, SS-adap. Steve Fisher, d. Delmer Daves.

ACTION: SUSPENSE: War Stories; Submarines; Race Against Time; Japanese as Enemy; Japan
(Gray Lady Down; The Bedford Incident)

Destiny of a Man, 1959, 98m, ★★★/$, Sovexportfilm-Mosfilm/NA. A Russian soldier escapes from a Nazi P.O.W. camp only to discover upon his return home that his family has been killed. Sergei Bondarchuk, Zinaida Kirienko, Pavlik

Boriskin. w. Y. Lukin, F. Shakhmagonov, SS-adap. Mikhail Sholokhov, d. Sergei Bondarchuk.

DRAMA: TRAGEDY: Escape Adventure; Reunions; Journies; Family Drama; World War II Stories; Russians; POWs; Germans as Enemy; Young Men; Soldiers
(Ballad of a Soldier)

Destry Rides Again, 1939, 94m, ★★★★/$$$$, U/MCA-U. An easy-going sheriff turns the other cheek once too often, finally deciding to stand up like a man and face his foes. James Stewart, Marlene Deitrich, Brian Donlevy, Charles Winninger, Samuel S. Hinds, Mischa Auer, Una Merkel, Billy Gilbert. w. Felix Jackson, Gertrude Purcell, Henry Myers, N-adap. Max Brand, d. George Marshall.

WESTERNS: COMEDY DRAMA: ROMANCE: Western Comedy; Men Proving Themselves; Cowards; Police Stories; Fighting Back

REMAKE: Destry (1954)
(High Noon; The Man Who Shot Liberty Valance)

The Detective (*Father Brown, Detective*), 1954, 91m, ★★★/$$, Ealing/Col. A priest who is also an amateur detective tracks down an antique thief in England. Alec Guinness, Peter Finch, Joan Greenwood, Cecil Parker, Bernard Lee. d. Robert Hamer.

MYSTERY: Comic Mystery; Priests; Thieves; Detective Stories; Detectives-Amateur; British Films

The Detective, 1968, 114m, ★★★/$$, 20th/CBS-Fox, R/S-P. After the mayor's gay son is murdered, a police detective goes into the gay subculture to find the killer-who may be a public official. Frank Sinatra, Lee Remick, Jacqueline Bisset, Ralph Meeker, Jack Klugman, Horace MacMahon, Lloyd Bochner, William Windom. w. Abby Mann, N-adap. Roderick Thorp, d. Gordon Douglas.

DRAMA: MURDER: MYSTERY: MURDER MYSTERY: Detective Stories; Detectives-Police; Corruption-Government; Conspiracy; Homosexual Secrets; Homophobia; Murders of Homosexuals; Gay Men; Underworld; Politicians; Ahead of Its Time
(Dress Gray; Cruising)
(Ed: Daring, especially with our notions of Sinatra, yet still not treating the gay men as full human beings)

Detective, 1985, 98m, ★★½/$, Ind-JLG/NA. Four separate groups of travelers staying in a Paris hotel get involved in a murder plot, which the hotel detective tries to solve. Claude Brasseur, Nathalie Baye, Johnny Hallyday. w. Alain Sarde, Philippe Setbon, Anne-Marie Mieville, Jean-Luc Godard, d. Jean-Luc Godard.

DRAMA: Art Films; MURDER: MYSTERY: MURDER MYSTERY: Detective Stories; Ensemble Films; Hotels; Paris; French Films

Detective Story, 1951, 103m, ★★★/$$$, Par/Par. In a New York precinct station, a strict authoritarian police detective uncovers shady goings on in his own family while doing battle with himself and ethics. Kirk Douglas, Eleanor Parker (BActress), William Bendix, Cathy O'Donnell, George Macready, Horace MacMahon, Joseph Wiseman, Lee Grant (BActress). w. Philip Yordan, Robert Wyler (BScr), P-adap. Sidney Kingsley, d. William Wyler (BDirector). Oscars: 4-0.

DRAMA: MELODRAMA: Character Studies; Police Stories; Detective Stories; Detectives-Police; Police Corruption; Abortion Dilemmas; Suspecting One's Self; Marriage Drama; Marriage on the Rocks; Ethics; Faded Hits; Forgotten Films; Stagelike Films; Hidden Gems
(Ed: Dated, though riveting at times like a serious and tragic *The Front Page*, but still lacking)

Detonator, 1993, 98m, ★★½/$$, Col/Col, R/P-S-V. A Russian General goes AWOL and steals a nuclear bomb and gets out of the country to Iraq on a commandeered train, and it's up to a U.N. negotiator to stop disaster. Pierce Brosnan, Patrick Stewart, Alexandra Paul, Ted Levine, Christopher Lee. w. d. David S. Jackson.

ACTION: SUSPENSE: Bombs-Atomic; Russians; Russians as Enemy; Chase Stories; Race Against Time
(The Fourth Protocol; Goldeneye)

Detour, 1947, 69m, ★★★½/$ (LR), Ind/Barr Films, A&E. A man (Tom Neal) who has picked up a hitchhiker (Ann Savage) in the desert may have killed a man to get the car he has, and when the woman he's picked up discovers this, she may be next. w. Martin Goldsmith, d. Edgar G. Ulmer.

SUSPENSE: MURDER MYSTERY: MYSTERY: Film Noir; Road Movies; Murderer-Debate to Reveal Killer;

Hitchhikers; Identities-Assumed; Nightmares; Nightmare Journies; Suspecting One's Self; Amnesia; Hidden Gems; Cult Films
(Angel Heart; A Double Life)

The Devil and Max Devlin, 1981, 95m, ★½/$, Disney/Disney. A slumlord is killed in an accident and goes to hell. If he can find three souls to offer, Satan will let him out. Elliott Gould, Bill Cosby, Susan Anspach, Adam Rich, Charles Shamata. w. Mary Rodgers, d. Steven Hilliard Stern.

COMEDY: Selling One's Soul; Satan; Hell; Dead-Back from the; One Last Chance; Disney Comedy; Coulda Been Good; Female Screenwriters
(Leonard, Part 6; Oh God, You Devil)
(Ed: Evidence, as are *Condorman* and *Trench Coat*, of the mess Disney was in in the early 80s)

The Devil and Daniel Webster, see All That Money Can Buy

The Devil and Miss Jones, 1941, 97m, ★★★/$$$, RKO/Turner. A department store tycoon pretends to be a clerk in order to check on service complaints and ends up falling for the lovely clerk he's checking on. Jean Arthur, Charles Coburn, Robert Cummings, Spring Byington, S. Z. Sakall, William Demarest. w. Norman Krasna, d. Sam Wood.

COMEDY: ROMANCE: Romantic Comedy; Romance-Older Men/Younger Women; Infatuations; Department Stores; Worker vs. Boss; Romance with Boss; Undercover; Hidden Gems
(The More the Merrier; The Shop Around the Corner)

Devil and the Deep, 1932, 73m, ★★½/$$, Par/NA. A possessive and high-strung submarine captain goes into a jealous rage over his wife's infidelities. Tallulah Bankhead, Charles Laughton, Gary Cooper, Cary Grant. w. Benn Levy, d. Marion Gering.

DRAMA: MELODRAMA: Marriage Drama; Marriage on the Rocks; Jealousy; Cheating Women; Submarines; Forgotten Films

The Devil at Four O'Clock, 1961, 126m, ★★½/$$, Col/Goodtimes. In an island leper colony, a volcano is about to explode. A motley crew of convicts and a broken-down old missionary help the leper children escape before the eruption. Spencer Tracy, Frank Sinatra, Kerwin Mathews, Jean-Piere Aumont, Gregoire

Aslan. w. Liam O'Brien, N-adap. Max Catto, d. Mervyn Le Roy.

DRAMA: Missionaries; Islands; Volcanoes; Escape Adventure; Forgotten Films

The Devil Came from Arkansas, 1970, 85m, ★½/$, CCC Films/NA. Various cults travel to Arkansas to find a mystical stone and unleash its powers. Fred Williams, Susann Korda, Horst Tappert, Ewa Stroemberg, Siefried Schurenberg. w. Paul Andre, Lladislas Fedor, d. Jess Frank (Jesus Franco).

SCI-FI: Fantasy; **HORROR:** Occult; Quests; Arkansas; Satan; Mountain People; Forgotten Films

The Devil Doll, 1936, 79m, ★★★/$$, MGM/MPI. An escapee from Devil's Island disguises himself as a beggar-woman and sells human voodoo "dolls" with a mission to go back and kill those who turned him in. Lionel Barrymore, Marueen O'Sullivan, Frank Lawton, Henry B.I. Walthall, Grace Ford. w. Tod Browning, Garrett Fort, Erich Von Stroheim, Guy Endore, N-adap. A. A. Merritt (*Burn Witch Burn*), d. Tod Browning.

HORROR: SCI-FI: Prison Drama; Possessions; **MURDER:** Disguises; Voodoo; Occult; Devil's Island; Hidden Gems; Coulda Been Great; Forgotten Films

Devil in a Blue Dress, 1995, 100m, ★★½/$, Tri-Star/Col-Tri, R/S-P-V. A man out of work in the 40s accepts a job to find a politician's girlfriend who's in hiding, but he has no idea what he may be getting into. Denzel Washington, Tom Sizemore, Jennifer Beals, Don Cheadle. w. d. Carl Franklin, N-adap. Walter Mosley.

MYSTERY: SUSPENSE: Detective Stories; Conspiracy; Missing Persons; 1940s; Black Men; Black Screenwriters; Black Directors
(One False Move; Chinatown; Virtuosity; The Late Show)
(Ed: He doesn't get into much, actually. What was supposed to be a black Chinatown doesn't make it around the corner)

Devil in the Flesh, 1946, 112m, ★★★/$$, Ind/Nos. While a French soldier is away at war, his wife has an affair with a high school student. Gerard Philippe, Micheline Presle, Denise Grey. N-adap. Raymond Radiquet, d. Claude Ataunt-Lara.

Devil in the Flesh, 1987, 110m, ★★/$, Sony-Orion/Sony, NC-17/ES-P-FFN-MFN. Update of the above with the husband as a terrorist in Italy. Maruschka Detmers, Federico Pitzalis. w. d. Marco Bellochio.
(Ed: Noted for a near-pornographic oral sex scene which is very shadowy)

DRAMA: Erotic Drama; Romantic Drama; Romance with Married Person; Coming of Age; Teachers; Romance with Teacher; Cheating Women; World War II Era

The Devil Is a Sissy, 1936, 92m, ★★½/$$, MGM/NA. A troubled youth from a "broken home" falls in with the wrong crowd but finds help among it. Freddie Bartholomew, Jackie Cooper, Mickey Rooney, Ian Hunter, Peggy Conklin, Gene Lockhart, Dorothy Peterson. w. John Lee Mahin, Richard Schayer, Roland Brown, d. W. S. Van Dyke.

MELODRAMA: CHILDREN'S: FAMILY: Juvenile Delinquents; Inner-City Life; Coming of Age; Boyhood; Men and Boys; Social Workers; Reformers
(Boys Town; Men of Boys Town)

The Devil Is a Woman, 1935, 82m, ★★★/$, Par/NA. In the port of Seville at the turn of the century, a vain woman is sought by all the men in town, but danger lurks behind the locks. Marlene Dietrich, Lionel Atwil, Cesar Romero, Edward Everett Horton, Alison Skipworth. w. John Dos Passos, S. K. Winston, N-adap. Pierre Louys (La Femme et le Pantin), d. Josef Von Sternberg.

MELODRAMA: ROMANCE: Dangerous Women; Sexy Women; Men Fighting over Women; Forgotten Films; Spain
(Desire; Morocco; The Blue Angel)
(Ed: Cliche of the Dietrich cliche . . .)

The Devils, 1971, 109m, ★★★½/$ (LR), UA/MGM-UA, R/P-FN. A nun (Vanessa Redgrave) who may be possessed seeks redemption in a fantastic Middle Ages world of debauchery. Oliver Reed, Dudley Sutton, Max Adrian. w. Ken Russell, N-adap. Aldous Huxley, P-adap. John Whiting, d. Ken Russel.

DRAMA: Art Film; Avant Garde Films; Fantasy; Possessions; Surrealism; Middle Ages; Religion; Historical Drama; Oppression; Priests; Nuns; Cult Films; Underrated; Hidden Gems; Novel and Play Adaptations; Outstanding Production Design

The Devil's Advocate, 1977, 109m, ★★½/$, Ind/NA. A candidate for sainthood is the subject of a postmortem investigation by a priest dying himself and a bit envious of his subject. John Mills, Stephane Audran, Jason Miller, Timothy West, Patrick Mower. w. N-adap. Morris West, d. Guy Green.

DRAMA: Priests; Death-Dealing with; Saintly People; Death-Impending; Coulda Been Good

The Devil's Bride (*The Devil Rides Out*), 1968, 95m, ★★★/$, WB-Hammer/NA, R/S-V. A friend of the Duc de Richleau is kidnapped and indoctrinated by a group of Satanists, and the Duc must come to the rescue. Christopher Lee, Charles Gray, Leon Greene, Gwen Ffrangcon Davies. w. Richard Matheson, N-adap. Dennis Wheatley, d. Terence Fisher.

HORROR: Satanism; Occult; Death-Personified; Escape Drama; Castles; Kidnappings; Royalty
(Rosemary's Baby; Eye of the Devil)

The Devil's Brigade, 1968, 132m, ★★/$, UA/MGM-UA. A US commander assembles a motley crew of roughnecks to fight in his French and Italian campaigns. William Holden, Cliff Robertson, Vince Edwards, Andrew Prine, Carroll O'Connor. w. William Roberts, d. Andrew V. McLaglen.

ACTION: War Stories; World War II Stories; Ensemble Films; Ensembles-Male; Special Teams; Forgotten Films

REMAKE/RETREAD: The Dirty Dozen
(The Dirty Dozen; Force Ten from Navarone)

The Devil's Disciple, 1959, 82m, ★★½/$, UA/MGM-UA. A man falsely accused of treachery bites his tongue to the moment of hanging to protect a pastor who was the real culprit. Burt Lancaster, Kirk Douglas, Laurence Olivier, Eva Le Gallienne, Janette Scott, Harry Andrews. w. John Deighton, Roland Kibbee, P-adap. Bernard Shaw, d. Guy Hamilton.

WESTERNS: DRAMA: Accused Unjustly; **MURDER:** Murder-Debate to Reveal Killer; Preachers/Ministers; Murderers-Nice; Ethics; Death-Impending; Executions; Coulda Been Great

The Devil's Eye, 1960, 90m, ★★½/$, Svensk Filmindustri/Embassy. The Devil comes to Earth to tempt a virtuous woman in a bucolic Swedish setting. Jarl Kulle,

Bibi Andersson, Nils Poppe, Stig Jarrel, Gunnar Bjornstrand. w. d. Ingmar Bergman.

COMEDY DRAMA: DRAMA: Marriages-Impending; Domestic Life; Virgins; Satan; Narrated Films; Writer-Directors; Bergmanesque

The Devil's Playground, 1976, 107m, ★★★/$ (LR). Boys at a boarding school in Australia have their sexual awakenings, mostly toward each other, leading to great tension and controversy. Arthur Dignam, Nick Tate, Simon Burke, Charles McCallum, John Frawley. w. d. Fred Schepisi.

DRAMA: TRAGEDY: Coming of Age; Sexuality; Homoeroticism; Gay Men; Gay Awakenings; Boyhood; Boarding Schools; Boys' School; Australian Films; Writer-Directors

(Dead Poet's Society; H . . . ; Consenting Adults)

The Devil's Wanton, 1949, 80m, ★★1/2/$, Terrafilm/NA. A group of filmmakers discuss the projects they're thinking about but abandon them all. Doris Svedlund, Birger Malmsten, Eva Henning, Hasse Ekman. w. d. Ingmar Bergman.

DRAMA: Moviemaking; Directors; Documentary Style; Documentaries; Intellectuals; Swedish Films; Forgotten Films; Writer-Directors; Bergmanesque

Devlin, 1992, 106m, ★★/$, Viacom/Viacom. When a politician is murdered, his brother-in-law, a city cop, is framed but fights back. Bryan Brown, Roma Downey, Lloyd Bridges, Whip Hubley. w. David Taylor, N-adap. Roderick Thorp, d. Rick Rosenthal.

DRAMA: Crime Drama; **MURDER:** Accused Unjustly; Framed?; Police Stories; Brothers; Fighting Back; Murder-Finding Real Killer

Devotion, 1946, 107m, ★★1/2/$$, RKO/Turner. The governess of a lawyer's son turns out to be deeply in love with him. Ann Harding, Leslie Howard, Robert Williams, O. P. Heggie, Dudley Digges. w. Graham John, Horace Jackson, N-adap. Pamela Wynne (*A Little Flat in the Temple*), d. Robert Milton.

MELODRAMA: ROMANCE: Infatuations; Babysitters; Romance-Older Women/Younger Men; British Films; England

(Adam Had Four Sons; Anna and the King of Siam)

Diabolique (B&W), 1955, 107m, Ind/MPI, ★★★★/$$$. Two women want to kill one's abusive husband, whom the other woman is also mistress to. But he won't die, and the plot thickens. Simone Signoret. w. Henri-Georges Clouzot, G. Geronomi, N-adap. Pierre Boileau, Thomas Narcejac, *The Woman Who Was*, d. Georges Clouzot.

SUSPENSE: MYSTERY: MURDER: Conspiracy; Infidelity; Illusions; Romance-Triangles; Mindgames; Hitchcockian; Love-Questionable; Clever Plots & Endings; Abused Women; Boarding Schools; Friendships-Female; French Films; French New Wave Films; Hidden Gems; Female Protagonists

REMAKE: 1996

(Deathtrap; The Wages of Fear; Dynasty of Fear; Blood Simple)

(Ed: From the writers of another novel that *Vertigo* was based upon, bringing into question where the real genius lies-the story structure or the filming of it? Or both? In both cases, there are great filmmakers at work, but both dealing with great stories from the same writers who have been forgotten)

Dial M for Murder, 1954, 105m, ★★★★/$$$, WB/WB. When a man decides to murder his wife for having an affair, the man he hires to do it gets killed instead and his wife is accused-and may yet die at the gallows anyway. Ray Milland, Grace Kelly, Robert Cummings. w. P-adap. Frederick Knott, d. Alfred Hitchcock.

SUSPENSE: MURDER MYSTERY: MYSTERY: Framed?; Perfect Crimes; Clever Plots & Endings; Murder of Spouse; Detective Stories; Detectives-Police; Accused Unjustly; Turning the Tables; Cheating Women; Revenge; Revenge on Cheaters; Jealousy; Romance-Triangles; Burglars; England; 3-D Movies; Hitchcockian; Telephone Terror

REMAKE: TV (1981)

(Guilty Conscience; Rear Window)

Dialogues with Madwomen, 1994, 90m, ★★★/$, Ind/NA, NR. Portraits of various women who are "entrapped" in their social positions, from asylums to prisons to suburbia, mostly as a result of mental illness. d. Allie Light.

Documentaries; Social Drama; Asylums; Women in Prison; Mental Illness; Women's Rights; Feminist Films; Lesbians; Female Directors

Diamond Head, 1962, 107m, ★★1/2/$$, Col/Col. A Hawaiian land baron rules his fruit plantation with an iron fist and his family feels the punch as well, no pun intended. Charlton Heston, Yvette Mimieux, George Chakiris, France Nuyen, James Darren, Aline MacMahon, Elizabeth Allen. w. Marguerite Roberts, N-adap. Peter Gilman, d. Guy Green.

MELODRAMA: ROMANCE: Power Struggles; Family Drama; Rich People; Stern Men; Islands; Hawaii; Plantation Life; Good Premise Unfulfilled; Forgotten Films; Female Screenwriters

(The Hawaiians)

Diamond Horseshoe, 1945, 104m, ★★★/$$$, 20th/NA. A medical student asks his love, a cabaret singer, to give up her career for him. Things don't go so easy. Betty Grable, Dick Haymes, William Gaxton, Phil Silvers, Beatrice Kay, Margaret Dumont. w. d. George Seaton, P-adap. Kenyon Nicholson (*The Barker*).

ROMANCE: MELODRAMA: MUSICALS: Music Movies; Dancers; Singers

(The Beautiful Blonde from Bashful Bend; Strawberry Blonde)

Diamond Jim, 1935, 93m, U/NA. The turn of the century industrialist who loved Lillian Russell is the subject of this apocryphal biopic. Edward Arnold, Jean Arthur, Binnie Barnes, Cesar Romero. w. Preston Sturges, d. A. Edward Sutherland Bridge.

COMEDY DRAMA: ROMANCE: Infatuations; Biographies; Biographies-Fictional; Romantic Drama; Actresses; Playboys

(The Great Ziegfeld; Blonde Venus)

Diamonds Are Forever, 1971, 119m, ★★★1/2/$$$$$, UA/MGM-UA, PG. Agent 007 goes to Vegas this time to do battle again with a would-be world ruler and winds up being chased by welding gadgets in tunnels in between babehopping. Sean Connery, Jill St. John. w. Richard Maibaum, Tom Mankiewicz, N-adap. Ian Fleming, d. Guy Hamilton.

ACTION: Action Comedy; Spy Films; Secret Agents; Playboys; James Bond; Undercover; Chase Movies; Las Vegas; Rule the World-Plots to

(Thunderball; Goldfinger; Dr. No)

Diamonds for Breakfast, 1968, 102m, ★★1/2/$, Par/NA. A down-on-his luck Russian nobleman plans to steal back his family jewels from a museum and then seduce his female accomplices. Marcello

Mastroianni, Rita Tushingham, Elaine Taylor, Warren Mitchell, Nora Nicholson, Bill Fraser. w. N. F. Simpson, Pierre Rouve, Ronald Harwood, d. Christopher Morahan.

COMEDY DRAMA: ROMANCE: Heist Stories; Capers; Romantic Comedy; Playboys; Revenge; Jewel Thieves; Russians; Coulda Been Great; Good Premise Unfulfilled

Diana: Her True Story, 1993, 180m, ★★½/$$$, CBS/Enterprise. Biography of Princess Di from her girlhood to her nervous breakdown and the public disintegration of her marriage to Prince Charles. Serena Scott Thomas, David Threlfall, Elizabeth Garvie, Davis Tracy. w. Stephen Zito, d. Kevin Connor.

MELODRAMA: Biographies; Marriage Drama; Princesses; Princes; Royalty; England; Fame-Rise to; Newlyweds; Scandals; Marriage on the Rocks; TV Movies

Diary for My Children, 1982, 107m, ★★★/$, Ind/NA. During the occupation of Hungary, a woman orphaned as a child recounts happier times to her children. Zsuzsa Czinkoczi, Annas Polony, Jan Nowicki, Annas Polony, Jan Nowicki. w. Marta Meszaros, Balazs Fakan, Andras Szeradas, d. Marta Meszaros.

DRAMA: Family Drama; Tearjerkers; Mothers-Struggling; Oppression; Orphans; Memories; Storytellers; Hidden Gems; Europeans-Eastern

A Diary for Timothy, 1945, 40m, ★★★½/$$, British Ministry of Information/NA. When a baby is born at the end of World War II, the narrator of his story wonders what's in store for him. Narrator: Michael Redgrave. w. E. M. Forster, d. Humphrey Jennings, Benedict Bogeaus.

DRAMA: MELODRAMA: Documentaries; Documentary Style; Babies-Having; Boyhood; World War II-Post Era England; Narrated Films; Time Capsules

The Diary of a Chambermaid, 1946, 86m, ★★★/$$, Meredith-Goddard/Republic. In the 1800s a maid in two households proves too alluring to be left to her chores. Paulette Goddard, Burgess Meredith, Hurd Hatfield, Francis Lederer. w. Burgess Meredith, N-adap. Octave Mirbeau, d. Jean Renoir.

The Diary of a Chambermaid, 1963, 98m, ★★½/$, Speva/Conoisseur. A take on the classic novel by the esteemed

Spanish surrealist, though this one isn't very surreal at all. Jeanne Moreau, Georges Geret, Michel Piccoli. w. Luis Bunuel, Jean-Claude Carriere, d. Luis Bunuel.

DRAMA: ROMANCE: Sexy Women; Servants; Romance with Servants; Rural Life

(Fanny Hill; The Amorous Adventures of Moll Flanders; Tristana)

The Diary of a Country Priest, 1950, 120m, ★★★/$, U.G.C./Ingram. A novice priest just out of the seminary isn't accepted by his congregation. Dejected and alone, he contracts a fatal illness. Claude Laydu, Jean Riveyre, Armand Guibert. w. d. Robert Bresson, N-adap. Georges Bernanos.

DRAMA: Character Studies; Priests; Religion; Death-Impending; Disease Stories; Depression; Allegorical Stories

Diary of a Mad Housewife, 1970, 94m, ★★★★/$$$, Universal/MCA-U, R/S-P-FFN-MRN. A bored woman (Carrie Snodgress, BActress) takes up a lecherous writer's (Frank Langella) invitation to have an affair and forget her anal husband (Richard Benjamin) but which is worse? w. Eleanor Perry, N-adap. Sue Kaufman, d. Frank Perry. Oscars: 1-0.

DRAMA: SATIRE: Character Studies; Biographies-Fictional; Romance-Doomed; Life Transitions; Alienation; Cheating Women; Elusive Men; Social Climbing; Lonely People; Depression; Women's Films; New York Life; Upper Class; Housewives; Husbands-Troublesome; Underrated; Hidden Gems; Quiet Little Films; Female Protagonists; Female Screenwriters

(Up the Sandbox; Alice Doesn't Live Here Anymore; An Unmarried Woman; A Woman Under the Influence; David and Lisa; The Attic)

(Ed: A modern classic)

The Diary of a Madman, 1962, 96m, ★★½/$, UA/MGM-UA. A courtroom drama based on the insanity defense. Vincent Price, Nancy Kovack, Chris Warfield. w. Robert E. Kent, d. Reginald Le Borg.

DRAMA: HORROR: MURDER: Courtroom Drama; Mental Illness; Character Studies; Coulda Been Good; Ahead of Its Time

The Diary of Anne Frank (B&W), 1959, 150m, ★★★½/$$$, UA/Fox. The true story of the girl whose family was hid-

den from the Nazis, as found out later in her diaries. Shelley Winters (**BSActress**), Millie Perkins, Ed Wynn (BSActor), Richard Beymer. w. P-adap. Frances Goodrich, Albert Hackett, NF-adap. Anne Frank, d. George Stevens (BDirector). BPicture, **BB&WArt**, **BB&WCin**, BOScore, BCostume. Oscars: 8-3.

DRAMA: MELODRAMA: TRAGEDY: Biographies; Tearjerkers; Girlhood; Hiding Out; Fugitives-Harboring; Ensemble Films; True Stories; Anti-Semitism; Jewish People; Jews-Saving; Oppression; Nazi Stories; World War II Stories; Novel and Play Adaptations; Stagelike Films; Female Screenwriters; Female Protagonists

REMAKE: The Attic (TV, 1988).

(Holocaust; The Assault; Europa, Europa; The Hiding Place)

Diary of a Hitman, 1991, 90m, ★★½/$$, Ind/Col, R/V-S-P. When a wealthy stockbroker wants his wife dead because of her drug addiction and her child dead because it isn't his, a hitman has to decide whether it's worth it, even though he needs the money. Forest Whitaker, James Belushi, Sherilyn Fenn, Sharon Stone, Seymour Cassel, Lois Chiles. w. Kenneth Pressman, N-adap. Pressman, Insider's Price, d. Roy London.

SUSPENSE: Crime Drama; **MURDER:** Hitmen; Drugs-Addictions; Stock Brokers; Murder of Spouse; Ethics; One Last Time; TV Movies

(Traces of Red; A Rage in Harlem; The Crying Game; China Moon)

Dick Tracy, 1990, 103m, ★★★/$$$$$, Touchstone/Touchstone, PG/V. The cartoon hero (Warren Beatty) meets a femme fatale (Madonna) battling evil gangsters (Al Pacino, BSActor; Dustin Hoffman). Glenne Headly, Mandy Patinkin, Charles Durning, Dick Van Dyke, William Forsythe. w. Jim Cash, Jack Epps, d. Warren Beatty. **BArt**, BCin, **BMakeup**, **BOSong**, BSound, BCostume. Oscars: 7-3.

ACTION: ADVENTURE: MYSTERY: MURDER: MURDER MYSTERY: Fantasy; Detective Stories; Film Noir-Modern; Detectives in Deep; Gangsters; Camp; Heroes-Comic; Dangerous Women; Villains-Classic; Disguises; Blockbusters

(Batman; Bladerunner; Heaven Can Wait)

(Ed: All style)

Did You Hear the One About the Traveling Saleslady?, 1967, 96m, ★★½/$, U/NA. A woman travels door to door selling player pianos that come unhinged when delivered. Phyllis Diller, Bob Denver, Joe Flynn, Jeanette Nolan. w. John Fenton Murray, d. Don Weis.

COMEDY: Comedy of Errors; Salesmen; Female Protagonists; 1900s; Comedians; Coulda Been Good

Die! Die! My Darling!, 1965, 97m, ★★½/$, Col/Col, R/V. When a young widow goes to stay in her dead husband's mother's creepy home in the English countryside, the old woman decides to blame her and seek vengeance. Stefanie Powers, Tallulah Bankhead, Peter Vaughan, Donald Sutherland. w. Richard Matheson, d. Silvio Narizzano.

SUSPENSE: Young Women; Widows; Generation Gap; Houses-Creepy; In-Laws-Troublesome; Mean Women; Evil Women; Avenging Death of Someone; Malicious Menaces; England; Camp; Curiosities; Gothic Style
(You'll Like My Mother; Whatever Happened to Aunt Alice?)

Die Hard, 1988, 131m, ★★★½/$$$$$, 20th/Fox, R/EV-P. A cop (Bruce Willis) is at the right place at the right time to save his wife (Bonnie Bedelia) from a gang of Eurotrash terrorists atop a skyscraper. w. Jeb Stuart, Steve E. deSouza, N-adap. Roderick Thorpe, *Nothing Lasts Forever*, d. John McTiernan.

ACTION: SUSPENSE: Hostage Situation; Police-Vigilante; Terrorists; Christmas; Heroes-Ordinary; Japanese People; Germans as Enemy; Die Hard Stories; High-Rise Settings; Sleeper Hits
(Under Siege; Passenger 57; Speed)

Die Hard 2, 1991, 124m, ★★½/$$$$, 20th/Fox, R/EP-EV-MRN. This time vigilante cop Willis happens to be at the airport when terrorists overtake it just as his wife's (Bonnie Bedelia) plane is about to land with the same old pesky reporter (William Atherton) aboard. w. Steven E. DeSouza, Doug Richardson, Walter Wager, 58 Minutes, d. Renny Harlin.

ACTION: SUSPENSE: Hostages; Crisis Situation; Cops-Vigilante; Terrorists; Christmas; Heroes-Superhuman; Airports; Die Hard Stories

SEQUEL TO: Die Hard
(Under Siege; Passenger 57; Speed; Airport)

Die Laughing, 1980, 108m, ★★/$, Orion-WB/WB, PG/V. A young musician learns of the plot behind the murder of a famous scientist and must run from the co-conspirators as well as the FBI. Robby Benson, Linda Grovenor, Charles Durning, Elsa Lanchester, Bud Cort. w. Jerry Segal, Robby Benson, Scott Parker, d. Jeff Werner.

COMEDY: Action Comedy; Chase Movies; Conspiracy; **MURDER:** FBI Agents; Scientists; Taxi Driver; Good Premise Unfulfilled; Coulda Been Good

REMAKE/RETREAD OF: The 39 Steps (The 39 Steps; Hanky Panky; North by Northwest; Saboteur)

Die Watching, 1993, 92m, ★½/VR, Trimark/Trimark, R/ES-FFN-MN. A soft-core video maker gets too obsessed with his bimbo models which leads to murder. Christopher Atkins, Vali Ashton, Tim Thomerson, Carlos Palomino. w. Kenneth J. Hall, d. Charles Davis.

SUSPENSE: Erotic Thriller; Obsessions; Pornography World; Photography; Bimbos; **MURDER:** Murders of Women; Voyeurs

RETREAD OF: Peeping Tom

A Different Story, 1978, 106m, ★★½/$, Avco-Embassy/New Line, R/S-P-MRN. A gay man falls for a lesbian, but then begins cheating just as they've adjusted. Perry King, Meg Foster, Valerie Curtin, Peter Donat. w. Henry Olek, d. Paul Aaron.

COMEDY DRAMA: ROMANCE: Romantic Comedy; Romance-Triangles; Roommates; Alternative Lifestyles; Gay Men; Lesbians; Bisexuality; Sexuality; Fashion World; Marriage of Convenience; Ahead of Its Time; Good Premise Unfulfilled
(Making Love; Threesome; Three of Hearts)
(Ed: Ultimately contrived wishful thinking and just not very good)

Digby, the Biggest Dog in the World, 1973, 88m, ★★½/$$, 20th/Prism. A dog accidently eats a vegetable growth hormone with comic results. Jim Dale, Spike Milligan, Angela Douglas, Milo O'Shea, Dinsdale Landen, Victor Spinetti. w. Michael Pertwee, d. Joseph McGrath.

SCI-FI: Fantasy; **CHILDREN'S: FAMILY:** Pet Stories; Animals-Mutant; Monsters-Mutant; Cult Films
(Honey, I Blew Up the Kid; Beethoven)

Diggstown, 1992, 98m, ★★/$, MGM/MGM-UA, R/EP-EV. A promoter and his aging fighter client go to a big boxing rally and bet a million that he can beat the ten best fighters. James Woods, Louis Gossett Jr., Bruce Dern, Oliver Platt. w. Steven McKay, N-adap. Leonard Wise, d. Michael Ritchie.

DRAMA: COMEDY DRAMA: Sports Movies; Boxing; Con Artists; Bets; Comebacks; Southerns; Corruption; Political Corruption; Small-town Life; Old-Fashioned Recent Films
(Bestseller; Cop; Smile; An Officer and a Gentleman; The Main Event)
(Ed: Harkens back to the 40s with updated profanity a-plenty)

Dillinger, 1945, 70m, ★★★/$$, Monogram/Fox. The life and hard times of public enemy number one. Lawrence Tierney, Edmund Lowe, Anne Jeffreys. w. Philip Yordan, d. Max Nosseck.

Dillinger, 1973, 107m, ★★★/$$, AIP/Vestron, Live. Dillinger's last year, as told with a sense of irony and cynicism and newly permissive violence of the 70s, not inappropriate for the 30s, however. Warren Oates, Ben Johnson, Michelle Phillips, Cloris Leachman, Harry Dean Stanton, Richard Dreyfuss. w. d. John Milius.

Writer-Directors

DRAMA: Crime Drama; Mob Stories; Mob Wars; Biographies; Criminal Biographies; Chicago; Prohibition Era
(Capone; The Untouchables)

Dim Sum: A Little Bit of Heart, 1985, 89m, ★★★/$, Ind/Imperial. In Chinatown, San Francisco, a young woman is pressured into finding a husband by her hypochondriac widowed mother, who is afraid she'll die without seeing her daughter married. w. Terrel Seltzer, d. Wayne Wang.

COMEDY DRAMA: Mothers-Troublesome; **ROMANCE:** Romantic Comedy; Marriage-Impending; Matchmakers; Chinese People; San Francisco; Female Protagonists
(Chan Is Missing; Life Is Cheap. . . .)

Diner, 1982, 110m, ★★★½/$$, MGM/MGM-UA, R/S. Several young men journey into adulthood, meeting regularly at a diner to discuss it. Steve Guttenberg, Daniel Stern, Ellen Barkin, Mickey Rourke, Timothy Daly. w. d. Barry Levinson (BOScr). Oscars: 1-0.

DRAMA: COMEDY DRAMA: Coming of Age; Ensemble Films; Ensembles-Male; Ensembles-Young People; Friendships-Male; Pre-Life Crisis; Settling Down; Young Men; 20-somethings; Restaurant

Settings; 1950s; Baltimore; Writer-Directors; Sleeper Hits; Cult Films
FEMALE FLIPSIDE: Mystic Pizza (Mystic Pizza; Avalon; Tin Men; The Bachelor Party [1957])
Dinner at Eight, 1933, 113m, ★★★¹/₂/$$$$, MGM/MGM-UA. Several rich people meet for dinner and discover much about themselves, especially since some will soon be poor. Marie Dressler, Lionel Barrymore, Jean Harlow, Billie Burke, Wallace Beery. w. Frances Marion, Herman J. Mankiewicz, P-adap. George S. Kaufman, Edna Ferber, d. George Cukor.
DRAMA: COMEDY DRAMA: SATIRE: Social Satire; Social Drama; Depression Era; Losing It All; Ensemble Films; Rich People; Secrets-Keeping; Class Conflicts; Dinner Parties; Female Screenwriters; Female Protagonists
REMAKE: TV (1985)
(The Discreet Charm of the Bourgeoisie; You Can't Take It With You; Grand Hotel; The Great Sinner)
Dino, 1957, 93m, ★★¹/₂/$, AA/Republic. A young Italian hood gets out of juvenile prison and has a hard time staying out of trouble. Sal Mineo, Brian Keith, Susan Kohner. w. P-adap. Reginald Rose, d. Thomas Carr.
DRAMA: MELODRAMA: Young Men; Young Men-Angry; Juvenile Delinquents; Social Workers; Forgotten Films
(Rebel Without a Cause; I Was a Teenage Mobster)
(Ed: Primarily for fans of Mineo)
The Dion Brothers, 1974, 96m, ★★★/$, Col/NA, R/V-P. Two brothers out of their steel mill jobs wind up on a crime spree which they might succeed at if they can stop arguing. Stacy Keach, Frederic Forrest, Margot Kidder, Barry Primus. w. Bill Kerby, Terence Malick, d. Jack Starrett.
COMEDY DRAMA: ACTION: Action Comedy; Black Comedy; Comedy-Morbid; Ordinary People Turned Criminal; Crime Sprees; Road Movies; Outlaw Road Movies; Brothers; Eccentric People; Hidden Gems; Overlooked at Release
(Freebie and the Bean; Slither; Bonnie and Clyde)
Dirty Dancing, 1987, 100m, ★★¹/₂/$$$$, Vestron/Vestron, PG/S. A wallflower (Jennifer Grey) meets a dancing hunk (Patrick Swayze) who whisks her cares away to the melodies' sound-track. w. Eleanor Bergstein, d. Emile Ardolino. **BOSong** ("The Time of My Life"). Oscars: 1-1.
ROMANCE: Dance Movies; **MELO-DRAMA:** Jewish People; Musicals; Music Movies; Dancing; Coming of Age; Wallflowers; Wallflowers & Hunks; Romance-Mismatched; 1960s; Sleeper Hits; Female Protagonists; Female Screenwriters
(The Way We Were; The Sterile Cuckoo; Strictly Ballroom)
The Dirty Dozen, 1967, 150m, ★★★/$$$$, MGM/MGM-UA, PG/V-P. A group of lifers in prison are made to go on a suicide mission. Lee Marvin, Ernest Borgnine, Robert Ryan, Charles Bronson, John Cassavetes (BSActor), George Kennedy, Richard Jaeckel, Telly Savalas, Donald Sutherland. w. Nunnally Johnson, Lukas Heller, N-adap. E. M. Nathanson, d. Robert Aldrich. Oscars: 1-0.
ACTION: COMEDY DRAMA: War Stories; Special Teams; Prison Drama; World War II Stories; Suicidal Tendencies; Ensemble Films; Ensembles-Male; Sleeper Hits
TV SERIES; TV SEQUEL: 1982.
(The Devil's Brigade; A Reason to Live, A Reason to Die; Force Ten from Navarone; Kelly's Heroes)
Dirty Harry, 1971, 102m, WB/WB, ★★★/$$$$, R/EV-P. A cop (Clint Eastwood) is tired of the system letting criminals go and decides to take matters into his own hands. w. Harry Julian Fink, Rita M. Fink, Dean Reisner, d. Don Siegel.
ACTION: Crime Drama; Murder-Learning to; Chase Movies; Detective Stories; Detectives-Police; Police Stories; Police-Vigilantes; Psycho-Killers; Transvestite Killers; San Francisco; San Francisco Cops; San Francisco Chases; Sleeper Hits
SEQUELS: Magnum Force, The Enforcer, Sudden Impact, The Dead Pool
(Bullitt; Freebie and the Bean; Death Wish)
Dirty Little Billy, 1972, 92m, ★★¹/₂/$, Col/NA. A psychological study of the young Billy the Kid, taking the point of view that his violent nature came about as a result of his mental retardation. Michael J. Pollard, Lee Purcell, Richard Evans. w. Charles Moss, Stan Dragoti, d. Stan Dragoti.
WESTERNS: DRAMA: Revisionist Films; Westerns-Neo; Mentally Disabled; Forgotten Films; Good Premise Unfulfilled
(Young Guns; Young Guns 2; Billy the Kid; Pat Garrett & Billy the Kid)
Dirty Rotten Scoundrels, 1988, 110m, ★★★/$$$, Orion/Vestron, PG-13. A debonair ladies' man (Michael Caine) and a goofy one (Steve Martin) team up and do battle to swindle a rich woman (Glenne Headly) on the Riviera. Barbara Harris, Dana Ivey, Meagen Fay. w. Dale Launer, S-adap. Stanley Donen, d. Frank Oz.
COMEDY: Comedy-Slapstick; Con Artists; Playboys; Bets; Romance-Triangles; Rich People; Murder Attempts-Comic; Prostitutes-Male; Riviera Life; Love-Questionable; Clever Plots & Endings; Turning the Tables
REMAKE OF: Bedtime Story
(The Fortune; A New Leaf; A Shock to the System)
The Disappearance of Aimee, 1976, 93m, ★★★¹/₂/$$$, NBC/Live. Story of famed Los Angeles fundamentalist female preacher Aimee Semple McPherson and how she mysteriously disappeared, then reappeared claiming to be abducted, but her mother said it was to have an affair. The subsequent scandal and trial were a highpoint of the 1920s. Faye Dunaway, Bette Davis, James Sloyan, James Woods, Severn Darden. d. Anthony Harvey.
DRAMA: MELODRAMA: Missing Persons; Cheating Women; Accused Unjustly; Preachers; Female Among Males; Mothers & Daughters; Scandals; Kidnappings; Romance with Married Person; True or Not?; True Stories; Biographies; Female Protagonists; TV Movies
(Agatha; The Handmaid's Tale; The Lindbergh Kidnapping)
The Disappearance of Christina, 1993, 95m, ★★¹/₂/$, U/MCA-U, PG-13/V. A black female detective is on the trail of a man whose rich wife mysteriously disappeared on a sailing trip and claims it was an accident. John Stamos, Kim Delaney, CCH Pounder, Robert Carradine. w. Camille Thomasson, d. Karen Arthur.
SUSPENSE: MURDER: MYSTERY: MURDER MYSTERY: Black Women; Murder of Spouse; Death-Accidental; Drownings; Female Protagonists; Female Screenwriters; Female Directors
Disaster at Silo 7, 1988, 92, ★★¹/₂/$$$, ABC/Trimark, PG. When a nuclear missile engine goes out of control

on a test in a silo in Arkansas, the Air Force tries desperately to avert nuclear disaster. Perry King, Patricia Charbonneau, Peter Boyle, Michael O'Keefe, Dennis Weaver. w. Douglas McIntosh, d. Larry Elikann.

DRAMA: Bombs-Atomic; Race Against Time; Accidents; True Stories; Arkansas; TV Movies
(Acceptable Risks; Warning Sign; War Games)

Disclosure, 1994, 120m, ★★★/$$$$, WB/WB, R/P-S. A computer expert gets a new boss who's an old girlfriend and who also insists they rekindle their personal relationship with their business one. But when he protests her groping advances, the good husband finds himself slapped with a sexual harassment suit when he was the one being harassed. Will the tables turn further? Demi Moore, Michael Douglas, Donald Sutherland, Caroline Goodall, Dennis Miller, Roma Maffia, Dylan Baker, Nicholas Sadler. w. Paul Attanasio, N-adap. Michael Crichton, d. Barry Levinson.

SUSPENSE: DRAMA: Psychological Thriller; Battle of the Sexes; Sexual Harassment; Men in Jeopardy; Corporate Life; Female in Male Domain; Turning the Tables; Liars; Evil Women; Virtual Reality
(Oleanna; Fatal Attraction; Business as Usual)

The Discreet Charm of the Bourgeoisie, 1972, 100m, ★★★★/$$$, 20th/Fox, PG. Wealthy French people are ready to have a dinner party, but there are some drug dealers about to interrupt their soiree. Stephane Audran. w. Luis Bunuel, Jean-Claude Carriere (BOScr), d. Luis Bunuel. **BFFilm.** Oscars: 2-0.

SATIRE: Art Films; Avant-Garde Films;
COMEDY: FARCE: Screwball Comedy; Tragi-Comedy; Black Comedy; Comedy-Morbid; Rich People; Class Conflicts; Surrealism; Dinner Parties; Drugs-Dealing; French Films
(The Exterminating Angel; The Phantom of Liberty; Dinner at Eight)

Dishonored, 1931, 91m, ★★★/$$, Par/MCA-U. An officer's wife falls on hard times when he dies and so she becomes a prostitute. A German officer she meets gets her into the spy corps. Marlene Dietrich, Victor McLaglen, Barry Norton. w. Daniel H. Rubin, d. Josef Von Sternberg.

MELODRAMA: TRAGEDY: Riches to Rags; Prostitutes-Low Class; Spies; Spy Films; Spies-Female; Germany; Female Protagonists

The Disorderly Orderly, 1964, 90m, ★★¹/₂/$$, Par/Par. A would-be doctor (Jerry Lewis) instead winds up in a mental institution where one surreal accident after another happens wherever he goes. w. d. Frank Tashlin.

COMEDY: Comedy-Gag; Comedy of Errors; Surrealism; Comedy-Slapstick; Mental Illness; Asylums; Character Comedy; Romance-Boy Wants Girl; Doctors; Hospitals; Accident Prone; Hidden Gems; Underrated
(The Bellboy; The Errand Boy; The Pink Panther)

Disorganized Crime, 1989, 101m, ★★¹/₂/$, Touchstone/Touchstone, PG-13/P. The leader of a band of incompetent crooks is in jail. When he flies the coop, he's got a foolproof plan for a bank robbery. Hoyt Axton, Corbin Bernsen, Ruben Blades, Fred Gwynne, Ed O'Neill, Lou Diamond Philips. w. J. H. Blanchon, N-adap. Pierre Very, d. Christian-Jaque.

COMEDY: Comedy of Errors; Heist Stories; Theives; Criminals-Stupid; Ensemble Films; Coulda Been Good; Good Premise Unfulfilled
(Big Deal on Madonna Street; Crackers; Quick Change)

The Displaced Person, 1976, 58m, ★★★¹/₂/$$, PBS/PBS. When Polish refugees enter a Georgia farming community in the 1940s, competition results between them and the locals, who have been resting on their laurels. Irene Worth, John Houseman, Henry Fonda, Shirley Stoler, Lane Smith, d. Glenn Jordan.

DRAMA: Immigrants; Farm Life; 1940s; Southerns; Fish out of Water Stories; Europeans-Eastern; TV Movies

Disraeli, 1929, 89m, ★★★/$$$, WB/MGM-UA. A biopic of the famous British prime minister in the turn of the century. George Ariliss (**BActor**), Joan Bennett, Florence Arliss, Anthony Bushell. w. Julian Josephson (BScr), P-adap. Louis N. Parker, d. Alfred E. Green. BPicture. Oscars: 3-1.

DRAMA: Biographies; Presidents; Politicians; Political Drama; Stagelike Films; British Films; England
(Young Winston; Goodbye, Mr. Chips)

Distant Drums, 1951, 101m, ★★¹/₂/$$, USP/NA. A military officer liberates POWs of the Seminoles in 1840s Florida. Gary Cooper, Mari Aldon, Richard Webb, Ray Teal, Arthur Hunnicutt. w. Niven Busch, Martin Rackin, d. Raoul Walsh.

DRAMA: ADVENTURE: Escape Adventure; Rescue Drama; POWs; Indians-American; Military Leaders; True Stories; Florida; Swamp Life

Distant Thunder, 1973, 100m, ★★★/$$, Balaka/Facets. In the forties in Bengal, a religious leader in a small community witnesses the beginnings of famine and what it does to the social fabric of a once-sane place. Sounitra Chatterjee, Babita, Ramesh Mukherjee, Chitra Banerjee. w. d. Satyajit Ray, N-adap. Bibhutibhusan Banerjee.

DRAMA: Social Drama; Homeless People; Poor People; India; Epidemics; Preachers/Ministers; Religion; Writer-Directors
(An Enemy of the People)

Distant Thunder, 1988, 114m, ★★/$, Par/Par, PG-13/P-V. A Vietnam vet who's living in the wilderness is visited by his long-lost son. John Lithgow, Ralph Macchio, Kerrie Keane, Janet Margolin. d. Rick Rosenberg.

DRAMA: Fathers & Sons; Children-Long-lost; Nature-Back to; Veterans-Vietnam

Disturbed, 1990, 96m, ★★/$, Live/Live, R/EV-P-S. An asylum director has a thing for one of his female patients who, luckily for him, is a bit of a nympho. Malcolm McDowell, Geoffrey Lewis, Pamela Gidley, Priscilla Pointer. w. Charles Winkler, Emerson Bixby, d. Winkler.

MELODRAMA: HORROR: Erotic Thriller; Asylums; Mental Illness; Sexy Women
(A Clockwork Orange)

Diva, 1982, 123m, ★★★★/$$$, UAC/MGM-UA, R/S-P. A bootleg tape of a concert by a black opera singer (Wilhelmina Wiggins Fernandez) who doesn't make recordings has been made by a devout young fan (Frederic Adrei), which puts him in jeopardy when the underworld wants it. w. Jean Van Hamme, Jean Jacques Beineix, d. Beineix.

SUSPENSE: DRAMA: Art Films; Chase Movies; Young Men; Fans-Crazed; Mob Stories; Fugitives from the Mob; French Films; Singers; Opera; Outstanding Cinematography; Cult Films; Sleeper Hits
(Exposed; Ready to Wear; Betty Blue)

Divine Madness, 1980, 93m, ★★★/$$, WB/WB, R/EP-S. A Bette Midler concert in which she does a retrospective of her career, music, and comical characters. Bette Midler. d. Michael Ritchie.
COMEDY: Comedy Performance; Comedians; Concert Films; Singers; One-Performer Shows
(The Rose; For the Boys)

Diving In, 1990, 92m, ★★/$, Par/Par, PG-13/S. A young Olympic diver suddenly gets a case of height fright and has to rely on his love interest to overcome it and jump in. Matt Adler, Kristy Swanson, Burt Young, Matt Lattanzi. d. Strathford Johnson.
MELODRAMA: ROMANCE: Sports Movies; Swimming; Olympics; Phobias
(American Anthem; Gymkata)

Divorce, American Style, 1967, 109m, ★★★/$$$, Col/NA. In California, a suburban couple think of divorcing, but can't afford it. Dick Van Dyke, Debbie Reynolds, Jean Simmons, Jason Robards Jr., Lee Grant, Tom Bosley. w. Norman Lear (BOScr), d. Bud Yorkin. Oscars: 1-0.
COMEDY: Marriage Comedy; Romance-Bickering; Marriage on the Rocks; Suburban Life; Making a Living; 1960s; Sleeper Hits
(How Sweet It Is; Divorce, Italian Style)

Divorce, Italian Style, 1961, 108m, ★★★/$$$, Lux-Vides-Galatea-Embassy/Hen's Tooth, Ingram. A wealthy Sicilian gets rid of his wife by hiring a hitman to seduce her, but the joke may be on him yet as he pursues a young lovely. Marcello Mastroianni (BActor), Daniela Rocca, Stefania Sandrelli. w. Ennio de Concini, Pietro Germi, Alfredo Gianetti (BOScr), d. Pietro Germi (BDirector). Oscars: 3-0.
COMEDY DRAMA: Black Comedy; Comedy-Light; MURDER: Murder Attempts-Comic; Hitmen; Murder of Spouse; Romance-Triangles; Romance-Boy Wants Girl; Cheating Men; Romance-Older Men/Younger Women; Dead-Back from the; Trials; Italian Films; Sleeper Hits
(How to Murder Your Wife; Marriage, Italian Style; Kind Hearts and Coronets; A New Leaf)
(Ed: Not exactly a hilarious farce, but very good in its own style)

The Divorce of Lady X, 1938, 92m, ★★★/$$$, London/Nos. In order to woo a lawyer, a woman pretends to be a candidate for divorce and solicits his "services." Laurence Olivier, Merle Oberon, Binnie Barnes, Ralph Richardson, Lajos Biro, Arthur Wimperis, Ian Dalrymple, P-adap. Gilbert Wakefield (*Counsel's Opinion*), d. Tim Whelan.
COMEDY DRAMA: ROMANCE: Romantic Comedy; Divorce; Lawyers; Mindgames; Liars; Romance-Reluctant; British Films
(That Hamilton Woman)

The Divorcee, 1930, 83m, ★★★/$$$, MGM/MGM-UA. A couple of young Libertines agree to accept each other's philandering and get married anyway. Only problem is, the husband isn't so keen on her affairs. She eventually takes up with another married man, but thinks better of the whole affair. Norma Shearer (BActress), Chester Morris, Conrad Nagel, Robert Montgomery. w. John Meehan, Nick Grinde, Zelda Sears (BScr), N-adap. Ursula Parrot (*Ex-Wife*), d. Robert Z. Leonard (BDirector). BPicture. Oscars: 4-1.
COMEDY DRAMA: ROMANCE: Divorce; Marriage on the Rocks; Marriage Drama; Cheating Women; Cheating Men; Romance with Married Person; Jealousy; Feminist Films; Women's Films; Female Protagonists
(The Awful Truth; The Marrying Man)

Dixie, 1943, 90m, ★★½/$$, Par/NA. A musical biopic about the old-time minstrel entertainer Dan Emmett. Bing Crosby, Dorothy Lamour, Marjorie Reynolds, Lynne Overman, Eddie Foy Jr., Billy de Wolfe, Raymond Walburn. w. Karl Turnberg, Darrell Ware, d. A. Edward Sutherland.
MUSICALS: Biographies; Music Movies; Singers; Dancers; Nostalgia; Southerns; Race Relations
(Birth of the Blues; The Jazz Singer)

D.O.A., 1950, 83m, ★★★½/$$, UA/Nos. A man must find out who injected him with a slow-acting poison, with only 24 hours before it's too late. Edmond O'Brien, Pamela Britton, Luther Adler. w. Russel Rouse, Clarence Greene, d. Rudolphe Mate.
SUSPENSE: MURDER: Poisons; Race Against Time; MYSTERY: MURDER MYSTERY: Chase Movie; Saving One's Self; Death-Impending; Film Noir; Underrated; Hidden Gems
REMAKES: Color Me Dead, D.O.A. (1988).

(Ed: A classic. Thoroughly original and riveting despite the hero's futility)

D.O.A., 1988, 97m, ★★/$, Touchstone/Touchstone, PG-13/S-P. A remake which unnecessarily complicates the streamlined plot of the original and becomes a ridiculous chase picture with the two leads' hands superglued together. Dennis Quaid, Meg Ryan, Charlotte Rampling, Daniel Stern. w. Charles Edward Pogue, SS-adap. Charles Edward Pogue, Russel Rouse, Clarence Green, d. Rocky Morton, Annabel Jankel.
SUSPENSE: MURDER: Poisons; Race Against Time; MYSTERY: MURDER MYSTERY: Chase Movie; Saving One's Self; Death-Impending; Cuff to Cuff; Unintentionally Funny; New Orleans; Female Directors
REMAKE OF: 1949 version; Color Me Dead
(Color Me Dead; Flesh and Bone)

Doc, 1971, 96m, ★★★/$$, UA/Fox. Doc Holliday supports Wyatt Earp in his fight with the Clanton gang, and fights nobly even though he's dying of tuberculosis. Stacy Keach, Harris Yulin, Faye Dunaway. w. Pete Hamill, d. Frank Perry.
WESTERNS: DRAMA: Character Studies; Biographies; Wyatt Earp; Westerns-Neo; Death-Impending; One Last Time
(Wyatt Earp; Tombstone; The Tin Star)

Doc Hollywood, 1991, 103m, ★★★½/$$$$, WB/WB, PG-13/S-P-FFN. A doctor on his way to L.A. crashes his car in a small town and stays put, despite the seeming backwardness. Michael J. Fox, Julie Warner, Barnard Hughes, Woody Harrelson, David Ogden Stiers, Bridget Fonda. w. Jeffrey Price, Peter S. Seaman, Daniel Pyne, N-adap. Neil B. Shulman (*What? . . . Dead Again*), d. Michael Caton-Jones.
COMEDY: COMEDY DRAMA: ROMANCE: Romantic Comedy; Fish out of Water Stories; North vs. South; City vs. Country; Stranded; Doctors; Cosmetic Surgery; Southerns; Small-town Life; Sleeper Hits; Hidden Gems; Capra-esque
(My Cousin Vinny; Northern Exposure TV Series)
(Ed: Best of Fox's little comedies-not saying much, but this is good and the Southern stereotypes get a twist)

The Doctor, 1991, 125m, ★★★/$$$, Touchstone/Touchstone, PG-13/P-S. An arrogant and somewhat cold surgeon becomes a better person after being on the "other side of the knife" at his own hospital as a cancer patient. William Hurt, Christine Lahti, Elizabeth Perkins, Mandy Patinkin, Adam Arkin. w. Robert Caswell, NF-adap. Ed Rosenbaum (*A Taste of My Own Medicine*), d. Randa Haines.

DRAMA: Death-Impending; Doctors; Disease Stories; Hospitals; Marriage Drama; Redemption; Midlife Crisis; Female Directors
(Ed: You've seen pieces of it all before, but it's better done here)

The Doctor and the Devils, 1985, 93m, ★★1/2/$, EMI/Fox, R/V-B&G. A Scottish doctor in the 1700s collects bodies from local graves for his experiments. Timothy Dalton, Jonathan Pryce, Twiggy, Julian Sands, Stephen Rea. w. Ronald Harwood, P-adap. Dylan Thomas, d. Freddie Frances.

HORROR: Scientists-Mad; Body Parts; Experiments; Gothic Style; Overlooked at Release; 1700s; Frankenstein Stories
(Frankenstein; The Body Snatcher; The Flesh and the Fiends; Burke and Hare)

Dr. Cyclops, 1940, 76m, ★★★/$$, Par/MCA-U. A group of explorers in the jungle are taken prisoner by an evil scientist who shrinks them down to doll-size creatures. Albert Dekker, Janice Logan, Victor Kilian, Thomas Coley, Charles Halton. w. Tom Kilpatrick, d. Ernest Schoedsack.

HORROR: SCI-FI: Fantasy; Kidnappings; Scientists-Mad; Experiments; Shrinking People; Little People; Ahead of Its Time; Hidden Gems; Cult Films
(Tom Thumb; The Incredible Shrinking Man; SHE; Darby O'Gill and the Little People)

Doctor Detroit, 1983, 91m, ★★/$$, U/MCA-U, R/P-S. A mild mannered professor becomes a fabulous pimp and mobster in the motor city. Dan Aykroyd, Donna Dixon, Fran Drescher, Howard Hesseman, Lynn Whitfield, Andrew Duggan, Kate Murtagh, Glenne Headly. w. Carl Gottlieb, d. Michael Pressman.

COMEDY: Professors; Pimps; Prostitutes-High Class; Mob Comedy; College Life; Bimbos; Sexy Women; Power-Rise to; Power-Rise to to Idiot; Ordinary Person Turned Prostitute
(The Couch Trip; The Nutty Professor)

Dr. Dolittle, 1967, 152m, ★★★/$$$, 20th/Fox, G. The singing veterinarian (Rex Harrison) takes to the south seas to talk and sing to his strange, mutant animal collection. Samantha Eggar, Anthony Newley, Richard Attenborough. w/songs Leslie Bricusse, N-adap. Hugh Lofting, d. Richard Fleischer. BPicture, BCinema, BArt, BEdit, BSound, **BOSong**, BOScore, BMScore, **BSFX.** Oscars: 9-2.

MUSICALS: CHILDREN'S: SCI-FI: Fantasy; **ADVENTURE:** Fairy Tales; Doctors; Veterinarians; Adventure at Sea; Animals-Mutant; Animals-Smart; Animals-Talking; Islands; Production Design-Outstanding
(Willy Wonka and the Chocolate Factory; Chitty Chitty Bang Bang; My Fair Lady)

Dr. Ehrlich's Magic Bullet, 1940, 103m, ★★★/$, WB/NA. A historic melodrama about the discovery of the cure for VD. Edward G. Robinson, Ruth Gordon, Otto Kruger, Donald Crisp, Maria Ouspenskaya, Montagu Love. w. John Huston, Heinz Herald, Norman Burnside, d. William Dieterle.

DRAMA: Cures-Search for; Doctors; Scientists; Sexuality; Historical Drama; Biographies; Forgotten Films
(The Story of Louis Pasteur; Madame Curie)

Dr. Faustus, 1967, 93m, ★★1/2/$, Col/Col. In the Middle Ages, an ascetic scholar is tempted by the Devil to give up his soul in exchange for riches and sensual pleasures. Richard Burton, Andreas Tuber, Ian Marter, Elizabeth Taylor. w. Nevill Coghill, P-adap. Christopher Marlowe, d. Richard Burton, Nevill Coghill.

DRAMA: TRAGEDY: Selling One's Soul; Satan; Evil Men; Greed; Middle Ages; Classic Literary Adaptations; Classic Tragedy; Legends; Actor Directors
(Eye of the Devil; All That Money Can Buy; Hammersmith Is Out)

Dr. Giggles, 1992, 96m, ★★/$, U/MCA-U, R/EV-P-S-B&G. A demented doctor escapes from the asylum and returns to his abandoned childhood home where teens like to congregate, making for convenient murders. Larry Drake, Holly Marie Combs, Cliff DeYoung. w. Graeme Whitler, Manny Coto, d. Coto.

HORROR: Black Comedy; Comedy-Morbid; Horror Comedy; Teenagers; Murders of Teenagers; Psycho-Killers; Asylums; Prison Escapes; Murders-One by One
(Halloween SERIES; Friday the 13th SERIES)

Dr. Heckyl and Mr. Hype, 1980, 99m, ★★/$, Cannon/Cannon. A homely, nerdy scientist becomes a cruel but handsome dude after drinking a formula he concocts in his lab. Oliver Reed, Sunny Johnson, Mel Wells, Maia Danziger. w. d. Charles B. Griffith.

COMEDY: HORROR: Horror Comedy; Comedy-Morbid; Scientists-Mad; Experiments; Elixirs/Cures; Dual Lives; Writer-Directors
(The Nutty Professor; Dr. Jekyll and Mr. Hyde)

Doctor in the House, 1954, 91m, ★★★/$$$, Rank/Par. Medical students in England in the fifties have academic as well as amorous struggles. Dirk Bogarde, Kenneth More, Donald Sinden, Donald Houston, James Robertson Justice. w. Nicholas Phipps, N-adap. Richard Gordon, d. Ralph Thomas.

COMEDY DRAMA: MELODRAMA: Doctors; Medical School; **ROMANCE:** Young People; Ensemble Films; British Films
(The Interns; Carry on Doctor)

Doctor Jekyll and Mr. Hyde, 1931, 98m, ★★★★/$$$, MGM/MGM-UA. The famous story of the genteel Victorian gentleman scientist who devises a potion that unleashes the beast within himself. Fredric March, Miriam Hopkins, Rose Hobart, Holmes Herbert. w. Samuel Hoffenstein, Percy Heath, N-adap. Robert Louis Stevenson, d. Rouben Mamoulian.

Dr. Jekyll and Mr. Hyde, 1941, 122m, ★★★/$, MGM/MGM-UA. A more psychologically oriented remake of above, but it didn't do very well. Spencer Tracy, Ingrid Bergman, Lana Turner, C. Aubrey Smith, Donald Crisp. w. John Lee Mahin, d. Victor Fleming.

DRAMA: HORROR: Psychological Drama; **ROMANCE:** Character Studies; Dual Lives; Cures/Elixirs; Scientists-Mad; Experiments; Secrets-Keeping; Classic Literary Adaptations
(Mary Reilly; Dead Ringers)
(Ed: Though this was not a success, Tracy and Bergman make it the most interesting version)

Dr. Jekyll and Sister Hyde, 1971, 97m, ★★1/2/$$, Hammer-EMI-MGM/Lebell, MGM-UA. Doctor Jekyll now becomes a woman, and a prostitute at that, when he takes his formula. Ralph Bates, Martine Beswick, Gerald Sim. w. Brian Clemens, d. Roy Ward Baker.

COMEDY DRAMA: HORROR: Horror Comedy; Men as Women; Dual Lives; Transsexuals; Revisionist Films; Doctors; Scientists-Mad; Prostitutes-Low Class; British Films

Dr. M., 1989, 116m, ★★/$, Ind/NA. In a vacation wonderland, an evil scientist injects people with a serum that makes them want to off themselves. Alan Bates, Jennifer Beals, Jan Niklas, Benoit Regent, William Berger. w. Sollace Mitchell, Thomas Buermeister, d. Claude Chabrol.

HORROR: Scientists-Mad; Poisons; Suicidal Tendencies; Vacations; Vacations-Nightmare

Doctor Mabuse, the Gambler, 1922, 101m, ★★★/$$, UFA/Nos. A sadistic madman tries to take over the world but is foiled. Rudolph Klein-Rogge, Alfred Abel, Gertrude Welcker, Paul Richter. w. Thea Von Harbou, Fritz Lang, N-adap. Norbert Jacques, d. Fritz Lang.

HORROR: Rule the World-Plots to; Hypnosis; Mental Illness; Gamblers; Surrealism

(Metropolis; The Cabinet of Dr. Caligari)

Dr. No, 1962, 111m, ★★★½/$$$, UA/MGM-UA. Agent 007 goes to the West Indies to stop a madman from taking over the world and meets a lovely in a bikini along the way. Sean Connery, Ursula Andress, Jack Lord. w. Richard Maibaum, Johanna Harwood, Berkely Mather, N-adap. Ian Fleming, d. Terence Young.

ACTION: ADVENTURE: Secret Agents; Rule the World-Plot to; Playboys; Caribbean; Islands; Sleeper Hits; James Bond

(From Russia With Love; Goldfinger)

Dr. Phibes Rises Again, 1972, 89m, ★★★/$$, AIP/Orion, Vestron, R/V-B&G. This time, the evil, vengeful doctor (Vincent Price) searches for an elixir to bring his dead wife-who he killed the surgical staff presiding over her dying moments for-back to life, travelling to Egypt and the sphinx to get it. w. Robert Fuest, Robert Blees, d. Robert Fuest.

HORROR: COMEDY: Horror Comedy; Black Comedy; Dead-Back from the; Cures/Elixirs; Egypt; Cult Films; Underrated; Hidden Gems

SEQUEL TO: The Abominable Dr. Phibes

(Theater of Blood; The Comedy of Terrors)

(Ed: A rare sequel as good or better than the first)

Doctor Quinn, Medicine Woman, 1992, 100m, ★★★/$$$, CBS/Fox. The TV pilot for the sleeper hit series about a beautiful lady doctor settling in a small Western town to practice medicine and get the town hunk (aka Little Hunk on the Prairie). Jane Seymour, Joe Lando, Diane Ladd.

MELODRAMA: Doctors; Female Among Males; **WESTERNS:** 1800s; Hunks; Sleeper Hits; TV Movies; Old-Fashioned Recent Films; Conservative-Value Films; Female Protagonists

(Christy [TV Series]; Blossoms in the Dust)

The Doctor's Dilemma, 1958, 99m, ★★★/$, MGM/NA. A group of British doctors around the turn of the century debate the case of a tubercular artist and his loving wife from an ethical standpoint. Leslie Caron, Dirk Bogarde, John Robinson, Alastair Sim, Robert Morley. w. Anatole de Grunwald, P-adap. Bernard Shaw, d. Anthony Asquith.

DRAMA: Character Studies; Doctors; Marriage Drama; **ROMANCE:** Ethics

Doctor's Wives, 1970, 102m, ★½/$$, Col/RCA-Col, R/S-FN. A doctor murders his unfaithful wife after she bets she can seduce every husband of a ladies' bridge club membership, causing everyone involved to examine their marriages. Richard Crenna, Janice Rule, Gene Hackman, John Colicos, Dyan Cannon, Carroll O'Connor, Ralph Bellamy. w. Daniel Taradash, N-adap. Frank G. Slaughter, d. George Schaefer.

MURDER: Bets; Promiscuity; Sexy Women; Suburban Life; Doctors; Playgirls; Good Premise Unfulfilled; Coulda Been Good

(Such Good Friends; The Chapman Report)

(Ed: What starts off promising turns out to be a dreary middle-aged soap opera with the most interesting character offed and no one seems to care)

Dr. Socrates, 1935, 70m, ★★★/$$, WB/NA. In a small town being overrun by gangsters, a local doctor inadvertently gets involved by caring for their wounded. Paul Muni, Ann Dvorak, Barton MacLane, Robert Barrat, John Eldridge, Hobart Cavanaugh, Mayo Methot. w. Robert Lord, N-adap. W. R. Burnett, d. William Dieterle.

DRAMA: MELODRAMA: Crime Drama; Mob Stories; Doctors; Ethics; Decisions-Big; Forgotten Films; Hidden Gems

(The Last Angry Man)

Dr. Strangelove: or How I Learned to Stop Worrying and Love the Bomb (B&W), 1964, 93m, ★★★★/$$$$, Col/RCA-Col. The government is afraid they've accidentally sent an atomic bomb to Russia and may not be able to retrieve it amid a series of bureaucratic snafus. Peter Sellers (BActor), George C. Scott, Keenan Wynn, Slim Pickens. w. Stanley Kubrick, Terry Southern, Peter George, N-adap. Peter George (Red Alert) (BAScr), d. Stanley Kubrick (BDirector). BPicture. Oscars: 4-0.

COMEDY: SATIRE: FARCE: Black Comedy; Comedy of Errors; Social Satire; Bombs-Atomic; Race Against Time; Apocalyptic Stories; Paranoia; Cold War Era; Cold War Error; Military Stories; Military Leaders; Pentagon; Misunderstandings; Accidents; Multiple Performances; Washington D.C.; Russians; Cult Films; Sleeper Hits

(Fail Safe; Whoops!; Apocalypse; The Mouse That Roared; Kind Hearts and Coronets; War Games)

Dr. Syn Alias Scarecrow, 1962, 98m, ★★½/$$, Disney/Disney. In the late 18th Century, the vicar of a small English seaside town is by night a swashbuckling smuggler. Patrick McGoohan, George Cole, Tony Britton, Geoffrey Keen, Kay Walsh, Patrick Wymark. w. Robert Westerby, N-adap. Russell Thorndike, Willam Buchanan (Christopher Syn), d. James Neilson.

DRAMA: ADVENTURE: Dual Lives; Thieves; Swashbucklers; Secrets-Keeping; 1700s; England; Legends; Robin Hood Stories

RETELLING: Captain Clegg.

(Treasure Island; The Adventures of Robin Hood)

(Ed: A more macabre story from Disney, with plenty of mood but not necessarily story)

The Doctor Takes a Wife, 1940, 89m, ★★★½/$$$, Col/Col. The author of Spinsters Aren't Spinach (Loretta Young) hitches a ride with a doctor (Ray Milland) who winds up posing as her husband when "America's #1 bachelor girl" is rumored to have gotten married-this, or risk a story claiming she had a strange man in her bedroom, unless she gets out of the fix by divorcing him after never really marrying him in order to write another bestseller, *Divorces Are Dynamite*. w. George Seaton, Ken Englund, d. Alexander Hall.

COMEDY: ROMANCE: Romantic Comedy; Screwball Comedy; **FARCE:** Comedy-Situation; Romance-Bickering; Romance-Opposites Attract; Romance-Reluctant; Romance-Triangles; Misunderstandings; Marriages-Fake; Marriages of Convenience; Career Women; Doctors; Forgotten Films; Pretending; Hidden Gems; Writers; Newlyweds
(Take a Letter, Darling; Libeled Lady; My Favorite Wife; A Night to Remember)
(Ed: Witty repartée abounds in this forgotten screwball long unavailable on video but well worth tracking down on TV. Gail Patrick played the jilted fiancee in both this and similar *My Favorite Wife*)

Doctor, You've Got to be Kidding, 1967, 93m, ★★/$$, MGM/NA. Three men woo a young girl in a maternity ward. Sandra Dee, George Hamilton, Celeste Holm, Bill Bixby, Dwayne Hickman, Mort Sahl. w. Phillip Shuken, N-adap. Patte Wheat Mahan, d. Peter Terkesbury.

COMEDY DRAMA: ROMANCE: Romantic Comedy; Mothers-Unwed; Babies-Having; Young Women; Men Fighting Over Women

Doctor Zhivago, 1965, 192m, ★★★★/$$$$$, MGM/MGM-UA, G. A writer (Omar Sharif) and his true love (Julie Christie) are separated during the onset of the Russian revolution and cross the countryside to survive, hopefully to be reunited. Rod Steiger, Geraldine Chaplin, Tom Courtenay (BSActor). w. Robert Bolt (**BAScr**), N-adap. Boris Pasternak, d. David Lean (BDirector). BPicture, **BCCin**, BCCost, **BCArt**, **BOScore, BSound**, BEditing. Oscars: 10-5.

DRAMA: ROMANCE: ADVENTURE: Romantic Drama; War Stories; Epics; Journies; Russia; Russian Revolution; Romance Reunited; Parallel Stories; Writers; Poets; Snow Settings; All-Star Casts; Cast of Thousands; Blockbusters; Scenery-Outstanding; Production Design-Outstanding
(Reds; A Passage to India; Lawrence of Arabia)

Dodge City, 1939, 104m, ★★★/$$$, WB/MGM-UA. The new sheriff of Dodge City means business, unlike his predecessors, and he aims to make the streets safe for women and children. Errol Flynn, Olivia de Havilland, Ann Sheridan, Bruce Cabot, Alan Hale, Frank McHugh. w. Robert Buckner, d. Michael Curtiz.

WESTERNS: Police Stories; Dodge City; Men Proving Themselves; Duels

Dodsworth, 1936, 101m, ★★★½/$$$, Goldwyn-UA/Goldwyn, HBO. A middle-aged middle-class American couple go to Europe and events force them to re-examine their relationship. Walter Huston (BActor), Mary Astor, Ruth Chatterton, David Niven, Maria Ouspenskaya (BSActress). w. Sidney Howard (BScr), N-adap. Sinclair Lewis, d. William Wyler (BDirector). BPicture, **BB&WArt**. 6-1.

DRAMA: ROMANCE: Marriage Drama; Marriage on the Rocks; Vacations; Vacations-European; Classic Literary Adaptations
(Arrowsmith)

Does This Mean We're Married?, 1990, 93m, ★★½/$, Col/Col, PG-13/S. A comedienne in Paris is going to be deported just when she's making it and has to find a husband. Patsy Kensit, Stephane Freiss. d. Carol Wiseman.

COMEDY: COMEDY DRAMA: Marriage Comedy; Marriage for Citizenship; Paris; Comedians; Female Protagonists; Female Directors; British Films
(Green Card; Paper Marriage)
(Ed: Sounds suspiciously like, uh . . . *Green Card?*)

Dog Day Afternoon, 1975, 130m, ★★★★/$$$$, WB/WB, R/EP-S-V. A man (Al Pacino, BActor) robs a bank, taking hostages until he gets money for an operation for a very interesting reason. John Cazale, Chris Sarandon (BSActor), Carol Kane, Charles Durning, James Broderick. w. Frank Pierson (**BAScr**), NF-adap. Patrick Mann, d. Sidney Lumet (BDirector). BPicture, BEdit. Oscars: 6-1.

DRAMA: TRAGEDY: Tragi-Comedy; Hostage Situations; Bank Robberies; Alternative Lifestyles; Gay Men; Men as Women; Transsexuals; Young Men-Angry; Riots; True Stories; Fighting the System
(And Justice For All; Fourteen Hours; The Man Upstairs; Killing Zoe; Cadillac Man)

Dogfight, 1991, 92m, ★★★/$ (LR), WB/WB, PG-13/P-S. A young marine (River Phoenix) is in a bet to bring the ugliest date to a party (Lili Taylor) and winds up finding out she's not so disgusting. w. Robert Comfort, d. Nancy Savoca.

DRAMA: ROMANCE: Romance-Mismatched; Wallflowers; Wallflowers and Hunks; Soldiers; Looksism; Waitresses; Young Men; Bets; Quiet Little Films; Overlooked at Release; Underrated; Hidden Gems; Female Directors
(Circle of Friends; The Sterile Cuckoo)

Dog of Flanders, 1959, 97m, ★★★/$$, 20th/Par. Misunderstood and unappreciated by his parents, a sensitive young boy runs away from home. But his dog leads his family to him and they all reconcile. David Ladd, Donald Crisp, Theodore Bikel, Max Croiset. w. Ted Sherdeman, N-adap. Ouida, d. James B. Clark.

CHILDREN'S: MELODRAMA: FAMILY: Pet Stories; Boyhood; Boy and His Dog; Runaways; Missing Children; Animals-Smart
(Misunderstood)

Dogs in Space, 1987, 109m, ★★★/$, 20th/Fox, R/P-S. A slice of life about punkers and would-be rockers in Australia in the late 70s. Michael Hutchence, Saskie Post. w. d. Richard Lowenstein.

DRAMA: SATIRE: Teenagers; Musicians; Rebels; Young Men-Angry; Australian Films
(Absolute Beginners; Starstruck; Young Einstein)

The Dogs of War, 1980, 118m, ★★½/$$, UA/MGM-UA, R/P-EV. A soldier of fortune becomes involved in the coup of a small African country. Christopher Walken, Tom Berenger, Colin Blakely, Hugh Millais. w. Gary DeVore, George Malko, N-adap. Frederick Forsyth, d. John Irvin.

ACTION: War Stories; Political Unrest; Mercenaries; Soldiers; Africa

La Dolce Vita, see L

Dollars, 1971, 119m, ★★★½/$$$, WB/WB, R/S-P. A suave American working in a bank in Germany (Warren Beatty) gets his kooky girlfriend (Goldie Hawn) to work with him on a clever bank heist scheme. Robert Webber, Gert Frobe, Scott Brady. w. d. Richard Brooks.

COMEDY DRAMA: SUSPENSE: Chase Movies; Heist Stories; Bank Robberies; Criminal Couples; Crime Pays;

Americans Abroad; Germany; Clever Plots & Endings; Writer-Directors (Perfect Friday; Bonnie and Clyde; A Man, a Woman, and a Bank)

A Doll's House, 1973, 95m, ★★★/$, Ind/MGM-UA. In the late 1800s, a staid Norwegian family falls apart as the woman begins to feel trapped by her controlling husband and the limited choices society offered women at the time. Claire Bloom, Anthony Hopkins, Ralph Richardson, Denholm Elliott, Anna Massey, Edith Evans. w. Christopher Hampton, P-adap. Henrik Ibsen, d. Patrick Garland.

A Doll's House, 1973, 106m, ★★★/$, Ind/Prism. More filmic and Hollywood version of the above. Jane Fonda, David Warner, Trevor Howard, Edward Fox, Delphine Seyrig. w. David Mercer, P-adap. Henrik Ibsen, d. Joseph Losey.

DRAMA: Social Drama; Oppression; Housewives; Scandinavia; Snow Settings; Feminist Films; Ahead of Its Time; Stagelike Films; Female Protagonists; Classic Literary Adaptations
(Ghosts; Hedda)

The Dolly Sisters, 1945, 114m, ★★★/$$$, 20th/NA. In the vaudeville era, two sisters from Hungary make it to the big time. Betty Grable, June Haver, John Payne, S. Z. Sakall, Reginald Gardner. w. John Larkin, Marian Spitzer, d. Irving Cummings.

MUSICALS: Vaudeville; Singers; Dancers; Immigrants; Sisters; Nostalgia
(The Strawberry Blonde)

Dolores Claiborne, 1995, 131m, ★★★1/2/$$$, Col/Col, R/P-V. A stern and cantankerous woman is accused of killing a rich old woman when the past comes back to haunt her-her successful, citified daughter returns, and it comes out that she was suspected of killing the daughter's father years before. Did she kill either of these people, and was she justified if she did? Will the daughter be able to save her? Kathy Bates, Jennifer Jason Leigh, David Strathairn, John C. Reilly, Eric Bogosian, Christopher Plummer. w. Tony Gilroy, N-adap. Stephen King, d. Taylor Hackford.

SUSPENSE: MYSTERY: MURDER: Accused Unjustly; Framed?; Psychological Thriller; Psychological Drama; Mothers & Daughters; Stern Women; Journalists; Flashbacks; Past-

Haunted by the; Murderers-Female; Abused Women; Incest; Sleeper Hits; Hitchcockian
(Misery; Ladybird, Ladybird; The Burning Bed; Mildred Pierce)
(Ed: Beautiful, moody, and riveting, with another incredible performance from Bates)

Dominick & Eugene, 1988, 96m, ★★★/$, Orion/Orion, PG. Mentally handicapped Dominick works hard as a garbage man to help put his smart but poor brother through medical school, and they feel the tensions and pulls of family and ambition when Eugene falls in love with another intern. Ray Liotta, Tom Hulce, Jamie Lee Curtis, Todd Graff, Bill Cobbs, David Straithairn. w. Alvin Sargent, d. Robert M. Young.

MELODRAMA: COMEDY DRAMA: Family Drama; Brothers; Twins; Mentally Disabled; Jealousy; Doctors; Friendships-Male; Smart vs. Dumb
(Rain Man; Benny and Joon)

Dominique, 1978, 100m, ★★1/2/$, NA, R/S. A neurotic woman believes that her husband is trying to drive her insane. No one believes her until she ends up dead. Afterward, she is seen around town. Cliff Robertson, Jean Simmons, Jenny Agutter, Simon Ward, Ron Moody, Judy Geeson. w. Edward and Valerie Abraham, N-adap. Harold Lawlor (*What Beckoning Ghost*), d. Michael Anderson.

SUSPENSE: MYSTERY: Murder of Spouse; Dead-Back from the; Insane-Plot to Drive; Mental Illness; Coulda Been Great; Hitchcockian
(Diabolique; Obsession)

The Domino Principle, 1977, 100m, ★★/$, 20th/Fox, R/V. A professional hitman is told he'll be free if he'll assassinate one last political figure, and his refusal puts everyone he knows in jeopardy, including his wife. Gene Hackman, Candice Bergen, Richard Widmark, Mickey Rooney, Edward Albert, Eli Wallach, Ken Swofford. w. Adam Kennedy, d. Stanley Kramer.

SUSPENSE: ACTION: Hitmen; Assassinations; One Last Time; Mob Stories; Chase Movies; Fugitives from the Mob; Women in Jeopardy; Coulda Been Good; Unintentionally Funny
(Ed: Some exciting moments, but overall, over-the-top, laugh-out-loud bad-especially when Candice sees the big truck coming her way by the cliff but it's too

late, and Gene guns down bad guy Mickey Rooney)

Dona Flor and Her Two Husbands, 1976, 110m, ★★★/$$, Ind/Fox-Lorber, R/S-FN-MN. After her husband dies, a young woman remarries but finds her late husband's ghost occupying her new marriage bed. Sonia Braga, Jose Wilker, Mauro Mendonca. w. d. Bruno Barreto, N-adap. Jorge Amado.

COMEDY DRAMA: ROMANCE: Erotic Comedy; Ghosts; Dead-Back from the; Widows; Starting Over; Romance-Triangles; Hidden Gems; South America
REMAKE/RETREAD: Kiss Me Goodbye (Blithe Spirit; Truly, Madly, Deeply)

Don Juan DeMarco, 1995, 97m, ★★★/$$$, New Line/New Line, PG-13/S-P. A young man escapes his tumultuous past by escaping into the fantasy world of playing a Latin lover character in real life. But when the psychiatric world has to decide whether he's sane or should be placed on heavy doses, it may ruin the magic he's created for his lovers and himself. Marlon Brando, Johnny Depp, Faye Dunaway, Rachel Ticotin, Bob Dishy, Talisa Soto, Marita Geraghty, Richard Sarafian, Tresa Hughes, Al Corley. w. d. Jeremy Leven. BOSong. "Have You Ever Really Loved a Woman?" Oscars: 1-0.

COMEDY DRAMA: ROMANCE: Romantic Comedy; Fantasy; Illusions/Hallucinations; Identities-Assumed; Mental Illness; Young Men; Secrets-Haunting; Psychologists; Psychologists as Detective; Marriage Drama; Rejuvenation; Writer-Directors
(Harvey; A Fine Madness; Equus)

Donovan's Brain, 1953, 81m, ★★1/2/$, UA/MGM-UA. A wealthy capitalist dies, but his brain is kept alive by a scientist who is forced by the brain into a zombie-like robotic state to serve it. Lew Ayres, Gene Evans, Nancy Davis, Steve Brodie. w. d. Felix Feist, N-adap. Curt Siodmak.

HORROR: SCI-FI: Brains; Scientists-Mad; Experiments; Rich People; Cult Films; Camp
(Ed: Starring First Lady Nancy Reagan; the premise would make an interesting explanation of some of the things in the Reagan Presidency)

Donovan's Reef, 1963, 108m, ★★1/2/$$$, Par/Par. In the South Pacific after World War II, veterans settling with native girls must protect the reputation of one of their lot whose daughter comes for a visit. John Wayne, Lee Marvin, Jack Warden, Elizabeth Allen, Dorothy Lamour, Cesar Romero. w. Frank Nugent, James Edward Grant, d. John Ford.

COMEDY DRAMA: Veterans; Soldiers; South Pacific; Islands; Fathers & Daughters; Scandals; Secrets-Keeping
(Don't Go Near the Water; Trouble Along the Way)

Don's Party, 1976, 90m, ★★★/$$, Ind/MPI, Facets, R/ES-P-FFN-MFN. A party at a suburban Australian home turns into a confrontative wife-swapping party where not everyone wants to join in. Ray Barrett, Clare Binney, Pat Bishop. w. P-adap. David Williamson, d. Bruce Beresford.

DRAMA: Ensemble Films; Dinner Parties; Swapping Partners; Coulda Been Great; Stagelike Films; Married Couples; Australian Films
(Who's Afraid of Virginia Woolf?; The Big Chill; The Decline of Westrn Civilization)

Don't Bother to Knock, 1952, 76m, ★★★/$, 20th/Fox. A psychotic babysitter threatens to kill the child in her care. Marilyn Monroe, Richard Widmark, Anne Bancroft, Lurene Tuttle, Jim Backus. w. Daniel Taradash, N-adap. Charlotte Armstrong, d. Cyril Frankel.

MELODRAMA: HORROR: Mental Illness; Babysitters; Babysitters-Evil; Psycho Killers; Murderers-Female; Sexy Women; Murderers-Nice; Children in Jeopardy; Curiosities

Don't Go Near the Water, 1957, 107m, ★★1/2/$$, MGM/MGM-UA. A navy PR unit on a South Pacific base has a tough time with the enlisted men as well as the natives and their amorous adventures. Glenn Ford, Fred Clark, Gia Scala, Romney Brent, Keenan Wynn, Russ Tamblyn. w. Dorothy Kingsley, George Wells, N-adap. William Brinkley.

COMEDY DRAMA: Military Movies; Ensemble Films; **ROMANCE:** Sailors; South Pacific; Islands; Female Screenwriters
(Donovan's Reef)

Don't Just Stand There, 1967, 99m, ★★1/2/$, U/NA. A timid man gets swept up in intrigue involving murder and kidnapping. Mary Tyler Moore, Robert Wagner, Barbara Rhoades. w. N-adap. Charles Williams (The Wrong Venus), d. Ron Winston.

COMEDY: Spoofs; **MURDER:** Kidnappings; Detective Stories; Spoofs-

Detective; Nerds; Men Proving Themselves; Women in Jeopardy; Coulda Been Good; Good Premise Unfulfilled; Forgotten Films

Don't Look Back, 1967, 95m, ★★★/$$, Par/Par. A documentary of the career-to-date of Bob Dylan, circa 1967. Bob Dylan, Joan Baez, Donovan. d. D. A. Pennebacker.

Documentaries; Rockumentaries; Rock Stars; Singers; Musicians; Biographies; 1960s; Anti-Establishment Films; Psychedelic Era

Don't Look Now, 1977, 110m, ★★★1/2/$, Par/Par, R/S. A couple goes to Venice to try and outlive the death of their child but it's difficult to escape it all. Julie Christie, Donald Sutherland, Hilary Mason. w. Chris Bryan, Allan Scott, N-adap. Daphne DuMaurier, d. Nicolas Roeg.

DRAMA: Psychological Drama; Erotic Drama; Death-Dealing with; Marriage Drama; Marriage on the Rocks; Nightmares; Fantasies; Illusions; Venice; Hidden Gems; Cult Films
(Eureka; Bad Timing)

Don't Make Waves, 1967, 97m, ★★1/2/$$, MGM/NA. An attractive young woman makes life hell for a Malibu pool salesman who likes to surf. Tony Curtis, Claudia Cardinale, Robert Webber, Jim Backus, Mort Sahl. w. Ira Wallach, George Kirgo, N-adap. Ira Wallach (Muscle Beach), d. Alexander Mackendrick.

COMEDY: Beach Movies; **ROMANCE:** Romantic Comedy; Sexy Women; Forgotten Films; Time Capsules
(Arrivaderci, Baby)

Don't Raise the Bridge, Lower the Water!, 1967, 100m, ★★1/2/$$, Col/Col. An American in England married to a British woman turns their home into a nightclub. Jerry Lewis, Terry-Thomas, Jacqueline Pearce, Bernard Cribbins. w. Max Wilk, d. Jerry Paris.

COMEDY: Comedy-Slapstick; Nightclubs; Fools-Bumbling; Americans Abroad; London; Mod Era; Marriage on the Rocks

Don't Tell Her It's Me, 1990, 101m, ★★/$, WEG/HBO. A romance novelist tries to help her little brother get the girl he wants by turning him into one of her novel cover boys. Steve Guttenberg, Jami Gertz, Shelley Long, Kyle MacLachlan, Madchen Amik. w. Sarah Bird, d. Malcolm Mowbray.

COMEDY: ROMANCE: Romantic Comedy; Looksism; Macho Men; Nerds; Nerds & Babes; Identities-Assumed; Romance Novelists; Matchmakers; Female Screenwriters; Good Premise Unfulfilled
(Cyrano de Bergerac; Roxanne)

Don't Tell Mom the Babysitter's Dead, 1991, 105m, ★★/$, WB-HBO/WB, PG-13/P-S. A teenager who looks like a bimbo but has some responsible nature about her supports the kids while mom's away on business and the old baby-sitter she hired has croaked and hidden the money they're supposed to live on. Christina Applegate, Joanna Cassidy, John Getz, Keith Coogan, David Duchovny. w. Neil Landau, Tara Ison, d. Stephen Herek.

COMEDY: Hide the Dead Body; While the Parents Are Away; Career Women; Babysitters; Teenagers; Teenage Movies; Making a Living; Suburban Life; Coulda Been Good
(Adventures in Babysitting; Weekend at Bernie's)
(Ed: Christina Applegate being serious isn't much fun, and where was Chris Columbus when they needed him?-probably wise avoiding this nowhere script. Every joke is missed except the old lady croaking and even that's done poorly)

The Doom Generation, 1995, 90m, ★★1/2/$, Goldwyn-Ind/Goldwyn, R/EP-S-FN-MN. Two teenagers, a girl and a guy, living on the edge go over it, winding up on a spree of mayhem and destruction with another guy, but are they really the ones at fault, or is society? James Duval, Rose McGowan, Jonathan Schaech. w. d. Gregg Araki.

DRAMA: SATIRE: Road Movies; Outlaw Road Movies; Crime Sprees; Alternative Lifestyles; Bisexuality; Romance-Triangles; Writer-Directors; Independent Films; Generation X
(Kids; The Living End; Gun Crazy [1992])

The Doors, 1991, 134m, ★★1/2/$$, U-Carolco/MCA-U, R/P-S-V-FFN. Story of Jim Morrison and his formation of the rock band The Doors and his descent in to drugs. Val Kilmer, Meg Ryan, Frank Whaley, Kevin Dillon, Kyle MacLachlan, Billy Idol, Kathleen Quinlan, Josh Evans, Michael Madsen. w. J. Randal Johnson, Oliver Stone, d. Stone.

DRAMA: Music Movies; Fame-Rise to; Psychedelic Era; Rock Stars; Singers;

Music Dies; Biographies; 1960s; Rise and Fall Stories; Coulda Been Great (Medium Cool; Born on the Fourth of July) (Ed: Too much music and atmosphere and not nearly enough insight and story. Numbing)

Doppelganger: The Evil Within, 1990, 105m, ★★/$, Ind/Fox, R/V-S. A fairly nice girl moves in with a nice guy as a roommate, but may in fact be a brutal, psychopathic killer. Drew Barrymore, George Newbern, Dennis Christopher, Sally Kellerman, Leslie Hope. w. d. Avi Nesher.
SUSPENSE: MURDER: Murderers-Female; Murderers-Nice; Accused Unjustly; Roommates from Hell; Evil Women; Evil Children; Psycho-Killers; Writer-Directors; Female Protagonists (Poison Ivy)

Do The Right Thing, 1989, 120m, ★★★/$$, Universal/MCA-U, R/EP-V-S. Tensions rise between blacks and Italians resulting in the burning of a pizza shop when an altercation occurs between the owner of the shop (Danny Aiello, BSActor) and a black guy who won't turn his boom box down. Spike Lee, Joie Lee, Ruby Dee, Ossie Davis, John Turturro, John Savage. w. d. Spike Lee (**BOScr**). Oscars: 2-0.
DRAMA: TRAGEDY: Message Film; Political Drama; Social Drama; Race Relations; Black vs. White; Fires; Riots; Young Men-Angry; New York Life; Working Class; Ordinary People Stories; Black Casts; Black Men; Italians; Black Directors; Black Screenwriters (Malcolm X; DROP Squad) (Ed: Time will tell as to whether the anger outweighs the art)

Double-Crossed, 1991, 111m, ★★/$$, WB/WB. An American drug smuggler with ties to the Medellin cartel in Nicaragua agrees to help U.S. officials expose links between the cartel and the Sandinista government in exchange for clemency. But his cover gets blown, and he ends up running for his life. Dennis Hopper, Robert Carradine, G. W. Bailey, Adrienne Barbeau.
SUSPENSE: Crime Drama; Chase Stories; Fugitives from the Mob; Informers; Drugs-Dealing; Central America; Double Crossings

Double Exposure: The Story of Margaret Bourke-White, 1989, 105m, ★★★/$$$$, Turner/Turner. The true story of the first official female photographer of

World War II. Farrah Fawcett, Frederic Forrest, Mitchell Ryan, David Huddleston, Jay Patterson, Ken Marshall. d. Lawrence Schiller.
DRAMA: ROMANCE: Biographies; True Stories; Female Among Males; Feisty Females; Photographers; Depression Era; World Travel; Episodic Stories; Female Protagonists; TV Movies (Gandhi)

Double Impact, 1991, 109m, ★★/$$, Tri-Star/Col-Tri, R/EV. Orphaned when their parents are murdered, twin brothers seek out the gangsters behind the heinous act. Jean-Claude Van Damme, Geoffrey Lewis, Alan Scafe. w. Sheldon Lettich, Jean-Claude Van Damme, Steve Meerson, Peter Krikes, d. Sheldon Lettich.
ACTION: Avenging Death of Someone; Revenge; Twins; Brothers; Multiple Performances; Unintentionally Funny; Camp (Sudden Death; Time Cop; Brotherly Love)

Double Indemnity (B&W), 1944, 107m, Par/Par, ★★★★/$$$$. A femme fatale (Barbara Stanwyck, BActress) cons her insurance man (Fred MacMurray) into an affair and into murdering her older husband. Edward G. Robinson. w. Charles Brackett, Billy Wilder (BOScr), d. Billy Wilder (BDirector). BPicture, BScore, BB&WCin. Oscars: 5-0.
SUSPENSE: ROMANCE: MURDER: TRAGEDY: Film Noir; Murder-Debate to Confess; Murder of Spouse; Romance-Doomed; Cheating Women; Dangerous Women; Mindgames; Love-Questionable; Framed?; Con Artists; Insurance Scams
REMAKE: TV (1974) (Body Heat; China Moon)

Double Jeopardy, 1992, 101m, ★★/$, Ind/Fox, R/S. A comfortably married man has his life turned upside-down when an old flame comes to town and turns up the heat. Bruce Boxleitner, Rachel Ward, Sela Ward, Sally Kirkland. d. Lawrence Schiller.
SUSPENSE: Erotic Drama; Dangerous Women; Romance with Married Person; Cheating Men; Romance-Reunited; TV Movies

A Double Life, 1947, 103m, ★★★½/$$, U/Republic. A Shakespearean actor gets so into the role of Othello that he imagines his lady friend is Desdemona and acts accordingly. Ronald Colman (**BActor**),

Shelley Winters, Signe Hasso, Edmond O'Brien. w. Ruth Gordon, Garson Kanin (BScr), d. George Cukor (BDirector). BOScore. Oscars: 4-2.
COMEDY DRAMA: SUSPENSE: MURDER: Tragi-Comedy; Dual Lives; Multiple Personalities; Actors; Crossing the Line; Obsessions; Fantasies; Illusions/Hallucinations; Theater Life; Suspecting One's Self; Amnesia (Unfaithfully Yours; Crimes of Passion; Othello)

The Double Life of Veronique, 1991, 98m, ★★★/$$, Ind/Par. A French violinist on a tour of Poland sees her "twin" through the window of a bus in this artsy film about two women living in these separate countries leading parallel lives. Irene Jacob, Halina Gryglaszewska, Kalina Jedrusik. w. Krzysztof Kieslowkski, Krzysztof Piesewicz, d. Krzysztof Kieslowski.
DRAMA: ROMANCE: Romantic Drama; Art Films; Avant-Garde Films; Character Studies; Parallel Stories; Lookalikes; French Films; Writer-Directors; Female Protagonists; Lyrical Films (Red; White; Blue)

The Double McGuffin, 1979, 100m, ★★½/$, Mulberry Square/Vestron, G. A group of children learn of an assassination plot and become junior spies. Ernest Borgnine, George Kennedy, Elke Sommer. w. d. Joe Camp.
CHILDREN'S: Capers; Assassinations; Spies; Spy Films; Conspiracy; Ensemble Films; Ensembles-Children; Comedy-Disneyesque; Writer-Directors

The Double O Kid, 1992, 95m, ★★½/$$, Prism/Prism, PG-13/V. A 17-year-old intern at a government spy agency is charged with safely delivering a package to Los Angeles. Along the way, using his video-gaming and computer skills, he discovers that an evil man wants what he has and will try anything to prevent its delivery. Corey Haim, Wallace Shawn, Brigitte Neilsen, Nicole Eggert, John Rhys-Davies, Basil Hoffman, Karen Black. w. Andrea Buck, Duncan McLachlan, d. Dunchan McLachlan.
ACTION: Action Comedy; CHILDREN'S: Chase Stories; Fugitives from a Murderer; Witness to Murder; Spies; Spoofs-Spy; Child Protagonists; Teenagers; Boys (Cloak and Dagger [1986]; License to Drive)

Double Threat, 1992, 94m, ★★/$, Concorde/Concorde. An aging bombshell makes a steamy movie with her younger beau in the lead and a "body double" who appears to be her double in her off-screen sex scenes as well. Sally Kirkland, Andrew Stevens, Lisa Shane, Richard Lynch, Tony Franciosa, Sherrie Rose, Chick Vennera. d. David A. Prior.

SUSPENSE: Erotic Thriller; Romance-Triangles; Sexy Women; Romance-Older Women/Younger Men; Lookalikes; Women Fighting over Men; Camp
(Body Double; Paint It Black)

Double Wedding, 1937, 87m, ★★★/$$, MGM/MGM-UA. An opportunist makes a play for the sister of the woman he really wants, merely to make her jealous and win her heart. William Powell, Myrna Loy, John Beal, Florence Rice. w. Jo Swerling, P-adap. Ferenc Molnar (*Great Love*), d. Richard Thorpe.

COMEDY: ROMANCE: Romantic Comedy; Playboys; Romance-Boy Wants Girl; Jealousy; Sisters; Weddings; Forgotten Films
(Libeled Lady; Holiday; The Philadelphia Story)

The Doughgirls, 1944, 102m, ★★★/$$, WB/NA. A couple on an illegal honeymoon are constantly interrupted before the festivities can begin. Jane Wyman, Alexis Smith, Jack Carson, Ann Sheridan, Eve Arden, Charles Ruggles. w. James V. Kern, Sam Hellman, P-adap. Joseph Fields, d. Kern.

COMEDY: FARCE: Bedroom Farce; Hotels; Honeymoons; Newlyweds; Comedy of Errors; Hidden Gems; Forgotten Films

The Dove, 1974, 105m, ★★¹/₂/$, Par/Par, G. The true story of a 16-year-old sailor's trip around the world in a 23-foot sloop. At the end of his journey, at the tender age of 21, he marries a local island girl whom he met along the way. Joseph Bottoms, Deborah Raffin, Dabney Coleman, Peter Gwynne. d. Charles Jarrott.

MELODRAMA: ADVENTURE: Sailors; World Travel; Sailing; Teenagers;
ROMANCE: Love-First; Coming of Age

Down and Out in Beverly Hills, 1986, 96m, ★★★★/$$$$, Touchstone/Touchstone, R/S-P-MRN. A Beverly Hills bum (Nick Nolte) almost drowns in a wealthy man's pool (Richard Dreyfuss). The man takes him in and the bum turns out to be good-looking enough to seduce everyone. Bette Midler, Tracy Nelson, Little Richard. w. Paul Mazursky, Leon Capetanos, d. Paul Mazursky.

COMEDY: SATIRE: Romance-Triangles; Fish out of Water Stories; Romance with Servant; Servants; Class Conflicts; Rich vs. Poor; Beverly Hills; Rich People; Homeless People; 1980s; Sleeper Hits
REMAKE OF: Boudu Saved from Drowning
(Ruthless People; Three Wishes)

Down Argentine Way, 1940, 94m, ★★★/$$$, 20th/Fox. An Argentine horse breeder woos an American woman and after they marry, she must make the adjustment to his culture. Betty Grable, Carmen Miranda, Don Ameche, Charlotte Greenwood, J. Carrol Naish, Henry Stephenson. w. Karl Tunberg, Darrell Ware, d. Irving Cummings.

ROMANCE: MUSICALS: Musical Romance; Fish out Water Stories; Marriage Comedy; Horse Racing; South American; Latin People; Female Protagonists
(Never a Dull Moment [1950]; Moon Over Miami)

Down by Law, 1986, 107m, ★★★/$, Island/Island, R/P-S. Two underground hipsters get framed and end up sharing a jail cell with an Italian who's learning English at his own pace, to say the least. Tom Waits, John Lurie, Roberto Benigni, Ellen Barkin, Billie Neal. w. d. Jim Jarmusch.

COMEDY DRAMA: Black Comedy; Art Films; Prison Drama; New Orleans; Film Noir-Modern; Quiet Little Films; Cult Films; Writer-Directors
(Stranger Than Paradise; Night on Earth; Mystery Train)

Down to Earth, 1947, 101m, ★★★/$$, Col/Col. A Greek muse helps a Broadway producer doing a musical with a Greek theme. Rita Hayworth, Larry Parks, Roland Culver, Edward Everett Horton, James Gleason. w. Edwin Blum, Don Hartman, d. Alexander Hall.

MUSICALS: ROMANCE: Theater Life; Muses; Ghosts; Angels; Heaven; Coulda Been Great; Forgotten Films
SEQUEL TO: Here Comes Mr. Jordan
(Here Comes Mr. Jordan; Gilda; Cover Girl)

Downhill Racer, 1969, 101m, ★★¹/₂/$$, Par/Par, PG. An American skier in Europe is totally obsessed with competition and winning and has no time for anything else, including emotional involvements. Robert Redford, Gene Hackman, Camilla Sparv, Timothy Kirk, Dabney Coleman. w. James Salter, N-adap. Oakley Hall, d. Michael Ritchie.

DRAMA: Character Studies; Men Proving Themselves; Sports Movies; Skiing; Snow Settings; Mountain Settings; Competitions; Olympics
(Aspen Extreme; The Electric Horseman)
(Ed: Miles above any skiing movie since but still lacking)

Do You Like Women?, 1964, 100m, ★★¹/₂/$, Ind/NA, B&G. Cannibals who prefer women are loose in Paris. Sophie Daumier, Guy Bedos. w. Roman Polanski, Gerard Brach, N-adap. Georges Bardawil, d. Jean Leon.

HORROR: MURDER: Murders of Women; Black Comedy; Cannibals; Comedy-Morbid; Paris; Serial Killers; Psycho Killers; Forgotten Films; French Films
(Repulsion; Delicatessen)

Dr., see Doctor

Dracula, see also **Bram Stoker's Dracula**

DRACULA SERIES

Dracula, 1931, 84m, ★★★¹/₂/$$$$, U/MCA-U. The famous story of the Transylvanian count who comes to London after sucking the blood out of a real estate agent who visits his Carpathian castle. Bela Lugosi, Helen Chandler, David Manners, Dwight Frye, Edward Van Sloan. w. Garrett Fort, P-adap. Hamilton Deane, John Balderston, N-adap. Bram Stoker, d. Tod Browning.

Dracula (*Horror of Dracula*), 1958, 82m, ★★★/$$$, Hammer-U/MCA-U. A remake in shocking technicolor by the inimitable Hammer studios. Peter Cushing, Christopher Lee, Melissa Stribling, Carol Marsh. w. Jimmy Sangster, N-adap. Bram Stoker, d. Terence Fisher.

Dracula, 1979, 112m, ★★★/$$, U/MCA-U, R/S-V. A more romantic retelling of the famous story which casts the Count more as a tragic figure, faithful to the play adaptations. Frank Langella, Laurence Olivier, Donald Pleasance, Kate Nellingan. w. W. D. Richter, d. John Badham.

Dracula AD 1972, 1972, 95m, ★★¹/₂/$$, Hammer-WB/NA. Dracula comes alive in 1972 and puts the bite on swingin' Londoners. Peter Cushing,

Christopher Lee, Stephanie Beacham. w. Don Houghton, d. Alan Gibson.

Dracula Has Risen from the Grave, 1968, 92m, ★★1/2/$, Hammer-WB/WB, R/V. Dracula rises again to reak more havoc until a local bishop drives him back to the grave. Christopher Lee, Rupert Davies, Veronica Carlson. w. John Elder (Anthony Hinds), d. Freddie Francis.

Dracula, Prince of Darkness, 1966, 90m, ★★1/2/$$, Hammer-WB/WB. Dracula's manservant helps the ailing Count by inviting travelers to stay the night and draws some of their blood. Christopher Lee, Philip Latham, Barbara Shelley, Thorley Walters, Andrew Keir. w. John Sansom, John Elder, d. Terence Fisher.

HORROR: SUSPENSE: ROMANCE: Romantic Drama; MURDER: Murders-One by One; Vampires; Women in Jeopardy; Men in Jeopardy; Selling One's Soul; England; Victorian Era; Classic Literary Adaptations; Novel and Play Adaptations
(Bram Stoker's Dracula)

Dracula's Daughter, 1936, 70m, ★★★/$$, U/MCA-U. When Dracula's body is brought from Transylvania to London, his daughter follows it and revives it once it arrives. Otto Kruger, Marguerite Churchill, Edward Van Sloan. w. Garrett Ford, d. Lambert Hillyer.

HORROR: SUSPENSE: ROMANCE: Romantic Drama; MURDER: Murders-One by One; Murderers-Female; Vampires; Men in Jeopardy; Selling One's Soul; Fathers & Daughters; England; Victorian Era; Revisionist Films; Classic Literary Adaptations; Female Protagonists

Dragnet, 1954, 93m, ★★1/2/$, Mark VII/Movies Unltd. A spinoff of the television series in which Sgt. Joe Friday delivers his deadpan monologues on the sorry state of L.A. as he solves crimes from the L.A.P.D. police blotter. Jack Webb, Ben Alexander, Richard Boone. w. Richard Breen, d. Jack Webb.

DRAMA: Crime Drama; Police Stories; Detective Stories; Detectives-Police; Los Angeles; Camp; Cult Films
REMAKE: Dragnet (TV Series)

Dragnet, 1987, 106m, ★★/$$$, U/MCA-U, PG-13/P-S. Sgt. Friday's inept nephew attempts to duplicate his famous uncle's style. Dan Aykroyd, Tom Hanks,

Christopher Plummer, Harry Morgan, Dabney Coleman. w. Dan Aykroyd, Alan Zweibel, Tom Mankiewicz, d. Tom Mankiewicz.

COMEDY: Comedy-Slapstick; Police Stories; Police Comedy; Detective Stories; Spoofs-Detective; Spoofs; TV Series; Los Angeles
(Turner and Hooch)

Dragon Seed, 1944, 144m, ★★1/2/$$, MGM/MGM-UA. When the Japanese army invades, Chinese dirt farmers fight back. Katharine Hepburn, Walter Huston, Turhan Bey, Akim Tamiroff, Hurd Hatfield, Agnes Moorehead, Aline MacMahon (BSActress). w. Marguerite Roberts, Jane Murfin, N-adap. Pearl S. Buck, d. Jack Conway. BB&WCin. Oscars: 2-0.

DRAMA: Political Drama; Costume Drama; Epics; China; Forgotten Films
(The Good Earth; The Inn of the Sixth Happiness)
(Ed: Kate the Great as a Chinese woman is amusing today, but it holds up fairly well)

Dragonslayer, 1981, 110m, ★★1/2/$$, Disney-Par/Par, PG. A young lad fights dragons and other assorted dangers with the help of his master's magic stone. Peter MacNichol, Caitlin Clarke, Ralph Richardson. w. Hal Barwood, Matthew Robbins, d. Matthew Robbins. BOScore, BSFX. Oscars: 2-0.

ADVENTURE: Fantasy; SCI-FI: Medieval Times; Dragons; Magic; Coulda Been Great
(The Reluctant Dragon [short cartoon]; The Black Cauldron; The Sword in the Stone)

Dragonwyck, 1946, 103m, ★★1/2/$$, 20th/NA. A simple country woman marries a wealthy distant cousin and learns through the gradual emergence of clues that he may have killed his first wife. Gene Tierney, Vincent Price, Glenn Langan, Walter Huston, Anne Revere. w. d. Joseph L. Mankiewicz.

SUSPENSE: MYSTERY: Romance-Dangerous; Dangerous Spouse; Dangerous Men; Secrets-Keeping; Past-Haunted by the; Cousins; Coulda Been Good; Writer-Directors
(Rebecca; Suspicion; The Two Mrs. Carrolls; Beyond the Secret Door)

Dramatic School, 1938, 80m, ★★1/2/$$, MGM/NA. At an acting school for young women, cat fights and petty

jealousies abound. Luise Rainer, Paulette Goddard, Alan Marshal, Lana Turner, Margaret Dumont. w. Ernst Vajda, Mary McCall Jr., P-adap. Hans Szekely (*School of Drama*), d. Robert B. Sinclair.

COMEDY DRAMA: MELODRAMA: Actresses; Ensemble Films; Ensembles-Female; Forgotten Films; Female Protagonists
REMAKE/RETREAD: Stage Door

The Draughtman's Contract, 1983, 108m, ★★★/$, UAC/MGM-UA, R/S-FFN. A draughtsman/architect makes a strange pact with an English noblewoman in which he exchanges landscaping designs for sex. Anthony Higgins, Janet Suzman, Anne Louise Lambert. w. d. Peter Greenaway.

DRAMA: ROMANCE: Romantic Drama; Erotic Drama; Artists; Art Films; 1700s; England; Writer-Directors
(Belly of an Architect; Prospero's Book)
(Ed: Greenaway's most accessible besides *Belly of an Architect*, another architect flick)

Dreamchild, 1985, 94m, ★★★/$, EMI/MGM-UA, PG. Alice Hargreaves, the inspiration for Lewis Carroll's *Alice in Wonderland*, comes to New York on the hundredth anniversary of his birth, and many painful memories are stirred and dealt with. Coral Browne, Peter Gallagher, Ian Holm, Jane Asher, Nicola Cowper. w. Dennis Potter, d. Gavin Miller.

DRAMA: Fantasy; Memories; CHILDREN'S: Fantasies; Elderly Women; Lyrical Films; Cult Films; Overlooked at Release
(Alice in Wonderland)

Dream Lover, 1986, 104m, ★★/$, MGM-UA/MGM-UA, R/P-S. A sleep cycle researcher is enlisted in a murder case when a female suspect has strange dreams. Kristy McNichol, Ben Masters, Paul Shenar. w. Jon Boorstin, d. Alan J. Pakula.

SUSPENSE: MURDER: Detective Stories; Psychological Drama; Psychological Thriller; Psychologist as Detective; Medical Detectives; Dreams; Nightmares; Coulda Been Good; Good Premise Unfulfilled

Dream Lover, 1994, 103m, ★★1/2/$, New Line/New Line, R/S-P-FFN-MN. After a painful divorce, a yuppie architect, succeptible to the charms of a beautiful, sexy woman, ignores her warnings about her unstable emotional state and marries her anyway. He realizes his big mistake too late, as her sordid and violently disturbed past catches up with both of them. James Spader, Madchen Amick, Frederic Lehne, Bess Armstrong, Larry Miller, Kathleen York, Blair Tefkin, Scott Coffey. w. d. Nicholas Kazan.

SUSPENSE: Erotic Drama; Erotic Thriller; Liars; Dangerous Spouses; Dangerous Women; Marriage Drama; Writer-Directors

The Dream Team, 1989, 113m, ★★1/2/$$, U/MCA-U, PG/P. Four mental patients escape and hit the town in New York. They stumble into a murder plot and stop it, becoming heroes. Michael Keaton, Christopher Lloyd, Peter Boyle. w. Jon Connolly, David Loucka, d. Howard Zieff.

COMEDY: MURDER: Murder-Discovering; Escape Adventure; Detective Stories; Detectives-Amateur; Mental Illness; Asylums; Eccentric People; Heroes-Unlikely; Unbelieved (Crazy People; The Couch Trip)
(Ed: It's hard to buy that they're mentally ill, and not just pretty stupid)

Dream Wife, 1953, 99m, ★★1/2/$$, MGM/NA. An American businessman, fed up with his "liberated" wife, decides to go for a "submissive" Arab woman-but it's not without complications. Cary Grant, Deborah Kerr, Walter Pidgeon. w. Sidney Sheldon, Herbert Baker, Alfred Levitt, d. Sidney Sheldon.

COMEDY: ROMANCE: Romantic Comedy; Romance-Bickering; Marriage Comedy; Divorce; Starting Over; Women's Rights; Arab People; Immigrants; Forgotten Films; Coulda Been Great; Good Premise Unfulfilled
(The Grass Is Always Greener; How to Murder Your Wife)

Dreams That Money Can Buy, 1946, 81m, ★★1/2/$, Art of the Century/NA. A surrealist film in which a drifter sells dreams to people he meets. w. d. Hans Richter (with Max Ernst, Man Ray, Fernand Leger, Marcel Duchamp and Alexander Calder).

DRAMA: Fantasy; What If . . . Stories; Art Films; Avant-Garde Films; Surrealism; Dreams; Wishes; Forgotten Films; Hidden Gems; Curiosities; Ahead of Its Time

Dreamscape, 1984, 99m, ★★1/2/$$, EMI/Imperial. A scientist discovers he can enter other people's dreams, and this

skill is used by the U.S. government. Dennis Quaid, Max Von Sydow, Christopher Plummer, Eddie Albert, Kate Capshaw. w. David Loughery, Joseph Ruben, Chuck Russell, d. Joseph Ruben.

SCI-FI: ADVENTURE: Dreams; Nightmares; Experiments; Scientists; Psychological Thriller; Government as Enemy
(Inner Space; Dream Lover [1986])

Die Dreigroschenoper, see **The Threepenny Opera**

Dressed to Kill, 1980, 116m, ★★★1/2/$$$$, AIP-Filmways/WB, R/ES-P-V-B&G. A woman (Angie Dickinson) is murdered after picking up a stranger and a hooker (Nancy Allen) sees the killer, after which she is then stalked by him-or her. Michael Caine, Keith Gordon, w. d. Brian DePalma.

SUSPENSE: MYSTERY: MURDER MYSTERY: Murder-Witness; Murders of Women; Women in Jeopardy; Transvestite Killers; Chase Movies; Psycho Killers; Psychologists; Avenging Death of Someone; Clever Plots & Endings; Nightmares; Female Protagonists; Protagonist Dies; Hitchcockian; Writer-Directors

REMAKE/RETREAD: Psycho
(Psycho; Body Double; Raising Cain)
(Ed: Best of the DePalma Hitchcock retreads)

The Dresser, 1983, 118m, ★★★1/2/$, Goldcrest-Col/RCA-Col, PG. An actor and the leader of a Shakespearean troupe has an interesting relationship with his effemintate dresser until he revolts. Albert Finney (BActor), Tom Courtenay (BActor), Edward Fox. w. P-adap. Ronald Harwood (BAScr), d. Peter Yates (BDirector). BPicture. Oscars: 5-0.

DRAMA: TRAGEDY: Friendships-Male; Stern Men; Servants; Theater Life; Actors; Worker vs. Boss; Betrayal; Oppression; Gay Men; Neurotic People; One Day Stories; Two Character Stories; Forgotten Films; Stagelike Films; Overlooked at Release; Hidden Gems (All About Eve; Withnail and I; Othello)
(Ed: One of the least-grossing Best Picture nominees ever, but Oscar did notice it, very deservedly)

The Dressmaker, 1988, 91m, ★★★/$, Rank-Film Four/Capitol Video. American soldiers hit the soil in England and irrate locals with their ways. Joan Plowright, Billie Whitelaw, Jane Horrocks, Tim

Ransom, Pete Postlethwaite, Tony Haygarth. w. John McGrath, N-adap. Beryl Bainbridge, d. Jim O'Brien.

DRAMA: World War II Stories; Family Drama; **ROMANCE:** Social Drama; Class Conflicts; Quiet Little Films; England; Americans Abroad; British Films (Yanks)

Drifting, 1982, 103m, ★★1/2/$, Ind/Facets, R/S-MN. An Israeli filmmaker struggles with his homosexuality in the sometimes repressive atmosphere of contemporary Jerusalem. Jonathan Sagalle, Ami Traub, Ben Levine, Dita Arel. w. d. Amos Guttman.

DRAMA: Character Studies; Autobiographical Stories; Gay Men; Israel; Bigots

Driftwood, 1947, 90m, ★★1/2/$$, Republic/NA. A bachelor doctor adopts a lonely orphan girl. Natalie Wood, Ruth Warrick, Walter Brennan, Dean Jagger. w. Mary Loos, d. Richard Sale.

MELODRAMA: CHILDREN'S: FAMILY: Girls; Orphans; Children-Adopted; Single Men; Doctors; Fathers-Surrogate; Fathers Alone; Forgotten Films; Female Screenwriters
(Little Miss Marker; Miracle on 34th Street)

Drive, He Said, 1970, 90m, ★★/$, Col/RCA-Col, R/P-V-S. A draft dodger helps a basketball star prove his incompetence for military service. Michael Margotta, William Tepper, Bruce Dern, Karen Black, Robert Towne, Henry Jaglom. w. Jeremy Larner, Jack Nicholson, d. Jack Nicholson.

DRAMA: SATIRE: Anti-Establishment Films; Anti-War Films; Vietnam Era; Basketball; Actor Directors
(Getting Straight; The Strawberry Statement)

The Driver, 1978, 91m, ★★1/2/$, EMI/Fox. Two old enemies, a getaway driver and a detective, play cat and mouse. Ryan O'Neal, Bruce Dern, Isabelle Adjani, Ronnee Blakley. w. d. Walter Hill.

ACTION: Action Drama; Crime Drama; Mindgames; Detectives-Private; Hitmen; Mob Stories; Men in Conflict; Writer-Directors

The Driver's Seat, 1973, 101m, ★★/$, Ind/Sultan, R/S. A whacked-out woman in bad polyester pantsuits goes to Rome to meet her lover, but they continually miss each other. Elizabeth Taylor, Ian

Bannen, Mona Washbourne, Andy Warhol. d. Giuseppe Patroni Griffi.
DRAMA: Psychological Drama; Art Films; Vacations-European; 1970s; Cult Films; Camp; Unintentionally Funny (Ash Wednesday; X, Y and Zee)

Driving Miss Daisy, 1989, 123m, ★★★★/$$$$, WB/WB, PG. An elderly Southern Jewish lady (Jessica Tandy, **BActress**) is given a black chauffeur (Morgan Freeman, BActor) by her son (Dan Aykroyd, BSActor) and an antagonistic, unique friendship develops between them over the years. w. P-adap. Alfred Uhry (**BAScr**), d. Bruce Beresford. **BPicture**, BArt, BCost, BSound, BMakeup. Oscars: 9-4.
DRAMA: COMEDY DRAMA: Friendships-Great; Race Relations; Friendships-Interracial; Southerns; Lonely People; Episodic Stories; Eccentric People; Elderly Women; Elderly People; Jewish People; Stern Women; Pulitzer Prize Adaptations; Sleeper Hits; Blockbusters; Time Capsules; Southerns-British Directors of (Fried Green Tomatoes; Guarding Tess; Camilla)

Drop Dead, Darling!, see **Arriverderci, Baby!**

Drop Dead Fred, 1991, 99m, ★★1/2/$, Ind/Live, PG/P. An old imaginary friend from childhood re-enters a grown woman's life, much to her chagrin and consternation. Phoebe Cates, Rik Mayall, Marsha Mason, Tim Matheson, Bridget Fonda, Carrie Fisher. w. Carlos Davis, Anthony Fingleton, Elizabeth Livingston, d. Ate de Jong.
COMEDY: CHILDREN'S: Fantasy; Invisibility; Childhood; Nuisances; Cult Films; Underrated; Overlooked at Release
(Ed: Annoying to many, hilarious to others)

DROP Squad, 1994, 86m, ★★/$, Gramercy-U/MCA-U, R/P-V. Black anarchists from the Deprogramming and Restoration of Pride Squad are kidnapping other blacks they feel have kowtowed to the white establishment, from drug dealers to preachers, and trying to de-brainwash them; but it all may backfire on them within their own community. Eriq La Salle, Vondie Curtis-Hall, Ving Rhames, Leonard Thomas, Michael Ralph, Billy Williams, Eric A. Payne, Crystal Fox, Vanessa Williams. w. David

Johnson, Butch Robinson, d. David Johnson.
SATIRE: ACTION: Action Comedy; Kidnappings; Drugs-Dealing; Inner City Life; Terrorists; Black vs. White; Black Casts; Black Men; Black Screenwriters; Black Directors; Curiosities (Juice; Come Back Charleston Blue; Cotton Comes to Harlem; Putney Swope; Dead Boyz Can't Fly)

Drop Zone, 1994, ★★/$$, Par/Par, R/EP-EV-S. When a government agent escorts a criminal from prison on a plane with other such baddies, a bomb goes off, which allows these fellows to parachute out to safety and obscurity. But the agent's brother, who's on the flight, is killed and blamed for the bungle that allowed this to happen. He sets out to recapture the bad guys and clear his brother's name. Wesley Snipes, Gary Busey, Yancy Butler, Michael Jeter, Corin Nemec, Kyle Secor, Luca Bercovici, Malcolm-Jamal Warner, Rex Linn. d. John Badham.
ACTION: Police Stories; Chase Stories; Avenging Death of Someone; Brothers; Drugs-Dealing; Prison Escapes; Skydiving; Bombs; Airplane Crashes (Passenger 57; Point Break)

Drowning by Numbers, 1988, 119m, ★★★/$, Ind/Live, R/ES-P-FFN-MFN. Three women with the same name all kill their husbands. Bernard Hill, Joan Plowright, Juliet Stevenson. w. d. Peter Greenaway.
DRAMA: Art Films; Avant-Garde Films; **MURDER:** Murder of Spouses; Drownings; Swimming; Erotic Drama; British Films; Writer-Directors (A Zed and Two Noughts; Prospero's Books)

The Drowning Pool, 1975, 108m, ★★1/2/$$, WB/WB, R/S. PI Lew Harper goes to Louisiana to help out an old flame who is being blackmailed but the mystery is about what. Paul Newman, Joanne Woodward, Gail Strickland, Melanie Griffith, Coral Browne, Tony Franciosa, Murray Hamilton, Linda Hayes, Richard Jaeckel. w. Tracy Keenan Wynn, Lorenzo Semple, Walter Hill, N-adap. John Ross MacDonald, d. Stuart Rosenberg.
MYSTERY: MURDER: MURDER MYSTERY: Detective Stories; Detectives in Deep; Conspiracy; Friends as Lovers; Romance-Reunited; Blackmail; Juvenile Delinquents; Suicidal Tendencies;

Drownings; Murderers Child; Murderers-Female; Southerns; New Orleans; Coulda Been Good
COMIC FLIPSIDE: Fletch Lives.
SEQUEL TO: Harper
(Night Moves; The Drowning Pool; Fletch Lives)
(Ed: What could have been interesting and mysterious is cliched and ultimately futile because of all the hoopla and drowning pool antics, especially when we find out who really did it)

Drugstore Cowboy, 1990, 100m, ★★★/$$$ (LR), R/S-P. A junkie (Matt Dillon) and his friends (Kelly Lynch, James Remar, James LeGros) rob drugstores to support their habit in early 70s Oregon. w. Daniel Yost, Gus Van Sant, N-adap. James Fogle, d. Gus Van Sant.
DRAMA: Art Films; Social Drama; Drugs-Addictions; Thieves; Hippies; Families-Extended; Swapping Partners; Anti-Establishment Films; Cult Films (The Boost; Leaving Las Vegas; Patty Hearst; My Own Private Idaho)

Drum, 1976, 100m, ★★/$$, DEG-Par/WB, R/ES-P-FFN-MFN. After the Civil War, a brothel gets into gear, mixing whites with black slaves. Warren Oates, Ken Norton, Isela Vega, Yaphet Kotto. w. Norman Wexler, N-adap. Kyle Onstott, d. Steve Carver.
MELODRAMA: Erotic Drama; **ROMANCE:** Romance-Interracial; Prostitutes-Low Class; Black vs. White; Civil War Era; Southerns; Plantation Life; Camp; Cult Films
SEQUEL TO: Mandingo

Drums Along the Mohawk, 1939, 103m, ★★★/$$$, 20th/Fox. In early American upstate New York, settlers beset by Indians defend themselves. Claudette Colbert, Henry Fonda, Edna May Oliver, John Carradine, Ward Bond. w. Lamar Trotti, Sonya Levien, N-adap. Walter Edmonds, d. John Ford.
WESTERNS: MELODRAMA: ADVENTURE: Indians-Conflict with; Saving Someone; Pioneers; Early America (Last of the Mohicans)

A Dry White Season, 1989, 107m, ★★1/2/$, MGM-UA/MGM-UA, PG-13/P-V. The story of the political education of a white South African as to the state of things in his country. Donald Sutherland, Janet Suzman, Zakes Mokae, Jurgen Prochnow, Susan Sarandon, Marlon Brando (BSActor). w. Colin Welland,

Euzhan Palcy, N-adap. Andre Brink, d. Euzhan Palcy. Oscars: 1-0.

DRAMA: Political Drama; Courtroom Drama; Character Studies; Race Relations; Black vs. White; South Africa; Apartheid; Quiet Little Films; Overlooked at Release (Cry Freedom; Bopha; Mandela)
(Ed: Brando received $3 million and an Oscar nomination for very little work, overshadowing what could have been a more sedately released film)

D2: The Mighty Ducks, 1994, 107m, ★★¹/₂/$$$, Disney/Disney, G. The same minor leaguer from the first film is again out of work, this time because of an injury, and he's lured back to coaching the kid's hockey team by the promise of endorsement money. But what he gets from the kids is "more important than money" (of course, he gets the money, too). Emilio Estevez, Michael Tucker, Jan Rubes, Kathryn Erbe, Shaun Weiss, Kenan Thompson, Ty O'Neal. w. Steven Brill, d. Sam Weisman.

ACTION: Action Comedy; Sports Movies; **CHILDREN'S:** Skating; Hockey; Coaches; Underdog Stories; Ethics; Men and Boys
SEQUEL TO: The Mighty Ducks
(The Bad News Bears SERIES; The Big Green)

Dubarry Was a Lady, 1943, 101m, ★★¹/₂/$$, MGM/MGM-UA. In contemporary New York, a woman has an imaginary life as a courtesan of Louis XIV. Gene Kelly, Lucille Ball, Red Skelton, Virginia O'Brien, Zero Mostel. w. Irving Brecher, B. G. De Sylva, Herbert Fields, d. Roy del Ruth.

COMEDY: ROMANCE: Romantic Comedy; Prostitutes-High Class; Fantasies; Fantasy; Time Travel; Dual Lives; Kings; Royalty; Castles; 1700s
(A Connecticut Yankee in King Arthur's Court; American Dreamer)

The Duchess and the Dirtwater Fox, 1976, 104m, ★★¹/₂/$$, 20th/CBS-Fox, PG/S. A con man teams up with a cabaret singer and galavants about the West on scam jobs-until the wrong guys go after them and they run for their lives. George Segal, Goldie Hawn, Conrad Janis, Thayer David. w. Melvin Frank, Barry Sandler, d. Melvin Frank.

WESTERNS: Western Comedy; **ROMANCE:** Romantic Comedy; Romance-Bickering; Con Artists; Heist Stories; Chase Movies; Coulda Been Great; Good Premise Unfulfilled

(W.W. and the Dixie Dancekings; Cat Ballou)
(Ed: What starts out promising soon disintegrates into a chase flick)

Duchess of Idaho, 1950, 98m, ★★¹/₂/$$, MGM/MGM-UA. Two female roommates get into it when one of the girls, trying to help her friend patch up her romance, ends up falling in love with the guy herself. Esther Williams, Van Johnson, John Lund, Paula Raymond, Amanda Blake, Eleanor Powell, Lena Horne. d. Robert Z. Leonard.

COMEDY: ROMANCE: Romantic Comedy; Swimming; Women Fighting over Men; Roommates; Skiing; Beauty Pageants
(My Friend Irma; Dangerous When Wet)

Duck Soup, 1933, 68m, ★★★★/$$$, Par/Par. Groucho becomes president of Fredonia, a fictional empire waging crazy war on its neighbors. Groucho Marx, Harpo Marx, Chico Marx, Zeppo Marx, Margaret Dumont. w. Bert Kalmar, Harry Ruby, Arthur Sheekman, Nat Perrin, d. Leo McCarey.

COMEDY: FARCE: Screwball Comedy; Power-Rise to, of Idiot; Presidents; Kingdoms; Misunderstandings; War Stories
(The Mouse That Roared; Animal Crackers)

Dudes, 1987, 90m, ★★¹/₂/$, New Century-Vista/Live. A bunch of rednecks attack three punk rockers traveling backroads on their way to California. Jon Cryer, Daniel Robecuk, Flea, Catherine Mary Stewart, Lee Ving. w. John Randall Johnson, d. Penelope Spheeris.

COMEDY DRAMA: Black Comedy; Road Movies; Journies; Nightmare Journies; Fish out of Water Stories; City vs. Country; North vs. South; Rednecks; Good Premise Unfulfilled; Coulda Been Good; Female Directors
(Easy Rider; Tapeheads; Hiding Out)

Duel, 1971, 88m, ★★★★/$$$$, $ (released in theaters in 1985), ABC-Universal/MCA-U, PG. A businessman traveling through the desert in a car (Dennis Weaver) is chased and bashed with the intent to kill by a large, ominous truck with no visible driver. w. Richard Matheson, d. Steven Spielberg.

SUSPENSE: ACTION: Chase Movies; Car Chases; Kill the Beast; Stalkers; Desert Settings; Duels; Truck Drivers; Cult Films; Sleeper Hits; Blockbusters

(Maximum Overdrive; Night Terror; Slither; The Hitcher; Christine)

Duel in the Sun, 1946, 135m, ★★★/$$$$$, Selznick-UA/Fox. Two brothers fight over a beautiful half-breed woman-and some land in Texas. Jennifer Jones (BActress), Joseph Cotten, Gregory Peck, Lionel Barrymore, Lillian Gish (BSActress), Walter Huston. w. David O. Selznick, Oliver H. P. Garrett, N-adap. Niven Busch, d. King Vidor, B. Reeves Eason, Otto Brower. Oscars: 2-0.

MELODRAMA: WESTERNS: ROMANCE: Romantic Drama; Men Fighting over Women; Epics; Romance-Triangles; Brothers; Cattle Ranchers; Texas; Desert Settings; Indians-American; Romance-Interracial; Romance-Forbidden; Blockbusters
(Gone With the Wind; Band of Angels)
(Ed: Rumored to have had half a dozen more directors at points, but it worked; the *GWTW* of Westerns)

The Duellists, 1977, 101m, ★★¹/₂/$, Par/Par. After sixteen years of dueling each other, two sworn enemies finally give up. Keith Carradine, Harvey Keitel, Albert Finney, Edward Fox. w. Gerald Vaughan-Hughes, SS-adap. Joseph Conrad (*The Point of Honour*), d. Ridley Scott.

DRAMA: Men in Conflict; Feuds; Duels; Gunfighters; Friendships-Male; Friends as Enemies; 1800s; Classic Literary Adaptations; Coulda Been Great

Duffy's Tavern, 1945, 97m, ★★¹/₂/$$, Par/NA. A failing bar gets a boost from a group of Hollywood stars, each dropping in for a minute. Ed Gardner, Victor Moore, Marjorie Reynolds, Barry Sullivan, Bing Crosby, Bob Hope, Alan Ladd, Dorothy Lamour, Veronica Lake, William Bendix. w. Melvin Frank, Norman Panama, d. Hal Walker.

COMEDY DRAMA: Mortgage Drama; Hollywood Life; Docudrama; Curiosities
(Stage Door Canteen)

Dumb and Dumber, 1994, 106m, ★★★/$$$$$, New Line/New Line, PG-13/P-S. An incredibly goofy and stupid chauffeur falls in love with a beautiful female passenger who leaves an attache case behind. He tries to return it to her, only to find that the kidnappers it was left for are after him for its contents-ransom money. He and his even more intellectually deficient buddy try to return the case and evade these nuisances while getting the girl. Jim Carrey, Jeff Daniels, Lauren Holley, Teri Garr, Mike Starr, Karen Duffy, Charles Rocket. w. Peter Farrelly, Bennett Yellin, Bobby Farrelly, d. Peter Farrelly.

COMEDY: FARCE: Buddy Films; Buddy Comedy; Romantic Comedy; Smart vs. Dumb; Chase Stories; Mob Comedy; Fugitives from a Murderer; Fugitives from the Mob; Kidnappings; Simple Minds; Criminals-Stupid; Blockbusters
(The Disorderly Orderly; Living It Up; The Mask; Ace Ventura)

Dumbo, 1941, 64m, ★★★★/$$$$, Disney/Disney, G. A classic of animation in which a misfit elephant learns to fly despite his hugely out of proportion ears. Voices of Sterling Holloway, Edward Brophy, Verna Felton. w. various, d. Ben Sharpsteen. **BScore,** BOSong. Oscars: 2-1.

CHILDREN'S: FAMILY: MELODRAMA: TRAGEDY: Cartoons; Circus Life; Animal Stories; Animals-Talking; Elephants; Fires
(Babe; Bambi)

Dune, 1984, 140m, ★★/$$, DEG-U/MCA-U, PG/S-V. Inhabitants of various planets are addicted to a drug that is guarded by huge man-eating worms, and other such bizarrities. Kyle MacLachlan, Francesca Annis, Jose Ferrer, Sian Phillips, Brad Dourif, Dean Stockwell, Freddie Jones, Sting, Linda Hunt, Jurgen Prochnow, Max Von Sydow. w. d. David Lynch, N-adap. Frank Herbert.

ADVENTURE: SCI-FI: Outer Space Movies; Fantasy; **HORROR:** War Stories; Animal Monsters; Production Design-Outstanding; Cult Films; Flops-Major
(Krull; Eraserhead; Stargate)
(Ed: The bestseller's audience came, not turned off prior to the release with the negative press, but it wasn't enough. Incoherent but lovely to look at)

The Dunera Boys, 1985, 150m, ★★/$, Ind/Sultan, Prism. A group of Jewish brothers from Vienna escape the Nazis but are suspected of spying when they seek asylum in England. They're deported to Australia, where they end up, after their prison terms, rebuilding their former Viennese glory. Bob Hoskins, Joe

Spano, Warren Mitchell, Joseph Furst, Moshe Kedem, Dita Cobb, John Meillon, Mary-Anne Fahey, Simon Chivers, Steven Vidler. d. Sam Lewin.

DRAMA: Spies; Accused Unjustly; Jewish People; Brothers; Nazi Stories; World War II Era; Traitors; Australia; Prison Drama; British Films

The Dunwich Horror, 1970, 90m, ★★¹/₂/$, AIP/Sultan. A young, naive girl goes off with a mysterious stranger to his family estate, where he has a beastly brother hidden in an upstairs room, among other weirdnesses. He also has plans for her . . . Dean Stockwell, Sandra Dee, Ed Begley, Sam Jaffe. w. Curtis Lee Hanson, Henry Rosenbaum, Ronald Silkosky, SS-adap. H. P. Lovecraft, d. Daniel Haller.

HORROR: Romance-Dangerous; Mental Illness; Human Monsters; Gothic Style; Castles; Houses-Creepy; Coulda Been Good; Forgotten Films
(Dead of Winter)

Dutch, 1991, 107m, ★★/$, 20th/Fox, PG/P. A bratty boy being raised by a single mom is whipped into shape during a cross-country trip with her down-to-earth blue-collar boyfriend. Ed O'Neill, Ethan Randall, Christopher McDonald, Ari Meyers. w. John Hughes, P-adap. LeRoi Jones, d. Anthony Harvey.

MELODRAMA: COMEDY DRAMA: CHILDREN'S: FAMILY: Road Movies; Fathers-Surrogate; Stepfathers; Children-Brats; Car Wrecks; Class Conflicts; Rich vs. Poor; Good Premise Unfulfilled
(Ed: Someone forgot, besides the jokes, that the parents are supposed to be annoying, not the kid, in a kid's picture)

Dying Room Only, 1973, 74m, ★★★/$$$$, Lorimar/ABC. A woman (Cloris Leachman) and her husband (Dabney Coleman) stop at a redneck roadside diner in the desert and while in the bathroom, he disappears for no apparent reason and no one seems to want to cooperate in finding him. Ned Beatty, Ross Martin. w. Richard Matheson, d. Philip Leacock.

SUSPENSE: MYSTERY: MURDER: MURDER MYSTERY: Missing Persons; Missing Person Thriller; Conspiracy;

Unbelieved; Good Premise Unfulfilled; Abandoned People; Stranded; Desert Settings; Rednecks; Female Protagonists; One Day Stories; TV Movies
(The Vanishing; Missing; Night Terror)

Dying Young, 1991, 111m, ★★/$$, 20th/CBS-Fox, PG. A nurse looking after a young man dying of cancer can't help falling in love with him, in spite of the inevitable tragedy involved. Julia Roberts, Campbell Scott, Vincent D'Onofrio, Ellen Burstyn, David Selby. w. Richard Friedenberg, N-adap. Marti Leimbach, d. Joel Schumacher.

MELODRAMA: ROMANCE: Romance-Reluctant; Disease Stories; AIDS Stories; Death-Impending; Dying Young; Nurses; Servants; Romance with Servant; Young Men; Coulda Been Good
(Love Story; Untamed Heart)
(Ed: What a title. Apparently was about AIDS originally-or should have been about AIDS, because the relationship seems contrived in order to convey a message, and there is none except that one last weekend with Julia makes life worth it)

Dynamite, 1929, 129m, ★★★/$$$, MGM/NA. A gold digger marries a wealthy man on death row, hoping to cash in. But his execution is stayed. Kay Johnson, Charles Bickford, Conrad Nagel, Julia Faye, Joel McCrea. w. Jeanie Macpherson, d. Cecil B. de Mille.

MELODRAMA: SATIRE: Prison Drama; **ROMANCE:** Love-Questionable; Marrying Up; Inheritances at Stake; Golddiggers; Executions; Death-Impending; Forgotten Films; Hidden Gems; Female Screenwriters
(She Done Him Wrong)

Dynasty of Fear, 1972, ★★/$$, Ind/Republic. The assistant headmaster at a British boarding school for boys seduces his boss's wife and together they plan his murder so that they can run away together. Peter Cushing, Joan Collins, Ralph Bates, Judy Geeson, James Cossins. w. d. Jimmy Sangster.

SUSPENSE: MURDER: Cheating Women; Murder of Spouse; Boys Schools; Writer-Directors
(Diabolique)

Films by Title

E

The Eagle Has Landed, 1976, 135m, ★★½/$$$, ITC-20th/Fox, R/V. Spies land upon a small British village during the height of World War II in the hopes of offing Churchill while on tour. Michael Caine, Donald Sutherland, Robert Duvall, Jenny Agutter, Anthony Quayle, Jean Marsh, Donald Pleasence. w. Tom Mankiewicz, N-adap. Jack Higgins, d. John Sturges.
ACTION: Spy Films; Spies; Assassinations; World War II; England; Lookalikes; Leaders; Conspiracy; Germans as Enemy
(Eye of the Needle; Battle of Britain)
Eagle in a Cage, 1970, 103m, ★★½/$, Ind/NA. A mercenary during the time of Napoleon rises in political power and winds up in charge of a new prisoner eventually-Napoleon himself. John Gielgud, Ralph Richardson, Kenneth Haigh, Billie Whitelaw, Moses Gunn. w. Millard Lampell, d. Fielder Cook.
DRAMA: Historical Drama; Napoleon; British Films
Eagle's Wing, 1979, 111m, ★★½/$, Ind/Media. A white stallion on the loose is sought by a white trapper and a Native American warrior. Martin Sheen, Sam Waterston, Harvey Keitel, Stephane Audran, Caroline Langrishe. w. John Briley, d. Anthony Harvey.

MELODRAMA: ADVENTURE: WESTERNS: Indians-American; Horses; Quests; Missing Persons; Desert Settings; Allegorical Stories; Coulda Been Great
(Ed: A great-looking film without much else to offer artistically)
The Earl of Chicago, 1939, 87m, ★★½/$$, MGM/NA. A mobster in Chicago inherits a position as a British earl, but his shady past catches up with him. Robert Montgomery, Edward Arnold, Edmund Gwenn. w. Lesser Samuels, N-adap. Brock Williams, d. Richard Thorpe.
DRAMA: Crime Drama; MURDER: Trials; Accused Unjustly; Mob Stories; Ordinary Person Becomes Royalty; Chicago; Past-Haunted by
(King Ralph; Little Lord Fauntleroy)
An Early Frost, 1985, 97m, ★★★/$$$$, Col-NBC/Col. A yuppie lawyer seems to have it all, until he discovers he is HIV positive. When he develops AIDS-related illnesses, he must "come-out" to his family and seek their help at the same time. Aidan Quinn, Gena Rowlands, Ben Gazzara, John Glover, D. W. Moffett, Sylvia Sidney. d. John Erman.
DRAMA: Disease Stories; Mothers & Sons; AIDS Stories; Bigots; Gay Men; Death-Impending; Life Lessons; Stern Women; Lawyers; TV Movies
(Andre's Mother; Summer Wishes, Winter

Dreams; Longtime Companion; Philadelphia)
(Ed: The first TV movie, or virtually any movie, dealing with AIDS)
Early Summer (Bakushu), 1951, 125m, ★★★/$$, Ind/Facets, Ingram. When a daughter decides not to marry the man she's been betrothed to, her family reacts violently, then slowly deteriorates. Setsuko Hara, Chishu Ryu. w. Kogo Noda, Yasujiro Ozu, d. Ozu.
DRAMA: Family Drama; Sagas; Episodic Stories; Marriage-Forced; Engagements-Breaking; Female Protagonists; Generation Gap; Japan; Japanese Films
Earth (Zemlya), 1930, 63m (Silent), ★★★½/NA, INd/Voyager, Critic's Choice. A farmer refuses to give up his land to the collective as the communists take over. Semyon Svashenko. w. d. Alexander Dovzhenko.
DRAMA: Social Drama; Quiet Little Films; Rebels; Communists; Farm Life; Russia; Russian Life; Government as Enemy; Classic Early Films; Writer-Directors; Film History
Earth Girls Are Easy, 1988, 100m, ★★½/$$, Vestron-DEG/Vestron, PG/S. Three male aliens crash in vacuous suburbia and learn to party with the babes hangin' by the pool. Geena Davis, Julie Brown, Jeff Goldbum, Damon Wayans, Jim Carrey, Michael McKean, Charles

Rocket. w. Brown, Charlie Coffey, Terrence McNally, d. Julien Temple.
COMEDY: Spoofs; **ROMANCE: MUSICALS:** Musical Comedy; Romantic Comedy; Music Video Style; Music Movies; Aliens-Outer Space, Good; Suburban Life; Hairdressers; California; Beach Movies
(Starstruck; Medusa: Dare to be Truthful; Absolute Beginners; Fast Times at Ridgemont High)
Earthquake, 1974, 123m, ★★☆/$$$$$, U/MCA-U, PG/V. The Big One hits L.A. and terrorizes all-star cast. Genevieve Bujold, Charlton Heston, Ava Gardner, George Kennedy, Victoria Principal, Lorne Green, Marjoe Gortner, Walter Matthau. w. George Fox, Mario, Puzo, d. Mark Robson. **BSound, BSFX,** BArt, BCin. Oscars: 4-2.
Disaster Movies; **DRAMA:** Interwoven Stories; Multiple Stories; All-Star Casts; Cast of Thousands; Ensemble Films; Los Angeles; California; Earthquakes; Guilty Pleasures; Female Protagonists
(The Big One; The Towering Inferno)
(Ed: When broadcast in two parts on TV, they cut right as the quake hits and the plane's about to land into it. Bad but fun. How can you fault Genevieve Bujold being chased by a tumbling house? No pun intended)
East Lynne, 1931, 102m, ★★½/$$$, 20th/NA. A woman is divorced by her husband, then winds up losing the lover at the root of the situation-but not before beginning to go blind. Ann Harding, Clive Brook, Conrad Nagel.
w. Bradley King, Tom Barry, N-adap. Mrs. Henry Wood, d. Frank Lloyd. BPicture. Oscars: 1-0.
DRAMA: MELODRAMA: Tearjerkers; **TRAGEDY: ROMANCE:** Romantic Drama; Romance-Doomed; Divorce; Romance-Triangles; Female Protagonists; England; Forgotten Films; Best Picture Nominees
(Ed: A classic, overwrought weepie in the Victorian tradition)
East of Eden, 1955, 115m, ★★★★/ $$$$, UA/CBS-Fox. A disillusioned young man (James Dean, BActor) rebells against his father and seeks out the truth about his mother while coming of age. Julie Harris, Jo Van Fleet (**BSActress**). w. Paul Osborn (BAScr), N-adap. John Steinbeck, d. Elia Kazan (BDirector). Oscars: 4-1.

East of Eden, 1980, 375m, ★★★/$$$$, WB/WB, Live. The famous Steinbeck tale remade as a television miniseries, focusing on the Cain and Abel story of two brothers vying for their father's affection and decrying their evil mother. Jane Seymour, Bruce Boxleitner, Warren Oates, Lloyd Bridges, Anne Baxter, Timothy Bottoms, Soon-Teck Oh, Karen Allen, Hart Bochner, Sam Bottoms, Howard Dugg, Richard Masur, Wendell Burton, Nicholas Pryor, Grace Zabriskie, M. Emmett Walsh, Matthew "Stymie" Beard. N-adap. John Steinbeck, d. Harvey Hart.
TV Movies; Miniseries
DRAMA: MELODRAMA: ROMANCE: Coming of Age; Farm Life; Alienation; Young Men; Angry Young Man; Secrets-Consuming; Children-Longlost; Prostitutes-Low Class; Mothers-Troublesome; Evil Women; Reunions; Young Men-Angry; California; Depression Era
REMAKE: TV miniseries (1985)
(Rebel Without a Cause; Giant; The Grapes of Wrath; Of Mice and Men; Splendor in the Grass)
East of Elephant Rock, 1976, 92m, ★★/$, Ind/Sultan. A rakish man in a tropical post for the British service is shot by a paramour upset at his philandering. Judi Bowker, Jeremy Kemp, John Christopher Cazenove. w. d. Don Boyd.
DRAMA: MURDER: Jealousy; British Films; Murderers-Female; Cheating Men; Romance with Married Person; Crimes of Passion; Infidelity Crimes; Female Protagonists
REMAKE/RETREAD: The Letter
(The Letter; White Mischief)
East Side, West Wide, 1949, 108m, ★★½/$$, MGM/MGM-UA. A wealthy New York man is torn between his wife and a mistress. James Mason, Barbara Stanwyck, Van Heflin, Ava Gardner, Gale Sondergaard, Cyd Charisse, Nancy Davis. w. Isobel Lennart, N-adap. Marcia Davenport, d. Mervyn LeRoy.
DRAMA: MELODRAMA: Soap Operas; Cheating Men; Romance-Triangles; Mistresses; New York Life
Easter Parade, 1948, 109m, ★★★/ $$$$, MGM/MGM-UA. A songwriter has to find a new partner and keep a romance going while anticipating the big parade. Fred Astaire, Judy Garland, Ann Miller, Peter Lawford. w. Sidney Sheldon,

Frances Goodrich, Albert Hackett, d. Charles Walters.
MUSICAL: ROMANCE: Musicians; Parades
(Three Little Words; The Pirate; The Big Clock; The Band Wagon)
Easy Living, 1937, 91m, ★★★½/$$$, Par/Par. When a fur is thrown out the window on Park Avenue, it lands on a shop girl (Jean Arthur) who then must explain how she got it while a wealthy man (Ray Milland) pursues her. w. Preston Sturges, d. Mitchell Liesen.
COMEDY: Screwball Comedy; **FARCE: ROMANCE:** Romantic Comedy; Romance-Boy Wants Girl; Misunderstandings; Social Climbing; Class Conflicts; Working Class; Female Protagonists; Lucky People; Hidden Gems; Writer-Directors
REMAKE/RETREAD: All in a Night's Work
(All in a Night's Work; That Touch of Mink; Palm Beach Story; The Lady Eve)
Easy Living, 1949, 77m, ★★½/$$, RKO/Turner. A football pro wants to retire but has problems with his wife. Victor Mature, Lucille Ball, Lizabeth Scott. w. Charles Schnee, SS-adap. Irwin Shaw, d. Jacquer Tourneur.
DRAMA: COMEDY DRAMA: Life Transitions; Football; Retirement; Wives-Troublesome; Class Conflicts
Easy Money, 1948, 93m, ★★/$$, Gainsborough/Media, Turner. Four people win big amounts in the football pools in England and deal with their winnings in different ways. Edward Rigby, Jack Warmer, Petula Clark. w. Muriel and Sydney Box, P-adap. Arnold Ridley, d. Bernard Knowles.
DRAMA: Multiple Stories; Lucky People; Lotteries; Social Climbing
Easy Money, 1983, 100m, ★★½/$$, Orion-WB/Orion, Vestron, PG/P-S. A slob of a baby photographer inherits money, only can he keep up the stipulation of stopping his bad habits? Rodney Dangerfield, Joe Pesci, Geraldine Fitzgerald. w. Dangerfield, Michael Endler, P.J. O'Rourke, Dennis Blair, d. James Signorelli.
COMEDY: Race Against Time; Inheritances at Stake; Rags to Riches; Snobs vs. Slobs; Cheating Men; Bets
(Back to School; Brewster's Millions)
Easy Rider, 1969, 94m, ★★★½/$$$$, Columbia/RCA-Col, R/P-S. Two hippies

(Dennis Hopper, Peter Fonda) head across country on motorcycles to New Orleans, meeting a large and polarized cross-section of America only to find an end to the road. Jack Nicholson (BSActor). w. Dennis Hopper, Terry Southern, Peter Fonda (BOScr), d. Dennis Hopper. Oscars: 2-0.

DRAMA: Road Movies; **TRAGEDY:** Anti-Establishment Film; Hippies; 1960s; Psychedelic Era; Motorcycles; New Orleans; Drugs; Alienation; Sleeper Hits; Young Men
(Hell's Angels; The Last Movie; 1969; Dudes; The Trip)

Easy to Love, 1953, 96m, ★★1/2/$$$, MGM/MGM-UA. A beautiful young thing infatuated with her boss can't get him to notice her until a handsome young singer starts wooing her. Esther Williams, Van Johnson, Tony Martin, John Bromfield, King Donovan, Carroll Baker. w. William Roberts, d. Charles Walters.

COMEDY: MUSICAL: Musical Comedy; Infatuions; Marrying the Boss; Singers; Romance-Triangles; Jealousy; Swimming
(Duchess of Idaho; Neptune's Daughter)
(Ed: Underwater choreography by Busby Berkeley)

Easy to Wed, 1946, 110m, ★★★/$$$$, MGM/MGM-UA. When a rich woman threatens to sue for libel, a reporter leaves his bride hanging again to con-vince this woman they meant no harm, but she's one step ahead-and his bride is only a few behind. Van Johnson, Esther Williams, Lucille Ball, Keenan Wynn. w. Dorothy Kingsley, Maurine Watkins, Howard Rogers, George Oppenheimer, d. Edward Buzzell.

COMEDY: FARCE: Screwball Comedy; 1930s; Journalists; Romantic Comedy; Impostors; Honeymoons; Marriages-Fake; Heiresses; Double Crossings; Female Screenwriters
REMAKE OF: Libeled Lady
(Libeled Lady; The Philadelphia Story)

Easy Virtue, 1927, 73m (B&W, Silent), ★★/$$, Gainsborough/Nos. A woman leaves her alcoholic husband for a younger man with suicidal tendencies and the stigma of both begins to take its toll. Isabel Jeans, Eric Bransby. w. Eliot Stannard, P-adap. Noel Coward, d. Alfred Hitchcock.

DRAMA: MELODRAMA: TRAGEDY: Social Drama; Ostracism; Divorce; Alcoholics; Depression; Social Climbing; Past-Haunted by; Suicidal Tendencies

Eat My Dust, 1976, 89m, ★★1/2/$$$, AIP/Sultan, PG/V. In a small California town, the sheriff's son decides to impress a popular girl by stealing a stockcar from the local racetrack and taking her for a spin. They end up leading the authorities (including his dad) on a wild chase through the streets. Ron Howard, Christopher Norris, Warren Kemmerling, Rance Howard, Clint Howard, Corbin Bernsen. w. d. Charles B. Griffith.

ACTION: Action Comedy; Car Chases; Chase Stories; Teenagers; Teenage Movies; Daddy's Girls
(Grand Theft Auto)

Eat the Peach, 1986, 90m, ★★1/2/$, Ind/Col, R. A group of young layabouts in a small town on the coast of Ireland, inspired by an Elvis Presley flick, become national motorcycle champs. Stephen Brennan, Eamon Morrissey, Catherine Byrne, Niall Toibin, Tony Doyle, Joe Lynch. w. Peter Omrod, John Kelleher, d. Peter Omrod.

COMEDY DRAMA: Motorcycles; Ordinary People Stories; Irish Films; Ireland
(The Commitments; Spetters)

Eat the Rich, 1987, 89m, ★★★/$, Col/Col, R. A quasi-political group of headbangers take over a London eatery and soon the *patrons* become the *spe-cialite du Maison*. Nosher Powell, Lanah Pellay, Fiona Richmond, Ronald Allen, Sandra Dome, Paul McCartney, Bill Wyman, Koo Stark, Miranda Richardson. d. Peter Richardson.

COMEDY: Black Comedy; Cannibalism-Funny; Restaurant Settings; Political Satire; Musicians; England; British Films; Cult Films
(Consuming Passions; The Cook, The Thief, His Wife, and Her Lover; Sweeney Todd)

Eaten Alive, 1976, 96m, ★1/2/$, Ind/Prism. Down South, a tour guide takes a group of unsuspecting campers to a crocodile pit, to laugh maniacally while they are devoured. Neville Brand, Mel Ferrer, Carolyn Jones, Marilyn Burns, Stuart Whitman, Robert Englund. d. Tobe Hooper.

HORROR: Comedy-Morbid; Alligators; Swamp Life; Murders-One by One

Eating Raoul, 1982, 83m, ★★★/$$$, Ind/Fox, R/S-P. A poor, sexually repressed couple find that when they kill a dinner guest who makes a pass at the wife, they've discovered a new way to finance that restaurant they've always dreamed about. Mary Woronov, Paul Bartel, Buck Henry, Ed Begley Jr., Edie McClurg, Robert Beltran, John Parragon. w. d. Mary Woronov, Paul Bartel.

COMEDY: Comedy-Morbid; Black Comedy; Cannibalism; Cannibalism-Funny; Murder-Comic Attempts; Murders-One by One; Sleeper Hits; Female Protagonists; Female Directors; Cult Films; Hidden Gems
(Scenes From the Class Struggle in Beverly Hills; Consuming Passions; Sweeney Todd)

Ebb Tide, 1937, 92m, ★★★/$$, Par/Par. Sailors and a maiden (Frances Farmer) are stranded on a Pacific Island with a mad scientist despot with strange ideas. Ray Milland, Oscar Homolka, Barry Fitzgerald. w. Bertram Millhauser, N-adap. R. L. Stevenson, Lloyd Osborne, d. James Hogan.

SUSPENSE: HORROR: SCI-FI: DRAMA: Stranded; Mad Scientists; Evil Men; Islands; Stranded on an Island; Female Among Males
REMAKE: Adventure Island (1946)
(Adventure Island; Island of Lost Souls; Mysterious Island; Island of Dr. Moreau)

The Ebony Tower, 1986, 80m, ★★★/$$, BBC/BBC, FN-MRN. An eccentric old artist lives in an old French chateau with two young women. When a handsome young traveler enters their midst, a sexual rivalry between the two men ensues. N-adap. John Fowles, d. Robert Knights.

DRAMA: Erotic Drama; Artists; Models; Art Films; Men Fighting over Women; Friendships-Intergenerational; Men in Conflict; Friends as Enemies; British Films
(Sirens)

Echo Park, 1986, 97m, ★★1/2/$ (LR), Ind/Barr, PG-13/S. A waitress and would-be actress (Susan Dey) rents out her extra room to a pizza man (Thomas Hulce) and soon sparks fly amid the eccentrics of their rundown L.A. neigh-borhood. w. Michael Ventura, d. Robert Dornhelm.

DRAMA: ROMANCE: COMEDY DRAMA: Roommates; Situation Comedy; Romance-Mismatched; Romance-Boy

Wants Girl; Mothers Single; Single Women; Female Protagonists; Los Angeles; Actresses

REMAKES/RETREADS: The Goodbye Girl

Echoes of a Summer, 1975, 98m, ★★1/2/$, Astral/NA. A young girl spends her last summer with her folks on the coast of Nova Scotia. Jodie Foster, Richard Harris, Lois Nettleton, Geraldine Fitzgerald, William Windom. w. Robert Joseph, d. Don Taylor.

DRAMA: MELODRAMA: TRAGEDY: Disease Movies; Tearjerkers; Canadian Films; Independent Films; Female Protagonists; Child Protagonists

The Eclipse, 1962, 125m, ★★★/$, Ind/Tapeworm. A woman living the chic life in Rome leaves one man to see another and the complications make her reconsider. Monica Vitti, Alain Delon. w. d. Michelangelo Antonioni.

DRAMA: ROMANCE: Romantic Drama; Romance-Triangles; Life Transitions; Art Films; Character Studies; Italian Films; Italy; Female Protagonists; Young; Quiet Little Films; Writer-Directors (L'avventura)

Ed and His Dead Mother, 1993, 93m, ★★/$, 20th/Fox. A middle-aged mama's boy can't take it when she dies, so he brings her back to life through witchcraft. Unfortunately, death hasn't been kind to her: she's become a psychopathic chain-saw killer with rather disgusting habits. Ned Beatty, Steve Buscemi, John Glover, Miriam Margolyes. w. Chuck Hughes, d. Jonathan Wacks.

COMEDY: HORROR: Horror Comedy; Mama's Boys; Mothers-Troublesome; Murderers-Female; Criminal Mothers; Dead-Back from the; Witchcraft; Psycho Killers; Camp

The Eddie Cantor Story, 1953, 116m, ★★1/2/$$, WB/WB. The rise to stardom of vaudeville and film funny man. Keefe Brasselle, Aline MacMahon. w. Jerome Weidman, Ted Sherdeman, Sidney Skolsky, d. Alfred Green.

DRAMA: Biographies; Rise to Fame; Hollywood Life; Hollywood Biographies; Comedians; Vaudeville; Jewish People (The Comic; Chaplin)

Eddie Macon's Run, 1983, 95m, ★★/$$, U/MCA-U, R/P-S. A young country boy (John Schneider) breaks out of prison and heads for the hills with a cop

on his tail (Kirk Douglas). w. d. Jeff Kanew, N-adap. James McLendon.

ACTION: Chase Movies; Fugitives from the Law; Accused Unjustly; Prison Escapes; Rednecks; Southerns

The Eddy Duchin Story, 1956, 123m, ★★1/2/$$, Col/Col. A famous pianist and his bout with leukemia are detailed from his rise to demise, hankies not included. Tyrone Power, Kim Novak, James Whitmore. w. Sam Taylor, Leo Katcher (BOStory), d. George Sidney. BCCin. Oscars: 2-0.

DRAMA: MELODRAMA: Biographies; Musicians; Music Dies; Tearjerkers; Disease Stories; Death-Impending (Love Story; Eric; Something for Joey)

Edge of Doom, 1950, 97m, ★★/$, Goldwyn-UA/NA. A young rebel who kills a priest tries to deal with the realities of his actions. Dana Andrews, Farley Granger, Paul Stewart. w. Philip Yordan, N-adap. Leo Brady, d. Mark Robson.

DRAMA: Crime Drama; **MURDER:** Guilty Conscience; Priests; Murder-Debate to Reveal Killer; Young Men (I Confess; Rebel Without a Cause)

Edge of the City, 1957, 85m, ★★★/$$$, MGM/MGM-UA. Life on the waterfront erupts into violence over racial tensions. Sidney Poitier, John Cassavetes, Jack Warden, Ruby Dee. w. P-adap. Robert Alan Arthur, d. Martin Ritt.

DRAMA: Social Drama; Race Relations; Black vs. White; Working Class; Rebels (On the Waterfront; Do the Right Thing)

Edison, the Man, 1940, 107m, ★★★/$$$, MGM/MGM-UA. The trials of the great inventor are chronicled, overcoming being poor with his innovativeness. Spencer Tracy, Charles Coburn, Rita Johnson. w. Dore Schary, Hugo Butler (BOStory), Talbot Jennings, Bradbury Foote, d. Clarence Brown. Oscars: 1-0.

DRAMA: Biographies; Rise to Fame; Inventors; Geniuses; Dreams (The Story of Alexander Graham Bell)

Educating Rita, 1983, 110m, ★★★/$$$, Col/RCA-Col, PG/P-S. A British working-class hairdresser (Julie Walters, BActress) goes to university to learn about literature and develops a relationship with a professor who takes her under his wing while drinking himself under (Michael Caine, BActor).

w. P-adap. Willy Russell (BOScr), d. Lewis Gilbert. Oscars: 3-0.

COMEDY DRAMA: COMEDY: ROMANCE: Romantic Comedy; Svengalis; Mentors/Role Models; College Life; Female Protagonists; Young Women; British Films; Dreams; Hairdressers (Pygmalion; My Fair Lady; Up Close and Personal; Georgy Girl; Personal Services; Shirley Valentine)

Edward, My Son, 1949, 112m, ★★★/$$$, MGM/MGM-UA. A wealthy man recalls all of the people he stepped on on the way and especially ponders his estranged relationship with his son. Spencer Tracy, Deborah Kerr (BActress), Ian Hunter, James Donald. w. Donald Ogden Stewart, P-adap. Robert Morley, d. George Cukor. Oscars: 1-0.

DRAMA: MELODRAMA: Evil Men; Fathers & Sons; Family Drama; England; Rich People; Narrated Films (An American Romance; From the Terrace)

Edward II, 1991, 90m, Palace/Col, R/ES-MFN. The King of England's love for another man leads to his demise. Steven Waddington, Kevin Collins, Andrew Tiernan. w. Derek Jarman, Stephen McBride, Ken Butler, P-adap. Christopher Marlowe, d. Jarman.

DRAMA: Avant Garde; Art Films; Gay Men; Historical Drama; Kings; England; Medieval Era; Revisionist Films (The Garden; Poison)

Edward Scissorhands, 1990, 100m, ★★★/$$$, 20th/Fox, PG. A mad scientist creates a boy as a companion, but dies before getting around to giving the boy hands. He becomes a sort of mascot when he enters the suburban world below the dark castle in which he grew up, but can never quite feel accepted. Johnny Depp, Winona Ryder, Dianne Wiest, Vincent Price, Anthony Michael Hall, Alan Arkin, Kathy Baker, Conchata Ferrell, Caroline Aaron, Dick Anthony Williams, Robert Oliveri, John Davidson. w. Caroline Thompson, Tim Burton, d. Tim Burton.

COMEDY: Fantasy; **ROMANCE:** Romantic Comedy; Teenagers; Love-First; Fairy Tales; **SCI-FI:** Suburban Life; **SATIRE:** Eccentric People; Castles; Cartoonlike Movies; Female Screenwriters; Production Design-Outstanding (Frankenweenie; Batman; Starman)

Ed Wood, 1994, 110m, ★★★½/$, Touchstone/Touchstone, PG-13. The "true story" of the angora-obsessed, women's-undergarment-wearing director of such famously bad grade-Z films of the fifties as *Plan 9 From Outer Space* and *Glen or Glenda (I Changed My Sex)*. Its emotional center is his touching father-son relationship with the aging, morphine-addicted Bela Lugosi. Johnny Depp, Sarah Jessica Parker, Martin Landau (**BSActor**), Bill Murray, Jim Myers, Patricia Arquette, Jeffrey Jones, Lisa Marie, Vincent D'Onoffrio. w. Scott Alexander, Larry Karaszewski, d. Tim Burton. **BMakeup.** Oscars: 2-2.
COMEDY: SATIRE: Comedy-Morbid; Movie Making; Hollywood Life; Hollywood Satire; Spoofs; Camp; Men as Women; Transvestites; Eccentric People; Drugs-Addictions; Vampires; Cult Films
(Young Frankenstein; Plan 9 from Outer Space; Glen or Glenda?)
The Effect of Gamma Rays on Man-in-the-Moon Marigolds, 1972, 99m, ★★★½/$$, FA-NG/WB, AMC, PG. A neurotic mother and widow (Joanne Woodward) has two daughters, one who detests her, then one who may be brilliant and whose success might give the mother some needed attention, too. But this might also bring out her own secrets from the past. w. Stewart Stern, P-adap. Paul Zindel, d. Paul Newman.
DRAMA: MELODRAMA: Secrets-Haunting; Family Drama; Mothers-Troublesome; Widows; Mothers Alone; Mothers Struggling; Mothers & Daughters; Parents vs. Children; Poor People; Neurotic People; Mental Illness; Depression; Pulitzer Prize Adaptations; Actor Directors; Hidden Gems; Overlooked at Release
(Stella Dallas; Stella; Rachel, Rachel)
The Efficiency Expert, 1992, 97m, ★★★/$, Par/Par, PG. A family-run moccasin factory in Australia is on the verge of bankruptcy because of its inefficiently managed and unruly labor force. They buckle down and hire an efficiency expert, who ruffles many feathers but eventually achieves the desired result. Anthony Hopkins, Ben Mendelsohn, Alwyn Kurts, Bruno Lawrence, Angela Punch McGregor, Russell Crowe, Rebecca Rigg, Toni Collette. w. Andrew Knight, d. Mark Joffe.

COMEDY DRAMA: SATIRE: Efficiency Experts; Australia; Corporations; Reformers; British Films; Overlooked at Release
(Battle of the Sexes; Cheaper by the Dozen)
The Egg and I (B&W), 1947, ★★★★/$$$$$, Universal/MCA-U, AMC. A city couple (Claudette Colbert, Fred MacMurray) moves to the country to raise chickens and have more than a little trouble adjusting. Began Ma and Pa Kettle characters, Marjorie Main (**BSActress**), Percy Kilbride. w. Chester Erskine, Fred Finkelhoffe, N-adap. Betty McDonald, d. Chester Erskine. Oscars: 1-0.
COMEDY: Romantic Comedy; Nature-Back to; City vs. Country; Country Life; Farm Life; Hillbillies; Jealous Wives; Women in Conflict; Blockbusters
(Funny Farm; Green Acres TV Series; Baby Boom; Mr. Blandings Builds His Dream House; The Money Pit
The Eiger Sanction, 1975, 125m, ★★★/$$$, U/MCA-U, R/S-FN. A professor (Clint Eastwood) re-enlists in the CIA for a mountain-climbing spy mission in the Alps which he may not survive getting to. George Kennedy, Vonetta McGee, Jack Cassidy. w. Warren Murphy, Hal Dresner, Rod Whitaker, N-adap. Trevanian, d. Clint Eastwood.
ACTION: SUSPENSE: Spy Films; Spies; CIA Agents; Romance-Interracial; Teachers; Mountain Climbing
(Cliffhanger; For Your Eyes Only; Breakout)
8½, 1963, 138m, ★★★★/$$$$, Embassy. A film director (Marcello Mastroianni) recalls his life and fantasizes about various women in his past as he finds himself at a crisis point. Claudia Cardinale, Anouk Aimee. w. Federico Fellini, Ennio Flaiano, Tullio Pinelli, d. Fellini.
DRAMA: Autobiographical; Directors; Movie Making; Italian Films; Italy; Fantasies; Avant Garde; Art Films; Beautiful People; Life Transitions; Flashbacks
(La Dolce Vita; Amarcord)
Eight Men Out, 1988, 119m, ★★★/$, Orion/Orion, PG. Story of the 1919 Chicago Black Sox baseball team and how they took money to lose the World Series, only to be found out. John Cusack, D.B. Sweeney, Christopher Lloyd, Clifton James, Michael Lerner,

John Mahoney, Charlie Sheen, David Straithairn. w. d. John Sayles, NF-adap. Eliot Asinof.
DRAMA: True Stories; Docudrama; Sports Movies; Baseball; Scandals; Bets; Ethics; 1900s; Chicago; Quiet Little Films; Writer-Directors
(The Natural; Field of Dreams)
8 Million Ways to Die, 1985, 115m, ★★½/$, PSM/Fox, R/V-P-S. An ex-cop working as a private eye is hired to bail a prostitute out of a difficult situation, but ends up being chased down by her pimp and his band of drug sellers and criminal cohorts. Jeff Bridges, Rosanna Arquette, Andy Garcia, Alexandra Paul. w. Oliver Stone, N-adap. Lawrence Block, d. Hal Ashby.
ACTION: Action Drama; Crime Drama; Film Noir-Modern; Police Stories; Detectives-Police; Prostitutes-High Class; Drugs-Dealing; Women in Jeopardy; Protecting Someone
Eight on the Lam, 1966, 107m, ★★½/$$, UA/NA. When a banker (Bob Hope) is suspected of stealing money, he has to run with his eight kids in tow. Phyllis Diller, Jonathan Winters, Jill St. John. w. Albert Lewin, Burt Styler, Bob Fisher, Arthur Marx, d. George Marshall.
COMEDY: Family Comedy; Chase Movies; Accused Unjustly; Thieves; Bank Robberies; Fugitives from the Law
(Boy Did I Get a Wrong Number!; I'll Take Sweden)
8 Seconds, 1994, 104m, ★★½/$, 20th/Fox, PG-13/S. The true story of Lane Frost, a young rodeo star, in love with a "good woman," who was killed in the ring at 25. Luke Perry, Cynthia Geary, Stephen Baldwin, James Rebhorn, Carrie Snodgress, Red Mitchell, Ronnie Clair Edwards. w. Monte Merrick, d. John G. Avildsen.
DRAMA: Sports Movies; Rodeos; Southwestern Life; True Stories;
TRAGEDY: ROMANCE: Romantic Drama; Romance-Doomed; Young Men; Underdog Stories
(Ed: And, of course, lasted about that long at the box office; directed by underdog story king Avildsen [*Rocky, Karate Kid, A Night in Heaven*])
84 Charing Cross Road, 1986, 97m, ★★★/$$, Col/RCA-Col, PG. A woman in New York (Anne Bancroft) begins a pen-pal romance with a man who sells rare books in London (Anthony Hopkins). w.

Hugh Whitemore, N/P-adap. Helene Hanff, d. David Jones.

ROMANCE: DRAMA: Romantic Drama; Old-Fashioned Films; Epistolaries; Romance-Middle-Aged; Lonely People (Love Letters [play]; Shadowlands)

84 Charlie Mopic, 1989, 95m, ★★1/2/ $$, Col/Col, R/V. A cameraman's journey into dangerous territory during the Vietnam war and how it affects him. Johnathan Emerson, Nicholas Cascone, Jason Tomlins. w. d. Patrick Duncan.

ACTION: DRAMA: Photographers; War Movies; Vietnam War; Docudrama; Writer-Directors

Eleanor and Franklin, 1976, 208m, ★★★1/2/$$$$, ABC/Time-Life. A made-for-television historical drama based on the lives and political careers of Franklin D. Roosevelt and his influential wife Eleanor. Jane Alexander, Edward Herrmann, Ed Flanders, Rosemary Murphy, MacKenzie Phillips, Pamela Franklin, Anna Lee, Lindsay Crouse, Linda Purl, Linda Kelsey. NF-adap. Joseph Lash, d. Daniel Petrie. Multiple Emmy winner.

DRAMA: Presidents; Marriage Drama; Biographies; Episodic Stories; Charismatic People; TV Movies (Sunrise at Campobello)

El Cid, 1961, 184m, ★★★/$$$$, AA/VCI. The epic, cast-of-thousands tale of a hero (Charlton Heston) who helped the Spaniards fight off the invasion of the Moors. Sophia Loren, Herbert Lom. w. Frederic Frank, Philip Yordan, d. Anthony Mann.

DRAMA: ADVENTURE: ACTION: Epics; Cast of Thousands; Medieval Era; Spain; International Casts; Production Design-Outstanding (Fall of the Roman Empire; Ben-Hur; The Agony and the Ecstasy; Exodus)

Electra Glide in Blue, 1973, 113m, ★★1/2/$$, UA/MGM-UA, R/P-S. A motorcycle cop in a small desert town reconsiders his life as he encounters loser after loser. Robert Blake, Mitch Ryan, Royal Dano. w. Robert Boris, d. James Geurcio.

DRAMA: COMEDY DRAMA: Depression; Life Transitions; Motorcycles; Police Stories; Small-town Life; Desert Life; Ordinary People Stories; Quiet Little Films; Forgotten Films

Electric Dreams, 1984, 112m, ★★/$$, MGM-UA/MGM-UA, PG. A nerdy computer guy falls in love and his computer becomes jealous of the woman. Lenny Von Dohlen, Virginia Madsen, Maxwell Caulfield, Bud Cort. w. Rusty Lemorande, d. Steve Barron.

COMEDY: COMEDY DRAMA: ROMANCE: SCI-FI: Fantasy; Computers; Man vs. Machine; Nerds; Nerds & Babes; Jealousy

The Electric Horseman, 1979, 120m, ★★★/$$$$, Col-U/MCA-U, PG. A cowboy advertising breakfast cereal on a famous horse in Vegas grows tired of the fraud and develops a relationship with a lady reporter who ultimately supports his chucking it all. Robert Redford, Jane Fonda, Valerie Perrine, Willie Nelson, John Saxon. w. Robert Garland, d. Sydney Pollack.

COMEDY DRAMA: ROMANCE: Romantic Comedy; Romance-Bickering; Old-Fashioned Films; Cowboys; Horses; Nature-Back to; Las Vegas; Advertising World; Ethics; Animal Rights (Comes a Horseman; Butch Cassidy and the Sundance Kid)

Elena and Her Men, 1956, 98m, ★★1/2/$, Ind/Facets. A Polish princess, down on her luck, has flings while in Paris. Ingrid Bergman, Jean Marais, Mel Ferrer, Jean Richard, Magali Noel, Pierre Bertin, Juliette Greco. d. Jean Renoir.

COMEDY DRAMA: ROMANCE: Romantic Drama; Princesses; Europeans-Eastern; Fish out of Water Stories; Free Spirits; Forgotten Films; French Films

Eleni, 1985, 117m, ★★★/$, CBS-WB/WB, PG. A journalist (John Malkovich) investigates how his mother stood up in the Greek civil war after World War II and became a martyr. Kate Nelligan, Linda Hunt. w. Steve Tesich, NF-adap. Nicholas Gage, d. Peter Yates.

DRAMA: MELODRAMA: True Stories; Biographies; World War II Era; Greece; Narrated Films; Flashbacks; Journalists

Elephant Boy, 1937, 91m, ★★★/$$$, Korda-UA/HBO. An Indian boy (Sabu, in his debut) helps government workers against the poachers. w. John Collier, Akos Tolnay, Marcia deSylva, N-adap. Rudyard Kipling, d. Robert Flaherty, Zoltan Korda.

DRAMA: ADVENTURE: Docudrama; Nature-Back to; India; Boys (The Jungle Book; The Thief of Bagdad)

The Elephant Man (B&W), 1980, PG, ★★★★/$$$, Par/Par, PG. The story of a man (John Hurt, BActor) so horribly disfigured by disease he hides behind a mask and the doctor (Anthony Hopkins) who tries to cure him and the woman who tries to comfort him (Anne Bancroft). w. Christopher DeVore, Eric Bergren, David Lynch (BOScr), d. David Lynch (BDirector). BPicture, BCinema, BArt, BCostume, BEditing. Oscars: 8-0.

DRAMA: MELODRAMA: Romance-Unrequited; Biographies; True Stories; Avant-Garde; Art Films; Disease Stories; Tearjerkers; Disabled People; England; Lyrical Films (The Elephant Man [stage taping version])

Elephant Walk, 1954, 103m, ★★★/$$$, Par/Par. Elizabeth Taylor goes to a tea plantation in India (Ceylon) with her new British husband, but she soon turns to another man to fight the boredom (but it doesn't help ours). Peter Finch, Dana Andrews. w. John Lee Mahin, N-adap. Robert Standish, d. William Dieterle.

DRAMA: ROMANCE: Romantic Drama; Romance-Triangles; Plantations; Newlyweds; Indias; Cheating Women; Elephants (Green Fire)

Eleven Harrowhouse, 1974, 108m, ★★★/$, 20th/Fox. A heist story told from the point of view of the the robbee rather than the robber, building into a farce. Charles Grodin, Candice Bergen, James Mason, Trevor Howard, John Gielgud, Jack Watson. w. Jeffrey Bloom, N-adap. Gerald Browne, d. Aram Avakian.

COMEDY DRAMA: FARCE: Capers; Heist Stories; Chase Movies; Clever Plots & Endings; Jewel Thieves; Black Comedy; Forgotten Films; Overlooked; Underrated (The Heartbreak Kid; Thieves)

El Mariachi, 1993, 81m, ★★★/$$, Col/Col, R/P-EV. A young musician is mistaken for a hitman in this famously low-budget but high-spirited action film shot in Mexico for $7,000 (supposedly, for initial costs). Carlos Gallardo, Consuelo Gomez, Peter Marquardt, Jaime de Hoyos, Reinoi Martinez, Ramiro Gomez. w. Carlos Gallardo, Robert Rodriguez, d. Robert Rodriguez.

ACTION: Action Comedy; Latin People; Musicians; Mexico; Identities-Mistaken; Hitmen; Misunderstandings; Chase Stories; Fugitives from a Murderer; Sleeper Hits

SEQUEL: Desperado. (From Dusk Till Dawn)

Elmer Gantry, 1960, 145m, ★★★½/ $$$$, UA/CBS-Fox. A midwestern preacher (Burt Lancaster, **BActor**) turns out to be hypocrite, as a prostitute (Shirley Jones, **BSActress**) can attest. Jean Simmons. w. Richard Brooks (**BAScr**), N-adap. Sinclair Lewis, d. Richard Brooks. BPicture, BOScore. Oscars: 5-3.
DRAMA: MELODRAMA: Message Films; Political Drama; Religion; Hypocrisy; Small-town Scandals; Midwesterns; Preachers; Cheating Men; Prostitutes-Low Class

El Norte, 1983, 139m, ★★★½/$$, AP-PBS/Fox, PG. A brother and sister from Guatemala flee the violence and make a dangerous journey to the United States. Zaide Silvia Gutierrez, David Villalpando, Ernest Gomez Cruz. w. Gregory Nava (BOScr), d. Gregory Nava. Oscars: 1-0.
DRAMA: Social Drama; Political Drama; Political Unrest; Journies; Escape Adventure; Oppression; Central America; Latin People; Dreams; Magic Realism; Brothers & Sisters; Hidden Gems; Spanish Films; Sleeper Hits
(Alsino and the Condor; Like Water for Chocolate; A Walk in the Clouds)

The Elusive Pimpernel, 1950, 109m, ★★★/$$, Ind/Homevision. A revised, comedic version of *The Scarlet Pimpernel* who tries to save French aristocrats from the guillotine during the Revolution. David Niven, Margaret Leighton, Cyril Cusack, Jack Hawkins. w. d. Michael Powell, Emeric Pressburger, N-adap. Baroness Orczy.
ADVENTURE: COMEDY: COMEDY DRAMA: Comic Adventure; Costume Drama; Historical Drama; French Revolution; Classics-Literary Adaptations; Revisionist Films
REMAKE OF: The Scarlet Pimpernel.

Elvira Madigan, 1967, 95m, ★★★/$$$, Ind/World Artists, R/S. A soldier meets a dancer and falls madly in love, running off into nature to run in fields together to be together forever . . . come whatever. Pia Degermark, Thommy Berggen. w. d. Bo Widerberg.
ROMANCE: DRAMA: MELODRAMA: Romantic Drama; Nature-Back to; Romance-Doomed; Tearjerkers; Suicidal Tendencies; Swedish Films; Writer-Directors; Sleeper Hits

Elvis: The Movie, 1979, 117m, ★★★/$$$$, ABC/Live, Vestron. A made-for-television biopic of Elvis, chronicling his rise from poverty to stardom and his introduction to the world of drugs, ending with his Vegas comeback. Kurt Russell, Season Hubley, Shelley Winters, Ed Begley Jr., Dennis Christopher, Pat Hingle, Bing Russell, Joe Mantegna. d. John Carpenter.
DRAMA: Biographies; Rock Stars; Singers; Southerns; Mothers & Sons; Fame-Rise to; 1950s; Famous People When Young; TV Movies; Episodic Stories
(Elvis, TV Series; Elvis [documentary])

Embassy, 1972, 90m, ★★½/$$, Hemdale/World Video. A Soviet agent holes up on the US Embassy in Beirut trying to avoid a KGB assassin who may infiltrate the compound. Chuck Connors, Richard Roundtree, Max Von Sydow, Ray Milland. w. William Fairchild, d. Gordon Hessler.
ACTION: SUSPENSE: Spy Films; Spies; KGB Agents; Middle East; Cold War Era; Assassinations

The Emerald Forest, 1985, 113m, ★★★/$$, Embassy/Col, PG-13/MN. A man posted in Brazil with a corporation goes exploring in the Amazon when his son is kidnapped by natives. Powers Boothe, Meg Foster, Charley Boorman. w. Rospo Pallenberg, d. John Boorman.
DRAMA: ADVENTURE: Searches; Missing Persons; Missing Children; Kidnappings; South America; Fathers & Sons; Amazon River
(The Searchers; Adam; Without a Trace)

The Emigrants, 1972, 191m, ★★★½/$$, Svensk-WB/WB. A family saga of Swedes coming to the New World to build a farm in Minnesota in the late 1800s. Liv Ullman, Max Von Sydow. w. Jan Troell, Bengt Forslund, N-adap. Vilhelm Moberg, d. Jan Troell.
DRAMA: Family Drama; Sagas; Journies; Pioneers; Immigrants; Swedish Films; Farm Life; Epics
SEQUEL TO: The New Land
(The New Land; Pelle the Conqueror)

Eminent Domain, 1991, 102m, ★★/$, Ind/Imperial, PG. A communist party official in Poland finds one day that his power's been usurped in a coup, and he must deal with the consequences. Donald Sutherland, Anne Archer, Paul Freeman,

Bernard Hepton, Francoise Michaud, Jodhi May. w. Andrzej Krakowski, Richard Greggson, d. John Irvin.
DRAMA: Spy Films; Political Drama; Communists; Iron Curtain-Behind the; Power Struggles
(Citizen X; The Projectionist)

Emma, 1932, 73m, ★★★/$$$, MGM/ NA. An older, feisty maid married into a hoity-toity family and learns to fit in. Marie Dressler, Richard Cromwell, Jean Hersholt, Myra Loy. w. Frances Marion, Leonard Praskins, Zelda Sears, d. Clarence Brown.
COMEDY DRAMA: MELODRAMA: Class Conflicts; Newlyweds; Social Climbing; Ostracism; Servants; Female Protagonists; Female Screenwriters
(Momma, There's a Man in Your Bed!; The Farmer's Daughter)

Emmanuelle, 1974, 94m, ★★/$$$, Ind/Col, R/ES-FN-MN. The new bride of a French diplomat in Thailand soon begins finding sexual outlets for herself-enough for three sequels. Sylvia Kristel. w. Jean-Louis Richard, d. Just Jaekin.
DRAMA: Erotic Drama; Sexuality; Promiscuity; Asia; Orgies; Female Protagonists; Sexy Women
SEQUELS: Emmanuelle II, III, IV . . .

The Emperor Waltz, 1948, 106m, ★★★/$$, Par/Par. A countess (Joan Fontaine) falls in love with an ordinary American salesman (Bing Crosby) in 1900s Vienna. Lucile Watson, Richard Haydn. w. Charles Brackett, Billy Wilder, d. Wilder.
DRAMA: COMEDY DRAMA: ROMANCE: Romance-Class Conflicts; Vienna; 1900s; Writer-Directors
(Ed: Notable primarily as a Wilder failure probably due mostly to miscasting)

Empire of the Ants, 1977, 89m, ★/$, AIP/Sultan. Real estate investors are attacked by mutant ants in the Florida swamps. Joan Collins, Robert Lansing. w. Jack Turley, SS-adap. H.G. Wells, d. Bert Gordon.
SCI-FI: HORROR: Animal Monsters; Insects; Florida; Revisionist Films; Unintentionally Funny
(Ants; Frogs; Them)

Empire of the Sun, 1987, 152m, ★★★/$$, Amblin-WB/WB, PG/V. A British boy in China is taken to an internment camp by the Japanese during World War II while battles swirl all around.

Christian Bales, Miranda Richardson, John Malkovich, Joe Pantoliano. w. Tom Stoppard, N-adap. J.G. Ballard, d. Steven Spielberg. BCin, BEdit. Oscars: 2-0.
DRAMA: Epics; War Movies; Boyhood; Child Protagonists; POWs; Autobiographical Stories; Concentration Camps; China; Historical Drama; World War II Stories; Asia; Flops-Major
(Genre glut [1987]; The Last Emperor; Hope and Glory)
(Ed: Strange that Spielberg would have gotten this done before *Schindler's List*, or at all, though he does approach the vision of Lean; too bad it was the same year as *Emperor* and not a better story.)
The Empire Strikes Back, 1980, 124m, ★★★/$$$$$, 20th/CBS-Fox, PG/V. Action abounds as Luke Skywalker unravels more of the mystery of Darth Vader while evading him on a frozen planet. Mark Hamill, Harrison Ford, Carrie Fisher, Billy Dee Williams, w. Leigh Brackett, Lawrence Kasdan, George Lucas, d. Irvin Kershner.
ACTION: ADVENTURE: SCIFI: Fantasy; Good vs. Evil; Outer Space Movies; Chase Stories; Snow Settings; Evil Men; Blockbusters
SEQUEL TO: Star Wars; **SEQUEL:** Return of the Jedi
(Ed: Only for fans of the series and action; surprisingly little else happening)
Enchanted April, 1992, 99m, ★★★/$$, Miramax/Miramax, PG. Four diverse women go to Italy for holiday from England and share sisterhood until their men show up and tensions begin. Miranda Richardson, Joan Plowright (BSActress), Polly Walker, Josie Lawrence, Alfred Molina. w. Peter Barnes, N-adap. Elizabeth von Arnim, d. Mike Newell. Oscars: 1-0.
COMEDY DRAMA: DRAMA: Ensemble Films; Ensembles-Female; Women's Films; Vacations; Italy; British Films; Quiet Little Films; Female Protagonists
(Tom and Viv; A Room with a View)
The Enchanted Cottage, 1945, 92m, ★★★/$$, RKO/Turner. Beast and the Beast, sort of, with a plain Jane falling for a man who's had an accident. Dorothy McGuire, Robert Young, Mildred Natwick, Herbert Marshall. w. DeWitt Bodeen, Herman Mankiewicz, d. John Cromwell. BOScore. Oscars: 1-0.

DRAMA: ROMANCE: Romantic Drama; Fairy Tales; Nerds; Wallflowers; Lonely People; Accidents; Looksism
(Beauty and the Beast; The Man Without a Face)
The Enchanted Forest, 1945, 77m, PRC/Nos. A hermit in a beautiful forest has the trees and animals for friends until a boy gets lost and he has to help him. Harry Davenport, Edmund Lowe, Billy Severn. w. Robert Lee Johnson, John leBar, Lou Brock, d. Lew Landers.
CHILDREN'S: FAMILY: Fantasy; Fairy Tales; Lonely People; Missing Persons; Saving Someone; Men and Boys
Encino Man, 1992, 88m, Hollywood/ Hollywood, ★★½/$$, PG-13/P. Two out-of-it suburban teenagers (Sean Astin, Pauly Shore) dig up a Stone Age teen (Brendan Fraser) and train him to be hip under the guise of being an exchange student. w. Shawn Schepps, George Zaloom, d. Les Mayfield.
COMEDY: SATIRE: Fish out of Water Stories; Simple Minds; Training the Savage; Childlike People; Suburbia; California; Cave Men; High School Life
(Splash!; Bio Dome; Son-in-Law)
Encore, 1952, 85m, ★★★/$, B-L/NA. The third collection of W. Somerset Maugham short stories to be filmed in the series that includes *Quartet* and *Trio*. Among the stories in this installment are "Winter Cruise," "The Ant and the Grasshopper," and "Gigolo and Gigolette." Nigel Patrick, Kay Walsh, Roland Culver, John Laurie, Glynis Johns, Ronald Squire, Noel Purcel, Peter Graves. w. (various), SS-adap. W. Somerset Maugham, d. Pat Jackson, Anthony Pelissier, Harold French.
DRAMA: MELODRAMA: ROMANCE: Romantic Drama; Multiple Stories; Hidden Gems; British Films
(Of Human Bondage)
The End, 1978, 100m, ★★★/$$$$, UA/CBS-Fox, PG. A selfish pig (Burt Reynolds) decides to change his ways when he finds out he's dying, if he doesn't wind up committing suicide first-a comedy. Sally Field, Dom de Luise, Strother Martin, Joanne Woodward, Norman Fell, Myrna Loy, David Steinberg, Robby Benson. w. Jerry Belson, d. Burt Reynolds.
COMEDY: Black Comedy; Comedy-Morbid; Death-Impending; Death-

Impending, False; Suicidal Tendencies; Life Transitions; Depression; Forgotten Films; Faded Hits
(Better Off Dead)
(Ed: A big hit and not as bad as you might think)
Endangered Species, 1982, 97m, ★★½/$$, MGM/MGM-UA, PG. A woman sheriff of a small Wyoming town (JoBeth Williams) becomes involved in the mysterious killing of cattle by satanists, UFOs, or the federal government. Robert Urich, Peter Coyote, Paul Dooley. w. Alan Rudolph, John Binder, Judson Klinger, Richard Woods, d. Rudolph.
MYSTERY: SUSPENSE: MURDER: SCI-FI: Conspiracy; Small-town Life; Farm Life
(Rage; Roswell)
The Endless Game, 1989, 123m, ★★/$, Ind/Prism. A British secret agent must solve the puzzle when his copatriot and lover dies in mysterious circumstances. Albert Finney, George Segal, Derek De Lint, Monica Guerittore, Ian Holm, John Standing, Anthony Quayle, Kristin Scott Thomas. d. Ennio Morricone.
MYSTERY: MURDER: MURDER MYSTERY: Conspiracy; Spies; British Films
Endless Love, 1981, 110m, ★½/$$, Polygram-FWA-Orion/Vestron, R/ES-FN-MRN. A good-looking boy has sex with a good-looking girl in his father's house-a lot-and when the father splits them up, well, it sparks revenge. Brooke Shields, Martin Hewitt, Shirley Knight, Richard Kiley, Beatrice Straight. w. Judith Rascoe, N-adap. Scott Spencer, d. Franco Zeffirelli.
MELODRAMA: TRAGEDY: ROMANCE: Romantic Drama; Erotic Drama; Love-First; Coming of Age; Romance-Doomed; Mental Illness; Revenge; Fires; Lover Family Dislikes; Unintentionally Funny; Female Screenwriters
(Romeo and Juliet; Havana)
(Ed: It becomes a real howler with the way the father dies of a heart attack)
Endless Summer, 1966, 95m, ★★½/$$$, Col/RCA-Col. A documentary that rode the surf craze of the 60s and has been around ever since. w.d. Bruce Brown. Documentary; California; 1960s; Sports Movies; Beach Movies; Cult Films; Surfers
(Big Wednesday)

End of the Game (*Deception*), 1976, 104m, ★★/$, Ind/NA. A policeman decides to exact revenge against the wealthy man who killed the woman between them years ago. Jacqueline Bisset, Jon Voight, Robert Shaw, Martin Ritt. w. Maximilian Schell, Friedrich Durrenmatt, N-adap. Durrenmatt, *The Judge and His Hangman*, d. Schell.
DRAMA: TRAGEDY: Mindgames; Revenge; Romance-Triangles; Retirement; Friends as Enemies
The End of Innocence, 1990, 102m, ★★¹/₂/$, Par/Par, PG. A co-dependent woman suffers a nervous breakdown trying to make everyone happy but herself. Dyan Cannon, John Heard, George Coe, Lola Mason, Rebecca Schaeffer, Stephen Meadows, Billie Bird, Michael Madsen, Madge Sinclair, Renee Taylor, Viveka Davis. w. d. Dyan Cannon.
COMEDY DRAMA: Character Studies; Nervous Breakdowns; Episodic Stories; Flashbacks; Women's Films; Female Protagonists; Female Screenwriters; Female Directors
(Hannah and Her Sisters)
End of the Line, 1987, 103m, ★★★/$, Orion/Orion, PG. When an old railroad in Arkansas is to be shut down, two former employees of the line steal a train and take one last journey across the country. Wilford Brimley, Levon Helm, Mary Steenburgen, Kevin Bacon, Holly Hunter, Barbara Barrie, Bob Balaban, Howard Morris, Bruce McGill, Clint Howard, Trey Wilson, Rita Jenrette. w. John Wohlbruck, d. Jay Russell.
COMEDY: COMEDY DRAMA: Retirement; Ordinary People Stories; Corporation as Enemy; Trains; Southerns; Elderly Men; Ensemble Films; Rednecks; Small-town Life; Arkansas; Coulda Been Great; Capra-esque
(Miss Firecracker; Mr. Deeds Goes to Town)
(Ed: Cute, but its simplicity misses the importance it could have achieved with its statements about changing times and growing old)
End of the Road, 1970, 110m, ★★★/$, AA/Fox, R/S-FN-MN. A young man (Stacy Keach) gets out of a mental hospital and gets a job teaching at a university, whereupon he proceeds to borrow fellow instructor's wives. James Earl Jones, Grayson Hall, Harris Yulin, Dorothy Tristan. w. Aram Avakian, Dennis

McGuire, Terry Southern, N-adap. John Barth, d. Avakian.
DRAMA: Black Comedy; Romance-Triangles; College Life; Professors; Mental Illness; Asylums; 1970s; Anti-establishment Films; Cult Films; Hidden Gems; Coulda Been Great
(The War Between the Tates; The Dion Brothers)
The End of the World . . . in Our Usual Bed in a Night Full of Rain, 1978, 104m, ★★¹/₂/$, WB/WB, R/S. An American photographer (Candice Bergen) meets up with a suave Italian journalist (Giancarlo Giannini) who happens to be a communist and have more expensive tastes than herself. w. d. Lina Wertmuller.
COMEDY DRAMA: ROMANCE: Romantic Comedy; Black Comedy; Americans Abroad; Romance on Vacation; Italian Films; Italy
(Swept Away; Lovers and Liars)
Enemies, A Love Story, 1989, 119m, ★★★/$$, 20th/Fox, R/P-S. A concentration camp survivor in America (Ron Silver) with a new wife and a mistress is surprised when his old wife turns up alive. Anjelica Huston (BSActress), Lena Olin (BSActress), Margaret Sophie Stein, Alan King. w. Roger Simon, Paul Mazursky, N-adap. Isaac Bashevis Singer, d. Mazursky. Oscars: 2-0.
DRAMA: ROMANCE: Romantic Drama; Romance-Triangles; Cheating Men; Nazi Stories; Concentration Camps; Jewish People; Immigrants; World War II Era; Bigamy; Dead-Back from the
(Sophie's Choice; Micki and Maude)
Enemy from Space, (*Quartermas II*), 1957, 85m, ★★★/$$, Ind-British/NA. At a top-secret military research laboratory, aliens plan their takeover of Earth. Brian Donlevy, John Longden, Sidney James, Bryan Forbes, William Franklyn. w. Nigel Kneale, Val Guest, (Teleplay)-adap. Nigel Kneale, d. Val Guest.
SCI-FI: HORROR: Aliens-Outer Space, Evil; Rule the World-Plot; Sci-Fi-1950s
SEQUEL TO: The Quatermass Experiment.
Enemy Mine, 1985, 108m, ★★/$$, 20th/Fox, PG-13. An outer space pilot (Dennis Quaid) crash lands on a strange planet and must deal with a strange lizard-like creature who captures him (Louis Gossett). w. Edward Khmara, Barry Longyear, d. Wolfgang Petersen.

DRAMA: SCI-FI: Outer Space Movies; Enemies Unite; Allegorical Stories; Race Relations; Flops-Major; Stagelike Films
(Hell in the Pacific)
An Enemy of the People, 1977, 103m, ★★¹/₂/$, FA-WB/NA. Adaptation of the Ibsen play about a doctor trying to warn the locals about a conspiracy/cover-up regarding contamination of their town spa. Steve McQueen, Charles Durning, Bibi Andersson, Richard Dysart. w. Alexander Jacobs, Arthur Miller, P-adap. Henrik Ibsen, d. George Schaefer.
An Enemy of the People, 1989, 100m, ★★¹/₂/$, Ind/NA. An Indian version of the Ibsen play. w. d. Satyajit Ray, P-adap. Henrik Ibsen.
Indian Films
DRAMA: Message Films; Political Films; Whistleblowers; Corruption-Government
(Silkwood; Lois Gibbs and the Love Canal)
Les Enfants Terribles, see L
The Enforcer, 1950, 87m, ★★★¹/₂/$$$, Republic/Republic. A DA is on the trail of a band of hitmen who may make him their next target. Humphrey Bogart, Everett Sloane, Zero Mostel. w. Martin Rackin, d. Bretaigne Windust.
ACTION: SUSPENSE: Crime Drama; Mob Stories; Lawyers as Detectives; Hitmen; Fugitives from the Law; Detectives-Police; Detective Stories
(The Untouchables)
The Enforcer, 1976, 96m, ★★★/$$$, WB/WB, R/EV. Macho vigilante cop Harry Callahan (Clint Eastwood) must deal with a new partner who's a woman while doing battle against organized crime. Tyne Daly, Harry Guardino, Bradford Dillman. w. Stirling Silliphant, Dean Riesner, d. James Fargo.
ACTION: Crime Drama; Battle of the Sexes; Detective Stories; Police Stories; Police-Vigilantes; Detectives-Police; Female Law Officers; San Francisco; Chase Movies; San Francisco Chases
SEQUELS: Dirty Harry SERIES.
(Hunter TV SERIES; The Gauntlet)
England Made Me, 1972, 100m, ★★★/$$, Hemdale/Hemdale, R/S. A spoiled young man (Michael York) meets a man through his sister who may be able to cater to his tastes. Peter Finch, Michael Hordern. w. Desmond Cory, Peter Duffell, N-adap. Graham Greene, d. Duffell.
DRAMA: MELODRAMA: Character Studies; Playboys; Romance-Triangles;

Bisexuality; Gay Men; British Films (Sunday, Bloody, Sunday; Something for Everyone; The Servant; Entertaining Mr. Sloane)

English Without Tears, see **Her Man Gibley**

Enid Is Sleeping, see **Over Her Dead Body**

Ensign Pulver, 1964, 104m, ★★1/2/$$, WB/WB. A sequel to *Mister Roberts* without the key original actors and the charm or strength. Robert Walker, Burl Ives, Walter Matthau, Millie Perkins, Tommy Sands, Larry Hagman. w. Joshua Logan, Peter Fiebelman, P-adap. Logan, Thomas Heggen, d. Logan.
COMEDY: COMEDY DRAMA: Military Comedy; Ensemble Films; Ensembles-Male
(Mister Roberts; The Wackiest Ship in the Army)

Enter Laughing, 1967, 111m, ★★★/$$, Col-7Arts/Col. A young Jewish man in the 30s decides to become an actor and runs across all kinds of strange characters. Reni Santoni, Jose Ferrer, Shelley Winters, Elaine May, Jack Gilford, Janet Margolin. w. Joseph Stein, Carl Reiner, P-adap. Reiner, d. Reiner.
COMEDY: COMEDY DRAMA: FARCE: Romantic Comedy; Theater Life; Actors; Depression Era; 1930s; New York Life; Jewish People; Stagelike Films
(Act One; Radio Days)

Enter the Dragon, 1973, 99m, ★★/$$$, WB/WB. A karate expert (Bruce Lee) is taken on by the British to fight drug dealers. John Saxon. w. Michael Allin, d. Robert Clouse.
ACTION: Spy Films; Spies; Martial Arts; Golf

The Entertainer, 1960, 96m, ★★★1/2/$$, UA/Tapeworm, Fox. A vaudevillian recalls his past triumphs as he attempts a comeback, which may not succeed. Laurence Olivier (BActor), Joan Plowright, Brenda deBanzie, Roger Livesay, Alan Bates, Albert Finney, Daniel Massey. w. John Osborne, Nigel Kneale, P-adap. Osborne, d. Tony Richardson.
DRAMA: MELODRAMA: Character Studies; Theater Life; Vaudeville; Comedians; Memories; British Films; Comebacks
TV REMAKE: 1976, starring Jack Lemmon.
(Lenny; Death of a Salesman)

Entertaining Mr. Sloane, 1970, 94m, ★★★/$$, Pathe-EMI/HBO, R/S. A very attractive, devious young man usurps the home of a middle-aged closeted gay man and his wanton sister. Beryl Reid, Harry Andrews, Peter McEnery, Alan Webb. w. Clive Exton, P-adap. Joe Orton, d. Douglas Hickox.
COMEDY: Black Comedy; COMEDY DRAMA: FARCE: Comedy-Morbid; Mindgames; Gay Men; Bisexuality; Babies-Having; Sexy Men; Dangerous Men; Roommates from Hell; British Films; Stagelike Films
(Brimstone and Treacle; Loot; England Made Me; Something for Everyone)

The Entity, 1982, 125m, ★★/$$, 20th/CBS-Fox, R/V-FN. A young woman (Barbara Hershey) who may be possessed and may have been raped by a poltergeist is placed under an experiment to try and trap it. Ron Silver. w. N-adap. Frank DeFelitta, d. Sidney J. Furie.
SCI-FI: HORROR: Psychological Drama; Women in Jeopardy; Rape/Rapists; Ghosts; Experiments; Female Protagonists; Unbelieved
(The Exorcist; Rosemary's Baby)

Entre-Nous, 1983, 112m, ★★★/$$$, UAC/MGM-UA, R/S. Among two middle-class families in postwar France, the mothers increasingly find their husbands less interesting and each other moreso. Isabelle Huppert, Miou-Miou, Guy Marchand. w. d. Diane Kurys. BFLFilm. Oscars 1-0.
DRAMA: Friendships-Female; Women's Films; Lesbians; Homo-eroticism; World War II-Postwar Era; Autobiographical Stories; True Stories; French Films; Female Protagonists; Female Screenwriters; Female Directors; Sleeper Hits

The Epic That Never Was, 1965, 74m, ★★1/2/$, Ind/Nos. A documentary about the ill-fated attempt by Joseph von Sternberg to make a big-budget film of "I, Claudius" in 1937. Charles Laughton, Flora Robson, Merle Oberon, Emlyn Williams, Robert Newton, Josef von Sternberg, Robert Graves.
Documentaries; Movie Makies; Filmumentaries; Dreams; Forgotten Films

Equinox, 1993, 110m, ★★/$, Triumph/Col, R. In the near future, twin brothers separated at birth lead very different lives: one is a chauffeur for a big-time mob boss, one a garage mechanic.

They are brought together by circumstances when it's discovered that they have an inheritance coming to them. Matthew Modine, Lara Flynn Boyle, Lori Singer, Marisa Tomei, Fred Ward, M. Emmett Walsh, Tyra Ferrell, Tate Donovan. w. d. Alan Rudolph.
DRAMA: Psychological Drama; Twins; Brothers; Inheritances at Stake; Twins-Evil; Art Films; Writer-Directors
(Dead Ringers)

Equus, 1977, 138m, ★★★1/2/$$, UA/MGM-UA, R/EV-FFN-MFN. A psychiatrist (Richard Burton, BActor) at a mental institution in England must unlock the mystery of a boy (Peter Firth, BSActor) who stabbed out the eyes of a horse and is now incoherent. w. P-adap. Peter Shaffer (BAScr), d. Sidney Lumet. Oscars: 3-0.
DRAMA: MURDER: MYSTERY: MURDER MYSTERY: Psychological Drama; Psychologists; Psychologists as Detectives; Mental Illness; Asylums; Coming of Age; Interior Monologues; Crossing the Line; Sexuality; Violence-Sudden
(Agnes of God; Silent Fall)
(Ed: The intensity of the play remains intact, without the surreal portrayal of the horses, though real animals make the crimes unbearable)

Eraserhead, 1976, 89m (B&W), ★★★/$$$, Ind/RCA-Col, R. An extremely bizarre man with hair sticking straight up has a series of nightmares in black and white with an extremely strange soundtrack. John Nance, Charlotte Stewart. w. d. David Lynch.
HORROR: Surrealism; Fantasy; Nightmares; Mental Illness; Eccentric People; Babies-Having; Human Eaters; Avant Garde; Art Films; Writer-Directors
(Elephant Man)

Erendira, 1983, 105m, ★★★/$$, Ind/Media. When a girl accidentally burns down her family's home, her stern grandmother sends her out to be a prostitute. Irene Papas, Claudia Ohana. w. Gabriel Garcia Marquez, d. Ruy Guerra.
DRAMA: TRAGEDY: Fantasy; Surrealism; Evil Women; Girlhood; Coming of Age; Innocence Lost; Fires; Accidents; Prostitutes-Child; Magic Realism; Spain; Spanish Films

Eric, 1975, 100m, ★★★/$$$$, CBS/Live. A young star athlete battles bravely to stay alive once it's discovered that he has leukemia, in this made-for-television weepie. Patricia Neal, John Savage, Claude Akins, Sian Barbara Allen, Mark Hamill, Tom Clancy. d. James Goldstone.

MELODRAMA: Disease Stories; Mothers & Sons; Sports Movies; Death-Impending; Young Men; TV Movies; True Stories (Brian's Song; Something for Joey; The Eddy Duchin Story)

(Ed: Better than average TV fare)

Erik the Viking, 1989, 108m, ★★/$, Orion/Orion, PG-13/P-S. A goofy Viking takes his men through uncharted and calamitous territory on a quest for comedy. Tim Robbins, Mickey Rooney, Eartha Kitt, Terry Jones, Imogen Stubbs, John Cleese. w. d. Terry Jones.

COMEDY: Comedy-Slapstick; Fantasy; Journies; Comedy of Errors; Medieval Times; Dragons; Vikings; Comedy-Skit; Writer-Directors

(Time Bandits; Yellowbeard)

Ernest Goes to Camp, 1987, 92m, ★★/$$$, Touchstone/Touchstone, PG/P. The idiotic hick named Ernest P. Worrell gets a job as a camp counselor and can't do anything right. Jim Varney, Victoria Racimo, John Vernon, Iron Eyes Cody, Lyle Alzado, Gailard Sartain, Daniel Butler, Hakeem Abdul-Samad. d. John Cherry.

Camping

Ernest Goes to Jail, 1990, 81m, ★★/$$, Touchstone/Touchsone, G. Ernest goes on jury duty and gets mistaken for an identical (but much smarter) crime boss and winds up in jail. Jim Varney, Gailard Sartain, Randall "Tex" Cobb, Bill Byrge, Barry Scott, Charles Napier. d. John Cherry.

Lookalikes

Ernest Rides Again, 1993, 93m, ★★/$$, Touchstone/Touchsone, G. The hickster hero of the series is back, helping his college history professor buddy find some jewels he thinks were hidden by the British in a Revolutionary War cannon. Jim Varney, Ron James, Duke Ernsberger, Jeffrey Pillars, Linda Kash, Tom Butler. w. John Cherry, William M. Akers, d. John Cherry.

Ernest Scared Stupid, 1991, 93m, ★★/$$, Touchstone/Touchsone, G. Ernest unwittingly unleashes a 200-year-old curse on his hometown when he opens a sacred tomb. Now he must find a way to put it back. Jim Varney, Eartha Kitt,

Austin Nagler, Jonas Moscartolo, Shay Astar. d. John Cherry.

COMEDY: Comedy-Slapstick; Fools-Bumbling; **CHILDREN'S:** Sleeper Hits

Ernest Saves Christmas, 1988, 91m, ★½/$$$, Touchstone/Disney, G. Santa Claus needs a replacement and the ultimate goofball hick, Ernest, is it. Jim Varney, Gailard Sartain. w. B. Kline, Ed Turner, d. John.

COMEDY: CHILDREN'S: FAMILY: Comedy-Slapstick; Nerds; Rednecks; Christmas; Santa Claus

SEQUEL TO: Ernest SERIES

The Ernest Green Story, 1993, 92m, ★★★/$$, Disney/Disney. The made-for-cable true story of a member of the famous "Little Rock Nine" who became a mascot for integration at the expense of having a sane life in high school. Morris Chestnut, C.C.H. Pounder, Gary Grubbs, Tina Lifford, Avery Brooks, Ruby Dee, Ossie Davis. d. Eric Laneuville.

DRAMA: Social Drama; High School Life; Black Men; Black Casts; Race Relations; Riots; Arkansas; Southerns; True Stories; Historical Drama; TV Movies

(Crisis at Central High; The Little Rock Nine [docu.])

The Errand Boy, 1961, 92m (B&W), ★★½/$$, Par/Par. A goofy peon for the studios in Hollywood winds up a comedian after knocking everything over along the way. Jerry Lewis, Brian Donlevy. w.d. Lewis.

COMEDY: Comedy-Slapstick; Comedy of Errors; Rise to Fame; Rise to Power of Idiot; Comedians; Hollywood Life; Good Premise Unfulfilled; Forgotten Films (The Bellboy; The Disorderly Orderly)

(Ed: Some good jokes and physical humor, but ultimately pretty much a bust)

Escape, 1940, 104m, ★★★/$$, MGM/MGM-UA. An American man returns to Europe at the outbreak of World War II and tries to get his mother out of a concentration camp before it's too late. Robert Taylor, Norma Shearer, Conrad Veidt, Nazimova, Bonita Granville. w. Arch Obler, Marguerite Roberts, N-adap. Ethel Vance, d. Mervyn le Roy.

DRAMA: MELODRAMA: Race Against Time; Mothers & Sons; Saving Someone; Rescue Drama; Concentration Camps; Nazi Stories; World War II Era; Germans as Enemy; Jews-Saving; Forgotten Films; Faded Hits

(Schindler's List; Eleni; Max and Helen)

(Ed: Ahead of its time then, dated now, but still stirring.)

The Escape Artist, 1982, 93m, ★★½/$, Z-UA/Live, PG. Tales of a boy magician extraordinaire. Griffin O'Neal, Raul Julia, Teri Garr, Joan Hackett, Desi Arnaz. w. Melissa Mathison, Stephen Zito, N-adap. David Wagner, d. Caleb Deschanel.

DRAMA: COMEDY DRAMA: Flashbacks; Magic/Magicians; Narrated Stories; Quiet Little Films

Escape from Alcatraz, 1979, 112m, ★★½/$$$$, Par/Par, PG/P-V. True story of a 1960 prison break from the island where the prisoners were never heard from again. Clint Eastwood, Patrick McGoohan, Roberts Blossom. w. Richard Tuggle, NF-adap. J. Campbell Bruce, d. Don Siegel.

ACTION: Action Drama; Escape Adventure; Prison Escapes; Prison Drama; True Stories; San Francisco; Faded Hits

(Murder in the Fire; The Birdman of Alcatraz)

Escape from Fort Bravo, 1953, 98m, ★★★/$$$, MGM/MGM-UA. A young woman helps her Confederate boyfriend escape from a Yankee POW camp in the wild west but will they also survive the Indians? William Holden, Eleanor Parker, John Forsythe, William Demarest. w. Frank Fenton, d. John Sturges.

DRAMA: WESTERN: ROMANCE: Escape Adventures; Prison Escapes; North vs. South; Civil War Era; Saving Someone (Andersonville)

Escape from New York, 1981, 99m, Embassy/New Line, R/EP-EV-S. In the future, New York has been turned into a giant penal colony and the President has been kidnapped and held there. Kurt Russell, Lee Van Cleef, Ernest Borgnine, Donald Pleasence, Season Hubley, Adrienne Barbeau, Harry Dean Stanton. w. John Carpenter, Nick Castle, d. Carpenter.

ACTION: SCI-FI: Futuristic Films; Apocalyptic Stories; Prison Drama; Kidnappings; Presidents; Race Against Time; New York Life

(Big Trouble in Little China)

Escape from the Dark, 1976, 104m, ★★½/$$, Disney/Disney, G. In early 1900s England, two boys foil a plot to turn horses into glue. Alastair Sim, Peter

Barkworth. w. Rosemary Anne Sisson, d. Charles Jarrott.

DRAMA: FAMILY: CHILDREN'S: Saving Someone/Animals; England; 1900s; Horses; Animal Rights; Female Screenwriters
(Miracle of the White Stallion)

Escape from the Planet of the Apes, 1971, 97m, ★★★/$$$, 20th/CBS-Fox, PG/V. Vera the Ape and friends land in a spaceship in modern-day America to tell the world of what is to come when the holocaust sets evolution back, and they are soon celebrities about to be assassinated. Kim Hunter, Roddy McDowell, Bradford Dillman, Ricardo Montalban, Eric Braeden. w. Paul Dehn, d. Don Taylor.

SCI-FI: DRAMA: TRAGEDY: Futuristic Films; Apocalypse Stories; Primates; Fish out of Water Stories; Conspiracy; Babies-Having; Government as Enemy; Experiments; Unbelieved Assassination Plots

SEQUEL in Planet of the Apes SERIES, Beneath the Planet of the Apes, Conquest of the Planet of the Apes
(Ed: A favorite of kids, this is more thoughtful and frightening than *Beneath* or *Conquest*)

Escape to Witch Mountain, 1975, 97m, ★★1/2/$$$, Disney/Disney, G. Two children who may be psychic aliens, not witches, are chased by an evil millionaire after their secret powers. Ray Milland, Eddie Albert, Kim Richards, Ike Eisenmann, Donald Pleasance. w. Robert M. Young, N-adap. Alexander Key, d. John Hough.

CHILDREN'S: ADVENTURE: Fantasy; **SCI-FI:** Race Against Time; Chase Movies; Orphans; Brothers & Sisters; Aliens-Outer Space, Good; Psychics
SEQUEL: Return to Witch Mountain

E.T.: The Extra-Terrestrial, 1982, 115m, ★★★★/$$$$$, Universal/MCA-U, PG. A boy (Henry Thomas) discovers a stray animal that turns out to be an alien creature, which he hides until the government steps in. Dee Wallace, Drew Barrymore, Peter Coyote. w. Melissa Mathison (BOScr), d. Steven Spielberg (BDirector). BPicture, **BCinema, BSFX, BSound,** BArt, BEditing, **BOScore.** Oscars: 9-4.

COMEDY DRAMA: ADVENTURE: SCI-FI: Fantasy; Comic Adventure; **CHILDREN'S: FAMILY:** Boyhood; Pet Stories; Aliens; Hiding Out; Secrets-Keeping; Government as Enemy; UFOs; Suburban Life; Child Protagonists; Blockbusters
(Old Yeller; Mac; Free Willy)

Eternally Yours, 1939, 95m, ★★1/2/$$, UA/Nos. A magician (David Niven) is so caught up in his trickery that his wife becomes jealous and tries to compete. Loretta Young, Broderick Crawford, Billie Burke, Zasu Pitts. w. Gene Towne, Graham Baker, d. Tay Garnett.

COMEDY: ROMANCE: Romantic Comedy; Jealousy; Magic/Magicians; Screwball Comedy; Husbands-Troublesome

Ethan Frome, 1992, 107m, ★★1/2/$, AP-Miramax/Miramax, PG-13. A shy, lonely farmer in New England caring for his stoic, invalid wife is shaken by forbidden lust when her beautiful cousin comes to help him care for her. Liam Neeson, Patricia Arquette, Joan Allen, Tate Donovan, Katharine Houghton, Stephen Mendillo. w. Richard Nelson, N-adap. Edith Wharton, d. John Madden.

DRAMA: ROMANCE: Romantic Drama; Romance-Forbidden; Romance-Triangles; Romance with Relative; New England; Marriage Drama; Marriage on the Rocks; Nurses; Classic Literary Adaptations
(The Age of Innocence; Jude the Obscure)

Etoile du Nord, see **Star of the North**

Eureka, 1982, 129m, ★★1/2/$, MGM-UA/MGM-UA, R/S-FN-MN. A mogul becomes involved with the mob, endangering everyone around him in this Surreal World. Gene Hackman, Theresa Russell, Rutger Hauer, Jane Lapotaire, Mickey Rourke. w. Paul Mayersberg, N-adap. Marshall Houts, *Who Killed Sir Harry Oakes?*, d. Nicolas Roeg.

SUSPENSE: DRAMA: Art Films; Surrealism; Mob Stories; Rich People-Decadent; Evil Men; Men in Conflict; Hitmen; Lyrical Films
(McCabe and Mrs. Miller; Bad Timing)

Europa, see **Zentropa**

Europa, Europa, 1991, 110m, ★★★1/2/$$$, Orion/Orion, R/V-S-MFN. A young boy captured in Poland by the Nazis pulls forward what's left of his foreskin to pretend not to be a circumcised Jew. Marco Hofschneider, Julie Delpy. w. d. Agznieska Holland (BAScr), NF-adap. Salomon Perel. Oscars: 1-0.

DRAMA: SUSPENSE: Chase Movies; Fugitives from the Law; Disguises; Undercovers; Nazi Stories; Jewish People; World War II; Germans as Enemy; Boyhood; Coming of Age; Female Screenwriters; Female Directors; Writer-Directors
(Olivier, Olivier)

The Europeans, 1979, 83m, ★★★/$, MI-Ind/Connoisseur. In pre–Civil War days of Boston, a wealthy woman comes to find a suitable husband in the New World, but only if she plays by the proper rules. Lee Remick, Robin Ellis, Lisa Eichhorn. w. Ruth Prawer Jhabvala, N-adap. Henry James, d. James Ivory. BCostume. Oscars: 1-0.

DRAMA: MELODRAMA: ROMANCE: Romantic Drama; Old-Fashioned Films; Social Drama; Comedy of Manners; Classics-Literary Adaptations; Social Climbing; Class Conflicts; Costume Drama; Quiet Little Films; Boston
(The Bostonians; Little Women; Portrait of a Lady)

Evel Knievel, 1971, 90m, ★1/2/$$$, MGM/MPI, PG. Docudrama about the stunt daredevil's death-defying stunts. George Hamilton, Sue Lyons. w. Alan Calliou, John Milius, d. Marvin Chomsky.

ACTION: Action Drama; Unintentionally Funny; True Stories; Docudrama; Motorcycles; Stuntmen

Evelyn Prentice, 1934, 78m, ★★/$$, RKO/Turner. A lawyer and his wise-cracking wife stand on shakey ground after he has an affair, setting her revenge plot in motion, with tragic results. Myrna Loy, William Powell, Harvey Stephens, Isabel Jewell, Una Merkel, Rosalind Russell, Henry Wadsworth, Edward Brophy, Pat O'Malley. w. Lenore Coffee, d. William K. Howard.

MELODRAMA: COMEDY DRAMA: ROMANCE: Marriage Drama; Romance with Married Person; Cheating Men; Marriage on the Rocks
(Libeled Lady; The Awful Truth)

Even Cowgirls Get the Blues, 1994, 98m, ★★/$, Fine Line/Fine Line, R/S-P-FN. The bizarre, surreal, and ridiculous adventures of a beautiful blond hitchhiker out west with the world's largest thumbs, so necessary to her hitching accumen. Uma Thurman, John Hurt, Rain Phoenix, Noriyuki "Pat" Morita, Keanu Reeves, Lorraine Bracco, Angie Dickinson, Sean Young, Crispin Glover, Ed Begley Jr., Carol Kane. w. Gus Van Sant, N-adap. Tom Robbins, d. Gus Van Sant.

COMEDY DRAMA: Fantasy; Art Films; Road Movies; Surrealism; Cult Films; Bisexuality; Lesbians; Hitchhikers; Flops-Major; Female Protagonists; 1970s
(My Own Private Idaho; Salmonberries)

Ever in My Heart, 1933, 70m, ★★½/$$, WB/NA. A patriotic woman discovers that her husband may be a German spy. Barbara Stanwyck, Otto Kruger, Ralph Bellamy. w. Bertrand Millhauser, Beulah Marie Dix, d. Archie Mayo.

DRAMA: SUSPENSE: MELODRAMA: Enemies-Sleeping with; Dangerous Men; Evil Men; Germans as Enemy; Spies; Women in Jeopardy; Patriotism

Eversmile, New Jersey, 1989, 88m, ★★/$, 20th/Fox, R. A dentist doing relief work in Argentina meets a woman in need of dental care, and the two fall in love-or something like that, amid riding motorcycles across the countryside. Daniel Day Lewis, Mirjana Jokovic. w. Jorge Goldenberg, d. Carlos Sorin.

DRAMA: ROMANCE: Surrealism; Fish out of Water Stories; Dentists; Art Films; South America; Argentina

Everybody's All American, 1988, 127m, ★★½/$$, WB/WB, PG-13/S-P-FRN. A man and his wife, after being the star quarterback and cheerleader of their high school, suffer disappointments and learn that life isn't all one big homecoming game, while a young man who adored the wife still pines for her. Jessica Lange, Dennis Quaid, Timothy Hutton, John Goodman, Carl Lumbly, Ray Baker, Savannah Smith. w. Douglas Day Stewart, N-adap. Dan Jenkins, d. Taylor Hackford.

MELODRAMA: ROMANCE: Romantic Drama; Football; Southerns; Romance-Triangles; Writers; Infatuations; 1950s; Episodic Stories; Ordinary People Stories; Coulda Been Good
(Semi-Tough; North Dallas Forty)

Everybody's Fine, 1990, 115m, ★★★/$$, Col/Col, PG. The father in a bitterly divided family travels all over Italy trying to reunite his five grown children. Marcello Mastroianni, Salvatore Cascio, Valeria Cavalli, Norma Martelli, Marino Cenna. w. Giuseppe Tornatore, Tonino Guerra, d. Giuseppe Tornatore.

DRAMA: Family Drama; Fathers & Daughters; Fathers & Sons; Reunions; Italy; Italian Films; Journies
(Cinema Paradiso)

Every Day's a Holiday, 1937, 79m, ★★★/$$$, Par/Par. A con artist sells the

Brooklyn Bridge over and over with her feminine wiles. Mae West, Edmund Lowe, Lloyd Nolan. w. Mae West, d. Edward Sutherland.

COMEDY: ROMANCE: Romantic Comedy; Sexy Women; Con Artists; Female Protagonists; Role Reversal
(Dynamite; She Done Him Wrong)

Every Girl Should Be Married, 1948, 84m, ★★★/$$$, RKO/Turner. A girl decides to catch a man however she can, and Cary Grant is the biggest catch to land, but he may be on to the gig. Betsy Drake, Franchot Tone, Diana Lynn. w. Stephen Avery, Don Hartman, d. Hartman.

COMEDY: ROMANCE: Romantic Comedy; Settling Down; Single Women; Single Men; Marriage-Impending; Virgins
(The Moon Is Blue; Sunday in New York)
(Ed: Worth it only for Grant and the fresh face of Drake)

Every Home Should Have One, 1970, 94m, ★★½/$$, B-L/NA. A ad exec tries to sell oatmeal with sex and winds up screwing up his own life in the process. Marty Feldman, Shelley Berman. w. Feldman, Barry Cook, Denis Norden, d. James Clark.

COMEDY: Comedy of Errors; Advertising World; British Films; TV Life
(How to Get Ahead in Advertising; Will Success Spoil Rock Hunter?)

Every Man for Himself (and God Against All), 1975, 110m, ★★★/$$, New Yorker/New Yorker, R/S. In the early 1800s, a man rises up out of the dungeon in which he was raised and appears at the age of 18 in the town square of Nuremberg, unable to stand up or speak. He becomes a nationally known oddity and must learn to cope with the world and the attention of strangers. Bruno S., Brigitte Mira, Walter Ladengast, Hans Musaus. w. d. Werner Herzog.

DRAMA: Historical Drama; **MYSTERY:** Drifters; Mute People; Ecentric People; German Films; Art Films

Every Time We Say Goodbye, 1985, 95m, ★★/$, Tri/Col-Tri, PG. An American soldier in Israel falls in love with a Jewish girl under strict religious rules. Tom Hanks, Christina Marsillach. w. Moshe Mizrahi, Rachel Fabie, Leah Appet, d. Mizrahi.

ROMANCE: DRAMA: MELODRAMA: Jewish People; Americans Abroad; Soldiers; Romance-Brief; Female Screenwriters

(Ed: Not even for Hanks fans)

Every Which Way but Loose, 1978, 114m, ★★½/$$$$$, WB/WB, PG/EV. A truckdriver (Clint Eastwood) with an orangutan and a kooky mother (Ruth Gordon) gets into brawls while on the road. Sondra Locke. w. Jeremy Kronsberg, d. James Fargo.

ACTION: COMEDY: Action Comedy; Rednecks; Boxing; Primates; Eccentric People; Faded Hits; Blockbusters

SEQUEL: Any Which Way You Can

Everybody Wins, 1990, 97, ★★/$, Orion/Orion, R/S. A prostitute (Debra Winger) in a small town hires a P.I. (Nick Nolte) to help clear someone she cares about, and he soon discovers more about the town than he bargained for. Will Patton, Judith Ivey, Jack Warden. w. Arthur Miller, d. Karel Reisz.

DRAMA: MYSTERY: Detective Stories; Detectives; in Deep; **ROMANCE:** Detectives-Private; Prostitutes-Low Class; Double Crossings; Flops-Major; Corruption; Film Noir-Modern; Small-Town Life; Quiet Little Films; Coulda Been Good; Southerns; Southerns-British Directors of
(Liebestraum)

Every Thing You Always Wanted to Know About Sex . . . , 1972, 87m, ★★★½/$$$, R/S-FN. Various skits about sexuality stitched together, parodying the famous book. Woody Allen, Lynn Redgrave, Anthony Quayle, Louise Lasser, Tony Randall, Burt Reynolds, Gene Wilder. w. d. Allen, NF-adap. Dr. David Reuben.

COMEDY: Spoofs; Erotic Comedy; Sexuality; Alternative Lifestyles; Comedy-Skits; Comedy-Slapstick; Fantasy; Multiple Stories
(Love and Death; Sleeper)

The Evictors, 1979, 92m, ★★/$$$, AIP/WB, R/EV-S. A couple moves into an old creepy house in the south and an ax murderer begins lurking. Michael Parks, Jessica Harper, Vic Morrow. w. Charles Pierce, Gary Rusoff, Paul Fink, d. Pierce.

HORROR: SUSPENSE: MURDER: Serial Killers; Haunted Houses; Southerns; Gothic Style; Murders-One by One
(The Town That Dreaded Sundown)

The Evil Dead, 1983, 85m, ★★½/$$$, Ind/Imperial, R/EV. Teenagers find a book that allows them to summon up demons-and more than they bargained for. Bruce Campbell, Ellen Sandweiss, Betsy Baker, Hal Delrich. w. d. Sam Raimi.

HORROR: MURDER: Murders-One by One; Occult; Demons; Teenagers; Teenage Movies; Murders of Teenagers; Writer-Directors
SEQUEL: Evil Dead 2.
(Army of Darkness; Darkman; Night of the Living Dead; Dawn of the Dead)

The Evil That Men Do, 1984, 90m, ★★/$$, ITC-Filmways/Orion, Vestron, R/EV-P. A hitman is sent to Central America to off an evil despot. Charles Bronson, Theresa Saldana, Jose Ferrer. w. David Lee Henry, John Crowther, N-adap. Lance Hill, d. J. Lee Thompson.

ACTION: Hitmen; Assassinations; Evil Men; Central America

Evil Under the Sun, 1982, 117m, ★★★/$$, EMI-U/HBO, PG. A movie star dies among the rich and jaded on the Riviera, and Poirot happens to be around to figure it all out. Peter Ustinov, James Mason, Diana Rigg, Maggie Smith, Colin Blakely, Roddy McDowell, Sylvia Miles. w. Anthony Schaffer, N-adap. Agatha Christie, d. Guy Hamilton.

MYSTERY: MURDER MYSTERY: Mystery-Whodunit; Riviera Life; Detective Stories; Detectives-Private; Agatha Christie; Rich People-Decadent; Actors Ensemble Films; 1930s
(Appointment with Death; Death on the Nile)

Excalibur, 1981, 140m, ★★★/$$$$, Orion-WB/WB, R/V-S-FN-MN. A more realistic telling of the King Arthur legend that was quite a big hit. Nigel Terry, Helen Mirren, Nicol Williamson, Cherie Lunghi. w. Rospo Pallenberg, John Boorman, d. Boorman. BCin. Oscars: 1-0.

ACTION: ADVENTURE: Fantasy; Mythology/Legends; Medieval Era; Good vs. Evil; England; British Films; Sleeper Hits; Camelot Stories; Faded Hits
(Camelot; Dragonslayer; Knights of the Round Table; The Sword in the Stone; First Knight)

Excessive Force, 1993, 87m, ★★/$$, Col/Col, R/EV. A $3 million drug deal is blown by the intrusion of some cops, so the leader of the gang involved goes after them one by one. Thomas Ian Griffith, Lance Henriksen, James Earl Jones, Charlotte Lewis, Tony Todd, Burt Young. w. Thomas Ian Griffith, d. Jon Hess.

ACTION: Martial Arts; Drugs-Dealing; Police vs. Mob; Police Stories; Police-Vigilante
(Above the Law; Under Seige)

The Execution of Private Slovik, 1974, 122m, ★★★/$$$, NBC/MCA-U. This made-for-television movie tells the true story of Eddie Slovik, a World War II inductee who had the dubious distinction of being the only U.S. soldier after the Civil War executed for desertion. Martin Sheen, Mariclare Costello, Ned Beatty, Gary Busey, Matt Clark, Ben Hammer, Warren Kemmerling. w. Richard Levinson, William Link, d. Lamont Johnson.

DRAMA: Historical Drama; Executions; Traitors; True Stories; TV Movies
(Andersonville)

The Executioner's Song, 1982, 157m, ★★★1/2/$$$, WB/Live, R/S-FN. The European version of the American television movie based on Norman Mailer's famous book about convicted killer Gary Gilmore. Tommy Lee Jones, Rosanna Arquette, Eli Wallach, Christine Lahti, Jenny Wright, Jordan Clark, Steven Keats. NF-adap. Norman Mailer, d. Lawrence Schiller. Multiple Emmy winner.

DRAMA: Crime Drama; Character Studies; **MURDER:** True Stories; Biographies; Marriage Drama; Marriage on the Rocks; Executions; Prison Drama; Pulitzer Prize Adaptations; TV Movies
(In Cold Blood; At Close Range)

Executive Suite, 1954, 104m, ★★★/$$$, MGM/MGM-UA. A corporate battle begins when the CEO dies, unraveling the personal and professional relationships within the boardroom. William Holden, Frederic March, June Allyson, Barbara Stanwyck, Walter Pidgeon, Shelley Winters, Louis Calhern, Nina Foch (BSActress). w. Ernest Lehman, N-adap. Cameron Hawley, d. Robert Wise. BB&WCin, BB&WArt, BB&WCostume. Oscars: 4-0.

DRAMA: MELODRAMA: Ensemble Films; Executive Life; Power Struggles; Inheritances at Stake; Rewards at Stake; Corporation as Enemy
SEQUEL: TV Series (1976)
(Patterns; The Bad Sleep Well; Network)
(Ed: A forerunner to the miniseries of the 70s and *LA Law*, where the behind-the-scenes soap opera often overtakes the supposed story)

Ex-Lady, 1933, 70m, ★★★/$$, WB/MGM-UA, S. A radical artist of the day (Bette Davis) doesn't believe in marriage until she falls in love. Gene Raymond. w. David Boehm, Edith Fitzgerald, Robert Riskin, d. Robert Florey.

DRAMA: ROMANCE: Romantic Drama; Sexuality; Single Women; 1930s; Artists; Rebels; Female Protagonists; Women's Films; Love-First; Female Screenwriters
(Woman of The Year; Dangerous; Jezebel)

The Ex– Mrs. Bradford, 1936, 87m, ★★★/$$, RKO/Nos, Media. The goofy wife of a doctor involves him in a murder mystery. William Powell, Jean Arthur, James Gleason. w. Anthony Veiller, James Edward Grant, d. Stephen Roberts.

COMEDY: MYSTERY: Comic Mystery; Screwball Comedy; **MURDER MYSTERY:** Mystery-Whodunits; Unbelieved; Doctors; Wives-Troublesome; Romance-Reunited; Ex-Spouse Trouble
(The Thin Man SERIES; A Night to Remember; Manhattan Murder Mystery)

Exodus, 1960, 220m, ★★★/$$$$, UA/CBS-Fox. The epic multiple stories of the beginnings of Israel and the Palestinian war that erupted as a result. Paul Newman, Eva Marie Saint, Ralph Richardson, Peter Lawford, Lee J. Cobb, Sal Mineo (BSActor), Hugh Griffith, John Derek. w. Dalton Trumbo, N-adap. Leon Uris, d. Otto Preminger. **BOScore**, BCCin. Oscars: 3-0.

DRAMA: ADVENTURE: Epics; War Movies; Multiple Stories; Interwoven Stories; Cast of Thousands; Pioneers; Israel; Jewish People; World War II Era; Military Movies; Spies; Rebels; Arab People; Middle East
(Masada; Golda Meir)
(Ed: The score lives on even if the movie doesn't)

The Exorcist, 1973, 122m, ★★★1/2/$$$$$, WB/WB, R/EV-EP-B&G-S. An actress (Ellen Burstyn, BActress) discovers her daughter (Linda Blair, BSActress) is possessed and has priests (Jason Miller, BSActor; Max Von Sydow) come to exorcise the demon. w. adap. William Peter Blatty (**BAScr**), d. William Friedkin (BDirector). BPicture, BCin, BEdit, **BSound**, BOScore. Oscars: 10-2.

HORROR: SUSPENSE: Supernatural Danger; Good vs. Evil; Satanism; Evil Children; Children-Problem; Priests;

Catholicism; Possessions; Mothers Alone; Actresses; Blockbusters

SEQUEL: The Exorcist II; **SPOOF:** Repossessed

(The Omen; Rosemary's Baby; The Entity)

The Exorcist II: The Heretic, 1977, 117m, ★★/$, WB/WB, R/EV-P-S. Poor little Ragin has been repossessed and the Father must visit again, only this time we know what's going to happen. Richard Burton, Linda Blair, Louise Fletcher, Max Von Sydow, James Earl Jones, Ned Beatty. w. William Goodhart, N/S-adap. William Peter Blatty, d. John Boorman.

HORROR: SUSPENSE: Supernatural Danger; Good vs. Evil; Satanism; Evil Children; Children-Problem; Priests; Possessions; Flops-Major

SEQUEL TO: The Exorcist; **SPOOF:** Repossessed

The Exorcist III, 1990, 110m, ★★/$$, 20th/CBS-Fox, R/EV-P. A detective (George C. Scott) investigates gruesome murders linked to a psychopath in prison who seems to have telepathic powers. Brad Dourif, Ed Flanders, Jason Miller, Nicol Williamson. w.d. N-adap. William Peter Blatty, *Legion*.

HORROR: SUSPENSE: Kill the Beast; Serial Killers; Trail of a Killer; Psychics; Telepathy; Blood & Gore; Convict Pursues Good Guy's Family; Detectives-Police; Mental Illness; Possessions; Cult Films

SEQUEL TO: The Exorcist

(Silence of the Lambs; Manhunter; Dead Certain)

(Ed: Has some merits of its own and is certainly better than the second one, though it's a completely different story just milking the name recognition)

Exotica, 1994, 103m, ★★★/$$, Miramax/Miramax-Touchstone, R/ES-P-FFN-MN. A peep-show stripper and her biggest fan develop a strange relationship while he continues his job as an auditor by day, letting loose at night. Bruce Greenwood, David Hemblen, Calvin Green, Don McKellar, Peter Krantz, Mia Kirshner, Arsinee Khanjian, Elias Koteas, Damon D'Oliveira, Sarah Polley, Victor Garber. w. Atom Egoyan, d. Atom Egoyan.

DRAMA: Art Films; Erotic Drama; Romance with Prostitute; Dual Lives; Strippers; Voyeurs; Gay Men; Extroverted vs. Introverted; Canada/Canadian Films; Writer-Directors

(The Adjuster; Law of Desire)

Experience Preferred, but Not Essential, 1983, 77m, ★★★/$, UAC/MGM-UA, PG/S-MRN. A naive British girl gets a summer job at a hotel on the coast of England and learns a few things as the staff living there goes through their routines during the day and during the night. Elizabeth Edmonds, Sue Wallace, Geraldine Griffith, Ron Bain. w. June Roberts, d. Peter Duffell.

COMEDY DRAMA: Comedy-Light; Hotels; Ensemble Films; Young Women Coming of Age; Wallflowers; Virgins; British Films; Hidden Gems; 1960s; Female Protagonists; Female Screenwriters

(Georgy Girl; The Snapper)

Experiment in Terror, 1962, 123m (B&W), ★★★/$$$, Col/RCA-Col. A lovely bank teller and her kid sister (Lee Remick, Stefanie Powers) are stalked by a madman who insists they help him commit a robbery when he may really be up to something else. Glenn Ford, Ross Martin. w. N-adap. The Gordons, *Operation Terror*, d. Blake Edwards.

SUSPENSE: MELODRAMA: Psychological Thriller; Women in Jeopardy; Stalkers; Bank Robberies; Sisters; Telephone Terror; Clever Plots & Endings; Protecting Someone; San Francisco

(Nick of Time; No Way to Treat a Lady)

Experiment Perilous, 1944, 91m, ★★½/$$, RKO/Media. A rich man with a beautiful wife becomes crazed at the attention she receives and may do something about it. Paul Lukas, Hedy Lamarr, George Brent. w. Warren Duff, N-adap. Margaret Carpenter, d. Jacques Tourneur.

MYSTERY: MURDER MYSTERY: MELODRAMA: ROMANCE: Jealousy; Marriage on the Rocks; Sexy Women; Evil Men; Rich People

The Experts, 1989, 83m, ★★½/$, Par/Par, PG-13/P-S. Two guys from New York (John Travolta, Arye Gross) think they've been recruited to help a new nightclub get off the ground when in fact they're getting involved with the KGB. Kelly Preston, Deborah Foreman, James Keach, Jan Rubes. w. Nick Thiel, Stephen Greene, Eric Alter, d. Dave Thomas.

COMEDY: COMEDY DRAMA: ROMANCE: Spies; Fish out of Water Stories; Mindgames; Russians as Enemy; KGB Agents; Double Crossings; Kidnappings; Misunderstandings; Cold War Era; Small-town Life; Good Premise Unfulfilled; Coulda Been Good

(Ed: Very bad timing for the release with the Berlin Wall falling, etc., but 1966 probably wouldn't have helped much either)

Explorers, 1985, 109m, ★★½/$$, Par/Par, PG. Suburban boys travel to outer space and discover a planet where all they do is watch our TV. River Phoenix, Ethan Hawke, Jason Presson. w. Eric Luke, d. Joe Dante.

SCI-FI: CHILDREN'S: FAMILY: Fantasy; Outer Space Movies; Boyhood; TV Life; Spoofs-TV; Aliens-Outer Space, Good

(The Goonies; Stand by Me)

Exposed, 1983, 99m, ★★★/$, MGM-UA/MGM-UA, R/S-V-FN-MRN. A fashion model becomes involved with a volatile violinist who is part of a terrorist organization which she may have become involved with unwittingly. Nastassja Kinski, Rudolph Nureyev, Harvey Keitel, Ian McShane, Bibi Andersson. w. d. James Toback.

SUSPENSE: DRAMA: ROMANCE: Erotic Drama; Spy Films; Spies; Terrorists; Fashion World; Models; Enemies-Sleeping with; Dangerous Men; Coulda Been Great; Lyrical Films; Art Films; Underrated; Writer-Directors

(Diva; Frantic; The Little Drummer Girl)

(Ed: Very European in style but a plot that's exciting in an American way which some may feel clash; watch Nureyev play Kinski with his bow)

Expresso Bongo, 1959, 111m, ★★½/$$, Ind/NA. A London music promoter finds a teen idol and makes him a star, perhaps before his time. Laurence Harvey, Cliff Richard, Sylvia Syms, Meier Tzelniker. w. P-adap. Wolf Mankowitz, d. Val Guest.

SATIRE: COMEDY DRAMA: Music Movies; **MELODRAMA:** Fame-Rise to; Singers; Svengalis; Beatnik Era; Teen Idols

(Absolute Beginners; Smashing Time; The Idol Maker; The Beat Generation)

The Exterminating Angel, 1962, 95m, ★★★½/$$, Ind/Ingram, Conoisseur. High-society people at a dinner party become trapped in the dining room and must face each other before finally getting out and having it happen all over again when they go to church, driven insane by the experience. Silvia Plnal, Enrique Rambal. w. d. Luis Bunuel.

SATIRE: COMEDY: Black Comedy;
COMEDY DRAMA: Allegorical Stories;
Dinner Parties; Rich People; Rich
People-Decadent; Mexico; Latin People;
Spanish Films; Cult Films; Writer-
Directors
(The Discreet Charm of the Bourgeoisie)
The Exterminator, 1980, 102m,
★★/$$, Ind/New Line, R/EV-P. A
Vietnam vet vows revenge when gang
members kill his buddy on the street.
Robert Ginty, Christopher George,
Samantha Eggar. w. d. James
Glickenhaus.
ACTION: Revenge; Vigilantes; Gangs-
Street; Homeless People; Vietnam Vets;
Blood & Gore; Murders-One by One;
Writer-Directors
The Exterminator 2, 1984, 90m,
★★/$$$, Cannon/MGM/UA. Apparently
he didn't kill everyone the first go-round.
Robert Ginty, Mario Van Peebles. w.
Mark Buntzman, William Sachs, d.
Buntzman.
ACTION: Revenge; Vigilantes; Gangs-
Street; Homeless People; Vietnam Vets;
Blood & Gore; Murders-One by One
(Death Wish; Rambo)
Extreme Justice, 1993, 96m, ★1/2/$,
Vidmark/Vidmark, R/V. The LAPD's
Special Investigations Section hunts down
violent criminals using dubious tactics
that border on the barbaric. Lou Diamond
Phillips, Scott Glenn, Yaphet Kotto, Ed
Lauter, Chelsea Field.
ACTION: Police Stories; Police-
Vigilantes; Los Angeles; Police Brutality
Extreme Prejudice, 1987, 104m,
Tri/Live, R/P-EV-S. A modern-day Texas
Ranger (Nick Nolte) goes after a drug
lord on the border. Powers Boothe, Rip
Torn, Maria Conchita Alonso. w. Deric
Washburn, Harry Kleiner, John Milius,
Fred Rexer, d. Walter Hill.
WESTERN: ACTION: Westerns-
Revisionist; Men in Conflict; Drugs-
Dealing; Good vs. Evil; Texas; Crossing
the Border
(High Noon; The Border; Farewell to the
King)
Extremities, 1986, 90m, ★★★/$$,
Atlantic/Par, R/V-S. A woman stalked by
a rapist takes matters into her own hands
and traps him but then must deal with the
consequences. Farrah Fawcett, Alfre
Woodard, Diana Scarwid, James Russo.
w. P-adap. William Mastrosimone, d.
Robert M. Young.

DRAMA: Message Films; Revenge;
Turning the Tables; Rape/Rapists;
Revenge on Rapists; Social Drama;
Women in Jeopardy; Men in Jeopardy;
Kill the Beast; Abused Women; Stalkers;
Stagelike Films; Underrated
(Death and the Maiden; The Burning
Bed; Hannie Caulder; Lipstick)
(Ed: May have been underrated due to
Fawcett's lead, though excellent, and the
praise she received in the similar
Burning Bed a few years before)
An Eye for an Eye, 1981, 104m,
★★/$$$, Embassy/New Line, R/EV-P. A
cop leaves the force but soon returns to
vigilante action to bust a drug ring.
Chuck Norris, Christopher Lee, Richard
Roundtree. w. William Gray, James
Bruner, d. Steve Carver.
ACTION: Vigilantes; Cops-Vigilantes;
Martial Arts; Drugs-Dealing; Revenge
(The Octagon; Good Guys Wear Black)
Eye of the Cat, 1969, 102m, ★★★/$,
U/NA. A guy who has a phobia of cats
winds up staying in a house full of them
with his creepy old aunt. Michael
Sarrazin, Eleanor Parker, Gayle
Hunnicutt. w. Joseph Stefano, d. David
Lowell.
HORROR: SUSPENSE: Psychological
Thriller; Phobias; Cats; Forgotten Films;
Underrated; Houses-Creepy
(Creepshow; Cat's Eye)
(Ed: From the writer of *Psycho* . . .)
Eye of the Devil, 1967, 92m, ★★1/2/$,
MGM/NA, R/V. A crazed French aristo-
crat (David Niven) becomes obsessed
with occult traditions in his ancestral cas-
tle. Deborah Kerr, Emlyn Williams,
Donald Pleasence, Sharon Tate, David
Hemmings. w. Robin Estridge, Dennis
Murphy, N-adap. Philip Loraine, d. J. Lee
Thompson.
HORROR: SUSPENSE: Castles; Houses-
Creepy; Occult; Satanism; Rich People-
Decadent; Flops-Major; Unintentionally
Funny; Cult Films; Forgotten Films
(The Black Cat)
Eye of the Needle, 1981, 110m,
★★★/$$, UA/MGM-UA, R/S-V-FN. A
German spy (Donald Sutherland) in
England during World War II escapes
capture and hides on a remote island
where a disabled husband and his wife
(Kate Nelligan) seducing her to avoid her
finding out. Christopher Cazenove, Ian
Bannen. w. Stanley Mann, N-adap. Ken
Follett, d. Richard Marquand.

SUSPENSE: Spy Films; **ROMANCE:**
Romance-Triangles; Spies; Love-
Questionable; Enemies-Sleeping with;
Parallel Stories; Hitmen; Woman Fights
Back; Women in Jeopardy; Disabled
People; World War II Era; Stranded on an
Island; Coulda Been Great
(Choice of Arms; The Stranger)
Eye of the Storm, 1991, 98m, ★★/$,
New Line/New Line, R/V. Two brothers,
proprietors of a highway motel, recall the
night ten years ago when their parents
were murdered and their younger brother
was blinded in this place. Now another
tragedy seems about to unfold, on the
same kind of stormy night. . . . Craig
Sheffer, Bradley Gregg, Lara Flynn Boyle,
Dennis Hopper, Leon Rippy. d. Yuri
Zeltser.
SUSPENSE: Crime Drama; **MYSTERY:**
MURDER: MURDER MYSTERY: Murder
of Parents; Brothers
Eyes in the Night, 1942, 80m,
★★★/$$, MGM/NA. A blind man is a
detective trying to find out whether the
man an heiress is planning to marry is
possibly a Nazi spy intent on nothing
more than infiltrating the American mili-
tary. Edward Arnold, Ann Harding,
Donna Reed, Allen Jenkins, Reginald
Denny. w. Guy Trosper, Howard Rogers,
N-adap. Baynard Kendrick, *The Odor of
Violets*, d. Fred Zinneman.
SUSPENSE: MYSTERY: Detective
Stories; Heiresses; Love-Questionable;
Spies; Germans as Enemy; Nazi Stories;
World War II Era; Blind People; Women
in Jeopardy; Overlooked; Underrated;
Forgotten Films
SEQUEL: The Hidden Eye (1944)
(The Stranger; Secret Beyond the Door;
Eye of the Needle)
(Ed: The director apparently made the
difference in what could have been a for-
gettable B flick)
Eyes of Laura Mars, 1978, 116m,
★★★/$$$, Col/Good, R/P-V-EFN. A
high-fashion photographer (Faye
Dunaway) begins having premonitions of
murders that are echoed in her sexy and
violent pictures, but soon the killer may
enter more than her imagination. Tommy
Lee Jones, Raul Julia, Rene Auberjonois.
w. John Carpenter, John Goodman, d.
Irvin Kerschner.
**THRILLER: MYSTERY: MURDER MYS-
TERY:** Psychological Thriller; Women in
Jeopardy; Murder-Discovering; Murders-

One by One; Enemy-Sleeping with the; Photographers; Fashion World; Beautiful People; Romance-Triangles; Accused Unjustly; Clever Plots & Endings; Psychics; Supernatural Danger; Unintentionally Funny
(Eyes of a Stranger; The Morning After; Criminal Law; The Clairvoyant)
(Ed: Intriguing premise and a good thriller despite a few implausibilities and clunks; ahead of its time for the women-in-jeopardy onslaught of the 80s)

Eyes Without a Face, see **The Horror Chamber of Dr. Faustus**

Eyewitness, 1970, 91m, ★★½/$, ITC/NA. A boy (Mark Lester) is the only witness to an assassination in a Mediterranean country, but not even his sister believes him until it's too late. Susan George, Lionel Jeffries, Jeremy Kemp. w. Ron Harwood, N-adap. Mark Heblen, d. John Hough.

SUSPENSE: MURDER: Assassinations; Witnesses to Murder; Unbelieved; Child Protagonists; Boy Cries Wolf; Chase Movies; Fugitives from the Mob; Mediterranean

REMAKES/RETREADS OF: The Window (Fallen Idol; The Window; Witness)

Eyewitness, 1981, 108m, ★★½/$$, 20th/CBS-Fox, PG/V-S. An eccentric janitor (William Hurt) is an eyewitness to a murder that his favorite TV reporter (Sigourney Weaver) is trying to solve. Christopher Plummer, Irene Worth, James Woods, Kenneth McMillan. w. Steve Tesich, d. Peter Yates.

MYSTERY: MURDER MYSTERY: MURDER: SUSPENSE: ROMANCE: Romance-Mismatched; Journalists; Working Class; Class Conflicts; Eccentric People; Female Protagonists
(Ed: A bizarre follow-up from the team who did *Breaking Away*; never seems to know what it wants to be-romance, thriller, quirky thriller. Originally titled *The Janitor Doesn't Dance*)

F

F. Scott Fitzgerald in Hollywood, 1976, 98m, ★★★/$$, NA. A made-for-television biopic of the famous writer and his severe depressions in Hollywood amid the stars, movie moguls, corruption, and conformity he was pressured into. He's helped through the degradation by his loving wife, Zelda. Jason Miller, Tuesday Weld, Susan Sarandon, Julia Foster, Dolores Sutton, Michael Lerner, James Woods. d. Anthony Page.
DRAMA: Hollywood Life; Hollywood Satire; Writers; 1930s; True Stories; Biographies; TV Movies
(Beloved Infidel; Power, Passion, and Murder/Tales from the Hollywood Hills; The Last Tycoon)
The Fabulous Baker Boys, 1989, 113m, ★★★¹/₂/$$, 20th/Fox, R/S-P. A brother duo lounge act (Jeff and Beau Bridges) needs a girl singer, so Suzy Diamond (Michelle Pfeiffer, BActress) walks in and changes their lives. Ellie Rabb, Jennifer Tilly. w. d. Steve Kloves (BOScr). Oscars: 2-0.
DRAMA: COMEDY DRAMA: ROMANCE: Romance-Triangles; Men Fighting Over Women; Friendships-Male; Brothers; Pianists; Singers; Feisty Females; Sexy Women; Quiet Little Films; Writer-Directors; Sleeper Hits
(Willie and Phil; Into the Night; The Brothers McMullen)

A Face in the Crowd (B&W), 1957, 125m, ★★★★/$$$, WB/WB. A homespun philosopher bumpkin singer from Arkansas (Andy Griffith) becomes a political folk hero and soon an egomaniac corrupted by the system. Patricia Neal, Lee Remick, Walter Matthau, Tony Franciosa. w. SS-adap. Budd Schulberg (*Your Arkansas Traveler*), d. Elia Kazan.
DRAMA: SATIRE: Political Drama; Media Satire; Biographies-Fictional; Fame-Rise to; Power-Rise to; Power-Rise to, of Idiot; Rise and Fall Stories; TV Life; Greed; Corruption; Rags to Riches; Charismatic People; Singers; Country Music; Ordinary People Stories; Politicians; Southerns; Arkansas; Hidden Gems; Cult Films
(Network; The Goddess; No Time for Sergeants)
Face to Face, 1976, 136m, ★★★¹/₂/$$$, Svensk Filmindustri-Par/Par, R/S. At her grandparents country home, a young female therapist comes apart, leading to an intense psychodrama. Liv Ullmann (BActress), Erland Josephson, Gunnar Bjornstrand, Aino Taube-Henrikson. w. d. Ingmar Bergman. (BDirector) Oscars: 2-0.
DRAMA: Psychological Drama; Art Films; Psychologists; Parents vs Children; Nervous Breakdowns; Young Women Midlife Crisis; Swedish Films;

Writer-Directors; Bergmanesque (Scenes from a Marriage; Persona)
Faces, 1968, 130m, ★★★/$$, Faces/Touchstone, R/P-S. A businessman in an alienated, neurotic suburban world goes through a painful divorce. John Marley, Gena Rowlands, Lynn Carlin, Seymour Cassel, Fred Draper. w. d. John Cassavetes.
DRAMA: Marriage Drama; Marriage on the Rocks; Art Films; Avant-Garde Films; Ensemble Films; Multiple Stories; Suburban Life; 1960s; Time Capsules; Hidden Gems; Improvisational Films; Writer-Directors
(Who's Afraid of Virginia Woolf?; Shadows)
The Facts of Life, 1960, 103m, ★★★/$$, UA/NA. An affair between two conventional middle-class married people ends badly for all concerned. Bob Hope, Lucille Ball, Ruth Hussey, Don Defore. w. Norman Panama, Melvin Frank (BOScr), d. Melvin Frank. BB&WCin, BOSong, BB&WArt. Oscars: 4-0.
COMEDY DRAMA: COMEDY: ROMANCE: Romance with Married Person; Sex Comedy; Romantic Comedy; Suburban Life; Romance-Middle-Aged; Romance-Doomed; Romance-Clandestine
(Brief Encounter; When Strangers Meet; Falling in Love)
Fahrenheit 451, 1966, 111m, ★★★★/$$, BBC-Universal/MCA-U. In a

futuristic society in which all non-government books are banned and burned, one of those who burns them (Oskar Werner) turns against his leaders and falls in love with a subversive reader of them (Julie Christie). Cyril Cusack. w. Francois Truffaut, Jean-Louis Richard, N-adap. Ray Bradbury, d. Francois Truffaut.

DRAMA: SCI-FI: Futuristic Films; **ROMANCE:** Fighting the System; Oppression; Censorship; Multiple Performances; Rebels; Fires; Fires-Arsonists; Betrayals; Wives-Troublesome; Escape Drama; Lookalikes; Brainwashing; Cult Films; Hidden Gems
(1984; Closet Land; Alphaville)

Fade to Black, 1980, 100m, ★★/$$, AIP/Media, R. A movie-obsessed loner loses his grip on reality, dressing like famous characters from classic films such as Dracula to stalk those who have hurt him. Dennis Christopher, Tim Thomerson, Linda Kerridge, Mickey Rourke, Melinda Fee. d. Vernon Zimmerman.

HORROR: SUSPENSE: MURDER: Serial Killers; Psycho Killers; Hollywood Life; Fans-Crazed; Transvestites; Cult Films

Fade to Black, 1993, 84m, ★★/$, Par/Par. A college professor has a nasty hobby: videotaping through his neighbors' windows. He discovers on one of his tapes that he's captured a murder! Due to his carelessness, the murderer finds out, and he's next! Timothy Busfield, Heather Locklear, Michael Beck, Louis Giambalvo, Cloris Leachman, David Byron. w. Douglas Barr, d. John McPherson.

SUSPENSE: MURDER: Voyeurs; Men in Jeopardy; Videotape Scandals; Neighbors-Troublesome; Professors
(Blow Up; Blow Out; Rear Window; The Conversation; Sliver)

Fail Safe, 1964, 111m, ★★★1/2/$$$, Col/RCA-Col. At the Pentagon, communications go awry, sending a jet fighter to Moscow carrying an atomic payload. This in turn sets off a terrifying and wholly believable chain of events that brings the world to the brink of utter destruction. Henry Fonda, Walter Matthau, Dan O'Herlihy, Frank Overton, Larry Hagman. w. Walter Bernstein, N-adap. Eugene Burdick, Harvey Wheeler, d. Sidney Lumet.

DRAMA: SUSPENSE: Apocalyptic Stories; Bombs-Atomic; Crisis Situations; Cold War Era; Misunderstandings; Washington D.C.; Pentagon; Presidents; Hidden Gems; Time Capsules; What If . . . Stories
(Dr. Strangelove; The Mouse That Roared; War Games; The Bedford Incident)

Fair Game, 1995, 100m, ★1/2/$, WB/WB, R/S-EV. After a beautiful woman (guess who) gets a rusty trawler in a divorce, the KGB is after her for its contents, and it's up to her hunky protector to save the day or be blown up. William Baldwin, Cindy Crawford, Steven Berkoff, Christopher McDonald. w. Charlie Fletcher, d. Andrew Sipes.

ACTION: Women in Jeopardy; Fugitives; KGB Agents; Protecting Someone; Chase Stories; Flops-Major

The Falcon and the Snowman, 1985, 123m, ★★★/$$, Orion/Orion, R/P. The true story of two sleazy computer hacks, one of them a drug dealer, who sold U.S. secrets to the Soviets in Mexico. Timothy Hutton, Sean Penn, David Suchet, Lori Singer, Pat Hingle. w. Steven Zaillian, NF-adap. Robert Lindsey, d. John Schlesinger.

DRAMA: Spy Films; Spies; Political Drama; Scandals; True Stories; Con Artists; Young Men; Corruption; Government Corruption; Whistleblowers; Traitors; Russians; Mexico; Computers; Nerds; Bratpack Movies
(Gotcha; The King of Comedy)
(Ed: The theme song, "This Is Not America," by David Bowie, lives on better than the film. One of the best from the Bratpack Era)

Fallen Angel, 1945, 97m, ★★★/$, 20th/NA. A philandering husband who tries to off his wife has the whole plot turn around on himself. Dana Andrews, Alice Faye, Linda Darnell, Charles Bickford, Anne Revere, Bruce Cabot, John Carradine. w. Harry Kleiner, N-adap. Marty Holland, d. Otto Preminger.

SUSPENSE: MURDER: Film Noir; Murder of Spouse; Turning the Tables; Cheating Men; Clever Plots & Endings; Good Premise Unfulfilled; Coulda Been Great; Forgotten Films; Dose of Own Medicine-Given
(Kiss and Tell; Laura; Whirlpool)

Fallen Idol (B&W), 1949, 94m, ★★★★/$$, B-L/Nos, Prism,. A boy knows a secret about his mother's lover, who is also the butler (Ralph Richardson), but with his wild imagina-tion, will they listen when he tells it and it's a matter of life and death? w. SS-adap. Graham Greene (BAScr), d. Carol Reed (BDirector). Oscars: 2-0.

DRAMA: SUSPENSE: MURDER: MYSTERY: MURDER MYSTERY: Secrets-Keeping; Secrets-Haunting; Boy Cries Wolf; Unbelieved; Child Protagonists; Murderer-Debate to Reveal; Stepfathers; British Films
(The Window; Eyewitness [1970]; The Client)

The Fallen Sparrow, 1943, 93m, ★★1/2/$, RKO/Media. Nazis looking for the Spanish flag of freedom hunt down an American veteran of the Spanish Civil War in New York. John Garfield, Maureen O'Hara, Walter Slezak, John Banner. w. Warren Duff, N-adap. Dorothy B. Hughes, d. Richard Wallace.

DRAMA: SUSPENSE: Spy Films; Film Noir; Nazi Stories; World War II Era; Coulda Been Good; Forgotten Films
(Spy in Black; The Stranger)

Falling in Love, 1984, 106m, ★★★1/2/$$, Par/Par, PG/S. Two suburbanite commuters (Robert De Niro, Meryl Streep) meet on the train to New York but don't get together until fate reunites them. w. Michael Cristofer, d. Ulu Grosbard.

ROMANCE: DRAMA: Romantic Drama; Ordinary People Stories; Cheating Men; Cheating Women; Romance with Married Person; Suburban Life; Marriage on the Rocks; Marriage Drama; Romance-On Again/Off Again; New York Life; Old Fashioned Recent Films; Wisecracking Sidekicks; Underrated
(Brief Encounter; John and Mary; Sleepless in Seattle; An Affair to Remember; Love Affair)

Falling in Love Again, 1980, 103m, ★★★/$, PG/S. International Picture Show/Sultan. A New Yorker somewhat "past his prime" wistfully looks back on his salad days and in the process gets re-energized. Elliott Gould, Susannah York, Stuart Paul, Kaye Ballard. w. Steven Paul, Ted Allan, Susannah York, d. Steven Paul.

DRAMA: ROMANCE: Romantic Drama; Romance-Reunited; Love-First; Nostalgia; Memories; Flashbacks; Rejuvenation; Redemption; Reunions; Old-Fashioned Recent Films; Hidden Gems
(Middle-Age Crazy)

The Fall of the House of Usher, 1928, 48m (silent), ★★★/$$$, Ind/NA. A brother and sister are the two remaining members of an old aristocratic family, and their house deteriorates around them as they deteriorate psychologically. It all culminates, as in so many Poe stories, in the sister being accidently buried alive-a show stopper that literally brings down the house. Marguerite Gance, Jean Dubucourt, Charles Lamy. w. d. Jean Epstein, Luis Bunuel, SS-adap. Edgar Allan Poe.

SUSPENSE: HORROR: Psychological Thriller; Art Films; Buried Alive; Rich People-Decadent; Houses-Creepy; Forgotten Films
(Ed: Notable as Bunuel's early work)

The Fall of the Roman Empire, 1964, 187m, ★★1/2/$$, Samuel Bronston-Par/VCI. Commodus goes insane after killing his father the Emperor Marcus Aurelius, and Rome is left without a ruler-an open invitation to the Goths and Barbarians who proceed to burn and pillage it. Alec Guinness, Christopher Plummer, Stephen Boyd, James Mason, Sophia Loren, John Ireland, Eric Porter, Mel Ferrer, Omar Sherif. w. Ben Barzman, Philip Yordan, d. Anthony Mann. BOScore. Oscars: 1-0.

DRAMA: Historical Drama; Epics; Cast of Thousands; Romance; Ancient Times; Political Unrest; Power Struggles; Royalty; Italy; Production Design-Outstanding; Flops-Major
(El Cid; The Agony and The Ecstasy)

Fame, 1980, 133m, ★★★/$$, MGM/MGM-UA, R/P-S. A fictitious "slice of life" from Manhattan's High School for the Performing Arts, where young hopefuls compete in the worlds of dance, singing and acting, meanwhile going through the usual teen angst and sexual blossoming. Irene Cara, Lee Curreri, Laura Dean, Paul McCrane, Barry Miller. w. Christopher Gore (BOScr), d. Alan Parker. BOSong "Fame," BOSong "Out Here on My Own." Oscars: 3-1.

DRAMA: MUSICALS: Music Movies; Dancers; Dance Movies; Singers; Teenagers; High School Life; Prodigies; Children-Gifted; New York Life; Coming of Age; Ensemble Films; Coulda Been Great
SEQUEL: TV SERIES (1983–87)
(Rich Kids; Flashdance)

(Ed: It should have taken off bigger at the box office, but the only thing that sold was a bit of a legend followed by a TV series and a big hit soundtrack)

The Family, 1987, 128m, ★★★/$, Veston/Vestron, PG. At a family reunion in a Roman apartment, the 80-year-old patriarch spins yarns of the family history. Vittorio Gassman, Fanny Ardant, Philippe Noiret, Stefania Sandrelli, Andrea Occhipinti, Jo Ciampa. w. Ettore Scola, Ruggero Maccari, Furio Scarpelli, d. Ettore Scola. BFLFilm. Oscars: 1-0.

DRAMA: Family Drama; Elderly Men; Reunions; Memories; Flashbacks; Episodic Stories; Italy; Italian Films
(My Father's Castle; Lies My Father Told Me; I Never Sang for My Father; Everybody's Fine)

A Family Affair, 1937, 69m, ★★★/$$$, MGM/NA. The Hardy family, whose father is a small-town judge, has its share of strife but always pulls through. Lionel Barrymore, Spring Byington, Mickey Rooney, Eric Linden. w. Kay Van Riper, P-adap. Aurania Rouverol, P-adap. (Skidding), d. George B. Seitz.

COMEDY: MELODRAMA: Family Comedy; Small-Town Life; American Myth; Andy Hardy; Judges; Forgotten Films
(Babes in Arms; The Human Comedy)

Family Business, 1989, 110m, ★★/$, Tri-Star/Tri-Star, R/P-V. A Scottish gangster teaches his son and grandson how it's done, but not everyone gets away. Sean Connery, Dustin Hoffman, Matthew Broderick, Rosana DeSoto, Victoria Jackson. w., N-adap. Vincent Patrick, d. Sidney Lumet.

DRAMA: Crime Drama; Heist Stories; Family Drama; Fathers & Sons; Friendships-Male; Ethics; Grandfathers-Fascinating
(The Anderson Tapes; At Close Range)
(Ed: A bore from start to finish, and believing these three are related is next to impossible)

Family Pictures, 1993, 240m, ★★★/$$$, ABC/ABC, PG. A female photojournalist recalls growing up in the fifties with five siblings, including an autistic brother who occupied her mother's attention to the exclusion of the four other children, and caused her father to blame her mother for the child's handicap. Angelica Huston, Sam Neill, Kyra Sedgewick, Dermot Mulroney, Gemma Barry, Tara Charendoff, Torri Higginson,

Jamie Harold. w. Jennifer Miller, N-adap. Sue Miller, d. Philip Saville.

DRAMA: Family Drama; Episodic Stories; Photographers; Mentally Disabled; Disabled People; Marriage Drama; Marriage on the Rocks; Divorce; Death-Dealing with; TV Movies; Miniseries; Female Protagonists; Female Screenwriters
(Crooked Hearts; Son Rise; A Day in the Death of Joe Egg; The Good Mother)

Family Plot, 1976, 126m, ★★★/$$, U/MCA-U, PG. A charlatan psychic pulls a scam on a wealthy family by "producing" an heir to the recently dead matriarch (actually a cohort of the psychic in on the scheme) and trying to run off with the money. Karen Black, Bruce Dern, Barbara Harris, William Devane. w. Ernest Lehman, N-adap. Victor Canning (*The Rainbird Pattern*), d. Alfred Hitchcock.

SUSPENSE: Comic Thriller; Heist Stories; Jewel Thieves; Chase Movies; Comedy-Light; Criminals-Stupid; Clever Plots & Endings; Con Artists; Fortune Tellers; Hidden Gems; Hitchcockian
(To Catch a Thief; Seance on a Wet Afternoon)
(Ed: More light comedy than thriller)

Family Upside Down, 1978, 100m, ★★★/$$$, Col/Col. A made-for-television movie in which an elderly couple struggle to stay together when the husband suffers a heart attack and is committed to a nursing home. Helen Hayes, Fred Astaire, Efrem Zimbalist Jr., Patty Duke. d. David Lowell Rich. Emmy winner.

MELODRAMA: DRAMA: Death-Impending; Tearjerkers; Elderly People; Family Drama; Marriage Drama; Disease Stories; TV Movies
(Right of Way; A Piano for Mrs. Cimino)

The Fan, 1981, 95m, ★★1/2/$, Par/Par, R/EV-S-B&G. An overzealous admirer of a Broadway star stalks her. She begins to fear for her safety when her assistant is slashed and others around her turn up dead. Lauren Bacall, James Garner, Maureen Stapleton, Hector Elizondo, Michael Biehn, Anna Maria Horsford. w. Priscilla Chapman, John Hartwell, d. Edward Bianchi.

SUSPENSE: HORROR: MURDER: Murder-Learning to; Fans-Crazed; Obsessions; Actresses; Women in Jeopardy; Psycho Killers; Murders-One by One; Stalkers; Theater Life; Camp;

Uninentionally Funny; Female Protagonists; Female Screenwriters (The Seduction)
(Ed: Campy and trashy with a few moments. Looks good and has a good musical number by Tim Rice and Andrew Lloyd Webber)

Fancy Pants, 1950, 92m, ★★★/$$$, Par/Par. Through a series of convoluted incidents, an English actor ends up in the Old West, running from outlaw cowboys. He must pose as a butler to escape detection. Bob Hope, Lucille Ball, Bruce Cabot, Jack Kirkwood, Lea Penman, Eric Blore. w. Edmund Hartman, Robert O'Brien, d. George Marshall.
COMEDY: WESTERN: Western Comedy; Fish out of Water Stories; Imposters-Actor; Impostors; Disguises; Servants; Misunderstandings; Identities-Mistaken; Fugitives; Chase Movies; Hiding Out
REMAKE OF The Ruggles of Red Gap
(The Ruggles of Red Gap; The Shakiest Gun in the West)

Fandango, 1985, 91m, ★★★/$, WB/WB, PG. During the Vietnam War five college seniors, leary of the impending draft, take a wild trip through Texas in a gesture of defiance and liberation. Judd Nelson, Kevin Costner, Sam Robards, Chuck Bush, Brian Cesak, Elizabeth Daily, Suzy Amis. w. d. Kevin Reynolds.
COMEDY: DRAMA: Road Movies; Road Movies-Guys in a Car; Texas; Vietnam Era; College Life; Skydiving; Young Men; Wild People; Pre-Life Crisis; Writer-Directors; Cult Films
(1969; Watch It; Coupe de Ville)

Fanny, 1961, 133m, ★★★/$$$, WB/WB. A series of vignettes about lovers and old fogies living in the port of Marseilles, hanging around a bar. Charles Boyer (BActor), Maurice Chevalier, Leslie Caron, Lionel Jeffries. w. Julius J. Epstein, P-adap. S. N. Behrman, Joshua Logan, S-adap. Marcel Pagnol (Marius, Fanny, Cesar), d. Joshua Logan. BPicture, BCCin, BMScore. Oscars: 4-0.
COMEDY DRAMA: ROMANCE: MUSICALS: Music Movies; Multiple Stories; Ensemble Films; Young Women; International Casts; Sailors; Faded Hits (Can-Can; Gigi; Lili)

Fanny and Alexander, 1983, 188m, ★★★1/2/$$$, Svensk Filmindustri-Embassy/Embassy, PG/S. The opulent life of a wealthy young boy with an overactive imagination (Alexander) is radically changed when his actor father dies and his mother marries an oppressive and sadistic Calvinist minister. He and his sister plan their escape from the literally dungeonlike house in which they're imprisoned with the minister and his forlorn, neurotic sister. Gunn Walgren, Ewa Froling, Jarl Kulle, Erland Josephson, Allan Edwall, Borje Ahlstedt, Gunnar Bjornstrand. w. d. Ingmar Bergman (BOScr, BDirector). **BFLFilm, BCinema, BArt, BCostume.** Oscars: 6-4.
DRAMA: Family Drama; Autobiographical Stories; Multiple Stories; Boyhood; Girlhood; Ensemble Films; Costume Drama; Memories; Nostalgia; Swedish Films; 1900s; Bergmanesque
(Ed: For the devout and Swedophiles. A little bit long for sheer entertainment)

Fanny Hill, 1965, 104m, ★★1/2/$$, Meyer/NA. A prostitute has sexual and other misadventures in the 1700s. Miriam Hopkins, Laetitia Roman, Walter Giller, Alex D'Arc, Helmut Weiss. w. Robert Heel, d. Russ Meyer.
COMEDY DRAMA: Comic Adventure; **FARCE:** Erotic Comedy; Costume Drama; Sexy Women; Promiscuity; Classic Literary Adaptations; 1700s; Cult Films (The Amorous Adventures of Moll Flanders)

Fantasia, 1940, 135m, ★★★★/$$$, Disney/Disney, G. A classic in the art of animation: a visual ballet of the beautiful to the humorous to the macabre, synchronized to classical music. d. Ben Sharpsteen.
Cartoons; **MUSICALS:** Musicals-Animated; Music Video Style; **CHILDREN'S: FAMILY**
(Bambi; Allegro Non Troppo)
(Ed: Probably the first music video)

Fantastic Voyage, 1966, 100m, ★★★/$$$, 20th/CBS-Fox. A top scientist embarking on a brilliant discovery develops a clot in the brain and a team of scientists are miniaturized so they can enter his bloodstream and perform the ultimate microsurgery. In their tiny vessel, however, they've unwittingly harbored a traitor. Stephen Boyd, Raquel Welch, Edmond O'Brien, Donald Pleasence, Arthur Kennedy. w. Harry Kleiner, d. Richard Fleischer.
SCI-FI: Fantasy; **ADVENTURE:** Shrinking People; Body Parts; Scientists; Geniuses; Traitors; Spies; Little People (Innerspace; Tom Thumb; Dr. Cyclops)

Far and Away, 1992, 140m, ★★1/2/$$$, U/MCA-U, PG/S. An Irishwoman leaves for America in the 1800s with her houseboy in tow. Once they arrive, they fall in love. Tom Cruise, Nicole Kidman, Thomas Gibson, Robert Prosky, Barbara Babcock, Cyril Cusack, Eileen Pollock. w. Bob Dolman, Ron Howard, d. Ron Howard. BCin, BOScore. Oscars: 2-0.
MELODRAMA: ROMANCE: Epics; Sagas; Family Drama; Romantic Drama; Romance with Servant; Immigrants; Irish People; Early America; Pioneers (The Manions of America; The Emigrants)

Faraway, So Close! (In Weiter Ferne, So Nah!), 1993, 146m, ★★1/2/$, Col/Col, PG-13. A sequel to Wender's 1988 Wings of Desire. This time Cassiel, the angel who didn't become human, observes the physical and mental landscape of Berlin after the Wall came down, again with the heartbreaking incapacity to affect the lives of those whose pain he feels. Otto Sander, Peter Falk, Horst Buchholz, Nastassia Kinski, Heinz Ruhmann, Bruno Ganz, Solveig Dommartin, Ruediger Vogler, Willem Dafoe, Lou Reed. w. Ulrich Zieger, Richard Reitinger, Wim Wenders, d. Wim Wenders.
DRAMA: COMEDY DRAMA: Fantasy; Angels; Reincarnation; Art Films; German Films; Berlin
SEQUEL TO: Wings of Desire

Far from Home: The Adventures of Yellow Dog, 1995, 81m, ★★★/$$, 20th/Fox, PG. A boy and his yellow dog wind up shipwrecked on an island off the coast of British Columbia while his parents search for them. Mimi Rogers, Bruce Davison, Jesse Bradford, Tom Bower, Joel Palmer, Dakotah, Josh Wannamaker, Margot Finley. w. d. Phillip Borsos.
ADVENTURE: CHILDREN'S: FAMILY: MELODRAMA: Boy and His Dog; Pet Stories; Stranded on an Island; Shipwrecked; Rescue Drama; Writer-Directors
(The Incredible Journey; Homeward Bound; Lassie; Dog of Flanders)

Far from the Madding Crowd, 1967, 175m, ★★★/$$, MGM/MGM-UA. A strong-willed young woman can't be hemmed in by her family and its Victorian mores and winds up torn between several men in the beautiful countryside. Julie Christie, Peter Finch, Alan Bates, Terence Stamp, Prunella Ransome. w. Frederick Raphael, N-adap. Thomas Hardy, d. John Schlesinger. BOScore, BCCostume. Oscars: 2-0.

DRAMA: ROMANCE: Romantic Drama; Marriage Drama; Episodic Stories; Rural Life; England; British Films; Classic Literary Adaptations
(Wuthering Heights; The Go-Between)
Farewell My Concubine, 1993, 157m, ★★★/$$$, Miramax/Miramax, PG-13. Two male stars of the Peking Opera fall in and out of love while the world around them changes drastically, from the last emperor to Mao Tse Tung. Leslie Cheung, Ahang Fengyi, Gong Li, Lu Qi, Ying Da, Ge You. w. Lilian Lee, Lu Wei, d. Chen Kaige. BFLFilm. Oscars: 1-0.

DRAMA: ROMANCE: Romantic Drama; Gay Men; China; War Stories; Opera; Oprea Singers; Romance-On Again, Off Again; Episodic Stories; Sleeper Hits; Taiwanese Films
(The Wedding Banquet; Shanghai Triad)
Farewell My Lovely, see **Murder My Sweet**.

Farewell, My Lovely, 1975, 118m, ★★★/$$, Avco/Sultan, R/V-S. Robert Mitchum, Charlotte Rampling, Sylvia Miles, John Ireland, Anthony Zerbe, Jack O'Halloran, Harry Dean Stanton, Sylvester Stallone, Cheryl "Rainbeaux" Smith. w. David Zelag Goodman, d. Dick Richards.

SUSPENSE: MYSTERY: MURDER: MURDER MYSTERY: Detective Stories; Detectives in Deep; Detectives-Private; Conspiracy; Los Angeles; Missing Persons; Searches; Film Noir
(Marlowe; The Big Sleep [1978])
A Farewell to Arms, 1932, 78m, ★★★/$$$$, Par/Par. In an Army hospital during World War I, a romance slowly develops between a nurse and her convalescing patient, a wounded ambulance driver. Gary Cooper, Helen Hayes, Adolphe Menjou, Mary Philips, Jack La Rue. w. Benjamin Glazer, H. P. Garrett, N-adap. Ernest Hemingway, d. Frank Borzage.

A Farewell to Arms, 1957, 150m, ★★★/$$, 20th/CBS-Fox. A miscast remake. Rock Hudson, Jennifer Jones, Vittorio de Sica, Alberto Sordi, Kurt Kasznar, Mercedes McCambridge, Oscar Homolka, Elaine Stritch, Victor Francen. w. Ben Hecht, d. Charles Vidor.

MELODRAMA: ROMANCE: Romantic Drama; World War I Era; Veterans; Hospitals; Soldiers; Nurses; Paris; Classic Literary Adaptations
(The Sun Also Rises; For Whom the Bell Tolls)
Farewell to the King, 1988, 117m, ★★½/$, Orion/Orion, R/P-V. An American in Borneo becomes the leader of a local tribe of headhunters and fights the Japanese with the British. Nick Nolte, Nigel Havers, Frank McRae, James Fox, Marilyn Tokuda, Marius Weyers, Choy Chang Wing. w. d. John Milius.

DRAMA: ADVENTURE: War Stories; World War II Stories; Islands; Kingdoms; Royalty-Sudden; Kings; South Pacific; Asia; Japanese as Enemy; Cannibalism; Flops-Major; Coulda Been Great; Writer-Directors
(Apocalypse Now; Heart of Darkness)
The Farmer Takes a Wife, 1953, 81m, ★★½/$$, 20th/Fox. A mysterious girl, wandering from town to town, is sheltered and helped by a quiet and gentle farmer. They eventually fall in love and marry. Betty Grable, Dale Robertson, Thelma Ritter, Eddie Foy Jr., John Carroll. w. Walter Bulloch, Sally Benson, Joseph Fields, d. Henry Levin.

ROMANCE: COMEDY DRAMA: MUSICALS: Musical Romance; City vs. Country; Farm Life; New in Town; Marriage Comedy; Newlyweds; Forgotten Films; Female Screenwriters
The Farmer's Daughter, 1947, 97m, ★★★½/$$$, RKO/Turner. A congressman's Swedish maid starts taking an interest in politics and becomes a folk heroine. Loretta Young (**BActress**), Joseph Cotten, Ethel Barrymore, Charles Bickford (**BSActor**), Rose Hobart, Rhys Williams, Harry Davenport. w. Allen Rivkin, Laura Kerr, d. H. C. Potter. Oscars: 2-1.

COMEDY DRAMA: ROMANCE: Power-Rise to; Political Campaigns; Politicians; Midwestern Life; Hidden Gems; Servants; Romance with Servant; Female Protagonists; Female Screenwriters
(Mr. Smith Goes to Washington; Being There; The Distinguished Gentleman; Adam Had Four Sons)
Fast Company, 1938, 75m, ★★★/$$, MGM/NA. A married couple who own a bookstore get implicated in a murder and have to figure out whodunit. Melvyn Douglas, Florence Rice, Clare Dodd,

Louis Calhern, George Zucco. w. Marco Page (Harry Kurnitz), d. Edward Buzzell.

COMEDY DRAMA: MURDER: MYSTERY: MURDER MYSTERY: Comic Mystery; Detective Stories; Detectives-Amateur; Detective Couples; Mystery-Whodunit
(A Night to Remember; The Thin Man)
Faster Pussycat! Kill! Kill!, 1965/1995, 83m, ★★★/$$, Strand/NA, R/S-V-FFN. A trio of renegade strippers take to their choppers, heading to the desert to rape and pillage and finding an All-American couple to subjugate to their enormous breasts and other weaponry. Tura Satana, Haji, Lori Williams, Susan Bernard, Stuart Lancaster, Paul Trinka, Dennis Busch, Ray Barlow, Mickey Foxx. w. d. Russ Meyer.

COMEDY: ACTION: Action Comedy; Kidnappings; Desert Settings; Motorcycles; Strippers; Bimbos; Camp; Cult Films; Hidden Gems; Writer-Directors
(Beyond the Valley of the Dolls)
(Ed: An acquired taste, but not as esoteric as it used to be)
Fast Times at Ridgemont High, 1982, 92m, ★★★/$$$, U/MCA-U, R/P-S-FN-MN. A more realistic and honest "teen film" than you usually see, involving the sexual awakenings of suburban youths-what else? Sean Penn, Jennifer Jason Leigh, Judge Reinhold, Phoebe Cates, Ray Walston, Robert Romanus. w., NF-adap. Cameron Crowe, d. Amy Heckerling.

COMEDY: COMEDY DRAMA: SATIRE: Teenage Movies; Teenagers; High School Life; Suburban Life; Los Angeles; Female Directors; Sleeper Hits; 1980s
(Dazed and Confused; The Breakfast Club)
Fatal Attraction, 1987, 102m/119m, ★★★½/$$$$$$, Par/Par, R/S-V-P-FN-MRN. A married man (Michael Douglas) has a fling with a woman (Glenn Close, BActress) who suddenly becomes insane when he won't see her again and goes on the attack. Anne Archer (BSActress). w. S-adap. James Dearden (BAScr), d. Adrian Lyne (BDirector). BPicture, BEdit. Oscars: 6-0.

SUSPENSE: DRAMA: Fatal Attractions; Obsessions; Men in Jeopardy; Women in Jeopardy; Revenge; Rogue Plots; Stalkers; Psycho Killers; Kill the Beast; Psychological Thriller; Romance-Brief;

Romance with Married Person; Saving Someone; Suicidal Tendencies; Dangerous Women; Blockbusters; Sleeper Hits

REMAKE: Diversion

REMAKE/RETREAD OF: Play Misty for Me

(Basic Instinct; The Temp; The Crush; Jagged Edge)

(Ed: Started a whole sub-genre, but its exploitative tendencies are undeniable)

Fatal Beauty, 1987, 104m, ★★/$$, MGM/MGM-UA, R/EV-EP-S. A black female cop doggedly pursues a drug dealer pushing "fatal beauty," a designer drug, through the streets of L.A., using various disguises and a lot of rough moves and talk along the way. Whoopi Goldberg, Sam Elliott, Ruben Blades, Harris Yulin, John P. Ryan, Jennifer Warren, Brad Dourif, Mike Jolly, Charles Hallahan. w. Hilary Henkin, Dean Riesner, Bill Svanoe, d. Tom Holland.

ACTION: Drugs-Dealing; Chase Stories; Police Stories; Detective Stories; Crime Drama; Detectives-Police; Detectives-Female; Law Officers-Female; Black Women; Female Among Males; Female Protagonists; Female Screenwriters

(Burglar)

Fatal Vision, 1984, 192m, ★★★/$$$$, NBC-Col/Col. A made-for-television movie based on the true case of Jeffrey MacDonald, a respectable doctor who almost got away with murdering his wife and children by making it appear as if a gang of hippy intruders had done it, though this verdict is still in doubt to some. Gary Cole, Karl Malden, Eva Marie Saint, Andy Griffith, Barry Newman. w. John Gay, NF-adap. Joel MacGuinness, d. David Greene.

MYSTERY: MURDER: MURDER MYSTERY: Fathers & Daughters; Murder of Spouse; **TRAGEDY:** Courtroom Drama; Doctors; True Stories; True or Not?; Avenging Death of Someone; TV Movies; Blockbusters

(Cruel Doubt; The Case of Dr. Sam Shepperd)

Fat City, 1972, 96m, ★★★/$, Col/RCA-Col, R/P-S. A former champion boxer tries to stage a comeback but winds up on skid row again. Stacy Keach, Jeff Bridges, Susan Tyrrell (BSActress), Candy Clark. w., N-adap. Leonard Gardner, d. John Huston. Oscars: 1-0.

DRAMA: Character Studies; Ensemble Films; Boxing; Small-town Life; Sports Movies; Working Class; Poor People; Rise and Fall Stories; Homeless People; Alcoholics; Hidden Gems; Overlooked at Release

(Requiem for a Heavyweight; Raging Bull)

Fate Is the Hunter, 1964, 106m, ★★★/$$$, 20th/NA. An airplane crashes and the pilot is among the victims. His good friend at the airline investigates what happened. Glenn Ford, Rod Taylor, Nehemiah Persoff, Nancy Kwan, Suzanne Pleshette, Jane Russell. w. Harold Medford, N-adap. Ernest K. Gann, d. Ralph Nelson. BCCin, BOSong. Oscars: 2-0.

DRAMA: MELODRAMA: Tearjerkers; Disaster Movies; Airlines; Airplane Crashes; Detective Stories; Pilots-Airline; Death-Dealing with

(Fearless; The High and the Mighty; Airport)

Father Goose, 1964, 116m, ★★★/$$$, U/MCA-U, G. A drifter on the South Seas during World War II comes across a teacher and her six little students who are fleeing battle. Cary Grant, Leslie Caron, Trevor Howard. w. Peter Stone, Frank Tarloff (BOScr), d. Ralph Nelson. Oscars: 1-1.

COMEDY: COMEDY DRAMA: Fathers-Surrogate; Rescue Drama; **ROMANCE:** Romantic Comedy; World War II Stories; Pacific Ocean/Islands; Teachers; Teachers & Students; Men and Babies; Faded Hits; Hidden Gems

(Father is a Bachelor; The Last Flight of Noah's Ark; Houseboat)

Father Hood, 1993, 94m, ★★/$, Touchstone/Touchstone, PG. A brave young girl leaves the children's home where she and her brother are being mistreated to go find her petty-thief dad and make a family again. Complications, such as the fact that her dad's being chased by the police, make it a bit difficult. Patrick Swayze, Halle Berry, Sabrina Lloyd, Brian Bonsall, Diane Ladd, Michael Ironside, Bob Gunton. w. Scott Spencer, d. Darrell Roodt.

COMEDY DRAMA: MELODRAMA: Family Comedy; Romance-Interracial; Black Women; Fathers & Daughters; Girls; Ex-Convicts

(Getting Even with Dad; Three Wishes)

Father Is a Bachelor, 1950, 85m, ★★½/$$, Col/NA. A bunch of orphans are taken under the wing of a grizzled cowboy. William Holden, Coleen Gray, Charles Winninger, Stuart Erwin, Sig Rumann. w. Aleen Leslie, James Edward Grant, d. Norman Foster, Abby Berlin.

COMEDY DRAMA: Tearjerkers; **WESTERNS:** Western Comedy; Men and Boyd; Men and Babies; Babies-Finding; Orphans; Cowboys; Forgotten Films; Female Screenwriters

(The Three Godfathers; The Cowboys)

Father of the Bride, 1950, 93m, ★★★½/$$$$, MGM/MGM-UA. As his daughter gets ready to get married, a father becomes more and more flustered with the preparations and expense. Spencer Tracy (BActor), Joan Bennett, Elizabeth Taylor, Don Taylor, Billie Burke, Moroni Olsen, Leo G. Carroll, Taylor Holmes. w. Frances Goodrich, Albert Hackett (BScr), N-adap. Edward Streeter, d. Vincente Minnelli. BPicture. Oscars: 3-0.

COMEDY: COMEDY DRAMA: Tearjerkers; Weddings; Marriage-Impending; Fathers & Daughters; Coming of Age; Parents vs. Children; Suburban Life; Fairy Tales

SEQUEL: Father's Little Dividend

(The Actress; Life with Father; Betsy's Wedding)

Father of the Bride, 1991, 105m, ★★★/$$$$, Touchstone/Touchstone, PG. Remake of the above, with a more affluent set of parents. Steve Martin, Diane Keaton, Kimberly Williams, Martin Short, Kieran Culkin. w. Frances Goodrich, Albert Hackett, Nancy Myers, Charles Shyer, N-adap. Edward Streeter, d. Charles Shyer.

COMEDY: COMEDY DRAMA: Tearjerkers; Weddings; Marriage-Impending; Fathers & Daughters; Coming of Age; Parents vs. Children; Suburban Life; Narrated Films; Old-Fashioned Recent Films; Fairy Tales; Sleeper Hits

SEQUEL: Father of the Bride 2

(The Actress; Life with Father; Betsy's Wedding; Parenthood)

(Ed: It's nice to be able to afford the dream situation that's here, but it's hardly realistic in any way, shape or form; Keaton is underused and underbilled)

Father of the Bride 2, 1995, 106m, ★★½/$$$, Touchstone/Touchstone, PG. In this remake of a sequel, the parents are not only dealing with becoming grandparents as their married child is expecting, but with becoming parents again themselves. Steve Martin, Diane

Keaton, Martin Short, Gedde Watanabe, Kimberly Williams, George Newbern, Kieran Culkin. w. Nancy Meyers & Charles Shyer, d. Shyer.
Babies-Having; Female Screenwriters
Fathers and Sons, 1992, 100m, ★★1/2/$, Col/Col, PG-13. A film director living in New Jersey re-examines his life of drunken revelry after his wife dies, and he decides to sober up. In the process, he gets to know his son, who has drug problems of his own. Jeff Goldblum, Rory Cochrane, Mitchell Marchand, Famke Janssen, Natasha Gregson Wagner, Ellen Greene, Samuel L. Jackson. w. d. Paul Mones.
DRAMA: Fathers & Sons; Director; Movie Making; Alcoholics; Life Transitions; Midlife Crisis; Widowers; Death-Dealing with; Drugs-Addictions; Writer-Directors
(Doing Time on Maple Drive; I Never Sang for My Father)
Fathom, 1967, 99m, ★★1/2/$$, 20th/CBS-Fox, PG/S. A Bond-like female spy cavorts around international locals, skydiving into dangerous situations and getting the bad guys. Raquel Welch, Tony Franciosa, Clive Revill, Ronald Fraser, Greti Chi, Richard Briers. w. Lorenzo Semple Jr., N-adap. Larry Forrester, d. Leslie Martinson.
ACTION: Secret Agents; Spies; Spies-Female; Spy Films; Beautiful People; Sexy Women; Skydiving; Coulda Been Good; Camp; Curiosities; Female Protagonists
(Deadlier Than the Male; The Biggest Bundle of Them All)
Fat Man and Little Boy, 1989, 127m, ★★-/$, Par/Par, PG. The Manhattan project in Los Alamos is examined in this historical-fictional tale of the battle between the brilliant but tormented scientist J. Robert Oppenheimer and the top brass of the U.S. military. Paul Newman, Dwight Schultz, Bonnie Bedelia, John Cusack, Laura Dern, John C. McGinley, Natasha Richardson, Ron Frazier. w. Bruce Robinson, Tony Garnett, Roland Joffe, d. Roland Joffe.
DRAMA: Historical Drama; Bombs-Atomic; Military Stories; Leaders-Military; Stern Men; World War II Stories; Biographies; Biographies-Fictional; New Mexico; Flops-Major
(Day One)
Fatso, 1980, 93m, ★★/$, 20th/CBS-Fox, PG. A corpulent nebb has trouble socially and tries to lose weight, but finds

it difficult. Dom DeLuise, Anne Bancroft, Ron Carey. w. d. Anne Bancroft.
COMEDY: Black Comedy; Depression; Weight Problems; Obsessions; Good Premise Unfulfilled; Female Screenwriters; Female Directors; Actor Directors; Writer-Directors
(Sugarbaby; Babycakes; Angus)
Faust, 1926, 100m, ★★★1/2/$$, silent, UFA/Nos. The famous fable of the man who sells his soul to the Devil in exchange for certain powers. Emil Jannings, Gosta Ekman, Camilla Horn, Yvette Guilbert, William Dieterle. w. Hans Kyser, d. F. W. Murnau.
DRAMA: Art Films; Soul-Selling One's; Satan; Legends; German Films
(Falstaff; All That Money Can Buy)
The Favor, 1994, 97m, ★★/$, Col/Col, R/S-P. A bored wife takes interest in her best friend's affair with a former flame of her own, and that interest becomes more than merely academic. Harley Jane Kozak, Elizabeth McGovern, Bill Pullman, Brad Pitt, Ken Wahl, Larry Miller, Holland Taylor. w. Josann McGibbon, d. Donald Petrie.
COMEDY: ROMANCE: Romantic Comedy; Friendships-Female; Romance-Triangles; Women Fighting Over Men; Nuisances; Female Protagonists; Female Screenwriters
(Moonlight and Valentino; Chantilly and Lace)
The Favour, the Watch, and the Very Big Fish, 1991, 87m, ★★1/2/$, Sovereign/Vidmark, R/S. A woman who dubs in sex sounds for porno films snags the creator of religious postcards who hires an ex-con to play Christ in one of his compositions. Bob Hoskins, Jeff Goldblum, Natasha Richardson, Michel Blanc, Jean-Pierre Cassel. w. d. Ben Lewin, SS-adap. Marcel Ayme (Rue-Saint Sulpice).
COMEDY: FARCE: Erotic Comedy; Pornography World; Con Artists; Impostors; Coulda Been Good; British Films
Fawlty Towers, 1977, 4 tapes at 90m each, 3 episodes per, ★★★★/$$$, BBC/Fox. The pilot episode and two more of the famous British television series, starring and created by Monty Python's John Cleese, about an inept hotel owner named Basil Fawlty, his shrewish wife, and the odd characters who hang about the place, including Manuel, the Spanish

bellhop. John Cleese, Prunella Scales, Connie Booth, Andrew Sachs. w. John Cleese, Connie Booth.
COMEDY: FARCE: Comedy of Errors; Mean Men; Hotels; Marriage Comedy; Misunderstandings; Mix-Ups; Battle of the Sexes; TV Series; British Films; Cult Films; Female Screenwriters
(A Fish Called Wanda; Clockwise)
The FBI Story, 1959, 149m, ★★/$$, WB/WB. A retired agent looks back at the highlights of his career. James Stewart, Vera Miles, Larry Pennell, Nick Adams, Murray Hamilton. w. Richard L. Breen, John Twist, d. Mervyn Le Roy.
ACTION: Crime Drama; Police Stories; Criminal Biographies; Flashbacks; Memories; Police-Retired; FBI Agents; Multiple Stories; Ku Klux Klan; Nazi Stories; Episodic Stories; Time Capsules; Ahead of Its Time
(Calling Northside 777; The FBI [TV Series]; Mississippi Burning)
(Ed: Ahead of Its time-this stuff was on every week not too long after and was more entertaining)
Fear, 1989, 95m, ★★/$, Vestron/Vestron, R/V-B&G. A detective with psychic powers hunts a killer who is also psychic. Ally Sheedy, Pruitt Taylor Vince, Lauren Hutton, Michael O'Keefe, Stan Shaw, John Agar. w. d. Rockne S. O'Bannon.
SUSPENSE: Detective Stories; MURDER: MURDER MYSTERY: Psychics; Detectives-Female; Trail of a Killer; Mindgames; Good Premise Unfulfilled; Writer-Directors; Female Protagonists
(Eyes of Laura Mars; The Clairvoyant)
The Fear Inside, 1992, 100m, ★★-/$$, 20th/Fox, R/V. A made-for-cable film about a housebound woman who hires a nice-seeming, clean-cut college kid to do her shopping and run errands and finds that he and his "brother" are up to something very bizarre. Christine Lahti, Jennifer Rubin, Dylan McDermott, David Ackroyd, Thomas Ian Nicholas, Paul Linke.
SUSPENSE: Disabled People in Jeopardy; Women in Jeopardy; Young Men; Murderers-Nice; Conspiracy; TV Movies
Fearless, 1993, 123m, ★★★1/2/$, WB/WB, PG-13/P. A man walks away from a plane crash and is haunted by the memories, unable to overcome them until he meets other survivors and they all deal with the deaths of who they were

with. Jeff Bridges, Rosie Perez (BSActress), Isabella Rosellini. w. N-adap. Rafael Yglesias, d. Peter Weir. Oscars: 1-0.

DRAMA: Character Studies; Disaster Movies; Airplane Crashes; Flashbacks; Depression; Alienation; Romantic Drama; Death-Dealing with; Redemption; Starting Over; Guilty Conscience; Overlooked at Release; Hidden Gems; Underrated; Quiet Little Films
(Fate Is the Hunter; Alive)
(Ed: An extremely realistic plane crash)

Fear in the Night, 1972, 85m, ★★¹/₂/$$, EMI/Sinister. Conspirators collaborate to drive a mentally unstable woman to murder. Peter Cushing, Judy Geeson, Joan Collins, Ralph Bates. w. Jimmy Sangster, Michael Syson, d. Jimmy Sangster.

SUSPENSE: HORROR: Murder-Persuaded/Coerced; Murder of Spouse; Mental Illness; Conspiracy; Insane-Plot to Drive; British Films

Fear of a Black Hat, 1994, 86m, ★★★/$, Goldwyn/Goldwyn, R/EP-S. A parody of black rap groups and their fans and managers, including a sociologist reporting on the central group's "meaning." Rusty Cundieff, Larry B. Scott, Mark Christopher Lawrence, Kasi Lemmons, Howie Gold, G. Smokey Campbell, Bob Mardis, Tim Hutchinson, Moon Jones, Faizon, Deezer D, Darin Scott. w. d. Rusty Cundieff.

COMEDY: Spoofs; Spoofs-Documentary; Rock Stars; Singers; Black Men; Writer-Directors
(This Is Spinal Tap; All You Need Is Cash)

Fear Strikes Out, 1957, 100m, ★★¹/₂/$$, Par/Par. A timid boy is pressured by his father into becoming a professional baseball player, and he can't stand the pressure. Anthony Perkins, Karl Malden, Norma Moore, Perry Wilson. w. Ted Berkman, Raphael Blau (based on the true story of Jim Piersal), d. Robert Mulligan.

DRAMA: Sports Movies; Baseball; Fathers & Sons; Boys; Young Men; Coming of Age; Men Proving Themselves; Parents vs. Children
(The Great Santini; Tall Story)

The Fearless Vampire Killers, or Pardon Me, Your Teeth Are in My Neck (Dance of the Vampires), 1967, 124m, ★★★/$$, MGM/MGM-UA. A pro-

fessor of folklore hunts vampires with his assistant. The vampires they meet aren't run-of-the-mill: one is gay, and another eats dogs . . . you get the picture. Jack MacGowran, Roman Polanski, Alfie Bass, Sharon Tate, Ferdy Mayne, Terry Downes. w. Gerard Brach, Roman Polanski, d. Roman Polanski.

HORROR: Horror Comedy; Vampires; Spoofs-Vampire; Professors; Eccentric People; Cannibalism; Monsters-Animal; Gay Men; French Films; Paris; Cult Films; Curiosities
(Repulsion; From Dusk Till Dawn)

Fedora, 1978, 110m, ★★★/$, Par/NA, PG/S. An actress from long ago comes out of retirement remarkably preserved and tries to make a comeback in the movies and in love, but it may not be meant to be. William Holden, Marthe Keller, Jose Ferrer, Henry Fonda, Michael York. w. IAL Diamond, Billy Wilder, SS-adap. Tom Tryon, *Crowned Heads*, d. Billy Wilder.

DRAMA: MELODRAMA: ROMANCE: Romantic Drama; Actresses; Comebacks; Aging; Hollywood Life; Time Sleepers; Flops-Major; Overlooked at Release; Hidden Gems; Curiosities; Coulda Been Great
(Sunset Boulevard; The Picture of Dorian Gray; Garbo Talks)

Felix the Cat: The Movie, 1989, 82m, ★★¹/₂/$, Transatlantic/Disney. The old comic strip character is revived and must travel to another dimension to rescue a princess. Voices of Chris Phillips, Maureen O'Connell, Peter Neuman, Alice Playton, Susan Montanaro. w. Don Oriolo, Pete Brown, d. Tibor Hernadi. Cartoons; Animal Stories; Cats; **CHILDREN'S: FAMILY:** Saving Someone; Princesses; Overlooked at Release

Fellow Traveler, 1989, 97m, ★★¹/₂/$$, Par/Par. In the fifties, during the McCarthy witch hunts, a screenwriter and an actor both get blacklisted and lose their livelihoods. Ron Silver, Hart Bochner, Daniel J. Travanti, Imogen Stubbs, Katherine Borowitz, Jonathan Hyde. d. Philip Saville.

DRAMA: Historical Drama; McCarthy Era; Writers; Communists; Cold War Era; Hollywood Life; Ostracism; Oppression; Writers; Actors; Avenging Death of Someone; TV Movies
(Guilty by Suspicion; The Front; Witchhunt)

The Female on the Beach, 1955, 97m, ★★¹/₂/$, U-I/NA. A slick, young stud puts the moves on a rich widow who's staying at the beach house next door. His intentions are less than honorable. Joan Crawford, Jeff Chandler, Jan Sterling, Cecil Kellaway, Natalie Schafer. w. Robert Hill, Richard Alan Simmons, d. Joseph Pevney.

ROMANCE: MELODRAMA: Romantic Drama; Romance-Older Women/Younger Men; Beach Movies; Beautiful People; Sexy Men; Prostitutes-Male; Camp; Curiosities; Unintentionally Funny
(Autumn Leaves; Moment to Moment; Love from a Stranger)

Female Trouble, 1974, 95m, ★★★/$$$, Ind/NA. John Waters' take on Jean Genet's "Crime is Beauty" theme: Divine, the 300-pound transvestite star of *Pink Flamingos*, starts going bad when she kills grandma with the Christmas tree, upset because she didn't get her cherished cha-cha heels. After reform school, she goes on a crime rampage, becoming a star criminal and delivering her Oscar speech from the electric chair. Divine, David Lochary, Mary Vivian Pearce, Mink Stole, Edith Massey, Danny Mills, Cookie Mueller, Susan Walsh. w. d. John Waters.

COMEDY: Spoofs; Men as Women; Transvestites; **MURDER:** Reform School; Murderers-Female; Women in Prison; Executions; Camp; Cult Films; Writer-Directors
(Pink Flamingos; Mondo Trasho; Polyester)

Femme Fatale, 1991, 96m, ★★/$ (VR), Republic/Republic, R/S-P. A newlywed husband spots his wife who's left him on his honeymoon in disguise as another woman, and delves into her "secret life." Colin Firth, Lisa Zane, Billy Zane, Scott Wilson, Lisa Blount. w. Michael Ferris, John D. Brancato, d. Andre Guttfreund.

SUSPENSE: Erotic Thriller; Newlyweds; Disguises; Dangerous Women; Double Crossings; Mindgames
(Desire and Hell at the Sunset Motel; Deceived)

FernGully: The Last Rainforest, 1992, 76m, ★★★/$$, 20th/CBS-Fox, G. An ecological fable about a group of oddball characters who save a forest from destruction. Voices of Tim Curry, Samantha Mathis, Christian Slater, Jonathan Ward, Robin Williams, Grace

Zabriskie, Cheech Marin, Tommy Chong, Tone-Loc. w. Jim Cox, Diana Young, d. Bill Kroyer.

Cartoons; Environmental Dilemmas; Message Films; **CHILDREN'S: FAMILY:** Rainforests; South America; Jungle Life; Animal Stories
(Balto; The Jungle Book)

Ferris Bueller's Day Off, 1986, 103m, ★★★1/2/$$$, Par/Par, PG/P. Eccentric free spirit Ferris takes his friends on a wild day in Chicago while playing hooky from high school, but will their parents or the insane principal find out? Matthew Broderick, Alan Ruck, Mia Sara, Jeffrey Jones, Cindy Pickett, Jennifer Grey. w. d. John Hughes.

COMEDY: FARCE: Chase Stories; Eccentric People; Free Spirits; Wild People; High School Life; Teenagers; Teenage Movies; Parents vs. Children; Parents are Gone; Parents are Gone from Chicago; Generation Gap; Chicago; Suburban Life; Narrated Films; Crossing the Line; Writer-Directors
(The Breakfast Club; Home Alone)

The Feud, 1990, 87m, ★★1/2/$, PBS-AP/Vidmark. Two families in a small town engage in all-out war until no one can remember what they're fighting about. Rene Auberjonois, Ron McLarty, Joe Grifasi, David Strathairn, Gale Mayron. d. Bill D'Elia.

COMEDY: COMEDY DRAMA: Family Comedy; Feuds; Small-Town Life; Coulda Been Good; TV Movies
(Cold Turkey; The Lolly Madonna War)

Fever Pitch, 1985, 95m, ★★/$, MGM-UA/MGM-UA, Fox, R/P-S. A sportswriter loses everything when he becomes addicted to gambling. Ryan O'Neal, Catherine Hicks, Giancarlo Giannini, Bridgette Anderson, Chad Everett, John Saxon, William Smith, Patrick Cassidy, Chad McQueen. w. d. Richard Brooks.

DRAMA: Gambling; Character Studies; Writers; Journalists; Losing it All; Risking it All; Obsessions; Flops-Major; Writer-Directors
(The Gambler; The Lady Gamble; The Driver)

A Few Good Men, 1992, 138m, ★★★/$$$$, Col/Col-Tri, R/P. Two marines are both accused of killing a cadet and must choose between taking the blame or implicating a high-ranking officer, and it's up to a rookie lawyer and his more experienced female colleague to try the case. Tom Cruise, Jack Nicholson (BSActor), Demi Moore, Kevin Bacon, Keifer Sutherland, Kevin Pollak, Christopher Guest. w. P-adap. Aaron Sorkin, d. Rob Reiner. BPicture, BEdit. Oscars: 3-0.

DRAMA: Courtroom Drama; Courts Martial; Military Stories; Trials; **MURDER:** Accused Unjustly; Death-Accidental; Conspiracy; Corruption; Government as Enemy; Leaders-Tyrant; Ethics; Lawyers; Blockbusters; Overrated
(The Caine Mutiny; The Bounty)
(Ed: Much ado about nothing but scenery chewing. Demi's character sets the plot into motion and then is told hot shot upstart Cruise gets the case, after which the obvious sexism is dropped and the courtroom histrionics begin. It continually seems to be heading toward a case of homophobic murder which makes the real reason for the cover-up seem all the more banal)

F for Fake, 1973, 85m, ★★1/2/$, Astrophore/NA. At a train station, the corpulent auteur gives a lecture on Art and Truth. w. Orson Welles, Oja Palinkas, d. Orson Welles.

Documentaries; One Person Shows; Art Films; Curiosities

Fiddler on the Roof, 1971, 180m, ★★★★/$$$$$, UA/CBS-Fox, G. In old Russia, a Jewish community faces the vicissitudes of life. The dead sing, a matchmaker joins two young people, and Tevye the milkman flees to America with his family once the pogroms start. Topol (BActor), Norma Crane, Leonard Frey (BSActor), Molly Picon. w. MP-adap. Joseph Stein, SS-adap. Sholom Aleichem (Tevye and His Daughters), d. Norman Jewison (BDirector). BPicture, **BAScore, BCin,** BArt, **BSound.** Oscars: 8-3.

MUSICALS: DRAMA: Musical Drama; Sagas; Family Drama; Small-town Life; Jewish People; Anti-Semitism; Life Transitions; Russians; Europeans-Eastern; 1900s; Blockbusters
(Yentl; Dr. Zhivago; Seven Brides for Seven Brothers; Zorba, The Greek)

The Field, 1990, 110m, ★★★/$, Granada-Miramax/Live, PG-13/P-V. An Irish farmer doggedly, and somewhat irrationally, defends a small unfruitful piece of land that an American developer wants to buy. Richard Harris (BActor), John Hurt, Tom Berenger, Sean Bean, Frances Tomelty, Brenda Fricker. w. d. Jim Sheridan, P-adap. John B. Keane. Oscars: 1-0.

DRAMA: Save the Farm; Mortgage Drama; Fighting the System; Corporation as Enemy; Americans as Enemy; Elderly Men; Irish People; Irish Films; Irish Land Battles
(Taffin; Cry the Beloved Country; Local Hero)

Field of Dreams, 1989, 106m, ★★★1/2/$$$$, U/MCA-U, PG. A farmer in Iowa (Kevin Costner) hears a little voice telling him to build a baseball field in the middle of his corn crop and ghosts of baseball players will come. Kevin Costner, Amy Madigan, James Earl Jones, Timothy Busfield, Ray Liotta, Burt Lancaster, Gaby Hoffmann, Frank Whaley. w. d. Phil Alden Robinson (BAScr), N-adap. W. P. Kinsella (Shoeless Joe). BPicture, BOScore. Oscars: 3-0.

COMEDY DRAMA: MELODRAMA: Fantasy; **FAMILY: CHILDREN'S:** Illusions/Hallucinations; Dreams; Baseball; Sports Movies; What If . . . Stories; American Myth; Capra-esque; Magic Realism; Ghosts; Dead-Back from the; Midwestern Life; Farm Life
(Bull Durham; Eight Men Out; Angels in the Outfield)

The Fiendish Plot of Dr. Fu Manchu, 1980, 108m, ★★/$, Orion-WB/WB, PG. The master criminal organizes a diamond heist. Peter Sellers, Helen Mirren, David Tomlinson, Sid Caesar, Simon Williams, Steve Franken, Clive Dunn. w. Jim Moloney, Rudy Dochtermann, d. Piers Haggard.

COMEDY: Heist Stories; Thieves; Comedy-Slapstick; Comedy-Character; Flops-Major
(Ed: Sellers' last and not his best)

Fiesta, 1947, 102m, ★★1/2/$$$, MGM/Voyager. A Mexican man wants his son to be a bullfighter, but the young fellow dreams of being a romantic musician. Esther Williams, Ricardo Montalban, Cyd Charisse, Mary Astor, John Carroll, Akim Tamiroff, Hugo Haas. w. George Bruce, Lester Cole, d. Richard Thorpe.

MUSICALS: ROMANCE: Musical Romance; Parents vs. Children; Bullfighting; Fathers & Sons; Mexico; Latin People; Forgotten Films
(Holiday in Mexico)

The Fifth Musketeer (*Behind the Iron Mask*), 1978, 106m, ★★1/2/$, Sascha-Wien Film/Col, PG. Two twin brothers fight for the crown of France. Beau Bridges, Sylvia Kristel, Ursula Andress, Cornel Wilde, Lloyd Bridges, Alan Hale Jr., Jose Ferrer, Rex Harrison, Olivia de Havilland, Helmut Dantine. w. David Ambrose, d. Ken Annakin.
ADVENTURE: Swashbucklers; Body Switching; Twins; Conspiracy; Mix-Ups; Misunderstandings; Princes; Royalty; Men in Conflict
REMAKE/RETREAD: The Man in the Iron Mask
Fifty/Fifty, 1993, 101m, ★★/$ (VR), WB/WB. Two independent soldiers of fortune who can't stand each other must work together in a covert operation for the CIA to overthrow a Southeast Asian dictator. Robert Hays, Peter Weller, Ramona Rahman, Charles Martin Smith. w. Dennis Shryack, d. Charles Martin Smith.
ACTION: Action Drama; War Stories; Mercenaries; CIA Agents; Asia
(The Dogs of War; The Amateur; Off Limits)
55 Days at Peking, 1963, 154m, ★★★/$$$, Samuel Bronston-UA/VCI. The events leading up to the Boxer rebellion and the Americans defending their embassy. Charlton Heston, David Niven, Ava Gardner, Flora Robson, Robert Helpmann, Leo Genn, Paul Lukas, Harry Andrews, Elizabeth Sellars, Massimo Serrato, Jacques Sernas. w. Philip Yordan, Bernard Gordon, d. Nicholas Ray, Andrew Marton. BOSong, BOScore. Oscars: 2-0.
ACTION: DRAMA: Action Drama; War Stories; Historical Drama; Americans Abroad; Asia; China
(Blood Alley; Shogun)
52 Pick-up, 1986, 114m, ★★1/2/$, Cannon/MGM-UA, R/EP-ES-FN. A group of blackmailers uses videotapes of an executive having sex with his mistress until the prime target's wife is kidnapped and a bomb is set. Roy Scheider, Ann-Margret, Vanity, John Glover, Robert Trebor, Lonny Chapman. w. Elmore Leonard, John Stepping, N-adap. Elmore Leonard, d. John Frankenheimer.
SUSPENSE: Revenge; Avenging Death of Loved One; Saving Somone; Kidnappings; Pornography World; Malicious Menaces; Blackmail; Videotape Scandals

(Assassination; Blindside; Relentless; Death Wish)
Fighting Back, 1982, 98m, ★★1/2/$, DEG-Par/Par, R/V-P. A corner deli owner takes matters into his own hands (with some help from the police and local businessmen) when his wife and mother are killed. Tom Skerritt, Michael Sarrazin, Patti LuPone, Yaphet Kotto, David Rasche. w. Tom Hedley, David Zelag Goodman, d. Lewis Teague.
DRAMA: Revenge; Avenging Death of Someone; Fighting the System; Inner City Life; Death-Dealing with; Vigilantes; Ordinary Person vs. Criminals; Coulda Been Good
(Death Wish; Law and Disorder; Outrage)
The Fighting Kentuckian, 1949, 100m, ★★/$$$, Republic/Republic. After the Battle of New Orleans in 1814, a soldier from Kentucky mosies on over to Alabama and falls in love with the daughter of a French general there. Her father disapproves until the Kentucky man proves himself by saving the community. John Wayne, Oliver Hardy, Vera Ralston, Marie Windsor, Philip Dorn, John Howard, Hugo Haas, Grant Withers. d. George Waggner.
MELODRAMA: ROMANCE: War Stories; War of 1812; War Battles; Soldiers; Men Proving Themselves; Faded Hits; Southerns
(Reap the Wild Wind; The Wake of the Red Witch)
Fighting Mad, 1976, 90m, ★★1/2/$, 20th./Vidmark. The son of a ranching family who went off to the city is drawn back in when his brother and father are murdered by a greedy developer who covets their land. Peter Fonda, Lynn Lowry, John Doucette, Philip Carey, Scott Glenn. w. d. Jonathan Demme.
WESTERNS: Westerns-Modern; Westerns-Revenge; Revenge; Avenging Death of Someone; Save the Farm; Corporation as Enemy; Fighting the System
The Fighting Seabees, 1944, 100m, ★★★/$$$, Republic/Republic. Construction workers sign up and fight the Japanese in World War II. John Wayne, Susan Hayward, Dennis O'Keefe, William Frawley, Duncan Renaldo, Addison Richards. w. Borden Chase, Aeneas Mackenzie, d. Edward Ludwig.
ACTION: War at Sea; Pilots-Military; War

Stories; World War II Stories; Pacific Ocean/Island; Japanese as Enemy (Action in the Atlantic; The Flying Tigers)
The File on Thelma Jordon, 1949, 100m, ★★★/$$, Par/NA, AMC. A woman who may or may not have committed murder develops a love affair with the district attorney prosecuting her case. Barbara Stanwyck, Wendell Corey, Paul Kelly, Joan Tetzel, Minor Watson, Barry Kelley. w. Ketti Frings, d. Robert Siodmak.
DRAMA: SUSPENSE: Courtroom Drama; MURDER: MURDER MYSTERY: MYSTERY: Romance with Suspect; Romance-Unprofessional; Romance with Lawyer; Accused Unjustly; Dangerous Women; Coulda Been Great; Murderers-Female; Female Screenwriters
(Jagged Edge; The Accused [1948])
Final Analysis, 1992, 124m, ★★/$$, WB/WB, R/V-S. A woman finds out that her therapist is having an affair with her married sister. Then her brother-in-law ends up dead. Whodunnit? Richard Gere, Kim Basinger, Uma Thurman, Eric Roberts. w. Wesley Strick, Robert Berger, d. Phil Joanou.
SUSPENSE: MURDER: MYSTERY: MURDER MYSTERY: Double Crossings; Psychologists; Romance with Psychologists; Romance-Unprofessional; Romance-Triangles; Mindgames; Murderers-Female; Evil Women; Sisters Sexy Women; Unintentionally Funny; Good Premise; Unfulfilled; Hitchcockian
REMAKE/RETREAD: Vertigo; Dark Mirror.
(Ed: A dumbbell did it. You figure it out)
The Final Conflict, 1981, 108m, ★★★/$$, 20th/CBS-Fox, R/P-V-FN. The third chapter in the Omen series, wherein Damian becomes the Ambassador to England in order to hatch an evil plot on the world. Sam Neill, Rossano Brazzi, Don Gordon, Lisa Harrow. w. Andrew Birkin, d. Graham Baker.
DRAMA: HORROR: SUSPENSE: Satan-Children of; Rule the World-Plot to; Power-Rise to; Politicians; Diplomats; Supernatural Danger; Satan
SEQUEL TO: The Omen, Damien: Omen II
The Final Countdown, 1980, 105m, ★★1/2/$$, UA/CBS-Fox, PG/V. The passengers of an aircraft carrier passing over Hawaii are transported into another

dimension when they come through the other end of a fierce storm. Kirk Douglas, Martin Sheen, Katharine Ross, James Farentino, Charles Durning. w. David Ambrose, Gerry Davis, Thomas Hunter, Peter Powell, d. Don Taylor.

SCI-FI: ACTION: ADVENTURE: Time Travel; Military Stories; Pearl Harbor; World War II Stories; Good Premise Unfulfilled
(The Philadelphia Experiment)

Finders Keepers, 1984, 96m, ★★★/$, CBS-WB/CBS-Fox, PG/P. When the passengers on a cross-country train learn that there's a big pile of loot stashed somewhere on board, all mayhem breaks loose. Michael O'Keefe, Beverly D'Angelo, Lou Gossett Jr., Pamela Stephenson, Ed Lauter, Brian Dennehy, John Schuck, Jim Carrey. w. Ronny Graham, Charles Dennis, Terence Marsh, N-adap. Charles Dennis (*The Next to Last Train Ride*), d. Richard Lester.

COMEDY: Capers; **FARCE:** Chase Stories; Trains; Finding Money; Treasure Hunts; Canada; Hidden Gems; Coulda Been Great
(Scavenger Hunt; It's a Mad, Mad, Mad, Mad World)
(Ed: Look for Jim Carrey in a small but outstanding bit part)

A Fine Madness, 1966, 104m, ★★★1/2/$$, WB/WB, PG. An incredibly wild and eccentric Scottish poet named Samson Shillitoe runs from the subpoenas of his ex-wife seeking alimony, freaks out the ladies' auxiliary, and winds up as a lobotomy experiment at an asylum while making out with his shrink's wife in a hot tub. Sean Connery, Jean Seberg, Joanne Woodward, Patrick O'Neal, Colleen Dewhurst. w., N-adap. Elliot Baker, d. Irvin Kershner.

COMEDY: FARCE: Chase Stories; Wild People; Eccentric People; Poets; Writers; New York Life; Time Capsules; Asylums; Psychologists; Experiments; Sexy Men; Playboys; Mental Illness; Scotland/Scottish People; Hidden Gems; Underrated
(Reuben, Reuben; Mr. Jones; The Fisher King)
(Ed: The novel *A Confederacy of Dunces* owes a lot to this in its satirical twist on it)

A Fine Mess, 1985, 88m, ★★/$, Col/RCA-Col. Two ineffectual private eyes stumble onto knowledge that gets

them into trouble with the mob. Ted Danson, Howie Mandel, Richard Mulligan, Stuart Margolin, Paul Sorvino. w. d. Blake Edwards.

COMEDY: Comedy-Slapstick; Detective Stories; Fools-Bumbling; Mob Comedy; Fugitives from the Mob; Coulda Been Good; Flops-Major
(Skin Deep; Wise Guys)
(Ed: Began Edwards' period of decline)

A Fine Romance, 1991, 100m, ★★★/$ (VR), Academy/Academy, PG/S. When a wealthy British woman in Paris finds her husband is cheating and an Italian man finds his younger daughter is cheating on him, the two find that each of their spouses are cheating with each other-and they proceed to cheat on the cheaters together, though not until after a battle. Julie Andrews, Marcello Mastroianni. P-adap. *Tchin-Tchin*, d. Gene Saks.

COMEDY: ROMANCE: Romantic Comedy; Cheating Men; Cheating Women; Paris; Marriage Comedy; Romance with Married Person; Romance-Middle-Aged; Romance Reluctant; Battle of the Sexes; Extroverted vs. Introverted; Alcoholics; Cheated Upon Meet; Swapping Partners; Old-Fashioned Recent Films; Overlooked at Release
(A Touch of Class)
(Ed: Marcello to Julie: "I want to see you naked in the desert singing to the moon!" Worth seeing)

Fine Things, 1990, 145m, ★★–/$$, NBC/World Vision. Bernie Fine's life is on the upswing: he's just married a beautiful woman with a smart, attractive daughter who likes him, and all's well-until his wife dies and her ex demands custody of their daughter. D. W. Moffett, Tracy Pollan, Judith Hoag, Cloris Leachman, Noley Thornton. w. Peter Lefcourt, d. Tom Moore.

MELODRAMA: Death-Dealing with; Fathers Alone; Widowers; Fathers & Daughters; Custody Battles; TV Movies

Finger of Guilt, 1956, 95m, ★★–/$$, Ind/NA. A film director in England is followed and hounded by a girl who claims to have been his mistress and threatens to wreck his life. Richard Basehart, Mary Murphy, Mervyn Johns, Constance Cummings. w. Peer Howard, N-adap., Howard, *Pay the Piper*, d. Joseph Walton.

SUSPENSE: MYSTERY: Directors; Impostors; Mistresses; Fatal Attractions;

Ahead of its Time; Coulda Been Good; British Films
(Fatal Attraction; Kitten with a Whip)

Fingers, 1977, 90m, ★★★/$, Gala/Turner, R/V-B&G. A gangster's son is a sensitive pianist with aspirations of playing concert halls, but can he resist the pressure to "join the family business"? The result is tragic. Harvey Keitel, Tisa Farrow, Jim Brown, Marian Seldes, Danny Aiello. w. d. James Toback.

DRAMA: Black Comedy; Mob Stories; Pianists; Body Parts; Violence-Sudden; Curiosities; Cult Films; Hidden Gems; Overlooked at Release; Writer-Directors

Finian's Rainbow, 1968, 140m, ★★★/$$, WB/WB, G. An American traveler in Ireland steals a leprechaun's crock of gold and takes it back home. Then his short green friend shows up to reclaim his property. Fred Astaire, Petula Clark, Tommy Steele, Don Francks, Keenan Wynn, Barbara Hancock, Al Freeman Jr. w. P-adap. E. Y. Harburg, Fred Saidy, d. Francis Ford Coppola.

MUSICALS: Fantasy; Musical Fantasy; Magic; Finding Money/Valuables; Americans Abroad; Revenge; Ireland; Irish People; Leprechauns; Hidden Gems
(Brigadoon; Luck of the Irish)

Finishing School, 1934, 73m, ★★1/2/$$, RKO/Turner. A young girl learning how to be a society lady falls for an intern at the local hospital. Frances Dee, Ginger Rogers, Billie Burke, Bruce Cabot, John Halliday, Beulah Bondi. w. Wanda Tuchock, Laird Doyle, d. George Nicholls Jr.

MELODRAMA: ROMANCE: Rich People; Doctors; Romance-Class Conflict; Hospitals; Forgotten Films

Firecreek, 1968, 104m, ★★1/2/$, WB/WB, G. Gunmen on the loose terrorize a small western town, so the locals take charge. James Stewart, Henry Fonda, Inger Stevens, Gary Lockwood, Dean Jagger, Ed Begley, Jay C. Flippen, Jack Elam. w. Calvin Clements, d. Vincent McEveety.

WESTERNS: Gunfighters; Small-town Life; Vigilantes; Men in Conflict; Forgotten Films

The Firefly, 1937, 131m, ★★★/$$$, MGM/MGM-UA. During the Napoleonic War, a Spanish enchantress flirts with the sailors while singing her way into one of their hearts. Jeanette MacDonald, Allan Jones, Warren William, Billy Gilbert, Henry Daniell, George Zucco, Douglass Dumbrille. w. Frances Goodrich, Albert Hackett, Ogden Nash, (Opera)-adap. Otto Harbach, d. Robert Z. Leonard.

MUSICALS: MELODRAMA: ROMANCE: Romantic Drama; Musical Romance; Costume Drama; Musicals-Operettas (Bittersweet; The Chocolate Soldier)

Firefox, 1982, 136m, ★★★/$$$$, WB/WB, PG/V. A spy/pilot dressed as a businessman goes to Moscow to steal a top-secret new fighter plane. Clint Eastwood, Freddie Jones, David Huffman, Warren Clarke, Ronald Lacey, Kenneth Colley, Nigel Hawthorne. w. Alex Lasker, Wendell Willman, N-adap. Craig Thomas, d. Clint Eastwood.

ACTION: Pilots-Daredevil; Pilots-Military; Russians as Enemy; Thieves; Spies
(Iron Eagle; Top Gun; Heartbreak Ridge)

A Fire in the Sky, 1993, 11m, ★★★/$$$, Par/Par, PG-13/V-P-MN. Several forest workers witness the abduction of one of their co-workers, supposedly by a UFO. D.B. Sweeney, Peter Berg, Craig Sheffer, Henry Thomas. w. Tracy Torme, d. Robert Lieberman.

DRAMA: SCI-FI: MYSTERY: UFOs; True Stories; True or Not?; Gossip/Rumors; Small-town Life; Rural Life; Rednecks; Southwestern Life; Working Class; Ordinary People Stories; Missing Persons; Accused Unjustly; Amnesia; Flashbacks; Coulda Been Great; Female Screenwriters
(UFOs: UFOria; Close Encounters of the Third Kind; A Cry in the Dark)

The Fireman's Ball, 1967, 73m, ★★★/$, Barrandov-Col/Col. In a small Czech town, plans for a fireman's ball are constantly going awry despite the locals' avid interest in it. Jan Vostrcil, Josef Kolb, Josef Svet, Frantisek Debelka. w. Milos Forman, Ivan Passer, Jaroslav Papousek, d. Milos Forman. BFLFilm. Oscars: 1-0.

COMEDY: COMEDY DRAMA: FARCE: Slice of Life Stories; Communists; Small-town Life; Czech Films; Hidden Gems

The Fire Next Time, 1993, 195m, ★★1/2/$$, Ind/Cabin Fever. Global warming, acid rain, and other effects of pollution create an ecological catastrophe in the United States in the year 2017. A family tries to make the trek to Canada, where the atmosphere is supposed to be more bearable. Craig T. Nelson, Bonnie Bedelia, Juergen Prochnow, Richard Farnsworth, Justin Whalin, Charles Haid. w. James Henderson, d. Tom McLoughlin.

DRAMA: Apocalyptic Stories; Environmental Dilemmas; Nature-Back to; Family Drama; Escape Drama; Starting Over; TV Movies
(The Mosquito Coast)

Fire Over England, 1937, 92m, ★★★/$$$, London Films/Nos. A seagoing epic of the British navy protecting England's shores from the Spanish Armada under the command of Elizabeth I. Flora Robson, Laurence Olivier, Leslie Banks, Vivien Leigh, Raymond Massey, James Mason. w. Clemence Dane, Sergei Nolbandov, N-adap. A. E. W. Mason, d. William K. Howard.

DRAMA: ACTION: ADVENTURE: War Stories; Elizabethan Era; Queen Elizabeth; Costume Drama; Historical Drama; Swashbucklers; British Films; Forgotten Films
(Elizabeth and Essex)

Firepower, 1979, 104m, ★★/$, ITC-UA/PM Entertainment. A research chemist finds out that a large shipment of drugs is contaminated, but he's killed before he can expose the pharmaceutical company. His wife then takes up the cause, with an old flame who also happens to be a gangster. Sophia Loren, James Coburn, Anthony Franciosa, O. J. Simpson, Eli Wallach, Vincent Gardenia, Victor Mature, George Grizzard. w. Gerard Wilson, d. Michael Winner.

ACTION: SUSPENSE: Action Drama; Chase Stories; Trail of a Killer; Avenging Death of Someone; Widows; Drugs-Dealing Conspiracy; Corporation as Enemy; Good Premise Unfulfilled

Firestarter, 1984, 115m, ★★/$$, U/MCA-U, PG-13/V. When the government learns of a young girl with the telekenetic power to start fires, they seek her out to use her as a weapon. Drew Barrymore, George C. Scott, David Keith, Martin Sheen, Freddie Jones, Heather Locklear, Art Carney, Louise Fletcher, Moses Gunn. w. Stanley Mann, N-adap. Stephen King, d. Mark L. Lester.

HORROR: Fires; Child Protagonists; Girls; Psychics
(Wilder Napalm; A Pyromaniac's Love Story; Cat's Eye)

(Ed: A big bestseller burned out fast on celluloid)

Firstborn, 1985, 105m, ★★★/$$, Par/Par, R/P-S. Everything was fine with a mother (Teri Garr) and her two adolescent boys (Chris Collet, Corey Haim) until their father remarried and she started dating a drug dealer (Peter Weller) who begins to destroy their lives with the abusive love he offers her. Robert Downey Jr., Sarah Jessica Parker. w. Ron Koslow, d. Michael Apted.

DRAMA: MELODRAMA: Mothers Alone; Family Drama; Divorce; Marriage Drama; Ordinary People Stories; Abused Women; Drugs; Mothers & Sons; Suburban Life; Teenagers; Young Men; Coming of Age; Stepfathers; Parents vs. Children; Could Been Great; Child Protagonists
(The Stepfather; Flight of the Doves)

First Blood, 1982, 94m, ★★★/$$$, Carolco-Orion/Orion, R/EV-P. A Vietnam veteran and mercenary soldier gets cornered in his small California town and strikes back. Sylvester Stallone, Richard Crenna, Brian Dennehy, David Caruso, Jack Starrett. w. Michael Kozoll, William Sackheim, Sylvester Stallone, N-adap. David Marell, d. Ted Kotcheff.

ACTION: Vietnam War; Veterans-Vietnam; Mercenaries; Vigilantes; Revenge; Fighting the System

SEQUEL: Rambo, Rambo III
(Missing in Action; Uncommon Valor)

The First Deadly Sin, 1980, 112m, ★★/$, Filmways/Vestron, R/V. A cop doggedly pursues a crazed slasher, but his obsession leads him to neglect his wife, who's dying in the city hospital. Frank Sinatra, Faye Dunaway, David Dukes, George Coe, Brenda Vaccaro, Martin Gabel. w. Mann Rubin, N-adap. Lawrence Sanders, d. Brian G. Hutton.

DRAMA: Crime Drama; **MELODRAMA:** Trail of a Killer; Psycho Killers; Police Stories; Detective Stories; Detectives-Police; Death-Impending; Comas; Flops-Major; Coulda Been Good
(Contract on Cherry Street; The Detective)

(Ed: The usually great Dunaway literally sleeps her way through this one, and her personal costume designer gets credit for the bed clothes)

First Knight, 1995, 131m, ★★1/2/$$$, Col/Col, PG-13/V-S. When lovely Guinevere is threatened by the evil Malagant, it's up to Sir Lancelot to save the day, but without the advent of magic, etc., in this version, unless the magic is love. Sean Connery, Richard Gere, Julia Ormond, Ben Cross, Sir John Gielgud, Liam Cunningham. w. William Nicholson, d. Jerry Zucker.

ADVENTURE: ROMANCE: Romantic Drama; Mean Men; Protecting Someone; Camelot Stories; Middle Ages; Revisionist Films; England
(Excalibur; Camelot; Robin and Marian)

First Love, 1939, 84m, ★★★/$$$, U/MCA-U. When her parents die, a teenage girl is taken in by her uncle and falls in love with the boy next door, the son of a prominent businessman. Deanna Durbin, Robert Stack, Eugene Pallette, Helen Parrish. w. Bruce Manning, Lionel House, d. Henry Koster.

MUSICALS: ROMANCE: Romantic Comedy; Musical Romance; Music Movies; Girls; Love-First; Orphans; Tearjerkers; Forgotten Films
(Mad About Music; Meet Me in St. Louis)

First Monday in October, 1981, 99m, ★★★/$$, Par/Par, PG/P. A comical, fictional account of the first woman appointed to the Supreme Court and the troubles she encounters with the old fogie men there in court and on the tennis court, for instance. Jill Clayburgh, Walter Matthau, Barnard Hughes, Jan Sterling, James Stephens. w. P-adap. Jerome Lawrence, Robert E. Lee, d. Ronald Neame.

SATIRE: COMEDY DRAMA: Political Satire; Judges; Supreme Court; Female Among Males; Battle of the Sexes; Womens' Rights; Washington D.C.; Generation Gap; Coulda Been Great; Good Premise Unfulfilled; Female Protagonists
(Kisses for My President; Semi-Tough)

First Name: Carmen, 1983, 95m, ★★/$, Ind/Connoisseur, Ingram, R/S-FFN-MFN. A contemporary Carmen robs banks to fund her terrorist group while posing as a filmmaker. During one bank heist, a guard is so taken with her that he follows her out, offering no resistance. Maruschka Detmers, Jacques Bonaffe, Jean-Luc Godard, Myriem Roussel, Christopher Odent. w. d. Jean-Luc Godard.

DRAMA: ROMANCE: Erotic Drama; Avant-Garde Films; Art Films; French Films; Young People; Beautiful People; Writer-Directors

The First Nudie Musical, 1975, 93m, ★★/$, Ind/Media. A failing Broadway producer puts on a 30s-style revue, but with a naked cast, in a desperate pitch for the lost audience. Cindy Williams, Stephen Nathan, Diana Canova, Bruce Kimmel. d. Mark Haggard.

MUSICALS: COMEDY: Musical Comedy; Spoofs-Musical; Theater Life; Putting on a Show; Nudists; Erotic Comedy; Cult Films; Curiosities
(Move; The Pornographers; Oh, Calcutta [stage taping])

The First of the Few (Spitfire), 1942, 117m, ★★1/2/$$, Melbourne-NA. The story of the invention of the spitfire jet fighter at the advent of World War II. Leslie Howard, David Niven, Rosamund John, Roland Culver. w. Anatole de Grunwald, Miles Malleson, Henry C. James, Katherine Strueby, d. Leslie Howard.

DRAMA: War Stories; World War II Stories; Pilots-Military; British Films; Female Screenwriters

The First Power, 1990, 98m, ★1/2/$, Col/Col, R/EV-B&G. A cop sensitive to the supernatural tracks down a serial killer who turns out not to be a live human being. Lou Diamond Phillips, Tracy Griffith, Jeff Kober, Mykel T. Williamson, Elizabeth Arlen. w. d. Robert Resnikoff.

SUSPENSE: Police Stories; Detective Stories; Detectives-Police; Serial Killers; Trail of a Killer; Supernatural Danger; Sataniam; Occult Psychics; Good Premise Unfulfilled; Writer-Directors
(The Prophecy; Seven; Angel Heart)

The First Time, 1968, 90m, ★★/$, UA/Fox, R/S. A group of teenage boys dream of sex and meet a real live girl with amnesia who thinks she's a prostitute. Jacqueline Bisset, Wes Stern, Rick Kelman, Wink Roberts, Sharon Acker. w. Jo Heims, Roger Smith, d. James Nielson.

COMEDY DRAMA: Erotic Comedy; Teenagers; Teenage Movies; Love-First; Virgins; Sexy Women; Prostitutes; Identities-Mistaken; Amnesia; Romance-Triangles; Men Fighting over Women; Coulda Been Good; Good Premise Unfulfilled
(Summer of '42; Class; The Grasshopper)

A Fish Called Wanda, 1988, 114m, ★★★★/$$$$, MGM/MGM-UA, PG-13/S-P. Americans and Brits team for a jewel heist, but a little old lady was a witness

and their leader is caught after he's hidden the gems, so the girl of the group (Jamie Lee Curtis) must romance the jewels' whereabouts from the silent leader's lawyer (John Cleese) while attempts are made to kill the old lady witness. Kevin Kline (**BSActor**), Michael Palin, Maria Aitken. w. John Cleese (**BOScr**), d. Charles Crichton (**BDirector**). Oscars: 3-1.

COMEDY: Capers; Heist Stories; Black Comedy; Action Comedy; **FARCE:** Comedy of Errors; Screwball Comedy; Chase Stories; Murder-Comic Attempts; Misunderstandings; Lawyers; Romance-Triangles; Simple Minds; Smart vs. Dumb; Crime Pays; Criminals-Stupid; Monty Pythoners; Sleeper Hits; British Films
(The Hot Rock; The Lavender Hill Mob; The Lady Killers; The Italian Job; Topkapi!)

The Fisher King, 1991, 135m, ★★★1/2/$$$, Tri-Star/Col-Tri, R/S-P-MN. A shock-jock DJ (Jeff Bridges) may have goaded a man into a killing spree, and a few years later, he learns the repercussions of that when he runs into a homeless man (Robin Williams). Mercedes Ruehl (**BSActress**). w. Richard LaGravenese (**BOScr**), d. Terry Gilliam. Oscars: 2-1.

DRAMA: Social Drama; Friendships-Male; Homeless People; Redemption; Starting Over; Saving Someone; Radio Life; Neurotic People; New York Life; Mental Illness; Nervous Breakdowns; Murderers-Mass; Guilty Conscience; Romance-Reluctant; Free Spirits
(The Saint of Fort Washington; A Fine Madness)

The Fish That Saved Pittsburgh, 1979, 104m, ★★/$, UA/Lorimar, WB, PG. The zodiac saves a losing Pittsburgh team when the manager starts hiring only Pisces. Julius Erving, Jonathan Winters, Meadowlark Lemon, Jack Kehoe, M. Emmet Walsh, Stockard Channing, Flip Wilson. w. Jaison Starkes, Edmond Stevens, d. Gilbert Moses.

COMEDY: Basketball; Sports Movies; Camp; Curiosities; 1970s

F.I.S.T., 1978, 145m, ★★1/2/$$, UA/CBS-Fox, R/V-P. An idealistic workman rises to become union boss and has to resist corrupting influences. Sylvester Stallone, Rod Steiger, Peter Boyle, Melinda Dillon, David Huffman, Tony Lo Bianco, Peter

Donat. w. Joe Eszterhas, Sylvester Stallone, d. Norman Jewison.

DRAMA: Corruption; Ethics; Working Class; Unions; Power-Rise to; Mob Stories; New York Life
(All the King's Men; Hoffa; On the Waterfront)
(Ed: One of Stallone's more thoughtful ventures, but also one of his least financially successful)

A Fistful of Dollars, 1964, 100m, ★★★/$$$, UA/CBS-Fox, V. In a corrupt Mexican town, all rats scatter as a mysterious gunman comes to town to clean things up. Clint Eastwood, Gian Maria Volonte, Marianne Koch. w. Sergio Leone, Duccio Tessari, d. Sergio Leone.
WESTERNS: Drifters; Westerns-Neo; Westerns-Spaghetti; New in Town; Mexico; Sleeper Hits; Vigilantes
SEQUELS: For a Few Dollars More; The Good, the Bad, and the Ugly.
(For a Few Dollars More; The Good, the Bad, and the Ugly; Hang 'em High)
(Ed: The film that started spaghetti westerns and launched Eastwood's and Leone's film careers)

A Fistful of Dynamite (*Duck, You Sucker*), 1971, 150m, ★★1/2/$, UA/MGM-UA. In turn of the century Mexico, an explosives expert for the IRA and a local outlaw join forces to rob a bank. Rod Steiger, James Coburn, Romolo Valli, Maria Monti. w. d. Sergio Leone.
WESTERNS: Heist Stories; Bank Robberies; Black Comedy; Mexico; Flops-Major; Coulda Been Good; Writer-Directors

Fitzcarraldo, 1982, 158m, ★★★/$, WB/WB. In the early 1900s, a wealthy and quirky Irishman has an obsessive and ridiculous, yet somehow heroic, quest to build an opera house in the jungles of Peru, but has to drag his large boat across land to get there. Klaus Kinski, Claudia Cardinale, Jose Lewgoy, Paul Hittscher. w. d. Werner Herzog.
ADVENTURE: DRAMA: Journies; Opera; Eccentric People; Mental Illness; Ships; Nightmare Journies; Amazon River; South America; Obsessions; River Trauma; Flops-Major; Allegorical Stories; Irish People; Writer-Directors
(Burden of Dreams; Sorcerer)

Fitzwilly, 1967, 102m, ★★1/2/$$, UA/NA. A rich woman has actually spent most of her inheritance, but her butler, Fitzwilly, hides this fact from her and

assembles the house staff into a criminal organization to fund her lifestyle. Dick Van Dyke, Edith Evans, Barbara Feldon, John McGiver, Harry Townes, Norman Fell, Cecil Kellaway, Sam Waterston. w. Isobel Lennart, N-adap. Poyntz Tyler (*A Garden of Cucumbers*), d. Delbert Mann.
COMEDY: COMEDY DRAMA: Servants; Elderly Women; Riches to Rags; Mob Stories; Mob Comedy; Good Premise Unfulfilled; Female Screenwriters
(Ed: A cute idea that grows old quickly)

Five Came Back, 1939, 75m, ★★★/$$, RKO/Turner. When they crashland in the jungle, ten people must run from head-hunters and their plane now will only carry five. Chester Morris, Lucille Ball, C. Aubrey Smith, Elizabeth Risdon, Wendy Barrie, John Carradine, Joseph Calleia, Allen Jenkins, Kent Taylor, Patric Knowles. w. Jerry Cady, Dalton Trumbo, Nathanael West, d. John Farrow.
DRAMA: ADVENTURE: Airplane Crashes; Survival Drama; Journies; Nightmare Journies; Murders/Deaths-One by One; Cannibalism; Africa; Jungle Life; Cult Films; Hidden Gems; Forgotten Films
REMAKE: Back to Eternity
(Back to Eternity; Sands of Kalahari; Flight of the Phoenix)

Five Card Stud, 1968, 103m, ★★1/2/$$, Par/Par, PG. A lynched man takes his revenge slowly on the five members of his lynching party. Dean Martin, Robert Mitchum, Inger Stevens, McDowell, Katherine Justice, John Anderson, Yaphet Kotto. w. Marguerite Roberts, N-adap. Ray Gaulden, d. Henry Hathaway.
WESTERNS: Westerns-Revenge; Revenge; Lynchings; Dead-Back from the; Convict's Revenge
(Hang 'em High; Cape Fear)

Five Corners, 1988, 93m, ★★★1/2/$, Handmade-Ind/MGM-UA, R/P-S-V. In early 60s New Jersey, old friends reunite after high school: one of them works for civil rights and one of them is a dangerous psychopath, which may lead to tragedy for everyone. Jodie Foster, Tim Robbins, Todd Graff, John Turturro. w. John Patrick Shanley, d. Tony Bill.
DRAMA: TRAGEDY: COMEDY DRAMA: Ensemble Films; Slice of Life Stories; Reunions; Friendships-Male; Rape/Rapists; Women in Jeopardy; New York Life; Inner City Life; 1960s; Hunchbacks; Time Capsules; Hidden Gems

(A Bronx Tale; Moonstruck; The Hunchback of Notre Dame; The Lords of Flatbush)
(Ed: Fascinating, but not as dense with detail and happenings as it could have been)

Five Days One Summer, 1982, 108m, ★★1/2/$, WB/WB, PG. In the thirties in the Alps, a Scottish doctor takes his mistress mountain climbing. Unfortunately for him, she falls in love with the younger, more handsome guide. Sean Connery, Betsy Brantley, Lambert Wilson, Jennifer Hilary, Isabel Dean, Anna Massey. w. Michael Austin, SS-adap. Kay Boyle (*Maiden Maiden*), d. Fred Zinnemann.
DRAMA: ROMANCE: ADVENTURE: Romantic Adventure; Alps; Mountain Climbing; Romance-Triangles; Doctors; Mistresses; Cheating Women; Scenery-Outstanding; Overlooked at Release
(Ed: About all the release time it got or deserved)

Five Easy Pieces, 1970, 98m, ★★★★/$$$, Columbia/RCA-Col, R/P. A young, disillusioned, angry young man (Jack Nicholson, BActor) wants to give it all up before he's even started, and the one thing he can do with consistency is play five simple piano pieces. Karen Black (BSActress), Susan Anspach, Lois Smith, Fannie Flagg, Sally Struthers, Toni Basil. w. Adrien Joyce (Carol Eastman) (BOScr), d. Bob Rafelson. (BDirector). BPicture. Oscars: 5-0.
DRAMA: Social Drama; Character Studies; Road Movies; Anti-Establishment Films; Young Men-Angry; Young Men; Alienation; Working Class; Oil People; Pianists; Quiet Little Films; Sleeper Hits; Female Screenwriters
(Easy Rider; East of Eden; One Flew Over the Cuckoo's Nest; Look Back in Anger)

Five Fingers, 1952, 108m, ★★★/$$, 20th/Fox. A true story of World War II involving military secrets of the British and double agents in Turkey working for the Germans. James Mason, Danielle Darrieux, Michael Rennie, Walter Hampden, Oscar Karlweis. w. Michael Wilson (BScr), NF-adap L. C. Moyzich (*Operation Cicero*), d. Joseph L. Mankiewicz (BDirector). Oscars: 2-0.
SUSPENSE: Spy Films; Spies; World War II Stories; Double Crossings; Traitors; Nazi Stories; Middle East; True Stories; Hidden Gems; Forgotten Films; Faded Hits
(The Tenth Man; The Third Man)

Five Graves to Cairo, 1943, 96m, ★★★1/2/$$, Par/NA, AMC. The British march on Rommel in North Africa and send secret missions to destroy his war chest. Franchot Tone, Anne Baxter, Erich Von Stroheim, Akim Tamiroff, Peter Van Eyck, Miles Mander. w. Charles Brackett, Billy Wilder, P-adap. Lajos Biro, d. Billy Wilder. BB&WArt, BEdit, BB&WCin. Oscars: 3-0.
SUSPENSE: ADVENTURE: Spy Films; Spies; Sabotage; War Stories; World War II Stories; Desert Settings; Middle East; Forgotten Films; Hidden Gems; International Casts; Africa
(Raid on Rommel; The Desert Fox)
The Five Heartbeats, 1991, 121m, ★★1/2/$$, 20th/Fox, PG/P. A black pop group rises and falls with the trends of the 60s and 70s, all the while dealing with racism and the usual showbiz sleaze. Robert Townsend, Michael Wright, Leon, Harry J. Lennix, Tico Wells. w. Robert Townsend, Kennan Ivory Wayans, d. Robert Townsend.
COMEDY DRAMA: Music Movies; Singers; Rock Bands; Musicians; Black Men; Ensembles-Male; Fame-Rise to; Biographies-Fictional; Black Screenwriters; Black Directors; 1960s; Nostalgia; Coulda Been Great
(Dreamgirls [musical]; The Hollywood Shuffle)
Five Miles to Midnight, 1962, 110m, ★★★/$$, UA/NA. A man who is assumed to be dead returns to his understandably shaken wife, forcing her to go along with the story and collect on his insurance policy. Sophia Loren, Anthony Perkins, Gig Young, Jean-Pierre Aumont, Yolande Turner. w. Peter Viertel, d. Anatole Litvak.
SUSPENSE: Romance-Dangerous; Dead-Back from the; Insurance Scams; Con Artists; Death-Faked; Hidden Gems; Coulda Been Great; Forgotten Films
(Shattered; Vertigo; Buried Alive)
Five Million Years to Earth (*Quartermass and the Pit*), 1967, 97m, ★★★/$$, Hammer/NA. Archaeologists digging under London discover magical skulls and people start dying mysteriously. Andrew Keir, James Donald, Barbara Shelley, Julian Glover, Duncan Lamont. w., TV-adap. Nigel Kneale, d. Roy Ward Baker.
SUSPENSE: HORROR: Archaeologists; Curses; MURDER: Murders-One by One; Satan; British Films

SEQUEL TO: The Enemy Above, The Quatermass Experiment
The Five Pennies, 1959, 117m, ★★1/2/$$$, Par/Par. Brass player Red Nichols' rise to fame in the jazz world. Danny Kaye, Barbara Bel Geddes, Louis Armstrong, Bob Crosby, Harry Guardino, Tuesday Weld, Ray Anthony. w. Jack Rose, Melville Shavelson, d. Melville Shavelson, BCCin, BMScore, BOSong. Oscars: 3-0.
DRAMA: Biographies; Musicians; Jazz Life; Fame-Rise to; Character Studies; Nostalgia; Faded Hits
Five Star Final, 1931, 89m, ★★★/$$$, WB/NA. In its ruthless search for the big scoop, a big city newspaper brings heartache into the lives of the subjects of its stories, but it all leads to inevitable repercussions. Edward G. Robinson, H. B. Warner, Marian Marsh, Anthony Bushell, George E. Stone, Ona Munson, Aline MacMahon, Boris Karloff. w. Robert Lord, Byron Morgan, P-adap. Louis Weitzenkorn, d. Mervyn Le Roy.
DRAMA: MELODRAMA: TRAGEDY: Ethics; Greed; Newspapers; Journalists; Forgotten Films; Hidden Gems; Faded Hits
(The Front Page; The Paper)
The Five Thousand Fingers of Doctor T, 1953, 88m, ★★★/$$, Col/Col. A boy who hates his oppressive piano teacher dreams of a prisonlike music camp where he and four hundred ninety-nine other boys are forced by his evil teacher to play on a huge piano. Hans Conried, Tommy Rettig, Peter Lind Hayes, Mary Healy. w. Dr. Seuss (Theodore Geisel), Alan Scott, d. Roy Rowland. BOScore. Oscars: 1-0.
Fantasy; SCI-FI: Boys; Oppression; Pianists; Surrealism; Dreams; Nightmares; Teachers & Students; Child Protagonists; Cult Films; Hidden Gems; Coulda Been Great
The Fixer, 1968, 130m, ★★★/$$, MGM/MGM-UA, R/S. In Tsarist Russia, a Jewish man hiding the fact acts as a go-between for criminal types and is always the one getting caught. When he's imprisoned without a trial, he finally realizes the value of his tribal identification as he becomes a Jewish folk hero. Alan Bates (BActor), Dirk Bogarde, Georgia Brown, Jack Gilford, Hugh Griffith, Ian Holm. w. Dalton Trumbo, N-adap. Bernard

Malamud, d. John Frankenheimer. Oscars: 1-0.
DRAMA: Social Drama; Character Studies; Oppression; Jewish People; Anti-Semitism; Accused Unjustly; Framed?; Heroes-Unwitting; Classic Literary Adaptations; Russia; Coulda Been Great; Forgotten Films
(King of Hearts; The Projectionist; Olivier, Olivier)
The Flame and the Arrow, 1950, 88m, ★★★/$$$, WB/WB. A Robin Hood–style swashbuckling adventurer fights tyranny in medieval Italy. Burt Lancaster, Virginia Mayo, Robert Douglas, Aline MacMahon, Frank Allenby, Nick Cravat. w. Waldo Salt, d. Jacques Tourneur. BCCin, BOScore. Oscars: 2-0.
ADVENTURE: ACTION: Action Comedy; Robin Hood Stories; Italy; Swashbucklers; Costume Drama; Rebels; Free Spirits; Forgotten Films; Hidden Gems
(The Crimson Pirate; The Black Rose)
The Flame of New Orleans, 1941, 79m, ★★1/2/$$$, U/NA. A German vixen settles to wreak havoc in the Crescent City. Marlene Dietrich, Roland Young, Bruce Cabot, Mischa Auer, Andy Devine, Frank Jenks, Eddie Quillan, Franklin Pangborn. w. Norman Krasna, d. Rene Clair.
MELODRAMA: COMEDY DRAMA: ROMANCE: Sexy Women; Free Spirits; New Orleans
(Desire; Blue Angel; Destry Rides Again)
Flame of the Barbary Coast, 1945, 97m, ★★★/$$$, Republic/Media. A cowboy traveling in San Francisco gets ensnared by a local chanteuse, but will romance weather the big quake? John Wayne, Ann Dvorak, Joseph Schildkraut, William Frawley. w. Borden Chase, d. Joseph Kane. BOScore. Oscars: 1-0.
MELODRAMA: ROMANCE: COMEDY DRAMA: Romance-Triangles; Romance-Reluctant; Singers; Cowboys; San Francisco; Earthquakes
(San Francisco; The Barbary Coast)
Flame Over India, 1959, 129m, ★★★/$$$, AA/Sultan. An young Indian prince and his British military escort make a dangerous journey through India by train. Kenneth More, Lauren Bacall, Herbert Lom, Ursula Jeans, Wilfrid Hyde White. w. Robin Estridge, d. J. Lee Thompson.

DRAMA: ADVENTURE: Trains; India; Princes; Journies
(A Passage to India; Bhowani Junction)
Flaming Star, 1960, 92m, ★★½/$$$, 20th/CBS-Fox. A half-breed is caught in the middle of conflicting sides of the Civil War within his own family. Elvis Presley, Dolores del Rio, Steve Forrest, Barbara Eden, John McIntire. w. Clair Huffaker, Nunnally Johnson, d. Don Siegel.
ACTION: WESTERNS: War Stories; Civil War; Indians-American; Southerns; Race Relations; Family Drama; Feuds; Curiosities
(King Creole)
The Flamingo Kid, 1984, 100m, ★★★/$$, 20th/CBS-Fox, PG/S. A good-looking but poor teenager tries to fit in with the rich kids he meets working at a beach club, especially to impress a special girl. Matt Dillon, Richard Crenna, Hector Elizondo, Jessica Walter, Fisher Stevens. w. Neal Marshall, Garry Marshall, d. Garry Marshall.
COMEDY DRAMA: ROMANCE: Romantic Comedy; Romance-Class Conflict; Coming of Age; Young Men; Teenagers; New York Life; Suburban Life; Rich vs. Poor; Country Club Life; Nostalgia
(A Night in the Life of Jimmy Reardon; Baby, It's You)
Flamingo Road, 1949, 94m, ★★★/$$$, WB/WB. A dancer with a carnival that sets up camp in a small Southern town ends up getting involved in politics through her liasons with local politicians. Joan Crawford, David Brian, Sidney Greenstreet, Zachary Scott, Gladys George, Virginia Huston, Fred Clark. w., N-adap. Robert Wilder, d. Michael Curtiz.
MELODRAMA: ROMANCE: Romantic Drama; Women in Conflict; Florida Dancers; New in Town; Southerns; Small-town Life; Small-town Scandals; Scandals; Sexy Women; Bimbos; Politicians; Political Corruption; Camp
REMAKE: TV Series (NBC, 1981)
(Queen Bee; Ada; Harriet Craig)
Flare Up, 1969, 98m, ★★/$, MGM/NA. After a possessive, jealous man's wife turns up dead, her friends are next in line because he holds them responsible for putting ideas in her head. Raquel Welch, James Stacy, Luke Askew, Don Chastain, Ron Rifkin. w. Mark Rodgers, d. James Neilson.

SUSPENSE: MURDER: Murder of Spouse; Dangerous Spouses; Revenge; Neighbors-Troublesome; Detective Stories; Detectives-Amateur; Detectives-Female; Sexy Women; Forgotten Films; Coulda Been Good; Female Protagonists
(Sudden Fear; Lady in Cement)
The Flash, 1990, 94m, ★★/$$, WB/WB. A forensic scientist is involved in a bizarre accident involving volatile chemicals and an opportune lightning strike, after which he becomes a superhero called The Flash, ready to use his new powers to fight crime on the streets of Central City. John Wesley Shipp, Amanda Pays, Michael Nader.
ACTION: SCI-FI: Comic Heroes; Vigilantes; **CHILDREN'S:** TV Movies
Flashback, 1989, 108m, ★★/$, Par/Par, PG/P. A drugged-out hippie hiding out in Latin America since the 60s gets a dose of culture shock when he's brought back to 80s America by a young FBI agent, who gets a bit of culture shock himself. Dennis Hopper, Kiefer Sutherland, Carol Kane, Cliff DeYoung, Paul Dooley, Michael McKean, Richard Masur, d. Franco Amurri.
COMEDY: Action Comedy; Chase Stories; FBI Agents; Hippies; Time Sleepers; Good Premise Unfulfilled
(Rude Awakening; Midnight Run)
Flashdance, 1983, 98m, ★★★/$$$$, Par/Par, R/S-P. In Pittsburgh, a female welder practices ballet every night and dreams of being a star dancer. Jennifer Beals, Michael Nouri, Lilia Skala, Sunny Johnson, Kyle T. Heffner, Belinda Bauer. w. Tom Hedley, Joe Eszterhas, d. Adrian Lyne. **BOSong**, "Flash-dance," BOSong, "Maniac," BCin, BEdit. Oscars: 4-1.
MELODRAMA: ROMANCE: Dance Movies; Dancers; Strippers; Music Movies; Female Protagonists; Women Proving Themselves; Working Class; Sexy Women; Sleeper Hits; Blockbusters
Flash Gordon, 1980, 115m, ★★/$$, DEG-U/MCA-U, PG/S-V. On the planet Mongo, Flash Gordon and his pals must escape the clutches of the evil Emperor Ming. Sam J. Jones, Melody Anderson, Topol, Max Von Sydow, Timothy Dalton, Brian Blessed, Peter Wyngarde. w. Lorenzo Semple Jr., (Comic-strip)-adap. Alex Raymond, d. Michael Hodges.
ACTION: Outer Space Movies; **SCI-FI:** Comic Heroes; Good vs. Evil; Sexy Men;

Sexy Women; Camp; Unintentionally Funny; Flops-Major
(Buck Rogers; Flesh Gordon)
Flashpoint, 1985, 94m, ★★/$, HBO-Tri-Star/HBO, PG-13/V-P. A group of corrupt border patrol guards at Canada find a stash of loot and decide to abscond with it. Kris Kristofferson, Treat Williams, Rip Torn, Kevin Conway. w. Dennis Shryack, Michael Butler, N-adap. George La Fountaine, d. William Tannen.
ACTION: Heist Stories; Police Corruption; Police Stories; Lucky People; Finding Money/Valuables; Canada
Flatliners, 1990, 114m, ★★★/$$$$, Col/Tri-Col, PG/S-P. A group of medical students in Chicago supervise each others' "clinical deaths" (when all life signs are flat on the EKG, hence the title). Their near-death experiences begin affecting their "normal" lives as well. Kiefer Sutherland, Julia Roberts, Kevin Bacon, William Baldwin, Oliver Platt, Kimberly Scott. w. Peter Filardi, d. Joel Schumacher.
DRAMA: SCI-FI: ADVENTURE: Scientists; Doctors; Medical School; Experiments; Dead-Back from the; Psychological Drama; Psychological Thriller
(Altered States)
A Flea in Her Ear, 1968, 94m, ★★★/$$, 20th/NA. A bed-hopping French farce set at the Hotel Coq d'Or where wives are trying to find out what their husbands are doing. Rex Harrison, Rachel Roberts, Rosemary Harris, Louis Jourdan, John Williams. w. John Mortimer, P-adap. George Feydeau (*La Puce a l'Oreille*), d. Jacques Charon.
COMEDY: FARCE: Farce-Bedroom; Marriage Comedy; Misunderstandings; Mix-Ups; Hotels; Cheating Men; Paris; Classic Literary Adaptations; Coulda Been Great
(Hotel Paradiso; The Honey Pot)
Flesh, see "Andy Warhol's Flesh"
Flesh and Blood, 1951, 102m, ★★½/$, B-L/NA. An inherited mental quirk causes the deterioration of a Scottish family. Richard Todd, Glynis Johns, Joan Greenwood, Andre Morell, Ursula Howells, Freda Jackson. w. Anatole de Grunwald, P-adap. James Birdie (*A Sleeping Clergyman*), d. Anthony Kimmins.
DRAMA: MELODRAMA: Psychological Drama; Mental Illness; Scotland; British Films; Forgotten Films

Flesh and Blood, 1985, 126m, ★★1/2/$, Orion/Orion, R/ES-FFN-MN-B&G. A sword-and-sorcery story in which a princess bride is kidnapped by an evil knight who forces himself on her. She eventually falls for this brute and sours on her promised groom. Rutger Hauer, Jennifer Jason Leigh, Tom Burlinson, Jack Thompson. w. Gerard Soeteman, Paul Verhoeven, d. Paul Verhoeven.
ACTION: Erotic Drama; Rape/Rapists; **ROMANCE:** Romance-Reluctant; Kidnappings; Kidnappers-Sympathizing with; Medieval Times; Sword & Sorcery (The Name of the Rose; Ladyhawke)

Flesh and Bone, 1993, 127m, ★★/$, Par/Par, R/S-V. A mysterious vending machine salesman enters the life of a West Texas woman and it later appears they've met before, under horrendous circumstances. Dennis Quaid, Meg Ryan, James Caan, Gwyneth Paltrow, Scott Wilson, Christopher Rydell. w. d. Steven Kloves.
DRAMA: MYSTERY: MURDER: MURDER MYSTERY: Flashbacks; Nightmares; Incest; Southwestern Life; **ROMANCE:** Writer-Directors; Flops-Major
(Fool for Love; Les Enfants Terribles; D.O.A. [1988])
(Ed: Boring to the bone)

Flesh and the Devil, 1926, 109m, ★★★/$$$$, MGM/MGM-UA, B&W, silent. Three men vie for the affections of a femme fatale who plays with their affections but ends up getting burned herself. Greta Garbo, John Gilbert, Lars Hanson, Marc McDermott, Barbara Kent. w. Benjamin Glazer, N-adap. Hermann Sudermann *(The Undying Past)*, d. Clarence Brown.
MELODRAMA: ROMANCE: Romantic Drama; Romance-Triangles; Men Fighting over Women; Sexy Women; Dose of Own Medicine-Given
(Romance; Love; Blue Angel; Desire)

Flesh Gordon, 1972, 70m, ★★/$$$, Ind/Media, R/ES-FFN-MFN. A "nudie-cutie" take-off on the popular science-fiction serial from the thirties. Jason Williams, Suzanne Fields, Joseph Hudgins, John Hoyt, Howard Zieff, Michael Benveniste, Candy Samples. d. Mike Light.
SCI-FI: Spoofs-Sci-Fi; Fantasy; Erotic Comedy; Comic Heroes; Cult Films
(Flash Gordon; The First Nudie Musical)

The Flesh of the Orchid, 1974, 100m, ★★1/2/$, Ind/NA. A greedy woman convinces her family to put her wealthy niece in a mental institution in order to handle her money, but the niece escapes with a man marked for death. Charlotte Rampling, Bruno Cremer, Edwige Feuillere, Alida Valli, Hans Christian Blech. w. Jean-Claude Carriere, Patrice Chereau, N-adap. James Hadley Chase, d. Patrice Chereau.
SUSPENSE: Psychological Thriller; Mob Stories; Mental Illness; Asylums; Committed-Wrongly; Hit Men; Fugitives from the Mob; Greed; Inheritances at Stake; French Films; Forgotten Films; Good Premise Unfulfilled; Female Protagonists
(Suddenly, Last Summer)

Fletch, 1985, 96m, ★★1/2/$$$, U/MCA-U, PG/P-V-S. A journalist who enjoys going undercover gets a little overzealous in his pursuit of a notorious criminal, winding up in hot water but with a babe in tow. Chevy Chase, Dana Wheeler-Nicholson, Tim Matheson, Joe Don Baker, Kenneth Mars, M. Emmett Walsh. w. Andrew Bergman, N-adap. Gregory McDonald, d. Michael Ritchie.
COMEDY DRAMA: Action Comedy; Detective Stories; Spoofs-Detective; Journalists; Journalists as Detectives; Undercover; Fools-Bumbling; Coulda Been Good
SEQUEL: Fletch Lives.
(Dead Men Don't Wear Plaid; Who's Harry Crumb?)

Fletch Lives, 1989, 95m, ★★★/$$$, U/MCA-U, PG-13/P-S. The reporter from the first film inherits an estate down South and immediately steps into the middle of another mystery involving Southern belles and corrupt TV preachers. Chevy Chase, Hal Holbrook, Julianne Phillips, Randall "Tex" Cobb, Cleavon Little. w. Leon Capetanos, d. Michael Ritchie.
COMEDY DRAMA: COMEDY: Action Comedy; Detective Stories; Spoofs-Detective; Comedy-Slapstick; Journalists; Journalists as Detectives; Undercover; Fools-Bumbling; Southerns; Plantation Life; Preachers; Coulda Been Good
SEQUEL TO: Fletch
COMIC FLIPSIDE TO: The Drowning Pool
(Ed: Better than the first and surprisingly so)

Flight of the Doves, 1971, 101m, ★★1/2/$, Col/NA. When their stepfather becomes oppressively tyrannical, two children, heirs to a great fortune, run away to their grandmother, but are pursued by an avaricious uncle after their inheritance. Ron Moody, Dorothy McGuire, Helen Raye, Jack Wild, Stanley Holloway. w. Frank Gabrielson, Ralph Nelson, N-adap. Walter Macken, d. Ralph Nelson.
DRAMA: SUSPENSE: MURDER: Murder of Spouse; Chase Movies; Stalkers; Inheritances at Stake; Evil Men; Stepfathers; Runaways; Elderly Women; Children-Adopted; Hiding Out; Child Protagonists; British Films; Ireland
REMAKE/RETREAD: Night of the Hunter
(Cape Fear; Radio Flyer; Firstborn)

Flight of the Intruder, 1991, 113m, ★★/$, Par/Par, PG-13/V-P. A fictionalized account of the bombing of Hanoi during the Vietnam war. Danny Glover, Willem Dafoe, Brad Johnson, Rosanna Arquette, Tom Sizemore, J. Kenneth Campbell. w. Robert Dillon, David Shaber, N-adap. Stephen Coonts, d. John Milius.
ACTION: War Stories; Vietnam War; Pilots-Military; War at Sea; Flops-Major
(The Firebirds; Bat 21; Air America)

Flight of the Navigator, 1986, 90m, ★★1/2/$, Disney/Disney, PG. A 12-year-old boy, missing for eight years, suddenly returns out of the blue without having grown older. He explains to his family and friends that he was abducted by aliens. Joey Cramer, Veronica Cartwright, Cliff De Young, Sarah Jessica Parker, Matt Adler, Howard Hesseman, Paul Mall (Paul Reubens). w. Michael Burton, Matt Macmanus, Mark H. Baker, d. Randal Kleiser.
SCI-FI: Fantasy; **CHILDREN'S: FAMILY: ACTION:** Action Comedy; Disney Comedy; Aliens-Outer Space, Good; UFOs; Kidnappings; Missing Children; Dead-Back from the; Good Premise Unfulfilled; Could Been Good

The Flight of the Phoenix, 1965, 149m, ★★★/$$$, 20th/Fox. When their airplane crash-lands in the desert, the passengers who survive are left to fight the elements and each other as they try to rebuild their plane. James Stewart, Richard Attenborough, Hardy Kruger, Peter Finch, Dan Duryea, Ernest

Borgnine, George Kennedy, Christian Marquand, Ian Bannen (BSActor). w. Lukas Heller, N-adap. Elleston Trevor, d. Robert Aldrich. BEdit. Oscars: 2-0.

DRAMA: ADVENTURE: Airplane Crashes; Survival Drama; Journies; Nightmare Journies; Desert Settings; Power Struggles; Ensemble Films; Ensembles-Male; Hidden Gems
(Sands of Kalahari; Five Came Back; Back to Eternity)

The Flim Flam Man, 1967, 104m, ★★★/$$, 20th/Fox. An army man goes AWOL and teams up with a con man to take the residents of their small town. George C. Scott, Michael Sarrazin, Sue Lyon, Harry Morgan, Jack Albertson, Alice Ghostley. w. William Rose, N-adap. Guy Owen, d. Irvin Kershner.

COMEDY DRAMA: Hiding Out; Con Artists; Chase Stories; Ordinary People Stories; New in Town; Soldiers; Small-town Life; Fugitives from the Law; Coulda Been Great; Quiet Little Films; Hidden Gems

The Flintstones, 1994, 92m, ★★/$$$$$, U/MCA-U, PG. The "prehistoric family" from the famed cartoon sitcom of the sixties comes to life with the aid of thirty-odd writers and some excellent art direction. Fred is "promoted" to boss at the quarry, only to find he's been duped by the real boss into taking the heat for his embezzling. John Goodman, Rick Moranis, Elizabeth Perkins, Rosie O'Donnell, Elizabeth Taylor, Kyle MacLachlan, Halle Berry, Jonathan Winters. w. Tom S. Parker, Jim Jennewein, Steven E. de Souza, d. Brian Levant.

COMEDY: CHILDREN'S: FAMILY: Cartoons; Cartoonlike Films; TV Series Movies; Prehistoric Times; Family Comedy; Marriage Comedy; Dinosaurs; Blockbusters; Power-Rise to, of Idiot
(Ed: Hyped into success, it's mostly a kid's show)

Flipper, 1963, 87m, ★★★/$$$, MGM/MGM-UA, G. In the Florida Keys, an airboat fisherman finds out that his son's best friend is a dolphin. Chuck Connors, Luke Halpin, Kathleen Maguire, Connie Scott. w. Arthur Weiss, d. James B. Clark.

CHILDREN'S: FAMILY: Pet Stories; Animal Stories; Dolphins; Animal Rights; Fishermen; Fathers & Sons; Fathers Alone; Florida Keys; Sleeper Hits

REMAKE: TV series, mid 60s, which is actually much better known than the film; 1996 version
(Free Willy; Day of the Dolphin)

Flirting, 1989/1993, 99m, ★★★/$, Ind/Vidmark, R/S-FN. In 1960s Australia, a shy romance develops between an Australian boy and a Ugandan girl in boarding school, which isn't always helped along by the racism of their peers. Noah Taylor, Thandie Newton, Nicole Kidman, Bartholomew Rose. w. d. John Duigan.

COMEDY DRAMA: ROMANCE: Romance-Interracial; Race Relations; Black vs. White; Love-First; Coming of Age; Boarding Schools; Teenagers; Young Men; Australian Films; Hidden Gems; Overlooked at Release; Coming of Age; Writer-Directors
SEQUEL TO: The Year My Voice Broke

Flood!, 1976, 100m, ★★/$$$, WB/WB. A town's dam bursts and the inhabitants must be rescued from drowning in the deluge. Robert Culp, Martin Milner, Barbara Hershey, Richard Basehart, Carol Lynley, McDowell, Cameron Mitchell, Teresa Wright. d. Earl Bellamy.

MELODRAMA: Disaster Stories; Floods; Rescue Drama; TV Movies

Flower Drum Song, 1961, 91m, ★★★/$$$, U/MCA-U. A romance develops between young residents of San Francisco's Chinatown and family complications arise. Nancy Kwan, James Shigeta, Juanita Hall, Myoshi Umeki, James Soo, Sen Yung. w. Joseph Fields, d. Henry Koster. BCCin, BMScore. Oscars: 2-0.

MUSICALS: ROMANCE: Musical Romance; Lover Family Dislikes; Immigrants; Asian-Americans; Chinese People; San Francisco; Forgotten Films; Faded Hits; Hidden Gems; Stagelike Films
(West Side Story; The World of Suzie Wong)

Flowers in the Attic, 1987, 92m, ★★1/2/$$, New World/New World, R/V. A psychotic old woman keeps her grandchildren locked up in her attic, and they grow into perfect little monsters. Louise Fletcher, Victoria Tennant, Jeb Stuart Adams. w. d. Jeffrey Bloom, N-adap. Virginia C. Andrews.

HORROR: SUSPENSE: Grandmothers; Abused Children; Revenge; Mental

Illness; Evil Women; Houses-Creepy; Coulda Been Good
(Ed: The big bestseller falls flat on screen, though it does have a following)

Fluffy, 1964, 92m, ★★1/2/$$, U-I/NA, G. A zoologist sets out to prove that a lion can be domesticated. Tony Randall, Shirley Jones, Edward Andrews, Ernest Truex, Howard Morris, Jim Backus. w. Samuel Rocca, d. Earl Bellamy.

CHILDREN'S: FAMILY: Animal Stories; Pet Stories; Scientists; Veterinarians
(Born Free; Clarence, The Cross-Eyed Lion)

Fluke, 1995, 96m, ★★/$, MGM/MGM-UA, PG. When a young man is killed, he's reincarnated into a dog who tries to find his family again-the young man's family, anyway. Matthew Modine, Nancy Travis, Eric Stoltz, Max Pomeranc, Ron Perlman, Bill Cobbs, Federico Pacifici, Jon Polito, Collin Wilcox Paxton. w. Carlo Carlei & James Carrington, N-adap. James Herbert, d. Carlo Carlei.

COMEDY DRAMA: CHILDREN'S: FAMILY: Dogs Reincarnation; Animals-Talking
(You Can Never Tell; Baxter; Homeward Bound)

The Fly, 1958, 94m, ★★★/$$$, 20th/CBS-Fox. A scientist develops a matter transmographier and decides to use it himself. The experiment is successful but for a fly that got caught in the contraption with him. His atoms and those of the fly get recombined and he becomes half-man, half-fly. Of course it all ends tragically, not only for the man but the fly as well. Vincent Price, David Hedison, Patricia Owens, Herbert Marshall. w. James Clavell, d. Kurt Neumann.

SEQUELS: Return of the Fly, Curse of the Fly.
REMAKE: The Fly (1986), The Fly II (1989)

The Fly, 1986, 100m, ★★★/$$$, 20th/CBS-Fox, R/S-V-MN-B&G. A remake of the above with more emphasis on special effects and the psycho-sexual deterioration of the scientist Seth Brundle. Jeff Goldblum, Geena Davis, John Getz. w. Charles Edward Pogue, David Cronenberg, d. David Cronenberg.

SCI-FI: ROMANCE: HORROR: Romance-Doomed; Babies-Having Scientists; Experiments; Humans into Animals; Insects; Sleeper Hits
(Altered States)

The Fly II, 1989, 105m, ★★½/$, 20th/CBS-Fox, R/V-P-S-B&G-FN-MFN. At the end of the first film, Seth Brundle's girlfriend was pregnant and he prevented her from aborting the child. Now his spawn is back to seek revenge on the scientist who was his guardian. Eric Stoltz, Daphne Zuniga, Lee Richardson, Harley Cross, Gary Chalk, Ann Marie Lee. w. Mick Garris, Jim and Ken Wheat, Rank Darabout, d. Chris Walas.

SCI-FI: ROMANCE: HORROR: Scientists; Experiments; Humans into Animals; Insects; Fathers & Sons; Family Traditions-Carrying on

Fly by Night, 1942, 74m, ★★½/$$, Par//NA. A man falsely accused of murdering a scientist must find the real killer and ends up uncovering a Nazi conspiracy. Richard Carlson, Nancy Kelly, Albert Basserman, Walter Kingsford, Martin Kosleek, Miles Mander. w. Jay Dratler, F. Hugh Herbert, d. Robert Siodmak.

SUSPENSE: MURDER: Murder-Clearing Oneself; Conspiracy; Chase Stories; Murder-Discovering; Hitchcockian; Nazi Stories; Accused Unjustly; Framed?; Forgotten Films; Coulda Been Good
REMAKE/RETREAD: The 39 Steps
(The 39 Steps; The Man Who Knew Too Much; Foreign Correspondent)

Flying Down to Rio, 1933, 89m, ★★★/$$$$, RKO/Turner. A couple meet on vacation in Rio where an American band makes a big splash. Everyone dances then. Dolores del Rio, Gene Raymond, Raul Roulien, Ginger Rogers, Fred Astaire, Blance Frederici. w. Cyril Hume, H. W. Hannemann, Erwin Gelsey, P-adap. Anne Caldwell, SS-adap. Louis Brock, d. Thornton Freeland. BOSong, The Carioca. Oscars: 1-0.

MUSICALS: ROMANCE: Musical Romance; Dance Movies; Brazil; Latin People; Astaire & Rogers
(Down Argentine Way; Romance on the High Seas)

Flying Leathernecks, 1951, 102m, ★★½/$$$, RKO/Turner. During World War II on Guadalcanal, two hardbitten Marines brawl and fight the Japs with equal gusto. John Wayne, Robert Ryan, Janis Carter, Don Taylor, Jay C. Flippen, William Herrigan, James Bell. w. James Edward Grant, d. Nicholas Ray.

ACTION: War Stories; World War II Stories; Pacific Ocean/Islands; Men in Conflict; Japanese as Enemy; War at Sea
(The Fighting Seabees; Flying Tigers)

Flying Tigers, 1942, 100m, ★★½/$$$, Republic/Republic. A group of fighter pilots battle the Japanese in the skies above China during World War II. John Wayne, John Carroll, Anna Lee, Paul Kelly, Mae Clarke. w. Kenneth Gamet, Barry Trivers, d. David Miller.

ACTION: War Stories; World War II Stories; Men in Conflict; Japanese as Enemy; Pilots-Military; Ensemble Films; Ensembles-Male; China
(Flying Leathernecks; The Fighting Seabees)

FM, 1978, 104m, ★★½/$$, U/MCA-U, PG/P-S. The manager with "integrity" fights encroaching commercialism at his FM radio station. Michael Brandon, Eileen Brennan, Alex Karras, Cleavon Little, Martin Mull. w. Ezra Sacks, d. John A. Alonzo.

COMEDY DRAMA: Fighting the System; Rebels; Music Movies; Radio Life; 1970s; Musicals-Disco Era; Disco Era; Time Capsules; Cult Films; Forgotten Films
(Pump Up the Volume; Talk Radio; SFW)
(Ed: Soundtrack was a hit)

The Fog, 1979, 91m, ★★★/$$$, Avco-Embassy/Col, R/V-B&G. An old ship is spotted off the shore of a small California town, rolling in with a fog. It turns out to be an ancient pirate ship filled with the ghosts of its former crew, who proceed to terrorize the townspeople. Adrienne Barbeau, Hal Holbrook, John Houseman, Janet Leigh, Jamie Lee Curtis, Tom Atkins. w. John Carpenter, Debra Hill, d. John Carpenter.

SUSPENSE: HORROR: Ghosts; Pirates; Dead-Back from the; Ships; Radio Life; Supernatural Danger; Women in Jeopardy
(The Island; 2000 Maniacs)
(Ed: Better than *The Island*, but not by much)

Fog over Frisco, 1934, 68m, ★★½/$$, WB/NA. A man stalks an heiress through the San Francisco fog and when she's murdered, a detective must find him. Bette Davis, Donald Woods, Margaret Lindsay, Lyle Talbot, Hugh Herbert, Arthur Byron, Douglass Dumbrille, Irving Pichel, Alan Hale. w. Robert N. Lee, N-adap. George Dyer, d. William Dieterle.

MYSTERY: MURDER: MURDER MYSTERY: Mystery-Whodunit; Detective Stories; Missing Persons; Comic Mystery; Heiresses; San Francisco; Curiosities; Ahead of Its Time
REMAKE: Spy Ship (1942)
(Ed: Known for its fast pace and tongue-in-cheek humor)

Folies Bergere, 1935, 84m, ★★–/$$, 20th/NA. A banker in Paris hires to a cabaret performer impersonate him in order to facilitate his liasons with a dancer at the Folies Bergere, but all sorts of confusion ensues when his mistress and his wife get fooled by the imposter. Maurice Chevalier, Merle Oberon, Ann Sothern, Eric Blore. w. Bess Meredyth, Hal Long, P-adap. Rudolph Lothar, Hans Adler (*The Red Cat*), d. Roy del Ruth.

COMEDY: ROMANCE: Romantic Comedy; Impostors; Lookalikes; Cheating Men; Mistresses; Women Fighting over Men; Dancers; Paris; Female Screenwriters; Forgotten Films
(Victor/Victoria; Moon over Parador)

Folks!, 1992, 106m, ★★/$, Penta-WB/WB, PG-13/S-P-V. A stockbroker is set up by a supposed friend and winds up losing his job when his elderly parents are in dire trouble down in Florida. The senile father comes back to live with him, mother in tow as well, and constant chaos is the result. The parents then decide to commit suicide not to be a burden to their son's already destroyed life-but there's one thing which might save them. Tom Selleck, Don Ameche, Anne Jackson, Christine Ebersole, Wendy Crewson, Michael Murphy. w. Robert Klane, d. Ted Kotcheff.

COMEDY: Comedy-Slapstick; Murphy's Law Stories; Comedy of Errors; Black Comedy; Comedy-Morbid; Elderly People; Parents vs. Children; Suicidal Tendencies; Euthanasia; Fathers-Troublesome; Retirement; Unemployment; Losing It All; Riches to Rags; Stock Brokers; Chicago; Coulda Been Good; Good Premise Unfulfilled
(Grace Quigley; The Money Pit; Cocoon)
(Ed: Some good moments don't add up to much. Should appeal to those who loved *The Money Pit*)

Follies in Concert, 1985, 90m, ★★★/$$, PBS-Ind/MVD. A record of a Lincoln Center performance of Sondheim's famous musical. Carol Burnett, Lee Remick, Betty Comden, Andre Gregory, Adolphe Green, Mandy Patinkin, Phyllis Newman, Elaine Stritch,

Licia Albanese. w. & music Steven Sondheim.

MUSICALS: Theater Life; Actresses; Women in Conflict; Behind the Scenes; Stage Tapings

Follow Me, Boys!, 1966, 132m, ★★¹/₂/$$$, Disney/Disney, G. In a small town, the headmaster at a boys school helps the students through their trials and tribulations while doing a little flag waving. Fred MacMurray, Vera Miles, Lillian Gish, Charlie Ruggles, Elliott Reid, Kurt Russell. w. Louis Pelletier, N-adap. Mackinlay Kantor, (*God and My Country*), d. Norman Tokar.

COMEDY DRAMA: MELODRAMA: Patriotic Films; Conservative Value Films; Small-town Life; Boys Schools; Men and Boys; Boys; Boy Scouts; Boarding Schools; Teachers; Teachers & Students; Disney Comedy; Forgotten Films; American Myth
(The Happiest Millionaire; Rally 'Round the Flag, Boys!)
(Ed: A little too much saccharin and a little too long)

Follow That Dream, 1962, 110m, ★★¹/₂/$$, UA/CBS-Fox. A family leaves their conventional life and moves onto the beaches of Florida. Elvis Presley, Arthur O'Connell, Joanna Moore, Anne Helm, Jack Kruschen. w. Charles Lederer, N-adap. Richard Powell, (*Pioneer Go Home*), d. Gordon Douglass.

COMEDY DRAMA: Music Movies; **MELODRAMA:** Family Comedy; New in Town; Starting Over; Florida; Forgotten Films
(Blue Hawaii; Clambake)
(Ed: Forgotten even as Elvis movies go)

Follow the Fleet, 1936, 110m, ★★★/$$$, RKO/Turner. Some sailors go to town on shore leave and meet some beautiful cabaret singers. The romance, music and dancing never end until they're back on the ship. Fred Astaire, Ginger Rogers, Randolph Scott, Harriet Hilliard, Astrid Allwyn, Harry Beresford, Lucille Ball, Betty Grable, Tony Martin. w. Dwight Taylor, P-adap. Hubert Osborne, Allan Scott, (*Shore Leave*), d. Mark Sandrich.

MUSICALS: Dance Movies; Dancers; **ROMANCE:** Musical Romance; Sailors; Shore Leave; Astaire & Rogers
(On the Town; One Hundred Men and a Girl)

The Food of the Gods, 1976, 88m, ★★¹/₂/$, AIP/Vestron, R/B&G-V.

Animals in a local forest have become gargantuan because of eating a strange substance that bubbles up from the ground. Marjoe Gortner, Pamela Franklin, Ida Lupino, Ralph Meeker, John McLiam. w. d. Bert I. Gordon, SS-adap. H. G. Wells.

HORROR: SCI-FI: Toxins; Environmental Dilemmas; Monsters-Mutant; Monsters-Animal
(Prophecy; Impulse; Night of the Lepus; Them!)

The Fool, 1990, 140m, ★★★/$, Ind/NA, PG. A Victorian businessman poses as a lowly clerk to prove a point about class and social status. Derek Jacobi, Cyril Cusack, Ruth Mitchell, Maria Aitken, Irina Brook, Paul Brooke, Richard Caldicot. w. Christine Edzard, Olivier Stockman, d. Christine Edzard.

SATIRE: Social Satire; Class Conflicts; Ordinary People Stories; Working Class; Disguises; Message Films; Time Capsules; England; Victorian Era; British Films; Female Screenwriters; Female Directors
(My Man Godfrey; Life Stinks!)

Fool for Love, 1985, 106m, ★★★/$, Cannon-MGM/MGM-UA, R/S-P-FN. An extremely dysfunctional couple, who are actually half-brother and -sister, meet again after a time in a fleabag motel which is owned by a man who may or may not be their father. Sam Shepard, Kim Basinger, Randy Quaid, Harry Dean Stanton. w. P-adap. Sam Shepard, d. Robert Altman.

DRAMA: COMEDY DRAMA: Art Films; **ROMANCE:** Romantic Drama; Romance-On Again/Off Again; Romance-Doomed; Incest; Desert Settings; Brothers & Sisters; Reunions
(Les Enfants Terribles; Flesh and Bone)

Foolin' Around, 1979, 101m, ★★¹/₂/$, Col/RCA-Col, PG/S. A poor little rich girl leaves home and falls for a country boy, but their marriage won't be so easy. Gary Busey, Annette O'Toole, John Calvin, Eddie Albert, Cloris Leachman, Tony Randall. w. Mike Kane, David Swift, d. Richard T. Heffron.

COMEDY: ROMANCE: Romantic Comedy; Lover Family Dislikes; Marriages-Impending; Romance-Class Conflicts; City vs. Country; Snobs vs. Slobs; Rednecks; North vs. South; Old-Fashioned Recent Films; Coulda Been Great; Good Premise Unfulfilled
(The Graduate)

Foolish Wives, 1921, 85m, ★★★/$$$$, U/Critic's Choice. (B&W, silent). A rake travels the tables in Monte Carlo looking for gullible rich women to seduce. Erich Von Stroheim, Mae Busch, Maud George, Cesare Gravina. w. d. Erich Von Stroheim.

MELODRAMA: ROMANCE: FARCE: Romance-Triangles; Playboys; Sexy Men; Dangerous Men; Con Artists; Monte Carlo; Hidden Gems; Writer-Directors

Fools for Scandal, 1938, 81m, ★★★/$$, WB/NA. A French diplomat is charmed by a beautiful actress, which leads to problems with her other beau. Carole Lombard, Fernand Gravet, Ralph Bellamy, Allen Jenkins. w. Herbert and Joseph Fields, P-adap. Nancy Hamilton, Rosemary Casey, James Shute (*Return Engagement*), d. Mervyn Le Roy.

COMEDY: ROMANCE: Romantic Comedy; Screwball Comedy; Actresses; Diplomats; Hollywood Life; Forgotten Films; Hidden Gems

Fools Parade, 1971, 98m, ★★¹/₂/$, Col/NA. A prisoner dilligently saves money and, when he's released, has quite a stash. But some bad guys find out he's put it somewhere and go after him. James Stewart, George Kennedy, Strother Martin, Anne Baxter, Kurt Russell. w. James Lee Barrett, N-adap. Davis Grubb, d. Andrew V. McLaglen.

SUSPENSE: COMEDY DRAMA: Crime Drama; Ex-Convicts; Chase Stories; Treasure Hunts; Finding the Loot; Fugitives from a Murderer; Forgotten Films; Hidden Gems; Overlooked at Release; 1930s

Footlight Parade, 1933, 104m, ★★★/$$$, WB/MGM-UA. A producer gets a show off the ground despite great obstacles and much bickering with the cast. James Cagney, Joan Blondell, Ruby Keeler, Dick Powell, Frank McHugh, Guy Kibbee, Ruth Donnelly, Hugh Herbert. w. Manuel Seff, James Seymour, d. Lloyd Bacon.

MUSICALS: COMEDY: Musical Comedy; Dance Movies; Screwball Comedy; Singers; Dancers; Actors; Actresses; Ensemble Films; Theater Life; Behind the Scenes; Putting on a Show; Race Against Time; Forgotten Films; Hidden Gems
(42nd Street; The Band Wagon)

Footloose, 1984, 107m, ★★¹/₂/$$$$, Par/Par, PG. Religious leaders in a small town ban dance, but a young rambunctious teenager rebels by dancing in barns and what-not. Kevin Bacon, Lori Singer, John Lithgow, Dianne Wiest, Christopher Penn. w. Dean Pitchford, d. Herbert Ross. BOSong, "Footloose," BOSong, "Let's Hear It for the Boy." Oscars: 2-0.

MUSICALS: COMEDY DRAMA: Teenage Movies; Teenagers; Bratpack Movies; Dance Movies; Music Video Style; Rebels; Small-town Life; Censorship; Oppression; Preachers; Southwestern Life; Curiosities
(Flashdance; Newsies)
(Ed: The soundtrack was huge, but the film is dated and silly, though it made a fortune, of course!)

For a Few Dollars More, 1965, 130m, ★★★/$$$$, UA/MGM-UA. In El Paso naturally greedy bounty hunters form a tentative alliance, but must always look over their shoulders. Clint Eastwood, Lee Van Cleef, Gian Maria Volonte, Klaus Kinski. w. d. Sergio Leone.

WESTERNS: Drifters; Westerns-Neo; Westerns-Spaghetti; Chase Stories; Journies; Texas; Bounty Hunters; Vigilantes; Writer-Directors
SEQUEL TO: A Fistful of Dollars
SEQUEL: The Good, the Bad, and the Ugly
(A Fistful of Dollars; The Good, the Bad, and the Ugly; Hang 'em High)

Forbidden, 1953, 85m, ★★1/2/$$, U-I/NA. A mobster hires a private detective to find his missing gal, but once he finds her, he ends up falling for her, putting himself in jeopardy. Tony Curtis, Joanne Dru, Lyle Bettger, Marvin Miller, Sen Yung. w. William Sackheim, Gil Doud, d. Rudolph Mate.

SUSPENSE: Film Noir; Mob Stories; Fugitives from the Mob; Mob Girls; Romance with Boss' Lover; Detective Stories; Missing Persons; Forgotten Films
REMAKE/RETREAD: Out of the Past
(Out of the Past; Second Chance)

The Forbidden Dance, 1990, 90m, ★★/$, Ind/Col, PG-13. A Brazilian princess entreats U.S. government officials to help her stop the destruction of her country's rainforest and does a mean Lambada to boot. Laura Herring, Jeff James, Sid Haig, Richard Lynch, Kid Creole & the Coconuts. d. Greydon Clark.

MELODRAMA: ROMANCE: Dance Movies; Music Movies; Erotic Drama; Nightclubs; Latin People
(The Lambada; Salsa)

Forbidden Games, 1952, 90m, ★★★/$$, Ind/Sultan, Nos. A group of children during growing up in France during World War II re-enact their fathers' battles on a smaller scale in backyard games with animals. A classic study of how children mirror the horrors of the world around them. Brigitte Fossey, Georges Poujouly, Amedee, Louis Herbert. d. Rene Clement.

DRAMA: Psychological Drama; Boys; Girls; Allegorical Stories; War Stories; World War II-Post Era; French Films
(Lord of the Flies; The Chocolate War)

Forbidden Planet, 1956, 98m, ★★★1/2/$$$, MGM/MGM-UA. A spaceship goes on a mission to an uncharted planet to find out what happened to members of a previous mission. Walter Pidgeon, Anne Francis, Leslie Nielsen, Warren Stevens, Jack Kelly, Earl Holliman. w. Cyril Hume, d. Fred M. Wilcox.

SCI-FI: SCI-FI 1950s: SUSPENSE: Outer Space Movies; Journies; Missing Persons; Monsters; Robots; Invisibility; Aliens-Outer Space, Evil; Cult Films; Hidden Gems
(Aliens; Robinson Crusoe on Mars)

The Forbin Project, 1969, 100m, ★★★/$, U/NA. The Pentagon computerizes its defense system, but the computer seems to have a mind of its own, joining forces with a Soviet computer to thwart its bosses. Eric Braeden, Gordon Pinsent, Susan Clark, William Schallert. w. James Bridges, N-adap. D. F. Jones (*Colossus*), d. Joseph Sargent.

SUSPENSE: Political Thriller; Military Stories; Pentagon; Computers; Computer Terror; Russia as Enemy; Cold War Era; Man vs. Machine; Race Against Time; Forgotten Films; Ahead of its Time
(War Games; Failsafe; Demon Seed)

Forever Female, 1953, 93m, ★★–/$$, Par/Par. An aging actress, smitten with a brilliant young playwright, persuades her Broadway producer husband to procure a work for her to star in. Trouble is, the lead role as written is a nineteen-year-old girl, and the part would be perfect for a young up-and-coming starlet who also has romantic designs on the young playwright. Ginger Rogers, William Holden, Paul Douglas, Pat Crowley, James Gleason, Jesse White, George Reeves, Marjorie Rambeau, King Donovan, Vic Perrin, Marion Ross. w. Julius J. Epstein, d. Irving Rapper.

MELODRAMA: COMEDY DRAMA: ROMANCE: Actresses; Writers; Theater Life; Women in Conflict; Women Fighting Over Men; Generation Gap; Forgotten Films; Infatuations
(All About Eve; Sunset Boulevard; Lily in Love)

Forever James Dean, 1988, 69m, ★★★/$, WB/WB. A documentary about the short life and career of the actor and his legions of obsessed fans around the world. d. Ara Chekmayan.
Documentaries; Biographies; Hollywood Biographies; Actors; James Dean
(9-30-55; East of Eden; Rebel without a Cause)

Forgotten Prisoners (*Forgotten Prisoners: The Amnesty Files*), 1990, 92m, ★★/$$, Turner/Turner. An Amnesty International official tries to get to the bottom of what's happening in Turkish jails, which includes horrendous torture and inhuman conditions, in this made-for-cable movie. Ron Silver, Roger Daltrey, Hector Elizondo. d. Robert Greenwald.

DRAMA: Prison Drama; Social Drama; Torture; Reformers; TV Movies
(Midnight Express)

For Love of Ivy, 1968, 100m, ★★1/2/$$, ABC-Cin/Fox, G. The hippie kids of a businessman hire a black con-man to woo their maid to keep her from quitting. Sidney Poitier, Abby Lincoln, Beau Bridges, Carroll O'Connor, Nan Martin. w. Robert Alan Arthur, Sidney Poitier, d. Daniel Mann. BOSong. Oscars: 1-0.

COMEDY: COMEDY DRAMA: ROMANCE: Romantic Comedy; Black Men; Black Women; Romance with Servant; Matchmakers; Dates-Hired; Blackmail; Servants; Curiosities; Good Premise Unfulfilled
(Corrina, Corrina; Warm December; Adam Had Four Sons; The Farmer's Daughter)

For Love or Money, 1963, 108m, ★★1/2/$$, U-I/MCA-U. A lawyer is appointed guardian of the three daughters of a wealthy old matriarch but ends up in love with one of them himself. Kirk Douglas, Mitzi Gaynor, Thelma Ritter, William Bendix, Gig Young. w. Larry Marks, Michael Morris, d. Michael Gordon.

MELODRAMA: COMEDY DRAMA: ROMANCE: Romantic Comedy; Lawyers;

Romance with Lawyer; Romance-Unprofessional; Sisters; Women Fighting over Men

For Love or Money, 1993, 89m, ★★¹/₂/$$, U/MCA-UA, R/S. A concierge dreams of opening his own luxury hotel, but ends up doing "favors" for the hotel owner. If he can outsmart his benefactor, he may be able to get what he wants-including the girl he has. Michael J. Fox, Gabrielle Anwar, Isaac Mizrahi, Anthony Higgins, Michael Tucker, Bobby Short, Bob Balaban, Udo Kier. w. Mark Rosenthal, d. Barry Sonnenfeld.

COMEDY DRAMA: ROMANCE: Romantic Comedy; Men Fighting Over Women; Mistresses; Hotels; Men Proving Themselves; Worker vs. Boss; Romance with Boss' Lover; Coulda Been Good
REMAKE/RETREAD: The Apartment (The Apartment; Life with Mikey; Doc Hollywood)
(Ed: The connections to the apartment are in the way it is revealed the girl is his boss' and in the way he's bound to serve him, though it leaves out [dumbs up] the more important elements of comedy and tragedy that made Wilder's film a classic)

For Me and My Gal, 1942, 104m, ★★★/$$$$, MGM/MGM-UA. A vaudeville singer is pursued by two men, each with their own appeal, but World War I is starting, so she'd better make up her mind, though she'd rather sing. Judy Garland, Gene Kelly, George Murphy, Marta Eggerth, Ben Blue. w. Richard Sherman, Sid Silvers, Fred Finkelhoffe, d. Busby Berkeley. BMScore. Oscars: 1-0.

MUSICALS: ROMANCE: COMEDY DRAMA: Musical Romance; Romance-Triangles; Romance-Choosing the Right Person; Vaudeville; World War I Era (Meet Me in St. Louis; The Big Clock)
(Ed: Received a big Broadway reworking/revival in the 80s)

For Pete's Sake, 1974, 90m, ★★★¹/₂/$$$, Rastar-Col/RCA-Col, PG/P-S. A working-class housewife (Barbra Streisand) wants to help her cabbie husband (Michael Sarrazin) out (first, she should get rid of the maid), so she takes a series of wacky, calamitous part-time jobs (selling bathroom products to attempted prostitution to bomb delivery), each one leading her further into debt and further into hock with the mob. Estelle Parsons, William Redfield, Molly Picon. w. Stanley Shapiro, Martin Richlin, d. Peter Yates.

COMEDY: FARCE: Chase Movies; Screwball Comedy; Comedy of Errors; Ordinary People Stories; Working Class; Fugitive from the Mob; Mob Comedy; Making a Living; New York Life; Taxi Drivers; Escalating Plots; Underrated (Fun with Dick and Jane; The Owl and the Pussycat; What's Up, Doc?)

For Queen and Country, 1988, 105m, ★★¹/₂/$, Atlantic/Par, PG. A black soldier finds life less than agreeable upon his return to England. Denzel Washington, Dorian Healy, Sean Chapman. w. Martin Stellman, Triz Worrell, d. Martin Stellman.

DRAMA: Character Studies; Black Soldiers; Black Men; Race Relations; England; Working Class; Poor People; Class Conflicts; Overlooked at Release (Mississippi Masala; Glory; A Soldier's Story)

For Richer, for Poorer, 1992, 90m, ★★/$$, HBO/HBO. A wealthy entrepreneur tries to teach his son the value of money by giving all of his away, but his plan backfires when he finds it much harder to "pull himself up by the bootstraps" the second time around. Jack Lemmon, Talia Shire, Joanna Gleason, Jonathan Silverman, Madeline Kahn, George Wyner. d. Jay Sandrich.

COMEDY: Family Comedy; Riches to Rags; Business Life; Restaurant Settings; Fathers & Sons; Life Lessons (Life Stinks; My Man Godfrey)

For the Boys, 1991, 145m, ★★★/$$, 20th/Fox, PG. An old song-and-dance team, a man and woman in their sixties, reminisce about their 40 years in show business, especially entertaining the troops from World War II to Viet Nam. Bette Midler (BActress), James Caan, George Segal, Patrick O'Neal, Christopher Rydell, Ayre Gross, Norman Fell, Bud Yorke. w. Marshall Brickman, Neil Jimenez, Lindy Laub. BMakeup. Oscars: 2-0.

MELODRAMA: COMEDY DRAMA: Marriage Drama; Episodic Stories; Flashbacks; Memories; Singers; Veterans; War Stories; World War II Era; Vietnam Era; Korean War; Female Protagonists; Nostalgia
(The Rose; The Road to Bali [Road SERIES])

For the Love of Benji, 1977, 84m, ★★¹/₂/$$, Mulberry Square/Disney. Benji goes on a trip with his family to the

Greek Islands and they lose him. Patsy Garrett, Cynthia Smith, Peter Bowles, Ed Nelson. w. Ben Vaughn, Joe Camp, d. Joe Camp.

CHILDREN'S: FAMILY: Pet Stories; Vacations; Greece; Ind Films (Oh, Heavenly Dog; Benji)

For Whom the Bell Tolls, 1943, 168m, ★★★¹/₂/$$$$, Par/Par. An American signs up for the Spanish Civil War and falls in love with a beautiful local woman just before going off to fight-perhaps to his death. Gary Cooper (BActor), Ingrid Bergman (BActress), Akim Tamiroff (**BSActor**), Arturo de Cordova, Arturo de Cordova, Katina Paxinou (**BSActress**), Vladimir Sokoloff. w. Dudley Nichols, N-adap. Ernest Hemingway, d. Sam Wood. BPicture, BCCin, BCArt, BEdit, BOScore. Oscars: 9-1.

DRAMA: War Stories; **ROMANCE:** Romantic Drama; Historical Drama; Mercenaries; Spanish Civil War; Spain; Rebels; Americans Abroad; Latin People; Classic Literary Adaptations (A Farewell to Arms; The Sun Also Rises)

For Your Eyes Only, 1981, 127m, ★★★/$$$$, UA/MGM-UA, PG/S-V. James Bond must dismantle a time bomb stuck in a submerged vessel off the coast of Greece, but will he be able to first untie himself from the beauties floating about? Roger Moore, Carole Bouquet, Topol, Lynn-Holly Johnson, Julian Glover. w. Richard Maibaum, Michael G. Wilson, d. John Glen. BOSong. Oscars: 1-0.

ACTION: ADVENTURE: Spy Films; Secret Agents; Playboys; James Bond; Undercover; Chase Movies; Rule the World-Plots to; Riviera Life; Mountain Climbing; Greece; Mediterranean (Octopussy; Moonraker; A View to a Kill; Breakout)

Force of Evil, 1948, 78m, ★★★¹/₂/$$, MGM/World Vision. A gangster working for a big crime boss tries to help his brother, a slightly less corrupt criminal running a numbers racket, before his boss takes him over. Tragedy results in this dark tale. John Garfield, Thomas Gomez, Beatrice Pearson, Marie Windsor. w. Abraham Polonsky, Ira Wolfert, N-adap., Ira Wolfert (*Tucker's People*), d. Abraham Polonsky.

SUSPENSE: Mob Stories; Film Noir; **TRAGEDY:** Fugitives from the Mob;

Hiding Out; Gambling; Brothers; Hidden Gems; Forgotten Films
(Kiss of Death; Blood and Sand; The Killers)

A Force of One, 1979, 90m, ★★/$$$, American Cinema/Media, R/EV. One man cleans up the streets of L.A. using his karate expertise. Chuck Norris, Jennifer O'Neill, Clu Glager, Ron O'Neal, James Whitmore Jr. w. Ernest Tidyman, Pat Johnson, d. Paul Aaron.
ACTION: Vigilantes; Martial Arts; Sleeper Hits
(Good Guys Wear Black; The Octagon)

Force Ten from Navarone, 1978, 118m, ★★1/2/$$, Col/WB. A special force in World War II has to get to a Yugoslavian bridge and blow it up before the Germans can cross it. Robert Shaw, Edward Fox, Franco Nero, Harrison Ford, Barbara Bach, Richard Kiel. w. Robin Chapman, N-adap. Alastair MacLean, d. Guy Hamilton.
ACTION: War Stories; Special Teams-Paramilitary; Sabotage; Nazi Stories; World War II Stories
(The Hornet's Nest; The Guns of Navarone; The Dirty Dozen)

A Foreign Affair, 1948, 116m, ★★★/$$, Par/Par, AMC. A congress-woman on a diplomatic trip with several other American officials to Berlin meets and falls for a sea captain much to the chagrin of his German mistress. Jean Arthur, Marlene Dietrich, John Lund, Millard Mitchell. w. Charles Brackett, Billy Wilder, Richard Breen, David Shaw (BOScr), d. Billy Wilder. BB&WCin. Oscars: 2-0.
COMEDY: COMEDY DRAMA: ROMANCE: Romantic Comedy; Romance-Triangles; World War II-Post Era; Politicians-Female; Fish out of Water Stories; Germany; Berlin; Hidden Gems; Female Protagonists
(The More the Merrier; The Devil and Miss Jones)

Foreign Correspondent, 1940, 119m, ★★★★/$$$, UA/WB. Journalist falls for a girl who's father is at the head of the spy ring he's trying to uncover after stumbling upon it after an assassin hit close to him. Joel McCrea, Laraine Day, Herbert Marshall, Albert Basserman (BSActor), Edmund Gwenn, George Sanders, Eduardo Ciannelli, Robert Benchley, Harry Davenport. w. Charles Bennett, Joan Harrison, James Hilton, Robert

Benchley (BScr), N-adap. Vincent Sheean *(Personal History)*, d. Alfred Hitchcock. BPicture, BB&WCin, BB&WArt. Oscars: 5-0.
SUSPENSE: MYSTERY: Detective Stories; Assassination Plots; Chase Stories; Conspiracy; Journalists as Detectives; Spy Films; Spies; Kidnappings; Children Saving Parents; Nazi Stories; World War II Stories; Unbelieved; Airplane Crashes; Female Screenwriters; Hidden Gems
REMAKE/RETREAD: Foreign Intrigue
(The 39 Steps; North by Northwest; Foreign Intrigue; Sullivan's Travels)

Foreign Intrigue, 1956, 100m, ★★1/2/$$, UA/NA. A reporter in Europe uncovers a blackmail plot when he investigates a murder. Robert Mitchum, Genevieve Page, Ingrid Thulin, Eugene Deckers. w. d. Sheldon Reynolds.
MYSTERY: MURDER: MURDER MYSTERY: Detective Stories; Journalists; Journalists as Detective; Blackmail; Conspiracy; Murder-Discovering; Writer-Directors
REMAKE/RETREAD OF: Foreign Correspondent
(Foreign Correspondent; Year of the Gun)

The Forest Rangers, 1942, 85m, ★★1/2/$$, Par/NA. A cosmopolitan woman goes off to the forest when she marries a ranger. She has trouble adjusting to the life, and a rival ranger makes it hard on both of them, until they forget their petty differences and pull together during a forest fire. Fred MacMurray, Paulette Goddard, Susan Hayward, Lynne Overman, Albert Dekker, Eugene Pallette. w. Harold Shumate, d. George Marshall.
MELODRAMA: COMEDY DRAMA: ROMANCE: Nature-Back to; Romance-Class Conflicts; City vs. Country; Fish out of Water Stories; Rescue Drama; Forgotten Films
(Northwest Mounted Police)

Forever Amber, 1947, 137m, ★★★/$$$, 20th/Fox. In the old England of Charles II, a beautiful tart/courtesan has amorous adventures, keeping her costumes on, as seeing them on is the main point of the film. Linda Darnell, Cornel Wilde, George Sanders, Richard Greene, Glenn Langan, Richard Haydn, Jessica Tandy, Leo G. Carroll, d. Otto Preminger. BOScore. Oscars: 1-0.
ROMANCE: MELODRAMA: Costume Drama; Romantic Drama; Prostitutes-

High Class; Romance with Prostitute; Royalty; Sexy Women; Promiscuity; 1700s; England; Unintentionally Funny (Frenchman's Creek; The King's Whore)
(Ed: Based on the scandalous bestseller of the 40s)

Forever and a Day, 1943, 104m, ★★★/$$, RKO/Tapeworm. A family saga set in England and spanning its history from the turn of the 19th century to World War II. Anna Neagle, Ray Milland, Claude Rains, C. Aubrey Smith, Dame May Whitty, Gene Lockhart, Edmund Gwenn, Ian Hunter, Jessie Matthews, Charles Laughton, Montagu Love, Cedric Hardwicke, Buster Keaton, Ida Lupino, Brian Aherne, Edward Everett Horton, Merle Oberon, Una O'Connor, Nigel Brudce, Roland Young, Gladys Cooper, Robert Cummings, Richard Haydn, Elsa Lanchester, Sara Allgood, Donald Crisp, Ruth Warrick, Herbert Marshall, Victor McLaglen. w. Charles Bennett, C. S. Forrester, Lawrence Hazard, Michael Hogan, W. P. Lipscomb, Alice Duer Miller, John Van Druten, Alan Campbell, Peter Godfrey, S. M. Herzig, Christopher Isherwood, Gene Lockhart, R. C. Sheriff, Claudine West, Norman Corwin, Jack Hartfield, James Hilton, Emmet Lavery, Frederick Lonsdale, Donald Ogden Stewart, Keith Winter, d. Rene Clair, Edmund Goulding, Cedric Hardwicke, Frank Lloyd, Victor Saville, Robert Stevenson, Herbert Wilcox.
MELODRAMA: Historical Drama; Costume Drama; Family Drama; Episodic Stories; Sagas; England; Multiple Stories; All-Star Casts; All-Star Cameos
(Roots; Random Harvest)
(Ed: Surely one the largest casts of character actor names ever assembled; also reputed to have the largest list of writers on board in history)

Forever Darling, 1956, 91m, ★★1/2/$$, MGM/MGM-UA. A guardian angel tries to help out a couple whose marriage is in trouble. Lucille Ball, Desi Arnaz, James Mason, John Emery, Louis Calhern, John Hoyt, Natalie Schafer. w. Helen Deutsch, d. Alexander Hall.
COMEDY: COMEDY DRAMA: Marriage Comedy; Marriage on the Rocks; Angels; Forgotten Films; Coulda Been Good; Curiosities
(The Long, Long Trailer; Angel on My Shoulder)

(Ed: What may have worked in the movies obviously didn't work in real life) **Forever Young**, 1992, 102m, ★★/$$, WB/WB, PG-13/P-S-MRN. During World War II, a top secret cryogenics experiment is abandoned, but a pilot involved in it remains frozen until modern day. Some kids find him, thaw him out, and teach him about life in the 90s. Mel Gibson, Jamie Lee Curtis, Elijah Wood, Isabel Glasser, George Wendt, Joe Morton. w. Jeffrey Abrams, d. Steve Miner.

MELODRAMA: SCI-FI: ROMANCE: Time Sleepers; Frozen People; Men and Boys; Fish out of Water Stories; Good Premise Unfulfilled; Old-Fashioned Recent Films (Late for Dinner; Iceman)

(Ed: Some say putrid, others say cute-it probably all depends on whether you're nuts about Mel)

For Keeps, 1988, 98m, ★★/$, Tri-Star/Col-Tri, PG/S. When two teens discover they're expecting, they get married and do everything right but face reality. Molly Ringwald, Randall Batinkoff, Kenneth Mars, Miriam Flynn, Conchata Ferrell, Sharon Brown. w. Denise deClue, Tim Kazursinsky, d. John G. Avildsen.

COMEDY DRAMA: ROMANCE: Marriage Comedy; Marriage Drama; Mothers-Unwed; Teenagers; Teenage Movies; Young People; Coming of Age; Pre-Life Crisis; Coulda Been Good; Female Screenwriters

(Fresh Horses; The Family Way)

The Formula, 1980, 117m, ★★½/$$, MGM/MGM-UA, R/P-S-V. An international plot to obtain a secret formula for turning coal into gas is discovered by a detective following a trail of deaths to Europe. George C. Scott, Marlon Brando, Marthe Keller, John Gielgud, Beatrice Straight. w., N-adap. Steven Shagan, d. John G. Avildsen. BCin. Oscars: 1-0.

SUSPENSE: MYSTERY: MURDER: MURDER MYSTERY: Conspiracy; Spies; Cures/Elixirs-Search for; Oil People; Coulda Been Good

(Three Days of the Condor; The Boys from Brazil)

Forrest Gump, 1994, 142m, ★★★/$$$$$, Par/Par, PG/S-V. Simple-minded Forrest makes his way through life, paralleling the history of last half-century, managing to turn disadvantage to ambition and success, often by sheer luck and happenstance. Tom Hanks (**BActor**),

Robin Wright, Sally Field, Gary Sinise (**BSActor**), Mykelti Williamson. w. Eric Roth (**BAScr**), N-adap. Winston Groom, d. Robert Zemeckis (**BDirector**). **BPicture, BEditing,** BCin, BSound, BSFX, BArt, BMakeup, BSoundFX, BOScore. Oscars: 13-6.

COMEDY: COMEDY DRAMA: MELODRAMA: SATIRE: ROMANCE: Simple Minds; Romance-Reluctant; Episodic Stories; Mothers & Sons; American Myth; Conservative Value Films; Old-Fashioned Recent Films; Football; Southerns; Narrated Films; Flashbacks; Vietnam Era; 1940s; 1950s; Psychedelic Era; Blockbusters; Sleeper Hits

Fort Apache, 1948, 127m, ★★★/$$$, RKO/Turner. A cavalry officer defends his territory and family from the Indians, but his family's providing problems he doesn't need as well. Henry Fonda, John Wayne, Shirley Temple, Pedro Armendariz, Ward Bond, Irene Rich, George O'Brien, John Agar, Victor McLaglen, Guy Kibbee. w. Frank S. Nugent, SS-adap. James Warner Bellah (*Massacre*), d. John Ford.

WESTERNS: Family Drama; Fathers & Daughters; Indians-American, Conflict with Cavalry; Faded Hits (Stagecoach; The Searchers)

Fort Apache, the Bronx, 1980, 123m, ★★★/$$$, Time Life-20th/CBS-Fox, R/EV-EP-S. A crusty, veteran cop in the rough New York burrough tries to make his hellish precinct a decent place to live, against all odds. Paul Newman, Ed Asner, Ken Wahl, Danny Aiello, Rachel Ticotin, Pam Grier. w. Heywood Gould, d. Daniel Petrie.

ACTION: Crime Drama; Police Stories; Drugs-Dealing; Gang-Street; Gangs-Black; Inner City Life; Multiple Stories; New York Life; Time Capsules; Ahead of its Time

(Across 110th Street; Assault on Precinct 13)

Fortress, 1993, 91m, ★★/$, Live/Live, R. In the future, people take population control very seriously. When a couple tries to have a second child, they are sent to a torture chamber called the Fortress, where a sadistic guard administers horrible punishments. Christopher Lambert, Kurtwood Smith, Loryn Locklin, Lincoln Kilpatrick. w. Steve Feinberg, Troy Nabors, Terry Curtis Fox, d. Stuart Gordon.

ACTION: SCI-FI: Environmental Dilemmas; Apocalyptic Stories; Futuristic Films; Babies-Having; Torture (Daybreak; The Handmaid's Tale; Soylent Green)

The Fortune, 1975, 88m, ★★★/$$, Par/Ind. Two hustlers (Jack Nicholson, Warren Beatty) try to murder a goofy heiress (Stockard Channing) who won't take the hint, managing to survive their attempts. w. Adrien Joyce (Carole Eastman), d. Mike Nichols.

COMEDY: Black Comedy; Screwball Comedy; Comedy-Light; Murder Attempts-Comic; Romance-Triangles; Con Artists; Ménage à Trois; Heiresses; Inheritances at Stake; 1930s; Flops-Major; Coulda Been Great; Underrated; Hidden Gems; Female Screenwriters (Lucky Lady; A New Leaf)

(Ed: Pretty good and holds up well. Shown on cable often. On video under the ridiculous title *Spite and Malice*)

Fortune and Men's Eyes, 1971, 102m, ★★★/$, MGM/MGM-UA, R/E-P-MRN. Canadian men in jail deal with their homosexuality and the brutal prison conditions. Wendell Burton, Michael Greer. w. P-adap. John Herbert, d. Harvey Hart.

DRAMA: Prison Drama; Gay Men; Bisexuality; Rape-Male; Reformers; Canadian Films; Canada; Ahead of Its Time

(Brubaker)

The Fortune Cookie, 1966, 125m, ★★★½/$$$, UA/MGM-UA, PG. A man who's broke (Jack Lemmon) fakes nearly broken neck injuries from an accident at the insistence of his shady lawyer acquaintance (Walter Matthau, **BSActor**). Cliff Osmond, Lurene Tuttle. w. Billy Wilder, IAL Diamond (BOScr), d. Billy Wilder. BB&WCin. Oscars: 3-1.

COMEDY DRAMA: SATIRE: Social Satire; Black Comedy; Corruption; Ethics; Accidents; Insurance Scams; Liars; Lawyers; Friends as Enemies; Hidden Gems

(The Odd Couple; Buddy, Buddy; Grumpy Old Men)

Fortunes of War, 1987, 160m, ★★★/$$$, BBC/Fox. In the last days before World War II, a British teacher living with his wife in the Balkans is swept up in the local independence movement, and, once the war starts, he and his marriage are on the line. Kenneth Branagh, Emma Thompson, Rupert Graves, Ronald

Pickup, Robert Stephens, Charles Kay, James Villers, Harry Burton, Ciaran Madden. w. Alan Plater, d. James Cellan Jones.

DRAMA: Historical Drama; Marriage Drama; War Stories; Teachers; Political Unrest; TV Movies; British Films

Forty Carats, 1973, 109m, ★★½/$$, Col/Col. After her divorce, a forty-something woman has a wild, fun fling on vacation in Greece. Liv Ullman, Edward Albert, Gene Kelly, Gilly "Green" Bush, Binnie Barnes, Nancy Walker, Deborah Raffin, Natalie Shafer. w. Leonard Gershe, P-adap. Pierre Barillet, Jean-Pierre Gredy, d. Milton Katselas.

MELODRAMA: ROMANCE: COMEDY DRAMA: Romantic Comedy; Romantic Drama; Vacation Romance; Romance-Older Women/Younger Men; Greece; Coulda Been Good
(Shirley Valentine; Ash Wednesday)

48 Hours, 1982, 96m, ★★★/$$$$, Par/Par, R/EP-EV-S. A black parolee and a renegade white cop team up to get the crooks former cohorts who did him wrong, but they've only got 48 hours to do it. Nick Nolte, Eddie Murphy, Annette O'Toole, Frank McRae. w. Roger Spottiswoode, Walter Hill, Larry Gross, Steven E. de Souza, d. Walter Hill.

ACTION: Action Comedy; Crime Drama; Police Stories; Comedy & Violence; Free Spirits; Black Comedy; Black vs. White; Black vs. White Together; Black Men; Informers; Buddy Cops; San Francisco

SEQUEL: Another 48 Hours
(Lethal Weapon; Bad Boys [1995])

Forty Guns, 1957, 80m, ★★½/$$, 20th/NA. A strong pioneer woman goes to bat for her outlaw brother when he's in a pinch. Barbara Stanwyck, Barry Sullivan, Dean Jagger, Gene Barry, John Ericson. w. d. Samuel Fuller.

WESTERNS: DRAMA: Family Drama; Feisty Females; Pioneers; Brothers & Sisters; Cattle Ranchers; Cattle Rustlers; Cattle Herded by Barbara Stanwyck; Writer-Directors

Forty Pounds of Trouble, 1963, 105m, ★★★/$$, U-I/NA. The sleazy manager of a casino neglects to pay alimony and his ex-wife puts a detective on his trail. At the same time, a six-year-old girl shows up on his doorstep and he must take care of her until he can find her family. Tony Curtis, Phil Silvers, Suzanne Pleshette,

Edward Andrews. w. Marion Hargrove, d. Norman Jewison.

COMEDY: COMEDY DRAMA: Men and Girls; Fathers & Daughters; Fugitives from the Law; Divorce; Custody Battles; Chase Stories; Forgotten Films
(Little Miss Marker; Just You and Me, Kid)

42nd Street, 1933, 89m, ★★★½/$$$$$, WB/WB. The source of many a backstage musical cliche-the Broadway producer who must pull the cast together against incredible odds, the leading lady who can't make opening night, giving her young untried understudy the break of her life, etc. Warner Baxter, Ruby Keeler, Bebe Daniels, George Brent, Una Merkel, Guy Kibbee, Dick Powell, Ginger Rogers, Ned Sparks. w. James Seymour, Rian James, N-adap. Bradford Ropes, d. Lloyd Bacon. BPicture. Oscars: 1-0.

MUSICALS: COMEDY: Musical Comedy; Fame-Rise to; Putting on a Show; Theater Life; Behind the Scenes; Understudies; Blockbusters

Foul Play, 1978, 116m, ★★★/$$$$, Par/Par, PG/V-S. A couple unwittingly get involved in a plot to murder the Pope on his visit to San Francisco. Chevy Chase, Goldie Hawn, Burgess Meredith, Rachel Roberts, Eugene Roche, Dudley Moore, Billy Barty. w. d. Colin Higgins. BOSong. Oscars: 1-0.

COMEDY: ROMANCE: Romantic Comedy; Action Comedy; Detective Couples; Comedy & Violence; Popes Capers; Chase Stories; Librarians; Fools-Bumbling; San Francisco Chases

The Fountainhead, 1949, 114m, ★★★½/$$$, WB/Key. An architect (Gary Cooper) sticks to his principles regarding a massive development, and when it's not built as he designed it, he blows it up, thus dividing the city in half-for him or for the big business and politicians who corrupted the project. Patricia Neal, Raymond Massey, Kent Smith, Robert Douglas, Henry Hull. w. N-adap. Ayn Rand, d. King Vidor.

DRAMA: Political Drama; **ROMANCE:** Romantic Drama; Message Films; Conformism; Corruption; Corporation as Enemy; Government as Enemy; Artists; Fighting the System; Ethics; Underdog Stories; Dreams; Illusions Destroyed; Scandals; Cult Films; Hidden Gems; Allegorical Stories; Female Screenwriters

(Mr. Deeds Goes to Town; And Justice for All)

Four Clowns, 1970, 96m, ★★★½/$, Robert Youngson Productions/NA. A collection of shorts from four silent film stars: Laurel and Hardy, Charley Chase and Buster Keaton. w. Robert Youngson.

COMEDY: Comedy-Character; Comedy-Slapstick; Silent Film Era; Compilation Films

Four Daughters, 1938, 90m, ★★★½/$$$, WB/WB. A small-town family has to deal with giving away its daughters, one by one. Claude Rains, John Garfield (BActor), Priscilla Lane, Rosemary Lane, Lola Lane, Gale Page, Jeffrey Lynn, Frank McHugh, May Robson. w. Julius Epstein, Lenore Coffee (BScr), N-adap. Fannie Hurst (Sister Act), d. Michael Curtiz (BDirector). BPicture. Oscars: 4-0.

MELODRAMA: COMEDY DRAMA: ROMANCE: Family Drama; Family Comedy; Small-town Life; Ensemble Films; Ensembles-Female; American Myth; Capra-esque; Faded Hits; Hidden Gems; Female Screenwriters; Female Protagonists

REMAKES: Daughters Courageous, Young at Heart

SEQUELS: Four Wives, Four Mothers
(Sense and Sensibility; The Old Maid)

The Four Feathers, 1929, 83m, ★★★/$$$, Par/NA, B&W, silent. A timid man in Africa is ridiculed for not signing up for the Sudanese campaign. His friends send him four white feathers-an African symbol of cowardice. Inspired to prove them wrong, he springs into action and rescues his best friend from imminent death. Richard Arlen, Fay Wray, Clive Brook, William Powell, George Fawcett, Theodore Von Eltz, Noah Beery. w. Howard Estabrook, N-adap. E. W. Mason, d. Lothar Mendes, Merian C. Cooper, Ernest Schoedsack.

The Four Feathers, 1939, 130m, ★★★★/$$$, London/Sultan. A talking remake of above also in early technicolor. Great action sequences. John Clements, Ralph Richardson, C. Aubrey Smith, June Duprez, Allan Jeayes, Donald Gray. w. R. C. Sherriff, Lajos Biro, Arthur Wimperis, d. Zoltan Korda.

ACTION: ADVENTURE: Ensembles-Male; Heroes-Unlikely; War Stories; Middle East; Men Proving Themselves;

Anti-War Stories; Cowards; Faded Hits; 1900s; Africa

REMAKE: Storm over the Nile, The Four Feathers (TV Movie, 1977)

(Storm over the Nile; Gunga Din; Gallipoli)

Four for Texas, 1963, 124m, ★★1/2/$$, WB/WB. Two outlaws involved in a stagecoach robbery each try to steal more than their share of the loot. Eventually they both open saloons in the same town and their rivalry goes legit. Dean Martin, Frank Sinatra, Anita Ekberg, Ursula Andress, Charles Bronson, Victor Buono, The Three Stooges. w. Teddi Sherman, Robert Aldrich, d. Robert Aldrich.

COMEDY: WESTERNS: Western Comedy; Heist Stories; Men in Conflict; Thieves; Fools-Bumbling; Texas; Rat Pack Movies; Female Screenwriters

(Bandolero; Five Card Stud)

Four Friends, 1981, 115m, ★★1/2/$, Filmways/WB. A Yugoslavian immigrant's son, his two male friends, and a girl (who wants to grow up to be Isadora Duncan) go through life together in a Midwestern working-class town and beyond. The men all vie for the attentions of the girl at one time or another. Craig Wasson, Jodi Thelen, Michael Huddleston, Jim Metzler. w. Steve Tesich, d. Arthur Penn.

COMEDY DRAMA: MELODRAMA: Autobiographical Stories; Episodic Stories; Ensemble Films; Friendships Between Sexes; Midwestern Life; Men Fighting Over Women; Overlooked at Release; Coulda Been Good

(Ed: From the writer of *Breaking Away*)

Four Frightened People, 1934, 78m, ★★1/2/$$, Par/NA. Rats bring plague to a ship at sea, killing everyone but four who escape on a lifeboat to face an uncertain fate. Claudette Colbert, Herbert Marshall, William Gargan, Mary Boland, Leo Carrillo, Nella Walker, Tetsu Komai. w. Bartlett Cormack, Lenore Coffee, N-adap. E. Arnot Robertson, d. Cecil B. de Mille.

DRAMA: Adventure at Sea; Survival Drama; Epidemics; Disease Stories; Murders/Deaths-One by One; Ships; Female Screenwriters

(Lifeboat; The Plague)

The Four Horsemen of the Apocalypse, 1961, 153m, ★★★/$$$, MGM/MGM-UA. In World War II, an heir to a cattle empire finally tests his mettle fighting for the French resistance. Glenn Ford, Ingrid Thulin, Charles Boyer, Paul Henreid, Lee J. Cobb, Paul Lukas, Karl Boehm, Yvette Mimieux. w. Robert Ardrey, John Gay, d. Vincente Minnelli.

MELODRAMA: DRAMA: Epics; War Stories; World War II Stories; Men Proving Themselves; Cattle Ranchers; Cowards; Argentina

The 400 Blows, 1959, 94m, ★★★★/$$$, Films du Carrosse/Home Vision. After he runs away from home, a determined but moody 12-year-old boy gets sent to a prison-like school for juvenile delinquents and must plan his escape. Jean-Pierre Leaud, Claire Maurier, Albert Remy. w. d. Francois Truffaut (BOScr). Oscars: 1-0.

DRAMA: Character Studies; Boyhood; Memories; Autobiographical Stories; Juvenile Delinquents; Child Protagonists; French Films; Hidden Gems; French New Wave Films; Quiet Little Films; Writer-Directors

SEQUELS: Stolen Kisses, Love on the Run, Bed and Board

(The Long Day Closes; Hope and Glory)

(Ed: A must-see for film students, but also very insightful and entertaining for anyone willing to endure subtitles)

The Four Musketeers, 1974, 103m, ★★★/$$$, 20th/CBS-Fox, PG/V-S. A sequel to *The Three Musketeers*. They are joined by a swashbuckling friend who helps them do battle with the evil Rochefort. Michael York, Oliver Reed, Frank Finlay, Richard Chamberlain, Raquel Welch, Faye Dunaway, Charlton Heston, Christopher Lee, Simon Ward, Geraldine Chaplin, Jean-Pierre Cassel. w. George MacDonald Fraser, d. Richard Lester.

ADVENTURE: ACTION: FARCE: Costume Drama; Women in Jeopardy; Evil Women; Evil Men; Ensemble Films; Swashbucklers; 1700s

SEQUEL TO: The Three Musketeers (1973)

(The Fifth Musketeer; The Count of Monte Cristo)

The Four-Poster, 1952, 103m, ★★1/2/$$, Col/NA. A marriage is chronicled through the years in a series of scenes set in the couple's bedroom. Rex Harrison, Lilli Palmer. w. Allan Scott, P-adap. Jan de Hartog, d. Irving Reis.

COMEDY DRAMA: Marriage Drama; Marriage Comedy; Marriage on the Rocks; Episodic Stories; Stagelike Films

(Same Time, Next Year; Bed and Board)

The Four Seasons, 1981, 108m, ★★★/$$$$, U/MCA-U, PG/P-S. Three couples always vacation together and have extra- and intra-marital problems. Alan Alda, Carol Burnett, Len Cariou, Sandy Dennis, Rita Moreno, Jack Weston, Bess Armstrong. w. d. Alan Alda.

COMEDY: COMEDY DRAMA: Ensemble Films; Marriage Comedy; Marriage Drama; Vacations; Skiing; Episodic Stories; Multiple Stories; Interwoven Stories; Sleeper Hits; Faded Hits; Hidden Gems; Actor Directors; Writer-Directors

(The Big Chill; The Return of the Secaucus Seven)

(Ed: Alda's best film)

Four Sons, 1940, 89m, ★★★/$, 20th/NA. During the rise of Hitler, a Czech family is split apart by the Nazis. Henry Deaniell, Eduard Franz, Valerie French, Grant Richards, Paul Cavanagh. w. Orville H. Hampton, d. Edward L. Cahn.

DRAMA: War Stories; Nazi Stories; World War II Stories; World War II Era; Europeans-Eastern; Forgotten Films; Time Capsules

(The Damned; The Garden of the Finzi-Continis)

Four's a Crowd, 1938, 91m, ★★1/2/$$, WB/NA. A PR man can't find a good angle on his client, an irascible millionaire, but in the process of getting to know his family, he falls in love with the curmudgeon's daughter. Errol Flynn, Rosalind Russell, Olivia de Havilland, Patric Knowles, Walter Connolly, Hugh Herbert, Melville Cooper, Franklin Pangborn, Herman Bing, Margaret Hamilton. w. Casey Robinson, Sig Herzig, d. Michael Curtiz.

COMEDY: ROMANCE: Romantic Comedy; Screwball Comedy; Romance with Boss' Child; Coulda Been Great; Good Premise Unfulfilled; Forgotten Films

Fourteen Hours, 1951, 92m, ★★★1/2/$, 20th/NA. A detective and several others try to talk a man out of jumping from a skyscraper over the course of fourteen hours. Richard Basehart, Paul Douglas, Barbara Bel Geddes, Grace Kelly, Debra Paget, Agnes Moorehead, Robert Keith, Howard da Silva. w. John Paxton, (Article)-adap. Joel Sayre, d. Henry Hathaway. BB&WArt. Oscars: 1-0.

DRAMA: TRAGEDY: Crisis Situations; Suicidal Tendencies; Docudrama; True Stories; Documentary Style; Psychological

Drama; Character Studies; Forgotten
Films; Hidden Gems
(Dog Day Afternoon; The Man Upstairs)
1492: Conquest of Paradise, 1992,
155m, ★★★/$$, Par/Par, PG-13/V.
Columbus seeks funding from Queen
Isabel of Spain for his controversial plan
to voyage to the New World. Gerard
Depardieu, Armand Assante, Sigourney
Weaver, Loren Dean, Angela Molina,
Fernando Rey, Michael Wincott, Tcheky
Karyo, Frank Langella. w. Roselyne
Bosch, d. Ridley Scott.
ADVENTURE: DRAMA: Epics; Historical
Drama; Costume Drama; True Stories;
Revisionist Films; Explorers; Spain;
Caribbean; Middle Ages; Overlooked at
Release; Flops-Major
(Christopher Columbus)
The Fourth Man, 1984, 102m, ★★★/
$$$, Goldwyn/Goldwyn, R/ES-V-B&G-
FFN-MFN. A bisexual writer interested
in the boyfriend of a beautiful woman
learns that he may be the last in her line
of husbands who die mysteriously-appar-
ently by castration. Jerome Krabbé,
Renee Soutendijk, Thom Hoffman, Dolf
De Vries, Geert De Jong. w. Gerard
Soeteman, N-adap. Gerard Reve, d. Paul
Verhoeven.
SUSPENSE: MYSTERY: Gay Men;
Bisexuality; Evil Women; Murderers-
Female; Paranoia; Psychological Thriller;
Nightmares; Chase Stories; Dream
Sequences; Fantasies; Cult Films;
Curiosities; Dutch Films
(The Fifth Floor; Spetters; Flesh and
Blood)
(Ed: One of the Basic Instinct director's
earlier and more bizarre efforts)
The Fourth Protocol, 1987, 119m,
★★1/2/$$, Lorimar-WB/WB, PG-13/V-P.
The world is brought to the brink of
nuclear disaster with a renegade atomic
bomb plot, but two master spies foil the
plot. Michael Caine, Pierce Brosnan,
Joanna Cassidy, Ned Beatty, Betsy
Brantley, Ian Richardson, Anton Rodgers.
w., N-adap. Frederick Forsyth, d. John
Mackenzie.
SUSPENSE: Spy Film; Spies; Bombs-
Atomic; Terrorists; Chase Stories; Race
Against Time; Apocalyptic Stories;
Coulda Been Great
(Special Bulletin; Livewire; The Holcroft
Covenant)
Fourth Story, 1990, 91m, ★★/$$,
Showtime/Media, R/V-S-MN. A beautiful

and sexy woman hires a detective to find
her missing husband, and various clues
make him wonder what she's up to. Mark
Harmon, Mimi Rogers, Cliff DeYoung,
Paul Gleason, M. Emmet Walsh. w.
Andrew Guerdat, d. Ivan Passer.
**SUSPENSE: MYSTERY: MURDER: MUR-
DER MYSTERY:** Missing Persons;
Dangerous Women; Detective Stories;
Detectives-Private; TV Movies
The Fourth War, 1990, 91m, ★★1/2/$
(VR), KodiakHB/HBO, R/V-P. An
American and Soviet commander, each
patroling the border between East
Germany and Czechoslovakia, develop a
personal vendetta. Roy Scheider, Jurgen
Prochnow, Tim Reid, Lara Harris, Harry
Dean Stanton, Dale Dye. w. Stephen
Peters, Kenneth Ross, N-adap. Stephen
Peters, d. John Frankenheimer.
SUSPENSE: Cold War Era; Russians as
Enemy; Men in Conflict; Leaders-
Military; Bombs-Atomic; Iron Curtain-
Behind the; Feuds Revenge
(Gulag; Red Heat; Russia House; Iron
Curtain)
Four Weddings and a Funeral, 1994,
118m, ★★★/$$$$$, Gramercy/MCA-U,
PG-13/P-S. A British thirty-something
bachelor bemoans his fate as all of his
friends marry, leaving him to suffer sin-
glehood alone. But the enchanting
American woman who keeps showing up
at these weddings changes his mind.
Trouble is, the next wedding is hers.
Hugh Grant, Andie MacDowell, Simon
Callow, Kristin Scott Thomas, James
Fleet, John Hannah, Charlotte Coleman,
David Bower. w. Richard Curtis, d. Mike
Newell. BPicture, BOScr. Oscars: 2-0.
COMEDY DRAMA: ROMANCE:
Romantic Drama; Romance-On Again/Off
Again; Romance-Choosing the Right
Person; Shy People; Elusive Women;
Weddings; Funerals; England; Americans
Abroad; Sleeper Hits
The Fox, 1968, 110m, ★★★/$$$,
WB/WB, R/S-P-FN. A salty old sailor
befriends two lesbians living on a farm.
Anne Heywood, Sandy Dennis, Keir
Dullea. w. Lewis John Carlino, Howard
Koch, N-adap. D. H. Lawrence, d. Mark
Rydell, BOScore. Oscars: 1-0.
DRAMA: Erotic Drama; Lesbians; Farm
Life; Rural Life; Sailors; Alternative
Lifestyles; Sleeper Hits; Faded Hits;
Hidden Gems; Ahead of Its Time
(Lianna; Desert Hearts; Priest of Love)

Fox and His Friends, 1975, 123m,
★★★/$$, Lorimar/Karl-Lorimar, R/ES-V-
MFN. A traveling circus performer and
gay adventurer who wins a lottery suffers
his downfall at the hands of a jerk.
Rainer Werner Fassbinder, Karl-Heinz
Boehm, Peter Chatel, Harry Bar, Ulla
Jacobsen. w. Rainer Werner Fassbinder,
Christian Hohoff, d. Rainer Werner
Fassbinder.
DRAMA: TRAGEDY: Art Films;
Lotteries; Rags to Riches; Betrayals;
Suicidal Tendencies; Suicidal Tendencies
of Homosexuals; Drugs-Addictions;
Dangerous Men; Gay Men; Gay
Awakenings; Gay & Lesbian Films;
Circus Life; German Films; Germany
(Taxi Zum Klo; Bad Influence)
The Fox and the Hound, 1981, 83m,
★★★/$$$, Disney/Disney, G. An ani-
mated feature about the two title crea-
tures growing up to realize that they are
different and growing apart. Voices of
Mickey Rooney, Kurt Russell, Pearl
Bailey, Jack Albertson, Sandy Duncan,
Jeanette Nolan. w. various, N-adap.
Daniel P. Mannix, d. Art Stevens, Ted
Berman, Richard Rich.
CHILDREN'S: FAMILY: Cartoons;
Animal Stories; Friendships-Great;
Coming of Age
(Bambi; Robin Hood [1973]; Oliver and
Company)
Foxes, 1980, 106m, ★★★/$, UA/CBS-
Fox, R/P-S. A group of suburban L.A.
girls struggle with the trials of teenage
life, including bouts with drugs. Jodie
Foster, Scott Baio, Sally Kellerman,
Randy Quaid, Adam Faith. w. Gerald
Ayres, d. Adrian Lyne.
DRAMA: Character Studies; Ensemble
Films; Ensembles-Female; Teenagers;
Teenage Movies; Coming of Age;
Friendships-Female; Suburban Life;
1970s; Slice of Life Stories; High School
Life; Cult Films; Overlooked at Release;
Time Capsules; Female Protagonists
(Dazed and Confused; Fast Times at
Ridgemont High; Lost Angels)
Foxfire, 1955, 92m, ★★/$, U-I/NA. A
cosmopolitan girl from Manhattan goes
out to Arizona and snags a halfbreed-
miner-desert-hunk. Jane Russell, Jeff
Chandler, Frieda Inescort, Dan Duryea.
w. Ketti Frings, N-adap. Anya Seton, d.
Joseph Pevney.
MELODRAMA: ROMANCE: Vacations;
Vacation Romance; Romance-Older

Women/Younger Men; Mining Towns; Desert Settings; Indians-American; Romance-Interracial; Forgotten Films; Unintentionally Funny; Female Protagonists; Female Screenwriters

Foxfire, 1987, 118m, ★★★1/2/$$$, CBS-Republic/Republic. In this made-for-television movie, an elderly widow in all her life in the Blue Ridge Mountains talking only to the ghost of her dead husband, but stubbornly resists her son's entreaties to move away from her isolated mountain home. Jessica Tandy, Hume Cronyn, John Denver, Gary Grubbs, Harriet Hall. d. Judd Taylor. Multiple Emmy winner.

DRAMA: MELODRAMA: Elderly Women; Mountain People; Southerns; Mothers & Sons; Storytellers; Ghosts; Illusions/Hallucinations; Widows; Ordinary People Stories; TV Movies; Hidden Gems

(Dance with the White Dog; Driving Miss Daisy; Camilla; Fried Green Tomatoes; The Trip to Bountiful)

Frances, 1982, 140m, ★★★/$$, EMI-Universal/MCA-U, R/P-S-FFN. The story of actress Frances Farmer (Jessica Lange, BActress) and her fall from a meteoric rise of stardom into a pit of mental institutions and rebellion, spurred on mostly by her mother (Kim Stanley, BSActress) and the unforgiving studio system. Sam Shepard, Jeffrey DeMunn, Bart Burns. w. Eric Bergren, Nicholas Kazan, Christopher Devore, d. Graeme Clifford. Oscars: 2-0.

DRAMA: TRAGEDY: Biographies; Hollywood Life; Hollywood Biographies; Rebels; Fighting the System; Rise and Fall Stories; Fame-Rise to; Committed-Wrongly; Feisty Females; Rags to Riches; Fame-Rise to; Mental Illness; Asylums; Actresses; 1930s; Narrated Films; Hidden Gems; Female Protagonists

(Will There Really Be a Morning?; The Goddess)

(Ed: Great performances from Lange and Stanley, but the story in the TV version, *Will There Really Be a Morning?*, based on Farmer's autobiography, is much more accurate. The Shepard character was pure fabrication. Look for Anjelica Huston screaming in one of the asylum scenes)

Francis, God's Jester, 1950, 75m, ★★★/$, Cineriz/NA. Saint Francis goes to Assisi and starts an order of monks.

Addo Fabrizi, Arabella Lamaitre, Brother Nazario Geraldi. w. Roberto Rossellini, Federicio Fellini, NF-adap. (*The Little Flowers of St. Francis, The Life of Brother Ginepro*), d. Roberto Rossellini.

DRAMA: Art Films; Priests; Monks; Historical Drama; Religion; Biographies; Italian Films; Neo-Realist Films; Forgotten Films; Hidden Gems

Francis the Talking Mule, 1949, 91m, ★★★/$$$, U/MCA-U. Fighting in Burma, a dim-witted G.I. starts talking to his mule and brings him home with him to the states after the War. Donald O'Connor, Patricia Medina, ZaSu Pitts, Ray Collins, John McIntire, Eduard Franz, Howland Chamberlin, Frank Faylen, Tony Curtis. w. Frank Skinner, d. Arthur Lubin.

COMEDY: Animals-Talking; Animal Stories; Horses; What If . . . Stories; Soldiers; Curiosities

SEQUELS: Francis Goes to the Races, Francis in the Navy, Francis Joins the WACS

(Mr. Ed TV Series; Babe)

Frankenhooker, 1990, 90m, ★★1/2/$ (VR), Shapiro/Shapiro-Glickenhaus, R/V-S-FN-B&G. After his girlfriend is minced and diced in a lawnmower accident, a mad scientist "reconstructs" her out of the bodies of dead prostitutes. James Lorintz, Patty Mullen, Charlotte Helmkamp, Shirley Stoler. w. Robert Martin, Frank Henenlotter, d. Frank Henenlotter.

HORROR: Black Comedy; Comedy-Morbid; Prostitutes-Low Class; Murders of Prostitutes; Women in Jeopardy; Murders of Women; Serial Killers; Murders-One by One; Body Parts; Monsters-Manmade; Scientists-Mad; Dead-Back from the; Camp; Coulda Been Great; Curiosities; Overlooked at Release

Frankenstein, 1931, 71m, ★★★★/$$$$, U/MCA-U. Dr. Frankenstein, obsessed with the mystery of life, creates a living being constructed from corpses and animated with electricity. Unfortunately, this inarticulate brute isn't exactly happy to be alive. Boris Karloff, Colin Clive, Mae Clarke, John Boles, Edward Van Sloan, Frederick Kerr, Dwight Frye. w. Garrett Fort, Francis Edward Faragoh, John L. Balderston, P-adap. Peggy Webling, N-adap. Mary Wollstonecraft Shelley, d. James Whale.

HORROR: Scientists-Mad; Monsters; Monsters-Manmade; Body Parts; Brain

Transplants; Dead-Back from the; Murders-One by One; Rogue Plots; Kill the Beast; Blockbusters

(Bride of Frankenstein; Young Frankenstein; Reanimator; Mary Shelley's Frankenstein)

Frankenstein and the Monster from Hell, 1973, 99m, ★★1/2/$, Hammer-Avco/Par, R/EV-B&G. The fabled doctor creates a hairy monster from an injured resident of a mental hospital. Peter Cushing, Shane Briant, Madeleine Smith, John Stratton, Bernard Lee, Dave Prowse. w. John Elder (Anthony Hinds), d. Terence Fisher.

HORROR: Scientists-Mad; Monsters; Monsters-Manmade; Body Parts; Dead-Back from the; Murders-One by One; Rogue Plots; Kill the Beast

Frankenstein Created Woman, 1967, 86m, ★★/$, WB/NA. The old Baron Von Frankenstein is back up to his old tricks, this time re-animating a dead girl with the soul of her lover. Peter Cushing, Thorley Walters, Susan Denberg, Robert Morris, Duncan Lamont. w. John Elder (Anthony Hinds), d. Terence Fisher.

HORROR: Scientists-Mad; Monsters; Monsters-Manmade; Body Parts; Dead-Back from the; Murders-One by One; Rogue Plots; Kill the Beast; Revisionist Films

(Re-Animator 2; Bride of Frankenstein)

Frankenstein Meets the Wolf Man, 1943, 73m, ★★1/2/$$, U/MCA-U. The Wolfman goes to Transylvania to find a cure and runs into Frankenstein's monster. Peter Cushing, Freddie Jones, Veronica Carlson, Simon Ward, Thorley Walters, Maxine Audley. w. Bert Batt, d. Terence Fisher.

HORROR: Monsters; Werewolves; Monsters-Manmade; Cures-Search for; Monsters Meet

Frankenstein '70, 1958, 83m, ★★/$, Allied Artists/NA. A television crew goes to Germany to get footage of Frankenstein's descendant at work. And he needs the money from the rights to the show. Boris Karloff, Tom Duggan, Jana Lund, Mike Lane. w. Richard Landau, G. Worthing Yates, d. Howard W. Koch.

HORROR: Scientists-Mad; Monsters; Monsters-Manmade; Body Parts; Dead-Back from the; Murders-One by One; Rogue Plots; Kill the Beast; TV Life; Movies Within Movies; Revisionist Films; Curiosities

Frankenstein Unbound, 1990, 85m, ★★★/$ (VR), 20th/Fox, R/V-S-B&G. A gathering of Victorian authors including Mary Shelley exist alongside her creation-Dr. Frankenstein. And a doctor from the future travels back to 19th-century Switzerland to find them all. John Hurt, Raul Julia, Bridget Fonda, Nick Brimble, Michael Hutchence. w. Roger Corman, F. X. Feeney, N-adap. Brian Aldiss, d. Roger Corman.

HORROR: Scientists-Mad; Monsters; Monsters-Manmade; Body Parts; Dead-Back from the; Murders-One by One; Rogue Plots; Kill the Beast; Time Travel; Writers; Revisionist Films; Overlooked at Release; Female Protagonists (Frankenstein; Haunted Summer; Gothic; Andy Warhol's Frankenstein; Mary Shelley's Frankenstein)

Frankie and Johnny, 1991, 116m, ★★★/$$$, Par/Par, R/P-S. A romance develops between an ex-convict (Al Pacino), just released after several years, and a reluctant waitress (Michelle Pfeiffer) at the diner where he gets a job. Kate Nelligan, Hector Elizondo, Nathan Lane, Jane Morris, Glenn Plummer. w. P-adap. Terrence McNally, d. Garry Marshall.

COMEDY DRAMA: ROMANCE: Romantic Comedy; Romantic Drama; Romance-Mismatched; Romance-Reluctant; Ex-Convicts; Starting Over; Ordinary People Stories; Working Class; Waitresses; Restaurant Settings; Wisecracking Sidekicks; New York Life (Ed: Slight with a few good moments, but with Kathy Bates repeating her stage lead would have helped tremendously. Pfeiffer being dowdy and dateless is only so believable)

Frantic, 1958, 92m, ★★/$, Ind/Nos. A man in love with his boss's wife plans his murder with her. They execute it, and she makes it look like suicide. Everything goes according to plan, until they find his car and gun have been used by teenagers in a robbery/murder, and he is accused of that crime. Maurice Ronet, Jeanne Moreau, George Poujouly. w. d. Louis Malle.

SUSPENSE: MURDER: Murder of Spouse; Cheating Women; Romance with Boss' Lover; Suicidal Tendencies; Clever Plots & Endings; Hidden Gems; Forgotten Films; Writer-Directors; French Films

(Double Indemnity; Body Heat; China Moon)

Frantic, 1988, 120m, ★★★/$$, WB/WB, PG-13/P-S-V-MRN. An American doctor in Paris at a cardiology convention is at a loss when his wife suddenly disappears. His search for her leads to Arab terrorists and a nuclear bomb detonator. Harrison Ford, Betty Buckley, Emmanuelle Seigner. w. Roman Polanski, Gerard Brach, d. Roman Polanski.

SUSPENSE: Missing Persons; Missing Person Thriller; Kidnappings; Bombs-Atomic; Terrorists; Saving Someone; Women in Jeopardy; Americans Abroad; Race Against Time; Doctors; Paris; Arab People; Hitchcockian (The Man Who Knew Too Much; The Fugitive [1993])

Fraternity Row, 1977, 101m, ★★★/$, Par/NA, R/P-S. An expose of dangerous fraternity initiation practices in the 50s. Peter Fox, Gregory Harrison, Scott Newman, Nancy Morgan, Wendy Phillips, Robert Emhardt, Cliff Robertson. w. Charles Gary Allison, d. Thomas J. Tobin.

DRAMA: COMEDY DRAMA: College Life; Young Men; Conformism; Fraternity Life; 1950s; Nostalgia; Overlooked at Release (Animal House; A Separate Peace) (Ed: The dramatic predecessor to *Animal House.* Nobody went)

Freaks, 1932, 64m, ★★★/$, MGM/MGM-UA. In a circus, the beauty queen/trapeze artist marries the midget for his money and kills him. But his "special" friends exact their horrible revenge on her, in one of the most chilling climaxes in cinema history. Wallace Ford, Olga Baclanova, Leila Hyams, Roscoe Ates. w. Willis Goldbeck, Leon Gordon, N-adap. Tod Robbins (*Spurs*), d. Tod Browning.

DRAMA: MELODRAMA: Psychological Drama; Surrealism; Revenge; Circus Life; Little People-Midgets; Cult Films; Curiosities; Hidden Gems (Shadows and Fog)

Freaked, 1993, 80m, ★★/$, 20th/Fox. A sleazy TV personality becomes the spokesman for a green, slimy, toxic fertilizer used in South America. When on a promotional tour down south, he's captured by a freak-show barker, who forces him to drink the fertilizer, making him into a freak himself. Alex Winter, Randy Quaid, Megan Ward, Michael Stoyanov,

Brooke Shields, Mr. T, Alex Zuckerman, Keanu Reeves. w. Alex Winter, Tim Burns, Tom Stern, d. Alex Winter.

SCI-FI: HORROR: Poisons; South America; Scientists-Mad (The Island of Lost Souls; The Island of Dr. Moreau; Dr. Cyclops)

Freaky Friday, 1976, 100m, ★★★/$$$, Disney/Disney, G. A mother and daughter change bodies and get into all sorts of hilarious trouble when the mom tries to cook at home and the daughter enters a skiing competition and is chased by the cops. Jodie Foster, Barbara Harris, John Astin, Patsy Kelly, Dick Van Patten, Sorrell Booke. w., N-adap. Mary Rodgers, d. Gary Nelson.

COMEDY: CHILDREN'S: FAMILY: Disney Comedy; Chase Stories; Magic; Body Switching; Mothers & Daughters; Curiosities (Vice Versa; Like Father, Like Son; Candleshoe) (Ed: Good performances from both Foster and Harris make this worth it)

Freddie as F.R.0.7., 1992, 91m, ★★ 1/2/$, Rank/Live. An animated take off on James Bond, with a French frog as a secret agent. Voices of Ben Kingsley, Jenny Agutter, Brian Blessed, Nigel Hawthorne, Edmund Kingsley, Phyllis Logan, Jonathan Pryce, Prunella Scales, Billie Whitelaw. w. Jon Acevski, David Ashton, d. Jon Acevski.

CHILDREN'S: FAMILY: Cartoons; Spoofs-Spy; Secret Agents; Overlooked at Release; Comedy-Disneyesque; British Films (The Rescuers; The Secret of NIMH)

Freddy's Dead: The Final Nightmare, 1991, 90m, ★★ 1/2/$$, New Line/New Line, R/S-P-EV-B&G. Freddie Kruger's daughter grows up to destroy her father, with the help of her narcoleptic dream buddies. Robert Englund, Lisa Zane, Shon Greenblatt, Lezlie Deane, Alice Cooper. w. Michael DeLuca, SS-adap. Rachel Talalay, d. Rachel Talalay.

HORROR: SCI-FI: Nightmares; Evil Men; Teenagers in Jeopardy; Murders of Teenagers; Teenagers; Teenage Movies; Cult Films; Sleeper Hits; Female Directors; Female Protagonists; Female Among Males; 3-D Movies

SEQUEL TO: Nightmare on Elm Street

Free and Easy, 1930, 75m, ★★ 1/2/$$, MGM/MGM-UA. A klutzy manager takes a beauty queen to Hollywood. Buster

Keaton, Anita Page, Robert Montgomery, Trixie Friganza. w. Al Boasberg, Richard Schayer, d. Edward Sedgwick.
COMEDY: ROMANCE: Romantic Comedy; Comedy-Slapstick; Beauty Pageants; Fools-Bumbling; Hollywood Satire; Forgotten Films
(The General)

A Free Soul, 1931, 91m, ★★¹/₂/$$, MGM/MGM-UA. A liberal lawyer allows his daughter to do what she wants, but is dismayed when she starts running around with a mobster. Lionel Barrymore (BActor), Norma Shearer (BActress), Leslie Howard, Clark Gable, Lucy Beaumont, James Gleason. w. John Meehan, N-adap. Adela Rogers St. John, d. Clarence Brown (BDirector). Oscars: 3-0.
MELODRAMA: Mob Stories; Lover Family Dislikes; Fathers & Daughters; Lawyers; Romance-Dangerous; Faded Hits
REMAKE: The Girl Who Had Everything
(The Divorcee; Bombshell)

Freebie and the Bean, 1974, 113m, ★★★/$$, WB/WB, R/P-S-V. A mobster's numbers racket is infiltrated by two somewhat inept cops and a series of car chases begins. Alan Arkin, James Caan, Loretta Swit, Jack Kruschen, Mike Kellin, Valerie Harper. w. Richard Kaufman, d. Richard Rush.
COMEDY: ACTION: Action Comedy; Police Stories; Police Comedy; Chase Stories; Buddy Cops; Car Chases; Car Wrecks; Mob Comedy; Gambling; Transvestite Killers; Coulda Been Great
(Super Cops; Slither; Law and Disorder; Fuzz)
(Ed: A bit of a send-up of Dirty Harry, not too bad)

Freejack, 1992, 108m, ★★¹/₂/$$, WB/WB, R/P-V. A racer in a fatal accident is taken to the future right before the moment of death and his body is used to house someone else's soul. Emilio Estevez, Mick Jagger, Rene Russo, Anthony Hopkins, Jonathan Banks, David Johannsen, Amanda Plummer. w. Steven Pressfield, Ronald Shusett, Dan Gilroy, N-adap. Robert Sheckley, d. Geoff Murphy.
ACTION: SCI-FI: Time Travel; Car Racing; Futuristic Films; Soul-Selling One's; Body Switching; Dead-Back from the; Good Premise Unfulfilled
(Total Recall; The Running Man [1987])

Free Willy, 1993, 112m, ★★–/$$$, WB/WB, G. A runaway boy identifies with a captive whale mistreated at an amusement park, so he decides to set him free. Jason James Richter, Lori Petty, Jayne Atkinson, August Schellenberg, Michael Madsen. w. Keith A. Walker, Corey Blechman, d. Simon Wincer.
CHILDREN'S: FAMILY: Animal Stories; Amusement Parks; Saving Someone; Nature-Back to; Whales; Sleeper Hits
SEQUEL: Free Willy 2
(E.T.; Flipper; André)
(Ed: In England, the title had to be changed because of the connotations of "willy")

Free Willy 2, 1995, 98m, ★★/$$$, WB/WB, PG. When the boy and his killer whale encounter an oil tanker spill, will everything get sticky or simply wash away? Jason James Richter, August Schellenberg, Jayne Atkinson, Jon Tenney, Elizabeth Pena, Michael Madsen. w. Karen Janszen, Corey Blechman, John Mattson, d. Dwight Little.
CHILDREN'S: Animal Stories; Environmental Dilemmas; Whales; Oil People; Female Screenwriters; Child Protagonists
(Dead Ahead; Flipper)

The French Connection, 1971, 104m, 20th/Fox, ★★★¹/₂/$$$$, R/V-P. A New York detective (Gene Hackman, **BActor**) uncovers a French heroin smuggling ring but he has to chase and catch them red-handed. Roy Scheider (BSActor). Fernando Rey, Tony Lo Bianco. w. Ernest Tidyman (**BAScr**), NF-adap. Robin Moore, d. William Friedkin (**BDirector**), **BPicture**, **BCin**, **BEdit**, BSound. Oscars: 8-5.
DRAMA: ACTION: Action Drama; Crime Drama; Police Stories; Detective Stories; Detectives-Police; Mob Stories; Drugs-Dealing; Chase Movies; Car Chases; Faded Hits
SEQUEL: The French Connection 2
(The Seven-Ups; Bullitt; The French Connection 2; To Live and Die in L.A.; Jade)
(Ed: Famous for its very long chase sequence, often imitated; seems cliche by today's TV standards)

French Connection II, 1975, 119m, ★★/$$, 20th/Fox, R/P-V. The cop from the first film, who shut down the New York operation almost entirely, goes to Marseilles to bring down the Man behind

it all. Gene Hackman, Fernando Rey, Bernard Fresson, Jean-Pierre Castaldi. w. Robert Dillon, Laurie Dillon, Alexander Jacobs, d. John Frankenheimer.
ACTION: Action Drama; Police Stories; Mob Stories; Crime Drama; Detective Stories; Detectives-Police; Drugs-Dealing; Undercover; Flops-Major
SEQUEL TO: The French Connection
(Ed: A logical sequel doesn't deliver)

The French Lieutenant's Woman, 1981, 123m, ★★★★/$$$, UA/MGM-UA, R/P-S. The story of a nobleman (Jeremy Irons) who's engaged in Victorian England to a society girl but becomes infatuated with a woman he sees (Meryl Streep, BActress) who turns out to have the reputation of being a French lieutenant's mistress and therefore forbidden to him. Irons and Streep also play the parts of actors playing the characters in a modern-day parallel story of the movie of first story being made. w. Harold Pinter (BAScr), N-adap. John Fowles, d. Karel Reisz. BCin, BCostume, BEdit. Oscars: 5-0.
DRAMA: ROMANCE: Romantic Drama; Love-Forbidden; Gossip; Prostitutes-Low Class; Missing Persons; Searches; Romance-Reunited; Marriage-Impending; Victorian Era; Class Conflicts; Spinsters; Scandals; Cheating Men; Engagements-Breaking; Parallel Stories; Movies within Movies; Actresses; Actors; England
(The Age of Innocence; Howards End; The Go-Between; Day for Night; The House of the Spirits; Swann in Love)

Frenchie, 1950, 80m, ★★¹/₂/$$, U-I/NA. A saloon singer goes to Bottleneck to hunt down her father's killers. Shelley Winters, Joel McCrea, Paul Kelly, Elsa Lanchester, Marie Windsor, John Emery, George Cleveland. w. Oscar Brodney, d. Louis King.
WESTERNS: Westerns-Revenge; Avenging Death of Someone; Sexy Women; Dancers; Revenge; Fathers & Daughters; Female Protagonists; Forgotten Films
(Hannie Caulder; Johnny Guitar; Destry Rides Again; Belle of the Yukon)
(Ed: A novelty in that it's a female-driven western)

Frenchman's Creek, 1945, 112m, ★★★/$$$, Par/NA, AMC. In 1600s England, a beautiful woman returns to her family in Cornwall to escape the unwanted advances of a lothario.

However, after not too long in her boring coastal town, she falls for a swashbuckling French pirate. Joan Fontaine, Arturo de Cordova, Basil Rathbone, Nigel Bruce, Cecil Kellaway, Ralph Forbes. w. Talbot Jennings, N-adap. Daphne du Maurier, d. Mitchell Leisen. **BCArt.** Oscars: 1-1.

MELODRAMA: ROMANCE: Costume Drama; Romance-Triangles; Romance-Choosing Right Person; Swashbucklers; Hiding Out; Restoration Period; Female Protagonists; Womens' Films; Production Design-Outstanding; Flops-Major
(Forever Amber)
(Ed: The most expensive film to that point-at only $10 million. A flop at that budget, but otherwise a decent entertainment)

French Postcards, 1979, 95m, ★★★/$$, Par/Par, G. Three American students do the "junior year abroad" thing in Paris, and make the most of it by falling in love. Miles Chaplin, Blanche Baker, Valerie Quennessen, Debra Winger, Mandy Patinkin, Marie-France Pisier. w. Gloria Katz, d. Willard Huyck.

COMEDY DRAMA: ROMANCE: CHILDREN'S: FAMILY: Teenagers; Americans Abroad; Teachers and Students; Paris
(Peppermint Soda; Once in Paris; A Little Romance)

Frenzy, 1972, 116m, ★★★1/2/$$$, U/MCA-U, R/P-S-V. A series of "necktie murders" points to an innocent military veteran in London as its prime suspect. He must find the real culprit as he eludes the police. Jon Finch, Alec McCowen, Barry Foster, Vivien Merchant, Anna Massey, Billie Whitelaw. w. Anthony Shaffer, N-adap. Arthur La Bern (Goodbye Piccadilly, Farewell Leicester Square), d. Alfred Hitchcock.

SUSPENSE: Black Comedy; Comedy-Morbid; Detective Stories; Detectives-Police; Fugitives from the Law; Serial Killers; Murders of Women; Murderers-Nice; Psycho-Killers; Trail of a Killer; Parallel Stories; England; Hidden Gems; Hitchcockian
(Psycho; The Boston Strangler; Henry: Portrait of a Serial Killer)

Fresh, 1994, ★★★/$, Miramax/Miramax, R/EP-S-EV. A child drug dealer and chess player gets in over his head very quickly in this inner city tale of black life on the streets. While "Fresh" as he is called would seem to mean well, getting out of the hole he was born into, the powers that

be in his own world won't allow it the way he's chosen. Sean Nelson, Giancarlo Esposito, Samuel L. Jackson, N'Bushe Wright, Ron Brice, Jean LaMarre, Cheryl Freeman. w. d. Boaz Yakin.

DRAMA: TRAGEDY: Boys; Children-Little Adults; Games Chess; Mob Stories; Child Protagonists; Black Men; Drugs-Dealing; Inner City Life; 'Hood Stories; Writer-Directors; Black Directors; Black Screenwriters; Black Casts/Films
(Menace II Society; Boyz N the Hood; Juice)

Fresh Horses, 1988, 103m, ★1/2/$, Weintraub-Col/Col-Tri, PG-13/S. An upper-class student apparently infatuated with poor white trash falls for a married 16-year-old named Jewel. Molly Ringwald, Andrew McCarthy, Patti D'Arbanville, Ben Stiller, Leon Russom. w., P-adap. Larry Ketron, d. David Anspaugh.

MELODRAMA: ROMANCE: Romantic Drama; Romance-Class Conflicts; Lover Family Dislikes; Horses; Unintentionally Funny; Camp; Bratpack Movies
(Pretty in Pink; Buster and Billie)
(Ed: Molly as country trash should be an unintended hoot, but even that possibility flags in this turgid exercise in mediocrity)

The Freshman, 1925, 75m, ★★★1/2/$$$, (B&W, silent), Harold Lloyd/Time Life. A geeky nerd in college accidently wins the big game for his football team. Harold Lloyd, Jobyna Ralston, Brooks Benedict. w. Sam Taylor, Ted Wilde, Tim Whelan, John Grey.

COMEDY: Comedy-Slapstick; Comedy of Errors; College Life; Fools-Bumbling; Football; Nerds; Accidents; Hidden Gems
(The World of Harold Lloyd)

The Freshman, 1990, 102m, ★★★/$$$, Tri-Star/Col-Tri, R/P-S. A film student and gangster film aficionado gets a job working for the mob and meets a real-life Don Corleone. Things are okay until he goes after the don's stuck-up daughter-though finding an iguana may save the day. Marlon Brando, Matthew Broderick, Bruno Kirby, Penelope Ann Miller, Frank Whaley, Jon Polito, Paul Benedict. w. d. Andrew Bergman.

COMEDY: SATIRE: Spoofs; Black Comedy; Mob Stories; Mob Comedy; Fugitives from the Mob; Romance with Boss' Child; Romance-Reluctant; Nerds; Film Students; Hidden Gems; Coulda Been Great; Writer-Directors
(The In-Laws; Honeymoon in Vegas)

Freud, 1962, 140m, ★★★/$, U-I/MCA-U. Dr. Freud is presented as a maverick bucking the establishment in the Vienese Academe as he investigates the psychosexual problems of several patients. Montgomery Clift, Larry Parks, Susannah York, Eileen Herlie. w. Charles Kaufman, Wolfgang Reinhardt (BOScr), d. John Huston. BOScore. Oscars: 2-0.

DRAMA: Psychologists; Psychological Drama; Rebels; Biographies; Incest; Sexual Problems; Sexuality; Dream Sequences; Surrealism; Mothers & Sons; Fathers & Sons; Secrets-Haunting; Freud; Vienna; Multiple Stories; Cult Films

Friday the Thirteenth, 1933, 84m, ★★★1/2/$$, Gainsborough/NA. On that fateful day . . . a group of people are victims of a bus crash. Their individual stories are told in flashbacks, and we learn how they all got to be so unlucky. Sonnie Hale, Cyril Smith, Eliot Makeham, Ursula Jeans, Emlyn Williams, Frank Lawton, Belle Chrystal, Max Miller, Robertson Hare. w. G. H. Moresby-White, Sidney Gilliat, Emlyn Williams, d. Victor Saville.

DRAMA: TRAGEDY: Disaster Movies; Accidents; Car Wrecks; Buses; Multiple Stories; Interwoven Stories; Forgotten Films; Flashbacks; British Films
(The Bridge of San Luis Rey)
(Ed: Probably the first slice of life disaster movie done as we know them today [without the comparable special effects, however], though The Bridge of San Luis Rey set the trend in books)

Friday the 13th, 1980, 95m, ★★★/$$$, Par/Par, R/S-PEV-B&G. A summer camp where a bunch of kids were killed years ago is reopened and the killings just start again. Betsy Palmer, Adrienne King, Jeannine Taylor, Robbi Morgan. w. Victor Miller, d. Sean S. Cunnigham.

Friday the 13th, Part II, 1981, 87m, ★★/$$$, Par/Par, R/S-PEV-B&G. More stupid and horny teenagers ignore all warnings and go off to Camp Crystal Lake to have sex and get killed. Amy Steel, John Furey, Adrienne King, Kristen Baker, Stu Charno. w. Ron Kurz, d. Steve Miner.

Friday the 13th, Part 3-D, 1982, 95m, ★★/$$$, Par/Par, R/S-PEV-B&G. More of the same with Jason killing all who enter his stomping grounds at Camp Crystal Lake. Dana Kimmell, Richard Brooker, Catherine Parks, Paul Kratka. w. Martin

Kitrosser, Carol Watson, d. Steve Miner.
3-D Movies

Friday the 13th: Final Chapter, 1984, 91m, ★★/$$$, Par/Par, R/S-PEV-B&G. Jason's body's been frozen for years, but he gets reanimated and kills again. E. Erich Anderson, Judie Aronson, Peter Barton, Kimberly Beck. w. Barney Cohen, d. Joseph Zito.
Time Sleepers; Frozen People

Friday the 13th Part V-A New Beginning, 1985, 92m, ★¹/²$$, Par/Par, R/S-PEV-B&G. More of the same, this time set at a hospital. The primary horror is that they lied about that "final chapter" bit. John Shepard, Shavar Ross, Richard Young. w. Martin Kitrosser, David Cohen, Danny Steinmann, d. Danny Steinmann.
Hospitals

Friday the 13th Part VI-Jason Lives, 1986, 93m, ★¹/²$$, Par/Par, R/S-PEV-B&G. Jason's corpse is reanimated once again and more teenagers are fed into the meat grinder. Thom Mathews, Jennifer Cooke, David Kagen, Renee Jones. w. d. Tom McLoughlin.

Friday the 13th Part VII-The New Blood, 1988, 90m, ★/$, Par/Par, R/S-PEV-B&G. A telepathic woman fights Jason in the woods. Lar Park Lincoln, Kevin Blair, Susan Blu, Terry Kiser, Kane Hodder. w. Daryl Haney, Manuel Fidello, d. John Carl.
Psychics

Friday the 13th Part VIII-Jason Takes Manhattan, 1989, 96m, Par. Jason's body lies at the bottom of the Hudson and is revived by an electrical shock. He is free again to kill lusty teenagers, this time in the Big Apple. Jensen Daggett, Scott Reeves, Barbara Bingham, Peter Mark Richman, Kane Hodder. w. d. Rob Hedden.
New York Life

HORROR: Murders of Teenagers; Teenagers; Teenage Movies; Teenage Horror Flicks of 1980s; Serial Killers; Psycho-Killers; Dead-Back from the; Camps; Camping; Murders-One by One; Kill the Beast; Rogue Plots
(The Town That Dreaded Sundown; Nightmare on Elm Street SERIES; Prom Night SERIES)

Fried Green Tomatoes, 1991, 132m, ★★★★/$$$$$, Universal/MCA-U, PG-13/P-S. A lonely, overweight Southern housewife (Kathy Bates) vists a rest home and meets an elderly woman (Jessica Tandy, BSActress) who begins telling her the story of two women (Mary Stuart Masterson, Mary Louise Parker) and a murder that occurred many years ago. Cicely Tyson. w. Fannie Flagg, Carol Sobieski (BAScr), N-adap. Fannie Flagg, d. Jon Avnet. Oscars: 2-0.
COMEDY: COMEDY DRAMA: MYSTERY: MURDER MYSTERY: Friendships-Female; Episodic Stories; Parallel Stories; Storytellers; Memories; Narrated Films; Midlife Crisis; Marriage on the Rocks; Starting Over; Weight Problems; Elderly Women; Free Spirits; Murderers-Female; Feisty Females; Homo-eroticism; Lesbians; Cannibalism; Cannibalism-Funny; Ku Klux Klan; Southerns; 1920s; Alabama; Female Protagonists; Women's Films; Sleeper Hits; Blockbusters
(The Color Purple; Camilla; Crimes of the Heart)

Friendly Fire, 1979, 146m, ★★★−/$$$$, ABC/Fox. The true story of a soldier in Vietnam who was killed by American gunfire somehow and his mother's search for the explanation and her fight to keep her other son from going over to fight, too. Carol Burnett, Ned Beatty, Sam Waterston, Timothy Hutton. w. Fay Kanin, d. David Greene. Multiple Emmy winner.
DRAMA: Social Drama; Vietnam Era; Death-Dealing with; Mothers & Sons; Reformers; Fighting the System; Ordinary People Stories; Farm Life; Midwestern Life; Female Protagonists

Friendly Persuasion, 1956, 139m, ★★★¹/²$$$, AA/NA. A Quaker family is torn between North and South at the outbreak of the Civil War and must deal with their own pacifist religious beliefs. Gary Cooper, Dorothy McGuire, Anthony Perkins (BSActor), Marjorie Main, Richard Eyer. w. Michael Wilson (BAScr), N-adap. Jessamyn West, d. William Wyler (BDirector). BPicture, BOSong. Oscars: 6-0.
DRAMA: Civil War Era; War Stories; Family Drama; Religion; Peaceful People; Ethics; Feuds; North vs. South; Sleeper Hits; Hidden Gems
(The Birch Interval; Chariots of Fire)

Friends and Husbands, 1982, 106m, Miracle-Ind/NA, R/S-FN. A psychological study of the destructive friendship between two women and how it affects their husbands. Hanna Schygulla, Angela Winklet, Peter Striebeck, Christine Fersen, Franz Buchrieser, Jochen Striebeck. w. d. Margarethe von Trotta.
DRAMA: TRAGEDY: Character Studies; Psychological Drama; Friendships-Female; Betrayals; Marriage Drama; Marriage on the Rocks; Art Films; German Films; Female Directors; Female Screenwriters; Writer-Directors
(The Marriage of Maria Braun; Entre Nous)

Friends Forever, 1986, 95m, ★★★/VR, Ind/Facets. A coming-of-age drama in which a high school student slowly discovers that he is gay and must deal with it in his longstanding friendships. d. Stefan Christian Henszelman.
DRAMA: Gay Men; Alternative Lifestyles; Teenagers; Social Drama; High School Life; Ostracism

The Friends of Eddie Coyle, 1973, 102m, ★★¹/²$, Par/NA, R/P-V. An older mobster turns informant, but a police sting may foil the scheme when he's exposed. Robert Mitchum, Peter Boyle, Richard Jordan, Steven Keats, Mitch Ryan, Alex Rocco. w. Paul Monash, N-adap. George V. Higgins, d. Peter Yates.
SUSPENSE: ACTION: Mob Stories; Informers; Fugitives from the Mob; Retirement; Manhunts; Forgotten Films
(The Informant; The French Connection)
(Ed: Okay and realistic)

Fright Night, 1985, 105m, ★★★/$$$, Col/RCA-Col, PG-13/P-S-V. A high school nerd, totally obsessed with horror films, is surprised to find that his new next-door neighbor is a vampire-but will anyone believe him? Chris Sarandon, William Ragsdale, Amanda Bearse, McDowell. w. d. Tom Holland.
HORROR: Horror Comedy; Vampires; Spoofs-Vampires; Boy Cries Wolf; Unbelieved; Neighbors-Troublesome; Nerds; Sleeper Hits; Writer-Directors
(Buffy, The Vampire Slayer)

Fright Night, Part 2, 1988, 104m, ★★/$ (VR), Col/RCA-Col, PG-13/P-S-V. Vampires move into a college town and have plenty of victims to go around. McDowell, Traci Lin, Julie Carmen, Jonathan Gries, Russell Clark. w. Tim Metcalfe, Miguel Tejada-Flores, Tommy Lee Wallace, d. Tommy Lee Wallace.
HORROR: Horror Comedy; Vampires; Spoofs-Vampires; Unbelieved; College Life

(Ed: Doesn't live up to the first, not that there's all that much to live up to)

The Frisco Kid, 1935, 77m, ★★¹/₂/$$$, WB/WB. A salty dog of the sea becomes king of the wharf in San Francisco. James Cagney, Margaret Lindsay, Ricardo Cortez, Lili Damita, Donald Woods, Barton MacLane, George E. Stone. w. Warren Duff, Seton I. Miller, d. Lloyd Bacon.
WESTERNS: West-Old; Sailors;
ROMANCE: Romantic Comedy; San Francisco; 1860s; Forgotten Films
(The Barbary Coast)

The Frisco Kid, 1979, 108m, ★★¹/₂/$$, WB/WB, PG. A rabbi struggles with outlaws, Indians, and sheriffs in the Old West. Gene Wilder, Harrison Ford, Ramon Bieri, Leo Fuchs, Penny Peyser. w. Michael Elias, Frank Shaw, d. Robert Aldrich.
COMEDY: WESTERNS: Western Comedy; Spoofs-Western; Comedy-Light; Jewish People; Fish out of Water Stories; New in Town; Indians-American, Conflict with; Heroes-Unwitting
(Blazing Saddles; The Ruggles of Red Gap)
(Ed: A light comic variation on *Blazing Saddles*, which is to say, what's the point if it's light?)

Fritz the Cat, 1973, 78m, ★★★/$$, UA/WB, X-R/ES-P. A semi-pornographic animated film based upon the hippy icon R. Crumb's famous underground comics. w. d. Ralph Bakshi, (comic strip)-adap. R. Crumb.
Cartoons; Erotic Comedy; Sexploitation; Psychedelic Era; 1970s; Cult Films
(Heavy Traffic; Cool World)

The Frog Prince, 1984, 90m, ★★★/$, WB/Cannon. In the 60s, an English girl studying in Paris makes it her mission to lose her virginity with a handsome Frenchman. Jane Snowden, Alexandre Sterling, Diana Blackburn. w. Brian Gilbert, Posy Simmonds, d. Brian Gilbert.
COMEDY DRAMA: ROMANCE: Romantic Comedy; Romantic Drama; Coming of Age; Young Women; Virgins; Sexy Men; Overlooked at Release
(Sunday in New York; Peppermint Soda)

Frogs, 1972, 91m, ★★★/$$$, AIP/WB. In a small Southern swamp town the frogs start acting funny. Other slimy creatures start acting following suit. Ray Milland, Joan Van Ark, Sam Elliott, Adam Roarke, Judy Pace. w. Robert Hutchinson, Robert Blees, d. George McGowan.

HORROR: Monsters-Animal; Swamp Settings; Murders-One by One; Cult Films; Sleeper Hits
(Jaws of Satan; Alligator)

From Here to Eternity, 1953, 118m, ★★★¹/₂/$$$$$$, Col/RCA-Col. Before, during, and after the Pearl Harbor bombing, soldiers in Honolulu are called into action and romance, all under great tension. Burt Lancaster (BActor), Deborah Kerr (BActress), Frank Sinatra (**BSActor**), Donna Reed (**BSActress**), Ernest Borgnine, Montgomery Clift (BActor). w. Daniel Taradash (**BAScr**), N-adap. James Jones, d. Fred Zinnemann (**BDirector**).
BPicture, BOScore, **BB&WCin**, **BEdit**, **BSound**, BB&WCostume. Oscars: 13-8.
DRAMA: MELODRAMA: ROMANCE: Romantic Drama; War Stories; World War II Era; World War II Stories; Military Stories; Ensemble Films; Romance with Married Person; Romance-Clandestine; Power Struggles; Prostitutes-Low Class; Soldiers; Pearl Harbor; Hawaii; Blockbusters
REMAKE: TV Miniseries (1979, NBC)
(Pearl [TV miniseries])

From Russia with Love, 1963, 118m, ★★★/$$$$, UA/MGM-UA. Russian spies are after James Bond to kill him in the Mediterranean. Sean Connery, Robert Shaw, Pedro Armendariz, Daniela Bianchi, Lotte Lenya. w. Richard Maibaum, Johanna Harwood, N-adap. Ian Fleming, d. Terence Young.
ACTION: Spy Films; Spies; Secret Agents; Mediterranean; Playboys; Russians as Enemy; Assassination Plots; Men in Jeopardy; James Bond; Female Screenwriters
(Dr. No; Moonraker; Goldfinger)
(Ed: Not as active as other Bonds, but more urbane)

From the Hip, 1987, 112m, ★★/$, DEG/DEG, PG-13/S-P. A professor is on trial for murder, defended by a Machiavellian, rebellious young lawyer. Judd Nelson, Elizabeth Perkins, John Hurt, Darren McGavin, Dan Monahan, David Alan Grier. w. David E. Kelley, Bob Clark, d. Bob Clark.
COMEDY DRAMA: SATIRE: MURDER: Courtroom Drama; Trials; Corruption; Lawyers; Rebels; Professors; Coulda Been Good
(And Justice for All; Criminal Law)

From the Life of the Marionettes, 1980, 104m, ★★★/$, ITC-AFD/Live,

R/S-P. A detective searches for the killer of a prostitute, believed to be a prominent businessman. Robert Atzorn, Christine Buchegger, Martin Benrath. w. d. Ingmar Bergman.
DRAMA: MYSTERY: MURDER: MURDER MYSTERY: Detective Stories; Art Films; Detectives-Private; Swedish Films; Scandinavia; Prostitutes-High Class; Murders of Prostitutes; Curiosities; Writer-Directors
(Klute)

From the Terrace, 1960, 144m, ★★★/$$$, 20th/CBS-Fox. The lives of upper-class Philadelphia families are examined when one young women considers marrying a man whose family is wealthy, but not wealthy enough. Paul Newman, Joanne Woodward, Myrna Loy, Ina Balin, Leon Ames, Felix Aylmer. w. Ernest Lehman, N-adap. John O'Hara, d. Mark Robson.
DRAMA: ROMANCE: Romantic Drama; Social Drama; Rich People; Class Conflicts; Romance-Class Conflicts; Episodic Stories; Marriage Drama; Philadelphia; Time Capsules; 1950s
(The Young Philadelphians; Peyton Place)
(Ed: Only for Newman & Woodward fans)

From This Day Forward, 1946, 95m, ★★★/$$, RKO/NA. A middle-aged New York couple remember the Depression and how the pulled through it all. Joan Fontaine, Mark Stevens, Rosemary de Camp, Henry Morgan, Wally Brown, Arline Judge, Bobby Driscoll. w. Hugo Butler, Garson Kanin, N-adap. Thomas Bell (*All Bridges Are Beautiful*), d. John Berry.
DRAMA: MELODRAMA: Social Drama; Depression Era; 1930s; Marriage Drama; New York Life; Time Capsules; Flashbacks; Memories; Forgotten Films; Hidden Gems

The Front, 1976, 95m, ★★★/$$, Col/RCA-Col, PG. During the McCarthy witchhunts, a blacklisted writer gets a "front" to submit his manuscripts. Woody Allen, Zero Mostel, Herschel Bernardi, Michael Murphy, Andrea Marcovicci, Lloyd Gough. w. Walter Bernstein (BOScr), d. Martin Ritt. Oscars: 1-0.
DRAMA: COMEDY DRAMA: Message Films; Social Drama; Historical Drama; McCarthy Era; Impostors; Writers; Hollywood Life; Communists; Paranoia
(Guilty by Suspicion; Trial; The Way We Were)

The Front Page, 1931, 101m, ★★★★/ $$$$, Howard Hughes/Nos. A hard-bitten newspaper reporter in Chicago is on the verge of retirement but is pulled back in by his tricky editor. Adolphe Menjou (BActor), Pat O'Brien, Mary Brian, Edward Everett Horton, Walter Cartlett, George E. Stone, Mae Clarke, Slim Summerville, Frank McHugh. w. Bartlett Cormack, Charles Lederer, P-adap. Charles MacArthur, Ben Hecht, d. Lewis Milestone (BDirector). BPicture. Oscars: 3-0.
REMAKES: His Girl Friday (1940), The Front Page (1974)
The Front Page, 1974, 105m, ★★★/$$, U-I/MCA-U, PG. A remake with language and themes updated to the 70s, though it's still set in the 30s. Walter Matthau, Jack Lemmon, Susan Sarandon, David Wayne, Carol Burnett, Vincent Gardenia, Austin Pendleton. w. Billy Wilder, I. A. L. Diamond, d. Billy Wilder.
COMEDY: FARCE: COMEDY DRAMA: Detective Stories; Fugitives from the Law; Fugitives-Harboring; Accused Unjustly; Journalists as Detectives; Race Against Time; Executions; Journalists; Newspapers; Romance-Reunited; Romance-Triangles; Ethics; Chicago; Stagelike Films
(His Girl Friday; Gaily, Gaily; Five-Star Final)
Frozen Assets, 1992, 93m, ★/$, Ind/Fox, PG. A corporate takeover king makes a faux-pas when he finds that the bank he just acquired does not hold money, but rather sperm. Being a sport, he decides to make a go of it anyway. Corbin Bernsen, Shelley Long, Larry Miller, Dody Goodman, Gerrit Graham, Paul Sand, Teri Copley, Matt Clark. w. Don Klein, Tom Kartozian, d. George Miller.
COMEDY: Babies-Having; Comedy-Situation
(Made in America)
The Fugitive, 1947, 104m, ★★¹/₂/$$, Argosy/Turner. In the Mexican country-side where the locals distrust the church, a corrupt priest is chased out of town. Henry Fonda, Dolores del Rio, Pedro Armendariz, J. Carrol Naish, Leo Carrillo, Ward Bond, Robert Armstrong. w. Dudley Nichols, N-adap. Graham Greene (*The Power and the Glory*), d. John Ford.
DRAMA: Chase Stories; Priests; Corruption; Informers; Fugitives; Religion;

Mexico; Forgotten Films; Flops-Major (The Informer)
The Fugitive: The Final Episode, 1967, 78m, ★★★/$$$$$, Quinn-Martin-ABC/. Dr. Richard Kimble, the fugitive of the famed series, finally meets up with the one-armed man whom he believed killed his wife, but can he prove it? And will he bring him to justice before he himself is killed? Tune in next time. . . . David Janssen, Barry Morse, Bill Ralsch, Diane Baker, Joseph Campanella, Michael Constantine.
SUSPENSE: Chase Stories; Fugitives from the Law; Fugitives from a Murderer; Prison Escapes; Accused Unjustly; Framed?; Conspiracy; Murder-Clearing Oneself; Manhunts; Chicago; Doctors; TV Series
The Fugitive, 1993, 140m, ★★★¹/₂/$$$$$$, WB/WB, PG/V-P. When a prominent doctor's wife is murdered, he walks in on the aftermath and sees a one-armed man fleeing the scene. He's caught by circumstantial evidence and con-victed-until he's able to escape and, as a fugitive, find the real culprit-and who's behind him. Harrison Ford, Tommy Lee Jones (BSActor), Sela Ward, Joe Pantoliano, Jerome Krabbé. d. Andy Davis. BPicture, BCin, BEdit, BSound, BSoundFX. Oscars: 7-1.
ACTION: SUSPENSE: Chase Stories; Fugitives; Fugitives from the Law; Prison Escapes; Accused Unjustly; Framed?; Conspiracy; Murder-Clearing Oneself; Searches; Chicago; Doctors; TV Series Movies; Blockbusters
(Three Days of the Condor; Total Recall; Frantic; The Shawshank Redemption; The Story of Dr. Sam Shepperd)
The Fugitive Kind, 1959, 122m, UA/MGM-UA, ★★★¹/₂/$$. A drifter (Marlon Brando) arrives in a small Mississippi town and begins seeing two women, the older Italian, married woman (Anna Magnani) who owns the general store and a wild, free spirit (Joanne Woodward), and soon winds up in great trouble. Victor Jory, Maureen Stapleton, R. G. Armstrong. w. Tennessee Williams, Meade Roberts, P-adap. Tennessee Williams (*Orpheus Descending*), d. Sidney Lumet.
DRAMA: TRAGEDY: ROMANCE: Romance-Triangles; Romance-Clandestine; Romance with Married Person; Romance-Older Women/Younger

Men; Ku Klux Klan; Drifters; New in Town; Italians; Free Spirits; Jealousy; Cheating Men; Mississippi; Tennessee Williamsesque
REMAKE: Orpheus Descending (TV, 1990)
(Sweet Bird of Youth; Wild Is the Wind)
Fugitive Lovers, 1933, 74m, ★★¹/₂/$$, MGM/NA. A prisoner plans his escape, breaks free, and travels cross-country by bus as police are alerted. Robert Montgomery, Madge Evans, Ted Healy and the Three Stooges, Nat Pendleton, C. Henry Gordon. w. Ferdinand Reyher, Frank Wead, d. Richard Boleslawski.
SUSPENSE: COMEDY DRAMA: ROMANCE: Romantic Comedy; Fugitives-Harboring; Fugitives from the Law; Prison Escapes; Buses; Road Movies; Outlaw Road Movies; Chase Stories; Forgotten Films
(North by Northwest; It Happened One Night)
Full Eclipse, 1993, 97m, ★★/$$$, HBO/HBO, R/S-V-B&G-FN-MN. A young black police officer is recruited by a sexy young woman to be part of a special crime unit. He subsequently discovers that they all take a serum which turns them into werewolves. Mario Van Peebles, Patsy Kensit, Bruce Payne, Anthony John Denison. d. Anthony Hickox.
SCI-FI: HORROR: Werewolves; Police Stories; Black Men; Conspiracy; TV Movies
Full Metal Jacket, 1987, 116m, ★★★¹/₂/$$$$, WB/WB, R/EP-EV-S. Almost two films, the first half concerned with the training of Marine recruits, the second half the standard "platoon-cut-off-from-command-and-left-to-die" story in Vietnam. Matthew Modine, Adam Baldwin, Vincent d'Onofrio, Lee Ermey, Arliss Howard. w. Stanley Kubrick, Michael Herr, Gustav Hasford (BAScr), N-adap. Gustav Hasford (*The Short Timers*), d. Stanley Kubrick. Oscars: 1-0.
DRAMA: SATIRE: Black Comedy; Comedy-Morbid; **TRAGEDY:** Avant-Garde Films; Comedy & Violence; Evil Men; Weight Problems; Surrealism; Nightmares; Nightmare Journies; Vietnam War; Soldiers; Sleeper Hits; Cult Films
(Casualties of War; A Clockwork Orange)
Full Moon in Blue Water, 1988, 95m, ★★¹/₂/$, TWE/Media, PG/S-P. Down in Texas, the owner of a local greasy spoon fights developers trying to steal his land

out from under him. Gene Hackman, Teri Garr, Burges Meredith, Elias Koteas, Kevin Cooney. w. Bill Bozzone, d. Peter Masterson.

COMEDY: COMEDY DRAMA: Comedy-Light; ROMANCE: Romantic Comedy; Eccentric People; Ordinary People Stories; Elderly Men; Small-town Life; Southerns; Fishermen; Mortgage Drama; Save the Land; Coulda Been Great
Full Moon in Paris, 1984, 102m, ★★★/$, Triumph-Col/RCA-Col, R/S-FFN-MRN. A free-spirited young woman won't settle down and instead flits between her boyfriend in the suburbs and her apartment in Paris. Pascale Ogier, Tcheky Karo, Fabrice Luchini, Virgine Thevenet, Christian Vadim, Laszlo Szabo. w. d. Eric Rohmer.

DRAMA: ROMANCE: Romance-Triangles; Erotic Drama; Urban Life; Suburban Life; Art Films; French Films; Writer-Directors
(Boyfriends and Girlfriends; Summer; Pauline at the Beach; Moon in the Gutter)
The Fuller Brush Girl, 1950, 85m, ★★★/$$, Col/Col. A door-to-door sales-woman accidently gets involved in a mur-der plot. Lucille Ball, Eddie Albert, Carl Benton Reid, Gale Robbins, Jeff Donnell. w. Frank Tashlin, d. Lloyd Bacon.

COMEDY: Comedy-Slapstick; MURDER: MYSTERY: MURDER MYSTERY: Comic Mystery; Saving Oneself; Accused Unjustly; Framed?; Murder-Clearing Oneself; Salesmen; FARCE: Misunderstandings; Female in Male Domain; Female Protagonists
FLIPSIDE OF: The Fuller Brush Man
The Fuller Brush Man, 1948, 93m, ★★★/$$$, Col/RCA-Col. A door-to-door salesman accidently gets involved in a murder plot. Red Skelton, Janet Blair, Don McGuire, Adele Jergens. w. Frank Tashlin, Devery Freeman, d. S. Sylvan Simon.

COMEDY: Comedy-Slapstick; MURDER: MYSTERY: MURDER MYSTERY: Comic Mystery; Saving Oneself; Accused Unjustly; Framed?; Murder-Clearing Oneself; Salesmen; FARCE: Misunderstandings
FLIPSIDE: Fuller Brush Girl
(I Dood It; My Favorite Brunette)
Fun Down There, 1988, 88m, ★★1/2/$ (LR), Metro/Waterbearer, R/S-P-MFN. A young man who discovers that he's gay escapes the opression of his small town

and goes to New York to make friends. Michael Waite, Nickolas Nagurney, Martin Goldin, Jeanne Sobrowski. w. Roger Stigliano, Michael Waite, d. Roger Stigliano.

COMEDY DRAMA: DRAMA: Gay Awakenings; Coming of Age; Young Men; Gay Men; Greenwich Village; Sexual Problems; Sexuality; Ordinary People Stories; Overlooked at Release; Quiet Little Films; Gay & Lesbian Films (Parting Glances; Lie Down With Dogs) (Ed: Rather ordinary and dull, but inter-esting to those who would empathize. A mainstream film with a surprise penile erection-probably a first to slip by)
Funny About Love, 1990, 107m, ★★/$, Par/Par, PG. An aging married man wants children, and after his wife fails to conceive, this becomes his excuse when he drools after a young nubile thing who is supposedly "fertile." Gene Wilder, Christine Lahti, Mary Stuart Masterson, Farrah Fawcett, Robert Prosky, Stephen Tobolowsky, Susan Ruttan. w. Norman Steinberg, David Frankel, d. Leonard Nimoy.

COMEDY: COMEDY DRAMA: ROMANCE: Romantic Comedy; Sex Comedy; Romance-Older Men/Younger Women; Babies-Having; Married Couples-Childless; Midlife Crisis (The Woman in Red; Micki and Maude)
Funeral in Berlin, 1967, 102m, ★★★/$$, Par/Par. A British spy, Harry Palmer, goes to Berlin to help a Soviet colonel come over the wall. Michael Caine, Oscar Homolka, Eva Renzi, Paul Hubschmid, Hugh Burden. w. Evan Jones, N-adap. Len Deighton (The Berlin Memorandum), d. Guy Hamilton.

SUSPENSE: ACTION: Spy Films; Spies; Secret Agents; Funerals; Iron Curtain-Escape from; Iron Curtain-Behind the; Russians as Enemy; Berlin; British Films; England
SEQUEL TO: The Ipcress File
SEQUEL: Billion Dollar Brain
(The Spy Who Came in from the Cold)
Funny Face, 1957, 103m, ★★★★/$$$$, Par/Par. A chic fashion magazine editor and her suave photographer search for the "quality woman" for a new feature, and end up finding a gawky anti-commercial bookstore clerk who turns out to be a graceful beauty unsurpassed. Fred Astaire, Audrey Hepburn, Kay Thompson, Michel Auclair. w. Leonard

Gershe, d. Stanley Donen. BCCin, BCArt. Oscars: 3-0.
MUSICALS: ROMANCE: Musical Romance; Fame-Rise to; Wallflowers; Models; Fashion World; Svengalis; Photographers; Journalists; Beatnik Era; Greenwich Village; New York Life; 1950s (Breakfast at Tiffany's; Roman Holiday; Paris When It Sizzles; Silk Stockings)
Funny Girl, 1968, 151m, Col/RCA-Col, ★★★★/$$$$, G. The rise to fame of comedienne and singer Fanny Brice (Barbra Streisand, BActress), from the streets of New York to the bright lights of Broadway, where adulation is easy but love isn't. Omar Sharif, Kay Medford (BSActress), Walter Pidgeon. w. MP-adap. Isobel Lennart, d. William Wyler. BPicture, BCin, BAScore, BOSong, "Funny Girl," BEdit, BSound. Oscars: 8-1.
MUSICALS: COMEDY: Musical Comedy; Musical Drama; COMEDY DRAMA: Biographies; Hollywood Biographies; Fame-Rise to; Feisty Females; Underdog Stories; Rags to Riches; Gambling; Marriage Drama; Marriage on the Rocks; Cheating Men; Theater Life; Female Protagonists; Female Screenwriters; 1920s; New York Life
SEQUEL: Funny Lady
(Funny Lady; Star!; On a Clear Day You Can See Forever; Hello, Dolly!)
Funny Lady, 1975, 137m, ★★★1/2/$$$$, Rastar-Col/RCA-Col, PG. The con-tinuation of the Fanny Brice story, as she becomes a radio star and finds a new heel of a love in songwriter Billy Rose. The story is more dramatic than Funny Girl, with less music and humor, but still effective. Roddy McDowell, Ben Vereen, Omar Sharif. w. Jay Presson Allen, Arnold Schulman, d. Herbert Ross. BOSong, "How Lucky Can You Get," BSScore, BCin. Oscars: 3-0.
DRAMA: MUSICALS: Musical Drama; COMEDY DRAMA: Biographies; Hollywood Biographies; Feisty Females; Marriage Drama; Marriage on the Rocks; Singers; Hollywood Life; Radio Life; Vaudeville; Cheating Men; 1930s; Female Protagonists; Female Screenwriters
SEQUEL TO: Funny Girl
A Funny Thing Happened on the Way to the Forum, 1966, 99m, ★★★1/2/$$, UA/CBS-Fox, PG. A slave in ancient Rome uses his cunning to buy liberty from his brutish master. Zero Mostel, Phil Silvers, Michael Crawford,

Jack Gilford, Michael Hordern, Buster Keaton, Patricia Jessel. w. Melvin Frank, Michael Pertwee, MP-adap. Burt Shevelove, Larry Gelbart (music/lyrics, Stephen Sondheim), d. Richard Lester. **BAScore.** Oscars: 1-1.
COMEDY: FARCE: Comedy-Slapstick; Spoofs; Slavery; Turning the Tables; Revenge; Misunderstandings; Romans; Ancient Times; Hidden Gems
(Ed: The Broadway version was an enormous hit, though this didn't fare so well at the box office)
Fun with Dick and Jane, 1976, 95m, ★★★/$$$$, Columbia/RCA-Col, PG/P. A couple on the verge of losing everything in a recession decides to fight back when welfare and unemployment money ends by robbing the phone company to applause and eventually the company that laid the husband off in the first place. Jane Fonda, George Segal, Ed McMahon, Dick Gautier, Alan Miller. w. David Giler, Jerry Belson, Mordecai Richler, SS-adap. Gerald Gaiser, d. Ted Kotcheff.
COMEDY: Social Satire; **SATIRE:** Capers; Heist Stories; Criminal Couples; Marriage Comedy; Ordinary People Stories; Suburban Life; Crime Pays; Making a Living; Unemployment; 1970s; Los Angeles; Time Capsules
(How to Beat the High Cost of Living; For Pete's Sake)
The Furies, 1950, 109m, ★★¹/2/$$, Par/NA, AMC. The headstrong daughter of a rancher fights tooth and nail with him to control her life. Barbara Stanwyck, Walter Huston, Wendell Corey, Judith Anderson, Gilbert Roland, Thomas Gomez, Beulah Bondi, Wallace Ford, Albert Dekker. w. Charles Schnee, N-adap. Niven Busch, d. Anthony Mann.
WESTERNS: DRAMA: MELODRAMA: Fathers & Daughters; Cattle Ranchers; Cattle Herded by Barbara Stanwyck; Electra Stories; Feisty Females; Forgotten Films; Female Protagonists
(Cattle Queen of Montana; The Maverick Queen)
Fury, 1936, ★★★¹/2/$$$, MGM/MGM-UA. When a stranger has the misfortune of passing through a small town just as a manhunt is underway, he gets mistaken for a murderer and is lynched. Later, believed to have died in a fire, he seeks his revenge. Spencer Tracy, Sylvia Sidney, Bruce Cabot, Walter Abel,

Edward Ellis, Walter Brennan, Frank Albertson. w. Bartlett Cormack, Fritz Lang, Norman Krasna (BOStory), d. Fritz Lang. Oscars: 1-0.
DRAMA: TRAGEDY: MURDER: Lynchings; Executions; Dead-Back from the; Murder-Clearing Oneself; Accused Unjustly; Revenge; New in Town; Identities-Mistaken; Rural Horrors; Hidden Gems; Faded Hits; Forgotten Films
(The Big House; I Am a Fugitive from a Chain Gang)
The Fury, 1978, 117m, ★★★/$$$, 20th/CBS-Fox, R/V-P. A man who was the subject of government experiments in telekenesis as a child is wanted for his psychic powers now that he's a man. Kirk Douglas, John Cassavetes, Carrie Snodgress, Charles Durning, Andrew Stevens, Amy Irving. w. N-adap. John Farris, d. Brian de Palma.
SUSPENSE: HORROR: Supernatural Danger; Psychics; Chase Stories; Terrorists; Brothers & Sisters; Scientists; Experiments; Hitchcockian; Cult Films
(Cat's Eye)
Futureworld, 1976, 107m, ★★¹/2/$$, AIP/WB, R/V-P. A sequel to Westworld in which the robots are used to stand in for prominent world leaders in an evil plot. Peter Fonda, Blythe Danner, Arthur Hill, Yul Brynner, John Ryan, Stuart Margolin. w. Mayo Simon, George Schenck, d. Richard T. Heffron.
SCI-FI: Fantasy; Political Thriller; Futuristic Films; Resorts; Robots; Androids; Politicians; Impostors; Assassination Plots
SEQUEL TO: Westworld
(Westworld; The Running Man; Logan's Run)
Fuzz, 1972, 93m, ★★★/$$$, UA/MGM-UA, R/EV-P-S. Stupid Boston cops have a hard time finding a rapist mainly because of their own incompetence. Burt Reynolds, Raquel Welch, Jack Weston, Yul Brynner, Tom Skerritt, James McEachin. w. Evan Hunter ("Ed McBain"), d. Richard A. Colla.
COMEDY: COMEDY DRAMA: FARCE: Black Comedy; Police Stories; Police Comedy; Criminals-Stupid; Police Brutality; Police Corruption; Faded Hits; Forgotten Films; Hidden Gems; Coulda Been Great; Boston
(Super Cops; Freebie and the Bean; Law and Disorder)

The Fuzzy Pink Nightgown, 1957, 88m, ★★¹/2/$$, UA/NA. A fanatic kidnaps his favorite starlet, and she ends up falling in love with him. Jane Russell, Ralph Meeker, Keenan Wynn, Fred Clark, Adolphe Menjou, Una Merkel. w. Richard Alan Simmons, N-adap. Sylvia Tate, d. Norman Taurog.
COMEDY: ROMANCE: Romantic Comedy; **FARCE:** Kidnappings; Kidnappers-Sympathizing; Kidnapping Celebrities; Actresses; Fans-Crazed; Curiosities
FLIPSIDE: The Collector, Misery
(Heartbreak Hotel; Gentlemen Prefer Blondes; Will Success Spoil Rock Hunter?)
(Ed: By today's standards, it's total fantasy-the kidnapper's, and the idea it could all be a comedy)
F/X, 1985, 106m, ★★★/$$$, Orion/Orion, PG-13/P-V-B&G. A Hollywood special effects man is hired to coordinate a fake assassination. But he soon finds himself the target of real assassins. Bryan Brown, Brian Dennehy, Diane Venora, Cliff De Young, Mason Adams, Jerry Orbach. w. Robert T. Megginson, Gregory Fleeman, d. Robert Mandel.
SUSPENSE: MURDER: Detective Stories; Detectives-Private; Stuntmen; Hollywood Life; Movie Making; Turning the Tables; Conspiracy; Chase Stories; Clever Plots & Endings; Framed?; Accused Unjustly; Double Crossings; Con Artists; Actors; Assassination Plots; Mob Stories; Fugitives from the Mob; Hitmen; Sleeper Hits
SEQUEL: F/X 2
(The Stunt Man)
F/X 2: The Deadly Art of Illusion, 1991, 108m, ★★¹/2/$, Orion/Orion, PG-13/P-V. A retired Hollywood effects man and a detective look for artifacts from the Italian Renaissance. Bryan Brown, Brian Dennehy, Rachel Ticotin, Joanna Gleason, Philip Bosco, Keven J. O'Connor, Tom Mason. w. d. Richard Franklin.
SUSPENSE: Heist Stories; Art Thieves; Searches; Detective Stories; Detectives-Private; Stuntmen; Hollywood Life; Movie Making; Turning the Tables; Conspiracy; Chase Stories; Clever Plots & Endings; Framed?; Accused Unjustly; Double Crossings; Con Artists; Actors
SEQUEL TO: F/X

G

Gable and Lombard, 1976, 131m, ★★/$, U/MCA-U, R/S. In his old age, the famous actor remembers his life with Carole Lombard before tragedy struck in a plane crash in '42. James Brolin, Jill Clayburgh, Allen Garfield, Red Buttons. w. Barry Sandler, d. Sidney J. Furie.
MELODRAMA: TRAGEDY: ROMANCE: Tearjerkers; Memories; Biographies; Hollywood Biographies; Hollywood Life; Actors; Actresses; Airplane Crashes; 1930s; Nostalgia; Flops-Major

Gabriel over the White House, 1933, 87m, ★★★/$$, MGM/MGM-UA. A gangster runs for President and once he's in the White House, he's mysteriously transformed. Walter Huston, Karen Morley, Franchot Tone, C. Henry Gordon. w. Carey Wilson, Bertram Bloch, N-adap. T. F. Tweed (*Rinehard*), d. Gregory La Cava.
COMEDY: COMEDY DRAMA: SATIRE: Mob Stories; Mob Comedy; Presidents; Presidential Comedy; Political Campaigns; Washington D.C.; Political Satire; Fish out of Water Stories; Hidden Gems; What If . . . Stories
(The Great McGinty; Dave)

Gabriela, 1983, 102m, MGM-UA/MGM-UA, ★★1/2/$ (LR), R/S-FFN. Older man who owns a bar (Marcello Mastroianni) hires a younger woman (Sonia Braga) and soon she uses her charm to get what she wants. Based on a famous South American soap opera character. w. Leopoldo Sarran, Bruno Barreto, N-adap. Jorge Amado, d. Bruno Barreto.
ROMANCE: MELODRAMA: Romantic Drama; Erotic Drama; Free Spirits; Sexy Women; South America; Latin People; Brazil

Gaby, 1956, 97m, ★★1/2/$$, MGM/NA. A soldier and a ballerina fall in love with the war over London as a backdrop. Leslie Caron, John Kerr, Cedric Hardwicke, Taina Elg, Margalo Gillmore. w. Albert Hackett, Frances Goodrich, d. Curtis Bernhardt.
MELODRAMA: ROMANCE: Tearjerkers; World War II Era; War at Home; Ballet Dancers; Soldiers; Female Screenwriters
REMAKE OF: Waterloo Bridge

Gaby, a True Story, 1987, 114m, ★★★/$, Col/Tri-Star, G. The uplifting story of a Hispanic girl with cerebral palsy who struggles with dignity against the ravages of the disease. Liv Ullman, Norma Aleandro (BSActress), Robert Loggia, Rachel Levin, Lawrence Monoson. w. Martin Salinas, Michael James Love, d. Luis Mandoki. Oscars: 1-0.
MELODRAMA: Tearjerkers; Disease Stories; Girls; Mexico; Latin People; International Casts; Overlooked at Release

Gaily, Gaily, 1969, 117m, ★★★/$$$, UA/Fox, PG/P. Autobiographical tale of famous playwright and screenwriter Ben Hecht's misadventurous early days as a reporter in Chicago in the thirties. Beau Bridges, Melina Mercouri, Brian Keith, George Kennedy, Hume Cronyn, Margot Kidder, Wilfrid Hyde White, Melodie Johnson. w. Abram S. Ginnes, NF-adap. Ben Hecht, d. Norman Jewison. BArt, BCostume, BSound. Oscars: 3-0.
COMEDY: FARCE: COMEDY DRAMA: Journalists; Newspapers; Young Men; Autobiographical Stories; Biographies; Nostalgia; Chicago; 1930s; Hidden Gems; Faded Hits; Forgotten Films
(The Front Page; His Girl Friday; Act One)
(Ed: Gay in the old sense of the word and unjustly forgotten)

The Gallant Hours, 1959, 115m, ★★1/2/$$, UA/MGM-UA. A biopic of the World War II admiral William F. Halsey and his famed military exploits. James Cagney, Dennis Weaver, Richard Jaeckel, Ward Costello, Carl Benton Reid. w. Beirne Lay Jr., Frank D. Gilroy, d. Robert Montgomery.
DRAMA: Military Stories; War Stories; Leaders-Military; Behind the Scenes; World War II Stories; Biographies

Gallipoli, 1981, 110m, ★★★1/2/$$$, Aus-Par/Par, R/V-MFN. Two soldiers (Mel Gibson, Mike Lee) trek across Australia to join the cavalry which leads them to battle in North Africa at a place called Gallipoli during World War I, but only one will survive. w. David Williamson, d. Peter Weir.

DRAMA: TRAGEDY: World War I Stories; War Stories; Friendships-Male; Soldiers; Journies; Desert Settings; Australian Films; Historical Drama
(The Red Badge of Courage; Breaker Morant; Paths of Glory)

Gambit, 1966, 109m, ★★★/$$$, U/MCA-U, PG/S. A cockney thief teams up with an Asian girl and strikes up an involved plan to rob a museum of a prized piece of sculpture. Michael Caine, Shirley MacLaine, Herbert Lom, John Abbott, Roger C. Carmel. w. Jack Davies, Alvin Sargent, d. Ronald Neame.

COMEDY DRAMA: ROMANCE: Romantic Comedy; Heist Stories; Art Thieves; Asia; England; Museums
(Topkapi!)

The Gambler, 1975, 111m, ★★¹/₂/$, Par/Par, R/S. A gambler is more addicted to the behavior than to winning. James Caan, Paul Sorvino, Lauren Hutton, Morris Carnovsky, Jacqueline Brookes, Burt Young. w. James Toback, d. Karel Reisz.

DRAMA: Gambling; Obsessions; Psychological Drama; Coulda Been Great; Flops-Major
(Fever Pitch; The Great Sinner; Rabbit Run)

Gambling Lady, 1934, 66m, ★★★/$$$, WB/WB. A gambler who can't pay his debts commits suicide. His daughter becomes a gambler as well and gets involved with much bigger crimes. Barbara Stanwyck, Joel McCrea, Pat O'Brien, Claire Dodd, C. Aubrey Smith. w. Ralph Block, Doris Malloy, d. Archie Mayo.

MELODRAMA: Crime Drama; Gambling; Fathers & Daughters; Suicidal Tendencies; Criminals-Female; Hidden Gems; Forgotten Films
(The Lady Gambles; Seduction of Gina [TV movie])

The Game Is Over, 1966, 96m, ★★¹/₂/$$, Ind/Media, R/S. A young woman (Jane Fonda) romances her older husband's son and deceit combusts with lust. w. d. Roger Vadim.

DRAMA: MELODRAMA: ROMANCE: Romantic Drama; Romance-Triangles; Romance-Older Men/Younger Women; Romance with Relative's Lover; French Films; Paris; Writer-Directors
(Damage; Class)

Game of Death, 1945, 72m, ★★¹/₂/$, RKO/NA. A man who invites a group of people to his estate to hunt them like wild animals. John Loder, Audrey Long, Edgar Barrier, Russell Wade. w. Norman Houston, d. Robert Wise.

ACTION: ADVENTURE: Men in Jeopardy; Manhunts; Murder-Invitation to; Chase Movies; Snipers
REMAKE OF: Most Dangerous Game
(No Escape; Ebb Tide)

Gandhi, 1982, 188m, ★★★/$$$$, Goldcrest-Col/RCA-Col, PG. The life of the great Indian leader Mahatma Gandhi (Ben Kingsley, **BActor**) is followed up until his assassination, but his greatness shouldn't be confused with this film. Ian Charleson, Candice Bergen. w. John Briley (**BOScr**), d. Richard Attenborough (**BDirector**). **BPicture, BCinema, BEditing, BArt, BCostume,** BSound, BOScore. Oscars: 10-8.

DRAMA: Biographies; Epics; Episodic Stories; International Cast; Cast of Thousands; Assassination Plots; India; Religion; Charismatic People; Faded Hits; Actor Directors
(Cry Freedom; Little Buddha)
(Ed: Surely one of the least watched Best Picture winners of recent years since its glory year passed; it seems many confused the greatness of the man for greatness of the film)

The Gang That Couldn't Shoot Straight, 1971, 96m, ★★/$, MGM/NA. The mob holds a race that ends in a bloody war. Jerry Orbach, Leigh Taylor-Young, Jo Van Fleet, Lionel Stander, Robert De Niro, Herve Villechaize, Joe Santos. w. Waldo Salt, N-adap. Jimmy Breslin, d. James Goldstone.

SATIRE: Black Comedy; Mob Stories; Mob Comedy; Criminals-Stupid; Race Against Time; Competition; Bicycles; Coulda Been Good; Flops-Major
The Gang's All Here, 1943, 103m, ★★★/$$$, 20th/Nos. A military man loves a boisterous singer and a society dame and can't decide between the two, until the choice is no longer his. Alice Faye, Carmen Miranda, James Ellison, Phil Baker, Benny Goodman, Charlotte Greenwood, Eugene Pallette, Edward Everett Horton. w. Walter Bullock, d. Busby Berkeley. BCArt. Oscars: 1-0.

MUSICALS: ROMANCE: Musical Romance; Romantic Comedy; Musical Comedy; Romance-Triangles; Dance Movies; Singers; Dancers; Social Climbing; Romance-Class Conflicts; Soldiers
(Down Argentine Way; Strawberry Blonde)

Garbo Talks, 1984, 103m, ★★¹/₂/$, MGM-UA/MGM-UA, PG/P-S. A mother's dying wish is that Greta Garbo come see her and speak in this light comedy about the son and his friends who try to make it happen. Anne Bancroft, Ron Silver, Carrie Fisher, Catherine Hicks, Howard Da Silva, Harvey Fierstein, Hermione Gingold. w. Larry Grusin, d. Sidney Lumet.

COMEDY: COMEDY DRAMA: Comedy-Light; Dying Wishes; Hospitals; Ensemble Films; Actresses; Fans-Crazed; Obsessions; Mothers & Sons; Hidden Gems; Overlooked at Release; Quiet Little Films
(Heartbreak Hotel; Fedora)

The Garden, 1990, 90m, ★★¹/₂/$, Ind/New Line, R/ES-MFN. An art film of religious images contrasted with homophobic persecution and the director himself in his garden make for an acquired taste-test. Kevin Collins, Roger Cook. w. d. Derek Jarman.

DRAMA: Art Films; Avant-Garde Films; Gay Men; Jesus Christ; Religion; Homophobia; Allegorical Stories; British Films; Cult Films; Writer-Directors
(Poison; Edward II)

Garden of Allah, 1936, 86m, ★★★/$$$, David O. Selznick-UA/Fox. A classy dame goes gets tired of "the life" and goes off to the Middle East to woos a monk. Marlene Dietrich, Charles Boyer, Basil Rathbone, Tilly Losch. w. W. P. Lipscomb, Lynn Riggs, N-adap. Robert Hitchens, d. Richard Bolwslawski. **BCCin** (special award), BOScore. Oscars: 2-1.

ROMANCE: MELODRAMA: ADVENTURE: Romantic Adventure; Desert Settings; Middle East; Monks; Romance-Mismatched
(Algiers; Desire; The Blue Angel)

Garden of Evil, 1954, 100m, ★★¹/₂/$$, 20th/NA. A gambler and a former sheriff panning for gold help a mountain woman rescue her husband from a mine but must fight Indians in the process. Susan Hayward, Gary Cooper, Richard Widmark, Hugh Marlowe, Cameron Mitchell. w. Frank Fenton, d. Henry Hathaway.

WESTERNS: Rescue Drama; Gold Mining; Indians-American, Conflict with; Gambling; Saving Someone; Romance-Triangles; Women in Jeopardy; Trapped in a Hole; Forgotten Films

The Garden of the Finzi-Continis, 1971, 95m, ★★★1/2/$$$, WB/Lorimar-WB, R. A Jewish family in Italy lives through the demise of its good fortune, culminating in World War II. Dominique Sanda, Lino Capolicchio, Helmut Berger, Romolo Valli, Fabio Testi. w. Tullio Pinelli, Valerio Zurlini, Franco Brusati, Ugo Pirro, Vittorio Bonicelli, Alain Katz, N-adap. Giorgio Bassani, d. Vittorio de Sica. **BFLFilm**, BOScr. Oscars: 2-1.
DRAMA: MELODRAMA: TRAGEDY: World War II Stories; Jewish People; Concentration Camps; Nazi Stories; Oppression; Family Drama; Italians; Italy; Italian Films; Hidden Gems
(The Damned; The Conformist)

Gardens of Stone, 1987, 112m, ★★1/2/$$, Col/Col-Tri, R/P. A drill sergeant is personally opposed to the Vietnam War, but must send his trainees off to fight nonetheless. James Caan, Angelica Huston, James Earl Jones, D. B. Sweeney, Dean Stockwell, Mary Stewart Masterson. w. Ronald Bass, N-adap. Nicholas Proffitt, d. Francis Ford Coppola.
DRAMA: War Stories; Military Stories; Vietnam War; Funerals; Death-Dealing with; Ethics; Leaders-Military; Anti-War Stories; Coulda Been Great
(Born on the Fourth of July; Friendly Fire)

The Garment Jungle, 1957, 88m, ★★★/$$, Col/NA. A family trying to run an honest clothing business in New York has to resist the mob's infiltration of its unions. Lee J. Cobb, Kerwin Mathews, Gia Scala, Richard Boone, Valerie French, Robert Loggia, Joseph Wiseman. w. Harry Kleiner, d. Robert Aldrich, Vincent Sherman.
DRAMA: MELODRAMA: Family Drama; Mob Stories; Fashion World; Business Life; Working Class; New York Life; Corruption; Unions; Strikes; Ethics; Decisions-Big
(On the Waterfront; Save the Tiger; Patterns)

Gas Food Lodging, 1991, 101m, ★★1/2/$, Mainline/Col, R/S-P. A single woman struggles to make a living for herself and her two daughters in a trailer in the desert. Brooke Adams, Ione Skye, Fairuza Balk, James Brolin, Robert Knepper, Donovan Lietch. w. d. Allison Anders, N-adap. Richard Peck (Don't Look and It Won't Hurt).
COMEDY DRAMA: DRAMA: Mothers-Struggling; Family Drama; Mothers Alone; Sisters; Mothers & Daughters; Desert Setting; Making a Living; Working Class; Coming of Age; Multiple Performances; Quiet Little Films

Gaslight (Angel Street), 1939, 84m, ★★★-/$$, Brit/Fox. A young bride is driven insane in order to serve his plot to find some jewels. Diana Wynyard, Anton Walbrook, Frank Pettingell. N-adap. Angel Street, Patrick Hamilton, d. Thorold Dickinson.
DRAMA: SUSPENSE: Psychological Drama; Illusions/Hallucinations; Mental Illness; Conspiracy; Insane-Plot to Drive; Newlyweds; Finding the Loot; Evil Men; Dangerous Spouse; Hitchcockian; Hidden Gems; Forgotten Films
REMAKE: Gaslight (1944)
(Gaslight (1944); Suspicion; Rebecca; Vertigo; Nightwalker)

Gaslight 1944, 144m, ★★★/$$$$, MGM/MGM-UA. A young bride (Ingrid Bergman, **BActress**) may be driven crazy by her new husband (Charles Boyer, BActor), but the question is why. Angela Lansbury (BSActress). w. John Van Druten, Walter Reisch, John L. Balderston, P-adap. Patrick Hamilton. d. George Cukor (BDirector). BPicture, BB&WCin. Oscars: 6-1.
DRAMA: SUSPENSE: Psychological Drama; Illusions/Hallucinations; Mental Illness; Conspiracy; Insane-Plot to Drive; Newlyweds; Evil Men; Dangerous Spouse; Hitchcockian
(Suspicion; Rebecca; Vertigo; Nightwalker)

Gassss: or It May Become Necessary to Destroy the World to Save It! 1970, 97m, ★★/$, AIP/NA. In the future, all people over the age of twenty-five are killed by a mysterious gas, leaving the planet to the groovy people. Robert Corff, Elaine Giftos, Pat Patterson, Graham Armitage, Alex Wilson, Ben Vereen, Bud Cort. w. Graham Armitage, d. Roger Corman.
SATIRE: COMEDY DRAMA: Sexual Revolution; Apocalyptic Stories; Futuristic Stories; Psychedelic Era; Aging; Epidemics; Generation Gap; Massacres; Young People; Hippies; 1970s; Time Capsules; Curiosities

The Gate, 1987, 92m, ★★1/2/$$, Vista/Live, R/V-B&G. Two young boys accidently open up a gate to hell in their back yard. Stephen Dorff, Christa Denton, Louis Tripp, Kelly Rowan, Jennifer Irwin, Scott Denton. w. Michael Nankin, d. Tibor Takacs.

The Gate II, 1992, 95m, ★★/$$, Alliance/Col, R/V-B&G. Three teenagers reopen the gate to Hell by reading up on demonology and summoning up evil spirits. Louis Tripp, Simon Reynolds, Pamela Segall, James Villemaire, Neil Munro. w. Michael Nankin, d. Tibor Takacs.
HORROR: Hell; Satan; Supernatural Danger; Occult; Suburban Life; Child Protagonists; Boys
(The Sentinel; Hellraiser SERIES)

Gate of Hell, 1953, 90m, ★★★/$$, Daiei/Sultan. A Samurai warrior wins a battle and demands his payment: a beautiful woman in the village. Unfortunately, she is married. Machiko Kyo, Kazuo Hasegawa, Isao Yamagata. w. d. Teinosuke Kinugasa. BFLFilm. Oscars: 1-0.
DRAMA: TRAGEDY: War Stories; Duels; Romance with Married Person; Fatal Attractions; Romance-Triangles; Martial Arts; Art Films; Japanese Films; Writer-Directors
(Ed: Its rare color for a Japanese film of its time is "sumptuous")

The Gathering, 1978, 94m, ★★★/$$$, ABC/World Vision. A dying man in upstate New York faces death while his family gathers for Christmas. Ed Asner, Maureen Stapleton, Lawrence Pressman, Stephanie Zimbalist, Gregory Harrison, Veronica Hamel, Gail Strickland. w. James Poe, d. Randal Kleiser.
DRAMA: Reunions; Death-Impending; Death-Dealing with; Family Drama; Stern Men; Mean Men; Christmas
(A Family Upside Down; A Delicate Balance)
(Ed: Emmy winner for best drama special)

A Gathering of Eagles, 1963, 115m, ★★1/2/$$$, U-I/MCA-U. A colonel ruffles some feathers when he implements stricter policies at the base in his command. Rock Hudson, Mary Peach, Rod Taylor, Barry Sullivan. w. Robert Pirosh, d. Delbert Mann.

ACTION: DRAMA: Action Drama; Power Struggles; War Stories; Military Stories; Military Leaders
REMAKE/RETREAD: Twelve O'Clock High
Gator, 1976, 116m, ★★½/$$$, UA/MGM-UA, R/S-P-V. A bootlegger is caught by government agents and forced to work undercover to catch other law-breakers. Burt Reynolds, Jack Weston, Lauren Hutton, Jerry Reed, Alice Ghostley, Mike Douglas. w. William Norton, d. Burt Reynolds.
ACTION: Crime Drama; Detective Stories; Undercover; Police Stories; Ex-Convicts; Informers; Southerns; Rednecks; Arkansas; Swamp Settings; Bootleggers; Actor Directors
SEQUEL TO: White Lightning.
(Ed: Basically a repeat of the first install-ment with this Reynolds character, but with an added romantic interest)
The Gauntlet, 1977, 109m, ★★★/$$$$, WB/WB, R/EV-P. A prostitute wanted dead by the gangsters she double-crossed is escorted cross-country by a crooked cop. They must both make it through the gauntlet of all kinds of armed men, good and bad, while fleeing on a bus which isn't really bulletproof. Clint Eastwood, Sondra Locke, Pat Hingle, William Prince. w. Michael Butler, Dennis Shryack, d. Clint Eastwood.
ACTION: Crime Drama; Police Stories; Police-Vigilante; Prostitutes-Low Class; Informers; Mob Stories; Fugitives from the Mob; Fugitives from the Law; Road Movies; Chase Stories; Protecting Someone; Witnesses-Protecting; Actor Directors; Buses
(Speed; Dirty Harry; Midnight Run)
The Gay Divorcee, 1934, 107m, ★★★★/$$$$, RKO/Turner. A woman on vacation on the English seaside to cele-brate her imminent divorce is pursued by a dancer whom she mistakes for a reporter. Fred Astaire, Ginger Rogers, Edward Everett Horton, Alice Brady, Erik Rhodes, Eric Blore, Lillian Miles, Betty Grable. w. George Marion Jr., Dorothy Yost, Edward Kaufman, MP-adap. Samuel Hoffenstein, Kenneth Webb, Cole Porter, P-adap. Dwight Taylor, J. Hartley Manners, d. Mark Sandrich. BPicture, BMScore, BArt, **BOSong** "The Contintental." Oscars: 4-1.
MUSICALS: ROMANCE: Musical Romance; Musical Comedy; Romantic Comedy; Identities-Mistaken;

Misunderstandings; Americans Abroad; Vacation Romance; Dancers; Astaire & Rogers; Divorce; Starting Over; Female Screenwriters
(Top Hat)
Gay Purree, 1962, 85m, ★★★/$$, UPA-WB/WB. An uppity farm cat from Normandy goes to Paris and but finds she's no match for the big bad city. Voices of Judy Garland, Robert Goulet, Hermione Gingold. w. Dorothy and Chuck Jones, d. Abe Levitow.
CHILDREN'S: FAMILY: Cartoons; **MUSI-CALS:** Musicals-Animated; Cats; City vs. Country; Fish out of Water Stories; Paris
The Gay Sisters, 1942, 110m, ★★★/$$, WB/NA. Three sisters in posh old New York try to stave off selling their mansion to skyscraper developers. Barbara Stanwyck, George Brent, Geraldine Fitzgerald, Donald Crisp, Gig Young, Nancy Coleman, Gene Lockhart. w. Leonore Coffee, N-adap. Stephen Longstreet, d. Irving Rapper.
MELODRAMA: Family Drama; Mortgage Drama; Rich People; New York Life; Corporation as Enemy; Greed; Sisters
(The Cherry Orchard [play])
The Gazebo, 1959, 102m, ★★★/$, MGM/MGM-UA. When a TV writer kills a blackmailer and buries him under the gazebo in his garden, problems arise, possibly including the body. Glenn Ford, Debbie Reynolds, Carl Reiner, John McGiver, Mabel Albertson, Zasu Pitts, Martin Landau. w. George Wells, P-adap. Alec Coppel, d. George Marshall.
SATIRE: MURDER: Black Comedy; Comedy-Writer; Hide the Dead Body;
FARCE: Writers; TV Life; Hollywood Life; Blackmail
(Deathtrap; Woman Screaming)
The Gene Krupa Story, 1959, 110m, ★★½/$$, Col/Col. Story of a bigtime jazz drummer who gets involved with drugs and worse, losing what he'd gained. Sal Mineo, Susan Kohner, James Darren, Susan Oliver, Shelly Mann, Buddy Lester, Yvonne Craig. w. Orin Jennings, d. Don Weis.
DRAMA: TRAGEDY: Biographies; Drugs-Addictions; Rise and Fall Stories; Fame-Rise to; Young Men; Musicians; Jazz Life; Beatnik Era; Teen Idols; Time Capsules; Forgotten Films; Curiosities
(Bird; All the Fine Young Cannibals)
(Ed: For fans of Mineo. The irony here is that the same reckless abandon that made Krupa a creative success also drove him

too far in his personal life, and because of the time, it's not addressed)
The General, 1926, 80m, B&W, silent, ★★★★/$$$, UA/Nos. During the Civil War, a confederate conductor has his train usurped by Union soldiers with his girlfriend still aboard, and devises many an elaborate scheme to get them both back. Buster Keaton, Marion Mack, Glen Cavander. w. Al Boasberg, Charles Smith, d. Buster Keaton, Clyde Bruckman.
COMEDY: Comedy-Slapstick; Civil War Era; Trains; Kidnappings; Revenge; Chase Stories; Hidden Gems
(Free and Easy)
General Della Rovere, 1961, 137m, ★★★/$, Zebra-Gaumont-Continental/Nos. An actor is hired to stand in for a dead general but gets so wrapped up in the role that he never "breaks character," even when facing the firing squad. Vittorio de Sica, Hannes Messemer, Sandra Milo, Giovanna Ralli, Anne Vernon. w. Sergio Amidei, Diego Fabbri, Indro Montanelli, Roberto Rossellini (BOScr), d. Roberto Rossellini. Oscars: 1-0.
SATIRE: DRAMA: TRAGEDY: Allegorical Stories; Art Films; Actors; Impostors; Impostors-Actors; Italian Films; Italy
COMEDY REMAKE: Moon Over Parador.
(On the Double; Moon Over Parador; The Magic Face; The Masquerader; Dave)
The General Died at Dawn, 1936, 93m, ★★★/$$$, Par/MCA-U. A soldier-for-hire in China fights with the resistors of an evil general to usurp his command. In the process, he falls in love with a beautiful spy. Gary Cooper, Madeleine Carroll, Akim Tamiroff (BSActor), Dudley Digges, Porter Hall, William Frawley. w. Clifford Odets, N-adap. Charles Booth, d. Lewis Milestone. BCin, BOScore. Oscars: 3-0.
ADVENTURE: War Stories; **ROMANCE: MELODRAMA:** Romantic Drama; Soldiers; Spies; Spies-Female; China; Mercenaries; Epics; Forogtten Films; Faded Hits; Hidden Gems
(For Whom the Bell Tolls)
Generation, 1969, 104m, ★★½/$$, Avco Embassy/Home Vision, PG/S. A businessman is aghast when he finds out his daughter wants to give birth at home. David Janssen, Kim Darby, Carl Reiner, Pete Duel, Andrew Prine, James Coco, Sam Waterston, Don Beddoe. w., P-adap. William Goodhart, d. George Schafer.

COMEDY: COMEDY DRAMA: Parents vs. Children; Generation Gap; Babies-Having; Alternative Lifestyles; 1960s; Hippies
(The Family Way; Butterflies Are Free)

Genevieve, 1953, 86m, ★★★/$$$$, GFD/Learning Corp. Two old friends and their wives go to Brighton's vintage car rally and on the way back engage in an impromptu race. Dinah Sheridan, John Gregson, Kay Kendall, Kenneth More, Geoffrey Keen, Joyce Grenfell, Reginald Beckwith, Arthur Wontner. w. William Rose (BOScr), d. Henry Cornelius. BOScore. Oscars: 2-0.

COMEDY: COMEDY DRAMA: ROMANCE: Romantic Comedy; Marriage Comedy; Friendships-Male; Feuds; Car Racing; Race Against Time; Costume Drama
(The Great Race; Those Magnificent Men in Their Flying Machines)
(Ed: A blockbuster in England, it didn't break records in America, but did do well and was imitated several times)

Genghis Khan, 1964, 126m, ★★1/2/$, Col/NA. The famous ruthless Mongolian general rises to prominence in the ancient world by bringing his enemies to their knees. Omar Sharif, Stephen Boyd, Francoise Dorleac, James Mason, Robert Morley, Telly Savalas, Woody Strode, Eli Wallach, Yvonne Mitchell. w. Clarke Reynolds, Beverly Cross, d. Henry Levin.
ADVENTURE: Historical Drama; Epics; Leaders-Tyrants; Royalty; Evil Men; War Stories; China; Ancient Times; Cast of Thousands; Flops-Major; Female Screenwriters
(The Conqueror)

Gentleman Jim, 1942, 104m, ★★1/2/$$$, WB/MGM-UA. In the gay nineties, the street boxer Jim Corbett goes professional. Errol Flynn, Alan Hale, Alexis Smith, John Loder, Jack Carson, Ward Bond, Wililam Frawley, Rhys Williams, Arthur Shields. w. Vincent Lawrence, Horace McCoy, NF-adap. James J. Corbett (The Roar of the Crowd), d. Raoul Walsh.
DRAMA: COMEDY DRAMA: Sports Movies; Boxing; Romance with Boxer; Biographies; Gay 90s; 1890s; Fame-Rise to; Free Spirits

Gentleman's Agreement, 1947, 118m, ★★★1/2/$$$$, 20th/Fox. In order to do a piece on anti-semitism, a WASPy reporter goes undercover as a Jew. Gregory Peck (BActor), Dorothy McGuire (BActress), John Garfield, Celeste Holm (BSActress), Anne Revere, June Havoc, Albert Dekker, Jane Wyatt, Dean Stockwell. w. Moss Hart (BScr), N-adap. Laura Z. Hobson, d. Elia Kazan (BDirector). BPicture, BEdit. Oscars: 7-3.
DRAMA: Social Drama; Message Films; Jewish People; Anti-Semitism; Undercover; Disguises; Detective Stories; Journalists as Detectives; Faded Hits
(Crossfire; Consenting Adult; Black Like Me)

Gentlemen Prefer Blondes, 1953, 91m, ★★★1/2/$$$$, 20th/CBS-Fox. A sharp showgirl-a brunette-takes her ditzy blonde friend with her to Paris to find husbands and gets miffed when her friend gets all the attention. Jane Russell, Marilyn Monroe, Charles Coburn. w. Charles Lederer, N-adap. Anita Loos, d. Howard Hawks.
COMEDY: MUSICALS: Musical Comedy; **ROMANCE:** Romantic Comedy; **SATIRE:** Marrying Up; Golddiggers; Dancers; Singers; Sexy Women; Women in Conflict; Female Protagonists
(The Fuzzy Pink Nightgown; There's No Business Like Show Business; How to Marry a Millionaire)

The Gentle Sex, 1943, 93m, ★★1/2/$$, Rank/NA. Leslie Howard narrates a propaganda film for British women encouraging them to sign up for a special service. Rosamund John, Joan Greenwood, Joan Gates, Jean Gillie, Lilli Palmer, Joyce Howard, Barbara Waring. w. Moie Charles, Aimee Stuart, Phyllis Rose, Roland Pertwee, d. Leslie Howard, Maurice Elvey.
Documentaries; World War II Era; British Films; Curiosities; Narrated Films

The George Raft Story, 1961, 105m, ★★1/2/$$, Allied Artists/NA. A biopic of the dancer with a mob past in New York who went to Hollywood to follow his star but couldn't stay out of trouble. Ray Danton, Julie London, Jayne Mansfield, Frank Gorshin, Neville Brand. w. Crane Wilbur, d. Joseph M. Newman.
MELODRAMA: Biographies; Crime Drama; Hollywood Biographies; Hollywood Life; Mob Stories; Actors; Fame-Rise to; Dancers; Fugitives from the Mob; Rebels
(The Cotton Club; Bugsy)

George Washington Slept Here, 1942, 93m, ★★★/$$, WB/WB. A city couple try to make a go of it in their new country house, badly in need of repairs. Jack Benny, Ann Sheridan, Percy Kilbride, Charles Coburn, Hatti McDaniel, William Tracy, Lee Patrick, John Emery. w. Everett Freeman, P-adap. George Kaufman, Moss Hart, d. William Keighley.
COMEDY: Comedy of Errors; House Havoc; City vs. Country; Fish Out of Water Stories; Marriage Comedy; Coulda Been Great; Hidden Gems
(The Money Pit; Mr. Blandings Builds His Dream House; In Society; Funny Farm)

George White's Scandals, 1934, 79m, ★★★/$$$$, 20th/Critic's Choice. A huge show full of dancing girls and vaudevillians of all stripes has its share of backstage intrigue and romance. George White, Rudy Vallee, Alice Faye, Jimmy Durante, Dxie Dunbar, Adrienne Ames, Cliff Edwards, Gertrude Michael, Gregory Ratoff. w. Jack Yellen (from the Broadway show directed by George White), d. Thornton Freeland, Harry Lachman, George White.

George White's 1935 Scandals, 1935, ★★★/$$$, 20th/NA. George White's Scandals discover a new starlet while touring through a small town. George White, Alice Faye, James Dunn, Eleanor Powell, Ned Sparks, Lyda Roberti, Cliff Edwards, Atline Judge. w. Jack Yellen, Patterson McNutt, d. George White.

George White's Scandals 1945, 1945, 95m, ★★1/2/$$, RKO/NA. Veterans of George White's Scandals from the thirties get together in the forties to put on a nostalgia show, and one of the chorus girls ends up missing. Joan Davis, Jack Haley, Philip Terry, Martha Holliday, Ethel Smith, Margaret Hamilton, Glenn Tryon, Jane Greer, Fritz Feld, Rufe Davis. w. Hugh Wedlock, Parke Levy, Howard Green, d. Felix E. Feist.
MUSICALS: COMEDY: Musical Comedy; Theater Life; Behind the Scenes; Dancers; Dance Movies; Sexy Women; Strippers; Vaudeville

Georgia, 1995, 106m, ★★★/$, R/P-S-FN-MRN. A frazzled young rock singer comes home to pull herself together-in the shadow of her settled, famous, folksinger sister. Jennifer Jason Leigh, Mare Winningham, Ted Levine, Max Perlich, John Doe, John C. Reilly. w. Barbara Turner, d. Ulu Grosbard.

DRAMA: Sisters; Singers; Character Studies; Family Drama; Independent Films; Overlooked at Release; Female Protagonists; Female Screenwriters (Ed: An interesting film that twenty years ago would have been given the big studio treatment. Written by Leigh's mother.)

Georgy Girl (B&W), 1966, 100m, ★★★★/$$$$, Col/RCA-Col, PG/S-MRN. A pudgy wallflower (Lynn Redgrave, BActress) with a sexy roommate (Charlotte Rampling) soon finds the roommate's boyfriend (Alan Bates) after her, as well as being chased by a wealthy old man (James Mason, BSActor). w. Margaret Foster, Peter Nichols, N-adap. Margaret Foster, d. Silvio Narizzano. BOSong, BB&WCin. Oscars: 4-0.

COMEDY: DRAMA: ROMANCE: Romantic Comedy; Romance-Triangles; Wallflowers; Wallflowers & Hunks; Romance with Friend's Lover; Coming of Age; Life Transitions; Babies-Having; Ordinary People Stories; Mean Women; Wild People; Free Spirits; Extroverted vs. Introverted; Mod Era; British Films; Sleeper Hits; Cult Films; Hidden Gems (The Sterile Cuckoo; Getting it Right; Rich in Love; Sugarbaby; Babycakes; Muriel's Wedding)
(Ed: A great film all around)

Geronimo, 1962, 101m, ★★1/2/$$, UA/MGM-UA. Geronimo and the Apaches under his command draw up a peace accord with the Cavalry but are double-crossed. Chuck Connors, Ross Martin, Kamala Devi. w. Pat Fielder, d. Arnold Laven.

WESTERNS: Cavalry vs. Indians; Betrayals; Traitors; Double Crossings; Indians-American, Conflict with; Indians-American; Custer's Last Stand; Historical Drama; Heroes-Unwitting

Geronimo, 1993, 115m, ★★/$, Col/Col, PG-13/V. Revisionist look at the great Indian warrior and his fight to keep the cavalry off of Indian reservations. Jason Patric, Wes Studi, Robert Duvall, Gene Hackman, Matt Damon. w. John Milius, Larry Gross, d. Walter Hill.

WESTERNS: DRAMA: Historical Drama; Westerns-Neo; Western-Revisionist; Cavalry vs. Indians; Betrayals; Traitors; Double Crossings; Indians-American, Conflict with; Indians-American; Custer's Last Stand; Heroes-Unwitting; Flops-Major

Gertrude, 1966, 115m, ★★1/2/$, Pathe/Facets. The middle-aged wife of a lawyer gets tired of her staid suburban life and takes up with a younger musician, but finds it unsatisfying after the initial excitement wears off. Nina Pens Rode, Bendt Rothe, Ebbe Rode. w. d. Carl Theodor Dreyer, P-adap. Hjalmar Soderberg.

MELODRAMA: ROMANCE: Romance-Triangles; Romance with Married Person; Romance-Clandestine; Romance-Older Women/Younger Men; Character Studies; Psychological Drama; Cheating Women; Female Protagonists; Scandinavia (The Idol; Indiscretion of an American Wife; Ash Wednesday)

Gervaise, 1956, 116m, ★★★/$, Festival. In the 1800s a washerwoman in Paris is distraught when her lover leaves her, but she rebuilds her life with another man. They open a laundry business together. Maria Schell, Francois Perier, Suzy Delair, Mathilde Casadeus. w. Jean Aurenche, Pierre Bost, N-adap. Emile Zola (L'Assommoir), d. Rene Clement. BFLFilm. Oscars: 1-0.

DRAMA: MELODRAMA: Historical Drama; Social Drama; **ROMANCE:** Alcoholics; Episodic Stories; Ordinary People Stories; 1800s; Paris; French Films

Get Carter, 1971, 112m, ★★★/$$$, MGM/MGM-UA, R/S-P-V-FFN-MRN. A gangster kills those responsible for his brother's death but meets with a tragic end himself. Michael Caine, John Osborne, Ian Hendry, Britt Ekland. w. d. Mike Hodges, N-adap. Ted Lewis (Jack's Return Home).

SUSPENSE: TRAGEDY: Crime Drama; **ACTION:** Mob Stories; Chase Stories; Avenging Death of Someone; Brothers; England; British Films; Hidden Gems; Faded Hits (The Billion Dollar Brain; The Ipcress File)

The Getaway, 1972, 122m, ★★★/$$$$, FA-NG/WB, R/EV-S. A bank robber (Steve McQueen) and his girlfriend (Ali MacGraw) pull a clever heist with a gang but don't have such an easy getaway to Mexico. Ben Johnson. w. Walter Hill, N-adap. Jim Thompson, d. Sam Peckinpah.
(Ed: Tension-filled and stylish with plenty of plot barriers and reversals; McQueen is at his stoic, excellent best. MacGraw holds her own, though awkward. Better than the remake. Much use is made of Sally Struthers's breasts)

The Getaway, 1994, 125m, ★★1/2/$, WB/WB, R/S-EV-P-FFN-MRN. This time, they rob a dog track. Alec Baldwin, Kim Basinger, d. Roger Donaldson. (Ed: Literal remake where, this time, everyone's cuter and slicker-but not as successful)

ACTION: ROMANCE: Crime Drama; **SUSPENSE:** Chase Movies; Heist Stories; Bank Robberies; Fugitives from the Mob; Fugitives from the Law; Criminal Couples; Crossing the Border; Clever Plots & Endings; Perfect Crimes; Crime Pays; Southwestern Life; Kidnappers-Sympathizing with; Kidnappings; Gun Molls; Jim Thompson-esque (Charley Varrick; Dollars; Bonnie and Clyde)

Get Out Your Handkerchiefs, 1978, 109m, ★★★-/$$$, UAC/WB, R/S-FN. When a husband can't satisfy his wife sexually, he asks a teacher to try his hand, but she's unhappy until she meets a teenager and complications arise. Gerard Depardieu, Carole Laure, Patrick Dewaere. w. d. Bertrand Blier. **BFLFilm.** Oscars: 1-1.

COMEDY: DRAMA: Erotic Drama; Erotic Comedy; Romance-Triangles; Sexual Problems; Marriage Comedy; Romance-Older Women/Younger Men; Teenagers; Teachers; Romance with Teacher; Child Molestation; French Films; Hidden Gems; Faded Hits; Writer-Directors (Beau Pere; Jules et Jim; Going Places)

Get Shorty, 1995, 105m, ★★★1/2/$$$$, MGM-UA/MGM-UA, R/P-S-V. When a loan shark comes to Hollywood to collect on a debt from a producer, the payoff is to make the guy a star. The only problem is that he doesn't realize the difference between acting like a bad guy and being one. John Travolta, Gene Hackman, Rene Russo, Danny De Vito, Dennis Farina, Delroy Lindo, James Gandolfini, Jon Gries, Renee Props, David Paymer. w. Scott Frank, N-adap. Elmore Leonard, d. Barry Sonnenfeld.

COMEDY DRAMA: Black Comedy; Mob Comedy; Hollywood Life; Hollywood Satire; Sleepers; Coulda Been Great (Bugsy; Pulp Fiction)

Getting Even with Dad, 1994, 108m, ★★/$$, MGM/MGM-UA, PG-13/P. When his criminal dad steals some dough, son hides it to make him go straight and spend time with him. Ted Danson,

Macaulay Culkin, Glenne Headly, Hector Elizondo, Saul Rubinek, Gailard Sartain. w. Tom Parker, Jim Jennewein, d. Howard Deutsch.

COMEDY: Fathers & Sons; Criminals-Stupid; Blackmail; Family Comedy; Finding the Loot; Flops-Major

Getting It Right, 1989, 101m, Virgin-MCEG/Virgin, ★★★/$$, PG-13/S. A 31-year-old male virgin hairdresser finally finds love, but perhaps from too many women. Jesse Birdsall, Lynn Redgrave. w. N-adap. Elizabeth Jane Howard, d. Randal Kleiser.

COMEDY: ROMANCE: Virgins; Coming of Age; Romance-Older Women/Younger Men; Sexual Problems; Single Men; Hairdressers; Dating Scene; British Films; Female Screenwriters; Old-Fashioned Recent Films

FLIPSIDE OF: Georgy Girl

(Georgy Girl; The Graduate; The Last American Virgin)

The Getting of Wisdom, 1977, 100m, ★★★/$$, Ind/Fox. In Australia at the turn of the century, a young girl of the outback is sent to Melbourne and wins a music scholarship. Susannah Fowle, Sheila Helpman, Patricia Kennedy, John Waters, Barry Humphries, Kerry Armstrong. w. Eleanor Witcombe, N-adap. Henry Handel Richardson (Ethel Richardson), d. Bruce Beresford.

DRAMA: COMEDY DRAMA: Pianists; Musicians; Boarding Schools; Girls' Schools; Young Women; Girls; Coming of Age; Australian Films; 1900s; Hidden Gems; Quiet Little Films; Female Protagonists; Female Screenwriters

(My Brilliant Career; We of the Never Never)

Getting Straight, 1970, 124m, ★★1/2/$$$, Col/RCA-Col, R/S-P. A left-wing activist of the 60s takes a teaching job at Berkeley and finds the students unbearably naive. Elliott Gould, Candice Bergen, Robert F. Lyons, Jeff Corey, Max Julien, Cecil Kellaway. w. Robert Kaufman, N-adap. Ken Kolb, d. Richard Rush.

COMEDY DRAMA: Anti-Establishment Films; College Life; Professors; Political Activisists; Rebels; 1960s; Vietnam Era; Time Capsules; Faded Hits

(The Strawberry Statement; Move)

Gettysburg, 1993, 254m, ★★★/$$$, TNT/Turner. A recreation of the great Civil War battle, focusing on the military

officers in charge-behind the scenes. Jeff Daniels, Martin Sheen, Tom Berenger, Richard Jordan, Sam Elliott, Stephen Lang, Maxwell Caulfield, C. Thomas Howell, Andrew Prine, Kevin Conway. w. d. Ronald Maxwell, N-adap. *The Killer Angels*, Michael Shaara.

DRAMA: Civil War Stories; War Battles; Epics; Cast of Thousands; Interwoven Stories; Multiple Stories; Pulitzer Prize Adaptations; Cult Films

(Andersonville; North and South)

Ghost, 1990, 123m, ★★★1/2/$$$$$, Par/Par, PG-13/S-P. A young couple (Patrick Swayze, Demi Moore) are separated when the husband is killed, but when he comes back through a two-bit psychic (Whoopi Goldberg, **BSActress**), will she believe it's him and help him avenge his murder? w. Bruce Joel Rubin (**BOScr**), d. Jerry Zucker. BPicture, BOScore, BEdit. Oscars: 5-2.

COMEDY DRAMA: MELODRAMA: ROMANCE: SUSPENSE: MURDER: MURDER MYSTERY: MYSTERY: Romantic Drama; Marriage Drama; Fantasy; Friends as Enemies; Dangerous Men; Revenge; Avenging Death of Someone; Saving Oneself; Protecting Someone; Conspiracy; Friends as Enemies; Black Women; Yuppies; Ghosts; Newlyweds; Fortunetellers; Supernatural Danger; Widows; Psychics; Sleeper Hits; Blockbusters

(Blithe Spirit; Kiss Me Goodbye)

The Ghost and Mr. Chicken, 1965, 90m, ★★★/$$$, U/MCA-U, G. A cowardly small-town reporter agrees to spend the night in a supposedly haunted house to write it up for his column. Once inside, he encounters all manner of "things that go bump in the night." Don Knotts, Skip Homeier, Joan Staley, Liam Redmond, Dick Sargent, Rita Shaw. w. James Fritzell, Everett Greenbaum, d. Alan Rafkin.

COMEDY: CHILDREN'S: FAMILY: Spoofs-Horror; Horror Comedy; Ghosts; Cowards; Nerds; Houses-Creepy; Supernatural Danger; Journalists; Small-Town Life; Comedy-Disneyesque; Sleeper Hits

The Ghost and Mrs. Muir, 1947, 104m, ★★★/$$$, 20th/CBS-Fox. A woman buys a home by the sea and finds afterward that it is haunted by the ghost of an old sea captain. She's not frightened away; in fact, she eventually falls in love with him. Gene Tierney, Rex Harrison,

George Sanders, Edna Best, Vanessa Brown, Natalie Wood. w. Philip Dunne, N-adap. R. A. Dick, d. Joseph L. Mankiewicz. BB&WCin. Oscars: 1-0.

MELODRAMA: COMEDY DRAMA: ROMANCE: Fantasy; Ghosts; Houses-Creepy; Romantic Drama; Romance-Reluctant; Widows; Haunted Houses; England; Sailors; Starting Over; Hidden Gems

The Ghost Breakers, 1940, 85m, ★★★1/2/$$$$, Par/Par. In the West Indies, a young woman inherits a haunted castle, and seeks out the help of a local "service." Bob Hope, Paulette Goddard, Paul Lukas, Willie Best, Richard Carlson, Lloyd Corrigan. w. Paul Dickey, Walter de Leon, P-adap. Paul Dickey, Charles W. Goddard, d. George Marshall.

COMEDY: Horror Comedy; Cowards; Ghosts; **ROMANCE:** Romantic Comedy; Caribbean; Houses-Creepy; Haunted Houses; Castles; Faded Hits; Hidden Gems; Forgotten Films

REMAKE: Scared Stiff

(Ghostbusters; The Cat and the Canary)

Ghostbusters, 1984, 107m, ★★★/$$$$$$, Col/RCA-Col, PG/P. A group of madcap ghost exterminators do battle with a legion of demonic ghoulies in this spoof of supernatural and Satanic movies. Dan Aykroyd, Bill Murray, Sigourney Weaver, Annie Potts, Harold Ramis. w. Dan Aykroyd, Harold Ramis, d. Ivan Reitman. BOSong. Oscars: 1-0.

Ghostbusters 2, 1989, 102m, ★★1/2/$$$$$, Col/RCA-Col, PG/P-S. The original gang has closed up shop when a new rash of ghosts and goblins start attacking New York, causing them to re-don their ghost-fighting smocks and anti-plasma guns. Bill Murray, Dan Aykroyd, Sigourney Weaver, Harold Ramis, Rick Moranis, Ernie Hudson, Annie Potts, Peter MacNichol, David Margulies. w. Harold Ramis, Dan Aykroyd, d. Ivan Reitman.

COMEDY: ACTION: Action Comedy; Spoof-Horror; Horror Comedy; Ghosts; Special Teams; Bounty Hunters; Psychics; Supernatural Danger; Blockbusters

(Poltergeist; The Exorcist; Ghostbreakers)

The Ghost Goes West, 1935, 85m, ★★★1/2/$$, London/HBO. A millionaire buys a Scottish castle and transports it to America, but the ghost that haunts it comes with. Robert Donat, Jean Parker,

Eugene Pallette, Elsa Lanchester, Ralph Bunker, Patricia Hilliard, Morton Selton. w. Robert E. Sherwood, Geoffrey Kerr, Eric Keown, d. Rene Clair.

COMEDY: Horror Comedy; Fantasy; Castles; Houses-Creepy; Haunted Houses; Ghosts; Nuisances; British Films; Hidden Gems; Forgotten Films

The Ghost in the Invisible Bikini, 1966, 82m, ★★1/2/$$, AIP/NA. A Hell's Angels–type gang hangs out at a haunted mansion and has to run from a re-animated corpse. Boris Karloff, Basil Rathbone, Patsy Kelly, Tommy Kirk, Deborah Walley, Aron Kincaid. w. Louis M. Heyward, Elwood Ullman, d. Don Weis.

COMEDY: Horror Comedy; Spoofs-Horror; Teenagers; Teenage Movies; Beach Movies; Motorcycles; Haunted Houses; Dead-Back from the; Sexy Women; Curiositites

Ghost in the Machine, 1993, 104m, ★★/$, Fox/Fox, R/V. A serial killer's soul winds going through a hospital's MRI system and into its computer network where it goes out and wreaks havoc via the Internet. Karen Allen, Chris Mulkey, Jessica Walter, Ric Ducommun. w. William Davies, William Osborne, d. Rachel Talalay.

HORROR: SCI-FI: Computers; Computer Terror; Telephone Terror; Serial Killers; Monsters-Machine; Female Directors

REMAKE/RETREAD: Shocker.

(Shocker; Hardware; Pulse)

Ghosts Can't Do It, 1990, 91m, ★/$, Col/Turner, R/S-FN-MRN. A sexpot wants to bring back the libido of her dead hubby through another man's . . . body. Bo Derek, Anthony Quinn, Don Murray. w. d. John Derek.

COMEDY: Erotic Comedy; Erotic Drama; Dead-Back from the; Camp

(Bolero; Ten)

Ghost Story, 1981, 110m, ★★★/$$, U/MCA-U, R/V-P. Four old men who get together to tell ghost stories have a guilty secret of their own, which comes back to "haunt" them. Fred Astaire, Melvyn Douglas, John Houseman, Douglas Fairbanks Jr., Craig Wasson, Patricia Neal, Alice Krige, Jacqueline Brookes. w. Larry Cohen, N-adap. Peter Straub, d. John Irvin.

SUSPENSE: HORROR: Ghosts; Haunted Houses; Reunions; Elderly Men; Ensemble Films; Ensembles-Male; Storytellers; Secrets-Haunting; Past-Haunted by the; Guilty Conscience; Friendships-Male

Ghosts . . . of the Civil Dead, 1988, 93m, ★★★/$ (VR), Ind/NA, R/EV-EP-S-MRN. In an Australia, prisoners rise up against horrible conditions. Dave Field, Mike Bishop, Chris De Rose, Nick Cave, Freddo Dierck, Vincent Gil, Dave Mason. w. Gene Conkie, John Hillcoat, Evan English, Nick Cave, Hugo Race, d. John Hillcoat.

DRAMA: Social Drama; **TRAGEDY:** Prison Drama; Fighting the System; Men in Conflict; Reformers; Documentary Style; Art Films; Australian Films; Coulda Been Great; Stagelike Films (Brubaker; Alien 3; Weeds)

Ghostwriter, 1984, 90m, ★★-/$, PBS-AP/PBS. Philip Roth's autobiographical tale of a writer coming to terms with his past, Jewish heritage, and sexual problems. Sam Wanamaker, Claire Bloom, Mark Linn Baker. w. N-adap. Philip Roth, d. Tristam Powell.

DRAMA: Autobiographical Stories; Biographies-Fictional; Writers; Jewish People; Sexual Problems; Midlife Crisis (Portnoy's Complaint)

The Ghoul, 1933, 79m, ★★★/$$, Ind/Sinister. An archaeologist returns from Egypt with a murderer in tow. Boris Karloff, Cedric Hardwicke, Ralph Richardson, Kathleen Harrison, Ernest Thesiger, Dorothy Hyson. w. Frank King, Leonard Hines, L. DuGarde Peach, Roland Pertwee, John Hastings Turner, Rupert Downing, N-adap. Frank King, d. T. Hayes Hunter.

HORROR: SUSPENSE: Archeologists; Mummies; **MURDER:** Murders-One by One; British Films; Forgotten Films

REMAKE: What a Carve Up (The Mummy; The Mummy's Shroud)

The Ghoul, 1975, 88m, ★★/$, 20th/Media. A former clergyman puts up a group of vacationing tourists whose car breaks down, then proceeds to kill them off one by one. Peter Cushing, Alexandra Bastedo, John Hurt, Gwen Watford, Don Henderson. w. John Elder, d. Freddie Francis.

HORROR: Preachers/Ministers; Serial Killers; Psycho Killers; Murders-One by One; **MURDER:** Stranded; Forgotten Films

Giant, 1956, 201m, ★★★/$$$$, WB/WB. A Texan cattle and oil clan over a period of several decades, centering around a romantic triangle. Rock Hudson (BActor), Elizabeth Taylor, James Dean (BActor), Mercedes McCambridge (BSActress), Carroll Baker, Chill Wills, Dennis Hopper, Sal Mineo, Rod Taylor, Judith Evelyn, Earl Holliman. w. Fred Guiol, Ivan Moffat, N-adap. Edna Ferber, d. George Stevens (**BDirector**). BPicture, BOScore, BCArt, BEdit, BCCostume. Oscars: 9-1.

MELODRAMA: DRAMA: ROMANCE: Romance-Triangles; Epics; Sagas; Family Drama; Cattle Ranchers; Oil People; Rags to Riches; Power-Rise to; Men Fighting Over Women; Texas; Blockbusters (So Big; Dallas TV Series; Texasville; East of Eden; Written on the Wind)

G.I. Blues, 1960, 104m, ★★1/2/$$$, Par/Fox. Elvis romances a dancer while stationed in Germany. Elvis Presley, Juliet Prowse, Robert Ivers, Leticia Roman, Arch Johnson. w. Edmund Beloin, Henry Garson, d. Norman Taurog.

ROMANCE: Music Movies; **MELODRAMA: MUSICALS:** Soldiers; Americans Abroad; Germany; Dancers

Gidget, 1959, 95m, ★★★/$$$, Col/RCA-Col. The popular all-American girl falls for a surfer. Her parents are against it until they find out that he's the son of their good friends. Sandra Dee, Cliff Robertson, James Darren, Arthur O'Connell. w. Gabrielle Upton, N-adap Frederick Kohner, d. Paul Wendkos.

COMEDY: COMEDY DRAMA: Romantic Comedy; Infatuations; Love-First; Girls; Teenagers; Teenage Movies; Young Women; Beach Movies; Surfers; American Myth; Suburban Life; Free Spirits; Female Protagonists

SEQUELS: Gidget Goes Hawaiian, Gidget Goes to Rome, TV Series (1965), ABC, TV Movies (1971, ABC).

Gigi, 1948, 109m, ★★★/$$, Codo/NA. Trained from a young age by her aunt to be a prostitute, a young woman is forced to marry a sleazy customer. Afterward, she is transformed and transforms her husband into a decent person. Daniel Delorme, Gaby Morlay, Yvonne de Bray, Frank Villard, Jean Tissier, Madeleine Rousset. w. Pierre Laroche, N-adap. Colette, d. Jacqueline Audry.

COMEDY DRAMA: ROMANCE: Romantic Comedy; Coming of Age; Young

Women; Girls; Prostitutes-High Class;
Paris; 1900s; Female Protagonists;
Female Directors

MUSICAL REMAKE: Gigi (1958)

Gigi, 1958, 119m, ★★★¹/2/$$$$,
MGM/MGM-UA. A beautiful young girl
(Leslie Caron) in gay Paree decides to try
and marry rather than become a courtesan. Maurice Chevalier (**Special Award**),
Louis Jourdan, Hermione Gingold, Eva
Gabor, John Abbott. w. Alan Jay Lerner
(**BAScr**), d. Vincente Minnelli
(**BDirector**). **BPicture, BCCinema,
BCArt, BCCostume, BAScore,
BOSong.** Oscars: 9-9. (8-8)

**MUSICAL: ROMANCE: COMEDY
DRAMA:** Musical Romance; Musical
Drama; Costume Drama; Romantic
Comedy; Coming of Age; Young Women;
Girls; Prostitutes-High Class; Paris;
1900s; Blockbusters; Production Design-
Outstanding

MUSICAL REMAKE: of 1948 version,
stageplay.

(Lili; Fanny; Moulin Rouge)

(Ed: The only major Oscar nominee to
win every award it was nominated for)

Gigot, 1962, 104m, ★★¹/2/$, 20th/NA.
A mute man who lives in a Parisian
boardinghouse and is a sometimes clown
helps a prostitute and her child. Jackie
Gleason, Katherine Kath, Gabrielle
Dorzat. w. John Patrick, Jackie Gleason,
d. Gene Kelly. BOScore. Oscars: 1-0.

MELODRAMA: Tearjerkers; Street Life;
Boardinghouses; Prostitutes-Low Class;
Deaf People; Mute People; Men and
Girls; Saving Someone; Paris; Coulda
Been Good; Flops-Major; Forgotten Films

(The Clown; Papa's Delicate Condition)

(Ed: A failed attempt at Chaplinism, but
not too bad on its own. Not really a comedy, however, as Gleason's starring may
suggest)

G.I. Joe, 1945, 108m, ★★★/$$,
UA/MGM-UA. Ernie Pyle's life and
wartime experiences: the true story of
a dignified war reporter who won fame
telling the story of common soldiers.
Burgess Meredith, Robert Mitchum
(BActor), Freddie Steele. w. Leopold
Atlas, Guy Endore, Philip Stevenson, NF-
adap. Ernie Pyle, d. William Wellman.
BOScore, BOSong. Oscars: 3-0.

DRAMA: MELODRAMA: War Stories;
World War II Stories; Soldiers;
Biographies; Journalists; True Stories;
Writers

Gilda, 1946, 110m, ★★★¹/2/$$$$,
Col/RCA-Col. An old drifting gambler
gets a job in a South American town
working for the husband of his old
flame . . . and that flame slowly rekindles,
threatening to explode in both their faces.
Rita Hayworth, Glenn Ford, George
Macready, Steve Geray, Joseph Calleia,
Gerald Mohr. w. Marion Parsonnet, E. A.
Ellington, d. Charles Vidor.

MELODRAMA: ROMANCE: Film Noir;
Romantic Drama; Romance-Triangles;
Romance-Dangerous; Romance
Reunited; Mob Stories; Mob Girls;
Dancers; Sexy Women; Elusive Women;
Hidden Gems; Blockbusters; Female
Screenwriters

(Cover Girl; Down to Earth; Miss Sadie
Thompson)

Gilda Live, 1980, 90m, ★★★¹/2/$$,
WB/WB, PG/P. A series of sketches from
Gilda Radner's Broadway show, including
more than just her *Saturday Night Live*
material. Gilda Radner. w. Gilda Radner,
d. Mike Nichols.

COMEDY: One Person Shows; Comedy-
Performance; Stage Filmings; Multiple
Performances; Comedy-Skit; Comedy-
Character; Hidden Gems

(Whoopi Goldberg Live; Saturday Night
Live TV Series)

The Gilded Lily, 1935, 85m, ★★¹/2/$$,
Par/NA. A poor but happy court stenographer meets her boyfriend on a park
bench-another poor but happy man, a
reporter. All is fine until she's wooed by
a suave Brit. Claudette Colbert, Fred
MacMurray, Ray Milland, C. Aubrey
Smith, Luis Alberni, Donald Meek. w.
Claude Binyon, d. Wesley Ruggles.

COMEDY DRAMA: ROMANCE:
Romantic Comedy; Romance-Triangles;
Poor People; Ordinary People Stories;
Depression Era; Time Capsules

The Gin Game, 1984, 82m, ★★★¹/2/$$,
RKO-cable/RKO, Turner. An elderly man
in a rest home back decades ago begins a
friendship with a woman who moves in by
playing a gin card game. Both retell their
lives to each other while a battle of the
sexes begins over the cards and death
stares them down. Hume Cronyn, Jessica
Tandy. d. Mike Nichols.

COMEDY: COMEDY DRAMA: Elderly
People; Romance-Elderly; Games Battle
of the Sexes; Romance-Bickering;
Memories; Stage Tapings; Hidden Gems

(Foxfire; To Dance with the White Dog)

(Ed: A multiple Tony winner on stage,
and well worth a peek)

Ginger and Fred, 1986, 126m,
★★★/$$, UAC/MGM-UA. A pair of
retired dancers are reunited for an
appearance on a television program and
find their glow has faded but not burned
out. Giulietta Masina, Marcello
Mastroianni, Franco Fabrizi, Frederick
Von Ledenberg. w. Federico Fellini,
Tonino Guerra, Tullio Pinelli, d. Federico
Fellini.

COMEDY DRAMA: DRAMA: Art Films;
Dance Movies; Dancers; Reunions; Elder
People; Romance Reunited; Italian Films

(Ed: Ginger Rogers sued for the similarities)

Ginger in the Morning, 1973, 90m,
★★/$, Ind/NA. A free spirited Southern
girl is picked up as a hitchhiker by an
older man. Sissy Spacek, Slim Pickens,
Monte Markham, Susan Oliver. d. Gordon
Wiles.

DRAMA: ROMANCE: Free Spirits;
Hitchhikers; Road Movies; Forgotten
Films

(Breezy; Petulia)

(Ed: Notable only as Spacek's first
major role)

The Girl Can't Help It, 1956, 99m,
★★¹/2/$$$, 20th/Fox. A gangster wants
his moll to be a Broadway star. He hires a
coach who has trouble discerning where
her "talents" lie. Jayne Mansfield, Tom
Ewell, Edmond O'Brien, Henry Jones,
John Emery, Julie London, Fats Domino,
Little Richard, The Platters. w. Frank
Tashlin, Herbert Baker, SS-adap. Garson
Kanin (*Do Re Mi*), d. Frank Tashlin.

COMEDY: ROMANCE: Romantic
Comedy; Mob Stories; Mob Comedy; Mob
Girls; Bimbos; Actresses; Svengalis;
Romance with Teacher; Nerds & Babes;
Sexy Women; Smart vs. Dumb; Camp;
Faded Hits

REMAKE/RETREAD: Born Yesterday
(Born Yesterday; Ball of Fire; Bullets
Over Broadway)

Girl Crazy, 1943, 99m, ★★★/$$$$,
MGM/MGM-UA. At a college out West,
the co-eds get together and chase each
other around the quads while singing
intermittently. Judy Garland, Mickey
Rooney, Guy Kibbee, Gil Stratton, Robert
E. Strickland, Rags Ragland, Tommy
Dorsey and his band. w. Fred F.
Finkelhoffe, P-adap. Guy Bolton, Jack
McGowan, d. William A. Seiter.

MUSICALS: COMEDY: Musical Comedy;
ROMANCE: Romantic Comedy; College
Life; Nostalgia; American Myth
REMAKE: Where the Boys Meet the Girls
The Girl from Petrovka, 1974, 104m,
★★/$, U/MCA-U. A foreign correspon-
dent in Russia falls for a beautiful
babushka ballerina with lots of eye-
shadow. Goldie Hawn, Hal Holbrook,
Anthony Hopkins, Gregoire Aslan, Anton
Dolin. w. Allan Scott, Chris Bryant, d.
Robert Ellis.
DRAMA: MELODRAMA: ROMANCE:
Romantic Drama; Russia; Russians;
Ballet; Americans Abroad; Romance-
Doomed; Journalists; Forgotten Films
(The Russia House)
The Girl from Tenth Avenue, 1935,
69m, ★★1/2/$$, WB/NA. A lawyer loses
his great love and marries the first girl
who gives him a positive sign. Bette
Davis, Ian Hunter, Colin Clive, Alison
Skipworth, Katherine Alexander, John
Eldredge. w. Charles Kenyon, P-adap.
Hubert Henry Davies, d. Alfred E. Green.
MELODRAMA: Lawyers; Romance with
Lawyer; Romance-Brief; Marriage Drama;
Womens' Films
(Dangerous; The Old Maid)
The Girl in the Red Velvet Swing,
1955, 109m, ★★1/2/$$, 20th/NA. A
wealthy man at the turn of the century in
New York goes crazy and shoots the for-
mer lover of his current mistress. Ray
Milland, Farley Granger, Joan Collins,
Glenda Farrell, Luther Adler, John Hoyt.
w. Walter Reisch, Charles Brackett, d.
Richard Fleischer.
DRAMA: MELODRAMA: TRAGEDY:
MURDER: Crimes of Passion; True
Stories; Mental Illness; Fatal Attractions;
Jealousy; 1900s
(Ed: Based on the famous and scandalous
case of the day where architect Stanford
White shot his mistress' boyfriend, also
included in *Ragtime*)
The Girl in the Watermelon, 1995,
94m, ★★★/$, Ind/NA, NR. A girl with
big dreams is upset when her mother
decides to re-marry just when she needs
money for college. With the help of a
boyfriend, she decides to break into her
mother's safe to steal her inheritance
early but instead finds a diary with men-
tions of two other men who may be her
father. She sets out to find them. Michele
Pawk, Lazaro Perez, Steven Stahl, James
Spencer Thierree, Meredith Scott Lynn,

Michael Allison, M. Joseph Poss. w. d.
Sergio M. Castilla.
COMEDY DRAMA: Dreams; Girls; Young
Women; Inheritances at Stake; Father-
Who's the?; Fathers & Daughters; Writer-
Directors; Ind Films
The Girl Most Likely, 1958, 98m,
★★1/2/$$, RKO/VCI. A woman acciden-
tally gets engaged to three men and must
deal with it. Jane Powell, Cliff Robertson,
Keith Andes, Tommy Noonan, Kaye
Ballard, Una Merkel. w. Devery Freeman,
d. Mitchell Leisen.
MUSICALS: COMEDY: Musical Comedy;
Romance-Triangles; Romance-Choosing
the Right Person; Cheating Women; Men
Fighting over Women; Engagements-
Breaking; Marriage-Impending; Female
Protagonists
FLIPSIDE: Worth Winning
REMAKE OF: Tom, Dick, and Harry
The Girl Most Likely to . . . , 1971,
95m, ★★★1/2/$$$$ (TV), ABC/ABC.
When a chubby co-ed returns to campus
after going to the fat farm and cosmetic
surgeon, she exacts revenge on all those
who snubbed her-including making an
unwitting, witless cheerleader do backflips
out a window to her death. But there's a
cop hot on her tail. Stockard Channing,
Edward Asner. w. d. Joan Rivers.
COMEDY: Black Comedy; TV Movies;
Comedy-Slapstick; Murders-One by One;
Death-Accidental; College Life; Revenge;
Weight Problems; Cosmetic Surgery;
Hidden Gems; Cult Films; Female
Protagonists; Female Screenwriters;
Female Directors; Writer-Directors
FLIPSIDE: Mother Love
(A Shock to the System; Rabbit Test)
A Girl Named Tamiko, 1962, 119m,
★★1/2/$$, Par/Par. A Eurasian photogra-
pher in Japan tries to use a woman to get
American citizenship but it backfires
with love. Laurence Harvey, France
Nuyen, Martha Hyer, Michael Wilder,
Miyoshi Umeki. w. Edward Anhalt, N-
adap. Ronald Kirkbride, d. John Sturges.
MELODRAMA: ROMANCE: Romantic
Drama; Americans Abroad; Marriage for
Citizenship; Marriage-Fake; Photogra-
phers; Romance-Interracial; Asian-
Americans; Japanese People; Japan
(The World of Suzie Wong; Green Card)
The Girl of the Golden West, 1938,
121m, ★★★/$$$, MGM/MGM-UA. A girl
in the Rockies falls for a wanted man
with mounties after him. Jeanette

McDonald, Nelson Eddy, Walter Pidgeon,
Leo Carrillo, Buddy Ebsen. w. Isobel
Dawn, Boyce DeGaw, d. Robert Z.
Leonard.
MUSICALS: MELODRAMA: ROMANCE:
Musical Romance; Fugitives from the
Law; Fugitives-Harboring; Canada;
Female Screenwriters; Female
Protagonists
(Rosalie; The Chocolate Soldier)
The Girl Who Couldn't Say No, 1968,
104m, ★★/$, NA. A young intern falls for
an Italian woman at sea near Italy.
George Segal, Virna Lisi, Lila Kedrova.
w. Franco Brusati, Ennio de Concini, d.
Franco Brusati.
COMEDY: ROMANCE: Romantic
Comedy; Doctors; Americans Abroad;
Italians; Ships; Mediterranean; Flops-
Major; Forgotten Films
(How to Murder Your Wife; Loving)
The Girl Who Had Everything, 1953,
69m, ★★1/2/$$, MGM/MGM-UA. A crimi-
nal lawyer is aghast when his daughter
falls for one of his sleazy clients. Elizabeth
Taylor, William Powell, Fernando Lamas,
Gig Young. w. Art Cohn, N-adap. Adela
Rogers St. John, d. Richard Thorpe.
MELODRAMA: ROMANCE: Fathers &
Daughters; Lover Family Dislikes;
Parents vs. Children; Lawyers; Romance-
Dangerous; Forgotten Films
REMAKE OF: A Free Soul
(Father of the Bride; National Velvet;
Daddy Longlegs)
Girl with Green Eyes, 1963, 91m,
★★★/$$, UA/NA. A guileless young neo-
phyte from Dublin is seduced by an
older, wiser writer. Peter Finch, Rita
Tushingham, Lynn Redgrave. w. N-adap.
Edna O'Brien (*The Lonely Girl*), d.
Desmond Davis.
DRAMA: ROMANCE: Romantic Drama;
Smart vs. Dumb; Romance-Mismatched;
Quiet Little Films; Lonely People;
Ordinary People Stories; Kitchen Sink
Drama; British Films; Ireland; Irish
People; Hidden Gems
(Georgy Girl; Smashing Time; A Taste of
Honey)
Girlfriends, 1978, 86m, ★★★/$$,
Ind/WB, R/S. A lesbian artist in New
York is dumped by her girlfriend and
considers going for men. Melanie Mayron,
Eli Wallach, Anita Skinner, Bob Balaban.
w. Vicki Polon, d. Claudia Weill.
COMEDY DRAMA: DRAMA: ROMANCE:
Gay Awakenings; Lesbians; Bisexuality;

Artists; Photographers; Starting Over; Life Transitions; Young Women; New York Life; Female Protagonists; Female Directors; Female Screenwriters
(Go Fish; Lianna; Three of Hearts)

Girls! Girls! Girls!, 1962, 106m, ★★1/2/$$$, Par/Par. A lounge singer/fisherman chases girls, but doesn't really need to since they're at his feet to hear his songs anyway. Elvis Presley, Stella Stevens, Laurel Goodwin, Jeremy Slate. w. Edward Anhalt, Allan Weiss, d. Norman Taurog.

COMEDY: MUSICALS: Music Movies; Romantic Comedy; Teenage Movies; Teenagers; Sexy Women; Singers; Teen Idols; Fishermen; Beach Movies; Women Fighting over Men; Faded Hits

Give Me a Sailor, 1938, 80m, ★★1/2/$$, Par/NA. A homely woman is jealous of her sister's luck with men, but ends up winning a best legs competition. Martha Raye, Bob Hope, Betty Grable, Jack Whiting, Clarence Kolb. w. Doris Anderson, Frank Butler, P-adap. Anne Nichols, d. Elliott Nugent.

COMEDY: ROMANCE: Romantic Comedy; Elusive Men; Wallflowers; Jealousy; Sisters; Feuds; Contests; Sailors; Forgotten Films

Give My Regards to Broad Street, 1984, 109m, ★★1/2/$, 20th/CBS-Fox, PG. A major pop star searches all over London for his missing tapes, while singing and dancing. Paul McCartney, Bryan Brown, Ringo Starr, Barbara Bach, Tracey Ullman, Ralph Richardson, George Martin. w. Paul McCartney, d. Peter Webb.

MUSICALS: Music Movies; Fantasy; Musical Fantasy; Music Video Style; Searches; London; Singers; Flops-Major; Coulda Been Good; Time Capsules

Give My Regards to Broadway, 1948, 89m, ★★★/$$, 20th/Fox. A vaudeville veteran tries to stage a comeback on Broadway. Dan Dailey, Charles Winninger, Fay Bainter, Charles Ruggles, Nancy Guild. w. Samuel Hoffenstein, Elizabeth Reinhardt, d. Lloyd Bacon.

MUSICALS: COMEDY: Musical Comedy; Vaudeville; Dancers; Singers; Family Comedy; Nostalgia; Female Screenwriters
(The Band Wagon; The Entertainer)

Give the Girl a Break, 1953, 84m, ★★/$$, MGM/MGM-UA. Three female dancers romance their way toward the lead in a big show via men associated with the production. Marge Champion, Gower Champion, Bob Fosse, Debbie Reynolds, Richard Anderson. d. Stanley Donen.

MUSICALS: Dance Movies; Theater Life; Behind the Scenes; Actresses; Dancers; Social Climbing; Woman Fighting Over Men; Golddiggers
(How to Marry a Millionaire; Three Blind Mice)

Gladiator, 1992, 102m, ★★1/2/$$, Col./Col-Tri, PG-13/V-P-S. A young white boxer befriends an up-and-coming black boxing star and they join forces against a sleazy promoter. James Marshall, Cuba Gooding Jr., Brian Dennehy, Robert Loggia, Ossie Davis, Cara Buono. w. Lyle Kessler, Robert Mark Kamen, Djordje Milicevic, d. Rowdy Herrington.

ACTION: Boxing; Sports Movies; Underdog Stories; Black vs. White; Friendships-Interracial; Corruption

Glamour Boy, 1941, 79m, ★★★/$$, Par/NA. A child actor whose star is on the decline must coach an up-and-comer and watch his fame increase. Jackie Cooper, Susanna Foster, Walter Abel, Darryl Hickman, Ann Gillis, William Demarest. w. Bradford Ropes, Val Burton, d. Ralph Murphy.

COMEDY: COMEDY DRAMA: SATIRE: Hollywood Satire; Hollywood Life; Actors; Children-Little Adults; Children-Brats; Fame-Rise to; Riches to Rags; Child Protagonists; Hidden Gems

The Glass Bottom Boat, 1966, 110m, ★★★/$$$, MGM/MGM-UA, G. A tourist show mermaid diver gets a job at NASA working for the scientist who fished her mermaid suit off of her derriere and that's when the trouble and the romance starts. Doris Day, Rod Taylor, Arthur Godfrey, Paul Lynde, John McGiver, Edward Andrews, Eric Fleming, Dom De Luise. w. Everett Freeman, d. Frank Tashlin.

COMEDY: ROMANCE: Romantic Comedy; Romance-Reluctant; Spies-Spoofs; Spies; Spy Films; Spies-Female; Detective Stories; Detectives-Amateur; Mermaids; Misunderstandings; Widows; Hidden Gems
(Caprice)

The Glass House, 1972, 92m, ★★★/$$, Ind/Hollywood Home. A college professor goes to prison for manslaughter and learns to adjust, even with his mild-mannered ways. Alan Alda, Vic Morrow, Billy Dee Williams, Dean Jagger, Clu Galagher. w. SS-adap. Truman Capote, d. Tom Gries.

DRAMA: Prison Drama; Accused Unjustly; Professors; Fish out of Water Stories; Psychological Drama; Character Studies; Forgotten Films; Hidden Gems; TV Movies

The Glass Key, 1935, 87m, ★★★/$$, Par/NA. The assistant to a somewhat shady, though basically decent, politician has to find the clue that will save him from going to prison for murder. Edward Arnold, George Raft, Claire Dodd, Rosalind Keith, Guinn Williams, Ray Milland. w. Kathryn Scola, Kubec Glasmon, Harry Ruskin, N-adap. Dashiell Hammett, d. Frank Tuttle. Female Screenwriters

The Glass Key, 1942, 85m, ★★★/$$$, Par/MCA-U. A well-done remake of above. Brian Donlevy, Alan Ladd, Veronica Lake, Bonita Granville, William Bendix, Richard Denning, Joseph Calleia. w. Jonathan Latimer, N-adap. Dashiell Hammett, d. Stuart Heisler.

SUSPENSE: Film Noir; Crime Drama; Political Drama; Politicians; **MURDER:** Accused Unjustly; Framed?; Corruption; Ethics; Saving Someone
(This Gun for Hire; The Blue Dahlia)

The Glass Menagerie, 1950, 107m, ★★★1/2/$$, WB/NA. A beleaguered widow (Gertrude Lawrence) with a crippled daughter (Jane Wyman) she wants to find a beau for and a disillusioned son (Kirk Douglas) try to cope and live normally. w. Tennessee Williams, Peter Berneis, P-adap. Tennessee Williams, d. Irving Rapper.

The Glass Menagerie, 1973, 100m, ★★★/$$$$$, ABC-TV/NA, Multi-Emmy winner. Katharine Hepburn, Joanna Miles, Sam Waterston, Michael Moriarty, w., P-adap. Tennessee Williams, d. Anthony Harvey.

The Glass Menagerie, 1987, 137m, ★★★/$, Cineplex-Universal/MCA-U, PG. Joanne Woodward, Karen Allen, John Malkovich, James Naughton. w. P-adap. Tennessee Williams, d. Paul Newman.

DRAMA: MELODRAMA: ROMANCE: TRAGEDY: Romance-Doomed; Romance-Reluctant; Tearjerkers; Family Drama; Mothers ALone; Mothers & Daughters; Disabled People; Matchmakers; Coming of Age; Young Men; Wallflowers; Narrated Films;

Illusions Destroyed; Poor People; Stagelike Films; Southerns; Classic Literary Adaptations; Tennessee Williams-esque
(Summer and Smoke; Rachel, Rachel)

Gleaming the Cube, 1988, 105m, ★★/$, Gladden/Live, PG/V-P. A California teenager hunts down on skateboard those who murdered his adoptive Vietnamese brother. Christian Slater, Steven Bauer, Richard Herd, Le Tuan, Min Luong, Art Chudabala, Ed Lauter, Peter Kwong. w. Michael Tolkin, d. Graeme Clifford.
ACTION: Chase Stories; Detective Stories; Teenagers; Teenage Movies;
CHILDREN'S: Suburban Life; Sports Movies; Avenging Death of Someone; Revenge; Manhunts; Roller Skating
(Pump Up the Volume; Prayer for the Rollerboys)

Glen or Glenda?, 1956, 61m, ★★½/$$, Par/Par. A highly "personal" film from the infamous cross-dressing bad-filmmaking auteur about what it meant in 50s America to be a transvestite. Narrated by Bela Lugosi, spouting incomprehensible dialogue like, "pull the string! Dance to that which one was made for!"; Lyle Talbot, Timothy Farrell, Bela Lugosi. w. d. Edward D. Wood Jr.
COMEDY: SATIRE: MELODRAMA: Transvestites; Transsexuals; Men as Women; Role Reversals; Unintentionally Funny; Camp; Cult Films; Narrated Films; Ind Films
(Ed Wood; Plan 9 from Outer Space)

Glengarry Glen Ross, 1992, 100m, ★★★½/$$, Fine Line/Fine Line, R/EP-S. Several shady real estate salesmen compete for a set of steak knives and their very livelihood. Al Pacino (BSActor), Jack Lemmon, Alec Baldwin, Ed Harris, Alan Arkin, Kevin Spacey, Jonathan Pryce. w. P-adap. David Mamet, d. James Foley. Oscars: 1-0.
DRAMA: Ensemble Films; Ensembles-Male; Character Studies; Salesmen; Business Life; Ethics; Corruption; Competitions; Race Against Time; Ordinary People Stories; Mean Men; Pulitzer Prize Adaptations
(Death of a Salesman; Save the Tiger; House of Games; Homicide)

The Glenn Miller Story, 1954, 116m, ★★★/$$$$, U-I/MCA-U. The story of the famous bandleader and genteel humanitarian whose plane mysteriously disappeared during World War II. James Stewart, June Allyson, Harry Morgan, Charles Drake, Frances Langford, Louis Armstrong, Gene Krupa. w. Valentine Davies, Oscar Brodney (BOScr), d. Anthony Mann. BOScore. Oscars: 2-0.
MELODRAMA: Biographies; **TRAGEDY:** Airplane Crashes; **MYSTERY:** True or Not?; World War II Stories; World War II Era; Musicians; Big Band Era; Music Dies; Female Screenwriters
(The Benny Goodman Story; The Spirit of St. Louis)

Gloria, 1980, 121m, ★★★★/$$, Columbia/RCA-Col, R/EV-P. When a gun moll/mobster's girlfriend (Gena Rowlands, BActress) learns about a hit on an accountant's family, she's asked to save the son, and in doing so, puts her own life in danger by takin the kid on the run to save him. w. d. John Cassavetes. Oscars: 1-0.
DRAMA: ACTION: MELODRAMA: Chase Movies; Fugitives from the Law; Fugitives from the Mob; Hitwomen; Mob Stories; Mob Girls; Mother and Son; Mothers-Surrogate; Saving Someone; Saving Oneself; Feisty Females; Female Protagonists; Female in Male Domain; New York Life; Hidden Gems
REMAKE/RETREAD: The Professional
(Ed: Excellent if a few rough edges. Rowlands carries it every step under her husband's brilliant eye)

Glory, 1989, 122m, ★★★/$$, Tri-Star/Col-Tri, PG-13/EV. The first black regiment of the civil war is led by a young Yankee (Matthew Broderick) into battle. Morgan Freeman, Denzel Washington (**BSActor**), Cary Elwes. w. Kevin Jarre, NF-adap. Lincoln Kirstein (Lay This Laurel), Peter Burchard (One Gallant Rush), Robert Gould Shaw (Letters), d. Edward Zwick. **BCin,** BArt, BSound, BEdit. Oscars: 5-2.
DRAMA: ACTION: Action Drama; Epics; True Stories; Civil War Era; War Stories; Black Casts; White Among Blacks; Black Men; Black Soldiers; Race Relations; Southerns
(A Soldier's Story; Bad Company [1972]; For Queen and Country; Posse)

Glory! Glory!, 1990, 152m, ★★★/$, Orion/Orion, PG-13/P-S. A raunchy Madonna-like rock singer is recruited by a TV preacher to help raise money, but raises something else. Ellen Greene, Richard Thomas, Barry Morse, James Whitmore. d. Lindsay Anderson.

SATIRE: COMEDY DRAMA: Religion; Preachers; TV Life; Coulda Been Great; Overlooked at Release; Hidden Gems
(Pass the Ammo; Americathon)

G-Men, 1935, 85m, ★★★/$$$, WB/WB. When a gangster is murdered, his lawyer friend becomes a G-man and goes after his killers. James Cagney, Ann Dvorak, Margaret Lindsay, Robert Armstrong, Barton MacLane, Lloyd Nolan, William Harrigan. w. Seton I. Miller, d. William Keighley.
MELODRAMA: ACTION: Crime Drama; Police vs. Mob; Mob Stories; FBI Agents; Warner Gangster Era; Lawyers; Police Stories; Avenging Death of Someone; Friendships-Male; Manhunts

The Gnome Mobile, 1967, 90m, ★★★/$$$, Disney/Disney, G. A wealthy family goes on a picnic and discovers a colony of gnomes in the forest who could use some help. Walter Brennan, Matthew Garber, Karen Dotrice, Richard Deacon, Ed Wynn, Jerome Cowan. w. Ellis Kadison, N-adap. Upton Sinclair, d. Robert Stevenson.
COMEDY: Fantasy; **CHILDREN'S: FAMILY:** Family Comedy; Disney Comedy; Little People
(Darby O'Gill and the Little People)

The Go-Between, 1970, 116m, ★★★½/$$, UA/MGM-UA. A little boy in turn-of-the-century England carries love letters back and forth between a farmer and his friend's sister. Alan Bates, Julie Christie, Michael Redgrave, Dominic Guard, Michael Gough, Margaret Leighton (BSActress), Edward Fox. w. Harold Pinter, N-adap. L. P. Hartley, d. Joseph Losey. Oscars: 1-0.
DRAMA: MELODRAMA: ROMANCE: Romantic Drama; Costume Drama; Boys; Romance-Triangles; Epistolaries; Farm Life; Rural Life; England; 1900s; Hidden Gems
(Far from the Madding Crowd)

Go Chase Yourself, 1938, 70m, ★★½/$$, RKO/Turner. A bank teller becomes an unwitting partner to some gangsters. Joe Penner, Lucille Ball, June Travis, Richard Lane, Fritz Feld, Tom Kennedy. w. Paul Yawitz, Bert Granet, d. Edward F. Cline.
COMEDY: Mob Stories; Mob Comedy; Heist Stories; Bank Robberies; Screwball Comedy; Forgotten Films
(The Affairs of Annabel; Foul Play)

God Bless the Child, 1988, 93m, ★★★/$$$, ABC/World Vision. A single mother and her child are forced onto the streets and become one of the homeless, even though it seems they shouldn't be. Mare Winningham, Dorian Harewood, Grace Johnston, Charlaine Woodard, Obba Babbatunde. w. Dennis Nemec, d. Larry Elikann.

DRAMA: Social Drama; Homeless People; Social Workers; Mothers-Struggling; Mothers Alone; TV Movies
(American Heart; Stone Pillow; The Saint of Fort Washington)

Go Fish, 1994, 90m, ★★/$$$, Goldwyn/Goldwyn, R/S-EP-FFN. A group of grunge-lesbians lives in Chicago's radical chic Wicker Park neighborhood go through the motions. d. Rose Troche.

COMEDY DRAMA: ROMANCE: Romantic Drama; Art Films; Lesbians; Chicago; Female Protagonists; Female Screenwriters; Female Directors; Sleeper Hits; Ind Films
(Bad Girls; Lianna; Desert Hearts)
(Ed: Clunky and murky from the underground, and yet charming if you can get into it. No better than most film students' first efforts, it caught on in the absence of anything else like it)

Go for Broke, 1951, 93m, ★★★/$$, MGM/Nos. Japanese-American soldiers convince their bigoted comrades that not all "Japs" are bad. Van Johnson, Lane Nakano, George Miki, Akira Fukunaga, Warner Anderson, Don Haggerty. w. d. Robert Pirosh. (BOScr). Oscars: 1-0.

DRAMA: War Stories; World War II Stories; Asian-Americans; Japanese as Enemy; Japanese People; Bigots; Race Relations; Curiosities; Hidden Gems; Ahead of Its Time

Go into Your Dance, 1935, 89m, ★★★/$$$, WB/NA. A star gets too big for his britches and is let down a notch, finally becoming humble enough to let happiness in. Al Jolson, Ruby Keeler, Glenda Farrell, Benny Rubin, Phil Regan, Barton MacLane, Sharon Lynne, Akim Tamiroff, Helen Morgan, Patsy Kelly. w. Earl Baldwin, d. Archie Mayo. BChoreography. Oscars: 1-0.

MUSICALS: COMEDY: COMEDY DRAMA: Musical Comedy; Hollywood Life; Hollywood Satire; Dose of Own Medicine-Given; Mean Men; Faded Hits; Forgotten Films
(The Jazz Singer; 42nd Street)

The Goalie's Anxiety at the Penalty Kick, 1971, 110m, ★★¹/₂/$, Ind/Facets, Ingram. A goalie past his prime is sent out of a game for playing poorly, and his shame and rage turns into a murderous impulse once he's off the field. Arthur Brauss, Kai Fischer, Erika Pluhar, Libgart Schwartz, Rudiger Vogler, Marie Bardischewski. w. d. Wim Wenders, SS-adap. Peter Handke.

DRAMA: TRAGEDY: MURDER: Sports Movies; Soccer; Nervous Breakdowns; German Films; Germany

God Is My Co-pilot, 1945, 89m, ★★¹/₂/$$, WB/NA. A group of fighter pilots fight each other and the Japs during World War II. Dennis Morgan, Dane Clark, Raymond Massey, Alan Hale, Andrea King, John Ridgeley, Stanley Ridges, Craig Stevens. w. Peter Milne, Abem Finkel, NF-adap. Col. Robert Lee Scott Jr., d. Robert Florey.

ACTION: War At Sea; World War II Stories; Pilots-Military; Japanese as Enemy; Patriotic Films; Men in Conflict

The Goddess (B&W), 1958, 105m, ★★★¹/₂/$$, Columbia/RCA-Col. A young woman from Tennessee (Kim Stanley) decides to leave her turbulent, ordinary life behind and make it in Hollywood, but things may not get much better. Lloyd Bridges, Steven Hill. w. Paddy Chayevsky (BOScr), d. John Cromwell.

DRAMA: Biographies-Fictional; Fame-Rise to; Dreams; Actresses; Sexy Women; Southerns; Small-town Life; Hollywood Life; 1950s; Abused Women; Children-Losing/Parting with; Episodic Stories; Hidden Gems; Cult Films
(Darling; Frances; Star!)

The Godfather, 1972, 175m, ★★★★/$$$$$, Par/Par, R/EV-S-P. A mafia don (Marlon Brando, **BActor**) is caught in a war between factions and must depend on his sons (Al Pacino, BSActor) (James Caan, BSActor) to save himself and the family. Robert Duvall (BSActor), Diane Keaton. w. Mario Puzo, Francis Ford Coppola (**BAScr**), N-adap. Puzo, d. Coppola (BDirector). **BPicture,** BCin, BCostume, BSound, **BEdit.** Oscars: 11-3.
Mob Stories; Mob Wars; Crime Drama;

DRAMA: ACTION: MURDER: Action Drama; Family Drama; Epics; Fathers & Sons; Assassination Plots; Female Among Males; Marriage on the Rocks; Power Struggles; Evil Men; Hitmen; Life Transitions; Brothers; Men in Conflict; Blockbusters

SEQUELS: The Godfather, Part II; The Godfather, Part III

COMIC FLIPSIDE: The Freshman

The Godfather, Part II, 1974, 200m, ★★★★/$$$$, Par/Par, R/EV-P-S. The saga continues as Michael Corleone (Al Pacino, BActor) takes over the family empire and must face several crises, including one with his brother (John Cazale). Talia Shire (BSActress), Michael V. Gazzo (BSActor), Lee Strasberg (BSActor), Diane Keaton, Robert De Niro (**BSActor**), Troy Donahue. w. Francis Ford Coppola, Mario Puzo (**BAScr**), S/N-adap. Mario Puzo, d. Francis Ford Coppola (**BDirector**). **BPicture, BOScore, BArt,** BCostume. Oscars: 11-6.
Mob Stories; Mob Wars; Crime Drama;

DRAMA: ACTION: MURDER: Action Drama; Family Drama; Epics; Fathers & Sons; Assassination Plots; Female Among Males; Marriage on the Rocks; Hitmen; Power Struggles; Evil Men; Life Transitions; Brothers; Men in Conflict; Cuba

PREQUEL: The Godfather

SEQUEL: The Godfather, Part III

The Godfather, Part III, 1990, 179m, ★★★/$$$, Par/Par, R/EV-S-P. Michael Corleone (Al Pacino) continues the family dynasty into present day by diversifying the family assets into corporations, all the while trying to stay alive and control his family. Diane Keaton, Andy Garcia (BSActor), Bridget Fonda, Sofia Coppola, Joe Mantegna, Helmut Berger, George Hamilton, Eli Wallach. w. Mario Puzo, Francis Ford Coppola, S-N-adap. Mario Puzo, d. Francis Ford Coppola (BDirector). BPicture, BOSong, BArt, BCin, BEdit. Oscars: 7-0.
Mob Stories; Mob Wars; Crime Drama;

DRAMA: ACTION: MURDER: Action Drama; Family Drama; Epics; Business Life; Fathers & Sons; Assassination Plots; Female Among Males; Marriage on the Rocks; Power Struggles; Hitmen; Evil Men; Life Transitions; Brothers; Men in Conflict; Mentors/Proteges; Popes
(GoodFellas; Casino; Bugsy; The Untouchables; The Cotton Club)

God's Little Acre (B&W), 1958, 110m, ★★★★/$$, UA/Prism. A poor farmer is obsessed with a supposed gold treasure buried on this land, which exacerbates the relations between his children. Aldo Ray, Robert Ryan, Buddy Hackett, Tina Louise, Jack Lord. w. N-adap. Erskine Caldwell, d. Anthony Mann.

DRAMA: MELODRAMA: Family Drama; Dreams; Obsessions; Religion; Southerns;

Treasure Hunts; Romance with Married Person; Romance-Triangles; Rural Life; Poor People; Parents vs. Children; Ordinary People Stories; Hidden Gems (Tobacco Road; The Egg and I; The Grapes of Wrath)

The Gods Must Be Crazy, 1981, 108m, ★★★/$$$, New Realm-20th/CBS-Fox, PG. A Kalahari bushman who speaks in clicks finds a Coke bottle which drops out of the sky (after being discarded by a jet-setter in a commercial plane), and attaches religious significance to it. N'xau, Marius Weyers, Sandra Prinsloo, Nic de Jager, Michael Thys. w. d. Jamie Uys.
COMEDY: Documentary Style; Simple Minds; Africans; Africa; Sleeper Hits; Cult Films; Independent Films; Writer-Directors

The Gods Must Be Crazy II, 1988, 98m, ★★1/2/$$, 20th/CBS-Fox, PG. The bushman from the first film meets a New Yorker in the desert of Africa who takes him home. N'xau, Lena Farugia, Hans Strydom, Eiros Nadies, Erick Bowen, Treasure Tshabalala, Pierre Van Pletzen, Lournes Swanepoel. w. d. Jamie Uys.
COMEDY: Documentary Style; Simple Minds; Africans; Africa; Fish out of Water Stories; Writer-Directors

Godspell, 1973, 102m, ★★★/$$, Col/NA, PG. Hippies sing and dance through the streets of New York relaying the story of Jesus, etc. Victor Garber, David Haskell, Lynn Thigpen, Robin Lamont, Jerry Sroka. w. David Greene, John Michael Tebelak, P-adap. Tebelak, d. Greene.
MUSICALS: DRAMA: MELODRAMA: Musical Drama; Musicals-Hippie; Biblical Stories; Jesus Christ; Hippies; 1970s; Curiosities; Forgotten Films; Overlooked at Release
(Jesus Christ Superstar; Hair)
(Ed: A big hit on stage with a few hit songs, this film sank like a stone. But it's still worth checking out if you can find it)

Godzilla, 1955, 80m, ★★/$$$, Toho/Vestron. An H-bomb explosion in Tokyo sets off a chain reaction in which a prehistoric monster is reanimated and wreaks havoc on the city. Raymond Burr, Takashi Shimura, Momoko Kochi. w. Takeo Murato, Inoshiro Honda, d. Inoshiro Honda.
(Ed: The Raymond Burr framing device of the American reporter was added for American release)

Godzilla versus Gigan, 1972, 89m, ★★/$$, Toho/Vestron. A comic-strip artist stops giant alien cockroaches with the help of Godzilla. Hiroshi Ishikawa, Tomoko Umeda, Yuriko Hishimi, Minora Takashima, Zan Fujita, Toshiaki Nishizawa, Kunio Murai. w. Shinichi Sekizawa, d. Jun Fukuda.

Godzilla versus Megalon, 1976, 80m, ★★/$$$, Toho/Nos. The leader of the Seatopians, an undersea race, sends his giant lobster pal to destroy Tokyo. Katsuhiko Sasaki, Yutaka Hayashi, Hiroyuki Kawase. w. Shinichi Sekizawa, d. Jun Fukuda.
HORROR: SCI-FI: ACTION: Monsters; Japan; Japanese Films; Cult Films
(Godzilla '85)

Goin' South, 1978, 109m, ★★★/$$, Par/Par, PG/S-P. An irrascible outlaw is reformed and saved from being hanged by the love of a good woman who gets up enough gumption to defend them both-after she finally gives in to him, that is. Jack Nicholson, Mary Steenburgen, Christopher Lloyd, John Belushi, Veronica Cartwright, Richard Bradford. w. John Herman Shaner, Al Ramrus, Charles Shyer, Alan Mandel, d. Jack Nicholson.
WESTERNS: COMEDY DRAMA: ROMANCE: Romantic Comedy; Western Comedy; Marriage Comedy; Virgins; Romance-Reluctant; Executions; Saving Someone; Pioneers; Newlyweds; Old-Fashioned Recent Films; Brides-Mail Order
(Mail Order Bride)

Goin' to Town, 1935, 74m, ★★★/$$$, Par/MCA-U. The daughter of a Texas oil baron moves up North and tries to fit in with the drawing-room crowd. Mae West, Paul Cavanagh, Ivan Lebedeff, Tito Coral, Marjorie Gateson, Fred Kohler Sr., Monroe Owsley. w. Mae West, d. Alexander Hall.
COMEDY: ROMANCE: Romantic Comedy; Sexy Women; Heiresses; Oil People; North vs. South; Fish out of Water Stories; Social Climbing; Forgotten Films; Hidden Gems; Female Protagonists; Female Screenwriters
(She Done Him Wrong; Dynamite)
(Ed: A little more tame for the dame, but still worth it for fans)

Going Home, 1971, 98m, ★★1/2/$, MGM/NA. A man kills his wife in a drunken rage, then goes to prison. Later,

when he's released, he tries to re-establish a relationship with his son even though old habits die hard. Robert Mitchum, Jan-Michael Vincent, Brenda Vaccaro. w. Lawrence Marcus, d. Herbert B. Leonard.
DRAMA: Fathers & Sons; Ex-Convicts; Starting Over; MURDER: Murder of Spouse; Alcoholics; Rural Life; Rednecks; Ordinary People Stories; Past-Haunted by the; Flashbacks; Coulda Been Good
(Flesh and Bone; The Mechanic)

Going in Style, 1979, 96m, ★★★1/2/$$$, WB/WB, PG/P-S. Three elderly men decide to pull one last heist in order to retire in style, but their health and guilt may do them in before they can enjoy it. George Burns, Lee Strasberg, Art Carney. w. d. Martin Brest.
COMEDY DRAMA: Heist Stories; Bank Robberies; Elderly Men; One Last Time; Clever Plots & Endings; Clever Escapes; Dying Wishes; Death-Impending; Friendships-Male; Hidden Gems; Sleeper Hits; Writer-Directors
(Seven Thieves; Perfect Gentlemen)

Going My Way, 1944, 126m, ★★★1/2/$$$$$, Par/Par. An old crusty pastor is wary of the new young priest who comes into his ghetto parish, but is eventually won over by him and his charming ways. Bing Crosby (**BActor**), Barry Fitzgerald (**BActor** & **BSActor**), Rise Stevens, Frank McHugh, Gene Lockhart, Porter Hall. w. Frank Butler, Fran Cavett, Leo McCarey (**BOStory, BScr**), d. Leo McCarey (**BDirector**). **BPicture. BOSong**, "Swingin' on a Star," **BB&WCin, BEdit.** Oscars: 10-6.
COMEDY DRAMA: MELODRAMA: Tearjerkers; Priests; Religion; Social Workers; Poor People; Generation Gap; Teachers; Teachers & Students; Blockbusters; Faded Hits
SEQUELS: The Bells of St. Mary's, Say One for Me
(Boys' Town; Lilies of the Field)
(Ed: Doesn't seem to hold up as well as some of its contemporaries, but in its day, it swept everything)

Going Places, see Les Valeuses

Gold, 1974, 124m, ★★1/2/$$, Hemdale-AA/NA, PG/S-P. Romance and intrigue in the gold mines of South Africa. Roger Moore, Susannah York, Ray Milland, Bradford Dillman, John Gielgud. w. Wilbur Smith, Stanley Price, N-adap.

Wilbur Smith (*Goldmine*), d. Peter Hunt. BOSong. Oscars: 1-0.
ACTION: ADVENTURE: ROMANCE: Romantic Adventure; Conspiracy; Rich People; Gold Mining; South Africa; Forgotten Films

Gold Diggers of Broadway, 1929, 98m, ★★★/$$$, WB/NA. Chorus girls in the big show are really looking for wealthy husbands. Nancy Welford, Conway Tearle, Winnie Lightner, Ann Pennington, Lilyan Tashman, William Bakewell, Nick Lucas. w. Robert Lord, P-adap. Avery Hopwood (*The Gold Diggers*), d. Roy del Ruth.

Gold Diggers of 1933, 1933, 96m, ★★★1/2/$$$$, WB/MGM-UA. A remake of the above with better songs and great production numbers choreographed by Busby Berkeley. Warren William, Joan Blondell, Aline MacMahon, Ruby Keeler, Dick Powell, Guy Kibbee, Ned Sparks, Ginger Rogers. w. Erwin Gelsey, James Seymour, David Boehm, Ben Markson, P-adap. Avery Hopwood (*The Gold Diggers*), d. Mervyn Le Roy.

Gold Diggers of 1935, 1935, 95m, ★★★/$$$, WB/MGM-UA. A New York society dame puts on a show in her country home and falls in with a shady producer. Dick Powell, Adolphe Menjou, Gloria Stuart, Alice Brady, Hugh Herbert, Glenda Farrell, Frank McHugh, Grant Mitchell, Wini Shaw. w. Manuel Seff, Peter Milne, Robert Lord, d. Busby Berkeley. BChoreography, **BOSong**, "Lullaby of Broadway." Oscars: 2-1.

Gold Diggers of 1937, 1936, 100m, ★★★/$$$, WB/NA. A bunch of hard-up Broadway producers look to a group of insurance salesmen to back their show, and run into difficulties when they want "creative input." Dick Powell, Joan Blondell, Glenda Farrell, Victor Moore, Lee Dixon, Osgood Perkins. w. Warren Duff, P-adap. Richard Maibaum, Michael Wallach, George Haight, d. Lloyd Bacon. BChoreography. Oscars: 1-0.

Gold Diggers in Paris, 1938, 95m, ★★★/$$, WB/NA. Three chorus girls in a show touring Europe hunt for wealthy husbands in Paris. Rudy Vallee, Rosemary Lane, Hugh Herbert, Allen Jenkins, Gloria Dickson, Fritz Feld, Curt Bois. w. Earl Baldwin, Warren Duff, d. Ray Enright.
MUSICALS: Dance Movies; **COMEDY:** Musical Comedy; Golddiggers; Dancers; Bimbos; Cult Films; Camp

The Gold Rush, 1925, 72m, ★★★1/2/$$$$, Charles Chaplin/Nos. In the cold, barren Yukon territory, a prospector spends a long time struggling, but finally strikes it rich. Charles Chaplin, Georgia Hale, Mack Swain, Tom Murray. w. d. Charles Chaplin.
COMEDY: Gold Mining; Comedy-Slapstick; Comedy of Errors; **ADVENTURE:** Comic Adventure; Comedy-Character; Rags to Riches; Canada; Snow Settings; Hidden Gems

The Golden Age of Comedy, 1957, 78m, ★★★★/$$, Ind/Lebell. The first compilation of its kind, involving the restoration of silent shorts, including those of Laurel and Hardy. Stan Laurel, Oliver Hardy, Harry Langdon, Ben Turpin, Will Rogers, Billy Bevan, Charlie Chase, Andy Clyde. w. d. Robert Youngson.
COMEDY: Comedy-Slapstick; Comedy-Character; Compilation Films; Forgotten Films; Ind Films
(The World of Harold Lloyd)

Golden Boy, 1939, 99m, ★★★/$$$, Col/RCA-Col. A kid on poverty row wants to be a violinist, but his boxing talents may take him further in this world. Barbara Stanwyck, William Holden, Adolphe Menjou, Joseph Calleia, Lee J. Cobb, Sam Levene, Don Beddoe. w. Lewis Meltzer, Daniel Taradash, Sarah Y. Mason, Victor Heerman, P-adap. Clifford Odets, d. Rouben Mamoulian. BOScore: 1-0.
DRAMA: MELODRAMA: ROMANCE: Social Drama; Social Climbing; Boxing; Sports Movies; Inner City Life; Rags to Riches; Young Men; Woman Behind the Man; Hidden Gems; Female Screenwriters; Female Protagonists
(Champion; The Leather Saint)

Golden Braid, 1990, 91m, ★★1/2/$, Ind/NA. A clockmaker obsessed with freezing time falls in love with a lock of hair he finds inside one of his classic time pieces. Chris Haywood, Gosia Dorowolska, Paul Chubb, Norman Kaye, Marion Heathfield, Monica Maughan, Robert Menzies, Jo Kennedy. w. Paul Cox, Barry Dickens, SS-adap. Guy de Maupassant (*La Chevelure*), d. Paul Cox.
DRAMA: Character Studies; Memories; Fantasy; Fantasies; Obsessions; Death-Dealing with; Australian Films; Hidden Gems; Overlooked at Release; Independent Films
(Somewhere in Time; A Woman's Tale)

The Golden Child, 1986, 96m, ★★/$$$, Par/Par, PG/P. A social worker looks for the Oriental boy whom myth foretells will bring peace to Earth, and so on. . . . Eddie Murphy, Charles Dance, Charlotte Lewis, Victor Wong. w. Dennis Feldman, d. Michael Ritchie.
ADVENTURE: Fantasy; **COMEDY: COMEDY DRAMA:** Comic Adventure; **SCI-FI:** China; Black Men; Legends; Social Workers; Flops-Major
(Ed: Murphy's name brought money in at first, but repeat business was not to be)

Golden Earrings, 1947, 95m, ★★1/2/$, Par/MCA-U. A gypsy woman uses her charms to get the formula for a poison gas from a Nazi official and return it to England with her beloved British Intelligence officer. Marlene Dietrich, Ray Milland, Murvyn Vye, Bruce Lester, Dennis Hoey, Reinhold Schunzel, Ivan Triesault. w. Abraham Polonsky, Frank Butler, Helen Deutsch, N-adap. Yolanda Foldes, d. Mitchell Leisen.
SUSPENSE: Spy Films; Spies; World War II Stories; Nazi Stories; Gypsies; Conspiracy; Unintentionally Funny; Forgotten Films; Female Screenwriters; Female Protagonists
(Mata Hari; Desire; Plenty)

Goldeneye, 1995, 130m, ★★/$$$$$, MGM-UA/MGM-UA, PG-13/S-EV. James Bond takes on a Russian general who has a satellite weapon which can take out anything on earth but finds a former Russian computer expert to be an unexpectedly loyal ally. Pierce Brosnan, Sean Bean, Izabella Scorupco, Famke Janssen, Joe Don Baker, Robbie Coltrane, Desmond Llewelyn, Samantha Bond, Judi Dench. w. Jeffrey Caine & Bruce Feirstein, d. Martin Campbell.
ACTION: ADVENTURE: Spy Films; Russia; KGB Agents; James Bond
(Moonraker; The Man with the Golden Gun)

Goldfinger, 1964, 112m, ★★★1/2/$$$$$$, UA/MGM-UA, S-V. A world master criminal who spray paints people to death with gold and loves to pet his angora cat plans to rob Fort Knox, and only Bond can stop him. Sean Connery, Honor Blackman, Gert Frobe, Harold Sakata, Shirley Eaton, Bernard Lee. w. Richard Maibaum, Paul Dehn, N-adap. Ian Fleming, d. Guy Hamilton.
ACTION: ADVENTURE: Spy Films; Secret Agents; Playboys; James Bond;

Undercover; Chase Stories; Rule the World-Plots to; Golf; Sexy Women; Bimbos; Blockbusters
(Dr. No; From Russia with Love)

Golden Gate, 1993, 95m, ★★−/$, Goldwyn-AP/Goldwyn, R/V-S. After a young detective sent to go after union activists in San Francisco's Chinatown during the McCarthy Era, he later runs into the daughter of a man he defamed by arrest. When she finds this out, the romance is on hold. Matt Dillon, Joan Chen, Bruno Kirby, Teri Polo. w. David Henry Hwang, d. John Madden.
DRAMA: Film Noir-Modern; **ROMANCE:** Romantic Drama; Police Stories; McCarthy Era; Communists; San Francisco; Coulda Been Good

Goldengirl, 1979, 104m, ★★/$, Avco/Col, PG/V. A scientist feeds his daughter an experimental concoction which turns her into a super-athlete, then enters her in the Olympics, but other countries want the formula. Susan Anton, James Coburn, Curt Jurgens, Leslie Caron, Robert Culp, James A. Watson Jr., Michael Lerner. w. John Kohn, N-adap. Peter Lear, d. Joseph Sargent.
SUSPENSE: Sports Movies; Track & Field; Olympics; Women in Jeopardy; Fathers & Daughters; Cartoonlike Films; Scientists; Experiments; Spies; Running; Female Protagonists; Unintentionally Funny

The Golden Seal, 1983, 94m, ★★1/2/$, Goldwyn/Goldwyn, G. A young boy befriends a seal and protects it from hunters. Steve Railsback, Michael Beck, Penelope Milford, Torquil Campbell. w. John Groves, N-adap. James Vance Marshall (*A River Ran out of Eden*), d. Frank Zuniga.
CHILDREN'S: FAMILY: Animal Stories; Pet Stories; Alaska; Hunters; Animal Rights; Boys; Child Protagonists
(Andre; Flipper; Free Willy)

Golden Years, 1991, 232m, ★★★/$$, CBS/Worldvision. A janitor is exposed to chemicals which create amazing results, changing aging processes and other bodily functions but the government wants in on it at all costs. Keith Szarabajka, Frances Sternhagen, Ed Lauter. w. N-adap. Stephen King.
SCI-FI: Aging; Aging-Reverse; Accidents; Government as Enemy; Oppression; TV Series; Stephen King
(It; The Langoliers; The Stand)

The Golden Voyage of Sinbad, 1973, 105m, ★★1/2/$$, Col/RCA-Col, G. Sinbad finds the map to buried treasure and must fight an evil magician who gets in his way. John Philip Law, Caroline Munro, Tom Baker, Douglas Wilmer, Gregoire Aslan. w. Brian Clemens, Ray Harryhausen, d. Gordon Hessler.
ACTION: ADVENTURE: Mythology; Monsters-Mythology; Treasure Hunts; Magic/Magicians; Forgotten Films
(Clash of the Titans)
(Ed: Failed to revive the Harryhausen series)

The Goldwyn Follies, 1938, 115m, ★★★/$$$, Goldwyn-UA/HBO. In 1930s Hollywood, a producer searches for a script girl who will represent the average moviegoer's views. This all leads to much dancing. Kenny Baker, Vera Zorina, The Ritz Brothers, Adolphe Menjou, Edgar Bergen and Charlie McCarthy, Helen Jepson, Phil Baker, Ella Logan, Bobby Clark. w. Ben Hecht, d. George Marshall. BArt, BMScore. Oscars: 2-0.
MUSICALS: COMEDY: Musical Comedy; Dance Movies; Dancers; Hollywood Life; Hollywood Satire; Searches; 1930s
(The George White Scandals)

The Golem, 1920, 75m, ★★★/$$, B&W, silent, UFA/Nos. The old Hebrew fable about a Rabbi who makes a man out of clay who comes alive and defends the Jews against a pogrom. Paul Wegener, Albert Steinruck, Ernst Deutsch. w. Paul Wegener, Henrik Galeen, d. Paul Wegener.
DRAMA: MELODRAMA: Fantasy; Jewish People; Jews-Saving; Legends; Forgotten Films

Go Naked in the World, 1960, 103m, ★★1/2/$$, MGM/NA. A millionaire and his son both fight over the same prostitute. Gina Lollobrigida, Tony Franciosa, Ernest Borgnine, Luana Pattern, Will Kuluva, Philip Ober. w. d. Ranald MacDougall.
MELODRAMA: ROMANCE: Romance-Triangles; Romance with Prostitute; Men Fighting over Women; Fathers & Sons; Parents vs. Children; Prostitutes-High Class; Rich People; Italians; Writer-Directors
(All Night Long; Sabrina)
(Ed: A lurid title does not necessarily make a lurid, exciting film)

Gone With the Wind, 1939, 222m, ★★★★/$$$$$$$, MGM/MGM-UA, G. A

Southern belle extraordinaire leaves a string of men in her path as she claws her way through the Civil War toward the one she really wants, but Scarlett O'Hara doesn't always get everything she wants. Clark Gable (**BActor**), Vivien Leigh (**BActress**), Olivia de Havilland (BSActress), Hattie McDaniel (**BSActress**), Leslie Howard, Evelyn Keeyes, Jane Darwell, Ward Bond, Thomas Mitchell, Butterfly McQueen. w. Sidney Howard (**BAScr**), N-adap. Margaret Mitchell, d. Victor Fleming (**BDirector**) (and George Cukor, Sam Wood). **BPicture**, BOScore, BSFX, **BCCin**, BCin (special award), **BCArt**, **BEdit**, BSound. Oscars: 14-9.
DRAMA: MELODRAMA: ROMANCE: Romantic Drama; War Stories; Civil War Era; Southerns; Romance-Reluctant; Historical Drama; Costume Drama; Episodic Stories; Epics; Plantation Life; Mean Women; Marriage Drama; Romance-On Again/Off Again; Sisters; Feuds; Women in Conflict; Servants; Black Women; Friendships-Interracial; Elusive Men; Rags to Riches; Reconstruction Era; Georgia; Fires; Blockbusters; Pulitzer Prize Adaptations; Production Design-Outstanding; Female Protagonists
SEQUELS: Musical stage version (1970), Scarlett (TV miniseries, 1994)
(Band of Angels; Jezebel; Raintree County)
(Ed: Still, in terms of number of tickets sold, undeniably the biggest box office hit ever in America)

The Gong Show Movie, 1980, 89m, ★1/2/$, Barris-U/NA, PG/P. A look behind the scenes of the (in)famous show and the life of its smarmy host. Chuck Barris, Robin Altman, Brian O'Mullin, Mabel King, James B. Douglas, Jaye P. Morgan. w. Chuck Barris, Robert Downey, d. Chuck Barris.
COMEDY: Documentaries; Documentary Style; Game Shows; Spoofs; Camp; Eccentric People; Forgotten Films; Overlooked at Release; Curiosities; TV Series Movies

Goodbye Again, 1961, 120m, ★★★/$$, UA/MGM-UA. An aging woman turns in her playboy lover for a younger model, a sensitive law student. Ingrid Bergman, Anthony Perkins, Yves Montand, Jessie Royce Landis. w. Samuel Taylor, N-adap. Francoise Sagan (*Aimez-vous Brahms*), d. Anatole Litvak.

MELODRAMA: ROMANCE: Romance-Older Women/Younger Men; Romantic Drama; Hidden Gems; Female Protagonists (Ash Wednesday; And Now My Love; Indiscreet)

Goodbye, Charlie, 1964, 116m, ★★★/$$, 20th/NA. An adulterous gangster is murdered by the husband of one of his flings. Afterwords, he's reincarnated as a she, and gets a glimpse of how the "other half" lives. Debbie Reynolds, Pat Boone, Walter Matthau, Tony Curtis. w. Harry Kurnitz, P-adap. George Axelrod, d. Vincente Minnelli.

COMEDY: Body Switching; Reincarnation; Dead-Back from the; Mob Stories; Mob Comedy; Men as Women; Role Reversal; Dose of Own Medicine-Given; Playboys; Cheating Men; Female Protagonists

REMAKE/RETREAD: Switch

Goodbye Columbus, 1969, 105m, ★★★/$$$$, Par/Par, R/S-P-FRN-MRN. A timid and poor, young Jewish male librarian in New York has an exciting affair with an upper-crusty girl on the Upper East Side, but it may not be all that he dreamed. Richard Benjamin, Ali MacGraw, Jack Klugman, Nan Martin, Michael Meyers, Lori Shelle. w. Arnold Schulman (BAScr), N-adap. Philip Roth, d. Larry Peerce. Oscars: 1-0.

COMEDY DRAMA: ROMANCE: Social Satire; Coming of Age; Young Men; Jewish People; Romance-Class Conflicts; Romance-Mismatched; Nerds; Nerds & Babes; Elusive Women; New York Life; Librarians; Country Club Life; Faded Hits (The Heartbreak Kid; Portnoy's Complaint)

Goodbye Gemini, 1970, 89m, ★★1/2/$, Cinerama/NA. In swinging London, a brother and sister in their twenties have a weird and dangerous symbiotic relationship. Judy Geeson, Martin Potter, Michael Redgrave, Alexis Kanner, Mike Pratt, Freddie Jones. w. Edmund Ward, N-adap. Jenni Hall (Ask Agamemnon), d. Alan Gibson.

MELODRAMA: Love-Forbidden; Beautiful People; Mod Era; London; Alternative Lifestyles; Incest; Brothers & Sisters; British Films; Overlooked at Release; Forgotten Films; Time Capsules; Independent Films; Female Protagonists (Fool for Love; The Idol)

The Goodbye Girl, 1977, 110m, ★★★★/$$$$$, MGM-WB/MGM-UA, PG/S-P. An actress (Marsha Mason, BActress) who's recently been left by her actor-lover needs to rent the extra bedroom out to make ends meet and winds up with another actor (Richard Dreyfuss, BActor), who says her lover rented the entire apartment out to him weeks before. Quinn Cummings (BSActress). w. N. Simon (BOScr), d. Herbert Ross, BPicture. Oscars: 5-1.

COMEDY: Romantic Comedy;

ROMANCE: Romance-Bickering; Comedy-Situation; Roommates; Roommates from Hell; Romance-Reluctant; Mothers Alone; Starting Over; Actors; New York Life; Theater Life; Happy Endings; Children-Little Adults; Blockbusters (The More the Merrier; Walk, Don't Run; Star-Spangled Girl; Echo Park; Only When I Laugh)

Goodbye, Mr. Chips, 1939, 114m, ★★★★/$$$, MGM/MGM-UA. A mild mannered teacher rises to headmaster, having a romance with a showgirl along the way, and then is remembered fondly after he dies. Robert Donat (BActor), Greer Garson (BActress), Paul Henreid, Lyn Harding, Austin Trevor. w. R. C. Sheriff, Claudine West, Eric Maschwitz (BOScr), N-adap. James Hilton, d. Sam Wood (BDirector). BPicture, BEdit. Oscars: 6-1.

Goodbye, Mr. Chips, 1969, 147m, ★★★/$$$, MGM/MGM-UA, PG. A remake with music, based on the above. Peter O'Toole (BActor), Petula Clark, Michael Bryant, Michael Redgrave, George Baker, Jack Hedley, Sian Philips, Alison Leggatt. w. Terence Rattigan, d. Herbert Ross. BMScore. Oscars: 2-0.

MELODRAMA: DRAMA: MUSICALS: Music Movies; Musical Drama;

ROMANCE: Romance with Teacher; Romance-Mismatched; Teachers; Teachers & Students; Nerds; Nerds & Babes; Boarding Schools; England; 1900s; Hidden Gems (Ball of Fire; The Prime of Miss Jean Brodie; The Browning Version; Mr. Holland's Opus)

Goodbye, My Fancy, 1951, 107m, ★★1/2/$$, WB/MGM-UA. A middle-aged congresswoman is given an honorary degree from her alma mater, and when there, she has a fling with an old flame.

Joan Crawford, Robert Young, Frank Lovejoy, Eve Arden, Janice Rule. w. Ivan Goff, Ben Roberts, P-adap. Fay Kanin, d. Vincent Sherman.

MELODRAMA: COMEDY DRAMA: ROMANCE: Romance-Reunited; Romance-Middle-Aged; Congressmen/Senators; Politicians; Politicians-Female; College Life; Reunions; Wisecracking Sidekicks; Female Protagonists (Mother Is a Freshman; Harriet Craig)

Goodbye, My Lady, 1956, 95m, ★★★/$$, WB/WB. A poor boy growing up in backwoods Mississippi befriends a wandering dog, but later finds out that it's a valuable pure-bred sought by its wealthy owner. Brandon de Wilde, Walter Brennan, Phil Harris, Sidney Poitier, William Hopper, Louise Beavers. w. Sid Fleischman, N-adap. James Street, d. William Wellman.

MELODRAMA: CHILDREN'S: FAMILY: Pet Stories; Rural Life; Rewards at Stake; Dogs; Boy and His Dog; Boys; Southerns; Forgotten Films; Child Protagonists (Old Yellow; The Biscuit Eater)

Goodbye, New York, 1985, 90m, ★★-/$, Vestron/Vestron, PG. A high-toned young woman winds up on the wrong flight and lands in Israel where she finds romance in the military, and so on. Julie Haggerty, Amos Kollek. w. d. Kollek.

COMEDY: Fish out of Water Stories; Israel; Stranded; Yuppies; Military Comedy; Desert Settings; Mix-Ups; Coulda Been Good (Private Benjamin) (Ed: What was supposed to be the Israeli Woody Allen's breakthrough had a good trailer but no pull)

The Goodbye People, 1984, 104m, ★★1/2/$ (LR), Col/Col, PG. On vacation at the beach, a couple of free-spirited middle-aged people meet and fall in love and do a lot of talking-they're from New York, after all. Martin Balsam, Judd Hirsch, Pamela Reed, Ron Silver, Michael Tucker, Gene Saks. w. d. P-adap. Herb Gardner.

COMEDY DRAMA: DRAMA: Romance-Middle Aged; Eccentric People; Character Studies; Elderly People; Jewish People; New York Life; Stagelike Films; Overlooked at Release; Coulda Been Good; Writer-Directors (Boardwalk; Outrage)

Goodbye, Pork Pie, 1980, 105m, Ind/Sultan. Three youngsters in New Zealand go joyriding through the country and get into a lot of trouble. Tony Barry, Kelly Johnson, Claire Oberman. w. Geoff Murphy, Ian Mune, d. Geoff Murphy.
ACTION: DRAMA: Action Drama; Outlaw Road Movies; Road Movies; Car Chases; Teenage Terrors; Juvenile Delinquents; New Zealand; Curiosities

The Good Companions, 1933, 113m, ★★★/$$, Gaumont/NA. A group of down-and-out performers join a pantomime troupe and travel from town to town spreading joy. Edmund Gwenn, Mary Glynne, John Gielgud, Jessie Matthews, Percy Parsons, Max Miller, Jack Hawkins, George Zucco. w. W. P. Lipscomb, Angus Macphail, Ian Dalrymple, P-adap. J. B. Priestley, Edward Knoblock, N-adap. J. B. Priestley.

The Good Companions, 1956, 104m, ★★¹/₂/$, ABP/NA. Remake of the above, not as good. Eric Portman, Celia Johnson, John Fraser, Janette Scott, Hugh Griffith, Bobby Howes, Rachel Roberts, John Salew, Thora Hird. w. T. J. Morrison, d. J. Lee-Thompson.
COMEDY DRAMA: Music Movies; Ensemble Films; Theater Life; Actors; Actresses; Vaudeville; Road Movies; Episodic Stories; British Films; Hidden Gems; Time Capsules

The Good Day for a Hanging, 1959, 85m, ★★/$, Col/NA. An outlaw is set to be lynched by an angry mob, but the fair-minded marshal tries to stop them. Fred MacMurray, Robert Vaughn, Maggie Hayes, Joan Blackman, James Drury. w. Daniel B. Ullman, Maurice Zimm, d. Nathan Juran.
WESTERNS: Lynchings; Executions; Accused Unjustly; Police Stories; Marshals
(The Ox Bow Incident)

The Good Die Young, 1954, 98m, ★★★/$$, Remus-Ind/NA. A mixed bag of thieves, all with personal lives and problems, try to escape it all with a heist. Laurence Harvey, Margaret Leighton, Gloria Grahame, Richard Basehart, Joan Collins, John Ireland, Rene Ray, Robert Morley. w. Vernon Harris, Lewis Gilbert, d. Lewis Gilbert.
MELODRAMA: COMEDY DRAMA: Heist Stories; Capers; Crime Drama; Ensemble Films; Thieves; Multiple Stories; Bank Robberies; Hidden Gems; Independent Films
(The Hot Rock; The Killing; Deadfall [1968])

The Good Earth, 1937, 138m, ★★★¹/₂/$$$$, MGM/MGM-UA. A poor couple who are rice farmers in China suffer through drought and pestilage but finally they become rich and the changes begin to break the family apart. Paul Muni, Luise Rainer (**BActress**), Walter Connolly, Tilly Losch, Jessie Ralph. w. Talbot Jennings, Tess Schlesinger, Claudine West, P-adap. Owen and Donald Davis, N-adap. Pearl S. Buck, d. Sidney Franklin (**BDirector**). **BPicture**, BCin, BEdit. Oscars: 5-2.
MELODRAMA: DRAMA: ROMANCE: Romance-Doomed; Marriage Drama; Social Drama; Epics; China; Chinese People; Rags to Riches; Poor People; Farm Life; Children-Brats; Greed; Production Design-Outstanding
(Dragon Seed; Inn of the Sixth Happiness; Keys to the Kingdom)

The Good Fairy, 1935, 90m, ★★★/$$$, U/NA. An usherette at a neighborhood theatre gets into a romantic entanglement with three rich men who want to do more than be seated. Margaret Sullavan, Herbert Marshall, Frank Morgan, Reginald Owen, Alan Hale, Beulah Bondi, Cesar Romero, Eric Blore. w. Preston Sturges, P-adap. Ferenc Monar, d. William Wyler.
COMEDY: ROMANCE: Romantic Comedy; Romance-Triangles; Movie Theaters; Young Women; Working Women; Men Fighting over Women; Forgotten Films; Hidden Gems
REMAKE: I'll Be Yours
(The Miracle of Morgan's Creek; Palm Beach Story)

The Good Father, 1987, 138m, ★★★/$, 20th/Fox, Media, PG-13/P-S. A motor-cycle-riding dad is becoming more and alienated from his son as tensions continue with he and his ex-wife and spill over into the problems of a friend. Anthony Hopkins, Joanne Whalley-Kilmer. d. Mike Newell.
DRAMA: Character Studies; Fathers; Fathers Alone; Alienation; Depression; Divorce; Custody Battles; Fathers & Sons; Overlooked at Release; Hidden Gems; Men's Films; TV Movies; British Films
(Kramer vs. Kramer; Author! Author!; See You in the Morning)

GoodFellas, 1990, 146m, ★★★★/$$$$, WB/WB, EP-EV-S-B&G. The rise of a neighborhood mobster (Ray Liotta) is chronicled as a cross-section of other gangsters in New York in the 1960s come to blows when drugs become a mainstay of their business. Robert De Niro (BActor), Joe Pesci (**BSActor**), Lorraine Bracco (BSActress), Harvey Keitel, Paul Sorvino. w. Henry Hill, Martin Scorsese (BAScr), NF-adap. Hill, d. Scorsese (BDirector). BPicture. Oscars: 6-1.
DRAMA: Crime Drama; **TRAGEDY:** Mob Stories; Police vs. Mob; Power-Rise to; **MURDER:** Betrayals; Informers; Witnesses-Protecting; Newlyweds; Marriage Drama; Dangerous Men; Evil Men; Mental Illness; Psycho Killers; Hitmen; 1960s; New York Life; Narrated Films
(A Bronx Tale; Casino; Mean Streets)
(Ed: Relentlessly realistic and oppressive, not as entertaining as *The Godfather*, but you get more of an understanding of the workings of mobsters and the lengths they'll go to)

The Good Fight, 1992, 91m, ★★¹/₂/$$, Lifetime/Prism. A woman lawyer is asked by a friend to defned him in suing a tobacco company for the cancer he developed. Christine Lahti, Terry O'Quinn, Kenneth Welsh. w. Beth Gutcheon, d. W. G. Snuffy Walden.
DRAMA: Courtroom Drama; Lawyers; Disease Stories; Ethics; Female Protagonists; Female Screenwriters; TV Movies

Good Guys Wear Black, 1977, 95m, ★★¹/₂/$$$, American Cinema/WB, PG/EV. A commando raid goes awry in Vietnam and is left to die, and its commander goes to Washington to ferret out their traitor. Chuck Norris, Anne Archer, James Franciscus, Lloyd Haynes, Dana Andrews, Jim Backus. w. Bruce Cohn, Mark Medoff, Joseph Fraley, d. Ted Post.
ACTION: Action Drama; Chase Stories; Vietnam War; Soldiers; Military Stories; Avenging Death of Someone; Martial Arts; Conspiracy; Sleeper Hits
(The Octagon; Code of Silence)
(Ed: First of many more for Norris to come)

A Good Man in Africa, 1994, 93m, ★★¹/₂/$, Gramercy-U/MCA-U, R/P-S. Corruption and greed threaten to undermine the strides made by a new, small African country as blacks rise up against the imperialist whites, but race may not be the dividing line so much as ethics. Sean Connery, Colin Friels, John Lithgow, Diana Rigg, Louis Gossett, Jr., Joanne Whalley-Kilmer, Sarah-Jane Fenton, Jeremy Crutchley. w. N-adap. William Boyd, d. Bruce Beresford.

DRAMA: Social Drama; Imperialist Problems; Ensemble Films; Africa; Ethics; Greed; Black vs. White; Race Relations; Coulda Been Great; Overlooked at Release; Quiet Little Films (Mister Johnson; Black and White in Color)
(Ed: Some good moments, but finally empty)

Good Morning, Babylon, 1987, 115m, ★★1/2/$, Vestron/Vestron, R/P-S. A group of Italian film makers go to Hollywood to save their sagging family fortunes. Vincent Spano, Joaquim de Almeida, Greta Scaacchi, Desiree Becker, Charles Dance. w. d. Paulo and Vittorio Taviani.

DRAMA: Silent Film Era; Immigrants; Dreams; Hollywood Life; Movie Making; Italians; Coulda Been Great; Good Premise Unfulfilled; 1900s; Writer-Directors; Independent Films
(Ed: What Coppola could have done with this. It has little perspective or scope)

Good Morning, Vietnam, 1987, 120m, ★★★1/2/$$$$$, Touchstone/Touchstone, PG/P-S. Primarily a frenetic wild monologue from Robin Williams, this is ostensibly the true story of an Armed Forces Radio disc jockey and how the Vietnam War affects him. Robin Williams (BActor), Forest Whitaker, Tung Tanh Tran, Chintara Sukapatana, Bruno Kirby. w. Mitch Markowitz, d. Barry Levinson. Oscars: 1-0.

COMEDY: COMEDY DRAMA: Radio Life; Vietnam War; Military Comedy; Rebels; Wild People; Comedy-Performance; Sleeper Hits; Blockbusters (The Fisher King; Dead Poet's Society; The Killing Fields)
(Ed: Even though it's still mostly Robin's monolgue, there's a good story and the character isn't just gratuitously thrown into the midst of it)

The Good Mother, 1988, 104m, ★★★/$$, Touchstone/Touchstone, PG-13/P-S. A single mother (Diane Keaton) with a little girl dates a liberal artist (Liam Neeson) and a bogus molestation scandal is the consequence that may cost her everything. w. Michael Bortman, N-adap. Sue Miller, d. Leonard Nimoy.

DRAMA: TRAGEDY: ROMANCE: Romantic Drama; Starting Over; Mothers ALone; Single Women; Ethics; Life Transitions; Mothers Alone; Custody Battles; Molestation; Artists; Children-Losing/Parting with; Womens' Films; Female Protagonists; Hidden Gems; Overlooked at Release; Flops-Major (Something About Amelia; Sophie's Choice; Family Pictures)
(Ed: Rushed to video with incredible speed, this film was misunderstood and had much more to it than the TV movie prurience of its subject matter)

Good Neighbor Sam, 1964, 130m, ★★★/$$$, Col/RCA-Col. A sexy French divorcee "hires" her next door neighbor to play her husband when she needs to appear married in order to get $15 million from her grandfather's codisil-infested will, but when they fake couple winds up in an ad campaign and her real estranged husband reappears, the plan goes awry. Jack Lemmon, Romy Schneider, Dorothy Provine, Senta Berger, Edward G. Robinson, Mike Connors, Edward Andrews, Louis Nye. w. James Fritzell, Everett Greenbaum, David Swift, N-adap. Jack Finney, d. David Swift.

COMEDY: FARCE: Marriages-Fake; Impostors; Neighbors-Troublesome; Inheritances at Stake; Rewards at Stake; Advertising World; Suburban Life; Relatives-Troublesome; Sexy Women; Hidden Gems
(The Apartment; Under the Yum-Yum Tree; Guest Wife)

Good News, 1947, 93m, ★★★/$$, MGM/MGM-UA. A football hero has to pass an exam or flunk out, so he sings and dances through this Roaring 20s raccoon-coat fest. June Allyson, Peter Lawford, Mel Torme. w. Betty Comden, Adolph Green, d. Charles Walters.

MUSICALS: Musical Comedy; Nostalgia; Roaring 20s; 1920s; Football; College Life; Forgotten Films; Female Screenwriters
(Margie)

Good Sam, 1948, 128m, ★★1/2/$$, Rainbow/Republic. A gregarious small-town businessman goes on the road to bankruptcy being charitable. Gary Cooper, Ann Sheridan, Ray Collins, Edmund Lowe, Joan Lorring. w. Ken Englund, d. Leo McCarey.

COMEDY: COMEDY DRAMA: Small-town Life; Rich People; Risking It All;

Saintly People; Capra-esque; Forgotten Films; Coulda Been Good
(For Richer, For Poorer; Mr. Deeds Goes to Town)

The Good Son, 1993, 87m, ★★/$$$, 20th/Fox, R/V. When an orphan goes to stay with relatives, his little cousin turns out to be a lying psychopath who, for some reason, is hell-bent on killing everyone around. Elijah Wood, Macaulay Culkin, Wendy Crewson, David Morse. w. Ian McEwan, d. Joseph Ruben.

SUSPENSE: Serial Killers; Murderers-Child; Evil Children; Liars; Boys; Orphans; Children-Brats; Framed?; Child Protagonists; Curiosities
(The Little Girl Who Lives Down the Lane; The Bad Seed; Bad Influence)
(Ed: Culkin isn't bad, but the motivations of the character and the situations are mostly totally gratuitous; nowhere near *The Little Girl Who Lives Down the Lane* or *The Bad Seed*)

The Good, the Bad, and the Ugly, 1966, 180m, ★★★/$$$$, UA/MGM-UA. An almost operatic spaghetti Western about three men competing to find a stash of money hidden by an outlaw compatriot. Clint Eastwood, Eli Wallach, Lee Van Cleef. w. Age Scarpelli, Luciano Vincenzoni, Sergio Leone, d. Sergio Leone.

WESTERNS: Westerns-Spaghetti; Treasure Hunts; Outlaw Road Movies; Searches; Lyrical Films
(Hang 'em High; For a Few Dollars More)
(Ed: The whistling score by Ennio Morricone is probably even more famous than the film)

Good Times, 1967, 92m, ★★1/2/$, Ind/NA. Sonny and Cher imagine themselves as the heroes of several different film genres . . . and sing a few songs. Sonny and Cher, George Sanders, Norman Alden, Larry Duran. w. Tony Barrett, d. William Friedkin.

COMEDY: Spoofs; Music Movies; Musicians; Singers; Fantasies; Curiosities; Cult Films

The Good Wife, 1987, 92m, ★★1/2/$, Ind/Imperial, R/S-FN-MRN. In the late 30s, a married woman in a conservative Australian outback community has a love affair with her husband's best friend who is visiting. Rachel Ward, Bryan Brown, Sam Neill, Steven Vidler. w. Peter Kenna, d. Ken Cameron.

DRAMA: ROMANCE: Romantic Drama; Cheating Women; Romance with Lover's

Friend; Romance-Triangles; Romance with Married Person; Marriage on the Rocks; Farm Life; 1930s; Australian Films; Ind. Films; Female Protagonists (The Country Life; The Thorn Birds)

The Goofy Movie, 1995, 90m, ★★★/$$, Disney/Disney, G. Goofy goofs his way through several adventures in this extended version of the afternoon series. Voices of Jason Marsden, Bill Farmer, Kellie Martin, Jenna Von Oy, Jim Cummings, Rob Paulsen, Wallace Shawn, Joanne Worley, Joey Lawrence, Julie Brown. d. Kevin Lima.
CHILDREN'S: COMEDY: Cartoons; TV Series Movies; Dogs; Fools-Bumbling; Fathers & Sons; Disney Comedy

The Goonies, 1985, 111m, ★★½/$$$, WB/WB, PG/V-P. When a group of suburban kids find a pirate treasure map, they set out to find the good and wind-up in a fantastic other world. Sean Astin, Josh Brolin, Jeff Cohen, Corey Feldman, Kerri Green, Martha Plimpton, Ke Huy Kwan. w. Chris Columbus, Steven Spielberg, d. Richard Donner.
ACTION: COMEDY: Action Comedy; Children's; **ADVENTURE:** Comic Adventure; Fantasy; **SCI-FI:** Journies; Monsters; Treasure Hunts; Coulda Been Great
(Explorers; Gremlins)

Gordon's War, 1973, 90m, ★★½/$, 20th/Fox. After returning from Vietnam, a black soldier has his own war at home in avenging his wife's death. Paul Winfield, Carl Lee, David Downing. w. Howard Friedlander, Ed Spielman, d. Ossie Davis.
DRAMA: Crimes of Passion; Avenging Death of Someone; Soldiers; Black Casts; Black Soldiers; Vietnam Era; Veterans-Vietnam; Forgotten Films; Overlooked at Release
(Green Eyes; Coming Home)

Gore Vidal's Billy The Kid: see Billy the Kid
Gore Vidal's Lincoln, 1988, 190m, ★★★/$$$, NBC/Avenue. The revisionist look at the president and his neurotic wife, exploring some details left out of the history books. Sam Waterston, Mary Tyler Moore, John Houseman, Cleavon Little, Richard Mulligan, Ruby Dee. w. Ernest Kilroy, NF-adap. Gore Vidal, d. Lamont Johnson.
DRAMA: Historical Drama; Marriage Drama; Revisionist Films; Presidents; Abraham Lincoln; Civil War Era; Assassination Plots; Eccentric People; TV Movies
(Young Mr. Lincoln; Abraham Lincoln)
(Ed: Remembered most for Moore's turn as the oft-forgotten first lady)

The Gorgeous Hussy, 1936, 105m, ★★★/$$$, MGM/MGM-UA. Andrew Jackson's mistress gets around. Joan Crawford, Lionel Barrymore, Franchot Tone, Melvyn Douglas, Robert Taylor, James Stewart, Alison Skipworth, Louis Calhern, Beulah Bondi (BSActress), Melville Cooper, Gene Lockhart. w. Ainsworth Morgan, Stephen Morehouse Avery, N-adap. Samuel Hopkins Adams, d. Clarence Brown. Oscars: 1-0.
MELODRAMA: ROMANCE: Historical Drama; Biographies; Costume Drama; Washington, D.C.; Southerns; Presidents; Civil War Era; Sexy Women; Soap Operas; Forgotten Films; Faded Hits; Curiosities
(Jezebel; Queen Bee; Gone With the Wind)

The Gorgon, 1964, 83m, ★★½/$$, Col/Goodtimes. In the German countryside at an old crumbling castle, Greek mythological monster gorgons rule the roost and frighten off potential visitors. Peter Cushing, Christopher Lee, Barbara Shelley, Richard Pasco, Patrick Troughton. w. John Gilling, SS-adap. J. Llewellyn Devine, d. Terence Fisher.
HORROR: Monsters; Monsters-Mythological Castles; Germany; Kill the Beast
(The Keep)

The Gorilla, 1939, 66m, ★★½/$$, 20th/Nos. When a series of murders happen, the real culprit blames it all on a gorilla. The Ritz Brothers, Bela Lugosi, Lionel Atwill, Patsy Kelly, Joseph Calleia, Anita Louise, Edward Norris. w. Rian James, Sid Silvers, P-adap. Ralph Spence, d. Allan Dwan.
HORROR: MURDER: Serial Killers; Primates; Forgotten Films
(Gorilla at Large; Mighty Joe Young)

Gorilla at Large, 1954, 93m, ★★½/$$, 20th/NA. A gorilla makes a good scapegoat for a murderer on the lamb. Anne Bancroft, Lee J. Cobb, Cameron Mitchell, Lee Marvin, Raymond Burr, Charlotte Austin, Warren Stevens. w. Leonard Praskins, Barney Slater, d. Harmon Jones.
SUSPENSE: MURDER: Fugitives from the Law; Primates; Circus Life; 3-D Movies; Curiosities
(The Gorilla; Mighty Joe Young)

Gorillas in the Mist, 1988, 129m, ★★★/$$$, Universal/MCA-U, PG/P-V. A research biologist studies gorillas and almost becomes a member of their community. Sigourney Weaver (BActress), Bryan Brown, Julie Harris, John Miluwi. w. Anna Hamilton Phelan (BAScr), story: Tab Murphy, NF-adap. Dian Fossey, NF-adap. Harold T. P. Hayes, d. Michael Apted. BOScore, BEdit, BSound. Oscars: 5-0.
DRAMA: Biographies; **TRAGEDY: MURDER: MYSTERY:** True Stories; Character Studies; Pioneers; Feisty Females; Obsessions; Africa; Primates; Scientists; Sleeper Hits; Female Protagonists

Gorky Park, 1983, 128m, ★★½/$, Orion/Orion, R/V-P-S-FN-MRN. A killer in Moscow uses techniques learned in fur stripping to skin his victims. William Hurt, Lee Marvin, Brian Dennehy, Ian Bannen, Joanna Pacula. w. Dennis Potter, N-adap. Martin Cruz Smith, d. Michael Apted.
SUSPENSE: MYSTERY: MURDER: MURDER MYSTERY: Detective Stories; Detectives-Police; Conspiracy; Russia; Americans & Russians; Overlooked at Release; Coulda Been Good
(The Russia House; Citizen X)
(Ed: The big bestseller gets watered down, and when one finds out what it's all about one wonders what the big deal was)

Gorp!, 1980, 90m, ★/$$, Ind/HBO, R/P-S. Summer camp shenanigans. Dennis Quaid, Rosanna Arquette. d. Joseph Ruben.
COMEDY: Teenagers; Teenage Movies; Camping; Bathroom Humor
(Meatballs; Little Darlings)

The Gospel According to St. Matthew, 1966, 135m, ★★★/$$, Arco-Walter Reade/Nos. The life of Christ filmed as a modern documentary. Enrique Irazoqui, Susanna Pasolini, Mario Socrate. w. d. Pier Paolo Pasolini. BB&WArt, BB&WCostume, BAScore. Oscars: 3-0.
DRAMA: Docudrama; Biographies; Documentaries; Documentary Style; Jesus Christ; Ancient Times; Biblical Stories; Revisionist Films; Curiosities; Hidden Gems; Writer-Directors
(The Last Temptation of Christ; Christ Stopped at Eboli)

Gotham, 1988, 97m, ★★½/$ (LR), R/S-V. A detective is hired by a man who's certain his dead wife is following him. Tommy Lee Jones, Virginia Madsen,

Colin Bruce, Frederic Forrest. w. d. Lloyd Fovielle.

SUSPENSE: MYSTERY: Detective Stories; Detectives-Private; Dead-Back from the; Good Premise Unfulfilled; Coulda Been Good; Writer-Directors

Gotcha!, 1985, 97m, ★★–/$$, U/MCA-UA, PG-13/S-V. College student is caught up in a real spy assassination situation after playing a game on campus. Anthony Edwards, Linda Fiorentino, Nick Corri, Alex Rocco. w. Dan Gordon, d. Jeff Kanew.

COMEDY: Comic Thriller; **SUSPENSE:** Spy Films; Spoofs-Spy; College Life; Young Men; Chase Movies; Coulda Been Good; Bratpack Movies

COMIC FLIPSIDE TO: The Marathon Man

(Year of the Gun; Risky Business)

Gothic, 1987, 87m, ★★★/$, Vestron/Vestron, R/ES-FN-MN. In 1800s Switzerland, Byron, Dr. Polidori, and Mary Shelley and her husband spend their vacation thinking up weird tales while taking opium and having elaborate sexual hallucinations. Gabriel Byrne, Julian Sands, Natasha Richardson, Miriam Cyr, Timothy Spall. w. Stephen Volk, d. Ken Russell.

HORROR: Fantasy; Erotic Drama; Revisionist Films; Art Films; Avant-Garde Films; Illusions/Hallucinations; Nightmares; Castles; Alternative Lifestyles

(Haunted Summer; Frankenstein Unbound; The Devils; Lair of the White Worm)

(Ed: *Haunted Summer* is the more traditional version of the same story, meaning that you can follow the story; *Frankenstein Unbound* is the other version in this late-80s genre glut)

Go West, 1940, 82m, ★★★/$$$, MGM/MGM-UA. The Marx Brothers invade the old West and bring their particular brand of chaos to bear on a dastardly villain. Groucho Marx, Harpo Marx, Chico Marx, John Carroll, Diana Lewis, Robert Barrat. w. Irving Brecher, d. Edward Buzzell.

COMEDY: Comedy-Slapstick; Western Comedy; **WESTERNS:** Spoofs-Western; Marx Brothers; Fish out of Water Stories

(Fancy Pants; Duck Soup; The Big Store)

Go West Young Man, 1936, 80m, ★★★/$$$, Par/Par. A beautiful and sexy star befriends a local farmboy when he helps her fix her car on the way to L.A. Mae West, Randolph Scott, Warren

William, Lyle Talbot, Alice Brady, Isabel Jewell, Elizabeth Patterson. w. Mae West, P-adap. Lawrence Riley (*Personal Appearance*), d. Henry Hathaway.

COMEDY: ROMANCE: Romantic Comedy; Older Women Seducers; Romance-Older Women/Younger Men; Actresses; Stranded; Sexy Women; Fish out of Water Stories; Coulda Been Great; Forgotten Films

COMIC FLIPSIDE OF: Sweet Bird of Youth

(She Done Him Wrong; Dynamite)

Grace Quigley, 1985, 87m, ★★★/$, Cannon-MGM/MGM-UA, PG/P-V. An elderly woman (Katharine Hepburn) hires a hitman (Nick Nolte) to knock her off, but before he does, she wants him to knock off her willing friends. Elizabeth Wilson, Wal⊥ .bel, Kit Le Fever, Chip Zuen. w. A. ⊥⊥rtin Zweiback, d. Anthony Harvey.

COMEDY: Black Comedy; Comedy-Morbid; Screwball Comedy; Social Satire; Suicidal Tendencies; Elderly People; Euthanasia; Hitmen; Mothers-Surrogate; Death-Dealing with; Mothers & Sons; Psychologists; Lonely People; New York Life; Overlooked at Release; Hidden Gems

(Harold and Maude; Whose Life Is It Anyway?; A Shock to the System)

The Graduate, 1967, 105m, ★★★★/$$$$$$, Embassy/Embassy, R/P-S. An alienated young man (Dustin Hoffman, BActor) goes after the daughter (Katharine Ross, BSActress) of the older woman he's lost his virginity to (Anne Bancroft, BActress). Norman Fell, William Daniels, Murray Hamilton, Elizabeth Wilson. w. Buck Henry, Calder Willingham (BAScr), N-adap. Charles Webb, d. Mike Nichols (**BDirector**). BPicture, BEditing. Oscars: 7-1.

COMEDY DRAMA: SATIRE: ROMANCE: Romance-Boy Wants Girl; Coming of Age; Obsessions; Young Men; Anti-Establishment Films; Life Transitions; Pre-life Crisis; Mean Women; Romance-Older Women/Younger Women; Romance-Triangles; Romance-Choosing the Right Person; Romance-Forbidden; Lover Family Dislikes; Marriage-Impending; Weddings; Fatal Attractions; Obsessions; Suburban Life; Rich People; California; Men Proving Themselves; 1960s; College Life; Blockbusters; Sleeper Hits; Time Capsules; Cult Films

(The Heartbreak Kid; Say Anything; Five Easy Pieces)

Graffiti Bridge, 1990, 95m, ★★/$, WB/WB. The pop star Prince falls out of favor trying to promote his dreamy hippy music as a rival clubowner plays a more uptempo style. Prince, Ingrid Chavez, Morris Day, Jerome Benton, Mavis Staples. w. d. Prince.

MUSICALS: Music Movies; Nightclubs; Singers; Musicians; Black Casts; Black Men; Black Directors; Writer-Directors

(Purple Rain; Under a Cherry Moon)

Grand Canyon, 1991, 134m, ★★★/$$, 20th/Fox, PG-13/P-S-V. A white lawyer gets stranded in the L.A. ghetto and is helped out by a black truck driver, and among all of their other friends, they try to bridge the gulf between their two worlds. Danny Glover, Kevin Kline, Steve Martin, Mary McDonnell, Mary-Louise Parker, Alfre Woodard. w. Meg and Lawrence Kasdan (BOScr), d. Lawrence Kasdan. Oscars: 1-0.

DRAMA: Social Drama; Social Satire; Los Angeles; Hollywood Life; Urban Life; Urban Horrors; Black vs. White; Race Relations; Friendships-Interracial; Class Conflicts; Earthquakes; Coulda Been Great; Female Screenwriters

(Short Cuts; A Family Thing)

The Grand Highway (Le Grand Chemin), 1987, 104m, ★★★/$, WB/WB, PG. A childless couple is rejuvinated when a nine-year-old boy spends the summer with them. Anemone, Richard Bohringer, Antoine Hubert, Vanessa Guedi, Christine Pascal, Raoul Billerey, Marie Matheron. w. d. Jean-Loup Hubert.

MELODRAMA: COMEDY DRAMA: Family Drama; Women-Childless; Vacations; Summer Vacations; Boys; Children-Adopted; Hidden Gems; Quiet Little Films; Writer-Directors

REMAKE: Paradise

Grand Hotel, 1932, 113m, ★★★½/$$$$$, MGM/MGM-UA. A cross section of the lives of the guests at the luxury hotel in Berlin, mostly all in crisis. Greta Garbo, John Barrymore, Lionel Barrymore, Joan Crawford, Wallace Beery, Jean Hersholt, Lewis Stone. w. William A. Drake, N-adap. Vicki Baum, d. Edmund Goulding. **BPicture.** Oscars: 1-1.

DRAMA: MELODRAMA: ROMANCE: Multiple Stories; Interwoven Stories; Hotels; German; Ballet; Jewel Thieves; Berlin; Blockbusters; All-Star Casts

(Dinner at Eight; Voyage of the Damned; Ship of Fools)

The Grand Illusion, 1937, 111m, ★★★★/$$, Realisations d'Art Cinematographique-World/Fox, Voyager. The tense relations in a German P.O.W. camp are explored in a very imaginative way. Pierre Fresnay, Erich Von Stroheim, Jean Gabin, Julien Carette, Marcel Dalio, Gaston Modot, Jean Daste, Dita Parlo. w. Jean Renoir, Charles Spaak, d. Jean Renoir. BPicture. Oscars: 1-0.
DRAMA: TRAGEDY: War Stories; World War I Stories; Fantasies; Surrealism; Art Films; Ensemble Films; POWs; Concentration Camps; Germans as Enemy; Germany; Hidden Gems; Cult Films; Film History
(Playing for Time; All Quiet on the Western Front)
(Ed: One of the few foreign films ever nominated for Best Picture)
Grand Prix, 1966, 176m, ★★★/$$$, MGM/MGM-UA, PG/S-V. A group of master motorists converge on Monte Carlo for the big race. James Garner, Eva Marie Saint, Brian Bedford, Yves Montand, Toshiro Mifune, Jessica Walter, Francoise Hardy, Adolfo Celi, Claude Dauphin, Genevieve Page. w. Robert Alan Aurthur, d. John Frankenheimer.
ACTION: Car Racing; **ROMANCE:** Road Movies; Multiple Stories
(Days of Thunder; Winning; Le Mans)
(Ed: Way too long for what it is, but it looks great for a while)
Grand Theft Auto, 1977, 84m, ★★/$$$, AIP/WB, PG/V. A couple steals a car to go to Vegas and get married and soon has a whole slew of people after them. Ron Howard, Nancy Morgan, Marion Ross. w. d. Ron Howard.
ACTION: Action Comedy; Chase Movies; Car Chases; Road Movies; Marriage-Elopments; Writer-Directors; Actor Directors; Sleeper Hits
(Eat My Dust; Cotton Candy)
Grandview, USA, 1984, 97m, ★★½/$$, CBS-WB/WB, PG/S-P. A teenager falls for the woman who runs a demolition derby in his small town and has a fling while still trying to smooth things out with his girl and not get into more trouble. C. Thomas Howell, Jamie Lee Curtis. d. Randal Kleiser.
COMEDY: ROMANCE: Coming of Age; Romance-Older Women/Younger Men; Music Video Style; Fantasies; Small-town

Life; Wild People; Teenagers; Boys; Coulda Been Good
(A Tiger's Tale; Class)
The Grapes of Wrath, 1940, 128m, ★★★★/$$$, 20th/CBS-Fox. In the great migration after the Oklahoma drought of the thirties, poor families travel to California for a better life. But not everyone makes it. Henry Fonda (BActor), Jane Darwell (**BSActress**), John Carradine, Charley Grapewin, Dorris Bowdon, Russell Simpson, Zeffie Tilbury, John Qualen, Grant Mitchell. w. Nunnally Johnson (BScr), N-adap. John Steinbeck, d. John Ford (**BDirector**). BEdit. Oscars: 6-2.
DRAMA: Sagas; Family Drama; Historical Drama; Depression Era; Social Drama; Journies; Midwestern Life; California; Road to California; Accused Unjustly; Poor People; Mothers & Sons; Allegorical Stories; Classic Literary Adaptations; Pulitzer Prize Adaptations
(Of Mice and Men; Tortilla Flat; God's Little Acre; Tobacco Road)
The Grass Is Always Greener over the Septic Tank, 1978, 98m, ★★★/$$$$, CBS/Prism. A city family moves to the suburbs and the wife has trouble adjusting to the less hectic and gossip-ridden lifestyle. Carol Burnett, Charles Grodin, Linda Gray, Alex Rocco, Eric Stoltz. w. N-adap. Erma Bombeck, d. Robert Day.
COMEDY: Fish out of Water Stories; Suburban Life; Marriage Comedy; Family Comedy; Autobiographical Stories; 1970s; Gossip; Female Protagonists; Writers; Female Screenwriters; TV Movies; Hidden Gems
The Grass Is Greener, 1960, 105m, ★★★/$$, Ind/Republic. A member of the British aristocracy is seduced by a vacationing American millionaire and each of their lovers don't find it so nice. Cary Grant, Deborah Kerr, Robert Mitchum, Jean Simmons, Moray Watson. w. P-adap. Hugh and Margaret Williams, d. Stanley Donen.
COMEDY DRAMA: ROMANCE: Romantic Comedy; Sex Comedy; Comedy of Manners; Romance-Triangles; Romance with Married Person; Married Couples; Cheating Men; Cheating Women; Rich People; England; Coulda Been Great
(Indiscreet; Marriage on the Rocks)
The Grasshopper, 1969, 98m, ★★½/$, NGP/WB, R/S-P. A young woman goes to hit the big time in Vegas and winds up

being a prostitute instead. Jacqueline Bisset, Jim Brown, Joseph Cotten, Corbett Monica. w. Jerry Belson, N-adap. Mark MacShane (*The Passing of Evil*), d. Jerry Parris.
DRAMA: Erotic Drama; Prostitutes-High Class; Prostitutes-Ordinary People Turned; Sexy Women; Character Studies; Young Women; Las Vegas; Forgotten Films; Curiosities
(Showgirls; Valley of the Dolls; First Love; Class; Secrets)
Graveyard Shift, 1987, 89m, ★★½/$$, Col/Col-Tri, R/EV-B&G. The caretakers of an old rundown mill find out that it's inhabited by a mysterious creature that won't go away. David Andrews, Kelly Wolf, Stephen Macht, Andrew Divoff, Brad Dourif, Robert Alan Beuth, Ilona Margolis. w. John Esposito, SS-adap. Stephen King, d. Ralph S. Singleton.
HORROR: Monsters; Rural Horrors; Rogue Plots; Kill the Beast; Human Eaters; Stephen King; Taxi Drivers
(Pet Sematary; Creep Show)
Gray Lady Down, 1978, 111m, ★★/$, U/MCA-U, PG/V-P. A submarine gets lodged in an cavern underwater and the crew must figure out what to do. Charlton Heston, David Carradine, Stacy Keach, Ned Beatty, Stephen McHattie, Ronny Cox, Dorian Harewood. w. James Whittaker, Howard Sackler, N-adap. David Levallee (*Event 1000*), d. David Greene.
DRAMA: Military Stories; Survival Drama; Crisis Situations; War Stories; Submarines; Underwater Adventure
(The Bedford Incident; Crimson Tide)
Grease, 1978, 110m, ★★★/$$$$$$, Par/Par, PG/S. Australian visitor doll (Olivia Newton-John) meets up with stud guy (John Travolta) and sings and dances her way through senior year at Rydell High. Sid Caesar, Stockard Channing, Didi Conn, Eve Arden, Dody Goodman, Alice Ghostley, Kevin Conway. w. Bronte Woodard, Allan Carr, P-adap. Warren Casey, Jim Jacobs, d. Randal Kleiser.
MUSICAL: COMEDY: Musical Comedy; **ROMANCE:** Romantic Comedy; 1950s; High School Life; Teenage Movies; Teenagers; Juvenile Delinquents; Rebels; Nostalgia; Exchange Students; Blockbusters; All-Star Casts; Female Protagonists
(American Graffiti; Hairspray; Bye Bye Birdie)

(Ed: Not exactly faithful to the Broadway version, plus the cast is old enough to be their own parents, but fun and great music. All-time musical grosser)

Grease 2, 1982, 114m, ★★/$, Par/Par, PG/S. This time the foreigner is the boy-an Englishman who comes to Rydell and steals the heart of a little blond cutie. Maxwell Caufield, Michelle Pfeiffer, Adrian Zmed, Lorna Luft, Eve Arden, Sid Caesar, Tab Hunter, Connie Stevens. w. Ken Finkleman, d. Patricia Birch.
MUSICAL: COMEDY: Musical Comedy; Dance Movies; ROMANCE: Romantic Comedy; 1950s; High School Life; Teenage Movies; Teenagers; Juvenile Delinquents; Rebels; Nostalgia; Exchange Students; Flops-Major; Female Directors; Female Protagonists
(Ed: More dancing and motorcycles in this one, but lousy music and mediocre everything else; Pfeiffer's first big break)

Greased Lightning, 1977, 94m, ★★1/2/$$, WB/WB, R/S-V-P. A black Virginia moonshine runner hones his skill at taking a curve and puts it to good use as a stock-car racer. Richard Pryor, Beau Bridges, Pam Grier, Cleavon Little, Vincent Gardenia. w. Kenneth Vose, Lawrence DuKore, Melvin Van Peebles, Leon Capetanos, d. Michael Schultz.
ACTION: COMEDY: Action Comedy; Black Men; Biographies; True Stories; Car Racing; Rednecks; Bootleggers; Mountain People; Southerns; Black vs. White; Black Among Whites; Curiosities
(Bustin' Loose; Thunder and Lightning)

Great Balls of Fire, 1989, 108m, ★★1/2/$, Orion/Orion, PG-13/S-P. Jerry Lee Lewis performs his barn-burnin' music and leaves the country under a cloud of scandal related to his marriage to his 15-year-old cousin. Dennis Quaid, Winona Ryder, John Doe, Joe Bob Briggs, Stephen Tobolowsky, Trey Wilson, Alec Baldwin, Steve Allen, Lisa Blount. w. Jack Baran, Jim McBride, NF-adap. Myra Lewis, Murray Silver, d. Jim McBride.
DRAMA: COMEDY DRAMA: Music Movies; Biographies; Musicians; Singers; Southerns; Rebels; Love-Forbidden; Romance with Relative; Romance-Older Men/Younger Women; 1950s; Rock Stars; Flops-Major; Overlooked at Release; Nostalgia
(The Buddy Holly Story; Elvis; Hail! Hail! Rock 'n Roll)

The Great Bank Hoax, 1978, 89m, ★★–/$, WB/WB, PG. Three bankers imbezzle money and cover-up with a heist. Richard Basehart, Ned Beatty, Burgess Meredith, Michael Murphy, Paul Sand. d. Joseph Jacoby.
COMEDY: Heist Stories; Bank Robberies; Thieves; Southerns; Cover-Ups; Hoaxes
(The Hot Rock; Thunderbolt and Lightfoot; Quick Change)

The Great Bank Robbery, 1969, 98m, ★★1/2/$, WB/NA. A group of outlaws dress up as priests and attempt to rob a bank. Kim Novak, Zero Mostel, Clint Walker, Claude Akins, Akim Tamiroff, Larry Storch, John Anderson, Elisha Cook Jr.. w. William Peter Blatty, N-adap. Frank O'Rourke, d. Hy Averback.
WESTERNS: COMEDY: Capers; Heist
ories; Western Comedy; Ensemble
ilms; Disguises; Disguised as Priest; Criminals-Stupid

The Great Caruso, 1951, 113m, 1951, 109m, ★★★/$$$, MGM/MGM-UA. Glossy biopic of the famous Italian opera star, starring perhaps an even more legendary Italian opera star. Mario Lanza, Ann Blyth, Dorothy Kirsten, Jarmila Novotna, Carl Benton Reid, Eduard Franz. w. Sonya Levien, William Ludwig, d. Richard Thorpe. BMScore, BCCostume. Oscars: 2-0.
MUSICALS: MELODRAMA: Opera; Opera Singers; Musical Drama; Biographies; ROMANCE: Musical Romance; Fame-Rise to; Singers; Italians; Female Screenwriters
(The Student Prince; Farinelli)

Great Catherine, 1968, 98m, ★★1/2/$, WB/NA. Catherine the Great catches the eye of an adventurous English sailor and chaos hits her kingdom. Jeanne Moreau, Peter O'Toole, Zero Mostel, Jack Hawkins, Marie Lohr, Akim Tamiroff, Kenneth Griffith. w. Hugh Leonard, P-adap. Bernard Shaw, d. Gordon Flemyng.
COMEDY: Comedy of Manners; Comedy-Slapstick; Queens; Royalty; Romance-Mismatched; Romance-Girl Wants Boy; Eccentric People; Leaders-Tyrants; Leaders-Female; Russian; Classic Literary Adaptations; Flops-Major; Coulda Been Good; Female Protagonists
(Rasputin and the Empress; Catherine the Great; Young Catherine)

Great Day in the Morning, 1956, 92m, ★★/$, RKO/NA. Denver is torn between North and South at the start of the Civil War. Robert Stack, Virginia Mayo, Ruth

Roman, Alex Nicol, Raymond Burr, Regis Toomey. w. Lesser Samuels, N-adap. Robert Hardy, d. Jacques Tourneur.
WESTERNS: Civil War Era; Feuds; Mountain People; Men in Conflict

The Great Dictator, 1940, 128m, ★★★1/2/$$$, UA/Fox. Chaplin's spoof of Hitler, the man who stole his moustache, where a little Jewish man is mistaken for a very similar-but fictitious-dictator, Adenoid Hynkel. Charles Chaplin, Paulette Goddard, Jack Oakie (BSActor), Reginald Gardiner. w. d. Charles Chaplin (BOScr, BDirector). BOScore. Oscars: 4-0.
COMEDY: SATIRE: Political Satire; Spoofs; Hitler; Nazi Stories; World War II Stories; Leaders-Tyrant; Jewish People; Identities-Mistaken; Hairdressers; Hidden Gems
(To Be or Not to Be; Modern Times)

The Great Escape, 1963, 173m, ★★★/$$$$$, UA/MGM-UA. In a German P.O.W. camp, an international band of allied soldiers plan their escape by motor-cycle and other means. James Garner, Steve McQueen, Richard Attenborough, James Donald, Charles Bronson, Donald Pleasence, James Coburn, David McCallum, Gordon Jackson, John Layton, Nigel Stock. w. James Clavell, W. R. Burnett, NF-adap. Paul Brickhill, d. John Sturges. BEditing. Oscars: 1-0.
ACTION: DRAMA: Action Drama; Escape Drama; POWs; Prison Drama; Prison Escape; Nazi Stories; World War II Stories; Motorcycles; Soldiers; All-Star Casts; Ensemble Films; Ensembles-Male; Germans as Enemy
(Victory; The Dirty Dozen)

The Great Escape 2: The Untold Story, 1988, 93m, ★★/$$$, NBC/Vidmark. A retelling and extension of the 1963 action classic, as an escapee turns Nazi, prompting those who have escaped a POW camp to go after him and others. Christopher Reeve, Judd Hirsch, Ian McShane, Judd Taylor, Charles Haid. d. Micahel Nader, Paul Wendkos.
ACTION: Escape Drama; POWs; Prison Escapes; World War II Stories; Nazi Stories; German as Enemy; True Stories
SEQUEL TO: The Great Escape

Great Expectations, 1947, 118m, ★★★★/$$$, U/Par, Learning Corp. A poor young boy on his own has a mysteri-ous benefactor who suddenly bestows riches upon him, leading him on exciting journeys. John Mills, Bernard Miles, Finlay Currie, Martita Hunt, Valerie Hobson, Jean Simmons, Alec Guinness, Francis L. Sullivan, Anthony Wager, Ivor Barnard, Freda Jackson, Hay Petrie. w. Ronald Neame, David Lean, Kay Walsh, Cecil McGivern, Anthony Havelock-Allan (BAScr), d. David Lean (BDirector). BPicture, **BB&WArt, BB&WCin.** Oscars: 5-2.

ADVENTURE: COMEDY DRAMA: Fantasy; Epics; Journies; Rags to Riches; Boys; Men and Boys; World Travel; All-Star Casts; Classic Literary Adaptations; British Films; Hidden Gems; Production Design-Outstanding
REMAKE OF: 1934 version
(Around the World in 80 Days; Treasure Island)

The Great Garrick, 1937, 91m, ★★★/$$, WB/NA. The famous English actor, David Garrick, goes to Paris and is the subject of a practical joke by the Comedie Francaise. Brian Aherne, Edward Everett Horton, Olivia de Havilland, Lionel Atwill, Melville Cooper, Luis Alberni, Etienne Girardot, Marie Wilson, Lana Turner, Albert Dekker, Fritz Leiber. w. Ernest Vajda, d. James Whale.

COMEDY: Comedy of Manners; **COMEDY DRAMA:** Actors; Practical Jokers; Theater Life; Paris; Biographies; Costume Drama; Forgotten Films; Hidden Gems

The Great Gatsby, 1949, 90m, ★★1/2/$$, Par/NA. A mobster living the good life gets a blast from the past from a jealous husband of one his mistresses. Alan Ladd, Macdonald Carey, Betty Field, Barry Sullivan, Howard da Silva. w. Richard Maibaum, N-adap. F. Scott Fitzgerald, d. Elliott Nugent.
SEQUEL TO: silent version, 1926
(Ed: Misses the mark)

The Great Gatsby, 1974, 146m, ★★★1/2/$$$, Par/Par, PG/S-V. A debonair man living in a mansion in West Egg, Long Island, has everyone enthralled with his charming ways-except the vengeful husband of one of his conquests. Robert Redford, Mia Farrow, Karen Black, Scott Wilson, Sam Waterston, Lois Chiles. w. Francis Ford Coppola, d. Jack Clayton. **BCostume, BOScore.** Oscars: 2-2.

DRAMA: Social Drama; **TRAGEDY: MURDER: ROMANCE:** Romance-Reluctant; Romance with Married Person; Jealousy; Crimes of Passion; Elusive Men; Beautiful People; Sexy Men; Playboys; Charismatic People; Rich People; Narrated Films; Coulda Been Great; Roaring 20s
REMAKE OF: 1926 and 1949 versions
(Day of the Locust; Tender Is the Night; F. Scott Fitzgerald in Hollywood)
(Ed: Though it was considered to be a flop at the time, it is a good film, and a very good-looking film, whose hype outweighed what it could have ever delivered; much more faithful to the original, though with some basic changes)

The Great Impostor, 1961, 112m, ★★★/$$, U-I/MCA-U. The true story of Ferdinand Waldo Demara, a marine who impersonated everyone from a monk to a Harvard researcher. Tony Curtis, Raymond Massey, Karl Malden, Edmond O'Brien, Arthur O'Connell, Gary Merrill, Frank Gorshin, Joan Blackman, Robert Middleton. w. Liam O'Brien, NF-adap. Robert Crichton, d. Robert Mulligan.

COMEDY DRAMA: True Stories; Biographies; Impostors; Disguises; Episodic Stories; Forgotten Films; Hidden Gems; Curiosities
(Critical Condition; The Mouse That Roared)

The Great Lie, 1941, 107m, ★★★1/2/$$$, WB/WB. A girl loves a married man, and when he is presumed dead in a plane crash, she steals his baby from his wife-but then he returns. Bette Davis, Mary Astor (**BSActress**), George Brent, Lucile Watson, Hattie McDaniel, Grant Mitchell. w. Leonore Coffee, N-adap. Polan Banks (*January Heights*), d. Edmund Goulding. Oscars: 1-1.

MELODRAMA: Tearjerkers; **TRAGEDY:** Dead-Back from the; Return of Spouse; Babies-Stealing; Mental Illness; Women in Conflict; Romance-Triangles; Airplane Crashes; Jealousy; Ethics; Pianists; Hidden Gems
(The Hand That Rocks the Cradle; Now, Voyager)

The Great Locomotive Chase, 1956, 85m, ★★1/2/$$, Disney/Disney. A spy for the Union commands a train sending supplies to the Confederacy during the Civil War. Fess Parker, Jeffrey Hunter, Jeff York, John Lupton, Kenneth Tobey. w. Lawrence Edward Watkin, d. Francis D. Lyon.

DRAMA: ADVENTURE: CHILDREN'S: FAMILY: Trains; Civil War Era; Spies; Spy Films; War Stories; Chase Stories; Fugitives from the Law; Traitors; Forgotten Films

The Great Lover, 1931, 77m, ★★1/2/$$, MGM/NA. A famous tenor is pursued by and pursues women. Adolphe Menjou, Irene Dunne, Neil Hamilton, Olga Baclanova. w. Gene Markey, d. Harry Beaumont.

COMEDY DRAMA: ROMANCE: Romantic Comedy; Cheating Men; Playboys; Opera; Opera Singers; Singers; Boy Scouts; Forgotten Films
(The Great Caruso; Break of Hearts)

The Great Lover, 1949, 80m, ★★★/$$, Par/Par, Col. A strangler is loose on a cruise chip and a bumbling worker manages to snag him while impressing a lady. Bob Hope, Rhonda Fleming, Roland Young, Jim Backus. Roland Culver. w. Edmund Beloin, Melville Shavelson, Jack Rose, d. Alexander Hall.

COMEDY: MURDER: MYSTERY: MURDER MYSTERY: Comic Mystery; Ships; Serial Killers; Black Comedy; Fools-Bumbling; Nerds; Nerds & Babes; Boy Scouts; Hidden Gems; Curiosities
(The Cat and the Canary; My Favorite Brunette)

The Great Manhunt (*State Secret*), 1950, 104m, ★★/$, British Lion/NA. In a fictitious dictatorship, soldiers under orders pursue the only man who knows that the dictator is dead. Douglas Fairbanks Jr., Glynis Johns, Herbert Lom, Jack Hawkins, Walter Rilla. w. d. Sidney Gilliat, also N-adap. (*Appointment with Fear*).

DRAMA: Military Stories; Leaders-Tyrant; War Stories; Soldiers; Death-Faked; Forgotten Films; Curiosities

The Great McGinty, 1940, 81m, ★★★1/2/$$$, Par/MCA-U. A petty thief and a bum get a political career off the ground, but it may not last. Brian Donlevy, Akim Tamiroff, Muriel Angelus, Louis Jean Heydt, Arthur Hoyt. w. d. Preston Sturges (**BOScr**). Oscars: 1-1.

COMEDY: SATIRE: Political Satire; Politicians; Political Corruption; Corruption; Political Campaigns; 1940s; Time Capsules; Thieves; Homeless People; Power-Rise to, of Idiot; Hidden Gems

The Great Moment, 1944, 83m, ★★1/2/$, Par/MCA-U. Dr. W. T. G. Morgan stumbles upon the invention of anaesthetics. Joel McCrea, Betty Field, William Demarest, Harry Carey, Franklin

Pangborn, Porter Hall, Grady Sutton. w. d. Preston Sturges.

DRAMA: MELODRAMA: Biographies; Doctors; Inventors; Scientists; Historical Drama; Medical Drama; Curiosities; Flops-Major; Writer-Directors

The Great Mouse Detective, 1986, 80m, ★★★/$$$, Disney/Disney, G. A mouse reads his Sherlock Holmes too seriously, becoming an amateur detective and foiling a plot by the nefarious Professor Rattigan, a rat, of course. Voices of Barrie Ingham, Vincent Price, Val Bettin, Alan Young. w. Pete Young, Steven Hulett, John Musker, Matthew O'Callaghan, Dave Michener, Vane Gerry, Ron Clements, Bruce M. Morris, Melvin Shaw, Burny Mattinson, N-adap. Eve Titus (*Basil of Baker Street*), d. John Musker.

CHILDREN'S: Cartoons; **MUSICALS:** Musicals-Animated; Detective Stories; Animal Stories; Sherlock Holmes; Revisionist Films; Rodents
(Oliver and Company; The Rescuers)

The Great Muppet Caper, 1981, 97m, ★★★/$$$, ITC/Disney, Henson. A jewel thief stealing the baseball diamond gives Kermit and Fozzie a run for their money. Diana Rigg, Charles Grodin, John Cleese, Robert Morley, Trevor Howard, Peter Ustinov, Jack Warden. w. Tom Patchett, Jay Tarses, Jerry Juhl, Jack Rose, d. Jim Henson.

COMEDY: CHILDREN'S: FAMILY: Heist Stories; Muppets; Animal Stories; Capers; Jewel Thieves; Chase Stories
(The Muppet Movie; The Muppets Take Manhattan)

The Great Northfield Minnesota Raid, 1972, 91m, ★★1/2/$, U/MCA-U, R/P-V. A band of outlaws are pardoned but revert back to their wicked ways and plan a bank robbery. Cliff Robertson, Robert Duvall, Luke Askew, Elisha Cook Jr. w. d. Philip Kaufman.

WESTERNS: Heist Stories; Westerns-Neo; Bank Robberies; Ensemble Films; Writer-Directors
(The Long Riders; Missouri Breaks; Thunderbolt and Lightfoot)

The Great Outdoors, 1988, 90m, ★★/$$$, Universal/MCA-U, PG/P. A camping trip goes awry when the father's in-laws decide to stay in an adjacent cabin. Dan Aykroyd, John Candy, Stephanie Faracy, Annette Bening, Chris Young, Ian Giatti, Rebecca Gordon. w. John Hughes, d. Howard Deutch.

COMEDY: CHILDREN'S: FAMILY: Comedy-Slapstick; Bathroom Humor; Nature-Back to; Fish out of Water Stories; Camping; Vacations; Nightmare Vacations; Coulda Been Good
(Nothing but Trouble; National Lampoon's Vacation)
(Ed: A few good laughs but mostly silly slapstick)

The Great Race, 1965, 150m, ★★★/$$$$, WB/WB. In 1908, a car race from New York to Paris attracts many a fanatic, among them Professor Fate and the Great Leslie who are in a great feuds as they try to outdo each other in air and car inventions-and win the lovely damsel in distress who is really a reporter on their tail. Jack Lemmon, Tony Curtis, Peter Falk, Natalie Wood, George Macready, Ross Martin, Vivian Vance, Dorothy Provine. w. Arthur Ross, d. Blake Edwards. BCCin, BOSong. Oscars: 2-0.

COMEDY: ACTION: Action Comedy; Comedy-Slapstick; Comedy of Errors; Car Racing Competitions; World Travel; Race Against Time; Fantasy; Car Chases; Inventors; Journalists; Undercover; Men Fighting Over Women; Russia; Snow Settings; Paris; 1900s; Balloons; Hidden Gems; Faded Hits; Cartoonlike Movies
(Around the World in 80 Days; Those Magnificent Men in Their Flying Machines; Genevieve)

The Great Santini, 1980, 116m, ★★★1/2/$$, Orion-WB/WB, R/P. A marine (Robert Duvall, BActor) home on leave begins to take out his frustrations on his son (Michael O'Keefe, BSActor) and wife (Blythe Danner). w. d. Lewis John Carlino, N-adap. Pat Conroy. Oscars: 2-0.

DRAMA: Character Studies; Fathers and Sons; Family Drama; Men Proving Themselves; Macho Men; Parents vs. Children; Fathers-Troublesome; Midlife Crisis; Mean Men; Practical Jokers; Soldiers; Alcoholics; Abused Children
(The Lords of Discipline; I Never Sang for My Father)

Great Scout and Cathouse Thursday, 1976, 102m, ★★1/2/$$, AIP/Live, R/S-P-V. A cowboy on a mission of vengeance takes time out to fall for a beautiful young prostitute with a heart of gold. Lee Marvin, Oliver Reed, Kay Lenz, Robert Culp, Elizabeth Ashley, Strother Martin, Sylvia Miles. w. Richard Shapiro, d. Don Taylor.

WESTERNS: Western Comedy; **ROMANCE:** Romantic Comedy; Romance with Prostitute; Prostitute with Heart of Gold; Romance-Older Men/Younger Women; Revenge; Curiosities
(The Duchess and the Dirtwater Fox; The Man Who Loved Cat Dancing)

The Great Sinner, 1949, 110m, ★★1/2/$$, MGM/NA. A promising young writer gambles it all away at the tables. Gregory Peck, Walter Huston, Ava Gardner, Agnes Moorehead, Ethel Barrymore, Melvyn Douglas, Frank Morgan. w. Ladislas Fodor, Christopher Isherwood, d. Robert Siodmak.

DRAMA: MELODRAMA: Character Studies; Writers Gambling; Losing It All; Risking It All; Obsessions; Forgotten Films
(Fever Pitch; The Gambler)

The Great Smokey Roadblock, 1976, 84m, Marvista-20th/Media, PG. An old truck driver barely making ends meet runs from his debtors in one last desperate ride, picking up strange characters along the way. Henry Fonda, Eileen Brennan, John Byner, Dub Taylor, Susan Sarandon, Dana House, Robert Englund, Melanie Mayron, Valerie Curtin. w. d. John Leone.

COMEDY: ACTION: Action Comedy; Chase Stories; Truck Drivers; Road Movies; Outlaw Road Movies; Fugitives from the Law; Fugitives; Elderly Men; Eccentric People; Hitchhikers; Curiosities; Writer-Directors
(Handle with Care; Convoy)

The Great Waldo Pepper, 1975, 107m, ★★1/2/$$, U/MCA-U, PG. After honing his skills in World War I, a flying ace does the air show circuit, becoming a stunt flyer, but life isn't so easy and the stunts don't always work. Robert Redford, Bo Svenson, Bo Brundlin, Susan Sarandon. w. William Goldman, d. George Roy Hill.

DRAMA: TRAGEDY: Character Studies; Pilots-Daredevil; Nostalgia; 1900s; Flops-Major
(Tarnished Angels; The Gypsy Moths)

The Great Waltz, 1938, 103m, ★★★1/2/$$$, MGM/MGM-UA. A musical biopic of the life of young Johann Strauss and his rise to fame in Vienna. Fernand Gravet, Luise Rainer, Miliza Korjus, Lionel Atwill, Hugh Herbert, Herman Bing, Curt Bois. w. Walter Reisch, Samuel Hoffenstein, SS-adap. Gottfried Reinhardt, d. Julien Duvivier.

The Great Waltz, 1972, 134m, ★★½/$, MGM/NA. Remake, modernized and opened up on real locations. Looks better but isn't as entertaining. Horst Buccholz, Nigel Patrick, Rosanno Brazzi. w. d. Andrew L. Stone.
DRAMA: MELODRAMA: MUSICALS: Music Movies; Costume Drama; Biographies; Music Composers; Dance Movies; Dancers; Vienna; Forgotten Films; Hidden Gems
(The Great Caruso; Immortal Beloved; Amadeus)
The Great White Hope, 1970, 101m, ★★★/$$, 20th/Fox, PG/V. A black champion boxer gains money and fame, but finds there are still barriers to what he can do, especially when he falls in love with a white woman. James Earl Jones (BActor), Jane Alexander (BActress), Lou Gilbert, Joel Fluellen, Chester Morris, Robert Webber, Hal Holbrook. w. P-adap. Howard Sackler, d. Martin Ritt. Oscars: 2-0.
DRAMA: Historical Drama; ROMANCE: Romantic Drama; Love-Forbidden; Romance-Interracial; Black vs. White; Boxing; Sports Movies; Race Relations; 1900s; Forgotten Films; Ahead of its Time; Hidden Gems
The Great Ziegfeld, 1936, 179m, ★★★½/$$$$$, MGM/MGM-UA. The biopic of the famous and influential producer of Broadway revues with musical numbers interspersed with his backstage life. William Powell, Luise Rainer (BActress), Myrna Loy, Frank Morgan, Reginald Owen, Nat Pendleton, Virginia Bruce, Ray Bolger, Fanny Brice. w. William Anthony McGuire (BScr), d. Robert Z. Leonard (BDirector).
BPicture, BArt, BChoreography. Oscars: 6-3.
MELODRAMA: MUSICALS: Musical Drama; Biographies; Theater Life; Marriage Drama; ROMANCE: Behind the Scenes; Dance Movies; Dancers; Episodic Stories; Blockbusters
(Ziegfeld Follies; Funny Girl; Yankee Doodle Dandy)
The Greatest, 1977, 101m, ★★/$, Co/Col. Muhammed Ali plays himself in this biopic, focusing more on his rise as a boxer than his religious convictions. Muhammed Ali, Ernest Borgnine, Roger E. Mosley, Lloyd Haynes, Malachi Throne, John Marley, Robert Duvall, James Earl Jones, Paul Winfield. w. Ring Lardner Jr., NF-adap. Muhammed Ali, d. Tom Gries.

DRAMA: COMEDY DRAMA: Docudrama; Biographies; Fame-Rise to; Boxing; Sports Movies; Unintentionally Funny; Curiosities; Forgotten Films; Flops-Major
The Greatest Show on Earth, 1952, 153m, ★★★½/$$$$$, Par/Par. Backstage tensions at the Ringling Brothers and Barnum and Bailey Circus culminate in a horrible train crash, but "the show must go on." Betty Hutton, Cornel Wilde, James Stewart, Charlton Heston, Dorothy Lamour, Gloria Grahame, John Kellogg. w. Fredric M. Frank, Theodore St. John, Frank Cavett (BOStory), & Barre Lyndon, d. Cecil B. de Mille (BDirector). BPicture, BEdit. 4-2.
MELODRAMA: TRAGEDY: FAMILY: Ensemble Films; Circus Life; Epics; Disaster Movies; Trains; All-Star Casts; Blockbusters
(Billy Rose's Jumbo; Heller in Pink Tights; Trapeze)
(Ed: Highly dated extravaganza that still works to a degree, especially for children, but it's not exactly what one would expect to win Best Picture, at least not today)
The Greatest Story Ever Told, 1965, 225m, ★★★/$$$$, UA/MGM-UA. A weaving together of Biblical tales all involved in the ascension of Christ. Max Von Sydow, Dorothy McGuire, Claude Rains, Charlton Heston, Sidney Poitier, Donald Pleasence, Roddy McDowell, Carroll Baker, Pat Boone, Sal Mineo, Angela Lansbury, Telly Savalas, Victor Buono, David McCallum, Jose Ferrer, Van Heflin. w. James Lee Barrett, George Stevens, d. Stevens.
DRAMA: Epics; Biblical Stories; Jesus Christ; Ancient Times; Middle East; Israel; Multiple Stories; Interwoven Stories; Cast of Thousands
(King of Kings; The Bible; Jesus of Nazareth)
Greed, 1924, 110m, ★★★½/$$$, MGM/MGM-UA. B&W, silent. A woman's greed prompts her husband, a dentist, to kill her. He later ends up handcuffed to her lover in Death Valley, and he must kill him to break free. Gibson Gowland, Zasu Pitts, Jean Hersholt, Chester Conklin, Dale Fuller. w. d. Erich Von Stroheim, N-adap. Frank Norris (McTeague).
SUSPENSE: MURDER: Crimes of Passion; Murder of Spouse; Jealousy; Cheating;

Women; Greed; Cheated Upon Meet; Survival Drama; Desert Settings; Ahead of its Time; Hidden Gems; Silent Films
Greedy, 1994, 109m, ★★-/$, U/MCA-U, PG-13/S-P. When a patriarch is about to kick the bucket and possibly leave his fortune to his bimbo of the month, relatives pop out of the woodwork to change his will regarding his will. Michael J. Fox, Kirk Douglas, Nancy Travis, Phil Hartman, Olivia D'Abo, Ed Begley Jr. w. Lowell Ganz, Babaloo Mandel, d. Johnathan Lynn.
COMEDY: Black Comedy; Greed; Death-Impending; Inheritances at Stake; Family Comedy; Rich People; Bimbos; Coulda Been Great; Flops-Major
(Daddy's Dyin'; Volpone; Passed Away)
(Ed: Another example of how today's Hollywood dumbs up what otherwise could have been a more intelligent and spry black comedy-and a hit)
The Greek Tycoon, 1978, 106m, ★★/$$, U/MCA-U, R/S-P. Veiled account of the life of Aristotle Onassis, focusing on his marriage to Jackie Kennedy. Anthony Quinn, Jacqueline Bisset, Raf Vallone, Edward Albert, James Franciscus. w. Mort Fine, d. J. Lee-Thompson.
MELODRAMA: ROMANCE: Romantic Drama; Biographies; Biographies-Fictional; Widows; Starting Over; Rich People; Greece; Ships; Flops-Major
The Green Berets, 1968, 141m, ★★/$$$, WB/WB, PG/V. A special team is sent in to Vietnam to shake things up and win. John Wayne, David Janssen, Jim Hutton, Aldo Ray, Raymond St. Jacques, Jack Soo, Bruce Cabot, Patrick Wayne, Irene Tsu. w. James Lee Barrett, N-adap. Robin Moore, d. John Wayne.
ACTION: War Stories; Vietnam War; Conservative Value Films; Patriotic Stories; Special Teams-Military
(Rambo; Navy SEALS; Missing in Action; Uncommon Valor)
(Ed: Much reviled at the time due to its pro-war stance and glorification of Vietnam; obviously wishful thinking on the creator and star's part)
Green Card, 1990, 113m, ★★★/$$$, Touchstone/Touchstone, PG/S. A woman (Andie MacDowell) who wants a New York apartment with a green house needs a spouse to get it, so she meets a Frenchman (Gerard Depardieu) who needs to get married to get green card, but a Platonic arrangement may not be

possible. w. d. Peter Weir (BOScr).
Oscars: 1-0

ROMANCE: COMEDY DRAMA:
Romantic Comedy; Marriage for
Citizenship; Marriage-Fake; Marriages of
Convenience; Immigrants; Romance-
Reluctant; Romance-Triangles;
Roommates; Comedy-Situation; New York
Life; Quiet Little Films; Hidden Gems
(Paper Marriage; Muriel's Wedding)

Green Dolphin Street, 1947, 141m,
★★★/$$$, MGM/MGM-UA. Two beauti-
ful sisters vie for the same young man in
New Zealand during the mid 1800s, but
when he ventures elsewhere to settle, in a
drunken stupor he requests the sister he
didn't like as much to join him, but as
she's okay, he doesn't quibble. Once she's
there, the results are earthquakes and
Indian attacks and driving the jilted sis-
ter back home into nunhood. Lana
Turner, Richard Hart, Edmund Gwenn,
Van Heflin, Donna Reed. w. Samson
Raphaelson, N-adap. Elizabeth Goudge,
d. Victor Saville. BB&WCin, BEdit.
BSFX. Oscars: 3-1.

MELODRAMA: ADVENTURE: Epics;
ROMANCE: Romantic Adventure;
Marriage Drama; Romance-Choosing
Right Person; Romance-Doomed; Sisters;
Women Fighting Over Men;
Misunderstandings; Mix-Ups;
Earthquakes; New Zealand; Nuns;
Pioneers
(The Piano)
(Ed: Came from a novel that won an
MGM writing competition; the title refers
to a ship and a boat in their town with lit-
tle signifigance)

Green Eyes, 1976, 100m, ★★★1/2/$$$,
CBS/Live. A black ex-GI goes back to
Vietnam to find his lost son he had with
a Vietnamese woman. Paul Winfield,
Johnathan Lippe, Rita Tushingham. d.
John Erman.

DRAMA: Vietnam; Vietnam Era;
Veterans-Vietnam; Orphans; Children-
Longlost; Romance-Interracial; Asian-
Americans; Black Men; Black vs. White;
TV Movies; Hidden Gems
(Gordon's War; The Killing Fields)

Green Fire, 1954, 100m, ★★★/$$$,
MGM/MGM-UA. Two emerald miners in
South American fight over jewels and the
beautiful woman who wears them. Grace
Kelly, Stewart Granger, Paul Douglas. w.
Ivan Goff, Ben Roberts, d. Andrew
Marton.

MELODRAMA: ROMANCE: Romance-
Triangles; Romance-Reluctant; Men
Fighting Over Women; Mining Towns;
South America; Hidden Gems; Forgotten
Films
(Mogambo)
(Ed: Only worth it as a forgotten Grace
Kelly movie)

Green for Danger, 1946, 100m,
★★★/$$, Rank/Nos. A clever killer
strikes at an army hospital in England
during World War II and may get away
with it. Alastair Sim, Sally Gray,
Rosamund John, Trevor Howard, Leo
Genn, Megs Jenkins, Judy Campbell,
Ronald Ward, Moore Marriott. w. Sidney
Gilliat, Claud Guerney, N-adap.
Christianna Brand, d. Sidney Gilliat.

**SUSPENSE: MURDER: MYSTERY: MUR-
DER MYSTERY:** Medical Thriller; Medical
Detectives; Detective Stories; Doctors;
Hospitals; World War II Era; British Films;
Hidden Gems; Clever Plots & Endings

The Green Goddess, 1930, 80m,
★★1/2/$$, WB/NA. Two British explorers
in India are held captive by a local female
ruler. George Arliss, Alice Joyce, H. B.
Warner, Ralph Forbes, David Tearle. w.
Charles Bennett, d. Rudolph Mate.

ADVENTURE: MELODRAMA: Hostage
Situations; Kidnappings; Explorers; India;
Leaders-Female; Curiosities; Forgotten
Films
REMAKE: Adventure in Iraq

Green Ice, 1981, 116m, ★★/$, ITC-
AFD/USA, PG/S-P. Thieves in Mexico are
after valuable emeralds and an adventur-
ing American joins their ranks. Ryan
O'Neal, Anne Archer, Omar Sharif, Philip
Stone. w. Edward Anhalt, Ray Hassett,
Anthony Simmons, Robert de Laurentis,
N-adap. Gerald Browne, d. Ernest Day.

ACTION: Heist Stories; **ROMANCE:** Jewel
Thieves; Mexico; Coulda Been Good

The Green Man, 1991, 150m, ★★★/$$,
BBC/A&E. The owner of a roadside inn
in England has ghosts floating about
which seem like only legends until murder occurs. Albert Finney, Sarah Berger,
Linda Marlowe. w. Malcolm Bradbury, N-
adap. Kingley Amis, d. Elijah Moshinsky.

**SUSPENSE: MYSTERY: MURDER: MUR-
DER MYSTERY:** Ghost Stories;
Alcoholics; Hotels; Race Against Time;
TV Movies
(The Dark Age; The Uninvited)

Green Mansions, 1959, 104m, ★★★/$$,
MGM/MGM-UA. An explorer in a fantasy

Amazon world discovers a "noble savage"
girl named Rema, who takes him to an
enchanted community in the jungle.
Anthony Perkins, Audrey Hepburn, Lee J.
Cobb, Henry Silva. w. Dorothy Kingsley,
N-adap. W. H. Hudson, d. Mel Ferrer.

ADVENTURE: Fantasy; **MELODRAMA:
ROMANCE:** Journies; Quests; Jungle
Life; Amazon River; Fairy Tales;
Curiosities; Allegorical Stories; Female
Screenwriters
(Ed: Strange by any standard)

The Green Pastures, 1936, 93m,
★★★1/2/$$$, WB/MGM-UA. Elderly
blacks down South tell their own unique
versions of Old Testament tales. Rex
Ingram, Oscar Polk, Eddie Anderson,
Frank Wilson, George Reed. w. P-adap.
Marc Connelly, SS-adap. Roark Bradford,
d. William Keighley, Marc Connelly.

COMEDY DRAMA: Storytellers; Black
Casts; Southerns; Biblical Stories; Elderly
People; Multiple Stories; Angels; Heaven;
Hidden Gems; Revisionist Films
(Hallelujah!; Song of the South; Cabin in
the Cotton)
(Ed: Controversial politically, but hard to
fault otherwise)

The Green Slime, 1968, 90m, ★★/$,
MGM/MGM-UA. An asteroid is headed
for Earth and before it has come an alien
blob green slime. Robert Horton, Richard
Jaeckel. d. Kinji Fukansaku.

SCI-FI: Camp; Meteors; Aliens-Outer
Space, Evil; Parasites; Cult Films;
Japanese Films
(What's Up, Tiger Lily?)
(Ed: Groovy theme song if nothing else)

The Green Years, 1946, 127m,
★★★/$$$, MGM/MGM-UA. A boy
undergoes a strict upbringing in Ireland
and later goes to America to live with his
free-spirited grandfather, who shows him
a whole new world. Charles Coburn
(BSActor), Dean Stockwell, Tom Drake,
Beverly Tyler, Hume Cronyn, Gladys
Cooper, Selena Royle, Jessica Tandy,
Richard Haydn. w. Robert Ardrey, Sonya
Levien, N-adap. A. J. Cronin, d. Victor
Saville. BB&WCin. Oscars: 2-0.

**MELODRAMA: COMEDY DRAMA:
CHILDREN'S: FAMILY:** Boys; Fish out
of Water Stories; Fathers-Surrogate;
Children-Adopted; Men and Boys;
Grandfathers-Fascinating; Ireland; Irish
People; Hidden Gems
(Lies My Father Told Me; Little Lord
Fauntleroy)

(Ed: Stockwell then starred in *The Boy with Green Hair*)

Greenwich Village, 1944, 82m, ★★¹/2/$$, 20th/NA. A country bumpkin making a living as a composer allows his classical piece to be given a jazz performance. Carmen Miranda, Don Ameche, William Bendix, Vivian Blaine, Felix Bressart, Tony and Sally De Marco, Betty Comden. w. Michael Fessier, Ernest Pagano, d. Walter Lang.

MUSICALS: COMEDY: Musical Comedy; Musicians; Greenwich Village; Fish out of Water Stories; City vs. Country; Jazz Life; Forgotten Films

Greetings, 1968, 88m, ★★¹/2/$, Ind/Vidmark, R/S-P. A coward tries every machination in the book to escape military service after he's drafted during the Vietnam War. Jonathan Warden, Robert de Niro, Gerrit Graham, Megan McCormik. w. Charles Hirsch, Brian de Palma, d. Brian de Palma.

COMEDY: Comedy of Errors; Cowards; Vietnam War; Vietnam War Era; Military Comedy; Overlooked at Release; Cult Films

(Hair; Home Movies)

Gregory's Girl, 1981, 91m, ★★★/$$$, Goldwyn/Goldwyn, PG/S. A Scottish boy falls for the tomboyish girl on their school's soccer team and a first love begins. Gordon John Sinclair, Dee Hepburn, Jake D'Arcy, Claire Grogin. w. d. Bill Forsyth.

COMEDY DRAMA: ROMANCE: Romantic Comedy; Love-First; Tomboys; Soccer; High School Life; Scotland; Sleeper Hits; Writer-Directors; Ind Films

(Circle of Friends; Georgy Girl)

Gremlins, 1984, 111m, ★★★/$$$$, Amblin-WB/WB, PG/V. A father brings home a little pet with special powers and special procreative abilities allowing it to multiply and wreak havoc on small-town America. Zach Galligan, Polly Holliday, Hoyt Axton. w. Chris Columbus, d. Joe Dante.

HORROR: COMEDY: Horror Comedy; Black Comedy; CHILDREN'S: Magic; Pet Stories; Monsters-Animal; Small-town Life; Christmas; Blockbusters

Gremlins 2: The New Batch, 1990, 105m, ★★★/$$, WB/WB, PG-13/V-B&G. The furry little mogwai from the first film proliferate at the lab of a mad scientist and take over a mall. w. Charlie Haas, d. Joe Dante.

HORROR: COMEDY: Horror Comedy; Black Comedy; CHILDREN'S: Magic; Pet Stories; Monsters-Animal; Movie Theaters; Overlooked at Release; Flops-Major; Hidden Gems

(The Goonies; The Golden Child; Critters)

(Ed: Disappeared off the box-office radar but in some ways is more wicked than the first)

The Grey Fox, 1982, 92m, ★★★/$$, UA/Fox. An incorrigible old outlaw, released from prison after a long sentence, returns to his life of crime. Richard Farnsworth (BSActor), Jackie Burroughs, Ken Pogue, Wayne Robson. w. John Hunter, d. Philip Borsos. Oscars: 1-0.

WESTERNS: Heist Stories; Ex-Convicts; Thieves; True Stories; Fugitives from the Law; Elderly Men; One Last Time; Hidden Gems; Canada; Canadian Films

(Comes a Horseman; Going in Style; Breaking In)

Greystoke: The Legend of Tarzan, 1984, 130m, ★★★/$$$$, WB/WB, PG/S-V-MRN. A more faithful, realistic telling of the Tarzan legend from the jungles of Africa to the manor of Lord Greystoke in England. Christopher Lambert, Ralph Richardson (BSActor), Andie MacDowell (dubbed by Glenn Close). w. P.H. Vazak (Robert Towne), Michael Austin (BAScr), N-adap. Edgar Rice Burroughs (*Tarzan of the Apes*), d. Hugh Hudson. Oscars: 2-0.

ADVENTURE: MELODRAMA: Fish out of Water Stories; Jungle Life; Primates; Raised by Animals; Comic Heroes; Legends; City vs. Country; Royalty-Sudden; Africa; England; Sleeper Hits

(Tarzan, the Ape Man)

(Ed: After a rousing, beautiful start, things get a little out of whack, and MacDowell's dubbing doesn't help matters. P. H. Vazak is reportedly Towne's dog's name)

Griffin and Phoenix, A Love Story, 1976, 110m, ★★-/$$$, ABC/Fox. Two people dying of cancer flee their families and have an affair while facing death. Peter Falk, Jill Clayburgh, Dorothy Tristan. d. Daryl Duke.

DRAMA: MELODRAMA: Disease Stories; ROMANCE: TRAGEDY: Romance with Married Person; Runaways; TV Movies; Old-Fashioned Recent Films

(Love Story; Dying Young)

The Grifters, 1990, 105m, ★★★★/$$$, HBO-Miramax/HBO, R/P-S-V-FN. A con artist (John Cusack) is beaten up and his mother (Anjelica Huston, BActress) comes to see him. Sparks fly between he and his duplicitous girlfriend (Annette Bening, BSActress), leading to a showdown. w. Donald Westlake (BAScr), adap. Jim Thompson, d. Stephen Frears (BDirector). Oscars: 4-0.

DRAMA: SUSPENSE: TRAGEDY: MURDER: Crime Drama; Film Noir-Modern; Con Artists; Heist Stories; Mothers & Sons; Romance-Triangles; Lover Family Dislikes; Bimbos; Mob Girls; Oedipal Stories; Body Switching; Jim Thompson-esque; Clever Plots & Endings; Los Angeles; Abused Women; Sleeper Hits

(After Dark, My Sweet; Delusion)

Grizzly, 1976, 91m, ★/$, Film Ventures Internationall/Media. A bear kills campers one by one in a national forest. Christopher George, Andrew Prine, Richard Jaeckel, Joan McCall. w. Harvey Flaxman, David Sheldon, d. William Girdler.

HORROR: SUSPENSE: Monsters-Animal; Animal Stories; Camping; Unintentionally Funny; Rogue Plots; Kill the Beast

(Jaws; Bigfoot)

Gross Anatomy, 1989, 107m, ★★¹/2/$, Touchstone/Touchstone, PG-13/P-S. The lives of several medical students making their way through the grind, one inspired by a female professor who's unable to help herself with her knowledge. Matthew Modine, Christine Lahti. w. Ron Nyswaner, d. ???

DRAMA: Medical School; Medical Drama; Doctors; Depression; Dreams; Teachers; Teachers & Students; Death-Impending; Disease Stories; Men Proving Themselves; Quiet Little Films; Coulda Been Good

(Vital Signs; The Interns; The New Interns; The Paper Chase)

(Ed: More realistic than *The Interns* or *Dr. Kildare*, but not particularly entertaining, either)

Groundhog Day, 1993, 123m, ★★★/$$$$, WB/WB, PG/P-S. A weatherman in Pittsburgh (Bill Murray) goes to cover a story on the famous groundhog hole on Groundhog Day and winds up reliving the same day in many different ways before his ordeal is over. Andie MacDowell, Chris Elliott, Stephen Tobolowsky. w. Harold Ramis, Daniel Rubin, d. Harold Ramis.

COMEDY: COMEDY DRAMA: ROMANCE: Romantic Comedy; Romance-Boy Wants Girl; Romance-

Reluctant; Capra-esque; American Myth; Small-town Life; Clever Plots & Endings; Episodic Stories; Flashbacks; Nightmares; Sleeper Hits

Ground Zero, 1987, 107m, ★★/$, Ind/Video Treasures, R. A photographer begins a dangerous journey unraveling the mystery of his father's death thirty years before. Colin Friels, Jack Thompson, Donald Pleasence, Natalie Bate. w. Jan Sardi, Mac Gudgeon, d. Michael Pattinson, Bruce Myles.

DRAMA: MYSTERY: Fathers & Sons; Photographers; Conspiracy; Death-Dealing with; British Films

The Groundstar Conspiracy, 1972, 96m, ★★1/2/$, U/MCA-U. A scientist at a secret government lab survives a horrible explosion but contracts amnesia. George Peppard, Michael Sarrazin, James Olson, Christine Belford, Tim O'Connor. w. Matthew Howard, N-adap. L. P. Davies (*The Alien*), d. Lamont Johnson.

SUSPENSE: MYSTERY: SCI-FI: Conspiracy; Amnesia; Detective Stories; Scientists; Experiments; Government as Enemy; Cosmetic Surgery

The Group, 1966, 150m, ★★★1/2/$$, UA/Fox. The journeys of several Vassar women's college graduates during the 30s as they begin their chic and unusual lives in New York. Joanna Pettet, Candice Bergen, Joan Hackett, Jessica Walter, Kathleen Widdoes, Elizabeth Hartman, Mary Robin-Redd, Larry Hagman, Richard Mulligan, Hal Holbrook, Robert Emhardt, James Broderick. w. Sidney Buchman, N-adap. Mary McCarthy, d. Sidney Lumet.

DRAMA: Ensemble Films; Ensembles-Female; College Life; Reunions; Lesbians; Rich People; Friendships-Female; Young Women; New York Life; 1930s; Beautiful People; Female Protagonists; Hidden Gems
(Old Acquaintance; Rich and Famous; Uncommon Women and Others; St. Elmo's Fire)
(Ed: This may not be great, but compare this to the brat pack garbage of the 80s and realize how far standards have dropped)

Grumpier Old Men, 1995, 105m, ★★★/$$$$, WB/WB, PG-13/P-S-MN. When a sexy Italian restauranteur (Sophia Loren) arrives in town, the feud between the old guys is revived even though their children are getting married

to each other and one of the guys has married a gorgeous sculptress/professor (Ann-Margret). Jack Lemmon, Walter Matthau, Sophia Loren, Ann-Margret, Daryl Hannah, Kevin Pollak, Burgess Meredith. w. Mark Steven Johnson, d. Howard Deutch.

COMEDY: Elderly Men; Men Fighting Over Women; Italians
(The Odd Couple; The Fortune Cookie; Kotch; Buddy, Buddy)

Grumpy Old Men, 1993, 104m, ★★★1/2/$$$$, WB/WB, PG-13/EP-S. Two feuding old men who happen to be neighbors have their world turned upside down when a younger 50-something bombshell moves in-literally-between them and vies for their attention. Jack Lemmon, Walter Matthau, Ann-Margret, Burgess Meredith, Daryl Hannah, Kevin Spacey, Kevin Pollak, Ossie Davis, Bucky Henry. w. Mark Steven Johnson, d. Donald Petrie.

COMEDY: ROMANCE: Romantic Comedy; Men Fighting Over Women; Romance-Older Men/Younger Women; Romance-Elderly; Elderly Men; Snow Settings; Midwestern Life; Small-Town Life; Feuds; Friendships-Male; Practical Jokers; Bathroom Humor; Sleeper Hits
SEQUEL: Grumpier Old Men
(The Fortune Cookie; The Odd Couple; Buddy, Buddy)

Guadalcanal Diary, 1943, 93m, ★★★/$$$, 20th/CBS-Fox. A key battle in the Pacific theatre of World War II, Marines must take this vital base from the Japs. Preston Foster, Lloyd Nolan, William Bendix, Richard Conte, Anthony Quinn, Richard Jaeckel, Roy Roberts, Minor Watson, Ralph Byrd, Miles Mander. w. Lamar Trotti, NF-adap. Richard Tregaskis, d. Lewis Seiler.

DRAMA: ACTION: Action Drama; War Stories; World War II Stories; True Stories; Soldiers; Japanese as Enemy
(The Sands of Iwo Jima; Midway)

The Guardian, 1990, 98m, ★★/$, U/MCA-U, R/V-P-FN. A nanny turns out to be a tree worshipping weirdo who wants to sacrifice her boss' kids to an oak. Jenny Seagrove, Dwier Brown, Carey Lowell, Brad Hull, Miguel Ferrer, Natalia Nogulich, Pamela Brull, Gary Swanson. w. Stephen Volk, Dan Greenburg, N-adap. Dan Greenburg (*The Nanny*), d. William Friedkin.

HORROR: SUSPENSE: Children in Jeopardy; Babysitters; Occult; Satanism; Evil Women; Babysitters-Evil; Camp; Unintentionally Funny
(The Hand That Rocks the Cradle; The Turn of the Screw [1991]; The Tie That Binds)

Guarding Tess, 1994, 98m, ★★-/$$$, Tri-Star/Col-Tri, PG-13/P-V. When a Secret Service agent has to stick it out guarding a cantankerous former First Lady, his loyalty to her is tested when she is kidnapped. Shirley MacLaine, Nicolas Cage, Austin Pendleton, Edward Albert. w. Peter Torokvei, Hugh Wilson, d. Wilson.

COMEDY DRAMA: MELODRAMA: Rescue Drama; Friendships Between Sexes; Bodyguards; Presidents; Secret Service; Stern Women; Mean Women; Kidnappings; Good Premise Unfulfilled; Coulda Been Great
(Driving Miss Daisy)
(Ed: Opened #1 then faded quickly due to the maudlin third act and lack of comedy, all else which was highly reminiscent of *Driving Miss Daisy* anyway. The actors are the only attraction)

The Guardsman, 1931, 83m, ★★★/$$$, MGM/MGM-UA. An actor poses as a stranger to try to woo his wife and test her moral character. Alfred Lunt, Lynn Fontaine, Roland Young, Zasu Pitts, Maude Eburne, Herman Bing, Ann Dvorak. w. Ernest Vajda, Claudine West, P-adap. Ferenc Molnar, d. Sidney Franklin.

COMEDY DRAMA: Marriage Comedy; Impostors; Actors; Cheating Women; Disguises; Faded Hits; Hidden Gems
MUSICAL REMAKE: The Chocolate Soldier
(Ed: A phenomenal success on stage; cute but very dated)

Guess Who's Coming to Dinner, 1967, 128m, ★★★1/2/$$$$$, Columbia/RCA-Col. A wealthy couple's white daughter brings home a sophisticated black man and they must deal with the fact the couple has married behind their backs. Katharine Hepburn (**BActress**), Spencer Tracy (BActor), Sidney Poitier, Katharine Houghton (BSActress), Beah Richards (BSActress), Isabel Sanford. w. William Rose (**BOScr**), d. Stanley Kramer (BDirector). BPicture, BArt, BEdit. Oscars: 9-2.

DRAMA: MELODRAMA: Marriage Drama; Social Drama; Race Relations; Romance-

Interracial; Romance-Middle-Aged; Parallel Stories; Black vs. White; Black Men; Newlyweds; Dinner Parties; One Day Stories; Blockbusters; Tracy & Hepburn (The Birdcage; La Cage Aux Folles; Norman, Is That You?; The Defiant Ones; Lilies of the Field; Adam's Rib; Desk Set; Goodbye, Columbus; White Palace)

(Ed: When you look at Hepburn's tear-filled eyes, it's as if she's powerless to do anything but say goodbye to Tracy as he gives his great speech toward the end. He died days after shooting ended)

Guest in the House, 1944, 121m, ★★1/2/$$, Hunt Stromberg-Ind/Nos. An apparently harmless woman enters the home of a middle class family and proceeds to tear their lives apart. Anne Baxter, Ralph Bellamy, Aline MacMahon, Ruth Warrick, Scott McKay, Jerome Cowan, Marie McDonald, Percy Kilbride, Margaret Hamilton. w. Ketti Frings, P-adap. Dale Eunson, Hegar Wilde (*Dear Evelyn*), d. John Brahm. BOScore. Oscars: 1-0.
SUSPENSE: MELODRAMA: Malicious Menaces; Roommates from Hell; Mean Women; Family Drama; Forgotten Films; Curiosities; Ahead of Its Time; Female Screenwriters
(Leave Her to Heaven; All About Eve; The Nanny)

Guest Wife, 1945, 90m, ★★★/$$, UA/Republic. A man "rents" the wife of his neighbors when he needs to be married for a business trip. Claudette Colbert, Don Ameche, Dick Foran, Charles Dingle, Grant Mitchell. w. Bruce Manning, John Klorer, d. Sam Wood. BOScore. Oscars: 1-0.
COMEDY: ROMANCE: Romantic Comedy; FARCE: Screwball Comedy; Marriage Comedy; Dates-Hired; Swapping Partners; Marriages-Fake; Misunderstandings; Forgotten Films; Coulda Been Great; Hidden Gems
(Good Neighbor Sam)

A Guide for the Married Man, 1967, 91m, ★★★/$$, 20th/Fox. A sleazeball tells his married friend how to play the field, but it doesn't work so easily. Walter Matthau, Inger Stevens, Robert Morse, Sue Anne Langdon, Lucille Ball, Art Carney, Jack Benny, Polly Bergen, Joey Bishop, Carl Reiner, Phil Silver, Jeffrey Hunter, Terry-Thomas. w. Frank Tarloff, d. Gene Kelly.

COMEDY: Marriage Comedy; Playboys; Cheating Men; Promiscuity; Dating Scene; Time Capsules; Actor Directors; Forgotten Films; Coulda Been Great; Hidden Gems
(Loving; A New Life; About Last Night; California Suite)

Guilty as Charged, 1991, 95m, ★★/$, Col/Col, R/V-P. A crazed megalomaniac hell-bent on avenging his enemies builds an electric chair in his home to dispatch them. Rod Steiger, Lauren Hutton, Heather Graham, Lyman Ward, Isaac Hayes, Zelda Rubinstein. w. Charles Gale, d. Sam Irvin.
HORROR: Psycho Killers; Vigilantes; Revenge; Rich People; Executions
(The Star Chamber)

Guilty as Sin, 1993, 110m, ★★★/$$$, Hollywood/Hollywood, R/P-V-S. A woman lawyer (Rebecca DeMornay) takes on a case in which a philandering gigolo (Don Johnson) is accused of throwing his wife out a window, but was it really suicide as he first claims, or is he the ultimate sociopath? (One of the better hybrids of its kind.) Jack Warden. w. Larry Cohen, d. Sidney Lumet.
SUSPENSE: Legal Thriller; Psychological Thriller; MURDER: MYSTERY: MURDER MYSTERY: Women in Jeopardy; Accused Unjustly; Framed?; Saving Oneself; Murderer-Debate to Reveal; Lawyer vs. Client; Perfect Crimes; Clever Plots & Endings; Liars; Cheating Men; Underrated; Sleeper Hits
REMAKES/RETREAD of: Jagged Edge, Criminal Law
(Jagged Edge; Criminal Law; Black Widow; Never Talk to Strangers; Primal Fear)
(Ed: Despite it's derivations, it manages to put an original and consistent twist on things)

Guilty by Suspicion, 1990, 105m, ★★★/$, WB/WB, PG. A film director is blacklisted during the McCarthy witch hunts and finds all of his friends turning on him out of fear. Robert De Niro, Annette Bening, George Wendt, Patricia Wettig, Sam Wanamaker. w. d. Irwin Winkler.
DRAMA: Social Drama; Hollywood Life; McCarthy Era; Ostracism; Conformism; Ethics; Writers; Writer-Directors
(The Front; Daniel; The Way We Were)
(Ed: Looks good and could've been great, but the fictitious story based on amalgamations lessens the impact)

Guilty Conscience, 1985, 100m, ★★★1/2/$$$, CBS-Viacom/Viacom. A man (Anthony Hopkins) cheating on his wife (Blythe Danner) may be in trouble when his mistress (Swoosie Kurtz) teams up with the wife to do him in. w. Richard Levinson, William Link, d. Glenn Jordan.
SUSPENSE: MURDER: Clever Plots & Endings; Lawyers; Cheating Men; Romance-Triangles; Marriage on the Rocks; Revenge; Deaths-Faked; Mistresses; Turning the Tables; TV Movies; Hidden Gems
(Murder By Natural Causes; Diabolique; Kiss and Tell)

Gulliver's Travels, 1939, 74m, ★★★/$$$, Par/Nos. An animated version of the popular picaresque novella of the hero's adventures in strange lands and among strange beings. d. Dave Fleischer, N-adap. Jonathan Swift.

Gulliver's Travels, 1976, 81m, ★★1/2/$, EMI-U/VCI. A watered-down, simple version. voices of Richard Harris, Catherine Schell, Norman Shelley. w. Don Black, d. Peter Hunt.
Cartoons; CHILDREN'S: FAMILY: SATIRE: ADVENTURE: Stranded on an Island; Shipwrecks; Animation-Partial; Little People; Classic Literary Adaptations
RETELLING: The Three Worlds of Gulliver
TV REMAKE: Miniseries (1996)

The Gumball Rally, 1976, 107m, ★★1/2/$$, WB/WB. A race from New York to Long Beach attracts folks of every (racing) stripe. Michael Sarrazin, Normann Burton, Gary Busey, John Durren, Susan Flannery. w. Leon Capetanos, d. Chuck Bail.
ACTION: COMEDY: Action Comedy; Car Racing; Competitions; Ensemble Films; Road Movies; Road to California
(Cannonball Run; Cherry 2000)

Gumshoe, 1972, 88m, ★★★/$, Col/NA. A Liverpudlian man has fantasies of being a Humphrey Bogart–like detective and gets to act them out on a real murder case at the bingo game he calls. Albert Finney, Billie Whitelaw, Fulton Mackay, Frank Finlay, Janice Rule. w. Neville Smith, d. Stephen Frears.
COMEDY DRAMA: MYSTERY: Comic Mystery; Fantasies; Detective Stories; Detectives-Private; Detectives-Amateur; British Films
(Billy Liar; Play It Again, Sam)

Gun Crazy, 1950, 87m, ★★★½/$$, U/MCA-U. A nasty young redneck girl wants the good life and gets a poor schmuck to shoot his way to it, but not without major repercussions. John Dall, Peggy Cummins, Morris Carnovsky, Berry Kroeger. w. Dalton Trumbo, Mackinlay Kantor, d. Joseph H. Lewis.

Gun Crazy, 1992, ★★½/$$, Showtime/Academy. Remake of the classic film noir B-flick where the bad girl taunts her boyfriend into a life of crime on the run. Drew Barrymore, James LeGros, Billy Drago, Ione Skye. w. Matthew Bright, d. Tamara Davis. Female Directors; TV Movies

ACTION: Crime Drama; **SUSPENSE:** Film Noir; Criminal Couples; Outlaw Road Movies; Road Movies; Evil Women; Criminals-Female; Dangerous Women; Romance-Dangerous; **MURDER:** Murder-Coerced; Fugitives from the Law; Chase Stories; Hiding Out; Thieves; Cult Films; Hidden Gems

REMAKE: TV (Showtime, 1992)
(Bonnie & Clyde; Badlands; True Romance; Kalifornia; They Live by Night)

A Gunfight, 1970, 90m, ★★½/$, Ind/Video Treasures, R/V. Two outlaws become celebrities. It reaches its apex when they stage a gunfight for money. Kirk Douglas, Johnny Cash, Karen Black, Raf Vallone. w. Harold Jack Bloom, d. Lamont Johnson.

WESTERNS: Gunfighters; Competitions; Duels; Westerns-Neo; Forgotten Films; Curiosities

Gun Fury, 1953, 83m, ★★½/$$, Col/Col. A man whose fiancee is kidnapped during a stagecoach hijacking goes after her abductors. Rock Hudson, Donna Reed, Phil Carey, Lee Marvin, Neville Brand. w. Irving Wallace, Roy Huggins, d. Raoul Walsh.

WESTERNS: Western-Revenge; Hijackings; Kidnappings; Rescue Drama; Chase Stories; Manhunts; Women in Jeopardy; Forgotten Films; 3-D Movies

Gunfight at the O.K. Corral, 1957, 122m, ★★★/$$$$, Par/Par. The events leading up to the famous showdown between the Clanton Gang and Wyatt Earp with Doc Holliday. Burt Lancaster, Kirk Douglas, Jo Van Fleet, Rhonda Fleming, John Ireland, Frank Faylen, Earl Holliman. w. Leon Uris, d. John Sturges.

WESTERNS: ACTION: Gunfighters; Men in Conflict; True Stories; Wyatt Earp; Duels; Faded Hits
(Wyatt Earp; Tombstone; The Tin Star)

The Gunfighter, 1950, 84m, ★★★/$$$, 20th/Fox. An aging outlaw tries to give it up but gets drawn into one last gun battle. Gregory Peck, Helen Westcott, Millard Mitchell, Jean Parker, Karl Malden, Skip Homeier, Mae Marsh. w. William Bowers, William Sellers, d. Henry King.

WESTERNS: Gunfighters; One Last Time; Retirement; Small-town Life; Starting Over; Forgotten Films

Gunga Din, 1939, 117m, ★★★½/$$$$$, RKO/Turner. Three army veterans seek excitement as fun-loving mercenaries try to stop an uprising in old India and are helped by their mascot waterboy, Gunga Din who ironically comes to the rescue. Cary Grant, Victor McLaglen, Douglas Fairbanks Jr., Sam Jaffe, Eduardo Ciannelli, Joan Fontaine, Montagu Love, Cecil Kallaway. w. Joel Sayre, Fred Guiol, Ben Hecht, Charles McArthur, (Poem)-adap. Rudyard Kipling, d. George Stevens.

ACTION: ADVENTURE: COMEDY: Action Comedy; Comic Adventure; War Stories; Political Unrest; Mercenaries; Soldiers; Boys; India; Heroes-Unlikely; Men and Boys; Ensemble Films; Ensembles-Male; Blockbusters
(The Four Feathers; The Rains Came; Lord Jim)

Gung Ho! 1943, 88m, ★★½/$$$, Par/Republic. In World War II, the U.S. Marines see action in the Pacific. Randolph Scott, Grace MacDonald, Alan Curtis, Noah Beery Jr., J. Carrol Naish, David Bruce, Peter Coe, Robert Mitchum. w. Lucien Hubbard, NF-adap. Captain W. S. LeFrancois USMC, d. Ray Enright.

ACTION: War Stories; World War II Stories; Pacific Ocean; Japanese as Enemy

Gung Ho, 1986, 111m, ★★½/$$, Par/Par, PG. A Japanese car manufacturer's factory in the U.S. hires managers from Japan and their style clashes with that of the American workers. Michael Keaton, Gedde Watanabe, George Wendt, Mimi Rogers, John Turturro. w. Lowell Ganz, Babaloo Mandel, d. Ron Howard.

COMEDY: COMEDY DRAMA: Power Struggles; Ordinary People Stories; Factory Life; Working Class; Japanese People; Japanese as Enemy; Coulda Been Good
(Alamo Bay; Blue Collar; Parenthood; Mr. Mom)

The Gun in Betty Lou's Handbag, 1992, 90m, ★★★/$, Hollywood/ Hollywood, PG-13/P-S-EV. A cute but uneven, bizarrely violent comedy about a librarian (Penelope Ann Miller) who finds a gun used to murder a mobster (whose toupee flies off when shot in the forehead) and packs it in her purse to show she can handle herself, but winds up also defiantly confessing to the murder because no one thinks she's capable of it. Alfre Woodard, Eric Thal, Cathy Moriarty. w. Grace Cary Bickley, d. Allan Moyle.

COMEDY: FARCE: MURDER: Black Comedy; Mob Stories; Mob Comedy; Ordinary People vs. Criminals; Young Women; Librarians; Identities-Mistaken; Accused Unjustly; Women Proving Themselves; Liars; Violence-Sudden; Ordinary People Stories; Small-town Life; Small-town Scandals; Wallflowers; Southerns; Rednecks; Comedy & Violence; Coulda Been Great; Female Protagonists; Female Screenwriters

REMAKE/RETREAD OF: True Confession (1937).
(Nothing Sacred)
(Ed: Totally marred by a third act with violence and a subsequent dark tone in what is otherwise a goofy, not satirical comedy-unlike, for instance, *Sugarland Express*)

The Gunrunner, 1984, 92m, ★/$, Ind/Sultan. A bootlegger gets involved in the Chinese rebellion during the 20s. Kevin Costner, Sara Botsford. d. Nardo Castillo.

DRAMA: Bootlegging; Political Unrest; Roaring 20s; Arms Dealers; Mob Stories; Forgotten Films; China

The Guns of Navarone, 1961, 157m, ★★★/$$$$, Col/RCA-Col. Commando soldiers stealth about World War II Europe trying to destroy Nazi weaponry. Gregory Peck, David Niven, Stanley Baker, Anthony Quinn, Anthony Quayle, James Darren Gia Scala, Richard Harris, Irene Papas, Bryan Forbes. w. Carl Foreman (BAScr), N-adap. Alistair Maclean, d. J. Lee-Thompson (BDirector). BPicture, BSFX, BOScore, BEdit, BSound. Oscars: 7-0.

ACTION: War Stories; World War II Stories; Special Teams-Military; Spies; Mountain Climbing; Nazi Story; Sabotage; Faded Hits
(Force Ten from Navarone [not really a sequel]; The Bridge on the River Kwai;

The Train; Battle of the Bulge; The Longest Day)

Guns of the Magnificent Seven, 1969, 106m, ★★/$, UA/MGM-UA. A Mexican bandit helps the poor people of his town. When he's captured by evil outlaws, seven soldiers of fortune search him out for the reward. George Kennedy, Monte Markham, Joe Don Baker, James Whitmore, Bernie Casey, Scott Thomas, Reni Santoni, Fernando Rey. w. Herman Hoffman, d. Paul Wendkos.

WESTERNS: ACTION: Action Drama; Mercenaries; Mexico; Revenge; Westerns-Revenge; Ensemble Films; Ensembles-Male; Rescue Drama; Robin Hood Stories
SEQUEL TO: The Magnificent Seven, The Return of the Magnificent Seven
REMAKE OF: Seven Samurai

Gus, 1976, 96m, ★★1/2/$$$, Disney/BV, G. A mule has a special talent for kicking field goals and is hired by a football team for just that purpose. Ed Asner, Don Knotts, Gary Grimes, Tim Conway, Liberty Williams, Bob Crane, Harold Gould, Tom Bosley, Dick Van Patten. w. Arthur Alsberg, Don Nelson, d. Vincent McEveety.

COMEDY: Sports Movies; Football; Animal Stories; **CHILDREN'S:** Faded Hits
(Ed: Big with the kids then, but there wasn't much else that summer)

The Guyana Tragedy: The Story of Jim Jones, 1980, 240m, ★★★/$$$$, CBS/VC Home Entertainment. The story of the rise of the infamous Peoples' Temple cult of San Francisco leading to its mass suicide in South America that shocked the world. Powers Boothe (Emmy winner), Ned Beatty, Randy Quaid, Brad Dourif, Brenda Vaccaro, LeVar Burton, Colleen Dewhurst, James Earl Jones. d. William Graham.

DRAMA: True Stories; Charismatic People; Docudrama; Cults; Religion; Suicidal Tendencies; Murder-Mass; Multiple Stories; Interwoven Stories; TV Movies; Miniseries
(Waco: The David Koresh Story)

A Guy Named Joe, 1943, 120m, ★★★/$$$, MGM/MGM-UA. After he's killed, an ace pilot's ghost comes back to haunt his girlfriend's new beau. Spencer Tracy, Irene Dunne, Ward Bond, Van Johnson, James Gleason, Lionel Barrymore, Barry Nelson, Don Defore. w. Dalton Trumbo, d. Victor Fleming.

COMEDY: COMEDY DRAMA: ROMANCE: Romantic Comedy; Ghosts; Revenge; Romance-Triangles; Widows; Pilots-Military; World War II Era; Jealousy; Nuisances; Hidden Gems
FLIPSIDE TO: Blithe Spirit; **REMAKE:** Always.
(Always; Ghost; Blithe Spirit; Kiss Me Goodbye)

Guys and Dolls, 1955, 150m, ★★★1/2/$$$$, Goldwyn-MGM/MGM-UA. A fast-talking suave and handsome gangster loves to gamble. He loves a challenge so much that he bets his pal he can seduce a chaste Salvation Army worker. In the process, he learns to quote the Bible and gets something he didn't bargain for-love. Marlon Brando, Frank Sinatra, Jean Simmons, Vivian Blaine, Stubby Kaye, B. S. Pully, Robert Keith, Sheldon Leonard, George E. Stone. w. d. Joseph L. Mankiewicz, MP-adap. Jo Swerling, Abe Burrows, SS-adap. Damon Runyon. BCCin, BMScore, BCArt, BCCostume. Oscars: 4-0.

MUSICALS: COMEDY: Musical Comedy; Mob Stories; Mob Comedy; Gambling; Bets; New York Life; Tough Guys & Religious Women; Battle of the Sexes; Street Life; Playboys; Bimbos; Wallflowers; Wallflowers & Hunks; Elusive Women; Virgins; Settling Down
(Pal Joey; Dangerous Liaisons; Dogfight)

Gymkata, 1985, 90m, ★1/2/$, MGM-UA/MGM-UA. PG-13/V. In a small Pacific-rim country, an American ninja arrives ostensibly to enter a physical contest, but he's really there on a secret mission for the U.S. government to install a satellite there. Kurt Thomas, Tetchie Agbayani, Richard Norton, Edward Bell.

w. Charles Robert Carner, N-adap. Dan Tyler Moore (*The Terrible Game*), d. Robert Clouse.

ACTION: Martial Arts; Sports Movies; Olympics; Undercovers; Secret Agents; Camp; Unintentionally Funny
(American Anthem; Diving In)

Gypsy, 1962, 149m, ★★★/$$$, WB/WB. The rise of stripper/dancer Gypsy Rose Lee and the big push her ultimate stage mother gave her in vaudeville, but she apparently pushed a bit too far. Rosalind Russell, Natalie Wood, Karl Malden, James Milhollin. w. Leonard Spigelgass, P-adap. Arthur Laurents, d. Mervyn Le Roy. BCCin, BMScore, BCCostume. Oscars: 3-0.

Gypsy, 1993, 140m, ★★★1/2/$$$$, CBS/Cabin Fever. Bette Midler, Peter Riegert, Ed Asner, Cynthia Gibb, Michael Jeter. w. Arthur Laurents, d. Emile Ardolino. A more faithful adaptation with a more vibrant and capable performer.

MUSICALS: MELODRAMA: Family Drama; Musical Drama; Strippers; Dancers; Stagemothers; Mothers & Daughters; Parents vs. Children; Episodic Stories; Vaudeville; Female Protagonists
(Auntie Mame; Imitation of Life; Funny Girl)

The Gypsy Moths, 1969, 110m, ★★★/$$, MGM/MGM-UA, R/P-S. A group of stunt skydivers work the air show circuit, but their leader finds himself grounded in love in one small town, though tragedy lurks overhead. Burt Lancaster, Deborah Kerr, Gene Hackman, Scott Wilson, William Windom, Bonnie Bedelia. w. William Hanley, N-adap. James Drought, d. John Frankenheimer.

DRAMA: Family Drama; Ordinary People Stories; **ROMANCE:** Romantic Drama; Romance-Middle-Aged; Pilots-Daredevil; Skydiving; Midwestern Life; Small-town Life; Forgotten Films
(The Great Waldo Pepper)

Hackers, 1995, 105m, ★★★/$$, UA/
MGM-UA, PG-13/P-S-V. Computer bank-
ing thieves use a whiz kid computer
hacker and his pals as the fall guys in
their ploy, but can they outhack the bad
guys? Jonny Lee Miller, Angelina Jolie,
Fisher Stevens, Jesse Bradford, Matthew
Lillard, Laurence Mason, Renoly
Santiago, Wordell Pierce, Lorraine
Bracco. w. Rafael Moreu, d. Iain Softley.
SUSPENSE: Chase Stories; Fugitives
from the Law; Teenagers; Bank
Robberies; Love-First; Computer Terror;
Computers; High School Life;
(Sneakers; The Net; War Games)
(Ed: The kids' plot and stars are good,
but the villains are ridiculous)
Hail, Hail, Rock n Roll, 1987, 121m,
★★★/$$, U/MCA-U, PG. Rockumentary
about the legendary rock n roll pioneer
Chuck Berry. Chuck Berry, Eric Clapton,
Etta James, Linda Ronstadt, Robert Cray,
Julian Lennon, Keith Richards, Bo
Diddley, Jerry Lee Lewis, John Lennon,
Bruce Springsteen, Kareem Abdul
Jabbar. d. Taylor Hackford.
Rockumentaries; Documentaries; Concert
Films; Biographies; Rock Stars;
Nostalgia; Singers; 1950s; Black Men
(Great Balls of Fire; FM; American Hot
Wax)
Hail the Conquering Hero, 1944,
101m, ★★★1/2/$$$, Par/Par. A soldier

for whom things didn't go so well in the
war comes home and winds up being
forced into playing hero when he really
didn't do anything heroic. Eddie Bracken,
William Demarest, Ella Raines, Franklin
Pangborn, Elizabeth Patterson, Raymond
Wlaburn, Alan Bridge. w. d. Preston
Sturges.
COMEDY: COMEDY DRAMA: Hoaxes;
Impostors; Soldiers; Heroes-Unwitting;
Heroes-False; Small-Town Life; Secrets-
Keeping; Liars; Hidden Gems
(Greetings; Nothing Sacred; Living It Up;
The Miracle of Morgan's Creek;
Christmas in July)
Hair, 1979, 121m, ★★★/$$, UA/CBS-
Fox, R/S-P-MRN. The long-running
musical about a group of hippies who
welcome a greenhorn off the farm into
their midst. John Savage, Treat Williams,
Beverly D'Angelo, Annie Golden, Nell
Carter, Charlotte Rae. w. Michael Weller,
MP-adap. Galt MacDermot (music) and
Gerome Ragni/James Rado (book), d.
Milos Forman.
MUSICALS: DRAMA: Social Drama;
Musical Drama; Musicals-Hippie; Anti-
Establishment Films; Anti-War Stories;
Vietnam Era; Rebels; 1960s; Psychedelic
Era; Coulda Been Great; Overlooked at
Release; Time Capsules
(Greetings; The Revolutionary)
(Ed: Probably a bit too late for the period

to appreciate itself and a bit too soon for
the nostalgia trip)
The Hairdresser's Husband, 1990,
80m, ★★★/$, Ind/Par, R/S. A homely
and lonely man is obsessed with marrying
a hairdresser to fulfill a long-held fantasy.
Jean Rochefort, Anne Galiena, Roland
Bertin, Maurice Chevit. w. Claude Klotz,
Patrice Leconte, d. Patrice Leconte.
DRAMA: Erotic Drama; Romantic Drama;
Obsessions; Sexual Kinkiness;
Infatuations; Hairdressers; Eccentric
People; Character Studies; French Films;
Curiosities; Hidden Gems; Female
Screenwriters; Female Directors
Hairspray, 1988, 90m, ★★★1/2/$$,
New Line/New Line, PG-13/S. A local
Baltimore version of *American Bandstand*
called the *Corny Collins Show* has always
been segregated, until an overweight girl
who gets ridiculed by the in-crowd leads
a movement to integrate it as a renegade
"hair hopper." Ricki Lake, Divine, Sonny
Bono, Debbie Harry, Ric Ocasek, Pia
Zadora. w. d. John Waters.
COMEDY: MUSICALS: Musical Comedy;
Music Movies; Dancers; Dance Movies;
Spoofs; Black Comedy; Bombs; Compe-
titions; Weight Problems; Men as Women;
Mothers & Daughters; Race Relations;
Bigots; Snobs vs. Slobs; Teen Idols; TV
Life; Nostalgia; Baltimore; 1960s
(Cry Baby; Bye Bye Birdie; Polyester)

The Hairy Ape, 1944, 91m, ★★1/2/$, Ind/Nos. The hulking fireman on a steamer is slighted by a dandy passenger and plans to murder him. William Bendix, Susan Hayward, John Loder, Dorothy Comingore, Roman Bohnen. w. Jules Levy, P-adap. Eugene O'Neill, d. Alfred Santell.

DRAMA: MURDER: Social Drama; Revenge; Snobs; Class Conflicts; Ships; Classic Literary Adaptations

Half a Sixpence, 1967, 148m, ★★★/$, Par/Par. A rags to riches story in which a working-class decorator inherits a fortune unexpectedly and goes social climbing. Tommy Steele, Julia Foster, Cyril Richard, Penelope Horner. w. P-adap. Beverley Cross, N-adap. H. G. Wells (*Kipps*), d. George Sidney.

MUSICALS: COMEDY DRAMA: Musical Comedy; Heirs; Rags to Riches; Social Climbing; Class Conflicts; Rich People; Rich vs. Poor; England; British Films; Edwardian Era

REMAKE OF: Kipps

Half Moon Street, 1986, 90m, ★★/$, Col/HBO, New Line, R/S-P-V-FFN-MN. An educated woman must sell her body to live comfortably. One of her customers leads her into Middle Eastern intrigue. Sigourney Weaver, Michael Caine, Patrick Kavanaugh, Keith Buckley. w. Bob Swaim, Edward Behr, N-adap. Paul Theroux (*Dr. Slaughter*), d. Bob Swaim.

SUSPENSE: Spy Films; Spies; Prostitutes-High Class; Intellectuals; Women in Jeapardy; Diplomats; Assassination Plots; England; Rich People; Coulda Been Good; Female Protagonists

(Blue Ice; Little Drummer Girl; Eyewitness)

(Ed: A muddled mess with good moments and atmosphere, but that's about it)

Hallelujah!, 1929, 106m, ★★★/$$$, MGM/MGM-UA. A freed slave who still must pick cotton to support himself decides to become a preacher after he accidently kills a man. Daniel Haynes, Nina Mae McKinney, William Fountaine, Fannie Belle De Knight. w. Wanda Tuchock, King Vidor, d. King Vidor (BDirector). Oscars: 1-0.

MELODRAMA: Music Movies; Black Casts; Black Men; Southerns; Death-Accidental; **MURDER:** Starting Over; Redemption; Preachers; Guilty Conscience; Slavery; Hidden Gems;

Curiosities; Female Screenwriters (Cabin in the Cotton; Green Pastures)

Hallelujah, I'm a Bum, 1933, 80m, ★★★/$$$, WB/Learning Corp. A bum living in Central Park during the Depression meets an amnesiac woman with whom he falls in love. He then proceeds to help her discover her past. Al Jolson, Harry Langdon, Madge Evans, Frank Morgan. w. S. N. Behrman, Ben Hecht, d. Lewis Milestone.

MELODRAMA: DRAMA: Homeless People; Amnesia; **ROMANCE:** Social Drama; Searches; Missing Persons; Depression Era; New York Life; Time Capsules; Forgotten Films

(Mister Buddwing; Central Park; My Man Godfrey)

The Hallelujah Trail, 1965, 167m, ★★1/2/$$, UA/MGM-UA. A wagon train encounters many obstacles, from Indians to irate farmers, on its way to Denver. Burt Lancaster, Lee Remick, Brian Keith, Jim Hutton, Donald Pleasance, Martin Landau. w. John Gay, N-adap. Bill Gulick, d. John Sturges.

WESTERNS: Wagon Trains; Indians-American, Conflict with; Journies; Epics; Family Drama; Forgotten Films; Historical Drama

Halloween, 1978, 91m, ★★★1/2/$$$$, Ind/Media, R/EV-B&G. Mike Myers, a man who was sent to an asylum for killing his parents as a boy escapes and goes on a killing rampage in his hometown. Donald Pleasence, Jamie Lee Curtis, Nancy Loomis, P. J. Soles. w. John Carpenter, Debra Hill, d. John Carpenter.

HORROR: Rogue Plots; Kill the Beast; Asylums; Prison Escapes; Women in Jeopardy; Psycho Killers; Stalkers; Halloween; Small-Town Life; Rural Horrors; Sleeper Hits; Blockbusters; Cult Films

(The Town That Dreaded Sundown; Friday the 13th SERIES; Asylum; Afraid of the Dark)

Halloween 2, 1981, 92m, ★★1/2/$$$, DEG/MCA-U, R/EV-B&G. Mike Myers escapes again after his second stint in the nuthouse. He kills more people. Donald Pleasence, Jamie Lee Curtis, Charles Cyphers, Jeffrey Kramer. w. John Carpenter, Debra Hill, d. Rick Rosenthal.

HORROR: Rogue Plots; Kill the Beast; Asylums; Prison Escapes; Women in Jeopardy; Psycho Killers; Stalkers; Halloween; Small-Town Life; Rural Horrors

Halloween 3: Season of the Witch, 1983, 98m, ★★/$$, DEG/Lorimar, MCA-U, R/EV-B&G. An evil Gepetto type makes possessed toys that cause people to act strangely and kill people. Tom Atkins, Stacey Nelkin, Dan O'Herlihy, Michael Currie. w. d. Tommy Lee Wallace.

HORROR: Monsters-Toys/Dolls as; **MURDER:** Serial Killers; Possessions; Psycho Killers; Witchcraft; Kill the Beast; Rogue Plots

(Child's Play; Trilogy of Terror)

Halloween 4: The Return of Michael Myers, 1988, 88m, ★★/$, 20th/Fox, R/EV-B&G. The original creep is back from a coma. Apparently that's why he couldn't make the third installment. Donald Pleasence, Ellie Cornell, Danielle Harris, Michael Pataki. w. Alan B. McElroy, Dhani Lipsius, Larry Rattner, Benjamin Ruffner, d. Dwight H. Little.

HORROR: Rogue Plots; Kill the Beast; Asylums; Prison Escapes; Women in Jeopardy; Psycho Killers; Stalkers; Small-Town Life; Rural Horrors; Comas

Halloween 5: The Revenge of Michael Myers, 1989, 96m, ★1/2/$, Ind/Fox, R/EV-B&G. A small girl has clairvoyant powers and is psychically connected to Mike Myers. She is used by police and others to track him down. Donald Pleasence, Danielle Harris, Wendy Kaplan, Ellie Cornell. w. Michael Jacobs, Dominique Othenin-Girard, Shem Bitterman, d. Dominique Othenin-Girard.

HORROR: Rogue Plots; Kill the Beast; Asylums; Prison Escapes; Women in Jeopardy; Psycho Killers; Stalkers; Small-Town Life; Rural Horrors; Psychics; Good Premise Unfulfilled; Female Directors; Female Screenwriters

Hamburger Hill, 1987, 110m, ★★1/2/$, Par/Par, R/EV-P. A troup of greenhorns gets "on-the-job training" in Vietnam with tragic results. Anthony Barrie, Michael Patick Boatman, Don Cheadle, Michael Dolan, Don James. w. Jim Carabatsos, d. John Irvin.

DRAMA: TRAGEDY: Ensemble Films; Ensembles-Male; War Stories; Vietnam War; Young Men

(Platoon; Hanoi Hilton; Green Eyes; The Killing Fields; The Deerhunter)

Hamlet, 1948, 142m, ★★★★/$$$, U/Par. The famous Shakespeare play in which an indecisive young man learns to take the bull by the horns and avenge his father's death. Laurence Olivier (**BActor**), Eileen Herlie, Basil Sydney, Jean Simmons (**BSActress**), Felix Aylmer, Stanley Holloway, Peter Cushing. w. Alan Dent, P-adap. William Shakespeare, d. Laurence Olivier (**BDirector**). **BPicture, BB&WArt,** BOScore, **BCostume.** Oscars: 7-4.

Hamlet, 1969, 119m, ★★★/$, Woodfall-Filmways-Columbia/Col. A lesser-known version of the famous play. Nicol Williamson, Anthony Hopkins, Gordon Jackson, Judy Parfitt, Marianne Faithfull. w. William Shakespeare, d. Tony Richardson.

Hamlet, 1991, 135m, ★★★/$$, WB/WB, PG-13/V. The famous story of the wishy-washy Danish prince who ultimately avenges his father's death by murdering his uncle. Mel Gibson, Glenn Close, Alan Bates, Paul Scofield, Ian Holm, Helena Bonham-Carter. w. Christopher De Vore, Franco Zeffirelli, P-adap. William Shakespeare, d. Franco Zeffirelli. BArt, BCostume. Oscars: 2-0.

DRAMA: TRAGEDY: MURDER: Family Drama; Avenging Death of Someone; Mothers & Sons; Stepfathers vs. Children; Parents vs. Children; Ghosts; Illusions/Hallucinations; Betrayals; Mental Illness; Nervous Breakdowns; Princes; Castles; Scandinavia; Classic Tragedy
(Othello; The Tempest)

Hammerhead, 1968, 99m, ★★1/2/$$, Col/RCA-Col, PG/V-S. A master criminal meets his match in a James Bond-like secret agent with a furrowed brow. Vince Edwards, Peter Vaughan, Judy Geeson, Diana Dors, Michael Bates, Beverly Adams. w. William Best, Herbert Baker, N-adap. James Mayo, d. David Miller.
ACTION: MYSTERY: Secret Agents; Spies; Playboys; Coulda Been Good; Forgotten Films
(The Wrecking Crew; In Like Flint)

Hammersmith Is Out, 1972, 114m, ★★1/2/$, Cinerama/Prism. A murderous psychopath becomes a powerful leader under the guidance of his caretaker at a mental hospital. Richard Burton, Elizabeth Taylor, Peter Ustinov, Beau Bridges, Leon Ames, George Raft. w. Stanford Whitmore, d. Peter Ustinov.
DRAMA: HORROR: MURDER: Black Comedy; Psycho Killers; Soul-Selling One's; Satan; Evil Men; Asylums; Svengalis; Leaders-Tyrant; Brainwashing;

Psychologists; Mental Illness; Coulda Been Good; Curiosities; Forgotten Films
(Mr. Frost; Faust; X, Y and Zee; Equus)

Hammett, 1982, 97m, ★★★/$, Orion/Orion, PG/V. The famous mystery writer Dashiel Hammett gets into a real-life entanglement that forms the basis of one of his books in San Francisco's Chinatown. Fredric Forrest, Peter Boyle, Marilu Henner, Roy Kinnear, Sylvia Sidney, Samuel Fuller. w. Ross Thomas, Dennis O'Flaherty, N-adap. Joe Gores, d. Wim Wenders.
MYSTERY: MURDER: MURDER MYSTERY: Detective Stories; Biographies-Fictional; Revisionist Films; Writers; San Francisco; Chinese People; Film Noir-Modern; Flops-Major; Overlooked at Release

The Hand, 1960, 104m, ★★1/2/$, Ind/Sinister. A man loses his hand and is later murdered-all of which fits the modus operandi of a psychopathic doctor. Derek Bond, Ronald Leigh-Hunt, Reed de Rouen, Ray Cooney. w. Ray Cooney, Tony Hilton, d. Henry Cass.

The Hand, 1981, 104m, ★★★/$, Orion-WB/Orion, R/EV-B&G. When a cartoonist's hand is severed, his enemies end up mysteriously strangled. Michael Caine, Andrea Marcovicci, Viveca Lindfors. w. d. Oliver Stone. Writer-Directors; **HORROR:** Psychological Thriller; Body Parts; Accidents; **MURDER:** Serial Killers; Murders-One by One; Revenge; Writers; Kill the Beast; Rogue Plots; Camp; Curiosities
(Body Parts; Fingers)

The Hand That Rocks the Cradle, 1992, 110m, ★★★1/2/$$$$, Touchstone/Touchstone, PG-13/EV-P. A yuppie mother who needs extra help finds what seems to be the perfect nanny. But how did the nanny find her? This mysterious babysitter turns out to have a huge grudge with her host family, which she bears out in horrifying ways. Rebecca De Mornay, Matt McCoy, Ernie Hudson. w. Amanda Silver, d. Curtis Hanson.
SUSPENSE: HORROR: MURDER: Psycho Killers; Psychological Thrillers; Murderers-Nice; Babysitters; Babysitters-Evil; Revenge; Revenge on Doctors; Avenging Death of Someone; Sexual Harassment; Suburban Life; Women in Conflict; Jealousy; Babies-Having; Female Protagonists; Murderers-Female; Sleeper Hits; Female Screenwriters

(The Babysitter; The Guardian; The Nanny)

A Handful of Dust, 1988, 118m, ★★★/$, Ind/Col, PG/S. The bored wife of the patriarch of a wealthy old family takes up with a young lad. James Wilby, Kristin Scott Thomas, Rupert Graves, Angelica Huston, Alec Guinness. w. Charles Sturridge, Tim Sullivan, Derek Granger, N-adap. Evelyn Waugh, d. Charles Sturridge.
DRAMA: ROMANCE: Romantic Drama; Romance with Married Person; **SATIRE:** Romance-Class Conflicts; Rich vs. Poor; New in Town; Romance-Older Women/Younger Men; Cheating Women; British Films; Quiet Little Films
(A Summer Story; Maurice; Howards End)

Handle with Care (*Citizen's Band*), 1977, 98m, ★★★/$, Par/Par, PG/P. A C.B. radio nut goes on a crusade against townsfolk who use it for prank calls. Paul LeMat, Candy Clark, Ann Wedgeworth, Ed Begley Jr. w. Paul Brickman, d. Jonathan Demme.
COMEDY: COMEDY DRAMA: Radio Life; Small-Town Life; Rednecks; Ordinary People Stories; Road Movies; Obsessions; Cult Films; Curiosities; Truck Drivers; Coulda Been Great; Hidden Gems
(The Great Smokey Roadblock; Convoy)

The Handmaid's Tale, 1990, 109m, ★★★/$$, Virgin-Miramax/Miramax, HBO, R/S-P. In a right-wing religiously controlled land bearing a striking resemblance to North Carolina, young women still able to have children after generations of toxic poisoning are recruited by elite couples to bear their children; but one particular woman doesn't want to go through with it completely. Natasha Richardson, Robert Duvall, Faye Dunaway, Aidan Quinn, Elizabeth McGovern, Victoria Tennant. w. Harold Pinter, N-adap. Margaret Atwood, d. Volker Schlondorff.
DRAMA: SCI-FI: Futuristic Films; Oppression; Religion; Religious Zealots; Preachers; Leaders-Military; Babies-Having; Mothers-Surrogate; Slavery; Women's Rights; Feminist Films; Female Protagonists; Coulda Been Great; Hidden Gems
(Fahrenheit 451)

Hands Across the Table, 1935, 81m, ★★★/$$$, Par/NA, AMC. A poor fellow pretending to be wealthy via a snooty girlfriend has a pretty manicurist who's set her eye on him but may not want him poor. Carole Lombard, Fred MacMurray, Ralph Bellamy, Astrid Allwyn, Ruth Donnelly, Marie Prevost, William Demarest. w. Norman Krasna, Vincent Lawrence, Herbert Fields, d. Mitchell Leisen.

COMEDY: ROMANCE: Romantic Comedy; Impostors; Rich vs. Poor; Liars; Romance-Mismatched; Romance-Reluctant; Romance-Triangles; Golddiggers; Marrying Up; Ordinary People Stories; Forgotten Films; Hidden Gems
(Breakfast at Tiffany's; The Princess Comes Across)

Hang 'em High, 1967, 114m, ★★★/ $$$, UA/MGM-UA. An outlaw seeks revenge on the gang that had him lynched-which he obvious survived. Clint Eastwood, Inger Stevens, Ed Begley, Pat Hingle. w. Leonard Freeman, Mel Goldberg, d. Ted Post.

WESTERNS: Westerns-Spaghetti; Westerns-Revenge; Revenge; Executions; Lynchings; Dead-Back from the; Vigilantes
(A Fistful of Dollars; For a Few Dollars More)
(Ed: Made by Hollywood, not Italy, but still full of meatballs)

Hangar 18, 1980, 97m, ★★/$$$, Sunn Classic/World Vision. The U.S. government conspires to hide a UFO once it crash-lands on Earth. Darren McGavin, Robert Vaughn, Gary Collins, Philip Abbott. w. Steven Thornley, d. James L. Conway.

SCI-FI: CHILDREN'S: FAMILY: UFOs; Aliens-Outer Space, Good; **MYSTERY:** True or Not?; Conspiracy; Government as Enemy
(Close Encounters; Independence Day)

Hangin' with the Homeboys, 1991, 89m, ★★1/2/$$, New Line/New Line. Four Latino and black teenagers from the Bronx go to Manhattan for a boys' night out, with mixed results. Doug E. Doug, Mario Joyner, John Leguizamo, Nestor Serrano. w. d. Joseph B. Vasquez.

COMEDY: Party Movies; Teenagers; Teenage Movies; Black Casts; Latin People; New York Life; Inner City Life
(House Party; The Jerky Boys)

The Hanging Tree, 1959, 106m, ★★1/2/$$, WB/WB. A doctor kills his unfaithful wife in a Montana miner's camp. Gary Cooper, Maria Schell, Karl Malden, George C. Scott. w. Wendell

Mayes, Halstead Welles, N-adap. Dorothy M. Johnson, d. Delmer Daves.

WESTERNS: MURDER: MELODRAMA: Crimes of Passion; Cheating Women; Murder of Spouse; Doctors; Lynchings; Mining Towns; Forgotten Films

Hangmen Also Die, 1943, 131m, ★★1/2/$, Ind/NA. The Nazis invade Czechoslovakia after an assassination of one of their own. Brian Donlevy, Anna Lee, Walter Brennan, Gene Lockhart, Dennis O'Keefe. w. John Wexley, Fritz Lang, Bertolt Brecht, d. Fritz Lang.

DRAMA: Historical Drama; War Stories; World War II Stories; Nazi Stories; Europe-Eastern; Germany; Assassination Plots; Forgotten Films
(Night Train to Munich; The North Star)

Hanky Panky, 1982, 107m, ★★1/2, Col/Col, PG/S-P. A gang of international terrorists and assassins pursue a female spy. She seeks help from a stranger in a taxi. Gene Wilder, Gilda Radner, Kathleen Quinlan, Richard Widmark. w. Henry Rosenbaum, David Taylor, d. Sydney Poitier.

COMEDY: Action Comedy; Capers; Fugitives from the law; Chase Stories; Conspiracy

REMAKE/RETREAD/FLIPSIDE: North by Northwest
(North by Northwest; Saboteur; Outrageous Fortune)

Hannah and Her Sisters, 1986, 106m, ★★★★/$$$, Orion/Orion, PG-13/P-S. A group of people centering around three sisters intermingle in romance, friendship, and over holidays during a period of time as they all attempt to settle with the right people and find themselves. Woody Allen, Mia Farrow, Dianne Wiest (**BSActress**), Michael Caine (**BSActor**), Carrie Fisher, Barbara Hershey, Maureen O'Sullivan, Max Von Sydow. w. d. Woody Allen (**BOScr**, BDirector). BArt, BEdit. Oscars: 6-3.

COMEDY: COMEDY DRAMA: ROMANCE: FARCE: Romance-On Again/Off Again; Romance-Reluctant; Romance-Triangles; Romance with Married Person; Romance-Clandestine; Women Fighting Over Men; Religion; Artists; Multiple Stories; Interwoven Stories; New York Life; Sleeper Hits
(Manhattan; Husbands and Wives; Crimes and Misdemeanors)

Hanna's War, 1988, 148m, ★★1/2/$, Cannon/Media. A female British secret

service agent during World War II is captured in Yugoslavia and discovered to be Jewish. Ellen Burstyn, Maruschka Detmers, Anthony Andrews, Donald Pleasance. w. d. Menahem Golan, NF-adap. Hanna Senesh (The Diaries of Hanna Senesh), Yoel Palgi (A Great Wind Cometh).

ACTION: TRAGEDY: Spy Films; Spies; Spies-Female; World War II Stories; True Stories; Jewish People; Anti-Semitism; Coulda Been Good

Hannie Caulder, 1971, 85m, ★★1/2/$$, Par/Par, PG/V. A tough western woman takes the law into her own hands when she's raped by three men and blows away everyone in her path. Raquel Welch, Robert Culp, Ernest Borgnine, Strother Martin, Christopher Lee. w. Z. X. Jones (Burt Kennedy, David Haft), d. Burt Kennedy.

WESTERNS: Revenge; Rape/Rapists; Revenge on Rapist; Westerns-Revenge; Criminals-Female; Vigilantes; Female Among Males; Unintentionally Funny; Camp; Curiosities; Role Reversal; Female Protagonists; Heroines
(The Quick and the Dead; Two Mules for Sister Sara; Bandolero)

Hanover Street, 1979, 108m, ★★1/2/$$, Col/RCA-Col, PG/S. During World War II, a fighter pilot and a Red Cross nurse meet and fall in love, solidifying their commitment by getting each other out of tough spots. Harrison Ford, Lesley-Anne Down, Christopher Plummer, Richard Masur. w. d. Peter Hyams.

ROMANCE: MELODRAMA: Pilots-Military; Nurses; World War II Stories; World War II Era; England; Old-Fashioned Recent Films; Writer-Directors
(The Clock; New York, New York; Waterloo Bridge)

Hans Christian Andersen, 1952, 112m, ★★★/$$$, Goldwyn-UA/Goldwyn. A musical biopic of the shoemaker who gets a job making slippers for the best dancer in Copenhagen and delights her with his stories. Danny Kaye, Zizi Jeanmaire, Farley Granger. w. Moss Hart, d. Charles Vidor.

COMEDY: MUSICALS: Musical Comedy; Biographies; Fairy Tales; Writers; **ROMANCE:** Musical Romance; Scandinavia

Hanussen, 1988, 117m, ★★★/$, Triumph/Col-Tri, PG/V-S. A psychic makes predictions which the Nazis use in

the war effort. Klaus Maria Brandauer, Erland Josephson. w. Istvan Szabo, Peter Dobai, d. Szabo. BFLFilm. Oscars: 1-0.
DRAMA: War Stories; World War II Era; Political Drama; Nazi Stories; Psychics; Future-Seeing the
(Mephisto; Colonel Redl)

The Happening, 1967, 101m, ★★★/$$, Col/RCA-Col, PG/V. When a wealthy businessman is kidnapped by a group of hippies for ransom, they're disappointed to discover that no one will pay up. Anthony Quinn, George Maharis, Michael Parks, Faye Dunaway, Robert Walker, Oscar Homolka, Milton Berle. w. Frank R. Pierson, James D. Buchanan, Ronald Austin, d. Eliot Silverstein.
COMEDY: Kidnappings; Comedy of Errors; Teenage Terrors; Florida; Mob Comedy; Hippies; Generation Gap; Curiosities
REMAKE/RETREAD: Ruthless People
(Ruthless People; Lord Love a Duck)

The Happiest Days of Your Life, 1950, 81m, ★★★/$$, British Lion/Home Vision. A girls' school and boys' school get their rosters mixed up to comic effect. Alastair Sim, Margaret Rutherford, Joyce Grenfell, Richard Wattis, Guy Middleton, Muriel Aked. w. Frank Launder, John Dighton, P-adap. John Dighton, d. Frank Launder.
COMEDY: FARCE: Comedy of Errors; Mix-Ups; Misunderstandings; Girls' Schools; Boys' Schools; World War II-Post Era; Forgotten Films; Hidden Gems

The Happiest Millionaire, 1967, 159m, ★★/$$, Disney/Disney, G. An eccentric tycoon pulls his family together in between his flamboyant adventures. Fred MacMurray, Tommy Steele, Greer Garson, John Davidson, Galdys Cooper, Lesley Anne Warrne, Geraldine Page, Hermione Baddeley. w. A. J. Carothers, P-adap. Kyle Crichton, NF-adap. Cornelia Drexel, *My Philadelphia Father*, d. Norman Tokar.
COMEDY DRAMA: FAMILY: Family Drama; Disney Comedy; Rich People; Eccentric People; Flops-Major; Forgotten Films
(Follow Me, Boys!; Bon Voyage; Greedy)

Happy Anniversary, 1959, 83m, ★★★/$$, UA/NA. When a TV set is purchased by a family, it causes unexpected problems. David Niven, Mitzi Gaynor, Carl Reiner, Loring Smith, Patty Duke. w. P-adap. Joseph Fields, Jerome Chodorov, *Anniversary Waltz*, d. David Miller.

COMEDY: Family Comedy; Marriage Comedy; Feuds; TV Life; Suburban Life; Forgotten Films; Overlooked at Release
Happy Birthday to Me, 1980, 111m, ★★¹/₂/$$$, Col/RCA-Col, R/EV-B&G. Seniors at a private school start dropping like flies when a psychotic girl gets her revenge. Melissa Sue Anderson, Glenn Ford, Laurence Dane, Sharon Acker. w. Timothy Bond, Peter Jobin, John Saxton, d. J. Lee-Thompson.
HORROR: MURDER: Serial Killers; Psycho Killers; Murders-One by One; Murderers-Female; Revenge; Murders of Teenagers; Teenagers; Teenage Movies; High School Life; Teen Horror Flicks of 80s
(Prom Night; Carrie)

Happy Birthday, Wanda June, 1971, 105m, ★★★/$, Col/NA. An explorer captured and held hostage on a mission is believed by his wife to be dead. He returns just as she's about to remarry. Rod Steiger, Susannah York, George Grizzard, Don Murray. w. P-adap. Kurt Vonnegut Jr., Mark Robson.
COMEDY DRAMA: Black Comedy; Return of Spouse; Missing Person; Dead-Back from the; Explorers; Romance-Triangles; Curiosities; Cult Films
(COMIC FLIPSIDE: My Favorite Wife; Move Over, Darling)

The Happy Ending, 1969, 112m, ★★★/$$, UA/Fox, PG/S. Sixteen years of unhappily married life are told in flash-backs. Jean Simmons (BActress), John Forsythe, Shirley Jones, Lloyd Bridges, Teresa Wright, Bobby Darin, Tina Louise. w. d. Richard Brooks. BSong. Oscars: 2-0.
DRAMA: Character Studies; Marriage Drama; Romance-Middle-Aged; Marriage on the Rocks; Memories; Flashbacks; Female Protagonists; Hidden Gems; Forgotten Films; Writer-Directors
(Scenes from a Marriage; Chapter Two)

The Happy Hooker, 1975, 98m, ★★¹/₂/$$, Ind/Vestron, R/ES-FN-P. The story of Xaviera Hollander, the famous Dutch woman who enjoyed being a high-class call girl in New York so much that she made a second career of writing about it. Lynn Redgrave, Jean-Pierre Aumont, Lovelady Powell. w. William Richert, NF-adap. Xaviera Hollander, d. Nicholas Sgarro.
COMEDY: Erotic Comedy; Prostitutes-High Class; Writers; Autobiographical Stories; Curiosities; Unintentionally

Funny; Coulda Been Good; Female Protagonists
(Whore; Personal Services)
Happy Land, 1943, 75m, ★★★/$$, 20th/NA. When a G.I. is killed in World War II, his grandfather's ghost repairs to his hometown to comfort his grieving relatives. Don Ameche, Frances Dee, Harry Carey, Ann Rutherford. w. Kathryn Scola, Julien Josephson, N-adap. Mackinlay Kantor, d. Irving Pichel.
COMEDY DRAMA: MELODRAMA: War Stories; World War II Stories; Ghosts; Death-Dealing with; Family Comedy; Family Drama; Forgotten Films; Female Screenwriters

Happy New Year (*La Bonne Année*), 1973, 115m, ★★★/$$, Films 13-Rizzoli/ Sultan. In a rather sadistic scheme to get to his cohorts, police release a thief on New Year's Eve and follow him. Lino Ventura, Francoise Fabian, Charles Gerard, Andre Falcon. w. d. Claude Lelouch.
COMEDY: Heist Stories; Jewel Thieves; New Year's Eve; Ex-Convicts; Reunions; Framed?; Double Crossings; French Films; Hidden Gems; Writer-Directors
(Les Trois Fugitifs; Three Fugitives)

Happy New Year, 1987, 85m, ★★★/$, Col/RCA-Col, PG-13/P. A jewel thief is released from prison after a long sentence and seeks out his old comrade in order for the two of them to pull one last big score down in Florida. Peter Falk, Charles Durning, Wendy Hughes, Tom Courtney. w. Warren Lane, d. John G. Avildsen.
COMEDY: Heist Stories; Jewel Thieves; New Year's Eve; Ex-Convicts; Reunions; Multiple Performances; Disguises; Foreign Film Remakes; Overlooked at Release; Hidden Gems; Coulda Been Great
(Les Trois Fugitifs; Three Fugitives)

The Happy Time, 1952, 94m, ★★★/$$, Col/NA. A family saga set in the twenties in Quebec revolving around the coming of age of its teenage members. Charles Boyer, Louis Jourdan, Bobby Driscoll, Marsha Hunt, Marcelo Dalio. w. Earl Felton, P-adap. Samuel A. Taylor, d. Richard Fleischer.
COMEDY DRAMA: Family Drama; Family Comedy; Sagas; Coming of Age; Young Men; Young Women; Love-First; Canada; Forgotten Films; Hidden Gems; Nostalgia

Hard Contract, 1969, 106m, ★★½/$$, 20th/NA. A hitman has trouble forming lasting relationships as he does his work in Europe. James Coburn, Lilli Palmer, Lee Remick, Burgess Meredith, Sterling Hayden, Karen Black. w. d. S. Lee Pogostin.
ACTION: Crime Drama; Character Studies; Hitmen; Sexual Problems; Mob Stories; Americans Abroad; Vacations-European; Coulda Been Great; Writer-Directors
(Dead Heat on a Merry-Go-Round)

Hard Country, 1981, 104m, ★★½/$$, AFD/NA, PG/V-S. Small-Town life is too boring for a sexy girl and her non-committal boyfriend/cowpoke, so she hightails it out of there. Jan-Michael Vincent, Kim Basinger, Michael Parks, Tanya Tucker. w. Michael Kane, d. David Greene.
DRAMA: MELODRAMA: Ordinary People Stories; Romance-Reluctant; Dreams; Romance-On Again/Off Again; Small-Town Life; Southwestern Life; Texas
(Katie: Portrait of a Centerfold)

A Hard Day's Night, 1964, 85m, ★★★★/$$$, UA/MGM-UA. Paul's grandfather gets on their case, but the free-wheeling Fab Four head off toward a TV show in London, encountering many odd adventures along the way. Paul McCartney, John Lennon, George Harrison, Ringo Starr, Victor Spinetti. w. Alun Owen (BOScr), d. Richard Lester. BMScore. Oscars: 2-0.
COMEDY: Music Video Style; Action Comedy; Chase Stories; Music Movies; Musicians; Rock Stars; TV Life; Race Against Time; Mod Era; British Films
(Help; Yellow Submarine; Let It Be)

Hardcore, 1978, 108m, ★★★/$$, Col/RCA-Col, R/S-P. The daughter of a strict Protestant man from Michigan becomes a porn actress in L.A. He comes looking for her and discovers the sordid world into which she's descended. George C. Scott, Peter Boyle, Season Hubley, Dick Sargent. w. d. Paul Schrader.
DRAMA: Character Studies; Missing Persons; Searches; Fathers & Daughters; Pornography World; Parents vs. Children; Generation Gap; Illusions Destroyed; Writer-Directors
(American Gigolo)

The Harder They Fall, 1956, 109m, ★★★/$$, Col/RCA-Col. A fixed fight is exposed by a scrupulous press agent but it leads him to question his decision. Humphrey Bogart, Rod Steiger, Jan Sterling, Mike Lane, Max Baer. w. Philip Yordan, N-adap. Budd Schulberg, d. Mark Robson. BB&WCin. Oscars: 1-0.
DRAMA: MELODRAMA: Crime Drama; Boxing; Corruption; Journalists; Whistleblowers; Ethics
(Requiem for a Heavyweight; The Sweet Smell of Success)
(Ed: Humphrey Bogart's last performance)

Hard Promises, 1991, 95m, ★★★/$, Col/RCA-Col, PG/S. A peripatetic fellow neglects his wife so much that he doesn't find out she's divorced him until he returns from a long business trip and finds she's planning to remarry. He then decides to take the relationship more seriously. Sissy Spacek, William Peterson, Brian Kerwin, Mare Winningham, Jeff Perry. w. Jule Selbo, d. Martin Davidson.
COMEDY DRAMA: ROMANCE: Romantic Comedy; Romance-On Again/Off Again; Marriage-Impending; Marriage on the Rocks; Reunions; Return of Spouse; Ordinary People Stories; Coulda Been Great; Overlooked at Release
REMAKE/RETREAD: The Philadelphia Story.
(The Philadelphia Story; Violets Are Blue)

Hard Times, 1975, 93m, ★★★/$$, Col/RCA-Col, R/V-P. An amateur boxer and his skid-row promoter help each other out in Depression-era New Orleans. Charles Bronson, James Coburn, Jill Ireland, Strother Martin. w. Walter Hill, Bryan Gindorff, Bruce Henstell, d. Walter Hill.
DRAMA: Sports Movies; Boxing; Depression Era; New Orleans
(Diggstown; Studs Lonigan; The Great White Hope)

Hard to Handle, 1933, 75m, ★★½/$$$, WB/NA. A PR man's rise to fame and fortune. James Cagney, Ruth Donnelly, Mary Brian, Allen Jenkins, Claire Dodd. w. Wilson Mizner, Robert Lord, d. Mervyn Le Roy.
COMEDY: COMEDY DRAMA: Power-Rise to; Rags to Riches; Forgotten Films; Faded Hits

Hard to Kill, 1989, 96m, ★★½/$$$, WB/WB, R/EV-P-S. A cop comes out of a coma and goes after the crooks who put him there when they killed his family. Steven Seagal, Kelly Le Brock, Bill Sadler. w. Steve McKay, d. Bruce Malmuth.
ACTION: Police Stories; Martial Arts; Revenge; Comas; Avenging Death of Someone; Sleeper Hits
(Above the Law; Death Wish)

Hardware, 1990, 92m, ★★★/$$, Ind/WB, R/EV-B&G. In a dystopic future, scrap dealers unwittingly unearth and reactivate a killer cyborg. Dylan McDermott, Stacey Travis, John Lynch, Iggy Pop. w. d. Richard Stanley.
HORROR: SCI-FI: Futuristic Films; Apocalyptic Stories; Man vs. Machine; Monsters-Manmade; Robots; Androids; Hitmen; Rogue Plots; Kill the Beast; Writer-Directors
(Blade Runner; The Terminator; Re-Animator)

The Hard Way, 1942, 109m, ★★★/$$, WB/WB. The back-stage story of a reluctant star whose career is pushed forward by her domineering sister. Ida Lupino (BActress, NYFC), Joan Leslie, Dennis Morgan, Jack Carson, Gladys George. w. Daniel Fuchs, Peter Viertel, d. Vincent Sherman.
DRAMA: MELODRAMA: Svengalis; Sisters Actresses; Fame-Rise to; Women in Conflict; Behind the Scenes; Theater Life; Hollywood Life; Hidden Gems; Faded Hits
(Anna; All About Eve; Stage Door)

The Hard Way, 1991, 111m, ★★★/$$, U/MCA-U, PG-13/P-V. A pampered young Hollywood star does "research" for his next role by teaming up with a hard-bitten New York cop and, of course, sparks fly. Michael J. Fox, James Woods, Stephen Lang, Annabella Sciorra, Delroy Lindo, Penny Marshall. w. Daniel Pyne, Lem Dobbs, Michael Kozoll, d. John Badham.
COMEDY: ACTION: Action Comedy; Buddy Films; Buddy Cops; Police Comedy; Police Stories; Hollywood Satire; Actors; Men in Conflict; Partners-Mismatched; Coulda Been Great; Overlooked at Release
(Into the Sun; Lethal Weapon; 48 Hours)

Harlem Nights, 1989, 116m, ★/$$, Par/Par, R/EP-EV-S. In Harlem in the 30s, two black club owners band together to thwart a mob takeover. Everyone gets into the fight. Eddie Murphy, Richard Pryor, Redd Foxx, Danny Aiello, Michael Lerner, Della Reese, Jasmine Guy. w. d. Eddie Murphy. BCostume. Oscars: 1-0.

COMEDY: ACTION: Action Comedy; Mob Stories; Mob Comedy; Nightclubs; Men in Conflict; Feuds; Black Casts; Black Directors; Black Screenwriters; Actor Directors; Inner City Life; 1930s; Flops-Major

(Ed: A mess from start to finish with the only bright spots including Della Reese)

Harley Davidson and the Marlboro Man, 1991, 98m, ★★★/$$, MGM/MGM-UA, R/P-V-S. Two eccentric renegades hold up a bank and give the money to a saloon owner to reopen, then wind up on a wild chase from the mob and authorities with explosions and all the rest. Mickey Rourke, Don Johnson, Chelsea Field, Daniel Baldwin, Giancarlo Esposito, Vanessa Williams. w. Don Michael Paul, d. Simon Wincer.

ACTION: COMEDY: Action Comedy; Chase Stories; Heist Stories; Mortgage Drama; Robin Hood Stories; Motorcycles; Desert Settings; Fugitives from the Law; Eccentric People; Hidden Gems; Overlooked at Release; Robin Hood Stories

(The Cowboy Way)

Harlow, 1965, 125m, ★★1/2/$$, Par/Par, PG/S. A man-behind-the-woman story of Jean Harlow and her Svengali-like agent, Arthur Landau. Carroll Baker, Peter Lawford, Mike Connors, Red Buttons, Martin Balsam. w. John Michael Hayes, d. Gordon Douglas.

MELODRAMA: Biographies; Actresses; Hollywood Life; Svengalis; Fame-Rise to; Hollywood Biographies; Forgotten Films; Coulda Been Good; Camp

(The Legend of Lylah Clare; The Goddess)

Harold and Maude, 1971, 92m, ★★★★/$$, Par/Par, R/S-P. A spoiled rich boy who thwarts his mother's attempts to fix him up with girls is obsessed with death. He finally meets the woman of his dreams at one of the funerals they both regularly attend, and she's 80 years old. Bud Cort, Ruth Gordon, Vivien Pickles, Cyril Cusak. w. Colin Higgins, d. Hal Ashby.

COMEDY: Black Comedy; Comedy-Morbid; Boys; Women and Boys; Elderly Women; Romance-Mismatched; Romance-Older Women/Younger Men; Romance-Elderly; Suicidal Tendencies; Suicidal Tendencies of Young People; Funerals; Cult Films; Hidden Gems

(Grace Quigley; The Graduate; Inside Daisy Clover; The Prince of Central Park)

Harold Lloyd's World of Comedy, 1962, 99m, ★★★1/2/$, Harold Lloyd/NA. A compilation of the best scenes from Lloyd's silent and sound shorts. Commentary by: Art Ross, w. Walter Scharf.

COMEDY: Comedy-Slapstick; Compilation Films; Comedy of Errors; Hidden Gems

Harper, 1966, 121m, ★★★/$$$, WB/WB, PG/V. When a wealthy man turns up missing, his wife hires a private detective to find him, and he gets caught up in a web of intrigue. Paul Newman, Lauren Bacall, Shelley Winters, Arthur Hill, Julie Harris, Janet Leigh, Robert Wagner, Strother Martin. w. William Goldman, N-adap. Ross MacDonald, d. Jack Smight.

MYSTERY: MURDER: MURDER MYSTERY: Detective Stories; Detectives in Deep; Conspiracy; Friends as Lovers; Romance-Reunited; Blackmail

SEQUEL: The Drowning Pool

(The Drowning Pool; The Big Sleep)

Harper Valley P.T.A., 1978, 93m, ★★★/$$$, April Fools/Vestron, G. A free-spirited woman in a mythical small town has to avenge those who gossip about her supposedly wicked ways. Barbara Eden, Ronny Cox, Nanette Fabray, Pat Paulsen. w. George Edwards, Barry Schneider, d. Richard Bennett.

COMEDY: American Myth; Small-Town Life; Small-Town Scandals; Scandals; Gossip/Rumors; Revenge; Turning the Tables; Corruptions; Sleeper Hits; Song Title Movies

(Chattanooga Choo-Choo; The Positively True Adventures of The Alleged Texas Cheerleader-Murdering Mom)

The Harrad Experiment, 1973, 97m, ★★1/2/$$, Cinerama/Vestron, R-X/ES-FFN-MFN. Professor Harrad uses his students as guinea pigs in his experiments on human sexuality. James Whitmore, Tippi Hedren, Don Johnson, Laurie Walters. w. Michael Werner, Ted Cassidy, N-adap. Robert H. Rimmer, d. Ted Post.

Harrad Summer, 1974, 105m, ★★/$, Cinerama/VCI, R/ES-MFN-FFN. After learning about human sexuality from professor Harrad all year, diligent students go home to practice. Robert Reiser, Laurie Walters, Richard Doran, Bill Dana. w. Morth Thaw, Steven Zacharias, d. Steven Hillard Stern.

MELODRAMA: Erotic Drama; Boarding Schools; College Life; Young People;

Experiments; Ensemble Films; Nudism; Curiosities; Sexuality; Sexual Revolution; Sexual Problems; Time Capsules

SEQUEL TO: The Harrad Experiment

Harriet Craig, 1950, 94m, ★★★/$$, Col/NA. A suburban housewife really is that-married to her house. But things soon change. Joan Crawford, Wendell Corey, Allyn Joslyn, Lucile Watson. w. Anne Froelick, James Gunn, P-adap. George Kelly, (Craig's Wife), d. Vincent Sherman.

MELODRAMA: Marriage Drama; Marriage on the Rocks; Women's Films; Domestic Life; Housewives; Suburban Life; Time Capsules; Woman Behind the Man; Female Protagonists

REMAKE OF: Craig's Wife

Harry and Son, 1984, 117m, ★★/$, Orion/Orion, PG. A construction worker and his son have to live together, causing tensions to flair. Paul Newman, Robby Benson, Ellen Barkin, Wilford Brimley. w. Ronald L. Buck, Paul Newman, N-adap. Raymond DeCapite (A Lost King), d. Paul Newman.

MELODRAMA: Character Studies; Fathers & Sons; Parents vs. Children; Family Drama; Working Class; Generation Gap; Flops-Major; Forgotten Films

(Nobody's Fool; Terms of Endearment [male counterpart])

Harry and the Hendersons, 1987, 110m, ★★1/2/$$, U/MCA-U, PG. A family on a camp-out encounters a gentle furry beast reminiscent of Bigfoot and winds up taking him in. John Lithgow, Melinda Dillon, David Suchet, Don Ameche. w. William Dear, William E. Martin, Ezra D. Rappaport, d. William Dear.

CHILDREN'S: FAMILY: Fantasy; **COMEDY:** Family Comedy; Roommates; Nuisances; Fish out of Water Stories; Monsters-Animal; Animal Stories; Pet Stories; Legends

(Bigfoot; The Legend of Boggy Creek)

Harry and Tonto, 1974, 115m, ★★★1/2/$$$, 20th/CBS-Fox, PG/S-P. A retired man living on social security gets evicted from his New York apartment and treks across country with his cat meeting an eccentric assortment of people along the way. Art Carney (**BActor**), Ellen Burstyn, Chief Dan George, Geraldine Fitzgerald, Larry Hagman, Melanie Mayron. w. Paul Mazursky, Josh Greenfield (**BOScr**), d. Paul Mazursky. Oscars: 2-1.

COMEDY DRAMA: MELODRAMA:
Elderly People; Elderly Men; Runaways;
Road Movies; Hitchhikers; Eccentric
People; Pet Stories; Cats; Sleeper Hits
(Kotch; Roommates)

Harry and Walter Go to New York,
1976, 120m, ★★¹/₂/$$, Col/RCA-Col,
PG/S-P. Two vaudevillians in Old New
York get mixed-up with a suffragette and
a heist plot involving blowing up a safe.
James Caan, Elliott Gould, Michael
Caine, Diane Keaton, Charles Durning,
Lesley Ann Warren, Jack Gilford. w. John
Byrum, Robert Kaufman, d. Mark Rydell.
COMEDY: Heist Stories; Capers;
Romance-Triangles; Vaudeville;
Friendships-Male; Buddy Films; 1900s;
Women's Rights; Coulda Been Great
(Freebie and the Bean; The Hot Rock;
The Great Train Robbery)

Harry in Your Pocket, 1973, 103m,
★★¹/₂/$$, UA/NA, PG/S-P-V. Three
pickpockets, ranging in age from old to
young, teach each other tricks as they
ply their trade. James Coburn, Walter
Pidgeon, Michael Sarrazin. w. Ron
Austin, James Buchanan, d. Bruce Geller.
COMEDY DRAMA: Crime Drama;
Capers; Thieves; Pickpockets;
Friendships-Male; Generation Gap;
Coulda Been Great

Harum Scarum, 1965, 95m, ★★/$$$,
MGM/MGM-UA. An American singer
and movie star are kidnapped on a pub-
licity tour of the Middle East. Elvis
Presley, Mary Ann Mobley, Fran Jeffries,
Michael Ansara, Theo Marcuse. w.
Gerald Drayson Adams, d. Bruce Geller.
MUSICALS: Music Movies; Singers;
Actresses; Kidnappings; Middle East;
Forgotten Films

Harvey, 1950, 104m, ★★★★/$$$$, U-
I/MCA-U. The famous story of an alco-
holic and his giant white rabbit friend
and how they elude the men in white
with nets. James Stewart (BActor),
Josephine Hull (**BSActress**), Victoria
Horne, Peggy Dow, Cecil Kellaway,
Charles Drake. w. Mary Chase, Oscar
Brodney, P-adap. Mary Chase, d. Henry
Koster. Oscars: 2-1.
COMEDY: Screwball Comedy; **FARCE:**
Mental Illness; Chase Stories; Invisibility;
Friendships-Male; Simple Minds;
Relatives-Troublesome; Inheritances at
Stake; Asylums; Psychiatrists; Rabbits;
Pulitzer Prize Adaptations
(A Fine Madness; Arsenic and Old Lace)

The Harvey Girls, 1946, 101m,
★★★¹/₂/$$$$, MGM/MGM-UA. The
famous chain of railroad-station restau-
rants in the West hired waitresses who
could also sing and dance. Judy Garland,
Ray Bolger, John Hodiak, Preston Foster,
Virginia O'Brien, Angela Lansbury. w.
Edmund Beloin, Nathaniel Curtis, d.
George Sidney. **BOSong,** "On the
Atchison, Topeka & the Sante Fe,"
BMScore. Oscars: 2-1.
MUSICALS: COMEDY: ROMANCE:
Musical Comedy; Musical Romance;
Trains; **WESTERNS:** Western Comedy;
Romantic Comedy; Waitresses; Singers;
1890s; Nostalgia
(The Dolly Sisters; Centennial Summer)

Has Anybody Seen My Gal?, 1952,
89m, ★★★/$$$, U-I/NA. An elderly rich
gentleman with no children tests his rela-
tives for their worthiness as heirs by
showing up at their doorstep disguised as
a poor man. Charles Coburn, Piper
Laurie, Rock Hudson, Gigi Perreau, Lynn
Bari, James Dean. w. Joseph Hoffman, d.
Douglas Sirk.
COMEDY: Family Comedy; Rich vs.
Poor; Rich People; Disguises; Poor
People; Homeless People; Inheritances
at Stake; Nostalgia; Roaring 20s; 1920s
(My Man Godfrey; Greedy; The More the
Merrier)

The Hasty Heart, 1949, 104m,
★★★/$$, ABP-WB/WB. In a Burmese
military hospital, an egotistical Scottish
soldier is detested by everyone, until they
learn he is dying. Richard Todd (BActor),
Patricia Neal, Ronald Reagan, Orlando
Martins. w. Ranald MacDougall, P-adap.
John Patrick, d. Vincent Sherman.
Oscars: 1-0.
DRAMA: MELODRAMA: Death-
Impending; Mean Men; Tearjerkers;
Disease Stories; Military Stories;
Scotland; British Films
(Bright Victory; Cobb; On Wings of
Eagles)

Hatari!, 1962, 158m, ★★★/$$$, Par/
Par. Competing to catch wild animals to
sell to zoos, an international band of
adventurers travels to Tanganyika and
learns the baby elephant walk. John
Wayne, Elsa Martinelli, Red Buttons,
Hardy Kruger. w. Leigh Brackett, d.
Howard Hawks. BCCin. Oscars: 1-0.
ADVENTURE: COMEDY: CHILDREN'S:
Comic Adventure; Safaris; Africa; Animal
Stories; Animal Rights; Hunters

(Born Free; Daktari [TV Series])
(Ed: The score launched the famous
instrumental "Baby Elephant Walk" by
Henry Mancini, which was not nominated
for an Oscar due to Mancini's *Days of
Wine and Roses* music winning that year
instead)

The Hatchet Man, 1932, 74m, ★★¹/₂/
$$, WB/NA. A Chinese-American hitman
in San Francisco is asked to kill his best
friend. He does so, but guilt prompts him
to take care of the murdered man's daugh-
ter. Edward G. Robinson, Loretta Young,
Dudley Digges. w. J. Grubb Alenxander,
P-adap. Achmed Abdullah, David
Belasco, d. William A. Wellman.
DRAMA: Crime Drama; Mob Stories;
Hitmen; **MURDER:** Friendships-Male;
Friends as Enemies; Guilty Conscience;
San Francisco; Chinese People; Asian-
Americans; Mob-Asian; Forgotten Films;
Good Premise Unfulfilled; Curiosities;
Warner Gangster Era

A Hatful of Rain, 1957, 108m, ★★★/
$$$, 20th/CBS-Fox. A soldier has a hard
time adjusting to life after World War II
and descends into drug abuse. Eva Marie
Saint, Don Murray, Anthony Franciosa
(BActor), Lloyd Nolan, Henry Silva. w.
Michael V. Gazzo, Alfred Hayes, P-adap.
Alfred Hayes, d. Fred Zinnemann.
DRAMA: MELODRAMA: Drugs-
Addictions; World War II-Post Era;
Veterans; Nervous Breakdowns; Ahead
of Its Time
(The Man with the Golden Arm; Career)

Haunted Honeymoon, 1986, 82m,
★★/$, Orion/Orion, PG-13/P-S. A radio
star and his new bride spend their honey-
moon at his family estate, which is inhab-
ited by transvestites and ghosts. Gene
Wilder, Gilda Radner, Dom DeLuise,
Jonathan Pryce. w. Gene Wilder, Terence
Marsh, d. Gene Wilder.
COMEDY: Horror Comedy; Haunted
Houses; Honeymoons; Newlyweds; Spoofs;
Werewolves; Ghosts; Coulda Been Good
(The Cat and the Canary; Scared Stiff)

The Haunted Palace, 1963, 85m,
★★¹/₂/$, AIP/HBO. An heir to a great
estate moves into his family mansion and
is haunted by a dead relative. Vincent
Price, Lon Chaney Jr., Debra Paget. w.
Charles Beaumont, SS-adap. H. P.
Lovecraft & Edgar Allan Poe, d. Roger
Corman.
HORROR: Black Comedy; Haunted
Houses; Relatives-Troublesome; Ghosts;

Coulda Been Good; Forgotten Films
(Fall of the House of Usher; Comedy of Terrors)

Haunted Summer, 1988, 106m, ★★1/2/$, Pathe-Cannon/MGM-UA, R/S-FN-MFN. In the Swiss Alps in the 1800s, Byron, Shelley, Mary Godwin, and her friends romp about nude in the creeks, do some illicit drugs available at the time, and have sex. Philip Anglim, Laura Dern, Alice Krige, Eric Stoltz. w. Lewis John Carlino, N-adap. Anne Edwards, d. Ivan Passer.

DRAMA: ROMANCE: Vacations; Vacation Romance; Erotic Drama; Biographies; Biographies-Fictional; Famous People When Young; Swapping Partners; Drugs-Addictions; Alternative Lifestyles; Coulda Been Good; Alps
(Gothic; Frankenstein Unbound; Mary Shelley's Frankenstein)
(Ed: This is the more ordinary, traditional version of the tale, as opposed to *Gothic*, though this contains more blatant nudity)

The Haunting, 1963, 112m, ★★★/$$, MGM/MGM-UA. Two women and a few psychic phenomena specialists spend the night in a haunted castle and soon come to believe in ghosts. Richard Johnson, Claire Bloom, Russ Tamblyn, Julie Harris. w. Nelson Gidding, N-adap. Shirley Jackson, *The Haunting of Hill House*, d. Robert Wise.

SUSPENSE: HORROR: Psychological Thriller; Psychics; Supernatural Danger; Ghosts; Haunted Houses; Hidden Gems; Female Protagonists
(The Uninvited; The House on Haunted Hill)
(Ed: No special effects, but still spooky)

Havana, 1990, 145m, ★★/$, U/MCA-U, PG-13/S-P. During Fidel Castro's rise under Batista, an American gambler in love with an exotic woman gets mixed up in revolutionary politics. Robert Redford, Lena Olin, Alan Arkin, Tomas Milian, Raul Julia. w. Judith Rascoe, David Rayfiel, d. Sydney Pollack.

DRAMA: ROMANCE: Romantic Drama; Gambling; Cuba; Political Drama; Political Unrest; Communists; Romance-Dangerous; Dangerous Women; Coulda Been Good; Flops-Major; Female Screenwriters
(Casablanca; The Year of Living Dangerously; Out of Africa; Indecent Proposal)
(Ed: It was supposed to be a modern *Casablanca*, but the only thing that came up was a blank-a, with a story that sleep-walks and dialogue that put it under)

Hawaii, 1966, 186m, ★★★/$$$$, UA/CBS-Fox, PG/S-FN. In the early 1800s, an American missionary goes to Hawaii and struggles with the locals while trying to start a family. Max Von Sydow, Julie Andrews, Richard Harris, Jocelyn La Garde (BSActress), Carroll O'Connor, Gene Hackman. w. Daniel Taradash, Dalton Trumbo, N-adap. James A. Michener, d. George Roy Hill. BCCin, BOScore, BOSong. Oscars: 4-0.

DRAMA: ADVENTURE: Marriage Drama; Historical Drama; Journies; Adventure at Sea; Explorers; Pioneers; Islands; Hawaii; Babies-Having; Scenery-Outstanding

SEQUEL: The Hawaiians.

The Hawaiians, 1970, 132m, ★★1/2/$$, UA/CBS-Fox. After an argument with his business partner, a young shipping executive quits his job and strikes oil off the coast of Hawaii. Charlton Heston, Tina Chen, Geraldine Chaplin. w. James R. Webb, d. Tom Gries.

DRAMA: Men in Conflict; Oil People; Power-Rise to; Historical Drama; Hawaii

SEQUEL TO: Hawaii
(Hawaii; Diamondhead)

Hawks, 1988, 109m, ★★1/2/$ (VR), Par/Par. In a cancer ward, two terminal patients run off together to enjoy life one last time. Timothy Dalton, Anthony Edwards, Robert Lang. w. Roy Clarke, d. Robert Ellis Miller.

COMEDY DRAMA: TRAGEDY: Tragi-Comedy; Black Comedy; Disease Stories; Death-Impending; One Last Time; TV Movies
(The Living End; Homer and Eddie; Boys on the Side)

He Knows You're Alone, 1980, 92m, ★★/$$, MGM/MGM-UA, R/EV-S-B&G. Teenage girls start dropping like flies and a mad slasher is pursued for the crimes. Don Scardino, Elizabeth Kemp, Tom Hanks. w. Scott Parker, d. Armand Mastroianni.

HORROR: Serial Killers; Weddings; Murders of Teenagers; Trail of a Killer; Teenage Horror Flicks of 1980s
(Prom Night; When a Stranger Calls)

He Married His Wife, 1940, 83m, ★★1/2/$$, 20th/NA. A divorced couple still love each other underneath all the bickering, so they decide to give it one more go. Joel McCrea, Nancy Kelly, Roland Young, Mary Boland, Cesar Romero, Lyle Talbot. w. Sam Hellman, Darrell Ware, Lynn Starling, John O'Hara, Erna Lazarus, Scott Darling, d. Roy Del Ruth.

COMEDY: ROMANCE: Romantic Comedy; Screwball Comedy; Marriage Comedy; Romance-On Again/Off Again; Romance-Bickering; Marrying Again; Forgotten Films; Coulda Been Good
(The Awful Truth; The Marrying Man)

He Said, She Said, 1991, 115m, ★★1/2/$, Par/Par, PG-13/S-P. A couple with a point/counterpoint-style talk show break up, and the story is told twice, once from each of their perspectives. Kevin Bacon, Elizabeth Perkins, Nathan Lane, Anthony LaPaglia, Sharon Stone. w. Brian Hohlfeld, d. Ken Kwapis, Marisa Silver.

COMEDY: ROMANCE: Romantic Comedy; Romance-Bickering; Marriage Comedy; TV Life; Talk Show Hosts; Parallel Stories; Coulda Been Good; Female Directors
(She's Having a Baby; The Cutting Edge)

He Was Her Man, 1934, 70m, ★★1/2/$$$, WB/NA. When his compadres leave him holding the bag, a safecracker joins forces with the right side of the law to track them down. James Cagney, Joan Blondell, Victor Jory, Frank Craven. w. Niven Busch, Tom Buckingham, d. Lloyd Bacon.

COMEDY DRAMA: Crime Drama; Ex-Convicts; Revenge; Convict's Revenge; Informers; Warner Gangster Era

Head, 1968, 85m, ★★★/$$, Col/RCA-Col, G. The Monkees' psychedelic head-trip movie, building off of their wacky TV show in the tradition of the Beatles' movies. The Monkees, Victor Mature, Annette Funicello, Timothy Carey. w. Jack Nicholson, Bob Rafaelson, d. Bob Rafaelson.

COMEDY: MUSICALS: Music Movies; Rock Stars; Musicians; Mod Era; Teen Idols; Cult Films; Music Video Style; TV Series Movies
(A Hard Day's Night; Help; The Monkees [TV Series])

Head Over Heels, see **Chilly Scenes of Winter.**

Health, 1979, 102m, ★★1/2/$ (LR), 20th/NA, PG. A convention of health food peddlers in Florida culminates in chaos in this satire of the 70's health food craze. Lauren Bacall, Glenda Jackson, James Garner, Dick Cavett, Carol Burnett, Paul Dooley, Henry Gibson. w. Robert Altman,

Paul Dooley, Frank Barhydt, d. Robert Altman.

COMEDY: SATIRE: Ensemble Films; Eccentric People; 1970s; Curiosities; Coulda Been Great; Hidden Gems; All-Star Cast

(A Wedding; Nashville; Ready to Wear; Honky Tonk Freeway)

(Ed: Actually unfinished, this was supposed to be a companion to *Nashville*, but doesn't quite cut the all-natural mustard)

Hear My Song, 1991, 105m, ★★★/$$, Palace-Miramax/Par. In Liverpool, a failing nightclub gets a boost when the manager hires Joseph Locke, a once-popular singer who fled to Ireland. But doubts arise as to the true identity of this mysterious stranger. Ned Beatty, Adrian Dunbar, Shirley Anne Field, Tara Fitzgerald, William Hootkins, Harold Berens. w. Peter Chelsom, Adrian Dunbar, d. Peter Chelsom.

COMEDY DRAMA: MELODRAMA: Impostors; Past-Haunted by the; Singers; Nightclubs; Mortgage Drama; British Films; Irish People; England; Sleeper Hits; Old-Fashioned Recent Films

The Hearse, 1980, 95m, ★★/$, Crown International/Media, R/V. The country estate a wealthy woman has just purchased is said to be haunted. She finds out for herself when she moves in. Trish Van Devere, Joseph Cotten, David Gautreaux, Donald Hotton, Perry Lang. w. Bill Bleich, d. George Bowers.

HORROR: SUSPENSE: Haunted Houses; Ghosts; Women in Jeopardy; Female Protagonists; Independent Films

Heart and Soul, 1993, 103m, ★★/$$, U/MCA-U, PG-13. A bus runs over a four different people in 1959 who then are reincarnated into one young fellow who then has to deal with all of their alter-egos. Robert Downey, Jr., Alfre Woodard, Kyra Sedgwick, Tom Sizemore, Charles Grodin. w. Brent Maddock, Erik Hansen, Gregory Hansen, S. S. Wilson, d. Ron Underwood.

COMEDY: Fantasy; Dead-Back from the; Angels; Ensemble Films; Old-Fashioned; Recent Films

RETREAD OF: All of Me

(All of Me; Heaven Can Wait; Angel on My Shoulder; Chances Are)

(Ed: *Herman's Head* TV series as a movie?)

Heart Beat, 1979, 109m, ★★★/$, Orion/Orion, R/S-P. The life and loves of Jack Kerouac are explored as he and two friends travel the country. John Heard, Nick Nolte, Sissy Spacek, Ray Sharkey, Tony Bill. w. John Byrum, d. John Byrum.

DRAMA: Character Studies; Biographies; Writers; Romance-Triangles; Menage a Trois; Beatnik Era; Nostalgia; 1950s; Hidden Gems; Curiosities; Quiet Little Films; Writer-Directors

(The Subterraneans; The Beat Generation)

The Heartbreak Kid, 1972, 106m, ★★★★/$$$, 20th/Media, PG/S-P. A bridegroom quickly becomes disgusted with his new bride and before their honeymoon is over he's chasing after the elusive, beautiful blonde he sees by the pool—but with her cantankerous, wealthy father, the grass may not be greener even though the hair is lighter. Charles Grodin, Cybill Shepherd, Elaine May, Jeannie Berlin (BSActress), Eddie Albert (BSActor). w. Neil Simon, SS-adap. Bruce Jay Friedman (*A Change of Plan*), d. Elaine May. Oscars: 2-0.

COMEDY DRAMA: ROMANCE: Romantic Comedy; **SATIRE:** Newlyweds; Honeymoons; Cheating Men; Weddings; Lover Family Dislikes; Elusive Women; Sexy Women; Vacations; Vacation Romance; Alienation; Romance-Boy Wants Girl; Marrying Up; In-Laws-Troublesome; American Dream; Neurotic People; Hidden Gems; Faded Hits; Female Directors

(The Graduate; Thieves; The Last Picture Show; Honeymoon)

(Ed: A comedy with guts and a fallible, real hero)

Heartbreak Ridge, 1986, 130m, ★★1/2/$$$, WB/WB, PG-13/EP-V. An over-the-hill drill sergeant is tough on his troops when they go into "battle" in Grenada, but off-base he tries to learn to be a "sensitive male" to his ex-wife. Clint Eastwood, Marsha Mason, Everett McGill, Moses Gunn. w. James Carabatsos, d. Clint Eastwood. BSound. Oscars: 1-0.

ACTION: COMEDY DRAMA: Military Stories; Stern Men; Mean Men; War Stories; Political Unrest; Marriage Drama; Marriage on the Rocks; Macho Men; Faded Hits

(An Officer and a Gentleman; The Great Santini)

Heartbreakers, 1984, 98m, ★★★/$, Orion/Orion, R/ES-P-FN-MRN. Two middle-aged men whose lives have taken very different paths get together and discuss their love lives and then share a woman. Peter Coyote, Nick Mancuso, Carole Laure, Max Gail, Kathryn Harrold. w. d. Bobby Roth.

DRAMA: MELODRAMA: Friendships-Male; Romance-Triangles; Menage a Trois; Men's Films; Midlife Crisis; Playboys; Ordinary People Stories; Los Angeles; Curiosities; Writer-Directors; Independent Films

(The Men's Club; That Championship Season)

(Ed: Has to be given credit for going where few stories about men have gone before—or few men will go—truly sensitive behavior)

Heartburn, 1986, 108m, ★★★/$$, Par/Par, R/S-P. A journalist (loosely based on writer Nora Ephron's ex, Carl Bernstein) marries a food critic (Ephron, loosely) and proceeds to cheat and cheat. Meryl Streep, Jack Nicholson, Jeff Daniels, Maureen Stapleton, Stockard Channing, Milos Forman. w. N-adap. Nora Ephron, d. Mike Nichols.

COMEDY DRAMA: Biographies-Fictional; Autobiographical; Character Studies; Marriage Drama; Cheating Men; Starting Over; Romance-On Again/Off Again; Weddings; Babies-Having; Washington, D.C.; Coulda Been Great; Female Protagonists; Female Screenwriters

(An Unmarried Woman; She-Devil; Postcards from the Edge)

(Ed: More than meets the eye initially, and would've been even more if they'd kept Meryl's Dorothy and the Wicked Witch fantasy sequence, where she does in the mistress)

Heart Condition, 1990, 95m, ★★/$, New Line/New Line, PG-13/P. A black man's heart is transplanted into the chest of an ultra-bigoted white guy, and he's haunted by the ghost of his donor. Bob Hoskins, Denzel Washington, Chloe Webb, Robert Apisa. w. d. James D. Parriott.

COMEDY: SATIRE: Possessions; Bigots; Black vs. White; Race Relations; Body Parts; Organ Donors; Police Stories; Police Comedy; Good Premise Unfulfilled; Writer-Directors

(All of Me)

(Ed: Truly dumb after a point)

The Heart Is a Lonely Hunter, 1968, 123m, ★★★1/2/$$$, WB/WB, PG/S. A young girl's struggling with coming of age are helped when a friendship with a unique deaf-mute man who moves into her house develops in the Deep South. Alan Arkin (BActor), Sondra Locke (BSActress), Stacy Keach, Laurinda Barrett, Chuck McCann, Cicely Tyson (BSActress). w. Thomas C. Ryan, N-adap. Carson McCullers, d. Robert Ellis Miller. Oscars: 3-0.

DRAMA: Character Studies; Friendships-Between Sexes; Coming of Age; Girls; Ostracism; Love-First; Teenagers; Mute People; Deaf People; Roommates; Southerns; Mississippi; Classic Literary Adaptations; Hidden Gems; Quiet Little Films
(The Member of the Wedding; Rich in Love)

Heartland, 1979, 96m, ★★★/$, Ind/HBO, PG. A pioneer woman in wild west Wyoming becomes a housekeeper to make ends meet. Conchata Ferrell, Rip Torn, Barry Primus, Lila Skala. w. Beth Ferris, d. Richard Pearce.
DRAMA: Character Studies; Family Drama; **WESTERNS:** Western-Neo; Western-Revisionist; Pioneers; Mothers-Struggling; Making a Living; Feisty Females; Cult Films; Quiet Little Films; Hidden Gems; Female Screenwriters; Female Protagonists
(O Pioneers!; Ballad of Josie)

Heart Like a Wheel, 1983, 113m, ★★1/2/$, 20th/CBS-Fox, PG/P. A woman's driving ambition to be a drag racer and to fight the men who won't let her. Bonnie Bedelia, Beau Bridges, Leo Rossi, Hoyt Axton, Bill McKinney. w. Ken Friedman, d. Jonathan Kaplan. BCostume. Oscars: 1-0.
DRAMA: Character Studies; Biographies; Women's Rights; Female in Male Domain; Car Racing; Rural Life; Rednecks; Ordinary People Stories; Female Protagonists
(Norma Rae)

Heart of Dixie, 1989, 105m, ★★1/2/$, Orion/Orion, PG. A group of college students in Alabama in the fifties deal with the ramifications of the civil rights movement and our one brave heroine helps the first blacks into the university. Ally Sheedy, Virginia Madsen, Phoebe Cates, Treat Williams. w. Tom McCown, N-adap. Anne Rivers Siddons (*Heartbreak Hotel*), d. Martin Davidson.
MELODRAMA: ROMANCE: Race Relations; Black vs. White; College Life; 1950s; Southerns; Biographies-Fictional;

Female Protagonists; Rebels; Sorority Life; Fighting the System; Coulda Been Good
(The Long Walk Home; Shag; My Little Girl)
(Ed: Politically correct white-girl do-gooder clap-trap, but it sure looks good)

Heart of Glass, 1976, 94m, ★★★/$, Werner Herzog/NA. A man who owns a glass factory learns the secret of manufacturing a rare glass from a mysterious shepherd. Josef Bierbichler, Stefan Guttler, Glemens Scheitz, Sonja Skiba. w. Werner Herzog, Herbert Achternbusch, d. Werner Herzog.
DRAMA: Fantasy; Social Drama; Allegorical Stories; Magic; Apocalyptic Stories; Factory Life; Curiosities; German Films

The Heart of the Matter, 1953, 105m, ★★★/$, BL-London/NA. An MP in an African colony has an affair when his wife goes home for a stay and then finds himself blackmailed and contemplating suicide. Trevor Howard, Maria Schell, Elizabeth Allan, Denholm Elliott, Peter Finch, Michael Hordern. w. Ian Dalrymple, Lesley Storm, N-adap. Graham Greene, d. George O'Ferrall.
MELODRAMA: SUSPENSE: Blackmail; Romance with Married Person; Cheating Men; Suicidal Tendencies; Africa; Imperialist Problems
(The Letter; Beyond the Limit)

Heart of the West, 1975, 74m, ★★/$, MGM/MGM-UA. In the early days of the talkies, a midwesterner goes to Hollywood and is marketed as a cowboy. Jeff Bridges, Alan Arkin, Andy Griffith, Blythe Danner, Donald Pleasence. w. Rob Thompson, d. Howard Zieff.
COMEDY: WESTERNS: Western Comedy; Hollywood Life; Hollywood Satire; Movie Making; Actors; Cowboys; Silent Film Era; Nostalgia; Forgotten Films
(Sunset)

Hearts of Darkness: A Filmmaker's Apocalypse, 1991, 96m, ★★★1/2/$$, Par/Par, P. A documentary about the tortuous, long, drawn-out process of filming *Apocolypse Now*. w. d. Fax Bahr, George Hickenlooper.
Filmumentaries; Documentaries; Movie Making; Hollywood Life; Directors; Actors; Jungle Life

Hearts of Fire, 1987, 95m, ★★1/2/$, Lorimar/WB. Over-the-hill rockers get a

vicarious thrill out of aiding the meteoric rise of a young starlet. Fiona Flanagan, Bob Dylan, Rupert Everett, Lesley Donaldson, Ian Dury, Richie Havens. w. Scott Richardson, Joe Esterhas, d. Richard Marquand.
MELODRAMA: Rockumentaries; Rock Stars; Musicians; Beautiful People; England; British Films; Overlooked at Release

Heat, 1987, 101m, ★★/$, Vista-New Century/Par, R/P-V. A winning gambler in Las Vegas is sought by the gangsters he won money from. Burt Reynolds, Karen Young, Peter MacNicol, Howard Hesseman. w., N-adap. William Goldman, d. R. M. Richards.
ACTION: Crime Drama; Gambling; Revenge; Fugitives from the Mob; Las Vegas; Coulda Been Good

Heat, 1995, 176m, ★★★/$$$, WB/WB, R/EP-EV-S. Pacino is a police detective who goes up against master criminal and murderer De Niro in a cat-and-mouse chase of wits. Al Pacino, Robert De Niro, Val Kilmer, Tom Sizemore, Jon Voight, Diane Venora, Ashley Judd. w. d. Michael Mann.
ACTION: Crime Drama; Cat-and-Mouse Stories; Police Stories; Men in Conflict; Writer-Directors
(Once Upon a Time in America; True Confessions; Manhunter)

Heat and Dust, 1982, 130m, ★★★/$, Merchant Ivory-U/MCA-U, PG/S. A young Englishwoman finds a personal view of the history of India is told in the letters of her great aunt and through a journey there. Julie Christie, Christopher Cazenove, Shashi Kapoor, Greta Scacchi, Nikolas Grace. w., N-adap. Ruth Prawer Jhabvala, d. James Ivory.
DRAMA: Journies; Quests; Family/Heritage-Search for; Reincarnation; India; Race Relations; Letters; Female Protagonists; British Films; Hidden Gems; Quiet Little Films
(Shakespeare Wallah; A Passage to India)

Heathers, 1988, 103m, ★★★/$$, New World/New World, R/P-V-S. A demented prankster who's new to a snobby high school and his girlfriend murder teenage girls and pass their deaths off as suicides. Winona Ryder, Christian Slater, Shannen Doherty, Lisanne Falk. w. Daniel Waters, d. Michael Lehmann.
COMEDY: Black Comedy; Comedy-Morbid; **MURDER:** Romance-Doomed;

Romance-Dangerous; Dangerous Men; Suicidal Tendencies; Suicidal Tendencies of Young People; Serial Killers; Murders of Teenagers; New in Town; Surrealism; Sleeper Hits

Heatwave, 1982, 95m, ★★1/2/$, Ind/NA. Australians work together to prevent a bigtime developer from ruining their neighborhood. Judy Davis, Richard Moir. w. Marc Rosenberg, Philip Noyce, d. Noyce.

DRAMA: Mortgage Drama; Save the Land; Fighting the System; Female Protagonists; Australian Films

Heaven and Earth, 1993, 142m, ★★1/2/$, WB/WB, R/S-V. Life of a Vietnamese woman whom an American soldier brings to America as his wife. But her life doesn't find peace just then. Tommy Lee Jones, Hiep Thi Le, Haing S. Ngor, Joan Chen. w. d. Oliver Stone, NF-adap. Le Ly Haslip.

DRAMA: MELODRAMA: Marriage Drama; Romance-Interracial; Vietnam; Vietnam Era; Soldiers

(Come See the Paradise; Platoon)

Heaven Can Wait, 1943, 112m, ★★★1/2/$$$, 20th/CBS-Fox. An aging playboys dies and goes to hell and then campaigns to go to heaven, but first has to prove himself. Don Ameche, Gene Tierney, Laird Cregar, Charles Coburn, Marjorie Main, Eugene Pallette, Louis Calhern. w. Samson Raphaelson, P-adap. Lazlo Bus-Fekete, Birthday, d. Ernst Lubitsch (BDirector). BPicture, BB&WCin. Oscars: 3-0.

COMEDY: COMEDY DRAMA: Fantasy; Death-Back from the; Angels; Hell; Heaven; Men Proving Themselves; Playboys; Hidden Gems; Faded Hits

(Heaven Can Wait [1978]; Here Comes Mr. Jordan; Defending Your Life)

Heaven Can Wait, 1978, 100m, ★★★1/2/$$$$$$, Par/Par, PG/S-P. A football star dies accidentally in a car wreck-accidentally because heaven jumped the gun. So they send him back, not as himself but as a rich man whose wife is trying to kill him. Warren Beatty (BActor), Julie Christie, Dyan Cannon (BSActress), Charles Grodin, Jack Warden (BSActor), Buck Henry, Vincent Gardenia, James Mason. w. Warren Beatty, Elaine May (BAScr), P-adap. Harry Segall, d. Warren Beatty, Buck Henry (BDirector). BPicture, BCin, BOScore, **BArt**. Oscars: 9-1.

COMEDY: COMEDY DRAMA: Screwball Comedy; Dead-Back from the; Heaven; Angels; Reincarnation; ROMANCE: Romantic Drama; MURDER: Murder Attempts-Comic; Football; Body Switching; Religion; Blockbusters

(Here Comes Mr. Jordan; Defending Your Life)

(Ed: A surprise blockbuster considering the subject matter, but not considering the talent; a remake of *Here Comes Mr. Jordan*, not *Heaven Can Wait*, though both are similar and some consider it an amalgamation of the two)

Heaven Help Us, 1985, 104m, ★★★/$, HBO-Tri-Star/HBO, PG-13/S-P-MRN. Several teenagers at boys' Catholic school in Brooklyn come of age in the early sixties finding romance and the chaos accompanying it. Andrew McCarthy, Donald Sutherland, John Heard, Mary Stuart Masterson, Kevin Dillon. w. Charles Purpura, d. Michael Dinner.

COMEDY: COMEDY DRAMA: Coming of Age; Love-First; Sexuality; Ensemble Films; Ensemble-Male; Boys' Schools; Religion; Priests; New York Life; Bratpack Movies; Hidden Gems

(Five Corners; Mischief)

Heaven Knows, Mr. Allison, 1957, 105m, ★★★1/2/$$$, 20th/CBS-Fox. A missionary nun and a hard-bitten marine who can't stand each other have to join forces to fight the Japs in the South Pacific when stranded on an island together. Robert Mitchum, Deborah Kerr (BActress). w. John Lee Mahin, John Huston (BAScr), N-adap. Charles Shaw, d. John Huston. Oscars: 2-0.

COMEDY DRAMA: War Stories; ROMANCE: Romantic Comedy; Romantic Drama; Romance-Opposites Attract; Tough Guys & Religious Women; World War II Stories; Battle of the Sexes; Stranded on an Island; Roommates; Islands; South Pacific; Spinsters; Nuns; Soldiers; Macho Men; Feisty Females; Hidden Gems; Female Protagonists

(The African Queen; Rooster Cogburn)

Heaven Only Knows, 1947, 98m, ★★/$, UA/NA. An outlaw cowboy gets a visit from a guardian angel who makes him mend his ways. Robert Cummings, Brian Donlevy, Marjorie Reynolds. w. Art Arthur, Rowland Leigh, d. Albert S. Rogell.

WESTERNS: Western Comedy; COMEDY DRAMA: Angels; Cowboys; Redemption

Heaven with a Gun, 1969, 101m, ★★1/2/$, MGM/MGM-UA, PG/V. In a small Western town, the new preacher has a past: he used to be a gun fighter. This fact becomes apparent soon enough. Glenn Ford, Carolyn Jones, David Carradine. w. Richard Carr, d. Lee Katzin.

WESTERNS: DRAMA: Preachers; Gunfighters; Past-Haunted by the; Murderers-Nice; Small-Town Life; Small-Town Scandals; Duels

Heavenly Pursuits, 1986, 91m, ★★1/2/$, Island/NA. Miracles begin occuring at a Scottish Catholic school and a skeptical teacher investigates. Tom Conti, Helen Mirren, Brian Pettifer, David Hayman, Dave Anderson, Jennifer Black. w. d. Charles Gormley.

COMEDY DRAMA: SATIRE: Religion; Religious Comedy; Miracles; Teachers; Scotland; Quiet Little Films; British Films; Writer-Directors

Heavens Above, 1963, 118m, ★★1/2/$$, British Lion/Facets. A tin-pot social-ist parson gets sent to an upper-crust village in England and tries to convert them. Somehow he ends up becoming a national hero and being sent into outer space. Peter Sellers, Isabel Jeans, Cecil Parker, Brock Peters, Ian Carmichael. w. Frank Harvey, John Boulting, d. John Boulting.

COMEDY: SATIRE: Social Satire; Power-Rise to; Politicians; Political Activists; Astronauts; Heroes-Unlikely; Forgotten Films

(I'm All Right, Jack; Only Two Can Play)

Heaven's Gate, 1980, 219m, ★★1/2/$, UA/MGM-UA, PG/V-P-S. In Wyoming in the late 1800s, cattle ranchers struggle to make their mark and keep rustlers and immigrants off their land. Kris Kristofferson, Christopher Walken, John Hurt, Sam Waterston, Brad Dourif, Isabelle Huppert, Joseph Cotten, Jeff Bridges. w. d. Michael Cimino.

WESTERNS: DRAMA: Epics; Ensemble Films; Cattle Ranchers; Cattle Rustlers; Montana Cattle Problems; Prostitutes with Heart of Gold; Small-Town Life; Flops-Major; Coulda Been Great; Writer-Directors

(McCabe and Mrs. Miller; Comes a Horseman)

(Ed: Such a major, unreleasable flop in its original, mammoth form, it toppled United Artists studio, hence that company's merger with MGM. It has gained stature since)

Heavy Metal, 1981, 90m, ★★1/2/$$, Col/RCA-Col, PG/S-P-V. After the magazine of the same name, a series of "adult" animated sex and science-fiction fantasies set to rock music. w. Dan Goldberg, Len Blum, Richard Corben, Angus McKie, Dan O'Bannon, Thomas Warkentin, Berni Wrightson, d. Gerald Potterton.
Cartoons; Musicals-Animated; Music Movies; Rock Stars; Party Movies; Cult Films
(Rock-a-Doodle-Doo; Cool World)

Heavyweights, 1994, 98m, ★★1/2/$, Caravan-Disney/Disney, PG/P. A fat farm for kids is taken over by a greedy yuppie who threatens to ruin the ironic fun the overweight kids there were having. Tom McGowan, Aaron Schwartz, Shaun Weiss, Tom Hodges, Leah Lail, Paul Feig, Kenan Thompson, David Bowe, Max Goldblatt, Robert Zalkind, Patrick LaBrecque, Jeffrey Tambor, Jerry Stiller, Anne Meara, Ben Stiller. w. Judd Apatow & Steven Brill, d. Brill.
COMEDY: CHILDREN'S: Camps; Weight Problems; Mortgage Drama
(Angus)

Hedda, 1975, 102m, ★★★1/2/$$, Brut-Embassy/Media. An adaptation of the famous proto-feminist Ibsen play about a pregnant woman who hates her husband and exacts a revenge ultimately more devastating to herself than him. Glenda Jackson (BActress), Peter Eyre, Timothy West, Jennie Linden, Patrick Stewart. w. d. Trevor Nunn, P-adap. Henrik Ibsen, *Hedda Gabler*. Oscars: 1-0.
DRAMA: Abortion Dilemmas; Mean Women; Power Struggles; Battle of the Sexes; Revenge; Romance-Reunited; Dose of Own Medicine-Given; Suicidal Tendencies; Homoeroticism; Scandinavia; Female Protagonists; Classic Literary Adaptations; Stagelike Films; Hidden Gems; British Films
(Miss Julie; A Doll's House)

Heidi, 1937, 88m, ★★★/$$$$, 20th/Fox. In a mountain village, a girl whose parents have died brightens the lonely world of her curmudgeonly uncle. Shirley Temple, Jean Hersholt, Arthur Treacher, Helen Westley. w. Walter Ferris, Julian Josephson, N-adap. Johanna Spyri, d. Allan Dwan.
COMEDY DRAMA: MELODRAMA: CHILDREN'S: Girls; Men and Girls;

Orphans; Alps; Fairy Tales; Child Protagonists
(Bright Eyes; A Little Princess)

Heimat, 1984, 924m, ★★★/$$, Edgar Reitz-WDR/NA. The residents of a German village deal with the enormous upheavals and changes from World War I to the 1980s. Marita Breuer, Michael Lesch, Dieter Schaad. w. Edgar Reitz, Peter Steinbach, d. Reitz.
DRAMA: Miniseries; War Stories; Small-Town Life; Germany; World War I Stories; World War II Stories; Nazi Stories; German Films; Epics; Episodic Stories; Multiple Stories; Interwoven Stories; Curiosities; Historical Drama
(Berlin Alexanderplatz)

The Heiress, 1949, 115m, ★★★1/2/$$$, Par/Par. An incorrigable rogue seduces a homely girl in Old New York merely to get at her money-but she has his number . . . eventually. Olivia de Havilland (**BActress**), Ralph Richardson (**BSActor**), Montgomery Clift, Miriam Hopkins, Vanessa Brown. w. P-adap. Augustus Goetz, N-adap. Henry James (*Washington Square*), d. William Wyler (**BDirector**). BPicture, **BB&Art, BB&WCostume, BOScore, BB&WCin.** 8-4.
DRAMA: MELODRAMA: Costume Drama; ROMANCE: Family Drama; Romantic Drama; Romance-Doomed; Lover Family Dislikes; Spinsters; Playboys; Con Artists; Heiresses; Golddiggers; Wallflowers; Wallflowers & Hunks; Hidden Gems
COMIC FLIPSIDE: A New Leaf
(Portrait of a Lady; The Age of Innocence; Suspicion; Masquerade; The Bostonians; The Europeans; To Each His Own)

The Helen Morgan Story, 1957, 118m, ★★1/2/$$, WB/WB. A biopic of the vaudeville star who rose to Broadway fame, all the while descending into alcoholism. Ann Blyth, Paul Newman, Richard Carlson, Gene Evans, Alan King, Walter Woolf King. w. Oscar Saul, Dean Riesner, Stephen Longstreet, Nelson Gidding, d. Michael Curtiz.
DRAMA: MELODRAMA: Biographies; Vaudeville; Singers; Fame-Rise to;
ROMANCE: Romantic Drama; Marriage Drama; Marriage on the Rocks; Alcoholics; Theater Life; Actresses; Female Protagonists; Forgotten Films
(I'll Cry Tomorrow; Start; Funny Girl)

Hell and High Water, 1954, 103m, ★★★/$$$, 20th/Fox. A privately funded paramilitary unit goes to Alaska to nip a budding Red Chinese plot against the U.S. Richard Widmark, Bella Darvi, Victor Francen, David Wayne, Cameron Mi small daily trials of the Twentieth Century. Marita Breuer, Michael Lesch, Dieter Schaad, Karin Keinzler, Eva Maria Bayerswaltes, Rudiger Wigang.
ACTION: ADVENTURE: War Stories; Military Stories; Cold War Era; Alaska; Snow Settings; Communists; Chinese People; Anarchists; Special Teams-Military; Faded Hits

Hell, Heaven, and Hoboken, 1958, 100m, ★★★/$, Ind/NA. An actor poses as the great General Montgomery to confuse the Germans in North Africa during World War II. John Mills, Cecil Parker, M. E. Clifton-James, Patrick Allen. w. Bryan Forbes, NF-adap. M. E. Clifton-James, d. John Guillermin.
COMEDY: War Stories; Military Comedy; World War II Stories; Impostors-Actors; Misunderstandings; Germans as Enemy; Desert Settings; Africa
(General Della Rovere; Moon Over Parador)

Hell in the Pacific, 1969, 104m, ★★★/$$, Cinerama/Fox. Two soldiers are stranded on a desert isle in the midst of World War II: an American pilot and a Japanese officer. Having to cooperate to survive, they slowly form a tenuous friendship. Lee Marvin, Toshiro Mifune. w. Alexander Jacobs, Eric Bercovici, d. John Boorman.
DRAMA: War Stories; World War II Stories; Japanese People; Soldies; Japanese as Enemy; Stranded on an Island; Race Relations; Friends as Enemies; Islands; Pacific Islands; Curiosities; Good Premise Unfulfilled
(Enemy Mine; Heaven Knows, Mr. Allison)

Hellbound: Hellraiser II, 1988, 93m, ★★/$$, New World/New World, R/EV-P-S-B&G. The chief doctor at a mental hospital conducts strange and sadistic experiments on his patients involving bloody mattresses which act as portals to hell. Clare Higgins, Ashley Lawrence, Kenneth Cranham, Imogen Boorman. w. Peter Atkins, SS-adap. Clive Barker, d. Tony Randel.
HORROR: SCI-FI: Psychiatrists; Asylums; Satan; Satanism; Hell; Widows;

Ghosts; Return of Spouse; Cult Films; Zombies

Hellcats of the Navy, 1957, 82m, ★★/$, Col/Goodtimes. A submarine crew braves the dangers of the deep and the kamikaze attacks of the Japanese to emerge victorious in the South Pacific. Ronald Reagan, Nancy Davis, Arthur Franz, Robert Arthur. w. David Lang, Raymond Marcus, NF-adap. Charles A. Lockwood, Hans Christian Adamson, d. Nathan Juran.

MELODRAMA: ACTION: Action Drama; War Stories; World War II Stories; Submarines; Japanese as Enemy; Pacific Ocean; War at Sea; Camp; Unintentionally Funny; Patriotic Films

Heller in Pink Tights, 1960, 100m, ★★★/$$, Par/Par. A traveling theater troupe has misadventures in the wild old West with a beautiful Italian star leading the way. Sophia Loren, Anthony Quinn, Steve Forrest, Eileen Heckart, Edmund Lowe, Margaret O'Brien, Ramon Novarro. w. Dudley Nichols, Walter Bernstein, N-adap. Louis L'Amour (*Heller with a Gun*), d. George Cukor.

COMEDY: WESTERNS: Western Comedy; Circus Life; Theater Life; Journies; Ensemble Films; Sexy Women; Curiosities; Hidden Gems; Forgotten Films

(The Greatest Show on Earth; Trapeze)

Hello Again, 1987, 96m, ★★½/$$, Touchstone/Touchstone, PG/P-S. A psychic brings her sister back a year after her death, caused by choking on an hors d'oeuvre, to check out what her hubby's been up to. She's none too pleased. Shelly Long, Judith Ivey, Thor Fields, Corbin Bernson, Gabriel Byrne, Sela Ward. w. Susan Isaacs, d. Frank Perry.

COMEDY: Marriage Comedy; Dead-Back from the; Return of Spouse; Widowers; Sisters; Psychics; Fortune Tellers; Eccentric People; Revenge; Cheating Men; Curiosities; Coulda Been Great; Female Protagonists; Female Screenwriters

(Blithe Spirit; She's Back; Move Over, Darling)

(Ed: The stars hold it together with a few good jokes along the way; only suitable for incidental cable viewing)

Hello Dolly, 1969, 129m, ★★★/$$$$, 20th/Fox. In New York in the Gay Nineties, a matchmaker whose husband has died goes after a rich businessman, deciding to help herself out to a prospect.

Barbra Streisand, Walter Matthau, Michael Crawford, Marianne McAndrew, Tommy Tune. w. Ernest Lehman, (musical)-adap. Jerry Herman, Michael Stewart, P-adap. Thornton Wilder (*The Matchmaker*), d. Gene Kelly. BPicture, BCin, **BMScore, BArt, BSound,** BCostume, BEdit. Oscars: 7-3.

MUSICALS: COMEDY: Musical Comedy; **ROMANCE:** Musical Romance; Matchmakers; Jewish People; 1890s; Romance-Older Men/Younger Women; Romance-Girl Wants Boy; Female Protagonists; Production Design-Outstanding

(The Matchmaker; Funny Girl)

(Ed: Considered a flop by many, mostly due to its swollen budget, it still brought in major box office, and if you can overlook Streisand playing a woman twice her age, it's not so bad at all)

Hello Down There, 1969, 98m, ★★½/$, MGM/NA. A scientist/architect who designs an underwater house becomes his own guinea pig and has to survive in it for at least a month to avoid embarrassment in the press for its probable failure. Tony Randall, Janet Leigh, Jim Backus, Roddy McDowell, Merv Griffin, Richard Dreyfuss. w. Frank Telford, John McGreevey, d. Jack Arnold.

COMEDY: CHILDREN'S: FAMILY: Underwater Adventure; Experiments; Scientists; Inventors; Family Comedy

Hello Frisco Hello, 1943, 98m, ★★★/$$$, 20th/Fox. A San Fransisco nightclub singer rises to superstardom. Alice Faye, John Payne, Jack Oakie, Lynn Bari, June Havoc, Ward Bond, Aubrey Mather, George Barbier. w. Robert Ellis, Helen Logan, Richard Macauley, d. Bruce Humberstone.

MUSICALS: Singers; San Francisco; Nostalgia; Fame-Rise to; Female Protagonists; Nightclubs; Faded Hits

(In Old Chicago; The Dolly Sisters)

Hellraiser, 1988, 93m, ★★½/$$, New World/New World, R/EV-S-P-B&G. After her lover dies, a woman engages in elaborate rituals involving bloody mattresses and an oriental puzzle box to bring him back from Hell. Unfortunately, she brings up a lot of other characters as well, and, since they haven't got any skin, they go searching for it. Andrew Robinson, Clare Higgins, Ashley Laurence, Sean Chapman, Oliver Smith. w. d., N-adap. Clive Barker (*The Hellbound Heart*).

HORROR: SCI-FI: Satan; Satanism; Hell; Widows; Ghosts; Return of Spouse; Cult Films; Zombies

Hellraiser III: Hell on Earth, 1992, ★★★½/$$, New World/New World, R/EV-P-S-B&G. Pinhead and his cohorts are brought back from Hell through a mysterious sculpture bought by a studly nightclub owner. He makes a pact with Pinhead but loses more than his soul in the bargain. Terry Farrell, Doug Bradley, Paula Marshall, Kevin Bernhardt, Ken Carpenter, Peter Boynton, Aimee Leigh. w. Peter Atkins, Tony Randel, d. Anthony Hickox.

HORROR: SCI-FI: Satan; Satanism; Hell; Widows; Ghosts; Return of Spouse; Cult Films; Zombies; Selling One's Soul

Hell's Angels, 1930, 135m, ★★★/$$$$, Howard Hughes/MCA-U. During World War I, two young friends join up and become star fighter pilots. Ben Lyon, James Hall, Jean Harlow, John Darrow. w. Howard Estabrook, Harry Behn, d. Howard Hughes.

ACTION: War Stories; Pilots-Military; World War I Stories; Friendships-Male; Blockbusters; Faded Hits; Forgotten Films

(Wings)

The Hellstrom Chronicle, 1971, 90m, ★★★/$$, David Wolper-WB/Col. A documentary (which coincided with the popular notion that bugs would soon take over the world) narrated by Dr. Nils Hellstrom, an entomologist who explains the insect world for you-its facinating facts and its dangers. Laurence Pressman. w. David Seltzer, d. Walon Green.

BDocumentary Feature. Oscars: 1-1. Documentaries; Animal Stories; Nature-Back to; Insects; Narrated Films; Curiosities; Sleeper Hits

Hellzapoppin, 1942, 84m, ★★★½/$$$, U/NA. A "puttin' on a show" story about two comics and Hollywood neophytes who try to make a movie. Ole Olsen, Chic Johnson, Hugh Herbert, Martha Raye, Mischa Auer, Robert Paige, Shemp Howard, Elisha Cook Jr, Richard Lane. w. Nat Perrin, Warren Wilson, d. H. C. Potter.

COMEDY: Putting on a Show; Moviemaking; Hollywood Life; Hollywood Satire; 1940s; Comedians; Comedy-Gag; Cult Films; Curiosities; Hidden Gems

Helter Skelter, 1949, 75m, ★★½/$, GFD/NA. The BBC helps out a young

woman of the upper classes when she develops a bad case of the hiccups. Carol Marsh, David Tomlinson, Mervyn Johns, Peter Hammond, Jimmy Edwards, Richard Hearne, Jon Pertwee, Terry-Thomas. w. Patrick Campbell, d. Ralph Thomas.
COMEDY: Documentaries; Spoofs; Heiresses; Curiosities; Eccentric People; TV Life; Radio Life; British Films

Helter Skelter, 1976, 194m, ★★★/ $$$$$, CBS/Fox, PG/V. The story of the Tate—La Bianca murders which exposed one of the most terrifying cults ever in American history-Charles Manson's "family." George DiCenzo, Steve Railsback, Marilyn Burns. d. Tom Gries.
DRAMA: Courtroom Drama; Murders-Mass; Psycho-Killers; Mental Illness; 1960s; Psychedelic Era; Serial Killers; Lawyers; Lawyers as Detectives; TV Movies
(Ed: One of the first big, realistic TV miniseries)

Hemingway's Adventures of a Young Man (*Adventures of a Young Man*), 1962, 145m, ★★★/$$, 20th/NA. A doctor's son with a repressive religious mother decides to head out into the wilderness to find himself, based loosely upon Hemingway's Nick Adams character. Richard Beymer, Diane Baker, Corinne Calvet, Fred Clark, Arthur Kennedy, Ricardo Montalgban, Susan Strasberg, Paul Newman, Jessica Tandy, Eli Wallach. w. A. E. Hotchner, SS-adap. Ernest Hemingway, d. Martin Ritt.
DRAMA: ADVENTURE: Young Men; Family Drama; Nature-Back to; Coming of Age; Teenagers; Hidden Gems; Forgotten Films; All-Star Casts

Henry and June, 1990, 136m, ★★★/$$, U/MCA-U, NC-17/ES-P-FFN-MRN. Sexy young Anais Nin, author of the famous erotic diaries, has an affair with author Henry Miller and his very young wife, June, leading to all kinds of entanglements. Fred Ward, Uma Thurman, Maria de Medeiros, Richard E. Grant, Kevin Spacey. w. Philip Kaufman, Rose Kaufman, NF-adap. Anais Nin, d. Philip Kaufman. BCin. Oscars: 1-0.
DRAMA: Erotic Drama; Alternative Lifestyles; ROMANCE: Romance-Triangles; Romantic Drama; Menage a Trois; Autobiographical Stories; Biographies; Paris; Wild People; Lesbians; Bisexuality; Roaring 20s; Writers
(The Moderns; Tropic of Cancer)

Henry V, 1944, 137m, ★★★/$$$, Rank-UA/Par. A beautiful opening up of Shakespeare's play: it starts in the Globe theatre, then we "enter" the world of the play as it becomes more filmic. The story concerns the King's romance with a French princess and his rejection of his old friend Falstaff. Laurence Olivier, Robert Newton, Leslie Banks, Esmond Knight, Renee Asherson, George Robey, Leo Gunn, Ernest Thesiger, Harcourt Williams, Felix Aylmer, John Laurie. w. Laurence Olivier, Alan Dent, P-adap. William Shakespeare, d. Laurence Olivier.

Henry V, 1989, 137m, ★★★1/2/$$$, Goldwyn/Goldwyn, PG-13/V. After losing his claim to the throne of France, Henry retakes it in battle, also clumsily winning the heart of the French princess in the process. Kenneth Branagh (BActor), Derek Jacobi, Simon Shepherd, James Larkin, Brian Blessed, James Simmons, Paul Gregory, Ian Holm, Paul Scofield, Emma Thompson. w. Kenneth Branagh, P-adap. William Shakespeare, d. Kenneth Branagh (BDirector). BCostume. Oscars: 3-1.
DRAMA: Epics; ROMANCE: Romantic Drama; Historical Drama; War Stories; War Battles Revenge; Young Men; Young Men-Angry; Friendships-Male; Kings; Royalty; Middle Ages; Classic Literary Adaptations; Shakespeare; British Films
(Richard III; Much Ado About Nothing)
(Ed: A darker, less jingoistic version than Olivier's, which was in part a rallying cry for the British troops in World War II)

Henry VIII and His Six Wives, 1972, 125m, ★★1/2/$, EMI/NA, PG/S. The title is self-explanatory. Told from the king's deathbed. Keith Mitchell, Frances Cuka, Charlotte Rampling, Jane Asher, Jenny Bos, Lynne Frederick, Barbara Leigh-Hunt, Donald Pleasance. w. Ian Thorne, d. Waris Hussein.
DRAMA: Costume Drama; Historical Drama; Marriage Drama; Kings; Bigamy; Executions; Evil Men; England; British Films
(Anne of the Thousand Days)

Henry: Portrait of a Serial Killer, 1990, 83m, ★★★1/2/$$$, Ind/MPI, R-NC-17/EV-P-S-B&G. A deranged young man and his pal run around murdering and torturing random, innocent victims. Michael Rooker, Tom Towles, Tracy Arnold. w. Richard Fire, John McNaughton, d. John McNaughton.

DRAMA: HORROR: Serial Killers; Psycho Killers; MURDER: Murderers-Mass; Murders of Women; True Stories; Biographies; Biographies-Fictional; Road Movies; Outlaw Road Movies; Buddy Films; Criminal Couples; Friendships-Male; Revenge; Jealousy; Violence-Sudden; Mental Illness; Sleeper Hits; Hidden Gems
(The Deliberate Stranger; Peeping Tom)
(Ed: Extremely controversial and disgustingly realistic, though not particularly gory; travels the story of infamous serial killer Henry Lee Lucas, though only pieces of what's not even known for certain. Often very hard to find)

Her Alibi, 1989, 94m, ★★1/2/$$, WB/WB, PG-13/P-S. A beautiful, accident-prone woman needs an alibi for murder which a mystery writer is sympathetic to, but when he gets an arrow in his backside. . . . Tom Selleck, Paulina Porizkova, William Daniels, Tess Harper, James Farentino, Hurd Hatfield, Patrick Wayne. w. Charlie Peters, d. Bruce Beresford.
COMEDY: MURDER: MYSTERY: MURDER MYSTERY: Comic Mystery; Comedy-Slapstick; Comedy of Errors; Accident Prone; Writers; Models; Sexy Women; ROMANCE: Romantic Comedy; Fugitives from the Law; Fugitives-Harboring; Murderers-Female; Coulda Been Good; Good Premise Unfulfilled
(Folks!; Three Men and a Baby)

Herbie Goes Bananas, 1980, 100m, ★★/$$, Disney/Disney, G. A couple take Herbie the Love Bug on a trip to South America, where he has many a chance to save them from comical predicaments. Charles Martin Smith, Stephan W. Burns, Cloris Leachman, John Vernon. w. Don Tait, d. Vincent McEveety.
CHILDREN'S: FAMILY: ACTION: Action Comedy; COMEDY: Comedy-Slapstick; Objects with Personalities; Car Racing; South America
SEQUEL TO: Herbie Goes to Monte Carlo; The Love Bug

Herbie Goes to Monte Carlo, 1977, 105m, ★★/$$$, Disney/Disney, G. The magical VW is at it again, this time entering the Monte Carlo Grand Prix. Dean Jones, Don Knotts, Julie Sommar, Roy Kinnear. w. Arthur Abberg, Don Nelson, d. Vincent McEveety.
CHILDREN'S: FAMILY: ACTION: Action Comedy; COMEDY: Comedy-Slapstick;

Objects with Personalities; Car Racing
Monte Carlo
SEQUEL TO: Herbie Rides Again, The
Love Bug.

Herbie Rides Again, 1974, 88m, ★★★/
$$$, Disney/Disney, G. Herbie gives a
slumlord his comeuppance when he mis-
treats an elderly woman. Helen Hayes,
Ken Berry, Stefanie Powers, John
McIntyre, Keenan Wynn, Huntz Hall.
w. Bill Walsh, d. Robert Stevenson.
CHILDREN'S: FAMILY: ACTION: Action
Comedy; **COMEDY:** Comedy-Slapstick;
Objects with Personalities; Car Racing;
Elderly Women; Mortgage Drama;
Corporation as Enemy

Hercules, 1957, 105m, ★★/$$$,
Ind/Vidmark. Jason and the Argonauts
solicit the help of Hercules in their quest
for the golden fleece. Steve Reeves,
Sylvia Koscina, Gianna Maria Canale,
Fabrizio Mione. w. Pietro Francisci,
Ennio de Concini, Gaio Frattini, d. Pietro
Francisci.

**Hercules in New York, (Hercules
Goes Bananas; Hercules-The Movie)**,
1969, 105m, ★/$, Ind/MPI. Hercules
joins the pro-wrestling circuit
in New York. Arnold Stang, Arnold
Schwarzenegger, Deborah Loomis, James
Karen, Ernest Graves. w. Aubrey
Wisberg, d. Arthur A. Seidelman.

Hercules Unchained, 1959, 105m,
★★/$$, Ind/MPI. The big lug has prob-
lems with royalty in his homeland, but
soon sets them straight. Steve Reeves,
Sylvia Koscina, Sylvia Lopez. w. Pietro
Francisci, Ennio di Concini, d. Francisci.
ACTION: Heroes-Super; Body Builders;
Ancient Times; Greece; Mythology;
Camp; Independent Films

Here Come the Girls (*Champagne for
Everybody*), 1953, 78m, ★★¹/2/$$,
Par/Par. A has-been vaudeville performer
gets a little glory and the girl while solv-
ing a backstage mystery. Bob Hope,
Rosemary Clooney, Tony Martin, Arlene
Dahl, Millard Mitchell, Fred Clark,
William Demarest, Robert Strauss.
w. Edmund Hartmann, Hal Kanter,
d. Claude Binyon.
**COMEDY: MURDER: MYSTERY: MUR-
DER MYSTERY:** Comic Mystery; 1890s;
Vaudeville; Theater Life

Here Comes Mr. Jordan, 1941, 93m,
★★★¹/2/$$$, Col/Col. A saxophone-
playing prizefighter is en route to a match
when his private plane crashes.

Unfortunately, his guardian angel jumps
the gun and snatches his soul up to
heaven prematurely: he was to have sur-
vived to live another forty years. When he
goes back to retrieve his body, he discov-
ers it's been cremated, so he must find a
new one. Robert Montgomery (BActor),
Evelyn Keyes, Rita Johnson, Claude
Rains, James Gleason (BSActor), Edward
Everett Horton, John Emery, Donald
MacBride, Halliwell Hobbes. w. Seton I.
Miller, Sidney Buchman (**BOStory,
BScr**), P-adap. Harry Segall, (Halfway to
Heaven), d. Alexander Hall (BDirector).
BPicture, BB&WCin. Oscars: 7-2.
COMEDY: COMEDY DRAMA: Fantasy;
Reincarnation; Dead-Back from the;
Heaven; Angels; Boxing; Airplane
Crashes; Body Switching; Hidden Gems;
Faded Hits
REMAKE: Heaven Can Wait
(Angel on My Shoulder; Down to Earth;
A Guy Named Joe; Heaven Only Knows;
The Horn Blows at Midnight; That's the
Spirit; Ghost)

Here Comes the Groom, 1951, 114m,
★★¹/2/$$, Par/Par. After World War II, an
idealistic foreign correspondent adopts
orphans and has some disciplinary prob-
lems. Bing Crosby, Jane Wyman,
Franchot Tone, Alexis Smith, James
Barton, Anna Maria Alberghetti. w.
Virginia Van Upp, Myles Connelly, Liam
O'Brian, Story: Robert Riskin (BOStory).
d. Frank Capra. **BOSong.** Oscars: 2-1.
COMEDY: COMEDY DRAMA: Family
Comedy; Marriage Comedy; Orphans;
Children-Adopted; Journalists; Fathers-
Troublesome
(Father Goose; Houseboat)

Here Comes the Navy, 1934, 86m,
★★¹/2/$$$, WB/NA. Two friends in the
Navy must navigate through rough waters
when one man is promoted to Petty
Officer and must command the other.
James Cagney, Pat O'Brien, Dorothy Tree,
Gloria Stuart, Frank McHugh. w. Ben
Markson, Earl Baldwin, d. Lloyd Bacon.
BPicture. Oscars: 1-0.
DRAMA: COMEDY DRAMA: Military
Stories; Military Comedy; Friendships-
Male; Friends as Enemies; Feuds; Faded
Hits; Forgotten Films

**Here We Go Round the Mulberry
Bush**, 1967, 96m, ★★★/$$, UA/NA,
R/S-P-FRN-MRN. A college student in
England drops out in order to devote
more time to losing his virginity. Barry

Evans, Judy Geeson, Angela Scoular,
Adrienne Posta, Vanessa Howard,
Denholm Elliott, Michael Bates. w.
Hunter Davies, Larry Kramer, N-adap.
Hunter Davies, d. Clive Donner.
COMEDY: ROMANCE: Romantic
Comedy; Erotic Comedy; Sex Comedy;
Virgins; England; College Life; Young
Men; Love-First; Forgotten Films; Time
Capsules; Mod Era; Hidden Gems
(Oxford Blues; A Yank at Eton)

Her Husband's Affairs, 1947, 83m,
★★¹/2/$$, Col/Goodtimes. A man and his
wife in advertising strike out on their own
to sell a hair-growing product with
calamitous results. Lucille Ball, Franchot
Tone, Edward Everett Horton, Mikhail
Rasumny, GeneRobert Barrat. w. Ben
Markson, Earl Baldwin, d. Lloyd Bacon.
COMEDY: ROMANCE: Romantic
Comedy; Partners-Married; Marriage
Comedy; Inventors; Comedy of Errors;
Forgotten Films
(Easy Living; Fuller Brush Girl)

Hero, 1992, 116m, ★★/$, Tri-Star/Col-
Tri, PG-13/P-S. After a plane crashes, a
down-and-out fellow/bum rescues several
of the passengers, including a TV news
reporter, but after he tells his pal and no
one else will believe him, the pal takes
the credit and becomes a celebrity. Dustin
Hoffman, Geena Davis, Andy Garcia, Joan
Cusack, Kevin J. O'Connor, Maury
Chaykin. w. David Webb Peoples, Laura
Ziskin, Alvin Sargent, d. Stephen Frears.
DRAMA: COMEDY DRAMA: SATIRE:
Airplane Crashes; Heroes-Unlikely;
Homeless People; Journalists; TV Life;
Fathers-Troublesome; Ethics; Liars;
Impostors; Identities-Assumed; Flops-
Major; Capra-esque; Old-Fashioned
Recent Films; Coulda Been Good
(Hail, The Conquering Hero; Nothing
Sacred)·
(Ed: It bogs down half-way through and
doesn't seem to know which way it's going
by the end)

**A Hero Ain't Nothin' but a
Sandwich**, 1977, 107m, ★★¹/2/$, New
World/New World, PG. A nobly suffering
black family survives life in the ghetto.
Cicely Tyson, Paul Winfield, Larry B.
Scott, Helen Martin, Glynn Turman. w.,
N-adap. Alice Childress, d. Ralph
Nelson.
DRAMA: COMEDY DRAMA: Black
Casts; Family Drama; Black Men; Black
Women; Inner City Life; Poor People;

Coulda Been Good; 1970s; Black Screenwriters; Black Directors; Female Screenwriters
(Claudine; Crooklyn; Cornbread Ernie and Me)

Hero at Large, 1980, 98m, ★★1/2/$$, MGM/MGM-UA, PG. An actor playing a superhero saves a child from a fire while in costume and becomes a folk hero. His fans turn on him, however, when he fails to live up to his superhero image. John Ritter, Anne Archer, Bert Convy, Kevin McCarthy, Harry Bellaver. w. A. J. Carothers, d. Martin Davidson.
COMEDY: ACTION: Action Comedy; Heroes-Unlikely; Secrets-Keeping; Dual Lives; ROMANCE: Romantic Comedy; Fires; Saving Someone; Sleeper Hits; Forgotten Films
(Meteor Man)

Heroes, 1977, 113m, ★★1/2/$$$, U/MCA-U, PG. A young woman falls for and domesticates a slightly off-kilter Vietnam veteran. Sally Field, Henry Winkler, Harrison Ford, Val Avery. w. James Carabatsos (David Freeman, uncredited), d. Jeremy Paul Kagan.
COMEDY: COMEDY DRAMA: ROMANCE: Romantic Comedy; Vietnam Veterans; Eccentric People; Marriage Comedy; Romance-Reluctant; Sleeper Hits; Forgotten Films; Faded Hits

The Heroes of Telemark, 1965, 131m, ★★1/2/$$, UA/NA. The allies solicit the help of Norwegian resistance fighters to capture a water plant. Kirk Douglas, Richard Harris, Ulla Jacobsson, Roy Dotrice, Michael Redgrave. w. Ivan Moffat, Ben Barzman, d. Anthony Mann.
ACTION: War Stories; World War II Stories; Scandinavia; Special Teams-Military

Hester Street, 1974, 89m, (B&W), ★★★1/2/$$, Midwest Films/Vestron, PG. A saga of the Eastern-European Jewish migration to the East Side of New York around the turn of the century, and one young woman's struggle with the New World. Steven Keats, Carol Kane (BActress), Mel Howard, Dorrie Kavanaugh, Doris Roberts. w. d. Joan Micklin Silver, SS-adap. Abraham Cahan (Yekl). Oscars: 1-0.
DRAMA: Immigrants; 1900s; Jewish People; New York Life; Young Women; Sleeper Hits; Cult Films; Forgotten Films; Hidden Gems; Female Protagonists; Female Screenwriters;

Female Directors; Writer-Directors (Chilly Scenes of Winter; Crossing Delancey; The Chosen; Yentl)

Hey, Good Lookin', 1982, 76m, ★★1/2/$$, WB/WB, PG/S. An animated film about the coming-of-age of two girl-obsessed guys in Brooklyn in the fifties. Voices of Richard Romanus, David Proval, Jesse Welles, Tina Bowman. w. d. Ralph Bakshi.
Cartoons; COMEDY DRAMA: Coming of Age; New York Life; Nostalgia; 1950s (The Lords of Flatbush; Fritz the Cat)

The Hidden, 1988, 97m, ★★★/$$, Ind/Media, R/P-S-V-B&G. Strange alien creatures take over bodies with wormlike tentacles, and it's up to detectives to figure who's been taken over and stop the parasites. Kyle MacLachlan, Michael Nouri, Claudia Christian, Clarence Felder, Clu Gulager, Richard Brooks. w. Bob Hunt, d. Jack Sholder.

The Hidden 2, 1994, 91m, ★★/$, New Line/New Line, R/EV. More of the same. Rafael Sbarge, Kate Hodge, Michael Nouri. w. d. Seth Pinkser.
Writer-Directors
HORROR: SCI-FI: SUSPENSE: MURDER: MYSTERY: MURDER MYSTERY: Aliens-Outer Space, Evil; Parasites; Detective Stories; Trail of a Killer; Hidden Gems
(Body Snatchers; Invasion of the Body Snatchers; The Puppet Masters)

Hidden Agenda, 1990, 109m, ★★★/$, Hemdale/HBO, R/P-V. In Ulster, the police collaborate with the bombers of IRA sympathizers and it's up to a woman caught in the middle to help figure out the connection. Brian Cox, Frances McDormand, Brad Dourif, Mai Zetterling, Bernard Bloch, Patrick Kavanagh. w. Jim Allen, d. Ken Loach.
DRAMA: Political Drama; Conspiracy; MYSTERY: Courtroom Drama; Trials; IRA; Ireland; Irish People; Avenging Death of Someone; Americans Abroad (In the Name of the Father; Michael Collins)
(Ed: More for political buffs than entertainment)

Hideaway, 1995, 102m, ★★1/2/$$, Tri-Star/Col-Tri, R/P-V-S. A man is brought back from the dead after a car crash that killed one of his daughters, and discovers he has psychic abilities. With these gifts he unfortunately has a connection to a serial killer who, transversely, can figure

out his thoughts as well, and learns of his other, living, daughter, who would make a good victim. Now to stop the serial killer from getting another child. Jeff Goldblum, Christine Lahti, Alicia Silverstone, Alfred Molina, Jeremy Sisto. w. Andrew Kevin Walker, Neal Jimenez, N-adap. Dean Koontz, d. Brett Leonard
HORROR: SUSPENSE: SCI-FI: Psychics; Serials Killers; Dead-Back from the; Car Crashes; Women in Jeopardy; Fathers & Daughters; Saving Someone; Coulda Been Great
(Fear; The Dark Half)

Hide in Plain Sight, 1980, 92m, ★★/$, MGM/MGM-UA, PG/P-V. When his ex-wife enters the witness protection program, a factory worker has a nightmare searching for his children. James Caan, Jill Eikenberry, Robert Viharo. w. Joseph Moncure March, d. James Caan.
DRAMA: MELODRAMA: Detective Stories; Ordinary People Stories; True Stories; Docudrama; Fathers & Sons; Fathers Alone; Missing Persons; Witnesses-Protecting; Searches; Good Premise Unfulfilled; Coulda Been Good; Actor Directors

Hider in the House, 1989, 108m, ★★1/2/$, Vestron/Vestron, PG. A family unknowingly harbors an accused murderer in its attic who is both courteous and seemingly safe. Gary Busey, Mimi Rogers, Michael McKean, Kurt Christopher Kinder, Candy Hutson, Elizabeth Ruscio, Chuck Lafont. w. Lem Dobbs, d. Matthew Patrick.
SUSPENSE: Fugitives from the Law; Roommates from Hell; Family Drama; Suburban Life; Hiding Out; Accused Unjustly; Murderers-Nice; Coulda Been Good; Curiosities

The High and the Mighty, 1954, 147m, ★★★/$$$, Wayne-WB/WB. One of the earliest disaster movies, about a commercial liner experiencing mechanical difficulties above the Pacific. John Wayne, Robert Newton, Robert Stack, Doe Avedon, Claire Trevor (BSActress), Laraine Day, Jan Sterling (BSActress), Phil Harris, Sidney Blackmer, John Howard. w., N-adap. Ernest K. Gann, d. William Wellman (BDirector). BOSong, BOScore. Oscars: 5-1.
DRAMA: MELODRAMA: SUSPENSE: Disaster Stories; Airplane Crashes; Pilots-Airline; Ahead of Its Time (Airport; Fate Is the Hunter)

High Anxiety, 1977, 94m, ★★★½/ $$$$, 20th/CBS-Fox, PG/P.. A psychologist believes he's being followed by murderers and he may not be merely paranoid as a group of deranged Hitchcock-spoof characters surround him. Mel Brooks, Madeline Kahn, Cloris Leachman, Harvey Korman, Ron Carey, Howard Morris, Dick Van Patten. w. Mel Brooks, Ron Clark, Rudy DeLuca, Barry Levinson, d. Mel Brooks.
COMEDY: Spoofs; SUSPENSE: Psychological Thriller; Psychologists; Hitchcockian; Eccentric People; Paranoia
(Young Frankenstein; Blazing Saddles; Silent Movie)

High-Ballin', 1978, 100m, ★★/$$, AIP/Vestron, PG. A truckdriver struggles against a huge firm to remain independent, all the while keeping hijackers and smokies at bay. Peter Fonda, Jerry Reed, Helen Shaver, Chris Wiggins. w. Paul Edwards, d. Peter Carter.
ACTION: COMEDY: Action Comedy; Truck Drivers; Thieves; Chase Stories; Hijackers
(Smokey and the Bandit; Handle with Care)

Higher Learning, 1995, 127m, ★★★/ $$$, Col/Col, R/EP-S-V. Several stories of life on a big state university campus as a freshman white girl and a black exchange student learn the ropes; tensions of all kinds, mostly about political correctness, rage all around them. Omar Epps, Kristy Swanson, Michael Rapaport, Ice Cube, Laurence Fishburne, Jason Wiles, Regina King, Jennifer Connelly, Tyra Banks. w. d. John Singleton.
DRAMA: Social Drama; Black Men; Black vs. White; Race Relations; College Life; 1990s; Multiple Stories; Rape/ Rapists; Exchange Students; Bigots; Writer-Directors; Black Directors; Black Screenwriters; Overlooked at Release
(PCU; Poetic Justice; Boyz n the Hood; Getting Straight; The Strawberry Statement)

High Heels, 1991, 108m, ★★★/$$, Orion/Par, Monterey, R/S. A newlywed learns that her husband is a former lover of her mother, an aging pop star. She also discovers that they have recently rekindled their affair. Victoria Abril, Marisa Paredes, Miguel Bose, Feodor Atkine, Pedro Diez del Corral. w. d. Pedro Almodovar.

COMEDY DRAMA: MELODRAMA: SATIRE: Sex Comedy; Erotic Comedy; ROMANCE: Romantic Comedy; Rock Stars; Singers; Marriage Comedy; Newlyweds; Cheating Men; Romance with Lover's Relative; Neurotic People; Eccentric People; Spanish Films; Cult Films; Writer-Directors
(Women on the Verge of a Nervous Breakdown; Kika; Tie Me Up! Tie Me Down!; Jamon, Jamon)

High Hopes, 1988, 112m, ★★½/$, BBC-Palace/Academy. A family whose members have gone down separate paths, to say the least, get together for the birthday of the matriarch. Philip Davis, Ruth Sheen, Edna Dore, Philip Jackson, Heather Tobias, Lesley Manville, David Bamber, Jason Watkins, Judith Scott. w. d. Mike Leigh.
COMEDY DRAMA: Family Comedy; Family Drama; Ensemble Films; Eccentric People; Parents vs. Children; Working Class; Feuds; British Films; Writer-Directors

Highlander, 1986, 111m, ★★½/$$$, EMI-Ind/Republic, R/EV. An immortal Scotsman fights his immortal nemesis throughout the ages, finally ending up in modern-day New York. Christopher Lambert, Roxanne Hart, Clancy Brown, Sean Connery. w. Gregory Widden, Peter Bellwood, Larry Ferguson, d. Russell Mulcahy.
ACTION: ADVENTURE: Sword & Sorcery; Time Travel; Chase Stories; Feuds; Men in Conflict; Scotland; Sleeper Hits
(Time After Time; Warlock)
(Ed: A flop in theaters in the States, it took off on video and overseas, spawning the sequels)

Highlander II-The Quickening, 1990, 100m, ★★/$$, Ind/Col, R/EV. Two more immortals fight in the future against the dictator of the Earth. Christopher Lambert, Sean Connery, Virginia Madsen, Michael Ironside, Allan Rich, John C. McGinley. w. Peter Bellwood, Brian Clemens, William Panzer, d. Russel Mulcahy.
Subways

Highlander III-The Final Dimension, 1995, 105m, ★★½/$$$, Ind/Col, R/EV. More battling to rule the world with high-tech sword-and-sorcery and time travel. Christopher Lambert, Mario Van Peebles, Deborah Unger. d. Andrew Morahan.

ACTION: ADVENTURE: Sword & Sorcery; Time Travel; Chase Stories; Feuds; Men in Conflict; Scotland; Rule the World-Plot to

Highpoint, 1984, 88m, ★★/$, New World/Sultan, R/V. A businessman gets involved in shady dealings and winds up being chased by the Mafia as well as the CIA. Richard Harris, Christopher Plummer, Beverly D'Angelo, Kate Reid, Peter Donat. w. Richard Guttman, Ian Sutherland, d. Peter Carter.
ACTION: SUSPENSE: Fugitives from the Law; Fugitives from the Mob; Mob Stories; CIA Agents

High Noon, 1952, 85m, ★★★★/$$$$, Kramer-UA/CBS-Fox. A lone lawman must battle all corrupt elements in a Western town, since he gets no help from the cowardly townsfolk, leading to a duel at noon in the center of town. Gary Cooper (BActor), Grace Kelly, Thomas Mitchell, Lloyd Bridges, Katy Jurado, Otto Kruger, Lon Chaney, Henry Morgan. w. Carl Foreman (BScr), SS-adap. John Cunningham (The Tin Star), d. Fred Zinnemann (BDirector). BPicture, BOScore, BOSong, BEdit. Oscars: 7-4.
DRAMA: WESTERNS: Men in Conflict; Men Proving Themselves; Marshals; Police Stories; Weddings; Marriage-Impending; Duels
REMAKE/RETREAD: Outland (High Noon in outer space)
(The Ox-Bow Incident; Mr. Deeds Goes to Town; The Duellists)

High Plains Drifter, 1972, 105m, ★★★/$$$, U/MCA-U, PG/V. A strange cowboy gallops into town on a revenge mission and all rats scatter. Clint Eastwood, Verna Bloom, Marianna Hill, Mitch Ryan, Jack Ging. w. Ernest Tidyman, d. Clint Eastwood.
WESTERNS: ACTION: Revenge; Cowboys; Vigilantes; Westerns-Revenge; Westerns-Spaghetti; Faded Hits
(A Fistful of Dollars; A Few Dollars More; Hang 'em High)

High Pressure, 1932, 74m, ★★★/$$, WB/NA. A speculative entrepreneur sinks everything he's got into rubber, but will his checks bounce instead? William Powell, Evelyn Brent, George Sidney, Guy Kibbee, Frank McHugh. w. Joseph Jackson, P-adap. Abem Kandel (Hot Money), d. Mervyn Le Roy.
COMEDY: Inventors; Rich People;

Risking It All; Losing It All; Con Artists; Forgotten Films; Hidden Gems

High Risk, 1981, 94m, ★★/$, American Cinema/Sultan. In order to fund a documentary film in South America, the director gets his friends to rob a drug lord. James Brolin, Cleavon Little, Lindsay Wagner, Ernest Borgnine, Bruce Davison, Chick Vennera, Anthony Quinn, James Coburn. w. d. Stewart Raffill.

ACTION: Action Comedy; Movie Making; Documentaries; South America Directors; Drugs-Dealing; Mob Stories; Thieves; Good Premise Unfulfilled; Writer-Directors; Independent Films

High Road to China, 1983, 105m, ★★1/2/$$$, Golden Harvest-WB/WB, PG. In the twenties, an adventurous and hard-drinking pilot in the Middle East hooks up with a cantankerous American heiress. Tom Selleck, Bess Armstrong, Jack Weston, Robert Morley, Wilford Brimley, Brian Blessed. w. Sandra Weintraub Roland, S. Lee Pogostin, N-adap. Jon Cleary, d. Brian G. Hutton.

ACTION: ADVENTURE: COMEDY: Comic Adventure; Action Comedy; **ROMANCE:** Romantic Comedy; Romance-Bickering; Old-Fashioned Recent Films; Heiresses; Feisty Females; Himalayas; Battle of the Sexes; Pilots-Daredevil; 1920s; Faded Hits; Curiosities (The Aviator; Raiders of the Lost Ark) (Ed: Selleck's first big feature after having to give up *Raiders of the Lost Ark* for *Magnum, PI* obligations, but it's nowhere near *Raiders* or the old-fashioned bickering romances it wants to be like)

High Season, 1987, 92m, ★★1/2/$, Ind/New Line, R/S-P-FRN. On vacation in Greece, a female photographer meets interesting people who become good friends and a few have romantic encounters. Jacqueline Bisset, James Fox, Irene Papas, Sebastian Shaw, Kenneth Branagh, Robert Stephens. w. Mark and Clare Peploe, d. Clare Peploe.

COMEDY DRAMA: Slice of Life Stories; Greece; Photographers; Vacations; Vacation Romance; Midlife Crisis; Ensemble Films; Female Protagonists; Quiet Little Films; Coulda Been Good; Independent Films; Female Screenwriters; Female Directors (A Month at the Lake; Summer Lovers)

High Sierra, 1941, 96m, ★★★/$$$, WB/WB. An aging gangster wants to pull one last job in the Sierras of California so he can retire. But things go awry, partially due to his entanglement with two women. Humphrey Bogart, Ida Lupino, Joan Leslie, Alan Curtis, Arthur Kennedy, Henry Hull. w. John Huston, W. R. Burnett, N-adap. W. R. Burnett, d. Raoul Walsh.

DRAMA: ACTION: Action Drama; Crime Drama; Mob Stories; One Last Time; Romance-Triangles; Retirement; Faded Hits; Hidden Gems

High Society, 1956, 107m, ★★★/$$$, MGM/MGM-UA. A musical remake of *The Philadelphia Story*, where a socialite is about to marry a new man when her old one comes into the picture along with an appealing reporter covering the big wedding to be-but who will wind up getting married? Bing Crosby, Grace Kelly, Frank Sinatra, Celeste Holm, Louis Armstrong, Sidney Blackmer, Margalo Gillmore, Louis Calhern, Lydia Reed. w. John Patrick, d. Charles Walters. BOSong, BMScore. Oscars: 2-0.

MUSICALS: Musical Romance; **ROMANCE:** Rich People; Romance-Triangles; Romantic Comedy; Men Fighting Over Women; Weddings; Marriage-Impending; Engagements-Breaking

MUSICAL REMAKE OF: The Philadelphia Story

(The Philadelphia Story; The Swan; Green Fire; Holiday)

(Ed: The story was Oscar-nominated but rescinded when *The Philadelphia Story* connection was made)

High Spirits, 1988, 96m, ★★/$, U/MCA-U, PG. The owner of a castle in Ireland fakes ghosts to drum up publicity and tourism. Unfortunately, this makes the real ghosts mad. Peter O'Toole, Donald McCann, Mary Koughlan, Liz Smith, Steve Guttenberg, Beverly D'Angelo, Jennifer Tilly, Peter Gallagher, Daryl Hannah, Liam Neeson, Ray McAnally. w. d. Neil Jordan.

COMEDY: Ghosts; Haunted Houses; Castles; Ireland Vacations; Sabotage; Animals-Talking; Flops-Major; Good Premise Unfulfilled

High Tide, 1987, 104m, ★★1/2/$, New Line/New Line, R/S-P. A woman who put her baby up for adoption years before to pursue a music career that never really took off meets her daughter, now a teenager, for the first time since. Judy Davis, Jan Adele, Claudia Karvan, Colin Friels, John Clayton, Frankie J. Holden. w. Laura Jones, d. Gillian Armstrong.

DRAMA: MELODRAMA: Mothers Alone; Reunions; Children-Long lost; Children-Adopted; Mothers & Daughters; Musicians; Dreams; Illusions Destroyed; Midlife Crisis; Female Screenwriters; Female Protagonists; Female Directors (B.F.'s Daughter; Min and Bill; Woman to Woman; White Banners)

High, Wide, and Handsome, 1937, 110m, ★★1/2/$$, Par/NA. A traveling cabaret in a rural community brings together a showgirl and a strapping young farmer. Irene Dunne, Randolph Scott, Dorothy Lamour, Raymond Walburn, Alan Hale, Elizabeth Patterson, Charles Bickford, William Frawley. w. Oscar Hammerstein II, d. Rouben Mamoulian.

ROMANCE: MELODRAMA: Romantic Drama; Farm Life; Romance-Mismatched; Rural Life; Dancers; Forgotten Films

Hilda Crane, 1956, 87m, ★★1/2/$$, 20th/NA. A woman's third marriage seems to be headed the way of her first two because she has little faith. Jean Simmons, Guy Madison, Jean-Pierre Aumont, Evelyn Varden, Judith Evelyn, Peggy Knudsen. w. d. Philip Dunne, P-adap. Samson Raphaelson.

MELODRAMA: Marriage Drama; Marriage on the Rocks; Neurotic People; Young Women; Divorce; Female Protagonists; Women's Films

The Hill, 1965, 122m, ★★★/$$, MGM/MGM-UA. In a military prison in World War II North Africa, the prisoners rebel over the deplorable conditions the British, of all people, have allowed to exist. Sean Connery, Harry Andrews, Michael Redgrave, Ian Bannen, Ossie Davis, Roy Kinnear. w. P-adap. Ray Rigby, d. Sidney Lumet.

DRAMA: War Stories; Prison Drama; Military Stories; Corruption; Rebels; World War II Stories; Africa; Desert Settings; Forgotten Films (Stalag 17; King of the Hill [1965])

The Hills Have Eyes, 1977, 90m, ★★/$$, New Realm/Starmaker, R/EV-B&G. A middle-class family get in their RV to take a vacation in the desert and are attacked by family of mysterious cave-dwelling psychopaths who survive on human flesh. John Steadman, Janus Blythe, Arthur King, Russ Grieve, Virginia Vincent. w. d. Wes Craven.

HORROR: Cannibalism; Cult Films; Desert Settings; Vacations; Nightmare Vacations; Independent Films

Hi, Mom!, 1969, 86m, ★★★/$$, Ind/NA, R/P-S. A young pornographer makes films using the oddball characters from his apartment building. Robert de Niro, Allen Garfield, Gerrit Graham, Jennifer Salt. w. d. Brian de Palma.

COMEDY: SATIRE: Pornography World; Eccentric People; Apartment Buildings; Time Capsules; Cult Films; Writer-Directors; Independent Films
(Move; Greetings; Promise Her Anything)

The Hindenburg, 1975, 125m, ★★★/$$$, U/MCA-U, PG/EV. An attempt to explain the story of the fateful flight of this zeppelin that exploded on camera in Lakehurst, New Jersey. This film alleges that it was rigged to do so by a terrorist. George C. Scott, Anne Bancroft, Burgess Meredith, William Atherton, Roy Thinnes, Gig Young, Charles Durning, Robert Clary, Rene Auberjonois. w. Nelson Gidding, N-adap. Michael M. Mooney, d. Robert Wise. BCin, BArt, BSound, **BSoundFX, BVisualFX.** Oscars: 5-2.

DRAMA: TRAGEDY: Disaster Stories; Balloons; Airplane Crashes; Sabotage; Terrorists; Germans as Enemy; Germany

Hired Wife, 1940, 96m, ★★★/$$, U/NA, AMC. When she learns her boss's company is failing, a secretary marries him so that he can place the company in her name-thereby sating her crush on him and saving his assets. Rosalind Russell, Brian Aherne, Virginia Bruce, Robert Benchley, John Carroll, Hobart Cavanaugh. w. Richard Connell, Gladys Lehman, d. William A. Seiter.

COMEDY: ROMANCE: Romantic Comedy; Office Comedy; Business Life; Secretaries; Marrying the Boss; Marriage of Convenience; Infatuations; Romance-Reluctant; Romance-Girl Wants Boy; Feisty Females; Female Protagonists; Female Screenwriters; Hidden Gems; Forgotten Films; Coulda Been Great
(My Dear Secretary; More Than a Secretary)

The Hireling, 1973, 108m, ★★1/2/$, Col/NA. A wealthy lady has an affair with her chauffeur in the roaring twenties. Sarah Miles, Robert Shaw, Peter Egan, Elizabeth Sellars, Caroline Mortimer. w. Wolf Mankowitz, N-adap. L. P. Hartley, d. Alan Bridges.

DRAMA: ROMANCE: Romantic Drama; Erotic Drama; Rich People; Chauffeurs; Servants; Romance with Servant; Romance with Married Person; Cheating Women; Roaring 20s; 1920s; British Films; Forgotten Films
(Sailor Who Fell from Grace . . .; Lady Caroline Lamb; White Mischief)

Hiroshima, Mon Amour, 1959, 91m, ★★★/$$, Pathe/Sultan, Voyager. In Hiroshima in the fifties, a French actress has an affair with a Japanese architect but their collective memories of war intrude on their romantic bliss. Emmanuele Riva, Eiji Okada. w. Marguerite Duras (BOScr), d. Alain Resnais. Oscars: 1-0.

DRAMA: ROMANCE: Romantic Drama; Romance-Interracial; Bombs-Atomic; Flashbacks; Memories; Past-Haunted by the; Veterans; War Stories; World War II-Post Era; Japanese People; French Films; French New Wave Films; Hidden Gems; Forgotten Films; Female Screenwriters

His Brother's Wife, 1936, 91m, ★★/$$, MGM/NA. A man helps his brother, a scientist, hide from his pursuers, but he has to disappear. Then the unscrupulous brother takes up with the scientist's girlfriend. Robert Taylor, Barbara Stanwyck, Joseph Calleia, John Eldridge, Jean Hersholt, Samuel S. Hinds, Leonard Mudie, Jed Prouty. w. Leon Gordon, John Meehan, George Aurbach, d. W. S. Van Dyke II.

DRAMA: MELODRAMA: ROMANCE: Romantic Drama; Romance-Triangles; Betrayals; Romance with Relative's Lover; Brothers; Fugitives; Scientists

His Girl Friday, 1940, 92m, ★★★★/$$$, Col/RCA-Col, Nos. A woman reporter finds her old beau on a story with her while planning to go away with her husband to be-but the story may rekindle old love while also staying an execution. Rosalind Russell, Cary Grant, Ralph Bellamy, Gene Lockhart, Porter Hall, Ernest Truex, Cliff Edwards, Clarence Kolb, Roscoe Karns, Frank Jenks, Billy Gilbert. w. Charles Lederer, P-adap. Charles MacArthur, Ben Hecht (*The Front Page*), d. Howard Hawks.

COMEDY: FARCE: Screwball Comedy; ROMANCE: Romantic Comedy; Journalists; Executions; Fugitives from the Law; Hiding Out; Romance-Bickering; Race Against Time; Romance-Reunited; Romance-Triangles;

Marriage-Impending; Engagements-Breaking
REMAKE OF: The Front Page
REMAKE: Switching Channels
(The Women; Auntie Mame)

His Majesty O'Keefe, 1954, 90m, ★★1/2/$$, WB/WB. A sailor on a remote island teaches the natives a few modern ideas and how to fight off the pirates. Burt Lancaster, Joan Rice. w. Borden Chase, James Hill, N-adap. Lawrence Kingman, Gerald Green, d. Byron Haskin.

ADVENTURE: Adventure at Sea; Islands; Sailors; Pirates; Forgotten Films
(Lilies of the Field; Robinson Crusoe)

Histoires Extraordinaires (*Spirits of the Dead*), 1968, 120m, ★★★/$, Les Films Marceau-AIP/Vestron, R/S. Three stories of Poe: Metzengerstein, William Wilson, and Toby Dammit, by three big directors of the hip and artsy sixties. Jane Fonda, Peter Fonda, Carla Marlier, James Robertson Justice, Alain Delon, Brigitte Bardot, Katia Christina, Terence Stamp, Salvo Randone. w. Roger Vaadim, Pascal Cousin, Clemment Biddlewood, Louis Malle, Federico Fellini, d. Vadim, Malle, Fellini.

HORROR: Art Films; Avant-Garde Films; Buried Alive; Classic Literary Adaptations; Revisionist Films; French Films; Italian Films; International Casts; Forgotten Film; Curiosities

History of the World, Part One, 1981, 92m, ★★★/$$$, Brooksfilms-20th/Fox, PG/P-S. A look at world history from the cavemen to the Spanish Inquisition, through Mel Brooks's scatalogical, stereotypical lens. Mel Brooks, Dom De Luise, Madeline Kahn, Cloris Leachman, Harvey Korman, Ron Carey, Sid Caesar, Pamela Stephenson, Henny Youngman. w. d. Mel Brooks.

COMEDY: Spoofs; Historical Drama; Comedy-Skit; Ancient Times; Rome; Spain; Jewish People; Bathroom Humor; Writer-Directors
(A Funny Thing Happened on the Way to the Forum; Bill and Ted's Excellent Adventure)
(Ed: Some big laughs for the politically incorrect; otherwise, a dud)

Hit!, 1973, 134m, ★★/$, Par/Par. After his daughter dies, an F.B.I. agent cracks open the drug ring that supplied her habit. Billy Dee Williams, Richard Pryor, Paul Hampton, Gwen Welles. w. Alan Trustman, David Wolf, d. Sidney J. Furie.

ACTION: Drugs-Dealing; Avenging Death of Someone; Fathers & Daughters; Vigilantes; Police-Vigilante; FBI Agents; Trail of a Killer; Black Men; Black Casts; Blaxploitation Era; Forgotten Films (Death Wish; Night of the Juggler; Black Caesar; Across 110th Street; Hit Man)

The Hit, 1984, 98m, ★★1/2/$, Island/Island, R/S-V-P. A mob snitch hiding in Spain is sought after by two Mafia operatives, leading to an existential chase of sorts. John Hurt, Terence Stamp, Tim Roth, Laura del Sol, Fernando Ray, Bill Hunter. w. Peter Prince, d. Stephen Frears.

ACTION: DRAMA: Action Drama; Crime Drama; Hitmen; Mob Stories; Chase Stories; Spain; British Films; Art Films (Ed: More visually interesting and arty than entertaining in any conventional way)

Hit Man, 1972, 90m, ★★/$, MGM/NA. A man who usually kills for money does one for free when his brother is killed by gangsters. Bernie Casey, Pam Grier, Lisa Moore, Bhetty Waldron, Sam Laws, Don Diamond. w. d. George Armitage, N-adap. Ted Lewis (*Jack's Return Home*).

ACTION: Crime Drama; Blaxploitation; Hitmen; Mob Stories; Avenging Death of Someone; Black Casts; Black Men

The Hit Parade, 1937, 77m, ★★1/2/$$, Republic/NA. A group of hopefuls are represented by an agent who tries to get them spots on a famous radio show. Frances Langford, Phil Regan, Louise Henry, Pert Kelton, Al Pearce, Ed Brophy, William Demarest, Duke Ellington and his Band, Eddy Duchin and his Band, Max Terhune, Monroe Owsley, Inez Courtney, The Tic Toc Girls. w. Bradford Ropes, Sam Ornitz, d. Gus Meins.

COMEDY: Putting on a Show; Radio Life; Ensemble Films; 1930s

Hit Parade of 1941, 1940, 83m, ★★1/2/$$, Republic/NA. An aspiring singer is miffed when her boyfriend, a radio station owner, dumps her for the daughter of a big advertiser. Kenny Baker, Frances Langford, Hugh Herbert, Mary Boland, Ann Miller, Patsy Kelly, Phil Silvers, Sterling Holloway, Donald MacBride, Barnett Parker, Franklin Pangborn, Six Hits and a Miss, Borrah Minevitch and his Harmonica Rascals. w. Bradford Ropes, F. Hugh Herbert, Maurice Leo, d. John H. Auer.

COMEDY: ROMANCE: Jealousy; Engagements-Breaking; Radio Life; Singers

Hit Parade of 1943, 1943, 90m, ★★★/$$$, Republic/NA. A songwriter steals his best ideas from other songs, until he sees the error of his ways and learns to trust his instincts. John Carroll, Susan Hayward, Gail Patrick, Eve Arden, Melville Cooper, Walter Catlett, Mary Treen, Tom Kennedy, Dorothy Dandridge, the Golden Gate Quartet, Count Basie and his orchestra. w. Frank Gill Jr., d. Albert S. Rogell.

MUSICALS: COMEDY: Musical Comedy; Radio Life; Songwriters; Musicians; Ethics; Liars; Thieves; Starting Over

Hit Parade of 1947, 1947, 90m, ★★1/2/$$, Republic/NA. A hack songwriter tries to step up to the big leagues. Eddie Albert, Constance Moore, Joan Edwards, Gil Lamb, Bill Goodwin, William Frawley, Richard Lane, Roy Rogers and Trigger, Woody Herman and his orchestra. w. Mary Loos, Parke Levy, d. Frank McDonald.

MUSICALS: COMEDY: Musical Comedy; Radio Life; Songwriters; Singers; Musicians

Hit the Deck, 1954, 112m, ★★1/2/$$, MGM/MGM-UA. Three sailors disembark in San Francisco and hit the town in search of girls. Tony Martin, Jane Powell, Ann Miller, Debbie Reynolds, Walter Pidgeon, Vic Damone, Gene Raymond. w. Sonya Levien, William Ludwig, (Musical)-adap. Herbert Fields, N-adap. Hubert Osborn (*Shore Leave*), d. Roy Rowland.

MUSICALS: Sailors; Shore Leave; San Francisco; **ROMANCE:** Romantic Comedy; Musical Romance

REMAKE/RETREAD: On the Town

The Hitler Gang, 1944, 101m, ★★★/$$, Par/NA. The historical drama of Hitler and his henchmen as they rise to power. Robert Watson, Martin Kosleck, Victor Varconi, Luis Van Rooten, Alexander Pope, Ivan Triesault, Helene Thimig, Reinhold Schunzel, Sig Rumann, Alexander Granach. w. Frances Goodrich, Albert Hackett, d. John Farrow.

DRAMA: Biographies; Hitler; Nazi Stories; Germans as Enemy; Germany; Historical Drama; War Stories; Power-Rise to; Episodic Stories; Leaders-Tyrant; Evil Men; Hidden Gems; Forgotten Films; Time Capsules; Female Screenwriters
(Inside the Third Reich; Hitler-The Last Ten Days)

Hitler-The Last Ten Days, 1973, 104m, ★★1/2/$, MGM/Par. After the fall of the Third Reich, Adolf Hitler and Eva Braun wait to off themselves in the infamous "bunker." Alec Guinness, Simon Ward, Doris Kunstmann, Adolfo Celi, Diane Cilento, Eric Porter, Joss Ackland. w. Ennio de Concini, Maria Pia Fusco, Wolfgang Reinhardt, Ivan Moffat, d. Ennio de Concini.

DRAMA: Biographies; Hitler; Nazi Stories; Germans as Enemy; Germany; Death-Impending; Historical Drama; War Stories; Power-Rise to; Episodic Stories; Leaders-Tyrant; Evil Men; Forgotten Films; Coulda Been Great; Time Capsules
(Inside the Third Reich; Mein Kampf; The Bunker)

Hobson's Choice, 1953, 107m, ★★★1/2/$$$, British Lion/New Line. In the early industrial age (the 1890s) in Lancashire, a domineering and intolerant bootblack is taught a lesson by his daughter and the son-in-law he doesn't consider smart enough to do it. Charles Laughton, Brenda de Banzie, John Mills, Richard Wattis, Helen Haye, Prunella Scales. w. Norman Spencer, Wynard Browne, P-adap. Harold Brighouse, d. David Lean.

COMEDY: COMEDY DRAMA: SATIRE: Con Artists; Turning the Tables; Working Class; Mindgames; Dose of Own Medicine-Given; Hidden Gems; Lover-Family Dislikes

TV REMAKE: 1982

Hoffa, 1992, 140m, ★★/$$, 20th/Fox, R/P-V. The infamous booster of the teamsters is given the rosey treatment in this biopic focusing on the good he did for American workers before allowing the mob to take sway. Eventually he's in too deep and when he tries to get out, he mysteriously "disappears." Jack Nicholson, Danny DeVito, Armand Assante, J. T. Walsh, John C. Reilly, Frank Whaley, Kevin Anderson, John P. Ryan, Robert Prosky, Cliff Gorman. w. David Mamet, d. Danny DeVito. BCin. Oscars: 1-0.

DRAMA: Biographies; Reformers; Leaders; Unions; Strikes; Mob Stories; Mob Wars; **MURDER:** Assassination Plots; Working Class; Power-Rise to; Flops-Major
(GoodFellas; Casino)

Hoffman, 1970, 113m, ★★★1/2/$, ABP/NA. A timid man in a midlife crisis can't get a date, so he blackmails a secretary into spending a week with him. Peter Sellers, Sinead Cusack, Jeremy Bulloch, Ruth Dunning. w. P-adap. Ernest Gebler, d. Alvin Rakoff.

COMEDY: Sex Comedy; Romantic Comedy; Blackmail; Nerds; Nerds & Babes; Secretaries; Forgotten Films

The Holcroft Covenant, 1985, 112m, ★★/$$, EMI-MGM-UA/MGM-UA, R/V. One of Hitler's henchmen leaves behind a document which could upset the world balance of power if used by the wrong people. Michael Caine, Anthony Andrews, Victoria Tennent, Lilli Palmer, Mario Andorf. w. George Axelrod, Edward Anhalt, John Hopkins, N-adap. Robert Ludlum, d. John Frankenheimer.

SUSPENSE: Spy Films; Spies; Nazi Stories; Hitler; Conspiracy; Political Drama; Political Thriller; Coulda Been Good; Unintentionally Funny

(The Whistleblower; The Boys from Brazil)
(Ed: Rather light-headed and boring, unfortunately)

Hold Back the Dawn, 1941, 115m, ★★★/$$$, Par/Par. An illegal alien from Mexico marries a grammar school teacher in the U.S. in order to gain citizenship, but he really loves another. Charles Boyer, Olivia de Havilland (BActress), Paulette Goddard, Victor Francen, Walter Abel, Curt Bois, Rosemary de Camp, Nestor Paiva, Mitchell Leisen. w. Charles Brackett, Billy Wilder (BScr), d. Mitchell Leisen. BPicture, BB&WCin, BOScore, BB&WArt. Oscars: 6-0.

MELODRAMA: ROMANCE: Romantic Drama; Marriage for Citizenship; Marriage of Convenience; Cheating Men; Mexicans; Teachers; Romance-Doomed; Women's Films

(Green Card; To Each His Own)

Hold Me, Thrill Me, Kiss Me, 1993, 95m, ★★★1/2/$, Ind/Live, R/EP-S-FN-MRN-V. Eli is running from Twinkles, a fatal attraction whom he then kills and hides out in a trailer park with the loot they stole from her parents. There, he meets an assortment of psychos, porn stars, and rednecks-and the love of his life. But first, he must escape the porn star and the revenge of Twinkles. Max Parrish, Sean Young, Adrienne Shelley, Diane Ladd, Bela Lehocsky, Ania Sull. w. d. Joel Herschman.

COMEDY: Screwball Comedy; **FARCE:** Fugitives from the Law; Hiding Out;

Disguises; Fatal Attractions; **ROMANCE:** Romantic Comedy; Pornography World; Rednecks; Writer-Directors; Cult Films; Hidden Gems; LA 90s Indies; Independent Films

(Blood and Concrete)

Hold That Ghost, 1941, 86m, ★★★/$$$, U/MCA-U. Various people break down in the country and take refuge in a house that turns out to be haunted. Bud Abbott, Lou Costello, Joan Davis, the Andrews Sisters, Richard Carlson, Ted Lewis and his band, Evelyn Ankers, Mischa Auer. w. Robert Lees, Fred Rinaldo, John Grant, d. Arthur Lubin.

COMEDY: HORROR: Horror Comedy; Haunted Houses; Houses-Creepy; Fools-Bumbling; Abbott & Costello; Stranded; Ghosts; Faded Hits; Hidden Gems

(Haunted Honeymoon, Ghostbreakers; Abbott and Costello SERIES)

Hold Your Man, 1933, 89m, ★★★/$$$, MGM/MGM-UA. A tough young broad falls in love with a con-man and gets pregnant, which leads to problems when he's jailed and she's alone. Jean Harlow, Clark Gable, Stuart Erwin, Dorothy Burgess, Muriel Kirkland, Paul Hurst. w. Anita Loos, Howard Emmett Rogers, d. Sam Wood.

COMEDY DRAMA: ROMANCE: Romantic Drama; Crime Drama; Prison Drama; Marriage Drama; Mothers Alone; Mothers-Struggling; Babies-Having; Con Artists; Feisty Females; Sexy Women; Sexy Men; Faded Hits; Hidden Gems; Female Screenwriters

(Red Dust; Bombshell; Saratoga)

A Hole in the Head, 1959, 120m, ★★★/$$$, UA/CBS-Fox. A struggling hotel owner in Miami almost loses his property and must swallow his pride to ask his wealthy brother for a loan. Frank Sinatra, Edward G. Robinson, Eleanor Parker, Eddie Hodges, Carolyn Jones, Thelma Ritter, Keenan Wynn, Joi Lansing. w. P-adap. Arnold Shulman, d. Frank Capra. BOSong. Oscars: 1-1.

COMEDY: COMEDY DRAMA: Mortgage Drama; Hotels; Fathers Alone; Fathers-Struggling; Brothers; Family Comedy; **FAMILY:** Faded Hits

(The Courtship of Eddie's Father)
(Ed: More famous for the theme song: "Whoops, there goes another rubber tree . . .")

Holiday, 1938, 93m, ★★★★/$$, Col/RCA-Col. A upwardly mobile working-class businessman falls for a wealthy socialite who invites him to the mansion to meet the family-including her skeptical father and freewheeling, sexy sister, whose adventurous nature proves to be more suitable. Cary Grant, Katharine Hepburn, Doris Nolan, Edward Everett Horton, Ruth Donnelly, Lew Ayres, Binnie Barnes. w. Donald Ogdan Stewart, P-adap. Philip Barry, d. George Cukor. BB&WArt. Oscars: 1-0.

COMEDY: ROMANCE: Romantic Comedy; **COMEDY DRAMA:** Comedy-Light; Romance-Triangles; Romance-Class Conflicts; Rich vs. Poor; Rich People; Romance with Lover's Relative; Free Spirits; Engagements-Breaking; Romance-Choosing Right Person; Stagelike Films

REMAKE OF: 1930 version
(The Philadelphia Story; Bringing Up Baby; Arthur)

Holiday for Sinners, 1952, 72m, ★★1/2/$$, MGM/NA. Three old friends reunite in New Orleans for Mardi Gras, but none is in much of a partying mood, all three having suffered tragedies in their lives. Gig Young, Keenan Wynn, Janice Rule, Richard Anderson, William Campbell, Michael Chekhov, Sandro Giglio, Edith Barrett, Porter Hall. w. A. I. Bezzerides, N-adap. Hamilton Basso, d. Gerald Mayer.

DRAMA: MELODRAMA: Friendships on the Rocks; Friendships-Male; Midlife Crisis; Ensemble Films; New Orleans; Curiosities; Coulda Been Good

Holiday in Mexico, 1946, 127m, ★★★/$$$$, MGM/MGM-UA. The American ambassador in Mexico is a trifle upset when his daughter falls for the popular local singer Jose Iturbi. Jane Powell, Walter Pidgeon, Ilona Massey, Jose Iturbi, Roddy McDowell. w. Isobel Lennart, d. George Sidney.

MUSICALS: ROMANCE: Musical Romance; Lover Family Dislike; Latin People; Singers; Diplomats; Mexico; Americans Abroad; Female Screenwriters

Holiday Inn, 1942, 101m, ★★★/$$$$, Par/Par. Two business partners who manage a hotel together both love the same woman, and they've just gotta sing about it-especially on a "White Christmas." Bing Crosby, Fred Astaire, Walter Abel, Marjorie Reynolds, Virginia Dale, Louise Beavers, Irving Bacon, James Bell. w. Claude Binyon, Elmer Rice (BOStory),

d. Mark Sandrich. **BO**Song "White Christmas," BMScore. Oscars: 3-1.

MUSICALS: COMEDY: Musical Comedy; **MELODRAMA: ROMANCE:** Romantic Comedy; Musical Romance; Christmas; Hotels; Romance-Triangles; Blockbusters

SEQUEL: White Christmas (1954).

The Holly and the Ivy, 1952, 83m, ★★½/$$, British Lion/NA. In a working-class community in northern England, Christmas celebrations bring family tensions to the fore. Ralph Richardson, Celia Johnson, Margaret Leighton, Denholm Elliott, John Gregson, Hugh Williams, Margaret Halstan, Maureen Delany, William Hartnell, Robert Flemyng, Roland Culver. w. Anatole de Grunwald, P-adap. Wynard Browne, d. George More O'Ferrall.

MELODRAMA: Family Drama; Reunions; Christmas; Small-Town Life; England; Rural Life; British Films; Forgotten Films

Hollywood Boulevard, 1936, 75m, ★★★/$$, Par/NA. A broken-down, drunken former star writes a tell-all autobiography, but suffers retribution when he "names names." John Halliday, Marsha Hunt, Robert Cummings, C. Henry Gordon, Frieda Inescort, Esther Dale, Gary Cooper, Francis X. Bushman, Maurice Costello, Mae Marsh, Charles Ray, Jane Novak, Bryant Washburn, Creighton Hale, Bert Roach. w. Marguerite Roberts, d. Robert Florey.

MELODRAMA: SATIRE: Hollywood Life; Hollywood Satire; Actors; Memories; Scandals; Writers; Dose of Own Medicine-Given; Alcoholics; Stuntmen; Curiosities; Female Screenwriters

Hollywood Boulevard, 1977, 83m, ★★/$, New World/WB. A fresh-faced young woman with stars in her eyes goes to work for a low-budget producer of shlocky horror and action pics. Candice Rialson, Mary Woronov, Rita George, Jeffrey Kramer, Dick Miller, Paul Bartel, Jonathan Kaplan, Charles B. Griffith. w. Patrick Hobby, d. Allan Arkush, Joe Dante.

MELODRAMA: HORROR: Hollywood Life; Hollywood Satire; Compilation Films; Actresses; Curiosities

(Inserts; Eating Raoul)

(Ed: Made on a shoestring with clips from other American International-New World films)

Hollywood Canteen, 1944, 123m, ★★★/$$$, WB/WB. Documentary movie within a movie about the stars' help entertaining the soldiers on leave during World War II. Joan Leslie, Robert Hutton, Dane Clark, Jack Benny, Bette Davis, John Garfield, Joan Crawford, Eddie Cantor, Paul Henreid, Ida Lupino, Barbara Stanwyck. w. d. Delmer Daves.

COMEDY: Documentary Style; Movies within Movies; Hollywood Life; All-Star Cameos; Putting on a Show; World War II Era; Curiosities; Time Capsules; Actors; Actresses

Hollywood Cavalcade, 1939, 96m, ★★★/$$$, 20th/Fox. A Hollywood producer rises through the ranks to become top dog at the studio. Don Ameche, Alice Faye, J. Edward Bromberg, Alan Curtis, Stuart Erwin, Jed Prouty, Buster Keaton, Mack Sennett, Donald Meek and the original Keystone Kops. w. Ernest Pascal, d. Irving Cummings.

MELODRAMA: Biographies-Fictional; Biographies; Hollywood Life; Directors; Movie Making; Power-Rise to; Faded Hits

(Ed: Supposedly based on Mack Sennett-although he appears in a cameo under his own name)

Hollywood Hotel, 1938, 109m, ★★★/$$, WB/NA. Star squabbles and budget problems beset a Hollywood radio show, but they pull through it all to become number one. Dick Powell, Rosemary Lane, Lola Lane, Hugh Herbert, Ted Healy, Glenda Farrell, Louella Parsons, Alan Mowbray, Frances Langford, Allyn Joslyn, Benny Goodman, Edgar Kennedy. w. Jerry Wald, Maurice Leo, Richard Macauley, d. Busby Berkeley.

COMEDY: MUSICAL: Musical Comedy; Actresses; Hotel; Radio Life; Putting on a Show; Fame-Rise to; Hollywood Life

(The Big Broadcast SERIES)

Hollywood or Bust, 1956, 95m, ★★★½/$$, Par/Par. A romeo and a boob, hence the "bust," head for the movies and instead only make a mockery. Dean Martin, Jerry Lewis, Pat Crowley, Maxie Rosenbloom, Anita Ekberg. w. Erna Lazarus, d. Frank Tashlin.

COMEDY: Hollywood Satire; Hollywood Life; Fools-Bumbling; Comedians; Playboys; Fame-Rise to; Actors; Road to California

(My Friend Irma; Scared Stiff)

(Ed: Last of the Martin-Lewis movies)

Hollywood Revue of 1929, 116m, ★★★/$$$, MGM/NA. A vaudevillian compendium featuring several of MGM's biggest stars at the dawn of talkies. Jack Benny, Buster Keaton, Joan Crawford, John Gilbert, Marion Davies, Norma Shearer, Marie Dressler, Lionel Barrymore, Bessie Love. w. Al Boasberg, Robert Hopkins, d. Charles Reisner. BPicture. Oscars: 1-0.

COMEDY: Vaudeville; Comedians; Comedy-Skit; All-Star Casts; Curiosities; Forgotten Films; Faded Hits; Stagelike Films

Hollywood Shuffle, 1987, 82m, ★★★/$$$, Goldwyn/Goldwyn, PG-13/P-S. A struggling black actor in Hollywood has to hide his proper English accent and affect a "homeboy" persona to get roles. Robert Townsend, Anne-Marie Johnson, Starletta Dupois, Helen Martin, Craigus R. Johnson, John Witherspoon, Keenen Ivory Wayans, Jimmy Woodard. w. Robert Townsend, Keenen Ivory Wayans, d. Robert Townsend.

COMEDY: Comedy-Skit; Black Casts; Black Men; Black Women; Actors; Actresses; Fame-Rise to; **SATIRE:** Hollywood Satire; Hollywood Life; Race Relations; Black vs. White; Ensemble Films; Sleeper Hits; Black Directors; Black Screenwriters

(I'm Gonna Git You, Sucka; Meteor Man)

(Ed: Famous for Townsend's financing via credit cards)

Holocaust 2000, 1977, 102m, ★½/$, Embassy/Embassy, New Line, R/V-P. The head of a nuclear power plant in the Middle East discovers that his son is the anti-Christ. Kirk Douglas, Simon Ward, Agostina Belli, Anthony Quayle, Virginia McKenna, Spiros Focas, Alexander Knox, Adolfo Celi. w. Sergio Donati, Alberto de Martino, Michael Robson, d. Alberto de Martino.

HORROR: SUSPENSE: Satanism; Apocalyptic Stories; Satan-Children of; Nuclear Energy; Fathers & Sons; Flops-Major

REMAKE/RETREAD OF: The Omen

Holy Matrimony, 1943, 87m, ★★★/$$, 20th/NA. A great British expatriot artist returns to be knighted, and when his valet dies on the journey, he arranges for him to be buried in his own name, so that he can live without the burden of fame and marry his love. Monty Woolley, Gracie Fields, Laird Cregar, Eric Blore, Una O'Connor. w. Nunnally Johnson, N-adap. Arnold Bennett, d. John Stahl.

MELODRAMA: ADVENTURE: ROMAN-TIC: Romantic Adventure; War Stories; War Battles; Identities-Assumed; Death-Faked; Artists; Royalty; Riches to Rags; Romance-Choosing the Right Person; British Films; Forgotten Films

Hombre, 1967, 111m, ★★★/$$, 20th/Fox. A reviled half-breed redeems himself in the eyes of stagecoach passengers being robbed when he saves their lives. Paul Newman, Diane Cilento, Fredric March, Richard Boone, Martin Balsam, Barbara Rush, Cameron Mitchell. w. Irving Ravetch, Harriet Frank, N-adap. Elmore Leonard, d. Martin Ritt.
WESTERNS: ACTION: Saving Someone; Redemption; Thieves; Hostage Situations; Heroes-Unlikely; Hidden Gems; Faded Hits

Home Alone, 1990, 102m, ★★★1/2/$$$$$, 20th/Fox, PG/V. When a precocious and clever boy is left home by his wealthy family while they fly with a gaggle of pre-teens to Paris-they're apparently rich-burglars terrorize the young lad, but what he has in store is literally unbelievable, but clever. Macauley Culkin, Joe Pesci, Daniel Stern, Catherine O'Hara, John Heard, Roberts Blossom, John Candy. w. John Hughes, d. Chris Columbus. BOSong, BOScore. Oscars: 2-0.
COMEDY: COMEDY DRAMA: Action Comedy; Boys; Men and Boys; Parents Are Gone; Parents Are Gone from Chicago; Elderly Men; Tearjerkers; Thieves; Turning the Tables; Runaways; Christmas; Children Alone; Cartoonlike Films; Blockbusters
SEQUEL: Home Alone 2
(Home Alone 2; Risky Business; Adventures in Babysitting; Uncle Buck)

Home Alone 2: Lost in New York, 1992, 120m, ★★1/2/$$$$$, 20th/Fox, PG/V. The kid from the first film gets separated once again from his huge family, this time in New York, where he runs into the same burglars from the first film (who didn't learn their lesson) and an old bag lady (as opposed to the old grandfather from the first). Macauley Culkin, Joe Pesci, Daniel Stern, Catherine O'Hara, John Heard, Brenda Fricker, Devin Ratray. w. John Hughes, d. Chris Columbus.
COMEDY: COMEDY DRAMA: Action Comedy; Boys; Men and Boys; Parents

are Gone; Parents are Gone from Chicago; Elderly Men; Thieves; Turning the Tables; Runaways; Christmas; Children Alone; Cartoonlike Films; New York Films; Blockbusters

Home from the Hill, 1959, 150m, ★★★/$$$, MGM/MGM-UA. A Southerner who likes the ladies, finds his son-one legitimate and the other not-following in his footsteps after returning from college. Robert Mitchum, George Hamilton, George Peppard, Eleanor Parker, Luana Patten, Everett Sloane, Constance Ford, Ray Teal. w. Irving Ravetch, Harriet Frank, N-adap. William Humphrey, d. Vincente Minnelli.
DRAMA: MELODRAMA: Family Drama; Southerns; Fathers & Sons; Playboys; Rich People; Romance-Reunited; Love-First; Parents vs. Children; Tennessee Williams-esque; Hidden Gems
(The Long, Hot Summer; Written on the Wind; All the Fine Young Cannibals)

Homeboy, 1988, 116m, ★1/2/$, 20th/Fox, R/P-S. A boxer past his prime readies himself for a big comeback bout. Mickey Rourke, Christopher Walken, Debra Feuer, Thomas Quinn, Kevin Conway, Anthony Alda. w. Eddie Cook, Mickey Rourke, d. Michael Seresin.
DRAMA: Sports Movies; Boxing; Comebacks; Starting Over

Homecoming, 1948, 113m, ★★1/2/$$$, MGM/MGM-UA. A rich doctor with a cushy suburban practice is called to service in World War II and has his life changed when an army nurse he falls in love has a tragedy. Clark Gable, Lana Turner, Anne Baxter, John Hodiak, Ray Collins, Gladys Cooper, Cameron Mitchell, Marshall Thompson. w. Paul Osborn, d. Mervyn Le Roy.
MELODRAMA: ROMANCE: Romantic Drama; Tearjerkers; War Stories; World War II Stories; Doctors; Nurses; Military Stories; Romance-Doomed

The Homecoming, 1973, 114m, ★★★1/2/$, AFT/NA. A retired butcher in London has his children move back in, and he and his sons start a very unorthodox family business with the only female supplying all the "service." Paul Rogers, Cyril Cusack, Michael Jayston, Ian Holm, Vivien Merchant, Terence Rigby. w., P-adap. Harold Pinter, d. Peter Hall.
DRAMA: Art Films; Avant-Garde Films; Family Drama; SATIRE: Black Comedy; Working Class; Reunions; Female Among

Males; Incest; Prostitutes-Ordinary People Turned; Allegorical Stories; Fathers & Sons; Sexual Harassment; Sexuality; Sexual Problems; Stagelike Films; Stage Filmings
(The Caretaker; Accident; Betrayal)

A Home of Our Own, 1994, 95m, ★★★/$$, PG. A woman with several children tries to turn a run-down house in a place they can live permanently after she's fired in a sexual harassment situation. Kathy Bates, Edward Furlong, Soon-Teck Oh, Tony Campisi, Clarissa Lassig, Sarah Schaub, Miles Feulner. w. Patrick Duncan, d. Tony Bill.
MELODRAMA: Family Drama; Mothers-Struggling; Mothers Alone; Making a Living; House Havoc; Small-Town Life; Siblings; Coming of Age; Mothers & Sons; Old-Fashioned Recent Films; Female Protagonists
(Heartland; American Heart)

Homicide, 1991, 102m, ★★★1/2/$, Col/Col, R/EP-V. A Jewish cop finds himself in the middle of an investigation of anti-Semitic crime and at the crossroads of deciding whether to go back to his religious roots or simply do his job. Joe Mantegna, William H. Macy, Natalija Nogulich, Ving Rhames, Rebecca Pidgeon, J. J. Johnson, Jack Wallace. w. d. David Mamet.
DRAMA: Crime Drama; Police Stories; Jewish People; Anti-Semitism; MURDER: MYSTERY: MURDER MYSTERY: Detective Stories; Detectives-Police; Ethics; Religion; Terrorists; Hidden Gems; Writer-Directors
(House of Games; Glengarry Glen Ross; Thunderheart)

Honey, I Blew Up the Kid, 1992, 89m, ★★★/$$$, Disney/Disney, G. An scientist experiments with an enlarging ray, which, of course, accidently goes off when pointed at his baby boy-who grows to 50 feet tall and wreaks havoc in Las Vegas. Rick Moranis, Marcia Strassman, Robert Oliveri, Daniel Shalikar, Joshua Shalikar, Lloyd Bridges, John Shea, Keri Russell, Amy O'Neil. w. Thom Eberhardt, Peter Eibling, Gary Goodrow, d. Randal Kleiser.
ACTION: ADVENTURE: Action Adventure; Comic Adventure; Fantasy; SCI-FI: CHILDREN'S: FAMILY: Giants; Babies; Family Comedy; Inventors; Las Vegas; Cartoonlike Films; Outstanding Art Direction; Old-Fashioned Recent Films

SEQUEL TO: Honey, I Shrunk the Kids (Baby's Day Out)

Honey, I Shrunk the Kids, 1989, 93m, ★★★/$$$$$, Disney/Disney, G. When the kids play with dad's experimental shrink-ray gun, which he thinks doesn't work, they suddenly find it does and are soon one-inch fugitives from bees and ants in the backyard when they're accidentally taken out with the garbage. It's up to dad to fix his machine to get them back to size-if he can ever find them. Rick Moranis, Matt Frewer, Marcia Strassman, Kristine Sutherland, Thomas Brown, Jared Rushton, Amy O'Neil, Robert Oliveri. w. Ed Naha, Tom Schulman, Stuart Gordon, Brian Yuzna, d. Joe Johnston.
ACTION: ADVENTURE: Action Adventure; Comic Adventure; Fantasy; **SCI-FI: CHILDREN'S: FAMILY:** Shrinking People; Chase Stories; Family Comedy; Inventors; Las Vegas; Cartoonlike Movies; Insects; Outstanding Art Direction; Blockbusters; Old-Fashioned Recent Films
(The Incredible Shrinking Man; Dr. Cyclops)

The Honey Pot, 1966, 150m, ★★★/$$, UA/MGM-UA. A millionaire plays a trick on three avaricious former lovers by pretending to be dying and watching the lengths they go to to have his hand in marriage. Unfortunately, the game goes too far, ending in real tragedy. Rex Harrison, Susan Hayward, Maggie Smith, Cliff Robertson, Capucine, Edie Adams, Adolfo Celi, Herschel Bernardi. w. d. Joseph L. Mankiewicz, P-adap. Frederick Knott (*Mr. Fox of Venice*), N-adap. Thomas Sterling (*The Evil of the Day*), P-adap. Ben Johnson (*Volpone*).
COMEDY: SATIRE: Black Comedy; **MURDER:** Tragi-Comedy; Women Fighting Over Men; Inheritances at Stake; Murder-Comic Attempts; Murder-Attempted; Clever Plots & Endings; Death-Impending, False; Revisionist Films; Classic Literary Adaptations
(Send Me No Flowers)

Honeymoon, 1947, 74m, ★★½/$$, RKO/Turner. The 18-year-old Shirley Temple goes to Mexico to elope but finds a better prospect once she arrives. Shirley Temple, Franchot Tone, Guy Madison, Lina Romay, Gene Lockhart, Grant Mitchell. w. Michael Kanin, Vicki Baum, d. William Keighley.

COMEDY DRAMA: ROMANCE: Romantic Comedy; Marriage-Impending; Marriage-Elopement; Mexico; Runaways; Ballet; Girls; Men and Girls; Romance-Older Men/Younger Women
(The Bachelor and the Bobby-Soxer; The Heartbreak Kid)

Honeymoon in Vegas, 1992, 96m, ★★★/$$, Tri-Star/Col-Tri, R/P-V. A struggling New York divorce detective and his fiancee go to Las Vegas and he gambles away their nest egg. The last thing he loses is his fiancee, whom he inadvertently gambles away to a big-shot mafioso type, who claims he wants her just for the weekend but takes her off to Hawaii. It's up to him to become a sky-diving Elvis and get her back. James Caan, Nicolas Cage, Sarah Jessica Parker, Pat Morita, Johnny Williams, Anne Bancroft, Peter Boyle. w. d. Andrew Bergman.
COMEDY: COMEDY DRAMA: ROMANCE: Romantic Comedy; Romance-Triangles; Newlyweds; Marriage on the Rocks; Gambling; Bets; Prostitutes-Ordinary People Turned; Las Vegas; Skydiving; Chase Stories; Coulda Been Good; Writer-Directors
COMIC FLIPSIDE OF: Indecent Proposal (Indecent Proposal; It Could Happen to You)
(Ed: Primarily for Cage fans; what could have been great soon peters out after the first act into cliches and stunts)

The Honeymoon Killers, 1969, 108m, ★★★/$$, Steibel-AIP/Vestron, R/S-V. A wild, frightening nurse and an Italian male prostitute go after lonely widows with dough to blow-before they get blown away themselves. Shirley Stoler, Tony Lo Bianco, Mary Jane Higby, Doris Roberts, Kip McArdle. w. d. Leonard Kastle.
SUSPENSE: SATIRE: COMEDY: Black Comedy; Tragi-Comedy; **MURDER:** Serial Killers; Murderers-Black Widow; Murders of Women; Prostitutes-Male; Nurses; Cult Films; Hidden Gems; Writer-Directors; Independent Films
(Eating Raoul; Black Widow; Boxcar Bertha)

The Honeymoon Machine, 1961, 91m, ★★/$$, MGM/MGM-UA. An enlisted man uses the Navy's computers to win big at the Venice Casino in Las Vegas. Steve McQueen, Brigid Bazlen, Jim Hutton, Paula Prentiss, Dean Jagger, Jack Weston,

Jack Mullaney. w. George Wells, P-adap. Lorenzo Stemple Jr. (*The Golden Fleecing*), d. Richard Thorpe.
COMEDY: COMEDY DRAMA: ROMANCE: Romantic Comedy; Computers; Gambling; Heist Stories; Las Vegas; Military Comedy; Sailors; Forgotten Films; Good Premise Unfulfilled

Honeysuckle Rose, 1980, 119m, ★★½/$$, WB/WB, PG/S-P. A grizzled old country singer misses his wife on the road and hits the drink hard, singing and having fun along the way. Willie Nelson, Dyan Cannon, Amy Irving, Slim Pickens. w. Carol Sobieski, William D. Wittliff, John Binder, d. Jerry Schatzberg.
COMEDY DRAMA: ROMANCE: Romantic Comedy; Romance-Triangles; Singers; Musicians; Country Singers; Road Movies
(Barbarosa; Pure Country; Baby, the Rain Must Fall)

Honky Tonk, 1941, 104m, ★★★/$$$, MGM/MGM-UA. Two people on the make in the wild west-a con man and a crooked judge's daughter-meet up and fall in love. Clark Gable, Lana Turner, Frank Morgan, Claire Trevor, Marjorie Main, Albert Dekker, Henry O'Neill, Chill Wills, Betty Blythe. w. Marguerite Roberts, John Sanford, d. Jack Conway.
COMEDY DRAMA: MELODRAMA: ROMANCE: Romantic Comedy; **WESTERNS:** Con Artists; Dose of Own Medicine-Given; Turning the Tables; Faded Hits
(The Lady Eve; Boom Town)

Honky Tonk Freeway, 1981, 107m, ★★½/$, EMI-U/MCA-U, PG. A small Florida town has a freeway comin' through and the kind of tourists that it attracts are not what were expected. William Devane, Beau Bridges, Teri Garr, Beverly D'Angelo, Hume Cronyn, Jessica Tandy, Howard Hesseman, Geraldine Page, George Dzundza. w. Edward Clinton, d. John Schlesinger.
COMEDY: FARCE: Ensemble Films; Car Wrecks; Southerns; Small-Town Life; Slice of Life; Eccentric People; Florida; Vacations; Flops-Major; Coulda Been Great; Curiosities
(Nashville; It's a Mad, Mad, Mad, Mad World; Health)

Honkytonk Man, 1982, 122m, ★★½/$, WB/WB, PG. During the Depression, a broken-down old country singer hits hard times and returns to his family farm for sustenance. Clint Eastwood, Kyle Eastwood, John McIntire, Verna Bloom, Alexa Kenin, Matt Clark. w., N-adap. Clancy Carlile, d. Clint Eastwood.

DRAMA: Depression Era; Family Drama; Fathers & Sons; Singers; Country Singers; Farm Life; Nature-Back to; Midlife Crisis; Quiet Little Films; Flops-Major; Curiosities; Coulda Been Great
(Tender Mercies; The Southerner)

The Hook, 1962, 98m, ★★1/2/$, MGM/NA. Three enlisted men in Korea are ordered by their superiors to kill a P.O.W. but have a hard time executing their orders. Kirk Douglas, Robert Walker, Nick Adams, Nehemiah Persoff. w. Henry Denker, N-adap. Vahe Katcha (The Hamecon), d. George Seaton.

DRAMA: War Stories; Korean War; POWs; Executions; Ethics; Murder-Learning to; Soldiers; Race Relations; Decisions-Big
(Casualties of War; The Bold and the Brave)

Hook, 1991, 144m, ★★1/2/$$$$, Tri-Star/Col-Tri, PG/V. Peter Pan has grown up and lives in the semi-modern world as a yuppie lawyer who's decided to grow up after all and has forgotten how to fly. Then he gets a visit from Tinkerbell, who tells him of trouble in Neverland. She gets him back into training and he battles his old nemesis, Captain Hook. Robin Williams, Dustin Hoffman, Julia Roberts, Bob Hoskins, Maggie Smith, Caroline Goodall, Charlie Korsmo, Phil Collins, David Crosby. w. Jim V. Hart, Malia Scotch Marmo, Nick Castle, P-adap. J. M. Barrie (Peter Pan), d. Steven Spielberg. BBArt, BOSong, BVFX. Oscars: 3-0.
ADVENTURE: Fantasy; **CHILDREN'S: FAMILY:** Fairy Tales; Childlike People; Kingdoms; Aging-reverse; Pirates; Roller Skating; Fathers-Fascinating; Time Travel; Flying People; Coulda Been Great; Faded Hits
(Peter Pan)
(Ed: All hype and not much else except a revamping of cliches without the energy that made the original tale a classic. Check out the Mary Martin stage version of Peter Pan.)

Hook, Line, and Sinker, 1968, 92m, ★★1/2/$$, Col/Col, Nos. A struggling salesman is told he is dying, so he goes on a mad shopping spree. Then he learns he's not actually dying and has to run from his creditors. Jerry Lewis, Peter Lawford, Anne Francis, Pedro Gonzales Gonzales. w. Rod Amateau, d. George Marshall.
COMEDY: Comedy-Slapstick; Death-Impending; Death-Impending, False; Fools-Bumbling
(Short Time; Send Me No Flowers)

Hoop Dreams, 1994, 165m, ★★★1/2/ $$$, Fine Line/New Line, PG. The story over a period of a few years of two black teenage basketball players and their fight to become good enough to play for a college team and make it out of their inner city beginnings. d. Steve James. BEditing. Oscars: 1-0.
Documentaries; Sports Movies; Basketball; American Dream; Dreams; Inner City Life; Poor People; Chicago; Black Men; Teenagers; High School Life; Sleeper Hits; Cult Films
(Ed: Originally shot on video and then transferred to film, the picture quality isn't so great, which may be one of the reasons it wasn't nominated for Best Documentary Feature by the Academy, but content-wise, it's excellent)

Hooper, 1978, 99m, ★★1/2/$$$$, WB/WB, PG/P-V. A middle-aged Hollywood stuntman wants to pull one really big, spectacular stunt off before he retires. This means many car chases and crashes. Burt Reynolds, Sally Field, Brian Keith, Jan-Michael Vincent, John Marley, Robert Klein, James Best, Adam West. w. Thomas Rickman, Bill Kerby, d. Hal Needham.
ACTION: COMEDY: Action Comedy; Car Chases; Car Crashes; Movie Making; Hollywood Life; Stuntmen; One Last Time; Retirement; 1970s
(The Stunt Man; Stroker Ace; The Cannonball Run)

Hoosiers, 1986, 114m, ★★★/$$, Orion/ Vestron, PG/P. At a small-town Indiana high school, the coach gains new inspiration to whip the basketball team into state champions. Gene Hackman, Barbara Hershey, Dennis Hopper, Sheb Wooley, Fern Persons. w. Angelo Pizzo, d. David Anspaugh.
DRAMA: COMEDY DRAMA: Underdog Stories; Sports Movies; Coaches; Basketball; Midwestern Life; Small-Town Life; High School Life; Sleeper Hits
(Blue Chips; Celtic Pride; Slap Shot)
(Ed: A little more realistic underdog tale

without too many of the hackneyed cliches)

Hope and Glory, 1987, 113m, ★★★1/2/$$, Col/Col, PG. World War II from the point of view of a little boy growing up in the suburbs of London. For him, war is exciting and fun, and he can't understand the adult's reactions. Sarah Miles, Susan Woolridge, Ian Bannen, David Hayman, Derrick O'Connor. w. d. John Boorman (BOScr, BDirector). BPicture, BCin, BArt. Oscars: 5-0.
DRAMA: Autobiographical Stories; Boyhood; Coming of Age; Illusions Destroyed; Family Drama; **FAMILY:** Memories-Childhood; War Stories; War at Home; World War II Stories; England; Child Protagonists; British Films; Hidden Gems
(The Long Day Closes; Empire of the Sun)

Hopscotch, 1980, 104m, ★★★/$$, Avco-Embassy/Embassy, Col, PG/P. Upon retirement, a CIA official writes a tell-all book which forces him to run around the world being pursued by the CIA and an international cast of spies. Walter Matthau, Glenda Jackson, Ned Beatty, Sam Waterston, Herbert Lom, George Baker. w. Brian Garfield, Bryan Forbes, N-adap. Brian Garfield, d. Ronald Neame.
COMEDY: ROMANCE: Romantic Comedy; Romance-Bickering; Capers; Spy Films; Spies; Spoofs-Spy; CIA Agents; Chase Stories; Fugitives; Hiding Out; Hidden Gems
(Housecalls; A Touch of Class; Spycatcher)
(Ed: A minor hit and a must-see for fans of Jackson or of her and Matthau's chemistry from House Calls)

The Horn Blows at Midnight, 1945, 80m, ★★★/$, WB/MGM-UA. Gabriel's horn is used by an angel on a mission to destroy the Earth, but calamity sidetracks the mission. Jack Benny, Alexis Smith, Dolores Moran, Allyn Joslyn, Guy Kibbee, Reginald Gardner, Franklin Pangborn, John Alexander, Margaret Dumont. w. Sam Hellman, James V. Kern, d. Raoul Walsh.
COMEDY: Comedy-Slapstick; Comedy of Errors; Angels; Heaven; Apocalyptic Stories; Comedians; Hidden Gems; Flops-Major
(Here Comes Mr. Jordan; Heaven Can Wait)

Hornet's Nest, 1969, 109m, ★★/$, UA/CBS-Fox, PG/V. Some Italian children play doctor on a U.S. Army explosives expert wounded in World War II. After he's fit again, they all go off together and destroy a dam held by the Nazis. Rock Hudson, Sergio Fantoni, Sylva Koscina, Jacques Sernas. w. S. S. Schweitzer, d. Phil Karlson.

ACTION: DRAMA: Action Drama; War Stories; World War II Stories; Sabotage; Heroes-Unlikely; Men and Boys; Italy; Italians; Curiosities
(Force Ten from Nararone; The Secret of Santa Vittoria)

Horror Express, 1972, 90m, ★★½/$$, AIP/Sinister, R/V. A scientist is carrying a petrified missing link in the luggage compartment of a passenger train traveling through China in 1906. All hell breaks loose when this petrified person comes to life and attacks passengers. Peter Cushing, Christopher Lee, Telly Savalas, Jorge Rigaud. w. Arnaud D'Usseau, Julian Halevy, d. Eugenio Martin.

HORROR: Primates; Monsters-Human; Monsters-Animal; Scientists; Murders-One by One; Trains; Rogue Plots

Horror Hotel (*City of the Dead*), 1960, 78m, ★★/$$, AIP/NA. A woman burned as a witch in Salem is undead and living in Massachusetts, running a hotel which supplies her with fresh victims. Patricia Jessel, Betta St. John, Christopher Lee, Dennis Lotis, Valentine Dyall, Venetia Stevenson, Norman Macowan, Fred Johnson. w. George Baxt, d. John Moxey.

HORROR: Witches; Dead-Back from the; Hotels; Murders-One by One; Forgotten Films

Horse Feathers, 1932, 69m, ★★★★/ $$$, Par/Par. The somewhat hucksterish president of a college uses unscrupulous means to ensure that their football team has a winning season, thus guaranteeing more funding. Groucho Marx, Chico Marx, Harpo Marx, Zeppo Marx, Thelma Todd, Robert Greig. w. Bert Kalmar, Harry Ruby, S. J. Perelman, Will B. Johnstone, d. Norman Z. McLeod.

COMEDY: Screwball Comedy; FARCE: Con Artists; College Life; Football; Professors
(Cocoanuts; Duck Soup; Room Service)

The Horse in the Grey Flannel Suit, 1969, 112m, ★★/$, Disney/Disney, G. A teenage boy allows his horse to be used

in an ad campaign for an indigestion remedy but begins to have second thoughts when things get out of hand. Dean Jones, Fred Clark, Diane Baker, Lloyd Bochner, Morey Amsterdam. w. Louis Pelletier, N-adap. Eric Hatch (*The Year of the Horse*), d. Norman Tokar.

COMEDY: COMEDY DRAMA: CHILDREN'S: Comedy-Disney; FAMILY: Horses; Animal Stories; Pet Stories; Advertising World; Boys; Forgotten Films
(Ed: One of Disney's few flops for kiddies)

The Horse Soldiers, 1959, 119m, ★★½/$$$, UA/CBS-Fox. In 1863, with the confederates approaching a strategic railroad bridge with a trainload of munitions, a Union cavalry officer must travel three hundred miles into their territory to blow it up before they reach it. John Wayne, William Holden, Constance Towers, Hoot Gibson. w. John Lee Mahin, Martin Rackin, d. John Ford.

WESTERNS: Civil War Era; Trains; Cavalry; War Stories; Sabotage; Ensembles-Male; Faded Hits; Forgotten Films
(The Bridge on the River Kwai; Alvarez Kelly)

The Horse's Mouth, 1958, 93m, ★★★½/$$, UA/HomeVision. An eccentric London artist causes much chaos for his beleaguered friends with his temperament and stubbornness. Alec Guinness, Ray Walsh, Renee Houston, Robert Coote, Arthur Macrae, Michael Gough, Ernest Thesiger. w. Alec Guinness (BAScr), N-adap. Joyce Cary, d. Ronald Neame. Oscars: 1-0.

COMEDY: COMEDY DRAMA: Artists; Eccentric People; Friendships on the Rocks; London; British Films; Hidden Gems
(A Fine Madness; Lust for Life)

The Hospital, 1971, 101m, ★★★★/$$$, UA/CBS-Fox, R/P-S. An urban Boston hospital is plagued by foul-ups leading to several deaths, and it's up to a doctor going through a terrible midlife crisis to bring things under control-if possible-while falling in love with a British hippie girl and finding out who's pulling the plug on certain patients. George C. Scott (BActor), Diana Rigg, Barnard Hughes, Nancy Marchand, Richard Dysart. w. Paddy Chayevsky (BOScr), d. Arthur Hiller. Oscars: 2-1.

COMEDY: COMEDY DRAMA: Black Comedy; SATIRE: Social Satire;

Hospitals; Doctors; Nurses; Hippies; Comedy of Errors; ROMANCE: Romantic Drama; Romance-Older Men/Younger Women; Redemption; Midlife Crisis; Suicidal Tendencies; Fathers & Daughters; Boston; Hidden Gems; Time Capsules
(Network; Brittania Hospital; Article 99)
(Ed: A much-imitated masterpiece)

Hot Lead and Cold Feet, 1978, 90m, ★★½/$$, Disney/Disney, G. Twin brothers have very different temperaments: one's a gunfighter, the other's a coward. They butt heads when each vies for control of the same town out west. Jim Dale, Karen Valentine, Don Knotts, Jack Elam, Darren McGaven, John Williams, Warren Vanders. w. Arthur Alsberg, Joe McEveety, Don Nelson, Rod Piffath, d. Robert Butler.

COMEDY: Comedy-Disney; CHILDREN'S: FAMILY: WESTERNS: Western Comedy; Twins; Men in Conflict; Feuds; Brothers; Marriage-Impending
(The Apple Dumpling Gang; The Shakiest Gun in the West)

Hot Millions, 1968, 106m, ★★★/$$$, MGM/MGM-UA, PG. A huckster creates "hollow tree" companies that don't actually exist in order to part investors with loads of cash and make off to South America. Peter Ustinov, Maggie Smith, Bob Newhart, Karl Malden, Robert Morley, Cesar Romero. w. Ira Wallach, Peter Ustinov (BOScr), d. Eric Till. Oscars: 1-0.

COMEDY: Heist Stories; Capers; Computers; Con Artists; Clever Plots & Endings; Hidden Gems
(Quick Change; Topkapi!; Dollars)

Hot Pursuit, 1987, 93m, ★★/$, Par-RKO/Par, PG/S-P. A teenager on a Caribbean vacation with his girlfriend and her family has to search for them when they get separated in transit. John Cusack, Robert Loggia, Wendy Gazelle, Jerry Stiller, Monte Markham, Shelley Fabares. w. Stephen Lisberger, Steven Carabatsos, d. Stephen Lisberger.

COMEDY: ROMANCE: Romantic Comedy; Romance-Boy Wants Girl; Vacations; Vacation Romance; Chase Stories; Caribbean; Missing Persons; Coulda Been Good
(Say Anything; The Last Resort)

The Hot Rock, 1972, 105m, ★★★½/$$$, 20th/CBS-Fox, PG. Four accomplices plan and execute an elaborate heist of a famous, heavily guarded diamond at the Brooklyn Museum. Robert Redford, George Segal, Zero Mostel, Paul Sand, Ron Leibman, Moses Gunn, William Redfield. w. William Goldman, N-adap. Donald E. Westlake, d. Peter Yates. BEdit. Oscars: 1-0.

COMEDY: Capers; Heist Stories; Jewel Thieves; Ex-Convicts; Comedy of Errors; Ensemble Films; Ensembles-Male; Museums; Crime Pays; Clever Plots & Endings; Hidden Gems

(Sneakers; Rififi; Topkapi!)

Hot Shots!, 1991, 85m, ★★★/$$$, 20th/Fox, PG/P-S. In a take-off on *Top Gun* and films of its genre, a maverick pilot has an identity crisis on a mission to bomb an atomic reactor (or the secondary target, an accordion factory). Charlie Sheen, Cary Elwes, Valeria Golino, Lloyd Bridges, Jon Cryer, Kevin Dunn, Bill Irwin, William O'Leary, Kristy Swanson, Efrem Zimbalist Jr. w. Jim Abrahams, Pat Proft, d. Jim Abrahams.

Hot Shots, Part Deux, 1993, 89m, ★★/$$$, 20th/Fox, PG-13/P-S. More of the gags on the base as the Admiral from the first is elected President and calls our hero into a Rambo-style mission in Iraq. Charlie Sheen, Lloyd Bridges, Valeria Golina, Miguel Ferrer. w. Pat Proft, Jim Abrahams, d. Abrahams.

Presidents; POWs; **COMEDY:** Spoofs; Military Comedy; Pilots-Military; Comedy-Slapstick; **ACTION:** Action Comedy; Fools-Bumbling; Cartoonlike Movies

(Top Gun; Airplane SERIES; Naked Gun SERIES)

Hot Spell, 1958, 86m, ★★½/$$, Par/Par. A married middle-aged man in a small town down South confronts the wrath of his family and townsfolk when he takes up with a twenty-year-old girl. Anthony Quinn, Shirley Booth, Shirley MacLaine, Earl Holliman, Eileen Heckart. w. James Poe, P-adap. Lonnie Coleman (*Next of Kin*), d. Daniel Mann.

DRAMA: MELODRAMA: Family Drama; Southerns; Tennessee Williams-esque; Small-Town Scandal; Scandals; Romance-Older Men/Younger Women; Cheating Men; Coulda Been Good; Forgotten Films; Mississippi

(The Dark at the Top of the Stairs; The Long, Hot Summer; Cat on a Hot Tin Roof)

The Hot Spot, 1990, 130m, ★★½/$$, Orion/Orion, PG-13/S-P-V. A smooth-

talking huckster and crook goes to work for a used-car dealer with the sexiest wife in town, and a doomed love-triangle ensues. Don Johnson, Virginia Madsen, Jennifer Connelly, Charles Martin Smith, William Sadler, Jerry Hardin, Barry Corbin, Jack Nance. w. Nona Tyson, Charles Williams, N-adap. Charles Williams (*Hell Hath No Fury*), d. Dennis Hopper.

DRAMA: ROMANCE: Erotic Drama; Erotic Thriller; Romance-Doomed; Romance-Triangles; Con Artists; Small-Town Life; Cheating Women; Jim Thompson-esque; Film Noir-Modern

(After Dark, My Sweet; Two-Moon Junction; The Long, Hot Summer [1985])

Hot Stuff, 1979, 91m, ★★½/$$$, Col/Col, PG/P-S. In order to meet their quota of arrests, the burglary division of an urban police force sets up traps, with unintended comic results. Dom DeLuise, Suzanne Pleshette, Ossie Davis, Jerry Reed, Luis Avalos, Marc Lawrence. w. Michael Kane, Donald E. Westlake, d. Dom DeLuise.

COMEDY: Police Comedy; Police Stories; Comedy-Slapstick; Comedy of Errors; Thieves; Turning the Tables; Faded Hits

(Fuzz; Super Cops)

Hotel, 1967, 124m, ★★★/$$$, WB/WB, PG/S-FRN. In New Orleans, the residents of a posh hotel play out their various soap operas in their respective rooms (and in the rooms of their neighbors). Rod Taylor, Catherine Spaak, Karl Malden, Melvyn Douglas, Merle Oberon, Richard Conte, Michael Rennie, Kevin McCarthy, Alfred Ryder. w. Wendell Mayes, N-adap. Arthur Hailey, d. Richard Quine.

DRAMA: MELODRAMA: Soap Operas; Multiple Stories; Interwoven Stories; Hotels; New Orleans; Faded Hits

(Grand Hotel; Doctors' Wives)

The Hotel New Hampshire, 1984, 108m, ★★★/$$, Orion/Orion, Vestron, R/S-P-MRN. A very eccentric family of children with a wayward father live at a hotel in New Hampshire and one in Paris, having very sexual escapades while growing up in a surreal world. Rob Lowe, Jodie Foster, Paul McCrane, Beau Bridges, Nastassja Kinski, Wallace Shawn, Wilford Brimley. w. d. Tony Richardson, N-adap. John Irving.

COMEDY DRAMA: Comedy-Light; Hotels; Family Comedy; Ensemble Films; Bratpack Movies; Young People;

Teenagers; Incest; Coming of Age; Episodic Stories; Surrealism; Curiosities; Coulda Been Great

(The World According to Garp)

Hotel Paradiso, 1966, 99m, ★★★½/$$, MGM/MGM-UA. A advertisement goes around about a hotel for midnight rendezvous in Gay Nineties Paris, giving Monsieur Boniface the chance to finally get his beautiful neighbor lady away from her overweight, boorish husband, so he also escape his overweight, overbearing wife. The only problem is, everyone else they know also winds up at the naughty hotel at the same time. Alec Guinness, Gina Lollobrigida, Marie Bell, Akim Tamiroff, Robert Morley, Derek Fowlds. w. Peter Glenville, Jean Claude Carriere, P-adap. Georges Feydeau (*L'Hotel du Libre Exchange*), d. Peter Glenville.

COMEDY: FARCE: Farce-Bedroom; Cheating Men; Cheating Women; Hotels; Multiple Stories; Interwoven Stories; Gay 90s; 1890s; Paris; Hidden Gems; Coulda Been Great

(Tom Jones; The Ambassadors; A Flea in Her Ear)

Houdini, 1953, 106m, ★★½/$$$, Par/Par. The famous magician from the 1890s dazzles the masses with his death-defying stunts, until the fateful day when he cheats death for the last time. Tony Curtis, Janet Leigh, Torin Thatcher, Sig Rumann, Angela Clarke. w. Philip Yordan, d. George Marshall.

DRAMA: COMEDY DRAMA: Biographies; Magic/Magicians; Risking It All; Death of Celebrity; 1900s; Fame-Rise to

TV REMAKE: 1976, ABC

The Hound of the Baskervilles, 1939, 86m, ★★★/$$$, 20th/Fox. A series of disappearances in London are attributed to a mysterious, otherworldly canine beast. Scotland Yard puts Sherlock Holmes on the case to get to the more down-to-earth explanation. Basil Rathbone, Nigel Bruce, Richard Greene, Wendy Barrie, Lionel Atwill, Morton Lowry, John Carradine, Ralph Forbes, E. E. Clive, Mary Gordon. w. Ernest Pascal, N-adap. Arthur Conan Doyle, d. Sidney Lanfield.

The Hound of the Baskervilles, 1959, 86m, ★★½/$$, UA/Hammer/MGM-UA. A remake with more blood, gore, and sex. Peter Cushing, Andre Morell, Christopher Lee, Marla Landi, Ewen Solon, Francis

de Wolff, Miles Malleson, John Le Mesurier. w. Peter Bryan, N-adap. Arthur Conan Doyle, d. Terence Fisher.
MYSTERY: MURDER: MURDER MYSTERY: Detective Stories; Sherlock Holmes; Monsters-Animal; Gothic Style; England; British Films
(The Adventures of Sherlock Holmes)
The Hound of the Baskervilles, 1977, 85m, ★★/$, Hemdale/Atlantic, PG. A comic take-off on the famous Sherlock Holmes story. Peter Cook, Dudley Moore, Denholm Elliott, Terry-Thomas, Joan Greenwood, Max Wall, Irene Handl, Kenneth Williams, Hugh Griffith, Roy Kinnear, Prunella Scales, Spike Milligan. w. Dudley Moore, Peter Cook, Paul Morrissey, d. Paul Morrissey.
COMEDY: Spoofs; Comic Mystery; MYSTERY: MURDER: MURDER MYSTERY: Detective Stories; Sherlock Holmes; Monsters-Animal; Gothic Style; England; British Films
(The Adventures of Sherlock Holmes' Smarter Brother; Without a Clue; They Might Be Giants)
Hour of the Gun, 1967, 101m, ★★1/2/$$, UA/MGM-UA, PG/V. A "revisionist Western" in which Wyatt Earp is portrayed as less than heroic in his obsessive, violent retribution on the Clanton gang. James Garner, Jason Robards Jr., Robert Ryan, Steve Ihnat, Michael Tolan, Frank Converse, Monte Markham, Jon Voight. w. Edward Anhalt, d. John Sturges.
WESTERNS: DRAMA: Biographies; Wyatt Earp; Westerns-Neo Revenge; Westerns-Revenge; Coulda Been Good (Wyatt Earp; Tombstone; The Tin Star)
House, 1986, 93m, ★★★/$$$, New World/New World, R/EV-B&G. A boy moves into the house in which his aunt died and is besieged by evil spirits. William Katt, George Wendt, Richard Moll, Kay Lenz. w. Ethan Wiley, d. Steve Miner.
(The House of Long Shadows)
House II: The Second Story, 1988, 88m, ★★/$$, New World/New World, R/EV-B&G. A couple are killed in their house in the sixties. Flash-forward to the present, when their Vietnam vet son moves back into that house and runs from ghosts while looking for the Aztec skull of their ancestors, buried on the grounds. Arye Gross, Jonathan Stark, Royal Dano, Bill Maher, Lar Park Lincoln, John Ratzenberger. w. d. Ethan Wiley.

House III (*The Horror Show*), 1989, 95m, ★★/$, NW/NW, R/EV-B&G. An executed killer is brought back to life through the miracle of electricity and goes after the cop who arrested him to terrorize his family. Lance Henriksen, Brion James, Rita Taggart, Dedee Pfeiffer, Thom Bray, Matt Clark, Lawrence Tierney. w. Alan Smithee, Leslie Bohem, d. James Isaac.
(Shocker)
House IV, 1992, 93m, ★1/2/$, New Line/Col, R/EV-B&G. The widow of a wealthy estate owner is the subject of a scare campaign by her brother-in-law, who tries to convince her that ghosts are after her in order to get the house to himself. Terry Treas, William Katt, Scott Burkhoilder, Melissa Clayton, Denny Dillon, Dabbs Greer, Mark Gash. w. Geof Miller, Deirdre Higgins, Jim Wynorski, R. J. Robinson, d. Lewis Abernathy.
HORROR: Haunted Houses; Houses-Creepy; MURDER: Murders-One by One; Possessions; Writers
(Ed: Started off well with the first installment but quickly faded away)
House Calls, 1978, 98m, ★★★1/2/$$$$, U/MCA-U, PG/S. A playboy, goofball doctor meets up with a feisty struggling mom, which eventually leads to romance. Walter Matthau, Glenda Jackson, Art Carney, Richard Benjamin, Candice Azzara, Thayer David, Dick O'Neill. w. Max Shulman, Julius J. Epstein, Alan Mandel, Charles Shyer, d. Howard Zieff.
COMEDY: ROMANCE: Romantic Comedy; Sex Comedy; Romance-Middle-Aged; Romance-Bickering; Romance-Reluctant; Feisty Females; Settling Down; Starting Over; Widows; Widowers; Doctors; Secretaries; Sleeper Hits; Hidden Gems; Faded Hits; Old-Fashioned Recent Films
(A Touch of Class; Hopscotch)
A House Divided, 1931, 70m, ★★★/$$, U/NA. When his wife dies, a wizened old fisherman meets a younger woman and falls in love. Unfortunately, she's got her eye on his son. Walter Huston, Kent Douglas, Helen Chandler, Vivian Oakland, Frank Hagney. w. John P. Clymer, Dale Van Every, John Huston, SS-adap. Olive Edens (*Heart and Hand*), d. William Wyler.
DRAMA: MELODRAMA: ROMANCE: Romance-Triangles; Romance-Older Men/Younger Women; Widowers; Fishermen; Forgotten Films; Romance

with Lover's Relative; Romance-Unrequited
Houseguest, 1995, 108m, ★★/$$, Hollywood/Hollywood, PG-13/P. A black con artist schemer has bottomed out and happens upon the chance to pose as a childhood white friend who doesn't remember enough to suspect he's an impostor, but soon, just like all the rest, the gig's up. Sinbad, Phil Hartman, Kim Greist, Chauncey Leopardi, Talia Seider, Kim Murphy, Paul Ben-Victor, Tony Longo, Jeffrey Jones, Stan Shaw, Ron Glass. w. Michael J. DiGaetano, Lawrence Gay, d. Randall Miller.
COMEDY: Con Artists; Reunions; Impostors; Identities-Assumed; Roommates from Hell; Nuisances; Black Men
(Opportunity Knocks; Six Degrees of Separation)
Household Saints, 1994, 112m, ★★1/2/$, Polygram/Polygram, PG. The lives of an Italian Catholic family that started with the husband winning the wife in a card game. Time passes, and their daughter grows up to become a nun. But soon, things begin to unravel as family crises and ambitions lead to conflicts. Tracey Ullman, Vincent D'Onofrio, Lili Taylor, Judith Malina, Michael Rispoli, Victor Argo, Michael Imperioli, Rachael Bella, Illeana Douglas, Joe Grifasi. w. Nancy Savoca, Richard Guay, d. Savoca.
COMEDY DRAMA: MELODRAMA: Family Drama; Episodic Stories; Italians; Religion; Nuns; Female Screenwriters; Female Directors; Female Protagonists
(Breathing Lessons; True Love; I Love You to Death; Used People)
(Ed: Esoteric appeal, which will probably lead to yawns)
A House Is Not a Home, 1964, 98m, ★★1/2/$$, Par/Par. Polly Adler, the infamous New York madam, gets the melodramatic Hollywood treatment. Her life is seen as tragic, rather than joyous. Shelly Winters, Robert Taylor, Cesar Romero, Ralph Taeger, Broderick Crawford. w. Russel Rouse, Clarence Greene, d. Russel Rouse.
DRAMA: MELODRAMA: TRAGEDY: Biographies; Madams; Prostitutes-High Class; Female Protagonists; True Stories; Forgotten Films
(Personal Services; A Walk on the Wild Side)
House of Cards, 1968, 100m, ★★1/2/$, U/NA. An American English teacher in

Paris gets swept up in international intrigue when he takes an assignment tutoring the widow of a French general. George Peppard, Inger Stevens, Orson Welles, Keith Mitchell, William Job, Maxine Audley, Peter Bayliss. w. James P. Bonner, N-adap. Stanley Ellin, d. John Gurney.

SUSPENSE: Spy Films; Spies; Americans Abroad; Innocent Bystanders; Teachers; Hitchcockian; Coulda Been Good
(The House on Carroll Street; Half-Moon Street)

House of Cards, 1994, 115m, ★★1/2/$, Polygram/Polygram, PG-13/S. A woman's daughter starts behaving in strange ways, such as being withdrawn, then having screaming fits, then climbing on the roof or in trees, building precarious houses of cards with great ease. She refuses to believe this apparent autism is a permanent phase, but the psychiatrist she takes the girl to has conflicting ideas. That doesn't stop them from finding the daughter's problems something they have in common, which could lead to more. Kathleen Turner, Tommy Lee Jones, Asha Menina, Shiloh Strong, Esther Rolle, Park Overall, Michael Horse, Anne Pitoniak. w. d. Michael Lessac.

DRAMA: Disease Stories; Mothers & Daughters; Girls; Mental Illness; Mentally Disabled; Psychiatrists; Writer-Directors; Quiet Little Films
(Silent Fall; Son-Rise; Miracle of Love)

House of Dracula, 1945, 67m, ★★1/2/$$, U/MCA-U. A kindly doctor goes berserk after being scared out of his wits by the Wolf Man, Dracula, and Frankenstein's monster. The Wolf Man lives happily ever after. Onslow Stevens, John Carradine, Lon Chaney Jr., Glenn Strange, Lionel Atwill, Martha O'Driscoll, Jane Adams. w. Edward T. Lowe, d. Erle C. Kenton.

HORROR: Spoofs-Horror; Vampires; Werewolves; Frankenstein; Mental Illness; Castles; Monsters
(Dracula; Bram Stoker's Dracula)

House of Frankenstein, 1944, 71m, ★★1/2/$$, U/MCA-U. A sequel of sorts to *Frankenstein Meets the Wolf Man,* in which the title stars were frozen stiff at the end, this one has them thawed out and ready for action. Boris Karloff, John Carradine, Lon Chaney Jr., George Zucco, J. Carrol Naish, Anne Gwynne, Elena Verdugo, Lionel Atwill, Sig Rumann,

Glenn Strange. w. Edward T. Lowe, Curt Siodmak, d. Erle C. Kenton.

HORROR: Spoofs-Horror; Frankenstein; Vampires; Werewolves; Scientists-Mad (Frankenstein; Mary Shelley's Frankenstein)

House of Games, 1987, 102m, ★★★/$$, Orion/Orion, R/P. A female pop-psychologist decides to write a book on con-men but gets in over her head. Just who's conning who is the question. Lindsay Crouse, Joe Mantegna, Mike Nussbaum, Lilia Skala. w. d. David Mamet.

DRAMA: SUSPENSE: Mindgames; Con Artists; Bets; Psychological Thriller; Psychological Drama; Psychologists; Gambling; Radio Life; Cat and Mouse; Hidden Gems; Cult Films; Writer-Directors
(Homicide; Glengarry Glen Ross)

The House of Rothschild, 1934, 87m, ★★1/2/$$, 20th/NA. The story of French/Jewish bankers who also started a famous vineyard in the days of Napoleon. George Arliss, Loretta Young, Boris Karloff, Robert Young, C. Aubrey Smith, Arthur Byron, Helen Westley, Reginald Owen, Florence Arliss, Alan Mowbray, Holmes Herbert. w. Nunnally Johnson, P-adap. George Humbert Westley, d. Alfred Werker.

DRAMA: Biographies; Family Drama; Historical Drama; Costume Drama; Napoleon; Jewish People; 1800s

The House of Seven Gables, 1940, 89m, ★★★/$$$, U/NA, AMC. In New England in the 1600s, in a respected family, a brother thwarts his sister's marriage in an attempt to sustain their strange, symbiotic bond. George Sanders, Margaret Lindsay, Vincent Price, Alan Napier, Nan Grey, Cecil Kellaway, Dick Foran, Miles Mander. w. Lester Cole, N-adap. Nathaniel Hawthorne, d. Joe May.

DRAMA: Family Drama; Brothers & Sisters; Mindgames; Marriage-Impending; Relatives-Troublesome; Romance-Triangles; Witches; Early America; 1600s; Hidden Gems
(The Scarlet Letter; The Crucible)

House of Strangers, 1949, 101m, ★★/$$, 20th/NA. An Italian banker keeps his family of three sons well ordered under a tight watch. But that order begins to break down as the crack in the facade of his life is revealed, and he's accused of illegal activities. Edward

G. Robinson, Richard Conte, Susan Hayward, Luther Adler, Paul Valentine, Efrem Zimbalist Jr., Debra Paget, Hope Emerson, Esther Minciotti, Diana Douglas. w. Philip Yordan, N-adap. Jerome Weidman, d. Joseph L. Mankiewicz.

DRAMA: Family Drama; Crime Drama; Mob Stories; Italians; Fathers & Sons; Stern Men; Ordinary People Turned Criminal; Secrets-Keeping
(All My Sons)

The House of the Spirits, 1994, 109m, ★★★/$$, Miramax/Miramax, R/S-EV-FN-MN. The saga of a Chilean aristocratic family over several decades centering around the evil patriarch (Jeremy Irons), his clairvoyant wife (Meryl Streep), their daughter (Winona Ryder) and his spinster sister (Glenn Close), leading up to the 1973 coup. Antonio Banderas, Vanessa Redgrave, Armin Mueller-Stahl, Maria Conchita Alonso. w. d. Bille August, N-adap. Isabel Allende.

DRAMA: Epics; Family Drama; Episodic Stories; South America; Rich People; Evil Men; Psychics; Fortune Tellers; Spinsters; Lover Family Dislikes; Political Unrest; Rape/Rapists; Magic Realism; Lyrical Films; Life Transitions; Ghosts; Reunions
(Indochine; Babette's Feast; Like Water for Chocolate; A Walk in the Clouds; Missing)
(Ed: A beautiful, enchanting film that doesn't fully make sense until the end, but the performances are so engaging they carry the story. A big hit in Europe)

House of the Long Shadows, 1983, 101m, ★★1/2/$, Cannon/MGM-UA, R/V. A writer, on a dare, takes up residence in a haunted house to write a Gothic novel in one night. Christopher Lee, Peter Cushing, Vincent Price, Desi Arnaz Jr., John Carradine, Sheila Keith, Julie Peasgood, Richard Todd. w. Michael Armstrong, P-adap. George M. Cohan (*Seven Keys to Baldpate*), N-adap. Earl Derr Biggers, d. Pete Walker.

HORROR: Haunted Houses; Gothic Style; Writers; Bets; Coulda Been Good
(House; The Haunting)

House of Usher, 1960, 85m, ★★★/$$, AIP/NA. The two remaining members of a once-distinguished family, a sleepwalking sister and her strange brother, disintegrate personally as the house they inhabit disintegrates physically around them, all of which reaches its apex on a night when the sister's narcolepsy is especially bad and the brother mistakenly buries her alive. Vincent Price; Myrna Fahey, Mark Damon, Harry Ellerbe. w. Richard Matheson, SS-adap. Edgar Allan Poe (*The Fall of the House of Usher*), d. Roger Corman.

House of Usher, 1990, 90m, ★★/$, 21st Century/Col, R/V-B&G. A poor unsuspecting girl is pressured by her boyfriend's uncle, Roderick Usher, to let him impregnate her. Oliver Reed, Donald Pleasence, Romy Windsor, Rufus Swart, Norman Coombes, Anne Stradi. w. Michael J. Murray, SS-adap. Edgar Allan Poe (*The Fall of the House of Usher*), d. Alan Birkinshaw.
HORROR: Buried Alive; Incest; Houses-Creepy; Rape/Rapists; Brothers & Sisters; Classic Literary Adaptations
(The Fall of the House of Usher)

House of Wax, 1953, 88m, ★★★/$$$, WB/WB. A mad genius wax sculptor is badly burned in a fire in his studio, so he exacts revenge on the world by using live models and pouring wax over their screaming heads. Vincent Price, Carolyn Jones, Paul Picerni, Phyllis Kirk, Frank Lovejoy. w. Crane Wilbur, d. Andre de Toth.
HORROR: Revenge; Artists; Mental Illness; Museums; 3-D Movies; Cult Films
(Theater of Blood; Waxwork)

House of Women, 1962, 105m, ★★1/2/$, WB/NA. A pregnant woman is the scapegoat for a crime she didn't commit, and she must bear her child in prison. Shirley Knight, Andrew Duggan, Constance Ford, Barbara Nichols, Margaret Hayes. w. Crane Wilbur, d. Walter Doniger.
DRAMA: Accused Unjustly; Framed?; Babies-Having; Prison Drama; Women in Prison; Social Drama; Female Protagonists; Young Women
(Caged; Love Child; Last Dance)

The House on Carroll Street, 1988, 100m, ★★★/$, Orion/Orion, PG. A writer for *Life* magazine at the height of the McCarthy communist witch-hunt sees strange goings-on in a neighboring house and finds herself uncovering a scheme to smuggle Nazis into the country. Kelly McGillis, Jeff Daniels, Mandy Patinkin, Christopher Rhode, Jessica Tandy, Jonathan Hogan. w. Walter Bernstein, d. Peter Yates.

SUSPENSE: Detective Stories; Detectives-Female; Detectives-Amateur; Chase Stories; Detectives in Deep; McCarthy Era; Nazi Stories; Communists; Germans as Enemy; Conspiracy; 1950s; FBI Agents; Coulda Been Great; Hitchcockian; Female Protagonists; Female Among Males
(The House on 92nd Street)
(Ed: Great-looking with some preposterous moments involving a bomb and some ketchup, but otherwise, very interesting)

House on Haunted Hill, 1958, 75m, ★★1/2/$$, AA/Fox. A millionaire throws a big bash in a house that was the sight of multiple murders. Vincent Price, Richard Long, Carol Ohmart, Alan Marshal, Elisha Cook Jr. w. Robb White, d. William Castle.
HORROR: Party Movies; **MURDER:** Murder-Invitation to; Camp; Cult Films
(The Haunting; Murder by Death; Ten Little Indians)
(Ed: Schlock producer William Castle used his "emergo" gimmick for this one, where skeletons, etc., dropped out of the ceiling of the theater)

The House on 92nd Street, 1945, 88m, ★★1/2/$$, 20th/NA. Nazis posing as normal Americans in New York to search for atomic secrets get found out by G-men doing their duty to God and country. William Eythe, Lloyd Nolan, Signe Hasso, Leo G. Carroll, Gene Lockhart, Lydia St. Clair, Harry Bellaver. w. Barre Lyndon, Charles G. Booth, John Monks Jr., d. Henry Hathaway.
DRAMA: Spy Films; Spies; Nazi Stories; World War II Stories; Bombs-Atomic; Patriotic Films
(The House on Carroll Street; Keeper of the Flame)

House Party, 1990, 104m, ★★★/$$$, New Line/New Line, PG-13/P-S. The rap-duo Kid n' Play and a group of black middle-class teenagers throw a big party and they each deal with love and life and class-conflicts within the black community in a non-preachy, realistic way. Kudos for the plug for safe sex, too. Christopher Reid, Robin Harris, Christopher Martin, Martin Lawrence, Tisha Campbell, A. J. Johnson. w. d. Reginald Hudlin.
Writer-Directors; Independent Films

House Party 2, 1991, 94m, ★★/$$, New Line/New Line, R/P-S. The rap duo from the first film engage in role playing at

their high-school: switching the brain and the brawn. Then they graduate, and consider their career opportunities. Christopher Reid, Christopher Martin, Tisha Campbell, Iman, Martin Lawrence, D. Christopher Judge, Queen Latifah. w. Rusty Cundieff, Daryl G. Nickens, d. Doug McHenry, George Jackson.
COMEDY: Buddy Films; Party Movies; Black Men; Sleeper Hits; Black Directors; Black Screenwriters

The House That Dripped Blood, 1970, 102m, ★★1/2/$$, Amicus/Prism, R/V-B&G. Four stories, all involving the same haunted house, are told to a Scotland Yard inspector investigating a murder there. John Bennett, Christopher Lee Peter Cushing, Denholm Elliott, Joanna Dunham, Nyree Dawn Porter, Jon Pertwee, Ingrid Pitt. w. Robert Bloch, d. Peter John.
HORROR: Multiple Stories; Haunted Houses; British Films; Independent Films
(Dead of Night; Trilogy of Terror)

Houseboat, 1958, 110m, ★★★/$$$, Par/Par. A middle-aged widower with three children hires a bubbly, vivacious, and sexy Italian maid who turns their life around, and they all decide to live on a houseboat. Cary Grant, Sophia Loren, Martha Hyer, Eduardo Ciannelli, Harry Guardino. w. Melville Shavelson, Jack Rose, d. Melville Shavelson.
COMEDY: ROMANCE: Romantic Comedy; Family Comedy; Fathers Alone; Sexy Women; Widowers; Romance with Servants; Babysitters; Italians
(Father Goose; Adam Had Four Sons)

Housekeeping, 1987, 115m, ★★★/$, Col/Col, PG. A strange and eccentric woman brings up her two nieces after her sister dies. Christine Lahti, Sara Walker, Andrea Burchill, Anne Pitoniak, Barbara Reese, Rill Smillie, Margo Pinvidic. w. d. Bill Forsythe, N-adap. Marilynne Robinson.
COMEDY DRAMA: Black Comedy; Eccentric People; Ordinary People Stories; Friendships-Female; Family Comedy; Orphans; Hidden Gems; Female Protagonists

Housesitter, 1992, 102m, ★★★1/2/$$$, U/MCA-U, PG/S. A free-spirited con artist decides an architect who's built a new house for his fiancee is the one for her, so she moves into his house and drives his fiancee away, but will true love blossom between them or will everything cave in? Steve Martin, Goldie Hawn, Dana Delany, Julie Harris, Donald Moffat, Peter MacNicol, Richard B. Shull, Laurel Cronin. w. Mark Stein, Brian Grazer, d. Frank Oz.

COMEDY: Screwball Comedy;
ROMANCE: Romantic Comedy; Eccentric People; Free Spirits; Engagements-Breaking; Marriage-Impending; Con Artists; Liars; Fatal Attractions; Hidden Gems; Underrated; Old-Fashioned Recent Films
COMIC FLIPSIDE OF: Fatal Attraction (Bringing Up Baby; Good Neighbor Sam)

How Do I Love Thee, 1970, 109m, ★★½/$, ABC/ABC. An eccentric professor of philosophy remembers his atheist father and the battles they used to have. Jackie Gleason, Maureen O'Hara, Shelley Winters, Rick Lenz, Rosemary Forsyth. w. Everett Freeman, N-adap. Peter De Vries (*Let Me Count the Ways*), d. Michael Gordon.

DRAMA: Fathers & Sons; Professors; Religion; Memories; Forgotten Films (I Never Sang for My Father)

How Green Was My Valley, 1941, 118m, ★★★/$$$$, 20th/Fox. A man remembers his childhood in a poor but happy Welsh mining community. Walter Pidgeon, Maureen O'Hara, Roddy McDowell, Donald Crisp (**BSActor**), Sara Allgood (BSActress), Anna Lee, John Loder, Barry Fitzgerald, Patric Knowles. w. Philip Dunne (BScr), N-adap. Richard Llewellyn, d. John Ford (**BDirector**). **BPicture, BB&WCin, BB&WArt,** BSound, BEdit, BScore. Oscars: 10-5.

MELODRAMA: Boyhood; Family Drama; Sagas; Episodic Stories; Coming of Age; Memories; Mining Towns; Epics; England (The Corn Is Green; Hope and Glory)

How I Got Into College, 1989, 89m, ★★½/$, 20th/Fox, PG-13/P-S. A brainy girl gets into a prestigious university, so the brainless party dude who loves her applies as well and finagles his way in. Anthony Edwards, Corey Parker, Lara Flynn Boyle, Finn Carter, Charles Rocket, Christopher Rydell, Brian Doyle-Murray. w. Terrel Seltzer, d. Savage Steve Holland.

COMEDY: College Life; High School Life; Students; Romance-Boy Wants Girl; Party Movies; Smart vs. Dumb; Romance-Opposites Attract (Better Off Dead; Making the Grade; PCU)

How I Won the War, 1967, 110m, ★★/$, UA/Fox. A soldier in World War II is hardened by the loss of his friends and becomes a killing machine. Michael Crawford, John Lennon, Roy Kinnear, Lee Montague, Jack McGowran, Michael Hordern, Jack Hedley, Karl Michael Vogler, Ronald Lacey, James Cossins, Alexander Knox. w. Charles Wood, N-adap. Patrick Ryan, d. Richard Lester.

DRAMA: War Stories; Soldiers; Death-Dealing with; Psycho-Killers; Nervous Breakdowns; Message Films; Peaceful People; Cult Films; Forgotten Films

How Sweet It Is, 1968, 98m, ★★/$$, WB/WB. A teenage boy and his girlfriend go off on a school-sponsored European vacation. They think they are alone, but his suspicious parents have followed them. James Garner, Debbie Reynolds, Maurice Ronet, Paul Lynde, Marcel Dalio, Terry-Thomas, Donald Losby, Hilarie Thompson. w. Garry Marshall, Jerry Belson, N-adap. Muriel Resnik (*The Girl in the Turquoise Bikini*), d. Jerry Paris.

COMEDY: Vacations-European; Parents vs. Children; Marriage Comedy; Generation Gap; Teenagers (Divorce, American Style; The Impossible Years)

How the West Was Won, 1963, 162m, ★★★½/$$$$$, MGM/MGM-UA. The history of the cowboys and the Indians, North and South, and the opening of the West, as seen through the eyes of a pioneer girl who grows to old age throughout the course of the film. Debbie Reynolds, Carroll Baker, Lee J. Cobb, Henry Fonda, Carolyn Jones, Karl Malden, Gregory Peck, George Peppard, Robert Preston, James Stewart, Eli Wallach, John Wayne, Richard Widmark, Brigid Bazlen, Walter Brennan, David Brian, Andy Devine, Raymond Massey, Agnes Moorehead, Henry Morgan, Thelma Ritter, Russ Tamblyn, Spencer Tracy. w. James R. Webb (**BOScr**), d. Henry Hathaway (first half), John Ford (Civil War sequence), George Marshall (train sequence). BPicture, BCCin, BCArt, **BSound, BEdit,** BOScore, BCCostume. Oscars: 7-3.

DRAMA: ADVENTURE: Historical Drama; **WESTERNS:** American Myth; Multiple Stories; Interwoven Stories; Epics; Episodic Stories; Blockbusters; Cowboys; Indians-American; Cavalry vs. Indians; Conflict with American Indians;

All-Star Casts; Cast of Thousands (The Alamo; Centennial TV miniseries; TV series remake [1979])

How to Be Very Very Popular, 1955, 89m, ★★/$, 20th/NA. Two belly dancers hide from the mob at a co-ed college. Betty Grable, Sheree North, Charles Coburn, Robert Cummings, Orson Bean, Fred Clark, Tommy Noonan. w. d. Nunnally Johnson.

COMEDY: Fugitives from the Mob; Hiding Out; College Life; Dancers; Forgotten Films; Writer-Directors (Ball of Fire; She's Working Her Way Through College)

How to Beat the High Cost of Living, 1980, 110m, ★★/$$, Filmways/Orion, PG. Three housewives scraping to make ends meet decide to rob banks instead of pinching pennies. Susan Saint James, Jane Curtin, Jessica Lange, Richard Benjamin, Fred Willard, Eddie Albert. w. Robert Kaufman, d. Robert Scheerer.

COMEDY: Making a Living; Suburban Life; Heist Stories; Housewives; Ensembles-Female; Curiosities (Fun with Dick and Jane; Perfect Gentlemen)

How to Get Ahead in Advertising, 1989, 96m, ★★★/$$, 20th/Fox, R/P-S. A copywriter at an ad agency in England develops a boil on his neck that starts giving him unwanted advice as it grows into, literally, his alter ego. Richard E. Grant, Rachel Ward, Richard Wilson, Jacqueline Tong, John Shrapnel, Susan Woodridge, Mick Ford, Jacqueline Pearce. w. d. Bruce Robinson.

COMEDY: Black Comedy; Surrealism; What If . . . Stories; Advertising World; British Films; Cult Films; Writer-Directors (Withnail & I)

How to Make an American Quilt, 1995, 109m, ★★★/$$, Col/Col, PG/S. Before her wedding a college student doing her thesis on quilting decides to spend the summer at her grandmother's, who has quilting parties. She finds a love at the pool but can't decide whether he's worth pursuing before she's married or not-or suddenly whether her fiancé's worth it either. Winona Ryder, Maya Angelou, Anne Bancroft, Ellen Burstyn, Samantha Mathis, Kate Nelligan, Jean Simmons, Lois Smith, Alfre Woodard, Jonathan Schaech, Dermot Mulroney,

Claire Danes, Loren Dean, Melinda Dillon, Joanna Going. w. Jane Anderson, N-adap. Whitney Otto, d. Jocelyn Moorhouse.

COMEDY DRAMA: DRAMA: Coming of Age; Ensembles-Female; Young Women; Mothers & Daughters; Women's Films; Marriage-Impending; Decisions-Big; Female Directors; Female Screenwriters; Female Protagonists
(Moonlight and Valentino; Welcome Home, Roxy Carmichael; Mystic Pizza)
How to Marry a Millionaire, 1953, 96m, ★★★/$$$, 20th/Fox. Three beautiful bombshells rent out a swingin' pad in Manhattan and proceed to lure rich men into their lair. Lauren Bacall, Marilyn Monroe, Betty Grable, William Powell, Cameron Mitchell, David Wayne, Rory Calhoun, Alex D'Arcy, Fred Clark. w. Nunally Johnson, d. Jean Negulesco.

COMEDY: ROMANCE: Romantic Comedy; Ensembles-Female; Friendships-Female; Marrying Up; Golddiggers; Sexy Women
(Three Blind Mice; Moon Over Miami; Three Little Girls in Blue; The Greeks Had a Word for Them)
How to Murder Your Wife, 1965, 118m, ★★★/$$$, UA/MGM-UA. A comic-strip author imagines murdering his wife in print, but when she disappears in reality, can he get off the hook? Jack Lemmon, Virna Lisi, Terry-Thomas, Eddie Mayehoff, Sidney Blackmer, Claire Trevor. w. George Axelrod, d. Richard Quine.

COMEDY: MURDER: Marriage Comedy; Murder of Spouse; Black Comedy; Murder-Comic Attempts; Missing Persons; Accused Unjustly; Courtroom Drama; Sexy Women; Comic Heroes; Writers
(Divorce, Italian Style; Shooting Elizabeth; I Take This Woman)
How to Save a Marriage and Ruin Your Life, 1968, 102m, ★★1/2/$$, Col/Col. In an attempt to save his best friend's strained marriage, a lawyer tries to convince him that his mistress is having an affair. Dean Martin, Eli Wallach, Stella Stevens, Anne Jackson, Betty Field, Jack Albertson, Katharine Bard. w. Stanley Shapiro, Nate Monaster, d. Fielder Cook.

COMEDY: ROMANCE: Romantic Comedy; Mistresses; Jealousy; Friendships-Male; Cheating Men; Marriage Comedy

(Marriage on the Rocks; Who's Been Sleeping in My Bed?)
How to Steal a Million, 1966, 127m, ★★★/$$$, Par/Par. A forger of famous works of art has trouble knock on his door when his daughter gets involved with a detective. Audrey Hepburn, Peter O'Toole, Charles Boyer, Hugh Griffith, Eli Wallach, Fernand Gravet, Marcel Dalio. w. Harry Kurnitz, d. William Wyler.

COMEDY: Capers; Heist Stories; Art Thieves; Fathers & Daughters; Con Artists; Mix-Ups; Detectives-Private; Cat and Mouse Stories
(Topkapi!; The Pink Panther SERIES; Paris When It Sizzles; Charade)
How to Succeed in Business without Really Trying, 1967, 121m, ★★★/$$, UA/MGM-UA. A window cleaner bluffs his way into the executive suite of a large Manhattan corporation in an incredibly short period of time, but it soon may unravel with song and dance. Robert Morse, Rudy Vallee, Michele Lee, Anthony Teague, Maureen Arthur, Murray Matheson. w. David Swift, (Musical)-adap. Abe Burrows, Jack Weinstock, Willie Gilbert, NF-adap. Shepherd Mead, d. David Swift.

MUSICALS: COMEDY: Musical Comedy; Business Life; New York Life; Wall Street; Power-Rise to; Power-Rise to of Idiot; Coulda Been Great; Pulitzer Prize Adaptations; Hidden Gems; Faded Hits
(The Secret of My Success; The Hudsucker Proxy)
Howard the Duck, 1986, 111m, ★★/$, U/MCA-U, PG. An intergalactic duck saves people in jeopardy, particularly a female rocker (though he almost toppled his studio with the flop he made). Lea Thompson, Jeffrey Jones, Paul Guilfoyle. w. Willard Huyck, Gloria Katz, Comic-Adap. Steve Gerber, d. Willard Huyck.

SCI-FI: COMEDY: Fantasy; **CHILDREN'S:** Comic Heroes; Animal Stories; Birds; Rock Stars; Female Protagonists; Flops-Major; Curiosities; Female Screenwriters
(Ed: Coproduced with George Lucas. The duo who along with Lucas made *American Graffiti* really laid one with this)
Howards End, 1992, 140m, ★★★★/$$$, Merchant Ivory-Sony/Col-Tri, PG. A spinster becomes friends with a woman who soon dies, after which the woman's widower proposes to the spinster. And as a poor man her new husband laid off

seeks help from the spinster, tragedy borne out of social class prejudice results. Emma Thompson (**BActress**), Anthony Hopkins, Vanessa Redgrave (BSActress), Helena Bonham Carter, James Wilby, Sam West, Jemma Redgrave, Prunella Scales, Simon Callow. w. Ruth Prawer Jhabvala (**BAScr**), N-adap. E. M. Forster, d. James Ivory (BDirector). BPicture, BCin, BArt, **BCostume.** Oscars: 8-3.

DRAMA: TRAGEDY: Social Drama; Multiple Stories; Interwoven Stories; Marriage Drama; Family Drama; Spinsters; Inheritances at Stake; Friendships-Female; Female Protagonists; Marriage of Convenience; Stern Men; Violence-Sudden; Class Conflicts; Rich vs. Poor; Edwardian Era; Classic Literary Adaptations; Female Screenwriters
(A Room with a View; Where Angels Fear to Tread; Maurice; The Bostonians; Sense and Sensibility)
The Howards of Virginia, 1940, 117m, ★★/$$$, Col/Col. In the 1700s, a land surveyor in Virginia gets swept up in the Revolutionary war. Cary Grant, Martha Scott, Cedric Hardwicke, Alan Marshal, Richard Carlson, Paul Kelly, Irving Bacon. w. Sidney Buchman, N-adap. Elizabeth Page (*The Tree of Liberty*), d. Frank Lloyd.

DRAMA: MELODRAMA: War Stories; Revolutionary War; Family Drama; Sagas; Historical Drama; Forgotten Films
The Howling, 1980, 90m, ★★/$$, Avco-Live/Live, R/EV-B&G. The anchorwoman on a local news show seeks a retreat from her life at an "encounter group"-type camp. Once she gets there, however, she finds that they take "getting in touch with your primal self" pretty damned seriously. Dee Wallace, Patrick MacNee, Dennis Dugan, Christopher Stone, Kevin McCarthy, John Carradine, Slim Pickens. w. John Sayles, Terence H. Winkless, N-adap. Gary Brandner, d. Joe Dante.

The Howling II . . . Your Sister Is a Werewolf, 1985, 90m, ★★/$$, Live/Live, R/EV-B&G. A folklorist goes to Transylvania in search of a female werewolf reputed to be the queen of a band of werewolves. Christopher Lee, Annie McEnroe, Reb Brown, Ferdy Mayne. w. Robert Sarno, Gary Brander, d. Philippe Mora.

The Howling III, 1987, 94m, ★★/$$, Live/Live, R/EV-B&G. Strange looking hybrid werewolves are sought by a mad scientist, who elicits the help of Dame Edna. Barry Otto, Imogen Annesley, Dasha Blahova, Max Fairchild, Ralph Cotterill, Barry Humphries, Michael Pate, Frank Thring. w. d. Philippe Mora, N-adap. Gary Brandner.

Howling IV: The Original Nightmare, 1988, 92m, ★★/$$, Live/Live, R/EV-B&G. A writer goes to a retreat with a group of werewolves. Romy Windsor, Michael T. Weiss, Anthony Hamilton, Suzanne Severeid, Lamya Derval, Clive Turner. w. Clive Turner, Freddie Rowe, d. John Hough.

Howling V: The Rebirth, 1989, 99m, ★★/$$, Live/Live, R/EV-B&G. Vacationers receive a summons to a castle in Budapest and proceed to get attacked by werewolves once they arrive. Ben Cole, William Shockley, Mark Siversen, Philip Davis, Elizabeth She, Victoria Catlin, Stephanie Faulkner, Clive Turner. w. Clive Turner, Freddie Rowe, d. John Hough.
HORROR: Werewolves; Murders-One by One
(Silver Bullet; Werewolf of London; Cujo)

Huckleberry Finn, 1939, 90m, ★★★½/ $$$$, MGM/MGM-UA. The famous Twain story about the motherless lad who flees from his abusive dad on a raft down the Mississippi with a runaway slave. Mickey Rooney, Walter Connolly, William Frawley, Rex Ingram. w. Hugo Butler, N-adap. Mark Twain (*The Adventures of Huckleberry Finn*), d. Richard Thorpe.
(See also under **The Adventures of Huckleberry Finn**)

Huckleberry Finn, 1960, 107m, ★★★/ $$, MGM/MGM-UA. A less vibrant remake. Eddie Hodges, Tony Randall, Archie Devine. w. James Lee, d. Michael Curtiz.

Huckleberry Finn, 1974, 118m, ★★/ $$, UA/Fox. A musical version of the famous Twain story of the adventurous, spunky lad. Jeff East, Paul Winfield, David Wayne, Harvey Korman, Arthur O'Connell, Gary Merrill, Natalie Trundy. w/w/ly Richard M. Sherman, Robert B. Sherman, d. J. Lee-Thompson.
ADVENTURE: Boyhood; 1800s; Journeys; Friendships-Interracial; Black Men; Classic Literary; Adaptations; American Myth

(The Adventures of Huckleberry Finn; The Adventures of Tom Sawyer; Tom and Huck)

The Hucksters, 1947, 115m, ★★★/$$$, MGM/MGM-UA. An adman goes off to World War II and when he returns to the States, he finds it harder to put up with the sleazy tactics of his cohorts. Clark Gable, Deborah Kerr, Ava Gardner, Sidney Greenstreet, Adolphe Menjou, Keenan Wynn, Edward Arnold, Aubrey Mather. w. Luther Davis, N-adap. Frederic Wakeman, d. Jack Conway.
DRAMA: Advertising World; New York Life; World War II-Post Era; Ethics; Corruption; Corporate Corruption; Business Life; Hidden Gems; Time Capsules
(The Man in the Grey Flannel Suit; Crazy People)

Hud, 1963, 112m, ★★★★/$$$, Par/Par. A realistic, modern western drama about a philandering cattle rancher's son named Hud and the woman who helps out around the house, all caught up in changing times on the Texas prairie. Paul Newman (BActor), Patricia Neal (**BActress**), Melvyn Douglas (**BSActor**), Brandon de Wilde. w. Irving Ravetch, Harriet Frank (BAScr), N-adap. Larry McMurtry (*Horseman Pass By*), d. Martin Ritt (BDirector). **BB&WCin.** BB&WArt. Oscars: 7-3.
DRAMA: WESTERNS: Westerns-Neo; Small-Town Life; Texas; Playboys; Rebels; Family Drama; Maids; Romance with Servant; Fathers & Sons; Parents vs. Children; Infatuations; Romance-Reluctant; Spinsters; Female Screenwriters; Hidden Gems
(The Last Picture Show; All Fall Down)

Hudson Hawk, 1991, 100m, ★★/$, Col/Col, PG/V. A master criminal is hired to steal an artifact from the Vatican using various nefarious and wacky spy gadgets and methods. Bruce Willis, Danny Aiello, Andie MacDowell, James Coburn, Richard E. Grant, Sandra Bernhard, David Caruso. w. Steven E. de Souza, Daniel Waters, Bruce Willis, Robert Kraft, d. Michael Lehmann.
ACTION: COMEDY: Action Comedy; Spies; Detective Stories; Chase Stories; Heist Stories; Jewel Thieves; Art Thieves; Spoofs-Spy; Coulda Been Good; Flops-Major
(Our Man Flint; In Like Flint; The Wrecking Crew)

Hudson's Bay, 1940, 95m, ★★/$$, 20th/NA. In the 1600s, a French-Canadian fur trapper forges through the American wilderness, making a path for the British. Paul Muni, Laird Cregar, Gene Tierney, John Sutton, Virginia Field, Vincent Price, Nigel Bruce, Morton Lowry, Robert Greig, Montagu Love. w. Lamar Trotti, d. Irving Pichel.
DRAMA: ADVENTURE: Historical Drama; War Stories; 1600s; Early America; Indians-American; Explorers
(The Black Rose; Northwest Passage)

The Hudsucker Proxy, 1994, 115m, ★★★/$, 20th/Fox, PG. A mailboy rises to the top of a surrealistic 1950s corporate empire with his invention of the hula hoop, but can he keep the position by outwitting the chairman and get the girl reporter in disguise who may or may not be out to expose the fact he's an idiot? Tim Robbins, Paul Newman, Jennifer Jason Leigh, Charles Durning, John Mahoney, Peter Gallagher. w. Joel Coen, Sam Raimi, Ethan Coen, d. Joel Coen.
COMEDY: COMEDY DRAMA: ROMANCE: Romantic Comedy; Business Life; Corporation as Enemy; 1950s; Inventors; Power-Rise to; Power-Rise to, of Idiot; Power Struggles; Stern Men; Evil Men; Outstanding Art Direction
(How to Succeed in Business Without Really Trying)

The Human Comedy, 1943, 117m, ★★★/$$$, MGM/MGM-UA. During World War II, a small-town messenger must be the bearer of bad news. Mickey Rooney (BActor), Frank Morgan, James Craig, Marsha Hunt, Jackie Jenkins, Fay Bainter, Ray Collins, Van Johnson, Donna Reed. w. Howard Estabrook, William Saroyan (**BOStory**), N-adap. William Saroyan, d. Clarence Brown (BDirector). BPicture. Oscars: 4-1.
MELODRAMA: World War II Stories; Small-Town Life; Death-Dealing with; American Myth; Pulitzer Prize Adaptations
(Babes in Arms; Andy Hardy SERIES)

The Human Factor, 1979, 114m, ★★★/$, MGM/MGM-UA, R/V A spy thriller in which a civilian is caught up in international espionage. Nicol Williamson, Richard Attenborough, Derek Jacobi, Robert Morley, John Gielgud, Ann Todd, Richard Vernon, Joop Doderer, Iman. w. Tom Stoppard, N-adap. Graham Greene, d. Otto Preminger.

SUSPENSE: Spy Films; Spies; Innocent Bystanders; Double Crossings; Overlooked at Release
(The Russia House; The Spy Who Came in from the Cold; Frantic)
(Ed: Not to be confused with the film of the same title from 1975)

Humoresque, 1946, 125m, ★★★/$$$, WB/WB. A poor but talented violinist becomes involved with his patroness. Joan Crawford, John Garfield, Oscar Levant, J. Carrol Naish, Joan Chandler, Tom D'Andrea, Craig Stevens, Ruth Nelson. w. Clifford Odets, Zachary Gold, N-adap. Fannie Hurst, d. Jean Negulesco.
MELODRAMA: ROMANCE: Romantic Drama; Musicians; Rich People; Tearjerkers
(Duet for One; Golden Boy)

The Hunchback of Notre Dame, 1923, 120m, B&W, silent, ★★★/$$$$, U/MCA-U. A deformed bell-ringer loves a gypsy girl from afar. Lon Chaney, Patsy Ruth Miller, Norman Kerry, Ernest Torrence, Gladys Brockwell, Kate Lester, Brandon Hurst, Tully Marhall. w. Percy Poore Sheehan, Edward T. Lowe Jr., N-adap. Victor Hugo (*Notre Dame de Paris*), d. Wallace Worsley.

The Hunchback of Notre Dame, 1939, 117m, ★★★/$$$$, RKO/Turner. A brilliant remake with great acting. Charles Laughton, Cedric Hardwicke, Maureen O'Hara, Edmund O'Brien, Thomas Mitchell, Harry Davenport, Walter Hampden, Alan Marshal. w. Sonya Levien, Bruno Frank, d. William Dieterle. BSound, BOScore. Oscars: 2-0.

The Hunchback of Notre Dame, 1956, 107m, ★★/$, NA. A bad, partially dubbed remake with an international cast. Anthony Quinn, Gina Lollobrigida, Jean Danet, Alain Cuny, Robert Hirsch. w. Jacques Prevert, Jean Aurenche, d. Jean Delanoy.

The Hunchback of Notre Dame, 1982, 102m, ★★★/$$$, Hallmark-CBS/Vidmark. Anthony Hopkins, Lesley Anne Down, John Gielgud, Derek Jacobi. d. Michael Tuchner.
TV Movies
MELODRAMA: ROMANCE: TRAGEDY: Romantic Drama; Romance-Doomed; Romance-Opposites Attract; Kidnappings; Fatal Attractions; Disabled People; Middle Ages; Saving Someone; Hunchbacks; Gypsies; Classic Literary Adaptations; Classic Tragedy

COMIC REMAKE: Big Man on Campus. (Five Corners)

The Hunger, 1983, 99m, ★★★¹/₂/$$, MGM/MGM-UA, R/S-FN-MRN-B&G-V. A hip, modern vampire couple must find new blood or die. However, the doctor the female vampire has found who is studying the aging process may be too smart for their 2,000-year-old game. Catherine Deneuve, Susan Sarandon, David Bowie, Cliff de Young. w. Ivan Davis, Michael Thomas, N-adap. Whitley Strieber, d. Tony Scott.
HORROR: SUSPENSE: Erotic Thriller; Erotic Drama; Vampires; Lesbians; Homoeroticism; Bisexuality; Doctors; Medical Detectives; Murders-One by One; **MURDER:** Aging; Flashbacks; Aging-Revers; Cures/Elixirs; Rich People-Decadent; Revisionist Films; Female Protagonists; Hidden Gems; Cult Films
(Interview with the Vampire; Repulsion; Pink Floyd—The Wall)
(Ed: Looks great, and for a Hollywood film is quite artistic and European. Unfortunately, director Scott hasn't lived up to his brother Ridley's track record as an inventive director, following with *Beverly Hills Cop 2, Revenge,* and *The Last Boy Scout*)

The Hunt for Red October, 1990, 137m, ★★★/$$$$$, Par/Par, PG-13/V-P. When a Soviet submarine commander wants to defect, the U.S. military isn't sure whether this stray sub is on the attack or just surrendering. Sean Connery, Alec Baldwin, Scott Glenn, Sam Neill, James Earl Jones, Joss Ackland, Richard Jordan, Peter Firth, Tim Curry. w. Larry Ferguson, Donald Stewart, N-adap. Tom Clancy, d. John McTiernan. BSound, BEdit, **BSound Edit.** Oscars: 3-1.
ACTION: Action Drama; **SUSPENSE:** Political Thriller; Chase Stories; Military Stories; CIA Agents; Spies; Russians; Russians as Enemy; Cold War Era; Submarines; Patriotic Films; Blockbusters
SEQUELS: Patriot Games; Clear and Present Danger
(Patriot Games; Clear and Present Danger; The Bedford Incident; Crimson Tide)

Hunted, 1952, 84m, ★★★/$, GFD/NA. A murderer on the lam shows his gentler side as he shelters and protects a young

boy running away from home. Dirk Bogarde, Jon Whiteley, Kay Walsh, Elizabeth Sellars, Frederick Piper, Geoffrey Keen, Julian Somers. w. Jack Whittingham, d. Charles Crichton.
SUSPENSE: MELODRAMA: Fugitives from the Law; Hiding out; Runaways; Men and Boys; Murderers-Nice; Manhunts
(Tiger Bay; Scene of the Crime)

The Hunter, 1980, 117m, ★★★/$$, Par/Par, PG/V. A bounty hunter has many grisly assignments, which eventually get under his skin as his wife's about to have a baby. Steve McQueen, Eli Wallach, Kathryn Harrold, LeVar Burton, Ben Johnson. w. Ted Leighton, Peter Hyams, NF-adap. Christopher Keane, and the life of Ralph Thorston, d. Buzz Kulik.
ACTION: Action Drama; **MELODRAMA:** Marriage Drama; Bounty Hunters; Manhunts; Trail of a Killers; Babies-Having; True Stories; Biographies; Curiosities
(Bullitt; The Getaway; Tom Horn)
(Ed: McQueen's last film, just after *Tom Horn*)

The Hurricane, 1937, 110m, ★★★/$$$$, Samuel Goldwyn-UA/Sultan. On a small South Pacific island with a corrupt governor, a huge sea storm forces former enemies to band together while star-crossed lovers unite. Dorothy Lamour, Jon Hall, C. Aubrey Smith, Mary Astor, Raymond Massey, Thomas Mitchell, John Carradine, Jerome Cowan. w. Dudley Nichols, Oliver H. P. Garrett, N-adap. Charles Nordhoff, James Norman Hall, d. John Ford.

Hurricane, 1979, 120m, ★★/$, DEG-U/MCA-U. A remake with all the De Laurentis flourish. Jason Robards, Mia Farrow, Trevor Howard, Max Von Sydow, Dayon Ka'ne, Timothy Bottoms, James Keach. w. Lorenzo Semple Jr., d. Jan Troell.
MELODRAMA: ADVENTURE: Disaster Movies; Hurricanes; South Pacific Islands; **ROMANCE:** Romantic Drama; Romance-Interracial; Government Corruption; Female Protagonists; Flops-Major

Hurry Sundown, 1967, 146m, ★★/$$, Par/Par, PG. A racial fable of the modern South, with all the blacks good and all the whites evil. Jane Fonda, Michael Caine, Rex Ingram, Diahann Carroll, Burgess Meredith, John Phillip Law, Robert

Hooks, Faye Dunaway, Beah Richards, George Kennedy, Madeleine Sherwood. w. Thomas C. Ryan, Horton Foote, N-adap. K. B. Gilden, d. Otto Preminger.

MELODRAMA: Social Drama; **DRAMA:** Race Relations; Black vs. White; Mississippi; Southerns; Ensemble Films; Courtroom Drama; Lawyers; All-Star Casts; Coulda Been Great
(The Defiant Ones; Intruder in the Dust; The Chase)

Husbands, 1970, 154m, ★★★/$, Col/Touchstone, PG. A group of middle-aged married men decide impulsively to fly off to London when a friend dies. Peter Falk, John Cassavetes, Ben Gazzara. w. d. John Cassavetes.

DRAMA: COMEDY DRAMA: Ensembles-Male; Men's Films; Midlife Crisis; Death-Dealing with; Friendships-Male; Marriage Drama; Actor Directors; Writer-Directors; Cult Films; Independent Films
(Bye Bye Braveman; Faces; Shadows)

Husbands and Wives, 1992, 108m, ★★★¹/₂/$$, Tri-Star/Col-Tri, R/S-FN. A middle-aged man begins to question his marriage when his married friends start splitting up, and he has an illicit affair with a much younger woman. Woody Allen, Judy Davis (BSActress), Mia Farrow, Juliette Lewis, Liam Neeson, Blythe Danner, Sydney Pollack, Lysette Anthony. w. d. Woody Allen (BOScore). Oscars: 2-0.

DRAMA: COMEDY DRAMA: Marriage Drama; Cheating Men; Cheating Women; Divorce; Swapping Partners; Midlife

Crisis; Romance with Teacher; Professor; Romance-Older Men/Younger Women; New York Life; Narrated Films; Documentary Style; Interviews; Actor Directors; Writer-Directors
(Another Woman; Hannah and Her Sisters)

Hush, Hush, Sweet Charlotte, 1964, 133m, ★★★/$$$, 20th/Fox, PG/V. An aged Southern belle is tormented by the thought that she murdered her fiance thirty-seven years before, but her guilt may not be justified. Bette Davis, Olivia de Havilland, Joseph Cotten, Cecil Kellaway, Victor Buono, William Campbell, Mary Astor, Agnes Moorehead (BSActress). w. Henry Farrell, Lukas Heller, d. Robert Aldrich. BB&WCin, BB&WArt, BEdit, BOScore, BB&WCostume, BOSong. Oscars: 7-0.

SUSPENSE: HORROR: Psychological Thriller; Insane-Plot to Drive; Inheritances at Stake; **MURDER:** Past-Haunted by the; Southerns; Women in Jeopardy; Houses-Creepy; Gothic Style; Conspiracy; Female Protagonists; Cult Films
(Whatever Happened to Baby Jane?; Gaslight; The Beguiled; Lady in a Cage)

Hustle, 1975, 118m, ★★¹/₂/$$, Par/Par, R/S-V. A high-ranking police officer lives with a prostitute and deals with his double life. Burt Reynolds, Catherine Deneuve, Ben Johnson, Paul Winfield, Eileen Brennan, Eddie Albert, Ernest Borgnine, Catherine Bach, Jack Carter. w. Steve Shagan, d. Robert Aldrich.

ACTION: Action Drama; Police Stories; Erotic Drama; Romance with Prostitute;

Dual Lives; Film Noir-Modern; Prostitutes-High Class; Coulda Been Good
(Fuzz; Sharky's Machine; Shamus)

The Hustler, 1961, 135m, ★★★¹/₂/$$$, 20th/Media, Fox. A pool shark falls in love and loses his knack. Paul Newman (BActor), Jackie Gleason (BSActor), George C. Scott (BSActor), Piper Laurie (BSActress), Myron McCormick, Murray Hamilton, Michael Constantine. w. Robert Rossen, Sidney Carroll (BAScr), N-adap. Walter Tevis, d. Robert Rossen (BDirector). BPicture, **BB&WCin, BB&WArt.** Oscars: 9-2.

DRAMA: Character Studies; Pool; Games; Con Artists; Life Transitions; Playboys; Settling Down; Men in Conflict; Competitions; Comebacks

SEQUEL: The Color of Money
(The Color of Money; The Baltimore Bullet; Hud)

Hysteria, 1965, 85m, ★★/$, MGM/MGM-UA. In a London hospital, an American suffering from amnesia is released, and his lack of memory gets him involved in a murder plot. Robert Webber, Lelia Goldoni, Anthony Newlands, Jennifer Jayne, Maurice Denham, Peter Woodthorpe. w. Jimmy Sangster, d. Freddie Francis.

SUSPENSE: Psychological Drama; **MYSTERY: MURDER: MURDER MYSTERY:** Amnesia; Americans Abroad; London; Mod Era; Coulda Been Great; Good Premise Unfulfilled
(Mister Buddwing; Blow-Up)

I

I Accuse, 1958, 99m, ★★★/$$, MGM/NA. A retelling of the Alfred Dreyfus trial for treason where the only man who would come to his defense was author Emile Zola. Jose Ferre, Anton Walbrook, Emlyn Williams, Viveca Lindfors, Leo Genn, Herbert Lom. w. Gore Vidal, d. Jose Ferrer.

DRAMA: Courtroom Drama; Historical Drama; Trials; Traitors; Accused Unjustly; Writers; 1890s

REMAKE/RETELLING OF: The Life of Emile Zola.

(The Life of Emile Zola; Prisoner of Honor)

(See also **J'Accuse**)

I Am a Camera, 1955, 99m, ★★★/$, Romulus-UA/Monterey. A young British girl lives the nightlife in pre-War Berlin and becomes an object of fascination for an American writer. Julie Harris, Laurence Harvey, Shelley Winters. w. John Collier, SS-adap. Christopher Isherwood, d. Henry Cornelius.

COMEDY DRAMA: ROMANCE: Autobiographical Stories; Romance-Reluctant; Romance-Unrequited; Free Spirits; Young Women; Feisty Females; Theater Life; Americans Abroad; Writers; Actresses; Dancers; Berlin

MUSICAL REMAKE: Cabaret; **RETELLING/SAME SOURCE:** The Sheltering Sky.

I Am a Fugitive from a Chain Gang, 1932, 90m, ★★★★/$$$, WB/WB. An innocent man (Paul Muni, BActor) is sent to prison camp and goes through the hell of a chain gang until he breaks free to run. Glenda Farrell, Preston Foster. w. Sheridan Gibney, Brown Holmes, Robert Burns, d. Mervyn Leroy. Best Picture. Oscars: 2-0.

DRAMA: TRAGEDY: Social Drama; Prison Drama; Prison Escapes; Chase Movies; Fugitives from the Law; Accused Unjustly; Innocent Bystanders; Documentary Style; Ahead of Its Time

(An Innocent Man; The Defiant Ones)

I Am the Law, 1938, 83m, ★★★/$$, Col/Col. A law professor goes back to practice trying to clean up the mob. Edward G. Robinson, Otto Kruger, John Beal. w. Jo Swerling, d. Alexander Hall.

DRAMA: Crime Drama; Mob Stories; Lawyers; Lawyers as Detectives; Political Drama; Politicians

I Believe in You, 1952, 95m, ★★★/$, Ealing/NA. British probation officers deal with and try to inspire their charges. Celia Johnson, Cecil Parker, Joan Collins, Laurence Harvey, Godfrey Tearle. w. Michael Relph, Basil Dearden, Jack Whittingham, Nicholas Phipps, d. Dearden.

DRAMA: MELODRAMA: Social Drama; Social Workers; Prison Drama; Juvenile Delinquents; British Films; Female Protagonists; Time Capsules

I Can Get It for You Wholesale (*Only the Best*), 1951, 89m, ★★½/$$, 20th/NA. A young woman makes it up through the ranks in the fashion industry and may leave some debris in her path. Susan Hayward, Dan Dailey, George Sanders, Sam Jaffe, Marvin Kaplan. w. Abraham Polonsky, N-adap. Jerome Weidman, d. Michael Gordon.

MELODRAMA: SATIRE: Soap Operas; Feisty Females; Power-Rise to; Fashion World; Career Women

(Backstreet; Ada; The Best of Everything)

(Ed: A bad TV movie before its time; only a smidgin of humor)

Ice Castles, 1978, 109m, ★★/$$$, Col/RCA-Col, PG. Lovers on the ice are put to the test when the girl skater is blinded, but not by love. Robbie Benson, Lynn-Holly Johnson, Colleen Dewhurst, Tom Kerritt, Jennifer Warren. w. Donald Wrye, Gary Baim, d. Donald Wrye. BOSong, "Through the Eyes of Love." Oscars: 1-0.

MELODRAMA: ROMANCE: Tearjerkers; Blind People; Accidents; Skating; Unintentionally Funny

(Voices; Dark Victory)

Iceman, 1984, 99m, ★★★/$$, U/MCA-U, PG. A preserved Neanderthal man is found in the ice of the Arctic and thawed out, but should the geologists who find him take him to society for dissection or leave him in the wild. Timothy Hutton, Lindsay Crouse, John Lone, Josef Sommer, Danny Glover. w. Chip Proser, John Drimmer, d. Fred Schepisi.

DRAMA: Social Drama; Ethics; Frozen People; Cavemen; Animal Rights; Nature-Back to; Time Sleepers; Fish out of Water Stories; Scientists; What If . . . Stories; Arctic; Snow Settings (Greystoke; Encino Man; Never Cry Wolf)

DRAMA: Episodic Stories; Snow Settings; Alaska; Fighting the System; Nature-Back to; Letters; Fishermen; Veterans; Soldiers; World War I Era; Flops-Major; Forgotten Films

Ice Palace, 1960, 143m, ★★/$, WB/WB. Two World War I veteran pals become fishermen in Alaska and must deal with the changes coming to their territory. w. Harry Kleiner, N-adap. Edna Ferber, d. Vincent Sherman.

DRAMA: Episodic Stories; Snow Settings; Alaska; Fighting the System; Nature-Back to; Letters; Fisherman; Veterans; Soldiers; World War I Era; Flops-Major; Forgotten Films
(Ed: Ferber's other novels may have been big hits-*Giant, Show Boat*-but this one suffers from freezer burn)

The Ice Pirates, 1984, 94m, ★1/2/$, MGM/MGM-UA, PG-13/S-P. On a far-away planet, ice and water are a precious resource and its up to our hero to keep the bad guys from getting it all. Robert Urich, Anjelica Huston, Mary Crosby, Ron Perlman, John Carradine. w. Stewart Raffill, Stanford Sherman, d. Raffill.

SCI-FI: Outer Space Movies; Conspiracy; Good vs. Evil; Corruption; Snow Settings; Pirates; Flops-Major
(Spacehunter; Solarbabies; Flash Gordon)

Ice Station Zebra, 1968, 118m, ★★★/ $$$, MGM/MGM-UA, PG/V. A military leader heads a rescue and discovery expedition in the future into the great region of ice at the end of the Earth. Rock Hudson. N-adap. Alistair McLean, d. John Sturges. BSFX, BCin. Oscars: 2-0.

SCI-FI: ADVENTURE: Snow Settings; Arctic; Race Against Time; Rescue Drama; Submarines
(The Bedford Incident; Scott of the Antarctic)

Ichabod and Mr. Toad/Legend of Sleepy Hollow, 1949, 68m, ★★★/$$$,

Disney/Disney, G. Children's fantasy (Mr. Toad from the *Wind in the Willows*) mixed with the scary *Legend of Sleepy Hollow* is a bit odd, but still good Disney fare. d. Jack Kinney, Clyde Geronimi, James Algar.

CHILDREN'S: FAMILY: HORROR: Stalkers; Fantasy; Animal Stories; Legends

The Icicle Thief, 1989, 85m, ★★★/$$, Ind/Fox-Lorber, R/S. When a film director is watching an art film of his and the actors begin changing their lines and actions, he enters the TV set to set things right. Maurizio Nichetti, Caterina Labini, Federico Rizzo. w. Maurizio Nichetti, Mauro Monti, d. Nichetti.

SATIRE: COMEDY: Art Films; Movie Making; Directors; Actors; Italian Films; Crossing the Line; What If . . . Stories
TITLE/SPOOF from the Bicycle Thief (Stay Tuned; The Purple Rose of Cairo; Amazon Women on the Moon; Kentucky Fried Movie; The Groove Tube)

I Confess, 1953, 94m, ★★★/$$, WB/WB. A priest (Montgomery Clift) hears the confession of a murderer but can't tell anyone, possibly even if he becomes the prime suspect himself. Anne Baxter, Brian Aherne, Karl Malden. w. George Tabori, William Archibald, P-adap. Paul Anthelme, d. Alfred Hitchcock.

SUSPENSE: DRAMA: MURDER: Murder-Debate to Reveal Killer; Priests; Accused Unjustly; Framed?; Saving Oneself; Race Against Time; Secrets-Keeping; Hitchcockian
(The Wrong Man; Stage Fright; Last Rites)
(Ed: Not prime Hitchcock, but still good)

I Could Go on Singing, 1963, 99m, ★★★/$$, UA/MGM-UA. An actress/ singer goes back to England to find an old love and to get to know the son she left with him, but trying to change her life for them proves difficult. Judy Garland, Dirk Bogarde, Aline MacMahon, Jack Klugman. w. Mayo Simon, d. Ronald Neame.

DRAMA: MELODRAMA: Music Movies; Children-Long Lost; Reunions; Singers; Actresses; Americans Abroad; England; Female Protagonists
(A Child Is Waiting; A Star Is Born [1954])

I Cover the Waterfront, 1933, 75m, ★★★/$$$, Reliance/Nos. A reporter on the dock beat uses a girl to get to what her father's really doing-smuggling. Claudette Colbert, Ben Lyon, Ernest

Torrence. w. Wells Root, Jack Jevne, Max Miller, d. James Cruze.

DRAMA: Crime Drama; **MELODRAMA: ROMANCE:** Journalists; Fathers & Daughters; Betrayals

I Died a Thousand Times, 1955, 109m, ★★/$, WB/WB. A thief plans one more heist-of a big hotel-but his pals aren't getting along. Jack Palance, Shelley Winters, Lori Nelson, Lee Marvin, Earl Holliman. w. W. R. Burnett, d. Stuart Heisler.

ACTION: Heist Stories; Crime Drama; Thieves; Friends as Enemies; One Last Time

REMAKE/RETREAD OF: High Sierra (The Killing; Rififi)

Idiot's Delight, 1939, 105m, ★★★/$$$, MGM/MGM-UA. A showman (Clark Gable) with an all-girl dance troop entertaining in pre-World War II Europe runs into an old girlfriend pretending to be royalty (Norma Shearer). Edward Arnold, Laura Hope Crews, Burgess Meredith, Charles Coburn, Joseph Schildkraut. w. P-adap. Robert Sherwood, d. Clarence Brown.

COMEDY: ROMANCE: Romantic Comedy; Impostors; Romance-Reunited; Musicians; Dancers; Theater Life; World War II Era
(Victor/Victoria; Honky Tonk; Ninotchka)

The Idol, 1966, 111m, ★★/$$, Embassy/ NA, R/S. A middle-aged woman falls for a sexy young hunk who's friends with her son and then both must deal with the repercussions. Jennifer Jones, Michael Parks, John Leyton. w. Millard Lampell, d. Daniel Petrie.

DRAMA: ROMANCE: Romantic Drama; Romance-Older Women/Younger Women; Romance with Relative's Lover; Mothers & Sons; Generation Gap; England; Mod Era; Female Protagonists
(Class; Damage; The Game Is Over; Indiscretion of an American Wife)

The Idolmaker, 1980, 119m, ★★/$, UA/MGM-UA, R/S-P. A songwriter cashes it in to become a singer's manager and promoter and live the glory from backstage. Ray Sharkey, Tovah Feldshuh, Peter Gallagher, Paul Land. w. Edward di Lorenzo, d. Taylor Hackford.

DRAMA: Fame-Rise to; Singers; Songwriters; Musicians; Svengalis; Behind the Scenes
(Eddie and the Cruisers; The Buddy Holly Story)

I Don't Buy Kisses Anymore, 1992, 112m, ★★1/2/$, Par/Par, PG. An overweight Jewish man falls for a pretty grad student who's doing a study on fat people. Jason Alexander, Nia Peeples, Laine Kazan, Eileen Brennan. w. Johnnie Lindsell, d. Robert Marcarelli.
COMEDY: COMEDY DRAMA:
ROMANCE: Romantic Comedy; Weight Problems; Students; Psychologists; Romance-Mismatched; Romance-Opposites Attract; Jewish People; Sexy Women; Looksism
(Babycakes; Fatso; Angus)

The I Don't Care Girl, 1953, 78m, ★★1/2/$$, 20th/NA. Biopic of USO-type singer Eva Tanguay, a star during World War I. Mitzi Gaynor, David Wayne, Oscar Levant, George Jessel. w. Walter Bullock, d. Lloyd Bacon.
MUSICALS: Music Movies; Biographies; Singers; ROMANCE: Romance-Triangles; World War I Era; Flashbacks; Memories; Narrated Films

I Don't Want to Talk About It, 1995, 102m, ★★★/$, Sony/Sony, PG-13/S. A girl with dwarfism in South America marries an elderly man who comes to her village, and a fairy-tale like marriage with inspiration for everyone involved is the result. Marcello Mastroianni, Luisina Brando, Alejandra Podesta, Betiana Blum, Monica Lacoste, Hernan Munoa, Miguel Serebrenik. w. Maria Luisa Bemberg, Jorge Goldenberg, d. Maria Luisa Bemberg
COMEDY DRAMA: Art Films; Fantasy; ROMANCE: Romance-Older Men/Younger Women; Magic Realism; Little People; 1930s; Argentina; Latin Films; Female Screenwriters; Female Directors
(House of the Spirits; Dark Eyes; Gabriela)

I Dood It!, 1943, 102m, ★★★/$$, MGM/MGM-UA. A goofy tailor has a crush on a starlet, and she'll be lucky he doesn't stumble and crush her in the process. Red Skelton, Eleanor Powell, Lena Horne, Jimmy Dorsey. w. Sig Herzig, Fred Saidy, d. Vincente Minnelli.
COMEDY: MUSICALS: Music Movies; Comedy-Slapstick; ROMANCE:
Infatuations; Actresses; Theater Life
(The Fuller Brush Man)

I'd Rather Be Rich, 1964, 96m, ★★★/$$, U/NA. When her rich grandfather seems to be dying, a girl introduces a man she finds as her fiance, but when grandpa recovers and can't wait for them to get married . . . Maurice Chevalier, Sandra Dee, Robert Goulet, Andy Williams, Gene Raymond, Hermione Gingold, Charles Ruggles. W. Oscar Brodney, Leo Townsend, Norman Krasna, d. Jack Smight.
COMEDY: ROMANCE: Romantic Comedy; Situation Comedy; FARCE:
Misunderstandings; Grandfathers-Fascinating; Matchmaking; Death-Impending; Dead-Back from the; Rich People; Heiresses; Inheritances at Stake; Impostors; Marriages-Fake; Marriage-Impending
REMAKE OF: It Started with Eve.
(Daddy Longlegs; Mad About Music)

I Dream of Jeannie, 1952, 90m, ★★/$$, Republic/Nos. Biopic of songwriter Stephen Foster, who had a thing for light brown hair. Bill Shirley, Ray Middleton, Muriel Lawrence, Rex Allen. w. Alan LeMay, d. Allan Dwan.
DRAMA: MELODRAMA: Biographies; Songwriters; Musicians; 1800s
SAME SOURCE: Swanee River.

I Dream Too Much, 1935, 95m, ★★1/2/$$, RKO/Turner. An American songwriter (Henry Fonda) falls for a French opera singer (Lily Pons) and they make something beautiful together. w. Edmund North, James Gow, d. John Cromwell.
ROMANCE: MELODRAMA: Music Movies; Singers; Songwriters; Musicians

if . . ., 1969, 111m, ★★★/$$, Par/Par, R/P-S-MN. Anarchy begins at a British boys' school led by one bizarre rebel (Malcolm McDowell). David Wood, Richard Warwick. w. David Sherwin, d. Lindsay Anderson.
DRAMA: Art Films; Boarding Schools; Boys Schools; Rebels; Political Unrest; Anti-Establishment Films; 1960s; British Films
SEQUELS: O Lucky Man; Brittania Hospital
(Taps; The Chocolate War)
COMEDY: ROMANCE: Marriage Comedy; Sex Comedy; Jealousy; Misunderstandings; Young Women; Female Protagonists
(I'd Rather Be Rich; Daddy Longlegs)

If I Had a Million, 1932, 88m, ★★★/$$$, Par/NA. A wealthy man gives a million bucks to several different people to see how they'll react. Told in vignettes. W.C. Fields, Charles Laughton, May Robson, Gary Cooper, George Raft, Frances Dee, Jack Oakie. w. Ernst Lubitsch, Claude Binyon, Joseph L. Mankiewicz, and a dozen others, d. Lubitsch, Norman Taurog, and five others.
COMEDY: Rags to Riches; Rich vs. Poor; Rich People; Money-Finding; Eccentric People; Multiple Stories; Interwoven Stories
(Brewster's Millions; I'll Give a Million)

If I Had My Way, 1940, 82m, ★★★/$$$, U/NA. Two washed-up vaudeville comedians come across and orphan girl and make her into a star, rejuvenating their careers in the process. Bing Crosby, Charles Wininger, Gloria Jean, El Brendel. w. William Conselman, James Kern, d. David Butler.
COMEDY DRAMA: FAMILY: Orphans; Comedians; Vaudeville; Fathers-Surrogate; Comebacks; Girls
(Little Miss Marker)

If It's Tuesday, This Must Be Belgium, 1969, 98m, ★★★/$$, UA/MGM-UA, PG. Americans on a bus tour of Europe wind up in all kinds of little adventures and romantic predicaments. Suzanne Pleshette, Ian McShane, Mildred Natwick, Michael Constantine, Murray Hamilton, Norman Fell, Peggy Cass, Pamel Britton, Marty Ingels. w. David Shaw, d. Mel Stuart.
COMEDY: COMEDY DRAMA: Multiple Stories; Ensemble Films; Vacations; Romance on Vacation; Vacations-European; Female Protagonists
(Bon Voyage; Three on a Date [TV movie]; Three Coins in the Fountain; Rome Adventure; Innocents in Paris)

If a Man Answers, 1962, 102m, ★★/$$, U/NA. A young woman tries to make her husband jealous by pretending she's in a Doris Day movie. Sandra Dee, Bobby Darin, Stephanie Powers, Cesar Romero. w. Richard Morris, N-adap. Winifred Wolfe, d. Henry Levin.
COMEDY:ROMANCE: Marriage Comedy; Sex Comedy; Jealousy; Misunderstandings; Young Women; Female Protagonists
(I'd Rather Be Rich; Daddy Longlegs)

If I Were King, 1938, 101m, ★★★/$$, Par/NA. Mindgames and pranks begin with the medieval French poet Francois Villon and King Louis XI, which sparks political unrest. Ronald Colman, Basil

Rathbone (BSActor), Frances Dee, Ellen Drew. w. Preston Sturges, d. Frank Lloyd. BScore, Bart. Oscars: 3-0.

COMEDY DRAMA: Historical Drama; Costume Drama; Political Unrest; Kings; Practical Jokers; Poets; Writers; Mindgames; Men in Conflict; Forgotten Films; Hidden Gems

(Cardinal Richelieu; The Madness of King George)

I Found Stella Parish, 1935, 85m, ★★★/$$$, WB/NA. An actress with a shady past doesn't want her kid to know what she did, which is why a blackmailer shows up to put the screws to the situation. Kay Francis, Paul Lukas, Ian Hunter, Sybil Jason. w. Casey Robinson, d. Mervyn LeRoy.

MELODRAMA: Newlyweds; War Brides; Soap Opera; Secrets-Haunting; Secrets-Keeping; Blackmail; Betrayals; Actresses; Female Protagonists; Forgotten Films; Hidden Gems

(Madame X; Born to Be Bad)

(Ed: Nasty backstabbing situation women seemed to love in its release, but is good fun still if you don't expect too much)

If Winter Comes, 1948, 97m, ★★½/$$, MGM/NA. A nice man in an English village takes in an unwed mother, but the town gossip finds out about it. Deborah Kerr, Walter Pidgeon, Janet Leigh, Angela Lansbury, May Whitty, Reginald Owen. w. Marguerite Roberts, Arthur Wimperis, N-adap. ASM Hutchinson, d. Victor Saville.

DRAMA: MELODRAMA: Small-Town Scandals; Scandals; Gossips; Mothers-Unwed; England; British Films; Female Screenwriters

If You Could Only Cook, 1935, 72m, ★★½/$, Col/NA. A rich man and a poor girl meet while he poses as a butler to win her affection. w. Hugh Herbert, Gertrude Purcell, Howard Green, d. William Seiter.

COMEDY: ROMANCE: Romantic Comedy; Romance-Reluctant; Servants; Rich vs. Poor; Female Screenwriters

(My Man Godfrey)

If You Knew Susie, 1948, 90m, ★★½/$$, RKO/Critic's Choice. A vaude-viller marries and retires to the English countryside to raise a family, but the performing bug bites. Eddie Cantor, Joan Davis, Bobby Driscoll, Charles Dingle. w. Warren Wilson, Oscar Brodney, d. Gordon Douglas.

COMEDY: FAMILY: Marriage Comedy; Vaudeville; Comedians; Settlin Down; Rural Life; Americans Abroad; Fish out of Water Stories

I, Jane Doe, 1948, 85m, ★★½/$$, Republic/NA. A soldier married a French girl during the war who, after he's married again to an American, comes back to get him. Ruth Hussey, John Carroll, Vera Ralston, Gene Lockhart. w. Lawrence Kimble, d. John Auer.

MELODRAMA: Newlyweds; War Brides; Romance-Triangles; Revenge; Bigamy; Soldiers; Americans Abroad; World War II-Post Era

I, the Jury, 1953, 87m, ★★/$$, Ind/NA. Mike Hammer, cool P.I., must avenge the death of his pal. Biff Elliott, Peggie Castle, Preston Foster, Elisha Cook, Jr. w. d. Harry Essex, N-adap. Mickey Spillane.

3-D Movies; Independent Films

I, the Jury, 1982, 109m, ★★½/$, American Cinema/Fox, R/V-P-FFN-MRN. Mike Hammer avenges death of his Vietnam vet pal. Armand Assante, Barbara Carrera, Alan King, Paul Sorvino. w. Larry Cohen, N-adap. Mickey Spillane, d. Rich Heffron.

ACTION: Crime Drama; **MYSTERY: MURDER: MURDER MYSTERY:** Detective Stories; Detectives-Private; Detectives in Deep; Film Noir; Film Noir-Modern; Avenging Death of Someone; Independent Films

Ikiru, 1952, 143m, ★★★½/$$, Toho/Home Vision, Connoisseur. A thief learns he's dying and, remembering his own childhood, he spends his last months building a playground for children. Takashi Shimura. w. Hideo Oguni, Shonubu Hashimoto, Akira Kurosawa, d. Kurosawa.

DRAMA: Death-Impending; Redemption; Thieves; Memories; Childhood; Japanese Films; Hidden Gems

(Americana; A Woman's Tale)

I Know Where I'm Going, 1945, 91m, ★★½/$$, GFD/Hemdale, Learning Corp. A young woman goes to Scotland to marry a rich old man but winds up stranded and meeting a young sailor instead. Wendy Hiller, Roger Livesay, Pamela Brown, Nancy Price, Finlay Curie. w. d. Michael Powell.

COMEDY DRAMA: MELODRAMA: ROMANCE: Romance-Older Men/Younger Women; Young Women; Feisty Females; Social Climbing; Marrying Up;

Scotland; Sailors; British Films; World War II Era

I Know Why the Caged Bird Sings, 1979, 100m, ★★★/$$, CBS/Live. Memoirs of writer/poet Maya Angelou and her childhood in south Arkansas, following her move to St. Louis with her family. Diahann Carroll, Ruby Dee, Esther Rolle, Constance Good, Roger Mosley, Paul Benjamin. NF-adap. Maya Angelou, d. Fielder Cook.

DRAMA: Character Studies; Autobiographical Stories; Memories; Writers; Female Screenwriters; Black Women; Black Casts; TV Movies; Narrated Films; Female Protagonists

(The Color Purple; Sounder; The Heart Is a Lonely Hunter)

Il Faut Vivre Dangereusement, see **You've Got to Live Dangerously**

I Like It Like That, 1994, 95m, ★★½/$, ?, R/P-S-V. A young Afro-Latino woman in The Bronx tries to deal with her children when her husband is arrested by getting a job with a record company and moving up a little in the world-if it doesn't tear apart all she's worked for already. Lauren Velez, Jon Seda, Rita Moreno, Jesse Borrego, Tomas Melly, Lisa Vidal, Griffin Dunne. w. d. Darnell Martin.

DRAMA: COMEDY DRAMA: Young Women; Making a Living; Marriage on the Rocks; Inner-City Life; Career Women; New York Life; Blackouts; Transsexuals; Female Screenwriters; Female Directors; Black Directors; Black Screenwriters; Latin People; Latin Casts/Films; Black Casts/Films; Female Protagonists; Writer-Directors; Independent Films

(Just Another Girl on the I.R.T.; Hollow Image)

I Live My Life, 1935, 85m, ★★½/$$$, MGM/MGM-UA. A rich girl who's grown weary of the party set finds an ordinary archaeologist charming. Joan Crawford, Brian Aherne, Frank Morgan, Aline MacMahon, Arthur Treacher, Hedda Hopper. w. Joseph L. Mankiewicz, SS-adap. A Carter Goodloe, *Claustrophobia*, d. W. S. Van Dyke.

ROMANCE: MELODRAMA: Class Conflicts; Rich vs. Poor; Romance-Reluctant; Romance-Follow Your Heart; Archaeologists

(Bringing Up Baby; The Lady Eve)

I'll Be Seeing You, 1944, 85m, ★★★/$$$, Selznick-UA/NA. A female

ex-con meets a soldier who's worse for the wear of war and love blossoms at Christmastime, despite the secrets each hides. Ginger Rogers, Joseph Cotten, Shirley Temple, SpringByington, Chill Wills. w. Marion Parsonnet, N-adap. Charles Martin, d. William Dieterle.
ROMANCE: MELODRAMA: Tearjerkers; Romance-Opposites Attract; Secrets-Haunting; Criminals-Female; Ex-Convicts; Soldiers; Christmas; World War II Era; Female Screenwriters; Female Protagonists; Forgotten Films
(Waterloo Bridge; Christmas in July)
I'll Cry Tomorrow, 1955, 119m, ★★1/2/$$$, MGM/MGM-UA. The biopic of Lillian Roth, a stage and screen star of the 20s and 30s, and her fall with alcohol. Susan Hayward (BActress), Eddie Albert, Jo Van Fleet, Richard Conte. w. Helen Deutsch, Jay Kennedy, NF-adap. Lillian Roth, Gerold Frank, d. Daniel Mann. BBWCin, BBWArt. Oscars: 3-0.
MELODRAMA: DRAMA: Biographies; Tearjerkers; Singers; Alcoholics; Actresses; Theater Life; Hollywood Life; Female Screenwriters; Female Protagonists
(Smash Up; The Story of a Woman; The Morning After; The Lost Weekend; Star!; The Star; Dangerous)
I'll Do Anything, 1994, 115m, ★★1/2/$, Col/Col, PG-13/S-P. An out of work actor winds up taking care of his little girl, who soon upstages him by getting major parts. Nick Nolte, Albert Brooks, Julie Kavner, Joely Richardson, Tracey Ullman. w. d. James L. Brooks.
COMEDY: SATIRE: Hollywood Satire; Hollywood Life; Actors; Actresses; Fathers & Daughters; Children-Little Adults; Children-Brats; Parents vs. Children; Unemployment; Fathers Alone; Directors; Movie Making; Flops-Major; Writer-Directors
(Paper Moon; Life with Mikey)
Illegal, 1955, 88m, ★★★/$$, WB/NA. A DA becomes a mob lawyer but can't deal with the compromises and deceit. However, the decision to walk away may be deadly. Edward G. Robinson, Nina Foch, Hugh Mrlowe, Ellen Corby, Jayne Mansfield. w. W.R. Burnett, James R. Webb, Frank Collins, d. Lewis Allen.
SUSPENSE: Crime Drama; Courtroom Drama; Trials; Mob Stories; Lawyers; Ethics; Betrayals; Men in Jeopardy
REMAKE OF: The Mouthpiece

Illegally Yours, 1987, 102m, ★★/VR, DEG/MGM-UA, PG/P-S. A nerdy juror (Rob Lowe) tries to set an accused woman free (Colleen Camp) he's fallen in love with, but she may just be leading him on. Kenneth Mars, Kim Myers. w. M. A. Stewart, Max Dickens, d. Peter Bogdonavich.
COMEDY: Screwball Comedy; **ROMANCE:** Romantic Comedy; Romance-Unrequited; Chase Movies; Accused Unjustly; Trials; Flops-Major; Florida
(Ed: Lowe actually shows great signs of talent here, but in such a mess, who can be sure?)
I'll Give a Million, 1938, 70m, ★★1/2/$$, 20th/NA. When a millionaire becomes a homeless person, he tells the press he'll give his money to people who perform genuine acts of kindness. Warner Baxter, Peter Lorre, Marjorie Weaver, Jean Hershlolt. w. Boris Ingster, Milton Sperling, d. Walter Land.
COMEDY DRAMA: SATIRE: Depression Era; Homeless People; Riches to Rags; Money-Recieving; Rich People; Ethics
(Brewster's Millions; If I Had a Million)
I'll Never Forget Whatshisname, 1967, 96m, ★★1/2/$, U/NA. An exec in England takes the high road and quits to run a literary journal, but when his big boss beckons him back, he reconsiders his altruism and integrity situation. Oliver Reed, Orson Welles, Harry Andrews, Marianne Faithfull. w. Peter Draper, d. Michael Winner.
SATIRE: COMEDY DRAMA: Ethics; Retiring; Advertising World; Young Men; 1960s; Mod Era; Anti-establishment Films; England; British Films
I'll See You in My Dreams, 1952, 112m, ★★1/2/$$, WB/WB. Songwriter Gus Kahn's life is chronicled with his songs. Doris Day, Danny Thomas, James Gleason. w. Melville Shavelson, Jack Rose, d. Michael Curtiz.
MUSICALS: Biographies; Songwriters; Theater Life; Singers; **ROMANCE:** Marriage Drama
(I Dream of Jeannie; I'll Be Seeing You)
I'll Take Sweden, 1965, 96m, ★★1/2/$$, UA/MGM-UA. An oil man (Bob Hope) goes to Sweden to break his daughter (Tuesday Weld) up with a hip boyfriend. Frankie Avalon, Dina Merrill, Jeremy Slate, John Qualen. w. Nat Perrin, Bob Fisher, Arthur Marx, d. Fred DeCordova.

COMEDY: Screwball Comedy; Lover Family Dislikes; Fathers & Daughters; Oil People; Sweden; Cult Films
(Boy, Did I Get a Wrong Number; Bachelor in Paradise)
(Ed: Has a bit of a following)
The Illustrated Man, 1969, 103m, ★★1/2/$$, WB/WB, R/S-MRN. A young man (Robert Drivas) encounters an older drifter (Rod Steiger) with a body covered with tattoos, each telling a different science-fiction story. Claire Bloom. w. Howard Kreitsek, N-adap. Ray Bradbury, d. Jack Smight.
DRAMA: Fantasy; **SCI-FI:** Multiple Stories; Storytellers; Young Men; Friendships-Male; Futuristic Films
Illustrious Corpses, 1975, 120m, ★★1/2/$$, UA/NA. Assassinations of Italian officials is part of a conspiracy by the right-wing government. Lino Ventura, Alain Cuny, Max Von Sydow, Fernando Rey. w. Francesco Rosi, Ronin Guerra, Lin Jannuzzi, N-adap. Leonardo Sciascia, d. Rosi.
DRAMA: Political Drama; **SUSPENSE:** Conspiracy; Assassinations; Political Unrest; Italy; Italian Films
(Year of the Gun)
I Love Melvin, 1953, 77m, ★★1/2/$$, MGM/MGM-UA. A rich girl in the chorus of a show has a crush in a nerdy fellow who sings his way into her heart. Donald O'Connor, Debbie Reynolds, Una Merkel. w. George Wells, d. Don Weis.
MUSICALS: ROMANCE: Musical Romance; Romance-Boy Wants Girls; Infatuations; Dancers; Photographers; Theater Life
(Ed: Follow-up for stars to *Singin' in the Rain*, but nowhere near that level)
I Love a Mystery, 1945, 68m, ★★1/2/$$, Col/NA. A man is offered big money if he'll hand over his head when he dies to a cult whose leader's mummified head is deteriorating. George Macready, Nina Foch. w. Charles O'Neal, d. Henry Levin.
SUSPENSE: HORROR: MYSTERY: Cults; Cult Films
(Ed: Based on the radio serial)
I Love My Wife, 1970, 95m, ★★1/2/$$, Col/MCA-U. A doctor has affairs with various women even though he has tremendous guilt. Elliott Gould, Brenda Vaccaro, Angel Tompkins. w. Robert Kaufman, d. Mel Stuart.
COMEDY DRAMA: COMEDY: SATIRE: Romance with Married Person; Marriage

Comedy; Marriage Drama; Doctors; Promiscuity; Guilty Conscience; Sexuality; Forgotten Films
(Loving; Move; Doctors' Wives)

I Love Trouble, 1947, 93m, ★★¹/2/$$, Col/NA. A political official's wife has a shady past that a PI is hired to uncover. Franchot Tone, Janet Blair, Janis Carter. w. N-adap. Roy Huggins, *The Double Take*, d. Sylvan Simon.

MYSTERY: SUSPENSE: Detective Stories; Detectives-Private; Secrets-Haunting; Politicians

I Love Trouble, 1994, 123m, ★★/$$, Col/Col-Tri, PG-13/S-FN. When two sparring reporters in Chicago reluctantly wind up on a story together, they find themselves fugitives from conspirators, and so on. . . . Nick Nolte, Julia Roberts, Saul Rubinek, Robert Loggia. w. Nancy Myers, Charles Shyer, d. Shyer.

COMEDY DRAMA: Action Comedy; Romance-Bickering; Journalists; Journalists as Detectives; Detective Stories; Romance-Older Men/Younger Women; Fugitives from a Murderer; Conspiracy; Chicago; Flops-Major; Coulda Been Good; Comedy & Violence; Female Screenwriters
(Foul Play)
(Ed: Though Nolte is twice Roberts' age, he carries it well; but this is hardly a match on any level, which further undermines the simplistic storyline and bickering)

I Love You Again, 1940, 99m, ★★★¹/2/$$, MGM/MGM-UA. A man who's happily married gets amnesia and then starts another life. William Powell, Myrna Loy, Frank McHugh, Edmund Lowe, Donald Douglas. w. Charles Lederer, George Oppenheimer, Harry Kurnitz, d. W. S. Van Dyke.

COMEDY: FARCE: Romance-Triangles; Identities-Mistaken; Amnesia; Dual Lives; Starting Over; Misunderstandings
(A Double Life; Mr. Buddwing; My Man Godfrey; Love Crazy)

I Love You, Alice B. Toklas, 1968, 93m, ★★★/$$, WB-7Arts/WB. A lawyer drops out and joins the flower children and has a wild time. Peter Sellers, Jo Van Fleet, Joyce Van Patten, Leigh Taylor-Young, Herb Edelman. w. Paul Mazursky, Larry Tucker, d. Hy Averback.

COMEDY: COMEDY DRAMA: Anti-Establishment Films; Hippies; Psychedelic Era; Lawyers; 1960s; Time Capsules
(The Magic Christian; Skidoo)

I Love You to Death, 1990, 96m, ★★★¹/2/$$, Tri-Star/Col-Tri, R/S-P. A woman (Tracey Ullman) tries to kill her philandering husband (Kevin Kline), but he won't die no matter how hard she tries. Joan Plowright, William Hurt, Keanu Reeves, River Phoenix, Victoria Jackson. w. John Kostmayer, d. Lawrence Kasdan.

COMEDY: Black Comedy; Marriage Comedy; Comedy-Morbid; **MURDER:** Comedy of Errors; Murder-Comic Attempts; Cheating Men; Incredible but Mostly True; True Stories; Working Class; Criminals-Stupid; Simple Minds; Underrated; Hidden Gems
(She-Devil; Switch; A Fish Called Wanda)

Images, 1972, 101m, ★★¹/2/$, Hemdale/NA, R/S. A mentally ill woman is haunted by the men in her life. Susannah York, Rene Auberjonois. w. d. Robert Altman. BOScore. Oscars: 1-0.

DRAMA: Character Studies; Memories; Flashbacks; Past-Haunted by the; Illusions/Hallucinations; Mental Illness; Nervous Breakdowns; Female Protagonists; Independent Films
(They Shoot Horses, Don't They?; I Never Promised You a Rose Garden)

Imaginary Crimes, 1994, 105m, ★★¹/2/$, PG-13/P. A salesman/con artist tries to maintain ties with his daughters after breaking free from his wife and descending into a life of ever-increasing scams. Harvey Keitel, Fairuza Balk, Elisabeth Moss, Chris Penn, Seymour Cassel, Kelly Lynch, Vincent D'Onofrio, Sam Fuller. w. Kristine Johnson Davia Nelson, N-adap. Sheila Ballantyne, d. Anthony Drazan.

DRAMA: Family Drama; Con Artists; Salesmen; Fathers & Daughters; Making a Living; Redemption
(The Bad Lieutenant; Death of a Salesman)

I'm All Right, Jack, 1959, 104m, ★★★/$$, B-L/Facets, FRN. An ordinary worker manages to start a nationwide strike within his factory, despite his ineptness. Peter Sellers, Ian Carmichael, Irene Handl, Richard Attengborough, Terry-Thomas, Margaret Rutherford. w. Frank Harvey, John Boulting, N-adap. Ian Hackney, *A Private Life*, d. John Boulting.

SATIRE: COMEDY: FARCE: Unions; Strikes; Heroes-Unlikely; Class Conflicts; Working Class; England; Nudists

I Married a Dead Man, 1983, 110m, ★★★/$, Ind/NA. In the wake of a train disaster, a woman assumes the identity of a wealthy woman victim to lead a new life, particularly for her child-to-be. Nathalie Baye, Franis Huster, Richard Bohringer. w. Patrick Laurent, Robin Davis, N-adap. William Irish, d. Robin Davis.

SUSPENSE: Film Noir-Modern; Identities-Assumed; Impostors; Babies-Having; Criminals-Female; Female Protagonists; French Films; Foreign Film Remakes

REMAKE OF: No Man of Her Own

I Married a Monster from Outer Space, 1958, 78m, ★★★/$$, Par/Par. A young husband is taken over by an alien force and soon his whole neighborhood is turned into zombies, except his wife, who must do battle alone. Tom Tryon, Gloria Talbott, Rober Ivers. w. Louis Vittes, d. Gene Fowler.

HORROR: SUSPENSE: Paranoia; Suburban Life; Newlyweds; Identities-Assumed; Aliens-Outer Space-Evil; Zombies
(Invasion of the Body Snatchers)

I Married a Witch, 1942, 82m, ★★★¹/2/$$, UA/WB. A witch and her father travel to the future to get at a descendant of the man who had them burned at a Salem stake, but romance, not revenge, is the result. Veronica Lake, Frederic March, Cecil Kellaway, Robert Benchley, Susan Hayward, Elizabeth Patterson. w. Robert Pirosh, Marc Connelly, N-adap. Thorne Smith, *The Passionate Witch*, d. Rene Clair.

COMEDY: ROMANCE: Romantic Comedy; Fires; Romance-Reluctant; Revenge; Witches; Warlocks; Time Travel
(Bell, Book and Candle; Maid of Salem)

I Married a Woman, 1956, 85m, ★★¹/2/$, RKO/VCI. A nerdy ad executive is married to a sexpot but neglects her, so she goes roaming. George Gobel, Diana Dors, Adlophe Menjou, Nita Talbot. w. Goodman Ace, d. Hal Kanter.

COMEDY: ROMANCE: Marriage Comedy; Sex Comedy; Romantic Comedy; Jealousy; Cheating Women; Advertising World

I'm Dancing as Fast as I Can, 1982, 106m, ★★¹/2/$, Par/Par, PG/S. A woman filmmaker (Jill Clayburgh) deals with her addiction to valium. Geraldine Page,

Nicol Williamson, Dianne Wiest, Joe Pesci. w. David Rabe, NF-adap. Barbara Gordon, d. Jack Hofsiss.

DRAMA: Biographies; Autobiographical Stories; Drugs-Addictions; Nervous Breakdowns; Midlife Crisis; Moviemaking; Directors; Female Directors; Female Protaognists
(A Woman Under the Influence; An Unmarried Woman)

I'm Gonna Git You Sucka, 1988, 89m, ★★★/$$$, MGM-UA/MGM-UA, PG-13/P-S. A parody of 70s blaxploitation-era action movies. Bernie Casey, Keenan Ivory Wayans, Isaac Hayes, Jim Brown, Dawnn Lewis, Janet DuBois. w. d. Keenan Ivory Wayans.

COMEDY: SATIRE: Spoofs; **ACTION:** Action Comedy; Blaxploitation Era; Black Casts; Black Screenwriters; Black Men; Black Directors; Inner City Life; 1970s; Writer-Directors
(Don't Be a Menace . . . ; A Low Down Dirty Shame)

Imitation of Life, 1934, 109m, ★★★/$$$, U/NA. A white woman sells the pancake recipe of her black nanny and becomes wealthy, keeping the nanny in her life, though the woman's mulatto daughter causes problems wanting to live her life as a white person. Claudette Colbert, Louise Beavers, Warren Williams, Rochelle Hudson, Alan Hale, Warren William. w. William Hulrbut, N-adap. Fannie Hurst, d. John Stahl. BPicture. Oscars: 1-0.

Imitation of Life, 1959, 124m, ★★★¹/₂/$$$, U/MCA-U. In the remake, the white woman is now an actress who makes it big, leaving her black nanny and her daughter in the shadows trying to get out. Lana Turner, Juanita Moore (BSActress), Susan Kohner (BSActress), Sandra Dee, John Gavin, Robert Alda. w. Eleanore Griffin, Allan Scott, d. Douglas Sirk. Oscars: 2-0.

DRAMA: MELODRAMA: TRAGEDY: Tearjerkers; Race Relations; Black vs. White; Fame-Rise to; Friendships-Female; Babysitters; Servants; Actresses; Female Protagonists; Female Screenwriters
(Gypsy; Peyton Place; Valley of the Dolls)
(Ed: One of the few remakes that was better and a bigger hit)

Immediate Family, 1988, 95m, ★★¹/₂/$$, Tri/Col-Tri, PG. A yuppie couple decides to adopt, but getting to know the baby's parents before birth causes

problems. Glenn Close, James Woods, Mary Stuart Masterson, Kevin Dillon, Jane Greer. w. Barbara Benedek, d. Johnathan Kaplan.

DRAMA: MELODRAMA: Babies-Having; Children-Adopted; Marriage Drama; Rich vs. Poor; Ethics; Yuppies; Female Protagonists; Female Screenwriters

Immortal Beloved, 1994, 123m, ★★★/$, Universal/MCA-U, PG-13/S. The life of Beethoven and his various women, including the mystery woman mentioned in his letters as his "immortal beloved," who may be a woman everyone knows or someone no one but Beethoven himself knows. Gary Oldman, Jeroen Krabbe, Isabella Rossellini, Johanna Ter Steege, Marco Hofschneider, Miriam Margolyes, Barry Humphries, Valeria Golino. w. d. Bernard Rose.

DRAMA: Historical Drama; Costume Drama; **ROMANCE:** Romantic Drama; Romance-Triangles; **MYSTERY:** Letters; Music Composers; Biographies; 1700s; Writer-Directors; Flashbacks
(Amadeus; Dangerous Liaisons; Farinelli)

The Immortal Sergeant, 1943, 90m, ★★¹/₂/$$, 20th/Fox. A war leader rallies his soldiers into battle in World War II North Africa and winds up being a victim of his own avarice. Henry Fonds, Thomas Mithell, Maureen O'Hara, Reginald Gardiner, Allyn Joseph, Melville Cooper. w. Lama Trotti, N-adap. John Brophy, d. John Stahl.

DRAMA: War Stories; World War II; **TRAGEDY:** Character Studies; Leaders; Soldiers; Africa
(Raid on Rommel; The Desert Fox)

The Immortal Story, 1968, 60m, ★★/$, Albina/NA. In old Macao a rich man tries to realize the stories of an old fisherman. Orson Welles, Jeanne Moreau, Roger Coggio. w. d. Welles.

DRAMA: Art Films; South Pacific; Legends; Fantasy; Fantasies; Storytellers; 1800s; Actor Directors; Writer-Directors; Independent Films
(Ed: Only for those studying the decline of Welles)

I'm No Angel, 1933, 88m, ★★★¹/₂/$$$$, Par/MCA-U. A sideshow star (Mae West) manages to prove herself innocent of a murder, but the celebrity it brings sends her into high society and romance. Mae West, Edward Arnold, Cary Grant, Gregory Ratoff. w. Mae West, d. Wesley Ruggles.

COMEDY: SATIRE: Rags to Riches; **MURDER:** Sex Comedy; Trials; Accused Unjustly; Fish out of Water Stories; Snobs vs. Slobs; Rich vs. Poor; Female Screenwriters; Female Protagonists
(She Done Him Wrong; Dynamite; Way Out West)

I, Mobster, 1958, 80m, ★★¹/₂/$, AIP/NA. A teenager from the wrong side of the tracks rises to be a mob leader. Steve Cochran, Lita Milan, Robert Strauss. w. Steve Fisher, N-adap. Joseph Hilton Smith, d. Roger Corman.

MELODRAMA: Crime Drama; Power-Rise to; Mob Stories; Young Men; Inner City Life; Forgotten Films; Curiosities
(Capone; Dillinger; The Outsiders)

I, Monster, 1970, 75m, ★★¹/₂/$, Ind/NA. A retelling of the Jekyll and Hyde tale. Christopher Lee, Peter Cushing. w. Milton Subostsky, d. Stephen Weeks.

HORROR: Scientists; Doctors; Scientists-Made; Experiments; Dual Lives; Monsters-Human

REMAKE/RETREAD OF: Dr. Jekyll and Mr. Hyde

Impact, 1949, 111m, ★★¹/₂/$, UA/Nos. A woman and her secret lover plan to do in her husband, but the husband has a few tricks up his own sleeve. Brian Donlevy, Ella Raines, Charles Coburn. w. Dorothy Reid, d. Arthur Lubin.

SUSPENSE: MURDER: Murder of Spouse; Romance-Triangles; Cheating Women; Film Noir; Clever Plots & Endings; Dead-Back from the; Female Screenwriters
(The Postman Always Rings Twice; Body Heat; Double Indemnity; Caught; Buried Alive)

The Impatient Years, 1944, 91m, ★★¹/₂/$$, Col/NA. A soldier home from the war has trouble getting used to married life. Lee Bowman, Jean Arthur, Charles Coburn, Edgar Buchanan, Jane Darwell. w. Virginia Van Upp, d. Irving Cummings.

COMEDY DRAMA: MELODRAMA: Marriage Drama; Pre-life Crisis; Young Men; Newlyweds; War Brides; Soldiers; World War II Era; War at Home; Female Screenwriters
(The Best Years of Our Lives)

The Importance of Being Earnest, 1952, 95m, ★★★¹/₂/$$$, Rank/Par. When going to a summer estate, much is discovered about two young men, each planning to get married, as to their true identities and class. Michael Redgrave, Michael Denison, Edith Evans, Margaret Rutherford, Joan Greenwood. w. d. Anthony Asquith, P-adap. Oscar Wilde.

COMEDY: Comedy of Manners; **FARCE:** Marriage-Impending; Class Conflicts; Impostors; Children-Long Lost; Stagelike Films; British Films; Classic Play Adaptations; 1890s

TV REMAKE: 1986, BBC (Bravo Channel)

The Impossible Years, 1968, 98m, ★★★/$$$, MGM/MGM-UA, G. A college psychology professor (James Stewart) has embarassing problems controlling his increasingly wild teenage daughter (Cristina Ferrare). Chad Everett, Lola Albright, Ozzie Nelson. w. George Wells, P-adap. Bob Fisher, Arthur Marx, d. Michael Gordon.

COMEDY: Coming of Age; Parents vs. Children; Fathers & Daughters; Teenagers; Generation Gap; Daddy's Girls; Fathers Controlling Daughters; Psychologists; Professors; California; 1960s

(She's Outta Control!; How Sweet It Is)

Impromptu, 1990, 107m, ★★★/$$, Hemdale/Hemdale, PG/S. The mannish female writer George Sand pursues composer Chopin from a country retreat to Paris. Judy Davis, Hugh Grant, Mandy Patinkin, Bernadette Peters, Julian Sands, Emma Thompson. w. Sarah Kernochan, d. James Lapine.

COMEDY DRAMA: ROMANCE: Romantic Comedy; Romance-Girl Wants Boys; Free Spirits; Nerds; Extroverted vs. Introverted; Writers; Musicians; Music Composers; Tomboys; Women as Men; Female Screenwriters; Female Protagonists; Coulda Been Great

RETELLING OF: A Song to Remember

(A Song to Remember; Immortal Beloved)

Improper Channels, 1979, 91m, ★★/$, Ind/Vestron. When a man takes his daughter to the hospital, he runs into all kinds of bureaucratic trouble and one particular woman. Alan Arkin, Mariette Hartley, Monica Parker. w. Morrie Rubinsky, Ian Sutherland, Adam Arkin, d. Eric Till.

COMEDY DRAMA: SATIRE: Black Comedy; **ROMANCE:** Battle of the Sexes; Hospitals; Fathers & Daughters; Coulda Been Good

An Impudent Girl, 1985, 97m, ★★1/2/$, Ind/NA. An adolescent girl

begins to come out of a fantasy world and see the reality before her about growing up. Charlotte Gainsbourg, Bernadette Lafont. w. Claude Miller, Luc Beraud, Bernard Stora, Annie Miller, d. Claude Miller.

DRAMA: MELODRAMA: Coming of Age; Girlhood; Teenagers

(The Member of the Wedding; Peppermint Soda; Pauline at the Beach; Desert Bloom)

Impulse, 1984, 99m, ★★1/2/$, ABC-20th/CBS-Fox, R/P-V-S-FN. Strange happenings that may be related to an earthquake and/or a conspiracy occur in a small California town when a young woman returns home with her boyfriend. Tim Matheson, Meg Tilly, Hume Cronyn, John Karlen. w. Bart Davis, Don Dunaway, d. Graham Baker.

SUSPENSE: MYSTERY: SCI-FI: Conspiracy; Environmental Dilemmas; Toxic Waste; Earthquakes; Small-Town Life; Epidemics; Mental Illness; Coulda Been Good; Forgotten Films

(The Stepford Wives; Body Snatchers; Prophecy)

Impulse, 1990, 108m, ★★/$, WB/WB, R/V-S. When a witness to a case vanishes, a cop knows what happened but keeps quiet, leading to danger for all. Jeff Fahey, Theresa Russell, George Dzundza, Alan Rosenberg, Lynn Thigpen. w. John deMaro, Leigh Chapman, d. Sondra Locke.

SUSPENSE: MURDER: Missing Persons; Detectives-Police; Witness to Murder; Female Directors; Female Screenwriters; Female Protagonists; Coulda Been Good

(Physical Evidence)

In the Army Now, 1994, 94m, ★★/$$, Hollywood/Hollywood, PG-13/P. Spaced out pseudo-surfer dude enlists for benefits and winds up in battle. Pauly Shore, Esai Morales, Lri Petter, David Alan Grier, Ernie Hudson. w. Dan Petrie, Jr., Ken Kaufman, Fairfax Bahr, Stu Kreiger, Adam Small, d. Petrie.

COMEDY: Comedy-Slapstick; Comedy-Character; Military Comedy; Fish out of Water Stories; Fools-Bumbling

(Private Benjamin; Stripes; Abbott and Costello in the Army; Son-in-Law; Biodome)

(Ed: Tired retread, period)

Inchon, 1981, 140m, ★/$, MGM-UA/MGM-UA, PG/V. An account of how General MacArthur was supposedly

affected by divine intervention (of the Moonies' kind, since Sun Yung Moon financed this film) during a battle in the Korean War. Laurence Olivier, Jacqueline Bisset, David Janssen, Ben Gazzara, Toshiro Mifiune, Rex Reed. w. Robin Moore, Laird Koenig, d. Terence Young.

DRAMA: ACTION: Epics; War Movies; Korean War; War Battles; Unintentionally Funny; Flops-Major

(MacArthur)

Incident at Oglala, 1992, 90m, ★★★/$, Ind/Live, PG. Documentary about the murders of two FBI agents for which American Indian Leonard Peltier has been imprisoned since, but which brings up many questions begging his innocence. w. Michael Apted.

Documentaries; **MURDER:** True Stories; Indians-American; FBI Agents; Accused Unjustly

(The Thin Blue Line; Thunderheart)

In Cold Blood, 1967, 134m, ★★★1/2/$$$, Columbia/RCA-Col, R/V-P. Two drifters murder a Kansas family for apparently no reason. Scott Wilson, Robert Blake. w. d. Richard Brooks (BAScr, BDir), N-adap. Truman Capote. BOScore, BCCin. Oscars: 4-0.

DRAMA: MURDER: SUSPENSE: Crime Drama; Film Noir; Murderers-Mass; Character Studies; Biographies-Fictional; True Stories; Evil Men; Criminal Couples; Midwestern Life; 1960s; Writer-Directors

(The Cradle Will Rock; Swoon; Badlands)

In the Cool of the Day, 1962, 91m, ★★1/2/$$, MGM/NA. The young wife of a publisher (Jane Fonda) travels to Greece where she has an affair with a friend (Peter Finch) of her husband's, who is constantly obligated to his own wife, the victim of a tragic accident (Angela Lansbury). Arthur Hill, Constance Cummings. w. Meade Roberts, N-adap. Susan Ertz, d. Robert Stevens.

DRAMA: MELODRAMA: TRAGEDY: ROMANCE: Romantic Drama; Romance-Older Men/Younger Women; Romance with Lover's Friend; Death-Impending; Americans Abroad; Vacations; Vacation Romance; Accidents; Past-Haunted by the

(The Chapman Report; Bonjour, Tristesse)

In Country, 1989, 115m, ★★1/2/$, WB/WB, PG-13/P-S. A young girl in Kentucky (Emily Lloyd) tries to learn about her father who died in Vietnam. Bruce Willis, Joan Allen, Judith Ivey,

Kevin Anderson. w. Frank Pierson, Cynthia Cidre, N-adap. Bobbie Ann Mason, d. Norman Jewison.

DRAMA: Coming of Age; Ordinary People Stories; Girlhood; Fathers & Daughters; Death-Dealing with; Vietnam Era; Rural Life; Southerns; Coulda Been Good; Female Protagonists; Female Screenwriters

(Desert Bloom; The Heart Is a Lonely Hunter)

The Incredible Journey, 1963, ★★★1/2/$$$, Disney/Disney, G. Two dogs and a cat cross the Northwest to get to their owners who've left them behind. Only animal stars. w. James Algar, N-adap. Sheila Burnford, d. Fletcher Markle.

CHILDREN'S: FAMILY: Animal Stories; Animals in Jeopardy; Pet Stories; Journies; Cats; Dogs; What If . . . Stories; Narrated Films

REMAKE: Homeward Bound.

(The Bear; Far from Home; Old Yeller)

(Ed: Amazingly well-done considering the lack of actors, like an art film for children)

The Incredible Journey of Dr. Meg Laurel, 1979, 143m, ★★★/$$$$, CBS-Col/Col. A young, charismatic female doctor returns to her home in Appalachia to help the mountain people during the Depression and finds a fascinating world she never fully appreciated. Lindsay Wagner, Dorothy McGuire, James Woods. d. Guy Green.

MELODRAMA: Doctors; Depression Era; Mountain People; Old-Fashioned Recent Films; TV Movies; Hidden Gems; Female Protagonists

(Dr. Quinn, Medicine Woman; Christy; Foxfire; Cross Creek)

(Ed: The original of this TV sub-genre, made at time when TV movies had matured to a level of intelligence and production values worth seeing; Wagner's best TV movie before becoming TV romance queen)

The Incredible Mr. Limpet, 1964, 99m, ★★/$$, WB/WB, G. A nerd is transformed into a cartoon fish, escaping society and falling in love, plus helping the war effort in fighting German subs-or something like that. Don Knotts, Jack Weston, Carole Cook. d. Arthur Lubin. Cartoons; Animation-Partial; Fish; **CHILDREN'S:** Nerds; Humans into Animal; World War II Stories; Germans as Enemy

The Incredible Sarah, 1976, 105m, ★★★/$$, Readers Digest-UA/Imperial, G. The life of the legendary 1900s actress Sarah Bernhardt up to her peak in her 30s. Glenda Jackson (BActress), Yvonne Mitchell, Daniel Massey, Douglas Wilmer. w. Ruth Worloff, d. Richard Fleischer. Oscars: 1-0.

DRAMA: MELODRAMA: Biographies; Actresses; Theater Life; Paris; 1900s; Female Protagonists; Old-Fashioned Recent Films

(Hedda; Star!)

The Incredible Shrinking Man, 1957, 81m, ★★★/$$$, U/MCA-U. When a mysterious mist covers a man on a boat in the ocean, he returns home having begun to shrink with no end in sight. Grant Williams, April Kent. w. Richard Matheson, d. Jack Arnold.

DRAMA: SCI-FI: Fantasy; **HORROR: SUSPENSE:** Survival Drama; Shrinking People; Environmental Dilemmas; Cats

(Dr. Cyclops; Honey, I Shrunk the Kids)

The Incredible Shrinking Woman, 1981, 88m, ★★/$$, Univ/MCA-U, PG. A housewife whose life is overrun with chemical house cleaners and what-not begins to shrink as a result. Lily Tomlin, Charles Grodin, Ned Beatty, Henry Gibson, Elizabeth Wilson. w. Jane Wagner, d. Joel Schumacher.

COMEDY DRAMA: SCI-FI: Spoofs; Revisionist Films; Allegorical Stories; Domestic Life; Suburban Life; Female Protagonists; Female Screenwriters

(Ed: Presumably also an allegory to the role of the housewife and women's subjugation, although not on any serious or successful level)

An Indecent Obsession, 1985, 100m, ★★1/2/$, Ind/Live, PG. A nurse is the object of all the soldiers' affection in her mental ward during World War II in Australia. Wendy Hughes, Gary Sweet, Johnathan Hyde. w. Denise Morgan, N-adap. Colleen McCullough, d. Lex Marinos.

MELODRAMA: ROMANCE: Romantic Drama; Asylums; Nurses; Soldiers; World War II Era; Australian Films

(A Farewell to Arms; The Getting of Wisdom)

(Ed: Despite having been a bestseller on the heels of *The Thorn Birds*, McCullough's blockbuster, this film sank quickly)

Indecent Proposal, 1993, 119m, Par/Par, ★★★/$$$$$. A young couple on the brink of bankruptcy (Demi Moore, Woody Harrelson) goes to Vegas to save their house when a rich gambler (Robert Redford) spies the wife and offers her a million dollars for one night. Who will she choose? w. Amy Jones, N-adap. Jack Engelhard, d. Adrian Lyne.

DRAMA: ROMANCE: MELODRAMA: Marriage Drama; Erotic Drama; Romantic Drama; Romance-Choosing the Right Person; Marriage on the Rocks; Romance-Triangles; Narrated Films; Young People; Gambling; Bets; Las Vegas; Female Protagonists; Female Screenwriters

COMIC FLIPSIDE: Honeymoon in Vegas

(Ed: Although the premise seems preposterous, this serious treatment of the premise did far better than the *Honeymoon in Vegas* partial send-up of it released just a few months later)

Indiana Jones and the Last Crusade, 1989, 127m, ★★★/$$$$$$, Par/Par, PG-13/V. Indiana tries to save his father, who's been captured by Nazis after getting close to the trail of the whereabouts of the Holy Grail. Harrison Ford, Sean Connery, Denholm Elliott, Alison Doody, John Rhys-Davies, Julian Glover, River Phoenix, Michael Byrne. w. Jeffrey Boam, George Lucas, Menno Meyjes, d. Steven Spielberg. BSound, **BSoundEdit,** BOScore. Oscars: 3-1.

ACTION: ADVENTURE: Action Comedy; Saving Someone; Kidnappings; Conspiracy; Chase Movies; Journies; Treasure Hunts; Thieves; Searches; Legends; Nazi Stories; Fathers & Sons

SEQUEL TO: Indiana Jones and the Temple of Doom

(Ed: Going back to the elements of the original, it's far superior to *Temple of Doom*)

Indiana Jones and the Temple of Doom, 1984, 118m, ★★★/$$$$$, Par/Par, PG-13/V-B&G. Indiana travels Asia in search of a much-coveted jewel while romancing a screaming blonde the director later married. Harrison Ford, Kate Capshaw, KeHuy Kwan, Philip Stone. w. Willard Huyck, Gloria Katz, George Lucas, d. Steven Spielberg.

ACTION: ADVENTURE: Action Comedy; Saving Someone; Conspiracy; Chase

Movies; Journeys; Treasure Hunts; Jewel Thieves; Searches; Legends; Nazi Stories; Asia; Female Screenwriters

SEQUEL TO (Prequel): Raiders of the Lost Ark

(Ed: Considering the track record of Huyck and Katz after *American Graffiti* with Lucas (*Best Defense, Howard the Duck*, etc.), is it any surprise this was so flat, though fast thanks to Spielberg?)

The Indian Fighter, 1955, 88m, ★★/$$, UA/MGM-UA. An Indian fighter protects a wagon train from renegade Sioux warriors. Kirk Douglas, Elsa Martinelli, Walter Matthau. w. Frank Davis, ben Hecht, d. Andre de Toth.

WESTERN: Wagon Trains; Protecting Someone; Indians-American

The Indian in the Cupboard, 1995, 97m, ★★/$$, Par-Col/Par, PG. A little boy finds in a cabinet an even littler Indian who the day before was just a toy. He discovers he can bring any toy to life but things get a little out of hand when they start interacting. Hal Scardino, Litefoot, Lindsay Crouse, Richard Jenkins, Rishi Bhat, Steve Coogan, David Keith. w. Melissa Mathison, N-adap. Lynne Reid Banks. d. Frank Oz.

ADVENTURE: Fantasy; **CHILDREN'S:** Indians-American; Objects with Personalities; Toys; Magic; Child Protagonists; Female Screenwriters

(Toy Story; E.T.)

(Ed: High hopes from the writer of *E.T.*, but no blockbuster here)

The Indian Runner, 1991, 126m, ★★/$, Tri/Col-Tri, R/V-S-P. A cop in a small town in the 1960s has trouble dealing with his criminal brother. David Morse, Viggo Mortenson, Dennis Hopper, Valerie Golina, Patricia Arquette, Charles Bronson, Sandy Dennis. w. d. Sean Penn.

DRAMA: Crime Drama; Character Studies; Brothers; Police Stories; Small-Town Life; 1960s; Actor Directors; Writer-Directors

(At Close Range; Dead Man Walking)

(Ed: Supposedly loosely based on the Bruce Springsteen song "Highway Patrolman")

Indiscreet, 1958, 100m, ★★★/$$$, U/Republic. An American ambassador falls in love with an actress in London's jet set but decides to keep his emotional distance by pretending to really be married. Cary Grant, Ingrid Bergman, Phyllis

Calvert, Cecil Parker. w. N-adap. Norman Krasna, d. Stanley Donen.

ROMANCE: COMEDY DRAMA: Romantic Comedy; Romance-Reluctant; Romance with Married Person; Cheating Men; Marriages-Fake; England; Rich People; Diplomats; Actresses

(The Grass Is Greener; Pillow Talk)

Indiscretion of an American Wife, 1954, 75m, ★★★/$$, Selznick-UA/Fox. An American woman and a younger Italian professor have an affair and try to say farewell, centering around a train station. Jennifer Jones, Montgomery Clift, Richard Beymer. w. Cesare Zavattini, Truman Capote, d. Vittorio DeSica.

DRAMA: ROMANCE: Romantic Drama; Art Films; Romance-Older Women/Younger Men; Romance with Married Person; Vacation Romance; Americans Abroad; Female Protagonists; Italy

(The Roman Spring of Mrs. Stone; The Idol; Brief Encounter; A Month by the Lake)

Indochine, 1992, 158m, $$$, French-Sony/Col-Tri, PG/V-S. A plantation owner's wife (Catherine Deneuve, BActress) struggles with the changes of pre-World War II Southeast Asia as her adopted daughter's tragic love affair and political alliances tear her family apart. Vincent Perez, Linh Dan Pham, Jean Yanne. w. Erik Orsenna, Louis Gardeal, Catherine Cohen, Regis Wargnier, d. Wargnier. **BFLFilm.** Oscars: 2-1.

DRAMA: Epics; Mothers & Sons; Flashbacks; Episodic Stories; World War II Era; Asia; Vietnam; Communists; Spies; Upper Class; POWs/MIAs; Female Protagonists; French Films; Female Screenwriters

(The House of the Spirits; Dr. Zhivago)

I Never Promised You a Rose Garden, 1977, ★★★/$$, New World/WB. A teenage girl with suicidal tendencies is locked up in an asylum in the 50s and must fight through the ordeal. Kathleen Quinlan, Bibi Andersson, Sylvia Sidney, Ben Piazza, Lorraine Gary. w. Gavin Lambert, Lewis John Carlino (BAScr), N-adap. Hannah Green, d. Anthony Page. Oscars: 1-0.

DRAMA: Social Drama; Suicidal Tendencies; Suicidal Tendencies of Young People; Teenagers; Girlhood; Young Women; Asylums; Mental Illness; Nightmares; Prison Drama; Psychological; Coming of Age

(The Bell Jar; Frances; Will There Really Be a Morning?; Bedlam)

I Never Sang for My Father, 1970, 92m, ★★★1/2/$$, Col/RCA-Col, PG/P-S. The mother of a widower who is trying to rebuild his life dies and he's suddenly married to his father instead, who doesn't want him to meet any women to replace or share him with. Gene Hackman (BActor), Melvyn Douglas (BActor), Dorothy Stickney, Estelle Parsons. w. P-adap. Robert Anderson, d. Gilbert Cates. Oscars: 3-0.

DRAMA: Family Drama; Fathers-Troublesome; Fathers & Sons; Romance-Middle Aged; Widowers; Death-Dealing with; Starting Over; Stern Men; Jealousy; Faded Hits; Forgotten Films; Hidden Gems

(Dad; Kotch; Da; How Do I Love Thee?)

Inferno, 1953, 83m, ★★★/$$, 20th/NA. A man whose wife is cheating on him breaks his leg in the desert and she and her lover leave him for dead. Robert Ryan, William Lundigan, Rhonda Fleming. w. Francis Cockrell, d. Roy Baker.

DRAMA: SUSPENSE: Romance-Triangles; Cheating Women; Murder of Spouse w/Lover; Desert Settings; Dead-Left for; 3-D Movies

The Informer, 1935, 91m, ★★★1/2/$$$, RKO/Turner. An IRA leader is ratted on by a peasant who wants money from the government to leave the country but may have a greater price to pay than he realized. Victor McLaglen (BActor), Wallace Ford, Preston Foster. w. Dudley Nichols (BAScr), N-adap. Liam O'Flaherty, d. John Ford (BDirector). BPicture, BEdit, BScore. Oscars: 6-4.

DRAMA: TRAGEDY: Social Drama; Ireland; IRA; Double Crossings; Traitors; Trials; Guilty Conscience

(In the Name of the Father; Hidden Agenda; Odd Man Out)

In the French Style, 1962, 105m, ★★★/$, Col/NA. An American young woman travels to Paris and has an affair with a teenager and an older man, covering all the bases. Jean Seberg, Stanley Baker, Phillipe Fouquet. w. Irwin Shaw, d. Robert Parrish.

DRAMA: ROMANCE: Romance-Older Women/Younger Men; Romance-Older Men/Younger Women; Romance-Triangles; Romantic Drama; Americans Abroad; Paris; Teenagers; Female Protagonists

(The Game Is Over; Damage; Bonjour, Tristesse)

In the Good Old Summertime, 1949, 102m, ★★★/$$$, MGM/MGM-UA. A shop girl writes to a man, via a matchmaker, who turns out to be her boss, whom she can't stand. Judy Garland, Van Johnson, Spring Byington, Buster Keaton. w. Albert Hackett, Frances Goodrich, Ivan Tors, P-adap. Miklos Laszlo, d. Robert Leonard.

MUSICALS: ROMANCE: MELODRAMA: Romance-Opposites Attract; Romance-Reluctant; Epistolaries; Working Class
MUSICAL REMAKE OF: The Shop Around the Corner.
(The Shop Around the Corner; I Sent a Letter to My Love; Meet Me in St. Louis)

In the Heat of the Night, 1967, 109m, ★★★1/2/$$$, UA/MGM-UA, PG/V. A bigoted sheriff doesn't welcome a black FBI man who arrives to help solve a murder in his small Mississippi town. Rod Steiger (**BActor**), Sidney Poitier, Warren Oates, William Schallert, Lee Grant. w. N-adap. Sterling Silliphant (**BAScr**), d. Norman Jewison (**BDirector**). **BPicture**, BSoundFX, **BSound, BEdit.** 7-5.

DRAMA: ACTION: Crime Drama; **MYSTERY: MURDER: MURDER MYSTERY:** Social Drama; Conspiracy; Race Relations; Black vs. White; Fish out of Water Stories; Black Men; City vs. Country; Small-Town Life; Southerns; Mississippi
SEQUELS: They Call Me Mr. Tibbs; The Organization; TV SERIES (1988–1994)
(Mississippi Burning; The Defiant Ones)

The Inheritance, 1976, 121m, ★★1/2/$$, Ind/Sultan. A wealthy Italian man disinherits his children, but his beautiful, scheming daughter-in-law may win his favor. Dominique Sanda, Anthony Quinn, Fabio Testi. w. UgoPirro, Sergio Bazzini, N-adap Gaetano Chelli, d. Mauro Bolognini.

DRAMA: MELODRAMA: Inheritances at Stake; Greed; Betrayals; Stern Men; Evil Women; Italy; 1800s

Inherit the Wind, 1960, 127m, ★★★1/2/$$$, UA/MGM-UA. The Scopes monkey trial is detailed in this old-fashioned sweat-and-ceiling-fans drama where creationism and Darwinism have their first major duel. Spencer Tracy (**BActor**), Fredric March, Gene Kelly, Dick York, Harry Morgan. w. Jonathan Douglas, Harold Smith (**BAScr**), P-adap.

Jerome Lawrence, Robert E. Lee, d. Stanley Kramer. BB&WCin, BEdit. Oscars: 4-0.
DRAMA: Social Drama; Courtroom Drama; Trials; Ethics; Historical Drama; Men in Conflict; Lawyers; True Stories; Southerns; Censorship
(To Kill a Mockingbird; As Summers Die)

The Inkwell, 1994, 112m, ★★/$, Col/Col, R/P-V. In 70s Martha's Vineyard a young man comes of age hanging around the wealthy black resort area called the Inkwell. Lorenz Tate, Joe Morton, Phyllis Stickney. w. Tom Ricostronza, Paris Qualles, d. Matty Rich.
MELODRAMA: Coming of Age; Black Casts; Black Men; Young Men; Resorts; Family Drama; Coulda Been Good; Black Screenwriters; Black Directors
(Straight out of Brooklyn; The Flamingo Kid)

The In-Laws, 1979, 103m, ★★★1/2/$$$$, WB/WB, PG/P. The father of the bride (Alan Arkin) gets mixed up with the groom's father (Peter Falk) who has the mob and counterfeiters after him. Somehow they both wind up in Central America before a firing squad and could miss the wedding. Nancy Dussault. w. Andrew Bergman, d. Arthur Hiller.
COMEDY: Comedy-Slapstick; Comedy of Errors; **FARCE:** Chase Movies; Mob Comedy; Fugitives from the Mob; Fugitives from the Law; Fathers & Daughters; Marriage-Impending; Innocent Bystanders; Weddings; Central America; Leaders-Tyrant; Dentists; Sleeper Hits
(Honeymoon in Vegas; The Freshman)

In Like Flint, 1967, 107m, ★★1/2?$$$, 20th/CBS-Fox. Secret agent Flint goes after a group of deadly female spies who have kidnapped the President and are doing terrible things to him. James Coburn, Lee J. Cobb, Anna Lee. w. Hal Fimberg, d. Gordon Douglas.
COMEDY: ACTION: Action Comedy; Spoofs; Spoofs-Spy; Secret Agents; Kidnappings; Spies-Female; Golf; Cult Films
SEQUEL TO: Our Man Flint
(The Liquidator; Matt Helm SERIES; James Bond SERIES)

In the Line of Fire, 1993, 129m, ★★★/$$$$, Col/Col-Tri, R/V-P. A Secret Service agent who still feels guilt about Kennedy's death in 1963 now has to protect the President 30 years later from a psycho-stalker who's taunting him personally. Clint Eastwood, Rene Russo, John

Malkovich (BSActor), Dylan McDermott, Gary Cole, Fred Dlaton Thompson, John Mahoney. w. Jeff MacGuire (BOScr), d. Wolfgang Petersen. BEdit. Oscars: 3-0.
SUSPENSE: Psychological Thriller; Psycho-Killers; Stalkers; Mindgames; Secret Service; Assassination Plots; Presidents; JFK; Men Proving Themselves; Redemption; Chase Stories; Race Against Time
(Day of the Jackal; The Parallax View)

In a Lonely Place, 1950, 93m, ★★★1/2/$$$, Col/RCA-Col. A screenwriter moves into an apartment complex in Hollywood and falls in love with a neighbor, but when suspicion arises he may have murdered a young woman, who will believe he's innocent? Humphrey Bogart, Gloria Grahame, Frank Lovejoy. w. Andrew Solt, N-adap. Dorothy Hughes, d. Nicholas Ray.
DRAMA: SUSPENSE: MYSTERY: MURDER: MURDER MYSTERY: ROMANCE: Film Noir; Writers; Hollywood Life; Unbelieved; Accused Unjustly; Underrated; Hidden Gems

In Love and War, 1991, 96m, ★★1/2/$, Vidmark/Vidmark, R/P-V. A POW returns home from Vietnam and tries to adjust. James Woods, Jane Alexander, Haing S. Ngor, Concetta Tomei. w. Carol Schneider, d. Paul Aaron.
DRAMA: Character Studies; Veterans-Vietnam; Reunions; POWs; Female Screenwriters
(Welcome Home; Coming Home; The Deerhunter)

In the Mouth of Madness, 95m, ★★1/2/$$, New Line/New Line, R/EV-B&G-P-S. When a Stephen King–like writer disappears, an insurance investigator searches him out, believing that one of his fictional towns really exists as a hiding place for him. It turns out it really does and that the line between fiction and fact has blurred as the writer has finished a new book which has the power to affect reality with murder and mayhem. Sam Neill, Julie Carmen, Jurgen Prochnow, Charlton Heston. w. Michael De Luca, d. John Carpenter.
HORROR: SUSPENSE: Writers; Fantasy; What If . . . Stories; Race Against Time; Good Premise Unfulfilled
(The Dark Half; Delirious; Hideaway)

In the Name of the Father, 1993, 133m, ★★★/$$$, U/MCA-U, R/P-V. A father and son are unjustly accused and imprisoned for IRA terrorists acts in Ireland, and it's not until a British female lawyer takes the case that there's any hope of release. Daniel Day Lewis (BActor), Emma Thompson (BSActress), Pete Postlethwaite (BSActor), John Lynch, Corin Redgrave. w. Terry George (BAScr), d. Sheridan (BDirector). BPicture, BOScore. Oscars: 7-0.

DRAMA: True Stories; Accused Unjustly; Prison Drama; Courtroom Drama; IRA; Terrorists; Fathers & Sons; Episodic Stories; Lawyers; Lawyers as Detective; Ireland; Irish Films

(An Innocent Man; The Informer; Hidden Agenda; My Left Foot)

In Name Only, 1939, 94m, ★★½/$$$, RKO/Turner. A man strays from his wife but when she won't give him a divorce, it complicates matters for his mistress. Cary Grant, Carole Lombard, Kay Francis, Charles Coburn. w. Richard Sherman, N-adap. Bessie Brewer, *Memory of Love*, d. John Cromwell.

DRAMA: MELODRAMA: ROMANCE: Romantic Drama; Marriage Drama; Cheating Men; Mistresses; Romance-Triangles

(Intersection)

The Inner Circle, 1991, 122m, ★★★/$, Col/Col, PG-13. The projectionist of the theater in the Kremlin under Stalin is sworn to secrecy about his job and what is seen-mostly Hollywood fare-and also finds himself oblivious to the terrible world around him. Tom Hulce, Lolita Davidovich, Bob Hoskins. w. Andrei Konchalovsky, Anatoli Usov, d. Konchalovsky.

DRAMA: Ordinary People Stories; Movie Theaters; Russia; Stalin; Leaders-Tyrant; Oppression; Secrets-Keeping

Innerspace, 1987, 120m, ★★½/$$$, Amblin-WB/WB, PG/V-MRN. A military pilot is shrunken in an experiment and put into a hypdermic needle which is then accidently jabbed into a goofy grocery boy who then must deal with a microscopic man in a spacecraft zooming through his veins, talking to him. Dennis Quaid, Martin Short, Meg Ryan, Kevin McCarthy. w. Jeffrey Boam, Chip Proser, d. Joe Dante. BSFX. Oscars: 1-1.

COMEDY: ACTION: Action Comedy; **SCI-FI:** Fantasy; Shrinking People; Mix-Ups; Experiments; Pilots-Military; Multiple Personalities; Body Parts; Good Premise Unfulfilled

(Fanstastic Voyage; D.O.A. [1988])

(Ed: A basic disappointment with good moments, mostly Short's)

The Innocent, 1995, 107m, ★★/$, NA. During the height of the cold war, a CIA operative goes to intercept messages at the East German border and winds up being used on both sides of the iron curtain. Campbell Scott, Anthony Hopkins, Isabella Rossellini, Hart Bochner, James Grant. w. Ian McEwan, d. John Schelsinger.

SUSPENSE: Spy Films; Spies; Cold War Era; Russians as Enemy; CIA Agents; Romance-Dangerous; Double Crossings

(The Spy Who Came in From the Cold; Torn Curtain; The Looking Glass War)

An Innocent Man, 1989, 113m, ★★/$$, Touchstone/Touchstone, PG-13/V. When a man is framed by corrupt police, he learns some tricks in prison to use against the cops later. Tom Selleck, F. Murray Abraham, Laila Robins, David Rasche, Todd Graff. w. Larry Brothers, d. Peter Yates.

DRAMA: MELODRAMA: Prison Drama; Turning the Tables; Revenge; Police Corruption; Ordinary People Turned Criminal; Framed?; Accused Unjustly

(I Am a Fugitive from a Chain Gang; In the Name of the Father; The Shawshank Redemption)

The Innocents, 1961, 99m, ★★★/$$, 20th/NA. An eccentric governess in a creepy ancient British home thinks the children she takes care of are possessed by spirits of servants who died there, but she may be imagining it all. Deborah Kerr, Megs Jenkins, Michael Redgrave, Pamela Franklin. w. William Archibald, Truman Capote, N-adap. Henry James (*The Turn of the Screw*), d. Jack Clayton.

SUSPENSE: HORROR: Character Studies; Fantasy; Ghosts; Babysitters; Possessions; Children; Houses-Creepy; Illusions/Hallucinations; British Films; Classic Literary Adaptations

REMAKE OF: The Turn of the Screw

(The Chalk Garden; The Canterbury Ghost)

Innocents in Paris, 1953, 102m, ★★★/$$, Romulus-UA/Nos. Several various British tourists have little adventures over a weekend in Paris. Alastair Sim, Margaret Rutherford, Jimmy Edwards, Claie Bloom, Laurence Harvey. w. Anatole deGrunwald, d. Gordon Parry.

COMEDY DRAMA: DRAMA: ADVEN-

TURE: ROMANCE: Ensemble Films; Vacations; Vacation Romance; Paris; British Films

(If This Is Tuesday, This Must Be Belgium)

Innocents of Paris, 1929, 69m, ★★½/$$$, Par/NA. A junk dealer in gay Paris saves a boy's life and a result meets a nice woman to sing with. Maurice Chevalier, Sylvia Beecher, Russell Simpson. w. Ethel Doherty, Ernest Vajda, P-adap. Charles Andrews (*Flea Market*), d. Richard Wallace.

MUSICAL: COMEDY: Musical Comedy; **ROMANCE:** Saving Someone; Ordinary People Stories; Paris; Female Screenwriters

(Ed: Chevalier's first film shown in America)

The Inn of the Sixth Happiness, 1958, 158m, ★★★/$$$, 20th/CBS-Fox. A British girl goes to remote China to become a missionary, the pinnacle of her career being the rescue of many children. Ingrid Bergman, Curt Jurgens, Robert Donat, Athene Seyler. w. Isobel Lennart, NF-adap. *The Small Woman*, the life of Gladys Aywald, Alan Burgess, d. Mark Robson (BDirector). Oscars: 1-0.

DRAMA: MELODRAMA: Tearjerkers; Biographies; True Stories; Saving Children; Rescue Drama; Missionaries; China; Happy Endings; Female Protagonists; Female Screenwriters

(The Bells of St. Mary's; Black Narcissus; The Good Earth; Keys to the Kingdom)

(Ed: Bergman isn't terribly convincing as a small British woman nor is the Welsh countryside for China, not overall, it's passable)

In Old Arizona, 1929, 95m, ★★★/$$$, 20th/NA. Cisco Kid does his thing in the wild west in one of the first talking westerns. Warner Baxter, Edmund Lowe, Dorothy Burgess. w. Tom Barry, SS-adap. O. Henry, d. Raoul Walsh, Irving Cummings (BDirector). BPicture, BAScr, BCin. Oscars: 4-0.

WESTERN: Comic Heroes; Legends; Good vs. Evil; Faded Hits

(The Cisco Kid; The Frisco Kid)

In Old Chicago, 1937, 115m, ★★★/$$$, 20th/CBS-Fox. Multiple stories, including a romance in the dance-hall district that all climax when Mrs. O'Leary's cow kicks over the lantern and the city burns. Tyrone Power, Alice Faye, Don Ameche, Alice Brady (**BSActress**), Andy Devine, Brian Donlevy, Sidney

Blackmer. w. Lamar Trotti, Sonya Levien, N-adap. Niven Busch (BOStory), *We the O'Learys*, d. Henry King. BPicture, BOScore. Oscars: 4-1.

DRAMA: MELODRAMA: ROMANCE: Multiple Stories; Ensemble Films; Fires; Disaster Movies; Dancers; Gambling; Chicago; 1870s; Female Screenwriters (San Francisco)

In Old Kentucky, 1935, 85m, ★★★/$$$, 20th/20th. Near Churchhill Downs, a family feud hinges on a horse race. Will Rogers, Bill Robinson, Dorothy Wilson. w. Sam Hellman, Gladys Lehmann, P-adap. Charles Dazey, d. George Marshall.

MELODRAMA: COMEDY DRAMA: Feuds; Southerns; Horse Racing; Female Screenwriters

In Our Time, 1944, 110m, ★★1/2/$$, WB/NA. An British girl marries Polish royalty in an attempt to infiltrate and defeat Nazis during the war. Ida Lupino, Paul Henreid, Nazimova, Nancy Coleman. w. Ellis St. Joseph, Howard Koch, d. Vincent Sherman.

DRAMA: Spy Films; Spies; Nazi Stories; World War II Stories; Marrying Up; England; Europeans-Eastern

In Person, 1935, 85m, ★★1/2/$$, RKO/Turner. A movie star tries to take a breather by heading to the country but can't get away from everything. Ginger Rogers, George Brent, Alan Mowbray, Grant Mitchell. w. Allan Scott, N-adap Samuel Hopkins Adams, d. William Seiter.

COMEDY: Fish out of Water Stories; Actresses; Hollywood Life; City vs. Country; Female Protagonists (Boy, Did I Get a Wrong Number; Never a Dull Moment {1950})

In Praise of Older Women, 1978, 108m, ★★1/2/$$, Embassy/Fox, R/ES-FN-MFN. A very sexy young Hungarian immigrant (Tom Berenger) manages to get many older women in bed, but that's about all that happens. Karen Black, Susan Strasberg, Helen Shaver, Alexandra Stewart. w. Paul Gottlieb, N-adap. Stephen Vizinczey, d. George Kaczender.

DRAMA: Erotic Drama; **ROMANCE:** Romantic Drama; Romance-Older Women/Younger Women; Character Studies; Sexy Men; Sexy Women; Independent Films (Loverboy; American Gigolo)

The Inquisitor (*Garde à Vu*), 1981, 90m, ★★1/2/$$, Ind/NA. A police detec-

tive suspects a prominent lawyer of murdering a child and corners him. Lino Ventura, Michel Serrault, Guy Marchand, Romy Schneider. w. Claude Miller, Jean Herman, Michel Audiard, N-adap. John Wainwright (*Brainwash*), d. Miller.

SUSPENSE: MYSTERY: MURDER: MURDER MYSTERY: Detective Stories; Detectives-Police; Lawyers; Murderers of Children; New Year's Eve; Coulda Been Great; Hidden Gems; French Films (M; The Atlanta Child Murders)

In the Realm of the Senses, 1979, 105m, ★★★/$$, Ind/Fox-Lorber, CVC, X,R/ES-FFN-MFN-V. A couple finds solace away from the oppression of pre-World War II Japan in bed with each other while terror reigns around them. Tatsuya Fuji, Eiko Matsuda. d. Nagia Oshima.

DRAMA: Social Drama; Erotic Drama; 1930s; Oppression; Japan; Japanese Films; Cult Films

SEQUEL: In the Realm of Passion

In Search of the Castaways, 1961, 100m, ★★★1/2/$$$$, Disney/Disney, G. When their father is lost, three kids get a professor with some tricks up his sleeve. Maurice Chevalier, Haley Mills, George Sanders, Wilfrid Hyde-White, Wilfrid Brumbell. w. Lowell S. Hawley, N-adap. Jules Verne, Captain Grant's Children, d. Robert Stevenson.

ADVENTURE: SCI FI: Fantasy; **CHILDREN'S: FAMILY:** Time Travel; Journeys; South America; Earthquakes; Floods Volcanoes; Disaster Movies; Cartoonlike Movies; Hidden Gems; Faded Hits; Blockbusters (Swiss Family Robinson; 20,000 Leagues Under the Sea)

In Search of Gregory, 1969, 90m, ★★1/2/$, U/NA, PG/S. A young woman goes to her father's wedding hoping to meet a man named Gregory and finds not only him but herself. Julie Christie, Michael Sarrazin, John Hurt, Adolfo Celi. w. Tonino Guerra, Lucile Laks, d. Peter Wood.

DRAMA: Art Films; Fathers & Daughters; Weddings; Allegorical Stories; Coulda Been Good; British Films; Female Protagonists; Female Screenwriters (Avanti!; Four Weddings and a Funeral; The Go-Between)

Inserts, 1976, 117m, ★★1/2/$, UA/Key-Fox, R/ES-P-FFN-MRN. The travails of a 1920s porn producer and his screwed-up

actors. Richard Dreyfuss, Veronica Cartwright, Jessica Harper, Bob Hoskins, Stephen Davies. w. d. John Byrum.

DRAMA: MELODRAMA: Character Studies; Silent Film Era; Hollywood Life; Moviemaking; Movies within Movies; Actors; Pornography World; 1920s; Writer-Directors (Move; Hardcore; The Big Party)

In a Shallow Grave, 1987, 92m, ★★1/2/$, AP-PBS-WB/WB, R/S-V. A disfigured World War II veteran returns to his Southern small town and tries to rekindle love with his disablement staring him in the mirror, while also dealing with bisexual tendencies. Michael Biehn, Petrick Dempsey, Maureen Mueller. N-adap. James Purdy, d. Kenneth Bowser.

DRAMA: MELODRAMA: Veterans; World War II-Post Era; Southerns; Bisexuality; Homoeroticism; Romance-Triangles; Disabled People; Looksism; Female Screenwriters; Independent Films (The Man Without a Face; Americana)

Inside Daisy Clover, 1965, 128m, ★★★/$$, WB/WB. A feisty tomboy on the docks cuts a record and Hollywood beckons, but will there be a happy ending? Natalie Wood, Robert Redford, Christopher Plummer, Ruth Gordon (BSActress), Roddy McDowell w. N-adap. Gavin Lambert, d. Robert Mulligan. BCArt, BCCostume. Oscars: 3-0.

DRAMA: COMEDY DRAMA: Black Comedy; Music Movies; Fantasy; Fame-Rise to; Hollywood Life; Actresses; Singers; Actors; Grandmothers-Fascinating; Suicidal Tendencies; Feisty Females; Tomboys; 1930s; Depression Era; Female Protagonists (Presenting Lily Mars; This Property Is Condemned; Funny Lady) (Ed: An oddity by any standard and quite good on many levels)

Inside Monkey Zetterland, 1992, 92m, ★★★/$, Ind/Prism. The title character goes home to his hippie dad, lesbian sister, neurotic mother, and a family all in dire need of mental help. He tries to rekindle a romance with a mean girlfriend but winds up alone and wondering about his own sanity. Steven Antin, Patricia Arquette, Martha Plimpton, Rupert Everett, Sofia Coppola, Sandra Bernhard, Tate Donovan, Katherine Helmond, Debi Mazar, Ricki Lake. w. Steven Antin, d. Jeffrey Levy.

COMEDY: COMEDY DRAMA: Family Comedy; Writers; Eccentric People; Hippies; Lesbians; Mean Women; Neurotic People; Art Films; Coulda Been Great; Curiosities; LA 90s Indies; Independent Films
(Floundering; Sleep with Me)

Inside Moves, 1980, 113m, ★★★/$$, ITC-AFD/Fox, R/S. A disabled young man who is often suicidal (John Savage) finds new friends in a bar where other disabled people meet. David Morse, Amy Wright, Diana Scarwid (BSActress), Harold Russell. w. Barry Levinson, Valerie Curtin, N-adap. Todd Walton, d. Richard Donner. Oscars: 1-0.
DRAMA: COMEDY DRAMA: TRAGEDY: Tragi-Comedy; Disabled People; Ensemble Films; Alcoholics; Suicidal Tendencies; Vietnam Veterans; Basketball; Friendships-Great; Forgotten Films; Hidden Gems
(The Deadliest Season; Tell Me That You Love Me, Junie Moon; Waterdance)

Inside Out, 1975, 97m, ★★½/$$, Ind/NA. A German, probably an ex-Nazi, gets Americans to help him in finding lost Nazi treasures. Telly Savalas, James Mason, Robert Culp, Aldo Ray, Gunter Meisner. w. Judd Bernard, Stephen Schneck, d. Peter Duffell.
ACTION: Treasure Hunts; Nazi Stories; Germans as Enemy; Emsemble Films; Ensembles-Male

Insignificance, 1985, 108m, ★★★/$, Island/WB, R/S. On a summer night in New York in 1953, Marilyn Monroe, Einstein, and friends get together in a hotel room. Theresa Russell, Gary Busey, Tony Curtis, Michael Emil. w. P-adap. Terry Johnson, d. Nicolas Roeg.
DRAMA: COMEDY DRAMA: Art Films; Avant-Garde; Allegorical Stories; Ensemble Films; Biographies-Fictional; Hotels; Stagelike Films; 1950s; Independent Films
(Four Rooms; IQ; Marilyn: The Untold Story)
(Ed: For Roeg fans, truly different and its success is entirely debatable)

In Society, 1944, 74m, ★★½/$$$, U/MCA-U. Abbott and Costello are plumbers who try to fix the pipes in a mansion but instead wreak havoc. w. John Grant, Hal Fimberg, Edmund Hartmann, d. Jean Yarbrough.
COMEDY: FARCE: Comedy of Errors; Snobs vs. Slobs; Abbott & Costello; House Havoc
(The Money Pit; Mr. Blandings Builds His Dream House; George Washington Slept Here)

The Inspector, see Lisa
An Inspector Calls, 1954, 79m, ★★★/$$, B-L/NA. After a girl dies in 1900s England, a prominent family is visited by an inspector who sets out to prove they all had a hand in her death. Alastair Sim, Jane Wenham, Arthur Young, Bryan Forbes. w. Desmond Davis, P-adap. J.B. Priestley, d. Guy Hamilton.
SUSPENSE: MYSTERY: MURDER: MURDER MYSTERY: Detective Stories; Detectives-Police; Death-Dealing with; Strangers in Town; Guilty Conscience; British Films; Hidden Gems
(Murder on the Orient Express)
(Ed: Revived very successfully in 1994 on Broadway with a more macabre edge)

Inspector Clouseau, 1968, 105m, ★★/$, UA/NA. The clumsy fool detective is hired to investigate a train robbery, but without Peter Sellers or Blake Edwards. Alan Arkin (as Clouseau), Delia Boccardo, Frank Finlay, Beryl Reid. w. Tom and Frank Waldman, d. Bud Yorkin.
COMEDY: Comedy of Errors; **FARCE:** Detective Stories; Fools-Bumbling; Bank Robberies; Trains; England
SEQUEL TO: The Pink Panther

The Inspector General (*Happy Times*), 1949, 101m, ★★★/$$, WB/MGM-UA. A traveling salesman in old Russia is mistaken for the Inspector who can cause many problems for the locals in a village. Danny Kaye, Walter Slezak, Barbara Bates, Elsa Lanchester, Alan Hale. w. Philip Rapp, Harry Kurnitz, P-adap. Nikolai Gogol, d. Henry Koster.
COMEDY: FARCE: Identities-Assumed; Identities-Mistaken; Innocent Bystanders; Small-Town Life; Russia; Classic Play Adaptations

Inspiration, 1930, 74m, ★★½/$$$, MGM/NA. An artists' model in Paris may ruin her lover's career with her reputation. Greta Garbo, Robert Montgomery, Lewis Stone, Marjorie Rambeau. w. Gene Markey, d. Clarence Brown.
MELODRAMA: ROMANCE: Romance-Doomed; Scandals; Models; Paris

In the Spirit, 1989, 94m, ★★/$, Academy/Academy, PG-13/S-P. When a couple into New Age mysticism moves to New York, a kooky fortune teller and a killer wind up in the cards. Elaine May, Marlo Thomas, Jeannie Berlin, Peter Falk, Melanie Griffith, Olympia Dukakis. w. Jeannie Berlin, Laurie Jones, d. Sandra Seacat.
COMEDY: Fugitives from a Killer; Fortune Tellers; Eccentric People; Female Protagonists; Female Screenwriters; Female Directors; Coulda Been Good; Independent Films

Interiors, 1978, 93m, ★★★★/$$$, UA/MGM-UA, PG/S. A depressed mother (Geraldine Page, BActress) of three daughters (Diane Keaton, Mary Beth Hurt, Kristin Griffith) is upset that her husband (E.G. Marshall) is considering remarrying. (Maureen Stapleton, BSActress). w. d. Woody Allen (BOScr). Oscars: 3-0.
DRAMA: TRAGEDY: Family Drama; Character Studies; Ensemble Films; Sisters; Bergmanesque; Family Conflicts; Reunions; Lonely People; Cold People; Mental Illness; Suicidal Tendencies; Alienation; Depression; Female Protagonists; Writer-Directors
(Another Woman; Autumn Sonata; Summer Wishes, Winter Dreams; September; Cries and Whispers; Diary of a Mad Housewife)

Interlude, 1957, 89m, ★★½/$$, U/NA. A girl visiting Germany romances a maestro but when he won't leave his mentally ill wife, the romance may be over. June Allyson, Rosanno Brazzi, Francoise Rosay, Jane Wyatt. w. Daniel Fuchs, Franklin Coen, d. Douglas Sirk.
Interlude, 1968, 113m, ★★½/$, Col/NA. Remake of above re-set in the mod London era. Oskar Werner, Barbara Ferris, John Cleese, Donald Sutherland, Virginia Maskell, Alan Webb. w. Lee Langley, Hugh Leonard, d. Kevin Billington.
ROMANCE: MELODRAMA: Tearjerkers; Romance-Triangles; Romance with Married Person; Romance-Doomed; Americans Abroad; Musicians; Mental Illness; Female Protagonists; Forgotten Films
REMAKE OF: When Tomorrow Comes, Intermezzo

Intermezzo, 1939, 69m, ★★★½/$$$$, Selznick-UA/Fox. A famous violinist has an affair with his Swedish accompanist, despite the presence of his wife. Ingrid Bergman, Leslie Howard, Edna Best,

Cecil Kellaway. w. George O'Neil, S-adap. Gosta Stevens, Gustav Molander, d. Gregory Ratoff. BScore. Oscars: 1-0.
ROMANCE: MELODRAMA: Romance-Triangles; Tearjerkers; Romance with Married Person; Romance-Doomed; Musicians; Female Protagonists
REMAKE OF: Swedish version, starring Bergman

Internal Affairs, 1990, 115m, ★★★/$$$, Par/Par, R/EV-EP-S-FN. A bad cop (Richard Gere) makes life hard for a pal working in internal affairs (Andy Garcia), who's on his tail while he's on the pal's wife. Laurie Metcalf, Nancy Travis, William Baldwin. w. Henry Bean, d. Mike Figgis.
DRAMA: Crime Drama; **SUSPENSE: MYSTERY: MURDER: MURDER MYSTERY:** Police Stories; Police-Corruption; Betrayals; Friends as Enemies; Evil Men; Lesbians; Female Law Officers; Coulda Been Great
(Ed: One of Gere's few very good performances, and a breakthrough for Garcia)

International House, 1933, 73m, ★★★/$$$, Par/MCA-U. A bunch of international travelers wind up quarantined in a Chinese hotel with a whacked-out doctor and other loonies. W.C. Fields, George Burns, Gracie Allen, Peggy Hopkins Joyce, Bela Lugosi, Rose Marie, Rudy Vallee, Sterling Holloway, Cab Calloway. w. Francis Martin, Walter deLeon, Lou Heifetz, Neil Brant, d. Edward Sutherland.
COMEDY: FARCE: Misunderstandings; Stranded; Epidemics; China; Hotels; International Casts; All-Star Casts

International Velvet, 1978, 125m, ★★1/2/$$, MGM/MGM-UA, G. A retelling as a sequel the *National Velvet* tale, where again an older woman trains a feisty girl to be an equestrian champ. Tatum O'Neal, Nanette Newman, Anthony Hopkins, Christopher Plummer. w. d. Bryan Forbes.
MELODRAMA: FAMILY: CHILDREN'S: Girlhood; Teachers and Students; Horses
SEQUEL TO: National Velvet

The Internecine Project, 1974, 89m, ★★1/2/$, 20th/Fox, PG. Several people are murder targets because they know too much about a Presidential candidate. James Coburn, Lee Grant, Harry Andrews, Keenan Wynn. w. Barry Levinson, Johnathan Lynn, N-adap. Mort Elkind, d. Ken Hughes.

SUSPENSE: MYSTERY: MURDER: MURDER MYSTERY: ACTION: Murders-One by One; Spies; Spy Films; Assassination Plots; Professors; Presidents; Politicians
(The Parallax View; Winter Kills; The Manchurian Candidate; In the Line of Fire)

The Interns, 1962, 130m, ★★1/2/$$$, Col/Col. The lives of several young doctors serving their time in residency. Cliff Robertson, Michael Callan, James MacArthur, Nick Adams, Suzy Parker, Buddy Ebsen, Telly Savalas. w. Walter Newman, David Swift, N-adap. Richard Frede, d. Swift.
DRAMA: MELODRAMA: Ensemble Films; Ensembles-Male; Doctors; Hospitals; Young Men; Young Women; Female Among Males
SEQUEL: The New Interns (1965), also TV SERIES The Interns
(Gross Anatomy; Vital Signs)

Interrogation, 1982/1990, 120m, ★★★/$, Ind/Kino Video. A singer in Poland is arrested and then tortured by the police, giving a harrowing portrayal of life behind the iron curtain. Krystyda Janda, Adam Ferency. w.d. Ryszard Bugajski.
DRAMA: TRAGEDY: Police Corruption; KGB Agents; Prison Drama; Accused Unjustly; Framed?; Torture; Singers; Polish Films; Europeans-Eastern; Foreign Films; Writer-Directors
(Ed: Release was delayed until 1990 because of ban in Poland)

Interrupted Melody, 1955, 106m, ★★★/$$$, MGM/MGM-UA. Australian opera singer Marjorie Lawrence's career is struck down at its peak by polio. Eleanor Parker (BActress), Glenn Ford, Roger Moore, Cecil Kellaway. w. William Ludwig, Sonya Levien (**BOScr**), d. Curtis Bernhardt. Oscars: 2-1.
DRAMA: MELODRAMA: Tearjerkers; Biographies; Disease Stories; Opera; Singers; Disabled People; Disabled but Nominated; Female Screenwriters; Female Protagonists
(An Affair to Remember; Passion Fish; The Other Side of the Mountain)

Intersection, 1994, 98m, ★★/$$, Par/Par, R/S. When an architect has a car crash and has to choose between his wife and his mistress. Richard Gere, Sharon Stone, Lolita Davidovich, Martin Landau, David Selby. w. Marshall

Brickman, David Rayfiel, d. Mark Rydell.
MELODRAMA: Marriage Drama; Car Wrecks; Romance-Choosing the Right Person; Romance-Triangles; Mistresses; Redemption; Starting Over; Foreign Film Remakes
REMAKE OF: Les Choses de la Vie (Regarding Henry; Loving)

Interview with the Vampire, 1994, 120m, ★★★/$$$$$, WB/WB, R/EV-P-S-B&G. Elegant New Orleans vampire Lestat seduces a plantation owner who's lost his wife and child and the two become vampire buddy/lovers, traveling about looking for more prey. Then a girl Lestat has recruited joins them as a surrogate daughter on their journeys to places such as Paris, who ultimately will grow to turn on and combat the invincible Lestat. Tom Cruise, Brad Pitt, Antonio Banderas, Stephen Rea, Christian Slater, Kirsten Dunst, Virginia McCollam, John McConnell, Mike Seelig. w. N-adap. Anne Rice, d. Neil Jordan. BOScore, BArt.
DRAMA: SUSPENSE: Erotic Drama; Erotic Thriller; Vampires; Costume Drama; Homoeroticism; Bisexuality; Gay Men; Sexy Men; Fathers-Surrogate; Children-Adopted; Girls; New Orleans; Paris; 1800s; Cult Films; Blockbusters; Female Screenwriters
(The Hunger; Dracula)

Intervista, 1987, 108m, ★★★/$$, Triumph/Col-Tri, PG. Federico Fellini takes the viewer through a journey of his past films and their stars. Federico Fellini, Marcello Mastroianni, Anita Ekberg. w. Fellini, Gianfranco Angelucci, d. Fellini.
Documentaries; Documentary Style; Autobiographical Stories; Narrated Films; Memories; Directors; Italian Films; Interviews
(Amarcord; 81/2)

The Intimate Stranger, see **Finger of Guilt**

Intolerance, 1916 (Silent), 115m, ★★★1/2/$$, D.W. Griffith/Kino. Four stories of great examples of intolerance from ancient times to the 1900s, all tied together with this common motif and theme. Mae Marsh, Lillian Gish, Constance Talmadge. w. d. D. W. Griffith.
DRAMA: TRAGEDY: Legends; Biblical Stories; Epics; Multiple Stories;

Interwoven Stories; Oppression; Ethics; Episodic Stories; Mothers Alone; Jesus Christ; Writer-Directors; Film History; Silent Films
(Birth of a Nation)

Into the Night, 1985m, 115m, ★★1/2/$, U/MCA-U, R/P-V-S. A man trying to get away from his wife picks up a mysterious woman with a number of people after her jewels. Jeff Goldblum, Michelle Pfeiffer, Richard Farnsworth, Irene Papas, Paul Mazursky, David Bowie. w. Ron Koslow, d. John Landis.
COMEDY: COMEDY DRAMA: Black Comedy; Chase Movies; Jewel Thieves; Fugitives from the Mob; Fugitives from the Law; Nerds & Babes; Road Movies; Outlaw Road Movies
(Something Wild; The Fabulous Baker Boys)

Into the Sun, 1991, 100m, ★★/VR, Trimark/Trimark, PG-13/V. A fighter pilot is assigned to teach an actor how to do the maneuvers. Anthony Michael Hall, Michael Pare, Terry Kiser, Michael St. Gerard. w. John Brancato, Michael Ferris, d. Fritz Keirsch.
ACTION: COMEDY: COMEDY DRAMA: Action Comedy; Pilots-Military; Actors; Men in Conflict; Good Premise Unfulfilled; Coulda Been Good
(The Hard Way [1991]; Iron Eagle SERIES)

Into the West, 1993, 97m, ★★★/$$, Touchstone/Disney, G. Two gypsy boys in Ireland are given a magical white horse, which is then wanted by any means by a horse trader, so they take it on the run to save it. Gabriel Byrne, Ellen Barkin, Colm Meaney, John Kavanaugh, Ciaran Fitzgerald, Riuadhri Conroy. w. Jim Sheridan, d. Mike Newell.
CHILDREN'S: FAMILY: Boys; Horses; Animal Stories; Fathers & Sons; Pet Stories; Saving Someone; Fugitives; Fantasy; Ireland; Magic Realism
(The Black Stallion; Black Beauty; The Miracle of the White Stallions)

The Intruder, 1961, 84m, ★★1/2/$, AIP/NA. A drifter comes to a small Southern town and soon racial troubles begin. William Shatner, Frank Maxwell, Jeanne Cooper. w. Charles Beaumont, d. Roger Corman.
DRAMA: Social Drama; Race Relations; Black vs. White; Strangers in Town; Drifters; Southerns; Young Men;

Independent Films
(The Long, Hot Summer)

Intruder in the Dust, 1949, 87m, ★★★★/$$, MGM/MGM-UA. When a black man is wrongly accused of a crime, a boy and an old lady join forces, compelled by witnessing certain things and circumstances, to find the real killer. Claude Jarman, Juano Hernandez, Elizabeth Patterson, Davis Brian, Porter Hall, Will Geer. w. Ben Maddow, N-adap. William Faulkner, d. Clarence Brown.
MYSTERY: SUSPENSE: MURDER: MURDER MYSTERY: DRAMA: Film Noir; Black Men; Race Relations; Black vs. White; Accused Unjustly; Wrong Man Thrillers; Southerns; Classic Literary Adaptations; Ahead of Its Time; Underrated; Forgotten Films; Hidden Gems; Child Protagonists
(A Time to Kill; To Kill a Mockingbird; As Summers Die)

Invaders from Mars, 1953, 82m, ★★1/2/$$, 20th/Media. Martians hypnotize earthlings to do their bidding. Helena Carter, Arthur Franz, Leif Erickson. w. Richard Blake, d. William Cameron Menzies.
SCI-FI: HORROR: Sci-Fi-; 1950s; Martians; Aliens-Outer Space, Evil; Hypnotism; 3-D Movies

Invaders from Mars, 1986, 100m, ★★/$, Cannon/Media, PG-13/V. In a rural town, a boy sees a spacecraft land in his backyard with evil creepies about to emerge. Karen Black, Hunter Carson, Timothy Bottoms, Louise Fletcher, Bud Cort. w. Dan O'Bannon, Don Jakoby, d. Tobe Hooper.
SCI-FI: HORROR: Martians; Aliens-Outer Space, Evil; Hypnotism; Rural Life; Boys
(The Martian Chronicles; Independence Day)

Invasion, 1966, 82m, ★★1/2/$, Allied/Movies Unltd. A small village in the English countryside is invaded by a spacecraft. Edward Judd, Valerie Gearon, Lyndon Brooke. w. Roger Marshall, d. Alan Bridges.
SCI-FI: HORROR: Aliens-Outer Space, Evil; Paranoia; England; Rural Life; Independent Films

Invasion of the Body Snatchers, 1956, 80m, ★★★★/$$$, Allied/Republic. A small town in California is slowly taken over by pods-beings that look like the people they subsume but who are really evil aliens. Where will it stop? Kevin

McCarthy, Dana Wynter, Larry Gates, King Donovan, Sam Peckinpah, Carolyn Jones, Virginia Christine. w. Daniel Mainwaring, Sam Peckinpah, N-adap. Jack Finney, d. Don Siegel.
SCI-FI: HORROR: Sci-Fi-; 1950s; Paranoia; Aliens-Outer Space, Evil; Parasites; Mental Illness; Murders-One by One; Fugitives; Small-Town Life; Conformism; Allegorical Stories; Cold War Era; Impostors; Cult Films; Sleeper Hits; Independent Films
REMADE: 1978 and 1993 (Body Snatchers)

Invasion of the Body Snatchers, 1978, 115m, ★★★/$$, UA/MGM-UA, R/V-FFN. This time the setting is San Francisco and the effects are better and the mood a bit darker and less effective. Donald Sutherland, Brooke Adams, Leonard Nimoy, Veronica Cartwright, Jeff Goldblum, Art Hindle, Kevin McCarthy, Don Siegel. w. W.D. Richter, S-adap. Daniel Mainwaring, d. Philip Kaufman.
SCI-FI: HORROR: Paranoia; Aliens-Outer Space, Evil; Parasites; Mental Illness; Impostors; Murders-One by One; Fugitives; Allegorical Stories; Conformism; San Francisco
REMAKE OF: 1956 version, REMAKE: 1993 (Body Snatchers)
(I Married a Monster from Outer Space)

Investigation of a Citizen Above Suspicion, 1971, 115m, ★★★/$$$, Par/Par, NA. A police detective murders his girlfriend and then has trouble with his conscience which eeks out in various ways. Gian Maria Volonte, Florinda Bolkan. w. Ugo Pirro, Elio Petri (BOScr), d. Petri. BFLFilm. Oscars: 2-1.
DRAMA: MURDER: SUSPENSE: MYSTERY: MURDER MYSTERY: Murder of Spouse/Lover; Crimes of Passion; Guilty Conscience; Character Studies; Murder-Debate to Reveal Killer; Suspecting Oneself; Police Stories; Detectives-Police; Police Corruption; Mistresses; Italian Films
(Crimes and Misdemeanors)

The Invisible Man, 1933, 71m, ★★★1/2/$$$, U/MCA-U. A scientist gets out of control with his invisibility formula, contemplating even murder. Claude Rains, Gloria Stuart, William Harrigan, Henry Travers, E.E. Clive. w. R.C. Sheriff, Philip Wylie, N-adap. H.G. Wells, d. James Whale.

The Invisible Man Returns, 1940, 81m, ★★★/$$$, U/MCA-U. A man accused of killing his brother uses invisibility to find the real killer. Vincent Price, Cedric Hardwicke, John Sutton, Cecil Kellaway, Alan Napier. w. Curt Siodmak, Lester Cole, Cedrick Belfrage, d. Joe May.

The Invisible Man's Revenge, 1944, 77m, ★★1/2/$$, A serial killer hides out with a doctor who has an invisibility formula. Jon Hall, Leon Errol, John Carradine, Gale Sondergaard. w. Bertram Millhauser, d. Ford Beebe.

SCI-FI: Fantasy; Invisibility; Ethics; MURDER: Revenge; Revenge on Doctors (The Invisible Woman; Memoirs of an Invisible Man)

The Invisible Ray, 1935, 79m, ★★1/2/$$, U/MCA-U. A mad scientist goes even madder with the power of his ray-who will stop him? Boris Karloff, Bela Lugosi, Frances Drake, Beulah Bondi, Frank Lawton. w. John Colton, Howard Higgin, Douglas Hodges, d. Lambert Hillyer.

SCI-FI: HORROR: Scientists; Scientists-Mad

The Invisible Woman, 1941, 72m, ★★1/2/$$, U/MCA-U. A goofy mad scientist turns a beautiful model invisible, and comedy results. John Barrymore, Virginia Bruce, Charles Ruggles, Oscar Homolka, Margaret Hamilton. w. Robert Lees, Fred Rinaldo, Gertrude Purcell, d. Edward Sutherland.

COMEDY: SCI-FI: Spoofs; Screwball Comedy; Comedy of Errors; Invisibility; Scientists-Mad; Models; Forgotten Films; Hidden Gems; Unintentionally Funny; Camp

Invitation, 1952, 81m, ★★1/2/$$, MGM/NA. An heiress believes she's dying and suddenly realizes things about her questionable hubby. Dorothy McGuire, Van Johnson, Ruth Roman, Louis Calhern. w. Paul Osborn, Jerome Weidman, d. Gottfried Reinhardt.

MELODRAMA: DRAMA: Tearjerkers; Heiresses; Death-Impending; Inheritances at Stake; Love-Questionable; Rich People

L'Invitation see L

Invitation to the Dance, 1954, 92m, ★★★/$$, MGM/MGM-UA. Three stories interwoven with ballet and mime-a pure musical, but not very successful in its day. Gene Kelly. w. d. Gene Kelly.

MUSICALS: Dance Movies; Ballet; Dancers; Fantasy; Art Films; Circus Life; Flops-Major; Forgotten Films; Writer-Directors (An American in Paris; Small Town Girl)

Invitation to Happiness, 1939, 95m, ★★1/2/$$, Par/NA. A socialite marries a working-class boxer and spars in the marital arena. Irene Dunne, Fred MacMurray, Charles Ruggles, Billy Cook. w. Claude Binyon, d. Wesley Ruggles.

COMEDY: ROMANCE: Romantic Comedy; Screwball Comedy; Marriage Comedy; Romance-Opposites Attract; Romance-Class Conflicts; Boxers; Rich vs. Poor; Female Protagonists; Forgotten Films (The Main Event; Never a Dull Moment [1950]; Overboard)

Invitation to the Wedding, 1985, 90m, ★★/$, Vestron/Vestron. A rich girl's wedding goes awry when the bishop marries her to the wrong man. Ralph Richardson, John Gielgud, Elizabeth Shepperd, Paul Nicholas. w. William Fairchild, d. Joseph Brooks.

COMEDY: SATIRE: Weddings; Comedy of Errors; Misunderstandings; Mix-Ups; Rich People; Preachers; Independent Films

In a Year with 13 Moons, 1978, 124m, ★★1/2/$, Ind/Karl-Lorimar. A man has a sex change operation in Germany and deals with the repercussions. Volker Spengler, Ingrid Caven. w. d. Rainer Werner Fassbinder.

DRAMA: Character Studies; Transsexuals; Art Films; German Films; Alternative Lifestyles; Writer-Directors (Second Serve; Fox and His Friends)

I Ought to Be in Pictures, 1982, 107m, ★★1/2/$$, 20th/CBS-Fox, PG. A would-be spunky actress heads for her washed-up writer father's place in California, where she interrupts his life but also brightens it up. Dinah Manoff, Walter Matthau, Ann-Margret, Lance Guest. w. P-adap. Neil Simon, d. Herbert Ross.

COMEDY DRAMA: COMEDY: MELODRAMA: Fathers & Daughters; Writers; Actresses; Feisty Females; Free Spirits; Romance-Middle Aged; Children-Long Lost; Hollywood Life; Narrated Films; Female Protagonists (Max Dugan Returns; Only When I Laugh) (Ed: A Tony Award–winning hit on Broadway, here it falls flat)

I Passed for White, 1960, 92m, ★★1/2/$, Allied/NA. A light-skinned young black woman heads for New York hoping to "pass for white," but soon finds it changes nothing. Sonya Wilde, James Franciscus, Pat Michon. w. d. Fred Wilcox.

DRAMA: Social Drama; Race Relations; Black as White; Black vs. White; Black Casts; Black Women; Romance-Interracial; Female Protagonists; Ahead of Its Time; Time Capsules; Hidden Gems; Writer-Directors; Independent Films (Showboat; Pinky; Imitation of Life; Black Like Me; Soul Man) (Ed: Though it's dated and the production values are fairly lacking, it's an interesting experiment-and title)

The Ipcress File, 1965, 109m, ★★★/$$$, U/MCA-U, V-S. A secret agent tracks down a missing scientist and uncovers a conspiracy involving his own people. Michael Caine, Nigel Green, Sue Lloyd. w. Bill Canaway, James Doran, N-adap. Len Deighton, d. Sidney J. Furie.

MYSTERY: SUSPENSE: Spy Films; Spies; Secret Agents; Conspiracy; Scientists; Kidnappings; Brainwashing; British Films

SEQUELS: Funeral in Berlin, Billion Dollar Brain. (Get Carter; The Spy Who Came in from the Cold)

I.Q., 1994, 96m, ★★★/$$$, Par/Par, PG. The niece of Albert Einstein is more of a scientist than a romantic young woman. But when an ordinary but imaginative mechanic falls in love with her and wants to show her what true love and chemistry is all about, it's up to her genius uncle to forget physics and tackle the mysteries of romantic chemistry and get the two together despite her boring fiance and her supposed disinterest. Tim Robbins, Meg Ryan, Walter Matthau, Lou Jacobi, Gene Saks, Joseph Maher, Stephen Fry, Tony Shalhoub, Frank Whaley, Charles Durning, Alice Playten, Helen Hanft. w. Andy Breckman, Michael Leeson, d. Fred Schepisi.

COMEDY: ROMANCE: Romantic Comedy; Matchmakers; Geniuses; Scientists; Extroverted vs. Introverted; Smart vs. Dumb; Romance-Class Conflicts; Romance-Reluctant; 1950s; Old-Fashioned Recent Films (When Harry Met Sally; French Kiss)

I Remember Mama, 1948, 134m, ★★★1/2/$$$$, RKO/Turner. A woman writer recalls her fascinating, hard-working mother and family growing up in turn-of-the-century San Francisco as Norwegian immigrants. Irene Dunne (BActress), Barbara Bel Geddes (BSActress), Oscar Homolka (BSActor), Edgar Bergen, Philip Dorn, Ellen Corby (BSActress), Florence Bates, Barbara O'Neil, Rudy Vallee. w. DeWitt Bodeen, P-adap. John Van Durten, N-adap. Kathryn Forbes, *Mama's Bank Account*, d. George Stevens. BB&WCin. Oscars: 5-0.
MELODRAMA: COMEDY DRAMA: FAMILY: Family Stories; Memories; Flashbacks; Mothers-Struggling; Writers; Sisters; Female Protagonists; Narrated Films; Immigrants; San Francisco; Scandinavians
(A Tree Grows in Brooklyn; The Emigrants)
Irene, 1940, 101m, ★★1/2/$$, RKO/Turner. A lowly shopgirl begins making her way into high society by singing and dancing. Anna Neagle, Ray Milland, Roland Young, May Robson, Billie Burke, Arthur Treacher. w. Alice Duer Miller, P-adap. James H. Montgomery, d. Herbert Wilcox.
MUSICALS: ROMANCE: Social Climbing; Class Conflicts; Ordinary People Stories; Working Class; Rich People; New York Life
REMAKE OF: 1926 silent version
Irish Eyes Are Smiling, 1944, 90m, ★★1/2/$$$, 20th/NA. Songwriter Ernest Ball's life is detailed with all its Ire. Dick Haymes, June Haver, Monty Wooley, Anthony Quinn. w. Earl Baldwin, John Tucker Battle, d. Gregory Ratoff.
MUSICALS: Biographies; Songwriters; Irish People; Ireland; 1890s; Music Composers
The Irish in Us, 1935, 84m, ★★1/2/$$, WB/NA. Three brothers in the Irish ghetto of New York live life with gusto. James Cagney, Pat O'Brien, Olivia de Havilland, Mary Gordon, Frank McHugh. w. Earl Baldwin, d. Lloyd Bacon.
COMEDY DRAMA: Brothers; Irish People; New York Life; Young Men; Ensemble Films; Ensembles-Male
(True Confessions; Manhattan Melodrama)
Irma La Douce, 1963, 146m, ★★★/$$$$, UA/MGM-UA, S. An ordinary guy who happens to be a vice cop (Jack

Lemmon) falls for a prostitute (Shirley MacLaine, BActress) who has a very jealous boyfriend who may kill him after he's lost his job over her. w. Billy Wilder, IAL Diamond, P-adap. d. Wilder. **BMScore,** BCCin. Oscars: 3-1.
ROMANCE: MUSICAL: COMEDY DRAMA: Musical Drama; Romance with Prostitute; Prostitute-Low Class; Romance-Reluctant; Romance-Triangles; Nerds; Nerds & Babes; Feisty Females; Paris; Stagelike Films
(Sweet Charity; The Apartment)
Iron Eagle, 1986, 119m, ★★/$$$, Tri/Col-Tri, PG-13/V-P. A young man learns to fly a fighter plane iorder to rescue his father in the Middle East. Jason Gedrick, Louis Gossett Jr., David Suchet. w. Kevin Elders, Sidney Furie, d. Furie.
ACTION: Military Movies; Pilots-Military; Rescue Drama; Young Men; Fathers & Sons; Teachers and Students; Middle East
Iron Eagle II, 1988, 100m, ★★/$$, Carolco/Live, PG-13/V. American and Russian fighter pilots work together in destroying a missile factory in the Middle East. Mark Humphrey, Louis Gossett Jr., Stuart Margolin. w. Kevin Elders, Sidney J. Furie, d. Furie.
ACTION: Military Movies; Pilots-Military; Russians; Americans & Russians; Middle East; Bombs-Atomic
(Aces: Iron Eagle III; Into the Sun)
The Iron Man, 1931, 73m, ★★★/$$$, U/NA. A rich girl prods her boxing husband on to greatness, so she can spend his money. Jean Harlow, Lew Ayres, Robert Armstrong. w. Francis Faragoh, N-adap. W.R. Burnett, d. Tod Browning.
DRAMA: MELODRAMA: Sports Movies; Boxing; Women Behind Men; Fame-Rise to
(Bombshell; Red Dust; Harriet Craig)
The Iron Mask (partially silent), 1929, 97m, ★★★/$$$, UA/Nos. The classic tale of the kidnapping of the prince of France, involving the Three Musketeers. Douglas Fairbanks, Nigel deBurlier, Belle Bennett. w. Elton Thomas (Fairbanks), N-adap. Alexandre Dumas (*Ten Years After*), d. Allan Dwan.
ACTION: Kidnappings; Swashbucklers; Princes; Impostors
REMAKE OF: The Man in the Iron Mask, The Three Musketeers
Iron Maze, 1991, 102m, ★★/$, Academy/Academy, R/EV-S. A Japanese

businessman is murdered in an American mining town, which leads to a violent conspiracy unravelling. Jeff Fahey, Bridget Fonda, Hiroshi Murakami. w. Tim Metcalfe, S-adap. *Rashomon*, SS-adap. Ryunosuke Akutagawa (*In a Grove*), d. Horoaki Yoshida.
ACTION: SUSPENSE: MURDER: MYSTERY: MURDER MYSTERY: Conspiracy; Mining Towns; Japanese People; Corporation as Enemy; Coulda Been Good; Foreign Film Remakes; Independent Films
REMAKE OF: Rashomon
(Rising Sun; Black Rain; The Yakuza)
The Iron Mistress, 1952, 107m, ★★1/2/$$, WB/NA. The trail of old-west Arkansas outlaw Jim Bowie as he travels into Texas with his infamous Bowie knife. Alan Ladd, Virginia Mayo, Douglas Dick, Joseph Calleia. w. James R. Webb, N-adap. Paul Wellman, d. Gordon Douglas.
WESTERN: Legends; Old West; Outlaw Road Movies; Journies; Arkansas; Texas
(The Last Command)
The Iron Petticoat, 1956, 96m, ★★★/$$, Par/NA. A Russian woman pilot is shown the ways of the west by an air force pilot, and perhaps even romance. Katharine Hepburn, Bob Hope, James Justice, Robert Helpman. w. Ben Hecht, Ralph Thomas.
COMEDY: COMEDY DRAMA: ROMANCE: Romantic Comedy; Russians; Russians & Americans; Pilots-Military; Forgotten Films; Underrated; Hidden Gems
(Ninotchka; Christopher Strong)
Ironweed, 1987, 143m, ★★★1/2/$$, Taft-Tri/HBO, R/S-P. A man who once dropped his baby years ago (Jack Nicholson, BActor) has become a homeless man in the depths of the Depression with only a few comrades, including a washed-up bar singer (Meryl Streep, BActress). w. N-adap. William Kennedy, d. Hector Babenco. Oscars: 2-0.
DRAMA: MELODRAMA: TRAGEDY: Homeless People; Depression Era; Depression; Past-Haunted by the; Singers; Ordinary People Stories; Flashbacks; Nervous Breakdowns
(Central Park; Scarecrow; Stone Pillow; The Purple Rose of Cairo)
Irreconcilable Differences, 1984, 113m, ★★★/$$, WB/WB, PG. A young girl (Drew Barrymore) decides to divorce her feuding Hollywood parents (Ryan

O'Neal, Shelley Long). w. Charles Shyer, Nancy Myer, d. Shyer.

COMEDY: COMEDY DRAMA: Divorce; Marriage on the Rocks; Marriage Drama; Child Protagonists; Custody Battles; Girlhood; Hollywood Life; Episodic Stories; Flashbacks; Writers Directors; Female Screenwriters

(Bright Eyes; Kramer vs. Kramer)

Isadora (*The Many Loves of Isadora*), 1968, 138m, ★★★1/2/$$, U/MCA-U, R/S. Biopic of the free spirited dancer Isadora Duncan as she mingles with many people until an untimely, sudden death. Vanessa Redgrave (BActress), Jason Robards, James Fox, Bessie Love. w. Melvyn Bragg, Clive Exton, d. Karel Reisz. Oscars: 1-0.

DRAMA: Biographies; **TRAGEDY:** Dancers; Theater Life; Alternative Lifestyles; Eccentric People; Free Spirits; 1920s; Violence-Sudden

(Nijinsky; The Moderns; Morgan!; Women in Love)

I Saw What You Did, 1965, 82m, ★★1/2/$$, Castle-U/MCA-U. A man murders a woman and thinks two teenage girls who are prank calling him know something about the murder (but they don't), and then sets out to find them-with the help of Joan Crawford. John Ireland, Leif Erickson. w. William McGivern, N-adap. Ursula Curtiss, d. William Castle.

SUSPENSE: HORROR: MURDER: Witness to Murder; Unbelieved; Telephone Terror; Teenagers; Girls; Good Premise Unfulfilled; Coulda Been Great

TV REMAKE: 1991

(Woman Screaming; Rear Window)

(Ed: A teenybopper thriller but not too bad)

I See a Dark Stranger, see **The Adventuress**

I Sent a Letter to My Love, 1981, 102m, ★★★/$$, Ind/NA. Two lonely elderly people take up pen pals, but neither of them realizes who they're really writing to. Simone Signoret, Jean Rochefort, Delphine Seyrig. w. Moshe Mizrahi, Gerard Brach, N-adap. Bernice Rubens, d. Mizrahi.

DRAMA: MELODRAMA: ROMANCE: Romantic Drama; Lonely People; Romance-Middle-Aged; Epistolaries; Misunderstandings; Personal Ads; Brothers & Sisters; Incest; French Films

(The Shop Around the Corner; The Miracle [1990])

Ishtar, 1987, 107m, ★★/$$, Col/Col-Tri, PG. Two vaudeville-types (Dustin Hoffman, Warren Beatty) head to Morocco for some reason and run into blind camels and Isabelle Adjani. w. d. Elaine May.

COMEDY: Spoofs; Actors; Comedians; Vaudeville; Buddy Films; Americans Abroad; Morocco; Unintentionally Funny; Flops-Major; Female Directors; Female Screenwriters; Writer-Directors

(Ed: Not the worst movie ever made, as some have said, but close, with surely one of the worst endings)

The Island, 1961, 92m, ★★★/$, Ind/Voyager. A Japanese family living on an island is interrupted by illness, but still not a word is spoken among them. Nobuko Otowa. w. d. Kaneto Shindo.

DRAMA: Family Stories; Death-Dealing with; Islands; Japanese Films; Writer-Directors

The Island, 1980, 114m, ★★/$$$, U/MCA-U, R/V-S-B&G. A man and his son are stranded on a Caribbean island as he searches out the mystery of several missing boats. But they soon become victims of pirates who still roam the seas, raping, pillaging, and murdering. Michael Caine, David Warner, Angela Punch McGregor, Frank Middlemass, Dudley Sutton, Clyde Jeavons. w. N-adap. Peter Benchley, d. Michael Ritchie.

ACTION: MURDER: MYSTERY: MURDER MYSTERY: Pirates; Time Travel; Islands; Missing Persons; Kidnappings; Stranded on an Island; Journalists; Fathers & Sons; Evil Men; Caribbean

(The Fog; Cutthroat Island)

The Island at the Top of the World, 1965/1974, 93m, ★★★/$$$, Disney/ Disney, G. When his son is lost, a wealthy man charters a zeppelin to take him to a mystical oasis in the arctic where the son is supposed to be. David Hartman, Donald Sinden, Jacques Martin, Mako. w. John Whedon, N-adap. Ian Cameron (*The Lost Ones*), d. Robert Stevenson. BArt. Oscars: 1-0.

ADVENTURE: Adventure at Sea; Journeys; Arctic; Missing Persons; Blimps; Fathers & Sons; Searches; Vikings; Whales

(The Land That Time Forgot; In Search of the Castaways; Around the World in 80 Days)

(Ed: Shelved for years, it was nominated for an Oscar in 1974)

Island in the Sun, 1957, 119m, ★★★/$$, 20th/Fox. Various relationships on a Caribbean island come to blows over racial and political situations that develop. James Mason, Joan Fontaine, John Williams, Harry Belafonte, Dorothy Dandridge, Joan Collins, Stephen Boyd, Diana Wynyard, Michael Rennie. w. Alfred Hayes, N-adap. Alec Waugh, d. Robert Rossen.

DRAMA: MELODRAMA: Ensemble Films; Betrayals; Political Unrest; Black vs. White; Black Men; Black Women; Islands; Caribbean; Forgotten Films

(Burn!; The Ugly American; The Comedians)

The Island of Dr. Moreau, 1977, 98m, ★★1/2/$$, AIP/WB. Burt Lancaster, Michael York, Nigel Davenport, Barbara Carrera, Richard Basehart. w. John Herman Shaner, Al Ramrus, SS-adap. H.G. Wells, d. Don Taylor.

REMAKE OF: The Island of Lost Souls, Mysterious Island, Ebb Tide

Island of Lost Souls, 1932, 74m, ★★★/$$, Par/MCA-U. Shipwreck victims are stranded on an island with giant mutant animals and an insane doctor who plans to experiment on his new guests next. Charles Laughton, Bela Lugosi, Richard Arlen, Kathleen Burke.

REMAKE: The Island of Dr. Moreau

SCI-FI: HORROR: Monsters-Mutant; Animal Monsters; Animals into Humans; Humans into Animals; Scientists-Mad; Stranded on an Island; Shipwrecks; Islands; South Pacific

(Mysterious Island; Ebb Tide)

Island of Love, 1963, 101m, ★★/$, WB/NA. A mobster wants to make his girl into a movie star, but when the movie turns out to be terrible, he chases the producers into hiding in Greece. Tony Randall, Robert Preston, Walter Matthau, Giorgia Moll. w. David Schwartz, d. Morton daCosta.

COMEDY: Mob Stories; Mob Comedy; Chase Movies; Mob Girls; Bimbos; Moviemaking; Con Artists; Hiding Out; Islands; Greece; Good Premise Unfulfilled; Forgotten Films

(Mistress; The Producers)

Islands in the Stream, 1977, 105m, ★★★/$$, Par/Par, PG. A gruff artist in the Caribbean has his three young sons down for the summer and tries to keep them out of trouble and himself on the wagon. George C. Scott, David Hemmings,

Gilbert Roland, Susan Tyrrell, Hart Bochner, Claire Bloom. w. Denne Bart Petitclerc, N-adap. Ernest Hemingway, d. Franklin Schaffner. BCin. Oscars: 1-0.

DRAMA: MELODRAMA: Family Drama; Autobiographical Stories; Fathers & Sons; Brothers; Fathers-Troublesome; Macho Men; Reunions; Back to Nature; Artists; Writers; Fishermen; Sharks; Caribbean

Isle of the Dead, 1945, 72m, ★★★/$$, Lewton-RKO/Turner. People hide on an island from an epidemic around the 1900s, but one of the people seeking refuge may be a vampire. Ardel Wray, Josef Mischel, d. Mark Robson.

HORROR: MURDER: Murders-One by One; Art Films; Vampires; Hiding Out; Stranded on an Island; Epidemics; Islands; Forgotten Films

(Nosferatu; White Zombie; Ebb Tide)

(Ed: A unique film, with less exploitative qualities than a mood and lighting reminiscent of *Nosferatu*)

Isn't It Romantic?, 1948, 87m, ★★½/$$, Par/NA. A military man's daughters in post–Civil War Indiana find love, and maybe he will, too. Veronica Lake, Rand Culver, Mona Freeman, Mary Hatcher, Billy deWolfe, Patric Knowles, Pearl Bailey. w. Theodore Strauss, Josef Mischel, Richard Breen, d. Norman Z. McLeod.

MUSICAL; MUSICAL ROMANCE: Multiple Stories; Ensemble Films; Ensembles-Female; Female Protagonists; Midwestern Life; Civil War Era; Sisters

(Seven Brides for Seven Brothers)

(Ed: Veronica Lake in a musical is a rarity)

Is Paris Burning? (B&W), 1965, 165m, ★★★/$$, Par/Par. An ensemble of interwoven stories centering around the liberation of Paris toward the end of World War II. Leslie Caron, Orson Welles, Charles Boyer, Yves Montand, Alain Delon, Gert Frobe, Jean-Pierre Cassell, Jean-Paul Belmondo, Kirk Douglas, Glenn Ford, Anthony Perkins, Simone Signoret, Robert Stack, George Chakiris. w. Francis Ford Coppola, Gore Vidal, NF-adap. Larry Collins & Dominque Lapeierre, d. Rene Clement. BB&WCin. Oscars: 1-0.

DRAMA: War Stories; World War II Stories; Ensemble Films; Multiple Stories; Interwoven Stories; Paris; International Casts; All-Star Casts; Female Screenwriters

I Stand Condemned (*Moscow Nights*), 1936, 75m, ★★½/$$, London Films/Nos. A condemned man is saved when his girlfriend seduces the executioner. Laurence Olivier, Penelope Dudley Ward, Harry Bauer, Robert Cochran. w. Erich Seipmann, N-adap. Pierre Benoit, d. Anthony Asquith.

MELODRAMA: MURDER: ROMANCE: Prison Drama; Executions; Saving Someone; Death-Impending

Is There Sex After Death?, 1971, 97m, ★★★/$, Ind/NA. A satire on the hip New York scene during the sexual revolution and porn industry's beginnings in the early 70s. Buck Henry, Holly Woodlawn, Alan Abel. d. Jeanne Abel, Alan Abel.

COMEDY: Documentary Style; **SATIRE:** Sexual Revolution; Psychedelic Era; Promiscuity; Pornography World; Cult Films; Female Directors; Time Capsules; Independent Films

(Hi, Mom!; Move; Andy Warhol's Flesh)

I Stole a Million, 1939, 89m, ★★½/$, U/NA. A cabbie screwed over by a loan company decides to take matters into his own hands and become a crook. George Raft, Claire Trevor, Dick Foran. w. Nathanael West, SS-adap. Lester Cole, d. Frank West.

DRAMA: Crime Drama; Making a Living; Thieves; Ordinary People Turned Criminal; Taxi Drivers; Turning the Tables; Mortgage Drama; Good Premise Unfulfilled; Coulda Been Great

It, 1927, 72m, ★★★/$$$$, Par/Connoisseur. A pretty shop girl takes the advice of a book on how to marry her boss. Clara Bow, Antonio Merno, Gary Cooper, Elinor Glyn. w. Hope Loring, Louis Lighton, NF-adap. Elinor Glyn, d. Clarence Badger.

COMEDY: ROMANCE: Romantic Comedy; Marrying Up; Marrying the Boss; Female Protagonists

It, 1990, 193m, ★★½/$$$$, ABC/WB. Children, now grown, relive a series of bizarre child murders and must admit what happened to them to stop what's happening now. John Ritter, Tim Reid, Richard Thomas, Annette O'Toole, Olivia Hussey, Tim Curry. w. N-adap. Stephen King, d. Tommy Lee Wallace.

HORROR: Murders of Children; Child Molestations; Secrets-Keeping; Ensemble Films; Small-Town Life; **MURDER:** Serial Killers; TV Movies; Stephen King

(Dolores Claiborne; The Atlanta Child Murders)

It Ain't Hay, 1943, 79m, ★★½/$$$, U/MCA-U. Two cabbies try to replace a prize racehorse after it dies at their hands. Bud Abbott, Lou Costello, Cecil Kellaway. w. Allen Boretz, John Grant, SS-adap. Damon Runyan, Princess O'Hara, d. Erie Kenton.

COMEDY: Comedy of Errors; Horses; Deaths-Accidental; Situation Comedy; Fools-Bumbling; Abbott & Costello; Good Premise Unfulfilled

(Abbott and Costello SERIES)

I Take This Woman, 1931, 74m, ★★½/$$, Par/NA. A cowboy lassoes a rich girl who comes to live on the range, but for how long? Gary Cooper, Carole Lombard. w. Vincent Lawrence, N-adap. Mary Rinehart, Lost Ecstasy, d. Marion Gering.

ROMANCE: COMEDY DRAMA: Marriage Comedy; Romance-Opposites Attract; Fish out of Water Stories; City vs. Country; Cowboys; Rich People; Rich vs. Poor; Female Directors

(The Cowboy and the Lady; Overboard)

I Take This Woman, 1939, 97m, ★★/$$, MGM/NA. A rich doctor marries a sexy woman from Europe but then tries to get out of it. Spencer Tracy, Hedy Lamarr, Laraine Day, Jack Carson, Marjorie Main. w. James McGuinness, Charles MacArthur, d. W. S. Van Dyke.

COMEDY DRAMA: MELODRAMA: ROMANCE: Marriage Comedy; Romance-Opposites Attract; Situation Comedy; Sexy Women

(How to Murder Your Wife)

(Ed: A flop all the way around for stars at their peaks, apparently because Louis B. Mayer decided to get involved personally, and it was reshot so much it has become known as *I Re-Take This Woman*)

The Italian Job, 1969, 100m, ★★★/$$$, Par/Par, PG/V. A team of ex-convicts pulls a heist Italy under connected to a prison warden in England, but the question is can the keep the goods? Michael Caine, Noel Coward, Benny Hill, Rosanno Brazzi. w. Troy Kennedy Martin, d. Peter Collinson.

COMEDY: ACTION: Action Comedy; Capers; Bank Robberies; Heist Stories; Chase Movies; Car Chases; Comedy of Errors; International Casts; Italy; British Films

(The Hot Rock; The Lavender Hill Mob; Deadfall; Silver Bears)

An Italian Straw Hat, 1927, 74m, ★★★/$$, Ind/Voyager. When a young man in a hurry to get to a wedding's horse eats a lady's hat, her boyfriend makes him replace it before letting him go. Albert Prejean. w. d. Rene Clair.
COMEDY: COMEDY DRAMA: Situation Comedy; Comedy of Errors; Accidents; Weddings; Race Against Time; Writer-Directors

It All Came True, 1940, 97m, ★★★/$$, WB/NA. A mobster hides out in a run-down boardinghouse and winds up helping everyone there. Humphrey Bogart, Ann Sheridan, Jeffrey Lynn, Zasu Pitts, Una O'Connor. w. Michael Fessier, Lawrence Kimble, SS-adap. Louis Bromfield (*Better Than Life*), d. Lewis Seiler.
COMEDY DRAMA: Hiding Out; Mob Stories; Boardinghouses; Heroes-Unlikely; Forgotten Films; Hidden Gems
(Key Largo; The Lodger; The Man Upstairs)

It Always Rains on Sunday, 1947, 92m, ★★★/$$, Ealing/NA. An escaped convict hides out in his girlfriend's house-only now she's married. Googie Withers, John McCallum, Jack Warner, Susan Shaw. w. Angus MacPhail, Robert Hamer, Henry Cornelius, N-adap. Arthur LaBern, d. Robert Hamer.
COMEDY DRAMA: MELODRAMA: Escaped Convicts; Prison Escapes; Hiding Out; Mistresses; British Films
(Seems Like Old Times; Talk of the Town)

It Came From Outer Space, 1953, 80m, ★★★/$$$, U/MCA-U. A spaceship lands in the desert and a young astronomer tracks it down-only the aliens on it have taken human form by then. Richard Carlson, Barbara Rush, Charles Drake, w. Harry Essex, SS-adap. Ray Bradbury, d. Jack Arnold.
SCI-FI: HORROR: Sci-Fi-; 1950s; Aliens-Outer Space, Evil; Parasites; Body Switching; Desert Settings; 3-D Movies
(The Day the Earth Stood Still; Invaders from Mars)

It Could Happen to You, 1994, 96m, ★★★/$$, Tri-Star/Col-Tri, PG. When a cop doesn't have enough money for his diner bill, he gives the waitress half of his lottery ticket, which, of course, turns out to be a winner and leads to his greedy wife's rebelling when the winnings are split and a romance develops with the

waitress. Nicolas Cage, Bridget Fonda, Rosie Perez, Red Buttons, Isaac Hayes, Stanley Tucci. w. Jane Anderson, Andrew Bergman, d. Bergman.
COMEDY: COMEDY DRAMA: ROMANCE: Romantic Comedy; Lotteries; Rags to Riches; Riches to Rags; Romance-Triangles; Incredible but Mostly True; Rise and Fall Stories; Greed; Ethics; Waitresses; Police Comedy; Old-Fashioned Recent Films; Coulda Been Great; True Stories; Female Screenwriters

It Grows on Trees, 1952, 84m, ★★★/$$, U/NA. A beleaguered mother discovers her lilac tree is sprouting dollar bills. Irene Dunne, Dean Jagger, Joan Evans, Richard Crenna. w. Leonard Praskins, Barney Slater, d. Arthur Lubin.
COMEDY: Fantasy; **CHILDREN'S: FAMILY:** Mothers-Struggling; Hidden Gems; Underrated; What If . . . Stories; Female Protagonists

It Had to Be You, 1947, 98m, ★★½/$$, Col/NA. A woman has three men after her but can't make up her mind which she wants, so she takes off on a lark and encounters an Indian who wants her, too. Ginger Rogers, Cornel Wilde, Percy Waram, Spring Byington, Thurston Hall. w. Norman Panama, Melvin Frank, d. Don Hartman, Rudolph Mate.
COMEDY: ROMANCE: Romantic Comedy; Romance-Triangles; Marriage-Impending; Engagements-Breaking; Female Protagonists

I Thank a Fool, 1962, 100m, ★★/$, MGMNA. A murderess comes to live with her prosecutor's family, but old habits die hard. Susan Hayward, Peter Finch, Diane Cilento, Cyril Cusack, Kieron Moore. w. Karl Tunberg, N-adap. Audrey Lindop, Robert Stevens.
DRAMA: SUSPENSE: MURDER: Murderers-Female; Roommates from Hell; Past-Haunted by the; Lawyers; Starting Over; Unintentionally Funny; Camp
(Ada; Backstreet)

It Happened Here, 1963, 99m, ★★★/$$, UA/NA. A what-if story about the Germans invading England during World War II and taking over a village. Sebastian Shaw, Pauline Murray, Fiona Lekland, Honor Fehrson. w. d. Kevin Brownlow, Andrew Mollo.
DRAMA: War Stories; Germans as Enemy; England; What If . . . Stories
(Red Dawn; Amerika; Fatherland)

It Happened in Brooklyn, 1947, 103m, ★★★/$$, MGM/MGM-UA. Several young musicians make their way up the club and theater ladder on the New York postwar scene. Frank Sinatra, Jimmy Durante, Kathryn Grayson, Peter Lawford, Gloria Grahame. w. Isobel Lennart, d. Richard Whorf.
COMEDY DRAMA: MUSICALS: Music Movies; Musicians; Singers; Fame-Rise to; New York Life; Ensemble Films; Forgotten Films; Hidden Gems; Female Screenwriters
(Birth of the Blues; All the Fine Young Cannibals)

It Happened One Night, 1934, 105m, ★★★★/$$$$$, Columbia/Col-Tri. A mad-cap heiress (Claudette Colbert, **BActress**) on the run from her publisher father hitches a ride with a journalist (Clark Gable, **BActor**) who knows who she is and she has to share a motel room with him. w. Robert Riskin (**BScr**), SS-adap. Night bus, Samuel Hopkins Adams, d. Frank Capra (**BDirector**). **BPicture.** Oscars: 5-5.
COMEDY: ROMANCE: Screwball Comedy; Romantic Comedy; Romance-Opposites Attract; Romance-Bickering; Road Movies; Heiresses-Madcap; Journalists; Hitchhikers; Secrets-Keeping; Runaways; Blockbusters
REMADE AS: You Can't Run Away from It
(Bringing Up Baby; Palm Beach Story; After Office Hours)

It Happened on Fifth Avenue, 1947, 115m, ★★½/$$, Allied/NA. A young woman finds squatters living in her father's mansion and sets out to help them when she finds they're not so bad. Gale Storm, Ann Harding, Charles Ruggles. Don Defore. w. Everett Freeman, Frederick Stephani, d. Roy Del Ruth.
COMEDY DRAMA: Homeless People; Rich vs. Poor; Female Protagonists
(Where the Heart Is; My Man Godfrey)

It Happened to Jane, 1959, 98m, ★★★/$$, Col/RCA-Col. A mother who raises lobsters for a living gets ticked at the local train, which is never on time and is hindering her business, so she takes on the bureacracy. Doris Day, Jack Lemmon, Ernie Kovacs, Steve Forrest. w. Norman Katkov, d. Richard Quine.
COMEDY: FARCE: Women Fighting the System; Fighting the System; Corporation

as Enemy; Mothers-Struggling; Trains; Fishermen; Trials; Female Protagonists; Good Premise Unfulfilled; Coulda Been Great

(Solid Gold Cadillac; End of the Line)

It Happened Tomorrow, 1944, 84m, ★★★/$$, UA/NA. A newspaper reporter meets a wise old fellow with the power to tell him the headlines of news before it happens, but will he abuse it? w. Dudley Nichols, Rene Clair, d. Rene Clair.

COMEDY DRAMA: Fantasy; Ethics; Time Travel; Future-Seeing the; Psychics; Journalists; Hidden Gems; Forgotten Films (Ed: A similar *Twilight Zone* episode was made)

It Happens Every Spring, 1949, 87m, ★★★/$$, 20th/Fox. With his invention of a anti-magnetic repellant for wood, a professor becomes a baseball star. Ray Milland, Jean Peters, Paul Douglas, Ed Begley, Alan Hale. w. Valentine Davies, d. Lloyd Bacon.

COMEDY: Fantasy; Baseball; Professors; Inventors; Magic; ROMANCE: Romantic Comedy; Fame-Rise to; Forgotten Films; Hidden Gems

(Angels in the Outfield; The Absent-Minded Professor)

It Happens Every Thursday, 1953, 80m, ★★1/2/$, U/NA. A small-town newspaper owner tries to boost circulation through divulging gossip and creating mayhem for attention. John Forsythe, Loretta Young, Jimmy Conlin, Edgar Buchanan, Jane Darwell. w. Dane Lussier, d. Joseph Pevney.

COMEDY: FARCE: Small-Town Scandals; Newspapers; Small-Town Life; Gossip/ Rumors; Good Premise Unfulfilled

(The Harper Valley PTA; The Miracle of Morgan's Creek)

It's Alive, 1974, 81m, ★★/$$$, WB/WB, R/V-B&G. A baby becomes a monster for a young couple. John Ryan, Sharon Farrell. w. d. Larry Cohen.

It's Alive II, 1978, 91m, ★★/$, WB/WB, R/V-B&G. The baby monster returns. w. d. Larry Cohen.

It's Alive III, 1988, 91m, ★★/$, WB/ WB, R/V-B&G. The baby's grown up and finds an island of like human monsters, then has a baby of his own. Michael Moriarty, Karen Black, Neal Isreal. w. d. Larry Cohen.

HORROR: Babies-Having; Monsters-Human; Monsters-Mutant; Deaths-One by One; Writer-Directors

(Rosemary's Baby II; The Godsend)

It's Always Fair Weather, 1955, 101m, ★★★/$$$, MGM/MGM-UA. Soldiers reunite after the war to find their lives are a bore, so they party in the Big Apple. Gene Kelly, Dan Dailey, Michael Kidd, Cyd Charisse. w. Betty Comden, Adolph Green (BStory/Scr), d. Gene Kelly, Stanley Donen. BMScore. Oscars: 2-0.

MUSICALS: Dance Movies; Dancers; Soldiers; Reunions; Roller Skating; New York Life; Female Screenwriters; World War II-Post Era

(On the Town; Anchors Aweigh)

It's in the Bag, 1945, 86m, ★★★/$$, UA/Republic. A flea-circus owner discovers he's sold a set of chairs where one of the little seats has something valuable hidden it and he has to get it back-but which one and sold to whom? Fred Allen, Don Ameche, Jack Benny, Robert Benchley, Rudy Vallee. w. Jay Dratler, Alma Reville, d. Richard Wallace.

COMEDY: MYSTERY: Race Against Time; Rewards at Stake; Treasure Hunts; Searches; Mix-Ups; Female Screenwriters

REMADE AS: Keep Your Seats, Please; The Twelve Chairs

It's a Big Country, 1952, 89m, ★★1/2/$$, MGM/NA. Seven stories over time depict pioneers and patriots in American history. Janet Leigh, Gene Kelly, Frederic March, Marjorie Main, William Powell, James Whitmore, Lewis Stone, Ethel Barrymore, Nancy Davis-Reagan. w. William Ludwig, Helen Deutsch, George Wells, Allen Rivkin, Dorothy Kingsley, Isobel Lennart, d. Richard Thorpe, Joh Sturges, Charles Vidor, Clarence Brown, William Wellman, Don Weis, Don Hartman.

DRAMA: MELODRAMA: Conservative Value Films; Patriotic Films; Historical Drama; Episodic Stories; Multiple Stories; Female Protagonists; Female Screenwriters

(How the West Was Won; Forever and a Day)

It's a Date, 1940, 100m, ★★★/$$$, U/MCA-U. The daughter of a Broadway star has a crush on an older man who's after her mother, the star. Deanna Durbin, Walter Pidgeon, Kay Francis, Eugene Pallette. w. Norman Krasna, d. William Seiter.

COMEDY: ROMANCE: Romantic Comedy; MUSICALS: Infatuations; Romance-Older Men/Younger Women;

Romance-Unrequited; Actresses; Mothers-Troublesome

(The Bachelor and the Bobby-Soxer; Mad About Music; It Started with Eve)

It's a Gift, 1933, 74m, ★★★/$$$, Par/MCA-U. A man buys an orange grove from the back of a magazine and moves to California to find pictures can lie. W.C. Fields, Kathleen Howard. w. Jack Cunningham, W.C. Fields, J.P. McEvoy, d. Norman Z. McLeod.

COMEDY: Comedy of Errors; Family Comedy; Fish out of Water Stories; Con Artists; California

(International House; The Dentist; The Egg and I; Funny Farm)

It's a Great Feeling, 1949, 85m, ★★★/$$$, WB/Fox. When actor Jack Carson can't find a director for his picture, he decides to do it himself in this movie within a movie. Jack Carson, Doris Day, Dennis Morgan, Cary Cooper, Joan Crawford, Errol Flynn, Danny Kaye, Patricia Neal, Edward G. Robinson, Jane Wyman, Ronald Reagan, Eleanor Parker. w. Jack Rose, Mel Shavelson, d. David Butler.

COMEDY: FARCE: SATIRE: Moviemaking; Movies within Movies; Hollywood Life; Hollywood Satire; Directors; Actors; Actresses; All-Star Cameos; Forgotten Films; Hidden Gems; Time Capsules

It Should Happen to You, 1954, 87m, ★★★1/2/$$$, Col/RCA-Col. A free-spirited New York model decides to go around the system and get famous overnight by putting her mug on a billboard, but things don't go so smoothly. Judy Holliday, Jack Lemmon, Peter Lawford, Michael O'Shea. w. Ruth Gordon, Garson Kanin, d. George Cukor.

COMEDY: Romantic Comedy; Eccentric People; Free Spirits; Feisty Females; Fame-Rise to; Models; Female Screenwriters; Hidden Gems

(Pfffft!; Solid Gold Cadillac; Bells Are Ringing)

It's Love I'm After, 1937, 90m, ★★★/$$$, WB/WB. A famous acting couple don't get along so well behind the scenes. Bette Davis, Leslie Howard, Olivia de Havilland, Patric Knowles, Spring Byington. w. Casey Robinson, d. Archie Mayo.

COMEDY: ROMANCE: Romantic Comedy; Romance-Bickering; Marriage Comedy; Marriage on the Rocks; Theater

Life; Actors; Actresses; Behind the Scenes

(The Guardsman; The Barkleys of Broadway)

It's a Mad Mad Mad Mad World!, 1963, 192m, ★★★★/$$$$$, UA/MGM-UA. A wild chase begins as a man dies in a wreck on a desert highway (Jimmy Durante), but not before telling everyone who's stopped to help him that there's a fortune "under the big W." The first who finds the spot gets whatever's buried there. Spencer Tracy, Jimmy Durante, Ethel Merman, Milton Berle, Sid Caesar, Buddy Hackett, Mickey Rooney, Dick Shawn, Phil Silvers, Terry-Thomas, Johnathan Winters, Edie Adams, Dorothy Provine, Peter Falk, William Demarest. w. William and Tania Rose, d. Stanley Kramer. BSound, BEdit, BOSong, BOScore, BCCin, **BSoundFX.** Oscars: 6-1.

COMEDY: ACTION: Action Comedy; FARCE: Chase Movies; Treasure Hunts; Race Against Time; Clever Plots & Endings; Rewards at Stake; All-Star Casts; Cast of Thousands; Female Screenwriters

(The Million Dollar Mystery; What's Up, Doc?; Scavenger Hunt; The Cannonball Run)

(Ed: The comic turn of Spencer Tracy is the high point, but rarely has such an all-star cast been so comedically talented)

It's My Turn, 1980, 90m, ★★1/2/$$, Col/RCA-Col, R/S-P. A professor is torn between a baseball player and her new stepbrother. Jill Clayburgh, Michael Douglas, Charles Grodin, Beverly Garland, Steven Hill. w. Eleanor Bergstein, d. Claudia Weill.

COMEDY DRAMA: ROMANCE: Romance-Triangles; Romance with Relative; Decisions-Big; Female Protagonists; Female Screenwriters; Female Directors

(Starting Over; Semi-Tough)

(Ed: A more comic and fluffy version of Clayburgh's classic, *An Unmarried Woman*)

It's Only Money, 1962, 84m, ★★1/2/$, Par/NA. A dufus gets in the way of helping his friend who's a small-time detective find the heir to some money who may be someone he knows. Jerry Lewis, Zachary Scott, Jack Weston, Joan O'Brien. w. John Fenton Murray, d. Frank Tashlin.

COMEDY: Comedy of Errors; Inheritances at Stake; Fools-Bumbling; Detective Stories; Forgotten Films

(Dumb and Dumber; California or Bust)

It's Pat, 1994, 77m, ★★/$, Touchstone/Touchstone, PG. The super-androgynous character from *Saturday Night Live* goes on an adventure and finds love with another androgyne. Julia Sweeney, David Foley, Charles Rocket. w. Julia Sweeney, Jim Emerson, d. Adam Bernstein.

COMEDY: Women as Men; Men as Women; Sexual Problems; Dating Scene; Saturday Night Live Movies; Comedy-Character; Flops-Major; Female Screenwriters; Female Protagonists

It's a Small World, 1935, 72m, ★★1/2/$$, 20th/NA. When a man and woman meet after a car crash, they soon find themselves falling in love. Spencer Tracy, Wendy Barrie. w. Sam Hellman, Gladys Lehmann, d. Irving Cummings.

COMEDY: ROMANCE: Romantic Comedy; Stranded; Situation Comedy; Car Wrecks; Southerns; Small-Town Life

It Started with Eve, 1941, 93m, ★★★/$$$, U/MCA-U. An rich old man who is dying has one last wish of seeing his grandson get married, but since he doesn't have a girlfriend, he gets a waitress to play the part-until the old man doesn't die after all. Deanna Durbin, Charles Laughton, Robert Cummings, Guy Kibbee. w. Norman Krasna, Leo Townsend, d. Henry Koster.

COMEDY: ROMANCE: Romantic Comedy; Romance-Reluctant; Dying Words; Death-Impendings; Dead-Back from the; Inheritances at Stake; Fathers & Sons; Grandfathers-Fascinating; Marriages-Fake; Engagements-Breaking; Impostors; Hired Dates; Waitresses; Rich vs. Poor; Rich People

REMAKE: I'd Rather Be Rich

(Daddy Longlegs; Mad About Music)

It Started with a Kiss, 1959, 104m, ★★1/2/$$, MGM/MGM-UA. An army man goes to Spain and his goofy wife follows him to make sure he's okay and not doing anything he shouldn't. Glenn Ford, Debbie Reynolds, Eva Gabor. w. Charles Lederer, d. George Marshal.

COMEDY: Marriage Comedy; Nuisances; Wives-Troublesome; Americans Abroad; Spain

(How Sweet It Is; The Lieutenant Wore Skirts)

It Started in Naples, 1960, 100m, ★★1/2/$$, Par/Par. A lawyer travels to Italy to settle his brother's estate and falls for a woman in his life. Clark Gable, Sophia Loren, Vittorio deSica. w. Melville Shavelson, Jack Rose, Sussi Cecchi D'Amico, d. Shavelson.

COMEDY DRAMA: ROMANCE: Romantic Comedy; Romance with Relative's Lover; Vacations; Vacation Romance; Funerals; Americans Abroad; Italy

(Avanti!; The Black Orchid)

It Takes Two, 1995, 100m, ★★/$$, WB/WB, G. Two twins meet for the first time at summer camp and decide to get their parents back together. Kirstie Alley, Steve Guttenberg, Mary-Kate Olsen, Ashley Olsen, Philip Bosco, Jane Sibbett. w. Deborah Dean Davis, d. Andy Tennant.

COMEDY: CHILDREN'S: Girls; Twins; Divorce; Summer Camp

REMAKE/RETREAD: The Parent Trap

(The Parent Trap; All I Want for Christmas)

It's a Wonderful Life, 1946, 129m, ★★★★/$$$$, RKO/Turner, various. A guardian angel stops a young man from jumping off of a bridge during the Depression by proving to him how much he's meant to people. James Stewart (BActor), Donna Reed, Henry Travers, Lionel Barrymore, Thomas Mitchell, Beulah Bondi, H.B. Warner, Gloria Grahame. w. Frances Goodrich, Albert Hackett, Frank Capra, d. Capra (BDirector). BPicture, BEdit, BSound. Oscars: 5-0.

COMEDY DRAMA: DRAMA: Character Studies; Suicidal Tendencies; Angels; Saving Someone; Depression Era; Flashbacks; Christmas; Small-Town Life; Bankers; Female Screenwriters

(A Christmas Carol; Scrooge)

It's a Wonderful World, 1939, 86m, ★★★/$$, MGM/NA. A young woman is kidnapped by a fugitive wanted for murder and decides to help him find the real killer to save her own hide, but may find more than that. Claudette Colbert, James Stewart, Guy Kibbee, Sidney Blackmer. w. Ben Hecht, Herman J. Mankiewicz, d. W.S. Van Dyke.

COMEDY: FARCE: ROMANCE: MYSTERY: MURDER: MURDER MYSTERY: Comic Mystery; Romantic Comedy; Kidnapper-Sympathizing with; Fugitives from the Law; Accused Unjustly; Framed?; Kidnappings; Sympathizing with Enemy; Female Protagonists (Backtrack; Midnight; Talk of the Town)

Ivanhoe, 1952, 105m, ★★★/$$$$, MGM/MGM-UA. The knights of chivalry ride tall in the saddle in merry old England with full regalia and armor to impress the ladies. Robert Taylor, Elizabeth Taylor, Joan Fontaine, Emlyn Williams, George Sanders. w. Noel Langley, Aeneas Mackenzie, d. Richard Thorpe. BPicture, BCCin, BOScore. Oscars: 3-0.
ACTION: DRAMA: ROMANCE: Epics; Medieval Times; Historical Drama; Costume Drama; Classic Literary Adaptations
(Prince Valiant; The Adventures of Robin Hood)

Ivan's Childhood, 1962, 95m, ★★★/$, Mosfilm/NA. An orphan boy manages to escape a concentration camp and join the partisans. Kolya Burlyaev. w. Vladimir Bogomolov, Mikahil Papava, d. Andrei Tarkovsky.
DRAMA: Revenge; Escape Drama; Concentration Camps; World War II Stories; Nazi Stories; Boys; Child Protagonists; Orphans; Russians; Russian Films

Ivan the Terrible, 1946, 188m, ★★★¹/2/$, Mosfilm/Nos. The rise and fall of the 16th-century czar of Russia. w. d. Sergei Eisenstein.
DRAMA: Epics; Leaders-Tyrants; Historical Drama; Costume Drama; Character Studies; Kings; Royalty; Russia; Russian Films; 1500s; Writer-Directors
(Strike; The Battleship Potemkin)

I've Heard the Mermaids Singing, 1987, 84m, ★★¹/2/$, Miramax/Miramax, R/S. An odd woman falls for her boss, an art gallery owner. Sheila McCarthy, Ann-Marie McDonald. w.d. Patricia Rozema.
DRAMA: COMEDY DRAMA: ROMANCE: Alternative Lifestyles; Lesbians; New York Life; Artists; Female Protagonists; Female Screenwriters; Female Directors; Writer-Directors; Independent Films
(Girlfriends; Lianna; Bar Girls)

I Vitelloni, 1953, 104m, ★★★¹/2/$$, Ind/Ingram. Several boys grow up in an Italian village, with only one leaving to seek a better life as the others keep with tradition, perhaps unhappily-the one who leaves being Fellini himself in this autobi-

ographical film. Alberto Sordi, Franco Interlenghi, Franco Fabrizi. w. Fellini, Ennio Flaiano, d. Federico Fellini.
DRAMA: Autobiographical Stories; Character Studies; Ensembles-Male; Small-Town Life; Coming of Age; Young Men; Slice of Life Stories; Multiple Stories; Episodic Stories; Italy; Italian Films; Hidden Gems
(Amarcord; Cinema Paradiso; 8¹/2)

Ivy, 1947, 99m, ★★¹/2/$$, U/NA. A woman who offs people with poison meets her match but may not know it. Joan Fontaine, Herbert Marshall, Patric Knowles, Lucile Watson. w. Charles bennett, N-adap. Mrs. Belloc Lowndes, d. Sam Wood.
DRAMA: SUSPENSE: MURDER: Murderers-Female; 1900s; Edwardian Era; Poison; Turning the Tables; Forgotten Films; Coulda Been Good; Female Protagonists
(Suspicion; Lucretia Borgia)

I Wake Up Screaming, 1941, 79m, ★★★/$$, 20th/Fox. A Hollywood starlet is murdered, and when a detective hits the case, her sister helps him find the trail. Betty Grable, Victor Mature, Carole Landis, Laird Cregar, William Gargan. w. Dwight Taylor, N-adap Steve Fisher, d. H. Bruce Humberstone.
SUSPENSE: MURDER: MYSTERY: MURDER MYSTERY: Film Noir; Trail of a Killer; Detective Stories; Detectives-Private; Detective Couples; Forgotten Films; Underrated; Hidden Gems; Hollywood Life
(The Seventh Victim; The Black Dahlia; Kiss Me Deadly)
(Ed: Probably misfired originally due to the baggage Grable carried with her and the film's dark nature. Well worth a look, or a read of the novel)

I Walk Alone, 1947, 98m, ★★¹/2/$$, Par/NA. An ex-con gets out of the big house and looks for vengeance. Burt Lancaster, Kirk Douglas, Lizabeth Scott, Wendell Corey, Kristine Miller. w. Charles Schnee, P-adap. Theodore Reeves (*Beggars Are Coming to Town*), d. Byron Haskin.
DRAMA: Crime Drama; Revenge; Convict's Revenge; Film Noir

I Walked with a Zombie, 1943, 68m, ★★★/$$, RKO/Media. A plantation owner in the Caribbean has a wife cursed with voodoo, so he hires a nurse to take care of her who may fall prey as well.

Frances Dee, James Ellison, Tom Conway. w. Curt Siodmak, Ardel Wray, d. Jacques Torneur.
HORROR: SUSPENSE: Nurses; Curses; Caribbean; Voodoo; Witchcraft; Zombies

I Walk the Line, 1970, 97m, ★★★/$$, Col/NA. A sheriff in backwoods Tennessee trades protection for moonshiners for sexual favors from their daughter-until a federal investigator arrives to see what's up. Gregory Peck, Tuesday Weld, Estelle Parsons, Ralph Meeker. w. Alvin Sargent, N-adap. Madison Jones, *An Exile*, d. John Frankenheimer.
DRAMA: ACTION: Police Stories; Police Corruption; FBI Agents; Rural Life; Prostitutes-Low Class; Blackmail; Bootleggers; Tennessee; Hillbillies; Rednecks
(The Bootleggers; The Lolly Madonna War)

I Wanna Hold Your Hand, 1978, 104m, ★★/$$, Amblin-U/MCA-U, PG. New Jersey teens can't wait for the Beatles to arrive and appear on Ed Sullivan. Nancy Allen, Bobby diCicco, Marc McClure. w. Robert Zemeckis, Bob Gale, d. Zemeckis.
COMEDY: COMEDY DRAMA: Teenage Movies; Teenagers; Musicians; Rock Groups; 1960s; Time Capsules
(Backbeat; 9-30-55)

I Wanted Wings, 1941, 131m, ★★¹/2/$$$, Par/NA. The young men go into the Air Force for World War II and find it isn't so bad. Ray Milland, William Holden, Brian Donlevy, Wayne Morris, Veronica Lake, Constance Moore. w. Richard Mailbaum, Beirne Lay Jr., Sig Herzig, d. Mitchell Leisen.
MELODRAMA: War Stories; Pilots-Military; Patriotic Films; World War II Stories; Soldiers; Dreams

I Want to Live!, 1958, 126m, ★★★★/$$$$, UA/MGM-UA. A wild woman (Susan Hayward, **BActress**) with a criminal past is framed as an accessory to murder, then sentenced to die unless her persistent cries for another trial and leniency are accepted, but her past leads to prejudice. w. Nelson Gidding, Don Mankiewicz (**BAScr**), d. Robert Wise (**BDirector**). BB&WCin, BEdit, BSound. Oscars: 6-1.
DRAMA: TRAGEDY: Crime Drama; **MURDER:** Murderers-Female; Film Noir; Accused Unjustly; Framed?;

Unbelieved; Biographies; Death-Impending; Courtroom Drama; Fighting the System; Dangerous Women; Starting Over; Dreams-Broken; Wild People; Women in Prison; Playgirls; Feisty Females; Underworld; Liars; Wisecracking Sidekicks; Female Protagonists
(Caged; Last Dance; Dead Man Walking)

I Want What I Want, 1971, 105m, ★★/$, Marayan/Prism, R/S. After a sex change, Roy is Wendy and got what he wanted. Anne Heywood, Paul Rogers, Harry Andrews. w. Gillian Freeman, N-adap Geoff Brown, d. John Dexter.
DRAMA: MELODRAMA: Transsexuals; Character Studies; Camp; Unintentionally Funny; Men as Women; Forgotten Films; Cult Films; Ahead of Its Time
(Dinah East; The Christine Jorgensen Story; Glen or Glenda?; Second Serve)

I Want You, 1951, 101m, ★★1/2/$$, Goldwyn-UA/Goldwyn. When young men are being drafted to Korea, a small-town family becomes especially affected by it. Dana Andrews, Dorothy McGuire, Farley Granger, Peggy Dow, Robert Keith, Martin Milner, Jim Backus. w. Irwin Shaw, d. Mark Robson.
DRAMA: Family Drama; War Stories; Korea War; 1950s; Time Capsules; Small-Town Life; Female Protagonists

I Was an Adventuress, 1940, 81m, ★★1/2/$$, 20th/NA. A ballerina (Vera Zorina) is decoy used in ploys by a couple of con artists, but how long will she stand for it? Erich von Stroheim, Peter Lorre, Richard Greene, Fritz Feld. w. Karl Tunberg, Don Ettlinger, John O'Hare, d. Gregory Ratloff.
COMEDY: COMEDY DRAMA: Con Artists; Dancers; Ballet; Female Protagonists

I Was a Communist for the FBI, 1951, 83m, ★★1/2/$, WB/NA. An FBI informant is undercover in a steel mill hoping to trap communists who might sabotage work. Frank Lovejoy, Dorothy Hart, Phil Carey. w. Crane Wilbur, Matt Cvetic, d. Gordon Douglas.
BDocumentary. Oscars: 1-0.
DRAMA: Social Drama; Docudrama; Documentary; Documentary Style; FBI Agents; Communists; McCarthy Era; Cold War Era; Undercover; Patriotic Films;

Time Capsules; 1950s; Camp; Unintentionally Funny; Cult Films
(Keeper of the Flame; The House on 92nd Street)
(Ed: Straddles documentary and fiction and is heavily dated, though interesting)

I Was Happy Here, see **Time Lost and Time Remembered**

I Was a Male War Bride, 1949, 105m, ★★★/$$$, 20th/CBS-Fox. A WAC in World War II marries a Frenchman and then has trouble getting him into the states because only female war brides, not male grooms, are allowed to come back. Result? Cary in drag. Cary Grant, Ann Sheridan, Marion Marhsall, Randy Stuart. w. Charles Lederer, Hagar Wilde, Leonard Spiegelgass, d. Howard Hawks.
COMEDY: FARCE: Marriage Comedy; Newlyweds; Americans Abroad; Immigrants; Marriage for Citizenship; Government as Enemy; Role Reversals; Men as Women; Undercover; World War II-Post Era; Hidden Gems; War Brides
(Tootsie; Bringing Up Baby; Charley's Aunt)
(Ed: Though not as good or fast-paced as other Hawks-Grant ventures like *Bringing up Baby* or *His Girl Friday*, still remembered for the wig Cary donned made of a horse tail)

I Was Monty's Double, see **Hell, Heaven, and Hoboken**

I Was a Spy, 1933, 89m, ★★1/2/$$, Gaumont/NA. In World War I, a nurse in Belgium becomes a spy. Madeleine Carroll, Conrad Veidt, Herbert Marshall, Edmund Gwenn, Nigel Bruce. w. W. P. Lipscomb, Ian Hay, NF-adap. Marthe McKenna, d. Victor Saville.
DRAMA: Spy Films; Spies; War Stories; World War I Stories; Nurses; Spies-Female; Female Protagonists

I Was a Teenage Frankenstein, 1957, 72m, ★★★/$$, AIP/NA. Dr. Frankenstein puts together a new monster and gives it a more handsome face by killing a teenager. Whit Bissell, Phyllis Coates, Gary Conway, Robert Burton. w. Kenneth Langtry, d. Herbert Strock.
HORROR: Horror Comedy; Black Comedy; Spoofs-Horror; Frankenstein; Monsters-Manmade; Teenagers; Teenage Movies; Scientists-Mad; Cult Films; British Films
(I Was a Teenage Werewolf)

I Was a Teenage Werewolf, 1957, 76m, ★★★/$$$, AIP/Col. A mad scientist finds a handsome young lad and makes him very hairy and hungry. Michael Landon, Whit Bissell, Yvonne Lime. w. Ralph Thornton, d. Gene Fowler.
HORROR: Horror Comedy; Black Comedy; Spoofs-Horror; Werewolves; Monsters-Manmade; Teenagers; Teenage Movies; Hypnosis; Scientists-Mad; Cult Films
REMAKE: Teen Wolf
(I Was a Teenage Frankenstein; Teen Wolf; Teen Wolf Too)

I Will . . . I Will . . . for Now, 1975, 108m, ★★1/2/$$, Brut-Embassy/Media, R/S. Divorced thirty-somethings during the sexual revolution break up then think about getting back together. Diane Keaton, Elliott Gould, Paul Sorvino, Victoria Principal, Candy Clark, Robert Alda. w. Norman Panama, Albert Lewin, d. Panama.
COMEDY: ROMANCE: Romantic Comedy; Marriage Comedy; Divorce; Single Men; Single Women; Sexual Revolution; Battle of the Sexes; 1970s
(The Marrying Man; I Love My Wife; Annie Hall)
(Ed: Not very good, and dated, but worth a peek for Keaton)

I Wonder Who's Kissing Her Now, 1947, 104m, ★★1/2/$$, 20th/NA. Songwriter Joseph Howard's life is chronicled with his songs. Mark Stevens, June Haver, Martha Stewart, Reginald Gardiner, William Frawley. w. Lewis R. Foster, d. Lloyd Bacon.
MUSICAL: Music Movies; Biographies; Songwriters; Musicians; 1890s; Nostalgia
(I Dream of Jeannie; Swanee River)

I, the Worst of All, 1990, 105m, ★★1/2/$, Ind/NA. A nun in 17th-century Mexico is forbidden by the church from studying or writing poetry or plays. Assumpta Serra, Dominique Sanda. w. Maria Luisa Bemberg, Antonio Larreta, NF-adap. Octavio Paz, *Sor Juana*, d. Maria Luisa Bemberg.
DRAMA: Historical Drama; Religion; Women's Rights; Nuns; Oppression; Mexico; Mexican Films; Independent Films
(Yentl; The Nun's Story)

Films by Title

J

Jabberwocky, 1977, 101m, ★★/$, Ind/Col, PG. In the middle ages a bumbling fool slays a dragon and becomes a local hero in his village. w. Charles Alverson, Terry Gilliam, d. Terry Gilliam.
COMEDY: Dragons; Middle Ages; Heroes-Unlikely; Spoofs
(Erik the Viking; Dragonslayer)
J'Accuse, 1939, 95m, ★★★/$, Ind/CVC. A pacifist invents a device that he hopes will end all wars, but it only fuels the flames. As a last resort, he summons the casualties of war out of their graves to condemn war to the face of humanity. Victor Francen, Jean Max, Renee Devilliers. w. d. Abel Gance.
DRAMA: SCI-FI: Peaceful People; Apocalyptic Stories; Dead-Back from the; Surrealism; Message Films; Heaven; Writer-Directors; Hidden Gems
(Grand Illusion; The Day the Earth Stood Still)
Jack and Sarah, 1996, 106m, ★★★/$ (VR), Polygram-Gramercy-U/Polygram, PG-13/P-S. A British yuppie has a bachelor lifestyle when he winds up with a baby, but luckily gets an American young woman to care for it while he keeps his nice job. However, not everyone in his life so accommodating and unless love comes between them, neither will this babysitter be. Richard E. Grant, Samantha Mathis, Judi Dench, Ian McKellan. w.d. Tim Sullivan.
COMEDY: COMEDY DRAMA: Romantic Comedy; Marriage Comedy; Alternative Lifestyles; Babies-Inheriting; Fathers Alone; Babysitters; British Films; Quiet Little Films; Writer-Directors
(Three Men and a Baby; Three Men and a Cradle; Georgy Girl; Rich in Love)
Jack and the Beanstalk, 1952, 78m, ★★★/$$, WB/WB. A babysitter reading the famous fable to his bratty charge dreams himself into the story, then wakes up-"or was it a dream?" Bud Abbott, Lou Costello, Buddy Baer, Dorothy Ford, William Farnum. w. Nat Curtis, d. Jean Yarbrough.
COMEDY: CHILDREN'S: Fantasy; Fairy Tales; Abbott & Costello; Fools-Bumbling; Giants; Boys; Babysitters; Storytellers
(The 30-Foot Bride of Candy Rock)
Jack London, 1943, 93m, ★★/$$, RKO/Nos. A fictionalized biopic of the adventurer-writer who braved the wilds of the Klondike and had other adventures that he turned into his famous novels and stories. Michael O'Shea, Susan Hayward, Osa Massen, Harry Davenport, Virginia Mayo, Jonathan Hale. w. Ernest Pascal, d. Alfred Santell.

ADVENTURE: Biographies; Writers Journeys; Snow Settings; Alaska
(Call of the Wild)
Jack of All Trades, 1936, 76m, ★★1/2/$, Ind/NA. A young upstart in an international corporation cons his way to the top. Jack Hulbert, Gina Malo, Robertson Hare, Athole Stewart, Felix Aylmer, H. F. Maltby. w. Jack Hulbert, Austin Melford, J. O. C. Orton, P-adap. Hubert Griffith, Paul Vulpuis (*Youth at the Helm*), d. Jack Hulbert, Robert Stevenson.
ACTION: Action Drama; Crime Drama; Power-Rise to; Business Life; Con Artists; Forgotten Films; British Films
(Head Office; Lloyd's of London; The Secret of My Success; How to Succeed in Business Without Really Trying)
Jack of Diamonds, 1967, 105m, ★★/$, MGM/NA. A young apprentice jewel thief has his "coming out" under the tutelage of a retired master thief. George Hamilton, Joseph Cotten, Marie Laforet, Maurice Evans, Wolfgang Preiss, Lilli Palmer, Carroll Baker, Zsa Zsa Gabor. w. Jack de Witt, Sandy Howard, d. Don Taylor.
COMEDY DRAMA: Heist Stories; Jewel Thieves; Proteges; Teachers; Playboys
(To Catch a Thief; Breaking In; The Pink Panther)

Jack the Giant Killer, 1961, 94m, ★★★/$$, MGM/MGM-UA. A young boy on a farm in England rises to the challenge when the lady he worships from afar is taken prisoner by the evil Demon Pendragon. Kerwin Matthews, Judi Meredith, Torin Thatcher, Don Beddoe, Walter Burke, Barry Kelley. w. Orville Hampton, Nathan Juran. d. Nathan Juran.
CHILDREN'S: FAMILY: Fantasy; Boys; Kidnappings; British Films; England

Jack the Ripper, 1958, 84m, ★★/$$, Par/Par. A massive search by Scotland Yard for the famous London killer of young prostitutes ends at the doorstep of a respected young surgeon. Ewen Solon, Lee Patterson, Eddie Byrne, Betty McDowell, John Le Mesurier. w. Jimmy Sangster, d. Robert S. Baker.
SUSPENSE: MYSTERY: MURDER: MURDER MYSTERY: Serial Killers; Murders of Prostitutes; Jack the Ripper; Detective Stories
(The Lodger; The Man Upstairs; Jack's Back)

Jacknife, 1988, 103m, ★★/$, Castle Hill/HBO, PG-13/S-P. A woman has a tumultuous affair with her brother's old army buddy, a Vietnam vet with a tortured memory and a drinking problem. Robert De Niro, Ed Harris, Kathy Baker, Charles Dutton, Elizabeth Franz, Tom Isbell, Loudon Wainwright III, Sloane Shelton, Ivan Brogger. w., P-adap. Stephen Metcalfe, d. David Jones.
DRAMA: ROMANCE: Romantic Drama; Men in Conflict; Romance-Triangles; Jealousy; Romance with Friend's Relative; Friendships-Male; Mental illness; Veterans-Vietnam; Alcoholics
(Coming Home; Welcome Home)

The Jackpot, 1950, 85m, ★★/$$, 20th/NA. A quiet, middle-class man becomes an instant celebrity by winning a radio contest, and it disrupts his attempts at living a normal life. James Stewart, Barbara Hale, James Gleason, Fred Clark, Alan Mowbray, Patricia Medina, Natalie Wood, Tommy Rettig, Robert Gist, Lyle Talbot. w. Phoebe and Henry Ephron, d. Walter Lang.
COMEDY DRAMA: Family Drama; Family Comedy; Lotteries; Contests; Ordinary People Stories; Rags to Riches
(Champagne for Caesar; Quiz Show)

Jack's Back, 1987, 97m, ★★★/$$, Ind/Par, R/EV-B&G. When two twin brothers are caught up in a Jack the Ripper case and one of them is accused, it's up to the other to one to get him off the hook-or wind up a victim himself. James Spader, Cynthia Gibb, Rod Loomis. d. Rowdy Herrington.
SUSPENSE: HORROR: Twins; Twins-Evil; Jack the Ripper; Serial Killers; Murders of Women; Women in Jeopardy; Murder-Debate to Reveal Killer; Psychologists; Brothers; Hidden Gems
(Dead Ringers; Time After Time; Jack the Ripper)

Jackson County Jail, 1978, 95m, ★★/$$, UA/New World. A female truck driver is attacked by a hitchhiker who rapes her. She's subsequently thrown in jail by police who don't believe her story, and to top it all off, she's raped in jail by the warden, before she bashes in his head with a stool, and so on. . . . Yvette Mimieux, Tommy Lee Jones, Robert Carradine, Frederic Cook, Severn Darden, Howard Hesseman. w. Donald Stewart, d. Michael Miller.
ACTION: Crime Drama; Prison Drama; Women in Prison; Women in Jeopardy; Rape/Rapists; Southerns; Hitchhikers; Truck Drivers; Unbelieved; Police Corruption; Rural Horrors
(Caged Fear; Brubaker)

Jacob's Ladder, 1990, 113m, ★★★/$, Tri-Star/Col-Tri, R/V-P. A Vietnam vet is besieged by apparitions on the subway, at parties, and everywhere he goes. He meets other vets with the same problem, all of whom were in his battalion, which he later learns was exposed to chemical warfare and drug experiments of some kind. Tim Robbins, Elizabeth Pena, Danny Aiello, Matt Craven, Jason Alexander, Patricia Kalember. w. Bruce Joel Rubin, d. Adrian Lyne.
DRAMA: Psychological Drama; MURDER: Nightmares; Veterans-Vietnam; Illusions/Hallucinations; Psychologists; Inner City Life; Nervous Breakdowns; Flashbacks; Coulda Been Great

Jade, 1995, ★1/2/$, Par/Par, R/P-S-FFN-MFN. When a man is murdered, is the wife of a friend of the detective/D.A. on the case the killer? David Caruso, Linda Fiorentino, Chazz Palminteri, Richard Crenna, Michael Biehn. w. Joe Eszterhas, d. William Friedkin.
SUSPENSE: Crime Drama; MURDER: MURDER MYSTERY: Chases-Car; San Francisco; Flops-Major

(Sliver; Basic Instinct; The Last Seduction)
(Ed: A muddled mess with a good car chase. It simply has no third act, but that wouldn't have helped)

Jagged Edge, 1985, 108m, ★★★1/2/$$$, Col/Col, R/V-S. A respectable man accused of a brutal rape and heinous murder is defended by a female lawyer who is utterly convinced of his innocence and developing a keen attraction for him, until startling evidence turns up causing her to reassess her position, both legally and personally. Jeff Bridges, Glenn Close, Peter Coyote, Robert Loggia, Leigh Taylor-Young, John Dehner. w. Joe Eszterhas, d. Richard Marquand.
SUSPENSE: MURDER: MURDER MYSTERY: MYSTERY: Lawyers; Lawyers as Detective; Romance-Unprofessional; Enemy-Sleeping with the; Lawyer vs. Client; Rape/Rapists; Murder of Spouse; Accused Unjustly; Women in Jeopardy; Sleeper Hits; Female Protagonists
REMAKE/RETREAD: Guilty as Sin
(Guilty as Sin; Basic Instinct; Betrayed [1989]; Sliver; Criminal Law; Defenseless)

Jailhouse Rock, 1957, 96m, ★★★/$$$, MGM/MGM-UA. An ex-con gets out of the clink and onto the stage with some wild gyrations. Elvis Presley, Judy Tyler, Mickey Shaughnessy, Dean Jones. w. Guy Trosper, d. Richard Thorpe.
MUSICALS: Rock Stars; Ex-Convicts; Prison Drama; Fame-Rise to; Rebels; Sexy Men; Cult Films
(Baby, the Rain Must Fall; King Creole)

Jakarta, 1988, 95m, ★★/$ (VR), Medusa-Troma/Troma, R/V-S. A CIA Agents travels to the Indonesian capital to put a stop to a drug cartel. Christopher Noth, Sue Francis Pai. w. Charles Kaufman, Ralph Soll, d. Kaufman.
ACTION: Action Drama; Drug-Dealing; American Abroad; Undercover; Asia; Independent Films
(The Year of Living Dangerously)

Jamaica Inn, 1939, 107m, ★★★/$$, UA/Nos. A young woman in old England winds up involved with mysterious smugglers on the coast. Charles Laughton, Maureen O'Hara, Leslie Banks, Robert Newton, Emlyn Williams. w. Sidney Gilliat, Joan Harrison, J.B. Priestly, N-adap. Daphne du Maurier, d. Alfred Hitchcock.

Jamaica Inn, 1982, 180m, ★★★/$$, Ind/New World. Jane Seymour, Patrick McGoohan. d. Lawrence Clark.
DRAMA: SUSPENSE: ROMANCE: Romantic Drama; Thieves; Girls; England; Gothic Style; Hitchcockian; Female Protagonists; Female Screenwriters
(I Was an Adventuress)

Jamaica Run, 1953, 92m, ★★/$, Par/NA. Sides of a family race to find papers that will decide who becomes heir to a fortune. Rya Milland, Arlene Dahl, Wendell Corey, Patric Knowles. w. d. Lewis Foster.
SUSPENSE: DRAMA: Inheritances at Stake; Family Drama; Writer-Directors
(Greedy)

Jane and the Lost City, 1988, 92m, ★★/$, Ind/New World, R/V-S. A stripper in World War II England becomes a spy. Maud Adams, Sam J. Jones, Jasper Carrott. w. Mervyn Haisman, Terry Marcel, Harry Robertson, d. Terry Marcel.
ACTION: Spoofs-Spy; Spies; Spies-Female; Erotic Comedy; Comic Heroes; Independent Films
(Mata Hari; Allan Quatermain and the Lost City of Gold)

Jane Eyre, 1934, 62m, 20th/NA. A poverty-stricken young girl in Victorian England is taken in by a wealthy family as governess, and sexual tensions arise between her and her broodingly handsome master. Virginia Bruce, Colin Clive, Beryl Mercer, Jameson Thomas. w. Adele Comandini, N-adap. Charlotte Bronte, d. Christy Cabanne.
Female Screenwriters; Female Directors

Jane Eyre, 1943, 96m, ★★★½/$$$, 20th/Fox. An orphan girl is taken in by a mysterious landowner and becomes governess and possibly lover to the master. Joan Fontaine, Orson Welles, Margaret O'Brien, Henry Danielle, Agnes Moorehead, Elizabeth Taylor, Sara Allgood, Peggy Ann Garner. w. Aldous Huxley, Robert Stevenson, John Houseman, N-adap. Charlotte Bronte, d. Robert Stevenson.

Jane Eyre, 1971, 100m, ★★★/$$$, BBC/NA. Susannah York, George C. Scott.
DRAMA: MELODRAMA: Girls; Orphans; Girls' Schools; Servants; Romance with Servant; Babysitters; Classic Literary Adaptations
REMAKE: 1996
(Wuthering Heights)

The January Man, 1989, 122m, ★★★/$$, MGM-UA/MGM-UA, R/S-P-V. A former detective (Kevin Kline) tries to redeem himself by catching a zodiac-type killer and romancing the mayor's daughter (Mary Elizabeth Mastrantonio), who may yet become a victim herself. Susan Sarandon, Alan Rickman, Rod Steiger, Danny Aiello. w. John Patrick Shanley, d. Norman Jewison.
MYSTERY: MURDER: MURDER MYSTERY: COMEDY: Comic Mystery; Black Comedy; Murders-One by One; Murders of Women; Romantic Comedy; Serial Killers; Trail of a Killer; Redemption; Free Spirits; Men Proving Themselves; Race Against Time; New York Life; Clever Plots & Endings; Coulda Been Great; Curiosities
(Apartment Zero; Shadows and Fog)
(Ed: Has major flaws and an uneven style, but it's still entertaining and interesting)

Jarrapellejos, 1987, 108m, ★★½/$, Ind/NA. In turn-of-the Century Spain, a small-town *jefe* tries to cover up his rape of a peasant woman and her daughter. Antonio Ferrandis, Juan Diego, Lydia Bosch, Amparo Larranaga, Joaquin Hinojosa, Miguel Rellan, Jose Coronado. w. Antonio Gimenez Rico, Manuel Gutierrez Aragon, N-adap. Felipe Trigo, d. Antonio Gimenez Rico.
DRAMA: Rape/Rapists; Conspiracy; Scandals; Small-town Scandals; 1900s; Spain; Spanish Films
(The Virgin Spring)

Jason and the Argonauts, 1963, 104m, ★★★/$$$, Col/RCA-Col, V. In Ancient Greece, warrior Jason voyages to find the Golden Fleece and encounters all kinds of animated monsters along the way. Todd Armstrong, Honor Blackman, Niall MacGinnis. w. Jan Read, Beverley Cross, d. Don Chaffey.
ACTION: ADVENTURE: Fantasy; Mythology; Ancient Times; Journeys; Animation-Stop; Cult Films
(The Golden Voyage of Sinbad; Clash of the Titans)

Jaws, 1975, 124m, ★★★★/$$$$$, Universal/MCA-U, PG/EV-B&G. A giant rogue shark is munching on swimmers at a summer resort, so it's up to the local sheriff (Roy Scheider), a marine biologist (Richard Dreyfuss), and a fisherman (Robert Shaw) to stop it. w. Peter Benchley, Carl Gottlieb, N-adap. Peter Benchley, d. Steven Spielberg. BPicture,

BCinema, **BEditing, BSound, BOScore.** Oscars: 5-3.
SUSPENSE: HORROR: ADVENTURE: ACTION: Adventure at Sea; Monsters-Animal; Hunters; Kill the Beast; Beach Movies; Human Eaters; Murders-One by One; Unbelieved; Men in Jeopardy; Sharks; Blockbusters
SEQUELS: Jaws 2, Jaws 3-D, Jaws 4 (Jaws 2; Orca; Moby Dick; Blue Water; White Death; The Beast [TV miniseries])

Jaws 2, 1978, 117m, ★★★/$$$$, U/MCA-U, PG/EV-B&G. Fun-loving and horny teenagers vacationing on Amity Beach just can't keep their feet from dangling underwater, and you-know-who is hungry. Roy Scheider, Lorraine Gary, Murray Hamilton, Joseph Mascolo, Collin Wilcox. w. Carl Gottlieb, Howard Sackler, Dorothy Tristan, d. Jeannot Szwarc.
Murders of Teenagers; Blockbusters

Jaws 3-D, 1983, 99m, ★★/$$, U/MCA-U, PG/EV-B&G. In an amusement park down in Florida, tourists are besieged by a giant man-eating shark. Dennis Quaid, Bess Armstrong, Simon MacCorkindale, Louis Gossett Jr., Lea Thompson. w. Richard Matheson, Carl Gottlieb, Guerdon Trueblood, d. Joe Alves.
3-D Movies

Jaws 4: The Revenge, 1987, 95m, ★/$, U/MCA-U, PG-13/EV-B&G. The Great White this time is after Brody's widow, seeing how he's eaten everyone else from the first film. Lorraine Gary, Lance Guest, Mario Van Peebles, Karen Young, Michael Caine. w. Michael de Guzman, d. Joseph Sargent.
SUSPENSE: HORROR: ADVENTURE: ACTION: Adventure at Sea; Monsters-Animal; Hunters; Kill the Beast; Human Eaters; Murders-One by One; Flops-Major; Revenge
(Orca)

The Jazz Singer, 1927, 89m, ★★★/$$$$, WB/WB. A Jewish boy makes it big in show business as a singing star in the first major sound film release. Al Jolson, May McAvoy, Warner Oland. w. Alfred A. Cohn, P-adap. Samson Raphaelson, d. Alan Crosland.
Blockbusters

The Jazz Singer, 1953, 107m, ★★/$, WB/WB. A corny remake of the above archetypal showbiz story. Danny Thomas, Peggy Lee, Mildred Dunnock. w. Frank Davis, Leonard Stern, Lewis Meltzer, d. Michael Curtiz.

The Jazz Singer, 1980, 115m, ★★¹/₂/ $$, EMI-U/MCA-U, PG/S. Updating with more emphasis on his marriage than his relationship with his mother, and curiously with the old-fashioned melodrama though with thoroughly modern music. Neil Diamond, Laurence Olivier, Lucie Arnaz, Catlin Adams, Sally Boyar. w. Herbert Baker, Stephen H. Foreman, d. Richard Fleischer.

MELODRAMA: Singers; Fathers & Sons; Jewish People; Marriage Drama; Fame-Rise to
(Ed: The soundtrack was a huge hit; the film was not)
(The Jolson Story; The Chosen; Yentl)

Je Vous Aime, 1981, 105m, ★★¹/₂/$, Ind/Connoisseur. A woman can't maintain a relationship, though she has ideals which would lead one to believe she would want to be more monogamous. Catherine Deneuve, Jean-Louis Trintignant, Gérard Depardieu, Christian Marquand. w. Claude Berri, Michel Grisolla, d. Claude Berri.

DRAMA: Character Studies; Promiscuity; Settling Down; Single Women; Women's Films; Female Protagonists; French Films
(Belle de Jour)

Jean de Florette, 1986, 121m, ★★★¹/₂/ $$$, Orion/Orion, PG. In 1920s France, two neighboring farmers' fight over water rights escalates into a feud. Yves Montand, Gerard Depardieu, Daniel Auteuil, Elisabeth Depardieu. w. Claude Berri, Gerard Brach, N-adapt. Marcel Pagnol, d. Claude Berri.

DRAMA: Feuds; Men in Conflict; Farm Life; Ordinary People Stories; Rabbits; French Films

SEQUEL TO: Manon of the Spring.
(Manon of the Spring; Manon des Sources)

Jefferson in Paris, 1995, 130m, ★★★¹/₂/$$$, MI-Touchstone/Touchstone, PG-13/S. Thomas Jefferson's political and romantic liaisons in 18th-century Paris, centering around his relationship with a mulatto slave girl. Nick Nolte, Greta Scacchi, Lambert Wilson, Simon Callow, Seth Gilliam, James Earl Jones, Michael Lonsdale, Thandie Newton, Gwyneth Paltrow, Charlotte de Turckheim, Elsa Zylberstein. w. Ruth Prawer Jhabvala, d. James Ivory.

DRAMA: ROMANCE: Love-Forbidden; Historical Drama; Paris; Presidents; Biographies; Romance-Interracial;

Costume Drama; Slavery; Revisionist Films; Female Screenwriters
(1776; The Journey of August King)

Jeffrey, 1995, 92m, ★★★/$$, Orion/ Orion, R/ES-P-MRN. Sweet, pretty Jeffrey roams the streets of gay New York trying to decide whether love can make it in his life anymore or not, what with the oppressive fear of AIDS. Matters get better and yet so much worse when a superhunk comes into his life-who happens to be infected. Steven Weber, Patrick Stewart, Michael T. Weiss, Bryan Batt, Sigourney Weaver, Nathan Lane, Christine Baranski, Kathy Najimy, Debra Monk, Olympia Dukakis w. P-adapt. Paul Rudnick, d. Christopher Ashley.

COMEDY: Gay Men; Alternative Lifestyles; Single Men; Dating Scene; AIDS Stories; All-Star Casts
(Lie Down with Dogs; Parting Glances; Fun Down There)
(Ed: Actually less cute than the play version, and Weber carries it extremely well)

Jennifer 8, 1992, 127m, ★★★/$$$, Par/Par. A forensics cop (Andy Garcia) returns home after a breakdown to investigate a serial killer case in which the victims are blind women like the one he falls in love with (Uma Thurman). Kathy Baker, Lance Henriksen. w. d. Bruce Robinson.

SUSPENSE: ROMANCE: Serial Killers;
MURDER: MYSTERY: MURDER:
Framed?; Murder-Clearing Oneself; Women in Jeopardy; Disabled People in Jeopardy; Blind People; Accused Unjustly; Snow Settings; Boarding Schools; Writer-Directors
(Silence of the Lambs; Blink; Wait Until Dark; Hear No Evil)

Jeremiah Johnson, 1972, 107m, ★★★¹/₂/$$$$, WB/WB. The adventures of a frontiersman (Robert Redford) as he crosses the Rockies in the late 1800s. Will Geer. w. Edward Anhalt, John Milius, d. Sydney Pollack.

WESTERN: DRAMA: ADVENTURE:
Journeys; Drifters; Westerns-Neo Pioneers; Explorers; Sleeper Hits
(Tell Them Willie Boy Is Here; High Plains Drifter; Pale Rider)

The Jerk, 1979, 94m, ★★★/$$$$$, U/MCA-U, R/EP-S. A white boy (Steve Martin) born to a black sharecropper's family in Mississippi leaves for the big time and, among other things, joins a carnival. Bernadette Peters. w. Carl Gottlieb, Steve Martin, d. Carl Reiner.

COMEDY: Romantic Comedy; Comedy-Slapstick; Spoofs; Fish out of Water Stories; Simple Minds; Mentally Disabled; White Among Blacks; Fame-Rise to; Power-Rise to, of Idiot; Circus Life; Underrated; Blockbusters; Sleeper Hits
(Ace Ventura; Dumb and Dumber; Living It Up)
(Ed: Often brilliant though uneven; underrated in its time, though a major box-office hit)

The Jerky Boys, 1994, 82m, ★/$, Caravan-Disney/Disney, R/EP-S. Two stupid practical jokers wind up with the mob after them. Johnny Brennan, Kamal, William Hickey, Alan Arkin. w. James Melkonian, Rich Wilkes, John G. Brennan Kamal Ahmed, d. James Melkonian.

COMEDY: Comedy-Character; Telephone Terror; Practical Jokers; Flops-Major
(Wise Guys; Dumb and Dumber; Houseguest)

Jersey Girl, 1992, 95m, ★★¹/₂/$, Col/Col, PG-13/S-P. A girl on the shores of Jersey dreams of snaring a sexy guy from New York City, but a plumber may fix his pipes instead. Jami Gertz, Joseph Bologna, Aida Tuturro, Dylan McDermott, Sheryl Lee. w. Gina Wendkos, d. David Burton Morris.

MELODRAMA: Character Studies; Ordinary People Stories; Young Women; Pre-Life Crisis; **ROMANCE:** Romantic Comedy; Dreams; Small-town Life; Romance-Triangles; Romance-Choosing the Right Person; Female Protagonists; Female Screenwriters
(Angie; Pretty Woman)

Jesus Christ, Superstar, 1973, 108m, ★★★/$$$, U/MCA-U, G. A rock opera on the superstar status of the Lord's son in the days leading up to his death. Ted Neeley, Carl Anderson, Yvonne Elliman, Josh Mostel. d. Norman Jewison. BSScore. Oscars: 1-0.

MUSICALS: Musical Drama; Musicals-Hippie; Rock Opera; Israel; Jesus Christ; Biblical Stories; Revisionist Films
(Godspell; Tommy; Fiddler on the Roof)
(Ed: A huge hit on stage, its lack of stars kept it from becoming the hit the Jewison-directed *Fiddler on the Roof* became two years before)

Jesus of Montreal, 1989, 119m, ★★★/$$, Orion/Orion, R/S-MFN. In a revisionist production of the last days of Christ, a young man gets caught up on the lead, as the story mirrors the real story of Jesus, with everyone having the same conflicts as in ancient times. Gilles Pelletier, Lothaire Bluteau, Catherine Wilkening. w. d. Denys Arcand. BFLFilm. Oscars: 1-0.

DRAMA: Allegorical Stories; Jesus Christ; Putting on a Show; Directors; Actors; Canadian Films; Writer-Directors (Hail Mary)

Jesus of Nazareth, 1977, 371m, ★★★/$$$$, NBC/Fox. An all-star mini-series of the last days of Christ. Robert Powell, Anne Bancroft, Ernest Borgnine, Claudia Cardinale, James Mason, Laurence Olivier, Anthony Quinn. d. Franco Zeffirelli.

DRAMA: Epics; Biblical Stories; Ancient Times; Jesus Christ; Death-Impending; Executions; TV Movies; All-Star Casts (King of Kings; The Greatest Story Ever Told)

Jet Pilot, 1950/1957, 112m, ★★/$, Hughes-U/MCA-U. An American pilot marries a defeated Russian female pilot and then suspects her of spying, so he defects back with her to Russia to find out what's up. John Wayne, Janet Leigh, Jay C. Flippen, Paul Fix. d. Josef von Sternberg.

MELODRAMA: Military Stories; Spy Films; Spies; Dangerous Spouses; Double Crossings; Russians as Enemy; Marriage on the Rocks; Flops-Major; Unintentionally Funny (The Iron Petticoat; Torn Curtain)

The Jetsons Movie, 1990, 82m, ★★1/2/$$, U/MCA-U, G. George Jetson gets promoted to running a planet and then having to save it from ecologically incorrect villains. d. William Hanna, Joseph Barbera.

CHILDREN'S: FAMILY: Cartoons; Environmental Dilemmas; Outer Space Movies; Nerds; Family Comedy; TV Series Movies

The Jewel in the Crown, 1984, 750m, ★★★/$$$, BBC/A&E. Story of the withdrawing of the British Empire from Africa after World War II and all of the various lives it effects. Peggy Ashcroft, Art Malik, Charles Dance, Susan Wooldridge, Tim Piggott-Smith. d. Christopher Morahan, Jim O'Brien. Multiple International Emmy winner.

DRAMA: Sagas; Epics; Africa; Ensemble Films; Episodic Stories; British Films; TV Movies; Miniseries (Out of Africa; Heat and Dust; Flame Over India; Indochine)

Jewel of the Nile, 1985, 104m, ★/$$$$$, 20th/CBS-Fox, PG/S. A continuation of the *Romancing the Stone* couple's adventures where the most interesting character, Kathleen Turner's, is changed and under-used in a rehash. w. Mark Rosenthal, Larry Konner, d. Lewis Teague.

COMEDY: ACTION: Action Comedy; **ROMANCE:** Romantic Comedy; Chase Movies; Treasure Hunts; Romance Novelists; Writers; Faded Hits **SEQUEL TO:** Romancing the Stone (Ed: Opened very big and stayed around a little while, but not even worth it for diehard fans or anyone else hoping for a spark like the first had)

Jezebel, 1938, 105m, ★★★/$$$$, WB/MGM-UA. A manipulative Southern belle in pre-Civil War Louisiana loses her man because of selfishness, but when he falls with malaria, she takes care of him and becomes a heroine to everyone. Bette Davis (**BActress**), George Brent, Henry Fonda, Maragaret Lindsay, Fay Bainter (**BSActress**), Spring Byington, Eddie Anderson, Donald Crisp. d. William Wyler. BPicture, BCin, BOScore. Oscars: 5-2.

MELODRAMA: ROMANCE: Romantic Drama; Romance-Reluctant; Epics; Civil War Era; Southerns; Feisty Females; Stern Women (Gone With the Wind; The Little Foxes)

JFK, 1991, 179m, WB/WB, ★★★1/2/$$$$. The story of Jim Garrison (Kevin Costner) and his conspiracy theory about the assassination of Kennedy. Tommy Lee Jones (BSActor), Joe Pesci, Kevin Bacon, Laurie Metcalf, Jack Lemmon, Donald Sutherland. w. Oliver Stone, Jim Garrison (BAScr), adap. Jim Garrison, d. Oliver Stone (BDirector). BPicture, BCinema, **BEditing, BSound,** BOScore. Oscars: 8-2.

DRAMA: Documentary Style; **MURDER MYSTERY:** Political Drama; **MYSTERY:** Biographies; True Stories; Conspiracy; Assassination Plots; 1960s; New Orleans; Texas; JFK; Presidents (Missing; Nixon)

The Jigsaw Man, 1984, 90m, ★★/$, Ind/HBO, PG. A double agent working the Russians goes into England to get a list of KGB agents left behind. Michael Caine, Laurence Olivier, Susan George, Robert Powell, Charles Gray. d. Terence Young.

DRAMA: Action Drama; Spy Films; Spies; Russians as Enemy; British Films; Cosmetic Surgery (The Spy Who Came in from the Cold; The Russia House; Spycatcher)

Jim Thorpe, All American, 1951, 105m, ★★1/2/$$$, WB/WB. Story of the American Indian who became a great athlete in several different sports, despite prejudices and odds. Burt Lancaster, Phyllis Thaxter, Charles Bickford. d. Michael Curtiz.

DRAMA: Sports Movies; Runners; Football; 1900s; Indians-American; Bigots; Fame-Rise to; Biographies; Olympics

Jimmy Hollywood, 1994, 110m, ★★/$, Tri-Star/Col-Tri, R/P-S. A loser actor in a motel in Hollywood becomes a vigilante in his rough neighborhood. Videotapes of his heroism get him the fame he's been longing for. Joe Pesci, Christian Slater, Victoria Abril. w.d. Barry Levinson.

COMEDY: SATIRE: Hollywood Life; Media Satire; Actors; Fame-Rise to; Heroes-Unlikely; Videotape Scandals; Vigilantes; Ordinary Person vs. Criminal; Video Proof; Flops-Major; Writer-Directors (Hero; Hero at Large)

Jinxed, 1982, 103m, ★★/$, MGM-UA/MGM-UA, R/EP-S. A Vegas bimbo pays a hitman to off her abusive boyfriend, but the hitman dies and the boyfriend finds out-plus there's money hidden somewhere. Bette Midler, Ken Wahl, Rip Torn. w. David Newman, Frank Gilroy, d. Don Siegel.

COMEDY: Romance-Bickering; Fugitives from the Mob; Gambling; Las Vegas; Bimbos; Singers; Abused Women; Treasure Hunts; Coulda Been Good; Flops-Major (Honeymoon in Vegas; Faithful; Ruthless People) (Ed: Only worth watching for Midler)

Jo Jo Dancer, Your Life Is Calling, 1986, 97m, ★★1/2/$$, Col/Col, R/EP-S-FN. A comedian is in drug detox and has to start over, trying to figure out where things went wrong. Richard Pryor, Debbie Allen, Art Evans, Fay Hauser, Paula Kelly, Diahanne Abbott. w. Richard Pryor, Rocco Urbisci, d. Pryor.

MELODRAMA: COMEDY DRAMA: Drugs-Addictions; Starting Over; Nervous Breakdowns; Black Men; Comedians; Actor Directors; Autobiographical Stories

(Clean and Sober; The Basketball Diaries)

Joan of Arc, 1948, 100m, ★★★/$$, Ind/Home Vision. The life of the great young French female saint whose beliefs led to tragedy. Ingrid Bergman, Jose Ferrer, John Ireland, Leif Erickson. d. Victor Fleming. BEdit, **BCCin**, BCArt, **BCCostume**, BScore. Oscars: 5-2.

MELODRAMA: DRAMA: Character Studies; Biographies; Legends; Saintly People; Leaders-Female; Religion; Illusions/Hallucinations; Middle Ages; Female Protagonists
(The Passion of Joan of Arc)

Joan of Paris, 1942, 91m, ★★★/$$, RKO/Turner. A French resistance female spy puts her life on the line so Allied pilots can be freed from the clutches of Nazis. Michele Morgan, Thomas Mitchell, Paul Henreid, May Robson, Alan Ladd. d. Robert Stevenson.

DRAMA: Action Drama; Spy Films; Spies; World War II Stories; Spies-Female; Female Protagonists; Saintly People; Saving Someone; Pilots-Military; Nazi Stories; Forgotten Films; Hidden Gems
(Plenty; Mata Hari)

Joe, 1970, 107m, ★★★/$$$, AIP/MGM-UA, R/P-S-FFN-MRN. When a rich girl's (Susan Sarandon) father intervenes in her relationship with a drug dealer, a bigoted working-class malcontent, Joe (Peter Boyle) becomes involved by chance. w. Dennis Patrick. d. John G. Avildsen.

DRAMA: MURDER: Bigots; Working Class; Drugs-Dealing; Rich vs. Poor; Snobs vs. Slobs; Friendships-Male; Fathers & Daughters; Lover Family Dislikes; Blackmail; Murderer-Debate to Reveal; Guilty Conscience; Hippies; 1970s; Sleeper Hits; Forgotten Films; Faded Hits
(Hardcore)

Joe Kidd, 1972, 88m, ★★/$$, U/MCA-U, PG/V. When a dispute breaks out of land rights in the old New Mexico, a loner comes into town to settle the matter. Clint Eastwood, Robert Duvall, John Saxon, Don Stroud. w. Elmore Leonard, d. John Sturges.

WESTERNS: Westerns-Spaghetti; Drifters; Men in Conflict; Feuds; Flops-Major
(High Plains Drifter; Pale Rider)

Joe Panther, 1976, 110m, ★★/$, WB/WB, G. A seminole Indian young man's adventures in the swamps wrestling alligators. A. Martinez, Brian Keith, Ricardo Montalban, Alan Feinstein. d. Paul Krasny.

FAMILY: ACTION: Wrestling; Indians-American; Swamp Life; Florida; Alligators

Joe vs. the Volcano, 1990, 102m, ★★/$$, Amblin-WB/WB, PG. A man named Joe (Tom Hanks) who believes he's dying sets off on a journey, encountering three very different women (Meg Ryan) in very different locales, winding up on an island with a volcano. w. d. John Patrick Shanley.

COMEDY: COMEDY DRAMA: Black Comedy; Comedy-Morbid; Vacations; Disease Stories; Alienation; Depression; Death-Impending; Surrealism; Volcanoes; Production Design-Outstanding; Multiple Performances; Writer-Directors
(Ed: Some great ideas and lines, but overall, a great-looking misfire. To its credit, there's virtually nothing like it)

Joey Breaker, 1993, 92m, ★★★/$, Par/Par, R/S-P. A cynical, huckster talent agent has some changes in his life with a romance with a Jamaican woman, an AIDS patient, and a trip to the Caribbean. Richard Edson, Cedelia Marley, Fred Fondren, Erik King. w. d. Steven Starr.

COMEDY DRAMA: SATIRE: Character Studies; Hollywood Satire; Vacations; Romance on Vacation; Romance-Interracial; AIDS Stories; Life Transitions; Independent Films
(Leaving Las Vegas; Local Hero)

John and Mary, 1969, 92m, ★★★/$$$, 20th/NA, R/S. A young man (Dustin Hoffman) and woman (Mia Farrow) meet and get together for a night, but then part and realize they don't know each other's names. Sunny Griffin, Tyne Daly. d. Peter Yates.

DRAMA: ROMANCE: Young People; Sexual Revolution; 1960s; One Day Stories; Romance-Brief; New York Life; Single Men; Single Women; Forgotten Films; Hidden Gems; Faded Hits

John Cleese on How to Irritate People, 1968, 65m, ★★★/$$, BBC/BBC. Various skits from the Monty Python leader John Cleese. Michael Palin, Graham Chapman, Connie Booth. w. d. John Cleese.

COMEDY: Comedy-Skits; British Films; TV Series; Monty Python; Writer-Directors
(Fawlty Towers; Clockwise; A Fish Called Wanda)

John Paul Jones, 1959, 126m, ★★½/$, WB/WB. Story of great Revolutionary War hero and his journies to Europe and Russia. Robert Stack, Charles Coburn, MacDonald Carey, Marisa Pavan, Bette Davis, Peter Cushing. w. John Farrow, Jesse Lasky, d. Farrow.

DRAMA: Historical Drama; Costume Drama; Adventure at Sea; Revolutionary War; 1700s

Johnny Angel, 1945, 79m, ★★★/$$$, RKO/Turner. When his father is murdered, a sailor sets out to find the killer. George Raft, Claire Trevor. d. Edwin Marin.

SUSPENSE: Film Noir; **MURDER: MURDER MYSTERY: MYSTERY:** Fathers & Sons; Murder of Parents; Ships; Sailors; Forgotten Films; Hidden Gems

Johnny Be Good, 1988, 91m, ★★/$$, Orion/Orion, R/S-FN-MN. College football greed tempts a high school star into possibly going against the folks back home. Anthony Michael Hall, Robert Downey Jr., Paul Gleason, Uma Thurman, Stuart Pankow.

DRAMA: Sports Movies; Ethics; Friendships on the Rocks; College Life; Football; Teenagers
(All the Right Moves; The Program)

Johnny Belinda, 1948, 103m, ★★★/$$$$, WB/WB. A deaf mute girl is raped and impregnated (Jane Wyman, **BActress**), and the doctor who helps her with the baby becomes a suspect. Lew Ayres, Charles Bickford (BSActor), Agnes Moorehead (BSActress). w. Irmgard Von Cube, Allenn Vincent (BScr), d. Jean Negulesco (BDirector). BPicture, BB&WCin, BB&WArt, BSound, BEdit, BScore. Oscars: 11-1.

DRAMA: MELODRAMA: ROMANCE: Disabled People in Jeopardy; Women in Jeopardy; Deaf People; Disabled but Nominated; Rapes/Rapists; Mothers-Unwed; Babies-Having; Scandals; Small-town Scandals; Female Protagonists; Female Screenwriters

TV REMAKE: 1984, starring Rosanna Arquette.
(Agnes of God; Hear No Evil; Public Eye [1971])

Johnny Dangerously, 1984, 90m, ★½/$, 20th/Fox, PG. A spoof on gangster flicks about a cowardly mobster who needed to pay his mother's medical bills

and got into a life of crime and can't figure out how to get out. Michael Keaton, Maureen Stapleton, Marilu Henner, Joe Piscopo, Danny DeVito, Griffin Dunne, Peter Boyle, Dom DeLuise. w. Norman Steinberg, d. Amy Heckerling.
COMEDY: Spoofs; Mob Comedy; Cowards; One Last Time; Mob Girls; 1930s; Coulda Been Good; Female Directors

Johnny Eager, 1942, 108m, ★★★/$$$, MGM/MGM-UA. The daughter of a D.A. falls in love with a gangster her daddy is after, leading to dangerous entanglements. Lana Turner, Robert Taylor, Van Heflin (**BSActor**), Edward Arnold. w. James Edward Grant, John Lee Mahin, d. Mervyn LeRoy. Oscars: 1-1.
DRAMA: Crime Drama; ROMANCE: Romance-Dangerous; Love Family Dislikes; Dangerous Men; Lawyers; Police vs. Mob; Film Noir; Hidden Gems

Johnny Guitar, 1953, 110m, ★★★1/2/$$, Republic/Republic. Hired-powered pistol-packin' dames hit the prairie when a loner with a guitar enters a town where the saloon owner is in a feud with a powerful, and female, foe. Joan Crawford, Mercedes McCambridge, Ernest Borgnine, Sterling Hayden, Ward Bond. w. Philip Yordan, d. Nicholas Ray.
WESTERNS: Westerns-Neo; Westerns-Revisionist; Women in Conflict; Drifters; Feisty Females; Dangerous Women; Feuds; Camp; Cult Films; Unintentionally Funny; Female Protagonists
(Lust in the Dust; Queen Bee; Flamingo Road)

Johnny Handsome, 1989, 94m, ★★★/$$, Tri-Star/Live, R/V-S. An ex-convict in New Orleans (Mickey Rourke) comes out and gets a new face so that he can exact revenge on those who set him up. Elizabeth McGovern, Ellen Barkin, Lance Henriksen, Forest Whitaker, Scott Wilson, Morgan Freeman. w. Ken Friedman, d. Walter Hill.
DRAMA: Crime Drama; Revenge; Ex-Convicts; Cosmetic Surgery; Starting Over; ROMANCE: Romance-Dangerous; Framed?; Film Noir-Modern; New Orleans
REMAKE/RETREAD OF: Dark Passage

Johnny Mnemonic, 1995, 107m, ★★/$, Tri-Star/Col-Tri, R/V-P-S. A young man with a computer drive slot in his head is sent to deliver a message to save the planet from disease in this futuristic journey. The only problem is his memory is overloaded and he must get rid of the excess before battling on in his mission. Keanu Reeves, Dina Meyer, Ice-T, Takeshi, Denis Akiyama, Dolph Lundgren, Henry Rollins. w. SS-adap. William Gibson, d. Robert Longo.
SCI-FI: Futuristic Films; Computers; Computer Terror; Cult Films; Flops-Major
(Blade Runner; Total Recall; Strange Days; The Terminal Man)

Johnny Stecchino, 1992, 100m, ★★★/$$, New Line/New Line, PG-13/S. A nerdy klutz is mistaken for a mobster when a beautiful woman lures him in-a dream come true, until he realizes she's the mobster's wife and she needs a double to be hit to cover for him. Roberto Benigni, Nicoletta Bracchi, Paola Bonaceli. w. d. Roberto Benigni.
COMEDY: Comedy-Slapstick; Comedy of Errors; Mob Comedy; Lookalikes; Identities-Mistaken; Framed?; Hitmen; Dangerous Women; Nerds; Coulda Been Great; Italian Films; Hidden Gems; Actor Directors; Writer-Directors
(Son of the Pink Panther; Never a Dull Moment [1968])

Johnny Suede, 1992, 97m, ★★★/$, Ind/Par, R/S-P. A wanna-be pop star with very big hair wanders around, romancing and crooning in a hipster world leading nowhere but artiness. Brad Pitt, Calvin Levels, Nick Cave, Tina Louise, Samuel L. Jackson. w. d. Tom DiCillo.
COMEDY DRAMA: Art Films; Surrealism; Beautiful People; Dreams; Singers; Sexy Men; Writer-Directors

A Joke of Destiny, 1984, 105m, ★★/$, Ind/Lorimar. An Italian bureaucrat is trapped in his super-modern limousine which has malfunctioned to the max just before a big speech. Ugo Tognazzi, Piera degli Esposti. w. d. Lina Wertmueller.
SATIRE: COMEDY DRAMA: Political Satire; Politicians; Race Against Time; Art Films; Italian Films; Female Screenwriters; Female Directors
(Seven Beauties; Swept Away)

Jolson Sings Again, 1949, 96m, ★★/$$$, Col/Col. The story continues of Al Jolson's comeback in the 40s during the war. Larry Parks, William Demarest, Barbara Hale, Bill Goodwin. d. Henry Levin.
SEQUEL TO: The Jolson Story

The Jolson Story, 1946, 126m, ★★★/$$$, Col/Col. Biopic of the famous singer from a boy singer to his big hit in *The Jazz Singer*. Larry Parks (BActor), Evelyn Keyes, William Demarest, Bill Goodwin, John Alexander. d. Alfred Green. BCCin, **BSound**, BEdit.
Oscars: 4-1.
MUSICALS: Biographies; Singers; Episodic Stories; Fame-Rise to; Comebacks; Hollywood Biographies; Time Capsules; 1920s; 1940s
(The Jazz Singer)

Joni, 1979, 75m, ★★/$$, Ind/Live, G. A young woman is injured and paralyzed and then becomes a painter. Joni Eareckson Tada, Bert Ramsen. d. James Collier.
MELODRAMA: Disabled People; Painters; Young Women; Sleeper Hits; Conservative Value Films; Religion
(The Other Side of the Mountain)

Joseph Andrews, 1977, 104m, ★★★/$$, Par/Par, R/FFN-MRN. The further adventures of the shirttail relative of Tom Jones, Joseph Andrew (Peter Firth), as Lady Booby (Ann-Margret) takes him in after he's been found naked in the road. Michael Hordern, Beryl Reid, Jim Dale, John Gielgud, Hugh Griffith, Peter Bull, Peggy Ashcroft, Wendy Craig, Karen Dotrice. w. Alan Scott, Chris Bryant, N-adap. Henry Fielding, d. Tony Richardson.
COMEDY: FARCE: ROMANCE: Romantic Comedy; Love-Forbidden; England; 1700s; Restoration Era; Older Women/Younger Men; Young Men; Coming of Age; Romance-First Love; Gypsies
SEQUEL TO: Tom Jones
(The Graduate; The Amorous Adventures of Moll Flanders; Fanny Hill)

The Josephine Baker Story, 1990, 97m, ★★★/$$$, HBO/HBO, PG-13/S-FN. The life of the black singer/dancer who became extremely famous in Europe during the 20s but would soon fall from grace. Lynn Whitfield, Ruben Blades, David Dukes, Craig T. Nelson, Louis Gossett. d. Brian Gibson. Multiple Emmy winner.
DRAMA: Biographies; Music Dies; Singers; Rise and Fall Stories; Fame-Rise to; Black Women; Bigots; Romance-Interracial; Americans Abroad; Roaring 20s; Sexy Women; TV Movies
(Lady Sings the Blues)

Josh and S.A.M., 1993, 97m, ★★/$, New Line/New Line, PG. Two brothers,

one of whom is convinced he's a robot, steal a Grand Prix and travel the country-side. Jacob Tierney, Noah Fliess, Martha Plimpton, Joan Allen, Christopher Walken. w. Frank Deese, d. Billy Weber.
CHILDREN'S: ACTION: Action Comedy; Road Movies; Boys; Robots; Brothers; Child Protagonists

Joshua Then and Now, 1985, 102m, ★★★/$, 20th/Fox. A writer's life comes apart as sexuality and his heritage cause problems with his marriage, so he begins some soul searching. James Woods, Alan Arkin, Michael Sarrazin, Gabrielle Lazure, Alexander Knox. w. N-adap. Mordecai Richler, d. Ted Kotcheff.
DRAMA: Character Studies; Midlife Crisis; Marriage on the Rocks; Writers; Gay Men; Scandals; Sexual Problems; Gay Awakenings; Bisexuality; Memories; Jewish People; Canadian Films; Hidden Gems
(The Ghostwriter; Portnoy's Complaint)

Jour de Fete, 1948, 79m, ★★★★/$$$, Ind/Sultan. A French postman tries to emulate the speediness of the American post office (!) in the postwar years, but things don't go so smoothly. Jacques Tati. w. d. Tati.
COMEDY: Comedy-Character; Comedy-Slapstick; Comedy of Errors; **FARCE:** Working Class; French Films; Hidden Gems; Actor-Directors; Writer-Directors
(Monsieur Hulot's Holiday; Playtime)

Journey for Margaret, 1942, 81m, ★★★/$$, UA/MGM-UA. A couple during the war in London who are expecting a baby deal with the terror all around them. Robert Young, Laraine Day, Fay Bainter, Margaret O'Brien. N-adap. William White, d. W. S. Van Dyke.
MELODRAMA: World War II Stories; Marriage Drama; Babies-Having; Young People; Americans Abroad; Journalists
(Penny Serenade, Made for Each Other)

Journey into Fear, 1942, 71m, ★★★/$$, RKO/Turner, RKO. An arms expert is smuggled across the Turkish border with the bad guys close behind but with treacherous seas ahead, not knowing who to trust. Joseph Cotten, Dolores DelRio, Orson Welles, Agnes Moorehead. d. Norman Foster.
DRAMA: SUSPENSE: Journeys; Spy Films; Spies; Psychological Drama; Undercover; Middle East; World War II Era; Arms Dealers; Hidden Gems
REMAKE: Journey into Fear (1974)

(The Third Man; The Lady from Shanghai)

The Journey of August King, 1995, 110m, ★★1/2/$, PG/V. In the early 1800s mountains of the Carolinas, a young man whose wife has died lives alone in the hills, when a male and female slave come his way in hiding. No one would care about interracial relationships this far back in the woods, but the problem is the woman's master is also her father and wants her back. Jason Patric, Thandie Newton, Larry Drake, Sam Waterston, Sara-Jane Wylde. w. John Ehle, d. John Duigan.
DRAMA: Historical Drama; **ROMANCE:** Romantic Drama; Romance-Interracial; Romance-Forbidden; Southerns; 1800s; Slavery; Saving Someone; Hiding Out; Abused Women; Incest; Overlooked at Release
(Jefferson in Paris; The Winter People; Sommersby)

Journey of Hope, 1990, 112m, ★★★/$$, WB/WB, HBO. A Kurdish family, oppressed by Sadam Hussein's regime, emigrates to Switzerland, but may run into more problems on the way than expected. w. d. Xavier Killer. BFLFilm. Oscars: 1-0.
DRAMA: MELODRAMA: Escape Drama; Journies; Family Drama; Oppression; Writer-Directors
(Night Crossing; America, America)

The Journey of Natty Gann, 1985, 101m, ★★★/$, Disney/Disney, PG. A girl and her pet wolf travel the country looking for her father during the Depression. Meredith Salenger, John Cusack, Ray Wise, Scatman Crothers, Lainie Kazan. w. Jerome Rosenberg, d. Jeremy Paul Kagan.
DRAMA: ADVENTURE: CHILDREN'S: FAMILY: Journeys; Girls; Pet Stories; Depression Era; Overlooked at Release; Hidden Gems; Child Protagonists; Female Protagonists

Journey to the Center of the Earth, 1959, 122m, ★★★/$$$, 20th/Fox. A professor and some students journey down into a cave which leads-guess where? James Mason, Pat Boone, Arlene Dahl, Diane Baker. d. Henry Levin.
ADVENTURE: SCI-FI: FAMILY: CHILDREN'S: Archaeologists; Professors; Ensemble Films; Faded Hits
(The Land That Time Forgot)

Journey to the Far Side of the Sun, 1969, 92m, ★★★/$$, U/MCA-U. An

astronaut goes out to a planet hidden on the far side of the sun which is exactly like earth, only everything is backwards in reverse polarity. Roy Thinnes, Ian Hendry, Lynn Loring. d. Robert Parrish.
SCI-FI: Astronauts; Outer Space Movies; Psychological Drama; What If . . . Stories; Earth-Center of

The Joy Luck Club, 1993, 136m, ★★★/$$, Touchstone/Touchstone, PG-13/S-V. The lives of three generations of Chinese-American women from their journey to America to their conflicts in a changing world. Tsai Chin, Kieu Chinh, France Nuyen, Rosalind Chao, Tamlyn Tomita, Andrew McCarthy, Chris Rich, Diane Baker. w. N-adap. Amy Tan, d. Wayne Wang.
DRAMA: MELODRAMA: Tearjerkers; Episodic Stories; Women's Films; Chinese People; China; Asian-Americans; Ensembles-Female; Female Protagonists; Female Screenwriters
(Waiting to Exhale; Eat a Bowl of Tea)

Joy of Living, 1938, 90m, ★★★/$$$, RKO, Turner. A reserved chanteuse is romanced by a randy playboy who may have to change his tune to get her. Irene Dunne, Douglas Fairbanks, Jr., Alice Brady, Jean Dixon, Lucille Ball. d. Tay Garnett.
COMEDY: MUSICALS: Musical Comedy; **ROMANCE:** Romantic Comedy; Screwball Comedy; Singers; Playboys; Romance-Boy Wants Girl; Extroverted vs. Introverted; Hidden Gems; Faded Hits
(The Awful Truth; Theodora Goes Wild)

Juarez, 1939, 132m, ★★★/$$, MGM/MGM-UA. The story of the Mexican revolutionary who overthrew the government and became President. Paul Muni, John Garfield, Bette Davis, Claude Rains, Gale Sondergaard. d. William Dieterle.
DRAMA: Political Unrest; War Stories; Mexico; Historical Drama; Men in Conflict
(Pancho Villa; Viva Zapata!)

Jude the Obscure, 1971, 130m, ★★★/$, 20th/Fox. A poor man in the English countryside wants to marry his cousin but must get the education to match her class. But while home, he meets a farm girl and can't resist her charms, winding up with a son named Father Time. His cousin marries unhappily, and after time the two think about getting together again, but without any money to live on. Robert Powell, Daphne Heard, Alex Marshall. w. Harry Green, d. Hugh David.

DRAMA: ROMANCE: Romantic Drama; Romance-Doomed; Episodic Stories; Smart vs. Dumb; College Life; Marriage Drama; City vs. Country; Romance-Class Conflicts; Class Conflicts; Poor People; Rich vs. Poor; England; British Films; Classic Literary Adaptations

(Tess; Maurice; Howards End)

Judge Dredd, 1995, 91m, ★★/$$, Hollywood/Hollywood, R/EV-P. A vigilante "judge" in a post-apocalyptic world is himself unjustly accused of a murder in his own corrupt world and has to do battle with the system as well as find the real killer. Sylvester Stallone, Armand Assante, Diane Lane, Rob Schneider, Joan Chen, Jurgen Prochnow, Max Von Sydow. w. William Wisher & Steven E. de Souza, d. Danny Cannon.

ACTION: SCI-FI: Accused Unjustly; Framed?; Murder-Clearing Oneself; Futuristic Films; Judges; Corruption; Vigilantes; Flops-Major

(Demolition Man; The Star Chamber; Strange Days)

(Ed: Another good premise gone to waste amid special effects)

Judgment at Nuremburg, 1961, 178m, ★★★1/2/$$$$, UA/MGM-UA. The horrors of the Nazi holocaust are recanted in war crimes trials. Burt Lancaster, Spencer Tracy, Maximiliam Schell (**BActor**), Judy Garland (**BSActress**), Richard Widmark, Montgomery Clift (**BSActor**), Marlene Dietrich. w. Abby Mann (**BAScr**), d. Stanley Kramer. BPicture, BB&WArt, BB&WCin, BB&WCostume, BEdit. Oscars: 9-2.

DRAMA: TRAGEDY: MELODRAMA: Historical Drama; Courtroom Drama; Nazi Stories; World War II-Post Era; Concentration Camps; Jewish People; True Stories; Ensemble Films

(Schindler's List; Shoah)

Judgment Night, 1993, 109m, ★★/$$, U/MCA-U, R/EV-P. Several guys wind up in the ghetto in a fancy motorhome and are chased by a psycho-killer through the sewers. Emilio Estevez, Stephen Dorff, Cuba Gooding, Denis Leary. w. Lewis Colick, d. Stephen Hopkins.

ACTION: SUSPENSE: Chase Stories; Urban Horror; Psycho-Killers; Fugitives from a Murderer; Ensembles-Male

Jud Suess, 1940, 100m, ★★★/NA, Nazi Party/Nos. Propaganda of the Nazis about a Jew who terrorizes Aryans, thereby justifying his extermination. Ferdinand Marian, Werner Krauss, Heinrich George. d. Veit Harlan.

DRAMA: Documentary Style; Nazi Stories; Political Drama; German Films; Jewish People

(Triumph of the Will; Olympischpiele)

Juggernaut, 1974, 109m, ★★1/2/$$, 20th/Fox. A bomb is about to go off on a luxury liner. Richard Harris, Omar Sharif, David Hemmings, Shirley Knight, Anthony Hopkins, Ian Holm. d. Richard Lester.

SUSPENSE: DRAMA: Race Against Time; Bombs; Ships; Disaster Stories; Terrorists

(Airport; Terror on a Train; Black Sunday)

Juice, 1992, 95m, ★★1/2/$$, Par/Par, R/EP-EV. Slice of life of street kids in Harlem. Omar Epps, Jermaine Hopkins. w. Gerard Brown, Ernest Dickerson, d. Dickerson.

DRAMA: Social Drama; Inner City Life; Boys; Black Men; Black Women; New York Life; Multiple Stories; Interwoven Stories; Coulda Been Great; Black Screenwriters; Black Directors

(Dead Boyz Can't Fly; Boyz N the Hood)

Jules and Jim, 1962, 104m, ★★★1/2/$$$, Ind/Fox. Two men are in love with the same woman in various ways over the years, leading to tragedy. Jeanne Moreau, Oskar Werner, Henri Serre. w. Jean Gruault, d. Francois Truffaut.

DRAMA: TRAGEDY: Erotic Drama; **ROMANCE:** Romantic Drama; Romance-Triangles; Ménage à Trois; Men Fighting Over Women; Friendships-Male; Cult Films; French Films

(Willie and Phil; A Small Circle of Friends; Going Places)

Julia, 1977, 118m, 20th/Fox, ★★★★/ $$$. The true story of Lillian Hellman (Jane Fonda, BActress) and her friendship with Julia (Vanessa Redgrave, **BSActress**) who was a resistance spy and needed Hellman's help as a courier, endangering both of their lives. Jason Robards (**BSActor**), Maximilian Schell (**BSActor**), Meryl Streep. w. Alvin Sargent (**BAScr**), NF adap. Lillian Hellman (*Pentimento*), d. Fred Zinneman (BDirector). BPicture, BCinema, BArt, BCostume, BOScore. Oscars: 11-3.

DRAMA: SUSPENSE: Spy Films; Spies-Female; Autobiographical; Friendships-

Great; Friendships-Female; Episodic Stories; Writers; Rich People; Famous People When Young; Young Homoeroticism; Lesbians; Female Protagonists

(The Children's Hour; Sister, Sister)

Julia and Julia, 1988, 98m, ★★/$, Ind/Fox, R/S. An American woman in Italy is thrust into two different worlds, one where her husband died and she has a new lover, and one where he's still alive. Kathleen Turner, Sting, Gabriel Byrne. d. Peter DelMonte.

DRAMA: Erotic Drama; Psychological Drama; Dual Lives; Illusions/ Hallucinations; Lookalikes; Female Protagonists

(Ed: Shot on early high-definition video, then transferred to film-and it shows)

Julia Misbehaves, 1948, 99m, ★★★/ $$, MGM/MGM-UA. After two decades away, a woman returns to her husband and daughter and tries to fit in again as the daughter's about to be married. Greer Garson, Walter Pidgeon, Peter Lawford, Cesar Romero, Elizabeth Taylor, Lucile Watson, Migel Bruce. d. Jack Conway.

COMEDY DRAMA: Marriage Comedy; Family Comedy; Return of Spouse; Weddings; Mothers & Daughters; Circus Life

(My Favorite Wife; Kramer vs. Kramer)

Juliet of the Spirits, 1965, 142m, ★★★/$$, UA/Vidmark. A woman tries to deal with her husband cheating on her, living in fairy tales to escape. Giuletta Masina, Valentina Cortese, Sylvia Koscina. w. Federico Fellini, Tullio Pinelli, Ennio Flaiano, Brunello Rondi, d. Fellini. BCCin, BCCostume. Oscars: 2-0.

COMEDY DRAMA: Fantasies; Cheating Men; Character Studies; Midlife Crisis; Italian Films; Surrealism; Art Films

Julius Caesar, 1953, 121m, ★★★1/2/ $$$, UA/MGM-UA. The great Shakespearean tragedy following closely to the original classic play. Marlon Brando (BActor), James Mason, John Gielgud, Greer Garson, Edmond O'Brien, Deborah Kerr, Louis Calhern. w. d. Joseph L Mankiewicz, P-adap. Shakespeare. BPicture, BB&WArt, BB&WCin, BOScore. Oscars: 5-0.

DRAMA: TRAGEDY: Ancient Times; Assassination Plots; Rome; Leaders-Tyrant; Kings; Men in Conflict; Greed; Government Corruption; Classic Literary Adaptations; Shakespeare

(Men of Respect; Othello; Caesar and Cleopatra)

Jumanji, 1995, 100m, ★★1/2/$$$$, Tri-Star/Col-Tri, PG/V. A boy finds an ancient board game buried, and he's tucked away until years later when the game is found again; he pops out, and the game's powers become unleashed, leading to adventures and an elephant coming through his new family's house. Robin Williams, Kirsten Dunst, David Alan Grier, Adam Hann-Byrd, Bonnie Hunt, Jonathan Hyde, Bebe Neuwirth, Bradley Pierce. w. Jonathan Hensleigh, Greg Taylor, Jim Strain, d. Joe Johnston.
ADVENTURE: Fantasy; CHILDREN'S: Games; Time Travel; Fantasies
(Toys; Mrs. Doubtfire; Hook)

Jumpin at the Boneyard, 1992, 107m, ★★1/2/$, 20th/Fox, R. Two poor and slightly deranged brothers have adventures among the depths of New York streetlife, sinking into a life of drugs and crime. Tim Roth, Alexis Arquette, Danitra Vance, Samuel L. Jackson. w. d. Jeff Stanzier.
DRAMA: Crime Drama; Inner City Life; Drugs-Addictions; Drugs-Dealing; Prostitutes-Low Class; New York Life; Brothers; Overlooked at Release; Writer-Directors; Independent Films
(Little Odessa; Federal Hill)

Jumpin' Jack Flash, 1986, 96m, ★★/$$, 20th/Fox, PG-13/EP. When a bank employee communicates with a computer hacker, she gets caught up in a conspiracy and finds herself on the lam from a killer, with sometimes hilarious results. Whoopi Goldberg, Stephen Collins, Carol Kane, Annie Potts, Johnathan Pryce, Jim Belushi, Jon Lovitz, Sara Botsford, Tracey Ullman, Michael McKean. w. David Franzoni, d. Penny Marshall.
COMEDY: Comedy-Slapstick; Comic Mystery; Comic Thriller; Chase Stories; Fugitives from a Murderers; Conspiracy; Computers; Innocent Bystanders; Coulda Been Great; All-Star Cameos; Black Women; Female Directors; Female Protagonists
(Burglar; Ghost; Fatal Beauty)

June Bride, 1948, 97m, ★★★/$$, MGM/MGM-UA. When a male-female writing team is sent to write about weddings together, sexual and gender tensions rise in comic ways. Bette Davis, Robert Montgomery, Fay Bainter, Tom

Tully, Mary Wickes. w. Ranald MacDougall, d. Bretaigne Windust.
COMEDY: ROMANCE: Romantic Comedy; Battle of the Sexes; Weddings; Writers; Partners-Married; Hidden Gems; Forgotten Films
(Best Friends; Adam's Rib)

The Jungle Book, 1967, 78m, ★★★★/$$$$, Disney/Disney, G. Mowgli, the Indian boy, and all the rest of the jungle cats and the cool cat bear, Baloo, sing and dance. Phil Harris, Sebastian Cabot, Louis Prima, George Sanders, Sterling Holloway. d. Wolfgang Retherman. BOSong ("The Bear Necessities"). Oscars: 1-0.
Cartoons; ADVENTURE: Nature-Back to; Animal Stories; Boys; Imperialist Problems; India; Raised by Animals

The Jungle Book, 1994, 100m, ★★★/$$$, Disney/Disney, G. A live action, back to the original adaptation of Kipling's classic about an Indian boy who befriends the animals amid Imperialists and then has to save them. Jason Scott Lee, John Cleese, Cary Elwes, Lena Headley, Sam Neill. w. Stephen Sommer, Ronald Yanover, Mark Gelman, N-adap. Rudyard Kipling, d. Sommer.
ADVENTURE: Nature-Back to; Animal Stories; Boys; Imperialist Problems; India; Raised by Animals
REMAKE OF: 1940 Korda version
(Kim; Winnie The Pooh)

Jungle Fever, 1991, 132m, ★★/$$$, U/MCA-U, R/S-P-FN. A black architect (Wesley Snipes) falls for an Italian woman (Annabella Sciorra) and sparks fly with friends and family. John Turturro, Samuel Jackson, Ossie Davis, Ruby Dee, Lonette McKee, Brad Dourif, Veronica Webb. w. d. Spike Lee.
DRAMA: ROMANCE: COMEDY DRAMA: Romance-Interracial; Black vs. White; New York Life; Social Drama; Romantic Drama; Message Films; Writer-Directors; Black Directors; Black Men; Black Screenwriters
(Love Field; Kings Go Forth)
(Ed: Too heavy-handed and clunky to be entertaining)

Junior, 1994, 117m, ★★1/2/$$, U/MCA-U, PG-13/P-S. A man is impregnated as part of an experiment by a female doctor and soon sees life from the other's half's point of view. Arnold Schwarzenegger, Emma Thompson, d. Ivan Reitman.
COMEDY: Babies-Having; Babies-Men

Having; Scientists; Experiments; Role Reversal; Men as Women; Flops-Major
(A Slightly Pregnant Man; Rabbit Test)

Junior Bonner, 1972, 100m, ★★★/$$, 20th/Fox, PG. A rodeo star tries to win a competition to help his father build a new ranch. Steve McQueen, Robert Preston, Ida Lupino, Ben Johnson, Joe Don Baker. d. Sam Peckinpah.
WESTERNS: DRAMA: Westerns-Modern; Rodeos; Cattle Ranchers
(8 Seconds; Tom Horn; Baby, the Rain Must Fall)

Jupiter's Darling, 1955, 96m, ★★/$$, MGM/MGM-UA. A musical spoof of ancient Romans. Esther Williams, George Sanders, Howard Keel, Gower Champion. d. George Sidney.
MUSICALS: COMEDY: Musical Comedy; Ancient Times; Rome; Spoofs; Forgotten Films
(Neptune's Daughter)

Jurassic Park, 1993, 127m, ★★★/$$$$$, U/MCA-U, PG/V-B&G. When a billionaire bio-engineers dinosaurs from ancient embryos found on an island, the planned amusement park/"petting zoo" is visited by paleontologists who become prey instead of just guests. Sam Neill, Laura Dern, Jeff Goldblum, Richard Attenborough. w. David Koepp, Michael Crichton, N-adap. Michael Crichton, d. Steven Spielberg. BSFX, BCin, BSound, BEdit, BSEdit, BOScore. Oscars: 6-3.
SUSPENSE: ACTION: Chase Stories; Dinosaurs; Animal Monsters; Kill the Beast; Islands; Scientists; Archaeologists/Paleontologists; Murders-One by One; Children in Jeopardy; Blockbusters
SEQUEL: The Lost World
(Jaws; Duel; The Land That Time Forgot; One Million B.C.; The Lost World)
(Ed: Thrilling and consistent, but not all there-the story ends rather abruptly without a third act-they're dead, let's leave-and the moment of discovery from the book is missing: an attack by a small dinosaur on a beach with a woman doctor set up as detective)

Just Another Girl on the IRT, 1993, 96m, ★★1/2$, Ind/Live, R/S-P. A young black girl comes of age in the inner city and wants to get out, but getting pregnant presents a problem. Arlyan Johnson, Kevin Thigpen. w. d. Leslie Harris.

COMEDY DRAMA: Babies-Having; Coming of Age; Girls; Teenagers; Black Casts; Black Women; Inner City Life; Ordinary People Stories; Female Screenwriters; Female Directors; Writer-Directors; Independent Films
(I Like It Like That; Kids)

Just Between Friends, 1986, 100m, ★★1/2/$$, Tri-Star/HBO, PG. When a woman's husband dies, she finds that her new friend she met through him was really his mistress-and she's pregnant with his child. Mary Tyler Moore, Christine Lahti, Ted Danson, Sam Waterston. w. d. Allan Burns.

MELODRAMA: Friendships-Female; Marriage Drama; Death-Dealing with; Romance-Triangles; Babies-Having; Widows; Starting Over; Writer-Directors; Female Protagonists
(Between Friends; Starting Over)

Just Cause, 1995, 105m, ★★1/2/$$$, WB/WB, R/P-S-V. A young black man is convicted of murdering a little black girl after raping her. Years later, a white law professor is begged by the man's grandmother to find the real killer. He agrees to try and soon finds himself in the underworld of South Florida with a black detective at once helping and then sparring with him over racial issues in a case which has more to it than first meets the eye. Sean Connery, Laurence Fishburne, Kate Capshaw, Blair Underwood, Ruby Dee, Ed Harris. w. Jeb Stuart, Peter Stone, N-adap. John Katzenbach, d. Arne Glimcher.

SUSPENSE: Detective Stories; **MURDER: MYSTERY: MURDER MYSTERY:** Accused Unjustly; Rape/Rapists; Molestation-Child; Murders of Children; Florida; Race Relations; Black Men; Black & White Together
(Primal Fear; Silence of the Lambs; Criminal Law)
(Ed: Echoes of Alan Dershowitz's real-life cases here, but not the psychological and

legal machinations that could have added to the suspense and suspension of disbelief, which is lacking)

Just One of the Girls, 1993, 94m, ★★/$, Vidmark/Vidmark, PG. When a new kid goes to his new school, he dresses as a girl to avoid the big bully he ticked off. Corey Haim, Nicole Eggert. d. Michael Keusch.

COMEDY: Men as Women; Undercover; Hiding Out; High School Life
(Some Like It Hot; Ladybugs)

Just One of the Guys, 1985, 100m, ★★/$$, Col/Col, PG. A teenager joins the football team to prove herself as a reporter. Joyce Hyser, Toni Hudson, Leigh McCloskey, Sherilyn Fenn. d. Lisa Gottlieb.

COMEDY: High School Life; Female Among Males; Female Directors; Female Protagonists; Teenagers; Teenage Movies

Just Tell Me What You Want, 1980, 112m, ★★★/$, WB/WB, R/P-S. When a mogul won't let his mistress become a movie producer, she walks and marries a young, totally opposite, artistic playwright. The mogul sets the wheels of revenge in motion, she attacks him at Bergdorf's, and war is declared. Can they make up and be friends? Ali MacGraw, Alan King, Myrna Loy, Kennan Wynn, Tony Roberts. w. Jay Presson Allen, d. Sidney Lumet.

COMEDY: COMEDY DRAMA: Comedy-Light; **ROMANCE:** Romantic Comedy; Romance-Bickering; Revenge; Mistresses; Cheating Men; Battle of the Sexes; Greed; Rich People; Power Struggles; Romance-Triangles; Underrated; Hidden Gems; Coulda Been Great; Flops-Major; Female Screenwriters; Female Protagonists
(Born Yesterday; Love Story; Mistress)
(Ed: Smells like an old-fashioned screwball comedy, but it's really an insightful story about a woman caught in a power struggle and getting what she wants)

Just You and Me, 1977, 90m, ★★★/$, Ind/Ind. A kooky woman drives cross-country with an uptight fellow and almost falls in love, with quite a bit of humor along the way. Louise Lasser, Charles Grodin. w. d. Louise Lasser.

COMEDY: ROMANCE: Romantic Comedy; Road Movies; Comedy-Situation; Eccentric People; Hidden Gems; Female Screenwriters; Female Directors; Female Protagonists; Independent Films; Writer-Directors
(Homer and Eddie; When Harry Met Sally)
(Ed: When Harry Met Sally owes its premise to this, though it fades after the first hour)

Justine, 1969, 115m, ★★1/2/$, 20th/Fox, R/S. A prostitute gets involved in Middle East arms dealers and politics through some of her clients. Anouk Aimee, Michael York, Dirk Bogarde. w. Laurence Marcus, N-adap. Lawrence Durrell (The Alexandria Quartet), d. George Cukor.

MELODRAMA: DRAMA: Spies; Prostitutes-High Class; Middle East; Political Drama; Coulda Been Good; Forgotten Films
(The Little Drummer Girl; Half Moon Street)

J.W. Coop, 1971, 112m, ★★1/2/$, Col/NA. A cowboy on the rodeo circuit gets into trouble with the law. After ten years in prison, he returns to his home town to tie up loose ends. Cliff Robertson, Cristina Ferrare, Geraldine Page, R. G. Armstrong. w. Cliff Robertson, Gary Cartwright, Bud Shrake, d. Cliff Robertson.

DRAMA: Ex-Convicts; Prison Drama; Rodeos; Cattle Ranchers; Small-town Life; Quiet Little Films; Actor-Directors
(Junior Bonner; Five Easy Pieces)

K

K-9, 1989, 111m, ★★½/$$$, Universal/MCA-U, PG/P. A cop gets a super dog to sniff out drugs. Jim Belushi, Mel Harris, Kevin Tighe, Ed O'Neill, Jerry Lee. w. Steven Siegel, Scott Myers, d. Rod Daniel.
COMEDY: Police Stories; Police Comedy; **ACTION:** Action Comedy; Pet Stories; Dog
(Turner and Hooch; CHOMPS; K-9000)
K-9000, 1989, 96m, ★★/$, Fries/Fries, PG. A cop gets a robotic dog to help bust drugs and crime. Chris Mulkey, Catherine Oxenberg, Dennis Haysbert, Thom McFadden, Jerry Houser. w. Stephen E. deSouza, Michael Part, d. Kim Manners.
ACTION: COMEDY: Action Comedy; Pet Stories; Dogs; Robots; Independent Films
(K-9; Turner and Hooch; CHOMPS)
K-2, 1992, 104m, ★★★/$, Par/Par, PG-13/P-V. Two friends go through hell climbing upward toward heaven in the Himalayas. Michael Biehn, Matt Craven, Raymond Barry. w. Patrick Myers, Scott Roberts, P-adap. Myers, d. Franc Roddam.
DRAMA: ADVENTURE: Survival Drama; Mountain Climbing; Snow Settings; Buddy Films; Friendships-Male; Himalayas
(The Snows of Kilimanjaro; Alive)
Kafka, 1991, 100m, B&W, ★★½/$, Par/Par, PG. Fictionalization of the writer Franz Kafka's adventure into a dark conspiracy in a dark and oppressive world, inspired by the writer's own works of surreal, psychological horror. Jeremy Irons, Theresa Russell, Joel Grey, Ian Holm, Joroen Krabbe, Armin Mueller-Stahl, Alec Guinness. w. Lem Dobbs, d. Steven Soderbergh.
HORROR: DRAMA: Psychological Drama; Surrealism; Writers Biographies-Fictional; Mindgames; Conspiracy; Castles; Oppressions; Coulda Been Great; Writer-Directors
(Shadows and Fog; The Trial [1962]; Zentropa)
(Ed: Disappointing next move for Soderbergh off of *Sex, Lies & Videotape* and Irons fresh from his Oscar for *Reversal of Fortune*)
Kagemusha, 1980, 160m, ★★★½/$$$, 20th/Fox, R/EV. When a warlord is killed in ancient Japan, another takes his place with a double that confuses the enemies, but leads to battle. Tatsura Makadai, Tsutomu Yamakuzi. w. Akira Kurosawa, Masato Ide, d. Kurosawa. BFLFilm, BArt. Oscars: 2-0.
ADVENTURE: DRAMA: ACTION: Historical Drama; Action Drama; Identities-Assumed; Epics; Cast of Thousands; War Stories; War Battles; Lookalikes; Japan; Japanese Films; Ancient Times
(Ran; Rashomon; The Seven Samurai)

Kaleidoscope, 1966, 103m, ★★★/$$, WB/WB. A playboy in Europe has a card scam he takes to all of the casinos while winning the ladies and rolling the dice. Warren Beatty, Susannah York, Clive Revill, Eric Porter. w. Robert and Jane Howard-Carrington, d. Jack Smight.
DRAMA: ROMANCE: Elusive Men; Con Artists; Playboys; Gambling; Casinos; Americans Abroad; Mod Era; Female Screenwriters
(Gambit; The Cincinnati Kid)
(Ed: Cool and cute, but not much else)
Kalifornia, 1993, 118m, ★★½/$, Gramercy-U/MCA-U, R/EV-EP-S-FN-MRN. A hip journalist couple writing a book on serial killer murder sites pick up a redneck (Brad Pitt) and his girl (Juliette Lewis) for their trip which may make them unwitting victims, too. David Duchovny. w. Tim Metcalfe, d. Dominic Sena.
DRAMA: HORROR: TRAGEDY: Serial Killers; Psycho-Killer; Trail of a Killer; Road Movies; Outlaw Road Movies; Psychological Drama; Psychological Thriller; Hitchhikers; Black Comedy; Comedy-Morbid; Art Films; Unintentionally Funny; Road to California; Cult Films
(True Romance; Natural Born Killers)
Kamikaze 89, 1983, 90m, ★★★/$, UAC/MGM-UA, R. Terrorist bombings are the focus of an investigation by a

German police detective who finds himself in a characteristically bizarre world from Fassbinder, though he only starred in this one. Rainer Werner Fassbinder, Gunther Kaufman. d. Wolf Gremm.

DRAMA: Psychological Drama; Bombs; Terrorists; Detective Stories; Detectives-Police; Art Films; German Films

Kangaroo, 1952, 84m, ★★1/2/$$, 20th/MCA-U. A drifter comes to an Australian outback ranch and tries to romance the owner's daughter by pretending to be a relative. Peter Lawford, Maureen O'Hara, Finlay Currie, Richard Boone. w. Harry Kleiner, d. Lewis Milestone.

ROMANCE: DRAMA: Drifters; Con Artists; Love-Questionable; Heirs; Children-Long Lost; Impostors; Cattle Ranchers; Australia

The Kansan, 1943, 79m, ★★1/2/$$, UA/Nos. A gunfighter winds up marshal of a small Western town and has to adjust to being on the other side of the law. Richard Dix, Albert Dekker, Jane Wyatt, Eugene Pallette. w. Harold Schumate, NF-adap. Frank Gruber, d. George Archainbaud.

WESTERNS: Police Stories; Marshals; Gunfighters; Starting Over; Turning the Tables

Kansas, 1988, 111m, ★★/$, Cannon-TWE/Media, PG/V. A young man wandering through guess where runs into trouble when falls in love and teams up unwittingly with a con man. Andrew McCarthy, Matt Dillon, Leslie Hope, Krya Sedgwick, Harry Northrup. w. Spencer Eastman, d. David Stevens.

DRAMA: Crime Drama; **SUSPENSE:** Con Artists; Drifters; **ROMANCE:** Friends Turned Enemies; Midwestern Life; Coulda Been Good
(Bad Influence)

Kansas City Bomber, 1972, 99m, ★★1/2/$$$, MGM/MGM-UA, R/P-V. A young woman (Raquel Welch) fights her way through life as a member of a very violent all-women's roller derby team, matching her arch nemesis while trying to find romance. Kevin McCarthy, Norman Alden, Jeanne Cooper. w. Tom Rickman, Calvin Clements, d. Jerrold Freedman.

DRAMA: ACTION: MELODRAMA: Female Protagonist; Role Reversal; Roller Skating; Feisty Females; Evil Women; Women in Conflict; Female Protagonists

(Hannie Caulder; All the Marbles; Rollerball)
(Ed: Not so bad, and unusual to have a female protagonist like Welch, not so bright but tough as nails, though still beautiful-which for some undermines what might have otherwise been there)

Kansas City Confidential, 1952, 98m, ★★1/2/$$, UA/MGM-UA. The perfect crime is executed by an old pro who used to be a good guy, teaming up with three partners who remain anonymous to each other until the big plan goes into action. Preston Foster, John Payne, Coleen Gray, Lee Van Cleef, Neville Brand, Jack Elam. w. George Bruce, Harry Essex, d. Phil Karlson.

ACTION: Crime Drama; Heist Stories; Perfect Crimes; Ordinary Person Turned Criminal; Clever Plots & Endings; Coulda Been Great
(The Thomas Crown Affair; The Killing; The Hot Rock; The Asphalt Jungle)

Kaos, 1984, 188m, ★★★/$, RAI-TV-UAC/MGM-UA. A mixture of varied stories by famous Italian Pirandello are interlaced by their setting in an Italian town. Maragrita Lozano, Claudio Bigagli. w. d. Paolo and Vittorio Taviani, P-adap. Pirandello.

COMEDY: DRAMA: HORROR: SUSPENSE: Multiple Stories; Interwoven Stories; Italy, Italian Films; Revisionist Films

The Karate Kid, 1984, 126m, ★★★/$$$$$, Columbia/RCA-Col, PG/V. A new kid in town runs from the streets to learn karate and fight back and win the girl, becoming a young champion under the tutelage of an elderly Asian man. Ralph Macchio, Pat Morita (BSActor), Elizabeth Shue, Martin Kove. w. Robert Mark Kamen, d. John G. Avildsen. Oscars: 1-0.

ACTION: MELODRAMA: ROMANCE: Coming of Age; Love-First; Sports Movies; Martial Arts; Underdog Stories; Teachers and Students; New in Town; Suburban Life; Asian-Americans; Los Angeles; Gangs-Street; Fighting Back; Blockbusters; Sleeper Hits
(Ed: The old *Rocky* formula with the *Rocky* director works again, though less artsily this go around)

The Karate Kid, Part II, 1986, 95m, ★★1/2/$$$, Col/RCA-Col, PG/V. The kid's teacher goes back to Japan where his father is dying and the kid falls in

love again while trying to win an international competition. Ralph Macchio, Pat Morita, Nobu McCarthy. w. Robert Mark Kamen, d. John G. Avildsen.

The Karate Kid, Part III, 1989, 105m, ★★/$$, Col/RCA-Col, PG-13/V. The kid goes at it again, but mainly just fights this time. Ralph Macchio, Pat Morita, Robyn Lively, Sean Kanan, Martin Kove, Thomas Ian Griffith. w. Robert Mark Kamen, d. John G. Avildsen.

ACTION: MELODRAMA: ROMANCE: Coming of Age; Love-First; Sports Movies; Martial Arts; Underdog Stories; Teachers and Students; Asian-Americans; Competitions
(The Power of One; Rocky SERIES)
(Ed: Just rehashes-without much hash-of the first one)

Katherine, 1975, 98m, ★★★/$$$, ABC-New World/New World. An heiress becomes a revolutionary terrorist in the late 60s and then goes on the lam until it all catches up to her. Sissy Spacek, Art Carney, Jane Wyatt, Henry Winkler, Julie Kavner. d. Jeremy Paul Kagan.

DRAMA: Biographies-Fictional; Terrorists; Heiresses; Riches to Rags; Political Drama; Young Women; Vietnam Era; 1970s; 1960s; TV Movies; Curiosities
(Patty Hearst; Running on Empty)
(Ed: An amalgamation of Patty Hearst and various other female terrorist/ activists of the day with a decidedly unsympathetic, though otherwise objective portrayal)

The Keep, 1983, 93m, ★★1/2/$, Par/Par, PG/V. Nazis try to take over a castle but find forces within greater than even the Feuhrer. Scott Glenn, Jurgen Prochnow, Alberta Watson, Robert Prosky, Gabriel Byrne, Ian McKellen. w. d. Michael Mann.

HORROR: SUSPENSE: Nazi Stories; Fantasy; **SCI-FI:** Gothic Style; Ghosts; Castles; Coulda Been Great; Good Premise Unfulfilled; Forgotten Films; Writer-Directors
(The Gorgon)

Keeper of the Flame, 1942, 100m, ★★★/$$, MGM/MGM-UA-Turner. A woman fears she was married to a communist and this is why he died, but a journalist is trying to make her face it. Katharine Hepburn, Spencer Tracy, Richard Whor, Margaret Wycherly, Donald Meek. w. Donald Ogden Stewart, N-adap. IAR Wylie, d. George Cukor.

DRAMA: MELODRAMA: Political Drama; Communists; McCarthy Era; World War II Era; Traitors; Secrets-Keeping; Suicidal Tendencies; Widows; Journalists; Patriotic Films; Coulda Been Great; Time Capsules; Tracy & Hepburn (Sabotage; Caught; I Was a Communist for the FBI)
(Ed: Compromised by the times, seeming to want to be fair-minded and yet at the same time red-baiting)

Keep the Change, 1992, 95m, ★★¹/₂/ $$, Turner/Turner. An artist down on his luck returns to his Montana hometown where his former love's father wants to get his family's property, leading to more problems than he thought he had. William Petersen, Lolita Davidovich, Rachael Ticotin, Buck Henry, Jack Palance, Fred Dalton Thompson. N-adap. Thomas McGuane, d. Andy Tennant.
DRAMA: Character Studies; Artists; Reunions; Romance-Reunited; Save the Farm; Midlife Crisis; Eccentric People; Ordinary People Stories; TV Movies
(Rancho de Luxe; 92 in the Shade)

Kelly's Heroes, 1970, 143m, ★★★/$$$, MGM/MGM-UA, PG/V. Soldiers in Europe during World War II kidnap a Nazi, thereby stumbling onto a stash of gold, leading to a confrontation. Clint Eastwood, Telly Savalas, Don Rickles, Donald Sutherland, Carroll O'Connor, Stuart Margolin. w. Troy Kennedy Martin, d. Brian Hutton.
ACTION: War Stories; Heist Stories; World War II Stories; Nazi Stories; Gold Mines; Chase Movies; Ensemble Films; Ensembles-Male; Soldiers
(The Dirty Dozen; The Heroes of Telemark)

The Kennel Murder Case, 1933, 73m, ★★★/$$$, WB/NA. Detective Philo Vance has to prove that a murder really occurred when everyone thinks a death was a suicide. William Powell, Mary Astor, Eugene Pallette, Ralph Morgan. w. Robert Lee, Peter Milner, N-adap. S. S. Van Dine, d. Michael Curtiz.
MYSTERY: Mystery-Whodunit; **MURDER: MURDER MYSTERY:** Detective Stories; Suicidal Tendencies; Dogs; Hidden Gems; Forgotten Films
REMAKE: Calling Philo Vance

The Kentuckian, 1955, 104m, ★★¹/₂/$$, UA/CBS-Fox. A hunter from the mountains moves to the Texas plains to start over with his boy. Burt Lancaster, Dianne

Foster, Diana Lynn, Walter Matthau, John McIntire, Una Merkel, John Carradine. w. A. B. Guthrie, N-adap. Felix Holt (*The Gabriel Horn*), d. Burt Lancaster.
WESTERNS: MELODRAMA: New in Town; Fish out of Water Stories; Fathers & Sons; Mountain People; Starting Over; Texas; Actor-Directors

Kentucky, 1938, 95m, ★★★/$$$, 20th/NA. Romance in the horse stables and rivalry between breeding families. Loretta Young, Richard Greene, Walter Brennan (BSActor), Karen Morley. w. Lamar Trotti, N-adap. John Taintor Foote, *The Look of Eagles*, d. David Butler. Oscars: 1-1.
MELODRAMA: COMEDY DRAMA: ROMANCE: Horses; Family Drama; Rivalries; Feuds
(In Old Kentucky)

Kentucky Fried Movie, 1977, 85m, ★★★/$$$, Alpha/Media, R/S-P. A series of parodies, spoofs, skits, etc., mostly of TV shows and commercials. Marilyn Joi, Saul Kahan, Marcy Goldman. w. David & Jerry Zucker, Jim Abrahams, d. John Landis.
COMEDY: Spoofs; Comedy-Skit; TV Life; Cult Films; Sleeper Hits
(The Groove Tube; Airplane; Amazon Women on the Moon; Stay Tuned)

Kentucky Moonshine, 1938, 87m, ★★★/$$$, 20th/NA. The Ritz Brothers, rivals to the Marx, pretend to be hillbillies in order to win a prize but are mistaken for the real thing by the real McCoys who want to finish off a feud. w. Art Arthur, M.M. Musselman, d. David Butler.
COMEDY: Comedy-Skit; Fools-Bumbling; Radio Life; Competition; Identities-Mistaken; Hillbillies; Feuds

Kes, 1969, 109m, ★★★/$, UA/NA. When his pet bird dies, a young boy begins to realize about life around him. David Bradley, Lynne Perrie, Colin Welland, Brian Glover. w. Barry Hines, Ken Loach, Tony Garnet, N-adap. Barry Hines (*A Kestrel for the Knave*), d. Loach.
DRAMA: Coming of Age; Childhood; Boyhood; Pet Stories; Death-Dealing With; Allegorical Stories; Cult Films; Forgotten Films; Hidden Gems; Ireland; Irish Films
(Careful, He Might Hear You; The Long Day Closes)

The Key, 1934, 71m, ★★¹/₂/$$, WB/NA. A British soldier has an affair with a superior officer's wife in Ireland. William

Powell, Edna Best, Colin Clive, Donald Crisp. w. Laird Doyle, P-adap. R. Gore-Brown, J. L. Hardy, d. Michael Curtiz.
MELODRAMA: ROMANCE: Romance with Married Person; Romance-Clandestine; Cheating Women; Ireland; Soldiers; Forgotten Films
(Reflections in a Golden Eye)

The Key, 1958, 134m, ★★¹/₂/$$, Col/RCA-Col. Sailors have a key to an apartment which they pass among each other, also sharing the girl who stays there. William Holden, Sophia Loren, Trevor Howard, Oscar Homolka, Kieron Moore. w. Carl Foreman, N-adap. Jan de Hartog (*Stella*), d. Carol Reed.
DRAMA: MELODRAMA: ROMANCE: Female Among Males; World War II Stories; Sailors; Allegorical Stories; Good Premise Unfulfilled; Coulda Been Good; Forgotten Films; Affair Lairs
(The Apartment; The Men's Club)

Key Exchange, 1985, 96m, ★★¹/₂/$, 20th/CBS-Fox, R/FRN-MRN. A yuppie couple debates whether to give each their the keys to their apartments for fear of real commitment. Ben Masters, Brooke Adams, Daniel Stern. w. P-adap. Kevin Wade, d. Barnett Kellman.
COMEDY DRAMA: ROMANCE: Romantic Comedy; Yuppies; New York Life; 1980s; Bicycles; Forgotten Films; Coulda Been Good
(About Last Night; Almost You)
(Ed: The stage hit didn't translate so well, and casting may have had a lot to do with it)

Key Largo, 1948, 101m, ★★★★/$$$, WB/CBS-Fox, PIA. A gangster holds visitors at a Key West area hotel hostage looking for their hit target while a hurricane is making its way on-land. Humphrey Bogart, Lauren Bacall, Claire Trevor (BSActress), w. Richard Brooks, John Huston, P-adap. Maxwell Anderson, d. John Huston. Oscars: 1-1.
DRAMA: SUSPENSE: Hostage Situations; Crime Drama; Mob Stories; One Day Stories; Ordinary People vs. Criminals; Race Against Time; Feisty Women; Hiding Out; Hurricanes; Florida Keys
(Desperate Hours; To Have and Have Not; The Petrified Forest)

Key to the City, 1950, 101m, ★★¹/₂/ $$, MGM/MGM-UA. A mayoral convention leads to romantic affairs for a few participants. Clark Gable, Loretta Young, Frank Morgan, James Gleason, Marilyn

Maxwell, Raymond Burr, Lewis Stone, Pamela Britton. w. Robert Crutcher, d. George Sidney.

COMEDY DRAMA: ROMANCE: Romantic Comedy; **FARCE:** Politicians; Romance with Married Person; Romance-Clandestine; Conventions; San Francisco; Coulda Been Great; Good Premise Unfulfilled; Forgotten Films

The Keys of the Kingdom, 1945, 137m, ★★★/$$$, 20th/CBS-Fox, IGP. A Scottish missionary goes on an adventure to China to save the workers and find glory. Gregory Peck (BActor), Thomas Mitchell, Vincent Price, Rose Stradner, Roddy McDowell, Peggy Ann Garner, Edmund Gwenn, Cedric Hardwicke, Anne Revere. w. Joseph L. Mankiewicz, Nunnally Johnson, N-adap. A.J. Cronin, d. John Stahl. BB&WArt, BB&WCin, BScore. Oscars: 5-0.

DRAMA: MELODRAMA: ADVENTURE: Epics; Missionaries; Religion; China (The Inn of the Sixth Happiness; The Razor's Edge)

Khartoum, 1966, 134m, ★★½/$$$, UA/MGM-UA. The story of General Gordon going into battle in North Africa in epic style. Charlton Heston, Laurence Olivier, Ralph Richardson, Richard Johnson, Hugh Williams, Alexander Knox, Nigel Green, Michael Hordern. w. Robert Ardrey (BOScr), d. Basil Dearden. Oscars: 1-0.

ACTION: DRAMA: Epics; War Stories; War Battles; World War I Stories; Biographies; Historical Drama; Leaders-Military; Africa; Desert Settings (Lawrence of Arabia; The Desert Fox; Raid on Rommel; The Hill)

Kickboxer, 1989, 103m, ★★/$$, Kings Road/WB, HBO, R/EV-P. A kickboxer goes after those who maimed his brothers-by maiming others. Jean Claude Van Damme, Dennis Alexio, Dennis Chan. w. Glenn Bruce, Mark DiSalle, Jean Claude Van Damme, d. DiSalle.

Kickboxer 2—The Road Back, 1990, 89m, ★★/$$, Kings Road/WB, HBO, R/EV-P. Back out of retirement, a young kickboxer goes after an Asian champ. No resemblance except in kicking to first one. Sasha Mitchell, Peter Boyle, Dennis Chan, John Diehl. w. David S. Goyer, d. Albert Pyun.

ACTION: Martial Arts; Revenge; Brothers; Sports Movies (Bloodfist; The Challenge)

Kicking and Screaming, 1995, 96m, ★★★/$, Trimark/Trimark, R/P-S. Four college guys out in the real world find it difficult to cope outside of campus, in the workplace, or in social life but have humorous, realistically portrayed diversions symptomatic of the TV generation. Josh Hamilton, Olivia d'Abo, Chris Eigeman, Parker Posey, Elliott Gould, Eric Stoltz. w. d. Noah Baumbach.

COMEDY: COMEDY DRAMA: Twenty-somethings; Men's Films; Friendships-Male; Ensembles-Male; Writer-Directors; Independent Films; Generation X (Reality Bites; Naked in New York; The Brothers McMullen; Metropolitan; Watch It; Barcelona)

The Kid, 1921, 52m (silent), ★★★★/$$$$, Ind/Facets. The tramp finds a baby but the mother comes back for it, leading possibly to romance. Charlie Chaplin, Jackie Coogan, Edna Purviance. w. d. Chaplin.

COMEDY: ROMANCE: Romantic Comedy; Tearjerkers; Comedy-Slapstick; Abandoned People; Children-Abandoned; Mothers-Unwed; Mothers-Struggling; Writer-Directors; Film History (City Lights; Modern Times)

Kid, 1990, 91m, ★★/$, Alpha Cine-Ind/Live. A young man goes back to avenge the death of his parents in a small western town. C. Thomas Howell, Sarah Trigger, Brian Austin Green, R. Lee Ermey. w. Leslie Boehm, d. John Mark Robinson.

WESTERNS: Avenging Death of Someone; Revenge; Young Men; Independent Films

The Kid Brother, 1927, 83m (Silent), ★★★★/$$$, Par/Time-Life. A young man out to prove himself gets into an endless series of hilarious predicaments. Harold Lloyd, Jobyna Ralston. w. John Grey, Tom Crizer, Red Wilde, d. Wilde, J. A. Howe, Lewis Milestone.

COMEDY: Comedy-Slapstick; Men Proving Themselves; Comedy of Errors (Harold Lloyd's World of Comedy)

A Kid for Two Farthings, 1955, 96m, ★★★/$$, London-Rank/Home Vision. In a seedy but colorful area of London, a boy has a pet goat with magical powers-or so it seems. Celia Johnson, Diana Dors, David Kossoff, Brenda deBanzie, Joe Robinson. w. Wolf Mankowitz, d. Carol Reed.

COMEDY DRAMA: Fantasy; Magic; Pet Stories; Capra-esque; London; Good Premise Unfulfilled; Coulda Been Great (Ed: A great-looking film, but not as great as it could have been, entertainment-wise)

The Kid from Brooklyn, 1946, 114m, ★★★/$$, Goldwyn-UA/Goldwyn. A nerdy fellow winds up a boxer and in a lot of trouble. Danny Kaye, Virginia Mayo, Vera-Ellen, Steve Cochran, Eve Arden, Walter Abel, Lionel Stander, Fay Bainter. w. Grover Jones, Frank Butler, Richard Connell, d. Norman Z. McLeod.

COMEDY: Comedy of Errors; Comedy-Slapstick; Sports Movies; Boxing; Nerds; Mob Stories; Mob Comedy; Heroes-Ordinary; Underdog Stories

REMAKE OF: The Milky Way (Harold Lloyd)

(The One and Only; Wonder Man)

The Kid from Left Field, 1953, 80m, ★★★/$$$, 20th/NA. The kid of a washed-up baseball player who's now selling peanuts in the stands helps the Padres make a big comeback during the season by parlaying his dad's advice. Dan Dailey, Billy Chapin, Anne Bancroft, Lloyd Bridges, Ray Collins, Richard Egan. w. Jack Sher, d. Harmon Jones.

COMEDY DRAMA: MELODRAMA: FAMILY: CHILDREN'S: Sports Movies; Baseball; Fathers & Sons; Comebacks; Underdog Stories

REMAKE: TV (1979)

(Rookie of the Year; Angels in the Outfield)

The Kid from Spain, 1932, 90m, ★★★/$$$, Goldwyn-UA/NA. An ordinary goof is thought to be a star bullfighter, so he takes advantage of the situation until he faces the horns of reality. Eddie Cantor, Lyda Roberti, Robert Young, Noah Beery, J. Carrol Naish, Paulette Goddard, Betty Grable. w. William McGuire, Bert Kalmar, Harry Ruby, d. Leo McCarey.

COMEDY: MUSICAL: Musical Comedy; Identities-Mistaken; Bullfighters; Fools-Bumbling; Comedians; Dance Movies (Kid Millions)

Kid Galahad, 1937, 101m, ★★★/$$$, WB/MGM-UA. A young bellhop is trained as a boxer until his svengali gets a little jealous and sparks fly. Edward G. Robinson, Bette Davis, Wayne Morris, Humprey Bogart, Harry Carey. w. Seton Miller, N-adap. Franis Wallace, d. Michael Curtiz.

MELODRAMA: Sports Movies; Boxing; Svengalis; Teachers and Students; Rags to Riches

SEQUEL: Kid from Kokomo; **REMAKE:** The Wagons Roll at Night
(The Wagons Roll at Night; Kid from Kokomo; Rocky; Karate Kid)

A Kid in King Arthur's Court, 1995, 90m, ★★1/2/$$, Disney/Disney, G/V. Merlin needs a knight from modern day to travel back and talk King Arthur into ruling Camelot correctly. Thomas Ian Nicholas, Joss Ackland, Art Malik, Paloma Baeza, Kate Winslet, Ron Moody, Daniel Craig. w. Michael Part & Robert L. Levy, d. Michael Gottlieb.
ADVENTURE: SCI-FI: COMEDY: CHILDREN'S: Boys; Time Travel; Camelot Stories
(A Yankee in King Arthur's Court; The Sword in the Stone)

Kid Millions, 1935, 90m, ★★/$$$, Goldwyn-UA/Sultan. A poor guy inherits a fortune and whoops it up singing and dancing. Eddie Cantor, Ethel Merman, Ann Sothern, George Murphy. w. George Oppenheimer, William Anthony McGuire, Nunnally Johnson, d. Roy del Ruth.
COMEDY: MUSICAL: Musical Comedy; Identities-Mistaken; Bullfighters; Fools-Bumbling; Comedians; Dance Movies
(The Kid from Spain)

Kidnapped, 1938, 93m, ★★★/$$$, 20th/NA. A boy is sold into slavery by his uncle and makes friends with a thief who helps him out. Warner Baxter, Freddie Bartholemew, Arleen Whelan, John Carradine, Nigel Bruce, Reginald Owen. w. Sonya Levien, Richard Sherman, Walter Ferris, N-adap. Robert Louis Stevenson, d. Alfred Walker.
Kidnapped, 1959, 95m, ★★★/$$$, Disney/Disney. More action-oriented, literally colorful remake. Peter Finch, James MacArthur, Bernard Lee, John Laurie, Finlay Currie, Peter O'Toole. w. d. Robert Stevenson, N-adap. Robert Louis Stevenson.
Kidnapped, 1971, 107m, ★★1/2/$$, Omnibus/NA. Less adventurous remake, but still passable due to the stars. Michael Caine, Trevor Howard, Jack Hawkins, Donald Pleasence, Freddie Jones. w. Jack Pulman, d. Delbert Mann.
ACTION: ADVENTURE: Kidnappings; Slavery; Orphans; Boys; Men and Boys; Friendship-Male; Thieves; Ordinary People Turned Criminal; Revenge; Classic Literary Adaptations
(Treasure Island)

The Kidnapping of the President, 1980, 113m, ★★1/2/$, Ind/Cinergi. Terrorists plot to kidnap our leader and must be stopped! Hal Holbrook, Ava Gardner, William Shatner, Van Johnson. w. Richard Murphy, N-adap. Charles Templeton, d. George Mendeluk.
SUSPENSE: ACTION: DRAMA: Action Drama; Kidnappings; Terrorists; Presidents; Conspiracy; Coulda Been Good; Independent Films

Kids, 1995, 95m, ★★★/$$, NC-17/ES-EP-V. A day in the life of inner-city teenagers talking about sex mostly, in between doing drugs, and not thinking much about the possible repercussions of either. Leo Fitzpatrick, Chloe Sevigny, Sarah Henderson, Justin Pierce, Sajan Bhagat, Billy Valdes, Billy Waldman, Javier Nunez. w. Harmony Korine, d. Larry Clark.
DRAMA: Social Drama; Inner-City Life; Ensemble Films; Ensembles-Children; Teenagers; AIDS Stories; New York Life; One-Day Stories; Documentary Style; Latin People; Improvisational Films; Female Screenwriters; Independent Films; Sleeper Hits
(I Like It Like That; Five Corners; A Bronx Tale; The Wanderers; Aaron and Angela)
(Ed: Much controversy surrounded whether this was a realistic portrayal of inner-city life or just compressed hype of everything bad and exploitative from the area)

Killer Elite, 1975, 120m, ★★1/2/$$, UA/MGM-UA, R/EV-S. A SWAT team for the CIA breaks all the rules to handle its assignments. James Caan, Robert Duvall, Arthur Hill, Gig Young, Mako, Bo Hopkins, Tom Clancy, Burt Young. w. Marc Norman, Stirling Silliphant, N-adap. Robert Rostand (*Monkey in the Middle*), d. Sam Peckinpah.
ACTION: Spy Films; Secret Agents; CIA Agents; Ensemble Films; Ensembles-Male; Conspiracy; Hitmen; Assassination Plots; Crime Pays; Special Teams-Military; Coulda Been Good
(Navy SEALS; The Domino Principle)

Killer Fish, 1979, 101m, ★★1/2/$, Ind/CBS-Fox, R/S-V. A thief hides his gang's stash in a lake with piranhas to guard it. Lee Majors, Karen Black, Margaux Hemingway, Marisa Berenson, James Franciscus. w. Michael Rogers, d. Antonio Margheriti.

ACTION: HORROR: Heist Stories; Deaths-One by One; Animal Monsters; Fish; Unintentionally Funny
(Piranha; The Deep)
(Ed: The joy here is most of the cast is eaten)

Killer Inside Me, 1976, 99m, ★★1/2/$, Ind/WB. The sheriff of a small Texas town is becoming increasingly crazed and about to begin murdering. Stacy Keach, Susan Tyrrell, Kenan Wynn, John Carradine. N-adap. Jim Thompson, d. Burt Kennedy.
SUSPENSE: Psychological Drama; **MURDER:** Serial Killers; Nervous Breakdowns; Crime Drama; Psycho-Killers; Police Stories; Police Brutality; Character Studies; Narrated Films; Small-town Life; Jim Thompson-esque
(Detour; Road Games; The Getaway)

Killer McCoy, 1947, 104m, ★★1/2/$, MGM/NA. A boxer gets caught up in a murder plot and has to prove his innocence. Mickey Rooney, Ann Blyth, Brian Donlevy, James Dunn, Sam Levene. w. Frederick Brennan, Thomas Lennon, George Bruce, George Oppenheimer, d. Roy Rowland.
SUSPENSE: Crime Drama; **MURDER: MYSTERY: MURDER MYSTERY:** Saving Oneself; Accused Unjustly; Framed?; Sports Movies; Boxing; Forgotten Films

Killer Nun, 1978, 90m, ★★/$, Ind/NA. A nun decides that when it comes to male patients in her asylum, there should be none. Anita Ekberg, Alida Valli, Joe Dallesandro. w. Giulio Berruti, Albert Tarallo, d. Berruti.
HORROR: MURDER: Serial Killers; Psycho Killers; Nuns; Murderers-Female; Asylums; Men in Jeopardy; Female Protagonists

The Killers, 1946, 105m, ★★★1/2/$$$, Universal/MCA-U. A cook called the Swede in a small town is wanted by the mob, and as they stalk him, the audience is told how it all came to this. Burt Lancaster, Ava Gardner, Edmond O'Brien, Albert Dekker, Sam Levene, Virginia Christine. w. Anthony Veiller (BScr), John Huston, SS-adap. Ernest Hemingway, d. Robert Siodmak (BDirector). BScore, BEdit. Oscars: 4-0.
DRAMA: SUSPENSE: Crime Drama; Film Noir; Simple Minds; Mob Stories; Hitmen; Death-Impending; Boxing; Flashbacks
(Force of Evil; Kiss of Death)

(Ed: Lancaster's big breakthrough, and though not a thriller by today's standards, still harrowing as we wait for the inevitable, wondering why)

The Killers, 1964, 95m, ★★1/2/$$$, Universal/MCA-U. Fairly lousy, campy remake of the above, credited as being the first TV movie but wound-up in theaters due to the gunfire. Ronald Reagan, Angie Dickinson, John Cassavetes, Claude Akins, Clu Galagher. w. Gene Coon, SS-adap. Ernest Hemingway, d. Don Siegel.

ACTION: DRAMA: Action Drama; Crime Drama; **SUSPENSE:** Hitmen; Mob Stories; Death-Impending; Flashbacks; Unintentionally Funny; Camp; TV Movies

Killer's Kiss, 1955, 67m, ★★★/$, MGM/MGM-UA. A boxer puts himself on the line with mob by helping out a woman being harassed by her mobster boyfriend. Frank Silvera, Irene Kane, Jamie Smith. w. d. Stanley Kubrick.

DRAMA: Crime Drama; **MELODRAMA: ROMANCE:** Saving Someone; Bodyguards; Protecting Someone; Mob Stories; Boxing; Art Films; Cult Films; Writer-Directors

(Requiem for a Heavyweight; The Leather Saint)

The Killing, 1956, 83m, ★★★1/2/$$, MGM/MGM-UA, VYG. A convict wanting get back in the biz decides to round up some pals to pull a heist on a racetrack. Sterling Hayden, Marie Windsor, Jay C. Flippen, Elisha Cook Jr., Vince Edwards. w. d. Stanley Kubrick, N-adap. Lionel White, Clean Break.

SUSPENSE: DRAMA: Crime Drama; Heist Stories; One Last Time; Ex-Convicts; Horse Racing; Car Racing; Race Against Time; Cult Films

(The Asphalt Jungle; Riffifi; The Getaway)

Killing Dad, 1989, 93m, ★★1/2/$, Palace/NA. A drop-out father comes home after twenty years and his bitter son decides to do him in-with the family's consent. Denholm Elliott, Julie Walters, Richard E. Grant, Anna Massey, Laura deSol. w. d. Michael Austin, N-adap. Anna Quinn (*Berg*).

SATIRE: Black Comedy; Social Satire; **MURDER:** Murder-Comic Attempts; Comedy-Morbid; Murder of Relative; Family Comedy; Fathers-Troublesome; Abandoned People; Reunions; British Films; Overlooked at Release; Coulda

Been Good; Good Premise; Unfulfilled; Female Directors

SERIOUS FLIPSIDE TO: Max Dugan Returns

(To Sleep with Anger)

The Killing Fields, 1984, 142m, ★★★/$$$, Ladd-WB/WB, PG/V-P. A reporter in Cambodia during the great massacres has a friend who disappears but treks hundreds of miles to safety. Sam Waterston (BActor), Haing S. Ngor (**BSActor**), Julian Sands, John Malkovich, Craig T. Nelson. w. Bruce Robinson (BAScr), NF-adap. Sidney Schanberg, d. Roland Joffe (BDirector). BPicture, **BCin**, **BEdit**. Oscars: 7-3.

DRAMA: MELODRAMA: Tearjerkers; True Stories; Docudramas; Survival Drama; Saving Someone; Concentration Camps; Leaders-Tyrant; Political Unrest; Asia; Americans Abroad; Journalists

(Green Eyes; Off Limits; Platoon)

A Killing in a Small Town, 1990, 95m, ★★★1/2/$$$$, CBS/Vidmark. A Bible school teacher (Barbara Hershey [Emmy winner]) has an affair with a churchgoer whose wife threatens her with an axe, which the teacher then uses to return the threat and carry it out. Brian Dennehy, Hal Holbrook. d. Stephen Guylenhaal.

DRAMA: MURDER: True Stories; Courtroom Drama; Murderers-Female; Crimes of Passion; Ordinary People Turned Criminal; Murderers-Nice; Romance with Married Person; Small-town Life; Texas; Female Protagonists; TV Movies

(The Legend of Lizzie Borden)

The Killing of a Chinese Bookie, 1976, 113m, ★★★/$, Cassavetes-Faces/Touchstone, R/EV-EP. A man is told to kill a Chinese bookie in order to pay a debt to the mob. Ben Gazzara, Timothy Carey, Seymour Cassel, Morgan Woodward. w. d. John Cassavetes.

DRAMA: Crime Drama; Hitmen; Mob Stories; Murder-Coerced to; Chinese People; Los Angeles; Mob-Asian; Underworld; Film Noir-Modern; Overlooked at Release; Underrated; Hidden Gems; Writer-Directors; Independent Films

(The Yakuza; Black Rain; The Killers)

The Killing of Sister George, 1969, 138m, ★★★/$$, 20th/Fox, R/S. The trials of a lesbian soap opera star. Beryl Reid, Susannah York, Coral Browne, Roland

Fraser. w. Lukas Heller, P-adap. Frank Marcus, d. Robert Aldrich.

DRAMA: Black Comedy; Lesbians; Alternative Lifestyles; Actresses; TV Life; Soap Opera Shows; Nervous Breakdowns; Cult Films; Female Protagonists

(The Dresser; The Fox)

Killing Zoe, 1994, 96m, ★★★/$, Ind/Live, R/EV-EP-S-FFN-B&G. A safe-cracker meets a prostitute named Zoe who then happens to work at the bank he and his scuzzy French pals are about to rob. But even with a lucky start, things soon go all wrong, with one last chance to go right. Eric Stoltz, Julie Delpy, Jean-Hugues, Anglade, Gary Kemp. w. d. Roger Avary.

DRAMA: TRAGEDY: Crime Drama; **ACTION:** Action Drama; Heist Stories; Bank Robberies; Paris; Americans Abroad; Hostage Situations; Romance with Prostitute; Prostitutes-High Class; Psycho Killers; Drugs-Addictions; AIDS Stories; Risking It All; Writer-Directors; Underrated; Independent Films

(Rififi; Pulp Fiction; The Killing; Dog Day Afternoon)

(Ed: A heist movie with a brain-a tragic but realistic brain)

Killjoy, 1981, 100m, ★★★/$$$$, Lorimar-CBS/USA. A man (Robert Culp) is missing a lady friend named Joy who may or may not be dead, but regardless, for whom an actress has been hired to make people believe is alive in this elaborate murder conspiracy tale. Kim Basinger, John Rubenstein, Stephen Macht, Nancy Marchand, Anne Wedgeworth. d. John Llewellyn Moxey.

SUSPENSE: MYSTERY: MURDER: MURDER MYSTERY: Conspiracy; Mystery-Whodunits; Clever Murders; Clever Plots & Endings; Escalating Plots; Faked Deaths; Impostors; Mistaken Identity; Missing Persons; Mothers & Sons; Doctors; Hospitals; Murderers-Female; Hidden Gems; TV Movies

(Consenting Adults)

(Ed: Very good TV movie worth catching)

Kill Me Again, 1989, 93m, ★★★/$$ (VR), MGM/MGM-UA, R/S-EV. A small-time detective in Nevada (Val Kilmer) is lured into a web of murder and deceit by a beautiful woman (Joanne Whalley-Kilmer) where nothing is quite what it seems. Michael Madsen, Pat Mulligan. w. John Dahl, David Warfield, d. Dahl.

SUSPENSE: MYSTERY: Detective Stories; Erotic Thriller; **ROMANCE:** Clever Plots & Endings; Dead-Back from the; Desert Settings; Jim Thompson-esque (The Grifters; Chinatown; Body Heat; Delusion; Red Rock West; The Last Seduction)

The Kill-Off, 1989, 97m, ★★½/$, Ind/NA. A small-town gossip won't keep the trap shut, so three men are called upon to shut it for good. Loretta Gross, Andrew Lee Barrett, Jackson Sims, Steve Monroe. w. d. Maggie Greenwald, N-adap. Jim Thompson.

SUSPENSE: MURDER: Black Comedy; Gossips; Small-town Life; Overlooked at Release; Jim Thompson-esque; Coulda Been Great; Good Premise Unfulfilled; Female Screenwriters; Female Directors; Independent Films

Kim, 1950, 112m, ★★★/$$, MGM/MGM-UA. An orphan boy in old India meets up with a colorful British secret agent and tags along for adventure. Errol Flynn, Dean Stockwell, Paul Lukas, Robert Douglas, Thomas Gomez, Cecil Kellaway, Reginald Owen. w. Leon Gordon, Helen Deutsch, Richard Schayer, d. Victor Saville, N-adap. Rudyard Kipling.

ADVENTURE: COMEDY DRAMA: Friendship-Male; Men and Boys; India; Indian People; Imperialist Problems; Secret Agents; Horses; Classic Literary Adaptations; Coulda Been Great (The Jungle Book; Gunga Din)

Kind Hearts and Coronets, 1949, 104m, ★★★★/$$, Ealing-EMI/EMI-HBO. A possible heir to a family fortune must first knock off the family members who could inherit first. Alec Guinness in multiple roles. Dennis Price, Valerie Hobson, Joan Greenwood, Miles Malleson. w. Robert Hamer, John Dighton, N-adap. Roy Horniman (*Noblesse Oblige*), d. Robert Hamer.

COMEDY: FARCE: Black Comedy; Comedy-Morbid; Murders-One by One; Murder Attempts-Comic; Inheritances at Stake; Multiple Performances; Hidden Gems (The Mouse That Roared; The Lady Killers)

A Kind of Loving, 1962, 112m, EMI/HBO. Two young people get married because of a baby on the way and then realize they don't love each other much at all. Alan Bates, June Richey, Thora Hird,

Bert Palmer. w. Keith Waterhouse, Willis Hall, N-adap. Stan Barstow, d. John Schlesinger.

DRAMA: ROMANCE: Coming of Age; Marriages-Forced; Kitchen Sink Drama; In-Laws-Troublesome; Working Class; Young People; Young Men; Time Capsules; England; British Films (Saturday Night and Sunday Morning; A Taste of Honey; This Sporting Life)

Kindergarten Cop, 1990, 111m, ★★/$$$$, U/U-MCA CCB, PG/V. An L.A. cop (Arnold Schwarzenegger) goes undercover in Oregon as a kindergarten teacher to nab the killer (Richard Tyson) whose son attends class there. Penelope Ann Miller. w. Murray Salem, Herschel Wingrod, Timothy Harris, d. Ivan Reitman.

COMEDY: COMEDY DRAMA: ACTION: Action Comedy; Detective Stories; **ROMANCE:** Romantic Comedy; Fish out of Water Stories; Teachers; School Life; Trail of a Killer; Fathers-Alone (Twins; Junior; Billy Madison) (Ed: Dumb but cute, sold completely on the contrast of Arnold and a bunch of screaming kiddies-too much violence for little kids)

The Kindred, 1987, 92m, ★★★/$$, Ind/Vestron, Live, R/V-B&G. A boy finds that his mother/scientist has cloned a being with his own tissue-a being that looks like him and likes to eat other people. Rod Steiger, Kim Hunter, David Allan Brooks, Talia Balsam, Amanda Pays, Timothy Gibbs. w. Jeffrey Obrow, Stephen Carpenter, Jo Stefano, John Penney, Earl Ghaffari, d. Obrow & Carpenter.

HORROR: Cannibals; Twins-Evil; Twins; Scientists-Mad; Mothers-Troublesome; Human Eaters; Monsters-Human; Cult Films; Overlooked at Release; Coulda Been Great; Hidden Gems (The Other; Re-animator; Chiller)

King, 1978, 272m, ★★★/$, NBC/NA. The life story of Martin Luther King Jr., focusing on his rise to prominence during the 50s. Paul Winfield, Cicely Tyson, Roscoe Lee Browne, Ossie Davis, Howard E. Rollins, Cliff DeYoung. w. d. Abby Mann.

DRAMA: Biographies; Saintly People; Charismatic People; Politicians; Preachers; Black Men; Black Casts; Historical Drama; Southerns; Race Relations; Assassination Plots;

Miniseries; TV Movies; Hidden Gems; Forgotten Films; Writer-Directors (Gandhi; Malcolm X) (Ed: After the release of *Malcolm X*, much was said as to why there was no film on King-perhaps not as exciting a story somehow, yet there was this TV miniseries which failed in the ratings on the heels of *Roots*, but which is worth a look)

The King and Four Queens, 1956, 86m, ★★½/$$, UA/MGM-UA. A fugitive from the law finds a ghost town, inhabited only by a woman and her three daughters who are there looking for money their criminal dad hid-which this fellow would like to romance his way into-if he can duel with the leader of the pack. Clark Gable, Eleanor Parker, Jo Van Fleet, Jean Wiles. d. Raoul Walsh.

MELODRAMA: Finding the Loot; Fugitives from the Law; Treasure Hunts; Male Among Females; Romance-Triangles; Romance with Relative's Lover; Dangerous Men; Dangerous Women; Good Premise Unfulfilled; Forgotten Films (Johnny Guitar; Boom Town; The Misfits)

The King and I, 1956, 133m, ★★★½/$$$$, 20th/CBS-Fox, RDG. The King of Siam gets a British governess who whips things in to shape, leading to romance for the stern king. Deborah Kerr (BActress), Yul Brynner (**BActor**), Rita Moreno, Martin Benson. w. Ernest Lehman, d. Walter Lang (BDirector), MP-adap. Richard Rodgers, Oscar Hammerstein. BPicture, **BCArt, BMScore**, BCCin, **BSound, BCCostume**. Oscars: 9-5.

MUSICALS: ROMANCE: Musical Romance; Babysitters; Kings; Royalty; Kingdoms; Stern Men; Fathers-Troublesome; Families-Large; Teachers; Asia; Production Design-Outstanding **MUSICAL VERSION OF:** Anna and the King of Siam

King Creole, 1958, 115m, ★★½/$$, Par/Fox. A drifter becomes a singing sensation in New Orleans, with the mob hot on his heels. Elvis Presley, Walter Matthau, Carolyn Jones, Dean Jagger, Paul Stewart, Dolores Hart. w. Herbert Baker, Michael V. Gazzo, N-adap. Harold Robbins (*A Stone for Danny Fisher*), d. Michael Curtiz.

MELODRAMA: Music Movies; Crime Drama; Mob Stories; Singers; New Orleans; Southerns; Coulda Been Great

(Ed: A great-looking film that just misses the mark-due to its star more than anything else, ironically)

King David, 1985, 114m, ★½/$, Par/Par, PG-13/S. Biography of the young man (Richard Gere) who took on Goliath and became king of Israel. Richard Gere, Edward Woodward, Denis Quilley, Cherie Lunghi, Alice Krige, Hurd Hatfield. w. Andrew Birkin, James Costigan, d. Bruce Beresford.
DRAMA: Biblical Stories; Ancient Times; Kings; Legends; Power-Rise to; Unintentionally Funny; Coulda Been Good; Flops-Major
(Ed: Gere's miscasting and the pace don't help matters, which are already pretty bad otherwise)
The Kingdom, 1995, 279m, ★★★/$$. Many surreal and supernatural things happen in a hospital built on sacred ground in Denmark in this miniseries from Danish TV that developed a cult following in Europe. Udo Kier, Otto Brandenburg, Kirsten Rolffes. w. Lars von Trier, Niels Vorsel, d. Lars von Trier.
SUSPENSE: HORROR: SCI-FI: Psychological Thriller; Hospital; Miniseries; Art Films; Ensemble Films; Danish Films; Cult Films
(Zentropa)
A King in New York, 1957, 109m, ★★/$, Attica-Ind/Fox. A poor, washed-up king from Europe tries to cope with his arrival in New York. Charlie Chaplin, Michael Chaplin, Oliver Johnston. w. d. Charles Chaplin.
COMEDY: COMEDY DRAMA: SATIRE: Fish out of Water Stories; Kings; New York Life; Flops-Major
(Coming to America; The Countess from Hong Kong)
King Kong, 1933, 105m, ★★★★/$$$$, RKO/Turner. A movie producer goes to find the fabled giant ape on his remote island and winds up causing the Empire State Building some problems. Fay Wray, Bruce Cabot, Robert Armstrong, Frank Reicher. w. James Creelman, Ruth Rose, SS-adap. Edgar Wallace, d. Merian C. Cooper.
King Kong, 1976, 135m, ★★★/$$$$, DEG-Par/Par, PG/S-V. More realistic remake at a more leisurely pace. Jessica Lange, Jeff Bridges, Charles Grodin, John Randolph, Rene Auberjonois, Julius Harris, Ed Lauter. w. Lorenzo Semple, d. John Guillermin.

ACTION: SCI-FI: ADVENTURE: Epics; Primates; Animal Monsters; Women in Joepardy; Islands; Hollywood Life; Empire State Building; Dinosaurs; High-Rise Settings
(Mighty Joe Young; Godzilla; Gorilla at Large)
King Lear, 1971, 137m, ★★½/$, Col/Nos. A king divides his kingdom between his daughters, leading to conflict between them and affecting his desire to die in peace. Paul Scofield, Irene Worth, Alan Webb, Tom Fleming, Cyril Cusack, Patrick Magee. w. d. Peter Brook, P-adap. William Shakespeare.
DRAMA: TRAGEDY: Fathers & Daughters; Kings; Royalty; Power Struggles; Inheritances at Stake; Stern Men; Greed; Classic Literary Adaptations; Classic Tragedy; Coulda Been Good
(Ran; Macbeth; The Tempest)
King Lear, 1987, 91m, ★½/$, Cannon/MGM-UA, PG. An aesthete in France wants to make a film about an old man and his four daughters, happening to mirror the famous play. Woody Allen, Molly Ringwald, Burgess Meredith, Peter Sellars, Jean-Luc Godard, Norman Mailer, Kate Mailer. w. d. Jean Luc Godard.
COMEDY DRAMA: Art Films; **SATIRE:** Fathers & Daughters; French Films; Flops-Major; Revisionist Films; Movies within Movies
The King of Comedy, 1983, 109m, ★★★★/$, 20th/CBS-Fox, R/P-S. An aspiring but bad comedian, Rupert Pupkin (Robert De Niro), and his demented friend (Sandra Bernhard) plan to kidnap a Johnny Carson–type talk show host (Jerry Lewis) in order to get attention. w. Paul D. Zimmerman, d. Martin Scorsese.
COMEDY: SATIRE: COMEDY DRAMA: Black Comedy; Stalkers; Kidnappings; Fans-Crazed; Mental Illness; Illusions Destroyed; TV Life; Comedians; Talk Shows; Flops-Major; Underrated; Overlooked at Release; Hidden Gems
(Taxi Driver; The Fan; Heartbreak Hotel)
(Ed: Inexplicably denounced and ignored in its original opening amid rumors of going grossly over-budget and overboard. A classic in the making whose story rings more and more true with every year)
King of Hearts, 1968, 101m, ★★★/$$, UA/MGM-UA, R/S. A soldier in World War II France wanders alone and comes

about a village full of what turns out to be mentally ill asylum inmates who've escaped and worship his sanity. Alan Bates, Genevieve Bujold, Jean-Claude Brialy. w. Daniel Boulanger, d. Phillipe de Broca.
COMEDY DRAMA: Fantasy; Mental Illness; Kings; Soldiers; World War II Era; Small-town Life; Psychologists; Allegorical Stories; Coulda Been Great; Hidden Gems
(Farewell to the King; One Flew Over the Cuckoo's Nest)
King of Jazz, 1930, 101m, ★★★/$$$$, U/MCA-U. A big musical revue to show of the advances of talkies. Bing Crosby, Paul Whiteman, John Boles, Laura La Plante, Walter Brennan, Charles MacArthur. w. Harry Ruskin, Charles MacArthur, d. John Anderson. BArt. Oscars: 1-0.
MUSICALS: Dance Movies; Dancers; Singers; Jazz Life; Hidden Gems
King of Kings, 1927, 115m, ★★★/$$$$, Pathe/Modern Sound. Epic story of Jesus told from Mary Magdalen's point of view, focussing on his miracles. H. B. Warner, Jacqueline Logan, Joseph Schildkraut. w. Jeanie Macpherson, d. Cecil B. DeMille.
DRAMA: MELODRAMA: Epics; Biographies; Biblical Stories; Jesus Christ; Ancient Times; Middle East; Cast of Thousands; Female Screenwriters
King of Kings, 1961, 170m, ★★★/$$$, MGM/MGM-UA. A more glossy version of the story of Jesus, more realistic than the gladiator-style epics of the previous years, but still all gloss. Jeffrey Hunter, Robert Ryan, Siobhan McKenna, Hurd Hatfield, Rip Torn, Harry Guardino, Viveca Lindfords. w. Philip Yordan, d. Nicholas Ray.
DRAMA: MELODRAMA: Epics; Biographies; Biblical Stories; Jesus Christ; Ancient Times; Middle East; Cast of Thousands
(The Robe; Jesus Christ; The Greatest Story Ever Told; Jesus of Nazareth)
The King of Marvin Gardens, 1972, 104m, ★★★/$, Col/Col-Tri, R/S-V. A disc jockey (Jack Nicholson) and his scheming con artist brother (Bruce Dern) return to the old days in the decayed Atlantic City and try to start over . . . or finish. Ellen Burstyn. w. Jacob Brackman, d. Bob Rafelson.
DRAMA: TRAGEDY: Brothers; Friendships-Male; Dreamers; Con Artists;

Atlantic City; Violence-Sudden; Allegorical Stories; Radio Life; American Dream; Murder of Spouse
(Atlantic City; True West; Fat City)
King of New York, 1990, 106m, ★★/$, Ind/Live, R/EV-P. A mobster gets out of prison and then takes over the local drug cartel in a murder spree. Christopher Walken, David Caruso, Larry Fishburne, Victor Argo, Wesley Snipes. w. Nicholas St. John, d. Abel Ferrara.
ACTION: Mob Stories; Drugs-Dealing; Mob Wars; Convict's Revenge; Ex-Convicts; Murder Sprees; Power-Rise to; Overlooked at Release; Coulda Been Good; Independent Films
(Scarface; McBain)
(Ed: With the talent involved, this is a surprising effort, though it doesn't really rise out of exploitation)
King of the Gypsies, 1978, 112m, ★★★/$, DEG-Par/Par, R/V-S. When a young gypsy king wants to marry the beautiful daughter of a rival band of "gypsies," conflict results in murder and loyalty plays a part in his fate. Eric Roberts, Susan Sarandon, Shelley Winters, Sterling Hayden, Brooke Shields, Judd Hirsch. w. d. Frank Pierson, N-adap. Peter Maas.
DRAMA: Crime Drama; ROMANCE: Romance-Doomed TRAGEDY: MURDER: Crimes of Passion; Gypsies; Con Artists; Underworld; Inner City Life; Coulda Been Good; Writer-Directors
(Pretty Baby; The Wanderers; Five Corners)
The King of The Hill, 1965, 122m, ★★1/2/$$, MGM/MGM-UA. A British P.O.W. camp in North Africa during World War II is the sight of a rebellion after the prisoners have taken all the abuse they can endure. Sean Connery, Harry Andrews, Michael Redgrave, Ian Bannen, Alfred Lynch, Ossie Davis, Roy Kinnear, Jack Watson, Ian Hendry. w. Ray Rigby, d. Sidney Lumet.
DRAMA: ACTION: Action Drama; POWs; World War II Stories; Prison Drama; Prison Escapes; Africa
(Victory; Stalag 17; The Hill)
King of the Hill, 1993, 102m, ★★★1/2/$, U/MCA-U, PG. True story of A.E. Hotchner, the writer who practically raised himself in Depression-era St. Louis. Jesse Bradford, Jeroen Krabbe, Lisa Eichhorn, Karen Allen, Spalding Gray, Elizabeth McGovern. w. d. Steven Soderbergh, NF-adap. A.E. Hotchner.

DRAMA: Character Studies; Boyhood; Autobiographical Stories; True Stories; Depression Era; Orphans; Fathers & Sons; Hotels; Memories; Overlooked at Release; Hidden Gems; Child Protagonists; Writer-Directors
King, Queen, Knave, 1972, 94m, ★★★/$, Ind/Sultan, R/S. The older wife of a man falls for his teenage nephew, resulting in rather interesting complications. Gina Lollobrigida, David Niven, John Moulder Brown. w. David Shaw, David Seltzer, N-adap. Vladimir Nabokov, d. Jerzy Skolimowski.
COMEDY DRAMA: ROMANCE: Romance-Doomed; Romance-Older Women/Younger Men; Romance with Relative; Romance-Clandestine; Teenagers; Coming of Age; Hidden Gems; Forgotten Films
FLIPSIDE TO: Lolita
(Lolita; Class; My Tutor; Homework; Murmur of the Heart; Love, Pain, and the Whole Damn Thing)
King Ralph, 1991, 96m, ★★1/2/$$$, U/MCA-U, PG/P. When the royal family of England is electrocuted while taking a family photo, it is discovered that the only living heir is a fat American slob (John Goodman). Peter O'Toole, John Hurt, Joely Richardson, Julian Glover. w. d. David S. Ward.
COMEDY: Inheritances at Stake; Royalty-Sudden; Heirs; Fish out of Water Stories; Snobs vs. Slobs; England; Kings; Americans Abroad; Coulda Been Good; Writer-Directors
(Little Lord Fauntleroy; The Prisoner of Zenda; Earl of Chicago)
King Rat, 1965, 134m, ★★★/$$, Col/Col. The story of an American POW in Singapore during World War II and his dealings to stay living decently. George Segal, Tom Courtenay, John Mills, James Fox, Denholm Elliott, Todd Armstrong, Patrick O'Neal. w. d. Bryan Forbes. BB&WCin. Oscars: 1-0.
DRAMA: Prison Drama; War Stories; World War II Stories; POWs; Soldiers; Asia
(Stalag 17; Midnight Express; The Killing Fields)
King Solomon's Mines, 1937, 80m, ★★★/$$$, Gainsborough/Nos. Explorers following the legend of King Solomon's treasure, moved from place to place for protection in ancient times, find a chieftain who claims he can help them locate

the location of it. Cedric Hardwicke, Paul Robeson, Roland Young, John Loder, Anna Lee. w. Michael Hoigan, AR Rawlinson, Roland Pertwee, Ralph Spence, Charles Bennett, N-adap. H. Rider Haggard, d. Robert Stevenson.
King Solomon's Mines, 1950, 102m, ★★★1/2/$$$$, MGM/MGM-UA. A more epic, sweeping version of the adventure. Stewart Granger, Deborah Kerr, Richard Carlson, Hugo Haas. w. Helen Deutsch, N-adap. H. Rider Haggard, d. Compton Bennett. BPicture, **BCCin, BEditing**. Oscars: 3-2.
Female Screenwriters
King Solomon's Mines, 1985, 101m, ★★/$$, Cannon/MGM-UA, PG/V. A comic-book style version, à la Indiana Jones. Clever twist on the staid plot but too silly. Richard Chamberlain, Sharon Stone, John Rhys-Davies, Herbert Lom. w. Gene Quintano, James Silke, d. J. Lee-Thompson.
ADVENTURE: Quests; Treasure Hunts; Journeys; Epics; Female Among Males; Africa; Legends
(Indiana Jones and the Last Crusade; Raiders of the Lost Ark; Congo)
Kingdom of the Spiders, 1977, 90m, ★★/$, Ind/VCI. Tarantulas run amok in Arizona. William Shatner, Tiffany Bolling, Woody Strode, Altovise Davis. w. Richard Robinson, Alan Caillou, d. John Cardos.
HORROR: SCI-FI: Insects; Spiders; Animal Monsters; Desert Settings
(Arachnophobia; Empire of the Ants)
(Ed: Check out *Arachnophobia*)
Kings and Desperate Men, 1983, 118m, ★★1/2/$, Ind/MPI. A controversial radio talk-show host is held hostage by terrorists. Patrick McGoohan, Alexis Kanner, Andrea Marcovicci, Margaret Trudeau,. w. Edmund Ward, Alexis Kanner, d. Alexis Kanner.
DRAMA: Hostage Situations; Terrorists; Political Drama; Radio Life; Coulda Been Good; Stagelike Films; Canadian Films; Independent Films
(Talk Radio; Betrayed)
Kings Go Forth, 1958, 109m, ★★1/2/$$, UA/MGM-UA. Two white American soldiers fall in love with a black French lady, leading to great conflict between them all. Frank Sinatra, Tony Curtis, Natalie Wood, Leora Dana, Karl Swenson. w. Merle Miller, N-adap. Joe David Brown, d. Delmer Daves.

DRAMA: Race Relations; Black vs. White; **ROMANCE:** Romance-Triangles; Romance-Doomed; Men Fighting Over Women; Soldiers; Black Women; Americans Abroad; Ahead of its Time; Forgotten Films; Overlooked at Release (A Patch of Blue; Jungle Fever; Love Field)

Kings of the Road, 1976, 176m, ★★1/2/$, Ind/Facets. Two guys on a bus remember their past and contemplate their lives. Rudigier Volger, Hanns Zichler. w. d. Wim Wenders.

DRAMA: Character Studies; Friendships-Male; Buses; Road Movies; Art Films; Avant-Garde Films; Writer-Directors (My Dinner with Andre; Wings of Desire)

Kings of the Sun, 1963, 108m, ★★1/2/$$, UA/NA. Ancient Mayan chieftain and his trek to find a new home for his tribe. Yul Brynner, George Chakiris, Shirley Anne Field, Richard Basehart, Barry Morse. w. Elliott Arnold, James R. Webb, d. J. Lee-Thompson.

ADVENTURE: Epics; Ancient Times; Indians-American; Leaders; Latin People; Legends; Mexico; Forgotten Films (Ed: Lovely to look at, good opening, but not much else to recommend)

Kings Row, 1941, 127m, ★★★★/$$$, MGM/MGM-UA. Story of a family ridden with mental illness and animosity in a small town at the turn of the century. Ann Sheridan, Robert Cummings, Ronald Reagan, Betty Field, Claude Rains, Charles Coburn, Nancy Coleman, Judith Anderson. w. Casey Robinson, N-adap. Harry Bellaman, d. Sam Wood (BDirector). BPicture, BB&WCin. Oscars: 3-0.

DRAMA: MELODRAMA: Family Drama; Small-town Life; Behind the Scenes; Brothers & Sisters; Abused Women; Stern Men; Midwestern Life; Mental Illness; Ensemble Films (The Magnificent Ambersons; Random Harvest)

The King's Whore, 1990, 138m, ★★★/$, Vidmark/Vidmark, R/S-FN-MRN. A beautiful woman is forced by circumstance to become a courtesan/mistress of a king in 1600s Europe. Timothy Dalton, Valeria Golino. w. Daniel Vigne, Frederic Raphael, Axel Corti, Derek Marlowe, N-adap. Jacques Tourneier, Jeanne, Putain du Roi, d. Corti.

MELODRAMA: ROMANCE: Erotic Drama; Romantic Drama; Costume Drama; Prostitutes-High Class; Mistresses; Kings; Royalty; Castles; French Films; Overlooked at Release (Queen Margot; Restoration)

Kinjite, Forbidden Subjects, 1989, 97m, ★★/$$, Cannon/MGM-UA, R/EV-S. A child prostitution ring is a police detective's goal to destroy. Charles Bronson, Perry Lopez, Peggy Lipton. w. Harold Nebenzal, d. J. Lee-Thompson.

ACTION: Police Stories; Detective Stories; Pornography World; Girls; Prostitutes-Child

Kipps (*The Remarkable Mr. Kipps*), 1941, 95m, ★★★1/2/$$, 20th/Nos CAB. In turn of the century England, a lowly interior decorator's assistant gets money that takes him into high society and some problems with friends. Michael Redgrave, Phyllis Calvert, Diana Wynyard, Michael Wilding, Arthur Riscoe, Hermione Baddely. w. Sidney Gilliat, N-adap. H. G. Wells, d. Carol Reed.

COMEDY DRAMA: Heirs; Rags to Riches; Social Climbing; Class Conflicts; Rich People; Rich vs. Poor; England; British Films; Edwardian Era; Hidden Gems

MUSICAL REMAKE: Half a Sixpence

Kismet, 1944, 100m, ★★1/2/$$, MGM/NA. In a fantastical Oriental world, a magician does battle with evil. Ronald Colman, Marlene Dietrich, James Craig, Edward Arnold, Hugh Herbert. w. John Meehan, d. William Dieterle.

MELODRAMA: Fantasy; **SCI-FI:** Legends; Good vs. Evil; Magic; Surrealism

Kismet, 1955, 113m, ★★★/$$$, MGM/MGM-UA, PIA FCT. Musical remake of the above, with more emphasis on romance. Howard Keel, Ann Blyuth, Dolores Gray, Vic Damone, Monty Woolley, Sebastian Cabot, Jay C. Flippen. w. MP-adap. Charles Lederer, Luther Davis, d. Vincente Minnelli.

MUSICALS: ROMANCE: Musical Romance; **MELODRAMA:** Fantasy; Musical Fantasy; **SCI-FI:** Legends; Good vs. Evil; Magic; Surrealism

The Kiss, 1929, 89m (silent), ★★1/2/$$$, MGM/MGM-UA. A woman having an affair is accused of murdering her jealous husband-perhaps before he was about to do her in for cheating. Greta Garbo, Lew Ayres, Conrad Nagel. w. Hans Kraly, Jacques Feyder.

MELODRAMA: MURDER: Accused Unjustly; Murder of Spouse; Jealousy; Cheating Women; Guilty Conscience (Ed: MGM and Garbo's last silent film)

The Kiss, 1988, 98m, ★★/$, Tri-Star/Col-Tri, R/V-S. A beautiful model becomes possessed by an evil force that inhabits a serpent creature. Joanna Pacula, Pamela Collyer, Meredith Salnger, Mimi Kuzyk, Jan Rubes. w. Stephen Volk, Tom Ropelewski, d. Pen Densham.

HORROR: SCI-FI: Animal Monsters; Snakes; Models; Fashion World; Africa; Coulda Been Good (The Sentinel; The Guardian; SSssss) (Ed: Could have been called *It Came Out of Africa*)

Kiss and Tell, 1945, 92m, ★★★/$$, Col/NA. A young girl pretends to be pregnant in a wacky scheme to protect another girl's reputation. Shirley Temple, Robert Benchley, Walter Abel, Katherine Alexander. w. P-adap. F. Hugh Herbert, d. Richard Wallace.

COMEDY: FARCE: Misunderstandings; Babies-Having Scandals; Identities-Assumed; Protecting Someone; Friendships-Female; Teenagers; Girls; Young Women; Female Protagonists

SEQUEL: A Kiss for Corliss (The Miracle of Morgan's Creek; The Bachelor and the Bobby-Soxer; Honeymoon)

A Kiss Before Dying, 1956, 94m, ★★★/$$, UA/NA (TBS). A young man rising to the top of his wife's father's corporation kills anyone in his way or who knows about his past secrets. Jeffrey Hunter, Joanne Woodward, Robert Wagner, Virginia Leith, Mary Astor. w. Lawrence Roman, N-adap Ira Levin, d. Gerd Oswald. Ahead of Its Time

A Kiss Before Dying, 1991, 93m, ★★★/$, Universal/MCA-U, R/V-B&G-S-MRN-FN. Remake of original, based on Ira Levin novel, with more of a serial killer and revenge edge, and a theme that's not carried off. Matt Dillon, Sean Young, Max Von Sydow, Diane Ladd. w. d. James Dearden, N-adap. Ira Levin.

SUSPENSE: DRAMA: MURDER: MURDER MYSTERY: Serial Killers; Romance-Dangerous; Secrets-Keeping; Twins; Identities-Assumed; Impostors; Enemy-Sleeping with the; Revenge; American Dream; Underrated; Coulda Been Great (The Scar; The Temp)

(Ed: Much potential in the actual subtext revealed at the end of the '91 version, but marred and diverted by traditional thriller conventions)

A Kiss for Corliss, 1949, 88m, ★★½/ $$, UA/NA. The girl from *Kiss and Tell* gets a crush on a much older man who doesn't know how to react. Shirley Temple, David Niven, Tom Tully, Darryl Hickman. w. Howard Dimsdale, d. Richard Wallace.

COMEDY: ROMANCE: Romantic Comedy; Infatuations; Girls; Teenagers; Romance-Older Men/Younger Women; Obsessions; Coulda Been Good

SEQUEL TO: Kiss and Tell

(The Bachelor and the Bobbysoxer; It Started with Eve)

A Kiss in the Dark, 1949, 87m, ★★½/$$, WB/NA. A stuffy concert pianist has to live in a boardinghouse full of eccentric misfits except for one love interest. David Niven, Jane Wyman, Broderick Crawford, Maria Ouspenkaya, Victor Moore. w. Harry Kurnitz, d. Delmer Daves.

COMEDY: COMEDY DRAMA: ROMANCE: Romantic Comedy; Nerds; Pianists; Musicians; Eccentric People; Boardinghouses; Coulda Been Good

(The L-Shaped Room; About Mrs. Leslie)

Kiss Me Deadly, 1955, 105m, ★★★½/ $$, MGM/MGM-UA. After finding a girl running for her life along a road (Cloris Leachman) who is eventually killed, a detective (Ralph Meeker) finds himself entangled in conspiracy involving Hollywood rats, nuclear testing, and a mysterious box. Albert Dekker, Paul Stewart, Maxene Cooper, Wesley Addy. w. A. I. Bezzerides, N-adap. Mickey Spillane, d. Robert Aldrich.

SUSPENSE: MURDER: MYSTERY: MURDER MYSTERY: Detective Stories; Detectives in Deep; Detectives-Private; Men in Jeopardy; Women in Jeopardy; Conspiracy; Clever Plots & Endings; Hollywood Life; 1950s; Nuclear Energy; Radiation; Hidden Gems; Cult Films (Farewell, My Lovely; Chinatown; The Big Knife)

Kiss Me Goodbye, 1982, 101m, ★★★/$$, 20th/CBS-Fox, PG. A widow finds her kooky dead husband lurking around the house just as soon as she's remarrying. Sally Field, James Caan, Jeff Bridges, Paul Dooley, Claire Trevor, Mildred Natwick, William Prince.

w. Charlie Peters, S-adap. Bruno Bareto, d. Robert Mulligan.

COMEDY DRAMA: ROMANCE: Romantic Comedy; Dead-Back from the; Widows; Ghosts; Romance-Triangles; Jealousy; Female Protagonists; Foreign Film Remakes; Coulda Been Great; Overlooked at Release

REMAKE OF: Dona Flor and Her Two Husbands

(Blithe Spirit; Ghost; Truly, Madly, Deeply)

Kiss Me Kate, 1953, 110m, ★★★½/ $$$, MGM/MGM-UA. A musical production of *Taming of the Shrew* mirrors the actual story of a bickering romance. Howard Keel, Kathryn Grayson, Ann Miller, Keenan Wynn, Bobby Van, James Whitmore, Bob Fosse. BMScore. Oscars: 1-0.

MUSICALS: ROMANCE: Musical Romance; Romance-Bickering; Romance-Reluctant; Elusive Women; Behind the Scenes; Theater Life; Actors; Actresses; Singers; Classic Literary Adaptations; Revisionist Films; 3-D Movies (Noises Off; The Bandwagon; The Barkleys of Broadway)

Kiss Me, Stupid!, 1964, 126m, MGM/MGM-UA. A Vegas singer (Dean Martin) is stuck in a small town and a local man wants him to hear his songs, but the singer may take his wife instead or in exchange. Kim Novak. w. Billy Wilder, I.A.L. Diamond, P-adap. Anna Bonacci, d. Wilder.

COMEDY: ROMANCE: Romantic Comedy; Romance-Triangles; Con Artists; Singers; Desert Settings; Small-town Life; Stranded (Doc Hollywood; A Chorus of Disapproval)

Kiss of Death, 1947, 98m, ★★★/$$$, 20th/CBS-Fox. An informer turns in his mob pals, but soon a hitman who will stop at nothing is sent to off him. Victor Mature, Richard Widmark (BSActor), Brian Donlevy, Colleen Gray, Karl Malden. w. Ben Hecht, Charles Lederer, E. Lipsky (BOStory), d. Henry Hathaway. Oscars: 2-0.

SUSPENSE: Crime Drama; Mob Stories; Informers; Hitmen; Revenge; Psycho Killers; Film Noir; Sleeper Hits; Hidden Gems

REMAKE: 1995

(Force of Evil; The Killers; Murder Inc.)

Kiss of Death, 1995, 106m, ★★★/$$, 20th/Fox, R/EV-P-S. A regular guy is trapped between the D.A. and the mob

when he's forced to go undercover to nab some family members-but he may be endangering who he's trying to save in the bargain by taking on the assignment. David Caruso, Nicolas Cage, Samuel L. Jackson, Kathryn Erbe, Helen Hunt, Michael Rapaport, Ving Rhames, Stanley Tucci, Nicolas Cage, Little Junior. d. Barbet Schroeder.

SUSPENSE: Crime Drama; Mob Stories; Informers; Hitmen; Revenge; Psycho Killers; Film Noir-Modern; Sleeper Hits; Hidden Gems

Kiss of Evil (*Kiss of the Vampire*), 1964, 88m, ★★½/$, Hammer/NA. A honeymooning couple in the early 1900s meets up with a vampire. Noel Willman, Clifford Evans, Edward deSouza. w. John Elder, d. Don Sharp.

HORROR: Vampires; Honeymoons; Newlyweds; Europeans-Eastern; British Films

(Dracula; The Dark; Old House)

Kiss of the Spider Woman, 1985, 119m, ★★★★/$$$, FilmDallas/Charter, New Line, R/S-P-MRN. A gay transvestite (William Hurt, **BActor**) is jailed with a subversive (Raul Julia) and through his fantasies, he soon seduces the macho cellmate before certain doom. w. Leonard Schrader (BAScr), adap. Manuel Puig, d. Hector Babenco (BDirector). BPicture. Oscars: 4-1.

DRAMA: ROMANCE: Prison Drama; Political Drama; Transvestites; Macho Men; Gay Men; Bisexuality; Homophobia; Two-Character Stories; Oppression; Illusions; Dreams; Betrayals; Independent Films; Surrealism; Fantasy; Enemies Unite; Magic; Realism; Sleeper Hits; Argentina

(Situation Hopeless but not Serious; Apartment Zero; Midnight Express; Like Water for Chocolate)

Kiss Shot, 1989, 98m, ★½/$, Academy/ Academy, PG. A black mother struggling to make ends meet becomes a pool hustler and finds romance. Whoopi Goldberg, Dorian Harewood, Dennis Franz. d. Jerry London.

COMEDY: Pool; Black Women; Mothers-Struggling; Making a Living; Overlooked at Release; Good Premise Unfulfilled; Female Protagonists

Kiss the Blood Off My Hands, 1948, 80m, ★★½/$$, U/NA. A sailor accused of murder finds refuge with a nurse, who may provide love but not complete safety.

Burt Lancaster, Joan Fontaine, Robert Newton. w. Leonardo Bercovici, N-adap. Gerald Butler, d. Norman Foster.

MELODRAMA: MURDER: Accused Unjustly; Framed?; Fugitives from the Law; **ROMANCE:** Nurses; England; Hiding Out; Forgotten Films

Kiss the Boys Goodbye, 1941, 85m, ★★★/$$$, Par/NA. A big Broadway show producer has a thing for one of the chorus line, but will she reciprocate? Don Ameche, Mary Martin, Oscar Levant, Raymond Walburn, Connie Boswell. w. Harry Tugend, Dwight Taylor, P-adap. Clare Boothe, d. Victor Schertzinger.

MUSICALS: ROMANCE: Musical Romance; Theater Life; Dancers; Behind the Scenes; Romance with Boss

Kiss Them for Me, 1957, 105m, ★★¹/2/$$, 20th/NA, AMC. Three Navy air pilots take a leave in San Francisco and run into a bombshell or two. Cary Grant, Jayne Mansfield, Suzy Parker, Ray Wlaston, Larry Blyden, Leif Erickson. w. Julius Epstein, N-adap. Shore Leave, Frederick Wakeman, d. Stanley Donen.

COMEDY: ROMANCE: Romantic Comedy; Multiple Stories; Sailors; Sexy Women; San Francisco; Forgotten Films; Coulda Been Great; Shore Leave

MUSICAL VERSION: Hit the Deck (Hit the Deck; On the Town)

Kiss Tomorrow Goodbye, 1950, 102m, ★★¹/2/$$, Cagney-Republic/Republic. A convict escapes from prison and has plans to outdo the crimes that put him there. James Cagney, Barbara Payton, Ward Bond, Luther Adler. w. Harry Brown, N-adap. Horace McCoy, d. Gordon Douglas.

ACTION: Crime Drama; Convict's Revenge; Prison Escapes; Heist Stories; Forgotten Films (White Heat; Angels with Dirty Faces)

Kisses for My President, 1964, 113m, ★★¹/2/$$, WB/WB. A lady President has the biggest problem at home-a husband who doesn't much like being in her shadow. Polly Bergen, Fred MacMurray, Arlene Dahl, Eli Wallach. w. Claude Binyon, Robert Kane, d. Curtis Bernhardt.

COMEDY: Marriage Comedy; Jealousy; Role Reversal; Battle of the Sexes; Presidents; Washington D.C.; Ahead of its Time; Curiosities; Female in Male Domain; Politicians; Politicians-Female; Female Protagonists (First Monday in October)

Kissin' Cousins, 1963, 96m, ★★/$$, MGM/MGM-UA. The government plans to put a military base in the Smoky Mountains, and one of their men finds his twin among the hillbillies there. Elvis Presley, Glenda Farrell, Arthur O'Connell, Jack Albertson. w. Gerald Drayson Adams, Gene Nelson, d. Nelson.

COMEDY: Government as Enemy; Mountain People; Hillbillies; Lookalikes (L'il Abner)

The Kissing Bandit, 1948, 102m, ★★¹/2/$$, MGM/NA. A young man has to live up to his father's infamous reputation in his old-west town and finds it rather trying, so he sings about it. Frank Sinatra, Kathryn Grayson, J. Carrol Naish, Mildred Natwick. w. Isobel Lennart, John Harding, d. Laslo Benedek.

MUSICALS: WESTERNS: Musical Westerns; Men Proving Themselves; Outlaws; Gunfighters; Fathers & Sons; Female Screenwriters; Forgotten Films

The Kitchen Toto, 1987, 95m, ★★★/$, Ind/WB. After a priest is murdered in 1950s Africa, a policeman reluctantly takes in the man's orphaned son. Bob Peck, Phyllis Logan. w. d. Harry Hook.

DRAMA: TRAGEDY: Fathers-Surrogate; Children-Adopted; Orphans; **MURDER:** Priests; Africa; Black Men; Writer-Directors; Independent Films (Carbon Copy)

Kitten with a Whip, 1964, 83m, ★★¹/2/$$, U/MCA-U. A reform school fugitive with a body that won't quit decides to hide out and drive insane a local politician who's wife is away-therefore the kitten can play. Ann-Margret, John Forsythe, Patricia Barry. w. d. Douglas Heyes, N-adap. Wade Miller.

DRAMA: MELODRAMA: Malicious Menaces; Nuisances; Nightmares; Blackmail; Evil Women; Juvenile Delinquents; Politicians; Camp (Ed: Great titles don't make great movies, though this has its camp moments, especially with Ann so bad but good)

Kitty, 1945, 103m, ★★★/$$, Par/NA. In old London, a poor street woman becomes a lady at the behest of a royal who has a thing for her. Paulette Goddard, Ray Milland, Cecil Kellaway, Constance Collier, Reginald Owen, Patric Knowles. w. Darrell Ware, Karl Tunberg, N-adap. Rosamund Marshall, d. Mitchell Leisen.

COMEDY DRAMA: ROMANCE: Svengalis; Rags to Riches; Class Conflicts;

Rich vs. Poor; Social Climbing; Marrying Up; Teachers and Students; England; 1800s; Forgotten Films; Hidden Gems (Pygmalion; My Fair Lady)

Kitty Foyle, 1940, 108m, ★★★/$$$$, RKO/Turner. A working girl has trouble with love and work but muddles through anyhow. Ginger Rogers (**BActress**), Dennis Morgan, James Craig, Gladys Cooper. w. Dalton Trumbo (BScr), Donald Ogden Stewart, N-adap. Christopher Morley, d. Sam Wood (BDirector). BPicture. Oscars: 4-1.

MELODRAMA: COMEDY DRAMA: ROMANCE: Tearjerkers; Working Class; Career Women; Single Women; Young Women; Making a Living; Female Protagonists; Faded Hits; Time Capsules (Bachelor Mother; The Major and the Minor)

The Klansman, 1974, 112m, ★★/$, Par/Par, R/V-P. A sheriff in the deepest of deep South takes on the KKK of Alabama. Lee Marvin, Richard Burton, Cameron Mitchell, O.J. Simpson, Lola Falana, Linda Evans. w. Millard Kaufman, Samuel Fuller, N-adap. William Huie, d. Terence Young.

ACTION: DRAMA: Action Drama; Race Relations; Bigots; Ku Klux Klan; Southerns; Fighting the System; Police Stories; Black vs. White; Police-Vigilantes; Vigilantes; Coulda Been Good (Mississippi Burning; Walking Tall)

Klute, 1971, 114m, ★★★★/$$$, WB/WB, R/S-P. A cynical callgirl (Jane Fonda, **BActress**) is being stalked by someone, and a detective named Klute (Donald Sutherland) on the trail of a murderer she may have serviced may be the only one who can save her. w. Dave & Andy Lewis (BOScr), d. Alan J. Pakula. Oscars: 2-1.

DRAMA: SUSPENSE: Film Noir-Modern; Psychological Thriller; **MURDER:** Detective Stories; Detectives-Private; Psychologists; Stalkers; Prostitutes-High Class; Surveillance; Women in Jeopardy; Feisty Females; Abused Women; Sexy Women; 1970s; Telephone Terror (The Morning After; Jennifer 8; Midnight Lace; Fear City; Street Smart; Irma La Douce; Sessions)

The Knack, 1965, 84m, ★★★¹/2/$$$, UA/MGM-UA. A young teacher rents out his house to a playboy and a virgin, and sparks fly in mod London. Michael Crawford, Ray Brooks, Rita Tushingham,

Donal Donelly. w. Charles Wood, P-adap. Ann Jellicoe, d. Richard Lester.
COMEDY DRAMA: Music Movies; ROMANCE: Romantic Comedy; FARCE: Roommates; Playboys; Virgins; Nerds; Young People; Teachers; Mod Era; Cult Films; British Films; London
(A Hard Day's Night; Georgy Girl; The L-Shaped Room; Smashing Time)

Knave of Hearts (*Lover Boy*), 1954, 103m, ★★★/$, Transcontinental/NA. A playboy who cheats on his wife finally has to come to terms with his many conquests. Gerard Philipe, Margaret Johnston, Joan Greenwood, Valerie Hobson. w. Rene Clement, Hugh Mills, d. Clement.
COMEDY DRAMA: ROMANCE: Romantic Comedy; Marriage Comedy; Marriage on the Rocks; Cheating Men; Jealousy; Starting Over; Redemption; Playboys; International Casts; British Films

Knickerbocker Holiday, 1944, 84m, ★★★/$$, UA/NA. An old one-legged curmudgeon sings his way around Early American New York on his way toward changing his ways late in life. Charles Coburn, Nelson Eddy, Constance Dowling, Shelley Winters. w. David Boehm, Hary Goldman, Roland Leigh, Thomas Lennon, N-adap. Washington Irving, d. Harry Joe Brown.
COMEDY DRAMA: MUSICALS: Music Movies; Elderly Men; Life Transitions; Early America; Disabled People; New York Life; Forgotten Films

Knife in the Water, 1962, 94m, ★★★/$, Ind/Fox. A wealthy young couple meet a hitchhiker and invite him for a weekend on their boat, only to find out he has mental problems. Leon Niemczyk, Jolanta Umecka. w. Jerzy Skolimowski, Roman Polanski, Jakub Goldberg, d. Polanski. BFLFilm. Oscars: 1-1.
SUSPENSE: MURDER: Psycho Killers; Art Films; Vacations; Nightmare Vacations; Hitchhikers; Malicious Menaces; Young People; Independent Films
(Dead Calm)

Knight Moves, 1992, 116m, ★★¹/₂/$$, Ind/Republic, R/S-V. A serial killer is out there and clues lead to a champion chess player at a big tournament. Christopher Lambert, Diane Lane, Tom Skerritt, Daniel Baldwin, Ferdinand Mayne. w. Brad Mirman, d. Carl Schenkel.
SUSPENSE: MURDER: Detective Stories; Serial Killers; Games; Chess Players;

Trail of a Killer; Mindgames; Coulda Been Good

Knight Without Armor, 1937, 107m, ★★★/$$, London/Sultan. A Brit in Russia during the Revolution helps a countess there to safety and love. Marlene Dietrich, Robert Donat. w. Lajos Biro, Arthur Wimperis, Frances Marion, N-adap. James Hilton, d. Jacques Feyder.
ROMANCE: MELODRAMA: Escape Adventure; Political Unrest; Saving Someone; Russia; Russians
(Desire; Blond Venus; Morocco)

Knightriders, 1981, 145m, ★★¹/₂/$, 20th/Media, R/V-S. Jousting on motorcycles entertains the alienated and angry of a nether world. Ed Harris, Gary Lahti. w. d. George Romero.
ACTION: SCI-FI: Motorcycles; Art Films; Futuristic World; Hippies; Camelot Stories; Cult Films

Knights of the Round Table, 1954, 106m, ★★★/$$$, MGM/MGM-UA. Lancelot returns reclaim his love, Guenevere, and exact revenge against Modred. Robert Taylor, Mel Ferrer, Ava Gardner, Anne Crawford, Stanley Baker. w. Talbot Jennings, Jan Lustig, Nowl Langley, d. Richard Thorpe.
ADVENTURE: Costume Drama; Legends; Mythology; ROMANCE: Revenge; Good vs. Evil; Magic; Medieval Times; Camelot Stories; England
(Excalibur; Camelot; The Sword in the Stone)

Knock on Any Door, 1949, 100m, ★★★/$$, Col/Col. A prominent lawyer defends a poor young man accused of murder as a charity case because he believes in him-or is it that he's so pretty? Humphrey Bogart, John Derek, George Macready. w. Daniel Taradash, John Monks, N-adap. Willard Motley, d. Nicholas Ray.
DRAMA: Courtroom Drama; MURDER: Accused Unjustly; Class Conflicts; Poor People; Social Drama; Forgotten Films
(Primal Fear; Criminal Law; The Accused [1948])

Knock on Wood, 1954, 103m, ★★★/$$$, Par/NA. A ventriloquist finds that bad guys are after his dummy-because it has stolen secret papers inside of it. Danny Kaye, Mai Zetterling, David Burns, Torin Thatcher. w. d. Norman Panama, Melvin Frank (BOScr). Oscars: 1-0.

COMEDY: Chase Movies; Fugitives from the Mob; Ventriloquists; Comedians; Fools-Bumbling; Hidden Gems
(Magic; The Man from the Diner's Club)

Knute Rockne: All-American, 1940, 98m, ★★★/$$$, WB/MGM-UA. The famous Notre Dame football coach's life is detailed, accent on the victories. Pat O'Brien, Ronald Reagan, Gale Page, Donald Crisp. w. Robert Buckner, d. Lloyd Bacon.
ACTION: MELODRAMA: Biographies; Sports Movies; Leaders-Great; Football

Kotch, 1971, 113m, ★★★¹/₂/$$$, ABC/CBS-Fox. An elderly man (Walter Matthau, BActor) takes a liking to a free-spirited young woman (Deborah Winters) about to have a baby and changes his life. w. John Paxton, N-adap. Katherin Topkins, d. Jack Lemmon. BOSong. Oscars: 2-0.
DRAMA: COMEDY DRAMA: MELO-DRAMA: Family Drama; FAMILY: Tearjerkers; Friendships-Great; Generation Gap; Romance-Older Men/Younger Women; Grandfathers-Fascination; Fathers-Surrogate; Mothers-Unwed; Mothers Alone; Elderly Men; Young Women; Life Transitions; Saving Someone; Actor Directors
(Harry and Tonto; Dad; Grumpy Old Men)

Koyaanisqatsi, 1983, 87m, ★★★/$$, Ind/Music Video Dist., Facets. A documentary of high-speed film of life from the deserts to the bustling cities all over the world showing how "life out of balance," as the title means, has occurred. w. Ron Fricke, Godfrey Reggio, Michael Hoenig, Alton Wadpole, d. Reggio.
Documentaries; Art Films; Avant-Garde Films; Social Drama; City vs. Country; Nature-Back to; Alienation; Music Video Style; Scenery-Outstanding; Independent Films
SEQUEL: Powaqqatsi

Krakatoa, East of Java, 1968, 136m, ★★¹/₂/$$, ABC-Cinerama/NA. A boat hurries to leave Singapore and avoid the eruption of the great mountain which affected the world. Maximilian Schell, Diane Baker, Brian Keith, Rosanno Brazzi, Sal Mineo. w. Clifford Gould, Bernard Gordon, d. Bernard Kowalski. BSFX. Oscars: 1-0.
ADVENTURE: DRAMA: Disaster Movies; Ships; Volcanoes; Race Against Time; Islands; Asia; Tidal Waves; Rescue Drama

(Ed: Krakatoa is west of Java, actually-unless you're heading from the wrong direction, which must be why they headed into the tidal wave)

Kramer vs. Kramer, 1979, 105m, ★★★★/$$$$$, Columbia/RCA-Col, PG. When a mother (Meryl Streep, **BSActress**) leaves her small son (Justin Henry, BSActor) and his father (Dustin Hoffman, **BActor**), the father must learn to play mother, too, until she comes back for custody and a battle begins. Jane Alexander (BSActress), Sam Wanamaker, Howard Duff, Jobeth Williams. w. Robert Benton (**BAScr**), N-adap. Avery Corman, d. Benton (**BDirector**). **BPicture**, BCin, BAScore. Oscars: 9-5.
DRAMA: MELODRAMA: Family Drama; Tearjerkers; Divorce; Custody Battles; Fathers Alone; Women Who Leave; Women Proving Themselves; Fathers & Sons; Marriage on the Rocks; Executives; Advertising World; New York Life; Time Capsules; Blockbusters
COMIC FLIPSIDE: Baby Boom
(The Champ; Baby Boom; Author! Author!)

The Krays, 1990, 119m, ★★★/$$, Miramax/HBO, R/S-P-EV-MRN. Twin mobsters rule 1950s England with their wild crimes and lifestyles. Gary Kemp, Martin Kemp, Billie Whitelaw, Susan Fleetwood. w. Philip Ridley, d. Peter Medak.

DRAMA: Crime Drama; **MURDER:** True Stories; Biographies; Twins; Brothers; Mothers-Troublesome; Psychological Drama; 1950s; British Films
(Dead Ringers; Let Him Have It)

The Kremlin Letter, 1970, 122m, ★★½/$$, 20th/CBS-Fox. An arms treaty signed by mistake is in the Russians' hands, so the CIA sends in operatives to retrieve it before real problems arise. Richard Boone, Orson Welles, Bibi Andersson, Max Von Sydow, Patrick O'Neal, George Sanders, Dean Jagger, Barbara Parkins, Lili Kedrova, John Huston. w. John Huston, Gladys Hill, N-adap. Noel Behn, d. Huston.
DRAMA: Spy Films; Spies; Mindgames; Misunderstandings; Russians; Cold War Era; Russia; CIA Agents; KGB Agents; International Casts; Female Screenwriters
(The Russia House; The Looking Glass War)

Krull, 1983, 121m, ★★½/$, Col/RCA-Col, PG/V. Medieval sorcery and swash-buckling on a faraway planet with a prince saving a princess from an evil kingdom and lots of riding on horses. Ken Marshall Lysette Anthony, Freddie Jones, Francesca Annis. w. Stanford Sherman, d. Peter Yates.
ADVENTURE: ACTION: SCI-FI: Fantasy; Outer Space Movies; Medieval Times; Quests; Treasure Hunts; Sword & Sorcery; Swashbucklers; Princes; Princesses; Little People-Midgets;

Overlooked at Release; Underrated (Willow; Dune; Star Wars SERIES)
Kuffs, 1991, 102m, ★★½/$$, Universal/MCA-U, PG-13/V-P-S. A young guy inherits a detective agency and then sets out to avenge the death of his brother who owned it. Christian Slater, Tony Goldwyn, Milla Jovovich, Bruce Boxleitner. w. Bruce Evans, Raynold Gideon, d. Evans.
ACTION: COMEDY: Action Comedy; Detective Stories; Avenging Death of Someone; Brothers; Detectives-Private; Detectives-Amateur; Crossing the Line; Narrated Films
(Pump Up the Volume; Gleaming the Cube)

Kung Fu, 1972, 75m, ★★★½/$$$$, ABC/WB, V. A young man in the wild west is attracted to a Chinese martial arts sanctuary and comes out an expert ready to defend the defenseless as he drifts about. David Carradine, d. Jerry Thorpe.
DRAMA: WESTERNS: Westerns-Neo; Martial Arts; Chinese People; Protecting Someone; Drifters; Sleeper Hits

Kwaidan, 1964, 164m, ★★★/$, Ind/Nos. Japanese ghost stories, four in a row. Rentaro Mikuni. w. Yoko Mizuki, d. Masaki Kobayashi. BFLFilm. Oscars: 1-0.
SUSPENSE: HORROR: Gothic Style; Ghosts; Storytellers; Japan; Japanese Films; Cult Films
(Ghost Story; Dead of Night)

L

La Balance, 1982, 102m, ★★★/$$$, UAC/Fox, R/S-EV-FN. A pimp and his main employee are coerced by the cops into informing in a major case which poses the question as to who is more corrupt-prostitutes or the cops? Nathalie Baye, Philippe Leotard, Richard Barry. w. M. Fabiani, Bob Swaim, d. Swaim.
SUSPENSE: THRILLER: Crime Drama; Prostitutes-Low Class; Erotic Drama; Erotic Thriller; Police Corruption; Double Crossings; French Films
(Internal Affairs; Fuzz; Cop)
La Bamba, 1987, 99m, ★★★/$$$, Col/Col, PG. Biography of the short life of Buddy Holly's co-star on the road, Ritchie Valens, a young hispanic rising star. Lou Diamond Phillips, Esai Morales, Joe Pantoliano, Brian Setzer, Elizabeth Pena, Rick Dees. w. d. Luis Valdez.
DRAMA: MELODRAMA: TRAGEDY: Biographies; Singers; Music Dies; Airplane Crashes; 1950s; Teen Idols; Latin People; Writer-Directors
(The Buddy Holly Story)
La Belle Noiseuse, 1990, 240m, ★★★1/2/$, New Yorker/New Yorker, NR. A painter in his twilight years has an unfinished painting that he is inspired to finish by a younger admirer's lover, but tensions between him and the model may prevent it. Michel Piccoli, Emmanuelle

Beart, Jane Birkin. N-adap. Honoré de Balzac, d. Jacques Rivette.
DRAMA: Character Studies; Artists-Famous; Painters; Models; **ROMANCE:** Romantic Drama; Episodic Stories; Romance-Older Men/Younger Women; Art Films; French Films
(Camille Claudelle; Moulin Rouge)
La Bete Humaine, 1938, 90m, ★★★1/2/$$, Ind/Nos. A working class fellow plots with a woman to kill her husband but a guilty conscience may undo the plan. Jean Gabin, Simone Simon, Julian Carette. N-adap. Emile Zola, d. Jean Renoir.
SUSPENSE: Psychological Drama; **MURDER:** Murder of Spouse; Cheating Women; Romance-Triangles; Film Noir
REMAKE: Human Desire (1954)
(The Postman Always Rings Twice; Obsessione)
La Boum, 1981, 100m, ★★1/2/$$$$ (in France) $ (in America), PG. A teenage soap opera where different teens meet at a big party in France. d. Claude Pinoteau.
MELODRAMA: French Films; Teenagers; Teenage Movies; Party Movies; Girlhood
(Boyfriends and Girlfriends)
(Ed: A big hit in France. For teens into foreign films)
Labyrinth, 1986, 101m, ★★1/2/$, Tri-Star/Col-Tri, PG/V. A wish backfires

when a girl hopes her brother will be kidnapped by demon-like goblins-and he is. The problem is, now she must rescue him from the maze of the title or be taken herself. Jennifer Connelly, David Bowie, Terry Jones. w. Terry Jones, d. Jim Henson.
CHILDREN'S: FAMILY: SCI-FI: Fantasy; Kidnappings; Brothers & Sisters; Chase Movies; Nightmares; Mindgames; Demons; Monsters-Mythology; Mythology; Overlooked at Release
(The Dark Crystal; Legend)
La Cage Aux Folles, 1979, 91m, ★★★★/$$$$$, UAC/MGM-UA, R/S. Two gay men living together have their son over for dinner since he's getting married to a girl, only her parents are coming and they have to try and keep their lifestyle a secret. Ugo Tognazzi, Michel Serrault. w. Francis Veber (BOScr), d. Edward Moulinaro (BDirector). Oscars: 2-0.
COMEDY: FARCE: Marriage Comedy; Secrets-Keeping; Marriage-Impending; Transvestites; Gay Men; Dinner Parties; French Films
SEQUELS: La Cage Aux Folles 2 and 3
REMAKE: The Birdcage
(Guess Who's Coming to Dinner; Norman, Is That You?; Torch Song Trilogy)
La Cage Aux Folles 2, 1981, 100m, ★★★/$$$, UA/MGM-UA, R/S. More mayhem involving mistaken identities,

spying with microfilm, and midlife crises. Ugo Tognazzi, Michel Serrault. w. Jean Poiret, Francis Veber, Marcello Danon, d. Edouardo Molinaro.

COMEDY: FARCE: Spies; Spoofs-Spies; Midlife Crisis; Marriage Comedy; Secrets-Keeping; Marriage-Impending; Transvestites; Gay Men; French Films

La Cage Aux Folles 3: The Wedding, 1985, UA/MGM-UA, ★★¹/₂/$$, PG-13/S. The gay couple may inherit some money, but only if one of them is married-not to the other, but a woman. Ugo Tognazzi, Michel Serrault. w. Marcello Danon, Phillippe Nicaud, Christine Carere, Jacques Audiard, Georges Lautner, Gerald Lamballe, d. Lautner.

COMEDY: FARCE: Inheritances at Stake; Secrets-Keeping; Marriage Comedy; Secrets-Keeping; Marriage-Impending; Marriages-Fake; Transvestites; Gay Men; French Films

The Lacemaker, 1977, 107m, ★★★/$, Janus/Voyager. A young woman becomes severely depressed when her first real romance comes to an end. Isabelle Huppert, Yves Beneyton. w. Pascal Laine, Calude Goretta, N-adap. Laine, d. Goretta.

DRAMA: Social Drama; Character Studies; Romance-Doomed; Depression; Young Women; French Films

La Chevre, 1976, 90m, ★★★¹/₂/$$, Ind/Facets, PG. When a corporate mogul's very unlucky daughter is missing, a detective is hired who then must enlist a very unlucky person to help in tracing her steps. Only problem is the luck rubs off. Gerard Depardieu, Pierre Richard. w. d. Francis Veber.

COMEDY: Screwball Comedy; **FARCE:** Detective Stories; Partners-Mismatched; Fools-Bumbling; Accident Prone; Missing Persons; Murphy's Law Stories; Unlucky People; Mexico; Buddy Cops; Hidden Gems; French Films; Writer-Directors

REMAKE: Pure Luck (nowhere near the finesse)

(Les Compères; A Pain in the A—; Les Trois Fugitifs)

La Chienne, 1931, 93m, ★★★¹/₂/$$, Ind/International Classics, Ingram. A husband on the verge finds romance with a hardened prostitute on the street of Paris but may regret it. Michel Simon, Janie Mareze, George Flament. w. Andre Girard, Jean Renoir, N-adap. Georges de la Fouchardiere, d. Renoir.

DRAMA: MELODRAMA: Psychological Drama; **ROMANCE:** Romance with a Prostitute; Cheating Men; Marriage on the Rocks; Nervous Breakdowns; Hidden Gems; French Films

COMIC FLIPSIDE: Irma La Douce

(Anna Christie; Crimes of Passion)

Lacombe, Lucien, 1974, 141m, ★★★¹/₂/$$, Ind/NA. When a teenage boy is turned down for service in the French Resistance, he turns to the Nazis instead, a choice he may regret. Pierre Blaise, Aurore Clement. w. Louis Malle, Aurore Clement, d. Malle.

DRAMA: War Stories; Nazi Stories; World War II Stories; Traitors; Soldiers; Decisions-Big; French Films; Writer-Directors

(Au Revoir, Les Enfants; Olivier, Olivier)

Ladies in Retirement, 1941, 92m, ★★★/$$, Col/NA. A maid decides to off her wealthy employer to help out her two mentally ill sisters. Ida Lupino, Louis Hayward, Elsa Lanchester, Isobel Elsom, Edith Barrett. w. Reginald Denham, Edward Percy, Garrett Fort, P-adap. Denham, Percy, d. Charles Vidor.

COMEDY DRAMA: TRAGEDY: HORROR: Horror Comedy; Black Comedy; **MURDER:** Worker vs. Boss; Mental Illness; Psycho Killers; Murderers-Nice; Hidden Gems; Female Protagonists

REMAKE: The Mad Room

(Arsenic and Old Lace; Who Slew Aunite Roo?; Whatever Happened to Baby Jane?)

Ladies' Man, 1947, 90m, ★★/$, Par/NA. A nerd strikes oil and suddenly has women all over him. Eddie Bracken, Virginia Welles. w. Ed Beloin, Jack Rose, Lewis Meltzer, d. William Russell.

COMEDY: Rags to Riches; Nerds & Babes; Nerds; Fish out of Water Stories; Good Premise Unfulfilled

(Hail, the Conquering Hero)

Ladies' Man, 1961, 106m, ★★¹/₂/$$, Par/Par. A valet at a hotel for actresses trips and falls head over heels for the tenants. Jerry Lewis, Helen Traubel, Jack Kruschen, Doodles Weaver. w. Jerry Lewis, Bill Richmond, d. Lewis.

COMEDY: Comedy-Slapstick; Fools-Bumbling; Nerds; Nerds & Babes; Hotels

(The Bellboy; The Disorderly Orderly)

Ladies Should Listen, 1934, 63m, ★★¹/₂/$$, Par/NA. A rich man needs help with his romance, and a nosy telephone operator wants to help. Cary Grant,

Frances Drake. w. Claude Binyon, Frank Butler, Guy Bolton, d. Frank Tuttle.

ROMANCE: MELODRAMA: Romantic Comedy; Matchmakers; Nuisances; Gossip

Ladies They Talk About, 1932, 69m, ★★★/$$, WB/MGM-UA. Sexy dames get put in the lock-up and fight it out. Barbara Stanwyck, Preston Foster, Lillian Roth. w. Sidney Sutherland, Brown Holmes, P-adap. Dorothy Mackaye (*Women in Prison*), d. Howard Bretherton, William Keighley.

COMEDY DRAMA: MELODRAMA: Prison Drama; Women in Prison; Feisty Females

(Caged; Born to Be Bad)

La Dolce Vita, 1961, 173m, ★★★¹/₂/$$$, Astor/Republic. A reporter-playboy roaming in the very chic circles of Roma goes on a picaresque journey meeting all kinds of eccentric people, gorgeous women, ending with an orgy and a monster on the beach. Marcello Mastroianni, Anita Ekberg, Anouk Aimee, Lex Barker. w. Ennio Flaiano, Federico Fellini, Tullio Pinelli, Brunella Rondi (BOScr), d. Fellini (BDirector). **BB&W Costume.** Oscars: 3-1.

DRAMA: SATIRE: Art Films; Cult Films; **ROMANCE:** Journalists; Beautiful People; Orgies; Playboys; Playgirls; Sexy Men; Sexy Women; Suicidal Tendencies; Rich People; Rome; Italian Films; Film History (8½; Blow-Up; Dark Eyes)

The Lady and the Tramp, 1955, 76m, ★★★★/$$$$$, Disney/Disney, G. A cocky dog of the streets falls for a beautiful uptown dog and tries to romance her despite their class differences. Voices: Peggy Lee, Bill Thompson, Stan Freberg, Barbara Luddy. d. Hamilton Locke, Clyde Geronomi, Wilfred Jackson.

Cartoons; **CHILDREN'S: FAMILY: ROMANCE:** Romantic Comedy; Pet Stories; Dogs; Cats

(Oliver and Company)

Lady Be Good, 1941, 111m, ★★¹/₂/$$, MGM/MGM-UA. A songwriting couple do a big musical. Eleanor Powell, Robert Young, Ann Sothern, Red Skelton, Dan Dailey, Lionel Barrymore, Reginald Owen, John Carroll. w. Jack McGowan, Kay van Riper, John McClain, d. Norman Z. McLeod.

MUSICALS: Partners-Married; Putting on a Show; Theater Life; Songwriters; Marriage; Comedy

Ladybird, Ladybird, 1995, 101m, ★★★/$, Goldwyn/Goldwyn, PG-13/S-P. A woman which children from fathers of four different races leads her life in much the same open-minded way. Unfortunately, she lost her child to foster homes and has a penchant for men who are also abusive. With her life in ruins, she meets an immigrant who needs her for citizenship, but will he love her in return? Crissy Rock, Vladimir Vega, Ray Winstone, Sandie Lavelle. w. Rona Munro, d. Ken Loach.
DRAMA: Abused Women; Children-Losing/Parting with; Marriage for Citizenship; Poor People; British Films; True Stories; Latin People; Black Women; Female Screenwriters; Female Protagonists

Lady Bugs, 1992, 92m, ★★/$$, Par/Par, PG-13/P. A coach stuck with a girl's soccer team (Rodney Dangerfield) uses a cute boy in drag as a secret weapon. Jackee Harry, Johnathan Brandis, Ilene Graff. w. Curtis Burch, d. Sidney J. Furie.
COMEDY: CHILDREN'S: Sports Movies; Teenagers; Teenage Movies; Role Reversal; Men as Women; Soccer
FLIPSIDE OF: Bad News Bears
(Bad News Bears SERIES; Just One of the Girls)
(Ed: Distasteful and stupid . . . equals a great pre-teen flick!)

Lady By Choice, 1934, 78m, ★★/$$$, Col/Col. A dancer takes on an old lady as a publicity ploy on Mother's Day, but it may backfire. Carole Lombard, May Robson, Walter Connolly. w. Jow Serling, Dwight Taylor, d. David Burton.
COMEDY: Dancers; Con Artists; Elderly Women; Hoaxes
(Lady for a Day; Hands Across the Table)

Lady Caroline Lamb, 1972, 123m, ★★1/2/$, IndPrism, PG. The wild lady embarrasses her royal husband by her outrageous behavior in this costume epic. Sarah Miles, Jon Finch, Richard Chamberlain, Maragaret Leighton, John Mills, Ralph Richardson, Laurence Olivier. w. d. Robert Bolt.
COMEDY DRAMA: Costume Drama; Biographies; Biographies-Fictional; Wild People; Feisty Females; Royalty; Scandals; 1800s; Female Protagonists
(Great Catherine; White Mischief)

Lady Chatterley's Lover, 1955, 101m, ★★/$, Ind/Nos, S. A woman in a mining town who is married to an impotent miner has an affair with a sexy man who rejuve-nates her. Danielle Darrieux, Leon Genn, Erno Orisa. w. Gaston Bonheur, Philip de Rothschild, Marc Allegret, N-adap. D. H. Lawrence, d. Allegret.

Lady Chatterley's Lover, 1981, 104m, ★★1/2/$$, Cannon/MGM-UA, R/ES-FFN-MN. Much more sexy, if not pornographic remake. Sylvia Kristel, Nicholas Clay, Shane Briant. w. Christopher Wicking, Just Jaeckin, d. Jaeckin.
ROMANCE: Romantic Drama; Erotic Drama; Sexy Women; Sexy Men; Sexuality; Scandals; Romance with Married Person; Cheating Women; Rejuvenation; Mining Towns; Classic Literary Adaptations
(Priest of Love; Women in Love)

The Lady Eve, 1941, 94m, ★★★★/$$$, Par/Par. A slow-witted millionaire (Henry Fonda) manages to take advantage of a con artist and his card-playing daughter (Barbara Stanwyck), who in turn seek revenge amid the fact she may be falling in love with him. Charles Coburn, Eugene Pallette, William Demarest, Eric Blore. w. d. Preston Sturges, P-adap. Monckton Hoffe (BOStory). Oscars: 1-0.
COMEDY: ROMANCE: Romantic Comedy; Enemies-Sleeping with; Con Artists; Gambling; Simple Minds; Lucky People; Battle of the Sexes; Revenge; Marriages-Fake; Love-Questionable; Nerds; Nerds & Babes; Turning the Tables; Ships; Feisty Females; Fathers & Daughters
(Ball of Fire; The Male Animal; Sullivan's Travels)

Lady for a Day, 1934, 95m, ★★★★/$$$, Col/RCA-Col. Gangsters help a homeless woman pretend to be wealthy for when her daughter comes to visit. May Robson (BActress), Warren William, Guy Kibbee, Glenda Farrell, Walter Connolly. w. Robert Riskin (BOScr), SS-adap. Damon Runyon (*Madame La Gimp*), d. Frank Capra (BDirector). BPicture. Oscars: 4-0.
COMEDY: COMEDY DRAMA: MELO-DRAMA: Tearjerkers; Mob Stories; Mob Comedy; Homeless People; Depression Era; Elderly Women
REMAKE: Pocketful of Miracles
(Lady's Choice)

The Lady from Shanghai, 1947, 87m, ★★★1/2/$$, Col/RCA-Col. An Irishman with a past (Orson Welles) rescues a woman from being raped (Rita Hayworth), who then repays him by giving him a job with her rich husband's globe-trotting shady friends; but the shady friends have a set-up in mind for this new friend. w. d. Orson Welles, N-adap. Sherwood King (*If I Die Before I Wake*).
DRAMA: MYSTERY: SUSPENSE: MUR-DER: MURDER MYSTERY: Film Noir; Saving Someone; Saving Oneself; Framed?; Accused Unjustly; Complicated Plots; Clever Plots & Endings; Deaths-Faked; Femme Fatales; World Travel; Sailing; Writer-Directors, Actor-Directors
(Journey into Fear; The Third Man)

The Lady Gambles, 1949, 99m, ★★1/2/$$, U/NA. A woman becomes a gambling addict and wrecks her marriage. Barbara Stanwyck, Robert Preston, Stephen McNally, Edith Barrett. w. Roy Huggins, S-adap. Lewis Meltzer, Oscar Saul, d. Michael Gordon.
DRAMA: MELODRAMA: Gambling; Obsessions; Marriage on the Rocks; Female Protagonists
(The Lady Eve; The Seduction of Gina; Fever Pitch; The Great Sinner)

Lady Godiva, 1955, 89m, ★★1/2/$$, U/NA. A woman gets her revenge in merry old England by riding through her village naked to spite a leader. George Nader, Maureen O'Hara, Victor McLaglen. w. Oscar Brodney, Harry Ruskin, d. Arthur Lubin.
COMEDY DRAMA: Historical Drama; Nudists; Rebels; Feisty Females; England

Ladyhawke, 1985, 124m, ★★1/2/$$, WB/WB, PG/V. A boy tries to reunite lovers who've been changed into a wolf and a bird, but they can't seem to become human again at the same time. Michelle Pfeiffer, Rutger Hauer, Matthew Broderick, Leo McKern. w. Edward Khmara, Michael Thomas, Tom Mankiewicz, d. Richard Donner.
COMEDY: ADVENTURE: Comic Adventure; Medieval Times; Humans into Animals; Animals into Humans;
ROMANCE: Romantic Comedy; Matchmakers; Boys; Teenagers; Sword & Sorcery; Fairy Tales; Animal Stories; Birds; Good Premise Unfulfilled
(Ed: If they'd stuck more to the fairy tale and less to the schtick . . .)

Lady in a Cage (B&W), 1964, 97m, ★★★/$$$, Par/Par, NR/V. A wealthy woman (Olivia de Havilland) who is disabled gets stuck in the birdcage-like elevator in her home when it breaks down, only to be plagued by a bum, his friend (Ann Sothern) and teenagers (James Caan) ready to ransack her house, steal her wine, and hold her hostage. Ann Sothern, Jeff Corey. w. Luther Davis, d. Walter Grauman.

SUSPENSE: DRAMA: HORROR: Burglars; Urban Horrors; Hostages; Trapped; Women in Jeopardy; Disabled People; Disabled People in Jeopardy; Female Protagonists; Teenagers; Teenage Terrors; Gothic Style; Camp (Grand Guignol: Whatever Happened to Baby Jane?; Hush, Hush, Sweet Charlotte; Disabled People in Jeopardy; Wait Until Dark; Hear No Evil; Teenage Terrors; The Happening; Orphans; Woman Screaming)
Lady in Cement, 1968, 93m, ★★1/2/$$, 20th/CBS-Fox, R/S-V. A P.I. happens across a dead bombshell blonde while on a morning swim in Florida and winds up on the case. Frank Sinatra, Raquel Welch, Richard Conte, Lainie Kazan, Martin Gabel. w. Marvin Albert, Jack Guss, d. Gordon Douglas.
MYSTERY: MURDER: MURDER MYSTERY: Detective Stories; Detectives-Private; Murder-Discovering; Conspiracy; Florida
SEQUEL TO: Tony Rome
(Tony Rome; The Detective; Fathom)
The Lady in Question, 1940, 81m, ★★★/$$, Col/Col. When a juror hangs his jury, acquitting a girl of murder, he gets a little worried about his decision when his son falls for her. Brian Aherne, Rita Hayworth, Glenn Ford, Irene Rich, George Coulouris, Lloyd Corrigan, Evelyn Keyes. w. Lewis Meltzer, Marcel Auchard, d. Charles Vidor.
SUSPENSE: MYSTERY: MURDER: MURDER MYSTERY: Men in Jeopardy; Dangerous Women; Love-Questionable; Romance-Dangerous; Juries; Trials; Fathers & Sons; Paris; Foreign Film Remakes; Hidden Gems; Coulda Been Great
REMAKE OF: Gribouille
(Black Widow; So I Married an Axe Murderer; Basic Instinct; Gilda; Cover Girl)
The Lady in Red, 1979, 93m, ★★1/2/$, New World/New World, R/S-V. Dillinger's mistress and her secret life with that dress. Pamela Sue Martin, Robert Conrad, Louise Fletcher. w. John Sayles, d. Lewis Teague.

DRAMA: Crime Drama; Mob Stories; Biographies; Biographies-Fictional; Sexy Women; Dangerous Women; Mistresses; Forgotten Films; Coulda Been Good (Dillinger)
The Lady in the Car with Glasses and a Gun, 1971, 105m, ★★/$, Col/NA, R/S. A woman in France decides to journey to the coast for a breather, but her strange journey may lead her into madness. Samantha Eggar, Oliver Reed, John McEnery, Stephane Audran. w. Richard Harris, Eleanor Perry, N-adap. Sebastien Japrisot, d. Anatole Litvak.
SUSPENSE: MYSTERY: Psychological Drama; Insane-Plot to Drive; Mental Illness; Illusions/Hallucinations; Journies; Vacations; Female Protagonists; Curiosities
Lady in the Dark, 1944, 100m, ★★★/$$, Par/NA. A woman with three men vying for her attention is also editor of a fashion magazine, and having nightmares, so she decides it's all too much and sees a shrink. Ginger Rogers, Warner Baxter, Ray Miland, Jon Hall, Mischa Auer, Barry Sullivan. w. Frances Goodrich, Albert Hackett, P-adap. Moss Hart, d. Mitchell Leisen.
MELODRAMA: ROMANCE: Psychological Drama; Romance-Triangles; Men Fighting over Women; Psychologists; Nightmares; Dreams; Nervous Breakdowns; Fashion World; Career Women; Forgotten Films; Female Protagonists; Female Screenwriters (Kitty Foyle; It Had to Be You)
Lady in the Iron Mask, 1952, 78m, ★★1/2/$, 20th/NA. In a twist on the old French legend, the English Princess Anne is kept under lock and key while her twin tries to succeed to the throne. Louis Hayward, Patricia Medina, Alan Hale Jr., Jud Holdren. w. Jack Pollexfen, Aubrey Wiseberg, d. Ralph Murphy.
MELODRAMA: Body Switching; Twins; Conspiracy; Mix-Ups; Misunderstandings; Princesses; Royalty; Revisionist Films; Female Protagonists
REMAKE/FLIPSIDE: The Man in the Iron Mask
The Lady in the Lake, 1946, 103m, ★★1/2/$$, MGM/MGM-UA. A detective tries to find a missing woman and we follow his every step. Robert Montgomery, Audrey Totter, Lloyd Nolan, Tom Tully. w. Steve Fisher, N-adap. Raymond Chandler, d. Montgomery.

SUSPENSE: MYSTERY: Missing Persons; Detective Stories; Detectives-Private; Searches; Film Noir
(Ed: Famous for its use of "P.O.V.," point of view, where the protagonist is never seen except in a mirror, but we see everything he does-a technique that was also the failing of the picture)
Lady in White, 1988, 113m, ★★★/$, New Visions/Live, PG. A boy sees the ghost a murdered girl and isn't believed, but he soon figures out who killed her and trouble starts. Lukas Haas, Len Cariou, Alex Rocco, Katherine Helmond, Jason Presson. w. d. Frank LaLoggia.
SUSPENSE: MURDER: MYSTERY: MURDER MYSTERY: Ghosts; Nightmares; Detectives-Amateur; Boyhood; Children in Jeopardy; Murder-Witness to; Murder-Debate to Reveal Killer; Unbelieved; Overlooked at Release; Hidden Gems; Writer-Directors; Child Protagonists (Witness; Afraid of the Dark)
The Lady Is Willing, 1942, 91m, ★★1/2/$$, RKO/Turner, Facets. When a childless actress winds up with a baby given to her, she has trouble with the reality of motherhood until a kindly pediatrician helps her out. Marlene Dietrich, Fred MacMurray, Aline MacMahon, Sterling Holloway. w. James Edward Grant, Albert McCleery, d. Mitchell Liesen.
COMEDY: Women-Childless; Actresses;
ROMANCE: Romantic Comedy; Mothers-Struggling; Babies-Finding; Orphans; Children-Adopted; Doctors; Role Reversals; Marriage of Convenience; Marriage Comedy; Coulda Been Great (Bundle of Joy; Bachelor Mother)
Lady Jane, 1986, 142m, ★★★/$, Par/Par, PG/S. The story of how a group of royal insiders tried to make the dead King Edward's cousin Queen in the 1500s. Helena Bonham Carter, Cary Elwes, John Wood, Michael Hordern, Jill Bennett, Jane Lapotaire, Joss Ackland. w. David Edgar, Chris Bryant, d. Trevor Nunn.
DRAMA: Historical Drama; Costume Drama; Queens; Royalty; Inheritances at Stake; England; Medieval Times; British Films
(Anne of the Thousand Days; Queen Margot)
Lady Killer, 1933, 76m, ★★★1/2/$$$$, WB/WB. A movie usher joins the mob and soon winds up a star in Hollywood,

but his past soon catches up with a bullet. James Cagney, Mae Clarke, Leslie Fenton, Margaret Lindsay. w. Ben Markson, N-adap. Rosalind Keating (*The Finger Man*), d. Roy del Ruth.

ACTION: DRAMA: Crime Drama; **COMEDY DRAMA:** Mob Stories; Fame-Rise to; Rags to Riches; Actors; Hollywood Life; Past-Haunted by the

(The George Raft Story; The Cotton Club)

Ladykiller, 1992, 93m, ★★/$(VR), Univ/MCA-U, R/P-V-S. A woman cop (Mimi Rogers) investigating a supposed suicide gets involved with a man (John Shea) claiming to be from a dating service she went to and using a name connected with the suicide. Will she fall for him or not? Alice Krige, Tom Irwin. d. Michael Scott.

SUSPENSE: MYSTERY: MURDER: MURDER MYSTERY: Detective Stories; Detectives in Deep; Crimes of Passion; Detectives-Police; Detectives-Female; Law Officers-Female; Women in Jeopardy; Psycho Killers; Romance with Married Person; Enemies-Sleeping with; Personal Ads; Romance-Dangerous; Cheating Men; Suicidal Tendencies; Female Protagonists; Lonely People; Single Women; Unbelieved; Clever Plots & Endings; Murderers-Female; TV Movies

(Defenseless; Blue Steel; Presumed Innocent)

(Ed: Original in many ways but with a few implausibilities, though a very interesting performance from Rogers)

The Ladykillers, 1955, 97m, ★★★1/2/ $$$, Ealing/EMI-HBO. A little old lady takes on a boarder in her house who brings his thief pals in to try and kill her and steal her things. Alec Guinness, Katie Johnson, Peter Sellers, Cecil Parker, Herbert Lom, Danny Green, Jack Warner. w. William Rose (BOScr), d. Alexander MacKendrick. Oscars: 1-0.

COMEDY: Black Comedy; Murder-Attempted; Murder-Comic Attempts; Elderly Women; Con Artists; Roommates from Hell; Thieves; British Films; Cult Films; Hidden Gems

(A Fish Called Wanda; The Lavender Hill Mob)

Lady L., 1965, 124m, ★★1/2/$, MGM/MGM-UA. An elderly woman remembers her days as a poor, but very sexy and active young Parisian woman. Sophia Loren, David Niven, Paul

Newman, Peter Ustinov, Claude Dauphin, Phillipe Noiret, Michel Piccoli. w. d. Peter Ustinov.

COMEDY DRAMA: ROMANCE: Romantic Comedy; Romantic Drama; Beautiful People; Multiple Stories; Sexy Women; Young Women; Memories; Flashbacks; Paris; Actor Directors; Writer-Directors; Flops-Major

(What a Way to Go; Lydia; The Millionairess)

(Ed: Good-looking but not much else)

Lady of Burlesque, 1943, 91m, ★★★/$$, RKO/Nos. An exotic dancer gets on the case of several murders backstage in her club. Barbara Stanwyck, Michael O'Shea, J. Edward Bromberg. w. James Gunn, N-adap. *The G-String Murders*, Gypsy Rose Lee, d. William Wellman. BMScore. Oscars: 1-0.

MYSTERY: COMEDY: Comic Mystery; **MURDER: MURDER MYSTERY:** Strippers; Dancers; Detective Stories; Detectives-Amateur; Detectives-Female; Murder-Discovering; Forgotten Films; Hidden Gems; Coulda Been Great; Female Protagonists

(The Mad Miss Manton)

Lady on a Train, 1945, 84m, ★★★/$$$, U/MCA-U. A young woman on a train out of New York sees a murder but no one will believe her. Deanna Durbin, Ralph Bellamy, David Bruce, Edward Everett Horton, Dan Duryea. w. Edmund Beloin, Robert O'Brien, N-adap. Leslie Charteris, d. Charles David.

MYSTERY: COMEDY: Comic Mystery; **MURDER: MURDER MYSTERY:** Murder-Witness to; Unbelieved; Trains; Hidden Gems; Coulda Been Great; Good Premise Unfulfilled

Lady Sings the Blues, 1972, 144m, ★★★/$$$, Par/Par, R/P-S. The sad life story of singer Billie Holiday from her humiliating beginning as a club girl to her rise to legend status. Diana Ross (BActress), Billy Dee Williams, Richard Pryor. w. Terence McCloy, Chris Clark, Suzanne dePasse (BOScr), d. Sidney J. Furie. BArt, BCostume, BAScore. Oscars: 5-0.

DRAMA: TRAGEDY: Biographies; Singers; Music Dies; Black Women; Black Casts; Jazz Life; Musicians; Episodic Stories; Fame-Rise to; Drugs; 1930s; Female Protagonists; Black Screenwriters; Female Screenwriters

(The Josephine Baker Story)

The Lady Takes a Chance, 1943, 86m, ★★1/2/$$, RKO/Turner. A secretary goes on vacation in Oregon and meets up with a tall cowboy. Jean Arthur, John Wayne, Charles Winninger. w. Robert Ardrey, d. William A. Seiter.

ROMANCE: WESTERN: Western Comedy; Romantic Comedy; Vacations; Vacation Romance; Cowboys; Secretaries; Romance-Opposites Attract

(The Cowboy and the Lady; Never a Dull Moment)

The Lady Takes a Flyer, 1958, 95m, ★★1/2/$$, U/MCA-U. The wife of a pilot stays at home with a baby and gets bored, then begins finding new ways to amuse herself. Lana Turner, Jeff Chandler, Richard Denning, Chuck Connors. w. Danny Arnold, d. Jack Arnold.

COMEDY DRAMA: Marriage Drama; Marriage on the Rocks; Housewives; Depression; Pilots-Airline; Forgotten Films

(Ed: Provocative title provoking little to nothing)

The Lady Vanishes, 1938, 97m, ★★★★/$$, Gaumont-Gainsborough-U/MCA-U. A young woman on a train going through pre-World War II Europe thinks she's seen a woman who has subsequently disappeared. When she expresses fear that something happened to her, no one will admit they saw her as well. Margaret Lockwood, Michael Redgrave, Dame May Whitty, Paul Lukas, Basil Radford. w. Sidney Gilliat, Frank Launder, N-adap. The Wheel Spins, d. Alfred Hitchcock.

The Lady Vanishes, 1979, 97m, ★★1/2/$, Embassy/Media. REMAKE of original in color, and without the same suspense. Cybill Shepherd, Elliott Gould, Angela Lansbury. w. George Axelrod, d. Anthony Page.

SUSPENSE: MYSTERY: Spies; Missing Persons; Missing Person Thriller; Conspiracy; Nazi Stories; British Films; World War II Era; Unbelieved; Female Protagonists; Clever Plots & Endings; Trains; Coulda Been Great; Hitchcockian

(Lady on a Train; The Vanishing)

(Ed: The 1979 version isn't up to the original, of course, but not really bad, either. The first real Missing Person thriller)

The Lady with a Dog, 1959, 86m, ★★★/$, Ind/Facets, Ingram. A couple of married people meet by chance in the park, but can't take the pressure of the secret. Iya Savvina, Alexei Batalov. SS-adap. Anton Chekhov, d. Yosif Heifitz.

MELODRAMA: ROMANCE: Romantic Drama; Cheating Women; Cheating Men; Romance-Clandestine; Romance-Doomed; Russians; Russian Films
(Moscow Does Not Believe in Tears; Brief Encounter; Falling in Love)

La Femme Nikita, 1990, 130m, ★★★¹/₂/$$$, Miramax/Miramax, R/EV-S-FN. A beautiful criminal doing life in a French prison is offered a change of identity if she'll become a hired assassin for French intelligence. Anne Parillaud, Jean-Hughes Anglade, Tcheky Karyo, Jeanne Moreau. w. d. Luc Besson.

ACTION: Spy Films; Spies; Secret Agents; Assassination Plots; Blackmail; Brainwashing; Murder-Coerced into; Murder-Learning to; Dangerous Women; Feisty Females; Hitwomen; Murderers-Female; Spies-Female; French Films; Female Protagonists; Writer-Directors
REMAKE: Point of No Return

Lair of the White Worm, 1988, 93m, ★★★/$$, Vestron/Vestron, R/S-P-FFN. A hip bisexual vampiress (Amanda Donohoe) has a pit in an ancient ruin in the English countryside and is planning on sacrificing a few young unsuspecting maidens to the snakelike monster living in it. Catherine Oxenberg, Sammi Davis, Hugh Grant. w. d. Ken Russell.

HORROR: Black Comedy; Horror Comedy; Vampires; Monsters; Snakes; Revisionist Films; British Films; Teenage Horror Movies; Virgins; Lesbians; Bisexuality; Writer-Directors
(Gothic; Crimes of Passion)

Lake Consequence, 1992, 85m, ★★¹/₂/VR, Republic/Republic, R/S-FN-MN. When a housewife winds up on a camping trip (not necessarily by her will) with a nature boy, she soon begins living out fantasies with he and another woman on the lake. Billy Zane, Joan Severance, May Karasun. w. Zalman King, d. Rafael Eisenmann.

MELODRAMA: Erotic Drama; Fantasies; Cheating Women; Nature-Back to; Romance-Triangles; Bisexuality; Housewives; Independent Films
(Two Moon Junction; Wild Orchid)

La Lectrice, 1988, 98m, ★★★/$$, Orion/Orion, R/S. People hire a beautiful woman to read stories to them but the lines between reader and lover become blurred in some of their minds. Miou-Miou, Regis Royer, Christian Ruche. w. Michel Deville, Rosalind Deville, N-adap. Raymond Jean, d. Michel Deville.

DRAMA: Character Studies; Sexy Women; Lonely People; Women and Boys; Infatuations; Quiet Little Films; French Films; Hidden Gems

La Marseillaise, 1938, 145m, ★★★/$, Ind/Nos. A French version of the French Revolution. Pierre Renoir, Lise Delemere. w. d. Jean Renoir.

DRAMA: War Stories; Political Unrest; French Revolution; Historical Drama; Costume Drama; Cast of Thousands; French Films; Writer-Directors
(A Tale of Two Cities)

La Maschera (The Mask), 1988, 90m, ★★¹/₂/$, Ind/NA. An actress in 1700s Italy has her eye on a masked man who comes to her on occasion, instead of being seduced by a rich man-sexiness winning over money. Helena Bonham Carter, Michael Maloney, Feodor Chaliapin. w. Adriano Apra, Fiorella Infascelli, Enzo Ungari, Ennio deConcini, d. Fiorelle Infascelli.

ROMANCE: MELODRAMA: Erotic Drama; Costume Drama; Romance-Triangles; Dangerous Men; Sexy Men; Actresses; Female Screenwriters; Female Directors
(The Wicked Lady; The Gambler)

Lamb, 1986, 110m, ★★★/$, Cannon/MGM-UA, PG. A priest runs off with a fourteen-year-old student from their extremely strict reform school in Ireland, but they won't get far or get away with it. Liam Neeson, Hugh O'Connor, Harry Towb, Ian Bannen, Frances Tomelty. w. N-adap. Bernard MacLaverty, d. Colin Gregg.

DRAMA: TRAGEDY: Priests; Religion; Men and Boys; Homoeroticism; Irish Films; Ireland; Overlooked at Release; Underrated
(Priest; The Boys of St. Vincent)

Lambada, 1990, 98m, ★¹/₂/$$, Cannon-WB/WB, PG-13/S-P. A teacher teaches by day, dances by night, all leading to a competition for he and his underdog students. J. Eddie Peck, Melora Hardin, Shabba-Doo, Ricky Paul Goldin. w. Joel Silberg, Sheldon Renan, d. Joel Silberg.

MELODRAMA: Dance Movies; Music Movies; Competitions; Teachers and Students; Unintentionally Funny
(The Forbidden Dance; Stand and Deliver)
(Ed: *Stand and Deliver* goes dancing)

Lancer Spy, 1937, 80m, ★★¹/₂/$$, Ind/NA. When a German spy is caught during World War I, an English double is found to replace him as a mole back home. George Sanders, Dolores del Rio, Peter Lorre, Joseph Schildkraut, Virginia Field. w. Philip Dunne, N-adap. Marthe McKenna, d. Gregory Ratoff.

SUSPENSE: Spy Films; Spies; Lookalikes; Undercover; Germans as Enemy; World War I Stories; Forgotten Films; Good Premise Unfulfilled
(Dave; Moon Over Parador; The Prisoner of Zenda)

The Land Before Time, 1988, 69m, ★★★/$$$, Amblin-U/MCA-U, G. A baby dinosaur loses his parents and finds a group of friends to help him to safety. w. Stu Kreiger, Judy Freudberg, Tony Geiss, d. Don Bluth.

Cartoons; **CHILDREN'S:** Dinosaurs; Families-Extended; Orphans; Childhood
SEQUELS: The Land Before Time II & III
(We're Back!)

The Land that Time Forgot, 1974, 91m, ★★★/$$, AIP/Vestron. During World War I, a ship is sunk and the survivors land on a deserted island full of dinosaurs. Doug McClure, John McEnery, Susan Penhaglion. w. James Cawthorne, Michael Moorcock, N-adap. Edgar Rice Burroughs, d. Kevin Connor.

SCI-FI: ACTION: ADVENTURE: Dinosaurs; Time Sleepers; Islands; Explorers; Shipwrecked; World War I Era; Submarines; Volcanoes
(The People that Time Forgot; Journey to the Center of the Earth; Jurassic Park)

The Landlord, 1970, 110m, ★★★¹/₂/$$, UA/NA, Showtime. A rich, white, young man buys an apartment house in an area of black Brooklyn supposedly being gentrified. But things aren't so easy to change, as his idealism begins to sink while he deals with his snooty parents, the neighbors, and begins to romance a beautiful black woman. Beau Bridges, Lee Grant, Pearl Bailey, Susan Anspach, Diana Sands. w. Bill Gunn, N-adap. Kristin Hunter, d. Hal Ashby.

SATIRE: COMEDY DRAMA: Inner City Life; Class Conflicts; Rich vs. Poor; Riches to Rags; Illusions Destroyed; Romance-Interracial; Race Relations;

White Among Blacks; Black Women; Young Men; Apartment Buildings; Rebels; Country Club Life; Snobs; Hidden Gems; Time Capsules
(The Super; My Little Girl; Desperate Characters)
(Ed: If it were made today, it would be incredibly goofy and not nearly so sly. It shows how far Hollywood had gone then, how far it went back, and how angry and violent at least films featuring black main characters came back as)

L'Année des Meduses, 1987, 100m, ★★/$$, Ind/New Yorker, R/S-FN-MRN. A young sexy girl on the topless beaches of the Riviera meets up with a young gigolo for soap opera. Valerie Kaprisky.
MELODRAMA: ROMANCE: Erotic Drama; Beach Movies; Beautiful People; Alternative Lifestyles; Prostitutes-Male; Riviera Life; Nudists; Soap Operas; French Films
(Aphrodite; Breathless [1983])

La Notte, 1960, 121m, ★★1/2/$$, Nepi-Ind/NA. An Italian novelist and his French wife have a midlife crisis together during a long night in Milan. Marcello Mastroianni, Jeanne Moreau, Monica Vitti, Bernhard Wicki. w. Michelangelo Antonioni, Ennio Flaiano, Antonio Guerra, d. Michelangelo Antonioni.
DRAMA: Marriage Drama; Nervous Breakdowns; Marriage on the Rocks; Writers; Italian Films; Art Films

La Nuit de Varennes, 1982, 133m, ★★★/$$$, Triumph/Col, R/S-FN-MRN. Some of the key American and French planners of the French Revolution ride in a coach together to meet King Louis XIV at Varennes, leading to some rather eccentric people and happenings. Jean-Louis Barrault, Marcello Mastroianni, Hanna Shygulla, Harvey Keitel. w. Sergio Amidei, Ettore Scola, d. Ettore Scola.
COMEDY DRAMA: Biographies-Fictional; Historical Drama; Costume Drama; Kings; Queens; Royalty; French Films; Hidden Gems
(Danton; La Marseillaise)

La Passante, 1983, 106m, ★★★/$$, Ind/Ingram. A normally pacifist man in Paraguay can't take the poverty and dictatorship any longer, so he assassinates a leader and we learn what led him to it. Michel Piccoli, Romy Schneider, Helmut Griern. d. Jacques Rouffo.
DRAMA: Political Drama; Art Films; South America; Peaceful People;

Assassination Plots; Flashbacks; Multiple Performances

Larceny, Inc., 1942, 95m, ★★1/2/$$$, WB/WB. When an ex-con decides to get back in the biz and rob a bank, he winds up having second thoughts. Edward G. Robinson, Jane Wyman, Broderick Crawford, Anthony Quinn, Jack Carson. w. Everett Freeman, Edwin Gilbert, P-adap. Laura & S. J. Perelman, *The Night Before Christmas*, d. Lloyd Bacon.
COMEDY DRAMA: Crime Drama; Heist Stories; Bank Robberies; One Last Time; Ex-Convicts; Guilty Conscience

La Ronde, 1950, 100m, ★★★/$$, Ind/Sultan. A wise old man narrates a story proving that love is a merry-go-round: a series of lovers form a chain that leads back to the original soldier that began the narrative by chasing after a prostitute. Anton Walbrook, Simone Signoret, Serge Reggiani, Simone Simon, Daniel Gelin, Danielle Darrieux, Fernand Gravey, Odette Joyeux, Jean-Louis Barrault, Isa Miranda, Gerard Philipe. w. Jacques Natanson, Max Ophuls, N-adap. Arthur Schnitzler, d. Max Ophuls.
Narrated Films

La Ronde, 1964, 110m, ★★1/2/$, Ind/NA. A remake of the above, losing much without the elderly narrator, set in Paris in 1913. Marie Dubois, Claude Giraud, Anna Karina, Jean-Claude Brialy, Jane Fonda, Maurice Ronet, Catherine Spaak, Bernard Noel, Francine Berge, Jean Sorel. w. Jean Anouilh, d. Roger Vadim.
DRAMA: COMEDY DRAMA: ROMANCE: Romantic Drama; FARCE: Multiple Stories; Slice of Life Stories; Interwoven Stories; Hand-Me-Down Stories; Romance with Prostitute; Soldiers; French Films; Hidden Gems; Narrated Films
(Children of Paradise)

Lassie, 1994, 97m, ★★★/$, Par/Par, G. The famous collie moves in with a family who has retreated to the Virginia countryside and faces updated 90s challenges with her suburban angst-ridden family. Lassie, Thomas Guiry, Helen Slater, Jon Tenney, Frederic Forrest, Richard Farnsworth. w. Matthew Jacobs, Gary Ross, Elizabeth Anderson, d. Daniel Petrie.
MELODRAMA: Pet Stories; Dogs; Family Drama; Saving Someone; Boy and His Dog

Lassie Come Home, 1943, 88m, ★★★1/2/$$$, MGM/MGM-UA. When an impoverished country family has to sell their prize dog, Lassie makes it all the way back home where she belongs. Roddy McDowell, Elizabeth Taylor, Donald Crisp, Edmund Gwenn, Dame May Whitty, Nigel Bruce, Else Lanchester. w. Hugo Butler, N-adap. Eric Knight, d. Fred Wilcox.
MELODRAMA: Tearjerkers; Pet Stories; Dogs; Journies; Reunions; Lassie
(Lassie; The Magic of Lassie; The Incredible Journey; Homeward Bound)
(Ed: Started everything)

Lassiter, 1984, 100m, ★★/$, WB/WB, R/S-P-FRN. A suave American detective heads to England for intrigue during the 30s to help out against the Germans. Tom Selleck, Jane Seymour, Lauren Hutton, Bob Hoskins, Joe Regalbuto, Ed Lauter. w. David Taylor, d. Roger Young.
SUSPENSE: Detective Stories; Detectives-Private; Germans as Enemy; Nazi Stories; American Abroad; England

The Last Action Hero, 1993, 131m, ★★/$, Tri-Star/Col-Tri, PG-13/V. A kid jumps into a movie screen with his favorite action star and has an adventure. Austin O'Brien, Arnold Schwarzenegger, Mercedes Ruehl, F. Murray Abraham, Charles Dance, Anthony Quinn. w. Shane Black, David Arnott, d. John McTiernan.
COMEDY: ACTION: Action Comedy; Spoofs; Chase Stories; Crossing the Line; Fantasy; Fans-Crazed; Child Protagonists; Hollywood Satire; Hollywood Life; Movie Making; Movie Theaters; All-Star Cameos; Flops-Major; Coulda Been Good
(Kindergarten Cop; The Purple Rose of Cairo)
(Ed: One of the most expensive films ever and a big flop to boot. The list of star cameos is dazzling, but it can't make up for fundamental flaws in the committee-thinked story)

The Last American Hero, 1973, 95m, ★★1/2/$, 20th/CBS-Fox, R/S-P. A modern-day moonshiner who likes to race cars adventures in the backwoods. Jeff Bridges, Valerie Perrine, Geraldine Fitzgerald, Ned Beatty, Gary Busey. w. William Roberts, d. Lamont Johnson.
COMEDY DRAMA: ACTION: Car Racing; Rednecks; Bootleggers; Southerns; Forgotten Films
(Stay Hungry; The Bootleggers)

The Last Angry Man, 1959, 100m, ★★★1/2/$$, Col/RCA-Col. A TV documentary crew comes to an elderly doctor's office in Brooklyn to chronicle his work with the poor and indigent, but he's not so willing to be explored or exploited. Paul Muni (BActor), David Wayne, Betsy Palmer, Luther Adler. w. N-adap. Gerald Green, d. Daniel Mann. BB&W Art. Oscars: 2-0.

DRAMA: SATIRE: Social Drama; Social Satire; Doctors; Saintly People; Stern Men; Social Workers; New York Life; Inner City Life; Time Capsules; Hidden Gems; Forgotten Films

The Last Boy Scout, 1991, 105m, ★★/$$$, WB/WB, R/EP-EV-S-FN. A detective (Bruce Willis) who's an ex-football player finds himself entangled in a cover-up of a plot to fix games and quite a bit more. Damon Wayans, Hally Berry. w. Shane Black, d. Tony Scott.

ACTION: MYSTERY: Buddy Cops; Buddy Films; Black & White Together; Detective Stories; Conspiracy; Film Noir-Modern; Gambling; Mob Stories; Car Chases; Car Crashes; Los Angeles; Coulda Been Good
(Striking Distance; Lethal Weapon)
(Ed: One of the highest-priced scripts ever turns out not to be up to writer's *Lethal Weapon*, and though it's empty, it does look great thanks to Scott)

The Last Command, 1928, 100m (silent), ★★★★/$$$, Par/Par. A Russian general nearly loses his mind when he's forced to become a movie extra in a movie about the battle he recently commanded in the Russian Revolution. Emil Jannings (**BActor**), William Powell, Evelyn Brent. w. John Goodrich, Lajos Biro (BOStory), d. Josef Von Sternberg. Oscars: 2-1.

SATIRE: Hollywood Satire; **COMEDY:** Actors; Moviemaking; Directors; Nervous Breakdowns; Russians; Soldiers; Leaders-Military; Hidden Gems; Media Satire; Ahead of its Time; Film History

The Last Command, 1955, 110m, ★★1/2/$$, Republic/Republic. Jim Bowie, maker of the infamous knife and other wild west legends, returns to Texas from Arkansas to fight in the Alamo. Ernest Borgnine, Sterling Hayden, Anna Maria Alberghetti, Arthur Hunnicutt, Richard Carolson, J. Carrol Naish. w. Warren Duff, d. Frank Lloyd.

WESTERNS: War Stories; War Battles; Alamo Stories; Biographies; Legends; Texas; West-Old; Rebels
(The Iron Mistress; The Alamo)

Last Days of Chez Nous, 1992, 96m, ★★★/$, New Line/New Line, R/S-FN-MN. A woman in Australia goes away on vacation, so her sister sleeps with her sexy French husband and her daughter takes up with a young visitor. Lisa Harrow, Bruno Ganz, Kerry Fox, Mirando Otto. w. Helen Garner, d. Gilliam Armstrong.

MELODRAMA: Erotic Drama; Soap Opera; Romance with Relative's Lover; Australian Films; Female Screenwriters; Female Directors; Female Protagonists
(Bonjour, Tristesse; Man of Flowers)

The Last Days of Pompeii, 1935, 96m, ★★★/$$, RKO/Turner. Stories of the people in the ancient village before the famous volcano is about to erupt. Preston Foster, Basil Rathbone, Alan Hale, Dorothy Wilson. w. Ruth Rose, Boris Ingster, N-adap. Lord Lytton, d. Merian Cooper.

DRAMA: Disaster Movies; Volcanoes; Ancient Times; Multiple Stories; Interwoven Stories; Italy
REMAKE: TV miniseries 1981.
(Krakatoa, East of Java)

The Last Detail, 1973, 104m, ★★★1/2/$$$, Col/RCA-Col, R/EP-S. Two soldiers escort a recruit, who's been caught stealing, to prison and have one last wild fling before it's all over. Jack Nicholson (BActor), Randy Quaid (BSActor), Otis Young, Clifton James, Carol Kane. w. Robert Towne (BOScr), N-adap. Darryl Ponicsan, d. Hal Ashby. Oscars: 3-0.

DRAMA: Military Stories; Friendships-Male; Soldiers; Young Men; Young Men-Angry; One Last Time; Thieves; 1970s
(One Flew Over the Cuckoo's Nest; Easy Rider)

The Last Emperor, 1987, 160m, ★★★/$$$, Col/RCA-Col, PG. The last one in China before Mao's revolution-from his time as a king tot to his last days in exile as a gardener. John Lone, Joan Chen, Peter O'Toole. w. Mark Peploe, Bernardo Bertolucci (**BAScr**), d. Bernardo Bertolucci (**BDirector**). **BPicture, BArt, BCin, BSound, BOScore, BEdit, BCostume.**
Oscars: 9-9, one of the biggest sweeps ever.

DRAMA: MELODRAMA: Epics; Cast of Thousands; Historical Drama; Political Drama; Costume Drama; China; Kings; Royalty; Rise and Fall Stories; Communists; Political Unrest; Episodic Stories; Faded Hits
(Empire of the Sun; Shanghai Triad; Raise the Red Lantern; Nicholas and Alexandra)
(Ed: Somewhat stilted though gorgeous)

Last Exit to Brooklyn, 1989, 98m, ★★★1/2/$, New Line/Col, R/EV-P-S. While workers strike in 1950s lower-class Brooklyn, a prostitute heads down a road to ruin. Jennifer Jason Leigh, Stephen Lang, Burt Young, Peter Dobson, Christopher Murray, Alexis Arquette, Jerry Orbach. w. Desmond Nakano, N-adap. Hubert Selby, d. Uli Edel.

DRAMA: TRAGEDY: Social Drama; Working Class; Prostitutes-Low Class; New York Life; Strikes; Unions; Underworld; Alternative Lifestyle; Homosexual Secrets; Gay Men; Gay Awakenings; Transvestites; Drugs-Addictions; Mob Stories; Gangs-Street; Inner City Life; Rape/Rapists; Overlooked at Release; Hidden Gems
(On the Waterfront; I Cover the Waterfront)

La Strada, 1954, 94m, ★★★1/2/$$$, Ponti-Ind/Sultan. A circus weightlifter buys an orphan girl to be his slave and travels the fantasylike Italian countryside. Guiletta Masina, Anthony Quinn, Richard Basehart. w. Federico Fellini, Ennio Flaiano, Tullio Pinelli (BOScr), d. Federico Fellini. (**BFLFilm**). Oscars: 2-1.

MELODRAMA: ROMANCE: Journies; Slice of Life Stories; Art Films; Circus Life; Slavery; Body Builders; Surrealism; Sleeper Hits; Hidden Gems
(La Guerre est Fine; 81/2; Juliet of the Spirits)

The Last Flight, 1931, 80m, ★★★/$$$, WB/NA. Soldiers recovering from World War I stay in Paris for some R&R. Richard Barthelmess, Helen Chandler, David Manners, Elliot Nugent. w. John Saunders, N-adap. Saunders, Single Lady, d. William Dieterle.

MELODRAMA: DRAMA: Pilots-Military; World War I Era; Paris; Americans Abroad; Medical Recovery

The Last Flight of Noah's Ark, 1980, 98m, ★★1/2/$$, Disney/Disney, G. A plane full of animals and orphans crash lands on a desert island, so the orphanage leader and the pilot fall in love. Elliott Gould, Genevieve Bujold, Ricky

Schroder, Vincent Gardenia. w. Steven Carabatsos, Sandy Glass, George Bloom, SS-adap. Ernest K. Gann, The Gremlin's Castle, d. Charles Jarrott.

CHILDREN'S: FAMILY: ROMANCE: Fantasy; Stranded on an Island; Airplane Crashes; Islands; Animal Stories
(Father Goose; The Castaway Cowboy)

The Last Hard Men, 1976, 97m, ★★1/2/$, 20th/NA. When a convict escapes from prison, he heads for the sheriff who put him there for a train robbery. Charlton Heston, James Coburn, Barbara Hershey, Christopher Mitchum, Michael Parks. w. Guerdon Trueblood, N-adap. Brian Gardfield, *Gun Down*, d. Andrew V. McLaglen.

WESTERN: Police Stories; Convict's Revenge; Prison Escape; Train Robberies; Overlooked at Release

Last House on the Left, 1972, 91m, ★★1/2/$$, Ind/Live, R/EV-B&G. When escaped criminals kidnap, rape, and murder a girl, her parents take off after them for vengeance. David Hess, Lacy Grantham, w. d. Wes Craven.

ACTION: SUSPENSE: Revenge; Avenging Death of Someone; Rape/Rapists; Revenge on Rapist; Prison Escapes; Writer-Directors

REMAKE/RETREAD, RETELLING: The Virgin Spring.
(Death Wish; Outrage; Fighting Back)

The Last Hunt, 1956, 103m, ★★★/$, MGM/MGM-UA. In the old West, buffalo hunters wind up in conflict over what seems trivial but winds up tragic. Stewart Granger, Robert Taylor, Debra Paget, Lloyd Nolan, Russ Tamblyn. w. d. Richard Brooks.

WESTERNS: Westerns-Neo; Men in Conflict; Hunters; Revenge; Chase Movies; Underrated; Forgotten Films; Ahead of its Time; Writer-Directors
(Unforgiven; Dances with Wolves)
(Ed: Has a harrowing, satirical ending where a gunman freezes to death waiting so long for his prey to come along)

The Last Hurrah, 1958, 92m, ★★★1/2/$$$, Col/RCA-Col. The head of a city's political machine fights one last campaign as new forces rise against him. Spencer Tracy, Jeffrey Hunter, Dianne Foster, Pat O'Brien, Basil Rathbone, Edward Brophy, Donald Crisp, James Gleason, John Carradine, Wallace Ford, Jane Darwell. w. Frank Nugent, N-adap. Edwin O'Connor, d. John Ford.

DRAMA: MELODRAMA: Political Drama; Political Campaigns; Politicians; Political Corruption; One Last Time; Retirement; All-Star Cameos; Stern Men; Charismatic People

REMAKE: TV, 1978, starring Carroll O'Connor, Mariette Hartley
(The Best Man; Beau James)

The Last Laugh, 1924, 73m, ★★★1/2/$$, UFA/Nos. When an elderly doorman of a hotel is demoted to washroom attendant, he suddenly comes upon some money and, hence, revenge. Emil Jannings, Max Hiller. w. Carl Mayer, d. F. W. Murnau.

SATIRE: Turning the Tables; Revenge; Rich vs. Poor; Worker vs. Boss; Working Class; Hotels

The Last Married Couple in America, 1979, 102m, ★★1/2/$$, U/MCA-U, R/S. During the sexual revolution, a couple in Los Angeles fights the temptations and prodding of their swinging friends, but it may not work. Natalie Wood, George Segal, Valerie Harper, Richard Benjamin, Arlene Golonka, Alan Arbus, Dom DeLuise. w. John Shaner, d. Gilbert Cates.

COMEDY: Sex Comedy; **SATIRE:** Marriage Comedy; Married Couple; Sexual Revolution; Divorce; Battle of the Sexes; 1970s; Los Angeles; Coulda Been Great; Good Premise Unfulfilled
(Serial; Chapter Two; A Change of Seasons; Bob & Ted & Carol & Alice; Loving Couples)

The Last Metro, 1980, 131m, ★★★1/2/$$, UAC/MGM-UA. At the onset of World War II, a Jewish movie theater manager hides for safety in the cellar down by the metro subway. Gerard Depardieu, Catherine Deneuve, Jean Poiret. w. Francois Truffaut, Suzanne Schiffman, d. Truffaut. (BFLFilm). Oscars: 1-0.

DRAMA: Art Films; **ROMANCE:** Protecting Someone; Anti-Semitism; Jewish People; Hiding Out; World War II Stories; Paris; Subways; Quiet Little Films; French Films
(The Shop on Main Street; Au Revoir, Les Enfants)

The Last Movie, 1971, 108m, ★★/$, U/VCI, R/S. Hip LA filmmakers go to South America to make a hip western and everything comes apart-including this appropriately titled movie. Dennis Hopper, Julie Adams, Peter Fonda, Kris

Kristofferson, Rod Cameron, Samuel Fuller. w. Stewart Stern, d. Dennis Hopper.

DRAMA: Art Films; Flops-Major; Movies within Movies; Moviemaking; Directors; Actors; Actresses; All-Star Casts
(Easy Rider; Living in Oblivion)

The Last of England, 1987, 87m, ★★★/$, Ind/Tapeworm. Disturbing images of modern England in art film packaging. w. d. Derek Jarman.
Documentaries; Art Films; Avant-Garde Films; England; Inner City Life; Alternative Lifestyles; Underworld; Cult Films; Writer-Directors
(Blue; Edward II; The Garden)

The Last of His Tribe, 1992, 90m, ★★★/$$, HBO/HBO, PG/V. In the early 1900s, an anthropologist finds the last Indian of his legendary tribe. Jon Voight, Graham Greene, David Ogden Stiers, Anne Archer. w. Stephen Harrigan, d. Harry Hook.

DRAMA: WESTERNS: Scientists; Sociologists; Indians-American; Legends; Quiet Little Films
(Dances with Wolves; Little Big Man)

The Last of Mrs. Cheyney, 1937, 98m, ★★1/2/$$, MGM/MGM-UA. A female con artist changes her ways a bit when she falls in love while trying to bilk a rich woman out of her dough. Joan Crawford, Robert Montgomery, William Powell, Frank Morgan, Nigel Bruce. w. Leon Gordon, Samson Raphaelson, Monckton Hoffe, d. Richard Boleslawski.

ROMANCE: COMEDY DRAMA: MELODRAMA: Con Artists; Criminals-Female; Life Transitions; Forgotten Films; Female Protagonists

REMAKE OF: 1929 version; **REMAKE:** The Law and the Lady
(Mildred Pierce; Possessed; The Women)

The Last of Sheila, 1973, 123m, ★★★/$$, WB/WB, R/S-P. A millionaire (James Coburn) invites several of his Hollywood friends (Raquel Welch, James Mason, Dyan Cannon, Richard Benjamin, Joan Hackett) to spend some time on his yacht in Italy, but he doesn't tell them how sinister the parlor games he has planned will be. w. Anthony Perkins, Stephen Sondheim, d. Herbert Ross.

MYSTERY: MURDER MYSTERY: Black Comedy; Deaths-One by One; Mystery-Whodunits; Murder-Invitation to; Vacations; Illusions/Hallucinations; Misunderstandings; Clever Plots &

Endings; Mindgames; Homosexual
Secrets; Secrets-Haunting; Hollywood
Life; Rich People; All-Star Casts;
Hidden Gems
(Ten Little Indians; Murder by Death)

Last of the Dogmen, 1995, ★★1/2/$,
Savoy/Savoy, PG/V. A mountain man must
look for a rare Indian tribe in order to
clear up a mystery and finds a female
anthropologist to help him out. But can
they stop bickering long enough to do the
job? Tom Berenger, Barbara Hershey,
Kurtwood Smith, Steve Reeves, Dawn
Lavand, Gregory Scott Cummins.
w. d. Tab Murphy.
DRAMA: ADVENTURE: Romance-
Bickering; Indians-American; **MYSTERY:**
Mountain Settings; Writer-Directors

The Last of the Mohicans, 1936, 91m,
★★★/$$$, WB/Nos. An adopted white
son of an Indian helps save some white
British pioneers from rival raging Indians,
while falling for one of the women.
Randolph Scott, Binnie Barnes, Bruce
Cabot. w. Philip Dunne, John Balderston,
Paul Perez, Daniel Moore, N-adap. James
Fenimore Cooper, d. George B. Seitz.

The Last of the Mohicans, 1992,
122m, ★★★/$$$$, WB/WB, R/EV-S. An
opulent remake, though a bit short of
story. Daniel Day Lewis, Madeleine
Stowe. w. Michael Mann, Christopher
Crowe, N-adap. James Fenimore Cooper,
d. Michael Mann. BSound. Oscars: 1-0.
ACTION: ADVENTURE: ROMANCE:
TRAGEDY: WESTERNS: Early America;
War Stories; Indians-American; Settlers
vs. Indians; Raised by Indians; Saving
Someone; Protecting Women; 1800s;
Classic Tragedy
(Dances with Wolves; The Light in the
Forest; Drums Along the Mohawk)

The Last of the Red Hot Lovers,
1972, 98m, ★★★/$$, Par/Par, R/S. A
middle-aged man wants to have an affair
and finds flings aren't so easy anymore.
Alan Arkin, Paula Prentiss, Sally
Kellerman, Renee Taylor. w. Neil Simon,
d. Gene Saks.
COMEDY: ROMANCE: Romantic
Comedy; Cheating Men; Romance with
Married Person; Sex Comedy; Midlife
Crisis; Romance-Middle-Aged; Forgotten
Films; Hidden Gems; Underrated
(Middle-Aged Crazy; Jake's Women)

Last of the Secret Agents, 1966, 90m,
★★1/2/$$, Par/NA. Two bumbling fools
wind up spies and causing a mess. Marty

Allen, Steve Rossi, Nancy Sinatra, John
Williams, Lou Jacobi. w. Mel Tokin,
d. Norman Abbott.
COMEDY: Comedy-Slapstick; Spies;
Spoofs-Spy; Fools-Bumbling; Secret
Agents; Comedians; Forgotten Films
(Martin & Lewis SERIES; Dumb and
Dumber)
(Ed: Only for Marty Allen hardcore
fans-are there any?; but it's really not
that bad)

The Last Outpost, 1935, 75m, ★★★/
$$, Par/NA. When a British military offi-
cer is kidnapped by Kurds in Iraq, a free-
lance secret agent goes into action. Cary
Grant, Claude Rains, Gertrude Michael,
Kathleen Burke, Akim Tamiroff. w. Philip
McDonald, Britten Austin, d. Charles
Barton, Louis Ganier.
ADVENTURE: Missing Persons;
Kidnappings; Rescue Drama; Secret
Agents; Middle East; Forgotten Films
(Gunga Din; The Wind and the Lion)

The Last Picture Show (B&W), 1971,
118m, ★★★★/$$$, Columbia/RCA-Col.
R/S-P-FFN-MFN. A small town in Texas
is fading with time as various people
leave and change while the tumble weeds
roll by and the only movie theater in town
closes. Jeff Bridges (BSActor), Cybill
Shepherd, Timothy Bottoms, Ben Johnson
(**BSActor**), Ellen Burstyn (BSActress),
Cloris Leachman (**BSActress**), Eileen
Brennan. w. Larry McMurtry, Peter
Bogdanovich (BAScr), N-adap. Larry
McMurtry, d. Peter Bogdanovich
(BDirector). BPicture, BCin. Oscars: 8-2.
DRAMA: ROMANCE: Ensemble Films;
Multiple Stories; Interwoven Stories; Slice
of Life Stories; Small-town Life; Elusive
Women; Teenagers; Life Transitions;
Coming of Age; Romance-Older
Women/Younger Men; Love-Firsts;
Virgins; Ordinary People Stories;
Southwestern Life; Texas; Neo-Realism;
All-Star Casts; Movie Theaters; Quiet
Little Films
SEQUEL: Texasville
(Texasville; Hud; Cinema Paradiso)

The Last Remake of Beau Geste,
1977, 85m, ★★1/2/$, U/MCA-U, PG/S.
Spoof of the original adventure, with
Marty Feldman as the cross-eyed goof
stuck in the foreign legion and after a
jewel. Marty Feldman, Michael York,
Ann-Margret, Peter Ustinov, Trevor
Howard, James Earl Jones, Henry
Gibson, Terry Thomas, Spike Milligan,

Hugh Griffith, Roy Kinnear. w. Marty
Feldman, Chris Allen, d. Feldman.
COMEDY: ADVENTURE: Comic
Adventure; Spoofs; Foreign Legion; Jewel
Thieves; Misunderstandings; Fools-
Bumbling; Coulda Been Good
(Ed: One great joke involving turning
some nipples)

Last Rites, 1988, 103m, ★★/$,
MGM/MGM-UA, R/EV-S-FFN-MFN. A
priest with mobster relatives becomes
involved with a young woman who may be
more than she appears when he tries to
save her from his own father's hitmen.
Tom Berenger, Daphne Zuniga, Chick
Venora, Anne Twomey, Paul Dooley, Dane
Clark. w. d. Donald Bellisario.
SUSPENSE: MURDER: Chase Movies;
Fugitives from the Mob; Mob Stories;
Hitmen; Women in Jeopardy; Priests;
Romance with Clergy; Dangerous Women;
Double Crossings; Mindgames; Mexico;
Good Premise Unfulfilled; Writer-
Directors
(Monsignor; The Thorn Birds; Someone to
Watch Over Me)

The Last Run, 1971, 92m, ★★1/2/$,
MGM/NA. A mobster hiding out in exile
in Portugal is forced to take one last job,
which may be the last, period. George C.
Scott, Tony Musante, Trish Van Devere.
w. Alan Sharp, d. Richard Fleischer.
SUSPENSE: Crime Drama; Mob Stories;
One Last Time; Retirement

The Last Seduction, 1994, 110m,
★★★1/2, October Films/NA, R/P-V-ES-
FFN-MRN. A drug dealer brings home a
big sale to pay off the mob who's after
him. But he's been a bit too abusive to his
wife, so she runs off with the money. She
starts a new life, but soon the old one
catches up with her and puts her new
beau in danger in a battle of wills and
money. Linda Fiorentino, Peter Berg, J. T.
Walsh, Bill Nunn, Bill Pullman. w. Steve
Barancik, d. John Dahl.
SUSPENSE: Erotic Thriller; Abused
Women; Dangerous Women; Dangerous
Men; Drugs-Dealing; Finding Money
Films; Noir-Modern; Double Crossings;
Betrayals; Cult Films; Sleeper Hits; TV
Movies
(Red Rock West; Kill Me Again)
(Ed: Famous for award-winning perfor-
mance of Fiorentino which was denied
Oscar eligibility because, even though
the film played in theaters, it debuted on
cable TV)

L. A. Story, 1991, 95m, ★★★/$$$, WB/WB, PG-13/S-P. A weatherman in L.A., where the weather never changes, tries to find romance among the pretentious and banal of la-la land. Steve Martin, Victoria Tennant, Sarah Jessica Parker, Marilu Henner, Richard E. Grant, Kevin Pollak, Patrick Stewart. w. Martin, d. Mick Jackson.

COMEDY: SATIRE: ROMANCE: Romantic Comedy; Ensemble Films; Eccentric People; Los Angeles; Snobs; Beautiful People; Coulda Been Great; Good Premise Unfulfilled

(Annie Hall; California Suite; Parenthood)

(Ed: Martin does Woody Allen from a less inspired intelligent L.A. point of view)

The Last Starfighter, 1984, 101m, ★★★/$$$, Lorimar-U/MCA-U, PG. Aliens from outer space kidnap a video game whizkid and take him to their planet to help them fight a great battle with an old wise fellow. Robert Preston, Lance Guest, Dan O'Herlihy, Catherine Mary Stewart, Barbara Bosson. w. Johnathan Beutel, d. Nick Castle.

ACTION: SCI-FI: Outer Space Movies; Video Games; Men and Boys; Young Men; Teenagers; Teenage Movies; Sleeper Hits

Last Summer, 1969, 97m, ★★★★/$$$, Allied-Cin/RCA-Col, R/S-V. A manipulative teenager (Barbara Hershey) on vacation at the beach with two boys (Bruce Davison, Richard Thomas) takes her frustrations out on a wallflower (Catherine Burns, BSActress), leading to tragedy. w. Eleanor Perry, N-adap., d. Frank Perry. Oscars: 1-0.

DRAMA: TRAGEDY: Character Studies; Teenagers; Sexy Women; Evil Women; Rape/Rapists; Wallflowers; Beach Movies; Conformism; Vacations; Summer Vacations; Juvenile Delinquents

(David and Lisa)

The Last Sunset, 1961, 112m, ★★1/2/$$, U/MCA-U. An outlaw murderer plays cat and mouse with the bounty hunter who is after him. Rock Hudson, Kirk Douglas, Dorothy Malone, Carol Lynley, Joseph Cotten, Neville Brand, Regis Toomey. w. Dalton Trumbo, N-adap. Howard Rigsby (*Showdown at Crazy Horse*), d. Robert Aldrich.

WESTERNS: Chase Movies; Trail of a Killer; Bounty Hunters; MURDER: Mindgames; Forgotten Films; Coulda Been Good

Last Tango in Paris, 1973, 129m, ★★★/$$$, UA/Key, R/ES-P-FFN-MN. After his wife dies, a man finds a hot young woman to share bathtubs with, etc., for a wild fling of abandonment. Marlon Brando (BActor), Maria Schneider, Jean-Pierre Leaud. w. Bernardo Bertolucci, Franco Arcalli, d. Bertolucci (BDirector). Oscars: 2-0.

DRAMA: Erotic Drama; Sexuality; Midlife Crisis; ROMANCE: Romantic Drama; Romance-Older Men/Younger Women; Death-Dealing with; Depression; Alienation; Cult Films; French Films

(Bad Timing; The Nightcomers)

The Last Temptation of Christ, 1988, 163m, ★★★/$$, U/MCA-U, R/S-MN. While being nailed to the cross, Jesus has fantasies of the life he never had as a normal person. Willem Dafoe, Harvey Keitel, Barbara Hershey, Harry Dean Stanton, David Bowie. w. Paul Schrader, N-adap. Nikos Kazantzakis, d. Martin Scorsese (BDirector). Oscars: 1-0.

DRAMA: Biblical Stories; Jesus Christ; Character Studies; Fantasies; Executions; Middle East; Desert Settings; Art Films; Cult Films

(King of Kings; The Robe; Christ Stopped at Eboli)

The Last Tycoon, 1976, 124m, ★★★/$, Par/Par, R/S-P. After his wife dies, a young Hollywood studio head (supposedly modeled after Irving Thalberg) meets a beautiful girl on the lot who reminds him of his wife-while the studio troubles swirl about him. Robert De Niro, Robert Mitchum, Jack Nicholson, Tony Curtis, Jeanne Moreau, Donald Pleasence, Ray Milland, Dana Andrews, John Carradine, Ingrid Boutling. w. Harold Pinter, N-adap. F. Scott Fitzgerald, d. Elia Kazan. BArt. Oscars: 1-0.

DRAMA: MELODRAMA: ROMANCE: Widowers; Hollywood Life; Hollywood Biographies; Stern Men; Biographies-Fictional; Death-Dealing with; Lookalikes; Infatuations; 1930s; Classic Literary Adaptations; Flops-Major; Underrated

(F. Scott Fitzgerald in Hollywood; Power, Passion and Murder; The Betsy; The Bad and the Beautiful)

The Last Valley, 1970, 128m, ★★★/$, ABC-Cin/ABC, PG/V. A thirty-year war epic where an academic takes to battle to defend a Swiss village from rapists and pillagers. Michael Caine, Omar Sharif,

Nigel Davenport, Florinda Bolkan. w. d. James Clavell.

ADVENTURE: ACTION: War Stories; War Battles; Men in Conflict; Middle Ages; Medieval Times; Vikings; Forgotten Films; Hidden Gems

(Conan the Barbarian; Braveheart)

The Last Voyage, 1960, 91m, ★★1/2/$$, MGM/MGM-UA. A ship has an explosion and begins to sink-and it does. Robert Stack, Dorothy Malone, Edmond O'Brien, George Sanders. w. d. Andrew Stone.

DRAMA: Disaster Movies; Shipwrecked; Ships; Writer-Directors

(A Night to Remember; The Titanic; Juggernaut)

(Ed: Good effects and sets, okay otherwise)

The Last Waltz, 1978, 115m, ★★★/$$, UA/MGM-UA. Rockumentary on the last concert of The Band. d. Martin Scorsese.

Rockumentaries; Documentaries; Musicians; Concert Films; Rock Stars; Cult Films

The Last Wave, 1977, 106m, ★★★/$, UA/RHI. A man in Australia begins having dreams about Aborigines and their prophecies about apocalypse by flood, providing a mystery he has to solve to rest. Richard Chamberlain, Olivia Hamnet. w. Peter Weir, Tony Morphett, Petru Popescu, d. Peter Weir.

SUSPENSE: MYSTERY: Psychological Drama; Apocalyptic Stories; Legends; Nightmares; Psychics; Australian Films; Cult Films; Hidden Gems

(Close Encounters of the Third Kind; Picnic at Hanging Rock)

Last Year at Marienbad, 1962, 95m, ★★★1/2/$$, Nos, Voyager. A man meets a woman in an old hotel with beautiful surroundings, who may be the same woman he met the year before on vacation, but he can't really remember. But it all looks so good you may not care. Delphine Seyrig, Giorgio Albertazzi. w. Alain Robbe-Grillet, d. Alain Resnais.

DRAMA: Art Films; Avant-Garde Films; ROMANCE: Romantic Drama; Vacations; Hotels; Memories; French Films; French New Waves Films; Cult Films

(81/2; La Dolce Vita; L'avventura; Providence)

Las Vegas Hillbillies, 1966, 85m, ★★/$, AIP/New Line, R/S. Adventures of hillbillies and their Vegas club with bimbos aplenty. Mamie Van Doren, Jayne Mansfield, Ferlin Husky, Sonny James. d. Arthur Pierce.

COMEDY: Erotic Comedy; Sex Comedy; Bimbos; Camp; Cult Films
SEQUEL: Hillbillies in a Haunted House
Late for Dinner, 1991, 93m, ★★★/$$, Col/Col-Tri, PG-13/S. Two men frozen in time during an experiment years ago are thawed out and meet their children, now the same age as they've been preserved as. Peter Berg, Brian Wimmer, Marcia Gay Harden, Kyle Secor, Peter Gallagher. w. Mark Andrus, d. W. D. Richter.
DRAMA: COMEDY DRAMA: SCI-FI: MELODRAMA: Family Drama; Experiments; Generation Gap; Incest; Fathers & Daughters; Time Sleepers; Desert Settings; Southwestern Life; Overlooked at Release; Hidden Gems
(Rude Awakening; Forever Young)
The Late George Apley, 1946, 96m, ★★★/$$, 20th/NA. Rich people in Boston in the good old days go through their daily paces with a little romance, a little comedy, etc. Ronald Colman, Edna Best, Vanessa Brown, Richard Haydn. w. Philip Dunne, N-adap. John Marquand, d. Joseph L. Mankiewicz.
COMEDY DRAMA: Family Drama; **FAMILY:** Rich People; Stern Men; Boston; Forgotten Films
(The Bostonians)
The Late Show, 1977, 93m, ★★★1/2/$$, WB/WB, PG/V. A kooky woman approaches a washed-up PI to help her find her cat, but when he finally relents, he winds up in far more of a mystery than he bargained for, especially at his age, Art Carney, Lily Tomlin, Joanna Cassidy, Billy Macy, Ruth Nelson, Howard Duff, Eugene Roche. w. d. Robert Benton (BOScr). Oscars: 1-0.
COMEDY DRAMA: MYSTERY: Comic Mystery; **MURDER: MURDER MYSTERY:** Black Comedy; Detective Stories; Spoofs-Detective; Detectives in Deep; Detectives-Private; Retirements; Comebacks; Elderly Men; Eccentric People; Animals in Jeopardy; Pet Stories; Cats; Hidden Gems
(The Black Marble; Ace Ventura, Pet Detective; Harry and Tonto)
(Ed: A darkly comic tale that is at once goofy and scary)
La Traviata, 1982, 109m, ★★★/$$$, Col/Col, PG. A successful screen adaptation of the famous Verdi opera, full of the tragedy of unrequited love and deathbed retributions. Placido Domingo, Teresa Stratas, Cornell MacNeil, Allan Monk,

Axell Gall. w. Francesco Maria Piave, Franco Zeffirelli, (Opera)-adap. Giuseppe Verdi, d. Franco Zeffirelli. BArt, BCostume. Oscars: 2-0.
MELODRAMA: TRAGEDY: MUSICALS: Opera; **ROMANCE:** Romance-Doomed; Dying Wishes; Classic Tragedy
(Carmen; Yes, Giorgio)
The Laughing Policeman, 1973, 112m, ★★★/$$, 20th/CBS-Fox, R/EV-P. A policeman investigating a murder of a bus driver (Walter Matthau), becomes alienated with the futility of finding the culprit, haunted by so many deaths. Bruce Dern, Lou Gossett Jr., w. Tom Rickman, N-adap. Maj Sjowall, Per Wahloo, d. David Walsh.
DRAMA: Crime Drama; Detective Stories; Police Stories; Detectives-Police; Detectives in Deep; Chase Movies; Murderers-Mass; Trail of a Killer; San Francisco Chases; San Francisco; Buses
(The Taking of Pelham 123)
Laughing Sinners, 1931, 71m, ★★1/2/$$, MGM/MGM-UA. A naughty girl of the streets decides to repent by joining the Salvation Army, but will it work? Joan Crawford, Clark Gable, Neil Hamilton, Marjorie Rambeau. w. Bess Meredyth, Martin Flavin, d. Harry Beaumont.
MELODRAMA: ROMANCE: Past-Haunted by the; Secrets-Keeping; Redemption; Female Screenwriters
(Bad Girl; The Last of Mrs. Cheyney)
Laughter, 1930, 99m, ★★★1/2/$$$, Par/NA. A former follies girl on the make marries a rich man, but still has a thing for a musician, which soon interferes with her meal ticket. Frederic March, Nancy Carroll, Frank Morgan, Glenn Anders. w. Donald Ogden Stewart (BOStory), d. Harry D'Abbabie D'Arrast. Oscars: 1-0.
COMEDY: ROMANCE: Romantic Comedy; Romance-Triangles; Romance-Reunited; Marrying Up; Dancers; Musicians; Marriage on the Rocks; Hidden Gems; Forgotten Films
(The Philadelphia Story; Holiday; Palm Beach Story)
Laughter in the Dark, 1969, 104m, ★★1/2/$, UA/NA. In the hip and trendy set, an art dealer is blinded in an accident and soon finds that the couple who have taken him in are despicable enough to kill. Nicol Williamson, Anna Karina, Jean-Claude Drouot, Peter Bowles. w. Edward Bond, N-adap. Vladimir Nabokov, d. Tony Richardson.

DRAMA: SUSPENSE: Black Comedy; Art Films; Mod Era; Beautiful People; Saving Someone; Accidents; Blind People; Riviera Life; Rich People; Coulda Been Good
(I Thank a Fool; The Hand That Rocks the Cradle)
Laura, 1944, 87m, ★★★★/$$$$, 20th/Fox. When a beautiful woman (Gene Tierney) loved by several men (Vincent Price, Clifton Webb) is murdered, the police detective (Dana Andrews) who's smitten with her legend must find the killer-until a surprise twist changes his focus. Clifton Webb (BSActor), w. Jay Dratler, Samuel Hoffenstein, Betty Reinhardt (BScr), N-adap. Vera Caspary, d. Otto Preminger (BDirector). BB&WArt, BB&WCin. Oscars: 5-1.
MYSTERY: MURDER: MURDER MYSTERY: MELODRAMA: Mystery-Whodunits; Film Noir; Detective Stories; Flashbacks; Infatuations; Romance-Triangles; Elusive Women; Cult Films; Female Screenwriters
(The Picture of Dorian Gray; Whirlpool; Leave Her to Heaven)
(Ed: A cult classic, but don't let anyone explain the ending before you see it)
Laurel Avenue, 1993, 156m, ★★★/$$, HBO/HBO, R/P. A working-class black family's life in Minnesota over the years, following the children's lives as they branch out into society. Mary Alice, Mel Winkler, Scott Lawrence, Malinda Williams. w. Michael Henry Brown, d. Carl Franklin.
DRAMA: Family Drama; Episodic Stories; Black Casts; Black Men; Black Women; Multiple Stories; Interwoven Stories; Working Class; Hidden Gems; Miniseries; TV Movies
(Boyz N the Hood; Juice; Claudine)
The Lavender Hill Mob, 1952, 78m, ★★★★/$$$, Ealing/Home Vision, EMI. A nerdy bank clerk (Alec Guiness, BActor) is actually the ironic mastermind of a gold heist. Stanley Holloway, Sidney James, Alfie Bass. w. T. E. B. Clarke (BOScr), d. Charles Crichton. Oscars: 2-1.
COMEDY: ACTION: Action Comedy; **COMEDY DRAMA:** Heist Stories; Capers; Chase Movies; **FARCE:** Comedy of Errors; Thieves; Bank Robberies; Nerds; Perfect Crimes; Crime Pays; Clever Plots & Endings; Cult Films; Hidden Gems
(A Fish Called Wanda; The Ladykillers;

The Wrong Arm of the Law; Quick
Change)
La Vie Continue, 1982, 93m, ★★★/$$,
Ind/Col, PG. A middle-aged widow finds
herself on her own with children to sup-
port. Annie Girardot, Jean-Pierre Cassel,
Michel Aumont. d. Moshe Mizrahi.
DRAMA: COMEDY DRAMA: ROMANCE:
Family Drama; Character Studies;
Widows; Mothers-Struggling; Mothers
Alone; Mothers & Sons; Brothers; Coming
of Age; Romance Older Women/Younger
Men; Love-First; Ethics; Lotteries;
Depression; Starting Over; French Films
REMAKE: Men Don't Leave (actually
better)
La Vie de Bohème, 1993, 100m,
★★★/$, Ind/New Yorker. The story of the
lives of several artists who are living on
the edge, with little money or inspiration,
but finding romance, however, fleeting.
Matti Pellonpaa, Andre Wilms, Jean
Pierre Leaud, Samuel Fuller, Louis
Malle. w. d. Aki Karismaki,
N-adap. Henri Mullet.
DRAMA: Character Studies; Slice of Life
Stories; Multiple Stories; Interwoven
Stories; ROMANCE: Romance-Doomed;
Artists; Paris; Poor People; Making a
Living; French Films; Hidden Gems;
Overlooked at Release
L'Avventura (B&W), 1960, 145m,
★★★1/2/$$$, WR/Cinematheque. A
woman disappears on an Italian island
while vacationing with friends. Her
absence makes the others question their
own existence. Claudia Cardinale.
w. d. Michelangelo Antonioni. BFFilm.
Oscars: 1-0.
DRAMA: Psychological Drama; Missing
Persons; Missing Person Thriller; Neo-
Realism; Avant-Garde Films; Italian
Films; Islands Mediterranean Vacations
(Blow-Up; Zabriskie Point; The Vanishing)
(Ed: Quite long and laborious, although to
great effect in pursuing a missing woman)
Law and Disorder, 1958, 76m, ★★★/$,
BL/NA. Thieves help out one of their own
to prevent his secret life from being
known by his son. Michael Redgrave,
Robert Morley, Joan Hickson, Lionel
Jeffries. w. T. E. B. Clarke, N-adap.
Smuggler's Choice, d. Charles Crichton.
COMEDY: Police Stories; Police Comedy;
Crime Drama; Capers; Heist Stories;
Thieves; Ensemble Films; Ensembles-
Male; Hidden Gems; Forgotten Films
(Fuzz, Super Cops; Freebie and the Bean;

The Wrong Arm of the Law; Big Deal on
Madonna Street)
Law and Disorder, 1974, 102m,
★★1/2/$, Col/Col, R/P-V. Elderly New
Yorkers band together against thugs in
the neighborhood. Ernest Borgnine,
Carroll O'Connor, Karen Black, Anne
Wedgeworth. w. Ivan Passer, William
Richert, Kenneth Fishman, d. Ivan
Passer.
COMEDY DRAMA: SATIRE: Crime
Drama; Police Stories; Police Comedy;
Vigilantes; Police-Vigilantes; New York
Life; Suburban Life; Ordinary Person vs.
Criminals
(Death Wish; Outrage; Fighting Back)
The Law and Jake Wade, 1958, 86m,
★★1/2/$$, MGM/MGM-UA. Problems
arise when a marshal helps out an old
pal who can't change his criminal ways.
Richard Widmark, Robert Taylor, Patricia
Owens. w. William Bowers, d. John
Sturges.
WESTERNS: Friendships-Male; Friends
as Enemies; Police Stories; Marshals;
Double Crossings; Forgotten Films
The Law and the Lady, 1951, 104m,
★★1/2/$$, MGM/NA. A female con artist
changes her ways a bit when she falls in
love while trying to bilk a rich woman out
of her dough. Greer Garson, Michael
Wilding, Fernando Lamas, Marjorie
Main, Hayden Rourke. w. Leonard
Spigelgass, Karl Tunberg, d. Edwin
Knopf.
ROMANCE: MELODRAMA: Con Artists;
Criminals-Female; Life Transitions;
Forgotten Films
REMAKE OF: 1929 and 1937 versions of
The Last of Mrs. Cheyney
Law of Desire, 1987, 107m, ★★★/$$,
Ind/Cinevista, R/S-MN. A gay film direc-
tor has mixed feelings about a romantic
attraction while trying to juggle chaos at
home with his brother who, via a sex-
change, has become a woman with an
adopted daughter. Eusebia Poncella,
Antonio Banderas, Carmen Maura, Bibi
Anderssen. w. d. Pedro Almodovar.
COMEDY: COMEDY DRAMA: Black
Comedy; Camp; Avant-Garde; Art Films;
Gay Men; Directors; Actors;
Transsexuals; Children-Adopted;
Families-Extended; Alternative
Lifestyles; Spanish Films; Spain; Writer-
Directors
(A Man Like Eva; Women on the Verge of
a Nervous Breakdown)

Lawman, 1970, 99m, ★★1/2/$,
UA/MGM-UA. Outlaws kill an old man
and the town marshal tracks them down
but has trouble bringing them to justice
with the townsfolk. Burt Lancaster,
Robert Ryan, Lee J. Cobb, Sheree North,
Robert Duvall, Joseph Wiseman, J. D.
Cannon. w. Gerald Wilson, d. Michael
Winner.
WESTERNS: Police Stories; MURDER:
Marshals; Trail of a Killer; Small-town
Life; Vigilantes; Ethics
The Lawnmower Man, 1992, 108m/
150m, ★★★/$$$, R/EV-S. A simple-
minded young man (Jeff Fahey) living in
a shack becomes the subject of a well-
intentioned scientist (Pierce Brosnan) and
his experiments into mind-altering drugs
and virtual reality. w. Brett Leonard,
Gimel Everett, SS-adap. Stephen King,
d. Brett Leonard.
SCI-FI: HORROR: Mentally Disabled
People; Simple Minds; Monsters-
Manmade; Human Monsters; Scientists;
Experiments; Allegorical Stories; Virtual
Reality; Cult Films
SEQUEL: The Lawnmower Man 2 (1994).
Lawrence of Arabia, 1962, 221m,
★★★★/$$$$, Col/RCA-Col. A British
adventurer seeks out an exciting life in
the deserts of the Middle East and
becomes an unlikely legendary figure
along the way. Peter O'Toole (BActor),
Omar Sharif (BSActor), Arthur Kennedy,
Claude Rains, Alec Guiness, Anthony
Quinn, Jose Ferrer, Jack Hawkins.
w. Robert Bolt (BAScr), d. David Lean
(**BDir**). **BPicture, BCCin, BOScore,
BSound, BCArt, BEdit.** Oscars: 10-7.
DRAMA: ADVENTURE: Epics; Historical
Drama; Biographies; Character Studies;
Free Spirits; Young Men; Arab People;
Charismatic People; World War I Era;
Middle East; Desert Settings; British
Films; Blockbusters
(A Passage to India; Murphy's War; The
Bridge on the River Kwai)
The Lawrenceville Stories, 1987,
180m, ★★★/$, AP-PBS/Disney. Slice of
life of the elite boys at the famous prep
school in New Jersey as they play around
and grow up, fulfilling the high expecta-
tions their parents have of them. Zach
Galligan, Edward Herrman, Nicolas
Rowe, Stephen Baldwin. w. SS-adap.
Owen Johnson, d. Robert Robert Iscove.
COMEDY DRAMA: Multiple Stories;
Interwoven Stories; Autobiographical

Stories; Rich People; Practical Jokers; Boarding Schools; Boys Schools; Coming of Age; Coulda Been Great
(Dead Poets Society; A Separate Peace)

LBJ: The Early Years, 1988, 144m, ★★★/$$$, CBS-Ind/Fries. Johnson's early years leading up to the White House in an excellent TV movie. Randy Quaid, Patti Lupone, Morgan Brittany, Kevin McCarthy, Barry Corbin. d. Peter Warner.

DRAMA: Biographies; Famous People When Young; Presidents; Texas; Power-Rise to; Politicians; Marriage Drama; TV Movies; Miniseries

Leadbelly, 1976, 126m, ★★1/2/$, Ind/NA. Biography of blues musician Huddie Ledbetter, known as "Leadbelly," following his rise out of the slums and prison. Roger E. Moseley, Paul Benjamin, Madge Sinclair. w. Ernest Knox, d. Gordon Parks.

DRAMA: Biographies; Music Movies; Black Men; Black Casts; Fame-Rise to; Forgotten Films; Black Directors; Black Screenwriters
(Bird; Crossroads)

The League of Gentlemen, 1960, 112m, ★★★/$, Rank/HomeVision. A military man decides to blackmail men he has information on into helping him with a heist. Jack Hawkins, Richard Attenborough, Roger Livesay, Nigel Patrick, Bryan Forbes, Kireon Moore, Nanette Newman. w. Bryan Forbes, N-adap. John Boland, d. Basil Dearden.

COMEDY DRAMA: Heist Stories; Capers; Bank Robberies; Blackmail; Secrets-Keeping; Soldiers; Hidden Gems
(The Hot Rock; The Thomas Crown Affair)

A League of Their Own, 1992, 128m, ★★1/2/$$$$, Col/Col-Tri, PG-13/P. From farm girls to streetwise types, an all-female baseball team is formed during World War II under a male leader (Tom Hanks). Geena Davis, Madonna, Rosie O'Donnell, Jon Lovitz, David Strathairn, Bill Pullman, Lori Petty. w. Lowell Ganz, Babaloo Mandel, Kim Wilson, Kelly Candaele, d. Penny Marshall.

COMEDY: COMEDY DRAMA: MELODRAMA: Women in Conflict; Male Among Females; Female in Male Domain; Ensemble Films; Ensembles-Female; Sports Movies; Baseball; World War II Era; 1940s; Flashbacks; Chicago; Women's Films Reunions; Female

Protagonists; Female Screenwriters; Female Directors
(Ed: More sentimental than slapstick)

Lean on Me, 1989, 108m, ★★1/2/$$$, WB/WB, PG-13/P. The story of a black principle (Morgan Freeman) and his crusade to straighten up his New Jersey high school. Beverly Todd, Robert Gillaume. w. Michael Schiffer, Douglas Seelig, d. John G. Avildsen.

DRAMA: MELODRAMA: Message Films; Social Drama; High School Life; Teachers; Black Casts; Black Men; Inner City Life; Stern Men; Reformers; Feelgood Movies; Sleeper Hits
(The Blackboard Jungle; To Sir With Love)

Leap of Faith, 1992, 110m, ★★1/2/$$, Par/Par, PG-13/S-P. A traveling preacher/con artist travels the midwest until getting stranded, guilt, and a few coincidental miracles make him reconsider what he's doing. Steve Martin, Debra Winger, Lolita Davidovich, Liam Neeson, Lukas Haas, Meatloaf. w. Janus Cercone, d. Richard Pearce.

COMEDY DRAMA: Religion; Preachers; Con Artists; Miracles; Redemption; Life Transitions; Guilty Conscience; Midwestern Life; Stranded; Coulda Been Good; Capra-esque
(Pass the Ammo; Americathon)
(Ed: Out of touch with the modern reality of such hucksters, who are far more folksy and clever, even though the computer tricks here are probably hipper than they should be. Typical Hollywood notions of what middle America is like but isn't)

The Learning Tree, 1969, 107m, ★★★/$$, NG/WB, PG. Director Gordon Parks' autobiographical tale of growing up in the south in the 20s and Depression days. Kyle Johnson, Alex Clarke, Estelle Evans, Dana Elcar. w. d. Gordon Parks.

DRAMA: Coming of Age; Autobiographical Stories; Southerners; Ahead of its Time; Forgotten Films; Black Men; Black Casts; Black Directors; Black Screenwriters; Writer-Directors; 1920s; Depression Era
(Sounder; Barn Burning; Roots; I Know Why the Caged Bird Sings)

The Leather Boys, 1963, 108m, ★★★/$$, BL/HBO, A&E. Two British teens get married in the throes of lust, but soon that subsides and the girl becomes depressed and the guy hooks up

with a bisexual motorcycle gang. Rita Tushingham, Dudley Sutton, Colin Campbell. w. Gillian Freeman, N-adap. Eliot George, d. Sidney J. Furie.

DRAMA: Kitchen Sink Drama; Working Class; Marriage Drama; Marriage on the Rocks; Teenagers; Motorcycles; Alternative Lifestyles; Gay Men; Gay Awakenings; Bisexuality; British Films
(A Taste of Honey; A Kind of Loving)

The Leather Saint, 1955, 86m, ★★1/2/$, Par/NA. In order to raise money for his parish, a priest becomes a boxer. Paul Douglas, John Derek, Cesar Romero, Ernest Truex. w. Norman Retchin, Alvin Ganzer, d. Alvin Ganzer.

MELODRAMA: Sports Movies; Priests; Boxing; Curiosities; Saintly People; Forgotten Films
(Let's Do It Again)

Leave Her to Heaven, 1945, 111m, ★★★/$$$$, 20th/Fox, AMC. A beautiful woman (Gene Tierney, BActress) causes great strife by her manipulations of those around the man she loves (Cornel Wilde), even to the point of murder. Jeanne Crain, Vincent Price. w. Jo Swerling, N-adap. Ben Williams, d. John Stahl. BCCin, BCArt. Oscars: 3-1.

DRAMA: TRAGEDY: SUSPENSE: MURDER: Courtroom Drama; Murderers-Female; Murders-Clever; Drownings; Suicidal Tendencies; Obsessions; Fatal Attractions; Evil Women; Psycho Killers; Ahead of its Time
(Mother Love; Mother's Boys)
(Ed: Ahead of its time in many ways with regard to subject matter and its treatment. Beautiful to look at, though not exactly as exciting or manipulative as today's similar tales)

Leaving Las Vegas, 1995, 112m, ★★★1/2/$$$, MGM-UA/MGM-UA, R/P-S. A former Hollywood agent has drunk himself into a hole in Vegas and may only be redeemed by the love of a good woman, who happens to be a prostitute. Nicolas Cage **(BActor)**, Elisabeth Shue (BActress), Julian Sands, Richard Lewis, Steven Weber, Kim Adams, Emily Procter, Stuart Regen, Valeria Golino, Mike Figgis, Danny Huston, Laurie Metcalf, Julian Lennon, Bob Rafelson, Marc Coppola, Lou Rawls. w. d. Mike Figgis (BDirector, BAScr), N-adap. John O'Brien. Oscars: 4-1.

DRAMA: ROMANCE: Romantic Drama; Alcoholism; Romance with Prostitute;

Prostitute with a Heart of Gold; Pimps; Romance-Doomed; Depression; Las Vegas; Sleeper Hits; Independent Films; Quiet Little Films; Addicted but Nominated (The Lost Weekend; Clean and Sober; Midnight Cowboy)

(Ed: Sadly, the writer of the novel this is based upon, who drew much of the story from his own life, took that life before the film was released)

Leaving Normal, 1992, 110m, ★★1/2/$, U/MCA-U, R/S-P. Two women take a road trip to a house one's ex-boyfriend left her to try and find themselves. Christine Lahti, Meg Tilly, Lenny Von Dohlen. w. Ed Solomon, d. Edward Zwick.

COMEDY DRAMA: MELODRAMA: Road Movies; Buddy Films; Friendships-Female; Midlife Crisis; Starting Over; Life Transitions; Female Protagonists (Boys on the Side; Thelma & Louise)

(Ed: Unfairly compared to *Thelma & Louise,* released on its heels, this could have been insightful but instead is self-indulgent and cliched)

Le Bal, 1982, 112m, ★★/$$, WB/WB. Snippets of the lives of the people who pass through a Parisian ballroom over fifty years. Jean Claude Penchenat, Chantal Chapron. w. Penechat, Ruggero Maccari, Furio Scapelli, Ettore Scola, d. Scola.

DRAMA: Episodic Stories; Slice of Life Stories; Dancers; Ensemble Films; Paris; French Films; Quiet Little Films

Le Cavaleur, 1978, 90m, ★★1/2/$$, Col/Col, R/S-FFN-MFN. A concert pianist begins fooling around and finds himself in some interesting French positions and lifestyles. Jean Rochefort, Lila Kedrova, Annie Girardot, Danielle Darrieux. d. Phillipe de Broca.

COMEDY: ROMANCE: Romantic Comedy; Playboys; Pianists; Cheating Men; Alternative Lifestyles; Midlife Crisis; Erotic Comedy; French Films

Le Corbeau, 1943, 92m, ★★★/$$, Ind/Nos. A blackmailer in a small French town sends threatening letters to various residents, creating a general atmosphere of fear until he's found out. Pierre Fresnay, Pierre Larquey, Ginette Leclerc, Helene Manson. w. Louis Chavance, d. Henri-Georges Clouzot.

SUSPENSE: Psychological Drama; Blackmail; Stalkers; Small-town Life; Small-town Scandals; French Films; Hidden Gems

(Blackmail)

The Left Hand of God, 1955, 87m, ★★★/$$, 20th/CBS-Fox. In postwar China, an American pilot on the run pretends to be a priest as a cover, then has to perform a miracle for the locals. Humphrey Bogart, Gene Tierney, Lee J. Cobb, E.G. Marshall, Agnes Moorehead. w. Alfred Hayes, N-adap. William Barrett, d. Edward Dmytryk.

MELODRAMA: War Stories; World War II Stories; Priests; Disguises; Disguised as Priest

(Waiting for the Light)

The Left-Handed Gun, 1958, 102m, ★★1/2/$$, WB/WB. Tale of Billy the Kid avenging the death of a friend. Paul Newman, John Dehner, Lita Milan, Hurd Hatfield. w. Leslie Stevens, TV-adap. Gore Vidal, d. Arthur Penn.

WESTERNS: Westerns-Neo; Billy the Kid; Avenging Death of Someone; Westerns-Revenge; Revenge; Young Men-Angry (Billy the Kid; Pat Garrett and Billy the Kid)

The Legacy, 1978, 102m, U/MCA-U, ★★/$$$, R/S. A woman visits her boss' mansion and becomes part of a plot of occultists involving a mysterious invalid who wants to put a ring on her finger. Katharine Ross, Sam Elliott, Roger Daltrey. w. Jim Sangster, Patrick Tiller, Paul Wheeler, d. Richard Marquand.

HORROR: SUSPENSE: MURDER: Inheritances at Stake; Occult; Houses-Creepy; Innocent Bystanders

Legal Eagles, 1986, 116m, ★★★/$$$, Par/Par, PG/S. A public defender up for D.A. (Robert Redford) has a client (Daryl Hannah) accused of murdering a man who stole a painting of her father's, but when he becomes romantically involved with this client, he also becomes entangled in a major art thievery scam and teams up with the kooky prosecuting attorney (Debra Winger) to solve it. w. Jim Cash, Jack Epps, d. Ivan Reitman.

MYSTERY: MURDER MYSTERY: Comic Mystery; Capers; Romantic Comedy; Conspiracy; Romance-Opposites Attract; Romance-Older Men/Younger Women; Accused Unjustly; Framed?; Lawyers; Art Thieves; Artists; Con Artists; Teams-Mismatched; Accident Prone; New York Life

(Adam's Rib; Hot Paint; Sneakers)

Legend, 1986, 94m, ★★1/2/$$, U/MCA-U, PG-13/V. A young man (Tom Cruise) takes his fair maiden on a journey to see

the last of the mythical unicorns in a fairy tale world that soon turns to great danger. Mia Sara, Tim Curry. w. William Hjortsberg, d. Ridley Scott. BMake-up. Oscars: 1-0.

FANTASY: SCI-FI: ADVENTURE: Sword & Sorcery; Fairy Tales; Journies; Satan; Mythology; Medieval Times; Flops-Major; Coulda Been Great (Krull; Ladyhawke; Labyrinth)

(Ed: Cruise's career might have been out of control had *Top Gun* not fallen on the heels of this well-meaning but bland opus)

The Legend of Billie Jean, 1985, 96m, ★★/$$, Tri/Col-Tri, PG. A young woman (Helen Slater) becomes an unwitting vigilante folk-hero while trying to save her brother. Keith Gordon, Christian Slater, Peter Coyote. w. Mark Rosenthal, Lawrence Konner, d. Matthew Robbins.

DRAMA: MELODRAMA: Chase Movies; Saving Someone; Protecting Someone; Brothers & Sisters; Vigilantes; Anti-Establishment Films; Heroes-Unlikely; Texas; Overlooked at Release; Female Protagonists

(The Sugarland Express; Billy Jack)

The Legend of Hell House, 1973, 94m, ★★★/$$, 20th/Fox. Psychic investigators come to a haunted house where others have been killed before-and will be again. Pamela Franklin, Roddy McDowell, Gayle Hunnicutt, Clive Revill. w. N-adap. Richard Matheson, d. John Hough.

HORROR: MURDER: Deaths-One by One; Haunted House; Psychics; Ghosts; Supernatural Dangers; Possessions; Hidden Gems

(Poltergeist; The Haunting)

The Legend of Lylah Clare, 1968, 130m, ★★★/$$, MGM/NA. A Hollywood director (Peter Finch) in the glory days brings an unknown would-be actress (Kim Novak) to town because of her resemblance to a star who died and who he's become obsessed with. Ernest Borgnine, Coral Browne, George Kennedy. w. Hugo Butler, Jean Rouverold, TV-adap. Robert Thom, Ed DeBlasio, d. Robert Aldrich.

DRAMA: MELODRAMA: MYSTERY: Hollywood Life; Directors; Actresses; Lookalikes; Obsessions; Cult Films; Camp; Hidden Gems; Underrated (Vertigo; Svengali; Sunset Boulevard; The Last Tycoon; The Goddess; Harlow)

Legend of the Holy Drinker, 1988, 129m, ★★★/$, Ind/NA. The story of a priest and the town drunk, giving charity and then trying to repay it. Rutger Hauer, Anthony Quayle, Sandrine Dumas. w. Tullio Kezich, Ermanno Olmi, N-adap. Joseph Roth, d. Ermanno Olmi.
MELODRAMA: Priests; Alcoholics; Fairy Tales; Ethics; Curiosities; Overlooked at Release

The Legend of the Lone Ranger, 1981, 98m, ★★1/2/$$, ITC-U/MCA-U, PG/V. Updating with more action of the masked avenger and his sidekick Tonto, the early days after being ambushed and recovering in an Indian village. Klinton Spilsbury, Michael Horse, Christopher Lloyd, Matt Clark. w. Ivan Goff, Ben Roberts, Michael Kane, William Roberts, d. William A. Fraker.
WESTERNS: ACTION: Comic Heroes; Indians-American; Revenge; Westerns-Revenge; Buddy Films
(The Lone Ranger SERIES)
(Ed: A failed revival attempt)

Legend of the Lost, 1957, 107m, ★★1/2/$$, UA/CBS-Fox. Two men search through the desert for a lost city with the aid of a native girl. John Wayne, Sophia Loren, Rosanno Brazzi. w. Robert Presnell, Ben Hecht. d. Henry Hathaway.
ADVENTURE: Quests; Journies; Desert Settings; Legends; Treasure Hunts; Africa; Forgotten Films
(King Solomon's Mine; Mountains of the Moon; The Black Robe)

Legends of the Fall, 1994, 145m, ★★★/$$$$, WB/WB, R/S-P-V. The story of an adventurous loner and his brother, and the brother's wife, over a span of years during World War I and after, always coming back to the West. Brad Pitt, Aidan Quinn, Anthony Hopkins, Julia Ormond. d. Edward Zwick. **BCin, BArt, BSound. Oscars: 3-1.**
DRAMA: ROMANCE: Romantic Drama; **ADVENTURE:** World War I Stories; **WESTERNS:** Westerns-Modern; Brothers; Men Fighting Over Women; Romance with Relative's Lover; Sleeper Hits; Old-Fashioned Recent Films; Scenery-Outstanding
(A River Runs Through It; Dances with Wolves)

Le Mans, 1971, 108m, ★★1/2/$$$, 20th/Fox, R/V-S. A car racer from America runs the famous race in France. Steve McQueen. w. Harry Kleiner, d. Lee Katzin.

ACTION: Car Racing; Sports Movies; Americans Abroad
(Grand Prix; Days of Thunder)
(Ed: Not much happens, much like *Days of Thunder*)

Le Million, 1931, 89m, ★★★1/2/$$$, Tobis/NA. A con artist and a regular artist frantically search for a lost lottery ticket, all to music. Annabella, Rene Lefevre, Paul Olivier. w. d. Rene Clair, MP-adap. Georges Berr, M. Guillemand.
COMEDY: MUSICALS: Musical Comedy; Searches; Race Against Time; Lotteries; Con Artists; Artists; Buddy Films; Forgotten Films; Hidden Gems; French Films; Paris
(It Could Happen to You)

The Lemon Drop Kid, 1951, 91m, ★★★/$$$, Par/Par. A mobster puts the heat on a bookie to come up with the money he lost on a bet at the track, but he may have to do some strange things to accomplish that. Bob Hope, Marilyn Maxwell, Lloyd Nolan, Jane Darwell, William Frawley. w. Edmund Hartmann, Frank Tashlin, Robert O'Brien, SS-adap. Damon Runyon, d. Sidney Lanfield.
COMEDY: Comedy of Errors; Mob Stories; Mob Comedy; Fugitives from the Mob; Horse Racing; Santa Claus; Christmas
(Little Miss Marker; Sorrowful Jones; Let It Ride)

Leningrad Cowboys Go to America, 1989, 78m, ★★★/$, Orion/Orion, R/S-P. A terrible rock band from Scandinavia travels America trying to break in. Matti Pellonpaa. w. d. Aki Kaurismaki.
SATIRE: Rockumentaries; Documentary Style; Rock Bands; Scandinavia; American Myth; Dreams; Foreign Misfits; Independent Films; Writer-Directors
(This Is Spinal Tap; Stroszek)

Lenny (B&W), 1974, 111m, ★★★★/$$$, UA/MGM-UA, R/EP-S-FN. The life story of controversial and somewhat decadent comedian Lenny Bruce (Dustin Hoffman, BActor), centering on his relationship with a stripper (Valerie Perrine, BActress) which couldn't save him from his own tenacity. w. P-adap. Julian Barry (BAScr), d. Bob Fosse (BDirector). BPicture, BCin. Oscars: 6-0.
DRAMA: Biographies; Comedians; Hollywood Life; Hollywood Biographies; Rise and Fall Stories; Drugs-Addictions; Strippers; Depression; Suicidal Tendencies; Lesbians; Young Men-Angry; Cult Films; Faded Hits

(Ed: Don't let the black and white keep you away)

Leonard, Part 6, 1987, 83m, ★/$, Col/Col, PG. Cosby in a spy spoof with lots of gadgets and no humor-at least that works, anyway. Bill Cosby, Gloria Foster, Tom Courtenay. w. Bill Cosby, Johnathan Reynolds, d. Paul Welland.
COMEDY: Spoofs-Spy; Spies; Secret Agents; Cartoonlike Films; Flops-Major; Rule the World-Plot to
(Ghost Dad)

Leon, the Pig Farmer, 1992, 104m, ★★1/2/$, Orion/Orion, PG-13/P. A stuffy, British Jewish man accidentally finds out his father is living in the country as a pig farmer. w. Gary Sinyor, Michael Norman, d. Vadim Jean, Gary Sinyor.
COMEDY: Fish out of Water Stories; Farmers; Farm Life; City vs. Country; Children-Long Lost; Jewish People; British Films

The Leopard, 1963, 205m, ★★★/$$. An Italian nobleman in ancient times deals with the political troubles of his family. Burt Lancaster, Claudia Cardinale, Alain Delon. w. d. Luchino Visconti, N-adap. Guiseppe de Lampedusa.
DRAMA: Epics; Rich People; Royalty; Family Dramas; Sagas; Ancient Times; Italian Films; Italy; Forgotten Films
(The Agony & The Ecstasy; The Damned; Death in Venice)
(Ed: A very beautiful film that has little conventional story to pull it through)

Leprechaun, 1993, 92m, ★★/$$, Vidmark/Vidmark, R/EV. A creepy little green man terrorizes farm people after a man goes to Ireland and steals a pot of gold, causing the little fellow to get his Ire up. Warwick Davis, Jennifer Aniston. w. d. Mark Jones.
HORROR: Little People; Magic; Revenge; Murder-One by One; Ireland; Treasure Hunts; Writer-Directors; Independent Films
(Luck of the Irish)

Les Bas-Fonds (*The Lower Depths*), 1936, 92m, ★★★/$$, Ind/NA. The conflicts of homeless men in France mirror the societal problems which got them where they are. Jean Gabin, Louis Jouvet. w. Jean Renoir, Charles Spaak, P-adap. Maxim Gorky, d. Jean Renoir.
DRAMA: Homeless People; Social Drama; Allegorical Stories; French Films
(Central Park; Sullivan's Travels)

Les Biches, 1968, 95m, ★★★½/$$$, Ind/Connoisseur, R/S. When a rich young woman seduces a female artist and takes her to the Riviera, the eroticism and romance between them comes to a halt when a man from the rich woman's past shows up. Stephane Audran, Jean Louis Trintignant, Jacqueline Sassard. w. d. Claude Chabrol.
DRAMA: ROMANCE: Erotic Drama; Romance-Triangles; Bisexuality; Lesbians; Alternative Lifestyles; Rich People; Rich People-Decadent; Riviera Life; French Films; Hidden Gems; Faded Hits; Cult Films; 1960s; Writer-Directors
(The Young Girls of Rochefort; Entre Nous)
Les Comperes, 1983, 92m, ★★★½/$$$, Ind/Media, PG. A woman convinces two former boyfriends to find her runaway son on the Riviera-two men who are completely at odds, one a savvy journalist and the other a suicidal klutz. Gerard Depardieu, Pierre Richard, Michael Aumont. w. d. Francis Veber.
COMEDY: Detective Stories; Detectives-Amateur; Journalists as Detectives; Romance-Triangles; Runaways; Missing Persons; Buddy Cops; Buddy Films; Extroverted vs. Introverted; Suicidal Tendencies; Macho Men vs. Nerd; Hidden Gems; French Films; Writer-Directors
(La Chevre; Les Trois Fugitifs; A Pain in the A—; Out on a Limb; Pure Luck; Buddy Buddy)
Les Enfants Terribles (The Strange Ones), 1950, 100m, ★★★/$$, Ind/Facets, Ingram. An incestuous relationship develops between a brother and sister. Nicole Stephane, Edouard Dermithe. w. d. Jean-Pierre Melville, N-adap. Jean Cocteau.
DRAMA: TRAGEDY: ROMANCE: Romance-Doomed; Incest; Brothers & Sisters; French Films; Avant-Garde; Hidden Gems; Art Films
(Beauty and the Beast (1946); Testament of Orpheus, Spanking the Monkey; Murmur of the Heart; Beau Pere; Alpine Fire)
Les Liaisons Dangereuses, 1959, 106m, ★★★/$$, Ind/NA, S. An updating of the French classic, in French, of the famous backstabbing tale, remade more faithfully in 1988 as Dangerous Liaisons. Gerard Philipe, Jeanne Moreau, Jean-Louis Trintignant. w. Roger Vailland, Roger Vadim, Claude Brule, N-adap. Choderlos de Laclos, d. Roger Vadim.

DRAMA: MELODRAMA: TRAGEDY: Revenge; Romance-Triangles; Evil Men; Evil Women; Paris; 1960s-Mod Era; Epistolaries; Revisionist Films; French Films; French New Wave Films; Classic Tragedy
REMAKE: Dangerous Liaisons, 1988. (Dangerous Game; Valmont)
Les Miserables, 1935, ★★★½/$$$, 20th/Fox. When a man steals a loaf of bread and is wrongly and too severely convicted, he spends years in prison, vowing to get out and get even. But once he does, a corrupt policeman makes his life hell. Fredric March, Charles Laughton, Cedric Hardwicke, Rochelle Hudson, Frances Drake. w. W. P. Lipscomb, N-adap. Victor Hugo, d. Richard Boleslawski. BPicture, BCin, BEdit. Oscars: 3-0.
Les Miserables, 1952, 106m, ★★★/$$, 20th/Fox, Voyager, Facets. Michael Rennie, Robert Newton, Edmund Gwenn, Debra Paget, Elsa Lanchester, Cameron Mitchell, Sylvia Sidney. w. Richard Murphy, d. Lewis Milestone.
REMAKES: (among 4 silent versions) 1978 TV remake, two French and one Italian version
DRAMA: Epics; Accused-Unjustly; Prison Drama; Stalkers; Thieves; Revenge; Ex-Convicts; Malicious Menaces; Historical Drama; Classic Literary Adaptations
(The Count of Monte Cristo; A Tale of Two Cities)
Les Miserables, 1995, 174m, ★★★/$$$, WB/WB, R/S-V. An updating of the classic tale to World War II with the hero a truck-driving former boxer who helps a Jewish family and becomes entangled in their tragedy. Jean-Paul Belmondo, Michel Boujenah, Alessandra Martines, Salome, Clementine Celarie, Philippe Leotard, Annie Girardot, Paul Belmondo. w. d. Claude Lelouch.
DRAMA: Multiple Stories; World War II Stories; Nazi Stories; Jewish People; Revisionist Films; Classic Literary Adaptations; Writer-Directors; French Films
(Richard III [1995]; The Diary of Anne Frank; Au Revoir, Les Enfants)
Less Than Zero, 1987, 98m, ★★½/$$, 20th/CBS-Fox, R/S-P-MRN. A rich and decadent clique of Beverly Hills offspring float through what there is of their lives beyond the material goodies. Andrew

McCarthy, Robert Downey, Jr. James Spader, Jami Gertz, Tony Bill. w. Harley Peyton, N-adap. Bret Easton Ellis, d. Marek Kanievska.
DRAMA: MELODRAMA: Rich People-Decadent; Rich People; Drugs-Addiction; Drugs-Dealing; Beverly Hills; Hollywood Life; Alienation; Young People; Bratpack Movies; Twentysomethings
(Bright Lights, Big City; St. Elmo's Fire; Lost Angels)
(Ed: What was a must-read as a slice-of-the-times becomes a preposterous, though beautiful, anti-drug crusade with only glimpses into what could have been a serious comment on a segment of society and the American Dream; but instead it's been Brat-packed. Downey is a stand-out)
A Lesson in Love, 1954, 95m, ★★★/$, Svensk/New Line. A gynecologist and his wife begin to split and see other people. Gunnar Bjornstrand, Eva Dahlbeck. w. d. Ingmar Bergman.
COMEDY DRAMA: Marriage on the Rocks; Romance with Married Person; Doctors; Swedish Films; Writer-Directors; Bergmanesque
(Ed: Early Bergman sex comedy, Scandinavian style)
Les Valseuses (Going Places), 1974, 118m, ★★½/$$, Ind/Col, R/S-V. Two pals take a girl on the lam for a life of crime. Gerard Depardieu, Miou-Miou, Patrick Dewaere, Jeanne Moreau. w. Bertrand Blier, Philippe Cumarcay, N-adap. Bertrand Blier, d. Bertrand Blier.
DRAMA: Action Drama; Crime Drama; Road Movies; Outlaw Road Movies; Buddy Films; Friendships-Male; Romance-Triangles; Writer-Directors; French Films
(Joyride; Goodbye Pork Pie; Menage)
Les Visiteurs du Soir, 1942/1945, 110m, ★★★½/$$, Ind/Ingram. The devil visits France in the Middle Ages and complicates a fairy tale romance. Arletty, Jules Berry. w. Jacques Prevert, Pierre Laroche, d. Marcel Carne.
COMEDY DRAMA: ROMANCE: Fantasy; Fairy Tales; Satan; Middle Ages; French Films; Art Films; Hidden Gems; Allegorical Films
(The Devil's Eye; The Advocate)
(Ed: Supposedly parallels the rise of Hitler and his meddling with the relationships of nations which sparked war)
Let Him Have It, 1991, 115m, ★★★/$$, New Line/New Line, R/V-P. A simple-

minded teenager is accused of a murder he may not have committed, but a witness claims to have heard him say the title line. Christopher Ecceston, Paul Reynolds, Tom Courtenay. w. Neal Purvis, Robert Wade, d. Peter Medak.

DRAMA: MURDER: Crime Drama; Accused Unjustly; Simple Minds; Mentally Disabled; 1950s; Kitchen Sink Drama; Social Drama

(In the Name of the Father; The Krays)

(Ed: A step above TV fare due to characterizations and style)

Let It Ride, 1989, 86m, ★★/$$, Par/Par, PG. A comedy about a horse race gambling problem that's hard to take as being funny, especially when his compulsion perhaps proves worthy. Richard Dreyfuss, Teri Garr, David Johansen, Jennifer Tilly, Michelle Phillips, Mary Woronov. w. Ernest Morton, Nancy Dowd, N-adap. Jay Cronley (*Good Vibes*), d. Joe Pykta.

COMEDY: COMEDY DRAMA: Gambling; Horse Racing; Midlife Crisis; Marriage on the Rocks; Obsessions; Dreams; Female Screenwriters

(The Great Sinner; The Lady Gambles; Fever Pitch)

Let No Man Write My Epitaph, 1960, 108m, ★★1/2/$, Col/NA. A kid from the slums with dreams of being a classical pianist falls by the wayside when the neighborhood mob corners him. James Darren, Shelley Winters, Burl Ives, Jean Seberg, Jeanne Cooper, Ricardo Montalban, Ella Fitzgerald. w. Robert Presnell, N-adap. Willard Motley, d. Philip Leacock.

DRAMA: MELODRAMA: Crime Drama; Mob Stories; Pianists; Inner City Life; Dreams; Forgotten Films; Coulda Been Good

(Golden Boy; A Bronx Tale)

Lethal Weapon, 1987, 110m, ★★★/$$$$, WB/WB, R/EV-P-MRN. A cop (Mel Gibson) with psychotic and suicidal tendencies is paired with a black cop nearing retirement (Danny Glover) who doesn't need any of his stuff-until the bad drug dealers almost get them and his daughter. Gary Busey, Darlene Love. w. Shane Black, d. Richard Donner.

ACTION: COMEDY: Action Comedy; Chase Movies; Police Stories; Detectives-Police; Drugs-Dealing; Buddy Cops; Buddy Films; Conspiracy; Chases-Car; Kidnappings; Women in Jeopardy; Revenge

(Ed: Too bad more emphasis wasn't played on the interesting dimensions to Mel's character, especially in the sequels)

Lethal Weapon 2, 1989, 111m, ★★★/$$$$, WB/WB, R/EV-EP. A continuation of the first, albeit at a faster pace with more emphasis on action and implausibility, with the drug dealers this time being South Africans with diplomatic immunity and the female in jeopardy being Mel's love interest (Patsy Kensit). Danny Glover, Joe Pesci. w. Jeffrey Boam, Shane Black, Warren Murphy, d. Richard Donner.

ACTION: COMEDY: Action Comedy; Chase Movies; Detectives-Police; Drugs-Dealing; Diplomats; Buddy Cops; Buddy Films; South Africa; Revenge; Women in Jeopardy

(Ed: Pesci makes the turmoil worth it, though he can be a bit much)

Lethal Weapon 3, 1992, 118m, ★★★1/2/$$$$, WB/WB, R/EV-P-S. Reinventing the story, this time the woman in jeopardy is a strong police officer (Rene Russo) who isn't in as much danger as Mel in their pursuit to catch cops selling confiscated weaponry. Mel Gibson, Danny Glover, Joe Pesci, Darlene Love, Traci Wolfe. w. Jeffrey Boam, Robert Mark Kamen, d. Richard Donner.

ACTION: COMEDY: Action Comedy; Chase Movies; **ROMANCE:** Police Stories; Detectives-Police; Police Corruption; Buddy Cops; Buddy Films; Arms Dealers; Bombs; Law Officers-Female; Romance-Unprofessional

(Ed: Russo is very impressive and her character rounds off the ridiculous edges which might have carried over from *2*)

(The Last Boy Scout; Bad Boys [1995]; 48 Hours)

Let's Dance, 1950, 112m, ★★1/2/$$, Par/Par. A dance team is reunited to stage a musical after breaking up years before. Fred Astaire, Betty Hutton, Roland Young, Ruth Warrick, Lucile Watson. w. Allan Scott, Maurice Zolotow, d. Norman Z. McLeod.

MUSICALS: ROMANCE: Musical Romance; Dancers; Dance Movies; Theater Life; Behind the Scenes; Reunions; Comebacks; Forgotten Films

(The Barkleys of Broadway)

Let's Do It Again, 1953, 95m, ★★1/2/$$, Col/NA. A couple decides to get divorced, then the husband gets jealous of the wife's new beau and sparks fly.

Jane Wyman, Ray Milland, Aldo Ray, Leon Ames. w. Mary Loos, Richard Sale, d. Alexander Hall.

MUSICALS: COMEDY: ROMANCE: Musical Comedy; Marriage Comedy; Marriage on the Rocks; Romance-Triangles; Divorce; Jealousy; Forgotten Films; Coulda Been Great; Female Screenwriters

MUSICAL REMAKE OF: The Awful Truth

(The Awful Truth; Let's Make It Legal)

Let's Do It Again, 1975, 113m, ★★1/2/$$$, WB/WB, R/P-S-V. Three black men decide to hypnotize a boxer in order to raise money for their church. Bill Cosby, Sidney Poitier, Calvin Lockhart, John Amos, Denise Nicholas, Ossie Davis, Jimmy Walker. w. Richard Wesley, d. Poitier.

COMEDY: Sports Movies; Boxing; Hypnotism; Black Casts; Black Men; Black Directors; Actor Directors

RETELLING/FLIPSIDE OF: The Leather Saint

(Uptown Saturday Night; Diggstown; The Leather Saint)

Let's Face It, 1943, 76m, ★★1/2/$$, Par/NA. A soldier infiltrates a women's health spa as part of a scam but finds out spies are on his tail wondering what he's up to. Bob Hope, Betty Hutton, Eve Arden, Zasu Pitts. w. Harry Tugend, MP-adap. Dorothy & Herbert Fields, Cole Porter, P-adap. Norma Mitchell, Russell Metcraft, d. Sidney Lanfield.

MUSICALS: COMEDY: Musical Comedy; Con Artists; Spies; Undercover; Male Among Females

Let's Get Lost, 1988, 120m, (B&W) ★★★/$$, Mainline/Col. The life in stylish documentary form of musician Chet Baker. w. Susan Stribling, d. Bruce Weber.

Documentaries; Art Films; Biographies; Musicians; Drugs-Addictions; Cheating Men; Sexy Men; 1950s; Memories

(Broken Noses; All the Fine Young Cannibals)

Let's Hope It's a Girl, 1985, 119m, ★★1/2/$, Ind/NA. On a European farm run by women, the matriarch hopes to continue the tradition. Liv Ullman, Catherine Deneuve, Phillipe Noiret, Bernard Blier. w. Leo Benvenuti, Tullio Pinelli, Suso Cecchi D'Amico, Pieros de Bernardi, Mario Monicelli, d. Monicelli.

COMEDY DRAMA: Farm Life; Farmers; Ensembles-Female; International Casts; Female Protagonists; Overlooked at Release
(Antonia's Line; The Wild Duck)

Let's Kill Uncle, 1966, 92m, ★★½/$$, U/MCA-U. A kid with a really mean uncle looming over him decides to get even and emancipate himself. Nigel Green, Mary Badham, Pat Cardi. w. Mark Rodger, N-adap. Rohan O'Grady, d. William Castle.

HORROR: Black Comedy; **MURDER:** Murderers-Child; Revenge; Murder of Relative; Uncles; Boys; Child Protagonists; Relatives-Troublesome

Let's Make It Legal, 1951, 77m, ★★★/$$, 20th/Fox. A married couple decide to get divorced after two decades, but when the wife's old boyfriend re-appears, things may re-spark. Claudette Colbert, MacDonald Carey, Zachary Scott, Barbara Bates, Robert Bates, Marilyn Monroe. w. Hugh Herbert, d. Richard Sale.

COMEDY: COMEDY DRAMA: Marriage Comedy; Divorce; Romance-On Again/Off Again; Marrying Again; Romance-Triangles; Jealousy; Romance-Reunited; Gambling; Forgotten Films; Hidden Gems
(The Marrying Man; The Awful Truth)

Let's Make Love, 1960, 118m, ★★★/$$, 20th/Fox. When a troublesome millionaire finds out he's being sent up in a show, he sneaks in and joins the cast to try and get even. This, of course, leads to romance. Yves Montand, Marilyn Monroe, Tony Randall, Wilfrid Hyde White, Frankie Vaughan, Bing Crosby, Milton Berle, Gene Kelly. w. Norman Krasna, d. George Cukor. BMScore. Oscars: 1-0.

MUSICALS: COMEDY: ROMANCE: Musical Comedy; Romantic Comedy; Theater Life; Turning the Tables; Revenge; Rich People; Romance-Older Men/Younger Women; Forgotten Films; Hidden Gems
(The Prince and the Showgirl)
(Ed: Worth it mostly for Monroe and Montand, though not tops)

Let's Scare Jessica to Death, 1971, 89m, ★★★/$$$, Par/Par, PG/V. Jessica (Zohra Lampert) comes home to a creepy mansion after leaving the asylum and the fun begins. Barton Heyman, Kevin O'Connor. w. Norman Jonas, Ralph Rose, d. John Hancock.

HORROR: SUSPENSE: CHILDREN'S: Insane-Plot to Drive; Mentally Ill; Nervous Breakdowns; Houses-Creepy; Illusions/Hallucinations
(Hush, Hush, Sweet Charlotte)

The Letter, 1929, 61m, ★★★/$$, Par/Par. Jeanne Eagels (BActress), Herbert Marshall, O. P. Heggie. Filmed version of stage play. w. P-adap. Somerset Maugham, d. Jean de Limur. Oscars: 1-0.

The Letter, 1940, 95m, ★★★/$$$$, WB/WB. A wealthy woman (Bette Davis, BActress) kills a man, supposedly in self-defense, but a letter may come back to haunt her. Herbert Marshall, James Stephenson (BSActor), Gale Sondergaard. w. Howard Koch, SS-adap. Somserset Maugham, d. William Wyler (BDirector). BPicture, BB&WCin, BScore, BEdit. Oscars: 7-0.

DRAMA: MELODRAMA: TRAGEDY: SUSPENSE: MURDER: MURDER MYSTERY: Murder in Self-Defense; Trials; Cheating Women; Blackmail; Secrets-Keeping; Murderers-Female; Accused Unjustly; Framed?; Letters; Plantation Life; Clever Plots & Endings; Evil Women; Revenge; Past-Haunted by the; Women's Films; Female Protagonists
REMAKE: East of Elephant Rock

Letter from an Unknown Woman, 1948, 89m, ★★★½/$$$, U/Republic. A beautiful film set in old Vienna about a woman (Joan Fontaine) pursuing a debonair pianist who may never be truly interested. Louis Jourdan. w. Howard Koch, N-adap. Stefan Zweig, d. Max Ophuls.

DRAMA: ROMANCE: MELODRAMA: Female Protagonists; Romance-Unrequited; Sexy Men; Musicians; Austria; Women's Films; Romance-Older Women/Younger Men

A Letter to Brezhnev, 1985, 95m, ★★★/$$, Palace/WB, PG-13/S. Two girls from Liverpool play around with some Russian sailors which eventually leads to an invitation to Moscow. Alfred Molina, Peter Firth, Margi Clarke, Tracy Lea, Alexandra Pigg. w. Franke Clarke, d. Chris Bernard.

DRAMA: COMEDY DRAMA: Class Conflicts; Working Class; Young Women; Female Protagonists; British Films; Russians; Allegorical Stories

A Letter to Three Wives, 1949, 103m, ★★★½/$$$$, 20th/Fox. Three upper-middle-class suburban wives (Jeanne Crain, Ann Sothern, Linda Darnell) get a letter that a friend of theirs has run off with one of their husbands, who, for various reasons told in a lengthy flashback, are all capable of such a thing. Jeffrey Young, Kirk Douglas, Paul Douglas, Barbara Lawrence. w. d. Joseph L. Mankiewicz (**BScr, BDirector**), SS-adap. John Klempner. BPicture. Oscars: 3-2.

DRAMA: COMEDY DRAMA: MELODRAMA: MYSTERY: Cheating Men; Cheating Women; Friends as Enemies; Women's Films; Ensemble Films; Ensembles-Female; Suburban Life; Class Conflicts; Yuppies; 1950s; Narrated Films; Flashbacks; Coulda Been Great; Faded Hits; Time Capsules; Writer-Directors
REMAKE: TV, 1986. **MALE FLIPSIDE:** Three Husbands
(Three Husbands; Doctors' Wives)

Letters from a Dead Man, 1985, 87m, ★★★/$, INd/NA, V. A Russian scientist tries to save survivors of a nuclear attack while writing a diary to his missing son. w. d. Konstantin Lopushansky.

DRAMA: TRAGEDY: Art Films; Apocalyptic Stories; Russians; Missing Persons; Doctors; Russian Films; Epistolaries; Writer-Directors

Leviathan, 1989, 98m, ★★/$$, DEG-MGM/MGM-UA, R/V. A deep sea monster attacks a mining crew. Peter Weller, Richard Crenna, Amanda Pays, Daniel Stern, Ernie Hudson, Meg Foster, Hector Elizondo. w. David Peoples, Jeb Stuart, d. George Cosmatos.

HORROR: SUSPENSE: SCI-FI: Monsters-Sea; Underwater Adventures; Submarines; Kill the Beast; Deaths One by One; Coulda Been Good; Unintentionally Funny
REMAKES/RETREADS: Alien
(Deep Star Six; The Abyss [1989])
(Ed: Supposed to be *Alien* underwater, but instead isn't even *The Abyss*. Hard to imagine the writer of *Unforgiven* is at least in part responsible for this)

Les Liaisons Dangereuses, see Les
Lianna, 1983, 112m, ★★★/$, Ind/Vestron, R/S-FN. A woman goes through major changes which lead her to a more honest lesbian lifestyle. Linda Griffiths, Jane Hallaren. w. d. John Sayles.

DRAMA: Character Studies; Lesbians; Gay Awakenings; Alternative Lifestyles; Women's Films; Homoeroticism;

Feminist Films; Writer-Directors; Female Protagonists

(Desert Hearts; Salmonberries; Personal Best)

Libeled Lady, 1936, 98m, ★★★★/$$$, MGM/MGM-UA. When a reporter (Spencer Tracy) is about to finally marry his girl (Jean Harlow), the paper slanders a capricious heiress (Myrna Loy) and he must marry off his girl to a romeo (William Powell) in an elaborate scheme to blackmail the heiress and prevent being sued, but it all begins to backfire. w. Maurine Watkins, George Oppenheimer, Howard Rogers, d. Jack Conway. BPicture. Oscars: 1-0.

COMEDY: FARCE: Screwball Comedy; Journalists; Romantic Comedy; Marriage-Impending; Marriages-Fake; Impostors; Honeymoons; Heiresses; Double Crossings; Blackmail; 1930s; Hidden Gems

REMAKE: Easy to Wed, Man's Favorite Sport?

(Easy to Wed; The Philadelphia Story; High Society; Holiday; Bringing Up Baby)

License to Kill, 1989, 133m, ★★★/$$$, MGM-UA/MGM-UA, PG-13/EV. Bond infiltrates a South American drug smuggling ring led by a bogus preacher (Wayne Newton) and other assorted heavies, eruptions, chases ensue. Carey Lowell, Robert Davi, Anthony Zerbe. w. Michael Wilson, Richard Maibaum, N-adap. John Gardner, d. John Glen.

ACTION: ADVENTURE: Spy Films; Secret Agents; James Bond; Undercover; Chase Movies; Rule the World-Plots to; Preachers; Con Artists; Drugs-Dealing; Mexico

(The Living Daylights; Goldeneye)

(Ed: The shark attack was a bit too real, and the whole film has a dark, bizarre quality not very Bondian, thus the first Bond flop in America)

Licensed to Kill: see **The Second Best Secret Agent in the Whole World**

Lie Down with Dogs, 1995, 86m, ★★/$$, Miramax/Miramax, R/P-ES-MN. A young gay man goes to the resort of Provincetown for the summer and finds an opportunistic Latin lover while trying to find a place to live, dishing all the time. Wally White, Bash Halow, Randy Becker. w. d. Wally White.

COMEDY: Sex Comedy; Narrated Films; Crossing the Line; Gay Men; Summer; Vacations; Actor-Directors; Writer-Directors

(Jeffrey; Fun Down There; Parting Glances)

(Ed: A beach movie for gay men, only everyone isn't so pretty and, though it's amusing, non-gay people may find it annoying even if they are tolerant. Why? It's pretty self-indulgent, not surprising considering it was written, directed, produced, and starred in by the same guy.)

Liebestraum, 1991, 113m/125m, ★★½/$ (LR), MGM/MGM-UA, R/P-S-FN-MN. An architectural writer (Kevin Anderson) goes to a small town to see his dying mother (Kim Novak) and begins uncovering secrets as he develops a romance with his friend's (Bill Pullman) wife (Pamela Gidley). w. d. Mike Figgis.

DRAMA: SUSPENSE: MYSTERY: MURDER: MURDER MYSTERY: Psychological Drama; Secrets-Haunted by; Mothers & Sons; Romance-Triangles; Romance with Friend's Lover; Small-town; Reunions; Hitchcockian; Writer-Directors

(Leaving Las Vegas; Orpheus Descending)

(Ed: A muddled process-oriented suspenser aiming for Hitchcock, settling for weirdness but not even up to Lynch)

Lies My Father Told Me, 1976, 102m, ★★★/$$, Col/Col, PG. A Jewish boy grows up with his grandfather in pre–Depression era Montreal. Yossi Yadin, Len Birman. w. N-adap. Ted Allan (BAScr), d. Jan Kadar. Oscars: 1-0.

DRAMA: COMEDY DRAMA: Coming of Age; Boyhood; Grandfathers-Fascinating; Fathers & Sons; Jewish People; Canadian Films

(The Chosen; Joshua; Then and Now; A Thousand Clowns)

The Lieutenant Wore Skirts, 1955, 99m, ★★★/$$, 20th/NA. A TV writer (Tom Ewell) joins the military and his young wife (Sheree North) tries to enlist to be with him, leading to humorous complications. Rita Moreno. w. Albert Beich, Frank Tashlin, d. Frank Tashlin.

COMEDY: ROMANCE: Romantic Comedy; **FARCE:** Military Movies; Military Comedy; Romance-Married Couples

(It Started with a Kiss)

The Life and Death of Colonel Blimp, 1943, 163m, ★★★/$$, E-L/Voyager. A British soldier's loves, as his career spans three wars and three women.

Roger Livesay, Anton Walbrook, Deborah Kerr. w. d. Michael Powell, Emeric Pressburger.

DRAMA: COMEDY DRAMA: ROMANCE: Romantic Comedy; Soldiers; Military Movies; World War II Era; World War I Era; Episodic Stories; Character Studies; British Films; Writer-Directors

Life and Nothing But, 1989, 135, ★★★/$, Orion/Orion, PG. Two women search for their beaux in post World War II France, facing the brutality of war and its aftermath. Phillipe Noiret, Sabine Azema. w. d. Bertrand Tavernier.

DRAMA: TRAGEDY: Searches; Missing Persons; World War II-Post Era; French Films; Overlooked at Release; Hidden Gems; Writer-Directors; Coulda Been Great

(Two Women; Indochine)

The Life and Times of Judge Roy Bean, 1972, 124m, ★★★/$$$, NG-First Artists/WB, PG/V. Vigilante Judge Bean in old Fort Smith, Arkansas wreaks havoc with his eccentric, extreme measures. Paul Newman, Ava Gardner, Jacqueline Bisset, Victoria Principal, Stacy Keach, Anthony Perkins, Roddy McDowell. w. John Milius, d. John Huston. BOSong. Oscars: 1-0.

WESTERN: Western Comedy; **COMEDY: COMEDY DRAMA:** West-Old; Judges; Stern Men; Eccentric People; Ensemble Films; Arkansas

(True Grit; Buffalo Bill and the Indians)

Life at the Top, 1965, 117m, ★★★/$$, Col/NA. Sequel to enormously successful *Room at the Top*, a class struggle drama, this shows what happens after getting to the top in the high society of London. Laurence Harvey, Jean Simmons, Honor Blackman, Margaret Johnson, Michael Craig. w. Mordecai Richler, d. Ted Kotcheff.

DRAMA: MELODRAMA: Class Conflicts; Social Drama; Mod Era; London; British Films; Sequels-Disappointing; Rise and Fall Stories; Cheating Men; Cheating Women; Romance with Married People; Marrying Up

SEQUEL TO: Room at the Top, 1959. **SEQUEL:** TV Series, Man at the Top, British.

(Room at the Top; Darling)

(Ed: Ironically, Harvey's other film of the same year, *Darling*, does a much better job showing a woman's rise and fall in one film rather than two)

Life Begins at 8:30, 1942, 85m, ★★★/$$, NA/NA. While drinking, an actor falls into a job as a Santa Claus. Monty Wooley, Ida Lupino, Cornel Wilde. w. Nunnally Johnson, P-adap. *The Light of Heart*, Emlyn Williams, d. Irving Pichel.
DRAMA: MELODRAMA: Tearjerkers; Rise and Fall Stories; Actors; Alcoholics; Christmas
(My Favorite Year; The Man Who Came to Dinner)
Life Force, 1985, 101m, ★★/$$, Cannon/MGM-UA, R/V-FN-MN. Vampires from outer space land in London and begin sucking up. Steve Railsback, Peter Firth, Frank Finlay. w. Dan O'Bannon, Don Jakoby, N-adap. *The Space Vampires*, Collin Wilson, d. Tobe Hooper.
HORROR: Black Comedy; Vampires; Aliens-Outer Space, Evil; Outer Space Movies; London; Unintentionally Funny
Life Is a Bed of Roses, 1983, 111m, ★★★/$, Ind/NA. An aristocrat in France starts a temple and invites his friends to join to rejuvenate themselves. Vittorio Gassman, Geraldine Chaplin, Fanny Ardant. w. Jean Gruault, d. Alain Resnais.
DRAMA: Fantasy; Art Films; Avant-Garde Films; French Films
Life Is Cheap, but Toilet Paper Is Expensive, 1990, 88m, ★★★/$ (LR), Ind/NA. A man from Hong Kong bringing a gift to a San Francisco drug dealer winds up in a lot of trouble due to his lack of understanding about America and the Asian subculture. Chan Kim Wan, Spencer Nakasako, Victor Wong. w. Spencer Nakasako, Amir Mokri, Wayne Wang, d. Wang.
DRAMA: SUSPENSE: TRAGEDY: COMEDY DRAMA: Black Comedy; Fish out of Water Stories; Asian-Americans; Chinese People; Art Films; Independent Films
(Chan Is Missing; Eat a Bowl of Tea)
Life Is Sweet, 1990, 103m, ★★/$$$, Palace/Republic. An middle-aged couple and their adult children still living at home struggle not to kill each other amid the resulting chaos. Alison Steadman, Jim Broadbent, Stephen Rea. w. d. Mike Lee. Numerous festival awards.
COMEDY: COMEDY DRAMA: Family Comedy; Eccentric People; Working Class; Character Studies; Parents vs. Children; Middle-Aged People; Midlife

Crisis; Pre-Life Crisis; Generation Gap; British Films; Art Films; Writer-Directors; Independent Films
(High Hopes; The Snapper)
The Life of Emile Zola, 1937, 116m, ★★★½/$$$$, WB/WB. The famous French writer Zola finds evidence in the famous case of Alfred Dreyfus which may prove he was unjustly accused. Paul Muni (**BActor**), Joseph Schildkraut (BSActor), Gale Sondergaard, Donald Crisp, Louis Calhern, Gloria Holden. w. Norman Reilly (BOStory, **BScr**), SS-adap. Heinz Herald, Geza Herczeg, d. William Dieterle (BDirector). **BPicture**, BScore, BArt. Oscars: 8-3.
DRAMA: MELODRAMA: MYSTERY: Courtroom Drama; Trials; Historical Drama; True Stories; Accused Unjustly; Framed?; Saving Someone; Writers; Detective Stories; Detectives-Amateur; Hidden Gems
(Prisoner of Honor)
A Life of Her Own, 1950, 108m, ★★½/$$, MGM/MGM-UA. A farm girl goes to the bright lights of New York to become a model and finds an older model for a friend and an older married man for an affair. Lana Turner, Ray Milland, Tom Ewell, Louis Calhern, Ann Dvorak. w. Isobel Lennart, George Cukor, d. Cukor.
MELODRAMA: Fame-Rise to; Models; Fashion World; **ROMANCE:** Romance with Married Person; Mistresses; Cheating Men; Friendships-Female; Single Women; Pre-Life Crisis; Young Women; Time Capsules; Camp; Soap Opera; 1950s; Female Protagonists; Female Screenwriters
(The Best of Everything; Peyton Place)
The Life of Riley, 1948, 87m, ★★★/$$$, U/NA. The travails of a working class fellow (William Bendix) trying to make a living. Adapted from the popular radio series, later a TV series with Jackie Gleason. James Gleason, Rosemary de Camp, Beulah Bondi. w. d. Irving Brechter.
COMEDY: DRAMA: COMEDY DRAMA: MELODRAMA: Class Conflicts; Making a Living; Working Class; Ordinary People Stories; Writer-Directors
Life Stinks, 1991, 95m, ★★/$$, MGM/MGM-UA, PG-13/S-P. A real estate mogul bets he can survive as homeless person for a month-not hard when Lesley Anne Warren is the baglady he finds. Mel Brooks, Jeffrey Tambor. w. Mel Brooks,

Rudy DeLuca, Steve Haberman, Ron Clark, d. Brooks.
COMEDY: SATIRE: Fish out of Water Stories; Screwball Comedy; Homeless People; Bets; Los Angeles; Rich vs. Poor; Class Conflicts; Comedy-Slapstick; Snobs vs. Slobs; Bathroom Humor; Coulda Been Good
(For Richer, For Poorer; My Man Godfrey)
(Ed: With this film failure, Brooks proves the point he was trying to make in the film-the rich can't understand or know)
Life Upside Down, 1964, 92m, ★★★/$$, AJ/NA. A young man likes being a loner so much, he winds up with nothing but four walls-but is freedom any more than a psychiatric ward? w. d. Alain Jessau.
COMEDY DRAMA: DRAMA: Character Studies; Young Men; Lonely People; Depression; Alienation; Drifters; Suicidal Tendencies; Suicidal Tendencies of Young People; Art Films; French Films; Writer-Directors
Life with Father, 1947, 118m, ★★★/$$$$, WB/WB, Nos. Pop lives life his own way, including his somewhat scandalous refusal to be baptized, in this turn-of-century tale which spawned a whole "those were the days" trend in the late 40s and early 50s. Based on the extremely long-running play. William Powell (BActor), Irene Dunne, Edmund Gwenn, Zasu Pitts, Elizabeth Taylor, Martin Milner. w. Donald Ogden Stewart, P-adap. Howard Lindsay, Russell Crouse, d. Michael Curtiz. BPicture, BScore, BCCin, BCArt. Oscars: 5-0.
DRAMA: COMEDY DRAMA: MELODRAMA: FAMILY: Family Drama; Fathers; 1900s; Eccentric People
(Cheaper by the Dozen; Father of the Bride; King's Row; The Barretts of Wimpole Street)
Lifeboat, 1944, 96m, ★★★★/$$, 20th/Key. A diverse group of people are trapped on a life boat after their ship is sunk during World War II and they have to put aside their differences in order to survive. Tallulah Bankhead, Walter Slezak, William Bendix, Hume Cronyn. w. Jo Swerling, John Steinbeck (BOStory), d. Alfred Hitchcock (BDirector). BCin. Oscars: 3-0.
DRAMA: TRAGEDY: Stranded; Trapped; Disaster Movies; Survival Drama; Slice of Life; Ensemble Films; Class Conflicts;

Shipwrecked; Stagelike Films; Hitchcockian
(Foreign Correspondent; Rope)
(Ed: Tallulah's tour de force)

Lifeguard, 1976, 96m, ★★★/$$, Par/Par, R/S-FN. A lifeguard (Sam Elliott) can't decide whether to pursue an affair with a teenager (Kathleen Quinlan) or give up the beach to be a married Porsche salesman. Anne Archer, Parker Stevenson, Stephen Young. w. Ron Koslow, d. Daniel Petrie.
DRAMA: Midlife Crisis; Character Studies; Young Men; Sexy Men; Settling Down; Life Transitions; Beach Movies; Romance-Older Men/Younger Women; Los Angeles; California; 1970s; Time Capsules; Female Protagonists; Female Screenwriters
(American Gigolo; Shampoo)
(Ed: Not all that much, but more than it had to be)

Life With Mikey, 1993, 91m, ★★ 1/2/$$. Touchstone/Touchstone, PG. To keep afloat, a former child star (Michael J. Fox) now runs his own child actor agency full of obnoxious brats he's trying to get jobs for when he's mugged by a little girl and finds his star. Nathan Lane, Cyndi Lauper. w. Marc Lawrence, d. James Lapine.
COMEDY: COMEDY DRAMA: SATIRE: Hollywood Life; Actors; Children-Little Adults; Children-Brats; Children-Adopted; Men and Girls; Fathers & Daughters; Pickpockets; Comebacks; Feisty Females; Coulda Been Great
(Paper Moon; Little Miss Marker)

The Light at the Edge of the World, 1971, 120m, ★★/$$, 20th/Media, PG. When pirates wreck a ship, a lighthouse keeper who sees what they've done is the victim of their revenge to keep him quiet. Kirk Douglas, Yul Brynner, Samantha Eggar. w. Tom Rowe, N-adap. Jules Verne, d. Kevin Billington.
ADVENTURE: Adventure at Sea; Ships; Journeys; Flops-Major; Coulda Been Good

The Light in the Forest, 1958, 92m, ★★★/$$$, Disney/Disney. James MacArthur, Carol Lynley, Jessica Tandy, Wendell Corey, Fess Parker, Joanne Dru. w. Lawrence Watkin, N-adap. Conrad Richter, d. Herschel Daugherty.
ADVENTURE: WESTERN: Indians-American; Early America; Raised by Indians; Journeys; Kidnappings; Fish out of Water Stories

(Last of the Mohicans; Little Big Man; Dances with Wolves)

Light in the Piazza, 1962, 101m, ★★★/$$$, MGM/NA. A mother (Olivia deHavilland) takes her daughter (Yvette Mimieux), who was kicked in the head by a pony as a child, to Europe and they both soon find love with a beautiful retarded boy and his father. George Hamilton, Rosanno Brazzi. w. Julius J. Epstein, N-adap. Elizabeth Spencer, d. Guy Green.
DRAMA: MELODRAMA: ROMANCE: Mentally Disabled; Simple Minds; Romance-Middle-Aged; Italy; Americans Abroad; Mothers & Daughters; Fathers & Sons; Vacations; Romance on Vacation
(Rome Adventure; Summertime; Three Coins in the Fountain)

Light Sleeper, 1991, 103m, ★★★/$$, Live, R/P-S-EV-FN-MRN. A drug dealer (Willem Dafoe) tries to get out of the business but may be framed for the murder (or suicide O.D.) of a friend (Dana Delaney). Susan Sarandon, David Clennon, Victor Garber, Mary Beth Hurt. w. d. Paul Schrader.
DRAMA: SUSPENSE: MYSTERY MURDER: TRAGEDY: Film Noir-Modern; Crime Drama; Drugs-Dealers; Drugs-Use; Life Transitions; One Last Time; Framed?; Accused Unjustly; New York Life; Writer-Directors
REMAKES/RETREADS: Schrader's own American Gigolo.
(American Gigolo; The Man with the Golden Arm)

The Light that Failed, 1939, 97m, ★★★/$$$, Par/NA. An artist who's going blind tries to finish a portrait of the lower-class girl he's fallen in love with before it's too late to see her. Ronald Colman, Walter Huston, Ida Lupino. w. Robert Caron, SS-adap. Rudyard Kipling, d. William Wellman.
DRAMA: MELODRAMA: ROMANCE: Obsessions; Tearjerkers; Blind People; Race Against Time; Last Wishes; Artists; London
(Portrait of Jennie; Bright Victory)

The Lighthorsemen, 1988, 110m, ★★/$$, RKO-WB/HBO, WB, PG-13. A World War I epic in which the cavalry battles against a barricaded city for free supplies and lives. Jon Blake, Peter Phelps, Anthony Andrews. w. Ian Jones, d. Simon Wincer.

ADVENTURE: ACTION: Action Drama; War Stories; World War I Stories; Australian Films
(Gallipoli; Breaker Morant)

Lightnin', 1930, 94m, ★★★/$$$, 20th/NA. Will Rogers stars as a bumpkin who helps other people settle their problems, while he has some of his own with his wife. Louise Dresser, Joel McCrea. w. P-adap. Frank Bacon, Winchell Smith, d. Henry King.
COMEDY: COMEDY DRAMA: Fish out of Water Stories; Country vs. City; Wives-Troublesome

Lightning Jack, 1994m, 101m, ★ 1/2/$, Savoy/HBO, PG-13/P. A cheesy outlaw in the wild west wants to become a legend, so, traveling with a mute black stooge/slave, he tries to become a criminal success to disappointing results. Paul Hogan Cuba Gooding Jr., Beverly D'Angelo, Roger Daltrey. w. Paul Hogan, d. Simon Wincer.
COMEDY: WESTERNS: Western Comedy; Black & White Together; Slavery; Mute People; Fools-Bumbling; Thieves; Criminals-Stupid; Good Premise Unfulfilled; Flops-Major
(Crocodile Dundee; Almost an Angel)

Lightning Over Water, 1980, 91m, ★★★/$ (LR), Ind/Imperial. Documentary on the last year of director Nicholas Ray's life while trying to hang on, suffering from cancer. w. d. Nicholas Ray, Wim Wenders.
Documentaries; Filmumentaries; Docudrama; Biographies; True Stories; Death-Impending; Comebacks; Hollywood Biographies; Directors; German Films

Lightning Strikes Twice, 1951, 91m, ★★ 1/2/$$, WB/NA. A woman tries to help clear her husband of murder but soon has her doubts about whether he's innocent or not. Ruth Roman, Richard Todd, Mercedes McCambridge, Zachary Scott. w. Leonore Coffee, N-adap. Margaret Echard, d. King Vidor.
DRAMA: SUSPENSE: MURDER: MURDER MYSTERY: Accused Unjustly; Romance-Dangerous; Enemies-Sleeping with; Female Screenwriters
(Deceived; Undercurrent)

Lights of New York, 1928, 57m, ★★ 1/2/$$$, WB/WB. A showgirl becomes a mobgirl and deals with the repercussions. Helene Costello, Cullen Landis. w. Hugh Herbert, Murray Roth, d. Bryan Foy.

DRAMA: Crime Drama; Mob Stories; Mob Girls; Dancers
(Ed: Notable as the first all-talking feature film)

The Lightship, 1985, 89m, ★★½/$, CBS-20th/Fox, R/P-V. A ship is held hostage by criminals on the run from authorities. Robert DuVall, Kalus Maria Brandauer. w. William Mai, David Taylor, N-adap. Siegfried Lenz, d. Jerzy Skolimowski.

DRAMA: SUSPENSE: Hostage Situations; Adventure at Sea; Mob Stories; Hiding Out; Ships
(Key Largo; The Island; Dead Calm)

Light Years, 1988, 83m, ★★/$, Miramax/Vidmark, PG. A sci-fi fantasy cartoon about a planet facing apocalypse. Voices of Glenn Close, Jennifer Grey, Christopher Plummer, Bridget Fonda, Paul Schaffer. w. Isaac Asimov, N-adap. Jean Pierre Andreven, d. Harvey Weinstein.

Cartoons; SCI-FI: Apocalyptic Stories; Outer Space Movies; Curiosities

Like Father, Like Son, 1988, 98m, Tri/Col-Tri, PG/P. A doctor (Dudley Moore) and his teenage son (Kirk Cameron) wind up body-switching to ridiculous results. w. Lorne Cameron, Steven Bloom, d. Rod Daniel.

COMEDY: Role Reversal; Body Switching; Men and Boys; Fathers & Sons; Unintentionally Funny
(GENRE GLUT [Body Switching]: Vice Versa; 18 Again; Big; [all in 1988])

Like Water for Chocolate, 1993, 105m, ★★★½/$$$$, Miramax/Touchstone, R/S-FFN-MFN. A lonely spinster cooks in her magical kitchen and the result is inspirational food and fantasies where sex and food are the ultimate dreams. Lumi Cavazos, Marco Leonardi. w. N-adap. Laura Esquivel, d. Alphonso Arau. BFLFilm. Oscars: 1-1.

DRAMA: Erotic Drama; Fantasies; Spinsters; Lonely People; Sisters; Magic Realism; Mexico; Sleeper Hits; Blockbusters; Female Protagonists; Female Screenwriters; Production Design-Outstanding; Latin Films
(A Walk in the Clouds; Babette's Feast; El Norte; Kiss of the Spider Woman; Old Gringo; The House of the Spirits)
(Ed: The biggest foreign language hit in American history, it also became an international phenomenon)

Li'l Abner, 1959, 113m, ★★★/$$, Par/Par. The cast of Al Capp's comic strip come to live, only in interior sets, however, to save their town of Dogpatch from becoming a nuclear test site. Peter Palmer, Leslie Parrish, Stubby Kaye, Stella Stevens. w. d. Melvin Frank, Norman Panama, P-adap. Johnny Mercer, Gene dePaul. BMScore. Oscars: 1-0.

MUSICAL: COMEDY: MUSICAL COMEDY: Save the Farm; Mortgage Dramas; Race Against Time; Nuclear Energy; Comic Book Characters; Hillbillies; Arkansas; Stagelike Films
(Kissin' Cousins)

Lili, 1953, 81m, ★★★★/$$$, MGM/MGM-UA. A fairy tale–like story of a girl who joins a traveling carnival in a surreal land and soon falls in love with the magician there. Leslie Caron (BActress), Mel Ferrer. w. Helen Deutsch (BAScr), N-adap. Paul Gallico, d. Charles Walters (BDirector). BCCin, BOScore, BArt. Oscars: 6-1.

MUSICAL: MUSICAL ROMANCE: ROMANCE: Young Women; Female Protagonists; Journies; Magic; Surrealism; Fairy Tales; Hidden Gems; Female Screenwriters
(Gigi; Brigadoon)

Lilies of the Field, 1963, 94m, ★★★★/$$$$, UA/MGM-UA,. A young black man (Sidney Poitier, BActor) winds up at an abbey in the desert building a new sanctuary for some white, reserved nuns, resulting in a major learning experience for all involved. Lilia Skala (BSActress). w. James Poe (BAScr), N-adap. William Barrett, d. Ralph Nelson. BPicture, BBWCin. Oscars: 5-1.

DRAMA: COMEDY DRAMA: Fish Out of Water Stories; Black Among Whites; Black Men; Black Protagonists; Nuns; City vs. Country; Religion; Conservative Values Films

SEQUEL: Christmas Lilies of the Field.
(Sister Act; The Defiant Ones; A Patch of Blue)

Lilith (B&W), 1964, 126m, ★★★½/$$, Col/Col. A young man (Warren Beatty) interns as a therapist at an asylum and falls for a beautiful woman there. Jean Seberg, Peter Fonda, Kim Hunter, Gene Hackman, Jessica Walter. w. d. Robert Rossen, N-adap. J. R. Salamanca.

DRAMA: ROMANCE: Romantic Drama; Mental Illness; Romance with Psychologist; Asylums; Psychologists; Young Men
(David and Lisa; Mickey One; Beautiful Dreamers; Splendor in the Grass)

Lilli Marlene, 1980, 116m, ★★★/$$$, Ind/Fox-Lorber, NA, R/S. A young German girl becomes famous during World War II for singing a popular song in a sexy way, à la Dietrich, which leads her into other interesting situations. Hanna Schuygulla, Giancarlo Giannini, Mel Ferrer, Karl Heinz. w. Manfred Purzer, Joshua Sinclair, Rainer Fassbinder, N-adap. *The Sky Has Many Colors*, Lale Anderson, d. Fassbinder.

DRAMA: MELODRAMA: ROMANCE: Rise to Fame; Singers; Female Protagonists; International Casts; World War II Era; Germany; German Films; Art Films
(Cabaret; Blonde Venus; Veronika Voss)

Lily in Love, 1985, 103m, ★★½/$$, Ind/Vestron, PG. An actor pretends to be a real Italian to get a part in a film that his wife wrote and he's been passed over for. Maggie Smith, Christopher Plummer, Elke Sommer, Adolph Green. w. Fran Cucci, d. Karoly Makk.

COMEDY: COMEDY DRAMA: Actors; Disguises; Italy; British Films; Writers; Turning the Tables; Good Premise Unfulfilled
(My Geisha)

Limbo, 1972, 111m, ★★★/$$, U/NA. Several young women await their husbands' fate in Vietnam, with only letters to give them hope. Kate Jackson, Stuart Margolin, Kathleen Nolan. w. Joan Micklin Silver, James Bridges, d. Mark Robson.

DRAMA: Vietnam Era; Soldiers; War at Home; Epistolaries; Women Behind the Man; Housewives; Female Protagonists; Young Women; Ahead of its Time; Hidden Gems
(Since You Went Away; Coming Home)

Limelight, 1952, 144m, ★★★½/$$, 20th/Fox. A vaudeville comedian whose life has gone downhill with his profession's passing falls in love with a ballerina and attempts a comeback. Charlie Chaplin, Claire Bloom, Buster Keaton, Sydney Chaplin, Norman Lloyd. w. d. Charlie Chaplin.

DRAMA: ROMANCE: MELODRAMA: Comedians; Comebacks; Vaudeville; Theater Life; Ballet; Dancers; Midlife Crisis; Hidden Gems; Writer-Directors

(The Entertainer; City Lights; Modern Times)

Limit Up, 1989, 88m, ★★½/$, MCEG/Vestron, PG-13. A stock broker (Nancy Allen) sells her soul to make it big on the Chicago stock exchange. Dean Stockwell, Brad Hall, Danitra Vance, Ray Charles. w. Richard Martini, Luanna Anders, d. Richard Martini.

COMEDY DRAMA: FANTASY: Selling One's Soul; Stock Brokers; Power-Rise to; Chicago; Overlooked at Release

The Lindbergh Kidnapping Case, 1975, 150m, ★★★/$$$$, Col/Col. The notorious case of the pilot's child who was stolen and murdered and the German who was possibly mistakenly accused. Anthony Hopkins, Cliff DeYoung, Joseph Cotten, Martin Balsam, Walter Pidgeon, Dean Jagger, Tony Roberts, Lawrence Luckinbill. d. Buzz Kulik.

DRAMA: True Stories; Docudrama; Kidnappings; Murderers of Children; Courtroom Drama; **MURDER:** Pilots-Airline; Accused Unjustly; TV Movies; Scandals; 1920s

(The Spirit of St. Louis; The Disappearance of Aimee; Adam)

The Linguini Incident, 1992, 99m, ★★/$, Ind/Imperial, R/P-S-V. Several hip eccentrics get together in a very hip restaurant and snipe and ponder life, or the absence of it. Rosanna Arquette, David Bowie, Buck Henry, Marlee Matlin, Julian Lennon, Iman. w. Richard Shepard, Tamar Brott, d. Shepard.

COMEDY: Comic Mystery; Eccentric People; Artists; Liars; Ensemble Films; Beautiful People; Deaf People; Restaurant Settings; Art Films; Curiosities; Coulda Been Good; Independent Films

(Slam Dance; The Cook, The Thief, His Wife and Her Lover)

Link, 1986, 103m, ★★/$, Cannon/NA, PG. A scientist (Terence Stamp) experiments with monkeys until one gets out of control. Elizabeth Shue. w. Everett deRoche, d. Richard Franklin.

HORROR: SCI-FI: Animal Monsters; Primates; Scientists; Cave People; Experiments

(Monkeyshines; Project X)

L'Invitation, 1973, 100m, ★★★/$, Ind/NA. A nerdy bachelor throws a party at a country house when his mother dies. Jean-Luc Bideau, Jean Champion. w. Claude Goretta, Michel Viala, d. Claude Goretta.

COMEDY DRAMA: Death-Dealing with; Nerds; Starting Over; Midlife Crisis; Parties; French Films

(Lonely Hearts [1981]; The Lacemaker)

The Lion in Winter, 1968, 134m, ★★★★/$$$, Embassy/Embassy, Col, PG/S. The medieval power struggle between the king of England (Peter O'Toole, BActor) and his estranged wife (Katharine Hepburn, **BActress**), Eleanor of Aquitaine, involving their feuding sons (Anthony Hopkins, Timothy Dalton, Nigel Terry). w. P-adap. James Goldman (**BAScr**), d. Anthony Harvey (BDirector). BPicture, **BOScore**, BCostume. Oscars: 7-3.

DRAMA: Historical Drama; Family Drama; Inheritances at Stake; Leaders; Middle Ages; Power Struggles; Kings; Queens; Royalty

(Becket; MacBeth; King Lear; The Madness of King George; Elizabeth and Essex)

(Ed: Dawn of a new age of historical and costume dramas-realism)

The Lion Is in the Streets, 1953, 88m, ★★★/$$, WB/WB. A con-man (James Cagney) becomes governor by going against the usual tide of rhetoric, but soon may become as corrupt as those he said he was against. Barbara Hale, Anne Francis. w. Luther Davis, N-adap. Adria Langley, d. Raoul Walsh.

DRAMA: SATIRE: Political Drama; Message Films; Power-Rise to; Politicians; Government Corruption; Ordinary People Stories; Con Artists; Overlooked; Forgotten Films

(All the King's Men; The Candidate; The Great McGinty; A Face in the Crowd)

Lion of the Desert, 1980, 163m, ★★/$, Ind/NA. A battle rages in North Africa financed by Arabs. Anthony Quinn, Oliver Reed, Irene Pappas, Rod Steiger, John Gielgud. w. H. A. L. Craig, d. Moustapha Akkad.

ACTION: War Stories; Africa; Desert Settings; Arab People; War Battles; Flops-Major

Lionheart, 1987, 104m, ★★/$, Orion/Orion, PG. A young knight saves children in medieval England from a slave trader, à la Robin Hood. Eric Stoltz, Gabriel Byrne. w. Menno Meyjes, Richard Outten, d. Franklin J. Schaffner.

ADVENTURE: CHILDREN'S: FAMILY: Historical Drama; Medieval Times; England; Saving Someone; Slavery

(The Adventures of Robin Hood; The Advocate)

Lipstick, 1976, 90m, ★★/$, Par/Par, R/EV-S-FN. Controversial failure ahead of its time in many ways about a girl who's raped but when no one will do anything, her sister sets a trap. Mariel Hemingway, Margaux Hemingway, Perry King, Chris Sarandon, Anne Bancroft. w. David Rayfiel, d. Lamont Johnson.

DRAMA: Erotic Thriller; Rape/Rapists; Revenge; Revenge on Rapist; Turning the Tables; Dose of Own Medicine-Given; Sisters; Sexy Women; Fashion World; Coulda Been Good; Flops-Major; Unintentionally Funny

(Extremities; Tattoo; Lady Beware)

The Liquidator, 1965, 104m, ★★★/$$$, MGM/NA. A spoof of James Bond starring Rod Taylor based on a character by the man who would eventually continue writing the Bond series. Trevor Howard, David Tomlinson, Jill St. John. w. Peter Yeldham, N-adap. John Gardner, d. Jack Cardiff.

COMEDY: Spoofs-Spy; **ACTION:** Action Comedy; Spies; Spy Films; British Films

(James Bond **SERIES**, Our Man Flint; In Like Flint; The Second Best Secret Agent in the World; Deadlier Than the Male; Hudson Hawk)

Lisa, 1961, 111m, ★★½/$$, 20th/NA. After World War II, a Dutch policeman rescues a Jewish girl from a Nazi still holding her and gets her to Palestine (Israel) for safety. Stephen Boyd, Dolores Hart, Leo McKern, Hugh Griffith, Donald Pleasence, Harry Andrews. w. Nelson Giddings, N-adap. Jan deHartog, d. Philip Dunne.

DRAMA: Rescue Drama; Women in Jeopardy; Nazi Stories; Jewish People; World War II-Post Era; Jews-Saving

(The Diary of Anne Frank; Town Without Pity; Two Women)

The List of Adrian Messenger (B&W), 1963, 98m, ★★★/$$, U/MCA-U. A serial killer with a thousand faces is trapped by an inspector at long last in the English countryside. George C. Scott, Kirk Douglas, Clive Brook, Gladys Cooper, Robert Mitchum, Frank Sinatra, Burt Lancaster, Tony Curtis. w. Anthony Veiller, N-adap. Philip MacDonald, d. John Huston.

DRAMA: MYSTERY: MURDER: MURDER MYSTERY: Detective Stories; Serial Killers; Trail of a Killer; Disguises;

England; All-Star Cameos; Clever Plots & Endings
(Day of the Jackal; No Way to Treat a Lady)
(Ed: Not exactly engaging but interesting; out of focus story-wise)

Listen to Me, 1989, 110m, ★/$, Tri-Star/Col-Tri, PG. Students take the abortion debate to Washington and romance develops. Kirk Cameron, Jami Gertz, Roy Scheider. w. d. Douglas Day Stewart.

DRAMA: ROMANCE: Message Films; Abortion; Teenagers; Teenage Movies; Supreme Court; Washington D.C.; High School Life; Competitions; Flops-Major; Unintentionally Funny; Writer-Directors
(Ed: A very saccharin, contrived, though well-intentioned, boring mess. Gertz is obviously too old for Cameron who has trouble living up to the lack of intelligence in his character.)

Listen Up: The Lives of Quincy Jones, 1990, 115m, ★★★/$$, WB/WB, PG-13/P. Fast-paced in sound bites documentary on Jones' fascinating life. d. Ellen Wiessbrod.
Documentaries; Biographies; True Stories; Fame-Rise to; Black Men; Inner City Life; Musicians; Female Directors
(Let's Get Lost; Round Midnight; Bird)

Lisztomania, 1975, 104m, ★★½/$$, WB/WB. A rock singer in modern times plays out the life of the classical composer. Roger Daltrey, Ringo Starr. w. d. Ken Russell.
MUSICAL: DRAMA: Biographies; Musicians; Revisionist Films; Avant Garde Films; Art Films; Singers; Rock Stars; Rock Operas; Allegorical Stories; Cult Films; Writer-Directors
(Tommy; McVicar)

The Little Ark, 1971, 86m, ★★½/$$, Cinema Center/NA, G. Two children escaping the war where their parents were killed take their pets with them, escaping in a flood on a houseboat to begin again. w. Joanna Crawford, N-adap. Jan deHartog, d. James B. Clark. Theodore Bikel. BOSong. Oscars: 1-0.
CHILDREN'S: FAMILY: DRAMA: Escape Adventures; Floods; Orphans; Allegorical Stories; Revisionist Films; Female Screenwriters

Little Big Horn, 1951, 86m, ★★½/$$, Republic/Moore. An earlier rendition of Custer's Last Stand and all. Lloyd Bridges, John Ireland, Hugh O'Brian. w. d. Charles Warren.

WESTERN: War Battles; Indians-American; Cavalry; Custer's Last Stand; Forgotten Films; Writer-Directors
(Little Big Man)

Little Big League, 1994, 119m, ★★/$$$, Touchstone/Touchstone, PG-13/P-S. A kid inherits a baseball team and encounters resistance from the players at first, but soon they hit it off. Luke Edwards, Jason Robards, Timothy Busfield, Dennis Farina, Jonathan Silverman, John Ashton. w. Gregory Pincus, Adam Scheinman, d. Scheinman.
COMEDY: Heirs; Inheritances at Stake; Sports Movies; Baseball; Men and Boys; Children-Little Adults; Children-Brats; Child Protagonists; What If . . . Stories
(Major League; Angels in the Outfield)

Little Big Man, 1970, 146m, ★★★★/$$$$, NG/Key, R/P-S-V. A young white boy is abducted and raised by an Indian tribe in the old west, but he grows up to be something of a klutz (Dustin Hoffman). Faye Dunaway, Chief Dan George (BSActor), Martin Balsam, Richard Mulligan. w. Calder Willingham, N-adap. Thomas Berger, d. Arthur Penn. Oscars: 1-0.
COMEDY: WESTERN: Spoofs-Westerns; SATIRE: Western Comedy; Fish out of Water Stories; Indians-American; Raised by Indians; Romance-Interracial; Romance-Older Women/Younger Men; Older Women Seducers; Simple Minds; Young Men; Flashbacks; Autobiographical Biographies-Fictional; Custer's Last Stand; Episodic Stories; Narrated Films
(Dances with Wolves; The Graduate; Tom Jones)

Little Buddha, 1994, 123m, ★★/$, Miramax/Touchstone, PG. When a boy is suspected of being the reincarnation of Buddha, his family travels to Tibet to check it out; and meanwhile, the story of Prince Siddhartha and his ancient quest to become Buddha is told. Keanu Reeves, Alex Wiesedanger, Chris Isaak, Bridget Fonda. w. Mark Peploe, Rudy Wurlitzer, d. Bernardo Betrolucci.
DRAMA: Fantasy; Religion; Reincarnation; Asia; God; Young Men; Boys; Child Protagonists; Art Films; Coulda Been Good; What if . . . Stories; Flops-Major

Little Caesar, 1931, 77m, ★★★½/$$$$, WB/WB, MGM-UA. A disguised biography of Al Capone and his rise to power in the mob. Edward G. Robinson, Douglas Fairbanks, Jr. w. Francis Faragoh, Robert E. Lee, N-adap. W. R. Burnett, d. Mervyn LeRoy.
DRAMA: ACTION: Mob Stories; Crime Drama; Warner Gangster Era; Power-Rise to; Rise and Fall Stories; Chicago; 1920s-Roaring; Biographies-Fictional
(Capone; Dillinger; The Little Giant)

Little Darlings, 1980, 92m, ★★½/$$$$, Par/Par, R/S-P. Two teenage girls at summer camp (Tatum O'Neal, Kristy McNichol) have bet on who can lose their virginity first. Matt Dillon, Armand Assante. w. Kimi Peck, Dalene Young, d. Ronald Maxwell.
COMEDY: Teenage Movies; Teenagers; Sex Comedy; Coming of Age; Girlhood; Camping; Virgins; Faded Hits; Sleeper Hits; 1970s; Time Capsules; Female Protagonists; Female Screenwriters
(The Last American Virgin; Meatballs)
(Ed: It grossed some $40 million at its release in '79-no small feat-but has become another novelty relic of the 70s)

Little Dorrit, 1987, 362m (2 parts), ★★★/$ (LR), Cannon/WB. The classic Dickens novel is given the miniseries treatment, but was released in a shorter feature film version in America. Alec Guinness (BSActor), Derek Jacobi, Joan Greenwood, Cyril Cusack, Robert Morley. w. d. Christine Edzard (BAScr), N-adap. Charles Dickens. Oscars: 1-0.
DRAMA: FAMILY: Costume Drama; Girlhood; Orphans; Female Protagonists; London; Classic Literary Adaptations; Female Screenwriters; Female Directors
(David Copperfield; Little Women)

The Little Drummer Girl, 1984, 130m, ★★½/$$, WB/WB, R/EV-P-MFN. An American actress doing theater in England (Diane Keaton) is talked into becoming a spy for the Israelis, under the seducing tones of a particular man (Yorgo Voyagis), despite her pro-Arab sentiments. Klaus Kinski, Sami Frey. w. Loring Mandel, N-adap. John LeCarre, d. George Roy Hill.
DRAMA: SUSPENSE: Spy Films; Spies; Spies-Female; Double Crossing; Conspiracy; Jewish People; Arab People; Terrorists; Undercover; Middle East; International Casts; Female Protagonists
(Patty Hearst; Hanna K.)
(Ed: Fans of the book were disappointed with the updating to modern times, though it was politically more relevant)

Little Fauss and Big Halsey, 1970, 99m, ★★/$, Par/Par, R/S. A motorcycle hunk and a motorcycle nerd ride across the desert. Robert Redford, Michael J. Pollard, Lauren Hutton, Noah Beery Jr. w. Charles Eastman, d. Sidney J. Furie.
DRAMA: Action Drama; Art Films; Motorcycles; Desert Settings; Hunks; Nerds
(Ed: Redford spends a great deal of time walking around without his shirt in the hot sun. If you're into that . . . Otherwise, no reason to bother)

The Little Foxes, 1941, 116m, ★★★★/$$$$, Goldwyn-UA/Goldwyn. The evil matriarch of a wealthy Southern family gets very upset when things don't work out the way she wants them to and tires of it once and for all, but her daughter may still be an obstacle once she's taken care of her husband. Bette Davis (BActress), Theresa Wright (BSActress), Patricia Collinge (BSActress), Herbert Marshall, Richard Carlson, Charles Dingle, Dan Duryea, Benton Reid. w. P. adap. Lillian Hellman (BScr), d. William Wyler (BDirector). BPicture, BEdit, BArt, BScore. Oscars: 9-0.
DRAMA: MELODRAMA: TRAGEDY: Family Drama; Family Conflicts; Inheritances at Stake; Evil Women; Mean Women; Mothers & Daughters; Civil War Era; Reconstruction Era; Southerns Gothic Style
SEQUEL: Another Part of the Forest (Jezebel; Gone With the Wind; Another Part of the Forest; Queen Bee)

The Little Giant, 1933, 74m, ★★¹/₂/$$, WB/WB. A gangster moves to California to use his money saved from bootlegging days to get into high society, but will it work? Edward G. Robinson, Mary Astor. w. Robert Lord, Wilson Mizner, d. Roy del Ruth.
COMEDY: Mob Stories; Warner Gangster Era; Mob Comedy; Class Conflicts; Social Climbing; 1920s-Roaring; Prohibition Era
(Mister Cory; My Blue Heaven; Little Caesar)

Little Giant, 1946, 91m, $$, U/MCA-U. Abbott and Costello sell vaccuums door to door à la the Fuller Brush Man, but don't play together as a team really, disseminating the comedy. Bud Abbott, Lou Costello, Elena Verdugo. w. Paul Jarrico, Richard Collins, Walter deLeon, d. William Seiter.

COMEDY: Salesmen; Abbott & Costello; Fools-Bumbling; Comedy of Errors (Abbott & Costello SERIES)

Little Giants, 1994, 107m, ★★★/$$$, WB/WB, PG. A band of small-town nerds and misfits go up against the champs in pee-wee football. Rick Moranis, Ed O'Neill, John Madden, Shawna Waldron, Mary Ellen Trainor, Mathew McCurley, Susanna Thompson, Brian Haley, Alexa Vega, Todd Bosley, Devon Sawa. w. James Ferguson, Robert Shallcross, Tommy Swerdlow, Michael Goldberg, d. Duwayne Dunham.
COMEDY: CHILDREN'S: Football; Underdog Stories; Small-town Life; Boys; Ensembles-Children; Ensembles-Male (The Mighty Ducks; D2; The Mighty Ducks; The Bad News Bears SERIES; The Sandlot)

The Little Girl Who Lives Down the Lane, 1976, 94m, ★★★/$$$, Ind/Vestron, Live, R/V. A little girl (Jodie Foster) who's not so little is hiding her mother's corpse in the basement after her father has died, and not wanting to be put in a foster home, must do whatever it takes to keep the nosy neighbors from looking down there and realizing she's an orphan. Alexis Smith, Martin Sheen, Scott Jacoby. w. N-adap. Laird Koenig, d. Nicholas Gessner.
HORROR: SUSPENSE: MURDER: Serial Killers; Murderers-Child; Murderers-Female; Murder of Parents; Molestation; Neighbors-Troublesome; Love-First; Virgins; Teenagers; Evil Women; Evil Children; Orphans; Murders-One by One; Saving Oneself; Child Protagonists; Underrated; Hidden Gems; Female Protagonists; Independent Films (The Bad Seed; Alice, Sweet Alice; Violette)

Little Gloria, Happy At Last, 1984, 180m, ★★★/$$$, NBC-Par/Par, A&E. The story of the Vanderbilt family's tug of war over the daughter of Gloria Morgan Vanderbilt, whose free-wheeling 1920s lifestyle became highly suspect and caused the loss of this little girl. Bette Davis, Angela Lansbury, Maureen Stapleton, Christopher Plummer, Martin Balsam. d. Waris Hussein.
DRAMA: MELODRAMA: True Stories; Custody Battles; Rich People; Rich People-Decadent; Alternative Lifestyles; Mothers-Struggling; Mothers & Daughters; Mothers-Troublesome; 1920s; 1930s; TV Movies; Miniseries

Little Lord Fauntleroy, 1936, 98m, ★★★/$$$$, Selznick-MGM/Nos. Freddie Bartholomew, C. Aubrey Smith, Mickey Rooney. w. Richard Schayer, Hugh Walpole, David Selznick, N-adap. Frances Hodgson Burnett, d. John Cromwell.

Little Lord Fauntleroy, 1980, 100m, ★★★/$$$, CBS/Fries. Alec Guinness, Ricky Schroeder. d. Jack Gold.
An American boy discovers he's heir to British wealth after his father has died and travels to the family castle.
DRAMA: MELODRAMA: Tearjerkers; Fathers & Sons; Grandfathers-Fascinating; Child Protagonists; Inheritances at Stake; Boyhood; Social Climbing; Royalty; Royalty-Sudden; Americans Abroad (The Little Princess; The Prince and the Pauper)

Little Man Tate, 1991, 131m, ★★★¹/₂/$$$, Orion/Orion, PG. A working-class mother (Jodie Foster) has a genius for a son (Adam Hann Byrd) and sends him to a school run by a woman who begins to compete with her (Dianne Wiest). w. Scott Frank, d. Jodie Foster.
DRAMA: MELODRAMA: COMEDY DRAMA: Mothers Alone; Mothers-Struggling; Prodigies; Geniuses; Children-Little Adults; Smart vs. Dumb; Class Conflicts; Working Class; Hidden Gems; Female Directors; Child Protagonists; Actor-Directors (Stella Dallas)

The Little Mermaid, 1989, 83m, ★★★★/$$$$$, Disney/Disney, G. A mermaid who wants desperately to be human falls in love with a handsome prince sailing through-but will an evil octopus queen keep her from her dreams? w. d. John Musker, Ron Clements, SS-adap. Hans Christian Andersen. **BOSong, BOScore.** Oscars: 2-2.
CHILDREN'S: FAMILY: ADVENTURE: Fantasy; Fairy Tales; Dreams; Adventure at Sea; Mermaids; Romance-Interracial; Fish; Octopi-Angry; Miniseries; Writer-Directors (Bedknobs & Broomsticks; Beauty and the Beast [1991])

The Little Minister, 1934, 110m, ★★¹/₂/$, RKO/Turner. A gypsy girl (Katharine Hepburn) is pursued by the local preacher in old Scotland, but turns out to be someone he wouldn't be so embarassed to have. John Beal, Alan

Hale, Donald Crisp. w. Jane Murfin, Sarah Y. Mason, Victor Heerman, N-adap. J. M. Barrie, d. Richard Wallace.

ROMANCE: COMEDY: Romantic Comedy; Romance-Forbidden; Gypsies; Free Spirits; Preachers/Ministers; Romance-Forbidden; Scotland; 1800s; Female Screenwriters; Female Protagonists
(Sylvia Scarlett; Spitfire; Little Women [1933])

Little Miss Marker, 1934, 80m, ★★★/$$$, Par/MCA-U. Shirley Temple, Adolphe Menjou, Charles Bickford. w. William Lipman, Sam Hellman, Gladys Lehman, SS-adap. Damon Runyan, d. Alexander Hall.

Little Miss Marker, 1980, 103m, ★★★/$$, U/MCA-U, PG. Walter Matthau, Julie Andrews, Tony Curtis, Bob Newhart, Sara Stimson, Lee Grant, Brian Dennehy. w. d. Walter Bernstein, SS-adap. Damon Runyan.
A wisecracking, grumpy gambler is forced to take on an abandoned little girl, who winds up helping to save him when he gets into trouble.

COMEDY: COMEDY DRAMA: MELODRAMA: Tearjerkers; Fathers & Daughters; Men and Girls; Children-Adopted; Babies-Finding; Abandoned People; Gambling; Girlhood; Horses; All-Star Casts

REMADE AS: Sorrowful Jones, 1949.
(Baby Boom; Bachelor Mother; Bundle of Joy; Lost Angel; Three Men & a Baby; Life with Mikey)

Little Murders, 1971, 108m, ★★★/$$, UA/Fox, R/V-S. When a man's (Elliott Gould) wife is killed in New York, he suddenly reconsiders his position in life. Marcia Rodd, Elizabeth Wilson, Vincent Gardenia, Alan Arkin. w. P-adap. Jules Feiffer, d. Alan Arkin.

DRAMA: Black Comedy; **SATIRE: COMEDY DRAMA:** Comedy-Morbid; **ROMANCE:** Romantic Comedy; Social Comedy; 1970s; New York Life; Violence-Sudden; Photographers; Coulda Been Great; Actor Directors
(The Prisoner of Second Avenue; The Out of Towners; Falling Down; Death Wish; Where's Poppa?)
(Ed: Though more of a romantic comedy, the turns it takes, if not also ridiculously jarring, are daring and worth taking note of)

A Little Night Music, 1977, 125m, ★★★/$$, Embassy/Sultan, PG/S. A man who's frustrated with his frigid wife is happy to see an old flame (Elizabeth Taylor) return to spark his interest. Diana Rigg, Len Cariou, Lesley-Anne Down, Hermione Gingold. w. P-adap. Hugh Wheeler, S-adap. Ingmar Bergman, *Smiles of a Summer Night*, d. Hal Prince. BAScore, BCostume. Oscars 2-1.

MUSICAL: MUSICAL DRAMA: ROMANCE: Romantic Comedy; Romance-Reunited; Virgins; Marriage on the Rocks; Actresses; Costume Drama; Coulda Been Great; Vienna; 1900s; Stagelike Films
(Smiles of a Summer Night; A Midsummer Night's Sex Comedy)
(Ed: Mostly known now for the classic "Send in the Clowns"; if you haven't seen or heard the stage version, you may think this fine, but many despise it, particularly Taylor's singing)

Little Noises, 1991, Monument/Prism, ★★★1/2/$ (LR). A would-be writer (Crispin Glover) decides to steal and sell a deaf boy's poetry to avoid the fate of being a loser like so many of his friends. Tatum O'Neal, John C. McGinley. w. d. Jane Spencer.

DRAMA: COMEDY DRAMA: Writers; Artists; Twentysomethings; Eccentric People; Art Films; Cult Films; Greed; Dreams; Homeless People; Deaf People; Fame-Rise to; Overlooked; Quiet Little Films; Coulda Been Great; Hidden Gems; Writer-Directors; Female Screenwriters; Female Directors; Independent Films
(Ed: A little gem with another fascinating, bizarre performance from Crispin Glover; a small film in every way, but a few big ideas-especially the debate over whether roaches can bite [between the eyes])

The Little Prince, 1974, 89m, ★★★/$$, Par/Par, G. The surreal fairy tale of a prince on a far planet who comes to learn about life on Earth, landing first in a desert and a musical. Richard Kiley, Steven Warner, Bob Fosse, Gene Wilder. w. Alan Jay Lerner, N-adap. Antoine de Saint-Exupéry, d. Stanley Donen. BAScore, BOSong. Oscars: 2-0.

MUSICAL: MUSICAL DRAMA: CHILDREN'S: Musical Fantasy; Fantasy; **SCI-FI:** Fairy Tales; Princes; Animals-Talking; Desert Settings
(Ed: A wee bit slow and strange for children, and too simple for adults)

A Little Princess, 1995, 100m, ★★★/$$, WB/WB, G. A girl goes to a boarding school during World War I and then becomes a maid when her father is missing in battle. She escapes into a world of her own fairy tales. Eleanor Bron, Liam Cunningham, Liesel Matthews, Rusty Schwimmer. w. Richard LaGravenese & Elizabeth Chandler, N-adap. Frances Hodgson Burnett, d. Alfonso Cuaron.

DRAMA: Fantasy; **CHILDREN'S:** Fantasies; Storytellers; Girlhood; Boarding Schools; Lonely People; India; Hidden Gems; Overlooked at Release; Female Protagonists; Child Protagonists; Female Screenwriters

REMAKE OF: Shirley Temple version, 1939
(Little Women; The Secret Garden; The Little Prince; Bright Eyes; Little Lord Fauntleroy)

The Little Princess, 1939, 93m, ★★★/$$$, 20th/Fox. The daughter of a businessman is left at a boarding school with too many rules she must rise above. Shirley Temple, Richard Greene, Anita Louise, Ian Hunter, Caesar Romero, Arthur Treacher. w. Ethel Hill, Walter Ferris, N-adap. Frances Hodgson Burnett, d. Walter Lang.

COMEDY DRAMA: MELODRAMA: Music Movies; Boarding Schools; Girlhood; Girls' Schools; Stern Men; Fighting the System; Americans Abroad; Victorian Era; Costume Drama; Hidden Gems
(Little Lord Fauntleroy; Bright Eyes)

The Little Rascals, 1994, 95m, ★★★/$$$, 20th/Fox, G. The old serial character revisited with Alfalfa running head on into feminism and love with Darla. Darryl Hannah, Whoopi Goldberg, Courtland Mead, Travis Tedford. w. Penelope Spheeris, Paul Guay, Steve Mazur, d. Spheeris.

COMEDY: CHILDREN'S: FAMILY: Battle of the Sexes; Comedy of Errors; Child Protagonists; Ensembles-Children; Boys; Girls; Children-Brats; TV Series Movies; Female Screenwriters; Female Directors
(The Sandlot)

A Little Romance, 1979, 93m, ★★★1/2/$$$, Orion-WB/WB, PG. An American diplomat's junior-high age daughter (Diane Lane) runs off with a cute French boy with the help of an old pickpocket (Laurence Olivier) on a bicycle who must find them when they get out of control on a European adventure. Sally Kellerman, Arthur Hill, David Dukes. w. Allan Burns (BAScr), N-adap. Patrick Cauvin, d. George Roy Hill. **BOScore.** Oscars: 2-1.

COMEDY: ROMANCE: COMEDY DRAMA: Romantic Comedy; Love-First; Romance-Forbidden; Marriage-Elopements; Elderly Men; Grandfathers-Fascinating; Con Artists; Thieves; Journeys; Missing Persons; Missing Children; Female Protagonists; Child Protagonists; Hidden Gems; Sleeper Hits; Old-Fashioned Recent Films
(Rich Kids; My Bodyguard; The Prince of Central Park; The Hideaways)

A Little Sex, 1982, 94m, ★★/$, MTM-CBS-U/MCA-U, R/P-S-FN. A yuppie couple (Kate Capshaw, Tim Matheson) have trouble when his philandering gets out of control. Edward Herrman, John Glover. w. Robert deLaurentiis, d. Bruce Paltrow.

COMEDY: ROMANCE: Romantic Comedy; Cheating Men; Marriage on the Rocks; Yuppies; Young People; Forgotten Films; Coulda Been Good
(About Last Night; Windy City; Worth Winning)
(Ed: A sexy TV movie that didn't make any B.O., at least of the dollars kind)

Little Shop of Horrors, 1960, 70m, ★★★/$, AIP/Nos. An underground low-budgeter about a flower shop worker, his man-eating venus flytrap, and a sadistic dentist and his masochistic patients (Jack Nicholson). Jonathan Haze, Jackie Joseph. w. Charles Griffith, d. Roger Corman.

HORROR: COMEDY: Horror Comedy; Black Comedy; Comedy-Morbid; Nerds; Wallflowers; Camp; Cult Films; Avant Garde Films; Independent Films

Little Shop of Horrors, 1986, 88m, ★★★¹/₂/$$$, G-WB/WB, PG/V. A nerdy florist (Rick Moranis) keeps a Motown-singing giant, man-eating venus flytrap plant in the back room while pursuing the love of a ditzy girl (Ellen Greene) in love with a sadistic dentist (Steve Martin). Will the nerd or the plant save the day? Vincent Gardenia. w. P-adap. Howard Ashman, S-adap. Charles Griffith, d. Frank Oz.

MUSICAL: COMEDY: Musical Comedy; **ROMANCE:** Romantic Comedy; Black Comedy; Comedy-Morbid; Nerds;

Wallflowers; Wallflowers & Nerds; Camp; Hidden Gems; Coulda Been Great; Stagelike Films
REMAKE OF: 1960 version
(Ed: The fact that it was too stagebound probably kept it from the being the big hit it should have been)

The Little Thief, 1989, 108m, ★★/$$, Miramax/HBO, PG-13. In post-war France, a teenage girl begins stealing to deal with her feelings, leading her on a small adventure of sorts. Charlotte Gainsbourg, Simon de la Brosse. w. Annie Millie, Claude Miller, SS-adap. Francois Truffaut, Claude deGivray, d. Truffaut, Claude Miller.

COMEDY DRAMA: Girls; Thieves; Pickpockets; World War II-Post Era; French Films; Female Protagonists; Female Screenwriters
(Ed: Miller was Truffaut's assistant and saw the film through after Truffaut's sudden death)

A Little Treasure, 1984, 95m, ★★/$, Tri-Star/Col-Tri, R/P-V-S. When a stripper goes to Mexico to look for her father, she winds up on a treasure hunt. Ted Danson, Margot Kidder, Burt Lancaster. w. d. Alan Sharp.

COMEDY: Comedy-Light; Treasure Hunts; Missing Persons; Fathers & Daughters; Romance-Bickering; Mexico; Strippers; Coulda Been Good; Flops-Major; Writer-Directors
(Ed: Supposed to be *Cheers* star Danson's first big foray into the movies, but wasn't)

Little Vegas, 1990, 90m, ★★¹/₂/$, Col/Col, R/S. When a guy inherits his girl's money, family members are out to get him. Michael Nouri, Anthony John Denison, John Sayles, Catherine O'Hara, Jay Thomas. w. d. Perry Lang.

COMEDY: FARCE: Inheritances at Stake; Lover Family Dislikes; Prostitutes-Male; Desert Settings; Coulda Been Good; Writer-Directors

Little Vera, 1988, 134m, ★★★/$$, Russian-Gorky/Miramax, R/FN-MN. A young woman sleeps around while her family struggles through daily life in pre-glasnost Russia. Natalya Negoda. w. Mariya Khlemik, d. Vasili Pichul.

DRAMA: Social Drama; Ordinary People Stories; Working Class; Russia; Russian Films; Promiscuity; Depression; Alienation; Female Protagonists; Female Screenwriters

Little Women, 1933, 115m, ★★★★/$$$$, RKO/Turner. With Katharine Hepburn leading as Jo, the charm of this version is undeniable, though sometimes annoyingly cute, as the four sisters deal with the changes around them in the mid-1800s with the civil war and growing up. Paul Lukas, Joan Bennett, Frances Dee, Spring Byington, Edna May Oliver. w. Sarah Mason, Victor Heerman, N-adap. Louisa May Alcott, d. George Cukor.

Little Women, 1949, 122m, ★★★/$$$, MGM/MGM-UA. June Allyson, Elizabeth Taylor, Peter Lawford, Janet Leigh, Mary Astor. w. Andrew Solt, Sarah Y. Mason, Victor Heerman, N-adap. Louisa May Alcott, d. Mervyn LeRoy.

Little Women, 1978, 200m, ★★★/$$$, NBC/NA. The third version, with more details in the longer running time. Meredith Baxter Birney, Susan Dey, Eve Plumb, Dorothy McGuire, Greer Garson, William Shatner. d. David Lowell Rich.

Little Women, 1994, 120m, ★★★/$$$, Col/Col, G. Fourth, most opulent version with a more realistic, less melodramatic (if that's possible) bent, but still not exactly modernized. Winona Ryder (BActress), Susan Sarandon, Samantha Mathis, Claire Danes, Trini Alvarado, Eric Stoltz. N-adap. Louisa May Alcott, d. Gillian Armstrong. BOScore, BCostume. Oscars: 3-0.

MELODRAMA: COMEDY DRAMA: FAMILY: CHILDREN'S: Tearjerkers; Ensemble Films; Ensembles-Female; 1800s; Civil War Era; Early America; New England; Free Spirits; Feisty Females; Classics-Literary Adaptations; Female Screenwriters; Female Directors; Female Protagonists
(The Europeans; Sense and Sensibility; Pride and Prejudice)

Live a Little, Love a Lot, 1968, 90m, ★★/$$, MGM/MGM-UA. Elvis takes pictures trying to make a living so he can sing to the babes. Elvis Presley, Michael Carey, Don Porter, Dick Sargent, Sterling Holloway. d. Norman Taurog.

MUSICAL: Musical Romance; **ROMANCE:** Romantic Comedy; Photographers; Singers; Unintentionally Funny

Live a Little, Steal a Lot (Murph the Surf), 1974, 102m, ★★¹/₂/$$, AIP/NA. Based on the real-life exploits of Murph the Surf, debonair jewel thief of the 60s, where the cops finally catch up to the gang and force them to return what they've taken-unless they can outwit the cops. Robert Conrad, Donna Mills, Don Stroud. w. Arthur Kean, Allan Dale Kuhn, d. Marvin Chomsky.

ACTION: Crime Drama; **COMEDY DRAMA:** Capers; Heist Stories; True Stories; Surfers; Jewel Thieves; Playboys; Florida

(The Hot Rock; To Catch a Thief)

Live and Let Die, 1973, 121m, ★★★/ $$$, UA/MGM-UA, PG/V-S. James Bond (Roger Moore's first) chases a black kingpin (Yaphet Kotto) from the Fillet of Soul bar in Harlem down to the Caribbean, winding up in voodoo intrigue. Jane Seymour. w. Tom Makiewicz, N-adap. Ian Fleming, d. Guy Hamilton. BOSong. Oscars: 1-0.

ACTION: ADVENTURE: Spy Films; Spies; James Bond SERIES; Caribbean; Occult; Voodoo; Black Men; Chases-Boat; Fortunetellers

(The Man with the Golden Gun; Moonraker; The Spy Who Loved Me)

(Ed: Better than some of those that followed with Moore, especially the humor involved, but still lacking that early Bond panache)

Live for Life, 1967, 130m, ★★★/$$, UA/NA. A French journalist (Yves Montand) falls for an American model (Candice Bergen) and contemplates leaving his wife. w. Pierre Uytterhoeven, Claude LeLouch, d. LeLouch. BFFilm. Oscars: 1-0.

ROMANCE: MELODRAMA: DRAMA: Romantic Drama; Americans Abroad; Fashion World; Romance with Married Person; Forgotten Films; French Films; 1960s

(In the Cool of the Day; The Game Is Over)

Live, Love and Learn, 1937, 78m, ★★½/$$, MGM/NA. A painter/playboy decides to settle down, but will he stay put? Robert Montgomery, Rosalind Russell, Robert Benchley, Monty Wooley. w. Charles Brackett, Cyril Hume, Richard Maibaum, d. George Fitzmaurice.

ROMANCE: COMEDY DRAMA: MELO-DRAMA: Marriage Drama; Romantic Comedy; Settling Down; Playboys; Artists; Single Men; Forgotten Films

(The Bachelor and the Bobby-Soxer; The Art of Love)

Live Now, Pay Later, 1962, 104m, ★★★/$, Regal-Ind/NA. A salesman in debt without a stable relationship keeps going on even though many setbacks occur. Ian Hendry, John Gregson. w. Jack Trevor Story, d. Jay Lewis.

SATIRE: DRAMA: Black Comedy; Working Class; Making a Living; Unlucky People; Kitchen Sink Drama; Salesmen; British Films

(Death of a Salesman; Imaginary Crimes)

Lives of a Bengal Lancer, 1934, 119m, ★★★/$$$$, Par/Par. The adventures of patrolmen in India during colonial days, taming tigers and what-not. Gary Cooper, Franchot Tone, Richard Cromwell. w. Waldemar Young, John Balderston, Achmed Abdullah, d. Henry Hathaway (BDirector). BPicture, BScr, BArt, BEdit. Oscars: 5-0.

ACTION: ADVENTURE: Special Teams; India; War Stories; War Battles; British Films; Faded Hits

(Gunga Din; The Jungle Book)

Live Wire, 1992, 85m, ★★½/$$, Showtime-Col/New Line, R/V-S. A bomb expert goes head to head with a terrorist with an undetectable explosive in his possession. Pierce Brosnan, Ben Cross, Ron Silver, Lisa Eilbacher. d. Christian Duguay.

ACTION: SUSPENSE: Bombs; Police Stories; Terrorists; Cat and Mouse; Race Against Time; Washington D.C.; TV Movies; Coulda Been Good

(Nighthawks [1981]; The Fourth Protocol)

The Living Corpse, 1928, 108m, (Silent), ★★★/NA, Russian/NA. A man whose wife is cheating on him wants to get out of the marriage, but when the church forbids it and he can't get it legally due to bureaucratic problems, he seeks other means. w. B. Gusman, Anatoly Marienhof, P-adap. Leo Tolstoy, d. Feodor Ozep.

DRAMA: TRAGEDY: SUSPENSE: Marriage on the Rocks; Divorce; Cheating Women; Russia; Russian Films; Suicidal Tendencies

The Living Daylights, 1987, 130m, ★★★/$$$, MGM-UA/MGM-UA, PG/V. A new James Bond (Timothy Dalton) infiltrates a drug and arms smuggling ring involving several international characters (Jeroen Krabbe, Joe Don Baker) while romancing a few beauties-with no real sex in the responsible era of AIDS (or much humor). John Rhys-Davies, Maryam

D'Abo. w. Richard Maibaum, Michael G. Wilson, d. John Glen.

ACTION: ADVENTURE: Spy Films; Spies; James Bond; Secret Agents; Drugs-Dealers; Arms Dealers

(License to Kill; Goldeneye)

The Living Desert, 1953, 72m, ★★★/$$$, Disney/Disney. Documentary à la Disney about desert critters. w. James Algar, Winston Hibler, Ted Sears, d. Algar. BFeatureDoc. Oscars: 1-1.

CHILDREN'S: FAMILY: Documentaries; Desert Settings; Animal Stories

The Living End, 1992, 84m, ★★½/$$, Mainline/Academy, R/P-S-MN. Two gay men who are both HIV-positive go on self-destructive crime spree on a trip through California. Mike Dytri, Craig Gilmore, Mary Woronov, Paul Bartel. w. d. Gregg Araki.

DRAMA: Road Movies; Outlaw Road Movies; Character Studies; One Last Time; Gay Men; AIDS Stories; California; Alienation; Coulda Been Great; Good Premise Unfulfilled; Time Capsules; Writer-Directors; Independent Films

(Thelma & Louise; The Doom Generation)

(Ed: The actors, though not the best, have a hip, modern look, though the production values make it look early 70s. Ultimately it's an interesting misfire)

Living in a Big Way, 1947, 103m, ★★½/$$, MGM/NA. A GI leaves his rich wife to start a home for war vets, while singing and dancing a bit, too. Gene Kelly, Marie McDonald, Spring Byington. w. Gregory LaCava, Irving Ravetch, d. LaCava.

MELODRAMA: COMEDY DRAMA: Music Movies; Veterans; World War II-Post Era; Message Films; Social Workers; Forgotten Films

Living in Oblivion, 1995, 91m, ★★★/$, Sony/Sony, R/P-S. A young director obsesses over shooting one scene in his independent film, much to the consternation of everyone else involved. Steve Buscemi, Catherine Keener, Dermot Mulroney, Danielle von Zerneck, James Le Gros. w. d. Tom Dicillo.

DRAMA: COMEDY DRAMA: Directors; One-Day Stories; Movie Making; Movies within Movies; Independent Films; Writer-Directors

(The Big Picture; Dangerous Game; Johnny Suede)

Living It Up, 1954, 95m, ★★★/$$$, Par/Par. An apparent nuclear poisoning victim in New Mexico (Jerry Lewis), a goofy gas pump boy is made a national hero by the press through a series of mis-understandings. Dean Martin, Janet Leigh, Edward Arnold, Sheree North. w. Jack Rose, Mel Shavelson, d. Norman Taurog.
COMEDY: SATIRE: FARCE: Comedy-Slapstick; Misunderstandings; Journalists; Nuclear Energy; Bombs-Atomic; New Mexico; Hoaxes
REMAKE/FLIPSIDE OF: Nothing Sacred. (The Atomic Kid; Nothing Sacred)
Lizzie, 1957, 81m, ★★/$$, MGM/NA. A woman develops multiple personalities after witnessing murder and being raped. Eleanor Parker, Richard Bone, Joan Blondell. w. Mel Dinelli, N-adap. Shirley Jackson (*The Bird's Nest*), d. Hugo Haas.
DRAMA: TRAGEDY: MURDER: Rape/Rapists; Multiple Personalities; Mental Illness; Asylums; Psychologists; Female Protagonists
RETREAD OF: The Three Faces of Eve (1957)
Lloyd's of London, 1936, 115m, ★★★/$$$, London/NA. A boy works his way up through the ranks of British big business, starting in the mailroom and soon runs the biggest insurance company in the world. Tyrone Power, Madeleine Carroll, George Sanders, Freddie Bartholomew. w. Ernest Pascal, Walter Ferris, N-adap. Curtis Kenyon, d. Henry King. BArt. Oscars: 1-0.
DRAMA: MELODRAMA: Social Climbing; Dreams; Power-Rise to; London; Biographies-Fictional; Historical Drama; Costume Drama; Faded Hits
Local Hero, 1983, 111m, ★★★¹/₂/$$ (LR), WB/WB, PG. A young businessman (Peter Reigert) is sent to a small town in coastal Scotland by his American oil company to offer to buy the entire area for oil drilling, but during the course of his stay begins to wonder about the ethics of ruining the community. Burt Lancaster, Denis Lawson. w. d. Bill Forsyth.
COMEDY DRAMA: Fish out of Water Stories; Corporation as Enemy; Class Conflicts; Small-town Life; Scotland; Country vs. City; Americans Abroad; Oil People; Irish Land Battles; Quiet Little Films; Writer-Directors; Hidden Gems (Whiskey Galore; The Maggie; Water)

Lock Up, 1989, 109m, ★★/$$$, Carolco/Live, R/EV-P. A prisoner does battle with a prison warden. Guess which one Stallone plays, guess which one wins. Sylvester Stallone, Donald Sutherland, John Amos. w. Richard Smith, Jeb Stuart, Henry Rosenbaum, d. John Flynn.
ACTION: Prison Drama; Accused Unjustly; Men in Conflict; Evil Men (Tango & Cash; Weeds; Brubaker)
Lock Up Your Daughters, 1969, 103m, ★★¹/₂/$$, Col/NA. In merry old England, a rich playboy and various other more ordinary men vy for various women, lead-ing to chaos and confusion. Christopher Plummer, Roy Kinnear, Susannah York, Glynis Johns, Ian Bannen, Jim Dale. w. Keith Waterhouse, Willis Hall, P-adap. Bernard Miles, N-adap: Henry Fielding, *Rape Upon Rape*, John Vanbrugh, *The Relapse*. d. Peter Coe.
FARCE: COMEDY: Farce-Bedroom; Erotic Comedy; Misunderstandings; Mistaken Identities; Promiscuity; Cheating Men; Playboys; 1700s; Novel and Play Adaptations; British Films; Rape/Rapists; Coulda Been Great (Tom Jones; The Amorous Adventures of Moll Flanders)
The Locket, 1944, 85m, ★★¹/₂/$$, RKO/RKO-Turner. A dangerous woman tries to exact revenge on a few men due to a secret contained in a locket. Laraine Day, Brian Aherne, Robert Mitchum. w. Sheridan Gibney, d. John Brahm.
DRAMA: SUSPENSE: Film Noir; Revenge; Evil Women; Dangerous Women; Dangerous Men; Secrets; Past-Haunted by; Female Protagonists
The Lodger (B&W), 1926, 84m, (Silent), Gainsborough/Nos. Ivor Novello, Marie Ault. w. Eliot Stannard, Alfred Hitchcock, N-adap. Mrs. Belloc Lowndes, d. Hitchcock.
The Lodger (The Phantom Fiend), 1932, 85m, ★★¹/₂/$$, Twickenham/NA. Ivor Novello, Elizabeth Allan, Jack Hawkins. w. Ivor Novello, Miles Mander, Paul Rotha, Fowler Mear, d. Maurice Elvey (set in contemporary period, not Ripper's).
The Lodger, 1944, 84m, ★★★/$$$, Ind/Nos. A stranger who stays in a board-inghouse may or may not be Jack the Ripper. Laird Cregar, Merle Oberon, George Sanders. w. Barre Lyndon, d. John Brahm.

SUSPENSE: MURDER: Accused Unjustly; Jack the Ripper; Serial Killers; Paranoia; London; British Films; Faded Hits
REMAKE: The Man in the Attic (The Man in the Attic; Jack the Ripper)
Logan's Run, 1976, 118m, ★★★/$$$$, MGM/MGM-UA, PG/V. In a futuristic bubble society, anyone over the age of 30 is sent away, but to heaven or hell? So a couple (Michael York, Jenny Agutter) escapes into the outside world to see what there truly is-unless they're caught first. Farrah Fawcett, Richard Jordan, Peter Ustinov. w. David Zelag Goodman, N-adap. William Nolan, d. Michael Anderson.
SCI-FI: ADVENTURE: SUSPENSE: Futuristic Films; Oppression; Conspiracy; Fugitives from the Law; Government as Enemy
REMAKE: TV Series, CBS 1977. (Solarbabies; Silent Running)
Lola, 1960, 91m, ★★★/$$, France/ Facets. A woman dancer (Anouk Aimee) has to choose between three men while finding herself. w. d. Jacques Demy.
ROMANCE: DRAMA: Coming of Age; Dancers; Romance-Triangles; Romance-Choosing the Right Person; French Films; French New Wave Films; Writer-Directors (A Man and a Woman; The Umbrellas of Cherbourg)
Lola, 1982, 113m, ★★¹/₂/$$, Rialto/ Karl-Lorimar, R/S-FN. The secret life of a lounge singer is explored through her sex life and friends. Barbara Sukowa, Armin Mueller-Stahl. w. Peter Marteschiemer, Pea Froelich, Rainer Fassbinder, d. Fassbinder.
DRAMA: Character Studies; Singers; Promiscuity; Sexuality; Female Protagonists; Germany; German Films (Veronika Voss; Lilli Marlene)
Lola Montes, 1955, 140m, ★★★/$$$, Col/Connoisseur, New Line. The legend of a courtesan's affair with the king of old Germany is recounted. Martine Carol, Anton Walbrook, Peter Ustinov, Oskar Werner. w. Max Ophuls, Annette Wademant, Franz Geiger, N-adap. Cecil Saint-Laurent, d. Max Ophuls.
DRAMA: ROMANCE: Romantic Drama; Costume Drama; Flashbacks; Narrated Films; Prostitutes-High Class; Kings; Female Screenwriters (The King's Whore; The Naked Maja)

Lolita, 1962, 152m, ★★★¹/₂/$$, MGM/MGM-UA, S. A middle-aged man (James Mason) becomes obsessed with a teenage nymphet (Sue Lyons) whose mother (Shelley Winters) is in the way of their getting together-not to mention the law. w. N-adap. Vladimir Nabokov (BAScr), d. Stanley Kubrick. Oscars: 1-0.

DRAMA: ROMANCE: SATIRE: Obsessions; Infatuations; Romance-Older Men/Younger Women; Virgins; Fugitives from the Law; In-Laws-Troublesome; Lover Family Dislikes; Cult Films (Baby Doll; The Lover; The Crush; Night of the Iguana)

The Lolly Madonna War, 1973, 105m, ★★¹/₂/$$, MGM/MGM-UA, R/EV. The tale of Tennessee hill people fighting over a piece of property-leading to a major feud and war. Rod Steiger, Robert Ryan, Jeff Bridges, Season Hubley. w. Rodney Carr-Smith, Sue Grafton, N-adap. Grafton, d. Richard Sarafian.

DRAMA: ACTION: Feuds; Rednecks; Hillbillies; Mountain People; Save the Farm; Forgotten Films (I Walk the Line; The Bootleggers)

London Belongs to Me (Dulcimer Street), 1948, 112m, ★★★/$$, B-L/NA. A boy gets arrested for murder in old London and his pals from his boardinghouse try to prove him innocent. Alastair Sim, Stephen Murray, Richard Attenborough, Joyce Carey, Hugh Griffith, Fay Compton. w. Sidney Gilliat, J. B. Williams, N-adap. Norman Collins, d. Sidney Gilliat.

COMEDY DRAMA: MURDER: MYSTERY: MURDER MYSTERY: Accused Unjustly; Juvenile Delinquents; Young Men; Boys; Ensemble Films; Ensembles-Male; Boardinghouses; Street Life; London; Hidden Gems

London Kills Me, 1991, 107m, ★★★/$ (LR), Rank-Polygram-Alive/Live, R/P-S. A drug dealer can hold onto his job as a waiter if he manages to fit in and not bring his sideline and friends into it. Justin Chadwick, Brad Dourif, Steven Mackintosh. w. d. Hanif Kureishi.

DRAMA: COMEDY DRAMA: Character Studies; Working Class; Poor People; Social Drama; Indian/Pakistani People; British Films; Drugs-Dealing; Ensemble Films; Overlooked at Release; Good Premise Unfulfilled; Writer-Directors (Sammie and Rosie Get Laid; My Beautiful Laundrette)

The Lone Ranger, 1955, 85m, ★★¹/₂/$$, Wrather-MGM/MGM-UA. The masked avenger of the wild west stops a white man from messing with an Indian reservation. Clayton Moore, Jay Silverheels, Bonita Granville. w. Herb Meadow, d. Stuart Heisler.

The Lone Ranger and the Lost City of Gold, 1958, 91m, ★★¹/₂/$$, Wrather-MGM/MGM-UA. The lone man goes on a murder mystery involving a gold medallion and some buried treasure. Clayton Moore, Jay Silverheels. w. Robert Schaefer, Eric Friewald, d. Lesley Selander.

ACTION: WESTERNS: Comic Heroes; CHILDREN'S: Treasure Hunts; Indians-American

TV SERIES, 1950s (The Legend of the Lone Ranger)

Lone Star, 1952, 90m, ★★¹/₂/$$, MGM/MGM-UA. A freelance adventurer journies down to Texas on orders from the President to talk Sam Houston into re-thinking his position against Mexico. Clark Gable, Ava Gardner, Lionel Barrymore, Broderick Crawford, Ed Begley, Beulah Bondi. w. Borden Chase, Howard Estabrook, d. Vincent Sherman.

WESTERNS: ADVENTURE: War Stories; War Battles; The Alamo; Early America; Texas; Forgotten Films (The Alamo; The Last Command)

Lone Wolf McQuade, 1983, 107m, ★★/$$$, Orion-WB/WB, R/V. A Texas Ranger (Chuck Norris) takes on cattle rustlers and thieves with a bit of a secret weapon. David Carradine, Barbara Carrera. w. B. J. Nelson, d. Steve Carver.

ACTION: WESTERN: Westerns-Modern; Martial Arts; Cattle Rustlers; Texas

TV Series: Walker, Texas Ranger.

The Loneliness of the Long Distance Runner, 1962, 104m, ★★★/$$, Woodfall-UA/WB. A runner (Tom Courtenay) thinks back on his life as he trains for marathons. Michael Redgrave. w. SS-adap. Alan Sillitoe, d. Tony

DRAMA: Character Studies; Running; Flashbacks; Young Men; Lonely People; Depression; British Films (Billy Liar; Running)

Lonely Are the Brave, 1962, 107m, ★★¹/₂/$$, U/MCA-U. A cowboy deals with changes on the range as new inventions compete with his usefulness. Kirk Douglas, Walter Matthau, Gena Rowlands, Carroll O'Connor, George

Kennedy. w. Dalton Trumbo, N-adap. Edward Abbey, *Brave Cowboy*, d. David Miller.

WESTERN: Westerns-Modern; DRAMA: Character Studies; Life Transitions; Man vs. Machine

The Lonely Guy, 1984, 90m, ★★★/$, Orion/Orion, PG/S. A writer (Steve Martin) tries to regroup with the help of a nerdy friend (Charles Grodin) and gets into the singles dating scene-barely. Judith Ivey, Merv Griffin, Dr. Joyce Brothers. w. Ed Weinberger, Stan Daniels, Neil Simon, N-adap. Bruce J. Friedman, *The Lonely Guy's Book of Life*, d. Arthur Hiller.

COMEDY: COMEDY DRAMA: Character Studies; ROMANCE: Romantic Comedy; SATIRE: Lonely People; Single Men; Dating Scene; Nerds; Starting Over; Life Transitions Underrated; Hidden Gems; Overlooked at Release (Marty; L.A. Story)

Lonely Hearts, 1981, 95m, ★★★/$ (LR), Ind/Sultan, PG. A man who's been living with his mother all of his life finally decides to have a life of his own when she dies. Norman Kaye, Wendy Hughes, John Finlayson. w. Paul Cox, John Clarke, d. Paul Cox.

DRAMA: COMEDY DRAMA: Starting Over; Single Men; Lonely People; Romance-Middle-Aged; Australian Films; Quiet Little Films (L'invitation)

The Lonely Lady, 1982, 92m, ★/$, U/MCA-U, R/ES-FN-MN. A starlet sleeps her way to the top by being on the bottom. Pia Zadora, Lloyd Bochner, Bibi Besch, Jared Martin, Anthony Holland. w. John Kershaw, Shawn Randall, N-adap. Harold Robbins, d. Peter Sasdy.

DRAMA: MELODRAMA: Rise to Fame; Actresses; Erotic Drama; Promiscuity; Unintentionally Funny; Time Capsules (Butterfly; The Lady in Red)

The Lonely Passion of Judith Hearne, 1987, 116m, Handmade-Alive/Cannon, WB, ★★★/$ (LR), PG. A lonely piano teacher lives out her days in Dublin, trying to find love and yet avoiding it. Maggie Smith, Bob Hoskins, Wendy Hiller, Prunella Scales. w. Peter Nelson, N-adap. Brian Moore, d. Jack Clayton.

DRAMA: ROMANCE: Romantic Drama; Romance-Middle-Aged; Romance-Opposites; Character Studies; Musicians; Ireland

(Lonelyhearts; The Prime of Miss Jean Brodie)

Lonesome Cowboys (Andy Warhol's), 1968, 105m, ★★½/$, Ind/NA, R/ES. A campy gay cowboy story with poor visual quality but interesting ideas. Taylor Mead, Joe Dallesandro. w. d. Paul Morrissey.

SATIRE: COMEDY: Gay Men; Cowboys; Westerns-Neo; Camp; Art Films; Cult Films; Avant Garde Films; Travestites; Alternative Lifestyles; Mod Era; Underground Films; Miniseries; Writer-Directors

(Andy Warhol SERIES)

The Long Day Closes, 1992, 84m, ★★★½/$$, Palace/Sony-Col-Tri, PG. A man recalls his life growing up as a middle-class boy in Liverpool-daily life, nightmares and all-in a beautiful visual style. Marjorie Yates, Leigh McCormack, Anthony Watson, Nicholas Lamont. w. d. Terence Davies.

DRAMA: Character Studies; Boyhood; Mothers & Sons; Coming of Age; Nightmares; Flashbacks; Lyrical Films; Quiet Little Films; British Films; Overlooked; Underrated; Writer-Directors (Hope and Glory; Kes; Careful, He Might Hear You; Au Revoir, Les Enfants)

Long Day's Journey Into Night, 1962, 170m, ★★★★/$$ (LR), WR/Republic. Eugene O'Neill's autobiographical saga of an acting family with a drunken, washed-up father (Ralph Richardson), an illustrious mother addicted to morphine (Katharine Hepburn, BActress), and two brothers (Dean Stockwell,), one of whom has consumption. w. P. adap. Eugene O'Neill, d. Sidney Lumet. Oscars: 1-0.

DRAMA: TRAGEDY: Family Drama; Autobiographical Stories; Brothers; Nervous Breakdowns; Mothers-Struggling; Depression; Drugs-Addiction; Actors; Theater Life; 1900s; Stagelike Films; Pulitzer Prize Adaptations; Independent Films

(Strange Interlude; Suddenly, Last Summer; Mourning Becomes Electra)

The Long Goodbye, 1973, 111m, ★★★/$, UA/MGM-UA, R/P-V-S. Elliott Gould as Philip Marlowe helping a friend who is being accused of murder in contemporary Los Angeles and Malibu. Nina Van Pallandt, Henry Gibson, Sterling Hayden. w. Leigh Brackett, N-adap. Raymond Chandler, d. Robert Altman.

MYSTERY: MURDER: MURDER MYSTERY: Detective Stories; Detectives-Private; Detectives in Deep; Revisionist Films; Los Angeles; Accused Unjustly; Philip Marlowe; Alienation; 1970s; Time Capsules; Cult Films

(Marlowe; S*P*Y*S)

(Ed: Controversial Altman interpretation updating the cliches to fit the disjointed, depressing world of modern L.A. and Malibu, though it's not particularly entertaining or meaningful; Arnold Schwarzenegger gets strip-searched)

The Long, Good Friday, 1980, 109m, ★★★/$$, EMI-U/EMI, HBO, R/P-V. A mob boss meets his nemesis after a series of bombings and shootings in London, but it may be the end of his empire. Bob Hoskins, Helen Mirren, Dave King, Pierce Brosnan, Derek Thompson. d. John MacKenzie.

DRAMA: Crime Drama; Action Drama; Mob Stories; Bombs; Mob Wars; Men in Conflict; London; British Films; Sleeper Hits; Faded Hits; Hidden Gems; Cult Films

(GoodFellas; Mona Lisa)

(Ed: Not as exciting as it may sound, but interesting)

The Long Gray Line, 1955, 138m, ★★½/$$, Col/Col. A track and field coach's life at West Point is detailed. Tyrone Power, Maureen O'Hara, Donald Crisp, Ward Bond. w. Edward Hope, NF-adap. Marty Mahler, *Bring up the Brass*, d. John Ford.

DRAMA: Biographies; Running; Coaches; Teachers and Students; Military Schools; Forgotten Films

(Ed: Why did this need to be detailed? Only notable to John Ford or West Point fans)

The Long Hot Summer, 1958, 118m, ★★★/$$$, UA/MGM-UA. A drifter (Paul Newman) comes to work on a plantation in Mississippi and finds himself involved with the owner's daughter (Joanne Woodward) and the other potboiling goings-on. Orson Welles, Angela Lansbury, Tony Franciosa, Lee Remick. w. Irving Ravetch, Harriet Frank, SS-adap. William Faulkner, d. Martin Ritt.

DRAMA: MELODRAMA: ROMANCE: Romantic Drama; Family Drama; Plantations; Southerns; Romance-Triangles; Coulda Been Great; Women Fighting over Men; Classic Literary Adaptations; Female Screenwriters

REMAKE: TV Version, 1985, starring Cybill Shepherd, Don Johnson.

(GENRE GLUT: Cat on a Hot Tin Roof, The Hot Spell, 1958)

(Cat on a Hot Tin Roof; The Hot Spell; The Sound and the Fury; Picnic)

(Ed: Forever lost in the shadow of *Cat*)

Long John Silver, 1953, 106m, ★★/$$, Ind/Monterey. The old peg-leg pirate returns with his young cohort to search for the treasure he's been looking for for years. Robert Newton, Conne Gilchrist, Kit Taylor, Rod Taylor. w. Martin Rackin, d. Byron Haskin.

ADVENTURE: CHILDREN'S: FAMILY: Treasure Hunts; Pirates Caribbean; Men and Boys; Forgotten Films

Long Live Life, 1984, 100m, ★★★/$ (LR), Ind/NA. An major investigation begins when several people disappear from home for several days and aren't sure what's happened in their post-apocalyptic world. Charlotte Rampling, Michel Piccoli, Jean-Louis Trintignant, Anouk Aimee. w. d. Claude LeLouch.

MYSTERY: DRAMA: MURDER MYSTERY: Mystery-Whodunits; Missing Persons; Amnesia; Apocalyptic Stories; Writer-Directors

The Long Long Trailer, 1954, 96m, ★★★/$$$$, MGM/MGM-UA. A couple with a very long trailer tries to make a cross-country trip and still keep their marriage together. Lucille Ball, Desi Arnaz, Marjorie Main, Keenan Wynn. w. Frances Goodrich, Albert Hackett, N-adap. Clinton Twiss, d. Vincente Minnelli.

COMEDY: ROMANCE: Romantic Comedy; Comedy-Slapstick; Road Movies; Marriage Comedy; Vacations; Vacation Nightmares; Comedy of Errors; Female Protagonists; Female Screenwriters

(Forever, Darling; Packin' It In)

The Long Night, 1947, 97m, ★★½/$$, RKO/NA. A man shoots the man his wife has been having an affair with and then tries to escape the wrath of the law. Henry Fonda, Barbara BelGeddes, Vincent Price. w. John Wexley, SS-adap. Jacques Viot, d. Anatole Litvak.

DRAMA: TRAGEDY: MURDER: SUSPENSE: Romance-Triangle; Crimes of Passion; Film Noir; Forgotten Films; Foreign Remakes

REMAKE OF: Le Jour se Leve

The Long Riders, 1980, 99m, ★★★/$$$, UA/MGM-UA, R/P-EV. Several different pairs of brothers band together in the old west and become a pack of outlaws, played mostly by real-life brothers. Stacy Keach, James Keach, David Carradine, Keith Carradine, Robert Carradine, Dennis Quaid, Randy Quaid. w. Bill Steven Smith, Stacy Keach, James Keach, d. Walter Hill.

WESTERN: Western-Neo; Brothers; Road Movies; Outlaw Road Movies; Bank Robberies; Ensemble Films; Ensembles-Male

The Long Ships, 1963, 126m, ★★½/ $$$, Col/NA. Vikings vs. Moors in the Middle Ages in the quest for gold on the high seas. Richard Widmark, Sidney Poitier, Russ Tamblyn. w. Berkley Mather, Beverley Cross, N-adap. Frank Bengtsson, d. Jack Cardiff.

ADVENTURE: Adventure at Sea; Middle Ages; Treasure Hunts; Vikings; Scandinavia; Epics
(The Vikings)

The Long Voyage Home, 1940, 104m, ★★½/$$$, WB/WB. The adventures of several ship workers while dry-docked and getting smashed. John Wayne, Thomas Mitchell, Ian Hunter, Ward Bond, Barry Fitzgerald, Mildred Natwick. w. Dudley Nichols, P-adap. Eugene O'Neill, d. John Ford.

DRAMA: Character Studies; Ships; Working Class; Ensembles-Male

The Longest Day, 1962, 169m, ★★★/ $$$$, 20th/CBS-Fox. D-Day at Normandy is examined from various perspectives in several stories. John Wayne, Robert Mitchum, Henry Fonda, Robert Ryan, Robert Steiger, Robert Wagner, Paul Anka, Fabian, Tommy Sands, Sal Mineo, Jeffrey Hunter, Roddy McDowell, Stuart Whitman, Red Buttons, Richard Burton, Peter Lawford, Sean Connery, Mel Ferrer. w. Cornelius Ryan, Romain Gary, James Jones, David Pursall, Jack Seddon, N-adap. Ryan, d. Andrew Marton, Ken Annakin, Bernhard Wicki. BPicture. **BBWCin**, BEdit, BB&WArt, **BSFX**. Oscars: 5-2.

DRAMA: TRAGEDY: War Stories; D-Day; War Battles; Historical Drama; Soldiers; Epics; All-Star Casts; All-Star Cameos; Cast of Thousands
(A Bridge Too Far; In Harm's Way)
(Ed: One of the few war movies ever nominated for Best Picture. Notice all of the teen idols as soldiers)

The Longest Yard, 1974, 122m, ★★★/ $$$$, Par/Par, R/P-S. A petty criminal

(Burt Reynolds) is forced to get a prison football team shaped-up to get himself out. Burt Reynolds, Eddie Albert, Michael Conrad. w. Tracy Keenan Wynn, d. Robert Aldrich.

ACTION: DRAMA: Sports Movies; Prison Drama; Football; Blackmail; Underdog Stories
(Weeds; The Jericho Mile)

Longtime Companion, 1989, 90m, ★★★/$$ (LR), AP-Goldwyn/Goldwyn, R/S. The lives of several young gay men are chronicled from the beginning of the AIDS epidemic through the late 1980s. Bruce Davison (BSActor), Dermot Mulroney, Patrick Cassidy, Stephen Caffrey, Mary-Louise Parker. w. Craig Lucas, d. Norman Rene. Oscars: 1-0.

DRAMA: Social Drama; Friendships-Male; Marriage Drama; AIDS Stories; Gay Men; Death-Dealing with; Epidemics; Deaths-One by One; Episodic Stories
(An Early Frost; Philadelphia; Parting Glances)

Look Back in Anger, 1959, 99m, ★★★½/$$, Woodfall-UA/Sultan. Richard Burton, Mary Ure, Claire Bloom, Edith Evans, Donald Pleasance. w. Nigel Kneale, P-adap. John Osborne, d. Tony Richardson.

Look Back in Anger, 1980, 100m, ★★½/$$, BBC/WB. Stage taping of the play. Malcolm McDowell, Lisa Banes, Fran Brill. d. Lindsay Anderson.

Look Back in Anger, 1989, 114m, ★★★/$$$, BBC/HBO. The quintessential angry young man grovels about his life while having an affair with his supposed best friend's wife. Another stage taping with superior production values, but not necessarily performances if one considers casting. Kenneth Branagh, Emma Thompson. d. David Jones.

DRAMA: Social Drama; Young Men-Angry; Working Class; Depression; Young Men; Romance with Friend's Lover; British Films; Working Class
(Room at the Top; Alfie)

Look in Any Window, 1961, 87m, ★★/$, Allied/NA. A rich teenager with a lot of time on his hands becomes a mentally ill voyeur. Paul Anka, Ruth Roman, Jack Cassidy. w. Laurence Mascott, d. William Alland.

DRAMA: Social Drama; Voyeurs; Sexual Problems; Sexual Kinkiness; Psychological Drama; Mental Illness;

Teenagers; Young Men; Juvenile Delinquents; Rich People; Forgotten Films; Coulda Been Good; Curiosities; Unintentionally Funny
(Peeping Tom; The Mark; Short Eyes)
(Ed: Not exactly a good transition to the screen for the teen idol)

Looker, 1980, 94m, ★★/$, Ladd-WB/WB, PG/S-FN. A cosmetic surgeon (Albert Finney) gets caught up in a conspiracy of scientists searching for perfect beauty and the murders of several models. Susan Dey, James Coburn, Leigh Taylor-Young, Tim Rossovich. w. d. Michael Crichton.

SUSPENSE: MURDER: MURDER MYSTERY: MYSTERY: SCI-FI: Advertising World; Murders-One by One; Fashion World; Conspiracy; Medical Detectives; Models; Cosmetic Surgery; Writer-Directors
(Wolfen; Coma)

Lookin' to Get Out, 1982, 105m, ★★½/$, Lorimar-WB/WB, R/P-S-FN. A couple of losers scam to win at gambling in Vegas in order to start over. Jon Voight, Ann-Margret, Burt Young. w. Jon Voight, Al Schwartz, d. Hal Ashby.

COMEDY: COMEDY DRAMA: One Last Time; Gambling; Las Vegas; Coulda Been Good

Looking for Love, 1964, 83m, ★★/$$$, MGM/MGM-UA. A girl singer tries to choose between a career and snagging Mr. Right at the pool. Connie Francis, Jim Hutton, Johnny Carson. w. Ruth Brooks Flippen, d. Don Weis.

ROMANCE: MELODRAMA: MUSICALS: Music Movies; Teenagers; Teenage Movies; Young Women; Female Protagonists; Singers; Career Women

Looking for Mr. Goodbar, 1977, 135m, ★★★★/$$$$, Par/Par, R/P-S-FN-MN. A teacher of the deaf (Diane Keaton) during the day spends her nights barhopping and then hopping into bed with strange and sometimes dangerous men. Tuesday Weld (BSActress), Richard Gere, Tom Berenger, William Atherton. w. Richard Brooks (BAScr), adap. Judith Rossner, d. Richard Brooks. Oscars: 2-0.

DRAMA: SUSPENSE: TRAGEDY: Psychological Drama; Psychological Thriller; Character Studies; Sexuality; Sexual Revolution; Obsessions; Stalkers; Promiscuity; Dual Lives; Female Among Males; Deaf People; Teachers; New York Life; Disco Era; Abused Women;

Dangerous Men; Romance Dangerous; Single Women; Violence-Sudden; Time Capsules; Evil Men; 1970s; Female Protagonists
(Montenegro; Saturday Night Fever)

The Looking Glass War, 1969, 107m, ★★½/$$, Col/RCA-Col, R/S-V. A young Polish man (Christopher Jones) is sent into East Germany to retrieve a secret film, but does he know his friends from his foes? Pia Degermark, Ralph Richardson, Anthony Hopkins, Susan George. w. d. Frank Pierson, N-adap. John LeCarre.
DRAMA: SUSPENSE: Spy Films; Spies; Iron Curtain-Behind the; Iron Curtain-Escape from; Undercover; Double Crossings; Berlin
(The Spy Who Came In from the Cold; The Russia House; Torn Curtain)

Look Who's Talking, 1989, 96m, ★★★/$$$$$, MCEG-Tri/Col-Tri, PG. An unwed mother's baby narrates his adventures from the womb to meeting his potential new father. Kirstie Alley, John Travolta, Olympia Dukakis, George Segal, voice of Bruce Willis. w. d. Amy Heckerling.
COMEDY: Mothers-Unwed; Babies-Having; Romance with Married Person; Taxi Drivers; Narrated Films; Sleeper Hits; Blockbusters; Female Screenwriters; Female Directors; Female Protagonists; Writer-Directors; Sidekicks-wisecracking

Look Who's Talking Now, 1992, 95m, ★★/$, Tri-Star/Col, PG. This time, the family's dogs begin talking to each other, bitching about what's going on. Voices of Diane Keaton, Danny DeVito; John Travolta, Kirstie Alley, Olympia Dukakis, George Segal, Lysette Anthony. w. Tom Ropelewski, Leslie Dixon, d. Ropelewski.
COMEDY: Animal Stories; Animals-Talking; Pet Stories; Family Comedy; Babies; Narrated Films; Female Screenwriters; Female Protagonists

Look Who's Talking Too, 1990, 81m, ★★/$$$, MCEG-Tri/Col-Tri, PG. The baby of the first is joined by the voice Roseanne Barr as his new sister, both dealing with the marriage of their parents. Kirstie Alley, John Travolta, Olympia Dukakis, voices of Bruce Willis, Mel Brooks, Damon Wayans. w. Amy Heckerling, Neal Israel, d. Amy Heckerling.
COMEDY: Newlyweds; Marriage on the Rocks; Narrated Films; Babies; Female

Protagonists; Female Screenwriters; Female Directors

Loophole, 1980, 105m, ★★/$, mdale/ Media, R. A bank robber plans a big heist of a London bank, if his partners will enable it to happen. Albert Finney, Martin Sheen, Susannah York, Johnathan Pryce, Robert Morley. w. Johnathan Hales, N-adap. Robert Pollock, d. John Quested.
COMEDY DRAMA: Heist Stories; Bank Robberies; Con Artists; British Films; Overlooked at Release

Loose Ankles, 1930, 66m, ★★★/$$, First-WB/NA. An heiress will lose her money if she's somehow involved in a scandal, and the other possible heirs plan to make this a reality. Loretta Young, Douglas Fairbanks, Jr. w. Gene Towne, P-adap. Sam Janney, d. Ted Wilde.
COMEDY: Screwball Comedy; Comedy of Errors; Inheritances at Stake; Heiresses; Scandals

Loot (Gimme My Money, Honey!), 1970, 101m, ★★★½/$$, EMI/HBO, NA, R/S-P. A nasty thief hides his mother's body in the house so he can use her coffin to hide money from one of his heists-but what if someone finds out about the money, or the body? Richard Attenborough, Lee Remick, Milo O'Shea. w. Ray Galton, Alan Simpson, P-adap. Joe Orton, d. Silvio Narrizzano.
COMEDY DRAMA: COMEDY: Black Comedy; Comedy-Morbid; Con Artists; Hide the Dead Body; Thieves; Comedy of Errors; Coulda Been Great; British Films; Overlooked at Release
(Entertaining Mr. Sloane; Greedy)

Lord Jim, 1964, 154m, ★★★/$$, Col/RCA-Col. A noble seaman travels the world having altruistic adventures, while also encountering danger, particularly in Southeast Asia. Peter O'Toole, James Mason, Eli Wallach, Paul Lukas, Jack Hawkins, Akim Tamiroff. w. d. Richard Brooks, N-adap. Joseph Conrad.
DRAMA: ADVENTURE: Epics; Adventures at Sea; World Travel; Classic Literary Adaptations; Coulda Been Great; Asia
(Lawrence of Arabia; Heart of Darkness)

Lord Love a Duck, 1966, 105m, ★★★½/$$, UA/MGM-UA, NA. Teenagers and their antics in southern California of the 60s from an adult, satirical perspective; precursor to *Fast Times at Ridgemont High*. Roddy McDowell,

Tuesday Weld, Lola Albright, Ruth Gordon, Harvey Korman. w. Larry Johnson, George Axelrod, d. Axelrod.
COMEDY: SATIRE: Teenagers; Teenage Movies; California; Beach Movies; Suburban Life; Young People; Mindgames; Ensemble Films; Hidden Gems; Time Capsules; Cult Films
(Fast Times at Ridgemont High; Beach Blanket Bingo; The Happening)

Lord of the Flies, 1963, 91m, ★★★/$$, Ind-Col/NA. James Aubrey, Tom Chapin. w. d. Peter Brook, N-adap. William Golding.

Lord of the Flies, 1990, 90m, ★★½/$, CR-Col/Tri-Col, PG-13/P. A plane crashes in the ocean and the teenage boys who survive start a small society of their own to survive, leading to much conflict. Chris Furth, Balthazar Getty, Badgett Dale, Danuel Pipoly. w. Sara Schiff, d. Harry Hook.
DRAMA: TRAGEDY: Allegorical Stories; Social Drama; Message Films; Boyhood; Men in Conflict; Ensemble Films; Ensembles-Male; Ensembles-Children; Stranded on an Island; Airplane Crashes; Islands; Female Screenwriters

Lord of the Rings, 1978, 133m, ★★★/ $$$, UA/Republic, G. An evil lord in the fantasy world of the hobbits loses his powerful ring and it's up to Bilbo Baggins, the central hobbit, to keep him from getting it back. w. Chris Conkling, Peter Beagle, N-adap. J.R.R. Tolkien, d. Ralph Bakshi.
Cartoons; **CHILDREN'S:** Fantasy; **SCI-FI:** Sword & Sorcery; Cult Films
(The Black Cauldron)

The Lords of Discipline, 1983, 103m, ★★½/$$, Par/Par, R/P-V. Tensions arise among cadets at a Citadel-like military institute. David Keith, Robert Protsky, Michael Biehn, Barbara Babcock, Rick Rossovich. w. Thomas Pope, Lloyd Fonvielle, N-adap. Pat Conroy, d. Franc Roddam.
DRAMA: Social Drama; Military Stories; Military Schools; Boarding Schools; Coming of Age; Men in Conflict; Young Men; Teenagers; Southerns; Secrets-Keeping; Conformism; Oppression
(A Few Good Men; Taps; Toy Soldiers)

The Lords of Flatbush, 1974, 86m, ★★★/$$$, Col/RCA-Col, R/P-S. Street toughs in 1950s Brooklyn live their sometimes eccentric lives and try to stay out of trouble while creating it for others. Perry King, Sylvester Stallone, Henry Winkler (began his Fonzie role), Paul Mace, Susan Blakely. w. Stephen Verona, Martin Davidson, Gayle Glecker, Sylvester Stallone, d. Verona, Davidson.

DRAMA: COMEDY DRAMA: Ensemble Films; Ensembles-Male; Gangs-White; Inner City Life; Nostalgia; 1950s; Sleeper Hits; Time Capsules
(The Wanderers; Diner; American Graffiti; Heaven Help Us; Five Corners)

Lorna Doone, 1934, 90m, ★★½/$$$, London/NA. In old Scotland a romance develops between a simple man and a young woman who turns out to be someone much more than he realized. Victoria Hopper, John Loder, Margaret Lockwood, Roy Emerson. w. Dorothy Farnum, Miles Malleson, Gordon Wellesley, N-adap. R.D. Blackmore, d. Basil Dean.

DRAMA: ROMANCE: Heiresses; Kidnappings; Mistaken Identities; Hiding Out; Scotland; 1600s
REMAKE: 1990 (Par)

Lorenzo's Oil, 1992, 137m, ★★★★/$$ (LR), Universal/MCA-U, PG. Parents of a child with a seemingly unbeatable degenerative disorder (ALD) use common sense and ingenuity to find what the medical establishment hadn't been able to-a treatment. Susan Sarandon (BActress), Nick Nolte, Peter Ustinov. w. George Kennedy, George Miller (BOScr), d. Kennedy, Miller. Oscars: 2-0.

DRAMA: MELODRAMA: Marriage Drama; Family Drama; Disease Stories; Fighting the System; Solutions/Cures-Search for; Detective Stories; Detectives-Amateur; Medical Detectives; Children-Saving; Disabled People; True Stories; Underrated; Overlooked; Hidden Gems
(Son-Rise, a Miracle of Love; House of Cards; The Karen Ann Quinlan Story)

Loser Takes All, 1956, 88m, ★★½/$$, British Lion/NA. A stuffy accountant takes his wife to Monte Carlo, but instead of having fun, they grow apart as greed and the bright lights distract them. Rosanno Brazzi, Glynis Johns, Robert Morley. w. N-adap. Graham Greene, d. Ken Annakin.

COMEDY DRAMA: Marriage on the Rocks; Gambling; Monte Carlo; Romance-Triangles

Losing Isaiah, 1995, 108m, ★★★/$$, Par/Par, R/P-S. A social worker raises a young baby neglected by a crack addicted young black woman. But when the black woman returns to reclaim her son, a black lawyer defends her rights to have the boy on the basis of race, since the social worker is white. Jessica Lange, Halle Berry, David Strathairn, Daisy Eagan, Cuba Gooding, Jr., Samuel L. Jackson, Regina Taylor, Marc John Jeffries, Joie Lee, La Tanya Richardson. w. Naomi Foner, N-adap. Seth Margolis, d. Stephen Gyllenhaal.

DRAMA: MELODRAMA: Black vs. White; Children-Adopted; Social Workers; Drugs-Addictions; Children-Losing/Parting with; Female Protagonists; Female Screenwriters
(White Banners)

Losin' It, 1982, 104m, ★★/$$, Ind/New Line, R/S-P. A carload of horny teenagers goes to Mexico with a married woman there for a divorce, with whom the lead wants to lose his virginity. Tom Cruise, Shelley Long, John Stockwell, Jackie Earl Haley. d. Curtis Hanson.

COMEDY: Sex Comedy; Erotic Comedy; Romance-Older Woman/Younger Men; Virgins; Teenagers; Teenage Movies; Crossing the Border; Road Movies; Road Movies-Guys in Convertibles; Unintentionally Funny; Curiosities; Independent Films
(Night Shift; My Tutor)
(Ed: Very interesting for the early Cruise and Long)

Lost (Tears For Simon), 1955, 89m, ★★½/$, Ind/NA. The police search for a missing child in England. David Farrar, David Knight. w. Janet Green, d. Guy Green.

DRAMA: Police Stories; Missing Persons; Missing Children; Kidnappings; British Films
(Without a Trace; Into Thin Air; Adam; Bunny Lake is Missing)

Lost and Found, 1979, 105m, ★★½/$$, Col/RCA-Col, PG. A widower (George Segal) meets up with a tenacious British woman (Glenda Jackson) at a ski resort and proceed to break each other's legs. Maureen Stapleton, Paul Sorvino. w. Melvin Frank, Jack Rose, d. Frank.

COMEDY: ROMANCE: Romantic Comedy; Romance-Opposites Attract; Romance-Bickering; Skiing; Widowers; Starting Over; Coulda Been Great
(A Touch of Class; House Calls; Hopscotch)
(Ed: A reteaming of the *A Touch of Class*

success, but the charm is lost in the sparring somehow, though still entertaining)

Lost Angel, 1943, 91m, ★★★/$$, MGM/NA. A reporter finds a cute little girl and winds up adopting her. Margaret O'Brien, James Craig, Marsha Hunt. w. Isobel Lennart, d. Roy Rowlands.

DRAMA: MELODRAMA: COMEDY DRAMA: SATIRE: Journalists; Children-Adopted; Children-Finding; Men and Girls; Fathers-Surrogate/Adopted; Forgotten Films; Female Screenwriters
(Little Miss Marker; Sorrowful Jones; Three Men & a Baby; Life with Mikey; Bachelor Mother)

Lost Angels, 1989, 116m, ★★★/$, Orion/Orion, R/P-S. A middle-class teenager in Los Angeles gets involved with drugs and his uncaring parents send him off to a private institution for children of the rich. But it doesn't necessarily do any good. Donald Sutherland, Adam Howovitz, Amy Locane, Don Bloomfield, Celia Weston, Graham Beckel, Patricia Richardson, Joseph d'Angerio. w. Michaell Weller, d. Hugh Hudson.

DRAMA: Social Drama; Los Angeles; Drugs-Addiction; Asylums; Teenagers; Aliens; Young Men; Young Men-Angry; Rebels
(Rebel Without a Cause; Less Than Zero)

Lost Boundaries, 1949, 105m, ★★/$, Ind/NA. A farmer and his wife discover they have black ancestors and must deal with their little town's reaction. Mel Ferrer, Beatrice Pearson. w. Virginia Shaler, Eugene Ling, d. Alfred Werker.

DRAMA: MELODRAMA: Race Relations; Secrets-Keeping; Secrets-Racial; Small-town Scandals; Secrets-Racial; Romance-Interracial; Forgotten Films; Ahead of its Time

The Lost Boys, 1987, 92m, ★★★/$$$, WB/WB, PG/V-P-S. Two boys (Jason Patric, Corey Haim) move with their mother (Dianne Wiest) to an idyllic coastal community and are soon beset by a gang of teenage biker vampires. Jami Gertz, Kiefer Sutherland, Barnard Hughes. w. Janice Fischer, Jeffrey Boam, James Jermias, d. Joel Schumacher.

HORROR: COMEDY DRAMA: Horror Comedy; Black Comedy; Vampires; Teenagers; Teenage Movies; New in Town; Small-town Life; Female Screenwriters

(The Hunger; Buffy, the Vampire Slayer; Near Dark; The Loveless)

Lost Command, 1966, 128m, ★★/$$, Col/RCA-Col. French paratroopers do their undercover work in Indo-China and Algeria developing an anti-war sentiment. Anthony Quinn, Alain Delon, George Segal, Claudia Cardinale. w. Nelson Gidding, N-adap. Jean Larteguy (*The Centurions*), d. Mark Robson.

DRAMA: ADVENTURE: War Stories; Spies; Spy Films; Undercover; Asia; Africa

The Lost Honor of Katharina Blum, 1975, 97m, ★★★/$$, Ind/Sultan, R/S-P-V. The man a woman's been seeing is wanted by the police and when he disappears, she becomes the target of the investigation. Angela Winkler, Mario Adorf, Deitar Lasser. d. Volker Schlondorff.

DRAMA: Fugitives from the Law; Political Drama; Accused Unjustly; Framed?; Romance-Dangerous; Dangerous Men; Innocent Bystanders; German Films; Female Protagonists

TV REMAKE: The Lost Honor of Katherine Beck

Lost Horizon, 1937, 130m, ★★★★/$$$$, Col/RCA-Col. Several people escape the Chinese revolution and are taken to Tibet to Shangri-La, a utopia where no war exists and no one ages, but can they deal with perfection? Ronald Colman, H.B. Warner (BSActor), Thomas Mitchell, Edward Everett Horton, Sam Jaffe, Jane Wyatt. w. Robert Riskin, N-adap. James Hilton, d. Frank Capra. BPicture, BOScore, BArt. Oscars: 4-1.

ADVENTURE: Fantasy; **DRAMA:** Utopias; Anti-War Films; Ensemble Films; Dreams; Aging-Reverse; Asia; China

REMAKE: 1973 version

Lost Horizon, 1973, 143m, ★★1/2/$, Col/RCA-Col, PG. Peter Finch, Liv Ullman, Sally Kellerman, Bobby Van, George Kennedy, Michael York, Olivia Hussey, John Gielgud, Charles Boyer. w. Larry Kramer, d. Charles Jarrott.

MUSICAL: Musical Drama; **ADVENTURE:** Fantasy; **DRAMA:** Utopias; Anti-War Films; Ensemble Films; Dreams; Aging-Reverse; Asia; China; Flops-Major; Unintentionally Funny; Guilty Pleasures; Production Design-Outstanding

Lost in America, 1985, 91m, ★★★/$$, G-WB/WB, PG. A yuppie couple (Albert Brooks, Julie Hagerty) toss their big city life away for a Winnebago and wind up in Vegas on the verge of losing their nest egg. w. Albert Brooks, Monica Johnson, d. Brooks.

COMEDY: COMEDY DRAMA: SATIRE: Road Movies; Risking it All; Losing it All; Las Vegas; Gambling; Yuppies; Vacations; Unemployment; American Dream; 1980s; Hidden Gems; Coulda Been Great; Female Screenwriters

Lost in Yonkers, 1993, 114m, ★★★/$$, Col/Col, PG. Two boys are sent to their cantankerous grandmother's house when their father goes away on business-a house that also includes their kooky spinster aunt who teaches them a thing or two. Mercedes Ruehl, Irene Worth, Richard Dreyfuss, Brad Stoll, Mike Damus, David Straithairn. w. P-adap. Neil Simon, d. Martha Coolidge.

COMEDY DRAMA: Family Comedy; Eccentric People; Jewish People; Spinsters; Women and Boys; Relatives-Troublesome; Lonely People; Roommates; Orphans; Boys; 1940s; Female Directors; Pulitzer Prize Adaptations; Narrated Films; Child Protagonists; Overlooked at Release

A Lost Lady, 1934, 71m, ★★1/2/$$, WB/WB. A romance between a younger woman (Barbara Stanwyck) and an older man develops during the Depression, but not without repercussions. Frank Morgan, Ricardo Cortez. w. Gene Markey, Kathryn Scola, N-adap. Willa Cather, d. Alfred Green.

DRAMA: MELODRAMA: ROMANCE: Romantic Drama; Romance-Older Men/Younger Woman; Single Women; Depression Era; Female Protagonists; Female Screenwriters

(Love in the Afternoon)

The Lost Language of Cranes, 1992, 90m, ★★★/$$, BBC-PBS/Fox, R/S-P-MN. A gay man has a major family crisis when he admits his sexuality, but his father is facing an even greater crisis. Brian Cox, Angus MacFayden, Eileen Atkins, Corey Parker, Cathy Tyson. N-adap. David Leavitt, d. Nigel Finch.

DRAMA: Gay Awakenings; Gay Men; Family Drama; Fathers & Sons; Secrets-Keeping; Secrets-Consuming; Homosexual Secrets; Mothers-Troublesome; Midlife Crisis; Nervous Breakdowns; British Films; TV Movies; Hidden Gems

(Consenting Adult; Andre's Mother; An Early Frost)

(Ed: The twists make this a step above the usual gay, coming-out melodrama)

The Lost Man, 1969, 113m, ★★/$, U/MCA-U, PG. A man goes into hiding after a robbery and finds himself in the middle of a civil rights dilemma. Sidney Poitier, Joanna Shimkus, Paul Winfield, Richard Dysart. w. d. Robert Alan Arthur.

DRAMA: SUSPENSE: Fugitives from the Law; Hiding Out; Thieves; Social Drama; Race Relations; Black Men; Black Casts; Romance-Interracial; Good Premise Unfulfilled; Writer-Directors

REMAKE/RETREAD OF: Odd Man Out

(Warm December; The Mark of the Hawk)

The Lost Moment, 1947, 89m, ★★★/$$, U/Republic. An American publisher goes to Venice to find a woman poet over one hundred years old in order to publish her love letter from youth. Robert Cummings, Susan Hayward, Agnes Moorehead. w. Leonardo Bercovici, N-adap. Henry James, *The Aspern Papers*, Martin Gabel.

DRAMA: MELODRAMA: ROMANCE: Romantic Drama; Americans Abroad; Writers; Poets; Elderly Women; Flashbacks; Forgotten Films; Hidden Gems

(Daisy Miller; Death in Venice)

The Lost Weekend, 1945, 101m, ★★★★/$$$$, Par/Par. During one long weekend, a young writer tries to deal with his alcoholism and subsequent hallucinations, struggling to hold on to dear life before it's too late. Ray Milland (BActor), Jane Wyman, Howard daSilva. w. Charles Brackett, Bill Wilder (**BScr**), N-adap. Charles Jackson, d. Bill Wilder (**BDirector**). **BPicture**, BCin, BScore, BEdit. Oscars: 7-4.

DRAMA: MELODRAMA: Message Films; Character Studies; Writers; Alcoholics; Depressions; Illusions; Nightmares; One Day Stories; New York Life; 1940s

(Days of Wine and Roses; Clean and Sober; Smash-up; Story of a Woman; Dangerous; The Morning After; Leaving Las Vegas)

Louisiana Purchase, 1941, 98m, ★★★/$$$, Par/Par. Political corruption abounds with music and scoundrels in

Louisiana at the point of purchase. Bob Hope, Vera Zorina, Victor Moore. w. Jerome Chodorov, Joseph Fiels, P-adap. Morris Ryskind, Irving Berlin, d. Irving Berlin.

MUSICAL: COMEDY: Musical Comedy; Political; Politicians; 1800s; Southerns; Costume Drama; Hidden Gems

Louisiana Story, 1948, 77m, ★★★/$, Ind/Home Vision. A boy who lives in the bayous of Louisiana watches oil drillers invade his world for industrial uses. Joseph Boudreaux. w. Robert and Frances Flaherty, d. Robert Flaherty. BOStory. Oscars: 1-0.

DRAMA: Documentaries; Docudrama; Documentary Style; Environmental Dilemmas; Message Films; Boyhood; Swamps; Cajuns; Louisiana; Oil People; Nature-Back to; Narrated Films
(Ed: Produced by Standard Oil, it's a sly attempt at propaganda, to show how oil drilling won't spoil such a beautiful environment)

Loulou, 1980, 105m, ★★1/2/$$, Gaumont-UA/New Yorker, R/S. A career woman falls for lazy working class guy and tries to make a go of it, despite other interests. Isabelle Huppert, Gerard Depardieu, Guy Marchand. w. Arlette Langmann, d. Maurice Pialat.

DRAMA: ROMANCE: Romantic Drama; Class Conflicts; Roommates; Working Class; Career Women; French Films; Quiet Little Films; Female Protagonists; Female Screenwriters
(Green Card; Too Beautiful for You; Momma, There's a Man in Your Bed)

Love, 1927, 84m (Silent), ★★★/$$$$, MGM/MGM-UA. A version of *Anna Karenina*, where a wealthy Russian woman leaves her cold husband and their son for her true love and finds herself doomed (Or not-there were two endings made.). Greta Garbo, John Gilbert. w. Frances Marion, Lorna Moon, N-adap. Leo Tolstoy, *Anna Karenina*, d. Edmund Goulding.

DRAMA: TRAGEDY: ROMANCE: MELO-DRAMA: Romantic Drama; Tearjerkers; Romance-Triangles; Romance-Choosing Right Person; Russians; Classic Literary Adaptations
REMAKES: Anna Karenina, 1935, 1985
(Anna Karenina; Romance; Anna Christie)

Love Affair, 1932, 68m, ★★★/$$$$, Col/NA. An heiress falls in love with a pilot. Humphrey Bogart, Dorothy Mackaill, Jack Kennedy. w. Jo Swerling, SS-adap. Ursula Parrott, d. Thornton Freeland.

ROMANCE: COMEDY DRAMA: Romantic Comedy; Romance-Opposites Attract; Heiresses; Class Conflicts; Working Class

Love Affair, 1939, 89m, ★★★1/2/$$$$, RKO/Turner, Nos. A Frenchman (Charles Boyer) meets an American woman on a transatlantic cruise and falls in love, but soon the tale turns toward tragedy and tears. Irene Dunne (BActress), Maria Ouspenkaya (BSActress). w. Delmer Daves, Donald Ogden Stewart, Mildred Cram, Leo McCarey (BOStory), d. McCarey. BPicture, BArt, BOSong. Oscars: 6-0.

ROMANCE: DRAMA: MELODRAMA: Romantic Drama; Tearjerkers; **TRAGEDY:** Romance-Reluctant; Americans Abroad; Disabled People; Romance on Vacation; Ships; Vacations-European; Empire State Building
REMAKES: An Affair to Remember; 1994 version

Love Affair, 1994, 105m, ★★★/$$, WB/WB, PG-13/P-S. A retelling of the classic weepy with some interesting new takes and beautiful scenery, where a fading sports hero crashlands with a singer on a Pacific Island and though both have fiances, they begin a long-term romance at a distance until tragedy almost tears them apart. Warren Beatty, Annette Bening, Katharine Hepburn, Garry Shandling, Chloe Webb, Pierce Brosnan, Kate Capshaw, Paul Mazursky, Brenda Vaccaro, Barry Miller, Harold Ramis, Taylor Dane. w. Robert Towne, Warren Beatty, S-adap. Delmer Daves and Donald Ogden Stewart. d. Glenn Gordon Caron.

DRAMA: MELODRAMA: ROMANCE: Tearjerkers; Romance-Reluctant; Airplane Crashes; Ships-Cruise; Disabled People; Romance on Vacation; Empire State Building; Old Fashioned Recent Films
REMAKE OF: 1932 and 1939 versions and *An Affair to Remember*
(Sleepless in Seattle; Bugsy)
(Ed: A leisurely old-fashioned romance done justice, but not particularly worthy of remaking. Hepburn is great in a small but memorable part and the chemistry seems genuine if under-developed

between the leads. Worth it for romance or Beatty fans)

Love Among the Ruins, 1975, 100m, ★★★★/$$$$, ABC-TV/Fox. A wealthy matron (Katharine Hepburn, BActress Emmy) who won't tell her age is sued by a young man who claims she reneged on an engagement, but she's forgotten the prosecutor in the case (Laurence Olivier, BActor Emmy) is an old, forgotten flame who might yet re-ignite. d. George Cukor.

COMEDY DRAMA: ROMANCE: Romantic Comedy; Romance-Older Women/Younger Men; Comedy of Manners; Trials; Romance Reunited; Romance-Elderly; Romance-Middle Aged; Romance-Reluctant; Romance-Bickering; Engagements-Breaking; Feisty Females; Marrying Up; Romance with Lawyer; Edwardian Era; London; Elderly People; Stagelike Films; Hidden Gems
(The Divorce of Lady X; The Glass Menagerie [1973])

Love and Bullets, 1978, 103m, ★★/$$, ITC-U/MCA-U, R/EV-S. A cop bent on revenge against a mobster brings his girlfriend back from seclusion in Europe to coerce him out. Charles Bronson, Jill Ireland, Rod Steiger, Strother Martin, Michael V. Gazzo. w. Wendell Mayes, John Melson, d. Stuart Rosenberg.

ACTION: Revenge; Mob Stories; Mob Girls; Kidnappings; Bounty Hunters; Police Stories; Detectives-Police
(Telefon; Murphy's Law; Death Wish)

Love and Death, 1975, 85m, ★★★★/$$$, UA/MGM-UA, PG/S. A mishmash spoof of Russian classics where it doesn't matter one bit if you don't have a clue as to the references, the situations of the nerdy fellow who's been sentenced to death remembering the girl who doesn't know he exists are universal and immediately hilarious. Woody Allen, Diane Keaton. w. d. Woody Allen.

COMEDY: Spoofs; Black Comedy; Comedy-Morbid; Comedy-Slapstick; Historical Drama; Nerds; Nerds and Babes; Romance-Unrequited; Death-Impending; Russians; 1800s; Writer-Directors
(Sleeper; The History of the World, Part One; The Twelve Chairs)

Love and Hisses, 1937, 84m, ★★1/2/$$, 20th/NA. A musician and a gossip columnist continue their bickering in this sequel. Walter Winchell, Ben Bernie,

Bert Lahr. w. Art Arthur, Curtis Kenyon, d. Sidney Lanfield.

COMEDY: Friends as Enemies; Feuds; Men in Conflict; Musicians; Big Band Era; Gossip; Rumors; Journalists

SEQUEL: Love Thy Neighbor

Love and Human Remains, 1995, 99m, ★★★/$$, Sony/Sony, R/S-V. A serial killer is on the loose, as a gay man and his female friend try to find love, or at least sex, without becoming victims. Thomas Gibson, Ruth Mitchell, Cameron Bancroft, Mia Kirshner, Joanne Vannicola, Matthew Ferguson, Rick Roberts. w. Brad Fraser, d. Denys Arcand.

DRAMA: SUSPENSE: Serial Killers; Friends as Enemies; Gay Men; Canada; Friendship Between Sexes; Independent Films

(The Adjuster; Exotica; Speaking Parts)

Love and Money, 1980, 95m, ★★/$, Lorimar-UA/NA, R/P-V-S. A man pursues a wealthy man's wife and finds himself in deep trouble with the men the husband gets his money from. Ray Sharkey, Ornella Muti, Klaus Kinski, Armand Assante. w. d. James Toback.

DRAMA: MELODRAMA: Crime Drama; Kidnappings; Mob Stories; Romance-Triangles; Enemy-Sympathizing with the; Writer-Directors

Love and Pain and the Whole Damn Thing, 1972, 113m, ★★★/$, Par/NA, PG/S. A young man in Spain (Timothy Bottoms) has an affair with an older woman who has many problems she's hiding. Maggie Smith. w. Alvin Sargent, d. Alan J. Pakula.

ROMANCE: COMEDY DRAMA: MELO-DRAMA: Romantic Drama; Tearjerker; Disease Stories; Romance-Older Women/Younger Men; Young Men; Americans Abroad; Romance on Vacation; Death-Impending; Spain; Coulda Been Great

(Summertime; Love Story; The Lonely Passion of Judith Hearne)

Love at First Bite, 1979, 96m, ★★★/$$$$, AIP/Orion, WB, PG/S-P. Count Dracula (George Hamilton) goes cargo class on a jet to New York hoping to rob blood banks and fall in love if not foiled by the crazy Von Helsing (Richard Benjamin). Susan St. James, Arte Johnson, Dick Shawn. w. Robert Kaufman, d. Stan Dragoti.

COMEDY: Spoofs; Spoofs-Vampire; Comedy-Slapstick; Comedy of Errors;

Unbelieved; Mental Illness; Vampires; Old-Fashioned Recent Films; Underrated; Sleeper Hits

(Dracula: Dead and Loving It; Zorro, the Gay Blade)

(Ed: Major hit at the time and justly so)

Love at Large, 1990, 97m, ★★★/$ (LR), Orion/Orion, R/S-P. A gruff and not so bright private detective goes after a man and the woman he's holding captive while his girlfriend puts a detective on his trail, too. Tom Berenger, Elizabeth Perkins, Anne Archer, Kate Capshaw, Annette O'Toole, Ann Magnuson. w. d. Alan Rudolph.

COMEDY DRAMA: Detective Stories; Detectives-Matrimonial; Romance-Triangles; Romance-Reluctant; Misunderstandings; Chase Movies; Double Crossings; Good Premise Unfulfilled; Coulda Been Great; Writer-Directors

(Last Rites)

Love Before Breakfast, 1936, 90m, ★★½/$$$, U/MCA-U. A rich young woman is pursued by two different men and has to decide who really loves her the most. Carole Lombard, Preston Foster, Cesar Romero. w. Herbert Fields, N-adap. Faith Baldwin, Spinster Dinner, d. Walter Lang.

COMEDY: ROMANCE: Romantic Comedy; Screwball Comedy; Romance-Choosing the Right Person; Romance-Triangles; Men Fighting Over Women; Forgotten Films

(The Awful Truth; Hands Across the Table)

The Love Bug, 1969, 107m, ★★★½/$$$$$, Disney/Disney, G. A VW Bug has a mind of its own as a race car driver soon finds-a meddlesome mind. David Tomlinson, Dean Jones, Michele Lee, Buddy Hackett. w. Bill Walsh, Don daGradi, d. Robert Stevenson.

COMEDY: CHILDREN'S: FAMILY: Chase Movies; Car Chases; Car Racing; Objects with Personalities; Comedy-Disneyesque; Sleeper Hits

SEQUELS: Herbie, The Love Bug; Herbie Rides Again; Herbie Goes to Monte Carlo

(Ed: One of the biggest hits of the year)

Love Crazy, 1941, 100m, ★★★½/$$$, MGM/MGM-UA. To stave off a divorce, a man does all kinds of things to keep his wife. William Powell, Myrna Loy, Gail Patrick, Jack Carson. w. William Ludwig, Charles Lederer, David Hertz, d. Jack Conway.

COMEDY: Screwball Comedy;

ROMANCE: Romantic Comedy; Divorce; Marriage Comedy; Marriage on the Rocks; Romance-Reunited; Hidden Gems

(The Awful Truth; I Love You Again)

Love Crimes, 1991, 90m, ★★/$, Sovereign/Miramax-HBO, R/S-V-FN. A DA in Atlanta travels to Savannah to go undercover as a model in order to trap a shady photographer raping his subjects. Sean Young, Patrick Bergin, James Read. w. Allan Moyle, Laurie Frank, d. Lizzie Borden.

DRAMA: SUSPENSE: Women in Jeopardy; Detective Stories; Lawyers as Detectives; Romance-Unprofessional; Undercover; Rape/Rapists; Photographers; Pornography World; Georgia; Southerns; Good Premise Unfulfilled; Coulda Been Great; Female Screenwriters; Female Directors; Female Protagonists

(Sleeping with the Enemy; Mirage [1994])

(Ed: Unflinching in its daringness, but misses the mark-a controversial one)

Love Field, 1992, 104m, ★★★/$, Orion/Orion, PG. At the time of JFK's assassination, a bubbly beautician (Michelle Pfeiffer, BActress) who idolizes Mrs. Kennedy wants to get to the funeral in Washington and along the way, meets a black man at the airport (Denis Haysbert) she has deal with her attraction to. w. Don Roos, d. Johnathan Kaplan. Oscars: 1-0.

DRAMA: MELODRAMA: Romance-Interracial; Road Movies; Funerals; Assassinations; Ordinary People Stories; 1960s; Hairdressers; Texas; JFK

(Jungle Fever; A Patch of Blue)

Love from a Stranger, 1936, 90m, ★★★/$$$, Ind/Nos. Ann Harding, Basil Rathbone, Bruce Seton. w. Frances Marion, P-adap. Frank Vosper, SS-adap. Agatha Christie (Philomel Cottage), d. Rowland Lee.

Love from a Stranger, 1947, 81m, ★★½/$$, Col/New World. A woman realizes a bit too late that her new husband may be psychotic. Sylvia Sidney, John Hodiak, Ann Richards. w. Philip MacDonald, d. Richard Whorf.

SUSPENSE: Enemy-Sleeping with the; Newlyweds; Dangerous Men; Romance-Dangerous; Agatha Christie; Women in Jeopardy; Female Protagonists

(Sabotage; Undercurrent; Rebecca; Suspicion)

The Love God?, 1969, 103m, ★★½/$$, U/MCA-U, PG/S. A nerdy scientist (Don Knotts) is mistaken to be a Hugh Hefner type and becomes a sex symbol, believe it or not. Not. w. d. Nat Hiken.
COMEDY: FARCE: Mistaken Identities; Misunderstandings; Sexy Men; Nerds; Nerds and Babes; Sexy Women; Pornography World; 1960s; Curiosities
RETREAD OF: Will Success Spoil Rock Hunter?
The Love Goddesses, 1965, 87m, ★★★/NA, Par/Par. A compendium of clips of sexy female stars up to that time. w. Saul Turell, Greme Ferguson.
Documentaries; Sexy Women; Actresses; Sexuality; Bimbos; Hollywood Life; Compilation Films
Love Has Many Faces, 1964, 104m, ★★/$$, Col/Goodtimes, PG/S. A wealthy woman (Lana Turner) marries a young hunk who apparently isn't enough, as the man she's having an affair with turns up dead and fingers begin pointing. Cliff Robertson, Hugh O'Brian, Stefanie Powers, Ruth Roman. w. Marguerite Roberts, d. Alexander Singer.
MELODRAMA: MURDER: MURDER MYSTERY: SUSPENSE: Accused Unjustly; Romance-Triangles; Romance-Older Women/Younger Men; Sexy Men; Gigolos; Unintentionally Funny
(Portrait in Black; Madame X; Autumn Leaves)
Love Hurts, 1989, 90m, ★★½/$, Vestron/Vestron, PG. A man returns home for a reunion with his parents and friends, but primarily with his children as they face a divorce. Jeff Daniels, Cloris Leachman, Cynthia Sikes, Judith Ivey, Amy Wright. w. Ron Nyswaner, d. Bud Yorkin.
COMEDY DRAMA: MELODRAMA: Fathers & Daughters; Fathers Alone; Divorces; Marriage on the Rocks; Reunions; Romance Reunited; Small-town Life; Starting Over; Coulda Been Good
(Short Time; Send Me No Flowers)
Love in a Goldfish Bowl, 1961, 88m, ★★/$$, Par/Par. Two teen idols (Fabian, Tommy Sands) take off for Hawaii for a family vacation and young love. Jan Sterling. w. d. Jack Sher.
COMEDY: ROMANCE: Love-First; Coming of Age; Romance on Vacation; Teenagers; Teenage Movies; Beach Movies; Family Comedy; Hawaii

Love in Bloom, 1934, 76m, ★★½/$$, Par/NA. A traveling show owner's daughter (Gracie Allen) meets up with a songwriting wisecracker (George Burns) and plants some love. w. J. P. McEvoy, Keene Thompson, d. Elliott Nugent.
COMEDY: ROMANCE: Romantic Comedy; Vaudeville; Screwball Comedy; Comedians; Songwriting
(The Burns and Allen Show, TV SERIES)
A Love in Germany, 1983, ★★★/$$, Gaumont-Col/RCA-Col, R/S-FN. A German woman (Hanna Schuygulla) falls for a younger Jewish POW she tries to help at the outbreak of World War II. Marie-Christine Barrault, Armin Mueller-Stahl. w. Boleslaw Michaelek, Agnieska Holland, N-adap. Rudolph Hochhuth, d. Andrez Wajda.
DRAMA: ROMANCE: Romantic Drama; Romance-Older Women/Younger Men; World War II Era; Jewish People; Jews-Saving; Nazi Stories; Germany; German Films; Saving Someone; Female Protagonists
(The Marriage of Maria Braun; Man of Iron)
Love in the Afternoon, 1957, 126m, ★★★/$$, Allied/Fox. A matrimonial detective's daughter warns a man cheating with a client's wife that the client is coming to get him and winds up falling for him herself. Audrey Hepburn, Gary Cooper, Maurice Chevallier. w. Billy Wilder, IAL Diamond, N-adap. Claude Anet, Ariane, d. Wilder.
DRAMA: ROMANCE: COMEDY DRAMA: Romantic Comedy; Romantic Drama; Detectives-Matrimonial; Cheating Men; Romance-Older Men/Younger Women; Paris; 1950s; Female Protagonists
(Roman Holiday; Funny Face)
Love Is a Ball, 1962, 112m, ★★/$$, UA/NA. A sophisticated Frenchman on the Riviera trains gigolos for his clients looking for love, but one of them decides to do more with the opportunity. Glenn Ford, Charles Boyer, Hope Lange, Richardo Montalban, Telly Savalas. w. David Swift, Tom Waldman, Frank Waldman, N-adap. Lindsay Hardy (The Grand Duke & Mr. Pimm), d. Swift.
COMEDY: ROMANCE: Romantic Comedy; Gigolos; Matchmakers; Riviera Life
(Bedtime Story; Dirty Rotten Scoundrels)
Love Is a Many-Splendored Thing, 1955, 102m, ★★★/$$$$, 20th/Fox. A journalist in Hong Kong during World

War II (William Holden) falls for a beautiful Eurasian woman doctor (Jennifer Jones, BActress) but it may not be able to last. w. John Patrick, N-adap. Han Suyin, d. Henry King. BPicture, BCCin, BCArt, **BOScore, BOSong.** Oscars: 6-2.
ROMANCE: MELODRAMA: Romantic Drama; Tearjerkers; **TRAGEDY:** Romance-Interracial; Romance-Doomed; Asians; Hong Kong; Journalists; Korean War; Unintentionally Funny; Faded Hits
(The World of Suzie Wong; Flower Drum Song; A Girl Named Tamiko)
Love Letters, 1945, 101m, ★★★/$$$, Par/Par. A young woman with amnesia (Jennifer Jones, BActress) rekindles a perhaps dangerous romance. Joseph Cotten, Ann Richards, Gladys Cooper. w. Ayn Rand, N-adap. Chris Massie, Pity My Simplicity, d. William Dieterle. BOScore, BOSong. Oscars: 3-0.
DRAMA: ROMANCE: MELODRAMA: Romantic Drama; Amnesia; Epistolaries; World War II Era; Letters; Trains; England; Small-town Life
(Portrait of Jennie; Undercurrent; Rebecca)
Love Letters, 1984, 90m, ★★★½/$(LR), AIP/New World, R/P-S-FN. A young woman (Jamie Lee Curtis) falls in love with an older, married man (James Keach) and while reading her dead mother's letters revealing an affair, she painfully ponders her own fate. Bonnie Bartlett, Amy Madigan. w. d. Amy Jones.
DRAMA: Young Women; **ROMANCE:** Romance with Married Person; Depression; Lonely People; Character Studies; Underrated; Overlooked; Women's Films; Letters; Female Protagonists; Female Screenwriters; Female Directors
(Rachel, Rachel; The Bridges of Madison County)
The Love Lottery, 1953, 83m, Ealing/NA, ★★★/$$. A movie star in England (David Nivens) is coaxed into becoming the prize in a raffle but may live to regret it. Herbert Lom, Peggy Cummins. w. Harry Kurnitz, d. Charles Crichton.
COMEDY: SATIRE: FARCE: Misunderstandings; Lotteries; Actors; British Films
The Love Machine, 1971, 110m, ★★/$$, Col/RCA-Col, R/S. An ambitious network TV reporter's libido jeopardizes

395

his goals and his conquests. John Philip Law, Dyan Cannon, Robert Ryan, Jackie Cooper, David Hemmings. w. Sam Taylor, N-adap. Jacqueline Susann, d. Jack Haley.

MELODRAMA: Erotic Drama; Soap Opera; Sexy Men; Journalists; TV Life; Promiscuity; Cheating Men; Unintentionally Funny; Time Capsules; Sexual Revolution; 1970s
(Once is Not Enough; The Burglars)

Love Matters, 1993, 97m, ★★1/2/$, Republic/Republic, R/S-FN-MN. A couple has problems when the man's best friend shows up with his mistress and announces his divorce, leading them to question their relationship. Griffin Dunne, Tony Goldwyn, Annette O'Toole, Gina Gershon. w. d. Eb Lottimer.

MELODRAMA: Marriage Drama; Erotic Drama; Marriage on the Rocks; Mistresses; Divorce; Married Couples; Writer-Directors; Yuppies
(Lake Consequence; Consenting Adults; The Last Married Couple in America)

Love Me or Leave Me, 1955, 122m, ★★★/$$$$, MGM/MGM-UA. A show girl named Ruth Etting in the roaring 20s (Doris Day) is pushed to stardom by a mobster (James Cagney, BActor), but it may be too much for either to bear. Cameron Mitchell, Tom Tully. w. Daniels Fuchs, Isobel Lennart (**BOStory**), BScr), d. Charles Vidor. BOScore, BOSong. Oscars: 5-1.

DRAMA: MELODRAMA: MUSICALS: Music Movies; Singers; 1920s-Roaring; Mob Stories; Biographies; Mob Girls; Music Dies; Hollywood Life; Fame-Rise to
(Citizen Kane; Bugsy; Casino)

Love Me Tender, 1956, 95m, ★★1/2/ $$$, 20th/CBS-Fox. Three brother civil war soldiers return home with valuable pilfered items they soon begin fighting over, and singing over. Elvis Presley, Richard Egan, Debra Paget, Neville Brand, Mildred Dunnock. w. Robert Buckner, d. Robert D. Webb.

WESTERNS: Music Movies; Civil War Era; Brothers; Soldiers; Men in Conflict; Curiosities; Southerns

Love Me Tonight, 1932, 104m, ★★★1/2/$$$, Par/Par. A musical about social climbing in gay Paris as a tailor makes it into high society by happenstance. Maurice Chevalier, Jeanette McDonald, Charles Butterworth, Charles Ruggles, Myrna Loy. w. Samuel Hoffenstein, Waldemar Young, George Marion, Rodgers & Hart, P-adap. Leopold Marchand, d. Rouben Mamoulian.

MUSICALS: COMEDY: Musical Comedy; Fashion World; Social Climbing; Paris; Hidden Gems
(Love Parade; The Merry Widow)

Love Nest, 1951, 84m, ★★1/2/$$, 20th/Fox. A writer and his wife run an apartment complex and find themselves immersed in the occupants' goings-on. William Lundigan, June Haver, Marilyn Monroe, Jack Paar. w. IAL Diamond, N-adap. Scott Corbett, d. Joseph Newman.

COMEDY: COMEDY DRAMA: Ensemble Films; Neighbors-Troublesome; Writers; Apartment Buildings
(No Down Payment; About Mrs. Leslie)

Love on the Dole, 1941, 100m, ★★★/$$, Ealing/NA. Slice of life of unemployed people in rural England, trying to build romances amid the tensions. Deborah Kerr, Clifford Evans, George Carney. w. Walter Greenwood, Barbara Emery, Rollo Gamble, N-adap. Greenwood, d. John Baxter.

DRAMA: Social Drama; **ROMANCE:** Romantic Drama; Farm Life; Unemployment; Making a Living; Working Class; England; Rural Life; World War II Era; British Films
(The Life and Death of Colonel Blimp)

Love on the Run, 1936, 81m, ★★★/ $$$, MGM/MGM-UA. Journalists working together help a madcap heiress get out of a wedding and crack a big story at the same time. Clark Gable, Joan Crawford, Franchot Tone, Reginald Owen. w. John Mahin, Manuel Seff, Gladys Hurlbut, d. W. S. VanDyke.

COMEDY: Screwball Comedy; **FARCE:** Marriages-Impending; Heiresses-Madcap; Journalists; Spies; Female Screenwriters
(It Happened One Night; After Office Hours)

Love on the Run, 1979, 95m, ★★★/$$, WB/WB, R/S. The boy from *The 400 Blows* continues to come of age dealing with romance and the usual angst. Jean-Pierre Leaud, Marie-France Pisier. w. Francois Truffaut, Pisier, Jean Aurel, Suzanne Schiffman, d. Truffaut.

DRAMA: ROMANCE: Young Men; Romantic Drama; Coming of Age; Character Studies; French Films; Female Screenwriters

SEQUEL TO: The 400 Blows

Love Parade, 1929, 112m, ★★★/$$$, Par/Par. An early sound musical about the marriage of a fictitious prince. Maurice Chevalier (BActor), Jeanette MacDonald. w. Ernest Vajda, Guy Bolton, N-adap. Leon Xanrof, Jules Chancel, *The Prince Consort*, d. Ernst Lubitsch (BDirector). BPicture, BCin, BArt. Oscars: 5-0.

MUSICAL: COMEDY: Musical Comedy; Operas; Princes; Weddings; Fairy Tales; Forgotten Films
(Love Me Tonight; The Merry Widow)

Love Potion #9, 1992, ★★/$, 20th/Fox, PG-13/P-S. Nerdy young scientist invents potion in animal experiment, love blossoms where it didn't before, but it gets out of hand. Tate Donovan, Sandra Bullock, Dale Midkiff, Anne Bancroft. w.d. Dale Launer.

COMEDY: ROMANCE: Romantic Comedy; Cures/Solutions-Search for; Romance-Reluctant; Chase Stories; Mix-Ups; Scientists; Nerds; Wallflowers; Extroverted vs. Introverted; Coulda Been Great; Good Premise Unfulfilled; Song Title Movies; Writer-Directors
(What's So Bad About Feeling Good?)
(Ed: The usually good Launer [*Ruthless People; My Cousin Vinny*] misfires here)

The Lover, 1992, 103m, ★★/$$, MGM/MGM-UA, NC-17, R/ES-FFN-MFN. A French girl in Indochina during the pre-war days falls in love with an older Chinese man but slowly may be becoming a prostitute. Jane March, Tony Lueng. Narrated by Jeanne Moreau. w. Gerard Brach, Jean Jacques Annaud, N-dap. Marguerite Duras, d. Annaud. BCin. Oscars: 1-0.

DRAMA: Erotic Drama; Romantic Drama; Romance-Older Men/Younger Women; Romance-Interracial; Love-First; Men and Girls; Scandals; Asia; 1920s; French Films; Female Protagonists; Sexy Women; Narrated Films
(Lolita; Color of Night)

Love Story, 1944, 112m, ★★1/2/$$, Gainsborough/NA. An injured, blinded soldier (Stewart Granger) falls in love with a lady pianist (Margaret Lockwood) who doesn't have long to live. w. Leslie Arliss, Doreen Montgomery, Rodney Ackland, N-adap. J.W. Drawbell, d. Arliss.

ROMANCE: MELODRAMA: Tearjerkers; Disease Stories; Death-Impending;

Musicians; Soldiers; World War II Era; British Films; Rural Life; England
(Duet for One; Waterloo Bridge)

Love Story, 1970, 99m, ★★★¹/2/ $$$$$$, Par/Par, PG. A Harvard rich kid in law school falls for a poor scholarship student with leukemia and never has to say he's sorry. Ryan O'Neal (BActor), Ali MacGraw (BActress), Ray Milland, Tommy Lee Jones, John Marley (BSActor). w. N-adap. Erich Segal (BAScr), d. Arthur Hiller (BDirector). BPicture, **BOScore**. Oscars: 7-1.
ROMANCE: **DRAMA: COMEDY DRAMA**: Romantic Drama; **MELODRAMA**: Disease Stories; Tearjerkers; Dying Young; Romance-Doomed; Death-Impending; Newlyweds; Law Students; Harvard; Blockbusters; Sleeper Hits
(Camille; Love Story [1944]; An Affair to Remember; Duet For One; Untamed Heart)

Love Streams, 1984, 141m, ★★★/$, Cannon/MGM-UA, R/S-P. A mentally ill woman (Gena Rowlands) whose marriage has ended after years moves in with her Peter Pan brother (John Cassavetes) and re-learns their past. w. Ted Allan, Cassavetes, P-adap. Allan, d. Cassavetes.
DRAMA: Character Studies; Brothers and Sisters; Divorce; Starting Over; Mental Illness; Playboys; Eccentric People
(A Woman Under the Influence; Faces; Minnie & Moskowitz; Opening Night)

Love Thy Neighbor, 1940, 81m, ★★¹/2/$$, Par/Par. Supposedly based on the actual feud between its stars of radio days. Jack Benny, Fred Allen, Mary Martin. w. William Morrow, Edmund Beloin, Ernest Pagano, d. Mark Sandrich.
COMEDY: Men in Conflict; Radio; Comedians; True Stories; Gossip; Feuds
SEQUEL: Love and Hisses

Love with the Proper Stranger, 1963, 100m, ★★★/$$$, Par/Par, S. A young shopgirl (Natalie Wood, BActress) is pregnant by a fellow she apparently doesn't know too well, but well enough, and contemplates an abortion unless he's come around (Steve McQueen). Tom Bosley, Edie Adams. w. Arnold Schulman (BOScr), d. Robert Mulligan. BB&WCin. Oscars: 3-0.
DRAMA: COMEDY DRAMA: ROMANCE: Romantic Comedy; Abortion Dilemmas; Mothers-Unwed; Young People; Promiscuity; Musicians; Working Class;

Ordinary People Stories; Marriages-Forced; Hidden Gems; Ahead of its Time
(The L-Shaped Room; To Find a Man; Splendor in the Grass)
(Ed: Refreshingly realistic for a Hollywood star vehicle of its day)

The Loved One, 1965, 118m, ★★★¹/2/ $$, MGM/MGM-UA. An everyman poet from England gets a job in a California cemetery and meets a lot of interesting and bizarre people. Robert Morse, John Gielgud, Rod Steiger, Liberace, Johnathan Winters, Dana Andrews, Milton Berle, James Coburn, Roddy McDowell, Tab Hunter. w. Terry Southern, Christopher Isherwood, N-adap. Evelyn Waugh, d. Tony Richardson.
SATIRE: COMEDY: Black Comedy;
COMEDY DRAMA: Comedy-Morbid; Funerals; Death-Dealing with; Hidden Gems; Cult Films
(Dr. Strangelove; Passed Away; The Busy Body)

The Loveless, 1983, 83m, ★★¹/2/$ (LR) Ind/Media, R/V-S-P. Bikers terrorize a small Southern town in the 50s-in an art-ful way. Willem Dafoe. w. d. Kathryn Bigelow.
DRAMA: ACTION: Rednecks; Motorcycles; Small-town Life; Cult Films; 1950s; Female Directors; Female Screenwriters; Writer-Directors
(Near Dark; The Lost Boys)

Lovely to Look At, 1953, 102m, ★★¹/2/$$$, MGM/MGM-UA. Broadway producers utilize Paris fashions in their musical numbers, romancing the models, too. Howard Keel, Kathryn Grayson, Ann Miller, Red Skelton, ZsaZsa Gabor. w. George Wells, Harry Ruby, d. Mervyn LeRoy.
MUSICAL: ROMANCE: Romantic Comedy; Musical Comedy; Fashion World; Models; Paris; Theater Life
(A New Kind of Love; Funny Face)

A Lovely Way to Die, 1968, 98m, ★★¹/2/$, U/NA. A bodyguard for a woman suspected of murder tries to prove her innocence and not get killed himself. Kirk Douglas, Sylvia Koscina, Eli Wallach, Marty Green, Sharon Farrell. w. A. J. Russell, d. David Lowell Rich.
SUSPENSE: MYSTERY: MURDER: MURDER MYSTERY: Black Comedy; **FARCE**: Bodyguards; Capers; Chase Movies; Clever Plots & Endings

Loverboy, 1989, 99m, ★★¹/2/$$, Tri/Col-Tri, PG-13/P-S. A pizza boy

(Patrick Dempsey) is mistaken for a gigolo and soon develops a clientele who like his romancing. Kate Jackson, Kirstie Alley, Carrie Fisher, Robert Ginty, Barbara Carrera, Robb Camiletti. w. Robin Schiff, Tom Ropelewski, Leslie Dixon, d. Joan Micklin Silver.
COMEDY: FARCE: Romantic Comedy; Erotic Comedy; Sex Comedy; Gigolos; Prostitutes-Male; Misunderstandings; Romance-Older Women/Younger Men; Young Men; Female Directors; Female Screenwriters
(Alvin Purple; A Night in the Life of Jimmy Reardon; Alfie; Some Girls)
(Ed: Silly and senseless with a few laughs. It plays on cable all the time . . .)

Lover Come Back, 1946, 90m, ★★¹/2/ $$, U/MCA-U. A journalist during the war returns home to find his wife has been preoccupying herself. Lucille Ball, George Brent, Vera Zorina. w. Michael Fessier, Ernest Pagano, d. William Salter.
COMEDY: ROMANCE: Romantic Comedy; Romance-Triangles; Return of Spouse; Cheating Women; Journalists; World War II Era; Misunderstandings; Photographers; Forgotten Films
(My Favorite Wife; Coming Home)

Lover Come Back, 1961, 107m, ★★★¹/2/$$$$$, U/MCA-U. A candy which makes you feel drunk is at the cen-ter of a battle of advertising executives, two of which (Rock Hudson, Doris Day) who may be in love, and even married, like it or not. Tony Randall, Jack Oakie, Edie Adams. w. Stanley Shapiro, Paul Henning (BOScr), d. Delbert Mann. Oscars: 1-0.
COMEDY: SATIRE: FARCE: ROMANCE: Romantic Comedy; Advertising World; Romance-Bickering; Race Against Time; Alcoholism; Marriages-Forced; Amnesia; Scientists
(Pillow Talk; Move Over, Darling)

Lovers and Other Strangers, 1970, 104m, ★★★/$$$, ABC-Cin/Fox, R/S-FN. The problems of the parents and in-laws of a newlywed couple mirror their own after the big wedding. Gig Young, Anne Jackson, Richard Castello (BActor), Bonnie Bedelia, Michael Brandon, Diane Keaton, Cloris Leachman, Beatrice Arthur. w. Renee Taylor, Joseph Bologna, David Zelag Goodman (BOScr), d. Cy Howard. **BOSong**, "For All We Know." Oscars: 3-1.

COMEDY: COMEDY DRAMA: FARCE: Sexuality; Marriage on the Rocks; Newlyweds; Weddings; Parents & Children; Young People; 1970s
(A Wedding; The Landlord; The Heartbreak Kid)

Loves of a Blonde, 1965, 82m, ★★★/ $$, Czech-Col/Col. A working-class girl wants a sexy musician but may have problems with his family. Hanna Brejchova, Vladimir Pucholt. w. Milos Forman, Jaroslav Papousek, Ivan Passer, d. Forman. BFFilm. Oscars: 1-0.

DRAMA: COMEDY DRAMA: ROMANCE: Romance-Class Conflicts; Musicians; Lover Family Dislikes; Europeans-Eastern; Czech Films

The Loves of Carmen, 1948, 99m, ★★1/2/$$, Col/Col. The basic tale of the opera where a soldier is tempted by a gypsy into killing her husband. Rita Hayworth, Glenn Ford, Victor Jory. w. Helen Deutsch, N-adap. Prosper Merimee, d. Charles Vidor.

MELODRAMA: TRAGEDY: MUSICALS: Sexy Women; Dangerous Women; Dancers; Murder-Coerced to; Spain; Female Screenwriters

Lovesick, 1983, 96m, ★★★/$$, Ladd-WB/WB, PG/S-P. A psychiatrist falls in love with a beautiful younger woman and then begins to doubt himself and the relationship, which is when the ghost of Freud appears to help him out. Dudley Moore, Elizabeth McGovern, Alec Guinness, John Huston, Larry Rivers, Wally Shawn, Gene Saks, Renee Taylor, Alan King. w. d. Marshall Brickman.

COMEDY: COMEDY DRAMA: ROMANCE: Romantic Comedy; Psychiatrists; Romance-Older Men/Younger Women; Ghosts; Fantasies; Eccentric People; Nervous Breakdowns; Freud; Coulda Been Great; Underrated; Writer-Directors
(Annie Hall; Alice; Simon)

Lovin' Molly, 1973, 98m, ★★★/$, UA/NA, R/S. Two men in Depression-era Texas have a woman between them, but neither really have a relationship with her beyond sex it seems. Blythe Danner, Anthony Perkins, Beau Bridges, Susan Sarandon, Edward Binns. w. Stephen Friedman, N-adap. *Leaving Cheyenne*, Larry McMurtry, d. Sidney Lumet.

COMEDY DRAMA: DRAMA: ROMANCE: Romantic Drama; Romance-Triangles; Friendships-Male; Men Fighting Over Women; Sexy Women; Small-town Life; Texas; Depression Era; Forgotten Films; Hidden Gems
(Hud; Jules and Jim; Lucky Lady)

Loving, 1970, 96m, ★★★/$$, Col/NA, R/S. A New York advertising artist is having trouble juggling a wife and mistress at the same time. George Segal, Eva Marie Saint, Nancie Phillips, Sterling Hayden, Keenan Wynn, Janis Young, David Doyle. w. Don Devlin, N-adap. *Brooks Wilson Ltd.*, J. M. Ryan, d. Irvin Kershner.

COMEDY: ROMANCE: Romantic Comedy; Marriage Comedy; Romance-Triangles; Mistresses; Cheating Men; Guilty Conscience; Midlife Crisis; Forgotten Films; Advertising World
(Blume in Love; A Touch of Class)

Loving Couples, 1980, 98m, ★★1/2/$, 20th/CBS-Fox, R/S-P. A married couple each decide to find a younger lover to liven things up. Shirley MacLaine, James Coburn, Susan Sarandon, Stephen Collins, Sally Kellerman. w. Martin Donovan, d. Jack Smight.

COMEDY: ROMANCE: Romantic Comedy; Marriage Comedy; Marriage on the Rocks; Alternative Lifestyles; Romance-Older Women/Younger Men; Romance-Older Men/Younger Women; Sexual Revolution; Swapping Partners
(The Last Married Couple in America; Bob & Ted & Carol & Alice; A Change of Seasons)

A Low Down Dirty Shame, 1995, 108m, ★★/$, Hollywood/Hollywood, R/EP-EV-S. A private detective tracks down drug dealers with the help of DEA agent and sexy, silly female sidekick. Keenan Ivory Wayans, Jada Pinkett, Charles S. Dutton, Salli Richardson, Andrew Divoff, Corwin Hawkins, Gary Cervantes, Gregory Sierra. w. d. Keenan Ivory Wayans.

ACTION: Action Comedy; Detective Stories; Film Noir-Modern; Drugs-dealing; Black Men; Black Casts; Black directors; Black screenwriters; Actor Directors; Song Title Movies
(Bad Boys)

The L-Shaped Room, 1963, 142m, ★★★1/2/$$, BL-Reade/TNT. A young woman in mod London moves into a boardinghouse in a seedier part of town intending to have an abortion but meets so many eccentric people there, she reconsiders her position in life. Leslie Caron (BActress), Tom Bell, Brock Peters, Cicely Courtneidge, Bernard Lee, Emlyn Williams. w. d. Bryan Forbes, N-adap. Lynne Banks. Oscars: 1-0.

COMEDY DRAMA: Slice of Life Stories; Ensemble Films; Eccentric People; Artists; Alternative Lifestyles; Boardinghouses; Lesbians; Writers; Black Among Whites; Mod Era; London; Abortion Dilemmas; Young Women; Families-Extended; Female Protagonists; Writer-Directors
(Georgy Girl; The Balcony; Promise Her Anything)

The Luck of the Irish, 1948, 99m, ★★★/$$$, 20th/Fox. A journalist visiting Ireland meets a meddlesome leprechaun who tries to fix his love life, but it's not so easy-and there's a few hitches. Tyrone Power, Cecil Kellaway (BSActor), Anne Baxter, Lee J. Cobb, Jayne Meadows, James Todd. w. Philip Dunne, N-adap. *There Was a Little Man*, Constance and Guy Jones, d. Henry Koster.

COMEDY: ROMANCE: Romantic Comedy; Magic; Matchmakers; Nuisances; Leprechauns; Little People; Ireland; Americans Abroad; Journalists; Hidden Gems; Coulda Been Great
(Finian's Rainbow; Leprechaun)

Lucky Lady, 1975, 118m, ★★/$$$, 20th/Fox, R/S-P. A kooky singer in Tijuana gets mixed up with two bootleggers and has a threesome. Liza Minnelli, Gene Hackman, Burt Reynolds, Michael Hordern, Robby Benson. w. Willard Huyck, Gloria Katz, d. Stanley Donen.

COMEDY DRAMA: ROMANCE: Romance-Triangles; Ménage à Trois; Bootleggers; 1930s; Mexico; Flops-Major
(The Fortune; Lovin' Molly)
(Ed: It did gross quite a bit of money, but the press was so incredibly bad, it can only be considered a turkey)

Lucky Me, 1954, 100m, ★★1/2/$$, WB/WB. A musical troupe gets stranded down in Florida, then things suddenly seem to go right and they put on a show. Doris Day, Robert Cummings, Phil Silvers, Eddie Foy, Nancy Walker, Martha Hyer. w. James O'Hanlon, Robert O'Brien, Irving Elinson, d. Jack Donohue.

MUSICALS: COMEDY: Musical Comedy; Stranded; Putting on a Show; Singers; Dancers; Forgotten Films

Lucky Night, 1939, 90m, ★★1/2/$$, MGM/NA. An heiress strikes out on her own into the real world and meets a man on a park bench who just may be what she's looking for. Myrna Loy, Robert Taylor, Joseph Allen, Marjorie Main, Charles Lane. w. Vincent Laurence, Grover Jones, d. Norman Taurog.

COMEDY: ROMANCE: Romantic Comedy; Heiresses; Romance-Girl Wants Boy; Romance-Class Conflicts; Good Premise Unfulfilled; Female Protagonists

The Lucky Star, 1980, 110m, ★★1/2/$, Ind/NA. In World War II, a Jewish boy with an obsession of Westerns winds up using some of his learned skills to capture a Nazi. Rod Steiger, Louise Fletcher, Brett Marx, Lou Jacobi. w. Max Fischer, Jack Rosenthal, d. Max Fischer.

COMEDY DRAMA: CHILDREN'S: FAMILY: Boys; Nazi Stories; Jewish People; Heroes-Unlikely; Child Protagonists; World War II Stories; Canadian Films
(Cloak and Dagger; Death Valley [1981])

The Lucky Stiff, 1948, 101m, ★★1/2/$, UA/Col. A singer wrongly convicted of murder and executed comes back to haunt the person who really did it and force a confession out of them. Dorothy Lamour, Brian Donlevy, Claire Trevor. w. d. Lewis Foster.

COMEDY: MURDER: Accused Unjustly; Framed?; Murderers-Female; Executions; Ghosts; Dead-Back from the; Good Premise Unfulfilled; Female Protagonists; Forgotten Films; Writer-Directors
(Ghost; Topper; Beetlejuice)

Lucretia Borgia, 1952, 105m, ★★1/2/$, Ind/NA. The story, not of the poisonings, but of her brother's use of her in political games. Martine Carroll, Pedro Armendariz. w. Cecil Saint-Laurent, Jacques Sigurd, Christian-Jacque, d. Christian-Jacque.

DRAMA: Political Drama; Historical Drama; Mindgames; Political Corruptions; Brothers and Sisters; Italian Films; Italy; Middle Ages; Forgotten Films

Lucy Gallant, 1955, 104m, ★★1/2/$$, Par/NA, AMC. A poor woman from Texas winds up a big fashion designer, but leaves her love behind, and it may be too late. Jane Wyman, Charlton Heston, Claire Trevor, Thelma Ritter, William Demarest, Wallace Ford. w. John Lee Mahin, Winston Miller, N-adap. Margaret Cousins, d. Robert Parrish.

MELODRAMA: ROMANCE: Power-Rise to; Romance Reunited; Rags to Riches; Fashion World; Texas
(So Big; Ruby Gentry; Back Street)

Ludwig, 1973, ★★1/2/$, MGM/NA, R/S. The mad count of Bavaria breaks his country building castles and begins to go even madder. Helmut Berger, Romy Schneider, Trevor Howard. w. Luchino Visconti, Enrico Medioli, d. Luchino Visconti. BCostume. Oscars: 1-0.

DRAMA: Historical Drama; Costume Drama; Character Studies; Rise and Fall Stories; Mental Illness; Kings; Castles; 1800s; Germany; Italian Films; International Casts
(The Madness of King George)
(Ed: Lovely to look at but tedious)

Lumiere, 1976, 101m, ★★★/$, Ind/Sultan, PG. Four actresses get together and begin chatting, but end up making some major decisions in their lives. Jeanne Moreau, Lucia Bose, Francine Racette, Caroline Cartier, Keith Carradine. d. Jeanne Moreau.

DRAMA: Actresses; One-Day Stories; Ensembles-Female; Art Films; Improvisational Films; Female Directors; Female Screenwriters; Female Protagonists; French Films

Lumiere d'Ete, 1943, 112m, ★★★/$, Ind/NA. Wealthy people whiling away their time in a resort in the Alps become involved in various ways with the working-class types in the local village. Madeleine Renaud, Pierre Brasseur. w. Jacques Prevert, Pierre Laroche, d. Jean Gremillion.

DRAMA: ROMANCE: Social Drama; Class Conflicts; Rich-Decadent; Resorts; Vacations; Working Class; French Films; Allegorical Stories; Alps; Female Protagonists
(Forbidden Games; The Discreet Charm of the Bourgeoisie)

Luna, 1979, 142, ★★1/2/$, Par/Par, R/S. An opera star (Jill Clayburgh) has an affair with a young man who is her son. Matthew Barry, Fred Gwynne. w. Guiseppe and Bernardo Bertolucci, Clare Peploe, d. Bernardo Bertolucci.

DRAMA: MELODRAMA: ROMANCE: TRAGEDY: Incest; Singers; Opera; Mothers & Sons; Oedipal Stories; Sexuality; Flops-Major; Forgotten Films; Coulda Been Good; Female Protagonists; Female Screenwriters
(Murmur of the Heart; Angela)
(Ed: Very odd but interesting attempt at forbidden subject; not the horrible flop embarrassment it was at the time, though

it may have contributed to Clayburgh's sudden decline)

Lunatics, A Love Story, 1992, 87m, ★★/$, Ind/NA. When a former mental patient calls a 900 number, one day he misdials and gets an equally unstable girl on the phone who pays a visit. Theodore Raime, Deborah Foreman, Bruce Campbell. w. d. Josh Beck.

COMEDY DRAMA: ROMANCE: Romantic Comedy; Mental Illness; Eccentric People; Los Angeles; Poor People; Coulda Been Great; Writer-Directors; Independent Films; LA 90s Indies

Lunch on the Grass, 1959, 91m, ★★★/$$, Ind/NA. A city dwelling scientist takes to the country and nature to find love and peace, but possibly deludes himself. Paul Meurisse, Catherine Rouvel. w. d. Jean Renoir.

DRAMA: ROMANCE: COMEDY DRAMA: Nature-Back to; Scientists; Romance-Class Conflict; Rural Life; French Films; Writer-Directors

Lured, 1947, 102m, ★★1/2/$$, UA/NA. A dancer in England (Lucille Ball) who may be a murder target herself, helps the police find the person she thinks is the killer. George Sanders, Charles Coburn, Boris Karloff. w. Leo Rosten, S-adap. Pieges, d. Douglas Sirk.

MURDER MYSTERY: MURDER: COMEDY DRAMA: Trail of a Killer; Innocent Bystanders; Murder-Discovering; Dancers; Americans Abroad; England
(Cornered; Midnight Lace)

Lust for Life, 1956, 122m, ★★★1/2/$$$, MGM/MGM-UA. The life of Vincent Van Gogh is chronicled in an inventive, very entertaining (if perhaps apocryphal) way. Kirk Douglas (BActor), Anthony Quinn (**BSActor**). w. Norman Corwin, N-adap. Irving Stone, d. Vincente Minnelli. BAScr, BCArt. Oscars: 4-1.

DRAMA: MELODRAMA: Biographies; Character Studies; Artists-Famous; Brothers; Hidden Gems
(Vincent & Theo; Van Gogh; The Light that Failed; The Agony and the Ecstasy)
(Ed: It's amazing how such a seemingly dull story-by today's movie standards-could be so entertaining)

Lust in the Dust, 1985, 85m, ★★★/$$, New World/New World, R/S-P-FN. When a sexy (you be the judge) whore in the old West accidentally kills a man with her incredibly strong thighs while in a certain position, it leads her on an odyssey on the lam to a town called Chile Verde. Tab Hunter, Divine, Lainie Kazan, Cesar Romero. w. Philip John Taylor, d. Paul Bartel.

COMEDY: Erotic Comedy; Screwball Comedy; Spoofs; **WESTERNS:** Western Comedy; Prostitutes-Low Class; Women in Conflict; Women Fighting Over Men; Men as Women; Camp

(Johnny Guitar; Eating Raoul)

(Ed: Because of Divine's starring role, many think this is a John Waters film; and though it's not quite as wicked as he would have made this, it's nearly there)

The Lusty Men, 1952, 113m, ★★/$$, RKO/VCI. Two men vy for the attention of a woman while trying to make a comeback on the rodeo circuit. Robert Mitchum, Susan Hayward, Arthur Kennedy, Arthur Hunnicutt. d. Nicholas Ray.

MELODRAMA: ROMANCE: Men Fighting Over Women; Romance-Triangles; Comebacks; Rodeos; Men Proving Themselves; Forgotten Films

(Junior Bonner; 8 Seconds)

Luther, 1973, 112m, ★★1/2/$, AFT-Embassy/NA, New Line, PG. A filmed play about Luther's teachings and how they led to a peasant revolt which would change history. Stacy Keach, Patrick Magee, Hugh Griffith, Julian Glover. w. Edward Anhalt, P-adap. John Osborne, d. Guy Green.

DRAMA: Biographies; Historical Drama; Charismatic People; Preachers/Ministers; Religion; Stagelike Films; Stage Filmings; Independent Films

Luv, 1967, 95m, ★★★/$, Col/RCA-Col. A man stops an old friend from jumping off of a bridge and brings him home which causes more trouble than he ever thought it would. Jack Lemmon, Peter Falk, Elaine May. w. Elliott Baker, P-adap. Murray Schisgal, d. Clive Donner.

COMEDY: Black Comedy; **FARCE:** Romance-Triangles; Suicidal Tendencies; Saving Someone; Nuisances; Forgotten Films

(Down and Out in Beverly Hills; The End)

Lydia, 1941, 104m, ★★1/2/$$, Korda-UA/Sultan. An aristocratic lady remembers all the men in her life. Merle Oberon, Joseph Cotten, Edna May Oliver. w. Ben Hecht, Samuel Hoffenstein, SS-adap. Julien Duvivier, Laszlo Bus-Fekete, d. Duvivier. BOScore. Oscars: 1-0.

MELODRAMA: ROMANCE: Narrated Films; Flashbacks; Memories

(Lady L; What a Way to Go; The Millionairess)

M

M, 1931, 118m, ★★★★/$$, Nero/
Sinister, Nos. A child murderer (Peter
Lorre) hides out on the wrong side of
town, but the local criminals decide to
earn a few points by finding him them-
selves. w. Thea Von Harbou, Paul
Falkenberg, Adolf Jansen, Karl Vash,
d. Fritz Lang.
SUSPENSE: HORROR: Art Films; Film
Noir; **MURDER:** Serial Killers; Murderers
of Children; Mental Illness; Fugitives
from the Law; Fugitives from the Mob;
German Films; Female Screenwriters
REMAKE: 1951
M, 1951, 82m, ★★1/2/$, Col/NA.
Remake of the child murderer tale, but
without the style or mood. David Wayne,
Howard daSilva, Luther Adler, Norman
Lloyd. w. Norman Reilly, Leo Katcher,
d. Joseph Losey.
SUSPENSE: HORROR: Art Films; Film
Noir; **MURDER:** Serial Killers; Murderers
of Children; Mental Illness; Fugitives
from the Law; Fugitives from the Mob;
Foreign Film Remakes
REMAKE OF: 1931 original.
M. Butterfly, 1993, 101m, ★★1/2/$,
WB/WB, R/S-MN. A French diplomat
goes to China and falls in love with an
opera singer who's not at all what she
seems. Jeremy Irons, John Lone, Barbara
Sukowa. w. P-adap. David Henry Hwang,
d. David Cronenberg.

DRAMA: ROMANCE: Romantic Drama;
Men as Women; Opera; Opera Singers;
Diplomats; Disguises; *Men as Women;*
Transvestites; Romance-Doomed; True
Stories; Chinese People; China; Coulda
Been Good
(The Crying Game; My Geisha)
(Ed: The big hit of Broadway bombs in
the wake of *The Crying Game*)
Ma and Pa Kettle, 1949, 75m, ★★★/
$$$, U/MCA-U. The hillbillies with the
mostest children win a contest and are
whisked off to the big city where their
new all-electric house awaits their
destruction. Marjorie Main, Percy
Kilbride, Richard Long. w. Herbert
Margolis, Louis Morheim, Al Lewis,
N-adap. *The Egg and I,* d. Charles
Lamont.
COMEDY: Comedy of Errors; Family
Comedy; Hillbillies; City vs. Country;
Fish out of Water Stories; Man vs.
Machine; Female Protagonists; Feisty
Females
SPINOFF/SEQUEL OF: The Egg & I.
SEQUELS: Ma and Pa Kettle at the Fair,
Ma and Pa Kettle Back on the Farm, Ma
and Pa Kettle Go to Town.
(The Egg & I; Dreamin' Out Loud [Lum
'n Abner])
Macaroni, 1985, 104m, ★★/$, Par/Par,
PG. A businessman returns to Italy in
remembrance of the war, whereupon he

is reunited with his freespirited but
troublesome old pal. Jack Lemmon,
Marcello Mastroianni. w. d. Ettore
Scola.
COMEDY: COMEDY DRAMA:
Friendships-Male; Reunions; Free
Spirited; Extroverted vs. Introverted;
Buddy Films; Italy; Americans Abroad;
Writer-Directors; Coulda Been Good
(Avanti!; Missing; A Fine Romance)
Macao, 1952, 81m, ★★1/2/$$, RKO/
Turner. A fugitive hides out in the Far
East port and meets a mysterious
chanteuse, then is met with a chance
to catch another fugitive and redeem
himself. Robert Mitchum, Jane Russell,
William Bendix, Gloria Grahame.
w. Bernard C. Shoenfeld, Stanley Rubin
d. Josef Von Sternberg (and Nicholas
Ray).
MELODRAMA: ROMANCE: Romance-
Dangerous; Film Noir; Fugitives from the
Law; Accused Unjustly; Asia; South
Pacific
(Out of the Past; Second Chance)
MacArthur, 1977, 130m, ★★/$$,
U/MCA-U, PG/V. The tale of the great,
cantankerous general-though not his life
story, just his battle stories near the end.
w. Hal Barwood, Matthew Robbins,
d. Joseph Sargent.
DRAMA: Biographies; War Battles; World
War II Stories; Korean War; Leaders-

Military; Leaders-Tyrant; Presidents;
Stern Men
(Inchon; Patton)

Machine Gun McCain, 1970, 94m,
★★/$, Col/Col, NA, R/V-P. The mob puts
a hit man out on the street in Vegas to
pay off a debt. John Cassavetes, Peter
Falk, Britt Ekland. w. Guiliano Montaldo,
Mino Roli, d. Guilano Montaldo.

ACTION: Crime Drama; Mob Stories;
Hitmen; Revenge; Las Vegas
(The Killing of a Chinese Bookie; The
Yakuza; The Friends of Eddie Coyle)

MacKenna's Gold, 1969, 136m,
★★¹/2/$$, Col/Goodtimes. On his
deathbed, an Indian gives the local sher-
iff a treasure map which then puts him in
jeopardy. Gregory Peck, Omar Sharif,
Telly Savalas, Keenan Wynn, Julie
Newmar, Eli Wallach, Edward G.
Robinson, Burgess Meredith, Anthony
Quayle, Lee J. Cobb. w. Carl Foreman,
N-adap. Will Henry, d. J. Lee-Thompson.

WESTERN: Treasure Hunts; Gold Mines;
Indians-American; All-Star Casts
(The Stalking Moon; Fool's Parade)

The Mackintosh Man, 1973, 99m,
★★¹/2/$$, WB/WB, PG/V-S. An ex-con is
blackmailed into espionage inside a
prison by the government. Paul Newman,
James Mason, Dominique Sanda, Harry
Andrews, Ian Bannen. w. Walter Hill,
N-adap. Desmond Bagley, *The Freedom
Trap*, d. John Huston.

DRAMA: SUSPENSE: Spy Films; Spies;
Conspiracy; Blackmail; Ex-Convicts;
Undercover; Secret Agents; Heist Stories;
Double Crossings; Prison Drama;
England; Mediterranean
(The Looking Glass War; 48 Hours; The
Secret War of Harry Frigg; The Drown-
ing Pool)

Mack the Knife, 1989, 121m, ★★/$,
Col/Col. A thief is in love with a young
girl set to macabre music from The
Threepenny Opera. Raul Julia, Roger
Daltrey, Richard Harris, Julie Walters,
Clive Revill, Julia Migenes Johnson.
d. Menahem Golan.

MUSICALS: DRAMA: Musical Drama;
Film Noir-Modern; Thieves; Dangerous
Men; Thieves

The Macomber Affair, 1947, 89m,
★★¹/2/$$, UA/NA. A macho game hunter
has a wife who strays for a more gentle
safari guide. Gregory Peck, Joan Bennett,
Robert Preston, Reginald Denny. w. Casey
Robinson, SS-adap. Ernest Hemingway,

"The Short Happy Life of Francis
Macomber," d. Zoltan Korda.

DRAMA: MELODRAMA: ROMANCE:
Romantic Drama; Romance-Triangles;
Romance with Married Person; Cheating
Women; Cuckolded; Macho Men;
Hunters; Safaris
(Red Dust; Mogambo; White Mischief)

Macon County Line, 1973, 89m,
★★/$$$, AIP/Sultan, R/V-P-S. Two red-
necks and their girl go up against a can-
tankerous sheriff. Alan Vint, Cheryl
Waters, Geoffrey Lewis, Max Baer. w.
Max Baer, Richard Compton, d. Richard
Compton.

ACTION: Crime Drama; Chase Movies;
Car Chases; Crime Sprees; Outlaw Road
Movies; Rednecks; Georgia; Southerns;
Police Corruption

SEQUEL: Return to Macon County.
(Walking Tall; Dirty Mary & Crazy Larry)
(Ed: Came at the beginning of the south-
ern redneck outlaw movie)

Mad About Music, 1938, 98m,
★★★/$$$, U/MCA-U. A lovely singing
orphan girl at a Swiss boarding school
finds a surrogate father figure. Deanne
Durbin, Herbert Marshall, Gail Patrick,
Arthur Treacher, William Frawley.
w. Bruce Manning, Felix Jackson,
d. Norman Taurog.

MUSICALS: Girlhood; Men and Girls;
Fathers-Surrogate; Orphans; Boarding
Schools
(It Started with Eve; Heidi)

Mad Dog and Glory, 1993, 97m,
★★★/$$, U/MCA-U, R/P-S-V. A police
photographer happens to save the life of a
mobster, so the mobster sends his beautiful girl to the cop as a reward-which will
be a friendly gesture just as long as they
don't get too friendly and make the mobster jealous. Robert De Niro, Bill Murray,
Uma Thurman, David Caruso, Kathy
Baker. w. Richard Price, d. John
McNaughton.

COMEDY DRAMA: Mob Stories; Mob
Comedy; **ROMANCE:** Romantic Comedy;
Romance-Triangles; Saving Someone;
Rewards at Stake; Mob Girls; Jealousy;
Chicago
(Born Yesterday; Married to the Mob)
(Ed: Okay, with some good moments)

Mad Love, 1935, 83m, ★★★/$$,
MGM/MGM-UA. When a pianist loses
his hands in an accident, a wacko doctor
who's got the hots for the pianist's wife
sews on the hands of a dead murderer.

Peter Lorre, Colin Clive, Frances Drake.
w. Guy Endore, P. J. Wolfson, John
Balderston, N-adap. Maurice Renard, *The
Hands of Orlac*, d. Karl Freund.

HORROR: TRAGEDY: Black Comedy;
Comedy-Morbid; Romance-Triangles;
Jealousy; Body Parts; Accidents;
Scientists-Mad; Experiments; Musi-
cians; Possessions; Forgotten Films;
Hidden Gems

REMAKE/RETREAD: Fingers.
(Fingers; The Hand; Body Parts)

Mad Love, 1995, 99m, ★★/$$,
U/MCA-U, PG-13/S-P. A manic-
depressive girl is befriended by a sensi-
tive young lad and takes him on a wild
ride, possibly to disaster. Chris
O'Donnell, Drew Barrymore, Joan Allen,
Kevin Dunn, Jude Ciccolella. Paula
Milne, d. Antonia Bird.

ROMANCE: MELODRAMA: Mental
Illness; Road Movies; Romance-Doomed;
Young People; Love-First
(Ed: A maudlin, over-the-top mess in
what otherwise could have been an inter-
esting portrait)

The Mad Magician, 1954, 72m,
★★¹/2/$$, Col/NA. Murder surrounds a
magic show on the rise. Vincent Price,
Eva Gabor, Mary Murphy, Patrick O'Neal.
w. Crane Wilbur, d. John Brahm.

HORROR: MURDER: Murders-One by
One; Magicians; Revenge; Jealousy;
Fame-Rise to; 3-D Movies
(Murder in the Wax Museum)

Mad Max, 1979, 100m, ★★★/$$$,
Ind/Live, R/EV-P-S. Gangs terrorize post-
apocalyptic Australia roadways and Max
becomes a hero going after them. Mel
Gibson, Joanne Samuel. w. James
McCausland, George Miller, d. George
Miller.

ACTION: SCI-FI: Futuristic Films; Chase
Movies; Car Chases; Gangs; Motorcycles;
Motorcycle Gangs; Apocalyptic Stories;
Australian Films

SEQUELS: The Road Warrior, Mad Max:
Beyond Thunderdome.
(A Clockwork Orange; Waterworld;
Tank Girl)

Mad Max Beyond Thunderdome,
1985, 106m, ★★★/$$$$, WB/WB, PG-
13/EV-P-S. Max breaks out of prison and
fights the gangs from taking over and
destroying everything in their post-
apocalyptic stories. Mel Gibson, Tina
Turner. w. Terry Hayes, George Miller,
d. George Miller.

ACTION: SCI-FI: Futuristic Films; Chase Movies; Car Chases; Gangs; Motorcycles; Prison Escapes; Apocalyptic Stories; Australian Films

SEQUEL TO: Mad Max, The Road Warrior.

Madame Bovary, 1949, 114m, ★★½/ $$, MGM/MGM-UA. A young, idealistic woman marries a man who disappoints her and then finds a lover, but it may all push her too far. Jennifer Jones, Van Heflin, James Mason, Louis Jourdan, Gene Lockhart, Gladys Cooper. w. Robert Ardrey, N-adap. Gustave Flaubert, d. Vincente Minnelli. BArt. Oscars: 1-0.

MELODRAMA: ROMANCE: TRAGEDY: Romantic Drama; Romance-Doomed; Romance with Married Person; Cheating Women; Suicidal Tendencies; Young Women; Midlife Crisis; Female Protagonists; Classic Literary Adaptations; Classic Tragedy
(The Awakening/Grand Isle; Anna Karenina)

Madame Butterfly, 1932, 88m, ★★★/ $$, Par/NA. After their romance, a Japanese girl must deal with an American soldier passing her over for an American girl. Cary Grant, Sylvia Sidney, Charles Ruggles. w. Josephine Lovett, Joseph M. March, P-adap. David Belasco, John Long, d. Marion Gering.

DRAMA: TRAGEDY: ROMANCE: MELODRAMA: Romance with Soldier; Romance-Doomed; Romance-Interracial; Japanese People; Japan; Americans Abroad; Female Protagonists; Suicidal Tendencies; Classic Tragedy
(Sayonara; A Girl Named Tamiko; The World of Suzie Wong)
(Ed: No opera in this one, just the story)

Madame Curie, 1943, 124m, ★★★/ $$$, MGM/MGM-UA. The female scientist and discoverer of radium's life story. Greer Garson (BActress), Walter Pidgeon (BActor), Henry Travers, Dame May Whitty, Van Johnson. w. Paul Osborn, Paul H. Rameau, NF-adap. Eve Curie, d. Mervyn Le Roy. BPicture, BCin, BScore, BArt. Oscars: 6-0.

DRAMA: Biographies; True Stories; Inventors; Scientists; Scientists-Female; Nuclear Energy; Female Protagonists
(The Story of Louis Pasteur; Mrs. Miniver)

Passion/Madame Dubarry, 1919, 85m, ★★★/$$$, UFA/NA. Pola Negri,

Emil Jannings.w. Fred Orbing, Hans Kraly, d. Ernst Lubitsch.
Silent Films

Madame Dubarry, 1934, 77m, ★★★/ $$$, WB/NA. Dolores DelRio, Reginald Owen, Anita Louise. w. Edward Chodorov, d. William Dieterle.

DRAMA: MELODRAMA: ROMANCE: Costume Drama; Historical Drama; Prostitutes-High Class; Kings

Madame Rosa, 1977, 120m, ★★★/$$, Ind/Vestron, R/S. An elderly lady who was once a notorious prostitute now runs a daycare center and plays foster mother but may find it hard to live down the past. Simone Signoret, Claude Dauphin. w. d. Moshe Mizrahi, N-adap. Emile Ajar. BFLFilm. Oscars: 1-1.

DRAMA: MELODRAMA: Starting Over; Dual Lives; Past-Haunted by the; Elderly Women; Prostitutes-High Class; French Films; Female Protagonists
(I Sent a Letter to My Love; A House Is Not a Home; Personal Services)

Madame Sousatzka, 1988, 122m, ★★★/$$, Cineplex/MCA-U, PG. An eccentric cantankerous Russian piano teacher in England tries dilligently to help a Pakistani student achieve greatness. Shirley MacLaine, Peggy Ashcroft, Twiggy, Shabana Azmi, Leigh Lawson. w. Ruth Prawer Jhabvala, John Schlesinger, N-adap. Bernice Rubens, d. John Schlesinger.

DRAMA: COMEDY DRAMA: MELO-DRAMA: Musicians; Teachers and Students; Eccentric People; Indian/ Pakistani People; Pianists; Stern Women; Russians; England; British Films; Female Screenwriters; Female Protagonists
(Mr. Holland's Opus; The Corn Is Green)

Madame X, 1929, 95m, ★★★/$$$, MGM/NA. Ruth Chatterton, Raymond Hackett, Mitchell Lewis, Sidney Toler, Lewis Stone. w. Willard Mack, P-adap. Alexandre Bisson, d. Lionel Barrymore.

Madame X, 1937, 72m, ★★½/$$, MGM/MGM-UA. Gladys George, John Beal, Reginald Owen, Ruth Hussey. w. John Meehan, d. Sam Wood.

Madame X, 1965, 100m, ★★½/$$, U/MCA-U. A woman survives what is seen as an accidental death and goes into hiding only to return to a new life and then be accused of murder. Lana Turner, John Forsythe, Ricardo Montalban, Constance Bennett, Burgess Meredith,

Keir Dullea. w. Jean Holloway, d. David Lowell Rich.

DRAMA: MELODRAMA: MURDER: Courtroom Drama; Trials; Tearjerkers; Accused Unjustly; Murderers-Female; Children-Long Lost; Identities-Assumed; Missing Persons; Past-Haunted by the; Mothers & Sons; Female Protagonists; Female Screenwriters
(White Banners; Portrait in Black)

Made for Each Other, 1938, 90m, ★★★/$$$, Selznick-UA/Nos. A young couple try to survive the death of their child. James Stewart, Carole Lombard, Charles Coburn, Lucile Watson, Harry Davenport. w. Jo Swerling, d. John Cromwell.

DRAMA: MELODRAMA: Tearjerkers; **COMEDY DRAMA:** Child-Death of; Death-Dealing with; Marriage Drama; Newlyweds; Young People; Lawyers; Making a Living
(Penny Serenade; Mr. and Mrs. Smith)

Made for Each Other, 1971, 107m, ★★½/$$, 20th/NA. Two neurotic people in New York meet and annoy each other but fall in love. Renée Taylor, Joe Bologna. w. Renée Taylor, Joe Bologna, d. Robert Bean.

COMEDY: COMEDY DRAMA: ROMANCE: Romantic Comedy; Neurotic People; Eccentric People; Stagelike Films; New York Life; Female Screenwriters; Female Protagonists
(Annie Hall; Little Murders)

Made in America, 1993, 111m, ★★½/ $$$, WB/WB, PG-13/S-P. When a black girl breaks into a sperm bank to find out her real father's identity, she's not prepared for him to be a white used car dealer-and neither is her mother. Whoopi Goldberg, Ted Danson, Will Smith, Nia Long, Paul Rodriqguez, Jennifer Tilly. w. Holly Goldberg Sloan, d. Richard Benjamin.

COMEDY: ROMANCE: Romantic Comedy; Family Comedy; Marriage Comedy; Romance-Interracial; Children-Longlost; Mothers Alone; Salesman; Black Women; Black vs. White; Fathers-Surrogate; Good Premise Unfulfilled; Coulda Been Great
(Frozen Assets; Carbon Copy)
(Ed: Often lame, especially for the energy the idea should have had, though the stars help)

Made in Heaven, 1987, 103m, ★★½/$, Lorimar-20th/HomeVision,

PG/S. A young man returns from heaven to meet with his girlfriend and tie things up. Timothy Hutton, Kelly McGillis, Maureen Stapleton, Don Murray, Debra Winger. w. Bruce A. Evans, Raynold Gideon, d. Alan Rudolph.

DRAMA: ROMANCE: Romantic Drama; **MELODRAMA:** Fantasy; Tearjerkers; Heaven; Angels; Romance-Reunited; Dead-Back from the; Young Men
(Heaven Can Wait; Defending Your Life)

Mademoiselle Fifi, 1944, 69m, ★★★/$, RKO/MGM-UA. A stagecoach in France is held up by Prussians during the Franco-Prussian war because of a courtesan on board with whom a Prussian soldier wants to have sex. The passengers try to convince her to do just that, but her initial refusal leads to problems for her. Simone Simon, Kurt Frueger, John Emery, Alan Napier, Jason Robards, Sr. w. Josef Mischel, Peter Ruric, SS-adap. w. Guy de Maupassant, *Boule de Suif/Mademoiselle Fifi,* d. Robert Wise.

DRAMA: MELODRAMA: Social Drama; Political Unrest; Kidnappings; Hijackings; Rape/Rapists; Prostitutes-High Class; Soldiers; Class Conflicts

Madhouse, 1974, 92m, ★★1/2/$, AIP/HBO. A horror movie star (Vincent Price) makes comeback and finds himself embroiled in murder. Peter Cushing. w. Greg Morrison, N-adap. Angus Hall, *Devilday,* d. Jim Clark.

HORROR: Horror Comedy; **MURDER: MYSTERY: MURDER MYSTERY:** Murders-One by One; Comebacks; Actors; Compilation Films
(Fright Night; Fright Night II; Theater of Blood)

Madhouse, 1990, 90m, ★★/$$, Orion/Orion, PG-13/S-P. A couple is besieged with visitors, leading to chaos. John Larroquette, Kirstie Alley, Alison LaPlaca, John Diehl, Dennis Miller, Robert Ginty. w. d. Tom Ropelewski.

COMEDY: FARCE: Roommates from Hell; Nuisances; Good Premise Unfulfilled; Coulda Been Good; Writer-Directors
(Houseguest; Sibling Rivalry)

Madigan, 1968, 100m, ★★★/$$, U/MCA-U, PG/V. A detective from Brooklyn goes to any length to get his man. Henry Fonda, Richard Widmark, Michael Dunn, Susan Clark, Inger Stevens, Harry Guardino, James

Whitmore, Sheree North, Don Stroud. w. Henri Simoun, Abraham Polonsky, N-adap. w. Richard Dougherty, *The Commissioner,* d. Don Siegel.

ACTION: DRAMA: Crime Drama; **TRAGEDY:** Police Stories; Chase Movies; Detective Stories; Detectives-Police; Manhunts; Trail of a Killer
(The French Connection; The Boston Strangler)

Madison Avenue, 1961, 94m, ★★/$, 20th/NA. An ad exec plots revenge on his boss. Dana Andrews, Jeanne Crain, Eleanor Parker, Eddie Albert, Kathleen Freeman. w. Norman Corwin, N-adap. Jeremy Kirk, *The Build-Up Boys,* d. Bruce Humberstone.

DRAMA: MELODRAMA: Revenge; Advertising World; Executive Life; Bosses-Bad; Good Premise Unfulfilled; Coulda Been Good
(The Man in the Grey Flannel Suit; Patterns)

The Mad Miss Manton, 1938, 80m, ★★★1/2/$$$, RKO/Turner. The daffy and persistent social Melsa Manton and her gaggle of debutante detectives keep discovering bodies and thwarting a handsome fella who at first believes Melsa had something to do with the first murder. Barbara Stanwyck, Henry Fonda, Sam Levene, Hattie McDaniel. w. Philip G. Epstein, d. Leigh Jason.

COMEDY: MURDER: MYSTERY: MURDER MYSTERY: Comic Mystery; Screwball Comedy; **ROMANCE:** Romantic Comedy; Detective Stories; Detectives-Amateur; Detectives-Female; Murder-Clearing Oneself; Murders-One by One; Murder-Discovering; Journalists; Fugitives from the Law; Feisty Females; Free Spirits; Unbelieved; Rich vs. Poor; Romance-Class Conflicts; Saving Oneself; Hidden Gems; Female Protagonists
(A Night to Remember; Lady of Burlesque)
(Ed: *Bringing up Baby* gone mystery)

Madness of the Heart, 1949, 105m, ★★1/2/$, GFD/NA. A rich Frenchman marries a beautiful blind girl and spites his jealous neighbor. Paul Dupuis, Margaret Lockwood, Kathleen Byron, Maxwell Reed. w. d. Charles Bennet, N-adap. Flora Sandstrom.

MELODRAMA: ROMANCE: SUSPENSE: Romantic Drama; Newlyweds; Blind People; Jealousy; Neighbors-Troublesome; Secrets-Haunting

The Mad Monkey, 1990, 108m, ★★1/2/$, Ind/MovieStore, R. A screenwriter abroad gets involved with a bizarre brother and sister living on the edge. Jeff Goldblum, Miranda Richardson, Anemone, Arielle Dombasle. w. Fernando Trueba, Manonlo Matji, N-adap. Christopher Frank, *The Dream of the Mad Monkey,* d. Fernando Trueba.

DRAMA: Erotic Drama; Art Films; Drugs; Americans Abroad; Siblings; Incest; Menage à Trois; Independent Films
(Siesta; The Comfort of Strangers; Mister Frost)

The Mad Room, 1969, 92m, ★★1/2/$, Col/NA, R/EV. A wealthy old woman is in danger because her assistant wants her money to support her mentally disabled siblings. Stella Stevens, Shelley Winters, Severn Darden. w. Bernard Girard, A. Z. Martin, d. Bernard Girard.

HORROR: MURDER: Black Comedy; Comedy-Morbid; Murder for Money; Elderly Women; Mentally Disabled
REMAKE/RIPOFF: Ladies in Retirement.
(Who Slew Auntie Roo?; What's the Matter with Helen?)

Mad Wednesday, 1947, 77m, ★★1/2/$, Hughes/NA. A nerdy accountant is fired after years on the job and goes wild. Harold Lloyd, Jimmy Conlin, Margaret Hamilton, Raymond Wilburn. w. d. Preston Sturges.

COMEDY: SATIRE: FARCE: Nervous Breakdowns; Wild People; Unemployment; Nerds; Forgotten Films; Good Premise Unfulfilled
(The Milky Way; The World of Harold Lloyd)
(Ed: A misfire and never really finished, but recut many times by others than Sturges)

The Madwoman of Chaillot, 1969, 142m, ★★★/$, WB/WB. A feisty and eccentric lady (Katharine Hepburn, who else?) fights plans by bureaucrats to drill for oil in Paris with the help of her equally bizarre friends. Yul Brynner, Edith Evans, Danny Kaye, Charles Boyer, Claude Dauphin, Paul Henreid, Nanette Newman, Margaret Leighton, Donald Pleasance, John Gavin, Oscar Homolka, Richard Chamberlain. w. Edward Anhalt, P-adap. Jean Giraudoux, d. Bryan Forbes.

COMEDY DRAMA: SATIRE: Fighting the System; Women Fighting the System; Eccentric People; Feisty Females;

Elderly Women; Female Protagonists; Paris; Classic Play Adaptations; All-Star Casts; Revisionist Films; Environmental Dilemmas; Oil People

Magic, 1978, 107m, ★★★/$$$, 20th/CBS-Fox, R/P-V-S. A ventriloquist takes a breather and heads to the country where his schizophrenic relationship with his dummy begins to take control of his desires for a woman. Anthony Hopkins, Ann-Margret, Burgess Meredith. w., N-adap. William Goldman, d. Richard Attenborough.

DRAMA: SUSPENSE: MURDER: ROMANCE: Hiding out; Vacations; Multiple Personalities; Comedians; Obsessions; Possessions; Nervous Breakdowns; Psycho Killers; Ventriloquists

(Knock on Wood; Silence of the Lambs)

The Magic Box, 1951, 118m, ★★★/$$, Ind/NA. Story of British cinema pioneer, William Friese Greene. Robert Donat, Margaret Johnson, Maria Schell, Richard Attenborough, Laurence Olivier, Leon Genn, Stanley Holloway, John McCallum, Margaret Rutherford, David Tomlinson, Emlyn Williams, Michael Redgrave. w. Eric Ambler, d. John Boulting.

DRAMA: Biographies; Historical Drama; Moviemaking; Inventors; Directors; British Films; All-Star Casts; All-Star Cameos

The Magic Christian, 1969, 95m, ★★¹/₂/$$, Ind/Republic. A wild millionaire takes a cruise and other little adventures trying to keep at bay the sycophants who crave his money. Peter Sellers, Ringo Starr, Richard Attenborough, Laurence Harvey, Christopher Lee, Roman Polanski, Spike Milligan, Yul Brynner, Raquel Welch, John Cleese, Graham Chapman. w. Terry Southern, Joseph McGrath, Peter Sellers, N-adap. w. Terry Southern, d. Joseph McGrath.

COMEDY: SATIRE: Art Films; Comedy-Skits; Bathroom Humor; Psychedelic Era; 1960s; Anti-Establishment Films; Cult Films; Forgotten Films; All-Star Cameos

(Candy; Let it Be; Help)

The Magic Face, 1951, 90m, ★★★/$, Col/NA. A man kills Hitler and then takes his place, leading to Germany's defeat. Luther Adler, Patricia Knight. w. Mort Briskin, Robert Smith, d. Frank Tuttle.

COMEDY: SATIRE: War Stories; World War II Stories; Hitler; Nazi Stories; Impostors; What If . . . Stories; Germany;

Good Premise Unfulfilled; Forgotten Films

(Moon Over Parador; Fatherland)

The Magic of Lassie, 1978, 99m, ★★¹/₂/$$, UA/MGM-UA, G. Lassie is sold away but knows where her true owner is. James Stewart, Alice Faye, Mickey Rooney, Pernell Roberts, Stephanie Zimbalist. w. Jean Holloway, Richard B. Sherman, Robert M. Sherman, d. Don Chaffey. BOSong. Oscars: 1-0.

CHILDREN'S: FAMILY: Pet Stories; Reunions; Grandfathers; Lassie Movies; Dogs

SEQUEL TO: Lassie Come Home

(Incredible Journey; Homeward Bound)

(Ed: Lassie starring in a remake of *Incredible Journey*)

Magic Town, 1947, 103m, ★★¹/₂/$, Republic/Republic. A polling company discovers the perfect All-American town whose opinions are directly representative of the country, but not necessarily everything else is. James Stewart, Jane Wyman, Kent Smith, Regis Toomey. w. Robert Riskin, d. William A. Wellman.

COMEDY DRAMA: COMEDY: SATIRE: Social Satire; American Dream; Small-town Life; Ordinary People Stories; Capra-esque; Good Premise Unfulfilled; Coulda Been Great; Forgotten Films; Hidden Gems

(It's a Wonderful Life; Cold Turkey)

The Magnificent Ambersons, 1945, 88m, ★★★★/$$, RKO/Turner. The decline of a great family in turn-of-the-century Indiana. Joseph Cotten, Agnes Moorehead (BSActress), Dolores Costello, Tim Holt, Anne Baxter, Ray Collins. w. d. Orson Welles, N-adap, Booth Tarkington. BPicture, BCin. Oscars: 3-0.

DRAMA: Family Drama; Riches to Rags; **TRAGEDY:** Avant-Garde Films; Rich People; Ensemble Films; American Dream; Midwestern Life; Young Men; 1900s; Narrated Films

REMAKE OF: Pampered Youth.

(King's Row; Another Part of the Forest; The Little Foxes; Alice Adams)

The Magnificent Doll, 1946, 95m, ★★/$$, U/NA. A connection between Dolly Madison, first lady, and Aaron Burr, the infamous traitor, is discovered. Ginger Rogers, David Niven, Burgess Meredith, Peggy Wood, Stephen McNally. w. Irving Stone, d. Frank Borzage.

DRAMA: Biographies; True or Not?;

Presidents; Historical Drama; Secrets-Keeping; Female Protagonists; Forgotten Films

Magnificent Obsession, 1935, 112m, ★★★/$$$$, U/NA. Irene Dunne, Robert Taylor, Ralph Morgan, Betty Furness, Arthur Treacher. w. George O'Neil, Sarah Y. Mason, Victor Heerman, N-adap. w. Lloyd C. Douglas, d. John M. Stahl.

Magnificent Obsession, 1954, 108m, ★★★¹/₂/$$$, U/MCA-U. When a woman and her husband are in an accident, he dies and she is blinded, and the young man circumstantially responsible for it vows to find a cure for her. Jane Wyman (BActress), Rock Hudson, Agnes Morehead, Barbara Rush, Otto Kruger. w. Robert Blees, d. Douglas Sirk. Oscars: 1-0.

MELODRAMA: Tearjerkers; **ROMANCE:** Medical Drama; Romantic Drama; Disease Stories; Blind People; Doctors; Romance-Reunited; Guilty Conscience; Obsessions; Accidents; Female Screenwriters; Women's Films

(Not as a Stranger; The Cure; Imitation of Life; Written on the Wind; Johnny Belinda)

The Magnificent Seven, 1960, 138m, ★★★¹/₂/$$$$, UA/CBS-Fox. Seven mercenaries are hired to protect a Mexican town from bad guys on the way. Yul Brynner, Steve McQueen. w. William Roberts (based on the *Seven Samurai*), d. John Sturges.

WESTERN: ACTION: Ensemble Films; Ensembles-Male; Mercenaries; Protecting Someone; Mexico; Hitmen; Foreign Film Remakes

REMAKE OF: *The Seven Samurai.*

(The Wild Bunch; The Professionals)

The Magnificent Yankee, 1950, 88m, ★★¹/₂/$$, MGM/MGM-UA. The life of supreme court judge Oliver Wendell Holmes. Louis Calhern (BActor), Ann Harding, Richard Anderson. w. Emmet Lavery, P-adap. w. Emmet Lavery, d. John Sturges. Oscars: 1-0.

DRAMA: Biographies; Judges; Lawyers; Politicians; Supreme Court

(First Monday in October; Talk of the Town)

Magnum Force, 1973, 124m, ★★★/$$$, WB/WB, R/EV-P. Dirty Harry's at it again, this time after his bad cop partner. Clint Eastwood, Hal Holbrook, Mitch Ryan, David Soul. w. John Milius, Michael Cimino, d. Ted Post.

ACTION: MURDER: Police Stories; Crime Drama; Detective Stories; Detectives-Police; Police Corruption; Police-Vigilante; Vigilantes; San Francisco
SEQUEL TO: Dirty Harry. **SEQUEL:** The Enforcer.
(The Gauntlet; Sudden Impact)
The Magus, 1968, 116m, ★★/$, 20th/NA. A British teacher goes to Greece to think and runs into a beautiful woman and a magician and much confusion. Michael Caine, Anthony Quinn, Candice Bergen, Anna Karina, Julian Glover. w. John Fowles, N-adap. John Fowles, d. Guy Green.
DRAMA: Fantasy; **MYSTERY:**
ROMANCE: Writers; Illusions; Art Films; Greece; Vacations
(The Ebony Tower; The French Lieutenant's Woman)
The Mahabharata, 1989, 171m, ★★¹/₂/$, Virgin/Facets. A man tells a boy the story of a great war in old India, based on the epic poem. Urs Biher, Ryszard Cieslak. w. Peter Brook, Jean-Claude Carrière, Marie-Hélène Estienne, P-adap. w. Jean-Claude Carrière, d. Peter Brook.
DRAMA: War Stories; Epics; Narrated Films; India
Mahler, 1974, 115m, ★★¹/₂/$, Ind/NA. The life of composer Gustav Mahler in fantasy form by the avant-garde Ken Russell. Robert Powell, Georgina Hale. w. d. Ken Russell.
DRAMA: Biographies; Art Films; Fantasy; Music-Composers; Musicians; British Films; Writer-Directors
(The Music Lovers; Amadeus; Gothic)
Mahogany, 1975, 109m, ★★¹/₂/$$$, Par/Par, R/S-P-FFN. The rise and confusion of a black fashion designer and model. Diana Ross, Anthony Perkins, Billy Dee Williams, Nina Foch. w. John Byrum, d. Berry Gordy. BOSong: "Do You Know Where You're Goin' To." Oscars: 1-0.
ROMANCE: MELODRAMA: Fame-Rise to; Fashion World; Models; Black Women; Cinderella Stories; Rape/Rapists; Unintentionally Funny; Camp; Underrated; Female Protagonists
(Lady Sings the Blues; Darling; Hollow Image)
(Ed: Not that bad, just takes itself too seriously)
Maid of Salem, 1937, 86m, ★★¹/₂/$$, Par/NA. A young woman in 1690s Salem is accused of witchcraft and defended

only by her boyfriend. Claudette Colbert, Fred MacMurray, Harvey Stephens, Gale Sondergaard, Louise Dresser. w. Bradley King, Walter Ferris, Durward Grinstead, d. Frank Lloyd.
DRAMA: MELODRAMA: ROMANCE: Accused Unjustly; Witchcraft; Saving Someone; 1600s; Early America
(The Crucible; The Scarlet Letter)
Maid to Order, 1987, 96m, ★★/$, New Visions/Live, PG-13/P. A stuck-up rich young woman winds up working as a maid in Malibu with only a fairy god-mother to save her. Ally Sheedy, Beverly D'Angelo, Michael Ontkean, Valerie Perrine, Dick Shawn, Tom Skerritt. w. Amy Jones, Perry Howze, Randy Howze, d. Amy Jones.
COMEDY: SATIRE: Fantasy; Wishes; Riches to Rags; Servants; Cinderella Stories; Good Premise Unfulfilled; Coulda Been Good; Female Protagonists; Female Directors; Female Screenwriters
(My Man Godfrey; Overboard)
The Maids, 1974, 95m, ★★★/$, Brut/NA. Two Parisian maids plot to kill their master and possibly each other. Glenda Jackson, Susannah York, Viven Merchant. w. Robert Enders, Christopher Miles, P-adap. Jean Genet, d. Christopher Miles.
DRAMA: Murder-Attempted; Revenge; Avant-Garde Films; Art Films; Servants; Rich vs. Poor; Paris; Stagelike Films; Independent Films
(The Homecoming; Nasty Habits; Querelle)
(Ed: Highly verbose. Notable for the performances or as an intro to Genet)
Mail Order Bride, 1963, 83m, ★★¹/₂/$, MGM/NA. A cowboy tries to find a wife for a younger cowpoke who won't settle down. Buddy Ebsen, Lois Nettleton, Keir Dullea, Warren Oates. w. d. Burt Kennedy.
WESTERN: Western Comedy;
ROMANCE: Cowboys; Marriage of Convenience; Brides-Mail Order; Matchmakers; Settling Down; Wild People; Writer-Directors
(Zandy's Bride; Paint Your Wagon)
The Main Event, 1979, 112m, ★★¹/₂/$$$$, WB/WB, PG/S-P. A cosmetic heiress learns she's broke and the only thing left she owns is the rights to a down and out boxer who happens to turn her on. w. Gail Parent, Andrew Smith, d. Howard Zieff.

COMEDY: ROMANCE: Romantic Comedy; Sports Movies; Boxing; Romance with Boxer; Riches to Rags; Battle of the Sexes; Romance-Bickering; Feisty Females; Female Protagonists; Good Premise Unfulfilled
(Moonlighting TV Series; The Prizefighter and the Lady; The Cowboy and the Lady; What's Up, Doc?; For Pete's Sake)
(Ed: Best thing about it was the title song)
Main Street to Broadway, 1953, 102m, ★★¹/₂/$, Ind/MPI. A playwright goes through the stages leading to a production, learning the ropes the hard way. Tom Morton, Mary Murphy. w. Samson Raphaelson, d. Tay Garnett.
DRAMA: MELODRAMA: Biographies-Fictional; Theater Life; Writers; Forgotten Films
(Act One; The Big Picture; Youngblood Hawke)
Maitresse, 1976, 112m, ★★★/$$, WB/WB, R/ES-FFN-MFN. A man gets involved in the bondage and torture sexual world of decadent France. Gerard Depardieu. w. d. Barbet Schroeder.
DRAMA: Erotic Drama; Sexual Kinkiness; Alternative Lifestyles; Torture; Sexual Problems; French Films; Curiosities; Writer-Directors
(Menage; Betty Blue; Tattoo)
The Major and the Minor, 1942, 100m, ★★★/$$$, Par/NA, AMC. A young woman poses as a girl to take a cheaper train ride but a soldier is onto her in more than one way. Ginger Rogers, Ray Milland, Rita Johnson, Robert Benchley. w. Charles Brackett, Billy Wilder, d. Billy Wilder.
COMEDY: ROMANCE: Romantic Comedy; Romance-Reluctant; Con Artists; Soldiers; Young Women; Disguises; Trains; Female Protagonists
(Bachelor Mother; It Happened One Night)
Major Barbara, 1941, 121m, ★★★¹/₂/$$, Ind/Learning Corp., HomeVision. The moral daughter of an arms dealer signs up with the Salvation Army in defiance but can't deal with them taking her father's money. Wendy Hiller, Rex Harrison, Robert Morley, Robert Newton, Emlyn Williams, Deborah Kerr. w. Anatole de Grunwald, Gabriel Pascal, P-adap. Bernard Shaw, d. Gabriel Pascal, Harold French, David Lean.
DRAMA: Social Drama; Fathers & Daughters; Parents vs. Children; Arms

Dealers; Ethics; Rebels; Young Women;
Female Protagonists
(Guys and Dolls; Music Box)

Major Dundee, 1965, 134m, ★★½/$$,
Col/Goodtimes. Cavalry men go out to
exterminate an Indian tribe. Charlton
Heston, Richard Harris, Jim Hutton,
James Coburn, Warren Oates, Slim
Pickens. w. Harry Julian Fink, Oscar
Saul, Sam Peckinpah, d. Sam Peckinpah.
WESTERN: ACTION: Indians-American;
Massacres; Cavalry

Major League, 1989, 106m, ★★½/$$$,
Par/Par, PG-13/P-MRN. The baseball
team doesn't like their new owner-a cantankerous woman who wants them to lose
for her financial gain. Tom Berenger,
Charlie Sheen, Corbin Bernsen, Margaret
Whitton, Rene Russo, Wesley Snipes.
w. d. David S. Ward.

COMEDY: Sports Movies; Baseball;
Ensembles-Male; Female Among Males;
Female in Male Domain; Battle of the
Sexes; Underdog Stories

SEQUEL: Major League 2 (1994).

REMAKE/RIPOFF OF: Take Me Out to
the Ball Game.

(Take Me Out to the Ball Game; Major
League 2; The Lemon Drop Kid)

Major League 2, 1994, 105m, ★½/$$,
WB/WB, PG-13/P-S. After being the
underdogs in the original, this time the
over the hill team is just done under.
Charlie Sheen, Tom Berenger, Corbin
Bernsen, Dennis Haysbert, David Keith,
Alison Doody, Margaret Whitton. w. R. J.
Stewart, d. David S. Ward.

COMEDY: Sports Movies; Comebacks;
Baseball; Ensembles-Male; Female
Among Males

Major Payne, 1995, 95m, ★★/$$,
Universal/MCA-U, PG-13/P-S. An over-
bearing, cantankerous drill sergeant
comes in to whip a junior ROTC team
into shape for competition, but personal-
ity conflicts and love may get in the way.
Damon Wayans, Karyn Parsons, Steven
Martini, Andrew Harrison Leeds,
William Hickey, Michael Ironside,
Albert Hall, Joda Blaire-Hershman,
Steven Coleman, Damien Wayans.
w. Dean Lorey, Damon Wayans, Gary
Rosen, d. Nick Castle.

COMEDY: Military Comedy; Stern Men;
Men and Boys; Underdog Stories;
Teenagers; Black Men; Black
Screenwriters
(Mo' Money; Sgt. Bilko)

A Majority of One, 1961, 156m, ★★/$,
WB/NA. A cruise is setting for a strange
romance between a Jewish widow and a
Japanese man. Rosalind Russell, Alec
Guinness. w. Leonard Spigelgass, P-adap.
w. Leonard Spigelgass, d. Mervyn Le Roy.
BCCin. Oscars: 1-0.

ROMANCE: COMEDY DRAMA: MELO-
DRAMA: Ships; Vacations; Vacation
Romance; Romance-Interracial; Japanese
People; Jewish People
(Love Is a Many-Splendored Thing; The
Lonely Passion of Judith Hearne)

Make Me an Offer, 1954, 88m,
★★½/$, Ind/Sultan. An antique shop
owner becomes obsessed with owning a
particular vase and will do anything to
get it. Peter Finch, Adrienne Corri, Meier
Tzeniker. w. W. P. Lipscomb, N-adap.
w. Wolf Mankowitz, d. Cyril Frankel.

COMEDY: COMEDY DRAMA: Jewish
People; Ordinary People Stories;
Obsessions; British Films

Make Mine Mink, 1960, 101m, ★★★/
$$, Rank/No. Rich Brits get a kick out of
stealing fur coats and then selling them to
give the money to charities. Terry-
Thomas, Athene Seyler, Billie Whitelaw.
w. Michael Pertwee, Peter Blackmore,
P-adap. Peter Coke, *Breath of Spring*,
d. Robert Asher.

COMEDY: FARCE: SATIRE: Rich
People; Rich vs. Poor; Robin Hood
Stories; Thieves
(School for Scoundrels; The Lavender
Hill Mob; The Wrong Arm of the Law)

Make Mine Music, 1946, 74m,
★★★/$$$, Disney/NA. Disney animated
shorts. w. various, d. various.

CHILDREN'S: FAMILY: Cartoons;
Multiple Stories; Compilation Films;
Music Movies
(Fantasia)

Making Love, 1982, 111m, ★★★/$$,
20th/CBS-Fox, R/S. A young doctor
leaves his wife for a male writer who then
may not want him. Michael Ontkean,
Harry Hamlin, Kate Jackson, Wendy
Hiller, Arthur Hill, Nancy Olson. w.
Barry Sandler, SS-adap. A. Scott Berg,
d. Arthur Hiller.

DRAMA: MELODRAMA: ROMANCE:
Romance-Triangles; Cheating Men;
Starting Over; Gay Men; Sexuality;
Marriage on the Rocks; Alternative
Lifestyles; Dual Lives; Doctors; Writers;
Los Angeles; Ahead of Its Time; Nar-
rated Films

(Ed: Making the protagonist the doctor
but having the writer narrate puts the
story out of balance, and the clichéd writ-
ing ruins the rest)

Making Mr. Right, 1987, 98m, ★★★/$,
Orion/Orion, PG/S. A kooky young
woman falls in love with a nerdy android
who may be able to do what flesh and
blood can't. John Malkovich, Ann
Magnuson, Glenne Headly, Ben Masters,
Laurie Metcalf, Polly Bergen, Hart
Bochner. w. Floyd Byars, Laurie Frank,
d. Susan Seidelman.

COMEDY: SATIRE: ROMANCE:
Romantic Comedy; Androids; Battle of
the Sexes; Advertising World; Female
Screenwriters; Female Directors; Female
Protagonists; Forgotten Films; Overlooked
at Release
(Starman; She-Devil)

Mala Noche, 1988, 78m, ★★★/$,
Ind/NA. A gay man falls in love with a
Mexican illegal alien who is apparently
straight. Tim Streeter, Doug Cooeyate.
w. d. Gus Van Sant, SS-adap. Walt Curtis.

DRAMA: ROMANCE: Character Studies;
Romance-Doomed; Romance-Reluctant;
Gay Men; Homophobia; Mexicans
(My Own Private Idaho; Law of Desire)

Malaya, 1949, 95m, ★★★/$$, MGM/
MGM-UA. A man becomes a rubber
smuggler during World War II for the
cause under Japanese occupation.
Spencer Tracy, James Stewart, Sidney
Greenstreet, Valentina Cortes, Lionel
Barrymore. w. Frank Fenton, d. Richard
Thorpe.

DRAMA: SUSPENSE: War Stories; World
War II Stories; Political Unrest; Japanese
as Enemy; Spies; Thieves; Ordinary
People Turned Criminal; Asia; South
Pacific

Malcolm, 1986, 86m, ★★½/$, Vestron/
Vestron, R. A mentally disabled young
man takes in some new roommates and
some new problems. Colin Friels, John
Hargeaves. w. David Parker, d. Nadia
Tass.

DRAMA: COMEDY DRAMA: Mentally
Disabled; Young Men; Australian Films;
Female Directors
(Tim; Tell Me that You Love Me,
Junie Moon)

Malcolm X, 1992, 201m, ★★★/$$$,
WB/WB, R/P-V-S. The life of controver-
sial black militant from his days as a
criminal to his triumphant reform and
beyond. Denzel Washington (BActor),

Angela Bassett, Albert Hall, Spike Lee, Lonette McKee. w. Arnold Perl, Spike Lee, NF-adap. Malcolm X, Alex Haley (*The Autobiography of Malcolm X*), d. Spike Lee.

DRAMA: Epics; Biographies; Autobiographical Stories; Black vs. White; Political Drama; Political Unrest; Episodic Stories; Power-Rise to; Historical Drama; Politicians; Charismatic People; Black Men (King [TV Miniseries]; Devil in a Blue Dress; Do the Right Thing; Mo' Better Blues)

The Male Animal, 1942, 101m, ★★★/ $$, WB/NA. When a nerdy college professor's wife takes a shine to a football player, he revamps himself a bit. Henry Fonda, Olivia deHavilland, Jack Carson, Hattie McDaniel. w. Julius J. and Philip G. Epstein, Stephen Morehouse Avery, P-adap. w. James Thurber and Elliott Nugent, d. Elliott Nugent.

COMEDY: COMEDY DRAMA: ROMANCE: Marriage Comedy; Battle of the Sexes; Nerds; Extroverted vs. Introverted; College Life; Professors; Jealousy; Life Transitions; Midlife Crisis (The Animal Kingdom; The Mad Miss Manton)

Malice, 1993, 107m, ★★★/$$$, Col/New Line, R/S-P. Women are being killed in a sleepy college town when a yuppie couple is visited by an old friend who's a surgeon with a possibly murderous scalpel. But when a malpractice suit develops involving his wife and the doctor-friend, the husband may be fooled by everyone, and it may be too late. Alec Baldwin, Bill Pullman, Nicole Kidman, Bebe Neuwirth, George C. Scott, Anne Bancroft, Peter Gallagher. w. Aaron Sorkin, Scott Frank, d. Harold Becker.

SUSPENSE: Psychological Thriller; **MURDER:** Murder of Spouse; Murders of Women; Serial Killers; College Life; Yuppies; Romance-Triangles; Friends as Enemies; Roommates from Hell; Dangerous Men; Insurance Scams; Doctors; Clever Plots & Endings; Coulda Been Great (Pacific Heights; The Last Seduction) (Ed: Worth a look. Could have been far more tired; originally called *Damages*, but the film *Damage* was already planned)

Mallrats, 1995, 90m, ★★1/2/$$, Miramax/Miramax, R/P-S. Life among the youth mall culture of suburbia in bits and spurts. Jeremy London, Jason Lee, Shannen Doherty, Claire Forlani, Ben Affleck, Joey Lauren Adams, Priscilla Barnes. w. d. Kevin Smith.

COMEDY: SATIRE: Suburban Life; Ensemble Films; Young People; Writer-Directors; Coulda Been Good (Clerks; Heathers; Dazed and Confused) (Ed: A few hilarious bits but not as full as *Clerks*)

Malone, 1987, 92m, ★★/$, Orion/Orion, R/V. A CIA hitman can't get away from the life no matter where he hides. Burt Reynolds, Cliff Robertson, Kenneth McMillan, Cynthia Gibb, Lauren Hutton. w. Christopher Frank, N-adap. William Wingate (*Shotgun*), d. Harley Corliss.

ACTION: Crime Drama; CIA Agents; Hitmen; One Last Time; Starting Over; Hiding Out; Coulda Been Good (Heat; Physical Evidence)

The Maltese Falcon, 1931, 80m, ★★★/ $$, WB/Ind. Ricardo Cortez, Bebe Daniels, Thelma Todd. w. Maude Fulton, Lucien Hubbard, Brow Holmes, N-adap. Dashiell Hammett, d. Roy Del Ruth.

REMAKES: Satan Met a Lady; The Maltese Falcon (1941).

Forgotten Films

The Maltese Falcon, 1941, 101m, ★★★★/$$$, WB/MGM-UA, Fox. Sam Spade is enlisted by the wife of his murdered partner and winds up in a bizarre race to claim an elusive antique bird statuette. Humphrey Bogart, Mary Astor, Sidney Greenstreet (BSActor), Elisha Cook, Lee Patrick, Peter Lorre, Ward Bond, Gladys George. w. d. John Huston (BOScr), N-adap. Dashiell Hammett. BPicture. Oscars: 3-0.

DRAMA: SUSPENSE: MYSTERY: MURDER: MURDER MYSTERY: Detective Stories; Detectives-Private; Detectives in Deep; Double Crossings; Treasure Hunts; Birds; Race Against Time; Film Noir (Casablanca; The Big Sleep [1946])

Mama, There's a Man in Your Bed, see Momma. . . .

The Mambo Kings, 1992, 104m, ★★★/$, WB/WB, R/S-V. Two Cuban brothers hit the Latin scene in 1940s New York and move together through the ups and downs of their careers and their women. Armand Assante, Antonio Banderas, Cathy Moriarty, Maruschka Detmers, Desi Arnaz, Jr., Roscoe Lee Browne, Tito Puente.

w. Cynthia Cidre, N-adap. Oscar Hijuelos (*The Mambo Kings Play Songs of Love*), d. Arne Glimcher. BOSong. Oscars: 1-0.

DRAMA: ROMANCE: Brothers; Friendships-Male; Latin People; Musicians; 1940s; New York Life; Cuba; Pulitzer Prize Adaptations; Female Screenwriters (Copacabana)

Mame, 1974, 131m, ★★/$, WB/WB, G. Musical version of film version of stage and novel version comes to screen with Lucille Ball, who cannot sing. Bea Arthur, Robert Preston, Bruce Davison, Joyce Van Patten. Paul Zindel, P-adap. Jerome Lawrence, Robert E. Lee, N-adap. Patrick Dennis, d. Gene Saks.

MUSICALS: COMEDY: Musical Comedy; Family Stories; Feisty Females; Christmas; Mothers-Surrogate; Novel and Play Adaptations; 1920s; Depression Era; Female Protagonists

MUSICAL REMAKE OF: Auntie Mame. (Ed: See the original, then if the music is what you want, buy the cast album with Angela Lansbury)

Mamma Roma, 1962/1995, 110m, ★★★1/2/$, Ind-Milestone/NA, NR/S. An aging prostitute is freed from her pimp and takes her son, who knows nothing of her profession, to Rome to start over. (But once there and having made a respectable name, her pimp returns to get blackmail money or let her son and everyone else know her secrets.) Things don't go so well. Anna Magnani, Ettore Garofolo, Franco Citti. w. d. Pier Paolo Pasolini.

DRAMA: MELODRAMA: TRAGEDY: Mothers & Sons; Starting Over; Prostitutes with a Heart of Gold; Pimps; Blackmail; Rome; Forgotten Films; Hidden Gems; Italian Films; Writer-Directors (Open City; The Rose Tattoo; Madame X)

A Man, a Woman and a Bank, 1979, 101m, ★★1/2/$, AIP/NewLine, R/S-V. Two men with expert knowledge put it to use to rob a bank with a woman. Donald Sutherland, Brooke Adams, Paul Mazursky. w. Raynold Gideon, Bruce A. Evans, Stuart Margolin, d. Noel Black.

DRAMA: Crime Drama; Heist Stories; Bank Robberies; Thieves; Canadian Films; Crime Pays (Silent Partner; Quick Change)

A Man About the House, 1947, 95m, ★★1/2/$$, B-L/Nos, Sinister. When two

British women travel to Italy to their villa, the sexy caretaker puts them under his spell and may yet take their money and poison one of them. Margaret Johnson, Dulcie Gray, Kieron Moore. w. J. B. Williams, Leslie Arliss, P-adap. John Perry, N-adap. Francis Brett Young, d. Leslie Arliss.

SUSPENSE: Murder-Attempted; Women in Jeopardy; Enemy-Sleeping with the; Servants; Inheritances at Stake; Poisons; Sisters; Italy; British Films; Novel and Play Adaptations
(Gaslight; Kind Lady; Rebecca)

Man Alive, 1945, 70m, ★★¹/₂/$$, RKO/NA. A man comes back from the dead as a ghost to mess things up for his wife and her new man. Pat O'Brien, Ellen Drew, Adolphe Menjou, Rudy Vallee. w. Edwin Blum, d. Ray Enright.

COMEDY: Ghosts; Dead-Back from the; Husbands-Troublesome

REMAKE/RETREAD OF: Blithe Spirit
(Kiss Me Goodbye; Blithe Spirit; Topper)

A Man and a Woman, 1966, 102m, ★★★¹/₂/$$$, WB/WB. A widow and a widower fall in love in chic, mod Paris on the LeMans tracks amid beautiful, multi-colored images. Anouk Aimee (BActress), Jean-Louis Trintignant. w. Claude LeLouch, Pierre Uytterhoeven (**BOScr**), d. LeLouch (BDirector). **BFLFilm.** Oscars: 4-2.

ROMANCE: DRAMA: MELODRAMA: Romantic Drama; Car Racing; Widows; Widowers; Starting Over; Marriage-Impending; Mod Era; Paris; French Films

SEQUEL: A Man and a Woman: Twenty Years Later.
(And Now, My Love; The Umbrellas of Cherbourg)
(Ed: The theme lives on far more famously than the film, but its following did demand a sequel . . .)

A Man and a Woman: Twenty Years Later, 1986, 120m, ★★¹/₂/$, WB/WB, PG. The romance picks up in their marriage much later with the same style, somehow more dated than when they first dated. Anouk Aimee, Jean-Louis Trintignant. w. Claude Lelouch, Pierre Uytterhoeven, Monique Lange, Jérôme Tonnerre, d. Claude Lelouch.

ROMANCE: DRAMA: Romantic Drama; Marriage Drama; Romance-Reunited; Romance-Middle-Aged; Paris; Car Racing; French Films

(Ed: Apparently much of the original audience couldn't remember enough about how they got together to care)

Man Bites Dog, 1992, 95m, ★★★/$, Ind/Fox-Lorber, R, NC-17/EV-B&G-S. A documentary follows a serial killer on his rounds, but it turns out the filmmakers have been hired by the killer and are paid by what he robs along the way. Benoit Poelvoorde, Remy Belvaux, Andre Borzei. w. Poelvoorde, Belvaux, Borzei, d. Poelvoorde, Belvaux, Borzei.

SATIRE: Media Satire; Black Comedy; Serial Killers; Documentaries; Documentary Style; Movie Making; Movies within Movies; Comedy-Morbid; Art Films; French Films (Belgian)
(Henry: Portrait of a Serial Killer; Natural Born Killers)

A Man Called Horse, 1970, 114m, ★★★/$$$, Cinema Center/Fox, R/EV-MN. In the early 1800s on the Great Plains, a British man is captured by renegade Indians and held like a slave until he eventually uses his wits to turn the tables. w. Jack di Witt, SS-adap. Dorothy M. Johnson, d. Elliot Silverstein.

WESTERN: DRAMA: Westerns-Neo; Indians-American; White Man Among Indians; Fish out of Water Stories; Character Studies; Slavery; Episodic Stories; Historical Drama; True Stories; Female Writers; Sleeper Hits; Revisionist Films

SEQUELS: Return of a Man Called Horse, 1976, Triumphs of a Man Called Horse, 1984.
(Man in the Wilderness; Dances with Wolves)

The Manchurian Candidate, 1962, 126m, ★★★★/$$$, UA/Par. A young man (Laurence Harvey) has been brainwashed in a political assassination conspiracy possibly involving his own mother (Angela Lansbury, BSActress). Frank Sinatra, Janet Leigh, Henry Silva. w. George Axelrod, N-adap. Ricahrd Condon, d. John Frankenheimer. Oscars: 1-0.

DRAMA: Spy Films; Spies; **MYSTERY: SUSPENSE: MURDER MYSTERY:** Psychological Drama; Political Thriller; Conspiracy; Assassinations; Communists; Korean War; Cold War Era; Anarchists; Brainwashing; Evil Women; Mothers & Sons
(The Parallax View; Winter Kills; Telefon)

(Ed: Withdrawn from circulation for twenty years due to parallels with Kennedy assassination)

A Man Could Get Killed, 1966, 98m, ★★¹/₂/$, U/MCA-U. An American businessman in Portugal is mistaken for a secret agent and has to go on the run. James Garner, Melina Mercouri, Sandra Dee, Tony Franciosa. w. T.E.B. Clarke, Richard Breen, N-adap. David Walker, *Diamonds are Danger*, d. Ronald Neame, Cliff Owen.

ACTION: COMEDY: Action Comedy; Spy Films; Spies; Spoofs-Spy; Secret Agents; Identities-Mistaken; Americans Abroad; Coulda Been Good; Forgotten Films
(Arabesque; Mr. Buddwing)

Mandela, 1987, 135m, ★★★/$$$, HBO/HBO. The early years of the great anti-apartheid leader up until his imprisonment on trumped-up charges in 1964. Danny Glover, Alfre Woodard, Julian Glover. d. Philip Saville.

DRAMA: Biographies; South Africa; Apartheid; Black vs. White; Black Casts; Black Men; Black Woman; Rebels; Political Unrest; Race Relations; Accused Unjustly; Framed?; Courtroom Drama; Prison Drama; Historical Drama; TV Movies
(Bopha!; Cry the Beloved Country; Cry Freedom)

Mandingo, 1975, 126m, ★★¹/₂/$$$, DEG-Par/Par, R/ES-P-FFN-MFN. The real goings-on on a dilapidated Southern plantation where the owners really mingle with the slaves. Perry King, James Mason, Susan George, Richard Ward, Brenda Sykes, Ken Norton. w. Norman Wexler, P-adap. w. Jack Kirkland, N-adap. w. Kyle Onstott, d. Richard Fleischer.

MELODRAMA: Erotic Drama; Black vs. White; Slavery; Plantations; Southerns; Civil War Era; Revisionist Films; Camp; Cult Films

SEQUEL: Drum.
(Drum; Roots; Queen)

A Man for All Seasons, 1966, 120m, ★★★¹/₂/$$$, Col/RCA-Col, PG. The story of Sir Thomas More's objection to King Henry VIII's divorce and his valiant try at saving his own life with reason under an unreasonable king. Paul Scofield (**BActor**), Wendy Hiller (BSActress), Susannah York, Robert Shaw (BSActor), John Hurt, Leo McKern, Orson Welles, Nigel Davenport, Corin

Redgrave. w. Robert Bolt (**BAScr**), P-adap. Robert Bolt, d. Fred Zinnemann (**BDirector**). **BPicture, BCCin, BCCostume.** Oscars: 8-6.

DRAMA: Historical Drama; Costume Drama; Kings; Divorce; Fighting the System; Trials; Rebels; England; Faded Hits

TV REMAKE: 1976.

(Cromwell; Becket; The Lion in Winter)

Man Friday, 1975, 115m, ★★/$, Avco/Fox. A re-telling of the Robinson Crusoe tale with Friday as an intelligent black man who supports Crusoe immeasurably. Peter O'Toole, Richard Roundtree. w. Adrian Mitchell, d. Jack Gold.

DRAMA: ADVENTURE: Survival Drama; Islands; Shipwrecked; Stranded on an Island; Race Relations; Black vs. White; Oppression; Slavery; Revisionist Films (The Adventures of Robinson Crusoe; Crusoe)

The Man from Colorado, 1949, 99m, ★★1/2/$$, Col/Col. A Civil War soldier settles out west and becomes a violent judge to maintain the law in his town. Glenn Ford, William Holden, Ellen Drew, Edgar Buchanan, Ray Collins. w. Robert D. Andrews, Ben Maddow, Borden Chase, d. Henry Levin.

WESTERNS: Judges; Civil War Era

The Man from Laramie, 1955, 104m, ★★★/$$$, Col/Col. A drifter is really out seeking the men who killed his brother. James Stewart, Arthur Kennedy, Donald Crisp, Cathy O'Donnell, Jack Elam. w. Philip Yordan, Frank Burt, d. Anthony Mann.

WESTERNS: Revenge; Westerns-Revenge; Avenging Death of Loved One; Drifters; Brothers; Men in Conflict; Trail of a Killer

The Man from Snowy River, 1982, 107m, ★★★/$$$, Disney/Disney, PG. A young boy grows up with a strong love of horses which follows him throughout his life. Kirk Douglas, Jack Thompson, Sigrid Thornton. w. John Dixon, Fred Cullen, POEM-Adap. w. A.B. Paterson, d. George Miller.

ADVENTURE: ACTION: WESTERNS: FAMILY: CHILDREN'S: Horses; Boys; Men and Boys; Child Protagonists; Australian Films; Australia; Sleeper Hits; Hidden Gems; Old-Fashioned Recent Films (The Black Stallion; Black Beauty)

The Man from the Diners' Club, 1963, 96m, ★★1/2/$$, Col/NA. A worker who accidentally gives a gangster a credit card has to get it back-if the mob doesn't get him first. Danny Kaye, Telly Savalas, Martha Hyer, Cara Williams, George Kennedy. w. William Peter Blatty, d. Frank Tashlin.

COMEDY: Mob Stories; Mob Comedy; Mix-ups; Misunderstandings; Fugitives from the Mob (Knock on Wood; Hiding Out)

Manhattan (B&W), 1979, 95m, ★★★★/$$$$, UA/MGM-UA, R/P-S. Several people's lives cross paths when a comedy writer (Woody Allen) quits his job and pursues an affair with his best friend's (Michael Murphy) mistress (Diane Keaton). The only problem is his teenage girlfriend, not to mention his lesbian ex-wife. Meryl Streep, Mariel Hemingway (**BSActress**), Anne Ditchburne, Andrea Marcovicci. w. d. Woody Allen (**BOScr**). Oscars: 2-0.

COMEDY: ROMANCE: Romantic Comedy; Romance-Older Men/Younger Women; Romance-Doomed; Romance with Friend's Lover; Secrets-Keeping; Romance-Triangles; Neurotic People; Lesbians; Multiple Stories; Ensemble Films; New York Life; Writer-Directors; Actor Directors; Cult Films (Annie Hall; Hannah and Her Sisters; Manhattan Murder Mystery; Husbands and Wives)

Manhattan Melodrama, 1934, 93m, ★★★1/2/$$$, MGM/MGM-UA. Two friends grow up out of the New York slums to become antagonists as D.A. and gangster. William Powell, Clark Gable, Myrna Loy, Leo Carrillo. w. Oliver H. P. Garrett, Joseph L. Mankiewicz, SS-adap. Arthur Caesar, d. W. S. Van Dyke.

DRAMA: MELODRAMA: Crime Drama; Mob Stories; Lawyers; Friends as Enemies; Inner City Life; Power-Rise to; Friendships-Male; Friendships-Great

REMAKE/RIPOFF: True Confessions. (True Confessions; Once Upon a Time in America; Angels with Dirty Faces)

Manhattan Murder Mystery, 1993, 94m, ★★★1/2/$$$, Tri-Star/Col-Tri, PG. The wife in a neurotic married couple (Diane Keaton, Woody Allen) is certain the death of a neighbor they just met was a murder and drags their friends in on a wild goose chase to prove it. Alan Alda, Anjelica Huston, Marshall Brickman. w. Woody Allen, d. Woody Allen.

COMEDY: MYSTERY: MURDER MYSTERY: FARCE: SUSPENSE: Black Comedy; Chase Movies; Comic Mystery; Comic Thriller; Hide the Dead Body; Female Protagonists; Detective Stories; Detectives-Amateur; Detectives-Female; Detective Couples; New York Life; Movie Theaters; Clever Plots & Endings; Double Crossings; Swapping Partners; Writer-Directors; Actor Directors (A Night to Remember; Rear Window; Compromising Positions; Consenting Adults; The Ghost and Mr. Chicken; The Lady from Shanghai)

Man Hunt, 1941, 98m, ★★/$$, 20th/NA. An assassin misses when trying to hit Hitler and then has to hide during the day and run at night to get back to England. Walter Pidgeon, Joan Bennett, George Sanders, John Carradine, Roddy McDowell. w. Dudley Nichols, N-adap. Geoffrey Household, *Rogue Male,* d. Fritz Lang.

SUSPENSE: Chase Movies; Assassinations; Spies; Spy Films; Germans as Enemy; Hitler; Murder-Attempted

REMAKE: Rogue Male (1974)

Manhunter, 1986, 120m, ★★1/2/$$, DEG/WB, R/EV-P-S. An FBI Agent specializing in serial killers deals with the infamous Hannibal Lecter in order to find his prey in this very different prequel to *Silence of the Lambs.* William Petersen, Kim Greist, Joan Allen, Dennis Farina, Stephen Lang, Tom Noonan. w. d. Michael Mann, N-adap. Thomas Harris, *Red Dragon.*

ACTION: Detective Stories; Detectives-Police; FBI Agents; **MYSTERY: MURDER: MURDER MYSTERY: SUSPENSE:** Serial Killers; Trail of a Killer

PREQUEL TO: Silence of the Lambs. (Band of the Hand; Heat [1995])

Maniac Cop, 1988, 85m, ★★/$$, Shapiro/TransWorld, R/EV-B&G. A deranged and deformed ex-cop picks and chooses who lives and dies on his rampages. w. Larry Cohen, d. William Lustig.

Maniac Cop 2, 1990, 88m, ★★/$$, Shapiro/Live, R/EV-B&G. A deranged and deformed ex-cop picks and chooses who lives and dies on his rampages. w. Larry Cohen, d. William Lustig.

ACTION: MURDER: Murders-One by One; Police Stories; Serial Killers; Revenge; Dead-Back from the

The Man I Married, 1940, 79m, ★★1/2/$, 20th/NA. An American woman marries a second generation German-American and takes a vacation to Germany with him only to find out he's a Nazi sympathizer. Joan Bennett, Francis Lederer, Lloyd Nolan, Otto Kruger. w. Oliver H. P. Garrett, N-adap. w. Oscar Shisgall (*Swastika*), d. Irving Pichel.

DRAMA: MELODRAMA: Conspiracy; Enemy-Sleeping with the; Germans as Enemy; World War II Era; Vacations; Vacations-European; Patriotic Films; Nazi Stories; Female Protagonists
(The Secret Beyond the Door)

The Man in Grey, 1943, 116m, ★★★/$$, GFD/NA. A girl of royal birth in old England helps a friend of lower class and meets with dire consequences. James Mason, Margaret Lockwood, Phyllis Calvert, Stewart Granger. w. Margaret Kennedy, Leslie Arliss, Doreen Montgomery, N-adap. Eleanor Smith, d. Leslie Arliss.

DRAMA: MELODRAMA: Costume Drama; Double Crossings; Betrayals; Rich vs. Poor; Social Climbing; Class Conflicts; Royalty; Female Protagonists; Female Screenwriters
(The Wicked Lady [1945]; Howards End)

Man in Love, 1987, 110m, ★★1/2/$, Col/Col, R/S-FN. An American actor has an affair while shooting in Italy which rejuvenates him but could jeopardize all he's worked for. Peter Coyote, Greta Scacchi, Jamie Lee Curtis, Peter Riegert, Claudia Cardinale. w. Diane Kurys, Olivier Schatzky, d. Diane Kurys.

DRAMA: ROMANCE: Romantic Drama; Erotic Drama; Actors; Moviemaking; Italy; Americans Abroad; Midlife Crisis; Female Directors; Female Screenwriters; Writer-Directors
(Quartet; Love Letters [1984])

The Man in the Attic, 1953, 82m, ★★/$$, 20th/NA. The man staying at a boardinghouse in late 1800s London could be the one who's slashing prostitutes. Jack Palance, Constance Smith, Frances Bavier. w. Robert Presnell Jr., Barre Lyndon, d. Hugo Fregonese.

SUSPENSE: MYSTERY: MURDER: MURDER MYSTERY: Serial Killers; Jack the Ripper; Boardinghouses; England; 1800s

REMAKE/RIPOFF: The Lodger.
(Jack the Ripper; The Lodger)

The Man in the Grey Flannel Suit, 1956, 152m, ★★★/$$$, 20th/CBS-Fox. A young executive has to choose between the fast lane in the affluent 50s of New York and Madison Avenue and living the life he's supposedly working so hard for with his family. w. d. Nunnally Johnson, N-adap. Sloan Wilson.

DRAMA: Social Drama; Power-Rise to; Advertising World; Executives; Young Men; Decisions-Big; Suburban Life; New York City Life; 1950s; Forgotten Films; Hidden Gems; Time Capsules
(Patterns; Gentleman's Agreement)

The Man in the Middle, 1964, 94m, ★★1/2/$$, 20th/NA. An American soldier is accused of murder in India during World War II. Robert Mitchum, Trevor Howard, Keenan Wynn, France Nuyen. w. Keith Waterhouse, Willis Hall, N-adap. Howard Fast, *The Winston Affair*, d. Guy Hamilton.

DRAMA: Courtroom Drama; **MURDER:** Accused Unjustly; Americans Abroad; Military Movies; Court Martials; India
(Casualties of War; Town Without Pity)

The Man in the Moon, 1991, 100m, ★★★/$$ (LR), MGM-UA/MGM, PG-13/S-FRN-MN. The story of an adolescent girl on a farm in Texas and the boy that she falls for, but who wants her older sister instead. Emily Warfield, Sam Waterston, Jason London, Tess Harper, Gail Strickland. w. Jenny Wingfield, d. Robert Mulligan.

DRAMA: MELODRAMA: Romantic Drama; Coming of Age; Romance-Triangles; Romance with Relative's Lover; Romance-Unrequited; Love-First; Girlhood; Teenagers; Women Fighting Over Men; Sisters; Rural Life; Farm Life; Texas; 1950s; Quiet Little Films; Child Protagonists; Female Protagonists; Old-Fashioned Recent Films; Female Screenwriters
(Rich in Love; Georgy Girl)

The Man in the White Suit, 1951, 81m, ★★★1/2/$$$, Ealing/HomeVision. An inventor comes up with a fabric that resists dirt and age but the unions and textile mills are none too happy about it. Alec Guinness, Joan Greenwood, Cecil Parker, Vida Hope, Ernest Thesiger. w. Roger MacDougall, John Dighton, Alexander Mackendrick

(BOScr), d. Alexander Mackendrick. Oscars: 1-0.

SATIRE: COMEDY: FARCE: Inventors; Scientists; Conspiracy; Fashion World; Forgotten Films; Hidden Gems
(I'm All Right, Jack)

Man in the Wilderness, 1971, 105m, ★★★/$$, WB/WB, PG/V. When a fur trapper is left for dead after a bear attack, he regains strength and must go it alone-but soon wants vengeance against those who left him. Richard Harris, John Huston, John Bindon. w. Jack De Witt, d. Richard Sarafian.

ADVENTURE: WESTERNS: DRAMA: Survival Drama; Revenge; 1800s
(A Man Called Horse; Dances with Wolves)

The Manitou, 1978, 104m, ★/$, 20th/Col, R/V-S. A woman is possessed with the tiny little spirit of an Aztec witchdoctor and her con artist boyfriend has to depossess her. Tony Curtis, Susan Strasberg, Michael Ansara, Stella Stevens, Burgess Meredith, Ann Sothern. w. William Girdler, Jon Cedar, Tom Pope, N-adap. Graham Masterton, d. William Girdler.

SCI-FI: HORROR: Possessions; Con Artists; Unintentionally Funny
(The Entity; The Exorcist)

A Man Like Eva, 1983, 89m, ★★★/$$, Ind/Fox-Lorber, Facets, R/S-FN-MN. A director marries his female star while bedding the male star-based on the life of Rainer Werner Fassbinder, and he's played by the actress one of the characters is based upon. Eva Mattes, Lisa Kreuzer, Werner Stocker. w. Radu Gabrea, Laurens Straub, d. Radu Gabrea.

SATIRE: DRAMA: Art Films; Avant-Garde Films; Black Comedy; Biographies; Directors; Actors; Actresses; Moviemaking; Movies within Movies; Women as Men; Gay Men; Bisexuality; German Films
(Law of Desire; Fox and His Friends)

Man Made Monster, 1940, 57m, ★★/$$, U/MCA-U. A scientist finds a man immune to electrocution and makes him into a robot to do his deeds. Lon Chaney Jr., Lionel Atwill. w. Joseph West, d. George Waggner.

SCI-FI: HORROR: Robots; Scientists; Experiments; Monsters-Manmade; Human Monsters
(Shocker; Frankenstein)

Mannequin, 1937, 95m, ★★1/2/$$$, MGM/MGM-UA. A woman leaves her crook of a husband and tries to work her way up in the world. Joan Crawford, Spencer Tracy, Alan Curtis. w. Lawrence Hazard, d. Frank Borzage.
DRAMA: MELODRAMA: ROMANCE: Ordinary People Stories; Career Women; Marriage on the Rocks; Marrying Up; Women's Films; Working Class; Female Protagonists
(Mildred Pierce; The Last of Mrs. Cheyney)

Mannequin, 1987, 89m, ★★/$$$, 20th/CBS-Fox, PG/P-S. A department store window dresser falls in love with a woman who is really one of the mannequins he sticks pins into. Andrew McCarthy, Kim Cattrall, Estelle Getty, James Spader, Meshach Taylor. w. Edward Rugoff, Michael Gottlieb, d. Michael Gottlieb.
COMEDY: Fantasy; ROMANCE: Romantic Comedy; Romance-Boy Wants Girl; Sexy Women; Chase Movies; Department Stores; Unbelieved; Sleeper Hits
REMAKE/RIPOFF OF: One Touch of Venus

Mannequin 2: On the Move, 1991, 95m, ★1/2/$, 20th/CBS-Fox, PG. A sequel without the originals (as if they'd be missed that much) where the hero discovers how the mannequin became a woman trapped in plastic-possession of the spirit of a peasant girl influenced by witchcraft. Billy Ragsdale, Kristy Swanson, Meshach Taylor, Terry Kizer, Stuart Pankin. w. Edward Rugoff, David Isaacs, Ken Levine, Betty Israel, d. Stewart Raffill.
COMEDY: Fantasy; ROMANCE: Romantic Comedy; Romance-Boy Wants Girl; Sexy Women; Chase Movies; Department Stores; Unbelieved; Sleeper Hits; Possessions; Female Screenwriters

Man of a Thousand Faces, 1957, 122m, ★★★/$$, U/MCA-U. The story of actor Lon Chaney in his silent film heyday. James Cagney, Dorothy Malone, Robert Evans, Roger Smith, Marjorie Rambeau, Jane Greer, Jim Backus. w. R. Wright Campbell, Ivan Goff, Ben Roberts (BOScr), d. Joseph Pevney. Oscars: 1-0.
DRAMA: Biographies; Hollywood Biographies; Fame-Rise to; Deaf People; Actors; Hollywood Life; Silent Film Era; Forgotten Films

(Yankee Doodle Dandy; Love Me or Leave Me)

Man of Aran, 1934, 75m, ★★★/$$, Gainsborough/HomeVision. The lives of townspeople in an Irish fishing village. Colman King, Maggie Dirane. w. Robert and Frances Flaherty, d. Robert Flaherty.
DRAMA: Documentaries; Documentary Style; Docudrama; Ordinary People Stories; Ireland; Fishermen; Forgotten Films
(The Informer; The Playboys)

Man of Flowers, 1983, 91m, ★★★/$$, Vestron/Vestron, R/S. The relationship among an Australian model and her coke-head artist boyfriend and an older lover of hers leads to tensions and possibly murder. Norman Kaye, Alyson Best, Chris Haywood, Werner Herzog. w. Paul Cox, Bob Ellis, d. Paul Cox.
SATIRE: COMEDY DRAMA: DRAMA: Erotic Drama; Romance-Triangles; Drugs; Rich vs. Poor; Beautiful People; Fashion World; Sexy Women; Violence-Sudden
(The Last Days of Chez-Nous; Cactus)

Man of Iron, 1981, 152m, ★★★/$, UAC/MGM-UA, R. Story of the Polish strikes of the early 80s and one of their leaders, loosely based on Lech Walesa. Jersy Radziwilowicz. w. Aleksander Scibor-Rylski, d. Andrzej Wajda.
DRAMA: Docudrama; Biographies-Fictional; Social Drama; Unions; Strikes; Oppression; Fighting the System; Leaders; Poland; Europeans-Eastern
SEQUEL/COMPANION TO: Man of Marble

Man of La Mancha, 1972, 132m, ★★★/$$, UA/MGM-UA, PG. A man in prison during the Spanish Inquisition begins recounting the tale of Don Quixote, which is then enacted with music. Sophia Loren, Peter O'Toole, James Coco, Harry Andrews. w. Dale Wasserman, M-P-adap. Dale Wasserman, Mitch Leigh, Loe Darion, d. Arthur Hiller. BMScore. Oscars: 1-0.
MUSICALS: DRAMA: MUSICAL DRAMA: ROMANCE: Romantic Drama; Dreams; Oppression; Spain; Middle Ages
(El Cid; Don Juan; Fiddler on the Roof)

Man of Marble, 1978, 165m, ★★★/$, New Yorker/New Yorker, NR. Polish film students put together a documentary on a political activist from the 50s. Jerzy Radziwilocicz. w. Aleksander Scibor-Rylski, d. Andrzej Wajda.

DRAMA: Docudrama; Documentary Style; Movies within Movies; Moviemaking; Social Drama; Political Unrest; Heroes-Ordinary; Film Students; Poland
SEQUEL: Man of Iron

A Man of No Importance, 1994, 98m, ★★★1/2/$, Sony/Col-Tri, R/S. A closeted gay bus driver in Dublin deals with his sexuality, his lost youth, and his lost loves while facing the possibility of dying without really having lived. Albert Finney, Brenda Fricker, Michael Gambon, Tara Fitzgerald, Rufus Sewell, Maureen Egan, Pat Killalea, Jonathan Rhys-Myers. w. Barry Devlin, d. Suri Krishnamma.
DRAMA: Character Studies; Social Drama; Gay Men; Gay Awakenings; Homophobia; Midlife Crisis; Infatuations; Buses; Ireland; British Films; Overlooked at Release; Hidden Gems
(The Lost Language of Cranes; The Sum of Us)

Man of the House, 1995, 98m, ★★1/2/$$$, Disney/Disney, PG/P. A boy whose mother is about to remarry a goofy older guy decides to scare him off but may have less luck than he'd hoped. Chevy Chase, Farrah Fawcett, Jonathan Taylor Thomas, George Wendt, David Shiner, Art LaFleur, Peter Appel, Richard Foronjy, Richard Portnow. w. James Orr, Jim Cruickshank, d. James Orr.
CHILDREN'S: Family Comedy; Accident Prone; Practical Jokers; Stepfathers-Troublesome; Sleeper Hits
(Tom and Huck; Firstborn)

Manon, 1949, 96m, ★★1/2/$, Alcina/Nos. In post-war France a promiscuous girl resorts to the underworld after it comes out she's been a collaborator. Cecile Aubry, Michel Auclair. w. H. G. Clouzot, J. Ferry, N-adap. w. L'Abbé Prévost, d. H. G. Clouzot.
DRAMA: Political Drama; TRAGEDY: Traitors; Young Women; World War II-Post Era; French Films; Female Protagonists
(Manon Lescaut; Gilda)

Manon des Sources, 1952, 190m, ★★/$, Pagnol/NA. Jacqueline Pagnol. w. d. Marcel Pagnol.
Writer-Directors.

Manon des Sources (Manon of the Spring), 1986, 114m, ★★★/$$, Orion/Orion, PG. Yves Montand, Daniel Auteuil, Emmanuelle Beart. w. Claude

Berri, Gérard Brach, S-adap. Marcel Pagnol, d. Claude Berri.
A young woman living in the hills avenges wrong done to her family and the rumors of her being a witch by cutting off a village's water supply.
DRAMA: MELODRAMA: Lyrical Films; Revenge; Rumors; Small-town Life; Rural Life; French Films
PREQUEL/SIMILAR: Jean de Florette.
Man on a Swing, 1975, 108m, ★★/$, Par/Par, R/V. A psychic helps cops in their murder investigation. Cliff Robertson, Joel Grey, Dorothy Tristan, Peter Masterson. w. David Goodman, d. Frank Perry.
MYSTERY: MURDER: MURDER MYSTERY: SUSPENSE: Detective Stories; Detectives-Police; Psychics; Good Premise Unfulfilled; Coulda Been Good; Forgotten Films
(Eyes of Laura Mars; The Clairvoyant)
Man on Fire, 1957, 95m, ★★/$, MGM/Vestron. A man refuses to give up his son when his wife divorces him. Bing Crosby, Inger Stevens, E.G. Marshall. w. d. Ronald MacDougall.
DRAMA: Marriage Drama; Divorce; Marriage on the Rocks; Custody Battles; Fathers & Sons; Midlife Crisis; Ahead of its Time; Forgotten Films; Coulda Been Good
(The Good Father; The Country Girl)
The Man on the Eiffel Tower, 1949, 82m, ★★1/2/$, A&T/Nos. Famous Inspector Maigret trails a killer in Paris to great heights. Charles Laughton, Burgess Meredith, Franchot Tone, Wilfrid Hyde White. w. Harry Brown, N-adap. Georges Simenon, *A Battle of Nerves*, d. Burgess Meredith.
MYSTERY: MURDER: MURDER MYSTERY: Detective Stories; Paris; Actor-Directors
The Man on the Flying Trapeze, 1935, 65m, ★★/$, Par/NA. A man with a great memory is used by his boss. W. C. Fields, Kathleen Howard. w. Ray Harris, Sam Hardy, Jack Cunningham, Bobby Vernon, Charles Bogle (W. C. Fields), d. Clyde Bruckman.
COMEDY: Comedians; Comedy-Skit; Bosses-Bad; Geniuses
Manpower, 1941, 70m, ★★★/$$, WB/NA. Construction workers are mesmerized by a showgirl, then driven to conflict. Edward G. Robinson, George

Raft, Marlene Dietrich, Alan Hale, Eve Arden, Ward Bond. w. Richard Macaulay, Jerry Wald, d. Raoul Walsh.
DRAMA: MELODRAMA: Men in Conflict; Men Fighting Over Women; Ensembles-Male; Working Class; Elusive Women; Sexy Women; Dancers
(Tiger Shark; Desire; Pittsburgh)
Man's Best Friend, 1993, 87m, ★★/$, New Line/New Line, R/V. A guard dog is experimented with, by giving him the genes of other very aggressive animals, but his owner may be the one he goes haywire on. Ally Sheedy, Lance Henriksen. w. d. John Lafia.
SCI-FI: HORROR: SUSPENSE: Animal Rights; Monsters-Animal; Dogs; Writer-Directors; Experiments; Female Protagonists
(Monkeyshines; White Dog)
Man's Castle, 1933, 70m, ★★★/$$, Col/NA. Love can still find a home in a homeless people's Hooverville during the Depression in New York. Spencer Tracy, Loretta Young, Marjorie Rambeau. w. Jo Swerling, P-adap. Lawrence Hazard, d. Frank Borzage.
MELODRAMA: ROMANCE: Poor People; Depression Era; Homeless People; New York Life
(Central Park; Fury)
Man's Favorite Sport?, 1963, 120m, ★★/$$, U/MCA-U. The allusion is to girl-chasing, and the irony is that the man doing it is Rock Hudson. So it's really probably fishing as a fishing-tackle sales-man has to learn how to fish. Paula Prentiss. w. John Fenton Murray, d. Howard Hawks.
COMEDY: ROMANCE: Romantic Comedy; **FARCE:** Screwball Comedy; Fishermen; Salesmen; Feisty Females; Competitions; Coulda Been Good; Forgotten Films
(Ed: A mish-mash of Hawks' earlier screwball comedies with bits lifted right out of *Bringing Up Baby, Libeled Lady* and *His Girl Friday*)
Mantrap, 1961, 93m, ★★/$, Par/NA. A man is tricked into a hijacking by a friend and jeopardizes his family's life. Jeffrey Hunter, David Janssen, Stella Stevens. w. Ed Waters, N-adap. John D. Macdonald, *Taint of the Tiger*, d. Edmond O'Brien.
DRAMA: SUSPENSE: Crime Drama; Friends as Enemies; Hijackings; Women

in Jeopardy; Betrayals; Double Crossings; Blackmail; Con Artists
Man Trouble, 1992, 100m, ★1/2/$, 20th/Fox, PG-13/S. A dog trainer (Jack Nicholson) sells a guard dog to a wealthy musician (Ellen Barkin) who has a stalker after her. Veronica Cartwright, Beverly D'Angelo, Michael McKean, Harry Dean Stanton. w. Carole Eastman, d. Bob Rafelson.
COMEDY: ROMANCE: Romantic Comedy; **MURDER: MYSTERY: MURDER MYSTERY:** Comic Mystery; Women in Jeopardy; Romance-Class Conflicts; Romance-Older Men/Younger Women; Flops-Major; Female Protagonists; Female Screenwriters
(Ed: Barkin is the only thing that works in this mess; Coulda Been Good if it was another movie altogether)
The Man Upstairs, 1958, 88m, ★★1/2/$, B-L/NA. A lonely man becomes psychotic in his boardinghouse and the result is violence and a standoff. Richard Attenborough, Bernard Lee, Dorothy Alison. w. Alan Falconer, d. Don Chaffey.
DRAMA: TRAGEDY: Lonely People; Hermits; Mental Illness; Violence-Sudden; Boardinghouses; British Films; Hostage Situations; Ahead of Its Time
(Fourteen Hours; Dog Day Afternoon)
The Man Who Broke the Bank at Monte Carlo, 1935, 67m, ★★★/$, 20th/NA. A cabbie wins a fortune at roulette, then has to decide how long he can make it last, if at all. Ronald Colman, Joan Bennett, Colin Clive, Nigel Bruce. w. Nunnally Johnson, d. Stephen Roberts.
COMEDY: COMEDY DRAMA: Gambling; Rise and Fall Stories; Rags to Riches; Monte Carlo; Taxi Drivers; Capra-esque
(Champagne for Caesar; If I Had a Million)
The Man Who Came to Dinner, 1941, 112m, ★★★★/$$$, WB/MGM-UA. A cantankerous radio star injures himself while on tour and staying in an ordinary family's home. He decides to sue the family while recuperating in their house, which leads to much conflict as he masterminds a romance, a lawsuit, and being catered to hand and foot. Monty Woolley, Bette Davis, Mary Wickes, Ann Sheridan, Jimmy Durante, Reginald Gardiner, Billie Burke, Mary Wickes, Grant Mitchell. w. Julius J. and Philip G. Epstein, P-adap.

George S. Kaufman, Moss Hart, d. William Keighley.

COMEDY: SATIRE: Black Comedy; Screwball Comedy; **FARCE:** Stranded; Comedy-Situation; Roommates from Hell; Nuisances; Suburban Life; Accidents; Forgotten Films; Ahead of Its Time; Hidden Gems; Stories That Begin Again (You Can't Take it With You; Sitting Pretty) (Ed: Supposedly based on Alexander Woolcott, played by Woolley, with an impersonation of Noel Coward. Excellent all-around, and the sting of the humor holds up even by today's standards. A whimsical fun comedy with a brain)

The Man Who Could Work Miracles, 1936, 82m, ★★★/$$, London/Sultan. An ordinary man discovers he has great powers but if they're misused, doom may result. Roland Young, Ralph Richardson, Edward Chapman, Ernest Thesiger, Joan Gardner, George Sanders. w. Lajos Biro, SS-adap. H. G. Wells, d. Lothar Mendes.

DRAMA: COMEDY DRAMA: Social Satire; Miracles; Magic; Psychics; Apocalyptic Stories; What If . . . Stories; British Films; Forgotten Films; Hidden Gems

The Man Who Fell to Earth, 1976, 138m, ★★★/$$$, Ind/Col, X & R/ES-FFN-MFN. A small, rock-star-like alien lands in America but finds the conventions of daily life daunting. David Bowie, Candy Clark, Rip Torn, Buck Henry. w. Paul Mayersburg, N-adap. Walter Tevis, d. Nicolas Roeg.

SATIRE: SCI-FI: Fantasy; **ROMANCE: DRAMA:** Romantic Drama; Erotic Drama; Art Films; Avant-Garde Films; Aliens-Outer Space, Good; Sleeper Hits; Alcoholics

(Just a Gigolo; Eureka; Starman)

The Man Who Haunted Himself, 1970, 94m, ★★½/$, ITC/NA. When a man returns home after recovering from a car wreck, he finds an impostor has taken over his life. Roger Moore, Hildegarde Neil, Freddie Jones. w. Basil Dearden, Michael Relph, SS-adap. w. Anthony Armstrong, *The Case of Mr. Pelham*, d. Basil Dearden.

DRAMA: SUSPENSE: MYSTERY: Cheating Women; Dead-Back from the; Lookalikes; Impostors; Ghosts; Multiple Performances

(Shattered; Mr. Buddwing)

The Man Who Knew Too Much, 1934, 84m, ★★★/$$, GFD-Gaumont/Nos, Sinister. Leslie Banks, Edna Best, Peter

Lorre. w. A. R. Rawlinson, Charles Bennett, D. B. Wyndham Lewis, Edwin Greenwood, Emlyn Williams, d. Alfred Hitchcock.

SUSPENSE: MYSTERY: Conspiracy; Assassinations; Kidnappings; Hitchcockian; Skiing

The Man Who Knew Too Much, 1956, 120m, ★★★½/$$$$, Par/MCA-U. While on vacation in Morocco, a couple's (James Stewart, Doris Day) son is kidnapped by assassins who fear a man has revealed damaging information to the husband before he died. Bernard Miles, Brenda deBanzie, Hillary Brooke, Daniel Gelin, Ralph Truman. w. John Michael Hayes, Angus MacPhail, d. Alfred Hitchcock.

BOSong, "Que Sera, Sera." Oscars: 1-1. Children-Saving; Americans Abroad; Innocent Bystanders; Ordinary People in Extraordinary Situations; Children in Jeopardy; Morocco; Hitchcockian

REMAKE OF: 1936 The Man Who Knew Too Much.

(Frantic; Rear Window; Rope; Vertigo)

The Man Who Lost Himself, 1941, 71m, ★★½/$, U/NA. When a man returns from a vacation, he winds up playing a millionaire who looks just like him in a scheme. Brian Aherne, Kay Francis, Henry Stephenson. w. Eddie Moran, N-adap. H. DeVere Stacpoole, d. Edward Ludwig.

COMEDY: FARCE: Identities-Mistaken; Impostors; Lookalikes; Coulda Been Good

(Dave; Moon Over Parador)

The Man Who Loved Cat Dancing, 1973, 114m, ★★/$$$, MGM/MGM-UA, R/S-V. Train robbers come across a wife who's run away from her husband and love blossoms while trains are robbed. Burt Reynolds, Sarah Miles, Lee J. Cobb, Jack Warden, George Hamilton, Bo Hopkins. w. Eleanor Perry, N-adap. w. Marilyn Dunham, d. Richard Sarafian.

WESTERNS: ROMANCE: Heist Stories; Thieves; Trains; Prostitutes-Low Class; Women Who Leave

(No Orchids for Miss Blandish; McCabe and Mrs. Miller)

(Ed: Infamous for an apparent murder which occurred on the set in Arizona)

The Man Who Loved Women, 1977, 119m, ★★★/$$, UAC/MGM-UA, R/S. Charles Denner, Brigitte Fossey, Leslie Caron, Nathalie Baye. w. Francois

Truffaut, Michel Fermaud, Suzanne Schiffman, d. Francois Truffaut. Female Screenwriters

The Man Who Loved Women, 1983, 108m, ★★★½/$$, Col/Col, R/S. A man runs around chasing women to the point of total exhaustion. Burt Reynolds, Julie Andrews, Kim Basinger, Marilu Henner, Cynthia Sikes, Jennifer Edwards. w. Blake Edwards, Milton Wexler, Geoff Edwards, d. Blake Edwards.

COMEDY: COMEDY DRAMA: ROMANCE: FARCE: Romantic Comedy; Playboys; Promiscuity; Sexuality; Elusive Women; Sexy Men; Sexy Women; Women Fighting Over Men

(Worth Winning; Skin Deep)

The Man Who Never Was, 1955, 102m, ★★★/$, 20th/Fox. To confuse the Germans, a British OSS officer drops a body with disinformation on his person for them to find. Clifton Webb, Robert Flemyng, Gloria Grahame, Stephen Boyd. w. Nigel Balchin, NF-adap. Ewen Montagu, d. Ronald Neame.

DRAMA: Spy Films; Spies; Secret Agents; World War II Stories; Germans as Enemy; Clever Plots & Endings; Coulda Been Great; Forgotten Films

(Night Train to Munich; The Spy in Black)

The Man Who Reclaimed His Head, 1934, 81m, ★★½/$$, U/NA. When a writer wants revenge on his publisher after much abuse, he finds a strange and gory way of achieving it. Claude Rains, Joan Bennett, Lionel Atwill. w. Jean Bart, Samuel Ornitz, P-adap. w. Jean Bart, d. Edward Ludwig.

HORROR: SCI-FI: MURDER: Revenge; Writers; Publishing World

The Man Who Shot Liberty Valance, 1962, 122m, ★★★/$$$, Par/Par. An ordinary man shoots an outlaw, or so it seems, because someone else really pulled the trigger, and the outlaw's hero status comes into question. James Stewart, John Wayne, Vera Miles, Lee Marvin, Edmond O'Brien, Andy Devine, Jeannette Nolan, Lee Van Cleef, Strother Martin. w. James Warner Bellah, Willis Goldbeck, d. John Ford.

WESTERN: DRAMA: COMEDY DRAMA: Identities-Mistaken; Friendships-Male; Protecting Someone; Ethics; Heroes-Ordinary; Heroes-Unlikely

(High Noon; The Ox-Bow Incident)

The Man Who Understood Women, 1959, 105m, ★★/$, 20th/NA. A film producer finally outdoes himself in the arrogance department and his wife's had enough, but can he do without her? Henry Fonda. w. d. Nunnally Johnson, N-adap. Romain Gary, *Colours of the Day*.

DRAMA: COMEDY DRAMA: Marriage Drama; Marriage on the Rocks; Hollywood Life; Directors; Moviemaking; Jerks; Forgotten Films

(Ed: An oddity for Fonda and fairly experimental)

The Man Who Watched Trains Go By (Paris Express), 1952, 80m, ★★¹/₂/$, Ind/NA. A lowly clerk imbezzles money then hops a train to travel, but his life ahead may soon be the same as his life behind him. Claude Rains, Marius Goring, Anouk Aimee, Herbert Lom. w. d. Harold French, N-adap. Georges Simenon.

SUSPENSE: MYSTERY: MURDER: MURDER MYSTERY: Heist Stories; Thieves; Embezzlers; Outlaw Road Movies; French Films

The Man Who Would Be King, 1974, 129m, ★★★/$$$, Allied/CBS-Fox, PG. Two men (Michael Caine, Sean Connery) go to the Middle East in the 1800s to become kings of a fictional country which is waiting for a white man like Alexander. Sean Connery, Michael Caine, Christopher Plummer. w. John Huston, Gladys Hill (BAScr), SS-adap. Rudyard Kipling, d. John Huston. BArt, BEdit, BCostume. Oscars: 4-0.

DRAMA: Epics; **ADVENTURE:** Treasure Hunts; Middle East; 1800s; Historical Drama; Costume Drama; Accidents; Identities-Mistaken; Men in Conflicts; Thieves; Con Artists; Writers; Legends/Mythology; Kings; Female Writers

(Mountains on the Moon; The Wind and the Lion; I Love a Mystery; Farewell to the King)

The Man with Bogart's Face, 1980, 106m, ★★/$, MSP-20th/CBS-Fox, PG. A PI gets lots of work but doesn't do it very well because of his resemblance to Bogie. Robert Sacchi, Misty Rowe, Michelle Phillips, Franco Nero, Olivia Hussey, Victor Buono, Herbert Lom, George Raft, Yvonne deCarlo. w. Andrew J. Fenady, N-adap. Andrew J. Fenady, d. Robert Day.

COMEDY DRAMA: Detective Stories; Detectives-Private; Lookalikes; Comedy of Errors; Nostalgia; All-Star Cameos; Hollywood Life; Coulda Been Good

The Man with Nine Lives, 1940, 73m, ★★¹/₂/$, Col/NA. A mad scientist thinks he has found the cure for cancer by freezing patients, but psychosis results when the thaw occurs. Boris Karloff, Byron Foulger. w. Karl Brown, SS-adap. w. Harold Shumate, d. Nick Grinde.

HORROR: SCI-FI: Ahead of Its Time; Experiments; Scientists-Mad; Mental Illness; Psycho Killers; Dead-Back from the

The Man with the Golden Arm, 1955, 119m, ★★¹/₂/$$$, Col/RCA-Col. Story of a Chicago street gambler who gets addicted to heroin and other drugs then tries to kick it. Frank Sinatra, Kim Novak, Eleanor Parker, Darren McGavin. w. Walter Newman, Lewis Meltzer, N-adap. Nelson Algren, d. Otto Preminger.

DRAMA: MELODRAMA: ROMANCE: Character Studies; Drugs-Addictions; Disease Stories; Gambling; Obsessions; Inner City Life; Ahead of Its Time; Coulda Been Great; Chicago; Unintentionally Funny

(The Basketball Diaries; Leaving Las Vegas)

(Ed: Much of this dated diatribe is laughable today)

The Man with the Golden Gun, 1974, 125m, ★★★/$$$, UA/MGM-UA, PG/S-V. James Bond travels to Asia to take out an assassin before he strikes again. Roger Moore, Christopher Lee, Britt Ekland, Maud Adams, Herve Villechaize, Clifton James. w. Richard Maibaum, Tom Mankiewicz, N-adap. w. Ian Fleming, d. Guy Hamilton.

ACTION: COMEDY: Action Comedy; Assassinations; Secret Agents; Chase Movies; Car Chases; Boat Chases; James Bond

(Live and Let Die; The Spy Who Loved Me)

(Ed: One of the lesser Bonds. Check out how ugly the AMC cars are)

The Man with Two Brains, 1983, 93m, ★★★¹/₂/$, WB/WB, PG/S-P. A surgeon married to a psychopathic beauty cheats on her with a brain in a jar with a sexy voice. Steve Martin, Kathleen Turner, David Warner, Merv Griffin, Paul Benedict, Sissy Spacek (as voice of brain). w. Carl Reiner, Steve Martin, George Gipe, d. Carl Reiner.

COMEDY: Screwball Comedy; **ROMANCE:** Romantic Comedy; Spoofs; Spoofs-SCI-FI;

Spoofs-Horror; **SCI-FI:** Black Comedy; Comedy-Morbid; Psycho-Killers; Murderers-Black Widows; Doctors; Love-Questionable; Cheating Men; Underrated; Hidden Gems

(So I Married an Ax Murderer; Young Frankenstein; Dead Man Don't Wear Plaid)

The Man with Two Faces, 1934, 72m, ★★¹/₂/$$, WB/NA. An actor disguises himself to avenge his sister. Edward G. Robinson, Mary Astor, Ricardo Cortez. w. Tom Reed, Niven Busch, P-adap. George S. Kaufman, Alexander Woollcott, *The Dark Tower*, d. Archie Mayo.

DRAMA: MELODRAMA: Crime Drama; Revenge; Disguises; Actors; Saving Someone; *Crime Pays;* Siblings; Actor-Impostors

The Man Within, see The Smugglers

The Man Without a Face, 1993, 115m, ★★/$, WB/WB, PG-13. A boy from a troubled home who's worried about passing a big test finds help from a man who's face is half destroyed and is inspirational because of his triumph over adversity. Mel Gibson, Nick Stahl. d. Mel Gibson.

MELODRAMA: Character Studies; Teachers; Teachers & Students; Lookism; Disabled People; Men and Boys; Boys; Good Premise Unfulfilled; Overlooked on Release; Actor-Directors

(The Elephant Man; Mask)

The Man Without a Star, 1955, 89m, ★★¹/₂/$$, U/MCA-U. Cattle wars on the big sky plains. Kirk Douglas, Jeanne Crain, Claire Trevor, Richard Boone. w. Borden Chase, D. D. Beauchamp, N-adap. w. Dee Linford, d. King Vidor.

WESTERNS: Cattle People; Men in Conflict

TV REMAKE: A Man Called Gannon.

Man, Woman and Child, 1982, 100m, ★★¹/₂/$, Par/Par, PG. A professor is shocked to learn he has a son by an affair years before and must deal with his wife's reaction. Martin Sheen, Blythe Danner, Craig T. Nelson, David Hemmings, Nathalie Neil. w. Erich Segal, David Selag Goodman, N-adap. Erich Segal, d. Dick Richards.

DRAMA: MELODRAMA: Tearjerkers; Marriage Drama; Marriage on the Rocks; Family Drama; Family Stories; Secrets-Keeping; Children-Long Lost; Cheating Men; Coulda Been Good; Forgotten Films

Map of the Human Heart, 1993, 109m, ★★★/$, Miramax/HBO, R/S-V. An Eskimo and his girlfriend deal with racism as youths and then are reunited in Germany during World War II, only for the boy to find the girl is now denying she's Eskimo. Meanwhile the world swirls about them. Jason Scott Lee, Annie Parillaud, Patrick Bergin, John Cusack, Jeanne Moreau. w. Vincent Ward, Louise Nowra, d. Ward.
DRAMA: MELODRAMA: ADVENTURE: Romantic Adventure; Romantic Drama; Romance-Reunited; Love-First; World War II Era; Snow Settings; Indians-American (Eskimo); Alaska; Race Relations; Romance-Interracial; Female Screenwriters
(Legends of the Fall; Dr. Zhivago)
(Ed: Great, unexpected visuals)

Marat/Sade (The Persecution and Assassination of Jean-Paul Marat as performed by the inmates of the Asylum of Clarenton under the direction of the Marquis de Sade), 1966, 116m, ★★★/$$, UA/MGM-UA. Life at the old nuthouse—sex, torture, death, and all. Patrick Magee, Glenda Jackson, Ian Richardson, Michael Williams, Clifford Rose. w. Adrian Mitchell, P-adap. Peter Weiss, d. Peter Brook.
DRAMA: Black Comedy; Art Films; Psychological Drama; Asylums; Mental Illness; Mindgames; Torture; Cult Films; Forgotten Films; Hidden Gems
(The Devils; King of Hearts)

Marathon Man, 1976, 126m, ★★★1/2/$$$$, Par/Par, R/S-P-V. A graduate student and runner (Dustin Hoffman) is dragged into a conspiracy involving Nazis (Laurence Olivier, BSActor) and hidden diamonds, when his brother (Roy Scheider) is killed and turns out to have been a spy. Marthe Keller, Fritz Weaver, William Devane. w. adap. William Goldman, d. John Schlesinger. Oscars: 1-0.
SUSPENSE: Spy Films; Spies; Chase Movies; Conspiracy; Nazi Stories; Innocent Bystanders; Running; Torture; Love-Questionable; Dangerous Women; College Life; Dentists
(The Odessa File; The Boys from Brazil)

March or Die, 1977, 107m, ★★/$, ITC/Fox, R/V-S. During World War I, Foreign Legion officers thwart the Arabs but succumb to love. Gene Hackman, Terence Hill, Catherine Deneuve, Max Von Sydow, Ian Holm. w. David Goodman, d. Dick Richards.
MELODRAMA: ROMANCE: Spoofs; War Stories; World War I Stories; Nostalgia; Soldiers; Desert Settings; Arab People; Foreign Legion

Mardi Gras, 1958, 107m, ★★/$$, 20th/NA. A movie star and a cadet fall in love among the confetti and floats. Pat Boone, Christine Carere, Sheree North, Tommy Sands, Gary Crosby, Barrie Chase. w. Winston Miller, Hal Kanter, d. Edmund Goulding.
MUSICAL: ROMANCE: MELODRAMA: Music Movies; Musical Romance; New Orleans; Soldiers; Actresses
(Bernardine; Murder at Mardi Gras)

Margie, 1946, 94m, ★★★/$$$, 20th/NA. A woman with a teenage daughter opens a trunk in the attic and begins recalling the roaring twenties and how she met Dad. Jeanne Crain, Glenn Langan, Alan Young, Lynn Bari, Conrad Janis. w. F. Hugh Herbert, SS-adap. Ruth McKinney, Richard Bransten, d. Henry King.
COMEDY: COMEDY DRAMA: ROMANCE: Romantic Comedy; Roaring 20s; 1920s; Flashbacks; Memories; Mothers & Daughters; Female Protagonists
(Pinky; A Letter to Three Wives)

Marie, 1985, 112m, ★★1/2/$, DEG-MGM/MGM-UA, PG. An abused wife gets her act together and becomes chair of the Tennessee parole board. Sissy Spacek, Jeff Daniels, Morgan Freeman, Fred Dalton Thompson. w. John Briley, NF-adap. Peter Maas, d. Roger Donaldson.
DRAMA: MELODRAMA: True Stories; Starting Over; Mothers & Children; Career Women; Abused Women; Mothers-Struggling; Mothers Alone; British Directors of Southerns; Southerns; Female Protagonists; Forgotten Films
(Raggedy Man; Brubaker; Norma Rae)
(Ed: This was the screenwriter's follow-up to Gandhi, also about a noble, ordinary person's rise but not any more entertaining)

Marie Antoinette, 1938, 160m, ★★★/$$$, MGM/MGM-UA. The life story of the queen who liked cake, centering around her last days holding court. Norma Shearer (BActress), Tyrone Power, John Barrymore, Anita Louise, Robert Morley (BSActor), Gladys George, Joseph Schildkraut, Reginald Gardiner. w. Claudine West, Donald Ogden Stewart, Ernest Vajda, d. W. S. Van Dyke. BArt, BScore. Oscars: 4-0.
DRAMA: MELODRAMA: TRAGEDY: Biographies; Costume Drama; Historical Drama; Royalty; Queens; Political Unrest; Executions

Marilyn, the Untold Story, 1981, 156m, ★★★/$$$$, ABC/ABC. TV movie on the rise and fall of the great Norma Jean, one of the best, if not the best yet. Catherine Hicks (Emmy nomination), Richard Basehart, Jason Miller, Sheree North. NF-adap. Norman Mailer, d. Jack Arnold, John Flynn, Lawrence Schiller.
DRAMA: Biographies; Hollywood Biographies; Actresses; Sexy Women; 1950s; TV Movies

Marius, 1931, 125m, ★★★1/2/$, Pagnol-Par/Nos. A young man decides not to follow his father into the seaside cafe business, but rather to become a sailor, despite his girlfriend's feelings. Raimu, Pierre Fresnay, Charpin. w. P-adap. Marcel Pagnol, d. Alexander Korda.
MELODRAMA: ROMANCE: Young Men; Decisions-Big; Riviera Life; Fathers & Sons; Forgotten Films; Cult Films
(Fanny)

Marjorie Morningstar, 1958, 123m, ★★1/2/$$, WB/WB, Republic. A young Jewish woman (Natalie Wood) has high hopes for a career in New York but is tempted with becoming a housewife. Gene Kelly, Claire Trevor, Everett Sloane, Ed Wyn, Carolyn Jones, Martin Balsam. w. Everett Freeman, N-adap. Herman Wouk, d. Irving Rapper. BOSong. Oscars: 1-0.
DRAMA: MELODRAMA: Young Women; Career Women; Housewives; New York Life; 1950s; Time Capsules; Jewish People; Women's Films; Decisions-Big
(Sex and the Single Girl; Hilda Crane)

The Mark, 1961, 127m, ★★★/$$, 20th/Video Treasures. A child molester gets out of prison but finds attitudes and habits die hard. Stuart Whitman (BActor), Maria Schell, Rod Steiger, Brenda de Banzie, Maurice Denham. w. Sidney Buchman, Stanley Mann, d. Guy Green. Oscars: 1-0.
DRAMA: MELODRAMA: Crime Drama; Social Drama; Prison Drama; Character Studies; Ex-Convicts; Molestation-Child; Rape/Rapists; Starting Over; Psychologists; Ahead of Its Time; Forgotten Films
(Look in Any Window; Murder, Inc.)

(Ed: A fascinating and daring film for its time)

The Mark of the Hawk, 1958, 84m, ★★1/2/$, U/Moore Video. A black man from Africa, but educated in America, returns to help his people fight for independence. Sidney Poitier, Juano Hernandez, Eartha Kitt. w. H. Kenn Carmichael, d. Michael Audley.
DRAMA: Political Unrest; Political Drama; Politicians; Black Men; Black Casts; Africa; Africans; Ahead of Its Time; Forgotten Films
(For Queen and Country; The Defiant Ones)

Mark of the Vampire, 1935, 61m, ★★★/$$, MGM/MGM-UA. A police detective hires men to dress up like vampires in a haunted house in order to go about solving a murder mystery. Lionel Barrymore, Jean Hersholt, Elizabeth Allan, Bela Lugosi, Lionel Atwill. w. Guy Endore, Bernard Schubert, d. Tod Browning.
HORROR: Horror Comedy; Spoofs-Vampire; MURDER: MYSTERY: MURDER MYSTERY: Comic Mystery; Impostors; Disguises; Undercovers; Detectives-Police; Haunted Houses
REMAKE OF: London After Midnight (silent)

The Mark of Zorro, 1920, 90m, ★★★/$$$$, Fairbanks-UA/Republic. Douglas Fairbanks, Noah Beery, Marguerite de la Motte. w. N-adap. Johnston McCulley, The Curse of Capistrano, d. Fred Niblo. Silent Films

The Mark of Zorro, 1940, 94m, ★★★1/2/$$$, 20th/Fox. Diego de Vega returns to his native California to find it under corrupt rule, so he becomes the superhero Zorro to save the day and rid his town of evil. Tyrone Power, Basil Rathbone, J. Edward Bromberg, Linda Darnell. w. John Foote, Garrett Fort, Bess Meredyth, d. Rouben Mamoulian.
ACTION: ADVENTURE: Heroes-Super; Political Unrest; Corruption; Leader-Tyrant; California; Mexico; Old West; Latin People
TV SERIES (Disney); COMEDY REMAKE: Zorro, the Gay Blade.
(Robin Hood; The Scarlet Pimpernel)

Marked for Death, 1990, 93m, ★★/$$$, 20th/CBS-Fox. A DEA agent gets back in the swing going after Jamaican drug dealers. Steven Seagal, Basil Wallace, Keith David, Joanna Pacula. w. Michael Grais, Mark Victor, d. Dwight Little.
ACTION: Drugs-Dealing; Martial Arts (Above the Law; Under Siege)

Marked Woman, 1937, 96m, ★★★/$$$, WB/WB. When the DA goes after a mobster, he gets a barmaid to testify against him but it may come back to haunt her. Bette Davis, Humphrey Bogart, Jane Bryan. w. Robert Rossen, Abem Finkel, d. Lloyd Bacon.
DRAMA: MELODRAMA: Crime Drama; Mob Stories; Courtroom Drama; Hitmen; Mob Girls; Women in Jeopardy; Female Protagonists
REMAKE: Lady Gangster.
(The Petrified Forest; The Juror)

Marlowe, 1969, 95m, ★★1/2/$, MGM/MGM-UA. Philip Marlowe is updated in a case trying to find a young woman's missing brother. James Garner, Rita Moreno, Sharon Farrell, Bruce Lee, Gayle Hunnicutt, Carroll O'Connor, William Daniels, Jackie Coogan. w. Stirling Silliphant, N-adap. Raymond Chandler, *The Little Sister*, d. Paul Bogart.
MYSTERY: Missing Persons; Detective Stories; Detectives-Private; Detectives in Deep; Siblings; Los Angeles; Revisionist Films
(The Long Goodbye; Harper)

Marnie, 1964, 130m, ★★★/$$, Universal/MCA-U. A young woman (Tippi Hedren) with a compulsion to steal and then lie about it meets up with a young man (Sean Connery) who wants to change her. w. Jay Presson Allen, N-adap. Winston Graham, d. Alfred Hitchcock.
DRAMA: MELODRAMA: MYSTERY: ROMANCE: Psychological Drama; Thieves; Liars; Dangerous Women; Saving Someone; Female Criminals; Hitchcockian; Female Screenwriters
(Petulia; The Birds)

Marooned, 1969, 134m, ★★1/2/$$, Col/RCA-Col, PG. When three astronauts are stranded in space, a race is run to save them. Gregory Peck, Richard Crenna, David Janssen, James Franciscus, Gene Hackman, Lee Grant, Mariette Hartley. w. Mayo Simon, N-adap. Martin Caidin, d. John Sturges.
DRAMA: Outer Space Movies; SCI-FI: Accidents; Crisis Situations; Stranded; Astronauts; Race Against Time; Saving Someone; Survival Drama; What If . . . Stories
(Capricorn One; Apollo 13)

The Marquise of O, 1976, 107m, ★★1/2/$, Janus/NA. When the Russians invade Italy in the late 1700s, somehow a wealthy local woman gets pregnant. Edith Clever, Bruno Ganz. w. d. Eric Rohmer, SS-adap. Heinrich von Kleist.
DRAMA: COMEDY DRAMA: Historical Drama; Babies-Having; Mothers Alone; Small-town Scandals; Political Unrest; Russians; Italians; Italy; French Films; International Casts
(The Miracle of Morgan's Creek; The Snapper)

The Marriage Go Round, 1961, 98m, ★★/$, 20th/NA. A Swedish girl wants a married American man to mate with her to produce the perfect child-only they don't get married. James Mason, Julie Newmar, Susan Hayward. w. P-adap. Leslie Stevens, d. Walter Lang.
COMEDY: ROMANCE: Romantic Comedy; Romance with Married Person; Romance-Triangles; Babies-Having; Fathers-Surrogate; Mothers Alone; Swedish People; Sexy Women; Good Premise Unfulfilled; Coulda Been Good
(Ed: A favorite plot of sitcoms in the 80s)

The Marriage of a Young Stockbroker, 1971, 95m, ★★★/$, 20th/NA. A yuppie gets bored with his seemingly perfect life and strays into the sexual revolution. Richard Benjamin, Joanna Shimkus, Elizabeth Ashley, Adam West. w. Lorenzo Semple, N-adap. Charles Webb, d. Lawrence Turman.
SATIRE: DRAMA: COMEDY DRAMA: Social Drama; Marriage Drama; Sexual Revolution; Cheating Men; Yuppies; Forgotten Films; Hidden Gems; Underrated
(The Graduate; The Heartbreak Kid; Diary of a Mad Housewife; You're a Big Boy Now; Portnoy's Complaint; Goodbye, Columbus)
(Ed: Benjamin plays the flipside from *Diary* and makes up for *Portnoy's Complaint*, though, unfortunately, no one remembers)

The Marriage of Maria Braun, 1978, 119m, ★★★/$$$, New Yorker/New Yorker, Col, R/S-P-FN. A new bride in post-war Germany marries a black American soldier and deals with the repercussions in melodramatic fashion. Hanna Schygulla, Klaus Lowitsch, Gottfried John. w. Peter Marthesheimer, Pea Frohloch, d. Rainer Werner Fassbinder.

DRAMA: MELODRAMA: TRAGEDY:
Marriage Drama; Black Comedy;
Romance-Interracial; Mothers Alone;
Newlyweds; Germany; World War II-Post
era; Female Protagonists; War Brides
(A Love in Germany; A Patch of Blue)
Marriage on the Rocks, 1965, 109m,
★★1/2/$$$, WB/NA. When a couple
decides to get divorced, they head to the
Mexican Riviera, but she somehow winds
up remarried to his best friend, which
makes him reconsider. Frank Sinatra,
Deborah Kerr, Dean Martin, Cesar
Romero, Hermione Baddely, Tony Bill,
Nancy Sinatra. w. Cy Howard, d. Jack
Donohue.
COMEDY: COMEDY DRAMA: Marriage
Comedy; Marriage on the Rocks; Divorce;
Friends as Enemies; Romance with
Lover's Friend; Mexico; Jealousy;
Swapping Partners
(The Grass Is Greener; Prudence and the
Pill)
Married to It, 1991/1993, ★★1/2/$,
Orion/Orion, R/S-P. Three couples meet
because of school and work and have din-
ner parties during which their relation-
ships are put through the mill. Cybill
Shepherd, Stockard Channing, Ron
Silver, Mary Stuart Masterson, Sean
Robert Leonard, Beau Bridges. w. Janet
Kovalcik, d. Arthur Hiller.
COMEDY: Marriage Comedy; Ensemble
Films; Married Couples; Cheating
Women; Cheating Men; Yuppies; Dinner
Parties; Generation Gaps; New York Life;
Female Protagonists; Female
Screenwriters
(The Last Married Couple in America;
Chances Are; Heartburn)
Married to the Mob, 1988, 103m,
★★★1/2/$$$, Orion/Orion, PG-13/P-V. A
mobster's wife (Michelle Pfeiffer) decides
to leave the life when her cheating hus-
band (Alec Baldwin) is killed, but his
don (Dean Stockwell, BSActor) decides
to follow her, and an FBI agent (Matthew
Modine) is following them both. w. Barry
Strugatz, Mark Burns, d. Johnathan
Demme. Oscars: 1-0.
COMEDY: Spoofs; Black Comedy;
MURDER: SATIRE: ROMANCE:
Romantic Comedy; Suburban Life; Mob
Stories; Mob Comedy; Mob Girls;
Fugitives from the Mob; Fugitives;
Cheating Men; Mothers Alone; FBI
Agents; Underrated
(The Freshman; Something Wild)

A Married Woman, 1964, 98m, ★★★/$,
Ind/Voyager. The wife of an airplane pilot
takes a lover who's an actor in this typi-
cally bizarre Godard epic. Macha Meril,
Bernard Noel. w. d. Jean-Luc Godard.
DRAMA: Avant-Garde Films; Art Films;
Character Studies; **ROMANCE:** Romance-
Triangles; Cheating Women; Female
Protagonists; French Films; Writer-
Directors
(Alphaville; First Name, Carmen)
The Marrying Kind, 1952, 93m,
★★★/$$, Col/RCA-Col. A couple whose
marriage is beginning to fall apart
recount their trouble to a judge and begin
reconsidering divorcing, realizing the
tough times were what bonded them. Judy
Holliday, Aldo Ray, Madge Kennedy,
Mickey Shaughnessy. w. Ruth Gordon,
Garson Kanin, d. George Cukor.
COMEDY: COMEDY DRAMA: Marriage
Comedy; Marriage on the Rocks;
Ordinary People Stories; Narrated Films;
Flashbacks; Working Class; Romance
Reunited; Female Screenwriters
(The Awful Truth; Adam's Rib; Phffft!)
The Marrying Man, 1991, 116m,
★★1/2/$$, Hollywood/Hollywood, PG-
13/S-P. A young man meets a bombshell
singer he just has to have, and has her
time and again, as they continually marry
and divorce and marry and divorce. But
what will the mobster's daughter he pro-
posed to first think? Alec Baldwin, Kim
Basinger, Elizabeth Shue, Robert Loggia,
Armand Assante, Paul Reiser, Risher
Stevens, Peter Dobson. w. Neil Simon,
d. Jerry Rees.
COMEDY: FARCE: Marriage Comedy;
Marrying Again; **ROMANCE:** Romantic
Comedy; Romance Reunited;
Newlyweds; Engagements-Breaking;
Marriage-Impending; Mob Stories; Mob
Comedy; Mob Girls; Fugitives from the
Mob; Las Vegas; Coulda Been Great;
Episodic Stories; Good Premise
Unfulfilled; 1940s; Old-Fashioned
Recent Films
(The Awful Truth; He Married His Wife;
The Getaway [1994])
(Ed: Infighting on the sets with the stars
led to a truncation of Simon's obvious
intent, but it's still passable)
Martin, 1978, 95m, ★★1/2/$, Laurel-
EMI/EMI, HBO, R/EV-B&G. A psychotic
young man either likes blood a lot or is a
vampire. John Amplas, Lincoln Maazel.
w. d. George Romero.

HORROR: Vampires; **SATIRE: MURDER:**
Murders-One by One; Black Comedy;
Radio Life; Psycho Killers; Mental
Illness; Young Men; Forgotten Films;
Writer-Directors
(Ed: Only for horror afficionados)
Martin Luther, 1953, 114m, ★★1/2/$,
Rochemont/Nos. The story of the founder
of the Lutheran movement and foe of
Catholicism. Niall MacGinnia, John
Ruddock. w. Allan Sloane, Lothar Wolff,
d. Irving Pichel. BB&WCin, BB&WArt.
Oscars: 2-0.
DRAMA: Biographies; Religion;
Historical Drama; Character Studies;
Episodic Stories
Martin's Day, 1985, 98m, ★★1/2/$,
MGM-UA/MGM-UA, Fox, G. An escaped
convict on the lam and a little boy
become allies, but it's not to last. Richard
Harris, Lindsay Wagner, James Coburn,
Justin Henry, Karen Black, John Ireland.
w. Allan Scott, Chris Bryant, d. Alan
Gibson.
DRAMA: MELODRAMA: Friendships-
Male; Canadian Films; Prison Escapes;
Fugitives from the Law; Men and Boys;
Illusions Destroyed; Coulda Been Good
(Convicts; A Perfect World; Tiger Bay;
Russkies; The Smuggler)
Marty, 1955, 91m, ★★★★/$$$, UA/
CBS-Fox. An unattractive butcher in New
York is afraid he'll never meet a girl until
one night at a dance he meets a similarly
introverted girl, but her ethnicity and
parents may interfere on both ends.
Ernest Borgnine (**BActor**), Betsy Blair
(**BSActress**), Esther Miniciotti, Joe
Mantell (**BSActor**), Jerry Paris. w. S/P-
adap. Paddy Chayefsky (**BAScr**), d.
Delbert Mann (**BDirector**). **BPicture**,
BB&WCin, BB&WArt. Oscars: 8-4.
DRAMA: MELODRAMA: ROMANCE:
Character Studies; Love-First; Nerds;
Virgins; Coming of Age; Looksism; Shy
People; Ordinary People Stories; Working
Class; Italians; Faded Hits; Hidden Gems
(The Lonely Guy; Lonelyhearts)
Mary Burns, Fugitive, 1935, 84m,
★★1/2/$$, Par/NA. A mob girl gets
caught up in a jam and winds up in
prison; but she soon escapes and starts
over. Sylvia Sidney, Melvyn Douglas,
Alan Baxter, Wallace Ford, Brian
Donlevy. w. Gene Towne, Graham Baker,
Louis Stevens, d. William Howard.
MELODRAMA: Mob Stories; Mob Girls;
Fugitives from the Law; Fugitives from the

Mob; Accused Unjustly; Framed?; Prison Drama; Women in Prison; Innocent Bystanders; Prison Escapes; Starting Over; Dreams; Female Protagonists; Depression Era; Allegorical Stories (That Certain Woman; I Want to Live!) (Ed: A good allegory for wanting to get out of the Depression)

Mary, Mary, 1963, 126m, ★★/$$, WB/NA. The tremendous Broadway hit is stillborn on screen with the jokes falling flat as a divorced couple tries to reunite, but an actor may steal the female of the duo away. Debbie Reynolds, Barry Nelson, Michael Rennie, Diane McBain. w. Richard Breen, P-adap. Jean Kerr, d. Mervyn LeRoy.

COMEDY: COMEDY DRAMA: ROMANCE: Romantic Comedy; Romance Reunited; Romance-Triangles; Divorce; Jealousy; Publishing World; Actors; Stagelike Films; Coulda Been Good (Please Don't Eat the Daisies; The Rat Race) (Ed: One of the longest running plays ever, with Barbara Bel Geddes, but the box office was short and sour for this as a movie)

Mary of Scotland, 1936, 123m, ★★★/$$, RKO/Turner. The last days of Mary Stuart as she refuses to give up her throne. Katharine Hepburn, Fredric March, Donald Crisp, Florence Eldridge, Douglas Watson, John Carradine. w. Dudley Nichols, P-adap. Maxwell Anderson, d. John Ford.

DRAMA: Biographies; TRAGEDY: Costume Drama; Historical Drama; Royalty; Queens; Scotland; Female Protagonists; Executions (Mary, Queen of Scots; The Little Minister)

Mary Poppins, 1964, 139m, ★★★★/ $$$$$$, Disney/Disney, G. A nanny (Julie Andrews, BActress) comes down out of the sky to care for two children who've driven every other nanny away. But that doesn't mean she'll be more lenient, and she certainly won't be boring. Dick Van Dyke, David Tomlinson, Glynis Johns, Ed Wynn, Hermione Baddeley, Matthew Garber, Karen Dotrice. w. Bill Walsh, Don DaGradi (BAScr), N-adap. P. L. Travers, d. Robert Stevenson (BDirector). BPicture, BCCinema, BCArt, BSound, BCCostume, **BOSong, BOScore**, BAScore, BSFX. **BEdit**. Oscars: 13-5 (tie 2nd place for all-time nomination champs)

MUSICAL: FANTASY: COMEDY: MUSICAL COMEDY: CHILDREN'S: FAMILY: Animation-Partial; Fantasies; Babysitters; Mothers-Surrogate; Stern Women; England; Edwardian Era; Female Protagonists; Narrated Films; Production Design-Outstanding (Bedknobs & Broomsticks; My Fair Lady; The Sound of Music) (Ed: Made millions more in subsequent releases, far outdoing its main competitor that year in grosses and Oscars, *My Fair Lady*. Nominated in both adapted and original score categories for Oscars. Julie got the role after being passed on for *Lady* after originating the role on Broadway)

Mary, Queen of Scots, 1971, 128m, ★★★/$$, U/MCA-U, PG. Mary Stuart fights for her throne in this lavish epic with more of an emphasis on Elizabeth and their family feud. Vanessa Redgrave (BActress), Glenda Jackson, Trevor Howard, Patrick McGoohan, Nigel Davenport. w. John Hale, d. Charles Jarrott. BOScore, BCostume, BSound, BArt. Oscars: 5-0.

DRAMA: Biographies; Epics; TRAGEDY: Costume Drama; Historical Drama; Royalty; Queens; Scotland; Female Protagonists; Executions; Revisionist Films (Mary of Scotland; Anne of the Thousand Days)

Masala, 1991, 106m, ★★1/2/$, Canada/Fox-Lorber. An Indian family in Toronto witnesses a Hindu miracle. Srinivas Krishna, Sakina Jaffrey. w. d. Krishna.

DRAMA: MELODRAMA: Miracles; Religions; Indian People; Canadian Films; Actor Directors; Writer-Directors

Masculine, Feminine, 1966, 103m, ★★★1/2/$$, Ind/New Yorker. A young soldier sows some wild oats in hip, mod Paris when he gets together with a wild chanteuse. Jean-Pierre Leaud, Marlene Jobert. d. Jean-Luc Godard.

DRAMA: ROMANCE: Romantic Drama; French New Wave; Art Films; Coming of Age; Mod Era; Paris; Soldiers; Singers; Wild People; French Films; Hidden Gems (Love on the Run; Alphaville)

MASH, 1970, 116m, ★★★1/2/$$$$, 20th/CBS-Fox, R/V-P-S-FFN. The shenanigans of a medical army outfit during the Korean War are chronicled. Elliott Gould, Donald Sutherland, Sally Kellerman (BSActress). w. Ring Lardner,

Jr. (BAScr), d. Robert Altman (BDirector). BPicture, BEdit. Oscars: 5-1.

SATIRE: COMEDY: Black Comedy; FARCE: Ensemble Films; COMEDY DRAMA: Comedy & Violence; Ensembles-Male; Female Among Males; Military Stories; Military Comedy; Doctors; Practical Jokers; Anti-Establishment Films; Anti-War Stories; Korean War; Blockbusters; Sleeper Hits; Faded Hits (Good Morning, Vietnam; M*A*S*H TV Series) (Ed: The more traditional, conventional TV show eclipsed the film's blockbuster status as an anti-establishment high point, but it's still very much worth seeing)

Mask, 1985, 120m, ★★★1/2/$$$, U/MCA-U, PG/P. A boy with a horrible, disfiguring disease has a mother, who, despite her uncouth behavior, fights for his dignity. Cher, Eric Stoltz, Sam Elliott, Estelle Getty, Laura Dern. w. Anna Hamilton Phelan, d. Peter Bogdonavich.

MELODRAMA: COMEDY: DRAMA: Tearjerkers; ROMANCE: Character Studies; Biographies; Mothers & Sons; Fighting the System; Disease Stories; Coming of Age; Disabled People; Love-First; Summer Camps; Motorcycle Gangs; Rednecks; Female Screenwriters; Female Protagonists (The Elephant Man; House of Cards) (Ed: One case where having a lot of angles and subplots helped what would otherwise be a manipulative story instead of an enlightening one)

The Mask, 1994, 100m, ★★★/$$$$$, New Line/New Line, PG-13/V-P. A nerdy banker is transformed into a wild superhero avenger when he finds a mystical mask in the river. With his alter ego and clever dog in tow, he does battle with gangsters and tries for the girl. Jim Carrey, Peter Riegert, Cameron Diaz, Amy Yasbeck, Richard Jeni. w. Mike Werb, d. Chuck Russell.

COMEDY: ACTION: Action Comedy; Fantasy; Superheroes; Comic Heroes; Nerds; Nerds & Babes; Romance-Boy Wants Girl; Mob Comedy; Mob Girls; Dual Lives; Dogs; Blockbusters; Sleeper Hits (Ace Ventura; Dumb and Dumber)

The Mask of Dimitrios, 1944, 99m, ★★★/$$, WB/NA. A writer from Holland goes on a journey to the Middle East and gets caught up in a web of spies and thieves. Peter Lorre, Sidney Greenstreet, Zachary Scott, Victor Francen, Florence Bates. w. Frank Gruber, N-adap. Eric Ambler, d. Jean Negulesco.

MYSTERY: SUSPENSE: Spy Films; Spies; Treasure Hunts; Middle East; Writers; Innocent Bystanders

The Mask of Fu Manchu, 1932, 70m, ★★★/$$$, MGM/MGM-UA. The master criminal catches the valiant Nayland Smith and cohorts in this feature which later was a serial. Boris Karloff, Myrna Loy, Lewis Stone, Karen Morley, Jean Hersholt. w. John Willard, Edgar Woolf, Irene Kahn, SS-adap. Sax Rohmer, d. Charles Brabin, Charles Vidor.

ADVENTURE: ACTION: SUSPENSE: Good vs. Evil; Evil Men; Torture; Female Screenwriters

(The Fiendish Plot of Fu Manchu)

Mask of the Avenger, 1951, 83m, ★★1/2/$$, Col/NA. A nobleman's son in old Italy avenges his father's death and goes after a traitor during the Austro-Italian war. John Derek, Anthony Quinn. w. Jesse Lasky, d. Phil Karlson.

ACTION: Avenging Death of Loved One; Revenge; Traitors; Young Men; Sexy Men; Royalty; Italy; 1800s

(Mark of Zorro; The Wicked Lady)

The Masque of the Red Death, 1964, 89m, ★★★/$$, AIP/Orion. An Italian prince involved in Satanism during the time of the great plague holds a great ball in his castle, unwittingly letting the metaphor for the red death inside. Vincent Price, Hazel Court, Jane Asher, Patrick Magee. w. Charles Beaumont, R. Wright Campbell, SS-adap. Edgar Allan Poe, d. Roger Corman.

HORROR: MURDER: TRAGEDY: Houses-Creepy; Evil Men; Gothic Style; Satanism; Epidemics; Middle Ages; Death-Personified; Allegorical Stories; Classic Literary Adaptations

(The House of Usher; Eye of the Devil)

Masquerade, 1965, 101m, ★★1/2/$, UA/NA. A Saudi prince is kidnapped by a British secret agent in a plot to calm tensions between the Arab emirates but dissent within causes problems for everyone. Cliff Robertson, Jack Hawkins, Charles Gray, Bill Fraser. w. Michael Relph, William Goldman, N-adap. Victor Canning, Castle Minerva, d. Basil Dearden.

ACTION: SUSPENSE: Spy Films; Spies; Secret Agents; Kidnappings; Middle East;

Princes; Traitors; Double Crossings; Arab People

Masquerade, 1988, 91m, ★★1/2/$$, MGM/MGM-UA, R/S-FFN-MRN. A playboy on the make marries a mousy heiress while keeping his gigolo status with other lovelies in the Hamptons, but will he murder his new wife for money or be murdered by an old foe who's onto him? Rob Lowe, Meg Tilly, Doug Savant, Kim Cattrall, Dana Delaney, John Glover. w. Dick Wolf, d. Bob Swaim.

SUSPENSE: MURDER: ROMANCE: Romantic Drama; Murder of Spouse; Prostitutes-Male; Love-Questionable; Marrying Up; Rich People; Wallflowers & Hunks; Coulda Been Good (Suspicion; Undercurrent; Deceived)

(Ed: A real clinker of an ending, dialogue and plot-wise, though that's not giving anything away; passable otherwise. Good John Barry score)

The Masquerader, 1933, 75m, ★★★/$$, Goldwyn/Goldwyn. When a politician with a drug problem goes awry, he's replaced by his lookalike cousin who's not that much alike. Ronald Colman, Elissa Landi, Halliwell Hobbes. w. Howard Estabrook, Moss Hart, P-adap. John Hunter Booth, N-adap. Katherine Thurston, d. Richard Wallace.

COMEDY: Screwball Comedy; Politicians; Impostors; Lookalikes; Drugs-Addictions; Ahead of Its Time; Hidden Gems; Forgotten Films; Novel and Play Adaptations

(Dave; A Double Life; The Man in the Iron Mask; Moon Over Parador; General Della Rovere)

Mass Appeal, 1984, 100m, ★★★/$$, U/MCA-U, PG/S. A stodgy old priest spars with a young seminary student over the changes the Catholic church should make. Jack Lemmon, Zeljko Ivanek, Charles Durning, Louise Latham. w. P-adap. Bill C. David, d. Glenn Jordan.

COMEDY: DRAMA: Religion; Priests Generation Gap; Video Hits

(Heaven Help Us)

(Ed: The enormously successful play transfers to the screen well-intact, though it didn't strike the same chord at the box-office as it did on stage or in the video store)

Mastergate (A Play on Words), 1991, 95m, Showtime/NA, ★★★/$$. A send-up of government hearings on scandals in

which government funds have been used to run a movie studio and other shenanigans. Ed Begley, Jr., David Ogden Stiers, Bruno Kirby, Tim Reid, Buck Henry, Robert Gillaume, James Coburn, Ken Howard, Richard Kiley, Dennis Weaver, Burgess Meredith. w. P-adap. L. Gelbart, d.

SATIRE: COMEDY: COMEDY DRAMA: Tragi-Comedy; Spoofs; **FARCE:** Courtroom Drama; Hollywood Life; Scandals; Corruption; Government as Enemy; Washington D.C.; Politicians; Clever Plots & Endings; All-Star Casts; Stage Tapings

The Master of Ballantree, 1953, 89m, ★★★/$, WB/WB. Two brothers in merry old England fight over who will join Prince Charles' rebellion. Errol Flynn, Anthony Steel, Roger Livesay. w. Herb Meadow, N-adap. Robert Louis Stevenson, d. William Keighley.

ADVENTURE: Political Unrest; Swashbucklers; Historical Drama; War Stories; Brothers; 1700s

Master of the World, 1961, 104m, ★★/$, AIP/Orion. In the 1800s, a mad scientist (Vincent Price) travels around in his special zeppelin-like invention to spread the word of peace, among other things. Charles Bronson, Henry Hull. w. Richard Matheson, N-adap. Jules Verne, d. William Whitney.

SCI-FI: ADVENTURE: Fantasy; Inventors; Scientists-Mad; War Stories; Anti-War Films; Balloons

(Around the World in 80 Days; Comedy of Terrors)

The Masters, 1975, 100m, ★★/$, Ind/NA. A new school teacher in a small town in Sicily becomes an innocent bystander to mob activities. Jennifer O'Neill, James Mason, Franco Nero. w. Leo Benevenuti, Piero DeBernardi, Luigi Zampa, Guiseppe Fava, d. Zampa.

SUSPENSE: Mob Stories; Innocent Bystanders; Women in Jeopardy; Teachers; Italy

Mata Hari, 1931, 92m, ★★★/$$$, MGM/MGM-UA. Greta Garbo, Ramon Navarro, Lionel Barrymore, Lewis Stone, Karen Morley. w. Benjamin Glazer, Leo Birinski, Doris Anderson, Gilbert Emery, d. George Fitzmaurice.

Mata Hari, Agent H21, 1964, 99m, ★★1/2/$$, Ind/NA. Jeanne Moreau, Jean-Louis Trintignant, Claude Rich. w. Jean-Louis Richards, Francois Truffaut, d. Jean-Louis Richard.

Mata Hari, 1985, 108m, ★★/$, Cannon-MGM-UA/MGM-UA, R/S-FN. Travails of the poor European girl and her exploits from exotic dancer to spy during World War I. Sylvia Kristel, Christopher Cazenove, Oliver Tobias. w. Joel Ziskin, d. Curtis Harrington.
MELODRAMA: SUSPENSE: Spy Films; Spies; Spies-Female; World War I Stories; Sexy Women; Dangerous Women; Dancers; Female Writers; Female Protagonists
(The Adventuress; Hanna's War; Odette)

The Match Factory Girl, 1991, 70m, ★★★/$, Svensk-Kino/Facets, Kino. A girl who works in a Scandinavian factory takes revenge on everyone who used and abused her. Kati Outinen, Elina Salo. w. d. Aki Kaurismaki.
COMEDY DRAMA: Black Comedy; Comedy-Morbid; Revenge; Factory Life; Working Class; Female Criminals; Female Protagonists; Abused Women; Ostracism; Evil Women; Swedish Films; Scandinavia
(The Girl Most Likely To . . .)

The Matchmaker, 1958, 101m, ★★¹/₂/$$, Par/Par. A nosy woman in turn of the century New York is hired as a match-maker for a man, but she soon decides she'll keep him for herself. Shirley Booth, Paul Ford, Anthony Perkins, Shirley MacLaine, Wallace Ford, Robert Morse, Perry Wilson. w. John Michael Hayes, P-adap. Thornton Wilder, d. Joseph Anthony.
COMEDY DRAMA: ROMANCE: Romantic Comedy; Matchmakers; Romance-Triangles; Protagonists; Nuisances; Crossing the Line; Jewish People; Narrated Films
MUSICAL REMAKE: Hello, Dolly!

Matewan, 1987, 133m, ★★★/$, Lorimar-WB/WB. In an early 1900s mining town, miners battle the owners in a strike that becomes very violent. Chris Cooper, Mary McDonnell, Will Oldham, David Strathairn, James Earl Jones, Bob Gunton, Ken Jenkins. w. d. John Sayles. BCin. Oscars: 1-0.
DRAMA: TRAGEDY: Political Drama; Historical Drama; Social Drama; True Stories; Mining Towns; Strikes; Unions; Factory Life; Working Class; Worker vs. Boss; Feuds; Mountain People; 1900s; Overlooked at Release; Hidden Gems; Writer-Directors
(Harlan County, USA; Blue Collar)

Matilda, 1978, 105m, ★★¹/₂/$, AIP/Vestron, G. A seedy agent finds a new client with a boxing kangaroo from Australia. Elliott Gould, Karen Carlson, Robert Mitchum, Harry Guardino, Clive Revill, Lionel Stander, Roy Clark. w. Albert S. Ruddy, Timothy Galfas, N-adap. Paul Gallico, d. Daniel Mann.
COMEDY: Sports Movies; Boxing; Animal Stories; Comebacks; Underdog Stories; Old-Fashioned Recent Films; Disneyesque Comedy; Coulda Been Great
(Ed: It's an under-kangaroo story)

Matinee, 1992, 98m, ★★★/$$, U/MCA-U, PG. A schlock movie king promotes a movie in south Florida on the eve of the Cuban Missile Crisis, where people begin to confuse the horrors of the movies with real life. John Goodman, Cathy Moriarty, Simon Fenton, Kellie Martin, John Sayles. d. Joe Dante.
COMEDY: Movie Making; Movie Theaters; Paranoia; Horror Comedy; Interwoven Stories; Multiple Stories; Teenagers; 1960s; Florida; Small-town Life; Southerns
(Ed Wood)

The Mating Game, 1959, 96m, ★★¹/₂/$$, MGM/MGM-UA. An IRS snoop delves into the life of a kooky farm family. Tony Randall, Debbie Reynolds, Paul Douglas, Fred Clark, Una Merkel. w. William Roberts, N-adap. H. E. Bates, *The Darling Buds of May*, d. George Marshall.
COMEDY: COMEDY DRAMA: ROMANCE: Romantic Comedy; Farm Life; Fish out of Water Stories; Government as Enemy; Eccentric People; Nerds

The Mating of Willie, 1948, 87m, ★★¹/₂/$, Col/NA. A young woman wants to adopt a baby in the 40s but needs a man to share it with, so she tries to talk a bus driver into it. Glenn Ford, Evelyn Keyes, Willard Parker. w. Louella MacFarlane, St. Clair McKelway, d. Henry Levin.
COMEDY DRAMA: MELODRAMA: ROMANCE: Romance-Reluctant; Marriage of Convenience; Children-Adopted; Working Class; Single Women; Mothers-Unwed; Ahead of Its Time; Female Protagonists; Female Screenwriters
(To Find a Man; Blue Denim)

The Mating Season, 1951, 101m, ★★★/$$, Par/Par, AMC. A man getting married to a prominent woman has his eccentric mother pop up without a dime,

so she settles for working for them as a cook. Thelma Ritter, Gene Tierney, John Lund, Miriam Hopkins, Jan Sterling. w. Walter Reisch, Charles Brackett, Richard Breen, d. Mitchell Liesen.
COMEDY DRAMA: MELODRAMA: ROMANCE: Marriage Drama; Marriage-Impending; Newlyweds; Mothers-Troublesome; Class Conflicts; Mothers & Sons; Female Protagonists
(Pickup on South Street; With a Song in My Heart)

A Matter of Time, 1976, 97m, ★★¹/₂/$, AIP/Vestron, G. An old countess in an ancient Italian pensione tells a young maid about her life through memory and fantasy. Liza Minnelli, Ingrid Bergman, Charles Boyer, Spiros Andros. w. John Gay, N-adap. Maurice Druon, *The Film of Memory*, d. Vincente Minnelli.
MELODRAMA: FAMILY: Fantasy; COMEDY DRAMA: Memories; Silent Film Era; Servants; Actresses; Unintentionally Funny; Hidden Gems; Camp; Old-Fashioned Recent Films; Narrated Films
(Sunset Boulevard; The Blue Bird; Travels with My Aunt; Just a Gigolo)
(Ed: Often incoherent but interesting for the stars and the ambiance)

Maurice, 1987, 140m, ★★★/$$, MI-Cinecom/Cinecom, R/S-MFN. A wealthy young man is faced with his own homo-sexuality, and the only man who will reci-procate his affections is an uneducated groundskeeper. James Wilby, Rupert Graves, Hugh Grant, Denholm Elliott, Ben Kingsley, Simon Callow, Billie Whitelaw. w. Kit Hesketh-Harvey, James Ivory, N-adap. E.M. Forster, d. Ivory. BCostume. Oscars: 1-0.
DRAMA: ROMANCE: Romantic Drama; Romance-Reluctant; Romance-Class Conflicts; Homoeroticism; Homophobia; Gay Men; Edwardian Era; Lyrical Films; British Films
(The Trial of Oscar Wilde; Howards End; A Room With a View; Another Country)

Maverick, 1994, 129m, ★★★/$$$$, WB/WB, PG. Comic shenanigans in a small western town as the card-playing Maverick has some trouble with old foes. Mel Gibson, Jodie Foster, James Garner, Graham Greene, James Coburn. w. William Goldman, d. Richard Donner.
COMEDY: WESTERNS: Western Comedy; Romantic Comedy; Police

Stories; Gambling; Duels; Chase Stories; TV Series Movies
(Cat Ballou; McClintock!; Poker Alice)
The Maverick Queen, 1955, 90m, ★★/$, Republic/Republic. A lady cattle rustler has a detective put on her trail, but he may not just arrest her. Barbara Stanwyck, Barry Sullivan, Scott Brady, Wallace Ford. w. Kenneth Gamet, DeVallon Scott, N-adap. Zane Grey, d. Joe Kane.
WESTERN: ROMANCE: Cattle People; Cattle Rustlers; Cattle Herded by Barbara Stanwyck; Female Protagonists; Detectives-Private
(The Furies; Cattle Queen of Montana)
Max and Helen, 1990, 94m, ★★★/$$, Turner/Turner. A woman is raped by a Nazi in a concentration camp and separated from her lover thereafter. Years later, the lover tracks her down for a startling revelation. Treat Williams, Alice Krige, Martin Landau, John Phillips. w. Corey Blachman, d. Philip Saville.
DRAMA: ROMANCE: Romance-Doomed; Nazi Stories; World War II Stories; Concentration Camps; Rape/Rapists; Episodic Stories; Clever Plots & Endings
(The Night Porter; Triumph of the Spirit; Dr. Zhivago; Sophie's Choice)
Max Dugan Returns, 1983, 98m, ★★★/$$, 20th/CBS-Fox, PG. A struggling mother with a teenage son finds her long-lost gambler father on her doorstep and he turns her life upside down-for the better it would seem. Marsha Mason, Matthew Broderick, Jason Robards, Donald Sutherland. w. Neil Simon, d. Herbert Ross.
COMEDY: COMEDY DRAMA: Family Comedy; Fantasy; Fairy Tales; Grandfathers-Fascinating; Mothers Alone; Mothers-Struggling; Poor People; Rags to Riches; Death-Impending; Reunions; Mothers & Sons; Fathers & Daughters; Gambling; Secrets-Keeping; Old-Fashioned Recent Films
(I Ought to Be in Pictures; Only When I Laugh)
Maxie, 1985, 98m, ★★/$, Orion/Orion, PG. The ghost of a failed silent film actress/flapper pops up in her old apartment when a young couple moves in and proceeds to possess the wife's body. Glenn Close, Mandy Patinkin, Ruth Gordon, Barnard Hughes, Valerie Curtin. w. Patricia Resnick, N-adap. Jack Finney (*Marion's Wall*), d. Paul Aaron.

COMEDY: Fantasy; Ghosts; Possessions; Roaring 20s; Silent Film Era; Female Protagonist; Female Screenwriters; Coulda Been Good
(Blithe Spirit; The Two Worlds of Jenny Logan)
Maximum Overdrive, 1986, 97m, ★★/$, DEG-WB/WB, R/EV. Machines go haywire in a small North Carolina town near the deLaurentiis studios there, especially the 18-wheelers. Emilio Estevez, Pat Hingle, Yeardley Smith. w. d. Stephen King.
HORROR: SCI-FI: Man vs. Machine; Monsters-Machines; Small-town Life; Nightmares; Writer-Directors; Stephen King.
REMAKE/RIPOFF: Duel.
(Pulse; Duel; Christine)
Maybe I'll Be Home in the Spring, 1971, 90m, ★★★/$$$$, ABC/ABC, VTR. A young woman runs away from home during the psychedelic drug days, but when she wants to go home, can she? Sally Field, Jackie Cooper, Eleanor Parker, David Carradine. d. Joseph Sargent.
DRAMA: Runaways; Family Drama; 1970s; Time Capsules; Psychedelic Era; Young Women; TV Movies; Hidden Gems
(Katherine; Where the Day Takes You)
(Ed: A big hit in the ratings when first aired as part of the legendary early 70s ABC movie of the week series)
Mayerling, 1935, 90m, ★★★/$$, MGM/Voyager, Facets. Charles Boyer, Danielle Darrieux, Marthe Regnier. w. Joseph Kessel, V. Cube, N-adap. Claude Anet, d. Anatole Litwak.
Mayerling, 1968, 141m, ★★½/$$, MGM/NA. The Hapsburg Emperor's son is driven into exile and possible death when the Empire crumbles in 1889. Omar Sharif, Catherine Deneuve, James Mason, Ava Gardner, James Robertson Justice. w. d. Terence Young.
DRAMA: TRAGEDY: MELODRAMA: Costume Drama; Historical Drama; Royalty; Suicidal Tendencies; Political Unrest; War Stories
(Dr. Zhivago; Ludwig)
The Mayflower Madam, 1987, 93m, ★★½/$$$$, CBS/Vidmark. Story of how Sidney Biddle Barrows went from fashion maven to earning a living as a high class madam. Candice Bergen, Chris Sarandon, Chita Rivera. d. Lou Antonio.

DRAMA: True Stories; Madams; Making a Living; Single Women; Ordinary Person Turned Criminal; Prostitutes-High Class
(Beverly Hills Madam; Personal Services)
May Fools (Milou in May), 1989, 108m, ★★★/$$, Orion/Orion, R/S-FN. When an elderly man's even older mother dies, he meets all of her family at the funeral, dealing with all of them and reminiscing. Michel Piccoli, Miou-Miou. w. Louis Malle, Jean-Claude Carriere, d. Malle.
DRAMA: COMEDY DRAMA: Family Drama; Death-Dealing with; Funerals; Elderly Men; Ensemble Films; Reunions; French Films
(Passed Away; Tatie Danielle; Daddy Nostalgie)
The Mayor of Hell, 1933, 90m, ★★½/$$$, WB/NA. A mobster reforms himself enough to become head of a reform school and keeps himself out of harm's way. James Cagney, Madge Evans, Allen Jenkins. w. Edward Chodorov, d. Archie Mayo.
DRAMA: Crime Drama; Juvenile Delinquents; Mob Stories; Ex-Convicts; Starting Over; Redemption; Warner Gangster Era
REMAKES/RIPOFFS: Crime School, Hell's Kitchen.
(The Big House; Boystown; Lean on Me)
Maytime, 1937, 132m, ★★★/$$, MGM/MGM-UA. An opera singer falls for another singer who is down on his luck, but her impresario is extremely jealous. Jeanette McDonald, Nelson Eddy, John Barrymore, Herman Bing. w. Noel Langley, P-adap. Rita Johnson Young, d. Robert Z. Leonard. BMScore. Oscars: 1-0.
MELODRAMA: TRAGEDY: ROMANCE: MURDER: Tearjerkers; Crimes of Passion; Romance-Triangles; Opera; Operettas; Jealousy
(Bittersweet; The Firefly; Unfaithfully Yours)
McBain, 1991, 102m, ★★/$, Shapiro/MCA-U, R/EV-P. A bizarre psuedo-superhero-mercenary-soldier helps a friend with a coup in Columbia. Christopher Walken, Maria Conchita Alonso. w. d. James Gkickenhaus.
ACTION: Political Unrest; Assassinations; Drugs-Dealing; South America
(King of New York; Dogs of War)
McCabe and Mrs. Miller, 1971, 120m, ★★★½/$$, WB/WB, R/V-S. An outlaw

comes to a Northwest mining town in the 1890s and becomes involved with a whore and her women, changing the town. Warren Beatty, Julie Christie (BActress), Shelley Duvall, Rene Auberjonois, John Schuck. w. Robert Altman, Brian McKay, N-adap. Edmund Naughton (*McCabe*), d. Robert Altman. Oscars: 1-0.

DRAMA: WESTERNS: ROMANCE: Art Films; Allegorical Stories; Prostitutes-Low Class; Pimps; Mining Towns; 1890s; Lyrical Films; Cult Films
(The Man Who Loved Cat Dancing; Heaven's Gate)

The McConnell Story, 1955, 107m, ★★/$$, WB/WB. The story of a flying ace during the Korean war and his untimely death. Alan Ladd, June Allyson, James Whitmore. w. Ted Sherdeman, Sam Rolfe, d. Gordon Douglas.

DRAMA: MELODRAMA: TRAGEDY: War Stories; Korean War; Pilots-Military; Death-Accidental

McLintock!, 1963, 127m, ★★★1/2/$$$, UA/Goodtimes, MPI. A man who practically owns his Arizona town commands everything until his feisty Irish wife returns and their bickering romance resumes full tilt. John Wayne, Maureen O'Hara, Yvonne DeCarlo, Patrick Wayne, Stefanie Powers, Chill Wills, Bruce Cabot, Jack Kruschen. w. James Grant, d. Andrew McLaglen.

COMEDY: WESTERN: Western Comedy; **ROMANCE:** Romantic Comedy; Romance-Bickering; Battle of the Sexes; Family Comedy; Mothers & Daughters; Feisty Females; Marriage-Impending; Desert Settings; Small-town Life; Hidden Gems; Faded Hits
(The Taming of the Shrew; The Quiet Man; Cat Ballou)
(Ed: Even for those who don't like westerns or Wayne)

The McMasters, 1969, 90m, ★★1/2/$, Ind/Xenon. A black young man who fought in the Civil War returns home to the South and tries to rebuild his life with the help of a white man, despite those who'd stop him. Brock Peters, Burl Ives, David Carradine, Nancy Kwan, Jack Palance, John Carradine. w. Harold Smith, d. Alf Kjellin.

DRAMA: Race Relations; Black vs. White; Black Men; Black Soldiers; Southerns; Reconstruction Era; Civil War Era
(Glory)

McQ, 1974, 111m, ★★1/2/$$, WB/WB, PG/V. A police detective hunts down the killer of his partner and friend. John Wayne, Eddie Albert, Diana Muldaur, Colleen Dewhurst, Clu Gulager, Julie Adams. w. Lawrence Roman, d. John Sturges.

ACTION: Detective Stories; Detectives-Police; Police Stories; Avenging Death of Friend; Trail of a Killer
(Brannigan)

McVicar, 1980, 112m, ★★1/2/$, Ind/Vestron, R/S-P. A young British criminal breaks out of prison but winds up in the reform system. Roger Daltrey, Adam Faith, Cheryl Campbell. w. John McVicar, Tom Clegg, d. Tom Clegg.

DRAMA: MELODRAMA: Docudrama; Crime Drama; Prison Drama; Prison Escapes; Biographies; True Stories; Ex-Convicts; Redemption; England; British Films
(Ed: Primarily an acting showcase attempt for Daltrey, but ultimately mediocre and overly long)

Me and Him, 1988, 90m, ★★/$ (VR), Col/RCA-Col, R/ES-P. A goofy man's penis begins to sass him at all the wrong times. Griffin Dunne, voice of penis: Mark Linn-Baker, Ellen Greene, Craig T. Nelson, Kelly Bishop, Carey Lowell. w. Warren D. Leight, Michael Junker, Doris Dorrie, N-adap. Alberto Moravia, *Lo e Lui*, d. Doris Dorrie.

COMEDY: COMEDY DRAMA: Comedy of Errors; Young Men; Sexuality; Architects; Fantasy; What If . . . Stories; Female Screenwriters; Female Directors; Coulda Been Good; Curiosities
(Men; All of Me)
(Ed: A similar fate would probably be the result of a man writing and directing a film about a talking vagina, which has apparently been done in porn form)

Me and My Gal, 1932, 79m, ★★★/$$, 20th/NA. A flatfoot goes after a diner waitress and a crook and everyone's happy. Spencer Tracy, Joan Bennett, George Walsh, Marion Burns. w. Arthur Kober, d. Raoul Walsh.

COMEDY: COMEDY DRAMA: ROMANCE: Romantic Comedy; Police Stories; Working Class
REMAKE: Pier 13.

Me and the Colonel, 1958, 110m, ★★/$, Col/NA. At the onset of the taking of France in World War II, a Polish commander who is anti-Semitic is forced to

flee with a Jewish refugee or stay and face consequences. Danny Kaye, Curt Jurgens, Akim Tamiroff. w. S. N. Berman, George Froeschel, P-adap. Franz Werfel, d. Peter Glenville.

COMEDY: COMEDY DRAMA: War Stories; Military Comedy; World War II Stories; Anti-Semitism; Jewish People; Fugitives; Jews-Saving
(Skokie; Hell in the Pacific; Kiss of the Spider Woman)

Me & Veronica, 1993, 97m, ★★/$, Col/Col, R/S-P. Two sisters reunite trying to put their lives back together after one has divorced and the other has been convicted of welfare fraud. Elizabeth McGovern, Patricia Wettig, Michael O'Keefe, John Heard. w. Leslie Lyles, d. Don Scardino.

DRAMA: Sisters; Criminals-Female; Starting Over; Friendships-Female; Working Class; Making a Living; Ordinary People Stories; Coulda Been Good; Overlooked at Release; Female Protagonists; Female Screenwriters
(Love Child; The Favor)

The Mean Season, 1985, 103m, ★★1/2/$$, Orion/Orion, PG-13/V-S. A journalist is contacted by a serial killer who may want his girlfriend next. Kurt Russell, Mariel Hemingway, Richard Jordan, Richard Masur, Joe Pantoliano. w. Leon Piedmont, N-adap. John Katzenbach (*In the Heat of the Summer*), d. Philip Borsos.

SUSPENSE: MURDER: MYSTERY: MURDER MYSTERY: Serial Killers; Stalkers; Women in Jeopardy; Men in Jeopardy; Journalists; Journalist as Detective; Detective Stories; Killer Calls Cop
(Relentless; Seven; No Way to Treat a Lady)

Mean Streets, 1973, 110m, ★★★1/2/$$, WB/WB, R/EP-V. A pool hall is the site for everything in the Italian neighborhood of four young men. Robert De Niro, Harvey Keitel, David Proval, Amy Robison. w. Martin Scorsese, Mardik Martin, d. Martin Scorsese.

DRAMA: MELODRAMA: Crime Drama; Character Studies; Gangs-White; Mob Stories; Ensemble Films; Ensembles-Male; Italians; New York Life; Cult Films; Hidden Gems
(GoodFellas; The Lords of Flatbush; The Wanderers; Taxi Driver)

Meatballs, 1979, 92m, ★★1/2/$$$$, Par/Par, PG/P-S. A goofy camp counselor

(Bill Murray) sets the tone for mayhem at a kids' summer camp. w. Len Blun, Dan Goldberg, Harold Ramis, Janis Allen, d. Ivan Reitman.

COMEDY: Party Movies; Summer Camp; Teenagers; Teenage Movies; Bathroom Humor; Comedy-Skit

SEQUELS: Meatballs 2, 3, & 4.

(Little Darlings; Gorp; Poison Ivy)

(Ed: It is what it is)

The Mechanic, 1972, 100m, ★★★/$$, UA/MGM-UA, Fox, R/EV-P-S. A hitman who specializes in "accidents" takes a young man under his wing, but he's not just a protege; he has a mission of his own. Charles Bronson, Jan-Michael Vincent, Keenan Wynn, Jill Ireland. w. Lewis John Carlino, d. Michael Winner.

ACTION: SUSPENSE: Crime Drama; Hitmen; Assassinations; Character Studies; Film Noir-Modern; Death-Accidental; Revenge; Teachers and Students; Proteges; Underrated; Forgotten Films; Coulda Been Great

(Breaking In)

A Medal for Benny, 1945, 77m, ★★1/2/$$, Par/NA. When an old man's son dies in battle, the town he lives in has a celebration. Dorothy Lamour, Arturo deCordova, J. Carrol Naish (BSActor), Frank McHugh. w. Frank Butler, John Steinbeck (BOStory), d. Irving Pichel. Oscars: 2-0.

MELODRAMA: SATIRE: Small-town Life; Death-Dealing with

Medicine Man, 1992, 105m, ★★1/2/$$$, Touchstone/Touchstone, PG/S. A scientist in the Amazon thinks he's found the cure for cancer, but he may get side-tracked with a goofy sidekick female assigned to him from New York. Sean Connery, Lorraine Bracco. w. Tom Schulman, Sally Robinson, d. John McTiernan.

COMEDY: COMEDY DRAMA: ROMANCE: Romantic Comedy; Romance-Bickering; Scientists; Jungle Life; Amazon River; Rain forests; Cures/Elixirs; Coulda Been Great; Female Screenwriters

(Ed: Some good romantic sparring moments, but ultimately a pretentious, bizarre concoction where both lovers are annoying [particularly Bracco, who thinks she's in a screwball comedy]-and yet it made money . . .)

Mediterraneo, 1992, 90m, ★★★/$$$, Miramax/Touchstone, R/S-FN-MN. A pla-toon of Italian soldiers gets stranded on a Mediterranean island during World War II and soon they'd rather stay than be rescued. d. Gabriele Salvatores.

COMEDY DRAMA: Comedy-Situation; Stranded on an Island; Fish out of Water Stories; Soldiers; Female Among Males; Menage à Trois; Mediterranean Islands; Italian Films

(Catch 22; Il Postino; Cinema Paradiso)

Medium Cool, 1969, 111m, ★★★/$, Par/Par, R/V-P-FFN-MFN. A TV camera-man during the Chicago Democratic convention riots in 1968 begins to come apart in similar fashion to his environment. Robert Forster, Verna Bloom, Peter Bonerz, Marianna Hill. d. Haskell Wexler.

DRAMA: Art Films; Avant-Garde Films; Documentary Style; Political Unrest; Riots; Journalists; TV Life; Young People; Young Men; Character Studies; Cult Films; Time Capsules; Anti-establishment Films; Psychedelic Era; 1960s; Chicago

(Wild in the Streets; The Strawberry Statement)

(Ed: Forster's breakthrough, long before winding up on *Falcon Crest*. Reputed to be the first major studio release with male frontal nudity-barely, though)

The Medusa Touch, 1978, 109m, ★★1/2/$, ITC/Fox, R/V. A writer begins having visions that he can cause or stop disasters from happening. Richard Burton, Lee Remick, Lino Ventura, Harry Andrews, Jeremy Brett. w. John Briley, N-adap. Peter Greenaway, d. Jack Gold.

SCI-FI: DRAMA: Fantasy; Disaster Movies; Nightmares; Illusions/Hallucinations; Psychics; Writers Airplane Crashes; Possessions; Underrated; Cult Films; Unintentionally Funny; Camp

(The Man Who Could Work Miracles; The Clairvoyant)

(Ed: Laughed at upon its release and barely released in America, this does have at least a campy charm)

Meet Danny Wilson, 1951, 83m, ★★/$$, U/MCA-U. A singer rises in the ranks by aligning with the mob. Frank Sinatra, Shelley Winters, Alex Nicol, Raymond Burr. w. Don McGuire, d. Joseph Pevney.

DRAMA: MELODRAMA: Singers; Mob Stories; Fame-Rise to; Biographies-Fictional; Nightclubs

(The Cotton Club; The George Raft Story)

Meet John Doe, 1941, ★★★/$$, Liberty/Prism, Nos. A female political activist and writer goes out and finds a supposed bum to represent "everyman" in a political campaign, but the intentions go very sour in their exploitation of him. w. Robert Riskin, story: Richard Connell, Robert Presnell (BOStory), d. Frank Capra. Oscars: 1-0.

SATIRE: DRAMA: COMEDY DRAMA: TRAGEDY: Political Drama; Social Drama; Ordinary People Stories; Political Campaigns; Newspapers; Journalists; Svengalis; Homeless People; Female Protagonists

(Mr. Deeds Goes to Town; Mr. Smith Goes to Washington; A Face in the Crowd)

(Ed: The writers of the original story sued because of the happy ending tacked on)

Meet Me After the Show, 1951, 88m, ★★1/2/$$, 20th/NA. A musical comedy actress thinks her husband is having an affair. Betty Grable, Macdonald Carey, Rory Calhoun, Eddie Albert, Irene Ryan. w. Mary Loos, Richard Sale, d. Sale.

MUSICALS: COMEDY: Musical Comedy; Theater Life; Actresses; Cheating Men; Paranoia; Jealousy; Accused Unjustly; Female Screenwriters

(Unfaithfully Yours)

Meet Me in Las Vegas, 1956, 112m, ★★/$, MGM/MGM-UA. A gambler believes a ballerina, who's in Las Vegas of all places, is bringing him good luck, so he sings about it. Dan Dailey, Cyd Charisse, Agnes Moorhead, Lili Darvas, Paul Henreid, Lena Horne, Frankie Laine. w. Isobel Lennart, d. Roy Rowland.

MUSICAL: ROMANCE: Musical Romance; Las Vegas; Gambling; Ballet Dancers; Lucky People; Female Writers

Meet Me in St. Louis, 1944, 113m, ★★★★/$$$$, MGM/MGM-UA. A girl sings on the St. Louis trolley around the time of the 1904 World's Fair about the trolley and the boy next door and her happy family life in general. Judy Garland, Margaret O'Brien, Tom Drake, Mary Astor, June Lockhart, Harry Davenport, Marjorie Main, Chill Wills. w. Irving Brecher, Fred Finkelhoffe (BScr), N-adap. Sally Benson, d. Vincente Minnelli. BCCin, BMDirection, BOSong, "The Trolley Song." Oscars: 4-0.

MUSICALS: FAMILY: Family Stories; Young Women; Love-First; American Dream; Fairy Tales; 1900s

(The Harvey Girls; In the Good Old Summertime)
(Ed: Several great, memorable songs and a dreamy Disney quality before Disney ever ventured into live action)
Meet the Applegates (The Applegates), 1990, 82m, ★★1/2/$, New World/New World, NA. A seemingly normal family in the suburbs is really a family of giant mutant insects who can transform themselves into humans. They're from the Amazon and they've come to America to avenge nuclear power. Ed Begley, Jr., Stockard Channing, Dabney Coleman, Boby Jacoby, Cami Cooper. w. Redbeard Simmons, Michael Lehmann, d. Lehmann.
COMEDY: SATIRE: SCI-FI: Fantasy; Disguises; Impostors; Monsters-Mutant; Insects; American Dream; Suburban Life; Coulda Been Good
(The Coneheads; Third Rock from the Sun, TV Series)
Meet the People, 1944, 100m, ★★/$$, MGM/NA. A highfalutin Broadway actress is tired of those trying to bring her down a notch, so she takes a job down at the docks to prove she's ordinary, though, of course, she's not. Lucille Ball, Dick Powell, Virginia O'Brien, Bert Lahr, June Allyson. w. S. N. Herzig, Fred Sandy, P-adap. Louis Lantas, Sol Barzman, Ben Barzman, d. Charles Reisner.
COMEDY: COMEDY DRAMA: Fish out of a Water Stories; Actresses; Snobs; Rich vs. Poor; Class Conflicts; Bets; Female Protagonists
(The Affairs of Annabel)
Meet the Stewarts, 1942, 74m, ★★1/2/$, Col/NA. A young married couple hits the skids when she needs more money for her lifestyle than he's able to supply. William Holden, Frances Dee, Grant Mitchell. w. Elizabeth Dunn, Karen DeWolf, d. Alfred Green.
COMEDY: COMEDY DRAMA: ROMANCE: Romantic Comedy; Marriage Comedy; Marriage on the Rocks; Rich vs. Poor; Romance-Class Conflicts; Female Screenwriters
(The Palm Beach Story; Made for Each Other)
Meeting Venus, 1990, 120m, ★★1/2/$, WB/WB, PG-13/S. The lead singer in an opera has a fling with the musical conductor, leading to complications for the whole show. Glenn Close, Niels

Arestrup. w. Istvan Szabo, Michael Hirst, d. Szabo.
DRAMA: COMEDY DRAMA: ROMANCE: Romance-Triangles; Romantic Drama; Art; Films; Character Studies; Opera Singers; Female Protagonists; Europeans-Eastern; Coulda Been Good
Mein Kampf, 1961, 118m, ★★★/$$, Svensk/Sultan. Newsreels detailing the rise of Hitler. w. d. Erwin Leiser. Documentaries; Nazi Stories; Hitler; World War II Stories; Germany
(Triumph of the Will; Olympispchiele)
Melancholia, 1989, 87m, ★★/$, Ind/NA. A German art critic gets mixed up in an assassination attempt. Jeroen Krabbe, Susannah York. w. Andi Engel, Lewis Rodia, d. Engel.
SUSPENSE: Spy Films; Spies; Assassinations; Germans; German Films; London; International Casts; Coulda Been Good
Melo, 1986, 112m, ★★★/$, Ind/NA. A woman cheating on her husband can't deal with the guilt. Sabine Azema, Fanny Ardant, Pierre Aditi. w. d. Alain Resnais, P-adap. Henry Bernstein.
DRAMA: MELODRAMA: ROMANCE: TRAGEDY: Cheating Women; Guilty Conscience; Romance with Married Person; Romance-Doomed; Suicidal Tendencies
Melody (S.W.A.L.K.), 1971, 106m, ★★1/2/$, Hemdale/Sultan. A romantic triangle develops among adolescents in school. Mark Lester, Jack Wild, Tracy Hyde. w. Alan Parker, d. Waris Hussein.
COMEDY DRAMA: CHILDREN'S: ROMANCE: Love-First; Friendships-Male; School Life; Teenagers; Boys; Forgotten Films
(Eyewitness; Some Kind of Wonderful)
Melvin and Howard, 1980, 95m, ★★★★/$, Universal/MCA-U, R/S-P-FN. When an average Joe named Melvin Dummar (Paul LeMat) gives Howard Hughes (Jason Robards, BSActor) a lift in the desert and is supposedly left in Hughes' will, his life turns upside down. Mary Steenburgen (**BSActress**). w. Bo Goldman (**BOScr**), d. Johnathan Demme. Oscars: 3-2.
COMEDY: COMEDY DRAMA: Black Comedy; Comedy-Light; Marriage Comedy; Ordinary People Stories; Inheritances at Stake; Rags to Riches Dreams; Working Class; Rich vs. Poor; Unbelieved; Game Shows; Hidden Gems

(UFOria; If I Had a Million; Howard Hughes)
(Ed: It never found an audience at the box office or video store, but it's definitely worth seeing from an artistic and an entertainment point of view)
The Member of the Wedding, (B&W), 1952, 91m, ★★★★/$$$, 20th/CBS-Fox. Carson McCuller's classic about a young girl (Julie Harris, BSActress) who confides in her family maid (Ethel Waters, BSActress) that she fantasizes about running off with her brother and his fiance once they're married, but she'll soon come face to face with reality. w. Edna and Edward Anhalt, N & P-adap. Carson McCullers, d. Fred Zinneman. Oscars: 2-0.
DRAMA: MELODRAMA: Friendships-Interracial; Women and Girls; Coming of Age; Life Transitions; Weddings; Girlhood; Dreams; Illusions Destroyed; Southerns; Novel and Play; Adaptations; Pulitzer Prize Adaptations
(The Heart is a Lonely Hunter; Desert Bloom; Pinky; The Chalk Garden)
Memoirs of a Survivor, 1981, 115m, ★★1/2/$, Ind/NA. In a dreary future world, a woman finds solace in an Old Victorian house, returning to the past in her mind. Julie Christie, Christopher Guard, Debbie Hutchings. w. Kerry Cracce, David Gladwell, N-adap. Doris Lessing, d. David Gladwell.
DRAMA: Futuristic Films; Surrealism; Fantasies; Apocalyptic Stories; Curiosities; Female Protagonists
Memoirs of an Invisible Man, 1992, 99m, ★★1/2/$$, WB/WB, PG-13/S-P. An executive (Chevy Chase) stumbles across an invisibility formula and has to go on the lam from corporate and CIA thugs led by a villain (Sam Neill), running into the arms of a much younger love interest (Daryl Hannah). w. Robert Collector, Dana Olsen, William Goldman, N-adap. H.F. Saint, d. John Carpenter.
SUSPENSE: COMEDY DRAMA: SCI-FI: Chase Movies; Fugitives from the Law; Experiments; Invisibility; Corporation as Enemy; Romance-Older Men/Younger Women; CIA; Special Effects; Narrated Films; Revisionist Films
(The Invisible Man SERIES)
(Ed: This updating of the tale is okay, but not especially exciting)
The Memphis Belle, 1990, 106m, ★★★/$$, WB/WB, PG. Military pilots prepare for their big mission in a bomber

flying over Germany during World War II. Matthew Modine, Eric Stoltz, Tate Donovan, Billy Zane, Sean Astin, D. B. Sweeney, Harry Connick, Jr., Courtney Gains. w. Monte Merrick, d. Michael Caton-Jones.

DRAMA: MELODRAMA: War Stories; Pilots-Military; Young Men; Ensemble Films; Ensembles-Male; Old-Fashioned Recent Films
(The Big Red One; The Enola Gay)
(Ed: The fact that it stars virtually every young up-and-coming actor in Hollywood doesn't make it any more entertaining)

Men, 1985, 99m, ★★★/$$, Ind/New Yorker. A husband finds out his wife is cheating, meets her lover and influences him, becoming good friends, much to her chagrin. Heiner Lauterbach. w. d. Doris Dorrie.

COMEDY: SATIRE: Romance-Triangles; Cheated Upon Meet; Battle of the Sexes; Friendships-Male; Cheating Women; Turning the Tables; Female Directors; Female Screenwriters; Writer-Directors; Independent Films
(Me and Him; Heartbreakers)

The Men, 1950, 85m, ★★★1/2/$$, Republic/Republic. Disabled veterans from World War II try to cope with life, helped more by their women than the VA. Marlon Brando, Teresa Wright, Everett Sloane, Jack Webb. w. Carl Foreman (BOScr), d. Fred Zinneman. Oscars: 1-0.

DRAMA: ROMANCE: Marriage Drama; Disabled People; Veterans; World War II-Post Era; Medical Recovery; Woman Behind the Man; Ahead of Its Time; Forgotten Films; Hidden Gems
(The Best Years of Our Lives)

Men Are Not Gods, 1936, 92m, ★★1/2/$, UA-London/Sultan. A man playing Othello in a production gets carried away and almost repeats the plot in real life. Miriam Hopkins, Sebastian Shaw, Rex Harrison, Gertrude Lawrence, Val Gielgud. w. G. B. Stern, Iris Wright, d. Walter Reisch.

DRAMA: MELODRAMA: TRAGEDY: MURDER: Murder of Spouse; Murder-Attempted; Mental Illness; Illusions/Hallucinations; Actors
(Othello; A Double Life)

Me, Natalie, 1969, 111m, ★★★/$$, Cinema Center/NA, PG. A wallflower with unattractive facial features moves into Greenwich Village and falls for a

sexy painter, but reality hits her in the face. Patty Duke, James Farentino, Martin Balsam, Elsa Lanchester, Nancy Marchand, Al Pacino (bit part). w. A. Martin Zweiback, d. Fred Coe.

COMEDY: COMEDY DRAMA: Coming of Age; Young Women; Greenwich Village; Mod Era; 1960s; Time Capsules; Artists; Wallflowers; Looksism; Wallflowers & Hunks; Virgins; Female Protagonists
(Billie; The Sterile Cuckoo)
(Ed: Duke's performance carries it)

Men at Work, 1990, 98m, ★★/$, Col/Col, PG. Two hip garbage men find a corpse, then set out to find who dumped it there. Charlie Sheen, Emilio Estevez, Leslie Hope, Keith David, John Getz. w. d. Emilio Estevez.

COMEDY: MURDER: MYSTERY: MURDER MYSTERY: Detective Stories; Detectives-Amateur; Murder-Discovering; Working Class

Men Don't Leave, 1990, 115m, ★★★1/2/$$, WB/WB, PG/S. A widow and her two sons move from the suburbs into Baltimore and she begins a new life, working and learning to love again while the kids adjust and learn about loyalty and sex. Jessica Lange, Chris O'Donnell, Charlie Korsmo, Joan Cusack, Arliss Howards, Tom Mason, Kathy Bates. w. Barbara Benedek, Paul Brickman, S-adap. La Vie Continue, d. Brickman.

DRAMA: COMEDY DRAMA: ROMANCE: Family Drama; Character Studies; Widows; Mothers-Struggling; Mothers Alone; Mothers & Sons; Brothers; Coming of Age; Romance Older Women/Younger Men; Love-First; Ethics; Lotteries; Depression; Starting Over; Baltimore; Foreign Film Remakes
REMAKE OF: La Vie Continue.
(Alice Doesn't Live Here Anymore; Blue Sky)

The Men in Her Life, 1941, 90m, ★★/$, Col/NA. A circus star makes her debut in love and into the ballet. Loretta Young, Conrad Veidt, Dean Jagger, Otto Kruger. w. Frederick Kohner, Michael Wilson, Paul Trivers, N-adap. Lady Eleanor Smith, Ballerina, d. Gregory Ratoff.

MELODRAMA: ROMANCE: Tearjerkers; Fame-Rise to; Rags to Riches; Dancers; Ballet; Circus Life; Women's Films

Men in White, 1934, 80m, ★★1/2/$$$, MGM/NA. A rich woman falls for a doc-

tor but can't deal with his schedule. Clark Gable, Myrna Loy, Jean Hersholt, Elizabeth Allan, Wallace Ford. w. Waldemar Young, P-adap. Sidney Kingsley, d. Richard Boleslawki.

DRAMA: ROMANCE: Romantic Drama; **MELODRAMA:** Marriage Drama; Doctors; Rich People

Men of Boys' Town, 1941, 106m, ★★★/$$$, MGM/MGM-UA. Father Flanagan helps out another batch of juvenile delinquents. Spencer Tracy, Mickey Rooney, Bobs Watson, Lee J. Cobb, Anne Revere. w. James McGuinness, d. Norman Taurog.

DRAMA: MELODRAMA: COMEDY DRAMA: Orphans; Fathers-Surrogate; Fathers & Sons; Men and Boys; Priests; Reformers; Boyhood; Juvenile Delinquents; Rebels
SEQUEL TO: Boys' Town.
(Going My Way; The Bells of St. Mary's)

Men of Respect, 1990, 113m, ★★/$, Col/Col, R/V. A young mobster receives a prediction he'll become mafia don soon and his wife wants him to see to it that the competition gets eliminated. John Turturro, Katherine Borowitz, Dennis Farina, Peter Boyle, Rod Steiger. w. d. William Reilly.

DRAMA: Crime Drama; **SUSPENSE:** Black Comedy; Mob Stories; Fortunetellers; Woman Behind the Man; Writer-Directors
(Macbeth; Joe Macbeth; Julius Caesar)

Men of the Fighting Lady, 1954, 80m, ★★★/$, MGM/MGM-UA. An aircraft carrier and its crew during the Korean War with actual battle footage. Van Johnson, Walter Pidgeon, Louis Calhern, Keenan Wynn, w. Art Cohn, d. Andrew Marton.

DRAMA: ACTION: Action Drama; War Stories; Korean War; Ensembles-Male; Documentary Style

Men with Wings, 1938, 106m, ★★/$, Par/NA. Early airline pilots fight over the love of a woman. Fred MacMurray, Ray Milland, Louise Campbell, Donald O'Connor. w. Robert Carson, d. William Wellman.

DRAMA: MELODRAMA ROMANCE: ACTION: Action Drama; Airplanes; Pilots-Airplane; Romance-Triangles; Men Fighting Over Women
SEQUEL/CONTINUATION TO: Wings.

The Menace, 1932, 64m, ★★1/2/$$, Col/NA. A criminal escapes prison, gets cosmetic surgery, then goes for revenge. Walter Byron, H.B. Warner, Bette Davis, Natalie Moorhead. w. Dorothy Howell, Charles Logue, Roy Chanslor, d. Roy William Neill.

ACTION: Crime Drama; Prison Escapes; Disguises; Revenge; Convict's Revenge; Female Writers
(Dark Passage; Johnny Handsome)
(Ed: Notable for early Bette Davis)

Menace II Society, 1993, 104m, ★★★1/2/$$, New Line/New Line, R/EV-EP-S. Black teens lost in an inner city, slice of life nightmare. Tyrin Turner, Larenz Tate, Samuel L. Jackson, Bill Duke. w. Tyrin Turner, d. Albert Hughes, Allen Hughes (twin brothers).

DRAMA: Crime Drama; Black Casts; Teenagers; Inner City Life; Gangs-Black; Black Men; Black Women; Black Screenwriters; Black Directors; Cult Films; Hidden Gems; Directed by Brothers; Independent Films
(Boyz N the Hood; Juice; Don't Be a Menace . . .)

Menage, 1986, 84m, ★★★1/2/$, Triumph/Col-Tri, R/S-P. A burglar breaks into the wrong home-or the right home, when the couple who lives there follow him around learning his tricks and having sexual and burglary adventures. Gerard Depardieu, Michel Blanc, Miou-Miou. w. d. Bertrand Blier.

COMEDY: Black Comedy; **ADVENTURE:** Thieves; Sexual Kinkiness; Alternative Lifestyles; Gay Men; Married Couples; Menage à Trois; French Films; Art Films; Hidden Gems; Overlooked at Release; Cult Films; Writer-Directors
(Going Places; Maitresse; The Ref)

The Men's Club, 1986, 100m, ★★1/2/$, Atlantic/Atlantic, R/P-S. Several male friends approaching mid-life rehash the past and try to figure out what's wrong with their lives. Roy Scheider, Frank Langella, Harvey Keitel, Treat Williams, Richard Jordan, David Dukes, Craig Wasson, Stockard Channing, Jennifer Jason Leigh. w. N-adap. Leonard Michaels, d. Peter Medak.

DRAMA: Ensemble Films; Ensembles-Male; Character Studies; Midlife Crisis; Female Among Males; Coulda Been Great; Overlooked at Release
(That Championship Season; Bachelor Party)

Mephisto, 1981, 144m, ★★★/$$, UAC/Republic, R/S. An actor and his

theater in pre-World War II Berlin are used by the Nazis, despite his liberal idealism. Klaus Maria Brandauer, Krystyna Janda. w. Peter Dobai, Istvan Szabo, N-adap. Klaus Mann, d. Szabo.

BFLFilm. Oscars: 1-1.

DRAMA: Social Drama; Nazi Stories; Actors; Theater Life; Berlin; Pianists; German Films; World War II Era; 1930s; Time Capsules
(The Last Metro; Colonel Redl)

The Mephisto Waltz, 1971, 109m, ★★1/2/$, 20th/Fox, R. A concert pianist sells his soul and is transported into a writer's body, leading to treachery. Alan Alda, Jacqueline Bisset, Curt Jurgens, Barbara Parkins. w. Ben Maddow, N-adap. Fred Mustard Stewart, d. Paul Wendkos.

HORROR: SUSPENSE: SCI-FI: Satanism; Selling One's Soul; Dead-Back from the; Reincarnation; Musicians; Writers

Mermaids, 1990, 110m, ★★★/$$, Orion/Orion, PG-13/P-S. A young woman with a free spirited mother can't decide whether to join the convent or lose her virginity, for fear of becoming like mom. Cher, Winona Ryder, Bob Hoskins, Michael Schoeffling, Christina Ricci, Caroline McWilliams. w. June Roberts, N-adap. Patty Dann, d. Richard Benjamin (Frank Oz, also).

COMEDY DRAMA: ROMANCE: Mothers & Daughters; Young Women; Teenagers; Coming of Age; Love-First; Free Spirits; Eccentric People; Small-town Life; Female Protagonists; Female Screenwriters
(Mask; How to Make an American Quilt)

Merrily We Live, 1938, 90m, ★★★/$$$, Roach-UA/NA. An eccentric family needs a chauffeur and unwittingly finds a writer who's posing as a bum who they think they're giving a break. Constance Bennett, Brian Aherne, Billie Burke, Alan Mowbray, Patsy Kelly, Bonita Granville, Marjorie Rambeau. w. Eddie Moran, Jack Jevne, d. Norman Z. McLeod.

COMEDY: Family Comedy; Eccentric People; Homeless People; Servants; Hidden Gems; Forgotten Films
(My Man Godfrey; Lady for a Day; Pocketful of Miracles; You Can't Take it With You)

Merry Andrew, 1958, 103m, ★★/$$, MGM/NA. A bookish history teacher joins a circus to get hold of a statue they have. Danny Kaye, Pier Angeli, Baccaloni, Noel Purcell. w. Isobel

Lennart, I.A.L. Diamond, SS-adap. Paul Gallico, d. Michael Kidd.

COMEDY: Circus Life; Treasure Hunts; Art Thieves; Nerds
(A Song Is Born)

Merry Christmas, Mr. Lawrence, 1983, 124m, ★★1/2/$, U/MCA-U, R. A British P.O.W. in a Japanese camp during World War II becomes the homoerotic mascot of the camp and the special favorite of the commanding officer. David Bowie, Tom Conti, Ryuichi Sakamoto, Takeshi, Jack Thompson. w. Nagisa Oshima with Paul Mayersberg, N-adap. Laurens van der Post, d. Nagisa Oshima.

DRAMA: Art Films; Avant-Garde Films; World War II Stories; Homoeroticism; Men in Conflict; Allegorical Stories; Japanese as Enemy; POWs; Prison Drama; Japanese Films

The Merry Widow, 1925, 111m, ★★★/$$$, MGM/NA. A king with sagging fortunes gets a member of his court to pursue a wealthy widow. Mae Murray, John Gilbert, Roy D'Arcy, Tully Marshall. w. Erich Von Stroheim, Benjamin Glazer, (Operetta)-adap. Victor Leon, Leo Stein, d. Erich Von Stroheim.

MELODRAMA ROMANCE: Marrying Up; Royalty; Kings; Widows; Love-Questionable; Silent Films

The Merry Widow, 1934, 99m, ★★★/$$$, MGM/MGM-UA. Remake of above with music. Maurice Chevalier, Jeanette MacDonald, Edward Everett Horton, Una Merkel. w. Samson Raphaelson, Ernest Vajda, (Operetta)-adap. Victor Leon, Leo Stein, d. Ernst Lubitsch.

The Merry Widow, 1952, 105m, ★★/$$, MGM/MGM-UA. Another remake. Fernando Lamas, Lana Turner, Richard Haydn, Una Merkel, Thomas Gomez. w. Sonya Levien, William Ludwig, d. Curtis Bernhardt.

MUSICALS: ROMANCE: Musical Romance; **MELODRAMA:** Marrying Up; Royalty; Kings; Widows; Love-Questionable

The Merry Wives of Reno, 1934, 61m, ★★★/$$, WB/NA. Three women drag their husbands to Nevada for cheap easy divorces. Margaret Lindsay, Donald Woods, Guy Kibbee. w. Robert Lord, d. H. Bruce Humberstone.

COMEDY: Screwball Comedy; Divorce; Marriage Comedy; Marriage on the Rocks; Romance-Reunited; Forgotten Films

Merton of the Movies, 1947, 82m, ★★1/2/$$, MGM/MGM-UA. A young hick goes to Hollywood and innocently stumbles into stardom. Red Skelton, Virginia O'Brien, Alan Mowbray, Gloria Grahame. w. George Wells, Alan Mowbray. w. George Wells, Lou Breslow, N-adap. Harry Leon Wilson, d. Robert Alton.
COMEDY: Fish out of Water Stories; Fame-Rise to; Comedians; Fools-Bumbling; Hollywood Life

A Message to Garcia, 1936, 86m, ★★1/2/$, 20th/NA. An American agent in Cuba during the Spanish-American war gets a message to the leader of the Revolution through a local girl. Wallace Beery, Barbara Stanwyck, John Boles, Alan Hale. w. W. P. Lipscomb, Gene Fowler, NF-adap. Andrew S. Rohan, d. George Marshall.
DRAMA: ROMANCE: Historical Drama; Political Unrest; Spies; War Stories; Cuba; 1890s

Meteor, 1979, 107m, ★★1/2/$$, AIP/WB, PG. Large fragments of an even larger meteor strike the Earth, portending the eventual collision with the big one-and earthquakes, tidal waves, fires, etc. Sean Connery, Natalie Wood, Karl Malden, Brian Keith, Martin Landau, Trevor Howard, Henry Fonda. w. Stanley Mann, Edmund H. North, d. Ronald Neame.
SCI-FI: Apocalyptic Stories; Disaster Movies; Meteors; Race Against Time; Scientists; Tidal Waves
(Fire in the Sky [1978]; The Day the Earth Caught Fire)

The Meteor Man, 1993, 100m, ★★/$, MGM/MGM-UA, PG. A black school teacher is hit by a meteor and gets special powers leading him to fly like superman, except that he's afraid of heights, etc. Robert Townsend, Robert Gillaume, Marla Gibbs, James Earl Jones, Frank Gorshin. w. d. Robert Townsend.
COMEDY: Spoofs; **ACTION:** Action Comedy; Teachers; Heroes-Unlikely; Comic Heroes; Nerds; Black Men; Black Casts; Black Screenwriters; Black Directors; Good Premise Unfulfilled; Writer-Directors
(Hero at Large; The Hollywood Shuffle)

Metropolis, 1926, 120m, ★★★★/$$$, UFA/Sinister, Nos. An allegorical tale in which a city's tyrannical ruling class lives in luxury while the workers that keep it running toil underground until the son of the city father teams up with an angelic woman to lead the workers in revolt. Briggitte Helm, Alfred Abel, Gustav Frohlich, Rudolf Klein-Rogge. w. Thea Von Harbou, d. Fritz Lang.
DRAMA: Art Films; Avant-Garde Films; Futuristic Films; Oppression; Androids; Floods; Workers vs. Boss; Rich vs. Poor; Political Unrest; Communists; Film History
(Things to Come; Modern Times)

Metropolitan, 1935, 79m, ★★1/2/$, 20th/NA. A backstage drama of the Metropolitan Opera in New York in which the star diva leaves in a huff to form her own company. Lawrence Tibbett, Alice Brady, Virginia Bruce, Cesar Romero. w. Bess Meredyth, George Marion Jr., d. Richard Boleslawski.
MELODRAMA: MUSICALS: Music Movies; Opera Singers; Feuds; Theater Life

Metropolitan, 1990, 98m, ★★★1/2/$$, AP-Goldwyn/Goldwyn, PG/S. A reserved middle class young man attends debutante functions with a group of people even though he's somewhat opposed to them and doesn't fit in. w. d. Whit Stillman (BOScr). Oscars: 1-0.
SATIRE: COMEDY: COMEDY DRAMA: Comedy of Manners; Romantic Comedy; Romance-Girl Wants Boy; Ensemble Films; Coming of Age; Young People; Love-Unrequited; Snobs; Rich People; New York Life; Shy People; Rich vs. Poor; Class Conflicts; Social Climbing; Intellectuals; Nerds; Wallflowers; Nerds & Wallflowers; Sleeper Hits; New England; Writer-Directors; Independent Films
(Barcelona; Hannah and Her Sisters)

Mexican Hayride, 1948, 77m, ★★/$$, U/MCA-U. At a bullfight in Mexico, two bumbling idiots get conned by shady types. Bud Abbott, Lou Costello, Virginia Grey, John Hubbard. w. Oscar Brodney, John Grant, P-adap. Herbert and Dorothy Fields, d. Charles Barton.
COMEDY: Fools-Bumbling; Con Artists; Bullfighting; Mexico; Abbott & Costello
(Abbott & Costello SERIES)

Miami Blues, 1990, 97m, ★★★/$, Orion/Orion, R/EP-EV-S. A criminal named Junior posing as a cop takes a hooker to the suburbs to live the normal life but just can't give up his ways. A real cop from his past is on his tail-if he can survive long enough himself. Alec Baldwin, Jennifer Jason Leigh, Fred Ward. w. d. George Armitage, N-adap. Charles Willeford.
DRAMA: Crime Drama; **SATIRE:** Detective Stories; Detectives-Police; Black Comedy; Comedy-Morbid; Chase Movies; Trail of a Killer; Newlyweds; Prostitutes-Low Class; Prostitutes with Heart of Gold; Romance with Prostitutes; Starting Over; Double Lives; Impostors; Miami

Mickey One, 1965, 93m, ★★★1/2/$, Col/NA. A struggling comedian on the seedy lounge circuit in the 60s faces reality while on the verge of losing it. Warren Beatty, Hurd Hatfield, Franchot Tone, Jeff Corey. w. Alan Surgal, d. Arthur Penn.
DRAMA: Character Studies; Young Men; Comedians; Nightclubs; Mod Era; Orgies; Pre-life Crisis; 1960s Underrated; Hidden Gems; Forgotten Films
(Lenny; Lilith)

Micki + Maude, 1984, 118m, ★★★/$$$, Col/RCA-Col, PG-13/S-MRN. A man gets his wife and mistress pregnant simultaneously and they're due at the same hospital at the same time and he's never told either one about the other. Dudley Moore, Amy Irving, Anne Reinking, Richard Mulligan, Wallace Shawn, John Pleshette. w. Johnathan Reynolds, d. Blake Edwards.
COMEDY: FARCE: Bigamy; Babies-Having; Cheating Men; Mistresses; TV Life; Secrets-Keeping
(Ten; The Man Who Loved Women)
(Ed: Amazing stretch for such a simple premise, though perhaps not amazing enough)

Middle Age Crazy, 1980, 91m, ★★1/2/$$, 20th/Fox, R/S-P. A 40-year old man's mid-life crisis finds unusual outlets. Bruce Dern, Ann-Margaret, Graham Jarvis. w. Carl Kleinschmitt, d. John Trent.
COMEDY: DRAMA: SATIRE: Midlife Crisis; Marriage on the Rocks; Cheating Men; Rejuvenation; Texas; Ordinary People Stories
(A New Life; Twice in a Lifetime)

Middle of the Night, 1959, 118m, ★★★1/2/$$, Col/RCA-Col. An older man in the fashion business meets a young woman who rekindles his spirit, but it may not be forever. Frederic March, Kim Novak, Lee Grant, Jan Norris. w. TV-adap. Paddy Chayefsky, d. Delbert Mann.
DRAMA: ROMANCE: Romantic Drama; Character Studies; Romance-Older Men/Younger Women; Fashion World;

Romance-Middle-Aged; Elderly Men; Redemption; Starting Over; Rejuvenation; Forgotten Films; Hidden Gems
(Marty; Breezy; Petulia)
(Ed: Reteaming of *Marty* writer and director)

Midnight, 1939, 95m, ★★★½/$$$, Par/NA, AMC. A rich man in Paris finds a young American woman who's stranded there and puts her up to seducing the gigolo his wife is seeing. Claudette Colbert, Don Ameche, John Barrymore, Francis Lederer, Mary Astor, Hedda Hopper. w. Billy Wilder, Charles Brackett, Edwin Mayer, Frank Schultz, d. Mitchell Liesen.
COMEDY: FARCE: Comedy of Manners; **ROMANCE:** Romantic Comedy; Screwball Comedy; Romance-Triangles; Mindgames; Cheating Women; Prostitutes-Male; Jealousy; Stranded; Female Protagonists; Paris
(The Palm Beach Story; Three of Hearts)

Midnight, 1989, 86m, ★★/$, Vidmark/Vidmark, R/S-P. A TV horror movie show hostess (Lynn Redgrave) is stalked, much like in the movies she shows. Tony Curtis, Steve Parrish, Rita Gam, Frank Gorshin. w. d. Norman Thaddeus.
COMEDY: HORROR: Horror Comedy; Spoofs-Horror; **MURDER:** Stalkers; Murder-Attempted; TV Life; Women in Jeopardy
(Fright Night; Elvira, Mistress of the Dark)

Midnight Cowboy, 1969, 113m, ★★★★/$$$, UA/MGM-UA, X & R/P-S-FN-MN. A drifter/male prostitute from Texas (Jon Voight, BActor) comes to New York to live on the seamy and wild side. He meets a friend in a mangy street character (Dustin Hoffman, BActor) and they dream of moving to Florida together. Brenda Vaccaro, Sylvia Miles (BSActress). w. Waldo Salt (**BAScr**), adap. John O'Herlihy, d. John Schlesinger (**BDirector**). **BPicture,** BOSong. Oscars: 7-3.
DRAMA: MELODRAMA: Friendships-Male; Buddy Films; Tearjerkers; Streetlife; Homeless People; New York Life; Underworld; Prostitutes-Male; Dreams; Simple Minds; Psychedelic Era; 1960s
(Rain Man; Scarecrow)

A Midnight Clear, 1992, 107m, ★★★/$, Col/Col, PG/V. At Christmastime in the last year of World War II, a dozen young soldiers are sent on a dangerous mission which may be their last. Peter Berg, Kevin Dillon, Arye Gross, Ethan Hawke, Gary Sinise, John C. McGinley, Frank Whaley. w. d. Keith Gordon, N-adap. William Wharton.
DRAMA: Fantasy; Surrealism; Soldiers; Young Men; Christmas; Snow Settings; Actor Directors; Ensembles-Male (Gallipoli; Platoon; The Naked and the Dead; Birdy)

Midnight Crossing, 1987, 104m, ★★/$, Vestron/Vestron, PG/V. Several people wind up at each other's throats on a trip to a Caribbean island, but really are out to get a supposed treasure. Faye Dunaway, Daniel J. Travanti, Kim Cattrall, Ned Beatty, John Laughlin. w. Roger Holzberg, Doug Weiser, d. Holzberg.
SUSPENSE: Women in Jeopardy; Treasure Hunts; Strandeds; Ships; Nightmares; Double Crossings; Blind People; Unintentionally Funny
(Dead Calm; Night Moves)
(Ed: Tagline-"Double Crossing, Triple Crossing-Midnight Crossing")

Midnight Express, 1978, ★★★½/$$$$, Columbia/RCA-Col, R/P-S-V-MRN. An American (Brad Davis) smuggling drugs out of Turkey is mistaken for a terrorist when caught, but the penalty for drugs is just as bad, as he spends the next several years in a hellacious prison. John Hurt (BSActor), Bo Hopkins, Randy Quaid. w. Oliver Stone (**BAScr**), d. Alan Parker (BDirector). BPicture, BSound, BEdit, **BOScore.** Oscars: 8-2.
DRAMA: Prison Drama; Accused Unjustly; Drugs-Dealing; Americans Abroad; Foreign Nightmares; Nightmares; Homo-eroticism; Middle East
(Brubaker; The Killing Fields; Fortune and Men's Eyes)

Midnight Lace, 1960, 108, ★★★/$$$, U/MCA-U. An American woman married to a wealthy Brit in London is stalked in the fog, at the train tracks, and on the phone, driving her to incessant crying and paranoia. Doris Day, Rex Harrison, Myrna Loy, John Gavin, Roddy McDowell, Herbert Marshall, Hermione Baddely. w. Ivan Goff, Ben Roberts, P-adap. Janet Green, *Matilda Shouted Fire*, d. David Miller.
SUSPENSE: MELODRAMA: Women in Jeopardy; Stalkers; Unbelieved; Enemy-Sleeping with the; Mindgames; Telephone Terror; Americans Abroad; London
TV REMAKE: 1984.
(Gaslight)

(Ed: Though the plot is a bit easy, and Doris is just a bit overwrought, it still works)

The Midnight Man, 1974, 117m, ★★/$, U/MCA-U. An ex-cop finally out of prison for killing his wife's lover becomes a security guard, but murder soon follows him again. Burt Lancaster, Susan Clark, Cameron Mitchell, Morgan Woodward. w. d. Roland Kibbee, Burt Lancaster, N-adap. David Anthony, *The Midnight & The Morning Man.*
SUSPENSE: Crime Drama; **MURDER: MYSTERY: MURDER MYSTERY:** Security Guards; Police-Former; Murder-Discovering; Ex-Cons; Starting Over; Actor Directors
(Scorpio; The Friends of Eddie Coyle)

Midnight Run, 1988, 125m, ★★★½/$$$, Universal/MCA-U, R/EP-V. A bounty hunter (Robert De Niro) is after a mob accountant (Charles Grodin), but when he finds him and his mouth, he may wish he hadn't. Dennis Farina, Joe Pantoliano, Karen Austin, Yaphet Kotto. w. Guy Gallo, d. Martin Brest.
COMEDY: ACTION: Action Comedy; Chase Movie; Mob Stories; Mob Comedy; Road Movie; Fugitives; Fugitives from the Mob; Fugitives from the Law; Partners-Unlikely; Partners-Antagonistic; Bounty Hunters; Clever Plots & Endings; Enemy-Sympathizing with; Traitors
(Pink Cadillac; Buck and the Preacher; Taking Care of Business)

A Midsummer Night's Dream, 1935, 133m, ★★★/$$, WB/MGM-UA. In a magical woods, two lovers are helped by a cupid in the Shakespeare classic. James Cagney, Dick Powell, Jean Muir, Olivia deHavilland, Arthur Treacher, Mickey Rooney, Anita Louise. w. Charles Kenyon, Mary McCall, P-adap. Shakespeare, d. Max Reinhardt.
COMEDY: ROMANCE: Romantic Comedy; Fantasy; Fairy Tales; Mythology; Classic Literary Adaptations; Female Screenwriters
(As You Like It; Much Ado About Nothing)

A Midsummer Night's Sex Comedy, 1982, 88m, ★★★/$, Orion-WB/WB, PG/S. An inventor invites several friends to a country retreat where they all begin to look at each other differently. Woody Allen, Mia Farrow, Mary Steenburgen, Tony Roberts, Jose Ferrer, Julie Hagerty. w. d. Allen.

**COMEDY: COMEDY DRAMA:
ROMANCE:** Romantic Comedy;
Romance-Reunited; Romance-
Unrequited; Marriage Comedy; Ensemble
Films; Vacations; Swapping Partners
(Wild Strawberries; Smiles of a Summer
Night; The Cherry Orchard)

Midway, 1976, 131m, ★★/$$$, U/MCA-
U, PG/V. The battle of guess what, told
from many different angles. Charlton
Heston, Henry Fonda, Robert Mitchum,
Glenn Ford, Edward Albert, James
Coburn, Robert Wagner, Hal Holbrook,
Roshiro Mifune, Robert Webber.
w. Donald Sanford, d. Jack Smight.
ACTION: War Stories; War at Sea; World
War II Stories; Multiple Stories;
Interwoven Stories; War Battles; Epics;
All-Star Casts
(Tora! Tora! Tora!; Gray Lady Down)
(Ed: Last of a breed)

Mighty Aphrodite, 1995, 94m,
★★★1/2/$$, Miramax/Miramax, R/P-S. A
man and his artsy wife adopt a baby boy
who grows to be an intelligent, interesting
kid. So Dad decides to find the birth
mother, but he doesn't bargain for hooker
and part-time porn actress. Woody Allen,
F. Murray Abraham, Mira Sorvino
(**BSActress**), Claire Bloom, Helena
Bonham Carter, Olympia Dukakis,
Michael Rapaport, David Ogden Stiers,
Jack Warden, Peter Weller. w. d. Allen,
BOScr. Oscars: 2-1.
COMEDY: COMEDY DRAMA: SATIRE:
Sexuality; Pornography; World;
Prostitutes; Children-Adopted; Romance
with Relative; Simple Minds; Nerds and
Bimbos; Bimbos; Sexy Women; Fathers &
Sons; Writer-Directors
(Play it Again, Sam; Broadway Danny
Rose; Radio Days)

The Mighty Ducks, 1992, 114m,
★★1/2/$$$$, Disney/Disney, PG/P. A
young coach leads a group of bratty pre-
teens to victory in the hockey rink.
Emilio Estevez, Joss Ackland, Lane
Smith. w. Steven Brill, Brian Hohlfiled,
d. Stephen Herek.
COMEDY: Sports Movies; Skating;
Underdogs Stories; Men and Boys;
Children-Brats; Boys; Hockey;
Ensembles-Male; Sleeper Hits
SEQUEL: D2, The Mighty Ducks 2.
(The Bad News Bears; The Big Green)

Mighty Joe Young, 1949, 94m,
★★1/2/$$$, RKO/Turner. A girl brings
back a pet gorilla from Africa which

grows up bigger than anyone ever
dreamed and begins stomping around and
on the town. Terry Moore, Ben Johnson,
Robert Armstrong. w. Ruth Rose, d.
Ernest Schoedsack. **BSFX.** Oscars: 1-1.
ACTION: SCI-FI: Monster Movies;
Animal Monsters; Pet Stories; Primates;
Africa; Female Screenwriters
(King Kong; Gorilla at Large)

**Mighty Morphin Power Rangers
Movie**, 1995, ★1/2/$$, 20th/Fox, PG/V.
The martial arts–obsessed teens do battle
with the weirdos from whatever space
they're from in this flop attempt to capi-
talize on the TV series. Jason David
Frank, Steve Cardenas, David Yost,
Johnny Yong Bosch, Amy Jo Johnson.
w. Arne Olsen, d. Bryan Spicer.
ACTION: CHILDREN'S: Martial Arts;
Young People; TV Series Movies

The Mighty Quinn, 1989, 98m,
★★1/2/$, MGM-UA/MGM-UA, R/S-P. A
Caribbean island's police chief investi-
gates a murder involving his kooky rasta-
farian friend, Maubee and a host of other
characters. Denzel Washington, Robert
Townsend, James Fox, Mimi Rogers, M.
Emmet Walsh, Sheryl Lee Ralph, Esther
Rolle. w. Hampton Fancher, N-adap.
A.H.Z. Carte (*Finding Maubee*), d. Carl
Shenkel.
**MYSTERY: MURDER: MURDER MYS-
TERY:** Detective Stories; Detectives-
Police; Caribbean; Islands Resorts; Black
Men; Ensemble Films; Eccentric People
(Devil in a Blue Dress)

Mignon Has Left, 1988, 90m, ★★★/$,
Ind/NA. When an Italian family has a
French cousin visit, it shakes things up
for the adolescent children facing sex and
adulthood. Stefania, Jean-Pierre Duriez,
Leonardo Ruta. w. Francesca Archibugi,
Gloria Malatesta, Claudia Sbargia,
d. Archibugi.
COMEDY DRAMA: Coming of Age;
Teenagers; **ROMANCE:** Love-First;
Character Studies; Italian Films; Rome;
Female Screenwriters; Female Directors
(Rambling Rose)

The Mikado, 1939, 91m, ★★★/$$,
GFD/NA. In the classic operetta, a shy
government official is made the royal exe-
cutioner and then discovers his first vic-
tim is the Emperor's son who's in
disguise. Martyn Green, John Barclay,
Sydney Granville. w. Geoffrey Toye, MP-
adap. Gilbert & Sullivan, d. Victor
Schertzinger.

MUSICALS: Operettas; Executioners;
Identities-Mistaken; Disguises; Ethics;
Japan; Japanese People

Mike's Murder, 1984, 109m, ★★★/$,
WB/WB, R/P-V. When her young free
spirited friend is killed in a drug deal, a
young woman becomes obsessed with how
he died-to the point that she may become
the next victim. Debra Winger, Darrell
Larson, Mark Keyloun, Paul Winfield. w.
d. James Bridges.
DRAMA: SUSPENSE: Psychological
Drama; **MURDER:** Obsessions; Death-
Dealing with; Drugs-Dealing; Friendships
Between Sexes; Ordinary People in
Extraordinary Situations; Young Women;
Women in Jeopardy; Writer-Directors;
Hidden Gems; Underrated; Female
Protagonists; Quiet Little Films
(Ed: Not a thriller, but an interesting take
on a personal to reaction to murder and
the consequences)

Mikey and Nicky, 1976, 118m,
★★1/2/$, Par-Castle Hill/Castle Hill,
R/V-P. Two old friends that are now mob-
ster-types have their problems, but are
they enough for one to kill the other on
assignment? Peter Falk, John Cassavetes,
Ned Beatty, Sandford Meisner, Joyce van
Patten, w. d. Elaine May.
COMEDY: Black Comedy; Mob Stories;
Mob Comedy; Hitmen; Friendships-Male;
Good Premise Unfulfilled; Coulda Been
Good; Female Screenwriters; Female
Directors; Writer-Directors
(Prizzi's Honor; The In-Laws; Wise Guys)
(Ed: Barely released in '76, then re-
released around 1984. A curiosity with
some good moments. The beginning of
May's decline after such great promise
with *A New Leaf* and *Heartbreak Kid*, cul-
minating in *Ishtar*.)

The Milagro Beanfield War, 1988,
118m, ★★★/$, U/MCA-U, PG-13/S-P.
Developers try to develop peasant farm-
ers' land in New Mexico, leading to a
revolt of sorts. Ruben Blades, Richard
Bradford, Melanie Griffith, Sonia Braga,
Julie Carmen, John Heard, M. Emmet
Walsh, Daniel Stern, Freddy Fender.
w. David Ward, John Nichols, N-adap.
Nichols, d. Robert Redford.
DRAMA: COMEDY DRAMA: Mortage
Drama; Save the Farm; Social Drama;
Latin People; Indians-American; New
Mexico; Southwestern Life; Corporation
as Enemy; Actor Directors
(The Field; Wild River)

Mildred Pierce, 1945, 109m, ★★★/ $$$$, WB/WB. A single mother (Joan Crawford, **BActress**) builds a chain of burger joints (Mildred's Fatburgers), also building a monster in the daughter (Anne Blythe, BSActress) for whom she wanted to provide better. The daughter's getting to be competition with the man in her life. Eve Arden (BSActress), Jack Carson, Zachary Scott, Bruce Bennett. w. Ranald McDougall, Catherine Turney (BAScr), N-adap. James M Cain, d. Michael Curtiz. BPicture, BB&WCin. Oscars: 6-1.
DRAMA: MURDER: MELODRAMA: TRAGEDY: Film Noir; Mothers Alone; Mothers-Struggling; Social Climbing; Rags to Riches; Power-Rise to; Mothers & Daughters; Love Questionable; Children-Brats; Incest; Accused Unjustly; Clever Plots & Endings (Stella Dallas; Min and Bill; Mannequin) (Ed: Still fun for everyone; catch the Carol Burnett spoof "Mildred Fierce" sometime)

Miles from Home, 1988, ★★1/2/$, Cinecom/Cinecom, PG/V-P. In destitution two brothers destroy their farm and then have to hit the road. Richard Gere, Kevin Anderson. w. Chris Gerolmo, d. Gary Sinise.
DRAMA: Save the Farm; Mortgage Dramas; Outlaw Road Movies; Fugitives; Fugitives from the Law; Fighting the System; Midwestern Life; Farm Life; Country People; Heroes-Unlikely; Actor Directors (Wisdom; Country; The Dion Brothers) (Ed: Richard Gere on the farm is a rather unlikely angle)

Milk Money, 1994, 105m, ★★1/2/$$, Par/Par, PG-13/S-P. A boy and his friends hire a hooker for lonely single dad and wind up with a big problem. Melanie Griffith, Michael Patrick Carter, Ed Harris, Malcolm McDowell. d. Richard Benjamin.
COMEDY: Fish out of Water Stories; Boys; Prostitutes-Low Class; Dating Scene; Hired Dates; Women and Boys; School Life; Good Premise Unfulfilled; Coulda Been Good (Sleepless in Seattle; Working Girl; Working Girls) (Ed: Really disgusting in reality, the only disease she has here is a case of the cutes)
The Milky Way, 1936, 88m, ★★★/$$, Par/Nos. A boxer who's a milkman by day

tangles with mobsters who want to do more than manipulate him. Harold Lloyd, Adolphe Menjou, Verree Teasdale, Lionel Stander. w. Grover Jones, Frank Butler, Richard Connell, P-adap. Lynn Root, d. Leo McCarey.
COMEDY: Comedy-Slapstick; Sports Movies; Mob Stories; Mob Comedy; Heroes-Ordinary; Underdog Stories
REMAKE: The Kid from Brooklyn.

The Milky Way, 1968, 102m, ★★★/$, Greenwich/Xenon, Connoisseur, Media. Two drifters take off on foot from France to a Spanish Catholic shrine, encountering many strange things along the way. w. Luis Bunuel, Jean-Claude Carriere, d. Louis Bunuel.
DRAMA: Art Films; Avant-Garde Films; Road Movies; Drifters; Homeless People; Surrealism; Jesus Christ (Tristana; Viridiana)

The Mill on the Floss, 1937, 94m, ★★★/$$, Ind/Nos. The mill owner, the land owner, and a romance equal a feud resulting in tragedy. Geraldine Fitzgerald, Frank Lawton, James Mason, Victoria Hopper. w. John Drinkwater, Garnett Weston, Austin Melford, Tim Whelan, N-adap. George Eliot, d. Tim Whelan.
DRAMA: MELODRAMA ROMANCE: TRAGEDY: Romantic Drama; Romance-Doomed; **MURDER:** Suicidal Tendencies; Lover Family Dislikes; Romance-Class Conflicts; Feuds; Wales; Classic Literary Adaptations (Romeo & Juliet; Wuthering Heights)

Millennium, 1989, 105m, ★★1/2/$, Gladden/Critic's Choice, PG-13/V-S-P. Planes keep crashing or disappearing and it turns out the stewardesses are really aliens setting up experiments and taking over bodies. Cheryl Ladd, Kris Kristofferson, Daniel J. Travanti, Robert Joy, Lloyd Bochner, Brent Carver. w. John Varley, N-adap. Varley, d. Michael Anderson.
ACTION: Fantasy; **SCI-FI: MYSTERY:** Outer Space Movies; Airplane Crashes; Aliens-Outer Space, Evil; Pilots-Airlines; Time Travel; Good Premise Unfulfilled; Coulda Been Good (Ed: Better than one would expect, although the worst of 50s cliches crop up)

Miller's Crossing, 1990, 115m, ★★1/2/$, 20th/CBS-Fox, R/EV-P-S. A man caught in between corrupt New Orleans politicians and the Irish mob finds himself with a great deal of power

and yet fighting for his own life when he lets a rat mobster go free instead of killing him. Gabriel Byrne, Albert Finney, Marcia Gay Harden, John Turturro, Jon Piloto. w. Joel Coen, Ethan Coen, d. Joel Coen.
DRAMA: Crime Drama; **MURDER: SUSPENSE:** Mob Stories; Mob Wars; Double Crossings; Double Lives; Political Corruption; Evil Men; Ethics; Coulda Been Great; Irish People; 1920s; Bootleggers; Prohibition Era (The Public Eye; The Untouchables) (Ed: Stylistically remarkable as usual for the Coens, but entertainment-wise, it's slow-going and Finney is under-used)

Million Dollar Baby, 1941, 100m, ★★1/2/$$, WB/NA. When a girl inherits a million bucks, everyone wants a piece of her. Priscilla Lane, Jeffrey Lynn, Ronald Reagan, May Robson, Lee Patrick. w. Richard MacCaulay, Jerry Wald, Casey Robinson, SS-adap. Leonard Spigelgass, *Miss Wheelwright Discovers America*, d. Curtis Bernhardt.
COMEDY: Inheritances at Stake; Heiresses; Young Women; Love-Questionable; Rags to Riches

Million Dollar Duck, 1971, 92m, ★★1/2/ $$, Disney/Disney, G. When a family's pet duck starts laying golden eggs, Disneyfied mobsters and Fort Knox Feds want to crack the case. Sandy Duncan, Dean Jones, Joe Flynn, Tony Roberts. w. Roswell Rogers, d. Vincent McEveety.
COMEDY: CHILDREN'S: FAMILY: Animals in Jeopardy; Pet Stories; Treasure Hunts; Gold Mines; Government as Enemy; Fugitives from the Mob
REMAKE/RETREAD: Mr. Drake's Duck (It Grows on Trees; Mr. Drake's Duck)

Million Dollar Legs, 1932, 64m, ★★★/ $$$, Par/NA. The horse racetrack is where Betty Grable, her famous legs, and her college pals are hanging out to see the legs of a particular horse. Betty Grable, John Hartley, Donald O'Connor, Buster Crabbe.
COMEDY: ROMANCE: Horse Racing; Sexy Women; Olympics; College Life

Million Dollar Mermaid, 1952, 115m, ★★1/2/$$$, MGM/MGM-UA. Story of famous swimmer Annette Kellerman, which gives Miss Williams a reason to be in the water, though perhaps not enough. Esther Williams, Victor Mature, Walter Pidgeon, David Brian. w. Everett Freeman, d. Mervyn leRoy.

MUSICALS: ROMANCE: Biographies; Swimming; Sports Movies; Australians; Female Protagonists
(The Duchess of Idaho; Dangerous When Wet)

The Millionaire, 1931, 80m, ★★★/$$, WB/NA. A rich man gets tired of the lush life and decides to be ordinary and work as a mechanic. George Arliss, Florence Arliss, Noah Beery, James Cagney.
w. Julien Josephson, Booth Tarkington, Earl Derr Briggers, d. John Adolfi.
COMEDY: COMEDY DRAMA: Riches to Rags; Ordinary People Stories; Rich vs. Poor; Depression Era
(For Richer, For Poorer; My Man Godfrey)

The Millionairess, 1960, 90m, ★★½/$$, 20th/NA. The richest woman in the world tires of her palace when a doctor from India comes into her life. Sophia Loren, Peter Sellers, Alastair Sims, Vittorio deSica. w. Wolf Mankowitz, P-adap. Bernard Shaw, d. Anthony Asquith.
COMEDY: COMEDY DRAMA: ROMANCE: Comedy of Manners; Rich People; Heiresses; Romance-Choosing the Right Person; Romance-Class Conflicts; Indian People; Female Protagonists; Flops-Major; Coulda Been Good
(Lady L.; What a Way to Go)
(Ed: Originally for Katharine Hepburn, Loren is miscast, though she and the sets look great. The irony is that because of her painting collection, Sophia is now reputed to be one of the wealthiest women in the world)

Millions Like Us, 1943, 103m, ★★★/$$$, GFD/NA. The saga of a British family enduring World War II and the surrounding death. Patricia Roc, Gordon Jackson, Moore Marriott. w. d. Frank Launder.
DRAMA: MELODRAMA: World War II Stories; War at Home; Family Drama; Death-Dealing with; Newlyweds; British Films; England; Writer-Directors

Min and Bill, 1931, 66m, ★★★★/$$$$, MGM/MGM-UA. With the help of Bill (Wallace Beery), a younger man working for her, the elderly Min (Marie Dressler, **BActress**) has kept a girl whose mother left her years ago. But when the girl's mother comes back out of the blue to embarrass the girl just as she's about to marry a rich man, Min may have to put a stop to it. Marjorie Rambeau, Dorothy Jordan, Donald Dillaway.

w. Frances Marion, Marion Jackson, P-adap. Lorna Moon, *Dark Star*, d. George Hill. Oscars: 1-1.
COMEDY DRAMA: MELODRAMA: Tearjerkers; **TRAGEDY:** Children-Adopted; Orphans; Mothers-Surrogate; Poor People; Social Climbing; Marriage-Impending; Mothers & Daughters; Mothers-Struggling; Crimes of Passion; Children-Saving; Children-Long Lost; Elderly Women; Underrated; Forgotten Films; Hidden Gems; Ahead of Its Time
(Stella Dallas; Stella; Mildred Pierce; Tugboat Annie)
(Ed: Dressler was ahead of her time and forgotten too soon after. Several excellent scenes and a tragic ending not soon forgotten)

Mina Tannenbaum, 1995, 128m, ★★½/$, New Yorker/New Yorker, NR. Two misfit Jewish girls grow up together, maintaining a lifetime friendship as times change and they with them. Romane Bohringer, Elsa Zylberstein, Florence Thomassin, Nils Tavernier, Stephane Slima, Chantal Krief, Jany Gastaldi, Dimitri Furdui. w. d. Martine Dugowson.
DRAMA: Friendships-Female; Coming of Age; Friendships-Lifetime; Jewish People; French Films; Narrated Films; Episodic Stories; Female Protagonists; Female Screenwriters; Female Directors
(One Sings, the Other Doesn't; Mirabelle and Rainette; Therese and Isabelle; Beaches)

The Mind Benders, 1963, 113m, ★★★/$, B-L/NA. A scientist undergoes sensory deprivation but when he turns evil, there maybe no stopping him. Dirk Bogarde, John Clements, Mary Ure. w. James Kenaway, d. Basil Dearden.
DRAMA: SCI-FI: HORROR: Scientists; Scientists-Mad; Experiments; Evil Men; British Films
(Altered States; Dr. Jekyll and Mr. Hyde)

The Mind of Mr. Soames, 1970, 98m, ★★½/$, Col/NA. A man wakes up from a coma after thirty years, but as a baby, starting over. Terence Stamp, Robert Vaughan, Nigel Davenport. w. John Hale, Edward Simpson, N-adap. Charles Maine, d. Alan Cooke.
SCI-FI: DRAMA: Avant-Garde Films; Reincarnation; Comas; Time Sleepers; Babies; Coulda Been Good
(Regarding Henry; Simon)

Mine Own Executioner, 1947, 108m, ★★★/$$, London/Nos. A mentally ill vet-

eran is under the care of a psychiatrist, but when he decides to kill his wife, can the doctor keep him from it? Burgess Meredith, Kieron Moore, Dulcie Gray. w. N-adap. Nigel Balchin, d. Anthony Kimmins.
DRAMA: Psychological Drama; **SUSPENSE: MURDER:** Murder of Spouse; Psychiatrists; Veterans; Mental Illness; World War II Era; British Films

Ministry of Fear, 1944, 85m, ★★★/$$, Par/NA. A mental patient in World War II England goes to a village where strange goings-on soon envelop him. Ray Milland, Marjorie Reynolds, Dan Duryea. w. Seton Miller, N-adap. Graham Greene, d. Fritz Lang.
SUSPENSE: MYSTERY: Conspiracy; Film Noir; World War II Era; Mental Illness; Veterans; England; Small-town Life; British Films; Coulda Been Great; Forgotten Films
(The Lost Weekend)

The Miniver Story, 1950, 104m, ★★½/$$$, MGM/MGM-UA. Mrs. Miniver of the award-winning same-titled film now valiantly carries on in England after the war, but only for so long, as disease fills the plot line out. Greer Garson, Walter Pidgeon, Cath O'Donnell, Leon Genn. w. Ronald Miller, George Froeschel, d. H.C. Potter.
MELODRAMA: Disease Stories; Tearjerkers; World War II-Post Era; Female Protagonists; England
SEQUEL TO: Mrs. Miniver.

Minnie & Moskowitz, 1971, 115m, ★★★/$, U/Touchstone, R/S. A romance develops between two eccentric, jaded people in L.A. Gena Rowlands, Seymour Cassel. w. d. John Cassevetes.
DRAMA: COMEDY DRAMA: ROMANCE: Eccentric People; Romance-Bickering; Character Studies; Friends as Lovers; Los Angeles; 1970s; Writer-Directors
(Faces; A Woman Under the Influence; Husbands; Love Streams; Images)

The Miracle, 1948, 40m, ★★★/$$, Tania/Nos. An Italian peasant is pursued and caught by the local shepherd, but she insists the child she has afterward is immaculate. Anna Magnani, Federico Fellini. w. Tullio Pinelli, Roberto Rossellini, Federico Fellini, d. Rossellini.
DRAMA: Fantasy; What If . . . Stories; Religion; Miracles; Nuns; Mothers-Unwed; Babies-Having; Who's the

Father?; Italian Films; Hidden Gems; Female Protagonists

(Agnes of God; Open City)

The Miracle, 1990, 97m, ★★1/2/$, Prestige-Miramax/Live, PG-13/S. A lustful teenager in Ireland is obsessed with an American actress in town who may be someone from his past. Beverly D'Angelo, Donald McCann, Nial Byrne. w. d. Neil Jordan.

COMEDY: COMEDY DRAMA: Romance; Romance-Boy Wants Girl; Romance-Older Women/Younger Men; Actresses; Americans Abroad; Mothers & Sons; Oedipal Stories; Love-First; Teenagers; Underrated; Quiet Little Films; Writer-Directors

(Spanking the Monkey; Angela; Murmur of the Heart; The Crying Game; Welcome Home; Roxy Carmichael)

(Ed: Starts off interestingly, then descends into melodrama and splinters apart)

Miracle in the Rain, 1954, 107m, ★★★/$$, WB/NA. A young woman falls in love with a soldier who is killed in the war. But they had a date for his return, and he does still keep it-only as a ghost. Jane Wyman, Van Johnson, Fred Clark, Eileen Heckart. w. Ben Hecht, d. Rudolph Mate.

ROMANCE: MELODRAMA: Tearjerkers; Fantasy; Ghosts; Romance-Doomed; Dead-Back from the; Romance-Reunited; Forgotten Films

(Ghost; The Ghost and Mrs. Muir)

Miracle Mile, 1989, 88m, ★★1/2/$, Hemdale/HBO, PG/V. As a nuclear attack is imminent, a young man spends his last moments running across a chaotic city. Anthony Edwards, Mare Winningham, John Agar, Kelly Minter, Denis Crosby. w. d. Steve deJarnatt.

DRAMA: SCI-FI: SUSPENSE: Race Against Time; Apocalyptic Stories; Bombs-Atomic; Disaster Movies; Death-Impending; Overlooked at Release; Writer-Directors

(The Day After; Testament)

Miracle of Morgan's Creek, 1944, 99m, ★★★★/$$$, Par/Par. A small-town girl (Betty Hutton) is pregnant, only she can't quite remember who the father might be. Eddie Bracken, William Demarest, Diana Lynn, Akim Tamiroff, Brian Donlevy. w. d. Preston Sturges.

COMEDY: SATIRE: Romantic Comedy; Race Against Time; Babies-Having;

Fathers-Troublesome; Who's the Father?; Small-town Scandals; Small-town Life; Misunderstandings; Amnesia; Young Women; Female Protagonists; Writer-Directors

(Agnes of God; Kiss and Tell; The Miracle)

The Miracle of the Bells, 1948, 120m, ★★1/2/$$, Republic/Republic. After a big movie star dies, a miracle reportedly takes place in a small town, but is it real or a hoax for publicity? Fred MacMurray, Alida Valli, Frank Sinatra, Lee J. Cobb. w. Ben Hecht, N-adap. Russell Janney, d. Irving Pichel.

COMEDY DRAMA: SATIRE: Miracles; Illusions; Small-town Life; Death-Dealing with; Actresses; Forgotten Films; Coulda Been Good

(9-30-55; Waiting for the Light)

The Miracle of the White Stallions, 1963, 118m, ★★1/2/$$, Disney/Disney, G. Prize horses are saved from the Nazis when they roll into Vienna. Robert Taylor, Lilli Palmer, Eddie Albert, Curt Jurgens. w. A. J. Carothers, d. Arthur Hiller.

FAMILY: CHILDREN'S: Animal Rights; Horses; Saving Someone; Nazi Stories; World War II Stories

Miracle on 34th Street, 1947, 94m, ★★★★/$$$$, 20th/CBS-Fox. A small girl (Natalie Wood) believes in Santa Claus and the man playing him at her mother's (Maureen O'Hara) department store might just be the real thing (Edmund Gwenn, BSActor). w. d. George Seaton (BScr), Valentine Davies (BOStory). BPicture. Oscars: 4-3.

REMAKE: 1974, TV Movie; 1994 version.

Miracle on 34th Street, 1994, 114m, ★★★/$, 20th/Fox, PG. The classic tale is retold, again, with the little girl who believed in Santa and may have actually found him at the local department store. Will her mommy fall for the lawyer prosecuting Santa for fraud? A 90s update with the focus more on the romance than the wonder of the child. Mara Wilson, Richard Attenborough, Elizabeth Perkins, Dylan McDermott, J. T. Walsh, James Remar, Robert Prosky, Jane Leeves, William Windom, Simon Jones. w. George Seaton, John Hughes, S-adap. George Seaton, Valentine Davies, d. Les Mayfield.

COMEDY DRAMA: Fantasy; CHILDREN'S: FAMILY: Dreams; Illusions;

What If . . . Stories; Christmas; Santa Claus; Department Stores

(Life Begins at 8:30)

The Miracle Woman, 1932, 90m, ★★★/$$, Col/NA. A woman preacher is also a con artist, or so it seems. An exaggeration of the Aimee Semple McPherson story. Barbara Stanwyck, Sam Hardy. w. Jo Swerling, P-adap. Robert Riskin, *Bless You, Sister*, d. Frank Capra.

SATIRE: COMEDY DRAMA: Preachers/Ministers; True or Not?; Biographies-Fictional; Con Artists; Female Criminals; Female Protagonists

(The Disappearance of Aimee)

The Miracle Worker, 1962, 106m, ★★★1/2/$$$, UA/CBS-Fox. The story of blind girl Helen Keller (Patty Duke, BSActress) and the teacher (Anne Bancroft, BActress) who taught her to write and read, focussing on the early years. w. P-adap. William Gibson (BAScr), d. Arthur Penn (BDirector). Oscars: 4-2.

DRAMA: MELODRAMA: Biographies; True Stories; Disease Stories; Underdog Stories; Blind People; Disabled People; Teachers; Teachers and Students; Friendships-Great; Girls; Female Protagonists

Miracles, 1985, 87m, ★★/$, Orion/Orion, PG. Bank robbers take the wrong people hostage and everyone winds up in Mexico and in a mess. Teri Garr, Tom Conti, Paul Rodriguez, Christopher Lloyd. w. d. Jim Kouf.

COMEDY: Action Comedy; Comedy of Errors; Bank Robberies; Kidnappings; Hostage Situations; Innocent Bystanders; Good Premise Unfulfilled; Coulda Been Good

Mirage, 1965, 109m, ★★★/$$, U/MCA-U, A&E. When a blackout happens in New York, a murder happens and a man loses his memory-or has he? Gregory Peck, Diane Baker, Walter Matthau, Jack Weston, George Kennedy, Kevin McCarthy. w. Peter Stone, N-adap. Walter Ericson, d. Edward Dmytryk.

SUSPENSE: MYSTERY: Fugitives; Conspiracy; Amnesia; Nightmares; Unbelieved; Blackouts; Clever Plots & Endings; Forgotten Films; Hidden Gems; Underrated

(Mr. Buddwing; North by Northwest)

Miranda, 1947, 80m, ★★★/$$, GFD/NA. A doctor goes fishing off the coast of England and catches a mermaid, then takes her to London in a wheelchair, pretending she's disabled to sneak her by. Glynis Johns, Griffith Jones, Margaret Rutherford, David Tomlinson. w. P-adap. Peter Blackmore, d. Ken Annakin.

COMEDY: COMEDY DRAMA: Fish Out of Water Stories; Mermaids; Good Premise Unfulfilled; Coulda Been Great; British Films; Forgotten Films; Hidden Gems

SEQUEL: Mad About Men.

(Splash!; Mad About Men)

The Mirror Crack'd, 1980, 105m, ★★★/$$, EMI-AFD/Republic, PG. When Hollywood descends upon an English village, a death occurs which turns out to be murder. Miss Marple is on the case, which involves a secret from long ago and an innocent bystander. Elizabeth Taylor, Angela Lansbury, Kim Novak, Rock Hudson, Geraldine Chaplin, Edward Fox, Tony Curtis, Marella Oppenheim. w. Johnathan Hales, Barry Sandler, N-adap. Agatha Christie, d. Guy Hamilton.

MYSTERY: MURDER: MURDER MYSTERY: Secrets-Keeping; Past-Haunted by the; Poisons; Feuds; Movie Making; Movies within Movies; Actresses; Actors; Hollywood Life; Elderly Women; Americans Abroad; England; All-Star Casts; Agatha Christie

(Evil Under the Sun; Death on the Nile)

(Ed: More comical than previous all-star Christie outings, but the mystery is still passable, though the suspense is lacking)

Mischief, 1985, 97m, ★★1/2/$, 20th/Fox, PG. A teenager in the 50s dreams of girls, cars, and getting out of town. Doug McKeon, Catherine Mary Stewart, Kelly Preston, Jamie Gertz, Terry O'Quinn. d. Mel Damski.

COMEDY: ROMANCE: Romantic Comedy; Romance-Boy Wants Girl; Love-First; Teenagers; Nostalgia; 1950s; Coming of Age; Forgotten Films

(The Return of Valentino; Heaven Help Us)

Misery, 1990, 107m, ★★★1/2/$$$$, CR-Columbia/RCA-Col, PG-13/V-P. A writer (James Caan) has a car wreck in a blizzard and is rescued by his most obsessed fan (Kathy Bates, **BActress**) who wants him to never leave. w. William Goldman, N-adap. Stephen King, d. Rob Reiner. Oscars: 1-1.

HORROR: SUSPENSE: DRAMA: Psychological Drama; Psychological Thriller; Romance-Unrequited; Hostage Situations; Fans-Crazed; Kidnappings; Mental Illness; Psycho-Killers;

Murderers-Female; Fatal Attractions; Writers; Snow Settings

(Dolores Claiborne; The Collector; The Beguiled; A Cold Day in the Park)

(Ed: The usual Reiner schmaltz is missing since it's not allowed by the story, but the tension is thick enough to cut)

The Misfits, 1961, 124m, ★★★/$$$, UA/CBS-Fox. Three eccentric cowboy-types rope wild horses in the desert, but when a neurotic sexpot comes their way, their small sense of existence is put to the test. Clark Gable, Marilyn Monroe, Montgomery Clift, Eli Wallach, Thelma Ritter, Estelle Winwood, Kevin McCarthy. w. Arthur Miller, d. John Huston.

DRAMA: MELODRAMA: Desert Settings; Bimbos; Character Studies; Horses; Art Films; Cult Films

(Ed: Most notable for Gable's death during filming, then soon after Clift and Monroe)

Mishima, 1985, 120m, ★★★/$, Zoetrope-WB/WB, R/S-V. The life celebrated Japanese writer Mishima and his tumultuous condition. Ken Ogata, Kanji Sawada. w. Paul Schrader, Leonard Schrader, d. Paul Schrader.

DRAMA: TRAGEDY: Biographies; Character Studies; Writers; Suicidal Tendencies; Japan; Writer-Directors

Miss Firecracker, 1989, 102m, ★★★1/2/$, Corsair/HBO, PG. A girl in Yazoo City (Holly Hunter) dreams of becoming Miss Firecracker like her visiting cousin (Mary Steenburgen), whose visiting brother (Tim Robbins) she's in love with, but who's also recently been released from an asylum w. P-adap. Beth Henley, d. Thomas Schlamme.

COMEDY: Black Comedy; Tragi-Comedy; Southerns; Underdog Stories; Beauty Pageants; Eccentric People; Life Transitions; Insanity-Questionable; Dreams; Small-town Life; Illusions Destroyed; Ostracism; Losing it All; Mean Women; Sisters; Infatuations; Cousins; Young Women; Quiet Little Films; Hidden Gems; Cult Films

(Crimes of the Heart; Wise Blood; True Stories)

Miss Grant Takes Richmond, 1949, 87m, ★★1/2/$$, Col/Col. A goofy young woman who's a terrible secretary turns out to be pretty good as an amateur, haphazard detective. Lucille Ball, William Holden, Janis Carter, James Gleason,

Gloria Henry. w. Nat Perrin, Devery Freeman, Frank Tashlin, d. Lloyd Bacon.

COMEDY: MYSTERY: Comic Mystery; Ordinary Person vs. Criminals; Detective Stories; Detectives-Amateur; Simple Minds; Secretaries; Innocent Bystanders; Thieves

(The Fuller Brush Girl)

Miss Robin Hood, 1952, 78m, ★★★/$, Ind/NA. An elderly British woman and some crooks protect other elderly people. Margaret Rutherford, Richard Hearne. w. Val Valentine, Patrick Campbell, Geoffrey Orme, d. John Guillermin.

COMEDY: MYSTERY: Comic Mystery; Ordinary Person vs. Criminals; Revisionist Films; Good Premise Unfulfilled; Robin Hood Stories

Miss Rose White, 1992, 95m, ★★★/$$$, CBS-Hallmark/Republic. A woman who has left her Polish-Jewish heritage behind with the war is visited by her sister who was thought to be dead but instead represents the past that haunts the remaining family members. Kyra Sedgwick, Amanda Plummer, Maximilian Schell, D.B. Sweeney, Maureen Stapleton. w. Anna Sandor, d. Joseph Sargent. Multiple Emmy winner.

DRAMA: Immigrants; Jewish People; Past-Haunted by the; Polish People; World War II-Post Era; TV Movies; Female Protagonists; Female Screenwriters

(Sophie's Choice; Max and Helen)

Miss Sadie Thompson, 1953, 91m, ★★★/$$, Col/Col. A prostitute on a South Seas island has an affair while singing in a saloon. Rita Hayworth, Jose Ferrer, Aldo Ray. w. Harry Kleiner, d. Curtis Bernardt. BOSong. Oscars: 1-0.

MELODRAMA: ROMANCE: Romantic Drama; **MUSICALS:** Music Movies; Sexy Women; Romance with Prostitute; Romance-Reluctant; South Pacific; Islands; 3-D Movies

REMAKES: Miss Sadie Thompson, (1928); Rain (1932)

Miss Susie Slagle's, 1946, 88m, ★★1/2/$, Par/NA. The stories of several young nurses in the Gibson Girl era, focusing on their lovelife ups and downs. Veronica Lake, Joan Caulfield, Lillian Gish, Lloyd Bridges. w. Anne Froelich, Hugo Butler, N-adap. Augusta Tucker, d. John Berry.

MELODRAMA: ROMANCE: Ensemble Films; Ensembles-Female; Nurses; Young Women; 1900s; Baltimore
(Ed: A departure for the vampish Lake)

Missing, 1982, 122m, ★★★★/$$, Universal/MCA-U, R/P-V-MRN. A man (John Shea) is taken during the coup in Chile and his wife (Sissy Spacek, BActress) and his father (Jack Lemmon, BActor) search for him w. Donald Stewart, Costa-Gavras (**BAScr**), d. Costa-Gavras. BPicture. Oscars: 4-1.

DRAMA: MYSTERY: MELODRAMA: Political Drama; Missing Persons; Missing Person Thriller; Government as Enemy; Political Unrest; Oppression; Anti-establishment Films; Nightmares
(The House of the Spirits; The Year of Living Dangerously; Z; Into Thin Air; Without a Trace; Adam)

Missing in Action, 1984, 101m, ★★/$$$, Cannon/MGM-UA, R/EV. A former POW goes on missions to retrieve others who are still in Vietnam. Chuck Norris, M. Emmet Walsh. w. James Bruner, d. Joseph Zito.

Missing in Action 2-The Beginning, 1985, 95m, ★★/$$, Cannon/MGM-UA, R/EV. Set before the previous film, this is the story of the original escape from the Vietnamese P.O.W. camp. Chuck Norris. w. Arthur Silver, Larry Levinson, Steve Bing, d. Lance Hool.
PREQUEL TO ABOVE.

ACTION: POWs: Missing Person; Missing in Action; Searches; Fathers & Sons; Vietnam; Vietnam Veterans
(First Blood; Rambo: First Blood Part II; Uncommon Valor)

Missing Pieces, 1991, 92m, ★★/$, Ind/NA. Two goofs, one a writer, the other a musician, try to solve a puzzle that could lead to hidden money, but the mob is after the money and them, too. Eric Idle, Robert Wuhl, Lauren Hutton, Bob Gunton, Richard Belzer, Bernie Kopell. w. d. Leonard Stern.

COMEDY: Chase Movies; Capers; Treasure Hunts; Writers Musicians; Buddy Films; Writer-Directors
(Splitting Heirs; Mistress; Wise Guys)

The Mission, 1986, 128m, ★★★/$$, Goldcrest-WB/WB, PG. A priest goes into the Amazon jungle to reform the natives but also must take charge of a criminal while the colonialists try to put a stop to their work. Jeremy Irons, Robert De Niro, Aidan Quinn, Ray McAnally, Liam Neeson. w. Robert Bolt, d. Roland Joffe (BDirector). BPicture, **BCin**, BEdit, BOScore, BCostume, BSound. Oscars: 7-1.

DRAMA: ADVENTURE: Epics; Priests; Reformers; Missionaries; South America; Amazon River; Jungle Life; Religion; Rainforests; Scenery-Outstanding; Lyrical Films; Coulda Been Great
(At Play in the Fields of the Lord)

The Missionary, 1983, 86m, ★★1/2/$, Handmade-Par/Par, R/S-FN. In the slums of early 1900s London, a missionary takes to the street to help prostitutes, but can't help himself. Michael Palin, Maggie Smith, Michael Hrdern, Trevor Howard, Denholm Elliott. w. Michael Palin, d. Richard Loncraine.

COMEDY: COMEDY DRAMA: Missionaries; Religion; Reformers; Prostitutes-Low Class; Romance with Prostitute; England; 1900s; Monty Pythoners; British Films; Coulda Been Good

Mississippi, 1935, 75m, ★★/$, Par/NA. A singer on a showboat has some skeletons in his closet he can't just sing away. Big Crosby, W. C. Fields, Joan Bennett, Gail Patrick. w. Herbert Fields, Chalude Binyon, SS-adap. Booth Tarkington, d. Edward Sutherland.

MUSICALS: MELODRAMA: Music Movies; Singers; Southerns; River Life; Mississippi

Mississippi Burning, 1988, 127m, ★★1/2/$$$, Tri-Star/RCA-Col, PG-13/V. Civil rights workers are murdered and a local Mississippi sheriff (Gene Hackman, BActor) must see to it that justice is done to those who've covered it up. Brad Dourif, Frances McDormand (BSActress). w. Chris Gerolmo, d. Alan Parker (BDirector). BPicture, **BCin**, BEdit, BSound. Oscars: 8-1.

DRAMA: MURDER: Historical Drama; Social Drama; Detective Stories; Detectives-Police; Conspiracy; Bigots; Race Relations; Southerns; Mississippi; Ku Klux Klan; FBI Agents; Unintentionally Funny; Southerns-British Directors of; Coulda Been Great; Overrated
(In the Heat of the Night; Attack on Terror; The Klansman)
(Ed: Pretty presposterous that all of this could happen in one small town in such a short period of time in such a way. Interesting the script was the only thing not nominated. "Rambo-ized history")

Miss Julie, 1950, 87m, ★★★1/2/$$, Ind/Col. When a wealthy young woman is seduced by a servant, she has to deal with the repercussions and depression. Anita Bjork, Ulf Palme, Anders Henrikson. w. d. Alf Sjoberg, P-adap. August Strindberg.

DRAMA: TRAGEDY: Romance-Class Conflicts; Romance-Doomed; Depression; Suicidal Tendencies; Female Protagonists; Swedish Films; Classic Play Adaptations
(Hedda; Anna Karenina)

Mississippi Masala, 1991, 113m, ★★1/2/$, Cinecom/Cinecom, PG/S. An Indian woman living in Mississippi of all places falls for a black man which upsets everyone they know. Denzel Washington, Roshan Seth, Sarita Choudbury, Charles Dutton, Joe Seneca. w. Sooni Taraporevala, d. Mira Nari.

ROMANCE: COMEDY DRAMA: MELO-DRAMA: Romantic Drama; Romance-Interracial; Lover; Family Dislikes; Black Men; Indian People; Mississippi; Rural Life; Small-town Life; Female Directors; Coulda Been Good
(For Queen and Country; Masala)

The Mississippi Mermaid, 1969, 123m, ★★★/$$, UA/MGM-UA. A Frenchman writes to a woman then asks her to come and visit, but when she turns out to be different than he'd hoped for . . . Jean-Paul Belmondo, Catherine Deneuve, Michel Bouquet. w. d. Francois Truffaut, N-adap. Waltz into Darkness, William Irish.

SUSPENSE: DRAMA: MURDER: MYS-TERY: MURDER MYSTERY: ROMANCE: Psychological Drama; Personal Ads; French Films; Coulda Been Good; Brides-Mail Order; Forgotten Films; Hidden Gems; Writer-Directors
(The Bride Wore Black; The Wild Child)

The Missouri Breaks, 1976, 126m, ★★/$, UA/MGM-UA, R/V-S. Ranchers and rustlers are in conflict over a number of things, leading to a duel in this neo-Western. Marlon Brando, Jack Nicholson, Randy Quaid, Kathleen Lloyd, Frederic Forrest, Harry Dean Stanton. w. Thomas McGuane, d. Arthur Penn.

WESTERNS: DRAMA: Westerns-Neo; Cattle People; Cattle Rustlers; Men in Conflict; Feuds; Duels; Flops-Major
(The Duellists; Heaven's Gate)

Mistress, 1991, 100m, ★★1/2/$, Ind/Live, R/P-S. A screenwriter's old screenplay is optioned and finally financed, but he has to cast all of the investors' mistresses. Robert Wuhl, Robert De Niro, Eli Wallach, Martin Landau, Sheryl Lee Ralph, Jean Smart, Danny Aiello, Laurie Metcalf. w. J. F. Lawton, Barry Primus, d. Primus.

COMEDY DRAMA: Movie Making; Mistresses; Writers Directors; Hollywood Life; Hollywood Satire; Mindgames; Coulda Been Great
(The Big Picture; Movers and Shakers)
(Ed: Has its moments, mostly from the actors, particularly Ralph and Smart, with De Niro doing a good character turn)

Misunderstood, 1984, 92m, ★★½/$, MGM/MGM-UA, G. Two young boys and their father have to adjust when their mother dies. Henry Thomas, Huckleberry Fox, Gene Hackman, Susan Anspach, Rip Torn. d. Jerry Schatzberg.

MELODRAMA: Family Drama; Fathers & Sons; Boys; Widowers; Tearjerkers

ALL Misters, see **MR.** even if it's spelled "Mister" in the title.

Mi Vida Loca, 1994, 92m, ★★/$, Ind. A look into the lives of tough female Latin gang members in L.A.'s Echo Park. Angel Aviles, Jesse Borrego. w. d. Alison Anders.

DRAMA: Documentary Style; Improvisational Films; Ordinary People Stories; Criminals-Female; Gangs-Latin; Ensembles-Female; Dangerous Women; Inner City Life; Latin People; Female Screenwriters; Female Directors; Female Protagonists; Writer-Directors
(Kids; Mi Familia)

Mixed Company, 1974, 109m, ★★/$, UA/NA. A couple adopt a multicultural family and try to deal with the conflicts between them which arise for racial reasons and for the fact that they are just plain children. Joseph Bologna, Barbara Harris, Lisa Gerritson. w. Melville Shavelson, Mort Lachman, d. Shavelson.

COMEDY DRAMA: FAMILY: Family Comedy; Marriage Comedy; Families-Large; Children-Adopted; Children-Brats; Race Relations; Basketball; Coaches; Coulda Been Good
(Yours, Mine & Ours; Room for One More)

Mixed Nuts, 1994, 97m, ★★★/$$, TriStar/Col-Tri, PG-13/P-S. A suicide prevention hotline is about to lose its lease just as Christmas and the suicide season approaches. Farce ensues among the var-

ious relationships between the people answering the line, which apparently aren't much better than those of the people calling for help. Steve Martin, Madeline Kahn, Robert Klein, Anthony LaPaglia, Juliette Lewis, Rob Reiner, Adam Sandler, Liev Schreiber, Rita Wilson, Parker Posey, Jon Stewart, Joely Fisher, Steven Wright, Garry Shandling, Victor Garber. w. Nora Ephron, Delia Ephron, S-adap. *Le Père Noel Est Une Ordure*, d. Nora Ephron.

COMEDY DRAMA: SATIRE: FARCE: Black Comedy; Suicidal Tendencies; Ensemble Films; Multiple Stories; Interwoven Stories; Foreign Film Remakes; Los Angeles; Coulda Been Good; Female Directors

FLIPSIDE: The Slender Thread.
(The End; A Pain in the A-; Beyond Therapy)
(Ed: Very good and the French shows)

Mo' Better Blues, 1990, 127m, ★★½/$$, UIP/MCA-U. An obsessively perfectionist trumpet player finds he's losing the love of his life to music, so he makes a choice. Denzel Washington, Spike Lee, Wesley Snipes, Joie Lee, Cynda Williams, Giancarlo Esposito. w. d. Spike Lee.

DRAMA: ROMANCE: Marriage Drama; Jazz Life; Musicians; Black Casts; Black Men; Young Men; Decisions-Big; Black Screenwriters; Black Directors; Writer-Directors
(Girl 6; School Daze; Bird; Leadbelly)

Mo' Money, 1992, 90m, ★★/$$, Col/Col-Tri, R/EP-V. A group of hustlers get a credit card under false pretenses, go on a wild shopping spree, and uncover an even bigger crook. Damon Wayans, Stacey Dash, Joe Santos, Marlon Wayans. w. Damon Wayans, d. Peter Macdonald.

COMEDY: Thieves; Criminals-Stupid; Con Artists; Black Men; Inner City Life; Black Screenwriters; Black Directors
(Major Payne; Don't Be a Menace . . .)

The Mob, 1951, 87m, ★★½/$, Col/NA. An undercover cop infiltrates the local Mafia and catches his man. Broderick Crawford, Richard Kiley, Ernest Borgnine, Neville Brand, Charles Bronson. w. William Bowers, d. Robert Parrish.

ACTION: Crime Drama; Mob Stories; Detective Stories; Detectives-Police; Undercover

Mobsters, 1991, 104m, ★★½/$, U/MCA-U, PG-13/S-P. A twenty-something *Godfather* with the young

Frank Costello, Lucky Luciano, Bugsy Siegel, and Meyer Lansky staking out their respective territories. Christian Slater, Patrick Dempsey, Richard Grieco, Costas Manddylor, F. Murray Abraham, Lara Flynn Boyle, Christopher Penn, Anthony Quinn. w. Michael Mahern, Nicholas Kazan, d. Michael Karbelnikoff.

DRAMA: Crime Drama; Criminal Biographies; Biographies; Ensemble Films; Ensembles-Male; Mob Stories; Famous People When Young; Power-Rise to; Men in Conflict; Bratpack Movies
(The Untouchables; Murder Inc.)

Moby Dick, 1956, 116m, ★★★/$$, WB/Fox, HomeVision. Captain Ahab is obsessed with killing the legendary whale that caused him to lose his leg. Gregory Peck, Richard Basehart, Friedrich Ledebur, Leo Genn, Orson Welles. w. Ray Bradbury, John Huston, N-adap. Herman Melville, d. John Huston.

ADVENTURE: DRAMA: Adventure at Sea; Ships; Fishermen; Animal Monsters; Quests; Obsessions; Whales; Classic Literary Adaptations
(Jaws; 20,000 Leagues Under the Sea)

The Model and the Marriage Broker, 1951, 103m, ★★½/$$, 20th/NA. A woman, who doesn't tell her friend she works at a matchmaking organization, helps her out in a clandestine way. Thelma Ritter, Jeanne Crain, Scott Brady, Zero Mostel. w. Charles Brackett, Walter Reisch, Richard Breen, d. George Cukor.

COMEDY: COMEDY DRAMA: Matchmakers; **ROMANCE:** Romantic Comedy; Secrets-Keeping; Models; Forgotten Films; Coulda Been Good; Good Premise Unfulfilled; Female Protagonists
(The Matchmaker; Hello, Dolly; The Mating Season)

The Moderns, 1988, 126m, ★★★/$, New Line/New Line, R/S. Slice of life about eccentric hipsters in roaring twenties Paris, interspersed with the lore of real-life writers and artists. Keith Carradine, Linda Fiorentino, John Lone, Genvieve Bujold, Geraldine Chaplin, Wallace Shawn. w. d. Alan Rudolph.

COMEDY DRAMA: Paris; Artists; Artists-Famous; Writers; Biographies-Fictional; Slice of Life Stories; Ensemble Films; Art Films; Hidden Gems
(Henry and June; The Sun Also Rises)

Modern Times (B&W, Silent), 1940, 87m, ★★★★/$$$, UA/MGM-UA. The little tramp takes on the industrial complex of machinery and bureaucracy. Charles Chaplin, Paulette Goddard. w. d. Charles Chaplin.

COMEDY: SATIRE: ROMANCE: Social Comedy; Social Satire; Romantic Comedy; Man vs. Machine; Corporation as Enemy; Working Class; Ordinary People Stories; Writer-Directors; Hidden Gems; Silent Films
(The Crowd; Desk Set; Metropolis; The Great Dictator)

Modesty Blaise, 1966, 119m, ★★/$, 20th/NA. The comic-book-based story of a female secret agent who has to protect a shipload of diamonds from international bandits. Monica Vitti, Dirk Bogarde, Terence Stamp, Harry Andrews, Michael Craig. w. Evan Jones, (Comic Strip)-adap. Peter O'Donnell, Jim Holdaway, d. Joseph Losey.
ACTION: Heist Stories; Secret Agents; Spies-Female; Heroes-Comic; Jewel Thieves; Coulda Been Good; Forgotten Films; British Films
(Deadlier Than the Male; Brenda Starr; Fathom)

Modigliani, 1958, 110m, ★★★/$, Ind/Facets. Life of the handsome modern artist around the turn of the century, centering on his relationships with tempestuous women. Gerard Phillipe, Lilli Palmer, Anouk Aimee, Lino Ventrua, Lila Kedrova. w. Max Ophuls, Henri Jeanson, Jacques Becker, d. Becker.
DRAMA: Biographies; Painters; Artists; Artists-Famous; 1900s; Episodic Stories; French Films; Forgotten Films; Hidden Gems
(Lust for Life; La Belle Noiseuse; Camille Claudelle; Goya)

Mogambo, 1953, 116m, ★★★1/2/$$$, MGM/MGM-UA. A man on safari in Kenya is visited by three friends from England and America and they all go hunting gorillas together. Clark Gable, Ava Gardner (BActress), Grace Kelly (BSActress). w. John Lee Mahin, d. John Ford. Oscars: 2-0.
COMEDY DRAMA: ADVENTURE: ROMANCE: Romantic-Triangles; Feisty Females; Women in Conflict; Women Fighting Over Men; Safaris; Africa
REMAKE OF: Red Dust; Congo Maisie.
(Red Dust; Green Fire; Night of the Iguana)

Mohammed, Messenger of God, 1976, 182m, ★★/$, Filmco/NA. A religious epic of the Islamic faith based on the Koran-the faithfulness extends to the Islamic tradition of never depicting Mohammed directly. Anthony Quinn, Irene Papas, Michael Ansara. w. H. A. L. Craig (with Arab advice), d. Moustapha Akkad.
DRAMA: Religion; Middle East; Epics; Flops-Major; Arab People

The Mole People, 1956, 78m, ★★/$, U/MCA-U. A group of explorers in Antarctica fall through a hole in the Earth and discover a race of mole people living underground. John Agar, Cythia Patrick, Hugh Beaumont, Alan Napier. w. Lazlo Gorog, d. Virgil Vogel.
SCI-FI: HORROR: Explorers; Center of the Earth; Little People; Animal Monsters; Unintentionally Funny; Cult Films
(Journey to the Center of the Earth)

The Molly Maguires, 1970, 123m, ★★1/2/$$, Par/Par, PG/V. A fact-based story of a private eye going undercover in a coal-mining town and ferreting out an underground society. Richard Harris, Sean Connery, Samantha Eggar. w. Walter Bernstein, d. Martin Ritt. BArt. Oscars: 1-0.
DRAMA: Social Drama; Detective Stories; Undercover; Unions; Political Unrest; Political Activists; Mining Towns; 1800s; Forgotten Films

Mom and Dad Save the World, 1992, 87m, ★/$, WB/HBO, PG. A suburban family is whisked away to a fantasy planet where the leader wants to destroy Earth, so, as the title says . . . Teri Garr, Jon Lovitz, Jeffrey Jones, Eric Idle, Wallace Shawn, Kathy Ireland. d. Greg Beeman.
COMEDY: Fantasy; **CHILDREN'S: FAMILY:** Family Comedy; Outer Space Movies; **SCI-FI:** Spoofs-SCI-FI; Flops-Major

Moment by Moment, 1979, 105m, ★★/$, Par/Par, R/S. A handsome stranger comes into the life of a bored suburban wife and they have an affair. John Travolta, Lily Tomlin, Andra Akers. w. d. Jane Wagner.
MELODRAMA: ROMANCE: Romantic Drama; Romance-Older Women/Younger Men; Love-Questionable; Beach Movies; Prostitutes-Male; Lonely People; Rich People; Flops-Major; Female Protagonists; Female Screenwriters; Female Directors; Writer-Directors
(Ed: Two boring people make a boring movie that, of course, was unbearable "moment by moment")

Moment to Moment, 1966, 108m, ★★1/2/$, U/NA. In the French Riviera, a housewife finds a body and must solve the mystery. Jean Seberg, Honor Blackman, Sean Garrison, Arthur Hill. w. John Lee Mahin, Alec Coppel, d. Mervyn Le Roy.
MYSTERY: MURDER: MURDER MYSTERY: Murder-Discovering; Riviera Life

Momma, There's a Man in Your Bed, 1990, 111m, ★★★1/2/$$$, Orion/Orion, HBO, PG/S. A black maid for a yogurt company helps get her boss off the hook for a frame-up food poisoning scandal, but can he help her when her son is arrested, and will they wind up falling in love against all odds and logic? Daniel Autieul, Firmine Richard. w. d. Coline Serreau.
COMEDY DRAMA: SATIRE: ROMANCE: Romantic Comedy; Mothers-Struggling; Servants; Romance-Interracial; Opposites Attract; Class Conflicts; Framed?; Scandals; French Films; Female Protagonists; Black Women; Writer-Directors; Underrated
(Too Beautiful for You; Corrina, Corrina)
(Ed: Funny, thoughtful, and poignant, something Hollywood seems incapable of combining without schmaltz)

Mommie Dearest, 1981, 129m, ★★★/$$, Par/Par, PG/P. The sensational biography of Joan Crawford by her adopted daughter, Cristina, following her career as her homelife became more and more bizarre. Faye Dunaway, Diana Scarwid, Steve Forrest, Howard daSilva. w. Frank Yablans, Frank Perry, Tracy Hotchner, Robert Getchell, d. Frank Perry.
DRAMA: Biographies; Hollywood Life; Hollywood Biographies; Autobiographical Stories; Black Comedy; Tragi-Comedy; Children-Adopted; Mothers-Troublesome; Abused Children; Evil Women; Mean Women; Mental Illness; Episodic Stories; Female Protagonists; Camp; Cult Films; Underrated
(The Wicked Lady; Network)
(Ed: Cult classic of "no more wire hangers" fame, but where Dunaway was too good for her own good)

Mona Lisa, 1986, 104m, ★★★1/2/$$$, Palace/HBO, R/P-S-V-FN. A cab driver (Bob Hoskins, BActor) gets an assignment to drive and protect a black call girl (Cathy Tyson), who he may be falling in love with. w. Neil Jordan, David Leland (BOScr), d. Jordan. Oscars: 2-0.

DRAMA: SUSPENSE: ROMANCE: Film Noir-Modern; Prostitutes-High Class; Romance with Prostitute; Romance-Interracial; Infatuations; Bodyguards; Protecting Someone; Unlikely Allies; Taxi Drivers; British Films
(The Bodyguard; The Crying Game)
Mondo Cane, 1963, 105m, ★★½/$$$, Cineriz/Sinister, Vidmark. An exploitation documentary with some of the most bizarre rituals and sights of the third world. w. d. Gualtiero Jacopetti. BOSong, "More". Oscars: 1-0.
Documentaries; World Travel; Cult Films; Sleeper Hits; Curiosities
(Ed: A sleeper cult film and a massive hit song out of nowhere)
Money for Nothing, 1993, 100m, ★★★/$, Touchstone/Touchstone, PG-13/S-P. When a dock worker finds a million in mob loot, the cops and the mob are after whoever found it, so it's a lose-lose situation unless he can get away. John Cusack, Debi Mazar, Michael Madsen, Fionnula Flannagan. w. Ramon Menendez, Carol Sobieski, d. Menendez.
COMEDY: Action Comedy; Fugitives from the Law; Fugitives from the Mob; Finding Money; Mob Stories; True Stories; Race Against Time; Working Class; Rags to Riches
(Blank Check; Gross Pointe Blank)
Money from Home, 1954, 100m, ★★½/$$, Par/Par. Martin & Lewis are a horse gambler and a veterinarian who wind up with a horse tied to the mob. Dean Martin, Jerry Lewis, Pat Crowley. w. Hal Kanter, DD-adap. Damon Runyon, d. George Marshall.
COMEDY: Comedy of Errors; Mob Stories; Mob Comedy; Horses; Horse Racing; Gamblers; Pet Stories; 3-D Movies
(California or Bust)
The Money Pit, 1986, 91m, ★★½/$$$, U/MCA-U, PG. Two yuppies find a mansion in the burbs dirt cheap, but there's a reason for the price. Tom Hanks, Shelley Long, Alexander Gudonov, Maureen Stapelton, Joe Mantegna, Philip Bosco, Josh Mostel. w. David Giler, d. Richard Benjamin.
COMEDY: Comedy of Errors; Comedy-Slapstick; Romance-Triangles; House Havoc; Marriage Comedy; Suburban Life; Yuppies; Coulda Been Great
(Mr. Blandings Builds His Dream House; George Washington Slept Here; In Society)

(Ed: Good bits and jokes don't make a complete picture)
The Money Train, 1995, 103m, ★★/$$, Col/Col, R/EV-P. Two disgruntled subway transit cops fight over a woman and try to decide whether or not they should rob the payroll train. Wesley Snipes, Woody Harrelson, Jennifer Lopez, Robert Blake, Chris Cooper. w. Doug Richardson & David Loughery, d. Joseph Ruben.
ACTION: Thieves; Bank Robberies; Subways; Men Fighting over Women; Buddy Films; Flops-Major
(White Men Can't Jump; The Taking of Pelham 1-2-3)
The Money Trap, 1966, 92m, ★★/$, MGM/NA. When a policeman with financial problems turns to a life of crime, it soon catches up with him. Glenn Ford, Rita Hayworth, Elke Sommer, Ricardo Montalban, Joseph Cotten. w. Walter Bernstein, N-adap. Lionel White, d. Burt Kennedy.
DRAMA: Crime Drama; Character Studies; Police Stories; Police Corruption; Ordinary Person Turned Criminal; Forgotten Films; Flops-Major; Coulda Been Good
Monkey Business, 1931, 81m, ★★★½/$$$, Par/MCA-U. The Marx Brothers stowaway on a cruise ship then crash a big party there and wind-up solving a crime. Groucho Marx, The Marx Brothers, Thelma Todd. w. S. J. Perlman, Will B. Johnstone, Arthur Sheekman, d. Norman Z. McLeod.
COMEDY: Comedy of Errors; Ships; Fools-Bumbling; Con Artists; Thieves
(Duck Soup; Room Service; Brain Donors)
Monkey Business, 1952, 97m, ★★★/$$, 20th/Fox. With the help of a chimp, a scientist accidentally invents a youth elixir and chaos follows. Cary Grant, Ginger Rogers, Charles Coburn, Marilyn Monroe, Hugh Marlowe. w. Ben Hecht, Charles Lederer, I. A. L. Diamond, d. Howard Hawks.
COMEDY: Screwball Comedy; Comedy-Slapstick; Aging-Reverse; Cures/Elixirs; Scientists; Primates; Hidden Gems; Forgotten Films
(Bringing Up Baby; Death Becomes Her)
(Ed: Not the energy and verve of Hawks' and Grant's Baby, but charming nonetheless)
Monkey Shines, 1988, 109m, ★★½/$$, Orion/Orion, R/S-MN. A young man is disabled in an accident and receives a

monkey to help around the house. But the monkey begins to murder. Jason Beghe, John Pankow, Kat McNeil, Joyce Van Patten. w. d. George Romero.
HORROR: MURDER: Murders-One by One; Animal Monsters; Animals-Smart; Experiments; Scientists; Primates; Disabled People; Disabled People in Jeopardy; Writer-Directors
(Link; Man's Best Friend)
Monkeys Go Home, 1966, 101m, ★★½/$$, Disney/Disney, G. A young American man inherits an olive plantation in France and trains chimps to help with the harvest. Dean Jones, Maurice Chevalier, Yvette Mimieux. w. Maurice Tombragel, N-adap. G. K. Wilkinson, d. Andrew V. McLaglen.
COMEDY: Fish out of Water Stories; Comedy-Disneyesque; Heirs; Primates; Farm Life; Forgotten Films
(The Ugly Dachshund; The Million Dollar Duck)
Mon Oncle D'Amerique, see My American Uncle.
Monkey Trouble, 1994, 95m, ★★★/$. A girl wanting attention when her parents have a new child winds up with a pick-pocketing monkey and a lot of trouble. Thora Birch, Harvey Keitel, Mimi Rogers. w. Franco Amuri, Stu Kreiger, d. Amuri.
COMEDY: CHILDREN'S: FAMILY: Family Comedy; Girls; Primates; Nuisances; Chase Stories; Pickpockets; Pet Stories; Comedy-Disneyesque
(Ed; The Barefoot Executive)
Monolith, 1993, 96m, ★★½/$, U/MCA-U, R/V. When a Russian in L.A. is accused of murder and disappears, two cops find themselves up against outer spacely forces. Bill Paxton, John Hurt, Lindsay Frost, Louis Gossett, Jr. w. Stephen Lister, d. John Eyres.
SUSPENSE: SCI-FI: Crime Drama; Aliens-Outer Space, Evil; Russians; Missing Person; Police Stories; Detective Stories; **MURDER: MYSTERY: MURDER MYSTERY:** Overlooked at Release
(Red Heat; Alien Nation)
Monsieur Beaucaire, 1946, 93m, ★★★/$$, Par/Par. The man who cuts the king's hair in the world of Versailles impersonates a member of the court for fun. Bob Hope, Joan Caulfield, Patric Knowles, Cecil Kellaway, Reginald Owen. w. Melvin Frank, Norman Panama, d. George Marshall.

COMEDY: ROMANCE: Romantic
Comedy; Costume Drama; Impostors;
Hairdressers; Kings; 1700s
(DuBarry was a Lady; The Court Jester)

Monsieur Hire, 1989, 82m, ★★★★/$$,
Orion/Orion, R/S-V. A lonely, homely,
balding middle-aged man has an obses-
sive love for the woman across the street
and sees things he shouldn't, leading to
tragedy. Michel Blanc, Sandrine
Bonnaire, Andre Wilms. w. Patrice
Leconte, Patrick Dewolf, N-adapt.
Georges Simenon (Les Fiancailles de M.
Hire), d. Patrice Leconte.
SUSPENSE: TRAGEDY: Psychological
Drama; Erotic Drama; Men and Girls;
Voyeurs; Abused Women; Suicidal
Tendencies; Lonely People;
Hitchcockian; Overlooked at Release;
Hidden Gems; French Films
(Rear Window; The Flesh of the Orchid)

Monsieur Hulot's Holiday, 1953, 91m
(Silent), ★★★★/$$$, Ind/NA, Bravo. A
middle-aged bachelor goes to a beachside
resort and wrecks everything he touches.
Jacques Tati, Nathalie Pascaud, Michele
Rolla, Valentine Camax. w. Jacques Tati,
Henri Marquet, d. Jacques Tati.
COMEDY: Comedy of Errors; Comedy-
Slapstick; Comedy-Light; Fools-
Bumbling; Relatives-Troublesome;
Uncles; Vacations; Mod Era; Tennis;
French Films; Hidden Gems; Silent Films
(Playtime; Mon Oncle)

Monsieur Verdoux, 1947, 125m,
★★★1/2/$$, Chaplin/Fox. To support his
wife, a timid bank teller "marries" and
kills rich women. Charles Chaplin,
Martha Raye, Isobel Elsom. w. d. Charles
Chaplin.
COMEDY: Black Comedy; SATIRE:
Comedy-Light; Comedy-Morbid; MUR-
DER: Serial Killers; Murderers-Black
Widow; Murders of Females; Murder
Attempts-Comic; Bigamy; Writer-
Directors
(Arriverderci, Baby!; A New Leaf)

Monsieur Vincent, 1947, 113m, ★★★/
$$, Ind/Moore Video. A nobleman in the
17th Century decides to give up all his
possessions and dedicate his life to the
poor. Pierre Fresnay, Aime Clairond, Jean
Debucourt. w. Jean-Bernard Luc, Jean
Anouilh, d. Maurice Cloche.
DRAMA: MELODRAMA: Riches to Rags;
Saintly People; Missionaries; Poor
People; Homeless People; 1600s
(For Richer, For Poorer; The Millionaire)

Monsignor, 1982, 121m, ★★1/2/$$,
20th/CBS-Fox, R/S. A cardinal in Ireland
raises funds for the Vatican through
nefarious means and has an illicit
romance on his way up. Christopher
Reeve, Genevieve Bujold, Fernando Rey,
Jason Miller. w. Abraham Polonsky,
Wendell Mayes, N-adapt. Jack Alain
Leger, d. Frank Perry.
DRAMA: ROMANCE: Romance-
Clandestine; Power-Rise to; Corruption;
Religion; Priests; Popes; Coulda Been
Good; Forgotten Films
(The Thorn Birds)

The Monster Club, 1980, 97m, ★★/$,
AIP/Live. An unfortunate soul is brought
to a monster club by a vampire. Vincent
Price, John Carradine, Anthony Steel,
Simon Ward, Donald Pleasance, Britt
Eckland. w. Edward and Valerie
Abraham, SS-adapt. R. Chetwynd-Hayes,
d. Roy Ward Baker.
HORROR: Horror Comedy; Spoofs-
Horror; Vampires; Monsters; Camp

Monster in a Box, 1991, 88m, ★★★/$,
New Line/New Line, ICA. Spalding Gray
in concert talking about the horror of fin-
ishing a novel-"the monster in a box" of
the title. Spalding Gray. w. P-adapt.
Spalding Gray, d. Nick Broomfield.
COMEDY: Comedy-Performance;
Storytellers; Writers; Stage Filmings; One
Person Shows
(Swimming to Cambodia)
(Ed: Apparently this was a more success-
ful story than that of the novel)

The Monster Squad, 1987, 81m,
★★1/2/$, Tri-Star/Vestron. A small town
is the hiding place of some major
Hollywood monsters. Stephen Macht,
Duncan Regehr, Andre Gower. w. Shane
Black, Fred Dekker, d. Fred Dekker.
HORROR: Horror Comedy; CHILDREN'S:
Monsters; Hiding Out; Overlooked at
Release

Montana, 1950, 76m, ★★1/2/$, WB/NA.
An Australian in Montana must fight the
locals to stake his claim. Errol Flynn,
Alexis Smith, S. Z. Sakall, Douglas
Kennedy. w. James R. Webb, Borden
Chase, Charles O'Neal, SS-adapt. Ernest
Haycox, d. Ray Enright.
WESTERNS: Men in Conflict; Save the
Farm; Strangers in Town

Montana Belle, 1952, 82m, ★★/$,
RKO/Turner. Belle Starr must act as a
decoy in a Dalton gang heist. Jane
Russell, George Brent, Scott Brady,

Forrest Tucker, Andy Devine. w. Horace
McCoy, Norman S. Hall, d. Allan Dwan.
WESTERNS: Heist Stories; Criminals-
Female; True Stories; Dangerous Women;
Female Among Males; Female in Male
Domain
(Belle Starr [TV Movie, ABC])

Monte Carlo, 1930, 94m, ★★★/$$$,
Par/NA. A woman playing the tables at
Monte Carlo gets wooed by her hairdresser
who later turns out to be a wealthy count
in disguise. Jack Buchanan, Jeanette
MacDonald, Zasu Pitts, Tyler Brooke.
w. Ernest Vajda, P-adapt. Hans Muller
(Blue Coast), N-adapt. Booth Tarkington
(Monsieur Beaucaire), d. Ernst Lubitsch.
COMEDY: ROMANCE: Romantic
Comedy; Impostors; Identities-Assumed;
Gambling; Monte Carlo; Forgotten Films
(Ed: Early talkie not quite up to
Lubitsch's later films)

The Monte Carlo Story, 1956, 101m,
★★1/2/$$, Ind/NA. A casino gigolo looks
for a wealthy woman to marry but ends up
falling for another poor hustler like him-
self, so they decide to hustle together.
Marlene Dietrich, Vittorio de Sica, Arthur
O'Connell, Mischa Auer. w. Samuel
Taylor, Marcello Girosi, Dino Risi,
d. Samuel Taylor.
COMEDY: ROMANCE: Romantic Comedy;
Con Artists; Gambling; Monte Carlo
(Bedtime Story; Object of Beauty)

Monte Walsh, 1970, 108m, ★★1/2/$,
20th/Fox, R/V. A "realistic" Western in
which aging cowboys deal with the real
hardships of cattle ranching and the petty
jealousies of small-town life. Lee Marvin,
Jack Palance, Jeanne Moreau, Mitch
Ryan. w. David Z. Goodman, Lukas
Heller, N-adapt. Jack Schaefer, d. William
A. Fraker.
WESTERNS: Cattle Ranchers; Men in
Conflict; Aging; Jealousy; Rural Life

Montenegro, 1981, 96m, ★★★/$,
Ind/NA, R/S. A bored housewife gets sex
and violence in one package when she
takes a vacation from her life and takes a
lover. Susan Anspach, Erland Josephson,
Bora Todorovic. w. d. Dusan Makavejev.
DRAMA: Character Studies; ROMANCE:
MURDER: Erotic Drama; Dangerous
Men; Murderers-Female; Mental Illness;
Nervous Breakdowns; Beautiful People;
Vacations-European; Scandinavia; Midlife
Crisis; Female Protagonists; Writer-
Directors; Hidden Gems; Cult Films
FLIPSIDE TO: Looking for Mr. Goodbar

A Month by the Lake, 1995, 115m, ★★★/$$, Miramax/Miramax, PG-13/S. Two middle-aged Brits vacationing in 1930s Italy fall in love, but a governess from America may lead the man to let his eye wander. So, the lady decides to cavort with a sexy young Italian to retaliate. The question isn't whether they'll get together but how. Vanessa Redgrave, Edward Fox, Uma Thurman, Alida Valli, Alessandro Gassman. w. Trevor Bentham, d. John Irvin.
COMEDY: Comedy-Light; Vacations; Vacations-European; ROMANCE: Romance on Vacation; 1930s British Films; Hidden Gems
(A Room with a View; High Season; Daisy Miller; Carrington)
A Month in the Country, 1987, 96m, ★★★/$, Ind/WB, PG. After World War I, two veterans find they aren't ready to re-enter society and go to a country cottage to recuperate. Colin Firth, Kenneth Branagh, Natasha Richardson. w. Simon Gray, N-adap. J. L. Carr, d. Pat O'Connor.
DRAMA: Character Studies; Veterans; Soldiers; World War II-Post Era; Medical Recovery; Nervous Breakdowns; Friendship-Male; British Films; Quiet Little Films; Overlooked at Release
(Ed: The subsequent rise of Branagh and Richardson will make this more interesting)
Monty Python and the Holy Grail, 1975, 90m, ★★★1/2/$$$, EMI-Col/Col, PG/P. The adventures of the knights of the round table as seen through the filter of the wacky British comedy troupe. Graham Chapman, John Cleese, Terry Gilliam, Eric Idle, Michael Palin, w. and starring Terry Jones d. Terry Gilliam, Terry Jones.
COMEDY: FARCE: ADVENTURE: Comic Adventure; Spoofs; Comedy-Slapstick; Comedy-Skit; Chase Movies; Biblical Stories; Quests; Camelot Stories; Ancient Times; British Films; Monty Pythoners
(Erik the Viking)
Monty Python's Life of Brian, 1979, 93m, ★★★/$$$, Handmade-Par/Par, R/P-S. A comedy about a case of mistaken identity involving Jesus, the Romans, and the "bright side of death." w. and starring John Cleese, Graham Chapman, Eric Idle, Michael Palin, Terry Gilliam, Terry Jones, d. Terry Jones.
COMEDY: FARCE: Spoofs; Comedy-Slapstick; Comedy-Skit; Religion; Jesus Christ; Middle East; Charismatic People;

Biblical Stories; Ancient Times; Biographies-Fictional; Multiple Performances; British Films; Monty Pythoners
(Wholly Moses; History of the World Part I)
(Ed: A worldwide hit, the religious aspect made release in America limited)
Monty Python's The Meaning of Life, 1983, 90m, ★★★/$$, Universal/MCA-U, PG/S-P. A series of vignettes related superficially by the theme of the meaning of life, sex, death, whatever. w. and starring John Cleese, Graham Chapman, Eric Idle, Michael Palin, Terry Gilliam, Terry Jones, d. Terry Jones.
COMEDY: FARCE: Spoofs; Comedy-Slapstick; Comedy-Skit; Sexuality; Aging-Reverse; Coming of Age; Death-Personified; British Films; Monty Pythoners
The Moon and Sixpence, 1943, 85m, ★★★1/2/$$, MGM/MGM-UA. Loosely based on the life of the painter Gauguin, the story of a conventional middle-class man who leaves his family to become an *artiste* in Paris and then the South Pacific. George Sanders, Herbert Marshall, Steve Geray, Doris Dudley. w. Albert Lewin, N-adap. d. Lewin.
DRAMA: Character Studies; Life Transitions; Historical Drama; Biographies; Artists; Artists-Famous; Rebels; South Pacific; Islands
TV REMAKE: CBS, 1982
(Lust for Life; Modigliani)
The Moon in the Gutter, 1983, 130m, ★★1/2/$, Triumph-Col/RCA-Col, R/S-FN. When his sister is raped by a longshoreman, a big, simple man scouts the docks for the culprit and ends up falling in love with a woman he meets there. Gerard Depardieu, Natassja Kinski, Victoria Abril, Milena Vukotic. w. Jean-Jacques Beneix, Olivier Mergault, N-adap. David Goodis, d. Jean-Jacques Beneix.
DRAMA: MYSTERY: Manhunts; ROMANCE: Erotic Drama; Rape/Rapists; Revenge; Art Films; French Films
(Too Beautiful for You; Betty Blue; Diva)
The Moon Is Blue, 1953, 95m, ★★★1/2/$$$$, WB/WB. A young woman (Maggie McNamara, BActress) sets out to find the right man to lose her virginity to, but has trouble deciding who (William Holden, David Nivens). w. P-adap. F. Hugh Herbert, d. Otto Preminger. BEdit, BOSong. Oscars: 3-0.

COMEDY: COMEDY DRAMA: ROMANCE: Romantic Comedy; Romance-Older Men/Younger Women; Romance-Triangles; Virgins; Sexuality; Coming of Age; Life Transitions; Decisions-Big
(Sabrina; Sunday in New York; Every Girl Should Be Married)
The Moon Is Down, 1943, 90m, ★★★/$, 20th/NA. The Nazis try to occupy a village in Norway but are thwarted by its tenacious residents. Henry Travers, Cedric Hardwicke, Lee J. Cobb, Dorris Bowden, Margaret Wycherly, Peter Van Eyck. w. Nunnally Johnson, N-adap. John Steinbeck, d. Irving Pichel.
DRAMA: Nazi Stories; World War II Stories; Fighting the System; Rebels; Small-town Life; Germans as Enemy; Scandinavia; Coulda Been Good
(The Secret of Santa Vittoria; The Heroes of Telemark)
Moonlight and Valentino, 1995, 107m, ★★1/2/$$, Col/Col, R/S-P. Several women chitchat about their problems with men and not much else. Elizabeth Perkins, Whoopi Goldberg, Jon Bon Jovi, Shadia Simmons, Gwyneth Paltrow, Kathleen Turner. w. Ellen Simon, d. David Anspaugh.
COMEDY DRAMA: Romantic Comedy; Ensembles-Female; Male Among Females; Women's Films; Female Protagonists; Female Screenwriters
(How to Make an American Quilt; Chantilly and Lace; Waiting to Exhale)
Moonlighting, 1982, 97m, ★★★/$, Ind/MCA-U, PG/S-P. Four immigrants from Poland build a house in England and have mixed feelings when they hear about the military crackdown at home. Jeremy Irons, Eugene Lipinski, Jiri Stanislaw. w. d. Jerzy Skolimowski.
DRAMA: Art Films; Character Studies; Immigrants; Political Unrest; Alienation; Working Class; Polish People; Europeans-Eastern; British Films; England
Moonlighting, 1985, 100m, ★★★/$$$, ABC/ABC, WB, NR/V. The pilot for the series, which is a pretty adept screwball-mystery-comedy that could have done well as a feature-amazingly enough for TV. Model Maddie is broke except for a detective agency and detective Dave begs her to keep it-and him with it-to make a living. Cybill Shepherd, Bruce Willis, Jim

McKrell, Allyce Beasley. w. d. Glenn
Gordon Caron.

COMEDY: Screwball Comedy; **FARCE:**
Comic Mystery; Romance-Bickering;
Romance-Mismatched; Models; Wild
People; Extroverted vs. Introverted;
Detective Stories; Detectives-Amateur;
Detectives-Female; Detective Couple;
TV Series; TV Movies; Writer-Directors;
Sleeper Hits
(The Main Event)

Moon Over Miami, 1941, 92m,
★★★/$$$, 20th/Fox. A pair of gold-
digging sisters travel to Florida to find
wealthy eligable bachelors. Don Ameche,
Betty Grable, Carole Landis, Robert
Cummings. w. Vincent Lawrence, Brown
Holmes, d. Walter Lang.
MUSICALS: Music Movies; Dancers;
Dance Movies; Gold diggers Digging;
Marrying Up; Social Climbing; Miami
MUSICAL REMAKE OF Three Blind
Mice.
(How to Marry a Millionaire; The Greeks
Had a Word for Them; Three Little Girls
in Blue; Gold Diggers of Broadway; Down
Argentine Way)

Moon Over Parador, 1988, 104m,
★★½/$, U/MCA-U, PG-13/P. An out of
work actor gets captured by Latin
American coup leaders and is forced to
impersonate the president of a fictitious
banana republic. Richard Dreyfus, Raul
Julia, Sonia Braga, Jonathan Winters,
Fernando Rey, Sammy Davis Jr., Michael
Greene. w. Leon Capetanos, Paul
Mazursky, Charles G. Booth, d. Paul
Mazursky.
COMEDY: Political Unrest; Kidnappings;
Actors; Impostors-Actor; Impostors; South
America; Lookalikes; Good Premise
Unfulfilled; Coulda Been Great
(General Della Rovere; The Magic Face;
The Masquerader; Dave)
(Ed: Dreyfus as the leader of a Caribbean
country somehow seems odd, and also
seems to begin undermining what could
have been rather Sturges-like)

Moon Pilot, 1961, 98m, ★★½/$$,
Disney/Disney. An astronaut finds a nice
alien girl to settle down with. Edmond
O'Brien, Tom Tyron, Brian Keith. w.
Maurice Tombragel, (Serial)-adap. Robert
Buckner, d. James Nelson.
FAMILY: CHILDREN'S: Romantic
Comedy; Outer Space Movies;
Astronauts; Comedy-Disneyesque;
Aliens-Outer Space, Good; Moon Settings

(Robinson Crusoe on Mars; The Cat from
Outer Space)

The Moon Spinners, 1964, 119m,
★★★/$$$, Disney/Disney. Jewel thieves
in Crete enlist the aid of a young girl on
vacation with her family. Hayley Mills,
Peter McEnery, Eli Wallach, Joan
Greenwood, Pola Negri. w. Michael
Dyne, N-adap. Mary Stewart, d. James
Neilson.
**COMEDY DRAMA: CHILDREN'S: FAM-
ILY:** Heist Stories; Jewel Thieves; Girls;
Vacations; Mediterranean; Child
Protagonists
(That Darn Cat!; The Boatniks)

Moonraker, 1979, 126m, ★★★/$$$$,
UA/MGM-UA, PG/S. James Bond must
rescue the space shuttle which has been
steered off course by an evil madman.
Roger Moore, Lois Chiles, Michael
Lonsdale, Richard Kiel. w. Christopher
Wood, N-adap. Ian Fleming, d. Lewis
Gilbert.
ACTION: Action Comedy; Chase Movies;
Outer Space Movies; Rule the World-Plot
to; Secret Agents; James Bond; Venice

Moonrise, 1948, 90m, ★★★/$,
Republic/Republic. As he comes of age,
a young man becomes more violent as he
is troubled by memories of his murderous
father. Gail Russell, Dane Clark, Ethel
Barrymore, Allyn Joslyn. w. Charles
Haas, d. Frank Borzage.
DRAMA: MURDER: Crime Drama;
Psychological Drama; Character Studies;
Memories; Nightmares; Coming of Age;
Young Men-Angry; Swamp Life; Ahead of
Its Time

The Moon's Our Home, 1936, 80m,
★★½/$$, Par/Barr Video. An adventurer
and an independent actress marry and
soon find its a huge tug-of-war between
their two powerful egos and ambitions.
Margaret Sullavan, Henry Fonda, Beulah
Bondi, Charles Butterworth, Margaret
Hamilton. w. Isabel Dawn, Boyce DeGaw,
N-adap, d. William A. Seiter.
ROMANCE: Romantic Comedy;
Romance-Opposites Attract; Romance-
Bickering; Marriage Comedy; Marriage on
the Rocks; Actresses; Free Spirits;
Forgotten Films
(A Star Is Born; The Way We Were)

The Moonshine War, 1970, 100m,
★★/$, MGM/NA. A bootlegger in the last
days of Prohibition tries to mend his
ways. Patrick McGoohan, Richard
Widmark, Alan Alda, Melodie Johnson.

w. N-adap. Elmore Leonard, d. Richard
Quine.
DRAMA: Crime Drama; Bootleggers;
Mountain People; Hillbillies; Prohibition
Era; Starting Over; Alcoholics
(I Walk the Line; The Bootleggers)

Moonstruck, 1987, 102m, ★★★★/
$$$$$, MGM/MGM-UA, PG/S. A spinster
(Cher, **BActress**) is engaged to an older
man, but his younger brother (Nicolas
Cage) soon steals her heart and makes
her feel young again; while her family
(Olympia Dukakis, **BSActress**) (Vincent
Gardenia, BSActor) is having dalliances
of their own. w. John Patrick Shanley
(**BOScr**), d. Norman Jewison (BDirector).
BPicture. Oscars: 6-3.
COMEDY: FARCE: Marriage Comedy;
Family Comedy; Spinsters; Romance-
Triangles; Engagements-Breaking;
Marriages-Impending; Cheating Women;
Romance with Lover's Relative; Starting
Over; New York Life; Italians
(True Love; Used People; Five Cor-
ners)

More American Graffiti, 1979, 111m,
★★½/$$, U/MCA-U, PG/S. A sequel to
the popular nostalgia piece, this time
moved-up to 1964, in which bored
teenagers do drugs, have sex, listen to
rock n' roll and drive too fast. Candy
Clark, Bo Hopkins, Ron Howard, Paul
Le Mat. w. d. B. W. L. Norton.
COMEDY: Coming of Age; Teenagers;
Teenage Movies; Ensemble Films;
Nostalgia; Small-town Life; Coulda Been
Good
SEQUEL TO: American Graffiti
(Ed: Only a mere shadow of the original)

More Than a Secretary, 1936, 80m,
★★½/$$, Col/NA. The boss starts to
notice her once a bookish secretary loses
her glasses. Jean Arthur, George Brent,
Lionel Stander, Ruth Donnelly, Reginald
Denny. w. Dale Van Every, Lynn Starling,
d. Alfred E. Green.
COMEDY: ROMANCE: Romantic Comedy;
Office Comedy; Marrying the Boss; Marry-
ing Up; Secretaries; Forgotten Films
(Easy Living; The More the Merrier; My
Dear Secretary; Take a Letter, Darling)

The More the Merrier, 1943, 104m,
★★★★/$$$$, Columbia/RCA-Col. A
young woman (Jean Arthur, BActress)
takes on a few boarders who turn out to
be men: a younger one (Joel McCrea) and
an older one (Charles Coburn, **BSActor**),
who plays matchmaker for her and the

younger fellow. w. Robert Russell, Frank Ross, Richard Flournoy, Lewis Foster (BOStory, BScr), d. George Stevens (BDirector). BPicture. Oscars: 6-1.

COMEDY: Romantic Comedy; Comedy-Situation; **ROMANCE:** Romance-Bickering; Matchmakers; Roommates; World War II Era; Washington D.C.; Female Among Males; Hidden Gems
REMAKE: Walk, Don't Run
(Walk, Don't Run; Talk of the Town)

Morgan! (*Morgan, A Suitable Case for Treatment*), 1966, 97m, ★★★1/2/$$, EMI-Ind/EMI, HBO, PG. In swinging London, a crazy artist with a love of gorillas nearly drives his wife over the brink. Vanessa Redgrave (BActress), David Warner, Robert Stephens, Irene Handl, Newton Blick. w. P-adap. David Mercer, d. Karel Reisz. Oscars: 1-0.

COMEDY: SATIRE: Character Studies; Free Spirits; Wild People; Marriage on the Rocks; Artists; Mental Illness; Mod Era; Young People; Anti-Establishment Films; Cult Films; Time Capsules; Hidden Gems
(Georgy Girl; Isadora; The Knack)

Morgan Stewart's Coming Home, 1987, 96m, ★★/$, HBO/HBO, PG-13. A politician brings his son home from boarding school to help with the family values campaign, but his son doesn't have such wholesome ideas. Jon Cryer, Lynn Redgrave, Nicholas Pryor. d. Alan Smithee.

COMEDY: Politicians; Family Comedy; Fathers & Sons; Parents vs. Children; Practical Jokers; Nuisances
(Hiding Out; The Black Sheep)

The Morning After, 1986, 103m, ★★★/$$$, Lorimar-20th/Fox, R/P-V-S-FN. An aging actress (Jane Fonda, BActress) with a past is apparently being framed for murder when she wakes up in bed with a dead guy. Raul Julia, Jeff Bridges. w. James Hickey. d. Sidney Lumet. Oscars: 1-0.

SUSPENSE: MYSTERY: MURDER: MURDER MYSTERY: Women in Jeopardy; Accused Unjustly; Framed?; Saving Oneself; Enemy-Sleeping with the; Stalkers; Conspiracy; Love-Questionable; Secrets-Haunted by; Los Angeles; Hollywood; Actresses; Alcoholics; Female Protagonists
(Jagged Edge; Klute; Defenseless)

Morning Glory, 1933, 74m, ★★★1/2/$$$, RKO/Turner. An aspiring young actress (Katharine Hepburn, **BActress**) knocks everyone off their feet with her charm and upstart initiative. w. Howard Green, P-adap. Zoe Akins, d. Lowell Sherman. Oscars: 1-1.

MELODRAMA: COMEDY DRAMA: Actresses; Theater Life; Fame-Rise to; Free Spirits; Feisty Females; Female Protagonists
REMAKE: Stage Struck
(Stage Struck; A Bill of Divorcement)

Morocco, 1930, 97m, ★★★/$$$, Par/MCA-U. A wanton hussie and cabaret singer goes through the lineup of eligible bachelors in Morocco but eventually settles down with Mr. Right. Marlene Dietrich, Gary Cooper, Adolphe Menjou, Ullrich Haupt, Juliette Compton. w. Jules Furthman, N-adap. Benno Vigny, (*Amy Jolly*), d. Josef Von Sternberg.

DRAMA: ROMANCE: Dancers; Sexy Women; Elusive Women; Morocco; Foreign Legion
(The Blue Angel; Blonde Venus; Casbah)
(Ed: Marlene's big break in America, and the themes would be repeated over and over . . .)

Mortal Thoughts, 1991, 103m, ★★★/$$, Col/Col-Tri, R/EP-S-V. When a woman's husband is murdered, both she and her best friend become suspects and may have to face to a few harsh realities. Demi Moore, Glenne Headly, Bruce Willis, John Pankow, Harvey Keitel, Billie Neal. w. William Reilly, Claude Kerven, d. Alan Rudolph.

SUSPENSE: MURDER: Psychological Drama; Abused Women; Murderers-Female; Friendship-Friends; Ethics; Murder-Debate to Reveal Killer; Working Class; New York Life
(Diabolique; The Burning Bed)

Moscow Does Not Believe in Tears, 1980, 148m, ★★★/$$, Mosfilm-Col/Col. Three middle-aged Muscovite women recall their respective affairs with the appropriate Russian dryness. w. Valentin Chernykh, d. Vladimir Menshov.
BFLFilm. Oscars: 1-1.

DRAMA: Character Studies; **ROMANCE:** Romantic Drama; Memories; Flashbacks; Russia; Russian Films
(Little Vera)

Moscow on the Hudson, 1984, 117m, ★★★/$$, Col/RCA-Col, R/S-FN-MRN. A Russian man hides out in Macy's and loses his tour group, thus starting a new life in America. Robin Williams, Maria Conchita Alonso, Cleavant Derricks. w. Paul Mazursky, Leon Capetanos, d. Paul Mazursky.

COMEDY DRAMA: SATIRE: Fish out of Water Stories; Immigrants; Life Transitions; American Myth; New York Life; Russians; Department Stores (Coming to America; Adventure for Two; The Fisher King)

The Mosquito Coast, 1986, 119m, ★★★1/2/$$, WB/WB, PG. A man (Harrison Ford) decides to take his family to Central America to get away from modern society and must face the realities of the jungle, if that's possible. River Phoenix, Helen Mirren. w. Paul Schrader, adap. Paul Theroux, d. Peter Weir.

DRAMA: ADVENTURE: Family Drama; Fathers and Sons; Nature-Back to; City vs. Country; Quests; Dreams; Hippies; Eccentric People; Central America; Narrated Films; Coulda Been Great

The Most Dangerous Game, 1932, 63m, ★★★1/2/$$$, RKO/Nos, Sinister. A group of people receive an invitation by an eccentric millionaire to come to his desert island and soon find that his intention is to hunt them for sport. Leslie Banks, Joel McCrea, Fay Wray, Robert Armstrong. w. James Creelman, SS-adap. Richard Connell, d. Ernest B. Schoedsack, Irving Pichel.

SUSPENSE: ACTION: MURDER: Murder-Invitation to; Chase Movies; Manhunts; Human Eaters; Fugitives; Fugitives from a Murderer; Hunters; Nightmares; Islands; Hidden Gems
REMAKE/RETREAD: The Hunted; Game of Death

Motel Hell, 1980, 106m, ★★/$$, UA/MGM-UA, R/EV-B&G. Motel proprietors are known for their great sausage, and their guests seem to mysteriously disappear . . . What could the connection be? w. Robert Jaffe, Steven-Charles Jaffe, d. Kevin Connor.

HORROR: MURDER: Murders-One by One; Cannibalism; Hotels; Nightmares; Vacation Nightmares
(Auntie Lee's Meat Pies)

Mother Carey's Chickens, 1938, 82m, ★★★/$$, RKO/NA. A turn-of-the-century family saga set in a small town. Anne Shirley, Ruby Keeler, Fay Bainter, James Ellison, Walter Brennan, Donnie Dunagan. w. S. K. Lauren, Gertrude Purcell, N-adap. Kate Douglas Wiggin, d. Rowland V. Lee.

COMEDY DRAMA: Family Drama; Ensemble Films; Farm Life; Small-town Life; Capra-esque; Female Screenwriters; Female Protagonists
REMAKE: Summer Magic, (1963)
(Ed: Originally offered to Katharine Hepburn, who declined)

Mother Is a Freshman, 1948, 80m, ★★½/$$, 20th/NA. A middle-aged woman goes back to college and finds herself in a love triangle with her daughter and a professor who is the mutual object of their affections. Loretta Young, Van Johnson, Rudy Vallee, Barbara Lawrence. w. Mary Loos, Richard Sale, d. Lloyd Bacon.
COMEDY: ROMANCE: Romantic Comedy; Romance-Triangles; Women Fighting Over Men; Parents vs. Children; College Life; Professors; Teachers & Students; Romance with Student; Back to School; Female Protagonists; Female Screenwriters
(She's Working Her Way Through College; Back to School)

Mother, Jugs & Speed, 1976, 99m, ★★½/$$$, 20th/Fox, R/S-P. A series of vignettes about ambulance drivers and the emergencies they handle. Bill Cosby, Raquel Welch, Harvey Keitel, Allen Garfield, Bruce Davison. w. Tom Mankiewicz, d. Peter Yates.
COMEDY: ACTION: Action Comedy; Comedy-Skit; Tragi-Comedy; Black Comedy; Inner City Life; Nurses; Hospitals; Sexy Women; Good Premise Unfulfilled
(Fuzz; Uptown Saturday Night)

Mother Lode, 1982, 101m, ★★½/$$, Vestron/Vestron. A gold miner has to protect his stake from other miners and looters. Charlton Heston, Nick Mancuso, Kim Basinger. w. Fraser Clarke Heston, Peter Snell, d. Charlton Heston.
WESTERNS: Men in Conflict; Gold Mining; Mining Towns

Mother Love, 1991, 160m, ★★★½/$$$, BBC-PBS/NA. A doting mother (Diana Rigg) loves her son (James Wilby) so much that she begins to plot against everyone who takes him away from her.
SUSPENSE: DRAMA: Psychological Thriller; Psychological Drama; **MURDER:** Murder-Clever; Perfect Crimes; Murders-One by One; Clever Plots & Endings; Mothers and Sons; Jealousy; British; Miniseries
(Leaver Her to Heaven; The Girl Most Likely to . . . ; Mother's Boys)

Mother's Boys, 1994, 95m, ★★/$, CBS-Miramax/Touchstone, R/P-S-V. Mother is a rich psycho who's returned to reclaim her children after leaving to marry a rich man who's now disappeared from the scene. Unfortunately, mother has a strange thing for oldest son and wants dad's new flame snuffed out. Jamie Lee Curtis, Peter Gallagher, Vanessa Redgrave, Joanne Whalley-Kilmer, Luke Edwards. w. Richard Hawley, Barry Schneider, d. Yves Simoneau.
HORROR: SUSPENSE: Psychological Thrillers; Psycho Killers; **MURDER:** Mothers-Troublesome; Stalkers; Evil Women; Incest; Mothers & Sons; Mama's Boys; Women Fighting Over Men; Custody Battles; Parents vs. Children; Kill the Beast; Rogue Plots; Coulda Been Good; Child Protagonists
HORROR FLIPSIDE TO: Kramer vs. Kramer.
(Ed: What could have been an interesting thriller is just a preposterous but very good looking mess with a good central performance from the son)

Mother Wore Tights, 1947, 109m, ★★★/$$$, 20th/NA. A family reminisces about their life on the vaudeville stage. Betty Grable, Dan Dailey, Mona Freeman, Connie Marshall, Vanessa Brown, Robert Arthur. w. Lamar Trotti, NF-adap. Miriam Young, d. Walter Lang.
COMEDY DRAMA: Family Comedy; Vaudeville; Comedians; Dancers; Nostalgia; Memories; Flashbacks

Mothra, 1962, 101m, ★★★/$$, Ind/Goodtimes, G. A giant insect-caterpillar thing invades Tokyo to rescue twin princesses, before evolving into a giant moth. Yumi Ito, Frankie Sakai. d. Inoshiro Honda.
SCI-FI: HORROR: Spoofs-Horror; Monsters-Animal; Monsters-Mutant; Insects; Rescue Adventure; Kidnappings; Princesses; Camp; Cult Films
(Godzilla; What's Up Tiger Lily?)

Mouchette, 1960, 80m, ★★★½/$, Ind/Facets. An adolescent girl seeks an escape from her alcoholic father and terminally ill mother by contemplating suicide. Nadine Nortier, Maria Cardinal. d. Robert Bresson.
DRAMA: TRAGEDY: Girls; Character Studies; Teenagers; Family Drama; Suicidal Tendencies; Death-Dealing with;

Alcoholics; French Films; French New Wave; Forgotten Films; Hidden Gems (The Bell Jar)

Moulin Rouge, 1952, 123m, ★★★★/$$$$, Romulus-UA/MGM-UA. The life story of diminutive painter Henri de Toulouse-Lautrec (Jose Ferrer, BActor) and the many beautiful women (Colette Marchand, BSActress) (Zsa Zsa Gabor) he encountered in his tortured but beautiful vision of the world. w. John Huston, Anthony Veiller, N-adap. Pierre La Mure, d. John Huston (BDirector). BPicture, BCArt, BEdit. Oscars: 6-1.
DRAMA: Character Studies; Biographies; Artists; Paris; Romance-Reunited; Love-First; Obsessions; Lyrical Films; Little People-Midgets; Disabled People; Prostitutes-High Class; Dancers; Nightclubs; Production Design-Outstanding
(Lust for Life; An American in Paris; Moon and Sixpence; Cyrano de Bergerac)
(Ed: A gorgeous must-see film with beautiful images and music)

The Mountain, 1956, 105m, ★★★/$$, Par/Par. A plane crash in a remote mountain pass becomes the center of conflict for two brothers, one who wants to loot it and one who must stop him. Spencer Tracy, Robert Wagner, Claire Trevor, William Demarest, E. G. Marshall. w. Ranald MacDougall, N-adap. Henri Troyat, d. Edward Dmytryk.
ADVENTURE: Survival Drama; Rescue Drama; Airplane Crashes; Heist Stories; Thieves; Brothers; Men in Conflict; Ethics; Mountain Climbing; Forgotten Films

The Mountain Eagle (Fear O' God), 1926, 72m, ★★½/$$, Gainsborough/NA. A girl gets fed up with slick city guys and falls in love with a mountain man. Nita Naldi, Bernard Goetzke, Malcolm Keene. w. Eliot Stannard, d. Alfred Hitchcock.
COMEDY DRAMA: ROMANCE: Runaways; City vs. Country; Young Women; Mountain People; Female Protagonists; Silent Films
(Ed: Notable only as early Hitchcock, and certainly not like what he's known for)

Mountains of the Moon, 1990, 140m, ★★★/$, Col/Live, PG-13/V. Two Victorian explorers leave comfort at home to find the beginning of the Nile River in deepest, darkest Africa. Patrick Bergin, Iain Glenn, Fiona Shaw, Richard E. Grant, Roger Rees. w. d. Bob Rafelson, N-adap. William Harrison, Burton and Speake.

DRAMA: ADVENTURE: Journies; Explorers; Africa; River Trauma; 1800s; Hidden Gems; Overlooked at Release; Outstanding Scenery
(Burke and Wills; The Man Who Would Be King)

Mourning Becomes Electra, 1947, 170m, ★★★¹/₂/$$, RKO/Turner. A Yankee family falls apart after the Civil War. Michael Redgrave (BActor), Rosalind Russell (BActress), Katina Paxinou, Kirk Douglas, Raymond Massey, Nancy Coleman. w. d. Dudley Nichols, P-adap. Eugene O'Neill, Sophocles.

DRAMA: TRAGEDY: MURDER: ROMANCE: Romance-Triangles; Family Drama; Mothers & Daughters; Parents vs. Children; Costume Drama; Civil War Era; Guilty Conscience; Stagelike Films; Literary Classic Adaptations
(The Little Foxes; Long Day's Journey into Night)

The Mouse That Roared, 1958, 83m, ★★★¹/₂/$$$, Col/RCA-Col. A small country in Europe declares war on the United States in order to get disaster relief aid to bail themselves out, but a bomb and a few other things complicate matters. Peter Sellers, Jean Seberg, Leo McKern, David Kossoff. w. Rober Macdougall, Stanley Mann, N-adap. Leonard Wibberley, d. Jack Arnold.

COMEDY: Comedy of Errors; Spoofs; Bombs-Atomic; Underdog Stories; Multiple Performances; Queens; Men as Women; Kingdoms; Power Struggles; British Films
(Kind Hearts and Coronets; After the Fox)

Move, 1970, 88m, ★★★/$, 20th/NA. An unsuccessful playwright starts writing pornography and makes enough money to move into a bigger apartment. But once he gets there he's haunted by his choice. Elliott Gould, Paula Prentiss, Genevieve Waite. w. Joel Lieber, Stanley Hart, N-adap. Joel Lieber, d. Stuart Rosenberg.

DRAMA: Writers; Pornography World; Decisions-Big; Ethics; Sexuality; 1970s; Sexual Revolution; Time Capsules; Coulda Been Great; Good Premise Unfulfilled; Forgotten Films; Overlooked at Release
(Hi, Mom!; Is There Sex After Death?)

Move Over, Darling, 1963, 103m, ★★★¹/₂/$$$$, U/MCA-U. A woman marooned on a remote tropical island for five years is rescued and returns to her husband. Trouble is, he just remarried. Doris Day, James Garner, Polly Bergen,

Thelma Ritter, Chuck Connors. w. Hal Kanter, Jack Sher, d. Michael Gordon.

COMEDY: ROMANCE: FARCE: Romantic Comedy; Marriage Comedy; Romance-Triangles; Return of Spouse; Missing Persons; Bigamy; Romance-Bickering; Romance-Reunited; Custody Battles; Divorce; Engagements-Breaking
(My Favorite Wife; Too Many Husbands; Our Wife; Three for the Show)

Movers and Shakers, 1985, 79m, ★★¹/₂/$, MGM/MGM-UA, PG/P. Hollywood types live out their neurotic lives, their domestic problems often upstaging or intermingling with the problems on the set. Walter Matthau, Charles Grodin, Vincent Gardenia, Tyne Daly, Gilda Radner, Steve Martin. w. Charles Grodin, d. William Asher.

SATIRE: COMEDY DRAMA: Comedy-Light; Hollywood Satire; Hollywood Life; Moviemaking; Directors; Writers; Actresses; Actors; Wives-Troublesome; Coulda Been Good; All-Star Casts
(The Big Picture; Grand Canyon)

Movie Movie, 1978, 106m, ★★¹/₂/$, ITC/Fox, PG/V. A double bill in the thirties style with a boxing picture *(Dynamite Hands)* and a dance revue a la Busby Berkeley *(Baxter's Beauties of 1933)*. George C. Scott, Trish Van Devere, Red Buttons, Eli Wallach, Michael Kidd, Barbara Harris, Barry Bostwick, Art Carney. w. Larry Gelbart, Sheldon Keller, d. Stanley Donen.

MELODRAMA: COMEDY DRAMA: MUSI-CALS: Sports Movies; Dance Movies; Boxing; Multiple Stories; 1930s; Nostalgia

Moving, 1988, 89m, ★★/$, WB/WB. A black traffic cop moves, with great chaos, from New Jersey to Idaho, where his style doesn't fit the substance. Richard Pryor, Beverly Todd, Randy Quaid, Dave Thomas, Dana Carvey, Morris Day. w. Andy Breckman, d. Alan Metter.

COMEDY: Fish out of Water Stories; Police Stories; Police Comedy; Life Transitions; Black Men; City vs. Country; House Havoc; Good Premise Unfulfilled
(Critical Condition; Bustin' Loose)

Moving Violation, 1976, 91m, ★★¹/₂/$$, 20th-AIP/Fox. A sheriff in a small town committs a murder. He would get off, but a group of teenagers witnessed it. Now he must hunt them down and shut them up for good. Stephen McHattie, Kay Lenz, Eddie Albert. w. David R. Osterhout, William Norton, d. Charles S. Dubin.

ACTION: MURDER: Police Corruption; Murder-Witness; Fugitives from the Law; Fugitives from a Murderer; Rednecks
(I Saw What You Did)

Moving Violations, 1985, 90m, ★★¹/₂/$$, 20th/Fox, PG-13/P-S. The idiots who attend traffic school are almost as stupid as the cops running it. John Murray, Jennifer Tilly, James Keach. w. Neal Israel, Pat Proft, d. Neal Israel.

COMEDY: Comedy-Slapstick; Comedy-Skit; Police Comedy; Car Wrecks; Car Chases; Fools-Bumbling; Coulda Been Good
(License to Drive; Police Academy)
(Ed: Bad, but a few big laughs)

Mr. and Mrs. Bridge, 1990, 124m, ★★★¹/₂/$, MI-Cineplex-Miramax/HBO, PG. The story of a stern, by-the-book couple living in Depression-era Kansas City, also covering their children's lives and in particular Mr. Bridge's inability to change or Mrs. Bridge's inability to cope completely. Paul Newman, Joanne Woodward (BActress), Kyra Sedgwick, Robert Sean Leonard, Blythe Danner, Simon Callow. w. Ruth Prawer Jhabvala, N-adap. Evan S. Connell, d. James Ivory. Oscars: 1-0.

DRAMA: COMEDY DRAMA: Family Drama; Marriage Drama; Character Studies; Parents vs. Children; Ordinary People Stories; Depression Era; Lawyers; Stern Men; Quiet Little Films; Midwestern Life; Hidden Gems; Overlooked at Release
(Nobody's Fool; Rachel, Rachel)

Mr. and Mrs. North, 1941, 68m, ★★¹/₂/$$, MGM/NA. A couple finds a dead body in their closet and the farce begins. Gracie Allen, William Post, Paul Kelly. w. S. K. Lauren, P-adap. Owen Davis, d. Robert Sinclair.

COMEDY: MURDER: MYSTERY: MUR-DER MYSTERY: Comic Mystery; Murder-Discovering; Spoofs-Detective; Detective Couples; Detectives-Amateur; Hide the Dead Body
(A Night to Remember; Thin Man SERIES)

Mr. and Mrs. Smith, 1941, 95m, ★★★/$$, RKO/Turner. A loving married couple in high society finds out their bethrothal wasn't legal, causing them to question everything. Carole Lombard, Robert Montgomery, Gene Raymond, Jack Carson, Lucile Watson. w. Norman Krasna, d. Alfred Hitchcock.

COMEDY DRAMA: ROMANCE: Romantic Comedy; Marriage Comedy; Mix-Ups; Marriages-Fake; Marriage on the Rocks (Guest Wife; Easy to Wed)
(Ed: Worth primarily to Hitchcock fans as a curious attempt at comedy that only makes it halfway)

Mr. Arkadin (Confidential Report), 1955, 99m, ★★1/2/$, Ind/NA. A tycoon in Spain hires an expatriot American detective to find his former associates. After he finds each one, they end up mysteriously dead. Orson Welles, Michael Redgrave, Katina Paxinou, Akim Tamiroff, Mischa Auer, Patricia Medina, Jack Watling, Peter Van Eyck, Paola Mori, Robert Arden. w. d. Orson Welles.
DRAMA: Psychological Drama; Mind-games; Conspiracy; **MURDER:** Missing Persons; Detective Stories; Murders-One by One; Writer-Directors; Spain; Curiosities
(Journey into Fear; The Third Man)

Mr. Belvedere Goes to College, 1949, 88m, ★★★/$$, 20th/NA. The eccentric intellectual babysitter of *Sitting Pretty* heads back to campus. Clifton Webb, Shirley Temple, Alan Young. w. Richard Sale, Mary Loos, Mary McCall, d. Elliott Nugent.
COMEDY: Romance-Middle-Aged; College Life; Back to School; Babysitters; Eccentric People; Widows
SEQUEL TO: Sitting Pretty; **SEQUEL:** Mr. Belvedere Rings the Bell.

Mr. Belvedere Rings the Bell, 1951, 87m, ★★1/2/$, 20th/NA. Mr. B. heads to a poor house of elderly people to test his theories of aging. Clifton Webb, Joanne Dru, Hugh Marlowe, Zero Mostel. w. Ronald MacDougall, P-adap. Robert McEnroe (*The Silver Whistle*), d. Henry Koster.
COMEDY: Elderly People; Eccentric People; Lonely People

Mr. Billion, 1977, 93m, ★★1/2/$$, 20th/Fox, R/S-V-P. A young man has to get to Frisco in order to get an inheritance with a lot of stipulations, but first he has to get the mob off of his tail. Terence Hill, Valerie Perrine, Jack Gleason, Slim Pickens, William Redfield, Chill Wills. w. Ken Friedman, Johnathan Kaplan, d. Jonathan Kaplan.
ACTION: Chase Movies; Inheritances at Stake; Heirs; Road Movies; Car Chases; San Francisco

Mr. Blandings Builds His Dream House, 1948, 84m, ★★★1/2/$$$, RKO/Turner. An ad executive in post-war crowded Manhattan decides to move to country Connecticut and buy an ancient but quaint fixer-upper that becomes much more of a nightmare than he ever dreamed. Cary Grant, Myrna Loy, Melvyn Douglas, Reginald Denny, Louise Beavers, Jason Robards. w. Norman Panama, Melvin Frank, N-adap. Eric Hodgins, d. H. C. Potter.
COMEDY: Comedy of Errors; Fish out of Water Stories; City vs. Country; Advertising World; New York Life; Rural Life; Nightmares; House Havoc
REMAKE/RIPOFFS: The Money Pit; Baby Boom.
(The Money Pit; Geoerge Washington Slept Here; In Society; Baby Boom; Mr. Hobbs Takes a Vacation)

Mister Buddwing, 1966, 99m, ★★★/$$, MGM/MGM-UA. A man wakes up on a bench and can't remember who he is or how he got there and proceeds to meet a cast of characters who lead him through his past and back home. James Garner, Katharine Ross, Suzanne Pleshette, Jean Simmons, Angela Lansbury, Jack Gilford. w. Dale Wasserman, N-adap, Evan Hunter, d. Delbert Mann.
DRAMA: MYSTERY: Psychological Drama; Amnesia; Character Studies; Multiple Stories; Flashbacks; Memories; Eccentric People; Journies; New York Life; Time Capsules; Coulda Been Great; Hidden Gems; Forgotten Films
(Hysteria; Mirage)
(Ed: An abrupt ending seems too pat for all the mystery and interest before. The character turns by the actress are very good)

Mister Cory, 1957, 92m, ★★1/2/$$, U/NA. A mobster tries to get into the country club life in the suburbs. Tony Curtis, Martha Hyer, Kathryn Grant, Charles Bickford. w. d. Blake Edwards.
COMEDY: COMEDY DRAMA: Fish out of Water Stories; Mob Stories; Starting Over; Gambling; Country Club Life; Suburban Life; City vs. Country; Writer-Directors
(My Blue Heaven; The Little Giant)

Mr. Deeds Goes to Town, 1936, ★★★1/2/$$$, Col/RCA-Col. When a small-town poet inherits a million dollars he becomes a celebrity and folk hero. Gary Cooper (BActor), Jean Arthur, Raymond Walburn, Lionel Stander, H. B. Warner. w. Robert Riskin (BScr), SS-adap. Clarence Budington Kelland

(*Opera Hat*), d. Frank Capra (**BDirector**). BPicture. Oscars: 4-0.
COMEDY: SATIRE: COMEDY DRAMA: Heroes-Ordinary; Writers; Poets; American Myth; Capra-esque
(Mr. Smith Goes to Washington; Meet John Doe)

Mr. Destiny, 1990, 105m, ★★/$, Touchstone/Touchstone, PG-13/P. A failed baseball player has a guardian angel who helps him live out his dreams. Jim Belushi, Michael Caine, Linda Hamilton, Jon Lovitz, Hart Bochner, Rene Russo. w. James Orr, Jim Cruikshank, d. James Orr.
COMEDY: Fantasy; Sports Movies; Baseball; Dreams; Angels; Midlife Crisis; Good Premise Unfulfilled
(Angels in the Outfield; Field of Dreams)

Mr. Drake's Duck, 1950, 85m, ★★★/$$, Fairbanks-Ind/NA. A duck lays an egg that has uranium in it somehow and soon every government wants it. Douglas Fairbanks, Jr., Yolande Donlan, Wilfrid Hyde White. w. d. Val Guest.
COMEDY DRAMA: SATIRE: Animal Stories; Animals in Jeopardy; Government as Enemy; Nuclear Energy; Writer-Directors
(The Million Dollar Duck)

Mister 880, 1950, 90m, ★★★/$$, 20th/NA. An old man is a counterfeiter with the treasury department after him. Edmund Gwenn (BSActor), Burt Lancaster, Dorothy McGuire. w. Robert Riskin, d. Edmund Goulding.
COMEDY: Fugitives from the Law; Counterfeiters; Eccentric People; Elderly Men; Hidden Gems; Forgotten Films
(Miracle on 34th Street [1947]; Paris Holiday)

Mr. Forbush & The Penguins, 1971, 101m, ★★/$, EMI/NA. A scientist has a crisis then awakening on a trip to study wildlife in Antarctica. John Hurt, Hayley Mills, Tony Britton. w. Anthony Shaffer, N-adap. Graham Billy, d. Roy Boulting.
DRAMA: ADVENTURE: Character Studies; Anarctica; Scientists; Animal Stories

Mister Frost, 1990, 104m, ★★/$, Ind/Imperial. An emissary of Satan goes after a doctor and makes his life hell. Jeff Goldblum, Alan Bates, Kathy Baker, Jean-Pierre Cassell. w. Phillippe Setbon, Brad Lynch, d. Phillippe Setbon.

DRAMA: SUSPENSE: HORROR: Selling One's Soul; Satan; Malicious Menaces; Doctors

Mr. Hobbs Takes a Vacation, 1962, 116m, ★★★/$$, 20th/Fox. When a man takes his family out of the city for the summer, the house they planned to stay in is a disaster and his children run amok. James Stewart, Maureen O'Hara, Fabian, John Saxon, Reginald Gardiner, John McGiver. w. Nunnally Johnson, N-adap Edward Streeter, d. Henry Koster.

COMEDY DRAMA: FAMILY: Family Comedy; Summer Vacations; Vacations; Teenagers; Parents vs. Children (Dear Brigitte; Summer Rental)

Mr. Johnson, 1990, 101m, ★★★/$, Avenue/Live, PG. A young man in Africa during the 20s goes up against the British imperials there and finds himself at a crossroads. Pierce Brosnan, Edward Woodward, Maynard Eziashi. w. William Boyd, N-adap. Joyce Cary, d. Bruce Beresford.

DRAMA: Character Studies; Ordinary People Stories; Africa; Quiet Little Films; Overlooked at Release (A Good Man in Africa; Taffin)

Mr. Jones, 1993, 102m, ★★1/2/$$, Col/Col, R/S-P. A manic depressive, but very attractive, man hits his midlife crisis hard by spazzing out and falling for his tough psychiatrist. But will this keep him from jumping off of the roof? Richard Gere, Lena Olin, Delroy Lindo, Anne Bancroft, Tom Irwin. w. Eric Roth, Michael Cristofer, d. Mike Figgis.

COMEDY DRAMA: ROMANCE: Romantic Drama; Psychiatrists; Romance with Psychologist; Mental Illness; Nervous Breakdowns; Free Spirits; Coulda Been Great (Charly; Frankie and Johnny; Breathless)

Mr. Klein, 1975, 122m, ★★★/$, Ind/Col, PG. When Jews escape France during the war, Mr. Klein buys valuables and art treasures for practically nothing, but then the tables are turned when he's mistaken as a Jew because a man has been using his identity. Alain Delon, Jeanne Moreau. d. Joseph Losey.

DRAMA: SATIRE: Jewish People; Identities-Mistaken; Nazi Stories; World War II Stories; Jews-Saving; Ethics; Dose of Own Medicine-Given; Turning the Tables; Hidden Gems; Clever Plots & Endings

Mr. Lucky, 1943, 98m, ★★★/$$$, RKO/Turner. A gambling man changes his angle and organizes a relief effort for war-torn Britain. Cary Grant, Laraine Day, Charles Bickford, Gladys Cooper, Henry Stephenson. w. Milton Holmes, Adrian Scott, d. H. C. Potter.

COMEDY DRAMA: MELODRAMA: ROMANCE: Romantic Comedy; Gambling; World War II Stories; Patriotic Films
REMAKE: Gambling House. **TV SERIES:** Mr. Lucky, 1958.

Mr. Mom, 1983, 91m, ★★★/$$$$, 20th/Vestron, PG. When a man is laid off, his wife goes back into advertising to pay the bills, leaving him at home to do the chores and deal with the kids. Michael Keaton, Teri Garr, Ann Jillian, Freddy Koehler, Martin Mull. w. John Hughes, d. Stan Dragoti.

COMEDY: Comedy-Slapstick; Comedy-Domestic; Suburban Life; Role Reversal; Male in Female Domain; Men as Women; Parents vs. Children; Career Women; Unemployment; Making a Living; Advertising World (Uncle Buck; Gung Ho)

Mr. Music, 1950, 113m, ★★1/2/$$, Par/NA. A songwriter has trouble concentrating and gets a young female assistant who's supposed to see to it he works, but of course, he mostly thinks about her. Bing Crosby, Nancy Olson, Charles Coburn, Ruth Hussey, Marge & Gower Champion, Peggy Lee, Groucho Marx. w. Arthur Sheekman, d. Richard Haydn.

MUSICALS: COMEDY: ROMANCE: Romantic Comedy; Romance-Older Men/Younger Women; Romance with Servant; Servants; Musicians
MUSICAL REMAKE OF: Accent on Youth

Mr. Nanny, 1993, 85m, ★★/$$, Col/Col, PG. A big wrestler who does not like children much winds up guarding two. Hulk Hogan, Sherman Hemsley, Mother Love, Madeline Zima. w. Ed Rugoff, Michael Gottlieb, d. Gottlieb.

COMEDY: ACTION: Action Comedy; Bodyguards; Men and Boys; Babysitters; Wrestling; Suburban Life; Fish out of Water Stories; Coulda Been Good (Kindergarten Cop)

Mr. North, 1988, 93m, ★★★/$, Hemdale/Hemdale, PG. A proper young man comes to the wealthy seaside resort of Newport in the roaring 20s and claims to be a faith healer. Anthony

Edwards, Lauren Bacall, Robert Mitchum, Harry Dean Stanton, Anjelica Huston, Mary Stuart Masterson, Virginia Madsen, David Warner, Tammy Grimes. w. Janet Roach, John Huston, James Costigan, N-adap. Thornton Wilder (Theophilus North), d. Danny Huston.

COMEDY DRAMA: SATIRE: Con Artists; Faith Healers; Magic; Magic Realism; Rich People; Charismatic People; Young Men; Resorts; 1920s; Female Screenwriters

Mr. Peabody and the Mermaid, 1948, 89m, ★★/$$, U/Republic. A man bored with his marriage fantasizes about an affair with a mermaid. William Powell, Ann Blyth, Irene Hervey. w. Nunnally Johnson, N-adap. Guy and Constance Jones, d. Irving Pichel.

COMEDY: ROMANCE: Romantic Comedy; Midlife Crisis; Fantasies; Mermaids; Illusions
REMAKE/RETREAD OF: Miranda (Miranda; Mad About Men; Splash!)

Mister Quilp, see The Old Curiosity Shop.

Mister Roberts, 1955, 123m, ★★★★/$$$$$, WB/WB. Relations between the sailors on a ship during World War II are tense and funny as they find amusing ways to deal with their stir-craziness. Henry Fonda, James Cagney, William Powell, Jack Lemmon (BSActor), Phil Carey, Betsy Palmer, Ward Bond. w. Frank Nugent, Joshua Logan, P-adap. Thomas Heggen and Joshua Logan, N-adap. Heggen, d. John Ford, Mervyn LeRoy. BPicture, BSound. Oscars: 3-0.

COMEDY: Military Movies; Military Comedy; Friendships-Male; Ships; Sailors; Novel and Play Adaptations (Ensign Pulver; The Wackiest Ship in the Army)

Mr. Saturday Night, 1992, 118m, ★★1/2/$, Col/Col, PG. The life story of a fictitious Jewish comedian on the Borscht Belt comedy circuit in the Catskills; from his rise to his twilight years. Billy Crystal, David Paymer (BSActor), Julie Warner, Helen Hunt, Ron Silver, Jerry Orbach. w. Billy Crystal, Babaloo Mandel, Lowell Ganz, d. Crystal. Oscars: 1-0.

COMEDY DRAMA: Biographies-Fictional; Comedians; Fame-Rise to; Episodic Stories; Brothers; Jewish

People; Comedy-Character; Actor Directors; Saturday Night Live Movies (The Sunshine Boys; City Slickers)

Mr. Smith Goes to Washington, 1939, 129m, ★★★★/$$$$. A young Congressman decides to go against the Washington machine and expose corruption, regardless of its impact on him. James Stewart (BActor), Claude Rains (BSActor), Jean Arthur, Thomas Mitchell, Edward Arnold, Harry Carey (BSActor), Guy Kibbee, H. B. Warner, Beulah Bondi. w. Sidney Buchman (BScr), Lewis Foster (**BOStory**), d. Frank Capra (BDirector). BPicture, BScore, BArt. Oscars: 9-1.

COMEDY DRAMA: Political Drama; **SATIRE:** Politicians; Corruption; Corruption-Political; Whistleblowers; Fighting The System; Young Men; Washington D.C.; American Myth; Capra-esque

REMAKE/RIPOFF: The Distinguished Gentleman.

(Mr. Deeds Goes to Town; It's a Wonderful Life; The Distinguished Gentleman)

Mr. Wonderful, 1993, 99m, ★★¹/₂/$, WB/WB, PG-13/S. A man tries to marry off his botanist ex-wife so he can invest the alimony money. Matt Dillon, Annabella Sciorra, William Hurt, Mary Louise Parker, Vincent D'Onfrio. w. Amy Schor, Vicki Polon, d. Anthony Minghella.

COMEDY DRAMA: Marriage Comedy; Marrying Again; Divorce; Finding New Mate for Spouse; Dating Scene; Starting Over

(Move Over, Darling)

Mrs. Brown, You've Got a Lovely Daughter, 1968, 95m, ★★¹/₂/$, MGM/MGM-UA. A London rock singer inherits a champion greyhound racer dog and heads to the track. Peter Noone & Herman's Hermits, Stanley Holloway, Mona Washbourne. w. Thaddeus Vane, d. Saul Swimmer.

COMEDY: Rock Stars; Heirs; Gambling; Pet Stories; Dogs; Mod Era; Time Capsules; Song Titles

(The Knack; Smashing Time; Help!)

Mrs. Doubtfire, 1993, 120m, ★★★/$$$$$$, 20th/Fox, PG/P. A loving dad (Robin Williams) and unemployed actor loses custody of his kids, so he masquerades as a British nanny and is unwittingly hired by his ex-wife (Sally Field), until his cover of great makeup is blown.

Pierce Brosnan. w. Leslie Dixon, N-adap. Anne (Alias Mrs. Doubtfire), d. Chris Columbus. BMakeup. Oscars: 1-1.

COMEDY: COMEDY DRAMA: FAMILY: CHILDREN'S: Family Comedy; Comedy-Slapstick; Tearjerkers; Divorce; Custody Battles; Actors; Fathers Alone; Impostors; Disguises; Elderly Women; San Francisco; Blockbusters

RETELLING OF: Tootsie.

(Ed: Some really big laughs, but ultimately fluffy contrived stuff on acid de Williams)

Mrs. Miniver, 1942, 134m, ★★★¹/₂/$$$$, MGM/MGM-UA. A woman during World War II in England survives everything triumphantly, despite the odds. Greer Garson (**BActress**), Walter Pidgeon (**BActor**), Teresa Wright (**BSActress**), Dame May Whitty (BSActress), Richard Ney, Reginald Owen, Henry Travers (BSActor). w. Arthur Wimperis, George Froeschel, James Hilton, Claudine West (**BAScr**), N-adap. Jan Struther, d. William Wyler (**BDirector**). **BPicture**, BEdit, BSFX, BSound, **BB&WCin**. Oscars: 12-6.

MELODRAMA: FAMILY: Family Drama; Tearjerkers; World War II Stories; War at Home; Saintly People; England; Female Protagonists; Faded Hits

SEQUEL: The Miniver Story.

(The Miniver Story; Hope and Glory; Since You Went Away)

(Ed: Another one of the handful of films nominated in all of the major Oscar categories)

Mrs. Parker and the Vicious Circle, 1994, 98m, ★★★/$, Fine Line/Fine Line, R/S-P. Famed and rapier-witted writer Dorothy Parker and her wild, high-style days of the twenties and thirties are detailed in this biopic, centering on her greatest romance and the inner turmoil which she hid with her humor. Jennifer Jason Leigh, Matthew Broderick, Campbell Scott. w. Alan Rudolph, Randy Sue Coburn, d. Rudolph.

COMEDY DRAMA: Biographies; **ROMANCE:** Romance-Reluctant; Writers; Hollywood Life; Hollywood Biographies; 1920s; 1930s; Comedians; Female Protagonists; Female Screenwriters; Overlooked at Release; Hidden Gems; Coulda Been Good

(Ed: Muddled in many ways)

Mrs. Parkington, 1944, 124m, ★★★/$$$, MGM/MGM-UA. Complications

arise for a wealthy woman when her maid marries an industrialist on the rise and tries to equal her former boss on the social circuit. Greer Garson (BActress), Walter Pidgeon, Edward Arnold, Agnes Moorehead (BSActress), Cecil Kellaway, Gladys Cooper, Peter Lawford. w. Robert Theoren, Polly James, N-adap. Louis Bromfield, d. Tay Garnett. Oscars: 2-0.

MELODRAMA: Social Climbing; Marrying Up; Marriage Drama; Turning the Tables; Rich People; Rich vs. Poor; Women in Conflict; Worker vs. Boss; Servants

(All About Eve; A Woman of Independent Means)

Mrs. Pollifax, Spy, 1970, 110m, ★★/$, Ind/NA. A middle-aged mother signs up at the CIA and is sent on a mission to Albania. Rosalind Russell, Darren McGavin. w. C. A. McKnight, N-adap. Dorothy Gilman, d. Leslie Martinson.

COMEDY DRAMA: Spy Films; Spies; Spies-Female; Secret Agents; CIA Agents; Camp; Unintentionally Funny

Mrs. Soffel, 1984, 110m, ★★★/$, MGM/MGM-UA, PG. A prison warden's wife, who ministers to prisoners, falls in love with a particularly handsome one who convinces her he's okay and prods her to help him escape and go on the lam with him. Diane Keaton, Mel Gibson, Matthew Modine, Edward Herrman, Trini Alvarado, Terry O'Quinn. w. Ron Nyswaner, d. Gillian Armstrong.

DRAMA: ROMANCE: Romantic Drama; Fugitives from the Law; Prison Escapes; Cheating Women; Missionaries; Dangerous Men; Romance-Dangerous; 1800s; True Stories; Female Protagonists; Female Directors

(Dead Man Walking)

Mrs. Wiggs of the Cabbage Patch, 1934, 80m, ★★★/$$, Par/Goodtimes. A poor family in the country tries to live respectably during the Depression. Pauline Lord, Zasu Pitts, W. C. Fields, Evelyn Venable, Donald Meek. w. William Slavens McNutt, Jane Storm, N-adap. Alice Hegan Rice, d. Norman Taurog.

REMAKE: 1942

COMEDY DRAMA: Family Comedy; Family Drama; Ensemble Films; Poor People; Rural Life; Depression Era

(Room for One More; Mother Carey's Chickens)

The Mudlark, 1950, 98m, ★★★/$$, 20th/NA. Queen Victoria has been holed up in her castle, *incommunicado* for fifteen years when a spunky working-class boy from a shipping community makes a pilgrimage to see her and charms her out of isolation. Alec Guinness, Irene Dunne, Andrew Ray, Anthony Steel, Finlay Currie, Edward Rigby. w. Nunnally Johnson, N-adap. Theodore Bonnet, d. Jean Negulesco.

COMEDY DRAMA: MELODRAMA: Ordinary People Stories; Working Class; Rich vs. Poor; Queens; Royalty; What If . . . Stories; England
(Elizabeth and Essex; The Virgin Queen)

The Mummy, 1932, 72m, ★★★/$$$, U/MCA-U. When an archaeologist unwittingly instigates a prophecy and brings an Egyptian pharaoh back to life, the mummy seeks out a woman who reminds him of his queen. Boris Karloff, Zita Johann, David Manners, Arthur Byron. w. John I. Balderston, d. Karl Freund.

HORROR: Mummies; Romance-Boy Wants Girl; Human Monsters; Dead-Back from the; Egypt; Archaeologists; Stalkers

The Mummy, 1959, 88m, ★★★/$$$, Hammer-WB/WB. In merry old England, a mummy brought back from Egypt by a team of archaeologists starts killing pretty young things. Peter Cushing, Christopher Lee, Yvonne Furneaux, Eddie Byrne. w. Jimmy Sangster, d. Terence Fisher.

HORROR: Mummies; MURDER: Murders-One by One; Murders of Women; Serial Killers; Human Monsters; Dead-Back from the; Egypt; Archaeologists; Stalkers

The Mummy's Hand, 1940, 67m, ★★★/$$, U/MCA-U. A modern cult revolving around the myths of ancient Egypt revives a mummy and seeks revenge on the archaeologists who desecrated his tomb. Dick Foran, Wallace Ford, George Zucco, Cecil Kellaway, Peggy Moran, Eduardo Ciannelli. w. Griffin Jay, Maxwell Shane, d. Christy Cabanne.

HORROR: Mummies; MURDER: Murders-One by One; Revenge; Human Monsters; Dead-Back from the; Egypt; Archaeologists; Stalkers

The Mummy's Shroud, 1966, 84m, ★★/$, Hammer-MGM/NA. A mummy who is revived kills those who unearthed him. John Phillips, Andre Morell, David Buck, Elizabeth Sellars. w. d. John Gilling.

HORROR: Mummies; MURDER: Murders-One by One; Human Monsters; Dead-Back from the; Egypt;

Archaeologists; Stalkers; Writer-Directors
Munchausen; see **Adventures of Baron Munchausen.**

A Muppet Christmas Carol, 1992, 120m, ★★★/$$, Disney/Disney, G. A retelling of *A Christmas Carol* with the Muppets. Michael Caine. d. Brian Henson.
COMEDY: MUSICALS: Musical Comedy; Fantasy; Puppets; Muppets; CHILDREN'S: FAMILY: Revisionist Films; Ghosts; Christmas; Stern Men; Evil Men; Redemption; Nightmares; Death-Impending; Turning the Tables; Message Films

The Muppet Movie, 1979, 94m, ★★★¹/₂/$$$$, ITC-AFD/Fox, G. Kermit & Fozzie hit the road to Hollywood and meet all of the other muppets, particularly Miss Piggy, along the way, singing songs and evading a frog-leg hunter. Steve Martin, Carol Kane, Madeline Kahn, Edgar Bergen, Milton Berle, Paul Williams, Charles Durning, Cloris Leachman, Orson Welles, Bob Hope, Dom DeLuise, Mel Brooks. d. James Frawley. BOSong. Oscars: 1-0.
COMEDY: MUSICALS: Musical Comedy; Fantasy; Puppets; Muppets; CHILDREN'S: FAMILY: Road Movies; Road to California; Animals in Jeopardy; All-Star Cameos; TV Series Movies

The Muppets Take Manhattan, 1984, 94m, ★★★/$$$, 20th/Fox, G. The Muppets head to Broadway with their show but have to fight off the perils of showbiz. Dabney Coleman, James Coco, Joan Rivers, Gregory Hines, Brooke Shields, Liza Minnelli. d. Frank Oz.
COMEDY: MUSICALS: Musical Comedy; Fantasy; Puppets; Muppets; CHILDREN'S: FAMILY: Theater Life; Putting on a Show; All-Star Cameos

Murder, 1930, 92m, ★★★/$$, British International/Republic. In the murder trial of a young woman only one juror believes in her innocence and sets out to find the real killer. Herbert Marshall, Norah Baring, Phyllis Konstam, Edward Chapman, Miles Mander. w. Alma Reville, N-adap. Clemence Dane, Helen Simpson (*Enter Sir John*), d. Alfred Hitchcock.
SUSPENSE: MURDER: MYSTERY: MURDER MYSTERY: Courtroom Drama; Murder-Finding the Real Killer; Unbelieved; Female Protagonists; Detectives-Amateur; Hitchcockian
(Blackmail; Stagefright; Trial by Jury)

Murder Ahoy, 1964, 74m, ★★★/$$, MGM/MGM-UA. When a naval cadet officer in training is killed, Mrs. Marple comes aboard to investigate. Margaret Rutherford, Lionel Jeffries, Stringer Davis, Charles Tingwell. w. David Pursall, Jack Seddon, N-adap. Agatha Christie, d. George Pollock.
MYSTERY: MURDER: MURDER MYSTERY: Detective Stories; Detectives-Female; Mystery-Whodunit?; British Films; Agatha Christie

Murder at the Gallop, 1963, 81m, ★★★/$$, MGM/MGM-UA. It's reported that an elderly man was frightened to death by his cat. But to Mrs. Marple this explanation seems a bit fishy. Margaret Rutherford, Flora Robson, Robert Morley, Stringer Davis. w. James P. Cavanagh, N-adap. Agatha Christie (*After the Funeral*), d. George Pollock.
MYSTERY: MURDER: MURDER MYSTERY: Detective Stories; Detectives-Female; Mystery-Whodunit?; British Films; Agatha Christie

Murder at the Vanities, 1934, 95m, ★★★/$$, Par/MCA-U. A backstage murder mystery at Earl Carroll's Vanities causes everyone to wonder about each other. Jack Oakie, Victor McLaglen, Carl Brisson, Kitty Carlisle, Dorothy Stickney, Gertrude Michael. w. Carey Wilson, Joseph Gollomb, Sam Hellman, d. Mitchell Leisen.
MYSTERY: MURDER: MURDER MYSTERY: Comic Mystery; MUSICALS: Dancers; Ensemble Films; Theater Life; Behind the Scenes

Murder by Death, 1976, 94m, ★★★★/$$$$, Col/RCA-Col, PG/P. An international group of top detectives are invited by an eccentric tycoon to his secluded mansion and must figure out the most complicated and farcical of murder plots imaginable. Peter Falk, Alec Guiness, Peter Sellers, Truman Capote, Elsa Lanchester, Eileen Brennan, James Coco, David Niven, Maggie Smith, Nancy Walker. w. Neil Simon, d. Robert Moore.
COMEDY: FARCE: Spoofs; Spoofs-Detective; MYSTERY: MURDER: MURDER MYSTERY: Detective Stories; Detectives-Female; Mystery-Whodunit?; Ensemble Films; Murder-Invitation to; All-Star Casts; Blockbusters
(The Cheap Detective)

Murder by Decree, 1978, 112m, ★★★/$$, Avco/New Line, PG. While

investigating the Jack the Ripper murders, Sherlock Holmes unearths a secret society behind the killings. Christopher Plummer, James Mason, Anthony Quale, David Hemmings, Susan Clark, John Gielgud, Donald Sutherland, Genevieve Bujold. w. John Hopkins, d. Bob Clark.
MYSTERY: MURDER: MURDER MYSTERY: Detective Stories; Mystery-Whodunit?; Serial Killers; Trail of a Killers; Jack the Ripper; Occult; Sherlock Holmes
(Crucifer of Blood; The Seven-Percent Solution)
Murder by Natural Causes, 1979, 96m, ★★★1/2/$$$, CBS/MCA-U. A woman and her sexy lover plot to kill her older husband by provoking a heart attack, but the joke may be on them. Katharine Ross, Barry Bostwick, Hal Holbrook, Richard Anderson.
w. Levinson & Link, d. Robert Day.
SUSPENSE: Psychological Thriller; **MURDER:** Murder of Spouse; Cheating Women; Romance-Triangles; Death-Accidental; Double Crossings; Clever Plots & Endings; Hidden Gems; TV Movies
(Guilty Conscience; Body Heat)
(Ed: Probably the best of all of the suspense murder TV movies by the *Columbo/Murder, She Wrote* producing team of Levinson & Link)
Murder by Phone, 1982, 79m, ★★/$, WB/WB, R/S-V. A professor's students are being killed by long distance. Richard Chamberlain, John Houseman, Sara Botsford. w. Michael Butler, John Kent Harrison, d. Michael Anderson.
HORROR: SUSPENSE: Telephone Terror; Professors; Flops-Major; Camp; Unintentionally Funny
(Telefon)
(Ed: From *Shogun* to this)
Murder by Television, 1935, 60m, ★★1/2/$, Imperial/Sinister, Nos. The inventor of the television is murdered and his twin brother takes over his life. Bela Lugosi, June Collyer, Huntley Gordon, George Meeker. w. Joseph O'Donnell, d. Clifford Sanforth.
HORROR: SCI-FI: MURDER: Twins; Lookalikes; Brothers; Identities-Assumed; TV Life; Forgotten Films
Murder, He Says, 1945, 91m, ★★★1/2/$$, Par/NA, AMC. An insurance salesman finds a family of hillbillies he thinks he can sucker out of their riches, but instead is forced to suffer all sorts of

indignities and marry their daughter-just before everyone starts glowing in the dark. Fred MacMurray, Marjorie Main, Helen Walker, Peter Whitney, Jean Heather.
w. Lou Breslow, d. George Marshall.
COMEDY: FARCE: MYSTERY: SCI-FI: Comic Mystery; Fish out of Water Stories; Mountain People; Hillbillies; Inheritances at Stake; Con Artists; Nuclear Radiation; Toxic Waste; Underrated; Hidden Gems
(The Egg & I; Ma and Pa Kettle)
Murder, Inc., 1960, 103m, ★★★/$$$, 20th/NA. Two crime organizations rise in Prohibition-era New York and an all-out gang war erupts. Stuart Whitman, Mai Britt, Henry Morgan, Peter Falk (BSActor), David J. Stewart. w. Irv Tunick, Mel Barr, d. Burt Balaban, Stuart Rosenberg. Oscars: 1-0.
ACTION: Action Drama; **COMEDY DRAMA:** Criminal Biographies; Mob Stories; Crime Drama; Mob Wars; Hitmen; Ensemble Films; Power-Rise to; Power Struggles; Bootleggers; Prohibition Era; True Stories
(Mobsters; The Untouchables)
Murder in New Hampshire, the Pamela Smart Story, 1991, 93m, ★★★/$$$$, Ind/Turner. The true story of the high school teacher who not only had an affair with a student but got him to kill her husband as well. Helen Hunt, Chad Allen, Larry Drake, Howard Hesseman, Ken Howard, Michael Learned. d. Joyce Chopra.
DRAMA: MURDER: Murderers-Female; Murder of Spouse; Romance-Unprofessional; Romance with Teacher; Teachers and Students; Hitmen; Liars; True Stories; Ordinary Person Turned Criminal; High School Life; Teenagers; Juvenile Delinquents; Female Directors
(To Die For; River's Edge; Fatal Vision)
Murder in Texas, 1981, 200m, ★★★/$$$, NBC-Ind/Hollywood Home Ent. A Texas society woman mysteriously dies and there are several possibilities as to how and why she died. Andy Griffith, Farrah Fawcett, Katharine Ross, Sam Elliott, Joan Collins, Craig T. Nelson. NF-adap. *Prescription Murder,* d. William Hale.
DRAMA: MURDER: MYSTERY: MURDER MYSTERY: Rich People; Texas; Doctors; Murder of Spouse; Evil Men; TV Movies; True Stories; Miniseries

Murder in the First, 1995, 122m, ★★★/$, WB/WB, R/P-V-MN. A youth who stole from a store with a post office substation in it was put away in Alcatraz, since it was technically a felony. He tried to escape but wound up in isolation for years. Then Norman Mailer campaigned for his release, which happened, but soon after, having been made a criminal in the system, he murdered a freed prisoner who informed against him in the escape attempt. But only a public defender believes he understands why and wants to help him. Christian Slater, Kevin Bacon, Gary Oldman, Embeth Davidtz, Brad Dourif, William H. Macy, F. Lee Ermey. w. Dan Gordon, d. Marc Rocco.
DRAMA: Prison Drama; Courtroom Drama; Torture; Accused Unjustly; **MURDER:** Government as Enemy; Flashbacks; True Stories; Alcatraz
(The Accused [1988]; Nuts; Criminal Law)
The Murder Man, 1935, 84m, ★★1/2/$$, 20th/NA. A journalist on the crime beat tries to steer the investigation away from himself. Spencer Tracy, Virginia Bruce, Lionel Atwill, James Stewart. w. Tim Whelan, John C. Higgins, d. Tim Whelan.
MYSTERY: MURDER: MURDER MYSTERY: Journalists; Saving Oneself; Accused Unjustly; Forgotten Films
(While the City Sleeps)
Murder Most Foul, 1964, 91m, ★★★/$$, MGM/MGM-UA. Mrs. Marple investigates a backstage murder at a community playhouse. Margaret Rutherford, Ron Moody, Charles Taingwell, Andrew Cruickshank, Meg Jenkins. w. David Pursall, Jack Seddon, N-adap. Agatha Christie *(Mrs. McGinty's Dead),* d. George Pollock.
MYSTERY: MURDER: MURDER MYSTERY: Detective Stories; Detectives-Female; Mystery-Whodunit?; Agatha Christie
The Murder of Mary Phagan, 1987, 251m, ★★★1/2/$$$$, NBC-Orion/Orion. A Jewish man in 1913 Georgia is accused of murdering a girl, and it's up to a suspicious lawyer to stop the wheels of "justice" to find the real killer. Jack Lemmon, Peter Gallagher, Richard Jordan, Paul Dooley, Rebecca Miller, Charles S. Dutton, Kathryn Walker. d. Billy Hale.
DRAMA: True Stories; Courtroom Drama; Lawyers; Lawyers as Detectives; Detective Stories; **MURDER: MYSTERY: MURDER MYSTERY:** Accused Unjustly;

Framed?; Jewish People; Anti-Semitism; Southerns; Bigots; 1900s; TV Movies
Murder on the Orient Express, 1974, 131m, ★★★/$$$$, Par/Par, PG. A group of international travelers on the famous train all become suspects when a murder occurs in one of the cars and Hercule Poirot must find out who done it-but there may be more than one culprit. Albert Finney (BActor), Ingrid Bergman (**BSActress**), Lauren Bacall, Wendy Hiller, Sean Connery, Vanessa Redgrave, Michael York, Martin Balsam, Richard Widmark, Jacqueline Bisset, John Gielgud, Anthony Perkins. w. Paul Dehn (BAScr), N-adap. Agatha Christie, d. Sidney Lumet. BCin, BOScore. Oscars: 5-1.
MYSTERY: MURDER: MURDER MYSTERY: Detective Stories; Mystery-Whodunit?; Ensemble Films; Trains; Snow Settings; All-Star Casts; International Casts; Rich People
(Death on the Nile; The Mirror Crack'd)
Murder My Sweet (*Farewell My Lovely*), 1944, 95m, ★★★/$$$, RKO/Turner. A private detective is hired by an ex-con to search for his missing girl-friend. The search leads him into the netherworld of big crime. Dick Powell, Claire Trevor, Anne Shirley, Mike Mazurki, Otto Kruger, Miles Mander. w. John Paxton, N-adap. Raymond Chandler.
SUSPENSE: MYSTERY: MURDER: MURDER MYSTERY: Detective Stories; Detectives in Deep; Detectives-Private; Conspiracy; Los Angeles; Missing Persons; Searches; Film Noir
Murder She Said, 1961, 87m, ★★★/$$, MGM/MGM-UA. Mrs. Marple sees a woman murdered in a passing train and investigates. Margaret Rutherford, Charles Tingwell, Muriel Pavlow, Arthur Kennedy. w. David Pursall, Jack Seddon, N-adap. Agatha Christie (*4:50 from Paddington*), d. George Pollock.
MYSTERY: MURDER: MURDER MYSTERY: Detective Stories; Detectives-Female; Mystery-Whodunit?; Trains; Agatha Christie
(The Lady Vanishes, Murder Ahoy)
Murderer's Row, 1966, 108m, Col. The hip superspy Matt Helm tracks down a madman who kidnaps a scientist and forces him to create a weapon of mass destruction. Dean Martin, Ann-Margaret, Karl Malden, Camilla Sparv, James Gregory. w. Herbert Baker, N-adap. Donald Hamilton, d. Henry Levin.

ACTION: Spoofs-Spy; Secret Agents; Kidnappings; Manhunts; Missing Persons; Searches; Rule the World-Plot to; Scientists; Mexico
(The Wrecking Crew; Hudson Hawk)
Murders in the Rue Morgue, 1932, 62m, ★★★/$$$, U/MCA-U. Many Londoners end up murdered and the culprit turns out to be a gorilla trained by a madman. Bela Lugosi, Sidney Fox, Leon Ames, Bert Roach. w. Tom Reed, Dale Van Every, John Huston, SS-adap. Edgar Allan Poe, d. Robert Florey.
HORROR: MURDER: Serial Killers; Primates; Animal Monsters; Evil Men; London
(Phantom of the Rue Morgue)
Murders in the Rue Morgue, 1971, 86m, ★★/$, AIP/New World. At a Grand Guignol theatre in Paris the famous Poe story is the main attraction as a backstage sadist kills people for real. Jason Robards, Jr., Herbert Lom, Lilli Palmer, John Lodge, Randolph Scott. w. Philip Wylie, Seton I. Miller, d. Edward Sutherland.
HORROR: MURDER: Serial Killers; Black Comedy; Evil Men; Behind the Scenes; Paris
(Phantom of the Rue Morgue)
Muriel, 1963, 116m, ★★★/$, Argos/Hen's Tooth, Facets. A young man and his widowed stepmother remember his father and their respective lovers. Delphine Seyrig, Jean-Pierre Kerien, Nita Klein, Jean-Baptiste Thierree. w. Jean Cayrol, d. Alain Resnais.
DRAMA: Art Films; Death-Dealing with; Fathers & Sons; Memories; French Films; Widows
Muriel's Wedding, 1995, 105m, ★★★/$$, Miramax/Miramax-Touchstone, PG-13/P-S-MRN. Seeming loser Muriel wants to get married at any cost, even though she can't hold down a decent job to pay for a wedding, even if she could get a date. But then she steals her parents' nest egg and is offered a hunk and a wedding. Will it work or make matters even worse? Toni Collette, Bill Hunter, Rachel Griffiths, Jeanie Drynan, Gennie Nevinson, Matt Day, Daniel Lapaine, Sophie Lee. w. d. P. J. Hogan.
COMEDY: ROMANCE: Romantic Comedy; Liars; Thieves; Marriages-Fake; Romance-Girl Wants Boy; Wallflowers; Wallflowers & Hunks; Romance-Mismatched; Weddings; Disease Stories;

Dreams; Female Protagonists; Australian Films; Woman in Conflict; Looksism (Georgy Girl; Strictly Ballroom; Four Weddings and a Funeral; Dirty Dancing)
(Ed: A little too cliched, but then again, with some twists)
Murmur of the Heart (Le Souffle au Coeur), 1971, 118m, ★★★½/$$$, Ind-Orion/Orion, R/S-FN-MRN. A frail boy with a heart murmur goes to a sanitarium with his youngish sexy Italian mother. Part of his "recovery" becomes entering the world of sex through his mother. Lea Massari, Benoit Ferreux, Daniel Gelin, Michel Lonsdale. w. d. Louis Malle (BOScr). Oscars: 1-0.
DRAMA: ROMANCE: Romantic Drama; Coming of Age; Incest; Mothers & Sons; Mama's Boys; Asylums; Boys; French Films; Cult Films; Writer-Directors
(Spanking the Monkey; Mother's Boys; Beau Pere)
Murphy's Law, 1986, 100m, ★★½/$$, Cannon/MGM-UA, R/EV-P. An alcoholic L.A. cop who doesn't go by the book is accused of his wife's murder. Charles Bronson, Carrie Snodgress, Kathleen Wilhoite. w. Gail Morgan Hickman, d. J. Lee-Thompson.
ACTION: MURDER: MYSTERY: MURDER MYSTERY: Murder of Spouse; Accused Unjustly; Police Stories; Alcoholics; Avenging Death of Someone; Trail of a Killer
(Ed: An attempt to revamp Bronson and the *Death Wish* fervor which is better than the "DW" sequels)
Murphy's Romance, 1985, 107m, ★★★/$$$, Col/RCA-Col, PG/S. A broken down old horse trainer moves into town and builds a new life with a middle-aged single mother and her son. Sally Field, James Garner (BActor), Brian Kerwin, Corey Haim. w. Harriet Frank, Jr., Irving Ravetch, d. Martin Ritt. BCin. Oscars: 2-0.
COMEDY DRAMA: ROMANCE: Romantic Comedy; Romance-Older Men/Younger Women; Mothers Alone; Mothers & Sons; Southwestern Life; Old-Fashioned Recent Films
(Alice Doesn't Live Here Anymore)
Murphy's War, 1971, 108m, ★★½/$, Hemdale-Par/Par. A British marine gunned down off the coast of Venezuela is determined to bomb the U-boat that got him. Peter O'Toole, Sian Phillips, Philippe Noiret, Horst Janson. w. Stirling Silliphant, N-adap. Max Catto, d. Peter Yates.

DRAMA: War Stories; Soldiers; Pilots-Military; Revenge; Germans as Enemy; Duels; Jungle Life; Forgotten Films; Coulda Been Great
(The African Queen; Lawrence of Arabia)
Muscle Beach Party, 1964, 94m, ★★★/$$, AIP/Video Treasures. It's bodybuilders vs. surfers in another beach party movie of the series. Frankie Avalon, Annette Funicello, Buddy Hackett, Don Rickles, Peter Lupus, Peter Lorre. d. William Asher.
COMEDY: MUSICALS: Musical Comedy; Beach Movies; Surfers; Body Builders; Camp; Cult Films; Men in Conflict
(Beach Blanket Bingo; Beach Party)
The Music Box, 1932, 30m, ★★★★/NA, MGM/MGM-UA. Laurel and Hardy play delivery men, and in the famous centerpiece, try to get a piano up a flight of stairs. Stan Laurel, Oliver Hardy. w. H. M. Walker, d. James Parrott.
COMEDY: Comedy-Slapstick; Comedy of Errors
Music Box, 1989, 126m, ★★★/$$, Carolco-UA/Live, PG-13/P. To exonerate her father of charges in a war crimes trial, a lawyer investigates his case and defends him in court, but may find evidence to make her reconsider. Jessica Lange (BActress), Armin Mueller-Stahl, Frederic Forrest, Donald Moffat, Lukas Haas. w. Joe Eszterhas, d. Costa-Gavras. Oscars: 1-0.
DRAMA: MYSTERY: Courtroom Drama; Lawyers; Fathers & Daughters; Illusions Destroyed; Nazi Stories; Ethics; Decisions-Big; Murder-Debate to Reveal Killer; Europeans-Eastern; Torture; Female Protagonists; Coulda Been Great
(Shadow of a Doubt; Class Action)
Music for Millions, 1944, 117m, ★★★/$$$, MGM/MGM-UA. A young girl must help her older sister, a singer in Jose Iturbi's orchestra, when she gets pregnant. Margaret O'Brien, June Allyson, Jose Iturbi, Jimmy Durante, Marsha Hunt. w. Myles Connelly, d. Henry Koster.
MUSICALS: MELODRAMA: Sisters; Girls; Young Women; Mothers-Unwed; Singers
(Mad about Music; Honeymoon)
Music in My Heart, 1940, 70m, ★★1/2/$$, Col/Col. An immigrant wants only one thing-to be a star on Broadway. When he's finally given his break he does become a star, preventing the immigra-

tion officials from deporting him. Rita Hayworth, Tony Martin, Edith Fellows, Alan Mowbray, George Tobias. w. James Edward Grant, d. Joseph Santley.
MUSICALS: ROMANCE: Singers; Dreams; Theater Life; Immigrants; Green Cards; Fame-Rise to
(Gilda; Cover Girl; Down to Earth)
The Music Lovers, 1970, 123m, ★★★/$$, UA/MGM-UA, R/S-MN. Tchaikovsky is forced to marry, though he's gay; his source of funding dries up and he drives his wife to the nuthouse. Richard Chamberlain, Glenda Jackson, Christopher Gable, Max Adrian. w. Melvyn Bragg, NF-adap. C. D. Bowen, Barbara Von Meck (*Beloved Friend*), d. Ken Russell.
DRAMA: Art Films; Character Studies; Biographies; Music Composers; Homosexual Secrets; Gay Men; Bisexuality; Marriage-Forced; Marriage on the Rocks; Mental Illness; Rise and Fall Stories; Camp; Hidden Gems; Ahead of Its Time
(Mahler; Nijinsky; Women in Love)
The Music Man, 1962, 151m, ★★★1/2/$$$$, WB/WB. A huckster comes to a small midwestern town and convinces them they need a band to keep their boys occupied and out of the poolhalls. While he's in town, he woos the local librarian, who sees through his wholesome facade. Robert Preston, Shirley Jones, Buddy Hackett, Hermione Gingold. w. Marion Hargrove, Meredith Wilson, d. Morton da Costa. BPicture, **BMScore**, BEdit, BCCostume, BSound, BCArt. Oscars: 6-1.
MUSICALS: ROMANCE: Cast of Thousands; Con Artists; Librarians; American Myth; Small-town Life; Midwestern Life; Blockbusters
(State Fair; Meet Me in St. Louis; Pollyanna)
The Music of Chance, 1993, 96m, ★★1/2/$, AP-PBS-Col/Col, R/P-S. When two hucksters lose a big poker game, they wind up slaves to a bizarre millionaire. James Spader, Mandy Patinkin, Charles Durning, Joel Grey, Christopher Penn, Samantha Mathis. w. Philip Haas, Belinda Haas, N-adap. Paul Auster, d. Philip Haas.
COMEDY DRAMA: Con Artists; Gambling; Slavery; Losing it All; Risking it All; Games; Art Films; Allegorical Stories; Coulda Been Good; Overlooked at Release; Female Screenwriters

The Music Room, 1958, 100m, ★★★/$, Satyajit Ray Productions-Ind/NA. A reclusive old aristocrat obsessed with classical music stages a musical evening in his home which becomes a sort of final cry against the onslaught of time. Chabi Biswas, Padman Devi, Pinaki Sen Gupta. w. d. Satyajit Ray, SS-adap. Tarasankar Banerjee.
DRAMA: Music Movies; Musicians; Elderly Men; Obsessions; Putting on a Show; Rich vs. Poor; Allegorical Stories; Indian Films; India
(The World of Apu; An Enemy People)
The Music Teacher, 1988, 98m, ★★1/2/$, Orion/Orion. Two music students of different schools have a contest under the tutelage of a faded star, leading to tensions between them all. Jose Van Dam, Anne Roussel, Philippe Volter, Sylvie Fennec, Patrick Bauchau. w. Gerard Corbiau, Andre Corbiau, Luc Jabon. d. Gerard Corbiau.
COMEDY DRAMA: Musicians; Pianists; Teachers; Teachers & Students; French Films
(The Competition; Madame Sousatzka; Mr. Holland's Opus)
Mutiny on the Bounty, 1935, 135m, ★★★★/$$$$, MGM/MGM-UA. The tyrannical captain Bly is so cruel to his crew on the way to South America that they are all but forced to mutiny. Charles Laughton (BActor), Clark Gable (BActor), Franchot Tone (BActor), Movita, Dudley Digges, Henry Stephenson, Donald Crisp. w. Talbot Jennings, Jules Furthman, Carey Wilson (BScr), NF-adap. Charles Nordhoff, James Hall, d. Frank Lloyd. **BPicture**, BEdit, BScore. Oscars: 7-1.
Mutiny on the Bounty, 1962, 185m, ★★★/$$$, MGM/MGM-UA. Remake of above with more violence and Marlon Brando. Trevor Howard, Richard Harris, Hugh Griffith, Tarita, Richard Haydn. w. Charles Lederer, d. Lewis Milstone. BPicture, BCCin, BOSong, BOScore, BSFX, BEdit, BCArt. Oscars: 7-0.
ADVENTURE: Adventure at Sea; Ships; Courts Martial; Men in Conflicts; Rebels; Power Struggles; Evil Men; Stern Men; South Pacific; Islands; True Stories; Outstanding Scenery
REMAKE: The Bounty
My American Uncle, 1980, 126m, ★★★/$$, Andrea-Ind/NA. Professor Henri Laborit explains three human lives in biologically reductionist terms-it's an

art film, see? Gerard Depardieu, Nicole Garcia, Roger Pierre. w. Jean Gruault (BOScr), NF-adap. Henri Laborit, d. Alain Resnais.

DRAMA: Art Films; Surrealism; Character Studies; French Films; Sleeper Hits; Uncles
(Providence)

My Beautiful Laundrette, 1986, ★★★1/2/$$$, BBC-Cinecom/Cinecom, Karl-Lorimar, WB, R/S-MN. A young Pakistani gay man (Saeed Jeffrey) has difficulty living his life while opening a new laundromat, and, failing, he hires a young tough (Daniel Day Lewis) to help with the neighborhood thugs. w. Hanief Kureishi (BOScr), d. Stephen Frears. Oscars: 1-0.
DRAMA: COMEDY DRAMA: ROMANCE: Parents vs. Children; Gay Men; Protecting Someone; Fish out of Water Stories; Making a Living; Homophobia; Indians/Pakistanis; British Films; Hidden Gems; Sleeper Hits
(My Bodyguard; London Kills Me)

My Best Friend's Girl, 1983, 100m, ★★1/2/$, Cannon/Col, PG/S. A man gets suspicious when leaving his girlfriend alone during the day, so he has his friend look after her with disastrous results. Coluche, Isabelle Huppert, Thierry L'hermitte, Farid Chopel. w. Bertrand Blier, Gerard Brach, d. Bertrand Blier.
COMEDY DRAMA: ROMANCE: Romance-Triangles; Romantic Comedy; Romance with Friend's Lover; Protecting Someone; Friendships-Male; Friends as Enemies; French Films
(Get Out Your Handkerchiefs; Deadfall; Beau Pere; Cousin, Cousine)

My Blood Runs Cold, 1965, 108m, ★★/$, WB/NA. A man convinces a woman he meets that she is the reincarnation of a dead seductress, but his motivations are suspect. Troy Donahue, Joey Heatherton, Barry Sullivan. w. John Mantley, d. William Conrad.
SUSPENSE: MYSTERY: ROMANCE: Reincarnation; Uninentionally Funny; Camp; Romance-Dangerous; Love-Questionable
(The Reincarnation of Peter Proud)

My Blue Heaven, 1950, 96m, ★★/$$, 20th/NA. A couple is having trouble having children. Betty Grable, Dan Dailey, Mitzi Gaynor, David Wayne, Jane Wyatt, Una Merkel. w. Lamar Trotti, Claude Binyon, d. Henry Koster.

COMEDY DRAMA: Marriage Comedy; Babies-Having; Women-Childless; Marriage on the Rocks
(Almost Pregnant; A Period of Adjustment)

My Blue Heaven, 1990, 95m, ★★1/2/$$, WB/WB, PG-13/S-P. A wacky gangster in the witness protection program has trouble adjusting to suburban life and starts finding ways to amuse himself. Steve Martin, Rick Moranis, Joan Cusack, Melanie Mayron, Carol Kane, Daniel Stern. w. Nora Ephron, d. Herbert Ross.
COMEDY: Fish out of Water Stories; Mob Stories; Mob Comedy; Witnesses-Protecting; Fugitives from the Mob; Baseball; Playboys; Marriage on the Rocks; Suburban Life; Good Premise Unfulfilled; Coulda Been Great; Female Screenwriters
(Mister Corey; The Little Giant; Cookie)

My Bodyguard, 1980, 96m, ★★★1/2/$$, 20th/Fox, PG/V. A skinny boy gets picked on in school until a hulking, friendly-giant type takes him under his wing. Chris Makepeace, Adam Baldwin, Ruth Gordon, Matt Dillon, Martin Mull, John Houseman. w. Alan Ormsby, d. Tony Bill.
COMEDY DRAMA: CHILDREN'S: FAMILY: Coming of Age; Protecting Someone; Friendships-Male; Nerds; Macho Men; Inner City Life; Chicago; Stranger in Town; Old-Fashioned Recent Films; Underrated; Forgotten Films; Hidden Gems
(My Beautiful Laundrette; A Little Romance)

My Brilliant Career, 1980, 100m, ★★★1/2/$$, Analysis/Vestron, G. At the turn of the century, a woman growing up on a farm in Australia dreams of life as a writer and makes it happen. Judy Davis, Sam Neill, Wendy Hughes, Robert Grubb, Max Cullen. w. Eleanor Whitcombe, N-adap. Miles Franklin, d. Gillian Armstrong.
DRAMA: Character Studies; Writers Dreams; Australian Films; Female Protagonists; Quiet Little Films; Sleeper Hits; Female Writers; Female Directors; Independent Films
(The Getting of Wisdom; We of the Never Never)
(Ed: Winner of a slew of Australian and British awards, a hit on the art house circuit, and the start of Judy Davis' career)

My Cousin Rachel, 1953, 98m, ★★★/$$$, 20th/CBS-Fox. An Englishman leaves family and country to marry an Italian woman. After he dies there, she travels to England and encounters a cold reception from his family, including his foster son. Olivia de Havilland, Richard Burton (BSActor), John Sutton, Audrey Dalton, Ronald Squire. w. Nunnally Johnson, N-adap. Daphne du Maurier, d. Henry Koster. BB&WCin, BB&WArt. Oscars: 3-0.
MELODRAMA: ROMANCE: Costume Drama; Romance with Relative; Stepmothers; Cousins; Accused Unjustly; Death-Dealing with; Widows
(Sister Carrie; Where Angels Fear to Tread; The Heiress)

My Cousin Vinny, 1992, 119m, ★★★/$$$$, 20th/Fox, PG-13/P. Two college boys from New York get arrested while driving through Alabama when they are mistaken for two convenience-store robber-murderers. Their cousin, an inept trial lawyer from New York, is sent for to defend them, but can they be saved from him? Joe Pesci, Ralph Macchio, Marisa Tomei (**BSActress**), Mitchell Whitfield, Fred Gwynne. w. Dale Launer, d. Jonathan Lynn. Oscars: 1-1.
COMEDY: MURDER: MYSTERY: MURDER MYSTERY: Courtroom Drama; Fish out of Water Stories; Accused Unjustly; Lawyers; Fools-Bumbling; Bimbos; North vs. South; City vs. Country; Romance-Older Men/ Younger Women; Southerns; Underrated; Sleeper Hits
(Doc Hollywood; The Super)
(Ed: Though the critics missed it, the audiences found it at the box-office and especially on video)

My Darling Clementine, 1946, 98m, ★★★1/2/$$$, 20th. Wyatt Earp comes to Tombstone to make the streets safe for decent citizens. Henry Fonda, Victore Mature, Walter Brennan, Linda Darnell. w. Samuel G. Engel, Winston Miller, NF-adap. Stuart N. Lake (Wyatt Earp, Frontier Marshall), d. John Ford.
WESTERNS: Men in Conflict; Police Stories; Duels; Gunfighters; American Myth; Wyatt Earp
(Wyatt Earp; Gunfight at the OK Corral)

My Dear Secretary, 1948, 96m, ★★1/2/$$, UA/Nos. A wife has reason to be jealous of her husband's secretary, since she once filled that position herself. Kirk Douglas, Laraine Day, Keenan

Wynn, Rudy Vallee. w. d. Charles Martin.

COMEDY: ROMANCE: Romantic Comedy; Jealousy; Secretaries
(Take a Letter, Darling; The Apartment)

My Dinner with Andre, 1981, 111m, ★★★½/$$, Ind/Home Vision. Two men with differing views on life and art discuss them over dinner in basically one long scene. Wallace Shawn, Andre Gregory. w. Wallace Shawn, Andre Gregory, d. Louis Malle.

COMEDY: Character Studies; Art Films; Intellectuals; Dinner Parties; One-Day Stories; Sleeper Hits; Curiosities; Cult Films

My Fair Lady, 1964, 107m, ★★★★/$$$$, WB/WB. A linguistics specialist (Rex Harrison, **BActor**) seeks out a street urchin (Audrey Hepburn) with a terrible cockney accent to teach her how to speak properly and act like a lady, but she may out-perform his wildest expectations. Theodore Bikel, Gladys Cooper (BSActress), Stanley Holloway (BSActor), Wilfrid Hyde White, Mona Washbourne, Jeremy Brett. w. MP-adap. Alan Jay Lerner (BAScr), P-adap. Bernard Shaw, *(Pygmalion)*, d. George Cukor (**BDirector**). **BPicture, BCCin, BCArt, BSound, BCEdit, BCCostume, BAScore.** Oscars: 12-8.

MUSICAL: ROMANCE: COMEDY: Musical Comedy; Musical Romance; Romantic Comedy; Comedy of Manners; Romance-Older Men/Younger Women; Svengalis; Romance-Class Conflicts; Rich vs. Poor; Experiments; Teachers; Teachers & Students; Edwardian Era; Young Women London; Stagelike Films; Blockbusters; Production Design-Outstanding; Classic Play Adaptations

MUSICAL REMAKE OF: Pygmalion (Mary Poppins; Funny Face; The King and I)

My Father Is Coming, 1991, 81m, ★★½/$, Ind/NA. A German woman tries out for a part in a porno and meets lots of strange people, including a lesbian who seduces her-all in New York! Alfred Edel, Shelley Kastner, Annie Sprinkle. w. Monika Treut, Bruce Benderson, Sarah Schulman, d. Monika Treut.

SATIRE: COMEDY DRAMA: Art Films; Alternative Lifestyles; Lesbians; Pornography World; Germans; Female Protagonists; Female Writers; Female Directors; Independent Films

(Ed: Underground and perhaps should stay there, although the director's documentaries and interviews are very interesting)

My Father the Hero, 1993, 90m, ★★/$$, Touchstone/Touchstone, PG. Divorced dad and daughter go on vacation and daughter pretends he's her boyfriend to impress a boy she wants. Chaos and stupidity abound. Gerard Depardieu, Katherine Heigl, Lauren Hutton, Faith Prince, Emma Thompson. w. Francis Veber, Charlie Peters, d. Steve Miner.

COMEDY: FAMILY: CHILDREN'S: Comedy-Disneyesque; Misunderstandings; Vacations; Comedy-Slapsticks; Romance-Girl Wants Boy; Fathers & Daughters; Jealousy; Coulda Been Good; Foreign Film Remakes

REMAKE OF: Mon Pere, Ce Heroes. (Superdad; She's Outta Control; Blame It on Rio)

My Father's Glory, 1991, 110m, ★★★/$, Orion/Orion, G. Marcel Pagnol's memoirs of boyhood in rural France in the 1900s and all of the people who surrounded him there. Julien Ciamaca, Phillipe Claubere. w. Lucette Andrei, d. Yves Robert.

DRAMA: Character Studies; **FAMILY:** Boys; Childhood; Memories-Childhood; Memories; Autobiographical Stories; 1900s; French Films; Female Screenwriters; Hidden Gems

SEQUEL: My Mother's Castle. (Sunday in the Country; The Long Day Closes)

My Favorite Blonde, 1942, 78m, ★★★½/$$$, Par/Par. A comedian saves a woman on a train from her would-be attacker and ends up in hot water himself. Bob Hope, Madeleine Carroll, Gale Sondergaard. w. Don Hartman, Frank Butler, Malvin Frank, Norman Panama, d. Sidney Lanfield.

COMEDY: FARCE: Spies; Comedy-Slapstick; Comedians; Saving Someone; Trains; Fugitives from a Murderer; Hidden Gems
(My Favorite Brunette)

My Favorite Brunette, 1947, 87m, ★★★/$$, Par/Nos. A kiddie photographer is mistaken for a detective and must run from mobster creeps. Bob Hope, Dorothy Lamour, Peter Lorre, Lon Chaney, Jr., John Hoyt. w. Edmund Beloin, Jack Rose, d. Elliot Nugent.

COMEDY: Chase Movies; Fugitives from the Mob; Mob Comedy; Photographers;

Identities-Mistaken; Spoofs-Detective; Narrated Films; Hidden Gems
(My Favorite Blonde)

My Favorite Spy, 1942, 86m, ★★½/$$, RKO/NA. A newlywed man is called away on a spy mission before he can get to his honeymoon. Kay Kyser, Ginny Simms, Ish Kabibble, Ellen Drew, Jane Wyman. w. Sig Herzig, William Bowers, d. Tay Garnett.

COMEDY: Spy Films; Spies; Spoofs-Spy; Newlyweds; Honeymoons

My Favorite Spy, 1951, 93m, ★★★/$$$, Par/NA. A comedian goes into the CIA to replace a lookalike spy and winds up on the lam. Bob Hope, Hedy Lamarr. w. Edmund Hartmann, Jack Sher, d. Norman Z. McLeod.

COMEDY: Chase Movies; Secret Agents; Spoofs-Spy; Spies; Lookalikes; Comedians; Identities-Assumed; Hidden Gems
(My Favorite Brunette)

My Favorite Wife, 1940, 88m, ★★★½/$$$, RKO/Turner. A man's (Cary Grant) wife (Irene Dunne) returns from being presumed dead after a shipwreck *and* after the man's already found a new woman, but they may yet find each other again. Gail Patrick, Randolph Scott. w. Sam & Bella Spewack, Leo McCarey (BOStory), d. Garson Kanin. BScore, BArt. Oscars: 3-0.

COMEDY: ROMANCE: Screwball Comedy; Romantic Comedy; **FARCE:** Marriage; Comedy; Bigamy; Romance-Bickering; Return of Spouse; Romance-Reunited; Secrets-Keeping; Custody Battles; Divorce; Missing Persons; Engagements-Breaking; Hidden Gems; Female Screenwriters

REMAKE: Move Over, Darling (Move Over, Darling; Too Many Husbands; Our Wife; Three for the Show)

My Favorite Year, 1982, 92m, ★★★½/$$, MGM/MGM-UA, PG. A washed-up alcoholic, old former matinee idol is asked to star in a TV series with disastrous results. Peter O'Toole (BActor), Mark Linn-Baker, Jessica Harper, Joseph Bologna. w. Norman Steinberg, Dennis Palumbo, d. Richard Benjamin. Oscars: 1-0.

COMEDY: Comedy-Slapstick; Comedy of Errors; Actors; Alcoholics; TV Life; 1950s; Nostalgia; Swashbucklers; Overlooked at Release; Cult Films; Hidden Gems; Underrated; Narrated Films

(On the Air; Laughter on the 23rd Floor [play])

(Ed: Mr. O'Toole presumably doing a send-up of himself in later years)

My Foolish Heart, 1949, 98m, ★★★/$$$, Goldwyn-UA/Goldwyn. A married woman who had an affair gets pregnant and must convince her husband that the child is his. Susan Hayward (BActress), Dana Andrews, Kent Smith, Robert Keith, Gigi Perreau. w. Julius J. and Philip G. Epstein, SS-adap. J. D. Salinger, d. Mark Robson. BOSong. Oscars: 2-0.

MELODRAMA: Marriage Drama; Marriage on the Rocks; Cheating Women; Babies-Having; Mothers-Unwed; Female Protagonists

(Ada; Back Street; Smash-Up . . .)

(Ed: Interesting to note it's based on a Salinger story)

My Forbidden Past, 1951, 81m, ★★★/$, RKO/Media. A woman with a past inherits money and then decides to go after the man she really wants by breaking up his marriage-until the wife is suddenly murdered and he is accused of doing it himself. Ava Gardner, Melvyn Douglas, Robert Mitchum, Janis Carter. w. Marion Parsonnet, N-adap. Polan Banks, d. Robert Stevenson.

MELODRAMA: MURDER: Accused Unjustly; Soap Operas; Marriage-Impending; Inheritances at Stake; Engagements-Breaking; Evil Women; Revenge; Secrets-Keeping; Sisters; Past-Haunted by the; New Orleans; Southerns; Camp; Coulda Been Great; Hidden Gems; Female Protagonists; Female Screenwriters

My Friend Flicka, 1943, 89m, ★★★/$$$$, 20th/Fox. A boy's best friend is his horse-a filly with a Swedish name. Roddy McDowell, Preston Foster, Rita Johnson, James Bell. w. Mary O'Hara, N-adap. Mary O'Hara, d. Harold Schuster.

CHILDREN'S: FAMILY: ADVENTURE: Pet Stories; Boyhood; Horses; Female Screenwriters

FLIPSIDE of National Velvet.

SEQUEL: Thunderhead: Son of Flicka (1945)

My Friend Irma, 1949, 103m, ★★★/$$$, Par/Par. A ditzy girl is persuaded by her slick boyfriend to let two soda jerks stay in her apartment. Marie Wilson, John Lund, Diana Lynn, Dean Martin,

Jerry Lewis, Don Defore. w. Cy Howard, Parke Levy, (Radio show)-adap. Cy Howard, d. George Marshall.

COMEDY: Comedy-Situation; Roommates; Fools-Bumbling; Comedians; Female Protagonists

SEQUEL: My Friend Irma Goes West.

(The More the Merrier; Walk, Don't Run)

(Ed: Notable for debut of Martin & Lewis comedy team)

My Friend Irma Goes West, 1950, 90m, ★★½/$$$, Par/Par. Steve and Seymour, Irma's goofy friends, go to Hollywood to become stars and meet strange people on the train west. John Lund, Marie Wilson, Dean Martin, Jerry Lewis, Diana Lynn. w. Cy Howard, Parke Levy, d. Hal Walker.

COMEDY: Hollywood Life; Fools-Bumbling; Comedians; Trains

SEQUEL TO: My Friend Irma

My Gal Sal, 1942, 103m, ★★★/$$$, 20th/NA. A musical biopic of the composer Paul Dreiser. Rita Hayworth, Victor Mature, John Sutton, Carole Landis. w. Seton I. Miller, Darrell Ware, Karl Turnbertg, NF-adap., Theodore Dreiser (My Brother Paul), d. Irving Cummings. BMScore, BCArt. Oscars: 2-1.

MUSICALS: ROMANCE: Music Movies; Biographies; Music Composers; ROMANCE: Fame-Rise to; Brothers; Nostalgia

My Geisha, 1962, 120m, ★★½/$$, Par/Par. A Hollywood director with a failing marriage goes to Japan and ends up casting his wife, disguised as a geisha, in the lead role. Shirley MacLaine, Yves Montand, Robert Cummings, Edward G. Robinson, Yoko Tani. w. Norman Krasna, d. Jack Cardiff.

MELODRAMA: ROMANCE: Marriage Comedy; Disguises; Jealousy; Hollywood Life; Moviemaking; Directors; Japan; Wives-Troublesome

(Lily in Love; Gambit)

(Ed: Sort of an elongated, not very funny I Love Lucy episode, with a melodramatic spin in Tokyo instead of the Tropicana)

My Girl, 1991, 102m, ★★½/$$$$, Col/Col-Tri, PG. A young boy's first love is the daughter of an undertaker and things go swimmingly-until the bees. Dan Aykroyd, Jamie Lee Curtis, Macauley Culkin, Anna Chlumsky, Richard Masur, Griffin Dunne. w. Laurice Elewany, d. Howard Zieff.

MELODRAMA: ROMANCE: CHILDREN'S: FAMILY: Love-First; TRAGEDY: Death-Dealing with; Female Screenwriters; Female Protagonists; Child Protagonists

(Paradise [1992]; The Man in the Moon)

(Ed: Bizarre on several levels, and the bees may upset little kids)

My Girl 2, 1993, 99m, ★★½/$$, Col/Col, PG. The girl of the first, sans Culkin (remember the bees?), searches for her real mother-her father's first wife, whom he can't remember anything about. Dan Aykroyd, Jamie Lee Curtis, Anna Chlumsky, Austin O'Brien, Richard Masur. w. Janet Kovalcik, d. Howard Zeiff.

MELODRAMA: ROMANCE: CHILDREN'S: FAMILY: Love-First; Children-Long lost; Family/Heritage-Search for; Death-Dealing with; Female Screenwriters; Female Protagonists; Child Protagonists

My Girl Tisa, 1948, 95, ★★★/$, United States Pictures/Republic. In the late 1800s, an immigrant girl is threatened with deportation and her politician boyfriend gets Teddy Roosevelt to intervene on her behalf. Lilli Palmer, Sam Wanamaker, Alan Hale, Stella Adler, Akim Tamiroff. w. Allen Boretz, P-adap. Lucille S. Prumbs, d. Elliott Nugent.

DRAMA: Immigrants; Politicians; Presidents

My Learned Friend, 1943, 76m, ★★★/$$, Ealing/NA. An ex-con plans to kill everyone who got him in the clink, ending with his crooked lawyer. Will Hay, Claude Hulbert, Mervyn Johns, Ernest Thesiger, Charles Victor. w. John Dighton, Angus Macphail, d. Basil Dearden.

ACTION: Crime Drama; Convict's Revenge; Revenge; Corruption; Accused Unjustly; Framed?; British Films

My Left Foot, 1989, 100m, ★★★½/$$$, Miramax/HBO, PG/P. Christy Brown, the Irish writer with cerebral palsy, learns to deal with his condition and the prejudices of those around him as he grows up to be a man. Daniel Day Lewis (BActor), Ray McAnally, Brenda Fricker (BSActress), Ruth McCabe, Fiona Shaw. w. Shane Connaughton, Jim Sheridan (BAScr), NF-adap. Christy Brown, d. Jim Sheridan (BDirector). BPicture. Oscars: 5-2.

DRAMA: Biographies; True Stories; Disease Movies; Disabled People; Artists;

Artists-Famous; Mothers-Struggling; Mothers & Sons; Rebels; Irish People; Irish Films; Independent Films
(Mask; Rain Man; Best Boy)

My Life, 1993, 114m, ★★¹/₂/$$, Col/Col, PG-13/S. An exec who isn't very popular finds out he's dying of pancreatic cancer just as his wife is expecting, so he leaves a video record of his last days. Michael Keaton, Nicole Kidman, Haing S. Ngor, Queen Latifah, Bradley Whitford. w. d. Bruce Joel Rubin.
MELODRAMA: Character Studies; Death-Impending; Yuppies; Marriage Drama; Babies-Having; Narrated Films; Life Transitions; Race Against Time; Writer-Directors
(Who Will Love My Children?; Short Time)

My Life as a Dog, 1987, 101m, ★★¹/₂/$$$, Svensk-Par/Par, PG/S. A young Swedish boy finds himself displaced like an unwanted dog after his mother dies and he has to cope and make new friends. w. Lasse Hallstrom, Reidear Jonsson, Brasse Brannstrom, Per Berglund (BAScr), N-adap. Reidar Jonsson, d. Hallstrom (BDirector). Oscars: 2-0.
DRAMA: Boyhood; Coming of Age; Life Transitions; Orphans; Children-Adopted; Mothers-Troublesome; Brothers; Memories; Quiet Little Films; Sleeper Hits; Swedish Films; Independent Films
(The Long Day Closes; Careful, He Might Hear You)
(Ed: This film's success in America seems to baffle the Swedes)

My Little Chickadee, 1939, 83m, ★★★/$$$, U/MCA-U. A bumbling con man and his lady friend beat a shady cowboy at his own game. Mae West, W. C. Fields, Joseph Calleia. w. Mae West, W. C. Fields, d. Edward Cline.
COMEDY: Turning the Tables; Con Artists; Criminal Couples; Cowboys; Sexy Women; Female Screenwriters; Female Protagonists
(She Done Him Wrong; The Dentist; International House)

My Little Girl, 1986, 117m, ★★¹/₂/$, Hemdale-M-I/Prism, PG. An upper-class girl works at a children's hospital and learns about the other side of life. James Earl Jones, Geraldine Page, Mary Stuart Masterson, Anne Meara, Pamela Payton Wright, Peter Michael Goetz, Peter Gallagher. w. Connie Kaiserman, Nan Mason, d. Connie Kaiserman.

COMEDY DRAMA: Social Drama; Social Satire; Class Conflicts; Rich vs. Poor; Saintly People; Hospitals; Illusions Destroyed; Young Women; Nurses; Overlooked at Release; Good Premise Unfulfilled; Female Directors; Female Screenwriters; Writer-Directors
(Stone Pillow; Up the Down Staircase)
(Ed: One of Geraldine Page's last films)

My Love Came Back, 1940, 85m, ★★¹/₂/$$$, WB/NA. A young violinist is the object of the affection of a benevolent millionaire who supports her career. Olivia de Havilland, Jeffrey Lynn, Charles Winninger, Eddie Albert, Jane Wyman. w. Robert Buckner, Ivan Goff, Earl Baldwin, d. Curtis Bernhardt.
ROMANCE: MELODRAMA: Musicians; Svengalis; Rich People; Faded Hits; Female Protagonists
(Golden Boy; Break of Hearts; Humoresque; Svengali)

My Lucky Star, 1938, 84m, ★★¹/₂/$$, 20th/Fox. A girl clerk in a shop gets into compromising positions with the owner's son when they skate together. Sonja Henie, Richard Greene, Joan Davis, Buddy Ebsen, Cesar Romero. w. Harry Tugend, Jack Yellen, d. Roy del Ruth.
ROMANCE: Romantic Comedy; Marrying Up; Skating

My Man Godfrey, 1936, 95m, ★★★★/$$$$, Universal/MCA-U, various. A butler (William Powell, BActor) is serving a mansion in which one sister (Carole Lombard, BActress) is in love with him and the other sister is out to get him because he seems to have more in his past than he's willing to say. Alice Brady (BSActress), Mischa Auer (BSActor), Jean Dixon. w. Morrie Ryskind, Eric Hatch, Gregory La Cava (BScr), d. Gregory La Cava (BDirector). Oscars: 6-0.
COMEDY: Screwball Comedy; FARCE: ROMANCE: Romance-Girl Wants Boy; Imposters; Disguises; Romance with Servant; Servants; Heiresses-Madcap; Homeless People; Rich People; New York Life; Depression Era
REMAKE: 1957 version
(Nothing Sacred)

My Man Godfrey, 1957, 92m, ★★¹/₂/$$, U-I/MCA-U. A remake in color and modernized. June Allyson, David Niven, Jessie Royce Landis, Jay Robinson, Robert Keith, Eva Gabor. w. Everett Freeman, Peter Berneis, William Bowers, d. Henry Koster.

COMEDY: ROMANCE: Romantic Comedy; Romance-Girl Wants Boy;
FARCE: Imposters; Disguises; Romance with Servant; Servants; Heiresses-Madcap; Homeless People; Rich People; New York Life
REMAKE of 1936 version

My Mother's Castle, 1991, 98m, ★★★¹/₂/$, Orion/Orion, G. Continuation of *My Father's Glory* with Marcel Pagnol's tales of his family and their summer vacations in a French fairytale land. Phillippe Caubere, Nathalie Roussel, Didier Pain. d. Yves Robert.
DRAMA: Character Studies; FAMILY: Boys; Childhood; Memories-Childhood; Memories; Autobiographical Stories; 1900s; French Films; Hidden Gems
SEQUEL TO: My Father's Glory.

My Name Is Julia Ross, 1945, 65m, ★★★/$, Col/NA. Kidnappers force their victim to impersonate an heiress in order to extort money from her family. Nina Foch, Dame May Whitty, George Macready. w. Muriel Roy Bolton, N-adap. Anthony Gilbert (*The Woman in Red*), d. Joseph H. Lewis.
DRAMA: Crime Drama; MELODRAMA: Kidnappings; Imposters; Heiresses
(Dead of Winter; Caroline?)

My Name Is Nobody, 1973, 116m, ★★¹/₂/$$, Ind/Hollywood Home Entertainment, R/V. A gunfighter facing his final sunset is persuaded to go out with a bang by a young foe. Henry Fonda, Terence Hill (Mario Girotti), Jean Martin, Piero Lulli. w. Ernesto Gastaldi, Fulvio Morsella, Ernesto Gastaldi, Sergio Leone, d. Tonino Valerii.
WESTERNS: Western-Spaghetti; Men in Conflict; Duels; Gunfighters; Death-Impending; Retirement; Mentors & Proteges

My New Gun, 1993, 93m, ★★★/$ (LR), Ind-Col/Col-Tri, PG-13/P-S. A young woman (Diane Lane) married to a doctor (Stephen Collins) gets a new gun and it leads her into several calamities, intrigue with the neighbors, and a romance with one of them, who steals her gun and may break up her marriage. Tess Harper, James LeGros. w. d. Stacy Cochran.
COMEDY DRAMA: Black Comedy; Comedy-Light; Ordinary People Stories; Romance-Clandestine; Detectives-Amateur; Eccentric People; Psycho Killers; Stalkers; Fatal Attractions; Country Singers; Weddings; Young

Women; Female Protagonists; Coulda Been Great; Overlooked at Release; Curiosities; Writer-Directors; Female Directors; Female Screenwriters (Ed: Much better and more ambitious than it had to be, may be too dark for some after a light start)

My Night at Maud's, 1969, 110m, ★★★/$$$, Cinema V/Media, R/S. A young man has an affair with a divorcee in his small French town, but can't marry her because of his Catholicism. Jean-Louis Trintignant, Marie-Christine Barrault, Francoise Fabian. w. d. Eric Rohmer (BOScr). BFLFilm. Oscars: 2-0.
DRAMA: ROMANCE: Romantic Drama; Romance-Triangles; Romance-Doomed; Ordinary People Stories; French Films; Writer-Directors; Sleeper Hits (Claire's Knee; Chloe in the Afternoon)

My Own Private Idaho, 1991, 102m, ★★★/$$, Fine Line/New Line, R/S-MN. Two male hustlers (River Phoenix, Keanu Reeves) go on a series of adventures from seedy hotels and homes of clients in Portland, Oregon, to the street life of Rome where everything comes apart. w. d. Gus Van Sant.
DRAMA: ROMANCE: Gay Men; Homo-eroticism; Alternative Lifestyles; Prostitutes-Male; Friends in Love; Friendships-Male; Friendships-Great; Road Movies; Drugs-Addictions; Suicidal Tendencies; Suicidal Tendencies of Homosexuals; Rome; Americans Abroad; Writer-Directors (Midnight Cowboy; Mala Noche)

My Reputation, 1946, 96m, ★★/$, WB/NA. A widow is considered by her nosy neighbors to be a bit too hasty in moving on with her life. Barbara Stanwyck, George Brent, Warner Anderson, Lucile Watson, Eve Arden. w. Catherine Turney, N-adap. Clare Jaynes *(Instruct My Sorrows)*, d. Curtis Bernhardt.
MELODRAMA: Small-town Life; Scandals; Widows; Starting Over; Neighbors-Troublesome; Female Protagonists; Female Screenwriters (Born to Be Bad; The Constant Nymph)

My Science Project, 1985, 91m, ★★½/$$, Touchstone/Touchstone, PG/S. A high school student finds a crashed UFO with a time machine in it, leading to some fun with his fellow teens. John Stockwell, Danielle Von Zerneck, Fisher Stevens, Raphael Sbarges, Richard Masur. w. d. Jonathan R. Betuel.

COMEDY: Teenagers; Teenage Movies; Comedy-Disneyesque; UFOs; Time Travel; Dinosaurs; Writer-Directors (Weird Science; Real Genius)

My Sin, 1931, 79m, ★★½/$$, Par/NA. A woman who has shot her husband gets help from her alcoholic lawyer. Tallulah Bankhead, Fredric March, Harry Davenport, Scott Kolk. w. Owen David, Adelaide Heilbron, SS-adap. Frederick Jackson, d. George Abbott.
DRAMA: TRAGEDY: ROMANCE: Romance with Lawyer; Alcoholics; Redemption; Forgotten Films (The Devil and the Deep; Dangerous)

My Sister Eileen, 1942, 96m, ★★★/$$$, Col/NA. Two midwestern girls have a strange wonderful time in wacky Greenwich Village meeting the friends of one of their sisters. Rosalind Russell (BActress), Janet Blair, Brian Aherne, Allyn Joslyn, George Tobias, Elizabeth Patterson. w. Ruth McKinney, Joseph Fields, Jerome Chodorov, N-adap. Ruth McKinney, d. Alexander Hall. Oscars: 1-0.
COMEDY: ROMANCE: Romantic Comedy; Young Women; Fish out of Water Stories; Female Protagonists; Female Screenwriters; Hidden Gems; Time Capsules; Greenwich Village
MUSICAL REMAKE: 1955.
(My Friend Irma; Sister Kenny)
(Ed: Russell makes it worth it)

My Sister Eileen, 1955, 108m, ★★★/$$, Col/Col. A musical version of the above. Betty Garrett, Janet Leigh, Jack Lemmon, Bob Fosse, Dick York. w. Blake Edwards, Richard Quine, P-adap. Joseph Fields, Jerome Chodorov, d. Richard Quine.
MUSICALS: COMEDY: Musical Comedy; ROMANCE: Romantic Comedy; Young Women; Fish out of Water Stories; Female Protagonists; Greenwich Village
MUSICAL REMAKE OF: 1942 version.

My Six Loves, 1963, 101m, ★★/$$, Par/NA. A Broadway star goes on hiatus in the country and ends up retiring when she falls in love with six local orphan kids and decides to adopt them. Debbie Reynolds, David Janssen, Cliff Robertson, Eileen Heckart. w. John Fante, Joseph Calvelli, William Wood, d. Gower Champion.
COMEDY DRAMA: MELODRAMA: Family Drama; FAMILY: Actresses; Vacations; Orphans; Children-Adopted; City vs. Country; Forgotten Films

(Bachelor Mother; Bundle of Joy; Father Goose)

My Son John, 1952, 122m, ★★½/$$, Par/NA. A red-baiting curiosity about a good Christian family that learns the shocking truth-one of its sons is a Communist! Helen Hayes, Robert Walker, Dean Jagger, Van Heflin, Minor Watson, Richard Jaeckel. w. Myles Connelly, Leo McCarey, d. Leo McCarey.
MELODRAMA: McCarthy Era; Communists; Conservative Value Films; Secrets-Keeping; Family Drama; Message Films; Unintentionally Funny; Forgotten Films (Keeper of the Flame; I Was a Communist for the FBI)

My Son, My Son, 1940, 117m, ★★½/$$, Edward Small/NA. A man rises from poverty to become wealthy and gives his son everything he never had. Unfortunately his son becomes a spoiled ingrate who spits in his eye. Brian Aherne, Madeleine Carroll, Louis Hayward, Laraine Day, Henry Hull. w. Lenore Coffee, N-adap. Howard Spring, d. Charles Vidor.
DRAMA: MELODRAMA: Power-Rise to; Fathers & Sons; Parents vs. Children's; Children-Brats; Female Screenwriters (Edward, My Son; Mildred Pierce)

My Stepmother Is an Alien, 1988, 108m, ★★/$, Weintraub-Col/Col-Tri, PG-13/S. A single father marries a beautiful woman, but his child soon makes the discovery of the title. Dan Aykroyd, Kim Basinger, Jon Lovitz, Alyson Hannigan. w. Herschel Weingrod, Timothy Harris, Jonathan Reynolds, d. Richard Benjamin.
COMEDY: SCI-FI: Aliens-Outer Space, Good; Sexy Women; Bimbos; Step-mothers; Unintentionally Funny; Flops-Major

My Sweet Little Village, 1985, 100m, ★★½/$, Cannon/NA. A retarded worker in Czechoslovakia has to leave his home town for Prague. Janos Ban, Marian Labuda, Rudolf Hrusinsky, Milena Dvorska. w. Zdenek Sverak, d. Jiri Menzel.
MELODRAMA: Mentally Disabled; Europeans-Eastern; City vs. Country; Czech Films

My Tutor, 1982, 97m, ★★½/$$, Crown/MCA-U, R/S-FN-MRN. A teenager loses his virginity with the help of an older woman, but his pal wants a lesson, too. Matt Lattanzi, Caren Kaye, Kevin McCarthy, Arlene Golonka. w. Joe Roberts, d. George Bowers.

COMEDY: Erotic Comedy; Teenagers; Teenage Movies; Romance-Older Woman/Younger Man; Virgins; Teachers & Students; Sexy Women; Sexy Men (Homework; Class; Private Lessons)

My Wife's Best Friend, 1952, 87m, ★★1/2/$, 20th/NA. A woman imagines how well female historical figures would have dealt with her situation when she learns her husband is having an affair. Anne Baxter, Macdonald Carey, Cecil Kellaway, Casey Adams. w. Isobel Lennart, d. Richard Sale.

MELODRAMA: COMEDY DRAMA: Fantasies; Cheating Men; Paranoia; Historical Drama; Feminist Films; Forgotten Films; Good Premise Unfulfilled; Female Screenwriters; Female Protagonists

FLIPSIDE TO: Unfaithfully Yours. (Unfaithfully Yours; Woman Times Seven)

My Wild Irish Rose, 1947, 101m, ★★1/2/$$, 20th/NA. Chauncey Olcott, the famous Irish tenor meets and woos Lillian Russell, wins her and loses her several times in this musical biopic. Dennis Morgan, Arlene Dahl, Andrea King, Alan Hale, George Tobias. w. Peter Milne, N-adap. Rita Ilcott, d. David Walter.

MUSICALS: Singers; **ROMANCE:** Musical Romance; Biographies; Romance-On and Off Again; Actresses; Nostalgia

Myra Breckinridge, 1970, 94m, ★★1/2/$$, 20th/Media, NA, R & X/ES-FN-MRN. A film critic gets a sex-change operation and makes it his/her mission in life to humiliate men. Mae West, Raquel Welch, John Huston, Rex Reed, Jim Backus, John Carradine. w. Mike Sarne, David Giler, N-adap. Gore Vidal, d. Mike Sarne.

COMEDY: SATIRE: Erotic Comedy; Men as Women; Transsexuals; Alternative Lifestyles; Gay Men; Lesbians; Hollywood Life; Doctors; Nurses; Cult Films; Revenge; Coulda Been Great; Hidden Gems; Curiosities; Time Capsules; Ahead of Its Time; Forgotten Films; Compilation Films

(Candy; Barbarella; Kansas City Bomber; Glen or Glenda?; Dinah East; Beyond the Valley of the Dolls)

(Ed: Fox disowned this one, though enough publicity with its incredible oddities could have made it as big of a hit, as the novel was. Pretty raunchy and naughty)

Mysterious Island, 1961, 101m, ★★★/$$, Col/Col. A group of confederate soldiers escape the Civil War in a hot air balloon and end up on an island inhabited by dinosaurs and shipwrecked Englishwomen. Joan Greenwood, Michael Craig, Herbert Lom. w. John Prebble, Dan Ullman, Crane Wilbur, N-adap. Jules Verne, d. Cy Endfield.

SCI-FI: HORROR: Monsters-Mutant; Monsters-Animal; Animals into Humans; Scientists-Mad; Stranded on an Island; Shipwrecks; Islands; South Pacific; Insects; Submarines; Octopi-Angry; Balloons

REMAKE: The Island of Dr. Moreau (Island of Lost Souls; Ebb Tide; Master of the World)

The Mystery of Edwin Drood, 1935, 85m, ★★★/$$, U/NA. Two men, a man and his drug-addicted uncle, woo the same woman. Claude Rains, Douglas Montgomery, Heather Angel, David Manners. w. John L. Balderston, Gladys Unger, Bradley King, Leopold Atlas, N-adap. Charles Dickens, d. Stuart Walker.

MELODRAMA: ROMANCE: Romance-Triangles; Men Fighting Over Women; Drugs-Addictions

MUSICAL REMAKE: Broadway version, 1985.

(Ed: The novel was unfinished and this is one attempt at completion, though the musical does it much better and differently)

Mystery of the Wax Museum, 1933, 77m, ★★★1/2/$$$, WB/MGM-UA. A mad artist badly burned in a fire opens a wax museum where the models are live humans he covers in molten wax. Lionel Atwill, Fay Wray, Glenda Farrell, Frank McHugh, Gavin Gordon, Allen Vincent. w. Don Mullally, Carl Erickson, P-adap. Charles S. Belden, d. Michael Curtiz.

HORROR: MURDER: Artists; Revenge; Wax Museums; Hidden Gems

(Murder in the Wax Museum; Waxworks)

Mystery Street, 1950, 93m, ★★★/$, MGM/NA. Detectives enlist the aide of forensic specialists from Harvard who gleen information from analyzing a victim's bones. Ricardo Montalban, Sally Forrest, Elsa Lanchester, Bruce Bennett, Jan Sterling. w. Sidney Boehm, Richard Brooks, Leonard Spigelgass (BOStory), d. John Sturges. Oscars: 1-0.

MYSTERY: MURDER: MURDER

MYSTERY: Detective Stories; Medical Detectives; Harvard; Curiosities; Hidden Gems; Forgotten Films (Gorky Park)

Mystery Train, 1989, 110m, ★★★/$, Orion/Orion, R/S-P. Elvis fans making pilgrimages to Memphis stay in the same fleabag hotel and their disparate stories intertwine. Masotoshi Nagase, Youki Kudoh, Screamin' Jay Hawkins, Cinque Lee, Rufus Thomas, Nicoletta Braschi, Elizabeth Bracco, Joe Stummer, Steve Buscemi. w. d. Jim Jarmusch.

COMEDY DRAMA: Art Films; Road Movies; Multiple Stories; Interwoven Stories; Fans-Crazed; Trains; Slice of Life Stories; Eccentric People; Japanese People; Good Premise; Unfulfilled; Writer-Directors; Independent Films (Down by Law; Stranger than Paradise)

Mystic Pizza, 1988, 104m, ★★★/$$$, Goldwyn/Goldwyn, PG/S. Three waitresses at a small-town pizza joint have love life troubles and confide in each other. Vincent Philip D'Onofrio, Annabeth Gish, William R. Moses, Julia Roberts, Lili Taylor, Conchata Ferrell. w. Amy Jones, Perry Howze, Randy Howze, Alfred Uhry, d. Donald Petrie.

COMEDY DRAMA: ROMANCE: Ensemble Films; Ensembles-Female; Restaurant Settings; Coming of Age; Liars; Cheating Men; Teenagers; Teenage Movies; Girls; Young Women; Virgins; Female Protagonists; Sleeper Hits; Female Screenwriters (Diner; Moonlight and Valentino; Satisfaction)

(Ed: Female version of *Diner* through and through, but also Julia Roberts' first big role-a much different one than her subsequent persona)

N

Nadine, 1987, 88m, ★★★/$, Tri-Star/ RCA-Col, PG/S. A murder investigation brings a bickering couple back from the brink of divorce when the wife is implicated in the small-town murder of a photographer who took some naughty photos of her. Jeff Bridges, Kim Basinger, Rip Torn, Jerry Stiller, Gwen Verdon, Glenne Headly. w. d. Robert Benton.
COMEDY: MYSTERY: MURDER: MURDER MYSTERY: Comic Mystery; Marriage Comedy; Murder-Discovering; Detective Stories; Detectives-Amateur; Hairdressers; Texas; Small-town Scandals; Pornography World; Photographers; Old-Fashioned Recent Films; Hidden Gems; Female Protagonists; Writer-Directors; Coulda Been Great
(A Night to Remember; The Ex-Mrs. Bradford; The Awful Truth)
Naked, 1993, 131m, ★★★/$, Fine Line/ Fine Line-Col, R/S-P. An out-of-work drifter stays with an ex-girlfriend, and in angry journey reflects on the decay of modern Britain and the anger of youth in artful, bizarre gray and purple London cityscapes. Davis Thewliss, Lesley Sharp, Caitlin Cartlidge. w. d. Mike Leigh.
DRAMA: Art Films; Depression; Young Men-Angry; Social Satire; Ensemble Films; Character Studies; London; British Films; Writer-Directors; Quiet Little Films
(High Hopes)

The Naked and the Dead, 1958, 131m, ★★1/2/$$, RKO/VCI. A platoon of green soldiers face the horrors of World War II. Aldo Ray, Cliff Robertson, Raymond Massey, William Campbell, Richard Jaeckel, James Best, Joey Bishop. w. Denis and Terry Sanders, N-adap. Norman Mailer, d. Raoul Walsh.
ACTION: War Stories; War Battles; World War II Stories; Soldiers; Ensembles-Male (Platoon; Midnight Clear; The Big Red One)
The Naked City, 1948, 96m, ★★★★/ $$$, U/MCA-U. A killer on the loose in New York City is the object of an all out manhunt by the NYPD; contains the famous line: "There are eight million stories in the naked city." Barry Fitzgerald, Don Taylor, Howard Duff. w. Malvin Wald, Albert Maltz, d. Jules Dassin.
SUSPENSE: Crime Drama; Police Stories; Detective Stories; Detectives-Police; Trail of a Killer; Serial Killers; Documentary Style; Time Capsules
(The January Man; The Boston Strangler)
The Naked Face, 1984, 106m, ★★1/2/$, Cannon/MGM-UA, R/V-P. A therapist in Chicago gets mixed up with the mob. Roger Moore, Rod Steiger, Elliott Gould, Anne Archer, Art Carney. w. d. Bryan Forbes, N-adap. Sidney Sheldon.
SUSPENSE: MYSTERY: Mob Stories; Fugitives from the Mob; Psychiatrists;

Saving Oneself; Chicago; Coulda Been Good
The Naked Gun: From the Files of Police Squad, 1988, 85m, ★★★1/2/ $$$$$, Par/Par, PG-13/S-EP. The thick-headed Lieutenant Frank Drebin of the LAPD is given the assignment of protecting the Queen of England on a visit to the states, but he may be more dangerous to her than the stalker. Leslie Nielsen, Priscilla Presley, Ricardo Montalban, George Kennedy, O. J. Simpson. w. Jerry Zucker, Jim Abrahams, David Zucker, Pat Proft, d. David Zucker.
COMEDY: Comedy-Gag; Comedy-Slapstick; Police Stories; Police Comedy; Spoofs; Detectives-Police; Spoofs-Detectives; Fools-Bumbling; Assassination Plots; Stalkers; Queens; Bathroom Humor; All-Star Cameos; Sleeper Hits
REMAKE OF: TV Series *Police Squad*, 1982.
The Naked Gun 2½: The Smell of Fear, 1991, 85m, ★★★/$$$$, Par/Par, PG-13/ EP-S. A group of international oilmen try to thwart a solar energy entrepreneur, and Lieutenant Frank Drebin stumbles in to set things right. Leslie Nielsen, Priscilla Presley, George Kennedy, O. J. Simpson, Robert Goulet, Richard Griffiths, Lloyd Bochner. w. David Zucker, Pat Proft, d. David Zucker.

COMEDY: Comedy-Gag; Comedy-Slapstick; Police Stories; Police Comedy; Spoofs; Detectives-Police; Spoofs-Detectives; Fools-Bumbling; Oil People; Conspiracy; Bathroom Humor; All-Star Cameos

(Ed: The plot is less effective than the first, but the gags are still there)

Naked Gun 33⅓, 1994, ★★★/$$$, Par/Par, PG-13/P-S. This time, there's a plot to bomb the Oscars and it's up to Frank Drebin to stop the show! Leslie Nielsen, Priscilla Presley, Anna Nicole Smith, Fred Ward, Kathleen Freeman, Raquel Welch, O. J. Simpson, George Kennedy, Pia Zadora, James Earl Jones. w. Pat Proft, Robert Locash, David Zucker, d. Peter Segal.

COMEDY: Comedy-Slapstick; Comedy-Gag; Police Stories; Police Comedy; Spoofs; Detectives-Police; Spoofs-Detectives; Fools-Bumbling; Hollywood Satire; Conspiracy; Bathroom Humor; All-Star Cameos; Oscars

(Ed: Not up to the first two helmed by ZAZ [the Zuckers brothers and Jim Abrahams] but worth it)

(Kentucky Fried Movie; Sledgehammer [TV Series]; Airplane; Dead Men Don't Wear Plaid)

Naked in New York, 1994, 91m, ★★/$, Ind/Sony, R/S-P-MFN. A playwright and a photographer fall in love but soon stray when their careers begin to rise; as they travel through the hip New York scene and all of its eccentricities. Eric Stoltz, Mary Louise Parker, Ralph Macchio, Jill Clayburgh, Tony Curtis, Kathleen Turner, Whoopi Goldberg, Timothy Dalton, William Styron, Eric Bogosian. w. Dan Algrant, John Warren, d. Dan Algrant.

COMEDY: SATIRE: ROMANCE: Romantic Comedy; Young Men; Young Women; Writers; Photographers; Slice of Life Stories; Neurotic People; Art World; New York Life; Homo-eroticism; Soap Opera Shows; Art Films; Hidden Gems; Overlooked at Release; All-Star Cameos; Quiet Little Films

(Ed: Not for those expecting the humor of Woody Allen or much of anything to happen. Mr. Stoltz reveals too much once again)

The Naked Jungle, 1954, 95m, ★★½/ $$, Par/Par. A genteel woman is betrothed by a family contract to a plantation owner residing in a banana republic, and she must make the requisite adjustments to her new environment-especially the ants. Charlton Heston, Eleanor Parker, William Conrad, Abraham Sofaer. w. Philip Yordan, Ranald MacDougall, SS-adap. Carl Stephenson (*Leningen Versus the Ants*), d. Byron Haskin.

MELODRAMA: ROMANCE: Romantic Drama; Fish out of Water Stories; Marriage of Convenience; Marriage Drama; Secrets-Keeping; Dangerous Spouse; Africa; Plantation Life; 1900s (Indochine; Elephant Walk; Out of Africa)

The Naked Kiss, 1964, 92m, ★★½/$, AA/Home Vision. The story of a woman of ill repute who tries to go legit. Constance Towers, Anthony Eisley, Michael Dante, Virginia Grey, Patsy Kelly. w. d. Samuel Fuller.

DRAMA: Social Drama; Prostitutes-Low Class; Underworld; Inner City Life; Class Conflicts; Redemption; Starting Over; Female Protagonists; Writer-Directors (A House Is Not a Home; Madame X; Personal Services)

Naked Lunch, 1991, 115m, ★★★/$, 20th/Fox, R/EP-S. An adaption which mixes biographical elements of William Burroughs' life; such as the "accidental" killing of his wife in a drunken William Tell party game and his struggles with homosexuality, with elements of his quasi-science fiction cult novel *Naked Lunch*. Peter Weller, Judy Davis, Ian Holm, Julian Sands, Roy Scheider, Monique Mercure. w. d. David Cronenberg, N-adap. William S. Burroughs.

HORROR: DRAMA: Art Films; Avant-Garde Films; Drugs-Addictions; Marriage Drama; Writers; Autobiographical Stories; Biographies; Death-Accidental; Wives-Troublesome; Alcoholics; Depression; Nervous Breakdowns; Surrealism; Insects; Fantasies; Illusions/Hallucinations; Curiosities; Cult Films

(Ed: Bizarre is not the word, not for the squeamish or those who prefer coherent plots)

The Naked Maja, 1959, 112m, ★★/$$, MGM/MGM-UA. A biopic of the famous artist Goya and the relationship to his patron, the Duchess of Alba. Anthony Franciosa, Ava Gardner, Amedeo Nazzari, Gino Gervi, Massimo Serrato. w. Giorgio Prosperi, Norman Corwin, Albert Lewin, Oscar Saul, d. Henry Koster.

DRAMA: ROMANCE: Romantic Drama; Biographies; Costume Drama; Artists-Famous; Spain

(Goya; Moon and Sixpence; Lust for Life)

The Naked Prey, 1966, 94m, ★★★/$$, Par/Par. A parable of racism in which a white hunter in Africa gets karmic payback when he himself is hunted by a local tribe. Cornel Wilde, Gert Van Den Berg, Ken Gampu. w. Clint Johnston, Don Peters (BOScr), d. Cornel Wilde. Oscars: 1-0.

ACTION: SUSPENSE: Hunters; Fugitives; Manhunts; Chase Movies; Africa; Hidden Gems; Actor Directors (White Hunter, Black Heart; Tales from the Hood)

The Naked Runner, 1967, 104m, ★★/$$, WB/WB, PG/V. Interpol volunteers a timid businessman into their spy corps to be an unwitting assassin. Frank Sinatra, Peter Vaughan, Derren Nesbitt, Edward Fox. w. Stanley Mann, N-adap. Francis Clifford, d. Sidney J. Furie.

SUSPENSE: Spy Films; Spies; Assassination Plots; Secret Agents; Conspiracy; Good Premise Unfulfilled (The Manchurian Candidate; The Parallax View)

The Naked Spur, 1953, 91m, ★★★/ $$$, MGM/MGM-UA, Time-Life. A bounty hunter and a fugitive of justice track each other across the Colorado rockies. James Stewart, Robert Ryan, Janet Leigh. w. Sam Rolfe, Harold Jack Bloom (BOScr), d. Anthony Mann. Oscars: 1-0.

WESTERNS: Bounty Hunters; Fugitives from the Law; Chase Movies; Hidden Gems

COMIC FLIPSIDE: Midnight Run

The Naked Street, 1955, 83m, ★★½/$, Edward Small/NA. A gangster bails his convicted murderer son-in-law out of jail but he kills again. Anthony Quinn, Anne Bancroft, Farley Granger, Peter Graves. w. Maxwell Shane, Leo Katcher, d. Maxwell Shane.

SUSPENSE: MURDER: Crime Drama; Mob Stories; Prison Drama; Ex-Convicts; Starting Over

Naked Tango, 1990, 92m, ★★★/$, Ind/NA, R/S. A bored housewife assumes the identity of a dead woman and moves to Buenos Aires to take up with a mobster tango dancer. Vincent D'Onofrio, Mathilda May, Esai Morales, Fernando Rey, Cipe Lincovsky, Josh Mostel. w. d. Leonard Schrader, SS-adap. Manuel Puig.

DRAMA: Art Films; Erotic Drama; Dance Movies; South America; Identities-Assumed; Mob Stories; Starting Over; Magic Realism; Female Protagonists; Argentina; Independent Films
(Kiss of the Spider Woman)

The Naked Truth (Your Past is Showing), 1957, 92m, ★★★/$$, Ind/Sultan. A Hollywood hanger-on gleans incriminating evidence about several stars and proceeds to blackmail them. Everything goes according to plan until they get together and plan his murder. Peter Sellers, Terry-Thomas, Peggy Mount, Dennis Price, Shirley Eaton. w. Michael Pertwee, d. Mario Zampi.
COMEDY: FARCE: Black Comedy; Gossip; Rumors; Blackmail; Journalists; Ethics; Hollywood Life; Hollywood Satire; Forgotten Films; Hidden Gems
(The Player; The Big Knife)

The Name of the Rose, 1986, 130m, ★★1/2/$$, 20th/CBS-Fox, R/S-FFN-MRN. A murder mystery set at a fourteenth-century Italian monastery which monks try to solve. Sean Connery, F. Murray Abraham, Christian Slater. w. Andrew Birkin, Gerard Brach, Howard Franklin, Alain Godard, N-adap. Umberto Eco, d. Jean-Jacques Annaud.
MYSTERY: MURDER: MURDER MYSTERY: Detective Stories; Detectives-Amateur; Monks; Middle Ages; Hunchbacks; Good Premise Unfulfilled; Flops-Major
(The Advocate)
(Ed: A bomb in America, but the novel's huge following turned up at the theater in Europe)

Nancy Goes to Rio, 1950, 99m, ★★1/2/$$, MGM/MGM-UA. A mother and daughter, both actresses, take a ship to Brazil to audition for a big part. Jane Powell, Ann Sothern, Carmen Miranda, Barry Sullivan, Louis Calhern, Fortunio Bonnanova, Hans Conried. w. Sidney Sheldon, d. Robert Z. Leonard.
MUSICALS: Singers; Mothers and Daughters; Parents vs. Children; Ships; Vacations
(Holiday in Mexico; Romance on the High Seas)

Nancy Steele Is Missing, 1937, 85m, ★★1/2/$, 20th/NA. A group of would-be kidnappers try to extort money from the wealthy parents of Miss Steele, even though they don't really have her. Victor McLaglen, Peter Lorre, June Lang, John Carradine. w. Gene Fowler, Hal Long, N-adap. C. F. Coe, d. George Marshall.
MELODRAMA: SUSPENSE: Kidnappings; Missing Persons; Con Artists; Hoaxes

The Nanny, 1965, 93m, ★★★/$$, Hammer-AIP/NA. No one believes a young boy who fears his seemingly perfect nanny until they discover that she's a psychopathic killer. Bette Davis, Jill Bennett, William Dix. w. Jimmy Sangster, N-adap. Evelyn Piper, d. Seth Holt.
SUSPENSE: HORROR: Psycho Killers; Babysitters; Babysitters-Evil; Unbelieved; Child Protagonists; Hidden Gems; British Films
(The Hand That Rocks the Cradle; The Guardian; The Babysitter; Don't Bother to Knock)

Nanook of the North, 1921, 57m, ★★★/$$$, Revillon Freres/NA. An eskimo family's daily life is explored in this pioneering early silent documentary. w. d. Robert Flaherty.
ADVENTURE: Silent Films; Disaster Movies; Snow Settings; Eskimos; Rescue Drama

Nanou, 1986, 110m, ★★1/2/$, Umbrella-Arion/NA. A French radical activist takes the heart of a vacationing British woman. Imogen Stubbs, Jean-Philippe Ecoffey, Daniel Day-Lewis. w. d. Conny Templeman.
MELODRAMA: ROMANCE: Vacations; Vacation Romance; Political Activists; Romance-Older Men/Younger Women; Love-First; Female Protagonists; Writer-Directors
(Swept Away; Salome's Last Dance)

Napoleon, 1927, 378m, ★★★1/2/$$, B&W, silent, Ind/MCA-U. An epic, sweeping biopic of the great French general and president including a spectacular restaging of the battle at Waterloo. Albert Djeudonne, Antonin Artaud, Pierre Batcheff. w. d. Abel Gance.
DRAMA: Silent Films; Epics; Napoleon; Historical Drama; Biographies; Cast of Thousands; Lyrical Films; Forgotten Films; Cult Films; Writer-Directors; Film; History
(Waterloo; Desiree)
(Ed: Originally unreleased due the advent of talkies, it was restored and released in the 80s)

Napoleon and Samantha, 1972, 91m, ★★1/2/$$, Disney/Disney, G. An orphan boy with a pet lion who is taken care of by an older man runs off when he dies. He takes his lion and girlfriend with him. Michael Douglas, Will Geer, Johnny Whittaker, Jodie Foster. w. Stewart Raffil, d. Bernard McEveety. BOScore. Oscars: 1-0.
ADVENTURE: CHILDREN'S: FAMILY: Orphans; Runaways; Pet Stories
(The Biscuit Eater [1971]; Candleshoe)

The Narrow Margin, 1952, 70m, ★★★1/2/$$, RKO/Turner. An informant in a witness protection program is escorted by train from Chicago to Los Angeles and must be protected from those who want him dead. Charles McGraw, Marie Windsor, Jacqueline White. w. Earl Fenton, d. Richard Fleischer.

Narrow Margin, 1990, 97m, ★★★/$, Carolco-Tri-Star/Col-Tri, R/V. Remake of above, with more action and peril, but not any better. Gene Hackman, Anne Archer, James B. Sikking, J. T. Walsh, M. Emmet Walsh. w. Earl Fenton, Jr., Martin Goldsmith, Jack Leonard, d. Peter Hyams.
SUSPENSE: Chase Movies; Fugitives from the Law; Fugitives from the Mob; Mob Stories; Police Stories; Witnesses-Protecting; Informers; Trains
(Midnight Run; Under Siege 2)

Nashville, 1975, 161m, ★★★★/$$$, ABC-Cin-Par/Par, R/P-S. A myriad of folksy, Southern characters meander their way around music city during the period before a political rally, each with their own story somehow relating to music. Lily Tomlin (BSActress), Keith Carradine, Ned Beatty, Ronee Blakely (BSActress), Geraldine Chaplin, Karen Black, Barbara Harris, Henry Jackson, Barbara Baxley, Jeff Goldblum,. w. Joan Tewkesbury, d. Robert Altman (BDirector). BPicture, BOSong. Oscars: 5-1.
SATIRE: FARCE: DRAMA: COMEDY DRAMA: Black Comedy; Political Drama; Assassination Plots; Interwoven Stories; Multiple Stories; All-Star Casts; Slice of Life; Southerns; Musicians; Country Singers; Singers; Dreams; Hidden Gems; Time Capsules; 1970s
(Short Cuts; Amateur Night at the Dixie Bar & Grill; Honkytonk Freeway; Ready to Wear)

The Nasty Girl, 1990, 92m, ★★★1/2/$$, Mainline-Miramax/HBO, PG-13. A student essay on her town's Nazi past ends up ruffling a lot of feathers and starting the political education of a German girl in a small town. Lena Stolze, Monika

Baumgartner, Michael Garh, Fred Stillkrauth. w. d. Michael Verhoeven. BFFilm. Oscars: 1-0.

DRAMA: SATIRE: Social Drama; Historical Drama; Secrets-Keeping; Scandals-Small-town; Germany; German Films; Hidden Gems; Writer-Directors (Ed: The title is provocative sexually, the film isn't, but politically . . . historically . . .)

Nasty Habits, 1976, 92m, ★★★/$, Brut-Embassy/Media. All the nuns in a convent compete ruthlessly for the top position when the abbess dies. Glenda Jackson, Melina Mercouri, Geraldine Page, Sandy Dennis, Rip Torn, Eli Wallach, Jerry Stiller. w. Robert Enders, N-adap. Muriel Spark (*The Abbess of Crewe*), d. Michael Lindsay-Hogg.

SATIRE: COMEDY: Black Comedy; Nuns; Power Struggles; Ensembles-Female; Allegorical Stories; Hidden Gems; Coulda Been Great; Female Protagonists; British Films (The Maids; Agnes of God)

Nate and Hayes, 1983, 100m, ★★1/2/$, Par/Par, PG. Swashbuckling adventures on the lam from pirates and slave traders. Tommy Lee Jones, Michael O'Keefe, Jenny Seagrove. d. Ferdinand Fairfax.

ADVENTURE: Chase Stories; Swashbucklers; Pirates; Slavery; Missionaries; South Pacific; Buddy Films; 1800s; Old-Fashioned Recent Films; Forgotten Films (Cutthroat Island)

National Lampoon's Animal House, 1978, 112m, ★★★/$$$$$, Universal/MCA-U, R/P-S-FN. Fraternity brothers go wild, wreaking havoc all over campus. Tim Matheson, John Belushi, Donald Sutherland. w. Harold Ramis, Chris Miller, Douglas Kenney, d. John Landis.

COMEDY: Party Movies; Teenage Movies; College Life; Fraternity Life; Wild People; Bathroom Humor; Sleeper Hits; Blockbusters (Bachelor Party; The Blues Brothers; PCU)

National Lampoon's Christmas Vacation, 1989, 97m, ★★★/$$$, WB/WB, PG-13/S-P. A family decides instead of their usual trip on Christmas, they will spend quality time at home. Big mistake. Chevy Chase, Beverly D'Angelo, Randy Quaid, Diane Ladd, E. G. Marshall, Julia Louis-Dreyfus. w. John Hughes, d. Jeremiah S. Chechik.

COMEDY: FARCE: Comedy-Slapstick; Christmas; Comedy of Errors; Family

Comedy; Fools-Bumbling; Feuds; Snow Settings

SEQUEL TO: European Vacation and Vacation.

National Lampoon's Class Reunion, 1982, 85m, ★★1/2/$$, ABC-20th/CBS-Fox, PG/S-P. A ten year reunion turns to mayhem as a murderer joins the revelers. Gerrit Graha, Michael Lerner, Fred McCarren. w. John Hughes, d. Michael Miller.

COMEDY: Psycho Killers; Reunions-Class; Spoofs; Spoofs-Horror; Horror Comedy; Comedy-Skit

National Lampoon's European Vacation, 1985, 94m, ★★★/$$$$, WBWB, PG-13/S-P-FN. The Griswald family goes to Europe, where Dad takes a semi-pornographic video of Mom which gets stolen in Italy. Later they see it's been turned into a soft-core hit. Chevy Chase, Beverly D'Angelo, Eric Idle. w. John Hughes, Robert Klane, d. Amy Heckerling.

COMEDY: Comedy of Errors; Vacations; Family Comedy; Fools-Bumbling; Video-tape Scandals; Scandals; Vacations-European; Female Directors (Bon Voyage; The Last Resort; Club Paradise)

National Lampoon's Movie Madness, 1981, 89m, ★★1/2/$, UA/NA. Three skit parodies of movie cliches. Robby Benson, Richard Widmark, Diane Ladd, Candy Clark, Christopher Lloyd. w. Tod Carroll, Shary Flenniken, Pat Mephitis, Gerald Sussman, Ellis Weiner, d. Bob Giraldi, Henry Jaglom.

COMEDY: Comedy-Skit; Spoofs; Moviemaking (Amazon Women on the Moon)

National Lampoon's Vacation, 1983, 98m, ★★★/$$$$, WB/WB, PG/P. A family travels cross-country, greeting and/or creating disasters at every turn, including having to carry their dead grandma on top of the station wagon. Chevy Chase, Imogene Coca, Beverly D'Angelo, Randy Quaid, Eddie Bracken. w. John Hughes, d. Harold Ramis.

COMEDY: Comedy-Slapstick; Comedy of Errors; Vacations; Family Comedy; Relatives-Troublesome; Fools-Bumbling; Sleeper Hits

SEQUELS: European Vacation; Christmas Vacation. (Funny Farm; Nothing but Trouble)

National Velvet, 1945, 125m, ★★★/$$$$, MGM/MGM-UA. A group of children succeed, where seasoned professionals fail, in training a horse to win a big race. Mickey Rooney, Elizabeth Taylor, Anne Revere, Donald Crisp, Angela Lansbury, Reginald Owen. w. Theodore Reeves, Helen Deutsch, N-adap. Enid Bagnold, d. Clarence Brown.

MELODRAMA: CHILDREN'S: FAMILY: Horses; Pet Stories; Girls; Child Protagonists; Women and Girls; Female Protagonists; Female Screenwriters

SEQUEL: International Velvet. (My Friend Flicka; Black Beauty; Seabiscuit)

Native Son, 1951, 91m, ★★★/$, Ind/Nos. The classic tale of the black chauffeur of a white family and the accidental death of their daughter for which he's held accountable. Stars author Richard Wright, Jean Wallace, Nicholas Joy. w. N-adap. Richard Wright, d. Pierre Chenal.

Independent Films

Native Son, 1986, 112m, ★★★/$, American Playhouse-Cinecom/Live, R/S-V. A young black man in thirties Chicago is humiliated by the lily-white daughter of the wealthy family he chauffeurs for, and passions get the best of him as he "accidently" kills her. Carroll Baker, Elizabeth McGovern, Oprah Winfrey, Akousuwa Busia, Matt Dillon, Art Evans, Geraldine Page. w. Richard Wesley, N-adap. Richard Wright, d. Jerrold Freedman.

DRAMA: TRAGEDY: MURDER: Social Drama; Death-Accidental; Race Relations; Bigots; Black vs. White; Crimes of Passion; Courtroom Drama; Trials; Black Men; Black Women; Mothers and Sons

The Natural, 1984, 137m, ★★★1/2/$$$, Tri-Star/Col-Tri, PG/V. A mythic look at "natural" talent involving a baseball player with almost mystical ability. Robert Redford, Robert Duvall, Glenn Close (BSActress), Kim Basinger, Wilford Brimley, Barbara Hershey, Joe Don Baker. w. Roger Towne, Phil Dusenberry, d. Barry Levinson. BOScore, BCin, BArt. Oscars: 4-0.

DRAMA: MELODRAMA: TRAGEDY: MURDER: Biographies-Fictional; Baseball; Sports Movies; Fame-Rise to; Rise and Fall Stories; Magic Realism; Lyrical Films; Flashbacks (Field of Dreams; Angels in the Outfield)

Natural Born Killers, 1994, 125m, ★★/$$, U/MCA-U, R/EV-EP-S-B&G. A couple of redneck serial killers become national celebrities in the tabloids for their reign of terror and its aftermath of coverage. Will they live happily ever after? Woody Harrelson, Juliette Lewis, Robert Downey, Jr., Ashley Judd, Tommy Lee Jones, Rodney Dangerfield, Rachel Ticotin. w. Quentin Tarantino, d. Oliver Stone.
COMEDY DRAMA: Black Comedy; SATIRE: Social Satire; Serial Killers; Criminal Couples; Crime Sprees; Media Satire; Journalists; Ethics; Rednecks; Murderers-Female; Comedy & Violence; Cult Films
(Kalifornia; True Romance; The Honeymoon Killers)
(Ed: Controversial, and intentionally so; raises the debate as to whether it's glorification of violence or analysis of it)

The Nature of the Beast, 1988, 95m, ★★1/2/$, Cannon/WB. In a depressed factory town, a mysterious creature kills the local animals and a group of young boys finds it, but who'll survive? Lynton Dearden, Paul Simpson, Tony Melody. w., N-adap. Janni Howker, d. Franco Rosso.
HORROR: SCI-FI: Monsters; Small-town Life; Working Class; Social Drama; Allegorical Stories; British Films
(Kes; Lord of the Flies)

Naughty But Nice, 1939, 90m, ★★1/2/$$, WB/NA. A professor who's a purist when it comes to classical music, stumbles onto the pop charts with a new composition. Dick Powell, Ann Sheridan, Ronald Reagan, Gale Page, Zasu Pitts. w. Jerry Wald, Richard Macaulay, d. Ray Enright.
MUSICALS: Music Movies; Musicians; Professors; Big Band Era; Fame-Rise to; Snobs

Naughty Marietta, 1935, 106m, ★★★/$$$, MGM/MGM-UA. The daughter of the royal family of France runs off to America and falls for an Indian. Jeanette MacDonald, Nelson Eddy, Frank Morgan, Elsa Lanchester. w. John Lee Mahin, Frances Goodrich, Albert Hackett, (Operetta)-adap. Rida Johnson Young, d. W. S. Van Dyke.
MUSICALS: ROMANCE: Musical Romance; Operettas; Romance-Interracial; Singers; Princesses; Runaways; Indians-American

(Bittersweet; The Firefly; The Chocolate Soldier; Roman Holiday)

The Naughty Nineties, 1945, 72m, ★★★/$$$, U/MCA-U. In the gay 90s, a showboat captain gets a boost from two comedians. Bud Abbott, Lou Costello, Henry Travers. w. Edmund L. Hartmann, John Grant, Edmund Joseph, Hal Fimburg, d. Jean Yarborough.
COMEDY: Comedians; Comedy-Skit; Showboats; 1890s; Gay 90s; Nostalgia; Baseball
(Abbott & Costello SERIES)
(Ed: Contains the famous "Who's On First" routine, the best thing in it)

The Navigator, 1924, 63m, B&W, silent, ★★★1/2/$$$, MGM/MGM-UA, NA. After the crew and all of the passengers jump ship, a foppish tycoon and his girlfriend are left to steer the ship ashore. Buster Keaton, Kathryn McGuire. w. Jean Havez, Clyde Bruckman, J. A. Mitchell, d. Buster Keaton.
COMEDY: Comedy-Slapstick; Comedy of Errors; Ships

Navy SEALS, 1990, 114m, ★★/$, Orion/Orion, PG-13/V-P. A special force of highly specialized soldiers within the Navy track down Arab terrorists in Lebanon. Charlie Sheen, Michael Biehn, Joanne Whalley-Kilmer, Bill Paxton. w. Chuck Pfarrer, Gary Goldman, d. Lewis Teague.
ACTION: Military Stories; Special Teams; Terrorists; Trail of a Killer; Arab People; Middle East
(Delta Force; Desert Storm; The Little Drummer Girl)

Nazi Agent, 1942, 84m, ★★1/2/$$, MGM/NA. Identical twins born in Germany become separated. One moves to America and one becomes a Nazi. During the war, they meet again, and the American brother is forced to work for the Germans. Conrad Veidt, Ann Ayars, Frank Reicher. w. Paul Gangelin, John Meehan, Jr., d. Jules Dassin.
DRAMA: War Stories; Nazi Stories; World War II Era; Twins; Brothers; Reunions
(The Great Impersonation; Dead Ringer; Dead Ringers; Max and Helen)

Near Dark, 1987, 94m, ★★1/2/$, Ind/HBO, R/V-S-B&G. An atmospheric modern vampire story in which a cult of bloodsuckers travels around Oklahoma in a Winnebago looking for victims. Adrian Pasdar, Jenny Wright, Lance Henrickson, Bill Paxton. w. Eric Red, Kathryn Bigelow, d. Kathryn Bigelow.

HORROR: Art Films; Vampires; Gangs; Southwestern Life; Female Screenwriters; Female Directors; Independent Films
(The Loveless; The Lost Boys)
(Ed: All night, no fright)

Necessary Roughness, 1991, 104m, ★★1/2/$$, Par/Par, PG-13/P-S-MRN. When the football coach at a state university loses all his star players in a scandal, he is forced to recruit among the better students, with disastrous results. Scott Bakula, Robert Loggia, Hector Elizondo. w. Rick Natkin, David Fuller, d. Stan Dragoti.
COMEDY: Sports Movies; Comedy of Errors; Football; Coaches; College Life; Scandals; Ethics; Good Premise Unfulfilled
(The Program; North Dallas Forty; Rudy)

Necromancy, 1973, 83m, ★/$, Cinerama/NA. A cult in a small town ensnares two of its younger residents into Satanism. Orson Welles, Pamela Franklin, Michael Ontkean. w. d. Bert I. Gordon.
HORROR: Satanism; Supernatural Danger; Small-town Life; Underworld; Occult; Cults; Curiosities; Writer-Directors; Independent Films

Needful Things, 1993, 120m, ★★1/2/$$, Col/Col, R.EV-B&G. The old curiosity shop in Maine is selling items which are possessed and cause great problems for those who purchase them-for it may be Satan's shop. Max Von Sydow, Ed Harris, Bonnie Bedelia, Amanda Plummer, J. T. Walsh. w. W. D. Richter, N-adap. Stephen King, d. Fraser Heston.
HORROR: Satan; Possessions; Police Stories; Evil Men; Supernatural Danger, Stephen King
(Creepshow; Tales from the Darkside)

Negatives, 1968, 98m, ★★1/2/$, Crispin-Ind/NA. An experimental narrative about three people's strange sexual fantasies involving the Red Baron and Dr. Crippen. Glenda Jackson, Peter McEnery, Diane Cilento, Maurice Denham. w. Peter Everett, Roger Lowry, N-adap. Peter Everett. d. Peter Medak.
DRAMA: Erotic Drama; Sexuality; Psychologists; Psychological Drama; Fantasies; Curiosities; Forgotten Films; Independent Films

Neighbors, 1981, 94m, ★★★/$$$, Col/RCA-Col, R/P-S. On a cul-de-sac in suburbia, a couch potato suddenly has to deal with a crazy neighbor and his sexy wife wreaking havoc, so he wreaks some himself. John Belushi, Dan Aykroyd, Cathy Moriarty, Kathryn Walker, Igors Gavon, Dru-Ann Chukron. w. Larry Gelbart, N-adap. Thomas Berger, d. John G. Avildsen.

COMEDY: Black Comedy; Feuds; Suburban Life; Neighbors-Troublesome; Wild People; Saturday Night Live Movies (The Burbs; The Blues Brothers)

Nell, 1994, 120m, ★★★/$$, 20th/Fox, PG-13/S-FN. A scientist comes to the North Carolina woods to investigate a young woman who's been found to have grown up alone in the mountains with the animals and developed her own language and way of life. Jodie Foster (BActress), Liam Neeson, Natasha Richardson, d. Michael Apted. Oscars: 1-0.

DRAMA: ROMANCE: Romantic Drama; Mountain People; Mentally Disabled; Simple Minds; Raised by Animals; Young Women; Sociologists; Southerns; Scenery-Outstanding; Disabled but Nominated ((The Wild Child; Spitfire; Rain Man)

Neptune's Daughter, 1949, 93m, ★★★/$$$$, MGM/MGM-UA. A female bathing suit mogul has a fling down in South America, in and out of the pool. Esther Williams, Ricardo Montalban, Betty Garrett, Keenan Wynn, Xavier Cugat and his Orchestra, Mel Blanc. w. Dorothy Kingsley, d. Edward Buzzell. **BOSong**, "Baby, It's Cold Outside." Oscars: 1-1.

MUSICALS: ROMANCE: Musical Romance; Musicals-Aquatic; Swimming; South America (Million Dollar Mermaid; The Duchess of Idaho) (Ed: The first of the 'aquatic' musicals)

The Net, 1995, 118m, ★★★/$$$, Col/Col, PG-13/P-V. When a young woman finds that she's lost her identity on every computer bank on which she's listed, she decides it must be because she stumbled across a conspiracy when she clicked on an icon of a web site on the computer. After that it's a race to stay alive before they erase her file completely. Sandra Bullock, Jeremy Northam, Dennis Miller, Diane Baker, Ken Howard. w. Irwin Winkler, Rob Cowan, d. Irwin Winkler.

SUSPENSE: Fugitives; Chase Stories; Enemy-Sleeping with; Computer Terror; Computers; Identities-Assumed; Female Protagonists

(Hackers; Three Days of the Condor; The Parallax View; Speed) (Ed: Could have easily been much better, but it's not bad)

Network, 1976, 120m, ★★★★/$$$, MGM/MGM-UA, R/P-V-S-FN. When a network anchorman (Peter Finch, **BActor**) threatens to commit suicide on the air, the programmer (Faye Dunaway, **BActress**) decides to exploit the publicity, much to the consternation of a newsman and friend (William Holden, BActor), the conflict of which may lead to tragedy for all concerned. Robert Duvall, Ned Beatty (BSActor), Beatrice Straight (**BSActress**). w. Paddy Chayefsky (**BOScr**), d. Sidney Lumet (BDirector). BPicture, BCinema, BEditing. Oscars: 10-4.

DRAMA: SATIRE: Black Comedy; Political Drama; **TRAGEDY:** TV Life; Hollywood Life; Message Films; Business Life; Executives; Journalists; Romance-Older Men/Younger Women; Suicidal Tendencies; Power Struggles; Corruption; Corporation as Enemy; Greed; Assassination Plots; Terrorists; Career Women; Evil Women; Mental Illness; Illusions/Hallucinations; Anti-Establishment Films; Hidden Gems (The Hospital; Talk Radio; A Face in the Crowd) (Ed: A landmark satirical and political achievement in film and the culmination of Chayefsky's spectacular writing career. A must-see)

Nevada Smith, 1966, 131m, ★★½/$$$, Avco-Par/Par, PG/V. In the old West an orphaned lad all grown-up now searches for the outlaws who killed his parents. When he finds them, he pays them back in a slow methodical revenge plot. Steve McQueen, Karl Malden, Brian Keith, Suzanne Pleshette, Arthur Kennedy, Howard da Silva. w. John Michael Hayes, N-adap. Harold Robbins (*The Carpetbaggers*), d. Henry Hathaway.

WESTERNS: Westerns-Revenge; Avenging Death of Someone; Revenge; Orphans; Manhunts; Chase Movies; Mindgames; Forgotten Films; Coulda Been Great (High Plains Drifter; The Ballad of Cable Hogue; Tom Horn)

Never a Dull Moment, 1950, 89m, ★★★/$$, RKO/Turner. When a citified female critic marries up with a cowboy and heads to his ranch, adjusting isn't so

easy. Irene Dunne, Fred MacMurray, William Demarest, Andy Devine, Natalie Wood. w. Lou Breslow, Doris Anderson, N-adap. Kay Swift, *Who Could Ask for Anything More?*, d. George Marshall.

COMEDY: ROMANCE: Romantic Comedy; Marriage Comedy; Newlyweds; Fish out of Water Stories; Critics; Female Protagonists; Cattle Ranchers; Cowboys; City vs. Country (The Egg & I; Please Don't Eat the Daisies; Funny Farm; The Cowboy and the Lady)

Never a Dull Moment, 1967, 100m, ★★★/$$, Disney/Disney, G. An out of work actor is a dead ringer for a mobster, causing him all sorts of complications. Dick Van Dyke, Edward G. Robinson, Dorothy Provine, Henry Silva, Joanna Moore, Slim Pickens. w. A. J. Carothers, N-adap. John Godey, d. Jerry Paris.

COMEDY: Mob Stories; Mob Comedy; Comedy-Disney-eque; Identities-Mistaken; Lookalikes; Actors; Fugitives from the Mob; Fugitives from the Law; Coulda Been Great; Good Premise Unfulfilled (Johnny Stecchino; Dave; Moon Over Parador)

Never Cry Wolf, 1983, 105m, ★★★/$$$, Disney/Disney, PG/MN. A lone biologist learns a lot about life from spending time with Arctic wolves. Charles Martin Smith, Brian Dennehy, Samson Jorah. w. Curtis Hanson, Sam Hamm, Richard Kletter, N-adap. Farley Mowat, d. Carroll Ballard.

ADVENTURE: COMEDY DRAMA: Nature-Back to; Scientists; Animal Stories; Lonely People; Stranded; Arctic; Sleeper Hits (Iceman; Call of the Wild)

Never Give a Sucker an Even Break, 1941, 70m, ★★★/$$$, U/MCA-U. W. C. Fields has the good fortune to meet a woman who's never seen a man before when he jumps off of a plane, and she somewhat unbelievably falls in love with him; among other typical and classic Fields' bits. W. C. Fields, Gloria Jean, Leon Errol, Butch and Buddy, Franklin Pangborn, Margaret Dumont. w. John T. Neville, Prescott Chaplin, Otis Criblecoblis (W. C. Fields), d. Edward Cline.

COMEDY: Comedy-Slapstick; Comedy of Errors; **ROMANCE:** Romantic Comedy; Love-First; Virgins; Hidden Gems

(My Little Chickadee; International House)
(Ed: Fields' last feature film; the saying is more famous than this film)

Never Let Go, 1960, 91m, ★★½/$, Rank-Ind/Sultan. When a bunch of gang members steal his car, a salesman confronts their leader. Richard Todd, Peter Sellers, Elizabeth Sellars, Adam Faith, Carol White. w. Alun Falconer, d. John Guillermin.

DRAMA: Crime Drama; Mob Stories; Gangs; Thieves; Ordinary Person vs. Criminal; British Films

Never Love a Stranger, 1958, 93m, ★★½/$$, AA/Republic. Two boyhood friends, one Catholic and one Jewish, drift toward opposite sides of the law as they grow older. They are brought back together when they must collaborate to nail a crook who's wronged them both. John Drew Barrymore, Steve McQueen, Robert Bray. w. Harold Robbins, Richard Day, N-adap. Harold Robbins, d. Robert Stevens.

DRAMA: Crime Drama; Good vs. Evil; Friendships-Male; Friends as Enemies; Enemies Unite; Episodic Stories; Jewish People; Forgotten Films
(Manhattan Melodrama; True Confessions)

Never on Sunday, 1960, 97m, ★★★/ $$$, Lopert-UA/MGM-UA, S. An Aegean enchantress steals the heart of an American academic on sabbatical in Greece, then he finds out her true profession and tries to reform her. Melina Mercouri (BActress), Jules Dassin, Georges Foundas, Titos Vandis, Despo Diamantidou. w. d. Jules Dassin (BOScr, BDirector). BOSong. Oscars: 4-1.

COMEDY DRAMA: ROMANCE: Romantic Comedy; Romance with Prostitute; Vacations; Vacation Romance; Professors; Nerds; Nerds and Babes; Reformers; Feisty Females; Greece; Faded Hits
(Pretty Woman; Pygmalion; Topkapi; Nights of Cabiria)
(Ed: Big hit song from a hit film, but the film itself hasn't withstood the test of time so well)

Never Say Die, 1939, 80m, ★★½/$$, Par/NA. A wealthy man, convinced he is dying, tries to make the most of his "last days." Martha Raye, Bob Hope, Andy Devine, Alan Mowbray. w. Don Hartman, Frank Butler, Preston Sturges, d. Elliott Nugent.

COMEDY: Paranoia; Hypochondriacs; Death-Impending; Death-Dealing with; Inheritances at Stake
(Send Me No Flowers; Short Time; Checking Out)

Never Say Goodbye, 1955, 96m, ★★½/$$, U-I/NA. During World War II, an army doctor in Berlin falls in love with a German concert pianist. Sadly, she is captured by the Russians and he gives up hope of finding her alive until they meet again in America. Rock Hudson, George Sanders, Cornell Borchers, David Janssen. w. Charles Hoffman, d. Jerry Hopper.

MELODRAMA: ROMANCE: War Stories; World War II Stories; Romance-Doomed; Romance-Reunited; Americans Abroad; Doctors; Pianists; Berlin
(Magnificent Obsession; The Unbearable Lightness of Being)

Never Say Never Again, 1983, 134m, ★★★½/$$$$, WB/WB. James Bond must stop another madman intent on taking over the world. This time, the arch villian is setting up shop on a state of the art underwater base. Sean Connery, Klaus Maria Brandauer, Max Von Sydow, Barbara Carrera, Kim Basinger, Edward Fox. w. Lorenzo Semple, Jr., Irvin Kershner.

ACTION: ADVENTURE: Action Comedy; Spy Films; Spies; Secret Agents; Kidnappings; James Bond; Undercover; Chase Movies; Rule the World-Plots to
(Thunderball; Diamonds Are Forever)
(Ed: More humorous, tongue in cheek, than previous Bonds, though the plot is very close to *Thunderball*'s)

Never So Few, 1959, 124m, ★★½/$$, MGM/MGM-UA. In Burma during the war, American soldiers are assigned to command a motley band of local guerillas. Frank Sinatra, Gina Lollobrigida, Peter Lawford, Steve McQueen, Charles Bronson. w. Millard Kaufman, N-adap. Tom Chamales, d. John Sturges.

ACTION: War Stories; World War II Stories; Military Stories; Special Teams; Terrorists; Asia; Forgotten Films

Never Take Sweets from a Stranger, 1960, 81m, ★★½/$, Hammer-Col/NA. An elderly gentleman must defend himself when accused of child molestation and becomes a pariah in his own small town. Gwen Watford, Patrick Allen, Felix Aylmer, Niall MacGinnis. w. John Hunter, P-adap. Roger Garis (The Pony Cart), d. Cyril Frankel.

DRAMA: Social Drama; Message Films; Molestation-Child; Abused Children; Ahead of its Time; Small-town Life; Small-town Scandals; Elderly Men; Men and Girls; Accused Unjustly; Forgotten Films
(Separate Tables; Something About Amelia; The Mark; Short Eyes)

Never Talk to Strangers, 1995, 102m, ★★½/$$, Tri-Star/Col-Tri, R/P-V-S. A shrink specializing in serial killers (another one) is being stalked but doesn't know by whom. It could be several different men, but most likely it's her new boyfriend she met in a store as a stranger. A torturous romance is the result. Rebecca DeMornay, Antonio Banderas, Harry Dean Stanton, Dennis Miller, Len Cariou. w. Lewis Green & Jordan Rush, d. Peter Hall.

SUSPENSE: Serial Killers; Enemy-Sleeping with the; Dangerous Men; Stalkers; Psychiatrists; Romance with Psychologist
(Guilty as Sin; Sleeping with the Enemy)

Never Too Late, 1965, 104m, ★★½/$, WB/WB. A woman getting on in years is surprised to learn that she's pregnant. Paul Ford, Maureen O'Sullivan, Connie Stevens, Jim Hutton, Lloyd Nolan. w., P-adap. Sumner Arthur Long, d. Bud Yorkin.

DRAMA: MELODRAMA: Character Studies; Decisions-Big; Abortion Dilemmas; Babies-Having; Babies-Having, Late in Life; Marriage Drama
(And Baby Makes Six; Prudence and the Pill; The Tenth Month)

The Neverending Story, 1984, 94m, ★★★/$$$, WB/WB, G. A boy enters a strange bookstore in New York where the elderly proprietor gives him a book that takes him into an alternate universe. The Great Unknown threatens the universe and a flying dog takes him on a journey. Barret Oliver, Gerald McRaney. w. d. Wolfgang Peterson, N-adap. Michael Ende.

ADVENTURE: SCI-FI: Fantasy; Outer Space Movies; CHILDREN'S: Invisibility; Animals-Talking; Journies; Good vs. Evil; Saving Someone; Boys; Child Protagonists; Female Screenwriters
(The Princess Bride; Krull)

The Neverending Story II: The Next Chapter, 1990, 89m, ★★½/$$$, WB/WB, G. An empress is in trouble in the alternate universe of the book. Our young hero must re-enter the world to save her. Jonathan Brandis, Kenny Morrison, Clarissa Burt, Alexandra Jones. w. Karin Howard, N-adap. Michael Ende, d. George Miller.

The New Barbarians, 1983, 91m, ★★/$, Ind/NA, R/V-S-P. In the near future, roving bands of homosexuals go around killing people unabated until two soldiers stop them. Fred Williamson, Timothy Brent, George Eastman, Anna Kanakis. w. Tito Carpi, Enzo Girolami, d. Enzo G. Castellari.

ACTION: MURDER: Murder Sprees; SCI-FI: Futuristic Films; Apocalyptic Stories; Soldiers; Trail of a Killer; Gangs; Homophobia; Gay Men; Murderers-Homosexual; Italian Films; Italy; Curiosities; Independent Films

The New Interns, 1964, 123m, ★★½/ $$, Col/NA. At an inner city hospital, a new group of young doctors go through the motions "Dr. Kildare" style, with the main story revolving around a tragic rape case. George Segal, Telly Savalas, Michael Callan, Dean Jones, Inger Stevens, Stefanie Powers. w. Wilton Schiller, d. John Rich.

MELODRAMA: Rape/Rapists; Young Men; Doctors; Medical School; Hospitals; Ensemble Films; Ensembles-Male; Female Among Males; Forgotten Films SEQUEL to The Interns. (The Interns; Gross Anatomy; Vital Signs)

New Jack City, 1991, 100m, ★★½/ $$$$, WB/WB, R/EP-EV-S. A cop goes undercover in the sordid world of Harlem drug kingpins, leading to a mob war and a wedding massacre. Wesley Snipes, Ice T, Allen Payne, Chris Rock, Mario Van Peebles, Judd Nelson. w. Thomas Lee Wright, Barry Michael Cooper, d. Mario Van Peebles.

ACTION: Crime Drama; Mob Stories; Mob Wars; Drugs-Dealing; Police Stories; Undercover; Betrayals; Weddings; Gangs-Black; Black Casts; Black Men; Black Directors; Black Screenwriters; Blaxploitation (Deep Cover; The Godfather; Across 110th Street) (Ed: Better than average for blaxploitation revival but still fairly routine plot; audiences died laughing at the preview where the list of black actors was shown and then . . . Judd Nelson)

A New Kind of Love, 1963, 110m, ★★★/$$, Par/Par, AMC. An American

fashion maven in Paris gets pursued by a dogged reporter who finally gets her to succumb to his charms, though both are playing mindgames. Paul Newman, Joanne Woodward, Maurice Chevalier, Thelma Ritter, George Tobias. w. d. Melville Shavelson.

COMEDY: ROMANCE: Romantic Comedy; Romance-Girl Wants Boy; Romance-Opposites Attract; Romance-Bickering; Fashion World; Journalists; Disguises; Paris; 1960s; Coulda Been Great; Writer-Directors (Rally Round the Flag, Boys; Paris When It Sizzles) (Ed: Husband and wife Newman and Woodward have great charisma, but it's all too fluffy, as were most of Newman's films of this period)

A New Leaf, 1971, 102m, ★★★★/$$$, Par/Par, PG. A rich, obnoxious man (Walter Matthau) with a butler finds he's spent all of his inheritance and no one but the butler seems to care, so he must marry for money or lose everything. But will the dopey heiress he finds (Elaine May) really fall for it? w. d. Elaine May, SS adap. Jack Ritchie, *The Green Heart*.

COMEDY: Black Comedy; MURDER: Murder-Comic Attempts; Race Against Time; Simple Minds; Heiresses; Rich People; Losing it All; Weddings; Marriage Comedy; Comedy Remakes; Marrying Up; Fantasies; Wallflowers; Nerds; Nerds & Wallflowers; Snobs; Female Screenwriters; Female Directors; Writer-Directors

COMIC FLIPSIDE OF: Suspicion. (Arthur; Suspicion; Monsieur Verdoux)

A New Life, 1988, 104m, ★★½/$$, Par/Par, R/S-P. A middle-aged couple (Alan Alda, Ann-Margret) break up and start dating other people, but things don't go so well for the man. Hal Linden, Veronica Hamel. w. d. Alan Alda.

DRAMA: COMEDY DRAMA: Midlife Crisis; Marriage Drama; Divorce; Starting Over; Friendships-Male; Coulda Been Good; Writer-Directors; Actor Directors (Starting Over; Middle-Age Crazy) (Ed: Mediocre)

New Nightmare (Wes Craven's), 1994, 112m, ★★/$$, New Line/New Line, R/EV, B&G. The makers of the *Nightmare on Elm Street* series play themselves in this real-life imitates horror-movie take on the story of a young woman consumed by nightmares of the

movie's character Freddy Krueger, which then gives *Nightmare* creator Wes Craven an excuse to revive the series and also give it a new perspective. Heather Langenkamp, Robert Englund, Miko Hughes, David Newsom, Matt Winston, Rob LaBelle, Wes Craven, Marianne Maddalena. w. d. Wes Craven.

HORROR: SCI-FI: Nightmares; Crossing the Line; Movie Making; Directors; Evil Men; Writer-Directors (Nightmare on Elm Street SERIES; The Dark Half; In the Mouth of Madness) (Ed: If at first other movie series don't succeed, sequelize, sequelize again)

New Orleans, 1947, 89m, ★★½/$$, Ind/NA. A fictionalized account of the birth of jazz in old Dixie with many real-life performers. Louis Armstrong and his All Stars, Arturo de Cordova, Dorothy Patrick, Billie Holliday, Meade Lux Lewis, Woody Herman and his Orchestra. w. Elliot Paul, Dick Irving Hyland, d. Arthur Lubin.

MUSICALS: Music Movies; Jazz Life; New Orleans; Black Casts; Documentary Style; Musicians; Forgotten Films (Birth of the Blues; Mardi Gras)

New Year's Day, 1989, 92m, ★★½/$, Jaglom-Rainbow/Par. A talkfest in which a writer moves to L.A. and gets involved in the lives of his female neighbors. Maggie Jakobson, Gwen Welles, Henry Jaglom. w. d. Henry Jaglom.

COMEDY: COMEDY DRAMA: Documentary Style; Ensemble Films; Ensembles-Female; Los Angeles; Apartment Buildings; Writer-Directors; Improvisational Films (Eating; Can She Bake a Cherry Pie?)

New York, New York, 1977, 153m, ★★★/$, UA/Fox, PG. The career of an aspiring jazz musician in New York is overshadowed by that of his girlfriend who attracts the attention of Hollywood producers. Liza Minnelli, Robert De Niro, Lionel Stander. w. Earl Mac Ruth, Mardik Martin, d. Martin Scorsese.

MELODRAMA: ROMANCE: Romantic Drama; Music Movies; Romance-Doomed; Singers; Musicians; World War II-Post Era; Fame-Rise to; Hidden Gems; Underrated (The Way We Were; The Clock) (Ed: Director's cut released in late 80s)

New York Stories, 1989, 124m, ★★½/$, Touchstone/Touchstone, PG-13/S-P. Three short films, all set in New

York: "Life Lessons" about a middle aged artist's affair with a younger woman, "Life Without Zoe" about a rich twelve-year-old girl dealing with her parent's divorce, and "Oedipus Wrecks" about a neurotic loner whose mother shows up on the skyline of New York, broadcasting her dating advice. Nick Nolte, Patrick O'Neal, Rosanna Arquette, Heather McComb, Talia Shire, Gia Coppola, Giancarlo Giannini, Woody Allen, Mia Farrow. w. Richard Price, Francis Coppola, Sofia Coppola, Woody Allen, d. Martin Scorsese, Francis Coppola, Woody Allen.

COMEDY DRAMA: Multiple Stories; Mothers & Daughters; Mothers & Sons; Romance-Older Men/Younger Women; Artists; Mothers-Troublesome; Greece; Dreams; Surrealism; Giants; Writer-Directors

(Ed: The only one of the three worth seeing is Woody Allen's)

Newsfront, 1978, 110m, ★★1/2/$, Ind/Sultan. Australian reporters for the newsreels in the fifties compete to get the best footage. Bill Hunter, Wendy Hughes, Gerald Kennedy. w. Philip Noyce, David Elfick, d. Philip Noyce.

DRAMA: SATIRE: Documentary Style; Journalists; TV Life; Competitions; Australian Films

Newsies, 1992, 121m, ★★1/2/$, Disney/Disney, G. Around the turn of the century, paperboys in New York go on strike to protest their exploitation by a corrupt publisher. Christian Bale, Bill Pullman, Ann-Margret, Robert Duvall. w. Bob Tzudiker, Noni White, d. Kenny Ortega.

MUSICALS: COMEDY: CHILDREN'S: FAMILY: Musical Comedy; Boys; Teenagers; Journalists; Newspapers; Dance Movies; Strikes; Old-Fashioned Recent Films

(Oliver!)

(Ed: The form was old-fashioned and noble, but the ideas behind it, the boy actors, and the writing were lackluster at best)

The Next of Kin, 1942, 102m, ★★1/2/$$, Ealing/NA. An instructional film in which, in a British platoon in World War II, loose lips sink ships. Mervyn Johns, Nova Pilbeam, Stephen Murray, Reginald Tate. w. Thorold Dickenson, Basil Bartlett, Angus Macphail, John Dighton, d. Thorold Dickenson.

Documentaries; Educational Films; World War II Stories; Military Stories; Patriotism; British Films

Next of Kin, 1989, 108m, ★★/$$, Lorimar-WB/WB, R/EV-P-MRN. A redneck and his big-city cop brother exact their revenge on the thugs who killed their other brother. Patrick Swayze, Liam Neeson, Adam Baldwin, Helen Hunt, Andreas Katsulas, Bill Paxton, Ben Stiller. w. Michael Jenning, Jeb Stuart, d. John Irvin.

ACTION: Revenge; Avenging Death of Someone; Brothers; Rednecks

(Death Wish; Roadhouse)

Next Stop, Greenwich Village, 1975, 111m, ★★★/$, 20th/Fox. In the fifties, a young Jewish boy growing up in the boroughs of New York dreams of joining the bohemian life of Greenwich Village. Lenny Baker, Shelley Winters, Ellen Greene, Lois Smith, Dori Brenner. w. d. Paul Mazursky.

COMEDY DRAMA: ROMANCE: Romance-Reluctant; Romance-Boy Wants Girl; Young Men; Dreams; Poets; Beatnik Era; New York Life; Greenwich Village; Jewish People; Autobiographical Stories; Writer-Directors

(Me, Natalie; Lenny; Greenwich Village; Radio Days)

Next Time We Love, 1936, 87m, ★★1/2/$$, U/NA. When a war reporter is out tracking stories, his wife invites gentlemen callers into their home. Margaret Sullavan, Ray Milland, James Stewart, Grant Mitchell. w. Melville Baker, SS-adap. Ursula Parrott, d. Edward H. Griffith.

ROMANCE: Marriage on the Rocks; Cheating Women; Journalists; Housewives

Niagara, 1952, 89m, ★★★/$$, 20th/Fox. A woman plans to get rid of her husband at Niagara Falls and take off with her lover. But her husband has a thing or two up his sleeve . . . Joseph Cotten, Jean Peters, Marilyn Monroe, Don Wilson, Casey Adams. w. Charles Brackett, Walter Reisch, Richard Breen, d. Henry Hathaway.

SUSPENSE: DRAMA: MURDER: Murder of Spouse; Dangerous Spouse; Sexy Women; Turning the Tables; Cheating Women; Hitchcockian; Hidden Gems; Jim Thompson-esque; Film Noir; Hidden Gems

(Desire and Hell at the Sunset Motel)

(Ed: Famous for nude silhouette of Monroe in the shower)

A Nice Little Bank That Should Be Robbed (How to Rob a Bank), 1958, 87m, ★★/$, 20th/NA. In a hair-brained, money-making scheme, two boobs decide to rob a bank in order to buy a racehorse. Mickey Rooney, Tom Ewell, Mickey Shaughnessy, Dina Merrill. w. Sidney Boehm, d. Henry Levin.

COMEDY DRAMA: Heist Stories; Thieves; Bank Robberies; Horse Racing; Buddy Films

(They Went Thataway and Thataway)

Nicholas and Alexandra, 1971, 189m, ★★★1/2/$$$, Col/RCA-Col, PG. The life of the last Russian Czar and his wife-the epic story of a bygone era, ending in the October Revolution and the tragic end of Russian royalty. Michael Jayston, Janet Suzman (BActress), Laurence Olivier, Tom Baker, Michael Redgrave, Alexander Knox. w. James Goldman, NF-adap. Robert K. Massie, d. Franklin Schaffner. BPicture, **BArt**, **BCostume**, BCin, BOScore. Oscars: 6-2.

DRAMA: TRAGEDY: Historical Drama; Costume Drama; Epics; Family Drama; Political Unrest; Russian Revolution; Russians; Kings; Queens; Royalty; Executions

(Doctor Zhivago; Reds; Anastasia)

Nicholas Nickleby, 1947, 108m, ★★★/$, Ealing/Prism. A poor schoolmaster has been expecting his inheritance all his life. When it's snatched out from under him, he decides to join a theatrical troupe and finally live for the moment. Derek Bond, Cedric Hardwicke, Alfred Drayton, Sybil Thorndike, Fay Compton. w. John Dighton, N-adap. Charles Dickens, d. Alberto Cavalcanti.

DRAMA: COMEDY DRAMA: Inheritances at Stake; Losing it All; Teachers; Actors; Theater Life; Dreams; Life Transitions; Starting Over; England; 1800s; Classic Literary Adaptations

(Oliver; David Copperfield)

Nick of Time, 1995, 105m, ★★★/$, U/MCA-U, PG-13/P-V. At noon one day a man and his daughter are accosted by criminals who tell the man he must assassinate the female governor of California or they'll kill his daughter-in two hours. Johnny Depp, Courtney Chase, Charles Dutton, Christopher Walken, Roma Maffia, Marsha Mason, Peter Strauss. w. Patrick Sheane Duncan, d. John Badham.

SUSPENSE: Race Against Time; One Day Stories; Politicians; Assassination Plots; Hitchcockian; Fathers & Daughters; Children in Jeopardy
(The Man Who Knew Too Much; Frantic; The Black Windmill)
(Ed: A good premise that unfortunately doesn't allow for much character development)
Nickelodeon, 1976, 122m, ★★1/2/$, Col/NA, PG. A take on the Hollywood of the early 1900s in which various film-makers try to make it. Fiction mixes with fact, and it all culminates in the opening of *Birth of a Nation*. Ryan O'Neal, Burt Reynolds, Tatum O'Neal, Brian Keith, Stella Stevens, John Ritter. w. W. D. Richter, Peter Bogdanovich, d. Peter Bogdanovich.
COMEDY: Comedy-Slapstick; Hollywood Life; Hollywood Satire; **SATIRE:** Moviemaking; Directors; Coulda Been Great; Flops-Major
(Paper Moon; Sunset; Heart of the West)
Night after Night, 1932, 76m, ★★★/ $$$, Par/MCA-U. A boxer retires and becomes a night-club proprietor. One of his tony customers catches his eye, and he tries to rise to her social level. George Raft, Constance Cummings, Wynne Gibson, Mae West. w. Vincent Laurence, N-adap. Louis Bromfield (*Single Night*), d. Archie Mayo.
COMEDY DRAMA: ROMANCE: Romance-Boy Wants Girl; Romance-Class Conflicts; Social Climbing; Nightclubs; Boxing
Night and Day, 1946, 132m, ★★1/2/$$, WB/MGM-UA. A musical biopic of famous Broadway composer Cole Porter, the Nebraska boy who grew up to epito-mize New York sophistication (but who looked absolutely nothing like the star). Cary Grant, Alexis Smith, Monty Woolley, Mary Martin, Ginny Simms, Jane Wyman, Eve Arden, Victor Francen, Alan Hale, Dorothy Malone. w. Charles Hoffman, Leo Townsend, William Bowers, d. Michael Curtiz.
MUSICALS: Biographies; Music Movies; Music Composers; Theater Life
(Rhapsody in Blue)
(Ed: Dubious docudrama; one of a list of gay bios made straight)
Night and Day, 1991, 100m, ★★★/$, Orion/Orion, R/S. A woman has sex with two men, one at night and one during the day, the point being that she feels no guilt

whatsoever and there is no moralistic ret-ribution. Guillaine Londez, Thomas Langmann, Francois Negret, Nicole Colchat, Pierre Laroche. w. d. Chantal Akerman.
DRAMA: Character Studies; Erotic Drama; Sexuality; Promiscuity; Sexy Women; French Films; Female Screenwriters; Female Directors; Female Protagonists; Writer-Directors
(Montenegro; Looking for Mr. Goodbar)
Night and the City, 1950, 101m, ★★★/$$, 20th/Fox. A promoter who makes his living fixing fights gets in trou-ble with the London mob. Richard Widmark, Gene Tierney, Googie Withers, Hugh Marlowe, Herbert Lom. w. Jo Eisinger, N-adap. Gerald Kersh, d. Jules Dassin.
DRAMA: TRAGEDY: Crime Drama; Mob Stories; Boxing; Americans Abroad; Con Artists; Wrestling
REMAKE: 1992 version.
(The Naked City)
Night and the City, 1992, 104m, ★★1/2/$$, 20th/Fox, R/P. A retelling of the 1950 version in modern New York with the boxing promoter as a lawyer who's having an affair with a restaurant owner's wife, whose husband is one of his financial backers, all leading to trouble down the line. Robert De Niro, Jessica Lange, Cliff Gorman, Jack Warden, Alan King, Eli Wallach. w. Richard Price, N-adap. Gerald Kersh, d. Irwin Winkler.
DRAMA: ROMANCE: Romantic Drama; Boxing; Lawyers; Mob Stories; Corruption; Ethics
REMAKE OF: 1950 version
(Guilty by Suspicion; A Bronx Tale)
(Ed: It doesn't seem to be going anywhere for the longest time, and when it gets there, it pretty much wasn't)
The Night Angel, 1931, 75m, ★★/$, Par/Fries. In Prague, a lawyer who's put a madam in jail falls in love with her daughter. All these "evil women" get to him and he descends into the realm of passions, eventually being driven to mur-der. Fredric March, Nancy Carroll, Alan Hale. w. d. Edmund Goulding.
ROMANCE: DRAMA: Romantic Drama; **MURDER: TRAGEDY:** Prostitutes-High Class; Romance with Prostitutes; Flops-Major; Writer-Directors
(The Blue Angel)
A Night at the Opera, 1935, 96m, ★★★★/$$$, MGM/MGM-UA. The Marx

Brothers' brand of anarchy found its apotheosis in this classic, in which they destroy an Opera production then work to rebuild it. Groucho Marx, Chico Marx, Harpo Marx, Margaret Dumont, Kitty Carlisle, Sig Rumann, d. George S. Kaufman, Morrie Ryskind, d. Sam Wood.
COMEDY: FARCE: Comedy of Errors; Comedy-Slapstick; Comedy-Character; Opera; Fools-Bumbling; Marx Brothers
(Duck Soup)
Nightbreed, 1990, 102m, ★★1/2/$$, 20th/Media. Another dimension of shape-changing beasts is discovered by a young man who has to run for his life or be con-sumed, but how does he get out? Craig Sheffer, Anne Bobby, David Cronenberg, Charles Haid. w. d. Clive Barker.
HORROR: SCI-FI: Nightmares; Humans into Animals; Fantasy; Monsters; Teenagers in Jeopardy; Writer-Directors
(Predator; Candyman; Wolfen)
Nightcomers, 1971, 96m, ★★★/$, Col/Col, R/V. A retelling of *The Turn of the Screw* with a modern psychological expla-nation: the children were molested by the gardener. Stephanie Beacham, Marlon Brando, Thora Hird, Harry Andrews. w. Michael Hastings, d. Michael Winner.
HORROR: SUSPENSE: Ghosts; Molestation-Child; Revisionist Films; Houses-Creepy; Haunted Houses; Curiosities
REMAKE OF: The Turn of the Screw.
(Something About Amelia; Flowers in the Attic; Last Tango in Paris)
Night Crossing, 1982, 106m, ★★1/2/$$, Disney/Disney, PG. A spectacular escape in a hot air balloon forms the centerpiece of this story of East Germans longing for freedom. John Hurt, Jane Alexander, Doug McKeon, Frank McKeon, Beau Bridges. w. John McGreevey, d. Delbert Mann.
DRAMA: MELODRAMA: FAMILY: Family Drama; Escape Drama; Rescue Drama; Cold War Era; Communists; Balloons; Iron Curtain-Escape from
(Journey of Hope)
Night Eyes, 1990, ★★/$$, Prism/Prism, R/S-FFN-MN. A surveillance man is watching his boss' sexy wife and he's being watched himself. Andrew Stevens, Tanya Roberts. d. Emilio Miraglio.
SUSPENSE: Erotic Thriller; Surveillance; Voyeurs; Romance with Boss' Lover; Romance-Dangerous; Jealousy
SEQUELS: Night Eyes 2; Night Eyes 3.
(Bedroom Eyes; The Seduction)

Nightfall, 1956, 78m, ★★½/$$, Col/Goodtimes. An artist witnesses the burying of loot by bank robbers. He's not interested in the money, but he's pursued for his knowledge. Anne Bancroft, Aldo Ray, Brian Keith, James Gregory. w. Stirling Silliphant, N-adap. David Goodis, d. Jacques Tourneur.
SUSPENSE: Police Stories; Chase Movies; Heist Stories; Bank Robberies; Fugitives from the Law; Fugitives from the Mob; Good Premise Unfulfilled

Night Gallery, 1969, 95m, ★★★½/$$$, U/MCA-U, V. Three tales of greed and being reborn centering around a woman who wants to buy some eyes to see again. Joan Crawford, Roddy McDowell, Tom Bosley, Ossie Davis, Barry Sullivan, Sam Jaffe. d. Steven Spielberg, Boris Sagal.
HORROR: SUSPENSE: Greed; Blind People; Buried Alive; Dead-Back from the; Nightmares; Body Parts; Female Protagonists; Supernatural Danger; TV Movies (The Twilight Zone; The Movie; Trilogy in Terror)
(Ed: Spielberg's impressive debut and the launch for the early 70s series)

Night Games, 1966, 105m, ★★★/$, Sandrews/Sultan. A timid man in his midthirties has trouble with women because he's reminded of his domineering dead mother. Ingrid Thulin, Keve Hjelm, Lena Brundin. w. d., N-adap. Mai Zetterling.
DRAMA: Character Studies; Psychological Drama; Sexuality; Nerds; Past-Haunted by the; Mothers-Troublesome; Female Screenwriters; Female Directors; Writer-Directors

The Night Has a Thousand Eyes, 1948, 80m, ★★½/$, Par/NA. A huckster with a mind-reading act begins to realize that he actually *can* predict the future. Edward G. Robinson, Gail Russell, John Lund, Virginia Bruce, William Demarest. w. Barre Lyndon, Jonathan Latimer, N-adap. Cornell Woolrich, d. John Farrow.
SCI-FI: Fantasy; Psychics; Con Artists (The Clairvoyant; The Medusa Touch; The Man Who Could Work Miracles)

The Night Has Eyes (Terror House), 1942, 79m, ★★★/$$, ABP/Nos. A man looks for his friend who disappeared on the Moors and meets a mysterious hermit living with his odd butler-then the danger begins. James Mason, Joyce Howard, Wilfrid Lawson, Mary Clare. w. Alan Kennington, d. Leslie Arliss.

SUSPENSE: Searches; Missing Persons; Missing Person Thriller; Gothic Style; England; British Films; Hidden Gems

Nighthawks, 1981, 99m, ★★★ U/MCA-U, R/V-P. An especially tricky lone terrorist is tracked by New York cops, leading to a harrowing conclusion. Sylvester Stallone, Billy Dee Williams, Rutger Hauer, Lindsay Wagner, Persis Khambatta. w. David Shaber, d. Bruce Malmuth.
ACTION: SUSPENSE: MURDER: Bombs; Police Stories; Trail of a Killer; Hostage Situations; Terrorists; Psycho-Killers; Cat and Mouse; Telephone Terror (Live Wire; The Fourth Protocol; Die Hard; Telefon; Assassins)

Nighthawks, 1978, 113m, ★★½/$, Cinegate/NA. A teacher deals with being openly gay and the societal issues involved. Ken Robertson. w. d. Ron Peck, Paul Hallam.

Nighthawks, 2: Strip Jack Naked, 1991, 94m, ★★/$, Ind/NA. The making of *Nighthawks*, which is nothing so great, since the original wasn't. John Brown, John Daimon, Nick Bolton. w. Ron Peck, Paul Hallam, d. Ron Peck.
DRAMA: Social Drama; Documentary Style; Underground; Gay Men; Teachers; Cult Films; Independent Films

A Night in Casablanca, 1946, 85m, ★★★/$$, MGM/NA. In North Africa, three eccentric Americans battle Nazis in hiding after the war. Who will win by their wits? Groucho Marx, Chico Marx, Harpo Marx, Sig Rumann, Lisette Verea. w. Joseph Fields, Roland Kibbee, Frank Tashlin, d. Archie Mayo.
COMEDY: FARCE: Comedy of Errors; Nazi Stories; World War II-Post Era; Marx Brothers (A Night at the Opera; The Big Store; Duck Soup)

A Night in Heaven, 1983, 85m, ★★/$, 20th/Fox, R/S-FN-MN. A professor finds out one of her students is a stripper on the sly, so she performs for him on the sly . . . Lesley Ann Warren, Christopher Atkins, Carrie Snodgress, Andy Garcia. w. Joan Tewksbury, d. John G. Avildsen.
COMEDY DRAMA: ROMANCE: Erotic Drama; Romance-Older Women/Younger Men; Strippers; Dual Lives; Professors; Romance with Teacher; Dancers; Prostitutes-Male; Sexy Men; Time Capsules; Camp; Female Protagonists; Female Screenwriters; Role Reversal (Ladies' Night; Blue Lagoon)

A Night in the Life of Jimmy Reardon, 1988, 95m, ★★½/$, 20th/Fox, PG-13/S. A high school playboy sticks around to romance the ladies and girls but may be seeing his life pass him by. So soon? River Phoenix, Anne Magnuson, Ione Skye, Meredith Salenger, Matthew Perry. d. William Richert.
COMEDY DRAMA: ROMANCE: Playboys; Coming of Age; Romance-Older Women/Younger Men; Teenagers; Teenage Movies; Romance-Class Conflicts; Promiscuity; Romance-Triangles; Boys; Young Men; Narrated Films; Crossing the Line; Curiosities; Forgotten Films (Loverboy; The Rachel Papers; Running on Empty)
(Ed: It begs an answer for who this was aimed at)

The Night Is Young, 1934, 82m, ★★½/$$, MGM/NA. A ballerina enchants a European nobleman. Evelyn Laye, Ramon Novarro, Una Merkel, Edward Everett Horton, Rosalind Russell, Charles Butterworth. w. Vicki Baum, d. Dudley Murphy.
MUSICALS: MELODRAMA: ROMANCE: Romantic Drama; Musical Romance; Dancers; Ballet; Royalty; Forgotten Films; Female Screenwriters (Waterloo Bridge; Grand Hotel)

The Night Is Young, 1986, 119m, ★★½/$, Ind/NA, R/S. In a futuristic, jaded world, thieves try to steal the cure to a disease which kills people who have sex without love. Juliette Binoche, Michel Piccoli, Denis Lavant. w. d. Leos Carax.
DRAMA: Art Films; Futuristic Films; Sexuality; Death by Sex; Epidemics; Cures/Elixirs; Thieves; Good Premise Unfulfilled; Writer-Directors; Independent Films (Liquid Sky)

Nightmare in the Sun, 1963, 81m, ★★/$, Afilmco/NA. When a wealthy man discovers his wife is having an affair with a roaming biker, he kills her and tries to pin the crime on him. John Derek, Ursula Andress, Arthur O'Connell, Aldo Ray. w. Ted Thomas, d. Marc Lawrence.
SUSPENSE: MURDER: Murder of Spouse; Cheating Women; Jealousy; Romance-Triangles (The Ultimate Thrill; Dial M for Murder)

The Nightmare Before Christmas, 1993, 105m, ★★★½/$$$, Touchstone/Touchstone, PG/V. A stop-animation musical about a group of Addams Family-like characters who try to take over Christmas with their ghoulish charm. w. Tim Burton, Caroline Thompson, Larry Thompson, d. Henry Selak.

FAMILY: CHILDREN'S: Cartoons; Animation-Stop; **MUSICALS:** Fantasy; Musical Fantasy; Black Comedy; Old-Fashioned Recent Films; Camp; Halloween; Christmas; Cult Films; Sleeper Hits

(James and the Giant Peach; The Addams Family; Frankenweenie; Edward Scissorhands; Batman [1989]; The Santa Clause)

A Nightmare on Elm Street, 1984, 91m, ★★★/$$$$, New Line/New Line, R/EV-B&G. A group of teenagers whose parents were all molested by Freddy Krueger find him showing up in their dreams, which become increasingly real. John Saxon, Ronee Blakley, Heather Langenkamp, Amanda Wyss, Nick Corri, Robert Englund. w. d. Wes Craven. Writer-Directors

A Nightmare on Elm Street Part Two: Freddy's Revenge, 1985, 84m, ★★1/2/$$$, New Line/New Line, R/V-B&G. Freddy possesses the body of a young boy. Mark Patton, Kim Myers, Hope Lange, Robert Englund. w. David Chaskin, d. Jack Sholder.

A Nightmare on Elm Street Part Three: Dream Warriors, 1987, 96m, ★★1/2/$$$, New Line/New Line, R/V-B&G. A group of teenagers who have trouble sleeping join forces in their dreams to battle Freddie. Heather Langenkamp, Patricia Arquette, Larry Fishburne, Robert Englund. w. Wes Craven, Bruce Wagner, d. Chuck Russell.

A Nightmare on Elm Street Part Four: The Dream Master, 1988, 93m, ★★/$$, New Line/New Line, R/V-B&G. A teenage girl finds that she has special powers in her dreams with which to do battle with Freddie. Robert Englund, Rodney Eastman, Danny Hassel. w. Brian Helgeland, Scott Pierce, William Kotzwinkle, d. Renny Harlin.

A Nightmare on Elm Street: The Dream Child, 1989, 89m, ★★/$$ New Line/New Line, R/V-B&G. A pregnant woman is hounded by Freddey, who wants to possess her child. Robert Englund, Lisa Wilcox, Kelly Jo Minter, Danny Hassel, Nick Mele. w. Leslie Bohem,

John Skipp, Craig Spector, d. Stephen Hopkins.
HORROR: SCI-FI: Nightmares; Evil Men; Teenagers in Jeopardy; Murders of Teenagers; Teenagers; Teenage Movies; Teen Horror Flicks of 80s; Cult Films; Sleeper Hits; Molestation-Child
SEQUEL: Freddy's Dead: The Final Nightmare.
(Friday the 13th SERIES; Bad Dreams)
(Ed: The first was a sleeper hit, pun intended)

Night, Mother, 1986, 96m, ★★★/$, Spelling-U/MCA-U, PG-13. A woman living with her mother decides for various reasons that life isn't worth it anymore, so her mother tries to stop her from the inevitable. Anne Bancroft, Sissy Spacek, Ed Berke, Carol Robbins. w. P-adap. Marsha Norman, d. Tom Moore.
DRAMA: TRAGEDY: Character Studies; Suicidal Tendencies; Mothers & Daughters; Lonely People; Stagelike Films; Coulda Been Great; Pulitzer Prize Adaptations; Female Protagonists; Female Screenwriters
(Crimes of the Heart; Right of Way)

Night Moves, 1975, 99m, ★★★/$, WB/WB, R/V-P-S-FFN. A detective (Gene Hackman) with his marriage on the rocks goes on a case to track down a teenage girl (Melanie Griffith) who's run away to Key West and become involved in a smuggling ring which may endanger his life and that of a woman he's met (Jennifer Warren). James Woods, Edward Binns, Harris Yulin. w. Alan Sharp, d. Arthur Penn.
SUSPENSE: MYSTERY: Crime Drama; Detective Stories; Detectives-Private; Detectives in Deep; Film Noir-Modern; Missing Persons; Teenagers; Art Thieves; Stuntmen; Florida Keys; Overrated
(The French Connection; Prime Cut; Midnight Crossing)
(Ed: Throwback to the old flatfoot tales, but it isn't nearly as clever and allegorical as some believe. The ending doesn't work and it's all as aimless as it portrays life for everyone in it to be)

Night Must Fall, 1937, 117m, ★★★1/2/$$$, MGM/MGM-UA-Turner, V. A very nice young man (Robert Montgomery) who's insinuated his way into a rich old lady's home as her caretaker may be responsible for a body found in the creek. Rosalind Russell. w. John Van Druten, P-adap. Emlyn Williams, d. Richard Thorpe.

Night Must Fall, 1964, 105m, 94m, ★★1/2/$, MGM/NA. A remake of the above, but not nearly as good. Albert Finney, Susan Hampshire, Mona Washbourne, Sheila Hancock, Michael Medwin, Joe Gladwin. w. Clive Exton, d. Karel Reisz.
British Films
SUSPENSE: MYSTERY: MURDER: MURDER MYSTERY: Serial Killers; Murders of Women; Murderers-Nice; Women in Jeopardy; England
(Psycho; Brimstone & Treacle)
(Ed: Tame by today's standards, but still creepy)

The Night My Number Came Up, 1954, 94m, ★★1/2/$, Ealing/NA. A man obsesses about dying in a plane crash and eventually finds himself in the situation he envisioned. Michael Redgrave, Alexander Knox, Sheila Sim, Denholm Elliott, Ursula Jeans. w. R. C. Sherriff, d. Leslie Norman.
SUSPENSE: DRAMA: Nightmares; Dreams; Psychics; What If . . . Stories; Airplane Crashes; Good Premise Unfulfilled; British Films
(Twilight Zone, The Movie; The Medusa Touch)

Night Nurse, 1931, 72m, ★★1/2/$$$, WB/MGM-UA. A home nurse must save the children in her charge from a nasty plot against them. Barbara Stanwyck, Ben Lyon, Joan Blondell, Clark Gable, Charles Winninger, Vera Lewis, Blanche Frederici. w. Oliver H. P. Garrett, N-adap. Dora Macy, d. William Wellman.
MELODRAMA: Nurses; Children in Jeopardy; Saving Someone; Conspiracy
(Miss Susie Slagle's)

Night of the Comet, 1984, 98m, ★★★/$$, Atlantic/Fox, PG. A comet hits the Earth and turns everyone that it doesn't kill into a zombie. Two sisters are the only people unaffected and they roam around trying to figure out what to do. Robert Beltran, Catharine Mary Stewart, Kelli Maroney, Sharon Farrell. w. d. Tom Eberhardt.
COMEDY: DRAMA: SCI-FI: Futuristic Films; Apocalyptic Stories; Sisters; Meteors; Zombies; Curiosities; Writer-Directors; Independent Films
(A Boy and His Dog; Omega Man; Earthgirls Are Easy)

The Night of the Following Day, 1969, 93m, ★★/$, U/MCA-U, R/S. Kidnappers snare a rich French girl who has some psychological surprises in store for her captors. Marlon Brando, Rita Moreno, Pamela Franklin. w. Robert Phippeny, Hubert Cornfield, d. Hubert Cornfield

MELODRAMA: SUSPENSE: Psychological Drama; Kidnappings; Turning the Tables; Flops-Major; Art Films; Curiosities

The Night of the Generals, 1967, 148m, ★★★/$, Col/Col, PG. A Nazi general goes berserk and murders prostitutes. A German secret agent tracks him down. Peter O'Toole, Omar Sharif, Tom Courtenay, Donald Pleasence, Joanna Pettet, Philippe Noiret, Christopher Plummer. w. Joseph Kessel, Paul Dehn, N-adap. Hans Helmut Kirst, d. Anatole Litvak.

SUSPENSE: MURDER: Serial Killers; Murders of Prostitutes; Nazi Stories; Secret Agents; Trail of a Killer; Mental Illness; Psycho Killers; World War II Stories; Forgotten Films; Coulda Been Great; Good Premise Unfulfilled

Night of the Hunter (B&W), 1955, 93m, ★★★★/$$. A psychotic preacher (Robert Mitchum) who's murdered his wife (Shelley Winters) goes on the rampage for hidden money and the children who witnessed his crime. Lillian Gish. w. James Agee, N-adap. Davis Grubb, d. Charles Laughton.

DRAMA: SUSPENSE: MURDER: Murder of Spouse; Fugitives from the Law; Fugitives from a Murderer; Chase Movies; Psycho-Killers; Stalkers; Witness to Murder; Treasure Hunts; Inheritances at Stake; Evil Men; Stepfathers; Runaways; Preachers; Religion; Rednecks; Con Artists; Elderly Women; Children-Adopted; Murderers of Children; Hiding Out; Midwestern Life; Farm Life; Gothic Style; Shelley Winters Drowns; Child Protagonists; Actor Directors; Hidden Gems (Cape Fear; Flight of the Doves; Fallen Idol)

Night of the Iguana (B&W), 1964, 125m, ★★★★/$$$, MGM/MGM-UA. An alcoholic, philandering preacher (Richard Burton) is a tourguide to Mexico who is both tempted and thwarted by the women he meets while trying to overcome his past. Deborah Kerr, Ava Gardner, Grayson Hall (BSActress), Sue Lyons. w. N-adap. Tennessee Williams, d. John Huston. BB&WCin. Oscars: 2-0.

DRAMA: MELODRAMA: Alcoholics; Starting Over; Redemption; Mean

Women; Free Spirits; Romance-Older Men/ Younger Women; Romance-Triangles; Preachers; Vacations; Vacation Romance; Women Fighting Over Men; Mexico; Tennessee Williams-esque (Lolita; Mogambo; The Rose Tattoo; Elmer Gantry)

Night of the Juggler, 1980, 100m, ★★/$, Col/Media. A man tracks down the kidnappers of his daughter through the streets of New York. James Brolin, Cliff Gorman, Richard Castellano, d. Robert Butler.

SUSPENSE: Chase Movies; Revenge; Kidnappings; Fathers & Daughters; Children in Jeopardy; Coulda Been Good (Death Wish; Hide in Plain Sight)

Night of the Lepus, 1972, 88m, ★★/$, MGM/NA, PG/V. Giant mutant jackrabbits terrorize ranchers who try to stay out of range of their droppings. Stuart Whitman, Rory Calhoun, Janet Leigh, DeForest Kelly.

HORROR: SUSPENSE: Monsters-Animal; Monsters-Mutant; Desert Settings; Rabbits; Veterinarians; Camp; Curiosities (Them!; Nightwing)

The Night of the Living Dead, 1968, 98m, ★★★/$$$, Ind/Republic, Nos, R/V-B&G. The oft-imitated tale of flesh eating zombies from the grave, done with a black comic touch. Judith O'Dea, Duane Jones, Karl Hardman, Keith Wayne. w. John A. Russo, d. George A. Romero.

(Ed: A hit midnight movie for twenty-five years)

Night of the Living Dead, 1990, 89m, ★★/$, Col/RCA-Col. A remake set in a barn, but not nearly as eerie. Tony Wood, Patricia Tallman, William Butler. w. George A. Romero, d. Tom Savini.

HORROR: SUSPENSE: Women in Jeopardy; Zombies; Apocalyptic Stories; Dead-Back from the; Cult Films; Sleeper Hits

(Evil Dead; Evil Dead 2; Carnival of Souls; Deranged)

The Night of the Shooting Stars, 1982, 106m, ★★★1/2/$$$, UAC/MGM-UA, R/S. A small Italian town divides over those supporting Mussolini and those defying the occupation, which eventually creates a war on a local level. Omero Antonutti, Maragarita Lozano. w. Tonino Guerra, Guilani DeNegri, Paolo Taviani, Vittorio Taviani, d. Taviani & Taviani.

DRAMA: Political Drama; World War II Stories; Men in Conflict; Small-town Life; Italy; Italian Films; Allegorical Stories; Directed by Brothers; Hidden Gems; Cult Films

(The Damned; The Garden of the Finzi-Continis; The Secret of Santa Vittoria)

Night on Earth, 1992, 129m, ★★★/$, Miramax/Miramax, R/P-S. On a single night, five taxi rides in different corners of the globe form this minimalist and atmospheric slice of life. Winona Ryder, Gena Rowlands, Giancarlo Esposito, Armin Mueller-Stahl, Rosie Perez, Isaach de Bankole, Beatrice Dalle, Roberto Benigni, Paolo Bonacelli, Matti Pellonpaa. w. d. Jim Jarmusch.

COMEDY: DRAMA: Character Studies; Taxi Drivers; Multiple Stories; Class Conflicts; Journies; Scandinavia; Beverly Hills; Feisty Females; World Travel; Writer-Directors

(Mystery Train; Down by Law)

Night People, 1954, 93m, ★★1/2/$$, 20th/NA. An army officer kidnapped by the Russians in Berlin is saved by his father. Gregory Peck, Broderick Crawford, Anita Bjork, Walter Abel, Buddy Ebsen, Peter Van Eyck. w. Nunnally Johnson, Tom Reed, Jed Harris (BOStory), d. Nunnally Johnson.

SUSPENSE: Kidnappings; Military Stories; Russians as Enemy; Russia; Berlin; Iron Curtain-Behind the; Good Premise Unfulfilled; Forgotten Films

The Night Porter, 1973, 118m, ★★1/2/$$, Ind/Sultan. A middle-aged married woman has a bizarre and abusive affair with the concierge of her building-the man she recognizes as the commandant of the concentration camp where she was imprisoned in the war. Dirk Bogarde, Charlotte Rampling, Philippe Leroy, Gabriele Ferzetti. w. Liliana Cavani, Italo Moscati, d. Liliana Cavani.

DRAMA: Art Films; Erotic Drama;

ROMANCE: Romance-Doomed; Mental Illness; S&M; Nazi Stories; Reunions; Abused Women; Curiosities; Cult Films; Female Directors; Female Screenwriters; Independent Films

(Max and Helen; The Damned; Salon Kitty)

Nights of Cabiria, 1957, 110m, ★★★1/2/$$$, DEG/Nos. A young, sweet prostitute wants to get off the street and start over with a respectable man, but her past may catch-up with her. Giulietta

Masina, Francois Perier, Dorian Gray. w. Federico Fellini, Ennio Flaiano, Tullio Pinelli, d. Federico Fellini. **BFLFilm.** Oscars: 1-1.

COMEDY: DRAMA: MELODRAMA: ROMANCE: Dreams; Prostitutes-Low Class; Past-Haunted by; Starting Over; Marrying Up; Rome; Italian Films
MUSICAL REMAKE: Sweet Charity.
(La Strada; Never on Sunday)

Night Shift, 1982, 106m, ★★★/$$, WB/WB, PG/P. An accountant becomes a guard at a morgue and his sleazy co-worker turns it into a brothel. Henry Winkler, Michael Keaton, Shelley Long, Gina Hecht. w. Lowell Ganz, Babaloo Mandel, d. Ron Howard.

COMEDY: Party Movies; Prostitutes-Low Class; Pimps; Funerals
(Risky Business; Losin' It)

The Night Stalker/ The Night Strangler, 1972/1974, 98m each, ★★★1/2/$$$$, ABC-U/MCA-U. Two of the pilots that started the cult sci-fi horror series of the 70s. The first involves a female vampire on the prowl in Las Vegas, and the second, a serial killer who sucks the blood out of his victims and leaves them under the streets of Seattle. Both have crack reporter Kolchak on the case. Darren McGavin, Simon Oakland, Carol Lynley. w. Richard Matheson, d. John Llewellyn Moxey.

HORROR: SCI-FI: Vampires; Serial Killers; Murderers-Female; Horror Comedy; Black Comedy; Detective Stories; Journalists as Detectives; Unbelieved; Vampires-Female; Murders of Women; Men in Jeopardy; Women in Jeopardy; TV Movies
SEQUEL: TV Series, The Night Stalker, 1974.
(Ed: Ratings blockbusters in their day)

Night Terror, 1974, 90m, ★★1/2/$$$$, Fries-NBC/Fries. A woman (Valerie Harper) witnesses a policeman's murder and the killer takes off after her in the night desert with her fuel gauge on empty.
SUSPENSE: Stalkers; Chase Movies; Witness to Murder; **MURDER:** Escalating Plots; Murderers-Cop; Desert Settings; Women in Jeopardy; Real Time Stories; One Day Stories; Female Protagonists; Good Premise Unfulfilled, TV Movies
(Duel; Dying Room Only; The Hitcher; The Victim)
(Ed: Idiot Plot: If the killer would just take one of many chances to kill her . . .)

The Night They Raided Minsky's, 1968, 99m, ★★★/$$, UA/Fox, R/S-FRN. Various colorful characters have problems on stage and off in a burlesque show during the roaring twenties. Jason Robards, Britt Ekland, Norman Wisdom, Forrest Tucker, Bert Lahr, Harry Andrews, Denholm Elliott, Elliott Gould. w. Arnold Schulman, Sidney Michaels, Norman Lear, NF-adap. Rowland Barber, d. William Friedkin.

COMEDY: DRAMA: Slice of Life Stories; Sexy Women; Strippers; Theater Life; Scandals; True Stories; Nostalgia; Coulda Been Great
(Smile; Lady of Burlesque)

A Night to Remember (B&W), 1943, 91m, ★★★★/$$$, Col./RCA-Col. A writer (Brian Aherne) and his wife (Loretta Young) rent an apartment so he can work on another mystery novel, but they don't know there's been a murder there already. w. Richard Flournoy, Jack Henley, d. Richard Wallace.

COMEDY: MYSTERY: MURDER MYSTERY: Comic Mystery; Romantic Comedy; Comic Thriller; Detective Stories; Detective Couples; Spoofs-Detective; Romance-Married Couples; Writers; Greenwich Village; Hidden Gems; Forgotten Films
(Manhattan Murder Mystery; The Thin Man SERIES; Hart to Hart TV SERIES; After Office Hours; The Ex-Mrs. Bradley; The Mad Miss Manton)

A Night to Remember, 1958, 123m, ★★★1/2/$$$, Col/Par. A historical drama retelling the story of the wreck of the Titanic. Kenneth More, Honor Blackman, Michael Goodlife, David McCallum, George Rose. w. Eric Ambler, N-adap. Walter Lord, d. Roy Baker.

DRAMA: TRAGEDY: Disaster Movies; Shipwrecked; Ships; Historical Drama; Docudrama; Ensemble Films; Multiple Stories; Interwoven Stories; Titanic Stories; All-Star Cameos
(Titanic; The Last Voyage)
(Ed: Details the terror up to the last minute, cutting between so many characters, their deaths are truly felt)

Night Train to Munich, 1940, 93m, ★★★/$$$, 20th/Nos. A Czech inventor interned at a concentration camp is the subject of a rescue attempt by a British agent posing as a Nazi. Margaret Lockwood, Rex Harrison, Basil Radford, Naunton Wayne, Paul Henreid. w. Frank

Launder, Sidney Gilliat, N-adap. Gordon Wellesley (BOStory) (*Report on a Fugitive*), d. Carol Reed. Oscars: 1-0.

DRAMA: MELODRAMA: SUSPENSE: Escape Drama; Rescue Drama; Concentration Camps; Trains; Nazi Stories; Germans as Enemy; World War II Stories; Germany; Fugitives from the Law (Schindler's List; Triumph of the Spirit)

Night unto Night, 1949, 85m, ★★1/2/$, WB/NA. A woman haunted by the ghost of her husband is helped by a kindly doctor with epilepsy, but mental illness lurks beneath the surface. Ronald Reagan, Viveca Lindofrs, Rosemary de Camp, Broderick Crawford, Osa Massen. w. Kathryn Scola, N-adap.; Philip Wylie, d. Don Siegel.

MELODRAMA: ROMANCE: Ghosts; Haunted Houses; Doctors; Mental Illness; Curiosities; Female Screenwriters; Female Protagonists

The Night Walker, 1965, 86m, ★★1/2/$, U-I/MCA-U. A woman whose husband died violently is tormented by dreams of a shadowy man who later shows up in her apartment. Robert Taylor, Barbara Stanwyck, Lloyd Bochner, Rochelle Hudson, Judi Meredith. w. Robert Bloch, d. William Castle.

HORROR: SUSPENSE: Psychological Drama; Haunted Houses; Ghosts; Insane-Plot to Drive; Revenge; Accidents; Past-Haunted by the; Nightmares; Illusions/Hallucinations; Cheating Women; Widows; Female Protagonists
(Night Watch; Gaslight)
(Ed: What's real and what's not is often difficult to figure out, but it just leads to confusion and a pat ending, not real suspense)

Night Watch, 1973, 98m, ★★1/2/$, Avco/Media, R/V-S. A woman whose husband has just died sees dead bodies in the hallways of her building. Is she imagining it? Elizabeth Taylor, Laurence Harvey, Billie Whitelaw, Robert Lang. w. Tony Williamson, P-adap. Lucille Fletcher, d. Brian G. Hutton.

SUSPENSE: Ghosts; Haunted Houses; Illusions/Hallucinations; Widows; Coulda Been Good
(Night Walker; Gaslight)

The Night We Never Met, 1993, 98m, ★★1/2/$, Miramax/HBO, R/S-P. One yuppie guy rents a place to get over a relationship, while another yuppie girl rents a place to get away from her husband, while still another guy wants to get away from his clingy girlfriend. All wind up in too close proximity. Matthew Broderick, Annabella Sciorra, Kevin Anderson, Jeanne Tripplehorn, Justine Bateman, Christine Baranski, Doris Roberts, Bill Campbell, Louise Lasser. w. Warren Leight, d. Evan Lurie.

COMEDY: COMEDY DRAMA: ROMANCE: Romantic Comedy; Roommates; Yuppies; Apartment Buildings; Multiple Stories; Young Men; Young Women; Starting Over; Coulda Been Good
(The Opposite Sex [1992]; Key Exchange)
(Ed: Okay, but not quite up to most of the cast's usual material)

Nightwing, 1979, 105m, ★★1/2/$$, Col/RCA-Col, PG/V. Scientists try to stop an onslaught of bats in the desert who are spreading a plague, but also killing their prey en masse. Nick Mancuso, David Warner, Kathryn Harrold, Stephen Macht, Strother Martin. w. Steve Shagan, Bud Shrake, N-adap. Martin Cruz Smith, d. Arthur Hiller.
Horror; Monsters; Animal; Desert Settings; Indians; American Scientists
(The Birds; Night of the Lepus)

Nine Months, 1995, 103m, ★★1/2/$$$, 20th/Fox, PG-13/S-P. When a child psychiatrist finds his girlfriend is pregnant, an obnoxious relative and a dark cloud of slapstick hover around him until he deals with the reality of the situation. Hugh Grant, Julianne Moore, Tom Arnold, Joan Cusack, Jeff Goldblum, Robin Williams, Mia Cottet, Joey Simmrin. S-adap. *Neuf Mois*, Patrick Braoude. w. d. Chris Columbus.
COMEDY: Comedy-Slapstick; Fathers; Psychiatrists; Engagements-Breaking; Babies-Having; Foreign Film Remakes; San Francisco; Writer-Directors
(She's Having a Baby; Four Weddings and a Funeral)
(Ed: Dumb but pretty)

1918, 1985, ★★★1/2/$, AP-PBS-Cinecom/Fox, G. The great Spanish flu strikes Waxahachie, Texas and affects many lives with those it kills. William Converse-Roberts, Hallie Foote, Matthew Broderick, Rochelle Oliver. w. Horton Foote, d. Ken Harrison.
DRAMA: MELODRAMA: Epidemics; Disease Stories; Small-town Life; 1900s; World War I Era; Texas; Southerns; Ordinary People Stories; Hidden Gems; Quiet Little Films;

SEQUEL TO: On Valentine's Day. (On Valentine's Day; The Trip to Bountiful)

1984, 1955, 91m, ★★★/$, British/NA. In the "future" of 1984, Winston Smith rebells against his fascistic brainwashing conformist society. Edmond O'Brien, Jan Sterling, Michael Redgrave. w. William P. Templeton, Ralph Bettinson, N-adap. George Orwell, d. Michael Anderson. (Ed: A faithful adaptation in terms of plot, but misses the mark in the story where the oppression of Big Brother on a small scale is abandoned for a simplistic, "love conquers all" theme)

1984, 1984, 110m, ★★★/$, Virgin/USA, R/S-FFN-MFN. A remake which treats Orwell's novel as a vision of what might have been in the 40s when it was first conceived, much like Russia. John Hurt, Richard Burton, Suzanna Hamilton, Cyril Cusack. w. d. Michael Radford, N-adap. George Orwell.
DRAMA: SCI-FI: Futuristic Films; Oppression; Romance-Clandestine; Government as Enemy; Voyeurs; Brainwashing; Paranoia; Allegorical Stories; Classic Literary Adaptations; Independent Films
(Fahrenheit 451; Alphaville; Metropolis)

1941, 1979, 118m, ★★★/$$$, Col-U/MCA-U, PG. During World War II, the threat of a lost Japanese submarine striking Los Angeles sends everyone and everything into complete chaos. Dan Aykroyd, Ned Beatty, John Belushi, Lorraine Gary, Murray Hamilton, Christopher Lee, Tim Matheson, Toshiro Mifune, Warren Oates. w. Robert Zemeckis, Bob Gale, d. Steven Spielberg. BCin. Oscars: 1-0.
COMEDY: ACTION: Action Comedy; **FARCE:** Comedy of Errors; World War II Stories; Military Stories; Paranoia; Los Angeles; Japanese as Enemy; Flops-Major
(The Russians Are Coming, The Russians Are Coming; Honkytonk Freeway)
(Ed: Rumored to be a flop, it actually grossed a large amount and is not a bad film at all)

1900, 1976, 200m, ★★★/$$, Par/Par, R/S-V-FFN-MN. A land-owning Italian family survives the rise of fascism and both world wars. Burt Lancaster, Robert De Niro, Gerard Depardieu, Dominique Sanda, Donald Sutherland, Sterling Hayden. w. Bernardo Bertolucci, Franco

Arcalli, Giuseppe Bertolucci, d. Bernardo Bertolucci.
DRAMA: Sagas; Family Drama; Epics; Political Drama; Historical Drama; World War I Era; World War II Era; Italians; Italy
(The Godfather; Once Upon a Time in America)

1969, 1988, 96m, ★★1/2/$, Atlantic/Par, PG/S-P. In a small town, two friends come of age against the backdrop of the Vietnam War. Robert Downey Jr., Kiefer Sutherland, Bruce Dern, Mariette Hartley, Winona Ryder, Joanna Cassidy. w. d. Ernest Thompson.
DRAMA: COMEDY DRAMA: Friendships-Male; Coming of Age; Small-town Life; Vietnam Era; Coulda Been Good; Writer-Directors; Independent Films
(Easy Rider; The Strawberry Statement; Flashback)

92 in the Shade, 1975, 88m, ★★★/$, UA/Fox, R/S-P. Two fishermen compete for the big prize down in Florida amid the many local eccentrics and colorful characters. Peter Fonda, Warren Oates, Margot Kidder, Elizabeth Ashley, Burgess Meredith, Harry Dean Stanton, Sylvia Miles, William Hickey. w. d., N-adap. Thomas McGuane.
COMEDY DRAMA: Character Studies; Eccentric People; Multiple Stories; Interwoven Stories; Competitions; Southerns; Small-town Life; Florida Keys; Fishermen; Hidden Gems; Underrated; Coulda Been Great; Writer-Directors
(Rancho Deluxe; Cold Feet; Criss-Cross; TV Series Key West)

99 and 44/100 Per Cent Dead, 1974, 98m, ★★/$, 20th/Fox. A gangster on the outs hires a consultant to drum up business. Richard Harris, Edmond O'Brien, Bradford Dillman, Chuck Connors. w. Robert Dillon, d. John Frankenheimer.
ACTION: Crime Drama; Mob Stories; Mob Wars; Black Comedy; Hitmen; Curiosities

Ninotchka, 1939, 110m, ★★★★/$$$$, MGM/MGM-UA. A stiff communist woman sent to Paris to sell some royal jewels is pursued by a Parisian philanderer who finds her all the more intriguing because of the incredible challenge. Greta Garbo (BActress), Melvyn Douglas, Sig Rumann, Ina Claire, Bela Lugosi. w. Charles Brackett, Billy Wilder, Walter Reisch, Melchior Lengyel (BOStory,

BScr), d. Ernst Lubitsch. BPicture.
Oscars: 4-0.

COMEDY: ROMANCE: Romantic
Comedy; **SATIRE:** Romance-Boy Wants
Girl; Romance-Reluctant; Battle of the
Sexes; Extroverted vs. Introverted;
Russians; Stern Women; Cold People;
Playboys; Paris; Communists
MUSICAL REMAKE: Silk Stockings.
(Silk Stockings; The Iron Petticoat)

The Ninth Configuration, 1980,
105m, ★★1/2/$, ITC-New World/New
World, R/P-V. On a military base, a psy-
chiatrist becomes the object of ridicule
and hateful pranks which slowly turn
serious in a surrealist manner. Stacy
Keach, Scott Wilson, Jason Miller, Ed
Flanders, Neville Brand, Moses Gunn. w.
d. William Peter Blatty.
SCI-FI: HORROR: Psychological Drama;
Psychiatrists; Military Stories; Identities-
Assumed; Ostracism; Practical Jokers;
Surrealism; Art Films; Cult Films;
Curiosities; Writer-Directors

Nitti, The Enforcer, 1988, 94m,
★★1/2/$$, Academy/Academy. Al
Capone's henchman's tale of violence
and crime in old Chicago. Anthony
LaPaglia, Trini Alvarado, Michael
Moriarty, Bruno Kirby. d. Michael
Switzer.
ACTION: Crime Drama; Mob Stories;
Hitmen; Al Capone; Chicago; 1930s;
Independent Films
(Capone; The Untouchables)

Nixon, 1995, 190m, ★★★/$$, Hollywood/
Hollywood, R/P-S. The life and times of
the only U.S. president to resign from
office, from his beginnings in Whittier,
California, to his exile. Anthony Hopkins
(BActor), Joan Allen (BSActress), Powers
Booth, Ed Harris, David Paymer, David
Hyde Pierce, James Woods, E. G.
Marshall, Mary Steenburgen, J. T. Walsh,
Madeline Kahn, John Diehl, Paul Sorvino,
Bob Hoskins. w. Stephen J. Rivele,
Christopher Wilkinson, & Oliver Stone, d.
Oliver Stone. Oscars: 2-0.
DRAMA: Biographies; Presidents; 1970s;
Rise and Fall Stories; Power-Rise to;
Scandals; Politicians; Woman Behind the
Man; Episodic Stories; Epics
(Secret Honor; JFK; All the President's
Men)

Nobody's Fool, 1986, 107m, ★★★/$,
Island/WB, PG/S. A lonely young woman
with too much spirit for her small town
falls for a techie with a traveling theatri-

cal troupe (rather than pine for the jock
she stuck chopsticks into the neck of on
prom night). Rosanna Arquette, Eric
Roberts, Mare Winningham, Jim Youngs,
Louise Fletcher. w. Beth Henley, d.
Evelyn Purcell.
COMEDY DRAMA: ROMANCE:
Romantic Comedy; Small-town Life;
Young Women; Drifters; Female
Protagonists; Female Screenwriters;
Female Directors; Independent Films
(Miss Firecracker; Rich in Love)

Nobody's Fool, 1994, 123m, ★★★1/2/
$$$, 20th/Fox, PG-13/P-S. An old
codger finds himself alone in his twilight
years but for a few old friends and a new
young woman who comes into his life,
but will it do any good? Paul Newman
(BActor), Bruce Willis, Melanie Griffith,
Jessica Tandy. w. d. Robert Benton.
Oscars: 1-0.
COMEDY DRAMA: DRAMA: Character
Studies; Elderly Men; Elderly People;
Romance-Older Men/Younger Women;
Rejuvenation; Life Transitions; Stern
Men
(The Verdict; Grumpy Old Men; Kotch)

Nobody's Perfect, 1968, 103m, ★★/$,
U/NA. A veteran who stole a Buddha
from a Japanese temple during the war
returns afterwards to make ammends.
Doug McClure, Nancy Kwan, Steve
Carlson, James Whitmore, David
Hartman. w. John D. G. Black, N-adap.
Allan R. Bosworth (The Crows of Edwina
Hill), d. Alan Rafkin.
COMEDY: Fish out of Water Stories;
Misunderstandings; Thieves; Reunions;
Japan; Americans Abroad

Nocturne, 1946, 87m, ★★★/$$, RKO/
Turner. A composer is murdered and a
detective investigates all leads-some
leading to rather satirical finds. George
Raft, Lynn Bari, Virginia Huston, Joseph
Pevney, Myrna Dell. w. Jonathan Latimer,
d. Edwin L. Marin.
SUSPENSE: Crime Drama; **MYSTERY:**
MURDER: MURDER MYSTERY:
Detective Stories; Detectives-Police;
Music Composers; Forgotten Films

No Deposit, No Return, 1976, 112m,
★★★/$$$, Disney/Disney, G. A million-
aire's grandchildren get lost in an airport
and end up tagging along with some
crooks who decide to take advantage of
the situation by kidnapping them. David
Niven, Darren McGavin, Don Knotts,
Herschel Bernardi, Barbara Feldon, Vic

Tayback. w. Arthur Alsberg, Don Nelson,
d. Norman Tokar.
COMEDY: Action Comedy; **CHILDREN'S:**
FAMILY: Chase Stories; Comedy-
Disneyesque; Thieves; Kidnappings;
Child Protagonists; Brothers & Sisters
(That Darn Cat; The Apple Dumpling
Gang)

No Down Payment, 1957, 105m,
★★★/$$, 20thNA. A group of residents
in an apartment complex in Los Angeles
in the fifties have turf wars and romantic
entanglements. Joanne Woodward, Tony
Randall, Jeffrey Hunter, Cameron
Mitchell, Barbara Rush, Pat Hingle,
Sheree North. w. Philip Yordan, N-adap.
John McPartland, d. Martin Ritt.
COMEDY DRAMA: MELODRAMA:
Ensemble Films; Multiple Stories;
Interwoven Stories; Apartment Buildings;
Forgotten Films; Hidden Gems
(The Love Nest; Under the Yum Yum Tree)

No Escape, 1936, 85m, ★★★/$$, Pathe
Welwyn/NA. As part of a criminal
scheme, two friends bluff that one of
them is dead. As the plot thickens, he
really *does* end up dead, and his accom-
plice is the prime suspect. Valerie
Hobson, Leslie Perrins, Robert Cochran,
Billy Milton. w., P-adap. George
Goodchild, Frank Witty (No Exit), d.
Norman Lee.
SUSPENSE: MURDER: Hoaxes; Accused
Unjustly; Framed; Deaths-Faked;
Practical Jokers; Clever Plots & Endings;
British Films

No Escape, 1994, 118m, ★★★/$,
Savoy/HBO, R/V. In the future a man is
sent to a primitive island penal colony
where dog eats dog-unless he can escape
to a sanctuary area. Ray Liotta, Lance
Henriksen, Stuart Wilson, Kevin Dillon,
Michael Lerner, Ernie Hudson.
w. Joel Gross, d. Martin Campbell.
ACTION: Chase Stories; Prison Drama;
Islands; Futuristic Films; Men in
Conflict; Race Against Time; Fugitives
from a Murderer; Fugitives from the Law
(The Most Dangerous Game; Manhunt)

No Escape, No Return, 1993, 93m,
★★1/2/$, PM Entertainment/PM, R/EV-S.
The FBI forces three corrupt cops to go
undercover in a drug ring, but things do
not go smoothly. Maxwell Caulfield,
Dustin Nguyen, John Saxon. w. d. Charles
Kanganis.
ACTION: Crime Drama; Police Stories;
Police Corruption; Police Brutality; Under-

cover FBI Agents; Drugs-Dealing; Mob Stories; Mob Wars; Independent Films (Deep Cover)

No Highway in the Sky, 1951, 98m, ★★★/$$, 20th/NA. In the middle of a long flight, passengers notice that the tail of the airplane is about to fall off. James Stewart, Marlene Dietrich, Glynis Johns. w. R. C. Sheriff, Oscar Millard, Alec Coppe, N-adap. Henry Koster.

DRAMA: SUSPENSE: Airplane Crashes; Disaster Movies; Multiple Stories; Pilots-Airline; Forgotten Films
(Airport; The High and the Mighty)

Noir et Blanc, 1986, 80m, ★★¹/₂/$, Ind/NA. A shy white accountant meets a black dominatrix who perfectly fills the void in his life. Francis Frappat, Jacques Martial, Josephine Fresson. w. d. Claire Devers, SS-adap. Tennessee Williams *(Desire and the Black Masseur)*.

COMEDY DRAMA: ROMANCE: Sexuality; Sexual Kinkiness; Romance-Interracial; Alternative Lifestyles; Tennessee Williams-esque, French Films; Female Screenwriters; Female Directors
(Maitresse; Momma, There's a Man in Your Bed)

Noises Off, 1992, 104m, ★★¹/₂/$, Touchstone/Touchstone, PG/S. A play of American actors playing in a British farce falls to pieces as the behind the scenes chaos begins to make that on the stage even worse. Carol Burnett, Michael Caine, Denholm Elliott, Julie Hagerty, Marilu Henner, Mark Linn-Baker, Christopher Reeve, John Ritter, Nicollette Sheridan. w. Marty Kaplan, P-adap. Michael Frayn, d. Peter Bogdanovich.

COMEDY: FARCE: Farce-Bedroom; Multiple Stories; Interwoven Stories; Actors; Actresses; Directors; Romance-Triangles; Cheating Men; Cheating Women; Cheated Upon Meet; Putting on a Show; Theater Life; Behind the Scenes; Flops-Major; Coulda Been Great
(Ed: What was a big hit on stage becomes a badly timed mess on screen with a cast of TV actors with no finesse, though Caine and Burnett do their best)

Nomads, 1985, 100m, ★★/$, PSO-Par/Par, R/V-S. After studying indigenous peoples all around the world, an anthropologist is haunted by their ghosts, even though he's in L. A. Pierce Brosnan, Lesley-Anne Down, Anna Maria Monticelli, Adam Ant. w. d. John McTiernan.

DRAMA: SCI-FI: Psychological Drama; Ghosts; Possessions; Nightmares; Curiosities; Coulda Been Good; Writer-Directors
(The Last Wave; The Serpent and the Rainbow)

No Man of Her Own, 1932, 98m, ★★★/$$$, Par/NA. A gambler bets he can get a girl, but after they marry he has to try to hide his avocation from her. Clark Gable, Carole Lombard, Dorothy Mackail, Grant Mitchell. w. Maurine Watkins, Milton H. Gropper, d. Wesley Ruggles.

COMEDY DRAMA: ROMANCE: Romantic Comedy; Marriage Comedy; Newlyweds; Bets; Gambling; Secrets-Keeping; Female Screenwriters
(Swing High, Swing Low; The Great Sinner)

No Man of Her Own, 1949, 98m, ★★¹/₂/$$, Par/MCA-U. An unwed woman about to give birth survives a train crash and afterwards claims to be the wife of a man who died. Barbara Stanwyck, John Lund, Lyle Bettger, Jane Cowl. w. Catharine Turney, Sally Benson, Mitchell Leisen, d. Mitchell Leisen.

MELODRAMA: Survival Drama; Disaster Movies; Trains; Mothers-Unwed; Impostors; Identities-Assumed; Female Screenwriters; Female Protagonists

No Man's Land, 1985, 110m, ★★¹/₂/$, Filmograph-Ind/NA. In the Swiss and French Alps, smugglers endure the harsh conditions in the vain hope for the one big score that will take them out of "the life." Jean-Philippe Ecoffey, Betty Berr, Marie-Luce Felber, Hugues Quester. w. d. Alain Tanner.

DRAMA: Character Studies; Thieves; Nervous Breakdowns; Depression; French Films; Switzerland; Alps; Writer-Directors

No Man's Land, 1987, 105m, ★★¹/₂/$, Orion/Orion, R/S-V. An undercover cop is trying to track down a car thief. On the way, he ends up falling in love with the thief's sister. D. B. Sweeney, Charlie Sheen, Lara Harris, Randy Quaid, Bill Duke, M. Emmett Walsh. w. Dick Wolf, d. Peter Werner.

ACTION: SUSPENSE: Police Stories; Undercover; Car Chases; Thieves; Romance-Unprofessional; Romance-Triangles; Men in Conflict
(The Chase [1994]; The Boys Next Door)
(Ed: Story like a Western, only without horses, just horsepower)

No Mercy, 1986, 105m, ★★/$$$, Tri-Star/RCA-Col, R/V-P-S. Undercover cops pose as hitmen and get into sticky situations when their bosses expect action. Then one of them runs off with the mobster's girl and hides out in the swamps. Richard Gere, Kim Basinger, Jeroen Krabbe, Terry Kinney, George Dzundza, William Atherton. w. Jim Carabatsos, d. Richard Pearce.

ACTION: Crime Drama; Police Stories; Undercover; Mob Stories; Hitmen; Impostors; Mob Girls; Fugitives from the Mob; Swamp Settings; New Orleans
(Out of the Past; Against All Odds)

No More Ladies, 1935, 79m, ★★¹/₂/$$, MGM/NA. A playboy snags a beautiful society dame under the misguided assumption that she can make him change his philandering ways. Joan Crawford, Robert Montgomery, Franchot Tone, Charles Ruggles, Edna May Oliver, Reginald Denny, Arthur Treacher. w. Donald Ogden Stewart, Horace Jackson, P-adap. A. E. Thomas, d. Edward H. Griffith, George Cukor.

MELODRAMA: COMEDY: ROMANCE: Romantic Comedy; Romance-Class Conflicts; Reformers; Playboys; Battle of the Sexes

FLIPSIDE OF: Pygmalion

None But the Brave, 1965, 105m, ★★★/$$, WB/WB. In the South Pacific during World War II, a U.S. marine transport plane crashes on a Japanese island, and those still alive must struggle to survive and avoid getting captured by Japanese troops. Frank Sinatra, Clint Walker, Tommy Sands, Tony Bill, Brad Dexter. w. John Twist, Katsuya Susaki, d. Frank Sinatra.

ACTION: DRAMA: Action Drama; War Stories; World War II Stories; Survival Drama; Airplane Crashes; Stranded; Soldiers; Islands-South Pacific; Japanese as Enemy; Coulda Been Great; Actor-Directors
(Hell in the Pacific; Heaven Knows, Mr. Allison)

None But the Lonely Heart, 1944, 113m, ★★★¹/₂/$$$, RKO/Turner. An itinerate cockney roaming around London begins taking life more seriously after his mother contracts a fatal illness. Cary Grant (BActor), Ethel Barrymore (**BSActress**), June Duprez, Barry Fitzgerald, Jane Wyatt. w. d. Clifford Odets, N-adap. Richard Llewellyn. BOScore, BEdit. Oscars: 4-1.

MELODRAMA: TRAGEDY: Disease Stories; Tearjerkers; Mothers & Sons; Death-Impending; Death-Dealing with; Life Transitions; Drifters; England
(The Subject Was Roses; Toys in the Attic)

No No Nanette, 1930, 90m, ★★½/$$$, WB/NA. A bible seller must hide three young women who come to his house from his nagging wife. Bernice Claire, Lucien Littlefield, Lilyan Tashman, Bert Roach, Zasu Pitts. w. Howard Emmett Rogers, P-adap. Otto Harbach and Frank Mandel, d. Clarence Badger.

No No Nanette, 90m, 1940, ★★½/$$, RKO/Nos. A remake of above musical. Anna Neagle, Richard Carlson, Victor Mature, Helen Broderick, Roland Young, Zasu Pitts, Eve Arden. w. Ken Englund, d. Herbert Wilcox.

COMEDY DRAMA: MUSICAL: ROMANCE: Romantic Comedy; Multiple Stories; Saving Someone; Religion; Cheating Men

No Orchids for Miss Blandish, 1948, 102m, ★½/$, Alliance/NA. The daughter of a tycoon is kidnapped for ransom and ends up falling for the deranged leader of the gang. Jack La Rue, Linden Travers, Hugh McDermott, Walter Crisham, Lily Molnar, Zoe Gail. w. d. St. John L. Clowes, N-adap. James Hadley Chase.

MELODRAMA: Crime Drama; Kidnappings; Mob Stories; Kidnappers-Sympathizing with; Flops-Major; Curiosities; Independent Films
(Backtrack; Patty Hearst)

Norman, Is That You?, 1976, 92m, ★★★/$, MGM/MGM-UA, R/S-P. A black couple in marital trouble finds out their son is not only gay, but that he's having an affair with a white man. Redd Foxx, Pearl Bailey, Dennis Dugan, Michael Warren, Tamara Dobson. w. P-adap. Ron Clark, Sam Bobrick, d. George Schlatter.

COMEDY: FARCE: Alternative Lifestyles; Gay Men; Gay Awakenings; Romance-Interracial; Black Casts; Black Men; Marriage on the Rocks; Lover Family Dislikes; Camp; Curiosities; Forgotten Films; Time Capsules; Ahead of its Time; Good Premise Unfulfilled
(La Cage Aux Folles; Guess Who's Coming to Dinner)
(Ed: Pretty bad in spots, but overall worth renting if you can find it, offensive and dated as it is)

Norma Rae, 1979, 113m, ★★★★/$$$, 20th/Fox, PG/S. A small-town woman (Sally Field, **BActress**) decides to join a union organizer (Ron Liebman) at her cotton mill despite her husband (Beau Bridges) and everyone in the town. w. Harriet & Irving Ravetch (BAScr), d. Martin Ritt. **BPicture, BOSong.** Oscars: 4-2.

DRAMA: Social Drama; Underdog Stories; Women Against the System; Fighting the System; Factory Workers; Working Class; Worker's Rights; Heroes-Ordinary; Whistleblowers; Prostitutes with Heart of Gold; Southerns; Unions; North Carolina; Mothers-Unwed; Romance-Triangles; North vs. South; Women Proving Themselves; Strikes; Women's Films; Sleeper Hits; Female Protagonists; Female Screenwriters; Sally Field Goes Southern
(Silkwood; Places in the Heart; The 5.20 an Hour Dream; Marie; Heart Like a Wheel)

No Room for the Groom, 1952, 82m, ★★½/$$, U/NA. A war bride who eloped on the sly moves back into her house without telling her family she's married. Then her husband comes back from the war. Tony Curtis, Piper Laurie, Don Defore, Spring Byington. w. Joseph Hoffman, Darwin H. Teilhet, d. Douglas Sirk.

COMEDY: Marriage Comedy; Comedy-Situation; Marriage-Elopements; Secrets-Keeping; Return of Spouse; In-Laws-Troublesome; Wives-Troublesome; Soldiers; Good Premise Unfulfilled; War Brides

North, 1994, 86m, ★★/$, Col/Col, PG. A kid who's tired of his parents goes on a world tour to find another pair of them. Elijah Wood, Bruce Willis, Jon Lovitz, Julia Louis-Dreyfus, Jason Alexander, Dan Aykroyd, Alan Arkin, Kathy Bates, Richard Belzer, Faith Ford, Alexander Godunov, Graham Greene, Kelly McGillis, Reba McEntire, Alan Rachins, John Ritter, Lauren Tom, Abe Vigoda, Mathew McCurley. w. Alan Zweibel & Andrew Scheinman, N-adap. Alan Zweibel, d. Rob Reiner.

COMEDY: ADVENTURE: Comic Adventure; Boys; Parents vs. Children; Quests; World Travel; Cartoonlike Movies; Flops-Major; Good Premise Unfulfilled; All-Star Casts
(Flirting with Disaster)

The North Avenue Irregulars, 1978, 99m, ★★½/$$, Disney/Disney, G. The FBI enlists the aid of a man of the cloth in exposing a gambling syndicate.

Edward Herrmann, Barbara Harris, Susan Clark, Karen Valentine, Michael Constantine, Cloris Leachman, Patsy Kelly, Alan Hale Jr. w. Don Tait, N-adap. Albert Fay Hill.

COMEDY: Ensemble Films; Ensembles-Female; Disguised as Priest

CHILDREN'S: FAMILY: Comedy-Disneyesque; Gambling; Undercover; Capers; FBI Agents
(That Darn Cat; Family Plot)
(Ed: A movie for kids without the kids)

North by Northwest, 1959, 136m, MGM/MGM-UA, ★★★★/$$$$. A businessman (Cary Grant) is framed for a murder and has to become a fugitive to find out who really did it, while becoming ensnared by a deceptive blonde with something up her sleeve *and* in her train berth. Eva Marie Saint, James Mason, Leo G. Carroll, Martin Landau, Jessie Royce Landis. w. Ernest Lehman (BScr), d. Alfred Hitchcock. BCArt, BEdit. Oscars: 3-0.

ACTION: ADVENTURE: MURDER: MYSTERY: MURDER MYSTERY: Action Comedy; Fugitives from the Law; Fugitives from a Murderer; Saving Yourself; Conspiracy; Accused Unjustly; Framed?; Road Movies; Chase Movies; Unbelieved; Insane-Plot to Drive; Kidnappings; Scientists-Mad; Daughters Saving Fathers; CIA Agents; Hitchcockian

REMAKE OF: Saboteur
(Saboteur; Three Days of the Condor; Total Recall; Hanky Panky; The 39 Steps; The Fugitive)

North Dallas Forty, 1979, 118m, ★★★/$$$, Par/Par, R/EP-S-FFN-MRN. An exposé of the sordid life of drugs and sex behind the scenes in the NFL. Nick Nolte, Mac Davis, Charles Durning, Dayle Haddon, Bo Swenson. w. Frank Yablans, Ted Kotcheff, Peter Gent, N-adap. Peter Gent, d. Ted Kotcheff.

COMEDY DRAMA: SATIRE: Sports Movies; Football; Macho Men
(Necessary Roughness; Semi-Tough; The Program)

North Star, 1943, 105m, ★★★/$$, Goldwyn-UA/Goldwyn. The Nazis fail to take over a small Russian village full of determined, feisty people. Anne Baxter, Farley Granger, Jane Withers, Dana Andrews, Walter Brennan, Erich Von Stroheim, Dean Jagger, Walter Huston. w. Lillian Hellman, d. Lewis Milestone.

MELODRAMA: Political Drama; War Stories; Nazi Stories; World War II Stories; Russians; Small-town Life; Fighting Back; Female Screenwriters; Patriotic Films; Female Protagonists
(Secret of Santa Vittoria; The Heroes of Telemark)

North to Alaska, 1960, 122m, ★★★/$$$, 20th/Fox. At the turn of the century, gold prospectors go to Alaska and end up fighting over women. John Wayne, Stewart Granger, Fabian, Capucine, Ernie Kovacs. w. John Lee Mahin, Martin Rackin, Claude Binyon, P-adap. Ladislas Fodor, d. Henry Hathaway.

ADVENTURE: WESTERNS: Comic Adventure; Men Fighting Over Women; Ensemble Films; Ensembles-Male; Gold Mining; Alaska
(Belle of the Yukon; Call of the Wild; Northwest Passage)

Northwest Mounted Police, 1940, 125m, ★★★/$$$$, Par/NA. A fugitive runs from Texas to Canada, pursued all the way by a dogged Texas ranger. Gary Cooper, Paulette Goddard, Madeleine Carroll, Preston Foster, Robert Preston, George Bancroft, Akim Tamiroff, Lon Chaney, Jr., Montagu Love. w. Alan Le May, Jesse Lasky, Jr., C. Gardner, Sullivan, d. Cecil B. de Mille. **BEdit, BCin, BOScore, BArt. Oscars: 4-1.**

ACTION: ADVENTURE: Chase Movies; Fugitives from the Law; Police Stories; Manhunts; Canadian Mounties; Journies; Crossing the Border
(The Pursuit of D. B. Cooper)

Northwest Passage (Part One, Rogers' Rangers), 1940, 126m, ★★★/$$$, MGM/MGM-UA. In colonial America, rangers battle Indians across the northern passage. Spencer Tracy, Robert Young, Ruth Hussey, Walter Brennan. w. Laurence Stallings, Talbot Jennings, N-adap. Kenneth Roberts, d. King Vidor.

WESTERNS: ACTION: War Stories; War Battles; Cavalry; Indians-American; West-Old
(A Light in the Forest)

Norwood, 1969, 95m, ★★½/$$, Par/Par, PG/V. A Vietnam vet has a hard time readjusting to life in his home town but finds his calling as a singer. Glen Campbell, Kim Darby, Joe Namath, Dom De Luise. w. Marguerite Roberts, d. Jack Haley Jr.

DRAMA: Vietnam Era; Veterans; Small-town Life; Singers; Ordinary People;

Stories; Texas; Southerns; Female Protagonists
(Baby, the Rain Must Fall; Tender Mercies)

No Sex, Please, We're British, 1973, 91m, ★★★/$$, Col/NA. A pornographic package is misaddressed and ends up at a bank, setting off a farcical chain of events. Ronnie Corbett, Arthur Lowe, Beryl Reid, Ian Ogilvy, Susan Penhaligon. w. Anthony Marriott, Johnnie Mortimer, Brian Cooke, P-adap. Anthony Marriott, Alistair Foot, d. Cliff Owen.

COMEDY: SATIRE: FARCE: Sex Comedy; Scandals; Pornography World; Misunderstandings; Mix-Ups; Letters; Stagelike Films; Hidden Gems
(Secret Admirer; Blame It on the Bellboy)
(Ed: One of the longest running plays in England's history-where its humor is most appropriate)

Nosferatu, 1921, 72m, (Silent) ★★★★/$$$, Prana-Ind/Nos. An unofficial adaptation of *Dracula* in which the hideous, mystical count dies from sunlight. Max Schreck, Gustav Von Wangenheim, Greta Schroder. w. Henrik Galeen, d. F. W. Murnau.

HORROR: Dracula; Vampires; Women in Jeopardy; Cult Films; Silent Films
(Dracula; Bram Stoker's Dracula)

No Small Affair, 1984, 102m, ★★/$, Col/Col, PG-13/P-S. An obsessed fan takes pictures of his favorite female rocker. Shades of Madonna before Madonna. Demi Moore, Jon Cryer, George Wendt, Jennifer Tilly, Tim Robbins. d. Jerry Schatzberg.

COMEDY DRAMA: ROMANCE: Obsessions; Fans-Crazed; Infatuations; Photographers; Rock Stars; Singers; Romance-Boy Wants Girl; Boys; Forgotten Films; Curiosities
(Heartbreak Hotel; The Fan)

No Surrender, 1985, 104m, ★★½/$, Dumbarton-Ind/Prism. In Liverpool, Catholic and Protestant Irish get into bar brawls. Michael Angelis, Avis Bunnage, James Ellis, Ray McAnally. w. Alan Bleasdale, d. Peter Smith.

SATIRE: Black Comedy; Men in Conflict; Political Satire; Irish People; England; British Films; Overlooked at Release

Not as a Stranger, 1955, 135m, ★★★/$$$$, UA/MGM-UA. A medical student gets an assignment in the country and must make the necessary adjustments. Robert Mitchum, Olivia de Havilland,

Broderick Crawford, Frank Sinatra, Gloria Grahame, Lon Chaney, Jr., Myron McCormick. w. Edna Edward Anhalt, N-adap. Morton Thompson, d. Stanley Kramer. BSound. Oscars: 1-0.

MELODRAMA: Character Studies; Doctors; Tearjerkers; Medical School; City vs. Country; Fish out of Water Stories; Female Screenwriters; Blockbusters; Sleeper Hits; Faded Hits; Forgotten Films
(Northern Exposure TV Series; The Story of Dr. Wassell; Arrowsmith; Magnificent Obsession)

No Time for Comedy, 1940, 93m, ★★★/$$, WB/NA. A writer of comedies gets depressed and can't crank the jokes out anymore-but things soon change. James Stewart, Rosalind Russell, Charles Ruggles, Genevieve Tobin. w. Julius J. and Philip G. Epstein, P-adap. S. N. Behrman, d. William Keighley.

COMEDY: Depression; Writers; Theater Life; Comedians; Good Premise Unfulfilled; Forgotten Films; Hidden Gems
(Delirious; My Favorite Year)

No Time for Love, 1943, 83m, ★★½/$$, Par/NA. A female photojournalist covering the digging of a tunnel under the Hudson falls for the sweaty muscleman who directs the crew. Claudette Colbert, Fred MacMurray, Ilka Chase, Richard Haydn, June Havoc. w. Claude Binyon, d. Mitchell Leisen. BB&WArt. Oscars: 1-0.

COMEDY DRAMA: ROMANCE: Comedy-Slapstick; Romantic Comedy; Journalists; Romance-Class Conflicts; Working Class; Romance-Reluctant; Career Women; Tunnels; Forgotten Films
(Absence of Malice; The Egg and I; Maid of Salem)

No Time for Sergeants, 1958, 111m, ★★★/$$$, WB/WB. A country boy joins up and has a hard time adjusting to army life. Andy Griffith, William Fawcett, Murray Hamilton, Nick Adams, Myron McCormick. w. John Lee Mahin, P-adap. Ira Levin, N-adap. Mac Hyman, d. Mervyn Le Roy.

COMEDY: SATIRE: Fish out of Water Stories; Military Stories; Military Comedy; Soldiers; Hillbillies; City vs. Country; Southerns; Hidden Gems
(In the Army Now; A Face in the Crowd)
(Ed: Based on hit play that started Andy Griffith and his hayseed, common sense characters)

Not of This Earth, 1956, 90m, ★★★/ $$$, AA/NA. A stranger comes into town and turns out to be a blood-sucking fiend from outer space. Paul Birch, Beverly Garland, Morgan Jones. w. Charles Griffith, Mark Hanna, d. Roger Corman. Sci-Fi-1950s

Not of This Earth, 1988, 92m, ★★/$, New World/MGM-UA, R/S-V-B&G. Remake of above starring ex-porn star Traci Lords, Arthur Roberts. w. d. Jim Wynorski.
HORROR: SCI-FI: Aliens-Outer Space, Evil; Human Eaters; Vampires; New in Town; Cult Films; Hidden Gems; Independent Films
(The Hidden; X-tro; Body Snatchers)

Not with My Wife You Don't, 1966, 119m, ★★/$, WB/NA. A soldier comes home and has suspicions that his best friend has dallied with his wife. Tony Curtis, George C. Scott, Virna Lisi, Carroll O'Connor. w. Norman Panama, Larry Gelbart, Peter Barnes, d. Norman Panama.
COMEDY: ROMANCE: Romantic Comedy; Romance-Triangles; Cheating Women; Jealousy; Friends as Enemies; Misunderstandings; Veterans; Good Premise Unfulfilled
(No Room for the Groom; Coming Home)

Not Without My Daughter, 1991, 114m, ★★½/$$, Cannon-MGM/MGM-UA, PG. A true story about an American woman whose Islamic husband won't allow her daughter and herself to leave once they arrive in his home country of Iran and are under its sexist law. Sally Field, Alfred Molina, Sheila Rosenthal, Roshan Seth, Soudabeh Farrokhnia. w. David W. Rintels, NF-adap. Betty Mahmoody, William Hoffer, d. Brian Gilbert.
MELODRAMA: Family Drama; Escape Drama; Rescue Drama; Marriage on the Rocks; Dangerous Spouses; Fighting the System; Mothers & Daughters; Custody Battles; Arab People; Middle East; Sexism; Coulda Been Great
(Into Thin Air; The Wind and the Lion)

Nothin' But a Man, 1964, 95m, ★★★/$, Ind/Touchstone. A working class black man falls for a preacher's daughter in his small town and tries to get a better job. But when his white bosses manipulate him, he quits and all may be ruined. Ivan Dixon, Abbey Lincoln, Gloria Foster, Yaphet Kotto. w. d. Michael Roemer.

DRAMA: Social Drama; ROMANCE: Romantic Drama; Marriage-Impending; Making a Living; Black vs. White; Bigots; Race Relations Strikes Black Men; Black Women; Black Casts; Black Screenwriters; Black Directors; Cult Films; Forgotten Films; Hidden Gems; Writer-Directors; Independent Films
(Almos' a Man)

Nothing But the Best, 1964, 99m, ★★★/$$, Anglo Amalgamated-Ind/NA. A lowly clerk rises in business by stepping on his peers, but will he get away with it like others do? Alan Bates, Denholm Elliott, Harry Andrews. w. Frederic Raphael, d. Clive Donner.
COMEDY: SATIRE: Working Class; Ordinary People Stories; Turning the Tables; Worker vs. Boss; Power-Rise to; Ethics; Business Life; British Films; Hidden Gems
(Patterns; The Rise and Rise of Michael Rimmer; Madison Avenue)

Nothing But the Truth, 1941, 90m, ★★½/$$, Par/NA. Taking a bet, a stock-broker tries to tell the truth and nothing but for a twenty-four hour period. Bob Hope, Paulette Goddard, Edward Arnold, Leif Erickson, Glenn Anders. w. Don Hartman, Ken Englund, P-adap. James Montgomery, N-adap. Frederic S. Isham, d. Elliott Nugent.
COMEDY: Bets; Stockbrokers; Race Against Time; Ethics
(My Favorite Blonde)
(Ed: Another premise *I Love Lucy* raided)

Nothing But Trouble, 1944, 70m, ★★½/$, MGM/MGM-UA. The hired help of a young king fumble into foiling a murder plot. Stan Laurel, Oliver Hardy, Mary Boland. w. Russel Rouse, Ray Golden, d. Sam Taylor.
COMEDY: Fools-Bumbling; Murder-Attempted; Murder-Comic Attempts; Poison; Princes; Servants; Heroes-Unlikely

Nothing But Trouble, 1991, 94m, ★/$, WB/WB, PG-13/P. After their car breaks down, a New York couple are detained in a small town run by a corrupt sheriff and his extremely bizarre family. Chevy Chase, Dan Aykroyd, John Candy, Demi Moore. w. Dan Aykroyd, Peter Aykroyd, d. Dan Aykroyd.
COMEDY: CHILDREN'S: Multiple Performances; Eccentric People; Stranded; Nightmares; Vacations-Nightmare; Flops-Major

(Ed: An embarrassment that only a small child could find amusing)

Nothing in Common, 1986, 118m, ★★★/$$$, Tri-Star/RCA-Col, PG. An advertising copywriter tries to reconcile with his dad after his mother walks out after thirty-six years of marriage. Tom Hanks, Jackie Gleason, Eva Marie Saint, Hector Elizondo, Barry Corbin. w. Rick Podell, Michael Preminger, d. Garry Marshall.
COMEDY DRAMA: Family Comedy; Fathers & Sons; Generation Gap; Divorce; Parents vs. Children; Advertising World
(Memories of Me; Dad; Da)
(Ed: Okay, but nothing great)

Nothing Sacred, 1937, 77m, ★★★★/ $$$, Selznick-UA/Nos. A girl supposedly dying of a rare, fatal disease becomes a media darling until it's learned that she was misdiagnosed. Carole Lombard, Fredric March, Walter Connolly, Charles Winninger, Hedda Hopper, Hattie McDaniel. w. Ben Hecht, SS-adap. James H. Street (*Letter to the Editor*), d. William Wellman.
SATIRE: COMEDY: Screwball Comedy; Disease Stories; Death-Impending; Death-Impending, False; Heroes-Unlikely; Impostors; Hoaxes; Capra-esque; Journalists; Newspapers; Hidden Gems
REMAKE: Living It Up
(Living It Up; Send Me No Flowers; My Man Godfrey)

Notorious (B&W), 1946, 101m, ★★★★/ $$$$, RKO/Fox. A woman (Ingrid Bergman) plans to marry a Nazi spy (Claude Rains, BSActor) in order to help her kidnapped father, and then marry the American spy (Cary Grant) whom she really loves. w. Ben Hecht (BOScr), d. Alfred Hitchcock. Oscars: 2-0.
SUSPENSE: ROMANCE: Spy Films; Spies; Nazi Stories; Romance-Dangerous; Poisons; Kidnappings; Daughters Saving Fathers
(Foreign Correspondent; North by Northwest)

The Notorious Landlady, 1962, 127m, ★★★/$$, Col/RCA-Col. An ambassador from the United States takes a room in a London flat where many murders occur. The prime suspect is his landlady but he helps her find the real culprit. Kim Novak, Jack Lemmon, Fred Astaire, Lionel Jeffries. w. Larry Gelbart, Richard Quine, d. Richard Quine.

COMEDY DRAMA: MURDER: MYSTERY: MURDER MYSTERY: Comic Mystery; ROMANCE: Romantic Comedy; Rumors; Accused Unjustly; London; Americans Abroad; Hidden Gems; Underrated
(A Night to Remember; Gaslight)

Nous Sommes Tous les Assassins (Are We All Murderers?), 1952, 108m, ★★★/$$, UGC-Ind/NA. A simple young lad is trained to kill during wartime. When he puts his skills to use after the war, he's caught and sentenced to death. Marcel Mouloudj, Raymond Pellegrin, Antoine Balpetre, Claude Laydu. w. Andre Cayatte, Charles Spaak, d. Andre Cayatte.
SATIRE: DRAMA: MURDER: Message Films; Mercenaries; Hitmen; Assassination Plots; Ethics; French Films; Good Premise Unfulfilled; Anti-War Films

Nouvelle Vague, 1990, 89m, ★★★/$, Ind/Facets. A class conflict develops between a king and his courtesan in this allegorical Godard opus. Alain Delon. w. d. Jean Luc Godard.
DRAMA: ROMANCE: Erotic Drama; Romance-Class Conflicts; Romance with Prostitute; Kings; Art Films; Allegorical Stories; Writer-Directors; French Films
(The King's Whore; King Lear [1987])

Now and Forever, 1934, 82m, ★★1/2/$$, Par/NA. The young daughter of a jewel thief chastizes him and his mistress and puts things right. Gary Cooper, Carole Lombard, Shirley Temple, Guy Standing. w. Vincent Lawrence, Sylvia Thalberg, d. Henry Hathaway.
COMEDY DRAMA: Jewel Thieves; Criminal Couples; Partners-Married; Family Comedy; Forgotten Films; Ethics; Fathers & Daughters
(Irreconcilable Differences)

Now and Then, 1995, 96m, ★★1/2/$$, Tri-Star/Col-Tri, PG. Several women get together and reminisce about the good ole days as pre-teens in the early 70s. Christina Ricci, Rosie O'Donnell, Thora Birch, Melanie Griffith, Gaby Hoffman, Demi Moore, Asleigh Aston Moore, Rita Wilson, Janeane Garofalo, Hank Azaria, Bonnie Hunt, Cloris Leachman. w. Marlene King, d. Lesli Linka Glatter.
COMEDY DRAMA: Memories; Childhood Memories; Girlhood; Coming of Age; 1970s; Female Protagonists; Female Directors; Female Screenwriters
(Stand By Me; The Babysitters Club)

No Way Out, 1950, 106m, ★★1/2/$$, 20th/NA. A black doctor loses a white patient whose racist brother then gets up in arms. Richard Widmark, Sidney Poitier, Linda Darnell, Stephen McNally, Ossie Davis, Ruby Dee. w. Joseph L. Mankiewicz, Lesser Samuels, d. Joseph L. Mankiewicz.
DRAMA: Social Drama; Black vs. White Race Relations; Revenge; Death-Dealing with; Doctors; Ethics; Bigots; Ahead of its Time
(Mark of the Hawk; The Defiant Ones)

No Way Out, 1987, 117m, ★★★1/2/$$$$, Orion/Orion, HBO, R/P-S-FFN. A naval officer (Kevin Costner) falls in love with a call girl (Sean Young) who's also the mistress of his boss (Gene Hackman), and is suddenly framed for her murder. Will Patton, Fred Dalton Thompson, w. d. Roger Donaldson, N-adapt. Kenneth Fearing, *The Big Clock.*
SUSPENSE: Chase Movies; Spy Films; Spies; Secret Agents; MURDER: MYSTERY: MURDER MYSTERY: ROMANCE: Romance-Dangerous; Cheating Women; Prostitutes-High Class; Romance with Prostitute; Accused Unjustly; Framed?; Saving Oneself; Clever Plots & Endings; Conspiracy; Military Stories; Suicidal Tendencies of Homosexuals; Pentagon; Washington D.C.; Russians
REMAKE OF: The Big Clock
(Three Days of the Condor; North by Northwest)

No Way to Treat a Lady, 1967, 113m, ★★★1/2/$$$, Par/Par, AMC, PG/V. A New York detective (George Segal) struggles to find a psychotic killer (Rod Steiger) with a thousand disguises before he kills another woman, who just might be the detective's girlfriend (Lee Remick). w. John Gay, N-adapt. William Goldman, d. Jack Smight.
SUSPENSE: MURDER: COMEDY DRAMA: Black Comedy; Psychological Thriller; Chase Movies; Impostors; Disguises; Detective Stories; Killer Calls Cop; Detectives-Police; Serial Killers; Trail of a Killer; Criminal Pursues Good Guy's Family; Multiple Performances; Clever Plots & Endings; Hidden Gems
(The Mean Season; Relentless)

Now I'll Tell, 1934, 72m, ★★1/2/$$, 20th/NA. A New York gambler of the roaring twenties is remembered by his widow. Spencer Tracy, Helen Twelvetrees, Hobart Cavanaugh, Alice Faye, Shirley Temple. w. d. Edwin Burke.

DRAMA: Biographies; Narrated Films; Mob Stories; Gambling; Roaring 20s; Prohibition Era; Memories; Forgotten Films; Writer-Directors
(Oldest Living Confederate Widow Tells All)

Now, Voyager, 1942, 117m, ★★★1/2/$$$$, WB/WB. An old maid is brought out of her shell by her psychoanalyst, but the things that sent her into her shell may arise again. Bette Davis (BActress), Claude Rains, Paul Henreid, Gladys Cooper (BSActress), Lee Patrick. w. Casey Robinson, N-adapt. Olive Higgins Prouty, d. Irving Rapper. BScore. Oscars: 3-1.
MELODRAMA: ROMANCE: Romance-Doomed; Psychological Drama; Psychologists; Spinsters; Wallflowers; Starting Over
(The Old Maid; The Rainmaker; Rachel, Rachel; Summertime)

Now You See Him, Now You Don't, 1972, 88m, ★★1/2/$$$, Disney/Disney, G. A couple of students at the mythical Medfield U. discover an invisibility potion which they use to thwart some mobsters. Kurt Russell, Cesar Romero, Joe Flynn, Jim Backus. w. Joseph L. McEveety, d. Robert Butler.
COMEDY: CHILDREN'S: FAMILY: Mob Stories; Mob Comedy; Ordinary Person vs. Criminal; Invisibility; College Life; Teenagers; Comedy-Disneyesque
(The Computer Wore Tennis Shoes; The Barefoot Executive; The Invisible Man)

The Nude Bomb, 1980, 94m, ★★/$$, U/MCA-U, PG. A madman wants to drop a bomb that will de-clothe everyone in the world and Maxwell Smart is the only man who can stop him. Don Adams, Sylvia Kristel, Dana Elcar, Rhonda Fleming. w. Arne Sultan, Bill Dana, Leonard B. Stern, d. Clive Donner.
COMEDY: Spy Films; Spoofs-Spy; Secret Agents; Bombs; Rule the World-Plot to; TV Series Movies

Nudo di Donna, 1983, 112m, ★★★/$$, Ind/Applause Video, R/S-FN. When a man gets tired of his longtime wife, he sees a photo of a woman nude who resembles his wife. It sparks him, and he chases after her to some rather humorous conclusions. Nino Manfredi, Jean-Pierre Cassel, Elenora Girogi. d. Manfredi.
COMEDY: ROMANCE: Romantic Comedy; Marriage Comedy; Cheating Men; Obsessions; Sexy Women; Italian Films; Hidden Gems

(The Woman in Red; Bread and Chocolate)

Number 17, 1932, 64m, ★★★/$$, Republic/Republic. A bum finds some stolen jewels and winds up a fugitive from a female ringleader who may have a change of heart. Leon M. Lion, Anne Grey, John Stuart, Barry Jones. w. Alfred Hitchcock, Alma Reville, Rodney Ackland, P-adap. J. Jefferson Farjeon, d. Alfred Hitchcock.

SUSPENSE: Fugitives from the Mob; Homeless People; Finding Money; Find the Loot; Chase Stories; Forgotten Films; British Films; Writer-Directors

Numero Deux, 1975, 90m, ★★½/$, Ind/Facets. A family is crumbling apart as everyone has their own frustrating problems. Sandrine Battistella, Pierre Oudry. w. Jean Luc Godard, Anne Marie Mieville, d. Godard.

DRAMA: Family Drama; Art Films; Nervous Breakdowns; Depression; Surrealism

Nuns on the Run, 1990, 92m, ★★½/$$, 20th/Fox, PG-13/P-S. Two thieves on the lam disguise themselves as nuns to escape the law. Eric Idle, Robbie Coltrane, Camille Coduri, Janet Suzman, Robert Morgan. w. d. Jonathan Lynn.

COMEDY: Comedy-Slapstick; Fugitives from the Law; Hiding Out; Disguises; Men as Women; Nuns; British Films (The Pope Must Diet; Sister Act; Nasty Habits)

The Nun's Story, 1959, 151m, ★★★½/$$$$, WB/WB. A girl in Belgium joins a convent and is sent to a mission in the Congo where she endures many hardships. It finally becomes too much and she contemplates leaving, if she can survive the rigors of Africa. Audrey Hepburn (BActress), Peter Finch, Edith Evans, Peggy Ashcroft, Dean Jagger, Colleen Dewhurst. w. Robert Anderson (BAScr),

NF-adap. Kathryn C. Hulme, d. Fred Zinnemann (BDirector). BPicture, BCCin, BOScore, BEdit. Oscars: 7-0.

DRAMA: MELODRAMA: Character Studies; Biographies; Saintly People; Disease Stories; Episodic Stories; Missionaries; Nurses; Nuns; Religion; Africa; Female Protagonists; Hidden Gems (The Song of Bernadette; The Sins of Rachel Cade; Agnes of God; Sister Kenny; Keys to the Kingdom)

Nurse, 1980, 105m, ★★/$$$$, CBS/Live. A widow goes to work as a nurse and reclaims her life. Based on the big bestseller. Michael Learned, Robert Reed, Antonio Fargas. N-adap. Peggy Anderson, d. David Lowell Rich.

DRAMA: Medical Drama; Starting Over; Nurses; Single Women; Widows; Midlife Crisis; TV Movies; TV Series

Nurse Edith Cavell, 1939, 95m, ★★★/$$, Ind/Nos. Story of the famous heroine who aided the Belgian underground during World War I. Edna May Oliver, George Sanders, Zasu Pitts. d. Herbert Wilcox.

MELODRAMA: World War I Stories; Nurses; Biographies; Women at War; Heroines; Peaceful People; Forgotten Films (Sister Kenny; Florence Nightingale)

Nutcracker - The Motion Picture, 1986, 85m, ★★★/$, Par/Par, G. A filmed dance concert by the Pacific Northwest Ballet of Tchaikovsky's famous ballet. Hugh Bigney, Vanessa Sharp, Patricia Barker. d. Caroll Ballard.

MUSICALS: Ballet; Dance Movies; CHILDREN'S: FAMILY: Stage Filmings; Fairy Tales; Child Protagonists

The Nutcracker, 1993, 93m, ★★/$, 20th/Fox, G. A retelling with George Balanchine choreography of the classic about Christmas and its effects on a boy. Macaulay Culkin, Jessica Lynn Cohen,

Darci Kistler. w. Susan Cooper, N-adap. E.T.A. Hoffman, d. Emile Ardolino.

MUSICALS: Dance Movies; Ballet; FAMILY: CHILDREN'S: Christmas; Magic; Child Protagonists; Female Screenwriters; Flops-Major

Nuts, 1987, 116m, ★★★/$$$, WB/WB, R/EP. A call girl (Barbra Streisand) kills a john (Leslie Nielsen) in self-defense and is put on trial for her sanity to avoid facing murder charges. Richard Dreyfuss, Karl Malden, Maureen Stapleton. w. Alvin Sargent, Daryl Ponicsan, Tom Topor, P-adap., Tom Topor, d. Martin Ritt.

DRAMA: Courtroom Drama; MURDER: Murder in Self-Defense; Social Drama; Character Studies; Mental Illness; Prostitutes-High Class; Incest; Secrets-Keeping; Past-Haunted by the; New York Life; Feisty Females; Female Protagonists (The Accused; The Snakepit; One Flew Over the Cuckoo's Nest)
(Ed: Didn't make the money Streisand pics usually do, but still did okay and is entertaining for her fans or those of mental illness stories)

The Nutty Professor, 1963, 107m, ★★★★/$$$, Par/Par. A comic variation of the *Dr. Jekyll and Mr Hyde* story, in which a bumbling, nerdy chemistry professor takes a potion which turns him into a suave gigolo. Jerry Lewis, Stella Stevens, Howard Morris, Kathleen Freeman. w. Jerry Lewis, Bill Richmond, d. Jerry Lewis.

COMEDY: Comedy-Gag; Comedy-Slapstick; Comedy-Character; Dual Lives; Multiple Performances; Nerds; Wild People; Professors; Scientists; Playboys; Extroverted vs. Introverted; Comedy Remakes; Underrated; Writer-Directors

COMIC FLIPSIDE: Dr. Jekyll & Mr. Hyde. (The Disorderly Orderly; The Errand Boy; The Bellboy; Dumb and Dumber)

O

Object of Beauty, 1991, 103m, ★★★/ $$, Avenue/Live, R/S. An American couple, broke but living high, have a famous Henry Moore sculpture stolen from their room by the deaf-mute maid at their London hotel, and then have to get it back since it's all they own. John Malkovich, Andie McDowell, Lolita Davidovitch, Rudi Davies, Joss Ackland, Bill Paterson, Ricci Harnett, Peter Riegert, Jack Shepherd. w. d. Michael Lindsay-Hogg.

COMEDY DRAMA: Art Thieves; Searches; Americans Abroad; Poor People; Mute People; Thieves; Con Artists; Partners-Married; Detective Stories; Detective Couples; Writer-Directors

Objective Burma, 1945, 142m, ★★1/2/ $$$, WB/WB. A variety of types form a platoon headed for Burma to face the hell of war. Errol Flynn, James Brown, William Prince, George Tobias, Henry Hull, Warner Anderson, John Alvin. w. Ranald MacDougall, Lester Cole, Alvah Bessie, d. Raoul Walsh.

ACTION: Action Drama; War Stories; Ensembles-Male; Asia; World War II Stories; Special Teams-Military

Oblomov, 1981, 145m, ★★★/$$, Ind-Cannon/WB, Tape Worm Video. A Russian aristocrat learns to have political and social convictions in his changing world. Oleg Tabakov. d. Nikita Mikhalikov.

DRAMA: Social Drama; Political Drama; Life Transitions; Young Men; Rich People; Class Conflicts; Russians; Russian Films; Art Films; Hidden Gems

The Oblong Box, 1969, 95m, ★★1/2/$, AIP/NA. In the 1800s, a man's brother is wounded and buried alive but somehow gets out and goes on a violent rampage. Vincent Price, Christopher Lee, Alastair Williamson, Hilary Dwyer, Peter Arne, Maxwell Shaw, Rupert Davies. w. Lawrence Huntington, d. Gordon Hessler.

HORROR: Buried Alive; Revenge; Dead-Back from the
(The Telltale Heart; The House of Usher)

Obsession, 1976, 98m, ★★★/$$$, Columbia/RCA-Col, R/S-V. A businessman (Cliff Robertson) mourning his wife and daughter thinks he's found the reincarnation of his wife (Genevieve Bujold), but his business partner (John Lithgow) has other ideas. w. Paul Schrader, d. Brian DePalma.

MYSTERY: SUSPENSE: Kidnappings; Flashbacks; Past-Haunted by; Widowers; Conspiracy; Lookalikes; Reincarnation; Incest; Mindgames; Betrayals; Starting Over; Friends as Enemies; Venice; New Orleans; Gothic Style; Hitchcockian

REMAKE/RETREAD of Vertigo.
(Vertigo; Dressed to Kill; Dominique)
(Ed: Though derivative, this is one of DePalma's Hitchcock 'homages' which works on its own terms, though not as profoundly as the original)

O.C. and Stiggs, 1987, 109m, ★★★/$, MGM/MGM-UA, PG-13/P-S. For the whole summer, two suburban Arizona teenagers drive their cantankerous neighbor crazy by constantly playing practical jokes on him and his family. Daniel H. Jenkins, Neill Barry, Paul Dooley, Jane Curtin, Jon Cryer, Ray Walston, Louis Nye, Tina Louise, Dennis Hopper, Melvin Van Peebles. w. Donald Cantrell, Ted Mann, Tod Carroll, d. Robert Altman.

COMEDY: Party Movies; Comedy-Slapstick; Bathroom Humor; Teenagers; Boys; Suburban Life; Nuisances; Juvenile Delinquents; Practical Jokers; Southwestern Life; Country Club Life; Hidden Gems; Curiosities; All Star Cameos (Caddyshack; Meatballs; Porky's)

The Octagon, 1980, 103m, ★★/$$$, Ind/Media, PG/EV. A bodyguard helps a woman with Ninjas after her. Chuck Norris, Karen Carlson, Lee Van Cleef. d. Eric Kerson.

ACTION: Bodyguards; Protecting Someone; Martial Arts
(Good Guys Wear Black)

October, 1927, 95m, B&W, silent, ★★★★/$, Ind/NA. A re-enactment of the October Revolution, which put the Bolsheviks into power in Russia. w. Sergei

M. Eisenstein, Grigory Alexandrov, d. Sergei M. Eisenstein.

DRAMA: War Stories; War Battles; Russian Revolution; Russians; Russian Films

(The Battleship Potemkin)

The October Man, 1947, 95m, ★★★/ $$$, B-L/Learning Corp. A man (John Mills) is accused of killing a young woman and must find proof of the real killer with the help of his girlfriend (Joan Greenwood). d. Roy Ward Baker.

SUSPENSE: MYSTERY: MURDER MYSTERY: MURDER: Fugitives from the Law; Saving Oneself; Framed?; Accused Unjustly; Murder-Clearing Oneself; Amnesia; Race Against Time; British Films; Hidden Gems; Hitchcockian

(Odd Man Out; The Fugitive)

Octopussy, 1983, 131m, ★★★/$$$$$, UA/MGM-UA, PG/S. A military zealot from Russia plans to launch an attack against NATO forces and Bond has to race to find out when and where and how to stop it. Roger Moore, Maud Adams, Louis Jourdan, Kristina Wayborn, Kabir Bedi, Desmond Llewellyn, Lois Maxwell. w. George MacDonald Fraser, Richard Maibaum, Michael G. Wilson, d. John Glen.

ACTION: Action Comedy; Chase Stories; Spies; Spy Films; Secret Agents; Bimbos; Sexy Women; Rule the World-Plot to; Russians; Leaders-Tyrant; Circus Life

(For Your Eyes Only; Moonraker; The Spy Who Loved Me; Goldeneye)

The Odd Couple, 1968, 105m, ★★★★/ $$$$$, Par/Par, G. A fastidious journalist needs a place to stay after his divorce, so he moves in with his sportswriter friend, a major slob in every way. Their two life-styles clash in often hilarious ways. Jack Lemmon, Walter Matthau, John Fiedler, Herb Edelman, David Sheiner, Larry Haines, Monica Evans, Carole Shelley, Iris Adrian. w. P-adap. Neil Simon (BAScr), d. Gene Saks. BEdit. Oscars: 2-0.

COMEDY: Comedy-Situation; Friendships-Male; Friends as Enemies; Roommates; Single Men; Extroverted vs. Introverted; Blockbusters

(The Goodbye Girl; Buddy Buddy; The Front Page [1974]; Grumpy Old Men)

Odd Man Out, 1946, 115m, ★★★/$$, Ind/Par. In Belfast, an IRA operative must hide from the British militia and is helped and hindered by his "comrades." James

Mason, Robert Newton, Kathleen Ryan, F. J. McCormick, Cyril Cusack, Robert Beatty, Fay Compton, Dan O'Herlihy, Denis O'Dea, Maureen Delany. w. F. L. Green, R. C. Sherriff, N-adap. F. L. Green, d. Carol Reed. BEdit. Oscars: 1-0.

SUSPENSE: Political Drama; Hiding out; Fugitives from the Law; Spies; Terrorists; IRA; British Films; Ireland; Hidden Gems

REMAKE OF: The Last Man.

(The Third Man; The October Man)

Ode to Billy Joe, 1976, 106m, ★★½/ $$, Col/RCA-Col, PG. In 1950s Mississippi, a thwarted teen romance ends in Billy Joe McCallister jumping off the Tallahachee bridge, as in the Bobbie Gentry song. Robby Benson, Glynnis O'Connor, Joan Hotchkiss, Sandy McPeak, James Best, Terence Goodman, Becky Brown. w. Herman Raucher, d. Max Baer.

MELODRAMA: ROMANCE: Romance-Doomed; Romance-Forbidden; Lover Family Dislikes; Suicidal Tendencies; Suicides of Teenagers; Southerns; Song Title Movies

The Odessa File, 1974, 129m, ★★★/$$, Col/RCA-Col, PG. A German journalist infiltrates a ring of Nazis in 1963. Jon Voight, Maria Schell, Maximilian Schell, Mary Tamm, Derek Jacobi, Peter Jeffrey, Noel Willman. w. Kenneth Ross, George Markstein, N-adap. Frederick Forsyth, d. Ronald Neame.

SUSPENSE: Political Drama; Spy Films; Spies; Nazi Stories; Undercover; Germans as Enemy; Journalists; Journalists as Detectives; Detective Stories

(The Boys from Brazil; Inside the Third Reich)

Odette, 1950, 123m, ★★½/$$, Ind/NA. During the war, a Frenchwoman with an English husband chooses to stay and work for the French resistance. For her efforts, she is imprisoned and tortured, while he tries to get help from outside. Anna Neagle, Trevor Howard, Peter Ustinov, Marius Goring. w. Warren Chetham Strode, NF-adap Jerrard Tickell, d. Herbert Wilcox.

DRAMA: MELODRAMA: War Stories; World War II-Resistance; World War II Stories; Torture; Spies; Spies-Female; Female Protagonists

Oedipus Rex, 1967, 110m, ★★★/$, Ind/Ingram, Facets. A radical version of the classic tale, with sections set in modern times. The familiar story is of the

man who discovers he's married his mother and killed his father, then rips out his eyes and wanders in the wilderness. Franco Citti, Silvana Mangano, Carmelo Bene, Julian Beck, Pier Paolo Pasolini, Alida Valli, Ninetto Davoli. w. d. Pier Paolo Pasolini, P-adap. Sophocles.

DRAMA: TRAGEDY: Incest; Oedipal Stories; Mothers & Sons; Stepfathers; Parent vs. Child; Greece; Ancient Times; Classic Literary Adaptations; Classic Tragedy

(Angela; The Miracle [1990]; Mother's Boys)

Of Human Bondage, 1934, 83m, ★★★½/$$$, RKO/Turner, Nos. An upperclass English medical student ruins himself with his obsessive love for an earthily sexy but manipulative waitress. Leslie Howard, Bette Davis, Frances Dee, Reginald Owen, Reginald Denny, Kay Johnson, Alan Hale. w. Lester Cohen, N-adap. W. Somerset Maugham, d. John Cromwell.

Of Human Bondage, 1946, 105m, ★★½/$, WB/MGM-UA. Remake of the above, without the style. Paul Henreid, Eleanor Parker, Alexis Smith, Edmund Gwenn, Patric Knowles, Janis Paige, Henry Stephenson. w. Catherine Turney, d. Edmund Goulding.

Female Screenwriters

Of Human Bondage, 1964, 99m, ★★½/$, MGM/MGM-UA. Remake with some nuance, but miscast. Laurence Harvey, Kim Novak, Nanette Newman, Roger Livesey, Jack Hedley, Robert Morley, Siobhan McKenna, Ronald Lacy. w. Bryan Forbes, d. Henry Hathaway.

MELODRAMA: ROMANCE: Romantic Drama; Romance-Class Conflicts; Waitresses; Mean Women; Romance-Doomed; Obsessions; Medical School; Doctors; Depression; Nervous Break-downs; Classic Literary Adaptations

(White Palace)

Of Human Hearts, 1938, 100m, ★★★/ $$$, MGM/MGM-UA. A small-town minister has trouble with his irreverent, non-believing son. Walter Huston, James Stewart, Beulah Bondi (BSActress), Gene Reynolds, Charles Coburn, Guy Kibbee, John Carradine, Gene Lockhart, Ann Rutherford. w. Bradbury Foote, N-adap. Honore Morrow (Benefits Forgot), d. Clarence Brown. Oscars: 1–0.

MELODRAMA: Small-town Life; American Myth; Preachers; Fathers & Sons;

Religion; Forgotten Films; Hidden Gems (Mass Appeal)

Of Love and Desire, 1963, 97m, ★★/$, Ind/NA. The lusty sister of an oil-company boss in Mexico seduces her brother's engineer. Merle Oberon, Steve Cochran, John Agar, Curt Jurgens. w. Laslo Gorag, Richard Rush, d. Richard Rush.
MELODRAMA: ROMANCE: Romance with Relative's Friend; Oil People

Of Mice and Men, 1939, 107m, ★★★★/ $$$, MGM/MGM-UA. A traveling farm laborer agreed on his aunt's deathbed to take care of his mentally retarded cousin; a big oaf who inadvertently harms people and gets them both into trouble. Burgess Meredith, Lon Chaney, Jr., Betty Field, Charles Bickford, Roman Bohnen, Bob Steele, Noah Beery, Jr.. w. Eugene Solow, N-adap. John Steinbeck, d. Lewis Milestone.

Of Mice and Men, 1993, 110m, PG-13/S-V. Gary Sinise, John Malkovich, Sherilyn Fenn, Casey Siezmasko, Joe Morton. w. Horton Foote, N-adap. John Steinbeck, d. Gary Sinise.
Actor Directors
DRAMA: TRAGEDY: Friendships-Male; Mentally Disabled; **ROMANCE:** Romance-Doomed; Infatuations; Rape/Rapists; Accused Unjustly; Farm Life; Depression Era; California; Violence-Sudden; Classic Literary Adaptations
(Tortilla Flat; The Grapes of Wrath)

Off and Running, 1991, 90m, ★★/$, U/MCA-U. An actress about to marry is distraught when her fiancée is murdered. And she's next, but why? She must find out before she winds up dead! Cyndi Lauper, David Keith, Johnny Pinto, David Thornton, Richard Belzer, Jose Perez, Anita Morris, Hazen Gifford. w. Mitch Glazer, d. Edward Bianchi.
COMEDY: Comic Mystery; **MURDER: MURDER MYSTERY: MYSTERY:** Fugitives from a Murderer; Chase Stories; Female Protagonists; Coulda Been Good
(Moon Over Miami; Vibes; Somebody Killed Her Husband)

Off Limits, see **Saigon.**

The Offence, 1972, 113m, ★★★/$, UA/MGM-UA, R/S. In England, a man accused of child molestation gets the shakedown from a ruthless Scotland Yard inspector. Sean Connery, Trevor Howard,

Ian Bannen, Vivien Merchant. w., P-adap. John Hopkins (This Story of Yours), d. Sidney Lumet.
DRAMA: Social Drama; Molestation-Child; Sexual Problems; Accused Unjustly; Police Stories; Police Brutality; British Films; Forgotten Films; Hidden Gems (The Mark; Short Eyes; Never Take Sweets from Strangers)

An Officer and a Gentleman, 1982, 126m, ★★★/$$$$$, Par/Par, R/S-EP-FFN-MRN. A young man (Richard Gere) in the military tries to prove himself to a tyrannical drill instructor (Louis Gossett, Jr., **BSActor**) and his working-class girlfriend (Debra Winger, **BActress**). David Keith, Lisa Blount, Lisa Eilbacher. w. Douglas Day Stewart (BOScr), d. Taylor Hackford. BEdit, BOScore, **BOSong.** Oscars: 6-2.
DRAMA: ROMANCE: Romantic Drama; Military Stories; Men Proving Themselves; Working Class; Young Men; Stern Men; Black Men; Feisty Females; Patriotic Films; Conservative Values Films
(Top Gun; Iron Eagle)

The Official Story, 1985, 115m, ★★★1/2/$$, Col/RCA-Col, R/V. A middle-class woman in Argentina learns that the little girl she adopted is the daughter of desaparecidos, political "dissidents" killed by the military regime. Her marriage falls apart as she discovers that her husband is complicitous and knew all along. Hector Alterio, Norma Aleandro, Chela Ruiz, Chuchuna Villafane, Hugo Arana, Patricio Contreras. w. Aida Bortnik, Luis Puenzo, d. Luiz Puenzo. **BFLFilm.** Oscars: 1-1.
DRAMA: TRAGEDY: Social Drama; Political Unrest; Oppression; Government Corruption; Fighting the System; Nightmares; Police Brutality; **MURDER:** Missing Person; Searches; Argentina; Female Protagonists; Hidden Gems; Female Screenwriters
(Missing; Apartment Zero; The House of the Spirits)

O'Hara's Wife, 1983, 87m, ★★1/2/$$$, CBS/Vestron. After his wife dies, a middle-aged man gets some help from her ghost. Ed Asner, Mariette Hartley, Jodie Foster, Perry Lang, Tom Bosley, Ray Walston. w. James Nasella, William S. Bartman, d. William S. Bartman.
COMEDY DRAMA: MELODRAMA: Ghosts; Widowers; TV Movies
(Topper SERIES; Kiss Me Goodbye; Ghost)

Oh, Dad, Poor Dad, Momma's Hung You in the Closet and I'm Feeling So Sad, 1966, 88m, ★★★/$, Par/Par. An eccentric matriarch who travels with the coffin of her dead husband goes on vacation with the family to the Caribbean where strange sets and morbid behavior abound. Rosalind Russell, Barbara Harris, Robert Morse, Johnathan Winters, Hugh Griffith, Lionel Jeffries. w. P-adap. Arthur Kopit, d. Richard Quine.
COMEDY: Black Comedy; Comedy-Morbid; Family Comedy; Eccentric People; Vacations; Cult Films; Curiosities; Hidden Gems; Cartoonlike Movies; Ahead of Its Time; Outstanding Production Design
(Auntie Mame)

Oh, God, 1977, 104m, ★★★/$$$$, WB/WB, PG. A timid grocery store manager is visited by God in the form of George Burns, who proceeds to show him how to show others how to live. George Burns, John Denver, Ralph Bellamy, Donald Pleasence, Teri Garr, William Daniels, Barnard Hughes, Paul Sorvino, Barry Sullivan, Dinah Shore, Jeff Corey, David Ogden Stiers. w. Larry Gelbart (BAScr), N-adap. Avery Corman, d. Carl Reiner. Oscars: 1–0.
COMEDY: God; Religion; Unbelieved; Suburban Life; Heaven; What If . . . Stories; Ethics; Blockbusters
(Almost an Angel; Defending Your Life; Heaven Can Wait; Here Comes Mr. Jordan)

Oh God Book Two, 1980, 94m, ★★/$$, WB/WB, PG. God visits a cute kid who tries to convince adults that He's there. George Burns, Suzanne Pleshette, David Birney, Louanne, Howard Duff, Hans Conreid, Wilfrid Hyde White. w. Josh Greenfield, Hal Goldman, Fred S. Fox, Seaman Jacobs, Melissa Miller, d. Gilbert Cates.
COMEDY: God; Religion; Unbelieved; Suburban Life; Heaven; What If . . . Stories; Ethics; Boys

Oh God, You Devil, 1984, 96m, ★★/$, WB/WB, PG. A would-be music star enlists the help of Satan to further his career, for the low, low price of his mortal soul. George Burns, Ted Wass, Ron Silver, Roxanne Hart, Eugene Roche. w. Andrew Bergman, d. Paul Bogart.
COMEDY: God; Religion; Unbelieved; Suburban Life; Heaven; What If . . .

Stories; Ethics; Soul-Selling One's; Satan; Rock Stars

Oh Heavenly Dog, 1980, 103m, ★★1/2/$$, 20th/Fox, G. A detective gets killed in mysterious circumstances and "comes back" as a dog, making it logistically problematic when he tries to find out who murdered him and why. Chevy Chase, Jane Seymour, Omar Sharif, Robert Morley, Alan Sues. w. Rod Browning, Joe Camp, d. Joe Camp.
COMEDY: MYSTERY: MURDER: MURDER MYSTERY: Comic Mystery; Detective Stories; Dead-Back from the; Dogs; Reincarnation; Humans into Animals
SEQUEL TO: Benji SERIES.
(All Dogs Go to Heaven; Benji)

Oh Men! Oh Women!, 1957, 90m, ★★★/$$$, 20th/Fox. A therapist learns during sessions on the couch that two of his patients are having affairs with his wife. David Niven, Ginger Rogers, Dan Dailey, Barbara Rush, Tony Randall. w. d. Nunnally Johnson, P-adap. Edward Chodorov.
COMEDY: Sex Comedy; Psychologists; Multiple Stories; FARCE: Romance-Triangles; Cheating Men; Bimbos; Sexy Women; Hidden Gems
(Three on a Couch; The Couch Trip; Sex and the Single Girl)

Oh, Mr. Porter, 1937, 84m, ★★1/2/$$, Ind/Nos. British gun-runners disguised as ghosts are apprehended when their train makes a stop by a ridiculous station guard and his cohorts. Will Hay, Moore Marriott, Graham Moffatt, David O'Toole, Dennis Wyndham, w. Marriott Edgar, Val Guest, J. O. C. Orton, Frank Launder, d. Marcel Varnel.
COMEDY DRAMA: Heist Stories; Trains; Ghosts; Criminals-Stupid; Good Premise Unfulfilled
(The Wrong Arm of the Law; The Lavender Hill Mob)

Oh, Rosalinda!, 1955, 105m, ★★1/2/$$, B-L/NA. A ladies' man galavanting about in occupied Vienna plays a joke on four officers using the coquettish wife of one of them. Anton Walbrook, Michael Redgrave, Anthony Quayle, Mel Ferrer, Dennis Price, Ludmilla Tcherina. w. d. Michael Powell, Emeric Pressburger.
COMEDY: COMEDY DRAMA: Romantic Comedy; Practical Jokers; Playboys; Good Premise Unfulfilled; Writer-Directors

Oh, What a Lovely War, 1969, 144m, ★★1/2/$$, Par/Par. A black-comic, British musical rumination on World War I. Ralph Richardson, Meriel Forbes, John Gielgud, Kenneth More, John Clements, Paul Daneman, Joe Melia, Jack Hawkins, John Mills, Maggie Smith, Michael Redgrave, Laurence Olivier, Susannah York, Dirk Bogarde, Phyllis Calvert, Vanessa Redgrave. w. Len Deighton, (Musical)-adap. Joan Littlewood, Charles Chilton, d. Richard Attenborough.
COMEDY DRAMA: Black Comedy; Military Comedy; War Stories; World War II Stories; All-Star Casts; MUSICALS: Musical Comedy; SATIRE: England; British Films

Oh, What a Night, 1992, 93m, ★★1/2/$, Col/Col, PG-13/S. A teenager has an affair with an older, married woman when his family moves to Canada. Corey Haim, Barbara Williams, Genevieve Bujold. d. Eric Till.
COMEDY DRAMA: ROMANCE: Romantic Comedy; Love-First; Coming of Age; Teenagers; Boys; Women and Boys; Canada; Canadian Films
(In the Mood; Summer of '42; Class)

Oklahoma!, 1955, 143m, ★★★1/2/$$$$, UA/Fox. A shy Oklahoma cowpoke finally gets his girl, despite the evil machinations of a sleazy ranchhand. Gordon Macrae, Shirley Jones, Rod Steiger, Gloria Grahame, Charlotte Greenwood, Gene Nelson, Eddie Albert. w. Sonya Levien, William Ludwig, (Musical)-adap. Oscar Hammerstein, P-adap. Lynn Riggs (Green Grow the Rushes), d. Fred Zinnemann.
BSound, BEdit, BMScore, BCCin. Oscars: 4-2.
MUSICALS: COMEDY DRAMA: Musical Comedy; ROMANCE: Romantic Comedy; Southwestern Life; Farm Life; Romance-Boy Wants Girl; Men Fighting Over Women; Female Screenwriters
(South Pacific; The Music Man; Giant)

Oklahoma Crude, 1973, 111m, ★★1/2/$$, Col/Fox. A female oil rigger gets some help from an itinerate veteran of the Oklahoma oil fields. Faye Dunaway, George C. Scott, John Mills, Jack Palance, Woodrow Parfrey. w. Marc Norman, d. Stanley Kramer.
DRAMA: ROMANCE: Romantic Drama; Oil People; Feisty Females; Battle of the Sexes; Romance-Older Men/Younger Women; 1900s; Coulda Been Great; Female Protagonists
(Places in the Heart; Tulsa; Cold Sassy Tree)

The Oklahoma Kid, 1939, 80m, ★★★/$$$, WB/WB. After his father is accused of a crime he didn't commit and badly lynched, an Oklahoma cowboy hunts down the men responsible and pays them back. James Cagney, Humphrey Bogart, Rosemary Lane, Donald Crisp, Harvey Stephens, Charles Middleton, Edward Pawley, Ward Bond. w. Warren Duff, Robert Buckner, Edward E. Paramore, d. Lloyd Bacon.
WESTERNS: Westerns-Revenge; Revenge; Accused Unjustly; Cowboys; Faded Hits

Old Acquaintance, 1943, 110m, ★★★/$$, WB/WB. Two female romance writers in a jealous fit begin to manipulate each other's love lives to evil ends. Bette Davis, Miriam Hopkins, Gig Young, John Loder, Dolores Moran, Philip Reed, Roscoe Karns, Anne Revere. w. John Van Druten, Lenore Coffee, P-adap. John Van Druten, d. Vincent Sherman.
COMEDY DRAMA: MELODRAMA: Women in Conflicts; Romance Novelists; Writers; Friendships-Female; Jealousy; Hidden Gems; Female Protagonists; Female Screenwriters
REMAKE: Rich and Famous.
(Rich and Famous; Beaches; The Turning Point)

The Old Curiosity Shop, 1975, 119m, ★★1/2/$, Reader's Digest/Republic, G. A shop owner in 1840s London owes money to a creep loanshark-type who wants something in his shop. w. Louis Kamp, Irene Kamp, N-adap. Charles Dickens, d. Michael Tuchner.
DRAMA: Mortgage Drama; Men in Conflict; Malicious Menaces; 1800s; London; British Films; Overlooked at Release; Independent Films
(Scrooge; A Christmas Carol; Oliver Twist)

The Old Dark House, 1932, 71m, ★★★/$$$, U/MCA-U. A group of vacationers break down outside a strange dark mansion and take refuge there, only to find it scarier on the inside. Melvyn Douglas, Charles Laughton, Raymond Massey, Boris Karloff, Ernest Thesiger, Eva Moore, Gloria Stuart, Lilian Bond, Brember Wills, John Dudgeon (Elspeth Dudgeon). w. Benn W. Levy, R. C. Sherriff, N-adap. J. B. Priestley (Benighted), d. James Whale.

The Old Dark House, 1962, 86m, ★★1/2/$$, Col-Hammer/Col. In England, a house called Femm Manor is visited by an American relative who is immediately set upon by the weird inhabitants within. Tom Poston, Janette Scott, Robert Morley, Joyce Grenfell, Mervyn Johns, Fenella Fielding, Peter Bull. w. Robert Dillon, d. William Castle.

HORROR: SUSPENSE: Houses-Creepy; Vacations-Nightmare; Ensemble Films; Hidden Gems

(The House on Haunted Hill; Dracula)

Old Dracula, 1974, 88m, ★★/$, Col/NA. A beauty contest is held in Dracula's castle because the Count needs pretty young things to revive his dead wife. David Niven, Teresa Graves, Peter Bayliss, Jennie Linden, Veronica Carlson.

HORROR: Horror Comedy; Spoofs-Vampire; Beauty Pageants; Castles; Vampires; Dead-Back from the; Bimbos; Elderly Men; Good Premise Unfulfilled

(Love at First Bite; Dracula: Dead and Loving It)

Old Gringo, 1989, 120m, ★★½/$, Col/Col-TriStar, PG-13/S-V. A fictionalized account of Ambrose Bierce's travels with his schoolteacher ladyfriend down in Mexico and their encounters with the revolutionary leader Pancho Villa. Jane Fonda, Gregory Peck, Jimmy Smits, Patricio Contreras, Jenny Gago, Gabriela Roel, Sergio Calderon. w. Aida Bortnik, Luis Puenzo, N-adap. Carlos Fuentes (Gringo Viejo), d. Luis Puenzo.

DRAMA: MELODRAMA: Epics; **ROMANCE:** Romantic Drama; Spinsters; Teachers; Romance with Teacher; Romance-Older Men/Younger Women; Elderly Men; Romance-Elderly; Mexico; Political Unrest; Biographies; True Stories; Coulda Been Great; Flops-Major; Female Protagonists; Latin People; Female Screenwriters

(Like Water for Chocolate; The Sheltering Sky)

The Old Maid, 1939, 95m, ★★★/$$, WB/WB, MGM-UA. A woman gets pregnant before the Civil War, and her lover is to marry her when he returns. When he dies, however, she is forced to give up her child to her barren cousin to raise. Bette Davis, Miriam Hopkins, George Brent, Jane Bryan, Donald Crisp, Louise Fazenda, Henry Stephenson, Jerome Cowan, William Lundigan, Rand Brooks. w. Casey Robinson, P-adap. Zoe Akins, N-adap. Edith Wharton, d. Edmund Goulding.

DRAMA: MELODRAMA: Babies-Having; Mothers-Unwed; Civil War Era; Babies-Having; Children-Losing/Parting with; Widows; Children-Adopted; Spinsters; Women-Childless; Forgotten Films; Novel & Play Adaptations

(Now, Voyager; Jezebel; White Banners)

The Old Man and the Sea, 1958, 89m, ★★★½/$$, WB/WB. An elderly Portuguese man is one with nature while fishing alone. Spencer Tracy (BActor), Felipe Pazos, Harry Bellaver. w. Peter Viertel, N-adap. Ernest Hemingway, d. John Sturges. BCCin, **BSound**, BOScore. Oscars: 4-1.

DRAMA: Character Studies; Fishermen; Lonely People; Elderly Men; Quiet Little Films; Classic Literary Adaptations; Hidden Gems; Faded Hits

(Captains Courageous)

Old Mother Riley, SERIES, 1937–1952, ★★★/$$$, B-L/Nos. The foibles and misadventures of an Irish washer-woman and her daughter. Kitty McShane, Arthur Lucan, d. Maclean Rogers. 1937: Old Mother Riley; 1938: Old Mother Riley in Paris; 1939: Old Mother Riley MP, Old Mother Riley Joins Up; 1940: Old Mother Riley in Business, Old Mother Riley's Ghosts; 1941: Old Mother Riley's Circus; 1942: Old Mother Riley in Society; 1943: Old Mother Riley Detective; 1944: Old Mother Riley at Home; 1945: Old Mother Riley Headmistress; 1947: Old Mother Riley's New Venture; 1949: Old Mother Riley's Jungle Treasure; 1952: Mother Riley Meets the Vampire.

COMEDY DRAMA: Feisty Females; Ordinary People Stories; Mothers & Daughters; Forgotten Films; Faded Hits; British Films

The Oldest Profession, 1967, 115m, ★★½/$$, AIP/New World. Six separate stories involving prostitutes. Michele Mercier, Elsa Martinelli, Jeanne Moreau, Jean-Claude Brialy, Raquel Welch, Nadia Gray, Anna Karina. w. Ennio Flaiano, Daniel Boulanger, George Tabet, Andre Tabet, Jean Aurenche, Jean-Luc Godard. d. Franco Indovina, Mauro Bolognini, Philippe de Broca, Michel Pfleghar, Claude Autant-Lara, Jean-Luc Godard.

COMEDY DRAMA: Multiple Stories; Prostitutes-High Class; Prostitutes-Low Class; International Casts; Coulda Been Good

(Woman Times Seven; Nights of Cabiria)

Old Yeller, 1957, ★★★½/$$$$, Disney/Disney, G. When a stray dog becomes part of the family, the family may be torn apart after the dog saves the son's life but contracts hydrophobia/rabies. Dorothy McGuire, Fess Parker, Tommy Kirk, Jeff York, Chuck Connors. d. Robert Stevenson, N-adap. Fred Gipson.

MELODRAMA: CHILDREN'S: FAMILY: Pet Stories; Animal Stories; Boy and His Dog; Dogs; Farm Life; Death-Dealing with; Tearjerkers

SEQUEL: Savage Sam.

(Savage Sam; The Biscuit Eater, Dog of Flanders; Where the Red Fern Grows; Bambi)

Oliver!, 1968, 146m, ★★★½/$$$$, Col/Col, G. A musical retelling of Dicken's famous Oliver Twist, about the orphan boy who falls in with a crowd of street thieves. Ron Moody (BActor), Oliver Reed, Harry Secombe, Mark Lester, Shani Wallis, Jack Wild (BSActor), Hugh Griffith, Joseph O'Conor, Leonard Rossiter, Hylda Baker, Peggy Mount, Megs Jenkins. w. Vernon Harris (BAScr), P-adap. Lionel Bart, N-adap. Charles Dickens (Oliver Twist), d. Carol Reed (**BDirector**). **BPicture**, BCin, BEdit, **BSound**, BArt, BCostume, **BMScore.** Oscars: 11-5.

MUSICALS: COMEDY DRAMA: Musical Comedy; Orphans; Thieves; Con Artists; Inner City Life; London; Boys; Juvenile Delinquents; Pickpockets; Classic Literary Adaptations; Novel and Play Adaptations; Blockbusters; MUSICAL VERSION of Oliver Twist.

(Oliver Twist; Newsies)

Oliver and Company, 1988, 74m, ★★★/$$$, Disney/Disney, G. A group of dogs takes on a small kitten after an initial skepticism, mimicking the classic Dickens tale, Oliver Twist. Voices of Joey Lawrence, Billy Joel, Cheech Marin, Richard Mulligan, Roscoe Lee Brown, Sheryl Lee Ralph, Dom DeLuise, Taurean Blacque, Carl Weintraub, Robert Loggia, William Glover, Bette Midler. w. Jim Cox, Timothy J. Disney, James Mangold, N-adap. Charles Dickens (Oliver Twist), d. George Scribner.

Cartoons; **CHILDREN'S: FAMILY:** Orphans; Dogs; Cats; Animal Stories; Thieves; **MUSICALS:** Musicals-Animated

(The Great Mouse Detective; The Rescuers)

Oliver Twist, 1948, 116m, ★★★½/$$$, Par/Par. In the Victorian era, an orphaned boy lives on the streets of London and finds comradeship among street hoodlums, until it leads him to trouble. When he really gets in a fix, he's rescued by a kindly old man. Alec Guinness, Robert Newton, Francis L. Sullivan, John Howard Davies, Kay Walsh, Anthony Newley, Henry Stephenson, Mary Clare, Gibb McLaughlin, Diana Dors. w. David Lean, Stanley Haynes, N-adap. Charles Dickens, d. David Lean.

Oliver Twist, 1982, 72m, ★★★/$$$, CBS-Hallmark/Republic. Remake with great performances and period detail. George C. Scott, Tim Curry, Anthony Harvey, Cherie Lunghi. w. James Goldman, d. Clive Donner.
TV Movies

MELODRAMA: Orphans; Thieves; Con Artists; Inner City Life; London; Boys; Juvenile Delinquents; Pickpockets; Classic Literary Adaptations
(The Old Curiosity Shop; Oliver!; Battlement de Couer)

Oliver's Story, 1978, 92m, ★★/$, Par/Par, PG/S. Continuing the story of *Love Story*, Oliver learns to love again, after a period of mourning, meeting up with a jogging partner. Ryan O'Neal, Candice Bergen, Nicola Pagett, Edward Binns, Ray Milland. w. Erich Segal, John Korty, d. John Korty.

MELODRAMA: ROMANCE: Starting Over; Widowers; Yuppies; Lawyers; Romance-Reluctant; Single Men
SEQUEL TO: Love Story
(Starting Over; Love Story; Sleepless in Seattle)

Olivier, Olivier, 1992, 109m, ★★★/$$, Triumph/Col, R/S. A young street hustler insinuates his way into a suburban French family by claiming to be their long-lost son. Francoise Cluzet, Brigitte Rouan, Jean-Francoise Stevenin, Gregoire Colin, Marina Golovine, Frederic Quiring. w. Agnieszka Holland, Yves Lapointe, Regis Debray, d. Agnieszka Holland.

DRAMA: Character Studies; Children-Longlost; Missing Persons; Boys; Juvenile Delinquents; True or Not?; Liars; French Films; Female Directors; Female Screenwriters
(Six Degrees of Separation; The Return of Martin Guerre; Sommersby; Princess Caraboo; Europa, Europa)

Olly Olly Oxen Free, 1978, 93m, ★★★/$, Ind/Time-Life, G. The haughty old maid who runs the local junkyard

helps a group of local children construct a hot-air balloon out of old rags. Katharine Hepburn, Kevin McKenzie, Dennis Dimster. w. Eugene Poinc, d. Richard A. Colla.

COMEDY DRAMA: Spinsters; Elderly Women; Women and Boys; Balloons; Eccentric People; Overlooked at Release; Hidden Gems; Coulda Been Great; Independent Films

O Lucky Man, 1973, 174m, ★★★/$$, WB/WB, R/P-S. A junior salesman rises to the top of the financial world, then decides to "give a little back" by doing good deeds. Malcom McDowell, Arthur Lowe, Ralph Richardson, Rachel Roberts, Helen Mirren, Mona Washbourne, Dandy Nichols. w. David Sherwin, d. Lindsay Anderson.

DRAMA: SATIRE: Social Satire; Social Drama; Black Comedy; Salesman; Saintly People; Young Men; Young Men-Angry; England; Multiple Performances; 1970s; British Films
SEQUEL TO: If . . . ; **SEQUEL:** Brittania Hospital.

Olympische Spiele, 1936, 107m, B&W, silent, ★★½/NA, Nazi Party/NA. The Berlin Olympics shown as the pinnacle of Aryan prowess by the master propagandist of the Third Reich. d./ed. Leni Riefenstahl.
Political Drama; Nazi Stories; Documentaries; World War II Era; German Films; Berlin; Olympics; Female Directors
(Triumph of the Will)

The Omega Man, 1971, 98m, ★★★/$$, WB/WB, R/V-S. In the Los Angeles of the future, a single man remains unscathed by a neutron bomb blast which has turned everyone else into vampires. Charlton Heston, Rosalind Cash, Anthony Zerbe. w. John William Corrington, Joyce M. Corrington, N-adap. Richard Matheson (*I Am Legend*), d. Boris Sagal.

SCI-FI: HORROR: Apocalyptic Stories; Bombs-Atomic; Vampires; Zombies; Black Women; Romance-Interracial; Cult Films; Hidden Gems
(Soylent Green; A Boy and His Dog)

The Omen, 1976, 111m, ★★★½/$$$$, 20th/Fox, R/V-B&G. The childless American ambassador to Great Britain unwittingly adopts the Antichrist (don't they do background checks?). Gregory Peck, Lee Remick, David Warner, Billie Whitelaw, Leo McKern, Harvey Stevens,

Patrick Troughton, Anthony Nicholls, Martin Benson. w. David Seltzer, d. Richard Donner. BOScore, BOSong. Oscars: 2-0.

HORROR: SCI-FI: SUSPENSE: Satan-Child of; Children-Adopted; Apocalyptic Stories; Race Against Time; Murders of Children; Murders-One by One; Men in Jeopardy; Detective Stories; Unbelieved; Diplomats; Rule the World-Plot to
SEQUELS: Damien: The Omen II; The Final Conflict: Omen III
(The Exorcist; Rosemary's Baby; The Seventh Sign)

Omen IV: The Awakening, 1991, 97m, ★★/$, 20th/Fox, R. A childless couple adopt a girl who turns out to be the daughter of the Antichrist. Faye Grant, Michael Woods, Michael Lerner, Madison Mason, Asia Vieria. w. Brian Taggert, d. Jorge Montesi, Dominique Othenin-Gerard.

HORROR: SCI-FI: SUSPENSE: Satan-Child of; Children-Adopted; Apocalyptic Stories; Race Against Time; Murders of Children; Murders-One by One; Detective Stories; Unbelieved; Rule the World-Plot to
SEQUEL TO: The Omen, Damien: Omen II, The Final Conflict: Omen III.
(It's Alive; Rosemary's Baby; The Godsend)

On a Clear Day You Can See Forever, 1970, 129m, ★★★/$$, Par/Par, PG. A zany New York girl goes to a French hypnotic therapist to quit smoking, but he learns that she's had past lives when he puts her under-scenarios she plays out to song and fantasy. Barbra Streisand, Yves Montand, Bob Newhart, Larry Blyden, Jack Nicholson, Simon Oakland. w. P-adap. Alan Jay Lerner, d. Vincente Minnelli.

COMEDY DRAMA: MUSICALS: Musical Comedy; Fantasies; Reincarnation; Psychologists; Episodic Stories; Multiple Stories; Hypnosis; Free Spirits; Neurotic People; Female Protagonists; Librarians; Costume Drama; Hidden Gems
(Hello, Dolly!; Funny Girl; Up the Sandbox)
(Ed: Not a flop, but not Streisand's biggest hit, either. Well worth it for her fans, otherwise, only of interest to see early Nicholson or Newhart)

On Approval, 1943, 80m, ★★★½/$$$, Ealing/Nos. In the Edwardian era, an American heiress traipses off to Scotland for a "trial wedding" to her beloved

English duke, whereupon she and her friend wind up trading partners on a trial basis. Clive Brook, Beatrice Lillie, Googie Withers, Roland Culver, O. B. Clarence, Lawrence Hanray, Hay Petrie. w. Clive Brook, Terence Young, P-adap. Frederick Lonsdale, d. Clive Brook.

COMEDY: FARCE: Swapping Partners; **ROMANCE:** Romantic Comedy; Weddings; Engagements-Breaking; Heiresses; Friendships-Female; Hidden Gems; Faded Hits; Female Protagonists (The Grass Is Greener)

Once Around, 1991, 114m, ★★★/$$, U/MCA-U, PG-13/P-S. A woman pushing "old maid" status in her mid-thirties finds a marriagable bachelor, but her family is turned off by his vulgar brashness, a hostility which soon changes when he dies. Richard Dreyfuss, Holly Hunter, Danny Aiello, Laura San Giacomo, Gena Rowlands, Roxanne Hart, Griffin Dunne. w. Malia Scotch Marmo, d. Lasse Hallstrom.

COMEDY DRAMA: MELODRAMA: Tearjerkers; **ROMANCE:** Romantic Drama; Spinsters; Newlyweds; Widows; Free Spirits; Marriage Drama; Marriage Comedy; Lover Family Dislikes; Romance-Choosing the Right Person; Starting Over; Death-Dealing with; Mothers & Daughters; Female Protagonists; Female Screenwriters (Terms of Endearment; Moonstruck; Home for the Holidays)

Once Bitten, 1985, 93m, ★★/$, Goldwyn/Goldwyn, PG/S. A group of teenagers are attacked by a female vampire who must suck the blood of three separate virgins by Halloween. Lauren Hutton, Jim Carrey, Karen Kopins, Cleavon Little. w. David Hines, Jeffrey Hause, Jonathan Roberts, d. Howard Storm.

COMEDY: Virgins; Women and Boys; Vampires; Spoofs-Vampire; Vampires-Female; Teenagers; Teenage Movies; Curiosities
(Vamp; The Lost Boys)

Once in a Blue Moon, 1936, 65m, ★★/$$, Par/NA. An American has misadventures traveling in Russia. Jimmy Savo, Nikita Balieff, Whitney Bourne, Cecilia Loftus. w. d. Ben Hecht.

COMEDY DRAMA: Russia; American Abroad; Vacations; Writer-Directors

Once in a Lifetime, 1933, 80m, ★★1/2/$$, U/NA. In the Hollywood of

yore, an unknown writer gets his big break and sells a script. Jack Oakie, Sidney Fox, Aline MacMahon, Russell Hopton, Zasu Pitts, Louise Fazenda, Gregory Ratoff, Onslow Stevens. w. Seton I. Miller, P-adap. Moss Hart, George S. Kaufman, d. Russell Mack.

COMEDY: Hollywood Life; Hollywood Satire; Writers; Forgotten Films

Once in Paris, 1978, 100m, ★★1/2/$, AIP/Media, PG/S. A neophyte American is shown the worldly ways of Paris by an interested British woman and her cynical but fatherly chauffeur. Wayne Rogers, Gayle Hunnicutt, Jack Lenoir, Philippe Hart, Tanya Lopert. w. d. Frank D. Gilroy.

MELODRAMA: ROMANCE: Romantic Drama; Midlife Crisis; Vacations-European; Paris; Romance on Vacation; Americans Abroad; Writer-Directors; Independent Films

Once Is Not Enough, 1975, 122m, ★★1/2/$$, Par/Par, R/S-P. A big-time Hollywood producer's wild lifestyle and friends begin to corrupt his daughter, much to his dismay. Kirk Douglas, Alexis Smith, David Janssen, George Hamilton, Melina Mercouri, Deborah Raffin, Brenda Vaccaro (BSActress), Gary Conway. w. Julius J. Epstein, N-adap. Jacqueline Susann, d. Guy Green. Oscars: 1-0.

MELODRAMA: Soap Operas; Hollywood Life; Directors; Fathers & Daughters; Coming of Age; Young Women; Sexy Women; Playboys; Female Protagonists (Valley of the Dolls; The Love Machine; The Other Side of Midnight; The Bad and the Beautiful; Scruples)

Once More with Feeling, 1960, 92m, ★★1/2/$$, Col/NA. The conductor of a major symphony orchestra has personal turmoils which fuel the passion of his work. Yul Brynner, Kay Kendall, Geoffrey Toone, Maxwell Shaw, Mervyn Johns, Martin Benson, Gregory Ratoff. w., P-adap. Harry Kurnitz, d. Stanley Donen.

COMEDY DRAMA: MELODRAMA: Musicians; Marriage Drama; Character Studies; Forgotten Films
(Unfaithfully Yours)

Once Upon a Crime, 1992, MGM/MGM-UA, ★★★1/2/$$. A lost dog with a reward on its head leads a group of motley Americans in Monte Carlo into the mystery of the murdered dog's owner, and suddenly they're all suspects. Richard Lewis, Sean Young, Cybill Shepherd, James Belushi, John Candy, Ornella Muti,

Giancarlo Giannini, George Hamilton. w. Nancy Meyers, Charles Shyer, S-adap. Rudolfo Sonega, d. Eugene Levy.

COMEDY: FARCE: MYSTERY: MURDER MYSTERY: Comic Mystery; Capers; Whodunit; Comedy of Errors; Hide the Dead Body; Identities-Mistaken; Misunderstandings; Dogs; Fighting Over Rewards; Accused Unjustly; Riviera Life; Monte Carlo; Foreign Film Remakes; Underrated; Hidden Gems; Old-Fashioned Recent Films

REMAKE OF: Criminals
(Blame It on the Bellboy; The Trouble with Harry)
(Ed: If you like a silly, fairly clever farce with a good cast, then this one fits the bill)

Once Upon a Dream, 1948, 84m, ★★1/2/$$, Ind/NA. A British woman has romantic dreams about her husband's friend, which later materialize. Googie Withers, Griffith Jones, Guy Middleton, Raymond Lovell, Hubert Gregg. w. Patrick Kirwan, Victor Katona, d. Ralph Thomas.

MELODRAMA: ROMANCE: Romantic Drama; Romantic Comedy; Cheating Women; Romance with Lover's Friend; Dreams; British Films

Once Upon a Honeymoon, 1942, 116m, ★★1/2/$$, RKO/Turner. A radio reporter and a married cabaret dancer have a dalliance and also beat the Nazis during World War II. Cary Grant, Ginger Rogers, Walter Slezak, Albert Dekker, Albert Basserman, Ferike Boros, Harry Shannon. w. Sheridan Gibney, Leo McCarey, d. Leo McCarey.

COMEDY DRAMA: ROMANCE: Romantic Comedy; Nazi Stories; Dangerous Romance; Dangerous Spouses; World War II Stories; Newlyweds; Forgotten Films; Good Premise Unfulfilled

COMIC FLIPSIDE of Suspicion, Undercurrent, Sabotage.
(A Foreign Affair; Under Suspicion)

Once Upon a Time, 1944, 89m, ★★/$, Col/NA. A hard-up Hollywood producer hits the jackpot with a young boy and his choreographed caterpillar act. Cary Grant, Janet Blair, James Gleason, Ted Donaldson, Howard Freeman, Art Baker, William Demarest, John Abbott. w. Lewis Meltzer, Oscar Saul, (Radio play)-adap. Norman Corwin, Lucile F. Hermann (*My Client Curley*), d. Alexander Hall.

COMEDY: Hollywood Life; Hollywood Satire; Boys; Men and Boys; Con Artists; Flops-Major; Coulda Been Good

Once Upon a Time in America, 1984, 228m, ★★★/$$, WB/WB, R/EV-P-S. The saga of a gangster family from 1922 to 1968, centering around the friendship of two boys who were delinquents together. Robert De Niro, James Woods, Elizabeth McGovern, Treat Williams, Tuesday Weld, Burt Young, Danny Aiello, William Forsythe. w. Leonardo Benvenuti, Piero de Bernardi, Enrico Medioli, Franco Arcalli, Franco Ferrini, Sergio Leone, N-adap. David Aaronson ("Harry Grey") *(The Hoods)*, d. Sergio Leone.

DRAMA: Crime Drama; Epics; Mob Stories; Juvenile Delinquents; Friendships-Male; Friends as Enemies; Bootleggers; Depression Era; Episodic Stories; Family Drama; Sagas; Cult Films (The Godfather SERIES; Angels with Dirty Faces; True Confessions; 1900; Once Upon a Time in the West)

Once Upon a Time in the West, 1969, 165m, ★★★¹/₂/$$, Par/Par, R/EV. A band of outlaws terrorizes a woman living alone in an isolated Western town. Henry Fonda, Claudia Cardinale, Jason Robards, Charles Bronson, Gabriele Ferzetti, Keenan Wynn, Paolo Stoppa, Lionel Stander, Jack Elam, Woody Strode. w. Sergio Leone, Sergio Donati, d. Sergio Leone.

WESTERNS: Epics; Westerns-Neo; Westerns-Spaghetti; Evil Men; **MURDER:** Hitmen; Ensembles-Male; Trains; Allegorical Stories; Women in Jeopardy; Writer-Directors
(Hang 'em High; For a Few Dollars More)

On Dangerous Ground, 1951, 82m, ★★★/$$, RKO/Turner. A retarded murderer's blind sister has a love affair with a cop. Robert Ryan, Ida Lupino, Ward Bond, Ed Begley, Cleo Moore, Charles Kemper. w. A. I. Bezzerides, N-adap. George Butler, d. Nicholas Ray.

MELODRAMA: Crime Drama; **ROMANCE:** Romantic Drama; Blind People; Police Stories; Dangerous Love; Dangerous Men; **MURDER:** Mentally Disabled
(Beware, My Lovely; I Wake Up Screaming)

On Deadly Ground, 1994, 102m, ★★/$$$, WB/WB, R/EV-P. When an evil oil magnate tries to pollute Alaska with his rigs, a martial arts expert who happens to

be around begins blowing up things to stop him. Steven Seagal, Michael Caine, Joan Chen, John C. McGinley. w. Ed Horowitz, d. Steven Seagal.

ACTION: Martial Arts; Environmental Dilemmas; Evil Men; Oil People; Alaska; Unintentionally Funny; Actor Directors (Under Siege; Above the Law)
(Ed: Seagal should've stuck to acting. Well, at least martial arts)

The One and Only, 1978, 98m, ★★¹/₂/$$$, Par/Par, PG. A performer obsessed with success sees his marriage fail as he then winds up in professional wrestling as a tossed-about joke. Henry Winkler, Kim Darby, Gene Saks, William Daniels, Polly Holiday, Herve Villechaize, Harold Gould, Richard Lane. w. Steve Gordon, d. Carl Reiner.

COMEDY: Actors; Marriage Comedy; Marriage on the Rocks; Wrestling; Sleeper Hits; Faded Hits
(Tootsie; Matilda; Heroes)

One Body Too Many, 1944, 74m, ★★¹/₂/$$, Par/Nos. A real estate insurance agent comes to the creepy house of a recluse, only to find the policy void, as his host's been murdered. Jack Haley, Bela Lugosi, Jean Parker, Bernard Nedell, Blanche Yurka, Douglas Fowley, Lyle Talbot. w. Winston Miller, Maxwell Shane, d. Frank McDonald.

COMEDY: MURDER: MYSTERY: MURDER MYSTERY: Comic Mystery; Murder-Discovering
(Murder, He Said; Dracula; The Old Dark House)

One Eyed Jacks, 1961, 141m, ★★★¹/₂/$$$, Par/Par. Two old enemies reunite in the old West, one still an outlaw and the other now a sheriff. Matters get even more complicated when the woman between them gets pregnant. Marlon Brando, Karl Malden, Pina Pellicer, Katy Jurado, Slim Pickens, Ben Johnson, Timothy Carey, Elisha Cook, Jr. w. Guy Trosper, Calder Willingham, N-adap. Charles Neider *(The Authentic Death of Hendry Jones)*, d. Marlon Brando.

WESTERNS: Westerns-Revenge; Revenge; Westerns-Neo; Friends as Enemies; Reunions; Feuds; Duels; Actor Directors; Cult Films
(High Noon; True Confessions; Angels with Dirty Faces; Manhattan Melodrama; Once Upon a Time in America)

One Flew Over the Cuckoo's Nest, 1975, UA/EMI-HBO, ★★★★/$$$$$.

A man (Jack Nicholson, **BActor**) is wrongly incarcerated in a mental ward full of men life has cast aside with an evil nurse (Louise Fletcher, **BActress**) making their lives even worse until something gives. Brad Dourif (BSActor), Danny DeVito, William Redfield, Vincent Schiavelli, Will Sampson. w. Lawrence Hauben, Bo Goldman (**BAScr**), N. & P. adap. Ken Kesey, d. Milos Forman (**BDirector**). **BPicture**, BEdit, BCin. Oscars: 9-5, second film ever to sweep top five categories (others: *It Happened One Night, Silence of the Lambs*).

DRAMA: MELODRAMA: TRAGEDY: Mental Illness; Asylums; Friendships-Male; Ensemble Films; Ensembles-Male; Female Among Males; Nurses; Prison Drama; Fighting the System; Evil Women; Stern Women; Indians-American; Suicidal Tendencies; Play & Novel Adaptations; Blockbusters; Sleeper Hits (Nuts; Crazy People; The Dream Team; Five Easy Pieces; The Last Detail; The Shawshank Redemption)

One Deadly Summer, 1983, 134m, ★★★/$$, U/MCA-U, R. A young woman returns to her hometown to exact revenge upon the men who raped her years before. Isabelle Adjani, Alain Souchon. d. Jean Becker.

DRAMA: Rape/Rapists; Revenge; Revenge on Rapist; Female Among Males; Mean Women; Young Women; French Films
(The Accused [1988]; Rider on the Storm; Hannie Caulder)

One False Move, 1992, 105m, ★★★¹/₂/$$, New Line/Col, R/EV-S-P. When a white redneck drug dealer and his black girlfriend kill several people in Los Angeles and flee to Arkansas to tie up their deal, the girlfriend finds herself trying to reclaim the son she had with the local sheriff there who's on to her secrets. Bill Paxton, Cynda Williams, Michael Beach, Billy Bob Thornton, Jim Metzler. w. Thornton, Tom Epperson, d. Carl Franklin.

SUSPENSE: Crime Drama; Chase Stories; Fugitives from the Law; Police vs. Mob; Police Stories; Drugs-Dealing; Romance-Interracial; Romance-Reunited; Children-Long lost; Southerns; Rednecks; Arkansas; Black Women; Sleeper Hits; Hidden Gems
(In the Heat of the Night; Laurel Avenue; Witness)

One Foot in Heaven, 1941, 108m, ★★1/2/$$, WB/NA. A Methodist minister serves his flock in a small town in the heartland. Fredric March, Martha Scott, Beulah Bondi, Gene Lockhart, Elisabeth Fraser, Harry Davenport, Laura Hope Crews, Grant Mitchell, Moroni Olsen, Ernest Cossart, Jerome Cowan. w. Casey Robinson, NF-adap. Hartzell Spence (a biography of his father), d. Irving Rapper.

MELODRAMA: Small-town Life; American Myth; Preachers; Saintly People; Biographies; True Stories; Midwestern Life; Forgotten Films
(Going My Way; The Bishop's Wife)

One from the Heart, 1982, 101m, ★★/$, Zoetrope-Col/Col, R/S. A musical with a film-noir feel about hard-boiled lovers in Vegas on the Fourth of July. Frederic Forrest, Teri Garr, Raul Julia, Nastasja Kinski, Lainie Kazan, Harry Dean Stanton. w. Armyan Bernstein, Francis Ford Coppola, d. Francis Ford Coppola.

MELODRAMA: ROMANCE: MUSICALS: Musical Romance; Las Vegas; Film Noir-Modern; Romance-Triangles; Art Films; Stagelike Films; Flops-Major; Production Design-Outstanding

One Good Cop, 1991, 105m, ★★/$, Hollywood/Hollywood, PG-13/V. When his partner is killed, a New York cop tries to adopt the three girls he left behind and runs into bureaucratic snags. Michael Keaton, Rene Russo, Anthony LaPaglia, Kevin Conway, Rachel Ticotin, Tony Plana, Benjamin Bratt. w. Heywood Gould, d. Ralf Bode.

MELODRAMA: Tearjerkers; Orphans; Police Stories; Children-Adopted; Men and Girls; Death-Dealing with; Old-Fashioned Recent Films
(Little Miss Marker; My Life; Clean and Sober; Losing Isaiah)

One Hour with You, 1932, 84m, ★★★/$$$, Par/NA. A Parisian doctor puts the moves on females from all walks of life, including many of his patients. Maurice Chevalier, Jeanette MacDonald, Genevieve Tobin, Roland Young, Charles Ruggles, George Barbier. w. Samson Raphaelson, P-adap. Lothar Schmidt (Only a Dream), d. George Cukor, Ernst Lubitsch.

COMEDY DRAMA: MELODRAMA: ROMANCE: Playboys; Doctors; Paris; Romance-Unprofessional; Faded Hits

101 Dalmatians, 1961, 79m, ★★★1/2/$$$$$, Disney/Disney, G. Cruela DeVille is stealing little dalmatians to make herself a fur, and all the street dogs of London band together to free her cuddly little prisoners. Voices of Rod Taylor, Cate Bauer, Betty Lou Gerson, J. Pat O'Malley. w. Bill Peet, N-adap. Dodie Smith, d. Wolfgang Reitherman, Hamilton S. Luske, Clyde Geronimi.

Cartoons; COMEDY: Black Comedy; Evil Women; Animal Stories; Pet Stories; Animals in Jeopardy; Dogs; Rescue Drama; Blockbusters
REMAKE: 1996.
(The Rescuers; Lady and the Tramp)
(Ed: Great moments, though it's rather short, with Miss Deville being one of the all-time great villains and her theme song equally legendary)

120 Days of Sodom, see Salo

One in a Million, 1936, 95m, ★★★/$$$, 20th/Fox. A poor Swiss girl is given a pair of skates by her humble inn-keeper father, and she grows up to be an Olympic champion skater. Sonja Henie, Don Ameche, The Ritz Brothers, Jean Hersholt, Ned Sparks, Arline Judge, Dixie Dunbar, Borrah Minnevitch and his Rascals, Monatagu Love. w. Leonard Praskins, Mark Kelly, d. Sidney Lanfield.

MELODRAMA: Skating; Girls; Fathers & Daughters; Olympics; Snow Settings; Faded Hits
(Thin Ice)

One Is a Lonely Number, 1972, 97m, ★★1/2/$, MGM/NA. A woman puts her life back together after her husband leaves her. Trish Van Devere, Monte Markham, Melvyn Douglas, Janet Leigh. w. David Seltzer, N-adap. Rebecca Morris, d. Mel Stuart.

DRAMA: Character Studies; Starting Over; Divorce; Single Women; 1970s; Forgotten Films
(The Rain People; Diary of a Mad Housewife; Play it as it Lays)

One Magic Christmas, 1985, 88m, ★★★/$, Disney/Disney, PG. It's Christmas time, and one family is having an especially bad holiday season when an angel in the guise of a bum drops in and brings good cheer back into their home. Mary Steenburgen, Gary Basaraba, Harry Dean Stanton, Arthur Hill. w. Thomas Meecham, d. Philip Borsos.

MELODRAMA: Christmas; Poor People; Ordinary People Stories; Angels; Homeless People; Depression; Mothers-Struggling; Hidden Gems; Overlooked at Release
(A Christmas Story; Three Wishes)

One Million BC, 1940, 80m, ★★1/2/$$, Ing/Media. During the Stone Age, tribes of cave-men make war while their wives make babies back in the caves. Some anachronistic dinosaurs are thrown in for good measure. Victor Mature, Carole Landis, Lon Chaney, Jr., John Hubbard, Nigel de Brulier, Conrad Nagel. w. Mickell Novak, George Baker, Joseph Frickert, d. Hal Roach, Jr., D. W. Griffith. Ahead of Its Time

One Million Years BC, 1966, 100m, ★★★/$$$, Hammer-MGM/NA. A remake of the above, with Raquel Welch providing some Neanderthal love interest in a bearskin bikini. John Richardson, Raquel Welch, Robert Brown, Percy Herbert, Martine Beswick. w. Michael Carreras, d. Don Chaffey.

ADVENTURE: ACTION: Prehistoric Times; Cavemen; Dinosaurs; Camp; Volcanoes; Unintentionally Funny
REMAKE of Man's Genesis, directed by D. W. Griffith.
(Cave Man; Quest for Fire)

One More River, 1934, 88m, ★★1/2/$$, U/NA. A married woman runs off with her lover, and he sends detectives and dogs after them. Colin Clive, Diana Wynyard, C. Aubrey Smith, Jane Wyatt, Lionel Atwill, Frank Lawton, Reginald Denny, Henry Stephenson, Alan Mowbray, E. E. Clive. w. R. C. Sheriff, N-adap. John Galsworthy, d. James Whale.

MELODRAMA: Romance with Married Person; Cheating Women; Romance-Triangles; Detectives-Matrimonial; Missing Persons; Forgotten Films

One More Spring, 1935, 87m, ★★1/2/$$, 20th/NA. During the Great Depression, three New Yorkers, down on their luck, meet in Central Park and decide to pool together their meager resources to make something happen. Janet Gaynor, Warner Baxter, Walter Woolf King, Grant Mitchell, Jane Darwell, Roger Imhof, John Qualen, Dick Foran, Stepin Fetchit. w. Edwin Burke, N-adap. Robert Nathan, d. Henry King.

MELODRAMA: Depression Era; Poor People; Homeless People; Time Capsules; Forgotten Films

(Central Park; Seventh Heaven; Street Angel)

One Night of Love, 1934, 95m, ★★★/$$$, Col/Col. A musical about an opera singer who struggles to get out from under the thumb of her oppressive and rigorous teacher. Grace Moore (BActress), Tullio Carminati, Lyle Talbot, Mona Barrie, Nydia Westman, Jessie Ralph, Luis Alberni, Jane Darwell. w. Dorothy Speare, Charles Beahan, S. K. Lauren, James Gow, Edmund North, d. Victor Schertzinger (BDirector), BPicture, **BScore**, BEdit, **BSound**. Oscars: 6–2.
MELODRAMA: MUSICALS: ROMANCE: Musical Romance; Opera; Opera Singers; Teachers; Teachers & Students; Stern Men; Female Screenwriters; Svengalis (Svengali; Metropolitan; My Love Came Back)

One of Our Dinosaurs Is Missing, 1975, 94m, ★★½/$$, Disney/Disney, G. In the 1920s, a top-secret microfilm is hidden in the skeleton of a dinosaur being shipped from China to the Museum of Natural History. Helen Hayes, Peter Ustinov, Derek Nimmo, Clive Revill, Joan Sims, Bernard Bresslaw, Roy Kinnear, Deryck Guyler, Richard Pearson. w. Bill Walsh, N-adap. David Forrest (The Great Dinosaur Robbery), d. Robert Stevenson.
COMEDY: CHILDREN'S: FAMILY: Archaeologists; Dinosaurs; Museums; Spies; Thieves
(Candleshoe; No Deposit, No Return)

One Sings, the Other Doesn't, 1977, 105m, ★★★/$$, Col/Col, R/S. Two women find solace in each other when trying to live on their own. Valerie Mairesse, Therese Liotard. w. d. Agnes Varda.
DRAMA: Friendships-Female; Homo-eroticism; Women's Films; Writer-Directors; Female Directors; Female Screenwriters; French Films; Quiet Little Films
(Entre Nous; Therese and Isabelle; Mirabelle and Rainette; Mina Tannenbaum)

One Sunday Afternoon, 1933, 93m, ★★½/$$$, Par/NA. In 1910, a dentist in Brooklyn begins to think he married the wrong girl when an old flame reappears. In the end, he discovers that he does indeed love his wife. Gary Cooper, Frances Fuller, Fay Wray, Neil Hamilton, Roscoe Karns. w. William Slavens

McNutt, Grover Jones, P-adap. James Hagan, d. Stephen Roberts.
MELODRAMA: ROMANCE: Romantic Drama; Cheating Men; Romance Reunited; Dentists; Romance-Triangles; Romance-Choosing the Right Person

The One That Got Away, 1957, 111m, ★★½/$$, Ind/NA. The true story of Franz Von Werra, a German fighter pilot who escaped from several different British P.O.W. camps. Hardy Kruger, Michael Goodliffe, Colin Gordon, Alec McCowen. w. Howard Clewes, NF-adap. Kendal Burt, James Leasor, d. Roy Baker.
DRAMA: Action Drama; War Stories; POWs; World War II Stories; True Stories; Germans; Germans as Enemy; Curiosities (Stalag 17; Victor; The Great Escape; Eye of the Needle)

One Trick Pony, 1980, 100m, ★★/$, WB/WB, PG/P-S. The story of a singer-songwriter and his marital problems which contrast the ups and downs of his career. Paul Simon, Joan Hackett, Blair Brown, Rip Torn, Mare Winningham. d. Robert M. Young.
MELODRAMA: Biographies-Fictional; Autobiographical Stories; Singers; Songwriters; Musicians; Midlife Crisis; Marriage Drama; Forgotten Films; Time Capsules
(Ed: Boring, but interesting inside view of late 70s Hollywood)

One Touch of Venus, 1948, 82m, ★★★/$$, U/Republic. A department store mannequin comes to life and falls in love with the window dresser who put her in Venus's garb. Ava Gardner, Robert Walker, Eve Arden, Dick Haymes, Olga San Juan, Tom Conway. w. Harry Kurnitz, Frank Tashlin, S. J. Perelman, Ogden Nash, d. William A. Seiter.
COMEDY DRAMA: ROMANCE: Romantic Comedy; Objects-Animated; Sexy Women; Fantasy; Fantasies; Department Stores (Mannequin [1987])

One, Two, Three!, 1961, 110m, ★★★½/$$$, Mirisch-UA/MGM-UA. The head of Coca-Cola in Berlin (James Cagney) during the rise of the wall tries to keep the president of the company's wild daughter from taking up with sexy communist. Horst Buchholz, Arlene Francis. w. Billy Wilder, I. A. L. Diamond, d. Billy Wilder. BB&WCin. Oscars: 1–0.
COMEDY: Race Against Time; Lovers Family Dislikes; Action Comedy; **FARCE:**

Undesirable Son-in-Laws; Communists; Berlin; Americans Abroad; Secrets-Keeping; Hidden Gems
(The Impossible Years; Bonjour, Tristesse)

One Way Passage, 1932, 69m, ★★½/$$$, WB/NA. Two doomed people, a criminal being deported to serve a life sentence and a girl with a fatal disease, fall in love when they meet on an ocean liner. William Powell, Kay Francis, Frank McHugh, Aline MacMahon, Warren Hymer, Herbert Mundin, Roscoe Karns, Stanley Fields. w. Wilson Mizer, Joseph Jackson, Robert Lord, d. Tay Garnett.
MELODRAMA: ROMANCE: TRAGEDY: Romantic Drama; Ships; Romance on Vacation; Romance-Doomed; Death-Impending; Tearjerkers; Faded Hits; Forgotten Films
(Love Affair; An Affair to Remember)

One Woman or Two, 1985, 100m, ★★½/$, Ind/Live, Vestron. An advertising woman tries to use a dinosaur digger's work for a campaign, but instead they wind-up in a chaotic romance. Sigourney Weaver, Gerard Depardieu, Dr. Ruth Westheimer, Michel Aumont. w. Elizabeth Rappeneau, Daniel Vigne, d. Daniel Vigne.
COMEDY: Screwball Comedy; **FARCE:** Dinosaurs; Archeologists/Paleontologists; Advertising World; SATIRE: ROMANCE: Romantic Comedy; Flops-Major; Coulda Been Great
REMAKE/RETREAD of Bringing Up Baby.

On Golden Pond, 1981, 109m, ★★★★/$$$$$, ITC-Universal/MCA-U, PG/P. A retired couple (Henry Fonda, **BActor**) (Katharine Hepburn, **BActress**) spend the summer on a New England pond. Their daughter (Jane Fonda, BSActress) comes to visit and face the past conflicts with her father and to leave her rebellious son (Doug McKeon) with them. Dabney Coleman. w. P-adap. Ernest Thompson (**BAScr**), d. Mark Rydell (BDirector). BPicture, BCin, BOScore, BSound, BEdit. Oscars: 10-3.
COMEDY DRAMA: MELODRAMA: ROMANCE: Family Stories; Fathers & Daughters; Elderly People; Elderly Men; Elderly Women; Death-Impending; Vacations; Reunions; Children-Brats; Blockbusters
(Driving Miss Daisy; Guess Who's Coming to Dinner; Once Around; The Portrait)

Ed: A surprise hit and surprisingly good in every way)

On Her Majesty's Secret Service, 1969, 140m, ★★★/$$$, UA/MGM-UA. The international supercriminal Blofeld is apprehended by Agent 007 in Switzerland, but not before he gets hitched and his love disappears. George Lazenby, Diana Rigg, Telly Savalas, Ilse Steppat, Gabriele Ferzetti, Yuri Borienko, Bernard Lee, Lois Maxwell. w. Richard Maibaum, N-adap. Ian Fleming, d. Peter Hunt.
ACTION: Spies; Secret Agents; Sexy Women; Snow Settings; Skiing; Weddings; Curiosities; James Bond
(For Your Eyes Only; Goldfinger)
(Ed: The lone Bond film of Lazenby's before Connery's first return; darker in tone)

Only You, 1994, 120m, ★★★/$$, Col/Col, PG-13/S. When a young woman about to be married hears the name of the man a fortune teller told her she would marry when she was nine, she follows the name all the way to Italy where she meets a man who may or may not have that name and/or the real Mr. Right. Marisa Tomei, Bonnie Hunt, Robert Downey, Jr., Fisher Stevens, Billy Zane. w. Diane Drake, d. Norman Jewison.
COMEDY: ROMANCE: Romantic Comedy; Romance-Choosing the Right Person; Engagements-Breaking; Romance on Vacations; Vacations; Fortunetellers; Italy; Impostors; Female Protagonists; Female Screenwriters
(Moonstruck; My Cousin Vinny)
(Ed: Tomei's character seems frivolous and inconsequential in her selfish quest, but Downey evens it out with Hunt stealing the whole picture)

On the Air, 1992, 168m, ★★★¹/2/$$, ABC-Spelling/World. The calamitous misadventures of *The Lester Guy Show* on the Zoblotnik Network, a live TV program of 1957 where nothing going right somehow goes right. Ian Buchanan, Miguel Ferrer, David L. Lander. w. Mark Frost, David Lynch, d. Lynch (pilot), various others.
COMEDY: FARCE: Comedy of Errors; Murphy's Law Stories; Black Comedy; Comedy-Slapstick; Comedy-Gag; Misunderstandings; Surrealism; Spoofs; Spoofs-TV; TV Series; TV Life; Actors; Actresses; 1950s; Hidden Gems; Cult Films
(My Favorite Year)

(Ed: One of those series too good for its own good, and yet more mainstream than you'd think; certainly worth some big laughs)

On the Avenue, 1937, 89m, ★★★/$$$, 20th/Fox. A wealthy and haughty society lady gets her hackles up when a Broadway play blatantly satirizes her. But the star of the show smooths things over and makes her fall in love with him. Dick Powell, Madeleine Carroll, The Ritz Brothers, George Barbier, Alice Faye, Walter Catlett, Joan Davis, E. E. Clive. w. Gene Markey, William Conselman, d. Roy del Ruth.
COMEDY: ROMANCE: Romantic Comedy; Theater Life; Actors; Rich People; SATIRE: Forgotten Films

On the Beach, 1959, 134m, ★★★/$$$, UA/Fox. After the nuclear war, a submarine gliding through the ocean's deepest recesses contains the only humans alive (at least one of them can dance). Gregory Peck, Ava Gardner, Fred Astaire, Anthony Perkins, Donna Anderson, John Tate, Lola Brooks. w. John Paxton, James Lee Barrett, N-adap. Nevil Shute, d. Stanley Kramer. BOScore, BEdit. Oscars: 2–0.
SCI-FI: DRAMA: Apocalyptic Stories; Bombs-Atomic; Submarines; Female Among Males; Military Stories; Cult Films
(The Omega Man; Waterworld; The Day After)

On the Double, 1961, 92m, ★★/$$, Par/NA. An army private with "acting skills" is asked to impersonate a British secret service agent during World War II. Danny Kaye, Dana Wynter, Wilfrid Hyde White, Diana Dors, Margaret Rutherford, Allan Cuthbertson, Jesse White. w. Jack Rose, Melville Shavelson, d. Melville Shavelson.
COMEDY: Impostors; Actors; World War II Stories; Military Comedy; Secret Agents; England
(General Della Rovere; Moon Over Parador)

On the Riviera, 1951, 90m, ★★★/$$$, 20th/Fox. A performer in a lounge act is cajoled into posing as a suave lady's man and local entrepreneur. Danny Kaye, Corinne Calvet, Gene Tierney, Marcel Dalio, Jean Murat. w. Valentine Davies, Phoebe and Henry Ephron, d. Walter Lang.
MUSICALS: ROMANCE: Musical Romance; Riviera Life; Playboys; Impostors; Faded Hits

On the Town, 1949, 98m, ★★★¹/2/$$$$, MGM/MGM-UA. Three sailors are on a mission during their shoreleave in New York City. They plan to see the sights, meet the girls and get hitched all within twenty-four hours! Gene Kelly, Frank Sinatra, Jules Munshin, Vera-Ellen, Betty Garrett, Ann Miller, Tom Dugan, Florence Bates, Alice Pearce. w. Betty Comden, Adolphe Green, (Ballet)-adap. Leonard Bernstein *(Fancy Free)*, d./ch. Gene Kelly and Stanley Donen.
MUSICALS: COMEDY: Musical Comedy; ROMANCE: Romance; Romantic Comedy; Ensembles-Male; Sailors; Shore Leave; New York Life; One Day Stories
(Anchors Aweigh; Follow the Fleet; Hit the Deck)

On the Waterfront, 1954, 108m, ★★★★/$$$$, Col/Col. A simple, brutish dockworker, and former prizefighter who took a fall for the local mob boss and thus ended his boxing career, is pushed over the edge when his brother, a mafioso, is killed by that same boss. He determines, alongside the local pro-union priest, to form a union at the docks and stand up to the mob. Marlon Brando (**BActor**), Eva Marie Saint (**BSActress**), Lee J. Cobb (BSActor), Rod Steiger (BSActor), Karl Malden (BSActor), Pat Henning, Leif Erickson, James Westerfield, John Hamilton. w., N-adap. Budd Schulberg (**BOScr**), d. Elia Kazan (**BDirector**). **BPicture, BB&WCin, BB&WArt, BEdit**, BScore. Oscars: 12–8.
DRAMA: MELODRAMA: Working Class; Ordinary People Stories; Boxing; Brothers; Men in Conflict; Mob Stories; Ethics; MURDER: Avenging Death of Someone; Men Proving Themselves
(East of Eden; Last Exit to Brooklyn; Boomerang; Norma Rae; F.I.S.T.)

On Your Toes, 1939, 94m, ★★★/$$$, WB/NA. A ballet company has its share of backstage melodrama. Vera Zorina, Eddie Albert, Alan Hale, Frank McHugh, James Gleason, Donald O'Connor, Gloria Dickson. w. Jerry Wald, Richard Macaulay, P-adap. George Abbott, d. Ray Enright.
MELODRAMA: MUSICALS: Musical Drama; Theater Life; Behind the Scenes; Dancers; Ballet
(42nd Street; Stage Door)

Once Were Warriors, 1994, 108m, ★★★¹/2/$$, Fine Line/Fine Line, R/EP-V-S. Life in the Mayori Indian slums of

New Zealand where a long-term marriage is both crumbling and yet held together by the abusive behavior of the working class husband. Rena Owen, Temuera Morrison, Anita Kerr-Bell, Taungaroa Emiie, Rachel Morris Jr., Joseph Kairau, Clifford Curtis, Pete Smith, George Henare. w. Alan Duff, Riwia Brown, d. Lee Tamahori.

DRAMA: Art Films; Abused Women; Marriage Drama; Marriage on the Rocks; Class Conflicts; Poor People; New Zealand Films; Female Screenwriters

The Onion Field, 1979, 126m, ★★★/$$, Avco/New Line, R/V-P. A policeman is thrown off the force when it is judged that he showed cowardice in handling a situation in which his partner was killed by a maniacal psychotic who subsequently menaces him from prison. John Savage, James Woods, Franklyn Seales, Ted Danson, Ronny Cox, David Huffman. w., N-adap. Joseph Wambaugh, d. Harold Becker.

DRAMA: Crime Drama; Police Stories; True Stories; **MURDER:** Prison Drama; Psycho Killers; Cowards; Accused Unjustly; Death-Dealing with; Avenging Death of Someone; Episodic Stories; Hidden Gems
(Cape Fear; Silence of the Lambs; The Choir Boys)
(Ed: A breakthrough performance as a psycho by Woods)

Only Angels Have Wings, 1939, 121m, ★★★½/$$$, Col/NA. Cargo plane pilots flying over the treacherous terrain of the Andes must deal with a loudmouth showgirl they find stranded at a drop-off point. Cary Grant, Jean Arthur, Rita Hayworth, Richard Barthlemess, Thomas Mitchell, Sig Rumann, Victor Kilian, John Carroll, Allyn Joslyn. w. Jules Furthman, Howard Hawks, d. Howard Hawks. BSFX. Oscars: 1-0.

COMEDY DRAMA: Romantic Comedy; Stranded; Saving Someone; Feisty Females; Female Among Males; Battle of the Sexes; Pilots-Airline; South America; Coulda Been Great; Forgotten Films; Hidden Gems; Faded Hits
(Talk of the Town; Air America; Indiana Jones and the Temple of Doom)

The Only Game in Town, 1969, 113m, ★★/$, 20th/NA. A Las Vegas showgirl loves her piano player, but his compulsive gambling drives them both to ruin. Elizabeth Taylor, Warren Beatty, Charles

Braswell, Hank Henry. w., P-adap. Frank D. Gilroy, d. George Stevens.

MELODRAMA: ROMANCE: Romantic Drama; Romance-Older Women/Younger Men; Gamblers; Dancers; Las Vegas; Pianists; Flops-Major; Stagelike Films
(Leaving Las Vegas)
(Ed: Hotel room bound and downright dumb)

Only the Lonely, 1991, 104m, ★★½/$$, 20th/Fox, PG. A middle-aged Chicago cop still living with his domineering mother begins a tentative relationship with a timid beautician working at the local funeral parlor, while the neighbor romances his cantankerous mother. John Candy, Maureen O'Hara, Ally Sheedy, Anthony Quinn, James Belushi, Kevin Dunn, Milo O'Shea, Bert Remsen, Macaulay Culkin. w. d. Chris Columbus.

COMEDY DRAMA: ROMANCE: Romantic Comedy; Romance-Elderly; Police Stories; Mothers & Sons; Mama's Boys; Irish People; Stern Women; Funerals; Life Transitions; Writer-Directors; Coulda Been Good
Melodramatic Flipside of the novel *A Confederacy of Dunces.*
(Uncle Buck)
(Ed: A great performance from O'Hara, who also looks great, dislikeable as her character is)

Only Two Can Play, 1962, 106m, ★★★/$$, Ealing/Col. A timid, somewhat henpecked, Welsh librarian obsesses about a sexy, "liberated" benefactor, married to a local politician. She eventually drives him out of his shell enough to have a shortlived affair with her which ends in disaster. Peter Sellers, Mai Zetterling, Virginia Maskell, Richard Attenborough, Raymond Huntley, John Le Mesurier, Kenneth Griffith. w. Bryan Forbes, N-adap. Kinglsey Amis *(That Uncertain Feeling),* d. Sidney Gilliat.

COMEDY DRAMA: ROMANCE: Romantic Comedy; Librarians; Playboys; Romance-Triangles; Cheating Women; Romance with Married Person; Small-town Life; England; British Films; Hidden Gems

Only When I Larf, 1968, 103m, ★★½/$$, Par/NA. A British threesome pull cons together and have a jolly good time doing it. Richard Attenborough, David Hemmings, Alexandra Stewart, Nicholas Pennell, Melissa Stribling, Terence Alexander, Edric Connor, Calvin

Lockhart, Clifton Jones. w. John Salmon, N-adap. Len Deighton, d. Basil Dearden.

COMEDY: Heist Stories; Ex-Convicts; Ensembles-Male; British Films; Forgotten Films
(The Wrong Arm of the Law; Going in Style)

Open City *(Roma, Citta Aperta),* 1945, 101m, ★★★★/$$, Ind/Nos. Italian Resistance fighters push the Nazis out of Rome near the end of World War II. A classic of neo-realism. Aldo Fabrizzi, Anna Magnani, Marcello Pagliero, Maria Michi. w. Sergio Amidei, Federico Fellini, d. Roberto Rossellini.

DRAMA: Art Films; World War II Stories; War Stories; Nazi Stories; Political Drama; Italy; Italian Films; Hidden Gems
(Bitter Rice; Paisan; The Bicycle Thief)

Opening Night, 1977/1993, ★★★/VR, Ind/Touchstone, PG. The trials of an actress opening a play on Broadway as her personal life and self doubts conflict with her performance. Gena Rowlands, John Cassavetes, Joan Blondell, Ben Gazzara, Zohra Lampert. w. d. John Cassavetes.

MELODRAMA: DRAMA: Character Studies; Actresses; Nervous Breakdowns; Neurotic People; Theater Life; Behind the Scenes; Hidden Gems; Forgotten Films; Writer-Directors; Independent Films; Female Protagonists
(A Woman Under the Influence; Minnie & Moskowitz; Chapter Two)

Operation Amsterdam, 1958, 104m, ★★/$$, Ind/Sultan. A stash of diamonds in Amsterdam is sought by the Nazis, and British spies must get to it first and prevent its theft. Peter Finch, Tony Britton, Eva Bartok, Alexander Knox, Malcom Keen, Tim Turner, John Horsley, Melvyn Hayes, Christopher Rhodes. w. Michael McCarthy, John Eldridge, NF-adap. David Walker *(Adventure in Diamonds),* d. Michael McCarthy.

ACTION: Heist Stories; Nazi Stories; Jewel Thieves; World War II Stories; Coulda Been Good; British Films
(The Train)

Operation CIA, 1965, 90m, ★★/$, AA/Fox. A message of vital importance to America's national security gets intercepted in Saigon and a top CIA agent is sent to retrieve it. Burt Reynolds, John Hoyt, Daniele Aubry, Kieu Chinh, Cyril Collick. w. Bill S. Ballinger, Peer J. Oppenheimer, d. Christian Nyby.

ACTION: CIA Agents; Vietnam War; Spies; Spy Films; Forgotten Films
Operation Crossbow, 1965, 116m, ★★1/2/$$, MGM/MGM-UA. During World War II, the Allies send a team of scientists parachuting down near the rocket factory in Peenemunde to dismantle the Nazi arsenal there. George Peppard, Tom Courtenay, John Mills, Sophia Loren, Lilli Palmer, Anthony Quayle, Patrick Wymark, Jeremy Kemp, Paul Henreid, Trevor Howard, Sylvia Sims, Richard Todd, Richard Johnson. w. Robert Imrie (Emeric Pressburger), Derry Quinn, Ray Rigby, d. Michael Anderson.
ACTION: War Stories; Nazi Stories; World War II Stories; Scientists; Special Teams-Military; British Films
(Force Ten from Navarone; The Heroes of Telemark)
Operation Dumbo Drop, 1995, 108m, ★★/$, Disney/Disney, PG-13/V. American servicemen try to replace an elephant for some Vietnamese peasants' religious rituals but have to airdrop it in to avoid conflict. Danny Glover, Ray Liotta, Denis Leary, Doug E. Doug, Corin Nemec, Tcheky Karyo, Dinh Thien Le. w. Gene Quintano & Jim Kouf, d. Simon Wincer.
COMEDY DRAMA: ADVENTURE: Vietnam; Soldiers; Military Stories; Elephants; Animal Stories
(Ed: The title further trivializes the setting)
Operation Mad Ball, 1957, ★★/$, Col/NA. Dancing is strictly forbidden among army recruits and army nurses at an encampment in Normandy during World War II, but a secret ball is planned anyway. Jack Lemmon, Ernie Kovacs, Kathryn Grant, Mickey Rooney, James Darren, Arthur O'Connell. w. Arthur Carter, Jed Harris, Blake Edwards, P-adap. Arthur Carter, d. Richard Quine.
COMEDY DRAMA: ROMANCE: Romantic Comedy; Dancers; World War II Stories; Soldiers; Nurses; Oppression; Forgotten Films
(Mister Roberts; The Wackiest Ship in the Army)
Operation Petticoat, 1959, 124m, ★★★1/2/$$$$, U/Republic. A damaged submarine in World War II is repaired just in time for a stranded regimen of nurses to climb aboard. Cary Grant, Tony Curtis, Joan O'Brien, Dina Merrill, Gene Evans, Arthur O'Connell, Richard Sargent. w. Stanley Shapiro, Maurice

Richlin, Paul King, Joseph Stone, d. Blake Edwards.
COMEDY: Military Comedy; Battle of the Sexes; Submarines; Nurses; Sailors; World War II Stories; Faded Hits; Blockbusters
O Pioneers!, 1991, 99m, ★★★/$$$$, CBS-Hallmark/Republic. A single woman runs a farm in the 1800s with her family reluctantly under her control-until love enters the picture. Jessica Lange, David Straithairn, Tom Aldredge. w. d. Glenn Jordan, N-adap. Willa Cather.
DRAMA: ROMANCE: Romantic Drama; Farm Life; Feisty Females; Midwestern Life; Spinsters; Single Women; Classic Literary Adaptations; Female Protagonists; TV Movies
(Sarah, Plain and Tall; The Substitute Wife; Heartland)
Opportunity Knocks, 1990, 105m, ★★/$, U/MCA-U, PG-13. When a mobster's after him, a con artist pretends to be the friend of a suburban family's son. Dana Carvey, Robert Loggia, Todd Graff, Milo O'Shea. w. Mitchell Kalin, Nat Bernstein, d. Donald Petrie.
COMEDY: Impostors; Con Artists; Fugitives from the Mob; Hiding Out; Suburban Life; Nuisances
RETREAD of Six Degrees of Separation, play version.
(Six Degrees of Separation; Houseguest)
The Opposite Sex, 1956, 116m, ★★1/2/$$, MGM/MGM-UA. A classy New York dame gives the boot to her philandering husband, amid several other stories of her friends and foes' woes with men-particularly the girl who stole her husband. June Allyson, Dolores Gray, Joan Collins, Ann Sheridan, Agnes Moorehead, Joan Blondell, Barbara Jo Allen, Charlotte Greenwood. w. Fay and Michael Kanin, P-adap. Clare Boothe, d. David Miller.
COMEDY: FARCE: Interwoven Stories; Multiple Stories; Cheating Men; Cheated Upon; Meet; Divorce; Starting Over; Women's Films; Women in Conflict; Women Fighting Over Men; Jealousy; Rumors; Friendships-Female; Ensemble Films; Ensembles-Female; Female Screenwriters; Female Protagonists; Women's Films
REMAKE OF The Women (with music).
The Opposite Sex and How to Live With Them, 1992, 86m, ★1/2/$, HBO/HBO, R/S-P. Yuppies in love turmoil, which is supposed to be endearing

but is really annoying. Arye Gross, Courtney Cox, Kevin Pollak, Julie Brown. w. Noah Stern, d. Matthew Meshekoff.
COMEDY DRAMA: ROMANCE: Romantic Comedy; Romance-On Again/Off Again; Battle of the Sexes; Yuppies; 20-Somethings; Crossing the Line; Narrated Films
(The Night We Never Met; Key Exchange)
(Ed: Worse than the series it apparently inspired with Cox, *Friends*. The characters are so one-dimensional and most of the actors so unimaginative, it never had a chance)
Orca—Killer Whale, 1977, 92m, ★★1/2/$$$, Par/Par, PG/EV. A killer whale off the coast of Newfoundland gets mad when its mate is harpooned by local fisherman and takes it personally. Richard Harris, Charlotte Rampling, Will Sampson, Keenan Wynn. w. Luciano Vincenzoni, Sergio Donati, d. Michael Anderson.
ACTION: Action Drama; SUSPENSE: Fish; Murders-One by One; Snow Settings; Revenge; Monsters-Animal; Fishermen; Whales; Unintentionally Funny
RETREAD OF: Jaws; RIPOFF: Jaws 4.
(Ed: As silly as the premise seems, it works as a *Jaws* retread and as a man vs. beast thriller; good score)
Orchestra Wives, 1942, 98m, ★★★/$$$, 20th/Fox. A swing band on tour comes to a small town in the heartland, and the trumpet player wins the heart of a local girl. Ann Rutherford, George Montgomery, Lynn Bari, Glenn Miller and his Orchestra, Carole Landis, Jackie Gleason, Cesar Romero. w. Karl Tunberg, Darrell Ware, d. Archie Mayo.
MUSICALS: Big Band Era; Musicians; ROMANCE: Romance-Boy Wants Girl; Small-town Life
Ordeal by Innocence, 1985, 88m, ★★1/2/$$, Cannon/MGM-UA, PG. Off exploring in the Antarctic, a British scientist is unaware that his friend has been framed for murder. When he returns, he tries to clear his friend's name. Donald Sutherland, Christopher Plummer, Faye Dunaway, Sarah Miles, Ian MacShane, Diana Quick, Annette Crosbie, Michael Elphick, Phoebe Nichols. w. Alexander Stuart, N-adap. Agatha Christie, d. Desmond Davis.
MYSTERY: MURDER: MURDER MYSTERY: Explorers; Framed?; Accused Unjustly; Murder-Clearing Oneself; Detective Stories; Detectives-Amateur;

TV Movies; Coulda Been Good; Agatha Christie
(Appointment with Death; Evil Under the Sun)
Ordinary People, 1980, 122m, ★★★★/ $$$$$, Par/Par, R/P. The death of his brother led a teenage boy of an affluent family (Timothy Hutton, **BSActor**) to attempt suicide, and he must now learn to live with his unforgiving mother (Mary Tyler Moore, BActress) and soul-seeking father (Donald Sutherland). Elizabeth McGovern, Judd Hirsch (BSActor), Dinah Manoff. w. Alvin Sargent (**BAScr**), N-adap. Judith Guest, d. Robert Redford (**BDirector**). BPicture. Oscars: 6-4.
DRAMA: TRAGEDY: Family Drama; Psychological Drama; Mothers & Sons; Fathers & Sons; Suicidal Tendencies; Death-Dealing With; Psychologists; Coming of Age; Love-First; Stern Women; Mean Women; Past-Haunted by the
(The Bell Jar; The Catcher in the Rye [novel])
(Ed: A faithful telling of the sleeper blockbuster novel of the 70s from first-time author Guest, elevating the story to profundity)
Orlando, 1992, 93m, ★★★/$$, New Line/Col, R/S. A human being lives for 400 years, beginning as a man in the court of Elizabeth I, but changing sex at the beginning of the 20th century. Tilda Swinton, Billy Zane, Lothaire Bluteau, John Wood, Charlotte Valandrey, Heathcote Williams, Quentin Crisp, Peter Eyre, Thom Hoffman, Jimmy Somerville, Dudley Sutton, Anna Healy. w. d. Sally Potter, N-adap. Virginia Woolf.
DRAMA: Allegorical Stories; Art Films; Historical Drama; Costume Drama; Women as Men; Role Reversals; Aging-Reverse; England; Female Protagonists; Female Screenwriters; Female Directors
(Impromptu; Queen Margot)
(Ed: For some, wonderful and opulent, but for others, unendurable)
Orphans, 1987, 120m, ★★★/$, Lorimar-WB/WB, R/P. Two brothers whose parents died have only each other, until they find a father figure among the local Mafia and tie him up. Albert Finney, Matthew Modine, Kevin Anderson, John Kellogg. w. P-adap. Lyle Kessler, d. Alan J. Pakula.
COMEDY DRAMA: Black Comedy; Social Drama; Mob Stories; Kidnappings; Orphans; Brothers; Stagelike Films; Flops-

Major; Coulda Been Great; Art Films
(The Happening; The King of Comedy)
Orpheus Descending, 1991, 117m, ★★★1/2/$$$, Turner/Turner, PG-13/S-MRN. A young drifter comes to a small southern town and falls for a mysterious Italian woman married to an ill store owner, a relationship which leads to a horrible end. Vanessa Redgrave, Kevin Anderson, Miriam Margolyes, Anne Twomey, Sloane Shelton. w. Peter Hall, Tennessee Williams, P-adap. Williams, d. Hall.
DRAMA: TRAGEDY: ROMANCE: Romance-Older Women/Younger Men; Romance with Married Person; Southerns; Immigrants; Mental Illness; Free Spirits; Romance-Doomed; Cheating Women; Jealous Husbands; Small-town Scandal; Hidden Gems; Tenessee Williams-esque; TV Movies
REMAKE OF The Fugitive Kind.
(The Rose Tattoo; Ballad of the Sad Cafe)
(Ed: The successful Broadway revival makes a fascinating transfer to the small screen, though Anderson seems not up to the level of Redgrave's lead)
The Oscar, 1965, 119m, ★★★/$$, Avco/Sultan, PG/S. The story of a big star and other little stars and the little people they all step on during the journey to the Oscar podium-except that there's an embarrassing twist for the shoo-in. Stephen Boyd, Elke Sommer, Jill St. John, Tony Bennett, Edie Adams, Milton Berle, Eleanor Parker, Joseph Cotten, Ernest Borgnine, Ed Begley, Walter Brennan, Broderick Crawford, James Dunn, Peter Lawford, (cameos) Bob Hope, Frank Sinatra. d. Russel Rouse.
MELODRAMA: Hollywood Life; Hollywood Satire; Power Struggles; Fame-Rise to; Actors; Actresses; Soap Operas; Double Crossings; Betrayals; Mean Women; Mean Men; Camp; The Oscars; Unintentionally Funny; Hidden Gems; All-Star Casts; All-Star Cameos; Cult Films
(The Bad and the Beautiful; Valley of the Dolls; California Suite)
Oscar, 1991, 109m, ★★/$, WB/WB, PG. A former mob hitman tries to go straight and set a good example for his daughters. Sylvester Stallone, Ornella Muti, Kirk Douglas, Peter Riegert, Chazz Palminteri, Vincent Spano, Marisa Tomei, Tim Curry, Don Ameche, Yvonne DeCarlo, Linda Gray. w. Michael Barrie, Jim Mulholland, P-adap. Claude Magnier, d. John Landis.

COMEDY: FARCE: Mob Comedy; Starting Over; Fathers & Daughters; Lover Family Dislikes; Daddy's Girls; Italians; Coulda Been Good; Foreign Film Remakes
Oscar Wilde, 1959, 96m, ★★1/2/$, Ind/NA. Recounting Wilde's later life, mostly dealing with his sodomy trial in the 1890s. Robert Morley, John Neville, Phyllis Calvert, Ralph Richardson, Dennis Price, Alexander Knox, Edward Chapman, Martin Benson, Robert Harris, Henry Oscar, William Devlin. w. Jo Esinger, d. Gregory Ratoff.
DRAMA: Biographies; Writers Trials; Courtroom Drama; 1890s; Gay Men; Homophobia; British Films
(The Trials of Oscar Wilde; Maurice)
(Ed: Shot and released at the same time as *The Trials of Oscar Wilde*, dealing with the same aspects of the same biography)
O.S.S., 1946, 107m, ★★1/2/$$$, Par/Par. During World War II, Americans parachute into occupied France on a special spy mission. Alan Ladd, Geraldine Fitzgerald, Patric Knowles, John Hoyt, Don Beddoe. w. Richard Maibaum, d. Irving Pichel.
ACTION: Spy Films; Spies; World War II Stories; Special Teams-Military
Ossessione, 1942/1975, 135m, ★★★1/2/$$, Ind/Ingram, Facets. A traveler in Italy staying in a provincial inn has an affair with the proprietor's wife. The cuckholded husband becomes obsessed with revenge, vowing to murder the intruder. Massimo Girotti, Clara Calamai, Elio Marcuzzo. w. Antonio Pietrangeli, Giuseppe de Santis, N-adap (uncredited) James M. Cain, *The Postman Always Rings Twice*, d. Luchino Visconti.
SUSPENSE: ROMANCE: Romance-Triangles; Romance with Married Person; Murder of Spouse; Dangerous Women; Cheating Women; Revenge; Film Noir; Neo-Realism; Cult Films; Hidden Gems
REMAKE/RETREAD OF: The Postman Always Rings Twice.
(The Postman Always Rings Twice [1945, 1981]; Le Dernier Tournant; Bitter Rice)
(Ed: Credited with starting the Italian Neo-Realist Movement, though many historians credit *Open City* in the post-war era of Italian film; unreleased in America until 1975 due to copyright problems with its unauthorized use of James M. Cain's story of *Postman*)
The Osterman Weekend, 1983, 102m, ★★/$$, 20th/Thorn-EMI, HBO, R/V-S. A

CIA chief confides his theory that his informants are actually Soviet spies to a television reporter that he trusts with the information. Rutger Hauer, John Hurt, Burt Lancaster, Craig T. Nelson, Dennis Hopper, Chris Sarandon, Meg Foster, Helen Shaver. w. Alan Sharp, Ian Masters, N-adap. Robert Ludlum, d. Sam Peckinpah.

SUSPENSE: Spy Films; Spies; CIA Agents; Russians as Enemy; KGB Agents; Journalists; Journalists as Detectives; Coulda Been Good

Otello, 1986, 120m, ★★★½/$, Ind/Media. A filmed version of Verdi's opera based on the famous Shakespeare tragedy in which the troubled Moore's jealous fantasies of his beautiful (white) wife's infidelities are fed by his evil "friend," Iago, until his rage cannot be contained. Placido Domingo, Katia Ricciarelli, Justino Diaz, Petra Malakova. w. d. Franco Zeffirelli, (Opera)-adap. Giuseppe Verdi, P-adap. William Shakespeare (*Othello*).

MUSICALS: Opera; Stage Filmings

Othello, 1951, 91m, ★★★/$, Ind/Academy. Orson Welles's reworking of the famous Shakespeare tragedy. Orson Welles, Michael MacLiammoir, Fay Compton, Robert Cook, Suzanne Cloutier, Michael Laurence, Hilton Edwards, Doris Dowling. w. d. Orson Welles, P-adap. William Shakespeare.

Othello, 1965, 166m, ★★★½/$$$, WB/NA. A filmed record of the Britain's National Shakespeare Theatre production with a stellar cast. Laurence Olivier (BActor), Frank Finlay (BSActor), Joyce Redman (BSActress), Maggie Smith (BSActress), Derek Jacobi, Robert Lang, Anthony Nicholls. w. William Shakespeare, d. Stuart Burge. Oscars: 4-0. Stage Filmings

DRAMA: TRAGEDY: MURDER: Murder of Spouse; Jealousy; Black Men; Mean Men; Liars; Conspiracy; Romance-Triangles; Betrayals; Shakespeare; Middle Ages; Venice; Classic Literary Adaptations; Classic Tragedy
(A Double Life)

The Other, 1972, 100m, ★★★½/$$, 20th/Fox, PG/V. A boy whose twin may or may not have died has macabre fantasies which lead to murder and the destruction of his otherwise idyllic world. Diana Muldaur, Uta Hagen, Chris Connelly,

Victor French. w. N-adap. Tom Tryon, d. Robert Mulligan.

HORROR: SUSPENSE: MURDER: Psychological Thriller; Evil Children; Twins; Twins-Evil; Murderers-Child; Illusions/Hallucinations; Surrealism; Boyhood; Midwestern Life; Grandmothers-Fascinating; Cult Films
(The Little Girl Who Lives Down the Lane; The Bad Seed; Dead Ringers)

Other People's Money, 1991, 101m, ★★½/$$, WB/WB, PG-13/S-P. A buyout king tries to drive the prices down on companies he wants, then take them over when they're weakest. He butts heads with an old-fashioned industrialist he targets and it becomes a war of old-school, make-money-by-earning-it capitalism vs. the new, get-rich-quick style, with a femme fatale in the midst. Danny DeVito, Gregory Peck, Penelope Ann Miller, Piper Laurie, Dean Jones, R. D. Call, Mo Gaffney, Bette Henritze. w. Alvin Sargent, P-adap. Jerry Sterner, d. Norman Jewison.

COMEDY DRAMA: ROMANCE: Romance-Reluctant; Battle of the Sexes; Romance-Unprofessional; Lawyers; Corporation as Enemy; Corporate Corruption; Business Life; Mean Men; Greed; Wall Street; Coulda Been Good
(Wall Street; Working Girl)
(Ed: Runs out of steam because both sides are rather dastardly and the actors don't do anything to make them more likeable-their greed and bland games become tiring)

The Other Side of Midnight, 1977, 166m, ★★/$$$, 20th/Fox, R/S-FN. During and after World War II a married woman in Paris loves an American fly boy, but when her husband returns, he's not too happy about it. Marie-France Pisier, John Beck, Susan Sarandon, Ral Vallone, Clu Gulager, Christian Marquand. w. Herman Raucher, Daniel Taradash, N-adap. Sidney Sheldon, d. Charles Jarrott.

MELODRAMA: ROMANCE: Romantic Drama; Erotic Drama; Soap Operas; World War II Stories; Romance-Triangles; Cheating Women; Paris; Americans Abroad; Romance with Married Person; Female Protagonists
(Mistral's Daughter)

The Other Side of the Mountian, 1975, 102m, ★★½/$$$$, U/MCA-U, PG. The true story of Olympic skier Jill

Kinmont, whose man stands by her when she is paralyzed in a skiing accident. Then tragedy strikes again when her husband dies in a plane crash. Marilyn Hassett, Beau Bridges, Belinda Montgomery, Nan Martin, William Bryant, Dabney Coleman. w. David Seltzer, NF-adap. E. G. Valens (*A Long Way Up*), d. Larry Peerce.

MELODRAMA: ROMANCE: TRAGEDY: Romantic Drama; Disease Stories; Disabled People; Skiing; Olympics; Tearjerkers; Women's Films; True Stories; Biographies; Female Protagonists; Sleeper Hits
(Joni; An Affair to Remember)

The Other Side of the Mountain Part Two, 1977, 99m, ★★/$$, U/MCA-U, PG. Handicapped former Olympic skier Jill Kinmont becomes a teacher and finds another man. Marilyn Hassett, Timothy Bottoms, Nan Martin, Belinda J. Montgomery. w. Douglas Day Stewart, d. Larry Pearce.

MELODRAMA: ROMANCE: Starting Over; Disabled People; True Stories; Biographies; Women's Films; Teachers; Female Protagonists

Our Dancing Daughters, 1928, 86m, B&W, silent, ★★½/$$$, MGM/MGM-UA. Two young flappers take opposite paths: one marries, while the other dies of alcohol poisoning at a wild party. Joan Crawford, John Mack Brown, Dorothy Sebastian, Anita Page, Nils Asther. w. Josephine Lovett, d. Harry Beaumont.

MELODRAMA: Sisters; Episodic Stories; Wild People; Dancers; Roaring 20s

Our Girl Friday, see **The Adventures of Sadie.**

Our Hearts Were Young and Gay, 1944, 81m, ★★/$$, Par/NA. Two flappers in the twenties run off to Paris together and have romantic adventures. Gail Russell, Diana Lynn, Charles Ruggles, Dorothy Gish, Beulah Bondi, James Brown, Bill Edwards, Jean Heather. w. Sheridan Gibney, NF-adap. Cornelia Otis Skinner, Emily Kimbrough, d. Lewis Allen.

MELODRAMA: ROMANCE: Romantic Drama; Romance on Vacation; Americans Abroad; Friendships-Female; Roaring 20s; Paris; Female Protagonists

Our Hospitality, 1923, 74m, B&W, silent, ★★★½/$$$, MGM/MGM-UA. In the 1850s down South, a landed gent

comes home to marry and gets stuck in the middle of a family feud. Buster Keaton, Natalie Talmadge, Joe Keaton, Buster Keaton, Jr., w. Jean Havez, Joseph Mitchell, Clyde Bruckman, d. Buster Keaton.
COMEDY: Comedy-Slapstick; Southerns; Feuds; Family Comedy; Marriage Comedy; Civil War Era; Hidden Gems
(The General)

Our Man Flint, 1965, 108m, ★★★/$$$, 20th/Fox. A mad scientist plans to bring the world to its knees by manipulating the weather. Only one secret agent is studly enough to stop him: our man Flint. James Coburn, Lee J. Cobb, Gila Golan, Edward Mulhare, Benson Fong, Sigrid Valdis. w. Hal Fimberg, Ben Starr, d. Daniel Mann.
ACTION: COMEDY: Action Comedy; Spies; Secret Agents; Chase Stories; Heist Stories; Rule the World Plot to; Scientists-Mad; Spoofs-Spy; Faded Hits; 1960s
SEQUEL: In Like Flint.
(Hudson Hawk; The Wrecking Crew)

Our Man in Havana, 1959, 112m, ★★★/$$, Col/NA. A British door-to-door vacuum cleaner salesman in Cuba allows himself to get involved in espionage, and finds himself quickly getting in over his head. Alec Guinness, Noel Coward, Burl Ives, Maureen O'Hara, Ernie Kovacs, Ralph Richardson, Jo Morrow, Paul Rogers, Gregoire Aslan, Duncan Macrae. w. N-adap. Graham Greene, d. Carol Reed.
COMEDY DRAMA: SUSPENSE: Spy Films; Spies; Spoofs-Spy; Ordinary People in Extraordinary Situations; Innocent Bystanders; Salesmen; British Films; Hidden Gems
(Fuller Brush Man; The Comedians)

Our Relations, 1936, 65m, ★★★1/2/$$$, MGM/Media. Two sailors charged with guarding a precious diamond ring meet their long-lost, recently married twins, and the proliferation of diamond rings gets quite confusing. Stan Laurel, Oliver Hardy, James Finlayson, Alan Hale, Sidney Toler, Daphne Pollard, Iris Adrian, Noel Madison, Ralf Harolde, Arthur Housman. w. Richard Connell, Felix Adler, Charles Rogers, Jack Jevne, SS-adap. W. W. Jacobs (The Money Box), d. Harry Lachman.
COMEDY: FARCE: Fools-Bumbling; Laurel & Hardy; Jewel Thieves; Faded Hits; Hidden Gems
(Bonnie Scotland; Big Business)

Our Town, 1940, 90m, ★★★1/2/$$$, UA/Nos. In a small New Hampshire town, the residents each have their own private dramas as a woman gives birth and a boy comes of age. Frank Craven, William Holden, Martha Scott (BActress), Thomas Mitchell, Fay Bainter, Guy Kibbee, Beulah Bondi, Stuart Erwin. w. Thornton Wilder, Frank Craven, Harry Chantlee, P-adap. Thornton Wilder, d. Sam Wood. BPicture, BB&WArt, BSound, BScore. Oscars: 5-0.
DRAMA: MELODRAMA: Small-town Life; New England; Interwoven Stories; Multiple Stories; Coming of Age; Babies-Having; Narrated Films; Stagelike Films; Pulitzer Prize Adaptations; Hidden Gems; Faded Hits
(Cold Sassy Tree; King's Row; Little Women)

Our Vines Have Tender Grapes, 1945, 105m, ★★★/$$$, MGM/MGM-UA. A Norweigian farming village in Wisconsin has its personal dramas as seen through the eyes of a young girl. Edward G. Robinson, Margaret O'Brien, James Craig, Agnes Moorehead, Jackie "Butch" Jenkins, Morris Carnovsky, Frances Gifford, Sara Haden. w. Dalton Trumbo, N-adap. George Victor Martin, d. Roy Rowland.
MELODRAMA: FAMILY: Family Drama; Girls; Farm Life; Immigrants; Coming of Age; American Myth; Capra-esque; Midwestern Life; Hidden Gems

Outbreak, 1995, 123m, ★★1/2/$$$$, WB/WB, R/P-V. A killer virus attacks soldiers fighting in 1960s central Africa and then resurfaces in some monkeys brought to the U.S. It's up to a crack epidemiologist to stop it before an atomic bomb must be dropped to control the spread! Dustin Hoffman, Rene Russo, Morgan Freeman, Kevin Spacey, Cuba Gooding, Jr., Donald Sutherland, Patrick Dempsey, Zakes Mokae. w. Laurence Dworet, Robert Roy Pool, d. Wolfgang Petersen.
SUSPENSE: ACTION: Chase Stories; Medical Thriller; Epidemics; Disease Stories; Race Against Time; Doctors; Scientists; Primates; Incredible but Mostly True; True Stories
(The Stand; The Andromeda Strain; Virus)

Out Cold, 1989, 92m, ★★/$, Ind/HBO, PG. A butcher thinks he's accidentally killed a co-worker and covers up the evi-dence. He later learns someone else may have committed the murder. John Lithgow, Teri Garr, Randy Quaid, Bruce McGill, Lisa Blount, Alan Blumenfield, Morgan Paull, Barbara Rhoades. w. Leonard Glasser, George Malko, d. Malcom Mowbray.
COMEDY: Black Comedy; Comedy-Morbid; MURDER: Murder-Clearing Oneself; Death-Accidental; Frozen People; Coulda Been Good

Out of Africa, 1985, 150m, ★★★★/$$$$$, Universal/MCA-U, PG/S. The true story of writer Isak Dinesen's (Meryl Streep, BActress) trip to build a coffee plantation with her husband (Klaus Maria Brandauer, BSActor) in Africa where she falls in love with the adventurer Denys Finch-Hatton (Robert Redford). w. Kurt Ludetke (BAScr), d. Sydney Pollack, (BDirector). BPicture, BCinema, BEditing, BArt, BCost, BSound, BOScore. Oscars: 11-7.
DRAMA: ROMANCE: Romantic Drama; Epics; Mortgage Drama; Women Fighting the System; Romance-Reluctant; Elusive Men; Romance-Triangles; Cheating Men; Cheating Women; Biographies; Feisty Females; Marriages of Convenience; Writers; Spinsters; Plantation Life; Save the Farm; Farm Life; New Year's Eve; Blockbusters
(Places in the Heart; O Pioneers; House of the Spirits; We of the Never, Never)

Out of Order, 1984, 88m, ★★/$, Vestron/Vestron, R. Four people stuck in a German high-rise's elevator must deal with their fear while trying to get out before it crashes several stories down. Gotz George, Renee Soutendijk, Wolfgang Kieling, Hannes Jaenicke, Klaus Wennemann, Ralph Richter. w. d. Carl Schenkel, N-adap. Wilhelm Heyne.
DRAMA: SUSPENSE: Trapped; Ensemble Films; German Films; Curiosities
(The Fourth Man; The Fifth Floor)

Out of the Blue, 1980, 94m, ★★★/$, Ind/Media, R/P-V. When a convict comes home to his hippie family, sparks fly between he and his feisty daughter. Dennis Hopper, Linda Manz, Raymond Burr. d. Hopper.
DRAMA: Family Drama; Fathers & Daughters; Ex-Convicts; Feisty Females; Hippies; Actor; Directors; Female Protagonists; Cult Films
(Backtrack; Easy Rider)

Out of the Dark, 1988, 89m, ★★/$, Ind/Col, R/S-P. A man dressed as a clown goes on a killing rampage, terrorizing phone-sex operators, so police try to discover his identity. Cameron Dye, Karen Black, Lynn Danielson, Karen Witter, Tracey Walter, Silvana Gallardo, Bud Cort, Geoffrey Lewis, Divine, Paul Bartel, Tab Hunter. w. J. Gregory De Felice, Zene W. Levitt, d. Michael Schroeder.
SUSPENSE: Comic Thrillers; Black Comedy; MURDER: Stalkers; Telephone Terror; Police Stories; Women in Jeopardy; Spoofs
(Call Me; Don't Answer the Phone; Apology)

Out of the Past, 1947, 102m, ★★★½/ $$$, RKO/Turner. A detective (Robert Mitchum) is hired by mobster friend (Kirk Douglas) to find the friend's girl (Jane Greer) down in Mexico, but when he finds her, he falls in love but also into deception and danger. Rhonda Fleming, Richard Webb, Steve Brodie, Virginia Houston, Dickie Moore. w., N-adap. Geoffrey Homes (*Build My Gallows High*), d. Jacques Tourneur.
DRAMA: ROMANCE: Film Noir; Romance-Dangerous; Dangerous Women; Romance with Friend's Lover; Romance-Triangles; Mob Stories; Detective Stories; Detectives in Deep; Betrayals; Hidden Gems; Cult Films
REMAKE: Against All Odds.
(Blowing Wild; Second Chance)

Out of This World, 1945, 96m, ★★½/$$, Par/NA. A messenger for Western Union is discovered singing on the job, and the rest is history. Eddie Bracken, Veronica Lake, Diana Lynn, Cass Daley, Parkyakarkus, Donald MacBride, Florence Bates, Carmen Cavallero, The Voice of Bing Crosby. w. Walter de Leon, Arthur Philips, d. Hal Walker.
COMEDY: WESTERNS: Western Comedy; MUSICAL: Singers; Fame-Rise to (Hail, the Conquering Hero)

The Out of Towners, 1970, 110m, ★★★★/$$$, Par/Par, PG. A couple from Ohio (Jack Lemmon, Sandy Dennis) goes on the ultimate trip of chaos when their plane has to land in Boston instead of New York and he has only a day to get back to New York for a job interview. Everything is on strike and their hotel reservation has been let go and they get mugged trying to find someplace to stay.

Anne Meara, Dolph Sweet, Billy Dee Williams. w. Neil Simon, d. Arthur Hiller.
COMEDY: SATIRE: Social Comedy; Comedy of Errors; Race Against Time; New York Life; Fish Out of Water Stories; Murphy's Law Stories; Marriage Comedy; Underrated
(Prisoner of Second Avenue; Quick Change; Planes, Trains and Automobiles)
(Ed: Lemmon tells a story about a woman at the New York premiere who was so outraged at the film's criminally negative portrayal of New York City, she patriotically stomped out of the theater and then was promptly mugged outside)

An Outcast of the Islands, 1951, 102m, ★★½/$, London/NA. A trader who just can't fit in in England goes to the Far East, but even there, he can't fit in. Trevor Howard, Ralph Richardson, Kerima, Robert Morley, Wendy Hiller, George Coulouris, Frederick Valk, Wilfrid Hyde White, Betty Ann Davies. w. William Fairchild, N-adap. Joseph Conrad, d. Carol Reed.
DRAMA: Character Studies; Journies; Asia; Ostracism; Islands; Drifters

The Outfit, 1973, 103m, ★★/$, MGM/NA. A man just released from prison must now run from the Mob. Robert Duvall, Karen Black, Robert Ryan, Joe Don Baker, Timothy Carey, Richard Jaeckel, Sheree North, Marie Windsor, Jane Greer, Elisha Cook Jr. w. d. John Flynn, N-adap. Richard Stark.
ACTION: Action Drama; Crime Drama; Fugitives from the Mob; Mob Stories; Ex-Convicts; Chase Stories; Coulda Been Good
(Midnight Man; Badge 373)

The Outfit, 1993, 92m, ★★½/$, U/MCA-U. A mob war begins in Depression era Chicago with an FBI agent in their midst. John Christian, Lance Henriksen, Billy Drago, Martin Kove. w. J. Christian Ingvordsen, Steven Kamen, Whitney Ransick, d. Ingvordsen.
ACTION: Action Drama; Crime Drama; Mob Stories; Mob Wars; FBI Agents; Depression Era

Outland, 1981, 109m, ★★½/$$$, WB/WB, R/V-MRN. A mining base in outer space is the locale for a futuristic gunfight at the OK Corral. Sean Connery, Peter Boyle, Francis Sternhagen, James B. Sikking, Kika Markham. w. d. Peter Hyams.

ACTION: SCI-FI: Outer Space Movies; Mining Towns; Duels; Detective Stories; Men in Conflict; MURDER: Writer-Directors
(High Noon; Gunfight at the OK Corral)

The Outlaw, 1943/1949, 126m, ★★½/$, Hughes/Nos. Billy the Kid, Doc Holliday, and Pat Garrett all vie for the same half-breed woman. Jack Beutel, Jane Russell, Thomas Mitchell, Walter Huston. w. Jules Furtham, d. Howard Hughes.
WESTERNS: Men Fighting Over Women; Billy the Kid; Indians-American; Sexy Women; Flops-Major
(Ed: Although it launched Jane Russell's career with her special bra, its release was cut short due to protests and disinterest in the film itself)

Outlaw Blues, 1977, 101m, ★★/$$, WB/WB, R/V-S. An ex-con and amateur songwriter hears a song of his on the radio and goes to find the man who stole it from him. Peter Fonda, Susan Saint James, John Crawford, James Callahan, Michael Lerner. w. B. W. L. Norton, d. Richard T. Heffron.
ACTION: Action Comedy; Revenge; Songwriters; Ex-Convicts; Chase Stories; Coulda Been Good

The Outlaw Josey Wales, 1976, 135m, ★★★/$$$$, WB/WB, PG/V. After his wife is brutally murdered by outlaws, a cowboy exacts his revenge, killing each of them one by one. Clint Eastwood, Chief Dan George, Sondra Locke, John Vernon, Bill McKinney. w. Phil Kaufman, Sonia Chernus, N-adap. Forrest Carter (*Gone to Texas*), d. Clint Eastwood.
WESTERNS: Revenge; Westerns-Revenge; Avenging Death of Someone; Murder of Spouse; Murder-One by One; Chase Stories; Manhunts; Vigilantes
(Hang 'em High; Pale Rider; Death Wish)

Outrage, 1950, 75m, ★★/$, Ind/NA. A woman who is raped almost loses her mind with anger. Mala Powers, Tod Andrews, Robert Clarke, Raymond Bond, Lilian Hamilton. w. Ida Lupino, Collier Young, Malvin Wald, d. Ida Lupino.
DRAMA: Social Drama; Rape/Rapists; Nervous Breakdowns;Ahead of Its Time; Female Protagonists; Female Directors; Female Screenwriters; Actor/Actress Directors
(The Accused [1948]; The Accused [1988])

The Outrage, 1964, 97m, ★★½/$, MGM/NA. A cowboy is murdered, and townsfolk all have differing views on how it happened. Paul Newman, Edward G. Robinson, Laurence Harvey, Claire Bloom, William Shatner, Albert Salmi. w. Michael Kanin, d. Martin Ritt.

WESTERNS: Westerns-Neo; MURDER: MYSTERY: MURDER MYSTERY: Detective Stories; Detectives-Amateur; Cowboys; Small-town Life; Good Premise Unfulfilled

(Hud; Missing; The OK-Bow Incident)

Outrageous Fortune, 1987, 100m, ★★★1/2/$$$, Touchstone/Touchstone, PG-13/EP-S. A man on the run from the CIA and KGB is the unfortunate object of affection for two competing actresses, who inadvertently get him into deeper trouble by chasing after him when they find out he's alive after supposedly dying in an explosion. Shelley Long, Bette Midler, Peter Coyote, Robert Prosky, John Schuck, Anthony Heald. w. Leslie Dixon, d. Arthur Hiller.

COMEDY: Action Comedy; Buddy Films; Friendships-Female; Women Fighting Over Men; Chase Stories; Actresses; KGB Agents; Race Against Time; Spoofs-Spy; Extroverted vs. Introverted; Smart vs. Dumb; Feisty Females; Female Protagonists; Female Screenwriters

(Ruthless People; Midnight Run; Hello Again)

(Ed: The chemistry between the two bickering leads is excellent and perhaps real, with Midler stealing most of the scenes, though the plot does get out of hand toward the end. Silly, often hilarious fun)

The Outside Man, 1972, 104m, ★★/$, UAMGM-UA, R/V. A Frenchman in LA kills a mob boss and must hide from would-be assassins. Jean-Louis Trintignant, Ann-Margret, Roy Scheider, Angie Dickinson, Georgia Engel, Felice Orlandi, Talia Shire. w. Jean-Claude Carriere, Jacques Deray, Ian McLellan Hunter, d. Jacques Deray.

ACTION: Action Drama; Fugitives from the Mob; Mob Stories; Hitmen; Coulda Been Good

The Outsider, 1961, 108m, ★★/$, U-I/NA. An Indian becomes a war hero, but still can't find acceptance in white society. Tony Curtis, James Franciscus, Bruce Bennett, Gregory Walcott, Vivian Nathan, Edmund Hashim, Stanley Adams. w. Stewart Stern, d. Delbert Mann.

WESTERNS: War Stories; Indians-American; Ethics; Peaceful People; Soldiers

The Outsiders, 1983, 91m, ★★★/$$$, WB/WB, PG. A group of teenagers form a gang and fight the "soches," the well-heeled kids from the rich side of town, in 50s Tulsa. Matt Dillon, Ralph Macchio, C. Thomas Howell, Patrick Swayze, Rob Lowe, Emilio Estevez, Tom Cruise, Diane Lane. w. Katherine Knutsen Rowell, N-adap. S. E. Hinton, d. Francis Ford Coppola.

DRAMA: ACTION: Action Drama; Gangs-Street; Rich vs. Poor; Teenagers; Ensembles-Male; Ensembles-Young People; Ensemble Films; Teenage Movies; All-Star Casts; Female Screenwriters

(Rumble Fish; The Wanderers; Five Corners)

Over Her Dead Body (Enid is Sleeping), 1989, 99m, ★★★/$, Vestron/Vestron, PG. A woman (Elizabeth Perkins) having an affair with her sister's husband (Judge Reinhold) accidently kills her and then has to get rid of the body with her brother-in-law, but it won't be easy. w. d. Maurice Phillips.

COMEDY: Black Comedy; Hide the Dead Body; Screwball Comedy; Comedy of Errors; MURDER: Romance with Relative's Lover; Death-Accidental; Small-town Life; Southwestern Life; Desert Life; Hidden Gems; Writer-Directors

(Blood Simple; The Trouble With Harry; Weekend at Bernie's SERIES)

Over the Brooklyn Bridge, 1983, 106m, ★★1/2/$, Cannon/MGM-UA, PG. A Jewish restaurant owner and his family have misadventures and struggle through life in Brooklyn. Elliott Gould, Margaux Hemingway, Sid Caesar, Shelley Winters, Burt Young, Carol Kane. w. Arnold Somkin, d. Menahem Golan.

MELODRAMA: COMEDY DRAMA: New York Life; Jewish People; Marriage Drama; Family Drama; Coulda Been Good

(Little Murders; Falling in Love Again)

Over the Top, 1987, 93m, ★1/2/$$, Cannon/WB, PG/V. An arm wrestling champion fights to prove to his son that he's a good father. Sylvester Stallone, Robert Loggia, Susan Blakely, Rick Zumwalt, David Mendenhall. w. Stirling Silliphant, Sylvester Stallone, d. Menahem Golan.

ACTION: Fathers & Sons; Men Proving Themselves; Wrestling; Unintentionally Funny

(Cobra; Rocky V; Every Which Way But Loose)

Over Twenty-One, 1945, 102m, ★★1/2/$$, Col/NA. A woman deals with her loneliness and the advances of neighbors when her husband's away at World War II. Irene Dunne, Alexander Knox, Charles Coburn, Jeff Donnell, Lee Patrick, Phil Brown, Cora Witherspoon. w. Sidney Buchman, P-adap. Ruth Gordon, d. Alexander Hall.

MELODRAMA: World War II Era; War at Home; Lonely People; Female Protagonists; Forgotten Films

Overboard, 1987, 112m, ★★★/$$, MGM-UA/MGM-UA, PG/P. A tyrannical heiress (Goldie Hawn) falls overboard her yacht, getting amnesia, and is rescued by her hunky but uncouth carpenter (Kurt Russell) who takes her to his country shack, filling her memory in by telling her she's his wife, who's dead, and that she's the mother of his brats. w. Leslie Dixon, d. Garry Marshall.

COMEDY: Comedy-Situation; Romance-Bickering; Romance-Mismatched; Fish out of Water Stories; Liars; Screwball Comedy; Riches to Rags; Amnesia; Rednecks; Mean Women; Heiresses; Mothers-Struggling; Children-Brats; Female Protagonists; Female Screenwriters

(Maid to Order; Private Benjamin)

The Overlanders, 1946, 91m, ★★★/$$, Ealing/Nos. In Australia during World War II, the Japanese invade, and a rancher must drive his cattle across the outback to keep them from procuring the beef. Chips Rafferty, John Heyward, Daphne Campbell. w. d. Harry Watt.

DRAMA: War Stories; Japanese as Enemy; World War II Stories; Cattle Ranchers; Australia; British Films; Writer-Directors

(The Secret of Santa Vittoria)

The Owl and the Pussycat, 1971, 96m, ★★★★/$$$, Columbia/RCA-Col, PG/P-S. A nerdy wanna-be writer (George Segal) complains about what he sees going on across the way of his seedy apartment building-in the room of a prostitute (Barbra Streisand), who when kicked out, comes to stay with him, leading to chaos, destruction, and perhaps love. Robert Klein. w. Buck Henry, P-adap. Bill Manhoff, d. Herbert Ross.

COMEDY: Romantic Comedy; Screwball Comedy; Romance-Bickering; Comedy of Errors; Romance-Opposites Attract; Extrovert vs. Introvert; Prostitutes-Low Class; Writers; Nerds; Nerds & Babes; Feisty Females; Smart vs. Dumb; New York Life; Underrated; Hidden Gems (What's Up, Doc?; For Pete's Sake; A Touch of Class)

The Ox-Bow Incident, 1943, 75m, ★★★★/$$$, 20th/Fox. A cowboy knows that three strangers are innocent of the crime of which they're accused, but can he convince the townsfolk before they are hung? Henry Fonda, Henry Morgan, Jane Darwell, Anthony Quinn, Dana Andrews, Mary Beth Hughes, William Eythe, Harry Davenport, Frank Conroy. w. Lamar Trotti, N-adap. Walter Van Tiburg Clark, d. William Wellman. BPicture. Oscars: 1-0.

DRAMA: WESTERNS: MURDER: Accused Unjustly; Executions; Murder-Debate to Reveal Killer; Saving Someone; Race Against Time; Social Drama; Ethics; Hidden Gems

Oxford Blues, 1984, 97m, ★★/$$, MGM/MGM-UA, PG. A smart-alecky California boy saves up his money and goes to Oxford, but must learn to play by their rules, especially when he fails to take his responsibilities on the rowing team seriously. Rob Lowe, Ally Sheedy, Alan Howard, Amanda Pays, Julian Sands, Julian Firth, Michael Gough, Aubrey Morris. w. d. Robert Boris.

COMEDY: ROMANCE: Romantic Comedy; Romance-Boy Wants Girl; Snobs vs. Slobs; Rich vs. Poor; College Life; Bratpack Movies; England; Writer-Directors; Americans Abroad (A Yank at Eton; The Rachel Papers; Youngblood; Making the Grade; Soul Man)

(Ed: They let this guy in? Even illegally?)

P

Pacific Heights, 1990, 103m, ★★★/ $$$, 20th/Fox, R/P. A yuppie couple (Matthew Modine, Melanie Griffith) buy a townhouse in San Francisco and rent part of it out to a wealthy businessman (Michael Keaton) who may be more than he seems, especially when he won't pay rent and barricades himself in, wreaking havoc. Mako, Nobu McCarthy, Laurie Metcalf, Carl Lumbly, Tippi Hedren. w. Daniel Pyne, d. John Schlesinger.
SUSPENSE: MYSTERY: Psychological Thrillers; Roommates From Hell; Malicious Menaces; Apartment Buildings; Psychotics; Yuppies; San Francisco; Risking it All; Female Protagonists (Malice; Single White Female; Apartment Zero)

The Pack, 1977, 99m, ★/$, WBWB, R/EV-B&G. Vacationing tourists on a secluded tropical island are besieged by a pack of wild dogs, who proceed to attack them one by one. Joe Don Baker, Hope Alexander Willis, Richard B. Shull, R. G. Armstrong. w. d. Robert Clouse, N-adap. Dave Fisher.
HORROR: Monsters-Animal; Dogs; Nightmare Vacations; Islands (Frogs; Empire of the Ants)

The Package, 1989, 108m, ★★¹/2/$$, Orion/Orion, PG-13/V. A sergeant must escort a prisoner for a transfer but loses him. His search for the runaway leads him into an underground assassination conspiracy. Gene Hackman, Joanna Cassidy, Tommy Lee Jones, Dennis Franz, Reni Santoni, Pam Grier, Kevin Crowley. w. John Bishop, d. Andrew Davis.
ACTION: SUSPENSE: Spy Films; Spies; CIA Agents; Military Stories; Fugitives from a Murderer; Conspiracy; Chase Stories; Assassination Plots (No Way Out; The Looking Glass War; Drop Zone)

The Pad, and How to Use It, 1966, 86m, ★★¹/2/$$, U/NA. A timid young bachelor striking out on his own gets some advice from more swinging pals before embarking on his first date. Brian Bedford, James Farentino, Julie Sommars, Edy Williams, Nick Navarro. w. Thomas C. Ryan, Benn Starr, P-adap. Peter Shaffer (The Private Ear), d. Brian C. Hutton.
COMEDY: Coming of Age; Teenagers; Teenage Movies; Playboys; Nerds; Nerds & Babes; Dating Scene; Shy People; Extroverted vs. Introverted (The Knack; Boeing, Boeing)

The Pagemaster, 1994, 75m, 20th-Turner/Turner, ★★/$, G. A boy goes into a video game fantasy world full of eccentric characters along the way, à la The Wizard of Oz, during which the young hero learns to appreciate reading. Macaulay Culkin, Ed Begley, Jr., Mel Harris, Christopher Lloyd, Patrick Stewart, Whoopi Goldberg, Frank Welker, Leonard Nimoy, George Hearn, Dorian Harewood, Ed Gilbert. w. David Casci, David Kirschner, Ernie Contreras.
CHILDREN'S: Fantasy; ADVENTURE: Cartoonlike Movies; Video Game Movies; Child Protagonists; Flops-Major (Little Monsters; Super Mario Brothers)

Pagliacci, see A Clown Must Laugh

Paid, 1930, 80m, ★★★/$$$, MGM/NA. A woman is accused of a crime she didn't commit. She knows the real culprits, and when she gets out of jail, she vows to make them pay. Joan Crawford, Kent Douglas, Robert Armstrong, Marie Prevost, John Miljan, Polly Moran. w. Charles MacArthur, Lucien Hubbard, P-adap. Bayard Veiller (Within the Law), d. Sam Wood.
MELODRAMA: Accused Unjustly; Framed?; Revenge; Criminals-Female; Prison Drama; Women in Prison; Faded Hits; Forgotten Films; Female Protagonists (The Last of Mrs. Cheyney; Mildred Pierce)

Paid in Full, 1949, 105m, ★★¹/2/$$, Par/NA. A woman entrusts her sister with the care of her child and it dies. Then her sister gets pregnant and is told she will die in childbirth. Lizabeth Scott, Diana

Lynn, Robert Cummings, Eve Arden, Ray Collins, Frank McHugh, Stanley Ridges, Louis Jean Heydt. w. Robert Blees, Charles Schnee, d. William Dieterle.

MELODRAMA: Feuds; Sisters; Tearjerkers; Babies-Having; Children-Adopted; Family Drama; Soap Operas; Women's Films

A Pain in the A . . . , 1973, 84m, ★★★½/$$, Ind/Col, PG. A hitman with a heart forgets about his prey long enough to help a man depressed about his marriage and life, and winds up in a chaotic mess. Lino Ventura, Jacques Brel. w. Edouard Molinaro, Francis Veber, P-adap. Le Contrat, Veber, d. Edouard Molinaro.

COMEDY: COMEDY DRAMA: Black Comedy; **FARCE:** Misunderstandings; Hitmen; Suicidal Tendencies; Depression; Saving Someone; French Films; Hidden Gems
(Le Chevre; Les Comperes; Les Trois Fugitifs)

Paint It Black, 1989, 101m, ★★½/$, Vestron/Vestron, R/S-P-V. A rich boy falls for an older woman and the art world, finding himself in a mysterious situation. Rick Rossovich, Sally Kirkland, Martin Landau, Doug Savant, Julie Carmen. w. d. Tim Hunter.

SUSPENSE: Erotic Thriller; **MYSTERY:** Artists; Rich People; Romance-Older Women/Younger Men; Writer-Directors

Paint Your Wagon, 1969, 164m, ★★★/$$$$, Par/Par, G. In the Gold Rush of the 1840s, two mormon cowboys in search of gold marry the same woman and "timeshare" her while singing and cavorting. Lee Marvin, Clint Eastwood, Jean Seberg, Harve Presnell, Ray Walston. w. Paddy Chayevsky, (Musical)-adap. Alan Jay Lerner, Frederick Loewe, d. Joshua Logan. BMScore. Oscars: 1-0.

MUSICALS: COMEDY DRAMA: ROMANCE: Musical Romance; Musical Comedy; Musical Westerns; **WESTERNS:** Western Comedy; Gold Mining; Female Among Males; West-Old; Bigamy; Romance-Triangles; Men Fighting Over Women; Curiosities
(Shenandoah; Oklahoma!)
(Ed: Clint Eastwood does his own "singing," and though it made money, this film is not exactly considered a success)

Painted Desert, 1938, 59m, ★★★/$$, RKO/NA. A rancher is prodded into becoming a prospector by his lady love,

but must fight the banker who wants to do him in. George O'Brien, Laraine Day, Ray Whitley, Fred Kohler, Sr., Stanley Fields, William V. Mong, Maude Allen. w. John Rathmell, Oliver Drake, Jack Cunningham, d. David Howard.

MELODRAMA: Mortgage Drama; Cattle Ranchers; **ROMANCE:** Gold Mining; Greed

The Painted Veil, 1934, 84m, ★★½/$$$, MGM/MGM-UA. In China with her doctor husband, a woman having an affair has pangs of conscience when an epidemic strikes and her husband needs her by his side to help with the care of the locals. Greta Garbo, George Brent, Herbert Marshall, Warner Oland, Jean Hersholt. w. John Meehan, Salka Viertel, Edith Fitzgerald, N-adap. W. Somerset Maugham, d. Richard Boleslawski.

MELODRAMA: Medical Drama; Doctors; Woman Behind the Man; China; Cheating Women; Epidemics; Forgotten Films
(Jezebel; Romance; Camille; Love; Anna Christie)

A Pair of Briefs, 1961, 90m, ★★½/$, Rank/NA. In England, a male and female barrister fall in love while battling each other in court. Michael Craig, Mary Peach, Brenda de Banzie, James Robertson Justice, Roland Culver, Liz Fraser, Ron Moody, Jameson Clark, Charles Heslop. w. Nicholas Phipps, P-adap. Harold Brooke, Kay Bannerman (How Say You), d. Ralph Thomas.

COMEDY: ROMANCE: Romantic Comedy; Romance-Bickering; Lawyers; Trials; British Films
(Adam's Rib; Legal Eagles)

Paisan, 1946, 115m, ★★★½/$$, Ind/Nos. Six small World War II battles in Italy are recounted, including a romance amid one where the lovers can't speak each other's language. William Tubbs, Gar Moore, Maria Michi and non-professionals. w. Federico Fellini, Roberto Rossellini, d. Roberto Rossellini.

DRAMA: War Stories; World War II Stories; **ROMANCE:** Mute People; Soldiers; Multiple Stories; Italian Films; Neo Realism; Art Films
(Open City; Bitter Rice; The Bicycle Thief; Hiroshima; Mon Amour)

The Pajama Game, 1957, 101m, ★★★½/$$$, WB/WB. A strike for higher pay at a pajama factory is waylaid when the female union leader falls for her

sexy boss. Doris Day, John Raitt, Eddie Foy, Jr., Reta Shaw, Carol Haney. w. George Abbott, Richard Bissell, NF-adap. Richard Bissell (Seven and a Half Cents), d. Stanley Donen.

MUSICALS: COMEDY: Musical Comedy; Unions; Strikes; Factory Life; Romance with Boss; Worker vs. Boss; Romance-Unprofessional; Novel and Play Adaptations; Faded Hits; Hidden Gems
(Norma Rae; Bells Are Ringing)

Pal Joey, 1957, 109m, ★★★½/$$$$, Col/Col. A New York night club owner rises to the top of his field through somewhat unscrupulous means, while his friend, who sends him regular letters, remains an unsuccessful musician in Chicago. Frank Sinatra, Rita Hayworth, Kim Novak, Bobby Sherwood, Hank Henry, Elizabeth Patterson, Barbara Nichols. w. Dorothy Kingsley, P-adap. John O'Hara, N-adap. John O'Hara, d. George Sidney. BCostume, BArt, BSound, BEdit. Oscars: 4-0.

MUSICALS: Musical Drama; **COMEDY DRAMA:** Nightclubs; Mob Comedy; Musicians; Marriage for Money; **ROMANCE:** Romantic Comedy; San Francisco; Female Screenwriters
(Carousel; Cover Girl; Gilda; The Man with the Golden Arm; All That Jazz)

Pale Rider, 1985, 115m, ★★★/$$$, WB/WB, R/V. Gold prospectors and their families are besieged by bandits until a lone stranger comes to their settlement to protect them. Clint Eastwood, Michael Moriarty, Carrie Snodgress, Christopher Penn, Richard Dysart, Richard Kiel. w. Michael Butler, Dennis Shryack, d. Clint Eastwood.

WESTERNS: Westerns-Neo; Protecting Someone; Drifters; Gold Mining; Thieves
(The Outlaw Josie Wales; Joe Kidd; Unforgiven)

The Paleface, 1948, 91m, ★★★/$$$$, Par/Par. Calamity Jane has to go incognito to catch a band of outlaws. Her best cover: marrying a nervous and cowardly dentist. Things get out of hand when he becomes a target as well. Bob Hope, Jane Russell, Robert Armstrong, Iris Adrian, Robert Watson, Jack Searle, Joe Vitale, Clem Bevans. w. Edmund Hartman, Frank Tashlin, d. Norman Z. McLeod. **BOSong** "Buttons and Bows." Oscars: 1-1.

COMEDY: WESTERNS: Western Comedy; Fish out of Water Stories; Undercover; Thieves; Bounty Hunters;

Battle of the Sexes; Law Officers-Female; Dentists; Cowards

(Fancy Pants; Calamity Jane; The Shakiest Gun in the West; The Ruggles of Red Gap)

The Palm Beach Story, 1942, 88m, ★★★★/$$$, Par/MCA-U. A young wife (Claudette Colbert) decides to leave her husband (Joel McCrea) for a millionaire they meet in Palm Beach because her husband couldn't afford their lavish lifestyle and didn't believe a wealthy weinie king had given her money out of simple kindness. Rudy Vallee, Mary Astor, Sig Arno, Robert Dudley, William Demarest, Jack Norton, Robert Greig, Franklin Pangborn. w. d. Preston Sturges.
COMEDY: Romantic Comedy; Screwball Comedy; Marriage Comedy; Marriage for Money; Swapping Partners; Romance-Triangles; Eccentric People; Rich People; Jetsetters; Identities-Assumed; Hidden Gems; Writer-Directors

(Easy Living; The Lady Eve; Midnight)

Panama Hattie, 1942, 79m, ★★/$$, MGM/MGM-UA. In Panama during World War II, a cabaret singer helps our boys capture some Nazis. Ann Sothern, Dan Dailey, Red Skelton, Marsha Hunt, Rags Ragland, Virginia O'Brien, Alan Mowbray, Carl Esmond. w. Jack McGowan, Wilkie Mahoney, (Musical)-adap. Herbert Fields, B. G. De Sylva, Cole Porter, d. Norman Z. McLeod.
MUSICALS: COMEDY: Musical Comedy; Nazi Stories; World War II Stories; Military Comedy; Singers; Soldiers

Pandemonium, 1982, 82m, ★★/$, UA/MGM-UA, PG/V. A spoof of teen slasher movies where cheerleaders are de-cheered. Ron Smothers, Carol Kane, Paul Reubens, Judge Reinhold, Tab Hunter, Eve Arden, Eileen Brennan. d. Alfred Sole.
COMEDY: Spoofs-Horror; **HORROR:** Horror Comedy; Serial Killers; Murders of Teenagers; Teenagers; Teenage Movies; Murders-One by One; Teenage Horror Flicks of 80s

(Saturday the 14th; Unmasked, Part 25)

Pandora and the Flying Dutchman, 1950, 122m, ★★1/2/$$, Romulus/NA. A beautiful but somewhat passionless American woman travels to Spain and is transformed when she falls in love with a ghost. She is so committed she decides to kill herself to be with him for eternity. James Mason, Ava Gardner, Harold

Warrender, Nigel Patrick, Sheila Sim, Mario Cabre, John Laurie, Pamela Kellino, Marius Goring. w. d. Albert Lewin.
MELODRAMA: ROMANCE: Ghosts; Americans Abroad; Romance on Vacation; Vacations-European; Female Protagonists; Forgotten Films; Writer-Directors

(The Ghost and Mrs. Muir)

Pandora's Box, 1929, 97m, B&W, silent, ★★★★/$$, Nero Film/Vidmark. After she murders her lover, a "bad woman" takes up the oldest profession, after which she's murdered by Jack the Ripper. Louise Brooks, Fritz Kortner, Franz Lederer, Gustav Diessl. w. G. W. Pabst, Laszlo Wajda, P-adap. Franz Wedekind (*Erdgeist and Pandora's Box*), d. G. W. Pabst.
SUSPENSE: TRAGEDY: MURDER: Prostitutes-Low Class; Prostitutes-Ordinary People Turned Murderers-Female; Serial Killers; Jack the Ripper; Murders of Women; Female Protagonists; Silent Films

Panic in Needle Park, 1971, 110m, ★★★/$, 20th/Fox, R/P-S-FN-MN. In a sleazy section of New York, a junkie and his girlfriend deal with the trials of lowlife drug culture, including violent drug pushers and cops. Al Pacino, Kitty Winn, Adam Vint, Richard Bright, Kiel Martin. w. Joan Didion, John Gregory Dunne, N-adap. James Mills, d. Jerry Schatzberg.
DRAMA: Drugs-Addictions; Drugs Dealing; 1970s; Psychedelic Era; Police Corruption; Police Brutality; Anti-Establishment Films; New York Life; Inner City Life

(Serpico; Joe; Cruising; Desperate Characters; The Strawberry Statement)

Panic in the Streets, 1950, 96m, ★★★/$$$, 20th/Fox. In New Orleans in the late 40s, a health inspector seeks out the person spreading bubonic plague as public hysteria mounts. Richard Widmark, Jack Palance, Paul Douglas, Barbara Bel Geddes, Zero Mostel. w. Richard Murphy, Edward and Edna Anhalt, **BOStory**. d. Elia Kazan. Oscars: 1-1.
DRAMA: Epidemics; Detective Stories; Medical Detectives; New Orleans; Faded Hits

(Boomerang; Outbreak)

Panic in the Year Zero, 1962, 93m, ★★1/2/$, AIP/New World. A lucky family is camping up in the mountains when an

atom bomb hits L.A., but they must live like primitives and rebuild society. Ray Milland, Jean Hagen, Frankie Avalon, Joan Freeman. w. Jay Simms, John Morton, d. Ray Milland.
SCI-FI: DRAMA: ADVENTURE: Apocalyptic Stories; Bombs-Atomic; Family Drama; Camping; Forgotten Films

(On the Beach; Testament; The Day After)

Papa's Delicate Condition, 1963, 98m, ★★★/$$$, Par/Par. In the early 1900s, in a backwater in Texas, a normally friendly father becomes beligerent when he hits too much of the sauce. Jackie Gleason, Glynis Johns, Charles Ruggles, Charles Lane, Laurel Goodwin, Juanita Moore, Elisha Cook, Jr. w. Jack Rose, NF-adap. Corinne Griffith, d. George Marshall. **BOSong**. Oscars: 1-1.
COMEDY: COMEDY DRAMA: Alcoholics; Fathers-Troublesome; Small-town Life; 1900s; Texas

(The Lost Weekend; Gigot; The Hustler; Life with Father)

The Paper, 1994, 112m, ★★1/2/$$, Col/Col, R/S-P. When a paper staff believes two black boys to be unjustly accused of a crime, the tensions of how to handle the story rise and infringe upon their personal lives. Michael Keaton, Glenn Close, Robert Duvall, Marisa Tomei, Jason Robards, Catherine O'Hara, Jason Alexander, Spalding Gray. w. David Koepp, Steven Koepp, d. Ron Howard.
DRAMA: COMEDY DRAMA: Newspapers; Journalists; Accused Unjustly; Power Struggles; Battle of the Sexes; Mean Women; Multiple Stories; Interwoven Stories; Marriage Drama

(The Front Page; Five Star Final; All the President's Men)

The Paper Chase, 1973, 111m, ★★★/$$$, 20th/CBS-Fox, R/P-S. A law student (Timothy Bottoms) butts heads with a stern professor (John Houseman, **BSActor**), and while struggling to make it in class, winds up dating the professor's daughter (Lindsay Wagner). w. d. James Bridges (BAScr), N-adap. John Jay Osborn. Oscars: 2-1.
DRAMA: ROMANCE: College Life; Lawyers; Law School; Stern Men; Professors; Pre-life Crisis; Young Men; Lovers; Family Dislikes; Romance with Boss' Child
SEQUEL: TV Series, 1978–79.

Paper Lion, 1968, 105m, ★★½/$$, 20th/NA. A writer sneaks into the Detroit Lions' line-up and sees what it's like. Alan Alda, Lauren Hutton, David Doyle, Sugar Ray Robinson. w. Lawrence Roman, d. Alex March.
DRAMA: COMEDY DRAMA: Journalists; Undercover; Sports Movies; Football; Fish out of Water Stories; Nerds vs. Macho Men

Paper Marriage, 1993, 88m, ★★/$, Academy/Academy, PG/S. When a woman comes from Poland with an English fellow who promptly dumps her, she finds a con artist to marry her so she can stay. Gary Kempy, Joanna Trepeschinska, Rita Tushingham. w. Marek Kreutz, Krsyztof Land, d. Lang.
COMEDY: ROMANCE: Romantic Comedy; Marriage for Citizenship; Marriage of Convenience; Polish People; Con Artists; Female Protagonists; British Films
(Green Card; Does This Mean We're Married?)

Paper Moon, 1973, 102m, ★★★★/ $$$$, Par/Par, PG. A con artist (Ryan O'Neal) hawking Bibles across the midwest in the Depression goes to a funeral and winds up with a feisty little girl (Tatum O'Neal, **BSActress**) who may be his daughter and more clever than himself. Madeline Kahn (BSactress). John Hillerman, Randy Quaid. w. Alvin Sargent (BAScr), N-adap. Joe David Brown (*Addie Pray*), d. Peter Bogdanovich. Oscars: 3-1.
COMEDY DRAMA: Road Movies; Con Artists; Fathers & Daughters; Men and Girls; Bootleggers; Fugitives from the Mob; Depression Era; Midwestern Life; Children-Little Adults; Feisty Females; Prostitutes-Low Class
REMAKE/SPINOFF: TV series, 1974, starring Jodie Foster.
(Nickelodeon; Little Miss Marker; Curly Sue)

Paper Tiger, 1975, 99m, ★★/$, Ind/Sultan. A Japanese boy and his English tutor both get involved in international intrigue. David Niven, Toshiro Mifune, Hardy Kruger, Ando, Ivan Desny, Irene Tsu, Miiko Taka, Ronald Fraser, Jeff Corey. w. Jack Davies, d. Ken Annakin.
COMEDY: Marital Arts; Spy Films; Spies; Indentities-Assumed; Teachers and Students; Forgotten Films

Paperhouse, 1988, 92m, ★★★/$, Vestron/Vestron, PG-13/V. A girl draws pictures of a house with a boy in the window, and enters the world of her drawing to free the boy from the house which may burn and kill him. Charlotte Burke, Ben Cross, Glenne Headley, Elliott Spiers, Gemma Jones. w. Matthew Jacobs, N-adap. Catherine Storr (*Marianne's Dream*), d. Bernard Rose.
HORROR: Fantasy; Nightmares; Girls; Boys; Hidden Gems; Overlooked at Release
(Afraid of the Dark; The Lady in White)

Papillon, 1973, 150m, ★★★/$$$$, Allied/Fox, PG. Story of French thief sent to Devil's Island and his unique friendship with a man there before planning an epic escape. Steve McQueen, Dustin Hoffman, Victor Jory, Anthony Zerbe. d. Franklin J. Schaffner, NF-adap. Henri Charriere.
DRAMA: ADVENTURE: Prison Drama; Prison Escapes; Islands; Thieves; Escape Adventure; Friendships-Male; Faded Hits
(Passage to Marseilles; Devil Doll)

The Paradine Case, 1947, 115m, ★★★/$$$, David O. Selznick-UA/Key. A defense attorney risks his professional career when he falls in love with his client in a murder case. Gregory Peck, Alida Valli, Ann Todd, Louis Jourdan, Charles Laughton, Charles Coburn, Ethel Barrymore, Leo G. Carroll. w. David O. Selznick, N-adap. Robert Hichens, d. Alfred Hitchcock.
DRAMA: SUSPENSE: MYSTERY: MURDER: MURDER MYSTERY: ROMANCE: Courtroom Drama; Trials; Lawyers; Romance-Unprofessional; Ethics; Hitchcockian
(Witness for the Prosecution)

Paradise, 1982, 96m, ★★/$, Embassy/Col, R/S-FN-MRN. A boy and girl in a secret oasis discover each other's secret parts. Phoebe Cates, Willie Aames, Richard Curnock. d. Stuart Gillard.
MELODRAMA: ROMANCE: Erotic Drama; Teenagers; Teenage Movies; Camp (The Blue Lagoon)

Paradise, 1991, 110m, ★★½/$$, Touchstone/Touchstone, PG. A childless couple receives a breath of fresh air one summer when a ten-year-old boy comes to visit. He meets a girl and has a great time. Melanie Griffith, Don Johnson, Elijah Wood, Thora Birch, Sheila McCarthy, Eve Gordon, Louise Latham,

Greg Travis, Sarah Trigger. w. d. Mary Ages Donoghue.
MELODRAMA: FAMILY: Family Drama; Women-Childless; Children-Adopted; ROMANCE: Love-First; Boys; Foreign Film Remakes
REMAKE OF Le Grand Chemin. (My Girl; The War)

Paradise Alley, 1978, 107m, ★★/$$, U/MCA-U, R/V. In the 40s, three brothers compete in the underground world of prize wrestling in New York's Hell's Kitchen. Sylvester Stallone, Kevin Conway, Anne Archer, Joe Spinell, Armand Assante, Lee Canalito. w. d. Sylvester Stallone.
MELODRAMA: Sports Movies; Wrestling; 1940s; Italians; Brothers; Writer-Directors
(F.I.S.T.; Cobra; Rocky SERIES)

The Parallax View, 1974, 102m, ★★★/$$, Par/Par, PG/V. A reporter (Warren Beatty) stumbles onto a few mysterious deaths and soon finds a trail leading to a large political assassination conspiracy. Paula Prentiss, William Daniels, Hume Cronyn, Walter McGinn. w. David Giler, Lorenzo Semple, Jr., N-adap. Loren Singer, d. Alan J. Pakula.
MYSTERY: SUSPENSE: MURDER MYSTERY: Murders-One by One; Conspiracy; Assassination Plots; Political Drama; Psychological Thriller; Journalists as Detectives; Journalists; Detective Stories; Coulda Been Great; Forgotten Films
(The Manchurian Candidate; Winter Kills; Three Days of the Condor; Saboteur; North by Northwest; The Naked Runner)

Paranoia, 1963, 80m, ★★/$, U-I/NA. A neurotic woman spirals into a depression, but is rescued at the point of attempting suicide by a man who claims to be her dead brother. Oliver Reed, Janette Scott, Alexander Davion, Sheila Burrell, Liliane Brousse, Maurice Denham. w. Jimmy Sagster, d. Freddie Francis.
MELODRAMA: MYSTERY: Impostors; Identities-Assumed; Suicidal Tendencies; Brothers & Sisters; Con Artists; British Films

Pardners, 1956, 88m, ★★★/$$$, Par/Par. A goofball from New York takes over as sheriff down in the desert; but if not for the help of a suave local, he may be run out on a rail and never get a girl. Jerry Lewis, Dean Martin, Lori Nelson, Agnes Moorehead, Lon Chaney, Lee Van

Cleef, Jack Elam. w. Sidney Sheldon, Jerry Davis. d. Norman Taurog.
COMEDY: Fish out of Water Stories; Fools-Bumbling; Southwestern Life; WESTERNS: Western Comedy; MUSICALS: Musical Comedy; Music Movies; Faded Hits
(Living It Up; California or Bust)

Pardon Mon Affaire, 1977, 108m, ★★★/$$, Gaumont/Sultan. A man in full-tilt mid-life crisis mode has a desperate affair, but is so clumsy about it that his wife is more amused than upset. Jean Rochefort, Claude Brasseur, Guy Bedos, Victor Lanoux, Danielle Delorme, Any Duperey. w. Jean-Loup Dabadie, Yves Robert, d. Yves Robert.
COMEDY DRAMA: Cheating Men; Comedy of Errors; Marriage Comedy; Midlife Crisis; Nerds; French Films
SEQUEL: Pardon Mon Affaire, Too!
(Le Cavaleur; The Tall Blond Man with One Black Shoe)

The Parent Trap, 1961, 129m, ★★★1/2/$$$$, Disney/Disney. At summer camp, the twin daughters of a separated couple who've accidentally met devise a plan to get them back together by switching identities. Hayley Mills, Maureen O'Hara, Brian Keith, Charles Ruggles, Leo G. Carroll, Una Merkel, Joanna Barnes, Cathleen Nesbitt, Ruth McDevitt, Nancy Kulp. w. d. David Swift, N-adap. Erich Kastner.
(Das Doppelte Lottchen)
COMEDY: CHILDREN'S: FAMILY: Comedy-Disney; Sisters; Twins; Body Switching; Identities-Assumed; Camping; Girls; Divorce; Child Protagonists; Blockbusters
Two TV Movie sequels.
(Three Smart Girls; All I Want for Christmas; The Man in the Iron Mask)

Parenthood, 1989, 124m, Universal/MCA-U, ★★★★/$$$$$. The foibles and trials of several parents raising small children as they deal with transitions in their own lives. Steve Martin, Mary Steenburgen, Dianne Wiest (BSActress), Rick Moranis, Jason Robards, Keanu Reeves, Tom Hulce. w. Lowell Ganz, Babaloo Mandell, d. Ron Howard. BOSong. Oscars: 2-0.
COMEDY DRAMA: COMEDY: FAMILY: Family Comedy; Ensemble Films; Parents vs. Children; Marriage Comedy; Fathers & Daughters; Mothers & Daughters;

Fathers & Sons; Mothers & Sons; Children-Problem; Mothers Alone; All-Star Casts; Suburban Life; Blockbusters
(Bye Bye Love; The Good Father; She's Having My Baby; All of Me)

Parents, 1988, 82m, ★★★/$, Vestron/Vestron, R/EV-B&G. A child in the suburbs in the fifties has enough normal problems growing up, let alone the fact that his parents are cannibals. Randy Quaid, Mary Beth Hurt, Sandy Dennis, Bryan Madorsky, Graham Jarvis. w. Christopher Hawthorne, d. Bob Balaban.
COMEDY: Family Comedy; Black Comedy; Human Eaters; Cannibals; Suburban Life; SATIRE: 1950s; Hidden Gems; Curiosities
(Motel Hell; The Cook, The Thief, His Wife & Her Lover)

Paris Blues, 1961, 98m, ★★★/$, UA/MGM-UA. A look at the private and public lives of American jazz musicians in Paris circa 1961. Paul Newman, Joanne Woodward, Sidney Poitier, Louis Armstrong, Diahann Carroll, Serge Reggiani, Barbara Laage. w. Jack Sher, Irene Kamp, Walter Bernstein, N-adap. Harold Flender, d. Martin Ritt.
DRAMA: ROMANCE: Romantic Drama; Jazz Life; Musicians; Americans Abroad; Paris; Forgotten Films
(Too Late Blues; Round Midnight; A New Kind of Love; The Hustler; All the Fine Young Cannibals)

Paris By Night, 1988, 103m, ★★/$, Virgin/Virgin, R. A British government official's personal daliances get the best of him and interfere with his public life. Charlotte Rampling, Michael Gambon, Robert Hardy, Iain Glen, Jane Asher, Andrew Ray, Niamh Cusack, Jonathan White. w. d. David Hare.
DRAMA: Art Films; Psychological Drama; Politicians; Marriage Drama; Nervous Breakdowns; Playboys; Dual Lives; British Films; Overlooked at Release; Writer-Directors
(Damage; Strapless; Wetherley)

Paris Holiday, 1957, 101m, ★★1/2/$$, UA/MCA-U. An American and a French comedian find the key to cracking a counterfeit ring in the script of the film they're shooting together in Paris. Bob Hope, Fernandel, Anita Ekberg, Martha Hyer, Andre Morell, Maurice Tenyac, Jean Murat, Preston Sturges. w. Edmund Beloin, Dean Riesner, d. Gerd Oswald.

COMEDY: Capers; Counterfeiters; Paris; Moviemaking; Comedians; Writers
(I'll Take Sweden; My Favorite Brunette)

Paris Is Burning, 1991, 71m, ★★★/$$$, 20th/Fox, R/S-P. Documentary dance movie about transvestites on the club scene of the 80s. Dorian Corey, Pepper Labeija, Venus Xtravaganza. d. Jennie Livingston.
Documentaries; Transvestites; Dance Movies; Nightclubs; New York Life; 1980s; Gay Men; Female Directors; Cult Films; Sleeper Hits
(To Wong Foo . . . ; Priscilla, Queen of the Desert)

Paris Model, 1953, 88m, ★★1/2/$$, NA. The disparate stories of four women in Paris, linked only by the fact that at some point in each, the woman buys the same gown. Paulette, Eva Gabor, Marilyn Maxwell, Barbara Lawrence, Tom Conway, Leif Erickson, Florence Bates, Cecil Kellaway, Robert Hutton. w. Robert Smith, d. Alfred E. Green.
MELODRAMA: Models; Fashion World; Hand Me Down Stories; Multiple Stories; Paris
(A New Kind of Love; The Yellow Rolls Royce)

Paris, Texas, 1984, 148m, ★★★/$$, 20th/Fox, R/P. A destitute drifter, separated from his wife, walks through the California desert to his brother's house where his son is staying. He and his son then journey to Texas to find his wife, and are horrified to find her working in a porno booth. Harry Dean Stanton, Dean Stockwell, Aurore Clement, Hunter Carson, Nastassja Kinski, Bernhard Wicki. w. Sam Shepard, d. Wim Wenders.
DRAMA: Art Films; Drifters; Texas; Prostitutes-Low Class; Mothers & Sons; Divorce
(The American Friend; The Starving Class)
(Ed: Much more pretense than reality, starting with Kinski's miscasting)

Paris Trout, 1991, 98m, ★★★1/2/$$$, HBO/HBO, R/V-P. A tyrannical store owner (Dennis Hopper) in Georgia in the 40s can't believe it's a crime to kill a black person when he suddenly finds himself on trial for murder. Barbara Hershey, Ed Harris, Ray McKinon, Tina Lifford, Darnita Henry, Eric Ware. w. N-adap. Pete Dexter, d. Stephen Gyllenhaal. Emmy winner.
DRAMA: Political Drama; Race Relations; White vs. Black; Evil Men;

Abusive Men; Bigots; White Supremacists; Southerns; TV Movies (Mississippi Burning; The Klansman; Cobb)

Paris When It Sizzles, 1963, 110m, ★★★/$$, Par/Par. A screenwriter and his secretary try out script ideas, which are presented as little "movies within a movie." William Holden, Audrey Hepburn, Gregoire Aslan, Noel Coward, Raymond Bussieres. w. George Axelrod, (Screenplay)-adap. Julien Duvivier, Henri Jeanson, d. Richard Quine.

COMEDY: Comedy-Light; ROMANCE: Romantic Comedy; Secretaries; Writers; Fantasies; Paris; Moviemaking; Hidden Gems

(Funny Face; How to Steal a Million; Delirious)

(Ed: May not be profound, but so beautiful, it's hard to resist)

Parlor, Bedroom and Bath, 1931, 72m, ★★/$$, MGM/NA. A henpecked husband becomes a landlord and is besieged by everyone in the building. Buster Keaton, Charlotte Greenwood, Reginald Denny, Cliff Edwards. w. Richard Schayer, Robert Hopkins, P-adap. Charles W. Bell, d. Edward Sedgwick.

COMEDY: Comedy-Slapstick; Apartment Buildings; Marriage Comedy; Fools-Bumbling; Forgotten Films

(The Tenant; The Super; No Down Payment)

Parnell, 1937, 115m, ★★¹/₂/$$$, MGM/NA. In the 1800s, an Irish politician nearly loses it all under the threat of a scandal because of a dalliance with a married woman. Clark Gable, Myrna Loy, Edmund Gwenn, Edna May Oliver, Alan Marshal, Donald Crisp, Billie Burke, Berton Churchill, Donald Meek, Montagu Love, George Zucco. w. John Van Druten, S. N. Berhman, P-adap. Elsie T. Schauffler, d. John M. Stahl.

MELODRAMA: Scandals; Politicans; Romance with Married Person; Cheating Men; Ireland; 1800s; Forgotten Films

Parsifal, 1982, 255m, ★★★/$$, Ind/NA. In Wagner's famous opera, King Arthur is dying and sends the knights of the round table to search for the Holy Grail that he might drink and rejuvenate. The innocent and simple Parsifal is the only knight pure enough to find it. Michael Kutter, Karin Krick, Edith Clever, Armin Jordan, Robert Lloyd, Aage Haugland. w.

Richard Wagner, d. Hans Jurgen Syberberg.

MUSICALS: Opera; TRAGEDY: Camelot Stories; Kings; Redemption; British Films

Parting Glances, 1986, 90m, ★★★/$, Ind/Fox, R/S-P. When a gay couple is about to split because of a move, one is distracted because of a friend's battle with AIDS. John Bolger, Steve Buscemi, Richard Ganoung, Adam Nathan. w. d. Bill Sherwood.

MELODRAMA: Gay Men; Gay Films; AIDS Stories; Marriage on the Rocks; Writer-Directors

(Fun Down There; Lie Down with Dogs; An Early Frost; Philadelphia)

(Ed: Okay, but nothing great)

The Party, 1968, 98m, ★★★/$, UA/MGM-UA. A chic Hollywood party goes awry when a klutzy Indian actor gets invited by mistake and wreaks havoc. Peter Sellers, Claudine Longet, Marge Champion, Fay McKenzie, Steve Franken, Buddy Lester. w. Blake Edwards, Rom and Frank Waldman, d. Blake Edwards.

COMEDY: Comedy-Slapstick; Comedy of Errors; Party Movies; Hollywood Satire; Indians; Fools-Bumbling; Hidden Gems; Forgotten Films; Overlooked at Release

(The Pink Panther; The Mouse That Roared)

The Party and the Guests, 1966, 71m, ★★★/$, NA. A political allegory about a garden wedding party in which a timid guest is shut out (just like a tyrannical political party). w. Ester Krumbachova, Jan Nemec, d. Jan Nemec.

DRAMA: SATIRE: Political Drama; Weddings; Ostracism; Curiosities; Art Films; Allegorical Stories; Female Screenwriters

Party Girl, 1958, 99m, ★★★/$$, MGM/MGM-UA. A mobster meets a dancer who convinces him to get out, but when he does, and turns witness for the government, they take the girl hostage. Robert Taylor, Cyd Charisse, Lee J. Cobb, John Ireland, Kent Smith. d. Nicholas Ray.

MUSICALS: MELODRAMA: Musical Drama; Musical Romance; Crime Drama; Mob Stories; Dancers; ROMANCE: Romantic Drama; Fugitives from the Mob; Hidden Gems; Forgotten Films; Hidden Gems

(Silk Stockings; Murder Inc.)

Party Girl, 1995, 98m, ★★★/$, First Look-Ind/NA, R/P-S. A wacky city girl throws a rent party for herself to curb a

pre-life crisis in this character study of a modern daffy dame. Parker Posey, Omar Townsend, Sasha von Scherler, Guillermo Diaz, Anthony DeSando, Donna Mitchell, Liev Schreiber, Nicole Bobbitt. w. Daisy von Scherler Mayer, Harry Birckmayer, & Sheila Gaffney, d. Mayer.

COMEDY: Young Women; Neurotic People; Pre-Life Crisis; New York Life; Character Studies; Female Protagonists; Female Screenwriters; Female Directors; Independent Films

The Party's Over, 1963, 94m, ★★¹/₂/$, Tricastle/NA. A suburban American family man investigates in the world of swinging London when his daughter dies in a "fall" from a balcony at a London party. Oliver Reed, Eddie Albert, Ann Lynn, Louise Sorel. w. Marc Behm, d. Guy Hamilton.

DRAMA: Mod Era; Death-Accidental; Fathers & Daughters; Detective Stories; Americans Abroad; England

(Joe; Blow-Up; Missing)

Pascali's Island, 1988, 104m, ★★★/$, Virgin/Live, PG-13. In the 1900s, on an island off the coast of Greece, a Turkish agent and a British confidence trickster play a game of cat-and-mouse. Ben Kingsley, Charles Dance, Helen Mirren, Stefan Gryff, George Marcull, Nadim Sawalha, T. P. McKenna. w. d. James Dearden, N-adap. Barry Unsworth.

SUSPENSE: Spy Films; Spies; Islands; 1900s; Mediterranean; Cat and Mouse Mindgames; Quiet Little Films

(Journey into Fear; Eye of the Needle)

The Passage, 1978, 98m, ★★/$, Hemdale/Hemdale. A scientist must escape from Nazi-occupied France during World War II and is escorted through the Pyrenees into Spain by a Basque shepherd. Anthony Quinn, James Mason, Malcolm McDowell, Patricia Neal, Kay Lenz, Paul Clemens, Christopher Lee. w. N-adap. Bruce Micolaysen (The Perilous Passage), d. J. Lee Thompson.

DRAMS: Escape Drama; Nazi Stories; World War II Stories; Scientists; Disguises

Pass the Ammo, 1988, 93m, ★★/$, Vista/Live. A TV preacher in Arkansas gets an old woman's last penny, but a couple who was expecting it as inheritance wants it back. Bill Paxton, Linda Koslowski, Annie Potts, Anthony Geary, Tim Curry. w. Neil Cohen, Joel Cohen, d. David Beaird.

COMEDY: SATIRE: Preachers; Inheritances at Stake; Religion; Turning the Tables; Corruption; TV Life; Mountain People; Arkansas; Southerns; Rednecks; Good Premise Unfulfilled (Americathon; The Jim & Tammy Faye Bakker Story [TV, 1989])

A Passage to India, 1984, 163m, ★★★★/$$$, Columbia/RCA-Col, PG. A young British woman (Judy Davis, BActress) travels to India with an older woman (Peggy Ashcroft, **BSActress**) and finds herself attracted to a young Indian tour guide (Victor Bannerjee), but is soon accusing him of rape when she may not be able to remember what really happened. Alec Guinness, Edward Fox. w. David Lean (BAScr), adap. E. M. Forster, d. David Lean (BDirector). BPicture, BCinema, BArt, BCostume, BEditing, BSound, **BOScore**. Oscars: 11-2.
DRAMA: Epics; ADVENTURE: Courtroom Drama; Young Women; Rape/Rapists; Vacations; India; Violence-Sudden; Accused Unjustly; Elderly Women; Illusions/Hallucinations; British
(To Kill a Mockingbird; Where Angels Fear to Tread; A Room with a View)

Passage to Marseilles, 1944, 110m, ★★★/$$$, WB/Fox. Prisoners on Devil's Island plan an elaborate escape and make the treacherous journey to Marseilles to join the Free French. Humphrey Bogart, Michele Morgan, Claude Rains, Philip Dorn, Sidney Greenstreet, Peter Lorre, Helmut Dantine, George Tobias, John Loder, Victor Francen, Eduardo Cianelli. w. Casey Robinson, Jack Moffit, Charles Nordhoff, James Hall, d. Michael Curtiz.
ADVENTURE: Prison Drama; Prison Escape; Journies; Thieves; Faded Hits; France
(Papillon; Devil Doll)

Passed Away, 1992, 96m, ★★/$, Hollywood/Hollywood, PG-13/P-S. A motley crew of relatives converge after the death of daddy and finds themselves in various comic situations and conflicts. William Petersen, Bob Hoskins, Tim Curry, Pamela Reed, Nancy Travis, Maureen Stapleton, Jack Warden, Peter Reigert, Teri Polo, Frances McDormand. w. d. Charlie Peters.
COMEDY: COMEDY DRAMA: Family Comedy; Funerals; Inheritances at Stake; Brothers & Sisters; Eccentric People;

Coulda Been Good; Writer-Directors (A Wedding; Greedy; Daddy's Dyin')
The Passenger, 1975, 119m, ★★★/$$, UA/MGM-UA, R. A television journalist staying in a hotel in a desert community swaps identities with a man who turns out to have been an African gun smuggler on the run from criminals. Jack Nicholson, Maria Schneider, Jenny Runacre, Ian Hendry. w. Mark Peploe, Peter Wollen, Michelangelo Antonioni, d. Michelangelo Antonioni.
DRAMA: Political Drama; Africa; Journalists; Journalists as Detectives; Art Films; Identities-Assumed; Arms Dealers; Conspiracy; Innocent Bystanders; Cult Films
(Last Tango in Paris; The Sheltering Sky)

Passenger 57, 1992, 84m, ★★1/2/$$$, WB/WB, R/EV-P. A slick terrorist takes over a plane while en route, and it's up to a renegade cop to get on the flight and take him over. Wesley Snipes, Tom Sizemore, Alex Dachter, Bruce Payne, Robert Hooks. w. David Loughery, d. Kevin Hooks.
ACTION: Airplanes; Terrorists; Police-Vigilante; Die Hard Plots; Evil Men; Black Men; Black Directors
(Die Hard; Cliffhanger; Under Siege; Executive Decision)
(Ed: Die Hard on a plane)

The Passing of the Third Floor Back, 1935, 90m, ★★1/2/$, Gaumont/Sultan. At a London boardinghouse, a mysterious stranger changes the lives of the residents with his selfless, Christlike acts of charity. Conrad Veidt, Rene Ray, Anna Lee, Frank Cellier, Mary Clare, Beatrix Leahmann, Cathleen Nesbitt, Sara Allgood. w. Michael Hogan, Alma Reville, P-adap. Jerome K. Jerome, d. Berthold Viertel.
MELODRAMA: Saintly People; MYSTERY: Life Transitions; Starting Over; Apartment Buildings; Curiosities

Passion, 1982, 88m, ★★1/2/$, New Yorker/NA. In France, a factory owner falls in love with an expatriate Polish film director. Isabelle Huppert, Hanna Schygulla, Michel Piccoli, Jerzy Radziwilowicz, Lazlo Szabo, Jean-Francois Stevenin, Patrick Bonnel, Sophie Loucachevsky. w. d. Jean-Luc Godard.
DRAMA: ROMANCE: Erotic Drama; Art Films; Factory Life; Directors; Polish People; French Films; Writer-Directors

(First Name Carmen; Every Man for Himself)
Passion Fish, 1992, 134m, ★★★/$$, Fine Line/Col, R/P. A bitter former soap star convalesces down South after an accident as she develops a lasting friendship with her earthy black nurse, who helps her get back in the game. Mary McDonnell (BActress), Alfre Woodard, David Strathairn, Vondie Curtis-Hall, Nora Dunn, Sheila Kelley, Angela Bassett, Leo Burmester. w. d. John Sayles (BOScr). Oscars: 2-0.
DRAMA: Character Studies; Disabled People; Nurses; Actresses; Soap Operas; Friendships-Female; Mean Women; Starting Over; Black & White Together; Black Women; Swamp Life; Writer-Directors; Female Protagonists
(The Other Side of the Mountain; Lianna)

The Passionate Plumber, 1932, 73m, ★★1/2/$$, MGM/NA. A woman thinks her suitor is too good for her, so she hires a gigolo to seduce her in his presence, hoping that will dissuade him. Buster Keaton, Jimmy Durante, Irene Purcell, Polly Moran, Gilbert Roland, Mona Maris. w. Laurence E. Johnson, P-adap. Frederick Lonsdale (Her Cardboard Lover), d. Edward Sedgwick.
COMEDY: Hired Dates; Jealousy; Marriage-Impending; Romance-Mismatched; Forgotten Films
(The General; Hands Across the Table)

The Passion of Joan of Arc, 1929, 114m, ★★★★/$$$, Ind/Nos, Voyager. The legendary story of the rebellious religious girl who was burned as a heretic. Maria Falconetti, Maurice Schultz. d. Carl Theodore Dreyer.
MELODRAMA: Epics; Religion; Historical Drama; Female Protagonists
(Joan of Arc)

Passport to Pimlico, 1949, 84m, ★★1/2/$$, Ealing/Nos, Prism. In England, after World War II, while the rest of the country continues with rationing, a neighborhood in London gets a reprieve when it's discovered to belong to France. Stanley Holloway, Margaret Rutherford, Basil Radford, Naunton Wayne, Hermione Baddeley, John Slater. w. T. E. B. Clarke, d. Henry Cornelius.
COMEDY: FARCE: Misunderstandings; England; World War II-Post Era; British Films
(A Private Function; The Mouse That Roared)

Past Midnight, 1991, 96m, ★★/$, Cinetel/Col, R/V-S. A social worker visits a prisoner convicted of murdering his pregnant wife and grows to believe in his innocence, and eventually to love him-but she may not be so bright. Rutger Hauer, Natasha Richardson, Clancy Brown. w. Frank Norwood, d. Jan Eliasberg.
SUSPENSE: Prison Drama; Romance-Dangerous; Accused Unjustly; Social Workers; MURDER: Dangerous Men; Overlooked at Release; Independent Films
(Knockback [BBC Series]; Dead Man Walking)

Pat and Mike, 1952, 95m, ★★★1/2/$$$, MGM/MGM-UA. A gutsy sports promoter takes on a new client-a woman tennis and golf whiz-who gives him far more than he bargained for. Spencer Tracy, Katharine Hepburn, Aldo Ray, William Ching, Sammy White. w. Ruth Gordon, Garson Kanin, d. George Cukor.
COMEDY: ROMANCE: Romantic Comedy; Romance-Bickering; Battle of the Sexes; Macho Men; Feisty Females; Sports Movies; Female Screenwriters; Female in Male Domain
(Adam's Rib; Desk Set; Woman of the Year)

Pat Garrett and Billy the Kid, 1973, 106m, ★★1/2/$, MGM/MGM-UA, R/V-S. The legendary historical standoff is presented by the master of the blood-and-guts Western. James Coburn, Kris Kristofferson, Bob Dylan, Richard Jaeckel, Slim Pickens, Chill Wills, Jason Robards, Jr. w. Rudolph Wurlitzer, d. Sam Peckinpah.
ACTION: WESTERNS: Westerns-Neo; Duels; Men in Conflict; Billy the Kid
(The Wild Bunch; Bring Me the Head of Alfredo Garcia; Billy the Kid; The Left-Handed Gun)

A Patch of Blue, 1965, 105m, ★★★1/2/$$$, MGM/MGM-UA. In the slums of New York, a blind white girl is touched by the act of kindness of a black man and she falls in love with him, not realizing he's black, and that her abusive mother won't stand for it. Sidney Poitier, Elizabeth Hartman (BActress), Shelley Winters (BSActress), Wallace Ford, Ivan Dixon. w. N-adap. Elizabeth Kata (Be Ready with Bells and Drums), d. Guy Green. BB&WArt, BB&WCin. Oscars: 4-1.

DRAMA: ROMANCE: Romantic Drama; Romance-Interracial; Romance-Forbidden; Black vs. White; Bigots; Blind People; Abused Women; Mothers-Troublesome; Black Men; Quiet Little Films; Hidden Gems; Faded Hits
(Johnny Belinda; Guess Who's Coming to Dinner; Sundays & Cybele; Sudie & Simpson)

Paternity, 1981, 93m, ★★1/2/$$, Par/Par, PG. A childless confirmed bachelor hires a surrogate mother to help him realize his dream of having a child. But things don't go as smoothly as he'd hoped. Burt Reynolds, Beverly D'Angelo, Norman Fell, Paul Dooley, Elizabeth Ashley, Lauren Hutton, Juanita Moore. w. Charlie Peters, d. David Steinberg.
COMEDY DRAMA: Fathers Alone; Babies-Having; Mothers-Surrogate; Romance-Choosing the Right Person; Single Men; Good Premise Unfulfilled
(Starting Over; Hired Wife)

Pathfinder, 1987, 86m, ★★★1/2/$$, Fox-Lorber/Fox-Lorber, PG. In the bleak, snowy landscape of Norway, a band of outlaws captures a boy and makes him lead them to his village so that they can rob its goods. Mikkel Gaup, Nils Utsi, Svein Scharffenberg, Helgi Skulason, Sverre Porsanger. w. d. Nils Gaup. BFLFilm. Oscars: 1-0.
DRAMA: Kidnappings; Thieves; Boys; Child Protagonists; Snow Settings; Scandinavia; Writer-Directors; Hidden Gems

Paths of Glory, 1957, 86m, ★★★1/2/$$, UA/MGM-UA. In 1916, French soldiers fight among the castles of Normandy and are betrayed by the ineptitude of their commanders. Kirk Douglas, Adolphe Menjou, George Macready, Wayne Morris, Richard Anderson, Timothy Carey. w. Stanley Kubrick, Calder Willingham, Jim Thompson, N-adap. Humphrey Cobb, d. Stanley Kubrick.
Action Drama; DRAMA: Power Struggles; Cowards; Men in Conflict; War Stories; World War I Stories; Anti-War Films; France; British Films; Hidden Gems
(Gallipoli; A Bridge Too Far; Midnight Clear)

Patriot Games, 1992, 117m, ★★★1/2/$$$$, Par/Par, PG-13/V-P. When an American military officer (Harrison Ford) foils an IRA terrorist attempt and kills one of the assailants, the dead man's brother avows revenge on the American

and his family, using every means necessary to get to America to do it. Anne Archer, Patrick Bergin, Sean Bean, Thora Birch, James Fox, Samuel L. Jackson, Polly Walker, James Earl Jones, Richard Harris, Hugh Fraser. w. W. Peter Iliff, Donald Stewart, Steven Zaillian, N-adap. Tom Clancy, d. Phillip Noyce.
SUSPENSE: ACTION: Spy Films; Spies; Revenge; Avenging Death of Loved One; Protecting Someone; Race Against Time; IRA; Terrorists; CIA Agents; Malicious Menaces; Criminal Pursues Good Guy's Family; Americans Abroad; Heroes-Ordinary
SEQUEL TO: The Hunt for Red October;
SEQUEL: Clear and Present Danger.
(Clear and Present Danger; Cape Fear; Fatal Attraction; The Hunt for Red October)

The Patsy, 1964, 101m, ★★1/2/$, Par/Par. A comedian dies and his desperate and greedy managers find a look-alike bellboy and try to train him to do the deceased comic's schtick. Jerry Lewis, Everett Sloane, Peter Lorre, John Carradine, Phil Harris, Hans Conreid, Ina Balin. w. d. Jerry Lewis.
COMEDY: Comedy of Errors; Fools-Bumbling; Comedy-Character; Lookalikes; Comedians
(Moon Over Parador; The Bellboy; The Errand Boy; On the Double)

Patterns, 1956, 88m, ★★★1/2/$, UA/MGM-UA, Nos. In the cutthroat world of New York big business in the fifties, a conniving boss orchestrates conflict between a young executive and an ineffectual old paper-pusher. Van Heflin, Everett Sloane, Ed Begley, Beatrice Straight, Elizabeth Wilson. w. P-adap. Rod Serling, d. Fielder Cook.
DRAMA: Character Studies; Social Drama; Executives; Business Life; Men in Conflict; Pwoer Struggles; Time Capsules; 1950s; Men's Films; Mindgames; Hidden Gems; Overlooked at Release; Stagelike Films
(Executive Suite; The Man in the Grey Flannel Suit; The Apartment; Madison Avenue)
(Ed: Probably coming after Executive Suite didn't help much, but well worth seeing)

Patti Rocks, 1987, 87m, ★★1/2/$, Ind/Prism, R/EP-S-MFN. A jockish brute is persuaded by his more sensitive married friend to see his pregnant girlfriend.

So on the road they go, griping all the way. Chris Mulkey, John Jenkins, Karen Landry, David L. Turk, Stephen Yoakam. w. David Burton Morris, Chris Mulkey, John Jenkins, Karen Landry, d. David Burton Morris.

COMEDY DRAMA: Character Studies; Buddy Films; Road Movies; Men's Films; Young Men; Friendships-Male; Midwestern Life; Macho Men; Mean Men; Independent Films; Female Screenwriters
(Withnail and I; The Brothers McMullen)

Patton, 1970, 171m, ★★★¹/₂/$$$$, 20th/CBS-Fox, PG/V. The story of the crusty and tyrannical general (George C. Scott, **BActor**) who led the European assault in World War II, chronicling his strange and somewhat deranged personal life after the war. w. Francis Ford Coppola, Edmund H. North (**BOScr**), d. Franklin J. Schaffner (**BDirector**). **BPicture, BArt, BSound, BEdit,** BOScore. Oscars: 8-7.

DRAMA: Biographies; War Movies; Military Movies; World War II Stories; Leaders-Military; Leaders-Tyrannical; Stern Men; Mean Men; Monologues-Interior; Narrated Films; Faded Hits
(MacArthur; The Hospital; Cobb)

Patty Hearst, 1988, 108m, ★★★/$, Atlantic/Par, R/V-P. The true story of heiress Patty Hearst (Natasha Richardson) who was kidnapped and then brainwashed into serving with her terrorist bankrobbing captors. William Forsythe, Ving Rhames, Frances Fisher, Jodi Long, Marek Johnson, Dana Delaney. w. Nicholas Kazan, NF-adap. Patty Hearst, Alvin Moscow (*Every Secret Thing*), d. Paul Schrader.

DRAMA: Biographies; True Stories; Terrorists; Kidnappings; Kidnappers-Sympathizing with; Heiresses; 1970s; Psychedelic Era
(Katherine)

Pauline at the Beach, 1983, 94m, ★★★/$$, Ind/Media, PG/S. A group of chic French people vacationing on the beach play musical beds and get hurt while the younger cousin of one of the women remains above the fray, watching them all with bemused detachment. Arielle Dombasle, Amanda Langlet, Pascal Greggory, Feodor Atkine, Simon de la Brosse, Rosette. w. d. Eric Rohmer.

COMEDY DRAMA: ROMANCE: Romantic Comedy; Cheating Men; Cheating Women; Multiple Stories;

Beach Movies; Romance on Vacation; Sexy Women; French Films; Writer-Directors
(Boyfriends and Girlfriends; Summer; Miami Rhapsody; L'Annee des Meduses)

The Pawnbroker, 1965, 114m, ★★★¹/₂/$$, Embassy/Republic. A Jewish man who owns a pawnshop in a harsh neighborhood in New York can't help remembering his experiences in the concentration camps which begins to drive him mad. Rod Steiger (**BActor**), Brock Peters, Geraldine Fitzgerald, Jaime Sanchez, Thelma Oliver, Juano Hernandez. w. David Friedkin, Morton Fine, N-adap. Edward Lewis Wallant, d. Sidney Lumet. Oscars: 1-0.

DRAMA: Character Studies; Nightmares; Flashbacks; Nervous Breakdowns; Past-Haunted by the; Ordinary People Stories; Jewish People; Concentration Camps; Film Noir-Modern; Hidden Gems
(The Shop on Main Street; The Pedestrian)

Payment Deferred, 1932, 75m, ★★¹/₂/$$, MGM/NA. A wealthy young man is murdered by his uncle for money. Charles Laughton, Maureen O'Sullivan, Ray Milland, Dorothy Peterson, Verree Teasdale, Billy Bevan, Halliwell Hobbes. w. Ernest Vajda, Claude West, P-adap. Jeffrey Dell, d. Lothar Mendes.

MELODRAMA: MURDER: Greed; Inheritances at Stake; Evil Men; British Films; Forgotten Films

Payment on Demand, 1951, 90m, ★★/$$, RKO/NA. A man asks his wife for a divorce, much to her shock. Bette Davis, Barry Sullivan, Jane Cowl, Kent Taylor, Betty Lynn, John Sutton, Otto Kruger, Frances Dee. w. Bruce Manning, Curtis Bernhardt, d. Curtis Bernhardt.

MELODRAMA: Marriage Drama; Marriage on the Rocks; Divorce; Cheating Men; Forgotten Films

The Pearl, 1948, 72m, ★★★/$$, RKO/Turner, Facets. In a small town in Mexico, an honest but poor shell diver finds a pearl which he thinks will make him rich. Instead, it ruins his life. Pedro Armendariz, Maria Elena Marques, Alfonso Bedoya. w. John Steinbeck, Emilio Fernandez, Kack Wagner, d. Emilio Fernandez.

DRAMA: Character Studies; Dreams; Greed; Poor People; Message Films; Classic Literary Adaptations
(Tortilla Flat; Cannery Row)

PCU (Politically Correct University), 1994, 90m, ★★¹/₂/$, 20th/Fox, PG-13/P-S. A freshman prep school student comes to a university and winds up the pawn of a fraternity house which is fighting against all of the warring special interest groups on campus. Jeremy Piven, Chris Young, David Spade, Jessica Walter, Megan Ward. w. Adam Leff, Zak Penn, d. Hart Bochner.

COMEDY: SATIRE: Social Satire; Party Movies; College Life; 1990s; Battle of the Sexes; Snobs vs. Slobs; Coulda Been Great
(Higher Learning; Animal House; With Honors)

The Pedestrian, 1973, 97m, ★★★/$, Ind/Sultan. When a mogul in modern day Germany is exposed as a former Nazi who led the execution of many people, his world crumbles. Maximilian Schell, Peggy Ashcroft, Lil Dagover, Elisabeth Bergner. d. Maximilian Schell. BFLFilm. Oscars: 1-0.

DRAMA: Nazi Stories; Social Drama; German Films; Art Films; Secrets-Keeping; Actor Directors; Hidden Gems
(Music Box; Judgment at Nuremburg)

Peeper, 1975, 87m, ★★/$, 20th/NA. In the late forties, a wealthy Los Angeles man hires an expatriate British detective to search for his missing daughter. Michael Caine, Natalie Wood, Kitty Winn, Thayer David, Liam Dunn. w. W. D. Richter, N-adap. Keith Laumer (*Deadfall*), d. Peter Hyams.

SUSPENSE: MYSTERY: Missing Persons; Missing Children; Detective Stories; 1940s; Film Noir-Modern; Flops-Major
(Two Jakes; Deadfall [1968]; The Black Windmill; The Late Show)

Peeping Tom, 1960, 88m, ★★★¹/₂/$$, London/HomeVision, PG/V. A strange young man who's secretly a voyeur loves to kill models he photographs and film their horrified expressions while doing it. Karl-Heinz Boehm, Moira Shearer, Anna Massey, Shirley Anne Field, Nigel Davenport. w. d. Michael Powell.

HORROR: SUSPENSE: Serial Killers; Psycho-Killers; Psychological Thriller; Women in Jeopardy; Murders-One by One; Murders of Women; Rape/Rapists; Photographers; Voyeurs; British Films; Female Protagonists; Writer-Directors; Hidden Gems
(Psycho; Eyes of a Stranger; Blow Up)
(Ed: Long on the shelf after its initial release, it was revived in the 80s with

much controversy and is often very hard to find on tape, though it is extremely tame compared to anything similar in the apparently misogynistic horror of today)

Pee-Wee's Big Adventure, 1985, 92m, ★★★/$$$, WB/WB, PG. The man-boy with a magical bicycle gets that bike stolen and goes on a wild goose chase to get it back. Paul Reubens, Elizabeth Daily, Mark Holton, Diane Salinger, Judd Omen, Jon Harris, Carmen Filpi, Tony Bill, James Brolin, Morgan Fairchild. w. Phil Hartman, Paul Reubens, Michael Verhol, d. Tim Burton.

COMEDY: CHILDREN'S: FAMILY: Chase Stories; Action Comedy; Eccentric People; Bicycles; Comedy-Character; Cartoonlike Movies

SEQUEL: Big Top Pee Wee.

Peg o' My Heart, 1933, 86m, ★★½/$$, MGM/NA. A member of Britain's royal family stuns the world by falling for an Irish common woman. Marion Davies, Onslow Stevens, Alan Mowbray, Robert Greig, Irene Browne, J. Farrell MacDonald, Juliette Compton. w. Frances Marion, P-adap. J. Hartley Manners.

MELODRAMA: ROMANCE: Royalty; Romance-Forbidden; Romance-Class Conflicts

Peggy Sue Got Married, 1986, 116m, ★★★½/$$$, Tri-Star/RCA-Col, PG/S. A depressed, middle-aged housewife (Kathleen Turner, BActress) travels back to her high school days where she might have the chance to break off the relationship leading to a miserable marriage. Nicolas Cage, Barbara Harris, Jim Carrey, Don Murray, Kevin J. O'Connor, Maureen O'Sullivan, Leon Ames. w. Jerry Leichtling, Arlene Sarner (BOScr), d. Francis Ford Coppola. BCostume. Oscars: 3-0.

COMEDY: COMEDY DRAMA: ROMANCE: Marriage Comedy; Marriage on the Rocks; Time Travel; High School Life; Coming of Age; Nostalgia; 1950s; Female Screenwriters; Female Protagonists

(Back to the Future)

(Ed: Though the time travel may be less plausible than other calendar-hoppers, it's the best at using the ideas of what might happen if one could do it all over again)

The Pelican Brief, 1993, 140m, ★★/$$$$, WB/WB, PG-13/V. An unwitting law student (Julia Roberts) stumbles

upon the identity of the assassins of two Supreme Court justices mentioned in the "bird brief" and goes on the run with a reporter (Denzel Washington). John Lithgow, John Heard, Anthony Heald, Robert Culp. w. Alan J. Pakula, N-adap. John Grisham, d. Alan J. Pakula.

SUSPENSE: MURDER: MYSTERY: MURDER MYSTERY: Conspiracy; Assassination Plots; Chase Movies; Lawyers; Judges; Government Corruption; Presidents; Female Among Males; Female Protagonists; Women in Jeopardy; Unintentionally Funny; Coulda Been Good; New Orleans

REMAKE/RETREAD: Three Days of the Condor.

(Three Days of the Condor; The Parallax View; The Firm; The Client)

(Ed: Preposterous and implausible, though slightly engaging. Best lines: "Who is this bird brief girl?," "We believe his death was not an accidental murder." Murders can be accidental? Pakula of *Klute*, *All the President's Men* and *Presumed Innocent* fame should have had a better script)

Pelle the Conqueror, 1987, 150m, ★★★½/$$$, Miramax, HBO, PG. At the turn of the century in Denmark, a poor Swedish immigrant works hard on a farm for little pay, and his son takes a lesson from watching his father struggle, vowing to be more independent. Max Von Sydow (BActor), Pelle Hvenegaard, Erik Paaske, Kristina Tornqvist, Morten Jorgensen, Alex Strobye, Astrid Villaume. w. d. Bille August, N-adap. Martin Anderson.

BFLFilm. Oscars: 2-1.

DRAMA: Epics; Journeys; Fathers & Sons; Boys; Cowards; Farm Life; Ordinary People Stories; Immigrants; Scandinavia; Hidden Gems; Danish Films

(Babette's Feast; The House of the Spirits)

Penelope, 1966, 98m, ★★/$, MGM/NA. A vice-president at a bank doesn't know his wife has a secret life-as a kleptomaniacal bank robber. Natalie Wood, Ian Bannen, Dick Shawn, Peter Falk, Jonathan Winters, Lila Kedrova, Lou Jacobi. w. George Wells, N-adap. E. V. Cunningham, d. Arthur Hiller.

COMEDY DRAMA: Bank Robberies; Thieves; Ordinary People Turned Criminal; Dual Lives; Housewives; Good Premise Unfulfilled

(Marnie; This Property Is Condemned)

Pennies from Heaven, 1936, 81m, ★★★/$$$, Col/NA. In New York during the Depression, a hobo takes pity on a poor street urchin and hides her from the local truant officer. Bing Crosby, Edith Fellows, Madge Evans, Louis Armstrong and his band. w. Katherine Leslie Moore, William Rankin, Jo Swerling, d. Norman Z. McLeod.

COMEDY DRAMA: MELODRAMA: Depression Era; MUSICALS: Musical Drama; Homeless People; Men and Girls; Female Screenwriters

(Little Miss Marker; Sundays & Cybele; Sudie and Simpson)

Pennies from Heaven, 1981, 108m, ★★★/$, MGM/MGM-UA, R/S-P. A sheet music salesman in Chicago endures the hardships of the Depression and escapes into the fantasy world of the musical numbers he promotes. Steve Martin, Bernadette Peters, Christopher Walken, Jessica Harper. w., (Teleplay)-adap. Dennis Potter, d. Herbert Ross.

MUSICALS: COMEDY DRAMA: Musical Fantasy; Fantasy; Dance Movies; Dancers; Salesmen; Depression Era; Marriage on the Rocks; Cult Films; Hidden Gems; Overlooked at Release; Flops-Major

(The Singing Detective)

Penny Serenade, 1941, 120m, ★★★/$$$, Col/Nos, Prism. A middle-aged woman looks back on her troubled marriage, including the death of two of her children, as she considers divorce. Cary Grant (BActor), Irene Dunne, Beulah Bondi, Edgar Buchanan, Ann Doran. w. Morrie Ryskind, d. George Stevens. Oscars: 1-0.

DRAMA: MELODRAMA: Divorce; Marriage Drama; Marriage on the Rocks; Memories; Flashbacks; Midlife Crisis; Female Protagonists; Tearjerkers

(Made for Each Other; The Happy Ending; The Perfect Marriage)

The Penthouse, 1967, 96m, ★★½/$, Par/.NA. Lovers using an apartment in a complex still under construction as a love pad are held hostage by a group of strangers. Suzy Kendall, Terence Morgan, Tony Beckley, Norman Rodway, Martine Beswick. w. d. Peter Collinson, P-adap. J. Scott Forbes.

SUSPENSE: Hostage Situations; Cheating Men; Mistresses; Apartment Buildings; British Films

(Cadillac Man; The Happening)

The People Against O'Hara, 1951, 102m, ★★★/$$, MGM/NA. A reformed alcoholic lawyer must make a huge personal sacrifice in order to prove his client's innocence. Spencer Tracy, Diana Lynn, Pat O'Brien, John Hodiak, James Arness, Arthur Shields, Eduardo Cianneli, Louise Lorimer.
DRAMA: Courtroom Drama; Lawyers; Alcoholics; Accused Unjustly; Character Studies
(The Verdict; The Last Hurrah)

The People Next Door, 1970, 93m, ★★1/2/$$, Avco/NA. A seemingly normal suburban family deals with their daughter's drug addiction. Eli Wallach, Deborah Winters, Julie Harris, Hal Holbrook, Cloris Leachman, Stephen McHattie, Nehemiah Persoff. w. (Teleplay)-adap. J. P. Miller, d. David Greene.
DRAMA: Drugs-Addictions; Suburban Life; Social Drama; Family Drama; Fathers & Daughters; TV Movies
(Sarah T, Her Last Chance [TV Movies]; Kotch)

The People That Time Forgot, 1977, 90m, ★★1/2/$$, AIP/NA. In 1916, an explorer disappears on an island populated with prehistoric creatures, and his friend goes back to search for him. Patrick Wayne, Sarah Douglas, Dana Gillespie, Doug McClure, Thorley Walters, Tony Britton. w. Patrick Tilley, d. Kevin Connor.
SCI-FI: ADVENTURE: Dinosaurs; Journies; Searches
SEQUEL TO: The Land That Time Forgot.
(The Lost World; Jurassic Park)

The People Under the Stairs, 1991, 102m, ★★1/2/$$, U/MCA-U, R/EV-B&G. A black thirteen-year-old boy enters the home of a rich white couple and is shocked to discover a whole community of boys and girls held captive whom the deranged couple have disfigured. Brandon Adams, Everett McGill, Wendy Robie, A. J. Langer, Vig Rhames, Sean Whalen. w. d. Wes Craven.
HORROR: Murders-One by One; Murders Children; Black vs. White Boys; Child Protagonists; Coulda Been Great; Allegorical Stories; Writer-Directors
(Parents; House; Nightmare on Elm Street)

People Will Talk, 1951, 110m, ★★★1/2/$$, 20th/Fox. A physician has an unorthodox bedside manner and gets very comfortable with an unwed pregnant patient. When his archenemy gets wind of this, it's off to the ethics board. Cary Grant, Jeanne Crain, Finlay Currie, Hume Cronyn, Walter Slezak, Sidney Blackmer. w. d. Joseph L. Mankiewicz.
COMEDY DRAMA: SATIRE: Medical Drama; Doctors; Romance-Unprofessional; Romance-Mismatched; Romance-Older Men/Younger Women; Mothers-Unwed; Men in Conflicts; Ethics; Hidden Gems; Writer-Directors
(None But the Lonely Heart; Not as a Stranger)

Pepe, 1960, 195m, ★★★/$$$, Col/NA. A poor Mexican immigrant living in L.A. becomes a *cause celebre* in Hollywood. Cantinflas, Dan Dailey, Shirley Jones, Ernie Kovacs, Jay North, William Demarest, Maurice Chevalier, Bing Crosby, Richard Conte, Bobby Darin, Sammy Davis, Jr., Jimmy Durante, Zsa Zsa Gabor, Judy Garland, Hedda Hopper, Joey Bishop, Peter Lawford, Janet Leigh, Jack Lemmon, Kim Novak, Andre Previn, Donna Reed, Debbie Reynolds, Greer Garson, Edward G. Robinson, Cesar Romero, Frank Sinatra, Billie Burke, Tony Curtis, Dean Martin, Charles Coburn. w. Dorothy Kingsley, Claude Binyon, d. George Sidney. BCArt, BCCin, BCCostume, BMScore, BOSong, BEdit, BSound. Oscars: 7-0.
COMEDY: MUSICALS: Musical Comedy; Fame-Rise to; Innocent Bystanders; Latin People; Hollywood Satire; Hollywood Life; Time Capsules; Faded Hits; Curiosities; All-Star Cameos; Female Screenwriters
(Being There; It's a Mad, Mad, Mad, Mad World)
(Ed: A most bizarre concoction)

Peppermint Soda, 1977, 97m, ★★★/$$, New Yorker/New Yorker, R/S. Two teenage sisters in 1960s Paris come of age by leaving their divorced mother behind for boys. Eleonore Klarwein, Odile Michel. w. d. Diane Kurys.
COMEDY DRAMA: Girls; Coming of Age; Teenagers; Love-First; Mothers & Daughters; Sisters; Female Protagonists; Child Protagonists; Female Screenwriters; Female Directors; Writer-Directors
(Entre Nous; One Sings, the Other Doesn't; Therese and Isabelle; Mirabelle and Rainette)

Perfect, 1985, 115m, ★★/$, Par/Par, PG/S. A cynical reporter doing a piece on health clubs interviews a sexy aerobics instructor. His slant is that there's too much emphasis on physical attractiveness in our culture, but he can't keep his mind on the point when she's jumping to the music and doing leg lifts in her skin-tight leotard. John Travolta, Jamie Lee Curtis, Carly Simon, Anne de Salvo, Marilu Henner, Laraine Newman. w. Aaron Latham, James Bridges, d. James Bridges.
COMEDY DRAMA: SATIRE: ROMANCE: Young People; Dating Scene; Looksism; Ethics; Journalists; Body Building; 1980s; Time Capsules; Unintentionally Funny; Flops-Major; Good Premise Unfulfilled; Writer-Directors
(Singles; Too Beautiful for You; Bright Lights, Big City; Pumping Iron; Staying Alive)

A Perfect Couple, 1979, 112m, ★★1/2/$, 20th/NA. A middle-aged man in a close-knit but sometimes claustrophobic Greek family signs up for a dating service and meets a vivacious jazz singer who changes his life. Paul Dooley, Marta Heflin, Titos Vandis, Belita Moreno, Henry Gibson, Dimitra Arliss. w. Robert Altman, Allan Nicholls, d. Robert Altman.
COMEDY DRAMA: Dating Scene; Starting Over; Midlife Crisis; Family Comedy; Singers; Overlooked at Release
(Slow Dancing in the Big City; Miami Rhapsody)

The Perfect Furlough, 1958, 93m, ★★1/2/$$, U-I/Barr Films. In a remote and isolated Army base in the Arctic circle, morale is very low. So one man in the unit is selected to enjoy a furlough in Paris and let the others experience it vicariously-it includes a sexy movie star. Tony Curtis, Janet Leigh, Elaine Stritch, Keenan Wynn, Troy Donahue, King Donovan, Linda Cristal. w. Stanley Shapiro, d. Blake Edwards.
COMEDY: ROMANCE: Romantic Comedy; Soliders; Actresses; Vacations; Romance on Vacation; Paris; Romance-Brief; Forgotten Films; Curiosities

The Perfect Marriage, 1946, 88m, ★★/$$, Par/MCA-U. A couple celebrating their tenth anniversary is told by all that they have the perfect marriage. All of which merely makes them question their union all the more, eventually starting a divorce. David Niven, Loretta Young, Eddie Albert, Nona Griffith, Virginia Field, Jerome Cowan, Rita Johnson,

Charles Ruggles, Nana Bryant, Zasu Pitts. w. Leonard Spigelgass, P-adap. Samson Raphaelson, d. Lewis Allen.
COMEDY DRAMA: Marriage Comedy; Divorce; Romance-Bickering; Forgotten Films
(Penny Serenade; The Happy Ending)
Perfect Strangers, 1950, 87m, ★★/$$, WB/NA. At a heated murder trial, the prosecutor and the defense attorney, a man and woman, succumb to the heated passion and fall in love. Ginger Rogers, Dennis Morgan, Thelma Ritter, Margalo Gillmore, Howard Freeman, Alan Reed, Paul Ford, George Chandler. w. Edith Sommer, P-adap. Charles MacArthur, Ben Hecht, d. Bretaigne Windust.
MELODRAMA: Courtroom Drama; Lawyers; **ROMANCE:** Romance-Unprofessional; **MURDER:** Trials; Female Screenwriters; Female Protagonists
(Adam's Rib; Legal Eagles; Jagged Edge; Storm Warning)
Performance, 1970, 105m, ★★★/$$, WB/WB, R/V-P-S. A young retired rock star gets a new roommate: a brutal mobster. James Fox, Mick Jagger, Anita Pallenberg, Michele Breton, Stanley Meadows, Allan Cuthbertson. w. Donald Cammell, d. Nicolas Roeg, Donald Cammell.
DRAMA: Art Films; Roommates; Roommate from Hell; Rock Stars; Mob Stories; Psychological Drama; Mod Era; 1970s; Dangerous Men; British Films; Hidden Gems; Cult Films
(Apartment Zero; The Tenant)
The Perils of Pauline, 1947, 96m, ★★/$$, Par/Nos. The silent film actress Pearl White gets into zany cliffhanger situations like those of her Saturday matinee serials. Betty Hutton, John Lund, Billy de Wolfe, William Demarest, Constance Collier, Frank Faylen, William Farnum, Paul Panzer, Snub Pollard, Creighton Hale, Chester Conklin, James Finlayson, Hank Mann, Bert Roach, Francis McDonald, Chester Clute. w. P. J. Wolfson, d. George Marshall.
MUSICALS: Biographies; Actresses; Silent Film Era; Hollywood Life; Female Protagonists; All-Star Cameos
(Fuller Brush Girl; The Miracle of Morgan's Creek)
Period of Adjustment, 1962, 122m, ★★★/$$, MGM/MGM-UA. When a soldier returns to his wife after his stint in the Korean War, she discovers to her dis-

may that his post-traumatic stress has affected his sexual performance; while an older couple's problems don't make staying together look so great. Tony Franciosa, Jane Fonda, Jim Hutton, Lois Nettleton. w. Isobel Lennart, P-adap. Tennessee Williams, d. George Roy Hill.
COMEDY: Marriage Comedy; **ROMANCE:** Romantic Comedy; Marriage on the Rocks; Soliders; Sexual Problems; Hidden Gems; Curiosities; Forgotten Films; Female Screenwriters; Female Protagonists
(Barefoot in the Park; Under the Yum Yum Tree)
(Ed: Williams' one true comedy is worth a look, particularly with the young Fonda as ingenue)
Permanent Record, 1988, 91m, ★★/$, Par/Par, PG-13/S-P. In high school, the kid with everything going for him commits suicide, shaking the other students and shocking their parents. Keanu Reeves, Alan Boyce, Michelle Meyrink, Jennifer Rubin, Barry Corbin, Kathy Baker, Pamela Gidley, Richard Bradford. w. Jarre Fees, Alice Liddle, Larry Ketron, d. Marisa Silver.
DRAMA: Suicidal Tendencies; High School Life; Teenagers; Social Drama; Ensemble Films; Coulda Been Good; Female Directors; Female Screenwriters
(Ordinary People; The Breakfast Club; River's Edge)
Perri, 1957, 75m, ★★★/$$$, Disney/NA. A live-action feature chronicling the life of a squirrel. w. Ralph Wright, Winston Hibler, N-adap. Felix Salten, d. Ralph Wright. BOScore. Oscars: 1-0.
CHILDREN'S: Animal Stories; Curiosities; Documentaries
Persona, 1966, 81m, ★★★★/$$$, Svensk Filmindustri-Embassy/MGM-UA. In a mental hospital, a nurse forms a dangerous symbiotic relationship with her patient, and in the end suffers a complete breakdown of personality, becoming a patient herself. Liv Ullman, Bibi Anderson, Margaretha Krook, Gunnar Bjornstrand. w. d. Ingmar Bergman.
DRAMA: Psychological Drama; Character Studies; Mental Illness; Nervous Breakdowns; Asylums; Nurses; Female Protagonists; Writer-Directors; Art Films; Swedish Films
(Face to Face; Cries and Whispers)
Personal Best, 1982, 122m, ★★1/2/$, WB/WB, R/ES-FFN-MFN. A lesbian

affair ensues between two track stars training for the Olympics. Mariel Hemingway, Scott Glenn, Patrice Donnelly, Kenny Moore, Jim Moody, Cliff DeYoung. w. d. Robert Towne.
DRAMA: Erotic Drama; Character Studies; Lesbians; Running; Olympics; Friendships-Female; Writer-Directors; Flops-Major; Female Protagonists
(Lianna)
(Ed: Dubbed "Chariots of Desire")
Personal Property, 1937, 84m, ★★1/2/$$$, MGM/MGM-UA. On an English estate, an American widow falls behind in her bills, and a bailiff sent to manage her affairs ends up winning her heart. Jean Harlow, Robert Taylor, Reginald Owen, Una O'Connor, Henrietta Crosman, E. E. Clive, Cora Witherspoon, Barnett Parker. w. Hugh Mills, Ernest Vajda, P-adap. H. M. Harwood (The Man in Possession), d. W. S. Van Dyke II.
MELODRAMA: ROMANCE: Romantic Drama; Widows; Sexy Men; Sexy Women; Faded Hits
REMAKE OF The Man in Possession.
(Red Dust; Saratoga; Libeled Lady)
Personal Services, 1987, 105m, ★★1/2/$, Vestron/Vestron, R/S-P-FN. The madame of a brothel in London deals with her lonely businessman clients and acts as a den mother to "wayward girls." Julie Walters, Alec McCowen, Shirley Stelfox, Danny Schiller, Victoria Hardcastle. w. F. Hugh Herbert, Erwin Gelsley, Gene Towne, Graham Baker, based on Cynthia Payne's life, d. Alan Crosland.
COMEDY DRAMA: Autobiographical Stories; Prostitutes-High Class; Madams; Feisty Females; Friendships-Female; Female Protagonists; True Stories; British Films
SEQUEL TO Wish You Were Here.
(A House is Not a Home; The Mayflower Madam; Beverly Hills Madam)
Pet Sematary, 1989, 103m, ★★/$$$$, Par/Par, R/EV-B&G. A family moves next door to an Indian burial ground which revives the dead bodies of those buried there. When their son dies, they must decide what to do. Dale Midkiff, Fred Gwynne, Denise Crosby, Brad Greenquist, Michael Lombard, Miko Hughes, Blaze Berdahl. w., N-adap. Stephen King, d. Mary Lambert. Sleeper Hits
(Ed: After a string of King flops, suddenly this one, for some reason, broke through)

Pet Sematary 2, 1992, 102m, ★1/2/$, Par/Par, R/EV-B&G. A new family moves next to the old boneyard and winds up with spooky goings-on. Anthony Edwards, Edward Furlong, Clancy Brown. w. Richard Outten, d. Mary Lambert.
HORROR: Animal Stories; Animal in Jeopardy; MURDER: New in Town; Supernatural Dangers; Dead-Back from the; Female Directors

Pete 'n Tillie, 1972, 100m, ★★★1/2/$$$, U/MCA-U, PG. Two eccentric, lonely, middle-aged people marry each other and try to live with each other's habits. But after having a child, things may not last forever. Walter Matthau, Carol Burnett, Geraldine Page (BSActress), Rene Auberjonois, Barry Nelson, Henry Jones. w. Julius J. Epstein (BAScr), N-adap. Peter de Vries (*Witch's Milk*), d. Martin Ritt. Oscars: 2-0.
COMEDY: COMEDY DRAMA: Marriage Comedy; Family Comedy; Eccentric People; Romance-Middle-Aged; Friendships-Female; Women in Conflict; Tearjerkers; Disease Stories
(Terms of Endearment; Penny Serenade)
(Ed: Similar in tone and structure to *Terms of Endearment*, except dealing with marriage instead of mother-daughter relationships)

Pete Kelly's Blues, 1955, 95m, ★★1/2/$$, WB/WB. A jazz musician in the roaring twenties finds himself entangled with and running from the mob. Jack Webb, Edmond O'Brien, Janet Leigh, Peggy Lee (BSActress), Andy Devine, Ella Fitzgerald, Lee Marvin, Martin Milner. w. Richard L. Breen, d. Jack Webb. Oscars: 1-0.
MELODRAMA: Crime Drama; Fugitives from the Mob; Jazz Life; Musicians; Roaring 20s; Forgotten Films

Peter Ibbetson, 1935, 100m, ★★★/$$$, Par/NA. A woman's "first love" returns to their home town after she's married. Then when her husband is murdered, the old flame is falsely accused, but there's hope they'll be together again. Gary Cooper, Ann Harding, Ida Lupino, John Halliday, Douglass Dumbrille, Virginia Weidler, Dickie Moore, Doris Lloyd. w. Vincent Lawrence, Waldemar Young, Constance Collier, N-adap. George du Maurier, d. Henry Hathaway.
MELODRAMA: ROMANCE: Romance-Reunited; Cheating Women; MURDER:

Accused-Unjustly; Romance-Triangles; Heaven; Love-First; Faded Hits (Ghost; Shadow of a Doubt; Talk of the Town)

Peter Pan, 1953, 76m, ★★★★/$$$, Disney/Disney, G. A green-suited flying boy from Never-Neverland takes a group of London children on a trip to his home and is helped by Tinkerbell when his powers fade. Voices of Bobbie Driscoll, Kathryn Beaumont, Hans Conreid, Bill Thompson, Heather Angel. (Supervisor) Ben Sharpsteen, d. Wilfred Jackson, Clyde Geronimi, Hamilton Luske.
CHILDREN'S: FAMILY: ADVENTURE: Cartoons; MUSICALS: Musicals-Animated; Flying People; Fairy Tales; Fantasy; Boys; Evil Men; Pirates (Hook)

Peter's Friends, 1992, 101m, ★★★/$, Miramax/HBO, R/S-P. At a beautiful English country home, an informal ten-year reunion of old college friends, including some Americans, gets somewhat nasty with everyone dishing the dirt on everyone else and hopping in bed with each other-or at least lots of trying to do so. Kenneth Branagh, Emma Thompson, Alphonsia Emmanuel, Stephen Fry, Hugh Laurie, Phyllida Law, Alex Lowe, Rita Rudner, Tony Slattery, Imelda Staunton, Richard Briers. w. Martin Bergman, Rita Rudner, d. Kenneth Branagh.
COMEDY: Sex Comedy; FARCE: Marriage Comedy; Ensemble Films; Reunions; Friendships Between Sexes; Romance-Reluctant; Gay Men; AIDS Stories; British Films; Hidden Gems; Overlooked at Release; Female Screenwriters; Coulda Been Great
(A Midsummer Night's Sex Comedy; Metropolitan; The Grass is Greener)
(Ed: Kenneth & Emma's Friends; The Brits do Woody Allen, but with marginal success)

Pete's Dragon, 1977, 127m, ★★★/$$$, Disney/Disney, G. An orphaned boy living with overbearing foster parents is visited by a huge animated dragon who helps him have adventures. Only he can see the dragon, causing many embarrassing situations. Sean Marshall, Mickey Rooney, Jim Dale, Helen Reddy, Red Buttons, Shelley Winters, Jim Backus, Joe E. Ross, Ben Wrigley. w. Malcolm Marmorstein, Seton I. Miller, S. S. Field, d. Don Chaffey. BOSong. Oscars: 1-0. (Harvey)

MUSICALS: COMEDY: Musical Comedy; Fantasy; Musical Fantasy; Dragons; Boys; Child Protagonists; Animation-Partial (Harvey; The Reluctant Dragon [cartoon])

The Petrified Forest, 1936, 83m, ★★★/$$$, WB/MGM-UA. Customers and employees at an isolated service station and cafe in the Arizona desert are held hostage by a vicious killer on the run from the law. Among them are the waitress who dreams of leaving this bleak landscape and a sensitive British writer with whom she's falling in love. Leslie Howard, Bette Davis, Humphrey Bogart, Genevieve Tobin, Dick Foran, Joe Sawyer, Porter Hall, Charley Grapewin. w. Charles Kenyon, Delmer Daves, P-adap. Robert E. Sherwood, d. Archie Mayo.
DRAMA: Crime Drama; Hostage Situations; Waitresses; Restaurant Settings; Desert Settings; Hidden Gems; Faded Hits; Stagelike Films; One Day Stories
(Key Largo; Desperate Hours)

Petulia, 1968, 105m, ★★★1/2/$$, WB/WB, PG. A free spirited young woman (Julie Christie) insinuates herself into a cynical, jaded (not to mention married) doctor's life (George C. Scott), but may wind-up disillusioning him even more. Richard Chamberlain, Joseph Cotten, Arthur Hill, Shirley Knight, Kathleen Widdoes, Pippa Scott. w. Lawrence B. Marcus, N-adap. John Haase (*Me and the Arch Kook Petulia*), d. Richard Lester.
DRAMA: ROMANCE: Romantic Drama; Romance-Older Men/Younger Women; Midlife Crisis; Doctors; Free Spirits; San Francisco; Suicidal Tendencies; Fantasies; Illusions/Hallucinations; Neurotic People; Flashbacks; Hidden Gems; Cult Films; Ahead of Its Time; Overlooked at Release
(The Hospital; Breezy; Darling)
(Ed: On many ten best of the 60s lists, it was ignored at its release and flopped)

Peyton Place, 1957, 157m, ★★★/$$$$$, 20th/CBS-Fox. Scandals and tragedy in the lives of those who live in the bestseller's legendary New England town. Lana Turner (BActress), Diane Varsi (BSActress), Hope Lange (BSActress), Arthur Kennedy (BSActor), Lee Philips, Lloyd Nolan, Russ Tamblyn (BSActor), Terry Moore, Barry Coe, David Nelson, Betty Field, Mildred Dunnock,

Leon Ames, Lorne Greene. w. John Michael Hayes (BAScr), N-adap. Grace Metalious, d. Mark Robson (BDirector). BPicture, BCin, BOScore. Oscars: 10-0.

DRAMA: MELODRAMA: Soap Operas; Scandals; Small-Town Scandals; Coming of Age; Multiple Stories; Mothers & Daughters; Secrets-Keeping; Mothers-Unwed; Interwoven Stories; Blockbusters
SEQUEL: Return to Peyton Place; TV Series, 1965–69.
(All the Fine Young Cannibals; Valley of the Dolls)
(Ed: Dated but still entertaining; one of Oscar's all-time losers)

Phantasm, 1979, 90m, ★★¹/₂/$$, Avco/Col, R/EV-B&G. A teenager has nightmares which become more and more real, until he can't re-enter his waking world at all. Michael Baldwin, Bill Thornbury, Reggie Bannister, Angus Scrimm. w. d. Don Coscarelli.
HORROR: SCI-FI: Nightmares; Fantasies; Teenagers; Teenage Movies; Cult Films; Writer-Directors
(A Nightmare on Elm Street; Bad Dreams)

Phantasm II, 1988, 97m, ★★/$$, U/MCA-U, R/EV-B&G. A teenager and his former nemesis from the first film combat a monster from a dream dimension who reanimates corpses and makes them his slaves. James Le Gros, Reggie Bannister, Angus Scrimm, Paula Irvine, Samantha Phillips, Kenneth Tigar, Ruth C. Engel. w. d. Don Coscarelli.
HORROR: SCI-FI: Nightmares; Teenagers; Teenage Movies; Writer-Directors

The Phantom of Liberty, 1974, 104m, ★★★¹/₂/$$, 20th/Xenon. A surrealistic look at the mores of the French *bourgeoisie*, in strange, thematically linked episodes ranging from the 1800s to modern-day Paris. Monica Vitti, Jean-Claude Brialy, Michel Piccoli, Jean Rochefort, Adolfo Celli, Michel Lonsdale, Adriana Asti, Bernard Verley, Muni, Philippe Brigaud. w. Luis Bunuel, Jean-Claude Carriere, d. Luis Bunuel.
DRAMA: Social Drama; Surrealism; Comedy of Manners; Class Conflicts; Art Films; Episodic Stories; French Films; Cult Films
(The Discreet Charm of the Bourgeoisie)

Phantom of the Opera, 1925, 94m, ★★★/$$$$, U/Nos., B&W, silent. The beautiful star soprano of the Paris Opera House is secretly coveted by a horribly scarred man who lives in the sewers underneath the structure. One night he determines to steal her away to his subterannean lair. Lon Chaney, Mary Philbin, Norman Kerry, Gibson Gowland. w. Raymond Shrock, Elliot Clawson, N-adap. Gaston Leroux, d. Rupert Julian.

The Phantom of the Opera, 1943, 92m, ★★★/$$$$, U/MCA-U. A talking version of the above, with a somewhat more urbane phantom. Claude Rains, Nelson Eddy, Susanna Foster, Edgar Barrier, Leo Carrillo, J. Edward Bromberg, Jane Farrar, Hume Cronyn. w. Erich Taylor, Samuel Hoffenstein, d. Arthur Lubin.

Phantom of the Opera, 1962, 90m, ★★/$, U-I-Hammer/NA. A remake in the Hammer mode of the sixties, with more shock and gore than its predecessors. Herbert Lom, Edward de Souza, Heather Sears, Thorley Walters, Michael Gough, Ian Wilson, Martin Miller, John Harvey, Miriam Karlin. w. Joh Elder, d. Terence Fisher.

Phantom of the Opera, 1989, 90m, ★★/$, New Line/Col, R/V-S. A singer in modern-day America bonks her head and wakes up in England in the Victorian Age, trying to escape the clutches of a brilliant musician horribly disfigured in an accident. Robert Englund, Jill Schoelen, Alex Hyde-White, Bill Nighy, Terence Harvey, Stephanie Lawrence, Nathan Lewis, Peter Clapham. w. Duke Sandefur, Gerry O'Hara, d. Dwight H. Little.
SUSPENSE: HORROR: TRAGEDY: Opera; Opera Singers; Women in Jeopardy; Monsters-Human; **MURDER:** Murders of Women; Murders-One by One
(The Hunchback of Notre Dame; Beauty and the Beast)

Phantom of Paradise, 1974, 91m, ★★¹/₂/$, 20th/Fox, R/V. A version of *Phantom of the Opera* with a rock and roll background rather than the original opera house setting. Paul Williams (AAN), William Finley, Jessica Harper, George Memmoli, Gerrit Graham. w. d. Brian de Palma.
SUSPENSE: Women in Jeopardy; **MURDER:** Murders of Women; Revisionist Films; Opera; Rock Stars; Writer-Directors

Phantom of the Rue Morgue, 1954, 84m, ★★¹/₂/$$, WB/NA. A series of murders of young women in turn of the century Paris turns out to have been the work of an ape escaped from the zoo. Karl Malden, Claude Dauphin, Steve Forrest, Patricia Medina, Allyn McLerie, Dolores Dorn. w. Harold Medford, James R. Webb, SS-adap. Edgar Allan Poe (*Murders in the Rue Morgue*), d. Roy del Ruth.
HORROR: MURDER: Serial Killers; Primates; Animal Monsters; Evil Men; London
REMAKE OF: The Murders in the Rue Morgue.

The Phantom President, 1932, 78m, ★★¹/₂/$$, Par/NA. A no-charisma candidate for the presidency is replaced by a look-alike huckster who gets the votes in his stead. George M. Cohan, Claudette Colbert, Jimmy Durante, George Barbier, Sidney Toler, Jameson Thomas, Paul Hurst, Alan Mowbray. w. Walter de Leon, Harlan Thompson, d. Norman Taurog.
COMEDY: SATIRE: Political Satire; Politicians; Impostors; Lookalikes; Con Artists; Forgotten Films
(Dave; The Great McGinty; Moon Over Parador)

The Phantom Tollbooth, 1969, 90m, ★★★/$$, MGM/MGM-UA, G. A young boy, disenchanted with normal life, enters a dreamworld through a mysterious tollbooth and combats such enemies as the Demons of Ignorance. Butch Patrick. w. Chuck Jones, Sam Rosen, N-adap. Norton Juster, d. Chuck Jones.
Cartoons; **CHILDREN'S: FAMILY:** Message Films; Fantasy; **ADVENTURE:** Boys; Child Protagonists; Cult Films; Hidden Gems
(Alice in Wonderland; The Wizard of Oz; Peter Pan; James and the Giant Peach)

Phar Lap, 1983, 118m, ★★¹/₂/$, 20th/Fox, PG. In Australia in the thirties, a racehorse wins its way to international fame, but then dies of unknown causes. Tom Burlinson, Martin Vaughan, Judy Morris, Celia de Burgh, Ron Leibman, Vincent Ball. w. David Williamson, d. Simon Wincer.
MELODRAMA: MYSTERY: Animal Stories; Horses; 1930s; Australia; True Stories

The Phenix City Story, 1955, 100m, ★★¹/₂/$, AA/NA. In a small town in Alabama, an idealistic young attorney fights the forces of corruption that run the local government. Richard Kiley, Edward Andrews, John McIntire, Kathryn Grant.

w. Crane Wilbur, Dan Mainwaring, d. Phil Karlson.

DRAMA: Social Drama; Courtroom Drama; Lawyers; Southerns; Race Relations; Bigots; Fighting the System; Government Corruption; Forgotten Films
(As Summers Die; To Kill a Mockingbird)

Phffft!, 1954, 91m, ★★½/$$, Col/Col. A couple gets divorced because their love is like a burned-out match (the sound of the title). They find life without each other is no bed of roses either. Jack Lemmon, Judy Holliday, Kim Novak, Jack Carson, Luella Gear, Donald Randolph, Donald Curtis. w. George Axelrod, d. Mark Robson.

COMEDY DRAMA: Marriage Comedy; Divorce; Marrying Again; Romance-On and Off Again
(The Marrying Kind; It Should Happen to You)

Philadelphia, 1993, 125m, ★★/$$$$, Tri-Star/Col-Tri, PG-13/P-S. A gay lawyer whizkid finds he has AIDS, but when he hides it and then his firm finds out, he's fired and must sue for his rights before he dies. Tom Hanks (**BActor**), Denzel Washington, Antonio Banderas, Jason Robards, Mary Steenburgen, Joanne Woodward, Obba Babbatunde. w. Ron Nyswaner (BOScr), d. Jonathan Demme. BOSong, (Philadelphia), **BOSong** (Streets of Philadelphia), BMakeup. Oscars: 6-2.

DRAMA: Social Drama; Character Studies; Courtroom Drama; Lawyers; Fighting the System; AIDS Stories; Homophobia; Gay Men; Disease Stories; Black vs. White; Philadelphia
(An Early Frost; Parting Glances)

The Philadelphia Experiment, 1984, 101m, ★★½/$$, New World/New World, PG. In 1943, on a Navy destroyer, a group of sailors enter a time tunnel, end up in 1984 and have to find a way back. Michael Pare, Nancy Allen, Eric Christmas, Bobby Di Cicco, Louise Latham. w. William Gray, Michael Janover, NF-adap. William I. Moore, Charles Berlitz, d. Stewart Raffill.

SCI-FI: ADVENTURE: Time Travel; Bombs-Atomic; World War II Stories; Germans as Enemy; Scientists-Mad; Experiments
SEQUEL: The Philadelphia Experiment 2, 1993.
(The Final Countdown)

The Phildelphia Story, 1940, 112m, ★★★★/$$$$, MGM/MGM-UA. A rich young woman (Katharine Hepburn, BActress) is planning to marry again after getting cold feet a few years before with a socially acceptable man (Cary Grant) who's still in her life. But when a reporter (James Stewart, **BActor**) and his side-kick (Ruth Hussey, BSActress) arrive to cover the grand social event, the woman begins to consider the reporter instead. Roland Young, John Halliday, Mary Nash, Virginia Weidler, John Howard, Henry Daniell. w. Donald Ogden Stewart (**BAScr**), P-adap. Philip Barry, d. George Cukor (BDirector). BPicture. Oscars: 6-2.

COMEDY: Romantic Comedy; Romance-Triangles; Marriage-Impending; Engagements-Breaking; Weddings; Romance-Choosing the Right Person; Heiresses; Rich People; Journalists; Divorce; Romance-Reluctant; Romance-Class Conflicts; Romance-On and Off Again; Philadelphia

MUSICAL REMAKE: High Society.
(Holiday; High Society)

Phobia, 1980, 90m, ★★½/$, Par/Par, R/S-V. Prisoners are released early if they agree to undergo psychological experiments on fear. Once out, they are murdered one at a time. Paul Michael Glaser, John Colicos, Susan Hogan, Alexandra Stewart, David Bolt. w. Lew Lehman, Jimmy Sangster, Peter Bellwood, d. John Huston.

SUSPENSE: Psychological Thriller; Psychologists; **MURDER:** Murders-One by One; Serial Killers; Coulda Been Great; Hitchockian; Flops-Major
(Coma; Winter Kills)

Physical Evidence, 1988, 99m, ★★/$, Col/Live, R/P-V. A retired policeman accused of murder is defended by a female attorney with dubious credentials. Burt Reynolds, Theresa Russell, Ned Beatty, Kay Lenz, Ted McGinley, Tom O'Brien, Kenneth Welsh, Ray Baker, Ken James, Michael P. Moran. w. Bill Phillips, Steve Ransohoff, d. Michael Crichton.

SUSPENSE: MURDER: MYSTERY: MURDER MYSTERY: Courtroom Drama; Legal Thrillers; Accused Unjustly/; Laywers; Police Stories; Coulda Been Good; Flops-Major
(Jagged Edge; Heat; Malone)

The Piano, 1993, 120m, ★★★½/$$$, Miramax/HBO, Live, R/ES-FFN-MFN. A mute woman travels to New Zealand in the 1800s with her daughter for an arranged marriage with a settler. But when another settler buys the piano she loved so much but which the husband wouldn't let her have, she takes up with this man in order to get it back. Holly Hunter (**BActress**) Harvey Keitel, Sam Neill, Anna Paquin (**BSActress**), Kerry Walker. w. d. Jane Campion (BDirector, **BOScr**). BPicture, BCin, BCostume, BEdit. Oscars: 8-3.

DRAMA: Erotic Drama; Mute People; Marriage of Convenience; Brides-Mail Order; Mothers & Daughters; Cheating Women; Quiet Little Films; Sleeper Hits; 1800s; New Zealand; Disabled but Nominated; Women's Films; Female Protagonists; Female Directors; Female Screenwriters; Writer-Directors
(The Go-Between; An Angel at My Table; Green Dolphin Street; Grand Isle)

Piccadilly Incident, 1946, 102m, ★★★/$$, ABP/NA. A British couple both enlist in World War II and are stationed on separate fronts. When news comes that the wife has drowned, the man is distraught, but goes on with his life after the war. Meanwhile, she has been hiding from the Germans and finally returns to England, only to find him remarried. Anna Neagle, Michael Wilding, Michael Laurence, Frances Mercer, Coral Browne, A. E. Matthews, Edward Rigby, Brenda Bruce. w. Nicholas Phipps, d. Herbert Wilcox.

MELODRAMA: Marriage Drama; World War II Stories; Dead-Back from the; Return of Spouse; Bigamy; World War II-Post Era; British Films
(My Favorite Wife; Move Over, Darling)

The Pickup Artist, 1987, 81m, ★★/$, 20th/Fox, R/S. A young playboy jerk romances women but could care less, until he really falls in love, with a girl connected to the mob. Robert Downey, Jr., Molly Ringwald, Harvey Keitel, Dennis Hopper, Danny Aiello, Lorraine Bracco, Vanessa Williams. w. d. James Toback.

COMEDY: ROMANCE: Romantic Comedy; Playboys; Romance-Reluctant; Promiscuity; Young Men; Crossing the Line; Narrated Films; Coulda Been Good; Writer-Directors

Pickup on South Street, 1953, 80m, ★★★/$$$, 20th/Fox. A pickpocket steals the wrong wallet from a female spy involved in an international network of espionage, and finds himself a moving target. Richard Widmark, Jean Peters,

Thelma Ritter, Richard Kiley. w. Samuel Fuller, Dwight Taylor, d. Samuel Fuller.
SUSPENSE: Chase Stories; Fugitives from a Murderer; Pickpockets; Thieves; Cold War Era; Communists; Innocent Bystanders; Spies; Spies-Female; Faded Hits; Hidden Gems

The Pickwick Papers, 1952, 115m, ★★1/2/$$, B-L/VCI. In England in the Victorian era, an eccentric men's group called the Pickwick Club has misadventures and mismanages its affairs until it is sued by a Mrs. Bardell for breach of contract. James Hayter, James Donald, Donald Wolfit, Hermione Baddeley, Hermione Gingold, Kathleen Harrison, Nigel Patrick, Alexander Gauge, Lionel Murton. w. d. Noel Langley. BCostume. Oscars: 1-0.
COMEDY DRAMA: Comedy of Manners; Ensembles-Male; Clubs; Female Among Males; Battle of the Sexes; Lawyers; Victorian Era; British Films; Classic Literary Adaptations

Picnic, 1955, 113m, ★★★/$$$$, Columbia/Tri-Col. Among the cornfields of the Midwest, the conservative locals are flustered by a mysterious, sexy hunk who wanders into town and proceeds to have his way with their young women. William Holden, Kim Novak, Rosalind Russell, Susan Strasberg, Arthur O'Connell (BSActor), Cliff Robertson, Betty Field, Verna Felton, Reta Shaw. w. Daniel Taradash, P-adap. William Inge, d. Joshua Logan. BPicture, **BcArt,** BEdit, BOScore. Oscars: 5-2.
MELODRAMA: ROMANCE: Romantic Drama; Tearjerkers; Midwestern Life; Drifters; Small-town Life; Sexy Men; Playboys; Women Fighting Over Men; Tennessee Williams-esque
(The Fugitive Kind; Splendor in the Grass; Bus Stop; The Long, Hot Summer)

Picnic at Hanging Rock, 1975, 115m, ★★★/$$, Ind/Vestron, PG. In Australia in 1900, a group from a girl's school goes on a picnic in the country and some never return. No one can quite explain the mystery. Rachel Roberts, Dominic Guard, Helen Morse, Jacki Weaver, Vivean Gray, Kirsty Child. w. Cliff Green, N-adap. Joan Lindsay, d. Peter Weir.
DRAMA: Psychological Drama; True Stories; **MYSTERY:** Missing Persons; Murders of Women; Ensembles-Female; Girls' Schools; Australian Films; Female Protagonists

(Missing; The Vanishing; The Getting of Wisdom)

Picture Mommy Dead, 1966, 88m, ★★/$, Embassy/New Line, PG/V. A young girl recovering from burns suffered in a house fire that killed her mother is released from the hospital to find her dad already remarried, unfortunately, to a homicidal maniac. Don Ameche, Martha Hyer, Zsa Zsa Gabor, Susan Gordon, Maxwell Reed, Signe Hasso, Wendell Corey. w. Robert Sherman, d. Bert I. Gordon.
HORROR: SUSPENSE: Psycho Killers; Murderers-Female; Stepmothers-Troublesome; Stepparents vs. Children; Fires
(The Stepfather; The Mad Room)

The Picture of Dorian Gray, 1945, 110m, ★★★★/$$$$, MGM/MGM-UA. Oscar Wilde's narcissistic tale of the beautiful, ageless man in the portrait (Hurd Hatfield) which mysteriously does show signs of age. Angela Lansbury (BSActress), George Sanders, Donna Reed, Peter Lawford. N-adap. Oscar Wilde, d. Albert Lewin. **BB&WCin,** BB&WArt. Oscars: 3-1.
DRAMA: MELODRAMA: MYSTERY: Fantasy; Sexy Men; Beautiful People; Aging; Young Men; Classic Literary Adaptations; London; Edwardian Era
REMAKE: 1971.
(Laura)

Pillow Talk, 1959, 102m, ★★★★/$$$$$, Universal/MCA-U. When an uptight decorator (Doris Day, BActress) has to share a party line with a ladies' man songwriter (Rock Hudson), sparks fly because he's always romancing yet another woman on the line. The songwriter decides to romance the decorator posing as the kind of man he thinks she wants. w. Stanley Shapiro, Maurice Richlin, Clarence Greene, Russell Rouse (**BOScr**), d. Michael Gordon. Oscars: 2-1.
COMEDY: Romantic Comedy; Sex Comedy; Battle of the Sexes; Romance-Opposites Attract; Romance-Bickering; Single Women; Wallflowers & Hunks; Impostors; Playboys; Musicians; Extrovert vs. Introvert; Telephone Terror; Blockbusters
(Lover Come Back; Send Me No Flowers; Move Over, Darling)

Pink Cadillac, 1989, 121m, ★★/$$, WB/WB, PG-13/V-P. A bondsman chases bail-jumpers in the said car with a

screaming blonde in the passenger seat whose husband is one of his prey. Clint Eastwood, Bernadette Peters, Michael Des Barres, William Hickey, Jim Carrey. w. John Eskow, d. Stephen Dorff.
COMEDY: ACTION: Action Comedy; Bounty Hunters; Chase Stories; Road Movies; Flops-Major
(Midnight Run; Every Which Way But Loose)

Pink Flamingos, 1972, 95m, ★★★/$$$, Ind/New Line, R/P-S. The famous transvestite Divine enters a contest to be the world's most digusting person and meets many more disgusting people along the way. Divine, David Lochary, Mink Stole. w. d. John Waters.
COMEDY: Spoofs; Competitions; Transvestites; Bathroom Humor; Camp; Writer-Directors; Cult Films; Independent Films
(Female Trouble; Hairspray; Polyester)

Pink Floyd: The Wall, 1982, 95m, ★★★/$$, MGM/MGM-UA, R/S-V. A surrealist music video taking the song of the alienation of a British schoolboy through his coming of age into major cynicism. Bob Geldof, Christine Hargreaves, Bob Hoskins. d. Alan Parker.
DRAMA: Fantasy; Music Videos; Music Video Style; Surrealism; Animation-Partial; Alienation; Coming of Age; Young Men; Young Men-Angry; Song Title Movies
(The Valley Obscured by Clouds)

The Pink Panther, 1964, 113m, ★★★★/$$$$, UA/MGM-UA. A suave jewel thief (David Niven) and his cool nephew (Robert Wagner) go to Europe to sweep a princess off her feet and steal her diamond from her display, but the famous Inspector Clouseau (Peter Sellers) is hot on their trail, even though the thief in is bed with his wife (Capucine). w. d. Blake Edwards. BOScore. Oscars: 1-0.
COMEDY: Heist Stories; Capers; **FARCE:** Comedy of Errors; Simple Minds; Fools-Bumbling; Comedy-Slapstick; Spoofs-Detective; Thieves; Americans Abroad
(Revenge of the Pink Panther; Return of the Pink Panther; Inspector Clouseau; A Shot in the Dark)

The Pink Panther Strikes Again, 1976, 103m, ★★★1/2/$$$$, UA/MGM-UA, Turner, PG. Clouseau tracks down his insanely evil boss who's escaped from the asylum and developed a death ray to take the world over. However, the boss has underestimated the power of

Clouseau's disguises and a beautiful Russian spy. Peter Sellers, Herbert Lom, Lesley Anne-Down, Colin Blakely. w. Frank Waldman, Edward Waldman, Blake Edwards, d. Blake Edwards. BOSong. Oscars: 1-0.

COMEDY: FARCE: Comedy of Errors; Fools-Bumbling; Detective Stories; Rule the World-Plot to; Asylums

Pinky, 1949, 102m, ★★★/$$$, 20th/Fox. A bi-racial girl whose mother is black tries to pass for white and bears the consequences on both sides of the racial fence. Jeanne Crain (BActress), Ethel Waters (BSActress), Ethel Barrymore. w. Philip Dunne, Dudley Nichols, d. Elia Kazan. Oscars: 2-0.

MELODRAMA: DRAMA: Social Drama; Race Relations; Black Women; Black vs. White; Forgotten Films; Faded Hits; Female Protagonists
(I Passed for White; Showboat; Imitation of Life)

Pinocchio, 1940, 87m, ★★★★/$$$$, Disney/Disney, G. Classic tale of the wooden puppet boy who comes to life but who tells too many tales and may be taken in by a sly fox and wind up a donkey. Voices of Dick Jones, Cliff Edwards, Evelyn Venable. d. Ben Sharptsteen. **BOScore, BOSong** (When You Wish Upon a Star). Oscars: 2-2.

CHILDREN'S: FAMILY: Fantasy; Cartoons; Musicals-Animated; **MUSICALS:** Objects with Personalities; Boys; Liars; Blockbusters
(Lili; Bambi; Peter Pan)

Pippi Longstocking, 1973, 99m, ★★★/$$$, Col/Movies, G. The red-pigtailed Swedish girl whose father is at sea wreaks havoc in her village with her mischief. Inger Nilsson. d. Olle Hellbron.

CHILDREN'S: ADVENTURE: Fantasy; Free Spirits; Scandinavia; Swedish Films; Female Protagonists; Child Protagonists; Girls; Sleeper Hits

REMAKE: 1985.
(Ed: Famous for its poor dubbing, this became a worldwide sensation, sending book sales skyrocketing)

Piranha, 1978, 90m, ★★½/$, Ind/WB, R/V-B&G. A lake in Texas has little critters with very sharp teeth who like the tourist meat. Bradford Dillman, Heather Menzies, Kevin McCarthy, Paul Bartel. w. John Sayles, d. Joe Dante.

HORROR: Spoofs; Spoofs-Horror Fish; Animal Monsters; Murders-One by One;

Tourists; Nightmare Vacations; Camp
(Killer Fish; Alligator)

The Pirate, 1948, 102m, ★★★/$$$, MGM/MGM-UA. On a Caribbean isle, an actor pretends to be a military hero in order to impress a girl. He also sings and dances. Judy Garland, Gene Kelly, Walter Slezak, Gladys Cooper, Reginald Owen. d. Vincente Minnelli.

MUSICALS: COMEDY: ROMANCE: Romantic Comedy; Musical Romance; Pirates; Caribbean; Romance-Reluctant; Disguises; Impostors; Actor Impostors; Actors
(Hail the Conquering Hero; The Clock)

The Pirate Movie, 1982, 98m, ★★/$, 20th/Fox, PG. Teen brats update the Pirates of Penzance tale with bad pop songs. Kristy McNichol, Christopher Atkins, Ted Hamilton. d. Ken Annakin.

COMEDY: Teenage Movies; Teenagers; Pirates; Revisionist Films; Curiosities

The Pirates of Penzance, 1983, 112m, ★★★/$, U/MCA-U, G. The Broadway version of the famous operetta where a young swashbuckler woos a fair maiden on the high seas. Kevin Kline, Linda Ronstadt, Angela Lansbury, Rex Smith, George Rose. d. Wilford Leach.

MUSICALS: Musicals-Operettas; **ROMANCE:** Musical Romance; Swashbucklers; Pirates; Stage Filmings

The Pit and the Pendulum, 1961, 90m, ★★★/$$$, AIP/WB. When his sister and her beau plan to drive a man insane, the man responds by torturing them with the help of his father-at first. Vincent Price, John Kerr, Barbara Steele. w. Richard Matheson, SS-adap. Edgar Allan Poe, d. Roger Corman.

The Pit and the Pendulum, 1991, 97m, ★★½/$, Par/Par, R/V. Re-set during the Spanish Inquisition and mixed with Poe's "Cast of Amantillado." Lance Henriksen, Rona De Ricci. w. Dennia Paoli, d. Stuart Gordon.

HORROR: SUSPENSE: MURDER: Torture; Insane-Plot to Drive; Revenge; Brothers & Sisters
(The House of Usher)

Pixote, 1981, 127m, ★★★½/$$, Col/Col, NR. An orphan travels the streets of Rio trying to survive amid the thousands of other legendary unwanted children. w. d. Hector Babenco.

DRAMA: Documentary Style; Inner City Life; Orphans; Runaways; Boys; Poor People; Homeless People; South

America; Cult Films; Hidden Gems; Writer-Directors
(Bye Bye Brazil; Kiss of the Spider Woman)

P.K. and the Kid, 1982, 89m, ★★/$, Sunn Classic/WB, PG. A girl runs away from home to escape her abusive stepfather and hitches a ride to L.A. with an arm wrestler headed toward a big prize contest there. Paul Le Mat, Molly Ringwald, Alex Rocco, Charles Hallahan, John Di Santi, Fionnula Flanagan, Leigh Hamilton, Esther Rolle. w. Neal Barbera, d. Lou Lombardo.

COMEDY DRAMA: Runaways; Hitchhikers; Men and Girls; Friendships Between Sexes; Forgotten Films

A Place in the Sun, 1951, 120m, ★★★★/$$$$, Par/Par. A young man (Montgomery Clift, BActor) who wants to move up in the world by marrying the daughter (Elizabeth Taylor) of the boss of a conglomerate is suddenly haunted by his ex (Shelley Winters, BActress), who's come to tell him she's pregnant and wants to get married. His dilemma becomes one of how to take care of her. w. Michael Wilson, Harry Brown (**BAScr**), N-adap. Theodore Dreiser (*An American Tragedy*), d. George Stevens (**BDirector**). BPicture, **BB&WCin**, BEdit, BOScore, **BB&WCostume**. Oscars: 9-5.

DRAMA: TRAGEDY MURDER: Murder of Spouse; Courtroom Drama; Social Climbing; Marrying Up; Drownings; Secrets-Haunted by; Shelley Winters Drowns; Classic Literary Adaptations
(An American Tragedy; Sister Carrie; Ethan Frome)
(Ed: Powerful, but one does wonder why the accidental death angle wasn't used by our hero who was seen dripping wet coming out of the lake by several witnesses, but then again, it's based on the true Eastman murder of the 1890s)

Places in the Heart, 1984, 113m, ★★★★/$$$, Tri-Star/RCA-Col, PG-13/S. When a sheriff is killed, his widow (Sally Field, **BActress**) is forced to take on renters (Danny Glover) (John Malkovich, BSActor) to make ends meet, but her debt is so large, she must harvest an entire cotton crop to pay her mortgage. Lindsay Crouse (BSActress), Ed Harris,. w. d. Robert Benton (**BOScr**, BDirector). BPicture, BArt, BCostume. Oscars: 7-2.

DRAMA: MELODRAMA: Mortgage Drama; Save the Farm; Underdog Stories;

Female Among Males; Women Fighting Back; Southerns; Small-town Life; Depression Era; Farm Life; Families-Extended; Slice of Life Stories; Interwoven Stories; Multiple Stories; Female Protagonists

(Country; The River; 1918; The Trip to Bountiful; Norma Rae; Out of Africa)

The Plague, 1992, 105m, ★★1/2/$, Ind/Live, R/V. A virus causes a South American city to be quarantined where the disease must either kill everyone or die itself before anyone is let go. William Hurt, Robert Duvall, Raul Julia, Sandrine Bonnaire. N-adap. Albert Camus, d. Luis Puenzo.

DRAMA: TRAGEDY: Social Drama; Message Films; Doctors; Disease Stories; Epidemics; Classic Literary Adapatations; Allegorical Stories; South America; Oppression

(1918; Kiss of the Spider Woman)

Plain Clothes, 1988, 98m, ★★1/2/$, Par/Par, PG. A detective goes to high school to try and solve a murder and remembers why he hated school so much. Arliss Howard, George Wendt, Suzy Amis, Diane Ladd, Seymour Cassel, Abe Vigoda, Robert Stack. d. Martha Coolidge.

COMEDY DRAMA: Detective Stories; **MURDER: MURDER MYSTERY: MYSTERY:** High School Life; Undercover; Female Directors

(Kindergarten Cop; Billy Madison; Valley Girl)

Plan 9 from Outer Space, 1956, 78m, ★(★★★)/$, Ed Wood Pictures/Media, Nos. UFOs and zombies stalk the night in this famously cheesy exercise in poor taste and just-so-plain-bad-it's-funny story. Bela Lugosi, Vampira, Tor Johnson, Lyle Talbot. d. Ed Wood.

SCI-FI: Sci-Fi-1950s; Camp; Spoofs; Spoofs-Sci-Fi; Cult Films; Unintentionally Funny; Independent Films

(Ed Wood; Glen or Glenda?)

Planes, Trains, and Automobiles, 1987, 93m, ★★★/$$$, Par/Par, PG-13/P. A businessman is stranded in the snow and must get to his holiday destination with an overweight goofball who manages to destroy everything in their path-including setting the car they're driving on fire. Steve Martin, John Candy, Edie McClurg, Kevin Bacon, Laila Robins, Michael McKean. w. d. John Hughes.

COMEDY: FARCE: Comedy of Errors; Race Against Time; Nightmare Vacations; Buddy Films; Fools-Bumbling; Writer-Directors; Thanksgiving

(The Outoftowners; Uncle Buck)

Planet of the Apes, 1968, 112m, ★★★1/2/$$$$, 20th/Fox, PG/V-MN. Astronauts from the not-too-distant future land on a planet run by speaking, walking apes-which turns out to be future earth, where humans are mute slaves. Charlton Heston, Roddy McDowall, Kim Hunter, Maurice Evans, Linda Harrison, James Whitmore. w. Rod Serling, Michael Wilson, d. Franklin J. Schaffner. BOScore, BCostume, **BMakeup**. Oscars: 3-1.

ACTION: ADVENTURE: SCI-FI: CHILDREN'S: FAMILY: Astronauts; Slavery; Primates; Fugitives from the Law; Mute People; Animals-Talking; Futuristic Films; Apocalyptic Stories; Sleeper Hits; Blockbusters

SEQUELS: Beneath the Planet of the Apes, Escape from the Planet of the Apes, Conquest of the Planet of the Apes, Battle for the Planet of the Apes.

Platinum Blonde, 1931, 86m, ★★★/$$$, Col/Col. A newspaperman marries a rich girl but doesn't like the new life. So he begins to turn the tables, much to his bride's chagrin. Loretta Young, Jean Harlow, Robert Williams, Louise Closser Hale. w. Jo Swerling, d. Frank Capra.

COMEDY: Screwball Comedy; Marriage Comedy; Romance-Class Conts; Rich vs. Poor; Journalists; Newspapers; Turning the Tables; Faded Hits

(Libeled Lady; Red Dust; Bombshell)

Platoon, 1986, 113m, ★★★★/$$$$, Hemdale-Orion/Orion-Vestron, R/P-V. A young man's (Charlie Sheen) diary of the horrors of a tour of duty in Vietnam. Tom Berenger (BSActor), Willem Dafoe (BSActor). w. d. Oliver Stone (**BOScr, BDirector**). **BPicture**, BCinema, BEditing, BSound. Oscars: 8-4.

DRAMA: War Stories; Military Stories; Autobiographical Stories; Narrated Films; Friendships-Male; Anti-War Films; Vietnam War; Epistolaries; Blockbusters; Sleeper Hits

(Apocalypse Now; The Deerhunter; Full Metal Jacket; Hamburger Hill; The Hanoi Hilton)

Play It Again, Sam, 1972, 85m, ★★★1/2/$$$, UA/Par, PG/S. A nerd in San Francisco obsessed with Bogart

wants his best friend's wife, and begins consulting the ghost of Bogart to muster the courage to get her. Woody Allen, Diane Keaton, Tony Roberts, Susan Anspach, Jennifer Salt, Viva. w. P-adap. Woody Allen, d. Herbert Ross.

COMEDY: ROMANCE: Romance with Married Person; Romance with Friend's Lover; Fantasies; Fans-Crazed; Nerds; Nerds & Babes; Sleeper Hits; Cult Films; San Francisco; 1970s

(Annie Hall; Sleeper; The Man with Bogart's Face)

Play Misty for Me, 1971, 102m, ★★★/$$$, U/MCA-U, R/S-V. A sexy radio d.j. has a secret admirer who loves the song 'Misty.' But when her infatuation grows to fatal attraction, his girlfriend may be in danger since she's between the admirer and his love. Clint Eastwood, Donna Mills, Jessica Walter. w. Jo Helms, Dean Reisner, d. Clint Eastwood.

DRAMA: SUSPENSE: Infatuations; Fatal Attractions; Radio Life; Romance-Triangles; Men in Jeopardy; Women in Jeopardy; Actor Directors; Sleeper Hits; Cult Films

(Fatal Attraction; The Crush)

(Ed: The similarities to *Fatal Attraction* are obvious-sixteen years before. Contained the blockbuster song, "The First Time Ever I Saw Your Face" by Roberta Flack)

The Playboys, 1992, 114m, ★★1/2/$, HBO/HBO, PG-13/S. An unwed mother in an Irish village sparks controversy when she seems to be courting several men at once. Robin Wright, Aidan Quinn, Albert Finney, Milo O'Shea, Alan Devlin. w. Shane Connaughton, Kerry Crabbe, d. Gilles Mackinnon.

DRAMA: ROMANCE: Romance-Triangles; Mothers-Struggling; Single Women; Ireland; Irish Films; Quiet Little Films; Scandals; Small-town Life; Small-town Scandals

(The Snapper)

The Player, 1992, 123m, ★★★★/$$$, Fine Line/New Line, R/S-P-FFN-MFN. A movie executive is being harassed by a writer he's ticked off. But when he tracks down who he thinks the writer is, he winds up killing him. Will he get away with it and live to make a movie of it? Tim Robbins, Greta Scacchi, Fred Ward, Whoopi Goldberg, Cynthia Stevenson, Dean Stockwell, Richard E. Grant, Vincent D'Onofrio, Lyle Lovett, Randall

Batinkoff, Dina Merrill. And a huge cast of stars. w. N-adap. Michael Tolkin (BAScr), d. Robert Altman (BDirector). BEditing. Oscars: 3-0.

SUSPENSE: MURDER: Black Comedy; SATIRE: Psychological Drama; Hollywood Life; Hollywood Satire; Murder-Debate to Confess; Mean Men; Identities-Mistaken; Police Stories; Crimes of Passion; Greed; Ethics; Good vs. Evil; Moviemaking; Clever Plots & Endings; Stalkers; Writers; All-Star Casts; All-Star Cameos; Sleeper Hits (The Big Knife; The Bad and the Beautiful)
(Ed: Surely the most realistic and comprehensive look at modern Hollywood and a fine psychological drama)

Players, 1979, 120m, ★★/$$, Par/Par, R/S-FN. An older woman inspires a sexy tennis star wannabe/gigolo to make it to Wimbledon. Ali MacGraw, Dean Paul Martin, Maximilian Schell, John McEnroe, Guillermo Vilas, Ilie Nastase. w. Arnold Schulman d. Anthony Harvey.

MELODRAMA: ROMANCE: Erotic Drama; Tennis; Romance-Older Women/Younger Men; Unintentionally Funny; Flops-Major

Playing for Time, 1980, 148m, ★★★1/2/$$$, CBS/NA. A concentration camp inmate begins a prison orchestra which plays despite the inevitabilities of the Nazis' plans. Vanessa Redgrave, Jane Alexander, Maud Adams, Verna Bloom, Melanie Mayron. w. Arthur Miller, d. Daniel Mann. Multiple Emmy winner.

DRAMA: TRAGEDY: Social Drama; Concentration Camps; Musicians; Nazi Stories; Female Protagonists; TV Movies; Hidden Gems
(Triumph of the Spirit; Victory; Sophie's Choice)

Playtime, 1967, 108m, ★★★/$$, Ind/New Line. The bewildered M. Hulot goes to the modern city this time and tries to cope. Jacques Tati. w. d. Tati.

COMEDY: Comedy-Light; City vs. Country; Urban Life; Comedy-Character; French Films; Cult Films

PREQUELS: Mon Oncle, Mr. Hulot's Holiday.
(Modern Times)

Plaza Suite, 1971, 114m, ★★★/$$$, Par/Par, PG/S. Several couples, all headed by men who look like Walter Matthau (in a multiple performance), deal with cheating, daughters afraid of getting married, and other assorted marital troubles-all in the Plaza Hotel. Barbara Harris, Lee Grant, Maureen Stapleton, Louise Sorel. w. P-adap. Neil Simon, d. Arthur Hiller.

COMEDY DRAMA: Marriage Drama; Marriage on the Rocks; Weddings; Hotels; Cheating Men; Cheating Women; Romance with Married Person; Midlife Crisis; Multiple Stories; Multiple Performances
(California Suite; The Last of the Red Hot Lovers; The War Between Men and Women)

Please Don't Eat the Daisies, 1960, 111m, ★★★/$$$$, MGM/MGM-UA. When a critic moves to the suburbs, his wife has trouble dealing with the freedom and problems of distance-it's harder to keep an eye on the hubby and that actress who wants a good review from him. Doris Day, David Niven, Janis Paige, Spring Byington, Richard Haydn, Patsy Kelly, Jack Weston. w. P-adap. Jean Kerr, d. Charles Walters.

COMEDY: FAMILY: Marriage Comedy; City vs. Country; Critics; Housewives; Suburban Life; Cheating Men; Jealousy; Actresses; Theater Life; New York Life; Autobiographical Stories; Putting on a Show; Female Screenwriters; Female Protagonists
SEQUEL: TV SERIES, 1965.
(Critic's Choice; Where Were You When the Lights Went Out?; Mary, Mary)
(Ed: Good Doris stuff. Very similar to several I Love Lucy episodes, or vice versa)

Plenty, 1985, 119m, ★★★1/2/$$, 20th/EMI-HBO, R/S. A woman's (Meryl Streep) struggles and deterioration dealing with the past of World War II and her work then in the Resistance is chronicled as her home country of England follows a similar post-war course with nothing to fight against anymore. Charles Dance, Tracey Ullman, John Gielgud, Sting. w. P-adap. David Hare, d. Fred Schepisi.

DRAMA: Character Studies; Stern Women; Marriage Drama; World War II Era; World War II-Post Era; Spies; Spies-Female; Mental Illness; Neurotic People; Nervous Breakdowns; Depression; Alienation; Life Transitions; Midlife Crisis; Wisecracking Sidekicks; 1950s; British; Past-Haunted by the; Female Protagonists; Hidden Gems
(Wetherby; Strapless; Blue Sky)

The Ploughman's Lunch, 1983, 107m, ★★★/$, Ind/Sultan, R/S-P-V. A ruthless journalist makes his way up the ladder only to find himself involved in a conspiracy. Jonathan Pryce, Charlie Dore, Rosemary Harris, Frank Finlay. d. Richard Eyre.

DRAMA: Journalists; Conspiracy; Ethics; Power-Rise to; British Films; Hidden Gems

Plutonium Circus, 1995, 73m, ★★★/$, Ind/NA. A look at the Pantex nuclear waste facility in Amarillo, which poses a grave threat to several states' water supplies, and the push to remove it. d. George Ratliff.

Documentaries; Environmental Dilemmas; Nuclear Energy; Texas; Government as Enemy; Message Films

Pocahontas, 1995, 87m, ★★★/$$$$$, Disney/Disney, G. Virginians in early colony days, including John Smith, who falls for an American Indian girl named Pocahontas. But after an Indian is shot and the governor learns that the Indians have some gold, a war ensues which puts the would-be lovers at odds. Voices of: Irene Bedard, Judy Kuhn, Mel Gibson, David Ogden Stiers, John Kassir, Russell Means, Christian Bale, Linda Hunt, Danny Mann. w. Carl Binder, Susannah Grant, Philip LaZebnik, & Mike Gabriel, d. Mike Gabriel & Eric Goldberg. BOMScore, BOSong. Oscars: 2-2.

Cartoons: CHILDREN'S: Indians-American; Early America; Romance-Interracial; Greed; Environmental Dilemmas; Female Screenwriters

Pocketful of Miracles, 1961, 136m, ★★★/$$$, 20th/Fox, MGM-UA. A poor woman who sells apples on the streets is taken on as a project by a mobster to make her look like a lady when her daughter comes to visit. Bette Davis, Glenn Ford, Hope Lange, Ann-Margret, Pater Falk (BSActor), Jack Elam, Edward Everett Horton, Thomas Mitchell. d. Frank Capra. BCCostume. Oscars: 2-0.

COMEDY: COMEDY DRAMA: Tearjerkers; Mob Comedy; Homeless People; Mothers & Daughters; Elderly Women; Capra-esque
REMAKE OF Lady for a Day (also directed by Capra).
(Lady for a Day; Robin and the Seven Hoods)

Poetic Justice, 1993, 109m, ★★1/2/$$, Col/Col, R/P-V-S. In the black inner

city, a teenage hairdresser's poetry gives her inspiration after her boyfriend is killed and her college plans are delayed. Janet Jackson, Tupac Shakhur, Tyra Ferrell, Regina King. w. d. John Singleton.
DRAMA: MURDER: Death-Dealing with; Inner City Life; Poets; Hairdressers; Teenagers; Black Casts; Black Women; Black Directors; Black Screenwriters; Female Protagonists; Writer-Directors (The Beat; Boyz 'n the Hood)

Point Blank, 1967, 92m, ★★/$$, MGM/MGM-UA, R/V-S. A gangster returns from exile to get his share of a job that went wrong. Lee Marvin, Angie Dickinson, Keenan Wynn, Carroll O'Connor, Lloyd Bochner, James B. Sikking. N-adap. *The Hunter*, d. John Boorman.
DRAMA: Crime Drama; Revenge; Mob Stories; Hollywood Life; Film Noir-Modern; Art Films; Cult Films; Hidden Gems
(The Killers; Bullitt)
(Ed: The Hollywood Hills rarely looked so artistic)

Point Break, 1991, 117m, ★★1/2/$$$, 20th/Fox, R/S-P-V. An FBI agent infiltrates a group of surfer/bankrobbers. Patrick Swayze, Keanu Reeves, Gary Busey, Lori Petty, John C. McGinley, James LeGros. w. Peter Iliff, d. Kathryn Bigelow.
ACTION: Crime Drama; Detective Stories; Bank Robberies; Surfers; Undercover; FBI Agents; Female Directors (Speed)

Point of No Return, 1993, 108m, ★★★/$$, WB/WB, R/EV-P-S. A young female murderer is taken in by a secret government group and brainwashed into submission as a hitwoman in order to save her from execution. But who's worse-her criminal pals or the government? Bridget Fonda, Gabriel Byrne, Anne Bancroft, Dermot Mulroney, Miguel Ferrer, Olivia D'Abo, Harvey Keitel, Richard Romanus. w. Robert Getchell, d. John Badham.
ACTION: Spy Films; Spies; Hitwomen; Secret Agents; Assassination Plots; Blackmail; Brainwashing; Murder-Coerced into; Dangerous Women; Feisty Females; Murderers-Female; Spies-Female; French Films; Female Protagonists; Foreign Film Remakes
REMAKE OF La Femme Nikita

The Pointsman, 1986, 95m, ★★★/$, Vestron/Vestron, R/S. A Norwegian woman gets stranded in Scotland with a loner who can't understand her but has designs on her. Jim Van Der Woude, Stephane Escoffier. d. Jos Stelling. BFLFilm (Norway). Oscars: 1-0.
DRAMA: Psychological Drama; **ROMANCE:** Stranded; Trains; Scotland; Art Films

Poison, 1991, 85m, ★★★/$, Ind/Fox-Lorber, R/S-V-MN. Interwoven tales of a gay men in an oppressive society's prison and a boy who murders his father, etc. Larry Maxwell, Edith Meeks, Susan Norman. w. d. Todd Haynes.
DRAMA: Art Films; Avant-Garde Films; Gay Men; Murder of Parents; Oppression; Prison Drama; Multiple Stories; Flashbacks; Writer-Directors; Independent Films
(Edward II; The Garden)

Poison Ivy, 1992, 91m, ★★/$$, New Line/New Line, R/S-FN. A sexy, over-sexed Lolita comes to visit her lesbian friend and goes after the much older dad. Drew Barrymore, Sarah Gilbert, Tom Skerritt, Cheryl Ladd. w. Katt Shea Ruben, Andy Ruben, d. Katt Shea Ruben.
DRAMA: Erotic Drama; Romance-Older Men/Younger Women; Romance with Friend's Relative; Sexy Women; Girls; Friendships-Female; Lesbians; Infatuations; Female Protagonists; Female Directors; Female Screenwriters; Narrated Films
(The Crush; Lolita; Doppelganger)

Police Academy, 1984, 96m, ★★1/2/$$$$, WB/WB, R/P-S. Every goofball in town wants to be a cop, it seems, and they're wreaking havoc on the academy in this first installment. Steve Guttenberg, Kim Cattrall, Bubba Smith, George Gaynes, Leslie Easterbrook. w. Hugh Wilson, Pat Proft, Neal Israel, d. Hugh Wilson.
COMEDY: Comedy-Gag; Comedy-Slapstick; Comedy of Errors; Police Comedy; Fools-Bumbling; Ensemble Films; Chase Stories; Sleeper Hits
SEQUELS: Police Academy 2–6, each in ascending order of descending quality. (Moving Violations)

Police Squad! Help Wanted!, 1982, 75m, ★★★/$$, Par/Par. The beginning of Frank Drebin of the *Naked Gun* series are in these episodes from the short-lived TV series. Leslie Nielsen, Alan North, Ed

Williams. w. d. Jerry Zucker, Jim Abrahams, David Zucker.
COMEDY: Police Comedy; Fools-Bumbling; Comedy of Errors; Comedy-Gag; TV Series; Cult Films
REMAKE: Naked Gun SERIES. (Sledgehammer TV Series; Police Academy)

Pollyanna, 1960, 134m, ★★★1/2/$$$, Disney/Disney. The ever-optimistic girl charms everyone in her fairy tale, all-American world. Hayley Mills (BJuvenile), Jane Wyman, Richard Egan, Karl Malden, Nancy Olson, Adolphe Menjou, Agnes Moorehead. d. David Swift. Oscars: 1-1.
CHILDREN'S: FAMILY: COMEDY DRAMA: MELODRAMA: Costume Drama; Women and Girls; Orphans; American Myth Girls; Ethics; Tearjerkers; 1900s; Small-town Life; Faded Hits
(The Parent Trap; Tiger Bay; The Chalk Garden)

Poltergeist, 1982, 114m, ★★★1/2/$$$$$, MGM/MGM-UA, PG/P-V-B&G. A real estate man learns his huge sub-division, including his own house, is sitting on top of a burial site when ghosts and ghoulies snatch his little girl into another dimension. Craig T. Nelson, Jobeth Williams, Beatrice Straight,. Zelda Rubinstein, Heather O'Rourke, James Karne, Dominique Dunne, Oliver Robbins. w. Steven Spielberg, Michael Grais, Mark Victor, d. Tobe Hooper.
HORROR: SCI-FI: SUSPENSE: Ghosts; Possessions; Supernatural Danger; Haunted Houses; Suburban Life; Kidnappings; Tornadoes; Salesmen; Blockbusters
SEQUELS: Poltergeist 2, Poltergeist 3.
SPOOF: Ghostbusters.
(The Exorcist; 2000 Maniacs)

Poltergeist 2, 1986, 92m, ★★1/2/$$, MGM/MGM-UA, PG-13/V-V-B&G. A new house, but same old troubles as Indian spirits haunt the Freeling family this time. Craig T. Nelson, Jobeth Williams, Heather O'Rourke, Geraldine Fitzgerald, John Beck, Will Sampson. w. Mark Victor, Michael Grais, d. Brian Gibson.
HORROR: SCI-FI: SUSPENSE: Ghosts; Possessions; Supernatural Danger; Haunted Houses; Suburban Life; Indians-American

Poltergeist 3, 1988, 97m, ★★/$, MGM/MGM-UA, R/V-B&G. This outing, the haunting is in the John Hancock skyscraper and only the little blonde girl is left to haunt, when she visits relatives. Tom Skerritt, Nancy Allen, Heather O'Rourke, Lara Flynn Boyle, Zelda Rubinstein. w. Brian Taggert, d. Gary Sherman.
HORROR: SCI-FI: SUSPENSE: Ghosts; Possessions; Supernatural Danger; Haunted Houses; High-Rise Settings
Polyester, 1981, 86m, ★★★/$$, Ind/Col, R/P-S. Transvestite housewife Divine wants that dream hunk in her boring cul-de-sac of a life, but isn't prepared for the consequences. Divine, Tab Hunter, Mink Stole, Edith Massey, David Samson. w. d. John Waters.
COMEDY: Spoofs; Suburban Life; Housewives; Wallflowers & Hunks; Men as Women; Cheating Women; Writer-Directors; Independent Films
(Pink Flamingo; Female Trouble)
The Poor Little Rich Girl, 1936, 79m, ★★★/$$$$, 20th/Fox. A rich girl runs away and joins some vaudevillians and becomes a little star. Shirley Temple, Jack Haley, Alice Faye, Jane Darwell, Gloria Stuart. d. Irving Cummings.
MUSICALS: MELODRAMA: Actresses; Vaudeville; Girls; Child Protagonists; Fame-Rise to
(Bright Eyes; A Little Princess)
The Pope Must Die(t), 1991, 87m, ★★/$, Ind/Media, R/S-P. An overweight oaf becomes the first Pope Dave by accident and ticks both the church and the mob off when he begins using funds for supposedly benevolent purposes-though that wasn't what it was intended for. Robbie Coltrane, Alex Rocco, Beverly D'Angelo, Herbert Lom, Paul Bartel. d. Peter Richardson.
COMEDY: FARCE: Popes; Religion; Impostors; Identities-Mistaken; Mob Comedy; Fugitives from the Mob
(Nuns on the Run; King Ralph)
The Pope of Greenwich Village, 1984, 122m, ★★/$$, MGM/MGM-UA, R/P-S-V. Two cousins deal in petty crime and fringe mob activities when their loyalty is put to the test. Mickey Rourke, Eric Roberts, Geraldine Page (BSActress), Daryl Hannah, Tony Musante, M. Emmet Walsh, Kenneth McMillan, Burt Young. w. Vincent Patrick, d. Stuart Rosenberg.

DRAMA: Crime Drama; Cousins; Friendships-Male; Mob Stories; Stern Women; Friendship on the Rocks; Coulda Been Great
(Mean Streets; Manhattan Melodrama; Public Enemy)
Popeye, 1980, 114m, ★★½/$$$, Par-Disney/Par, PG. The musical adventures of the spinach-craving sea man, his love, Olive Oyl, baby, Sweetpea, and his nemesis, Bluto. Robin Williams, Shelley Duvall, Ray Walston, Paul Dooley, Bill Irwin, Linda Hunt, Paul Smith. w. Jules Feiffer, d. Robert Altman.
MUSICAL: COMEDY DRAMA: Comedy-Life; Cartoon Heroes; ROMANCE: Babies-Having; Curiosities; Flops-Major
(Ed: It made some money, but with the critics and history, it was pretty much a turkey)
Popi, 1969, 115m, ★★½/$, Ind/NA. The life of a Puerto Rican custodian in the slums and his dreams of getting rich, or at least of his children getting rich. Alan Arkin, Rita Moreno. d. Arthur Hiller.
COMEDY DRAMA: Family Comedy; Dreams; Ordinary People Stories; Working Class; Poor People; Latin People; Inner City Life
Pork Chop Hill, 1959, 97m, ★★★/$$, MGM/MGM-UA. The last hours of the Korean War are detailed. Gregory Peck, Harry Guardino, George Peppard, James Edwards, Robert Blake, Martin Landau, Norman Fell. d. Lewis Milestone.
DRAMA: ACTION: Action Drama; War Stories; War Battles; Korean War; Ensemble Films; Ensembles-Male; Soldiers; Forgotten Films
(The Bridges at Toko-Ri; The Bold and the Brave)
Porky's, 1982, 94m, ★★★/$$$$$, 20th/Fox, R/ES-EP-FN-MRN. During the repressed 50s, anything will turn a bunch of horny teenagers on, and everyone seems to be doing something sexual to prove it. Dan Monahan, Boyd Gaines, Scott Colomby, Mark Harrier, Kim Cattrall, Susan Clark, Alex Karras. w. d. Bob Clark. Sleeper Hits; Blockbusters; Writer-Directors
Porky's 2, 1983, 100m, ★★/$$$, 20th/Fox, R/S-P-FN-MRN. More shenanigans involving streaking, the KKK, drive-ins, and other such fun. Bill Wiley, Dan Monahan, Scott Colomby. w. Alan Ormsby, Bob Clark, d. Bob Clark.

Porky's Revenge, 1985, 95m, ★½/$, 20th/Fox, R/ES-P-FN-MN. Time to graduate, but first, the big basketball game is about to be thrown, unless the kids can rally against the bookies and Porky himself. Dan Monahan, Wyatt Knight, Nancy Parsons, Scott Colomby, d. James Komack.
COMEDY: Erotic Comedy; Party Movies; 1950s Teenagers; Teenage Movies; High School Life; Florida
(Fast Times at Ridgemont High; Private School)
The Pornographers, 1966, 128m, ★★★/$, Ind/Tapeworm, Ingram. A Japanese filmmaker dabbles in porn while having fantasies about the daughter of the woman he lives with. Shiochi Ozawa, Massaomi Konda. d. Shoei Imamura.
DRAMA: COMEDY DRAMA: Erotic Drama; Infatuations; Japanese Films; Pornography World
(In the Realm of the Senses; Move; Promise Her Anything)
Port of Call, 1948, 100m, ★★★/$, Ind/New Line. A sailor docks in old Sweden and falls for a woman with a past. Ivine Christine Jonsson, Bengt Eklund. w. d. Ingmar Bergman.
DRAMA: ROMANCE: MELODRAMA: Romance-Doomed; Secrets-Keeping; Swedish Films; Writer-Directors
(Romance; Anna Christie)
The Portrait, 1993, 89m, ★★★/$$$, Turner/Turner, PG. A daughter who's an artist returns home to her well-to-do but disillusioned parents and wants to paint them. Unfortunately, they want to sell the house and tensions unload-but not too explosively. Lauren Bacall, Gregory Peck, Cecilia Peck, Paul McCrane, Mitchell Laurance. w. Lynn Roth, P-adap. Tina Howe, *Painting Churches*, d. Arthur Penn.
COMEDY DRAMA: MELODRAMA: Family Drama; Mothers & Daughters; Elderly People; Retirement; Painters; TV Movies
(On Golden Pond; Guess Who's Coming to Dinner)
Portrait of Jennie, 1948, 86m, ★★★½/$$$, 20th/CBS-Fox. A painter (Joseph Cotten) meets a girl in the park one day (Jennifer Jones) who may or may not be real but who does inspire him to continue painting, though he may be destroyed by falling in love in the

process. Ethel Barrymore, Lillian Gish, David Wayne, Cecil Kellaway. d. William Dieterle. BB&WCin, **BSFX**. Oscars: 2-1.

DRAMA: ROMANCE: Fantasy; Illusions; Surrealism; Dreams; Ghosts; Artists; Painters; Depression Era; Cult Films; Hidden Gems
(The Ebony Tower; Love Letters [1945])

The Poseidon Adventure, 1972, 117m, ★★★/$$$$$, 20th/Fox, PG/V. A New Year's Eve cruise in the Mediterranean is met with disaster when a tidal wave capsizes the ship and only a handful survive by crawling to the bottom of the ship to escape. Gene Hackman, Shelley Winters (BSActress), Carol Lynley, Roddy McDowall, Stella Stevens, Jack Albertson, Red Buttons, Ernest Borgnine. w. Wendell Mayes, Stirling Silliphant, d. Ronald Neame. BEdit, BOScore, **BOSong**, BSound, BCostume, BArt, BCin. Oscars: 8-1.

ACTION: ADVENTURE: MELODRAMA: SUSPENSE: Survival Drama; Escape Drama; Ships; Disaster Movies; Shelley Winters Drowns; Ensemble Films; Blockbusters; Faded Hits
(The Towering Inferno; Juggernaut; Airport 77)

The Positively True Adventures of the Alleged Texas Cheerleader-Murdering Mom, 1993, 99m, ★★★★/$$$$, HBO/HBO, R/P-S. The true story of the neurotic mother whose drive to make her daughter a cheerleader resulted in her trying to hire a hitman to knock off the main competition's mother. Holly Hunter (Emmy), Beau Bridges, Gregg Henry, Swoosie Kurtz, Matt Frewer. w. Jane Anderson (Emmy), d. Michael Ritchie. Multiple Emmy winner.

COMEDY: COMEDY DRAMA: SATIRE: Black Comedy; Murder-Attempted; Mental Illness; Evil Women; Scandals; Small-town Life; Small-town Scandals; Southerns; Housewives; Texas; True Stories; Girls; Women in Conflict; Mothers & Daughters; Rednecks; TV Movies; Hidden Gems; Female Protagonists; Female Screenwriters
(Miss Firecracker; Smile; I Love You to Death)

Posse, 1975, 94m, ★★★/$, Par/Par, PG/V. When a corrupt lawman goes after a bandit, it may be for more reasons than justice. Kirk Douglas, Bruce Dern, James Stacy, Bo Hopkins, David Canary. w. William Roberts, d. Kirk Douglas.

WESTERNS: ACTION: Action Drama; Police Stories; Police Corruption; Ethics; Forgotten Films; Overlooked at Release; Actor Directors

Posse, 1993, 113m, ★★¹/₂/$$, Polygram-U/Polygram, R/V-P. A pastiche of Western cliches with a black cast, showing that there were indeed black cowboys, but with white cowboys out to stop their freedom. Mario Van Peebles, Blair Underwood, Stephen Baldwin, Billy Zane, Charles Lane, Big Daddy Kane. w. Sy Richardson, Dario Scardapane, d. Mario Van Peebles.

WESTERNS: Westerns-Neo; Westerns-Revisionist; Black Men; Cowboys; Men in Conflict; Race Relations; Black vs. White; Black Casts; Black Directors; Black Screenwriters; Ensemble Films; Ensembles-Male
(New Jack City; Bad Company; Glory)

Possessed, 1947, 109m, ★★★/$$$, MGM/MGM-UA. A woman gets out of a mental institution and tries to start over as a nurse, but can't quite figure out how she got into the state she's in or where she's going. A few mysterious twists don't help matters. Joan Crawford (BActress), Van Heflin, Raymond Massey, Geraldine Brooks. SS-adap. Rita Weiman, One Man's Secret, d. Curtis Bernhardt. Oscars: 1-0.

MELODRAMA: Character Studies; Asylums; Mental Illness; Amnesia; Marriage Drama; Starting Over; Nurses; Female Protagonists
(Mr. Buddwing; Sudden Fear)

The Possession of Joel Delaney, 1972, 105m, ★★/$, Par/Par, R/S-V-MN. When an ancient occult spirit haunts a woman's brother, very strange things begin happening and soon a hostage situation with kinky aspects develops. Shirley MacLaine, Perry King, Michael Hordern. d. Waris Hussein.

DRAMA: Supernatural Danger; **SCI-FI:** Possessions; Brothers & Sisters; Forgotten Films; Curiosities
(The Exorcist; All of Me; Repossessed)

Postcards from the Edge, 1990, 101m, ★★★¹/₂/$$$$, Col/Col, R/S-P. A drug-addicted actress (Meryl Streep, BActress) is at a crisis point with her faltering career, her questionable boyfriend (Dennis Quaid), and her alcoholic mother (Shirley MacLaine). Richard Dreyfuss, Gene Hackman, Annette Bening, Rob Reiner. w. N-adap. Carrie Fisher, d.

Mike Nichols. BDirector, BOSong. Oscars: 2-0.

COMEDY DRAMA: Autobiographical Stories; Mothers & Daughters; Midlife Crises; Alcoholics; Comebacks; Drugs-Addictions; Nervous Breakdowns; Depression; Alienation; Hollywood Life; Hollywood Satire; Actresses; All-Star Casts; All-Star Cameos
(Terms of Endearment; Play It as It Lays; Heartburn)

The Postman (Il Postino), 1995, 105m, ★★★¹/₂/$$$, Miramax/Miramax, PG/S. When the writer Pablo Neruda visits a small Italian island and makes friends with the simple postman there, the postman is transformed in love, thinking, and life in general. Massimo Troisi (BActor), Philippe Noiret, Maria Grazia Cucinotta, Linda Moretti. w. Anna Pavignano, Michael Radford, Furio Scarpelli, Giacomo Scarpelli, & Massimo Troisi (BAScr) N-adap. *Burning Patience*, Antonio Skarmeta, d. Michael Radford (BDirector). BPicture, **BDScore**. Oscars: 5-1.

DRAMA: ROMANCE: Romantic Drama; Writers; Islands; Lyrical Films; Italian Films; Sleeper Hits; Female Screenwriters
(Mediterraneo; Everybody's Fine; Cinema Paradiso; Amarcord)
(Ed: The lead, Massimo Troisi, died from heart failure the day after the film was completed. Only the fourth foreign language film ever nominated for Best Picture (after *Grand Illusion* [1938], *Z* [1969], and *Cries and Whispers* [1973])

The Postman Always Ring Twice, 1945, 113m, ★★★★/$$$$, MGM/MGM-UA. A restaurant owner's wife (Lana Turner) has a wandering eye for a man (John Garfield) and soon convinces him to join her in killing her husband. Cecil Kellaway, Hume Cronyn, Leon Ames. N-adap. J. M. Cain, d. Tay Garnett. Film Noir

The Postman Always Rings Twice, 1981, 123m, ★★★/$, Par/Par. Remake of classic film noir with Jessica Lange and Jack Nicholson, where Lange takes a less dominant role. w. David Mamet, N-adap. J. M. Cain, d. Bob Rafelson. Film Noir-Modern; Flops-Major

SUSPENSE: MURDER: ROMANCE: Erotic Drama; Dangerous Women; Dangerous Men; Murder of Spouse; Murder-Coerced to; Film Noir

(Body Heat; Double Indemnity; Obsessione)

Powaqqatsi, Life in Transformation, 1988, 95m, ★★★/$. The sped-up beautiful cinematography of the first (Koyannisquatsi) this time travels to the third world countries and other foreign places. d. Godfrey Reggio.
Art Films; Documentaries; Music Video Style; Outstanding Scenery; Cult Films
SEQUEL TO: Koyaanisqatsi

Power, 1986, 111m, ★★/$, WB/WB, R/S-P. A mediaa consultant for high-powered politicians is forced to ponder the ethics of his job when a woman enters his life. Richard Gere, Julie Christie, Kate Capshaw, Gene Hackman, Denzel Washington, Michael Learned, Beatrice Straight, Fritz Weaver. w. David Himmelstein, d. Sidney Lumet.
DRAMA: Political Campaigns; Politicians; Political Drama; Power-Rise to; Greed; Ethics; 1980s; Coulda Been Good
(Primal Fear; Bob Roberts; The Best Man)

The Power of One, 1992, 126m, ★★/$$, WB/WB. A white orphan in 1940s South Africa learns to stand up for himself against the nasty Germans there, with the aid of a black boxing coach. Stephen Dorff, Armin Mueller-Stahl, Morgan Freeman, John Gielgud, John Osborne, Fay Masterson. w. Robert Mark Kamen, d. John G. Avildsen.
MELODRAMA: Underdog Stories; coming of Age; Race Relations; Black vs. White; South Africa; 1940s
(Gladiator; Streets of Gold)

Power, Passion, and Murder, 1983, 105m, ★★★/$$ (TV-VR), AP-PBS/Vidmark, R/S. An intermingling of F. Scott Fitzgerald stories about 1930s Hollywood, centering around a studio boss in crisis and an actress (Michelle Pfeiffer) who has an affair with an average man she gets into a car accident with (Brian Kerwin), eventually bringing tragedy to his life. Darren McGavin, Stella Stevens, Lois Chiles. SS-adap. F. Scott Fitzgerald, d. Paul Bogart, Leon Ichaso.
DRAMA: MURDER: Multiple Stories; Hollywood Life; ROMANCE: Romance-Doomed; Romance with Married Person; Actresses; Moviemaking; TV Movies; Hidden Gems
(The Last Tycoon; F. Scott Fitzgerald in Hollywood)

Powwow Highway, 1989, 105m, Ind/WB, R/P-V. Indian activists try to defend and improve the way of life on the reservation. A. Martinez, Gary Farmer, Amanda Wyss, Graham Greene. d. Joanelle Romero, Jonathan Wacks.
DRAMA: Native Americans; Indians-American; Government as Enemy; Corruption; Framed?; Southwestern Life; Female Directors; Independent Films
(The Milagro Beanfield War; Thunderheart)

A Prayer for the Dying, 1987, 104m, ★★1/2/$, Goldwyn/Goldwyn. An IRA hitman has to pull one last job and hides in the church after a priest witnesses it. Mickey Rourke, Alan Bates, Sammi Davis-Voss, Liam Neeson, Bob Hoskins, Alison Doody. w. Edmund Ward, Martin Lynch, d. Mike Hodges.
DRAMA: IRA; Hitmen; Witness to Murder; MURDER: One Last Time; Hiding Out; Ireland; Irish Films
(Odd Man Out; Last Rites)

Predator, 1987, 107m, ★★1/2/$$$, 20th/Fox, R/V-P-B&G. CIA mercenaries head into the Mexican jungle to unwittingly do battle with an unseen alien force. Arnold Schwarzenegger, Jesse Ventura, Bill Duke, Carl Weathers, Shane Black, Sonny Landham. w. Jim Thomas, John Thomas, d. John McTiernan.
ACTION: HORROR: SUSPENSE: Monsters; Aliens-Outer Space, Evil; Jungles; Mexico; CIA Age; Mercenaries; Invisible People
(Aliens; Alien; Wolfen; Sniper)

Predator 2, 1990, 105m, ★★/$$, 20th/Fox, R/P-V. A black L.A. cop this time does battle with the unseen force. Danny Glover, Gary Busey, Ruben Blades, Bill Paxton, Robert Davi, Adam Baldwin, Maria Conchita Alonso. w. Jim Thomas, John Thomas, d. Stephen Hoskins.
ACTION: Aliens-Outer Space, Evil; Los Angeles; Police Stories; Black Men; Invisible People

Prelude to a Kiss, 1992, 105m, ★★/$, 20th/Fox, PG-13/S. A young couple madly in love are thrown a curve when she turns into an old Jewish man. Alec Baldwin, Meg Ryan, Patty Duke, Sydney Walker, Ned Beatty, Kathy Bates, Stanley Tucci. w. P-adap. Craig Lucas, d. Norman Rene.
COMEDY DRAMA: ROMANCE: Romantic Comedy; Marriage-Impending;

Honeymoons; Body Switching; Looksism; Aging; Magic Realism; Elderly Men; Flops-Major; Coulda Been Great
(Ed: Oy vey . . . What was a Broadway hit play in a time when there were no hit plays became a major summer release dud)

The Preppie Murder, 1989, 100m, ★★1/2/$$$$, Turner/Turner. True story of rich boy Robert Chambers who strangled his girlfriend in Central Park while having kinky sex. William Baldwin, Lara Flynn Boyle, Danny Aiello, Joanna Kerns, William Devane. d. John Herzfeld.
DRAMA: True Stories; MURDER: Sexual Kinkiness; Young People; Murderers-Nice; Sexy Men; TV Movies

Presenting Lily Mars, 1943, 105m, ★★★/$$$, MGM/MGM-UA. A girl from a small town makes it up the ranks in New York, but will she find love? Judy Garland, Van Heflin, Fay Bainter, Richard Carlson, Tommy Dorsey. d. Norman Taurog.
COMEDY DRAMA: MELODRAMA: Fame-Rise to; Singers; Actresses; Young Women; Female Protagonists; Hidden Gems
(Morning Glory; The Actress)

The President's Analyst, 1967, 104m, ★★★/$, Par/Par, AMC. A psychiatrist is recruited to listen to the president, but when he begins to question things he winds up on the lam from secret agents who claim he's lost his mind. James Coburn, Godfrey Cambridge, Severn Darden, Pat Harrington, William Daniels, Joan Delaney, Will Geer. w. d. Theodore J. Flicker.
COMEDY DRAMA: SATIRE: Secret Agents; Fugitives; Government as Enemy; Fantasies; Presidents; Psychiatrists; Art Films; 1960s Psychedelic Era; Cult Films; Forgotten Films; Curiosities; Writer-Directors
(The Parallax View; Winter Kills; In Like Flint)

Presumed Innocent, 1990, 127m, ★★★1/2/$$$$, WB/WB, R/S-V-P. A lawyer (Harrison Ford) having an affair with a colleague (Greta Scacchi) finds his lover's been murdered, with all the signs pointing to himself. Bonnie Bedelia, Brian Dennehy, Raul Julia, John Spencer. w. Frank Pierson, N-adap. Scott Turow, d. Alan J. Pakula.
SUSPENSE: MURDER: MYSTERY: MURDER MYSTERY: Legal Thrillers; Lawyers as Detectives; Lawyers; Murder-Clearing

Oneself; Whodunit; Framed?; Romance-Triangles; Revenge; *Revenge on Cheaters*; Romance-Clandestine; Clever Plots & Endings
(The Fugitive; Burden of Proof)

Pretty Baby, 1978, 109m, ★★★1/2/$, Par/Par, R/S-FN. A bordello in old New Orleans is the scene where a young prostitute raises her daughter into the trade as a man pursues the daughter's sexuality before its time. Brooke Shields, Susan Sarandon, Keith Carradine, Diana Scarwid. w. d. Louis Malle. BOScore. Oscars: 1-0.
DRAMA: Erotic Drama; **ROMANCE:** Prostitutes-Low Class; New Orleans; Mothers & Daughters; Men and Girls; Sexual Kinkiness; Romance-Older Men/Younger Women; Cult Films; Writer-Directors
(King of the Gypsies; Lolita)

Pretty Poison, 1968, 96m, ★★★1/2/$$, 20th/Fox, Ingram. A very wicked teenage girl wants her mother bumped off and recruits a naive young man to do it. But will they get away with it? Tuesday Weld, Anthony Perkins, Beverly Garland, Ken Kercheval, John Randolph. w. d. Noel Black. Numerous critics' awards.
COMEDY DRAMA: Black Comedy; Murder of Parents; Murder-Coercing/Forcing into; Stories Which Begin Again; Evil Women; Teenagers; Cult Films; Hidden Gems; Forgotten Films; Writer-Directors
(Chicago Joe and the Showgirl; Last Summer)

Pretty Woman, 1990, 117m, ★★★/ $$$$$$, Touchstone/Touchstone, R/S-P. A zillionaire picks up a neophyte hooker who knows how to fix a Ferrari and pays her for a week of hanky panky and then actually promises to marry her. Richard Gere, Julia Roberts (BActress), Laura San Giacomo, Jason Alexander, Ralph Bellamy, Hector Elizondo, Elinor Donahue. w. J. F. Lawton, d. Garry Marshall. Oscars: 1-0.
COMEDY: ROMANCE: Romantic Comedy; Prostitutes-Low Class; Romance with Prostitute; Rich People; Romance-Mismatched; Beverly Hills; Dreams; Free Spirits; American Dream; Blockbusters; Sleeper Hits
(That Touch of Mink; The Happy Hooker)

Prick Up Your Ears, 1987, 110m, ★★★/$, Ind/Avenue, NA, R/S-P. Story of playwright Joe Orton and his jealous lover who eventually ended Orton's life. Gary Oldman, Alfred Molina, Vanessa Redgrave, Julie Walters, Lindsay Duncan, Wallace Shawn. w. Alan Bennett, d. Stephen Frears.
DRAMA: TRAGEDY: MURDER: Murder of Spouse; Tragi-Comedy; Crimes of Passion; True Stories; Writers; Gay Men; Jealousy; British Films; Hidden Gems
(Withnail & I; My Beautiful Laundrette; Sid and Nancy; We Think the World of You)

Pride and Prejudice, 1940, 114m, ★★★/$$$, MGM/MGM-UA. In Victorian-era England, a young woman decides not to pursue the man her parents have chosen for her, risking the consequences. Greer Garson, Laurence Olivier, Edmund Gwenn, Edna May Oliver, Mary Boland, Maureen O'Sullivan, Ann Rutherford. d. Robert Z. Leonard. **BB&WArt.**
DRAMA: MELODRAMA: Costume Drama; **ROMANCE:** Romance-Choosing the Right Person; Marriage-Impending; Female Protagonists; Feisty Females; Victorian Era; Classic Literary Adaptations
REMAKE: BBC/A&E 1996
(Sense and Sensibility; Howards End)

The Pride and the Passion, 1957, 132m, ★★/$$, MGM/MGM-UA. Resistance fighters in the Spanish Revolution do battle. Cary Grant, Frank Sinatra, Sophia Loren. w. Edward Anhalt, d. Stanley Kramer.
ACTION: Action Drama; War Stories; War Battles; Spanish Revolution; Historical Drama; Forgotten Films
(For Whom the Bell Tolls; A Farewell to Arms)

The Pride of the Yankees, 1942, 128m, ★★★1/2/$$$$, 20th/Fox. Rise and demise through disease of baseball great Lou Gehrig. Myasthenia Gravis was the disease which then became known by Lou Gehrig's disease. Gary Cooper, Teresa Wright (BActress), Babe Ruth, Walter Brennan, Dan Duryea. w. Paul Gallico (BOStory) Herman J. Mankiewicz, Jo Swerling, d. Sam Wood. BPicture, BSound, **BEdit**, BOScore, BArt, BB&WCin. Oscars: 9-1.
MELODRAMA: ROMANCE: Disease Stories; Marriage Drama; Biographies; Baseball; Crying in Baseball; True Stories; 1940s; Sports Movies
(Bang the Drum Slowly; The Babe)

Priest, 1995, 105m, ★★★1/2/$, Miramax/ Miramax-Touchstone, R/S-P. A priest in Britain begins his life in the clergy by confronting a priest having an affair with a woman, but then soon finds himself searching his own needs and the result is a trip to a gay bar and much confusion after. Linus Roache, Tom Wilkinson, Cathy Tyson, Robert Carlyle. w. Jimmy McGovern, d. Antonia Bird.
DRAMA: Priests; Sexual Problems; Gay Men; Gay Awakenings; Romance with Clergy; British Films; Female Directors
(The Lost Language of Cranes; The Boys of St. Vincent; A Man of No Importance; Lamb)

Priest of Love, 1981, 125m, ★★1/2/$, Ind/HBO, R/S. The last days of author D. H. Lawrence, famed for his erotic passages, as he struggles with tuberculosis. Ian McKellen, Janet Suzman, John Gielgud, Helen Mirren. d. Christopher Miles.
DRAMA: Marriage Drama; Biographies; Death-Impending; Disease Stories; Writers
(Women in Love; Tropic of Cancer; Lady Chatterley's Lover; Sons and Lovers; Henry and June)

Primary Motive, 1992, 93m, ★★/VR, 20th/Fox, R/S-P-V. A press secretary for a politician discovers the lies of the opposition, but no one believes him. Judd Nelson, Sally Kirkland, Richard Jordan, Justine Bateman, John Savage. w. Daniel Adams, William Snowden, d. Daniel Adams.
SUSPENSE: Conspiracy; Political Drama; Political Campaigns; Politicians; Ethics; Detective Stories; Unbelieved; Coulda Been Good

Prime Cut, 1972, 86m, ★★1/2/$$, 20th/Fox, R/P-V. All kinds of illicit behavior is covered up around the meat factories until one man digs into it. Gene Hackman, Lee Marvin, Sissy Spacek, Angel Tompkins. w. Robert Dillon, d. Michael Ritchie.
DRAMA: ACTION: MURDER: Detective Stories; Conspiracy; Corporate Corruption; Mob Stories; Forgotten Films
(Night Moves; The French Connection)

The Prime of Miss Jean Brodie, 1969, 116m, ★★★1/2/$$, 20th/CBS-Fox, PG. A Scottish girls' school teacher may get herself into trouble with her radical political and psychological ideals. Maggie Smith (**BActress**), Pamela Franklin, Robert

Stephens. Celia Johnson, Jane Carr. w. Jay Presson Allen, N-adap. Muriel Spark, d. Ronald Neame. BOSong (Jean). Oscars: 2-1.

DRAMA: Free Spirits; Feisty Females; Teachers; Teachers & Students; 1920s; Girls' Schools; Rebels; Stern Women; British Films; Faded Hits; Female Protagonists
(The Lonely Passion of Judith Hearne; These Three; Goodbye, Mr. Chips)

Prime Suspect, 1992, 240m, ★★★1/2/ $$$, Ind-BBC/Fox-Lorber. Female police detective Jan Tennison takes over a case from a male detective and soon believes the murderer she's after is a serial killer. Helen Mirren, Tom Bell, Zoe Wanamaker, Ralph Fiennes. w. N-adap. Lynda LaPlante, d. Christopher Menaul.

MYSTERY: MURDER: MURDER MYSTERY: Detective Stories; Detectives-Police; Detectives-Female; Trail of a Killer; Serial Killers; Miniseries; TV Movies; British Films; Cult Films; Female Protagonists; Female Screenwriters
(Silence of the Lambs)

The Prince and the Pauper, 1937, 118m, ★★★/$$$, 20th/Fox. Mark Twain's classic about the young King of England who trades places with a lookalike boy from the streets of London. Errol Flynn, Claude Rains, Alan Hale, Billy Mauch. d. William Keighley.

ADVENTURE: Comic Adventure; Lookalikes; Rich vs. Poor; Swashbucklers; Kings; Impostors; Body Switching; Costume Drama; Classic Literary Adaptations
REMAKE: Crossed Swords.
(The Prisoner of Zenda; The Man in the Iron Mask; Little Lord Fauntleroy)

The Prince and the Showgirl, 1957, 127m, ★★★/$$, WB/WB. An obscure European prince visiting London goes after an American actress who doesn't quite get the whole picture. Laurence Olivier, Marilyn Monroe, Sybil Thorndike. w. N-adap. Terence Rattigan, d. Laurence Olivier.

COMEDY DRAMA: ROMANCE: Romantic Comedy; Sexy Women; Actresses; Princes; Actor Directors; 1900s; Coulda Been Great; Actor Directors; Forgotten Films

The Prince of Central Park, 1977, 76m, ★★★1/2/$$, Ind/Live. Two orphans live in a tree in Central Park and find an elderly woman to take them in, but their magical, if unlikely world, in the park may be too much to leave behind. T. J. Hargrave, Ruth Gordon, Lisa Richards, Brooke Shields, Dan Hedaya. N-adap. Evan Rhodes, d. Harvey Hart.

COMEDY DRAMA: CHILDREN'S: FAMILY: Fantasy; Orphans; Elderly Women; Women and Boys; New York Life; Cult Films; Hidden Gems; TV Movies; Child Protagonists
REMAKE: Broadway, as a musical.
(The Hideaways; My Bodyguard)

Prince of Darkness, 1987, 102m, ★★/$$, U/MCA-U, R/EV-S-B&G. A chemical at a university lab contains essence d'Satan. Donald Pleasence, Lisa Blount, Jameson Parker. w.d. John Carpenter.

HORROR: Satan; Experiments; Murders-One by One; Soul-Selling One's; Writer-Directors

Prince of the City, 1981, 167m, ★★★/$, Ladd-WB/WB, R/P-V. True of story of a New York police officer trying to stop misuse of drug contraband by fellow police officers. Treat Williams, Jerry Orbach, Lindsay Crouse, Lance Henriksen, Richard Forojny. w. Jay Presson Allen, Sidney Lumet, d. Sidney Lumet.

DRAMA: Social Drama; Police Stories; Police Corruption; Government Corruption; True Stories; Female Screenwriters; Hidden Gems; Overlooked at Release
(Serpico; The French Connection)

The Prince of Tides, 1991, 132m, ★★★★/$$$$, Columbia/Col-Tri, R/S-P. A man going through a midlife crisis himself (Nick Nolte, BActor) must go to New York to help his sister who's attempted suicide again (Melinda Dillon), and try to unlock the past with the help of her psychiatrist (Barbra Streisand), though he may be falling in love. Kate Nelligan (BSActress), Blythe Danner, Jason Gould, George Carlin, Jeroen Krabbe. w. Pat Conroy, Becky Johnston (BAScr), N-adap. Pat Conroy, d. Barbra Streisand. BPicture, BOScore, BCin, BEdit. Oscars: 7-0.

DRAMA: MELODRAMA: ROMANCE: Midlife Crisis; Mental Illness; Secrets-Haunting; Rape/Rapists; Rape-Male; Brothers & Sisters; Redemption; Saving Someone; Psychologists; Romance with Psychologist; Romance-Brief; Romance-

Opposites Attract; New York Life; Southerns; City vs. Country; North vs. South; Female Directors; Female Screenwriters
(Conrack; The Great Santini; Ordinary People)

Prince Valiant, 1954, 100m, ★★1/2/ $$$, 20th/Fox. When Dad, the king, is exiled by a despot, the cute young prince goes to King Arthur for help. Robert Wagner, James Mason, Janet Leigh, Victor McLaglen, Debra Paget, Sterling Hayden, Donald Crisp, Brian Aherne. w. Dudley Nichols, d. Henry Hathaway.

DRAMA: ADVENTURE: Power Struggles; Medieval Times; Kings; Princes; Swashbucklers; Costume Drama; Camelot Stories
(The Sword in the Stone)

The Princess and the Pirate, 1944, 94m, ★★★/$$$, Par/HBO, Sultan. A court jester who's ticked off some pirates falls for a princess while on the lam. Bob Hope, Virginia Mayo, Walter Slezak, Walter Brennan, Victor McLaglen, Bing Crosby. d. David Bulter.

COMEDY: Pirates; **ROMANCE:** Romantic Comedy; Romance-Reluctant; Fugitives from the Mob; Caribbean; Fools-Bumbling
(Monsieur Beaucaire; The Court Jester)

The Princess Bride, 1987, 96m, ★★★/$$, Col/Col, PG. A grandfather sits his grandson down for a wild, anachronistic tale of a boy and girl who do battle with an evil kingdom in order to get back together. Cary Elwes, Robin Wright, Mandy Patinkin, Peter Falk, Wallace Shawn, Carol Kane, Fred Savage, Christopher Guest, Billy Crystal, Peter Cook. w. N-adap. William Goldman, d. Rob Reiner.

COMEDY: Fantasy; **ADVENTURE:** Fairy Tales; Comic Adventure; Storytellers; Men and Boys; Narrated Films; Princes; Princesses; Men in Conflict; Men Fighting Over Women; Saving Someone; Cartoonlike Movies
(The Neverending Story)

Princess Caraboo, 1994, 102m, ★★★/ VR, Col/Col, PG. When a gypsy-like girl wanders into an early 1800s English town speaking only some strange language, everyone's quick to pronounce her royalty from afar, when what she may be is something far more humble. Phoebe Cates, Stephen Rea, Kevin Kline. d. Michael Austin.

COMEDY DRAMA: True Stories; Incredible but Mostly True; Impostors; Princesses; Servants; Class Conflicts; 1800s; England
(Six Degrees of Separation; Olivier, Olivier; The Return of Martin Guerre; Sommersby)

Prison Stories: Women on the Inside, 1991, 94m, ★★★/$$, Showtime/Prism, R/P-S-V. A trilogy of life in the women's prison, revolving around two women thieves, a murderer about to be released, and a woman troubled by what's happening to her family while she's on the inside. Annabella Sciorra, Rae Dawn Chong, Lolita Davidovich, Rachel Ticotin, Grace Zabriskie. d. Penelope Spheeris, Donna Deitch, Joan Micklin Silver.

DRAMA: Multiple Stories; TV Movies; Women in Prison; Prison Drama; Women in Conflict; Friendships-Female; Criminals-Female; Female Protagonists; Female Screenwriters; Female Directors
(Caged; Caged Fear; Love Child)

The Prisoner, 1955, 91m, ★★★/$$, Col/Col. Story of a Hungarian Cardinal imprisoned behind the Iron Curtain. Alec Guinness, Jack Hawkins. d. Peter Glenville.

DRAMA: Political Drama; Religion; Priests; Iron Curtain-Behind the; Cold War Era; World War II Stories; British Films

The Prisoner: Arrival, 1968, 52m, ★★★/$$$, BBC-Ind/MPI. Pilot for the cult British series where a man has been imprisoned in a seemingly picture-perfect island exile where he struggles to figure out how and why he got there. Patrick McGoohan, Guy Doleman, Leo McKern, Virginia Maskell. d. Don Chaffey.

DRAMA: SCI-FI: Futuristic Films; Oppression; Prison Drama; Psychological Drama; Cult Films; British Films; TV Series
(Total Recall; Fahrenheit 451)
(Ed: The entire series is available on tape)

Prisoner of Honor, 1991, 90m, ★★★/$$$, HBO/HBO, PG. True story of a Jewish military officer in France accused of treason and those who believe he's innocent and a target of anti-Semitism. Richard Dreyfuss, Oliver Reed, Peter Firth, Jeremy Kemp, Lindsay Anderson. d. Ken Russell.

DRAMA: True Stories; Courtroom Drama; Traitors; Accused Unjustly; Framed?;

Anti-Semitism; Jewish People; France; 1800s; TV Movies
(The Life of Emile Zola)
(Ed: Dreyfuss stars in this story of his own ancestor)

Prisoner of Second Avenue, 1974, 98m, ★★★1/2/$$, WB/WB, PG/P. When a middle-aged executive is laid-off and the city of New York seems to be closing in on him, his wife tries to find a job while keeping him from having a breakdown. Jack Lemmon, Anne Bancroft, Elizabeth Wilson, Gene Saks, Sylvester Stallone, F. Murray Abraham. w. P-adap. Neil Simon, d. Melvin Frank.

COMEDY: COMEDY DRAMA: SATIRE: Social Satire; Nervous Breakdowns; Unemployment; Midlife Crisis; Marriage Drama; Marriage on the Rocks; New York Life
(The Out of Towners; The Fortune Cookie)

Prisoner of Zenda, 1937, 101m, ★★★1/2/$$$, MGM/MGM-UA. Ronald Colman, Douglas Fairbanks, Madeleine Carroll, David Niven, Raymond Massey, Mary Astor, Aubrey Smith. w. Donald Ogden Stewart, John Balderston, d. John Cromwell.

Prisoner of Zenda, 1952, 101m, ★★1/2/$$$, MGM/MGM-UA. Stewart Granger, Deborah Kerr, Louis Calhern, James Mason, Jane Greer, Lewis Stone. d. Richard Thorpe.

Prisoner of Zenda, 1979, 108m, ★★1/2/$$, U/MCA-U, PG/S-P. Spoof on the classic. Peter Sellers, Jeremy Kemp, Lynne Frederick, Lionel Jeffries, Elke Sommer. w. Dick Clement, Ian LaFrenais, d. Richard Quine.

COMEDY: Spoofs
An everyman is forced to pose as his cousin, the king from a little country, after said royal has been kidnapped and the anarchists are lurking. The only problem is he falls for the queen.

ADVENTURE: COMEDY DRAMA: Comic Adventure; Costume Drama; Body Switching; Impostors; **ROMANCE:** Romance with Relative's Lover; Royalty; Kings; Queens; Classic Literary Adaptations
(Dave; The Phantom President; Moon Over Parador)

The Private Affairs of Bel Ami, 1947, 112m, ★★★/$$, Republic/Republic. A playboy rises in social circles in gay 90s Paris. George Sanders, Angela Lansbury, Ann Dvorak, Frances Dee, John

Carradine, Susan Douglas. w. d. Albert Lewis.

COMEDY DRAMA: Playboys; Social Climbing; Cheating Men; Sexy Men; Paris; Costume Drama; Writer-Directors; Forgotten Films

Private Benjamin, 1980, 110m, ★★★1/2/$$$$$, WB/WB, R/S-P. A pampered rich girl runs away to join the army when her husband dies on their wedding night. But the pictures of luxury condos and lies the military use lead to a big shock for the princess when she finds herself in basic training under the thumb of a tyrannical female drill sergeant. Goldie Hawn (BActress), Eileen Brennan (BSActress), Albert Brooks, Robert Webber, Armand Assante, Barbara Barrie, Mary Kay Place, Sally Kirkland, Craig T. Nelson, Harry Dean Stanton, Sam Wanamaker. w. Nancy Meyers, Charles Shyer (BOScr), d. Howard Zieff. Oscars: 3-0.

COMEDY: Fish out of Water Stories; Military Comedy; Female in Male Domain; Mix-Ups; Simple Minds; Mean Women; Soldiers; Marriage-Impending; What If . . . Stories; Jewish People; Rich People; Female Protagonists; Female Screenwriters; Sleeper Hits; Blockbusters
(Protocol; Goodbye, New York; Troop Beverly Hills)

A Private Function, 1984, 96m, ★★★/$$, Island/Par, PG. During the height of rationing during the war, a poor British man steals a pig for his family to eat, but will guilt save the porker? Michael Palin, Maggie Smith, Liz Smith, Denholm Elliott, Bill Paterson, w. Alan Bennett, d. Malcolm Mowbray.

COMEDY: SATIRE: World War II Stories; Poor People; Decisions-Big; Animal Rights; Family Comedy; Hidden Gems

The Private Life of Henry VIII, 1933, 97m, ★★★1/2/$$$, Gainsborough-UA/HBO, Nos, Prism. The notorious king's many wives and their disappearances are detailed. Charles Laughton, Binnie Barnes, Elsa Lanchester, Robert Donat, Merle Oberon, Wendy Barrie. w. Arthur Wimperis, Lajos Biro, d. Alexander Korda.

DRAMA: Historical Drama; Marriage Drama; Evil Men; Marriage on the Rocks; Executions; Women in Jeopardy; Biographies; Kings; England; British Films
(Anne of the Thousand Days)

The Private Life of Sherlock Holmes, 1970, 125m, ★★★/$, 20th/Fox, PG. A look into the mystery of what Sherlock did after the mysteries were solved. Robert Stephens, Colin Blakely, Genevieve Page, Christopher Lee, Stanley Holloway. w. I.A.L. Diamond, Billy Wilder, d. Billy Wilder.
COMEDY DRAMA: Revisionist Films; Sherlock Holmes; Detective Stories; Detectives-Private; Behind the Scenes; Curiosities; Overlooked at Release
(The Seven Percent Solution; Without a Clue)

Private Lives, 1931, 92m, ★★★/$$$$, MGM/MGM-UA. When old flames honeymoon with new mates at the same hotel, their relationship begins to take the forefront once again-if the new spouses will allow it. Norma Shearer, Robert Montgomery, Reginald Denny, Una Merkel, Jean Hersholt. P-adap. Noel Coward, d. Sidney Franklin.
COMEDY: ROMANCE: Romantic Comedy; Romance-Bickering; Romance-Reluctant; Romance with Married Person; Swapping Partners; Cheating Men; Cheating Women; Honeymoons; Hotels; Stagelike Films
(Twentieth Century; The Guardsman; The Barkleys of Broadway)

The Private Lives of Elizabeth & Essex, 1939, 106m, ★★★/$$$, WB/Fox, MGM-UA. The affair between the virgin queen and her dashing earl is detailed, as the queen has to choose between love and going to war. Bette Davis, Errol Flynn, Nanette Fabray, Olivia de Havilland, Donald Crisp, Leo G. Carroll. d. Michael Curtiz. BB&WCin, BArt, BOScore, BEdit. Oscars: 4-0.
DRAMA: ROMANCE: Romantic Drama; Romance-Reluctant; Historical Drama; Costume Drama; Stern Women; Wallflowers & Hunks; Queens; Romance-Mismatched; Decisions-Big; Elizabethan Era
(The Virgin Queen; Elizabeth R.)

A Private Matter, 1992, 89m, ★★★/$$$, HBO/HBO, PG-13/S. The true story of an American woman's trek to Sweden to legally abort her baby believed to be defective from thalidomide. Sissy Spacek, Aidan Quinn, Estelle Parsons, Sheila McCarthy, Leon Russom, William H. Macy. w. William Nicholson, d. Joan Micklin Silver.
DRAMA: Social Drama; True Stories; Decisions-Big; Abortion Dilemmas;

Marriage Drama; 1960s; Female Protagonists; TV Movies; Female Directors
(Roe vs. Wade)

Private School, 1983, 89m, ★★/$$, U/MCA-U, R/ES-P-FN. Two girls go after a hunk from a boys' school down the road and wind up in a series of shenanigans. Phoebe Cates, Betsy Russell, Kathleen Wilhoite, Ray Walston, Matthew Modine, Jonathan Prince. d. Noel Black.
COMEDY: Erotic Comedy; Teenage Movies; Teenagers; Romance-Girl Wants Boy; Girls' Schools; Female Protagonists
(Fast Times at Ridgemont High; Little Darlings)

The Prize, 1963, 135m, ★★★/$$$, UA/MGM-UA-Turner. A Nobel Prize laureate in literature who's also a playboy (Paul Newman) is on the run from spies and thugs when he stumbles upon a conspiracy in Stockholm. Elke Sommer, Edward G. Robinson, Diane Baker, Leo G. Carroll. w. Ernest Lehman, N-adap. Irving Wallace, d. Mark Robson.
COMEDY DRAMA: THRILLER: Comic Thriller; Comic Mystery; Chase Stories; Conspiracy; Detectives-Amateur; Kidnappings; Impostors; Lookalikes; Mindgames; Unbelieved; Men in Jeopardy; Americans Abroad; Writers Romance-Reluctant; Romance-Opposites Attract; Playboys; Contests-Competitions; Scientists; Nudists; Faded Hits; Forgotten Films; Sweden; Hitchcockian
REMAKE/RETREAD: North by Northwest.
(North by Northwest; Charade; Arabesque; Saboteur; The Mackintosh Man)
(Ed: Probably suffered some in original release on the heels of N by NW four years before which it owes much to, but is actually more elegant and witty, though less action at first. Where N by NW is like Saboteur, The Prize isn't)

The Prizefighter and the Lady, 1933, 102m, ★★★/$$$, MGM/MGM-UA. Real-life boxing champ Max Baer, Sr. stars as a boxer who goes after a chanteuse who finds it hard to stay with him. Myrna Loy, Otto Kurger, Walter Huston. d. W. S. Van Dyke.
MELODRAMA: Boxing; Sports Movies; **ROMANCE:** Romance-Mismatched Actresses; Romance-Reluctant; Faded Hits
(The Cowboy and the Lady; The Champ; The Main Event; Designing Woman)

Prizzi's Honor, 1985, 130m, ★★★★/$$$, 20th/Vestron, R/P-V-S. When a hitman for the mob (Jack Nicholson, BActor) falls for a woman he meets, he doesn't know she's also a hitwoman (Kathleen Turner), but his ex (Anjelica Huston, **BSActress**) soons exposes his new love's identity and the games begin as the romance dissolves. William Hickey (BSActor), Robert Loggia, Robert Alda. w. Janet Roach, Richard Condon (BAScr), N-adap. Richard Condon, d. John Huston (BDirector). BPicture. Oscars: 6-1.
COMEDY DRAMA: Black Comedy; Mob Stories; Mob Comedy; Romance-Triangles; Hitmen; Hitwomen; Weddings; Double-Crossings; Mindgames; Clever Plots & Endings; New York vs. L.A.; Sleeper Hits
(Married to the Mob)

Problem Child, 1990, 81m, ★★¹/₂/$$, U/MCA-U, PG/P. A monster child bounces from house to house until one unwitting family adopts him and wishes they hadn't. John Ritter, Michael Oliver, Jack Warden, Amy Yasbeck, Michael Richards, Gilbert Gottfried. w. Scott Alexander, Larry Karaszewski, d. Dennis Dugan.

Problem Child II, 1991, 91m, ★★/$, U/MCA-U, PG-13/P. More of the same as Dad gets remarried to a rich woman with more expensive props to ruin. John Ritter, Michael Oliver, Laraine Newman, Amy Yasbeck, Jack Warden, Gilbert Gottfried, Charlene Tilton. w. Scott Alexander, Larry Karaszewski, d. Brian Levant.
COMEDY: Comedy of Errors; Children-Adopted; Children-Brats; Evil Children; Comedy-Slapstick

The Prodigal, 1955, 113m, ★★¹/₂/$$, MGM/MGM-UA. The greedy son from the Bible is given the Hollywood treatment as we await his return. Lana Turner, Louis Calhern, Edmund Purdom, Audrey Dalton, Neville Brand. d. Richard Thorpe.
MELODRAMA: Biblical Stories; Fathers & Sons; Greed; Ethics; Forgotten Films

The Producers, 1968, 90m, ★★★/$$$, Embassy/Embassy-Col, PG. A theater producer (Zero Mostel) finds a way to make a fortune with the help of an accountant (Gene Wilder, BSActor), only it's not by producing a hit but a flop; except that the play and playwright they choose may not cooperate. Dick Shawn,

Kenneth Mars, Estelle Winwood. w. d. Mel Brooks (BOScr). Oscars: 2-1.

COMEDY: Comedy of Errors; Actors; Directors; Putting on a Show; Elderly Women; Spoofs; Theater Life; Scams; Con Artists; Writer-Directors; Sleeper Hits; Cult Films

(The Twelve Chairs; Silent Movie)

The Professional, 1994, 112m, ★★★/$$, Col/Col, R/S-P-EV. The peaceful life of a nice hitman and his little girl is interrupted when a corrupt DEA agent tracks them down and wants to tear them apart to advance himself. Jean Reno, Gary Oldman, Natalie Portman, Danny Aiello. w. d. Luc Besson.

SUSPENSE: ACTION: DRAMA: Action Drama; Mob Stories; Hitmen; Men and Girls; Fathers & Daughters; Writer-Directors

(La Femme Nikita; Point of No Return; Romeo is Bleeding; Gloria)

(Ed: Owes most to Gloria)

The Professionals, 1966, 117m, ★★★1/2/$$$, Col/Col, PG/EV. Four men sign up to rescue a wealthy cattle baron's wife from Mexican kidnappers, ending in a bloody confrontation. Burt Lancaster, Lee Marvin, Claudia Cardinale, Jack Palance, Robert Ryan, Ralph Bellamy. w. d. Richard Brooks.

WESTERNS: Mercenaries; Kidnappings; Rescue Drama; Mexico; Desert Settings; Ensemble Films; Ensembles-Male; Sleeper Hits; Cult Films; Writer-Driectors

(The Magnificent Seven; The Wild Bunch)

The Program, 1993, 110m, ★★1/2/$$, Touchstone/Touchstone, R/S-P-MN. A football coach guns for the championship as his players get into a lot of trouble behind the scenes. James Caan, Kristy Swanson, Halle Berry, Craig Sheffer, Omar Epps. w. David S. Ward, Aaron Latham, d. David S. Ward.

COMEDY: Sports Movies; College Life; Coaches; Football; Ensembles-Male; Ensemble Films; Female Among Males; Practical Jokers; Party Movies

(Necessary Roughness; Rudy; North Dallas Forty)

The Projectionist, 1971, 84m, ★★★/$, AIP/Vestron, Live, PG/P. A projectionist in a slum theater begins to be unable to tell the movies he watches from the life he leads. Rodney Dangerfield, Chuck McCann, Ina Balin. w. d. Harry Hurwitz.

DRAMA: Allegorical Stories; Movie Theaters; Cult Films; Hidden Gems; Writer-Directors

(Variety; The Inner Circle; The Purple Rose of Cairo)

The Promoter (The Card), 1952, 91m, ★★★/$$, Ind./Hemdale. A resourceful young lad in an office job in England dreams up several wacky moneymaking schemes. Alec Guinness, Glynis Johns, Petula Clark, Valerie Hobson. w. Eric Ambler, N-adap. Arnold Bennett, d. Ronald Neame.

COMEDY: Making a Living; Dreams; Office Comedy; Business Life; Inventors; British Films

Prom Night, 1980, 81m, ★★/$$$, Avco/New Line, R/EV-P-S-B&G. A killer is on the loose on the big school night and the queen is the main target. Jamie Lee Curtis, Leslie Nielsen. d. Paul Lynch.

HORROR: Serial Killers; Murderers-Mass; Women in Jeopardy; Murders-One by One; High School Life; Teen Horror Flicks of 80s

SEQUELS: Prom Night 2, Prom Night 3, Prom Night 4.

(Halloween SERIES; Happy Birthday to Me; Carrie)

The Promise, 1978, 97m, ★★1/2/$$, U/MCA-U, PG/S. Young lovers are torn apart by a car wreck and not helped when the guy's mother offers to pay for the girl's surgery-if she'll leave him for good. Stephen Collins, Kathleen Quinlan, Beatrice Straight, Laurence Luckinbill, William Prince. w. Garry Michael White, d. Gilbert Cates. BOSong. Oscars: 1-0.

MELODRAMA: ROMANCE: Romantic Drama; Accidents; Car Crashes; Lover Family Dislikes; Blackmail

Promise Her Anything, 1966, 98m, ★★★/$$, Par/Par. A baby photographer with seamier hobbies (Warren Beatty) falls for the lovely French woman next door (Leslie Caron) but has to baby-sit her little son and keep her child psychiatrist (Bob Cummings) off of her if he wants to make the big proposal. Keenan Wynn, Hermione Gingold, Lionel Stander, Cathleen Nesbitt. w. William Peter Blatty, d. Arthur Hiller.

COMEDY: ROMANCE: Romantic Comedy; Romance-Reluctant; Photographers; Pornography World; Babies; Mothers Alone; Romance with Boss; Babysitters; Hidden Gems; Curiosities; 1960s; Time Capsules

(My Favorite Brunette; Shampoo; Move)

(Ed: Cute and very passable, plus has a good theme song by Tom Jones)

Promised Land, 1988, 110m, ★★1/2/$, Vestron/Vestron, R/S-P. Two high school pals are reunited by a tragedy in their small Western town and soon realize how their lives haven't gone as planned. Keifer Sutherland, Meg Ryan, Tracy Pollan, Jason Gedrick. Deborah Richter, Googy Gress, Jay Underwood, Sandra Seacat. w. d. Michael Hoffman.

DRAMA: Friendships Between Sexes; Ensemble Films; Death-Dealing with; Friendships-Male; Small-town Life; Reunions; Southwestern Life; Overlooked at Release; Writer-Directors

(1969; Desert Bloom)

(Ed: Contains a good cast, particularly Meg Ryan's pre-dated, unintended impersonation of Tonya Harding)

Promises in the Dark, 1979, 118m, ★★1/2/$, WB/WB, PG. A woman doctor does everything she can for a teenage girl with cancer under her care. Marsha Mason, Ned Beatty, Donald Moffat, Kathleen Beller, Susan Clark, Michael Brandon. d. Jerome Hellman.

MELODRAMA: Disease Stories; Saving Someone; Obsessions; Doctors; Women and Girls; Overlooked at Release

(Six Weeks; Audrey Rose)

Promises! Promises!, 1963, 90m, ★★/$$, 20th/NA. A couple having trouble having a baby goes on a cruise and winds up swapping partners with another couple. When both women get pregnant, who's the father? Jayne Mansfield, Tommy Noonan, Fritz Feld, Marie McDonald, d. King Donovan.

COMEDY: Sex Comedy; Swapping Partners; Bimbos; Sexy Women; Ships-Cruise; Father-Who's the?; Babies-Having; Women-Childless; Forgotten Films; Good Premise; Unfulfilled

(Will Success Spoil Rock Hunter?)

Proof, 1991, 90m, ★★★/$, Fine Line/New Line, R/S-P. A blind photographer meets a mysterious friend who comes between he and his housekeeper. Hugo Weaving, Genevieve Picot, Russell Crowe. w. d. Jocelyn Moorhouse.

DRAMA: Art Films; Psychological Drama; Romance-Triangles; Bisexuality; Homo-eroticism; Blind People; Photographers; Australian Films; Female Directors; Female Screenwriters; Independent Films

(Man of Flowers; The Sum of Us)

Prophecy, 1979, 102m, ★★/$$, Par/Par, PG/V. Toxic waste has created a monster in the woods of Maine. Talia Shire, Robert Foxworth, Armand Assante, Richard Dysart. w. David Seltzer, d. John Frankenheimer.
HORROR: Environmental Dilemmas; Toxic Waste; Monsters-Mutant; Legends; Forgotten Films
(Impulse [1985]; Swamp Thing)

Prospero's Books, 1991, 129m, ★★★/$, Ind/Fox, R/S-FFN-MFN. An avant-garde, highly visual and erotic rendition of Shakespeare's The Tempest, narrated by John Gielgud. Michel Blanc, Erland Josephson. w. d. Peter Greenaway.
DRAMA: Art Films; Avant-Garde Films; Erotic Drama; Narrated Films; Classic Play Adaptations; Revisionist Films; British Films; Writer-Directors
(Tempest; Drowning by Numbers; Poison; Edward II; The Garden)

Protocol, 1984, 100m, ★★¹/₂/$$, WB/WB, PG/V. A dingaling waitress in Washington, D.C. winds up in the middle of Middle East intrigue when she takes a bullet in the behind when a dignitary is the target of an assassin. Goldie Hawn, Chris Sarandon, Andre Gregory, Cliff DeYoug, Ed Begley, Jr., Gail Strickland, Kenneth Mars, Kenneth McMillan, Amanda Bearse. w. Charles Shyer, Buck Henry, d. Herbert Ross.
COMEDY: Innocent Bystanders; Heroes-Unlikely; Simple Minds; Free Spirits; Waitresses; Middle East; Assassination Plots
(Private Benjamin; Cactus Flower)

Providence, 1977, 104m, ★★★/$, New World/Col, R/S-B&G. A writer fantasizes, or maybe not, about his death, his autopsy, his widow's new life, and his last novel. John Gielgud, Ellen Burstyn, David Warner, Dirk Bogarde, Elaine Stritch. d. Alain Resnais.
DRAMA: Art Films; Avant-Garde Films; Writers Fantasies; Death-Impending; Widows; Crossing the Line
(Mon Oncle d'Amerique)
(Ed: Confusing but interesting, though not for just anyone)

Prowler, 1951, 92m, ★★¹/₂/$$, 20th/NA. A cop answers a burglary call, seduces the married woman there, and then plots to stage another burglary in order to bump off her rich husband-only she doesn't realize this until it's too late for her own sake. Van Heflin, Evelyn

Keyes, John Maxwell, Katherine Warren. d. Joseph Losey.
SUSPENSE: Film Noir; MURDER: Police Stories; Police Corruption; Murder of Spouse; Romance-Triangles; Women in Jeopardy; Evil Men; Thieves; Forgotten Films
(China Moon; Body Heat; Double Indemnity)

Psycho, 1960, 109m, ★★★★/$$$$, Universal/MCA-U, V. A woman (Janet Leigh, BSActress) steals some money and runs to hide at a remote motel. She contemplates returning it, but a deranged young man named Norman Bates (Anthony Perkins) has checked her out in the shower and doesn't intend to let her check out. Vera Miles, John Gavin, Martin Balsam. w. Joseph Stefano, d. Alfred Hitchcock (BDirector). BB&WArt, BB&WCin. Oscars: 4-0.
HORROR: SUSPENSE: MURDER: Thieves; Psycho Killers; Psychological Thriller; Serial Killers; Murders of Women; Criminals-Female; Female Protagonists; Protagonist is Killed; Cult Films
SEQUELS: Psycho 2, Psycho 3, Psycho 4. (Dressed to Kill; Pretty Poison)

Psycho 2, 1983, 113m, ★★¹/₂/$$, U/MCA-U, R/EV-B&G. Norman gets out of prison and the murders start happening again as his original victim's sister tries to prove he needs to be put away for them. Anthony Perkins, Vera Miles, Meg Tilly, Robert Loggia, Dennis Franz. w. Tom Holland, d. Richard Franklin.

Psycho 3, 1986, 93m, ★★/$$, U/MCA-U, R/EV-B&G. A mysterious young woman comes into Norman's life and the killing starts again, with a whole set of new mindgames. Anthony Perkins, Diana Scarwid, Jeff Fahey, Robert Maxwell. w. Charles Edward Pogue, d. Anthony Perkins.

Psycho 4, 1990, 96m, ★★★/$$, Showtime/MCA-U, R/EV-B&G. A radio call-in show is the setting for Norman's confessions about his original crime and his life with his mother that led to his murders, which may ruin the new life he's started in the suburbs. Anthony Perkins, Henry Thomas, C.C.H. Pounder, Olivia Hussey, Warren Frost. w. Joseph Stefano, d. Mick Garris.
Narrated Films; Flashbacks; Radio Life; Hidden Gems

HORROR: SUSPENSE: Serial Killers; Psycho Killers; Murders-One by One; Mental Illness; Fantasies; Mothers & Sons
(Ed: From one of the writers of the original and in many ways, the only one even near it in quality)

Psych-Out, 1968, 95m, ★★¹/₂/$, AIP/HBO, R/S-P. A deaf girl tries to find her runaway brother during the Summer of Love in San Francisco's Haight-Ashbury district. Jack Nicholson, Susan Strasberg, Bruce Dern, Henry Jaglom. w. d. Richard Rush.
DRAMA: Hippies; Runaways; Searches; Deaf People; San Francisco; Psychedelic Era; 1960s; Writer-Directors; Cult Films; Time Capsules
(The Tip; Five Easy Pieces; Joe)

Puberty Blues, 1981, 86m, ★★¹/₂/$, Ind/MCA-U, R/S. Two Aussie girls get into surfing in order to have a social life. Beil Schofield, Jad Capelja. d. Bruce Beresford.
COMEDY DRAMA: Coming of Age; Teenagers; Girls; Social Climbing; Surfers; Australian Films
(Little Darlings; Private School; Muriel's Wedding)

Public Enemy, 1931, 85m, ★★★¹/₂/$$$$, WB/MGM-UA. During prohibition, two Irish lads rise in the ranks of the mob with women at their sides. But when a mob war breaks out, its every man and woman for him or herself. James Cagney, Joan Blondell, Edward Woods, Leslie Fenton, Jean Harlow. d. William Wellman.
ACTION: DRAMA: Action Drama; Warner Gangster Era; Mob Stories; Power-Rise to; Mob Wars; Mob Girls; Blockbusters; Faded Hits; Cult Films
(Angels with Dirty Faces; Manhattan Melodrama; Manpower)
(Ed: Contains the famous grapefruit in the face scene)

The Public Eye, 1992, 98m, ★★★¹/₂/$$, U/MCA-U, R/V. Crime photographer Bernzy will do just about anything for an artistic, seemingly realistic photo of life on the streets in a gothic, 40s, big city. But when he becomes entangled in a plot to launder gas rationing stamps, his love for a beautiful widow running a nightclub for the mob may make him one of the crime victims he usually takes pictures of. Joe Pesci, Barbara Hershey, Stanley Tucci, Richard Forojny, Richard Riehle. w. d. Howard Franklin.

DRAMA: SUSPENSE: MYSTERY:
Conspiracy; Photographers; Romance-Reluctant; Infatutations; Nerds & Babes; Sexy Women; Mob Stories; Outstanding Production Design; Hidden Gems; Overlooked at Release; Writer-Directors
Pudd'nhead Wilson, 1987, 87m, ★★1/2/$$, AP-PBS/MCA-U. A small-town lawyer in the 1800s discovers a mulatto baby has been switched with a white baby by a slave and tries to straighten the mess out. Ken Howard. d. Alan Bridges.
DRAMA: MELODRAMA: Babies-Switched; Mix-Ups; Slavery; Black Women; Race Relations; Classic Literary Adaptations; 1800s; TV Movies
(Switched at Birth; The Adventures of Tom Sawyer)
Pulp Fiction, 1994, 153m, ★★★1/2/$$$$, Miramax/Miramax, HBO, R/EP-ES-EV-FN-MN. A clique of slick criminals make their rounds of crime when one meets a unique, dangerous woman which then sends their efforts into overdrive, ending in a clash of all the brewing tensions. John Travolta (BActor), Uma Thurman (BSActress), Samuel L. Jackson (BSActor), Amanda Plummer, Harvey Keitel, Christopher Walken, Eric Stoltz, Rosanna Arquette, Bruce Willis. w. d. Quentin Tarantino (**BOScr**, BDirector), BPicture. Oscars: 6-1.
COMEDY DRAMA: ACTION: Action Comedy; Black Comedy; Crime Drama; Film Noir-Modern; Heist Stories; Romance-Dangerous; Wild People; Dangerous Women; Drugs-Addictions; Buddy Films; Black & White Together; Alternative Lifestyles; 1970s; Writer-Directors; Cult Films; Sleeper Hits
(Rififi; Killing Zoe; Kiss Me Deadly; Reservoir Dogs)
Pulse, 1988, 91m, ★★1/2/$, Col/RCA-Col, PG-13/V. Household appliances start going haywire in suburbia when a boy visiting his dad gets left alone at home. Will the family get diced and sliced by the Cuisinart? Cliff deYoung, Joey Lawrence. w. d. Paul Golding.
HORROR: SUSPENSE: SCI-FI: Paranoia; Suburbia; Child Protagonists; Home Alone; Fathers & Sons; Writer-Directors
(Poltergeist; The Incredible Shrinking Woman)
(Ed: Original but implausible premise with a few good scares.)
Pump Up the Volume, 1990, 105m, ★★1/2/$, Col/Col, R/P-S. A slick, young radio talk show host becomes a cult hero broadcasting from an illegal radio station which is decidedly against his high school's rules. Christian Slater, Scott Paulin, Ellen Greene, Samantha Mathis, Mimi Kennedy. w. d. Allan Moyle.
COMEDY DRAMA: Teenagers; Teenage Movies; Radio Life; High School Life; Rebels; Young Men-Angry; Writer-Directors
(Airheads; Kuffs; SFW)
Pumping Iron, 1976, 90m, ★★1/2/$$$, Col/Col, PG. Documentary on the early wave of pro body-building which began Schwarzenegger's career. Arnold Schwarzenegger, Franco Columbo, Mike Katz, Lou Ferrigno. d. George Butler.
Pumping Iron 2: The Women, 1985, 107m, ★★1/2/$, Vestron/Vestron. Documentary on the upsurge of female pro body builders. Lori Bowen, Bev Francis, Rachel McLish. d. George Butler.
Documentaries; Body Building; Cult Films; Sports Movies
(Stay Hungry; Perfect)
Pumpkinhead, 1988, 89m, ★★/$$, MGM/MGM-UA, R/EV-B&G. A farmer conjures up a Satanic pumpkin monster to avenge his son's death, but the pumpkin gets carried away with itself. Lance Henriksen, Kerry Remsen, Jeff East. w. Gary Gerani, Mark Carducci, d. Stan Winston.
HORROR: Supernatural Danger; Revenge; Farm Life; Satan; Avenging Death of Someone; Fathers & Sons
(Rawhead Rex; Halloween SERIES)
Punchline, 1988, 100m, ★★1/2/$$, Col/Col, PG-13/P-S. A medical student tries to make it as a comedian, while a housewife battles her husband and her children to get a break on stage, too. Sally Field, Tom Hanks, John Goodman, Mark Rydell, Kim Griest, Barry Sobel, Paul Mazursky, Damon Wayans. w. d. David Seltzer.
COMEDY DRAMA: MELODRAMA: Comedians; Mothers-Struggling; Marriage Drama; Medical School; Friendship Between Sexes; Writer-Directors
(This Is My Life; The Entertainer)
Puppet Master, 1989, 90m, ★★/$$, Full Moon/Par, R/V-B&G. Evil puppets protect their maker's secrets from psychics who've come to figure them out. Paul LeMat, William Hickey. d. David Schmoeller.

HORROR: Puppets; Psychics; Supernatural Danger; Cult Films
The Puppetmasters, 1994, 111m, ★★★/$$, R/P-V-S-MRN. CIA Agents investigate a UFO landing where alien forces have taken parasitic holds on the local townspeople and then assume their bodies-and maybe everyone else's if they're not stopped. Donald Sutherland, Eric Thal, Julie Warner, Yaphet Kotto, Keith David, Will Patton, Richard Belzer, Marshall Bell, Tom Mason. w. Ted Elliott, Terry Rossio, David S. Goyer, N-adap. Robert A. Heinlein, d. Stuart Orme.
SCI-FI: HORROR: Paranoia; Aliens-Outer Space, Evil; Parasites; Mental Illness; Zombies; Deaths-One by One; Fugitives; Small-town Life; Allegorical Stories
REMAKE/RETELLING OF: Invasion of the Body Snatchers.
(Invasion of the Body Snatchers (1956, 1978); Body Snatchers; The Hidden; The Hidden 2; Alien; Invaders from Mars)
(Ed: A tired plot goes back to the origin, Heinlein's novel, and is done justice, but mostly because the story works so well, regardless of the treatment)
Pure Country, 1992, 113m, ★★/$$, WB/WB, PG. A country singer wants to return to the normal life but finds it hard due to the fans and his managers. George Strait, Isabel Glasser, Lesley Ann Warren, Rory Calhoun. w. Rex McGee, d. Christopher Cain.
MELODRAMA: Country Singers; Singers; City vs. Country
(Tender Mercies; Honeysuckle Rose)
A Pure Formality, 1995, 107m, ★★1/2/$, Sony/Sony, PG-13/P-V. A man is found by the police but can't remember exactly who he is, but it appears he may have been involved in a murder-or is it all a nightmare in a surreal world? Gerard Depardieu, Roman Polanski. w. Giuseppe Tornatore, Pascale Quignard, d. Tornatore.
DRAMA: MYSTERY: MURDER: Accused Unjustly; French Films
(Death and the Maiden; The Bourne Identity; The Trial)
Pure Luck, 1990, 92m, ★★/$, Universal/MCA-U, PG-13/P. A detective (Danny Glover) is assigned to track down a wealthy man's clumsy, unlucky daughter with a likewise unlucky man (Martin Short), whose bad luck gets them both in major situations. Martin Short, Danny

Glover, Sheila Kelley, Scott Wilson, Sam Wanamaker. w. Herschel Weingrod, Timothy Harris, S-adap. Francis Veber, d. Nadia Tass.

COMEDY: Screwball Comedy; **FARCE:** Detective Stories; Partners-Mismatched; Fools-Bumbling; Accident Prone; Missing Persons; Murphy's Law Stories; Mexico; Unlucky People; Foreign Film Remakes; Teams-Mismatched; Buddy Films; Female Directors; Flops-Major; Coulda Been Good; Cartoonlike Movies

REMAKE OF La Chevre (The Goat)

The Purple Rose of Cairo, 1985, 82m, ★★★★/$$$, Orion/Orion, PG. A bored housewife (Mia Farrow) in the Depression leaves her husband (Danny Aiello) regu-larly to go to the movies, and one day her matinee idol (Jeff Daniels) actually pops off the screen and joins her in real life. Dianne Wiest, Danny Aiello. w. d. Woody Allen. BOScr. Oscars: 1-0. Best Picture, British Academy Awards.

COMEDY: ROMANCE: Romance-Doomed; Romantic Comedy; **SATIRE:** Media Satire; Fantasy; Fish out of Water Stories; Depression Era; Poor People; What If . . . Stories; Housewives; Actors; Illusions/Hallucinations; Crossing the Line; Writer-Directors

RETREAD: The Last Action Hero. (Sherlock Jr. [Charlie Chaplin short]; Alice; Radio Days; Bullets Over Broadway)

Pygmalion, 1938, 96m, ★★★½/$$$, Col/Col. The original tale of upper-crusty Henry Higgins and his flower-girl waif he intends to turn into a lady, if not also his lover. Leslie Howard (BActor), Wendy Hiller (BActress), Wilfred Lawson, Marie Lohr. w. Cecil Lewis, Ian Dalrymple, W. P. Lipscomb, George Bernard Shaw (**BScr**) (**BAScr**), P-adap. Shaw, d. Leslie Howard, Anthony Asquith. BPicture. Oscars: 6-2.

COMEDY DRAMA: ROMANCE: Romantic Drama; Svengalis; Experiments; Class Conflicts; Romance-Class Conflicts; British Films; Classic Play Adaptations

MUSICAL REMAKE: My Fair Lady. (My Fair Lady; Educating Rita; Svengali)

Q

Q (The Winged Serpent), 1982, 92m, ★★¹/₂/$, U/MCA-U, R/V-B&G. Human sacrifices conjure up an Aztec monster in New York City who begins eating the locals. Michael Moriarty, Candy Clark, David Carradine, Richard Roundtree. w. d. Larry Cohen.

HORROR: Monsters; Legends; Human Eaters; Dragons; Supernatural Danger; Detective Stories; New York Life

Q & A, 1990, 132m, ★★★/$$, Orion/ Orion, R/EP-V-S. A neophyte D. A. fresh out of law school is appalled when he discovers a coverup at the local precinct involving a murder by a big, bigoted cop. Nick Nolte, Timothy Hutton, Armand Assante, Patrick O'Neal, Lee Richardson, Luis Guzman, Charles Dutton, Jenny Lumet. w. d. Sidney Lumet.

DRAMA: Crime Drama; **MURDER:** Social Drama; Police Stories; Romance-Interracial; Marriage on the Rocks; Police Corruption; Police Brutality; Bigots; Race Relations; Conspiracy; Whistleblowers; Writer-Directors

(Prince of the City; Serpico)

Quackser Fortune Has a Cousin in the Bronx, 1970, 90m, ★★¹/₂/$, Ind/VCI. An American student visits her cousin in Dublin and finds him to be a street bum, but they become good friends and learn from each other. Gene Wilder, Margot Kidder, Eileen Colgen, Seamus Ford. w. Gabriel Walsh, d. Waris Hussein.

COMEDY DRAMA: Exchange Students; Homeless People; Cousins; Irish People; Ireland; Curiosities

Quadrophenia, 1979, 120m, ★★¹/₂/$$, Col/Col, R. The Who's "concept album" of the sixties forms a loose basis for this story of the events leading up to the huge "rumble" between the Mods and Rockers on Brighton beach in 1964. Phil Daniels, Mark Wingett, Philip Davis, Leslie Ash, Garry Cooper, Toyah Wilcox, Sting. w. Dave Humphries, Martin Stellman, Franc Roddam, d. Franc Roddam.

Music Movies; Musicians; Rock Stars; Gangs-Street; England; Mod Era; 1960s; Time Capsules; British Films; Cult Films; Curiosities

(Tommy; Lisztomania)

Quality Street, 1937, 84m, ★★★/$, RKO/Turner. After a long absence at the Napoleonic War, a soldier comes home to find that his once beautiful lover is now old and ugly, so she pretends to be her cousin to hide her embarrassment. Katharine Hepburn, Franchot Tone, Fay Bainter, Eric Blore, Cora Witherspoon, Estelle Winwood, Florence Lake, Joan Fontaine. w. Mortimer Offner, Allan Scott, P-adap. J. M. Barrie, d. George Stevens.

MELODRAMA: ROMANCE: Return of Spouse; Impostors; Identities-Assumed; Cousins; Costume Drama; Overlooked at Release; Forgotten Films

(The Little Minister; Break of Hearts)

Quartet, 1948, 120m, ★★★/$$, GFD/NA. Four stories by Somerset Maugham: *The Facts of Life, The Alien Corn, The Kite, The Colonel's Lady*. Basil Radford, Naunton Wayne, Mai Zetterling, Jack Watling, Dirk Bogarde, Irene Browne, George Cole, Honor Blackman, Cecil Parker, Linden Travers, Nora Swinburne, Ernest Thesiger, Wilfrid Hyde White. w. R. C. Sheriff, SS-adap. W. Somerset Maugham, d. Ralph Smart.

DRAMA: COMEDY DRAMA: MELO-DRAMA: ROMANCE: Multiple Stories; Hidden Gems; Forgotten Films; British Films

(Trio; Encore; Of Human Bondage; Rain)

Quartet, 1981, 101m, ★★★/$, 20th/CBS-Fox, R/P-S-FN. A woman whose husband is in prison gets lonely and enters into a *ménage à trois*. Isabel Adjani, Maggie Smith, Alan Bates, Anthony Higgins. w. Ruth Prawer Jhabvala, N-adap. Jean Rhys, d. James Ivory.

DRAMA: ROMANCE: Romantic Drama; Erotic Drama; Ménage à Trois; Romance-Triangles; Riviera Life; Beautiful People; Hidden Gems; Female Screenwriters

(Henry and June; The Moderns)

The Quatermass Experiment (The Creeping Unknown), 1955, 82m, ★★★/$$.

Astronauts returning from a space voyage bring back a deadly virus. Brian Donlevy, Jack Warner, Margia Dean, Richard Wordsworth, David King Wood, Thora Hird, Gordon Jackson. w. Richard Landau, Val Guest, (Teleplay)-adap. Nigel Kneale, d. Val Guest.

SCI-FI: Epidemics; Aliens-Outer Space, Evil; Astronauts; Deaths-One by One; Experiments

SEQUELS: Enemy From Space, Five Million Years to Earth.

(The Andromeda Strain; Liquid Sky; Enemy From Space; Five Million Years to Earth)

Queen Bee, 1955, 95m, ★★★/$, Col/NA. A Southern matriarch controls her family and everyone else she encounters with a white-gloved iron fist. Joan Crawford, Barry Sullivan, Betsy Palmer, John Ireland, Fay Wray. w. d. Ranald MacDougall.

MELODRAMA: Power Struggles; Family Drama; Feisty Females; Mean Women; Southerns; Plantation Life; Camp; Hidden Gems; Curiosities; Writer-Directors; Female Protagonists

(The Little Foxes; Flamingo Road; Another Part of the Forest)

Queen Christina, 1933, 101m, ★★★1/2/$$$$, MGM/MGM-UA. A seventeenth-century Swedish queen is appalled at the thought of marriage and to ensure that it won't happen she runs around in men's clothing. But it doesn't dissuade a somewhat confused Spanish official. Greta Garbo, John Gilbert, Ian Keith, Lewis Stone, C. Aubrey Smith, Reginald Owen, Elizabeth Young. w. Salka Viertel, H. M. Harwood, S. N. Behrman, d. Rouben Mamoulian.

DRAMA: MELODRAMA: ROMANCE: Romantic Drama; Romance-Boy Wants Girl; Romance-Reluctant; Historical Drama; True Stories; Spinsters; Women as Men; Tomboys; Queens; Royalty; Scandinavia; Elusive Women

(The Abdication; Anna Christie)

Queen of Destiny (Sixty Glorious Years), 1938, 95m, ★★★/$$, Imperator/NA. A lavish historical costume drama of the life of Queen Victoria. Anna Neagle, Anton Walbrook, C. Aubrey Smith, Walter Rilla, Charles Carson. w. Robert Vansittart, Miles Malleson, Charles de Grandcourt, d. Herbert Wilcox.

DRAMA: Biographies; Costume Drama;

Historical Drama; Queens; England; British Films

SEQUEL TO: Victoria the Great.

Queen of Hearts, 1989, 112m, ★★★/$$, Ind/HBO. A family saga of Italians in London and the coming of age of the young boy who learns his father is a compulsive gambler. Vittorio Duse, Joseph Long, Anita Zagarita, Eileen Way, Vittorio Amandola, Roberto Scateni, Stefano Spagnoli. w. Tony Grisoni, d. Jon Amiel.

MELODRAMA: COMEDY DRAMA: Family Drama; Coming of Age; Gambling; Illusions Destroyed; Italians; London; British Films

Queen of Outer Space, 1958, 89m, ★★/$, 20th/Fox. Bimbos on Venus take advantage of the boy astronauts who land in their lair. Zsa Zsa Gabor, Eric Fleming, Laurie Mitchell, Paul Birch. d. Edward Bernds.

SCI-FI: Spoofs-Sci-Fi; Camp; Bimbos; Role Reversal; Outer Space Movies; Astronauts; Female Protagonists; Leaders-Female

(Cat Women on the Moon, Santa Claus on Mars)

Queen of the Stardust Ballroom, 1975, 98m, ★★★/$$, CBS/Prism. A lonely middle-aged woman goes to a ballroom dance and meets a man to start over with. Maureen Stapleton, Charles Durning, Charlotte Rae, Michael Brandon. d. Sam O'Steen.

DRAMA: Character Studies; ROMANCE: Romantic Drama; Romance-Middle-Aged; Lonely People; Dance Movies; Starting Over; Ordinary People Stories; Female Protagonists; TV Movies

(Lonelyhearts)

Queens Logic, 1991, 102m, ★★1/2/VR, Vista/Live, R/S-P-MRN. Several old friends meet once again in their New York neighborhood; they're just over 30 and some are moving up while others move down. Kevin Bacon, Joe Mantegna, Ken Olin, Jamie Lee Curtis, Chloe Webb, Tony Spiridakis. w. d. Tony Spiridakis.

COMEDY DRAMA: Ensemble Films; New York Life; Reunions; Friendships-Male; Midlife Crisis; Writer-Directors; Improvisational Films

(The Big Chill; Parallel Lives; St. Elmo's Fire; Indian Summer; True Love)

Querelle, 1983, 106m, ★★1/2/$, Triumph/Col, R/S-MN. A sailor on a ship in France finds himself caught in smuggling intrigue, double-crossing, and gay

eroticism. Brad Davis, Jeanne Moreau, Franco Nero. N-adap. Jean Genet, d. Rainer Werner Fassbinder.

DRAMA: Erotic Drama; Homo-eroticism; Smuggling; Mindgames; Men in Conflict; Gay Men; Sailors; Ships; French Films; Art Films; Cult Films

(Fox and His Friends; Midnight Express)

Quest for Fire, 1981, 100m, ★★★/$$$, ICC-20th/Fox, R/S-V-FN-MN. A group of Neanderthals are frozen out of their caves and try to get two sticks to rub together, among other things . . . Everett McGill, Ron Perlman, Rae Dawn Chong, Nameer El-Kadi. w. Gerard Brach, N-adap. J. H. Rosny (La Guerre du Feu), d. Jean-Jacques Annaud.

DRAMA: ADVENTURE: Prehistoric Times; Cavemen; Mute People; Small-town Life; Nature-Back to; Curiosities

(Clan of the Cave Bear; Caveman)

(Ed: Anthony Burgess invented the Neanderthal language used in the film, and anthropologist Desmond Morris choreographed the actors' movements)

Quick, 1993, 95m, ★★★/VR, Academy/Academy, R/EV-P-S-FN. A hitwoman named Quick (Teri Polo) is in a relationship with a bad cop (Jeff Fahey) when an opportunity comes along, via a mob accountant who's stolen some money (Martin Donovan) and needs witness protection from the cop. The mob needs her to get him. Though in the end, she may need him more amid the double-crossings. w. Frederick Bailey, d. Rick King.

ACTION: Film Noir-Modern; Kidnapper-Sympathizing with; Crime Drama; Black Comedy; Hitmen; Clever Plots & Endings; Double Crossings; Drugs-Dealing; Hitwomen; LA 90s Indies; Female Protagonists

(Midnight Run; Blood and Concrete; Gloria)

(Ed: The romance which develops begins to detract from a good action premise and fairly fascinating characters)

The Quick and the Dead, 1995, 123m, ★★1/2/$$, Col/Col, R/V-P. A woman goes on the rampage to avenge the death of dad in a town called Redemption, but can she outshoot the bad guys? Sharon Stone, Gene Hackman, Leonardo DiCaprio, Russell Crowe, Kevin Conway, Lance Henriksen. w. Simon Moore, John Sayles, d. Sam Raimi.

WESTERNS: ACTION: Action Drama; Westerns-Revisionist; Westerns-Neo;

Avenging Death of Someone; Revenge; Westerns-Revenge; Gunfighters; Female Protagonists; Hitwomen; Female Among Males
(Hannie Caulder; Johnny Guitar)

Quick Change, 1990, 88m, ★★★/$$$, WB/WB, PG/P. A trio of bank robbers (Bill Murray, Geena Davis, Randy Quaid) bumble their way out of New York with their loot as one calamitous thing after another besets them. Jason Robards. w. Howard Franklin, N-adap. Jay Cronley, d. Howard Franklin, Bill Murray.

COMEDY: Heist Stories; Capers; Comedy of Errors; Murphy's Law Stories; Criminals-Stupid; Nightmare Journies; Bank Robberies; New York Life
(New York Nightmares: The Outof-towners; Heist Comedies: The Lavender Hill Mob; A Fish Called Wanda)

Quick Millions, 1931, 69m, ★★★/$$, 20th/NA. A truck driver is slowly sucked into the mob that runs the union and eventually becomes a boss. Spencer Tracy, Marguerite Churchill, Sally Eilers, Robert Burns, John Wray, George Raft. w. Courtney Terett, Rowland Brown, John Wray, d. Rowland Brown.

DRAMA: Crime Drama; Mob Stories; Ordinary People vs. Criminal; Corruption; Ordinary People Turned Criminal; Truck Drivers; Forgotten Films
(Fury; The Big House)

Quicksand, 1950, 79m, ★★/$, UA/Nos. A blue-collar worker's girlfriend wants more out of life, so he starts committing petty robberies. Unfortunately, he merely succeeds in getting himself in trouble, and still can't please her. Mickey Rooney, Jeanne Cagney, Barbara Bates, Peter Lorre. w. Robert Smith, d. Irving Pichel.

MELODRAMA: Marriage Drama; Crime Drama; Working Class; Thieves; Ordinary People Turned Criminal
(A Nice Little Bank That Should Be Robbed)

Quicksilver, 1986, 106m, ★★/$$, Col/Col, PG. A young stockbroker in Frisco has little adventures delivering packages on his bike; set to pop music. Kevin Bacon, Jami Gertz, Paul Rodriguez, Larry Fishburne. w. d. Tom Donnelly.

COMEDY DRAMA: ACTION: Bicycles; Stockbrokers; Yuppies; Young Men; Bratpack Movies; Writer-Directors
(Footloose; Breaking Away)

The Quiet American, 1957, 122m, ★★★/$, UA/NA. During the Korean War, an American anti-Communist thinks he knows how to end the fighting, but he is betrayed by the reporter whose life he saves. Michael Redgrave, Audie Murphy, Claude Dauphin. w. d. Joseph L. Mankiewicz, N-adap. Graham Greene.

DRAMA: War Stories; Political Drama; Saving Somone; Journalists; Korean War; Communists; Fighting the System; Betrayals; Coulda Been Great
(The Comedians; Beyond the Limit)

The Quiet Man, 1952, 129m, ★★★★/$$$$, Republic/Republic. An Irish boxer retires to his native land and lands a fiery Irish lass-but has trouble dealing with her stormy temper. John Wayne, Maureen O'Hara, Barry Fitzgerald, Victor McLaglen (BSActor), Ward Bond. w. Frank Nugent (BScr), SS-adap. Maurice Walsh, d. John Ford (**BDirector**). BPicture, **BCCin.** Oscars: 5-2.

DRAMA: ROMANCE: Romantic Drama; Ireland; Irish People; Epics; Romance-Reluctant; Feisty Female; Boxing; Reunions; Small-town Life; Scenery-Outstanding
(Ed: An absolutely beautiful film, all the more so with O'Hara, even for those who don't like Wayne)

Quiet Wedding, 1940, 80m, ★★★1/2/$$, Par/NA. A family tries to put on a simple wedding, which spins out of their control, getting more and more complicated. Margaret Lockwood, Derek Farr, A. E. Matthews, Marjorie Fielding, Athene Seyler, Peggy Ashcroft, Margaretta Scott. w. Terence Rattigan, Anatole de Grunwald, P-adap. Esther McCracken, d. Anthony Asquith.

COMEDY DRAMA: SATIRE: FARCE: Weddings; Marriage-Impending; Family Comedy; British Films; Hidden Gems
(Father of the Bride; A Wedding; Betsy's Wedding; The Catered Affair)

Quigley Down Under, 1990, 120m, ★★1/2/$, MGM/MGM-UA, PG-13/P-S-V. In Australia in the 1860s, a ranch hand quits after an argument with the boss and goes on a shooting spree of vengeance. Tom Selleck, Laura San Giacomo, Alan Rickman, Chris Haywood, Ron Hadrick, Tony Bonner, Roger Ward. w. John Hill, d. Simon Wincer.

WESTERNS: Westerns-Revenge; Westerns-Revisionist; Revenge; Gunfighters; Australia
(The Sacketts; The Shadow Riders)

Quintet, 1979, 118m, ★★1/2/$, 20th/CBS-Fox, PG/V. In the future in a city made of ice, the residents play a game of pretend death, but one man is playing for real. Paul Newman, Vittorio Gassman, Fernando Rey, Bibi Anderson, Brigitte Fossey, Nina Van Pallandt. w. Frank Barhydt, Robert Altman, Patricia Resnick, d. Robert Altman.

DRAMA: SCI-FI: Futuristic Films; Psychological Thriller; Apocalytpic Stories; Duels; Snow Settings; Mindgames; Coulda Been Good; Flops-Major; Curiosities; Cult Films; Female Screenwriters
(Rollerball; Winter Kills)

Quiz Show, 1994, 132m, ★★★1/2/$$, Hollywood/Hollywood, PG-13/P. The true story of the quiz show scandal where NBC gave the answers to a prominent professor who could have won on his own merits, but the money was too great to resist. The story was too good to resist for a Washington bureaucrat who uncovered it. Ralph Fiennes, Paul Scofield (BSActor), Rob Morrow, David Paymer, Elizabeth Wilson, John Turturro. w. Paul Attanasio (BAScr), d. Robert Redford (BDirector). BPicture. Oscars: 4-0.

DRAMA: MYSTERY: Journalists as Detectives; Game Shows; Ensemble Films; Games; Scandals; Liars; Greed; Corporate Corruption; Professors; Fathers & Sons; Ethics; 1950s; True Stories; TV Life; Actor Directors
(Champagne for Caesar; All the President's Men)

Quo Vadis, 1951, 171m, ★★★/$$$$$, MGM/MGM-UA. During the reign of Nero, a Roman subject falls in love with a Christian girl and they both must pay in the forum with the lions. Robert Taylor, Deborah Kerr, Peter Ustinov (BSActor), Leo Genn (BSActor), Finaly Currie. w. John Lee Mahin, S. N. Behrman, Sonya Levien, d. Mervyn Le Roy. BPicture, BB&WCin, BOScore, BB&WArt, BEdit. Oscars: 7-0.

DRAMA: TRAGEDY: ROMANCE: Romance-Doomed; Historical Drama; Epics; Love-Forbidden; Romans; Religion; Ancient Times
(Sign of the Cross; Spartacus; Ben-Hur)

R

Rabbit, Run, 1970, 94m, ★★/$, WB/WB, R/P-S. A man whose wife just got pregnant leaves her for a whore. James Caan, Anjanette Comer, Arthur Hill, Jack Albertson, Carrie Snodgrass. w. Howard B. Kreitsek, N-adap. John Updike, d. Jack Smight.
DRAMA: Character Studies; Marriage on the Rocks; Cheating Men; Romance with Prostitute; Coulda Been Good; Flops-Major
(The Gambler; Look Back in Anger)
Rabbit Test, 1978, 84m, ★★¹/₂/$, Avco Embassy/Sultan, R/S-P. After having sex with an aggressive prostitute who demands that she be on top, a lonely man becomes pregnant. Billy Crystal, Joan Prather, Alex Rocco, Doris Roberts, Edward Ansara, Imogene Coca, Jane Connell, Roddy McDowell, Joan Rivers. w. Jay Redack, Joan Rivers, d. Joan Rivers.
COMEDY: Black Comedy; Babies-Having; Role Reversal; Men as Women; Good Premise; Unfulfilled; Curiosities; Female Screenwriters; Female Directors; Babies-Men Having
(Junior; A Slightly Pregnant Man; The Girl Most Likely To . . .)
(Ed: A few good jokes)
Rabid Grannies, 1988, 88m, ★★/$, Troma/Media, R/EV-B&G. Two old ladies invite their extended family to their estate and become disgusting harpies, murder-

ing and eating them one by one. Elie Lison, Catherine Aymerie, Jacques Mayar, Francoise Moens, Robert du Bois, Guy Van Riet. w. d. Emmanuel Kervyn.
HORROR: Horror Comedy; Black Comedy; Comedy-Morbid; Elderly Women; MURDER: Murders-One by One; Curiosities; Writer-Directors
(Ladies in Retirement; Arsenic and Old Lace; Motel Hell)
(Ed: *Arsenic and Old Lace* on acid, bad acid)
The Rachel Papers, 1989, 95m, ★★★/$, Virgin-20th/Fox. At Oxford, an American exchange student is pursued by and sometimes succumbs to a local boy who's trying to get accepted by her and the college. Dexter Fletcher, Ione Skye, Jonathan Pryce, James Spader, Bill Paterson, Jared Harris. w. d. Damian Harris, N-adap. Martin Amis.
COMEDY DRAMA: ROMANCE: Romantic Comedy; Romance-Class Conflicts; Romance-Boy Wants Girls; Elusive Women; Exchange Students; College Life; Americans Abroad; England; Young People; Overlooked at Release
(Say Anything; Alfie)
Rachel, Rachel, 1968, 101m, ★★★★/$$$, WB/WB, PG/S. A lonely woman (Joanne Woodward, BActress) contemplates her place in life and finds a lover

(James Olson) to break free from her domineering mother. Estelle Parsons (BSActress), Kate Harrington, Geraldine Fitzgerald, Donald Moffat. w. Stewart Stern (BAScr), N-adap. Margaret Lawrence (*A Jest of God*), d. Paul Newman **(BDirector, NYFC). B**Picture. Oscars: 4-0.
DRAMA: ROMANCE: Coming of Age; Love-First; Midlife Crises; Lonely People; Spinsters; Life Transitions; Mothers & Daughters; Past-Haunted by the; Fantasies; Monologues-Interior; Narrated Films; Elusive Men; Hidden Gems; Actor Directors; Quiet Little Films
(Summertime; The Prime of Miss Jean Brodie; Summer Wishes; Winter Dreams; Mr. and Mrs. Bridge; The Rainmaker; Looking for Mr. Goodbar)
(Ed: A classic performance and character study-a must see. The snub of Newman for Best Director with the Oscars was alleviated by his win with the New York Film Critics and the Best Picture Oscar nod)
Racing with the Moon, 1984, 108m, ★★/$, Par/Par, R/S-MRN. In 1942, two young Marines await the day their company will be shipped off to war, but a developing romance may make that tougher. Sean Penn, Elizabeth McGovern, Nicolas Cage, John Karlen, Max Showalter. w. Steven Kloves, d. Richard Benjamin.

DRAMA: ROMANCE: Coming of Age; Love-First; Small-town Life; World War II Era; 1940s; Nostalgia
(In the Mood; Since You Went Away)

The Rack, 1956, 100m, ★★1/2/$$, MGM/NA. During the Korean War, an American prisoner is tortured into giving away state secrets. After the war, he's court-martialed. Paul Newman, Walter Pidgeon, Edmond O'Brien, Lee Marvin, Cloris Leachman, Wendell Corey. w. Stewart Stern, P-adap. Rod Serling, d. Arnold Laven.

DRAMA: Courtroom Drama; Military Stories; Korean War; Traitors; Forgotten Films; Torture
(The Caine Mutiny Court-Martial; The Deerhunter)

Radio Days, 1987, 85m, ★★★1/2/$$, Orion/Orion, PG/S. As World War II is getting under way, families in New York have little crises and humorous misadventures. Mia Farrow, Dianne Wiest, Seth Green, Julie Kavner, Josh Mostel, Michael Tucker, Wallace Shawn. w. d. Woody Allen (BOScr). BArt. Oscars: 2-0.

COMEDY: Family Comedy; Ensemble Films; Nostalgia; Radio Life; 1940s; New York Life; World War II Era; Peeping Toms; Spinsters; Simple Minds; Bimbos; Boys Memories; Jewish People; Child Protagonists; Narrated Films; Writer-Directors
(The Purple Rose of Cairo; Annie Hall)

Radio Flyer, 1992, 114m, ★★/$, Col/Col, PG. Two boys escape from their alcoholic, abusive stepfather through the fantasy of their red wagon. Elijah Wood, Joseph Mazzello, Lorraine Bracco, Adam Baldwin, John Jeard, Ben Johnson. w. David Mickey Evans, d. Richard Donner.

MELODRAMA: Fantasy; CHILDREN'S: FAMILY: Family Drama; Fantasies; Dreams; Boys; 1960s; Abusive Men; Stepparents vs. Children; Mean Men; Brothers
(The Sandlot; Stand By Me; Firstborn)

Radioland Murders, 1994, 112m, ★★1/2/$, PG. Staff members are being offed at a radio network debuting it's big show, while the star is about to be left by his wife. A frenetic farce ensues in the attempt to find the culprit and get the show on the air, but, of course, things don't go so smoothly. Mary Stuart Masterson, Brian Benben, Ned Beatty, George Burns, Scott Michael Campbell, Brion James, Michael Lerner, Michael McKean, Jeffrey Tambor, Stephen Tobolowsky, Christopher Lloyd, Corbin Bernsen, Bobcat Goldthwaite, Robert Klein, Harvey Korman, Leighann Lord, Dylan Baker, Peter MacNicol, Anne DeSalvo, Larry Miller, Anita Morris, Robert Walden. w. Willard Huyck, Gloria Katz, Jeff Reno and Ron Osborn, SS-adap. George Lucas, d. Mel Smith

COMEDY: FARCE: MURDER: MYS-TERY: MURDER MYSTERY: Comic Mystery; Comic Thriller; Radio Life; Race Against Time; Coulda Been Great; 1940s; Female Screenwriters
(Tune in Tomorrow; The Big Broadcast SERIES)
(Ed: A twenty-year-old script finally got made, but probably should have stayed on the dusty shelf. Cute and frenetic but not particularly substantial)

Rafferty and the Gold Dust Twins, 1975, 91m, ★★★/$, WB/WB, R/P-S. A man is kidnapped by two female kooks who want to get to New Orleans, but the tables get turned through a little flirtation. Alan Arkin, Sally Kellerman, MacKenzie Phillips, Charles Martin Smith, Harry Dean Stanton. d. Dick Richards.

COMEDY: Kidnappings; Kidnappers-Sympathizing with; Romance-Triangles; Hitchhikers; Road Movies; New Orleans; Criminal Couples; Criminals-Female; Men In Jeopardy; Hidden Gems; Forgotten Films
(Slither; Ruthless People; Freebie and the Bean)

Raffles, 1939, 72m, ★★★/$$$, Samuel Goldwyn-UA/Goldwyn. In Britain, a famous cricket player nicknamed "Raffles" is also secretly a thief. David Niven, Olivia de Havilland, Dudley Digges, May Whitty, Douglas Walton. w. John Van Druten, Sydney Howard, N-adap. E. W. Hornung (*Raffles the Amateur Craksman*), d. Sam Wood.

COMEDY DRAMA: Crime Drama; Capers; Thieves; Playboys; Dual Lives; Forgotten Films; Faded Hits; Hidden Gems
REMAKE OF: 1930 version starring Ronald Colman.
(The Adventures of Arsene Lupin; To Catch a Thief)

Rage, 1972, 99m, ★★1/2/$, WB/WB, PG. After a chemical spill in the forest near a top secret military contractor's factory, a boy dies. His father is determined to find out who's responsible. George C. Scott, Richard Basehart, Martin Sheen, Barnard Hughes, Stephen Young. w. Philip Friedman, Dan Kleinman, d. George C. Scott.

DRAMA: Message Films; Government as Enemy; Conspiracy; Fighting the System; Avenging Someone's Death; Toxic Poisoning; Farm Life; Fathers & Sons
(Endangered Species; Warning Sign; The Cassandra Crossing; Impulse)

A Rage in Harlem, 1991, 108m, ★★★/$$$, Miramax/Miramax, HBO, PG/S-P-V. A gangster hides his loot in a casket and gets a stupid mortician's apprentice to keep it at a funeral home, leading to all sorts of complications. Forest Whitaker, Gregory Hines, Robin Givens, Zakes Mokae, Danny Glover, Badja Djola, Ron Taylor. w. John Toles-Bey, Bobby Crawford, N-adap. Chester Himes, d. Bill Duke.

COMEDY: Heist Stories; Mob Stories; Mob Comedy; 1950s; Black Casts; Black Men; Black Women; Sexy Women; Nerds; Nerds & Babes; Black Directors; Hidden Gems; Sleeper Hits
(The Busy Body; Come Back Charleston Blue)

A Rage to Live, 1965, 101m, ★★1/2/$, UA/NA. A woman who wants to have sex all the time has many flings in college followed by an unhappy marriage to a doltish nerd. Suzanne Pleshette, Bradford Dillman, Ben Gazzara, Peter Graves, Bethel Leslie, James Gregory, Ruth White. w. John T. Kelley, N-adap. John O'Hara, d. Walter Grauman.

DRAMA: Character Studies; Sexuality; Sexual Problems; Promiscuity; Sexy Women; College Life; Marriage Drama; Cheating Women; Coulda Been Good; Curiosities
(The Constant Nymph; Looking for Mr. Goodbar)

Raggedy Man, 1981, 94m, ★★1/2/$, U/MCA-U, PG. After her husband dies, a single mother is helped with her children by a mysterious stranger. Sissy Spacek, Eric Roberts, Sam Shepard, William Sanderson, Tracey Walter, R. G. Armstrong. w. William D. Wittliff, d. Jack Fisk.

DRAMA: MELODRAMA: Mothers-Struggling; Family Drama; Small-town Life; Protecting Someone; New in Town; Drifters; Texas; 1940s; Quiet Little Films; Overlooked at Release; Southerns

(Three Wishes; One Magic Christmas; Marie)

Raging Bull, 1980, 119m, ★★★/$$, UA/MGM-UA, R/EP-EV-S-FN. The story of boxer Jake LaMotta (Robert De Niro, BActor), his rise and fall, his marriages, and his ultimate fate. Cathy Moriarty (BSActress), Joe Pesci (BSActor). Theresa Saldano, Frank Vincent, Nicholas Colosanto. w. Paul Schrader, Mardik Martin, NF-Adap. Jake LaMotta, d. Martin Scorsese (BDirector). BPicture, BCinema, **BEdit**, BSound. Oscars: 8-2.
DRAMA: Character Studies; Biographies; Boxing; Sports Movies; Fame-Rise to; Rise and Fall Stories; Abusive Men; Marriage Drama; Marriage on the Rocks; Macho Men; Italians; Episodic Stories (Somebody Up There Likes Me; Champion; Good Fellas; Casino)
(Ed: Voted best film of the 80s in *Premiere* magazine's critics' poll)

The Raging Moon, 1970, 111m, ★★★/$, EMI/NA, PG/S. Two handicapped people fall in love at a sanitorium. Malcolm McDowell, Nanette Newman, Georgia Brown, Bernard Lee, Gerald Sim, Michael Flanders. w. d. Bryan Forbes, N-adap. Peter Marshall.
DRAMA: ROMANCE: Romantic Drama; Asylums; Mental Illness; Forgotten Films; Coulda Been Great; Curiosities; British Films
(Lilith; David & Lisa; Tell Me That You Love Me, Junie Moon; Disturbed)

Ragtime, 1981, 155m, ★★★¹/₂/$$, Par/Par, R/S-FFN. The fictionalization of a terrorist attempt in turn-of-the-century New York and the many lives intertwined leading to an explosive culmination, which includes crimes of passion. James Cagney, Howard Rollins (BSActor), Mary Steenburgen, Debbie Allen, Elizabeth McGovern (BSActress), Norman Mailer, Pat O'Brien,. w. Michael Weller (BAScr), N-adap. E. L. Doctorow, d. Milos Forman. BCin, BOScore, BOSong, BArt. Oscars: 7-0.
DRAMA: Historical Drama; TRAGEDY: Costume Drama; Biographies-Fictional; Slice of Life; Multiple Stories; Interwoven Stories; Babies-Finding; Crimes of Passion; Cheating Men; Dancers; Terrorists; Bombs; Coulda Been Great (Billy Bathgate; Reds; Nashville)

Raid on Rommel, 1971, 99m, ★★/$, U/MCA-U, PG/V. In Tobruk during World War II, a British officer and a motley crew of liberated P.O.W.s take on Rommel and his highly trained troops. Richard Burton, John Colicos, Clinton Greyn, Wolfgang Preiss. w. Richard Bluel, d. Henry Hathaway.
ACTION: War Stories; World War II Stories; Nazi Stories; Germans as Enemy; POWs; Prison Escapes; Forgotten Films (The Desert Fox; The Desert Rat)

Raiders of the Lost Ark, 1981, 115m, ★★★★/$$$$$, Par/Par, PG/V. A seemingly nerdy archaeology professor named Indiana Jones (Harrison Ford) goes on a quest to find the long lost ark of the covenant before the Nazis get to it and harm his girl (Karen Allen). John Rhys-Davies. w. Lawrence Kasdan, Philip Kaufman, George Lucas (BOScr), d. Steven Spielberg (BDirector). BPicture, BCinema, **BArt, BEdit, BSound,** BOScore. Oscars: 8-3.
ADVENTURE: ACTION: Action Comedy; Comic Adventure; Treasure Hunts; MYSTERY: Biblical Stories; Quests; Chase Movies; Epics; Legends; Mythology; Professors; Feisty Females; 1930s; Nazi Stories; Germans as Enemy; Middle East; South America; World Travel
SEQUELS: Indiana Jones & The Temple of Doom, Indiana Jones & The Last Crusade
(Stargate; Allan Quatermain and the Lost City of Gold; Romancing the Stone)

The Railway Children, 1970, 108m, ★★★/$$$, EMI/NA, G. When an Englishman is convicted of treason during the Edwardian era, his children must travel by train with their mother all over England on a mission to prove his innocence. Dinah Sheridan, William Mervyn, Jenny Agutter, Bernard Cribbins. w. d. Lionel Jeffries, N-adap. E. Nesbit.
CHILDREN'S: FAMILY: DRAMA: Historical Drama; Spies; Traitors; Accused Unjustly; Framed?; Children Saving Parents; Journies; England; Trains; British Films; Hidden Gems
(Ed: Not to be confused with the American children's classic book, *The Boxcar Children*)

Rain, 1932, 92m, ★★★/$$$, UA/Nos, VCI. A missionary in Pago Pago can't control his carnal urges, and pursues a prostitute. Meanwhile an epidemic is going around the island. Joan Crawford, Walter Huston, William Gargan, Beulah Bondi, Matt Moore, Guy Kibbee. w. Maxwell Anderson, P-adap. John Colton,

Clemence Randolph, SS-adap. W. Somerset Maugham, d. Lewis Milestone.
MELODRAMA: ROMANCE: Romantic Drama; Romance with Prostitutes; Love-Forbidden; Romance-Opposites Attract; Preachers; Islands; Pacific Islands; Stranded on an Island; Sexy Women; Nerds; Nerds & Babes; Hidden Gems
REMAKE OF: Sadie Thompson, 1928, REMAKE: Miss Sadie Thompson, 1953.
COMIC FLIPSIDE: Crimes of Passion.
(Miss Sadie Thompson; Of Human Bondage)

The Rainbow, 1988, 111m, ★★★/$, Vestron/Vestron, R/ES-FFN-MN. A country girl must decide between marrying her local boyfriend and going off to follow her ambition at college-in between a lesbian dalliance. Sammi Davis, Paul McGann, Amanda Donohoe, Christopher Gable, David Hemmings, Glenda Jackson, Dudley Sutton. w. Ken Russell, Vivian Russell, N-adap. D. H. Lawrence, d. Ken Russell.
DRAMA: ROMANCE: Erotic Drama; Romantic Drama; Fantasies; Sexuality; Bisexuality; Lesbians; Love-First; Coming of Age; Romance-Choosing Right Person; Hidden Gems
(Women in Love; The Fox)

The Rainmaker, 1956, 121m, ★★★/$$$, Par/Par. In turn-of-the-century Kansas, a charlatan hires himself out to farmers as a rainmaker, but ends up enchanting a spinster with dreams of delusion. Katharine Hepburn (BActress), Burt Lancaster, Wendell Corey, Lloyd Bridges, Earl Holliman, Cameron Prud'homme, Wallace Ford. w. P-adap, N. Richard Nash, d. Joseph Anthony. BOScore. Oscars: 2-0.
DRAMA: ROMANCE: Romantic Drama; MELODRAMA: Tearjerkers; Con Artists; New in Town; Drifters; Small-town Life; Midwestern Life; Spinsters; Wallflowers; Wallflowers & Hunks; Love-First (Summertime; Rachel, Rachel; Now, Voyager)

Rain Man, 1988, 133m, ★★★/$$$$$, MGM-UA/MGM-UA, PG/S. A young man (Tom Cruise) goes to visit his long lost brother (Dustin Hoffman, BActor) in an asylum and decides to take him on a cross-country trip to get to know him. Valeria Golina. w. Ronald Bass, Barry Morrow (BOScr), d. Barry Levinson (BDirector). BPicture, BCin, BEdit, BArt, BOScore. Oscars: 8-4.

DRAMA: MELODRAMA: Tearjerkers; Road Movies; Journies; Brothers; Friendships-Male; Mentally Disabled; Geniuses; Simple Minds; Childlike People; Disabled but Nominated; Sleeper Hits; Quiet Little Films; Blockbusters
(Dominick & Eugene; Sundays & Cybele; Midnight Cowboy)
(Ed: The melodramatic nature and Hoffman's charming performance drove it home at the box office, but it was quite a surprise for such a stark, slow-moving, and simple story)

The Rain People, 1969, 101m, ★★½/$, WB/WB, PG/S. A woman leaves her husband and drives around the country aimlessly. She picks up a mentally deficient hitchhiker who becomes her friend as she tries to find herself. Shirley Knight, James Caan, Robert Duvall, Tom Aldredge, Marya Zimmet. w. d. Francis Ford Coppola.

DRAMA: Character Studies; Romance-Reluctant; Protecting Someone; Nervous Breakdowns; Pre-Life Crisis; Young Women; Housewives; Runaways; Road Movies; Mentally Disabled People; Forgotten Films; Quiet Little Films; Curiosities; Writer-Directors
(Alice Doesn't Live Here Anymore; Diary of a Mad Housewife)

The Rains Came, 1939, 103m, ★★★/$$$$, 20th/Fox. Foppish colonials in India during the Raj finally make themselves useful when disaster strikes in the form of a deluge which creates flooding all over the countryside. Myrna Loy, George Brent, Tyrone Power, Brenda Joyce, Maria Ouspenskaya, Joseph Schildkraut, Nigel Bruce. w. Philip Dune, Julien Josephson, N-adap. Louis Bromfield, d. Clarence Brown. **BSFX**, BEdit, BOScore. Oscars: 3-1.

MELODRAMA: Disaster Movies; Imperialist Problems; Floods; India; Earthquakes; Faded Hits; Ahead of Its Time

Raintree County, 1957, 166m, ★★★/$$$$, MGM/MGM-UA. During the Civil War, a headstrong southern belle, who always gets what she wants, picks her man, but once married, finds him boring. Montgomery Clift, Elizabeth Taylor (BActress), Eva Marie Saint, Nigel Patrick, Lee Marvin, Rod Taylor, Agnes Moorehead, Walter Abel, Rhys Williams. w. Millard Kaufman, N-adap. Ross Lockridge, d. Edward Dmytryk. BCostume, BArt, BOScore. Oscars: 4-0.

MELODRAMA: ROMANCE: Costume Drama; Marriage Drama; Marriage on the Rocks; Feisty Females; Mean Women; Southerns; Faded Hits
(Gone With the Wind; Jezebel; Darling)

Raise the Red Lantern, 1991, 125m, ★★★/$$, Orion/Orion, R. An austere lord in turn of the century China has four wives, the youngest of whom is a poor country girl who is cut off from her family and must endure the jealousy and hostility of his other brides. Gong Li, Ma Jingwu, He Caidei, Cao Cuifeng, Jin Shuyuan, Kong Li. w. Ni Zhen, Su Tong, d. Zhang Yimou. BFLFilm. Oscars: 1-0.

DRAMA: Art Films; Royalty; Bigamy; Women in Conflict; Women Fighting Over Men; Prostitutes-High Class; Female Protagonists; Taiwanese Films; Chinese Films
(Shanghai Triad)

Raise the Titanic!, 1980, 122m, ★★/$, ITC/Fox. A group of tycoons raise money to uncover what they believe is valuable treasure buried underwater with the Titanic. Jason Robards, Richard Jordan, Alec Guinness, David Selby, Anne Archer, J. D. Cannon. w. Adam Kennedy, Eric Hughes, N-adap. Clive Cussler, d. Jerry Jameson.

ADVENTURE: Ensemble Films; Rescue Drama; Treasure Hunts; Ships; Shipwrecked; Titanic Stories; Flops-Major
(Ed: Sinks and stinks)

Raisin in the Sun, 1961, 128m, ★★★/$$$, Col/RCA-Col. A middle-class black family moves up to the suburbs of Chicago and has trouble adjusting. Sidney Poitier, Ruby Dee, Claudia McNeil, Diana Sands, Ivan Dixon, Lou Gossett. w. P-adap. Lorraine Hansberry, d. Daniel Petrie.

DRAMA: Family Drama; Social Drama; Social Climbing; Black Casts; Black Men; Black Women; Black vs. White; Race Relations; Suburban Life; Chicago; Stagelike Films; Black Screenwriters; Black Directors; Hidden Gems; Female Screenwriters; Faded Hits
(Nothin' But a Man; Almos' a Man; Laurel Avenue)

Raising Arizona, 1987, 94m, ★★★★/$$, 20th/CBS-Fox, PG/P-S-V. An ex-convict (Nicolas Cage) marries a barren policewoman (Holly Hunter) and decides to kidnap one of a wealthy man's several babies to give to her, but chaos and an endless chase is the result. Frances McDormand, John Goodman. w. Joel & Ethan Coen, d. Joel Coen.

COMEDY: FARCE: Action Comedy; Chase Movies; Babies-Having; Kidnappings; Rednecks; Rural Life; Law Officers-Female; Women-Childless; Southwestern Life
(Fargo; Stars and Bars)

Raising Cain, 1992, 92m, ★★/$$, WB/WB, R/P-EV. A child psychologist (John Lithgow) is haunted by the past and the reappearance of his evil twin, who may drive him to do unspeakable things to children. Lolita Davidovich, Steven Bauer, Frances Sternhagen, Mel Harris, Teri Austin. w. d. Brian DePalma.

SUSPENSE: HORROR: MURDER: Psychological Thrillers; Psycho Killers; Serial Killers; Evil Men; Twins; Psychologists; Murderers of Children; Illusions/Hallucinations; Multiple Personalities; Fantasies; Clever Plots & Endings; Writer-Directors
(M; Dead Ringers; Dressed to Kill)
(Ed: A muddled mess with a few good ideas and gimmicks, though the trailer looked good)

Rally Round the Flag, Boys, 1958, 106m, ★★★/$$$, 20th/CBS-Fox. A military base is planned for a site and the locals get up in arms, but a housewife has to keep a strumpet in a convertible away from her husband in the meantime. Paul Newman, Joanne Woodward, Joan Collins, Jack Carson, Dwayne Hickman, Tuesday Weld, Gale Gordon, Murvyn Vye. w. Claude Binyon, Leo McCarey, N-adap. Max Shulman, d. Leo McCarey.

COMEDY: COMEDY DRAMA: Marriage Comedy; Family Comedy; Sexy Women; Suburban Life; American Myth; Military Comedy; Fighting the System; Women Fighting Over Men; Boy Scouts; Men and Boys
(A New Kind of Love; Follow Me, Boys!)

Rambling Rose, 1991, 112m, ★★★★/$$, 7Arts-Carolco/Live, PG/S-P. A genteel southern family (Robert Duvall, Diane Ladd [BSActress], Lukas Haas) needs a housegirl and the beautiful tow-headed young lady who arrives (Laura Dern, BActress) turns out to be a nymphomaniac, much to the adolescent son's delight. w. N-adap. Calder Willingham, d. Martha Coolidge. Oscars: 2-0.

COMEDY DRAMA: DRAMA: Coming of Age; Promiscuity; Romance-Older Men/Younger Women; Teenagers; Boys;

Love-First; Infatuations; Small-town Life; Southerns; Sexy Women; Depression Era; Womens' Rights; Female Directors; Narrated Films
(Mignon Has Left; This Property is Condemned)
(Ed: Mother and daughter Oscar nominees in a year dominated by portrayals of Southern characters)

Rambo: First Blood Part Two, 1985, 92m, ★★½/$$$$$, Carolco-Tri-Star/LIVE, PG-13/EV-P. Rambo returns to Vietnam to rescue a group of M.I.A.s in a P.O.W. camp long after the war is over. Sylvester Stallone, Richard Crenna, Charles Napier, Julia Nickson, Steven Berkoff. w. Sylvester Stallone, James Cameron, d. George Pan Cosmatos.
ACTION: ADVENTURE: Journeys; Rescue Adventure; Vietnam War; POWs/MIAs; Sleeper Hits; Blockbusters
(Missing in Action; Uncommon Valor)

Rambo III, 1988, 101m, ★½/$$, Carolco-Tri-Star/LIVE, PG-13/EV-P. When his friend is captured by the Soviet Army, Rambo goes to Afghanistan and wages a one-man war to get him out. Sylvester Stallone, Richard Crenna, Marc de Jonge, Kurtwood Smith, Spiros Focas. w. Sylvester Stallone, Sheldon Lettich, d. Peter MacDonald.
ACTION: ADVENTURE: Rescue Adventure; POWs; Middle East; Flops-Major
(Ed: The gig was up once audiences started laughing at the coming attraction trailers)

Rampage, 1987, 92m, ★★★/$, Par/Par, R/EV-B&G. A good-looking serial killer has the cops and a DA hot on his trail, but he intends to use his Satanism against the DA's family. Alex MacArthur, Michael Biehn, Nicholas Campbell, Deborah Van Valkenburgh. w. d. William Friedkin, NF-adap. William Wood. Based on the story of Richard Chase.
SUSPENSE: Psychological Thriller; Serial Killers; Trail of a Killer; Lawyers; Lawyers as Detectives; Criminal Pursues Good Guy's Family; Satanism; Occult; True Stories
(Silence of the Lambs; Relentless)
(Ed: An effective true story fictionalization that's not as thrilling as totally fictional similar films, but in some ways more frightening simply because it did happen)

Ran, 1985, 161m, ★★★★/$$$, Orion/Orion, PG/EV-S. A Japanese lord in the days of the Samurai is banished from his kingdom and must live in exile with a fool, as his three sons fight over his inheritance. w. Akira Kurosawa, P-adap. William Shakespeare (*King Lear*), d. Akira Kurosawa (BDirector). BCin, **BCostume**, BArt, **BFLFilm**. Oscars: 5-2.
DRAMA: TRAGEDY: Epics; War Stories; Historical Drama; Power Struggles; Inheritances at Stake; Brothers; Fathers & Sons; Parents vs. Children; Men in Conflict; Royalty; Japanese Films; Revisionist Films; Classic Tragedy; Shakespeare
REMAKE OF: King Lear.

Rancho De Luxe, 1974, 95m, ★★★/$, UA/MGM-UA, R/S-P. Some dimwitted cowpokes hit the town, get drunk, and land in jail in their slice-of-life small town. Sam Waterston, Jeff Bridges, Elizabeth Ashley, Charlene Dallas, Slim Pickens. w. Thomas McGuane, d. Frank Perry.
COMEDY DRAMA: Black Comedy; Cattle Rustlers; WESTERNS: Western Comedy; Western-Modern; Small-town Life; Alcoholics; Slice of Life Stories; Hidden Gems; Overlooked at Release
(92 in the Shade; Cold Feet)

Rancho Notorious, 1952, 89m, ★★★/$, Ind/VCI. A man pursues his girlfriend's killer but gets sidetracked with a mysterious chanteuse. Arthur Kennedy, Marlene Dietrich, William Frawley, Jack Elam. w. Daniel Taradash, d. Fritz Lang.
MELODRAMA: SUSPENSE: ROMANCE: Romantic Drama; Film Noir; Trail of a Killer; Murder of Spouse; Dangerous Women; Singers; Forgotten Films
(I Wake Up Screaming; Stage Fright)

Random Harvest, 1942, 126m, ★★★½/$$$, MGM/MGM-UA. During World War I, a soldier becomes amnesiac in the fallout of a mortar explosion. He's committed to an asylum after the war. After being released, he falls in love with a cabaret singer. They marry, and then a traumatic event makes him realize he's actually a wealthy and married heir. His wife plays along, not knowing whether to believe him or not. Ronald Colman (BActor), Greer Garson, Susan Peters (BSActress), Philip Dorn, Reginald Owen, Henry Travers. w. Claudine West, George Froeschel, Arthur Wimperis (BScr), N-adap. James Hilton, d. Mervyn Le Roy (BDirector). BPicture, BCArt, BOScore. Oscars: 7-0.

MELODRAMA: Marriage Drama; Amnesia; Mentally Disabled; Asylums; Episodic Stories; Veterans; World War I Era; Singers; Heirs; Illusions/Hallucinations
(King's Row; Mr. Buddwing)

Ransom, 1975, 98m, ★★½/$, B-L/NA. In Norway, terrorists kidnap a British official, prompting the international community to get involved. Sean Connery, Ian McShane, Norman Bristow, John Cording, Isabel Dean, William Fox, Robert Harris. w. Paul Wheeler, d. Caspar Wrede.
ACTION: SUSPENSE: Spy Films; Spies; Kidnappings; Diplomats; Scandinavia; Overlooked at Release; Forgotten Films

Rapid Fire, 1992, 95m, ★★½/$$$, 20th/Fox, PG-13/EV-P. A mob hit has only one witness: a Chinese-American college student who also happens to be an expert at karate. The FBI soon approaches the lad and solicits his help in exposing a drug ring in which the murder victim was involved. Brandon Lee, Powers Boothe, Nick Mancuso, Raymond J. Barry, Kate Hodge, Tzi Ma. w. Alan McElroy, Cindy Cirile, d. Dwight H. Little.
ACTION: MURDER: Mob Stories; Witness to Murder; Witnesses-Protecting; Martial Arts; College Life; FBI Agents; Drugs-Dealing; Fugitives from the Mob
(The Crow; Enter the Dragon)

The Rapture, 1990, 100m, MGM/Fine Line, ★★★★/$, (LR/VR). A woman in Los Angeles (Mimi Rogers), tired of her hedonistic, empty lifestyle, decides to make a change, so she joins a Christian cult and marries a converted preacher, but all isn't so good being born again. w.d. Michael Tolkin.
DRAMA: TRAGEDY: MURDER: Murderers of Children; Single Women; Promiscuity; Sexuality; Religion; Alternative Lifestyles; Cults; Preachers; Wild People; Starting Over; Los Angeles; Ordinary People in Extraordinary Situations; Apocalyptic Stories; Desert Settings; Hidden Gems; Overlooked at Release; Writer-Directors; Female Protagonists

The Rare Breed, 1966, 97m, ★★½/$$, U/MCA-U. An American rancherwoman goes to England to take a prize bull back to St. Louis to breed with her longhorn cattle and everyone gets up in arms. James Stewart, Maureen O'Hara, Brian Keith, Juliet Mills, Don Galloway, David

Brian. w. Ric Hardman, d. Andrew V. McLaglen.

WESTERNS: Western Comedy; Cattle Ranchers; **ROMANCE:** Romantic Comedy; Farm Life

Rashomon, 1951, 83m, ★★★1/2/$$$, Daiei-Ind/Sultan. The story of a thief's attack of a nobleman is told by four witnesses, including a ghost. Each narrator has a very different view of what actually happened. Toshiro Mifune, Machiko Kyo, Masayuki Mori, Takashi Shimura. w. d. Akira Kurosawa. **BFLFilm**, BB&WArt. Oscars: 2-1.

DRAMA: Art Films; Fantasy; Ghosts; Rape/Rapists; Thieves; Women in Jeopardy; Multiple Stories; Narrated Films; Hidden Gems; Writer-Directors

REMAKE: The Outrage, The Iron Maze

Rasputin and the Empress, 1932, 133m, ★★★/$$$, MGM/MGM-UA. Catherine the Great's court is ruled by the Svengali-like Rasputin, her lover, who puts her up to all manner of evil. John Barrymore, Ethel Barrymore, Lionel Barrymore, Diana Winyard, Ralph Morgan, Edward Arnold, C. Henry Gordon. w. Charles McArthur, d. Richard Boleslawski.

MELODRAMA: Costume Drama; Historical Drama; Queens; Svengalis; Evil Women; Royalty; Russians
(Great Catherine; Young Catherine)

The Rat Race, 1960, 105m, ★★★/$$, Par/Par. Two young hopefuls, a jazz musician and a hostess in a nightclub, try to make it in New York, but they make the mistake of sharing an apartment. Tony Curtis, Debbie Reynolds, Jack Oakie, Kay Medford, Don Rickles. w. P-adap. Garson Kanin, d. Robert Mulligan.

COMEDY: COMEDY DRAMA:

ROMANCE: Romantic Comedy; Romance-Bickering; Making a Living; Young People; Roommates; Musicians; Jazz Life; Nightclubs; New York Life; Ordinary People Stories; Working Class; Forgotten Films; Hidden Gems; Coulda Been Great; Stagelike Films
(The More the Merrier; Under the Yum Yum Tree; Period of Adjustment; Mary, Mary)

Ratboy, 1986, 104m, ★★/$, WB/WB, G. The fable of an alien boy who looks like a rat and is ridiculed by his peers, but finally finds a place in the world. Sondra Locke, Robert Townsend, Christopher

Hewett, Larry Hankin. w. Rob Thompson, d. Sondra Locke.

DRAMA: CHILDREN'S: FAMILY:
Fantasy; Ostracism; Fairy Tales; Conformism; Rodents; Humans into Animals; Curiosities; Overlooked at Release; Female Directors; Ostracism (Mask)

The Raven, 1935, 61m, ★★★/$$$, U/MCA-U. A gangster on the lam makes an unfortunate choice of hiding places: the mansion of a mad scientist obsessed with Poe's torture devices. It so happens he was looking for a guinea pig . . . Bela Lugosi, Boris Karloff, Samuel S. Hinds, Irene Ware, Lester Matthews. w. David Boehm, d. Lew Landers.

HORROR: Fugitives from the Law; Scientists-Mad; Experiments; Torture; Cosmetic Surgery
(The Pit and the Pendulum)

The Raven, 1963, 86m, ★★1/2/$$, AIP/Lebell Video. Two mystical wizards have an all-out magic war. Vincent Price, Peter Lorre, Boris Karloff, Hazel Court, Jack Nicholson. w. Richard Matheson, d. Roger Corman.

HORROR: SCI-FI: Scientists-Mad; Feuds; Magic; Men in Conflict
(Master of the World; Comedy of Terrors)

Raw Deal, 1986, 106m, ★★/$$, DEG/Lorimar-WB, PG/P-V. Chicago's ruling mob gets an uninvited guest: a muscle-bound FBI man masquerading as a mobster. Arnold Schwarzenegger, Kathryn Harrold, Sam Wanamaker, Paul Shenar, Ed Lauter, Darren McGavin. w. Garry M. DeVore, Norman Wexler, d. John Irvin.

ACTION: Crime Drama; Mob Stories; Body Builders; FBI Agents; Detective Stories; Undercover; Chicago
(Commando; True Lies; The Terminator)

Rawhead Rex, 1987, 86m, ★★/$$, Vestron/Vestron, R/EV-B&G. A couple traveling in Ireland stay at a farmhouse which houses an unearthly beast from Hell. He proceeds to devour them and others in his way. David Dukes, Kelly Piper, Ronan Wilmot, Niall Toibin, Heiinrich Von Schellendoft, Niall O'Brien. w. Clive Barker, d. George Pavlou.

HORROR: Monsters; Ireland; Hell; Supernatural Danger; Nightmare Vacations; Independent Films

Rawhide, 1950, 86m, ★★★/$$$, 20th/Fox. Escaped convicts hijack a stagecoach and go on the lam. Tyrone

Power, Susan Hayward, Hugh Marlowe, Jack Elam, Dean Jagger, Edgar Buchanan, Jeff Corey. w. Dudley Nichols, d. Henry Hathaway.

WESTERNS: Hijackings; Kidnappings; Prison Escapes; Outlaw Road Movies

Razorback, 1984, 95m, ★★/$, UAA/WB, R-V. In the Australian outback, a man is accused of killing his grandson, but the boy was actually killed by a wild dog. Gregory Harrison, Aarkie Whiteley, Bill Kerr, Chris Haywood. w. Everett De Roche, N-adap. Peter Brennan, d. Russell Mulcahy.

DRAMA: MELODRAMA: MURDER:
Death-Accidental; Accused Unjustly; Avenging Death of Someone; Monsters-Animal; Australia
(A Cry in the Dark)

The Razor's Edge, 1946, 146m, ★★★1/2/$$$$, Fox/Fox. A man of means wanders the world in between the wars, finally finding some sort of personal truth he can connect with in Eastern mysticism, with romance also playing a major part. Tyrone Power, Gene Tierney, Clifton Webb (BSActor), Herbert Marshall, John Payne, Anne Baxter (**BSActress**), Frank Latimore, Elsa Lanchester. w. Lamar Trotti, N-adap. W. Somerset Maugham, d. Edmund Goulding. BPicture, BCArt. Oscars: 4-1.

The Razor's Edge, 1984, 128m, ★★1/2/$, WB/WB, PG. Bill Murray stars in an uninspired remake of the classic. Theresa Russell, Denholm Elliott, Catherine Hicks, Peter Vaughan, Faith Brook. w. John Byrum, Bill Murray, N-adap. W. Somerset Maugham, d. John Byrum.

DRAMA: ADVENTURE: ROMANCE:
Romantic Adventure; Asia; Himalayas; Quests; Journies; Religion; Pre-Life Crisis; Young Men
(Dodsworth; Keys to the Kingdom; Lord Jim)

Ready to Wear, 1994, 132m, ★★★/$$, Miramax/Miramax-Touchstone, R/P-S-FFN. Fashion reporters, models, designers, marketers, and a man accused of murdering a man who really choked on his snack all converge during the ready to wear season in gay Paree. Greed mixes with integrity-filled artistes, beautiful people with the preposterous, and love long dead with lust for a weekend, all coming together in a tasty slice of life in the fast and pretentious lane. Sophia

Loren, Marcello Mastroianni, Tim Robbins, Julia Roberts, Tracey Ullman, Forest Whitaker, Danny Aiello, Anouk Aimee, Lauren Bacall, Kim Basinger, Michel Blanc, Jean-Pierre Cassel, Rossy de Palma, Rupert Everett, Teri Garr, Richard E. Grant, Linda Hunt, Sally Kellerman, Ute Lemper, Stephen Rea, Sam Robards, Jean Rochefort, Lili Taylor, Lyle Lovett. w. Robert Altman, Barbara Shulgasserd, d. Robert Altman.

COMEDY: Art Films; Comedy-Light; **SATIRE: FARCE:** Fashion World; Greed; Multiple Stories; Interwoven Stories; Erotic Comedy; Paris; Romance-Reunited; Romance-Brief; Gay Men; Bisexuality; Underrated; All-Star Cast; Female Screenwriters
(Nashville; Unzipped; The Player)
(Ed: More of a droll satire than a rollicking farce, and once you accept that, it's mostly entertaining, enlightening, and rather brilliant if a bit tired. If it had been made in France by a Frenchman it would have received the attention it deserves)

Reality Bites, 1993, 104m, ★★/$$, Gramercy/MCA-U, PG-13/S-P. Several twenty-somethings live together and try to keep their jobs and not drive each other crazy. Central figure Ryder meets a yuppie from New York who can help her career-even after she hit his Saab-but there's the loser-musician who got fired for stealing a Snickers who may win out. Winona Ryder, Ethan Hawke, Ben Stiller, Swoosie Kurtz, Janeane Garafalo, Steve Zahn, John Mahoney, Jeanne Tripplehorn, Evan Dando. w. Helen Childress, d. Ben Stiller.

COMEDY: DRAMA: ROMANCE: Romance-Choosing the Right Person; Romance-Girl Wants Boy; 20-somethings; Roommates; Making a Living; Unemployment; Ensemble Films; Ensembles-Young People; Female Protagonists; Female Screenwriters; Actor Directors
(Singles; Threesome; Party Girl; How to Make an American Quilt)
(Ed: This movie bites)

Real Life, 1979, 99m, ★★★/$$, Par/Par, PG/P. A documentary crew enters the home of an "average American family" and learns just how weird we really are, as the presence of the crew and director create more events than they "report." Albert Brooks, Charles Grodin, Frances Lee McCain, J. A. Preston, Matthew

Tobin. w. Albert Brooks, Monica Johnson, Harry Shearer, d. Albert Brooks.
DRAMA: SATIRE: Family Drama; Documentaries; Documentary Style; Movies within Movies; Moviemaking; Suburban Life; Ordinary People Stories; Spoofs; Voyeurs
(An American Family (PBS Documentary); Modern Romance)

The Real McCoy, 1993, 104m, ★★/$, U/MCA-U, PG-13/S-P. A lady cat burglar-bank robber gets out of the clink and tries to go straight by raising her kid, but her old pals kidnap her to blackmail her into pulling another heist. Kim Basinger, Val Kilmer, Terence Stamp, Zach English. w. William Davies, William Osborne, d. Russell Mulcahy.
SUSPENSE: Heist Stories; Capers; Bank Robberies; Thieves; Criminals-Female; Blackmail; Kidnappings; Ex-Convicts; Starting Over; One Last Time; Female Protagonists; Coulda Been Good
(To Catch a Thief; Burglar)

Real Men, 1987, 96m, ★ 1/2/$, MGM-UA/MGM-UA, PG-13/P-V. An insurance salesman is recruited by the CIA, ostensibly as a messenger to a foreign ally. But he ends up being a sitting duck for other agents who haven't been "briefed." James Belushi, John Ritter, Barbara Barrie, Bill Morey, Isa Anderson, Gale Barle, Mark Herrier. w. d. Dennis Feldman.
COMEDY: ACTION: Action Comedy; Misunderstandings; CIA Agents; Undercover

Re-Animator, 1985, 86m, ★★ 1/2/$$, Empire/Empire, Vestron, R/EV-B&G. A madcap mad scientist brings people back from the dead, and they aren't too happy about it. Jeffrey Combs, Bruce Abbott, Barbara Crampton, David Gale. w. Dennis Paoli, William J. Norris, Stuart Gordon, SS-adap. H. P. Lovecraft (Herbert West-Re-animator), d. Stuart Gordon.
(Frankenstein)

Re-Animator 2, 1989, 96m, ★★ 1/2/$$, Empire/Vestron, R/EV-B&G. This time the doctor builds a woman to keep him company, but is attacked by jealous and violent re-animated corpses he had lying aroud the lab. Bruce Abbott, Claude Earl Jones, Fabiana Udenio, David Gale, Kathleen Kimmont, Jeffrey Combs, Mel Stewart, Michael Strasser. w. Woody Keith, Rick Fry, SS-adap. H. P. Lovecraft (Herbert West-Re-animator), d. Brian Yuzna.

(Bride of Frankenstein; The Bride)
HORROR: SCI-FI: Frankenstein Stories; Body Parts; Scientists-Mad; Experiments; Black Comedy; Horror Comedy

Reap the Wild Wind, 1942, 124m, ★★★/$$, Par/Par. Sailors in the stormy Atlantic put in on the Georgia coast and vie for the attentions of a particular southern belle. Ray Milland, John Wayne, Paulette Goddard, Raymond Massey, Robert Preston, Lynne Overman, Susan Hayward, Charles Bickford, Walter Hampden, Hedda Hopper. w. Alan le May, Jesse Lasky, Jr., d. Cecil B. de Mille. BCCin, BCArt. Oscars: 2-0.
MELODRAMA: ROMANCE: Southerns; Sailors; Plantation Life; Men Fighting Over Women; Romance-Triangles; Octopi-Angry; Forgotten Films
(Gone With the Wind; Green Dolphin Street)

Rear Window, 1954, Par/MCA-Universal, ★★★★/$$$$. A bedridden photographer (James Stewart) looks out his window at the backs of neighboring apartment buildings and thinks a murder has occurred. Grace Kelly, Thelma Ritter, Wendell Corey, Raymond Burr. w. John Mitchell Hayes (BScr), SS-adap. Cornell Woolrich, d. Alfred Hitchcock (BDirector). BSound, BCCin. Oscars: 4-0.
SUSPENSE: MYSTERY: MURDER MYSTERY: Murder-Discovering; Women in Jeopardy; Disabled People; Unbelieved; Voyeurism; Photographers; Murder-Discovering; New York Life; Surveillance; Apartment Buildings; Cult Films; Hitchcockian
(Manhattan Murder Mystery; Body Double; Somebody's Watching Me; Sliver; Monsieur Hire)

Rebecca, 1940, 130m, ★★★ 1/2/$$$$, RKO/CBS-Fox. A young woman (Joan Fontaine, BActress) marries a rich British man (Laurence Olivier, BActor) with a mansion containing some dark secrets relating to his first wife whom she knows nothing about. Judith Anderson (BSActress). w. Robert E. Sherwood, Joan Harrison (BScr), N-adap. Daphne DuMaurier, d. Alfred Hitchcock (BDirector). **BPicture, BB&WCin,** BEdit, BOScore, BB&WArt. Oscars: 11-2.
DRAMA: SUSPENSE: MYSTERY: Murder-Discovering; Murder of Spouse; Psychological Drama; Psychological Thriller; Marriage Drama; Dangerous Spouses; Mindgames; Secrets-Haunting;

Newlyweds; Houses-Creepy; Hitchcockian (The Secret Beyond the Door; Suspicion; The Two Mrs. Carrolls; Undercurrent; Suspicion)

Rebecca of Sunnybrook Farm, 1932, 75m, ★★½/$$$, 20th/NA. An optimistic young girl with a persuasive smile wins over her grumpy aunt and reforms a non-believer when she's sent off to the farm. Marian Nixon, Ralph Bellamy, Mae Marsh, Louise Closser Hale, Alan Hale, Charlotte Henry. w. S. N. Behrman, Sonya Levien, N-adap. Kate Douglas Wiggin and Charlotte Thompson, d. Alfred Santell.

MELODRAMA: Young Women; Girls; Farm Life; Charismatic People; Religion; Child Protagonists

PREVIOUS VERSION: 1917.

Rebecca of Sunnybrook Farm, 1938, 80m, ★★/$$$, 20th/Fox. A remake which totally recasts the story as Rebecca is exploited by an avaricious radio producer who wants to make her a star. Shirley Temple, Randolph Scott, Jack Haley, Gloria Stuart, Phyllis Brooks, Helen Westley, Slim Summerville, Bill Robinson. w. Karl Tunberg, Don Ettlinger, N-adap. Kate Douglas Wiggin and Charlotte Thompson. d. Allan Dwan.

MELODRAMA: Girls; Radio Life; Singers; Child Protagonists

(I'll Do Anything; Our Vines Have Tender Grapes)

Rebecca's Daughters, 1991, 97m, ★★★/$, Mayfair/NA. In the 1800s, farmers in Wales protest the toll-gate tariffs imposed by the local government by marching around in women's clothing. Peter O'Toole, Paul Rhys, Joely Richardson, Keith Allen, Simon Dormandy, Dafydd Hywel, Sue Roderick. w. Guy Jenkin, Karl Francis, Dylan Thomas, d. Karl Francis.

COMEDY: SATIRE: Comedy-Light; Men as Women; Political Unrest; Strikes; Victorian Era; Rich vs Poor; British Films; Small-town Life

Rebel Rousers, 1969, 81m, ★★/$$, AIP/Media, R/V-S. Bikers fight over pregnant girl. Jack Nicholson, Cameron Mitchell, Bruce Dern, Diane Ladd, Harry Dean Stanton. d. Martin Cohen.

ACTION: Action Drama; Motorcycles; Psychedelic Era; Babies-Having; Men Fighting Over Women; Competitions; Cult Films; Forgotten Films

(Hell's Angels; The Wild Ones)

Rebel Without a Cause, 1955, 111m, ★★★★/$$$$, WB/WB. A suburban kid who's moved from town to town by his traveling businessman dad comes to L.A. and gets in with the "wrong crowd"-this time a bunch of other disaffected children of the middle class, who play "chicken" on the edges of cliffs and hide out in abandoned buildings weilding guns. James Dean, Natalie Wood (BSActress), Sal Mineo (BSActor), Jim Backus, Ann Doran, Dennis Hopper. w. Stewart Stern, Story: Nicholas Ray (BOStory), d. Nicholas Ray. Oscars: 3-0.

DRAMA: Men Proving Themselves; Parents vs. Children; Coming of Age; Homo-eroticism; Suburban Life; Los Angeles; High School Life; Rebels; Young Men-Angry

(Lost Angels; East of Eden)

Reckless, 1935, 96m, ★★½/$$$, MGM/MGM-UA. A backstage drama of the life of Libby Holman, a singer who married a millionaire, to the utter dispair of the manager who nursed a lifelong infatuation for her. Jean Harlow, William Powell, Franchot Tone, May Robson, Ted Healy, Nat Pendleton, Rosalind Russell, Henry Stephenson. w. P. J. Wolfson, d. Victor Fleming.

MELODRAMA: ROMANCE: Biographies; Singers; Marrying Up; Fame-Rise to; 1920s; Fatal Attractions; Romance-Unrequited; Elusive Women; True Stories

Reckless, 1984, 100m, ★★½/$$, MGM/MGM-UA, R/S-P. A motorcycle-riding, pouting rebel sweeps a small-town rich girl off her feet. Aidan Quinn, Darryl Hannah. w. Chris Columbus, d. James Foley.

MELODRAMA: ROMANCE: Romance-Reluctant; Love-Forbidden; Romance-Class; Conflicts; Lover Family Dislikes; Rebels; Love-First; Coming of Age; Teenagers; Young Men; Young Men-Angry; Mining Towns; Coulda Been Good

(Picnic; Desperately Seeking Susan)

(Ed: If only this film had started off like it ends)

Reckless, 1995, 92m, ★★★/$, AP-Goldwyn/Goldwyn, PG-13/P-S. A mousy woman finds herself on a snowy adventure when her younger husband pushes her out of a window to escape the hitman he's hired to kill her. Mia Farrow, Scott Glenn, Mary-Louise Parker, Tony Goldwyn, Eileen Brennan, Giancarlo

Esposito, Stephen Dorff. w. P-adap. Craig Lucas, d. Norman Rene.

COMEDY: Black Comedy; Hitmen; MURDER: Murder-Attempted; Murder of Spouse; One Day Stories; Snow Settings; Female Protagonists

(Faithful; Alice)

The Reckless Moment, 1949, 82m, ★★½/$, Col/Learning Corp. In a moment of passion and mistaken identity, a mother kills her daughter's admirer and is later stalked by a blackmailer who knows the truth. Joan Bennett, James Mason, Geraldine Brooks, Henry O'Neill, Shepperd Strudwick. w. Henry Garson, R. W. Soderborg, N-adap. Elizabeth Sanxay Holding (The Blank Wall), d. Max Ophuls.

SUSPENSE: MURDER: Blackmail; Death-Accidental; Accused Unjustly; Stalkers; Indentities-Mistaken; Mothers & Daughters; Crimes of Passion; Good Premise Unfulfilled

(Mildred Pierce)

The Red Badge of Courage, 1951, 69m, ★★★/$$$, MGM/MGM-UA. During the Civil War a young recruit gets his first taste of battle and is transformed from a timid boy to a man. Audie Murphy, Bill Mauldin, Douglas Dick, Royal Dano, John Dierkes, Andy Devine, Arthur Hunnicutt. w. d. John Huston, N-adap. Stephen Crane.

DRAMA: War Stories; Cowards; Men Proving Themselves; Coming of Age Boys; Young Men; Civil War Era; Classic Literary Adaptations

(All Quiet on the Western Front; Platoon)

The Red Balloon, 1956, 34m, ★★★★/$$$, Films Montouris-Col/Col, G. A small, lonely boy finds himself being followed by a red balloon, but once he has it, it may escape him forever. Pascal Lamorisse. w. d. Albert Lamorisse.

(BOScr). Oscars: 1-1.

DRAMA: Allegorical Stories; Boys; Balloons; Child Protagonists; CHILDREN'S: FAMILY: Art Films; Sleeper Hits; French Films; Writer-Directors

(The White Balloon)

Red Dawn, 1984, 114m, ★★/$$$, MGM-UA/MGM-UA, PG-13/P-V. In Colorado, members of the local high school football team thwart an invasion by the Soviet Army joined with the Cubans. Patrick Swayze, C. Thomas Howell, Lea Thompson, Charlie Sheen, Darren Dalton, Jennifer Grey, Ben Johnson, Harry Dean Stanton, Powers

Boothe. w. Kevin Reynolds, John Milius, d. John Milius.

ACTION: Cold War Era; Russians as Enemy; Conservative Value Films; War Stories; Political Unrest; What If . . . Stories (Amerika; The Russians Are Coming . . .)

The Red Desert, 1964, 120m, ★★★/$, Ind/Connoisseur, Facets. A housewife in Italy has a breakdown and goes to find herself, and a man, in the industrial area of Northern Italy. Shot with monchrome color filters. Monica Vitti, Richard Harris, Carlos Chionette. w. d. Michelangelo Antonioni.

DRAMA: Art Films; Character Studies; Housewives; Nervous Breakdowns; Writer Directors; Italian Films; Cult Films (L'Avventura; Blow-Up; Zabriskie Point)

Red Dust, 1932, 86m, ★★★1/2/$$$, MGM/MGM-UA. In Indo-China, a love triangle forms between the owner of a rubber plantation, the wife of the engineer, and a local prostitute. Clark Gable, Jean Harlow, Mary Astor, Gene Raymond, Donald Crisp, Tully Marshall, Forrester Harvey. w. John Lee Mahin, P-adap. Wilson Collison, d. Victor Fleming.

MELODRAMA: ROMANCE: Romance-Triangles; Women Fighting Over Men; Asia; Plantation Life; Prostitutes-Romance with

REMAKE: Mogambo.

(Mogambo; Bombshell; Platinum Blonde)

Red Garters, 1954, 91m, ★★★/$$, Par/Par. A musical spoof of Westerns like *High Noon*, with the requisite big showdown in the town square and mysterious outlaws coming into town, etc. Rosemary Clooney, Guy Mitchell, Gene Barry, Jack Carson, Pat Crowley, Cass Daley, Frank Faylen, Reginald Owen. w. Michael Fessier, d. George Marshall.

WESTERNS: MUSICALS: Singers; Spoofs; Duels; Forgotten Films (Belle of the Yukon)

Red Headed Woman, 1932, 74m, ★★1/2/$$$, MGM/MGM-UA. A simple corner shop clerk is pursued by her boss, who travels in high society. After they marry, she finds herself often embarrassed and not fitting in to his social circle. Jean Harlow, Chester Morris, Lewis Stone, Leila Hyams, Una Merkel, Henry Stephenson, Charles Boyer, May Robson. w. Anita Loows, N-adap. Katharine Brush, d. Jack Conway.

MELODRAMA: ROMANCE: Marriage Drama; Marrying Up; Rich vs. Poor;

Ordinary People Stories; Fish out of Water Stories; Forgotten Films; Hidden Gems; Faded Hits

(Of Human Bondage; White Palace)

Red Heat, 1988, 104m, ★★1/2/$$$, Tri-Star/Col-Tri, PG-13/V-P-MRN. In order to stop an international band of drug dealers, a Soviet cop comes to Chicago and is teamed up with a local man in blue. Their styles obviously clash, but eventually each learns to respect the others mode of operation. Arnold Schwarzenegger, James Belushi, Peter Boyle, Ed O'Ross, Larry Fishburne, Gina Gershon, Richard Bright. w. Harry Kleiner, Walter Hill, Troy Kennedy Martin, d. Walter Hill.

ACTION: Fish out of Water Stories; Police Stories; Undercover; Drugs-Dealing; Buddy Films; Buddy Cops; Russians; Russians & Americans; Chicago (Beverly Hills Cop; Terminator 2)

The Red House, 1947, 100m, ★★★/$$, UA/Nos, Sinister. A farmer hangs on to the creepy old dilapidated house because it holds the secret to his haunted past (it's where he killed his parents). Edward G. Robinson, Judith Anderson, Lon McCallister, Allene Roberts, Rory Calhoun, Julie London, Ona Munson. w. d. Delmer Daves, N-adap. George Agnew.

SUSPENSE: MYSTERY: Houses-Creepy; Secrets-Haunting; Secrets-Keeping;

MURDER: MURDER MYSTERY: Guilty Conscience; Fathers-Troublesome; Hidden Gems; Cult Films (Ed: Great creepy atmosphere)

The Red Inn, 1951, 95m, ★★★/$$, Memnon/NA. Stagecoach travelers are murdered one by one in a country hostel, where the owner is a deranged psychopath. Some manage to escape, but fall down a ravine. Fernandel, Francoise Rosay, Carette, Gregoire Aslan. w. Jean Aurenche, Pierre Bost, d. Claude Autant-Lara.

SUSPENSE: HORROR: Black Comedy; Horror Comedy; **MURDER:** Murders-One by One; Nightmares; Hidden Gems; Forgotten Films

Red Kiss, 1985, 110m, ★★★/$, Ind/Fox-Lorber, R/S. A Polish immigrant girl in post-war France falls for an older photographer, but political convictions and family may tear them apart. Charlotte Valandrey, Marthe Keller, Lambert Wilson. w. d. Vera Belmont.

DRAMA: ROMANCE: Romantic Drama; Romance-Older Men/Younger Women;

Love-First; Young Women; Girls; Lover Family Dislikes; Political Drama; Polish People; Immigrants; Writer Directors; Female Directors; Female Screenwriters; French Films; Overlooked at Release

Red Line 7000, 1965, 110m, ★★/$$, Par/Par, PG. Adventures of a stock-car racer, on and off the track. James Caan, Laura Devon, Gail Hire, Charlene Holt, John Robert Crawford. w. George Kirgo, d. Howard Hawks.

ACTION: Playboys; Car Racing; Biographies-Fictional (All American Boy; Grand Prix)

The Red Pony, 1949, 88m, ★★★/$$, Republic/Republic. A boy thinks his farmer father is all-powerful, but is disillusioned when he can't prevent his red pony from dying of a mysterious illness. Myrna Loy, Robert Mitchum, Peter Miles, Louis Calhern, Shepperd Strudwick, Margaret Hamilton. w. John Steinbeck, d. Lewis Milestone.

The Red Pony, 1976, ★★★/$$$, CBS/BFA. Henry Fonda, Maureen O'Hara. d. Robert Totten.
TV Movies

DRAMA: MELODRAMA: Tearjerkers; Animal Stories; Pet Stories; Disease Stories; Fathers & Sons; Illusions Destroyed; Horses; Farm Life; Classic Literary Adaptations (Old Yeller; The Pearl)

Red River, 1948, 133m, ★★★1/2/$$$, UA/MGM-UA. The early pioneers blaze the Chisholm Trail out of the western wilds, battling Indians and the elements along the way. John Wayne, Montgomery Clift, Joanne Dru, Walter Brennan, Colleen Gray, John Ireland, Noah Beery, Jr., Harry Carey, Jr. w. Borden Chase, Charles Schnee (BOStory), d. Howard Hawks. BEdit. Oscars: 2-0.

WESTERNS: ADVENTURE: Journies; Wagon Trains; Pioneers; Cattle Ranchers; Indians-American, Conflict with

Red Rock West, 1993, 98m, ★★★/$, HBO/HBO, Col, R/S-P-V. When a drifter comes into town, he's mistaken for a hit man coming to town and can't get out of the plot without endangering himself. He winds up going to the house of the man who's been killed and confesses to his wife-but she may be the last person he should have told. Nicolas Cage, Lara Flynn Boyle, Dennis Hopper, J. T. Walsh, Dwight Yoakam. w. d. John Dahl.

SUSPENSE: MURDER: Hitmen; Men in Jeopardy; Dangerous Women; Double Crossings; Identities-Mistaken; Clever Plots & Endings; Innocent Bystanders; Drifters; Film Noir-Modern; Sleeper Hits; Writer-Directors; TV Movies
(Kill Me Again; The Last Seduction)
(Ed: Took off on cable, then in a few theaters, gaining critical attention, but not ticket sales)

The Red Shoe Diaries (Part I), 1992, 105m, ★★1/2/$$, Showtime/Republic, R/ES-FN-MN. A woman's lover discovers her erotic diaries after her suicide and finds out about her shoe salesman and the red shoes. First installment of the erotic Showtime series. David Duchovny, Billy Wirth, Brigitte Bako. d. Zalman King.
ROMANCE: Romantic Drama; Erotic Drama; Narrated Films; Memories; Romance-Clandestine; Salesmen; Secrets-Keeping; Suicidal Tendencies; TV Movies; Miniseries
(Wild Orchid; Two Moon Junction)

The Red Shoes, 1948, 136m, ★★★★/$$, GFD/Par. A dance student rises to prima ballerina, but becomes distraught when her lover forces her to choose between career and family life. Anton Walbrook, Moira Shearer, Marius Goring, Robert Helpmann, Albert Basserman, Frederick Ashton, Ludmilla Tcherina. w. d. Michael Powell, Story: Powell, Emeric Pressburger (BOStory). BPicture, **BCArt,** BEdit, **BOScore.** Oscars: 5-1.
DRAMA: MUSICALS: Dance Movies; Dancers; Ballet; **ROMANCE:** Decisions-Big; Fantasies; British Films; Hidden Gems; Female Protagonists; Production Design-Outstanding
(An American in Paris; Lili; Invitation to Dance)

Red Sky at Morning, 1970, 113m, ★★★/$$, U/MCA-U, PG. When their father is away at World War II, a family who recently moved to New Mexico finds the residents of the local base constantly playing musical beds, and trying to get them to join in. Claire Bloom, Richard Thomas, Richard Crenna, Catherine Burns, Desi Arnaz, Jr., John Colicos, Harry Guardino. w. Marguerite Roberts, N-adap. Richard Bradford, d. James Goldstone.
DRAMA: COMEDY DRAMA: Fish out of Water Stories; **ROMANCE:** Family Drama; Slice of Life Stories; Coming of Age; Small-town Life; Cheating Men;

Cheating Women; Military Stories; New Mexico; Female Screenwriters
(Last Summer; Doctors' Wives; Peyton Place)

Red Sonja, 1985, 89m, ★★/$$, MGM-UA/MGM-UA, PG-13/P-S-EV. In "ancient times," a redheaded, swordfighting sorceress overtakes an evil queen as part of her plot to avenge her sister's death. Brigitte Nielsen, Arnold Schwarzenegger, Sandahl Bergman, Paul Smith, Ronald Lacey. w. Clive Exton, George MacDonald Fraser, SS-adap. Robert E. Howard, d. Richard Fleischer.
ACTION: Sword & Sorcery; Avenging Death of Someone; Dangerous Women; Female Among Males; Ancient Times
(Conan, the Barbarian)

Red Sorghum, 1987, 92m, ★★★/$, New Yorker/New Yorker. A Chinese man narrates the story of the love affair between his grandparents against the backdrop of the early, violent days of the Cultural Revolution. Gong Li, Jiang Wen, Teng Rujun, Liu Ju, Qian Ming, Ji Chunhua, Zhai Chunhua. w. Chen Jianyu, Zhu Wei, Mo Yan, d. Zhang Yimou.
DRAMA: ROMANCE: Historical Drama; Political Drama; Political Unrest; True Stories; Chinese People; China
(The Last Emperor; The Joy Luck Club)

Reds, 1981, 196m, ★★★★/$$$, Par/Par, PG/S-P. The journey of American communist John Reed (Warren Beatty, BActor) and his wife Louise (Diane Keaton, BActress) to Russia to be a part of the 1917 Revolution, which proves to be a much greater undertaking than they ever believed. Jack Nicholson (BSActor), Maureen Stapleton (**BSActress**), Gene Hackman, Jerzy Kosinski. w. Warren Beatty, Trevor Griffiths, (BAScr), NF-adap. John Reed (*Ten Days That Shook the World*), d. Warren Beatty
(**BDirector**). BPicture, **BCinema,** BEditing, BArt, BCostume, BSound. Oscars: 12-3.
DRAMA: ROMANCE: Epics; Historical Drama; Romantic Drama; Biographies; True Stories; Writers; Political Activists; Political Unrest; Rebels; Americans Abroad; Russia; Russian Revolution; Communists; Intellectuals; Interviews; Greenwich Village
(Doctor Zhivago; Ragtime)

Reefer Madness (aka Tell Your Children), 1938, 67m, ★★★/$, Ind/Nos. Anti-marijuana propaganda from the 30s

become camp today. Dave O'Brien, Dorothy Short. d. Louis Gasnier. Documentaries; Drugs-Addictions; Message Films; Camp; Cult Films; Unintentionally Funny
(Heavy Petting; Atomic Cafe)

The Ref, 1994, 97m, ★★★1/2/$$, Touchstone/Touchstone, R/P. When a burglar decides to rob a house, he doesn't know he's walked into the house of a bickering couple on the verge of divorce and that the whole family's coming over for dinner. Pretty soon, he winds up as referee and will do anything to get away. Denis Leary, Judy Davis, Kevin Spacey, Glynis Johns, Christine Baranski. w. Richard LaGravenese, Marie Weiss, d. Ted Demme.
COMEDY: Screwball Comedy; Marriage Comedy; Romance-Bickering; Marriage on the Rocks; Thieves; Turning the Tables; Christmas; Overlooked at Release; Hidden Gems; Underrated; Female Screenwriters
(Ed: Consistently funny with great performances and acidic wit)

The Reflecting Skin, 1990, 95m, ★★1/2/$, Virgin-BBC/NA. A young boy sent to a family house in the country believes a mysterious, strange woman is murdering all of the children in the small town nearby. Viggo Mortensen, Lindsay Duncan, Jeremy Cooper, Sheila Moore, Duncan Fraser, David Longworth, Robert Koons, David Bloom. w. d. Philip Ridley.
HORROR: MURDER: Paranoia; Murderers-Female; Serial Killers; Murders of Children; Unbelieved; Black Comedy; American Myth; Small-town Life; British Films; Writer-Directors; Curiosities

Reflections in a Golden Eye, 1967, 108m, ★★★/$, WB-Seven Arts/WB, R/S-MRN. At a military base in the sixties during peacetime, everyone goes nuts: a private rides around naked taunting a closeted military man, his wife cuts off her nipples with garden clippers, and everyone's sleeping with everyone but their spouses. Marlon Brando, Elizabeth Taylor, Brian Keith, Julie Harris, Robert Forster. w. Chapman Mortimer, Gladys Hill, N-adap. Carson McCullers, d. John Huston.
DRAMA: Psychological Drama; **MELO-DRAMA:** Sexual Problems; Marriage on the Rocks; Gay Awakenings; Gay Men; Military Stories; Homophobia; Jealousy;

Mental Illness; Nervous Breakdowns; Cult Films; Hidden Gems
(The Sergeant; Last Tango in Paris; Ballad of the Sad Cafe)

Regarding Henry, 1991, 108m, ★★¹/₂/ $$$, Par/Par, PG/S-V. A ruthless lawyer (Harrison Ford) is shot one day in a robbery and loses all his mental functions, cutting his career short, but in his recovery he learns more about what was really going on in his life than he bargained for. Annette Bening, Rebecca Miller, Bill Nunn, Donald Moffat. w. Jeffrey Abrams, d. Mike Nichols.

DRAMA: MELODRAMA: Medical Drama; Marriage Drama; Marriage on the Rocks; Mean Men; Starting Over; Violence-Sudden; Mentally Disabled; Childlike People; Fathers-Fascinating; Cheating Men; Cheating Women; Fathers & Daughters; Lawyers; Donald Moffat as Lawyer/Father Figure
(Forever Young; Rain Man)

Rehearsal for Murder, 1982, 96m, ★★★/$$$, CBS/Republic. When the lead actress is murdered on the big Broadway opening night, it's up to a detective to figure out whodunit in the cast. Robert Preston, Lynn Redgrave, Patrick Macnee, Lawrence Pressman, Jeff Goldblum, William Daniels. w. Levinson & Link, d. David Greene.

MURDER: MYSTERY: MURDER MYSTERY: Actors; Actresses; Theater Life; Mystery-Whodunit?; Ensemble Films; Critics; TV Movies; Hidden Gems
(Murder by Natural Causes; Guilty Conscience; Murder Most Foul)

The Reincarnation of Peter Proud, 1974, 104m, ★★¹/₂/$$$, Avco Embassy/ Vestron, R/S-V-MN. In Amherst, Massachusetts, a history professor is disturbed by memories of what he realizes was his past life. Michael Sarrazin, Jennifer O'Neill, Margot Kidder, Cornelia Sharpe, Paul Hecht. w., N-adap. Max Ehrlich, d. J. Lee-Thompson.

SUSPENSE: MURDER: MURDER MYSTERY: MYSTERY: Drownings; Nightmares; Past-haunted by the; Reincarnation; Good Premise Unfulfilled; Unintentionally Funny
(Shattered; On a Clear Day You Can See Forever; The Groundstar Conspiracy)

The Reivers, 1969, 111m, ★★★/$$, Cinema Center/Key, PG. At the turn of the century in Mississippi, a workman on a family farm borrows their car and goes

to Memphis with the grandson and a black stable worker. Steve McQueen, Sharon Farrell, Will Geer, Rupert Crosse, Mitch Vogel, Michael Constantine, Juano Hernandez, Clifton James. w. Irving Ravetch, Harriet Frank, Jr., N-adap. William Faulkner, d. Mark Rydell.

COMEDY DRAMA: Road Movies; Friendships-Interracial; Small-town Life; Southerns; Mississippi; Hidden Gems; Forgotten Films; Classic Literary Adaptations
(Intruder in the Dust; The Sound and the Fury; The Long, Hot Summer; The Adventures of Huckleberry Finn)

Relentless, 1989, 92m, ★★/$$, Col/Col, R/EV-B&G-P. A cop trainee who was rejected gets revenge by using police procedures in his murders and terrorizing a cop's family. Judd Nelson, Meg Foster, Robert Loggia, Leo Rossi. d. William Lustig.

Relentless 2, 1991, 84m, ★★/$$, Col/Col, R/EV-B&G-P. The cop from the first tracks another killer, this time one who's into the occult. Leo Rossi, Meg Foster, Ray Sharkey. d. Michael Schroeder.

Relentless 3, 1993, 84m, ★★/$, Col/Col, R/EV-B&G-P. A serial killer is sending body parts of his female victims to the cops. Leo Rossi, William Forsythe. d. James Lemmo.

SUSPENSE: MURDER: Serial Killers; Trail of a Killer; Police Stories; Chase Stories; Criminal Pursues Good Guy's Family
(Rampage; Cape Fear; No Way to Treat a Lady)

The Reluctant Debutante, 1958, 96m, ★★¹/₂/$$, MGM/MGM-UA. A couple from the British noble family have trouble after they send their daughter off to college in the U.S. and she comes back with strange customs. Rex Harrison, Kay Kendall, Sandra Dee, Peter Myers, Angela Lansbury, John Saxon, Diane Clare. w., P-adap. William Douglas Home, d. Vincente Minnelli.

COMEDY DRAMA: Fish out of Water Stories; Class Conflicts; Rich vs. Poor; Forgotten Films; Social Climbing; Generation Gap; Parents vs. Children; England
(The Impossible Years; A Summer Place)

The Remains of the Day, 1993, 137m, ★★★¹/₂/$$, MI-Col/Col-Tri, PG. An extremely fastidious and cold butler of a

manor is forced to open up and deal with the possibility of love, death, and saving Jewish German refugees at Darlington Hall, his castle to keep clean. Anthony Hopkins (BActor), Emma Thompson (BActress), Christopher Reeve, Edward Fox, Hugh Grant. w. Ruth Prawer Jhabvala (BAScr), d. James Ivory (BDirector). BPicture, BArt, BOScore, BCostume. Oscars: 8-0.

DRAMA: MELODRAMA: Social Drama; Anti-Semitism; Saving Someone; Repression; Romance-Reluctant; Romance-Unrequited; Servants; Romance with Servant; Friends in Love; Cold People; World War II Era; Germans as Enemy; Jewish People; England; British Films
(Howards End; Sense and Sensibility)

Rembrandt, 1936, 85m, ★★★¹/₂/$$, London Films/Sultan. In the 17th century, the famous Dutch master paints and lives and loves. Charles Laughton, Elsa Lanchester, Gertrude Lawrence, Edward Chapman, Walter Hudd, Roger Liversey, Herbert Lomas, Raymond Huntley. w. Lajos Biro, June Head, Carl Zuckmayer, d. Alexander Korda.

DRAMA: Biographies; Historical Drama; Costume Drama; Artists-Famous; Painters; Episodic Stories; 1600s
(Moon and Sixpence; Moulin Rouge)

Remember Last Night?, 1936, 80m, ★★★/$$, U/NA. A raucous party is barely recalled by the hungover participants the next day. But they are forced to jog their memories when it appears one of the guests was murdered. Robert Young, Edward Arnold, Arthur Treacher, Constance Cummings, Robert Armstrong, Sally Eilers, Reginald Denny, Jack La Rue, Gregory Ratoff. w. Harry Clork, Dan Totheroh, Doris Malloy, N-adap. Adam Hobhouse (The Hangover Murders), d. James Whale.

COMEDY: MURDER: MURDER MYSTERY: Comic Mystery; Murder-Invitation to; Rich People; Black Comedy; Ensemble Films; Amnesia; Hidden Gems; Forgotten Films
(The Wild Party; The Thin Man; A Night to Remember)

Remember My Name, 1978, 94m, ★★¹/₂/$, Col/Col, NA. A woman takes the rap for a murder her man committed, but he forgets about her while she's in prison. When she's released twelve years later, she comes after him to make him

pay. Geraldine Chaplin, Anthony Perkins, Moses Gunn, Berry Berenson, Jeff Goldblum. w. d. Alan Rudolph.
DRAMA: Crime Drama; Revenge; Framed?; Accused Unjustly; Turning the Tables; Prison Drama; Murderers-Female; Criminals-Female; Convict's Revenge; Cult Films; Writer-Directors; Female Protagonists
(Hannie Caulder; The Quick and the Dead; The Hand That Rocks the Cradle)
Remo Williams: The Adventure Begins, 1985, 121m, ★★/$, Orion/Orion, PG-13/V-P. The CIA recruits a tough New York cop and trains him in martial arts and sics him on an international arms dealer. Fred Ward, Joel Grey, Wilford Brimley, J. A. Preston, Charles Cioffi, Kate Mulgrew, George Coe. w. Christopher Wood, N-adap. Richard Sapir, Warren Murphy (*Destroyer* series), d. Guy Hamilton.
ACTION: CIA Agents; Martial Arts; Arms Dealers; Spoofs; Secret Agents
Renaissance Man, 1994, 124m, ★★/$, 20th/Fox, PG-13/P. A short, out of work ad executive takes on teaching military recruits Shakespeare-and they comply, if he'll go through bootcamp with them. Danny DeVito, Marky Mark Wahlberg, Gregory Hines, James Remar, Ed Begley, Jr., Cliff Robertson. w. Jim Burnstein, Ned Maudlin, d. Penny Marshall.
COMEDY: COMEDY DRAMA: Fish out of Water Stories; Military Comedy; Teachers; Teachers and Students; Flops-Major; Good Premise Unfulfilled; Female Directors
(Dead Poet's Society; Stripes; Jack the Bear; Major Payne)
Rendez-Vous, 1985, 83m, ★★★/$$, Cannon/Tape Worm, R/S-FN-MN. An actress in a local company in the French provinces moves to Paris to break into the scene, but is dragged down by a cynical and bitter actor with whom she falls in love. Juliette Binoche, Lambert Wilson, Wadeck Stanczak, Jean-Louis Trintignant, Dominique Lavanant. w. Andre Techine, Olivier Assayas, d. Andre Techine (BDir, Cannes).
DRAMA: ROMANCE: Character Studies; Actors; Actresses; Paris; French Films; 20-Somethings; Young People; Hidden Gems; Overlooked at Release
(Blue; Damage)
Renegades, 1989, 105m, ★★/$, U/MCA-U, R/V-P. A young Navajo teams up with a maverick cop out West to

search for a sacred Indian object. Kiefer Sutherland, Lou Diamond Phillips, Jami Gertz, Rob Knepper, Bill Smitrovich, Peter MacNeill. w. David Rich, d. Jack Sholder.
ACTION: MYSTERY: Treasure Hunts; Journies; Quests; Indians-American; Native Americans; Police Stories; Buddy Films; Teams-Mismatched
(Thunderheart; The First Power)
Rent-a-Dick, 1972, 94m, ★★★/NA, BBC/NA. Skits revolving around detective spoofs, etc., by Monty Pythoners. James Booth, Spike Milligan, Julie Ege. w. Graham Chapman, John Cleese, d. Jim Clark.
COMEDY: Comedy-Skits; Detective Stories; Spoofs-Detective; British Films; Forgotten Films; Monty Pythoners
Rented Lips, 1988, 82m, ★★/$, Academy/Academy, R/ES-FN. Two documentary filmmakers are coerced by a PBS producer into taking over a porn movie in trouble. Martin Mull, Dick Shawn, Jennifer Tilly, Kenneth Mars. w. Robert Downer.
COMEDY: Pornography World; Documentaries; Movie Making; Blackmail; Fish out of Water Stories; Good Premise Unfulfilled; Writer-Directors; Independent Films
(Too Much Sun; Is There Sex After Death?)
Repentance, 1987, 151m, ★★★/$, Ind/Media, PG. A woman continually digs up the grave of a despicable man from her Russian town and is put on trial. Avalandi Makharadze. d. Tengiz Abuldaze. BFLFilm. Oscars: 1-0.
SATIRE: Black Comedy; Comedy-Morbid; Courtroom Drama; Trials; Russian Films; Russia; Allegorical Stories; Art Films
Repo Man, 1984, 92m, ★★★/$$, U/MCA-U, R/P-S. A wry look at suburban alienation involving repossessors of cars with mystical powers and disaffected youths out West whose parents give their college funds to televangelists. Harry Dean Stanton, Emilio Estevez, Tracey Walter, Olivia Barash, Sy Richardson. w. d. Alex Cox.
SATIRE: COMEDY DRAMA: SCI-FI: Allegorical Stories; Suburban Life; Alienation; Aliens-Outer Space, Good; Magic; Cult Films; Overlooked at Release; Writer-Directors; Independent Films
(UFOria; Sid and Nancy)

Report to the Commissioner, 1975, 112m, ★★1/2/$, UA/MGM-UA, R/P-V. A young tough murders a woman who turns out to have been an undercover cop and then he goes on the lam in the inner city. Michael Moriarty, Richard Gere, Susan Blakely, Hector Elizondo, Yaphet Kotto. w. Abby Mann, d. Milton Katselas.
SUSPENSE: Police Stories; MURDER: Murder of Police; Fugitives from the Law; Trail of a Killer; Crime Drama; Film Noir-Modern; Forgotten Films
(Breathless; Bloodbrothers; Looking for Mr. Goodbar; Prizzi's Honor)
Repossessed, 1990, 84m, ★★/$, Ind/Live, R/P-S-V-B&G. A demonic girl tries to possess the entire audience of a televangelist's program while he tries to exorcise her. Linda Blair, Ned Beatty, Leslie Nielsen, Anthony Starke, Thom J. Sharp, Lana Schwab. w. d. Bob Logan.
HORROR: COMEDY: Spoofs; Spoofs-Horror; Horror Comedy; Possessions; Satanism; Religion; Preachers; TV Life; Good Premise Unfulfilled; Writer-Directors
SPOOF OF: The Exorcist.
(Dracula: Dead and Loving It; The Naked Gun)
Repulsion, 1965, 105m, ★★★1/2/$$$, Ind/Vidmark, R/S-V. A young woman in France can't deal with her sexual impulses and begins to come apart at the seams in various ways. Catherine Deneuve, Yvonne Furneaux, Ian Hendry. w. Roman Polanski, Gerard Brach, d. Roman Polanski.
DRAMA: Psychological Drama; Psychological Thriller; Character Studies; Sexual Problems; Young Women; Sexy Women; Spinsters; Nervous Breakdowns; Cult Films; French Films; Hidden Gems
(Belle du Jour; Looking for Mr. Goodbar)
Requiem for a Heavyweight, 1956, 90m, ★★★1/2/$$$, Playhouse 90/Disney. A boxer risks going blind to fight one more round to help his manager pay off bookies. Jack Palance, Keenan Wynn, Kim Hunter, Ed Wynn. w. Rod Serling, d. Ralph Nelson.
Stage Tapings
Requiem for a Heavyweight, 1962, 87m, ★★★/$$, Col/RCA-Col. A boxer fights even though he's a worn-out has-been. Anthony Quinn, Jackie Gleason, Mickey Rooney, Julie Harris, Stan Adams, Jack Dempsey, Mohammed Ali. w. S-TV-adap. Rod Serling, d. Ralph Nelson.

DRAMA: Character Studies; Sports
Movies; Boxers; Rise and Fall Stories;
Depression; Comebacks; One Last Time;
Gambling; Friendships-Male; Hidden
Gems
(Champion; Golden Boy; The Great White
Hope; The Hustler)
The Rescue, 1988, 97m, ★/$, Touchstone/
Touchstone, PG. Kids of Navy SEALS go
to the rescue when their dads are taken
hostage. Marc Price, Charles Haid, Kevin
Dillon, Edward Albert. w. Jim Thomas,
John Thomas, d. Ferdinand Fairfax.
ACTION: Rescue Drama; Special Teams-
Military; Saving Someone; Hostage
Situations; Government as Enemy;
Teenagers; Teenage Movies; Flops-Major
(Uncommon Valor; Navy SEALS)
(Ed. Rambo Jr. The first big flop of the
Touchstone regime which had an incredi-
ble streak of hits from 1986-87)
Rescue Me, 1993, 99m, ★★/$, WB/
WB, PG-13. When an old flame is kid-
napped, martial arts expert Dudikoff goes
after the bad guys. Michael Dudikoff,
Stephen Dorff, Amy Dolenz, Dee Wallace
Stone. w. Michael Snyder, d. Arthur
Siedelman.
ACTION: Martial Arts; Romance-
Reunited; Kidnappings; Rescue Drama;
Overlooked at Release
(Hard Target; Above the Law)
The Rescuers, 1977, 77m, ★★★/$$$,
Disney/Disney, G. A girl being held
prisoner in Louisiana's bayous is the
subject of a rescue mission by the
Mouse Rescue Aid Society. Voices of
Bob Newhart, Eva Gabor, Geraldine
Page, Joe Flynn, Jim Jordan, John
McIntire. w. Larry Clemmons, Ken
Anderson, SS-adap. Margery Sharp, d.
Wolfgang Reitherman.
CHILDREN'S: ADVENTURE: Cartoons;
Kidnappings; Rescue Adventures; Swamp
Life; Animal Stories; Rodents
(101 Dalmations; Oliver and Company)
The Rescuers Down Under, 1990,
77m, ★★★/$$, Disney/Disney, G. An
eagle and a boy get trapped in the mid-
dle of the Australian outback, and the
Mouse Rescue Aid Society must come to
their rescue. Voices of Bob Newhart, Eva
Gabor, John Candy, Tristan Rogers,
Adam Ryen, George C. Scott, Wayne
Robson, Douglas Seale, Peter Firth. w.
Jim Cox, Karey Kirkpatrick, Byron
Simpson, Joe Ranft, d. Hendel Butoy,
Mike Gabriel.

CHILDREN'S: ADVENTURE: Cartoons;
Kidnappings; Rescue Adventures;
Animal Stories; Rodents; Australia
Reservoir Dogs, 1991, 99m, ★★★1/2/
$$$, Miramax/Live, R/EV-EP-B&G. A
jewelry store heist, meticulously planned,
goes horribly wrong, and the survivors of
the subsequent police shootout try to fig-
ure out who was the traitor in the midst of
their extremely violent and psychotic
gang. Harvey Keitel, Tim Roth, Michael
Madsen, Chris Penn, Steve Buscemi,
Lawrence Tierney, Randy Brooks, Kirk
Baltz, Eddie Bunker, Quentin Tarantino.
w. d. Quentin Tarantino.
DRAMA: ACTION: Action Drama; Crime
Drama; Heist Stories; Jewel Thieves;
TRAGEDY: Ensemble Films; Ensembles-
Male; Los Angeles; Cult Films; Sleeper
Hits; Writer-Directors; Independent Films
(True Romance; Pulp Fiction; The
Killing; Rififi)
Restoration, 1995, 113m, ★★★/$$,
Miramax/Miramax, R/ES-MN-FN. A young
medical student in Restoration-era
England is called upon by the king to be
a court jester of sorts, only orgies are the
fun, not just jokes. But when he's ordered
to marry a royal young lass, the stipulation
that he can't touch her may be too much to
bear. Robert Downey, Jr., Sam Neill, David
Thewlis, Polly Walker, Meg Ryan, Ian
McKellen, Hugh Grant. w. Rupert Walters,
N-adap. Rose Tremain, d. Michael
Hoffman. BArt, BCostume. Oscars: 2-2.
COMEDY DRAMA: Wild People; Free
Spirits; England; 1700s; Kings; Orgies;
Restoration Era; All-Star Casts;
Outstanding Production Design
(The Court Jester; Tom Jones; The
Madness of King George; Amadeus)
Resurrection, 1980, 103m, ★★★1/2/$,
U/MCA-U, PG. A woman survives a horri-
ble car accident seemingly by a miracle
and finds herself with amazing healing
powers afterwards. Ellen Burstyn
(BActress), Sam Shepard, Richard
Farnsworth, Eva LeGallienne (BSActress),
Roberts Blossom, Clifford David. w. Lewis
John Carlino, d. Daniel Petrie. Oscars: 2-0.
DRAMA: Character Studies; Accidents;
Medical Drama; Miracles; Religion;
Ordinary People Stories; Heaven;
Preachers; Reincarnation; Southerns;
Texas; Female; Protagonists; Quiet Little
Films
Return from Witch Mountain, 1978,
93m, ★★1/2/$$, Disney/Disney, G. Two

alien kids return to Earth after a few
years away for a vacation from their home
planet. Once here, their special powers
attract some thieves who use them to help
them pull heists. Bette Davis, Christopher
Lee, Ike Eisenmann, Kim Richards, Jack
Soo. w. Malcolm Marmorstein, d. John
Hough.
CHILDREN'S: ADVENTURE: Kidnap-
pings; Chase Stories; Aliens-Outer Space,
Good; Brothers & Sisters; Witches; Magic
SEQUEL TO: Escape to Witch Mountain.
Return of a Man Called Horse, 1976,
125m, ★★1/2/$$, UA/Key, R/V-S. The
Englishman taken in by the American
Indian tribe from the first film returns to
help them out when their land is threat-
ened. Richard Harris, Gale Sondergaard,
Geoffrey Lewis, Bill Lucking, Jorge Luke.
w. Jack de Witt, d. Irvin Kershner.
WESTERNS: DRAMA: Raised by
Indians; Indians-American; Mortgage
Drama; Save the Land; Indians-
American, Conflict with; Fish out of
Water Stories
SEQUEL TO: A Man Called Horse.
(Man in the Wilderness)
Return of Dracula, 1958, 77m,
★★★/$, UA/MGM-UA. A stranger comes
to a small town claiming to be a commu-
nist dissident artist. It later turns out that
he's actually a vampire. Francis Lederer,
Norma Eberhardt, Ray Stricklyn, Jimmie
Baird, John Wengraf. w. Pat Fielder, d.
Paul Landres.
HORROR: SUSPENSE: Small-town Life;
Identities-Assumed; Vampires; Hidden
Gems; Forgotten Films
The Return of Martin Guerre, 1983,
123m, ★★★1/2/$$$, Orion/Orion, Sultan,
R/S. In a remarkably well-evoked 16th
century French village, a soldier returns
from eight years absence claiming to be
the long-lost husband of a local woman.
At first the townspeople accept him, but
we are never sure if his wife believes he
is Martin Guerre or not. Eventually,
incongruous details eek out and he is
tried as an imposter. Gerard Depardieu,
Nathalie Baye, Sylvie Meda, Maurice
Barrier. w. Jean-Claude Carriere, Daniel
Vigne, d. Daniel Vigne.
DRAMA: ROMANCE: MYSTERY: MELO-
DRAMA: Romantic Drama; Return of
Spouse; Costume Drama; 1500s; Middle
Ages; Dead-Back from the; Impostors;
Identities-Assumed; Romance-Triangles;
French Films; Coulda Been Great

REMAKE: Sommersby.
(Sommersby; Jean de Florette; All the Mornings in the World)

The Return of Spinal Tap, 110m, ★★1/2/$, Ind/MPI. Return of the spoof on heavy metal bands with a concert film of the mock group's real show. Christopher Guest, Michael McKean, Harry Shearer. w. d. Guest, McKean, Shearer.
Concert Films; Spoofs; Rock Stars; Musicians
SEQUEL TO: This is Spinal Tap
(Fear of a Black Hat; All You Need is Cash; The Decline of Western Civilization)

Return of Superfly, 1990, 95m, ★★/$, Crash Pictures/NA. A drug pusher who gets clean goes after each member of his old gang, one at a time. Nathan Purdee, Margaret Avery, Leonard Thomas, Christopher Curry. w. Anthony Wisdom, d. Sig Shore.
ACTION: Crime Drama; Action Drama; Black Casts; Black Men; Drugs-Dealing; Starting Over; Revenge; Blaxploitation Era; Black Screenwriters; Black Directors; Independent Films
SEQUEL TO: Superfly.

Return of the Fly, 1959, 80m, ★★/$$, 20th/Fox. The son of the matter transmografier inventor proves to be a chip off the old block as he makes the same mistake as his dad, becoming a human fly as well. Vincent Price, Brett Halsey, John Sutton, Dan Seymour. w.d. Edward Bernds.
HORROR: SCI-FI: Humans into Animals; Insects; Fathers & Sons; Scientists; Experiments; Cult Films; Writer-Directors
SEQUEL TO: The Fly (1958)

Return of the Jedi, 1983, 132m, ★★★/$$$$$$, 20th/Fox, PG/V. Luke Skywalker and Han Solo join forces with some friends and do battle with Darth Vader and Jabba the Hutt in this, the sixth episode chronologically of the *Star Wars* saga, but only the third film made yet. Mark Hamill, Harrison Ford, Carrie Fisher, Billy Dee Williams, Anthony Daniels. w. Lawrence Kasdan, George Lucas, d. Richard Marquand.
ACTION: ADVENTURE: Outer Space Movies; Fathers & Sons; Children-Longlost; Good vs. Evil; Duels; Chase Stories; Blockbusters
SEQUEL TO: Star Wars, The Empire Strikes Back.

The Return of the Living Dead, 1985, 90m, ★★1/2/$$, Orion/Orion, R/EV-P-S-B&G. Punk-rocking zombies start rising from their graves and go in search of brains to eat. Clu Gulager, James Karen, Don Calfa, Thom Matthews. w. Dan O'Bannon, Rudy Ricci, John Russo, Russell Streiner, d. Dan O'Bannon.

The Return of the Living Dead Part II, 1987, 89m, ★★/$$, Orion/Orion, R/EV-P-B&G. A small town is invaded by the brain-eating zombies from the first film. James Karen, Thom Matthews, Dana Ashbrook, Marsha Dietlein, Suzanne Snyder, Philip Bruns. w.d. Ken Widerhorn.
HORROR: Black Comedy; Horror Comedy; Dead-Back from the; Zombies; Cannibals; Cult Films; Writer-Directors
SEQUEL TO: Night of the Living Dead, sort of.
(Evil Dead; Evil Dead 2; Army of Darkness)

The Return of the Musketeers, 1989, 101m, ★★/$, U/MCA-U. When Milady de Winter is murdered, her daughter seeks revenge on the Musketeers responsible. Michael York, Oliver Reed, Frank Finlay, C. Thomas Howell, Kim Cattrall, Geraldine Chaplin, Roy Kinnear, Christopher Lee, Philippe Noiret, Richard Chamberlain, Jean-Pierre Cassel. w. George MacDonald Fraser, N-adap. Alexandre Dumas *(Vingt Ans Apres)*, d. Richard Lester.
ACTION: ADVENTURE: Avenging Death of Someone; Swashbucklers; Vigilantes; Classic Literary Adaptations
(The Three Musketeers [1974]; The Four Musketeers [1975])

Return of the Pink Panther, 1973, 113m, ★★★1/2/$$$$, UA/MGM-UA, PG. The famous diamond, the pink panther, is stolen once again from the Royal Museum, and Inspector Clouseau is put on the case. Peter Sellers, Christopher Plummer, Herbert Lom, Catherine Schell, Peter Arne, David Lodge. w. Frank Waldman, Blake Edwards, d. Blake Edwards.
COMEDY: Comedy-Slapstick; Fools-Bumbling; **FARCE:** Misunderstandings; Jewel Thieves; Detective Stories; Police Stories; Detectives-Police; Mental Illness; Revenge
(The Pink Panther; Revenge of the Pink Panther)
(Ed: The classic physical comedy bits, especially with the vacuum and the parrot, make this a must-see despite the lack of overall plot)

The Return of the Scarlet Pimpernel, 1937, 94m, ★★★/$$$, London/NA. During the French Revolution, the famed caped and hooded nobleman saves his family and other nobles from the guillotine. Barry K. Barnes, Sophie Stewart, Margaretta Scott, James Mason, Henry Oscar, Francis Lister, Anthony Bushell. w. Lajos Biro, Arthur Wimperis, Adrien Brunel, d. Hans Schwartz.
ADVENTURE: ROMANCE: Romantic Adventure; Saving Someone; Executions; Classic Literary Adaptations
SEQUEL TO: The Scarlet Pimpernel, The Elusive Pimpernel.

Return of the Secaucus Seven, 1978, 95m, ★★★1/2/$$$, Ind./Cinecom, R/P-S-MFN. Several college pals get back together during the summer for a getaway in the hills of New Jersey and talk about their ordinary lives—played by very ordinary actors. David Straithairn, John Sayles. w. d. John Sayles.
DRAMA: COMEDY DRAMA: Ensemble Films; Ensembles-Young People; Young People; Ordinary People Stories; Vacations; Camping; College Life; Reunions-Class; Friendships Between Sexes; Time Capsules; 1970s; Intellectuals; Quiet Little Films; Sleeper Hits; Cult Films; Hidden Gems; Writer-Directors; Independent Films
REMAKES/RETREADS: The Big Chill.
(The Big Chill; Indian Summer; Between the Lines)
(Ed: Although the premise of *The Big Chill* was different—gathering for a funeral—the sub-genre was created by *Secaucus Seven*, Sayles' first hit in the arthouse market; also one of the first blatant uses of full-frontal male nudity—with virtually no female at all)

The Return of the Seven, 1966, 95m, ★★1/2/$$$, UA/MGM-UA, R/P-V. The gunmen from *The Magnificent Seven* reband when farmers are kidnapped and need their help. Yul Brynner, Robert Fuller, Julian Mateos, Warren Oates, Claude Atkins, Virgilio Texeira, Emilio Fernandez, Jordan Christopher. w. Larry Cohen, d. Burt Kennedy.
WESTERNS: Vigilantes; Protecting Someone; Kidnappings; Gunfighters; Rescue Adventure
SEQUEL TO: The Magnificent Seven.
(The Professionals)

The Return of the Soldier, 1982/1985, 102m, ★★★/$, Ind/NA. Returning shell-shocked from the first World War, a soldier forgets that he's married, although he remembers his first love. Alan Bates, Ann-Margret, Julie Christie, Glenda Jackson, Jeremy Kemp, Edward de Souza, Ian Holm. w. Hugh Whitemore, N-adap. Rebecca West, d. Alan Bridges.

DRAMA: MELODRAMA: ROMANCE: Romance-Triangles; Return of Spouse; Soldiers; Amnesia; Marriage Drama; Women Fighting Over Men; British Films; Independent Films
(The Return of Martin Guerre)

The Return of the Vampire, 1943, 69m, ★★★/$$, Col/Goodtimes. During the bombing of London, Dracula shows up in the subway tunnels amid the huddled masses. Bela Lugosi, Nina Foch, Frieda Inescort, Miles Mander, Matt Willis, Roland Varno, Ottola Nesmith. w. Griffin Jay, d. Lew Landers.

HORROR: SUSPENSE: Vampires; War Stories; London; British Films; Forgotten Films; Curiosities
(Dracula [1930])

Return to Macon County, 1975, 89m, ★★/$$, AIP/Vestron, R/S-P-V. It's the 1950s again in the Georgia county ruled by an evil cop, where two young bucks hook up with a waitress and get into trouble-again. Nick Nolte, Don Johnson, Robin Mattson, Robert Viharo. w. d. Richard Compton.

ACTION: COMEDY DRAMA: Action Comedy; Road Movies; Outlaw Road Movies; Southerns; ROMANCE: Romance-Triangles; Chase Stories; Rednecks; Georgia
SEQUEL: to Macon County Line
(Dirty Mary and Crazy Larry)

Return to Oz, 1985, 110m, ★★1/2/$, Disney/Disney, PG/V. After going to Oz, Dorothy exhibits symptoms of post-traumatic stress disorder and undergoes shock therapy. Fairuza Balk, Jean Marsh, Nicol Williamson, Piper Laurie, Matt Clark, Emma Ridley. w. Walter Murch, Gill Dennis, d. Walter Murch.

SCI-FI: Fantasy; Journies; Animation-Stop; Surrealism; CHILDREN'S: Art Films; Torture; Girls; Child Protagonists; Objects with Personalities; Cult Films; Curiosities; Forgotten Films; Flops-Major
SEQUEL TO: The Wizard of Oz.
(Nightmare Before Christmas; James and the Giant Peach)
(Ed: Too dark for the children, too childish for the adults; they should've waited

for Tim Burton's touch; does have some interesting special effects)

Return to Peyton Place, 1961, 122m, ★★1/2/$$$, 20th/Fox, S. The daughter of Constance Mackenzie writes a novel about her mother and her circle of bed-hopping friends at Peyton Place, and the cycle perpetuates itself. Jeff Chandler, Carol Lynley, Eleanor Parker, Mary Astor, Robert Sterling, Tuesday Weld. w. Ronald Alexander, d. Jose Ferrer.

MELODRAMA: Soap Opera; Small-town Life; Small-town Scandals; Writers; True or Not?; Cheating Men; Cheating Women; Young Women; Female Protagonists
SEQUEL TO: Peyton Place.
(The Best of Everything; The Nasty Girl)
(Ed: What may have happened to author Grace Metalious when her real book was published in real life?)

Return to the Blue Lagoon, 1991, 98m, ★1/2/$, Col/Col-Tri-Star. A mother and her daughter are marooned on a remote island with a beautiful orphan boy, and the daughter and the boy grow up naked in the jungle, learning about love. Milla Jovovich, Brian Krause, Lisa Pelikan, Courtney Phillips. w. Leslie Stevens, N-adap. Henry de Vere Stacpoole (The Garden of God), d. William A. Graham.

MELODRAMA: ROMANCE: Islands; Stranded on an Island; Love-First; Episodic Stories; Shipwrecked; Erotic Drama
(SEQUEL: of The Blue Lagoon)

Reuben, Reuben, 1983, 101m, ★★★/$$, Orion/Orion, PG/P-S. A British poet-in-residence at a quiet and quaint New England college rubs people the wrong way with his loud drunken antics-though one young woman may not mind. Tom Conti (BActor), Kelly McGillis, Roberts Blossom, Cynthia Harris, Joel Fabiani. w. Julius J. Epstein (BAScr), P-adap. Herman Shumlin (Spofford), N-adap. Peter de Vries, d. Robert Ellis. Oscars: 2-0.

COMEDY DRAMA: ROMANCE: Eccentric People; Alcoholics; Professors; College Life; Lover Family Dislikes; Romance-Reluctant; Poets; Writers; Romance-Older Men/Younger Women; Suicidal Tendencies; Hidden Gems
(A Fine Madness; Arthur)

Reunion, 1989, 110m, ★★1/2/$, Fries/Fries. A Jewish lawyer returns to Germany after the war and remembers a

childhood friendship destroyed by the Nazis. Jason Robards, Christien Anholt, Samuel West, Francoise Fabian, Maureen Kerwin. w. Harold Pinter, N-adap. Fred Uhlman, d. Jerry Schatzberg.

DRAMA: Character Studies; Art Films; Jewish People; Anti-Semitism; Memories; Friendship on the Rocks; Betrayals; Germany; World War II Stories; Nazi Stories
(Au Revoir Les Enfants; Max and Helen; Miss Rose White; The Pawnbroker)

Revenge, 1989, 124m, ★★/$, Col/Col-Tri-Star, R/S-P-V-FN. Down in Mexico, a female pilot is left to die by her husband and she teams up with his mistress to do him in. Kevin Costner, Anthony Quinn, Madeleine Stowe, Tom Milian, Joaquin Martinez, Sally Kirkland, Miguel Ferrer. w. Jim Harrison, Jeffrey Fiskin, N-adap. Jim Harrison, d. Tony Scott.

MELODRAMA: ROMANCE: Revenge; Revenge on Cheater; Romantic Drama; Romance-Triangles; Abused Women; Dangerous Women; Jealousy; Fires; Mexico
(Out of the Past; Against All Odds)
(Ed: Lovely to look at, but that's about it with this senseless, pseudo-art, pseudo film noir)

The Revenge of Billy the Kid, 1992, 87m, ★★/$, Ind/NA, R/EV-B&G. The half-goat son of a farmer eats his family members one by one. Michael Balfour, Samantha Perkins, Jackie D. Broad, Trevor Peake, Michael Ripper. w. Tim Dennison, Jim Groom, Richard Matthews, d. Jim Groom.

HORROR: MURDER: Monsers-Animal; Cannibals; Humans into Animals; Farm Life; Black Comedy; Curiosities; Revenge

The Revenge of Frankenstein, 1958, 89m, ★★1/2/$$, Hammer-Col/NA. The townspeople are about to execute Baron Frankenstein, but he escapes and continues his experiments, this time creating a monster with the brain of a psycho midget. Peter Cushing, Michael Gwynn, Oscar Quitak, Francis Matthews, Lionel Jeffries, John Stuart. w. Jimmy Sangster, Hurford Janes, d. Terence Fisher.

HORROR: SCI-FI: Little People; Psycho Killers; Frankenstein Stories; Experiments; Executions; Scientists-Mad; Monsters; Monsters-Manmade; Revenge

The Revenge of the Pink Panther, 1978, 98m, ★★★1/2/$$$$, UA/CBS-Fox, PG. Clouseau travels to Hong Kong and has a fling while on the trail of a drug smuggling ring. Peter Sellers, Herbert Lom, Robert Webber, Dyan Cannon, Burt Kwouk, Paul Stewart, Robert Loggia. w. Frank Waldman, Ron Clarke, Blake Edwards, d. Blake Edwards.

COMEDY: FARCE: Spoofs; Detective Stories; Spoofs-Detective; Chase Stories; Detectives-Police; Fools-Bumbling; Hong Kong; Drugs-Dealing; Undercover; Revenge
(Return of the Pink Panther; The Pink Panther Strikes Again)

The Revengers, 1972, 108m, ★★½/$, Cinema Center/WB, PG/V. After his wife and family are murdered by Indians, a rancher gathers a group of local men into a posse to hunt down those responsible. William Holden, Ernest Borgnine, Susan Hayward, Woody Strode, Roger Hanin. w. Wendell Mayes, d. Daniel Mann.

WESTERNS: Avenging Death of Someone; Revenge; Westerns-Revenge; Indians-American, Conflict with; Indians-American; MURDER: Murder of Spouse
(Death Wish; The Dirty Dozen)

Reversal of Fortune, 1990, 111m, ★★★★/$$, WB/WB, R/P. The true story of Klaus Von Bulow (Jeremy Irons, BActor), accused of poisoning his comatose wife Sunny (Glenn Close) and the lawyer, Alan Dershowitz (Ron Silver), who handled his appeal after he was convicted. w. Nicholas Kazan (BAScr), NF-adap. Alan Dershowitz, d. Barbet Schroeder. Oscars: 2-1.

DRAMA: Courtroom Drama; MYSTERY: MURDER: Psychological Drama; Mindgames; Comas; Accused Unjustly; Framed?; True Stories; Biographies; Character Studies; Rich People; Lawyers; Mean Men; Flashbacks

The Revolt of Job, 1983, 98m, ★★★/$, UA/MGM-UA. A Christian boy narrates the story of the Jewish farmer couple who adopted him and had to hide from the Nazis. Ference Zenthe, Hedi Temessy, Gabor Feher, Peter Rudolph, Leticia Cano. w. Katalin Petenyi, Imre Gyongyossi, Barna Kabay, d. Imre Gyongyossi.

DRAMA: Documentary Style; True Stories; Europeans-Eastern; Jewish People; Hiding Out; Nazi Stories; Jews-Saving; Farm Life; Female Screenwriters

Revolution, 1985, 125m, ★★/$, WB/WB, R/V-S. A drifter passes through scenes of the American Revolution look-ing for a woman and going into battle with his son. Al Pacino, Nastassja Kinski, Donald Sutherland, Annie Lennox, Joan Plowright. w. Robert Dillon, d. Hugh Hudson.

DRAMA: Epics; Revolutionary War; 1700s; Episodic Stories; Journies; Searches; Fathers & Sons; Slice of Life Stories; Coulda Been Good; Flops-Major
(Ed: Epic-ly slow)

The Revolutionary, 1970, 101m, ★★½/$, UA/NA, R/P-S-V. The biography of a fictitious revolutionary in an unspecified time and place, detailing his evolution from leaflet distributor to assassination organizer. Jon Voight, Jennifer Salt, Robert Duvall. w. Hans Konigsberger, d. Paul Williams.

DRAMA: Biographies-Fictional; Terrorists; Political Unrest; Young Men-Angry; Futuristic Films; Assassination Plots; Forgotten Films; Curiosities
(Katherine; The Strawberry Statement)

Rhapsody, 1954, 116m, ★★½/$$$, MGM/MGM-UA. Two musicians pursue the same woman and hope to make beautiful music together, but she just toys with them, playing on their weaknesses. Elizabeth Taylor, Vittorio Gassman, John Ericson, Louis Calhern, Michael Chekhov. w. Fay and Michael Kanin, N-adap. Henry Handel Richardson (*Maurice Guest*), d. Charles Vidor.

MELODRAMA: ROMANCE: Romantic Drama; Musicians; Romance-Triangles; Men Fighting Over Women; Elusive Women; Forgotten Films; Faded Hits; Female Screenwriters
(Love is Better Than Ever; Three Little Words)

Rhapsody in August, 1990, 97m, ★★★/$, Orion/Orion, PG. A young Japanese-American man returns to Japan to visit his grandmother, triggering her memories of the bomb at Nagasaki. Richard Gere, Sachiko Murase, Hisashi Igawa, Narumi Kayashima, Tomoko Ohtakara, Mitsunori Isaki, Toshie Negishi. w. d. Akira Kurosawa.

DRAMA: Character Studies; Japan; Japanese People; Asian-Americans; Bombs-Atomic; Memories; Nightmares; Curiosities; Art Films; Japanese Films; Writer-Directors
(Black Rain [1988]; Ran; Hiroshima; Mon Amour)

Rhapsody in Blue, 1945, 139m, ★★★/$$$, WB/MGM-UA. A musical biopic of the life and rise to fame of the composer George Gershwin. Robert Alda, Joan Leslie, Alexis Smith, Charles Coburn, Julie Bishop, Albert Basserman, Oscar Levant, Herbert Rudley, Rosemary de Camp, Al Jolson, Paul Whiteman, George White, Hazel Scott. w. Howard Koch, Elliot Paul, d. Irving Rapper. BMScore. Oscars: 1-0.

MELODRAMA: Biographies; Music Movies; Musicians; Music Composers; Theater Life
(Night and Day; Swanee River)

Rhinestone, 1984, 111m, ★★/$$, 20th/Fox, PG-13/S-P. A successful singer bets her manager that she can teach anyone to sing and make them a star, and proves her point with a dim-witted cabbie. Dolly Parton, Sylvester Stallone, Richard Farnsworth, Ron Leibman, Tim Thomerson. w. Phil Alden Robinson, Sylvester Stallone, d. Bob Clark.

COMEDY: Singers; Svengalis; Taxi Drivers; Country Singers; ROMANCE: Romance-Reluctant; Romantic Comedy; Romance-Class Conflicts; Bets; Female Protagonists; Coulda Been Great; Good Premise Unfulfilled; Flops-Major; Female Protagonists
(Trading Places; The Main Event)
(Ed: Dolly holds her own, but Sly is too much like the character to put the satirical edge in it; plagued with production and star problems)

Rhythm on the Range, 1936, 87m, ★★★/$$$, Par/NA. On a ranch in the wild West, the owner's daughter is kidnapped by outlaws, and a hired hand goes after them to rescue her. Bing Crosby, Martha Raye, Frances Farmer, Bob Burns, Lucile Watson, Samuel S. Hinds, George E. Stone. w. John C. Moffett, Sidney Salkow, Walter de Leon, Francis Martin, d. Norman Taurog.

MUSICALS: WESTERNS: COMEDY: Musical Comedy; Western Comedy; Singers; Kidnappings; Rescue Adventure; Faded Hits; Hidden Gems

Rich and Famous, 1981, 117m, ★★★/$$, MGM/MGM-UA, R/S-P-MRN. After college, two good friends reconnect. One has become a famous and respected novelist, and when she helps her friend into the publishing business, little does she know she's created her greatest competition. Jacqueline Bisset, Candice Bergen, David Selby, Hart Bochner, Steven Hill, Meg Ryan. Matt Lattanzi. w. Gerald

Ayres, P-adap. John Van Druten, *Old Acquaintance*, d. George Cukor.

DRAMA: COMEDY DRAMA: Friendships-Great; Friendships-Female; Friendships on the Rocks; Writers; Women in Conflict; Feuds; Jealousy; Female Protagonists; Hidden Gems

REMAKE OF: Old Acquaintance.

(Old Acquaintance; The Turning Point; Beaches)

Rich in Love, 1993, 123m, ★★★/$, MGM/MGM-UA, PG/S. When mom leaves an ordinary Southern family, dad and sis look for her, but suddenly older sis shows up with her pretty boyfriend. Younger sis and boyfriend hit it off, while also falling for a local boy. Will mom ever come home before dad finds someone new and will older sis ever have that baby? Albert Finney, Kathryn Erbe, Kyle MacLachlan, Suzy Amis, Alfre Woodard, Ethan Hawke, Jill Clayburgh, Piper Laurie. w. Alfred Uhry, d. Bruce Beresford.

DRAMA: COMEDY DRAMA: Family Drama; **ROMANCE:** Romantic Drama; Romance-Triangles; Romance with Relative's Lover; Babies-Having; Coming of Age; Girls; Young Women; Women Who Leave; Fathers Alone; Southerns; Quiet Little Films; South Carolina; Foreign; Directors of Southerns; Female Protagonists

(Georgy Girl; Desert Bloom; The Heart is a Lonely Hunter)

(Ed: Follow up for writer and director to *Driving Miss Daisy*, and though it's a good film, it's not up to that level)

Rich Kids, 1979, 96m, ★★★/$, MGM/MGM-UA, PG/S-P. A well-to-do teenage girl and boy develop a romance while their screwed-up parents play around. Trini Alvarado, Jeremy Levy, Kathryn Walker, John Lithgow, Terry Kiser, David Selby. w. Judith Ross, d. Robert M. Young.

COMEDY DRAMA: ROMANCE: Love-First; Multiple Stories; Teenagers; Rich Kids; Children-Little Adults; New York Life; Divorce; Quiet Little Films; Time Capsules; Hidden Gems; Overlooked at Release; Female Protagonists; Child Protagonists; Female Screenwriters

(A Little Romance; Moonstruck)

(Ed: Treats kids like human beings with adequate intelligence, though perhaps too much freedom. Overshadowed by hit *A Little Romance* same year. Produced by

Robert Altman, and has similar plot twists to the later *Moonstruck* when everyone who's cheating on each other literally bumps into discovering it after rounding a corner on the street)

Richard III, 1955, 161m, ★★★★/$$$, London Films/Col. The famous Shakespeare history of the hunchback king's rise to power and defeat in battle. Laurence Olivier (BActor), Claire Bloom, Ralph Richardson, Cedric Hardwicke, Stanley Baker, Alec Clunes, John Gielgud, Clive Morton. w. Laurence Olivier, Alan Dent, P-adap. William Shakespeare, d. Laurence Olivier. Oscars: 1-0.

DRAMA: Historical Drama; Rise and Fall Stories; Royalty; Kings; Middle Ages; Shakespeare; Disabled People; Hunchbacks

Richard III, 1995, 105m, ★★★/$, UA/MGM-UA, R/P-V-S. The power struggles of a king amid civil war in England is updated to the depths of the Depression. Ian McKellen, Annette Bening, Robert Downey, Jr., Maggie Smith, Nigel Hawthorne, John Wood, Kristin Scott Thomas, Jim Broadbent, Jim Carter, Bill Paterson, Adrian Dunbar. w. Ian McKellen, Richard Loncraine, P-adap. William Shakespeare, d. Richard Loncraine.

DRAMA: Kings; Power Struggles; Men in Conflict; Mean Men; Leaders-Tyrant; British Films; Depression Era; 1930s; Revisionist Films; Shakespeare

(Les Miserables [1995]; Henry V; King Lear)

The Richest Girl in the World, 1934, 80m, ★★★/$$, RKO/NA. A wealthy young woman tired of gold digging suitors poses as her secretary to find a man who loves her for herself. Miriam Hopkins, Joel McCrea, Fay Wray, Henry Stephenson, Reginald Denny, Beryl Mercer. w. Norman Krasna (BOStory), d. William A. Seiter. Oscars: 1-0.

COMEDY: COMEDY DRAMA: ROMANCE: Romantic Comedy; Heiresses; Undercover; Identities-Assumed; Gold diggers; Rich vs. Poor; Hidden Gems

Rich, Young and Pretty, 1951, 95m, ★★★/$$$, MGM/MGM-UA. Texan father and daughter are in gay Paree to sing and dance and find the girl's mother. Jane Powell, Danielle Darrieux, Wendell Corey, Vic Damone, Fernando Lamas, Una Merkel, Richard Anderson. w.

Sidney Sheldon, Dorothy Cooper, d. Norman Taurog.

MUSICALS: Family Comedy; Children-Long Lost; Fathers & Daughters; Texas; Paris; Vacations-European; Forgotten Films; Hidden Gems

(Holiday in Mexico; Nancy Goes to Rio)

Richie Rich, 1994, 95m, ★★½/$$, WB/WB, PG. The incredibly rich boy with too much time on his hands has some wild adventures with his pals before his family's accountant tries to embezzle it away. Macaulay Culkin, John Larroquette, Edward Herrmann, Jonathan Hyde, Christine Ebersole, Michael McShane, Stephi Lineburg. w. Tom S. Parker Jim Jennewein, d. Donald Petrie.

ACTION: Action Comedy; Fantasy;

CHILDREN'S: Boys; Rich People; Inheritances at Stake; Embezzlers; Comic Heroes; Flops-Major

(Ed: Not bad, but not very good. Kids won't notice it too much, though)

Ricochet, 1991, 102m, ★★/$$, WB/HBO, R/EV-EP-ES-FN-MRN. A murderer sent to prison for a long sentence hunts down the prosecutor who put him away once he's released. Denzel Washington, John Lithgow, Ice T, Kevin Pollak, Lindsay Wagner, Mary Ellen Trainer, Josh Evans. w. Steven E. De Souza, Fred Dekker, Menno Meyjes, d. Russell Mulcahey.

ACTION: Revenge; Convict's Revenge; Psycho Killers; Gay Men; Murderers-Homosexual; Criminal Pursues Good Guy's Family; Framed; Scandals; Men in Conflict; Black vs. White; Curiosities; Flops-Major; Unintentionally Funny

(The Adventures of Buckaroo Banzai . . .; Virtuosity)

Ride 'Em Cowboy, 1941, 82m, ★★/$$, U/MCA-U. Two New York hot dog vendors venture out West and get jobs on a ranch. Bud Abbott, Lou Costello, Dick Foran, Anne Gwynne, Samuel S. Hinds, Richard Lane, Johnny Mack Brown, Ella Fitzgerald. w. True Boardman, John Grant, d. Arthur Lubin.

COMEDY: Fish out of Water Stories; **WESTERNS:** Western Comedy; Fools-Bumbling; Abbott & Costello

(Cityslickers; Abbott & Costello SERIES)

Ride the High Country, 1962, 94m, ★★★/$, MGM/MGM-UA. Two retired officers are hired to guard a gold shipment from a mine to a bank, but one isn't so scrupulous. Joel McCrea, Randolph

Scott, Edgar Buchanan, Mariette Hartley, James Drury. w. N. B. Stone, Jr., d. Sam Peckinpah.

WESTERNS: Protecting Someone; Heist Stories; Friends as Enemies; Gold Mining; Forgotten Films; Journies; Hidden Gems
(Rio Lobo; The Wages of Fear; Sorcerer)

Ride the Pink Horse, 1947, 101m, ★★1/2/$, U-I/NA. A military man retires and revisits his old town to avenge his friend's death. Robert Montgomery, Wanda Hendrix, Andrea King, Thomas Gomez (**BSActor**), Fred Clark, Art Smith. w. Charles Lederer, N-adap. Dorothy B. Hughes, d. Robert Montgomery. Oscars: 1-0.

SUSPENSE: DRAMA: Crime Drama; Film Noir; Avenging Someone's Death; New in Town; Southwestern Life; New Mexico
(The Lady in the Lake; Bad Day at Black Rock)

Rider on the Rain, 1969, 119m, ★★1/2/$, Ind/Monarch, R/V. After being raped, a woman murders her attacker and tries to cover it up. Charles Bronson, Marlene Jobert, Annie Cordy, Jill Ireland, Gabriele Tinti, Jean Gavern, Jean Piat. w. Sebastian Japrisot, d. Rene Clement.

DRAMA: SUSPENSE: Revenge; **MURDER:** Rape/Rapists; Revenge on Rapist; Murderers-Female; Turning the Tables; Detective Stories; Forgotten Films; Curiosities
(The Accused [1948]; Outrage; Extremities)

Riding High, 1950, 112m, ★★★/$$$, Par/Par. A remake of *Broadway Bill,* about a horse breeder who won't let his horse race until he's good and ready, when he finally comes through in the Imperial Derby. Bing Crosby, Coleen Gray, Charles Bickford, Raymond Walburn, James Gleason, Oliver Hardy, Frances Gifford, William Demarest, Ward Bond, Percy Kilbride, Harry Davenport, Margaret Hamilton, Douglas Dumbrille, Gene Lockhart. w. Robert Riskin, d. Frank Capra.

COMEDY: FARCE: American Myth; Capra-esque; Horse Racing; **ROMANCE:** Romantic; Comedy

REMAKE OF: Broadway Bill.

Riff-Raff, 1935, 80m, ★★1/2/$$$, MGM/MGM-UA. Two dock workers fight over a sexy woman on the California coast. Similar to Steinbeck's *Sweet Thursday* novella. Jean Harlow, Spencer Tracy,

Joseph Calleia, Mickey Rooney, d. J. Walter Ruben.

MELODRAMA: ROMANCE: Men Fighting Over Women; Fishermen; Working Class; Poor People; Depression Era; Forgotten Films
(Cannery Row [based on Sweet Thursday])

Riff-Raff, 1947, 80m, ★★★/$, Ind/Turner. A dying man gives a pal who's a con artist a map to oil wells, but others want it. Edmond O'Brien, Walter Slezak, Anne Jeffreys. d. Ted Tetzlaff.

SUSPENSE: Film Noir; Oil People; Treasure Hunts; Dying Wishes; Forgotten Films; Hidden Gems; Coulda Been Great

Riff-Raff, 1990, 95m, ★★1/2/$, BFI-Orion/Orion, R/P. A construction site in England is unsafe, and when one of the workers dies, his co-workers rebel against their bosses. Robert Carlyle, Emer McCourt, Jimmy Coleman, George Moss, Ricky Tomlinson, David Finch, Richard Belgrave, Ade Sapara, Derek Young. w. Bill Jesse, d. Ken Loach.

DRAMA: Social Drama; **COMEDY DRAMA:** Ensemble Films; Strikes Working Class; British Films; Curiosities
(Moonlighting [1982])
(Ed: Subtitled due to the thick dialect)

Rififi, 1955, 116m, ★★★/$$, Pathe/Nos. After a jewelry store heist, the gang responsible falls apart and are gunned down one by one. Jean Servais, Carl Mohner, Robert Manuel, Marie Sabouret, Perlo Vita (Jules Dassin). w. Rene Wheeler, Jules Dassin, Auguste le Breton, N-adap. Auguste le Breton, d. Jules Dassin.

ACTION: Crime Drama; Heist Stories; Jewel Thieves; **TRAGEDY:** Ensemble Films; Ensembles-Male; French Films
(Reservoir Dogs; The Killing; The Asphalt Jungle; Odd Man Out)

Right of Way, 1985, 102m, ★★★/$$$, HBO/HBO. An elderly couple plans suicide when the woman begins dying. Bette David, James Stewart, Melinda Dillon. d. George Schaefer.

DRAMA: TRAGEDY: Death-Impending; Elderly People; Romance-Elderly; Marriage Drama; Suicidal Tendencies; Euthanasia; TV Movies
(Night, Mother)

The Right Stuff, 1983, 193m, ★★★/$$, Ladd-WB/WB, R/P-S. A historical film of the recruiting and training and eventual launching of the first astronauts. Sam Shepard (BSActor), Scott Glenn, Ed

Harris, Dennis Quaid, Fred Ward, Barbara Hershey, Kim Stanley, Veronica Cartwright. w. d. Philip Kaufman, NF-adap. Tom Wolfe. BPicture, **BCin, BOScore, BEdit, BSound, BSound Edit.** Oscars: 8-4.

DRAMA: SATIRE: COMEDY DRAMA: Epics; Historical Drama; Astronauts; Ensemble Films; Ensembles-Male; Faded Hits; Curiosities; Forgotten Films
(Apollo 13; Space; Countdown)

The Right to Love, 1930, 79m, ★★1/2/$$, Par/NA. A mother supports her illegitimate daughter, a missionary halfway across the world. Ruth Chatterton, Paul Lukas, David Manners, Irving Pichel, George Baxter. w. Zoe Atkins, N-adap. Susan Glaspell *(Brook Adams),* d. Richard Wallace.

MELODRAMA: Mothers-Struggling; Missionaries; Tearjerkers; Mothers & Daughters; Children-Longlost; Mothers-Unwed; Scandals; Forgotten Films
(Stella Dallas; Stella; Min and Bill)

Rikky and Pete, 1988, 103m, ★★1/2/$, MGM/MGM-UA, PG-13/P-S. Kooky brother and sister scientist-inventor types go into the Australian outback for a little adventure with like eccentrics. Nina Landis, Stephen Kearney. w. David Parker, d. Nadia Tass.

COMEDY DRAMA: Comedy-Light; Inventors; Scientists; Brothers & Sisters; Journies; Eccentric People; Australian Films; Female Directors

Ring of the Musketeers, 1993, 86m, ★★1/2/$, Col/Col, PG. Descendants of the swashbucklers rescue a kidnapped boy and battle the mob. David Hasselhoff, Alison Doody, Thomas Gottschalk, Cheech Marin, Corbin Bernsen. w. Joel Surrow, d. John Paragon.

ACTION: Action Comedy; Revisionist Films; Kidnappings; Rescue Drama; Swashbucklers

REMAKE OF: The Three Musketeers

Rio Bravo, 1959, 141m, ★★★1/2/$$$$, WB/WB. Two misfit lawmen get their act together and clean up the Western town in their charge. John Wayne, Dean Martin, Ricky Nelson, Angie Dickinson, Walter Brennan, Ward Bond, Harry Carey, Jr., Bob Steele. w. Jules Furthman, Leigh Brackett, d. Howard Hawks.

WESTERNS: Small-town Life; Turning the Tables; Starting Over; Protecting Someone; Eccentric People; Faded Hits; Cult Films

SEQUEL: El Dorado

(Fort Apache; Assault on Precinct 13)

Rio Grande, 1950, 105m, ★★1/2/$$$, Republic/Republic. In the 1800s, a border patrol unit of the U.S. Cavalry tries to keep Mexican Indians from crossing the great river. John Wayne, Maureen O'Hara, Ben Johnson, Claude Jarman, Jr., Harry Carey, Jr., Chill Wills, J. Carol Naish, Victor McLaglen. w. James Kevin McGuinness, James Warner Bellah, d. John Ford.

WESTERNS: West-Old; Indians-American, Conflict with; Cavalry; Indians-American; Mexico; Crossing the Border; Texas

(The Border; Borderline)

Rio Lobo, 1970, 114m, ★★1/2/$$$, Cinema Center/Fox. Toward the end of the Civil War, a Union officer saves a gold shipment from theft by bandits and exposes a double agent in the Yankee ranks. John Wayne, Jorge Rivero, Jennifer O'Neill, Jack Elam, Victor French, Chris Mitchum. w. Leigh Brackett, Burton Wohl, d. Howard Hawks.

WESTERNS: Civil War Era; Heist Stories; Gold Mining; Traitors; North vs. South; Journies

(Ride the High Country; El Dorado)

The Rise and Fall of Legs Diamond, 1960, 101m, ★★1/2/$$, WB/WB. In New York in the roaring twenties, a gangster rises to prominence in the mob. Ray Danton, Karen Steele Elaine Stewart, Jesse White, Simon Oakland, Robert Lowery, Warren Oates, Judson Pratt. w. Joseph Landon, d. Budd Boettischer.

ACTION: Crime Drama; Criminal Biographies; Mob Stories; Rise and Fall Stories; Roaring 20s; 1920s; Evil Men

(Public Enemy; Capone; Dillinger)

The Rise and Rise of Michael Rimmer, 1970, 101m, ★★1/2/$, WB/NA. A British advertising agency hires an efficiency expert as its president and CEO and he rises with comic rapidity through a succession of loftier jobs until he's finally a cabinet minister. Peter Cook, John Cleese, Arthur Lowe, Denholm Elliott, Ronald Fraser, Vanessa Howard, George A. Cooper, Harold Pinter, James Cossins, Dudley Foster, Ronnie Corbett. w. Peter Cook, John Cleese, Kevin Billington, Graham Chapman, d. Kevin Billington.

COMEDY: FARCE: SATIRE: Advertising World; Power-Rise to; Power-Rise to, of Idiot; Curiosities; Cult Films; Forgotten Films; British Films; Efficiency Experts

(The Hudsucker Proxy; Being There; Nothing But the Best)

The Rise of Louis XIV, 1966, 100m, ★★★/$, Ind/Ingram. A pseudo-documentary of the life of the flambouyant "Sun King," of the late 18th century, whose foppish ways and opulent parties raise the hackles of the starving peasants and, in part, lead to the French Revolution. Jean-Michel Patte, Raymond Jourdan, Silvagni, Katharine Renn, Dominique Vincent, Pierre Barrat. w. Jean Gruault, Philippe Erlanger, d. Roberto Rossellini.

DRAMA: Docudrama; Documentary Style; Biographies; Royalty; Kings; French; Revolution; 1700s; French Films

Rising Sun, 1993, 128m, ★★1/2/$$$, 20th/Fox, R/P-V-FN-MRN. A Japanese takeover of an American corporation leads to greed and a murder which two L.A. police detectives investigate (Sean Connery, Wesley Snipes). Tia Carerre, Kevin Anderson, Ray Wise. w. Philip Kaufman, Michael Crichton, N-adap. Crichton, d. Kaufman.

SUSPENSE: MYSTERY: MURDER MYSTERY: Detective Stories; Detectives-Police; Conspiracy; Corruption; Mystery-Whodunits; Scandals; Mob Stories; Mob-Asian; Martial Arts; Relationships-Interracial; Buddy Cops; Politicians; Los Angeles; Japanese; Video Proof; Coulda Been Good

(No Way Out; Sliver; Black Rain [1989])

(Ed: Hype over content; very routine with really dumb dialogue)

Risk, 1995, 85m, ★★★/$, NA, R/S-P-FFN-MN. The story of an artist's model and the drifter who has to have her and the people in both of their lives, who like themselves, seem to be going nowhere fast. Karen Sillas, David Ilku, Molly Price, Jack Gwaltney, Christie MacFadyen, Phillip Clarke, Charlie Levi. w. d. Deirdre Fishel

DRAMA: Art Films; Artists; Erotic Drama; Drifters; Sexy Men; Ensemble Films; Alienation; Hidden Gems; Female Protagonists; Female Directors; Female Screenwriters; Quiet Little Films; Independent Films

(Betty Blue; Leaving Las Vegas)

Risky Business, 1983, 99m, ★★★★/ $$$$$, G-WB/WB, R/P-S-FFN. A teen hoping to get into Princeton (Tom Cruise) winds up in a jam when his parents go away and a call girl he falls for (Rebecca DeMornay) turns their home into a whore/party house—just when the Princeton rep (Richard Masur) shows up. Bronson Pinchot. w. d. Paul Brickman.

COMEDY: COMEDY DRAMA: **ROMANCE:** Party Movies; Teenage Movies; Prostitutes-High Class; Suburban Life; Teenagers; Boyhood; Coming of Age; Race Against Time; Parents are Gone; Parents are Gone from Chicago; Narrated Films; Chicago; Writer-Directors

(Ed: A true anomaly: an intelligent, artistic teen party movie)

Rita, Sue and Bob, Too, 1987, 95m, ★★★/$$, Lorimar/WB, R/S. In a working-class community in England, teenage baby-sitters are the subject of sexual advances by the father of their "sittees." Michelle Holmes, Siobhan Finneran, George Costigan, Lesley Sharp. w., P-adap. Andrea Dunbar (The Arbour and Rita, Sue and Bob Too), d. Alan Clarke.

SATIRE: COMEDY DRAMA: Erotic Comedy; Social Satire; Sexuality; Sexual Problems; Romance-Older Men/Younger Women; Baby-sitters; British Films; Sexual Harassment; Working Class

(Poison Ivy; Lolita; Georgy Girl; Sammie and Rosie Get Laid)

The Ritz, 1976, 90m, ★★★/$, WB/WB, R/S-P-MRN. A farce of errors occurs when a family man takes refuge from the mob in what he doesn't realize at first is a gay bathhouse in 70s New York. Jack Weston, Rita Moreno, Jerry Stiller, Kaye Ballard, Bessie Love, George Coulouris, F. Murray Abraham, Treat Williams. w. P-adap. Terrence McNally, d. Richard Lester.

COMEDY: FARCE: Comedy of Errors; Gay Men; Fish out of Water Stories; Mob; Comedy; Fugitives from the Mob; Hiding Out; Chase Stories; Homophobia; 1970s; Sexual Revolution; New York Life; Hidden Gems

(Hotel Paradiso; The Birdcage)

(Ed: A very big hit on stage, it bombed as a movie, but it's not bad at all and not just for gay people by any means)

The River, 1951, 87m, ★★★1/2/$$, WB/HomeVision. A small group of British colonials try to have a normal life in India on the Ganges. Nora Swinburne, Esmond Knight, Arthur Shields, Adrienne Corri. w. Rumer Godden, N-adap. Rumer Godden, d. Jean Renoir.

DRAMA: Imperialist Problems; India; Indian People; Asia; Hidden Gems; Art Films; Scenery-Outstanding; Female Screenwriters
(Black Narcissus)

The River, 1984, 122m, ★★½/$, U/MCA-U, PG. A farm family struggles to keep an overflowing river from flooding their farm. Mel Gibson, Sissy Spacek (BActress), Shane Bailey, Becky Jo Lynch, Scott Glenn, Billy Green Bush. w. Robert Dillon, Julian Barry, d. Mark Rydell. BSound Edit, BCin, BOScore. Oscars: 4-0.
DRAMA: MELODRAMA: Farm Life; Save the Farm; Mortgage Drama; Family Drama; Floods; Southerns; Marriage Drama; Marriage on the Rocks
(Country; Places in the Heart)

The River Niger, 1976, 105m, ★★★/$, Ind/Continental. Life in the ghetto, based upon the Pulitzer Prize play of the 70s. James Earl Jones, Cicely Tyson, Glynn Turman, Louis Gossett, Roger E. Mosley. d. Krishna Shah.
DRAMA: Black Casts; Black Men; Black Women; Family Drama; Inner City Life; 1970s; Forgotten Films; Overlooked at Release; Art Films; Pulitzer Prize Adaptations; Independent Films
(The Piano Lesson; Fences; Claudine)

River of No Return, 1954, 91m, ★★½/$$, 20th/Fox. A man whose wife has died raises his ten-year-old son alone until he meets a saloon singer with a valuable gold claim they must fight for. They wind up on a harrowing river raft trip. Robert Mitchum, Marilyn Monroe, Tommy Rettig, Rory Calhoun, Murvyn Vye. w. Frank Fenton, d. Otto Preminger.
DRAMA: ROMANCE: ADVENTURE: Romantic Adventure; River Trauma; Forgotten Films; Fathers Alone; Fathers & Sons; Singers; Gold Mining
(Rooster Cogburn; The River Wild; Bus Stop)

River Rat, 1984, 93m, ★★/$, Par/Par, PG-13/S-V. A released prisoner runs from his opressive parol officer on a white-water rafting trip with the daughter he never got to know. Tommy Lee Jones, Nancy Lea Owen, Brian Dennehy, Martha Plimpton. w. d. Tom Rickman.
DRAMA: ADVENTURE: Fathers & Daughters; Ex-Convicts; River Trauma; Southerns; Fugitives from the Law; Children-Idle lost; Writer-Directors

A River Runs Through It, 1992, 123m, ★★★½/$$$, Col/Col, PG-13/S-MRN.

Two brothers with widely contrasting views on religion and life in general find common ground in their mutual love for fly-fishing and the attentions of a girl. Brad Pitt, Craig Sheffer, Tom Skerritt, Brenda Blethyn, Emily Lloyd, Susan Taylor. w. Richard Friedenberg (BAScr), N-adap. Norman Maclean, d. Robert Redford. BCin, BOScore. Oscars: 3-1.
DRAMA: ADVENTURE: Small-town Life; Nature-Back to; Nostalgia; **ROMANCE:** Coming of Age; Romance-Triangles; Brothers; Family Drama; Men Fighting Over Women; Fathers & Sons; Autobiographical Stories; Scenery-Outstanding; Sleeper Hits; Lyrical Films
(Legends of the Fall; The River Wild)

River's Edge, 1986, 99m, ★★★½/$$, Island/Island, R/P-S-FN. A bunch of disaffected youths have to choose between loyalty to their violent and off-balance friend who killed his girlfriend by the river's edge, and loyalty to her memory and their buried sense of morality. Crispin Glover, Keanu Reeves, Ione Skye, David Roebuck, Dennis Hopper, Joshua Miller. w. Neal Jiminez, d. Tim Hunter.
DRAMA: Social Drama; **SATIRE:** Social Satire; Young People; Teenagers; Death-Dealing with; Alienation; Murder-Discovering; Rape/Rapists; Liars; Conspiracy; California; Suburban Life; Hidden Gems; Cult Films; Time Capsules
(Permanent Record; Murder in New Hampshire; Little Noises; To Die For; The Last of Sheila)

The River Wild, 1994, 108m, ★★★/$$$$, U/MCA-U, PG-13/P-S-FRN. A mother and former river-raft guide takes her family, including her reluctant husband, for a trip down a river that gets very dangerous if one doesn't stop at a certain point. Unfortunately, bank robbers have also selected the river as a getaway by raft and need mom's expertise to get them past that point to safety-theirs, not hers. Meryl Streep, Kevin Bacon, David Strathairn, Joseph Mazzello, John C. Reilly, Stephanie Sawyer, Buffy the dog, Elizabeth Hoffman, Victor H. Galloway, Diane Delano, Thomas F. Duffy, William Lucking. w. Denis O'Neill, d. Curtis Hanson.
ACTION: ADVENTURE: SUSPENSE: Family Drama; Mothers & Sons; River Trauma; Bank Robberies; Malicious Menaces; Race Against Time; Hostage

Situations; Vacation Nightmares; Heroines; River Trauma; Female in Male Domain; Female Protagonists; Scenery-Outstanding
(Shoot to Kill; Rooster Cogburn; Dead Ahead [TV Movie])
(Ed: Realistic suspense held for a not-so-realistic time, buoyed by Streep and Bacon, the latter a little too cartoony in a situation already stretched)

The Road Back, 1937, 105m, ★★★/$$, U/NA. When World War I is over, soldiers find it hard to re-enter their peacetime lives. Richard Cromwell, John King, Slim Summerville, Andy Devine, Barbara Read, Louise Fazenda, Noah Beery, Jr., Lionel Atwill, John Emery, Etienne Girardot, Spring Byington. w. R. C. Sheriff, Charles Kenyon, N-adap. Erich Maria Remarque, d. James Whale.
DRAMA: War Stories; Germans as Enemy; Soldiers; World War I Stories; Social; Drama; Germany; Veterans; Forgotten Films
SEQUEL TO: All Quiet on the Western Front.
(All Quiet on the Western Front; The Best Years of Our Lives; Born on the Fourth of July)

Road Games, 1981, 110m, ★★½/$, Avco/Col, R/V-P-S. A murderer running from the law hitches a ride with an unfortunate and unsuspecting truck driver. Stacy Keach, Jamie Lee Curtis, Marion Edwards, Grant Page. w. Everett De Roche, d. Richard Franklin.
SUSPENSE: HORROR: Serial Killers; **MURDER:** Hitchhikers; Australia; Road Movies; Outlaw Road Movies; Fugitives from the Law; Truck Drivers; Art Films
(The Hitcher; Henry; Portrait of a Serial Killer; The Vanishing; Man Bites Dog)

Road House, 1989, 114m, ★★/$$$, UA/MGM-UA, R/S-P-EV-MRN. A local saloon keeper down South hires a karate champion to help defend him against the local gangsters. Patrick Swayze, Kelly Lynch, Sam Elliott, Ben Gazzara, Marshall Teague, Julie Michaels, Red West. w. David Lee Henry, Hilary Henkin, d. Rowdy Herrington.
ACTION: Martial Arts; Mob Stories; Rednecks; Men in Conflict; Bodyguards; Southerns; Texas
(Next of Kin; Hard Target)

Roadside Prophets, 1992, 96m, ★★½/$, Fine Line/New Line, R/S-P. A working-class biker goes to Vegas for a

90s *Easy Rider* homage. John Doe, Adam Horovitz, David Carradine, Timothy Leary, John Cusack. w. d. Abbe Wool.

COMEDY DRAMA: Road Movies; Motorcycles; Las Vegas; Journies; Eccentric People; Buddy Films; Coulda Been Good

Road to Bali, 1952, 91m, ★★¹/₂/$$$, Par/MCA-U. In the South Pacific, Bing and Bob encounter hostile natives and beautiful women. Bing Crosby, Bob Hope, Dorothy Lamour, Murvyn Vye, Peter Coe. w. Frank Butler, Hal Kanter, William Morrow, d. Hal Walker.
Pacific Islands

Road to Hong Kong, 1962, 91m, ★/$, UA/MGM-UA. Bing and Bob meet a lovely woman in the oriental capital. Bob Hope, Bing Crosby, Crosby, Dorothy Lamour, Joan Collins, Robert Morley, Walter Gotell, Felix Aylmer, Peter Sellers, David Niven, Frank Sinatra, Dean Martin, Jerry Colonna. w. Norman Panama, Melvin Frank, d. Norman Panama.
Hong Kong

Road to Morocco, 1942, 83m, ★★★/ $$$$, Par/MCA-U. In the lair of an Arab sultan, Bing and Bob must rescue a beautiful maiden held hostage. Bob Hope, Bing Crosby, Dorothy Lamour, Anthony Quinn, Dona Drake. w. Frank Butler, Don Hartman (BOScr), d. David Butler. Oscars: 1-0.
Arab People; Animals-Talking

Road to Rio, 1947, 100m, ★★★/$$$, Par/MCA-U. In the Brazilian capital, an heiress is hypnotized by her kidnappers and Bing and Bob must come to the rescue. Bob Hope, Bing Crosby, Dorothy Lamour, Gale Sondergaard, Frank Faylen, The Wiere Brothers, the Andrews Sisters. w. Edmund Beloin, Jack Rose, d. Norman Z. McLeod. BMScore. Oscars: 1-0.
South America; Hypnosis

Road to Singapore, 1940, 84m, ★★¹/₂/ $$$, Par/MCA-U. Two wealthy philanderers get tired of the high life and head off to Singapore, but end up fighting over an enchantress whose father rules her island. Bing Crosby, Bob Hope, Dorothy Lamour, Charles Coburn, Judith Barrett, Anthony Quinn. w. Don Hartman, Frank Butler, Harry Hervey, d. Victor Schertzinger.
Asia

Road to Utopia, 1945, 89m, ★★★/$$$, Par/MCA-U. Two poor drifters go to the Klondike during the gold rush in search

of riches. Bob Hope, Bing Crosby, Dorothy Lamour, Douglas Dumbrille, Hillary Brooke, Jack La Rue. w. Norman Panama, Melvin Frank, d. Hal Walker.
Utopia; Gold Mining; Animals-Talking

Road to Zanzibar, 1941, ★★★/$$$$, Par/MCA-U. The whole crew goes to Africa on safari and narrowly averts being devoured by animals and natives. Bob Hope, Bing Crosby, Dorothy Lamour, Una Merkel, Eric Blore. w. Frank Butler, Don Hartman, d. Victor Schertzinger.
Safari; Africa

COMEDY: Road Movies; Buddy Films; Comedians; **ADVENTURE:** Comic Adventure; Chase Stories; **ROMANCE:** Romantic Comedy; Romance-Boy Wants Girl; Hope & Crosby

The Road to Wellville, 1994, 117m, ★★★/$$, Col/Col, PG-13/P-S-FN-MRN. A group of turn-of-the-century health enthusiasts try out the Kellogg health sanitarium where all kinds of strange machines and concoctions will supposedly cure them of their various strange and eccentric ailments from impotence to frigidity, or corpulence to flatulence, or all and more. Anthony Hopkins, Bridget Fonda, Matthew Broderick, John Cusack, Dana Carvey, Michael Lerner, Traci Lind, Jacob Reynolds, Alexander Slanksnis, George Nannarello, Denise S. Bass. w. d. Alan Parker, N-adap. T. Coraghessan Boyle

COMEDY: FARCE: Screwball Comedy; Ensemble Films; Costume Drama; Resorts; Weight Problems; Sexual Problems; Marriage on the Rocks; Stern Women; Stern Men; Bathroom Humor; Inventors; Hidden Gems; Coulda Been Great; Overlooked at Release

The Road Warrior (Mad Max 2), 1981, 96m, ★★★/$$$, WB/WB, PG/EV-P. In post-apocalyptic Australia, Max intervenes in a war between the gangs controlling gas and the cops. Mel Gibson, Bruce Spence. w. Terry Hayes, George Miller, Brian Hannant, d. George Miller.

ACTION: SCI-FI: Futuristic Films; Chase Stories; Car Chases; Gangs; Motorcycles; Motorcycle Gangs; Apocalyptic Stories; Australian Films

SEQUEL TO: Mad Max; **SEQUEL:** Mad Max: Beyond Thunderdome.
(Waterworld; Tank Girl; Solarbabies)

Roanoak, 1986, 180m, ★★★/$, AP-PBS/PBS. The mystery of the first American settlement ever, which did not

succumb either to an Indian attack or epidemic. Will Sampson, Victoria Racimo. d. Jan Eggleson.

DRAMA: MYSTERY: Missing Persons; True or Not?; Early America; Historical Drama; Indians-American; Indian-American, Conflict with; TV Movies

The Roaring Twenties, 1939, 106m, ★★★¹/₂/$$$$, WB/MGM-UA. A veteran comes back from World War I and gets involved in bootlegging during Prohibition which leads to a major gang war. James Cagney, Humphrey Bogart, Priscilla Lane, Jeffrey Lynn, Gladys George, Frank McHugh, Paul Kelly, Elizabeth Risdon. w. Jerry Wald, Richard Macaulay, Robert Rossen, Mark Hellinger, d. Raoul Walsh.

ACTION: Action Drama; Crime Drama; Mob Stories; Warner Gangster Era; Prohibition Era; Roaring 20s; 1920s; Bootleggers; Veterans; World War I Era; Power-Rise to
(Public Enemy; Man Power)

The Robe, 1953, 135m, ★★★/$$$$$, 20th/CBS-Fox. Jesus's robe has mystical significance and is kept by his accolytes after his crucifixion. Richard Burton (BActor), Jean Simmons, Michael Rennie, Victor Mature, Jay Robinson, Torin Thatcher, Dean Jagger, Richard Boone, Jeff Morrow, Ernest Thesiger. w. Philip Dunne, N-adap. Lloyd C. Douglas, d. Henry Koster. BPicture, **BCArt**, BCCin, **BCCostume**. Oscars: 5-2.

DRAMA: Epics; Historical Drama; Jesus Christ; Religion; Middle East; Executions; Legends; Blockbusters; Spectacles; Cast of Thousands; Production Design-Outstanding
(King of Kings; The Greatest Story Ever Told)

Roberta, 1935, 105m, ★★★/$$$, RKO/ Turner. In a Parisian fashion house, feathers are ruffled when an American heiress takes over the operations. Irene Dunne, Fred Astaire, Ginger Rogers, Randolph Scott, Helen Westley, Claire Dodd. w. Jane Murfin, Sam Mintz, Allan Scott, P-adap. Otto Harbach, N-adap. Alice Duer Miller *(Gowns by Roberta)*, d. William A. Seiter. BOSong, "Lovely to Look At." Oscars: 1-0.

COMEDY: MUSICAL: Musical Comedy; Fashion World; Power-Rise to; Career Women; Womens' Films; Dance Movies; Paris; Social Climbing; Class Conflicts; Astaire & Rogers; Women Proving

Themselves; Female Screenwriters; Female Protagonists

REMAKE: Lovely to Look At.

Robert et Robert, 1979, 95m, ★★★/ $$, Col/Col, R/S. Two nerds try computer dating and find their own company more interesting than the women they were waiting for. Charles Denner, Jacques Villeret. w. d. Claude Lelouch.

COMEDY DRAMA: Nerds; Friendships-Male; Dating Scene; Computers; Homo-eroticism; French Films; Writer-Directors (Men; Les Comperes)

Robin and Marian, 1976, 107m, ★★★/$, Col/RCA-Col, PG. Marian waits for Robin to return from the Crusades. When he does, he finds life at home depressing, and must struggle with the Sheriff of Nottingham. Sean Connery, Audrey Hepburn. w. James Goldman, d. Richard Lester.

COMEDY DRAMA: ROMANCE: Romantic Comedy; Robin Hood Stories; Medieval Times; Forgotten Films; Hidden Gems
(First Knight; Robin Hood: Prince of Thieves)
(Ed: Worth seeing because of the stars)

Robin and the Seven Hoods, 1964, 123m, ★★¹/₂/$$$, WB/WB. In roaring twenties Chicago, a thief gets together a band of cohorts to steal from the rich and give to the poor. Frank Sinatra, Dean Martin, Bing Crosby, Sammy Davis, Jr., Peter Falk, Barbara Rush, Edward G. Robinson, Victor Buono, Barry Kelley, Jack La Rue, Allen Jenkins, Sig Rumann, Hans Conreid. w. David Schwartz, d. Gordon Douglas.

COMEDY: Spoofs; Mob Stories; Mob Comedy; Robin Hood Stories; Revisionist Films; Roaring 20s; Chicago; Thieves; Rat Pack Movies
(Pocketful of Miracles; Pal Joey)

Robin Hood, 1922, 127m, B&W, silent, ★★★/$$$, Fairbanks-UA/ Robin Hood steals from the rich and gives to the poor, much to the chagrin of the Sheriff of Nottingham and Prince John. Douglas Fairbanks, Wallace Beery, Alan Hale, Enid Bennett. w. Douglas Fairbanks, d. Allan Dwan.

Robin Hood, 1973, 83m, ★★★/$$$, Disney/Disney, G. Cartoon version of the famous legend with each character a dif-ferent animal. Voices of Brian Bedford, Peter Ustinov, Terry-Thomas, Phil Harris, Andy Devine, Pat Buttram. w. Larry

Clemmons, Ken Anderson, others, d. Wolfgang Reitherman.

Robin Hood, 1990, 104m, ★★¹/₂/$$$, 20th/Fox. Robert Hode, a Saxon noble-man, is wrongly condemned, and com-mits himself to stealing from the rich and giving to the poor. Patrick Bergin, Uma Thurman, Jurgen Prochnow, Edward Fox, Jeroen Krabbe, Owen Teale, David Morrissey, Alex North. w. Mark Allen Smith, John McGrath, d. John Irvin.

Robin Hood: Prince of Thieves, 1991, 143m, ★★¹/₂/$$$$, WB/WB, PG-13V. After the Crusades, Robin of Locksley returns to find his father has been killed by the Sheriff of Nottingham. He decides to steal from the rich and give to the poor to spite him. Kevin Costner, Morgan Freeman, Mary Elizabeth Mastrantonio, Christian Slater, Alan Rickman, Sean Connery, Geraldine McEwan, Brian Blessed. w. Pen Densham, John Watson, d. Kevin Reynolds.

ACTION: ADVENTURE: Legends; Medieval Times; Robin Hood Stories; Thieves; **ROMANCE:** Romance-Boy Wants Girl; Saving Someone; Romance-Reluctant; Men in Conflict; Swashbucklers; Revenge
(The Adventures of Robin Hood; Robin and Marian)

Robin Hood, Men in Tights, 1993, 105m, ★★¹/₂/$$, 20th/Fox, PG-13/P-S. Spoof on the classic tale with bathroom humor and sight gags. Cary Elwes, Richard Lewis, Mel Brooks, Roger Rees, Amy Yasbeck, Tracey Ullman, Eric Allen Kramer. w. Mel Brooks, David Shapiro, d. Mel Brooks.

COMEDY: Spoofs; Robin Hood Stories; Comedy-Gag; Comedy-Slapstick; Bathroom Humor; Coulda Been Good; Writer-Directors
(A Connecticut Yankee in King Arthur's Court; Dracula: Dead and Loving It)

Robinson Crusoe on Mars, 1964, 110m, ★★★/$$, Par/Par, G. An astronaut is stranded on mars and tries to survive while awaiting the rescue party. Paul Mantee, Adam West, Vic Lundin. w. Melchior, John C. Higgins, d. Byron Haskin.

ADVENTURES: SCI-FI: Astronauts; Outer Space Movies; Revisionist Films; Friendships-Male; Stranded; Futuristic Films
(The Adventures of Robinson Crusoe)

Robocop, 1987, 103m, ★★★/$$$$, Orion/Orion, R/EV-EP-B&G. Detroit of the future contracts out their police force to a corporation that offers them a mechanical super-cop to fight druglords and dealers. Peter Weller, Nancy Allen, Ronny Cox, Kurtwood Smith, Dan O'Herlihy, Miguel Ferrer.. w. Edward Neumeier, Michael Minder, d. Paul Verhoeven.

Robocop 2, 1990, 118m, Orion. A new, larger model of the robotic future cop goes haywire, becoming a walking time-bomb. The old robocop must take over and defuse it. Peter Weller, Nancy Allen, Dan O'Herlihy, Belinda Bauer, Tom Noonan, Gabriel Damon, Felton Perry, Willard Pugh. w. Frank Miller, Walon Green, d. Irvin Kershner.

ACTION: Crime Drama; Black Comedy; **SCI FI:** Futuristic Films; Comedy-Morbid; Robots; Man vs. Machine; Corruption; Drugs-Dealing; Androids
SEQUELS: Robocop 3, Robocop TV Series.
(Cyborg; Universal Soldier)
(Ed: The violence was controversial, but its extremities and juxtaposition are so obvious, how can it be anything but an overstretched parody?)

Rob Roy, 1995, 134m, ★★★/$$$, UA/MGM-UA, R/S-V-FN-MRN. The mostly true story of rebel Robert MacGregor who borrowed money from a rich man to buy cattle to sell at a profit in order to feed the poor starving people of his area. But his plans run afoul of a cou-ple of local villains who plan to make matters worse before they become better. With the help of a good woman, Rob swashbuckles and ravages forth. Liam Neeson, Jessica Lange, John Hurt, Tim Roth (**BS Actor**), Eric Stoltz, Brian Cox. w. Alan Sharp, N-adap. d. Michael Caton-Jones. Oscars: 1-0.

ADVENTURE: ACTION: MELODRAMA: ROMANCE: Romantic Drama; Robin Hood Stories; Class Conflicts; Evil Men; Poor People; Saintly People; Scotland; 1700s; Sleeper Hits
(Braveheart; Michael Collins; The Big Man)

Rock a Bye Baby, 1958, 107m, ★★★/ $$, Par/Par. A nebbish obsessed with a beautiful starlet agrees to take care of her triplets from a former marriage, which leads to much confusion when he's assumed to be the father. Jerry Lewis,

Marilyn Maxwell, Reginald Gardiner, Salvatore Baccaloni, Hans Conreid, Isobel Elsom, James Gleason, Connie Stevens. w. d. Frank Tashlin.

COMEDY: Comedy of Errors; Babysitters; Misunderstandings; Actresses; Bimbos; Fools-Bumbling; Nerds; Nerds & Babes; Forgotten Films; Faded Hits; Hidden Gems; Coulda Been Great; Writer-Directors

(The Miracle of Morgan's Creek; Sitting Pretty)

Rock-a Doodle, 1990, 74m, ★★/$, PG/V. An owl with magical powers changes a farmboy into a cat and the cat-boy must travel to a magical rooster to make everything right again. Voices of Phil Harris, Glen Campbell, Eddie Deezen, Kathryn Holcomb, Toby Scott Ganger, Christopher Plummer, Sandy Duncan. w. David N. Weiss, Don Bluth, John Pomeroy, T. J. Kuenster, David Steinberg, Gary Goldman, d. Don Bluth.

Cartoons; **CHILDREN'S: MUSICALS:** Musicals-Animated; **SCI-FI:** Fantasy; Music; Movies; Magic; Animal Stories; Humans into Animals; Journies

(Rat Boy; The Secret of NIMH)

Rock Around the Clock, 1956, 74m, ★★★/$$, Col. Bill Haley and the Comets perform a new amalgamation of rhythm & blues and rockabilly called "rock and roll"; teenagers everywhere are dancing in the aisles. Bill Haley and the Comets, The Platters, Little Richard, Tony Martinez and his Band, Freddie Bell and the Bellboys, Johnny Johnson, Alan Freed, Lisa Gaye, Alix Talton. w. Robert E. Kent, James B. Gordon, d. Fred F. Sears.

MUSICALS: Music Movies; Rock Stars; Nostalgia; Teenagers; Teenage Movies; 1950s; Fame-Rise to

(Great Balls of Fire; Hail, Hail Rock 'n Roll)

Rock n' Roll High School, 1979, 93m, ★★1/2/$, New World/New World, PG/P-S. A strict disciplinarian principal bans everything until the high school students are driven crazy and go hog wild with an all-out rock and roll party in the halls. P. J. Soles, Vincent Van Patten, Clint Howard, Dey Young, Mary Woronov, Paul Bartel, Dick Miller, Grady Sutton, The Ramones. w. Russ Dvonch, Joseph McBride, Richard Whitley, Allan Arkush, Joe Dante, d. Allan Arkush.

COMEDY: Teenagers; Teenage Movies; Party Movies; High School Life; 1970s;

Rebels; Generation Gap; Oppression; Spoofs; Coulda Been Great

(Cooley High; Grease)

(Ed: Parody of 50s films like *The Blackboard Jungle*)

The Rocketeer, 1991, 108m, ★★1/2/ $$$, Disney/Disney, PG/V. At the start of World War II, a pilot finds an experimental jet pack which he uses to fly over enemy lines and thwart the Nazis. Bill Campbell, Jennifer Connelly, Alan Arkin, Timothy Dalton, Paul Sorvino, Terry O'Quinn, Ed Lauter, James Handy. w. Danny Bilson, Paul De Meo, (Graphic Novel)-adap. Dave Stevens, d. Joe Johnston.

ACTION: FAMILY: ADVENTURE: SCI-FI: World War II Era; Good vs. Evil; Nazi Stories; Experiments; Heroes-Comic; Flying People; Coulda Been Great

(Dick Tracy)

Rocket Gibraltar, 1988, 92m, ★★★/$, Col/Col, PG. A grandfather's wish is dealt with on his birthday at his beach estate. Burt Lancaster, Macauley Culkin, Bill Pullman, John Glover, Patricia Clarkson. w. Amos Poe, d. Daniel Petrie.

MELODRAMA: Family Drama; Grandfathers-Fascinating; Fathers & Sons; Men and Boys; Dying; Wishes; Dreams

Rocket to the Moon, 1986, 118m, ★★★/$, AP-PBS/PBS. A dentist in the Depression has to deal with the facts of his life as he hits thirty. John Malkovich, Judy Davis, Eli Wallach. w. P-adap. Clifford Odets, d. John Jacobs.

DRAMA: Pre-Life Crisis; Young Men; Dentists; Depression; Depression Era; Stage Tapings

(Golden Boy; The Moon is Our Home)

Rock Hudson's Home Movies, 1993, 63m, ★★★/$, Ind/Water Bearer, S. Clips from Hudson's movies narrated to show the ironies of the star's gay personal life and the characters he played, with some absolutely uncanny, coincidental results. Eric Farr. w. d. Mark Rappaport. Documentaries; Actors; Gay Men; Gay Films; Hidden Gems; Homo-eroticism

Rocky, 1976, 119m, ★★★1/2/$$$$$, UA/CBS-Fox, PG/P-S-V. An amateur boxer's dream in life is to go fifteen rounds with the heavyweight champion of the world. Through extensive training and a series of practice fights, he readies himself and achieves his dream. As his self-esteem improves, so does that of the

woman in his life. Sylvester Stallone (BActor), Burgess Meredith (BSActor), Talia Shire (BActress), Burt Young (BSActor), Carl Weathers, Thayer David. w. Sylvester Stallone (BOScr), d. John G. Avildsen (**BDirector**). **BPicture,** BOSong, BSound, **BEdit.** Oscars: 9-3.

DRAMA: ACTION: Action Drama; Sports Movies; Underdog Stories; Fame-Rise to; Boxing; Dreams; Simple Minds;

ROMANCE: Romantic Drama; Romance-Boy Wants Girl; Romance with Boxers; Men Proving Themselves; Competitions; Philadelphia; Sleeper Hits; Faded Hits

(The Karate Kid; The Power of One; Champion; Raging Bull; Requiem for a Heavyweight)

Rocky II, 1979, 119m, ★★1/2/$$$$, UA/CBS-Fox, PG/V-P. Rocky becomes a champion, marries his sweetheart from the first film and they must both weather his subsequent downfall. Sylvester Stallone, Talia Shire, Burt Young, Carl Weathers, Burgess Meredith. w. d. Sylvester Stallone.

DRAMA: ACTION: Action Drama; Sports Movies; Underdog Stories; Fame-Rise to; Boxing; Dreams; Simple Minds; Marriage Drama; Comebacks; Men Proving Themselves; Competitions; Philadelphia; Faded Hits

Rocky III, 1982, 99m, ★★★/$$$$$, UA/CBS-Fox, PG/P-V. A hard-hitting, ambitious young boxer beats a now complacent Rocky in the first round, prompting our hero to retrain and "get hungry" again. Sylvester Stallone, Talia Shire, Burt Young, Burgess Meredith, Carl Weathers, Tony Burton, Mr. T, Hulk Hogan. w. d. Sylvester Stallone. BOSong, Eye of the Tiger. Oscars: 1-0.

DRAMA: ACTION: Action Drama; Sports Movies; Underdog Stories; Fame-Rise to; Boxing; Dreams; Simple Minds; Comebacks; Men Proving Themselves; Competitions; Philadelphia; Faded Hits

Rocky IV, 1985, 91m, ★★1/2/$$$$, MGM-UA/MGM-UA, PG/P-V. A Soviet champion squares off against Rocky for the battle of the superpowers. Sylvester Stallone, Dolph Lungren, Carl Weathers, Talia Shire, Burt Young, Brigitte Nielsen. w. d. Sylvester Stallone.

DRAMA: ACTION: Action Drama; Sports Movies; Underdog Stories; Fame-Rise to; Boxing; Dreams; Simple Minds; Competitions; Comebacks; Russians & Americans; Cold War Era; Philadelphia

Rocky V, 1990, 104m, ★★/$$, MGM-UA/MGM-UA, PG/P-V. After years of boxing, Rocky suffers from brain damage and trains a young boxer to follow his path to retardation. Sylvester Stallone, Talia Shire, Burt Young, Sage Stallone, Burgess Meredith, Tommy Morrison, Richard Gant, Tony Burton. w. Sylvester Stallone, d. John G. Avildsen.
DRAMA: Sports Movies; Underdog Stories; Fame-Rise to; Boxing; Dreams; Simple Minds; Fathers & Sons; Mentally Disabled
(Over the Top)
(Ed: Stallone starred with his own son for this one)
The Rocky Horror Picture Show, 1975, 100m, ★★★/$$$$, 20th/CBS-Fox, R/S-P-FN-MRN. A nerdy all-American waspy couple break down in a rainstorm, and take refuge in the dark mansion of a psychotic doctor who is trying to make a man out of spare parts. Tim Curry, Susan Sarandon, Barry Bostwick, Richard O'Brien, Patricia Quinn, Little Nell, Jonathan Adams, Peter Hinwood, Meatloaf, Charles Gray. w. Richard O'Brien, Jim Sharman, P-adap. Richard O'Brien (The Rocky Horror Show), d. Jim Sharman.
COMEDY: MUSICAL: Musical Comedy; SATIRE: Spoofs; Horror Comedy; Spoofs-Horror; SCI-FI: Experiments; Tranvestites; Transsexuals; Gay Men; Alternative Lifestyles; Erotic Comedy; Hunchbacks; Camp; Cult Films; Sleeper Hits
SEQUEL: Shock Treatment.
(Ed: Though a failure when originally released, the midnight movie circuit took the gross over $100 million after almost twenty years)
Roger & Me, 1989, 90m, ★★★/$$$, WB/WB. A documentary about a reporter intermittently trying to ask Roger Smith, CEO of General Motors, about his decision to move a plant from Flint, Michigan to Mexico and its effect on the blue-collar workers he *does* successfully interview there. w. d. Michael Moore.
COMEDY: SATIRE: Documentaries; Social Satire; Corporate Corruption; Working Class; Unemployment; Factory Life; American Dream; Sleeper Hits; Rich vs. Poor; Interviews; Curiosities
Rollerball, 1975, 129m, ★★½/$$, UA/CBS-Fox, R/S-P-V. In the future, an oppressive regime allows its residents only one release: a violent game played to

the death. James Caan, John Houseman, Maud Adams, John Beck, Moses Gunn. w. William Harrison, d. Norman Jewison.
ACTION: Competitions; Futuristic Films; Allegorical Stories; Skating; Sports Movies; Executions; Apocalyptic Stories; Oppression; Forgotten Films
(Gumball Rally; Death Race 2000; Kansas City Bomber)
Roller Boogie, 1978, 103m, ★★/$, UA/MGM-UA, PG. Roller skating appeals to runaways who have to save the rink from a developer. Linda Blair, Jim Bray, Beverly Garland. w. Barry Schneider, d. Mark Lester.
MELODRAMA: Music Movies; Roller Skating; Musicals-Disco Era; Disco Era; 1970s; Mortgage Drama; Teenagers; Teenage Movies; Generation Gap
(Xanadu)
Rolling Thunder, 1977, 94m, ★★½/$, AIP/Vestron. A P.O.W. returns from the war in Vietnam after being liberated and finds his wife and son are dead. He uses the techniques he learned as a soldier in the jungle to find their killers and avenge their death. William Devane, Tommy Lee Jones, Linda Haynes, Lisa Richards, Dabney Coleman, James Best. w. Heywood Gould, Paul Schrader, d. John Flynn.
ACTION: DRAMA: Crime Drama; Revenge; Avenging Death of Someone; Southerns; POWs; Veterans-Vietnam; Forgotten Films; Curiosities
(Distant Thunder; The Deerhunter)
Rollover, 1981, 115m, ★★½/$$, Orion/Orion, R/S-P. When the president of a large bank is murdered, his wife and a reporter uncover the international ring of corrupt bankers and criminal types responsible and their conspiracy which could wreck the stock markets around the world. Jane Fonda, Kris Kristofferson, Hume Cronyn, Josef Sommer, Bob Gunton. w. David Shaber, d. Alan J. Pakula.
SUSPENSE: DRAMA: Social Drama; Conspiracy; MURDER: MYSTERY: MURDER: MYSTERY: Actresses; Journalists; Journalists at Detectives; Stock Brokers; Coulda Been Great; Good Premise Unfulfilled; Female Protagonists
(The China Syndrome)
(Ed: The premise is too abstract and unexplained for most people to get, but it was a good try)
Roman Holiday, 1953, 118m, ★★★★/$$$$, Par/Par. When a princess (Audrey

Hepburn, **BActress**) runs off for a day away from the drudgery of being a monarch, a reporter (Gregory Peck, BActor) finds her and shows her the town and perhaps even love. Eddie Albert (BSActor), Hartley Power. w. Ian McLellan Hunter, Dalton Trumbo, John Dighton (**BO Story**, BOScr), d. William Wyler (BDirector). BPicture, **BB&WCostume**, BB&WCin, BB&WArt, BEdit. Oscars: 11-3.
COMEDY DRAMA: ROMANCE: Romantic Comedy; Comedy-Light; Fairy Tales; Princesses; Royalty; Fugitives; Romance-Older Men/Younger Women; Rome
(Love in the Afternoon; Funny Face)
(Ed: Dalton Trumbo was the original author of the Oscar winning story, but as he was blacklisted, he could not be given the credit, which Hunter received as a front; see the film *The Front*)
Roman Scandals, 1933, 93m, ★★★/$$$, Samuel Goldwyn/Goldwyn. A musical about a man who imagines he's back in ancient Rome. Eddie Cantor, Gloria Stuart, Ruth Etting, Edward Arnold, Alan Mowbray, Verree Teasdale. w. William Anthony McGuire, George Oppenheimer, Arthur Sheekman, Nat Perrin, George S. Kaufman, Robert E. Sherwood, d. Frank Tuttle.
COMEDY: MUSICALS: Music Comedy; Comedy-Slapstick; Rome; Dreams; Fantasies; Time Travel; Fools-Bumbling; Ancient Times
(A Funny Thing Happened on the Way to the Forum)
The Roman Spring of Mrs. Stone, 1961, 104m, ★★★½/$$, WB-7 Arts/WB, S. An American actress convalescing in Rome after her husband's death takes the help of a madame who sends her a sexy young stud named Paolo who she falls for, but true love is as elusive as a comeback. Vivien Leigh, Warren Beatty, Lotte Lenya (BSActress), Jeremy Spenser, Coral Browne, Ernest Thesiger. w. Gavin Lambert, N-adap. Tennessee Williams, d. Jose Quintero. Oscars: 1-0.
DRAMA: MELODRAMA: ROMANCE: Romance-Older Women/Younger Men; Elusive Men; Sexy Men; Infatuations; Prostitutes-Male; Aging; Actresses; Widows; Rome; Madames; Mental Illness; Nervous Breakdowns; Tennessee Williams-esque; Hidden Gems
(Sweet Bird of Youth; A Streetcar Named Desire)

Romance, 1930, 76m, ★★★/$$$$, MGM/MGM-UA. The mistress of a tycoon, herself an opera singer, tempts a man of the cloth into forsaking his vow of chastity. Greta Garbo, Lewis Stone, Gavin Gordon, Elliott Nugent, Clara Blandick, Florence Lake, Henry Armetta. w. Bess Meredyth, Edwin Justus Mayer, P-adap. Edward Sheldon, d. Clarence Brown.
MELODRAMA: ROMANCE: Romantic Drama; Opera; Romance-Reluctant; Religion; Scandals; Opera; Opera Singers; Mistresses; Romance-Triangles; Cheating Women; Priests; Virgins; Elusive Men; Female Protagonists; Female Screenwriters
(Love; Anna Christie; Rain)
Romance on the High Seas, 1948, 99m, ★★★/$$$, WB/Fox. A woman suspects her husband is up to no good on a cruise, so she sends a spy, but all may not be as shady as it seems because everyone finds someone. Jack Carson, Janis Paige, Don Defore, Doris Day, Oscar Levant, S. Z. Sakall, Eric Blore, Franklin Pangborn, Fortunio Bonanova. w. Julius J. and Philip G. Epstein, I. A. L. Diamond, d. Michael Curtiz.
COMEDY: ROMANCE: Romantic Comedy; **MUSICALS:** Musical Comedy; Musical Romance; Cheating Men; Jealousy; Misunderstandings; Ships; Singers; Romance-Triangles; Hidden Gems; Faded Hits; Ensemble Films
(Nancy Goes to Rio; High Society; Moon Over Miami)
Romancing the Stone, 1984, 106m, ★★★1/2/$$$$, 20th/CBS-Fox, PG/S-P-FN. When a romance novelist's sister is kidnapped, she (Kathleen Turner, **BActress, NYFC**) heads to South America to find her, bringing along a treasure map, and possibly living out one of her books when she meets an adventurer (Michael Douglas) who saves her. Danny DeVito, Zack Norman, Alfonso Arau. w. Diane Thomas, d. Robert Zemeckis.
ADVENTURE: COMEDY: ROMANCE: Romantic Comedy; Romantic Adventure; Comic Adventure; Fish out of Water Stories; Chase Stories; Spoofs; Romance Novelists; Romance-Bickering; Writers; Kidnappings; Treasure Hunts; Fugitives; Fugitives from a Murderer; Road Movies; Sleeper Hits
SEQUEL: Jewel of the Nile.
(American Dreamer; Jewel of the Nile)

Romanoff and Juliet, 1961, 103m, ★★1/2/$, U-I/NA. In the small country of Concordia, the Americans and Soviets vie for political control while the son and daughter of ambassadors carry on a romance on the sly. Peter Ustinov, Sandra Dee, John Gavin, Akim Tamiroff, Tamara Shayne, John Philips, Alix Talton, Peter Jones. w. d. P-adap. Peter Ustinov.
COMEDY: COMEDY DRAMA: ROMANCE: Romantic Comedy; Russians & Americans; Russians as Enemy; Kingdoms; Royalty; Revisionist Films; Feuds; Lover Family Dislikes; Cold War Era; Power Struggles; Diplomats
Romantic Comedy, 1983, 102m, ★★1/2/$, MGM-UA/MGM-UA, R/S-P. A timid New England schoolteacher helps a Broadway playwright/producer, but they don't get much writing done. Dudley Moore, Mary Steenburgen, Frances Sternhagen, Janet Eilber, Robyn Douglass, Ron Leibman. w. P-adap. Bernard Slade, d. Arthur Hiller.
COMEDY: ROMANCE: Romantic Comedy; **COMEDY DRAMA:** Romantic-Bickering; Writers; Theater Life; Romance-Mismatched Teachers; Autobiographical Stories; Stagelike Films; Forgotten Films
(Unfaithfully Yours; Best Friends)
(Ed: A big hit on Broadway, it falls flat on screen without much style or chemistry coming through)
The Romantic Englishwoman, 1975, 116m, ★★★/$, Avco-Embassy/WB, R/S-P. A middle-aged woman has an affair in Baden Baden while her husband, a novelist, is writing a parallel story at home. Glenda Jackson, Michael Caine, Helmut Berger, Marcus Richardson, Kate Nelligan, Rene Kolldehoff, Michel Lonsdale. w. Tom Stoppard, Thomas Wiseman, N-adap. Thomas Wiseman, d. Joseph Losey.
DRAMA: Character Studies; Marriage on the Rocks; Marriage Drama; Midlife Crisis; Writers; Vacations; Vacation Romance; Cheating Women; Quiet Little Films
(Sunday, Bloody Sunday; The French Lieutenant's Woman; Women in Love; Hedda)
Rome Express, 1932, 94m, ★★★1/2/ $$$, Gaumont/NA. An express train to Rome carries criminals and their potential victims. Conrad Veidt, Gordon Harker, Esther Ralston, Joan Barry,

Harold Huth, Cedric Hardwicke. w. CLifford Grey, Sidney Gilliat, Frank Vosper, Ralph Stock. d. Walter Forde.
SUSPENSE: MYSTERY: Double Crossings; Conspiracy; Missing Persons; Trains; Spies; Spy Films; Ensemble Films; Rome; British Films; Forgotten Films; Hidden Gems
(The Lady Vanishes; Night Train to Munich; Murder on the Orient Express)
Romeo & Juliet, 1936, 127m, ★★★/ $$$$, MGM/MGM-UA. Shakespeare's doomed star-crossed lovers' tale of tragedy. Leslie Howard, Norma Shearer (BActress), John Barrymore, Basil Rathbone (BSActor), Edna May Oliver, Henry Kolker, Reginald Denny. w. Talbot Jennings, P-adap. William Shakespeare, d. George Cukor. BPicture, BArt.
Romeo and Juliet, 1954, 138m, ★★★/$$$, Rank/NA. A remake with even more post-pubescent leads. Laurence Harvey, Susan Shentall, Aldo Zollo, Enzo Fiermonte, Flora Robson, Mervyn Johns, Sebastian Cabot, Giulio Garbinetti, John Gielgud. w. d. Renato Castellani.
Romeo and Juliet, 1968, 152m, ★★★★/$$$$, Par/Par, PG/S-MRN. A more realistic version of the classic romance by Shakespeare about the two young lovers (Leonard Whiting, Olivia Hussey) whose parents don't want them together. w. Franco Brusati, Masolino D'Amico, P-adap. William Shakespeare, d. Franco Zeffirelli (BDirector). BPicture, BCostumes, BCin. Oscars: 4-2.
ROMANCE: DRAMA: Romantic Drama; Romance-Doomed; **TRAGEDY:** Suicidal Tendencies; **MELODRAMA:** Suicidal Tendencies of Young People; Feuds; Family Drama; Lover; Family Dislikes; Italy; Shakespearean; Young People; Love-First; Classic Literary Adaptations; Classic Tragedy
(The Taming of the Shrew; Aaron and Angela)
Romeo Is Bleeding, 1994, 105m, ★★1/2/$, Polygram-Gramercy/MCA-U, R/P-S-EV. A down and out police detective living a secret life is assigned to transport a Russian mob girl but then is also ordered to kill her by a mobster who offers him big money. Gary Oldman, Lena Olin, Annabella Sciorra, Juliette Lewis, Roy Scheider, Will Patton. w. Hilary Henkin, d. Peter Medak.
DRAMA: Crime Drama; **SUSPENSE:** Art Film; Film Noir-Modern; Detective

Stories; Detectives in Deep; Romance with Suspect Dangerous Women; Murderers-Female; Hitwomen; Evil Women; Criminals-Female; Sexy Women; Cheating Men; Fantasies; Narrated Films; Coulda Been Good; Curiosities; Female Screenwriters
(Fallen Angels; The Hit; Criminal Law)

Romero, 1989, 105m, ★★½/$, WB/WB, PG/V. Down in El Salvador, a priest at a Catholic mission is forced by circumstances to become increasingly political the longer he stays there. Raul Julia, Richard Jordan, Ana Alicia, Eddie Velez, Alejandro Bracho, Tony Plana, Harold Gould. w. John Sacret Young, d. John Duigan.
DRAMA: Political Drama; Political Unrest; Priests; Religion; Central America; Latin People; Docudrama; Biographies; True Stories

Romper Stomper, 1992, 92m, ★★★/$$, Academy/Academy, R/EV-EP-S. In Melbourne a neo-fascist group is viewed from the inside, as merely teens who want to be involved in a group of some kind. The Vietnamese residents of their neighborhood might not agree. Russell Crowe, Daniel Pollock, Jacqueline McKenzie, Alex Scott, Leigh Russell. w. d. Geoffrey Wright.
ACTION: DRAMA: Action Drama; Social Drama; Nazi Stories; Australian Films; Vietnam; Race Relations; Bigots; Immigrants; Writer-Directors

The Rookie, 1990, 121m, ★★/$$, WB/WB, PG-13/V-P-S. A cocky young rookie cop trains with a hard-bitten older partner who teaches him how to be a cop and a man, and so on . . . Clint Eastwood, Charlie Sheen, Raul Julia, Sonia Braga, Tom Skerrit, Lara Flynn Boyle, Pepe Serna. w. Boaz Yakin, Scott Spiegel, d. Clint Eastwood.
ACTION: Action Drama; Police Stories; Mentors/Proteges; Teachers/Students; Young Men; Generation Gap
(The Dead Pool; The Presidio)

Room at the Top, 1959, 117m, ★★★★/$$$, Continental/MPI, NA. A young man (Laurence Harvey, BActor) tries to use his looks and finesse to move up the ladder from meager beginnings to the top of a factory empire, but romance may get in the way. Simone Signoret (**BActress**), Hermione Baddely (**BSActress**), Donald Wolfit, Heather Sears, Donald Houston. w. Neil Paterson (**BAScr**), N-adap. John

Braine, d. Jack Clayton (BDirector). BPicture. Oscars: 6-2.
DRAMA: ROMANCE: Kitchen Sink Drama; Romantic Drama; Social Drama; Working Class; Rich vs. Poor; Social Climbing; Class Conflicts; Romance-Clandestine; Romance-Doomed; Romance-Triangles; Romance-Choosing the Right Person; Marrying Up; Cheating Women; Sexuality; Hidden Gems; Faded Hits; British Films; Sleeper Hits
SEQUEL: Life at the Top.
(A Place in the Sun; The Heartbreak Kid; Darling)

Roommates, 1995, 99m, ★★★/$$, Hollywood/Hollywood, PG/P. A grandfather takes in his orphaned grandson and as the years go by, their love-hate relationship reverses itself as he needs to be cared for like a child himself. Peter Falk, D.B. Sweeney, Julianne Moore, Jan Rubes, Ellen Burstyn. d. Peter Yates.
MELODRAMA: COMEDY DRAMA: Grandfathers-Fascinating; Roommates; Men and Boys; Children-Adopted; Episodic Stories; Tearjerkers
(Lies My Father Told Me; I Never Sang for My Father)

Room Service, 1938, 78m, ★★★½/$$$, RKO/Turner. The Marx Brothers hole up in a hotel suite they can't pay for while they look for backers for a Broadway show they want to put up. Groucho Marx, Chico Marx, Harpo Marx, Lucille Ball, Donald MacBride, Frank Albertson, Ann Miller. w. Morrie Ryskind, P-adap. John Murray, Allen Boretz, d. William A. Seiter.
COMEDY: Comedy-Slapstick; **FARCE:** Hotels; Comedians; Ensemble Films; Marx Brothers; Theater Life; Putting on a Show; Vaudeville
(Duck Soup; Animal Crackers)

A Room with a View, 1986, 115m, ★★★★/$$$$, M-I-Cinecom/CBS-Fox, NR/MFN. When a young British woman (Helena Bonham-Carter) and her aunt (Maggie Smith, BSActress) travel to Florence, she meets a dashing young man (Julian Sands) who it turns out has mutual acquaintances in England and continues pursuing her when they return home, much to the aunt's consternation. w. Ruth Prawer Jhabvala (**BAScr**), adap. E.M. Forster, d. James Ivory (BDirector). BPicture, **BArt**, **BCostume**. Oscars: 6-3.
COMEDY DRAMA: ROMANCE: Comedy of Manners; Comedy-Light; Ensemble

Films; Violence-Sudden; Romance-Boy Wants Girl; Romance-Reluctant; Class Conflicts; Rich vs. Poor; Coming of Age; Lovers Family Dislikes; British Films; Edwardian Era; Sleeper Hits
(Where Angels Fear to Tread; Howards End; Maurice; A Month by the Lake)

Rooster Cogburn, 1975, 108m, ★★★/$$$, U/MCA-U, PG/V. A craggy old marshal reluctantly accepts the aid of a religious woman in hunting down the trail of a ruthless band of outlaws. John Wayne, Katharine Hepburn, Anthony Zerbe, Richard Jordan, John McIntyre, Strother Martin. w. Martin Julien, d. Stuart Miller.
ADVENTURE: ROMANCE: WESTERNS: Romance-Bickering; Romance-Opposites Attract; Romance-Elderly; Elderly People; One Last Time; Missionaries; River Trauma
REMAKE/RETREAD: The African Queen.
SEQUEL TO: True Grit.
(The African Queen; True Grit)

Roots, 1977, 570m, ★★★★/$$$$$, ABC-WB/WB; **Roots, the Next Generation**, 1979, 685m, ★★★/$$$, ABC-WB/WB. The story of author Alex Haley's family from their roots in Africa, through their years of slavery. Levar Burton, Edward Asner, Chuck Connors, Lloyd Bridges, O.J. Simpson, Sandy Duncan, Ben Vereen, Cicely Tyson, Lorne Greene, Burl Ives. Both multiple Emmy winners. d. David Greene.
DRAMA: Episodic Stories; Historical Drama; Family Drama; Sagas; Black Casts; Black men; Black Women; Slavery; Black vs. White Southerns; Plantation Life; Miniseries; TV Movies; Blockbusters
SEQUEL: Roots, the Gift.
(Roots, the Gift; Queen; Mandingo)
(Ed: Several original Roots episodes have held all-time ratings records for twenty years)

Roots, the Gift, 1988, 94m, ★★½/$$, WB/WB. Kunte Kinte tries to escape via the underground railroad and winds up helping others to freedom. Louis Gossett, Jr., Levar Burton, Michael Learned, Kate Mulgrew, Shaun Cassidy. d. Kevin Hooks.
MELODRAMA: Christmas; Slavery; Saving Someone; Black Casts; Black Men; Black Directors; TV Movies

The Roots of Heaven, 1958, 125m, ★★½/$$, 20th/NA. A nature lover in central Africa in the fifties tries to protect the elephants from poachers who slaugh-

ter them for their tusks. Trevor Howard, Juliette Greco, Paul Lukas, Herbert Lom, Gregoire Aslan, Friedrich Ledebur. w. Romain Gary, Patrick Leigh-Fermor, N-adap. Romain Gary, d. John Huston.
DRAMA: Animal Rights; Hunters; Safaris; Africa; Nature-Back to; Forgotten Films
(Elephant Walk; Born Free; Hatari)
Rope, 1948, 80m, ★★★/$, RKO/MCA-U. A homosexual couple of college boys murders a friend merely to prove the crackpot theory of one of their professors. They then throw a party including the professor and serve drinks from atop the trunk in which the body is hidden. James Stewart, John Dall, Farley Granger, Joan Chandler, Cedric Hardwicke, Constance Collier, Douglas Dick. w. Arthur Laurents, P-adap. Patrick Hamilton, d. Alfred Hitchcock.
SUSPENSE: MURDER: MURDER MYS-TERY: MYSTERY: Detective Stories; Gay Men; Murderers-Homosexual; True Stories; Mental Illness; One-Day Stories; Cult Films; Hitchcockian
(Swoon; Compulsion; Rear Window)
(Ed: Based on the Leopold and Loeb case of Chicago)
Rope of Sand, 1949, 105m, ★★1/2/$$, Par/NA. In a private, guarded area in South Africa, several international sleuths search for hidden diamonds. Burt Lancaster, Paul Henreid, Claude Rains, Peter Lorre, Corinne Calvet, Sam Jaffe. w. Walter Doniger, d. William Dieterle.
ADVENTURE: Treasure Hunts; Jewel Thieves; **ROMANCE:** Romantic Drama; Detective Stories; Journies; Quests; South Africa; Africa; Desert Settings; Forgotten Films
(King Solomon's Mines; Gold)
Rosalie Goes Shopping, 1989, 93m, ★★★/$, Vidmark/Vidmark, PG. A German woman living in Arizona maxes out all of her myriad credit cards in order to keep her family in consumer goods. Marianne Sagebrecht, Brad Davis, Judge Reinhold, William Harlander, Erika Blumberger. w. Percy Adlon, Eleonore Adlon, Christopher Doherty, d. Percy Adlon.
COMEDY DRAMA: SATIRE: Small-town Life; Housewives; Fish out of Water Stories; Germans; Arkansas; Rednecks; Farm Life; Losing it All; American Dream; Obsessions
(Sugarbaby; Baghdad Cafe)

The Rosary Murders, 1987, 105m, ★★1/2/$, Samuel Goldwyn/Goldwyn, R/V. A psychopathic murderer, upset about his harsh Catholic upbringing, kills officials of the church in grizzly ways parodying the morbid ceremonies of the hated institution. Donald Sutherland, Charles Durning, Josef Sommer, Belinda Bauer. w. Elmore Leonard, Fred Walton, d. Fred Walton.
SUSPENSE: MURDER: MYSTERY: MURDER MYSTERY: Priests; Religion; Revenge
(Seven; Dead Certain)
The Rose, 1979, 134m, ★★★1/2/$$$, 20th/CBS-Fox, R/P-S. The slow descent into Hell of a rock singer, aided by her manager and his abetting of her drug habit, loosely based on the life of Janis Joplin. Bette Midler (BActress), Alan Bates, Frederic Forrest (BSActor), Harry Dean Stanton, Barry Primus. w. Bill Kerby, Bo Goodman, d. Mark Rydell. BEdit, BSound. Oscars: 4-0.
DRAMA: Music Movies; Rock Stars; Singers; Biographies-Fictional; Suicidal Tendencies; Drugs-Addictions; Lesbians; Romance-Doomed; Bodyguards; Music Dies; Nostalgia; Female Protagonists; Faded Hits; Underrated
(A Star is Born [1976]; The Bodyguard; Lady Sings the Blues; For the Boys)
(Ed: Midler is fantastic and the film is realistic, something which was cast aside for the vaguely similar *The Bodyguard*)
Rosebud, 1975, 126m, ★★/$, UA/MGM-UA. The Palestine Liberation Army kidnaps a group of wealthy girls and extorts money from their families. Peter O'Toole, Richard Attenborough, Cliff Gorman, Claude Dauphin, John V. Lindsay, Peter Lawford, Raf Vallone. w. Erik Lee Preminger, N-adap. Joan Hemingway, Paul Bonnecarrere, d. Otto Preminger.
SUSPENSE: ACTION: Kidnappings; Middle East; Rich People; Women in Jeopardy; Flops-Major
(The Little Drummer Girl; The Wind and the Lion)
Rose Marie, 1936, 113m, ★★1/2/$$$, MGM/MGM-UA. An outlaw runs into the woods and is caught by a heroic Canadian Mountie, who also wins the heart of his beloved. Nelson Eddy, Jeanette MacDonald, James Stewart, Reginald Owen, Allan Jones, Gilda Gray, Alan Mowbray, Una O'Connor, David

Niven. w. Frances Goodrich, Albert Hackett, Alice Duer Miller, P-adap. Otto Harbach, Oscar Hammerstein II, d. W. S. Van Dyke.
Rose Marie, 1954, 115m, ★★1/2/$$, MGM/MGM-UA. A remake of the above with less charisma in the cast. Howard Keel, Ann Blyth, Fernando Lamas, Bert Lahr, Marjorie Main, Ray Collins. w. Ronald Millar, d. Mervyn Le Roy.
MELODRAMA: ROMANCE: MUSICALS: Musical Drama; Musical-Operettas; Musical Romance; Canada; Police Stories; Fugitives from the Law; Romance-Boy Wants Girl; Faded Hits
(Firefly; The Chocolate Soldier)
Rosemary's Baby, 1968, 137m, ★★★1/2/$$$$$, WB/WB, R/S. A new wife (Mia Farrow) living with her actor husband (John Cassavetes) in a creepy apartment building soon begins having horrible nightmares about the conception of her child, involving what is perhaps Satan. Ruth Gordon (BSActress), Charles Grodin. w. Roman Polanski (BAScr), N-adap. Ira Levin, d. Roman Polanski. Oscars: 2-1.
SUSPENSE: HORROR: MYSTERY: Psychological Thriller; Conspiracy; Friends as Enemies; Women in Jeopardy; Satanism; Satan-Child of; Mothers-Struggling; Newlyweds; Babies-Having; Rape/Rapists; Illusions/Hallucinations; Dream Sequences; Nightmares; Unbelieved; Insane-Plot to Make; Poisons; Illusions Destroyed; Houses-Creepy; Elderly Women; Selling One's Soul; Occult; Witchcraft; Young Women; Female Protagonists; Sleeper Hits
SEQUEL: Look What's Happened to Rosemary's Baby (Rosemary's Baby 2).
(The Omen; The Seventh Sign; It's Alive)
(Ed: Talk about flipsides [of the immaculate conception]. What good does it do for her to tell these people to "Go to hell"? At the birth, the question "What is it?" was never more appropriate. "This isn't a nightmare-this is really happening!")
Rosencrantz and Guildenstern Are Dead, 1990, 118m, ★★1/2/$, Cineplex-U/MCA-U, PG-13/P. While the events of the play *Hamlet* take place offstage, two of its characters bide their time while waiting to help their Danish prince. Gary Oldman, Tim Roth, Richard Dreyfuss, Joanna Roth, Iain Glen, Donald Sumpter, Joanna Miles, Ian Richardson. w. d., P-adap. Tom Stoppard.

COMEDY DRAMA: SATIRE: Theater Life; Movies within Movies; Behind the Scenes; Revisionist Films; Art Films; Princes; Friendships-Male; Middle Ages (Hamlet; The Dresser)

The Rose of Washington Square, 1939, 86m, ★★★/$$$, 20th. A Broadway comedienne is beloved by her fans and seems to "have it all," but at home she must suffer abuse from her loutish husband. Alice Faye, Tyrone Power, Al Jolson, Hobart Cavanaugh, William Frawley, Joyce Compton, Louis Prima and his band. w. Nunnally Johnson, d. Gregory Ratoff.

MELODRAMA: ROMANCE: Marriage Drama; Marriage on the Rocks; Biographies; Hollywood Biographies; Biographies-Fictional; True Stories; Theater Life; Actresses; Abused Men; Gambling; Forgotten Films; Faded Hits
REMAKE/RETELLING: Funny Girl
(Funny Girl; Funny Lady; Star!)

The Rose Tattoo, 1955, 117m, ★★★1/2/$$$, Par/CBS-Fox. When an Italian woman's husband is killed, she (Anna Magnani, **BActress**) discovers he's also been cheating and her undying loyalty is shaken, and when a free-wheeling young man (Burt Lancaster) comes into her life and gets a rose tattoo just like her husband had, she has to decide whether to move on or not. Marisa Pavan (BSActress). w. John Michael Hayes, P-adap. Tennessee Williams, d. Daniel Mann (BDirector). BPicture, BOScore, BEdit, **BB&WCin, BB&WArt.** Oscars: 8-3.

DRAMA: MELODRAMA: ROMANCE: Romantic Comedy; Romance-Reluctant; Starting Over; Widows; Cheating Men; Italians; Wild People; Free Spirits; Southerns; Mississippi; Fish out of Water Stories; Tennessee Williams-esque
(Alice Doesn't Live Here Anymore; The Fugitive Kind; Orpheus Descending; Wild is the Wind)

Rosie, 1967, 98m, ★★/$, U/MCA-U. A wealthy old woman is spending money so fast that her daughters, fearing their inheritance will dissappear, consider having her committed. Rosalind Russell, Brian Aherne, Sandra Dee, Vanessa Brown, Audrey Meadows, James Farentino, Leslie Nielsen, Margaret Hamilton, Reginald Owen, Juanita Moore, Virginia Grey. w. Samuel Taylor, P-adap. Ruth Gordon, P-adap. Philippe

Heriat (*Les Joies de la Famille*), d. David Lowell Rich.

COMEDY DRAMA: Mothers & Daughters; Rich People; Losing it All; Inheritances at Stake; Asylums; Committed-Wrongly; Nervous Breakdowns; Midlife Crisis
(Auntie Mame; Gypsy; Interiors)

Rough Cut, 1980, 112m, ★★1/2/$$, Par/Par, PG/S-V. An old inspector at Scotland Yard is about to retire when his nemesis, a jewel thief, finally convinces him to turn to the other side of the law. Burt Reynolds, Lesley-Anne Down, David Niven, Timothy West, Patrick Magee, Joss Ackland. w. Francis Burns, N-adap. Derek Lambert (*Touch the Lion's Paw*), d. Don Siegel.

COMEDY DRAMA: ROMANCE: Romantic Comedy; Heist Stories; Jewel Thieves; Police Corruption; England; Forgotten Films; Coulda Been Good
(Hustle; Malone; Heat; To Catch a Thief)
(Ed: All class, a change for Reynolds, but no plot)

Roujin-Z, 1995, 80m, ★★★/$, Central Park Media, NR. A wild animated tale from Japan centered around nuclear powered beds for the elderly raises many issues about how senior citizens are treated as half-dead and like numbers. Voices: Allan Wegner, Toni Barry, Barbara Barnes, Adam Henderson, Jana Carpenter, Ian Thompson, John Jay Fitzgerald. w. Katsuhiro Otomod, d. Toshiaki Hontani.

Cartoon **CHILDREN'S SCI-FI:** Japanese Films; Cult Films

Round Midnight, 1986, 133m, ★★★/$$, WB/WB, R/S-P. Bud Powell and Lester Young play their cool jazz in the bars of Paris in this pseudo-biography. Dexter Gordon (BActor), Francois Cluzet, Gabrielle Haker, John Berry, Martin Scorsese. w. Bertrand Tavernier, David Rayfiel, d. Bertrand Tavernier. **BOScore.** Oscars: 2-1.

DRAMA: Art Films; Jazz Life; Biographies; Black Men; Americans Abroad; Paris; Quiet Little Films; Sleeper Hits; French Films
(Bird; Leadbelly)

The Rounders, 1965, 85m, ★★/$, MGM/MGM-UA. Two outlaws on the verge of retiring always have to pull one more job. Henry Fonda, Glenn Ford, Chill Wills, Sue Ann Langdon, Edgar Buchanan. w. d. Burt Kennedy, N-adap. Max Evans.

WESTERNS: Friendships-Male; One Last Time; Retirement; Heist Stories; Bank Robberies

Roustabout, 1964, 101m, ★★/$$, Par/Par. A carnival is joined by a wanderer who happens to sing like a famous rock star and proceeds to charm everyone with his effusive personality. Elvis Presley, Barbara Stanwyck, Sue Ann Langdon, Joan Freeman, Leif Erickson. w. Allan Weiss, Anthony Lawrence, d. John Rich.

COMEDY DRAMA: Music Movies; Singers; Circus Life; Elvis Movies; Curiosities; Camp

Roxanne, 1987, 107m, ★★★1/2/$$$, Col/RCA-Col, PG-13/S. A fireman with an enormous schnoz loves a beautiful and intelligent astronomer, but agrees to help his dumb but hunky friend by writing her love letters in his name. She falls in love with the writer of the letters, thinking it's the hunk. Will she ever know who the real author is? Steve Martin, Daryl Hannah, Rick Rossovich, Shelley Duvall, John Kapelos, Fred Willard, Michael J. Pollard. w. Steve Martin (**BASer**), P-adap. Edmond Rostand (*Cyrano de Bergerac*), d. Fred Schepisi. Oscars: 1-0.

COMEDY: ROMANCE: Romantic Comedy; Romance-Boy Wants Girl; Romance-Reluctant; Nerds & Babes; Undercover; Impostors; Body Parts; Romance-Older Men/Younger Women; Fires; Small-town Life; Revisionist Films
REMAKE: Cyrano deBergerac
(The Truth About Cats & Dogs; The Front)

Roxie Hart, 1942, 72m, ★★1/2/$$, 20th/NA. A Chicago gangster moll takes the blame for a murder she didn't commit, and later gets revenge on the lout who asked her to do it. Ginger Rogers, George Montgomery, Adolphe Menjou, Lynne Overman, Nigel Bruce, Spring Byington, Sara Allgood, William Fawley. w. Nunnally Johnson, P-adap. Maurine Watkins (*Chicago*), d. William Wellman.

DRAMA: Crime Drama; Mob Stories; Accused Unjustly; Mob Girls; **MURDER:** Revenge; Double Crossings; Liars; Framed?; Chicago; Roaring 20s; 1920s

The Royal Family of Broadway, 1930, 82m, ★★★/$$, Par/NA. A satire of the Barrymore family, with all of their excesses and drunken carrying-on. Fredric March (BActor), Henrietta Crosman, Ina Claire, Mary Brian,

Charles Starrett, Frank Conroy. w. Herman J. Mankiewicz, Gertrude Purcell, P-adap. George S. Kaufman, Edna Ferber, d. George Cukor. Oscars: 1-0.

COMEDY: SATIRE: Theater Life; Family Comedy; Actors; Actresses; Biographies-Fictional; Forgotten Films; Curiosities; Hidden Gems
(The Barkleys of Broadway; The Guardsman)

Royal Flash, 1975, 118m, ★★/$, 20th/NA. A flashy dandy in the 19th Century meets all the major figures of the era in his swashbuckling adventures around the world. Malcolm McDowell, Oliver Reed, Alan Bates, Florinda Bolkan, Britt Ekland, Lionel Jeffries, Tom Bell, Joss Ackland, Leon Greene, Alastair Sim. w., N-adap. George Macdonald Fraser, d. Richard Lester.

COMEDY: ADVENTURE: Comic Adventure; **SATIRE:** Journeys; Historical Drama; Swashbucklers; 1800s; Curiosities; Good Premise Unfulfilled
(Bill & Ted's Excellent Adventure; Crossed Swords; The Three Musketeers)

A Royal Scandal, 1945, 94m, ★★/$, 20th/NA. Catherine the Great's many affairs which scandalized the Russian court. Tallulah Bankhead, Charles Coburn, Anne Baxter, William Eythe, Vincent Price, Mischa Auer, Sig Rumann, Vladimir Sokoloff. w. Edwin Justus Mayer, P-adap. Lajos Biro, Melchior Lengyel, d. Otto Preminger.

DRAMA: MELODRAMA: Queens; Russians; Royalty; Cheating Women; Promiscuity; Historical Drama; Costume Drama
(Great Catherine; Young Catherine; Catherine the Great; Rasputin and the Empress)

Royal Wedding, 1951, 93m, ★★★/$$$, MGM/MGM-UA. The Prince of Wales finds a bride and the press congregate for their elaborate nuptials. Fred Astaire, Jane Powell, Sarah Churchill, Peter Lawford, Keenan Wynn. w. Alan Jay Lerner, d. Stanley Donen.

MUSICALS: COMEDY: Musical Comedy; **ROMANCE:** Romantic Comedy; Musical Romance; Costume Drama; Romance-Boy Wants Girl; Princes; Royalty; Marriage-Impending; Weddings; Faded Hits; Hidden Gems
(Funny Face; Paris Holiday; Holiday in Mexico; Roman Holiday)

RPM (Revolutions Per Minute), 1970, 97m, ★★/$, Col/Col, R/P-S-V. A leftist professor almost incites his students to revolution. Anthony Quinn, Ann-Margret, Gary Lockwood, Paul Winfield, Alan Hewitt. w. Erich Segal, d. Stanley Kramer.

DRAMA: Political Unreast; Political Drama; Rebels; Professors; College Life; 1970s; Riots
(The Strawberry Statement; Getting Straight; The Revolutionary)

Rubin & Ed, 1992, 82m, ★★★/$, Ind/Col, PG-13/P. A real estate salesman wanna-be wants to rip-off his friend, but the friend wants him to help bury his cat which died eons ago—which lands them in the desert somehow. Crispin Glover, Howard Hesseman, Karen Black. w. d. Trent Harris.

COMEDY: Black Comedy; Comedy-Light; Eccentric People; Nerds; Cats; Pet Stories; Desert Settings; Buddy Films; Curiosities; Writer-Directors
(Little Voices; Tapeheads)

Ruby, 1992, 101m, ★★1/2/$, Col/Col, R/P-V. The life of Jack Ruby, the Texas nightclub owner who killed Lee Harvey Oswald, is examined, with special focus on his mob and CIA connections. Danny Aiello, Sherilyn Fenn, Frank Orsatti, Jeffrey Nordling, Jane Hamilton, Maurice Bernard, Joe Viterelli. w., P-adap. Stephen Davis (Love Field), d. John MacKenzie.

DRAMA: MYSTERY: MURDER: MURDER MYSTERY: Assassion Plots; Biographies; True or Not?; Mob Stories; JFK Stories; Conspiracy; Strippers
(JFK)

Ruby Gentry, 1952, 82m, ★★★/$$, 20th/Fox. A woman raised as a male by her messed-up parents for mysterious reasons rebels as a young girl, but eventually loses her lover in a shootout and becomes a sea captain. Jennifer Jones, Charlton Heston, Karl Malden, Josephine Hutchinson. w. Sylvia Richards, d. King Vidor.

MELODRAMA: Power-Rise to; Rebels; Women as Men; Sexy Women; Revenge; Southerns; Camp; Curiosities; Forgotten Films; Feisty Females; Female Protagonists; Episodic Stories; Female Screenwriters
(Spitfire; Sylvia Scarlett; Yentl)
(Ed: What?! Pure Southern slapstick melodrama)

Ruby in Paradise, 1993, 115m, ★★★/$$, Republic/Republic, R/S-P. A girl goes to Florida and gets a job in a shop where she is constantly hit on by the owner's son and other beach studs. Soon she decides to keep to herself. Ashley Judd, Todd Field, Bentley Mitchum, Dorothy Lyman. w.d. Victor Nunez.

DRAMA: Character Studies; Young Women; Coming of Age; Beach Movies; Florida; Southerns; Female Protagonists; Sleeper Hits; Writer-Directors
(Desert Bloom; Sweet Lorraine)

Rude Awakening, 1989, 101m, ★★/$, Russo-Vestron/Vestron, Live, R/P-S. Two hippies hide out in Central America in a fog of pot and good intentions, then return to late-eighties America, disgusted at the materialism and corruption they encounter. Cheech Marin, Eric Roberts, Julie Hagerty, Robert Carradine, Buck Henry, Louise Lasser, Cindy Williams. w. Neil Levy, Richard LaGravenese, d. Aaron Russo, David Greenwalt.

COMEDY: SATIRE: Hippies; Time Sleepers; 1960s; Fish out of Water Stories; Good Premise Unfulfilled
(Flashback; Shrimp on the Barbie)

Rudy, 1993, 112m, ★★1/2/$$, Col/Col, PG. A short, underweight boy dreams of being on the Notre Dame football team and persists for years. Sean Astin, Ned Beatty, Lili Taylor, Charles S. Dutton, Jason Miller, Robert Prosky. w. Angelo Pizzo, d. David Anspaugh.

MELODRAMA: Dreams; Football; College Life; Sports Movies; Underdog Stories; True Stories; Biographies; Ordinary People Stories
(The Karate Kid; Paper Lion; Knute Rockne)

The Ruggles of Red Gap, 1935, 90m, ★★★1/2/$$$, Par/. A rancher out West hires a British butler, and the two very different men have a great effect on each other and the members of the rancher's family. Charles Laughton, Mary Boland, Charles Ruggles, ZaSu Pitts, Roland Young, Leila Hyams. w. Walter de Leon, Harlan Thompson, Humphrey Pearson, N-adap. Harry Leon Wilson, d. Leo McCarey.

COMEDY: Fish out of Water Stories; Servants; Family Comedy; **WESTERNS:** Western Comedy; Rural Life; Cattle Ranchers; Faded Hits; Hidden Gems; Snobs vs. Slobs
REMAKE: Fancy Pants.

(Fancy Pants; The Shakiest Gun in the West)

Rules of the Game, 1939, 110m, ★★★★/$$, Ind/Nos. Near the beginning of World War II, French aristocrats have one last romp before tanks roll in. Marcel Dalio, Nora Gregor, Jean Renoir, Julien Carette, Gaston Modot, Mila Parely. w. d. Jean Renoir.

COMEDY DRAMA: SATIRE: Rich People-Decadent; FARCE: Farce-Bedroom; Ensemble Films; Servants; Class Conflicts; Allegorical Films; French Films; Film History; Writer-Directors; Hidden Gems

RETREAD: Scenes from the Class Struggle in Beverly Hills.

(Dinner at Eight; Scenes from the Class Struggle in Beverly Hills; The Discreet Charm of the Bourgeoisie)

The Ruling Class, 1972, 155m, ★★★/$$, Avco-Embassy/Embassy, PG/P-S. The megalomaniacal Mad Jack becomes king, succeeding his father, the Earl of Gurney, a fetishistic pervert. Peter O'Toole (BActor), Harry Andrews, Arthur Lowe, Alastair Sim, Coral Browne, Michael Bryant. w., P-adap. Peter Barnes, d. Peter Medak. Oscars: 1-0.

COMEDY: DRAMA: SATIRE: Jesus Christ; Mental Illness; Impostors; Royalty; Inheritances at Stake; Hidden Gems; Curiosities; Stagelike Films; Sexual Problems; Jack the Ripper; Eccentric People; Free Spirits; Wild People

Rumble Fish, 1983, 94m, B&W, ★★★/$, U/MCA-U, PG/V. In Oklahoma in the fifties, a sensitive kid who works in a pet store deals with pressure to join a gang and identifies with the pugnacious fish of the title that even fights its own reflection. Matt Dillon, Mickey Rourke, Diane Lane, Dennis Hopper, Diana Scarwid. w. d. Francis Ford Coppola, N-adap. S. E. Hinton.

DRAMA: Film Noir-Modern; Gangs-Street; Midwestern Life; Cult Films; Coming of Age; Teenagers; Teenage Movies; Young Men

(The Outsiders; Tex; Five Corners; The Wanderers)

Run, 1991, 91m, ★/$, Hollywood/Hollywood, R/S-V. A dopey, supposedly brilliant law student, drives a car to to Atlantic City and winds up on the lam from the mob when he kisses the wrong girl. Patrick Dempsey, Kelly Preston. d. Geoff Burrowes.

SUSPENSE: Fugitives from the Mob; Mob Stories; Innocent Bystanders; Chase Stories; Unintentionally Funny

(The Fugitive; Three Days of the Condor)

(Ed: Another stinker from the Dempsey Dumpster. Goofy like a comedy, but not a comedy. Cliches abound and scenes are straight of other fugitive flicks like *Three Days of the Condor*. You pray the "hero" will get what his stupidity deserves. Take the title's advice and run-away from it)

Run for the Sun, 1956, 99m, ★★1/2/$, UA/NA. Two writers, one a man and one a woman, find themselves on the run from vicious Nazis and hiding in the jungles of Mexico. Richard Widmark, Jane Greer, Trevor Howard. w. Dudley Nichols, Roy Boulting, d. Roy Boulting.

ACTION: Chase Stories; Nazi Stories; Mexico; Jungle Life; Forgotten Films

REMAKE OF: The Most Dangerous Game, Game of Death..

(Most Dangerous Game; Sniper; Game of Death; The Boys from Brazil)

A Run for Your Money, 1949, 83m, ★★1/2/$$, Ealing/NA. A group of rowdy Welsh fans of their local rugby team go to London for the big match and get into a lot of trouble with fans of the London team and other locals they encounter. Alec Guinness, Meredith Edwards, Moira Lister, Donald Houston, Hugh Griffith, Clive Morton, Joyce Grenfell. w. Richard Hughes, Charles Frend, Leslie Norman, d. Charles Frend.

COMEDY: FARCE: Chase Stories; Multiple Stories; Interwoven Stories; Sports Movies; British Films

Run Silent Run Deep, 1958, 93m, ★★1/2/$$, UA/MGM-UA. Tensions rise in the claustrophobic atmosphere of a submarine off the coast of Tokyo. Clark Gable, Burt Lancaster, Jack Warden, Brad Dexter, Nick Cravat, Joe Maross, H. M. Wynant. w. John Gay, d. Robert Wise.

DRAMA: War Stories; Submarines; World War II Stories; Power Struggles; Men in Conflict

(Das Boot; Gray Lady Down; Crimson Tide)

(Ed: A much better title than a movie)

Runaway, 1984, 100m, ★★/$$, Tri-Star/Col, PG-13/P-V. An inventor lets his robot escape the lab before it's completely perfected and must find it before it does real damage. Tom Selleck, Cynthia Rhodes, Gene L. Simmons,

Kirstie Alley, Stan Shaw. w. d. Michael Crichton.

ACTION: SCI-FI: Robots; Experiments; Chase Stories; Race Against Time; Forgotten Films; Rogue Plots; Spiders; Frankenstein Stories; Writer-Directors (Man's Best Friend; Hardware)

Runaway Train, 1985, 111m, ★★/$$, Cannon/MGM-UA, R/P. Prisoners being transported through the Alaskan wilderness take over a train whose brakes have failed. Jon Voight (BActor), Eric Roberts (BSActor), Rebecca DeMornay, Kyle T. Heffner. w. Djordje Milicevic, Paul Zindel, Edward Bunker, (Screenplay)-adap. Akira Kurosawa, d. Andrei Konchalovsky. BEdit. Oscars: 3-0.

DRAMA: ACTION: Action Drama; Trains; Race Against Time; Snow Settings; Disaster Stories; Prison Escapes; Hidden Gems

(Ed: The performanances are almost caricatures, but worked well enough for Oscar)

The Runner Stumbles, 1979, 110m, ★★/$, MSP-20th/Fox. In the 20s, a nun is murdered, and a priest in her parish is suspected, since it was known that they had an attraction for each other. Dick Van Dyke, Kathleen Quinlan, Maureen Stapleton, Ray Bolger, Tammy Grimes, Beau Bridges. w., P-adap. Milan Stitt, d. Stanley Kramer.

DRAMA: MELODRAMA: MURDER: Accused Unjustly; Framed?; Priests; Nuns; Romance-Clandestine; True Stories; Coulda Been Good

(I Confess; The Rosary Murders)

The Running Man, 1963, 103m, ★★1/2/$$, Col/NA. A commercial airline pilot fakes his own death and goes to Spain to rendezvous with his wife after she collects on his life insurance policy. Laurence Harvey, Alan Bates, Lee Remick, Felix Aylmer, Eleanor Summerfield, Allan Cuthbertson. w. John Mortimer, N-adap. Shelley Smith (*The Ballad of the Running Man*), d. Carol Reed.

SUSPENSE: MURDER: MYSTERY: MURDER MYSTERY: Deaths-Faked; Pilots-Airline; Spain; Insurance Scams; Perfect Crimes; Fugitives from the Law

The Running Man, 1987, 101m, ★★★/$$$, Tri-Star/Col-Tri, Vestron, PG-13/V-P. In the future, a game show hits the airwaves in which the contestants must run from professional killers through the streets of L.A. Arnold Schwarzenegger,

Maria Conchita Alonso, Yaphet Kotto, Jim Brown, Jesse Ventura, Erland Van Lidth, Marvin J. McIntyre, Mick Fleetwood, Richard Dawson. w. Steven E. de Souza, N-adap. Stephen King, d. Paul Michael Glaser.

ACTION: Chase Stories; **SCI-FI:** TV Life; Futuristic Films; Hitmen; Fugitives from a Murderer; Games; Game Shows; Mindgames; Race Against Time
(Most Dangerous Game; Rollerball; Logan's Run)

Running Mates, 1992, 88m, ★★★/$$$, HBO/HBO, PG-13/S-P. When a politician runs for the presidency, his wife has some problems with it-and he has some problems with her, especially when the long-forgotten sixties short film of her rolling naked in a flag turns up. Diane Keaton, Ed Harris, Ed Begley, Jr., Ben Masters, Russ Tamblyn. w. A. L. Appling, d. Michael Lindsay-Hogg.

COMEDY: Political Satire; **SATIRE:** Marriage Comedy; Political Campaigns; Politicians; Politicans' Wives; Presidents; Marriage on the Rocks; Scandals; Coulda Been Great; Hidden Gems; TV Movies
COMIC FLIPSIDE: of State of the Union.
(Speechless)

Running on Empty, 1988, 116m, ★★★1/2/$, Lorimar-WB/WB, PG-13/P-S. A couple running from the FBI (Christine Lahti, Judd Hirsch) for a bombing in the 60s has to create new identities for themselves constantly, but when their music prodigy son (River Phoenix, BSActor) wants to attend Juilliard, he may have to part ways with them to have a future of his own. Martha Plimpton, Ed Crowley, David Margulies. w. Naomi Foner (BOScr), d. Sidney Lumet. Oscars: 2-0.

DRAMA: MELODRAMA: Family Drama; Fugitives; Fugitives from the Law; Accused Unjustly; Government as Enemy; FBI Agents; Terrorists; Hippies; Coming of Age; Love-First; Young Men; Musicians; Parents vs. Children; Pianists; Quiet Little Films; Hidden Gems
(The Revolutionary; Katherine)

Running Scared, 1986, 106m, ★★★/$$$, MGM-UA/MGM-UA, PG-13/P-V. Two mismatched cops are partnered up to find a crook and bumble their way to success in their mission. Gregory Hines, Billy Crystal, Steven Bauer, Joe Pantoliano, Tracy Reed. w. Guy Devore,

Jimmy Huston, d. Peter Hyams.
COMEDY: Police Stories; Buddy Cops; Buddy Films; Police Comedy; Comedy of Errors; Friendships-Interracial; Black & White Cops; Accident Prone; Chicago
(Lethal Weapon; Pure Luck)
(Ed: Billy Crystal's first feature film hit)

Rush, 1992, 120m, ★★★/$$, MGM/MGM-UA, R/P-S-V. In the 70s, two undercover cops on a mission to infiltrate a drug ring can't escape becoming addicts themselves. Jason Patrick, Jennifer Jason Leigh, Sam Elliott, Max Perlich, Gregg Allmann, Tony Frank. w. Pete Dexter, NF-adap. Kim Wozencraft, d. Lili Fini Zanuck.

DRAMA: Crime Drama; Police Stories; Undercover; Drugs-Dealing; Drugs-Addictions; Enemy-Sympathizing with; Female Protagonists; Law Officers-Female; Texas; Rednecks; Female Directors
(Deep Cover; Serpico; The Prince of the City)

The Russia House, 1990, 123m, ★★1/2/$$, MGM-UA/MGM-UA, PG-13/S-P. A former spy (Sean Connery) is brought out of retirement to go to Russia and discover what a woman working in publishing (Michelle Pfeiffer) has discovered-her comrades are up to something sinister. Roy Scheider, James Fox, John Mahoney, Ken Russel, Klaus Maria Brandauer. w. Tom Stoppard, N-adap. J. LeCarre, d. Fred Schepisi.

DRAMA: Spy Films; **ROMANCE: MYS-TERY:** Romance-Older Men/Younger Women; Spies; Undercover; Mindgames; Russia; Communists; KGB Agents; CIA Agents; Cold War Era
(The Spy Who Came in from the Cold; The Looking Glass War)
(Ed: Plodding, but can hold one's interest if so inclined)

The Russians Are Coming, The Russians Are Coming, 1966, 126m, ★★★1/2/$$$$, UA/CBS-Fox. A Soviet submarine must make an emergency landing on a resort island off the coast of Connecticut, and chaos and hilarious panic follow in their wake. Carl Reiner, Eva Marie Saint, Alan Arkin (BActor), John Philip Law, Paul Ford, Tessie O'Shea, Brian Keith, Jonathan Winters, Theodore Bikel. w. William Rose (BAScr), N-adap. Nathaniel Benchley (*The Off-Islanders*), d. Norman Jewison.

BPicture, BEdit. Oscars: 4-0.

COMEDY: FARCE: Comedy of Errors; Cold War Error; What If . . . Stories; Russians as Enemy; Submarines; Islands; Small-town Life; American Myth; Patriotic Films; Sleeper Hits
(It's a Mad, Mad, Mad, Mad World; Cold Turkey)

Russkies, 1987, 98m, ★★/$, WB/WB, PG. Two kids find a Russian sailor who's defected and become pals on the waterfront. Whip Hubley, Leaf Phoenix, Peter Billingsley. d. Rick Rosenthal.

CHILDREN'S: ADVENTURE: Saving Someones; Russians; Fugitives from the Law; Fugitives-Harboring
(Tiger Bay)

Ruthless People, 1986, 97m, ★★★1/2/$$$$, Touchstone/Touchstone, R/EP-S. When a rich man's wife (Bette Midler) is kidnapped, he (Danny DeVito) may not want to pay the ransom to get her back, much to the glee of his mistress (Anita Morris). Judge Reinhold, Helen Slater, Bill Pullman. w. Dane Launer, d. David and Jerry Zucker.

COMEDY: FARCE: Kidnappings; Mean Women; Mean Men; Rich People; Mistresses; Inheritances at Stake; Enemy-Sympathizing with; Kidnappers-Sympathizing with; Ensemble Films; Sleeper Hits
REMAKE/RETREAD OF: The Happening
(The Happening; Down and Out in Beverly Hills; Outrageous Fortune; Big Business)

Ryan's Daughter, 1970, 206m, ★★★/$$$$, MGM/MGM-UA, PG/S. In 1916 Ireland, a British officer steals the heart of the wife of a local schoolmaster, much to the consternation of the locals. Sarah Miles (BActress), Robert Mitchum, Chris Jones, John Mills (**BSActor**), Trevor Howard, Leo McKern. w. Robert Bolt, d. David Lean. **BCin**, BSound. Oscars: 4-2.

DRAMA: Epics; Ireland; Sagas;
ROMANCE: Romantic Drama; Lover Family Dislikes; Romance-Reluctant; Romance-Triangles; Scandals; World War I Era; Alcoholics; Cheating Women; Teachers; Small-town Life; Hunchbacks; Scenery-Outstanding; Faded Hits
(Dr. Zhivago; A Passage to India; The French Lieutenant's Woman; The Playboys)

S

Saber Jet, 1953, 96m, ★★/$$, UA-Krueger Productions/NA. During the Korean War, a pilot fights a battle on the ground but his domestic troubles interfere with the completion of his duty. Robert Stack, Coleen Gray, Richard Arlen, Julie Bishop, Leon Ames, Amanda Blake. w. Dale Eunson, Katherine Albert, d. Louis King.
ACTION: MELODRAMA: War Stories; Pilot-Military; Korean War; Marriage Drama; Marriage on the Rocks; Female Screenwriters
Sabotage, 1936, 76m, ★★½/$$, Ind/Nos. A woman (Sylvia Sidney) suspects her husband (Oscar Homolka) may be a terrorist bomber and has to decide what to do. w. Charles Bennett, Ian Hay, Helen Simpson, E. V. H. Emmett, N-adap. Joseph Conrad *(The Secret Agent)*, d. Alfred Hitchcock.
SUSPENSE: MYSTERY: Debate to Reveal Killer; Romance-Dangerous; Dangerous Spouses; Terrorists; Bombs; British; Evil Men; Female Screenwriters; Hitchockian *(Suspicion; Betrayed; Decieved; Keeper of the Flame)*
Saboteur, 1942, 108m, ★★★★/$$$, Universal/MCA-U. A man (Robert Cummings) is framed for the fiery death of his friend at a defense plant in California during World War II. He has to go on the run to save himself, but also

must figure out how to infiltrate the conspiratorial anarchist organization he believes is out to get him. w. Alfred Hitchcock, Peter Viertel, d. Alfred Hitchcock.
SUSPENSE: MYSTERY: MURDER MYSTERY: Chase Movie; Conspiracy; Fugitives; Fugitives from the Law; Saving Yourself; Accused Unjustly; Framed?; Anarchists; Hitchockian
Unofficial Remake: North by Northwest. *(North by Northwest; Three Days of the Condor; Total Recall; The Fugitive)*
Sabrina, 1954, 113m, ★★★½/$$$$$, Par/Par. The chauffeur's daughter (Audrey Hepburn, BActress) is pursued by both of the older brothers (Humphrey Bogart, William Holden) who will inherit the estate she lives on. w. Billy Wilder, Samuel Taylor, Ernest Lehman (BScr), P-adap. Samuel Taylor, d. Billy Wilder (BDirector). BB&WCin, BB&WArt, **B&WCostume.** Oscars: 6-1.
ROMANCE: Romantic Comedy; Romance-Triangles; Romance-Older Men/Younger Women; Young Women; Men Fighting Over Women; Brothers; Rich People; Rich vs. Poor; Romance-Class Conflicts; Marrying Up; Servants; Free Spirits; Young Women Coming of Age
(Roman Holiday; Funny Face)
Sabrina, 1995, 135m, ★★★/$$$, Par/Par, PG/S. In this remake of the Audrey

Hepburn classic, when the now-glamorous daughter of two wealthy brothers' chauffeur comes back, the brothers find themselves vying for her affections. Harrison Ford, Julia Ormond, Greg Kinnear, Nancy Marchand, John Wood, Richard Crenna, Angie Dickinson, Lauren Holly, Dana Ivey. w. Barbara Benedek & David Rayfiel, S-adap. Billy Wilder, Samuel Taylor, & Ernest Lehman, d. Sydney Pollack. BOSong, BCDScore. Oscars: 2-0.
COMEDY DRAMA: ROMANCE: Romantic Comedy; Romance with Servants; Brothers; Men Fighting Over Women; Female Screenwriters
(Ed: This proves casting is everything and that Audrey is irreplaceable, despite good performances here from everyone and a generally very good film)
Sacco and Vanzetti, 1971, 120m, ★★½/$$, Ind/NA. Two Italian immigrants' true story of being railroaded by prejudice into an execution for murder in 1920s Boston. Gian Volonte, Riccardo Cucciola, Milo' O'Shea, Cyril Cusack. d. Guiliani Montaldo.
DRAMA: MURDER: Accused Unjustly; Courtroom Drama; Bigots; Italians; Immigrants; Executions; True Stories; 1920s; Boston; Independent Films
The Sacrifice, 1986, 149m, ★★½/$, Svensk/Ingram. A writer living in a country home promises God that he will live

in exile and not speak if He will avert nuclear disaster. Erland Josephson, Susan Fleetwood, Valerie Mairesse, Allan Edwall, Gudrun Gisladottir. w. d. Andrei Tarkovsky.

DRAMA: Nuclear Energy; Apocalyptic Stories; Political Drama; God; Religion; Obsessions; Writers; Swedish Films; Writer-Directors

The Sad Sack, 1957, 98m, ★★¹/2/$$, Par/Par A dufus becomes a general inductee, much to the chagrin of his commanding officers. Jerry Lewis, David Wayne, Phyllis Kirk, Peter Lorre. w. Edmund Beloin, Nate Monaster, (Comic Strip-adap.) George Baker, d. George Marshall.

COMEDY: Military Comedy; Soldiers; Fools-Bumbling; Power-Rise to, of Idiot
(In the Army Now; Living It Up)

Sadie McKee, 1934, 90m, ★★¹/2/$$, MGM/NA. Three men vie for the affections of a beautiful but simple maid. Joan Crawford, Franchot Tone, Edward Arnold, Jean Dixon, Akim Tamiroff. w. John Meehan, SS-adap. Vina Delmar, d. Clerence Brown.

MELODRAMA: ROMANCE: Men Fighting Over Women; Romance-Triangles; Servant; Working Class

Sadie Thompson, 1928, 97m (B&W, Silent), ★★★¹/2/$$$$UA/MGM-UA. On a South Pacific island, a prostitute proves too much temptation for a zealous missionary to bear. Gloria Swanson, Lionel Barrymore, Blanche Frederici, Raoul Walsh. w. G. Gardner Sullivan, SS-adap. Somerset Maugham, d. Raoul Walsh.

DRAMA: ROMANCE: Prostitutes-Low Class; Romance with Prostitute; Islands; South Pacific; Religious Men and Prostitutes

REMAKES: Rain, Miss Sadie Thompson.
(Crimes of Passion; Love)

Safe, 1995, 119m, ★★★¹/2/$, Gramercy/U, R/S-P. A perfect housewife carries her compulsive nature into all nature as she decides that she's been contaminated by her domestic surroundings. So, she heads for a germ-free environment, but will it cure her or make her less stable? Julianne Moore, Xander Berkeley. w. d. Todd Haynes.

DRAMA: Mental Illness; Obsessions; Environmental Dilemmas; Writer-Directors; Cult Films; Quiet Little Films
(David and Lisa; The Incredible Shrinking Woman)

Safe Passage, 1994, 97m, ★★★/$$, New Line/New Line, PG/P. A mother with seven boys and a rocky marriage receives news her eldest son may have been killed in the bombing of a military installation in the Middle East. She tries to hold the family together while waiting to hear, facing how much of her own life she's given to these boys. Susan Sarandon, Sam Shepard, Robert Sean Leonard, Nick Stahl, Jason London, Sean Astin, Marcia Gay Harden, Matt Keeslar, Philip Bosco, Philip Arthur Ross, Steven Robert Ross. w. Deena Goldstone, N-adap. Ellyn Bache, d. Robert Allan Ackerman.

MELODRAMA: Character Studies; Family Drama; Mothers-Struggling; Mothers & Sons; Blind People; Soldiers; Crisis Situations; Marriage on the Rocks; Death-Dealing with; Children-Losing/Parting with; Female Protagonists; Female Screenwriters
(Lorenzo's Oil)

Safety Last, 1923, 70m, B&W, silent, ★★★¹/2/$$$$, Harold Lloyd/NA. To show off for his girlfriend, a young country hayseed enters a contest to climb a skyscraper. Harold Lloyd, Mildred Davis, Noah Young. w. Harold Lloyd, Sam Taylor, Tim Whelan, Hal Roach, d. Sam Taylor, Fred Newmeyer.

COMEDY: ROMANCE: Comedy-Slapstick; Comedy of Errors; City vs. Country; Competitions
(Ed: Contains one of the most famous images in film history: Harold Lloyd hanging off a highrise clock)

Sahara, 1943, 97m, ★★★/$$$, Col/RCA-Col. During World War II, a motley crew of allied soldiers stranded in the desert struggle to survive at all costs, battling the Nazis as well as dehydration. Humphrey Bogart, Bruce Bennett, Lloyd Bridges, Rex Ingram. w. John Howard Lawson, Zoltan Korda, d. Zoltan Korda. BCin. Oscars: 2-0.

DRAMA: War Stories; World War II Stories; Ensembles-Male; Nazi Stories; Germans as Enemy; Africa; Desert Settings
(King of the Hill; Desert Rats)

Sailor Beware, 1952, 103m, ★★¹/2/$$, Par/Par. Martin & Lewis join the navy to predictable results. Jerry Lewis, Dean Martin, Leif Erickson, Corinne Calvet. w. James Allardice, Martin Rackin, P-adap Kenyon Nicholson, Charles Robinson, d. Hal Walker.

COMEDY: Comedians; Comedy-Slapstick; Fools-Bumbling; Buddy Films; Military Comedy
(Abbott & Costello in the Navy; Sad Sack)

The Sailor Who Fell from Grace with the Sea, 1976, 105m, ★★¹/2/$, Avco, X & R/ES-FFN-MRN. A boy, jealous of his widowed mother's lover, mentally prepares and may finally act on his wish to castrate him. Sarah Miles, Kris Kristofferson, Jonathan Kahn, Earl Rhodes. w. d. Lewis John Carlino, N-adap. Yukio Mishima.

DRAMA: ROMANCE: Romantic Drama; Erotic Drama; Sailors; Fantasies; Mothers & Sons; Parents vs. Children; Jealousy; Child Protagonists; Boyhood; Stepfathers; Violence-Sudden
(Lady Caroline Lamb; Firstborn)

Saigon, see Off Limits

Saint Benny, the Dip, 1951, 80m, ★★¹/2/$$, Ind/Nos. Small-time crooks running from the law disguise themselves as priests, then unwittingly start acting the part. Freddie Barholomew, Roland Young, Dick Haymes, Lionel Stander, Nina Foch. w. John Roeburt, d. Edgar G. Ulmer.

COMEDY DRAMA: Crime Drama; Criminals-Stupid; Juvenile Delinquents; Impostors; Priests; Disguises; Disguised as Priest; Hiding Out; Fugitives from the Law
(We're No Angels; Sister Act; Nuns on the Run)

St. Elmo's Fire, 1985, 107m, Columbia/RCA-Col, ★★¹/2/$$$. Yuppies just out of Georgetown try to deal with life and relationships, but only ever so superficially. Andrew McCarthy, Rob Lowe, Judd Nelson, Ally Sheedy, Demi Moore, Emilio Estevez, Mare Winningham, Andie MacDowell. w. Joel Schumacher, Carl Kurlander, d. Joel Schumacher. BOSong. Oscars: 1-0.

DRAMA: MELODRAMA: COMEDY DRAMA: Ensemble Films; Ensembles-Young People; Bratpack Movies; 20-Somethings; Pre-Life Crisis; Friendships-Male; Friendships-Female; Washington D.C.; College Life; Young People
(The Breakfast Club; About Last Night)
(Ed: Pretty and charming enough if you ignore the immaturity of it)

St. Ive's, 1976, 94m, ★★¹/2/$, WB/WB, R/V. A web of intrigue entangles a former crime-beat reporter when he uncovers a murder plot. Charles Bronson, Harry Guardino, John Houseman, Jacqueline Bisset, Maximilian Schell. w. Barry Beckerman, N-adap. Oliver Bleeck (*The Procane Chronicle*), d. J. Lee Thompson.

MYSTERY: MURDER: MURDER MYSTERY: SUSPENSE: Conspiracy; Journalists; Clever Plots & Endings
(Telefon; Death Wish)

Saint Jack, 1979, 112m, ★★½/$, New World/Vestron, R/ES-P-V. A drifting "slacker" winds up in Singapore, finding his true vocation as a pimp. Ben Gazarra, Denholm Elliott, James Villiers, Peter Bogdanovich. w. Peter Bogdanovich, Howard Sackler, Paul Theroux, N-adap. Paul Theroux, d. Peter Bogdanovich.

DRAMA: COMEDY DRAMA: Black Comedy; Drifters; Midlife Crisis; Pimps; Americans; Abroad; Asia
(The Killing of a Chinese Bookie; Broadway musical, Miss Saigon)

Saint Joan, 1957, 110m, ★★½/$$, WB/WB. The story of the proto-feminist heroine, burned at the stake for fighting in the Crusades. Jean Seberg, Anton Walbrook, Richard Widmark, John Gielgud, Harry Andrews, w. Graham Greene, P-adap. Bernard Shaw, d. Otto Preminger.

DRAMA: TRAGEDY: Political Drama; Fighting the System; Religion; Executions; Feminist Films; Classic Literary Adaptations; Middle Ages; Female Protagonists
(Joan of Arc; The Crucible)

St. Louis Blues, 1958, 93m, ★★★/$$, Par/Par. The life story of W. C. Handy and his rise as a blues musician in Memphis. Nat King Cole, Eartha Kitt, Cab Calloway, Mahalia Jackson, Ruby Dee, Ella Fitzgerald, Pearl Bailey. w. Seton Miller, Warren Duff, d. Allen Resiner.

DRAMA: Music Movies; Biographies; Black Casts; Black Men; Southerns; Musicians; Singers; Fame-Rise to
(Birth of the Blues; Cabin in the Sky; Leadbelly; Bird)

St. Martin's Lane, 1938, 85m, ★★★/$$, Ind/NA. An older man without much hope falls for a young actress who becomes a star and may not let him attend to her anymore. Charles Laughton, Vivien Leigh, Rex Harrison, Tyrone Guthrie. w. Clarence Dane, d. Tim Whelan.

ROMANCE: DRAMA: COMEDY DRAMA: Romance-Older Men/Younger Women; Romance-Unrequited; Romance-Doomed; Infatuations; Dancers; Actresses; Theater Life; British Films
(The Blue Angel; Citizen Kane)

The Saint of Fort Washington, 1993, 104m, ★★/$, WB/WB, R/P. A schizophrenic patient is sent to a homeless shelter where he meets a savvy Vietnam veteran who shows him the ropes. Matt Dillon, Danny Glover, Nina Siezmasko. w. Lyle Kessler, d. Tim Hunter.

DRAMA: MELODRAMA: Social Drama; Homeless People; Mental Illness; Buddy Films; Black & White Together; Veterans-Vietnam; Inner City Life; Simple Minds
(The Fisher King; Stone Pillow)

St. Valentine's Day Massacre, 1967, 100m, ★★★/$$, 20th/CBS-Fox. Al Capone's (Jason Robards) life is detailed leading up to the infamous gang-war shoot out between his men and Bugsy Moran's. Jason Robards, George Segal, Ralph Meeker, Bruce Dern, John Agar. w. Howard Browne, d. Roger Corman.

DRAMA: Crime Drama; **ACTION:** Mob Stories; Mob Wars; Biographies; Assassination Plots; Hitmen; Chicago; Evil Men
(Scarface; The Untouchables; Capone; Dillinger)

Sakharov, 1984, 120m, ★★★/$$$, HBO/HBO, Prism. The Russian scientist who designed the first H-bomb's story of oppression and imprisonment when he goes against the Soviet government who owed him so much. Jason Robards, Glenda Jackson. d. Jack Gold.

DRAMA: Biographies; Scientists; Bombs-Atomic; Political Drama; Political Unrest; Rebels; Russians; TV Movies

Salaam Bombay!, 1988, 114m, ★★★/$$$, Cinecom/Cinecom, NA. A group of orphaned children cope with life in the seedy streets of Bombay amid prostitutes and drug dealers. Shafiq Syed, Raghubir Yadav, Nana Patekar, Irshad Hasni, Aneeta Kanwar, Hansa Vithal. w. Sooni Taraporevala, d. Mira Nair. BLFFilm. Oscars: 1-0.

DRAMA: Docudrama; Documentary Style; Ensemble Films; Art Films; Orphans; Childhood; Poor People; Homeless People; India; Drugs-Dealing; Prostitutes; Inner City Life; Female Directors
(The World of Apu; Pixote)
(Ed: Noted for its realism and the fact that the "actors" were actually street children from Bombay)

The Salamander, 1981, 101m, ★★½/$, Ind/New Line, R/V. Italian fascists plan a coup to takeover the government in Rome. Franco Nero, Anthony Quinn, Martin Balsam, Claudia Cardinale, Christopher Lee. w. Robert Katz, Rod Serling, N-adap. Morris West, d. Peter Zinner.

DRAMA: Political Drama; Political Unrest; Anarchists; Italy
(Year of the Gun)

Salem's Lot, 1979, 112m, ★★★/$$$$, CBS/WB. A vampire is on the loose in New England and a hunter (David Soul) and his teenage sidekick (Lance Kerwin) must try to stop him, but first they have to take care of his sentinel (James Mason). w. Paul Monash, N-adap. Stephen King, d. Tobe Hooper.

HORROR: SCI-FI: Vampires; **SUSPENSE:** Fathers & Sons; New England; Miniseries
(It; Sleepwalkers; Buffy, the Vampire Slayer)
(Ed: Ahead of Its Time with King and the early 90s vampire and King craze)

Sally of the Sawdust, 1925, 91m (B&W, Silent), UA/Nos. A girl growing up in the circus learns that she is adopted, much to the consternation of her "father" who is a juggler. W. C. Fields, Carol Dempster, Alfred Lunt, Effie Shannon, Erville Anderson. w. Forrest Halsey, P-adap. Dorothy Donnelly, d. D. W. Griffith.

DRAMA: MELODRAMA: COMEDY DRAMA: Orphans; Children-Adopted; Circus Life

Salmonberries, 1991, 95m, ★★/$, Ind/Facets, R/S. A lesbian relationship ensues between a woman, orphaned as a child, and a German, expatriot librarian in Alaska. k.d. lang, Rosel Zech, Chuck Connors, Christel Merian. w. Percy Adlon, Felix O. Adlon, d. Percy Adlon.

DRAMA: ROMANCE: Romantic Drama; Ordinary People Stories; Lesbians; Aternative Lifestyles; Librarians; Alaska
(Desert Hearts; Lianna; Personal Best)

Salo: 120 Days of Sodom, 1975, 117m, ★★/$, WB/HollywoodHome, X & R/ES-B&G-EP-FFN-MFN. Germans torture and train Italians at a sado-masochistic camp during the war, subjecting them to some of the most disgusting and unthinkable things. w. d. Pier Paolo Pasolini.

DRAMA: World War II Era; Erotic Drama; Psychological Drama;

Concentration Camps; Torture; Nazi
Stories; Sado-Masochism; Writer-
Directors
(Salon Kitty; Fellini's Satyricon)

Salome, 1953, 103m, ★★1/2/$$$, Col/
RCA-Col. The story of the famous bib-
lical princess of Galilee who must dance
to save the life of John the Baptist. Rita
Hayworth, Charles Laughton, Cedric
Hardwicke, Alan Badel. w. Harry Kleiner,
Jesse Lasky, Jr., d. William Dieterle.
DRAMA: Costume Drama; Biblical
Stories; Historical Drama; Saving
Someone; Dancers

Salome, Where She Danced, 1945,
90m, ★★/$$, Universal/Nos. A European
dancer during World War II is thought to
be a spy. She escapes to Arizona and puts
down roots in a small town. Yvonne de
Carlo, Rod Cameron, Albert Dekker,
Walter Slezak. w. Laurence Stallings, SS-
adap. Michael J. Phillips, d. Charles
Lamont.
DRAMA: MELODRAMA: Spy Films;
Spies; Spies-Female; Accused Unjustly;
Hiding Out; Starting Over; Disguises;
Dancers; Desert Settings; Unintentionally
Funny; Cult Films

Salome's Last Dance, 1988, 90m,
★★★/$, Vestron/Vestron, R/S-P-FN-MN.
What if Oscar Wilde went to see a
raunchy performance of *Salome* in a
brothel? Glenda Jackson, Nicholas Grace,
Imogen Stubbs. w. d. Ken Russell, P-
adap. Oscar Wilde (*Salome*).
COMEDY DRAMA: SATIRE: Theater
Life; Dancers; Art Films; Avant-Garde
Films; British Films; What If . . . Stories
(Gothic; The Rainbow; The Music Lovers;
The Boy Friend)

Salon Kitty, 1978, 127m, ★★1/2/$,
20th, X & R/ES-P-FFN-MFN. Nazis use
a Berlin madame and her call girls to spy
on civilians and conspirators during
World War II-amid the torture and sex
camps they're conducting. Helmut
Berger, Ingrid Thulin, Teresa Ann Savoy,
John Ireland. w. Ennio de Concini, Maria
Pia Fusco, Tinto Brass, d. Tinto Brass.
DRAMA: Erotic Drama; Psychological
Drama; Spies; Nazi Stories; World War II
Stories; Berlin; Prostitutes; Concentration
Camps; Torture
(Salo: 120 Days of Sodom)

Salsa, 1988, 97m, ★★/$$, Cannon/
MGM-UA, PG-13/S. A salsa dance con-
test becomes the *raison d'etre* of a garage
mechanic and his girlfriend. Bobby Rosa,

Rodney Harvey, Magali Alvarado,
Miranda Garrison, Moon Orona, Angela
Alvarado. w. Boaz Davidson, Tomas
Benitez, Shepherd Goldman, SS-adap.
Boaz Davidson, Eli Tabor, d. Boaz
Davidson.
ROMANCE: MELODRAMA: Dance
Movies; Dancers; Competitions; Latin
People
(Lambada)

Salt and Pepper, 1968, 101m, ★★/$,
MGM/NA. Against the backdrop of
swinging London, two hipsters solve a
murder. Sammy Davis, Jr., Peter Lawford,
Michael Bates, Ilona Rodgers, Graham
Stark, Ernest Clark. w. Michael Pertwee,
d. Richard Donner.
MYSTERY: MURDER: MURDER MYS-
TERY: Comic Mystery; Detective Stories;
Buddy Films; Ahead of Its Time;
Friendships-Interracial; Mod Era;
England; London; Rat Pack; Movies

Salty O'Rourke, 1945, 100m, ★★1/2/
$$, Par/Par. The matron of a grammar
school takes in a con man, and teaches
him a gentler, more honest way of life.
Alan Ladd, Gail Russell, William
Demarest, Bruce Cabot. w. Milton
Holmes (BOStory), d. Raoul Walsh.
Oscars: 1-0.
DRAMA: COMEDY DRAMA: ROMANCE:
Svengalis; Starting Over; Redemption;
Teachers and Students; Con Artists
(The Man Upstairs [1992])

Salvador, 1986, 123m, ★★★1/2/$$,
Hemdale/Hemdale, Vestron, R/P-V. A
gonzo journalist (James Woods, BActor)
and his friend go on a story in El
Salvador during the civil war and realize
how much trouble they're surrounded by.
James Belushi, John Savage. w. d. Oliver
Stone (BOScr). Oscars: 2-0
DRAMA: Docudrama; Political Drama;
Political Unrest; Central America; War
Stories; Journalists; Friendships-Male;
Writer-Directors
(Under Fire; Platoon)

Samantha, 1992, 101m, ★★★/$,
Academy/Academy, PG. An eccentric girl
has a crack-up on her birthday, then
searches for her real parents and tries to
find love with a friend, but both hopes
are fleeting. Martha Plimpton, Dermott
Mulroney, Hector Elizondo, Mary Kay
Place, Ione Skye.
COMEDY DRAMA: ROMANCE: CHIL-
DREN'S: FAMILY: Romance-Reluctant;
Friends as Lovers; Young Women;

Eccentric People; Searches;
Family/Heritage-Search for; Children-
Adopted; Musicians

Same Time, Next Year, 1978, 119m,
★★★/$$$, Universal/MCA-U, PG/S. A
man and a woman, married to other peo-
ple, continue their once-a-year ren-
dezvous for twenty-five years; their
relationship grows and their hairstyles
change over time. Ellen Burstyn
(BActress), Alan Alda. w. P-adap.
Bernard Slade (BAScr), d. Robert
Mulligan. BCin, BOSong. Oscars: 4-0.
COMEDY: ROMANCE: Romantic
Comedy; COMEDY DRAMA: Episodic
Stories; Friends as Lovers; Romance with
Married Person; Cheating Men; Cheating
Women; Vacation Romance
(Romantic Comedy; Indiscreet)

Sammy and Rosie Get Laid, 1987,
100m, ★★★/$$, Island/WB, R/S-EP-FN-
MRN. A group of Pakistani and English
bohemians in an abandoned part of
London sleep around as the city goes up
in smoke (sometimes literally). Shashi
Kapoor, Claire Bloom, Ayub Khan Din,
Frances Barber, Roland Gift. w. Hanif
Kureishi, d. Stephen Frears.
COMEDY DRAMA: ROMANCE:
Ensemble Films; Promiscuity; Romance-
Triangles; Young People; Inner City Life;
London; England; British Films
(My Beautiful Laundrette; Rita, Sue &
Bob, Too)
(Ed: The "get laid" part was originally
left off of ads in America)

Samson and Delilah, 1949, 128m,
★★1/2/$$$$, Par/Par. The famous biblical
tale of a "woman scorned." Delilah's hell-
ish fury sends Samson, shorn of his fabu-
lous locks, to his enemies, where he must
cope with all sorts of trouble, and hold up
a crumbling temple with his bare hands.
Hedy Lamarr, Victor Mature, Angela
Lansbury, George Sanders, Fay Holden,
Russ Tamblyn. w. Jesse L. Lasky, Jr.,
Fredric M. Frank, d. Cecil B. de Mille.
BCArt, BCCin, BScore. Oscars: 3-1.
MELODRAMA: ACTION: ROMANCE:
Romance-Doomed; Epics; Biblical
Stories; Ancient Times; Stern Women;
Jealousy; Revenge; Blockbusters;
Spectacles; Faded Hits
(Solomon and Sheba; Sodom &
Gomorrah)

The Samurai, 1967, 97m, ★★★/$$,
Ind/NA. A woman unknowingly falls for a
hit man, then witnesses him perpetrating

a murder, and must keep it from him while she tries to solve the crime. Alain Delon, Francois Perier, Nathalie Delon, Caty Rosier. w. d. Jean-Pierre Melville.

SUSPENSE: Crime Drama; **MYSTERY: MURDER: MURDER MYSTERY:** Film Noir-Modern; Art Films; Mob Stories; Detective Stories; Detectives-Female; Detectives-Amateur; Murder-Debate to Reveal Killer; Hitmen; Romance with Hitman; French Films; Overlooked at Release; Underrated; Hidden Gems; Forgotten Films; Writer-Directors

San Antonio, 1945, 105m, ★★/$$$, WB/WB. A saloon owner has a grudge to bear with a local cowboy, a standoff resulting in the requisite duel on main street. Errol Flynn, Alexis Smith, Paul Kelly, Victor Francen, S. Z. Sakall. w. Alan le May, W. R. Burnett, d. David Butler.

WESTERN: Men in Conflict; Western Duels; Westerns-City Titles; Revenge

San Francisco, 1936, 116m, ★★★★/ $$$$$, MGM/MGM-UA. A priest (Spencer Tracy, BActor), a gambler (Clark Gable), and a singer (Jeanette McDonald) are caught in the great quake of 1906. Probably the first real disaster movie. Clark Gable, Spencer Tracy, Jeanette McDonald, Jack Holt, Jessie Ralph. w. Anita Loos, BOStory, SS-adap. Robert Hopkins, d. W. S. Van Dyke (BDirector). BADirector, BPicture, **BSound.** Oscars: 6-1.

DRAMA: MELODRAMA: TRAGEDY: ROMANCE: Romance-Triangles; Survival Drama; Disaster Movies; Earthquakes; Slice of Life Stories; Interwoven Stories; Multiple Stories; Saving Someone; Priests Friendships-Male; Singers; Gambling; Female Screenwriters; San Francisco (Earthquake; In Old Chicago; Honky Tonk)

The San Francisco Story, 1952, 90m, ★★½/$$, WB/WB. A traveler on his way to China in the 1800s stops in San Francisco to do some rabble-rousing, and ends up falling in love with a local girl. Joel McCrea, Yvonne de Carlo, Sidney Blackmer, Florence Bates. w. D. D. Beauchamp, N-adap. Richard Summers, d. Robert Parrish.

DRAMA: COMEDY DRAMA: ROMANCE: Political Drama; Politicians; San Francisco; Drifters

San Quentin, 1937, 70m, ★★½/$$, WB/WB. On her numerous prison visits to her brother, a young woman gradually

grows fond of the warden. They fall in love, and she tries to convince him to help her brother get released. Pat O'Brien, Ann Sheridan, Humphrey Bogart, Barton MacLane. w. Peter Milne, Humphrey Cobb, SS-adap. John Bright, Robert Tasker, d. Lloyd Bacon.

ROMANCE: DRAMA: Prison Drama; Saving Someone; Love-Questionable; Female Protagonist (Mrs. Soffel)

Sanctuary, 1960, 90m, ★★½/$$, 20th. During Prohibition, a bootlegger seduces the daughter of the governor and proceeds to ruin her life in Faulknerland. Lee Remick, Bradford Dillman, Yves Montand, Odetta, Strother Martin, Reta Shaw. w. James Poe, N-adap. William Faulkner, d. Tony Richardson.

DRAMA: MELODRAMA: ROMANCE: Abused Women; Marrying Up; Con Artists; Bootleggers; Southerns; Mississippi; Politicians; Forgotten Films (The Long, Hot Summer; The Sound and the Fury; The Reivers; Sweet Bird of Youth)

Sandakan No. 8, 1974, 121m, ★★★/ $$, Ind/Facets. A Japanese female journalist holds a woman who was a prostitute in old Borneo against her will and both learn from each other's lives, the archaic and oppressed vs. the liberated and modern. Jinuyo Tanaka, Yoko Takaskashi.

DRAMA: Friendships-Female; Generation Gaps; Journalists; Character Studies; Art Films; Japanese Films; Female Protagonists

The Sandlot, 1993, 101m, ★★★/$$, 20th/Fox, PG/P. A group of neighborhood boys play ball next to a junkyard where a big evil dogs lurks. They bond, they bunt, they run from the dog . . . Tom Guiry, Mike Vitar, Karen Allen, James Earl Jones, Denis Leary, Brooke Adams. w. David Mickey Evans, Robert Gunter, d. Evans.

COMEDY: CHILDREN'S: FAMILY: Nostalgia; 1950s; Ensemble Films; Ensembles-Male; Ensembles-Children; Baseball; Boys; Dogs; Mean Men (Stand By Me; Radio Flyer)

The Sand Pebbles, 1966, 179m, ★★★/$$$, 20th/CBS-Fox, PG. In the twenties, trouble ensues when a navy patrol in China floats into a hostile warlord's territory. Steve McQueen (BActor), Candice Bergen, Richard Attenborough,

Richard Crenna, Mako (BSActor), Larry Gates. w. Robert Anderson, N-adap. Richard McKenna, d. Robert Wise. BPicture, BOScore, BCCin. Oscars: 6-0.

DRAMA: War Stories; **ROMANCE:** Historical Drama; Power Struggles; Asia; 1920s (Bullitt; The Great Escape)

The Sandpiper, 1965, 116m, ★★★/$$$, MGM/MGM-UA. When an unwed artist mother living on the California coast is forced to send her son to boarding school, he becomes a project for the clergyman in charge as well as a way to get to the mother. Elizabeth Taylor, Richard Burton, Eva Marie Saint, Charles Bronson. w. Dalton Trumbo, Michael Wilson, d. Vincente Minnelli.

DRAMA: ROMANCE: MELODRAMA: Romantic Drama; Mothers & Sons; Preachers/Ministers; Artists; Mothers-Unwed; Free Sprits; Atheists; Beach Movies; California (The VIPs; Who's Afraid of Virginia Woolf?)

The Sands of Iwo Jima, 1949, 110m, ★★★/$$$$, Republic/Republic. A tough, seemingly heartless marine sergeant whips his raw recruits into shape. When they go into battle, they realize their training has been a form of "tough love." John Wayne, John Agar, Adele Mara, Forrest Tucker, Arthur Franz, Julie Bishop, Richard Jaeckel. w. Harry Brown, James Edward Grant, d. Allan Dwan.

DRAMA: ACTION: War Stories; World War II Stories; Soldiers; Stern Men; Conservative Value Films (An Officer and a Gentleman; Heartbreak Ridge)

Sands of the Kalahari, 1965, 119m, ★★½/$$, Ind/NA, A&E. A plane crash in the desert leaves its survivors stranded, searching for sustenance and running from baboons. Stanley Baker, Stuart Whitman, Harry Andrews, Susannah York, Theodore Bikel, Barry Low. w. d. Cy Endfield, N-adap. William Mulvihill.

DRAMA: ADVENTURE: Survival Drama; Stranded; Airplane Crashes; Power Struggles; Men in Conflict; Desert Settings; Africa (Flight of the Phoenix; Five Came Back)

Santa Claus, The Movie, 1985, 112m, ★★/$$. Salkind-TriStar/Col-Tri, G. A group of elves grant an old woodworker immortality if he'll take over the duties of Santa Claus. His first assignment is a search and rescue operation involving the captive dwarf of an evil toy manufacturer. David Huddleston, Dudley Moore, John Lithgow, Burges Meredith, Christian Fitzpatrick. w. David Newman, d. Jeannot Szwarc.

CHILDREN'S: FAMILY: Fantasy; Santa Claus; Christmas; Flops-Major; Servants; Good vs. Evil; Arctic; Race Against Time; Selling One's Soul; Toys
(Ed: Too dumb for adults, too boring for children)

The Santa Clause, 1994, 95m, ★★★/ $$$$$, PG-13/P. When a divorced and alienated Dad finds a man who's fallen off of a roof in a Santa suit, he tries on the suit and is unwittingly locked into the calamitous duties of Santa himself, but also winds up endearing himself to his son in the process. Tim Allen, Judge Reinhold, Wendy Crewson, Eric Lloyd, David Krumholtz, Joyce Guy, Zach McLemore, Nic Knight, Scott Wickware. w. Leo Benvenuti, Steve Rudnick, d. John Pasquin.

COMEDY: Family Comedy; Fathers & Sons; Christmas; Santa Claus; Cartoonlike Movies; Blockbusters; Sleeper Hits

Santa Fe, 1951, 89m, ★★1/2/$$, Col/NA. A tale of four brothers on the Santa Fe Trail: three are tempted to become outlaws; the one "good brother" acts as their conscience, and must intervene when things get out of hand. Randolph Scott, Jerome Courtland, Janis Carter, Roy Roberts. w. Kenneth Gamet, d. Irving Pichel.

WESTERN: Family Stories; Men in Conflict; Westerns-City Titles; Brothers; Good vs. Evil

Santa Fe Trail, 1940, 110m, ★★★/$$$, WB/MGM-UA. A protracted manhunt by the cavalry results in the apprehension of the outlaw, John Brown. Errol Flynn, Olivia de Havilland, Raymond Massey, Ronald Reagan, Alan Hale, Van Heflin, Gene Reynolds. w. Robert Buckner, d. Michael Curtiz.

WESTERNS: Manhunts; Bounty Hunters; Chase Movies; Biographies; True Stories; Fugitives from the Law; Cavalry

Santa Sangre, 1989, 123m, ★★1/2/$, Mainline/Republic. A boy must use his arms as substitutes for his mothers', which were chopped off by his father in a fit of jealous rage. Axel Jodorowsky, Faviola Elenka Tapia, Teo Jodorowsky.

w. Robert Leoni, Alejandro Jodorowsky, Claudio Argento, d. Alejandro Jodorowsky.

DRAMA: Art Films; Avant-Garde Films; Surrealism; Mothers & Sons; Comedy-Morbid; Body Parts; Italian Films
(Eraserhead; ZOO; Boxing Helena)

Sapphire, 1959, 92m, ★★1/2/$, Rank/NA. A Scotland Yard inspector investigating the murder of a music student in London uncovers its racial motivation. Nigel Patrick, Michael Craig, Yvonne Mitchell, Paul Massie, Bernard Miles. w. Janet Green, d. Basil Dearden.

MYSTERY: MURDER: MURDER MYSTERY: SUSPENSE: Detective Stories; Detectives-Police; Police Stories; Race Relations; Black vs. White; British Films; Clever Plots & Endings; Forgotten Films. Overlooked at Release
(In the Heat of the Night)

Sarafina!, 1992, 116m, ★★1/2/$$, Touchstone/Touchstone, PG. In Soweto, South Africa, a young girl's political education is encouraged and enhanced by her strong-willed history teacher and her own experience of imprisonment. Leleti Khumalo, Whoopi Goldberg, Miriam Makeba, John Kani, Dumisani Diamini, Mbongeni Ngema. w. William Nicholson, Mbongeni Ngema, MP-adap. Mbongeni Ngema, d. Darrell James Roodt.

DRAMA: MELODRAMA: MUSICALS: Musical Drama; Music Movies; Apartheid; South Africa; Black Casts; Black Women; Women and Girls; Teachers and Students; Race Relations; Black Screenwriters; Black Directors; Female Protagonists; Female Screenwriters
(Bopha!; Clara's Heart; A World Apart)

Sarah, Plain and Tall, 1991, 100m, ★★★1/2/$$$$, Hallmark-CBS/Hallmark. A spinster (Glenn Close, BActress Emmy) answers a request for a nanny position in Kansas in pre-World War I era, but the stern father (Christopher Walken) may be more than she bargained for. d. Glenn Jordan.

DRAMA: ROMANCE: MELODRAMA: FAMILY: Family Drama; Spinsters; Fathers Alone; Mothers-Surrogate; Brides-Mail Order; Midwesterns; 1900s; Old-Fashioned; Recent Films; Female Protagonists; TV Movies; Blockbusters
SEQUEL: Skylark.
(Skylark; The Substitute Wife; O Pioneers!)

Saratoga, 1937, 102m, ★★1/2/$$, MGM/MGM-UA. The daughter of a horse breeder, who's down on her luck, gets help from a local bookie in rebuilding her daddy's sagging fortunes. Clark Gable, Jean Harlow, Lionel Barrymore, Frank Morgan, Walter Pidgeon, Una Merkel. w. Anita Loos, Robert Hopkins, d. Jack Conway.

COMEDY DRAMA: ROMANCE: Romantic Commedy; Horses/Horse Racing; Gambling; Riches to Rags; Female Protagonists; Sexy Women; Female Screenwriters
(Bombshell; Platinum Blonde)
(Ed: Harlow's last film; she died during filming, so the film is definitely lacking)

Saratoga Trunk, 1943, 135m, ★★1/2/$$$, WB/NA. A cowboy, hiring himself out as protection for a railroad, gets snagged by a beautiful but wild woman just arriving in New Orleans. Ingrid Bergman, Gary Cooper, Flora Robson, Jerry Austin, Florence Bates, John Abbott. w. Casey Robinson, N-adap. Edna Ferber, d. Sam Wood.

MELODRAMA: ROMANCE: DRAMA: Dangerous Women; Love-Questionable; New Orleans; Secrets-Haunted by; Secrets-Keeping; Wild People; Free Spirits; Cowboys; Coulda Been Good
(For Whom the Bell Tolls)

Saskatchewan, 1954, 87m, ★★1/2/$$, U/NA. In the Canadian Rockies, a woman attacked by Indians is helped by a handsome mountie and falls in love. Alan Ladd, Shelley Winters, J. Carrol Naish, Hugh O'Brian, Robert Douglas, Richard Long. w. Gil Doud, d. Raoul Walsh.

DRAMA: MELODRAMA: ROMANCE: WESTERNS: Saving Someone; Protecting Someone; Canada

The Satan Bug, 1965, 114m, ★★/$, Mirisch-UA/NA. A madman steals a disgusting virus from a government laboratory in the desert, and they must get to him before he unleashes it on the world. George Maharis, Richard Basehart, Anne Francis, Dana Andrews, Ed Asner. w. James Clavell, Edward Anhalt, N-adap. Alilstair MacLean, d. John Sturges.

ACTION: SUSPENSE: Race Against Time; Epidemics; Secret Agents; Rule the World-Plot to; Good vs. Evil
(Outrageous Fortune; The Andromeda Strain)

Satan Met a Lady, 1936, 74m, ★★1/2/$$, WB/MGM-UA. Detectives must beat a band of criminals in locating a rare artifact. Bette Davis, Warren William, Alison Skipworth, Arthur Treacher, Wini Shaw, Marie Wilson, Porter Hall. w. Brown Holmes, d. William Dieterle.

DRAMA: MYSTERY: Detective Stories; Detectives-Private; Race Against Time; Treasure Hunts; Film Noir
RETREAD/VERSION OF: The Maltese Falcon.

Satisfaction (Sweet Little Rock 'n' Roller), 1988, 93m, ★★/$, 20th/CBS-Fox, PG. A mainly female rock band wins a "battle of the bands" contest and pair-up with trendy studs at the club where they perform. Justine Bateman, Liam Neeson, Trini Alvarado, Scott Coffey, Julia Roberts, Debbie Harry. w. Charles Purpura, d. Joan Freeman.

COMEDY DRAMA: MELODRAMA: Musicians; Female in Male Domain; Rock Stars; Underdog Stories; Stars When Young; Female Protagonists; Coulda Been Good
(Mystic Pizza; Tokyo Pop)
(Ed: Provides anything but)

Saturday Night and Sunday Morning, 1960, 89m, ★★★1/2/$$, Woodfall-UA/NA. Frustrated with his existence and nagged by his wife, a blue-collar worker in the north of England has an affair with a married woman. After events blow up in his face, he falls back into his old routine. Albert Finney, Shirley Anne Field, Rachel Roberts. w., N-adap. Alan Sillitoe, d. Karel Reisz.

DRAMA: Ordinary People Stories; Romance with Married Person; Cheating Men; Young Men; Pre-life Crisis; Kitchen Sink Drama; Marriage Drama; Working Class; British Films; Ahead of Its Time; Hidden Gems
(A Kind of Loving; Charlie Bubbles)
(Ed: Finney's breakthrough and started a new trend in realism)

Saturday Night Fever, 1977, 119m, ★★★/$$$$$, Par/Par, R & PG/P-S. An Italian kid growing up in Brooklyn escapes the drudgery of his working-class existence in the fantasy world of the disco. He falls for a dancer who wants to *really* escape Brooklyn and make a better life for herself in Manhattan. John Travolta (BActor), Karen Lynn Gorney, Barry Miller,

Joseph Cali, Paul Pape, Bruce Ornstein. w. Norman Wexler, SS-adap. Nik Cohn, d. John Badham. Oscars: 1-0.

DRAMA: MELODRAMA: MUSICALS: Music Movies; Musicals-Disco Era; Disco Era; Dancers; Dance Movies; New York Life; Ordinary People Stories; Working Class; Italians; Time Capsules; Blockbusters; Sleeper Hits
SEQUEL: Staying Alive
(Ed: Yes, Travolta was indeed nominated)

Saturn 3, 1980, 88m, ★★/$, ITC-AFD/Fox, PG/V-MRN. The mental disintegration of a mad scientist on a space station orbiting Saturn is mirrored by his robot creation. Kirk Douglas, Farrah Fawcett, Harvey Keitel, Ed Bishop. w. Martin Amis, SS-adap. John Barry, d. Stanley Donen.

DRAMA: HORROR: SCI-FI: Outer Space Movies; Man vs. Machine; Men in Conflict; Androids; Unintentionally Funny; Female Among Males
(Demon Seed; 2001)

Satyricon (Fellini), 1970, 129m, ★★★1/2/$$, UAC/MGM-UA, R/ES-MN. A Roman student has sexual escapades, along with the usual surrealistic interludes we've come to dub "Fellini-esque." Martin Potter, Hiram Keller, Salvo Randone, Max Born. w. Federico Fellini, Bernandino Zapponi, d. Federico Fellini (BDirector). Oscars: 1-0.

DRAMA: Erotic Drama; Art Films; Avant-Garde Films; Ancient Times; Gay Men; Bisexuality; Sexuality; Promsicuity; Orgies; Rome; Italian Films
(Salo; Decameron)

The Savage, 1952, 95m, ★★1/2/$$, Par/NA. A young boy who's taken captive by Indians is raised in their culture, and when he is reunited with his relatives years later, has trouble re-adjusting to white society. Charlton Heston, Susan Morrow, Peter Hanson, Joan Taylor, Richard Rober. w. Sidney Boehm, N-adap. L. L. Foreman, d. George Marshall.

WESTERNS: Boyhood; Kidnapped; Fish out of Water Stories; Raised by Indians
(Dances with Wolves; Last of the Mohicans)

Savage Intruder, 1968/1973, 90m, ★★/$, U/MCA-U. A psychopathic killer hires herself out as a private nurse for an aging Hollywood star. Miriam Hopkins, John David Garfield, Gale Sondergaard, Florence Lake, Lester Mathews, Riza Royce. w. d. Donald Wolfe.

HORROR: Elderly Women; Actresses; Hollywood Life; Disabled People; Nurses; Evil Women; Writer-Directors
(Whatever Happened to Baby Jane?; Night Must Fall; Sunset Boulevard)

Savage Sam, 1962, 103m, ★★1/2/$$, Disney/Disney, G. A boy-and-his-dog story set in the turn-of-the-century American plains, in which the mangy mutt seems to be good for nothing until it proves efficient at hunting down stray Indians. Brian Keith, Tommy Kirk, Kevin Corcoran, Dewey Martin, Jeff York. w. Fred Gipson, William Tunberg, d. Norman Tokar.

CHILDREN'S: FAMILY: DRAMA: MELO-DRAMA: Pets Stories; Boys; Boy and His Dog; Dogs; Indians-American; Indians-American, Conflict with; Manhunts; Curiosities
SEQUEL TO: Old Yeller.
(Old Yeller; The Biscuit Eater; Where the Red Fern Grows)

Savages, 1972, 106m, ★★1/2/$, Angelika-MI/Connoisseur, R/S-V-FN-MN. A deserted mansion becomes refuge for a group of "forest people," and once inside, they gradually become "civilized." Lewis Stadlen, Anne Francine, Thayer David. w. George Swift Trow, Michael O'Donoghue, d. James Ivory.

DRAMA: Art Films; Avant-Garde Films; Allegorical Stories; Social Satire; Coulda Been Good; Independent Films

Save the Tiger, 1973, 101m, ★★★★/$$$, Par/Par, R/P-S. A businessman has a mid-life crisis in which he grows gradually more disgusted with his life and that of modern society in general. And when his business is in trouble, he plots something he never thought he would. Jack Lemmon (BActor), Jack Gilford (BSActor), Laurie Heineman. w. Steve Shagan (BAScr), d. John G. Avildsen. Oscars: 3-1.

DRAMA: Social Drama; Character Studies; Ethics; Fires; Mid-life Crisis; Alienation; American Dream; Business Life; Fashion World; Forgotten Films; Hidden Gems; Faded Hits
(Death of a Salesman; Imaginary Crimes; Glengarry Glen Ross; The Garment Jungle; Patterns; The Man in the Gray Flannel Suit)

Saving Grace, 1986, 112m, Col./Embassy, PG. The pope goes incognito among the hoi polloi. Tom Conti, Fernando Rey, Erland Josephson,

Giancarlo Giannini, Donald Hewlett. w. Joaquin Montana, N-adap. Celia Gittelson, d. Robert M. Young.
COMEDY: COMEDY DRAMA: Popes; Ordinary People Stories; Disguises; Impostors; Fish out of Water Stories; Coulda Been Great
(The Pope Must Diet; Reuben, Reuben)
Sawdust and Tinsel (The Naked Night), 1953, 92m, ★★★/$, Svensk/New Line. Romantic triangles and backstage intrigue plague the members of a traveling circus. Harriet Andersson, Ake Gronberg, Hasse Ekman, Annika Tretow. w. d. Ingmar Bergman.
DRAMA: ROMANCE: Romantic Drama; Circus Life; Swedish Films; Writer-Directors; Bergmanesque
(After the Rehearsal; Shadows & Fog)
Say Amen, Somebody!, 1983, 100m, ★★★/$$, UA/MGM-UA, NA. A documentary about the gospel music community in Chicago. Minor drama develops between a gospel-singing mother and her nonreligious son. d. George Nierenberg. Documentary; Religion; Singers; Preachers/ministers; Black Casts; Black Women; Chicago; Inner City Life
Say Anything, 1989, 100m, ★★★¹/₂/ $$$, 20th/Fox, PG/S-P. A college-bound valedictorian dates an athlete with more modest (and local) ambitions-he wants to go into kickboxing, he says. Her father is worried she'll forego college to stay with him. John Cusack, Ione Skye, John Mahoney, Lili Taylor, Jason Gould, Joan Cusack. w. d. Cameron Crowe.
COMEDY: COMEDY DRAMA: ROMANCE: Romantic Comedy; Romance-Boy Wants Girl; Romance-Class Conflicts; Bratpack Movies; Young Men; Teenagers; Teenage Movies; Extroverted vs. Introverted; Suburban Life; Free Spirits; Hidden Gems; Underrated
(The Rachel Papers; Better Off Dead)
Say Hello to Yesterday, 1970, 92m, ★★¹/₂/$, Ind/Prism. On a shopping trip to London, a housewife is seduced by a young hipster. Jean Simmons, Leonard Whiting, Evelyn Laye, John Lee. w. Alvin Rakoff, Peter King, d. Alvin Rakoff.
ROMANCE: DRAMA: Romantic Drama; Romance-Older Women/Younger Men; Vacation Romance; One Day Stories; London; Mod Era; British Films
(The Idol; Indiscretion of An American Wife; John and Mary)

Say One for Me, 1959, 117m, ★★/$, 20th/NA. A priest explores the sinful world of the theater district in New York. Bing Crosby, Robert Wagner, Debbie Reynolds, Ray Walston, Sebastian Cabot. w. Robert O'Brien, d. Frank Tashlin.
DRAMA: MELODRAMA: Priests; Theater Life; Ethics; Fish out of Water Stories; Underworld; Coulda Been Good
FLIPSIDE TO: Going My Way.
Sayonara, 1957, 157m, ★★★¹/₂/$$$, WB/WB. After World War II in Toyko, an Air Force man and a Japanese actress fall in love, but things aren't all as nice as they seem. Marlon Brando (BActor), Miyoshi Umeki (**BSActress**), Miiko Taka, Red Buttons (**BSActor**), Ricardo Montalban, James Garner. w. Paul Osborn (BAScr), N-adap. James A. Michener, d. Joshua Logan (BDirector), BPicture, **BSound**, **BCin**, **BArt**, BEdit. Oscars: 10-4.
DRAMA: TRAGEDY: MELODRAMA: ROMANCE: Romance-Doomed; Romantic Drama; Romance-Interracial; Japan; Japanese People; Military Stories; Pilots-Military; Suicidal Tedencies; Actresses; World War II Stories; Men Fighting Over Women
Scalawag, 1973, 93m, ★★/$, Ind/NA. In 1800s Mexico, a young boy teams up with a peg-legged pirate to search for treasure. Kirk Douglas, Mark Lester, Neville Brand, Lesley-Anne Down, Phil Brown. w. Albert Maltz, Sid Fleischman, d. Kirk Douglas.
WESTERNS: ADVENTURE: Treasure Hunts; Men and Boys; Boys; Desert Settings; Disabled People
REMAKES/RETREADS: Treasure Island. (Treasure Island; Long John Silver; Against a Crooked Sky)
The Scalphunters, 1968, 102m, ★★¹/₂/$$, MGM/MGM-UA, PG/V. A freed slave and a grizzled old cowboy fight a band of ruthless outlaws who scalp and kill Indians. Burt Lancaster, Ossie Davis, Telly Savalas, Shelley Winters. w. William Norton, d. Sydney Pollack.
WESTERNS: MURDER: Manhunts; Men in Conflict; Duels; Cowboys; Indians-American; Turning the Tables; Buddy Films; Black & White Together
(The Skin Trade; Posse)
Scandal, 1989, 115m, ★★★/$$$, Hemdale/Miramax, HBO, R/ES-P-FN-MN. The story of two call girl/dancers and the orgies with British politicians

which got them all in hot water. John Hurt, Joanne Whalley-Kilmer, Ian McKellen, Bridget Fonda, Leslie Phillips, Britt Ekland, Roland Gift. w. Michael Thomas, d. Michael Caton-Jones.
DRAMA: Erotic Drama; Social Drama; Romance with Married Person; Political Drama; True Stories; Scandals; Politicians; Prostitutes-High Class; Spies; Orgies; British Films; England; Mod Era; 1960s; Female Protagonists
(Strapless; No Sex, Please, We're British)
A Scandal in Paris (Thieves' Holiday), 1946, 100m, ★★¹/₂/$$, UA/NA. A legendary and notorious thief in Paris, Vidocq, eventually quits his life of crime to use the knowledge he's gained through experience in his new role as the chief of police. George Sanders, Signe Hasso, Carole Landis, Akim Tamiroff, Gene Lockhart. w. Ellis St. Joseph, d. Douglas Sirk.
DRAMA: Costume Drama; Playboys; Thieves; Police Stories; Reformed
Scandal Sheet, 1952, 81m, ★★/$, Col/NA. A big-city tabloid, hot on the trail of a murderer, finds the prime suspect on its own staff. Broderick Crawford, John Derek, Donna Reed, Rosemary de Camp, Henry Morgan. w. Ted Sherdeman, Eugene Ling, James Poe, N-adap. Samuel Fuller, d. Phil Karlson.
MYSTERY: MURDER: MURDER MYSTERY: Journalist Detectives; Journalists; Scandals; Coulda Been Good
(Five-Star Final; Edge of the City)
Scandalous!, 1984, 92m, ★★/$, Hemdale/Vestron, R/S-P. After a television anchorman's wife is murdered, he meets two shady characters while working on a story. Accumulating clues indicate they may have had something to do with her death. Robert Hays, John Gielgud, Pamela Stephenson, M. Emmet Walsh, Nancy Wood, Jim Dale. w. Rob Cohen, John Byrum, d. Rob Cohen.
MYSTERY: Comic Mystery; **MURDER: MURDER MYSTERY:** Black Comedy; Detective Stories; Detectives-Amateur; Comedy-Morbid; Murder of Spouse; Avenging; Death of Loved One
Scandalous John, 1971, 113m, ★★¹/₂/$, Disney/Disney, G. A defunct ranch harbors an old coot who refuses to let the powers that be condemn his property. Brian Keith, Alfonso Arau, Michele Carey, Rick Lenz, Henry Morgan. w. Bill Walsh, Don da Gradi, N-adap. Richard Gardner, d. Robert Butler.

DRAMA: Mortgage Drama; Save the Farm; Elderly Men; Cattle People; Forgotten Films; Government as Enemy (The River; Country; Places in the Heart; Hush, Hush, Sweet Charlotte)

Scanner Cop, 1994, 94m, ★½/$, Republic/Republic, R/EV-S. When a mad scientist escapes from prison, he goes after the cop who caught him by programming zombies to kill cops-particularly his enemy. Daniel Quinn, Darlanne Flugle, Richard Lynch, Mark Rolston. w. John Bryant, George Saunders, d. Pierce David.

HORROR: SCI-FI: Scientists-Mad; Police Stories; Murders of Police; Psycho Killers; Revenge; Criminal Pursues Good Guy's Family

Scanners, 1980, 102m, ★★½/$$, Filmplan-Col/Col, R/EV-B&G. A race of telepathic and telekinetic people emerges in Canada, forming a quasi-political alliance. Oh yeah, and they blow up people's heads, too. Jennifer O'Neill, Patrick McGoohan, Stephen Lack, Michael Ironside. w. d. David Cronenberg.

HORROR: SCI-FI: Human Monsters; Deaths-One by One; Surrealism; Psychics; Writer-Directors; Cult Films; Exploding Heads
(Videodrome; Trancers; Deadlock)

Scanners II, The New Order, 1991, 104m, ★★/$, Ind/Media. The telepathic head-busters are back. This time, a corrupt city official tries to use them to help him extend his power. David Hewlett, Yvan Ponton, Deborah Raffin, Isabelle Majias, Raoul Trujillo, Vlasta Brana. w. B. J. Nelson, d. Christian Duguay.

HORROR: SCI-FI: Human Monsters; Deaths-One by One; Surrealism; Psychics

The Scapegoat, 1958, 92m, ★★★/$, MGM/NA. A man on vacation in the Riviera is tricked into playing the part of his lookalike in a scheme that pretends to be one thing, but really is murder. Alec Guinness, Bette Davis, Irene Worth, Pamela Brown. w. Gore Vidal, Robert Hamer, N-adap. Daphne DuMaurier, d. Robert Hamer.

SUSPENSE: MURDER: Lookalikes; Nerds; Con Artists; Clever Plots & Endings; Vacations; Riviera Life; Coulda Been Great; Hitchcockian; Forgotten Films; Hidden Gems
(Body Heat; Dave; Shattered)

The Scar, 1948, 83m, ★★★/$, Eagle-Lion/Republic. A convict kills his thera-

pist, for whom he is a dead ringer, and takes over his life. Unfortunately, he hadn't bargained on the fact that the therapist had a few skeletons in his closet as well. Joan Bennett, Paul Henreid, Eduard Franz, Leslie Brooks, John Qualen, Mabel Paige. w. Daniel Fuchs, N-adap. Murray Forbes, d. Steve Sekely.

SUSPENSE: MURDER: Double Lives; Impostors; Lookalikes; Psychiatrists; Secrets-Keeping; Ex-Convicts; Turning the Tables; Coulda Been Great; Forgotten Films
(A Kiss Before Dying; Dark Mirror)

Scaramouche, 1952, 115m, ★★★½/$$$, MGM/MGM-UA, Voyager. A swashbuckling adventure during the French Revolution, in which a fencing nobleman, disguised as an actor, seeks vengeance upon the evil marquis who murdered his friend. Stewart Granger, Mel Ferrer, Eleanor Parker, Janet Leigh, Nina Foch. w. Ronald Millar, George Froeschel, N-adap. Rafael Sabatini, d. George Sidney.

ACTION: DRAMA: MURDER: ADVENTURE: Costume Drama; Revenge; Avenging Death of Someone; Actors; Disguises; Swashbucklers; French Revolution
(The Scarlet Pimpernel; The Count of Monte Cristo; Les Miserables)
(Ed: Reputed to have the "longest swordfight in cinema history," clocking in at 6½ minutes)

Scarecrow, 1973, 115m, ★★½/$, WB/WB, R/P-S. Two drifters hitchhiking across America encounter various characters and adventures along the way. Gene Hackman, Al Pacino. w. Garry Michael White, d. Jerry Schatzberg.

DRAMA: Character Studies; Slice of Life Stories; Friendships-Male; Homeless People; Drifters; Road Movies; Hitchhikers; Buddy Films; 1970s; Coulda Been Good
(Midnight Cowboy; The Saint of Fort Washington)
(Ed: The dry flipside of Midnight Cowboy, in some ways more realistic and yet less telling)

Scared Stiff, 1953, 108m, ★★½/$$, Par/Par. A comedy and song-and-dance duo vy for the attentions of a young woman who inherited a haunted castle off the coast of Cuba. Dean Martin, Jerry Lewis, Lizabeth Scott, Carmen Miranda, Dorothy Malone. w. Herbert Baker,

Walter de Leon, d. George Marshall, Ed Simmons, Norman Lear.

COMEDY: ROMANCE: Romantic Comedy; Comedians; Horror Comedy; Ghosts; Caribbean; Ships; Castles; Houses-Creepy; Haunted Houses

REMAKE OF: The Ghost Breakers
(Ed: Most notable for Lewis' Carmen Miranda routine with the record getting stuck)

Scarface, 1932, 90m, ★★★½/$$$$, Hughes/MCA-U. A Chicago gangster, based on Al Capone, ruthlessly muscles his way to the top of the gangland heap. Paul Muni, Ann Dvorak, George Raft, Boris Karloff, Osgood Perkins, Karen Morley. w. Ben Hecht, Seton I. Miller, John Lee Mahin, W. R. Burnett, Fred Pasley, N-adap. Armitage Traill, d. Howard Hawks.

ACTION: Crime Drama; Criminal Biographies; Mob Stories; Mob Wars; Power-Rise to; Power Struggles; Biographies-Fictional; Evil Men; Bootlegging; Chicago; 1930s; Al Capone (Capone; The Untouchables)

Scarface, 1983, 170m, ★★½/$$$, Universal/MCA-U, R/EV-EP-FN. A violent, foul-mouthed remake of above classic with Al Pacino, this time as a Cuban gangster in Miami, and with the added element of drugs. Al Pacino, Steven Bauer, Michelle Pfeiffer, Mary Elizabeth Mastrantonio, Robert Loggia. w. Oliver Stone, d. Brian de Palma.

ACTION: Crime Drama; Criminal Biographies; Mob Stories; Mob Wars; Power-Rise to; Power Struggles; Biographies-Fictional; Drugs-Dealing; Evil Men; Miami; 1980s; Al Capone (Year of the Dragon; The Untouchables)

The Scarface Mob/The Untouchables Pilot, 1962, 120m, ★★★/$$$, Desilu-Quinn Martin/Par. Al Capone runs his operations from inside Alcatraz, and Chicago cop Eliot Ness fights to close them down. Robert Stack, Neville Brand, Keenan Wynn, Barbara Nichols, Joe Mantell, Pat Crowley. w. Paul Monash, N-adap. Eliot Ness (The Untouchables), d. Phil Karlson.

ACTION: Crime Drama; Criminal Biographies; Detective Stories; Police vs. Mob; Mob Wars; Police Stories; Detectives-Police; Good vs. Evil; Chicago; 1920s; Bootlegging; Al Capone; TV Series; TV Pilots; Alcatraz (The Untouchables; Nitti; The Enforcer)

The Scarlet Claw, 1944, 74m, ★★★/$$, Universal/Fox. Sherlock Holmes must ferret out the perpetrator of a series of ghastly murders in a Canadian mountain village. Basil Rathbone, Nigel Bruce, Miles Mander, Gerald Hamer, Paul Cavanagh. w. Edmund L. Hartmann, Roy William Neill, d. Roy William Neill.
MYSTERY: MURDER: MURDER MYSTERY: Detective Stories; Murders-One by One; Serial Killers; Canada; Sherlock Holmes

The Scarlet Empress, 1934, 109m, ★★★/$$, Par/MCA-U. A loose interpretation of the historical facts of the life of Catherine the Great. Marlene Dietrich, John Lodge, Sam Jaffe, Louise Dresser, C. Aubrey Smith. w. Manuel Komroff, d. Josef Von Sternberg.
DRAMA: Costume Drama; Historical Drama; Biographies; Queens; Royalty; Russians; Female Protagonists; Catherine the Great
(Catherine the Great; Rasputin and the Empress)

The Scarlet Letter, 1926, B&W, silent, 90m, ★★★/$$$, MGM/NA. The classic American tragedy of a "good woman" who must suffer rather than reveal that the father of her illegitimate son is the local priest. Lillian Gish, Lars Hanson, Karl Dane, Henry B. Walthall. w. Frances Marion, N-adap. Nathaniel Hawthorne, d. Victor Sjostrom.

The Scarlet Letter, 1934, 69m (Darmour/Majestic). One of many remakes of the classic tale of the adulterous woman made to wear a huge red "A" on her chest in the public square in Puritan New England. Colleen Moore, Hardie Albright, Henry B. Walthall, Alan Hale. w. Leonard Fields, David Silverstein, N-adap. Nathaniel Hawthorne, d. Robert G. Vignola.
OTHER VERSIONS: 1973, 1980.
An unwed mother in old New England is branded an adulteress and wears a red A on her chest because of her unwillingness to tell that the father is the town minister.
DRAMA: MELODRAMA: TRAGEDY: Cheating Women; Cheating Men; Romance with Married Person; Sexuality; Mothers-Unwed; Secrets-Keeping; Female Protagonists; 1600s; New England; Early America; Classic Literary Adaptations; Classic Tragedy
(The Crucible; Maid of Salem)

The Scarlet Letter, 1995, 135m, ★★1/2/$, Tri-Star/Col-Tri, R/S-FFN-MN. A colonial woman who has come to America without her husband falls for a religious man and has a child by him, for which she's forced to wear a scarlet "A" on her blouse for being an adulteress. She bears the burden of her sins, but will she forever? Demi Moore, Gary Oldman, Robert Duvall, Lisa Jolliff-Andoh, Edward Hardwicke, Robert Prosky, Roy Dotrice, Joan Plowright, Malcolm Storry, Jim Bearden, Larissa Lapchinski, Amy Wright, Dana Ivey, Diane Salinger. w. Douglas Day Stewart, d. Roland Joffe.
DRAMA: Erotic Drama; Message Films; Cheating Women; Romance-Forbidden; Early America; Ostracism; Allegorical Stories; Revisionist Films; Female Protagonists
(Ed: What could have been an interesting parallel to today's religious conflicts has gained a reputation as an erotic Harlequin opus)

The Scarlet Pimpernel, 1934, 98m, ★★★1/2/$$$, London/Nos. A swash-buckling Englishman in a red cape helps French nobles escape the guillotine during the revolution. Leslie Howard, Merle Oberon, Raymond Massey, Nigel Bruce. w. Robert E. Sherwood, Sam Berman, Arthur Wimperis Lajos Biro, N-adap. Baroness Orczy, d. Harold Young.
ACTION: ADVENTURE: Swashbucklers; Costume Drama; Escape Adventure; Saving Someone; French Revolution; Rich People; Royalty; Executions
REMAKE: The Elusive Pimpernel.
(A Tale of Two Cities; Les Miserables)
(Ed: Sort of Robin Hood in reverse)

Scarlet Street, 1945, 103m, ★★★/$$, Universal/Nos. A "john" kills the prostitute he frequents, but the murder is pinned on her pimp. Edward G. Robinson, Joan Bennett, Dan Duryea, Jess Barker. w. Dudley Nichols, P-adap. George de la Fouchardiere, S-adap. *La Chienne*, d. Fritz Lang.
DRAMA: MURDER: Accused Unjustly; Framed?; Prostitutes-Low Class; Pimps; Unbelieved; Crime Pays; Underrated; Ahead of Its Time; Forgotten Films; Hidden Gems; Foreign Film Remakes
REMAKE OF: *La Chienne* by Jean Renoir.
(Ed: Maybe you'll prefer the original French version, but this is pretty daring

for its time. However, if it hadn't been the French to do it first, would it have been done by Hollywood?-because it's reputed to be the first major Hollywood release where crime paid)

Scavenger Hunt, 1979, 117m, ★★/$, 20th/Fox, PG. A millionaire's will states whoever gathers all of the items on his scavenger list gets his fortune, so a bunch of loonies are off and running. Cloris Leachman, Cleavon Little, Vincent Price, Richard Benjamin, James Coco, Ruth Buzzi, Tony Randall, Robert Morley, Roddy McDowell. w. Steven A. Vail, Henry Harper, d. Michael Schultz.
COMEDY: Screwball Comedy; FARCE: Treasure Hunts; Inheritances at Stake; Feuds; Ensemble Films; Eccentric People; Criminals-Stupid; Coulda Been Good
(It's a Mad, Mad, Mad, Mad World; Million Dollar Mystery)

Scene of the Crime, 1987, 90m, ★★★/$, Triumph/Col, R/S, V. A fugitive hiding in a small town is led by a son to his mother, who is then seduced by the dangerous drifter, leading to a big dilemma. Catherine Deneuve, Danielle Darrieux, Victor Lanoux. d. Andre Techine.
DRAMA: Fugitives from the Law; Hiding Out; Fugitives-Harboring; Small-town Life; Romance-Dangerous; Men and Boys; Mothers & Sons; Widows; Sexy Men; Hidden Gems
(Choice of Arms)
(Ed: A bit slow to be very entertaining by American standards, even with the premise)

Scenes from a Marriage, 1973, 168m, ★★★1/2/$$$, Col/Col, R/S. In Sweden, a marriage begins crumbling in excruciating, realistic detail. Liv Ullman, Erland Josephson, Bibi Anderson. w. d. Ingmar Bergman.
DRAMA: Psychological Drama; Marriage Drama; Marriage on the Rocks; Ordinary People Stories; Swedish Films; Writer-Directors; Art Films; Hidden Gems; Faded Hits; Bergmanesque
(Face to Face; Persona; Cries and Whispers)

Scenes from the Class Struggle in Beverly Hills, 1989, 102m, ★★★/$$, Cinecom/Cinecom, R/S-P-FN-MN. A TV actress (Jacqueline Bisset) has an assortment of friends and servants after each other when they gather for a party. Ray Sharkey, Ed Begley, Jr., Ametia Walker,

Robert Beltran, Mary Woronov, Paul Bartel. w. Bruce Wagner, Paul Bartel, d. Paul Bartel.

COMEDY: FARCE: Bedroom Farce; **SATIRE:** Erotic Comedy; Rich People; Servants; Class Conflicts; Bathroom Humor; Beverly Hills; Actresses; Coulda Been Great; Underrated; Independent Films

REMAKE/RETREAD OF: Rules of the Game

(Eating Raoul; Lust in the Dust; Down and Out in Beverly Hills)

(Ed: Just misses the mark)

Scenes from a Mall, 1990, 87m, ★★½/ $$, Touchstone/Touchstone, R/P-S. A jaded, middle-aged couple's marriage begins coming apart when secrets are revealed and confrontations are made on a day-long trip to the mall. Woody Allen, Bette Midler. w. Roger L. Simon, Paul Mazursky, d. Paul Mazursky.

COMEDY DRAMA: Marriage Comedy; Marriage on the Rocks; Cheating Men; Romance-Bickering; Neurotic People; Secrets-Haunting; Mid-Life Crisis; Hollywood Life; One Day Stories

(Scenes from a Marriage; Husbands and Wives)

(Ed: Not up to Allen's own work, but still worth seeing if you're a fan of either star)

Scent of a Woman, 1992, 157m, ★★★½/$$$$, U/MCA-U, PG/P-S. A young boarding school student in a program to help the handicapped gets sent to the house of a blind World War II vet who proceeds to teach him about life and has him experience a bit too much of it. Al Pacino (**BActor**), Chris O'Donnell, James Rebhorn, Gabrielle Anwar, Philip S. Hoffman, Richard Venture. w. Bo Goldman (AScr), N-adap. *Il Buio il Miele*, Giovanni Arpino, S-adap, *Profumo di Donna*, d. Martin Brest (**BDirector**). BPicture. Oscars: 4-1.

COMEDY DRAMA: MELODRAMA: Men and Boys; Fathers-Surrogate; Teenagers; Young Men; Coming of Age; Blind People; Disabled People; Stern Men; Boarding Schools; Vacations; Suicidal Tendencies; Mid-life Crisis; New England; New York Life; Old-Fashioned; Recent Films

(And Justice for All)

(Ed: The finale is a bit much but the crowds cheered)

The Scent of Green Papaya, 1993, 100m, ★★★/$, Miramax/Touchstone,

R/S. The life of a peasant girl in Vietnam as she goes to the city and becomes a servant to the aristocracy. Tran Nu Yen-Khe, Le Man San. w. Tran Anh Hung, Patricia Petit, d. Tran Anh Hung. BFLFilm. Oscars: 1-0.

DRAMA: Servants; City vs. Country; Class Conflicts; Young Women; Coming of Age; Female Protagonists; 1950s; French Films; Vietnam; Female Screenwriters

(Ed: Made in France on a soundstage but by a Vietnamese native)

Scent of Mystery (Holiday in Spain), 1959, 125m, ★★/$$, Cinerama-Todd/NA. The story of a girl in Spain, the people who want to murder her, and her vacationing English protector. Denholm Elliott, Peter Lorre, Beverly Bentley, Paul Lukas, Elizabeth Taylor. w. William Rose, d. Jack Cardiff.

MYSTERY: SUSPENSE: Women in Jeopardy; Girls; Young Women; Spain; Vacations; Camp; Forgotten Films

(Ed: First to use the gimmick of smell-o-vision using scratch-n-sniff cards in the theater)

Schindler's List, 1993, 195m, ★★★★/ $$$$$$, U/MCA-U, R/S-EV. True story of the opportunistic Oskar Schindler, a manufacturer during World War II in Germany who, by using Jews as slave labor, then finds himself in a position to save their lives by placing their names on a list which he demands to the Nazis he retain as employees, despite the concentration camp round-up. Liam Neeson (BActor), Ben Kingsley, Ralph Fiennes (BSActor), Priscilla Pointer, Jonathan Sagalle, Embeth Davidtz. w. Steve Zaillian (**BAScr**), N-adap. Thomas Keneally (a nonfiction novel), d. Steven Spielberg (**BDirector**). Oscars: **BPicture, BCin, BEdit,** BSound, **BArt, BOScore,** BCostume, BMakeup. Oscars: 12-7.

DRAMA: TRAGEDY: MELODRAMA: Tearjerkers; World War II Stories; Saving Someone; Jews-Saving; Jewish People; Nazi Stories; Anti-Semitism; Concentration Camps; Ethics; Business Life; Clever Plots & Endings; Race Against Time; Heroes-Unlikely; Sleeper Hits; Blockbusters

(The Raoul Wallenberg Story; The White Rose; The Diary of Anne Frank)

School Daze, 1988, 120m, ★★★/$$, Columbia/RCA-Col, PG-13/P-S. Life at a black college with battling factions within

set to music and dance. Larry Fishburne, Spike Lee, Giancarlo Esposito, Tisha Campbell, Ossie Davis, Joe Seneca, Tyra Ferrell, Branford Marsalis. w. d. Spike Lee.

COMEDY DRAMA: MUSICALS: Musical Drama; **SATIRE:** Black Casts; Race Relations; College Life; Fraternity Life; Sorority Life; Coulda Been Great; Black Screenwriters; Black Directors; Writer-Directors; Buppies

(She's Gotta Have It; Higher Learning; PCU)

(Ed: The main racial situation touched upon here and virtually nowhere else is the differences between lighter and darker skinned blacks)

School for Husbands, 1930, 73m, ★★½/$, Wainright/NA. Adored by his scores of female fans, a writer of romances becomes the thorn in the side of their husbands. Rex Harrison, Henry Kendall, Romney Brent. w. Frederick Jackson, Gordon Aherry, Austin Melford, P-adap. Frederick Jackson, d. Andrew Marton.

COMEDY: Comedy of Manners; Misunderstandings; Romance Novelists; Writers; Sexy Men

The School for Scandal, 1930, 73m, ★★/$, Albion/NA. Two brothers get into trouble because the "bad" one is assumed to be good, and vice-versa. Madeleine Carroll, Basil Gill, Henry Hewitt, Ian Fleming. w. Jean Jay, P-adap. Richard Brinsley Sheridan, d. Maurice Elvey.

FARCE: COMEDY: Comedy of Manners; Brothers; Identities-Mistaken; Mix-ups; Classic Literary Adaptations; Coulda Been Great

(Steal Little, Steal Big; Brotherly Love)

School for Scoundrels, 1960, 94m, ★★★/$$, APB-Guardsman/NA. Con artists at a boarding school in England have some clever fund-raising plans. Ian Carmichael, Alastair Sim, Terry-Thomas, Janette Scott. w. Patricia Mayes, Hal E. Chester, N-adap. Stephen Potter, d. Robert Hamer.

COMEDY: FARCE: Con Artists; Boarding Schools; British Films; Hidden Gems; Forgotten Films; Female Screenwriters

School Ties, 1992, 107m, ★★½/$$, Par/Par, PG/P-MRN. In the fifties, a boy wins a scholarship to a New England prep school and must conceal the fact that he is Jewish once he gets there. Brendan Fraser, Matt Damon, Chris O'Donnell, Amy Locane, Ed Lauter. w. Dick Wolf, Darryl Ponicsan, d. Robert Mandel.

DRAMA: Social Drama; Message Films; Anti-Semitism; Jewish People; Romance-Class; Conflicts; Coming of Age; Ostracism; Bigots; Football; Young Men; Teeangers; Boarding Schools; Mining Towns; Coulda Been Good; 1950s (Gentleman's Agreement; Crossfire; Au Revoir Les Enfants; Olivier, Olivier) (Ed: Cliches abound, and the point is lessened because never once does the script try to get at the origins or conformist nature of the prejudice. If you didn't know about anti-Semitism, this real problem might seem all the more superfluous and therefore dismissable as something which only happened back then)

Schtonk!, 1992, 111m, ★★★/$$, Bavarian Film. A German huckster, claiming to have found Hitler's lost diaries, is revealed to have actually produced them himself. Götz George, Uwe Ochsenknecht, Christiane Hörbiger, Dagmar Manzel. w. Helmut Dietl, Ulrich Limmer, d. Helmut Dietl. BFLFilm. Oscars: 1-0.

COMEDY: Black Comedy; **FARCE:** Impostors; Con Artists; Hoaxes; Scandals; Newspapers; German Films; Germany; Hitler (Ed: Excellent for those with the acquired taste)

Scorchers, 1991, 81m, ★★/VR, Ind/Fox, R/P-S. In a small southern town, the local prostitute and other assorted miscreants gather at the local bar to sort out their problems amid the goings on outside, including a married couple where the wife is a little afraid of the wedding night. Faye Dunaway, Denholm Elliott, James Earl Jones, Emily Lloyd, Jennifer Tilly, Luke Perry. w. d. P-adap. David Beaird.

COMEDY DRAMA: MELODRAMA: Small-town Life; Southerns; Eccentric People; Multiple Stories; Interwoven Stories; Virgins; Newlyweds; Prostitutes-Low Class; Coulda Been Good; Tennessee; Williams-esque; Writer-Directors; Independent Films (Ed: The disjointed nature destroys what good lines and performances there are)

Scorpio, 1972, 114m, ★★½/$, UA/MGM-UA, R/V. A tale of intrigue and betrayal in the ranks of the CIA. Burt Lancaster, Alain Delon, Paul Scofield, Gayle Hunnicutt. w. David W. Rintels, Gerald Wilson, d. Michael Winner.

Spy Films; **SUSPENSE:** Spies; CIA Agents; Fugitives; Chase Movies; Betrayal; Double Crossings; Coulda Been Good (Midnight Man; The Human Factor [1979])

Scotland Yard, 1941, 68m, ★★½/$$, 20th/NA. During the war, a Nazi who happens to be the spitting image of a bank executive in London takes his place and embezzles large sums in the name of Der Furher. Nancy Kelly, Edmund Gwenn, Henry Wilcoxon, Melville Cooper, Norma Varden. w. Samuel G. Engel, John Balderston, P-adap. Deniston Clift, d. Norman Foster.

SUSPENSE: DRAMA: Heist Stories; Bank Robberies; Lookalikes; Impostors; Nazi Stoires; Spies; World War II Stories (The Man Who Watched Trains Go By; The Stranger)

Scott of the Antarctic, 1948, 110m, ★★★/$, Ealing/Nos. The true story of the perilous journey of Captain Scott to the South Pole. John Mills, James Robertson Justice, Derek Bond. w. Ivor Montagu, Walter Meade, Mary Hayley Bell, d. Charles Frend.

ADVENTURE: DRAMA: Journies; Explorers; Scientists; Anarctica

The Scoundrel, 1935, 74m, ★★★/$$, Par/NA. When a man-about-town and popular author dies, his ghost decides he's not finished learning about life and love. Noel Coward, Alexander Woolcott, Julie Haydon, Eduardo Ciannelli. w. d. Ben Hecht.

DRAMA: Fantasy; Ghosts; Dead-Back from the; Life Transitions; Writers; Writer-Directors (Blithe Spirit; Topper)

The Scout, 1994, 95m, ★★½/$, 20th/Fox, PG-13/P. A Yankees scout who's about to lose his job finds a way to keep it by finding an incredible pitcher-but the guy has a few screws loose and may undo everything. Albert Brooks, Brendan Fraser, Dianne Weist, Lane Smith, Michael Rappaport, Steve Garvey, Bob Costas, Anne Twomey, Tony Bennett. w. Albert Brooks, Andrew Bergman, Monica Johnson, d. Michael Ritchie.

COMEDY: COMEDY DRAMA: Sports Movies; Baseball; Simple Minds; Unemployment; Race Against Time; One Last Chance; Coulda Been Great; Overlooked at Release; Female Screenwriters (Ed: Chalk up another pretty good flop for both Fraser and Ritchie; but also one too many baseball movies in a year that saw the season strike out)

Scream and Scream Again!, 1969, 95m, ★★½/$, AIP/Vestron, Live. A deranged madman creates beings out of human remains who go around killing people for sustenance. Vincent Price, Christopher Lee, Peter Cushing, Alfred Marks, David Lodge. w. Christopher Wicking, N-adap. Peter Saxon (The Disoriented Man), d. Gordon Hessler.

HORROR: Scientists-Mad; Body Parts; Experiments; Human Monsters; **MURDER:** Serial Killers; Murders-One by One (Frankenstein; The Doctor and the Devils)

Screaming Mimi, 1958, 79m, ★★/$, Col./NA. A neurotic dancer continually relives an assault, eventually coming to a shocking revelation. Anita Ekberg, Phil Carey, Harry Townes, Gypsy Rose Lee, Alan Gifford. w. Robert Blees, N-adap. Robert Brown, d. Gerd Oswald.

DRAMA: Rape/Rapists; Psychological Drama; Women Fighting Back; **MURDER:** Nightmares; Suspecting Oneself; Flashbacks; Dancers; Strippers

Scrooge, 1951, see A Christmas Carol

Scrooge (A Christmas Carol), 1935, 78m, ★★★/$$$, Twickenham/Critic's Choice. The classic Dickens tale of a stingy old financier who learns the value of charity when three ghosts visit him on Christmas Eve. Seymour Hicks, Donald Calthrop, Athene Styler, Barbara Everest. w. Seymour Hicks, H. Fowler Mear, N-adap. Charles Dickens (A Christmas Carol), d. Henry Edwards.

DRAMA: MELODRAMA: Fantasy; Nightmares; Stern Men; Flashbacks; Ghosts; Christmas; Bosses-Bad; Redemption

REMAKE: 1951, A Christmas Carol, **MUSICAL REMAKE**, 1970. (Scrooge, 1970; A Christmas Carol; Scrooged)

Scrooge, 1970, 113m, 86m, ★★★/$$, Cinema Center/Fox. A musical version of the classic Dickens tale. Albert Finney, Michael Medwin, Alec Guinness, Edith Evans, Kenneth More. w. Leslie Bricusse, N-adap. Charles Dickens, d. Ronald Neame.

MUSICALS: DRAMA: Musical Drama; Musical Fantasy; Fantasy; Nightmares; Stern Men; Flashbacks; Ghosts; Bosses-Bad; Christmas; Redemption

MUSICAL REMAKE OF: 1935 and 1951 versions.

(Scrooge; A Christmas Carol; Scrooged)

Scrooged, 1988, 101m, ★★★/$$$, Par/Par, PG-13/P. A modern-day version of the classic, with Bill Murray as a cynical TV executive. Bill Murray, Karen Allen, John Forsythe, Robert Mitchum, Carol Kane, Alfre Woodard. w. Mitch Glazer, Michael O'Donoghue, d. Richard Donner.

COMEDY: COMEDY DRAMA: Tragi-Comedy; **SATIRE:** TV Life; Ghosts; Bosses-Bad; Evil Men; Stern Men; Executive Life; Revisionist Films; Coulda Been Great

(What About Bob?; Groundhog Day)

The Sea Beast, 1926, 125m, ★★★/$$$, B&W, silent, WB/NA. The tale of Captain Ahab and the whale, with a slapped-on happy ending. John Barrymore, Dolores Costello, George O'Hara, Mike Donlin. w. Bess Meredyth, N-adap. Herman Melville *(Moby Dick)*, d. Millard Webb.

ADVENTURE: Adventure at Sea; Ships; Obsessions; Fisherman; Classic Literary Adaptations; Female Screenwriters

REMAKE: Moby Dick.

(Ed: Notable only for early special effects sequences)

The Sea Chase, 1955, 117m, ★★¹/₂/$$$, WB/WB. In the early days of World War II, a German ship has to beat a hasty retreat from Australia back to its native shores. John Wayne, Lana Turner, David Farrar, Tab Hunter, James Arness. w. James Warner Bellah, John Twist, N-adap. Andrew Geer, d. John Farrow.

ADVENTURE: Adventure at Sea; World War II Stories; War Stories; Ships; Australia; Race Against Time; Chase Movies; Journies; Australia

Sea Devils, 1937, 88m, ★★/$$, RKO/Media. The adventures of the Coast Guard in its early days. Victor McLaglen, Preston Foster, Ida Lupino, Donald Woods. w. Frank Wead, John Twist and P. J. Wolfson, d. Ben Stoloff.

ADVENTURE: Adventures at Sea; Military Movies; Police Stories

Sea Devils, 1953, 90m, ★★/$$, Coronado-Ind/Media. Napoleon's plans to invade England are thwarted by seafaring spies. Yvonne de Carlo, Rock Hudson,

Maxwell Reed, Denis O'Dea. w. Borden Chase, d. Raoul Walsh.

ADVENTURE: Spy Films; Spies; War Stories; Swashbucklers; 1800s; Napoleon (Waterloo; Desiree)

The Sea Gull, 1968, 141m, ★★★/$, WB/NA. A saga of the shifting romantic and personal allegiences of an aristocratic Russian family at the turn of the century. James Mason, Simone Signoret, Vanessa Redgrave, David Warner, Denholm Elliott. w. Moura Budberg, P-adap. Anton Checkhov, d. Sidney Lumet.

DRAMA: Family Drama; Family Stories; Ensemble Films; Feuds; Rich People; Russians; Classic Literary Adaptations; Stagelike Films; Forgotten Films; Hidden Gems

(Fanny and Alexander; The Brothers Karamazov)

The Sea Hawk, 1940, 122m, ★★★¹/₂/$$$$, WBMGM-UA. Brave English captains fight the Spanish, using all necessary means, and are urged on by Elizabeth I. Errol Flynn, Flora Robson, Brenda Marshall, Henry Daniell, Claude Rains, Donald Crisp, Alan Hale. w. Seton I. Miller, Howard Koch, d. Michael Curtiz.

ADVENTURE: War Stories; Swashbucklers; Queens; England; Elizabethan Era

Sea of Grass, 1947, 131m, ★★★/$$, MGM/MGM-UA. A cattleman in the New Mexico-Texas region is visited by a woman who finds it hard to get close to him, as does his family, since business comes first. Spencer Tracy, Katharine Hepburn, Melvyn Douglas, Phyllis Thaxter, Robert Walker, Edgar Buchanan, Harry Carey. w. Marguerite Roberts, Vincent Lawrence, N-adap. Conrad Richter, d. Elia Kazan.

DRAMA: WESTERNS: Cattle People; Female Among Males; **ROMANCE:** Romance-Reluctant; Farm Life; Obsessions; Stern Men; New Mexico; 1900s; Female Screenwriters; Female Protagonists; Quiet Little Films; Tracy & Hepburn (Out of Africa; Cattle Queen of Montana)

(Ed: Only for Tracy & Hepburn fans; interesting at times, but rather slow-moving)

Sea of Love, 1989, 112m, ★★★/$$$, Universal/MCA-U, R/P-EV-S-FN. A cop (Al Pacino) on the trail of an apparent female serial killer of men she meets through personal ads may have fallen in love with his prey (Ellen Barkin). Al Pacino, Ellen Barkin, John Goodman,

Michael Rooker. w. N-adap. Richard Price, d. Harold Becker.

SUSPENSE: MYSTERY: MURDER MYSTERY: Serial Killers; Murderers-Female; Detective Stories; Detectives-Police; Police Stories; Detectives in Deep; Mystery-Whodunit; Dangerous Women; Romance-Dangerous; Love-Questionable; Personal Ads

(Basic Instinct; Jagged Edge)

The Sea Wife, 1957, 82m, ★★¹/₂/$$, 20th/NA. After a shipwreck in Singapore, a British man falls for a woman who he doesn't know is a nun. Richard Burton, Joan Collins, Basil Sydney. w. George Burke, N-adap. J.M. Scott, d. Bob McNaught.

DRAMA: ROMANCE: Romance-Doomed; Romance-Reluctant; Romance with Clergy; Nuns; Shipwrecked; British Films (Heaven Knows, Mr. Allison)

(Ed: Joan Collins as a nun?! That alone makes it worth checking out)

The Sea Wolf, 1941, 90m, ★★★¹/₂/$$$, WB/MGM-UA. When a ferry crashes in San Francisco Bay, the survivors are rescued by the captain of a commercial ship who turns out to be a murderous psychopath. Edward G. Robinson, Alexander Knox, Ida Lupino, John Garfield, Gene Lockhart, Barry Fitzgerald, Howard da Silva. w. Robert Rossen, N-adap. Jack London, d. Michael Curtiz.

DRAMA: SUSPENSE: Rescue Drama; Shipwrecked; Secrets-Keeping; Dual Lives; Murderers-Nice; Heroes-Unlikely

REMAKE OF: (4 silent versions);

REMAKES: Barricade (a Western), Wolf Larsen, Wolf of the Seven Seas.

The Sea Wolves, 1980, 120m, Lorimar-20th/WB. During World War II, a group of British retirees in India jump into the fray and capture a Nazi for the queen. Gregory Peck, Roger Moore, Trevor Howard, David Niven, Barbara Kellerman, Terence Longdon. w. Reginald Rose, N-adap. James Leasor *(Boarding Party)*, d. Andrew McLaglen.

ACTION: War Stories; Mercenaries; Spies; Manhunts; Bounty Hunters; Nazi Stories; Germans as Enemy; World War II Stories

(Ffolkes; The Wild Geese)

Seance on a Wet Afternoon, 1964, 115m, ★★★/$$, Artixo/HomeVision. A child is kidnapped by a middle-aged couple as part of a pathetic scheme to prove the "psychic" powers of the woman. Kim

Stanley (BActress), Richard Attenborough, Nanette Newman. w. d. Bryan Forbes. Oscars: 1-0.

DRAMA: SUSPENSE: Kidnappings; Children in Jeopardy; Hoaxes; Con Artists; Fortune-tellers; Psychics; Criminals-Female; British Films; Female Protagonists; Coulda Been Great; Forgotten Films; Hidden Gems; Writer-Directors, Independent Films
(Family Plot)
(Ed: Great title, good film)

The Search, 1948, 105m, ★★★¹/₂/$$$, MGM/MGM-UA. A war orphan in Germany is taken under the wing of a kindly American G.I. Montgomery Clift (BActor), Aline MacMahon, Ivan Jandl (**BJuvenile**), Wendell Corey. w. Richard Schweizer, David Wechsler, Paul Jarrico (**BOStory**, BScr), d. Fred Zinnemann (BDirector). Oscars: 5-2.

DRAMA: MELODRAMA: Tearjerkers; Searches; Manhunts; Missing Persons; Missing Children; Men and Boys; Soldiers; World War II Era; Sleeper Hits; Forgotten Films; Hidden Gems

The Search for Bridey Murphy, 1956, 84m, Par/Par. A Colorado housewife in the fifties "discovered" under hypnosis that she was the young Bridey, an Irish girl, in another life. This first nationally publicized case of claimed reincarnation is examined from a psychological viewpoint. Teresa Wright, Louis Hayward. w. d. Noel Langley.

DRAMA: Psychological Drama; Searches; Psychics; Reincarnation; Nightmares; Flashbacks; Ordinary People Stories; Hypnosis; Writer-Directors; Incredible but Mostly True
(The Reincarnation of Peter Proud)

The Searchers, 1956, 119m, ★★★¹/₂/$$$, WB/WB, Time-Life. A Southern veteran of the Civil War embarks on a mission of vengeance, hunting down the Indians who killed his brother and kidnapped his niece. John Wayne, Jeffrey Hunter, Natalie Wood, Vera Miles, Ward Bond. w. Frank S. Nugent, N-adap. Alan le May, d. John Ford.

WESTERNS: Searches; Missing Persons; Journies; Manhunts; Avenging Death of Loved One; Revenge; Indians-American; Civil War Era; Allegorical Stories; Lyrical Films; Cult Films
(Stagecoach; Fort Apache; The Magnificent Seven)

(Ed: Much acclaimed by film historians and history buffs, but others feel there's too much credit given to it)

Searching for Bobby Fischer, 1993, 111m, ★★★/$$, Par/Par, PG. A chess whiz who's only seven has a dad who wants him to succeed but also to live a regular life. This is hard to do with the demanding eccentrics who enter his life, wanting him to be the next Fischer. Joe Mantegna, Max Pomeranc, Joan Allen, Ben Kingsley, Larry Fishburne, Robert Stephens, David Paymer. w. d. Steve Zaillian, NF-adap. Fred Waitzkin.

DRAMA: MELODRAMA: Family Drama; Chess Games Geniuses; Children-Little Adults; Proteges; Boys; Fathers & Sons; Men and Boys; Fame-Rise to; Overlooked at Release; Hidden Gems (Little Man Tate)

Sebastiane, 1979, 90m, ★★★/$, Ind/Facets, R/S-MN. The tale of a soldier in an unnamed kingdom, who is exiled and put to death by his commanding officer when he refuses to sleep with him. Leonardo Treviglio, Barney James, Neil Kennedy, Richard Warwick. w. Derek Jarman, James Waley, d. Derek Jarman, Paul Humfress.

DRAMA: TRAGEDY: Gay Men; Homo-eroticism; Ostracism; Executions; Revenge; Sexual Harassment; Soldiers
(The Sergeant; Reflections in a Golden Eye; Poison)
(Ed: Sexual harassment is putting it mildly)

Second Best Secret Agent in the Whole Wide World (License to Kill), 1965, 93m, ★★¹/₂/$, Col/New Line. Russians are out to steal the Swede's antigravity device for which Swedes are most famous and a Bond-like agent is out to stop them. Tom Adams, Veronica Hurst. w. d. Lindsay Shaonteff.

ACTION: Spoofs-Spy; **COMEDY:** Action Comedy; Spy Films; Spies; Secret Agents; Coulda Been Great; Good Premise Unfulfilled; Sweden; Forgotten Films; Writer-Directors
(The Liquidator; In Like Flint)

Second Chance, 1953, 82m, ★★¹/₂/$, Republic/Media. A boxer (Robert Mitchum) goes to Mexico to protect a gangster's girl with a hitman on their tail (Jack Palance). Linda Darnell, Roy Roberts. w. Oscar Millard, Sidney Boehm, SS-adap. D. M. Marshman, d. Rudolph Mate.

DRAMA: SUSPENSE: ROMANCE:

Romance-Dangerous; Mob Stories; Mob Girls; Hitmen; Women in Jeopardy; Men In Jeopardy; Chase Movies; Survival Drama; Boxing; Mexico; 3-D Movies
(Last Rites; Out of the Past; The Fugitive [1947])
(Ed: Slow going for the first half, but then the third act is a harrowing scene on an air tram which is about to snap its line)

Second Chorus, 1940, 83m, ★★/$$, Par./Nos. A woman who manages two trumpeters has big plans for them on Broadway. Fred Astaire, Burgess Meredith, Paulette Goddard, Charles Butterworth, Artie Shaw and his Band, Jimmy Conlon. w. Elaine Ryan, Ian McClellan Hunter, Frank Cavett, d. H. C. Potter.

MUSICALS: MELODRAMA: Musicians; Fame-Rise to; Theater Life; Woman Behind the Man; Female Protagonists; Female Screenwriters

Second Fiddle, 1939, 86m, ★★¹/₂/$$, 20th/Fox. A talent scout goes on a search which ends in Minnesota where he finds skating beauty Henie and wants to make her a star. Her guardian resists, but when she gets to L.A. she's duped by her co-star and may prove the pundits right about the evils of tinsel town. Sonja Henie, Tyrone Power, Rudy Vallee, Edna May Oliver, Lyle Talbot. d. Sidney Canfield.

MUSICALS: ROMANCE: Musical Romance; Hollywood Life; Hollywood Satire; Searches; Fame-Rise to; City vs. Country; Actresses; Skating; Forgotten Films
(Thin Ice; Sun Valley Serenade)

Secret Ceremony, 1969, 109m, ★★¹/₂/$, 20th/Barr Video, R/S. An older prostitute looks like the dead mother of the girl she meets, and the girl looks like her dead daughter, leading to some complicated psychological situations. Elizabeth Taylor, Mia Farrow, Pamela Brown, Robert Mitchum. d. Joseph Losey.

DRAMA: Psychological Drama; Lookalikes; Mothers & Daughters; Dead-Back from the; Friendships-Female; Mindgames; Forgotten Films; Good Premises Unfulfilled; Curiosities; Female Protagonists

Second Honeymoon, 1937, 79m, ★★¹/₂/$$, 20th/NA. A man, still in love with his ex, tries to rekindle a romance with her. Tyrone Power, Loretta Young, Stuart Erwin, Lyle Talbot. w. Kathryn

Scola, Darrell Ware, SS-adap. Philip Wylie, d. Walter Lang.

COMEDY: ROMANCE: Romantic Comedy; Marriage on the Rocks; Marriage Comedy; Romance-Boy Wants Girl; Coulda Been Good; Good Premise Unfulfilled; Forgotten Films; Female Screenwriters

(The Awful Truth; The Marrying Man)

Seconds, 1966, 106m, ★★★/$$, Par/NA, AMC. Rich people are onto a service whereby one's death is faked and then one is brought back to life much healthier-unless something goes wrong. Rock Hudson, John Randolph, Will Geer, Jeff Corey, Richard Anderson, Murray Hamilton. w. Lewis John Carlino. N-adap. David Ely, d. John Frankenheimer. BB&WCin. Oscars: 1-0.

SUSPENSE: SCI-FI: SATIRE: Black Comedy; Fantasy; Elixirs/Cures; Death-Faked; Experiments; Dead-Back from the; Cosmetic Surgery; Forgotten Films; Hidden Gems

(Death Becomes Her; Total Recall)

(Ed: Truly unusual)

Second Sight, 1989, 85m, ★★/$, WB/WB, PG./P. A cop has to take on a hippie-dippy psychic and a nun to solve a case. Only problem is, the psychic's powers sometimes blow up buildings by mistake. John Larroquette, Bronson Pinchot, Bess Armstrong, Stuart Pankin. w. Patricia Resnick, Tom Schulman, d. Joel Zwick.

COMEDY: Comedy Of Errors; Psychics; **MYSTERY:** Detective Stories; Detectives-Police; Nuns; Good Premise Unfulfilled; Coulda Been Good

(Vibes)

(Ed: A goofy mess from otherwise good writers and a prominent sitcom director)

Second Thoughts, 1982, 98m, ★★/$, MTM-U/HBO, PG/S. A rake, in prison, charms his lawyer girlfriend into getting him out on a technicality. She's non-plussed when he dumps her upon his release. Lucie Arnaz, Craig Wasson, Ken Howard. w. Steve Brown, d. Lawrence Turman.

COMEDY DRAMA: ROMANCE: Love-Questionable; Playboys; Jerks; Lawyers; Female Protagonists; Coulda Been Good

Secret Admirer, 1985, 98m, ★★1/2/$$, EMI/HBO, PG/S. When a teenagers unsigned love letter is lost, it goes through a trail of people's hands who all take it to mean what they want it to. C. Thomas

Howell, Kelly Preston, Cliff deYoung, Dee Wallace, Fred Ward, Casey Siezmasko, Corey Haim, Leigh Taylor-Young. d. David Greenwalt.

COMEDY: FARCE: Mix-Ups; Hand-Me-Down Stories; Letters; High School Life; Suburban Life; Teenagers; Teenage Movies; Coulda Been Great; Good Premises Unfulfilled

(No Sex, Please We're British; A Tiger's Tale; Grandview USA)

The Secret Agent, 1936, 86m, ★★★/$$, Gaumont British/Nos. A man falls into the occupation of spying and is forced to kill someone on an early assignment. John Gielgud, Robert Young, Peter Lorre. w. Charles Bennett, P-adap. Campbell Dixon, SS-adap. Somerset Maugham (Ashenden), d. Alfred Hitchcock.

SUSPENSE: Spy Films; Spies; **MURDER:** Murder-Coerced; Secret Agents; British Films; Forgotten Films; Hidden Gems

(Spy in Black)

(Ed: Good early Hitchcock, though not as polished as later Hollywood work)

The Secret Beyond the Door, 1948, 98m, ★★★/$$, NTA/Republic. A woman (Joan Bennett) marries who she thinks is the perfect man (Michael Redgrave) until he behaves strangely and she finds out his mansion includes rooms full of things he's collected from actual murder scenes and she may be living in the next room to be added. w. Sylvia Richards, SS-adap. Rufus King, d. Fritz Lang.

SUSPENSE: MURDER: MYSTERY: MURDER MYSTERY: Film Noir; Women in Jeopardy; Romance-Dangerous; Love-Questionable; Secrets-Haunted by; Secrets-Keeping; Unbelieved; Newlyweds; Love-Questionable; Houses-Creepy; Narrated Films; Hidden Gems; Forgotten Films; Female Protagonists; Female Screenwriters

(Undercurrent; Rebecca; Suspicion)

(Ed: Good atmosphere but kooky unraveling may make it hard to buy)

Secret Friends, 1991, 97m, ★★1/2/VR, Ind/NA. A middle-aged British artist, having an anxiety attack on a train, can't distinguish between what's really happening and what's not, including the possibility that his wife's a murderer. Alan Bates, Gina Bellman, Frances Barber, Tony Doyle. w. d. N-adap. Dennis Potter (Ticket to Ride).

SUSPENSE: MURDER: Nightmares; Fantasies; Murder of Spouse; Midlife

Crisis; Nervous Breakdowns; Character Studies; Overlooked at Release; Hidden Gems

The Secret Garden, 1949, 92m, ★★★/$$, MGM/MGM-UA. Margaret O'Brien, Herbert Marshall, Gladys Cooper, Elsa Lanchester, Dean Stockwell. w. Robert Ardrey, N-adap. Frances Hodgson Burnett, d. Fred M. Wilcox.

The Secret Garden, 1984, 107m, ★★1/2/$$, BBC/Movies Unltd. Sarah Andrews, David Patterson. d. Katrina Murray.

Female Screenwriters

The Secret Garden, 1987, 100m, ★★★/$$$, Hallmark/Republic. Gennie James, Barret Oliver, Michael Hordern, Derek Jacobi, Billie Whitelaw, Julian Glover, Colin Firth.

The Secret Garden, 1993, 102m, ★★★/$$, WB/WB, G. A crochety old man is rejuvenated when his charming, vivacious young niece comes to visit, showing him the magic which exists literally in his own backyard. Kate Maberly, Maggie Smith, Haydon Prowse, Andrew Knott. w. Caroline Thompson, d. Agnieszka Holland.

CHILDREN'S: FAMILY: Fantasy; Mean Men; Redemption; Girls; Fantasies; Hunchbacks; Female Protagonists; Child Protagonists

(A Little Princess; Little Lord Fauntleroy)

Secret Honor, 1984, 90m, ★★★/$, Castle Hill/Vestron, Live. The story of the last days of Nixon before his resignation as he sinks into the abyss of history. Philip Baker Hall. w. P-adap. Arnold Stone, Donald Freed, d. Robert Altman.

DRAMA: SATIRE: Political Satire; Character Studies; Historical Drama; Political Drama; Presidents; Depression; One Person Shows; Stage Filmings

(Nixon)

The Secret Life of an American Wife, 1968, 92m, ★★1/2/$, 20th/Fox. A woman, wasting away in suburbia, embarks on a quest to find and win the love of a movie star. Walter Matthau, Anne Jackson, Patrick O'Neal, Edy Williams. w. d. George Axelrod.

SATIRE: COMEDY DRAMA: Dreams; Infatuations; Fantasies; Suburban Life; Actors; Fans-Crazed; Coulda Been Great; Good Premise Unfulfilled; Writer-Directors

(The Secret Life of Walter Mitty; Woman Times Seven; Up the Sandbox)

(Ed: Given the writer's other scripts, *Lord Love a Duck*, *The Loved One*, *Breakfast at Tiffany's*, and others, this is okay, but the potential for far more was there)

The Secret Life of Walter Mitty, 1947, 105m, ★★★/$$$, Samuel Goldwyn-UA/HBO. A reticent young man imagines himself in various superhero scenarios. Ultimately he gets the chance to act the part of hero in real life. Danny Kaye, Virginia Mayo, Boris Karloff, Florence Bates, Fay Bainter, Thurston Hall. w. Ken Englund, Everett Freeman, SS-adap. James Thurber, d. Norman Z. McLeod.
COMEDY: Fantasy; Fantasies; Dreams; Dual Lives
(Wonder Man; Hero at Large, Up the Sandbox)

The Secret of My Success, 1987, 110m, ★★/$$$$, Univ/MCA-U, PG/P-S. A young man from Kansas (Michael J. Fox) goes to Manhattan to work for his uncle (Richard Jordan) and finds his aunt (Margaret Whitton) after him, and the girl of his dreams (Helen Slater) eluding him. w. Jim Cash, Jack Epps, A. J. Carothers, d. Herbert Ross.
COMEDY: FARCE: ROMANCE: Romantic Comedy; Fish out of Water Stories; Romance-Boy Wants Girl; Romance with Relatives; Career Ambitions; New York Life; Power-Rise to; Executive Life; Business Life; Young Men; City vs. Country; Good Premise Unfulfilled; Coulda Been Good
(The Apartment; Bright Lights; Big City; Head Office; The Rise and Rise of Michael Rimmer)
(Ed: The swift direction and starpower hold this lowbrow, insipid thing together)

The Secret of NIMH, 1982, 83m, ★★★/$$, UA/MGM-UA. Nicodemus, leader of a band of rats mutated by government experiments, helps a widowed mouse who was forced from her home. They journey to find a new place to live. w. Don Bluth, John Pomeroy, Gary Foldman, Will Finn, N-adap. Robert C. O'Brien (*Mrs. Frisby and the Rats of NIMH*), d. Don Bluth.
CHILDREN'S: FAMILY: Cartoons; Animal Stories; Mortgage Drama; Journies; Starting Over; Rodents
(Watership Down)
(Ed: In some ways, a bit too adult for tots to get, and judging by the box office, they didn't)

The Secret of Roan Inish, 1995, 102m, ★★★½/$, First Look Pictures/NA, PG. A baby boy floating in a little boat on the Irish Sea, a girl hearing tales of Selkies which her relatives are rumorored to have mated with, who are half-man and half-seal, and the echoes of centuries of legends which seem to be coming true—all make for a wonderful tale of childhood fantasy and folly set off the coast of the Emerald Isle. Jeni Courtney, Eileen Colgan, Mick Lally, Richard Sheridan, John Lynch. w. d. John Sayles N-adap. Rosalie K. Fry.
DRAMA: Fantasy; Fairy Tales; Dreams; Girls; Humans into Animals; Islands; Legends; Ireland; Writer-Directors; Overlooked at Release

The Secret of Santa Vittoria, 1969, 140m, ★★★/$$$, UA/NA. During World War II, a village in Italy conspires to hide its wine from the Germans occupying their sector. They outwit them, but for how long? Anthony Quinn, Anna Magnani, Virna Lisi, Hardy Kruger. w. William Rose, Ben Maddow, N-adap. Robert Crichton, d. Stanley Kramer.
DRAMA: Family Drama; Fighting the System; Hiding Out; Nazi Stories; World War II Stories; Small-town Life; Secrets-Keeping; Italy
(The Heroes of Telemark; The Overlanders)

The Secret Partner, 1961, 91m, ★★★/$, MGM/NA. A dentist is into blackmailing until a stranger from the mob shows up in disguise and makes him rob one of his blackmail victims, leading to tragedy. Stewart Granger, Haya Harareet, Bernard Lee. w. Davis Pursall, Jack Seddon, d. Basil Dearden.
SUSPENSE: MYSTERY: Double Crossing; Betrayals; Blackmail; Mob Stories; Thieves; Murder-Coerced to; Turning the Tables; Underrated; Forgotten Films; Hidden Gems; Coulda Been Great; British Films

The Secret People, 1951, 96m, ★★½/$, Ealing/NA. In the thirties in England, a group of European exiles form an anarchist group. Valentina Cortese, Serge Reggiani, Audrey Hepburn, Irene Worth. w. Thorold Dickinson, Wolfgang Wilhelm, d. Thorold Dickinson.
DRAMA: Spy Films; Spies; Anarchists; Political Drama; World War II-Post Era; Rebels; Young People; British Films
(Ed: Worth it for the idea of seeing Audrey in a world of subversives)

Secret Places, 1984, 98m, ★★½/$, Virgin/CBS-Fox. An English and a German girl become fast friends in a British boarding school. Then World War II breaks out, and world events impinge on their friendship. Marie-Therese Relin, Tara MacGowran, Claudine Auger, Jenny Agutter. w. d. Zelda Brown, N-adap. Janice Elliott.
DRAMA: ROMANCE: Psychological Drama; Coming of Age; Character Studies; Young Women; Female Protagonists; Romance-Dangerous; Female Screenwriters; Female Directors
(Au Revoir Les Enfants; Alan and Naomi)

The Secret Policeman's Ball, 1979, 100m, ★★★/$, MGM/MGM-UA, R/P-S.

The Secret Policeman's Other Ball, 1982, ★★★/$$, MGM/MGM-UA, R/P-S. John Cleese, Graham Chapman, Michael Palin, Terry Jones, Peter Townshend, Sting, Billy Connolly, Bob Geldof, Eric Clapton, Jeff Beck. w. Michael Palin, d. Julien Temple.

The Secret Policeman's Private Parts, ★★½/$$, MGM/MGM-UA, R/P-S. John Cleese, Michael Palin, Terry Jones, Pete Townshend. d. Roger Graef.

The Secret Policeman's Third Ball, 1987, ★★/$, MGM/MGM-UA, R/P-S.
COMEDY: Comedy-Gag; Comedy-Character; Comedy-Skit; Monty Pythoners; British Films; Ensembles-Male

The Secret War of Harry Frigg, 1967, 110m, ★★½/$$, U-MCA. During World War II, an American soldier must rescue five generals who've become P.O.W.'s. Paul Newman, John Williams, Sylva Koscina, Tom Bosley, Vito Scotti. w. Peter Stone, Frank Tarloff, d. Jack Smight.
SATIRE: COMEDY: Military Comedy; Military Movies; Heroes-Unlikely; Soldiers; World War II Stories; War Stories; Escape Drama; Saving Someone
(Situation Hopeless, but Not Serious; Sergeant York; Uncommon Valor; Rambo)

Secrets, 1933, 85m, ★★½/$$$, UA/NA. A man cheats on his wife. She loves him anyway. Mary Pickford, Leslie Howard, C. Aubrey Smith. w. Frances Marion, P-adap. Rudolf Besier, May Edgington, d. Frank Borzage.
MELODRAMA: ROMANCE: COMEDY DRAMA: Marriage Drama; Marriage on the Rocks; Cheating Men
REMAKE OF: 1923 silent version.
(Something to Talk About)

The Seduction of Joe Tynan, 1979, 107m, ★★★/$$, Univ/MCA-U, R/S. A New York Senator (Alan Alda) is going through a midlife crisis, a marriage crisis, and a political crisis as he considers having an affair with a Southern political strategist (Meryl Streep) and leaving his wife (Barbara Harris). w. Alan Alda, d. Jerry Schatzberg.
DRAMA: ROMANCE: Marriage Drama; Cheating Men; Romance-Clandestine; Politicans; Politicians' Wives; Romance with Married Person; Romance-Older Men/Younger Women; Mistresses; Midlife Crisis; North vs. South; Career Women
(The Candidate; Running Mates; State of the Union; A New Life)
The Seduction of Mimi, 1972, 92m, ★★★/$$, 20th/Fox, R/S. A rural immigrant gets mixed up in Italian political strife, resulting in farcical complications. Giancarlo Giannini, Mariangela Melato. w. d. Lina Wertmuller.
COMEDY DRAMA: SATIRE: Political Satire; **FARCE:** Misunderstandings; Innocent Bystanders; Communistis; Mob Stories; Mob Comedy; City vs. Country; Italy; Italian Films; Hidden Gems; Forgotten Films
SEQUEL/REMAKE: Which Way is Up?
(Seven Beauties; Swept Away)
See How She Runs, 1978, 92m, ★★★/$$$, CBS/NA. A divorcee hitting midlife takes on jogging to getting over the hump, but the family isn't so keen on her newfound athleticism. Joanne Woodward, John Considine. d. Richard Heffron. Emmy for Woodward.
DRAMA: Character Studies; Midlife Crisis; Starting Over; Running; Sports Movies; TV Movies
See No Evil, 1971, 90m, ★★★/$, Col/Col, R/V-S. A blind young woman is trapped in a big, creepy house when she discovers the bodies of her family-and she's the last one to be added to the group. Mia Farrow, Dorothy Allison, Robin Bailey. w. Brian Clemens, d. Richard Fleischer.
SUSPENSE: Psychological Thriller; Psycho Killers; Women in Jeopardy; Disabled in Jeopardy; Blind People; Gothic Style; Houses-Creepy; **MURDER:** Murders-One by One; Hidden Gems; Forgotten Films
(Hear No Evil; Jennifer 8; Wait Until Dark; Blink)

See No Evil, Hear No Evil, 1989, 103m, ★★/$$, Col/Col-Tri, PG-13/P. After being accused of murder, two buddies go after the real killer-the only problem is, one's blind and the other's deaf. Richard Pryor, Gene Wilder, Kevin Spacey, Anthony Zerbe, Joan Severance. w. Earl Barret, Arne Sultan, Eliot Wald, Andrew Kurtzman, Gene Wilder, Marvin Worth, d. Arthur Hiller.
COMEDY: Comedy of Errors; **MURDER: MYSTERY: MURDER MYSTERY:** Blind People; Deaf People; Buddy Films; Accused Unjustly; Framed?; Fugitives from the Law; Saving Oneself; Good Premise Unfulfilled; Coulda Been Good
(Sir Crazy; Silver Streak)
See You in the Morning, 1989, 119m, ★★★/$$, WB/WB, PG-13/S. A divorced psychiatrist (Jeff Bridges) deals with his ex and his children's changes with his new love interest and her children. Alice Krige, Farrah Fawcett, Linda Lavin. w. d. Alan J. Pakula.
DRAMA: MELODRAMA: ROMANCE: Family Drama; Divorce; Starting Over; Fathers; Stepmothers; Parents vs. Children; Coulda Been Great; Writer-Directors
(Author, Author; Kramer vs. Kramer; Yours, Mine & Ours)
(Ed: Not particularly enlightening or entertaining, but interesting nonetheless, primarly due to the performances)
Seems Like Old Times, 1980, 121m, ★★★1/2/$$$$, Columbia/RCA-Col, PG. A writer (Chevy Chase) is taken hostage and used as a front for a bank robbery, then dumped. He hides out at the home of his ex-wife (Goldie Hawn), whose new husband (Charles Grodin) is the D.A. and the governor's coming for dinner. w. Neil Simon, d. Jay Sandrich.
COMEDY: FARCE: Fugitives; Fugitives from the Law; Fugitives-Harboring; Secrets-Keeping; Romance-Reunited; Ex-Spouse Trouble; Lawyers; Bank Robberies; Kidnappings; Hiding Out; Accused Unjustly; Framed?; Female Protagonists
RETREAD/REMAKE OF: Talk of the Town
(Best Friends; Foul Play)
Seize the Day, 1986, 93m, ★★★/$$, PBS/HBO. A midlife crisis besets an ordinary fellow who feels like a failure but isn't certain of what it means or what he should do. Robin Williams, Joseph

Wiseman, Glenne Headly, Tony Roberts, Jerry Stiller. SS-adap. Saul Bellow. d. Fielder Cook.
DRAMA: Character Studies; Midlife Crisis; Alienation; Losing it All; Depression; TV Movies; Quiet Little Films
(Dead Poets Society; Look Back in Anger)
Semi-Tough, 1977, 108m, ★★★/$$$$, UA/CBS-Fox, R/P-S. A couple of pro-football players fight for the attentions of their manager's daughter, even going to the self-help groups that she likes. Burt Reynolds, Kris Kristofferson, Jill Clayburgh, Bert Convy, Robert Preston, Lotte Lenya. w. Walter Bernstein, N-adap. Dan Jenkins, d. Michael Ritchie.
COMEDY: ROMANCE: Romantic Comedy; Romance-Triangles; Romance-Boy Wants Girl; Men Fighting Over Women; Football; Macho Men; Neurotic People; Underrated
(It's My Turn; North Dallas Forty)
The Senator Was Indiscreet, 1947, 97m, ★★★/$$, U-I/Republic. An ineffectual and bumbling senator makes a stab at the Oval Office, with the help of his publicist. William Powell, Ella Raines, Peter Lind Hayes, Hans Conreid. w. Charles MacArthur, SS-adap. Edwin Lanham, d. George S. Kaufman.
COMEDY: SATIRE: FARCE: Political Satire; Politicians; Senators; Presidents; Political Campaigns; Power-Rise to, of Idiot; Fools-Bumbling; Forgotten Films; Coulda Been Great; Hidden Gems
(State of the Union; Mr. Smith Goes to Washington; Running Mates; Power)
Send Me No Flowers, 1964, 100m, ★★★1/2/$$$$$, Universal/MCA-U. A man who thinks he's dying helps his wife find a suitable replacement husband, but she thinks he's up to something else. Doris Day, Rock Hudson, Tony Randall, Paul Lynde, Clint Walker. w. Julius Epstein, P-adap. Norman Barrasch, Carroll Moore, d. Norman Jewison.
COMEDY: FARCE: ROMANCE: Romantic Comedy; Marriage Comedy; Sex Comedy; Romance-Triangles; Finding New Mate for Spouse; Misunderstandings; Death-Impending; Widows; Mix-Ups; Neurotic People; Turning the Tables
(Never Say Die; Short Time; Move Over, Darling)
The Sender, 1982, 92m, ★★1/2/$, Par/Par, R/V. A psychiatrist (Kathryn Harrold) discovers a patient in a sleep experiment who can transfer his night-

mares to other patients. Zeljko Ivanek. w. d. Roger Christian.

HORROR: SUSPENSE: Psychological Thriller; Nightmares; Psychologists; Experiments; Forgotten Films; Coulda Been Good; Good Premise Unfulfilled; Writer-Directors
(Eyes of Laura Mars; Nightmare on Elm Street SERIES; Eyes of a Stranger; Dream Lover [1986])

Sense and Sensibility, 1995, 135m, ★★★¹/₂/$$$, Col/Col, PG. Two sisters whose father has died find themselves poor and living in the country away from their social circle in London. Each sister falls for a man, but will either turn out to be the right one? Emma Thompson (BActress), Alan Rickman, Kate Winslet (BSActress), Hugh Grant, James Fleet, Tom Wilkinson, Harriet Walter, Gemma Jones, Emile Francois, Elizabeth Spriggs, Robert Hardy, Ian Brimble, Isabelle Amyes, Imogen Stubbs. w. Emma Thompson (BAScr), N-adap. Jane Austen, d. Ang Lee. BPicture, BCin, BDScore, BCostume. Oscars: 7-1.

COMEDY DRAMA: ROMANCE: Romantic Drama; Comedy of Manners; Sisters; Romance-Reluctant; Cheating Men; 1800s; Classic Literary Adaptations; Female Protagonists
(Pride and Prejudice; Howards End; The Bostonians; Emma)
(Ed: In any other year, this film would have been an also-ran at the Academy Awards. The BBC-A&E miniseries "Pride and Prejudice" is almost as good, and ultimately, though both are excellent, there is little beyond the romance to take home)

Sentimental Journey, 1946, 94m, ★★¹/₂/$$, 20th/NA. A dying woman finds an orphan girl to occupy the affections of her husband. Maureen O'Hara, John Payne, William Bendix, Cedric Hardwicke, Connie Marshall. w. Samuel Hoffenstein, Elizabeth Reinhardt, SS-adap. Nelia Gardner White, d. Walter Lang.

MELODRAMA: ROMANCE: Tearjerkers; Death-Impending; Romance-Triangles; Widowers; Dying Wishes; Disease Stories; Orphans; Unintentionally Funny
REMAKE: The Gift of Love

The Sentinel, 1976, 92m, ★★★/$$, Universal/MCA-U,. R/V-S. An old apartment building is haunted by the ghosts of its former tenants, all of whom went to Hell. When a passage to Hell opens in the building, one of its current tenants, an attractive but possibly mentally unstable young model, is appointed sentinel at the border. Chris Sarandon, Cristina Raines, Martin Balsam, John Carradine, Jose Ferrer, Ava Gardner, Arthur Kennedy, Burges Meredith, Sylvia Miles. w. Michael Winner, Jeffrey Konvitz, N-adap. Jeffrey Konvitz, d. Michael Winner.

HORROR: SUSPENSE: MYSTERY: Missing Persons; Psychological Thriller; Satanism; Hell; Occult Models; Unbelieved; Forgotten Films; Underrated
(The Kiss; The Exorcist; Burnt Offerings; The Gate; Salem's Lot)

Separate but Equal, 1991, 194m, ★★★¹/₂/$$$$, ABC/Republic. The landmark trial of Brown vs. the Board of Education, brought about after a black girl wished to go to the white school in her Kansas town, culminating at the Supreme Court. Sidney Poitier, Burt Lancaster, Richard Kiley, Cleavon Little, John McMartin, Lynn Thigpen. w. d. George Stevens. Multiple Emmy winner.

DRAMA: Courtroom Drama; Race Relations; Bigots; Busses/Bussing; Black Men; Black vs. White; Supreme Court; Lawyers; Historical Drama; Writer-Directors; TV Movies; Miniseries
(The Ernest Green Story; Crisis at Central High)

A Separate Peace, 1974, 104m, ★★¹/₂/$$, Par/Par-KUI, PG. A boy in a boarding school in New England must cope with the trauma, and eventually find meaning, in his best friend's untimely death. Parker Stevenson, John Heyl. d. Larry Peerce.

DRAMA: MELODRAMA: TRAGEDY: Accidents; Homo-eroticism; Coming of Age; Ethics; Death-Dealing With; Friendships-Great; Friendships-Male; Teenagers; Boys; Boarding Schools; Classic Literary Adaptations
(School Ties; Dead Poets Society; Ordinary People)
(Ed: Read by most junior high kids, this glossy production doesn't quite live up to the density of the book, therefore it's not seen by many of the same)

Separate Tables, 1958, 99m, ★★★/$$$$, UA/MGM-UA. At a posh English seaside hotel four people's lives intertwine when one man is accused of having been a molester. David Niven (BActor), Burt Lancaster, Rita Hayworth, Deborah Kerr (BActress). Wendy Hiller (BSActress). w. Terrence Rattigan, John Gay (BAScr), P-adap. Terence Rattigan, d. Delbert Mann. BPicture, BB&WCin, BOScore. Oscars: 7-2.

DRAMA: MELODRAMA: Social Drama; Ensemble Films; Molestation; Repression; Sexual Problems; Hotels; Multiple Stories; Interwoven Stories; Repression; Neurotic People; England
(The Mark)
(Ed: The cryptic nature of Niven's crime given the time and its rather superficial handling makes it very dated)

September, 1987, 82m, ★★★/$, Orion/Orion, PG-13/S. Several people's lives come together at a New England country home; at the center of which is a conflict between a daughter (Mia Farrow) and her actress mother (Elaine Stritch). Dianne Wiest, Denholm Elliott, Sam Waterston. w. d. Woody Allen.

DRAMA: Family Drama; Character Studies; Ensemble Films; Mothers & Daughters; Bergmanesque; Children-Neglected; Actresses; Female Protagonists; Overlooked at Release; Writer-Directors
(Autumn Sonata; Another Woman)

September Affair, 1950, 104m, ★★¹/₂/$$, Par/Par. A plane crash off the coast of Capri liberates two lovers married to others to "start over" when the news reports claim no survivors. Joseph Cotten, Joan Fontaine, Francoise Rosay, Jessica Tandy. w. Robert Thoeren, d. William Dieterle.

ROMANCE: DRAMA: MELODRAMA: Romantic Drama; Survival Drama; Hiding Out; Dead-Back from the; Misunderstandings; Romance-Clandestine; Romance with Married Person; Airplane Crashes; Cheating Men; Cheating Women

September 30, 1955 see 9/30/55
The Sergeant, 1968, 108m, ★★★/$, WB/WB, R/S. In 1950s France, an army sergeant struggles to fight, and eventually succumbs to, his attraction to men. Rod Steiger, John Philip Law, Frank Latimore, Ludmila Mikael. w. P-adap. Dennis Murphy, d. John Flynn.

DRAMA: Character Studies; **TRAGEDY:** Gay Men; Homo-eroticism; Ahead of Its Time; Forgotten Films; Hidden Gems; Macho Men; Stern Men; Repression; Nervous Breakdowns; Midlife Crisis
(Reflections in a Golden Eye; The Lost Language of Cranes; The Pawnbroker)

(Ed: Steiger's performance is powerful as usual; probably suffered "coming out" on the heels of *Reflections*)

Sergeant Pepper's Lonely Hearts Club Band, 1978, 111m, ★★/$$, Universal/MCA-U, PG. Villians try to thwart an up-and-coming band with a new sound. Peter Frampton, Barry Gibb, Robin Gibb, Maurice Gibb, George Burns, Donald Pleasence, Alice Cooper, Steve Martin, Earth Wind and Fire. w. Henry Edwards, d. Michael Schultz.
MUSICALS: Music Movies; Musicals-Disco Era; Disco Era; Rock Groups; Small-town Life; American Myth; Flops-Major; Time Capsules; Camp; Cult Films; 1970s

Sergeant York, 1941, 134m, ★★★1/2/ $$$$, WB/WB. A country boy from Tennessee (Gary Cooper, **BActor**) goes to Europe and through common sense and gumption becomes a World War I hero. Walter Brennan (BSActor), Joan Leslie, George Tobais, Margaret Wycherly (BSActress) David Bruce, Ward Bond. w. Abem Finkel, Harry Chandler, Howard Koch, John Huston (BScr), d. Howard Hawks (BDirector). BPicture, BCin, BScore, BArt, BEdit. Oscars: 10-1.
COMEDY DRAMA: War Stories; World War I Stories; Biographies; True Stories; Noble Fools; Heroes-Ordinary; Simple Minds; Soldiers; Country People; Germans as Enemy; Hillbillies
(Forrest Gump; Being There; The Story of Dr. Wassell)

Serial, 1980, 86m, ★★1/2/$$, Par/Par, R/P-S. The satirical tale of a group of wealthy Californians and their mores, including trendy self-help and cultish orientations. Martin Mull, Tuesday Weld, Jennifer McAllister, Sam Chew, Jr., Sally Kellerman, Christopher Lee, Tom Smothers. w. Rich Eustis, Michael Elias, N-adap. Cyra McFadden, d. Bill Persky.
SATIRE: COMEDY: COMEDY DRAMA: FARCE: Suburban Life; Rich People; California; Cheating Men; Cheating Women; Cults; Swapping Partners; Alternative Lifestyles; Underrated; Coulda Been Great; Forgotten Films; Hidden Gems; 1970s; Time Capsules
(Bob & Ted & Carol & Alice; The Last Married Couple in America)

Serial Mom, 1994, 93m, ★★★/$, Savoy/HBO, R/EP-S-V. When the seemingly perfect mom turns out to be a foul-mouthed, murderous psychopath, the kids have a dilemma on their hands. Kathleen Turner, Ricki Lake, Sam Waterston, Matthew Lillard, Mink Stole, Traci Lords, Suzanne Somers, Joan Rivers, Patty Hearst. w. d. John Waters.
COMEDY: Spoofs-Horror; Serial Killers; Black Comedy; Comedy-Morbid; Dual Lives; Murderer-Debate to Reveal; Murderers-Female; Suburban Life; Murders-One by One; Chase Stories; Family Comedy; Writer-Directors; Female Protagonists; Could Been Great; Good Premise; Unfulfilled; Cult Films
(Hairspray; Cry Baby; Polyester)

The Serpent and the Rainbow, 1988, 98m, ★★/$$, U/MCA-U,. R/EV-B&G-S. A research scientist working for a pharmaceutical company travels to Haiti to find a drug that makes people into zombies. He gets involved with a local female doctor, who leads him into the nether world of Haitian voodoo. Bill Pullman, Cathy Tyson, Zakes Mokae, Paul Winfield. w. d. Wes Craven.
HORROR: SUSPENSE: Occult; Zombies; Nightmares; Caribbean; Scientists; Drugs; Writer-Directors
(The Believers)

The Serpent's Egg, 1978, 120m, ★★1/2/$, DEG/Live. An American trapeze artist/gymnast in Berlin must hide from the Nazis during the rise of the Third Reich. David Carradine, Liv Ullmann, Gert Frobe, James Whitmore. w. d. Ingmar Bergman.
DRAMA: TRAGEDY: Escape Drama; Hiding Out; World War II Stories; War Stories; Nazi Stories; Circus Life; Flops-Major; International Casts; Writer-Directors; Berlin
(Ed: Only for Bergman students)

Serpico, 1973, 129m, ★★★1/2/$$$, Par/Par, R/P-V-S. An eccentric police officer (Al Pacino, BActor) exposes corruption with the NYPD, risking his own life. F. Murray Abraham. w. Frank Pierson (BAScr), NF-adap. Peter Maas, d. Sidney Lumet. Oscars: 2-0.
DRAMA: Crime Drama; Biographies; True Stories; Police Stories; Police Corruption; Detectives-Police; Undercover; Whistleblowers; Fighting the System; New York Life
(Prince of the City; Internal Affairs; The Whistleblower; Rush)

The Servant, 1963, 115m, ★★★1/2/$, EMI/HBO. The cunning servant of a foppish young aristocrat conspires with his sister to take control of his fortunes. Dirk Bogarde, James Fox, Sarah Miles, Wendy Craig. w. Harold Pinter, N-adap. Robin Maugham, d. Joseph Losey.
COMEDY DRAMA: Black Comedy;
SATIRE: Art Films; Inheritances at Stake; Malicious Menaces; Servants; Rich People; Turning the Tables; Incest; Revenge; Mindgames; Thieves; British Films
(Entertaining Mr. Sloane; Something for Everyone; The Homecoming; The Caretaker)

The Set-Up, 1949, 72m, ★★★/$, RKO/Media. A gangland leader tries to fix the fight of a seasoned boxer, but the old man has more integrity than Mr. Big Shot counted on. Robert Ryan, Audrey Totter, George Tobias, Alan Baxter, Wallace Ford. w. Art Cohn, Poem-adap. Joseph Moncure, d. Robert Wise.
DRAMA: Crime Drama; Mob Stories; Boxing; Bets; Gambling; Forgotten Films; Underrated; Hidden Gems
(Requiem for a Heavyweight; Champion)

Seven, 1995, 131m, ★★★/$$$$, R/EV-P-B&G. Two cops are daunted by a serial killer, each of whose victims are killed for their indulgence in one of the seven deadly sins. But will catching the killer ease their agony? Brad Pitt, Morgan Freeman, Gwyneth Paltrow, R. Lee Ermey, John C. McGinley, Kevin Spacey. w. Andrew Kevin Walker, d. David Fincher. BEdit. Oscars: 1-0.
MYSTERY: SUSPENSE: Detective Stories; Detectives-Police; Cat and Mouse Stories; Black & White Together; Serial Killers; Killer Calls Cop; Film Noir-Modern
(Silence of the Lambs; Manhunter; Twelve Monkeys)
(Ed: Surely the darkest movie ever made, in more ways than one. You be the judge as to the thrills and the meaning)

Seven Beauties, 1976, 115m, ★★★1/2/ $$$, Col/RCA-Col, APD, R/V-S. A man survives the horrors of World War II and rises to prominence in the gangster world which springs up after the war. Then he proceeds to go through a number of women. Giancarlo Giannini (BActor), Fernando Rey, Shirley Stoler, Piero di Iorio. w. d. Lina Wertmuller (BDirector). BFLFilm. Oscars: 3-0.
COMEDY DRAMA: SATIRE: Black Comedy; Survival Drama; Concentration Camps; Female Screenwriters; Female Directors; Italian Films

(Swept Away)
(Ed: First time, before Jane Campion for *The Piano*, that a woman was nominated for an Oscar as Best Director)

Seven Brides for Seven Brothers, 1954, 103m, ★★/$$$$, MGM/MGM-UA. Seven cowboy brothers come of age and go looking for wives in neighboring towns. Howard Keel, Jane Powell, Jeff Richards, Russ Tamblyn. w. Frances Goodrich, Albert Hackett (BAScr), SS-adap. Stephen Vincent Benet *(Sobbin' Women)*, d. Stanley Donen. BPicture, BEdit, BCCin, **BMScore**. Oscars: 5-1.

MUSICALS: ROMANCE: Musical Romance; Ensemble Films; Marriage Comedy; Newlyweds; Marriage-Impending; Coming of Age; Young People; Brothers; Sisters; Female Screenwriters
Dramatic TV SERIES: 1987.
(Oklahoma!)

Seven Chances, 1925, 69m (Silent), ★★★/$$$, Keaton/NA. A timid man must gather up his courage, for if he can find a wife within a few hours, he'll inherit seven million dollars. Buster Keaton, Ruth Dwyer, Ray Barnes. w. Clyde Bruckman, Jean Havez, Joseph A. Mitchell, P-adap. Roi Cooper Megrue, d. Buster Keaton.

COMEDY: Comedy-Slapstick; Nerds; Shy People; Inheritances at Stake; Marriage-Impending; Race Against Time
(Seven Days Leave)

Seven Days in May, 1964, 118m, ★★★/$$$, 7-Arts-Par/Par. A hawkish army general plans a military takeover when he feels the president's dove policies are weakening America's standing in the world. Kirk Douglas, Burt Lancaster, Fredric March, Ava Gardner, Martin Balsam, Edmond O'Brien (BSActor), John Houseman. w. Rod Serling, N-adap. Fletcher Knebel, Charles W. Bailey II, d. John Frankenheimer. BB&WArt. Oscars: 2-0.

DRAMA: Psychological Drama; **MYSTERY**: Conspiracy; Anarchists; Presidents; Military Stories; Political Unrest; Macho Men; Washington D.C.; Pentagon; Forgotten Films; Hidden Gems

Seven Days Leave, 1942, 87m, ★★½, RKO/Turner. A sailor has seven days to get married, or he'll lose his one hundred thousand dollar inheritance. Lucille Ball, Victor Mature, Harold Peary, Mary Cortes, Wallace Ford. w. William Bowers,

Ralph Spence, Curtis Kenyon, Kenneth Earl, d. Tim Whelan.

COMEDY: ROMANCE: Romantic Comedy; Marriage-Impending; Inheritances at Stake; Race Against Time
(Seven Chances; Brewster's Millions)

The Seven Faces of Dr. Lao, 1964, 101m, ★★★/$$$, MGM/MGM-UA. A traveling circus comes to a small Southwestern town. The difference between this circus and others is that all the mythical creatures in it are real, including the master of the circus, an elderly Chinese man who can *really* see the humdrum futures of the townspeople. Tony Randall, Arthur O'Connell, John Ericson, Barbara Eden. w. Charles Beaumont, N-adap. Charles G. Finney *(The Circus of Dr. Lao)*, d. George Pal. BSFX, **BMakeup**. Oscars: 2-1.

SCI-FI: Fantasy; **CHILDREN'S: FAMILY**: COMEDY: Disguises; WESTERNS: Western Comedy; Scientists-Mad; Circus Life; Magic; Librarians; Psychics; Multiple Performances; Cult Films; Hidden Gems
(Something Wicked This Way Comes)

The Seven Little Foys, 1955, 95m, Par/Col. Biographies of vaudeville star Eddie Foy and his siblings (Bob Hope). Milly Vitale, George Tobias, Angela Clarke, Herbert Heyes, James Cagney (repeating role as George M. Cohan from *Yankee Doodle Dandy*). w. Melville Shavelson, Jack Rose (BOScr), d. Melville Shavelson.

COMEDY: Biographies; Family Comedy; Family Stories; Vaudeville; Comedians

The Seven Percent Solution, 1976, 114m, ★★★½/$$$, Univ/MCA-U, PG. A revision of the Sherlock Holmes myth in which he's portrayed as a cocaine-addicted paranoid who's taken to Freud by Watson to be cured. Nicol Williamson, Robert Duvall, Alan Arkin, Vanessa Redgrave, Laurence Olivier, Samantha Eggar, Joel Grey. w. N-adap. Nicholas Meyer (BAScr), d. Herbert Ross. Oscars: 1-0.

MYSTERY: DRAMA: Psychological Drama; Chase Movies; Detective Stories; Detectives-Private; Psychologists; Freud; Dreams; Nightmares; Hypnosis; Drug-Addictions; Sherlock Holmes; Revisionist Films
(The Private Life of Sherlock Holmes)

Seven Samurai, 1954, 155m, ★★★★/$$$, Toho/Nos. In medieval Japan, samurai warriors hire themselves out to small

farming villages to protect them from marauding bandits. Toshiro Mifune, Takashi Shimura, Kuninori Kodo. w. Akira Kurosawa, Shinobu Hashoto, Hideo Oguni, d. Akira Kurosawa.

ACTION: DRAMA: Mercenaries; Men in Conflict; Protecting Someone; Japanese Films; Japan
(REMAKES: The Magnificent Seven; Battle Beyond the Stars)

Seven Sinners, 1940, 83m, ★★½/$$, Universal/Nos. A nightclub singer is bounced from island to island for igniting the passions of the sailors in this South Pacific extravaganza. Marlene Dietrich, John Wayne, Albert Decker, Broderick Crawford. w. John Meehan, Harry Tugend, d. Tay Garnett.

DRAMA: ROMANCE: Soldiers; Nighclubs; Singers; Promiscuity; Sexy Women; South Pacific; Islands; World War II Era

Seven Thieves, 1960, 102m, ★★½/$$, 20th/CBS-Fox. A heist movie in which an elderly petty thief on the verge of retirement plans one last job-robbing a Monte Carlo casino. Edward G. Robinson, Rod Steiger, Joan Collins, Eli Wallach, Michael Dante, Sebastian Cabot. w. Sidney Boehm, N-adap. Max Catto *(Lions at the Kill)*, d. Henry Hathaway.

Heist Stories; **COMEDY DRAMA**: Character Studies; One Last Time; Elderly Men; Retirement; Gambling; Monte Carlo
(Going in Style; Breaking In)

The Seven-Ups, 1974, 109m, ★★½/$$, 20th/CBS-Fox, R/V-P. A special force within the NYPD is equipped and trained to hunt down the toughest gangsters. Roy Scheider, Victor Arnold, Jerry Leon, Tony Lo Bianco, Richard Lynch. w. Albert Ruben, Alexander Jacobs, d. Philip D'Antoni.

ACTION: Chase Movies; Car Chases; Car Wrecks; Police Stories; Mob Stories; Police vs. Mob
(The French Connection; Super Cops; Fuzz)
(Ed: Some of the car stunts were amazing for the time)

Seven Women, 1966, 100m, ★★★/$, MGM/NA. A bunch of hoodlums terrorize a group of American women on a mission in China. Anne Bancroft, Flora Robson, Margaret Leighton, Sue Lyon, Eddie Albert. w. Janet Green, John McCormick,

SS-adap. Norah Lofts (*Chinese Finale*), d. John Ford.

DRAMA: Missionaries; Women in Jeopardy; China; Thieves; Hostage Situations; Ensemble Films; Ensembles-Female; Coulda Been Great; Female Protagonists
(Black Narcissus; Inn of the Sixth Happiness; A Town Like Alice)

The Seven-Year Itch, 1955, 105m, ★★★1/2/$$$, 20thCBS-Fox. A married man's mid-life crisis while his family's away isn't helped when Marilyn Monroe moves in upstairs, puts her panties in the freezer, and stands over subway vents with loose skirts. Tom Ewell, Marilyn Monroe, Sonny Tufts, Evelyn Keyes, Oscar Homolka, Victor Moore. w. Billy Wilder, George Axelrod, P-adap. George Axelrod, d. Billy Wilder.

COMEDY: ROMANCE: Infatuations; Romance-Unrequited; Romance-Older Men/Younger Women; Sexy Women; Simple Minds; Elusive Women; Bimbos; Midlife Crisis; Nerds; Nerds & Babes; Fantasies; Dreams; Neighbors-Troublesome
(The Woman in Red; Ten; How to Marry a Millionaire; Some Like It Hot)

Seventeen, 1940, 76m, ★★★/$$, Par/NA. An episodic look at the awkwardness of adolescence as personified in a midwestern boy growing up in the forties. Jackie Cooper, Betty Field, Otto Kruger. w. Agnes Christine Johnston, Stuart Palmer, N-adap. Booth Tarkington, d. Louis King.

DRAMA: COMEDY DRAMA: Coming of Age; Teenagers; Boys; Small-town Life; Midwestern Life; 1900s; Episodic Stories; Female Screenwriters; Time Capsules

TV REMAKE, PBS
(Alice Adams)

1776, 1972, 141m, ★★★/$, Col/RCA-Col, PG/P. A musical which attempted to demystify the founding fathers, portraying them as flesh-and-blood humans with weaknesses aplenty-by singing their way through the Declaration of Independence. William Daniels, Howard da Silva, Ken Howard, Blythe Danner. w. P-adap. Peter Stone, d. Peter Hunt. BCin. Oscars: 1-0.

MUSICALS: DRAMA: Musical Drama; Historical Drama; Early America; Politicians; Political Drama; Presidents Flops-Major
(Jefferson in Paris)

(Ed: A big Broadway success, this rather somber version didn't fare so well as a film)

The Seventh Cavalry, 1956, 75m, ★★/$$, Col/Nos. A timid man must prove himself after Custer's last stand by retrieving Custer's body from Indian territory. Randolph Scott, Barbara Hale, Jay C. Flippen, Jeanette Nolan. w. Peter Packer, d. Joseph H. Lewis.

WESTERNS: Custer's Last Stand; Shy People; Heroes-Unlikely; Journies; War Battles; Cavalry; Indians-American

The Seventh Cross, 1944, 112m, ★★★/$$$, MGM/MGM-UA. In a concentration camp, seven inmates plan their escape. Who will survive if any? Spencer Tracy, Signe Hasso, Hume Cronyn, Jessica Tandy, Agnes Moorehead, Felix Bressart. w. Helen Deutsch, N-adap. Anna Seghers, d. Fred Zinnemann.

DRAMA: Prison Escape; Escape Drama; Survival Drama; Concentration Camps; Jewish People; Nazi Stories; Germans as Enemy; Executions; Female Screenwriters; Ahead of Its Time
(Stalag 17; The Great Escape; Night Train to Munich; Schindler's List)
(Ed: Timely and realistic for its day)

The Seventh Dawn, 1964, 123m, ★★1/2/$$, UA/NA. In 1950s Malaysia, a plantation owner discovers a friend is a terrorist leading the political coup there. William Holden, Tetsuro Tamba, Capucine, Susannah York, Michael Goodliffe. w. Karl Tunberg, N-adap. Michael Keon (*The Durian Tree*), d. Lewis Gilbert.

DRAMA: Political Unrest; Asia; Plantations; Friends as Enemies; Allies-Unlikely; Terrorists; Imperialist Problems
(Indochine; The Year of Living Dangerously)

Seventh Heaven, 1927, 93m, ★★★/$$$$, 20th/NA. Janet Gaynor **(BActress)**, Charles Farrell, Gladys Brockwell, David Butler. w. Benjamin Glazer **(BScr)**, P-adap. Austin Strong, d. Frank Borzage **(BDirector)**. BPicture, BArt. Oscars: 5-3.

Seventh Heaven, 1937, 102m, ★★1/2/$$, 20th/NA. Remake of above, with pumped-up pathos. James Stewart, Simone Simon, Jean Hersholt, Gale Sondergaard, J. Edward Bromberg, Gregory Ratoff. w. Melville Baker, d. Henry King.

A street urchin takes refuge in the Parisian flat of a city worker. They fall in love-a love so perfect it can withstand anything, even him being blinded at war.

ROMANCE: MELODRAMA: Tearjerkers; War Stories; World War I Stories; Blind People; Paris
(Street Angel)

The Seventh Seal, 1956, 96m, ★★★★/$$, Svensk-Ind/Vidmark, Sultan, Voyager. During the Middle Ages in a plague-ridden unnamed country, a knight must win a game of chess with Death to keep his friends alive. Max Von Sydow, Bengt Ekerot, Gunnar Bjornstrand, Bibi Andersson. w. d. Ingmar Bergman.

DRAMA: Avant-Garde Films; Art Films; Death-Dealing with; Death-Personified; Epidemics; Middle Ages; Mindgames; Saving Someone; Selling One's Soul; Bets; Allegorical Stories; Writer-Directors; Cult Films; Film History
(The Plague; Through a Glass Darkly)

The Seventh Sign, 1988, 105m, ★★1/2/$$, Tri-Star/Tri-Col. PG-13. Biblical omens signify that a woman's unborn child may be the final sign of the Apocalypse. Demi Moore, Jurgen Prochnow, Michael Biehn, John Heard. w. Clifford Green, Ellen Green, d. Carl Schultz.

SUSPENSE: SCI-FI: Apocalyptic Stories; Biblical Stories; Babies-Having Satan-Child of; Coulda Been Good; Good Premise Unfulfilled
(Rosemary's Baby; The Omen)
(Ed: The basic idea works and does lead to some suspense, but overall, the story's implausibility undermines what's there)

The Seventh Veil, 1945, 94m, ★★★/$$$, Par/Nos. A romantic rhombus in which four men vie for the affections of a concert pianist. James Mason, Ann Todd, Herbert Lom, Albert Lieven, Hugh McDermott, Yvone Owen, David Horne. w. Muriel and Sydney Box, d. Compton Bennett.

DRAMA: MELODRAMA: ROMANCE: Romance-Triangles; Musicians; Pianists; Men Fighting Over Women; British Films; Female Screenwriters
(One Night of Love; My Love Came Back)

The Seventh Victim, 1943, 71m, ★★★/$, RKO/Turner. A woman searches for her sister who's gotten into a Satanic cult. Kim Hunter, Tom Conway, Jean Brooks, Hugh Beaumont. w. Charles O'Neal, De Witt Bodeen, d. Mark Robson.

SUSPENSE: DRAMA: Satanism; Missing Persons; Searches; Sisters; Female Protagonists; Ahead of Its Time; Forgotten Films; Hidden Gems (Rosemary's Baby; The Believers; Hardcorer)

The Seventh Voyage of Sinbad, 1958, 94m, ★★★/$$$, Col/RCA-Col. Sinbad's going to get married. The only trouble is, his wife's been shrunk to parrot-size by a villainous wizard, and he must find the magical egg that will restore her. Kerwin Mathews, Kathryn Grant, Torin Thatcher. w. Kenneth Kolb, d. Nathan Juran.
ACTION: ADVENTURE: Mythology; Shrinking People; Humans into Animals; Animation-Partial; Animation-Stop; Ancient Times
(Clash of the Titans; Jason and the Argonauts)

A Severed Head, 1970, 98m, ★★1/2/$, Col/NA. A woman cheats on her husband, who thinks she doesn't know about his long-term affair. Lee Remick, Richard Attenborough, Ian Holm, Claire Bloom. w. Frederic Raphael, N-adap. Iris Murdoch, d. Dick Clement.
DRAMA: ROMANCE: Romantic Drama; Cheating Men; Cheating Women; Revenge; Revenge on Cheaters; Romance-Clandestine; Marriage on the Rocks; Marriage Drama; Coulda Been Good
(The War Between the Tates; Diary of a Mad Housewife)
(Ed: The title is figurative)

Sex, Lies, and Videotape, 1989, 101m, ★★★1/2/$$$, Miramax/HBO, R/P-S-FN. A young man (James Spader) with a penchant for voyeuristic videos and lies returns to his hometown and interrupts his best friend's (Peter Gallagher) affair with his wife's (Andie MacDowell) sister (Laura San Giacomo), exposing their own lies. w. d. Steven Soderbergh (BOScr). Oscars: 1-0.
DRAMA: Psychological Drama;
ROMANCE: Mindgames; Cheating Men; Romance with Friend's Lover; Sisters; Romance with Relative's Lover; Liars; Videotape Scandals; Videotape Scandals Starring James Spader; Sleeper Hits; Independent Films)
(Dangerous Liaisons; Manhattan; Husbands & Wives)

Sex and the Single Girl, 1964, 114m, ★★1/2/$$$, WB/WB, PG/S. An intrepid journalist meets his match in the female sexologist he'd hoped to dethrone by posing as someone else. Natalie Wood, Tony Curtis, Henry Fonda, Lauren Bacall, Mel Ferrer. w. Joseph Heller, David R. Schwarz, N-adap. Helen Gurley Brown, d. Richard Quine.
COMEDY: Sex Comedy; **ROMANCE:** Romantic Comedy; Sexuality; Battle of the Sexes; Virgins; Impostors; Car Chases; Psychologists; Female Protagonists
(Pillow Talk; Three on a Couch; Oh, Men! Oh, Women!)
(Ed: Gets pretty silly toward the end)

Sextette, 1978, 91m, ★★1/2/$, 20th/Media, R/S. A former Hollywood bombshell, married many times (and now an octogenarian), is bothered by former husbands on her current honeymoon. Mae West, Tony Curtis, Ringo Starr, Dom DeLuise, Timothy Dalton, George Hamilton, Alice Cooper, Rona Barrett, Walter Pidgeon, Tom Selleck. w. Herbert Baker, P-adap. Mae West, d. Ken Hughes.
COMEDY: Sex Comedy; Romance-Older Women; Sexy Women; Sexy Men; Bimboys; Newlyweds; Camp; Cult Films; Coulda Been Great; Good Premise Unfulfilled
(Myra Breckinridge)
(Ed: Has to be seen to be believed)

Sexton Blake and the Hooded Terror, 1938, 70m, ★★1/2/$$, George King/Sinister. A supposedly upstanding citizen and "man of means" turns out to be the leader of a gang of criminals. George Curzon, Tod Slaughter, Greta Gynt, Charles Oliver. w. A. R. Rawlinson, d. George King.
MYSTERY: Crime Drama; Detective Stories; Good vs. Evil; Dual Lives; Ordinary People Turned Criminal

S.F.W., 1995, 92m, ★★1/2/$, Gramercy-U/MCA-U, R/P-S-FN. Hostages released from a month-long stand-off become celebrities but soon the greed of the book deals, talk show appearances, and T-shirt sales consume their entire families, particularly one young man named Spab, who finds himself suicidal with anarchist tendencies, speaking the title: "So F---ing What." Stephen Dorff, Reese Witherspoon, Jake Busey, Joey Lauren Adams, Pamela Gidley. w. Danny Rubin, Jeffrey Levy, N-adap. Andrew Wellman, d. Jeffrey Levy.
SATIRE: COMEDY: COMEDY DRAMA: Media Satire; Hostage Situations; Greed; Good Premise Unfulfilled

(Pump Up the Volume; Airheads; Natural Born Killers)
(Ed: In some ways the idea, though not the treatment, is too intelligent to appeal to the young audience it was obviously aimed at)

The Shadow, 1933/1936, 74m, ★★1/2/$$, UA/Nos. A mysterious stranger blackmails and murders his way through London and the detective work of the police leads them to a shocking suspect. Henry Kendall, Elizabeth Allan, Felix Aylmer, John Turnbull. w. H. Fowler Mear, Terence Egan, Donald Stuart, d. George A. Cooper.
SUSPENSE: MURDER: Detective Stories; Detectives-Police; Blackmail; British Films; Forgotten Films

The Shadow, 1940, SERIAL (15 eps.), ★★1/2/$$, Col/NA. Based on the popular CBS radio show, Lamont Cranston, millionaire playboy, poses as the Shadow at night in order to fight crime. d. James W. Horne.

The Shadow, 1994, 97m, ★★★1/2/$$, U/MCA-U, PG-13/P-S. A drug dealer redeemed by mystic Tibetan powers is thrown into a life of fighting crime as penance. But this time, he also has to fight an evil Asian mastermind, intent on ruling the world with the new atomic bomb (it's set in the 40s), with only psychic powers and wit to help him. Alec Baldwin, Penelope Ann Miller, Peter Boyle, Ian McKellen, Tim Curry, Jonathan Winters. w. David Koepp, d. Russell Mulcahy.
ACTION: ADVENTURE: SCI-FI: Film Noir-Modern; Detective Stories; Comic Heroes; Rich People; Dual Lives; Occult; Magic; Production Design-Outstanding; Hidden Gems; Underrated
(Batman; The Saint; The Juror)
(Ed: A witty, clever, thinking man's super hero with fantastic sets and a thoroughly original villain, as villains go . . . Had the misfortune of being released at the same time as *Forrest Gump*)

The Shadow Box, 1980, 96m, ★★★1/2/$$$, ABC/Karl-Lorimar, PG. A hospice retreat for cancer victims is the setting for several people and their loved ones to deal with facing the end, particularly one middle-aged couple. Joanne Woodward, Christopher Plummer, James Broderick. w. P-adap. Michael Cristofer, d. Paul Newman. Emmy winner.

DRAMA: Multiple Stories; Death-Impending; Death-Dealing with; Hospitals; Disease Stories; Marriage Drama; Writers; Elderly People; Romance-Middle-Aged; Actor Directors; Pulitzer Prize Adaptations

FLIPSIDE OF: California Suite, Plaza Suite.

(Breathing Lessons; Longtime Companion)

Shadowlands, 1993, 125m, ★★★¹/₂/ $$, Savoy/HBO, PG. The love story of writer C. S. Lewis and the American woman he married upon learning she was dying of cancer. Anthony Hopkins, Debra Winger (BActress), Ian McKellen, w. P-adap., d. Richard Attenborough. Oscars: 1-0.

DRAMA: ROMANCE: Romantic Drama; Tearjerkers; Disease Stories; Romance-Doomed; Death-Impending; Death-Dealing with; Americans Abroad; Conservative Value Films; Religion; Old-Fashioned Recent Films; 1950s; British Films; Actor Directors

REMAKE OF/EARLIER VERSION: 1985, BBC.

Shadow of a Doubt, 1943, 107m, ★★★★/$$, Universal/MCA-U. A teenage girl (Teresa Wright) living in an idyllic small-town world is shaken by the idea that her favorite visiting uncle (Joseph Cotten) could be the Merry Widow Killer of rich old women. w. Thornton Wilder, Sally Benson, Alma Reville, SS-adap. Gordon McDonell, d. Alfred Hitchcock. BOStory. Oscars: 1-0.

SUSPENSE: MURDER: MYSTERY: MURDER MYSTERY: Psychological Thriller; Women in Jeopardy; Coming of Age; Serial Killers; Illusions Destroyed; Dual Lives; Secrets-Haunting; Infatuations; Small-town Life; American Myth; Hidden Gems; Hitchcockian

REMADE: *Step Down to Terror*, 1959; **TV REMAKE,** 1991.

(Music Box)

Shadow of the Thin Man, 1941, 97m, ★★★/$$$, MGM/MGM-UA. Murder among the horses at the track. William Powell, Myrna Loy, Barry Nelson, Donna Reed, Sam Levene. d. W. S. Van Dyke.

MYSTERY: MURDER: MURDER MYSTERY: Detective Stories; Detective Couples; Marriage Comedy; Partners-Married; Comic Mystery; Horses

SEQUEL TO: The Thin Man

The Shadow Riders, 1982, 96m, ★★¹/₂/ $$$, CBS/Vidmark. Two brothers who fought on opposite sides of the Civil War come back from battle to find their other brother's girl has been taken as a bargaining tool to free Confederate P.O.W.s. Katharine Ross, Sam Elliott, Tom Selleck, Ben Johnson. d. Andrew McLaglen.

WESTERNS: Rescue Drama; Kidnappings; P.O.W.s; Civil War Era; Brothers; Feuds; Enemies Unite; Women in Jeopardy; TV Movies

SEQUEL TO: The Sacketts.

Shadows, 1959, 81m, ★★★/$, Cassavetes-Faces/Touchstone, NA. An improvised exploration of the lives of young black people in fifties Manhattan. Ben Carruthers, Leila Goldoni, Hugh Hurd, Rupert Crosse, Anthony Ray. w. the cast, d. John Cassavetes.

DRAMA: Avant-Garde Films; Art Films; Documentary Style; Docudrama; Street Life; Black Casts; 1950s; Time Capsules; Ahead of Its Time; New York Life; Improvisational Films

(Faces; Husbands; Minnie & Moskowitz)

Shadows and Fog, 1992, 85m, ★★¹/₂/$, Orion/Orion. PG. In a Kafkaesque nightmare, an ordinary man is drawn into a neighborhood vigilante group hunting for a hulking murderer. Everyone seems to know the "plan" except for our hero, who is left in the dark, literally as well as figuratively. Woody Allen, Mia Farrow, John Malkovitch, Madonna, Donald Pleasence, Lily Tomlin, Jodie Foster, Kathy Bates, John Cusack, Fred Gwynne. w. d. Woody Allen.

DRAMA: MURDER: Art Films; Serial Killers; Magic; Paranoia; Character Studies; Circus Life; 1900s; Coulda Been Good; Writer-Directors; Flops-Major

(Kafka; The Trial; Freaks)

(Ed: Snooze . . .)

Shadows of our Forgotten Ancestors, 1964, 99m, ★★¹/₂/$, Dovzhenko Film Studios/Connoisseur. Two young lovers discover that their fathers were vicious enemies and that the woman's father killed the man's. Ivan Nikolaichuk, Larisa Kadochnikova, Tatiana Bestayeva. w. Sergo Paradjanov, Ivan Chendei, d. Sergo Paradjanov.

DRAMA: MELODRAMA: ROMANCE: TRAGEDY: Romance-Doomed; Romance-Class Conflicts; Russian Films; Russians

Shaft, 1971, 98m, ★★★/$$$, MGM/ MGM-UA, R/V-S. A super cool black

urban detective breaks up the operations of a local gangster. Richard Roundtree, Moses Gunn, Charles Cioffi. w. Ernest Tidyman, John D. F. Black, d. Gordon Parks. **BOSong.** Oscars: 1-1.

ACTION: Detective Stories; Detectives-Private; Mob Stories; Black Men; Black Casts; Inner City Life; Drugs-Dealing; Black Screenwriters; Black Directors; Blaxploitation

(Superfly; Hitman)

Shaft in Africa, 1973, 112m, ★★/$, MGM/MGM-UA, R/V. An Ethiopian ruler solicits Shaft's help in combating slave-owning capitalists. Richard Roundtree, Frank Finlay, Vonetta McGee. w. Stirling Silliphant, d. John Guillermin.

ACTION: Detective Stories; Detectives-Private; Mob Stories; Black Men; Black Casts; Africa; Blaxploitation

Shaft's Big Score, 1972, 105m, ★★¹/₂/$$, MGM/MGM-UA,. R/V-S. A gangster makes the mistake of killing one of Shaft's best friends. Richard Roundtree, Moses Gunn, Drew Bunini Brown. w. Ernest Tidyman, d. Gordon Parks.

ACTION: Detective Stories; Detectives-Private; Mob Stories; Black Men; Black Casts; Avenging Death of Loved One; Manhunts; Inner City Life; Black Screenwriters; Black Directors; Blaxploitation

Shag, 1989, 96m, ★★★/$$, Hemdale/ HBO, PG/S. Several young southern belles take a trip to Myrtle Beach, South Carolina to find boys and enter a dance contest. Phoebe Cates, Scott Coffey, Bridget Fonda, Tyrone Power III. w. Robin Swicord, Lanier Laney, Terry Sweeney, d. Zelda Barron.

COMEDY: COMEDY DRAMA: ROMANCE: Coming of Age; Ensemble Films; Ensembles-Female; Beach Movies; Young Women; Southerns; Sorority Life; Female Protagonists; Female Directors; Female Screenwriters

(Mystic Pizza; Where the Boys Are)

The Shaggy D.A., 1976, 90m, ★★★/$$$, Disney/Disney, G. A young lawyer becomes a dog and gets into politics. Dean Jones, Tim Conway, Suzanne Pleshette, Jo Anne Worley, Vic Tayback, Keenan Wynn, Dick Van Patten. w. Don Tait, d. Robert Stevenson.

COMEDY: Humans into Animals; Comedy-Disneyesque; Lawyers; Politicians; Dogs

SEQUEL TO: The Shaggy Dog.

The Shaggy Dog, 1959, 101m, ★★★1/2/ $$$$, Disney/Disney, G. In order to infiltrate a band of criminals, a teen winds up turning himself into a dog. Fred MacMurray, Jean Hagen, Tommy Kirk, Cecil Kellaway, Annette Funicello. w. Bill Walsh, Lillie Hayward, N-adap. Felix Salten (*The Hound of Florence*), d. Charles Barton.

COMEDY: Disguises; Humans into Animals; Comedy-Disneyesque; Politicians; Child Protagonists; Teenagers; Boys; Boy and His Dog; Dogs; Blockbusters; Faded Hits

SEQUEL: The Shaggy D.A.

(The Absent Minded Professor; That Darn Cat)

Shakedown, 1988, 96m, ★★/$$, U/MCA-U, R/P-V-S. A D.A. and a cop go undercover to stop police corrupton and get in over their heads. Peter Weller, Sam Elliott, Patricia Charbonneau, Antonio Fargas, Blanche Baker. w. d. James Glickenhaus.

ACTION: Crime Drama; Lawyers; Police Stories; Detectives-Police; Police Corruption; Writer-Directors

Shake Hands with the Devil, 1959, 110m, ★★1/2/$$, UA/MGM-UA. In 1920s Ireland a doctor who's secretly in the IRA begins to turn to violence as a solution. James Cagney, Glynis Johns, Dana Wynter, Michael Redgrave, Sybil Thorndike, Cyril Cusack, Richard Harris, Ray McAnally. w. Ben Roberts, Ivan Goff, N-adap. Rearden Connor, d. Michael Anderson.

DRAMA: Crime Drama; Political Unrest; Terrorists; IRA; Doctors; Ordinary People Turned Criminal; Ireland

(Hidden Agenda; Odd Man Out)

Shaker Run, 1985, 91m, ★★/VR, Mirage-Ind/Sultan, PG. A New Zealander who must run from evil pharmacists is aided by two American stunt drivers. Cliff Robertson, Leif Garrett, Lisa Harrow. w. James Kouf, Jr., Henry Fownes, Bruce Morrison, d. Bruce Morrison.

ACTION: SUSPENSE: Conspiracy; Chase Movies; Fugitives from the Mob; Fugitives from the Law; Car Chases

Shakespeare Wallah, 1965, 125m, ★★★/$, MI-Ind/Sultan. A touring Shakespeare company from England has various adventures, romantic and otherwise, in India. Felicity Kendal, Shashi Kapoor, Laura Liddell, Geoffrey Kendal,

Madhur Jaffrey, Uptal Dutt. w. Ruth Prawer Jhabvala, James Ivory, d. James Ivory.

COMEDY DRAMA: ROMANCE: Theater Life; Actors; British Films; Indian People; India; Hidden Gems

(Heat and Dust)

Shakes the Clown, 1992, 83m, ★★/$, Col/Col, R/P-S. An alcoholic clown is framed for murder and goes into hiding with the aid of his bowling star girl who wants to get him off the bottle. Bobcat Godthwait, Julie Brown, Blake Clark, Adam Sandler, Paul Dooley, Florence Henderson. w. d. Bobcat Goldthwait.

COMEDY: Black Comedy; Circus Life; **MURDER:** Framed?; Accused Unjustly; Fugitives from the Law; Fugitives-Harboring; Bathroom Humor; Coulda Been Good; Writer-Directors

(The Clown; The Comic; Hot to Trot)

(Ed: Has its moments, especially with Florence Henderson, but otherwise a big misfire)

The Shakiest Gun in the West, 1968, 101m, ★★1/2/$$, Universal/MCA-U, G. A dentist is forced to carry a six-shooter and defend his town from marauding bandits. Don Knotts, Barbara Rhoades, Jackie Coogan. w. Jim Fritzell, Everett Greenbaum, d. Alan Rafkin.

COMEDY: WESTERNS: Western Comedy; **CHILDREN'S: FAMILY:** Comedy of Errors; Heroes-Unlikely; Fools-Bumbling; Nerds; Turning the Tables

(The Ruggles of Red Gap; Fancy Pants; The Apple Dumpling Gang)

Shaking the Tree, 1990, 107m, ★★1/2/$, Academy/Academy, R/S-P. A reunion sparks reminiscences of growing pains and joys for a group of old school friends. Arye Gross, Gale Hansen, Doug Savant, Steven Wilde, Courtney Cox. w. Duane Clark, Steven Wilde, d. Duane Clark.

COMEDY DRAMA: Ensemble Films; Young People; Friendships-Great; Reunions; 20-Somethings; Memories; Pre-life Crisis; Independent Films

(Indian Summer; The Big Chill; The Return of the Secaucus Seven; Queens Logic)

(Ed: Epitome of the cliched genre of young people reunions)

Shaiako, 1968, 118m, ★★/$$, 20th/Fox. In New Mexico in the late 1800s, a group of Europeans out hunting

are massacred by local Indians. Sean Connery, Brigitte Bardot, Jack Hawkins, Stephen Boyd, Peter Van Eyck. w. J. J. Griffith, Hal Hopper, Scot Finch, N-adap. Louis L'Amour, d. Edward Dmytryk.

WESTERNS: ACTION: Massacres; Indians-American; International Casts; West-Old

Shallow Grave, 1995, 88m, ★★★1/2/ $$, Gramercy/MCA-U, R/EV-B&G-P-S. Three young and hip roomies interview for a fourth to share their hip and trendy space. But the one they choose soon turns up dead in his room with a whole bunch of money stashed there. After the grind they put their applicants through, they seemed to have completely failed on the safety of a new roommate issue as they're soon assailed by more dangers any other roommate from hell could have brought. Kerry Fox, Christopher Eccleston, Ewan McGregor, Ken Stott, Keith Allen, Colin McCredie, Victoria Nairn, Gary Lewis, Jean Marie Coffey. w. John Hodge, d. Danny Boyle.

SUSPENSE: MURDER: Finding Money; Hide the Dead Body; Fugitives from a Murderer; Ensemble Films; Young People; Roommates from Hell; Clever Plots & Endings; Scotland; British Films; Cult Films; Sleeper Hits; Hitchcockian

(Apartment Zero; Frenzy; Blood Simple)

Shall We Dance?, 1937, 116m, ★★★1/2/$$$$, RKO/Turner. In order to compete in a dance contest, a couple of dancers pretend to be married. They eventually like the game so much they tie the knot for real. Fred Astaire, Ginger Rogers, Edward Everett Horton. w. Allan Scott, Ernest Pagano, d. Mark Sandrich.

MUSICALS: Dance Movies; Married-Fake; **ROMANCE:** Romantic Comedy; Dancers; Competitions; Roller Skating; Astaire & Rogers

(Top Hat; Flying Down to Rio)

Shame, 1961, 84m, ★★★/$, AIP/Nos. A redneck protests and provokes desegregationists in the early days of bussing in the midwest. William Shatner, Jeanne Cooper. d. Roger Corman.

DRAMA: Social Drama; Bigots; Race Relations; Bussing/Busses; Rednecks; Political Drama; Character Studies; Mean Men; Forgotten Films; Independent Films Curiosities

(Paris Trout; Crisis at Central High)

The Shame, 1968, 103m, ★★★½/$, UA/MGM-UA, R/S. Elitist concert musicians who are married flee together from their oppressed country but soon the battles catch up with them, causing them to question their place in the world. Max Von Sydow, Liv Ullman. w. d. Ingmar Bergman.
DRAMA: War Stories; Oppression; Allegorical Stories-; Art Films; Musicians; Marriage Drama; Fugitives; Political Drama; Political Unrest; Surrealism; Swedish Films; Writer-Directors; Hidden Gems
(Scenes from a Marriage; Face to Face)
Shame, 1987, 94m, ★★★/$, Barron Films-UAA Films/Republic, R/V-S. A rapist is protected by the silence of his small outback town until a female lawyer comes to town and exposes him. Deborra-Lee Furness, Tony Barry, Simone Buchanan, Gillian Jones. w. Beverly Blankenship, Michael Brindley, d. Steve Jodrell.
DRAMA: Courtroom Drama; Manhunts; Detective Stories; Detectives-Female; Lawyers as Detectives; Rape/Rapists; Small-town Life; Secrets-Keeping; Hiding Out; Conspiracy; Female Protagonists; Australian Films; Female Screenwriters
(The Accused)
Shampoo, 1975, 110m, ★★★★/$$$$, Columbia/RCA-Col, R/P-S-FN-MRN. A Beverly Hills hairdresser (Warren Beatty) trying to get a shop of his own also gets himself into trouble by bedding most of his clients (Julie Christie, Goldie Hawn, Lee Grant (**BSActress**), Carrie Fisher). w. Robert Towne, Warren Beatty (BOScr), d. Hal Ashby. Oscars: 2-1.
DRAMA: Erotic Drama; **SATIRE:** Interwoven Stories; Playboys; Prostitutes-Male; Sexy Men; Sexy Women; Beautiful People; Hairdressers; Beverly Hills; Dreams; Mistresses; Romance-Triangles; 1960s; Anti-establishment Films
(American Gigolo; Lifeguard)
Shamus, 1972, 98m, ★★½/$$$, Col/Goodtimes, R/V. A millionaire's jewels are stolen and he hires a private eye to recover them in this updating of Chandler and Spillane type mysteries. Burt Reynolds, Dyan Cannon, John Ryan, Joe Santos, Giorgio Tozzi. w. Barry Beckerman, d. Buzz Kulik.
MYSTERY: Detective Stories; Detectives-Privates; Jewel Thieves; Revisionist Films; Film Noir-Modern
Rough Cut

(The Long Goodbye; Marlow; The Burglars)
Shane, 1953, 117m, ★★★½/$$$$, Par/Par, Time-Life. A Western pioneer family in trouble gets helped by a wandering stranger, who becomes a part of their family and is idolized by the son. Alan Ladd, Jean Arthur, Van Heflin, Jack Palance (BSActor), Brandon de Wilde. w. A. B. Guthrie, Jr. (BScr), N-adap. Jack Schaefer, d. George Stevens (BDirector), BPicture. **BCCin**, Oscars: 5-1.
WESTERNS: DRAMA: MELODRAMA: Men and Boys; Boys; Drifters; Heroes-Ordinary; Illusions Destroyed; Blockbusters
(The Man Who Shot Liberty Valance; Fallen Idol; The Ox-Bow Incident)
Shanghai Express, 1932, 84m, ★★★/$$$, Par/MCA-U. On a train in China, a British military man and his old lover rekindle their romance while at the next station, train robbers await. Marlene Dietrich, Clive Brook, Warner Oland, Anna May Wong, Eugene Pallette. w. Jules Furthman, d. Josef Von Sternberg.
DRAMA: SUSPENSE: ROMANCE: Romance-Reunited; Thieves; Trains; China
(Blonde Venus; The Blue Angel; Desire)
The Shanghai Gesture, 1942, 97m, ★★½/$$, Republic/MFVideo. A philandering husband is accused by his wife, the owner of a Shanghai nightclub, of raising their daughter to be a lost soul. Ona Munson, Victore Mature, Walter Huston, Gene Tierney, Albert Basserman, Phyllis Brooks. w. Josef Von Sternberg, Geza Herczeg, Karl Vollmoeller, Jules Furthman, P-adap. John Colton, d. Josef Von Sternberg. BB&WArt, BScore. Oscars: 2-0.
MELODRAMA: Cheating Men; Mothers & Daughters; Promiscuity; Nightclubs; China; Unintentionally Funny; Forgotten Films
Shanghai Surprise, 1986, 97m, ★/$, Handmade-Vestron/Vestron, PG/S. An adventurer-for-hire must track down a shipment of opium before a band of criminals gets ahold of it. Madonna, Sean Penn, Paul Freeman. w. John Kohn, Robert Bentley, N-adap. Tony Kenrick (*Faraday's Flowers*), d. Jim Goddard.
COMEDY DRAMA: Capers; Heist Stories; Chase Movies; China; Americans Abroad; Good Premise Unfulfilled; Flops-Major; Unintentionally Funny

(Ed: Deadly boring when it should be anything but)
Shanghai Triad, 1995, 125m, ★★★/$$, Sony/Sony, R/S. The life of a prostitute and the compromises she has to make in a world of crime, mirrored through the naive eyes of a country boy she befriends. Gong Li, Li Baotian, Li Xuejian, Shun Chun, Wang Xiao Xiao. w. Bi Feiyu, N-adap. Li Xiao, d. Zhang Yimou.
DRAMA: Character Studies; Prostitutes-Low Class; Romance with Prostitute; City vs. Country; Female Protagonists; Chinese Films
(Raise the Red Lantern)
Shark!, 1969, 88m, ★★/$$, U/Republic. After a gun dealer's boat sinks in the Persian Gulf, it's repaired by some treasure-hunting divers who encounter underwater danger. Burt Reynolds, Arthur Kennedy, Barry Sullivan, Silvia Pinal. w. Samuel Fuller, John Kingsbridge, N-adap. Victor Canning (*His Bones are Coral*), d. Samuel Fuller.
ADVENTURE: Treasure Hunts; Adventure At Sea; Animal Monsters; Sharks Middle East; Underwater Adventure
(The Deep; The Sharkhunters)
(Ed: Famous for a diver actually being attacked and killed during filming. The first death on a Reynolds film. The second one was *The Man Who Loved Cat Dancing*)
Sharky's Machine, 1981, 119m, ★★★/$$$, Orion-WB/WB, R/S-V-FN. A maverick cop gets to hand-pick a team for a new vice-squad unit. Burt Reynolds, Vittorio Gassman, Brian Keith, Charles Durning, Earl Holliman. w. Gerald Di Pego, N-adap. William Diehl, d. Burt Reynolds.
ACTION: Police Stories; Police-Vigilante; Car Chases; Prostitutes-Low Class; Female Among Males
(Stick; Hustle; Shamus; Heat; Malone)
Shattered, 1991, 98m, ★★½/$, MGM/MGM-UA, R/V-P-S. A man suffering from amnesia after a near-fatal accident hires a detective to find out who he is. Tom Berenger, Greta Scaachi, Bob Hoskins, Joanne Whalley-Kilmer, Corbin Bernsen. w. d. Wolfgang Petersen, N-adap. Richard Neely (*The Plastic Nightmare*).
SUSPENSE: MYSTERY: MURDER: MURDER MYSTERY: Suspecting Oneself; Amnesia; Lookalikes; Identities-Assumed;

Nightmares; Accidents; Past-Haunted by; Secrets-Keeping; Cheating Women; Cosmetic Surgery; Coulda Been Great (Liebestraum; Intersection; Angel Heart) (Ed: If you stick with it, you may get it, but it's muddled nature makes it difficult)

The Shawshank Redemption, 142m, ★★★1/2/$$, Col/Col, R/EP-V-S-MRN. A man convicted of murdering his wife goes to prison in 1947 and finds life hell. As the years go by, he makes allies and crusades to establish a prison library, but he has more secrets than anyone knows. Tim Robbins, Morgan Freeman (BActor), Bob Gunton. w. d. Frank Darabont (BAScr), SS-adap. Stephen King. BPicture, BEditing, BOScore, BCin, BSound. Oscars: 7-0.

DRAMA: Prison Drama; Accused Unjustly; **MURDER:** Murder of Spouse; Friendships-Male; Government as Enemy; Greed; Government Corruption; Narrated Films; 1940s; Episodic Stories; Rape/Rapists; Rape-Male; Black Men; Friendships-Interracial; Black & White Together; Librarians; Clever Plots & Endings; Incredible but Mostly True; Stephen King
(Short Eyes; One Flew Over the Cuckoo's Nest; The Birdman of Alcatraz; 20,000 Years at Sing-Sing)

She, 1935, 89m, ★★★/$$, RKO/NA. An ancient legend has it that the queen of a lost civilization will remain immortal until she falls in love, which happens when an archaeologist comes upon her ruined domain. Randolph Scott, Nigel Bruce, Helen Gahagan. w. Ruth Rose, Dudley Nichols, N-adap. H. Rider Haggard, d. Irving Pichel, Lansing G. Holden. BChoreography. Oscars: 1-0. Female Screenwriters

She, 1965, 105m, ★★/$, ABP-Hammer/ NA. Remake of above with more gore. Peter Cushing, Ursula Andress, Christopher Lee, John Richardson. w. David T. Chantler, N-adap. H. Rider Haggard, d. Robert Day.

ADVENTURE: ROMANCE: Fantasy; **SCI-FI:** Archaeologists Aging-Reverse; Soul-Selling One's; Arctic; Snow Settings; Volcanoes
(Sheena, Queen of the Jungle; Congo)
(Ed: This remake is set in the original story's setting of Africa)

She Couldn't Say No, 1952, 89m, ★★1/2/$$, RKO/Critic's Choice. A woman who turns out to become an heiress

returns to the small town where she grew up to repay all those who helped her. Jean Simmons, Robert Mitchum, Arthur Hunnicutt, Edgar Buchanan, Wallace Ford. w. D.D. Beauchamp, William Bowers, Richard Flournoy, d. Lloyd Bacon.

COMEDY DRAMA: MELODRAMA: Heiresses; Small-town Life; Reunions; **ROMANCE:** Romance-Reunited; Capra-esque

She-Devil, 1989, 99m, ★★★/$$, Orion/Orion, PG-13/S-P. A dowdy housewife (Roseanne Barr) loses her husband (Ed Begley, Jr.) to a beautiful romance novelist (Meryl Streep) and exacts a clever and laborious revenge on him. w. Barry Strugatz, Mark R. Burns, N-adap. Fay Weldon (The Life and Loves of a She-Devil), d. Susan Seidelman.

COMEDY: SATIRE: Women in Conflict; Romance Novelists; Cheating Men; Women Fighting Over Men; Jealousy; Starting Over; Rich vs. Poor; Parallel Stories; Coulda Been Great; Female Directors; Female Protagonists; Underrated
BBC TV version, 1987.
(Married to the Mob; Death Becomes Her)
(Ed: The primary problem is that the two rival female leads never actually confront each other and have it out, which misled audiences by having them choking each other in ads)

She Done Him Wrong, 1933, 68m, ★★★1/2/$$$$, Par/MCA-U. An undercover cop tries to dig up the dirty secrets of a female barkeep in the 1890s and they end up falling in love. Mae West, Cary Grant, Owen Moore, Gilbert Roland, Noah Beery. w. P-adap., Mae West (Diamond Lil), d. Lowell Sherman.

COMEDY: ROMANCE: Romantic Comedy; Secrets-Keeping; Romance-Reluctant; Detective Stories; Detectives-Police; Undercover; Sexy Women; Feisty Females; 1890s; Female Protagonists
(My Little Chickadee; Dynamite; Sextette)
(Ed: Some great lines and West lusting after Grant is tantilizingly hilarious)

She Loves Me Not, 1934, 85m, ★★★/$$, Par/NA. A dancer in a revue witnesses a murder, then hides from the murderers at a men's college. Bing Crosby, Miriam Hopkins, Kitty Carlisle, Edward Nugent. w. Ben Glazer, P-adap. Howard Lindsay, N-adap. Edward Hope, d. Elliott Nugent.

COMEDY: Murder-Witness; Hiding Out; College Life; Female Among Males; Female Protagonists; Fugitives; Fugitives from a Murderer
(Ball of Fire; Lady of Burlesque)

She Wore a Yellow Ribbon, 1949, 93m, ★★★/$$$$, RKO/Turner. A cavalry officer wants to retire but duty calls in the form of a beautiful woman. John Wayne, Joanne Dru, John Agar, Ben Johnson, Harry Carey, Jr. w. Frank Nugent, Laurence Stallings, SS-adap. James Warner Bellah, d. John Ford. BCCin. Oscars: 1-0.

DRAMA: WESTERN: MELODRAMA: Military Stories; Soldiers; Cavalry; Retirement
(The Red Badge of Courage; The Quiet Man)

Sheena, Queen of the Jungle, 1984, 117m, ★★/$, Col/RCA-Col, Goodtimes, PG/FN. A white orphan girl is taken in by an African tribe, and becomes a sort of female Tarzan. Tanya Roberts, Ted Wass, Donovan Scott. w. David Newman, Lorenzo Semple, Jr., d. John Guillermin.

ACTION: ADVENTURE: SCI-FI: Psychics; Cartoon Heroes; Raised by Animals; Jungle Life; Africa; Female Protagonists
(Tarzan, the Ape Man [1981]; SHE)

The Sheepman, 1958, 91m, ★★★/$$, MGM/MGM-UA. A farmer has trouble adjusting to city life. Glenn Ford, Shirley MacLaine, Leslie Nielsen. w. William Bowers, James Edward Grant (BOScr), d. George Marshall. Oscars: 1-0.

COMEDY DRAMA: Farmers; Farm Life; Fish out of Water Stories; Western Comedy; City vs. Country

The Sheik, 1921, 73m, ★★★/$$$$$, Par/Par, GPV. A British noblewoman falls in love with a darkly handsome Arabian sheik, and millions of females swooned. Rudolph Valentino, Agnes Ayres, Adolphe Menjou, Walter Long. w. Monte M. Katterjohn, N-adap. E. M. Hull, d. George Melford.

ROMANCE: MELODRAMA: ADVENTURE: Romance-Class Conflicts; Sexy Men; Arab People; Blockbusters
SEQUEL: Son of the Sheik.

She'll Be Wearing Pink Pajamas, 1985, 90m, ★★1/2/$, Virgin/Virgin, WB, PG. A group of suburban women have comical misadventures trying to survive an "outward bound"-type camping trip. Julie Walters, Anthony Higgins, Jane

Evers, Janet Henfrey, Paula Jacobs. w. Eva Hardy, d. John Goldschmidt.

COMEDY: Camping; Comedy of Errors; Fish out of Water Stories; British Films; Female Screenwriters
(Strangers in Good Company; The Mating Season [1980]; Educating Rita; Personal Services)

The Shell Seekers, 1989, 94m, ★★★/ $$$$, CBS/Republic. A widow recovering from heart surgery returns to her home in England. Angela Lansbury, Sam Wanamaker, Patricia Hodge, Irene Worth. w. John Pielmeier, d. Waris Hussein.

DRAMA: MELODRAMA: Memories; Reunions; Elderly Women; Widows; England; TV Movies
(The Trip to Bountiful; The Mirror Crack'd)

The Sheltering Sky, 1990, 139m, ★★1/2/$, WB/WB-PIA-FCT. A lost-generation writer and his wife go to Algeria in hopes of "finding themselves." What they find is a harsh land and an uninviting culture. Debra Winger, John Malkovich, Campbell Scott, Amina Annabi, Paul Bowles. w. Mark Peploe, Bernardo Bertolucci, N-adap. Paul Bowles, d. Bernardo Bertolucci.

DRAMA: ROMANCE: Romance-Triangles; Ménage a Trois; Art Films; Autobiographical Stories; Journies; Vacations; Vacation Romance; Desert Settings; Africa; Flops-Major; 1930s
(Cabaret; I Am a Camera; Little Buddha)
(Ed: Big snoozer once the sand has dulled one's senses. Based on autobiographical adventures of same people as *I am a Camera* and *Cabaret* were based upon in Bowles' and Christopher Isherwood's stories.)

Shenandoah, 1965, 105m, ★★★/$$$, U/MCA-U, G. A family in rural Virginia during the 1800s is torn apart by the Civil War but slowly rebuilds afterwards. James Stewart, Rosemary Forsyth, Doug McClure, Katharine Ross. w. James Lee Barrett, d. Andrew V. McLaglen. BSound. Oscars: 1-0.

DRAMA: MELODRAMA: Family Drama; **FAMILY:** War Battles; Civil War Era; Southerns; Mountain People; Rural Life
(Friendly Persuasion; The Lolly Madonna War)

Shepherd of the Hills, 1941, 98m, ★★★/$$$, Par/NA, AMC. A group of rugged mountain men are bothered by a stranger who interrupts their bucolic lives. John Wayne, Betty Field, Harry Carey, Buelah Bondi, James Barton. w. Grover Jones, Stuart Anthony, N-adap. Harold Bell Wright, Jr., d. Henry Hathaway.

MELODRAMA: Ensemble Films; Ensembles-Male; Hillbillies; Mountain People; Drifters; Rural Life

Sherlock Holmes, 1932, 68m, ★★1/2/$$, 20th/NA. Chicago gangsters invade London and the famous detective must deal with them. Clive Brook, Reginald Owen, Ernest Torrence, Miriam Jordan. w. Bertram Milhauser, d. William K. Howard.

MYSTERY: Detective Stories; Detectives-Private; Sherlock Holmes

Sherlock Holmes Faces Death, 1943, 68m, ★★★/$$, 20th/Fox. In an old-age home for war veterans a series of bizarre murders occur and Sherlock Holmes is brought in on the case. Basil Rathbone, Nigel Bruce, Hillary Brooke, Halliwell Hobbes, Dennis Hoey. w. Bertram Millhauser, SS-adap. Arthur Conan Doyle *(The Musgrave Ritual)*, d. Roy William Neill.

Sherlock Holmes and the Secret Weapon, 1942, 68m, ★★★/$$, Universal/Republic. During World War II, Sherlock Holmes must help the Allied Forces thwart a Nazi spy ring. Basil Rathbone, Nigel Bruce, Lionel Atwill, Karen Verne. w. Edward T. Lowe, W. Scott Darling, Edmund L. Hartmann, N-adap. Arthur Conan Doyle *(The Dancing Man)*, d. Roy William Neill.

Sherlock Holmes and the Spider Woman, 1944, 62m, ★★★/$$, Universal/MCA-U. An evil woman kills her victims with spiders to collect on their insurance policies. Sherlock Holmes finds her out. Basil Rathbone, Nigel Bruce, Gale Sondergaard, Dennis Hoey, Vernon Downing. w. Bertram Milhauser, d. Roy William Neill.

Sherlock Holmes: The Spider Woman Strikes Back, 1946, 70m, ★★1/2/$$, Universal/MCA-U. A sequel to the above film in which the spider woman uses another woman as her double. Gale Sondergaard, Brenda Joyce, Rondo Hatton, Milburn Stone, Kirby Grant, Hobart Cavanaugh. w. Eric Taylor, d. Arthur Lubin.

Sherlock Holmes and the Voice of Terror, 1942, 65m, ★★★/$$, Universal/Fox. During World War II, Sherlock Holmes helps the Allies by revealing a double-agent in the British government. Basil Rathbone, Nigel Bruce, Hillary Brooke, Reginald Denny, Thomas Gomez. w. Lynn Riggs, SS-adap. Arthur Conan Doyle *(His Last Bow)*, d. John Rawlins.

Sherlock Holmes in Washington, 1943, 71m, ★★1/2/$$, 20th/Fox. Sherlock is brought to the Capitol to ferret out Nazi spies in Washington during World War II. Basil Rathbone, Nigel Bruce, Henry Daniell, George Zucco. w. Bertram Millhauser, Lynn Riggs, d. Roy William Neill.

SHERLOCK SERIES:
MYSTERY: Detective Stories; Detectives-Private; Sherlock Holmes **SEE ALSO:** Sherlock Holmes category listing.
(The Private Life of Sherlock Holmes; They Might Be Giants; Without a Clue; Young Sherlock Holmes)

She's Gotta Have It, 1986, 84m (B&W), 20th/Fox, R/S-FN. A woman who is pursued by three men decides, rather than choose, she'll have them all. Tracy Camilla Jones, Tommy Redmon Hicks, Joie Lee, Spike Lee. w. d. Spike Lee.

COMEDY: COMEDY DRAMA: ROMANCE: Romantic Comedy; Men Fighting Over Women; Sexy Women; Macho Men; Battle of the Sexes; Inner City Life; Black Casts; Black Men; Black Women; Sleeper Hits; Black Screenwriters; Black Directors; Writer-Directors
(School Daze)

She's Having a Baby, 1988, 106m, ★★1/2/$$, Par/Par, PG/S. A young man trying to make a homelife in the suburbs panics when the onset of pregnancy means more responsibilities and a demanding wife. Kevin Bacon, Elizabeth McGovern. w. d. John Hughes.

COMEDY: COMEDY DRAMA: Babies-Having; Marriage Comedy; Newlyweds; Young People; Young Men; Suburban Life; Pre-Life Crisis; Writer-Directors
(Nine Months; Uncle Buck)

She's Out of Control, 1989, 95m, ★1/2/$, Weintraub-Col/RCA-Col, PG-13/S. A man raising a teenage daughter by himself becomes overwhelmed by the complications arising from her burgeoning sexuality, so he chases after her whenever he can to make sure she's not being naughty. Tony Danza, Catherine Hicks, Wallace Shawn. w. Seth Winston, Michael J. Nathanson, d. Stan Dragoti.

COMEDY: Fathers & Daughters; Coming of Age; Teenagers; Girls; Fathers Alone;

Daddy's Girls; Parents vs. Children (The Impossible Years; My Father, the Hero)

She's Working Her Way Through College, 1952, 101m, War. A stripper who decides to get her degree breathes life into a buttoned-down professor. Virginia Mayo, Ronald Reagan, Don Defore, Gene Nelson. w. Peter Milne, P-adap. James Thurber (*The Male Animal*), d. Bruce Humberstone.

COMEDY: COMEDY DRAMA: ROMANCE: Marriage Comedy; Battle of the Sexes; Nerds; Extroverted vs. Introverted; College Life; Professors; Jealousy; Life Transitions; Midlife Crisis **REMAKE OF:** The Male Animal.
(The Male Animal; Mother is a Freshman)
(Ed: This version of the hit Thurber play places more emphasis on the female character. There's an ironic speech by Reagan about how everyone, no matter who or how poor, should have full access to a college education)

The Shining, 1980, 143m, 1980, 143m, ★★★/$$$$, WB/WB, R/V-P. A blocked writer, hoping to rejuvenate himself, takes a winter job as the custodian of an old Maine hotel. But once there, he and his family begin to feel the odd effects of this apparently haunted place as he begins to lose his grip on reality. Jack Nicholson, Shelley Duvall, Danny Lloyd, Barry Nelson, Scatman Crothers. w. Stanley Kubrick, Diane Johnson, N-adap, Stephen King, d. Stanley Kubrick.
HORROR: SUSPENSE: Serial Killers; Stranded; Snow Settings; Hotels; Chase Movies; Mental Illness; Psycho Killers; Marriage on the Rocks; Female Screen-writers; Coulda Been Great; Stephen King (Dead of Winter; Misery; Wolf; Batman)
The Shining Hour, 1936, 76m, ★★1/2/$$$, MGM/MGM-UA. A wealthy and stodgy man goes after a bad-girl dancer he spies and friends don't like it. Joan Crawford, Margaret Sullavan, Melvyn Douglas, Robert Young, Fay Bainter. w. Ogden Nash, Jane Murfin, d. Frank Borzage.
MELODRAMA: ROMANCE: Romance-Mismatched; Romance-Class Conflicts; Rich People; Dancers; Lover Family Dislikes; Forgotten Films
Shining Through, 1991, 150m, ★★/$, 20th/Fox, R/V-P. By going undercover as a governess, a half-Jewish secretary helps the Americans fight the Nazi's in war-torn

Berlin. Michael Douglas, Melanie Griffith, Liam Neeson, John Gielgud. w. d. David Seltzer, N-adap. Susan Isaacs.
MELODRAMA: ROMANCE: Spy Films; Spies; Germans as Enemy; Berlin; World War II Stories; Nazi Stories; Undercover; Jewish People; Jews-Saving; Impostors; Chase Movies; Hiding Out; Escape Drama; Flops-Major
(Ed: Ridiculous from start to finish with major implausibilities and clinker lines, let alone inconsistencies with Griffith's and Douglas' command of German)
Ship of Fools, 1965, 149m, ★★★1/2/ $$$, Col/RCA-Col. In 1933, the lives of the ecclectic group of passengers on a cruise from Mexico to Germany are explored as they intersect and confront each other. Vivien Leigh, Simone Signoret (BActress), Oskar Werner (BActor), Jose Ferrer, Lee Marvin, Michael Dunn (BSActor), George Segal. w. Abby Mann (BAScr), N-adap, Katherine Anne Porter, d. Stanley Kramer. BPicture, BB&WCin, BB&WArt, BB&WCostume. Oscars: 7-2.
DRAMA: Social Drama; Ensemble Films; Multiple Stories; Interwoven Stories; Ships; Vacations; Journies; Jewish People; Anti-Semitism; All-Star Casts
(Voyage of the Damned; Grand Hotel)
(Ed: Strong, though dated and somehow seems contemporary to the 60s more than the 30s)
Shirley Valentine, 1989, 108m, ★★★/$, Par/Par, R/P-S-FFN-MRN. A British housewife (Pauline Collins, BActress) leaves her dreary suburban life for a trip to Greece to find herself. Tom Conti, Julia McKenzie, Alison Steadman, Bernard Hill. w. P-adap. Willy Russell, d. Lewis Gilbert. Oscars: 1-0.
COMEDY: COMEDY DRAMA: ROMANCE: Romantic Comedy; Romance-Middle-Aged; Romance on Vacation; Life Transitions; Starting Over; Vacation Romance; Midlife Crisis; Mediterranean; Female Protagonists; British Films
(Summertime; Alfie [same team]; Twenty-One; Educating Rita [same team])
(Ed: Collins reprises her Tony-winning, one-woman Broadway show)
Shock Corridor, 1963, 101m, ★★★/$, Col/HomeVision. A reporter (Peter Breck) checks into a mental institution to solve a murder where the only witness wasn't

believed. Peter Breck, Constance Towers, Gene Evans, James Best. w. d. Samuel Fuller.
SUSPENSE: MURDER: MYSTERY: MURDER MYSTERY: Asylums; Undercover; Mental Illness; Insane-Plot to Drive; Unbelieved; Detective Stories; Journalists as Detectives; Evil Men; Film Noir-Modern; Forgotten Films; Hidden Gems; Writer-Directors
(Bedlam; Asylum; Shock Treatment)
A Shock to the System, 1990, 88m, ★★★/$, Corsair/HBO, R/V-P. A man having a mid-life crisis decides to murder his wife and everyone else that bothers him-in clever and interesting ways. Michael Caine, Elizabeth McGovern, Peter Riegart, Swoosie Kurtz, Will Patton. w. Andrew Klavan, N-adap. Simon Brett, d. Jan Egleson.
COMEDY: Black Comedy; **MURDER:** Serial Killers; Murders-One by One; Murder-Comic Attempts; Nervous Breakdowns; Revenge; Clever Plots & Endings Underrated; Hidden Gems; Overlooked at Release
(A New Leaf; Mother Love)
Shock Treatment, 1964, 94m, ★★1/2/$, WB/Fox. In an insane asylum, a murderer is on the rampage. Lauren Bacall, Roddy MacDowall, Carol Lynley, Ossie Davis, Stuart Whitman. w. Sidney Boehm, d. Denis Sanders.
HORROR: MURDER: Serial Killers; Murders-One by One; Asylums; Psycho Killers; Forgotten Films; Camp
(Shock Corridor; Bedlam; Asylum)
Shock Treatment, 1981, 94m, ★/$, 20th/CBS-Fox, R/S-P. A sequel to *The Rocky Horror Picture Show,* with the same white-bread couple, this time perpetually replaying a sadistic game show. Jessica Harper, Cliff De Young, Richard O'Brien. w. Richard O'Brien, Jim Sharman, d. Jim Sharman.
COMEDY: Black Comedy; **MUSICAL:** Music Movies; Horror Comedy; Spoofs-Horror; Forgotten Films; Overlooked at Release
SEQUEL TO: The Rocky Horror Picture Show
(Ed: There are lots of fans of Rocky Horror who don't have a clue this exists and are probably better off for it)
Shocker, 1989, 111m, ★★1/2/$$, Universal/MCA-U, R/EV-P-S-B&G. A serial killer lives on after the electric chair as a sort of force field who can

enter people's bodies through television or electrical appliances. Michael Murphy, Peter Berg, Cami Cooper, Mitch Pileggi, John Tesh. w. d. Wes Craven.

HORROR: MURDER: Serial Killers; Murders-One by One; Framed; Accused Unjustly; Chase Movies; Prison Escape; Dead-Back from the; Executions; Convict's Revenge; Human Monsters; Teenagers; Writer-Directors
(The Walking Dead; Pulse)

The Shocking Miss Pilgrim, 1946, 85m, ★★1/2/$$, 20th/CBS-Fox. A female stenographer in 1890s Boston becomes a suffragette. Betty Grable, Dick Haymes, Anne Revere, Gene Lockhart, Elizabeth Patterson. w. d. George Seaton.

COMEDY: COMEDY DRAMA: Women's Rights; Secretaries; Heroes-Unlikely; Boston; 1890s; Female Protagonists; Writer-Directors; Scandals
(The Dolly Sisters; Strawberry Blonde)

The Shoes of the Fisherman, 1968, 160m, ★★★/$$, MGM/MGM-UA. A Russian bishop in the gulag for twenty years is finally freed and goes on to become Pope. Anthony Quinn, David Janssen, Laurence Olivier, Oskar Werner, John Gielgud, Vittorio de Sica. w. John Patrick, James Kennaway, N-adap. Morris West, d. Michael Anderson. BOScore, BArt. Oscars: 2-0.

DRAMA: Costume Drama; Epics; Episodic Stories; Popes; Religion; Power-Rise to; Biographies-Fictional; Russians
(The Cardinal; The Big Fisherman)

Shoeshine, 1946, 90m, ★★★1/2/$$, Alfa-Ind/Facets. During World War II, Rome is occupied and the necessities of life are scarce. Two shoeshine boys take advantage of the situation and get into the black market, but they soon find they're in over their heads. Franco Interlenghi, Rinaldo Smordoni. w. Cesare Zavattini, Sergio Amide, Adolfo Franci (BOScr), d. Vittorio deSica. BFLFilm. Oscars: 2-1.

DRAMA: TRAGEDY: World War II Era; Italy; Ordinary People Turned Criminal; Nazi Stories; Oppression; Fascism; Film History
(The Bicycle Thief; Open City)

Shogun Assassin, 1980, 89m, ★★/$, Katsu/MCA-U. Lone Wolf, a Japanese comic-book character, goes around killing people with his huge sword and martial-arts prowess. Tomisaburo Wakayama, Masahiro Tomikawa, Kayo Matsuo, Minoru Ohki. w. Kazuo Koike, Robert Houston, David Weisman, d. Kenji Misumi, Robert Houston.

ACTION: MURDER: Serial Killers; Comic Heroes; Evil Men; Martial Arts; Japanese Films; Japan

Shoot the Moon, 1981, 123m, ★★★1/2/$$, MGM/MGM-UA, R/S-P. In an upper-crust family, the parents' divorce slowly crumbles the facade of civility that they had worked so hard to maintain. Albert Finney, Diane Keaton, Karen Allen, Peter Weller. w. Bo Goldman, d. Alan Parker.

DRAMA: Character Studies; Marriage Drama; Marriage on the Rocks; Divorce; Battle of the Sexes; Custody Battles; Writers; Rich People; Quiet Little Films; Underrated; Hidden Gems

COMIC FLIPSIDE: War of the Roses.
(Firstborn; Kramer vs. Kramer; Divorce Wars; The War Between the Tates)
(Ed: May take a second viewing for emotional impact to be evident. The moments are in the characters, not the plot)

Shoot the Piano Player, 1962, 84m, ★★★/$$, Films de la Pleiade/Nos. When gangsters kill his girlfriend after his involvement with them, a piano-bar entertainer fights back. Charles Aznavour, Nicole Berger, Marie Dubois, Michele Mercier. w. Marcel Moussy, Francois Truffaut, N-adap. David Goodis (*Down There*), d. Francois Truffaut.

DRAMA: SUSPENSE: Art Films; Film Noir-Modern; Avenging Death of a Loved One; Pianists; French Films; French New Wave Films
(Breathless)

Shoot to Kill, 1988, 110m, ★★1/2/$$$, Touchstone/Touchstone, PG-13/V. A rugged hiker helps the FBI track down a murderer in the mountains. Sidney Poitier, Tom Berenger, Kirstie Alley, Clancy Brown, Frederick Coffin, Richard Masur. w. Harv Zimmell, Michael Burton, Daniel Petrie, Jr., d. Roger Spottiswoode.

ACTION: MURDER: Trail of a Killer; Chase Movies; Manhunts; Mountains; FBI Agents; Black Men
(The River Wild)

The Shooting, 1966, 82m, ★★★/$, AIP/Media. A bountyhunter is led on a chase through the desert by woman, who may have set him up. Warren Oates, Millie Perkins, Jack Nicholson. d. Monte Hellman.

ACTION: Action Drama; Bounty Hunters; Dangerous Women; Mindgames; Clever Plots & Endings; Desert Settings; Cult Films; Curiosities
(Ride in the Whirlwind)

The Shooting Party, 1985, 97m, ★★★/$, Ind/NA. As World War I is about to break out, the elites of the English countryside gather for a pheasant hunt and an era passes on. James Mason, Dorothy Tutin, Edward Fox, John Gielgud. w. Julian Bond, N-adap. Isabel Colegate, d. Alan Bridges.

DRAMA: Ensemble Films; World War I Era; Rich People; Hunters; England; British Films

The Shootist, 1976, 100m, ★★★/$$, Par/Par, AMC, PG. An aging gun fighter learns that he's dying and goes back to his home town to settle old scores and fall in love once more with his landlady. John Wayne, Lauren Bacall, James Stewart, Ron Howard, John Carradine, Scatman Crothers. w. Miles Hood Swarthout, Scott Hale, N-adap. Glendon Swarthout, d. Don Siegel.

DRAMA: MELODRAMA: ROMANCE: WESTERN: Death-Impending; Gunfighters; Retirement; Romance-Elderly; Elderly Men; One Last Time
(True Grit; Rooster Cogburn)
(Ed: May appeal to those interested in the romantic angle only)

The Shop Around the Corner, 1938, 101m, ★★★★/$$$, MGM/MGM-UA. In old Budapest before the war, a shop-keeper and the lovely young woman who spurns his advances bicker while writing to mysterious pen pals. James Stewart, Margaret Sullavan, Frank Morgan, Joseph Schildkraut, Sara Haden, Felix Bressart. w. Samson Raphaelson, P-adap. Nikolaus Laszlo, d. Ernst Lubitsch.

DRAMA: MELODRAMA: ROMANCE: COMEDY DRAMA: Pen pals; Epistolaries; Romance-Bickering; Romance-Reluctant; Europeans-Eastern; Clever Plots & Endings; Department Stores; Depression Era; Hidden Gems

MUSICAL REMAKE: In the Good Old Summertime.
(I Sent A Letter to My Love; 84 Charing Cross Road)
(Ed: A classic that holds up very well today)

The Shop on Main Street, 1965, 111m, ★★★1/2/$$, Ceskoslovensky Film/Col. During the occupation, a Czech carpenter hides an elderly Jewish woman from the Nazis but then can't accommodate her in her fragile condition. Ida Kaminska (BActress); Jozef Kroner, Hana Slivkova. w. Ladislav Grosman, Jan Kadar, Einar Klos, d. Jan Kadar. **BFLFilm.** Oscars: 2-1.

DRAMA: Hiding Out; Survival Drama; Nazi Stories; World War II Stories; Jews-Saving; Jewish People; Europeans-Eastern; Germans as Enemy; Department Stores
(The Diary of Anne Frank; The Attic; The White Rose; The Pawnbroker; The Last Metro)

Short Circuit, 1986, 98m, ★★1/2/$$$, Tri-Star/Col-Tri, PG. A government robotics lab accidently produces a robot with a personality which escapes the lab and proceeds to get into all sorts of trouble. Ally Sheedy, Steve Guttenberg, Fisher Stevens, Austin Pendleton, G. W. Bailey. w. S. S. Wilson, Brent Maddock, d. John Badham.

COMEDY: Comedy of Errors; Robots; Pet Stories; Matchmakers; Kidnappings; Chase Movies
(Man's Best Friend; Electric Dreams)

Short Circuit 2, 1988, 110m, ★★/$, Tri-Star/Col-Tri, PG. This time the robot loses its creator and is held hostage by thieves who want it to help them in a jewel heist. Fisher Stevens, Michael McKean, Cynthia Gibb. w. S. S. Wilson, Brent Maddock, d. Kenneth Johnson.

COMEDY: Comedy of Errors; Kidnappings; Robots; Jewel Thieves

Short Cuts, 1993, 183m, ★★★★/$$, Fine Line/New Line, R/S-P-V-FFN-MFN. A cross-section of life in Los Angeles, from a suicidal violinist to a waitress who runs into a boy on his birthday, to a phone-sex operator, to divorce feuds and fishermen who find a dead body. Tim Robbins, Lily Tomlin, Andie McDowell, Matthew Modine, Fred Ward, Jack Lemmon, Jennifer Jason Leigh, Robert Downey, Jr., Lili Taylor, Brice Davison, Lori Singer, Julianne Moore, Madeleine Stowe, Anne Archer, Huey Lewis, Chris Penn, Tom Waits, Estelle Altman. w. Robert Altman, Frank Barhydt, SS-adapt, Raymond Carver, d. Robert Altman (BDirector). Oscars: 1-0.

DRAMA: COMEDY DRAMA: Interwoven Stories; Multiple Stories; All-Star Casts; Slice of Life Stories; Death-Dealing with; Accidents; Marriage Drama; Marriage on the Rocks; Cheating Men; Suicidal Tendencies; Suburban Life; Los Angeles; Earthquakes; All-Star Casts

(Nashville; Slaves of New York; Ready to Wear; Welcome to L.A.)

Short Eyes, 1979, 100m, ★★★1/2/$, Ind/Live, R/S-EV. A child molester encounters horrors in prison when the other men mark him. Bruce Davison, Miguel Pinero, Nathan George, Curtis Mayfield. w. P-adap. Miguel Piñero, d. Robert M. Young.

DRAMA: Social Drama; Prison Drama; Molestation-Child; Men In Jeopardy; Mental Illness; Ensembles-Male; Rape-Male; Hidden Gems; Cult Films
(The Mark; The Shawshank Redemption; Brubaker)

A Short Film About Killing, 1988, 84m, ★★★/$, Gala/NA. A teenage boy commits a murder in the heat of passion that he regrets immediately afterward and a lawyer opposed to the death penalty defends him. Miroslawa Baka, Krzysztof Globisz, Jan Tesarz. w. Krzysztof Piesiewicz, Krzystof Kieslowski, d. Krzystof Kieslowski.

DRAMA: MURDER: Courtroom Drama; Crimes of Passion; Young Men; Teenagers; Boys; Executions; Polish Films; Europeans-Eastern; Overlooked at Release; Hidden Gems
(Ed: Part of Kieslowski's Decalogue, a ten-film series made for Polish television on the ten commandments).

Short Time, 1990, 100m, ★★/$, 20th/Live, PG/P. A cop who is told he has a fatal disease becomes reckless in his police work so that he can die in the line of duty, thereby ensuring his family an extra bundle of insurance money. Dabney Coleman, Matt Frewer, Teri Garr, Barry Corbin. w. John Blumenthal, Michael Berry, d. Gregg Champion.

COMEDY: Action Comedy; Chase Movies; Car Chases; Black Comedy; Comedy-Morbid; Race Against Time; Police Stories; Death-Impending; Inheritances at Stake; Suicidal Tendencies
(Send Me No Flowers; Never Say Die)

A Shot in the Dark, 1964, 101m, ★★★★/$$$, UA/Fox, MGM-UA, S. In a lover's quarrel, a man gets shot. Bumbling Inspector Clouseau is brought on the case, and stumbles into the solution to this crime while stumbling into a beautiful blonde fleeing from a nudist camp. Peter Sellers, Elke Sommers, Herbert Lom, George Sanders, Tracy Reed. w. Blake Edwards, William Peter Blatty, d. Blake Edwards.

COMEDY: Comedy-Slapstick; **FARCE: MURDER:** Comic Mystery; Detective Stories; Detectives-Police; Fools-Bumbling; Chase Movies; Nudists

SEQUELS: The Pink Panther SERIES.
(The Pink Panther; Inspector Clouseau)

Shout, 1991, 93m, ★★/$, U/MCA-U, PG-13. A small Texas town goes through changes with the advent of rock 'n' roll. John Travolta, James Walters, Richard Jordan, Linda Fiorentino. d. Jeffrey Hornaday.

MUSICALS: Music Movies; Dance Movies; Rock Stars; Small-town Life; Texas; 1950s; Nostalgia; Flops-Major; Curiosities

Showboat, 1936, 110m, ★★★1/2/$$, Universal/MGM-UA. An old-time Mississippi showboat provides the backdrop for romance and life's trials. Irene Dunne, Allan Jones, Helen Morgan, Paul Robeson, Charles Winninger, Hattie McDaniel. w. M-adapt., Oscar Hammerstein II, N-adapt. Edna Ferber, d. James Whale.

REMAKE OF: 1929 version.

Showboat, 1951, 108m, ★★★/$$$, MGM/MGM-UA. A remake of above with more colorful and elaborate set pieces and dance numbers. Kathryn Grayson, Howard Keel, Ava Gardner, William Warfield, Joe E. Brown, Agnes Moorehead. w. John Lee Mahin, d. George Sidney.

MUSICALS: MELODRAMA: Musical Drama; **ROMANCE:** Romantic Drama; Southerns; Race Relations; Black Women; Black Men; Secrets-Racial; Romance-Interracial; Secrets-Racial; Ships; Theater Life; Ensemble Films; Actors; Actresses; Singers
(Cabin in the Cotton; Stormy Weather; Oklahoma!; Giant; So Big)
(State Fair)

Show Business, 1944, 92m, ★★★/$$, RKO/Turner. In the days of vaudeville, four friends have their career and private-life ups and downs. Eddie Cantor, Joan Davis, George Murphy, Constance Moore. w. Joseph Quillan, Dorothy Bennett, d. Edwin L. Martin.

COMEDY: MELODRAMA: Comedian; Vaudeville; Ensemble Films; Ensembles-Male

Showdown, 1972, 99m, ★★1/2/$, Universal/MCA-U. Two childhood friends' paths diverge. They reemet as grown men when one is an outlaw and the other the sheriff of a small Western town. Rock

Hudson, Dean Martin, Susan Clark, Donald Moffat. w. Theodore Taylor, d. George Stevens.

WESTERNS: Men in Conflict; Friends as Enemies; Police Stories
(The Seventh Dawn; Extreme Justice)
(Ed: Rock's only real Western)

Showgirls, 1995, 124m, ★★/$$, MGM-UA/MGM-UA, NC-17/ES-EP-V-FFN-MRN. Upstart dancer Nomi makes her way up the ladder and slides down the dancing pole with Vegas stardom and men on her mind. Elizabeth Berkley, Kyle MacLachlan, Gina Gershon, Glenn Plummer, Robert Davi, Alan Rachins, Gina Ravera. w. Joe Eszterhas, d. Paul Verhoeven.

MELODRAMA: Fame-Rise to; Young Women; Dancers; Strippers; Las Vegas; Female Protagonists; Unintentionally Funny; Flops-Major
(Valley of the Dolls; All About Eve; Anna; Striptease)
(Ed: Bad but not the worst. Must be viewed from a camp perspective)

The Show-Off, 1934, 80m, ★★★/$$$, MGM/NA. A bumbling fool meddles in the affairs of his in-laws with near-disastrous results. Spencer Tracy, Madge Evans, Clara Blandick, Henry Wadsworth. w. Herman Mankeiwicz, P-adap. George Kelly, d. Charles Reisner.

COMEDY DRAMA: SATIRE: Lover Family Dislikes; Comedy of Manners; Fools-Bumbling; Newlyweds; Young Men; Nuisances; Forgotten Films; Hidden Gems
(Fury; The Big House; Boys' Town)
(Ed: Spencer Tracy's breakthrough film at MGM)

A Show of Force, 1990, 93m, ★★/$, Par/Par, R/V-P-S. A political murder in Brazil is covered by a female American reporter who doesn't know the law doesn't favor women. Amy Irving, Erik Estrada, Robert Duvall, Lou Diamond Phillips, Andy Garcia. w. Evan Jones, d. Bruno Barreto.

DRAMA: Political Drama; **MURDER:** Journalists; Journalists as Detectives; Detective Stories; Conspiracy; Coulda Been Good; Latin People

The Shrimp on the Barbie, 1989, 86m, ★★/$, Vestron/Vestron, R/P-S. A rich Aussie girl hires a Latin man from L.A. to pose as her boyfriend to tick her father off when he won't let her marry the guy she really wants. The fish out of water winds up on the grill in his confu-

sion. Cheech Marin, Emma Samms, Vernon Welles. d. Alan Smithee.

COMEDY: Fish out of Water Stories; Lover Family Dislikes; Hired Dates; Australia; Good Premise Unfulfilled
(Born in East L.A.; Rude Awakening)

Shy People, 1986, 116m, ★★★/$ (LR), Cannon/WB, PG-13/S. A New York writer (Jill Clayburgh) gets the bright idea to look up her uncle in the deep bayous of south Louisiana with her daughter (Martha Plimpton) and learns a few lessons. Barbara Hershey, Don Swayze, Merrit Butrick, John Philbin. w. Gerard Brach, Marjorie David, Andrei Konchaslovsky, d. Andrei Konchalovsky..

DRAMA: MELODRAMA: TRAGEDY: Family Drama; Quiet Little Films; Southerns; City vs. Country; Cajun Swamp Life; Fish out of Water Stories; Writers; Journalists; Mothers & Daughters; Mothers & Sons; Mothers Alone; Heritage/Family-Search for; Reunions-Family; Mortgage Drama; Rural Life; Rednecks; Nightmare Vacations; Cajuns; Ghosts; Past-Haunted by the; Incest; Overlooked at Release; Hidden Gems
(Belizaire, the Cajun; Lousiana Story; Deliverance; The River Wild)

Sibling Rivalry, 1990, 88m, ★★1/2/$$, Tri-Star/Col-Tri, SUE. PG-13/S-P. A woman tells her sister, who is unhappy in her marriage, to have an affair. She does so, unfortunately, with her sister's husband. Kirstie Alley, Bill Pullman, Carrie Fisher, Jami Gertz, Scott Bakula, Sam Elliott, Ed O'Neill. w. Martha Goldhirsh, d. Carl Reiner.

COMEDY: FARCE: Sex Comedy; Sisters Swapping Partners; Romance with Married Person; Romance with Relative's Lover; Good Premise Unfulfilled; Coulda Been Good; Female Protagonists; Female Screenwriters
(Madhouse)
(Ed: The pacing is lethargic and the jokes apparent in the script were missed for the most part)

The Sicilian, 1987, 146m, ★★★/$, 20th/Live, R/EV-S. Salvatore Giuliano, a Sicilian Robin Hood, is betrayed by his merry band of thieves in this Godfather-esque opus. Christophe Lambert, Terence Stamp, Joss Ackland, John Turturro, Richard Blauer, Aldo Ray. w. Steve Shagan, N-adap. Mario Puzo, d. Michael Cimino.

DRAMA: ACTION: Crime Drama; Mob Stories; Mob Wars; Robin Hood Stories; Betrayals; Double Crossing; Italy; Coulda Been Great
(The Godfather SERIES; Year of the Dragon; Subway; Highlander)
(Ed: As usual with Cimino, some beautiful shots and sweeping camera moves, but unfortunately lacking in cohesive storyline)

Sid and Nancy, 1986, 111m, ★★★/$, Embassy/New Line, R/EP-S-V. The infamous Sid Vicious of the Sex Pistols and his American girlfriend Nancy Spungen follow each other down a nihilistic path of sex, drugs, and rock 'n' roll, but mostly drugs. Gary Oldman, Chloe Webb, David Hayman. w. Alex Cox, Abbe Wool, d. Alex Cox.

DRAMA: Character Studies; Rock Stars; Musicians; Music Dies; Suicidal Tendencies; Drugs-Addictions; Young Men-Angry; Romance-Doomed
(Quadrophenia; Repo Man; Breaking Glass)

Side Out, 1990, 100m, ★★/$, Tri-Star/Col-Tri, PG-13/S. A guy wants to go the distance in volleyball and the serious surfer yuppies he meets want to, too. C. Thomas Howell, Peter Horton, Kathy Ireland, Courtney Thorne-Smith, Harley Jane Kozak. d. Peter Israelson.

MELODRAMA: Sports Movies; Beach Movies; Competitions; Unintentionally Funny; Surfers
(Endless Summer; North Shore)
(Ed: Nothing. Not even exploitation. Takes itself too seriously to be taken humorously)

Sidewalks of London, 1938, 85m, ★★★/$$, Mayflower/Nos. An older man, a street performer without much hope of success, falls for a young dancer who becomes a star and may not let him attend to her anymore. Charles Laughton, Vivien Leigh, Rex Harrison, Tyrone Guthrie. w. Clarence Dane, d. Tim Whelan.

ROMANCE: DRAMA: COMEDY DRAMA: Romance-Older Men/Younger Women; Romance-Unrequited; Romance-Doomed; Infatuations; Dancers; Actresses; Theater Life; British Films
(Waterloo Bridge; The Blue Angel; Svengali; Pygmalion)

Siegfried, 1924, 100m, ★★★★/$$, Ind/Nos. A medieval dragonslayer rescues a princess from a wicked queen in this telling of the German legend. Paul Richter. d. Fritz Lang.

ADVENTURE: Medieval Times; Dragons; Epics; Princesses; Queens; Evil Women; Men Proving Themselves; Legends; German Films; Hidden Gems

Siesta, 1987, 97m, ★★★/$ (LR), Lorimar-WB/WB, R/S-V-FFN-MN. A stuntwoman (Ellen Barkin) goes through a dreamlike state of amnesia, half-remembering a wild time on a film in Spain and eventually a murder. Jodie Foster, Julian Sands, Gabriel Byrne. w. Patricia Louisiana Knop, N-adap. Patrice Chaplin, d. Mary Lambert.

DRAMA: Art Films; Erotic Drama; **MYSTERY: MURDER:** Dream Sequences; Illusions/Hallucinations; Amnesia; Flashbacks; Nightmares; Suspecting Oneself; Beautiful People; Stuntmen; Female Protagonists; Female Directors; Female Screenwriters; Hidden Gems

(Angel Heart; The Comfort of Strangers; The Mad Monkey)

The Sign of the Cross, 1932, 123m, ★★★¹/₂/$$$, Par/NA, AMC. In ancient Rome, as Nero is condemning the Christians to the lion's den, a soldier takes the bold step of converting and leading a Christian revolt. Fredric March, Elissa Landi, Charles Laughton, Claudette Colbert, Ian Keith. w. Waldemar Young, Sidney Buchman, P-adap. Wilson Barrett, d. Cecil B. de Mille.

DRAMA: MELODRAMA: Epics; Cast of Thousands; Ancient Times; Biblical Stories; Forgotten Films; Hidden Gems; Spectacles; Production Design-Outstanding

(Cleopatra [1934]; The Ten Commandments)

(Ed: A lot of innuendo and debauchery for its day)

Silas Marner, 1985, 92m, ★★★/$$, BBC/Fox. The classic story about the ordinary man accused of treason and thereafter exiled. Ben Kingsley, Jenny Agutter, Patsy Kensit. d. Giles Foster.

DRAMA: Historical Drama; Traitors; Accused Unjustly; Prison Drama; Lonely People; Classic Literary Adaptations

The Silence, 1963, 95m, Svensk Filmindustri/Sultan. Two lonely women act out their neuroses in a hotel in a military-occupied city. Ingrid Thulin, Gunnel Lindblom. w. d. Ingmar Bergman.

DRAMA: Art Films; Avant-Garde Films; Swedish Films; Hotels; Nervous Breakdowns; Female Protagonists; Writer-Directors

(Persona; Cries and Whispers)

Silence of the Lambs, 1991, 123m, ★★★★/$$$$$$, Orion/Orion, R/P-EV-B&G-S. An FBI agent (Jodie Foster, **BActress**) is on the trail of a serial killer using the knowledge of another serial killer, a former psychologist (Anthony Hopkins, **BActor**) who plays with her mind in exchange for what he knows. Scott Glenn, Anthony Heald. w. Ted Tally (**BAScr**), N-adap. Thomas Harris, d. Jonathan Demme (**BDirector**). **BPicture,** BEdit, BSound. Oscars: 7-5.

SUSPENSE: MYSTERY: Psychological Thriller; Chase Movies; **MURDER MYSTERY:** Serial Killers; Trail of a Killer; FBI Agents; Detective Stories; Detectives-Female; Detectives in Deep; Women in Jeopardy; Cannibalism; Mindgames; Female Protagonists; Sex Crimes; Blockbusters; Heroines

(Jennifer Eight; Seven)

Silence of the North, 1981, 94m, ★★★/$, Universal/MCA-U, PG. In the early 1900s, a Canadian fur trapper on a trip to the city to sell his wares falls for a city girl, and persuades her to join him in his mountain home. Ellen Burstyn, Tom Skerritt, Gordon Pinsent, Jennifer McKinney. w. Patricia Louisiana Knop, N-adap. Olive Frederickson, Ben East, d. Allan Winton King.

DRAMA: ADVENTURE: WESTERNS: ROMANCE: Pioneers; Canada; Hunters; 1900s; Mountain People; Female Protagonists; Female Screenwriters

(Call of the Wild; Heartland; Resurrection)

The Silencers, 1966, 103m, ★★¹/₂/$$$, Col/RCA-Col. A take-off on the Bond films, with a suave secret agent (Dean Martin) and wacked-out comic-book villains struggling to control the free world. Dean Martin, Stella Stevens, Victor Buono, Daliah Lavi, Cyd Charisse. w. Oscar Saul, N-adap. Donald Hamilton, d. Phil Karlson.

ACTION: Spy Films; Spies; Secret Agents; Spoofs-Spy; Playboys; Rule the World-Plot to

(In Like Flint; The Liquidator)

SEQUELS: Murderers Row; The Ambushers; and Wrecking Crew.

Silent Fall, 1994, 102m, ★★/$, WB/WB, R/P-V. An autistic, mentally disabled young boy is the only witness to his parents' murder and it's up to a psychiatrist to break his code of silence to figure out whodunit. Richard Dreyfuss, John Lithgow, Linda Hamilton, J. T. Walsh, Ben Faulkner, Liv Tyler. w. Akiva Goldman, d. Bruce Beresford.

SUSPENSE: MYSTERY: Psychological Thriller; Psychological Drama; Psychologist as Detective; Detective Stories; Boys; Men and Boys; **MURDER:** Murder of Parents; Nightmares; Mentally Disabled; Coulda Been Good; Female Screenwriters

(Equus; Witness)

(Ed: Gimmicky, offensive, implausible, and stupid; the kid can supposedly mimic anyone's voice, including the killer's)

Silent Movie, 1976, 88m, ★★★¹/₂/$$$$, 20th/CBS-Fox, PG. A drunken washed-up producer tries to drum up support for a silent movie, which he thinks will really take off. Mel Brooks, Marty Feldman, Dom DeLuise, Bernadette Peters, Sid Caesar, Henny Youngman, Anne Bancroft, Paul Newman, Burt Reynolds, James Caan, Liza Minnelli, Marcel Marceau. w. Mel Brooks, Ron Clark, Rudy de Luca, Barry Levinson, d. Mel Brooks.

COMEDY: Comedy-Slapstick; Silent Film Era; Comedy of Errors; Hollywood Life; Spoofs; All-Star Cameos

(Young Frankenstein; The Producers)

(Ed: Marcel Marceau says the only spoken line: No!)

Silent Partner, 1979, 103m, ★★★/$$, Ind/Vestron, R/V-S-B&G. A mild-mannered banker (Elliott Gould) is able to make off with what a bank robber (Christopher Plummer) thought he had in the bag, but he soon has to deal with the robber's revenge. Elliott Gould, Susannah York. w. Curtis Hanson, N-adap. Anders Bodelson (*Think of a Number*), d. David Dukes.

SUSPENSE: Chase Movies; Heist Stories; Bank Robberies; Double Crossings; Stalkers; Ordinary Person Turned Criminal; Turning the Tables; Revenge; Stalker; Mindgames; Love-Questionable; Rags to Riches; Canadian Films; Hitchcockian; Underrated; Hidden Gems; Independent Films

(Money for Nothing)

Silent Running, 1971, 90m, ★★★/$$, Universal/MCA-U, PG. A lone astronaut accompanied by three robots is floating through space in a mobile terrarium. Their plan is to replenish a decimated earth's vegetation when it's safe to return, if they can survive when they wind up all alone. Bruce Dern, Cliff Potts, Ron Rifkin, Jesse Vint. w. Deric Washburn, Mike Cimino, Steve Bochco, d. Douglas Trumbull.

SCI-FI: DRAMA: Outer Space Movies; Man vs. Machine; Robots; Experiments; Scientists; Apocalyptic Stories; Lonely People
(Dark Star; 2001; THX 1138)

Silent Tongue, 1992, 101m, ★★¹/₂/VR, Ind/Vidmark, PG-13/P-S. A young man in the surreal West has lost his Indian wife and embarks on a journey of discovery as family members bicker and try to find him a new wife, among spirits and the occult. River Phoenix, Alan Bates, Dermot Mulroney, Richard Harris, Shiela Tousey. w. d. Sam Shepard.

WESTERNS: Westerns-Neo; Art Films; Surrealism; Eccentric People; Family Drama; Widowers; Indians-American; Romance-Interracial; Curiosities; Art Films; Writer-Directors; Overlooked at Release

Silhouette, 1991, 89m, ★★¹/₂/$$, U/MCA-U, R/V-S. A woman visiting a small Texas town witnesses the murder of a girl but only sees the shadow of the killer. Faye Dunaway, David Rasche, John Terry, Carlos Gomez. d. Carl Schenkel.

SUSPENSE: MURDER: Witness to Murder; Fugitives from a Murderer; **MYSTERY: MURDER MYSTERY:** Women in Jeopardy; Texas; TV Movies
REMAKE OF: Storm Warning

Silk Stockings, 1957, 117m, ★★★/$$$, MGM/MGM-UA, Turner. A Hollywood studio commissions an expatriate Soviet composer to write a musical and a female M.P. is sent from mother Russia to stop him. Fred Astaire, Cyd Charisse, Peter Lorre, Janis Paige. w. Leonard Gershe, Leonard Spigelgass, P-adap. George S. Kaufman, Leueen McGrath, Abe Burrows, P-adap. Melchior Lengyel, d. Rouben Mamoulian.

MUSICALS: ROMANCE: Romance-Reluctant; Spies; Musicians; Music Composers; Communists; Russians; Stern Women
MUSICAL REMAKE OF: Ninotchka.
(Band Wagon; Funny Face; Les Girls)

Silkwood, 1983, 131m, ★★★★/$$$$, ABC-20th/CBS-Fox, SUE, R/S-P. The true story of Karen Silkwood (Meryl

Streep, BActress) and her discovery of and fight to disclose dangers at a nuclear fuel factory and the repercussions which occur. Cher (BSActress), Kurt Russell, Craig T. Nelson. w. Alice Arlen, Nora Ephron (BOScr), d. Mike Nichols (BDirector). BArt. Oscars: 5-0.

DRAMA: Social Drama; **SUSPENSE:** Message Films; Conspiracy; Whistleblowers; Corporation as Enemy; Ordinary Heros; Corruption; Detectives-Amateur; Friendships-Female; Lesbians; Unions; Nuclear Energy; Midwestern Life; Small-town Life; Working Class; Women Fighting the System; Female Protagonists; Oklahoma
(Norma Rae; The China Syndrome)

Silver Bears, 1976, 113m, ★★★/$$, EMI-U/USA, NA. A gambling investor from Vegas has schemes all over Europe and a crew to help him make good on them. Michael Caine, Cybill Shepherd, Louis Jourdan, Martin Balsam, David Warner, Stephane Audran, Jay Leno, Tom Smothers. w. Peter Stone, N-adap. Paul Erdman, d. Ivan Passer.

Heist Stories; **COMEDY:** Capers; Bank Robberies; Ensemble Films; Con Artists; Gambling; Monte Carlo; Riviera Life
(The Italian Job; The Brinks Job; The Hot Rock)

Silver Bullet, 1985, 95m, ★★/$$, Par/Par, PG-13/V-B&G. Stephen King updates the werewolf from a child's point of view in a small town. Corey Haim, Gary Busey, Megan Follows. w. Stephen King, *Cycle of the Werewolf*, d. Daniel Attias.

HORROR: Werewolves; Child Protagonists; Boys; Unbelieved; Revisionist Films; Stephen King
(Sleepwalkers; Wolfen; An American Werewolf in London)
(Ed: Almost as if John Hughes has reworked *The Boy Who Cried Wolf*)

The Silver Chalice, 1954, 135m, ★★/$$$, WB/WB. In Biblical times, a slave is chosen by Luke because of his silversmithing talents to make the chalice for the Last Supper. Paul Newman, Pier Angeli, Jack Palance, Virginia Mayo, Walter Hampden, Lorne Greene, E. G. Marshall. w. Lesser Samuels, N-adap. Thomas B. Costain, d. Victor Saville.

DRAMA: Biblical Stories; Epics; Ancient Times; Religion; Jesus Christ; Middle East; Jewish People; Unintentionally Funny
(The Robe; The Greatest Story Ever Told)

Silver City, 1984, 110m, ★★¹/₂/$, Ind-Lorimar/WB. In an immigrant camp in 1940s Australia, a married Polish woman has an affair with a married man and both must deal with various forms of bigotry and racism. Gosia Dorowolska, Ivar Kants, Anna Jemison, Steve Bisley, Ewa Brok, Joel Cohen. w. Sophia Turkiewicz, Thomas Keneally, d. Sophia Turkiewicz.

DRAMA: Bigots; Immigrants; Romance with Married Person; Cheating Men; Polish People; Europeans-Eastern; Australia; Female Screenwriters; Female Directors

Silver Lode, 1954, 92m, ★★¹/₂/$, RKO/Turner. A stranger claiming to be a U.S. Marshal rides into Silver Lode claiming orders to arrest a prominent citizen of this Western mining town, but is later unmasked as an impostor with a personal vendetta. John Payne, Dan Duryea, Lizabeth Scott, Dolores Moran. w. Karen de Wolf, d. Allan Dwan.

WESTERNS: Police Stories; Impostors; Drifters; Strangers in Town; Mining Towns; Framed?; Marshals; Female Screenwriters
(Sommersby)

The Silver Streak, 1976, 113m, ★★★/$$$$, 20th/CBS-Fox, R/S-P. A publishing executive on a cross-country train discovers a body and must hide from the murderers. Cross-country calamity ensues. Gene Wilder, Jill Clayburgh, Richard Pryor, Patrick McGoohan, Ned Beatty. w. Colin Higgins, d. Arthur Hiller.

COMEDY: Comedy-Slapstick; Hide the Dead Body; **MURDER:** Murder-Discovering; Mystery-Whodunit?; Trains; Road Movies; Chase Movies
(Stir Crazy; Another You)

Silverado, 1985, 132m, ★★¹/₂/$$, Col/RCA-Col. PG/V. Pioneering cowboys seek their fortunes as homesteaders in the West in the late 1800s. Kevin Kline, Scott Glenn, Kevin Costner, Danny Glover, John Cleese, Rosanna Arquette, Brian Dennehy, Linda Hunt, Jeff Goldblum. w. Lawrence and Mark Kasdan, d. Lawrence Kasdan.

WESTERNS: ACTION: DRAMA: Cowboys; Pioneers; Cowboys; Ensemble Films; All-Star Casts; 1890s; Coulda Been Great
(Wyatt Earp [1994]; Pale Rider; Unforgiven)
(Ed: A lack of focus, as in *Wyatt Earp*, made by the same team, seems to be the primary problem, although this one as

opposed to Earp was cut extensively; still didn't help much)

Simba, 1955, 98m, ★★¹/₂/$, GFD/Group Film, IND. In Kenya, a colonial farmer fights the local tribes for control of his land. Dirk Bogarde, Donald Sinden, Virginia McKenna, Basil Sydney. w. John Baines, d. Brian Desmond Hurst.

DRAMA: Mortgage Drama; Save the Farm; Plantations; Africa; Imperialist Problems; British Films

Simon, 1980, 97m, ★★¹/₂/$, Orion-WB/WB, PG. Scientists hoping to cash in as discoverers of an extraterrestrial being, hypnotize a psychology professor into believing that he's not of this earth. Alan Arkin, Madeline Kahn, Austin Pendleton, Judy Graubert, William Finley, Fred Gwynne. w. d. Marshall Brickman.

COMEDY: Simple Minds; Hypnotism; Experiments; Psychologists; Scientists; Brainwashing; Writer-Directors
(Lovesick; Starman)

Simon and Laura, 1955, 91m, ★★★/$$, GFD/NA. A real-life married couple that play one on TV are in fact not as happily married as the public thinks they are, and their real life begins to intrude on their happy little sitcom. Peter Finch, Kay Kendall, Ian Carmichael, Alan Wheatley, Richard Wattis, Muriel Pavlow. d. Alan Melville.

COMEDY: Marriage Comedy; Behind the Scenes; TV Life; Marriage on the Rocks; Romance-Bickering; 1950s; British Films
(Breakfast with Les and Bes [play])

Simple Men, 1992, 105m, ★★¹/₂/$, New Line/New Line, R/S-V. Two brothers go after their long lost father who turns out to be on the FBI's most wanted list and in hiding. They meet eccentric women on the way which changes their plans. Robert Burke, William Sage, Karen Silas, Martin Donovan. w. d. Hal Hartley.

COMEDY DRAMA: Comedy-Light; Eccentric People; Children-Long lost; Parents vs. Children; Searches; Brothers; **ROMANCE:** Romantic Comedy; Fugitives from the Law; Fathers-Troublesome; Art Films; Writer-Directors
(Surviving Desire; Trust)

A Simple Story, 1980, 110m, ★★★/$$, Col/Col, R/S. A woman goes through a midlife crisis and breaks up with a lover after an abortion. Romy Schneider, Bruno Cremer. d. Claude Sautet.

DRAMA: Character Studies; Midlife Crisis; Abortion Dilemmas; Starting Over; Female Protagonists; French Films; Quiet Little Films

A Simple Twist of Fate, 1994, 106m, ★★¹/₂/$, Touchstone/Touchstone, PG-13/P. A man finds out his wife's child is not his and takes off on his own, only to have her die and the child return to him through mysterious circumstances, while his brother sinks into drugs and murder, and he comes into a fortune which is then stolen. He learns to cope with each twist and carry on-just when the real father of the child reappears. Steve Martin, Gabriel Byrne, Catherine O'Hara, Stephen Baldwin, Laura Linney, Alana Austin, Alyssa Austin, Amelia Campbell, Michael des Barres, Byron Jennings. w. Steve Martin, N-adap. *Silas Marner*, d. Gillies MacKinnon.

DRAMA: MELODRAMA: TRAGEDY: Fathers-Surrogate; Men and Girls; Children-Adopted; Relatives-Troublesome; Drugs-Dealing; Inheritances at Stake; Single Men; Fathers-Struggling; Custody Battles; Curiosities; Revisionist Films; Classic Literary Adaptations
(Kramer vs. Kramer; Losing Isaiah)

Sinatra, 1992, 245m, ★★★/$$$$, WB/WB. The life story of who else coming up out of the Jersey slums to stardom during wartime, tracing his life up through the 60s. Philip Casnoff, Olympia Dukakis, Joe Santos, Nina Siezmasko, Rod Steiger, Bob Gunton, Marcia Gay Harden. w. William Mastrosimone, d. James Sadwith.
(Multiple Emmy Winner)

DRAMA: Biographies; Fame-Rise to; Hollywood Biographies; Famous People When Young; Singers; Italians; Episodic Stories; TV Movies; Miniseries

Since You Went Away, 1944, 172m, ★★★¹/₂/$$$$, UA/Fox. The family of an American soldier copes with his absence and the trials of life during wartime. Claudette Colbert (BActress), Joseph Cotten, Jennifer Jones (BSActress), Shirley Temple, Monty Woolley (BSActor), Agnes Moorehead, Lionel Barrymore, Guy Madison, Robert Walker, Hattie McDaniel, Keenan Wynn. w. David O. Selznick (BScr), NF-adap. Margaret Buell Wilder, d. John Cromwell. BPicture, **BScore**, BB&WArt, BB&WCin, BEdit. Oscars: 9-1.

DRAMA: MELODRAMA: World War II Era; War at Home; Family Drama;

Soldiers; Patriotic Films; Time Capsules; Female Protagonists
(The Best Years of Our Lives; Mrs. Miniver)

Sing, 1988, 98m, ★★/$, Col/RCA-Col, PG. In a school about to be shut down for lack of funds, the students organize a talent show to put the budget back together. Lorraine Bracco, Peter Dobson, Jessica Steen, Louise Lasser, Patti LaBelle. w. Dean Pitchford, d. Richard Baskin.

COMEDY DRAMA: MUSICALS: Music Movies; Mortgage Drama; Teachers; Teachers & Students; Putting on a Show; High School Life; Coulda Been Good; Old-Fashioned Recent Films
(Beat Street; Babes in Arms; Fame)

Sing, You Sinners, 1938, 88m, ★★★/$$$, Par/NA. A racehorse owner and his family root for their underdog horse until he finally pulls through. Bing Crosby, Donald O'Connor, Fred MacMurray, Elizabeth Patterson, Ellen Drew. w. Claude Binyon, d. Wesley Ruggles.

COMEDY DRAMA: MUSICALS: Musical Comedy; Horse Racing; Family Comedy; Underdog Stories; Pet Stories

Sing as We Go, 1934, 80m, ★★¹/₂/$$, Ind/NA. A young woman laid off from her mill job in the north of England gets various summer jobs and attendant adventures. Gracie Fields, John Loder, Frank Pettingell, Dorothy Hyson. w. J. B. Priestley, Gordon Wellesley, d. Basil Dean.

COMEDY DRAMA: Ordinary People Stories; Coming of Age; Summer Vacations; Young Women; British Films; Forgotten Films
(Experience Preferred but not Essential)

Sing Baby Sing, 1936, 87m, ★★★/$$$, 20th/NA. A washed-up alcoholic actor modeled after Lionel Barrymore falls hard for a nightclub singer modeled after Elaine Barrie. Alice Faye, Adolphe Menjou, Gregory Ratoff, Patsy Kelly, Ted Healy, Montagu Love. w. Milton Sperling, Jack Yellen, Harry Tugend, d. Sidney Lanfield.

COMEDY: SATIRE: ROMANCE: Romantic Comedy; Romance-Reluctant; Actors; Singers; True or Not?; Alcoholics; Nuisances

The Singing Fool, 1928, 110m, ★★★/$$$$, WB/NA. A singer loses his footing in the public arena after his son dies. Al Jolson, Davey Lee, Betty Bronson, Josephine Dunn, Arthur Housman. w. C. Graham Baker, P-adap. Leslie S. Barrows, d. Lloyd Bacon.

DRAMA: MELODRAMA: Singers; Music Dies; Death-Dealing with; Death of A Child; Comebacks; Rise and Fall Stories (The Jazz Singer; The Jolson Story)

Singing in the Rain, 1952, 102m, ★★★★/$$$$, MGM/MGM-UA. A silent screen goddess suffers when the talkies come in because of her grating, nasal voice. She's superseded in stardom by the "nice girl" who dubs her lines. The rest is history, on and off screen. Gene Kelly, Donald O'Connor, Debbie Reynolds, Millard Mitchell, Jean Hagen (BSActress), Rita Moreno, Cyd Charisse, Douglas Fowley. w. Adolph Green, Betty Comden, d/ch. Gene Kelly, Stanley Donen. BMScore. Oscars: 2-0.

MUSICALS: COMEDY: Musical Comedy; SATIRE: Silent Film Era; Hollywood Life; Understudies; Fame-Rise to; Actresses; Nuisances; Dancers; Dance Movies
REVIVED: on Broadway, late 1980s.
(Band Wagon; An American in Paris)
(Ed: A classic in every way, though there's no justification for the Oscar snub)

The Singing Nun, 1966, 98m, ★★¹/2/$$$, MGM/MGM-UA, G. A nun who composes tunes hits the road and finds success outside the confines of her convent. Debbie Reynolds, Greer Garson, Ricardo Montalban, Agnes Moorehead, Chad Everett, Katharine Ross, Ed Sullivan. w. Sally Benson, John Furia, d. Henry Koster. BOScore. Oscars: 1-0.

MELODRAMA: Biographies; Singers; Nuns; Religion; Fame-Rise to; True Stories
(The Sound of Music; Sister Act)
(Ed: Based on life of Belgian nun who had big early 60s pop hit, "Dominique." Obvious attempt to cash in on *The Sound of Music*'s phenomenal box office sweep, and for the most part, it worked, though it's not really worth a look now)

Singles, 1992, 100m, ★★/$$, WB/WB, PG-13/S. Boring twenty-somethings whining about their stagnant lives in Seattle—one's an architect with grandiose plans, another's a musician, and the others don't know what they want. Campbell Scott, Matt Dillon, Bridget Fonda, Kyra Sedgwick, Sheila Kelley, Bill Pullman, James LeGros, Jeremy Piven, Eric Stoltz, Tom Skerritt, Peter Horton. w. d. Cameron Crowe.

COMEDY DRAMA: 20-Somethings; Musicians; Young People; Pre-Life Crisis; Ensemble Films; Ensembles-Young People; Multiple Stories; Simple Minds; Coulda Been Good; Writer-Directors; Generation X
(Reality Bites; St. Elmo's Fire; Bodies, Rest & Motion; Sleep With Me)
(Ed: Though there are unique problems for Generation X, the problems here are hardly worth caring about, let alone sitting through two hours for)

Single White Female, 1992, 99m, ★★¹/2/$$$, Col/Col-Tri, R/V-S-B&G-FFN-MRN. A big-city yuppie woman threatens to kick her wacko roommate out once her own boyfriend decides to move back in and soon realizes the extent to which people will go for a good apartment in New York. Bridget Fonda, Jennifer Jason Leigh, Steven Weber, Peter Friedman. w. Don Roos, N-adap. John Lutz (*SWF Seeks Same*), d. Barbet Schroeder.

SUSPENSE: Roommates from Hell; MURDER: Murders-One by One; Women in Jeopardy; Serial Killers; Psycho-Killers; Murderers-Female; New York Life; Fashion World; Apartment Buildings; Twins; Secrets-Keeping; Lookalikes; Unintentionally Funny; Female Protagonists
(Apartment Zero; The Hand that Rocks the Cradle; The Tenant; The Crush; The Temp)
(Ed: Preposterous, but has its scary, well-lit moments. Confusing as to whether it was really supposed to be a spoof or not)

The Sin of Madelon Claudet, 1931, 74m, ★★★/$$$, MGM/MGM-UA. The illegitimate child of a "wayward woman" is taken from her by the state. Helen Hayes, Robert Young, Neil Hamilton, Lewis Stone, Marie Prevost. w. Charles MacArthur, P-adap. Edward Knoblock, d. Edgar Selwyn.

MELODRAMA: Social Drama; TRAGEDY: Mothers-Unwed; Mothers Alone; Orphans; Social Workers; Prostitutes-Low-Class; Promiscuity; Female Protagonists
(White Banners; Bad Girl; Losing Isaiah)

Sins of Rachel Cade, 1960, 123m, ★★¹/2/$$, WB/NA. A Red Cross nurse in the Belgian Congo cares for a downed pilot and they eventually fall in love. The result is a child out of wedlock. Angie Dickinson, Roger Moore, Peter Finch, Errol John, Woody Strode. w. Edward Anhalt, N-adap. Charles Mercer, d. Gordon Douglas.

DRAMA: MELODRAMA: ROMANCE: Romance-Doomed; Mothers Alone; Mothers Unwed; Nurses; Missionaries; Africa

Sirens, 1994, 96m, ★★★/$$, Miramax/Miramax, R/S-FFN-MFN. A prudish couple goes to an artists' colony in Australia where nude models pose all the day long and taunt the couple's sexuality. Hugh Grant, Tara Fitzgerald, Sam Neill, Elle Macpherson, Mark Gerber, Kate Fischer. w. d. John Duigan.

COMEDY DRAMA: Erotic Drama; Artists; Models; Sexual Problems; Coming of Age; Vacation Romance; Art Films; Hidden Gems; Australian Films; Writer-Directors; Lyrical Films; Scenery-Outstanding
(The Ebony Tower)

Sister Act, 1992, 100m, ★★★¹/2/$$$$$$, Touchstone/Touchstone, PG. A singer who witnesses a mob hit must hide or be snuffed out herself, so the cops decide the perfect disguise would be as a nun. While hiding in the convent, she teaches the choir a thing or two. Whoopi Goldberg, Maggie Smith, Kathy Najimy, Wendy Makkena, Mary Wickes, Harvey Keitel. w. Joseph Howard, d. Emile Ardolino.

COMEDY: Fugitives from the Mob; Fugitives from a Murderer; Ensembles-Females; Hiding Out; Black Women; Fish out of Water Stories; Music Movies; Nuns; Popes; Teachers & Students; Singers; Old-Fashioned Recent Films; Blockbusters; Sleeper Hits; Female Protagonists
(The Sound of Music; Ball of Fire; Lilies of the Field)

Sister Act 2, 1993, 107m, ★★/$$, Touchstone/Touchstone, PG. The nun on the run returns to the convent to whip a choir into shape for the state finals. Whoopi Goldberg, Kathy Najimy, James Coburn, Maggie Smith, Mary Wickes, Barnard Hughes, Sheryl Lee Ralph, Michael Jeter. w. James Orr, Jim Cruickshank, Judi Ann Mason, d. Bill Duke.

COMEDY: MELODRAMA: Nuns; Singers; Ensembles-Female; Competitions; Underdog Stories; Female Protagonists; Black Women; Black Among Whites; Female Screenwriters
(Ed: Tired retread without even treading the same water)

Sister Kenny, 1946, 116m, ★★★/$$$, RKO/Turner. A biopic of the Catholic nurse who started treating people for polio. Rosalind Russell (BActress),

Alexander Knox, Dean Jagger, Philip Merivale, Beulah Bondi. w. Dudley Nichols, Alexander Knox, Mary McCarthy, NF-adap. Mary Kenny, *They Shall Walk*, d. Dudley Nichols. Oscars: 1-0.

MELODRAMA: DRAMA: Biographies; Autobiographical Stories; Disease Stories; Nurses; Saving Someone; Saintly People; Australia; Female Protagonists
(The Nun's Story; Keys to the Kingdom)

The Sisters, 1938, 98m, ★★¹/₂/$$, WB/NA. In a small Western town, the fortunes of three sisters in marriage and life are chronicled. Bette Davis, Errol Flynn, Anita Louise, Ian Hunter, Donald Crisp, Beulah Bondi, Jane Bryan, Alan Hale. w. Milton Krims, N-adap. Myron Brinig, d. Anatole Litvak.

MELODRAMA: ROMANCE: Sisters; Marriage-Impending; Episodic Stories; Marriage Drama; Small-town Life

Sisters, 1973, 92m, ★★★/$$, WB/Wb, R/V-S-B&G. A woman starts to think that her dead Siamese twin sister is still alive, yet by the end of the film we wonder whether she ever had a sister at all. Margot Kidder, Jennifer Salt, Charles Durning, Bill Finley. w. Brian De Palma, Louisa Rose, d. Brian De Palma.

HORROR: SUSPENSE: MYSTERY: Twins; Lookalikes; Fantasies; Nightmares; Dead-Back from the; Cult Films
(The Other; Dead Ringer)

Sister, Sister, 1987, 103m, ★★¹/₂/$, New World/New World, R/S-V. When a mysterious young man comes to visit a dark, remote southern mansion in the swamps, a woman and her young sister may either be protected by him or killed by him. Jennifer Jason Leigh, Eric Stoltz, Judith Ivey. w. Joel Coen, d. Bill Condon.

HORROR: SUSPENSE: Women in Jeopardy; Psycho Killers; Past-Haunted by the; Sisters; Houses-Creepy; Swamp Life; Southerns; Gothic Style
(Hush, Hush, Sweet Charlotte; The Beguiled; Angel Heart)
(Ed: All mood and no action)

Sitting Ducks, 1978, 88m, ★★¹/₂/$$, Sunny Side Up/Media. A couple of women hired to bump off two thieves find it easy work as they meet up with and seduce their unwitting victims on the way to Florida. Michael E. Jaglom, Zack Norman, Patrice Townsend, Irene Forrest, Richard Romanus. w. d. Henry Jaglom.

COMEDY: Black Comedy; Mob Stories; Mob Comedy; Hitmen; Hitwomen; Enemy-Sleeping with the; Murderers-Female; Journies; Road Movies; Cult Films; Writer-Directors; Independent Films
(Prizzi's Honor; Eating; Can She Bake a Cherry Pie?)

Sitting Pretty, 1948, 84m, ★★★¹/₂/$$, 20th/NA. A fastidious, to say the least, male nanny is hired by a suburban couple and they are shocked when he produces an exposé novel about them and their neighbors. Clifton Webb (BActor), Robert Young, Maureen O'Hara, Richard Haydn, Louise Allbritton, Ed Begley. Oscars: 1-0.

COMEDY: SATIRE: Comedy-Domestic; Family Comedy; **FAMILY:** Babysitters; Fish out of Water Stories; Scandals; Small-town Scandals; Writers; Suburban Life; Stern Men; Nuisances; Male in Female Domain; Sleeper Hits
(The Man Who Came to Dinner; Laura Lansing Slept Here [TV])

SEQUELS: Mr. Belvedere Goes to College; Mr. Belvedere Rings the Bell.

Sitting Target, 1972, 92m, ★★/$, MGM/NA. A killer is ratted on and ends up doing time. But woe to those who betrayed him when he gets out. Oliver Reed, Jill St. John, Edward Woodward, Frank Finlay, Freddie Jones. w. Alexander Jacobs, N-adap. Lawrence Henderson, d. Douglas Hickox.

ACTION: Crime Drama; Revenge; Convict's Revenge; Prison Drama
(Remember My Name)

Situation Hopeless But Not Serious, 1965, 97m, ★★★/$, Par/Par. After the Allies declare victory, a German civilian keeps two American pilots prisoners of war and doesn't tell them it's over. Alec Guinness, Robert Redford, Mike Connors, Anita Hoefer. w. Silvia Reinhardt, N-adap. Robert Shaw (*The Hiding Place*). d. Gottfried Reinhardt.

COMEDY DRAMA: SATIRE: Black Comedy; Tragi-Comedy; Hostage Situations; Prison Drama; Secrets-Keeping; P.O.W.s; World War II Stories; Germans as Enemy; Mental Illness; Eccentric People; Forgotten Films; Hidden Gems; Underrated; Female Screenwriters
(The Collector; Kiss of the Spider Woman)
(Ed: What the story lacks after the good premise is Guinness' performance)

Six Degrees of Separation, 1993, 121m, ★★★★/$$$, MGM/MGM-UA, R/P-S-MFN. A rich white art dealer and his wife (Donald Sutherland, Stockard Channing) are charmed by a suave young black man (Will Smith) claiming to be Sidney Poitier's son, after he first claims he was mugged. When he moves in, the result is an upheaval of the family and their social life. Mary Beth Hurt, Bruce Davison, Richard Masur, Anthony Michael Hall. w. P-adap. John Guare, d. Fred Schepisi.

COMEDY: COMEDY DRAMA: FARCE: SATIRE: Social Satire; Rich People; Class Conflicts; Gay Men; Black Men; Liars; Con Artists; Impostors; Greed; Snobs; Illusions Destroyed; Race Relations; Artists; New York Life; Suicidal Tendencies; Suicidal Tendencies of Homosexuals; Flashbacks; Female Protagonists
(Slaves of New York; Olivier, Olivier; Houseguest)
(Ed: Could've been another *Bonfire of the Vanities*, but instead, it's a faithful, opened-up, complete, and provocative, often hilarious satire)

Six in Paris, 1968, 93m, ★★★/$, New Yorker/New Yorker. Six short avant-garde films by New Wave filmmakers. Barbara Wilkin, Barbet Schroeder, Stephane Audran, Claude Chabrol, Nadine Ballot. w. d. Jean Douchet, George Keller, Jean Rouch, Jean Daniel Pollet, Eric Rohmer, Jean-Luc Godard, Claude Chabrol.

DRAMA: COMEDY DRAMA: Multiple Stories; French Films; French New Wave Films; Art Films; Writer-Directors; Forgotten Films

Six Pack, 1982, 110m, ★★/$$, 20th/CBS-Fox, G. Six orphans steal the heart of an independent stock-car racer. Kenny Rogers, Diane Lane, Erin Gray, Barry Corbin. w. Mike Marvin, Alex Matter, d. Daniel Petrie.

FAMILY: CHILDREN'S: Family Comedy; Fathers-Surrogate; Orphans; Car Racing; Southerns; Country Singers; Singers

Six Weeks, 1982, 107m, ★★¹/₂/$$, Polygram-20th/Col, PG. When she learns her daughter is dying of leukemia, an executive woman puts her considerable resources to use to make the last part of her life as fulfilling as possible. Dudley Moore, Mary Tyler Moore, Katherine Healy. w. David Seltzer, N-adap. Fred Mustard Stewart, d. Tony Bill.

MELODRAMA: Tearjerkers; Death-Impending; Death-Dealing with; Mothers & Daughters; Death of a Child; Fashion World; Rich People; Rich Kids
(The Christmas Tree; The Ryan White Story [TV]; Promises in the Dark)
Skidoo, 1968, 98m, ★/$, Par/NA. Gangsters join hippies in a love-in. Jackie Gleason, Carol Channing, Groucho Marx, Frankie Avalon, Fred Clark, Michael Constantine, Frank Gorshin, John Philip Law, Peter Lawford, Burgess Meredith, Cesar Romero, Mickey Rooney. w. Doran William Cannon, d. Otto Preminger.
SATIRE: COMEDY: Generation Gap; Mob Stories; Hippies; Parents vs. Children; Psychedelic Era; 1960s; Unintentionally Funny; Forgotten Films; Camp; All-Star Casts; Flops-Major
(Some Kind of a Nut)
(Ed: Old fogies' idea of what the summer of love was about)
Skin Deep, 1989, 102m, ★★1/2/$$, 20th/Media, R/P-S-FN-MN. A writer with writer's block (John Ritter) can't keep any of his relationships going either, and the chaotic result is literally a shock to his system and a tidal wave. Alyson Reed, Julianne Phillips, Vincent Gardenia. w. d. Blake Edwards.
COMEDY: COMEDY DRAMA: FARCE: Black Comedy; Comedy-Slapstick; Cheating Men; Revenge; Revenge on Cheaters; Women Fighting Back; Midlife Crisis; Writers; Hollywood Life; Marriage-Impending; Earthquakes; Los Angeles
(Switch; The Man Who Loved Women; S.O.B.)
(Ed: That old Edwards theme of women avenging philanderers goes out of control this time; the glow-in-the-dark condom scene and the blind man scenes are classics, though, and worth checking out if you fast-forward the rest)
The Skin Game, 1971, 102m, ★★1/2/$$, WB/WB, PG. A black and white team of con men hustle their way around the old West. James Garner, Lou Gossett, Jr., Susan Clark, Brenda Sykes, Ed Asner. w. Peter Stone, Richard Alan Simmons, d. Paul Bogart.
COMEDY: COMEDY DRAMA: WESTERNS: Western Comedy; Con Artists; Ensemble Films; Black vs. White; Race Relations; Slavery; Civil War Era
(The Scalphunters)
Skippy, 1931, 88m, ★★★/$$$, Par/NA. A health inspector, hated and feared by

the local merchants of skid row, gains favor when his son befriends the slum dwellers in his inspection area. Jackie Cooper (**BActor/Juvenile**), Robert Coogan, Mitzi Green, Jackie Searl. w. Joseph L. Mankiewicz, Norman McLeod (**BScr**), (Comic Strip)-adap. Percy Crosby, d. Norman Taurog (**BDirector**). BPicture. Oscars: 4-1.
COMEDY DRAMA: FAMILY: CHILDREN'S: Boys; Social Workers; Inner City Life; Depression Era; Child Protagonists; Children-Little Adults
(The Champ; The Kid)
Ski School, 1991, 88m, ★★/VR, Movie Store Entertainment/HBO, R/S-P. Rival hot dog skiers challenge each other to a competition, then try to cheat their way to a win. Dean Cameron, Tom Breznahan, Patrick Laborteaux, Charlie Sprading. w. David Mitchell, d. Damian Lee.
COMEDY: Party Movies; Sports Movies; Teenagers; Teenage Movies; Young People; Young Men; Skiing; Snow Settings; College Life; Fraternity Life; Bimbos; Competitions; Double Crossings; Snobs vs. Slobs
(Summer School; Hot Dog; Aspen Extreme; Meatballs)
(Ed: Several cast members from *Summer School* appear and do the same babe-crazed routine)
Skullduggery, 1969, 105m, ★★/$, Universal/Media. In New Guinea, a native tribe is invaded by archaeologists and adventurers who argue over their "find." Burt Reynolds, Susan Clark, Roger C. Carmel, Edward Fox. w. Nelson Gidding, d. Gordon Douglas.
DRAMA: ADVENTURE: Archaeologists; Scientists; Asia; Jungle Life; Men in Conflict; Power Struggles; Cave People
(Link; Congo)
Sky Devils, 1931, 89m, ★★1/2/$$, Caddo-Howard Hughes/NA. In World War I, the day is saved by two would-be draft dodgers who stumble into fighting for their country. Spencer Tracy, William Boyd, Ann Dvorak, George Cooper. w. Joseph Moncure March, Edward Sutherland, d. Edward Sutherland.
ACTION: World War I Stories; Pilots-Military; Heroes-Unlikely; Forgotten Films
Skyjacked, 1972, 101m, ★★1/2/$$$, MGM/MGM-UA, R/V. The passengers panic as the commercial jet liner they've taken on what they thought would be a

cross-country trip is forced to fly to Moscow by a man with a bomb. Charlton Heston, Yvette Mimieux, James Brolin, Claude Atkins, Rosey Grier, Walter Pidgeon, Leslie Uggams. w. Stanley R. Greenberg, N-adap. David Harper (*Hijacked*), d. John Guillermin.
ACTION: SUSPENSE: Hijackings; Airplanes; Kidnappings; Hostage Situations; Russians; Bombs
(White Nights; Airport; Passenger 57; The Pursuit of D.B. Cooper)
Skylark, 1941, 94m, ★★1/2/$$, Par/NA. A woman, for a change, has a midlife crisis and then an affair to spice up her hum-drum life, in which she is ignored by her workaholic husband. Claudette Colbert, Ray Milland, Brian Aherne, Binnie Barnes, Walter Abel. w. Z. Myers, P-adap. Samson Raphaelson, d. Mark Sandrich.
MELODRAMA: ROMANCE: Romance with Married Person; Cheating Women; Midlife Crisis; Rejuvenation; Female Protagonists
(Brief Encounter; Strangers When We Meet)
The Sky's the Limit, 1943, 89m, ★★1/2/$$, RKO/Turner. A female photo-journalist during the war is pursued by a suave flyboy on leave. Fred Astaire, Joan Leslie, Robert Benchley, Robert Ryan, Elizabeth Patterson. w. Frank Fenton, Lynn Root, d. Edward H. Griffith.
ROMANCE: Romantic Comedy; **COMEDY:** Pilots-Military; Photographers; Romance-Boy Wants Girl; Journalists; Forgotten Films; Coulda Been Good
(Ed: Wanted to be more but didn't make it)
Slacker, 1991, 97m, ★★★/$, Ind/Orion, R/P. A non-narrative film in which a series of characters in Austin, Texas address the camera and each other, expounding their strange theories and generally avoiding reality. Richard Linklater, Rudy Basquez, Jean Caffeine, Jan Hockey. w. d. Richard Linklater.
DRAMA: COMEDY DRAMA: SATIRE: Art Films; Young People; Alienation; Pre-Life Crisis; Documentary Style; Texas; Suburban Life; 20-Somethings; Sleeper Hits; Crossing the Line; Writer-Directors; One Day Stories; Generation X
(Dazed and Confused; Reality Bites)
Slamdance, 1987, 99m, ★★1/2/$, Island/Fox, R/P-S-V. A crooked cop frames a mild-mannered comic strip writer for murder. Tom Hulce, Mary

Elizabeth Mastrantonio, Virginia Madsen, Adam Ant, Harry Dean Stanton. w. Don Opper, d. Wayne Wang.

SUSPENSE: MURDER: Film Noir-Modern; Framed?; Accused Unjustly; Saving Oneself; Writers; Coulda Been Good
(Unlawful Entry; Echo Park)

Slap Shot, 1977, 124m, ★★★/$$$, Universal/MCA-U, PG/P. A hockey team on the skids is "helped" by its coach, who resorts to every trick in the book to get them back on the winning side. Paul Newman, Michael Ontkean, Lindsay Crouse, Jennifer Warren, Strother Martin. w. Nancy Dowd, d. George Roy Hill.

ACTION: COMEDY DRAMA: Sports Movies; Hockey; Skating; Coaches; Underdog Stories; Female Screenwriters
(Hoosiers; Blue Chips; The Mighty Ducks)

Slaughterhouse Five, 1972, 104m, ★★1/2/$, Universal/MCA-U, R/S-FN. A man has visions of future life on a sexless planet, alternating with "memories" of his service in World War II, which may be pure fantasies. Michael Sacks, Ron Leibman, Eugene Roche, Sharon Gans, Valerie Perrine, Sorrell Booke. w. Stephen Geller, N-adap. Kurt Vonnegut, Jr., d. George Roy Hill.

DRAMA: COMEDY DRAMA: Fantasy; **SCI-FI:** Fantasies; Outer Space Movies; Memories; Alienation; Concentration Camps; Anti-War Films; Anti-Establishment Films; Cult Films; Coulda Been Great
(Silent Running; Who Is Harry Kellerman . . .; Dark Star; Up the Sandbox)

Slaughter on Tenth Avenue, 1957, 103m, U-I/NA. The investigation of dockworker murders in New York ultimately leads to the mob. Richard Egan, Jan Sterling, Dan Duryea, Julie Adams, Walter Matthau, Charles McGraw. w. Lawrence Roman, N-adap. William J. Keating (*The Man Who Rocked the Boat*), d. Arnold Laven.

DRAMA: Crime Drama; Mob Stories; **MURDER:** Detective Stories; Detectives-Police; Police Stories; Working Class **MUSICAL REMAKE** on Broadway.
(On the Waterfront; Last Exit to Brooklyn)

Slaves of New York, 1989, 125m, Tri-Star/Col-Tri, ★★★/$, R/P-S. A waifish young woman (Bernadette Peters) stuck in a relationship primarily because she can't afford an apartment of her own travels through and around the lives of many artists and fashion people as she tries to gain independence selling her own hats. Mercedes Ruehl, Nick Corri, Mary Beth Hurt, Chris Sarandon, Tama Janowitz, w. SS-adap. Tama Janowitz, d. James Ivory.

COMEDY DRAMA: SATIRE: Slice of Life; Interwoven Stories; Multiple Stories; New York Life; Artists; Fashion World; Greenwich Village; Beautiful People; All-Star Cameos; Single Women; Young Women; Female Protagonists; Foreign-Like Films; Coulda Been Great; Overlooked at Release; Underrated; Female Screenwriters
(Naked in New York; Short Cuts; Bright Lights, Big City; Six Degrees of Separation; All the Vermeers in New York; Party Girl)
(Ed: If you like intertwining stories about odd but ordinary people and don't have to have a big finish, it's an interesting look at an eccentric slice of life)

Sleeper, 1973, 88m, ★★★1/2/$$$, UA/MGM-UA, R/S. A man from Greenwich Village in the 70s (Woody Allen) wakes up a century later in a rural sci-fi world where sex is done by machine and he's to be experimented upon. Diane Keaton, John Beck. w. Woody Allen, Marshall Brickman, d. Woody Allen.

COMEDY: ROMANCE: SCI-FI: SATIRE: Spoofs; Spoofs-Sci-Fi; Chase Movies; Romantic Comedy; Screwball Comedy; Sexual Problems; Fugitives from the Law; Oppression; Brainwashing; Amnesia; Nerds; Dead-Back from the; Time Sleepers; Oppression; Futuristic Films; Beauty Pageants; Robots; Cult Films; Writer-Directors
(Late for Dinner; Forever Young; Spaceballs; Love and Death; Play it Again, Sam)

Sleeping Beauty, 1959, 75m, ★★★1/2/$$$$, Disney/Disney, G. Gothic variation on the fairy tale of the sleeping princess and Prince Charming vs. the wicked witch. Voices of Mary Costa, Bill Shirley, Eleanor Audley. d. Clyde Geronimi. BOScore. Oscars: 1-0.

CHILDREN'S: FAMILY: Cartoons; **ROMANCE: SUSPENSE:** Good vs. Evil; Time Sleepers; Fairy Tales; Gothic Style; Princesses; Princes; Dragons; Witches; Evil Women
(Cinderella; The Little Mermaid)
(Ed: In many ways, a very adult cartoon, yet not too scary for kids)

The Sleeping Car Murders, 1965, 95m, ★★1/2/$, Ind/NA. On a cross-France train trip, a young woman is found dead in her chamber and the clues lead to several suspects. Yves Montand, Simone Signoret, Pierre Mondy, Catherine Allegret, Jacques Perrin. w. d. Costa-Garvras, N-adap. Sebastien Japrisot.

MYSTERY: MURDER: MURDER MYSTERY: Mystery-Whodunits; Detective Stories; Trains; French Films; Coulda Been Great; Forgotten Films
(Murder on the Orient Express)

Sleeping With the Enemy, 1991, 20th/Fox, ★★/$$$$$. A young woman (Julia Roberts) fakes her death and runs away from her abusive, domineering husband (Patrick Bergin), who soon begins tracking her down to her new life in Iowa with a new boy friend (Kevin Anderson). w. Ronald Bass, N-adap. Nancy Price, d. Joseph Ruben.

SUSPENSE: Chase Movies; Women in Jeopardy; Enemies-Sleeping with; Deaths-Faked; Stalkers; Evil Men; Abused Women; Fugitives; Fugitives from a Murderer; Starting Over; Dual Lives; Identities-Assumed; Hiding Out; Stern Men; Starting Over; Blockbusters
(The Burning Bed; The Stepfather; Deceived; Suspicion)
(Ed: All style [not much] and no substance. The reasons she leaves are hardly worthy-he seems to be just a stern, very fastidious jerk. The big climax is incredibly predictable and ridiculous, yet audiences ate it up, somehow)

Sleepless in Seattle, 1993, 106m, ★★★1/2/$$$$$, Tri/Col-Tri, PG. A widower's (Tom Hanks) son goes on a talk radio show to find his father a new wife and among thousands of women who respond, one from Baltimore (Meg Ryan) may be the one-if they ever meet. w. Nora Ephron, David S. Ward, Larry Atlas, Jeffrey Arch (BOScr), d. Nora Ephron. BOSong. Oscars: 2-0.

ROMANCE: MELODRAMA: COMEDY DRAMA: Tearjerkers; Widowers; Romance-Choosing Right Person; Single Men; Single Women; Wisecracking Sidekicks; Baltimore; Seattle; Parallel Stories; New Year's Eve; Empire State Building; Sleeper Hits; Blockbusters; Underrated; Old-Fashioned Recent Films
(Love Affair; An Affair to Remember; When Harry Met Sally; When a Man Loves a Woman)

Sleepwalkers, 1992, 89m, ★★1/2/$$$, Col/Col-Tri-Star, R/EV-B&G-S. The new neighbors in a suburban community, a

601

mother and son, turn out to be shape-shifting humanoids with an appetite. Brian Krause, Madchen Amick, Alice Krige, Jim Haynie, Ron Perlman, Joe Dante, Stephen King, Clive Barker, Tobe Hooper. w. Stephen King, d. Mick Garris.

HORROR: Humans into Animals; Human Monsters; Human Eaters; Werewolves; Nightmares; Strangers in Town; Mothers & Sons; Invisibility; Secrets-Keeping; Stephen King

(Silver Bullet; Cujo; Wolfen)

Sleep With Me, 1994, 87m, ★★½/$, UA/MGM-UA, R/S-EP-FN. Two of a trio decide to get married, leaving an odd man out-who decides over time he wanted the girl more than his friend. Tensions develop and soon begin to eat away at the friendship and the marriage, both. Eric Stoltz, Meg Tilly, Craig Sheffer, June Lockhart, Thomas Gibson, Adrienne Shelley, Quentin Tarantino. w. Duane Dell Amico, Roger Heddne, Neal Jimenez, Joe Keenan, Rory Kelly, Michael Steinberg, d. Rory Kelly.

DRAMA: Marriage Drama; Men Fighting Over Women; Romance-Triangles; Friendships-Male; Friends as Enemies; Cheating Women; Quiet Little Films; LA 90s Indies; 20-Somethings; Generation X; Young People; Ensemble Films; Improvisational Films

(Bodies, Rest & Motion; Reality Bites; Naked in New York; Inside Monkey Zetterland)

(Ed: Another blah story about pretty twenty-somethings [again in LA] with no real problems and certainly no real solutions)

The Slender Thread, 1965, 98m, ★★★/$$, Par/Par, PG. A social worker answers calls from a woman who finally confesses she's really going to commit suicide, so he tries to track her down in time. Sidney Poitier, Anne Bancroft, Steven Hill, Telly Savalas. w. Stirling Silliphant, d. Sydney Pollack. BB&WArt, BB&WCostume. Oscars: 2-0.

DRAMA: SUSPENSE: Psychological Drama; Race Against Time; Suicidal Tendencies; Social Workers; Midlife Crisis; Character Studies; Women in Jeopardy; Saving Someone; Black Men; Ahead of Its Time; Telephone Problems

COMIC FLIPSIDE: Mixed Nuts.

Sleuth, 1972, 139m, 20th/CBS-Fox, ★★★★/$$$, PG. The perfect murder is devised by a mystery writer, but he ulti-mately gets entangled in his own plot twists in a duel with a young man. Laurence Olivier (BActor), Michael Caine (BActor). w. P-adap. Anthony Shaffer, d. Joseph L. Mankiewicz (BDirector). Oscars: 3-0.

SUSPENSE: MURDER: COMEDY DRAMA: Men in Conflicts; Cat and Mouse; Mindgames; Writers; Turning the Tables; Clever Plots & Endings; Stagelike Films

(Deathtrap; Staircase)

A Slight Case of Murder, 1938, 85m, ★★★½/$$, WB/NA. When a bootlegger attempts to come clean, his partners try to kill him. Edward G. Robinson, Jane Bryan, Willard Parker, Ruth Donnelly, Allen Jenkins, John Litel, Harold Huber. w. Earl Baldwin, Joseph Schrank, P-adap. Damon Runyon, Howard Lindsay, d. Lloyd Bacon.

COMEDY: Black Comedy; **FARCE: MURDER:** Comedy-Morbid; Men in Conflict; Friends as Enemies; Power Struggles; Ethics; Starting Over

REMAKE: Stop, You're Killing Me.

The Slipper and the Rose, 1977, 146m, ★★★/$$, Par/Par, G. A new treatment of the story of Cinderella as a live-action musical-romance. Gemma Craven, Richard Chamberlain, Kenneth More, Michael Hordern, Margaret Lockwood, Christopher Gable. w. Bryan Forbes, Robert Sherman, d. Bryan Forbes. BOScore, BOSong. Oscars: 2-0.

MUSICAL: ROMANCE: Musical Romance; **FAMILY: CHILDREN'S:** Fairy Tales; Princes; Cinderella Stories; Race Against Time; Dreams; Royalty; Stepmothers; Sisters; Evil Women

(The Nutcracker; Cinderella)

Slipstream, 1989, 92m, ★★½/VR, Ind/Video Treasures. In a post-apocalyptic world, a young man hunts down a bounty hunter who's corrupt. Mark Hamill, Bill Paxton, Bob Peck, Ben Kingsley, F. Murray Abraham. d. Steven Liesberger.

ACTION: SCI-FI: Apocalyptic Stories; Bounty Hunters; Manhunts; Chase Stories

(Bladerunner; The Road Warrior; Mad Max)

Slither, 1973, 96m, ★★★½/$$, MGM/MGM-UA, R/V-P. When an ex-con is released from jail and his old pal clues him in to the whereabouts of some loot, he finds a large, black sinister RV on his tail while he seems to be going on a camping trip with friends, but is really heading for the dough. James Caan, Peter Boyle, Sally Kellerman, Louise Lasser. w. W. D. Richter, d. Howard Zieff.

COMEDY DRAMA: Action Comedy; Black Comedy; Chase Movies; Car Chases; Treasure Hunts; Ex-Convicts; Mob Stories; Eccentric People; Double Crossings; Underrated; Forgotten Films; Overlooked at Release

(Thunderbolt & Lightfoot; Fool's Parade)

(Ed: The writing and eccentric performances carry this one)

Sliver, 1993, 106m, ★★★/$$$, Par/Par, R/ES-FFN-MFN-P-V. A woman moves into a fancy apartment building where someone is watching every move by camera-even when people begin to be murdered. Sharon Stone, Billy Baldwin, Tom Berenger, Martin Landau, C.C.H. Pounder, Polly Walker, Nina Foch. w. Joe Eszterhas, N-adap. Ira Levin, d. Philip Noyce.

SUSPENSE: MURDER: MYSTERY: MURDER MYSTERY: Erotic Thriller; Mystery-Whodunit?; Women in Jeopardy; Apartment Buildings; Voyeurs; Sexy Women; Sexy Men; Dangerous Romance; Enemy-Sleeping with; Dangerous Men; Coulda Been Great; Video Proof

(Basic Instinct; Rear Window; Jade)

(Ed: Though there are major problems, Stone holds the screen even as a heroine and, overall, it's not terrible)

Slow Dancing in the Big City, 1978, 110m, ★★½/$, UA/MGM-UA, PG/P. A newspaper writer becomes enthralled with inner city stories and a romance with a ballerina. Paul Sorvino, Anne Ditchburn, Nicholas Coster. w. Barra Grant, d. John G. Avildsen.

MELODRAMA: ROMANCE: Journalists; Inner City Life; Newspapers; Ballet; Death-Dealing with; Tearjerkers

Small Change, 1976, 105m, ★★★½/$$, Films du Carosse-UAC/MGM-UA. Prepubescent friends in a small French town go through their individual growing pains, including first love and the mistreatment at the hands of their parents. Geory Desmouceaux, Philippe Goldman, Claudio Deluca. w. Francois Truffaut, Suzanne Schiffman, d. Francois Truffaut.

DRAMA: COMEDY DRAMA: Ensemble Films; Ensemble-Children; Coming of Age; Teenagers; Love-First; Parents vs. Children; Abused Children; French Films; Female Screenwriters

(Peppermint Soda; Rich Kids; The 400 Blows)

A Small Circle of Friends, 1980, 112m, ★★¹/₂/$, U-I/Fox. Against the background of the social upheavals of the sixties, a group of Harvard men go through their ups and downs. Brad Davis, Karen Allen, Jameson Parker, Shelley Long, John Friedrich. w. Ezra Sacks, d. Rob Cohen.

COMEDY DRAMA: MELODRAMA: ROMANCE: Romance-Triangles; Vietnam Era; Anti-War Films; 1960s; 1970s; College Life; Harvard; Coulda Been Good (Four Friends; Willie & Phil) (Ed: Pretty superficial, and not even very pretty)

Small Sacrifices, 1989, 159m, ★★★/ $$$$, ABC/Fries. True story of a mother who apparently murdered her children but denies it, despite the evidence. Farrah Fawcett, Ryan O'Neal, John Shea, Emily Perkins. w. Joyce Eliason, d. David Greene.

DRAMA: TRAGEDY: True Stories; True or Not?; Child Abuse; Murders of Children; Evil Women; Mental Illness; Courtroom Drama; TV Movies (The Burning Bed; Medea [play])

Small Town Girl, 1936, 90m, ★★★/$$$, MGM/NA. A revelling stranger in a small town proposes marriage to a local girl when drunk. In the morning, when he's sober, she tries to snag him for real. Janet Gaynor, Robert Taylor, James Stewart, Binnie Barnes, Frank Craven, Elizabeth Patterson. w. John Lee Mahin, Edith Fitzgerald, N-adap. Ben Ames Williamson, d. William A. Wellman.

COMEDY: ROMANCE: Romantic Comedy; Small-town Life; Romance-Girl Wants Boy; Marriage-Forced; Alcoholics; Female Protagonists; Female Screenwriters (Lover Come Back [1961])

Small Town Girl, 1953, 93m, ★★★¹/₂/ $$, MGM/MGM-UA. Musical remake of above. w. Dorothy Cooper, Dorothy Kingsley, d. Leslie Kardos. BOSong. Oscars: 1-0.

MUSICALS: ROMANCE: Musical Romance; Dance Movies; Dancers; Small-town Life; Romance-Girl Wants Boy; Marriage-Forced; Alcoholics; Female Screenwriters; Female Protagonists (Ed: Notable for spectacular dance sequences)

A Small Town in Texas, 1976, ★★/$, AIP/Live. After years in prison, an unjustly accused man returns to his home

town to wreak havoc on those who did him wrong. Timothy Bottoms, Susan George, Bo Hopkins, Art Hindle. w. William Norton, d. Jack Starett.

ACTION: Revenge; Convict's Revenge; Framed?; Small-town Life; Texas; Rednecks (Cape Fear; Sitting Target; The Last Picture Show)

Smart Woman, 1948, 93m, ★★¹/₂/$, Monogram/NA. A D.A. and a lady lawyer become romantically entangled with and without their legal briefs. Constance Bennett, Brian Aherne, Barry Sullivan, Michael O'Shea, James Gleason, Otto Kruger. w. Alvah Bessie, Louise Morheim, Herbert Margolis, d. Edward A. Blatt.

COMEDY DRAMA: ROMANCE: Romantic Comedy; Romance-Bickering; Lawyers; Lawyers in Love; Coulda Been Good; Female Screenwriters (Adam's Rib; Legal Eagles) (Ed: Good actors in mediocre material)

Smashing Time, 1967, 96m, ★★★/$, Par/NA. Two rowdy young women hit the town in swinging London; one becomes a pop star, the other gets revenge. Rita Tushingham, Lynn Redgrave, Ian Carmichael, Anna Quayle, Michael York. w. George Melly, d. Desmond Davis.

COMEDY: SATIRE: Rock Stars; Singers; Fame-Rise to; Mod Era; London; Revenge; Young People; Women in Conflict; Wallflowers; Time Capsules; Hidden Gems; Forgotten Films; Female Protagonists (Mrs. Brown, You've Got a Lovely Daughter; The Knack; Georgy Girl) (Ed: Often funny but silly. Redgrave is wonderful as a cow who gets the big head)

Smash Palace, 1981, 108m, ★★¹/₂/$$, Ind/Vestron, R/S-P-FFN-MRN. When his wife leaves him, a car junkyard proprietor goes to more pieces than his wrecks. Bruno Lawrence, Anna Jemison, Keith Aberdein, Greer Robson. w. d. Roger Donaldson.

DRAMA: Erotic Drama; Marriage Drama; Marriage on the Rocks; New Zealand; Working Class; Writer-Directors (Ed: Made a smash on the arthouse circuit, but it's not clear why-not much sex, not much action, not much story)

Smash-Up, the Story of a Woman, 1947, 113m, ★★¹/₂/$$$, Universal/MCA-U. A female Lost Weekend, giving

Hayward plenty of scenery to chew up toward an Oscar nomination. Susan Hayward (BActress), Lee Bowman, Eddie Albert, Marsha Hunt, Carl Esmond, Carleton Young, Charles D. Brown. w. John Howard Lawson, d. Stuart Heisler. Oscars: 2-0.

FLIPSIDE: The Lost Weekend (I'll Cry Tomorrow; The Lost Weekend; Dangerous; The Morning After; Days of Wine and Roses) (Ed: Not to be confused with Smash-Up on Interstate 5)

Smile, 1975, 113m, ★★★¹/₂/$$, UA/CBS-Fox, PG. The seedy underbelly and backstage backbiting of the Young Miss America pageant is explored. Bruce Dern, Barbara Feldon, Michael Kidd, Geoffrey Lewis. w. Jerry Belson, d. Michael Ritchie.

COMEDY: SATIRE: Beauty Pageants; Women in Conflict; Voyeurs; Marriage on the Rocks; Behind the Scenes; Teenagers; Girls; Young Women; American Myth; Underrated; Hidden Gems; Overlooked at Release; Cult Films;

MUSICAL REMAKE: on Broadway (failed). (Miss All-American Beauty; To Wong Foo . . .)

Smiles of a Summer Night, 1955, 105m, ★★★¹/₂/$$$, Svensk Film-industri/Home Vision. A traveling barrister runs into an old mistress. He's now married, but accepts her invitation for himself and his wife to stay with her in her country home. Romantic complications ensue. Gunnar Bjornstrand, Eva Dahlbeck, Ulla Jacobsson, Harriet Andersson. w. d. Ingmar Bergman.

COMEDY: COMEDY DRAMA: ROMANCE: Romantic Comedy; Romance-Reunited; Romance-Unrequited; Marriage Comedy; Ensemble Films; Vacations; Swedish Films; Art Films; Writer-Directors

MUSICAL REMAKE: A Little Night Music (A Midsummer Night's Sex Comedy; Wild Strawberries) (Ed: One of Bergman's more accessible)

The Smiling Lieutenant, 1931, 88m, ★★★¹/₂/$$, Par/NA. A princess takes up with a lowly Viennese guard, whose mistress is understandably upset. Maurice Chevalier, Miriam Hopkins, Claudette Colbert, Charles Ruggles, George Barbier. w. Ernest Vajda, Samson Raphaelson, MP-adap. (A Waltz Dream). d. Ernst Lubitsch. BPicture. Oscars: 1-0.

**COMEDY: COMEDY DRAMA:
ROMANCE:** Romantic Comedy;
Romance-Triangles; Romance-Class
Conflicts; **MUSICALS:** Music Movies;
Jealousy; Princesses; Soldiers; Vienna;
Hidden Gems

Smilin' Through, 1932, 97m,
★★★/$$$, MGM/MGM-UA, Facets. In
the Victorian Era, a woman is accidently
killed on her wedding day, and the effects
of this incident ripple through three gen-
erations of her family. Norma Shearer,
Leslie Howard, Fredric March, O. P.
Heggie. w. Ernest Vajda, Claudine West,
Donald Ogden Stewart, J. B. Fagan, P-
adap. Jane Cowl, Jane Murfin, d. Sidney
Franklin.

Smilin' Through, 1941, 100m,
★★1/2/$$$, MGM/MGM-UA. Remake of
above. Jeanette MacDonald, Gene Ray-
mond, Brian Aherne, Ian Hunter, Frances
Robinson. w. Donald Ogden Stewart, John
Balderston, d. Frank Borzage.

MELODRAMA: TRAGEDY: Tearjerkers;
Death-Dealing with; Episodic Stories;
Costume Drama; 1800s; Accidents;
England

Smithereens, 1982, 90m, ★★1/2/$,
Ind/Media, R/S-P. The groupie of a punk
rock band in New York wants to be their
manager, but ultimately gets snubbed by
them. Susan Berman, Brad Rinn, Richard
Hell, Roger Jet. w. Susan Seidelman, Ron
Nyswaner, Peter Askin, d. Susan
Seidelman.

DRAMA: Art Films; Cult Films; Rock
Stars; Musicians; Fans-Crazed;
Alienation; Young People; Female
Screenwriters; Female Directors; Female
Protagonists; Time Capsules;
Independent Films
(Desperately Seeking Susan)

Smokey and the Bandit, 1977, 97m,
★★★/$$$$$$, Universal/MCA-U, PG/P-
V. The small-town sheriff named Buford
T. Justice whose fiancee runs off, gets
understandably upset when a wandering
bootlegger who's younger and sexier picks
her up, so he chases them . . . and chases
them. Burt Reynolds, Jackie Gleason,
Sally Field, Jerry Reed, Paul Williams. w.
James Lee Barrett, Charles Shyer, Alan
Mandel, d. Hal Needham.

ACTION: COMEDY: Action Comedy;
Chase Movies; Car Chases; Car Wrecks;
Road Movies; Outlaw Road Movies;
Fugitives from the Law; Romance-
Triangles; Jealousy; Police Corruption;

Southerns; Rednecks; Bootlegging;
Blockbusters; Sleeper Hits
(WW & The Dixie Dancekings; High-
Ballin'; The Cannonball Run; Hooper)

Smokey and the Bandit II, 1980,
101m, ★★1/2/$$$, Universal/MCA-U,
PG/P-S. A Republican convention is
ready to get off the ground, except they're
waiting for the delivery of their mascot-an
elephant who happens to be pregnant,
supposed to be delivered by a truck driver (Burt Reynolds) who's once again
being chased by his nemesis, Buford T.
Justice (Jackie Gleason). Sally Field,
Jerry Reed, Dom DeLuise, Paul Williams.
w. Jerry Belson, Brock Yates, d. Hal
Needham.

ACTION: COMEDY: Action Comedy;
Chase Movies; Car Chases; Car Crashes;
Road Movies; Outlaw Road Movies;
Fugitives from the Law; Police
Corruption; Identities-Mistaken;
Southerns; Rednecks; Bootleggers;
Blockbusters

Smokey and the Bandit III, 1983,
88m, ★★/$$, Universal/MCA, PG/P.
Sheriff Buford T. Justice ("Smokey") mis-
takes a trucker passing through his small
town for the Bandit (who didn't want to be
in this sequel). Jackie Gleason, Jerry
Reed, Mike Henry, Pat McCormick, Burt
Reynolds. w. Stuart Birnbaum, David
Dashev, d. Dick Lowry.

ACTION: COMEDY: Action Comedy;
Chase Movies; Car Chases; Car Crashes;
Road Movies; Outlaw Road Movies;
Fugitives from the Law; Police
Corruption; Southerns; Rednecks;
Bootleggers

Smooth Talk, 1986, 90m, ★★★1/2/$$,
AP-PBS/Goldwyn. A teenage girl (Laura
Dern) is followed by a smooth talking
redneck man (Treat Williams) who has
the intent of deflowering her. Mary Kay
Place, Levon Helm. w. Tom Cole, SS-
adap. Joyce Carol Oates, d. Joyce Chopra.

DRAMA: ROMANCE: Coming of Age;
Erotic Drama; Life Transitions; Love-
Dangerous; Romance-Older Men/Younger
Women; Love-First; Virgins; Sexy Men;
Dangerous Men; Rednecks; Teenagers;
Girls; Young Women; Mothers-
Troublesome; Female Protagonists;
Female Directors; Independent Films
(36 Fillette; Lolita)

The Smugglers, 1947, 88m, ★★1/2/$,
GFD/NA. An orphan finds a man who
takes a liking to him but turns out not to

be the good big brother, but a thief.
Michael Redgrave, Richard Attenborough,
Jean Kent, Joan Greenwood. w. Muriel and
Sydney Box, N-adap. Graham Greene, d.
Bernard Knowles.

DRAMA: MELODRAMA: Protecting
Someone; Illusions Destroyed; Thieves;
Secrets; Orphans; Boys; Child
Protagonists
(Fallen Idol; The Window; Tiger Bay)

The Snakepit, 1948, 108m, ★★★/$$,
20th/Fox. An exposé of the horrors of the
insane asylum and a plea for more
humane treatment of the mentally ill.
The story concerns a middle-class girl
sent to an institution after her break-
down. Olivia de Havilland (BActress),
Leo Genn, Mark Stevens, Celeste Holm,
Glenn Langan, Leif Erikson, Beulah
Bondi. w. Frank Partos, Millen Brand
(BAScr), N-adap. Mary Jane Ward, d.
Anatole Litvak (BDirector). BPicture,
BScore. Oscars: 5-0.

DRAMA: MELODRAMA: Social Drama;
Mental Illness; Asylums; Nervous
Breakdowns; Depression; Psychiatrists;
Illusions/Hallucinations; Young Women;
1940s; Female Protagonists; Coulda Been
Great; Ahead of Its Time
(I Never Promised You A Rose Garden;
Bedlam)
(Ed: Although ahead of its time then, it's
rather dated now)

The Snapper, 1993, 90m, ★★★/$,
Miramax/Touchstone, PG-13/S-P. A
young Irish woman is pregnant and her
family finds out; but the big secret is who
the father might be. Tina Kellegher, Colm
Meaney, Ruth McCabe. w. Roddy Doyle,
d. Stephen Frears.

COMEDY DRAMA: Babies-Having;
Mothers Alone; **MYSTERY:** Family
Comedy; Parents vs. Children; Father?-
Who's the; Irish Films; Ireland
(The Family Way; The Miracle of
Morgan's Creek)

Sneakers, 1992, 135m, ★★★/$$$,
Universal/MCA-U, PG-13/P. A fugitive
from the FBI (Robert Redford) runs a
high-tech security team which comes
upon a microchip which can decipher
government computer codes and endan-
ger national security-and their lives.
Sidney Poitier, Mary McDonnell, Ben
Kingsley, Dan Aykroyd, River Phoenix,
David Straithairn. w. Phil Alden
Robinson, Lawrence Lasker, Walter F.
Parkes, d. Phil Alden Robinson.

SUSPENSE: MYSTERY: Comic Thriller; Capers; Heist Stories; Ensemble Films; Spies; Surveillance; Fugitives from the Law; Double Crossings; Secrets-Keeping; Traitors; Friends as Enemies; Turning the Tables; Friends Reunited; Geniuses; Computers; Blind People; Female Among Males

(The Hot Rock; Silver Bears; Hackers)

The Sniper, 1952, 87m, ★★★/$$, Col/NA. A madman with a rifle goes on a shooting rampage. His predilection is for gorgeous blondes. Adolphe Menjou, Arthur Franz, Gerald Mohr, Richard Kiley. w. Harry Brown, Edna & Edward Anhalt (BOStory), d. Edward Dmytryk. Oscars: 1-0.

DRAMA: MURDER: Crime Drama; Police Stories; Trail of a Killer; Detective Stories; Detectives-Police; Murders of Women; Serial Killers; Psycho Killers; Documentary Style; Snipers; Ahead of Its Time; Forgotten Films

Sniper (The Deadly Tower), 1975, 85m, ★★★/$$$$, CBS/Xenon Video. True story of the man with a brain tumor who cracked and began firing a rifle from atop a high-rise on the University of Texas campus, killing several people. Kurt Russell (in an attempt to break his Disney image), Richard Yniguez, John Forsythe, Ned Beatty, Pernell Roberts. d. Jerry Jameson.

SUSPENSE: True Stories; **MURDER:** Murderers-Mass; **TRAGEDY:** Serial Killers; Mental Illness; Nervous Breakdowns; Texas; College Life; TV Movies

Sniper, 1993, 98m, ★★★/$$, Col/Col, R/P-V. A Marine sniper in Panama is joined by a young, cocky marksman to stealth through the jungle and take out a guerilla rebel, but the journey becomes a duel where no one knows who's after who. Tom Berenger, Billy Zane, J.T. Walsh. w. Michael Frost Beckner, Crash Leyland, d. Luis Llosa.

ACTION: SUSPENSE: Psychological Thriller; Chase Movies; Secret Agents; Political Unrest; Double Crossings; Snipers; Central America; Jungle Life; Cat and Mouse Stories

(The Most Dangerous Game)

(Ed: Better than one expects from the genre)

The Snows of Kilimanjaro, 1952, 117m, ★★★/$$$, 20th/Goodtimes, Nos. A wounded hunter recalls his life's loves

and adventures as he lies bleeding in the mountains waiting for help. Gregory Peck, Susan Hayward, Ava Gardner, Hildegard Neff, Leo G. Carroll. w. Casey Robinson, SS-adap. Ernest Hemingway, d. Henry King.

DRAMA: ADVENTURE: Survival Drama; Memories; Flashbacks; Mountain Climbing; Explorers; Snow Settings; Africa; Ernest Hemingway

(K-Z; White Hunter, Black Heart; The Last Hunt)

Snow White & The Seven Dwarfs, 1937, 82m, ★★★★/$$$$$$, Disney/Disney, G. The classic fairy tale of a princess living with seven little men who is poisoned by a jealous queen, and can only be brought back to life by the kiss of a handsome prince. Voices of Adriana Caselotti, Harry Stockwell, Lucille La Verne, Billy Gilbert. w. Ted Sears, Otto Englander, Earl Hurd, Dorothy Ann Blank, Richard Creedon, Dick Richard, Merrill de Maris, Webb Smith, SS-adap. The Brothers Grimm, d. David Hand.

CHILDREN'S: FAMILY: ROMANCE: SUSPENSE: Cartoons; Fairy Tales; Evil Women; Queens; Good vs. Evil; Little People; Princes; Dead-Back from the; Poison; Female Among Males; Blockbusters; Sleeper Hits

(Bambi; Sleeping Beauty; Cinderella)

(Ed: One of the biggest hits ever in sheer number of ticket sales in initial release, not to mention over the sixty years since)

Snow White and the Three Stooges, 1961, 107m, ★★½/$$, 20th/NA. An adaptation of the famous fairy tale with stooges instead of dwarves and an Olympic skating star as the sweetheart. Carol Heiss, Moe Howard, Larry Fine, Joe de Rita, Edson Stroll. w. Noel Langley, Elwood Ullman, d. Walter Lang.

COMEDY: Fairy Tales; Comedy-Slapstick; Fools-Bumbling; Female Among Males; Skating; Revisionist Films

Soapdish, 1991, 97m, Par/Par, ★★★/$$$, PG-13/S-P. A soap opera actress (Sally Field) is in crisis mode as her ex-husband (Kevin Kline) and niece (Elisabeth Shue), who's secretly her daughter, are falling in love while she's struggling to stay star of her show. Whoopi Goldberg, Robert Downey, Jr., Carrie Fisher, Cathy Moriarty, Teri Hatcher, Garry Marshall. w. Robert Harling, Andrew Bergman, d. Michael Hoffman.

COMEDY: FARCE: Screwball Comedy; Ensemble Films; Soap Opera Shows; Children-Long Lost; Incest; Secrets-Keeping; Romance-Reunited; Romance-Older Men/Younger Women; Electra Complex; Neurotic People; Actresses; Actors; TV Life; Transsexuals; Underrated; Hidden Gems; Coulda Been Great

(Tootsie; Steel Magnolias; Tom Jones)

(Ed: Falls flat in places due to pacing, though there's enough one-liners and a great finale to pay it all off)

S.O.B., 1981, 121m, ★★★/$$, Lorimar-UA/Fox, WB, R/P-S-FFN. A big-time Hollywood director loses everything when he banks on an old-fashioned musical in the cynical, modern 80s. He then decides to "sex it up." Julie Andrews, Richard Mulligan, Robert Preston, William Holden, Robert Vaughn, Larry Hagman, Shelley Winters, Loretta Swit, Robert Loggia. w. d. Blake Edwards.

SATIRE: COMEDY: COMEDY DRAMA: FARCE: Spoofs-Musical; Tragi-Comedy; Comedy-Slapstick; Death-Dealing with; Hollywood Life; Marriage on the Rocks; Ensemble Films; Directors; Actors; Gossip; Depression; Suicidal Tendencies; Underrated; Coulda Been Great; Hidden Gems; All-Star Casts; Writer-Directors

(Movers and Shakers; The Big Picture; Welcome to L.A.; Skin Deep)

(Ed: Noted for Julie Andrews' baring her breasts. Stands for "standard operational bull." Vaguely autobiographical version of director and wife/star Andrews' problems with *Darling Lili*)

So Big, 1932, 80m, ★★★/$$$, WB/NA. A country school marm grows weary of the hard life on her husband's farm with her unruly son and escapes into the arms of a dashing sculptor in town. Barbara Stanwyck, George Brent, Dickie Moore, Guy Kibbee, Bette Davis, Hardie Albright. w. J. Grubb Alexander, Robert Lord, N-adap. Edna Ferber, d. William Wellman.

So Big, 1953, 101m, ★★½/$$, WB/WB. A remake of the above. Jane Wyman, Sterling Hayden, Richard Beymer, Nancy Olson, Steve Forrest. w. John Twist, d. Robert Wise.

ROMANCE: MELODRAMA: Romance-Triangles; Cheating Women; Women Who Leave; Artists; Teachers; Farm Life; Midlife Crisis; Depression

(Lucy Gallant; State Fair; Giant; Ada)

Society, 1989, 99m, ★★½/VR, Republic/Republic, R/V-B&G. A normal boy discovers he's the spawn of rich people who are really monsters who eat poor people for snacks. Bill Warlock, Davin DeVasquez, Evan Richards, Ben Meyerson. w. Woody Keith, Rick Fry, d. Brian Yuzna.

HORROR: Black Comedy; Comedy-Morbid; **SATIRE:** Social Satire; Class Conflicts; Rich vs. Poor; Cannibalism; Coulda Been Good
(Soylent Green; Parents; Delicatessen)

So Dear to My Heart, 1948, ★★★/$$$, Disney/Disney, G. At the turn of the century, a pioneer farm family has its trials and tribulations, set to music with intermittent animation (it's Disney!). Burl Ives, Beulah Bondi, Harry Carrey, Luana Patten. w. John Tucker Battle, N-adap. Sterling North *(Midnight and Jeremiah)*, d. Harold Schuster.

COMEDY DRAMA: MELODRAMA: CHILDREN'S: FAMILY: Family Comedy; Farm Life; Conservative Value Films; 1900s; Nostalgia; Animation-Partial
(Friendly Persuasion; Song of the South)

Sodom and Gomorrah, 1962, 154m, ★★/$$, Titanus-20th/Fox. Lot rallies his tribe to take over the sinful cities of Sodom and Gomorrah. Stewart Granger, Stanley Baker, Pier Angeli, Anouk Aimee. w. Hugo Butler, Giorgio Prosperi, d. Robert Aldrich.

ACTION: Biblical Stories; Power Struggles; Middle East; Ancient Times; Apocalyptic Stories; Spectacles
(Solomon and Sheba; David and Bathsheba)

So Fine, 1981, 91m, ★★★/$$, Lorimar-WB/WB, R/P-S-FFN-MRN. When his father gets mixed up with gangsters, a mild-mannered college professor must figure out how to bail him out of trouble. Somehow, the result is a line of jeans with see-through plastic cheeks. Ryan O'Neal, Jack Warden, Mariangela Melato, Richard Kiel, Fred Gwynne. w. d. Andrew Bergman.

COMEDY: SATIRE: Mob Stories; Mob Comedy; Professors; Fathers & Sons; Nerds & Babes; Fashion World; Underrated; Forgotten Films; Writer-Directors
(The Freshman; What's Up, Doc?; The Main Event)

The Soft Skin, 1964, 118m, ★★★/$$, Films du Carrosse-UAC/Fox. A man in midlife crisis mode leaves his wife for a younger woman. He realizes too late that he's thrown his life away. Jean Desailly, Francois Dorleac, Nelly Benedetti. w. Francois Truffaut, Jean-Louis Richard, d. Francois Truffaut.

DRAMA: MELODRAMA: Character Studies; Art Films; Cheating Men; Midlife Crisis; Marriage on the Rocks; Romance-Older Man/Younger Women; French Films
(Twice in a Lifetime; Middle Age Crazy; Le Cavaleuir; Too Beautiful for You)

Solarbabies, 1986, 94m, ★★/$, MGM/MGM-UA, PG/V. A band of kids who are refugees in a far away land with little water use magic to help them fight the system. Jami Gertz, Richard Jordan, Jason Patirc, Lukas Haas, James LeGros, Peter DeLuise, Sarah Douglas, Charles Durning. w. Walon Green, Douglas Metrov, d. Alan Johnson.

SCI-FI: ACTION: Futuristic Films; Apocalyptic Stories; Roller Skating; Fighting the System; Corruption-Government; Coulda Been Good
(Spacehunter; Waterworld)
(Ed: Very odd but interesting looking assortment)

Solaris, 1972, 165m, ★★★/$, Mosfilm/Fox-Lorber. A space station is invaded by an alien force which creates realistic illusions out of the astronaut's memories. Natalya Bondachuk, Donatas Banionis, Yuri Yarvet. w. Andrei Tarkovsky, Friedrich Gorenstein, N-adap. Stanislaw Lem, d. Andrei Tarkovsky.

SCI-FI: HORROR: Outer Space Movies; Astronauts; Aliens-Outer Space, Evil; Nightmares; Russians Films; Russians; Forgotten Films; Overlooked at Release
(Predator; Dark Star)

Soldier Blue, 1970, 114m, ★★½/$, Avco/Col, PG. Indians seeking gold attack a group of cavalry officers leaving only two survivors who walk through the desert to get to a safe haven. Candice Bergen, Peter Strauss, Donald Pleasence. w. John Gay, N-adap. Theodore V. Olsen *(Arrow in the Sun)*, d. Ralph Nelson.

ADVENTURE: WESTERNS: Journies; Survival Drama; Treasure Hunts; Indians-Americans; Forgotten Films

Soldier in the Rain, 1963, 87m, ★★½/$$, AA/Fox. Two military men about to disembark have a night on the town which ends tragically. Steve McQueen, Jackie Gleason, Tuesday Weld, Tony Bill, Tom Poston, Ed Nelson. w. Blake Edwards, Maurice Richlin, N-adap. William Goldman, d. Ralph Nelson.

DRAMA: TRAGEDY: COMEDY DRAMA: Tragi-Comedy; Soldiers; One-Day Stories; Forgotten Films; Coulda Been Good
(Casualties of War; Town Without Pity)

Soldier of Fortune, 1955, 96m, ★★½/$$, 20th/Fox. When her husband, a photo-journalist, disappears in China, a woman goes to Hong Kong in order to find a bounty hunter to search for him. Clark Gable, Susan Hayward, Gene Barry, Alex D'Arcy, Michael Rennie. w. Ernest K. Gann, N-adap. Ernest K. Gann, d. Edward Dmytryk.

DRAMA: MELODRAMA: Bounty Hunters; Missing Persons; Searches; Photographers; Asia; Hong Kong; Americans Abroad
(Missing; Inn of the Sixth Happiness)

A Soldier's Story, 1984, 101m, ★★★/$$$, CBS-Col/RCA-Col, PG/P. When an infamous drill sergeant is killed at a black military post in Louisiana during World War II, a special investigator comes to solve the case. Howard Rollins, Adolph Caesar (BSActor), David Alan Grier, Denzel Washington. w. P-adap. Charles Fuller (BAScr), d. Norman Jewison. BPicture. Oscars: 3-0.

DRAMA: Courtroom Drama; **MURDER MYSTERY: MYSTERY:** Lawyer as Detective; Military Stories; Soldiers; Black Soldiers; Black Casts; Black Men; Ensemble Films; Southerns; World War II Era; Pulitzer Prize Adaptations; Black Screenwriters
(A Few Good Men; Glory)

The Solid Gold Cadillac, 1956, 99m, ★★★½/$$$, Col/NA. A young woman who owns stock in a fat-cat's corporation gives him what for. Judy Holliday, Paul Douglas, John Williams, Fred Clark, Hiram Sherman, Ray Collins. w. Abe Burrows, P-adap. George S. Kaufman, Howard Teichmann, d. Richard Quine. BArt. Oscars: 1-0.

COMEDY: COMEDY DRAMA: Office Comedy; Corporate Life; Rich vs. Poor; Executives; Secretaries; Fighting the System; Women Fighting the System; Heroes-Unlikely; Capra-esque; Female Protagonists
(Working Girl; Born Yesterday; Bells Are Ringing)

Solomon and Sheba, 1959, 142m, ★★½/$$, UA/MGM-UA. The biblical story of a man scorned by his father who seeks revenge on his brother. Yul Brynner, Gina Lollobrigida, George Sanders, Marisa Pavan. w. Anthony Viller, Paul Dudley, George Bruce, d. King Vidor.

DRAMA: Biblical Stories; Epics; Spectacles; Cast of Thousands; Fathers & Sons; Revenge; Brothers
(David and Bathsheba; Sodom and Gomorrah)

So Long at the Fair, 1950, 86m, ★★★/ $$, Rank/NA. A sister and brother are separated at the 1889 Paris Exposition and she can't convince anyone he ever existed. Jean Simmons, Dirk Bogarde, David Tomlinson, Marcel Poncin, Cathleen Nesbitt, Honor Blackman. w. Hugh Mills, Anthony Thorne, d. Terence Fisher, Anthony Darnborough.

DRAMA: SUSPENSE: Psychological Drama; Missing Persons; Missing Person Thriller; Unbelieved; Searches; Brothers & Sisters; Paris; 1890s; Forgotten Films; Hidden Gems; Female Protagonists
(Without a Trace; Missing; Bunny Lake is Missing; The Lady Vanishes)

Somebody Killed Her Husband, 1978, 96m, ★★1/2/$, Col/NA, PG. A young new bride must solve the murder of her husband with the help of a department store manager who wants her. Farrah Fawcett Majors, Jeff Bridges, John Wood, Tammy Grimes. w. Reginald Rose, d. Lamont Johnson.

SUSPENSE: Comic Thriller; MURDER: MYSTERY: MURDER MYSTERY: Comic Mystery; ROMANCE: Comedy-Light; Department Stores; Newlyweds; Murder of Spouse
(Ed: Odd that it seems a bit better than when first out, though there's still not much)

Somebody Up There Likes Me, 1956, 112m, ★★★/$$$, MGM/MGM-UA. A poor kid growing up on skid row becomes a champion boxer. Paul Newman, Pier Angeli, Everett Sloane, Eileen Heckart, Sal Mineo, Robert Loggia. w. Ernest Lehman, d. Robert Wise. BB&WArt, BB&WCin, BEdit. Oscars: 3-2.

DRAMA: Biographies; COMEDY DRAMA: Sports Movies; Boxing; Fame-Rise to; Inner City Life; Italians
(Raging Bull; Rocky; Champion)
(Ed: Life story of Rocky Graziano)

Some Came Running, 1958, 136m, ★★★/$$$, MGM/MGM-UA. After doing his military service, a writer takes up with lowlifes in his home town. Frank

Sinatra, Dean Martin, Shirley MacLaine, (BActress), Martha Hyer (BSActress), Arthur Kennedy (BSActor). w. John Patrick, Arthur Sheekman, N-adap. James Jones, d. Vincente Minnelli. BOSong, BCostume. Oscars: 5-0.

DRAMA: MELODRAMA: ROMANCE: Ensemble Films; Pre-life Crisis; Writers; Small-town Life; Midwestern Life; Ratpack Movies; Female Among Males
(The Men; From Here to Eternity; Americana; Born on the Fourth of July)

Some Girls, 1988, 93m, ★★1/2/$, MGM/ MGM-UA, R/S-FN-MFN. A young American in love with a French-Canadian girl goes to spend Christmas with her family in Quebec, and ends up taking care of her ailing grandmother, but not before running around her house naked. Patrick Dempsey, Jennifer Connelly, Sheila Kelley, Lance Edwards, Lila Kedrova, Andre Gregory. w. Rupert Walters, d. Michael Hoffman.

COMEDY DRAMA: ROMANCE: Romantic Comedy; Romance-Boy Wants Girl; Bratpack Movies; Canada
(The Rachel Papers; Happy Together)
(Ed: A great looking film but unfortunately no different from the slew of other Dempsey and sub-Bratpack movies)

Some Kind of a Nut, 1969, 89m, ★★1/2/$, UA/NA, PG. When a conservative bank teller gets stung by a bee on the chin, he grows a beard to cover it up, and is thought to be a hippie, leading to protests and a parody of the late 60s. Dick Van Dyke, Angie Dickinson, Rosemary Forsyth, Zohra Lampert. w. d. Garson Kanin.

COMEDY: SATIRE: Anti-Establishment Films; Heroes-Unlikely; Accidents; 1960s; Coulda Been Good; Good Premise Unfulfilled; Time Capsules
(Never a Dull Moment; Skidoo)

Some Kind of Hero, 1981, 97m, ★★1/2/$, Par/Par, R/P. Long after the Vietnam War is over and he's presumed dead, a prisoner of war returns and tries to put the pieces of his life back together. Richard Pryor. w. James Kirkwood, Robert Boris, N-adap. James Kirkwood, d. Michael Pressman.

COMEDY DRAMA: MELODRAMA: Veterans; Dead-Back from the; Time Sleepers; Vietnam Veterans; POWs; Black Men
(Welcome Home; Bustin' Loose; Green Eyes; Coming Home)

Some Kind of Wonderful, 1987, 95m, ★★1/2/$$, Par/Par, PG. A romantic triangle among teenagers ends up with the right people coupling. Eric Stoltz, Mary Stuart Masterson, Craig Sheffer, John Ashton, Lea Thompson, Elias Koteas. w. John Hughes, d. Howard Deutch.

ROMANCE: COMEDY DRAMA: Romance-Triangles; Young People; Teenagers; Teenage Movies; Romance-Choosing the Right Person; Tomboys; High School Life; Musicians; Coulda Been Good
(Pretty in Pink; Sixteen Candles)

Some Like It Hot, 1959, 123m, ★★★★/ $$$$$, UA/MGM-UA. Two musicians in the roaring 20s (Jack Lemmon, Tony Curtis) are witness to a mob hit and are forced to dress as women and join an all-girl band in order to flee. Only problem is, they both fall for the same bombshell (Marilyn Monroe) who thinks they're both women. Joe E. Brown, George Raft, Pat O'Brien, Nehemiah Persoff. w. Billy Wilder, I. A. L. Diamond, d. Billy Wilder.

COMEDY: Screwball Comedy; FARCE: Romantic Comedy; Romance-Boy Wants Girl; Mob Stories; Mob Comedy; Fugitives from the Mob; Fugitives from a Murderer; Witness to Murder; Role Reversals; Chase Movies; Men as Women; Transvestites; Bimbos; Sexy Women; Misunderstandings; Identities-Mistaken; Disguises; Prohibition Era; Blockbusters
(Tootsie; Sister Act; Victor/Victoria; Bosom Buddies TV SERIES)
(Ed: Much imitated classic, pure and simple)

Someone to Love, 1987, 105m, ★★★/$, ICA-International Rainbow/Par, R/S-P. A director throws a Valentine's Day party and interviews his friends about their love lives in this documentary. Orson Welles, Henry Jaglom, Andrea Marcovicci, Michael Emil, Sally Kellerman, Stephen Bishop. d. Henry Jaglom.

Documentaries; ROMANCE: DRAMA: Docudrama; Crossing the Line; Dinner Parties; Improvisational Films; Independent Films
(Eating; Can She Bake a Cherry Pie?)

Someone to Watch Over Me, 1987, 106m, ★★1/2/$$, Col/RCA-Col, R/S. A wealthy woman (Mimi Rogers) being stalked needs a bodyguard, so enter working class police detective hero (Tom Berenger) who soons falls for her as he follows her around. Lorraine Bracco,

Jerry Orbach, John Rubinstein. w. Howard Franklin, d. Ridley Scott.

DRAMA: ROMANCE: MELODRAMA: Romantic Drama; Romance-Triangles; Detectives-Police; Police Stories; Saving Someone; Bodyguards; Protecting Someone; Witnesses-Protecting; Romance-Class Crossed; Rich People; Women in Jeopardy; Cheating Men; Coulda Been Great (The Bodyguard)
(Ed: Great looking but the romance is hard to buy)

Something for Everyone, 1970, 110m, ★★½/$, National General/Key, Fox, R/S. A widowed Austrian countess is charmed by a traveling rogue into letting him stay with her. Angela Lansbury, Michael York, Anthony Corlan, Heidelinde Weis. w. Hugh Wheeler, N-adap. Harry Kressing (The Cook), d. Harold Prince.

COMEDY: COMEDY DRAMA: Black Comedy; Romance-Triangles; Malicious Menaces; Nuisances; Drifters; Gay Men; Bisexuality; Mothers & Sons; Ahead of Its Time; Royalty; Austria
(Entertaining Mr. Sloane; Brimstone & Treacle; The Servant; Cabaret)

Something to Talk About, 1995, 105m, ★★½/$$$, WB/WB, R/S-P. When a young southern housewife catches her hubby cheating, she debates the possibility of taking him back. Julia Roberts, Dennis Quaid, Robert Duvall, Gena Rowlands, Kyra Sedgwick, Brett Cullen. w. Callie Khouri, d. Lasse Hallstrom.

COMEDY-DRAMA: Marriage Drama; Mothers & Daughters; Southerns; Young Women; Cheating Men; Housewives; Horses; Female Protagonists; Female Screenwriters
(Steel Magnolias; Thelma and Louise; Heartburn)

Something Wicked This Way Comes, 1983, 95m, ★★½/$, Disney/Disney, PG/V. In a small town in Illinois, a traveling carnival comes with strange magical powers. Jason Robards, Jonathan Pryce, Diane Ladd, Pam Grier, Royal Dano. w. N-adap. Ray Bradbury, d. Jack Clayton.

HORROR: SUSPENSE: SCI-FI: Magic; Cures/Elixirs; Librarians; Circus Life; Coulda Been Good
(The Seven Faces of Dr. Lao; The Illustrated Man)

Something Wild, 1961, 112m, ★★½/$, UA/NA. After a woman is raped, she moves in with an auto repairman and re-adjusts to normal life. Carroll Baker, Ralph Meeker, Mildred Dunnock, Charles Watts, Jean Stapleton. w. Jack Garfein, Alex Karmel, N-adap. Alex Karmel (Mary Ann), d. Jack Garfein.

DRAMA: Social Drama; Rape/Rapists; **MELODRAMA: ROMANCE:** Starting Over; Female Protagonists; Forgotten Films; Coulda Been Great; Ahead of Its Time
(The Accused; Cry Rape)

Something Wild, 1986, 112m, ★★★½/$$, Orion/Orion, R/EV-S-P-FN-MRN. A mild-mannered businessman (Jeff Daniels) meets up with a free-wheeling wild girl (Melanie Griffith) who takes him on an unexpected leave of absence and senses, only to be pursued by her psychotic boyfriend (Ray Liotta). w. E. Max Frye, d. Jonathan Demme.

COMEDY DRAMA: Black Comedy; **ROMANCE:** Tragi-Comedy; Film Noir-Modern; Screwball Comedy; Men Proving Themselves; Wild People; Free Spirits; Con Artists; Reunions-Class; Marriage-Fake; Romance-Triangles; Jealous Men; Road Movies; Love-Dangerous; Dangerous Women; Dangerous Men; Evil Men; Men Fighting Over Women; Underrated; Hidden Gems
(Into the Night; What's Up, Doc?)

Sometimes a Great Notion, 1971, 114m, ★★★/$$, Universal/MCA-U, PG. An outspoken and ruggedly determined family of woodsmen causes trouble for a big lumber company in an Oregon town. Paul Newman, Henry Fonda, Lee Remick, Richard Jaeckel (BSActor), Michael Sarrazin. w. John Gay, N-adap. Ken Kesey, d. Paul Newman. BOSong. Oscars: 2-0.

DRAMA: TRAGEDY: Family Drama; Life Transitions; Fighting the System; Working Class; Mountain People; Rural Life; Coulda Been Great; Actor Directors

Somewhere I'll Find You, 1942, 108m, ★★½/$$$, MGM/MGM-UA. Two brothers, both covering World War II for the U.S. wire service, track down the mutual object of their affections in China, and the fight for her favor continues anew. Clark Gable, Lana Turner, Robert Sterling, Patricia Dane, Reginald Owen. w. Marguerite Roberts, SS-adap. Charles Hoffman, d. Wesley Ruggles.

MELODRAMA: ROMANCE: Romance-Triangles; Brothers; Men in Conflict; Men Fighting Over Women; World War II Stories; Asia; China; Journalists

Somewhere in Time, 1980, 104m, ★★★/$$, Universal/MCA-U, PG. A writer who believes himself to be reincarnated goes back in time to rekindle a romance he had in his former life with a beautiful actress around the turn of the century. Christopher Reeve, Christopher Plummer, Jane Seymour, Teresa Wright. w. N-adap. Richard Matheson (Bid Time Return), d. Jeannot Szwarc. BOScore, BCostume. Oscars: 2-0.

MELODRAMA: ROMANCE: Romantic Drama; Romance-Boy Wants Girl; Romance-Older Women/Younger Men; Time Travel; Reincarnation; Infatuations; Obsessions; Dreams; Actresses; Lyrical Films; Writers What If . . . Stories; Hotel; Hidden Gems; Old-Fashioned Recent Films
(Berkeley Square; Time After Time)

Sommersby, 1993, 115m, ★★★/$$$, WB/WB, PG-13/S. A man returns from the Civil War (Richard Gere) to his wife (Jodie Foster) and farm, but she's not sure he's the man who left her several years before. Bill Pullman. d. Jon Amiel.

ROMANCE: DRAMA: MELODRAMA: Romantic Drama; Return of Spouse; Costume Drama; Civil War Era; Dead-Back from the; Impostors; Romance-Triangles; Identities-Assumed; Ku Klux Klan; Southerns; Foreign Film Remakes; Coulda Been Great

REMAKE OF: The Return of Martin Guerre

A Song Is Born, 1948, 113m, ★★½/$$, Goldwyn-UA/Goldwyn. A stripper must hide from the mob in a library where they're working on a dictionary of slang; the arrangement turns out to be mutually beneficial. Danny Kaye, Virginia Mayo, Hugh Herbert, Steve Cochran, Felix Bressart, J. Edward Bromberg, Louis Armstrong, Benny Goodman, Lionel Hampton, Tommy Dorsey. w. Harry Tugend, d. Howard Hawks.

MUSICAL: COMEDY: Musical Comedy; **ROMANCE:** Musical Romance; Romantic Comedy; Romance-Opposites Attract; Hiding Out; Fugitives from the Mob; Mob Comedy; Smart vs. Dumb; Extroverted vs. Introverted; Strippers; Professors; Nerds; Mob Girls; Free Spirits; Wild People; Shy People

MUSICAL REMAKE OF: Ball of Fire. (Ed: Why remake this and why so soon after the original in 1941?)

The Song of Bernadette, 1943, 156m, ★★★/$$$$, 20th/Fox. A poor, simple, country girl sees the Virgin Mary in the south of France, and Lourdes is born. Jennifer Jones (**BActress**), William Eythe, Charles Bickford (BSActor), Vincent Price, Lee J. Cobb, Gladys Cooper (BSActress), Anne Revere (BSActress). w. George Seaton (BScr), N-adap. Franz Werfel, d. Henry King (BDirector). BPicture, BSound, BEdit, **BB&WArt, BB&WCin, BScore**. Oscars: 12-4.
MELODRAMA: Historical Drama; Religion; Ordinary People Stories; Miracles; Illusion/Hallucinations; Saintly People; Nuns; Priests
(The Nun's Story; Sister Kenny; Keys to the Kingdom; The Bells of St. Mary's)
Song of Love, 1947, 118m, ★★★/$$, MGM/MGM-UA. A biopic of Brahms and Schumann, who were friends, centering around Schuman's wife, Clara. Katharine Hepburn, Paul Henreid, Robert Walker, Henry Daniel, Leo G. Carroll. w. Ivan Tors, Irmgard Von Cube, Allen Vincent, Robert Ardrey, d. Clarence Brown.
MELODRAMA: Music Composers; Musicians; Woman Behind the Man; Friendships-Great; Friendships-Male; Forgotten Films
(Break of Hearts; Impromptu)
(Ed: Mostly worth it only to Hepburn fans)
Song of Norway, 1970, 141m, ★★¹/₂/$$, ABC/Fox, G. Grieg the Viking has many musical adventures in his beautiful Norwegian countryside. Toralv Maurstad, Florence Henderson, Christina Schollin, Frank Poretta, Harry Secombe, Edward G. Robinson, Robert Morley, Oscar Homolka. w. d. Andrew Stone.
MUSICALS: Fantasy; Biographies; Music Composers; Scandinavia; Small-Town Life; Scenery-Outstanding
(The Sound of Music; Finian's Rainbow)
Song of the Islands, 1942, 75m, ★★¹/₂/$$, 20th/Fox. In the South Pacific, the son of a Texas cattle rancher is snagged by a beautiful Irish lass. Betty Grable, Victore Mature, Jack Oakie, Thomas Mitchell, Hilo Hattie. w. Joseph Schrank, Robert Pirosh, Robert Ellis, Helen Logan, d. Walter Lang.
MUSICALS: ROMANCE: Musical Romance; Romance-Girl Wants Boy; Islands; South Pacific
Song of the South, 1946, 94m, ★★★¹/₂/$$$, Disney/NA, G. Uncle Remus, an elderly black servant, tells his family's children stories about Brer Rabbit and the tar baby and other delightful animated creatures. Ruth Warrick, Bobby Driscoll, James Baskett, Luana Patten, Lucile Watson, Hattie McDaniel. w. Dalton Raymond, d. Harve Foster. **BOSong**, "Zippity Doo-dah," BScore. Oscars: 2-1.
COMEDY DRAMA: CHILDREN'S: FAMILY: MUSICALS: Musical Cartoons; Animation-Partial; Storytellers; Black Men; Southerns; Civil War Era; Plantation Life; Rabbits; Hidden Gems
(So Dear to My Heart; Gone With the Wind)
(Ed: A beautiful film which has ostensibly been withheld from release, unlike other similar films of the period, because of accusations of, or fears of, racial stereotyping)
Song of the Thin Man, 1947, 86m, ★★★/$$, MGM/MGM-UA. The last of the series with Nick and Nora after killer of a big band leader. William Powell, Myrna Loy, Kennan Wynn, Dean Stockwell, Gloria Grahame, Jayne Meadows. d. Edward Buzzell.
MYSTERY: Comic Mystery; **MURDER: MURDER MYSTERY**: Detective Stories; Detective Couples; Big Band Era
(The Thin Man; The Thin Man Goes Home)
A Song to Remember, 1944, 113m, ★★★/$$$, Col/Col. Chopin's life and romance with George Sand is given the Hollywood treatment in this costume biopic. Cornel Wilde (BActor), Merle Oberon, Paul Muni, Stephen Bekassy, Nina Foch, George Coulouris, George Macready. w. Sidney Buchman, Ernst Marischka (BOStory), d. Charles Vidor. BCCin, BScore, BEdit. Oscars: 5-0.
DRAMA: MELODRAMA: ROMANCE: Biographies; Music Composers; Musicians; Costume Drama; Romance-Reluctant; Tomboys; Writers; Female Screenwriters
(Impromptu; Song of Love)
Song Without End, 1960, 142m, ★★¹/₂/$, Col/Col. Franz Liszt's trysts and life. Dirk Bogarde, Capucine, Genevieve Page, Patricia Morison, Ivan Desny, Martita Hunt. w. Oscar Millard, d. Charles Vidor, George Cukor.
MELODRAMA: ROMANCE: Biographies; Music Composers; Musicians; Costume Drama; Coulda Been Good
Songwriter, 1984, 94m, ★★¹/₂/$, Tri-Star/Col-Tri, PG/S. Two country-singing partners have professional and personal ups and downs. Kris Kristofferson, Willie Nelson, Melinda Dillon, Rip Torn, Lesley Ann Warren. w. Bud Shrake, d. Alan Rudolph. BSongScore. Oscars: 1-0.
MELODRAMA: DRAMA: Musicians; Songwriters; Country Singers; Country Music; Friendships-Male
(Honeysuckle Rose; Barbarosa)
Son of Dracula, 1943, 80m, ★★★/$$, Universal/MCA-U. In the South, a mysterious stranger named Alucard moves onto a plantation and proceeds to feast on Southern belles. w. Lon Chaney, Jr., Louise Allbritton, Robert Paige, Samuel S. Hinds, Evelyn Ankers. w. Eric Taylor, d. Robert Siodmak.
HORROR: Vampires; Southerns; Plantation Life; Revisionist Films; Forgotten Films; Hidden Gems; Camp; Cult Films; Female Screenwriters
(Inteview with the Vampire; Dracula)
Son of Frankenstein, 1939, 99m, ★★★/$$$, Universal/MCA-U. The second sequel to Frankenstein, in which his son takes up daddy's hobbies, aided this time by a crippled shepherd. Basil Rathbone, Boris Karloff, Bela Lugosi, Lionel Atwill, Edgar Norton. w. Willis Cooper, d. Rowland V. Lee.
HORROR: Monsters-Manmade; Frankensteins; Fathers & Sons; Body Parts; Murders-One by One
Son of Kong, 1933, 69m, ★★¹/₂/$$$, RKO/Media. Carl Denham, the producer who brought Kong to Broadway, is chased out of New York by his backers seeking repayment for Kong's destruction. So he goes back to Kong Island and finds baby Kong. Robert Armstrong, Helen Mack, Frank Reicher, John Marston, Victor Wong. w. Ruth Rose, d. Ernest B. Schoedsack.
ACTION: ADVENTURE: Animal Monsters; Islands; Primates; Coulda Been Good; Female Screenwriters
SEQUEL TO: King Kong
(Ed: Might have made a good satire)
Son of Lassie, 1945, 100m, ★★¹/₂/$$, MGM/MGM-UA. Lassie fights the Nazis. Peter Lawford, Donald Crisp, June Lockhart, Nigel Bruce, Leon Ames, Nils Asther. w. Jeanne Bartlett, d. S. Sylvan Simon.
FAMILY: CHILDREN'S: Pet Stories; Dogs; Nazi Stories; World War II Era; Heroes-Unlikely; Child Protagonists; Scandinavia

Son of Paleface, 1952, 95m, ★★★/$$$, Par/Par. A female outlaw is sought after by a lovable goof and a suave government man. Bob Hope, Roy Rogers, Jane Russell, Trigger. w. Frank Tashlin, Joseph Quillan, Robert L. Welch, d. Frank Tashlin. BOSong. Oscars: 1-0.
COMEDY: Comedy-Slapstick; **WEST-ERNS:** Western Comedy; Criminals-Female; **ROMANCE:** Romantic Comedy; Men Fighting Over Women; Nerds; Fools-Bumbling
SEQUEL TO Paleface.
(Fancy Pants; Calamity Jane)
Son of Sinbad, 1955, 88m, ★★½/$$, RKO/VCI. The Caliph finds Sinbad and Omar Khayyam tresspassing in his domain and imprisons them both. They must escape and return with the secret of green fire. Dale Robertson, Vincent Price, Sally Forrest. w. Aubrey Wisberg, Jack Pollexfen, d. Ted Tetzlaff.
ADVENTURE: ACTION: Mythology; Escape Adventure; Cures/Elixirs; Ancient Times; Middle East; Arab People
Sons and Lovers, 1960, 103m, ★★★½/$$$, 20th/NA. A young working class man comes of age and falls in love in Nottingham. Dean Stockwell, Trevor Howard (BActor), Wendy Hiller, Mary Ure (BSActress), Donald Pleasence. w. Gavin Lambert, T. E. B. Clarke (BAScr), N-adap. D. H. Lawrence, d. Jack Cardiff (BDirector). BPicture, **BB&WCin,** BB&WArt. Oscars: 7-0.
DRAMA: MELODRAMA: Character Studies; Coming of Age; Young Men; Working Class; Mining Towns; England; Small-town Life; Classic Literary Adaptations
(Jude the Obscure; Women in Love)
The Sons of Katie Elder, 1965, 122m, ★★½/$$$, Par/Par. Four outlaw brothers reconnect at their mother's funeral and get into more trouble. John Wayne, Dean Martin, Michael Anderson, Jr., Earl Holliman, Martha Hyer, Jeremy Slate, James Gregory, George Kennedy. w. Allan Weiss, William H. Wright, Harry Essex, d. Henry Hathaway.
WESTERNS: COMEDY DRAMA: Funerals; Reunions; Brothers; Men in Conflict; Fathers & Sons
Sons of the Desert, 1934, 68m, ★★★½/$$$, Hal Roach/Media. Laurel and Hardy tell their wives that they're going on a health cruise, but actually slip off to Chicago. Stan Laurel, Oliver Hardy,

Charlie Chase, Mae Busch. w. Frank Craven, Byron Morgan, d. William A. Seiter.
COMEDY: Comedy of Errors; Comedy-Slapstick; Forgotten Films; Vacations; Chicago
(The Piano; Bonnie Scotland)
Sophia Loren, Her Own Story, 1980, 150m, ★★½/$$$, NBC/HBO. Loren plays not only herself but her mother as she rises out of the slums of Naples to stardom. Sophia Loren, Armand Assante, Ed Flanders, John Gavin. w. Joanne Crawford, NF-adap. A.E. Hotchner, d. Mel Stuart.
MELODRAMA: Fame-Rise to; Biographies; Autobiographical Stories; Autobiographical Stars; Actresses; Hollywood Biographies; Curiosities; Italians; Rags to Riches; Mothers & Daughters; Multiple Performances; TV Movies
(Aurora; Two Women)
Sophie's Choice, 1982, 152m, ★★★★/$$$, ITC-Universal/MCA-U, R/S-V. A young Southern writer (Peter MacNicol) rents a room below a manic man (Kevin Kline) and his girlfriend (Meryl Streep, **BActress**) who turns out to have a dark past from World War II and is haunted by those secrets. w. d. Alan J. Pakula (BAScr), N-adap. William Styron. BArt, BCost, BOScore. Oscars: 5-1.
DRAMA: ROMANCE: TRAGEDY: Secrets-Haunting; Children-Parting with; Romance-Doomed; Romance-Triangles; Jealousy; Mental Illness; World War II-Post Era; Nazi Stories; Concentration Camps; Immigrants; Writers; Infatuations; Virgins; Tennessee Williams-esque; Writers; Narrated Films
(Enemies; A Love Story)
(Ed: Though it deviates in tone and plot from the great novel, it still resonates strongly, due mostly to Streep's legendary performance)
Sophisticated Gents, 1981, 200m, ★★★/$$, PBS/Xenon. A black sports club has a reunion and the evolution of the black man's role in modern society is seen in the changes over the years. Paul Winfield, Rosie Grier, Bernie Casey, Rosalind Cash, Denise Nicholas, Alfre Woodard. w. Melvin Van Peebles, N-adap. *The Junior Bachelor Society*, John Williams, d. Harry Falk.
DRAMA: Episodic Stories; Reunions; Ensembles-Male; Black Men; Black

Casts; Race Relations; Multiple Stories; TV Movies; Black Screenwriters; Buppies
(A Gathering of Old Men; The Color Purple)
So Proudly We Hail, 1943, 125m, ★★★/$$$, Par/NA. The army nurses who served so gallantly in World War II are given their due in this war movie focusing on the enlisted women for a change. Claudette Colbert, Paulette Goddard (BSActress), Veronica Lake, George Reeves, Barbara Britton, Walter Abel, Sonny Tufts. w. Allan Scott (BScr), d. Mark Sandrich. BB&WCin. Oscars: 3-0.
MELODRAMA: War Stories; World War II Stories; Women at War; Nurses; Women's Films; Female Protagonists; Patriotic Films
(China Beach)
Sorcerer, 1977, 121m, ★★/$$, Universal/MCA-U, R/V. A group of desperate men in Latin America are willing to drive trucks loaded with nitro-glycerine across a dangerous mountain pass in hopes of reaping a large reward. Roy Scheider, Bruno Cremer, Francisco Rabal, Amidou. w. Walon Green, N-adap. George Arnaud, d. William Friedkin. BSound. Oscars: 1-0.
SUSPENSE: ADVENTURE: Rewards at Stake; Man vs. Machine; Men in Conflict; Quests; Journies; Nightmare Journies; Nightmares; Central America; Truck Drivers; Oil People; Coulda Been Great; Foreign Film Remakes; Flops-Major
REMAKE OF: Wages of Fear, by Henri-Georges Clouzot
(Ed: For those who haven't seen the original, some of the basic premise may be enough to hang onto for a while, but otherwise, forget it)
So Red the Rose, 1935, 82m, ★★½/$$, Par/NA. In the mid-1800s, a Southern family is tested by but ultimately struggles through the Civil War. Margaret Sullavan, Randolph Scott, Walter Connolly, Elizabeth Patterson. w. Laurence Stallings, Maxwell Anderson, Edwin Justus Mayer, N-adap. Stark Young, d. King Vidor.
MELODRAMA: War Stories; Civil War Era; Family Drama; Southerns; Plantations
(Gone With the Wind; Shenandoah)
Sorrowful Jones, 1949, 88m, ★★★/$$, Par/Par. A bookie and his small-time gangster cohorts befriend a street waif and become her extended family. Bob Hope, Lucille Ball, William Demarest,

Bruce Cabot, Mary Jane Saunders. w. Melville Shavelson, Edmund Hartmann, Jack Rose, SS-adap. Damon Runyan, d. Sidney Lanfield.

COMEDY: COMEDY DRAMA: Tearjerkers; Orphans; Girls; Fathers-Surrogate; Con Artists; Mob Comedy; Horses
REMAKE: Little Miss Marker.
(Little Miss Marker; Lost Angel; Life with Mikey; Three Men & a Baby)

Sorry, Wrong Number, 1948, 89m, ★★★★/$$$, RKO/Goldwyn. A bedfast, wealthy woman (Barbara Stanwyck, BActress) is receiving strange phone calls, while overhearing others, and is able to piece together her husband's (Burt Lancaster) shady dealings which may have put her life in jeopardy. w. P-adap. Lucille Fletcher, d. Anatole Litvak. Oscars: 1-0.
SUSPENSE: Race Against Time; Film Noir; Women in Jeopardy; Eavesdropping; Disabled People; Disabled People in Jeopardy; Disabled but Nominated; Mob Stories; Saving Yourself; Telephone Terror; Female Screenwriters; Female Protagonists; Hidden Gems
REMADE: TV, 1987.
(Wait Until Dark; La Souffle au Coeur, see *M* for *Murder; Murmur of the Heart*)

Soul Man, 1986, 101m, ★★¹/2/$$$, New World/New World, PG-13/P-S. In order to afford law school an upper-class white college student dies his skin black to get a minority scholarship. C. Thomas Howell, Rae Dawn Chong, Arye Gross, Melora Hardin, Leslie Nielsen. w. Carol Black, d. Steve Miner.
COMEDY: SATIRE: Impostors; Race Relations; Black vs. White; White as Black; Law School; Lawyers; What If . . . Stories; Disguises; Sleeper Hits; Female Screenwriters
(Carbon Copy; Black Like Me; Trading Places; I Passed for White; True Identity)

Souls at Sea, 1937, 93m, ★★★/$$, Par/NA. When his ship becomes grounded on an intelligence mission, a naval officer in the 1800s has to make a difficult decision in which lives will be lost either way. When he and part of his crew are returned to safety, he faces a courtmartial trial. Gary Cooper, George Raft, Frances Dee, Henry Wilcoxon, Harry Carey. w. Grover Jones, Dale Van Every, d. Henry Hathaway. BScore, BArt. Oscars: 2-0.

ADVENTURE: Adventure at Sea;
DRAMA: Survival Drama; Death-Impending; Shipwrecks; Ships; Spies; Sailors; Decisions-Big; Ethics; 1800s
(Mutiny on the Bounty; The Caine Mutiny; Court Martial)

The Sound and the Fury, 1959, 117m, ★★¹/2/$$, 20th/CBS-Fox. The sensitive son of a once-prominent Southern plantation owner fallen on hard times reflects on what we would now call his "dysfunctional family." Yul Brynner, Joanne Woodward, Margaret Leighton, Stuart Whitman, Ethel Waters, Jack Warden. w. Irving Ravetch, Harriet Frank, Jr., N-adap. William Faulkner, d. Martin Ritt.
DRAMA: MELODRAMA: Family Drama; Episodic Stories; Mental Illness; Eccentric People; Southerns; Plantations; Mississippi; Coulda Been Great; Classic Literary Adaptations
(The Cherry Orchard; The Long, Hot Summer; Sanctuary)
(Ed: Watered-down misfire with everything fairly askew, starting with Brynner's miscasting)

Sounder, 1972, 105m, ★★★★/$$$, 20th/CBS-Fox, G. A family story in which the son of a black sharecropper in the Depression-era South befriends a stray dog. Paul Winfield (BActor), Cicely Tyson (BActress), Kevin Hooks, Carmen Matthews, Taj Mahal. w. Lonnie Elder III (BAScr), N-adap. William H. Armstrong, d. Martin Ritt. BPicture. Oscars: 4-0.
DRAMA: MELODRAMA: Tearjerkers; Pet Stories; Dogs; Family Drama; Depression Era; Southerns; Black Casts; Black Men; Black Women; Poor People; Poor Kids; Black Screenwriters
(Old Yeller; The Color Purple; Almost a Man)

The Sound of Music, 1965, 128m, ★★★¹/2/$$$$$, 20th/Fox, G. A singing nanny (Julie Andrews, BActress) teaches several unruly, stuffy children of a captain (Christopher Plummer) how to let loose and have fun, even though she, herself, was kicked out of an abbey for it. Eleanor Parker, Peggy Wood (BSActress), Heather Menzies, Richard Haydn, Anna Lee, Marni Nixon. w. Ernest Lehman (BAScr), MP-adap. Rodgers & Hammerstein, d. Robert Wise (**BDirector**). **BPicture**, BCCinema, **BEdit**, BCArt, BCCostume, **BSound**, **BMScore**. Oscars: 10-5.

MUSICAL: ROMANCE: Musical Romance;
COMEDY DRAMA: FAMILY: Family Comedy; Escape Adventure; Babysitters; Free Spirits; Nuns; World War II Era; Nazi Stories; Germans as Enemy; Blockbusters; Scenery-Outstanding; Alps; Austria
(The King and I; Song of Norway; Sister Act; Mary Poppins)

Soup for One, 1982, 84m, ★★¹/2/$, WB/WB, R/S-P. A Jewish nerd wants a WASPy pretty woman, but she doesn't want him-at first. Saul Rubinek, Marcia Strassman, Gerrit Graham, Andrew Martin. w. d. Jonathan Kaufer.
COMEDY: COMEDY DRAMA: Romance-Boy Wants Girl; Romance-Reluctant; Elusive Women; Jewish People; Nerds; Nerds & Babes; Neurotic People; New York Life; Curiosities; Writer-Directors
(Annie Hall; I Don't Buy Kisses Anymore)
(Ed: Compared to Woody Allen, but mostly because of the Jewish connection)

South Central, 1992, 99m, ★★/$$, WB/WB, R/EP-EV-S. A con gets out of prison and goes back to the Los Angeles slum to get to know his son who's now on the same criminal track. Glenn Plummer, Carl Lumbly, Christian Coleman. w. d. Steve Anderson, N-adap. *Crips*, Donald Baker.
DRAMA: Crime Drama; Fathers & Sons; Ex-Convicts; Black Casts; Black Men; Black Screenwriters; Black Directors; Gangs-Black
(Boys in the Hood; Juice; Zebrahead)

Southern Comfort, 1981, 106m, ★★★/$, 20th/Fox, Sultan, R/P-V. A group of greenhorns from the National Guard play wargames in the Louisiana swamps which end up taking on a frightening reality when local Cajuns take up arms against them. Keith Carradine, Powers Boothe, Fred Ward. w. Michael Kane, Walter Hill, David Giler, d. Walter Hill.
DRAMA: TRAGEDY: Survival Drama; Nightmares; Nightmare Journies; Men in Conflict; Rednecks; Southerns; Swamp Life; Louisiana; Forgotten Films; Hidden Gems; Overlooked at Release
(Deliverance; Bad Company [1972])

The Southerner, 1945, 91m, ★★★¹/2/$$, UA/Nos, Prism. A dirt-poor farmer struggles to make ends meet as his crops fail and other troubles fall upon his head. Zachary Scott, Betty Field, Beulah Bondi, J. Carroll Naish, Percy Kilbride, Blanche Yurka. w. d. Jean Renoir (BDirector). BScore. Oscars: 2-0.

DRAMA: MELODRAMA: Tearjerkers; Poor People; Farm Life; Farmers; Ordinary People Stories; Making a Living; Southerns; Capra-esque; Southerns-Foreign Directors of; Forgotten Film; Hidden Gems
(The Grapes of Wrath; God's Little Acre)
The Southern Star, 1969, 105m, ★★★/$$, Col/NA. A poor American traveling in West Africa at the turn of the century finds a famed diamond and is chased by a motley band of fortune seekers for it. An ostrich helps out. George Segal, Ursula Andress, Orson Welles, Ian Hendry, Michael Constantine. w. David Purshall, Jack Seddon, N-adap. Jules Verne, d. Sidney Hayers.
COMEDY DRAMA: ADVENTURE: Comic Adventure; Treasure Hunts; Jewel Thieves; Africa; Forgotten Films; Hidden Gems; 1900s
(Gold; Congo; The Pink Jungle)
A Southern Yankee, 1948, 90m, ★★★/$$, MGM/MGM-UA. A southern civilian during the Civil War finds himself in the northern camp and decides to spy for the boys down home. Red Skelton, Brian Donlevy, Arlene Dahl, George Coulouris, Lloyd Gough, John Ireland. w. Harry Tugend, d. Edward Sedgewick.
COMEDY: Spy Films; Spies; Spoofs-Spy; Southerns; Impostors; Undercover; North vs. South; Civil War Era
REMAKE OF: The General, by Buster Keaton.
(I Dood It; Fuller Brush Man; Fletch Lives)
South Pacific, 1958, 170m, ★★★/$$$$, Magna-UA/Fox. On the island of Bali, a French expatriot woos an American Navy nurse. Things are going along swimmingly until she discovers he has mixed-race children from a previous marriage, and her bigotry comes out. Mitzi Gaynor, Rossano Brazzi, Ray Walston, John Kerr, Juanita Hall. w. Paul Osborn, Richard Rogers, Oscar Hammerstein II, Joshua Logan, SS-adap. James A. Michener (Tales of the South Pacific), d. Joshua Logan. BCCin, BMScore, **BSound.**
Oscars: 3-1.
MUSICALS: ROMANCE: Musical Romance; Musical Drama; World War II Stories; Soldiers; South Pacific; Islands; Race Relations; Romance-Interracial; Female Among Males; Bigots; Pulitzer Prize Adaptations
(Oklahoma; State Fair; Carousel)

(Ed: Not all so serious as the synopsis may sound)
Soylent Green, 1973, 97m, ★★★/$$$, MGM/MGM-UA, PG/V-B&G. In the future, New York is so overcrowded that the government resorts to unheard-of remedies. Charlton Heston, Edward G. Robinson, Leigh Taylor-Young, Chuck Connors, Brock Peters, Joseph Cotten. w. Stanley R. Greenberg, N-adap. Harry Harrison (Make Room, Make Room), d. Richard Fleischer.
SCI-FI: MYSTERY: MURDER: MURDER MYSTERY: SATIRE: Social Drama; Social Satire; Message Films; Detective Stories; Apocalyptic Stories; Futuristic Films; Cannibalism; Government as Enemy; Poor People; New York Life; Inner City Life; Survival Drama
(The Omega Man; Consuming Passions)
Spaceballs, 1987, 96m, ★★¹/₂/$$, MGM-UA/MGM-UA, PG-13/P. A planet of goons overtakes the planet Druidia and tries to suck its atmosphere out. A cast of zany spoof characters from sci-fi epics tries to save the day. Mel Brooks, John Candy, Rick Moranis, Bill Pullman, Daphne Zuniga, Dom DeLuise, John Hurt, Joan Rivers (as the voice of Dot Matrix). w. Mel Brooks, Thomas Meehan, Ronny Graham, d. Mel Brooks.
COMEDY: Spoofs; Outer Space Movies; Comedy of Errors; Androids; Bathroom Humor; All-Star Cast
(Spoof of Star Wars)
Spaced Invaders, 1989, 100m, ★★¹/₂/$$$, Disney/Disney, PG. A bunch of bumbling aliens badly botch their attempt at taking over the Earth. Douglas Barr, Royal Dano, Ariana Richards, J. J. Anderson. w. Patrick Read Johnson, Scott Alexander, d. Patrick Read Johnson.
CHILDREN'S: FAMILY: Spoofs; Outer Space Movies; Aliens-Outer Space, Good; Fools-Bumbling; UFOs; Rule the World-Plot to; Little People; Sleeper Hits
Spacehunter, Adventures in the Forbidden Zone, 1983, 90m, ★/$$, Col/RCA-Col, PG. A hero (Peter Strauss) goes to another planet to rescue some women with the help of an urchin (Molly Ringwald). Ernie Hudson, Andrea Marcovicci, Michael Ironside. w. David Preston, Edith Rey, Dan Goldbert, Len Blum, d. Lamont Johnson.
SCI-FI: ADVENTURE: Comic Adventure; Wisecracking Sidekicks; Outer Space

Movies; Rescue Adventure; Kidnappings; 3-D Movies
(Buck Rogers in the 25th Century; Solarbabies)
(Ed: A terrible mess with bad special effects and a dumb story. Strauss' big breakthrough attempt in features was this?)
Spanking the Monkey, 1994, 99m, ★★★¹/₂/$$, Fine Line/Fine Line, R/ES-FN-MN-P. A college student returns home for a brief visit and winds up taking care of his bedfast mother while his stern, cold father goes to work. He's trapped and unsure of his sexuality, only further frustrated by a baiting girlfriend. The result is his realization of his attraction to his mother. Jeremy Davies, Elizabeth Newitt, Benjamin Hendrickson, Alberta Watson, Carla Gallo, Liberty Jean. w. d. David O. Russell.
DRAMA: Erotic Drama; Psychological Drama; Incest; Mothers & Sons; Oedipal Stories; Sexual Problems; Coming of Age; Young Men; Suicidal Tendencies; Incest; Sleeper Hits; Cult Films; Writer-Directors; Independent Films
(The Miracle; Angela; The Graduate; Ordinary People; Murmur of the Heart)
Sparkle, 1976, 98m, ★★¹/₂/$, WB/WB, PG. Three black girls rise to superstardom in the 60s. Hmm . . . Lonette McKee, Irene Cara, Philip Michael Thomas, Dawn Smith, Dorian Harewood. w. Joel Schumacher, d. Sam O'Steen.
MELODRAMA: Music Movies; Singers; Fame-Rise to; Black Women; Black Casts; Biographies-Fictional; Ensembles-Female; Forgotten Films; Curiosities; Female Protagonists
(Dreamgirls [Broadway musical]; The Five Heartbeats)
Spartacus, 1960, 196m, ★★★¹/₂/$$$$, Universal/MCA-U, PG/S. A slave in ancient Rome leads a revolt that ends in tragedy. Kirk Douglas, Laurence Olivier, Charles Laughton, Tony Curtis, Jean Simmons, Peter Ustinov (**BSActor**). w. Dalton Trumbo, N-adap. Howard Fast, d. Stanley Kubrick. **BCCin, BCArt, BCCostume,** BOScore, BEdit. Oscars: 6-4.
DRAMA: ADVENTURE: ACTION: TRAGEDY: Epics; Spectacles; Biblical Stories; Ancient Times; Political Unrest; Homo-eroticism; Friendships-Male; Slavery; Rebels; Heroes-Unlikely; Blockbusters; Production Design-Outstanding

(Ben-Hur; Fall of the Roman Empire; Becket)

Spawn of the North, 1938, ★★1/2/$$$, Par/NA. A group of Alaskan fishermen fight back when their waters are invaded by a Russian boat. George Raft, Henry Fonda, Dorothy Lamour, John Barrymore, Akim Tamiroff, Louise Platt. w. Talbot Jennings, Jules Furthman, d. Henry Hathaway.

DRAMA: MELODRAMA: Men in Conflict; Animal Rights; Hunters; Fishermen; Alaska

REMAKE: Alaska Seas, 1951.

Speak Easily, 1932, 83m, ★★1/2/$$, MGM/MGM-UA, Nos. A mild-mannered college professor is bequeathed a Broadway musical in the will of a long-lost relative and becomes enamored of the footlights. Buster Keaton, Jimmy Durante, Hedda Hopper. w. Ralph Spence, Lawrence E. Johnson, N-adap. Clarence Budington Kelland (Footlights), d. Edward Sedgewick.

COMEDY: Comedy-Slapstick; Heirs; Inheritances at Stake; Theater Life; Professors; Fish out of Water Stories; Forgotten Films

(Ed: A rare chance to hear Keaton speak!)

Speaking Parts, 1989, 92m, ★★★/$, Academy/Fox-Lorber, R/ES-FN-MN. A bisexual love triangle ensues between a screenwriter, a maid, and an aspiring actor. Michael McManus, Arsinee Khanjian, Gabrielle Rose, Tony Nardi, David Hemblen. w. d. Atom Egoyan.

DRAMA: ROMANCE: Art Films; Romance-Triangles; Ménage a Trois; Bisexuality; Gay Men; Writers; Actors; Canadian Films; Overlooked at Release; Writer-Directors

(The Adjuster; Law of Desire; A Man Like Eva; Exotica)

Special Bulletin, 1983, 105m, ★★★1/2/$$, NBC/WB. Terrorists have an atomic bomb which they explode in Charleston, South Carolina while news-casters are live on TV. Kathryn Walker, Ed Flanders, Chris Allport, Roxanne Hart. w. Marshall Herskovitz, Ed Zwick, d. Ed Zwick. Emmy winner.

DRAMA: TRAGEDY: Documentary Style; Bombs-Atomic; Journalists; Terrorists; Message Films; TV Movies; Hidden Gems

(The Day After; Testament)

(Ed: Excellent, harrowing, realistic portrayal which actually had people believing it was a live broadcast)

A Special Day, 1977, 105m, ★★★/$$$, Col/Col, PG/S. A housewife and a gay man have an affair of love when Hitler comes to visit during the war, but the glory only lasts that day as the reality of their love and the war around them sets in. Sophia Loren, Marcello Mastroianni (BActor). w. d. Ettore Scola. BFLFilm. Oscars: 2-0.

COMEDY DRAMA: ROMANCE: Romantic Comedy; Romance-Mismatched; Romance-Doomed; World War II Stories; One-Day Stories; Gay Men; Housewives; Hidden Gems; Faded Hits; Italian Films; Writer-Directors

(Marriage, Italian Style; Blood Feud)

Special Delivery, 1976, 99m, ★★1/2/$$, AIP/Vestron, PG. Three Vietnam vets plan a heist which gets screwed up and the money falls into the wrong hands. Bo Svenson, Cybill Shepherd, Vic Tayback, Deidre Hall, Jeff Goldblum. d. Paul Wendkos.

COMEDY DRAMA: Heist Stories; Capers; Criminals-Stupid; Comedy of Errors; Veterans-Vietnam

(Silver Bears; The Hot Rock; Quick Change)

The Specialist, 1994, 103m, ★★/$$$, WB/WB, R/S-P-EV-FN-MN. Sexy Stone wants the thugs who murdered her parents murdered and teases bomb specialist Stallone into blowing them up. The only problem is, he's reluctant to do the job and she goes in to get them herself. Sylvester Stallone, Sharon Stone, James Woods, Eric Roberts, Rod Steiger. w. Alexandra Seros, d. Luis Llosa.

ACTION: SUSPENSE: Murder of Parents; Bombs; Mob Stories; Erotic Thriller; Avenging Death of Someone; Detectives-Police; Double Crossings; Female Screenwriters; Miami

(Assassins; Nighthawks)

(Ed: Great score but dumb, dumb movie with dumb, dumb dialogue and only the mood set by the music to make it bearable)

Species, 1995, 101m, ★★1/2/$$$$, MGM/MGM-UA, R/S-FFN-EV-B&G. When a creature from outer space lands, a team of scientists chasing it discovers it has taken over the body of a beautiful young woman who will stop at nothing to mate-and will stop anything it mates with. Ben Kingsley, Michael Madsen, Alfred Molina, Forest Whitaker, Marg Helgenberger, Whip Hubley, Michele Williams, Natasha Henstridge. w. Dennis Feldman, d. Roger Donaldson.

SCI-FI: HORROR: Monsters-Human; Aliens-Outer Space; Evil; Evil Women; Sexy Women; Rogue Plots; Scientists; Race Against Time; Death By Sex

(The Thing; Alien Nation; Predator; The Borrower)

(Ed: A great premise falls apart midway through and is further done in by terrible special effects toward the end)

Speechless, 1994, 98m, ★★1/2/$$, MGM/MGM-UA, PG-13/S. Two political speechwriters (à la James Carville and Mary Matalin) from opposing parties spar with words and then wind up in bed-but before they realize they're political enemies. Michael Keaton, Geena Davis, Christopher Reeve, Bonnie Bedelia, Ernie Hudson, Charles Martin Smith, Gailard Sartain, Ray Baker. w. Robert King, d. Ron Underwood.

COMEDY: ROMANCE: Romantic Comedy; Romance-Bickering; Battle of the Sexes; Political Satire; Political Campaigns; Writers; Good Premise Unfulfilled; Coulda Been Great

(Woman of the Year; Best Friends; State of the Union; Running Mates)

(Ed: Often shrill, silly, and goofy without the finesse of the films it's imitating; they seem to just bicker to bicker)

Speed, 1994, 115m, ★★★/$$$$$, 20th/Fox, R/EV-P. A young surfer dude cop is tormented by an ex-cop who plants a bomb on a bus which will go off if it exceeds 50 miles an hour, leading to a non-stop cat-and-mouse race against time. Keanu Reeves, Sandra Bullock, Dennis Hopper, Joe Morton, Jeff Daniels, Glenn Plummer. w. Graham Yost, d. Jan DeBont.

ACTION: Race Against Time; Chase Stories; Car Chases; Car Crashes; Bombs; Police-Corruption; Police Stories; Psycho Killers; Rescue Drama; Men in Conflict; Hostage Situations; Subways; Buses; Die Hard Stories; Blockbusters

(Die Hard SERIES; Passenger 57; Lethal Weapon SERIES; The Net)

Speedway, 1968, 90m, ★★/$$, MGM/MGM-UA. Elvis hits the racetrack to get away from a lovely IRS agent hot on his tail, who may fall for his songs. Elvis Presley, Nancy Sinatra, Bill Bixby, Gale Gordon, William Schallert, Teri Garr. d. Norman Taurog.

ACTION: ROMANCE: MUSICALS: Music Movies; Car Racing; Fugitives from the Law; Singers

Spellbinder, 1988, 96m, ★★/$, 20th/Fox, R/S-V. A lawyer saves a woman from a rapist only to have her drag him into the occult and its danger. Timothy Daly, Kelly Preston, Rick Rossovich, Audra Lindley. w. Tracy Torme, d. Janet Greek.
SUSPENSE: HORROR: Rape/Rapists; Dangerous Romance; Saving Someone; Witches; Satanism; Lawyers; Female Directors; Female Screenwriters

Spellbound, 1945, 111m, ★★★¹/₂/$$$, Selznick-UA/CBS-Fox. A man (Gregory Peck) may have committed a murder or have been framed, but he doesn't remember what happened, so it's up to a psychiatrist (Ingrid Bergman) to figure out what's blocking him and prove his innocence. Leo G. Carroll, Michael Chekhov (BSActor). w. Ben Hecht, Angus MacPhail, N-adap. Francis Beeding (The House of Dr. Edwardes), d. Alfred Hitchcock (BDirector). BPicture, BScore, BB&WCin. Oscars: 5-1.
DRAMA: ROMANCE: Psychological Drama; MURDER: MYSTERY: MURDER MYSTERY: Psychologists as Detectives; Romance with Psychologist; Romance-Unprofessional; Framed?; Accused Unjustly; Identities-Assumed; Hypnotism; Amnesia; Medical Drama; Race Against Time; Secrets-Haunting; Ethics; Suspecting Oneself; Murder-Debate to Reveal Killer; Skiing; Nightmares; Dreams; Female Protagonists
(Marnie; Notorious)

Spencer's Mountain, 1963, 121m, ★★★/$$$, WB/WB, G. During the Depression, a rural southern family copes with hard times and gets through on love and hard work. Henry Fonda, Maureen O'Hara, James MacArthur, Donald Crisp, Wally Cox, Mimsy Farmer. w. d. Delmer Daves, N-adap. Earl Hamner Jr.
MELODRAMA: COMEDY DRAMA: Family Drama; Family Comedy; Families-Large; Mountain People; Depression Era; Southerns
REMAKE: The Homecoming and The Waltons, TV SERIES.
(Shenandoah; The Southerner)

Spetters, 1980, 115m, ★★¹/₂/$$, Goldwyn/Goldwyn, R/S-P-FFN-MFN. Three motocross bikers share the same woman, a blond bombshell who gives them hot meals from the side of the track. Hans Van Tongeren, Renee Soutendijk, Toon Agterberg, Maarten Spanjer. w. Gerard Soeteman, d. Paul Verhoeven.

COMEDY DRAMA: ROMANCE: MELO-DRAMA: Romance-Triangles; Men Fighting Over Women; Young Men; Sexy Women; Motorcycles; Dutch Films
(The Fourth Man; Turkish Delight)
(Ed: Includes an amusing or shocking, depending on how you look at it, scene where the boys measure their penises. From the director who later went on to Basic Instinct fame and its famous genitalia display scene)

Sphinx, 1980, 118m, ★★/$, Orion-WB/WB, PG/V. A mystery/adventure in which an archaeologist discovers the secret of an ancient Egyptian treasure. Lesley-Anne Down, Frank Langella, Maurice Ronet, John Gielgud, Vic Tablian, Martin Benson, John Rhys-Davies. w. John Byrum, N-adap. Robin Cook, d. Franklin J. Schaffner.
SCI-FI: SUSPENSE: ADVENTURE: MYSTERY: Women in Jeopardy; Curses; Archaeologists; Egypt; Mummies; Coulda Been Good
(The Awakening; The Mummy)

The Spider's Stratagem, 1970, 97m, ★★★/$, Radiotelevisione Italiana-Red Film/New Yorker. A man who believed his father to be a war hero killed by fascists is disillusioned to find that he was, in fact, a traitor to the Resistance, killed by his own comrades. Giulio Brogi, Alida Valli, Tino Scotti, Pino Campanini. w. Bernardo Bertolucci, Eduardo de Gregorio, Marilu Parolini, SS-adap. Jorge Lujis Borges (The Theme of the Traitor and the Hero), d. Bernardo Bertolucci.
DRAMA: Illusions Destroyed; Fathers & Sons; Traitors; World War II Stories; Heroes-False; Italian Films; Art Films

Spies Like Us, 1985, 109m, ★★¹/₂/$$$$, WB/WB, PG/P. Two fools are mistaken as spies and wind up in a mess in the Middle East. Chevy Chase, Dan Aykroyd, Steve Forrest, Donna Dixon, Bruce Davison. w. Dan Aykroyd, Lowell Ganz, Babaloo Mandel, d. John Landis.
COMEDY: Spoof-Spy; Spies; Comedy of Errors; Fools-Bumbling; Identities-Mistaken; Coulda Been Good
(Hope & Crosby Road to . . . SERIES; S*P*Y*S)

Spinout, 1966, 93m, ★★/$$, MGM/MGM-UA. Elvis on the racetrack again. Elvis Presley, Shelly Fabares, Carl Betz, Diane McBain, Cecil Kellaway, Una Merkel. d. Norman Taurog.

ACTION: ROMANCE: MUSICALS: Music Movies; Car Racing; Singers

The Spiral Staircase, 1946, 83m, ★★★¹/₂/$$$, RKO/Fox. A psychopath on the rampage kills handicapped girls in a quaint New England town. Dorothy McGuire, George Brent, Kent Smith, Ethel Barrymore (BSActress), Rhys Williams. w. Mel Dineli, N-adap. Ethel Lina White (Some Must Watch), d. Robert Siodmack. Oscars: 1-0.
(Ed [1946 version]: One of the first contemporary style Women in Jeopardy or Disabled People in Jeopardy/Killer on the Loose tales and quite effective)

The Spiral Staircase, 1975, 89m, ★★¹/₂/$, WB/WB. A modern-day remake of above in color. Jacqueline Bisset, Christopher Plummer, Sam Wanamaker, Mildred Dunnock. w. Andrew Meredith, d. Peter Collinson.
SUSPENSE: MURDER: MYSTERY: MURDER MYSTERY: Women in Jeopardy; Disabled People in Jeopardy; Mute People; Serial Killers; Murders of Women; Houses-Creepy
(Hear No Evil; Night Must Fall)
(Ed [1975 version]: It falls flat, failing to create the same incredible mood and paranoia of the original)

Spirit of '76, 1991, 82m, ★★/$, Ind/NA. Time travelers come from the future planning to land in 1776 but instead wind up in 1976 at the height of disco. David Cassidy, Olivia D'Abo, Leif Garrett, Julie Brown. w. d. Lucas Reiner.
COMEDY: SCI-FI: Spoofs-Sci-Fi; Time Travel; Disco Era; 1970s; Writer-Directors; Coulda Been Good

The Spirit of St. Louis, 1957, 135m, ★★¹/₂/$$$, WB/WB. Charles Limbergh's historic record-breaking flight from New York to Paris is chronicled in this biopic. James Stewart, Murray Hamilton, Marc Connelly. w. Billy Wilder, Wendell Mayes, NF-adap. Charles Limbergh, d. Billy Wilder.
DRAMA: ADVENTURE: COMEDY DRAMA: Biographies; Pilots; Historical Drama; Race Against Time; 1920s
(The Lindbergh Kidnapping; The Glenn Miller Story)
(Ed: An oddity from Mr. Wilder-a mediocre film)

Spirit Rider, 1993, 120m, ★★★/$, Disney/Disney, G. An American Indian boy who's a foster child is taken back to his tribe as a teenager but has trouble adjusting. Herbie Barnes, Adam Beech, Graham Greene.

MELODRAMA: Teenagers; Orphans; Indians-American; Native Americans; Reunions; City vs. Country

Spirits of the Dead, see **Histoires Extraordinaires.**

Spitfire, 1934, 88m, ★★★/$$, RKO/Turner. A country gal from the Ozarks gets the fire and brimstone in her and alienates her community with her bogus faith healing and carrying on. Katharine Hepburn, Robert Young, Ralph Bellamy, Martha Sleeper, Louis Mason. w. Jane Murfin, P-adap. Lula Vollmer (*Triggeri*), d. John Cromwell.

COMEDY DRAMA: ROMANCE: City vs. Country; Religion; Free Spirits; Young Women; Girls; Hillbillies; Arkansas; Female Protagonists; Female Screenwriters

(Sylvia Scarlett; Ruby Gentry)

(Ed: A strange Hepburn film, but she makes it worth a look)

Splash!, 1984, 110m, ★★★1/2/$$$$, Touchstone/Touchstone, PG/FRN. A yuppie falls for a whacked-out mermaid with problems adjusting to life on dry land (and in New York). Tom Hanks, Daryl Hannah, Eugene Levy, John Candy, Dody Goodman, Shecky Greene. w. Lowell Ganz, Babaloo Mandel, Bruce Jay Friedman, Brian Glazer, d. Ron Howard.

COMEDY: Fish out of Water Stories; Mermaids; Romance-Mismatched; Sexy Women; Simple Minds; Chase Movies; Unbelieved; Scientists-Mad; Experiments; Government as Enemy; Sleeper Hits

(Miranda; Mr. Peabody & the Mermaid)

(Ed: The concept is not new, as much as they'd like to think so, but the updating is)

Splendor in the Grass, 1961, 124m, ★★★★/$$$$, WB/WB. A young girl (Natalie Wood, BActress) is head over heels in love with the town heartthrob (Warren Beatty) who, when the depression hits, leaves for college, putting her into a lonely tailspin. Pat Hingle, Audrey Christie, Sandy Dennis, Zohra Lampert, Barbara Loden. w. William Inge (BOScr), d. Elia Kazan. Oscars: 2-1.

DRAMA: MELODRAMA: Coming of Age; Love-First; Romantic Drama; Romance-Class Conflicts; Romance-Doomed; Teenagers; Young Women; Episodic Stories; Mental Illness; Nervous Breakdowns; Depression; Depression Era; Midwestern Life; Small-town Life;

Tennessee Williams-esque; Female Protagonists; Underrated; Hidden Gems (Summer and Smoke; Picnic; Bus Stop; Love with the Proper Stranger; Lilith)

Split Image, 1982, 111m, ★★1/2/$, Polygram-Ind/Sultan, R/S. An all-American jock gets indoctrinated by a cult and his family struggles to get him out. Michael O'Keefe, Karen Allen, James Woods, Elizabeth Ashley, Brian Dennehy, Peter Fonda. w. Scott Spencer, Robert Kaufman, Robert Mark Kamen, d. Ted Kotcheff.

DRAMA: Social Drama; Docudrama; Message Films; Cults; Brainwashing; Young Men; Religion

(Ticket to Heaven; Serial)

Split Second, 1991, 90m, ★★/$, HBO/HBO, R/P-EV-B&G. In the not-too-distant future, a London cop hunts down a monster on a killing rampage. Rutger Hauer, Kim Cattrall, Neil Duncan, Michael J. Pollard. w. Gary Scott Thompson, d. Tony Maylam.

ACTION: Police Stories; Trail of a Killer; Manhunt; Futuristic Films; Monsters; Kill the Beast; Serial Killer; London

REMAKE/RETREAD OF: Bladerunner.

Splitting Heirs, 1993, 87m, ★★/$, U/MCA-U, PG-13/S-P. A man who was abandoned in the 60s by his super mod parents returns to the family castle when he learns of his real heritage, but other relatives don't want to share the place. Eric Idle, Barbara Hershey, John Cleese, Rick Moranis. w. Eric Idle, d. Robert M. Young.

COMEDY: Inheritances at Stake; Children-Long Lost; Mothers-Troublesome; Royalty; Royalty-Sudden; Rich People; Children-Abandoned; Monty Pythoners

(Greedy; Nuns on the Run)

(Ed: Idle is older than his mother, played by Hershey, which was apparently supposed to be funny. What would have been funnier was to cut the lead out)

The Spoilers, 1942, 88m, ★★★/$$$, U/MCA-U. When goldminers are ripped-off, they set out for revenge in the Old Yukon. John Wayne, Randolph Scott, Marlene Dietrich, Harry Carey. d. Ray Enright.

ADVENTURE: WESTERNS: Gold Mining; Revenge; Con Artists; 1890s; Men in Conflict; Faded Hits

Spring Break, 1983, 101m, ★1/2/$$, Col/Col, R/S-FN. Four college boys go to Florida for break and meet the babes, but

have trouble with their boyfriends. Perry Lang, Steve Bassett. d. Sean S. Cunningham.

COMEDY: Erotic Comedy; Teenagers; Teenage Movies; Vacations; Party Movies (Fraternity Vacation; Where the Boys Are '84)

Springtime in the Rockies, 1942, 91m, ★★1/2/$$$, 20th/Fox. Several people on vacation in the Rockies fall in love when the snow thaws. Betty Grable, John Payne, Carmen Miranda, Edward Everett Horton, Cesar Romero. w. Walter Bullock, Ken Englund, d. Irving Cummings.

MUSICALS: ROMANCE: Musical Romance; Vacations; Vacation Romance; Mountain People; Snow Settings; Ensemble Films

(Ed: Nice title, ho-hum musical)

The Spy in Black (U-Boat 29), 1939, 82m, ★★★/$$, Ind/Embassy, Nos. German spies during the war wonder who's double-crossing whom. Conrad Veidt, Valerie Hobson, Hay Petrie, Helen Haye, Sebastian Shaw. w. Emeric Pressburger, Roland Pertwee, N-adap. J. Storer Clouston, d. Michael Powell.

SUSPENSE: MYSTERY: Spy Films; Spies; World War II Stories; Submarines; Double Crossings; Mindgames; Germans as Enemy; Forgotten Films

(Das Boot; The Devil and the Deep)

Spymaker, The Secret Life of Ian Fleming, 1990, 96m, ★★★/$$, Turner/Turner. Tales of Fleming's early days in the British Secret Service. Jason Connery, Kristin Scott Thomas, Patricia Hodge. d. Ferdinand Fairfax.

ACTION: Spy Films; Spies; Secret Agents; Biographies; Biographies-Fictional; Writers; 1940s; James Bond

S*P*Y*S, 1974, 100m, ★★/$, UA/Fox, R/S-P. A bunch of maverick cutups who somehow got into the CIA hunt down KGB agents in Europe and China. Elliott Gould, Donald Sutherland, Zouzou, Joss Ackland, Kenneth Griffith. w. Malcolm Marmorstein, Lawrence J. Cohen, Fred Freeman, d. Irwin Kershner.

ACTION: COMEDY: Action Comedy; Spoofs-Spy; CIA Agents; KGB Agents; Cold War Era; Buddy Films; Flops-Major (M*A*S*H; Spies Like Us)

The Spy Who Came in from the Cold, 1965, 112m, ★★★/$$, Par/Par. A British master spy gets even with his East German nemesis in an unorthodox fashion. Richard Burton (BActor), Claire

615

Bloom, Oskar Werner, Peter Van Eyck, Sam Wanamaker, Rupert Davies, Cyril Cusack. w. Paul Dehn, Guy Trosper, N-adap. John Le Carré, d. Martin Ritt. Oscars: 1-0.

DRAMA: Spy Films; Spies; Revenge; Mindgames; Communists; Berlin; Cold War Era; Iron Curtain-Behind the (The Russia House; The Looking Glass War)
(Ed: Interesting, realistic, and a great, cold atmosphere, but not particularly entertaining)

The Spy Who Loved Me, 1977, 125m, ★★★/$$$$, UA/MGM-UA, PG. A mad-man builds a huge underwater base from which to launch his takeover of the world, and James Bond must join forces with a beautiful Russian spy. Roger Moore, Barbara Bach, Curt Jurgens, Richard Kiel, Caroline Munro, Walter Gotell. w. Christopher Wood, Richard Maibaum, N-adap. Ian Fleming, d. Lewis Gilbert. BOSong. Oscars: 1-0.

ACTION: Action Comedy; Secret Agents; Spy Films; Spies; Rule the World-Plot to; Underwater Adventure; James Bond; Russians; Cold War Era
(Moonraker; For Your Eyes Only)

Squanto: A Warrior's Tale, 1994, 102m, ★★1/2/$$, Disney/Disney, PG/V. The story of the Indian/Native American who befriended the pilgrims just in time for Thanksgiving and his travails with the new ways of the white man. Adam Beach, Michael Gambon, Nathaniel Parker, Mandy Patinkin. w. Darlene Caraviotto, d. Xavier Koller.

CHILDREN'S: FAMILY: Early America; Indians-American; 1600s; Female Screenwriters
(Pocahontas)

Square Dance, 1986, 112m, ★★★/$, NBC-Island/NA, PG. A dreamy girl in a small Texas town leaves her grandfather to live with her stern mother and has a romance with a young retarded man. Jason Robards, Jane Alexander, Winona Ryder, Rob Lowe, Deborah Richter. w. N-adap. Alan Hines, d. Daniel Petrie.

COMEDY DRAMA: MELODRAMA: Girls; Mentally Disabled; Love-First; Parents vs. Children; Mothers-Troublesome; Teen-agers; Grandfathers; Rural Life; Texas; Forgotten Films; Female Protagonists
(Welcome Home, Roxy Carmichael)

The Squaw Man, 1931, 106m, ★★1/2/$$$, MGM/NA. An Indian woman bears

the child of a British soldier which leads to ostracism and tragedy. Warner Baxter, Lupe Velez, Charles Bickford, Eleanor Boardman, Roland Young, Paul Cavanagh, Raymond Hatton. w. Lucien Hubbard, Lenore Coffee, P-adap. Edwin Milton Royle, d. Cecil B. de Mille.

WESTERN: DRAMA: TRAGEDY: Romance-Interracial; Mothers-Unwed; Ostracism; Suicidal Tendencies; Indians-American

REMAKE OF: two silent versions, 1914 and 1918.

The Squeeze, 1987, 101m, ★/$, Tri-Star/HBO, PG-13/S. A con artist uncovers a plot by the mob to fix the lottery. Michael Keaton, Rae Dawn Chong, John Davidson, Joe Pantoliano. d. Roger Young.

COMEDY: Mob Comedy; Con Artists; Lotteries; Flops-Major

St., see **Saint** listings.

Stacy's Knights, 1983, 95m, ★★/$, Ind/Vestron. A wallflower has a flair for the cards and several fellows try to take advantage of her. Andra Millian, Kevin Costner. w. Michael Blake, d. Jim Wilson.

COMEDY DRAMA: Gambling; Female Among Males; Games; Wallflowers; Ensembles-Male

Stagecoach, 1939, 99m, ★★★★/$$$$, UA/WB, Vestron. A stagecoach passing through the hostile wilderness of the West brings out the best and worst in the characters who board it and then must defend themselves from an Indian attack. John Wayne, Claire Trevor, Thomas Mitchell (**BSActor**), George Bancroft, Andy Devine, John Carradine, Donald Meek. w. Dudley Nichols, SS-adap. Ernest Haycox (Stage to Lordsburg), d. John Ford (BDirector). BPicture, **BScore**, BCin, BArt, BEdit. Oscars: 7-2. Film History

Stagecoach, 1966, 114m, ★★/$$, 20th/CBS-Fox. A remake of above, and a failure. Ann-Margret, Alex Cord, Bing Crosby, Van Heflin, Slim Pickens, Stefanie Powers, Red Buttons, Keenan Wynn. w. Joseph Landon, SS-adap. Ernest Haycox (Stage to Lordsburg), d. Gordon Douglas.

WESTERN: DRAMA: Character Studies; Survival Drama; Ensemble Films; Journies; Epics; Wagon Trains; Indians-American
(Lifeboat; Grand Hotel; Fort Apache; The Searchers)

Stage Door, 1937, 93m, ★★★★/$$$, RKO/Turner. A hotel filled with aspiring

actresses, some of whom are making it (Katharine Hepburn, Ginger Rogers) and some of whom aren't so lucky (Lucille Ball, Ann Miller, Andrea Leeds [BSActress]). w. Morrie Ryskind, Anthony Veiller (BScr), P-adap. Edna Ferber, George S. Kaufman, d. Gregory LaCava. (BDirector). BPicture. Oscars: 4-0.

DRAMA: COMEDY DRAMA: MELO-DRAMA: TRAGEDY: Ensemble Films; Ensembles-Female; Actresses; Theater Life; Suicidal Tendencies; Dreams; Illusions Destroyed; Fame-Rise to; Young Women; Hidden Gems; Female Protagonists
(Dramatic School; The Women)

Stage Door Canteen, 1943, 132m, ★★★/$$, Sol Lesser-UA/Nos, Prism. A group of entertainers keep the boys hopping all night during a break from the war. Tallulah Bankhead, Ray Bolger, Helen Hayes, George Jessel, and an all-star cast of cameos. w. Delmer Daves, d. Frank Borzage.

Documentary; Docudrama; **MUSICALS:** Putting on a Show; Theater Life; All-Star Casts; World War II Stories; War at Home; Time Capsules

Stage Fright, 1950, 110m, ★★★/$$, WB/WB. The girlfriend of an actor on the run, accused of murder, takes an inside job as a maid for the actress he says really did it. She'll soon find out whether he's right. Marlene Dietrich, Jane Wyman, Richard Todd, Alastair Sim, Michael Wilding. w. Whitfield Cook, N-adap. Selwyn Jepson (Man Running), d. Alfred Hitchcock.

SUSPENSE: MURDER: MYSTERY: MUR-DER MYSTERY: Detective Stories; Detectives-Amateur; Detectives-Female; Theater Life; Undercover; Actresses; Actors; Murderers-Female; Female Protagonists; Hitchcockian
(Shadow of a Doubt; I Confess; Witness for the Prosecution; The Velvet Touch)
(Ed: Not prime Hitch, but okay)

Stage Struck, 1957, 95m, ★★★/$, RKO/VCI. A small-town girl with Big Apple dreams hits Broadway, eager to become a star. Susan Strasberg, Henry Fonda, Herbert Marshall, Joan Greenwood, Christopher Plummer. w. Ruth and Augustus Goetz, P-adap. Zoe Akins, d. Sidney Lumet.

COMEDY DRAMA: Young Women; Actresses; Free Spirits; Fame-Rise to;

Feisty Females; Female Screenwriters; Female Protagonists; Coulda Been Great
REMAKE OF: Morning Glory, 1933.
(Ed: Miss Strasberg, daughter of renowned acting teacher Lee Strasberg, didn't go on to the stardom that original star Katharine Hepburn did)

Staircase, 1969, 101m, ★★★/$, 20th/NA. Two gay hairdressers (Rex Harrison, Richard Burton) face growing older, and possibly apart. Cathleen Nesbitt. w. P-adap. Charles Dyer, d. Stanley Donen.
COMEDY DRAMA: MELODRAMA: ROMANCE: Gay Men; Hairdressers; Men in Conflict; Marriage Drama; Camp; Cult Films; Forgotten Films; Flops-Major; Hidden Gems; Stagelike Films; British Films; Coulda Been Great
(The Dresser; The Killing of Sister George)

Stairway to Heaven (A Matter of Life and Death), 1946, 104m, ★★/$$$, GFD/NA. A military pilot with brain damage from the war has surgery to help him out, but he fantasizes about life after death anyway. David Niven, Roger Livesay, Kim Hunter, Marius Goring, Raymond Massey. w. d. Michael Powell, Emeric Pressburger.
DRAMA: MELODRAMA: Disease Stories; Pilots-Military; Disabled People; World War II-Post Era; Medical Drama; Heaven; Fantasies; Ahead of Its Time; British Films; Writer-Directors
(The Life and Death of Colonel Blimp; The Singing Detective)

Stakeout, 1987, 115m, ★★★/$$$, Touchstone Touchstone, PG-13/S-P. A stakeout lasts so long that a cop has time to fall in love with a murder suspect before it's over. But when they're peeping in her bedroom, they're ahead of the game. Richard Dreyfuss, Emilio Estevez, Madeleine Stowe, Aidan Quinn, Dan Lauria. w. Jim Kouf, d. John Badham.
COMEDY: ACTION: Action Comedy; Police Stories; Detectives-Police; Undercover; Romance with Suspect; Protecting Someone; Sexy Women; Men Fighting Over Women; Sleeper Hits
SEQUEL: Another Stakeout
(Cops and Robbersons)
(Ed: Stowe's breakthrough, and a surprise hit, period)

Stakeout 2, see **Another Stakeout.**
Stalag 17, 1953, 120m, ★★★½/$$$$, Par/Par. In a Nazi P.O.W. camp, American G.I.s contemplate their fate and plan escapes. William Holden (**BActor**), Don

Taylor, Otto Preminger, Robert Strauss (BSActor), Harvey Lembeck, Peter Graves. w. Billy Wilder, Edwin Blum, P-adap. Donald Bevan, Edmund Trzinski, d. Billy Wilder (BDirector). Oscars: 3-1.
DRAMA: COMEDY DRAMA: World War II Stories; Ensemble Films; Ensembles-Male; POWs; Survival Drama; Prison Drama; Prison Escapes; Concentration Camps; Germans as Enemy; Faded Hits
RETREAD: Hogan's Heroes, TV SERIES.
(Desperate Journey; The Great Escape)

Stalin, 1992, 173m, ★★★/$$$, MGM-HBO/MGM-UA. Story of the tyrant of Russia whose power spanned generations of murder and oppression. Robert Duvall, Julia Ormond, Joan Plowright, Jeroen Krabbe, Maximilian Schell, Frank Finlay. w. Paul Monash, d. Ivan Passer.
DRAMA: Biographies; Leaders-Tyrant; Russia Oppression; Episodic Stories; Murderers-Mass; TV Movies

The Stalking Moon, 1968, 109m, ★★½/$, National General/WB, PG/V. A cavalryman on the verge of retirement performs one last act of heroism as he saves a pioneer woman from an Apache attack. Gregory Peck, Eva Marie Saint, Robert Forster, Frank Silvera.
WESTERNS: SUSPENSE: Protecting Someone; Saving Someone; Women in Jeopardy; Pioneers; Indians-American

The Stand, 1994, 360m, ★★★/$$$$, ABC/Republic. A virus escapes a government center and kills all but a small handful of people who then must do battle with a Satanic force setting up shop in Vegas. Rob Lowe, Molly Ringwald, Gary Sinise, Laura San Giacomo, Corky Nemec, Miguel Ferrer, Jamey Sheridan, Ruby Dee, Ed Harris, Kathy Bates. w. N-adap. Stephen King, d. Mick Garris.
SCI-FI: SUSPENSE: Epidemics; Apocalyptic Stories; Multiple Stories; Interwoven Stories; Bombs-Atomic; Good vs. Evil; Satan; Religion; Dangerous Women; Possessions; Stephen King
(Outbreak; The Plague; The Dead Zone)

Stand and Deliver, 1988, 104m, ★★★/$$$, American Playhouse-WB/WB, PG/P. In a barrio in East L.A., rough latino gangbangers are taught the value of algebra by a "tough-loving" committed teacher. Edward James Olmos (BActor), Lou Diamond Phillips, Rosana De Soto, Andy Garcia, Ingrid Olio. w. Ramon Menendez, Tom Musca, d. Ramon Menendez. Oscars: 1-0.

COMEDY DRAMA: Docudrama; True Stories; High School Life; Teachers; Teachers & Students; Saintly People; Latin People; Inner City Life
(The Blackboard Jungle; Dangerous Minds)

Stand by Me, 1986, 89m, ★★★½/$$$, Col/RCA-Col, PG/P. A group of adolescent boys bond, grow, and have a sobering, maturing experience as they learn about death on a fateful journey along a railroad track where they find something shocking. Wil Wheaton, River Phoenix, Corey Feldman, Jerry O'Connell, Kiefer Sutherland, Richard Dreyfuss. w. Raynold Gideon (BAScr), SS-adap. Stephen King (*The Body*), d. Rob Reiner. Oscars: 1-0.
COMEDY DRAMA: ADVENTURE: MURDER: Storytellers; Murder-Discovering; Boys; Coming of Age; Small-town Life; Rural Life; Memories; Writers; Fantasies; Narrated Films; Flashbacks; Stephen King; Sleeper Hits
(The Sandlot; Explorers; The Goonies)

Stand In, 1937, 90m, ★★★/$, Walter Wanger-UA/NA. A faltering Hollywood studio hires a consultant to tell them how to run things more efficiently, with humorous results. Leslie Howard, Joan Blondell, Humphrey Bogart, Alan Mowbray. w. Gene Towne, Graham Baker, (Serial)-adap. Clarence Budington Kelland, d. Tay Garnett.
COMEDY: SATIRE: Hollywood Life; Corporate Life; Nuisances; Nerds; Nerds & Babes; Efficiency Experts; Coulda Been Great; Forgotten Films
(Battle of the Sexes; The Efficiency Expert; Movers and Shakers; The Errand Boy)
(Ed: Of more interest to Hollywood or big corporation insiders)

Stand Up and Be Counted, 1971, 99m, ★★½/$, Col/NA. A female reporter on the international beat goes back home to the states and becomes a "women's libber." Jacqueline Bisset, Stella Stevens, Steve Lawrence, Gary Lockwood, Loretta Swit. w. Bernard Slade, d. Jackie Cooper.
COMEDY DRAMA: SATIRE: Social Satire; Political Activists; Journalists; Feminist Films; Womens' Rights; 1970s; Time Capsules; Coulda Been Good; Forgotten Films

Stand Up and Cheer, 1934, 80m, ★★★/$$$$, 20th/Fox. In the fictitious government, the Secretary of Entertainment gets a big show together with a little girl as the big star. Shirley Temple, Warner Baxter, Madge Evans, Nigel Bruce, Stepin Fetchit. w. Will Rogers, Ralph Spence, d. Hamilton McFadden.

MUSICALS: Depression Era; Putting on a Show; Dance Movies; Child Protagonists; Girls; Blockbusters; Faded Hits

Stanley & Iris, 1989, 105m, ★★★/$, MGM/MGM-UA, PG-13/S. A widow who's a former schoolteacher now working in a factory teaches an illiterate man to read after he loses his job. It takes a while, but he changes, and they soon fall in love. Jane Fonda, Robert De Niro, Swoosie Kurtz, Martha Plimpton. w. Harriet Frank, Jr., Irving Ravetch, N-adap. Pat Barker *(Union Street)*, d. Martin Ritt.

DRAMA: ROMANCE: Family Drama; Romantic Drama; Romance with Teacher; Romance-Middle-Aged; Working Class; Teachers; Teachers & Students; Mentally Disabled; Making a Living; Ordinary People Stories; Life Transitions; Old-Fashioned Recent Films; Quiet Little Films; Female Protagonists; Underrated; Overlooked at Release; Hidden Gems; Female Screenwriters
(Jackknife, Charly; Tim)

Stanley & Livingstone, 1939, 101m, ★★★¹/²/$$$, 20th/Fox. A modern-day newspaper man goes to Africa and finds the famous Victorian explorer. Spencer Tracy, Cedric Hardwicke, Richard Greene, Nancy Kelly, Walter Brennan, Charles Coburn. w. Philip Dunne, Julien Josephson, d. Henry King.

ADVENTURE: DRAMA: Explorers; Missing Persons; Searches; Africa; Faded Hits; Forgotten Films; Hidden Gems
(Mountains on the Moon; Gorillas in the Mist)

The Star, 1952, 91m, ★★¹/²/$$, 20th/NA. A star past her prime gets back into life. Bette Davis (BActress), Sterling Hayden, Natalie Wood, Warner Anderson. w. Katherine Albert, Dale Eunson, d. Stuart Heisler. Oscars: 1-0.

MELODRAMA: Character Studies; Hollywood Life; Midlife Crisis; Actresses; Comebacks; Female Protagonists; Female Screenwriters
(All About Eve)
(Ed: Mirrored problems Davis was facing at the time. Supposedly originally for Joan Crawford, another Oscar nomination Crawford probably resented Davis getting

[Whatever Happened to Baby Jane? being at least one more])

Star!, 1968, 194m, ★★★/$, 20th/Fox. A rags-to-riches tale of a cabaret singer who rises up the ranks by paying her dues. Julie Andrews, Richard Crenna, Michael Craig, Daniel Massey (BSActor), Bruce Forsyth. w. William Fairchild, d. Robert Wise. BCin, BArt, BCostume, BOSong, BMScore, BSound. Oscars: 7-0.

MUSICALS: DRAMA: Musical Drama; Biographies; Hollywood Life; Hollywood Biographies; Actresses; Singers; Theater Life; Rags to Riches; Fame-Rise to; Vaudeville; England; Female Protagonists; Flops-Major
(Funny Girl; Darling Lili)
(Ed: A film behind its time, though not bad, really. Compare it to another biopic the same year-*Isadora*)

The Star Chamber, 1983, 109m, ★★¹/²/$$, 20th/CBS-Fox, PG/V. When murderers and severe criminals are let off on technicalities, the judges who presided over their cases have them killed. Michael Douglas, Hal Holbrook, Yaphet Kotto, Sharon Gless. w. Roderick Taylor, Peter Hyams, d. Peter Hyams.

SUSPENSE: MURDER: MYSTERY: MURDER MYSTERY: Conspiracy; Social Satire; Judges; Lawyers; Government as Enemy; Vigilantes; Hitmen; Good Premise Unfulfilled; Coulda Been Great
(Strange Days)

Stardust Memories, 1980, 88m (B&W), ★★★/$$, UA/MGM-UA, R/S. A film director (Woody Allen), disillusioned with his career, goes to a bizarre film festival full of bizarre people honoring him, while his relationship with a woman (Charlotte Rampling) begins to change. w. d. Woody Allen.

DRAMA: Character Studies; Art Films; Avant-Garde; Directors; Movie Making; All-Star Cameos; Alienation; Depression; Life Transitions; Writer-Directors; Interviews
(La Dolce Vita; 8½; Day For Night)
(Ed: Not so funny, but worth it)

Star 80, 1983, 103m, ★★¹/²/$, WB/WB, R/S-V-P-FFN-MRN. The true story of Dorothy Stratten, the *Playboy* centerfold who was murdered by her jealous husband. Mariel Hemingway, Eric Roberts, Cliff Robertson, Carroll Baker. w. d. Bob Fosse.

DRAMA: TRAGEDY: Biographies; Murder of Spouse; Abused Women;

Simple Minds; Bimbos; Sexy Women; Dangerous Men; Love-Questionable; Fatal Attractions; Obsessions; Playboys; Mental Illness; Coulda Been Good; Writer-Directors
(Portrait of a Centerfold)

Stargate, 1994, 125m, ★★★/$$$, MGM-UA/MGM-UA, PG-13/P-S-V. A renegade Egyptologist is brought in to decipher a hidden code to a Rosetta Stone-like wheel which, if programmed correctly with the stars, should open a gate to the alternate universe which brought us the pyramids and UFOs. It works, and once in this other world, the Egyptologist and a military entourage encounter the heartless god Ra who may not only stop them from returning but destroy the world they were returning to. James Spader, Kurt Russell, Jaye Davidson. w. Dean Devlin, Roland Emmerich, d. Roland Emmerich.

ACTION: ADVENTURE: SCI-FI: Outer Space Movies; Evil Men; God; Egypt; Archaeologists; Special Teams-Military; Macho Men vs. Nerd; Bombs-Atomic; Coulda Been Great
(Raiders of the Lost Ark; Krull)
(Ed: Starts off very promising but degenerates into a third-act-long chase and senseless ending)

A Star Is Born, 1937, 111m, ★★★¹/²/$$$, David O. Selznick-UA/Nos. A young aspiring actress marries a fading matinee idol. His star falls as hers rises, causing tensions in their marriage. Janet Gaynor (BActress), Fredric March (BActor), Adolphe Menjou, Lionel Stander, Andy Devine. w. Dorothy Parker, Alan Campbell, Robert Carson, William Wellman (**BOStory**), d. William A. Wellman (**BDirector**), **BCCin** (Special award). Oscars: 7-2.

DRAMA: TRAGEDY: MELODRAMA: ROMANCE: Romantic Drama; Fame-Rise to; Actresses; Marriage Drama; Marriage on the Rocks; Actors; Suicidal Tendencies; Female Protagonists; Female Screenwriters; Faded Hits; Forgotten Films; Hidden Gems; The Oscars
REMAKE: 1954, 1976.

A Star Is Born, 1954, 181m, ★★★¹/²/$$$, WB/WB. A musical remake of the famous classic above-with the actress also a great singer and the husband even more despondent. Judy Garland (BActress), James Mason (BActor), Charles Bickford, Jack Carson, Tommy

Noonan. w. Moss Hart, d. George Cukor. BCArt, BCCostume, BMScore, BOSong, "The Man That Got Away." Oscars: 6-0.

DRAMA: TRAGEDY: MUSICALS: Music Movies; **MELODRAMA: ROMANCE:** Romantic Drama; Fame-Rise to; Singers; Actresses; Marriage Drama; Marriage on the Rocks; Actors; Suicidal Tendencies; Female Protagonists; The Oscars
REMAKE OF: 1937 version; **REMAKE:** 1976.

A Star Is Born, 1976, 140m, ★★★/ $$$$$, WB/WB, R/S-P. A new, somewhat grittier version with new great music and a new star who sticks mainly to music, but the same old melodrama. Barbra Streisand, Kris Kristofferson, Paul Mazursky, Gary Busey. w. John Gregory Dunne, Joan Didion, Frank Pierson, d. Frank Pierson. **BOSong,** "Evergreen," BOScore, BCin. Oscars: 3-1.

DRAMA: MELODRAMA: ROMANCE: Romantic Drama; Music Movies; Fame-Rise to; Singers; Marriage Drama; Marriage on the Rocks; Actors; Suicidal Tendencies; Depression; Female Protagonists; Blockbusters

Starman, 1984, 115m, ★★★/$$, Col/RCA-Col, PG/S. An alien takes the form of a rural Wisconsin woman's dead husband. At first she's shocked, but eventually they fall in love. Jeff Bridges (BActor), Karen Allen, Charles Martin Smith, Richard Jaekel. w. Bruce A. Evans, Raynold Gideon, d. John Carpenter. Oscars: 1-0.

COMEDY DRAMA: ROMANCE: Aliens-Outer Space, Good; Simple Minds; Fish out of Water Stories; Dead-Back from the; Reincarnation; Impostors; Rural Life
(Ghost; Kiss Me Goodbye; Three Wishes; Visit to a Small Planet; The Man Who Fell to Earth)

Star of Midnight, 1935, 90m, ★★★/ $$, RKO/Turner. A Broadway actress disappears mysteriously and a suave raconteur is brought on the case. William Powell, Ginger Rogers, Paul Kelly, Gene Lockhart, Ralph Morgan, Leslie Fenton. w. Howard J. Green, Anthony Veiller, Edward Kaufman, d. Stephen Roberts.

COMEDY: MYSTERY: Screwball Comedy; Missing Persons; Detective Stories; Comic Mystery; Women in Jeopardy; Actresses; Forgotten Films; Hidden Gems
(The Thin Man; A Night to Remember)

Stars and Bars, 1988, 94m, ★★/$ (LR), Col/RCA-Col, R/S-P-MRN. A British art expert (Daniel Day Lewis) is sent to backwoods Georgia to track down a long lost Renoir owned by a bunch of rednecks, placing him in the middle of a feud and wrecking his love life. Joan Cusack, Martha Plimpton, Harry Dean Stanton, Laurie Metcalf, Will Patton, Glenne Headly, Steven Wright. w. N-adap. William Boyd, d. Pat O'Connor.

COMEDY: FARCE: Fish out of Water Stories; Comedy of Errors, Murphy's Law Stories; Chase Movies; Treasure Hunts; Feuds; Rednecks; Country Life; North vs. South; City vs. Country; Eccentric People; Southerns; Georgia; Underrated; Coulda Been Great; Hidden Gems (Murder, He Says; Wise Blood; Daddy's Dyin')
(Ed. Some big laughs if you like subtle humor mixed with slapstick or hick humor; disappointing ending)

Stars and Stripes Forever, 1952, 89m, ★★★/$$, 20th/Fox. Biography of patriotic composer John Philips Sousa as his young protege romances around. Clifton Webb, Robert Wagner, Ruth Hussey, Debra Paget. d. Henry Koster

MUSICALS: MELODRAMA: ROMANCE: Musical Romance; Biographies; Music Composers; Nostalgia; Patriotic Films; 1890s

The Star Spangled Girl, 1971, 92m, ★★/$, Par/Par, PG. A writer in an apartment row in Los Angeles gets a kooky neighbor he's smitten by, but so is his roommate. Sandy Duncan, Tony Roberts, Todd Susman, Elizabeth Allen. w. Arnold Margolin, Jim Parker, P-adap. Neil Simon, d. Jerry Paris.

COMEDY: ROMANCE: Romantic Comedy; Free Spirits; Men Fighting Over Women; Roommates; Neighbors-Troublesome; Writers; Forgotten Films; Flops-Major
(Ed: Dismally bad adaptation of one of Simon's few mediocre if not downright dumb and boring plays-though he didn't adapt it. It does, however, seem to make the rounds a lot at the community theater level)

Star Spangled Rhythm, 1942, 99m, ★★★/$$, Par/NA. A studio lot guard at Paramount pretends to his son that he's a big producer and when his son's navy ship comes to port in Los Angeles he must prove it-luckily he gets help from the contract players on the lot at the time.

Betty Hutton, Eddie Bracken, Victor Moore, Walter Abel, Bob Hope, Bing Crosby, Paulette Goddard, Veronica Lake, Dorothy Lamour, Vera Zorina, Fred MacMurray, Ray Milland, Dick Powell, Cecil B. de Mille, Preston Sturges, Alan Ladd, Rochester, Susan Hayward. w. Harry Tugend, d. George Marshall.

COMEDY: FARCE: Impostors; Hollywood Life; Ordinary People Stories; All-Star Cameos; Fantasies; Forgotten Films

Starstruck, 1982, 102m, ★★½/$, Ind/Sultan. In Australia, a young boy becomes his brother's punk band's manager in order to save the family business, winding up in a parody of Esther Williams movies. Jo Kennedy, Ross O'Donovan, Margo Lee, Max Cullen. w. Stephen MacLean, d. Gillian Armstrong.

COMEDY: SATIRE: MUSICALS: Music Movies; Putting on a Show; Mortgage Drama; Spoofs; Fame-Rise to; Singers; Brothers; Forgotten Films; Female Directors; Australian Films
(Young Einstein; Dogs in Space)

Starting Over, 1979, 106m, ★★★½/ $$$$, Par/Par, R/S-P. A middle-aged man flirts with returning to his ex-wife who is great songwriter but a bad singer, but he's also been set up with a kindergarten teacher with a sense of humor. Burt Reynolds, Jill Clayburgh (BActress), Candice Bergen (BSActress), Frances Sternhagen, Charles Durning, Austin Pendleton. w. James L. Brooks, N-adap. Dan Wakefield, d. Alan J. Pakula. Oscars: 2-0.

COMEDY: COMEDY DRAMA: ROMANCE: Romance-Triangles; Starting Over; Midlife Crisis; Psychologists; Divorce; Songwriters; Singers; Teachers
(Best Friends; It's My Turn)
(Ed: Heartfelt, sensitive and funny, it's also Reynolds' best performance-though it was downhill after this)

Star Trek: The Motion Picture, 1979, 132m, ★★½/$$$$$, Par/Par, PG/V. Kirk resumes command of the U.S.S. Enterprise and fights a faceless and ultimately boring enemy. William Shatner, Leonard Nimoy, DeForest Kelley, Persis Khambatta. w. Harry Livingstone, Alan Dean Foster, d. Robert Wise. BOScore, BSFX, BArt. Oscars: 3-0.

ACTION: ADVENTURE: Outer Space Movies; Journies; Searches; Ensemble; Films; Female Among Males; TV Series Movies; Blockbusters

Star Trek II: The Wrath of Khan, 1982, 114m, ★★1/2/$$$$, Par/Par, PG/B&G, V. Ricardo Montalban is an evil warlord discovered by the crew of the Enterprise in outer space and he has creepy scorpion things that crawl in one's ears. William Shatner, Leonard Nimoy, DeForest Kelley. w. Jack B. Sowards, d. Nicholas Meyer.
ACTION: ADVENTURE: Outer Space Movies; Journeys; Searches; Ensemble Films; TV Series Movies; Good vs. Evil (Ed: A little better than the first; close your eyes when the things crawl in his ears)

Star Trek III: The Search for Spock, 1984, 105m, ★★1/2/$$$, Par/Par, PG/V. Spock is presumed dead but his spirit lives on in the body of a Vulcan child. William Shatner, DeForest Kelley, James Doohan, Leonard Nimoy. w. Harve Bennett, d. Leonard Nimoy.
ACTION: ADVENTURE: Outer Space Movies; Journeys; Searches; Missing Persons; Reincarnation; Dead-Back from the; Ensemble Films; TV Series Movies (Ed: A little worse than the last one)

Star Trek IV: The Voyage Home, 1986, 119m, ★★★/$$$$$, Par/Par, PG. Starfleet Command on Earth summons the crew of the Enterprise to a trial for mutiny. When back on Earth, they experience major culture shock and save the whale. William Shatner, Leonard Nimoy, DeForest Kelley, James Doohan, George Takei, Catherine Hicks. w. Harve Bennett, Steve Meerson, Peter Krikes, Nicholas Meyer, d. Leonard Nimoy. BCin, BOScore. Oscars: 2-0.
ACTION: ADVENTURE: ROMANCE: Outer Space Movies; Fish out of Water Stories; Animal Rights; Ensemble Films; Whales; Time Travel; Female Among Males; TV Series Movies (Ed: Much better than the others)

Star Trek V: The Final Frontier, 1989, 107m, ★★1/2/$$$, Par/Par, PG. A mystical and strange planet is rumored to be heaven. Kirk and the Enterprise crew decide to find out and basically have a camping trip. William Shatner, Leonard Nimoy, DeForest Kelley, James Doohan, Walter Koenig, George Takei. w. David Loughery, William Shatner, Harve Bennett, David Loughery, d. William Shatner.
ACTION: ADVENTURE: Outer Space Movies; Journeys; Searches; Ensemble Films; TV Series Movies; Camping (Ed: Back to being a little worse and the lowest grosser of all)

Star Trek VI: The Undiscovered Country, 1991, 110m, ★★★/$$$, UIP/Par. Kirk and McCoy are found guilty of murdering a Klingon, but Spock must find the real culprits. William Shatner, Leonard Nimoy, DeForest Kelley, James Doohan, Walter Koenig, George Takei, Christian Slater, Christopher Plummer. w. Nicholas Meyer, Denny Martin Flynn, Leonard Nimoy, Lawrence Konner, Mark Rosenthal, d. Nicholas Meyer.
ACTION: ADVENTURE: MURDER: MYSTERY: Detective Stories; Outer Space Moyies; Journeys; Searches; Ensemble Films; TV Series Movies (Ed: Again, a little better and more conventional, with a real story for once)

Star Trek Generations, 1994, 110m, ★★/$$$, Par/Par, PG/P-V. The new Enterprise goes on a rescue mission to save two ships caught in a time warp which introduces it to a new, deceptive villain with close ties to Klingons and years later comes back to haunt the crew in this adventure joining cast members of the first TV series with that of the second. Patrick Stewart, William Shatner, Jonathan Frakes, Brent Spiner, LeVar Burton, Michael Dorn, Gates McFadden, Marina Sirtis, Whoopi Goldberg, Malcolm McDowell, James Doohan, Walter Koenig, Barbara March, Gwynyth Walsh, Alan Ruck. w. Ronald D. Moore, Brannon Braga, d. David Carson
ACTION: ADVENTURE: SCI-FI: Outer Space Movies; Rescue Drama; Time Travel; Evil Men; TV Series Movies (Ed: Only for fans of the TV show. Others will be confused and asleep)

Start the Revolution Without Me, 1969, 90m, ★★★/$, WB/WB. The French Revolution is stumbled into by two sets of twins. Donald Sutherland, Gene Wilder, Hugh Griffith, Jack McGowran, Billie Whitelaw, Victor Spinetti. d. Bud Yorkin.
COMEDY: FARCE: Comedy-Slapstick; Spoofs; Misunderstandings; Impostors; Mix-Ups; Twins; French Revolution; Coulda Been Great; Ahead of Its Time (Big Business; The Boys from Syracuse)

Star Wars, 1977, 121m, ★★★1/2/$$$$$$, 20th/Fox, PG/V. A young man, Luke Skywalker (Mark Hamill), searches for the kidnapped Princess Leia (Carrie Fisher) and comes up against the dreaded evil Darth Vader (James Earl Jones/John Prowse). Alec Guinness (BSActor), Harrison Ford, Billy Dee Williams. w. d. George Lucas (BDirector). BPicture, **BCinema, BArt, BCostume, BEditing, BSound, BSFX, BOScore.** Oscars: 10-7.
ADVENTURE: SCI-FI: ACTION: ADVENTURE: Outer Space Movies; Chase Movies; Kidnappings; Women in Jeopardy; Good vs. Evil; Female Among Males; Robots; Sleeper Hits; Blockbusters; Cult Films
SEQUELS: The Empire Strikes Back; Return of the Jedi.
SPOOFS: Spaceballs.
(The Empire Strikes Back; The Return of the Jedi; Krull; Willow; Alien)

State Fair, 1933, 98m, ★★★/$$$, 20th/NA. A family goes to the fair, each with different reasons for being there. The kids find romance as dad shows his prize pig. Will Rogers, Janet Gaynor, Lew Ayres, Sally Eilers, Norman Foster, Louise Dresser. w. Paul Green, Sonya Levien, N-adap. Phil Stong, d. Henry King.
MELODRAMA: COMEDY DRAMA: FAMILY: Family Comedy; ROMANCE: Love-First; Multiple Stories; Ensemble Films; Competitions; Female Protagonists

State Fair, 1945, 100m, ★★★/$$$, 20th/Fox. A remake of above as a musical. Charles Winninger, Jeanne Crain, Dana Andrews, Vivian Blaine, Dick Haymes, Fay Bainter. w./lyrics Oscar Hammerstein II, d. Walter Lang.

State Fair, 1962, 118m, ★★1/2/$$, 20th/Fox. A second remake updated with an eye toward contemporary fashions and music. Pat Boone, Alice Faye, Tom Ewell, Ann-Margret, Bobby Darin. w. Richard Breen, d. José Ferrer.
MUSICAL: ROMANCE: Musical Romance; MELODRAMA: COMEDY DRAMA: FAMILY: Family Comedy; Love-First; Multiple Stories; Ensemble Films; Competitions; Actor Directors (Showboat; Oklahoma!)

State of Grace, 1990, 134m, ★★1/2/$, Orion/Orion, R/EV-EP-S. An Irish New York cop goes undercover in an Irish gang from his childhood neighborhood that has dealings with the Mafia. Sean Penn, Ed Harris, Gary Oldman, Robin Wright, John Turturro. w. Dennis McIntyre, d. Phil Joanou.

ACTION: Action Drama; Crime Drama; Mob Stories; Detectives-Police; Inner City Life; Undercover; Friends as Enemies; Irish People; Coulda Been Good
(Prince of the City; Manhattan Melodrama)

State of Siege, 1973, 119m, ★★★/$, Col/Col, R/V. International USA-ID investigator disappears in Uruguay and theories abound as to what happened. Yves Montand, Renato Salvatori. w. d. Costa-Gavras.

DRAMA: Political Drama; Conspiracy; Missing Persons; Assassination Plots; True or Not?; South American; Writer-Directors
(Z; Missing; JFK)

State of the Union, 1948, 110m, ★★★¹/₂/$$$, MGM/MGM-UA. A bickering couple separate, then get back together for political reasons when the husband decides to run for president, but the man has some things to face up to. Spencer Tracy, Katharine Hepburn, Adolphe Menjou, Van Johnson, Angela Lansbury. w. Anthony Veiller, Myles Connelly, P-adap. Howard Lindsay, Russell Crouse, d. Frank Capra.

DRAMA: MELODRAMA: COMEDY DRAMA: SATIRE: Romance-Bickering; Marriage Drama; Marriage on the Rocks; Politicians' Wives; Politicians; Political Campaigns; Washington D.C.; Woman Behind the Man; Decisions-Big; Ethics; Corruption-Political; Tracy & Hepburn; Pulitzer Prize Adaptations
(The Best Man; Woman of the Year)

The State of Things, 1982, 120m, ★★¹/₂/$, Ind/Ingram. At work on a film in Portugal, a crew and director is abandoned by their producer. The director follows him to Los Angeles to confront him about it. Isabel Weingarten, Rebecca Pauly, Patrick Bauchau, Paul Getty III, Samuel Fuller, Roger Corman. w. Wim Wenders, Robert Kramer, d. Wim Wenders.

DRAMA: Art Film; Movie Making; Directors; Power Struggles; German Films; Abandoned People; Stranded
(Living in Oblivion; Dangerous Game; The American Friend)

The Statue, 1970, 89m, ★★¹/₂/$, Cinerama/Prism, R/S-MRN. An artist makes a sculpture of her husband-an exact likeness in every respect except for the area a fig leaf would cover. His phallic jealousy gets the best of him as he

tries to find out who the endowment belongs to. David Niven, Virna Lisi, Robert Vaughn, John Cleese. w. Alec Coppel, Denis Norden, d. Rod Amateau.

COMEDY: FARCE: Artists; Nudists; Sexuality; Identities-Mistaken; Impostors; Cheating Women; Jealousy; Coulda Been Good; Idiot Plots; Camp; Hidden Gems; Unintentionally Funny
(Ed: Not pornographic, but you still have to see it to believe it)

Stay Hungry, 1976, 102m, ★★¹/₂/$$, UA/Fox, R/S-FN. A poor Alabama boy suddenly inherits a fortune and decides to live it up, much to the chagrin of the locals. Jeff Bridges, Sally Field, Arnold Schwarzenegger, Robert Englund. w. Charles Gaines, Bob Rafaelson, N-adap. Charles Gaines, d. Bob Rafaelson.

COMEDY DRAMA: ROMANCE: Heirs; Inheritances at Stake; Southerns; Body Builders; Playboys; Young Men
(All-American Boy; Pumping Iron)

Staying Alive, 1983, 96m, ★★/$$$, Par/Par, R/P-S. Tony Manero gets pumped up and dances in a show for a comeback. John Travolta, Cynthia Rhodes, Finola Hughes, Steve Inwood. w. Sylvester Stallone, Norman Wexler, d. Sylvester Stallone.

MELODRAMA: Dance Movies; Dancers; Music Movies; Disco Era; Comebacks; Playboys

SEQUEL TO: Saturday Night Fever

Staying Together, 1989, 91m, ★★¹/₂/$, Hemdale/HBO, PG-13/P-S. A coming-of-age story about three brothers growing up in a small southern town. Sean Astin, Stockard Channing, Melinda Dillon, Levon Helm, Dermot Mulroney. w. Monte Merrick, d. Lee Grant.

DRAMA: MELODRAMA: ROMANCE: Coming of Age; Brothers; Teenagers; Young Men; Ensemble Films; Ensembles-Male; Small-town Life; North Carolina; Coulda Been Good; Female Directors
(Breaking the Rules; Queens Logic)

Stay Tuned, 1992, 87m, ★★/$, WB/WB, PG/P. A lame satire on TV in which a couple are forced to watch bad programs as penance for their sins. John Ritter, Pam Dawber, Jeffrey Jones, David Thom. w. Tom Parker, Jim Jennewin, d. Peter Hyams.

COMEDY: SATIRE: TV Life; Game Shows; Spoofs-TV; Hollywood Satire; Comedy-Skit; Nightmares; Fantasies;

Crossing the Line; Hell; Coulda Been Good; Good Premise Unfulfilled
(Americathon; The Groove Tube; Amazon Women on the Moon)

The Steagle, 1972, 101m, ★★/$, Col/Col. A mad scientist lives out fantasies on the eve of the Cuban Missile Crisis. Richard Benjamin, Cloris Leachman. d. Paul Sylbert.

COMEDY DRAMA: Fantasy; Fantasies; Scientists-Mad; Curiosities; Cold War Era; Cuban Missle Crisis

Steal Big, Steal Little, 1995, 130m, ★★/$, Savoy/Savoy, PG-13/P-S. Two twin brothers, one of whom is good and the other greedy, vie for an inheritance. Andy Garcia, Alan Arkin, Holland Taylor, Rachel Ticotin, David Ogden Stiers, Richard Bradford, Kevin McCarthy, Charles Rocket, Ally Walker, Joe Pantoliano. d. Andrew Davis.

DRAMA: Brothers; Twins; Inheritances at Stake; Greed; Flops-Major; Multiple Performances
(A Stolen Life; Brotherly Love; The Other)

Stealing Heaven, 1988, 109m, ★★¹/₂/$$, Ind/Live, R/S-FFN-MFN. The legend of Abelard and Heloise in 1200s Paris who have an affair which is forbidden by her uncle and leads to tragedy for Abelard. Derek DeLint, Kim Thomson, Denholm Elliott, Rachel Kempson. w. Chris Bryant, d. Clive Donner.

MELODRAMA: Historical Drama; **ROMANCE: TRAGEDY:** Romantic Drama; Erotic Drama; Rape-Male; Middle Ages; Romance-Forbidden; Lover Family Dislikes; Legends
(The Advocate; Name of the Rose)

Steamboat Bill Jr., 1928, 80m, 71m (silent), ★★★/$$$, UA/Nos. A bookish young lad takes over his grizzled sailor father's boat. His ineptitude endears him to a local girl. There's also a spectacular cyclone finale. Buster Keaton, Ernest Torrence, Marion Byron. w. Carl Harbaugh, Buster Keaton, d. Charles Riesner.

COMEDY: Comedy-Slapstick; Comedy of Errors; **ROMANCE:** Nerds; Nerds & Babes; Sailing
(The General; The Cameraman; Free and Easy)

Steaming, 1985, 95m, ★★★/$, Col/New World, R/S-FFN. Several British women talk about everything while lounging in the steam room. Vanessa Redgrave, Sarah Miles, Diana Dors, Patti Love, Brenda

Bruce. w. Patricia Losey, P-adap. Nell Dunn, d. Joseph Losey.

COMEDY DRAMA: Ensemble Films; Ensembles-Female; Women's Films; Stagelike Films; British Films; Female Screenwriters; Female Protagonists (Steam Room [PBS, 1972]; Chantilly Lace; Personal Best)

Steel, 1979, 101m, ★★/$, Col/Vestron. A young woman pledges to finish the building her father, a civil engineer, was constructing when he was killed. Lee Majors, Jennifer O'Neill, Art Carney, George Kennedy. w. Leigh Chapman, d. Steve Carver.

MELODRAMA: Race Against Time; Mortgage Drama; Death-Dealing with; Female Protagonists

Steel Magnolias, 1989, 118m, ★★★½/ $$$$$, Tri-Star/RCA-Col, PG-13/S-P-MRN. A mother (Sally Field) and her daughter (Julia Roberts, BSActress) get ready for the big wedding while their small-town friends help out, all the while worried about the daughter's medical condition. Dolly Parton, Shirley MacLaine, Darryl Hannah, Olympia Dukakis, Tom Skerritt. w. P-adap. Ropert Harling, d. Herbert Ross. Oscars: 1-0.

COMEDY: COMEDY DRAMA: MELODRAMA: TRAGEDY: Disease Stories; Mothers & Daughters; Ensemble Films; Ensembles-Female; Friendships-Female; Tearjerkers; Southerns; Small-town Life; Ordinary People Stories; Gossips; Rumors; Women's Films; Louisiana; Sally Field Goes Southern; Hairdressers; Blockbusters; Female Protagonists (Crimes of the Heart; The Women; Terms of Endearment; Rich in Love)

(Ed: Fast-paced and funny, though catty to some, manipulative to others, it still creates its own wonderful world and with a great acting ensemble, though the weak link is the one who got the Oscar nomination, sounding like she has cott-uhn in huh moth)

Steelyard Blues, 1972, 92m, ★★/$, WB/WB, R/P. A D.A. with a working-class background is ashamed of his low-life ex-con brother and his hooker girlfriend. Donald Sutherland, Jane Fonda, Peter Boyle, Howard Hesseman. w. David S. Ward, d. Alan Myerson.

COMEDY DRAMA: Ordinary People Stories; Working Class; Class Conflicts; Brothers & Sisters; Con Artists; Prostitutes with a Heart of Gold; Ex-Convicts

Stella, 1990, 109m, ★★½/$$, Touchstone/Touchstone, PG-13/S-P. Remake of Stella Dallas set in the 60s and 70s. Bette Midler, John Goodman, Trini Alvarado, Stephen Collins, Marsha Mason. w. Robert Getchell, N-adap. Olive Higgins Prouty (Stella Dallas), d. John Erman.

DRAMA: MELODRAMA: Tearjerkers; Mothers Alone; Mothers-Struggling; Mothers-Unwed; Mothers & Daughters; Social Climbing; Marrying Up; Saintly People; Female Protagonists (Mildred Pierce; Min and Bill; White Banners)

Stella Dallas, 1925, 110m, B&W, silent, Samuel Goldwyn/NA. The tragic tale of a woman who loses her daughter and husband and must face life alone, supporting her daughter anonymously. Belle Bennett, Ronald Colman, Lois Moran, Jean Hersholt, Douglas Fairbanks, Jr., Alice Joyce. w. Frances Marion, N-adap. Olive Higgins Prouty, d. Henry King.

Stella Dallas, 1937, 106m, Goldwyn-UA/Goldwyn, Sultan, ★★★½/$$$$. A woman (Barbara Stanwyck, BActress) struggles to provide a better future for her daughter than she had, but it may mean staying in the background while the daughter moves up the social ladder. w. Victor Heerman, Sarah Y. Mason, N-adap. Olive Higgins Prouty, d. King Vidor.

Female Screenwriters

Step Down to Terror, 1959, 76m, ★★½/$, U-I/NA. A long lost relative returns to the bosom of his family and home town. He's welcomed with open arms, but they soon get suspicious that he's a recently escaped psychopathic killer. Charles Drake, Coleen Miller, Rod Taylor, Jocelyn Brando. w. Mel Dinelli, Czenzi Ormonde, Chris Cooper, d. Harry Keller.

SUSPENSE: MURDER: MYSTERY: MURDER MYSTERY: Psychological Thriller; Women in Jeopardy; Coming of Age; Serial Killers; Mental Illness; Illusions Destroyed; Dual Lives; Secrets-Haunting; Infatuations; Small-town Life; Hitchcockian

REMAKES/RETREADS: Shadow of a Doubt.

(Shadow of a Doubt; Music Box)

(Ed: Should've left well enough alone)

The Stepfather, 1986, 88m, ★★★/$$$, Ind/Embassy, R/EV. When her mother

marries the seemingly perfect man, a teenage girl begins to suspect he's actually a murderous lunatic. Terry O'Quinn, Jill Schoelen, Shelley Hack. w. Donald E. Westlake, d. Joseph Ruben.

HORROR: SATIRE: SUSPENSE: Family Drama; Stepparents vs. Children; Stepfathers; Dangerous Men; Evil Men; Psycho Killers; Suburban Life; Malicious Menaces; American Myth; Allegorical Stories; Hidden Gems; Sleeper Hits (Picture Mommy Dead; Firstborn; The Hand That Rocks the Cradle)

The Stepfather 2: Make Room for Daddy, 1989, 93m, ★★/$, Col/Col, R/EV-B&G. Terry O'Quinn, Meg Foster, Caroline Williams. d. Jeff Burr.

The Stepfather 3: Father's Day, 1992, 110m, ★½/$, Vidmark/Vidmark, R/EV-B&G. Robert Wightman, Priscilla Barnes, Season Hubley. d. Guy Mager.

HORROR: SATIRE: SUSPENSE: Family Drama; Parents vs. Children; Dangerous Man; Stepfathers; Evil Men; Psycho Killers; Suburban Life; American Myth

The Stepford Wives, 1975, 105m, ★★★/$$$, Col/NA, PG/S. A new resident in a well-off suburb discovers that there's either something in the water or the husbands are in on something making the women automatons. Katharine Ross, Paula Prentiss, Nanette Newman, Peter Masterson, Tina Louise. w. William Goldman, N-adap. Ira Levin, d. Bryan Forbes.

SUSPENSE: MYSTERY: SCI-FI: Conspiracy; Detectives-Female; Detectives-Amateur; Suburban Life; Sexism; Robots; Time Capsules; 1970s; American Myth; Androids; Allegorical Stories; Coulda Been Great

SEQUELS: TV: Revenge of the Stepford Wives.

(Ed: A guilty pleasure, but from a good novelist and screenwriter. Unfortunately, the ending should have been more realistic and therefore harrowing)

Stephen King's Golden Years; It; The Stand; The Tommyknockers: see individual titles.

Stepping Out, 1991, 110m, ★★½/$, Par/Par, PG. An aging tap dancer gets a motley crew of misfit, mostly female, dance students ready for a big show. Liza Minnelli, Shelley Winters, Robyn Stevan, Bill Irwin, Ellen Greene, Andrew Martin, Julie Walters. w., P-adap. Richard Harris, d. Lewis Gilbert.

COMEDY: COMEDY DRAMA: Ordinary People Stories; Dancers; Dance Movies; Teachers; Teachers & Students; Putting on a Show; Comebacks; Coulda Been Good; Stagelike Films; Overlooked at Release; Old-Fashioned Recent Films (Strictly Ballroom; Educating Rita)

The Sterile Cuckoo, 1969, 107m, ★★★¹/₂/$$$, Par/Par, R/S. An awkward and shy girl comes of age sexually at a New England college in the 60s, though it may not change her life for the better. Liza Minnelli (BActress), Tim McIntire, Wendell Burton, Austin Green. w. Alvin Sargent, N-adap. John Nichols, d. Alan J. Pakula. BOSong, "Come Saturday Morning." Oscars: 2-0.

COMEDY DRAMA: ROMANCE: Tearjerkers; **MELODRAMA:** Romantic Comedy; Romantic Drama; Shy People; Wallflowers; Nerds; Nerds & Wallflowers; Virgins; Eccentric People; Free Spirits; College Life; New England; Old-Fashioned Recent Films (Cabaret; Rachel, Rachel; Circle of Friends; Georgy Girl)

Stevie, 1978/1981, 102m, ★★★¹/₂/$$, First Artists-Goldwyn/Sultan, PG. A poetess lives out her solitary and somewhat eccentric life in a London suburb. Glenda Jackson, Mona Washbourne, Trevor Howard. w. P-adap. Hugh Whitemore, d. Robert Enders.

DRAMA: Character Studies; Women Alone; Lonely People; Eccentric People; Mothers & Daughters; Writers; Poets; Narrated Films; Crossing the Line; Quiet Little Films; Female Protagonists; British Films; Hidden Gems (Rachel, Rachel)

Stick, 1985, 109m, ★★/$, Universal/MCA-U, R/P-V-S. When he gets out of prison, a hardened criminal goes to Miami to hunt down the killers of his friend. Burt Reynolds, Candice Bergen, George Segal, Charles Durning. w. Elmore Leonard, Joseph C. Stinson, N-adap. Elmore Leonard, d. Burt Reynolds.

ACTION: Crime Drama; Revenge; Convict's Revenge; Avenging Death of Loved One; Manhunts; Mob Stories; Female Among Males; Miami

(Ed: Better than other Reynolds outings in the 80s, but that's not saying much)

Sticky Fingers, 1988, 88m, ★★/$, Ind/Media. Two female rock musicians without much hope of success spend money left with them which belongs to a drug dealer. Helen Slater, Melanie Mayron, Danitra Vance, Eileen Brennan, Carole Kane, Christopher Guest. w. Catlin Adams, Melanie Mayron, d. Catlin Adams.

COMEDY: Chase Movies; Comedy of Errors; Drugs-Dealing; Mob Comedy; Fugitives from the Mob; Musicians; Female Screenwriters; Female Directors; Female Protagonists; Coulda Been Good; Good Premise Unfulfilled; Independent Films

(Outrageous Fortune; The Lemon Sisters; True Romance; Money for Nothing)

Still of the Night, 1982, 91m, ★★★/$$, MGM-UA/MGM-UA, R/V. When his patient is murdered, a psychiatrist becomes the prime suspect but also the prime target for being the next victim. Roy Scheider, Meryl Streep, Jessica Tandy. w. Robert Benton, David Newman, d. Robert Benton.

SUSPENSE: MURDER: MYSTERY: MURDER MYSTERY: Mystery-Whodunit?; Psychological Thriller; Serial Killers; Detective Stories; Psychiatrists; Psychiatrist as Detective; Men in Jeopardy; Dangerous Women; Murderers-Female; Underrated; Overlooked at Release; Hidden Gems; Coulda Been Great

(Vertigo; Psycho; Dressed to Kill; Obsession)

(Ed: Streep's other release the same week, *Sophie's Choice*, completely overshadowed any attention this might have received, and it did deserve some. It's more stylish than the DePalma/Hitchcock reprises, though lacking in the third act, despite a few chilling moments)

The Sting, 1973, 129m, ★★★¹/₂/ $$$$$, Universal/MCA-U, PG. Two con artists (Paul Newman, Robert Redford [BActor]) try to pull a job on another con artist (Robert Shaw, BSActor) to avenge the death of a friend he caused, but humorous complications arise. w. David S. Ward (**BOScr**), d. George Roy Hill, (**BDirector**). **BPicture**, BCin, **BArt, BCostume, BEditing,** BSound, **BAScore.** Oscars: 10-7.

COMEDY DRAMA: COMEDY: Buddy Films; Heist Stories; Con Artists; Avenging Death of Loved One; Revenge; Mindgames; Clever Plots & Endings; Depression Era; 1930s

SEQUEL: The Sting 2.

(Butch Cassidy & The Sundance Kid; Paper Moon)

The Sting 2, 1982, 102m, ★★/$, Universal/MCA-U, PG/P. The gangster that was stung in the first film plots revenge on those who did the stinging. Jackie Gleason, Mac Davis, Teri Garr, Karl Malden, Oliver Reed. w. David S. Ward, d. Jeremy Paul Kagan.

COMEDY DRAMA: COMEDY: Con Artists; Revenge; Mindgames; Turning the Tables; Depression Era; 1930s

(Ed: Completely new cast and basically nothing to do with the first one)

Stir Crazy, 1980, 111m, ★★¹/₂/$$$$$, Col/RCA-Col, PG/P. Two out of work actors and general cutups are mistaken for bank robbers and sent to prison, where they must use their wiles to get out. Gene Wilder, Richard Pryor, George Stanford Brown, JoBeth Williams. w. Bruce Jay Friedman, d. Sidney Poitier.

COMEDY: FARCE: Prison Drama; Prison Escape; Comedy of Errors; Comedy-Slapstick; Buddy Films; Accused Unjustly; Framed?; Friendships-Interracial; Black Directors; Blockbusters; Faded Hits

REMAKE: TV SERIES, 1984.

(Three Fugitives; Another You; Silver Streak)

(Ed: Only funny in places, but made over $100 million in 1980)

Stolen Hours, 1963, 101m, ★★/$, MGM/MGM-UA. An heiress is dying and has but a short time to see life and love . . . Susan Hayward, Michael Craig, Diane Baker. w. Jessamynn West, Joseph Hayes, d. Daniel Petrie.

MELODRAMA: Death-Impending; Disease Stories; Tearjerkers; **ROMANCE:** Romantic Drama; Heiresses; Blind People; Female Protagonists; Female Screenwriters; Forgotten Films

REMAKE OF: Dark Victory.

(Dark Victory; Ada; Magnificent Obsession; Love Story; Dying Young)

Stolen Kisses, 1968, 91m, ★★★¹/₂/$$, Films du Carrosse-UAC/MGM-UA. A young loser can't get a job or a girl but plugs along anyway. Jean-Pierre Leaud, Delphine Seyrig, Michel Lonsdale. w. Francois Truffaut, Claude de Givray, Bernard Revon, d. Francois Truffaut. BFLFilm. Oscars: 1-0.

COMEDY DRAMA: MELODRAMA: Young Men; Coming of Age; Nerds; Pre-Life Crisis; French Films

SEQUEL TO: The 400 Blows.

(The 400 Blows; Love on the Run)

A Stolen Life, 1939, 91m, ★★★/$$, Par./NA. A woman assumes the identity of her dead twin in order to fool her husband. Elisabeth Bergner, Michael Redgrave, Wilfrid Lawson. w. Margaret Kennedy, George Barraud, N-adap. Karel J. Benes, d. Paul Czinner.

A Stolen Life, 1946, 107m, ★★★/$$, WB/MGM-UA. A remake of above set in New England. Bette Davis, Glenn Ford, Dane Clark, Walter Brennan, Charles Ruggles, Bruce Bennett. w. Catherine Turney, d. Curtis Bernhardt.
SUSPENSE: DRAMA: Psychological Drama; Twins; Identities-Assumed; Dual Lives; Dead-Back from the; Sisters; Clever Plots & Endings; Mindgames; Female Protagonists; Female Screenwriters
(Dark Mirror; The Lady in the Iron Mask; The Man in the Iron Mask; Dead Ringer)

Stone Cold, 1991, 91m, ★1/2/$$, Col/Col, R/EV-P-S. Biker terrorists have to be stopped by an equally stone-cold, brained musclehead. Brian Bosworth, Lance Henriksen, William Forsythe. d. Craig Baxley.
ACTION: Men in Conflict; Bombs; Terrorists; Motorcycles; Body Builders; Unintentionally Funny

The Stooge, 1952, 100m, ★★1/2/$$$, Par/Par. In the thirties, an egocentric lounge singer is upstaged by his zany cohort. Dean Martin, Jerry Lewis, Polly Bergen, Marie McDonald. w. Fred Finkelhoffe, Martin Rackin, d. Norman Taurog.
COMEDY: Comedians; Comedy-Skit; Vaudeville; Singers; Men in Conflict; Understudies; Fame-Rise to; Buddy Films
(Scared Stiff; My Friend Irma; California or Bust)

Stop Making Sense, 1985, 96m, ★★★/$$, Island-Alive/Col. Concert of the alternative rock group, Talking Heads, much more stylish and evocative than most concert films. David Byrne, Talking Heads. d. Jonathan Demme.
Concert Films; Rock Groups; Musicians; Art Films; Cult Films; Sleeper Hits

Stop! Or My Mom Will Shoot, 1992, 87m, ★★/$, U/MCA-U, PG-13/P. An L.A. cop gets by with a little help from his gun-toting elderly mom. Sylvester Stallone, Estelle Getty, JoBeth Williams, Roger Rees, Martin Ferrero. w. Blake Snyder, William Osborne, William Davies, d. Roger Spottiswoode.

COMEDY: Police Stories; Police Comedy; Mothers & Sons; Mothers-Troublesome; Elderly Women; Good Premise Unfulfilled; Coulda Been Good (Oscar)
(Ed: Getty would be the only reason to see this)

The Stork Club, 1945, 98m, ★★/$$, 20th/Fox. A shopgirl saves the life of a mogul who then thanks her with gifts that her soldier boy doesn't like much. So they sing and dance. Betty Hutton, Barry Fitzgerald, Robert Benchley. d. Hal Walker.
MUSICALS: ROMANCE: Musical Romance; Saving Someone; Romance-Triangles; Rich People; Soldiers; Forgotten Films; Nightclubs

Storm in a Teacup, 1937, 87m, ★★★/$$$, Korda-Ealing/Nos. When an old lady refuses to pay her dog license, a media frenzy and minor revolt ensues. Vivien Leigh, Rex Harrison, Cecil Parker, Sara Allgood, Ursula Jeans. w. Ian Dalrymple, Donald Bull, P-adap. Bruno Frank, d. Ian Dalrymple.
COMEDY: SATIRE: Social Satire; Heroes-Unlikely; Fighting the System; Elderly Women; Capra-esque; British Films

Storm Warning, 1950, 93m, ★★★/$$, WB/WB. When a sophisticated city woman goes to a small Southern town to visit her sister, she witnesses a Ku Klux Klan incident and then realizes it was her brother-in-law she saw lift up his sheet. Ginger Rogers, Doris Day, Ronald Reagan, Steve Cochran, Hugh Sanders. w. Daniel Fuchs, Richard Brooks, d. Stuart Heisler.
DRAMA: SUSPENSE: Social Drama; MURDER: Witness to Murder; Murder-Debate to Reveal Killer; Lover Family Dislikes; Ku Klux Klan; Bigots; Lynchings; Race Relations; Southerns; Small-town Life; Oppression; Ahead of Its Time
REMAKE: Silhouette.
(Mississippi Burning; Silhouette)
(Ed: Same basic premise of *Streetcar Named Desire*, only Stanley gets his comeuppance here, and there's nowhere near the same level of drama and emotion)

Stormy Monday, 1987, 93m, ★★1/2/$, Palace-Par/Par, R/V-S. American gangsters hit the British Isles and ruffle some feathers trying to take over a local club in

Newcastle. Melanie Griffith, Tommy Lee Jones, Sting. w. d. Mike Figgis.
DRAMA: Crime Drama; Film Noir-Modern; Mob Stories; Mob Wars; Americans Abroad; British Films; Coulda Been Great; Writer-Directors

Stormy Weather, 1943, 77m, ★★★1/2/$$$, 20th/Fox. A musical biopic with a cast of great black talent from the era celebrating the career and music of Bill Robinson. Bill Robinson, Lena Horne, Fats Waller, Ada Brown, Cab Calloway, The Nicholas Brothers. w. Frederick Jackson, Ted Koehler, d. Andrew Stone.
MUSICALS: Biographies; MELODRAMA: Black Casts; Music Composers; Musicians; Jazz Life; Black Men
(Cabin in the Sky; Panama Hattie)

The Story of Adele H., 1975, 98m, ★★★/$$, Films du Carrosse-New World/New World, PG. The true story of Victor Hugo's daughter, who followed her lover to Nova Scotia, all the while writing letters. Isabelle Adjani (BActress), Bruce Robinson, Sylvia Marriott. w. Francois Truffaut, Jean Gruault, Suzanne Schiffman, d. Francois Truffaut. Oscars: 1-0.
DRAMA: ROMANCE: Biographies; True Stories; Young Women; Epistolaries; Letters Canada; French Films; Female Protagonists; Female Screenwriters
(Camille Claudelle)

The Story of Alexander Graham Bell, 1939, 97m, ★★★/$$$, 20th/NA. The "Graham-father" of the phone marries a deaf girl and eventually goes deaf himself. How's that for irony? Don Ameche, Henry Fonda, Loretta Young, Charles Coburn, Gene Lockhart. w. Lamar Trotti, d. Irving Cummings.
MELODRAMA: ROMANCE: Biographies; Historical Drama; Inventors; Deaf People; True Stories; 1890s

The Story of Boys and Girls, 1991, 92m, ★★★/$, Ind/Fox-Lorber. Two families join over wedding festivities and learn a lot about each other-perhaps too much. Lucrezia della Rovere, Massimo Bonnetti, Davide Bechini. w. d. Pupi Avanti.
MELODRAMA: Family Drama; Reunions; Weddings; Ensemble Films; 1930s; Italian Films; Overlooked at Release; Writer-Directors
(Cousin, Cousine; Everybody's Fine)

The Story of Dr. Wassell, 1944, 140m, ★★★/$$, Par/NA. A country doctor from Arkansas stationed in the South Pacific saves many lives during wartime. Gary Cooper, Laraine Day, Signe Hasso, Dennis O'Keefe, Carol Thurston. w. Alan le May, Charles Bennett, NF-adap. James Hilton, d. Cecil B. de Mille.

COMEDY DRAMA: MELODRAMA: Biographies; True Stories; Doctors; World War II Stories; Saintly People; Fish out of Water Stories; Mountain People; Arkansas
(Sergeant York; Not as a Stranger; Arrowsmith)

The Story of G.I. Joe, see G for **G.I. Joe**

The Story of Louis Pasteur, 1936, 85m, ★★★1/2/$$$, WB/MGM-UA. In the 19th century in France, the famous discoverer of penicillin fights the prejudices of the ignorant peasants in curing disease. Paul Muni (**BActor**), Josephine Hutchinson, Anita Louise. w. Sheridan Gibney, Pierre Collings (**BOStory, BScr**), d. William Dieterle. BPicture. Oscars: 4-3.

DRAMA: MELODRAMA: Biographies; Scientists; Saintly People; Cures/Solutions-Search for; Cures/Elixirs; Doctors; Saintly People
(Madame Curie; Lorenzo's Oil)

The Story of Robin Hood and His Merry Men, 1952, 84m, ★★★/$$, Disney/Disney. The famous noble thief who protests excessive taxation steals from the rich and gives to the poor. Richard Todd, Joan Rice, James Hayter, Hubert Gregg. w. Laurence E. Watkin, d. Ken Annakin.

ADVENTURE: Robin Hood Stories; Medieval Times; Class Conflicts; Rich vs. Poor; British Films; Forgotten Films
(The Adventures of Robin Hood)

The Story of Three Loves, 1953, 122m, ★★1/2/$$, MGM/NA. On an ocean liner, three couples have climactic moments in their respective relationships. Ethel Barrymore, James Mason, Moira Shearer, Pier Angeli, Leslie Caron, Kirk Douglas, Farley Granger, Agnes Moorehead, Zsa Zsa Gabor. w. John Collier, Jan Lustig, George Froeschel, d. Gottfried Reinhardt. BCArt. Oscars: 1-0.

ROMANCE: MELODRAMA: Marriage Drama; Marriage on the Rocks; Vacations; Vacation Romance; Multiple Stories; Interwoven Stories; Ships
(Grand Hotel; An Affair to Remember; Love Affair; Romance on the High Seas)

The Story of Vernon and Irene Castle, 1939, 93m, ★★★/$$$, RKO/Turner. The true story of the married cou-

ple who made a name for themselves on the Vaudeville circuit before tragedy struck in the first World War. Fred Astaire, Ginger Rogers, Edna May Oliver, Walter Brennan. w. Richard Sherman, Oscar Hammerstein II, Dorothy Yost, NF-adap. Irene Castle, d. H. C. Potter.

MUSICALS: Dance Movies; Music Movies; ROMANCE: Musical Romance; Musical Drama; MELODRAMA: TRAGEDY: Biographies; Partners-Married; World War I Stories; Death-Dealing With; Soldiers; Fame-Rise to; Astaire & Rogers
(Flying Down to Rio; Top Hat)

The Story of Will Rogers, 1950, 109m, ★★/$$, WB/NA. A rodeo act who became a star under the wing of Ziegfeld and started a weekly radio broadcast. Will Rogers, Jr., Jane Wyman, James Gleason, Eddie Cantor. w. Frank Davis, Stanley Roberts, d. Michael Curtiz.

COMEDY DRAMA: TRAGEDY: Biographies; Hollywood Biographies; Comedians; Storytellers; Fame-Rise to; Airplane Crashes; Hollywood Life; Rodeos
(Ed: No offense to the son, but audiences probably stayed away in deference to the original, and justly so)

Storyville, 1992, 112m, ★★/$, Col/Col, R/S-FFN-MRN-V. A young politician in New Orleans has an affair with an Asian woman which gets him into big trouble and accused of murder when sex tapes of him and the girl surface. James Spader, Joanne Whalley-Kilmer, Jason Robards, Charlotte Lewis, Michael Warren, Piper Laurie. w. d. Mark Frost.

SUSPENSE: MURDER: Framed?; Accused Unjustly; Videotape Scandals; Videotape Scandals Starring James Spader; New Orleans; Political Campaigns; Politicians; Asian-Americans; Romance-Interracial; Scandals; Coulda Been Good; Southerns
(Bad Influence; Sex, Lies & Videotape; True Colors)

Straight out of Brooklyn, 1991, 83m, ★★★/$, AP-Goldwyn/Goldwyn, R/P-V. A young black boy growing up in Brooklyn is determined to get out of the ghetto and persuades some friends to rob a store to finance his plans. George T. Odom, Ann D. Sanders, Lawrence Gilliard, Jr., Barbara Sanon, Matty Rich. w. d. Matty Rich.

DRAMA: Crime Drama; MELODRAMA: Inner City Life; Coming of Age; Black

Men; Boys; Black Casts; New York Life; Good Premise Unfulfilled; Coulda Been Great; Hidden Gems; Black Screenwriters; Black Directors; Writer-Directors
(Juice; Boyz 'n the Hood)
(Ed: Rich was only 19 when this was begun. Overrated to an extent, not up to the level of *Boyz 'n the Hood,* by black writer/director John Singleton-also in his early 20's when it was made)

Straight Talk, 1992, 91m, ★★★/$$, Hollywood/Hollywood, PG/P. A woman with a gift for gab leaves Arkansas for Chicago to get some sort of job, but winds up a talk show radio sensation when she's mistaken for a psychologist. Dolly Parton, James Woods, Griffin Dunne, Michael Madsen, Deirdre O'Connell, John Sayles, Spalding Gray. w. Craig Bolotin, Patricia Resnick, d. Barnet Kellman.

COMEDY: ROMANCE: Romantic Comedy; Fish out of Water Stories; City vs. Country; Psychologists; Radio Life; Fame-Rise to; Heroes-Unlikely; Identities-Mistaken; Old-Fashioned Recent Films; Chicago
(The Couch Trip; Talk Radio; Nothing Sacred)

Straight Time, 1978, 114m, ★★★/$, WB/WB, R/P-V. An ex-con can't deal with being shadowed by his persistent parole officer, and as the other attendant pressures of "going straight" become too much, he slips back into a life of crime. Dustin Hoffman, Theresa Russell, Gary Busey, Harry Dean Stanton. w. Alvin Sargent, Edward Bunker, Jeffrey Boam, N-adap. Edward Bunker (*No Beast So Fierce*), d. Ulu Grosbard.

DRAMA: Crime Drama; Ex-Convicts; Prison Drama; Redemption; Starting Over; Forgotten Films; Overlooked at Release; Underrated; Hidden Gems
(Carlito's Way; Family Business)

Strait Jacket, 1963, 92m, ★★1/2/$$, Col/Col. An axe murderess is set free to commit more axe murders. Joan Crawford, Diane Baker, Leif Erickson, Howard St. John, Rochele Hudson, George Kennedy. w. Robert Bloch, d. William Castle.

HORROR: MURDER: Serial Killers; Murderers-Female; Asylums; Mental Illness; Camp; Cult Films; Unintentionally Funny; Female Protagonists
(Berserk!; The Caretakers; So I Married an Axe Murderer)

Strange Bargain, 1949, 68m, ★★★/$, RKO/NA. A bookkeeper about to lose his job is told by his boss he'll get two years' salary if he'll help make the boss' suicide look like murder-only he doesn't know the boss is setting up his partner in the process. Jeffrey Lynn, Henry Morgan, Martha Scott, Katherine Emery. w. Lillie Hayward, d. Will Price.
SUSPENSE: MURDER: MYSTERY: MURDER MYSTERY: Detective Stories; Detectives-Police; Accused Unjustly; Framed?; Suicidal Tendencies; Unemployment; Greed; Inheritances at Stake; Nerds; Clever Plots & Endings; Hidden Gems

Strange Bedfellows, 1965, 99m, ★★½/$$, U-I/NA. Two expatriates in London, an American businessman and his lusty Italian wife, have trouble relating with each other and the foreign culture they inhabit which leads to a bedroom farce. Rock Hudson, Gina Lollobrigida, Gig Young, Edward Judd, Howard St. John, Arthur Haynes. w. Melvin Frank, Michael Pertwee, d. Melvin Frank.
COMEDY: FARCE: Sex Comedy; Bedroom Farce; Cheating Men; Cheating Women; Americans Abroad; London; Coulda Been Great; Good Premise Unfulfilled
(Come September; How to Murder Your Wife)

Strange Brew, 1983, 90m, ★★/$, MGM/MGM-UA, PG. Two dumb Canadians invade a brewery looking for free beer and meet up with two mental patients. Who's crazier and more stupid? Dave Thomas, Rick Moranis, Max Von Sydow, Paul Dooley, Lynne Griffin. w. Rick Moranis, Dave Thomas, Steven De Jarnatt, d. Dave Thomas, Rick Moranis.
COMEDY: Comedy-Skit; Simple Minds; Mental Illness; Alcoholics; Canada

Strange Cargo, 1940, 105m, ★★★/$$, MGM/MGM-UA. On Devil's Island, several prisoners plan and execute a prison escape and meet a Christlike figure who shows them a better way of life. Clark Gable, Joan Crawford, Ian Hunter, Peter Lorre, Paul Lukas, Albert Dekker. w. Lawrence Hazard, N-adap. Richard Sale, *(Not Too Narrow, Not Too Deep)*, d. Frank Borzage.
DRAMA: MELODRAMA: Prison Escapes; Prison Drama; Devil's Island; Charismatic People; Unintentionally Funny; Camp; Hidden Gems

(Papillon; Devil Doll)
(Ed: A strange but interesting anomaly)
Strange Days, 1995, 135m, ★★★/$$, 20th/Fox, R/P-ES-EV-B&G. An ex-cop in futuristic LA is in the black market of selling other people's memories for the entertainment purposes of the bored. But when he sells the wrong memory and gets caught up in other intrigue, he's forced to face the oppressive reality of the oppressive LA that's not so different from that of today. Ralph Fiennes, Angela Bassett, Juliette Lewis, Tom Sizemore, Michael Wincott, Vincent D'Onofrio. w. James Cameron & Jay Cocks, d. Kathryn Bigelow.
SCI-FI: SUSPENSE: ACTION: Computer Terror; Computers; Memories; Thieves; Virtual Reality; Female Directors
(Virtuosity; Blade Runner; Total Recall; Johnny Mnemonic)

Strange Interlude, 1932, 110m, ★★★/$$$, MGM/MGM-UA. Norma Shearer, Clark Gable, May Robson, Robert Young, Maureen O'Sullivan. d. Robert Z. Leonard.
Strange Interlude, 1990, 190m, ★★★½/$, Ind/Fries. A wealthy woman wants to have a baby but when she discovers insanity runs in her husband's family, she decides to get another man to perform the duty, with repercussion, of course. Based on Eugene O'Neill's classic play. Glenda Jackson, Jose Ferrer, David Dukes, Ken Howard. d. Herbert Wise. Tony-winning production.
Stage Tapings
DRAMA: Marriage Drama; Scandals; Fathers-Surrogate; Babies-Having; Women-Childless; Cheating Women; Ahead of Its Time; Classic Literary Adaptations
(Hedda; Ghosts; Long Day's Journey into Night)

Strange Invaders, 1983, 93m, ★★½/$, Orion/Orion, PG-13/V. A small Midwestern town's inhabitants are replaced by humanoids from outer space. Paul Le Mat, Nancy Allen, Diana Scarwid, Michael Lerner, Louise Fletcher. w. William Condon, Michael Laughlin, d. Michael Laughlin.
SCI-FI: SATIRE: Spoofs; Aliens-Outer Space-Evil; Paranoia; Small-town Life
(Invaders from Mars; Invasion of the Body Snatchers)

The Strange Loves of Martha Ivers, 1946, 116m, ★★★/$$, Par/Nos. A young girl with a haunted past grows up and

marries an ineffectual lawyer. Then, an old boyfriend who knows of her checkered past comes into town and stirs up trouble. Barbara Stanwyck, Van Heflin, Kirk Douglas. w. Robert Rossen, Jack Patrick (BOStory), d. Lewis Milestone. Oscars: 1-0.
DRAMA: MELODRAMA: MURDER: Secrets-Keeping; Past-Haunted by the; Blackmail; Reunions; Female Protagonists
(The Two Mrs. Carrolls; Ada; The File on Thelma Jordan)

The Strange One, 1957, 99m, Monogram/NA. At a military school down south, an eccentric young cadet stirs up trouble with his sadistic, rebellious tendencies. Ben Gazzara, George Peppard, Mark Richman, Pat Hingle, Arthur Storch, Paul Richards. w. Calder Willingham, N-adap. Calder Willingham *(End As a Man)*, d. Jack Garfein.
DRAMA: Military Movies; Conformism; Rebels; Ostracism; Young Men-Angry; Young Men; Teenagers; Evil Men; Boarding Schools; Military Schools; Southerns; Forgotten Films; Hidden Gems
(If; The Lords of Discipline; The Wild One; Rebel Without a Cause)

The Stranger, 1946, 95m, ★★★/$$, RKO/Nos, Prism. A Nazi criminal hides in a New England town and marries an unsuspecting woman, but a detective is hot on his trail. Orson Welles, Loretta Young, Edward G. Robinson. w. Anthony Veiller, Victor Trivas, Decia Dunning (BOStory), d. Orson Welles. Oscars: 1-0.
SUSPENSE: DRAMA: MURDER: Detective Stories; Chase Movies; Nazi Stories; Hiding Out; Trail of a Killer; Enemy-Sleeping with the; Romance-Dangerous; Women in Jeopardy; Newlyweds; New England
(The House on 92nd Street; Marathon Man)

A Stranger Among Us, 1992, 109m, ★★★/$$, Hollywood/Hollywood, PG-13/V. A female cop goes undercover to catch a criminal believed to be lurking in a Hassidic Jewish community in Brooklyn. Only problem is, she falls for one of the men there. Melanie Griffith, Eric Thal, John Pankow, Tracy Pollan, Mia Sara, Jamey Sheridan. w. Robert Avereen, d. Sidney Lumet.
SUSPENSE: MYSTERY: MURDER: MURDER MYSTERY: Police Stories; Law

Officers-Female; Undercover; Jewish People; Fish Out of Water Stories; Romance-Forbidden; Romance-Reluctant; Female Protagonists (Witness; The Chosen)

(Ed: Interesting romance and fairly interesting mystery, the former being the compelling force, so whodunit fans beware)

A Stranger Is Watching, 1981, 92m, ★★1/2/$, MGM/MGM-UA, PG/V. The daughter of a woman who was raped and murdered is stalked by the culprit. Kate Mulgrew, Rip Torn, James Naughton. w. Earl McRaugh, Victor Miller, N-adap. Mary Higgins Clark, d. Sean S. Cunningham.

SUSPENSE: Women in Jeopardy; Children in Jeopardy; **MURDER:** Trail of a Killer; Rape/Rapists; Revenge on Rapist; Stalkers; Kill the Best; Subways; Coulda Been Great; Forgotten Films (The Cradle Will Fall; An Eye for an Eye)

(Ed: The huge bestseller gets the treatment from *Friday the 13th* director and fails)

Strangers in Good Company (The Company of Strangers), 1990, 101m, ★★★/$$, Touchstone/Touchstone, PG. When an old bus carrying seven even older women breaks down in the country, they must "rough it," and they get to learn about themselves and regain a sense of youthful adventure in the process. Alice Diabo, Constance Garneau, Winifred Holden, Cissy Meddings, Mary Meigs, Catherine Roche, Michelle Sweeney, Beth Webber. w. Gloria Demers, Cynthia Scott, David Wilson, Sally Bochner, d. Cynthia Scott.

ADVENTURE: COMEDY DRAMA: Ensembles-Female; Ensemble Films; Elderly Women; Vacations; Journies; Nightmare Vacations; Busses; Australian Films; Hidden Gems; Female Protagonists; Female Screenwriters; Female Directors (Travelling North; A Woman's Tale)

Strangers on a Train, 1950, 101m, ★★★★/$$$, WB/WB. A psychotic rich man (Robert Walker) tries to get a tennis pro (Farley Granger) to kill his father if the man will kill his nuisance wife. w. Raymond Chandler, Czenzi Oromonde, N-adap. Patricia Highsmith, d. Alfred Hitchcock. BB&WCin. Oscars: 1-0.

SUSPENSE: MURDER: Murder of Spouse; Psychological Thriller; Psycho-Killers; Mental Illness; Race Against

Time; Accused Unjustly; Murder-Clearing Oneself; Framed?; Murders-Exchanging; Turning the Tables; Double Crossings; Betrayals; Blackmail; Tennis; Malicious Menaces; Hitchcockian

COMIC REMAKE: Throw Momma from the Train.

REMAKE/RETREAD: Bad Influence. (Rope; Shadow of a Doubt; Bad Influence; Throw Momma from the Train)

Strangers, the Story of a Mother and Daughter, 1979, 90m, ★★★/$$$, CBS/Time-Life. A widow lives alone in pain when her daughter comes to help out, but neither really wants to be there. Bette Davis (Emmy winner), Gena Rowlands, Donald Moffat. d. Milton Katselas.

DRAMA: MELODRAMA: Tearjerkers; Mothers & Daughters; Reunions; Family Drama; Women's Films; Female Protagonists; Widows; Generation Gap; TV Movies

(Terms of Endearment; Something to Talk About)

Strangers When We Meet, 1960, 117m, ★★★/$$$, Col/Col. Wealthy neighbors in Bel-Air have an affair, but both are married to other people. They figure it out. Kirk Douglas, Kim Novak, Ernie Kovacs, Walter Matthau, Barbara Rush, Kent Smith, Helen Gallagher. w. N-adap. Even Hunter, d. Richard Quine.

ROMANCE: MELODRAMA: Romantic Drama; Romance with Married Person; Cheating Men; Cheating Women; Neighbors; Beverly Hills; Rich People; Faded Hits

(Falling in Love; Brief Encounter; Skylark; An Affair to Remember)

Stranger Than Paradise, 1985, 99m (B&W), ★★★/$$, Goldwyn/Goldwyn, R/P. A saxophone player takes his Hungarian friends on a road trip to Cleveland in the snow. John Lurie, Ezsther Balint, John Edson. w. d. Jim Jarmusch.

COMEDY DRAMA: Black Comedy; Eccentric People; Art Films; Road Movies; Immigrants; Europeans-Eastern; Sleeper Hits

(Down by Law; Mystery Train; Eraserhead)

Strapless, 1989, 100m, ★★1/2/$, Virgin-Miramax/Miramax, R/S. Two eccentric American sisters in London try their hand at relationships in the fashion world. Blair Brown, Bridget Fonda, Bruno Ganz, Alan Howard. w. d. David Hare.

DRAMA: Art Films; Sisters; London; Fashion World; Americans Abroad; Writer-Directors (Scandal; Plenty; Wetherby)

(Ed: Interesting for fans of the actresses or Hare, but not much else. Nowhere near Hare's *Wetherby* or *Plenty*)

Strategic Air Command, 1955, 114m, ★★1/2/$$$, Par/Par. The air force beckons a baseball player back to flight. James Stewart, June Allyson, Frank Lovejoy, Barry Sullivan. w. Valentine Davies, Beirne Lay (BOStory), d. Anthony Mann. Oscars: 1-0.

ACTION: DRAMA: Action Drama; War Stories; War Battles; Pilots-Military; World War II Stories; Baseball; Patriotic Films

(Air Force; The Bridges at Toko-Ri)

The Stratton Story, 1949, 106m, ★★1/2/$$$, MGM/MGM-UA. An obsessed fan starts at baseball late, becomes good at it, then has a tragic accident. James Stewart, June Allyson, Frank Morgan, Agnes Moorehead, Bill Williams. w. Douglas Morrow, Guy Trooper (BOStory), d. Sam Wood. Oscars: 1-1.

DRAMA: MELODRAMA: TRAGEDY: ROMANCE: Marriage Drama; Tearjerkers; Disease Stories; Baseball; Crying in Baseball; Dreams; Illusions Destroyed

(Bang the Drum Slowly; Pride of the Yankees; The Lou Gehrig Story; Rudy)

The Strawberry Blonde, 1941, 97m, ★★★/$$$, WB/MGM-UA. In the early 1900s, a dentist thinks back and wonders if he married the right girl. James Cagney, Olivia deHavilland, Rita Hayworth, Alan Hale, Jack Carson, Una O'Connor. w. Julius & Philip Epstein, d. Raoul Walsh.

ROMANCE: COMEDY DRAMA: Romance-Triangles; Romance-Choosing the Right Person; Memories; Decisions-Big; 1900s; Dentists; Nostalgia

REMAKE OF: One Sunday Afternoon. (The Dolly Sisters; Yankee Doodle Dandy)

The Strawberry Statement, 1970, 109m, ★★1/2/$$$, MGM/MGM-UA, R/S-P. At a university, students take over a building to protest the government and the Vietnam war. Bruce Davison, Kim Darby, Bud Cort. w. Israel Horowitz, N-adap. James Simon Kunen, d. Stuart Hagmann.

DRAMA: Anti-Establishment Films; Vietnam Era; Young Men-Angry; College

Life; Political Unrest; Riots; Time Capsules; Forgotten Films; Hidden Gems
(Getting Straight; The Revolutionary; Higher Learning; Generation)

Straw Dogs, 1971, 118m, ★★★¹/₂/$$, NG/WB, R/S-EV. An American writer moves to rural England and antagonizes bit by bit the local hooligans, resulting in tragedy. Dustin Hoffman, Susan George, David Warner, Peter Vaughan, Colin Welland. w. David Goodman, Sam Peckinpah, d. Peckinpah. BScore. Oscars: 1-0.
DRAMA: TRAGEDY: Fish out of Water Stories; Rape/Rapists; Nightmares; Ordinary Person Turned Criminal; Saving Someone; Saving Oneself; Revenge; Revenge on Rapist; Writers; Americans Abroad; Violence-Sudden; Rural Life; Rednecks; England
(Southern Comfort; Deliverance; Straight Time)

Streamers, 1983, 118m, ★★★/$, Ind/Media, R/P. At an army barrack at the onset of the Vietnam war, tension begins to flare among soldiers waiting to go into battle. Matthew Modine, Michael Wright, Mitchell Lichtenstein, David Alan Grier, George Dzundza. w. P-adap. David Rabe, d. Robert Altman.
DRAMA: Ensemble Films; Ensembles-Male; Young Men; Young Men-Angry; Vietnam War; Vietnam Era; Soldiers; Anti-War Films
(Casualties of War; Baby Blue Marine; Tribes; Full Metal Jacket)
(Ed: Insight not usually found in such subject matter)

Street Angel, 1928, 101m (part sound), ★★★/$$$$, 20th/NA. A prostitute with a heart of gold winds up out of the biz and in the circus. Which is worse? Janet Gaynor, Charles Farrell. w. Marion Orth, P-adap. Monckton Hoffe, d. Frank Borzage.
MELODRAMA: Tearjerkers; Prostitutes with a Heart of Gold; Circus Life; Life Transitions; Unintentionally Funny; Camp; Female Protagonists
(Seventh Heaven; A Star Is Born [1937])

A Streetcar Named Desire, 1951, 122m, ★★★★/$$$$, WB/WB. A woman who's lost everything (Vivien Leigh, BActress) comes to stay with her sister (Kim Hunter, BSActress) out of desperation, but her brother-in-law (Marlon Brando, BActor) doesn't buy her tragedy, then creates one for her. Karl Malden

(BSActor). w. P-adap. Tennessee Williams (BScr), d. Elia Kazan (BDirector). BPicture, BScore, BB&WCin, **BB&WArt**. Oscars: 10-3.
A Streetcar Named Desire, 1984, 94m, ★★★¹/₂/$$$$, ABC/NA. A more opened-up version shot on location in New Orleans. Ann-Margret, Treat Williams, Beverly D'Angelo, d. John Erman.
TV Movies
A Streetcar Named Desire, 1995, 135m, ★★★¹/₂/$$$$, CBS/NA. A more faithful adaptation of Williams' first stage version, shot on stage sets. Jessica Lange, Alec Baldwin, John Goodman.
Jessica Lange Goes Southern; TV Movies
DRAMA: MELODRAMA: TRAGEDY: Mental Illness; Nervous Breakdowns; Illusions; Romance-Triangles; Evil Men; Homosexual Secrets; Past-Haunted by the; Rape/Rapists; New Orleans; Southerns; Female Protagonists; Classic Play Adaptations; Tennessee Williams-esque
(Cat on a Hot Tin Roof; Sweet Bird of Youth; The Fugitive Kind; Summer and Smoke)

Street Fighter, 1994, 106m, ★★/$$, U/MCA-U, PG-13/EV. The superhero from the video game does battle against an evil villain who has kidnapped foreign dignitaries for ransom. Jean-Claude Van Damme, Raul Julia, Ming-Na Wen, Damian Chapa, Kylie Minogue, Simon Callow. w. d. Steven E. de Souza.
ACTION: Video Game Movies; CHILDREN'S: Heroes-Superhuman; Cartoonlike Movies; Kidnappings; Flops-Major
(Mortal Kombat; Judge Dredd; Super Mario Brothers)

Street Scene, 1931, 80m, ★★★/$$$, Goldwyn-UA/Goldwyn. Tragedy results for a woman cheating on her husband on a street in lower-class New York, as all of the other stories of the neighbors are told. Sylvia Sidney, William Collier. w. P-adap. Elmer Rice, d. King Vidor.
DRAMA: TRAGEDY: MELODRAMA: Slice of Life Stories; Multiple Stories; Interwoven Stories; Cheating Women; Crimes of Passion; Inner City Life; New York Life; Time Capsules; Depression Era; Female Protagonists
(Dead End; Bad Girl; Winterset)

Street Smart, 1987, 95m, ★★★/$$, Cannon/MGM-UA, R/EP-V-S-FN-MRN. A reporter goes to Times Square to interview

pimps and prostitutes, and he gets more involved than he thought he'd ever get. Christopher Reeve, Kathy Baker (BSActress), Morgan Freeman (BSActor), Mimi Rogers, Jay Patterson. w. David Freeman, d. Jerry Schatzberg. Oscars: 2-0.
DRAMA: Crime Drama; Journalists; Inner City Life; Prostitutes-Low Class; Pimps; Underworld; Sleeper Hits

Streets of Fire, 1984, 94m, ★★¹/₂/$, U/MCA-U, PG/S. A rock star gets kidnapped and a goodlooking detective tries to get her back, amid a lot of music. Michael Pare, Diane Ladd, Amy Madigan, Rick Moranis, Willem Dafoe. w. Walter Hill, Larry Gross, d. Walter Hill.
ACTION: DRAMA: ROMANCE: Music Video Style; Music Movies; Detective Stories; Rock Stars; Singers; Kidnappings; Film Noir-Modern; Coulda Been Good; Flops-Major

Streets of Gold, 1986, 95m, ★★¹/₂/$, 20th/CBS-Fox, PG-13/V. An Eastern European immigrant becomes a boxing coach for street kids in the inner city. Klaus Maria Brandauer, Adrian Pasdar, Wesley Snipes, Angela Molina. w. Heywood Gould, Richard Price, Tom Cole, d. Joe Roth.
ACTION: Sports Movies; Boxing; Underdog Stories; Inner City Life; Feelgood Movies; Europeans-Eastern; Immigrants; Coulda Been Good; Overlooked at Release
(Gladiator; Rocky)

Strictly Ballroom, 1992, 94m, ★★★¹/₂/$$, Miramax/Touchstone, PG. A rebellious ballroom dancer finds a partner to spar and dance with into competition and romance. Paul Mercurio, Tara Morice, Bill Hunter, Pat Thomason. w. Baz Luhrmann, Craig Pearce, P-adap. Baz Luhrmann, Andrew Lovell, d. Baz Luhrmann.
COMEDY: ROMANCE: Romantic Comedy; Dance Movies; Dancers; Music Video Style; Competitions; Sleeper Hits; Australian Films; Hidden Gems; Old-Fashioned Recent Films
(Dirty Dancing; Muriel's Wedding; Stepping Out)

Strictly Business, 1992, 87m, ★★★/$$, WB/WB, P-S. A black, yuppie, lawyer nerd (Joseph Phillips) wants a dancer from a hip-hop club (Halle Berry), and his cool mailroom pal (Tommy Davidson) is going to help him get her, but in the process, gets him into trouble that could jeopardize everything he's earned. w. Thomas Hudlin, Reginald Hudlin, d. Kevin Hooks.

DRAMA: ROMANCE: Romance-Boy Wants Girl; Double-Crossings; Black Casts; Black Men; Buppies; Lawyers; Yuppies; Nerds; Extrovert vs. Introvert; Underdog Stories; Nightclubs; Black Screenwriters; Black Directors (Boomerang; House Party)
(Ed: Slick and fairly well written with a good sense of humor, though ultimately nothing particularly important, except for the portrayal of class-mixing of various black characters.)

Strike, 1924, 70m, ★★★1/2/$, Goskino/ Nos. A strike occurs in pre-revolution Russia and is squashed by the police. w. d. Sergei Eisenstein.

DRAMA: TRAGEDY: Documentary Style; Strikes; Unions; Oppression; Political Unrest; Factory Life; Russian Films; Writer-Directors; Film History; Silent Films
(The Battleship Potemkin)
(Ed: Film historian's classic; finale from *Apocalypse Now* borrowed from slaughter scenes here)

Strike Up the Band, 1940, 120m, ★★★/ $$$, MGM/MGM-UA. Youngsters in a high school band prepare for a big contest, hence the title. Judy Garland, Mickey Rooney, Paul Whiteman. w. Fred Finkle-hoffe, John Monks, d. Busby Berkeley.

MUSICALS: High School Life; Musicians; Competitions; Small-town Life
(Andy Hardy SERIES)

Striking Distance, 1993, 101m, ★★1/2/$, Col/Col, R/EV-P. A cop whose father is killed insists that another cop did it. Bruce Willis, Sarah Jessica Parker, Dennis Farina, Robert Pastorelli, Timothy Busfield, John Mahoney. d. Marty Kaplan, Rowdy Herrington, d. Randy Herrington.

ACTION: MURDER: MYSTERY: MUR-DER MYSTERY: Serial Killers; Police Stories; Murder of Police; Avenging Death of Someone; Unbelieved; Flops-Major
(Die Hard; The Last Boy Scout; Cop)

Stripes, 1981, 106m, ★★★/$$$$, Col/RCA-Col, R/S-P-FN. Goofballs enter the army and do things they'd never get away with in reality. Bill Murray, John Candy, Harold Ramis, Warren Oates, P. J. Soles, John Larroquette, Sean Young. w. Len Blum, Dan Goldberg, Harold Ramis, d. Ivan Reitman.

COMEDY: Military Movies; Military Comedy; Comedy-Skit; Fools-Bumbling; Bathroom Humor; Female Among Males; Soldiers
(Private Benjamin; Abbott & Costello SERIES; The Sad Sack; Meatballs; Police Academy SERIES; In the Army Now; Caddyshack)

The Stripper, 1963, 95m, ★★★/$$, 20th/Fox, Key. A washed-up exotic dancer goes back home to Kansas and a teenage mechanic falls for her, but it's not meant to be. Joanne Woodward, Richard Beymer, Claire Trevor, Carol Lynley, Robert Webber, Gypsy Rose Lee, Michael J. Pollard. d. Franklin J. Schaffner.

DRAMA: MELODRAMA: ROMANCE: Romance-Older Women/Younger Men; Romance-Doomed; Strippers; Midlife Crisis; Bimbos; Infatuations; Small-town Life; Midwestern Life; Hidden Gems; Tennessee Williams-esque
(Summer of '42; A Tiger's Tale)
(Ed: Not of great quality, but interesting nonetheless)

Stroker Ace, 1983, 96m, ★★/$, U/MCA-U, PG/S-P. An action-comedy revolving around a race-car driver and a chicken franchise empire sponsoring him. Burt Reynolds, Ned Beatty, Jim Nabors, Parker Stevenson, Loni Anderson. w. Hugh Wilson, Hall Needham, N-adap. William Neely & Robert Ottum, *Stand on It*, d. Hal Needham.

ACTION: COMEDY: Action Comedy; Car Racing; Bimbos; Good Premise; Unfulfilled
(Cannonball Run; Hooper)
(Ed: When the jokes don't work in a comedy, it's a problem)

Stromboli, 1951, 81m, ★★1/2/$, Ind/ VCI. An Eastern European woman marries an Italian fisherman in order to escape the Russians, but the marriage is too much of a sham to bear. Ingrid Bergman, Mario Vitale. d. Roberto Rossellini.

DRAMA: Art Films; Marriage for Citizenship; Marriage Drama; Marriage on the Rocks; Europeans-Eastern; Fishermen; Quiet Little Films; Neo-Realism; Italian Films

Stroszek, 1977, 108m, ★★★/$, New Yorker/New Yorker, R/S. Three lower-class con-artist Germans emigrate to America and wind-up in a trailer, unable to figure out the American dream. Bruno S., Eva Mattes, Clemens Scheitz. w. d. Werner Herzog.

DRAMA: Immigrants; Prostitutes-Low Class; Thieves; Con Artists; Quiet Little Films; German Films; American Myth; Writer-Directors

The Stud, 1978, 90m, ★★/$$, EMI/HBO, R/ES-FN-MN. A woman who owns a sex nightclub hires a gigolo to take care of things. Joan Collins, Oliver Tobias, w. N-adap. Jackie Collins, d. Wuentin Masters.

MELODRAMA: Erotic Drama; Prostitutes-Male; Nightclubs; Sexual Revolution; British Films; Camp
SEQUEL: The Bitch.

The Stuff, 1985, 93m, ★★/$, New World/ New World, R/V-B&G. Two fast-food moguls find out their concoctions together turn townsfolk in to murderous zombies. Michael Moriarty, Andrea Marcovicci, Garrett Morris, Paul Sorvino, Danny Aiello, Brooke Adams. w. d. Larry Cohen.

HORROR: Monsters-Human; Zombies; Poisons; Epidemics; Writer-Directors; Camp; Drugs-Addictions
(The Blob; The Prophecy)

The Stuntman, 1980, 129m, ★★★/$$, 20th/CBS-Fox, R/. A stuntman (Steve Railsback) may be used for a real-life murder situation instead of a fictional movie situation. Peter O'Toole (BActor), Barbara Hershey, Steve Railsback, Alex Rocco. w. Lawrence Marcus (BAScr), N-adap. Paul Broadeur, d. Richard Rush (BDirector). Oscars: 3-0.

DRAMA: SUSPENSE: MURDER: SATIRE: Framed?; Psychological Drama; Mindgames; Accidents; Conspiracy; Movies within Movies; Moviemaking; Hollywood Life; Hollywood Satire; Directors; Actors; Actresses; Illusions; Stuntmen; Hitchcockian
(FX; FX 2; Hooper)

The Subject Was Roses, 1968, 107m, ★★★1/2/$$, MGM/MGM-UA, PG. When a soldier returns home from war, he realizes he has completely changed and he can't deal with his parents. Martin Sheen, Patricia Neal (BActress), Jack Albertson (**BSActor**), Don Saxon, Elaine Williams. w. Frank Gilroy, d. Ulu Grosbard. Oscars: 2-1.

DRAMA: Character Studies; Family Drama; Young Men; Alienation; Life Transitions; Reunions; Vietnam War; Vietnam Era; Soldiers; Veterans; Parents vs. Children; Generation Gap; 1960s; Stagelike Films; Pulitzer Prize Adaptations; Forgotten Films; Hidden Gems

(Coming Home; All My Sons; Return of the Soldier; Da)

The Substitute, 1993, 86m, ★★/$, Par/Par, R/S-P-B&G-FN-MRN. A high school teacher likes to seduce and murder her pupils, but a few don't go down so easily. Amanda Donohoe, Dalton James, Marky Mark Wahlberg. w. Cynthia Verlaine, d. Martin Donovan.

HORROR: MURDER: Serial Killers; Teenagers; Teenage Movies; Black Comedy; Murders-One by One; Murder-Learning to; Romance with Teacher; Teachers & Students; High School Life; Coulda Been Good; Female Protagonists; Female Screenwriters; Independent Films
(Cutting Class; The Class of Miss MacMichael)

The Subterraneans, 1960, 89m, ★★★/$, MGM/NA. San Francisco beat generation types hang out in clubs, drink coffee and mix and mingle while being hip and writing poetry, among other things. George Peppard, Leslie Caron, Janie Rule, Roddy McDowell, Anne Seymour, Jim Hutton. w. Robert Thom, N-adap. Jack Kerouac, d. Ranald MacDougall.

DRAMA: MELODRAMA: Art Films; Ensemble Films; Beatnik Era; Beautiful People; Poets; Writers; Artists; San Francisco; Forgotten Films; Hidden Gems; Time Capsules; Coulda Been Great
(All the Fine Young Cannibals; Breakfast at Tiffany's; The Beat Generation)
(Ed: Not great, but fascinating)

Suburban Commando, 1991, 90m, ★★/$$, New Line/New Line, PG/V. Champion wrestler Hulk Hogan stars as an alien who's a bounty hunter with a mission on earth, and he's stationed himself with a typical family. Hulk Hogan, Christopher Lloyd, Shelley Duvall. w. Frank Capello, d. Burt Kennedy.

ACTION: COMEDY: Action Comedy; Fish out of Water Stories; Aliens-Outer Space, Good; Bounty Hunters; Suburban Life; Comic Heroes; Body Builders
COMIC FLIPSIDE OF: The Terminator.
(Mr. Nanny; No Holds Barred)

Suburbia, 1983, 99m, ★★★/$, Ind/Vestron. Alienated teenagers in guess where decide to set up their own digs and rules to live by. Chris Pederson, Bill Coyne, Jennifer Clay. w. d. Penelope Spheeris.

DRAMA: SATIRE: Social Drama; Music Movies; Parents vs. Children; Generation Gap; Alienation; Rebels; Teenagers; Rock Stars; Dreams; Anti-Establishment Films; Female Screenwriters; Female Directors; Writer-Directors
(The Decline of Western Civilization)

Subway, 1985, 104m, ★★1/2/$$, Island/Fox. An exotic French hero hides out in the Paris metro subway when doing battle with the mob. Christopher Lambert, Isabelle Adjani, Richard Bohringer. w. d. Luc Besson.

ACTION: ROMANCE: MELODRAMA: Art Films; Comic Heroes; Heroes-Unlikely; Eccentric People; Subways; French Films; Paris; Writer-Directors
(Darkman; Hero at Large)
(Ed: Definitely different)

Success Is the Best Revenge, 1984, 91m, ★★1/2/$, Ind/Imperial. A Polish immigrant becomes a theater director but in his pursuit of the perfect show, neglects his son. Michael York, Joanna Szczerbic, Michael Lyndon, Jerry Skol, John Hurt, Anouk Aimee. w. Jerzy Skolimowski, Michael Lyndon, d. Jerzy Skolimowski.

MELODRAMA: Fathers & Sons; Family Drama; Theater Life; Directors; England; Europeans-Eastern; Polish People
(Moonlighting [1982])

Such Good Friends, 1971, 102m, ★★★/$$, Par/NA, R/S. A wealthy man is dying in a hospital and his wife tries to get help from his friends to try and figure out a solution while she deals with bureaucracy. Dyan Cannon, James Coco, Jennifer O'Neill, Nina Foch, Ken Howard, Laurence Luckinbill, Louise Lasser, Burgess Meredith, Rita Gam, Sam Levene. w. Elaine May, N-adap. Lois Gould, d. Otto Preminger.

COMEDY DRAMA: SATIRE: Black Comedy; Sex Comedy; Saving Someone; Hospitals; Doctors; Ensemble Films; Rich People; New York Life; All-Star Casts; Female Screenwriters; Female Protagonists
(The Happy Ending; The Love Machine; Doctor's Wives)

Sudden Death, 1995, 110m, ★★/$$, U/MCA-U, PG-13/P-EV-S. A fire fighter winds up in a terrorist attempt to hold hostage the spectators of the Stanley Cup finals unless the terrorists' demands are met. Jean-Claude Van Damme, Powers Boothe, Raymond J. Barry, Whittni

Wright, Ross Malinger, Dorian Harewood, Kate McNeil. w. Gene Quintano, d. Peter Hyams

ACTION: Hostage Situations; Die Hard Stories; Hockey; Race Against Time; Bombs
(Two-Minute Warning; Black Sunday)

Sudden Fear, 1952, 111m, ★★★1/2/$$, RKO/NA. A woman writer (Joan Crawford, BActress) who is also very wealthy is afraid her bizarre husband (Jack Palance, BSActor) is trying to kill her. Gloria Grahame, Bruce Bennett, Mike Connors. w. Lenore Coffee, Robert Smith, d. David Miller. BB&WCin. Oscars: 3-0.

SUSPENSE: Psychological Thriller; Women in Jeopardy; Murder of Spouse; Writers; Heiresses; Forgotten Films; Hidden Gems; Female Protagonists; Female Screenwriters
(Suspicion; Rebecca; Undercurrent; Deceived; Possessed; The Big Knife)

Sudden Impact, 1983, 117m, ★★1/2/$$$, WB/WB, R/V-P. A woman is killing men who raped her and Dirty Harry is out to find her. Clint Eastwood, Sondra Locke, Pat Hingle, Bradford Dillman, Paul Drake. w. Joseph Stinson, d. Clint Eastwood.

ACTION: Police Stories; Detective Stories; Detectives-Police; Rape/Rapists; Revenge; Revenge on Rapist; Women Fighting Back; Serial Killers; Murders-One by One; Men in Jeopardy; Murderers-Female; San Francisco
(Extremities; Outrage; The Accused [1948])
(Ed: Spawned the phrase, uttered with guns drawn, "Go ahead, make my day")

Suddenly, Last Summer, 1959, 114m, ★★★★/$$$$, Columbia/RCA-Col. A rich woman (Katharine Hepburn, BActress) decides to avenge her son's death by having the girl she feels is responsible (Elizabeth Taylor, BActress) lobotomized by a doctor (Montgomery Clift) she wants to endow with further "treatments." w. Gore Vidal, P-adap. Tennessee Williams, d. Joseph L. Mankiewicz. BB&WArt. Oscars: 3-0.

DRAMA: MELODRAMA: TRAGEDY: Mental Illness; Psychiatrists; Psychological Drama; Homosexual Secrets; Committed-Wrongly; Asylums; Avenging Death of Someone; Mothers & Sons; Flashbacks; Nightmares; Relatives-Troublesome; Rich People; New Orleans;

Southerns; Stagelike Films; Tennessee Williams-esque

REMAKE: PBS, 1993, with Rob Lowe, Maggie Smith.

(A Streetcar Named Desire; The Snakepit; The Fugitive Kind; Orpheus Descending; Sweet Bird of Youth)

(Ed: An art film made accessible with three great performances and a haunting score)

Sudie and Simpson, 1990, 95m, ★★★/$$$, Lifetime/Worldvision. A white girl in 1940s rural Georgia becomes friends with a black man who lives out in the woods. But when townspeople hear about it, racial tensions and accusations of molestation threaten their innocent relationship. Sara Gilbert, Louis Gossett, Frances Fisher. w. Sara Flanigan Carter, Ken Koser, d. Joan Tewksbury.

DRAMA: Friendships Between Sexes; Friendships-Interracial; Men and Girls; Girls; Black Men; Small-town Life; Small-town Scandals; Southerns; 1940s; Georgia; TV Movies; Hidden Gems; Female Protagonists; Child Protagonists; Female Directors; Female Screenwriters

(Wildflower; Cold Sassy Tree)

Suez, 1938, 104m, ★★★/$$, 20th/Fox. The story of the building of the Suez Canal in the Middle East and the man who led it, Ferdinand Lesseps. Tyrone Power, Annabella, Loretta Young, Joseph Schildkraut, Sidney Blackmer, Nigel Bruce. w. Philip Dunne, Julien Josephson, d. Allan Dwan. BScore, BCin. Oscars: 2-0.

ADVENTURE: Biographies; **MELO-DRAMA:** Historical Drama; Middle East; Desert Settings; Epics; Cast of Thousands

Sugarbaby, 1984, 87m, ★★★/$$, Ind/Lorimar-WB. An overweight but pleasant German woman goes after a young, better looking train conductor and knocks him for a loop. Marianne Sagebrecht, Eisi Gulp, Toni Berger. w. d. Percy Adlon.

COMEDY: COMEDY DRAMA: Art Films; Black Comedy; **ROMANCE:** Romantic Comedy; Romance-Girl Wants Boy; Romance-Older Women/Younger Men; Wallflowers & Hunks; German Films; Germany; Writer-Directors; Independent Films

(Bagdad Cafe; Rosalie Goes Shopping; Babycakes)

Sugar Hill, 1994, 123m, ★★/$$, 20th/Fox, R/EP-EV-S. Two black drug-dealer brothers in Harlem think about getting out of the biz when one falls for an actress. Wesley Snipes, Micheel Wright, Theresa Randle, Clarence Williams III, Abe Vigoda, Ernie Hudson, Leslie Uggams. w. Barry Michael Cooper, d. Leon Ichaso.

ACTION: Action Drama; Crime Drama; Drugs-Dealing; Black Men; Black Casts; Brothers; One Last Time; Retirement

(Boiling Point; Passenger 57)

The Sugarland Express, 1974, 110m, ★★★★/$$, Universal/MCA-U, PG/P. A woman (Goldie Hawn) whose baby has been taken away by social services breaks out of jail to take the baby back, but a statewide chase soon ensues. w. Hal Barwood, Matthew Robbins, d. Steven Spielberg.

COMEDY DRAMA: TRAGEDY: Tragi-Comedy; **ACTION:** Action Comedy; Escape Adventure; Chase Movie; Road Movies; Outlaw Road Movies; Ordinary People Stories; Fugitives from the Law; Rednecks; Texas; True Stories; Escalating Plots; Child-Losing a; Female Protagonists; Underrated; Hidden Gems

(Thelma & Louise; Bonnie and Clyde)

The Suicide Club, 1988, 92m, ★★/$, Academy/Academy, R/S-P. A rich young woman enters a hip secret club with lots of mindgames and more at stake than the comraderie may be worth. Mariel Hemingway, Robert Joy, Lenny Henry, Madeleine Potter. d. James Bruce.

DRAMA: SUSPENSE: Psychological Drama; Mindgames; Games; Young Women Risking it All; Curiosities; Suicidal Tendencies; Independent Films

Sullivan's Travels, 1942, 90m, ★★★★/$$$, Par/Par. A Hollywood director (Joel McCrea) of frivolous movies sets out to live the really gritty side of life as a homeless person, but there's more grit than he realized. Veronica Lake, William Demarest, Robert Warwick, Franklin Pangborn. w. d. Preston Sturges.

COMEDY: COMEDY DRAMA: FARCE: Action Comedy; Screwball Comedy; Social Drama; Depression Era; Road Movies; Dual Lives; Undercover; Hollywood Life; Directors; Homeless People; Riches to Rags; Dead-Back from the; Mistaken Identities; Hidden Gems; Writer-Directors

(The Lady Eve; Palm Beach Story)

(Ed: A classic on many levels, plain and simple)

Summer, 1986, 90m, ★★★/$, Orion/Orion, Facets. A young woman travels to the lights of Paris to find love while the tourist season is on. Marie Riviere, Eric Hamm, Lisa Heredia. w. d. Eric Rohmer.

DRAMA: Vacations; Vacation Romance; **ROMANCE:** Writer-Directors; French Films; Quiet Little Films

(Boyfriends and Girlfriends; Pauline at the Beach)

Summer and Smoke, 1961, 118m, ★★★/$$, Par/Par. An uptight spinster (Geraldine Page, BActress) may have found love at last when a handsome prodigal son returns home (Laurence Harvey), but will she be able to change enough to make it work? Rita Moreno, Earl Holliman, Pamela Tiffin, Una Merkel (BSActress). w. James Poe, Meade Roberts, P-adap. Tennessee Williams, d. Peter Glenville. BOScore. Oscars: 3-0.

DRAMA: MELODRAMA: Love-First; Spinsters; Wallflowers; Virgins; World War I Era; Infatuations; Love-Unrequited; Playboys; Mississippi; Southerns; Female Protagonists; Tennessee Williams-esque

(Rachel, Rachel; The Sterile Cuckoo; The Rainmaker; Summertime; A Streetcar Named Desire; Sweet Bird of Youth; Dear Heart)

Summer of '42, 1971, 103m, ★★★½/$$$$, WB/WB, R/S. A teenage boy spends the summer on the New England coast and develops a crush on a friendly war widow who shows him a few things. Gary Grimes, Jennifer O'Neill, Jerry Houser. w. Herman Raucher (BOScr), d. Robert Mulligan. BOScore, BCin, BEdit. Oscars: 4-1.

COMEDY DRAMA: DRAMA: MELO-DRAMA: ROMANCE: Coming of Age; Character Studies; Memories; Romance-Older Women/Younger Men; Infatuations; Virgins; Life Transitions; Sleeper Hits; Beach Movies

SEQUEL: Class of '44.

(The Stripper; Class; Last Summer)

The Summer of My German Soldier, 1978, 98m, ★★★/$$$, NBC/MTI Video. A Jewish girl down south finds a German P.O.W. who's escaped from Europe and protects him, letting only her family maid know. Kristy McNichol, Esther Rolle (Emmy winner), Bruce Davison. N-adap. Bette Green, d. Michael Tuchner.

MELODRAMA: ROMANCE: Fugitives from the Law; Fugitives-Harboring; P.O.W.s; World War II-Post Era; Germans as Enemy; Jewish People; Girls; Love-First; TV Movies; Hidden Gems
(Tiger Bay; Whistle Down the Wind)

A Summer Place, 1959, 130m, ★★½/ $$$, WB/WB. A girl goes to the Maine coast for the summer and falls in love with a blond adonis, but one of their mothers doesn't approve. Sandra Dee, Troy Donohue, Richard Egan, Arthur Kennedy, Dorothy McGuire, Constance Ford, Beulah Bondi. w. d. Delmer Daves.

ROMANCE: MELODRAMA: Summer Vacations; Vacations; Vacation Romance; Writer-Directors
(I'd Rather Be Rich; Gidget)

A Summer Story, 1988, 97m, ★★½/$, ITC-Ind/Media, PG. An upper class young man remembers back to a country romance with a working class girl that wasn't meant to be. James Wilby, Imogen Stubbs, Ken Colley, Sophie Ward, Susannah York. w. Penelope Mortimer, SS-adap. John Galsworthy, *The Apple Cart*, d. Piers Haggard.

ROMANCE: MELODRAMA: Romance-Class Conflicts; Romance-Triangles; Costume Drama; Vacation Romance; Summer Vacation; Quiet Little Films; British Films; Female Screenwriters
(A Room with a View; Maurice; A Handful of Dust; Jude the Obscure)

Summertime, 1955, 99m, ★★★★/$$$, UA/Janus-Goldwyn. A lonely woman from America (Katharine Hepburn, BActress) goes to Venice and falls in love with an Italian (Rosanno Brazzi), but nothing lasts forever, though the incredible beautiful images do. w. P-adap. Arthur Laurents, d. David Lean (BDirector). Oscars: 2-0.

DRAMA: ROMANCE: MELODRAMA: Romantic Drama; Tearjerkers; Lonely People; Spinsters; Romance-Brief; Romance with Married People; Mistresses; Romance on Vacation; Vacations; Italy; Venice; Scenery-Outstanding; Americans Abroad; Female Protagonists
(Rachel, Rachel; Dear Heart; The Rainmaker)
(Ed: One of the most beautiful films ever made-and in technicolor)

Summer Wishes, Winter Dreams, 1973, 88m, ★★★½/$$, Columbia/RCA-Col, PG/S. A cold, middle-aged woman (Joanne Woodward, BActress) can't deal with the illness of her mother (Sylvia Sidney, BSActress) or the gayness of her son, and she begins to slowly fall apart. w. Stewart Stern, d. Gilbert Cates. Oscars: 2-0.

DRAMA: Character Studies; Marriage Drama; Family Drama; Lonely People; Midlife Crisis; Nervous Breakdowns; Homosexual Secrets; Homophobia; Mothers & Daughters; Mothers & Sons; Death-Dealing With; Americans Abroad; Past-Haunted by the; Hidden Gems; Quiet Little Films; Forgotten Films; Female Protagonists

REMAKE/RETREAD: Andre's Mother.
(Andre's Mother; Interiors; Rachel, Rachel; The Effect of Gamma Rays on Man-in-the-Moon Marigolds)
(Ed: Sylvia Sidney's the grandmother here, too, as she was in *Andre's Mother*)

The Sum of Us, 1995, 95m, ★★★½/$, Goldwyn/Goldwyn, R/P-S. An almost overly-understanding Australian father of a gay young man plays the domineering mother role, trying to make sure his son is careful and sensible with who he sees. But this ironic approval may be more than the son can take. Jack Thompson, Russell Crowe, John Polson, Deborah Kennedy, Joss Moroney, Mitch Mathews, Julie Herbert, Des James, Mick Campbell, Donny Muntz, Jan Adele. w. David Stevens, d. Kevin Dowling, Geoff Burton

COMEDY DRAMA: SATIRE: Family Comedy; Fathers & Sons; Gay Men; Eccentric People; What If . . . Stories; Australian Films
(The Lost Language of Cranes; Priscilla, Queen of the Desert)

The Sun Also Rises, 1957, 129m, ★★★/$$$, 20th/NA. A depressed journalist meets up with a sexy woman in post–World War I Paris and proceeds to make the rounds of Paris and Europe with the artists and writers who would become the lost generation. Tyrone Power, Ava Gardner, Errol Flynn, Eddie Albert, Mel Ferrer, Robert Evans, Juliette Greco, Gregory Ratoff. w. Peter Viertel, N-adap. Ernest Hemingway, d. Henry King.

DRAMA: ADVENTURE: Ensemble Films; Episodic Stories; Beautiful People; Writers; Artists; Journalists; Paris; World War I Era; Rich People; 1920s; Bullfighting; All-Star Casts; Classic Literary Adaptations

REMAKE: TV miniseries, 1984.
(The Moderns; A Farewell to Arms)

Sunburn, 1979, 98m, ★★/$, Hemdale/Par, PG/S-V. A murderer is vacationing in Acapulco and an insurance investigator has a scam of his own planned to catch him. Charles Grodin, Farrah Fawcett, Joan Collins, Art Carney, Eleanor Parker, William Daniels, John Hillerman, Keenan Wynn. w. John Daly, Stephen Oliver, James Booth, N-adap. Stanley Ellin, *The Bind*, d. Richard Sarafin.

COMEDY DRAMA: MURDER: Trail of a Killer; Con Artists; Impostors; Undercover; Mexico; Coulda Been Good
(Somebody Killed Her Husband)
(Ed: Vehicle for Fawcett isn't much of anything but sun)

Sunday, Bloody Sunday, 1971, 110m, ★★★½/$$, UA/Key, R/S-P-FFN-MRN. A doctor (Peter Finch, BActor) is in love with a young man (Murray Head) who is also in love with a woman (Glenda Jackson, BActress). w. Penelope Gilliatt (BOScr), d. John Schlesinger (BDirector). Oscars: 4-0.

DRAMA: ROMANCE: Character Studies; Romance-Triangles; Romance-Older Women/Younger Men; Alternative Lifestyles; Gay Men; Bisexuality; Doctors; Free Spirits; Artists; British Films
(The Lost Language of Cranes; The Music Lovers; Making Love)

Sunday in New York, 1964, 105m, ★★★/$$$, MGM/NA. A young woman heads to Manhattan for the weekend basically to lose her virginity, but her brother is out to stop her. Jane Fonda, Cliff Robertson, Rod Taylor, Robert Culp, Jim Backus. w. P-adap. Norman Krasna, d. Peter Tewksbury.

COMEDY: ROMANCE: Romantic Comedy; Sex Comedy; Virgins; Brothers & Sisters; Protecting Someone; Playboys; Pilots-Airline; Young Women; New York Life; Female Protagonists; Forgotten Films; Hidden Gems
(The Moon is Blue; Any Wednesday; A Period of Adjustment; The Chapman Report)

Sunday in the Country, 1984, 94m, ★★★/$$, MGM-UA. An old man who is a painter gets a visit from his family in old country France, where they all come together as if posing for a painting. Louis Ducreux, Sabina Azema, Michel Aumont. w. Bertrand & Colo Tavernier, N-adap. Pierre Bost, d. Bertrand Tavernier.

DRAMA: MELODRAMA: Family Drama; Vacations; Rural Life; Artists; Elderly Men; Quiet Little Films; French Films (My Father's Castle; May Fools; 'Round Midnight)

Sundays and Cybele, 1962, 110m, ★★★1/2/$, Ind-Walter Reade/Nos. A military pilot with mental and memory problems wanders about and develops a relationship with a girl on the street whose father has put her in a convent, but when people misconstrue their friendship for more, major problems arise. Hardy Kruger, Nicole Courcel. w. Serge Bourgignon, Antoine Tudal (BAScr), N-adap. Bernard Echasseriaux, d. Serge Bourgignon. **BFLFilm**, BOScore. Oscars: 3-1.

DRAMA: MELODRAMA: TRAGEDY: Tearjerkers; Men and Girls; Friendships-Great; Misunderstandings; Mentally Disabled; Street Life; Pilots-Military; Amnesia; Girls; Paris; French Films; French New Wave Films; Hidden Gems; Forgotten Films
(David and Lisa; Sudie and Simpson)

Sundown, 1941, 91m, ★★1/2/$$, Wanger-UA/Nos. A young woman goes into the troop services during World War II in North Africa. Gene Tierney, Bruce Abot, George Sanders, Harry Carey, Reginald Gardner. w. Barre Lyndon, d. Henry Hathaway. BCin, BScore, BArt. Oscars: 3-0.

DRAMA: MELODRAMA: ADVENTURE: World War II Stories; Soldiers; Female Among Males; Desert Settings; Africa

The Sundowners, 1960, 133m, ★★★/$$$, WB/WB. A family pioneers the outback of Australia to ranch sheep and encounters many problems. Robert Mitchum, Deborah Kerr (BActress), Glynis Johns (BSActress), Peter Ustinov, Michael Anderson, Dina Merrill, Wylie Watson. w. Isobel Lennart (BAScr), N-adap. Jon Cleary, d. Fred Zinneman (BDirector). BPicture. Oscars: 5-0.

ADVENTURE: DRAMA: Family Drama; Journies; Pioneers; Life Transitions; Farm Life; 1920s; Australia; Faded Hits; Forgotten Films; Hidden Gems; Female Screenwriters
(The Thorn Birds; Under Capricorn)
(Ed: A Best Picture nominee then, but forgotten now, though it's worth a view if you like the stars of family sagas)

Sunflower, 1970, 101m, ★★1/2/$$, National General/NA. Lovers are torn apart during World War II then try to become reunited. Sophia Loren, Marcello Mastroianni. w. Tonino Guerra, Cesare Zavattini, Georgiy Mdivani, d. Vittorio DeSica.

ROMANCE: MELODRAMA: Romantic Drama; World War II Stories; Romance-Doomed; Romance-Reunited; Italian Films
(Doctor Zhivago; A Special Day; A Map of the Human Heart; Two Women)

Sunrise at Campobello, 1960, 143m, ★★★/$$$, WB/WB. The early career of Franklin Roosevelt is chronicled as he deals with the onset of polio, romances Eleanor, and decides to go into politics. Ralph Bellamy, Greer Garson (BActress), Ann Shoemaker, Hume Cronyn, Jean Hagen. w. P-adap. Dore Schary, d. Vincent Donehue. BCArt, BSound, BCCostume. Oscars: 4-0.

DRAMA: ROMANCE: Biographies; Disease Stories; Famous People When Young; Presidents; Historical Drama; Episodic Stories; Stagelike Films
(Wilson; Eleanor and Franklin)

Sunset, 1988, 107m, ★★/$, Tri-Star/Col-Tri, PG. During the silent film era, Wyatt Earp is a consultant on a film about himself when he gets together with Tom Mix to solve a murder. James Garner, Bruce Willis, Malcolm McDowell, Mariel Hemingway, Kathleen Quinlan, Jennifer Edwards, Patricia Hodge, M. Emmet Walsh. w. d. Blake Edwards.

COMEDY: MYSTERY: MURDER: MURDER MYSTERY: WESTERNS: Comic Mystery; Hollywood Life; Actors; Biographies-Fictional; Buddy Films; Silent Film Era; Writer-Directors
(Nickelodeon; Heart of the West)

Sunset Boulevard, 1950, 110m, ★★★★/$$$$, Par/Par. A writer (William Holden, BActor) takes a side job from an old silent movie queen (Gloria Swanson, BActress) and her strange butler (Erich Von Stroheim, BSActor) which requires far more than he ever bargained for. Nancy Olson (BSActress), Fred Clark, Jack Webb, Cecil B. DeMille, H.B. Warner, Buster Keaton, Hedda Hopper. w. Billy Wilder, I.A.L. Diamond (**BOScr**), d. Billy Wilder (BDirector). BPicture. **BScore**, BEdit, **BB&WArt**, BB&WCin. Oscars: 11-3.

DRAMA: MURDER: TRAGEDY: MYSTERY: Murder-Whodunit; Crimes of Passion; Film Noir; Hollywood Life;

Mental Illness; Illusions/Hallucinations; Illusions Destroyed; Prostitutes-Male; Writers; Actresses; Romance-Unrequited; Comebacks; Murderers-Female; Narrated Films; Flashbacks; Writer-Directors

MUSICAL REMAKE: on Broadway, 1994.
(The Roman Spring of Mrs. Stone; Double Indemnity; Valentino; Fedora)
(Ed: A classic. One of only a handful of films nominated in every major Oscar category)

The Sunshine Boys, 1975, 111m, ★★★1/2/$$$, MGM/MGM-UA, PG. When a TV special on vaudeville wants to reunite a famous comedy team who are still in the middle of a decades-long feud, the two reconsider, but only for so long. Walter Matthau (BActor), George Burns (**BSActor**), Richard Benjamin. w. P-adap. Neil Simon (BAScr), d. Herbert Ross. Oscars: 3-1.

COMEDY: COMEDY DRAMA: Comedians; Vaudeville; Feuds; Friendships-Great; Friendships-Male; Elderly Men; TV Life; Comebacks; Reunions
(Grumpy Old Men; The Odd Couple; Buddy, Buddy; Kotch)
(Ed: What was to be Burns' big comeback, after which he became a TV fixture, was originally intended for Jack Benny, who unfortunately died before filming)

The Super, 1991, 85m, ★★1/2/$$, Largo-20th/Fox, R/P. When a slumlord is confronted about his dilapidated apartment building, he's forced to live in the place himself and things change. Joe Pesci, Vincent Gardenia, Madolyn Smith-Osborne, Ruben Blades, Paul Benjamin, Carole Shelley. w. Sam Simon, d. Rod Daniel.

COMEDY: SATIRE: Social Satire; Fish out of Water Stories; Jerks; Snobs vs. Slobs; Inner City Life; Apartment Buildings; Turning the Tables; Good Premise Unfulfilled; Coulda Been Good
(Jimmy Hollywood; The Landlord; My Cousin Vinny)
(Ed: Pesci's performance is the only real thing to see)

Super Cops, 1974, 94m, ★★1/2/$$, UA/NA. Two buddy cops get suspended for going too far, so they go even further and pretend to be cops to take their vigilante-ism even further. Ron Leibman, David Selby, Pat Hingle, Sheila Frazier. w. Lorenzo Semple, NF-adap. L.H. Whittemore, d. Gordon Parks.

ACTION: COMEDY: Action Comedy; Police Stories; Police Corruption; Vigilantes; Vigilantes-Police; Buddy Cops; Buddy Films; Ahead of Its Time; Black Directors
(Freebie and the Bean; Law and Disorder; Fuzz)

SuperDad, 1974, 95m, ★★½/$$$, Disney/Disney, G. An overprotective father does everything like the teens in order to keep an eye on his daughter. Bob Crane, Barbara Rush, Kurt Russell, Kathleen Cody, Joe Flynn. w. Joseph McEveety, d. Vincent McEveety.

CHILDREN'S: FAMILY: COMEDY: Disney Comedy; Family Comedy; Fathers-Troublesome; Fathers & Daughters; Summer Vacations
(She's Outta Control; My Father, the Hero)

Superfly, 1972, 98m, ★★★/$$$, WB/WB, R/P-V-S. The infamous cocaine dealer of Harlem and his adventures in dealing. Ron O'Neal, Carl Lee, Shiela Frazier. w. Philip Fenty, d. Gordon Parks.

ACTION: COMEDY: Action Comedy; Black Comedy; Drugs-Dealing; Black Casts; Black Men; Inner City Life; Cult Films; Blaxploitation Era; Black Screenwriters; Black Directors
SEQUEL: Return of Superfly.
(Shaft SERIES; Black Caesar; New Jack City)

Supergirl, 1984, 124m, ★★½/$$, WB/WB, G. An elegant, chic witch gets ahold of Kryptonite and taunts Supergirl with it. Helen Slater, Faye Dunaway, Peter O'Toole, Mia Farrow, Brenda Vaccaro, Peter Cook, Simon Ward, Marc McClure, Hart Bochner, David Healy. w. David Odell, d. Jeannot Szwarc.

ACTION: CHILDREN'S: Action Comedy; Fantasy; Super Heroes; Comic Heroes; Witches; Good vs. Evil; Flying People; Underrated; Overlooked at Release; Flops-Major; Female Protagonists
SEQUEL in Superman SERIES.

Superman, 1978, 142m, ★★★/$$$$$, WB/WB, PG. From the early years of Clark Kent on planet Krypton to his life on the Daily Planet newspaper when he fights to keep his cover but has to fight the forces of evil which have caught up with him. Christopher Reeve, Marlon Brando, Gene Hackman, Jackie Cooper, Margot Kidder, Glenn Ford, Phyllis Thaxter, Trevor Howard, Ned Beatty, Susannah York, Valerie Perrine. w. Mario Puzo, David Newman, Robert Benton, Leslie Newman, d. Richard Donner. BOScore, BEdit, BSound, **BSFX**. Oscars: 4-1.

ACTION: ADVENTURE: SCI-FI: Fantasy; Comic Heroes; Super Heroes; Rule the World-Plot to; Journalists; Newspapers; Dual Lives; Secrets-Keeping; Flying People; Earthquakes

Superman 2, 1980, 127m, ★★★/$$$$, WB/WB, PG. Three villains come to Earth with a bomb and it's up to Superman, who may or may not tie the not with Lois Lane, to stop it. Christopher Reeve, Margot Kidder, Gene Hackman, Ned Beatty, Jackie Cooper, Sarah Douglas, Valerie Perrine, Terence Stamp, E.G. Marshall, Susannah York. w. Mario Puzo, David Newman, Leslie Newman, d. Richard Lester.

ACTION: ADVENTURE: SCI-FI: Fantasy; Comic Heroes; Super Heroes; Rule the World-Plot to; Journalists; Newspapers; Dual Lives; Secrets-Keeping; Flying People; Arctic

Superman 3, 1983, 125m, ★★½/$$$, WB/WB, PG. This time, some bad Kryptonite gets to Superman, and he loses his powers until a little boy begs him to help the planet. Christopher Reeve, Richard Pryor, Jackie Cooper, Margot Kidder, Annette O'Toole, Marc McClure, Annie Ross, Robert Vaughan. w. David Newman, Leslie Newman, d. Richard Lester.

ACTION: ADVENTURE: SCI-FI: Fantasy; Comic Heroes; Super Heroes; Rule the World-Plot to; Journalists; Newspapers; Dual Lives; Secrets-Keeping; Flying People; Environmental Dilemmas

Superman 4, 1987, 89m, ★★/$, Cannon-WB/WB, PG. Superman decides to stop the nuclear arms race. Christopher Reeve, Gene Hackman, Jackie Cooper, Mariel Hemingway, Margot Kidder, Marc McClure, Sam Wanamaker. w. Lawrence Konner, Mark Rosenthal, Christopher Reeve, d. Sidney J. Furie.

ACTION: ADVENTURE: SCI-FI: Fantasy; Comic Heroes; Super Heroes; Rule the World-Plot to; Journalists; Newspapers; Dual Lives; Secrets-Keeping; Flying People; Bombs-Atomic; Cold War Era; Arms Dealers

Super Mario Brothers, 1993, 104m, ★½/$, Hollywood/Hollywood, PG. The video game about plumbers trying to res-cue a princess comes to life, or supposedly so. Bob Hoskins, John Leguizamo, Samantha Mathis, Fisher Stevens. w. Terry Runte, Parker Bennett, Edward Solomon, d. Rocky Morton, Annabel Jankel.

ADVENTURE: ACTION: Video Game Movies; Games; Cartoonlike Movies; Flops-Major; Female Directors
(Ed: Another one of the incredibly long list of Hollywood Pictures turkeys)

Superstar, The Life and Times of Andy Warhol, 1990, 87m, ★★★/$$, Ind/Vestron, R/S. Biography and interviews with those who knew the modern art superstar who died tragically after a gall bladder surgery. Tom Wolfe, Sylvia Miles, David Hockney, Taylor Mead, Dennis Hopper. d. Chuck Workman. Documentaries; Biographies; Artists-Famous; Beautiful People; New York Life; Psychedelic Era; Mod Era; Time Capsules; Interviews; Hidden Gems
(Andy Warhol SERIES)

Support Your Local Gunfighter, 1971, 92m, ★★½/$$, UA/MGM-UA, PG. When a con artist robs a train, he's mistaken as a famous gunfighter and then decides to use it to his advantage. James Garner, Suzanne Pleshette, Joan Blondell, Jack Elam, Chuck Connors, Harry Morgan. w. James Grant, d. Burt Kennedy.

WESTERN: COMEDY: Western Comedy; Con Artists; Gunfighters; Identities-Mistaken
(The Skin Trade)

Support Your Local Sheriff, 1968, 92m, ★★★/$$$, UA/MGM-UA, PG/V. A sheriff in a gold rush town has all kinds of problems with the kooks and con artists that show up. James Garner, Joan Hackett, Walter Brennan, Jack Elam, Henry Morgan, Bruce Dern. w. William Bowers, d. Burt Kennedy.

WESTERN: COMEDY: Western Comedy; Gold Mines; Con Artists; Ensemble Films; Sleeper Hits

Suppose They Gave a War and Nobody Came, 1969, 114m, ★★/$, ABC-20th/Fox, PG. Three screwed-up servicemen become heroes incidentally, then screw that up in a military base town. Tony Curtis, Brian Keith, Ernest Borgnine, Ivan Dixon, Suzanne Pleshette, Tom Ewell, Don Ameche, Bradford Dillman. w. Don McGuire, Hal Captain, d. Hy Averback.

COMEDY: Military Comedy; SATIRE: FARCE: Soldiers; Flops-Major
(Tank; 1941; The Russians Are Coming, The Russians Are Coming; Hail the Conquering Hero)

The Sure Thing, 1985, 94m, ★★★/$$$, Embassy/Embassy, PG-13/S. A college boy travels cross-country to get to a gorgeous blonde that will have sex with him for sure-but he winds up hitchhiking with a brunette who makes him reconsider his plan. John Cusack, Daphne Zuniga, Anthony Edwards, Boyd Gaines, Tim Robbins, Lisa Jane Persky, Viveca Lindfors. w. Steven Bloom, Jonathan Roberts, d. Rob Reiner.

COMEDY: Romantic Comedy; Romance-Boy Wants Girl; Romance-Reluctant; Road Movies; Romance-Bickering; Teen-agers; Teenage Movies; Battle of the Sexes; Hitchhiking; College Life; Young Men; Young Women; Road to California; Sleeper Hits
(It Happened One Night; Fandango; Say Anything)

Surrender, 1987, 95m, ★★½/$, Cannon-WB/WB, PG-13/S-FRN-MRN. After being tied up nude in a robbery hostage situation, a writer and an artist fall for each other, despite the younger man she's involved with. Sally Field, Michael Caine, Steve Guttenberg, Peter Boyle, Jackie Cooper, Julie Kavner, Louise Lasser. w. d. Jerry Belson.

COMEDY DRAMA: ROMANCE: Romantic Comedy; Sex Comedy; Romance-Triangles; Romance-Reluctant; Romance-Older Women/Younger Men; Romance-Chance Meetings; Hostage Situations; Nudists; Los Angeles; Writers; Artists; Good Premise Unfulfilled; Coulda Been Good; Writer-Directors

Survive, 1976, 86m, ★★½/$$$, RSO-Par/Par. Low-budget Latin film dubbed for America about the sensational story of an Argentine rugby team whose plane crashed in the Andes and the survivors resorted to cannibalism until their rescue. Hugo Sitlitz, Norma Lazareno. w. d. Reen Cardona.

DRAMA: TRAGEDY: True Stories; Survival Drama; Rescue Drama; Stranded; Airplane Crashes; Disaster Movies; Ensemble Films; Ensembles-Male; South America; Cannibalism; Sleeper Hits; Writer-Directors
REMAKE: Alive.

Surviving Desire, 1991, 86m, ★★/$, AP-PBS/Fox-Lorber, R/S. An English professor falls in love with an Audrey Hepburn-esque Asian student who then begins playing mindgames. Martin Donovan, Mary Ward, Matt Mallow. w. d. Hal Hartley.

DRAMA: ROMANCE: Romantic Drama; Psychological Drama; Romance with Teacher; Professors; Teachers & Students; Romance-Interracial; Asian-Americans; Art Films; Quiet Little Films; Writer-Directors; Independent Films
(Simple Men; Trust)

The Survivors, 1983, 102m, ★★/$$, Col/RCA-Col, PG/P. When two men are targets of a hit man, they hide out in the mountains during snow season and in their paranoia, almost kill each other. Walter Matthau, Robin Williams, Jerry Reed, James Wainwright. w. Michael Leeson, d. Michael Ritchie.

COMEDY: COMEDY DRAMA: Black Comedy; Fugitives from the Mob; Hiding Out; Hitmen; Paranoia
(Deal of the Century; Best Defense; Bananas)

Susan and God, 1940, 117m, ★★★/$$, MGM/MGM-UA. A trendy rich woman becomes very religious, but then her old hypocritical ways rear their head. Joan Crawford, Fredric March, Ruth Hussey, John Carroll, Rita Hayworth, Nigel Bruce, Marjorie Main. w. Anita Loos, P-adap. Rachel Crothers, d. George Cukor.

COMEDY DRAMA: Religion; Life Transitions; Rich People; Ethics; Female Protagonists
(The Rapture; The Disappearance of America)
(Ed: A rare thing for Hollywood to get into, and even more ironic considering its star)

Susan Lenox, Her Fall and Rise, 1931, 76m, ★★★/$$$, MGM/MGM-UA. A young woman leaves the farm for the bright lights of the city to seek fame and fortune when she's betrothed to an uncouth jerk. Greta Garbo, Clark Gable, Jean Hersholt, John Miljan, Alan Hale. w. Wanda Tuchock, N-adap. David Graham, d. Robert Z. Leonard.

MELODRAMA: ROMANCE: Fish out of Water Stories; Marriages-Forced; Runaways; City vs. Country; Young Women; Starting Over; Forgotten Films; Female Screenwriters; Female Protagonists
(A Star Is Born; Camille; Morning Glory)

Susan Slept Here, 1954, 98m, ★★½/$$, RKO/VCI. A screenwriter writes a film about juvenile delinquents and then has to practice what he preaches by taking on a girl with rebellious tendencies. Dick Powell, Debbie Reynolds, Anne Francis. w. Alex Gottlieb, d. Frank Tashlin.

COMEDY: SATIRE: Juvenile Delinquents; Rebels; Feisty Females; Hollywood Life; Writers; Turning the Tables; Forgotten Films
(Inside Daisy Clover; Tammy)

Suspect, 1987, 121m, ★★½/$$$, Col/RCA-Col, PG-13/P. A woman lawyer takes on a case defending a mute homeless person and then discovers high-level corruption and a cover-up of the murder. She is aided by a jury member who has a thing for her. Cher, Dennis Quaid, Liam Neeson, John Mahoney, Joe Mantegna, Philip Bosco, E. Katherine Kerr. w. Eric Roth, d. Peter Yates.

SUSPENSE: MURDER: MYSTERY: MURDER MYSTERY: Conspiracy; Government; Corruption; Corruption Cover-ups; Lawyers as Detectives; Lawyers; Female Protagonists; Mute People; Homeless People
(Jagged Edge; Class Action)

Suspicion, 1941, 99m, ★★★★/$$$, RKO/Turner. A young heiress (Joan Fontaine, BActress) begins to believe her new, mysterious husband (Cary Grant) may actually be trying to kill her for her money. w. d. Alfred Hitchcock. BPicture. Oscars: 2-1.

SUSPENSE: Psychological Drama; Marriage Drama; Insane-Plots to Make; Women in Jeopardy; Murder of Spouse; Love-Questionable; Romance-Dangerous; Dangerous Men; Liars; Heiresses; Hitchcockian
COMEDY REMAKE: A New Leaf.
REMAKE: PBS, 1984.
(Rebecca; Undercurrent; Sudden Fear; Deceived)

Suspiria, 1976, 97m, ★★★/$$, Ind/Hollywood Home. An American student in Italy stumbles onto a serial killer and Satanism situation. Jessica Harper, Joan Bennett, Alida Valli. w. Dario Argento, Dario Nicolodi, d. Dario Argento.

HORROR: SUSPENSE: MURDER: Murders-One By One; Women in Jeopardy; Young Women; Italy; Italian Films; Cult Films; Underrated; Forgotten Films; Hitchcockian
(The Seventh Victim)

Suzy, 1936, 95m, ★★★/$$, MGM/MGM-UA. A World War I hero marries a dancer only to find her husband, who was reported dead in the war, has come back to find her. Jean Harlow, Cary Grant, Franchot Tone, Lewis Stone. w. Dorothy Parker, Alan Campbell, Horace Jackson, Lenore Coffee, N-adap. Herbert Gorman, d. George Fitzmaurice.

MELODRAMA: COMEDY DRAMA: ROMANCE: Romance-Triangles; Return of Spouse; Dead-Back from the; Newly-weds; Jealousy; World War I Era; Pilots-Military; Female Screenwriters
(Bombshell; Platinum Blonde)

Svengali, 1931, 81m, ★★★/$$$, WB/Nos, Sinister. When a hypnotist makes a girl a great opera singer, he hopes she'll grow to love him in thanks, but love is fleeting. John Barrymore, Marian Marsh, Donald Crisp. w. J. Grubb Alexander, N-adap. George du Maurier, Trilby, d. Archie Mayo.

Svengali, 1983, 96m, ★★★/$$$, CBS/NA. A young female singer wants a voice coach and finds a demanding man to push her along. Peter O'Toole, Jodie Foster, Elizabeth Ashley, Holly Hunter. d. Anthony Harvey.

ROMANCE: MELODRAMA: Romance-Unrequited; Romance with Teachers; Infatuations; Hypnotism; Opera; Singers; Paris; 1890s
(One Night of Love; Mesmerized)

Swamp Thing, 1981, 91m, ★★½/$$, New Line/Col, PG. When a scientist doing a horticulture experiment is turned into a half-man-half-plant "thing," he finds he has super powers. Louis Jourdan, Adrienne Barbeau, Ray Wise, David Hess. w. d. Wes Craven.

SCI-FI: HORROR: Super Heroes; Comic Heroes; Humans into Animals; Monsters-Mutant; Experiments; Scientists; Rule the World-Plot to; Swamp Life; Writer-Directors

SEQUEL: Swamp Thing 2, Swamp Thing TV SERIES.

Swamp Water (The Man Who Came Back), 1941, 90m, ★★★/$$, 20th/NA. A man wanted by the law hides out in the southern swamps and lives a normal but mysterious life with the locals. Walter Huston, Walter Brennan, Anne Baxter, Dana Andrews, John Carradine, Ward Bond. w. Dudley Nichols, Vereen Bell, d. Jean Renoir.

MELODRAMA: Ordinary People Stories; Fugitives from the Law; Hiding Out; Secrets-Keeping; Quiet Little Films;

Southerns; Swamp Life; Southerns-Foreign Directors of

REMAKE: Lure of the Wilderness. (Cross Creek; The Southerner; Louisiana Story)

The Swan, 1956, 108m, ★★★/$$, MGM/MGM-UA. The prince of Hungary is looking for a wife and a beautiful young woman is the choice (Grace Kelly). Alec Guinness, Louis Jourdan, Agnes Moorehead, Brian Aherne, Leo G. Carroll, Estelle Winwood. w. John Dighton, P-adap. Ferenc Molnar, d. Charles Vidor.

ROMANCE: COMEDY DRAMA: Fairy Tales; Marriage-Impending; Royalty; Princes; Princesses; Europeans-Eastern; Scenery-Outstanding
(Roman Holiday; High Society; The Prince and the Showgirl)
(Ed: Princess Grace's last film, and an appropriate one at that)

Swann in Love, 1984, 111m, ★★★/$$, Orion/Orion, R/S-FN. A beautiful woman with enticing bosoms becomes the obsession of Proust's lusty character, as Swann forsakes the whorehouses for his lust of one woman. Jeremy Irons, Ornella Muti, Alain Delon, Fanny Ardant, Marie-Christine Barrault. w. Peter Brook, Jean-Claude Carriere, Marie-Helene Estienne, N-adap. Marcel Proust, d. Volker Schlondorff.

DRAMA: Character Studies; **ROMANCE:** Erotic Drama; Romantic Drama; Costume Drama; Obsessions; Infatuations; Writers; Rich People; Paris; 1800s
(Letter from an Unknown Woman; Death in Venice; Damage)

The Swan Princess, 1994, 90m, ★★★/$$, New Line/New Line, G. A prince and princess of swans betrothed against their will find their marriage on the rocks when the princess leaves and descends into dangerous territory where she is physically altered by magic. It's then that the prince realizes he truly does love her and sets out to save her and prove it. Voices: Jack Palance, Howard McGillin, Michelle Nicastro, Liz Callaway, John Cleese, Steven Wright, Steve Vinovich, Mark Harelik, James Arrington, Davis Gaines, Joel McKinnon Miller, Dakin Matthews, Sandy Duncan. w. Brian Nissen. Story by Richard Rich, Brian Nissen, d. Richard Rich.

Cartoons; **CHILDREN'S:** Fairy Tales; Fantasy; Animal Stories; Birds;

ROMANCE: Saving Someone; Animals into Humans; Princes; Princesses (Thumbelina; A Little Princess)

The Swarm, 1978, 116m, ★★/$$, WB/WB, PG/V. The killer bees wreck a train and kill lots of people. Michael Caine, Katharine Ross, Lee Grant, Richard Chamberlain, Richard Widmark, Henry Fonda, Olivia deHavilland, Fred MacMurray, Ben Johnson, José Ferrer, Patty Duke, Bradford Dillman, Cameron Mitchell, Slim Pickens. w. Stirling Silliphant, N-adap. Arthur Herzog, d. Irwin Allen. BCostume. Oscars: 1-0.

MELODRAMA: TRAGEDY: Disaster Movies; All-Star Casts; Insects; Animal Monsters; Unintentionally Funny; Flops-Major
(Killer Bees; Savage Bees; When Time Ran Out)
(Ed: Funny, they still haven't killed us all yet. Nominated for Best Costume Design? In fact, costume designer Paul Zastup-nevich was actually also nominated for *The Poseidon Adventure* and *When Time Ran Out*, two other Irwin Allen disaster epics, but only the latter was a disaster at the box office)

Swashbuckler, 1976, 101m, ★★/$, U/MCA-U. A damsel in distress is helped out by pirates who normally are foes. Robert Shaw, Genevieve Bujold, James Earl Jones, Peter Boyle, Beau Bridges, Geoffrey Holder. w. Jeffrey Bloom, d. James Goldstone.

ACTION: ADVENTURE: Women in Jeopardy; Costume Drama; Swash-bucklers; Pirates; Enemies Unite; Old-Fashioned Recent Films
(Crossed Swords; The Three Musketeers; Scaramouche; The Scarlet Pimpernel)

Sweeney Todd, Demon Barber of Fleet Street, 1936, 68m, ★★★/$$, Ind/NA. An early film version of the old stage play where a barber cuts up his customers and sells them as pie to unwitting customers. Tod Slaughter (an interesting name for this), Bruce Seton, Even Lister. w. Frederick Hayward, H.F. Maltby, P-adap. George Dilbin-Pitt, d. George King.

COMEDY DRAMA: Black Comedy; **MUR-DER:** Comedy-Morbid; Serial Killers; Murderers-Nice; Hairdressers; Cannibalism; Cannibalism-Funny; Forgotten Films; Hidden Gems

MUSICAL REMAKE: on Broadway, 1978.
(Consuming Passions; Auntie Lee's Meat Pies)

Sweet Bird of Youth, 1962, 120m, ★★★1/2/$$$, MGM/MGM-UA. A Hollywood actress wanting to hide out until a picture premiere blows over takes up with a gigolo in her Florida motel. He believes she'll put him in pictures, but his past is catching up with him, thanks to the Governor. Paul Newman, Geraldine Page (BActress), Shirley Knight (BSActress), Ed Begley (**BSActor**), Rip Torn, Mildred Dunnock, Madeleine Sherwood. w. d. Richard Brooks. Oscars: 3-1.

DRAMA: MELODRAMA: TRAGEDY: Hiding Out; Nervous Breakdowns; Midlife Crisis; Young Men; Mothers-Unwed; Secrets-Keeping; Past-Haunted by the; Actresses; Prostitutes-Male; Dreams; Illusions Destroyed; Comebacks; Betrayals; Politicians; Florida; Tennessee Williams-esque

TV REMAKE: 1989 with Elizabeth Taylor, Mark Harmon, d. Nicolas Roeg. (The Roman Spring of Mrs. Stone; Sanctuary; Summer and Smoke; A Streetcar Named Desire)

Sweet Charity, 1969, 149m, ★★★/$$, U/MCA-U, PG/S. A dancer/prostitute named Charity sings and dances her way through New York, hoping to find love somehow. Shirley MacLaine, Ricardo Montalban, John McMartin, Chita Rivera, Paul Kelly, Stubby Kaye, Sammy Davis, Jr. w. Peter Stone, MP-adap. Neil Simon, S-adap. Federico Fellini, d. Bob Fosse. BMScore. Oscars: 1-0.

MUSICALS: COMEDY DRAMA: ROMANCE: Prostitutes-Low Class; Prostitutes with a Heart of Gold; Dancers; New York Life; Dreams; Illusions Destroyed; Free Spirits; Female Protagonists

REMAKE OF: Nights of Cabiria (Irma La Douce; The Best Little Whorehouse in Texas; Can-Can)

Sweet Dreams, 1985, 115m, ★★★/$, Tri-Star/HBO, PG/V. The rise and sudden end of the career of charismatic country singer Patsy Cline. Jessica Lange (BActress), Ed Harris, Anne Wedgeworth, David Clennon, James Staley. w. Robert Getchell, d. Karel Reisz. Oscars: 1-0.

DRAMA: Biographies; Fame-Rise to; Music Dies; Singers; Country Music; Marriage Drama; Abused Women; Airplane Crashes; Violence-Sudden; Southerns; Southerns-British Directors; Feisty Females; Underrated; Hidden Gems; Female Protagonists; Jessica Lange Goes Southern

(Coal Miner's Daughter; Blue Sky; Tender Mercies)

Sweethearts, 1938, 120m, ★★★/$$$$, MGM/MGM-UA. A couple who stars in stage musicals bickers their way back into love. Jeanette McDonald, Nelson Eddy, Frank Morgan, Ray Bolger, Mischa Auer, Reginald Gardiner, Lucile Watson. w. Dorothy Parker, Alan Campbell, d. W.S. Van Dyke. BCCin, **BMScore.** Oscars: 2-1.

MUSICALS: ROMANCE: Musical Romance; Romance-Bickering; Theater Life; Battle of the Sexes; Actors; Actresses; Female Protagonists; Female Screenwriters; Faded Hits (Firefly; The Chocolate Soldier)

Sweethearts Dance, 1988, 101m, ★★1/2/$, Tri-Star/Col-Tri, PG-13/S. Two couples in Vermont have marital problems and try to figure them out. Susan Sarandon, Jeff Daniels, Don Johnson, Elizabeth Perkins, Kate Reid, Justin Henry. w. Ernest Thompson, d. Robert Greenwald.

COMEDY DRAMA: ROMANCE: Marriage Drama; Marriage on the Rocks; Married Couples; New England; Snow Settings; Overlooked at Release; Old-Fashioned Recent Films (Married to It; The Four Seasons) (Ed: Good cast, mediocre everything else)

Sweetie, 1989, 100m, ★★★/$$, Ind/Live, R/S-P. A woman whose marriage is in trouble gets a visit by her rather odd sister which turns things around, perhaps for the better. Genevieve Lemon, Karen Colston, Tom Lycos, Jon Darling. w. Gerard Lee, Jane Campion, d. Jane Campion.

COMEDY DRAMA: Family Comedy; Sisters; Marriage on the Rocks; Eccentric People; Bathroom Humor; Female Screenwriters; Female Directors; Female Protagonists; Writer-Directors; New Zealand; Independent Films (Muriel's Wedding; The Piano)

Sweet Liberty, 1986, 107m, ★★1/2/$$, U/MCA-U, PG/S-MRN. When a film crew lands in a village for an American Revolution movie, tensions rise on and off the set for the director. Alan Alda, Michelle Pfeiffer, Michael Caine, Lillian Gish, Bob Hoskins, Saul Rubinek, Lois Chiles. w. d. Alan Alda.

COMEDY: COMEDY DRAMA: SATIRE: Movies within Movies; Moviemaking;

Directors; Actors; Actresses; Ensemble Films; New England; Good Premise Unfulfilled; Coulda Been Great; Writer-Directors (Ed: One wonders what Woody Allen could have done with this)

Sweet Lorraine, 1987, 91m, ★★★/$, Par/Par, PG. A teenager spends the summer with her grandmother at her old inn in the Catskill Mountains and soaks in the local eccentrics. Maureen Stapleton, Trini Alvarado, Lee Richardson. w. Michael Zettler, Shelly Altman, d. Steve Gomer.

COMEDY DRAMA: Coming of Age; Grandmothers-Fascinating; Mothers & Daughters; Hotels; Summer Vacations; Hidden Gems; Quiet Little Films (Ruby in Paradise; Desert Bloom)

Sweet November, 1968, 113m, ★★1/2/$, WB/NA. A woman with the dreaded fatal movie disease takes on a different boyfriend every month to make the most out of her time left, until one fellow stops her. Sandy Dennis, Anthony Newley, Theodore Bikel. w. Herman Raucher, d. Robert Ellis Miller.

COMEDY DRAMA: ROMANCE: Romance-Reluctant; Death-Impending; Disease Stories; Promiscuity; Stagelike Films; Good Premise Unfulfilled (Untamed Heart; Love Story; Dark Victory)

Sweet Rosie O'Grady, 1943, 79m, ★★★/$$$, 20th/Rex Miller Video. A gay 90s dancing sensation has a sensational past the tabloids are digging up on, but can she stop them? Betty Grable, Robert Young, Adolphe Menjou, Reginald Gardiner. w. Ken Englund, d. Irving Cummings.

MUSICALS: COMEDY: Musical Comedy; Secrets-Keeping; Past-Haunted by the; Dancers; Newspapers; Turning the Tables; 1890s

REMAKE OF: Love is News; **REMAKE:** That Wonderful Urge. (The Shocking Miss Pilgrim; The Dolly Sisters)

The Sweet Smell of Success, 1957, 96m, ★★★1/2/$, UA/MGM-UA. An unethical journalist becomes involved in a plot to get a friend of his sister away from her husband before danger results. Burt Lancaster, Tony Curtis, Martin Milner, Susan Harrison, Emile Meyer, Sam Levene, Barbara Nichols. w. Clifford Odets, Ernest Lehman, d. Alexander MacKendrick.

DRAMA: SATIRE: Corruption; Greed; Journalists; Ethics; Brothers & Sisters; Marriage on the Rocks; Film Noir; Forgotten Films; Hidden Gems; Overlooked at Release
(Five Star Final; Executive Suite; Edge of the City; Detective Story)
(Ed: A bit confusing at first, but the details soon add up)

Swept Away, 1975, 116m, ★★★★/$$$, Columbia/RCA-Col, R/S-P. A rich Italian woman (Mariangela Melato) is stranded on an island with a poor shipmate (Giancarlo Giannini) and sparks fly. w. d. Lina Wertmueller.

COMEDY: ROMANCE: Romantic Comedy; Screwball Comedy; Romance-Bickering; Romance-Reluctant; Romance-Opposites Attract; Battle of the Sexes; Stranded on an Island; Islands; Rich vs. Poor; Snobs vs. Slobs; Class Conflicts; Mean Women; Macho Men; Italian Films; Female Directors; Female Screenwriters; Writer-Directors; Underrated; Hidden Gems; Old-Fashioned Recent Films
(A Touch of Class; Seven Beauties)

The Swimmer, 1968, 94m, ★★★/$, Col/RCA-Col, R/S. The strange story of a man who swims his neighborhood's pools in succession, meeting people along the way, but finally gets home to reality. Burt Lancaster, Janice Rule, Kim Hunter, Diana Muldaur, Marge Champion. w. Eleanor Perry, SS-adap. John Cheever, d. Frank Perry.

DRAMA: Psychological Drama; Character Studies; Art Films; Suburban Life; Midlife Crisis; Illusions Destroyed; Swimming; Allegorical Stories; Hidden Gems; Female Screenwriters
(The Gypsy Moths; Happy Birthday, Wanda June; David and Lisa; Diary of a Mad Housewife)

Swimming to Cambodia, 1987, 87m, ★★★/$$, Cinecom/Cinecom, PG. Actor Spaulding Gray recalls his experiences filming *The Killing Fields*, milking it for every bit. w. P-adap. Spaulding Gray, d. Jonathan Demme.

COMEDY: Comedians; Storytellers; Memories; Stage Tapings; One Person Shows; Stage Filmings
(Monster in a Box)

The Swing, 1983, 133m, ★★★/$, Ind/NA. An elderly woman writer remembers her family life in Germany with fondness. Anja Jaenicke, Rolf Bing. w. d. Percy Adlon.

COMEDY DRAMA: FAMILY: Family Comedy; Memories; Flashbacks; Storytellers; Elderly Women; Writers; Grandmothers-Fascinating; Female Protagonists; German Films; Writer-Directors
(Fanny & Alexander)

Swing High, Swing Low, 1937, 97m, ★★½/$$$, Par/Nos. A jazz musician is rescued from the brink by his wife. Carole Lombard, Fred MacMurray, Charles Butterworth, Dorothy Lamour, Anthony Quinn. w. Virginia Van Upp, Oscar Hammerstein, P-adap. George Walters, *Burlesque*, d. Mitchell Leisen.

COMEDY DRAMA: ROMANCE: Marriage Drama; Jazz Life Musicians; Suicidal Tendencies; Alcoholics; Depression; Woman Behind the Man; Female Screenwriters; Female Protagonists
(Bird; A Star is Born; The Country Girl)

Swing Kids, 1993, 114m, ★/$, Hollywood/Hollywood, PG-13/V. As the Nazis take power, kids dance to the swing time and then get sucked in or escape, all to a beat, of course. Robert Sean Leonard, Christian Bale, Frank Whaley, Barbara Hershey, Kenneth Branagh. w. Jonathan Feldman, d. Thomas Carter.

MELODRAMA: Music Movies; Dance Movies; Big Band Era; Nazi Stories; Oppression; Germany; Escape Drama; Teenagers; Black Directors; Unintentionally Funny; Flops-Major
(Cabaret)
(Ed: From the same studio as *Newsies*. Branagh apparently just had to play a Nazi and didn't read the whole script)

Swing Shift, 1984, 100m, ★★½/$, U/MCA-U, PG/S. Rosie the Riveter falls in love with a co-worker during World War II. Goldie Hawn, Kurt Russell, Christine Lahti (BSActress), Fred Ward, Ed Harris. w. Nancy Dowd, Ron Nyswaner, Bo Goldman, d. Jonathan Demme. Oscars: 1-0.

COMEDY DRAMA: ROMANCE: Romantic Comedy; Romance-Triangles; Friendships-Female; Factory Life; War At Home; World War II Stories; Female Protagonists; Coulda Been Good; Female Screenwriters
(Ed: Controversy erupted among all involved as to the lack of release by the studio after protracted battles about the script and editing)

Swing Time, 1936, 96m, ★★★½/$$$, RKO/Turner. When a male-female dance

duo has trouble getting in sync on the floor, and off, it turns out he has a girl back home he won't let go of. Fred Astaire, Ginger Rogers, Victor Moore, Betty Furness. w. Howard Lindsay, Allan Scott, d. George Stevens. **BO**Song, "The Way You Look Tonight," **B**Dance Direction. Oscars: 2-1.

MUSICALS: ROMANCE: Musical Romance; Dance Movies; Dancers; Romance-Triangles; Romance-Reluctant; Astaire & Rogers
(Top Hat; Flying Down to Rio)

The Swiss Family Robinson, 1960, 126m, ★★½/$$$$$, Disney/Disney, G. They're shipwrecked and have to live in a tree (which later was made into a Disney World attraction). John Mills, Dorothy McGuire, James McArthur, Tommy Kirk, Sessue Hayakawa. w. Lowell S. Hawley, d. Ken Annakin.

ADVENTURE: FAMILY: CHILDREN'S: Family Drama; Survival Drama; Stranded; Islands; Shipwrecked; Blockbusters; Sleeper Hits
(In Search of the Castaways; Castaway; The Mosquito Coast)
(Ed: Renowned actor John Mills' greatest box-office hit)

Switch, 1991, 103m, ★★½/$$, Col/Col-Tri, R/S-P-FN-MRN. A philandering playboy is killed by the women he's been two-timing and is reincarnated as a woman (Ellen Barkin) to teach him a lesson. JoBeth Williams, Jimmy Smits, Lorraine Bracco. w. d. Blake Edwards.

COMEDY DRAMA: MELODRAMA: SATIRE: ROMANCE: Men as Women; Body Switching; Role Reversal; Surrealism; Sex Change; Dose of Own Medicine-Given; Turning the Tables; Babies-Having; Babies-Men Having; Lesbians; Alternative Lifestyles; Dual Lives; Fashion World; Advertising World; Cheating Men; Cheated Upon Meet; Revenge; Revenge on Cheaters; Reincarnation; Playboys; Satan; Writer-Directors

REMAKE/RETREAD OF: Goodbye, Charlie.
(The Man Who Loved Women; Tootsie)

Switching Channels, 1988, 105m, ★★/$, Col/RCA-Col, PG/P. A remake of *His Girl Friday* set at a CNN-like cable network, where a female anchor who's ready to be married to a neurotic preppie takes on one last story which changes everything due to working with her macho partner. Kathleen Turner, Burt Reynolds, Christopher Reeve, Ned Beatty, Henry Gibson. w. Jonathan Reynolds, P-adap. Charles MacArthur, Ben Hecht, *The Front Page*, d. Ted Kotcheff.

COMEDY: FARCE: ROMANCE: Romantic Comedy; Screwball Comedy; Race Against Time; Marriage-Impending; Executions; TV Life; Journalists; Revisionist Films; Old-Fashioned Recent Films

REMAKE OF: The Front Page, 1932, 1974, & His Girl Friday.

(Ed: Gets a case of the sillies too early on and looses its timing, even with tried and true material)

Swoon, 1992, 80m, ★★★/$, Argos, R/S-P. The Leopold & Loeb story retold. Two Jewish gay lovers kidnap and kill a boy in a dare situation and scandalize 1920s Chicago, also inadvertently furthering years of bad stereotypes of gay and Jewish men. Daniel Schlachet, Craig Chester, Ron Vawter. w. Tom Kalin, Hilton Als, d. Tom Kalin.

DRAMA: Art Films; Courtroom Drama; **MURDER:** Gay Men; Gay Films; Homosexual Murderers; Murders of Children; Jewish People; Revisionist Films; Chicago; 1920s; Writer-Directors; True Stories

REMAKE OF (Retelling): Rope, Compulsion.

(Rope; Compulsion; The Cradle)

The Sword & the Sorcerer, 1982, 99m, ★★1/2/$$$, U/MCA-U, R/V. A kingdom is at stake when a prince and a dictator do mystic battle. Lee Horsley, Kathleen Beller, Simon MacCorkindale, George Maharis. w. Tom Karnowski, Albert Pyun, John Stuckmeyer, d. Pyun.

ACTION: SCI-FI: Fantasy; Sword & Sorcery; Magic; Good vs. Evil; Kingdoms; Princes; Leaders-Tyrant; Medieval Times; Sleeper Hits

(The Beastmaster; The Sword in the Stone)

The Sword in the Stone, 1963, 80m, ★★★/$$$, Disney/Disney, G. Cartoon version of the King Arthur legend where the young boy Arthur is the only one with the power to remove the sword stuck in the stone. w. Bill Peet, N-adap. T. H. White, *The Once and Future King*, d. Wolfgang Reitherman.

ACTION: ADVENTURE: CHILDREN'S: FAMILY: Cartoon; Fantasy; Magic Boys; Princes; Mythology/Legends; Medieval Times; England; Camelot Stories

(Excalibur; Sword of Lancelot; Prince Valiant)

Sword of Lancelot, (Lancelot and Guinevere), 1962, 117m, ★★/$$, Emblem-U/MCA-U. Retelling of the Arthurian legend, centering on Guinevere's ascension to the throne. Cornel Wilde, Jean Wallace, Brian Aherne. w. Richard Schayer, Jefferson Pascal, d. Cornel Wilde.

ADVENTURE: ROMANCE: Romantic Drama; Costume Drama; Legends; Royalty; Kings; Camelot Stories; Actor Directors

(Excalibur; Camelot; First Knight)

Sword of the Valiant, 1984, 101m, ★★/$, Cannon-MGM-UA/MGM-UA, PG/V. Medieval sword & sorcery tale of Gawain vs. the Green Knight is retold. Sean Connery, Miles O'Keefe, Trevor Howard, Leigh Lawson, Peter Cushing, Lila Kedrova, John Rhys-Davies. w. Stephen Weeks, Philip Breen, Howard Pen, d. Weeks.

ACTION: Fantasy; Sword & Sorcery; Good vs Evil; Duels; Mythology/Legends; Medieval Times; England; British Films

(First Knight; Robin and Marian)

Sybil, 1976, 122m, ★★★/$$$$, NBC/Fox. True story of an abused little girl who grew up to develop sixteen separate personalities which her psychiatrist works with her to unravel. Sally Field (Emmy winner), Joanne Woodward, Brad Davis. d. Daniel Petrie.

DRAMA: True Stories; Psychological Drama; Multiple Personalities; Psychologists; Psychologists as Detectives; Abused Children; Evil Women; Female Protagonists; TV Movies; Blockbusters

(The Three Faces of Eve (where Woodward played the personalities); Lizzie)

(Ed: A huge ratings winner and Emmy winner, as well as Field's breakthrough after her *Gidget/Flying Nun* years)

Sylvia and the Ghost (Sylvia and the Phantom), 1944, 93m, ★★★/$, Ind/New Line. A teenage girl sees the ghost of a man who died fighting for her grandmother in her father's family castle, but no one wants to believe the stories she learns. Odette Joyeux, Francois Perier, Jacques Tati. w. Jean Aurenche, P-adap. Alfred Adam, d. Claude Autant-Lara.

COMEDY DRAMA: ROMANCE: Ghosts; Fantasy; Castles; Unbelieved; Girls; Female Protagonists; Forgotten Films; Hidden Gems; Coulda Been Great; French Films

(The Ghost and Mrs. Muir; The Uninvited; Canterbury Tales)

Sylvia Scarlett, 1935, 94m, ★★★1/2/$, RKO/Turner. A free-spirited young woman wants to run away with her con artist father to France, but needs to pretend to be a boy to do it. This gets her into many awkward situations in her country habitat. Katharine Hepburn, Cary Grant, Edmund Gwenn, Brian Aherne. w. Gladys Unger, John Collier, Mortimer Offner, N-adap. Compton MacKenzie, d. George Cukor.

COMEDY: Screwball Comedy; **COMEDY DRAMA:** Fairy Tales; Women as Men; Tomboys; Disguises; Fathers & Daughters; Ensemble Films; Gypsies; Con Artists; Ahead of Its Time; Cult Films; Overlooked at Release; Hidden Gems; Female Screenwriters; Female Protagonists

(The Little Minister; Quality Street; Tootsie; Yentl)

(Ed: Much imitated and admired, though it somehow misses whatever mark it was supposed to hit)

Films by Title

T

Table for Five, 1983, 124m, ★★¹/₂/$, CBS-WB/CBS-Fox, PG. A divorced dad takes his kids on a European cruise in order to tell them their mom's been killed, while also meeting a nice French woman who has interest in him. Jon Voight, Richard Crenna, Marie-Christine Barrault, Millie Perkins, Roxana Zal. w. David Seltzer, d. Robert Lieberman.
MELODRAMA: Tearjerkers; Family Drama; **FAMILY:** Fathers Alone; Widowers; Ships; Vacations-European; Fathers & Daughters; Death-Dealing
(Author, Author; The Champ [1979]; See You in the Morning)
Tabu, 1931, 80m, ★★★/$$, Colorart/ Lumiere Video. A fable about a young boy fisherman in Tahiti. w. d. F.W. Murnau. **BCin**. Oscars: 1-1.
DRAMA: ADVENTURE: Islands; Pacific Islands; Fishermen; Boys; Writer-Directors
(Hurricane)
Taffin, 1988, 96m, ★★¹/₂/$, Vestron/ Vestron, PG-13/P-V. A man battles a chemical company wanting to build a factory in an Irish village. Pierce Brosnan, Alison Doody, Ray McAnally, Jeremy Child. w. David Ambrose. d. Francis Megahy.
DRAMA: SUSPENSE: Revenge; Save the Farm/Land; Corporation as Enemy; Fighting the System; Irish Land Battles; Ireland; Irish Films

(Local Hero; The Field; Rob Roy)
Tai Pan, 1986, 127m, ★★/$, DEG-Par/Par, PG. A European galavants around the orient and winds up in hot water romantically and politically. Bryan Brown, Joan Chen, John Stanton. w. John Briley, Stanley Mann, N-adap. James Clavell, d. Daryl Duke.
MELODRAMA: ADVENTURE: ROMANCE: Romantic Adventure; Epics; Hong Kong; China; Costume Drama; 1800s; Flops-Major
(Shogun; The Last Emperor; Blood Alley)
Take a Letter, Darling, 1942, 94m, ★★★/$$$, Par/NA, AMC. A woman executive hires a secretary and winds up with a handsome man, and possibly a romance. Rosalind Russell, Fred MacMurray, MacDonald Carey, Cecil Kellaway, Constance Moore. w. Claude Binyon, d. Mitchell Leisen. BB&WCin, BB&WArt, BOScore. Oscars: 3-0.
COMEDY: ROMANCE: Romantic Comedy; Battle of the Sexes; Office Comedy; Executives; Business Life; Romance-Reluctant; Male in Female Domain; Female in Male Domain; Role Reversal; Hidden Gems; Faded Hits; Female Protagonists
(Hired Wife; Help Wanted: Male)
Take Her, She's Mine, 1963, 98m, ★★★/$$$, 20th/CBS-Fox. A middle-aged lawyer tries to keep his rowdy daughter

out of boy trouble and political activism, but it backfires. James Stewart, Sandra Dee, Robert Morley, Audrey Meadows, John McGiver. w. Nunnally Johnson, P-adap. Phoebe & Henry Ephron, d. Henry Koster.
COMEDY: FAMILY: Family Comedy; Teenagers; Free Spirits; Daddy's Girls; Lawyers; Generation Gap; Fathers & Daughters; Fathers Controlling Daughters; Parents vs. Children
(The Impossible Years; She's Outta Control; Gidget)
Take Me Out to the Ball Game, 1949, 93m, ★★★/$$$, MGM/MGM-UA. When a woman takes over a baseball team, the all-male team doesn't like the idea. Gene Kelly, Frank Sinatra, Esther Williams, Betty Garrett, Edward Arnold, Richard Lane. w. Harry Tugend, George Wells, d. Busby Berkeley.
COMEDY: MUSICALS: Musical Comedy; Sports Movies; Baseball; Battle of the Sexes; Female Among Males
REMAKE/RETREAD: Major League.
(Major League; The Lemon Drop Kid)
Take the Money and Run, 1968, 85m, ★★★¹/₂/$$, UA/MGM-UA, PG/S-P. A nerdy delinquent grows up to be a notorious bank robber on the run. Woody Allen, Janet Margolin. w. d. Woody Allen.
COMEDY: Nerds; Nerds & Babes; Heist Stories; Fugitives from the Law; Juvenile

Delinquents; Bank Robberies; Criminals-Stupid; Cult Films; Writer-Directors (Bananas; Quick Change; Zelig; The Delicate Delinquent)

Take This Job and Shove It, 1981, 100m, ★★/$$, Embassy/Col, PG/P-S. An efficiency expert tries to straighten out a brewery but decides to act out the title. Robert Hays, Barbara Hershey, Art Carney, Penelope Milford, Johnny Paycheck. w. Barry Schneider, d. Gus Trikonis.
COMEDY: Song Title Movies; Country Singers; Factory Life; Class Conflicts; Efficiency Experts; Fighting the System (Blue Collar; Lost in America; The Dion Brothers)

Taking Care of Business, 1990, 108m, ★ 1/2/$$, Hollywood/Hollywood, PG-13/S-P. When a businessman loses his address book, a just released ex-convict picks it up and takes over his life. Jim Belushi, Charles Grodin, Anne deSalvo, Hector Elizondo, Veronica Hamel. w. Jill Mazursky, Jeffrey Abrams, d. Arthur Hiller.
COMEDY: Identities-Assumed; Con Artists; Body Switching; Finding Valuables; Ex-Convicts; Rich vs. Poor; Snobs vs. Slobs; Good Premise Unfulfilled; Los Angeles; Female Screenwriters
REMAKE/RETREAD OF: Trading Places. (Life Stinks!; Midnight Run; A Stolen Life)
(Ed: Bad even as these mediocre rip-off comedies go)

The Taking of Beverly Hills, 1991, 96m, ★★/VR, New Line/Col, R/EV-P. A crazy billionaire decides to create a toxic spill in B-Hills and take all the rich folks' money while they're evacuated, but a supercop comes to the rescue. Ken Wahl, Matt Frewer, Harley Jane Kozak, Robert Davi. w. d. Sidney J. Furie.
ACTION: Action Comedy; Hostage Situations; Rich People; Beverly Hills; Police Stories; Police-Vigilante

The Taking of Pelham 123, 1974, 104m, ★★★/$$, UA/MGM-UA, R/V-P. Terrorists hold a subway train hostage and take it on a wild ride through the bowels of New York awaiting ransom money for their passengers. Walter Matthau, Robert Shaw, Martin Balsam, Hector Elizondo, James Broderick. w. Peter Stone, N-adap. John Godey, d. Joseph Sargent.

ACTION: SUSPENSE: Crime Drama; Police Stories; Terrorists; Hostage Situations; Kidnappings; Subways; Race Against Time; New York Life; Urban Horrors
(Money Train; Short Walk to Daylight; Nighthawks; The Laughing Policeman)

Taking Off, 1971, 92m, ★★★/$, U/MCA-U, R/P-S. When uptight suburban parents seek out their wayward daughter in the big, bad city, they get taken in by the scene themselves. Lynn Carlin, Buck Henry, Linnea Heacock. w. Milos Forman, John Guare, Jean-Claude Carriere, John Klein, d. Milos Forman.
COMEDY: COMEDY DRAMA: Fish out of Water Stories; Generation Gap; Missing Persons; Parents vs. Children; Extroverted vs. Introverted; Psychedelic Era; 1970s; Sexual Revolution; Cult Films; Forgotten Films; Hidden Gems (Hardcore; Hi, Mom!; Joe; The Party's Over)

Tale of a Vampire, 1992, 102m, ★★ 1/2/$ (VR), Vidmark/Vidmark, R/S-P-B&G. A man whose wife has been seduced and abandoned by a vampire tracks the sucker down. Julian Sands, Suzanna Hamilton, Kenneth Cranham. w. Shimako Sato, Jane Corbett, d. Shimeko Sato.
HORROR: Vampires; Erotic Thriller; Jealousy; Avenging Death of Someone; London; Beautiful People; Female Screenwriters
(Warlock; Husbands and Lovers)

A Tale of Two Cities, 1935, 121m, ★★★ 1/2/$$$, MGM/MGM-UA. A British lawyer winds up in a heroic and tragic position when the French Revolution explodes full force and a man he knows is being wrongly executed. Ronald Colman, Elizabeth Allan, Basil Rathbone, Edna May Oliver, Reginald Owen. w. W. P. Lipscomb, S. N. Behrman, N-adap. Charles Dickens, d. Jack Conway. BPicture, BEdit. Oscars: 2-0.

A Tale of Two Cities, 1958, 117m, ★★★/$$, Rank/Sultan. Dirk Bogarde, Dorothy Tutin, Christopher Lee, Donald Pleasence, Ian Bannen. w. T.E.B. Clarke, d. Ralph Thomas.

A Tale of Two Cities, 1982, 140m, ★★★ 1/2/$$$, Hallmark/Hallmark. Chris Sarandon, Dame May Robson, Billie Whitelaw. w. John Gay, d. Jim Goddard.
DRAMA: Costume Drama; Historical Drama; Epics; TRAGEDY: French

Revolution; Accused Unjustly; Saving Someone; Executions; Evil Women; Political Unrest; Classic Literary Adaptations; Classic Tragedy (Scaramouche; Les Miserables; David Copperfield)

A Talent for Loving, 1969, 101m, ★★ 1/2/$, Par/NA. Jet-setting playboys have trouble balancing their love lives with their sex lives over the years. Richard Widmark, Cesar Romero, Topol. w. N-adap. Richard Condon, d. Richard Quine.
DRAMA: Character Studies; Playboys; Beautiful People; Episodic Stories; Marriage on the Rocks; Cheating Men; Overlooked at Release

Talent for the Game, 1991, 91m, ★★/$, Par/Par, PG. A talent scout recruits a whiz kid only to have the team exploit him with seemingly no way to rectify it. Edward James Olmos, Lorraine Bracco, Jeff Corbett, Jamey Sheridan, Terry Kinney. w. David Himmelstein, Tom Donnelly, Larry Ferguson, d. Robert M. Young.
MELODRAMA: Baseball; Sports Movies; Proteges; Ethics; FAMILY: Overlooked at Release
(The Scout; The Search for Bobby Fischer)

Tales from the Crypt, 1972, 92m, ★★ 1/2/$$, Ind/HBO, R/EV. When several people get stuck in the catacombs, a mysterious monk with occult connections takes them on a journey through several stories of horror. Ralph Richardson, Geoffrey Balydon, Peter Cushing, Joan Collins, Roy Dotrice. w. Milton Subonsky, SS-adap. William Gaines, d. Freddie Francis.
HORROR: Multiple Stories; Monks; Satanism; Occult; Storytellers
(Asylum; Tales from the Crypt [TV SERIES])

Tales from the Darkside: The Movie, 1991, 93m, ★★ 1/2/$$, Par/Par, R/P-V-B&G. Several stories told by a kid about to be cooked for dinner by Deborah Harry. Matthew Lawrence, Christian Slater, Steve Buscemi, William Hickey, James Remar, Rae Dawn Chong. w. Michael McDowell, George Romero, SS-adap. Stephen King, Arthur Conan Doyle, d. John Harrison.
HORROR: Multiple Stories; Cannibalism; Satanism; Cats; Buried Alive; Boys; Narrated Films; Storytellers
(Creepshow; Tales from the Hood)

Tales from the Hood, 1995, 98m, ★★★/$$, Savoy/Savoy, R/EV-P-B&G. Drug thieves are forced by a mortician to listen to four tales of horror from the ghetto: three white cops kill a black activist and reap the wrath of the supernatural; a boy who's being abused says a monster at home is doing it and it may very well be true; a racist politician gets a dose of his own medicine; and a drive-by shooter is brainwashed. Clarence Williams III, Joe Torry, De'Aundre Bonds, Sam Monroe, Wings Hauser, Tom Wright, Anthony Griffith, Michael Massee, Duane Whitaker, David Alan Grier, Corbin Bernsen, Rosalind Cash. w. Rusty Cundieff & Darin Scott, d. Rusty Cundieff.

HORROR: Multiple Stories; Storytellers; Racism; Dose of Own Medicine-Given; Funerals; Brainwashing; Black Casts; Black Men; Gangs-Black; Blood and Gore
(Tales from the Darkside; Creepshow; A Clockwork Orange; Blacula)

Tales of Hoffman, 1951, 127m, ★★★/$$, BL-London/HomeVision. In three separate stories, the poet Hoffman has romances, and, sinking into lust, flirts with the ultimate evil. Robert Rounseville, Robert Helpmann, Pamela Brown, Moira Shearer. w. d. Michael Powell, Emeric Pressburger. BCArt. Oscars: 1-0.

DRAMA: MUSICALS: Musical Drama; Fantasy; Musical Fantasy; **ROMANCE:** Romantic Drama; Musical Romance; Surrealism; Dance Movies; Elusive Women; Sexy Women; Satan; Opera; Ballet; Writer-Directors
(The Red Shoes; Swann in Love; Faust)

Tales of Manhattan, 1942, 118m, ★★★/$$, 20th/NA. As a coat passes from owner to owner in New York, the stories of the owners are relayed. Charles Boyer, Rita Hayworth, Thomas Mitchell, Eugene Pallette, Ginger Rogers, Henry Fonda, Cesar Romero, Gail Patrick, Roland Young, Elsa Lanchester, Edward G. Robinson, George Sanders, Ethel Waters, Eddie Anderson, Charles Laughton. w. Ben Hecht, Ference Molar, Donald Ogden Stewart, Samuel Hoffenstein, Alan Campbell, Ladislas Fodor, Laslo Vadnay, Laszlo Gorog, Lamar Trotti, Henry Blankfort, d. Julien Duvivier.

COMEDY DRAMA: Multiple Stories; Interwoven Stories; Hand Me Down Stories; New York Life; All-Star Casts

(Flesh and Fantasy; Carnet de Bal; 20 Bucks; The Yellow Rolls Royce)

Tales of Terror, 1962, 90m, ★★★/$$, AIP/Orion. Several stories, one involving a man who walls up his wife, a girl, and her mummy mommy and hypnotism. Vincent Price, Peter Lorre, Basil Rathbone, Debra Paget. w. Richard Matheson, SS-adap. Edgar Allan Poe, d. Roger Corman.

HORROR: Multiple Stories; Buried Alive; Mummies; Mothers & Daughters; Marriage on the Rocks; Murder of Spouse; Hypnotism
(Comedy of Terrors; The Masque of the Red Death; The Pit and the Pendulum; The House of Usher)

Talk of the Town, 1942, 118m, ★★★½/$$$, Col/RCA-Col. When a man is wrongly accused of setting a fatal fire, he hides out at a former girlfriend's house that's been rented by a Supreme Court nominee who couldn't handle the scandal. It's up to them all to cover their tracks and find the real killer, but there may not have been a killing at all. Cary Grant, Ronald Colman, Jean Arthur, Edgar Buchanan, Charles Dingle. w. Irwin Shaw, Sidney Buchman (BOStory, BScr), d. George Stevens. BPicture, BB&WArt, BB&WCin, BEdit, BOScore. Oscars: 7-0.

COMEDY: COMEDY DRAMA: ROMANCE: Romantic Comedy; Fugitives from the Law; Framed?; Accused Unjustly; Romance-Reunited; Romance-Reluctant; Romance-Triangles; Roommates; Fugitives-Harboring; Judges; Supreme Court; Fighting the System; Fires-Arson; Clever Plots & Endings; Female Protagonists; Hidden Gems; Faded Hits

REMAKE/RETREAD: Seems Like Old Times
(Seems Like Old Times; The More the Merrier)

Talk Radio, 1987, 109m, ★★★½/$$, Cineplex-U/MCA-U, R/V-EP. A late night radio show host (Eric Bogosian) may have created more controversy than he can survive. Ellen Greene, Alec Baldwin. w. P-adap. Eric Bogosian, NF-adap. *The Life and Murder of Alan Berg*, Stephen Singular, d. Oliver Stone.

DRAMA: TRAGEDY: SATIRE: Social Satire; Social Drama; Radio Life; Rebels; Young Men-Angry; **MURDER:** Assassination Plots; Terrorists; Bigots;

Slice of Life Stories; Stagelike Films; Novel & Play Adaptations
(Network; Betrayed; Kings and Desperate Men)

Tall, Dark & Handsome, 1941, 78m, ★★½/$$, 20th/NA. A mobster tries to go legit and enter high society. Cesar Romero, Virginia Gilmore, Milton Berle. w. Karl Tunberg, Darrell Ware, d. H. Bruce Humberstone.

COMEDY DRAMA: Mob Stories; Mob Comedy; Starting Over; Social Climbing; Chicago; Roaring 20s
(Mister Cory; The Little Giant; My Blue Heaven)

The Tall Guy, 1989, 92m, ★★★/$, Virgin/Col, PG-13/S-P. An American in England tries for stardom in a musical based on *The Elephant Man*, hoping to break free from his comedy partner. Jeff Goldblum, Emma Thompson, Rowan Atkinson. w. Richard Curtis, d. Mel Smith.

COMEDY: MUSICALS: Music Movies; Theater Life; Actor; Comedian; **ROMANCE:** Romantic Comedy; Americans Abroad; England; Elephants; British Films

The Tall Men, 1955, 122m, ★★½/$$, 20th/Fox. After the Civil War several men set north to Montana to mine gold and wind up in conflict. Clark Gable, Jane Russell, Robert Ryan, Cameron Mitchell. w. Sidney Boehm, Frank Nugent, N-adap. Clay Fisher, d. Raoul Walsh.

WESTERNS: Civil War Era; Gold Mining; Men in Conflict; Journies; Men Fighting Over Women; Forgotten Films
(A King and Four Queens; Boomtown; Treasure of the Sierra Madre)

Tall Story, 1960, 91m, ★★½/$$, WB/WB. A basketball player gets married in college and encounters changes which affect his game. Anthony Perkins, Jane Fonda, Ray Walston, Anne Jackson, Murray Hamilton. w. Julius J. Epstein, N-adap. Howard Nemoor, *The Homecoming*, d. Joshua Logan.

COMEDY DRAMA: Character Studies; Basketball; Sports Movies; Marriage Drama; Pre-Life Crisis; Young Men; Life Transitions; College Life; Forgotten Films; Curiosities

The Tall Target, 1951, 78m, ★★★/$$, MGM/NA. A policeman in Washington during Lincoln's administration tries to prevent an assassination plot against the president to prove himself worthy after being demoted. Dick Powell, Adolphe

Menjou, Paul Raymond, Marshall Thompson, Will Geer, Ruby Dee. w. George Worthing Yates, Art Cohn, d. Anthony Mann.

DRAMA: SUSPENSE: Race Against Time; Historical Drama; Assassination Plot; Abraham Lincoln; Presidents; Police Stories; Men Proving Themselves; Civil War Era; Trains; Biographies-Fictional; Forgotten Films; Hidden Gems (The Lincoln Conspiracy; Abraham Lincoln)

The Tall Blond Man with One Black Shoe (*Le Grand Blond avec une Chaussure Noire*), 1973, 89m, ★★★/$$$, Col/Col, PG/S. A secret service man claims that a klutzy violinist is actually a master spy in order to get his superior to chase after him. Pierre Richard, Bernard Blier, Jean Rochefort, Mireille Darc, Jean Carmet, Colette Castel. w. Yves Robert, Francis Veber, d. Yves Robert.

COMEDY: FARCE: Chase Stories; Framed?; Accused Unjustly; Fugitives from the Law; Secret Agents; Spies; Identities-Mistaken; Accident Prone; French Films; Cult Films; Hidden Gems

REMAKE: The Man with One Red Shoe. (Les Comperes; La Chevre; Out on a Limb)

Tamango, 1959, 98m, ★★/$, Ind/Live. A slave ship captain takes a black mistress on a trip from Africa while the slaves plan to mutiny. Curt Jurgens, Dorothy Dandridge. d. John Berry.

DRAMA: Slavery; Romance-Interracial; Black Women; Black vs. White; Ships; 1800s; Curiosities; Forgotten Films (Mark of the Hawk; Bright Road; The Journey of August King; Queen)

The Tamarind Seed, 1974, 125m, ★★½/$, Lorimar-UA/CBS-Fox, R/P-S-V. A woman (Julie Andrews) becomes entangled in a spy plot when she's asked to join in foreign intrigue with a debonair mystery man (Omar Sharif). w. d. Blake Edwards.

DRAMA: SUSPENSE: Spy Films; **ROMANCE: MYSTERY:** Romance-Dangerous; Dangerous Men; Women in Jeopardy; Undercover; Spies-Female; Caribbean; Female Protagonists; Writer-Directors
(Ed: Looks good but no excitement)

The Taming of the Shrew, 1967, 122m, ★★★/$$, Col/RCA-Col, PG. Petruchio tries to tame the love of his life into submissive love, but it's not so easy. Richard Burton, Elizabeth Taylor, Michael York, Cyril Cusack, Michael Hordern. w. Suso Cecchi D'Amico, Paul Dehn, Franco Zeffirelli, d. Zeffirelli.

COMEDY: COMEDY DRAMA: Comedy of Manners; Battle of the Sexes; Abusive Men; Classic Literary Adaptations; Marriage Comedy; Spinsters; Elusive Women; Mean Men; Middle Ages; Costume Drama; Revisionist Films

MUSICAL REMAKE: Kiss Me Kate.

Tammy and the Bachelor, 1957, 89m, ★★★/$$$$, MGM/MGM-UA. A feisty tomboy down South falls in love with a pilot who has to crash land nearby and starts thinking about going to the city while singing on the docks of the river. Debbie Reynolds, Walter Brennan, Leslie Nielsen, Mala Powers, Fay Wray, Mildred Natwick. w. Oscar Brodney, SS-adap. Cid Ricketts Summer, d. Joseph Pevney.

MELODRAMA: Music Movies; **MUSICALS:** Musical Romance; **COMEDY DRAMA: ROMANCE:** Romantic Comedy; Stranded; Pilots-Airline; Southerns; Tomboys; Hillbillies; Rural Life; Female Protagonists

SEQUELS: Tammy and the Doctor; Tammy and the Millionaire; Tammy Tell Me True (played by Sandra Dee and Debbie Watson, not Reynolds) (Susan Slept Here; Gidget)

Tampopo, 1986, 117m, ★★★/$$, Republic/Republic, R/S. A Japanese woman becomes obsessed with cooking noodles and food in general in a slice of life story about Tokyo with a Western spice. Tsutomu Yamazaki, Nobuko Miyamoto, Ken Watanabe. w. d. Juzo Itami.

COMEDY: Spoofs; Spoofs-Westerns; Western Comedy; Food Stories; Restaurant Settings; Slice of Life Stories; Multiple Stories; Cult Films; Japanese Films; Japan; Female Protagonists; Writer-Directors
(Ed: "The first Japanese noodle Western")

Tango & Cash, 1989, 101m, ★★/$$$, WB/WB, R/EP-EV-MRN. Two cops are framed for murder and go to jail until they escape to exact revenge. Sylvester Stallone, Kurt Russell, Jack Palance, Teri Hatcher, Michael J. Pollard. w. Randy Feldman, d. Andrei Konchalovsky.

ACTION: Action Comedy; Crime Drama; **MURDER: MURDER MYSTERY: MYSTERY:** Police Stories; Detective Stories; Detectives-Police; Framed?; Accused Unjustly; Murder-Clearing Oneself; Police Corruption; Revenge; Prison Drama; Prison Escapes; Chase Stories; Fugitives from the Law; Coulda Been Good
(Lock-Up; Demolition Man; Judge Dredd)
(Ed: Too cute and cliched to be good)

Tank, 1984, 113m, ★★/$, Lorimar-U/MCA-U, PG/V. A war veteran restores a war tank to break his framed son out of jail. James Garner, Shirley Jones, C. Thomas Howell, Dorian Harewood, d. Marvin Chomsky.

COMEDY DRAMA: ACTION: Action Comedy; Accused Unjustly; Framed?; Prison Escapes; Vigilantes; Fathers & Sons; Veterans; Small-town Life; Good Premise Unfulfilled

Tank Girl, 1995, 94m, ★★½/$, UA/MGM-UA, R/S-P. In the future, earth has been hit by a comet and decimated. Tank Girl is a girl with a tank, who roams the barren wastelands trying to save what's left of civilization while running into various and sundry eccentric, manic characters and one evil villain. Lori Petty, Ice-T, Naomi Watts, Don Harvey, Reg E. Cathey, Scott Coffey, Jeff Kober, Malcolm McDowell. w. Tedi Sarafian, Comic-adap. Alan Martin & Jamie Hewlett, d. Rachel Talalay.

ACTION: ADVENTURE: SCI-FI: Apocalyptic Stories; Female in Male Domain; Comic Heroes; Female Protagonists; Female Directors
(The Road Warrior; Waterworld)

Tanner '88, 1988, 120m, ★★★/$, PBS/PBS, Disney. Satire of a politician's rise in the Democratic party under the Reagan era. Michael Murphy, Pamela Reed, Cynthia Nixon. w. Garry Trudeau, d. Robert Altman. Emmy winner.

SATIRE: Political Satire; Politicians; Political Campaigns; TV Movies
(Bob Roberts; The Candidate; Power)

Tap, 1989, 101m, ★★½/$, Tri-Star/Col-Tri, PG. A jewel thief returns to dancing and tries to revive tap. Gregory Hines, Sammy Davis, Jr., Joe Morton, Suzanne Douglas, Savion Glover. w. d. Nick Castle.

MUSICALS: Music Movies; Dancers; Dance Movies; Jewel Thieves; Black Casts; Black Men; Comebacks; Theater Life; Old-Fashioned Recent Films; Writer-Directors
(Beat Street; Sweet Charity; Salt and Pepper)

Taps, 1981, 126m, ★★★/$$$$, 20th/CBS-Fox, PG/P-EV. A boys' military school goes to extremes with their ammunition to keep condos from taking the place of their alma mater. Timothy Hutton, Sean Penn, Tom Cruise, George C. Scott, Ronny Cox. w. Darryl Ponicsan, Robert Mark Kamen, N-adap. Devery Freeman, *Father Sky*, d. Harold Becker.
DRAMA: TRAGEDY: ACTION: Action Drama; Military Schools; Mortgage Drama; Military Stories; Teenagers; Boys' Schools; Boys; Young Men; Save the Land; Ensembles-Male; Ensemble Films; Crisis Situations; Fighting the System; Obsessions; Curiosities; Bratpack Movies
(Toy Soldiers; The Lords of Discipline)
(Ed: A preposterous outcome of a preposterous premise if you think about it-but then, these are military zealots . . . as perceived by Hollywood)
Taras Bulba, 1962, 124m, ★★½/$$, UA/MGM-UA. A family saga about Russian cossacks, centering around a father-son dispute in the midst of war. Yul Brynner, Tony Curtis, Christine Kaufmann, Sam Wanamaker. w. Wlado Salt, Karl Tunberg, N-adap. Nikolai Gogol, d. J. Lee-Thompson. BOScore. Oscars: 1-0.
DRAMA: Epics; War Stories; Family Drama; Sagas; Russians; Fathers & Sons; Parents vs. Children; Forgotten Films
(The Brothers Karamazov; Dr. Zhivago)
Target, 1985, 117m, ★★/$, CBS-WB/WB, PG/V-P. When mom is kidnapped, CIA-agent dad and son head to Europe to do battle with the terrorists who've attached a bomb to her. Gene Hackman, Matt Dillon, Gayle Hunnicutt, Josef Sommer. w. Howard Berk, Don Peterson, d. Arthur Penn.
SUSPENSE: ACTION: Action Drama; Kidnappings; Saving Someone; Terrorists; Children Saving Parents; Bombs; Women in Jeopardy; Coulda Been Good; Unintentionally Funny
(Frantic; The Package; 52 Pick-up)
Targets, 1967, 90m, ★★★/$, Par/Par. A horror movie actor on the skids gets a shot at sort of comeback by going after a sniper in a drive-in movie. Boris Karloff, Tim O'Kelly, James Brown. w. d. Peter Bogdanovich.
SUSPENSE: MELODRAMA: Horror Comedy; Spoofs; Comebacks; Actors; Elderly Men; Curiosities; Movie Theaters;

Snipers; Heroes-Unlikely; Writer-Directors
(Fright Night; Midnight [1989])
The Tarnished Angels, 1957, 91m, ★★/$$, U/NA. A journalist doing a story on an air daredevil family falls in love with their daughter and thinks about joining up. Rock Hudson, Dorothy Malone, Robert Stack, Jack Carson. w. George Zuckerman, d. Douglas Sirk.
MELODRAMA: ROMANCE: ACTION: Family Drama; Romance-Reluctant; Pilots-Daredevil; Circus Life; Journalists; Flops-Major; Curiosities
(Written on the Wind; The Gypsy Moths)
(Ed: Contains most of the cast of the previous year's hit, *Written on the Wind*, but while that one still plays the afternoon matinees, this one crashed and burned)
Tarzan, the Ape Man, 1981, 105m, ★★/$$$, MGM/MGM-UA, R/ES-V-FFN-MRN. A bimbo crash lands in just the right place to find the hunky Tarzan and his ape friends to do kinky things with in the jungle. Bo Derek, Miles O'Keefe. w. d. John Derek.
MELODRAMA: ADVENTURE: Spoofs; Comic Adventure; Erotic Comedy; Jungle Life; Bimbos; Primates; Raised by Animals; Stranded; Africa; Cartoonlike Movies; Camp; Unintentionally Funny; Curiosities
(Greystoke; Ten; Congo)
Tarzan, The Ape Man, 1932, 99m, ★★★/$$$$, MGM/MGM-UA. The original Tarzan, where he meets Jane and learns to be more human than ape like those he was raised by. Johnny Weissmuller, Maureen O'Sullivan. d. W. S. Van Dyke
REMAKES: 1959 version; 1981 spoof, Greystoke.
(Greystoke; The Legend of Tarzan)
Tarzan and His Mate, 1934, 105m, ★★★/$$$, MGM/MGM-UA. Tarzan gets a little closer to Jane. Johnny Weissmuller, Maureen O'Sullivan. d. Cedrick Gibbons.
Tarzan Escapes, 1936, 90m, ★★★/$$$, MGM/Fox. Johnny Weissmuller, Maureen O'Sullivan.
Tarzan's New York Adventure, 1942, 71m, ★★★/$$$, MGM/MGM-UA. Johnny Weissmuller, Maureen O'Sullivan. d. Richard Thorpe.
REMAKE/RETREAD: Crocodile Dundee.
ADVENTURE: Fish out of Water Stories; Jungle Life; Raised by Animals; Primates; Stranded; Superhuman Heroes;

Comic Heroes; Nature-Back to; Africa
(Crocodile Dundee; The Cowboy Way)
OTHER TARZAN TITLES: 1933: Tarzan the Fearless, 1935: The New Adventures of Tarzan, 1938: Tarzan's Revenge, 1939: Tarzan Finds a Son, 1941: Tarzan's Secret Treasure, 1943: Tarzan Triumphs, 1945: Tarzan and the Amazons, 1946: Tarzan and the Leopard Woman, 1947: Tarzan and the Huntress, 1948: Tarzan and the Mermaids, 1949: Tarzan's Magic Fountain, 1950: Tarzan and the Slave Girl, 1951: Tarzan's Peril, 1952: Tarzan's Savage Fury, 1953: Tarzan and the She-Devil, 1955: Tarzan's Hidden Jungle, 1957: Tarzan and the Lost Safari, 1958: Tarzan's Fight for Life, 1959: Tarzan the Ape Man, 1960: Tarzan the Magnificent, 1962: Tarzan Goes to India, 1963: Tarzan's Three Challenges, 1966: Tarzan and the Valley of Gold, 1967: Tarzan and the Great River, 1968: Tarzan and the Jungle Boy.
A Taste for Killing, 1992, 87m, ★★½/VR, U/MCA-U, R/V-P. Two rich kids get a oil rig job and wind up making friends with a killer. Jason Bateman, Henry Thomas, Michael Biehn. w. Dan Bronson, d. Lou Antonio.
SUSPENSE: MURDER: Psycho Killers; Blackmail; Class Conflicts; Oil People; Working Class; Rich Kids; TV Movies
(Bad Influence; I Saw What You Did)
A Taste of Honey, 1961, 100m, ★★★½/$$$, B-L/NA. A pregnant girl has problems with her wayward mother, her black boyfriend, and her gay best friend in her small English town. Rita Tushingham, Dora Bryan, Murray Melvin, Robert Stephens. w. Shelagh Delaney, Tony Richardson, P-adap. Delaney, d. Richardson.
COMEDY DRAMA: MELODRAMA: ROMANCE: Romance-Interracial; Coming of Age; Young Women; Romantic Drama; Kitchen Sink Drama; Slice of Life Stories; Alternative Lifestyles; Gay Men; Small-town Life; England; British Films
(A Kind of Loving; The Leather Boys; Rita, Sue and Bob, Too; Georgy Girl; A Patch of Blue)
Taste the Blood of Dracula, 1970, 95m, ★★/$, Hammer-WB/WB, R/V-S-B&G. A man tries to bring Dracula back to Victorian era England with the help of some businessmen captivated by the mystique. Christopher Lee, Geoffrey Keen. w. John Elder, d. Peter Sasdy.

HORROR: Vampires; Dracula; Dead-Back from the; Revisionist Films; Victorian Era

Tatie Danielle, 1990, 112m, ★★★/$$, Ind/Live, PG. An old lady moves in with her nephew's family and makes life miserable for everyone. Tsilla Chelton, Catherine Jacob, Isabelle Nanty, Neige Dolsky. w. Florence Quentin, d. Etienne Chatillez.

COMEDY: Black Comedy; Tragi-Comedy; **COMEDY DRAMA:** Family Comedy; Elderly Women; Roommates; Roommates from Hell; Relatives-Troublesome; Mean Women; French Films; Hidden Gems; Female Screenwriters; Female Protagonists

(Daddy Nostalgia; Guarding Tess; Tell Me a Riddle)

Tattoo, 1980, 103m, ★★/$$, 20th/CBS-Fox, R/ES-P-FN-MRN. A depraved romance begins with tattooing between a model and the creep who kidnaps her. Bruce Dern, Maud Adams, Leonard Frey. w. Joyce Bunuel, d. Bob Brooks.

MELODRAMA: SUSPENSE: Erotic Thriller; Erotic Drama; Kidnappings; Turning the Tables; **MURDER:** Rape/Rapists; Violence-Sudden; Fashion World; Models; Fans-Crazed; Obsessions; Curiosities; Flops-Major; Coulda Been Good; Female Screenwriters

(Lipstick; The Collector; Misery; Extremities)

Taxi Driver, 1976, 114m, ★★★★/$$$, Columbia/RCA-Col, R/EP-S-V. A lowlife taxi driver (Robert De Niro, BActor) falls in love with a campaign worker (Cybill Shepherd) for a presidential candidate who then becomes his target for assassination. Jodie Foster (BSActress), Harvey Keitel. w. Mardik Mardik, Paul Schrader, d. Martin Scorsese. BPicture, BOScore. Oscars: 4-0.

DRAMA: SUSPENSE: Political Drama; Political Thrillers; Social Drama; Film Noir-Modern; Romance-Unrequited; Romance-Doomed; Assassination Plots; Mental Illness; Illusions/Hallucinations; Stalkers; Fatal Attractions; New York Life; Psycho Killers; Prostitutes-Child; Working Class; Taxi Drivers

(The King of Comedy)

A Taxing Woman, 1987, 130m, ★★★/$$, Ind/Fox-Lorber, R/S. A mysterious and sexy female tax inspector investigates a man suspected of evasion and begins playing some greedy mindgames. Nobuko Miyamoto, Tsutomu Yamazaki. w. d. Juzo Itami.

COMEDY DRAMA: Black Comedy; Psychological Drama; Greed; Corruption; Mindgames; Japanese Films; Japan; Writer-Directors

SEQUEL: A Taxing Woman's Return. (A Taxing Woman's Return; Tokyo Decadence)

Taxi zum Klo, 1981, 98m, ★★★/$$$, Ind/Cinevista. Story of a gay man in Germany who can't keep a relationship going and resorts to finding men in sordid places after he loses his teaching job to keep some semblance of a life. Bernd Broaderup, Frank Ripploh. d. Frank Ripploh.

DRAMA: Character Studies; Gay Men; Gay Films; Autobiographical Stories; Homophobia; Single Men; Depression; German Films; Hidden Gems

(Fox and His Friends; A Man Like Eva)

Tea and Sympathy, 1956, 122m, ★★★/$$, MGM/MGM-UA. A school teacher recalls a sensitive young boy she once had as a student and the ridicule he endured for being suspected of being gay and weak. Deborah Kerr, John Kerr, Leif Erickson, Edward Andrews, Darryl Hickman. w. P-adap. Robert Anderson, d. Vincente Minnelli.

DRAMA: MELODRAMA: Love-First; Romance-Older Women/Younger Men; Memories; Narrated Films; Women and Boys; Teachers; Teachers & Students; Romance with Teacher; Macho Men; Boarding Schools; Boys' Schools; Conformism; Gay Men; Boys; Homophobia; Homo-eroticism; Gay Awakenings; Sexual Problems; Curiosities; Hidden Gems; Ahead of its Time; Time Capsules

(Summer of '42; The Third Sex; The Devil's Playground)

(Ed: Unpopular today because of its ostensible stance that boys thought to be gay can be cured with the title's elements, but its daringness for the time can't be ignored, nor its ideas)

Tea for Two, 1950, 97m, ★★★/$$$, WB/WB. A wealthy man who's lost almost all of his money promises his musical star daughter he'll give her his last chunk of dough if she can say no to every question posed to her for a day. Doris Day, Gordon McRae, Gene Nelson, Eve Arden. w. Harry Clork, d. David Butler.

MUSICALS: COMEDY: Musical Comedy; Bets; Fathers & Daughters; Risking it All; Theater Life; Putting on a Show; One Day Stories; Forgotten Films

Teachers, 1984, 106m, ★★★/$$$, MGM/MGM-UA, PG-13/S-P. Trials and tribulations at an average inner city high school, centering around one teacher who's tired of the red tape and stagnancy. Nick Nolte, Jobeth Williams, Ralph Macchio, Richard Mulligan, Allen Garfield, Royal Dano, Judd Hirsch. w. W.R. McKinney, d. Arthur Hiller.

COMEDY: COMEDY DRAMA: SATIRE: Social Satire; Black Comedy; Teachers; Teachers & Students; Rebels; High School Life; Inner City Life; Reformers; Coulda Been Great

(Lean on Me; Up the Down Staircase; The Blackboard Jungle; Dangerous Minds)

(Ed: Quite a few funny moments, but not nearly the constructive satirical jab it could have been)

Teacher's Pet, 1958, 120m, ★★★/$$$, Par/Par. A bigtime newspaper editor falls in love with a woman who happens to be a journalism teacher, so he attends her class and begins contradicting what she says based on his real life of experience, heading for a bickering romance. Clark Gable, Doris Day, Gig Young (BSActor), Mamie Van Doren, Nick Adams. w. Fay Kanin, Michael Kanin (BOScr), d. George Seaton. Oscars: 2-0.

COMEDY: ROMANCE: Romantic Comedy; Romance-Bickering; Newspapers; Teachers; Romance with Teachers; Teachers & Students; Journalists; Romance-Older Men/Younger Women; Romance-Reluctant; Infatuations; Wisecracking Sidekicks; Elusive Women; Hidden Gems; Female Screenwriters

(Woman of the Year; Pillow Talk; Tunnel of Love)

The Teahouse of the August Moon, 1956, 123m, ★★★/$$$, MGM/MGM-UA. American soldiers try to fit in with the Japanese in Okinawa during the war, but it's not so easy. Marlon Brando, Glenn Ford, Eddie Albert, Paul Ford, Henry Morgan. w. P-adap. John Patrick, d. Daniel Mann.

COMEDY: COMEDY DRAMA: ROMANCE: Romantic Comedy; Fish out of Water Stories; Romance-Interracial; Asian-Americans; Ensemble Films;

Ensembles-Male; Soldiers; Military Stories; World War II Stories; Japan; Japanese People
(Sayonara; South Pacific)

Tears in the Rain, 1988, 100m, ★★/$$, BBC/BFS. An American woman travels to England to give a letter from her dead mother to a lord who may have enemies hoping to use her. Sharon Stone, Christopher Cazenove, Leigh Lawson. d. Don Sharp.
MELODRAMA: SUSPENSE: Romance-Forbidden; Romance-Dangerous; Death-Impending; Inheritances at Stake; British Films; Americans Abroad; Female Protagonists
(Sleeping Dogs; Basic Instinct)

Teen Wolf, 1985, 91m, ★★1/2/$$$, Atlantic/Atlantic, PG. A teen turns his hairiness problem into an asset on the basketball court. Michael J. Fox, James Hampton, Scott Paulin. w. Joseph Loeb, Matthew Weisman, d. Rod Daniel.
Basketball

Teen Wolf Too, 1987, 94m, ★1/2/$$, Atlantic/Atlantic, PG-13/S-P. This go around, a different star, but a different sport-boxing. Jason Bateman, Kim Darby, John Astin, Paul Sand, James Hampton. w. R. Timothy King, Joseph Loeb, Matthew Weisman, d. Christopher Leitch.
COMEDY: Action Comedy; Werewolves; Horror Comedy; Spoofs-Horror; Teenagers; Teenage Movies; Boxing; Sports Movies; Sleeper Hits
(I Was a Teenage Werewolf; An American Werewolf in London)

Teenage Mutant Ninja Turtles, 1990, 93m, ★★1/2/$$$$$$, New Line/New Line, PG/V. The masked turtles take on a band of Japanese ninja warriors while eating pizza in the sewers. Judith Hoag, Elias Koteas, Josh Pais, Michelan Sisti. w. Todd Langen, Bobby Herbeck, Comic-adap. Kevin Eastman, Peter Laird, d. Steve Barron.

Teenage Mutant Ninja Turtles 2, 1991, 87m, ★★1/2/$$$$, New Line/New Line, PG/V. The quartet returns to do battle with the evil Shredder character. Paige Turco, David Warner, Michaelan Sisti, Leif Tilden, Kenn Troum. w. Todd Langen, d. Michael Pressman.

Teenage Mutant Ninja Turtles 3, 1992, ★★/$$$, New Line/New Line, PG/V. More of the above. w. d. Stuart Gillard.

ACTION: COMEDY: Action Comedy; Martial Arts; **CHILDREN'S:** Animal Stories; Cartoonlike Movies; Comic Heroes; Animals-Mutant; Special Teams; Rodents
(TV Series Version)

Teenage Rebel, 1956, 94m, ★★1/2/$$, 20th/NA. A teenage bad seed visits her rich mother and proceeds to cause all kinds of problems. Ginger Rogers, Michael Rennie, Mildred Natwick, Betty Lou Keim, Louise Beavers. w. Walter Reisch, Charles Brakcett, P-adap. Edith Sommer, d. Edmund Goulding. BB&W Art. Oscars: 1-0.
MELODRAMA: SUSPENSE: Teenagers; Rebels; Children-Brats; Evil Women; Evil Children; Mothers & Daughters; Malicious Menaces
(Mildred Pierce; **[TK]**)

Telefon, 1977, 103m, ★★★/$$, MGM/MGM-UA, R/V-P. A KGB agent is sent abroad to stop Russian radicals trying to sabotage arms talks through long distance terrorism. Charles Bronson, Lee Remick, Tyne Daly, Donald Pleasence, Sheree North, Patrick Magee. w. Peter Hyams, Stirling Silliphant, N-adap Walter Wager, d. Don Siegel.
SUSPENSE: Spy Films; Spies; Terrorism; Cold War Era; KGB Agents; Russians; Telephone Terror
(Murder by Phone; Nighthawks)

Tell Me a Riddle, 1980, 90m, ★★★/$, Filmways/Media, PG/S. An elderly woman moves in with her family and everyone has to deal with the changes. Lila Kedrova, Brooke Adams, Melvyn Douglas, Zalman King. w. Kate Eliason, Alev Lytle, N-adap. Tillie, d. Lee Grant.
COMEDY DRAMA: Family Comedy; Elderly Women; Relatives-Troublesome; Romance-Elderly; Elderly Men; Elderly People; Immigrants; Female Protagonists; Female Directors; Female Screenwriters; Hidden Gems; Overlooked at Release
(The Goodbye People; Tatie Danielle)

Tell Me That You Love Me, Junie Moon, 1970, 113m, ★★1/2/$, Par/Par, R/S-P. A neurotic young woman takes up with a gay, paraplegic, epileptic guy and they move into a house together, trying to make up for their wrecked lives. Liza Minnelli, Ken Howard, Leonard Frey, Robert Moore, James Coco, Kay Thompson, Fred Williamson. w. N-adap. Marjorie Kellogg, d. Otto Preminger.

MELODRAMA: ROMANCE: TRAGEDY: Lonely People; Ensemble Films; Nerds; Wallflowers; Disabled People; Families-Extended; Roommates; Eccentric People; Neurotic People; Forgotten Films; Curiosities; Coulda Been Good; Female Screenwriters; Female Protagonists
(The Sterile Cuckoo; Cabaret; A Taste of Honey)

Tell Them Willie Boy Is Here, 1969, 97m, ★★1/2/$$, U/MCA-U, PG/V. An Indian who later became a cowboy returns to his hometown and encounters bigots who won't accept him, so after faking his death, he seeks revenge. Robert Redford, Robert Blake, Katharine Ross, Susan Clark, Barry Sullivan, Chalres McGraw. w. d. Abraham Polonsky.
WESTERNS: Westerns-Revenge; Revenge; Indians-American; Indians-American, Conflict with; Reunions; Bigots; Deaths-Faked; Dead-Back from the; Coulda Been Good; 1900s; Writer-Directors
(Ulzana's Raid; Thunderheart)

The Temp, 1993, 99m, ★★/$$, Par/Par, R/EV-S-P-B&G. When a yuppie at a food corporation in Portland gets a new temp, she tries to take over his job and poison the cookies they're marketing plus frame him for murder. Timothy Hutton, Faye Dunaway, Lara Flynn Boyle, Dwight Schultz, Oliver Platt. w. Kevin Falls, d. Tom Holland.
SUSPENSE: Kill the Beast; Psycho Killers; Secretaries; Advertising World; **MURDER:** Murders-One by One; Framed?; Malicious Menaces; Unintentionally Funny; Camp
(Body Language; Red Rock West; The Hand That Rocks the Cradle; The Crush)
(Ed: Only entertaining from the camp standpoint. They would have done much better to have Dunaway play the nut-at least it would have had something going for it)

Tempest, 1982, 142m, ★★1/2/$$, Col/RCA-Col, PG/S-P. A man leaves the city and his failing marriage for a Greek isle with his daughter to live with an assortment of characters, all parallelling Shakespeare's The Tempest. John Cassavetes, Gena Rowlands, Susan Sarandon, Molly Ringwald, Vittorio Gassman, Raul Julia, Jerry Hardin. w. Paul Mazursky, Leon Capetano, P-adap. William Shakespeare, d. Mazursky.
DRAMA: ROMANCE: Romantic Drama; Character Studies; Marriage on the

Rocks; Cheating Women; Starting Over; Nature-Back to; Islands; Greece; Allegorical Stories; Revisionist Films; Coulda Been Great; Forgotten Films

Ten, 1979, 122m, ★★★/$$$$$, Orion-WB/WB, R/S-P-FFN-MRN. A music composer in the Hollywood Hills who likes to spy on his sexy neighbors becomes infatuated with a young beauty on her honeymoon and suddenly is consumed by fantasies he hopes to turn into reality. Dudley Moore, Julie Andrews, Bo Derek, Dee Wallace, Robert Webber, Sam J. Jones. w. d. Blake Edwards. BOSong, BOScore. Oscars: 2-0.

COMEDY: ROMANCE: Romantic Comedy; Erotic Comedy; Screwball Comedy; Romance-Reluctant; Engagements-Breaking; Obsessions; Infatuations; Elusive Women; Midlife Crisis; Sexy Women; Nerds; Nerds & Babes Sexuality; Sleeper Hits; Blockbusters

(Claire's Knee; The Woman in Red)

The Tenant, 1976, 126m, ★★★/$, Par/Par, R/P-S-V. A young man in the midst of a breakdown moves into an apartment building and soon becomes convinced everyone there is out to get him. Roman Polanski, Melvyn Douglas, Isabelle Adjani, Shelley Winters, Jo Van Fleet, Lila Kedrova. w. Roman Polanski, Gerard Brach, N-adap. Roland Topor, d. Polanski.

SUSPENSE: Psychological Drama; Psychological Thriller; Character Studies; Roommates from Hell; Nervous Breakdowns; Paranoia; Apartment Buildings; Insane-Plot to Drive; Mental Illness; Illusions/Hallucinations; Hidden Gems; Overlooked at Release; Cult Films

(Apartment Zero; Single White Female; Repulsion)

The Ten Commandments, 1956, 219m, ★★★½/$$$$$$, Par/Par. The Biblical story of the parting of the Red Sea as Moses leads the Israelites to their promised land, et al. Charlton Heston, Yul Brynner, Edward G. Robinson, Anne Baxter, Nina Foch, Yvonne DeCarlo, Judith Anderson, John Derek, H.B. Warner, John Carradine, Vincent Price, Debra Paget. w. Aeneas Mackenzie, Jesse Lasky, Jack Gariss, Frederick Frank, d. Cecil B. DeMille. BPicture, BCCin, BCArt, BSound, BEdit, BCCostume, **BSFX**. Oscars: 7-1.

ADVENTURE: MELODRAMA: Epics; Cast of Thousands; All-Star Casts; Biblical Stories; Middle East; God;

Saving Someone; Leaders-Great; Journies; Spectacles; Blockbusters; Production Design-Outstanding

SPOOF: Wholly Moses.

(The Robe; King of Kings; Ben Hur)

Ten Days Wonder, 1972, 101m, ★★/$, Ind/Connoisseur. A wealthy, decadent family self-destructs as a son sleeps with his stepmother and murder is the result. Orson Welles, Anthony Perkins, Marlene Joubert. w. d. Claude Chabrol, N-adap. Ellery Queen.

SUSPENSE: MYSTERY MURDER: MURDER: MYSTERY: Romance-Forbidden; Incest; Curiosities; French Films; Independent Films

(Spanking the Monkey; Angela)

Tender Is the Night, 1961, 146m, ★★★/$$, 20th/CBS-Fox. When a psychiatrist marries his melancholy patient, problems arise on a tour of Europe. Jennifer Jones, Jason Robards, Joan Fontaine, Tom Ewell, Jill St. John, Paul Lukas. w. Ivan Moffat, N-adap. F. Scott Fitzgerald, d. Henry King. BOSong. Oscars: 1-0.

DRAMA: MELODRAMA: ROMANCE: Romance with Psychologist; Romance-Unprofessional; Vacations; Mental Illness; Nervous Breakdowns; Psychiatrists; Vacations-European; Classic Literary Adaptations

REMAKE: TV Miniseries, 1986.

(The Great Gatsby; Beloved Infidel)

Tender Mercies, 1983, 90m, ★★★★/$$, EMI-U/MCA-U, PG/S-V-P. A country singer (Robert DuVall, **BActor**) on the skids winds up drunk at a motel run by a widow (Tess Harper) and her young son, who both soon help him get back on his feet and deal with the death of his daughter and his lack of ambition. Ellen Barkin, Betty Buckley, Wilford Brimley, Lenny Von Dolen. w. Horton Foote (**BOScr**), d. Bruce Beresford (**BDirector**). BPicture, BOSong. Oscars: 5-2.

DRAMA: ROMANCE: Romantic Drama; Starting Over; Comebacks; Alcoholics; Country Singers; Singers; Death-Dealing With; Children-Parting with; Stepfathers; Redemption; Rural Life; Texas; Religion; Quiet Little Films; Overlooked at Release; Hidden Gems; Foreign Directors of Southerns

(Baby; the Rain Must Fall; The Prince of Tides; 1918; Convicts; St. Valentine's Day)

(Ed: A masterpiece of the genre, which though uniquely American, seems European rather than Hollywooden)

The Tender Trap, 1955, 111m, ★★★/$$$, MGM/MGM-UA. A playboy showbiz agent goes through one too many women when he runs up against a seemingly innocent young actress with a few tricks up her sleeve. Frank Sinatra, Debbie Reynolds, David Wayne, Celeste Holm, Lola Albright, Carolyn Jones. w. Julius J. Epstein, P-adap. Max Schulman, Robert Paul Smith, d. Charles Walters. BOSong. Oscars: 1-0.

COMEDY: ROMANCE: Romantic Comedy; Playboys; Turning the Tables; Cheating Men; Dose of Own Medicine-Given; Theater Life; Hollywood Life; Actresses; Coulda Been Great; Faded Hits

(Pal Joey; Dirty Rotten Scoundrels; Bedtime Story)

Ten Little Indians, 1966, 91m, ★★★/$$, UA/New Line. A diverse group of ten people invited to an Austrian chalet begin to disappear one by one every time the lights get cut. Hugh O'Brian, Shirley Eaton, Wilfrid Hyde-White, Dennis Price, Stanley Holloway, Fabian, Leo Genn. w. Peter Yeldham, Harry Towers, N-adap. Agatha Christie, d. George Pollock.

SUSPENSE: MYSTERY: MURDER: MURDER MYSTERY: Mystery-Whodunit; Murders-One by One; Murder-Invitation to; Alps; Ensemble Films; Austria; Agatha Christie

REMAKE OF: And Then There Were None, 1945.

(And Then There Were None; Murder by Death)

Tentacles, 1976, 102m, ★★/$, Ind/Live, R/V-B&G. Something in the sea sucks the flesh off of its swimming victims and they wash ashore as bones-what could it be? A bad movie, perhaps? No, an angry octopus! Shelley Winters, John Huston, Bo Hopkins, Henry Fonda, Claude Akins. w. Jerome Max, Tito Carpi, Steve Carabatsos, Soni Molteni, d. Sonia Assonitis.

HORROR: Rogue Plots; Kill the Beast; Beach Movies; Octopi-Angry; Monsters-Animal; Flops-Major; Unintentionally Funny; Female Directors

Ten Thousand Bedrooms, 1956, 114m, ★★½/$$, MGM/NA, Turner. A rich American buys a hotel in Rome and

finds the women seem to come with it. Dean Martin, Eva Bartok, Anna Maria Alberghetti, Paul Henried. w. Laslo Vadnay, Art Cohn, William Ludwig, Leonard Spigelgass, d. Richard Thorpe.
COMEDY: ROMANCE: Romantic Comedy; **FARCE:** Rome; Hotels; Rich People; Playboys; Coulda Been Good
(Come September; Toys in the Attic; Hotel Paradiso)

The Tenth Man, 1988, 99m, ★★★/$, MGM/MGM-UA. Nazi P.O.W.s exchange identities and in the deal, one's family will be supported by the other's money on the outside. But once free and the deal commenced, an impostor appears, throwing a wrench into the works. Anthony Hopkins, Derek Jacobi, Kristin Scott Thomas, Cyril Cusack. d. Jack Gold, N-adap. Graham Greene.
SUSPENSE: World War II Stories; P.O.W.s; Nazi Stories; Identities-Assumed; Impostors; Clever Plots & Endings; TV Movies; Hidden Gems
(The Third Man; The Innocent; A Kiss Before Dying)

Tequila Sunrise, 1988, 115m, ★★1/2/$$$, WB/WB, R/S-P-V-FRN-MRN. A drug dealer on the reform, but not really, wants a woman his old friend the narcotics cop wants, too, and everyone winds up in a big drug chase mess where it's not clear who's really up to what. Mel Gibson, Michelle Pfeiffer, Kurt Russell, Raul Julia, Arliss Howard, Arye Gross. w. d. Robert Towne. BCin. Oscars: 1-0.
SUSPENSE: ACTION: Action Drama; Crime Drama; Romantic Drama; Friendships-Male; Drugs-Dealing; **ROMANCE:** Romance-Triangles; Ethics; Betrayals; Double Crossings; Police-Former; Coulda Been Great; Faded Hits; Writer-Directors
(Out of the Past; Against All Odds)
(Ed: Though it looks and sounds great, there's really nothing there; and the audience doesn't know one way or another, since they've been numbed by all the plot twists)

Teresa, 1951, 101m, ★★★/$$, MGM/NA. A soldier comes back from war in Europe with an Italian wife and his mother doesn't really approve at first. John Ericson, Patricia Collinge, Peggy Ann Garner. w. Stewart Stern, Arthur Hayes (BOStory), d. Fred Zinneman. Oscars: 1-0.

MELODRAMA: ROMANCE: COMEDY DRAMA: Romantic Drama; Marriage Drama; Family Drama; Mothers & Sons; Lover Family Dislikes; Italians; Soldiers; World War II-Post Era; War Brides
(Frieda)

Terminal Bliss, 1991, 94m, ★/$, Cannon/Cannon, R/S. Rich kids and drugs mix, but when a girl comes between two friends, everything may not seem worth it. Luke Perry, Timothy Owen, Estee Chandler. w. d. Jordan Allen.
MELODRAMA: Men Fighting Over Women; High School Life; Rich Kids; Drugs-Dealing; Drugs-Addictions; Writer-Directors

The Terminal Man, 1974, 104m, ★★1/2/$, WB/WB, R/P-S-V. A man with a microchip in his brain becomes an uncontrollable maniac. George Segal, Joan Hackett, Richard Dysart, Jill Clayburgh, Donald Moffat. w. d. Mike Hodges.
SCI-FI: HORROR: MURDER: Psycho Killers; Murders-One by One; Rogue Plots; Human Monsters; Kill the Beast; Experiments; Scientists; Computers; Man vs. Machine; Ahead of its Time; Curiosities; Forgotten Films; Flops-Major; Writer-Directors
(Johnny Mnemonic; Westworld)

Terminal Velocity, 1994, 102m, ★★/$$, 20th/Fox, PG-13/P-V-S. Seduced by a sexy sky diver, a young would-be secret agent plunges into a plot of Russian spies, gold bullion, and cars falling from the sky. Charlie Sheen, Nastassja Kinski, James Gandolfini, Christopher McDonald. w. David Twohy, d. Deran Sarafian.
ACTION: Skydiving; Dangerous Women; Bank Robberies; Spies; Secret Agents; Russians as Enemy
(Point Break; Passenger 57; Die Hard 2)

The Terminator, 1984, 108m, ★★★1/2/$$$$, Orion/Orion, R/EV-P-S-MRN. A man (Michael Biehn) comes to earth from the future to stop a killing machine (Arnold Schwarzenegger) from killing the mother (Linda Hamilton) of a future great leader who could change history. w. James Cameron, Gale Anne Hurd, d. James Cameron.
ACTION: SUSPENSE: SCI-FI: MURDER: Chase Movies; Murders-One by One; Hitmen; Stalkers; Race Against Time; Futuristic Films; Women in Jeopardy;

Androids; Time Travel; Bounty Hunters; Sleeper Hits; Writer-Directors
SEQUEL: Terminator 2.
(Commando; Cyborg; Time Cop)
(Ed: After a lawsuit, the origin of the story is in doubt, since it bears a striking resemblance to a Harlan Ellison story)

Terminator 2: Judgment Day, 1991, 135m, ★★★/$$$$$, Carolco-Tri-Star/Live, PG-13/EV-P. The android returns to save the young future warrior and his mother (who he was charged to kill in the original) from a morphing evil force taking the shape of a police officer-all to avert nuclear disaster. Arnold Schwarzenegger, Linda Hamilton, Edward Furlong, Robert Patrick, Joe Morton. w. James Cameron, William Wisher, d. James Cameron. BCin, BMakeup, **BVisualFX, BSound, BSoundFX.** Oscars: 6-3.
ACTION: SUSPENSE: SCI-FI: Chase Movies; Survival Drama; Message Films; Bombs-Atomic; Apocalyptic Stories; Race Against Time; Androids; Time Travel; Bounty Hunters; Futuristic Films; Enemies Unite; Men and Boys; Saving Someone; Hitwomen; Blockbusters; Writer-Directors
(The Abyss; The Last Action Hero)

Term of Trial, 1962, 130m, ★★★/$, NA. A stern schoolmaster in rural England is accused of sexual misconduct with a sexy strumpet teen who may cause him to wreck his life, if the scandal doesn't before he self-destructs. Laurence Olivier, Simone Signoret, Sarah Miles, Hugh Griffith, Terence Stamp, Roland Culver. w. d. Peter Glenville, N-adap. James Barlow, *The Burden of Proof.*
DRAMA: Social Drama; Kitchen Sink Drama; Rape/Rapists; Teachers; Teachers & Students; Romance with Teachers; Sexual Harassment; Accused Unjustly; Scandals; England; Forgotten Films; Overlooked at Release; Ahead of its Time; Hidden Gems; British Films
(The Browning Version; The Prime of Miss Jean Brodie; The Boys of St. Vincents)

Terms of Endearment, 1983, 132m, ★★★★/$$$$$$, Par/Par, PG/S. An anti-social mother (Shirley MacLaine, **BActress**) and her rebellious daughter (Debra Winger, BActress) learn to get along over the years before time splits them apart. Jeff Daniels, Jack Nicholson (**BSActor**), John Lithgow (BSActor),

Danny DeVito, Lisa Hart Carroll. w. d. James L. Brooks (**BAScr, BDirector**), adap. Larry McMurtry. **BPicture**, BArt, BOScore. Oscars: 9-5.

COMEDY DRAMA: MELODRAMA: Mothers & Daughters; Family Drama; Episodic Stories; Tearjerkers; Disease Stories; Romance-Middle-Aged; Romance-Reluctant; Parallel Stories; Marriage Drama; Death-Impending; Dying Young; Ordinary People; Cheating Men; Southerns; Spinsters; Widows; Mothers & Sons; Playboys; Astronauts; Texas; Midwestern Life; Blockbusters; Sleeper Hits
(Strangers: A Story of a Mother and a Daughter; Harry & Son; Steel Magnolias) (Ed: Though some feminists have criticized it, apparently for no more reason than the fact neither of the women have a career, it made *Premiere* magazine's poll of the ten best of the 80s; only fuddy-duddies or those who would rather not be bothered with ordinary women would be bored)

Terror By Night, 1946, 60m, ★★★/$$$, U/NA. Sherlock Holmes solves some murders on a train while also solving a jewel heist. Basil Rathbone, Nigel Bruce. w. Frank Gurber, d. Roy William Neill.

MYSTERY: MURDER: MURDER MYSTERY: Detective Stories; Detectives-Private; Sherlock Holmes; Trains; Jewel Thieves; British Films

Terror on a Train, 1952, 72m, ★★-/$$, MGM/NA. A cargo train traveling across England has a bomb onboard, and the conductor must decide what to do. Glenn Ford, Anne Vernon, Maurice Denham, Harcourt Williams, Harold Warrender, Bill Fraser, John Horsley, Victor Maddern. w. N-adap. Ken Bennett (*Death at Attention*), d. Ted Tetzlaff.

SUSPENSE: Bombs; Trains; Race Against Time; Terrorists; Ahead of its Time
(Airport; The Cassandra Crossing; Juggernaut)

Terror Train, 1980, 97m, ★★/$$, 20th/CBS-Fox, R/EV-B&G. A party on a train is thwarted in their revelry by a psycho killer lurking in the berths. Ben Johnson, Jamie Lee Curtis, David Copperfield, Hart Bochner. w. T. Y. Drake, d. Roger Spottiswoode.

HORROR: MURDER: Murders-One by One; Psycho Killers; Party Movies; Trains; Forgotten Films
(Halloween; Prom Night)

The Terry Fox Story, 1983, 97m, ★★½/$$$, HBO/HBO, PG. A young runner dying of cancer, having had one leg already amputated, runs across Canada in one last attempt to save himself or go out in a blaze of glory. Eric Fryar, Robert Duvall, Christopher Makepeace, Rosalind Chao. w. Edward Hume, d. Ralph Thomas.

MELODRAMA: True Stories; Docudrama; Tearjerkers; Road Movies; Coaches; Friendships-Male; Young Men; Dying Young; Running; Sports Movies; Saving Oneself; Death-Impending; Canada; TV Movies
(American Flyers; Bang the Drum Slowly)

Tess, 1980, 180m, ★★★½/$$$, Col/RCA-Col, PG/S. A poor girl from the English countryside in Victorian times tries to prove she was born into wealth and then given away, but soon becomes pregnant by a young man who may be her relative. Natassja Kinski, Leigh Lawson, Peter Firth, John Collin. w. Roman Polanski, Gerard Brach, John Brownjohn, N-adap. Thomas Hardy (*Tess of the D'Urbervilles*), d. Roman Polanski (BDirector). BPicture, **BCin, BCostume**, BOScore, **BArt**. Oscars: 6-3.

DRAMA: MELODRAMA: Costume Drama; **ROMANCE:** Romantic Drama; Children-Long Lost; Children-Adopted; Mothers-Unwed; Scandals; Small-town Scandals; International Casts; England; Victorian Era; Lyrical Films; Female Protagonists; Classic Literary Adaptations; Faded Hits; Hidden Gems
(Jude the Obscure; Princess Caraboo; Sense and Sensibility)

Test Pilot, 1938, 118m, ★★★/$$$$, MGM/MGM-UA. A pilot with erratic tendencies in the air gets himself into a jam but has the help of his wife and best friend. Clark Gable, Spencer Tracy, Myrna Loy, Lionel Barrymore, Marjorie Main. w. Waldemar Young, Vincent Lawrence, Frank Wead (BOStory), d. Victor Fleming. BPicture, BEdit. Oscars: 3-0.

MELODRAMA: COMEDY DRAMA: ROMANCE: Romance-Triangles; Friendships-Male; Friendships-Great; Crisis Situations; Pilots-Airline; Saving Someone; Faded Hits; Hidden Gems
(Boom Town; Honky Tonk; San Francisco)

Testament, 1983, 90m, ★★★/$$, AP-Par/Par, PG/V. A San Francisco suburban family watches from their living

room in horror as a nuclear attack hits. Jane Alexander (BActress), William Devane, Ross Harris, Roxana Zal, Lukas Haas, Lilia Skala. w. John Sacret Young, Carol Amen, d. Lynne Littman. Oscars: 1-0.

DRAMA: MELODRAMA: Message Films; Anti-War Stories; Apocalyptic Stories; Bombs-Atomic; Suburban Life; Ordinary People Stories; Female Screenwriters; Female Directors; Female Protagonists
(The Day After [TV Movie]; Miracle Mile)

Testament of Orpheus (Orphee), 1959, 83m, ★★★/$, Ind/Connoiseur. A poet dies in the 1700s and wakes up in the 50s trying to figure out who he really is with the help of a mysterious woman. Jean Cocteau, Edouard Demithe, Maria Cesares. w. d. Jean Cocteau.

DRAMA: Art Films; Avant-Garde Films; Surrealism; Time Travel; Illusions/Hallucinations; Poets; Beatnik Era; Amnesia; Beautiful People; Homo-eroticism; Paris; Lyrical Films; Hidden Gems; Cult Films; Writer-Directors
(Beauty and the Beast [1946]; La Dolce Vita)

Tex, 1982, 103m, ★★★/$, Disney/Disney, PG/P. Two orphan brothers living together in Oklahoma come of age. Matt Dillon, Jim Metzler, Meg Tilly, Bill McKinney, Ben Johnson, Emilio Estevez. w. d. Tim Hunter, N-adap. S. E. Hinton.

DRAMA: Coming of Age; Character Studies; Boys; Young Men; Brothers; Orphans; Rural Life; Southwestern Life; Hidden Gems; Overlooked at Release
(That Was Then, This Is Now; Rumblefish)

Texas, 1941, 94m, ★★½/$$, Col/Col. Two southern Civil War vets set up cattle ranches in Texas and encounter some big problems. William Holden, Glenn Ford, Claire Trevor, George Bancroft, Edgar Buchanan. w. Horace McCoy, Lewis Meltzer, Michael Blankfort, d. George Marshall.

WESTERNS: Cattle Ranchers; Friendships-Male; Men in Conflict; Reconstruction Era; Civil War Era; Texas; Forgotten Films
(Alvarez Kelly; Duel in the Sun)

Texas Across the River, 1966, 101m, ★★½/$$, U/MCA-U. Three men, a Texan, a Spaniard, and an Indian, travel together, each on the lam for various reasons. Dean Martin, Alain Delon, Joey Bishop, Peter Graves, Rosemary Forsyth,

Tina Marquand, Andrew Prine, Michael Ansara. w. Wells Root, Harold Greene, Ben Starr, d. Michael Gordon.

WESTERNS: Western Comedy; Fugitives from the Law; Texas; Crossing the Border; Forgotten Films

(Five Card Stud; Bandolero)

The Texas Chainsaw Massacre, 1974, 81m, ★★½/$$$, Vortex/MPI, R/EV-B&G. Several people venture into a dark, rural cemetery and wind up being chased by a psycho killer with a chainsaw. Marilyn Burns, Allen Danziger, William Vail. w. Kim Henkel, Tobe Hooper, d. Tobe Hooper.

HORROR: Psycho Killers; **MURDER:** Murders-One by One; Texas; Rural Horrors; Cannibalism; Chase Stories; Cult Films

The Texas Chainsaw Massacre, Part 2, 1986, 95m, ★★/$, Cannon-MGM-UA/MGM-UA, R/EV-B&G. More of the same in a more slick fashion, this time with the killers hiding out in an amusement park. Dennis Hopper, Caroline Williams, Bill Johnson. w. L. M. Kit Carson, d. Tobe Hooper.

HORROR: Psycho Killers; **MURDER:** Murders-One by One; Texas; Rural Horrors; Chase Stories

Texasville, 1990, 125m, ★★½/$$, Columbia/RCA-Col, PG-13/S-P. The cast of the original reunites and much has changed in the oil rich plains of west Texas, but relationships between them haven't. Jeff Bridges, Cybill Shepherd, Timothy Bottoms, Annie Potts, William McNamara. w. d. Peter Bogdanovich. N-adap. Larry McMurtry.

COMEDY DRAMA: DRAMA: Slice of Life Stories; Reunions; Romance-Reunited; Southerns; Small-town Life; Oil People; Rich People; Ordinary People Stories; 1980s; Coulda Been Good

SEQUEL TO: The Last Picture Show. (Ed: Almost a cartoon compared to the first, though it does have its moments. Shepherd's character and ability has most noticeably grown, though Potts steals the scenes)

Thank God It's Friday, 1978, 89m, ★★/$$, Col/RCA-Col, PG/P-S. A DJ's life in a Hollywood disco as an excuse for a soundtrack-and it worked. Valerie Landsburg, Terri Nunn, Chick Vennera, Donna Summer, The Commodores. w. Barry Bernstein, d. Robert Klane.

BOSong, "Last Dance." Oscars: 1-1.

MUSICALS: Music Movies; Musicals-Disco; Disco Era; 1970s; Nightclubs; Radio Life; Singers; Ensemble Films; Curiosities; Time Capsules

(American Hot Wax; FM)

Thank Your Lucky Stars, 1943, 127m, ★★★/$$$, WB/MGM-UA. Military all-star musical with title song. Eddie Cantor, Dinah Shore, Bette Davis, Ann Sheridan, Humphrey Bogart, Errol Flynn, Ida Lupino, John Garfield, Edward Everett Horton, Olivis deHavilland. w. Norman Panama, d. David Butler.

MUSICALS: Military Comedy; World War II Era; All-Star Casts; All-Star Cameos

That Certain Age, 1938, 100m, ★★★/$$$, U/MCA-U. A young girl singer falls for an older, unattainable man. Deanna Durbin, Melvyn Douglas, Jackie Cooper, Irene Rich. w. Bruce Manning, d. Edward Ludwig.

MUSICALS: COMEDY: ROMANCE: Musical Romance; Musical Comedy; Romantic Comedy; Infatuations; Romance-Older Men/Younger Women; Girls; Men and Girls; Faded Hits; Hidden Gems

(The Bachelor and the Bobby-Soxer; Mad About Music)

That Certain Feeling, 1956, 102m, ★★★/$$, Par/Par. A comic book artist gets a ghost writer to help jazz up his work, but it causes romantic complications since the writer is his secretary's ex. Bob Hope, George Sanders, Eva Marie Saint, Pearl Bailey, Al Capp. w. Norman Panama, Melvin Frank, IAL Diamond, William Altman, P-adap. *King of Hearts*, Jean Kerr, Eleanor Brooke, d. Panama, Frank.

COMEDY: ROMANCE: Romantic Comedy; Writers; Romance-Reunited; Romance-Triangles; Impostors; Forgotten Films

(The Front; How to Murder Your Wife)

That Certain Woman, 1937, 91m, ★★★/$$$, WB/WB. A mob girl tries to reform herself but is tempted to go back in for a job one last time. Bette Davis, Henry Fonda, Ian Hunter, Anita Louise, Donald Crisp. w. d. Edmund Goulding.

MELODRAMA: Crime Drama; Mob Stories; Mob Girls; One Last Time; Widows; Starting Over; Female Protagonists; Criminals-Female; Forgotten Films; Writer-Directors

(Bureau of Missing Persons; Bad Girl)

That Championship Season, 1982, 108m, ★★★/$, Cannon/MGM-UA, PG/P-S. A basketball team from twenty-five years before gets back together to try and

relive their past glory but find the years in between haven't been so kind. Bruce Dern, Stacy Keach, Robert Mitchum, Martin Sheen, Paul Sorvino, Athur Franz. w. P-adap. d. Jason Miller.

DRAMA: Ensemble Films; Ensembles-Male; Basketball; Reunions; Memories; Men's Films; Coulda Been Great; Pulitzer Prize Adaptations; Hidden Gems; Writer-Directors; Stagelike Films

(The Mens' Club; The Bachelor Party [1957]; Thursday's Game; Watch It)

(Ed: What was a big hit on stage is an okay film but loses much of its original impact)

That Cold Day in the Park, 1969, 115m, ★★½/$, Ind/Republic, PG. A lonely woman rescues a young man out of the cold and takes him in, presumably as a seduction, but soons makes him an unwilling prisoner. Sandy Dennis, Michael Burns, Suzanne Benton, Luana Anders. w. Gillian Freeman, N-adap. Richard Miles, d. Robert Altman.

DRAMA: Psychological Drama; Trapped; Hostage Situations; Kidnappings; Older Women Seducers; Romance-Unrequited; Fatal Attractions; Independent Films

(The Collector; Misery; The Beguiled)

That Darn Cat!, 1965, 116m, ★★★/$$$$, Disney/Disney, G. When some bank robbers have a kidnapped woman in their hide-out, a bothersome cat belonging to an All-American British teen (Hayley Mills) inadvertently leads this amateur sleuth to the bad guys. Dean Jones, Grayson Hall, Roddy McDowell, Nevill Brand, Elsa Lanchester, William Demarest, Frank Gorshin, Ed Wynn. w. The Gordons, Bill Walsh, N-adap. *Undercover Cat*, The Gordons, d. Robert Stevenson.

COMEDY: COMEDY DRAMA: CHILDREN'S: FAMILY: MYSTERY: Heist Stories; Animal Stories; Bank Robberies; Detective Stories; Detectives-Female; Detectives-Amateur; Capers; Cats; Comic Mystery; Kidnappings; Faded Hits; Teenagers; Female Protagonists; Nuisances

(Tiger Bay; The Moonspinners; The Shaggy Dog)

That Forsyte Woman, 1949, 114m, ★★★/$$, MGM/MGM-UA. A wealthy woman falls in love with her niece's handsome fiance, leading others to proclaim this title. Greer Garson, Errol Flynn, Robert Young, Janet Leigh, Walter

Pidgeon, Aubrey Mather. w. Jan Lustig, Ivan Tors, James Williams, N-adap. James Galsworthy (*A Man of Property*), d. Compton Bennett.

MELODRAMA: ROMANCE: Love-Forbidden; Romantic Drama; Family Drama; Romance-Clandestine; Scandals; Rich People; Costume Drama; Inheritances at Stake; Marriage on the Rocks; Cheating Women; Marriage-Impending; Romance-Older Women/Younger Men
(*Forever Amber; Frenchman's Creek*)

That Hamilton Woman, 1941, 128m, ★★★/$$$, UA/HBO. Lord Nelson has an affair with a lady named Hamilton and sparks a veddy British scandal. Laurence Olivier, Vivien Leigh, Gladys Cooper, Sara Allgood. w. Walter Reisch, R.C. Sherriff, d. Alexander Korda. BCCin, BCArt. Oscars: 2-0.

MELODRAMA: ROMANCE: Romantic Drama; Romance-Clandestine; True Stories; Scandals; Royalty; British Films
(*Love Among the Ruins; The Divorce of Lady X*)

That Kind of Woman, 1959, 92m, ★★1/2/$$, Par/NA, AMC. A sexy Italian woman on a train in World War II sparks the interest of a hunky young American soldier, but not much else. Sophia Loren, Tab Hunter, George Sanders, Jack Warden, Keenan Wynn. w. Walter Bernstein, d. Sidney Lumet.

DRAMA: ROMANCE: Romantic Drama; Romance-Clandestine; Sexy Women; Soldiers; World War II Era; Italians; Elusive Women; Forgotten Films

REMAKE OF: Shopworn Angel.
(*The Black Orchid; Houseboat*)

That Lady in Ermine, 1948, 89m, ★★1/2/$$$, 20th/NA. A musical about European women and their fights against coups and what-not, set to music. Betty Grable, Douglas Fairbanks, Jr., Cesar Romero, Walter Abel. w. Samson Raphaelson, d. Ernst Lubitsch. BOsong. Oscars: 1-0.

MUSICALS: COMEDY: Musical Comedy; Historical Drama; Political Unrest; Female Protagonists

That Man from Rio, 1964, 120m, ★★★1/2/$$$, Lopert-UA/MGM-UA. A French pilot tries to save his girlfriend by helping her on a worldwide goose chase, mostly in Brazil, to find some stolen antiquities. Jean Paul Belmondo, Jean Servais, Francoise Dorleac. w. J.P.

Rappeneau, Ariane Mnouchkine, Daniel Boulanger, Phillipe de Broca (BOScr), d. Phillipe de Broca. Oscars: 1-0.

COMEDY: ACTION: ADVENTURE: Action Comedy; Comic Adventure; Heist Stories; Chase Stories; Thieves; World Travel; Brazil; South America; French Films; Sleeper Hits; Hidden Gems
(*Romancing the Stone; In Like Flint*)
(Ed: Much more contemporary, American, and imitated than you'd think)

That Night in Rio, 1941, 90m, ★★★/$$$, 20th/NA. A count is "indisposed," and a double takes his place. Only his wife can tell it's not him-down in Rio, where women wear fruit on their heads. Don Ameche, Alice Faye, Carmen Miranda, S. Z. Sakall, J. Carrol Naish, Curt Bois. w. George Seaton, Bess Meredyth, Hal Long, P-adap. Rudolph Lothar, Hans Adler, d. Irving Cummings.

MUSICALS: COMEDY: Musical Comedy; Impostors; Lookalikes; South America; Royalty; Faded Hits; Hidden Gems; Female Screenwriters
(*Dave; General Della Rovere; Moon Over Parador*)

That Obscure Object of Desire, 1977, 103m, ★★★1/2/$$, Col/Col, R/S. A man is constantly thwarted by his lover, a woman who even seems to mysteriously change form (she's played by two different actresses). Fernando Rey, Carole Bouquet, Angela Molina, Julien Bertheau. w. Luis Bunuel, Jean-Claude Carriere (BAScr), N-adap. Pierre Louys (*La Femme et le Pantin*), d. Luis Bunuel. BFLFilm. Oscars: 2-0.

COMEDY DRAMA: ROMANCE: Romantic Comedy; Romantic Drama; Body Switching; Elusive Women; Multiple Performances; Misunderstandings; Servants; Art Films; French Films; Hidden Gems
(*Fahrenheit 451; Too Beautiful for You*)

That Touch of Mink, 1962, 99m, ★★★/$$$$, U-I/MCA-U. A "gentleman bachelor" of means (and "experience") pursues a younger woman, who seems to have neither-after his limousine splashes her with mud and she protests her way into a Caribbean cruise. Cary Grant, Doris Day, Gig Young, Audrey Meadows, Dick Sargent, John Astin. w. Stanley Shapiro, Nate Monaster (BOScr), d. Delbert Mann. Oscars: 1-0.

COMEDY: ROMANCE: Romantic Comedy; Rich People; Accidents; Romance-

Reluctant; Romance-Older Men/Younger Women; Secretaries; Sex Comedy
(*Easy Living; All in a Night's Work; Caprice*)

That Uncertain Feeling, 1941, 84m, ★★★1/2/$$, UA/Nos. A woman's husband must nobly endure her chronic hiccups and insomnia, but begins to lose it when she invites her eccentric concert pianist friend to live in their house. Merle Oberon, Melvyn Douglas, Burgess Meredith, Alan Mowbray, Olive Blakeney, Harry Davenport, Eve Arden, Sig Rumann. w. Donald Ogden Stewart, Walter Reisch, P-adap. Victorien Sardou, Emile de Najac (*Divorcons*), d. Ernst Lubitsch. BOScore. Oscars: 1-0.

COMEDY: COMEDY DRAMA: ROMANCE: Screwball Comedy; Romantic Comedy; Romance-Triangles; Eccentric People; Musicians; Pianists; Hypochondriacs; Hidden Gems; Forgotten Films
(*Adam's Rib; My Man Godfrey*)
(Ed: Full of brilliant little touches)

That Was Then . . . This Is Now, 1985, 102m, ★★/$$, Par/Par, PG-13/S. A group of kids growing up in present-day Tulsa go through the motions-centering around a male friendship and rebellious tendencies. Emilio Estevez, Craig Sheffer, Kim Delaney, Jill Schoelen, Morgan Freeman, Barbara Babcock. w. Emilio Estevez, N-adap. S. E. Hinton, d. Christopher Cain.

MELODRAMA: Coming of Age; Teenagers; Teenage Movies; Rebels; Juvenile Delinquents; Southwestern Life; Friendships-Male; Wild People
(*Tex; Rumble Fish; Stand by Me*)
(Ed: The least successful of the S.E. Hinton adaptations)

That's Adequate, 1990, 82m, ★★-/VR, Hemdale/Hemdale, R/P. Spoof on a movie studio and the disdain for quality of most of its product. Tony Randall, Robert Downey, Jr., Bruce Willis, Robert Townsend, Stuart Pankin, Peter Reigert, James Coco, Susan Dey, Renee Taylor. w. d. Harry Hurwitz.

COMEDY: Spoofs; Hollywood Satire; **SATIRE:** Moviemaking; Actors; Directors; Overlooked at Release; Writer-Directors
(*Movers and Shakers; The Big Picture; S.O.B.*)

That's Dancin'!, 1985, 105m, ★★★/$$, MGM-UA/MGM-UA, G. Excerpts from Astaire and Rogers, Gene Kelly, Eleanor

Powell, and Busby Berkeley films. Narrators: Gene Kelly, Sammy Davis, Jr., Mikhail Baryshnikov, Liza Minnelli, Ray Bolger.

MUSICALS: Dance Movies; Dancers; Compilation Films; Nostalgia; Filmumentaries; Astaire & Rogers (That's Entertainment SERIES; Tap)

That's Entertainment, 1974, 137m, ★★★¹/2/$$$, MGM/MGM-UA, G. A snapshot of some of the highlights of the MGM musical in its heydey. Narrators: Fred Astaire, Gene Kelly, Elizabeth Taylor, James Stewart, Bing Crosby, Liza Minnelli, Donald O'Connor, Debbie Reynolds, Mickey Rooney, Frank Sinatra. w. d. Jack Haley, Jr.

That's Entertainment Part 2, 1976, 133m, ★★★/$$, MGM/MGM-UA, G. Adding comedy and drama to the mix, this still primarily focuses on the MGM musicals. Introduced by Fred Astaire and Gene Kelly. d. Gene Kelly.

That's Entertainment Part 3, 1994, 102m, ★★¹/2/$, MGM-UA.

MUSICALS: Music Movies; Dance Movies; Compilation Films; Filmumentaries; Nostalgia

That's Life!, 1986, 102m, ★★★/$, Col/Col, PG-13/P-S. On the verge of turning sixty, an architect looks back at his life and contemplates his mortality. Jack Lemmon, Julie Andrews, Sally Kellerman, Robert Loggia, Jennifer Edwards. w. Milton Wexler, Blake Edwards, d. Blake Edwards.

COMEDY DRAMA: Marriage Drama; **MELODRAMA:** Marriage on the Rocks; Cheating Men; Disease Stories; Death-Impending; Romance-Middle-Aged; Midlife Crisis; Overlooked at Release; Hidden Gems; Hollywood Life; Los Angeles
(Save the Tiger; Skin Deep; Middle Age Crazy)

Theater of Blood, 1972, 120m, ★★★/$$$, MGM/MGM-U, R/V-B&G. An actor (Vincent Price) angry at a critic's circle for never awarding him Best Actor decides to off each one of those who voted against him with clever reenactments from famous Shakespearean death scenes. Diana Rigg, Ian Hendry, Harry Andrews, Coral Browne, Robert Coote, Jack Hawkins, Michael Hordern, Arthur Lowe, Robert Morley, Dennis Price, Diana Dors, Milo O'Shea, Eric Sykes. w. Anthony Greville-Bell, d. Douglas Hickox.

HORROR: MURDER: Horror Comedy; Black Comedy; Murder-Clever; Serial Killers; Deaths One by One; Revenge; Theater Life; Actors; Hidden Gems
(Rehearsal for Murder; The Abominable Dr. Phibes; The Return of Dr. Phibes; Comedy of Terrors)

Thelma & Louise, 1991, 123m, ★★★¹/2/$$$$, MGM/MGM-UA, PG-13/EV-P-S. Two women friends from Arkansas (Susan Sarandon, BActress) (Geena Davis, BActress) go on the run when one is almost raped and the other kills the rapist, but will anyone believe their story of how it all happened? Harvey Keitel, Brad Pitt, Michael Madsen. w. Callie Khouri (**BScr**), d. Ridley Scott (**BDirector**). BEdit, BCin. Oscars: 6-1.

DRAMA: COMEDY DRAMA: ACTION: Action Drama; Action Comedy; Buddy Films; Buddy Films-Female; Crime Drama; Road Movies; Outlaw Road Movies; **MURDER:** Social Drama; Murderers-Female; Rape/Rapists; Accused Unjustly; Fugitives from the Law; Crossing the Border; Friendships-Female; Criminals-Female; Arkansas; Southerns; Foreign Directors of Southerns; Female Screenwriters; Female Protagonists; Sleeper Hits; Susan Sarandon Goes Southern

SPOOF: To Wong Foo . . .
(The Sugarland Express; Leaving Normal; Boys on the Side; Bonnie and Clyde)

Them!, 1954, 94m, ★★★/$$, WB/WB. After a nuclear test in the New Mexico desert, a race of giant ants emerges from the ground and terrorizes the populace. Edmund Gwenn, James Whitmore, Joan Weldon, James Arness, Onslow Stevens. w. Ted Sherdeman, George Worthing Yates, d. Gordon Douglas.

SCI-FI: Sci-Fi-; 1950s; **HORROR:** Animals-Mutant; Monsters-Animal; Insects; Monsters-Mutant; Desert Settings; Bombs-Atomic; Paranoia; Experiments
(Tremors; Night of the Lepus)

Theodora Goes Wild, 1936, 94m, ★★★/$$$, Col/Col. A mild-mannered young woman writes a steamy book that gets her small town all atwitter. Irene Dunne (BActress), Melvyn Douglas, Thomas Mitchell, Thurston Hall, Rosalind Keith, Spring Byington, Elizabeth Risdon, Nana Bryant. w. Sidney Buchman, Mary McCarthy, d. Richard Boleslawski. BEdit. Oscars: 2-0.

COMEDY: COMEDY DRAMA: Small-town Life; Small-town Scandals; Scandals; Writers; Rumors; Screwball Comedy; Forgotten Films; Faded Hits; Wild People; Female Protagonists
(Return to Peyton Place)

Therese and Isabelle, 1968, 102m, ★★★/$$, Ind/Connoiseur. Two French schoolgirls take a vacation and start exploring more than the landscape. Essy Persson, Anna Gael. d. Radley Metzger.

DRAMA: Character Studies; Gay Awakenings; Coming of Age; Young Women; Girls; Lesbians; French Films
(One Sings, The Other Doesn't; The Fox)

There Was a Crooked Man, 1970, 126m, ★★¹/2/$$, WB/WB, PG/V. An ex-con seeks the loot he hid when he gets out of prison, but the warden who put him there has an eagle eye on him all the time. Kirk Douglas, Henry Fonda, Hume Cronyn, Warren Oates, Burgess Meredith, John Randolph, Arthur O'Connell, Martin Gabel, Alan Hale. w. David Newman, Robert Benton, d. Joseph L. Mankiewicz.

WESTERNS: COMEDY DRAMA: Ex-Convicts; Treasure Hunts; Fugitives from the Law; Chase Stories; Finding the Loot
(Thunderbolt & Lightfoot; Fool's Parade)

There's a Girl in My Soup, 1970, 96m, ★★★/$$$, Col/Col, R/S-P. A skirt-chasing British television star has the tables turned on him when *he's* exploited by a "bird" for a change. Peter Sellers, Goldie Hawn, Tony Britton, John Comer, Diana Dors. w., P-adap. Terence Frisby, d. Roy del Ruth.

COMEDY: ROMANCE: Romantic Comedy; Playboys; Romance-Older Men/Younger Women; Mod Era; London; 1960s; Psychedelic Era; TV Life; Vacation Romance; Turning the Tables; Sexy Women; Bimbos; Hidden Gems; Faded Hits
(I Love You, Alice B. Toklas; Shampoo)

There's No Business Like Show Business, 1954, 117m, ★★★/$$$, 20th/Fox. A performing family on the vaudeville circuit has its trials and tribulations, but "the show must go on." Ethel Merman, Dan Dailey, Marilyn Monroe, Donald O'Connor, Johnny Ray, Mitzi Gaynor, Hugh O'Brian, Frank McHugh. w. Phoebe and Henry Ephron, story: Lamar Trotti (BOStory), d. Walter Lang. BMScore. Oscars: 2-0.

MUSICALS: Theater Life; Family Drama;

COMEDY DRAMA: Actresses; Actors; Vaudeville; Feisty Females; Female Protagonists; Ensemble Films
(Call Me Madam; The Barkleys of Broadway; The Band Wagon)
These Three, 1936, 93m, ★★★/$$$, Goldwyn-UA/Goldwyn. A snotty little schoolgirl bent on revenge ruins the lives of two schoolteachers by accusing them of having extra-marital affairs. Merle Oberon, Miriam Hopkins, Joel McCrea, Bonita Granville (**BJuvenile**), Catherine Doucet, Alma Kruger, Marcia Mae Jones, Margaret Hamilton, Walter Brennan. w. P-adap. Lillian Hellman (*The Children's Hour*), d. William Wyler. Oscars: 1-1.
MELODRAMA: DRAMA: Romance-Triangles; Love-Forbidden; Friendships-Female; Girls; Schools; Rumors; Scandals; Cheating Women; Cheating Men; Romance-Clandestine; Romance with Married Person; Nuisances; Liars; Accused Unjustly; Female Protagonists
REMAKE/RETELLING: The Children's Hour.
(The Children's Hour; The Prime of Miss Jean Brodie; The Browning Version)
They, 1993, 100m, ★★★/$$, Showtime/Col, PG. An architect has nightmares of his daughter's death down South and seeks out the help of a mystic to help him learn more and keep his other daughter from dying. Patrick Bergin, Valerie Mahaffey, Vanessa Redgrave. w. Edithe Swensen, d. John Korty.
DRAMA: Death-Dealing with; Psychics; Blind People; Fathers & Daughters; Nightmares; Southerns; TV Movies; Female Screenwriters
(Don't Look Now)
They All Laughed, 1982, 115m, ★★1/2/$, Time-Life-20th/Fox, PG/S. Two detectives fall in and out of love with the same woman, a colleague of theirs, as they all work on cases together. Audrey Hepburn, Ben Gazzara, John Ritter, Dorothy Stratten, Colleen Camp, Patti Hansen. w. d. Peter Bogdanovich.
COMEDY: Comedy-Light; **ROMANCE:** Romantic Comedy; **FARCE:** Detective Stories; Detectives-Matrimonial; Cheating Men; Cheating Women; Multiple Stories; Interwoven Stories; Bimbos; Sexy Women; Flops-Major; Coulda Been Good; Writer-Directors
They Call Me Mr. Tibbs!, 1970, 108m, ★★/$$, UA/MGM-UA, R/P-S-V. A San Francisco Bible-thumping preacher may

in fact be a murderer, and the local lieutenant is going to find out. Sidney Poitier, Martin Landau, Barbara McNair, Anthony Zerbe, Jeff Corey, Juano Hernandez, Ed Asner. w. Alan R. Trustman, James R. Webb, d. Gordon Douglas.
ACTION: DRAMA: Crime Drama; Police Stories; Detective Stories; **MURDER: MYSTERY: MURDER MYSTERY:** Black Casts; Black Men; Detectives-Police; San Francisco; Black Directors
SEQUEL TO: In the Heat of the Night.
SEQUEL: The Organization.
They Died with Their Boots On, 1941, 140m, ★★★/$$$, WB/WB. The famous tale of Custer's last stand at Little Big Horn. Errol Flynn, Olivia de Havilland, Arthur Kennedy, Charles Grapewin, Anthony Quinn, Sidney Greenstreet, Gene Lockhart, John Litel, Walter Hampden, Hattie McDaniel. w. Wally Kline, Aeneas Mackenzie, d. Raoul Walsh.
WESTERNS: TRAGEDY: ACTION: Action Drama; Epics; Cavalry; Indians-American, Conflict with; Custer's Last Stand; Faded Hits
They Drive by Night, 1938, 84m, ★★★/$$, Jackson-Ind./NA. In England, a convict escapes from prison and seeks the help of local truck drivers to prove he was innocent in the first place, while silk stocking strangler lurks. Emlyn Williams, Ernest Thesiger, Allan Jeayes. N-adap. James Curtis, Derek Twist, d. Raoul Walsh.
SUSPENSE: MURDER: MYSTERY: MURDER MYSTERY: Serial Killers; Ahead of its Time; Truck Drivers; Murder-Clearing One's Name; England; British Films; Hidden Gems; Forgotten Films
They Drive by Night, 1940, 97m, ★★★/$$$, WB/WB. When his brother is killed in a trucking accident, a truck driver decides to try to get out of the line by pulling off a job with his no-good gangster girlfriend. George Raft, Humphrey Bogart, Ann Sheridan, Ida Lupino, Gale Page, Alan Hale, Roscoe Karns, John Litel, Henry O'Neill, George Tobias. w. Jerry Wald, Richard Macaulay, N-adap. A. I. Bezzerides (*Long Haul*), d. Raoul Walsh.
SUSPENSE: Mob Stories; **MURDER:** Dangerous Women; Romance-Dangerous; Heist Stories; Warner Gangster Era; Crime Drama; Truck Drivers; Death-Accidental; Mob Girls; Film Noir; Hidden Gems
(Kiss of Death [1994]; Gun Crazy; They Live by Night)

1940, 96m, ★★★1/2/$$$, RKO/Turner. A mail-order marriage goes awry when a waitress travels to California and realizes the man she's marrying is not the strapping handsome one in the picture, but a much more homely and gruff one, and furthermore, that the man in the picture is actually a foreman at her new husband's vineyard. Charles Laughton, Carole Lombard, William Gargan (**BSActor**), Harry Carey, Frank Fay. w. Robert Ardrey, P-adap. Sidney Howard, d. Garson Kanin. Oscars: 1-0.
COMEDY: ROMANCE: Romantic Comedy; Marriage of Convenience; Screwball Comedy; Mix-Ups; Misunderstandings; Impostors; Romance-Reluctant; Weight Problems; Personal Ads; Brides-Mail Order; Looksism; Hidden Gems; Faded Hits
(Cyrano de Bergerac; Roxanne; I Sent a Letter to My Love)
They Live, 1988, 94m, ★★/$$, U/MCA-U, R/P-V. Aliens are taking over America, and they look just like . . . Yuppies! They infiltrate our minds through subliminal advertising, and you can only tell them from humans by wearing special x-ray specs. Roddy Piper, Keith David, Meg Foster, George "Buck" Flower, Peter Jason, Raymond St. Jacques, Jason Robards III. w. Frank Armitage, SS-adap. Ray Nelson (*Eight O'Clock in the Morning*), d. John Carpenter.
SCI-FI: ACTION: Paranoia; Aliens-Outer Space, Evil; Yuppies; Impostors; Fugitives; Fugitives from the Law; Chase Stories; Brainwashing; Coulda Been Good
(Invasion of the Body Snatchers; The Puppet Masters; Alien Nation)
(Ed: Some scenes are direct rip-offs of *Three Days of the Condor*, and the rest is a mish-mash of 50s sci-fi cliches)
They Live by Night, 1948, 96m, ★★★/$$, RKO/Turner. A man accidently kills someone, but can't prove his innocence. The only ones who believe in him are other criminals, who help him escape from prison, only to become the criminal that society labeled him to begin with. Farley Granger, Cathy O'Donnell, Howard da Silva, Helen Craig. w. Charles Schnee, N-adap. Edward Anderson, d. Nicholas Ray.
SUSPENSE: Film Noir; **MURDER:** Deaths-Accidental; Murder-Clearing One's Name; Fugitives from the Law;

Chase Stories; Accused Unjustly; Thieves; Prison Escapes; Ahead of its Time; Road Movies; Outlaw Road Movies; Criminal Couple; Ordinary Person Turned Criminal; Hidden Gems
REMAKE: Thieves Like Us, 1974.
(Gun Crazy; Badlands; Bonnie and Clyde; Aloha Bobby and Rose; Chicago Joe and the Showgirl; Kalifornia)
They Made Me a Criminal, 1939, 92m, ★★★/$$, WB/WB. A boxer fears he's killed his opponent with a fatal blow to the head, so he retreats from boxing and society, becoming a vagabond out West. John Garfield, Claude Rains, Gloria Dickson, May Robson, Billy Halop, Bobby Jordan, Leo Gorcey, Huntz Hall, Gabriel Dell, Ann Sheridan. w. Sig Herzig, d. Busby Berkeley.
DRAMA: MELODRAMA: MURDER: Death-Accidental; Accused Unjustly; Boxing; Sports Movies; Guilty Conscience; Homeless People; Drifters; Starting Over; Forgotten Films
They Might Be Giants, 1972, 89m, ★★★/$, U/MCA-U, PG. A lawyer in 70s America has daydreams in which he is Sherlock Holmes, solving crimes in Victorian England. Fantasy converges with reality when he is treated by a female Dr. Watson. George C. Scott, Joanne Woodward, Jack Gilford, Lester Rawlins. w. P-adap. James Goldman, d. Anthony Harvey.
COMEDY DRAMA: Black Comedy; Fantasies; Detective Stories; Detectives-Amateur; Detectives-Private; Amnesia; Illusions/Hallucinations; Identities-Assumed; Psychologists; Romance with Psychologist; Psychologist as Detective; Sherlock Holmes; Hidden Gems; Forgotten Films
TV Series Version, 1973.
(The Private Life of Sherlock Holmes; Without a Clue)
They Only Kill Their Masters, 1972, 98m, ★★/$, MGM/MGM-UA, R/V-P. A series of murders baffles even the local town's police chief, until he begins to decipher the pattern involved. James Garner, Katharine Ross, Hal Holbrook, June Allyson, Harry Guardino, Tom Ewell, Peter Lawford, Ann Rutherford, Chris Connelly, Edmund O'Brien, Art Metrano, Arthur O'Connell. w. Lane Slate, d. James Goldstone.
ACTION: DRAMA: Action Drama; **SUSPENSE: MYSTERY: MURDER: MURDER**

MYSTERY: Serial Killers; Dogs; Animal Stories; Veterinarians; Monsters-Animal; Conspiracy; Coulda Been Good
They Shoot Horses, Don't They?, 1969, 129m, ★★★★/$$$, ABC-Cin/Fox, R/S-P-V. During the Depression, contestants in a six-day "dance marathon" become consumed with their despair in the ordeal, leading to madness and death. Gig Young (**BSActor**), Jane Fonda (**BActress**), Susannah York (**BSActress**), Michael Sarrazin, Red Buttons, Bonnie Bedelia, Bruce Dern. w. James Poe, Robert E. Thompson (**BAScr**), N-adap. Horace McCoy, d. Sydney Pollack (**BDirector**). BCostume, BMScore, BEdit, BArt. Oscars: 9-1.
DRAMA: TRAGEDY: Depression Era; Dance Movies; Competitions; Race Against Time; Suicidal Tendencies; **ROMANCE:** Romance-Doomed; Mental Illness; Nervous Breakdowns; Alienation; Depression; Dreams; Illusions-Destroyed; Past-Haunted by the; Unemployment; Nightmares; Hidden Gems; Quiet Little Films
(Day of the Locust; The Great Gatsby)
(Ed: A near masterpiece, and underrated, though it is the most nominated film ever not to also get the Best Picture nod)
They Won't Believe Me, 1947, 95m, ★★★/$$, RKO/Turner. A slick ladykiller is accused of the real thing, simply because he was in the wrong bed at the wrong time. Robert Young, Susan Hayward, Rita Johnson, Jane Greer, Tom Powers, Don Beddoe, Frank Ferguson. w. Jonathan Latimer, d. Irving Pichel.
SUSPENSE: Comic Mystery; **COMEDY DRAMA: MYSTERY: MURDER: MURDER MYSTERY:** Accused Unjustly; Framed?; Playboys; Hidden Gems; Coulda Been Great
They Won't Forget, 1937, 94m, ★★★1/2/$$, WB/WB. In a small southern town, a girl is brutally murdered, and her killer becomes the object of an intensive manhunt by a lynching party. Claude Rains, Gloria Dickson, Edward Norris, Otto Kruger, Allyn Joslyn, Linda Perry, Elisha Cook, Jr., Lana Turner, Cy Kendall, Elizabeth Risdon. w. Robert Rossen, Aben Kandel, N-adap. Ward Greene (*Death in the Deep South*), d. Mervyn Le Roy.
DRAMA: TRAGEDY: MURDER: Accused Unjustly; Framed?; Southerns; Lynchings; Manhunts; Scandals; Small-town Life;

Rape/Rapists; Ahead of its Time; Forgotten Films; Hidden Gems
(To Kill a Mockingbird; Intruder in the Dust; Storm Warning; Silhouette)
The Thief, 1952, 86m, ★★1/2/$, Popkin-UA/VCI. A government scientist with nuclear secrets is sought by the FBI after he disappears, they fear to sell secrets to the Russians. Ray Milland, Martin Gabel, Rita Gam, Harry Bronson, John McKutcheon. w. Clarence Greene, Russel Rouse, d. Russel Rouse.
SUSPENSE: Cold War Era; Communists; Spy Films; Spies; Traitors; FBI Agents; Chase Stories; Fugitives from the Law; Nuclear Energy; Bombs-Atomic; Curiosities; Forgotten Films
(The House on 92nd Street; The House on Carroll Street)
(Ed: No dialogue in the entire film, but it's not entirely silent)
The Thief of Bagdad, 1924, 135m, B&W, silent, ★★★1/2/$$$$, UA/HBO, NOS. The evil Caliph of Bagdad rules by corrupt means; ironically, the only honorable man in his kingdom, and the one who must overthrow him, is a thief. Douglas Fairbanks, Snitz Edwards, Charles Belcher, Anna May Wong, Julanne Johnston, Etta Lee, Brandon Hurst, Sojin. w. Lotta Woods, Douglas Fairbanks, d. Raoul Walsh.
REMADE in 1940.
The Thief of Baghdad, 1940, 106m, ★★★1/2/$$$$, UA/SUE, MLB. An evil man assumes the throne from the rightful King of Baghdad, and a small boy must help the real king return to power. Conrad Veidt, Sabu, John Justin, June Duprez, Morton Selten, Miles Malleson, Rex Ingram, Mary Morris. w. Miles Malleson, Lajos Biro, d. Michael Powell, Ludwig Berger, Tim Whelan. **BCCin, BCArt**, BOScore. Oscars: 3-2.
ACTION: ADVENTURE: Fantasy; Desert Settings; Magic; Middle East; Kingdoms; Royalty; Kings; Evil Men; Corruption; Child Protagonists; Boys; Heroes-Unlikely; Faded Hits; Hidden Gems; Production Design-Outstanding
(The Jungle Book; Aladdin; Kim)
Thief of Hearts, 1984, 100m, ★★/$$, Par/Par, R-X/ES-FFN-MN. A man robbing a woman's house comes across her diary, which he uses to blackmail her into a sordid relationship of mutual fantasies. Steven Bauer, Barbara Williams, John Getz, George Wendt, David Caruso,

Christine Ebersole. w. d. Douglas Day Stewart.

SUSPENSE: ROMANCE: Romantic Drama; Erotic Drama; Thieves; Jewel Thieves; Fantasies; Cheating Women; Blackmail; Sexy Men; Writer-Directors (American Gigolo)

The Thief Who Came to Dinner, 1973, 105m, ★★/$$, WB/WB, PG/S-V. A computer nerd working as a programmer comes up with an elaborate scheme to rob a jewelry store. Ryan O'Neal, Jacqueline Bisset, Warren Oates, Jill Clayburgh, Charles Cioffi. w. Walter Hill, N-adap. Terence L. Smith, d. Bud Yorkin.

COMEDY DRAMA: Heist Stories; Thieves; **ROMANCE:** Romantic Comedy; Computers; Nerds; Jewel Thieves; Ordinary Person Turned Criminal (Raffles; The Hot Rock; Hot Millions)

Thieves Like Us, 1974, 123m, ★★★/$, UA/CBX-Fox, R/S. During the Depression, three fugitives from justice hide out at the house of a sympathetic farmer. Their fate is sealed when one of the convicts falls in love with the farmer's daughter. Keith Carradine, Shelley Duvall, John Schuck, Bert Remsen, Louise Fletcher, Tom Skerritt. w. Calder Willingham, Joan Tewkesbury, Robert Altman, N-adap. Edward Anderson, d. Robert Altman.

DRAMA: COMEDY DRAMA: ROMANCE: Romantic Drama; Crime Drama; Road Movies; Outlaw Road Movies; Depression Era; Fugitives from the Law; Southerns; Forgotten Films; Curiosities

REMAKE of They Live By Night, 1948.

The Thin Blue Line, 1988, 101m, ★★★/$$$, AP-BFI-HBO/HBO, R/P-V. A documentary which freed its subject, wrongly accused of a murder in Texas, and in the process dissected the flaws of small-town American "justice." w. d. Errol Morris.

Documentaries; **MURDER:** True Stories; Accused Unjustly; Police Corruption; Texas; Interviews; Sleeper Hits (The Wrong Man; An Innocent Man)

Thin Ice, 1937, 78m, ★★¹/₂/$$$, 20th/Fox. A prince visiting a Swiss ski resort in the Alps falls for his skating instructor, a local beauty (and a great skater, too). Sonja Henie, Tyrone Power, Arthur Treacher, Raymond Walburn, Joan Davis, Sig Rumann, Alan Hale, Melville Cooper. w. Boris Ingster, Milton Sperling, N-adap. Attilla Orbok (*Der*

Komet), d. Sidney Lanfield. BChoreography. Oscars: 1-0.

MUSICALS: ROMANCE: Musical Romance; Skating; Curiosities; Teachers and Students; Alps; Princes; Faded Hits (Sun Valley Serenade; One in a Million)

The Thin Man, 1934, 93m, ★★★¹/₂/$$$$, MGM/MGM-UA. An urbane husband-and-wife-and wire-haired terrier detective team scour Manhattan for a murderer, in-between exchanging quips and swigging a concoction from their fully-stocked liquor cabinets. William Powell (BActor), Myrna Loy, Maureen O'Sullivan, Nat Pendleton, Minna Gombell, Edward Ellis, Porter Hall, Henry Wadsworth, William Henry, Harold Huber, Cesar Romero, Edward Brophy. w. Frances Goodrich, Albert Hackett (BScr), N-adap. Dashiell Hammett, d. W. S. Van Dyke (BDirector). BPicture. Oscars: 4-0.

SEQUELS: After the Thin Man, 1939, Another Thin Man, 1939, Shadow of the Thin Man, 1941, The Thin Man Goes Home, 1944, Song of the Thin Man, 1947.

COMEDY: MYSTERY: MURDER: MURDER MYSTERY: Comic Mystery; Screwball Comedy; Detective Stories; Detectives-Amateur; Detective Couples; Rich People; Dogs; Mystery-Whodunits; Female Screenwriters (A Night to Remember; After Office Hours)

The Thing, 1951, 87m, ★★★¹/₂/$$$, RKO/Turner. In the Arctic Circle, a government expedition of scientists unwittingly unfreeze a being from another planet made of vegetable matter, which seemingly can't be killed, and proceeds to attack them one by one. Robert Cornthwaite, Kenneth Tobey, Margaret Sheridan, Bill Self, Dewey Martin, James Arness (as the Thing). w. Charles Lederer, SS-adap. J. W. Campbell Jr. (*Who Goes There*), d. Christian Nyby (with a "ghost director," either Howard Hawks or Orson Welles, legend has it).

SCI-FI: Sci-Fi-; 1950s; **HORROR:** Aliens-Outer Space, Evil; Arctic; Snow Settings; Explorers; Monsters; Paranoia; Murders-One by One; Stalkers; Allegorical Stories; Cold War Era

REMAKE: 1982. (Aliens; Invaders from Mars; The Abominable Snowman)

The Thing, 1982, 109m, ★★★/$$$, U/MCA-U, PG/V-P. A remake of the above, more faithful to the original short

story, in which the "thing" inhabits the bodies of various members of the expedition. Kurt Russell, Wilford Brimley, T. K. Carter, David Clennon, Richard Dysart, Richard Masur. w. Bill Lancaster, d. John Carpenter.

SCI-FI: HORROR: Aliens-Outer Space, Evil; Antarctic; Snow Settings; Explorers; Monsters; Paranoia; Murders-One by One; Parasites; Stalkers (Aliens; Congo; The Beast)

Thing Called Love, 1993, 116m, ★★-/VR, Par/Par, R/P-S. Several would-be neo-country singers schlep around Nashville falling in and out of love and luck. River Phoenix, Samantha Mathis, Sandra Bullock, Dermot Mulroney, K.T. Oslin. w. Allan Moyle, Carol Heikkinen, d. Peter Bogdanovich.

COMEDY DRAMA: Singers; Country Singers; Songwriters; Ensemble Films; Ensembles-Young People; 20-Somethings; **ROMANCE:** Romantic Drama; Female Screenwriters (Singles; Reality Bites; Songwriter) (Ed: Phoenix's last role, released on video soon after his death. Worth a look)

Things Are Tough All Over, 1982, 92m, ★★/$$, Col/RCA-Col, R/EP-S. Two bumbling potheads are entrusted by a wealthy Arab tycoon to drive his limo carrying five million dollars cash to Las Vegas. Richard "Cheech" Marin, Tommy Chong, Shelby Fields, Rikki Marin, Evelyn Guerrero, John Steadman, Rip Taylor. w. Cheech Marin, Tommy Chong, d. Thomas K. Avidsen.

COMEDY: Drugs-Addictions; Bathroom Humor; Latin People; California; Arab People; Fools-Bumbling; Road Movies; Las Vegas (Cheech & Chong's Still Smokin')

Things Change, 1988, 100m, ★★★/$$, Col./Tri-Star, PG. A nervous and incompetent two-bit hustler for the Chicago mob is assigned guard duty for an elderly cobbler who's to act as a double for their boss. Don Ameche, Joe Mantegna, Robert Prosky, J. J. Johnston, Ricky Jay, Mike Nussbaum, Jack Wallace, Dan Conway. w. David Mamet, Shel Silverstein, d. David Mamet.

COMEDY DRAMA: Mob Stories; Mob Comedy; Impostors; Lookalikes; Elderly Men; Con Artists; Quiet Little Films; Hidden Gems; Chicago; Writer-Directors (General Della Rovere; Dave; Johnny Stecchino)

Things to Come, 1936, 113m, ★★★★/ $$$, London/Nos, Prism. In 1940, there is a great war, and, after years of plague, a new, joyless but safe society is built, which produces the first rocketship to the moon. Raymond Massey, Edward Chapman, Ralph Richardson, Margaretta Scott, Cedric Hardwicke, Sophie Stewart, Derrick de Marney, John Clements. w., N-adap. H. G. Wells (*The Shape of Things to Come*), d. William Cameron Menzies.
SCI-FI: Fantasy; Futuristic Films; **DRAMA:** Dreams; Ahead of its Time; Cult Films; Epics; Hidden Gems
(Metropolis; Modern Times)
Things to Do in Denver When You're Dead, 1995, 204m, ★★ 1/2/$, Miramax/ Miramax, R/EP-V-S. A priest who went with the Mob is on the mend and has started a video bank where people can learn from taped advice of people who have since died. When a mobster implores him to do one more job, who else will wind up dead? Andy Garcia, Christopher Walken, Gabriel Anwar, Treat Williams, Christopher Lloyd, Bill Nunn, William Forsythe, Fairuza Balk, Steve Buscemi. w. Scott Rosenberg, d. Gary Fleder.
ACTION: Black Comedy; Heist Stories; Crime Drama; Mob Stories; Criminals-Stupid; Death-Dealing with; Disabled People; One Last Time
(The Usual Suspects; Fallen Angels; Pulp Fiction)
The Third Man, 1949, 100m, ★★★ 1/2/ $$, BL-London-UA/Republic, SNC. An American Westerns writer goes to Vienna after World War II to locate his old friend, who seems to have disappeared. Events conspire to force this apolitical man to choose sides in the morally complex universe of post-war Europe, with its black markets and unscrupulous profiteers. Joseph Cotten, Trevor Howard, Alida Valli, Orson Welles, Bernard Lee, Wilfrid Hyde White, Ernst Deutsch, Siegfried Breuer, Erich Ponto, Paul Hoerbiger. w. Graham Greene, d. Carol Reed (**BDirector**). BEdit, **BB&WCin**. Oscars: 3-2.
SUSPENSE: MYSTERY: Conspiracy; World War II-Post Era; Missing Persons; Writers; Innocent Bystanders; Con Artists; Spies; Spy Films; Cult Films; Intellectuals; Film History
(The Manchurian Candidate; Odd Man Out; The Tenth Man; Journey into Fear)

(Ed: More style and substance than entertainment, and therefore not as accessible as Hitchcock, though still a must-see)
The Third Sex, 1959, 80m, ★★-/$, Ind/Sinister. An all-American family tries to turn their gay son straight. Paul Dehlke, Paula Welsey.
DRAMA: 1950s; Gay Men; Gay Awakenings; Homophobia; Camp; Curiosities; Conformism
(Glen or Glenda?; Tea and Sympathy)
13 Rue Madeleine, 1946, 95m, ★★ 1/2/$$, 20th/Fox. A group of G-Men in France find a secret Nazi armory and blow it up before the Nazis use its bombs against the allies. James Cagney, Annabella, Richard Conte, Frank Latimore, Walter Abel, Melville Cooper, Sam Jaffe, Blanche Yurka. w. John Monks, Jr., Sy Bartlett, d. Henry Hathaway.
ACTION: Action Drama; Spies; Spy Films; **SUSPENSE:** Nazi Stories; World War II Stories; Bombs; Sabotage
(The House on 92nd Street; Heroes of Telemark; The Hornet's Nest; Force Ten from Navarone)
30 is a Dangerous Age, Cynthia, 1968, 85m, ★★-/$$, Ind/NA. Nerdy but cute young English man decides to get the girl of his dreams and everything else at any cost. Dudley Moore, Suzy Kendall. w. Dudley Moore, d. Joseph McGrath.
COMEDY: Race Against Time; Midlife Crisis; Young Men; Dreams; Elusive Women; Pianists; Forgotten Films; Curiosities; British Films; Independent Films
(Bedazzled; Ten)
32 Short Films about Glenn Gould, 1993, 93m, ★★/$$. Eccentric Canadian pianist's life is profiled in structure referring to Bach's Goldberg Variations, which Gould became famous for recording (the high point before his untimely death). Colm Feore, Gale Garnett. w. Don McKellar, d. Francois Girard, d. Francois Girard.
DRAMA: Biographies; Pianists; Music Composers; Eccentric People; Canadian Films; Art Films
36 Fillette, 1988, 88m, ★★★/$$, Fox-Lorber/Fox-Lorber, R/S. A girl growing out of her size thirty-six blouse is about to try and seduce a much older playboy to prove she's got what it takes. Delphine Zentout, Eiteene Chicot, Jean-Pierre Leaud. d. Catherine Breillat.

DRAMA: Character Studies; **ROMANCE:** Romance-Reluctant; Romance-Older Men/Younger Women; Girls; Coming of Age; French Films; Female Directors
(Smooth Talk; My Father the Hero)
The Thirty-Nine Steps, 1935, 81m, ★★★★/$$$, Gaumont-British/CNG, NOS. A female spy is murdered, and her would-be lover is suspected, but, as authorities chase him down, he must chase the real culprit. Robert Donat, Madeleine Carroll, Godfrey Tearle, Lucie Mannheim, Peggy Ashcroft, John Laurie, Wylie Watson, Helen Haye, Frank Cellier. w. Charles Bennett, Alma Reville, N-adap. John Buchan, d. Alfred Hitchcock.
The Thirty-Nine Steps, 1959, 93m, ★★ 1/2/$, Rank/NA. An almost scene-for-scene remake of the original, yet without the dazzle or pace. Kenneth More, Taina Elg, Barry Jones, Faith Brook, Brenda de Banzie, Duncan Lamont, James Hayter, Michael Goodliffe, Reginald Beckwith. w. Frank Harvey, d. Ralph Thomas.
The Thirty-Nine Steps, 1978, 102m, ★★ 1/2/$, Rank/NA. A remake set in the thirties, and generally faithful to the original. Robert Powell, Karen Dotrice, John Mills, Eric Porter, David Warner, George Baker, Ronald Pickup, Timothy West, Donald Pickering, Andrew Keir, Robert Flemyng, Miles Anderson. w. Michael Robson, d. Don Sharp.
SUSPENSE: Spy Films; Spies; **MURDER: MYSTERY: MURDER MYSTERY:** Conspiracy; Accused Unjustly; Framed?; Chase Stories; Fugitives from the Law; Murder-Clearing Oneself; Hitchcockian
REMAKES: 1959, 1978.
(North by Northwest; Saboteur; Foreign Correspondent; The Fugitive; The Wrong Man; Three Days of the Condor)
(Ed: Though the first is a bit dated and not up to some of Hitchcock's later work, it's definitely the best of these three)
Thirty Seconds Over Tokyo, 1944, 138m, ★★★/$$$, MGM/MGM-UA. A chronicle of the painstaking planning and gut-wrenching execution of the American attack on Japan during World War II. Spencer Tracy, Van Johnson, Robert Walker, Phyllis Thaxter, Tim Murdock, Don Defore, Robert Mitchum. w. Dalton Trumbo, d. Mervyn Le Roy. BB&WCin. Oscars: 1-0.
ACTION: DRAMA: Action Drama; War Stories; Pilots-Military; Japan; Japanese as Enemy

This Above All, 1942, 110m, ★★★/$$$, 20th/NA. An army nurse falls in love with a deserter and conscientous objector, who finally comes around and proves himself during an air raid. Tyrone Power, Joan Fontaine, Thomas Mitchell, Henry Stephenson, Nigel Bruce, Gladys Cooper, Melville Cooper. w. R. C. Sherriff, N-adap. Eric Knight, d. Anatole Litvak.

MELODRAMA: ROMANCE: War Stories; Nurses; Peaceful People; Men Proving Themselves; Romance-Opposites Attract; Patriotic Films; Faded Hits; Forgotten Films
(Two People; A Farewell to Arms)

This Boy's Life, 1993, 115m, ★★★1/2/$$, WB/WB, PG-13/S-P-V. A single mother with a teenage son moves away from her abusive boyfriend only to find a stern, macho disciplinarian who not only takes his aggressions out on her, but her son as well. Robert De Niro, Ellen Barkin, Leonardo DiCaprio. w. Robert Getchell, NF-adap. Tobias Wolff, d. Michael Caton-Jones.

DRAMA: Marriage Drama; Stepparents vs. Children; Stepfathers; Abused Women; Abused Children; Boys; Boyhood; Teenagers; Coming of Age; Mothers-Struggling; Autobiographical Stories; Biographies; Stern Men; Macho Men; Boy Scouts; 1950s; Hidden Gems
(Alice Doesn't Live Here Anymore; Firstborn; The Stepfather)

This Could Be the Night, 1958, 105m, ★★-/$$, MGM/MGM-UA. Two mob boys run a nightclub and take on an innocent secretary who falls for the worse of the two while the other gets jealous-all set to music and comedy. Anthony Franciosa, Jean Simmons, Paul Douglas, Joan Blondell, ZaSu Pitts. d. Robert Wise.

MUSICALS: COMEDY: Musical Comedy; ROMANCE: Romantic Comedy; Musical Romance; Men Fighting Over Women; Nightclubs; Secretaries; Bad Men and Religious Women; Mob Comedy
(Guys and Dolls; Pal Joey; The Tender Trap)

This Gun for Hire, 1942, 81m, ★★★/$$$, Par/Par. A hitman becomes involved in a conspiracy and isn't sure who to trust, but intends to find out who's behind the plot. Alan Ladd, Veronica Lake, Robert Preston, Laird Cregar, Tully Marshall, Mikhail Rasumny, Marc Lawrence. w. Albert Maltz, W. R. Burnett, N-adap. Graham Greene (A Gun for Sale), d. Frank Tuttle.

ACTION: SUSPENSE: Conspiracy; MYSTERY: MURDER: MURDER MYSTERY: Hitmen; Mob Stories; Fugitives from the Law; Film Noir
REMAKE: 1990 with Robert Wagner.
(The Blue Dahlia; The Glass Key; Three Days of the Condor)

This Happy Breed, 1947, 114m, ★★★/$$$, Eagle-Lion/Homevision. A family's trials and tribulations between the two wars in England. Robert Newton, Celia Johnson, John Mills, Kay Walsh, Stanley Holloway, narr. Laurence Olivier. w. d. David Lean, P-adap. Noel Coward.

MELODRAMA: Family Drama; World War II Era; Multiple Stories; Ensemble Films; Narrated Films; Hidden Gems; British Films; England; Faded Hits
(Cavalcade; Forever and a Day; King's Row)

This Happy Feeling, 1958, 92m, ★★1/2/$$, U-I/Barr Video. A washed-up actor has a rejuvenating fling with his secretary. Curt Jurgens, Debbie Reynolds, John Saxon, Alexis Smith, Mary Astor, Estelle Winwood. w. d. Blake Edwards.

COMEDY DRAMA: ROMANCE: Romantic Comedy; Actors; Midlife Crisis; Secretaries; Romance-Older Men/Younger Women; Writers-Directors
(Susan Slept Here; Paris When It Sizzles)

This Is My Life, 1992, 94m, ★★★/$$, 20th/Fox, PG. A single mother with two daughters entering their awkward adolescence tries to make it as a comedian on the stand-up circuit. Julie Kavner, Samantha Mathis, Gaby Hoffman, Carrie Fisher, Dan Aykroyd, Bob Nelson, Marita Geraghty. w. Nora Ephron, Delia Ephron, N-adap. Meg Wolitzer (This Is Your Life), d. Nora Ephron.

COMEDY: COMEDY DRAMA: Comedians; Mothers-Struggling; Fame-Rise to; Mothers & Daughters; Female Protagonists; Female Directors; Female Screenwriters; Writer-Directors
(Punchline)

This Is Spinal Tap, 1984, 82m, ★★★/$$, Embassy/Embassy, New Line, R/P-S. A pseudo-documentary about a fictitious British heavy metal band, which lambasts the whole rock establishment, exposing the vacuousness of these "creative geniuses" in hilarious vignettes. Christopher Guest, Michael McKean, Harry Shearer, Rob Reiner, R. J. Parnell, David Kaff, Tony Hendra, Bruno Kirby. w. Christopher Guest, Michael McKean, Harry Shearer, Rob Reiner, d. Rob Reiner.

COMEDY: Rockumentaries; Spoofs; Concert Films; Spoofs-Documentary; Rock Stars; Biographies-Fictional; Musicians; 1980s; Simple Minds
(All You Need is Cash; The Decline of Western Civilization; Fear of a Black Hat)

This Is the Army, 1943, 121m, ★★★/$$$$, WB/WB. During World War II, inductees with various talents put on a show for the boys. George Murphy, Joan Leslie, Irving Berlin, George Tobias, Alan Hale, Charles Butterworth, Rosemary de Camp, Dolores Costello, Una Merkel, Stanley Ridges, Ruth Donnelly, Kate Smith, Frances Langford, Gertrude Niesen, Ronald Reagan, Joe Louis. w. Casey Robinson, Claude Binyon, d. Michael Curtiz. BCArt, BOScore. Oscars: 2-1.

MUSICALS: War Stories; World War II Stories; Putting on a Show; All-Star Casts; All-Star Cameos
(Stage Door Canteen; Thousands Cheer)

This Island Earth, 1955, 86m, ★★★/$$, U-I/MCA-U. A top-secret scientific research center recruits the most brilliant minds in America to work for . . . *aliens from outer space!!!* Jeff Morrow, Faith Domergue, Rex Reason, Lance Fuller, Russell Johnson, Robert Nicholas, Karl Lindt. w. Franklin Coen, Edward G. O'Callaghan, N-adap. Raymond F. Jones, d. Joseph Newman.

SCI-FI: Sci-Fi-; 1950s; Aliens-Outer Space, Evil; UFOs; Experiments; Intellectuals; Scientists; Forgotten Films
(The Day the Earth Stood Still)

This Is My Affair, 1937, 102m, ★★1/2/$$, 20th/NA. Story of President McKinley's assassination and the romance developing out of the search for the culprit. Robert Taylor, Barbara Stanwyck, Victor McLaglen, Brian Donlevy, Sidney Blackmer. w. Allen Rivkin, Lamar Trotti, d. William Seiter.

DRAMA: ROMANCE: Romantic Drama; Presidents; Historical Drama; Political Drama; Assassination Plots; True Stories; 1890s; Forgotten Films

This Land Is Mine, 1943, 103m, ★★★/$$$, RKO/Turner. The citizens of a small village in Europe fight the Nazis, forcing ordinary citizens to become heroes.

Charles Laughton, Maureen O'Hara, George Sanders, Walter Slezak, Una O'Connor, Kent Smith, Philip Merrivale, Thurston Hall, George Coulouris. w. Dudley Nichols, d. Jean Renoir.

DRAMA: MELODRAMA: Patriotic Films; Nazi Stories; Political Drama; Heroes-Ordinary; Small-town Life
(Heroes of Telemark; The North Star)

This Property Is Condemned, 1966, 110m, ★★★/$$, Par/Par, S. A young woman (Natalie Wood) sleeps around until one young man (Robert Redford) comes into town and tries to change her path of destruction. Natalie Wood, Robert Redford, Mary Badham, Kate Reid, Charles Bronson, Jon Provost, John Harding, Alan Baxter, Robert Blake. w. Francis Ford Coppola, Fred Coe, Edith Sommer, P-adap. Tennessee Williams, d. Sydney Pollack.

DRAMA: MELODRAMA: ROMANCE: Romance-Reluctant; Romantic Drama; Free Spirits; Wild People; Past-Haunted by the; Southerns; Prostitutes-Low Class; Promiscuity; Wild People; Elusive Women; Drifters; Depression Era; New Orleans; Female Screenwriters; Tennessee Williams-esque
(Walk on the Wild Side; Splendor in the Grass)

This Sporting Life, 1963, 134m, ★★★½/$$, Continental-Rank/Par. In the North of England, a rough-and-tumble miner makes it as a rugby player, but his tendency to pick fights and get drunk keep him from fully enjoying his success. Richard Harris (BActor), Rachel Roberts (BActress), Alan Badel, William Hartnell, Colin Blakely, Vanda Godsell, Arthur Lowe. w., N-adap. David Storey, d. Lindsay Anderson. Oscars: 2-0.

DRAMA: Kitchen Sink Drama; **ROMANCE:** Romantic Drama; Alcoholics; Sports Movies; Young Men; Young Men-Angry; Wild People; Mining Towns; Working Class; British Films; Sleeper Hits; Hidden Gems
(Saturday Night and Sunday Morning; A Kind of Loving)

This Thing Called Love, 1941, 98m, ★★★/$$$, Col/NA. A savvy, cynical businesswoman attempts an experiment in "open marriage," believing it best when husband and wife are good friends, but not lovers. Of course her plan hits a few snags when the old human emotion of jealousy comes into play . . . Rosalind

Russell, Melvyn Douglas, Binnie Barnes, Allyn Joslyn, Gloria Dickson, Lee J. Cobb, Gloria Holden, Don Beddoe. w. George Seaton, Ken Englund, P. J. Wolfson, d. Alexander Hall.

COMEDY: ROMANCE: Romantic Comedy; Marriage Comedy; Marriage of Convenience; Partners-Married; Alternative Lifestyles; Ahead of Time; Career Women; Feisty Females; Cheating Men; Cheating Women; Hidden Gems; Forgotten Films; Feamle Protagonists
(Hired Wife; Take a Letter, Darling; Bob&Carol&Ted&Alice)

The Thomas Crown Affair, 1968, 102m, UA/MGM-UA, ★★★½/$$$. A playboy bank robber (Steve McQueen) is found out by a beautiful insurance investigator (Faye Dunaway), but before she seduces him into giving up, he may pull one over on her. Paul Burke, Jack Weston, Yaphet Kotto. w. Alan R. Trustman, d. Norman Jewison. **BOSong**, "The Windmills of Your Mind." Oscars: 1-1.

DRAMA: ROMANCE: Bank Robberies; Heist Stories; Romantic Drama; Psychological Drama; Romance-Unprofessional; Insurance Scams; Crime Pays; Playboys; Clever Plots & Endings; Female Protagonists
(Bullitt)
(Ed: Slick and rather dated, it's still effective)

Thoroughly Modern Millie, 1967, 138m, ★★★/$$$$, U/MCA-U., G. In the twenties, a small-town girl goes to New York and follows all the latest trends. Oh yeah, and she also uncovers a white slave trade fronting as a Chinese laundry. Julie Andrews, Mary Tyler Moore, John Gavin, James Fox, Carol Channing (BSActress), Beatrice Lillie, Jack Soo, Pat Morita, Anthony Dexter. w. Richard Morris, d. George Roy Hill. **BMScore**, BOSong, BOScore. Oscars: 4-1.

MUSICALS: COMEDY: Musical Comedy; Slavery; Missing Persons; Spoofs; Young Women; Simple Minds; Women in Jeopardy; **MYSTERY:** Detectives-Amateur; Elusive Men; Sexy Men; Infatuations; Roaring 20s; 1920s; Chinese People; Faded Hits; Hidden Gems
(The Boy Friend; Star!; Margie; Darling Lili)

Those Daring Young Men in Their Jaunty Jalopies, 1969, 125m, ★★½/$, Par/Par, G. Contestants in the Monte Carlo Rally use every trick in the book to

thwart their opponents. Peter Cook, Dudley Moore, Tony Curtis, Bourvil, Walter Chiari, Terry-Thomas, Gert Frobe, Susan Hampshire, Jack Hawkins, Eric Sykes. w. Jack Davies, Ken Annakin, d. Ken Annakin.

COMEDY: ACTION: Action Comedy; Car Racing; Nostalgia; 1900s; Monte Carlo; Forgotten Films
(Those Magnificent Young Men in Their Flying Machines; The Great Race; Genevieve)

Those Magnificent Men in Their Flying Machines, or How I Flew from London to Paris in 25 Hours and 11 Minutes, 1965, 133m, ★★★/$$$, 20th/Fox, G. A prize is offered by a London paper for the man who can get to Paris first, attracting airmen from around the globe. Sarah Miles, Stuart Whitman, Robert Morley, Eric Sykes, Terry-Thomas, James Fox, Alberto Sordi, Gert Frobe, Jean-Pierre Cassel, Karl Michael Vogler, Irina Demich, Benny Hill, Flora Robson, Sam Wanamaker, Red Skelton, Fred Emney, Cicely Courtneidge, Gordon Jackson, John Le Mesurier. w. Jack Davies, Ken Annakin (BOScr), d. Ken Annakin. Oscars: 1-0.

COMEDY: ACTION: Action Comedy; **FARCE:** Competitions; Women in Jeopardy; **ROMANCE:** Romantic Comedy; Airplanes; World Travel; Nostalgia; Balloons; 1900s; British Films
(Those Daring Young Men in the Their Jaunting Jalopies; The Great Race; Genevieve)
(Ed: Highly similar to The Great Race, and released at the same time, though each has its high and low spots—and this is about an air race, not a car race)

Those Were the Days, 1940, 74m, ★★½/$$, Par/NA. A middle-aged couple, on the occasion of their fortieth anniversary, remember meeting in college. William Holden, Bonita Granville, Ezra Stone, Judith Barrett, Vaughan Glazer, Lucien Littlefield, Richard Denning. w. Don Hartman, SS-adap. George Fitch, d. J. Theodore Reed.

MELODRAMA: COMEDY DRAMA: ROMANCE: Romantic Drama; Marriage Drama; Love-First; Nostalgia; 1900s; Memories; Romance-Middle-Aged

A Thousand Clowns, 1965, 115m, ★★★½/$$$, UA/CBS-Fox, PG/S. A non-conformist who refuses to work leads his orphaned nephew around Manhattan on daily adventures, until the social workers and the school board pay him a visit which may lead him to romance and his rethinking his position. Jason Robards, Martin Balsam (**BSActor**), Barry Gordon, Barbara Harris, William Daniels, Gene Saks. w. Herb Gardner (**BAScr**), P-adap. Herb Gardner, d. Fred Coe. BPicture, BOScore. Oscars: 4-1.

COMEDY DRAMA: ROMANCE: Romantic Comedy; Free Spirits; Wild People; Fathers-Surrogate; Orphans; Fathers & Sons; Social Workers; New York Life; Unemployment; Life Transitions; Forgotten Films; Faded Hits; Hidden Gems
(The Goodbye People; You're a Big Boy Now; Lies My Father Told Me)

The Thousand Eyes of Dr. Mabuse, 1960, 103m, ★★1/2/$, Ind/Criterion. A very late addition to Lang's silent series, about the sadistic "doctor" who performs experiments on unwitting victims. Dawn Addams, Peter Van Eyck, Gert Frobe, Wolfgang Preiss, Werner Peters. w. Fritz Lang, Jeinz Oskar Wuttig, d. Fritz Lang.

HORROR: SUSPENSE: Experiments; Scientists-Mad; Torture; Cult Films
SEQUEL TO: Dr. Mabuse
(The Cabinet of Dr. Caligari)

A Thousand Pieces of Gold, 1991, 105m, ★★★/$$, PBS/Hemdale. A Chinese woman is sold by her father into a marriage arrangement in 1900s America where she winds up a prostitute. Rosalind Chao, Dennis Dun, Chris Cooper. w. Anne Makepeace, d. Nancy Kelly.

DRAMA: WESTERNS: Westerns-Neo; Character Studies; Prostitutes with a Heart of Gold; Slavery; Marriage of Convenience; Female Protagonists; TV Movies; Chinese People; China; 1900s; Female Directors; Female Screenwriters
(Shanghai Triad; Raise the Red Lantern; Heaven and Earth)

Thousands Cheer, 1943, 126m, ★★★/$$$, MGM/MGM-UA. The troops decide to put on a show at the base to boost morale. Kathryn Grayson, Gene Kelly, John Boles, Mary Astor, Jose Iturbi, Kay Kyser and his Orchestra, Lionel Barrymore, Margaret O'Brien, June Allyson, Mickey Rooney, Judy Garland, Red Skelton, Eleanor Powell, Bob Crosby and his Orchestra, Lena Horne, Frank Morgan. w. Paul Jarrico, Richard Collins, d. George Sidney. BCArt, BMScore, BCCin. Oscars: 3-0.

MUSICALS: COMEDY: Musical Comedy; World War II Stories; Putting on a Show; Soldiers; All-Star Casts; All-Star Cameos; Faded Hits
(This Is the Army)

Three Amigos, 1986, 105m, ★★/$$, Orion/Orion, PG-13/P. Three timid movie cowboys have to play the real thing when the run-down town they're stuck in gets invaded by a band of thieves. Chevy Chase, Steve Martin, Martin Short, Patrice Martinez, Alfonso Arau. w. Steve Martin, Lorne Michaels, Randy Newman, d. John Landis.

COMEDY: Spoofs; **WESTERNS:** Western Comedy; Spoofs-Western; Mexico; Latin People; Fools-Bumbling
COMIC FLIPSIDE OF The Magnificent Seven.
(Zorro; The Gay Blade; Three Caballeros)

Three Blind Mice, 1938, 75m, ★★★/$$$, 20th/NA. Three inexperienced young girls fresh off their Kansas farms go to the big bad city in search of wealthy husbands. Loretta Young, Joel McCrea, David Niven, Stuart Erwin, Marjorie Weaver, Pauline Moore, Binnie Barnes, Jane Darwell, Leonid Kinskey. w. Brown Holmes, Lynn Starling, d. William A. Seiter.

COMEDY: ROMANCE: Romantic Comedy; Marrying Up; Golddiggers; Friendships-Female; Three Girls Want Men; Ensemble Films; Ensembles-Female; Multiple Stories; Rich People; Girls in Love; Young Women; Forgotten Films; Hidden Gems; Female Screenwriters; Female Protagonists
REMAKE OF: Three Little Girls in Blue.
REMAKE: How to Marry a Millionaire.
(How to Marry a Millionaire; Three Little Girls in Blue; The Greeks Had a Word for Them; Moon Over Miami; Three Coins in the Fountain; The Pleasure Seekers)

The Three Caballeros, 1945, 70m, ★★★1/2/$$$, Disney/Disney, G. A group of short documentaries on various South American countries, hosted by Donald Duck and his pals, in support of the "good neighbor policy." w. various, d. various.
Cartoons; Animation-Partial; Mexico; Latin People; South America; Documentaries

Three Came Home, 1950, 106m, ★★★/$$, 20th/Nos. The true story of the internment of the writer Agnes Newton

Keith and her daring escape attempt from a Japanese prison camp in Borneo during World War II. Claudette Colbert, Patric Knowles, Sessue Hayakawa, Florence Desmond, Sylvia Andrew, Phyllis Morris. w. Nunnally Johnson, NF-adap. Agnes Newton Keith, d. Jean Negulesco.

DRAMA: Escape Adventure; Rescue Drama; POWs; War Stories; World War II Stories; Japanese as Enemy; Writers; Female Protagonists; Asia; Forgotten Films; True Stories; Docudrama
(A Town Like Alice; The Bridge Over the River Kwai)

Three Coins in the Fountain, 1954, 102m, ★★★/$$$$, 20th/Fox. Three women on vacation in Rome each make the same wish: to find a handsome man to sweep them off their feet. It happens, to varying degrees. Clifton Webb, Dorothy McGuire, Louis Jourdan, Jean Peters, Rossano Brazzi, Maggie McNamara, Howard St. John, Kathryn Givney, Cathleen Nesbitt. w. John Patrick, N-adap. John H. Secondari, d. Jean Negulesco. BPicture, **BCCin**, **BOSong**. Oscars: 3-2.

MELODRAMA: ROMANCE: Romantic Drama; **COMEDY DRAMA:** Vacation Romance; Wishes; Marrying Up; Golddiggers; Girls in Love; Italy; Faded Hits; Three Girls Want Men
(The Pleasure Seekers; How to Marry a Millionaire; Three Blind Mice; Only You; Roman Holiday)

Three Comrades, 1938, 98m, ★★★/$$, MGM/MGM-UA. Three friends in Europe in the 1920s suffer through, with a little levity provided by the sole object of all three's attention, a local tubercular girl. Margaret Sullavan (**BActress**), Robert Taylor, Robert Young, Franchot Tone, Guy Kibbee, Lionel Atwill, Henry Hull, Charley Grapewin. w. F. Scott Fitzgerald, Edward A. Paramore, N-adap. Erich Maria Remarque, d. Frank Borzage. Oscars: 1-0.

MELODRAMA: Disease Stories; Men Fighting Over Women; **ROMANCE:** Romantic Drama; Tearjerkers; Friendships-Male; Romance-Triangles; Roaring 20s; 1920s; Americans Abroad; Free Spirits; Forgotten Films; Hidden Gems; Curiosities

Three Cornered Moon, 1933, 72m, ★★1/2/$$$, Par/NA. During the Depression, a formerly privileged family is shocked when its members must search for work. Claudette Colbert, Mary Boland, Richard Arlen, Wallace Ford, Lyda Roberti, Tom Brown, Hardie Albright. w. S. K. Lauren, Ray Harris, P-adap. Gertrude Tonkonogy, d. Elliott Nugent.

COMEDY DRAMA: MELODRAMA: Family Comedy; Family Drama; Depression Era; Ordinary People Stories; Unemployment; Riches to Rags; Forgotten Films
(You Can't Take it With You; Dinner at Eight; The Grapes of Wrath)

Three Days of the Condor, 1975, 119m, ★★★★/$$$$, Par/Par, R/P-V-S. A CIA researcher (Robert Redford) stumbles onto information which gets everyone in his office killed but himself, sending him on the run until he can figure out whether to trust his own bosses or not, all the while being followed by a hitman (Max Von Sydow). Faye Dunaway, Cliff Robertson, Max Von Sydow, John Houseman, Walter McGinn. w. Lorenzo Semple, Jr., David Rayfiel, N-adap. James Grady (*Six Days of the Condor*), d. Sydney Pollack. BEdit. Oscars: 1-0.

SUSPENSE: MURDER: Murderers-Mass; Hitmen; **MYSTERY: MURDER MYSTERY:** Murder-Clearing Oneself; Race Against Time; Chase Movies; Spies; Spy Films; CIA Agents; Fugitives; Fugitives from the Law; Fugitives from a Murderer; Conspiracy; Corruption; Hostage Situations; Stalker; Mindgames; Kidnapper-Sympathizing with; Kidnappings
(North by Northwest; Saboteur; Total Recall)

The Three Faces of Eve, 1957, 95m, ★★★1/2/$$$, 20th/Fox. A woman is discovered by her psychiatrist to have three distinct personalities, each of which is unaware of the other. Joanne Woodward (**BActress**), Lee J. Cobb, David Wayne, Nancy Kulp, Edwin Jerome. w. Nunnally Johnson, NF-adap. Corbett H. Thigpen M.D., Hervey M. Cleckley M.D., d. Nunnally Johnson. Oscars: 1-1.

DRAMA: Disease Stories; Mental Illness; Psychologists; Multiple Personalities; Marriage on the Rocks; True Stories; Docudrama; Female Protagonists
(Sybil [Mini Series]; Lizzie)

Three for the Road, 1987, 98m, ★★/$, MCEG-Vista/HBO, PG-13/P. A political aide to a governor is given the job of driving his runaway daughter to a reform school but many stupid things happen

along the way. Charlie Sheen, Alan Ruck, Sally Kellerman, Kerri Green. w. Tim Metcalfe, d. B.W.L. Norton.
COMEDY: Chase Stories; Road Movies; Road Movies-Transporting Girls; Feisty Females; Juvenile Delinquents; Politicians; Coulda Been Good
(The Chase [1994])

Three Fugitives, 1989, 96m, ★★★1/2/$$$, Touchstone/Touchstone, PG-13/p-V. When a bank robber (Nick Nolte) is released from prison, he goes to the bank to cash a check, but he walks in on an inept robber (Martin Short) stealing money for his daughter. Jason Robards, Sarah Rowland Doroff, James Earl Jones, Alan Ruck, Kenneth McMillan, David Arnott, Bruce McGill. w. d. Francis Veber.
COMEDY: FARCE: Screwball Comedy; Capers; Comedy of Errors; Mix-Ups; Accused Unjustly; Starting Over; Fugitives; Fugitives from the Law; Heist Stories; Chase Stories; Bank Robberies; Ex-Convicts; Children-Saving; Teams-Mismatched; Foreign Film Remakes; Writer-Directors
REMAKE OF: *Les Trois Fugitives.*
(Little Miss Marker; Les Comperes; La Chevre; Out on a Limb)

Three Godfathers, 1948, 106m, ★★★/$$$, MGM/MGM-UA. A baby orphan is found in the desert by three bandits, who learn sympathy and kindness . . . and so on. John Wayne, Pedro Armendariz, Harry Carey, Jr., Ward Bond. w. Laurence Stallings, Frank S. Nugent, Frank B. Kyne, d. John Ford.
COMEDY DRAMA: WESTERNS: Western Comedy; **MELODRAMA:** Men and Babies; Babies-Finding; Babies; Ensemble Films; Ensembles-Male; Friendships-Male; Fathers-Surrogate; Orphans; Desert Settings
REMAKE OF 6 earlier versions, mostly silent.
(Three Men and a Baby)

The 300 Spartans, 1962, 114m, ★★/$$, 20th/NA. The warring culture of Sparta whips the rest of the Grecian isles into shape in order to stop the Persian onslaught at Thermopylae. Richard Egan, Ralph Richardson, David Farrar, Diane Baker, Barry Coe, Donald Houston, Kieron Moore, John Crawford, Robert Brown. w. George St. George, d. Rudolph Mate.
ACTION: Ancient Times; Greece; Mythology; War Stories
(Ulysses)

Three Husbands, 1950, 76m, ★★/$, UA/Nos. Three men's marriages go haywire when they each recieve essentially the same letter from a friend who just died, which chronicles the affairs he had with each of their wives. Emlyn Williams, Eve Arden, Howard da Silva, Ruth Warrick, Shepperd Strudwick, Vanessa Brown, Billie Burke, Jonathan Hale. w. Vera Caspary, Edward Eliscu, d. Irving Reis.
MELODRAMA: Cheating Women; Cheating Men; Romance-Triangles; Secrets-Keeping; Marriage on the Rocks; Forgotten Films; Female Screenwriters
REMAKE/RETREAD/FLIPSIDE OF: A Letter to Three Wives.
(A Letter to Three Wives; Marriage on the Rocks)

Three Little Words, 1950, 102m, ★★★/$$$$, MGM/MGM-UA. A musical biopic of the lives, loves, and music of composers Bert Kalmar and Harry Ruby. Fred Astaire, Red Skelton, Vera-Ellen, Arlene Dahl, Keenan Wynn, Gale Robbins, Gloria de Haven, Phil Regan, Debbie Reynolds. w. George Wells, d. Richard Thorpe. BMScore. Oscars: 1-0.
MUSICALS: ROMANCE: Musical Romance; Biographies; Music Composers; Singers
(Day and Night; Rhapsody in Blue)

The Three Lives of Thomasina, 1963, ★★★/$$, Disney/Disney, G. In 1912, a local Scottish girl cures more animals than the local vet by merely loving them back to health-in particular, one mystical cat named Thomasina. Susan Hampshire, Patrick McGoohan, Karen Dotrice, Vincent Winter, Laurence Naismith, Finlay Currie, Wilfrid Brambell. w. Robert Westerby, N-adap. Paul Gallico (*Thomasina*), d. Don Chaffey.
CHILDREN'S: FAMILY: Magic; Fantasy; Scotland; Animal Stories; Pet Stories; Cats; Reincarnation; Veterinarians; 1900s; Girls; Circus Life; Child Protagonists
(All Creatures Great and Small)

Three Men and a Baby, 1987, 102m, ★★★/$$$$$$, Touchstone/Touchstone, PG. Three philandering dudes with a swank bachelor pad are taught a "lesson in life" when they're stuck with a baby that shows up mysteriously at their doorstep and they can't locate any family. Tom Selleck, Steve Guttenberg, Ted Danson, Nancy Travis. w. James Orr, Jim Cruickshank, d. Leonard Nimoy.

COMEDY: COMEDY DRAMA: Tear-jerkers; Fathers-Surrogate; Orphans; Babies-Finding; Playboys; Ensemble Films; Drugs-Dealing; Men and Babies; Ensembles-Male; Blockbusters; Sleeper Hits; Foreign Film Remakes

REMAKE OF: Three Men and a Cradle (*Trois Hommes et un Couffin*), 1985.

SEQUEL: Three Men and a Little Lady. (Three Godfathers; Little Miss Marker; Bachelor Mother; Jack and Sarah)

Three Men and a Cradle (*Trois Hommes et un Couffin*), 1985, 107m, ★★★/$$, Goldwyn/Goldwyn, PG. A former girlfriend gets fed up and leaves her baby on the doorstep of her jerky ex-boyfriend, who lives with two other swinging bachelors. Roland Giraud, Michel Boujenah, Andre Dussollier, Philippine Leroy Beaulieu. w. d. Coline Serreau. BFLFilm. Oscars: 1-0.

COMEDY: COMEDY DRAMA: Tearjerkers; Fathers-Surrogate; Orphans; Babies-Finding; Men and Babies; Playboys; Ensemble Films; Drugs-Dealing; Ensembles-Male; French Films; Writer-Directors

REMAKE: Three Men and a Baby.

Three Men and a Little Lady, 1990, 100m, ★★/$$$, Touchstone/Touchstone, PG. The mother of the baby of the first film wants to marry an Englishman, but would take the child (now a pre-teen girl) to England with her, which neither the girl nor the three men want. Tom Selleck, Steve Guttenberg, Ted Danson, Nancy Travis, Robin Weisman, Christopher Cazenove, Sheila Hancock, Fiona Shaw. w. Charlie Peters, Sara Parriott, Josan McGibbon, d. Emilio Ardolino.

COMEDY: COMEDY DRAMA: Fathers-Surrogate; Orphans; Ensemble Films; Ensembles-Male; Playboys; Mothers-Struggling; Children-Long-lost; Tearjerkers; Girls; Men and Girls; Female Screenwriters; Female Among Males

The Three Musketeers, 1935, 97m, ★★★/$$, RKO/Turner. The dueling, fighting threesome has swashbuckling adventures. Walter Abel, Paul Lukas, Moroni Olsen, Onslow Stevens, Margot Grahame, Heather Angel, Ian Keith, Miles Mander, Nigel de Brulier. w. Dudley Nichols, Rowland V. Lee, d. Rowland V. Lee.

The Three Musketeers, 1939, 73m, ★★★/$$$, 20th/Fox. A take-off on the familiar tale with singing instead of swashbuckling. Don Ameche, The Ritz Brothers, Binnie Barnes, Joseph Schildkraut, Lionel Atwill, Miles Mander, Gloria Stuart, Pauline Moore, John Carradine. w. M. M. Musselman, William A. Drake, Sam Wellman, d. Allan Dwan.

MUSICALS: Comic Adventure

The Three Musketeers, 1948, 125m, ★★★/$$$$, MGM/MGM-UA. An exciting remake of the 1935 film, with serious action sequences and beautifully choreographed swordfights. Gene Kelly, Lana Turner, June Allyson, Frank Morgan, Van Heflin, Angela Lansbury, Vincent Price, Keenan Wynn, John Sutton, Gig Young, Robert Coote, Reginald Owen, Ian Keith, Patricia Medina. w. Robert Ardrey, d. George Sidney. BCCin. Oscars: 1-0.

ACTION: ADVENTURE: Ensemble Films; Ensembles Male; Royalty; Evil Men; Kidnappings; Saving Someone; Women in Jeopardy; Swashbucklers; Popes/Cardinals; Classic Literary Adaptations; 1700s

REMAKES: 1973, 1993.

The Three Musketeers, 1973, 107m, ★★★1/2/$$$$, 20th/Fox, PG/V. A more farcical telling of the story of the famous trio of swashbuckling avengers and their battles with an evil cardinal, a nasty queen, and damsels in distress. Michael York, Oliver Reed, Richard Chamberlain, Frank Finlay, Raquel Welch, Geraldine Chaplin, Spike Milligan, Faye Dunaway, Charlton Heston, Christopher Lee, Jean-Pierre Cassel. w. George MacDonald Fraser, d. Richard Lester.

ACTION: ADVENTURE: Action Comedy; Comic Adventure; **FARCE:** Swashbucklers; Costume Drama; 1700s; Women in Jeopardy; Ensemble Films; Popes/Cardinals; Ensembles-Male; Revisionist Films

(Ring of the Musketeers; The Fifth Musketeer)

The Three Musketeers, 1993, 96m, ★★-/$$$, Disney/Disney, G/V. A more comical, children-oriented version Disneyfied and brat-packed. Charlie Sheen, Oliver Platt, Rebecca DeMornay, Keifer Sutherland, Chris O'Donnell, Tim Curry, Gabrielle Anwar, Julia Delpy. w. David Loughery, d. Stephen Herek.

CHILDREN'S: FAMILY: ACTION: ADVENTURE: Action Comedy; Comic Adventure; **FARCE:** Swashbucklers; Costume Drama; 1700s; Women in Jeopardy; Ensemble Films; Ensembles-Male; Popes/Cardinals; Revisionist Films; Bratpack Movies

Three Ninjas, 1992, 84m, ★★1/2/$$$, Touchstone/Touchstone, G. Boys who are the sons of an FBI agent and martial arts experts don black ninja garb and go after some evil arms dealers. Victor Wong, Michael Treanor, Max Elliott Slade. w. Edward Emanuel, Kenny Kim, d. Jon Turteltaub.

CHILDREN'S: COMEDY: ACTION: Disney Comedy; Action Comedy; Martial Arts; Ensembles-Children; Arms Dealers; Boys; Child Protagonists

(Sidekicks; Teenage Mutant Ninja Turtles)

Three Ninjas Kick Back, 1994, 95m, ★★/$, Disney/Disney, PG/V. Teenage brothers do battle over a sword their ninja grandfather had stolen from him. Victor Wong, Max Elliott Salde, Sean Fox, Dustin Nguyen. w. Mark Saltzman, d. Charles Kanganis.

CHILDREN'S: COMEDY: ACTION: Disney Comedy; Action Comedy; Martial Arts; Ensembles-Children; Arms Dealers; Boys; Child Protagonists

Three O'Clock High, 1987, 97m, ★★/$, U/MCA-U, PG/V. A high school reporter has to interview the big, new tough on campus and winds up under his thumb and fist. Casey Siezmasko, Anne Ryan, Richard Tyson, Jeffrey Tambor. w. Richard C. Matheson, d. Phil Joanou.

COMEDY: Action Comedy; High School Life; Nerds vs. Macho Men; New Kid in Town; Journalists; Curiosities; Duels; Teenagers; Teenage Movies

(My Bodyguard; Five Corners)

(Ed: Spielberg protege Joanou's first feature and it's virtually all camera gimmicks, covering for what wouldn't even be a very interesting short film)

Three of Hearts, 1993, 102m, ★★★/$, New Line/New Line, R/S-FN-MN. When two lesbians break up, one heading supposedly for men, the other hires a male prostitute to seduce her and make her hate men so she'll come back. Sherilyn Fenn, William Baldwin, Kelly Lynch, Joe Pantoliano, Gail Strickland. w. Philip Epstein, Adam Greenman, d. Yurek Bogayevicz.

COMEDY: COMEDY DRAMA: ROMANCE: Romantic Comedy; Lesbians; Bisexuality; Prostitutes-Male; Hired Dates; Romance-Triangles; Coulda Been Great

(Threesome; Beyond Therapy)
(Ed: What may be a sappy ending is well worth the trip getting there with interesting performances, a few ideas, and definitely not your run-of-the-mill situation)

Three on a Couch, 1966, 109m, ★★/$$, Col/NA. An artist about to marry a psychiatrist thinks he can cure her patients of their sexual problems in his own, unorthodox way. Jerry Lewis, Janet Leigh, James Best, Mary Ann Mobley, Gila Golan, Leslie Parrish, Kathleen Freeman, Fritz Feld. w. Bob Ross, Samuel A. Taylor, Arne Sultan, Marvin Worth, d. Jerry Lewis.

COMEDY: Sex Comedy; Psychologists; Young Women; Playboys; Fools-Bumbling; ROMANCE: Romantic Comedy; Marriage-Impending; Sexual Problems; Virgins; Multiple Performances; Forgotten Films; Coulda Been Good
(Sex and the Single Girl; The Nutty Professor; Boeing Boeing; Ladies Man [1961]; Oh Men! Oh Women!)

The Threepenny Opera (*Die Dreigroschenoper*), 1931, 114m, ★★★/$, WB/NA. A group of cabaret singers and lowlifes in Weimar Germany get romantically entangled. Lotte Lenya, Rudolf Forster, Fritz Rasp, Caroline Neher. w. Bela Balazs, Leo Lania, Ladislas Vajda, P-adap. Bertolt Brecht.

DRAMA: ROMANCE: Romantic Drama; MUSICALS: Ensemble Films; Stagelike Films; German Films; Art Films
(Mack the Knife)

The Three Sisters, 1970, 165m, ★★★1/2/$, Clore/NA. Three wealthy Russian sisters living in their dead father's country estate dream of abandoning it for the lure of the big city and true love, but things don't go so easily. Laurence Olivier, Joan Plowright, Jeanne Watts, Louise Purnell, Derek Jacobi, Alan Bates, Ronald Pickup. w. Anton Checkov (translated by Moura Budberg), d. Laurence Olivier.

DRAMA: Family Drama; Sisters; Dreams; Ensemble Films; Young Women; Fathers & Daughters; Russians; Classic Literary Adaptations; Stage Filmings; Stagelike Films; 1900s; Forgotten Films; Hidden Gems; Actor Directors
(King Lear; The Cherry Orchard; The Seagull)

Three Smart Girls, 1936, 86m, ★★★/$$$$, U/MCA-U. Three daughters of separated parents connive to get them back together. Deanna Durbin, Barbara Read, Nan Grey, Charles Winninger, Binnie Barnes, Ray Milland, Alice Brady, Mischa Auer, Ernest Cossart, Hobart Cavanaugh. w. Adele Commandini, Austin Parker (BOStory), d. Henry Koster. BPicture. Oscars: 2-0.

COMEDY: ROMANCE: Romantic Comedy; Parents vs. Children; Girls; Marriage on the Rocks; Romance-Reunited; Matchmakers; Child Protagonists; Female Screenwriters; Female Protagonists
REMAKE: Three Daring Daughters.
SEQUEL: Three Smart Girls Grow Up.
(The Parent Trap; All I Want for Christmas)

Three Smart Girls Grow Up, 1939, 87m, ★★★/$$$, U/MCA-U. Sequel to the above, in which the girls get interested in boys, and the smartest of the three sisters does all the matchmaking. Deanna Durbin, Helen Parrish, Nan Grey, Charles Winninger, Robert Cummings, William Lundigan, Ernest Cossart, Nella Walker. w. Bruce Manning, Felix Jackson, d. Henry Koster.

COMEDY: ROMANCE: Romantic Comedy; Matchmakers; Girls; Dating Scene; Coming of Age; Female Protagonists

Threesome, 1994, 93m, ★★★/$, 20th/Fox, R/ES-FFN-MN-P. When two guys have to share a dorm room with a girl, things are at first tense but soon develop into more as the title suggests. Only problem is, the girl likes the guy who has a secret-he likes the other guy. Lara Flynn Boyle, Josh Charles, Stephen Baldwin, Alexis Arquette. w. d. Andrew Fleming.

COMEDY DRAMA: ROMANCE: Romantic Drama; Erotic Drama; Romance-Triangles; Bisexuality; Gay Men; Gay Awakenings; Romance-Unrequited; Battle of the Sexes; College Life; Alternative Lifestyles; Underrated; Overlooked at Release; Narrated Films; Coming of Age; Writer-Directors
(Three of Hearts)
(Ed: What may seem cliched territory is given a fresh, intelligent-for Hollywood-treatment and is surprisingly daring with ideas and sexuality)

Three Wishes, 1995, 105m, ★★1/2/$, Tri-Star/Col-Tri, PG. A woman rescues an injured man who may have special powers and take her family a further step.

Patrick Swayze, Mary Elizabeth Mastrantonio, Joseph Mazzello, Seth Mumy, David Marshal Grant, Jay O. Sanders, Michael O'Keefe, John Diehl, Diane Venora, Bill Mumy. w. Elizabeth Anderson, d. Martha Coolidge.

COMEDY DRAMA: Fantasy; Wishes; Drifters; Magic; Female Protagonists; Female Directors; Female Screenwriters
(I Dream of Jeannie; Star Man; Down and Out in Beverly Hills)

The Three Worlds of Gulliver, 1959, 100m, ★★/$, Col/Col. An adaptation of the famous Swift novel of Gulliver's fantastic journeys among strange people. Kerwin Mathews, Basil Sydney, Mary Ellis, Jo Morrow, June Thorburn, Gregoire Aslan. w. Arthur Ross, Jack Sher, d. Jack Sher.

ADVENTURE: Fantasy; Allegorical Stories; Little People; Giants; Hostage Situations; Classic Literary Adaptations
(Gulliver's Travels; The World of Gulliver)

Threshold, 1983, 97m, ★★-/$, 20th/Fox, PG. A doctor implants the first artificial heart on a young woman he's infatuated with. Donald Sutherland, Jeff Goldblum, Mare Winningham. d. Richard Pearce.

DRAMA: MELODRAMA: Doctors; Medical Drama; Infatuations; Canadian Films

Thrill of a Romance, 1945, 105m, ★★/$$, MGM/MGM-UA. A G.I. back from the front in World War II steals the heart of a local swimming champion. Esther Williams, Van Johnson, Lauritz Melchior, Frances Gifford, Henry Travers, Spring Byington, Tommy Dorsey. w. Richard Connell, Gladys Lehmann, d. Richard Thorpe.

MUSICALS: ROMANCE: Musical Romance; Swimming; Soldiers; World War II Era; Forgotten Films
(Neptune's Daughter; Duchess of Idaho)

The Thrill of It All, 1963, 104m, ★★★/$$$$, U-I/MCA-U. A gynecologist can't take the pressure when his wife becomes a model in a ubiquitous ad campaign. Doris Day, James Garner, Arlene Francis, Edward Andrews, Reginald Owen, Zasu Pitts, Elliott Reid. w. Carl Reiner, d. Norman Jewison.

COMEDY: ROMANCE: Romantic Comedy; Sex Comedy; Marriage Comedy; Advertising World; Husbands-Troublesome; Fame-Rise to; Jealousy; Career Women; Battle of the Sexes;

Housewives; TV Life; Hidden Gems; Faded Hits
(Send Me No Flowers; Good Neighbor Sam; Move Over, Darling)

Throne of Blood, 1957, 105m, ★★★-/$$, Toho/Home Vision. A samurai warrior is inspired by a witch to kill his master, in an ancient Japanese take on *Macbeth*. Toshiro Mifune, Isuzu Yamada. w. Hideo Oguni, Shinobu Hashimoto, Ryuzo Kikushima, Akira Kurosawa, P-adap. William Shakespeare (*Macbeth*), d. Akira Kurosawa.

DRAMA: TRAGEDY: Witches; MURDER: Murder-Attempted; Revisionist Films; Japanese Films; Classic Literary Adaptations; Shakespeare; Martial Arts; Hidden Gems; Classic Tragedy
(Rashomon; Ran; Macbeth)

Through a Glass Darkly, 1961, 91m, ★★★/$$, Embassy/Embassy, Nos, Sultan. Four people stay together on a remote island and feel alienated from themselves and God. Harriet Anderson, Gunnar Bjornstrand, Max Von Sydow, Lars Passgard. w. d. Ingmar Bergman (BOScr). BFLFilm. Oscars: 2-1.

DRAMA: Surrealism; Art Films; Islands; Stranded; Alienation; Lonely People; Swedish Films; Forgotten Films; Faded Hits; Curiosities; Writer-Directors
(Persona; L'Avventura)
(Ed: Won the Oscar, but it makes one wonder if the voters got it, or if it was simply one of those awed beyond understanding applauds)

Throw Momma from the Train, 1987, 88m, ★★★/$$$, Orion/Orion, PG-13/P-V. A middle-aged man living with his obnoxious mother is inspired, after watching *Strangers on a Train*, to persuade his professor (who complains of his nagging wife) to swap murders. Danny DeVito, Billy Crystal, Anne Ramsey (BSActress), Kim Greist, Kate Mulgrew. w. Stu Silver, d. Danny DeVito. Oscars: 1-0.

COMEDY: MURDER: Clever Plots & Endings; Blackmail; Murder of Spouse; Misunderstandings; Mothers-Troublesome; Mama's Boys; Trains; Writers; Sleeper Hits
COMIC REMAKE OF: Strangers on a Train.
(Strangers on a Train)

Thumbelina, 1994, 86m, ★★-/$$, WB/WB, G. Disneyized Don Bluth cartoon of a little girl who travels in the dream land

of a fairy tale book, set to music.
w. d. Don Bluth, Gary Goldman, music by Barry Manilow, Jack Feldman, Bruce Sussman, William Ross.

CHILDREN'S: MUSICALS: Musicals-Animated; Cartoons; Fantasy; Fairy Tales; Girls; Child Protagonists
(The Swan Princess; Alice in Wonderland)

Thunder and Lightning, 1977, 93m, ★★1/2/$$, AIP-20th/CBS-Fox, R/S-P-V. A southern bootlegger finds himself in competition with his girlfriend's father, leading to a great many chases on land and water. David Carradine, Kate Jackson, Roger C. Carmel, Sterling Holloway, Ed Barth. w. William Hjortsberg, d. Corey Allen.

ACTION: COMEDY: Action Comedy; Southerns; Rednecks; Bootlegging; Lover; Family Dislikes; Feuds; Chase Stories; Car Chases; Boat Chases
(The Moonshine War; I Walk the Line; Greased Lightning)

Thunder Bay, 1953, 102m, ★★1/2/$$, U-I/MCA-U. A wealthy prospector almost goes broke and loses his reputation trying to drill for oil off the Louisiana gulf coast. James Stewart, Joanne Dru, Dan Duryea, Jay C. Flippen, Anthony Moreno, Gilbert Roland, Marcia Henderson. w. Gil Doud, John Michael Hayes, d. Anthony Mann.

DRAMA: ACTION: Action Drama; Risking it All; Oil People; Louisiana; Swamp Life; Marriage on the Rocks; Forgotten Films

Thunderball, 1965, 132m, ★★★1/2/$$$$$, UA/MGM-UA, PG/V-S. James Bond underwater to thwart a plot to rule the world from down under. Sean Connery, Adolfo Celi, Claudine Auger, Luciana Paluzzi, Rik Van Nutter, Bernard Lee, Lois Maxwell, Martine Beswick. w. Richard Maibaum, John Hopkins, N-adap. Ian Fleming, d Terence Young. BSFX. Oscars: 1-1.

ACTION: Spies; Spy Films; Rule the World-Plot to; Underwater Adventure; James Bond; Secret Agents; Bimbos; Blockbusters
(Never Say Never Again; Goldfinger)

Thunderbirds, 1942, 79m, ★★/$, 20th/NA. An Arizona training base for fighter pilots in World War II is the setting for this melodrama of clashing egos and lady loves on the ground. Gene Tierney, Preston Foster, John Sutton, Jack Holt, May Whitty, George Barbier,

Richard Haydn, Reginald Denny, Ted North. w. Lamar Trotti, d. William A. Wellman.

MELODRAMA: ROMANCE: Romance-Triangles; Pilots-Military; Desert Settings; World War II Era; Female Protagonists; Men Fighting Over Women

Thunderbolt and Lightfoot, 1974, 115m, ★★★1/2/$$$, UA/MGM-UA, R/P-EV. An ex-con (Clint Eastwood) meets up with a wild drifter (Jeff Bridges, BSActor) and after stealing some cars, decides to repeat the great heist of his career and add it to the take which was hidden years ago and is now missing, but it may not go so well this time. George Kennedy. w. d. Michael Cimino. Oscars: 1-0.

DRAMA: ACTION: Action Drama; Heist Stories; Thieves; Bank Robberies; Men as Women; Free Spirits; Wisecracking Sidekicks; Friendships-Male; Buddy Films; Drifters; Writer-Directors
(The Hot Rock; A Man, a Woman, and a Bank)

Thunderhead, Son of Flicka, 1945, 78m, ★★1/2/$$, 20th/Fox. A sequel to *My Friend Flicka* and other such horse tales. Roddy McDowell, Preston Foster, Rita Johnson, James Bell, Carleton Young. w. Dwight Cummins, Dorothy Yost, N-adap. Mary O'Hara, d. Louis King.

CHILDREN'S: FAMILY: Pet Stories; Animal Stories; Horses; Boys
SEQUEL TO My Friend Flicka.
(My Friend Flicka; National Velvet; Black Beauty)

Thunderheart, 1992, 119m, ★★1/2/$$, Col/Col, R/P-S-V. A half-Sioux FBI agent confronts his roots and the racism of his organization when he discovers a conspiracy revolving around the murder of a man on an Arizona reservation which may have been perpetrated by an FBI agent. Val Kilmer, Sam Shepard, Graham Greene, Fred Ward, Fred Dalton Thompson, Sheila Tousey, Chief Ted Thin Elk, John Trudell, Julius Drum, Sarah Brave. w. John Fusco, d. Michael Apted.

DRAMA: SUSPENSE: MYSTERY: MURDER: MURDER MYSTERY: FBI Agents; Native Americans; Indians-American; Conspiracy
(Incident at Oglala; Renegades; The Powwow Highway)

Thunder Road, 1958, 92m, ★★1/2/$$, UA/MGM-UA. Bootleggers in the hills down South do battle with some Chicago gangsters trying to muscle in on their territory. Robert Mitchum, Gene Barry, Jacques Aubuchon, Keely Smith. w. James Arlee Philips, Walter Wise, d. Arthur Ripley.

ACTION: Crime Drama; Action Drama; Bootlegging; Hillbillies; Mob Stories; Ordinary People vs. Criminals; Chicago; Southerns; Feuds; Forgotten Films

Thunder Rock, 1942, 112m, ★★★/$$, Charter/NA. A man escapes the horrors of the Depression to live in a lighthouse where he's then haunted by the ghosts of drowning victims. Michael Redgrave, Lilli Palmer, Barbara Mullen, James Mason, Frederick Cooper. w. Jeffrey Dell, Bernard Miles, P-adap. Robert Ardrey, d. Roy Boulting.

SUSPENSE: MYSTERY: Ghost Stories; Depression Era; Lonely People; Drownings; Art Films; Hidden Gems; Forgotten Films; Coulda Been Great
(Dead of Night; The Uninvited; Ghost Story)

Thursday's Game, 1974, 99m, ★★★/$$$, MTM-ABC/Vidmark. Two businessmen talk about their lives over a poker game every week. Bob Newhart, Gene Wilder, Cloris Leachman, Nancy Walker, Valerie Harper, Rob Reiner. w. d. James L. Brooks.

COMEDY DRAMA: Character Studies; Marriage Drama; Business Life; Men's Films; TV Movies; Time Capsules; Gambling; Forgotten Films; Hidden Gems; Writer-Directors
(Bachelor Party [1957]; That Championship Season)

THX 1138, 1970, 95m, ★★★/$, WB/WB, PG. In the future, people live in cells, controlled by drugs, and can only have sex when it is deemed by the master computer that it is necessary to produce offspring. The children resulting from their joyless unions are then raised collectively by the community. But there are few who want to challenge the system. Robert Duvall, Donald Pleasence, Pedro Colley, Maggie McOmie, Ian Wolfe. w. George Lucas, Walter Murch, d. George Lucas.

SCI-FI: DRAMA: Oppression; Sexual Problems; Futuristic Films; Drugs-Addictions; Babies-Having; Computers; Fighting the System; Rebels; Government as Enemy
(The Handmaid's Tale; Silent Running)

Tick, Tick, Tick . . ., 1969, 100m, ★★/$, MGM/NA. In the South during the 60s, a small town gets its first black sheriff, leading to all sorts of tensions and racial problems when a murder occurs. Jim Brown, George Kennedy, Fredric March, Lynn Carlin, Don Stroud, Clifton James. w. James Lee Barrett, d. Ralph Nelson.

SUSPENSE: DRAMA: MURDER: Police Stories; Race Relations; Detective Stories; Detectives-Police; Black Men; Black Among Whites; Southerns; Forgotten Films; Curiosities
(In the Heat of the Night)

Ticket to Heaven, 1981, 108m, ★★½/$, UAC/MGM-UA, R/S-P. A drifter is love-bombed by a religious cult, and his parents try to "deprogram" him. Nick Mancuso, Saul Rubinek, Meg Foster, Kim Cattrall. w. Ralph L. Thomas, Anne Cameron, NF-adap. Josh Freed (*Moonwebs*), d. Ralph L. Thomas.

DRAMA: Cults; Occult; Mental Illness; Brainwashing; Drifters; Young Men; Parents vs. Children; Saving Someone; 1970s
(Split Image; Synanon; Serial)

Tickle Me, 1965, 90m, ★★/$$, UA/Fox. Elvis goes to the rodeo and sings. Elvis Presley, Julie Adams. d. Norman Taurog.

MUSICALS: ROMANCE: Musical Romance; Rodeos; Singers; Curiosities; Forgotten Films

Tie Me Up! Tie Me Down!, 1989, 102m, ★★★/$$, Orion/Orion, R-X/ES-FN-MN. A mentally unbalanced man attacks a porno actress and ties her up in her apartment, eventually reminding her of the time they met before his stint in the psycho ward, and ultimately convincing her to marry him. Victoria Abril, Antonio Banderas, Loles Leon, Francisco Rabal, Julieta Serrano, Maria Barranco, Rossy De Palma, Lola Cardona. w. d. Pedro Almodovar.

COMEDY DRAMA: ROMANCE: Romantic Drama; Eccentric People; Wild People; Elusive Women; Mental Illness; Rape/Rapists; Erotic Comedy; Erotic Drama; Sexuality; Sexual Kinkiness; Pornography World; Spanish Films; Art Films; Cult Films; Writer-Directors
(Women on the Verge of a Nervous Breakdown; Kika; High Heels)

The Tie That Binds, 1995, 98m, ★★/$$, Hollywood/Hollywood, R/V-P-S. A criminal couple give up their daughter for adoption and then decide they want her back because of what she knows about their crimes, so the new adoptive couple becomes the target of terror. Daryl

Hannah, Keith Carradine, Moira Kelly, Vincent Spano, Julia Devin, Cynda Williams. w. Michael Auerbach, d. Wesley Strick.

SUSPENSE: Children-Adopted; Criminal Couples; Malicious Menaces
(The Hand that Rocks the Cradle; Daddy's Gone A-Hunting)

Tiger Bay, 1959, 105m, ★★★/$$$, Par/Par, G. A little girl (Hayley Mills in her debut) witnesses a foreign sailor kill his girlfriend and manages to steal the murder weapon to impress her friends, but the murderer (Horst Buchholz) comes back to steal her. John Mills, Megs Jenkins, Anthony Dawson, Yvonne Mitchell. w. John Hawkesworth, Shelley Smith, d. J. Lee-Thompson.

SUSPENSE: DRAMA: MURDER: CHILDREN'S: FAMILY: Witness to Murder; Murderer-Debate to Reveal; Kidnappings; Kidnappers-Sympathizing with; Female Protagonists; Child Protagonists; Women in Jeopardy; Children in Jeopardy; British Films; Sleeper Hits; Hidden Gems

REMAKES/RETREADS: The Gun in Betty Lou's Handbag.
(Whistle Down the Wind; Witness; The Gun in Betty Lou's Handbag; Russkies; Eye of the Needle)

Tiger Warsaw, 1988, 90m, ★★/$, Vestron/Vestron, R/S-P-V. A cleaned-up drug addict returns to the town where he shot his father while high, fifteen years before. Patrick Swayze, Barbara Williams, Piper Laurie, Lee Richardson, Mary McDonnell, Bobby DiCicco. w. Roy London, d. Amin Q. Chaudhri.

DRAMA: MELODRAMA: Drugs-Addictions; **MURDER:** Past-Haunted by the; Reunions; Young Men; Starting Over; Coulda Been Good

A Tiger's Tale, 1987, 97m, ★★★/$$, Atlantic/Par, R/S-P-FRN-MRN. A high school boy gets his middle-aged lover pregnant, and they both must deal with the consequences and the stares of the conservative residents of their town-especially since the older woman is the mother of the girl he took to the prom! Ann-Margaret, C. Thomas Howell, Charles Durning, Kelly Preston, William Zabka, Ann Wedgeworth, James Noble. w. d. Peter Douglas, N-adap. Allen Hanney III (*Love and Other Natural Disasters*).

COMEDY: ROMANCE: Romantic Comedy; Romance-Older Women/Younger Men; Teenagers; Babies-

Having; Romance-Triangles; Mothers & Daughters; Parents vs. Children; Coming of Age; Small-town Life; Small-town Scandal; Texas; Writer-Directors
(Grandview USA; Summer of '42)
(Ed: Not so bad, especially due Miss Margret, and much better than Howell's *Grandview* three years before)

Tightrope, 1984, 114m, ★★★/$$$, WB/WB, R/P-S-V-B&G. A detective investigating a string of grizzly rape/murders begins to question his own behavior, almost to the point of wondering whether *he* could be the man he's looking for. Clint Eastwood, Genevieve Bujold, Dan Hedaya, Alison Eastwood, Jennifer Beck. w. d. Richard Tuggle.
SUSPENSE: MYSTERY: MURDER: MURDER MYSTERY: Detective Stories; Detectives-Police; Police Stories; Detectives in Deep; Suspecting Oneself; Murders of Prostitutes; Serial Killers; Gay Men; Sexual Kinkiness; Homophobia; Avenging Death of Someone; New Orleans; Writer-Directors
(The Detective [1968]; Dirty Harry; Angel Heart)
(Ed: Over the top near the end, but otherwise a surprisingly deep look into a seedy, mysterious world, presenting two points of view. A bit of penance from Eastwood for the egregious stereotypes of gays from Dirty Harry?)

Till Death Us Do Part, 1968, 100m, ★★★/$, BL-ABF/NA. A thirty-year slice of the marriage of a cantankerous, racist, working-class Londoner. Warren Mitchell, Dandy Nichols, Anthony Booth, Una Stubbs, Liam Redmond, Bill Maynard, Sam Kydd, Brian Blessed. w. Johnny Speight, d. Norman Cohen.
COMEDY: SATIRE: Bigots; Race Relations; Family Comedy; Fathers-Troublesome; TV Series Movies; British Films; Forgotten Films; Hidden Gems
REMAKE: All in the Family TV SERIES; SEQUEL: The Alf Garnett Saga.
(Look Back in Anger)

Till the Clouds Roll By, 1946, 137m, ★★★/$$$$, MGM/MGM-UA. A musical biopic of the famed early Broadway composer Jerome Kern. Robert Walker, Judy Garland, Lucille Bremer, Van Heflin, Mary Nash, Dinah Shore, Van Johnson, June Allyson, Tony Martin, Kathryn Grayson, Lena Horne, Frank Sinatra, Virginia O'Brien. w. Myles Connolly, Jean Holloway, d. Richard Whorf.

DRAMA: MELODRAMA: Biographies; MUSICALS: Music Movies; Music Composers; Theater Life; Faded Hits (Night and Day; Three Little Words; Rhapsody in Blue)

Till the End of Time, 1946, 105m, ★★1/2/$$, RKO/Turner. In a small Rockwellian American town, two GIs returning from World War II have problems readjusting and getting back together with their girlfriends. Dorothy McGuire, Robert Mitchum, Guy Madison. w. Allen Rivkin, d. Edward Dmytryk.
DRAMA: MELODRAMA: Veterans; World War II-Post Era; War at Home; Small-town Life
(The Best Years of Our Lives; Coming Home)

Tillie and Gus, 1933, 61m, ★★★/$$$, Par/NA. A brother and sister are in danger of losing their inheritance, until their two card-shark uncles amble into town and help them reclaim it (and also win a paddle-boat race). W. C. Fields, Alison Skipworth, Baby Le Roy, Jacqueline Wells, Clifford Jones, Clarence Wilson, Edgar Kennedy, Barton MacLane. w. Walter de Leon, Francis Martin, d. Francis Martin.
COMEDY: Inheritances at Stake; Brothers & Sisters; Greed; Con Artists; Family Comedy; Eccentric People; Forgotten Films; Hidden Gems
(My Little Chickadee; Never Give a Sucker an Even Break)

Tillie's Punctured Romance, 1914, Silent, 73m, ★★★/$$$$, UA/Nos. It's cityslicker vs. farmgirl in this comedy which launched its stars to the big time. Charlie Chaplin, Marie Dressler, Mabel Normand. d. Mack Sennett.
COMEDY: Comedy-Slapstick; Con Artists; City vs. Country; Faded Hits
(The Kid; Modern Times)

Tim, 1979, 98m, ★★1/2/$$, Pisces/Media, R/S. A strong but simple construction worker helping to fix a widow's house develops a relationship with her. Piper Laurie, Mel Gibson, Alwyn Kurtis, Pat Evison, Peter Gwynne, Deborah Kennedy. w. d. Michael Pate, N-adap. Colleen McCullough.
DRAMA: ROMANCE: Romantic Drama; Love-First; Widows; Romance-Older Women/Younger Men; Mentally Disabled; Simple Minds; Wallflowers & Hunks; Australian Films; Curiosities
(Charly; Tea and Sympathy; Summer of '42)

Time After Time, 1979, 112m, ★★★1/2/$$, Orion-WB/WB, PG/S-P-V. In Victorian London, Jack the Ripper takes refuge in H.G. Wells' time machine, traveling to 1979, and it's up to H.G. himself to time travel after him to stop more killings of women-maybe even his own woman. Malcolm McDowell, David Warner, Mary Steenburgen, Charles Cioffi, Kent Williams. w. Nicholas Meyer, Karl Alexander, Steve Hayes, d. Nicholas Meyer.
SCI-FI: ADVENTURE: ROMANCE: Romantic Drama; SUSPENSE: Women in Jeopardy; Murders of Women; Murders of Prostitutes; Detectives-Amateur; Detective Stories; Trail of a Killer; Chase Stories; Race Against Time; Time Travel; Serial Killers; Saving Someone; Revisionist Films; Jack the Ripper; London; San Francisco; Hidden Gems; Cult Films
(Jack's Back; Warlock)

Time Bandits, 1981, 113m, ★★★/$$$, Handmade-ITC-Par/Par, PG/V. A magical band of dwarves invade the suburban London room of a young boy and take him on a time-travelling adventure. John Cleese, Sean Connery, Ian Holm, Ralph Richardson, David Warner, Shelley Duvall, Katherine Helmond, Michael Palin, Peter Vaughan, David Rappaport. w. Michael Palin, Terry Gilliam, d. Terry Gilliam.
ADVENTURE: SCI-FI: Fantasy; Little People; Time Travel; Boys; Magic; Little People-Midgets; Monty Pythoners; Child Protagonists; British Films
(The Adventures of Baron Munchausen [1988])

Time Cop, 1994, 103m, ★★/$$$, Col/Col, PG-13/V-P-FN-MRN. The muscles from Brussels is a policeman who goes back in time to stop a politician from changing history. Jean-Claude Van Damme, Ron Silver, Mia Sara, Bruce McGill. w. Mark Verheiden, d. Peter Hyams.
ACTION: Time Travel; Police Stories; SCI-FI: Politicians; Government Corruption
(The Terminator; Time Runner)

A Time for Loving, 1971, 104m, Ind/NA. Various couples in the same apartment building in Paris have their *tete a tetes*. Joanna Shimkus, Mel Ferrer, Britt Ekland, Philippe Noiret, Lila Kedrova, Robert Dhery, Mark Burns,

Susan Hampshire. w. Jean Anouilh, d. Christopher Miles.

COMEDY DRAMA: ROMANCE: Romantic Comedy; Romantic Drama; Multiple Stories; Interwoven Stories; Marriage Drama; Cheating Men; Cheating Women; Apartment Buildings; Paris

The Time Machine, 1960, 103m, ★★★/$$$$, MGM/MGM-UA. In Victorian England, a scientist builds a time-machine, which after several unsucessful prototypes, finally works. Rod Taylor, Yvette Mimieux, Alan Young, Sebastian Cabot, Tom Helmore, Whit Bissell, Doris Lloyd. w. David Duncan, N-adap. H. G. Wells, d. George Pal. **BSFX**. Oscars: 1-1.
SCI-FI: Time Travel; Victorian Era; Scientists; Experiments; **ACTION: ADVENTURE:** Journies; Faded Hits; Chase Stories
(Time After Time; The Land That Time Forgot)

A Time of Destiny, 1988, 118m, ★★/$, Col/Col, R/S. During World War II, a GI causes tragedy to befall the immigrant family whose daughter he marries. His brother-in-law then vows revenge. William Hurt, Timothy Hutton, Melissa Leo, Franciso Rabal, Concha Hidalgo, Stockard Channing, Megan Follows, Frederick Coffin. w. Gregory Nava, Anna Thomas, d. Gregory Nava.
DRAMA: MELODRAMA: Revenge; Avenging Death of Someone; World War II Stories; Soldiers; Death-Accidental; Men in Conflict; Coulda Been Good; Overlooked at Release; Flops-Major
(El Norte; A Walk in the Clouds)
(Ed: Nothing to say, but it sure looks good. Signalled the beginning of decline for Hurt's career)

The Time of Your Life, 1948, 109m, ★★★/$, Cagney-UA/Nos. A group of eccentric barflies cogitate on the state of the world as they douse themselves at a Frisco Bay bar. James Cagney, William Bendix, Wayne Morris, Jeanne Cagney, Gale Page, Broderick Crawford, James Barton, Ward Bond, Paul Draper, James Lydon, Richard Erdman, Natalie Schaefer. w. Nathaniel Curtis, P-adap. William Saroyan, d. H. C. Potter.
DRAMA: COMEDY DRAMA: Ordinary People Stories; San Francisco; Improvisational Films; Eccentric People; Intellectuals; Curiosities
(Barfly; The Barbary Coast; The Bachelor Party)

Timerider, 1983, 93m, ★★/$, Ind/NA, PG. A biker riding in the desert travels back in time to the wild west where he's used unwittingly in a science experiment. Fred Ward, Belinda Bauer, Peter Coyote, Richard Masur, Ed Lauter, d. William Dear.
ACTION: SCI-FI: Time Travel; Motorcycles; **WESTERNS:** Experiments
(The Philadelphia Experiment)

Time Runner, 1992, 90m, ★★-/VR, New Line/Col. To avoid alien war in the future, a young man travels back to change history. Mark Hamill, Rae Dawn Chong. d. Michael Mazo.
ACTION: SCI-FI: Aliens-Outer Space, Evil; Time Travel
(Terminator; Time Cop)

The Times of Harvey Milk, 1983, 90m, ★★★/$$, Ind/Tapeworm. Story of the gay politician who was assassinated with Mayor Moscone in San Francisco at the height of the gay liberation move-ment. d. Robert Epstein.
Documentaries; True Stories; Politicians; Assassination Plots; Gay Men; Gay Films; San Francisco; Ind Films

A Time to Love & A Time to Die, 1958, 133m, ★★-/$$, U/Barr. A German soldier falls for a girl during the war, but battle tears them apart. John Gavin, Liselotte Pulver, Jock Mahoney, Keenan Wynn, Klaus Kinski, Jim Hutton. N-adap. Erich Maria Remarquez, d. Douglas Sirk.
MELODRAMA: War Stories; World War II Stories; War Brides; Germany; Nazi Stories; **ROMANCE:** Romance-Doomed; Newlyweds; Tearjerkers; Forgotten Films
(A Farewell to Arms; The Sun Also Rises; Teresa)

Time Without Pity, 1957, 88m, ★★★/$, Ind/NA. With his son on trial for murder, a washed-up old alcoholic travels to London to find the evidence that will exonerate him. Michael Redgrave, Alec McCowen, Leo McKern, Renee Houston, Ann Todd, Peter Cushing, Paul Daneman, Lois Maxwell, George Devine, Richard Wordsworth, Joan Plowright. w. Ben Barzman, P-adap. Emlyn Williams (*Someone Waiting*), d. Joseph Losey.
DRAMA: MURDER: Saving Someone; MYSTERY: MURDER MYSTERY: Murder-Clearing Oneself; Accused Unjustly; Alcoholics; Fathers & Sons; British Films; Forgotten Films; Curiosities
(In the Name of the Father; Odd Man Out; The Informer)

Timebomb, 1991, 96m, ★★1/2/$, MGM/MGM-UA, R/V-P. An outspoken left-wing politician is the subject of a covert CIA assassination attempt, and a former hitman and watchmaker is the only man who can stop it. Michael Beihn, Patsy Kensit, Tracy Scroggins, Robert Culp, Richard Jordan, Raymond St. Jacques. w. d. Avi Nesher.
ACTION: SUSPENSE: Hitmen; Assassination Plots; CIA Agents; Political Drama; Conspiracy; Race Against Time; Saving Someone; Good Premise Unfulfilled; Coulda Been Great; Overlooked at Release; Writer-Directors
(The Manchurian Candidate; Winter Kills)

Times Square, 1980, 113m, ★★/$, EMI-U/MCA-U, PG/P. Against the back-drop of the New York "punk" scene, two misfit kids form a club act and take off. Tim Curry, Trini Alvarado, Robin Johnson, Peter Coffield, Herbert Berghof, David Margulies. w. Jacob Brackman, Alan Moyle, Leanne Unger, d. Alan Moyle.
MUSICALS: Music Movies; Fame-Rise to; Rock Stars; 1980s; New York Life; Curiosities; Overlooked at Release; Forgotten Films
(Fame; Beat Street)

The Tin Drum, 1979, 142m, ★★★1/2/$$$, UA/MGM-UA, R/S-B&G-FFN-MRN. A little boy wishes he'd never grow up and has an accident which stunts his growth, but it can't stop the deteriora-tion of his mother's life and the surreal German world he has to continue in—as a dwarf in a circus. David Bennent, Mario Adorf, Angela Winkler, Daniel Olbrychski. w. Jean-Claude Carriere, Franz Seitz, Volker Schlondorff, N-adap. Gunter Grass. **BFLFilm**. Oscars: 1-1.
DRAMA: Art Films; Surrealism; Little People; Psychological Drama; Coming of Age; Nervous Breakdowns; Suicidal Tendencies; Mental Illness; Boys; Child Protagonists; World War II Era; German Films; Germany; Nazi Stories; Little People-Midgets; Cult Films; Circus Life; Hidden Gems
(I Don't Want to Talk About It; Village of the Damned; Children of the Damned)
(Ed: Weird, but compelling and haunting)

Tin Men, 1987, 112m, ★★★/$$$, Touchstone/Touchstone, PG/P. Two scrap-metal salesmen in sixties Baltimore com-pete and feud in business and life in general. Richard Dreyfuss, Danny DeVito, Barbara Hershey, John Mahoney, Jackie Gayle, Stanley Brock. w. d. Barry Levinson.

COMEDY DRAMA: Feuds; Friendships-Male; Men Fighting Over Women; Marriage on the Rocks; Nerds & Babes; Salesmen; Baltimore; 1950s; Writer-Directors

(Diner; The Feud; Avalon; Wiseguys)

Tin Pan Alley, 1940, 95m, ★★★1/2/$$$, 20th/Fox. Two showgirls vie for the attentions of the same composer as they perform throughout the country during World War I and after. Alice Faye, Betty Grable, John Payne, Jack Oakie, Allen Jenkins, Esther Ralston, The Nicholas Brothers, John Loder, Elisha Cook, Jr. w. Robert Ellis, Helen Logan, d. Walter Lang.

BOScore. Oscars: 1-1.

MUSICALS: ROMANCE: Musical Romance; Theater Life; Dance Movies; Dancers; Singers; World War I Era; Vaudeville; Women Fighting Over Men; Music Composers; Faded Hits

The Tin Star, 1957, 93m, ★★★/$$$, Par/Par. The young greenhorn sheriff of a wild West town solicits the help of an older gun-for-hire, a former sheriff himself. Henry Fonda, Anthony Perkins, Betsy Palmer, Michel Ray, Neville Brand, John McIntire. w. Dudley Nichols (BOScr), Barney Slater, Joel Kane (BOStory), d. Anthony Mann. Oscars: 2-0.

WESTERNS: Police Stories; Marshals; Gunfighters; Hitmen; Mentors and Proteges; Thieves; Bank Robberies; Manhunts; Faded Hits

(Warlock [1958]; High Noon; Gunfight at the OK Corral)

'Tis a Pity She's a Whore (*Addio, Fratello Crudele*), 1971, 109m, ★★★/$, Ind/Academy, R/S. A man cuckolded by his brother-in-law goes mad with jealousy. Charlotte Rampling, Oliver Tobias, Fabio Testi, Antonio Falsi, Rik Battaglia, Angela Luce, Rino Imperio. w. Giuseppe Patroni Griffi, Alfio Valdarnini, Carlo Carunchio, P-adap. John Ford, d. Giuseppe Patroni Griffi.

DRAMA: TRAGEDY: Cheating Women; Babies-Having; Jealousy; Revenge; Revenge on Cheaters; Romance with Lover's Friend; Prostitutes-Ordinary People Turned; In-Laws-Troublesome; Italian Films; Classic Literary Adaptations; Forgotten Films; Stagelike Films

Titanic, 1953, 98m, ★★★/$$$, 20th/Fox. The famous shipwreck of 1912 is chronicled through the eyes of various passengers on board. Clifton Webb, Barbara Stanwyck, Robert Wagner, Audrey Dalton, Thelma Ritter, Brian Aherne, Richard Basehart, Allyn Joslyn. w. Charles Brackett, Walter Reisch, Richard Breen (**BScr**), d. Jean Negulesco. BB&WArt. Oscars: 2-1.

DRAMA: MELODRAMA: TRAGEDY: Disaster Stories; Shipwrecks; Ships; True Stories; Multiple Stories; Titanic Stories; Drowning

(A Night to Remember [1958]; The Last Voyage; The Unsinkable Molly Brown)

The Titfield Thunderbolt, 1952, 84m, ★★★/$$, Ealing-EMI/NA. A railroad on its last legs is saved by a local British community as they chip in to take it over themselves. Stanley Holloway, George Relph, John Gregson, Godfrey Tearle, Edie Martin, Naunton Wayne, Gabrielle Brune, Hugh Griffith, Sidney James. w. T.E.B. Clarke, d. Charles Crichton.

COMEDY: FARCE: Social Satire; Mortgage Drama; Ensemble Films; Trains; Small-town Life; Fighting the System; Time Capsules; British Films; England; Hidden Gems; Forgotten Films

(End of the Line; It Happened to Jane)

To Be or Not to Be, 1942, 99m, ★★★★/$$$, Korda-UA/MGM-UA. An acting troupe in Poland during the war subvert from within by doing farcical takeoffs on the Nazis in their plays. Jack Benny, Carole Lombard, Robert Stack, Stanley Ridges, Felix Bressart, Lionel Atwill, Sig Rumann, Tom Dugan, Charles Halton. w. Edwin Justus Mayer, Ernst Lubitsch, Melchior Lengyel, d. Ernst Lubitsch. BOScore. Oscars: 1-0.

To Be or Not to Be, 1983, 107m, ★★1/2/$$, 20th/CBS-Fox, PG/P. Remake of the above, much less fun or funny. Mel Brooks, Anne Bancroft, Tim Matheson, Charles Durning (BSActor), Jose Ferrer, George Gaynes, Christopher Lloyd, James Haake. w. Thomas Meehan, Ronnie Graham, d. Alan Johnson. Oscars: 1-0.

COMEDY: FARCE: Actors; Actresses; Theater Life; Nazi Stories; Hitler; World War II Stories; Europeans-Eastern; Spoofs; Putting on a Show

(The Great Dictator; Cabaret)

To Catch a Killer, 1992, 95m, ★★★/$$$, Ind/Worldvision. Story of a serial killer of young men, John Wayne

Gacy, who moonlighted as a clown and painted his victims as well. Brian Dennehy (Emmy winner), Michael Riley, Margot Kidder, Meg Foster. d. Eric Till.

DRAMA: Serial Killers; True Stories; Psycho Killers; Circus Life; **MURDER:** Murders-One by One; Gay Men; Murders of Homosexuals; TV Movies

(Chiefs; Silence of the Lambs; The Atlanta Child Murders)

To Catch a Thief, 1955, 97m, ★★★1/2/$$$$, Par/Par. A suave ex-cat burglar on the Riviera meets up with a beautiful American socialite whose mother's jewels are stolen at the same time as a rash of burglaries with his trademarks happen-will she love him or catch him? Cary Grant, Grace Kelly, Jessie Royce Landis, John Williams, Charles Vanel, Brigitte Auber. w. John Michael Hayes, N-adap. David Dodge, d. Alfred Hitchcock. BCCin, BCArt, BCCostume. Oscars: 3-1.

SUSPENSE: ROMANCE: MYSTERY: Romantic Drama; Dangerous Romance; Dangerous Men; Accused Unjustly; Framed?; Thieves; Jewel Thieves; Riviera Life; Cat and Mouse Stories; Rich People; Sexy Men; Sexy Women; Saving Oneself; Hitchcockian

(The Thief Who Came to Dinner; Arsene Lupin)

To Dance with the White Dog, 1994, 98m, ★★★/$$$$, Hallmark-CBS/Republic. When an elderly man's wife dies, a beautiful white dog comes to visit him and leads him on a journey, possibly embodying the spirit of his wife. Hume Cronyn (Emmy winner), Jessica Tandy, Christine Baranski, Amy Wright, Esther Rolle. w. Susan Cooper, d. Glenn Jordan.

DRAMA: MELODRAMA: Death-Dealing with; Widowers; Dogs; Illusions/Hallucinations; Possessions; Elderly Men; Romance-Elderly; Female Screenwriters; TV Movies

To Die For, 1995, 103m, ★★★1/2/$$$, 20th/Fox, R/S-P-V. A ruthless weather girl talks a young lover and his pals into killing her husband, but will her new-found celebrity get her off the hook and keep her out of the chair? Nicole Kidman (Golden Globe winner), Matt Dillon, Joaquin Phoenix, Alison Folland, Casey Affleck, Illeana Douglas, Dan Hedaya, Holland Taylor. w. Buck Henry, NF-adap. Joyce Maynard, d. Gus Van Sant.

COMEDY: SATIRE: Black Comedy; Comedy-Morbid; MURDER: Murder of Spouse; Murder-Coerced to; TV Life (The Positively True Adventures of the Alleged Texas Cheerleader Murdering Mom; Murder in New Hampshire; Pretty Poison)

To Each His Own, 1946, 100m, ★★★/ $$$, Par/Par. After the war, a woman who was forced to give up her illegitimate son twenty years before runs into him in London. He's now a handsome young soldier who knows nothing of her and thinks his adoptive parents are his own. Olivia de Havilland (**BActress**), John Lund, Roland Culver, Mary Anderson, Philip Terry, Bill Goodwin, Virginia Welles, Virginia Horne. w. Charles Brackett (**BOStory**), Jacques Thery, d. Mitchell Leisen. Oscars: 2-1.

DRAMA: MELODRAMA: Tearjerkers; ROMANCE: Romantic Drama; Mothers & Sons; Children-Long Lost; Orphans; Children-Adopted; Mothers Alone; Mothers-Unwed; World War I Era; World War II Era; Women's Films England; Faded Hits; Forgotten Films; Female Protagonists

(White Banners; Stella Dallas; Madame X)

To Find a Man, 1971, 93m, ★★1/2/$, Col/Col, R/S. A rich young woman is disowned by her conservative family after becoming pregnant, and seeks help from a nice guy. Pamela Martin, Darrell O'Connor, Lloyd Bridges, Phyllis Newman, Tom Ewell, Tom Bosley. w. Arnold Schulman, N-adap. S. J. Wilson, d. Buzz Kulik.

MELODRAMA: ROMANCE: Romantic Drama; Babies-Having; Mothers-Unwed; Ostracism; Decisions-Big; Marriage of Convenience; Rich People; Riches to Rags; Young Women; Female Protagonists; Forgotten Films; Time Capsules

(Kotch; Blue Denim; A Taste of Honey)

To Forget Venice, 1980, 90m, ★★★/$$, Col/Col, R/S. Three gay men and a lesbian have a unique friendship situation as they enter a midlife crisis on a vacation. Erland Josephson, Mariangela Melato, David Pontremoli. d. Franco Brusati. **BFLFilm**. Oscars: 1-1.

DRAMA: COMEDY DRAMA: Alternative Lifestyles; Gay Men; Lesbians; Friendship Between Sexes; Marriage Drama; Vacations; Venice; Italian Films; Hidden Gems

To Have and Have Not, 1945, 100m, ★★★1/2/$$$, WB/WB. Conscience eeks out from beneath the surface of a cynical American boat captain in Martinique, when he has to take a moral stand against the Nazis, although he claims not to care as long as he's paid. Humphrey Bogart, Lauren Bacall, Walter Brennan, Hoagy Carmichael, Dolores Moran, Sheldon Leonard, Dan Seymour, Marcel Dalio. w. Jules Furthman, William Faulkner, N-adap. Ernest Hemingway, d. Howard Hawks.

DRAMA: ROMANCE: Political Drama; Romance-Older Men/Younger Women; Guilty Conscience; Nazi Stories; Patriotic Films; Decisions-Big; Men Proving Themselves; Classic Literary Adaptations

REMAKES: The Breaking Point, Gun Runners.

(Key Largo; Casablanca; The Breaking Point)

To Hell and Back, 1955, 106m, ★★1/2/$$$, U-I/MCA-U. A biopic of Audie Murphy, starring World War II's most decorated hero as himself. Audie Murphy, Marshall Thompson, Charles Drake, Gregg Palmer, Jack Kelly, Paul Picerni, Susan Kohner. w. Gil Doud, NF-adap. Audie Murphy, d. Jesse Hibbs.

DRAMA: Hollywood Biographies; War Stories; World War II Stories; War Battles; Heroes-Ordinary; Biographies; Soldiers; True Stories; Autobiographical Stories

To Kill a Clown, 1971, 104m, ★★/$, Palomar-20th/Media, R/S-V. A mild-mannered artist moves with his wife to a quiet island off the New England coast, where they are menaced by a Vietnam vet with a pack of wild dogs. Alan Alda, Blythe Danner, Heath Lamberts, Eric Clavering. w. George Bloomfield, I.C. Rappaport, N-adap. Algis Budgys (Master of the Hounds), d. George Bloomfield.

SUSPENSE: HORROR: Malicious Menaces; Beach Movies; Nightmare Vacations; Vietnam Veterans; Unintentionally Funny; Camp; Evil Men; Forgotten Films; Coulda Been Good

(Straw Dogs; Whispers in the Dark; W)

(Ed: Has its moments, but whenever Alan Alda plays a psycho, it's funny)

To Kill a Mockingbird, 1962, 129m, ★★★/$$$$, U-I/MCA-U. The story of a young girl (Mary Badham, BSActress) in Depression-era Alabama whose lawyer father (Gregory Peck, **BActor**) defends a

black man accused of raping a white trash woman, and the girl may become the target of revenge by the woman's family. Rosemary Murphy, Brock Peters, narrated by Kim Stanley. w. Horton Foote (**BAScr**), N-adap. Harper Lee, d. Ricahrd Mulligan (BDirector). BPicture, BOScore, BB&WCin, **BB&WArt**. Oscars: 9-3.

DRAMA: CHILDREN'S: Courtroom Drama; Rape/Rapists; Black vs. White; Race Relations; Bigots; Liars; Accused Unjustly; Framed?; Girls; Brothers & Sisters; Ordinary People Stories; Fathers & Daughters; Southerns; Childhood; Depression Era; Memories; Narrated Films; Pulitzer Prize Adaptations; Child Protagonists; Female Protagonists

(A Passage to India; Trial)

To Kill a Priest, 1988, 113m, ★★1/2/$, Col/Col. A Polish priest, supportive of the Solidarity movement, gets incarcerated by the corrupt local police, and his comrades come to his defense. Christopher Lambert, Ed Harris, Joss Ackland, Tim Roth, Timothy Spall, Peter Postlethwaite, Cherie Lunghi, Joanne Whalley, David Suchet. w. Agnieszka Holland, Jean-Yves Pitoun, d. Agnieszka Holland.

DRAMA: Biographies; Rebels; Priests; Religion; Communists; Oppression; Police Corruption; Police Brutality; True or Not?; True Stories; Polish Films; Europeans-Eastern; Overlooked at Release

(Man of Iron; Romero)

To Live and Die in L.A., 1985, 116m, ★★★/$$, MGM/MGM-UA, R/S-EV-EP-FFN-MRN. A counterfeiter kills the wrong man, and the man's best friend, a secret service agent, comes after the criminal with a vengeance. William L. Petersen, Willem Dafoe, John Pankow, Debra Feuer, Dean Stockwell, John Turturro, Darlane Fleugel. w. William Friedkin, Gerald Petievich, N-adap. Gerald Petievich, d. William Friedkin.

ACTION: Police Stories; Detective Stories; Detectives-Police; Chase Stories; Drugs-Dealing; Counterfeiters; Avenging Death of Someone; Revenge; Cops-Vigilante; Secret Service; Los Angeles; 1980s

(The French Connection; Manhunter; Deep Cover)

To Paris with Love, 1954, 78m, ★★★/$$, GFD/NA. A young man and his widowed father search for brides for themselves and each other on a trip to

Paris. Alec Guinness, Vernon Gray, Odile Versois, Jacques Francois, Elina Labourdette, Austin Trevor. w. Robert Buckner, d. Robert Hamer.
MELODRAMA: ROMANCE: Romantic Drama; Romantic Comedy; Fathers & Sons; Matchmakers; Paris; British Films; Hidden Gems; Forgotten Films; Curiosities
(Light in the Piazza; Three Coins in the Fountain)
(Ed: Unexpectedly pretty and rather slight for such talent)
To Sir with Love, 1967, 105m, ★★★/ $$$$, Col/RCA-Col. A black teacher gets a job in a rough London neighborhood, where he encounters racism and roudiness, and also a young white girl who has a crush on him. Sidney Poitier, Christian Roberts, Judy Geeson, Suzy Kendall, Lulu, Faith Brook, Geoffrey Bayldon, Patricia Routledge. w. d. James Clavell.
DRAMA: MELODRAMA: ROMANCE: Romance with Teacher; Infatuations; Black Among Whites; Teachers; Teachers & Students; Inner City Life; Teachers in Inner City; High School Life; British Films; London; Writer-Directors
SEQUEL: 1996, TV Movie
(Dangerous Minds; Blackboard Jungle)
To Sleep with Anger, 1990, 102m, ★★★/$, Sony/Sony, R/P. A middle-class black family living in Los Angeles is visited by a southern relative, who brings them back in touch with the place they tried to forget when they moved "onward and upward." Danny Glover, Paul Butler, Mary Alice, Carl Lumbly, Vonetta McGee, Richard Brooks, Sheryl Lee Ralph, Ethel Ayler, Julius Harris. w. d. Charles Burnett.
COMEDY DRAMA: Black Comedy; Black Casts; Family Drama; Family Comedy; Black Men; Social Drama; Social Satire; Rags to Riches; Family Heritage; Los Angeles; 1950s; Black Screenwriters; Black Directors; Writer-Directors; Ind Films
(A Raisin in the Sun)
To Wong Foo, Thanks for Everything, Julie Newmar, 1995, 108m, ★★1/2/$$$, U/MCA-U, PG-13/P-S-V. Three drag queens hit the road for a beauty pageant but are besieged by ignoramuses in the towns they stop in and the fact that one thinks he/she may have killed a potential rapist. Wesley Snipes, Patrick Swayze, John Leguizamo,

Stockard Channing, Blythe Danner, Arliss Howard, Jack London, Quentin Crisp, Joey Arias, Chris Penn, Melinda Dillon, Beth Grant, Julie Newmar, RuPaul. w. Douglas Carter Beane, d. Beeban Kidron.
COMEDY: Ensembles-Male; Road Movies; Road Movies-Guys in Convertibles; Rednecks; City vs. Country; Gay Men; Rapists; Transvestites; Beauty Pageants; Female Directors; Comic Flipside of Thelma and Louise.
(Boys on the Side; Priscilla; Queen of the Desert; Paris is Burning; The Birdcage)
(Ed: What could have been brilliant is only a passable pastiche of cliches, most coincidentally from more successful films in the same year–*Boys* and *Priscilla*)
The Toast of New Orleans, 1950, 97m, ★★/$$, MGM/MGM-UA. A young girl from the swamps of Louisiana becomes an opera star in New Orleans. Kathryn Grayson, David Niven, Mario Lanza, J. Carroll Naish, James Mitchell, Richard Hageman, Clinton Sundberg, Sig Arno. w. Sy Gomberg, George Wells, d. Norman Taurog.
MELODRAMA: ROMANCE: Opera; Opera Singers; New Orleans; Costume Drama; Rags to Riches; Fame-Rise to
The Toast of New York, 1937, 109m, ★★★/$$$, RKO/Turner. A traveling con artist/salesman makes his way up the ladder in the early days of Wall Street. Edward Arnold, Cary Grant, Frances Farmer, Jack Oakie, Donald Meek, Clarence Kolb, Thelma Leeds. w. Dudley Nichols, John Twist, Joel Sayre, d. Rowland V. Lee.
DRAMA: Power-Rise to; Biographies; Con Artists; Salesmen; Stock Brokers; Wall Street; Time Capsules; New York Life; 1800s
Tobacco Road, 1941, 84m, ★★★1/2/ $$$, 20th/NA. Georgia dirt farmers fight to save their land from the financiers, amid farcical stories of their personal lives. Charley Grapewin, Elizabeth Patterson, Dana Andrews, Gene Tierney, Marjorie Rambeau, Ward Bond, William Tracy, Zeffie Tilbury, Slim Summerville, Grant Mitchell, Russell Simpson. w. Nunnally Johnson, P-adap. Jack Kirkland, N-adap. Erskine Caldwell, d. John Ford.
COMEDY: COMEDY DRAMA: Ordinary People Stories; Poor People; Mortgage Drama; Save the Farm; Fighting the

System; Rednecks; Rural Life; Southerns; Georgia; Forgotten Films; Hidden Gems; Faded Hits
(God's Little Acre; The Southerner; L'il Abner)
(Ed: Based on the blockbuster novel and play, the film may seem dated, but is still entertaining)
Tobruk, 1967, 110m, ★★/$$, U/MCA-U. A British major in North Africa during World War II gets together a troop of German Jews to bomb a Nazi fueling station. Rock Hudson, George Peppard, Nigel Green, Guy Stockwell, Jack Watson, Liam Redmond, Leo Gordon, Norman Rossington. w. Leo V. Gordon, d. Arthur Hiller.
ACTION: Sabotage; War Stories; World War II Stories; Spies; Africa; Desert Settings; Jewish People; Nazi Stories; British People; Forgotten Films
(Force Ten from Navarone; Khartoum; The Desert Rats; Raid on Rommel; The Hornet's Nest)
Today We Live, 1933, 113m, ★★/$$$, MGM/MGM-UA. A rich girl is pursued by three suitors, all of whom end up having to fight in World War I, leading to tragedy. Joan Crawford, Gary Cooper, Robert Young, Francot Tone, Roscoe Karns, Louise Closser Hale, Rollo Lloyd. w. Edith Fitzgerald, Dwight Taylor, William Faulkner, SS-adap. William Faulkner (*Turnabout*), d. Howard Hawks.
MELODRAMA: ROMANCE: Romantic Drama; Tearjerkers; **TRAGEDY:** Romance-Triangles; Romance Doomed; World War I Stories; War at Home
Together Again, 1944, 93m, ★★/$$, Col/NA. A widow has a statue made of her late husband, the town mayor, to stand in the square of their quaint New England town but eventually learns to let go. Charles Boyer, Irene Dunne, Charles Coburn, Mona Freeman, Jerome Courtland, Elizabeth Patterson, Charles Dingle, Walter Baldwin. w. Virginia Van Upp, F. Hugh Herbert, d. Charles Vidor.
COMEDY DRAMA: ROMANCE: Romantic Comedy; Widows; Death-Dealing with; Forgotten Films; Female Screenwriters
Tokyo Decadence, 1991, 92m, ★★★/ $$, NC-17/ES-FFN-MN. A hooker into S&M surprises herself by falling for a john, but can't find him. Miho Nikaido, Tenmei Kano. w. d. N-adap. Ryu Murakami.

DRAMA: Erotic Drama; Searches; Prostitutes-High Class; Sexual Kinkiness; Drugs-Addictions; Female Protagonists; Japanese Films; Art Films
(A Taxing Woman)

Tokyo Joe, 1949, 88m, ★★/$$, Col. An American is forced to leave behind his wife and his nightclub in Tokyo during the war. Afterward, he returns to get them both back, but finds things have changed. Humphrey Bogart, Florence Marly, Alexander Knox, Sessue Hayakawa, Lora Lee Michel, Jerome Courtland. w. Cyril Hume, Bertram Millhauser, d. Stuart Heisler.

DRAMA: MELODRAMA: ROMANCE: Romantic Drama; Marriage Drama; Romance-Interracial; Americans Abroad; Romance-Doomed; Social Drama; Ahead of its Time; Japanese as Enemy; Japanese People
(Come See the Paradise; Green Eyes)

Tokyo Pop, 1988, 99m, ★★/$, Fries-Lorimar/WB, R/S-P. A New York female punk singer on tour in Japan falls in love with a Japanese rocker. Carrie Hamilton, Yutaka Tadokoro, Daisuke Oyama, Hiroshi Kabayashi, Hiroshi Sugita, Satoshi Kanai. w. Fran Rubel Kuzui, Lynn Grossman, d. Fran Rubel Kuzui.

COMEDY DRAMA: ROMANCE: Romantic Comedy; Singers; Feisty Females; Rock Stars; Dreams; Romance-Interracial; Americans Abroad; Japanese People; Japan; Female Protagonists

Tokyo Story, 1953, 135m, ★★★½/$$, Shochiku/New Yorker. An aging couple from a small town in Japan excitedly prepare to visit their children in Tokyo, but are disappointed when they arrive and find they have no time for them. Chisu Ryu, Chieko Higashiyama, Setsuko Hara, Haruko Sugimura, Nobuo Nakamura, So Yamamura. w. Kogo Noda, Yasujiro Ozu, d. Yasujiro Ozu.

COMEDY DRAMA: Social Satire; Social Drama; Family Comedy; Family Drama; Generation Gaps; City vs. Country; Elderly People; Grandmothers; Grandfathers; Japanese Films; Japanese People; Hidden Gems; Time Capsules

Tom and Huck, 1995, 93m, ★★½/$$, Disney/Disney, PG/V. A mishmash of the Tom Sawyer and Huckleberry Finn tales, mostly built around searching with Injun Joe for the treasure. Jonathan Taylor Thomas, Brad Renfro, Eric Schweig, Amy Wright, Rachael Leigh Cook. w. Stephen

Sommers and David Loughery, N-adap. Mark Twain (*The Adventures of Tom Sawyer*), d. Peter Hewitt.

COMEDY: ADVENTURE: Comic Adventure; **CHILDREN'S:** Boys; Revisionist Films
(The Adventures of Tom Sawyer; The Adventures of Huckleberry Finn)

Tom & Viv, 1994, 123m, ★★★/$, Miramax/Miramax, PG-13/S. American writer T. S. Eliot's secretive love affair with an Englishwoman named Vivian, whose erratic behavior began to undermine the relationship. Willem Dafoe, Miranda Richardson (BActress). d. Brian Gilbert. Oscars: 1-0.

DRAMA: ROMANCE: Romantic Drama; Biographies; Writers; American Abroad; Eccentric People; Romance-Clandestine; Romance-On Again/Off Again; British Films
(Tender is the Night; Beloved Infidel)

Tom, Dick and Harry, 1941, 86m, ★★★/$$$, RKO/Turner. A popular girl can't decide which boyfriend to choose from among her three suitors. Ginger Rogers, Burgess Meredith, Alan Marshal, George Murphy, Phil Silvers, Joe Cunningham, Jane Seymour, Lenore Lonergan. w. Paul Jarrico (BOScr), d. Garson Kanin. Oscars: 1-0.

COMEDY: COMEDY DRAMA: ROMANCE: Romantic Comedy; Men Fighting Over Women; Romance-Triangles; Screwball Comedy; Misunderstandings; Decisions-Big; Small-town Life; American Myth; Hidden Gems; Faded Hits
(The Primrose Path; Once Upon a Honeymoon)

Tom Horn, 1979, 97m, ★★½/$$, WB/WB, R/V-S. A former cavalry rider, hard on his luck, takes a job as a detective, but gets framed for murder. Steve McQueen, Linda Evans, Richard Farnsworth, Billy Green Bush, Slim Pickens, Elisha Cook, Jr. w. Thomas McGuane, Bid Shrake, NF-adap. Tom Horn's diaries, d. William Wiard.

WESTERNS: DRAMA: Detective Stories; **MURDER:** Accused Unjustly; Framed?; **TRAGEDY:** Executions; True Stories; True or Not?; Autobiographical Stories; Biographies
(Nevada Smith; Junior Bonner)

Tom Jones, 1963, 131m, ★★★★/$$$$$, UA/Goldwyn, S. The bawdy tale of the wayward bastard Tom Jones (Albert

Finney, BActor) and his many women, one of whom may or may not be his long-lost mother and the other who may be a cousin, but will they figure it all out and save him before he's hanged? Hugh Griffith (BSActor), Joyce Redman (BSActress), Diane Cilento (BSActress), Suzannah York (BSActress). w. John Osborne (BAScr), N. adap. Henry Fielding, d. Tony Richardson (BDirector). BPicture, BOscore, BCArt. Oscars: 10-4.

COMEDY: FARCE: ROMANCE: Romantic Comedy; Erotic Comedy; Identities-Mistaken; Misunderstandings; Mix-Ups; Playboys; Cheating Men; Executions; Race Against Time; Young Men; Sexy Men; Orphans; Road Movies; Children-Longlost; Clever Plots & Endings; British Films; Restoration Period; Blockbusters; Hidden Gems

SEQUEL: Joseph Andrews
(Joseph Andrews; Hotel Paradiso; The Amorous Adventures of Moll Flanders)

Tom Sawyer, 1973, 103m, ★★★/$$$, Reader's Digest-UA/MGM-UA, G. The famed Twain hero whose adventures on the Mississippi with Huckleberry Finn have inspired boys all over the world (with musical numbers). Johnnie Whitaker, Celeste Holm, Warren Oates, Jeff East, Jodie Foster. w/m/ly Richard and Robert Sherman, d. Don Taylor. BOSong, BOSong. Oscars: 2-0.

ADVENTURE: COMEDY: COMEDY DRAMA: CHILDREN'S: FAMILY: MUSICALS: Musical Comedy; Comic Adventure; Rebels; Boys; Nuisances; Children-Brats; Child Protagonists; Runaways; Rescue Drama; Children in Jeopardy; Classic Literary Adaptations; Faded Hits
(The Adventures of Tom Sawyer; The Adventures of Huckleberry Finn; Tom and Huck)

Tom Thumb, 1958, 98m, ★★★/$$$, MGM/MGM-UA. Thieves meet their match in a dwarflike, tiny superhero who lives in the forest. Russ Tamblyn, Jessi Matthews, Peter Sellers, Terry Thomas, Alan Young, June Thorburn, Bernard Miles. w. Ladislas Fodor, d. George Pal.

CHILDREN'S: FAMILY: Fantasy; Fairy Tales; Little People; Heroes-Unlikely; Thieves; Faded Hits
(Darby O'Gill and the Little People)

The Tomb of Ligea, 1964, 81m, ★★★/$$, AIP/HBO. In the Victorian Era, a nobleman keeps his wife's lifeless body

and turns her into a cat, then Lady Rowena. Vincent Price, Elizabeth Shepherd, John Westbrook, Oliver Johnston, Richard Johnson, Derek Francis. w. Robert Towne, SS-adap. Edgar Allan Poe, d. Roger Corman.
HORROR: Fantasy; Magic; Buried Alive; Humans into Animals; Cats; Dead-Back from the; Victorian Era
(The House of Usher; Spirits of the Dead)

Tombstone, 1993, 130m, ★★/$$, Hollywood/Hollywood, R/EV. Another Wyatt Earp tale, retelling the gunfight at the O.K. Corral and his relationship with Doc Holliday. Kurt Russell, Val Kilmer, Michael Biehn, Sam Elliott, Dana Delaney, Bill Paxton, Stephen Lang, Jason Priestley, Powers Boothe, Billy Zane. w. Kevin Jarre, d. George Cosmatos.
WESTERNS: Westerns-Neo; Wyatt Earp; Revisionist Films; Men in Conflict; Gunfighters; Police Stories; All-Star Casts
(Wyatt Earp [same year]; Gunfight at the O.K. Corral)

Tommy, 1975, 108m, ★★★1/2/$$$, Col/RCA-Col, R/S-P. After a traumatic event, a boy becomes willingly deaf, dumb, and blind. The only way he can "communicate" is through a pinball machine, which he can play better than anyone. He of course becomes a rock messiah, and eventually learns to see, hear, and speak again. Roger Daltrey, Ann-Margret (BActress), Oliver Reed, Elton John, Eric Clapton, Keith Moon. w. Ken Russell, (Rock Opera)-adap. Pete Townshend and the Who, d. Ken Russell. BAScore. Oscars: 2-0.
MUSICALS: Rock Stars; Rock Opera; Music Movies; Surrealism; Avant-Garde Films; Music Video Style; Ahead of its Time; Fantasy; Biographies-Fictional; Fame-Rise to; Asylums; Mental Illness; Oedipal Stories; World War II Stories; Episodic Stories; Mothers & Sons; England; British Films; Coming of Age; Boys; Cult Films
(Pink Floyd, The Wall; Quadrophenia)
(Ed: A big hit on Broadway, 1993, as a stage musical, though it works very well on screen)

Tommy Boy, 1995, 95m, ★1/2/$$, Par/Par, PG-13/P-S. When overweight slob frat-rat Tommy finally gets out of college after almost a decade, he returns to his hometown where his father owns the last open factory. But when Dad dies, son must save the business-with the aid of his pals

from college who are no more competent than he is. Chris Farley, David Spade, Rob Lowe, Bo Derek, Brian Dennehy, Julie Warner, Sean McCann. w. Bonnie Turner, Terry Turner, Fred Wolf, d. Peter Segal.
COMEDY: Party Movies; Fraternity Life; Fathers & Sons; Factory Life; Men Proving Themselves; Female Screenwriters; Bathroom Humor; Salesmen; Saturday Night Live Movies
(The Black Sheep; Beverly Hills Ninja; Billy Madison; Wayne's World)

The Tommyknockers, 1993, 120m, ★★-/$$$, ABC/Vidmark. Writers in the woods of Maine are terrorized by UFOs that begin to possess people. Jimmy Smits, Marg Helgenberger, Joanna Cassidy, E.G. Marshall, Traci Lords, Cliff DeYoung. w. Larry Cohen, N-adap. Stephen King, d. John Power.
HORROR: SCI-FI: UFOs: Aliens-Outer Space, Evil; Missing Persons; Possessions; Small-town Life; Writers; Stephen King; TV Movies; Miniseries
(It; The Stand; The Langoliers)

Tomorrow Is Forever, 1946, 105m, ★★-/$$, MGM/MGM-UA. When her husband is presumed dead in World War I, she remarries, but guess who shows up and isn't too happy. Claudette Colbert, Orson Welles, George Brent, Natalie Wood. d. Irving Pichel.
MELODRAMA: ROMANCE: Marriage Drama; Romance-Triangles; Bigamy; Dead-Back from the; World War I Stories; Soldiers; Men Fighting Over Women
(My Favorite Wife; Coming Home)

Tonight and Every Night, 1945, 92m, ★★1/2/$$, Col/Col. During the Blitz, London cabaret dancers prove the "show must go on" and live and love their way through. Rita Hayworth, Lee Bowman, Janet Blair, Marc Platt, Leslie Brooks, Dusty Anderson, Florence Bates, Ernest Cossart. w. Lesser Samuels, Abem Finkel, P-adap. Lesley Storm (Heart of a City), d. Lesley Storm.
MUSICALS: Dance Movies; Dancers; World War II Stories; War Stories; Theater Life; England; Female Protagonists; Forgotten Films
(Cover Girl; Gilda; Down to Earth)

Tony Rome, 1967, 111m, ★★★/$$$, 20th/CBS-Fox, R/V-S. In Miami, a sleazy storefront detective hires himself out as a guard for a rich man's daughter, but gets more than he bargained for when a murder occurs. Frank Sinatra, Jill St. John,

Richard Conte, Gena Rowlands, Simon Oakland, Jeffrey Lynn, Lloyd Bochner, Sue Lyon. w. Richard L. Breen, N-adap. Marvin H. Albert (Miami Mayhem), d. Gordon Douglas.
SUSPENSE: MURDER: MYSTERY: MURDER MYSTERY: Detective Stories; Detectives-Private; Detectives-Amateur; Bodyguards; Murder-Discovering; Detectives in Deep; Florida
SEQUEL: Lady in Cement.
(Lady in Cement; The Detective)

Too Beautiful for You, 1988, 91m, ★★★/$$, Orion/Orion, R/S. When a wheeler-dealer French car mogul with a beautiful wife falls for his ordinary secretary, even he's surprised-especially when he realizes it doesn't take as much money and effort. Gerard Depardieu, Josiane Balasko, Carole Bouquet. w. d. Bertrand Blier.
DRAMA: ROMANCE: Romantic Drama; Romance-Mismatched; Looksism; Cheating Men; Secretaries; Romance with Boss; Writer-Directors; French Films; Salesmen
(Momma, There's a Man in Your Bed; Sugarbaby)

Too Late Blues, 1961, 100m, ★★1/2/$$, Par/Par. An artiste of a jazz musician resists the pressure to "go commercial" and nurses along his neurotic girlfriend. Stella Stevens, Bobby Darin, John Cassavetes, Everett Chambers, Nick Dennis, Rupert Crosse, Vince Edwards. w. John Cassavetes, Richard Carr, d. John Cassavetes.
DRAMA: Jazz Life; Musicians; **ROMANCE:** Romantic Drama; Young Men; Beatnik Era; Forgotten Films; Curiosities; Writer-Directors
(All the Fine Young Cannibals; Mickey One)

Too Late the Hero, 1969, 144m, ★★1/2/$$, Palomar-20th/CBS-Fox, R/V-P. The true story of the showdown between the Allies and the Japanese on a tiny island in the Pacific. Michael Caine, Cliff Robertson, Ian Bannen, Henry Fonda, Harry Andrews, Denholm Elliott, Ronald Fraser, Percy Herbert. w. Robert Aldrich, Lukas Heller, d. Robert Aldrich.
ACTION: DRAMA: Action Drama; War Stories; World War II Stories; War Battles; Pacific Islands; War at Sea

Too Many Husbands, 1940, 84m, ★★★/$$$, Col/Col. A woman's husband is believed drowned in a shipwreck. After a while she remarries, then he shows up after spending years on a desert isle. Jean Arthur, Melvyn Douglas, Fred MacMurray, Harry Davenport, Dorothy Peterson, Melville Cooper, Edgar Buchanan. w. Claude Binyon, P-adap. W. Somerset Maugham (*Home and Beauty*), d. Wesley Ruggles.

COMEDY: Screwball Comedy; Marriage Comedy; Return of Spouse; **ROMANCE:** Romantic Comedy; Romance-Triangles; Dead-Back from the; Misunderstandings; Secrets-Keeping; Shipwrecks; Islands; Men Fighting Over Women; Forgotten Films

REMAKE/RETREAD OF (same year): My Favorite Wife; **REMAKE:** Three for the Show.

(Three for the Show; My Favorite Wife; Move Over, Darling; Our Wife)

(Ed: Okay, but *My Favorite Wife* is much better)

Tootsie, 1982, 116m, ★★★★/$$$$$$, Columbia, RCA-Col, PG/S-P. An out-of-work actor (Dustin Hoffman, BActor) decides to go for auditions as an actress and gets a job on a soap opera, only he can't tell the actress on the show (Jessica Lange, **BSActress**) who he's crazy about that he's really a man-or her father, who's in love with him/her. Teri Garr (BSActress), Sydney Pollack, Bill Murray, Dabney Coleman, Charles Durning. w. Larry Gelbart, Murray Schisgal (BOScr), d. Sydney Pollack (BDirector). BPicture, BCin, BEdit, BSound, BOSong. Oscars: 10-1.

COMEDY: FARCE: ROMANCE: Romantic Comedy; Role Reversals; Sex Changes; Men as Women; Actors; TV Life; New York Life; Misunderstandings; Identities-Assumed; Disguises; Fame-Rise to; Impostors; Romance-Triangles; Romance-Unrequited; Romance-Reluctant; Infatuations; Blockbusters (Victor/Victoria; Yentl; Switch; Dave)

Top Gun, 1986, 110m, ★★★/$$$$$$, Par/Par, PG-13/S-P. Navy fighter pilots use expensive equipment to hot dog for the girls, with the top gun vying for the attention of the impossibly sexy lady flight instructor. Tom Cruise, Kelly McGillis, Val Kilmer, Anthony Edwards, Tom Skerritt. w. Jim Cash, Jack Epps, Jr., d. Tony Scott. BEdit, BSEdit, **BOSong.** Oscars: 1-0.

ACTION: ROMANCE: Pilots-Military; Military Stories; Romance-Reluctant;

Teachers; Teachers & Students; Romance with Teacher; Sexy Men; Sexy Women; Men Fighting Over Women; Men Proving Themselves; Bratpack Movies; 1980s; Conservative Value Films; Blockbusters; Faded Hits

(An Officer and a Gentleman; Days of Thunder)

Top Hat, 1935, 100m, ★★★★/$$$, RKO/Turner. Two would-be lovers chase each other around London, and finally end up in each other's arms in Monte Carlo. Fred Astaire, Ginger Rogers, Edward Everett Horton, Helen Broderick, Eric Blore, Erik Rhodes. w. Dwight Taylor, Allan Scott, d. Mark Sandrich. BPicture, BArt, BOSong, BChoreography. Oscars: 4-0.

MUSICALS: Dance Movies; Dancers; **ROMANCE:** Romantic Comedy; Romance-Reluctant; London; Monte Carlo; Astaire & Rogers

(Swing Time; Flying Down to Rio)

Top of the Town, 1937, 86m, ★★½/$$, U/NA. A famous swing club in New York is up in arms when the daughter of the owner wants to take over the main stage to put on an artsy ballet. George Murphy, Doris Nolan, Hugh Herbert, Gregory Ratoff, Ella Logan, Gertrude Niesen, Henry Armetta, Mischa Auer, Samuel S. Hinds, Peggy Ryan. w. Brown Holmes, Charles Grayson, Lou Brock, d. Ralph Murphy.

MUSICALS: Dance Movies; Dancers; Nightclubs; Ballet; Big Band Era; Forgotten Films

Top Secret!, 1984, 90m, ★★★/$$, Par/Par, PG/P-S. An American rock star goes to Germany and is enlisted as a spy to help fight the Nazis, winding up on a wild goose chase with a myriad of slapstick crazies. Val Kilmer, Lucy Gutteridge, Peter Cushing, Jeremy Kemp, Warren Clarke, Michael Gough, Omar Sharif, Christopher Villiers. w. Jim Abrahams, David Zucker, Jerry Zucker, Martyn Burke, d. Jim Abrahams.

COMEDY: Comedy-Gag; Comedy-Slapstick; Spoofs; Rock Stars; Nazi Stories; Spies; Spy Films; Americans Abroad; Teen Idols

(Naked Gun; Airplane!)

Top Secret Affair, 1956, 100m, ★★½/$$, WB/NA. A female military correspondent sets out to do an exposé on a man she believes to be a corrupt military official, but ends up liking him-a lot.

Kirk Douglas, Susan Hayward, Jim Backus, Paul Stewart, John Cromwell, Roland Winters. w. Roland Kibbee, Allan Scott, N-adap. John P. Marquand (*Melville Goodwin USA*), d. H. C. Potter.

COMEDY DRAMA: SATIRE: ROMANCE: Romantic Comedy; Military Stories; Journalists; Romance-Reluctant; Romance-Unprofessional; Corruption; Female Protagonists; Forgotten Films (Absence of Malice; My Dear Secretary)

Topaz, 1969, 124m, ★★½/$, U/MCA-U, PG. In 1962, a Russian spy ring is infiltrated by the CIA using a French double-agent. Frederick Stafford, John Forsythe, John Vernon, Roscoe Lee Browne, Danny Robin, Karin Dor, Michel Piccoli, Philippe Noiret. w. Samuel Taylor, N-adap. Leon Uris, d. Alfred Hitchcock.

SUSPENSE: Spies; Spy Films; Cold War Era; Secret Agents; **MURDER:** Assassination Plots; Russians; Russians as Enemy; Latin People; Double Crossings; Flops-Major; Forgotten Films; Hitchockian

(Torn Curtain; The Looking Glass War)

Topaze, 1933, 78m, ★★½/$$, RKO/Ingram. An English school's timid headmaster is a doormat to bullies until he finally stands up to being used. John Barrymore, Myrna Loy, Jobyna Howland, Jackie Searl. w. Ben Hecht, P-adap. Marcel Pagnol, d. Harry d'Abbabie d'Arrast.

DRAMA: Teachers; Teachers & Students; Boys' Schools; Boarding Schools; Men Proving Themselves; Nerds; England

Topkapi!, 1964, 119m, ★★★/$$$, UA/CBS-Fox. The Istanbul museum is staked out by master thieves from around the world, intent on stealing its treasures with clever and kooky means. Melina Mercouri, Maximilian Schell, Peter Ustinov (**BSActor**), Robert Morley, Akim Tamiroff, Gilles Segal, Jess Hahn. w. Monja Danischewsky, N-adap. Eric Ambler (*The Light of Day*), d. Jules Dassin. Oscars: 1-1.

COMEDY DRAMA: Heist Stories; Museums; Jewel Thieves; Art Thieves; Ensemble Films; Middle East; Female Among Males; Eccentric People; Faded Hits; Narrated Films

(The Hot Rock; How to Steal a Million)

Topper, 1937, 96m, ★★★½/$$$, MGM/MGM-UA, Media. A respected banker is visited by a family of ghosts who won't go away, and whom only he can see. Cary

Grant, Constance Bennett, Roland Young (BSActor), Billie Burke, Alan Mowbray, Eugene Pallette, Arthur Lake, Hedda Hopper. w. Jack Jevne, Erich Hatch, Eddie Moran, N-adap. Thorne Smith (*The Jovial Ghosts*), d. Norman Z. McLeod. Oscars: 1-0.

Topper Returns, 1941, 87m, ★★★/$$$, MGM/MGM-UA, Media. A female ghost puts her head together with Topper to figure out who murdered her. Roland Young, Joan Blondell, Eddie Anderson, Carole Landis, Dennis O'Keefe, H. B. Warner, Billie Burke, Donald McBride, Rafaela Ottiano. w. Jonathan Latimer, Gordon Douglas, with additional dialogue by Paul Gerard Smith, d. Roy del Ruth.
Avenging Death of Someone

Topper Takes a Trip, 1939, 85m, ★★½/$$$, MGM/Media. Topper and his wife go on vacation to the French Riviera, where Mrs. Kirby, one of his ghosts, spies a lusty Frenchman trying to seduce poor lady Topper, and saves her honor in time. Constance Bennett, Roland Young, Billie Burke, Alan Mowbray, Verree Teasdale, Franklin Pangborn, Alexander D'Arcy. w. Eddie Moran, Jack Jevne, Corey Ford, d. Norman Z. McLeod.
COMEDY: Screwball Comedy; Ghosts; Fantasy; Bankers; Dead-Back from the; Illusions/Hallucinations; Nuisances; Marriage Comedy; Hidden Gems; Faded Hits
REMAKE/RETREAD: Beetlejuice.
REMAKE: TV Series, 1950s & 1979.
(Beetlejuice; Blithe Spirits; The Ghost and Mrs. Muir)

Tora! Tora! Tora!, 1970, 144m, ★★½/ $$$, 20th/Fox, PG/V. The Japanese and American sides of the Pearl Harbor story. Martin Balsam, Joseph Cotten, James Whitmore, Jason Robards, Edward Andrews, Leon Ames, George Macready, Soh Yamamura, Takahiro Tamura. w. Larry Forrester, Hideo Oguni, Ryuzo Kikushima, d. Richard Fleischer.
BSVFX, BSound, BEdit, BCin, BArt. Oscars: 5-1.
ACTION: War Stories; War Battles; Multiple Stories; Epics; War at Sea; World War II Stories; Pearl Harbor; Japanese as Enemy; Japanese People; Hawaii
(Midway; Hell in the Pacific; The Sands of Iwo Jima; Guadalcanal Diary)

Torch Song, 1953, 90m, ★★★/$$$, MGM/MGM-UA. A blind concert pianist falls for a tempestuous Broadway star.

Joan Crawford, Michael Wilding, Gig Young, Marjorie Rambeau (BSActress), Henry Morgan, Dorothy Patrick. w. John Michael Hayes, Jan Lustig, SS-adap. I. A. R. Wylie (*Why Should I Cry?*), d. Charles Walters. Oscars: 1-0.
MELODRAMA: ROMANCE: Tearjerkers; Romantic Drama; Blind People; Theater Life; Actresses; Feisty Females; Pianists; Faded Hits; Forgotten Films; Hidden Gems
(Dark Victory; Bright Victory)

Torch Song Trilogy, 1988, 119m, ★★★/$, New Line/New Line, R/S-P-V. A gay drag queen confronts love in the age of AIDS, gay bashing, and the trial of coming out to his mother. Harvey Fierstein, Anne Bancroft, Matthew Broderick, Brian Kerwin, Karen Young, Eddie Castrodad, Ken Page, Charles Pierce, Axel Vera. w., P-adap. Harvey Fierstein, d. Paul Bogart.
DRAMA: ROMANCE: TRAGEDY: Gay Men; Transvestites; Mothers & Sons; Violence-Sudden; Actors; Mothers-Troublesome; Unintentionally Funny; Alternative Lifestyles; 1980s; Episodic Stories
(Parting Glances; The Birdcage; The Dresser)

Torn Curtain, 1966, 119m, ★★★/$$$, U/MCA-U, PG. A man defects into East Germany. When his girlfriend follows him, she's dismayed to learn that he was actually a double-agent, and she's now put them both in jeopardy. Paul Newman, Julie Andrews, Wolfgang Kieling, Ludwig Donath, Lila Kedrova, Hans-Joerg Felmy, Tamara Toumanova. w. Brian Moore, d. Alfred Hitchcock.
SUSPENSE: MYSTERY: Spies; Spy Films; Iron Curtain-Behind the; Iron Curtain-Escape from the; Cold War Era; Chase Stories; Secret Agents; ROMANCE: Secrets-Keeping; Faded Hits
(The Spy Who Came in From the Cold; The Looking Glass War; Topaz)
(Ed: Not Hitchcock's best, but still better than a lot of similar films)

Torrents of Spring, 1989, 101m, ★★½/$$, Orion/NA. A pretty but unassuming Italian pastry cook loves a wealthy Russian nobleman, and believes he loves her. Little does she know he's toying with her affections, being unfaithful at every turn. Timothy Hutton, Nastassja Kinski, Valeria Golino, William Forsythe, Urbano Barberini, Francesca

De Sapio, Jacques Herlin. w. Jerzy Skolimowski, Arcangelo Bonaccorso, N-adap. Ivan Turgenev, d. Jerzy Skolimowski.
MELODRAMA: ROMANCE: Romantic Drama; Cheating Men; Italian Films; Polish Films; International Casts; Costume Drama; Overlooked at Release

Tortilla Flat, 1942, 106m, ★★★/$$, MGM/MGM-UA. Half-Mexican peasants in California struggle to make ends meet and avoid deportation. Spencer Tracy, Hedy Lamarr, John Garfield, Frank Morgan, Akim Tamiroff, Connie Gilchrist, John Qualen, Sheldon Leonard, Donald Meek, Allen Jenkins, Henry O'Neill. w. John Lee Mahin, Benjamin Glazier, N-adap. John Steinbeck, d. Victor Fleming.
DRAMA: Family Drama; Race Relations; Immigrants; Farm Life; Depression Era; Poor People; California; Latin People; Social Drama; Classic Literary Adaptations; Forgotten Films; Hidden Gems; Time Capsules
(Of Mice and Men; The Grapes of Wrath; The Pearl)

Total Eclipse, 1995, 110m, ★★★/$, Fine Line/New Line, R/S-MN. The story of the two young male French poets who fell in love despite the fact that the older (Verlaine) was married and the younger (Rimbaud) was only sixteen. Their relationship develops over the years until their fates diverge. Leonardo DiCaprio, David Thewlis, Romane Bohringer, Dominique Blanc. w. Christopher Hampton, d. Agnieszka Holland.
DRAMA: ROMANCE: Romantic Drama; Poets; Writers; Gay Men; Bisexuality; Romance-Reluctant; France; Biographies
(Carrington; Swann in Love; Another Country)

Total Recall, 1990, 109m, ★★★/$$$$$, Carolco-Tri-Star/Live, PG-13/P-EV. A suburban man of the future realizes his life hasn't been quite so quiet when he goes to a "travel" agency specializing in virtual reality "trips" and "remembers" his former life as a secret agent on Mars. Only, is he dreaming now, or was he then? Arnold Schwarzenegger, Rachel Ticotin, Sharon Stone, Ronny Cox, Michael Ironside, Marshall Bell, Mel Johnson, Jr., Michael Champion, Roy Brocksmith, Ray Baker, Rosemary Dunsmore, Priscilla Allen. w. Ronald Shusett, Dan O'Bannon, Gary Goldman, SS-adap. Philip K. Dick (*We Can*

Remember It For You Wholesale), d. Paul Verhoeven. **BVSFX**. Oscars: 1-1.

ACTION: SCI-FI: Outer Space Movies; Experiments; Revenge; Time Travel; Memories; Brainwashing; Chase Stories; Fugitives from the Law; Divorces; Mean Women; Secret Agents; Amnesia; Taxi Drivers; Virtual Reality; Blockbusters (*Three Days of the Condor; The Fugitive; Seconds; Strange Days; Virtuosity*)

Toto le Heros, 1991, 91m, ★★★/$$, Ind/Par, PG-13/V-S. A bitter man remembers his trauma as a boy when his best friend stole his one true love. Now, as an old man, he plans to murder that man. Michel Bouquet, Jo De Backer, Thomas Godet, Gisela Uhlen, Mireille Perrier, Sandrine Blancke, Peter Bohlke, Didier Ferney, Hugo Harold Harrison. w. Jaco van Dormael, Laurette Vankeerberghen, Pascal Lonhay, Didier de Neck, d. Jaco van Dormael.

SUSPENSE: DRAMA: Revenge; Memories; Romance with Friend's Lover; Romance-Doomed; **MURDER:** Elderly Men; Episodic Stories; Flashbacks; Feuds; Friendships on the Rocks; Friendships-Male; Friends as Enemies; French Films; International Casts; Hidden Gems

A Touch of Class, 1973, 106m, ★★★★/$$$, Embassy/Media, R/S-P. A businessman (George Segal, BActor) takes a mistress (Glenda Jackson, **BActress**) on vacation, who's far from easy, then his best friends turn up and may blow his cover. Paul Sorvino. w. M. Frank, (BOScr), d. M. Frank (BDirector). BPicture, BOSong. Oscars: 5-1.

COMEDY: Romantic Comedy; Romance-Bickering; Romance-Opposites Attract; Romance with Married Person; Cheating Men; Romance-Clandestine; Mistresses; Feisty Females; Vacation; Romance; Nightmare Vacations; British Films; Sleeper Hits; Faded Hits; Hidden Gems (*Lost and Found; The Owl and the Pussycat; House Calls*)

(Ed: A real gem and a real throw-back to the days of screwball)

Touch of Evil, 1958, 114m, ★★★/$$, U-I/MCA-U. Newlyweds in Mexico-a Mexican narcotics officer in Texas and his wife, are ensnared in the trap of the local corrupt sheriff in the border town they hoped to leave after a few weeks. Charlton Heston, Orson Welles, Janet Leigh, Marlene Dietrich, Akim Tamiroff,

Joseph Calleia, Ray Collins, Dennis Weaver. w. d. Orson Welles.

DRAMA: TRAGEDY: Film Noir; Corruption; Police Corruption; Conspiracy; Crossing the Border; Bombs; Accused Unjustly; Framed?; Mexico; Latin People; Drugs-Dealing; Cult Films; Writer-Directors (*Journey into Fear; The Lady from Shanghai*)

Tough Guys, 1986, 104m, ★★★/$$$, Touchstone/Touchstone, PG/P-V. After thirty years in prison, two old train robbers find the retirement home boring and go back to their former trade. Burt Lancaster, Kirk Douglas, Charles Durning, Alexis Smith, Eli Wallach. w. James Orr, Jim Cruikshank, d. Jeff Kanew.

COMEDY: ACTION: Action Comedy; Heist Stories; Trains; Capers; Elderly Men; Buddy Films; Ex-Convicts; Reunions; Retirement; Old-Fashioned Recent Films (*Going in Style; Atlantic City*)

Tough Guys Don't Dance, 1987, 108m, ★★/$, Cannon/MGM-UA, R/S-P-V. A would-be Philip Marlowe, a small-town businessman in Massachussets, inadvertently gets involved with drug traffickers while doing an "investigation." Ryan O'Neal, Isabella Rossellini, Debra Sandlund, Wings Hauser, Lawrence Tierney. w. d. N-adap. Norman Mailer.

COMEDY DRAMA: SATIRE: Spoofs; Spoofs-Detective; Detective Stories; Detectives-Amateur; Film Noir-Modern; Flops-Major; Writer-Directors

Tovarich, 1937, 98m, ★★★/$$$, WB/NA. During the Russian Revolution, a noble couple flee to Paris and must accept jobs as domestics in a strange household. Claudette Colbert, Charles Boyer, Basil Rathbone, Anita Louise, Melville Cooper, Isabel Jeans, Maurice Murphy, Morris Carnovsky, Gregory Gaye, Montagu Love, Fritz Feld. w. Casey Robinson, P-adap. Robert E. Sherwood, P-adap. Jacques Deval, d. Anatole Litvak.

COMEDY: COMEDY DRAMA: Riches to Rags; Rich People; Poor People; Rich vs. Poor; Social Satire; Royalty; Russians; Russian Revolution; Servants; Faded Hits; Forgotten Films (*Midnight; Anastasia*)

Tower of London, 1939, 92m, ★★★½/ $$$, U/MCA-U. Richard III murders his way to the throne of England through his

evil accomplice, Mord the executioner. Basil Rathbone, Boris Karloff, Barbara O'Neil, Ian Hunter, Vincent Price, Nan Grey, John Sutton, Leo G. Carroll, Miles Mander. w. Robert N. Lee, d. Rowland V. Lee.

SUSPENSE: HORROR: MURDER: Historical Drama; True Stories; True or Not; Serial Killers; Power-Rise to; Evil Men; Kings; Royalty; England; Hidden Gems; Forgotten Films (*Richard III*)

Tower of London, 1962, 79m, ★★★/$$, AIP/MGM-UA. A retelling of the same historical facts as above, with more gore. Vincent Price, Michael Pate, Joan Freeman, Robert Brown, Justice Eatson, Sara Salby, Richard McCauly, Bruce Gordon. w. Leo V. Gordon, Amos Powell, James B. Gordon, d. Roger Corman.

SUSPENSE: HORROR: MURDER: Historical Drama; True Stories; True or Not; Serial Killers; Power-Rise to; Evil Men; Kings; Royalty

REMAKE OF: 1939 version.

The Towering Inferno, 1974, 165m, ★★★/$$$$$, 20th-WB/CBS-Fox, PG/V. At the unveiling party of the world's tallest skyscraper, a fire starts on a lower floor, trapping partyers in the penthouse. Paul Newman, Steve McQueen, William Holden, Faye Dunaway, Fred Astaire (BSActor), Susan Blakely, Richard Chamberlain, Robert Vaughn, Jennifer Jones, O.J. Simpson, Robert Wagner. w. Stirling Silliphant, N-adap. Richard Martin Stern (*The Tower*), Thomas M. Scortia, Frank Robinson (*The Glass Inferno*), d. John Guillermin, Irwin Allen. BPicture, BCin, BEdit, BOSong, BOScore, BArt, BSound. Oscars: 8-3.

ACTION: DRAMA: Action Drama; Disaster Stories; Corruption; Survival Drama; Rescue Drama; Fires; High Rise Settings; Multiple Stories; Ensemble Films; Men in Jeopardy; Women in Jeopardy; All-Star Casts; Blockbusters; Faded Hits (*The Poseidon Adventure; Earthquake*)

A Town Like Alice (The Rape of Malaya), 1956, 117m, ★★★/$$$. Among a female prison camp in Malaya, Japanese soldiers are rough, but the women band together to survive. Virginia McKenna, Peter Finch, Takagi, Marie Lohr, Maureen Swanson, Jean Anderson, Renee Houston, Nora Nicholson.

w. W. P. Lipscomb, Richard Mason, N-adap. Nevil Shute, d. Jack Lee.

A Town Like Alice, 1985, 300m, ★★★/$$, New World/New World. Bryan Brown, Helen Morse. d. David Stevens. TV Movies; Miniseries

DRAMA: War Stories; World War II Stories; P.O.W.s; Prison Drama; Women in Prison; True Stories; Docudrama; Japanese as Enemy; Australia; British Films; Female Protagonists; Hidden Gems; Ahead of its Time
(Women of Valor; Stalag 17; Three Came Home)
(Ed: A big hit in British countries, it didn't fare so well in America)

Town, 1956, 96m, ★★★/$$, Col/NA. In a genteel British community, a tennis club holds a dance and afterwards, a girl is murdered. Scotland Yard sends a man over to check it out and a whodunit develops. John Mills, Charles Coburn, Derek Farr, Barbara Bates, Alec McCowen, Margaretta Scott, Fay Compton. w. Ken Hughes, Robert Westerby, d. John Guillermin.
MYSTERY: MURDER: MURDER MYSTERY: Mystery-Whodunits; Police Stories; Detective Stories; Detectives-Police; England; Small-town Life; British Films; Hidden Gems

The Town That Dreaded Sundown, 1976, 96m, ★★★/$$$, WB/WB, R/EV. The true story of one of the first sexual serial killers in America, set in 1940s Texarkana, and the lawman (Ben Johnson) who comes to town to track him down. w. d. Charles B. Pierce.
SUSPENSE: MURDERS: MURDER MYSTERY: Serial Killers; MYSTERY: Trail of a Killer; True Stories; Murders of Teenagers; Southerns; 1940s; Arkansas; Writer-Directors
(Friday the 13th SERIES; The Evictors)
(Ed: At the beginning of a whole new genre with some truly horrifying moments and others out of place)

Town Without Pity, 1961, 103m, ★★★/$$, UA/CBS-Fox. After a German girl is raped by four American soldiers, their sleazy lawyer's tactics in court lead to more trouble than imagined. Kirk Douglas, E. G. Marshall, Christine Kaufmann, Barbara Rutting, Robert Blake, Richard Jaeckel. w. Silvia Reinhardt, George Hurdalek, N-adap. Manfred Gregor (*The Verdict*), d. Gottfried Reinhardt. BOSong. Oscars: 1-0.

DRAMA: TRAGEDY: Rape/Rapists; Germany; Soldiers; World War II-Post Era; Courtroom Drama; Lawyers; Ethics; Corruption; Suicidal Tendencies; Ahead of its Time; Girls; Men and Girls; Female Screenwriters
(To Kill a Mockingbird; Trial)

The Toxic Avenger, 1985, 76m, ★★/$$, Troma/Troma, R/P-V-B&G. A simple-minded geek is transformed into a plug-ugly superhero when he falls into a vat of radioactive waste. Andree Maranda, Mitchell Cohen, Pat Ryan, Jr., Jennifer Babtist, Cindy Manion, Robert Prichard, Gary Schneider. w. Joe Ritter, Lloyd Kaufman, d. Michael Herz, Samuel Weil.

The Toxic Avenger, Part II, 1989, 95m, ★★/$, Troma/Troma, R/P-V-B&G. A chemical company embarrassed by the mutant they have created attempts to kill the Toxic Avenger. Ron Fazio, John Altamura, Phoebe Legere, Rich Collins, Rikiya Yasuoka, Tsutomu Sekine, Mayako Katsuragi. w. Gay Partington Terry, Lloyd Kaufman, d. Michael Herz, Lloyd Kaufman.

**The Toxic Avenger Part III:
Temptation of Toxie**, 1989, 89m, ★¹/₂/$, Troma/Troma, R/V-P-B&G. Our superhero tries going legit, and "selling out," but returns to "form" as an ugly, oozing mess. Ron Fazio, John Altamura, Phoebe Legere, Rick Collins, Lisa Gaye, Jessica Dublin, Tsutomu Sekine. w. Gay Partington Terry, Lloyd Kaufman, d. Lloyd Kaufman, Michael Herz.
HORROR: SCI-FI: ACTION: Heroes-Unlikely; Monsters-Human; Monsters-Mutant; Toxic Waste; Environmental Dilemmas; Corporation as Enemy; Nerds; Revenge

Toy Soldiers, 1991, 112m, ★★/$$, Col/Col, PG-13/P-V. A South American drug dealer kidnaps some rich American teenagers at a military school for ransom, but they prove too smart for their captors. Sean Astin, Wil Wheaton, Keith Coogan, Andrew Divoff, R. Lee Ermey, Mason Adams, Denholm Elliott, Louis Gossett, Jr., George Perez. w. Daniel Petrie, Jr., David Koepp, N-adap. William P. Kennedy, d. Daniel Petrie.
ACTION: Military Stories; Kidnappings; Turning the Tables; Ensemble Films; Military Schools; Boys' Schools; Drugs-Dealing; Teenagers; Teenage Movies; Boys; Ensembles-Male; Good Premise

Unfulfilled; Unintentionally Funny
(Taps; The Rescue)

Toys, 1992, 121m, ★★/$$, 20th/Fox, PG. A military man takes over a toy company and starts producing evil, military hardware-inspired toys and its up to some do-gooders to stop it. Robin Williams, Michael Gambon, Joan Cusack, Robin Wright, LL Cool J, Donald O'Connor, Jack Warden. w. Valerie Curtin, Barry Levinson, d. Barry Levinson.
COMEDY DRAMA: Fantasy; Allegorical Stories; Toy Makers; Factory Life; Arms Dealers; Illusions Destroyed; Androids; Flops-Major
(Ed: Great art direction, but nothing else)

Toys in the Attic, 1963, 90m, ★★★/$$, UA/MGM-UA. Two old maids deal with the return of their younger playboy brother in their run-down old New Orleans home. Geraldine Page, Wendy Hiller, Dean Martin, Yvette Mimieux, Gene Teirney, Larry Gates. w. James Poe, P-adap. Lillian Hellman, d. George Roy Hill. BB&WCostume. Oscars: 1-0.
DRAMA: MELODRAMA: Family Drama; Reunions; Playboys; Spinsters; Sisters; Brothers & Sisters; Tennessee Williams-esque; Life Transitions; New Orleans; Hidden Gems
(Summer and Smoke; Ten Thousand Bedrooms)
(Ed: Underrated, though not particularly meaningful, and Martin isn't bad)

Toy Story, 1995, 81m, ★★★/$$$$$, Disney/Disney, G. A little boy's traditional-type toys are threatened by a new, high-tech spaceman toy. But soon they get along and do battle against the neighborhood brat who threatens their way of . . . being toys. Voices of Tom Hanks, Tim Allen, Don Rickles, Jim Varney, Wallace Shawn, John Ratzenberger, Annie Potts, John Morris, Erik Von Detten, Laurie Metcalf, R. Lee Ermey, Sarah Freeman, Penn Jillette. w. Joss Whedon, Andrew Stanton, Joel Cohen & Alec Sokolow (BOScr), d. John Lasseter.
CHILDREN'S: Cartoon; Animation-Computer; Toys; Objects with Personalities; Children-Brats; Blockbusters
(Indian in the Cupboard; Nightmare Before Christmas; James and the Giant Peach)

Traces of Red, 1992, 105m, ★★/$, Goldwyn/Goldwyn, R/P-S-V. A cop on the trail of a murderer is suspected himself when all of the victims turn out to be former lovers of his. James Belushi, Lorraine Bracco, Tony Goldwyn, William Russ, Faye Grant. w. Jim Piddock, d. Andy Wolk.

SUSPENSE: MURDER: Detective Stories; Murders of Women; Police Stories; Detectives-Police; Accused Unjustly; Framed?; Suspecting Oneself; Trail of a Killer; Women in Jeopardy; Prostitutes-Low Class; Southerns; Florida
(China Moon; Body Heat)

Track 29, 1988, 91m, ★★1/2/$, Handmade-Ind/MGM-UA, R/P-S. An American woman lives a dull life in the suburbs, where her model train obsessed husband ignores her, until one day her long lost "son" shows up, an angry young British man who comes to reclaim his "lost American childhood." Whether or not he's real, or a product of her overheated imagination is never quite clear. Theresa Russell, Gary Oldham, Christopher Lloyd, Sarah Bernhard, Colleen Camp, Seymour Cassell. w. Dennis Potter, d. Nicolas Roeg.

DRAMA: Art Films; Avant-Garde Films; Surrealism; Suburban Life; Southerns; Children-Long lost; Incest; Mothers & Sons; Wild People; Fantasies; Cult Films
(The Man Who Fell to Earth; Cold Heaven)

Trade Winds, 1939, 93m, ★★★/$$, Wanger-UA/NA. A detective pursues a suspected murderess to the Far East, where he finds, to her delighted surprise as well as his, that she may be innocent. Fredric March, Joan Bennett, Ralph Bellamy, Ann Sothern, Sidney Blackmer, Thomas Mitchell, Robert Elliott. w. Dorothy Parker, Alan Campbell, Frank R. Adams, d. Tay Garnett.

COMEDY DRAMA: ROMANCE: Romantic Comedy; **MYSTERY: MURDER: MURDER MYSTERY:** Comic Mystery; Detective Stories; Accused Unjustly; Americans Abroad; Asia; Fugitives from the Law; Murderers-Female; Female Protagonists; Coulda Been Great; Female Screenwriters

Trader Horn, 1930, 120m, ★★1/2/$$$, MGM/MGM-UA. A white man trading goods in Africa must deal with "native troubles." Harry Carey, Edwina Booth, Duncan Renaldo, Mutia Omoolu, C. Aubrey Smith. w. Richard Schayer, Dale Van Every, Thomas Neville, N-adap. Alfred Aloysius Horn, Etheldreda Lewis, d. W. S. Van Dyke.

ADVENTURE: DRAMA: Africa; Political Unrest; Forgotten Films

Trading Places, 1983, 116m, ★★★1/2/$$$$, Par/Par, R/P-S-FFN. Two wealthy men in a club engage in a gentleman's bet over the old nature vs. nurture argument. In order to prove the nurture side, they find a homeless man and make him into a stockbroker, unwittingly impoverishing a nasty, arrogant stockbroker in the process-the goal they really had in mind. Dan Aykroyd, Eddie Murphy, Ralph Bellamy, Don Ameche, Denholm Elliott, Jamie Lee Curtis, Kristin Holby. w. Timothy Harris, Herschel Weingrod, d. John Landis.

COMEDY: SATIRE: Social Satire; Comedy-Character; Screwball Comedy; Role Reversals; Rags to Riches; Riches to Rags; Stock Brokers; Snobs vs. Slobs; Black Men; Black vs. White; Black Among Whites; Ethics; Elderly Men; Body Switching; Identities-Assumed; Bets; Dose of own Medicine-Given; Turning the Tables; Philadelphia; Old-Fashioned Recent Films; Prostitutes with a Heart of Gold

REMAKE/RETREAD: Taking Care of Business.
(48 Hours; The Distinguished Gentleman)

Traffik, 1990, 360m, ★★★/$, BBC/PBS. Three drug dealers run their goods from Africa and Asia into Europe and affect various people of all societal levels. Lindsay Duncan, Bill Paterson, Jamal Shah. d. Alastair Reid.

DRAMA: Social Drama; Multiple Stories; Interwoven Stories; Drugs-Dealing; Drugs-Addictions; British Films; TV Movies; Asia

The Tragedy of a Ridiculous Man, 1981, 116m, ★★1/2/$, Ladd-WB/WB, R/S. An Italian dairy farmer's life comes loose at the seams when his son is kidnapped by terrorists and he must either pay ransom or suffer the consequences. Ugo Tognazzi, Anouk Aimee, Laura Morante, Victor Cavallo, Olympia Carlisi, Riccardo Tognazzi, Vittorio Caprioli. w. d. Bernardo Bertolucci.

DRAMA: Kidnappings; Art Films; Political Drama; Terrorists; Ordinary People in Extraordinary Situations; Italy; Italian Films; Overlooked at Release; Forgotten Films; Coulda Been Great; Writer-Directors
(Target; Frantic)

The Trail of the Lonesome Pine, 1936, 102m, ★★★/$$, Par/NA. A girl who left her family in the Ozarks returns when her brother's killed in a family feud. Sylvia Sidney, Fred MacMurray, Henry Fonda, Fred Stone, Nigel Bruce, Beulah Bondi, Robert Barrat, Spanky McFarland, Fuzzy Knight. w. Grover Jones, Horace McCoy, Harvey Thew, N-adap. John Fox, Jr., d. Henry Hathaway. BOSong. Oscars: 1-0.

DRAMA: Family Drama; Feuds; Brothers & Sisters; Funerals; Death-Dealing with; Reunions; Mountain People; Female Protagonists; Forgotten Films; Arkansas

Trail of the Pink Panther, 1982, 97m, ★★/$, MGM-UA/MGM-UA, PG-13. After Peter Sellers' death, the filmmakers tried using clips from older films in a pseudo-*Citizen Kane* plot where Clouseau's old friends and enemy's remember him after he's reported missing at sea. Peter Sellers, Joanna Lumley, Herbert Lom, David Niven, Richard Mulligan, Capucine, Robert Loggia, Harvey Korman, Burt Kwouk. w. Frank and Tom Waldman, Blake Edwards, Geoffrey Edwards, d. Blake Edwards.

COMEDY: Comedy-Slapstick; Compilation Films; Memories; Interviews; Missing Persons; Curiosities
(Curse of the Pink Panther; Pink Panther SERIES)

The Train, 1964, 140m, ★★★-/$$$, UA/MGM-UA. A trainload of art treasures from France is headed toward Nazi Germany, and one man, suddenly in the French Resistance, must stop it before it arrives. Burt Lancaster, Paul Scofield, Jeanne Moreau, Michael Simon, Wolfgang Preiss, Suzanne Flon. w. Franklin Coen, Frank Davis, Walter Bernstein (BOScr), d. John Frankenheimer. Oscars: 1-0.

ACTION: SUSPENSE: Race Against Time; Trains; Art Thieves; World War II Stories; Nazi Stories; Hidden Gems; Forgotten Films
(The Cassandra Crossing; Schindler's List)

Transmutations, 1985, 103m, ★/$, Vestron/Vestron, R/EV-B&G. An experimental drug leaves the college students who take it disfigured, Hyde-like addicts who then go after the drug's inventors. Denholm Elliott, Steven Berkoff, Miranda Richardson. w. James Caplin, Clive Barker, d. George Pavlou.

HORROR: Zombies; Drugs-Addictions; Experiments; Monsters-Human; Scientists-Mad; Flops-Major

The Trap, 1958, 84m, ★★½/$$, Par/NA. A lawyer winds up helping a murderer cross the border but he may wind up in more trouble than the fugitive. Richard Widmark, Lee J. Cobb, Tina Louise, Earl Holliman, Lorne Green. w. Richard Alan Simmons, Norman Panama, d. Norman Panama.

SUSPENSE: ACTION: Chase Stories; Fugitives from the Law; Double Crossings; Lawyers vs. Clients; Crossing the Border; Forgotten Films

Trapeze, 1956, 105m, ★★★/$$$, UA/MGM-UA. Two trapeze artists, a long-standing team, feel the heat and tension when a third member joins-a sexy female. Burt Lancaster, Tony Curtis, Gina Lollobrigida, Thomas Gomez, Johnny Puleo, Katy Jurado, Sidney James. w. James R. Webb, d. Carol Reed.

DRAMA: MELODRAMA: ROMANCE: Romance-Reluctant; Romance-Triangles; Circus Life; Men Fighting Over Women; Friendships Between Sexes; Friendships-Male; Feuds

(Heller in Pink Tights; Billy Rose's Jumbo; The Greatest Show on Earth)

Trapped in Paradise, 1994, 111m, ★★/$, 20th/Fox, PG-13/P-V. A fellow and his two stupid criminal brothers who've just been paroled go to rob a backwards bank in a small town, but screw it up and ruin their getaway plans. Nicolas Cage, Jon Lovitz, Dana Carvey, John Ashton, Donald Moffat, Madchen Amick, Richard Jenkins, John Bergantine, Florence Stanley, Angela Paton, Paul Lazar, Sean McCann. w. d. George Gallo.

COMEDY: Criminals-Stupid; Bank Robberies; Brothers; Improvisational Films; Liars; Thieves; Small-town Life; Good Premise Unfulfilled; Writer-Directors

(Three Fugitives; Disorganized Crime; Law and Disorder)

Trash (Andy Warhol's Trash), 1970, 103m, ★★½/$, Par/Par, R/ES-FN-MN. An impotent (or perhaps gay?) drug addict is the object of affection of his female friends, all of whom try to "cure" him. Joe Dallesandro, Geri Miller, Holly Woodlawn, Bruce Pecheur, Jane Forth, Michael Sklar. w. d. Paul Morrissey.

DRAMA: Art Films; Documentary Style; Sexual Problems; Erotic Drama; Time Capsules; Psychedelic Era; Drugs-Addictions; 1960s; Writer-Directors

Traveling North, 1986, 96m, ★★★/$$, Ind/NA, PG. A healthy and spry seventy-year-old man makes the trip from Melbourne to Queensland to retire, but on the way, his health gives out. Leo McKern, Julia Blake, Graham Kennedy, Henri Szeps. w. P-adap. David Williamson, d. Carl Schultz.

DRAMA: MELODRAMA: Elderly Men; Death-Dealing with; Death-Impending; Retirement; Australian Films

(Strangers in Good Company; On Golden Pond; Harry and Tonto)

Travels with My Aunt, 1972, 109m, ★★★/$$, MGM/MGM-UA, PG/S-P. After the death of his supposed mother, a middle-aged banker meets his long-lost, flamboyant, elderly, sex-starved aunt and proceeds to travel Europe with her, getting in and out of various scrapes. Maggie Smith (BActress), Alec McCowen, Lou Gossett, Robert Stephens, Cindy Williams. w. Jay Presson Allen, Hugh Wheeler, N-adap. Graham Greene, d. George Cukor. BCin, BArt, **BCostume.** Oscars: 4-1.

COMEDY: COMEDY DRAMA: Screwball Comedy; Eccentric People; Children-Long-lost; ADVENTURE: Comic Adventure; Treasure Hunts; Trains; Vacations; Relatives-Troublesome; Nerds; Extroverted vs. Introverted; Sexy Women; Elderly Women; Memories; Flashbacks; Romance-Interracial; Old-Fashioned Recent Films; Alternative Lifestyles; Coulda Been Great; Hidden Gems; Feisty Females; Female Screenwriters

(Auntie Mame; The Prime of Miss Jean Brodie)

(Ed: Originally started shooting with Katharine Hepburn, who was perfect for the part, but Smith pulls it off, though one wishes the film had stuck more to the spirit and scope of the book)

T.R. Baskin, 1971, 89m, ★★½/$, Par/Par, R/P-V. A lonely secretary meets a businessman in Chicago and tries to fall in love, though her loneliness may be for a reason. Candice Bergen, James Caan, Peter Boyle, Marcia Rodd. w. Peter Hyams, d. Herbert Ross.

DRAMA: MELODRAMA: ROMANCE: Romantic Drama; Pre-Life Crisis; Young Women; Lonely People; Single Women; Chicago; Overlooked at Release; Curiosities

(Sheila Levine is Dead and Living in New York; Dear Heart)

(Ed: The problem here is the very beautiful Miss Bergen being believable as lonely or not being able to find a good date, and then Mr. Caan being able to be trusted)

Treasure Island, 1934, 105m, ★★★/$$$, MGM/MGM-UA. A young boy and an old captain find a map to a buried treasure, and travel in search of it. Wallace Beery, Jackie Cooper, Lewis Stone, Lionel Barrymore, Otto Kruger, Douglass Dumbrille, Nigel Bruce, Chic Sale. w. John Lee Mahin, N-adap. Robert Louis Stevenson, d. Victor Fleming.

Treasure Island, 1950, 96m, ★★★/$$$, RKO-Disney/Disney, G. A technicolor remake with a great star turn. Robert Newton, Bobby Driscoll, Walter Fitzgerald, Basil Sydney, Denis O'Dea, Geoffrey Wilkinson, Ralph Truman. w. Lawrence Edward Watkin, N-adap. Robert Louis Stevenson, d. Byron Haskin.

Treasure Island, 1971, 95m, ★★/$, WB/Disney. An internationally co-produced remake with no pep. Orson Welles, Kim Burfield, Lionel Stander, Walter Slezak, Rik Battaglia. w. Wolf Mankowitz, O. W. Jeeves (Welles), N-adap. Robert Louis Stevenson, d. John Hough.

Treasure Island, 1990, 132m, ★★★/$$, WB/WB, G. A faithful remake, but lacking any magic. Charlton Heston, Christian Bale, Oliver Reed, Christopher Lee, Richard Johnson, Julian Glover, Clive Wood, John Benfield, Isla Blair. w. d. Fraser C. Heston, N-adap. Robert Louis Stevenson.

Treasure Island, 1991, 115m, ★★½/$, Cannon/MGM-UA, Turner, PG. In modern-day France, a boy dreams himself into the world of Robert Louis Stevenson's famous adventure. Melvil Poupaud, Martin Landau, Vic Tayback, Lou Castel, Jeffrey Kime, Anna Karina, Jean-Pierre Leaud. w. d. Raul Ruiz, N-adap. Robert Louis Stevenson (Treasure Island).

Fantasies; Dreams; Revisionist Films

ADVENTURE: ACTION: Treasure Hunts; Swashbucklers; Pirates; Men and Boys; Adventure at Sea; Boys; Child Protagonists; Classic Literary Adaptations (Great Expectations; Kidnapped)

Treasure of Matecumbe, 1976, 116m, ★★½/$$$, Disney/Disney, G. In the Florida Keys, two boys find an old pirate map and follow it to buried treasure but a hurricane dampens their plans. Robert Foxworth, Joan Hackett, Peter Ustinov, Vic Morrow, Jane Wyatt, Johnny Duran, Billy Attmore. w. Don Tait, d. Vincent McEveety.

ADVENTURE: CHILDREN'S: FAMILY: Treasure Hunts; Florida; Boys; Child Protagonists

The Treasure of the Sierra Madre, 1948, 126m, ★★★½/$$$, WB/WB. Three men in Mexico, down on their luck, search for gold and are undone by their greed while stranded in the remote mountains. Humphrey Bogart, Walter Huston (**BSActor**), Tim Holt, Alfonso Bedoya, John Huston, Bruce Bennett, Barton MacLane. w. d. John Huston (**BAScr, BDirector**), N-adap. B. Traven. BPicture. Oscars: 4-3.

DRAMA: ADVENTURE: WESTERNS: TRAGEDY: Power Struggles; Men in Conflict; Greed; Treasure Hunts; Gold Mining; Mexico; Quests; Allegorical Stories; Writer-Directors
(The Wages of Fear; The Sorcerer)

A Tree Grows in Brooklyn, 1945, 128m, ★★★½/$$$, 20th/Fox. An Irish family in turn-of-the-century New York has its ups and downs, but injects rays of sunshine into the dreary and bleak streets around them, especially when that tree sprouts. Peggy Ann Garner (**BJuvenile**), James Dunn (**BSActor**), Dorothy McGuire, Joan Blondell, Lloyd Nolan, Ted Donaldson, James Gleason, Ruth Nelson. w. Tess Slesinger, Frank Davis (**BScr**), N-adap. Betty Smith, d. Elia Kazan. Oscars: 3-2.

DRAMA: MELODRAMA: Family Drama; Tearjerkers; Poor People; Alcoholics; Coming of Age; Ensemble Films; New York Life; Ordinary People Stories; Dreams; Immigrants; Irish People; Faded Hits; Hidden Gems; Girls; Child Protagonists; Sleeper Hits
(I Remember Mama; Alan and Naomi)

The Tree of Wooden Clogs, 1978, 186m, ★★★/$, Ind/Fox-Lorber. In 1800s European peasant country, several peasant families struggle through their desultory lives. w. d. Ermanno Olmi. (Cannes Festival winner)

DRAMA: Documentary Style; Art Films; Poor People; Historical Drama; Farm Life; Italian Films; Ensemble Films; Multiple Stories; Curiosities; Writer-Directors

Tremors, 1989, 96m, ★★★/$$, U/MCA-U, PG-13/P-V. A small western town is attacked by giant underground man-eating worms, which cause tremors in their wake. Kevin Bacon, Fred Ward, Finn Carter, Michael Gross, Reba McEntire, Bobby Jacoby, Charlotte Stewart, Tony Genaro. w. S. S. Wilson, Brent Maddock, Ron Underwood, d. Ron Underwood.

HORROR: SUSPENSE: Spoofs; Spoofs-Horror; Horror Comedy; Monsters-Mutant; Snakes; Desert Settings; Murders-One by One; Earthquakes; Cult Films
(Jaws; Blood Beach)

Trespass, 1992, 104m, ★★/$$, U/MCA-U, R/EP-V. Two firemen go into deepest, darkest east St. Louis looking for gold treasure supposedly stolen and stashed there but wind up in a gang war in the process. Ice Cube, Ice-T, William Sadler, Bill Paxton. w. Robert Zemeckis, Bob Gale, d. Walter Hill.

ACTION: Treasure Hunts; Fires; Gangs-Black; Urban Horrors; Inner City Life; Mob Wars; Black Men; Black vs. White; Rednecks
(Ed: Curious entry from Zemeckis and Gale, usually involved in much more substantial projects)

Trial, 1955, 109m, ★★★/$$$, MGM/MGM-UA. A Mexican teenage boy is accused of raping a white woman by local bigots, and a liberal young lawyer comes to his defense against the myriad of fascist types of the 50s. Glenn Ford, Dorothy McGuire, Arthur Kennedy, John Hodiak, Katy Jurado, Rafael Campos, Juano Hernandez, Robert Middleton, John Hoyt. w., N-adap. Don M. Mankiewicz, d. Mark Robson.

DRAMA: Courtroom Drama; Social Drama; Bigots; Oppression; McCarthy Era; Race Relations; Latin People; Rape/Rapists; Accused Unjustly; Framed?; 1950s; Teenagers; Boys; Lawyers; Forgotten Films; Time Capsules
(To Kill a Mockingbird; A Passage to India; Town Without Pity)

The Trial, 1962, 120m, ★★★/$, Ind/Nos. A man is awakened by police who arrest him on unspecified charges, and he must defend himself, although he never learns of his crime. Orson Welles, Jeanne Moreau, Anthony Perkins, Madeleine Robinson, Elsa Martinelli, Suzanne Flon, Akim Tamiroff, Romy Schneider. w. d.

Orson Welles, N-adap. Franz Kafka. Cult Films

The Trial, 1993, 120m, ★★-/$, Orion/Orion, R. Kyle MacLachlan, Anthony Hopkins, Jason Robards, Polly Walker, Alfred Molina. w. Harold Pinter, d. David Jones.

DRAMA: Art Films; Avant-Garde Films; Oppression; Futuristic Films; Police Corruption; Framed?; Accused Unjustly; Nightmares; Saving Oneself; Classic Literary; Adaptations; Hidden Gems (1984; Closet Land; Kafka; Shadows & Fog)

Trial and Error (The Dock Brief), 1962, 88m, ★★/$, MGM/NA. A man up on murder charges soon realizes he has a buffoon for a lawyer. Peter Sellers, Richard Attenborough, David Lodge, Frank Pettingell. w. John Mortimer, Pierre Rouve, P-adap. John Mortimer, d. James Hill.

COMEDY DRAMA: Courtroom Drama; **MURDER:** Accused Unjustly; Framed?; Lawyers; British Films
(The Wrong Arm of the Law; My Cousin Vinny)

The Trials of Oscar Wilde (The Man With the Green Carnation), 1960, 123m, ★★★/$$, Ealing/NA. The true story of Wilde's trial on charges of sodomy, which he began by taking the Marquis of Queensbury to court for libel. Peter Finch, Yvonne Mitchell, John Fraser, Lionel Jeffries, Nigel Patrick, James Mason, Emrys Jones, Maxine Audley, Paul Rogers, James Booth. w. d. Ken Hughes.

DRAMA: Biographies; Trials; Courtroom Drama; Scandals; Sexual Problems; Gay Men; Writers; True Stories; Sexuality; Oppression; Historical Drama; British Films; England; Hidden Gems; Writer-Directors
(Maurice; Victim)

Tribes, 1970, 90m, ★★★/$$$$, ABC-MGM/MGM-UA. A hippie goes into the Marines and gets stripped of more than his love beads, but he fights back in small ways. Jan-Michael Vincent, Darren McGavin, Earl Holliman. d. Joseph Sargent.

COMEDY DRAMA: SATIRE: Military Stories; Military Comedy; Vietnam Era; Hippies; Fish out of Water Stories; Peaceful People; Fighting the System; Anti-establishment Films; TV Movies; Cult Films; Hidden Gems
(Baby Blue Marine; Full Metal Jacket)

Tribute, 1980, 122m, ★★★/$$, 20th/CBS-Fox, PG. A Broadway agent learns he is dying just as he's getting to know his son, who grew up with his mother. Jack Lemmon (BActor), Lee Remick, Robby Benson, Colleen Dewhurst, Kim Cattrall. w. P-adap. Bernard Slade, d. Bob Clark. Oscars: 1-0.

DRAMA: MELODRAMA: Tearjerkers; Death-Impending; Death-Dealing with; Theater Life; Fathers & Sons; Fathers-Troublesome; Children-Long lost
(Dad, Save the Tiger; Da)

Trilogy of Terror, 1975, 100m, ★★★/$$$, ABC/ABC, Fox. Three terrifying stories involving women, including the famous tiki doll one receives as the gift that keeps on giving-and killing. Karen Black. w. Richard Matheson, d. John Llewelyn Moxey.

HORROR: SUSPENSE: Women in Jeopardy; Monsters-Dolls; Cannibalism; Romance with Teacher; TV Movies; Multiple Stories; Multiple Performances
REMAKE/RETREAD: Child's Play.
(Dead of Night [1977]; Tales from the Crypt)

The Trip, 1967, 85m, ★★★/$$, AIP/Vestron, R/S-P. A television commercial director has freaky hallucinations when he decides to tune in, drop out, and drop acid. Peter Fonda, Susan Strasberg, Bruce Dern, Salli Sachse, Dennis Hopper. w. Jack Nicholson, d. Roger Corman.

DRAMA: Psychedelic Era; Drugs-Addictions; TV Life; 1960s; Time Capsules; Nightmares; Illusions/Hallucinations; Directors; Hollywood Life; Fantasies; Cult Films
(Head; The Lost Weekend; Easy Rider)

The Trip to Bountiful, 1985, 106m, ★★★★/$$, Island/Island, PG. An elderly woman (Geraldine Page, BActress) longs to leave her place in her son's (John Heard) home with his nagging wife (Carlin Glynn) to take the bus back to her old home town, but things have changed. w. P/TV-adap. Horton Foote (BAScr), d. Peter Masterson. Oscars: 2-1.

COMEDY DRAMA: DRAMA: Reunions; Journies; Elderly Women; Wives-Troublesome; Southerns; Texas; Country Life; Mothers & Sons; Dreams; Death-Impending; Ordinary People Stories; 1950s; Time Capsules; Small-town Life; Hidden Gems
REMAKE OF TV: Version, 1956.

(The Shell Seekers; 1918; Tender Mercies)
(Ed: A bravura performance from Page at the zenith of her career, with excellent performances from Glynn and Heard, as well, working with a classic script)

Tristana, 1970, 105m, ★★★★1/2/$$, Ind/Ingram, Connoisseur. An aristocrat with sagging fortunes seduces the wrong woman and pays dearly. Catherine Deneuve, Fernando Rey, Franco Nero, Lola Gaos, Antonio Casas, Jesus Fernandez. w. Luis Bunuel, Julio Alejandro, N-adap. Benito Perez Galdos, d. Luis Bunuel.

DRAMA: Art Films; TRAGEDY: Black Comedy; ROMANCE: Romance-Doomed; Romance-Dangerous; Dangerous Women; Sexy Women; Romance-Older Men/Younger Women; Rich People; Risking it All; French Films; International Casts; Hidden Gems; Faded Hits
(Vividiana; The Discreet Charm of the Bourgeouisie)

Triumph of the Spirit, 1989, 120m, ★★1/2/$, Col/Col, R/P-V. The true story of a Jewish boxer forced by the Nazis to literally fight for his life at Auschwitz. Willem Dafoe, Edward James Olmos, Robert Loggia, Wendy Gazelle, Kelly Wolf, Costas Mandylor, Kario Salem. w. Andrzej Krakowski, Laurence Heath, Shimon Arama, Zion Haen, d. Robert M. Young.

DRAMA: Nazi Stories; Concentration Camps; True Stories; Boxing; Saving Oneself; Jewish People; Coudla Been Great; Overlooked at Release
(Playing for Time; Schindler's List; Max and Helen; Night Train to Munich)

Triumph of the Will, 1936, 120m, ★★★1/2/$, Nazi Party/Nos, Voyager. A "documentary" of the Nazi party's Nuremberg rally in 1934 which was in fact an orchestrated, symmetrically composed piece of art as propaganda and made a demigod of Hitler. d. Leni Reifenstahl.

Documentaries; Art Films; Nazi Stories; Oppression; Germany; German Films; Hitler; Cult Films; Time Capsules; Female Directors
(Olympische Spiel; The Life & Times of Leni Reifenstahl)

Triumphs of a Man Called Horse, 1982, 89m, ★★/$, Ind/NA. The white man raised among the Sioux returns for

more adventures. Richard Harris, Michael Beck, Ana De Sade, Vaughn Armstrong, Buck Taylor. w. Ken Blackwell, Carlos Aured, Jack De Witt, d. John Hough.

DRAMA: WESTERNS: ADVENTURE: Indians-Raised by; Indians-American; Westerns-Spaghetti; Protagonist is Killed
(Man in the Wilderness)

Trog, 1970, 91m, ★★/$, WB/NA, PG/V. A female scientist trains a missing link found in a manhole to behave in a more "civilized" manner. Joan Crawford, Michael Gough, Bernard Kay, David Griffin. w. Aben Kandel, d. Freddie Francis.

HORROR: SCI-FI: Primates; Scientists; Experiments; Monsters-Human; Cult Films; Curiosities; Cave People; Unintentionally Funny
(Link; Berserk!)

The Trojan War, 1961, 105m, ★★1/2/$, Ind/NA. The ancient Greek siege of Troy, using the famous Trojan Horse, is reenacted for the silver screen. Steve Reeves, John Drew Barrymore, Juliette Mayniel, Hedy Vessel. w. Ugo Liberatore, Giorgio Stegani, Federico Zardi, Giorgio Ferroni, d. Giorgio Ferroni.

ACTION: Ancient Times; Greece; Mythology; War Stories; War Battles; Legends; Body Builders; Horses
(Hercules; Ulysses)

The Trojan Women, 1971, 111m, ★★★/$, Ind/Film for Humanities. When the Greeks invade Troy in their wooden horse, the women must try to defend their chastity and their lives. Katharine Hepburn, Vanessa Redgrave, Genevieve Bujold, Irene Papas, Patrick Magee, Brian Blessed, Pauline Letts. w. d. Michael Cacoyannis, P-adap. Euripides.

DRAMA: Ancient Times; Greece; Ensemble Films; Ensembles-Female; War Stories; Historical Drama; War at Home; Feisty Females; Classic Literary Adaptations; Horses; Hidden Gems; Forgotten Films; Female Protagonists; Ind Films
(The Trojan War; The Warrior's Husband)

Tron, 1982, 96m, ★★1/2/$$$, Disney/Disney, PG/V. A programmer who designs computer games must enter the world of his most sophisticated creation to thwart an enemy. Jeff Bridges, Bruce Boxleitner, David Warner, Barnard Hughes. w. d. Steven Lisberger. BSound, BCostume. Oscars: 2-0.

680

SCI-FI: ACTION: Fantasy; Computers; Video Game Movies; Animation-Partial; Writer-Directors; Faded Hits (Super Mario Brothers; Virtuosity; The Lawnmower Man)

Troop Beverly Hills, 1989, 106m, ★★1/2/$$, Col/Col, PG. A Beverly Hills girl scout troup has a morale problem until the den mother starts giving out merit badges in shopping. Shelley Long, Craig T. Nelson, Betty Thomas, Mary Gross, Stephanie Beacham, David Gautreaux. w. Pamela Norris, Margaret Grieco Oberman, Ava Ostern Fries, d. Jeff Kanew.

COMEDY: CHILDREN'S: FAMILY: Spoofs; Girls; Beverly Hills; Rich People; Fish out of Water Stories; Camp; Race Against Time; Competitions; Role Reversal; Women in Conflict; Female Protagonists; Female Screenwriters
FEMALE FLIPSIDE OF: Meatballs.
(Clueless; Hello Again)
(Ed: Not as bad as it may seem)

Tropic of Cancer, 1970, 88m, ★★1/2/$, Par/Par, R/ES-P. In Paris in the twenties, a poor but charismatic American writer charms his way into hot meals and hot beds. Rip Torn, James Callahan, Ellen Burstyn, David Bauer, Laurence Ligneres, Phil Brown. w. Joseph Strick, Betty Botley, N-adap. Henry Miller, d. Joseph Strick.

DRAMA: Autobiographical Stories; Erotic Drama; Playboys; Americans Abroad; Poor People; Alternative Lifestyles; Roaring 20s; 1920s; Paris; Writers; Classic Literary Adaptations; Curiosities; Forgotten Films; Female Screenwriters
(Henry and June; The Moderns; The Sun Also Rises; A Farewell to Arms)

Trouble Along the Way, 1953, 110m, ★★★/$$, WB/WB. In order to get his daughter's love back, a big football coach takes a job at her small Catholic college. John Wayne, Donna Reed, Charles Coburn, Rom Tully, Leif Erickson. w. Jack Rose, Melville Shavelson, d. Michael Curtiz.

COMEDY DRAMA: MELODRAMA: College Life; Football; Fathers & Daughters; Custody Battles; Fish out of Water Stories; Coaches; Macho Men; Men and Girls; Forogtten Films; Hidden Gems; Curiosities
(Ed: A departure for Wayne, with good writers, though a little too sappy)

Trouble for Two, 1936, 75m, ★★★/$$, MGM/NA. In London to be married, a continental prince finds himself by hap-

penstance enmeshed in a murder conspiracy. Robert Montgomery, Rosalind Russell, Reginald Owen, Frank Morgan, Louis Hayward, E. E. Clive, Walter Kingsford. w. Manuel Seff, Edward Paramore, Jr., SS-adap. Robert Louis Stevenson (*New Arabian Nights*), d. J. Walter Rubin.

SUSPENSE: MYSTERY: Black Comedy; MURDER: MURDER MYSTERY: Innocent Bystanders; Princes; Marriages-Impending; Conspiracy; England; Forgotten Films; Hidden Gems
(Night Must Fall)

Trouble in Mind, 1986, 111m, ★★1/2/$$, Charter/New Line, R/V-P-S. In a hip, futuristic, white light world, a cop gets mixed up with the mob, rockers, and a girl caught in between the two. Kris Kristofferson, Lori Singer, Genevieve Bujold, Keith Carradine, Joe Morton, Divine. w. d. Alan Rudolph.

COMEDY DRAMA: ROMANCE: Mob Stories; Police Stories; Futuristic Films; Art Films; Writer-Directors; Independent Films
(Choose Me; The Moderns)

Trouble in Paradise, 1932, 86m, ★★★1/2/$$$, Par/NA. A member of a band of jewel thieves taking up residence in the house of a Parisian society lady begins to fall in love with her, leading to all sorts of complications. Herbert Marshall, Miriam Hopkins, Kay Francis, Edward Everett Horton, Charles Ruggles, C. Aubrey Smith, Robert Greig. w. Samson Raphaelson, Grover Jones, P-adap. Laszlo Aladar (*The Honest Finder*), d. Ernst Lubitsch.

COMEDY: COMEDY DRAMA: ROMANCE: Romantic Comedy; Screwball Comedy; Comedy-Light; Thieves; Hostage Situations; Paris
(The Lady Killers)

The Trouble with Angels, 1966, 112m, ★★1/2/$$, Col/Col, G. Two young women in the convent are always cutting up, but the mother superior has been watching. Rosalind Russell, Hayley Mills, June Harding, Marge Redmond, Binnie Barnes, Gypsy Rose Lee, Camilla Sparv, Mary Wickes, Margalo Gillmore. w. Blanche Hanalis, N-adap. Jane Trahey (*Life with Mother Superior*), d. Ida Lupino.

COMEDY: CHILDREN'S: FAMILY: Nuns; Nuisances; Stern Women; Girls; Female Protagonists; Female Directors; Female Screenwriters

SEQUEL: Where Angels Go, Trouble Follows.

The Trouble with Girls, 1969, 105m, ★★/$, MGM/MGM-UA, PG. The leader of a traveling medicine show helps solve a murder in the town where they've pitched their tent. Elvis Presley, Marlyn Mason, Nicole Jaffe, Sheree North, Edward Andrews, John Carradine, Vincent Price, Joyce Van Patten. w. Arnold and Lois Peyser, N-adap. Day Keene, Dwight Babcock (*The Chatauqua*), d. Peter Tewksbury.

COMEDY DRAMA: MURDER: MYSTERY: MURDER MYSTERY: Con-Arists; 1920s; Salesmen; Small-town Life; ROMANCE: Romantic Comedy; Music Movies; Curiosities; Unintentionally Funny

The Trouble with Harry, 1955, 99m, ★★★/$$, Par/Par. The trouble with Harry is . . . he's dead. Various townsfolk in a quaint little New England town have guilty consciences, and their own individual reasons for digging him up and burying him again. Edmund Gwenn, Mildred Natwick, John Forsythe, Shirley MacLaine, Mildred Dunnock. w. John Michael Hayes, N-adap. Jack Trevor Story, d. Alfred Hitchcock.

COMEDY DRAMA: Black Comedy; Comedy-Morbid; Hide the Dead Body; Small-town Life; New England; MURDER: MYSTERY: MURDER MYSTERY: Hidden Gems
(Over Her Dead Body; Weekend at Bernie's)

True Believer, 1989, 103m, ★★1/2/$$, Col/Col, R/P-V. A hardened, cynical attorney still living in the 60s is reaquainted with the zeal that once inspired him when he's persuaded to take on a wrongful-imprisonment case involving racism with an Asian client. James Woods, Robert Downey, Jr., Margaret Colin, Yuji Okumoto, Kurtwood Smith, Tom Bower, Miguel Fernandez. w. Wesley Strick, d. Joseph Ruben.

DRAMA: Courtroom Drama; Lawyers; Lawyers vs. Clients; Ethics; Hippies; Accused Unjustly; Race Relations; Asian-Americans

True Colors, 1991, 115m, ★★★/$, Col/Col, R/P. Two old college friends are reunited when the poorer, upstart one runs for political office but loses what ethics he had and its up to the other to do something about it. James Spader, John Cusack. w. Kevin Wade, d. Herbert Ross.

DRAMA: Political Drama; Politicians; Political Campaigns; Friends as Enemies; Friendships on the Rocks; Friendships-Male; Ethics; Greed; Scandals; Coulda Been Great; Overlooked at Release
(The Candidate; Storyville)

True Confession, 1937, 85m, ★★★/$$$, Par/NA. A zany, compulsively daydreaming lady confesses to a murder she dreamed she may have committed, and her hapless husband, a staid attorney, is forced to concoct her defense. Carole Lombard, Fred MacMurray, John Barrymore, Una Merkel, Porter Hall, Edgar Kennedy, Lynne Overman, Fritz Feld, Irving Bacon. w. Claude Binyon, P-adap. Louis Verneuil, George Berr (*Mon Crime*), d. Wesley Ruggles.

COMEDY: MURDER: MYSTERY: MURDER MYSTERY: Screwball Comedy; Comic Mystery; Murderers-Female; Fantasies; Accused Unjustly; Dreams; Women Proving Themselves; Hidden Gems; Forgotten Films; Female Protagonists
REMAKE/RETREAD: The Gun in Betty Lou's Handbag.
(The Gun in Betty Lou's Handbag)

True Confessions, 1981, 108m, ★★★/$$, UA/MGM-UA, R/P-V. Two estranged brothers, one a priest and one a cop, remeet under dire circumstances when the cop investigates a murder that, to his shock and dismay, may have been perpetrated by his brother, the priest. Robert Duvall, Robert De Niro, Charles Durning, Kenneth McMillan, Ed Flanders, Cyril Cusack, Burgess Meredith. w. John Gregory Dunne, Joan Didion, N-adap. John Gregory Dunne, d. Ulu Grosbard.

DRAMA: MURDER: MYSTERY: MURDER MYSTERY: Murders of Females; Suspecting Oneself; Brothers; Ethics; Men in Conflict; Priests; Police Stories; Coulda Been Great; 1940s; True Stories
(Angels with Dirty Faces; Once Upon a Time in America; The Black Dahlia; Chinatown)

The True Glory, 1945, 90m, ★★★½/$$, Ind/NA. Re-edited newsreels of the last year of World War II, from D-Day to V-Day. w. Eric Maschwitz, Arthur Macrae, Jenny Nicholson, Gerald Kersh, Guy Trosper, d. Carol Reed, Garson Kanin.
Documentaries; World War II Stories; War Battles

True Grit, 1969, 128m, ★★★/$$$$, Par/Par, PG. After a girl's father is murdered, she enlists the help of a grizzled old shootist to kill the men who did it, tracking them down in the wilds of old Arkansas. John Wayne (**BActor**), Kim Darby, Glen Campbell, Dennis Hopper, Jeremy Slate, Robert Duvall, Strother Martin, Jeff Corey. w. Marguerite Roberts, N-adap. Charles Portis, d. Henry Hathaway. BOSong. Oscars: 2-1.

ADVENTURE: WESTERNS: Avenging Death of Someone; **MURDER:** Bounty Hunters; Manhunts; West-Old; Arkansas; Mountain People; Elderly Men; Female Screenwriters
SEQUEL: Rooster Cogburn
(The Shootist; McClintock!)

True Identity, 1991, 93m, ★★/$, WB/WB, PG-13/P-S. A black London actor running from the mob disguises himself as a white man to avoid detection. Lenny Henry, Frank Langella, Charles Lane, J. T. Walsh, Anne-Marie Johnson, Andreas Katsulas, Michael McKean, Peggy Lipton. w. Andy Breckman, d. Charles Lane.

COMEDY: Identities-Assumed; Black as White; Fish out of Water Stories; Black Men; Good Premise Unfulfilled; Mob Stories; Fugitives from the Mob; Mob Comedy
(Johnny Stecchino; Soul Man; Black Like Me)

True Lies, 1994, 121m, ★★★/$$$$$, Tri-Star/Col-Tri, R/EV-P-S. A secret agent has a cover and sneaks around without even his wife knowing what international chase adventures he goes on. But when she starts following him, an impostor double-agent shows up to woo her and find out what he's up to. Arnold Schwarzenegger, Jamie Lee Curtis, Bill Paxton, Tom Arnold, Tia Carrera, Charlton Heston. w. d. James Cameron, S-adap. *La Total*.

ACTION: ADVENTURE: Action Comedy; Marriage Comedy; Dual Lives; Chase Stories; Bombs-Atomic; Impostors; Spies; Secret Agents; Spy Films; Jealousy; Blockbusters; Foreign Film Remakes
REMAKE OF: (barely) La Total.

True Love, 1989, 100m, ★★★/$$, UA/MGM-UA, R/P-S. In the Bronx, a young hunk and his bride to be have second thoughts when he starts to back out. Annabella Sciorra, Ron Eldard, Aida Turturro, Roger Rignack, Star Jasper,

Michael J. Wolfe, Kelly Cinnante, Rick Shapiro. w. Nancy Savoca, Richard Guay, d. Nancy Savoca.

COMEDY DRAMA: ROMANCE: Romantic Comedy; Marriage-Impending; Engagements-Breaking; Italians; New York Life; Ordinary People Stories; Working Class; Female Protagonists; Female Screenwriters; Female Directors; Sleeper Hits; Hidden Gems; Quiet Little Films; Writer-Directors; Independent Films
(Moonstruck; Queens Logic; Five Corners)

True Romance, 1993, 116m, ★★-/$$, WB/WB, R/EP-EV-S-B&G. The son of a cop and a hooker meet up, steal drug money, and head to California (of course) to spend the dough and deal some dope. But the nasties soon catch up. Christian Slater, Patricia Arquette, Gary Oldman, Bronson Pinchot, Dennis Hopper, Christopher Walken, Brad Pitt, Val Kilmer, Christopher Penn, Michael Rappaport, Saul Rubinek, Conchata Ferrell. w. Quentin Tarantino, d. Tony Scott.

ACTION: Action Drama; Crime Drama; Road Movies; Road to California; Criminal Couples; Money-Finding; Fugitives from the Mob; Prostitutes-Low Class; Romance with Prostitute; Comedy & Violence
(Kalifornia; Reservoir Dogs; Pulp Fiction)

True Stories, 1986, 89m, ★★★/$$, Orion-Orion, PG/P. David Byrne introduces the inhabitants of Virgil, Texas, as if they are creatures from another planet under his microscope living out their ordinary but still bizarre lives in tract houses and tacky malls. David Byrne, John Goodman, Annie McEnroe, Jo Harvey Allen, Spalding Gray, Alix Elias, Swoosie Kurtz. w. Stephen Tobolowsky, Beth Henley, David Byrne, d. David Byrne.

COMEDY: Spoofs; Documentary Style; **SATIRE:** Social Satire; Eccentric People; Small-town Life; Legends; Ordinary People Stories; Working Class; Southerns; Texas; Hidden Gems

Truly, Madly, Deeply, 1990, 106m, ★★★/$$, Goldwyn/Goldwyn, PG/S. A woman loses the husband she was madly in love with, and his ghost comes back to help her through the grieving process. Juliet Stevenson, Alan Rickman, Bill Patterson, Michael Maloney, Jenny Howe, Carolyn Choa, Christopher Rozycki. w. d. Anthony Minghella.

COMEDY DRAMA: MELODRAMA: Comedy-Light; **ROMANCE:** Romantic Comedy; Ghosts; Dead-Back from the; Return of Spouse; Widows; Death-Dealing with; Hidden Gems; Writer-Directors (Ghost; Blithe Spirit; Kiss Me Goodbye)

Trust, 1990, 106m, ★★¹/₂/$, Republic/Republic. An unwed soon-to-be teenage mother meets a psycho geek who carries a grenade with him wherever he goes, and naturally takes him home to start a family. Adrienne Shelly, Martin Donovan, Marritt Nelson, John MacKay, Edie Falco, Gary Sauer, Matt Malloy. w. d. Hal Hartley.

COMEDY DRAMA: Black Comedy; **ROMANCE:** Romantic Comedy; Art Films; Nerds; Mothers-Unwed; Babies-Having; Mental Illness; Curiosities; Writer-Directors
(Surviving Desire; Simple Men; Hold Me; Thrill Me; Kiss Me; Quick; Blood and Concrete)
(Ed: Style and substance are inequal here)

Truth or Dare, 1991, 119m, B&W, ★★★/$$$, Ind/Live, R/P-S. Madonna's 1990 World Tour documented for the camera's (as well as everything else she does during, before, and after her performances). Madonna, Warren Beatty and others. d. Alex Keshishian.
Rocumentaries; Documentaries; Autobiographical Stories; Biographies; Behind the Scenes; Rock Stars; Singers; Feisty Females; Female Protagonists; Cult Films
SPOOF: Dare to Be Truthful (Julie Brown).

Tucker: The Man and His Dream, 1988, 115m, ★★★/$$, Par/Par, PG. A car designer with a cycloptic car years ahead of its time is quashed by the Detroit powers that be. Jeff Bridges, Joan Allen, Martin Landau (BSActor), Frederic Forrest, Mako, Elias Koteas, Christian Slater, Lloyd Bridges, Dean Stockwell. w. Arnold Schulman, David Seidler, d. Francis Ford Coppola. BArt, BCostume. Oscars: 3-0.
DRAMA: Biographies; True Stories; Inventors; Dreams; American Dream; Fighting the System; Car Racing; 1940s; Illusions Destroyed; Charismatic People
(Quiz Show; Edison the Man)

Tuff Turf, 1985, 112m, ★★/$$, New World/New World, PG-13/S-P-V. A preppie wanna-be fights his way through the young toughs in his new neighborhood to get the girl. James Spader, Kim Richards, Paul Mones, Robert Downey, Jr., Matt Clark. w. Jette Rinck, Greg Collins O'Neill, Murray Michaels, d. Fritz Kiersch.
ACTION: Teenagers; Teenage Movies; ROMANCE: Romance-Boy Wants Girl; Men Proving Themselves; New in Town

Tugboat Annie, 1933, 88m, ★★★¹/₂/$$$, MGM/MGM-UA. A cantankerous old lady saloon owner on the waterfront and her younger drinking pal help out some young lovers while flirting a bit themselves. Marie Dressler, Wallace Beery, Robert Young, Maureen O'Sullivan, Willard Robertson, Paul Hurst. w. Zelda Sears, Eve Greene, SS-adap. Norman Reilly Raine, d. Mervyn Le Roy.
COMEDY: ROMANCE: Comedy-Slapstick; Romantic Comedy; Romance-Bickering; Working Class; Feisty Females; Elderly Women; Hidden Gems; Faded Hits; Female Protagonists
(Min and Bill; Tillie's Punctured Romance)

Tugboat Annie Sails Again, 1940, 75m, ★★/$$, WB/NA. Cantankerous old waterfront Annie defends her turf against competing interests. Marjorie Rambeau, Alan Hale, Jane Wyman, Ronald Reagan, Clarence Kolb, Charles Halton, Victor Kilian. w. Walter De Leon, d. Lewis Seiler.
COMEDY: Elderly Women; Stern Women; Feisty Females; Working Class; Mortgage Drama; Female Protagonists

Tulsa, 1949, 88m, ★★¹/₂/$$, E-L-Wanger-UA/Media. A ranchman's daughter strikes oil on her inherited land and makes a killing. Susan Hayward, Robert Preston, Pedro Armendariz, Lloyd Gough, Chill Wills, Ed Begley. w. Frank Nugent, Curtis Kenyon, d. Stuart Heisler.
MELODRAMA: Power-Rise to; Oil People; Southwestern Life; Feisty Females; Female Among Males; Career Women; Rich People; Rags to Riches; Female Protagonists
(Oklahoma Crude; Giant; Pittsburgh)

Tune in Tomorrow, 1990, 104m, ★★★/$, Cinecom/Cinecom, PG-13/P-S. While a young man and his older aunt are on the brink of an affair, a whacked-out radio soap opera writer with a distaste for Albanians can't distinguish fantasy from reality. Barbara Hershey, Keanu Reeves, Peter Falk, Bill McCutheon, Patricia Clarkson, Richard Portnow, Jerome Dempsey. w. William Boyd, N-adap. Mario Vargas Llosa (*Aunt Julia and the Scriptwriter*), d. Jon Amiel.
COMEDY: COMEDY DRAMA; ROMANCE: FARCE: Romantic Comedy; Romance-Older Women/Younger Men; 1940s; Radio Life; Writers; Misunderstandings; Soap Opera Shows; Fantasies; Eccentric People; New Orleans; Coulda Been Great
(Radio Days; Radioland Murders)

Tunes of Glory, 1960, 107m, ★★★/$$, UA/MGM-UA. A strict disciplinarian takes over as Commanding Officer of a British regiment formerly run in slipshod fashion by a boisterous drunk. Alec Guinness, John Mills, Susannah York, Dennis Price, Kay Walsh, Duncan Macrae, Gordon Jackson, John Fraser, Allan Cuthbertson. w. N-adap. James Kennaway (BAScr), d. Ronald Neame. Oscars: 1-0.
DRAMA: Military Stories; Stern Men; Reformers; Alcoholics; Soldiers; British Films; England; Hidden Gems; Forgotten Films

The Tunnel of Love, 1958, 98m, ★★/$$, MGM/MGM-UA. A couple wanting to adopt runs into a snag when the husband can't remember if, one night while drunk, he seduced the lovely representative from the orphanage. Richard Widmark, Doris Day, Gig Young, Gia Scala, Elizabeth Fraser, Elizabeth Wilson. w., P-adap. Joseph Fields, N-adap. Peter de Vries, d. Gene Kelly.
COMEDY: Black Comedy; Misunderstandings; Alcoholics; Amnesia; Orphans; Children-Adopted; Coulda Been Good; Forgotten Films
(Teacher's Pet; Immediate Family)

Turkish Delight, 1973, 106m, ★★★/$$$, Ind-WB/USA, NA, R/ES-FFN-MFN. A Dutch angry young man artist has an abusive relationship with a girl whose mother hates him, but when their tortured relationship finally seems to be working, she goes catatonic. Monique van de Ven, Rutger Hauer, Tonny Huurdeman, Wim van den Brink, Dolf de Vries. w. Gerard Soeteman, N-adap. Jan Wolkers, d. Paul Verhoeven. BFLFilm. Oscars: 1-0.
DRAMA: Erotic Drama; Psychological Drama; Mental Illness; Romance-Doomed; Abused Women; Young Men; Young Men-Angry; Artists; Sexual Revolution; Drugs-Addictions; Lover

Family Dislikes; Scandinavia; Dutch Films; Cult Films; 1970s
(Betty Blue; Dandelions; The Fourth Man)

Turnabout, 1940, 83m, ★★★/$$, Par/NA. A married couple each complain that the other sex has it easier, so, with the help of a little movie magic, they switch bodies to see how the other half does it. Adolphe Menjou, John Hubbard, Carole Landis, Mary Astor, Verree Teasdale, Donald Meek, William Gargan, Joyce Compton. w. Mickell Novak, Berne Giler, John McLain, N-adap. Thorne Smith, d. Hal Roach.
COMEDY: Fantasy; Body Switching; Battle of the Sexes; Romance-Bickering; Marriage Comedy; Role Reversal; Babies-Having; Ahead of its Time; Forgotten Films; Hidden Gems; Curiosities
REMAKE: TV Series, NBC, 1978.
(Switch; Adam's Rib; Goodbye, Charlie; Freaky Friday; Vice Versa)

Turner & Hooch, 1989, 99m, ★★/$$$$, Touchstone/Touchstone, PG-13/P. A large slobbering dog is the only witness to a murder a goofy cop has to solve, if he can stay with the mongrel long enough to do that without it destroying everything in sight. Tom Hanks, Mare Winningham, Craig T. Nelson, John McIntire. w. Dennis Shryack, Michael Blodgett, Daniel Petrie, Jr., Jim Cash, Jack Epps, d. Roger Spottiswoode.
COMEDY: Comedy-Slapstick; Police Stories; MURDER: MYSTERY: MURDER MYSTERY: Animal Stories; Dogs; Nuisances; Comedy of Errors; Detective Stories; Detectives-Police
(K-9; Beethoven)

The Turning Point, 1952, 85m, ★★½/$$, Par/NA. The state appoints a young, idealistic attorney to bring the local mob to justice. William Holden, Alexis Smith, Edmond O'Brien, Tom Tully, Ray Teal. w. Warren Duff, d. William Dieterle.
DRAMA: Courtroom Drama; Mob Stories; Lawyers; Illusions Destroyed; Trials; Forgotten Films

The Turning Point, 1977, 119m, ★★★★/$$$$, 20th/CBS-Fox, PG/S-P. Two old friends are reunited and yet torn apart when the daughter (Leslie Browne, BSActress) of the friend who didn't pursue a ballet career (Shirley MacLaine, BActress) becomes a younger rival to the other who did (Anne Bancroft, BActress). Mikhail Baryshnikov (BSActor). w. N-adap. Arthur Laurents (BAScr), d.

Herbert Ross (BDirector). BPicture, BCinema, BArt, BCostume, BEditing. Oscars: 11-0, all-time loser, tied with *The Color Purple*.
DRAMA: ROMANCE: Romantic Drama; Dance Movies; Ballet; Dancers; Friendships-Female; Reunions; Friendships-Lifetime; Friends as Enemies; Feuds; Mothers & Daughters; Jealousy; Mean Women; Women in Conflict; Women's Films; Female Protagonists
(Beaches; Terms of Endearment)

Turtle Beach, 1992, 88m, ★★½/$, Ind/NA. A female reporter, tired of domesticity, leaves her family to go to Malaysia and tell the world about the plight of the Vietnamese boat people but winds up in a political controversy. Greta Scacchi, Joan Chen, Jack Thompson, Art Malik, Norman Kaye, Victoria Longley, Martin Jacobs, William McInnes, George Whaley. w. Ann Turner, N-adap. Blanche d'Alpuget, d. Stephen Wallace.
DRAMA: Political Drama; Journalists; Journalists as Detectives; Witness to Murder; Asia; Australian Films; Female Protagonists
(The Year of Living Dangerously)

Turtle Diary, 1985, 97m, ★★★/$, Ind/Vestron, Live. Two zany Londoners decide, for various reasons, to liberate the turtles from the London zoo. Glenda Jackson, Ben Kingsley, Richard Johnson, Michael Gambon, Rosemary Leach, Eleanor Bron, Harriet Walter, Nigel Hawthorne, Michael Aldridge. w. Harold Pinter, N-adap. Russell Hoban, d. John Irvin.
COMEDY DRAMA: ROMANCE: Romantic Drama; Rescue Drama; Eccentric People; Animal Stories; Animal Rights; England; London; Overlooked at Release; British Films

Twelve Angry Men, 1957, 95m, ★★★★/$$$, UA/CBS-Fox. The jury is unanimous in a murder case, until one man stands against the crowd and makes them rethink their positions. Henry Fonda, Lee J. Cobb, E. G. Marshall, Jack Warden, Ed Begley, Martin Balsam, John Fiedler, Jack Klugman, George Voskovec, Robert Webber, Edward Binns, Joseph Sweeney. w., P-adap. Reginald Rose (BAScr), d. Sidney Lumet (BDirector). BPicture. Oscars: 3-0.
DRAMA: Courtroom Drama; Social Drama; Trials; Ensemble Films;

Ensembles-Male; MURDER: MYSTERY: MURDER MYSTERY: Detectives-Amateur; Rebels; Fighting the System; Juries; Stagelike Films; Hidden Gems; Faded Hits
(Trial by Jury; The Juror)

The Twelve Chairs, 1970, 93m, ★★★/$$, Embasssy/Media, PG. A clerk of modest means in old Russia sells off the twelve chairs that were his inheritance, then learns that one of them contained precious jewels. He now must search all over Russia to find it. Ron Moody, Frank Langella, Dom De Luise, Bridget Brice, Diana Coupland, Mel Brooks. w. Mel Brooks, N-adap. Ilya Ilf, Evgeny Petrov, d. Mel Brooks.
COMEDY: FARCE: Comedy-Slapstick; Comedy-Character; Russia; Inheritances at Stake; Jewel Thieves; Chase Stories; Forgotten Films
(Twelve Plus One [based on same book, the same year]; It's in the Bag; Keep Your Seats, Please)

Twelve Monkeys, 1995, 130m, ★★★/$$$$, U/MCA-U, R/P-V. In the aftermath of a virus spread by monkeys, the future looks bleak and it's up to a man whose memory is fuzzy to go back in time and see if he or the mental patient and the woman he meets can help him to find a cure. Bruce Willis, Madeleine Stowe, Brad Pitt, Christopher Plummer, Frank Gorshin, Jon Seda, David Morse. w. David Peoples & Janet Peoples, S-adap. *La Jetée*, Chris Marker, d. Terry Gilliam.
SCI-FI: ADVENTURE: MYSTERY: Time Travel; Race Against Time; Futuristic Films; Disease Stories; Epidemics; Foreign Film Remakes; Cures-Search for
(Brazil; The Omega Man; The Terminator)

Twelve O'Clock High, 1949, 132m, ★★★/$$$$, 20th/Fox. A bomb squadron leader in World War II begins a nervous breakdown as the pressure of his post starts to get to him. Gregory Peck (BActor), Hugh Marlowe, Gary Merrill, Millard Mitchell, Dean Jagger (BSActor), Robert Arthur, Paul Stewart, John Kellogg. w. Sy Bartlett, Beirne Lay, Jr., d. Henry King. BPicture, BSound. Oscars: 4-2.
DRAMA: ACTION: Action Drama; War Stories; War Battles; World War II Stories; Soldiers; Pilots-Military; Bombs; Death-Dealing with; Ethics; Nervous Breakdowns; Faded Hits
(Spellbound; Breaking the Sound Barrier)

Twelve Plus One, 1969, 108m, ★★½/$, Ind/NA. A barber of modest means sells off the twelve chairs that were his inheritance from his aunt, then learns that one of them contained precious jewels. Sharon Tate, Vittorio Gassman, Orson Welles, Vittorio De Sica, Terry-Thomas, Mylene Demongeot, Gregoire Aslan, Tim Brooke-Taylor, Lionel Jeffries. w. Marc Behm, Dennis Norden, Nicolas Gessner, N-adap. Ilya Ilf, Evgeny Petrov (*Twelve Chairs*), d. Nicolas Gessner.

COMEDY: FARCE: Comedy-Slapstick; Comedy-Character; Inheritances at Stake; Jewel Thieves; Chase Stories; Forgotten Films; Ind Films

(The Twelve Chairs; It's in the Bag; Keep Your Seats, Please)

Twentieth Century, 1934, 91m, ★★★/$$$, Col/Col. The protege of a big-time Broadway producer gets a mind of her own, once she's "fully trained" and wreaks a little romantic havoc on the train of the title while on tour. John Barrymore, Carole Lombard, Roscoe Karns, Walter Connolly, Ralph Forbes, Etienne Girardot, Charles Lane, Edgar Kennedy. w. Ben Hecht, Charles MacArthur, P-adap. Charles Bruce, Millholland (*Napoleon of Broadway*), d. Howard Hawks.

COMEDY: Screwball Comedy; Theater Life; Behind the Scenes; Actresses; Directors; Trains; Bimbos; Feisty Females; Svengalis; Mentors/Proteges; Understudies; Faded Hits; Hidden Gems; Stagelike Films

REMAKE: Broadway Musical, 1978.

(Born Yesterday; 42nd Street; Bullets Over Broadway)

(Ed: Dated and a bit slow, but still has its great moments)

Twenty Bucks, 1993, 91m, ★★½/$, Col/Col, PG-13/S. A twenty-dollar bill floats from owner to owner as a young man tries to marry into a wealthy family and is beset with problems and two crooks find themselves in deep trouble, among several other side stories. Brendan Fraser, Linda Hunt, David Rasche, Gladys Knight, Elizabeth Shue, Steve Buscemi, Spalding Gray, Christopher Lloyd, William H. Macy, George Morfogen. w. Leslie Boehm, Eric Boehm, d. Keva Rosenfeld.

COMEDY DRAMA: Multiple Stories; Interwoven Stories; Hand Me Down Stories; Money-Finding; Weddings; Marriage-Impending; Romance-Class

Conflict; Ordinary People Stories; Coulda Been Great; Curiosities; Quiet Little Films; Female Directors

(Ed: The script was written by Eric Boehm in the 30s, whose son Leslie updated it, as it was never made then. It is dated and rather French, meaning it's slow and quiet)

21, 1991, 101m, ★★½/$$, Ind/Academy, R/S-P. A British girl in New York, having just turned twenty-one, recalls her boyfriends and their many annoyances—such as heroin addictions—but she still loved them all, somehow. Patsy Kensit, Jack Shepherd, Patrick Ryecart, Maynard Eziashi, Rufus Sewell, Sophie Thompson, Susan Woodridge. w. Zoe Heller, Don Boyd, d. Don Boyd.

DRAMA: COMEDY DRAMA: Character Studies; Young Women; Dating Scene; Memories; Flashbacks; Drugs-Addictions; Pre-Life Crisis; Narrated Films; Crossing the Line; Female Protagonists; Curiosities; British People; Female Screenwriters

FEMALE FLIPSIDE OF: Alfie.

21 Days, 1937, 75m, ★★½/$$, London/Facets. A woman cheating with a handsome young man is found out by her husband. In the fight with her husband, the lover kills him, leading to a big trial and only twenty-one days of freedom. Laurence Olivier, Vivien Leigh, Leslie Banks. w. Graham Greene, Basil Dean, d. Dean.

MELODRAMA: ROMANCE: Romantic Drama; Cheating Women; Jealousy; **MURDER:** Death-Accidental; Men in Conflict; Trials; Romance-Doomed; Forgotten Films

(That Hamilton Woman; The Divorce of Lady X)

29th Street, 1991, 101m, ★★½/$, 20th/Fox, PG. An Italian-American actor wins the first big lottery in New York and winds up going through major changes with his family as a result. Danny Aiello, Anthony LaPaglia, Lainie Kazan, Frank Pesce. w. George Gallo, NF-adap. Frank Pesce & James Franciscus, d. George Gallo.

COMEDY DRAMA: Lotteries; Rags to Riches; Actors; New York Life; Italians; Family Drama; True Stories

(The Lottery; It Could Happen to You)

20,000 Leagues Under the Sea, 1954, 122m, ★★★½/$$$$$, Disney/Disney. In the Victorian era, Captain Nemo rescues a team of scientists shipwrecked off the

shore. They are fascinated by the futuristic submarine he commands, but his evil plans are about to be put to an end by our hero and an angry octopus. Kirk Douglas, James Mason, Paul Lukas, Peter Lorre, Robert J. Wilke, Carlton Young, Ted de Corsia. w. Earl Felton, N-adap. Jules Verne, d. Richard Fleischer.

ADVENTURE: SCI-FI: Underwater Adventure; Fantasy; Scientists-Mad; Inventors; Shipwrecked; Submarines; Octopi-Angry; 1800s; Victorian Era; Sailors; Classic Literary Adaptations; Production Design-Outstanding

REMAKE IN OUTER SPACE: The Black Hole.

(Journey to the Center of the Earth; In Search of the Castaways; The Black Hole)

Twenty Thousand Years in Sing Sing, 1933, 77m, ★★★½/$$$, WB/WB. A tough criminal meticulously plans his escape from the famous prison, with his girlfriend as his getaway driver. Everything goes according to plan, until she shoots a man in the heat of the moment. Being chivalrous, he takes the blame, and is right back where he started. Spencer Tracy, Bette Davis, Arthur Byron, Lyle Talbot, Louis Calhern, Warren Hymer, Sheila Terry, Edward McNamara. w. Wilson Mizner, Brown Holmes, NF-adap. Lewis E. Lawes, d. Michael Curtiz.

ACTION: Action Drama; **MELODRAMA:** Crime Drama; Prison Drama; Prison Escapes; Mob Stories; Mob Girls; Murderers-Female; **ROMANCE:** Saving Someone; Woman Behind the Man; Warner Gangster Era; Faded Hits; Forgotten Films

(The Big House; Fury; Escape from Alcatraz; The Shawshank Redemption)

Twenty-Three Paces to Baker Street, 1956, 103m, ★★★/$$, 20th/NA. A blind man hears a murder plot being discussed in a London pub, and investigates despite his handicap and the dangers to his life. Van Johnson, Vera Miles, Cecil Parker, Patricia Laffan, Maurice Denham, Estelle Winwood, Liam Redmond. w. Nigel Balchin, N-adap. Philip MacDonald, d. Henry Hathaway.

SUSPENSE: MYSTERY: MURDER: MURDER MYSTERY: Blind People; Murder-Discovering; Detective Stories; Detectives-Amateur; Men in Jeopardy; Innocent Bystanders; Disabled People in Jeopardy; England; Good Premise

Unfulfilled; Forgotten Films
(Wait Until Dark; Jennifer Eight; Blink; Hear No Evil)

Twice in a Lifetime, 1985, 117m, ★★★/$$, Yorkin/Vestron, PG-13/S-P. A middle-aged man runs away from his longtime wife, who's not aging so well, for a bombshell, leading to the disruption of his entire family around the time of his daughter's wedding. Gene Hackman, Ellen Burstyn, Ann-Margret, Amy Madigan (BSActress), Ally Sheedy. w. P-adap. Colin Welland (*Kisses at 50*), d. Bud Yorkin. Oscars: 1-0.
COMEDY DRAMA: DRAMA: ROMANCE: Romantic Drama; Family Drama; Marriage Drama; Romance with Married Person; Cheating Men; Divorce; Weddings; Fathers & Daughters; Working Class; Ordinary People Stories; Starting Over; Midlife Crisis; Women Fighting Over Men; Hairdressers; Housewives; Parents vs. Children; Hidden Gems; Forgotten Films
(All Night Long; Middle Age Crazy)

Twilight for the Gods, 1958, 120m, ★★/$$, U-I/MCA-U. A captain and his ship have their last voyage together, from Mexico to Tahiti. Rock Hudson, Cyd Charisse, Arthur Kennedy, Leif Erickson, Charles McGraw, Ernest Treux, Richard Haydn, Wallace Ford, Vladimir Sokoloff. w., N-adap. Ernest K. Gann, d. Joseph Pevney.
ADVENTURE: Adventure at Sea; Ships; Pacific Islands; Mexico; Ensemble Films; Forgotten Films

Twilight Zone: The Movie, 1983, 101m, ★★★/$$$, WB/WB, PG-13/P-V. Four tales from the original Rod Serling series, expanded into "mini-movies," ranging from cartoons coming to life, a man freaking out on an airliner with hallucinations, elderly people becoming young, and Vietnam nightmares. Dan Aykroyd, Vic Morrow, Scatman Crothers, Bill Quinn, Kathleen Quinlan, Kevin McCarthy, John Lithgow. w. John Landis, George Clayton Johnson, Richard Matheson, Josh Rogan, Rod Serling, d. John Landis, Steven Spielberg, Joe Dante, George Miller.
SCI-FI: HORROR: Multiple Stories; Fantasy; Cartoonlike Movies; TV Series Movies; Elderly People; Monsters; Animation-Partial; Illusions/Hallucinations; Airplane Crashes; Vietnam War

Twilight's Last Gleaming, 1977, 146m, ★★1/2/$$, Lorimar-20th/Fox, PG. A psychotic former general takes over a nuclear launching site and demands that the president expose the skeletons in his closet. Burt Lancaster, Richard Widmark, Charles Durning, Melvyn Douglas, Paul Winfield, Burt Young, Joseph Cotten, Roscoe Lee Brown, Gerald S. O'Loughlin, Charles Aidman. w. Ronald M. Cohen, Edward Heubsch, N-adap. Walter Wager (*Viper Three*), d. Robert Aldrich.
SUSPENSE: Political Thriller; Political Drama; Race Against Time; Presidents; Blackmail; Military Stories; Leaders-Tyrant; Mental Illness; Nervous Breakdowns; Military Leaders; Bombs-Atomic; Terrorists; Good Premise Unfulfilled; Apocalyptic Stories
(The Hunt for Red October; Dr. Strangelove; Failsafe; Special Bulletin; Crimson Tide; Under Siege)

Twin Beds, 1942, 84m, ★★1/2/$, Small-UA/NA. A drunk wreaks havoc and drives the young married couple next door crazy with the resulting complications of his antics. George Brent, Joan Bennett, Mischa Auer, Una Merkel, Glenda Farrell, Ernest Truex, Margaret Hamilton, Charles Coleman. w. Curtis Kenyon, Kenneth Earl, E. Edwin Moran, P-adap. Margaret Mayo, Edward Salisbury Field, d. Tim Whelan.
COMEDY: FARCE: Bedroom Farce; **ROMANCE:** Romantic Comedy; Marriage Comedy; Marriage on the Rocks; Neighbors-Troublesome; Alcoholics; Coulda Been Great; Forgotten Films

Twin Peaks, 1989, 113m, ★★★/$$$$, ABC/World Vision, NR/S-V. A girl is murdered under bizarre circumstances in a small northwestern town, and an eccentric donut-eating FBI agent comes to town to investigate. Kyle MacLachlan, Michael Ontkean, Madchen Amick, Dana Ashbrook, Richard Beymer, Lara Flynn Boyle, Sherilyn Fenn, Warren Frost, Joan Chen, Piper Laurie. w. Mark Frost, David Lynch, d. David Lynch.
TV Series; Cult Films

Twin Peaks: Fire Walk with Me, 1992, 134m, ★★1/2/$, New Line/New Line, R/S-P-V. The backstory of the murder of Laura Palmer, detailing her involvement with sex, drugs, and the occult. Sheryl Lee, Ray Wise, Madchen Amick, Dana Ashbrook, Phoebe Augustine, David Bowie, Eric DaRue,

Miguel Ferrer, Chris Isaak, Kyle MacLachlan, James Marshall, Jurgen Prochnow, Harry Dean Stanton, Kiefer Sutherland, David Lynch. w. David Lynch, Robert Engels, d. David Lynch.
SUSPENSE: MURDER: MYSTERY: MURDER MYSTERY: Detective Stories; Detectives-Police; FBI Agents; Small-town Life; Rape/Rapists; Incest; Small-town Scandals; Scandals; Rumors; Teenagers; Cult Films

Twins, 1988, 107m, ★★1/2/$$$$, U/MCA-U, PG/P-S. A thirty-six-year-old genetically engineered government experiment-the perfect man-finds out he has a "twin" who got all the rejected genes, so they get together and try to find mommy. Arnold Schwarzenegger, Danny DeVito, Kelly Preston, Chloe Webb, Bonnie Bartlett, Marshall Bell, Trey Wilson, David Caruso, Hugh O'Brian. w. William Davies, William Osborne, Timothy Harris, Herschel Weingrod, d. Ivan Reitman.
COMEDY: ACTION: Action Comedy; Quests; Children-Long-lost; Twins; Brothers; Teams-Mismatched; Family Heritage-Search for; Bodybuilders; Experiments; Blockbusters; Faded Hits
(Junior; The Boys from Syracuse; Big Business)
(Ed: High concept formula premise at its lowest with little more than the juxtaposition of its incredibly physically divergent stars)

Twins of Evil, 1971, 87m, ★★1/2/$, Hammer-WB/NA, Lebell Video. In Austria, identical twins join a coven of vampires and spooky things begin to happen. Madeleine Collinson, Mary Collinson, Peter Cushing, Kathleen Byron, Dennis Price, Isobel Black. w. Tudor Gates, d. John Hough.
HORROR: Vampires; Twins; Twins-Evil; Satanism; 1800s; Austria
(Goodbye Gemini; Dracula's Daughter)

Twinsanity, see **Goodbye Gemini**

Twisted, 1986, 87m, ★★/$, Ind/NA, R/S-P. A nerdy science expert uses his wares to inflict pain upon those who ostracize him. Christian Slater, Tandy Cronyn, Lois Smith. d. Adam Holender.
HORROR: SCI-FI: Murders-One by One; Malicious Menaces; Psycho Killers; Curiosities; Ostracism; Nerds; Revenge

Twisted Nerve, 1968, 118m, ★★/$, BL/NA. A spoiled, psychotic young man is miffed when his mother remarries, so he dresses up as his mongoloid brother to kill his stepfather. Hayley Mills, Hywel Bennett, Phyllis Calvert, Billie Whitelaw, Frank Finlay, Barry Foster, Salmaan Peer. w. Leo Marks, Roy Boulting, d. Roy Boulting.

SUSPENSE: HORROR: MURDER: Murder-Attempted; Murder of Parent; Parents vs. Children; Stepparents vs. Children; Mentally Disabled; Impostors; Identities-Assumed; Revenge; Psycho-Killers; Young Men-Angry
(Daddy's Gone A-Hunting; Color Mommy Dead)

Two Against the World, 1936, 64m, ★★/$$, WB/NA. A yellow rag of a newspaper dishes the dirt with impunity until one story gets to two sensitive souls, and they committ suicide. Humphrey Bogart, Beverly Roberts, Helen MacKellar, Henry O'Neill, Linda Perry, Virginia Brissac. w. Michel Jacoby, P-adap. Louis Weitzenkorn, d. William McGann.

MELODRAMA: Newspapers; Journalists; Ethics; Suicidal Tendencies; Scandals; Forgotten Films
REMAKE/RETREAD OF: Five-Star Final.
(Five-Star Final; The Turning Point [1952])

Two-Faced Woman, 1941, 90m, ★★★/$$, MGM/MGM-UA. A female ski instructor poses as her more bubbly twin sister to try to win back her husband, whose affections are waning. Greta Garbo, Melvyn Douglas, Constance Bennett, Roland Young, Robert Sterling, Ruth Gordon, George Cleveland. w. W. N. Behrman, Salka Viertel, George Oppenheimer, P-adap. Ludwig Fulda, d. George Cukor.

COMEDY: ROMANCE: Romantic Comedy; Screwball Comedy; Twins; Identities-Assumed; Extroverted vs. Introverted; Skiing; Romance-Girl Wants Boy; Marriage on the Rocks; Impostors; Curiosities; Coulda Been Great
(Ed: This might explain why Garbo left)

Two for the Road, 1967, 113m, ★★★1/2/$$, 20th/Fox, PG. A married couple (Audrey Hepburn, Albert Finney) takes a trip across Europe remembering a similar trip years before when they were first together, mirroring the changes in their relationship over the years. Williams Daniels. w. Frederic Raphael (BOScr), d. Stanley Donen. Oscars: 1-0.

DRAMA: Marriage Drama; **ROMANCE:** Romance-Bickering; Vacations; Road Movies; Marriage on the Rocks; Vacations-European; Flashbacks; Memories; Midlife Crisis; Episodic Stories; Alienation; Cult Films; Overlooked Release
(The Happy Ending)

Two for the Seesaw, 1962, 120m, ★★★/$$$, UA/CBS-Fox. A lawyer from Omaha traveling in New York with his estranged wife has a tumultuous affair with a ballet teacher. Robert Mitchum, Shirley MacLaine. w. Isobel Lennart, P-adap. William Gibson, d. Robert Wise. BOSong. Oscars: 1-0.

DRAMA: ROMANCE: Romantic Drama; **COMEDY DRAMA:** Starting Over; Life Transitions; Divorce; Romance with Married Person; Dancers; Lawyers; Time Capsules; Female Screenwriters
(Career; Love with the Proper Stranger)

Two Girls and a Sailor, 1944, 124m, ★★★/$$$, MGM/MGM-UA. Another musical about sailors on shore-leave involving the love-triangle of the title, though this is above average. June Allyson, Gloria de Haven, Van Johnson, Xavier Cugat and his Orchestra, Jimmy Durante, Tom Drake, Lena Horne, Carlos Ramirez, Harry James and his Orchestra, Jose Iturbi, Gracie Allen, Virginia O'Brien, Albert Coates. w. Richard Connell, Gladys Lehman (BScr), d. Richard Thorpe. Oscars: 1-0.

MUSICALS: COMEDY: Musical Comedy; **ROMANCE:** Romance-Triangles; Musical Romance; Dancers; Sailors Shore Leave; Faded Hits; Hidden Gems; Female Protagonists; Female Screenwriters
(On the Town; Hit the Deck)

The Two Jakes, 1990, 138m, ★★/$$, Par/Par, R/P-S-V. Jake Gittes of *Chinatown* fame is haunted by the case of that first film involving a mysterious girl, who reappears in another conspiracy involving real estate development and cover-ups. Jack Nicholson, Harvey Keitel, Meg Tilly, Madeleine Stowe, Eli Wallach, Ruben Blades, Frederic Forrest, David Keith, Richard Farnsworth. w. Robert Towne, d. Jack Nicholson.

DRAMA: MYSTERY: MURDER: MURDER MYSTERY: Conspiracy; Detective Stories; Detectives in Deep; Film Noir-Modern; Los Angeles; 1940s; Elusive

Women; Earthquakes; Actor Directors; Coulda Been Great; Flops-Major
SEQUEL TO: Chinatown.
(Ed: Great looking but thoroughly muddled. It started production with Nicholson and Kelly McGillis in 1985 and changes were made before it began again in 1990—there should have been more . . . or less)

Two Lane Blacktop, 1971, 103m, ★★/$$, U/MCA-U, R/P-S. A pair of eccentrics race their rebuilt old hot rods through the southwestern desert. James Taylor, Warren Oates, Laurie Bird, Dennis Wilson. w. Rudolph Wurlitzer, Will Corry, d. Monte Hellman.

ACTION: DRAMA: Action Drama; Young Men; Hippies; Psychedelic Era; Car Racing; Alienation; Eccentric People; Southwestern Life; Desert Settings; Forgotten Films
(Easy Rider; Big Fauss and Little Halsey)

Two Minute Warning, 1976, 115m, ★★1/2/$$, U/MCA-U, R/P-V. At the Superbowl, a sniper terrorizes the crowd, and must be stopped—in time! Charlton Heston, John Cassavetes, Martin Balsam, Beau Bridges, David Janssen, Marilyn Hassett, Jack Klugman, Gena Rowlands, Walter Pidgeon, Brock Peters, Mitch Ryan. w. Edward Hume, N-adap. George LaFounataine, d. Larry Peerce.

SUSPENSE: ACTION: Snipers; Terrorists; Super Bowl; Murderers-Mass; Psycho-Killers; Race Against Time; Football
(Black Sunday; Nighthawks; Sudden Death)

Two Moon Junction, 1988, 105m, ★★/$$, Col/RCA-Col, R/ES-FFN-MRN. Even though she's about to marry, a wealthy southern belle can't help falling into the bed of a sexy carnival worker and taking off all her clothes—except her heels. Sherilyn Fenn, Richard Tyson, Louise Fletcher, Burl Ives, Kristy McNichol, Martin Hewitt, Juanita Moore, Millie Perkins, Don Galloway. w. d. Zalman King.

MELODRAMA: Erotic Drama; **ROMANCE:** Romantic Drama; Southerns; Love-Forbidden; Marriage-Impending; Sexy Women; Sexy Men; Romance-Class Conflicts; Southerns
SEQUEL: Return to Two Moon Junction.
(Wild Orchid; 9½ Weeks; The Red Shoe Diaries)

The Two Mrs. Carrolls, 1945 (released 1947), 99m, ★★★/$$, WB/WB. A deranged artist paints his wive's portraits just as he's about to poison them. Barbara Stanwyck, Humphrey Bogart, Alexis Smith, Nigel Bruce, Isobel Elsom, Pat O'Moore, Peter Godfrey. w. Thomas Job, P-adap. Martin Vale, d. Peter Godfrey.

SUSPENSE: Murder of Spouse; Dangerous Spouse; **MURDER:** Poison; Women in Jeopardy; Artists; Curiosities (Rebecca; The Secret Beyond the Door; Undercurrent; Suspicion)
(Ed: Only worth it for the stars)

Two Mules for Sister Sara, 1970, 116m, ★★★/$$$, U/MCA-U, PG/V. A renegade gunman witnesses the attempted rape of a nun, and kills the three men involved. But the "nun" turns out to be something altogether different, leading them both on an interesting journey. Clint Eastwood, Shirley MacLaine, Manolo Fabregas, Alberto Morin. w. Albert Maltz, Budd Boeticher, d. Don Siegel.

WESTERNS: COMEDY DRAMA: Western Comedy; Prostitutes-Low Class; Nuns; Saving Someone; Rape/Rapists; Revenge; Revenge on Rapist; Westerns-Revenge; Journies; Tough Guys & Religious Women; Disguises; Vigilantes
(Rooster Cogburn; Hannie Caulder; Hang 'em High)

Two of a Kind, 1983, 87m, ★/$, 20th/Fox, PG. God wants to have another flood, but four angels band together to find two human beings who think more of each other than themselves-or something like that. John Travolta, Olivia Newton-John, Charles Durning, Oliver Reed, Beatrice Straight, Scatman Crothers. w. d. John Herzfeld.

COMEDY DRAMA: Fantasy; Angels; Heaven; **ROMANCE:** Romantic Comedy; Flops-Major; Curiosities
(Grease; Heart and Souls)

Two or Three Things I Know About Her, 1967, 95m, ★★★/$$, Ind/New Yorker, NA. In Paris, a young mother must work as a prostitute to support her two children and her middle-class way of life. Jean-Luc Godard (narrator), Marina Vlady, Anny Duperey, Roger Montsoret, Jean Narboni, Christophe Bourseiller, Marie Bourseiller. w. d. Jean-Luc Godard.

DRAMA: Art Films; Character Studies; Housewives; Mothers-Struggling; Prostitutes-Ordinary People Turned; Prostitutes-High Class; Time Capsules; Secrets-Keeping; Dual Lives; Paris; French Films; French New Wave Films; Writer-Directors

Two People, 1973, 100m, ★★1/2/$, U/NA. A female photographer for a fashion magazine falls for an army deserter. Peter Fonda, Lindsay Wagner, Estelle Parsons, Alan Fudge. w. Richard de Roy, Robert Wise.

DRAMA: Character Studies; **ROMANCE:** Romantic Drama; Romance-Brief; Soldiers; Vietnam Era; Peaceful People; Fashion World; Quiet Little Films; 1970s
(John and Mary; The Paper Chase)

2001: A Space Odyssey, 1968, 141m, ★★★★/$$$$$, MGM/MGM-UA. A film essay on man's cosmic struggle to reach Godhead, from the Neanderthal's first tool to the space stations of the future. Gary Lockwood, Keir Dullea, William Sylvester, Leonard Rossiter, Robert Beatty, Daniel Richter, Douglas Rain (voice of HAL). w. Stanley Kubrick, Arthur C. Clarke, SS-adap. Arthur C. Clarke (The Sentinel), d. Stanley Kubrick.

SCI-FI: Outer Space Movies; **ADVENTURE:** Epics; Computers; Man vs. Machine; Art Films; Blockbusters; Alienation; Lonely People; Cult Films

SEQUEL: 2010.
(Ed: One of the few films which can be labeled both an art film and a blockbuster)

2010, 1984, 114m, ★★1/2/$$$, MGM-UA/MGM-UA, PG/V-P. The abandoned ship Discovery is reboarded and astronauts search for the meaning of the monolith. Roy Scheider, John Lithgow, Helen Mirren, Bob Balaban, Keir Dullea, Dana Elcar, Madolyn Smith. w. d. Peter Hyams, N-adap. Arthur C. Clarke.

SCI-FI: Outer Space Movies; **ADVENTURE:** Journies; Searches; **MYSTERY:** Coulda Been Great

SEQUEL TO: 2001.

2000 Maniacs, 1964, 75m, ★★★/$, Ind/Rhino Video. Southern Civil War soldiers' ghosts attack Yankee tourists who invade their haunt. Thomas Wood, Connie Mason, Ben Moore. w. d. Herschell Gordon Lewis.

HORROR: Ghosts; Revenge; Civil War Era; Soldiers; North vs. South; Southerns; Writer-Directors; Camp; Cult Films
(Night of the Living Dead; Dawn of the Dead)

Two Way Stretch, 1960, 87m, ★★★/$$, BL/NA. Three prisoners plan an elaborate break in order to rob a maharajah, but things don't go smoothly in the getaway. Peter Sellers, Lionel Jeffries, Wilfrid Hyde White, Bernard Cribbins, David Lodge, Maurice Denham, Beryl Reid, Liz Fraser, Irene Handl, George Woodbridge. w. John Warren, Len Heath, d. Robert Day.

COMEDY: FARCE: Capers; Heist Stories; Jewel Thieves; Prison Escapes; Royalty; Indian People; British Films; Hidden Gems
(Convict 99; The Italian Job; The Wrong Arm of the Law)

Two Weeks in Another Town, 1962, 107m, ★★★/$, MGM/MGM-UA. A washed-up Hollywood director finds backers in Rome who still believe in him, but can he overcome hauntings from the past and a drinking problem? Kirk Douglas, Edward G. Robinson, Cyd Charisse, Daliah Lavi, George Hamilton, Claire Trevor, Rosanna Schiaffino, James Gregory, George Macready. w. Charles Schnee, N-adap. Irwin Shaw, d. Vincente Minnelli.

DRAMA: Character Studies; Hollywood Life; Hollywood Satire; Directors; Actors; Actresses; Moviemaking; Rome; Cult Films; Hidden Gems; Forgotten Films; Flops-Major
(The Bad and the Beautiful; The Big Knife; The Oscar; The Lost Weekend; Leaving Las Vegas)

Two Women, 1961, 110m, ★★★1/2/$$$, UA/MGM-UA. A young woman and her daughter travel war-torn Italy any way they can, trying to stay alive and to get help from the invading troops. Sophia Loren (BActress), Eleonora Brown, Jean-Paul Belmondo, Raf Vallone. w. Cesare Zavattini, Vittorio de Sica, N-adap. Alberto Moravia, d. de Sica. Oscars: 1-1.

DRAMA: MELODRAMA: TRAGEDY: Mothers & Daughters; Mothers-Struggling; War Stories; War at Home; World War II Stories; Journies; Protecting Someone; Escape Drama; Rape/Rapists; Italians; Italian Films; Sleeper Hits; Hidden Gems; Faded Hits; Female Protagonists
(Open City; Yesterday, Today & Tomorrow)
(Ed: Loren's tour de force is the only foreign language performance to ever win an Oscar)

The Two Worlds of Jenny Logan, 1979, 97m, ★★★/$$$, CBS/Fries, Live. A woman puts on a dress she finds in her house and travels back to Victorian times when the dress was made in that house. She finds another lover there and can't decide whether, or how, to return. Lindsay Wagner, Marc Singer, Alan Feinstein, Linda Gray, Constance McCashin, Joan Darling. d. Frank de Felitta.

MELODRAMA: ROMANCE: Romantic Drama; Time Travel; Victorian Era; Dual Lives; Romance-Choosing the Right Person; Female Protagonists; TV Movies

U

UFOria, 1982, 92m, ★★★/$, U/MCA-U, PG. Ordinary people in a small desert town start seeing very extraordinary things in the sky, which leads to a cult-like following in town, changing the life of a checkout girl. Cindy Williams, Fred Ward, Harry Dean Stanton. d. John Binder.
COMEDY DRAMA: Comedy-Light; Small-town Life; UFOs; Ordinary People Stories; Unbelieved; Desert Settings; Southwestern Life
(Melvin & Howard; True Stories; Close Encounters)
Ugetsu Monogatari, 1953, 94m, ★★★/$, Ind/Sultan. Two ambitious artisans in the 16th century destroy themselves and their families. Masayuki Mori, Machiko Kyo, Sakae Ozawa. w. Masayuki Kawaguchi, from a 17th-century collection by Akinara Ueda (*Tales of a Pale and Mysterious Moon after the Rain*), d. Kenji Mizoguchi.
DRAMA: TRAGEDY: Family Drama; Historical Drama; Episodic Stories; Japan; Japanese Films
(Throne of Blood; Ran; Rashomon)
The Ugly American, 1962, 120m, ★★1/2/$$, U/MCA-U. An ambassador in Asia must deal with a Communist uprising and his lack of power. Marlon Brando, Ejii Okada, Sandra Church, Pat Hingle, Arthur Hill, Kukrit Pramoj. w. Stewart Stern, N-adap. William J. Lederer.

DRAMA: Political Drama; Political Unrest; Social Drama; Rich vs. Poor; Imperialist Problems; Communists; Cold War Era; Diplomats; Asia; Forgotten Films; Americans as Enemy
(Burn!; The Year of Living Dangerously; Indochine)
The Ugly Dachshund, 1965, 93m, ★★★/$$$, Disney/Disney, G. A baby Great Dane wiggles its way into a family of Dachshunds that a couple rushes to the hospital for the birth like it was a baby of their own. Dean Jones, Suzanne Pleshette, Charles Ruggles, Mako. w. Albert Aley, N-adap. G. B. Stern, d. Norman Tokar.
COMEDY: CHILDREN'S: FAMILY: Family Comedy; Pet Stories; Dogs; Marriage Comedy; Suburban Life; Sleeper Hits; Forgotten Films
(101 Dalmatians; Blackbeard's Ghost)
UHF, 1989, 97m, ★-/$, Orion/Orion, PG-13/P. A goofball gets a job running a cheapo TV station and takes on the networks. Weird Al Yankovic, Kevin McCarthy, Victoria Jackson, Michael Richard, Anthony Geary, David Bowie. d. Jay Levey.
COMEDY: Spoofs; Spoofs-TV; TV Life; Nerds; Underdog Stories
(Stay Tuned; Americathon)
Ulysses, 1954, 103m, ★★1/2/$, Lux Film-DEG/WB. Cassandra puts a curse on

Ulysses and he sets sail on a quest to pass several tests, including the killing of the Cyclops. Kirk Douglas, Silvana Mangano, Anthony Quinn, Rosanna Podesta. w. Franco Brusati, Mario Camerini, Ennio de Concini, Hugh Gray, Ben Hecht, Ivo Perelli, Irwin Shaw, (Poem)-adap. Homer, (*The Odyssey*), d. Mario Camerini.
ACTION: ADVENTURE: Adventure at Sea; Mythology; Ancient Times; Curses; Evil Witches; Forgotten Films
(The Vikings; The Long Ships; The Trojan Women)
Ulysses, 1967, 132m, ★★★/$, Reade/Strick, PG/P. A young Irish poet and a Jewish journalist spend a day in Dublin, encountering all sorts of odd sorts. Maurice Roeves, Milo O'Shea, Barbara Jefford. w. Joseph Strick, Fred Haines (BAScr), N-adap. James Joyce, d. Joseph Strick. Oscars: 1-0.
DRAMA: Character Studies; Friendships-Male; Irish People; Jewish People; Poets; Journalists; One Day Stories; Classic Lieterary Adaptations; Forgotten Films
(The Dead; Portrait of the Artist)
(Ed: The literal plot pulled from the ramblingly long classic, watered down but hardly what the book was admired for. The mild profanity was a big deal on its initial release)
Ulzana's Raid, 1972, 103m, ★★/$, Universal/MCA-U, R/V. A group of cow-

boys and Indians allign to avenge a vicious Apache attack. Burt Lancaster, Bruce Davison, Lorge Luke, Richard Jaeckel. w. Alan Sharp, d. Robert Aldrich.

WESTERN: Men in Conflict; War Battles; Revenge; Westerns-Revenge; Avenging; Death of Someone; Forgotten Films

Umberto D., 1952, 89m, ★★★/$, Dear Films/Nos, Sultan. A poor man in Italy living on the old-age pension loves his dog and almost gets evicted because of taking care of it. Carlo Battista, Maria Pia Casilio, Lina Gennari. w. Cesare Zavattini (BOStory), Vittorio de Sica, d. Vittorio de Sica. Oscars: 1-0.

COMEDY DRAMA: DRAMA: Character Studies; Pet Stories; Dogs; Elderly Men; Italian Films; Hidden Gems; Quiet Little Films

(We Think the World of You; Harry and Tonto)

The Umbrellas of Cherbourg, 1965, 92m, ★★★-/$$$, Parc-AIP/Live. A brief but intense liason between a gas station attendant and a local shopgirl gets her pregnant, but he's off in the army by the time she knows. She marries another man to save face, and years later meets up with the father of her child. Catherine Deneuve, Anne Vernon, Nino Castelnuovo. w. d. Jacques Demy (BOScr). BOScore, BAScore, BOSong, BFLFilm (1964). Oscars: 5-0.

MELODRAMA: ROMANCE: Romantic Drama; Romance-Reunited; Tearjerkers; Mothers-Unwed; Babies-Having; Working Class; Soldiers; Sleeper Hits; French Films; Forgotten Films; Hidden Gems; Lyrical Films; Writer-Directors

(Love with the Proper Stranger; The Young Girls of Rochefort)

The Unbearable Lightness of Being, 1987, 171m, ★★★/$$, Zaentz-Orion/Orion, R/ES-FFN-MRN. During and after the occupation of Prague, a love triangle between a Czech brain surgeon and two women plays itself out. Daniel Day Lewis, Juliette Binoche, Lena Olin. w. Jean-Claude Carriere, Philip Kaufman (BAScr), N-adap. Milan Kundera, d. Philip Kaufman. BCin. Oscars: 2-0.

DRAMA: Erotic Drama; Character Studies; **ROMANCE:** Romantic Drama; Romance-Triangles; Escape Drama; Cold War Era; Political Drama; Political Unrest; Oppression; Communists; Europeans-Eastern; Quiet Little Films

(Night Crossing; Henry and June)

(Ed: It's a long little film and unbearable for some)

The Unbelievable Truth, 1989, 90m, ★★★¹/₂/$, Vidmark/Vidmark, R/S. The day-dreaming, bookish daughter of a mechanic falls for the mysterious stranger who gets a job at her dad's garage. He turns out to be an escaped murderer. Adrienne Shelly, Robert Burke, Christopher Cooke, Julia McNeal. w. d. Hal Hartley.

DRAMA: Art Films; **ROMANCE:** Romance-Dangerous; **MURDER:** Secrets-Keeping; Drifters; Strangers in Town; Young Women; Female Protagonists; Overlooked at Release; Writer-Directors

(Smooth Talk; Trust; Simple Men; Hold Me, Thrill Me, Kiss Me)

(Ed: Better than most of Hartley's later ones-this has a story)

The Unborn, 1991, 85m, ★★/$, Col/Col, R. A woman gets inseminated but what grows inside her isn't what she planned on. Brooke Adams, Jeff Hayenge, K. Callan. d. Rodman Flander.

HORROR: Abortion Dilemmas; Babies-Having; Monsters-Human

(It's Alive; Rosemary's Baby; The Entity)

Un Chien Andalou (*An Andalusian Dog*), 1928, 20m, ★★★★/NA, Ind/Hollywood Home. The classic surrealist film with the famous slicing of an eyeball scene among other startling images—a dead horse, a severed hand, ants eating a man's hand, you know . . . . Pierre Batcheeff, Simon Marevil. d. Luis Bunuel, Salvador Dali.

HORROR: Art Films; Surrealism; French Films; Film History

Uncle Buck, 1989, 100m, ★★★¹/₂/$$$, U/MCA-U, PG-13/P-S. A fat slob is entrusted with the care of his sister's children who rebel and then grow to like him, all while he fights off the insane advances of a neighbor and the grumblings of his girlfriend. John Candy, Jean Louisa Kelly, Gaby Hoffman, Macaulay Culkin, Amy Madigan, Laurie Metcalf. w. d. John Hughes.

COMEDY: COMEDY DRAMA: FAMILY: CHILDREN'S: Family Comedy; Babysitters; Teenagers; Snobs vs. Slobs; Uncles; Parents are Gone; Parents are Gone from Chicago; Suburban Life; Infatuations; Bathroom Humor; Underrated; Relatives-Troublesome; Writer-Directors

(Home Alone; Sitting Pretty; Planes, Trains and Automobiles)

(Ed: Candy's funniest, poignant best and the role that started Macaulay Culkin going)

Uncle Tom's Cabin, 1914, 54m, ★★/$$$$, Ind/Facets. Mary Eline, Irving Cummings. d. William Robert Daly. Silent Films

Uncle Tom's Cabin, 1969, 120m, ★★/$, Ind/Xenon. Herbert Lom, John Kitzmiller, O.W. Fischer. d. Geza con Radvanyi.

Uncle Tom's Cabin, 1987, 110m, ★★★/$, Ind/Worldvision. Kate Burton, Avery Brooks, Bruce Dern, Paula Kelly, Phylicia Rashad, Kathryn Walker, Edward Woodward. d. Stan Latham TV Movies

>Story of the underground railroad in the old South and white people who helped blacks get across the Kentucky border to safety.

MELODRAMA: Slavery; Southerns; Saving Someone; Black vs. White; Race Relations; Black Men; Classic Literary Adaptations

(A Woman Called Moses; Roots)

Un Coeur en Hiver, 1993, 100m, ★★★/$, Ind/Republic, R/S. Friends run a music business, but a romance with one beautiful young woman threatens to tear everything apart, and poses the question as to the difference between true artists and simple craftsmen. Emmanuelle Beart, Daniel Auteil, Andre Dussolier. w. Yves Ullman, Jacques Fieschi, Jerome Tonnerre, d. Claude Sautet.

DRAMA: ROMANCE: Romantic Drama; Men Fighting Over Women; Romance-Triangles; Friendships-Male; Stern Men; Musicians; French Films

(Bitter Moon; Boyfriends and Girlfriends)

Uncommon Valor, 1983, 105m, ★★/$$, Par/Par, R/V-P. A former military man goes looking for his M.I.A. son in Vietnam. Gene Hackman, Robert Stack, Fred Ward, Patrick Swayze. w. Joe Gayton, d. Ted Kotcheff.

ACTION: War Stories; Missing Persons; Searches; Missing in Action; P.O.W.s; Fathers & Sons; Avenging Death of Someone; Vietnam Veterans; Vietnam War

(First Blood; Rambo: First Blood 2; Missing in Action; Air America)

Unconquered, 1947, 146m, ★★/$$, Par/NA. In England, a female convict is sent to the American penal colony in the

1800s. She reforms and marries an army man from Virginia. Paulette Goddard, Gary Cooper, Boris Karloff, Howard da Silva, Ward Bond. w. Charles Bennett, Frederic M. Frank, Jesse Lasky, Jr., N-adap. Neil H. Swanson, d. Cecil B. de Mille.

MELODRAMA: ROMANCE: Tearjerkers; Criminals-Female; Prison Drama; Reformers; Redemption; Starting Over; Early America; Forgotten Films; Female Protagonists

(So Proudly We Hail; Ada; The Last of Mrs. Cheyney)

The Undefeated, 1969, 119m, ★★/$$, 20th NA. A general for the North and a Confederate General meet on the Rio Grande after the Civil War and find that old grudges die hard. John Wayne, Rock Hudson, Lee Merriwether. w. James Lee Barrett, d. Andrew V. McLaglen.

WESTERNS: Men in Conflicts; North vs. South; Civil War Era; Feuds; Duels; Forgotten Films

(Ed: The Duke and Rock together at last, and one of the Duke's few flops of the era-Rock had many. Luckily, Wayne had *True Grit* the same year)

Under Capricorn, 1949, 117, ★★1/2/$, Transatlantic-RKO/Vestron. An Englishman visits his cousin in Australia and finds her entangled in a vicious web woven by her sadistic husband. Ingrid Bergman, Joseph Cotten, Michael Wilding. w. James Birdie, N-adap. Helen Simpson, d. Alfred Hitchcock.

MELODRAMA: Psychological Drama; Costume Drama; Abused Women; Australia; Female Protagonists; Forgotten Films; Flops-Major; Hitchcockian

(The Sundowners; Frenchman's Creek; Adam Had Four Sons)

(Ed: A real rarity-boring Hitchcock)

Undercover Blues, 1993, 90m, ★★-/$, MGM/MGM-UA, PG-13/P-V. Two slick secret agents who are married take on a case in New Orleans while on vacation, then do battle with arms dealers and goofy thugs. Kathleen Turner, Dennis Quaid, Fiona Shaw, Stanley Tucci, Tom Arnold, Park Overall, Saul Rubinek. w. Ian Abrams, d. Herbert Ross.

COMEDY: ACTION: Action Comedy; Detective Couples; Secret Agents; Married Couples; Cartoonlike Films; Spoofs-Spy; Spies; New Orleans; Arms Dealers

(Foul Play; The Thin Man; The Big Easy)

(Ed: What was supposed to be an update of Nick and Nora of *Thin Man* fame is a dumbed-up children's flick instead)

Under Fire, 1983, 127m, ★★★/$$, Orion/Orion, R/P-V. In Nicaragua, American reporters go undercover on both the Sandanista and Contra sides. Gene Hackman, Nick Nolte, Joanna Cassidy, Jean-Louis Trintignant, Ed Harris, Richard Masur. w. Ron Shelton, Clayton Frohman, d. Roger Spottiswoode.

DRAMA: ACTION: War Stories; Journalists; Spies; Central America; Communists; Undercover; Photographers (Salvador)

Under Milk Wood, 1971, 88m, ★★★/$, 20th/Fox, PG. Dylan Thomas's view of life in his small Welsh fishing village. Richard Burton, Elizabeth Taylor, Peter O'Toole, Glynis Johns, Vivien Merchant. w. d. Andrew Sinclair, P-adap. Dylan Thomas.

DRAMA: Character Studies; **ROMANCE:** Biographies; Autobiographical Stories; Writers; Poets; Ordinary People Stories; Fishermen; Small-town Life; England; Quiet Little Films; Forgotten Films; Underrated; Hidden Gems

(Local Hero; The Corn Is Green; The Field)

Under Siege, 1992, 102m, ★★★/$$$$, WB/WB, R/EP-EV. When a nuclear military ship is hijacked by terrorists, the cook and a stripper (?) manage to thwart them. Steven Seagal, Tommy Lee Jones, Gary Busey, Eirka Eleniak, Patrick O'Neal. w. J. F. Lawton, d. Andrew Davis. BSound, BSoundEdit. Oscars: 2-0.

ACTION: Terrorists; Hijackings; Ships; Bombs-Atomic; Heroes-Unlikely; Die-Hard plots; Sleeper Hits

(Die Hard; Die Hard 2; Speed; Juggernaut)

(Ed: *Die Hard* on a ship)

Under Siege 2, 1995, 98m, ★★1/2/$$, WB/WB, R/V-P. In this sequel to the *Die Hard* ripoff, Navy SEAL Casey is on a train with his niece when, lo and behold, terrorists take over the train and try to control the world with a satellite dish on board. Steven Seagal, Eric Bogosian, Katherine Heigl, Morris Chestnut, Everett McGill, Nick Mancuso. w. Richard Hatem & Matt Reeves, d. Geoff Murphy.

ACTION: SUSPENSE: Terrorists; Rule the World-Plot to; Pentagon; Trains; Die-Hard Stories; Race Against Time

(Under Siege; Die Hard SERIES; The Cassandra Crossing)

(Ed: Sequel to the sleeper on the ship, but this time there's no humor and nothing new in a rip-off of a rip-off)

Under Suspicion, 1991, 100m, ★★/$, Col/Col, R/P-S-FFN-MN. A detective having an affair with his client's mistress is accused of their murders when he's caught with her and escapes just before the murder. The man's wife comes into the picture to get him to figure out who did it. Liam Neeson, Laura San Giacomo, Kenneth Cranham, Maggie O'Neil, Alan Talbot. w. d. Simon Moore.

SUSPENSE: MURDER: MYSTERY: MURDER MYSTERY: Conspiracy; Detective Stories; Detectives in Deep; Romance-Unprofessional; Accused Unjustly; Saving Oneself; Framed?; Film Noir-Modern; England; 1950s; Overlooked at Release; Good Premise Unfulfilled; Writer-Directors

(Double Indemnity; Body Heat)

(Ed: Not up to what it's imitating, with a muddled plot and miscast leading lady all dressed up but in need of elocution lessons)

Under the Cherry Moon, 1986, 100m, (B&W), ★1/2/$, WB/WB, PG-13/S. A singer goes to Monte Carlo during the 40s and meets a lovely but capricious white British woman. Not much else. Prince, Kristin Scott Thomas, Francesca Annis, Jerome Betnon. d. Prince.

MELODRAMA: Music Movies; Singers; Black Men; Romance-Interracial; Monte Carlo; 1940s; Flops-Major; Unintentionally Funny

(Graffiti Bridge; Purple Rain)

Under the Rainbow, 1981, 95m, ★★1/2/$, Orion-WB/Orion, PG. During the filming of *The Wizard of Oz*, the midgets are interspersed with Nazi spies and misfits in love. Chevy Chase, Carrie Fisher, Billy Barty, Eve Arden, Joseph Maher. w. Pat McCormick, Harry Hurwitz, Martin Smith, Pat Bradley, Fred Bauer, d. Steve Rash.

COMEDY: SATIRE: FARCE: Actors; Actresses; Eccentric People; Behind the Scenes; Little People-Midgets; Hollywood Life; Movie Making; Movies within Movies; Coulda Been Good; Good Premise Unfulfilled; Forgotten Films

(Won Ton Ton the Dog Who Saved Hollywood; Nickelodeon; The Wizard of Oz)

(Ed: Beware of movies with millions of writers—except *Tootsie*)

Under the Volcano, 1984, 111m, ★★★/$, U/MCA-U, R/S. An alcoholic Brit is stuck in Mexico during a nervous breakdown as his beautiful ex-wife comes to visit and falls for a young man. Albert Finney (BActor), Jacqueline Bisset, Anthony Andrews, Katy Jurado. w. Guy Gallo, N-adap. Malcolm Lowry, d. John Huston. BOScore. Oscars: 2-0.

DRAMA: TRAGEDY: Character Studies; Nervous Breakdowns; Midlife Crisis; Alcoholics; Jealousy; Cuckolded Mexico; Volcanos; Allegorical Stories; Classic Literary Adaptations

(Night of the Iguana; The Green Man)

Under the Yum Yum Tree, 1963, 110m, ★★★/$$$, Col/RCA-Col. Two unmarried young people move in together and a nosy landlord wants to know what's up. Jack Lemmon, Carol Lynley, Dean Jones, Imogene Coca, Edie Adams, Paul Lynde, Robert Lansing. w. Lawrence Romanc, David Swift, d. David Swift.

COMEDY: FARCE: ROMANCE: Romantic Comedy; Living Together; Roommates; Newlyweds; Young People; Neighbors-Nosy; Landlords; Nuisances; Apartment Buildings; Hidden Gems; Underrated; Stagelike Films

(Good Neighbor Sam; Sunday in New York; A Period of Adjustment; Barefoot in the Park; It Happened One Night; Happy Together)

(Ed: So it's not brilliant-it works and Lemmon is hilarious in a character turn)

Under Two Flags, 111m, ★★1/2/$$, 20th/NA. A foreign legion soldier in trouble gets help from a waitress who likes him. Ronald Colman, Claudette Colbert, Rosalind Russell, Victor McLaglen, J. Edward Bromberg, Gregory Ratoff. w. W. P. Lipscomb, Walter Ferris, N-adap., *Ouida*, d. Frank Lloyd.

ADVENTURE: War Stories; **ROMANCE: MELODRAMA:** Foreign Legion; Soldiers; Waitresses; All-Star Casts

(Destry Rides Again)

Undercurrent, 1945, 127m, ★★★/$$, MGM/MGM-UA-Turner. When a woman (Katharine Hepburn) marries an industrial magnate (Robert Taylor), she soon begins encountering secrecy surrounding the disappearance of his brother and when she tries to find out about him, it may lead to more than she bargained for. Robert Mitchum, Marjorie Main, Edmund

Gwenn, Jayne Meadows. w. Edward Chodorov, Thelma Strabel, d. Vincente Minnelli.

SUSPENSE: DRAMA: MYSTERY: Psychological Drama; Missing Persons; Women in Jeopardy; Enemies-Sleeping with; Secrets-Haunted by; Brothers; Rich People; Forgotten Films; Female Screenwriters; Female Protagonists (Rebecca; Deceived; Suspicion; The Secret Beyond the Door)

(Ed: A fascinating find for Hepburn fans, a departure in many ways-and she's fascinating as long as she doesn't cry.)

Underworld, USA, 1960, 99m, ★★★/$, Col/Col. When his father his killed by the mob, a young man plots revenge in the dark streets of the city. Cliff Robertson, Beatrice Kay, Larry Gates. w. d. Samuel Fuller.

DRAMA: ACTION: Crime Drama; Mob Stories; Revenge; Avenging Death of Loved One; Film Noir; Inner City Life; Young Men; Young Men-Angry; Writer-Directors

(Shock Treatment; Murder Inc.)

The Unfaithful, 1947, 109m, ★★1/2/$$, WB/NA. When her husband leaves for a while, a woman gets into a little trouble, namely murder. Ann Sheridan, Zachary Scott, Lew Ayres, Eve Arden. w. David Goodis, James Gunn, d. Vincent Sherman.

SUSPENSE: MELODRAMA: MURDER: Crimes of Passion; **TRAGEDY:** Romance-Triangles; Cheating Women; Cuckolded

REMAKE/RETREAD: The Letter.

Unfaithfully Yours, 1948, 105m, ★★★1/2/$$, 20th/CBS-Fox. When a maestro fantasizes that his wife is cheating, he concocts several different ways of doing her in. Rex Harrison, Linda Darnell, Barbara Lawrence, Rudy Vallee, Kurt Krueger, Lionel Stander, Edgar Kennedy. w. d. Preston Sturges.

Writer-Directors; Cult Films

Unfaithfully Yours, 1984, 95m, ★★1/2/$$, 20th/CBS-Fox, PG. This time, there's only one plot to kill the wife, instead of three. Dudley Moore, Nastassja Kinski, Armand Assante, Albert Brooks, Cassie Yates. w. Valerie Curtin, Barry Levinson, Robert Klane, d. Howard Zieff.

COMEDY: Black Comedy; Comedy-Morbid; Murder of Spouse; Murder-Attempted; Fantasies; Paranoia; Cheating Women; Musicians; Female Screenwriters

REMAKE OF: 1948 version.

(A Shock to the System; A New Leaf)

An Unfinished Piece for a Player Piano, 1977, 100m, ★★★/$, Ind/Connoisseur. In pre-Revolution Russia, a general's widow has family and friends over, which becomes a sort of calm before the storm. Alexander Kalyagri. d. Nikita Mikhailov.

MELODRAMA: ROMANCE: Family Drama; Reunions; Multiple Stories; 1900s; Russia; Russian Films; Hidden Gems

The Unforgiven, 1960, 125m, ★★1/2/$$, UA/NA. Problems arise when a supposed half-breed daughter of a rancher encounters racism. Audrey Hepburn, Burt Lancaster, Audie Murphy, Lillian Gish, Charles Bickford, Doug McClure, John Saxon. w. Ben Maddow, N-adap. Alan Le May, d. John Huston.

DRAMA: WESTERNS: Men in Conflict; Protecting Someone; Race Relations; Bigots; Cattle Ranchers; Young Women; Fathers & Daughters; Indians-American

(Vera Cruz; Ulzana's Raid)

Unforgiven, 1992, 131m, ★★★1/2/$$$$$, WB/WB, R/S-V. When a hooker is slashed by a man who's small endowment she laughed at, a bounty hunter is hired by the brothel to kill him, but first the hunter has to deal with the locals. Clint Eastwood (BActor), Gene Hackman (BSActor), Morgan Freeman, Richard Harris, Jaimz Woolvett, Saul Rubinek, Frances Fisher, Anna Thomason. w. David Webb Peoples (BOScr), d. Clint Eastwood (BDirector). BPicture, BEdit, BSound, BCin, BArt. Oscars: 9-4.

WESTERNS: DRAMA: Westerns-Neo; Revisionist Films; Bounty Hunters; Manhunt; Prostitutes-Low Class; Cowboys; Westerns-Revenge; Revenge; Ethics; Black Cowboys; Police Corruption; Making a Living; Fathers Alone; Sleeper Hits; Actor Directors

(The Outlaw Josey Wales; Pale Rider)

The Unholy, 1987, 102m, ★★/$, Vestron/Vestron, PG-13/V. A priest goes to a church to perform an exorcism and runs into demons and lust. Ben Cross, Ned Beatty, William Russ, Jill Carroll, Hal Holbrook, Trevor Howard. w. Philip Yordan, Fernando Fonseca, d. Camilo Vilo.

HORROR: SCI-FI: Supernatural Danger; Priests; Satan; Possessions; Exorcisms; Religion; Good vs. Evil; Coulda Been Good

(The Exorcist; The Exorcist II; The Rosary Murders)

The Uninvited, 1944, 98m, ★★★¹/₂/$$, Par/MCA-U. A young woman goes to the home of a brother and sister to find her mother's ghost haunting the house. The brother and sister don't understand the evil intent. Ruth Hussey, Ray Milland, Gail Russell, Donald Crisp, Dorothy Stickney. w. Dodie Smith, N-adap. Dorothy Macardle (*Uneasy Freehold*), d. Lewis Allen.

SUSPENSE: HORROR: Ghosts; Houses-Creepy; Possessions; Haunted Houses; Death-Dealing with; Brothers & Sisters; Sleeper Hits; Forgotten Films; Hidden Gems; Female Screenwriters; Female Protagonists
(The Haunting; Dead of Night)

Union Pacific, 1939, 133m, ★★★/$$$, Par/NA. Epic surrounding the building of great railroads out west and the people in charge, those who did the labor, as well as Indians in the way. Barbara Stanwyck, Joel McCrea, Akim Tamiroff, Robert Preston, Brian Donlevy, Anthony Quinn, Evelyn Keyes. w. Walter deLeon, Gardner Sullivan, Jesse Lasky, d. Cecil B. DeMille.

DRAMA: ADVENTURE: WESTERNS: Epics; Trains; Historical Drama; Ensemble Films; Cast of Thousands; Worker vs. Boss; Indians-American

Union Station, 1950, 80m, ★★★/$$, Par/Barr Video, MCA-U. Kidnappers decide they want the money dropped at the train station, which the story then centers around. William Holden, Barry Fitzgerald, Nancy Olson, Lyle Bettger, Jan Sterling. w. Sidney Boehm, N-adap. Thomas Walsh, d. Rudolph Mate.

SUSPENSE: MELODRAMA: Kidnappings; Race Against Time; Saving Someone; Trains; Forgotten Films
(Naked City; Cohen and Tate)

Universal Soldier, 1992, 103m, ★★/$$$, Carolco-Tri-Star/Live, PG-13/EV. Vietnam casualties are put back together as half-man/half-machine and become mercenaries, but the wiring isn't so good. Jean-Claude Van Damme, Dolph Lundgren, Jerry Orbach. w. Ricahrd Rothstein, Christopher Leitch, Dean Devlin, d. Roland Emmerich.

ACTION: SCI-FI: Dead-back from the; Man vs. Machine; Vietnam Veterans
(Cyborg; Robocop SERIES)

Unlawful Entry, 1992, 111m, ★★★/$$$, 20th/CBS-Fox, R/S-V-P. A yuppie couple's home is broken into and the good-looking cop that answers their call

decides he wants the wife and sets out to systematically destroy the husband. Ray Liotta, Kurt Russell, Madeleine Stowe, Roger E. Mosley. w. Lewis Colick, George D. Putnam, John Katchmer, d. Jonathan Kaplan.

SUSPENSE: ACTION: Psychological Drama; Police Corruption; Friends as Enemies; Rogue Plots; Framed?; Accused Unjustly; Malicious Menaces; Kill the Beast
(The Hand that Rocks the Cradle; Blindside)
(Ed: As this genre goes, one of the better)

An Unmarried Woman, 1978, 120m, ★★★★/$$$, 20th/Fox, R/S-P. When a woman (Jill Clayburgh, BActress) finds her husband's been cheating and wants to leave her, she goes through a major transition and learns how to be independent. Michael Murphy, Alan Bates. w. d. Paul Mazursky (BOScr). BPicture. Oscars: 3-0.

DRAMA: ROMANCE: Character Studies; Marriage Drama; Life Transitions; Single Women; Starting Over; Midlife Crises; Cheating Men; Female Protagonists; Women's Films; Writer-Directors
(Alice Doesn't Live Here Anymore; Starting Over; It's My Turn; I'm Dancing as Fast as I Can; The Rain People)

The Unnamable, 1988, 97m, ★★/$, Vidmark/Vidmark, R/EV-B&G. College students discover a haunting near campus by a demon who likes to not only haunt but kill. Mark Stephenson, Alexandra Durrell. d. Jean-Paul Oullette.

The Unnamable Returns, 1992, 92m, ★★¹/₂/VR, Prism/Prism, R/EV-B&G. College students get into the occult and unleash a demon onto campus. John Rhys-Davies, Mark Stephenson, David Warner. w. d. Jean-Paul Ouellette, N-adap. H.P. Lovecraft.

HORROR: SCI-FI: Supernatural Dangers; **MURDERS:** Murders One by One; Demons; Possessions; Occult; College Life; British Films; Coulda Been Good; Overlooked at Release

Unnatural Causes, 1986, 96m, ★★★/$$$, NBC/NA. A Vietnam vet suffers complications of Agent Orange defoliant and tries to bring attention to it with the help of a nurse before it's too late for others. John Ritter, Alfre Woodard, Patti Labelle, John Sayles. w. John Sayles, d. Lamont Johnson.

DRAMA: Medical Drama; Fighting the System; Disease Stories; Veterans-

Vietnam; Nurses; Romance-Interracial; Friendship-Interracial; TV Movies; True Stories
(Coming Home; Waterdance)

The Unseen, 1945, 82m, ★★¹/₂/$, Par/NA. The nanny of an American couple living in London thinks the house next door holds some deep, dark secrets. Joel McCrea, Gail Russell, Herbert Marshall. w. Hagar Wilde, Raymond Chlandler, d. Lewis Allen.

SUSPENSE: Ghost Stories; **MURDER:** Houses-Creepy; Babysitters; London; Forgotten Films
(Gaslight; The Uninvited; Turn of the Screw)

The Unsinkable Molly Brown, 1964, 128m, ★★★¹/₂/$$$, MGM/MGM-UA, G. The musical biography of the tenacious tomboy who struck it rich in Colorado and then saved a lifeboat full of people on the Titanic. Debbie Reynolds (BActress), Harve Pernell, Ed Begley, Jack Kruschen, Hermione Baddely. w. Helen Deutsch, MP-adap. Richard Morris, d. Charles Walters. BMScore, BCCostume, BSound, BCArt, BCCin. Oscars: 6-0.

MUSICALS: WESTERNS: Western Comedy; **COMEDY:** Musical Comedy; Biographies; Epics; Episodic Stories; Feisty Females; Orphans; Rags to Riches; Rich vs. Poor; Snobs vs. Slobs; Shipwrecked; Mountain People; Titanic Stories; Heroes-Unlikely; 1900s; Drownings; Underrated; Female Protagonists; Female Screenwriters
(Annie Get Your Gun; Calamity Jane; Auntie Mame; Mame; Hit the Deck; The Singing Nun)
(Ed: Reynolds' big performance and an underrated picture)

Unstrung Heroes, 1995, 120m, ★★★/$$, Hollywood/Hollywood, PG. An eccentric Jewish family in the 60s, from the point of view of a gentile mother who married into the group. Her son is challenged to unite with the family when she becomes deathly ill and he wants to move in with his uncles. Andie MacDowell, John Turturro, Michael Richards, Maury Chaykin, Nathan Watt. w. Richard LaGravanese, N-adap. Franz Lidz, d. Diane Keaton. BDScore.

DRAMA: COMEDY DRAMA: Disease Stories; Family Drama; Mothers & Daughters; Jewish People; Boyhood; Female Protagonists; Female Directors
(A Thousand Clowns; Green Card)

An Unsuitable Job for a Woman, 1982, 90m, ★★★/VR, Gold Crest-BBC/BBC. A young woman detective tries to discover why a boy killed himself and then begins to wonder what really happened, when she becomes obsessed with his story. Pippa Guard, Billie Whitelaw, Paul Freeman, Dominic Guard. w. Elizabeth McKay, Brain Scobie, Christopher Petit, N. adap. P. D. James, d. Christopher Petit.
MYSTERY: Detective Stories; Detectives-Female; Young Men; Infatuations; Suicidal Tendencies; Obsessions; Quiet Little Films; British Films; Coulda Been Great; Good Premise Unfulfilled; Female Among Males; Female Protagonists; Female Screenwriters; TV Movies
(Wetherby)
(Ed: Slow and murky but worth it to P. D. James fans)
The Unsuspected, 1947, 103m, ★★1/2/$, WB/NA. A radio mystery writer murders, then winds up hearing clues to the crime on his show. Claude Rains, Joan Caulfield, Constance Bennett, Hurd Hatfield, Fred Clark. w. Ranald MacDougall, N-adap. Charlott Armstrong, d. Michael Curtiz.
SUSPENSE: MURDER: Murderer Stalked; Murder-Debate to Reveal Killer; Radio Life; Writers; Turning the Tables; Good Premise Unfulfilled; Forgotten Films; Coulda Been Great
(The Radioland Murders; The Big Broadcast SERIES)
Untamed Heart, 1992, 102m, ★★-/$$, MGM/MGM-UA, PG. When a diner gets a new cook, the waitress doesn't realize he's odd because he has a baboon heart and may die soon. She falls in love just in time . . . Marisa Tomei, Christian Slater, Rosie Perez, Kyle Secor. w. Tom Sierchio, d. Harold Ramis.
MELODRAMA: ROMANCE: Romantic Drama; Romance-Reluctant; Ordinary People Stories; Young People; Tearjerkers; Romance-Doomed; Disease Stories; Waitresses; Restaurant Settings; Saving Someone; Female Protagonists
(Love Story; Dying Young)
(Ed: A little too sappy and manipulative, but has its fans)
Until the End of the World, 1991, 158m, ★★★/$, WB/WB, PG-13/S. In a futuristic world, while a nuclear satellite readies to drop on Earth, a woman follows a man with multiple personalities to his father who's invented a device which helps blind people to see. William Hurt, Solveig Dommartin, Sam Neill, Max von Sydow, Jeanne Moreau. w. Peter Carey, Wim Wenders, d. Wenders.
DRAMA: SCI-FI: Art Films; Avant-Garde Films; Futuristic Films; Apocalyptic Stories; Blind People; Inventors; Eccentric People; Bombs-Atomic; Overlooked at Release
(Wings of Desire; Far Away So Close)
(Ed: Has a really good soundtrack if the film is too boring for you)
The Untouchables, 1987, 119m, ★★★/$$$$, Par/Par, PG-13/V-P. Classic crimefighter Elliot Ness (Kevin Costner) goes after Al Capone (Robert De Niro) in an attempt to smash his Chicago crime ring and winds up jeopardizing family and friends. Sean Connery (**BSActor**), Andy Garcia, Charles Martin Smith, Richard Bradford. w. David Mamet, d. Brian DePalma. BArt, BCostume, BOScore. Oscars: 4-1.
DRAMA: ACTION: Crime Drama; Criminal Biographies; Al Capone; Detective Stories; Detectives-Police; Mob Stories; Mob Wars; Prohibition Era; Bootleggers; 1920s; Chicago; TV Series Movies
REMAKE OF: TV Series, early 1960s; REMAKE: TV series, 1991–1994.
(The Scarface Mob; Scarface; Al Capone; Dillinger)
The Untouchables Series Pilot, see The Scarface Mob
Unzipped, 1995, 76m, ★★★/$$, Miramax/Miramax, R/S-FN. The life of the fast fashion lane with designer Isaac Mizrahi and the models is exposed. But not too far. Isaac Mizrahi, Eartha Kitt, Kate Moss, Linda Evangelista, Cindy Crawford, Naomi Campbell, Christy Turlington, Sandra Bernhard, Mark Morris, Ellen Barkin, Richard Gere. d. Douglas Keeve.
Documentaries; Fashion World; Models; Beautiful People
(Ready to Wear)
Up in Arms, 1944, 106m, ★★★/$$, Goldwyn-UA/Goldwyn. A neurotic idiot hypochondriac joins the arm and somehow survives. Danny Kaye, Dinah Shore, Constance Dowling, Louis Calhern. w. Don Hartman, Robert Pirosh, Allen Boretz, d. Elliot Bugent. BOSong, BMScore. Oscars: 2-0.
COMEDY: Comedy-Slapstick; Fools-Bumbling; Fish out of Water Stories; Military Comedy; World War II Era; Nerds
(Private Benjamin; Stripes; In the Army Now; The Delicate Delinquent)
Up in Smoke (*Cheech and Chong in . . .*), 1978, 86m, ★★★/$$$$, Par/Par, R/S-P. Two Latino L.A. potheads smoke their lives away laughing all the while. Cheech Marin, Tommy Chong, Strother Martin, Edie Adams, Stacy Keach, Tom Skerritt. w. Tommy Chong, Cheech Marin, d. Lou Adler.
COMEDY: Comedians; Comedy-Skit; Musicians; Drugs; Fools-Bumbling; Los Angeles; Latin People; Sleeper Hits
Up the Academy, 1980, 86m, ★★/$, WB/WB, R/S-P. Four boys go to a reform school which seems wilder than what sent them there. Ron Liebman, Ralph Macchio, Tom Poston, Barbara Bach. d. Robert Downey.
COMEDY: Teenagers; Teenage Movies; Erotic Comedy; Boarding Schools; Ensembles-Male; Bathroom Humor
(National Lampoon's Animal House; PCU)
(Ed: *Mad Magazine*'s foray into Lampoon territory)
Up the Creek, 1958, 83m, ★★1/2/$, Byron-Ind/Monarch. A run-down British naval base gets a new commander, an inept lieutenant who's been demoted to this lowly assignment. Peter Sellers, David Tomlinson, Wilfird Hyde White. w. d. Val Guest.
COMEDY: COMEDY DRAMA: Men in Conflict; Power-Rise to of Idiot; Military Comedy; Fools-Bumbling; British Films; Writer-Directors
(Renaissance Man; Major Payne)
Up the Creek, 1984, 95m, ★★★/$, Orion/Vestron, PG. Yuppies go rafting and wind up in a competition against old rivals. Tim Matheson, Jennifer Runyon, Stephen Furst, John Hillerman, Jeana Tomasina. d. Robert Butler.
COMEDY: Comedy-Slapstick; River Trauma; Ensemble Films; Yuppies; Competitions; Bathroom Humor; Camping
(Revenge of the Nerds; Indian Summer)
Up the Down Staircase, 1967, 124m, ★★★1/2/$$$, WB/WB, PG. An idealistic schoolteacher enters a job at an inner city school and tries not to become disillusioned. Sandy Dennis, Patrick Bedford, Eileen Heckart, Ruth White, Lionel Jeffries. w. Tad Mosel, N-adap. Bel Kaufman, d. Robert Mulligan.

DRAMA: Social Drama; Teachers; School Life; Race Relations; Illusions Destroyed; Inner City Life; Time Capsules; Female Protagonists

Up the Sandbox, 1972, 98m, ★★★¹/₂/ $$, WB/WB, R/S-P. The wife of a college professor begins living in a world of fantasy, dreaming of a wild and free life, when she learns she's pregnant a second time. Barbra Streisand, David Selby, Ariane Heller, Jane Hoffman. w. Paul Zindel, N-adap. Anne Richardson Rolphe, d. Irwin Kirshner.

COMEDY DRAMA: DRAMA: Character Studies; Marriage Drama; Psychological Drama; Fantasies; Dual Lives; College Life; Young Women; Mothers-Struggling; Pre-Life Crisis; Female Protagonists; Feminist Films; Ahead of its Time; Underrated; Hidden Gems
(Diary of a Mad Housewife; Looking for Mr. Goodbar)

Uptown Saturday Night, 1974, 104m, ★★¹/₂/$$$, WB/WB, R/S-P. A group of friends, card-playing middle-aged black men, have their lottery ticket stolen, and when they find out it's a winner, they search for the culprit. Sidney Poitier, Bill Cosby, Harry Belafonte, Flip Wilson, Richard Pryor, Rosalind Cash. w. Richard Wesley, d. Sidney Poitier.

COMEDY: Ensembles-Male; Lotteries; Searches; Thieves; Turning the Tables; Black Men; Black Casts; Inner City Life; Blaxploitation Era; Black Screenwriters; Black Directors

Uranus, 1990, 99m, ★★★/$, Miramax/ HBO, R/S-V. A provincial French town has its own "mini-war" right after V-day, tensions between Fascists, Communists, members of the Resistance, and collaborators boiling over in the strained "peace" that follows. Philippe Noiret, Gerard Depardieu, Jean-Pierre Marielle, Michel Blanc. w. Claude Berri, Arlette Langman, N-adap. Marcel Ayme, d. Claude Berri.

DRAMA: Social Drama; Political Drama; Political Unrest; Historical Drama; Small-town Life; French Films

Urban Cowboy, 1980, 135m, ★★¹/₂/$$$, Par/Par, PG/S-P. A country boy in the city finds that skills such as the Texas two-step and (mechanical) bull-riding can be just as useful there. John Travolta, Debra Winger, Scott Glenn. w. James Bridges, N-adap. Aaron Latham, d. James Bridges.

COMEDY DRAMA: ROMANCE: Music Movies; Country Music; Nightclubs; Young Men; Feisty Females; Cowboys; Ordinary People Stories; Texas; Forgotten Films
(Ed: Notable primarily for riding the crest of a country music fad after disco and the debut of Debra Winger)

Urga, see **Close to Eden**

Used Cars, 1980, 111m, ★★★/$, Col/ RCA-Col, R/P-S-FFN. A war between a small-time used car salesman and his takeover-minded bigger rival is decided by a star salesman at the smaller lot who wants to win over the boss's daughter. Kurt Russell, Gerrit Graham, Frank McRae, Deborah Harmon. w. Robert Zemeckis, Bob Gale, d. Robert Zemeckis.

COMEDY: Comedy-Slapstick; Black Comedy; Romance with Boss's Child; Men in Conflict; Competitions; Small-town Life; Rednecks; Salesmen; Ordinary People Stories; Bimbos; Underrated; Overlooked at Release; Cult Films; Hidden Gems
(Smile; Cadillac Man; Foolin' Around;

Used People, 1992, 122m, ★★-/$$, 20th/20th, PG/S. The matriarch of a Jewish family in Queens, N.Y. (Shirley MacLaine) contemplates the pursuit of a suitor (Marcello Mastroianni) amid the chaos her neurotic daughters (Kathy Bates, Marcia Gay Harden) create. Jessica Tandy, Sylvia Sidney. w. Todd Graff, d. Beeban Kidron.

DRAMA: COMEDY DRAMA: RO-MANCE: Romantic Comedy; Romance-Middle-Aged; Romance-Elderly; Mothers & Daughters; Mothers & Sons; Widows; Jewish People; New York Life; 1960s; Eccentric People; Stern Women; Italians
(Only the Lonely; Moonstruck; Angie; Terms of Endearment)
(Ed: Doesn't live up to the *Moonstruck* promise but has its moments.)

The Usual Suspects, 1995, 105m, ★★★¹/₂/$$, 20th/Fox, R/V-EP. After twenty-seven men are killed in a botched cocaine heist on a pier, there are few witnesses left to tell the tale and even fewer leads to who may have set them up in this mind game of twists and turns. Kevin Spacey (**BSActor**), Stephen Baldwin, Gabriel Byrne, Benico Del Toro, Kevin Pollak, Chazz Palminteri, Pete Postlethwaite, Suzy Amis, Giancarlo Esposito, Dan Hedaya, Paul Bartel, Christine Estabrook. w. Christopher McQuarrie (**BOScr**), d. Bryan Singer. Oscars: 2-2.

SUSPENSE: MYSTERY: Crime Drama; **MURDER:** Murders-Mass; Simple Minds; Flashbacks; Ensemble Films; Ensembles-Male; Clever Plots & Endings; Perfect Crimes; Mindgames; Cult Films
(Reservoir Dogs; Rififi; Killing Zoe; Seven)

Utz, 1992, 115m, ★★★/$, BBC-Academy/Academy. An American art merchant loses track of a precious collection of porcelain figurines and must find them. Armin Mueller-Stahl, Brenda Fricker, Peter Riegert, Paul Scofield, Gaye Brown. w. Hugh Whitemore, N-adap. Bruce Chatwin, d. George Sluizer.

COMEDY DRAMA: MYSTERY: Treasure Hunts; Thieves; Art Thieves; Searches; Overlooked at Release

V

Vacation from Marriage (Perfect Strangers), 1946, 102m, ★★★/$$$, MGM/NA. A frumpy housewife and her bored husband, a lowly clerk, sign up for service in World War II, and their new-found sense of purpose invigorates their marriage. Robert Donat, Deborah Kerr, Glynis Johns, Ann Todd, Roland Culver, Elliot Mason, Eliot Makeham, Brefni O'Rourke, Edward Rigby. w. Clarence Dane, Anthony Pelissier (**BOStory**), d. Alexander Korda. Oscars: 1-1.
MELODRAMA: ROMANCE: Marriage Drama; War Stories; World War II Stories; Redemption; Patriotic Films; British Films; Faded Hits

Vagabond, 1985, 104m, ★★★¹/₂/$$, Cine-Tamaris-Ind/New Yorker, Ingram, R/S. A story told in flashbacks of the events leading to the early death of a drifter abandoned by her drug buddies in a snow bank. Sandrine Bonnaire, Macha Meril, Stephanie Freiss, Laurence Cortadellas. w. d. Agnes Varda.
DRAMA: TRAGEDY: Character Studies; Drifters; Ordinary People Stories; Dying Young; Drugs-Addictions; Homeless People; Abandoned People; Flashbacks; Quiet Little Films; Female Screenwriters; Female Directors; Female Protagonists; Hidden Gems; Writer-Directors
(Christiane F.; The Double Life of Veronique)

The Valachi Papers, 1972, 127m, ★★¹/₂/$$, Euro France-DEG/NA, R/V. The fact-based story of the criminal activities and eventual capture of a minor gangster as told to the FBI. Charles Bronson, Fred Valleca, Gerald S. O'Loughlin, Lino Ventura. w. Stephen Geller, NF-adap. Peter Maas, d. Terence Young.
DRAMA: Crime Drama; Criminal Biographies; Mob Stories; Mob Wars; Flashbacks; Memories; FBI Agents; Episodic Stories
(Murder Inc.; GoodFellas)

Valdez Is Coming, 1971, 90m, ★★★/$$, MGM/MGM-UA, PG. A sexy Mexican-American moves into a small western town and romances a few of the ladies, until the white men get addled. Burt Lancaster, Susan Clark, Richard Jordan, Hector Elizondo. w. David Rayfiel, d. Edwin Stern.
WESTERNS: DRAMA: Romance-Interracial; Latin People; Small-town Scandals; Men in Conflict; Race Relations; Bigots; Jealousy
(Ulzana's Raid)

Valentino, 1951, 105m, ★★/$, Col/NA. A biopic of the life of the famous international sex symbol of the silent screen chronicling his childhood in Italy and rise to fame in Hollywood. Anthony Dexter, Eleanor Parker, Richard Carlson, Patricia Medina. w. George Bruce, d. Lewis Allen.
MELODRAMA: Biographies; Hollywood Biographies; Hollywood Life; Sexy Men; Dying Young; Actors; Silent Film Era
RETELLING: 1977.

Valentino, 1977, 127m, ★★¹/₂/$, UAMGM-UA, R/S-FN-MN. At his funeral, Valentino's friends and acquaintances have varying memories of the man, not all flattering. Rudolf Nureyev, Leslie Caron, Michelle Phillips, Carol Kane, Felicity Kendal. w. Ken Russell, Mardik Martin, NF-adap. Brad Steiger, Chaw Mank, d. Ken Russell.
DRAMA: Art Films; Character Studies; Erotic Drama; Biographies; Hollywood Biographies; Actors; Sexy Men; Memories; Flashbacks; Friends as Enemies; Silent Film Era; Underrated
RETELLING: of 1951 version.
(Nijinksy; The Music Lovers; Exposed)

Valentino Returns, 1989, 90m, ★★/$, Owl-Vidmark/Vidmark, R/S. A lowly geek scrapes up the money for a pink Cadillac to impress his lady love. Barry Tubb, Frederic Forrest, Veronica Cartwright, Jenny Wright. w. Leonard Gardner, SS-adap. Leonard Gardner (*Christ Has Returned to Earth and Preaches Here Nightly*), d. Peter Hoffman.
COMEDY DRAMA: ROMANCE: Coming of Age; Young Men; Teenagers; Nerds;

Nerds & Babes; Small-town Life; 1950s (Mischief; A Tiger's Tale; Grandview USA)

Valley Girl, 1983, 95m, ★★-/$$$, Vestron/Vestron, R/S-P. Ditzy but spunky girl wants a bad boy but they're from opposite sides of the Valley tracks. Deborah Foreman, Nicolas Cage, Colleen Camp, Frederic Forrest. d. Martha Coolidge.

COMEDY: ROMANCE: Romantic Comedy; Los Angeles; Simple Minds; Feisty Females; Romance-Class Conflicts; Suburban Life; Female Protagonists; Female Directors
(Vals; Foxes; My Chauffeur)

The Valley Obscured by the Clouds, 1972, 106m, ★★-/$$, WB/WB. Hippie type goes to New Guinea in search of nature set to Pink Floyd music. d. Barbet Schroeder.

Documentaries; Journies; Hippies; South America; Nature-Back to; Cult Films
(Pink Floyd: The Wall)

The Valley of Decision, 1945, 119m, ★★1/2/$$$, MGM/MGM-UA. In turn-of-the-century Pittsburgh, the son of a strict Protestant businessman elopes with his family's Irish maid and all hell breaks loose. Greer Garson, Gregory Peck, Lionel Barrymore, Donald Crisp, Preston Foster. w. John Meehan, Sonya Levien, N-adap. Marcia Davenport, d. Tay Garnett.

MELODRAMA: ROMANCE: Lover Family Dislikes; Romance-Class Conflicts; Marriage-Elopements; Romance with Servants; Servants; Rich People; Rich vs. Poor
(Sabrina; Mr. Skeffington; Roman Holiday)

Valley of the Dolls, 1967, 123m, ★★★/$$$$$, 20th/CBS-Fox, PG/S. A small-town New England girl gets into showbiz and meets up with a singer and an eventual skinflick star, all of whom are doomed in one way or another—most with the sleeping pills known as "dolls"—and are feuding with an aging, jealous Broadway star. Barbara Parkins, Patty Duke, Susan Hayward, Paul Burke, Sharon Tate, Martin Milner, Lee Grant. w. Helen Deutsch, Dorothy Kingsley, N-adap. Jacqueline Susann, d. Mark Robson. BOSong. Oscars: 1-0.

MELODRAMA: Ensemble Films; Ensembles-Female; Soap Operas; Fame-Rise to; Feuds; Women in Conflict; Mean Women; Hollywood Satire; Hollywood Life; Singers; Actresses; Nervous Breakdowns; Drugs-Addictions; Young Women; Generation Gaps; Camp; Unintentionally Funny; Time Capsules; Blockbusters; Female Protagonists; Female Screenwriters; Narrated Films

UNOFFICIAL SEQUEL: Beyond the Valley of the Dolls.

REMAKE: TV Miniseries, 1984.
(All About Eve; The Love Machine; Once Is Not Enough; Show Girls)
(Ed: An epic melodrama. Based on one of the best-selling books of all time, it has its great comic moments and lines of pure camp, and then some of the worst dreck ever)

Valley of the Kings, 1954, 86m, ★★/$$, MGM/NA. Looters try to get gold from a Pharaoh's tomb but are thwarted by vigilant archaeologists. Robert Taylor, Eleanor Parker, Carlos Thompson, Kurt Kasznar. w. Robert Pirosh, Karl Tunberg, d. Robert Pirosh.

DRAMA: SUSPENSE: Archaeologists; Egypt; Curses; Art Thieves; Jewel Thieves
(The Awakening; King Solomon's Mines; Indiana Jones and the Last Crusade)

Valmont, 1989, 137m, ★★1/2/$ (LR), Orion/Orion, R/S-FN. Arrogant aristocrats with too much time on their hands play a game of seduction with a virginal woman of simpler motivations, resulting in treachery and tragedy. Colin Firth, Annette Bening, Meg Tilly, Fairuza Balk. w. Jean-Claude Carriere, N-adap. Choderlos de Laclos (Les Liaisons Dangereuses), d. Milos Forman.

DRAMA: Erotic Drama; Costume Drama; Character Studies; Mindgames; Betrayals; Double Crossings; Virgins; Evil Women; 1700s; Classic Literary Adaptations; Flops-Major

OTHER VERSIONS: Dangerous Liaisons; Les Liasons Dangereuses
(Dangerous Liaisons; Les Liaisons Dangereuses)
(Ed: Suffered coming on the heels of the immensely successful *Dangerous Liaisons*, this is more focused on the character of Valmont and is quite different in tone from either of the other versions)

Vampira, see **Old Dracula**

Vamp, 1986, 93m, ★★/$, New World/New World, R/S-P. Two college buddies head into seamy nightclubs and find a black cross-dressing vampire of sorts. Grace Jones, Chris Makepeace, Gedde Watanabe. d. Richard Wenk.

HORROR: Horror Comedy; Vampires; Vampires-Female; Spoofs-Vampire; Nightclubs; Transvestites
(Once Bitten; Vampire's Kiss)

A Vampire in Brooklyn, 1995, 105m, ★★/$, Par/Par, R/EP-S-V-B&G. A vampire is lurking about but may have met his match in a tough-minded young woman. The question is, "Was this supposed to be funny?," because it isn't. Eddie Murphy, Angela Bassett, Allen Payne, Kadeem Hardison, Zakes Mokae, Joanna Cassidy, Jerry Hall. w. Charlie Murphy, Michael Lucker & Chris Parker, d. Wes Craven.

HORROR: Horror Comedy; Vampires; New York Life; Black Men; Black Casts; Flops-Major
(Blacula; Dracula; Love at First Bite; Tales from the Hood)

Vampire's Kiss, 1989, 103m, ★★1/2/$, Hemdale/Hemdale, R/S-P. A publisher starts to believe he's a vampire and buys a set of fangs to act the part. Nicolas Cage, Maria Conchita Alonso, Jennifer Beals, Elizabeth Ashley, Kasi Lemmons. w. Joseph Minion, d. Robert Bierman.

COMEDY: Vampires; Spoofs-Vampires; Black Comedy; Mental Illness; Fantasies; Nervous Breakdowns; Coulda Been Great; Good Premise Unfulfilled; Overlooked at Release
(Raising Arizona; Amos and Andrew; Vampire in Brooklyn)

Vampire Lovers, 1970, 91m, ★★1/2/$, Hammer-AIP-MGM/MGM-UA, R/S-FN. A female vampire makes her way through the homes of rich Londoners, primarily seducing women. Ingrid Pitt, Peter Cushing, Pippa Steele. w. Tudor Gates, Harry Fine, Michael Styles, SS-adap. Sheridan LeFanu, *Carmilla*, d. Roy Ward Baker.

HORROR: Vampires; Vampires-Female; MURDERS: Murders of Females; Murderers-Female; Lesbians; Bisexuality; Forgotten Films; Ahead of its Time; Female Protagonists
(Dracula's Daughter; The Night Stalker)

Van Gogh, 1991, 158m, ★★1/2/$, Artificial Eye. The famous artist psychologically deteriorates in the last few months of his life. Jacques Dutronc, Alexandra London, Bernard Le Coq, Gerard Sety, Corrine Bourdon. w. d. Maurice Pialat.

DRAMA: Biographies; Character Studies; Death-Impending; Mental Illness; Artists-

Famous; Brothers; Writer-Directors
(Vincent & Theo; Lust for Life)
The Vanishing, 1988, 106m, ★★★/$,
Ind/Fox-Lorber, R/V. A man searches for
his girlfriend after she mysteriously disappears during a brief vacation. After
three years, his search leads him to her
kidnapper. Bernard-Pierre Donnadieu,
Gene Bervoets, Johanna Ter Steege.
w. N-adap. Tim Krabbe (*The Golden
Egg*), d. George Sluizier.
French Films; Hidden Gems
The Vanishing, 1993, 110m, ★-/$,
20th/Fox, R/S-V-B&G. Remake by the
same director, but not as effective-in fact,
laughable in places. Jeff Bridges, Keifer
Sutherland, Nancy Travis, Sandra
Bullock, Park Overall. w. Todd Graff, S-
adap. Tim Krabbe, d. Georges Sluzier.
Foreign Film Remakes; Coulda Been
Great; Unintentionally Funny
SUSPENSE: MYSTERY: Missing Persons;
Missing Person Thriller; Searches; Serial
Killers; Nightmares; Avenging Death of
Loved One
REMAKE: 1994 American version
(Missing; Dying Room Only)
(Ed: The American version is lousy, but
the original is haunting and yet irritating,
albeit bizarre from the conventional
American standpoint of what should hap-
pen when the killer is found)
Vanishing Point, 1971, 107m, ★★1/2/
$$, 20th, R/P-S. A retired race car driver
gets hooked on downers and steals to
support his habit, ultimately leading
police on a high-speed chase in the
desert. Barry Newman, Cleavon Little,
Dean Jagger, Victoria Medlin. w.
Guillermo Cain, d. Richard Sarafin.
ACTION: Chase Movies; Drugs-
Addictions; Rebels; Anti-Establishment
Films; Sleeper Hits; Forgotten Films;
Underrated
Vanity Fair, 1932, 78m, ★★1/2/$, Allied
Artists/Nos. The exploits of Becky Sharp
updated to 1930s America. Myrna Loy,
Conway Tearle, Barbara Kent, Walter
Byron. w. F. Hugh Herbert, N-adap. W.
M. Thackeray, d. Chetser M. Franklin.
MELODRAMA: ROMANCE: Young
Women; Classic Literary Adaptations;
Flops-Major
(Becky Sharp [1935]; Barry Lyndon)
Variety, 1983, 101m, ★★★/$, Ind/
Media, R/S-FN. A young woman sells
tickets at a porn theater for extra money
and soon finds herself fascinated with the

men who go there and then what they
watch—after being initially repulsed.
Sandy McLeod, Will Patton. w. d. Bette
Gordon.
DRAMA: Pornography World; Women's
Films; Young Women; Voyeurs; Art Films;
Message Films; Social Drama; Battle of
the Sexes; Writer-Directors; Female
Protagonists; Female Screenwriters;
Female Directors; Hidden Gems; Coulda
Been Great; Ind Films
(Not a Love Story; The Projectionist; Move)
The Velvet Touch, 1948, 97m, ★★1/2/
$$, RKO/Turner. When a theatrical pro-
ducer is murdered, his leading lady is the
last suspected, but a detective's trail may
lead her way. Rosalind Russell, Leo
Genn, Sidney Greenstreet. w. Leo Rosten,
d. John Gage.
**SUSPENSE: MURDER: MYSTERY: MUR-
DER MYSTERY:** Murder-Debate to
Reveal Killer; Detective Stories;
Actresses; Guilty Consciences;
Murderers-Female; Female Protagonists
(Stage Fright; Rehearsal for Murder)
Venom, 1982, 92m, ★★1/2/$, Par/Par,
R/V. Kidnappers of a rich boy are foiled
by a poisonous snake loose in the house
they take over. Oliver Reed, Sarah Miles,
Cornelia Sharpe, Susan George, Sterling
Hayden, Klaus Kinski. w. Robert
Carrington, N-adap. Alan Scholefield,
d. Piers Haggard.
SUSPENSE: HORROR: Kidnappings;
Children in Jeopardy; Snakes; Animal
Monsters; Servants; London; Rogue Plots;
Camp; Unintentionally Funny; Coulda
Been Great
(Jaws of Satan; Sssss . . .)
(Ed: It would have been much better as a
black comic send-up)
Vera Cruz, 1953, 94m, ★★★/$$$, UA/
MGM-UA. A group of vagabonds in
Mexico take up arms against the Emperor
Maximilian. Gary Cooper, Burt Lancaster,
Denise Darcel, Cesar Romero, George
Macready, Ernest Borgnine, Charles
Bronson. w. Roland Kibbee, James R.
Webb, Borden Chase, d. Robert Aldrich.
DRAMA: WESTERNS: War Stories; War
Battles; Political Unrest; Mexico; Latin
People
(The Alamo; Ulzana's Raid; Viva Zapata;
Pancho Villa; The Professionals; The
Wild Bunch)
The Verdict, 1982, 128m, ★★★★/$$$$,
20th/CBS-Fox, R/P. A down and out
lawyer (Paul Newman, BActor) needs a

case to get him back on his feet. When a
wrongful death suit arises, he may have
what he needs, but the woman he falls for
(Charlotte Rampling) may destroy it all.
Lindsay Crouse, James Mason (BSActor).
w. David Mamet (BAScr), N-adap. Barry
Reed, d. Sidney Lumet (BDirector).
Oscars: 5-0.
DRAMA: Character Studies; Courtroom
Drama; Detective Stories; Lawyers;
Lawyers as Detectives; Redemption;
Starting Over; Depression; Romance-
Dangerous; Betrayals; Saving Oneself;
One Last Chance; Alcoholics; Boston
(Nobody's Fool; Absence of Malice)
Veronika Voss, 1982, 104m, ★★★/$$,
Maura/Applause Video. An actress tries
to make a comeback by going to a psychi-
atrist to get her motivated, but the shrink
may be out to undo her completely. Rosel
Zech, Hilmar Thate, Anne Marie
Duringer. w. Peter Marhesheimer, Per
Frohlich, Rainer Werner Fassbinder,
d. Rainer Werner Fassbinder.
DRAMA: Art Films; Character Studies;
Crazy Shrinks; Psychiatrists; Actresses;
Betrayals; Comebacks; German Films;
Female Protagonists; Writer-Directors
(The Marriage of Maria Braun; A Man
Like Eva)
Vertigo, 1958, 128m, ★★★★/$$,
Par/MCA-U. A police detective (James
Stewart) whose fear of falling kept him
from saving a fellow officer is hired to
investigate the mysterious doings of the
wife (Kim Novak) of a wealthy old friend,
but his phobia may trip him up when it
comes time to save her. w. Alec Coppel,
Samuel Taylor, N-adap. Pierre Boileau,
Thomas Narcejac (*D'entre les Morts*), d.
Alfred Hitchcock. BSound, BArt. Oscars:
2-0.
**MYSTERY: SUSPENSE: MURDER:
ROMANCE:** Romance-Dangerous; Love-
Questionable; Detective Stories;
Detectives-Private; Detectives in Deep;
Police-Former; Redemption; Starting
Over; Phobias; Framed?; Conspiracy;
Lookalikes; Dead-Back from the; Death-
Faked; San Francisco; Clever Plots &
Endings; Production Design-Outstanding
(Rear Window; To Catch a Thief;
Obsession; Still of the Night; Body
Double; Basic Instinct)
Vibes, 1988, 99m, ★★1/2/$, Imagine-
U/MCA-U, PG. A couple in Ecuador hires
a psychic to help them find El Dorado.
but all they find is chaos and creeps on

their heels. Cindi Lauper, Jeff Goldblum, Julian Sands, Peter Falk. w. Lowell Ganz, Babaloo Mandell, d. Ken Kwapis.

COMEDY: ROMANCE: Romantic Comedy; Treasure Hunts; Pyschics; Supernatural Danger; South America; Coulda Been Good; Flops-Major
(Second Sight; Romancing the Stone)

Vice Versa, 1988, 98m, ★★★/$$, Col/RCA-Col, PG. A boy and his dad exchange personalities with attendant problems for both. Judge Reinhold, Fred Savage, Corine Bohrer. w. Dick Clement, Ian La Frenais, d. Brian Gilbert.

COMEDY: Comedy-Slapstick; Fathers & Sons; Body Switching; Generation Gap; Overlooked at Release

REMAKE/RETREAD OF: Freaky Friday.
(Freaky Friday; Big; Like Father, Like Son)
(Ed: Better than *Like Father*, but still more like *Freaky Friday* than *Big*)

Vicki, 1953, 85m, ★★½/$$, 20th/NA. When a model is murdered, a single-minded detective goes after her boyfriend, but her sister tries to exonerate him. Jeanne Crain, Jean Peters, Richard Boone, Elliott Reid, Aaron Spelling. w. Dwight Taylor, d. Harry Horner.

SUSPENSE: MYSTERY: MURDER: MURDER MYSTERY: Detective Stories; Accused Unjustly; Detectives-Amateur; Hollywood Life; Time Capsules; Female Protagonists; Forgotten Films

REMAKE OF: I Wake Up Screaming.

Victim, 1961, 100m, ★★★½/$, Rank/Sultan, Bravo Network. A blackmailer threatens a closeted lawyer, who in turn decides to find out about this person and expose him instead. Dirk Bogarde, Sylvia Syms, John Barrie, Norman Bird, Peter McEnery, Charles Lloyd Pack. w. Janet Green, John McCormick, d. Basil Dearden.

DRAMA: MYSTERY: Malicious Menaces; Blackmail; Gay Men; Homophobia; Lawyers; Turning the Tables; Ahead of its Time; Hidden Gems; Female Screenwriters
(Another Country; Maurice; Consenting Adults; Philadelphia)

Victor/Victoria, 1982, 134m, ★★★★/$$$, MGM/MGM-UA, PG/S. A female singer in thirties Paris finds more success posing as a female impersonator. This becomes confusing to a man who is attracted to her/him, and subsequently confuses everyone else. Julie Andrews (BActress), James Garner, Robert Preston (BSActor), Lesley Anne Warren (BSActress), John Rhys-Davies, Alex Karras, Tracy Reed, Graham Stark. w. d. Blake Edwards (BAScr), S-adap. (*Viktor*). BArt, BCostume, **BSScore**. Oscars: 7–1.

COMEDY: FARCE: ROMANCE: Bedroom Farce; Romance-Reluctant; Misunderstandings; Impostors; Identities-Assumed; Identities-Mistaken; Singers; Mob; Comedy; Bimbos; Bisexuality; Gay Men; Women as Men; Paris; 1930s; Female Protagonists; Foreign Film Remakes; Writer-Directors

REMAKE/RETELLING OF: Viktor/Viktoria.
(Tootsie; Yentl; S.O.B.)
(Ed: Edwards at the top of his form before the decline)

The Victors, 1963, 175m, ★★½/$$, Col/NA. In World War II, a young untried troop learns about war the hard way. George Peppard, George Hamilton, Albert Finney, Melina Mercouri, Eli Wallach, Vince Edwards, Jeanne Moreau, Elke Sommer, Peter Fonda. w. Carl Foreman, N-adap. Alexander Baron (*The Human Kind*), d. Carl Foreman.

ACTION: War Stories; World War II Stories; **TRAGEDY:** Soldiers; Ensemble Films; Ensembles-Male
(The Big Red One)

Victory, 1981, 117m, ★★★/$$, Lorimar-UA/CBS-Fox, PG. A group of soccer players all held in the same German P.O.W. camp attempt to escape during a match staged by the Nazis for amusement. Sylvester Stallone, Michael Caine, Pele, Bobby Moore, Max Von Sydow. w. Evan Jones, Yabo Yablonsky, d. John Huston.

DRAMA: ACTION: Escape Drama; Escape Adventure; Prison Drama; Prison Escape; Sports Movies; Underdog Stories; Soccer; Nazi Stories; World War II Stories; Ensemble Films; Ensembles-Male; Forgotten Films; Coulda Been Great
(The Great Escape; Triumph of the Spirit)
(Ed: What would an underdog story be without Stallone? But that's probably what kept this somewhat loftier tale from going further at the time)

Videodrome, 1982, 89m, ★★/$, Filmplan International-U/MCA-U, R/EV-B&G. A cable company starts a new channel which acts like a sexual drug to those who view it. James Woods, Sonja Smits, Deborah Harry, Peter Dvorsky. w. d. David Cronenberg.

HORROR: SCI-FI: TV Life; Drugs-Addictions; Crossing the Line; Obsessions; Man vs. Machine; Pornography World; Voyeurs; Writer-Directors
(Scanners; Stay Tuned)

A View from the Bridge, 1961, 117m, ★★★½/$, Transcontinental-Ind/NA. A blue-collar worker is in love with his wife's niece, a fact which only becomes clear to everyone, including himself, when she announces her engagement to someone else. Raf Vallone, Maureen Stapleton, Carol Lawrence, Jean Sorel. w. Norman Rosten, P-adap. Arthur Miller, d. Sidney Lumet.

DRAMA: MELODRAMA: TRAGEDY: Romance-Unrequited; Obsessions; Depression; Suicidal Tendencies; Marriage-Impending; Romance with Relative; Coulda Been Great; Forgotten Films; Flops-Major; Ind Films
(Death of a Salesman; A Streetcar Named Desire)

A View to a Kill, 1985, 121m, ★★½/$$$, MGM-UA/MGM-UA, PG/V. James Bond fights a white-haired weirdo with plans to destroy San Francisco by triggering an earthquake-unless he gets ransom money. Roger Moore, Christopher Walken, Grace Jones, Fiona Fullerton. w. Richard Maibaum, Michael G. Wilson, d. John Glen. BOSong. Oscars: 1-0.

ACTION: Action Comedy; Secret Agents; Rule the World-Plots to; Earthquakes; Hostage Situations; Romance-Interracial
(Ed: The last view of Roger Moore as Bond)

The Vikings, 1958, 116m, ★★★/$$$$, UA/MGM-UA. Two vikings who are half-brothers fight for control of a kingdom on and off the longships. Orson Welles, Kirk Douglas, Tony Curtis, Ernest Borgnine, Janet Leigh. w. Calder Willingham, N-adap. Edison Marshall (*The Viking*), d. Richard Fleischer.

ACTION: DRAMA: Adventure at Sea; **ADVENTURE:** Men in Conflict; Historical Drama; War Stories; Brothers; Feuds; Vikings; Ancient Times; Scandinavia
(The Long Ships; Ulysses)

Village of the Damned, 1960, 78m, ★★★/$$$, MGM/MGM-UA. In a small English village, women give birth simultaneously and their children grow into superintelligent little monsters with Nazi-like tendencies. George Sanders, Barbara

Shelley, Michael Gwynn, Martin Stephens, Laurence Naismith. w. Stirling Silliphant, Wolf Rilla, Geoffrey Barclay, N-adap. John Wyndham (*The Midwich Cuckoos*), d. Wolf Rilla.

SCI-FI: SUSPENSE: HORROR: Psychological Thriller; Children-Brats; Children-Little; Adults; Oppression; England; Small-town Life; Cult Films; Hidden Gems; Allegorical Stories

SEQUEL: Children of the Damned.

REMAKE: 1995.

(Children of the Damned; The Children [1980]; The Reflecting Skin)

The Villain, 1978, 93m, ★★/$, Col/Col, PG. Western spoof of old-fashioned damsel in distress films like Mack Sennett comedies. Ann-Margret, Kirk Douglas, Arnold Schwarzenegger, Paul Lynde, Ruth Buzzi, Foster Brooks, Strother Martin. d. Hal Needham.

COMEDY: Spoofs; Kidnappings; Women in Jeopardy; **WESTERNS:** Western Comedy; Comedy-Slapstick; Cartoonlike Movies

Vincent and Theo, 1990, 140m, ★★★/$$, Ind/Ingram, others. Theo Van Gogh is the more practical of the two and tries to get his brother's art shown in the gallery where he works. Neither the gallery nor Vincent will compromise. Tim Roth, Paul Rhys, Johanna Ter Steege. w. Julian Mitchell, d. Robert Altman.

DRAMA: Art Films; Character Studies; Biographies; Artists-Famous; Brothers; Saving Someone; Friendships-Great; Ethics; Depression

(Van Gogh; Lust for Life; Goya)

The Violent Men, 1955, 96m, ★★1/2/$$, Col/Col. A mean old cripple has his hands full keeping squatters from his cattle land, unaware of what his younger wife is up to. Edward G. Robinson, Barbara Stanwyck, Glenn Ford, Brian Keith, Dianne Foster. w. Harry Kleiner, N-adap. Donald Hamilton, d. Rudolph Mate.

MELODRAMA: WESTERN: Cattle People; Marriage on the Rocks; Cuckolded; Romance-Triangles; Cheating Women; Romance-Older Men/Younger Women; Coulda Been Great; Cattle Herded by Barbara Stanwyck

(Cattle Queen of Montana; The Furies)

Violets Are Blue, 1986, 86m, ★★1/2/$, Col/Col, PG-13/S. A traveling journalist returns home to find her old high school boyfriend there, interested but married.

Yet when her job calls, will she answer? Sissy Spacek, Kevin Kline, Bonnie Bedelia. w. Naomi Foner, d. Jack Fisk.

MELODRAMA: ROMANCE: Romantic Drama; Romance-Reunited; Romance-Reluctant; Photographers; Cheating Men; Reunions; Journalists; Female Protagonists; Female Screenwriters; Forgotten Films

(Hard Promises)

Violette, 1978, 122m, ★★★/$$, New Yorker/New Yorker, R/V-S. A young woman decides to poison her parents to get her inheritance a little faster, but things don't go as planned. Isabelle Huppert, Stephane Audran. w. d. Claude Chabrol.

DRAMA: MURDER: Murder of Parents; Inheritances at Stake; Poison; Murderers-Female; 1930s; French Films; True Stories; Female Protagonists; Writer-Directors

(The Lacemaker)

The VIPs, 1963, 119m, ★★★/$$$, MGM/MGM-UA. Passengers on an international flight get stranded by fog at London Airport and two of them end up falling in love while the others bicker and get to know each other's problems. Richard Burton, Elizabeth Taylor, Maggie Smith, Rod Taylor, Margaret Rutherford (**BSActress**), Louis Jordan, Orson Welles, David Frost. w. Terence Rattigan, d. Anthony Asquith. Oscars: 1-1.

COMEDY DRAMA: ROMANCE: Ensemble Films; Multiple Stories; Interwoven Stories; Airports; Stranded; Beautiful People; Elderly Women; Forgotten Films; Hidden Gems; Stagelike Films; Faded Hits

(The Comedians; Ship of Fools; Airport)

The Virgin and the Gypsy, 1970, 95m, ★★1/2/$, Kenwood-Ind/Vestron, R/S-FN. In Edwardian England, a preacher's daughter falls for a fortune-teller gypsy traveling through town. Joanna Shimkus, Franco Nero, Honor Blackman, Fay Compton. w. Alan Plater, SS-adap. D. H. Lawrence, d. Christopher Miles.

DRAMA: Erotic Drama; **ROMANCE:** Gypsies; Sexy Men; Fortune Tellers; Virgins; 1920s; Female Protagonists

(Lady Chatterley's Lover; Women in Love)

The Virgin Queen, 1955, 92m, ★★★/$$, 20th/Fox, AMC. Sir Walter Raleigh's troublesome wooing of Queen Elizabeth is retold. Bette Davis, Richard Todd, Joan

Collins, Herbert Marshall, Jay Robinson, Dan O'Herlihy. w. Harry Brown, Mindret Lord, d. Henry Koster.

DRAMA: ROMANCE: Historical Drama; Biographies; Romance-Reluctant; Queens; Queen Elizabeth; Stern Women; Virgins; Elizabethan Era

(Elizabeth & Essex; Elizabeth R.)

The Virgin Soldiers, 1969, 96m, ★★★/$$, Col/Col, R/S-V. British army boys new to the scene are stationed in Singapore and soon find out, in comical ways, what they've gotten into. Nigel Patrick, Hywel Bennett, Lynn Redgrave, Nigel Davenport, Rachel Kempson. w. John Hopkins, N-adap. Leslie Thomas, d. John Dexter.

COMEDY DRAMA: Military Stories; Military Comedy; Soldiers; Young Men; Virgins; Fish out of Water Stories; British Films

SEQUEL: Stand Up, Virgin Soldiers.

The Virgin Spring, 1960, 87m, ★★★1/2/$$, Svensk-Embassy/Embassy, Sultan. In old Sweden, a young girl is raped and killed, and when her assailants are killed themselves, something magical happens. Max Von Sydow, Brigitta Valberg. w. Ulla Isaakson, d. Ingmar Bergman.

DRAMA: TRAGEDY: Rape/Rapists; Revenge; Revenge on Rapist; Avenging Death of Someone; Legends; Medieval Times; Swedish Films; Female Screenwriters

(The Seventh Seal)

Virginia City, 1940, 121m, ★★★/$$$, WB/MGM-UA. In Civil War era Nevada, a Confederate spy poses as a saloon performer, and it's up to the hero to stop the conspiracy she's a part of involving a gold delivery. Errol Flynn, Randolph Scott, Miriam Hopkins, Humphrey Bogart, Frank McHugh, Alan Hale. w. Robert Buckner, d. Michael Curtiz.

WESTERNS: Westerns-City Titles; Heist Stories; Conspiracy; North vs. South; Spies; Impostors

Viridiana, 1961, 91m, ★★★-/$$, Ind/Nos. A young woman hoping to be a nun takes revenge on her father for his wicked ways. Silvia Pinal, Fernando Rey. w. Luis Bunuel, Julio Alajandro, d. Bunuel.

COMEDY DRAMA: Black Comedy; Art Films; Avant-Garde Films; Surrealism; Religion; Nuns; Revenge; Homeless People; Mexico; Spanish Films

(Tristana; A Woman Without Love)

Virtuosity, 1995, 120m, ★★/$$, Par/Par, R/V-P-S-MRN. When a virtual reality experiment goes awry, a good-looking but psychotic young man emerges and proceeds to take on a law officer in futuristic L.A. in a cat-and-mouse tale where one often wishes the cops would lose. Denzel Washington, Kelly Lynch, Russell Crowe, Stephen Spinella, William Forsythe, William Fletcher, Costas Mandylor, Kevin J. O'Connor, Traci Lords, Miracle Unique Vincent. w. Eric Bernt, d. Brett Leonard.

ACTION: SCI-FI: Chase Stories; Computers; Video Games; Frankenstein Stories; Cat and Mouse Stories; Black Men; Flops-Major; Virtual Reality (Lawnmower Man; Strange Days) (Ed: The only meritorious part of this mess is the performance of Crowe as the villain)

Vision Quest, 1984, 100m, ★★1/2/$, WB/WB, R/S-P-MRN. A high school wrestler is in love with an older woman artist while training like the young Indian boys did on their vision quest to manhood. Matthew Modine, Linda Fiorentino, Ronnie Cox, Daphne Zuniga, Madonna. w. Daryl Ponicsan, d. Harold Becker.

DRAMA: ROMANCE: Coming of Age; Wrestling; Boys; Teenagers; Teenage Movies; Bratpack Movies

The Visit, 1964, 100m, ★★1/2/$, 20th/NA. A wealthy woman with a vendetta puts up a reward to anyone who will kill the man she scorned and says she no longer wants. Ingrid Bergman, Anthony Quinn, Paola Stoppa, Valentina Cortese. w. Ben Barzman, P-adap. Friedrich Durrenmatt, d. Bernhard Wicki.

DRAMA: COMEDY DRAMA: Black Comedy; Revenge; Hitmen; Rewards at Stake; Female Protagonists; International Casts; Coulda Been Good

Visit to a Small Planet, 1960, 101m, ★★★/$$$, Par/Par. A goofy alien winds up in suburbia and tries to stick it out while wreaking general havoc. Jerry Lewis, Loan Blackman, Earl Holliman, Fred Clark. w. Edmund Beloin, Henry Grason, P-adap. Gore Vidal, d. Norman Taurog.

COMEDY: SATIRE: ROMANCE: Romantic Comedy; Comedy of Errors; Comedy-Slapstick; Fish out of Water Stories; Aliens-Outer Space, Good; Fools-Bumbling; Suburban Life; Hidden Gems; Underrated

REMAKES/RETREADS: My Favorite Martian SERIES, Mork & Mindy SERIES.

(Splash!; My Blue Heaven [1990]; Starman)
(Ed: Though many cringe at how this was Jerry Lewis-ized, it still works on many levels. But on the other hand, many Lewis fans may find it too tame)

Viva Las Vegas, 1964, 85m, ★★/$$$, MGM/MGM-UA. A race car driver/pop singer hits Vegas and takes Ann-Margret for a ride. Elvis Presley, Ann-Margret, William Demarest, Jack Carson. w. Sally Benson, d. George Sidney.

MUSICALS: Music Movies; ROMANCE: Singers; Motorcycles; Car Racing; Las Vegas; Camp; Time Capsules; Female Screenwriters

Viva Maria!, 1965, 120m, ★★1/2/$, UA/MGM-UA. A young IRA woman goes to Central America to mingle with other activist types. Brigitte Bardot, Jeanne Moreau, George Hamilton, Paulette Dubost. w. Louis Malle, Lean-Claude Carriere, d. Louis Malle.

COMEDY DRAMA: SATIRE: Political Unrest; Political Activists; Terrorists; Anarchists; Central America; French Films; International Casts; Central America

Viva Villa!, 1934, 115m, ★★★/$$$, MGM/MGM-UA. Story of Pancho Villa and his Robin Hood efforts in old Mexico, trying for anarchy in the process. Wallace Beery, Fay Wray, Stuart Erwin, Leo Carrillo. w. Ben Hecht, d. Jack Conway.

ADVENTURE: True Stories; Biographies; Government as Enemy; Rebels; Robin Hood Stories; Mexico; Faded Hits (Viva Zapata)

Viva Zapata, 1952, 113m, ★★★/$$$, 20th/Fox. During the Mexican Revolution, a leader is betrayed by his friend, changing history. Marlon Brando (BActor), Anthony Quinn (BSActor), Jean Peters, Joseph Wiseman, Margo, Frank Silvera. w. John Steinbeck (BOScr), d. Elia Kazan. BScore, BB&WArt. Oscars: 5-1.

DRAMA: ACTION: War Stories; Epics; Historical Drama; Political Unrest; Friends as Enemies; Friendships-Male; Latin People; Mexico (Pancho Villa; One-Eyed Jacks; Viva Villa!)

Vivacious Lady, 1938, 90m, ★★1/2/$$, RKO/Media. When a sexy showgirl marries a timid professor scientist, he takes her home to his parents and the trouble starts. Ginger Rogers, James Stewart, Charles

Coburn, Beulah Bondi. w. P. J. Wolfson, Ernest Pagano, d. George Stevens.

COMEDY: ROMANCE: Romantic Comedy; Marriage Comedy; Lover Family Dislikes; In-Laws-Troublesome; Romance-Class Conflict; Dancers; Professors; Nerds & Babes (Teresa; White Palace; Ball of Fire)

V.I. Warshawski, 1991, 89m, ★★/$, Hollywood/Hollywood, PG-13/V-P. When an insurance executive is murdered, the female detective Warshawski is put on the case and she uncovers corporate-level corruption. Kathleen Turner, Jay O. Sanders, Charles Durning, Angela Goethals. w. Edward Taylor, David Aaron Cohen, Nick Thiel, N-adap. Sara Paretsky (*Infirmnity Only*), d. Jeff Kanew.

MYSTERY: MURDER: MURDER MYSTERY: Detective Stories; Detectives-Private; Detectives-Female; Feisty Females; Conspiracy; Corporate Corruption; Female Protagonists; Coulda Been Good; Flops-Major (Undercover Blues) (Ed: Unfortunately, her uncovering doesn't lead to much)

Voices, 1978, 107m, ★★-/$$, MGM/MGM-UA, PG. A fellow who wants to be a rock star falls for a woman who turns out to be deaf and can't appreciate the main thing he has going. Amy Irving, Michael Ontkean. d. Richard Markowitz.

MELODRAMA: ROMANCE: Romantic Drama; Deaf People; Singers; Romance-Boy Wants Girl; Romance-Mismatched; Tearjerkers; Forgotten Films (A Patch of Blue; Ice Castles)

Volpone, 1939, 95m, ★★★/$, Ind/Nos. When a rich man is dying, he decides to put his family to the test over the will before he even makes it-leading to greedy complications. Harry Baur, Louis Jouvet. P-adap. Ben Jonson, d. Maurice Torneur.

COMEDY: COMEDY DRAMA: Black Comedy; Inheritances at Stake; Death-Impending; Greed; Classic Literary Adaptations; French Films; Stage Filming

COMIC UPDATE: Greedy. (Stage Version, 1973)

Voltaire, 1933, 72m, ★★★/$$, WB/NA. Legendary actor of his day, George Arliss, plays the French humorist and philosopher. George Arliss, Doris Kenyon, Regina Woen. w. Paul Green, Maude Howell, N-adap. George Gibbs, Lawrence Dudley, d. John Adolfi.

COMEDY DRAMA: SATIRE:
Biographies; Writers; Stagelike Films;
Female Screenwriters

Von Ryan's Express, 1965, 117m,
★★★/$$$, 20th/CBS-Fox. An American
leads English P.O.W.s on a harrowing
train escape out of an Italian prison camp
during World War II. Frank Sinatra,
Trevor Howard, Sergio Fantoni, Edward
Mulhare, James Brolin. w. Endell Mayes,
Joseph Landon, N-adap. Davis
Westheimer, d. Mark Robson.

ACTION: SUSPENSE: ADVENTURE:
Escape Adventures; Prison Escapes;
Chase Movies; P.O.W.s; Heroes-Unlikely;
Trains; World War II Stories; Italy;
Forgotten Films; Hidden Gems
(The Great Escape; Stalag 17; Schindler's
List)
(Ed: Not quite what would be done with it
today using nonstop action, no matter
how ridiculous, but all the more realistic
and harrowing for it)

Voyage of the Damned, 1976, 155m,
★★★/$$, ITC-Embassy/Fox, R/P-V. A
cruise liner full of German Jews escapes
Germany at the outbreak of the war, but
when they are to dock in Cuba, they are
turned around. Faye Dunaway, Max Von
Sydow, Lee Grant (BSActress), Oskar
Werner, Malcolm McDowell, James
Mason, Orson Welles, Katharine Ross,
Sam Wanamaker, Julie Harris, Luther
Adler, Nehemiah Persoff, Maria Schell,
Jose Ferrer, Janet Suzman, Denholm
Elliott, Fernando Rey. w. Steve Shagan,
David Butler (BAScr), NF-adap. Gordon
Thomas, Max Morgan-Witts, d. Stuart
Rosenberg. BOScore. Oscars: 3-0.

DRAMA: TRAGEDY: True Stories;
Docudrama; Ensemble Films; Multiple
Stories; Interwoven Stories; Death-
Impendings; Suicidal Tendencies; Ships;
Jewish People; Germans as Enemy; All-
Star Casts
(Schindler's List; Ship of Fools; The

Damned; The Cassandra Crossing)
(Ed: Much more tragic and harrowing
than *Ship of Fools*, but not as interesting
characters)

Voyager, 1991, 110m, ★★★/$,
Academy/Academy, R/S-P. A young man
remembers his drifting life, from the first
girl he got pregnant and abandoned to
the mysterious woman he meets in
Europe who has a revelation that
changes his life. Sam Shepard, Julie
Delpy, Barbara Sukowa. w. Volker
Schlondorff, Rudy Wurlitzer, d. Volker
Schlondorff, N-adap. Max Frisch (*Homo
Faber*).

DRAMA: Character Studies; TRAGEDY:
Young Men; Episodic Stories; Oedipal
Stories; Men's Films; Memories;
Flashbacks; Narrated Films; Art Films;
German Films; Overlooked at Release
(Paris, Texas)

W

W, 1973, 95m, ★★/$, Crosby/Vestron, R/V-S. A young woman is tormented and stalked by her first husband at a beach house. Twiggy, Michael Witney, Eugene Roche, Dirk Benedict, John Vernon. w. Gerald di Pego, James Kelly, d. Richard Quine.
SUSPENSE: THRILLERS: Women in Jeopardy; Stalkers; Psycho Killers; Revenge; Ind Films
(Ed: Pretty bad, but then again, ahead of the trend)
W.C. Fields and Me, 1976, 112m, ★★/$$, Univ/U-MCA, PG. Biography of the comedian's rise to stardom late in life (Rod Steiger). Valerie Perrine, Jack Cassidy, Bernadette Peters. w. Bob Merrill, NF-adap. Carlotta Monti, d. Arthur Hiller.
DRAMA: Biographies; **COMEDY DRAMA:** Hollywood Life; Hollywood Biographies; Fame-Rise to; Actors
(Ed: Steiger's performance is the only thing worth bothering for.)
The W. Plan, 1930, 105m, ★★¹/₂/$$$, British International/NA. A British spy works undercover in Germany to destroy their infrastructure. Brian Aherne, Madeleine Carroll. w. Victor Saville, Miles Malleson, Frank Launder, N-adap. Graham Seton, d. Victor Saville.
DRAMA: Spy Films; Spies; British Films; Germans as Enemy; World War I Era

WUSA, 1970, 117m, ★★★/$$, Par/Par, R/P-S. A drifter becomes a rabble-rouser at a very conservative radio station down South. Paul Newman, Joanne Woodward, Laurence Harvey, Anthony Perkins, Cloris Leachman. w. N-adap. Robert Stone (*Hall of Mirrors*), d. Stuart Rosenberg.
DRAMA: SATIRE: Political Satire; Drifters; Fame-Rise to; Rebels; Radio Life; Southerns; Hidden Gems; Time Capsules; 1970s; Forgotten Films; Overlooked at Release
(A Face in the Crowd; Talk Radio; Kings and Desperate Men)
(Ed: A bit slow-paced to be entertaining, but definitely thought-provoking and ahead of its time.)
W.W. & The Dixie Dancekings, 1975, 94m, ★★¹/₂/$$$, R/P-S. A thief (Burt Reynolds) uses a band as a cover on the road while on a robbing spree through the South. Art Carney, Jerry Reed, Ned Beatty. w. Tom Rickman, d. John G. Avildsen.
COMEDY DRAMA: ACTION: Action Comedy; Road Movies; Outlaw Road Movies; Thieves; Forgotten Films; Southerns; Musicians; 1950s
(Smokey and the Bandit SERIES)
(Ed: Predecessor to *Smokey*, but better written, with more story)
Wabash Avenue, 1950, 92m, ★★/$$, 20th/NA. A dancer at the Chicago World's Fair of 1892 (Betty Grable) finds herself

in a love triangle. Victor Mature, Phil Harris, Reginald Gardner. w. Harry Tugend, Charles Lederer, d. Henry Koster.
ROMANCE: MELODRAMA: Romance-Triangles; Dancers; Chicago; 1890s
(Aaron Slick from Punkin Crick; Strawberry Blonde; The Dolly Sisters)
The Wackiest Ship in the Army, 1960, 99m, ★★★/$$$, Col/Col. A crew of goofy soldier-sailors manages to confuse and outwit the Japanese in the South Pacific. Jack Lemmon, Ricky Nelson. w. Richard Murphy, Herbert Carlson, d. Richard Murphy.
COMEDY: FARCE: Comedy of Errors; Underdog Stories; World War II Stories; Military; Comedy; Sea Adventure; Slapstick Comedy; Japanese as Enemy
(Operation Petticoat; McHale's Navy SERIES; Mister Roberts; Ensign Pulver)
(Ed: Goofy in a Disney way, better due to Lemmon.)
Waco, 1966, 85m, ★★/$$, Par/Par, V. A gunfighter comes into the cowpoke Texas town to set things right. Howard Keel, Jane Russell, Brian Donlevy. w. Steve Fisher, N-adap. Harry Sanford, Max Lamb (Emporia), d. R. G. Springsteen.
WESTERN: DRAMA: Western-Revenge; Texas; Western-City Titles; Revenge
The Wages of Fear, 1953, 140m, ★★★★/$$$, Ind/Sinister, Hollywood Home. In Central America, several truck

drivers are talked into taking very dangerous nitro-glycerin across treacherous roads leading to a nightmare they couldn't have imagined. Yves Montand, Folco Lulli, Charles Vanel. w. d. Henri Clouzot, N-adap. Georges Arnaud.

SUSPENSE: DRAMA: ADVENTURE: Psychological Drama; Journies; Oil People; Truck Drivers Quests; Central America; French Films; Film History

REMAKE: Sorcerer.

(Sorcerer; The Captains and the Kings; Treasure of the Sierra Madre; Diabolique)

(Ed: An all-time classic, especially in the suspense department; original and worth waiting for the end)

Wagonmaster, 1950, 86m, ★★1/2/$$, RKO/Turner. A wagon train of Mormons encounters problems en route to Utah. Ben Johnson, Joanne Dru, Harry Carey, Jr., Ward Bond. w. Frank Nugent, Patrick Ford, d. John Ford.

WESTERN: Journies; Men in Conflict; Wagon Trains

(Ed: Only of interest as a Ford film)

Waikiki Wedding, 1937, 89m, ★★★/ $$$, Par/Par. A Pineapple Queen contest in Hawaii provides the backdrop for music and romance. Bing Crosby, Shirley Ross, Bob Burns, Martha Raye, Anthony Quinn. w. Frank Butler, Walter de Leon, Don Hartman, Francis Martin, d. Frank Tuttle.

MUSICALS: Beauty Pageants; Hawaii; **ROMANCE:** Romantic Comedy

(Pennies from Heaven; Road to Singapore)

Wait 'Til the Sun Shines, Nellie, 1952, 108m, 20th/NA. The ups and downs, trims and close-shaves, of a small-town barber during the quartet-singing turn-of-the-century era. David Wayne, Jean Peters, Hugh Marlowe, Albert Dekker, Alan Hale, Jr. w. Allan Scott, N-adap. w. Ferdinand Reyher, d. Henry King.

COMEDY DRAMA: MELODRAMA: Small-town Life; Ordinary People Stories; 1900s; Nostalgia; Singers

Wait Until Dark, 1967, 108m, ★★★1/2/ $$$, WB/WB, PG/V. A blind woman (Audrey Hepburn, BActress) living alone is unaware her photographer husband has brought a doll stuffed with heroin into her basement apartment; and that the drug dealers who lost it have found where she and the doll are. Alan Arkin, Richard Crenna, Efrem Zimbalist, Jr. w. Robert and Jane Howard-Carrington, P-adap.

Frederick Knott, d. Terence Young. Oscars: 1-0.

SUSPENSE: THRILLERS: Women in Jeopardy; Blind People; Disabled People in Jeopardy; Drug Dealers; Turning the Tables; Female Screenwriters; Disabled but Nominated; Female Protagonists

(Jennifer 8; Hear No Evil)

Wait Until Spring, Bandini, 1990, 104m, ★★★/$, Ind/WB, PG-13/S. An Italian family moves west during the 20s to a small Colorado town where the father has a sexy woman vying for his attention as they try to adjust to the new style of life and climate. Joe Mantegna, Faye Dunaway, Burt Young, Ornella Muti, Alex Vincent. d. Dominique Deruddere.

COMEDY DRAMA: MELODRAMA: ROMANCE: Romantic Drama; Family Drama; Fish out of Water Stories; Cheating Men; Romance with Married Person; Immigrants; Italians; Hidden Gems

(Cold Sassy Tree; Scorchers)

Waiting for the Light, 1991, 94m, ★★1/2/$, Triumph-Col/Col-Tri, PG. A woman (Teri Garr) and her kooky aunt (Shirley MacLaine) run a diner in a small town during the Cuban Missile Crisis when a prank turns into a media circus. Vincent Schiavelli, Colin Baumgartner, Clancy Brown. w. d. Christopher Monger.

COMEDY: COMEDY DRAMA: Illusions; Small-town Life; Ordinary People Stories; Eccentric People; Hoaxes; Single Women; Mothers-Struggling; Con Artists; Miracles?; Angels; Cuban Missile Crisis; Coulda Been Good; Writer-Directors

(UFOria)

(Ed: Cute and quirky, but not much else)

Waiting to Exhale, 1995, 120m, ★★★/ $$$$, 20th/Fox, R/P-S. Four affluent black female friends go through the motions as each tries to find the right man. Whitney Houston, Angela Bassett, Loretta Devine, Lela Rochon, Gregory Hines, Dennis Haysbert, Mykelti Williamson. w. Terry McMillan & Ronald Bass, N-adap. Terry McMillan, d. Forest Whitaker.

DRAMA: COMEDY DRAMA: Ensemble Films; Ensembles-Female; Black Women; Black Casts; Divorce; Cheating Men; Women's Films; Black Directors; Black Screenwriters; Sleepers; Female Screenwriters; Female Protagonists

(Boys on Side; Steel Magnolias; Moonlight and Valentino; The Color Purple; Hollow Image; The Bodyguard; What's Love Got to Do With It?)

Wake Island, 1942, 78m, ★★1/2/$$, Par/Par. A small Pacific island is assaulted and marines fight to hold it. Brian Donlevy, Macdonald Carey, Robert Preston, William Bendix, Walter Abel. w. W. R. Burnett, Frank Butler, d. John Farrow.

War Movies; **ACTION:** World War II Movies; Soldiers; Pacific Islands; Islands

Wake of the Red Witch, 1948, 106m, ★★★/$$$, Republic/Republic. The fighting between the captain and owner of a ship, both in love with a dying woman, threatens to abort their mission of seeking treasure in the East Indies. John Wayne, Luther Adler, Gail Russell, Gig Young. w. Harry Brown, Kenneth Garnet, N-adap. Garland Roark, d. Edward Ludwig.

ADVENTURE: DRAMA: MELODRAMA: Pacific Islands; Treasure Hunts; Men in Conflict; **ROMANCE:** Tearjerkers; Romance-Triangles; Death-Impending

(Blood Alley; Mutiny on the Bounty)

(Ed: Slow moving, but visually interesting and remarkably sensitive at points)

Walk, Don't Run, 1966, 114m, ★★1/2/ $$, Col/RCA-Col, PG. During the Tokyo Olympics, all the hotels are booked, so two men have to share an apartment with a woman. Cary Grant, Samantha Eggar, Jim Hutton, John Standing, Miiko Taka. w. Sol Saks, S-adap. Talk of the Town, d. Charles Walters.

COMEDY: COMEDY DRAMA: ROMANCE: Romantic Comedy; Matchmakers; Romance-Bickering; Roommates; Female Among Males; Japan; Olympics

REMAKE OF The More the Merrier.

(The More the Merrier; Under the Yum Yum Tree)

A Walk in the Clouds, 1995, 100m, ★★1/2/$$$, 20th/Fox, PG-13/S. A young World War II soldier returns home to his young wife whom he knew only briefly before leaving. He leaves again and meets a young woman who's pregnant and needs a husband, or at least a man who will pretend to be that on a visit to her parents, but will love find a way through the veils? Keanu Reeves, Aitana Sanchez-Gijon, Anthony Quinn, Giancarlo Giannini, Angelica Aragon. w. Robert Mark Kamen, Mark Miller & Harvey Weitzman, S-adap. Quattro Passi Fra Le Nuvole, Piero Tellini, Cesare Zavattini, Vittorio de Benedetti, d. Alfonso Arau.

ROMANCE: MELODRAMA: Marriage-Fake; Mothers-Unwed; Soldiers; World War II Era; Magic Realism; Latin People; Foreign Film Remakes
(Like Water for Chocolate; El Norte; A Time of Destiny)

A Walk in the Spring Rain, 1969, 98m, ★★½/$, Col/NA. A professor's wife falls in love with a local man on vacation in mountain country. Ingrid Bergman, Anthony Quinn, Fritz Weaver, Katherine Crawford. w. Stirling Silliphant, N-adap, w. Richard Maddox, d. Guy Green.

ROMANCE: DRAMA: MELODRAMA: Romantic Drama; Romance-Middle-Aged; Forgotten Films; Overlooked at Release; Underrated
(The Visit; Shirley Valentine)
(Ed: Not up to Bergman's previous, but still worth it for fans of her or Quinn)

A Walk in the Sun, 1946, 117m, ★★★/$$, MGM/Nos. The Salerno landings of 1943, as seen through the eyes of a single army patrol who went through it. Dana Andrews, Richard Conte, Sterling Holloway, Lloyd Bridges. w. Robert Rossen, N-adap. Harry Brown, d. Lewis Milestone.

War Movies: **ACTION:** World War II Stories; Flashbacks; Soldiers

Walk on the Wild Side, 1962, 114m, ★★★/$$$, Col/RCA-Col. A dirt farmer in the thirties finds his first love working in a "house of ill repute" in New Orleans with flashy and glamorous women as her friends and enemies. Jane Fonda, Capucine, Barbara Stanwyck, Laurence Harvey, Ann Baxter. w. John Fante, Edmund Morris, N-adap. Nelson Algren, d. Edward Dmytryk.

MELODRAMA: ROMANCE: DRAMA: Romantic Drama; Prostitutes-High Class; Past-Haunted by; Romance Reunited; Love-First; Depression Era; New Orleans
(All the Fine Young Cannibals; This Property Condemned; A House Is Not a Home)
(Ed: Pretty trashy but pretty)

Walkabout, 1970, 100m, ★★½/$, Roadshow-Ind/NA, R/V. A man's young children are lead by Aborigines to safety after he kills himself in the Australian outback. Jenny Agutter, Lucien John, David Gumpilil. w. Edward Bond, N-adap. James Vance Marshall, d. Nicolas Roeg.

DRAMA: ADVENTURE: Art Films; Rescue Drama; Journies; Fathers;

Depression; Suicidal Tendencies; Australian Films; Aborigines
(The Last Wave)

Walker, 1987, 94m, ★★/$, U/MCA-U, R/P-S-V. An American explorer in the late 1800s sets himself up as dictator of Nicaragua. Ed Harris, Richard Masur, Rene Auberjonois, Peter Boyle, Marlee Matlin. w. Rudy Wurlitzer, d. Alex Cox.

DRAMA: Art Films; Surrealism; Revisionist Films; Central America; Politicians; Political Drama; Explorers; Leaders-Tyrants; Latin People; 1890s; Flops-Major; Curiosities
(Ed: Interesting curio for the anachronistic injections and commentaries)

The Walking Dead, 1936, 66m, ★★½/$$, WB/WB. An electrocuted man returns to life to avenge himself. Boris Karloff, Edmund Gwenn, Marguerite Churchill, Ricardo Cortez. w. Ewart Adamson, Peter Milne, Robert Andrews, Lillie Hayward, d. Michael Curtiz.

HORROR: Dead-Back from the; Executions; Revenge; Accused Unjustly; Framed?
(Shocker; The Crow)

The Walking Stick, 1970, 101m, MGM/MGM-UA. A shy young woman with polio falls in love with a painter who is also a con artist plotting a robbery. Samantha Eggar, David Hemmings. w. George Bluestone, N-adap. Winston Graham, d. Eric Till.

DRAMA: MELODRAMA: ROMANCE: Disease Stories; Tearjerkers; Romance-Doomed; Con Artists; Betrayals; British Films

Wall Street, 1987, 124m, ★★★/$$$, 20th/CBS-Fox, R/P-S-FFN. A young man (Charlie Sheen) wanting to become a business mogul convinces his idol, a billionaire named Gordon Gecko (Michael Douglas, **BActor**) to take him under his wing, only to discover his corruption and face deciding whether to become a part of it or not. Daryl Hannah, Sean Young, Martin Sheen, Terence Stamp. w. d. Oliver Stone. Oscars: 1-1.

DRAMA: Social Drama; Message Films; Power Struggles; Greed; Business Life; Executives; Corporation as Enemy; Corporate Corruption; Corruption; Rich People; Social Climbers; Stock Brokers; Yuppies; Ethics; Writer-Directors; 1980s
(Other People's Money; Working Girl; Disclosure)

(Ed: Over the top and pounding in parts, it's also a good time capsule of the 80s)

Waltz Across Texas, 1982, 99m, ★★/$, Aster/Vestron, R/P-S-MRN. A warm Texas oilman melts the ice on a cold female geologist who's helping him find black gold. Anne Archer, Terry Jastrow, Noah Beery, Mary Kay Place. w. Bill Svanoe, d. Ernest Day.

ROMANCE: COMEDY: Romantic Comedy; Romance-Bickering; Romance-Opposites Attract; Oil People; Texas
(Never a Dull Moment)

The Wanderers, 1979, 117m, ★★★/$$, Par/Par, R/EV-P. Teenage street gangs in early 60s Bronx New York battle it out while growing up. Ken Wahl, John Friedrich, Karen Allen. w. Rose and Philip Kaufman, N-adap. w. Richard Price, d. Philip Kaufman.

DRAMA: ACTION: Teenage Movies; Teenagers; Coming of Age; Gangs-White; Inner City Life; New York Life; Poor People; Time Capsules
(The Lords of Flatbush; Five Corners; A Bronx Tale; The Warriors; Paradise Alley; FIST; West Side Story; True Love; My Bodyguard)
(Ed: Early in the genre and more naturalistic)

The Wandering Jew, 1933, 111m, ★★★/$, Gaumont-Twickenham-Ind/ Glenn Video Vistas. As punishment, a Jewish man is condemned to live forever but must also face the Spanish Inquisition. w. H. Fowler Mear, P-adap. E. Temple Thurston, d. Maurice Elvey.

DRAMA: Fantasy; Surrealism; Anti-Semitism; Jewish People; Episodic Stories; Middle Ages

Wanted Dead or Alive, 1986, 104m, ★-/$, New World/New World, R/EV-P. A bounty hunter goes after a terrorist who stole his girl, as always seems to happen. Rutger Hauer, Gene Simmons, Robert Gillaume. w. Brian Taggert, d. Gary Sherman.

ACTION: Bounty Hunters; Trail of a Killer; Terrorists; Avenging Death of Someone; Chase Stories

The War, 1994, 127m, ★★/$, WB/WB, PG-13/P-V. A boy comes of age in Vietnam-era Mississippi with his veteran father who's down on his luck and down on the war. Elijah Wood, Kevin Costner, Mare Winningham, Lexi Randall, Leon Sills, Adam Henderson. w. Kathy McWorter, d. Jon Avnet.

DRAMA: MELODRAMA: Coming of Age; Fathers & Sons; Boys; Boyhood; Vietnam Era; Veterans-Vietnam; Peaceful People; Southerns; 1970s; Mississippi; Flops-Major; Female Screenwriters
(A Perfect World)

The War Against Mrs. Hadley, 1942, 86m, ★★½/$$, MGM/NA. A middle-aged Washington socialite finds World War II puts a damper on her social life and tries to carry on despite it. Fay Bainter, Edward Arnold, Richard Ney, Jean Rogers, Sara Allgood. w. George Oppenheimer, d. Harold S. Bucquet.

MELODRAMA: DRAMA: Character Studies; World War II Era; Washington D.C.; Social Climbing; Rich People
(White Banners; Auntie Mame; Mrs. Miniver)

War and Peace, 1956, 208m, ★★½/$$$, DEG-Par/Par. During the time of Napoleon's invasion, a Russian family's trials and tribulations are observed. Audrey Hepburn, Henry Fonda, Mel Ferrer, Herbert Lom, John Mills, Oscar Homolka, Anita Ekberg, Vittorio Gassman. w. Bridget Boland, Robert Westerby, King Vidor, Mario Camerini, Ennio de Concini, Ivo Perelli, N-adap. Leo Tolstoy, d. King Vidor (BDirector). BCCin. Oscars: 2-0.

DRAMA: MELODRAMA: Epics; Family Drama; Royalty; Costume Drama; Historical Drama; War Movies; Multiple Stories; All-Star Casts; Cast of Thousands; Russia; Classic Literary Adaptations
(The Brothers Karamazov; Dr. Zhivago; Rasputin and the Empress)
(Ed: A Hollywood version of the classic, but with Audrey, who cares about accuracy?)

War and Peace, 1967, 507m, ★★★/$, Mosfilm/Kultur Video. The effect of the Napoleonic invasion and its aftermath on a single, large Russian family. w. Sergei Bondarchuk, Vasili Solovyov, N-adap. Leo Tolstoy, d. Sergei Bondarchuk.

DRAMA: War Movies; War Battles; Epics; Family Drama; Royalty; Historical Drama; Multiple Stories; Cast of Thousands; Russia; Russian Films; Classic Literary Adaptations
(Dr. Zhivago)
(Ed: Immensely long, but the battles scenes are legendary; apparently one of the most expensive films ever made)

The War Between Men and Women, 1972, 105m, ★★★/$$, NG/WB, PG. A recently divorced woman's ex-husband torments her current one, a legally blind cartoonist modeled after James Thurber. Jack Lemmon, Barbara Harris, Jason Robards, Jr. w. Mel Shavelson, Danny Arnold, SS-adap. James Thurber, d. Mel Shavelson.

COMEDY DRAMA: COMEDY: ROMANCE: Romantic Comedy; Romance-Middle-Aged; Romance-Triangles; Marriage Comedy; Battle of the Sexes; Writers; Nerds; Coulda Been Great
(Little Murders; The Awful Truth)
(Ed: A peculiar Lemmon performance, and Harris is good)

War Games, 1983, 113m, ★★★½/$$$$, MGM/MGM-UA, PG. A teenage computer "hacker" taps into the Pentagon's nuclear defense computer system thinking he's playing a game, and causes panic at high levels in Washington. Matthew Broderick, Dabney Coleman, John Wood, Ally Sheedy, Barry Corbin. w. Lawrence Lasker, Walter F. Parkes (BOScr), d. John Badham. BCin. Oscars: 2-0.

DRAMA: SUSPENSE: Cold War Era; Cold War Error; Race Against Time; Chase Stories; Teenagers; Geniuses; Computers; Man vs. Machine; Russians as Enemy; Message Films; Political Thriller; Apocalyptic Stories; Sleeper Hits
(Hackers; The Forbin Project; Failsafe)
(Ed: A good idea that delivers and manages to be intelligent in what is essentially a kid's picture)

The War Lord, 1965, 121m, ★★★/$$, Universal/MCA-U. Druids give a Norman knight trouble while he tries to conquer ancient England. Charlton Heston, Richard Boone, Rosemary Forsyth, Maurice Evans, Guy Stockwell, James Farentino. w. John Collier, Millard Kaufman. w. P-adap. Leslie Stevens, *The Lovers*, d. Franklin J. Schaffner.

ADVENTURE: Costume Drama; Historical Drama; Medieval Times; Cults; Sword and Sorcery; Forgotten Films; England
(The Last Valley; Braveheart)

The War Lover, 1962, 105m, ★★½/$$, Col/Goodtimes. During World War II, an ace pilot's obsessions try the patience of the woman in his life. Steve McQueen, Shirley Anne Field, Robert Wagner, Michael Crawford. w. Howard Koch, N-adap. John Hersey, d. Philip Leacock.

DRAMA: War Movies; World War II Movies; Marriage on the Rocks;

Obsessions; Pilots-Military; Soldiers; Young Men
(The Right Stuff)

The War of the Roses, 1989, 116m, ★★★/$$$$$, 20th/Fox, R/EV-P-S. A couple decides to divorce, but no one's willing to give up the house without a major fight. Kathleen Turner, Michael Douglas, Danny DeVito, Marianne Sagebrecht, Sean Astin. w. Michael Leeson, N. adap. Warren Adler, d. Danny DeVito.

Black Comedy; Tragi-Comedy; COMEDY DRAMA: TRAGEDY: Marriage Drama; Marriage Comedy; Romance-Bickering; Divorce; Marriage on the Rocks; Murder-Comic Attempts
(Divorce Wars: A Love Story)
(Ed: A few good jokes, but all in all, much trashing about nothing)

The War of the Worlds, 1953, 85m, ★★★½/$$$, Par/Par. Martians invade the Earth, humans flee from spectacular special effects. Gene Barry, Ann Robinson. w. Barre Lyndon, N-adap, w. H. G. Wells, d. Byron Haskin.

SCI-FI: Sci-Fi-1950s; HORROR: SUSPENSE: THRILLER: Deaths-One by One; Aliens-Outer Space, Evil; Martians; Apocalyptic Stories; Paranoia
(Invaders from Mars; Independence Day)

War Party, 1989, 97m, ★★½/$, Hemdale/HBO. A real battle ensues after a Blackfoot Indian is killed by a white man during a reenactment of a historical massacre. Billy Wirth, Kevin Dillon, Tim Sampson, Jimmie Ray Weeks, M. Emmet Walsh. w. Spencer Eastman, d. Franc Roddam.

DRAMA: Men in Conflict; Deaths-Accidental; Indians-American; Native Americans
(Powwow Highway; Incident at Oglala; Thunderheart)

Warlock, 1959, 123m, ★★/$$, 20th/CBS-Fox. A gun-for-hire takes over as unofficial sheriff for a western town besieged by violence. Henry Fonda, Richard Widmark, Anthony Quinn, Dorothy Malone, Wallace Ford, DeForrest Kelley. w. Robert Alan Aurthur, N-adap. Oakley Hall, d. Edward Dmytryk.

WESTERNS: Hitmen; Men in Conflict; Vigilantes
(Ed: Nothing to do with witches)

Warlock, 1988, 102m, ★★★/$$, Trimark/New World, PG-13/S-EV. An emissary of Satan (Julian Sands) is transported into modern day America via an antique with a secret, followed by his hunter from way back when (Richard E. Grant) and a modern-day girl helping him (Lori Singer). Kevin O'Brien, David Carpenter. w. David T. Twohy, d. Steve Miner.

SCI-FI: Fantasy **ACTION:** Chase Stories; Time Travel; Women in Jeopardy; Bounty Hunters; Satan; Apocalyptic Stories; Murders-One by One; Witchcraft; Ind Films
(Time After Time; Highlander)
(Ed: A cheap Spielberg-esque romp that works)

A Warm December, 1972, 101m, ★★1/2/$$, First Artists-NG/WB, PG. An American widower in London falls in love with the niece of an African diplomat who has a dark secret. Sidney Poitier, Esther Anderson, George Baker, Johnny Sekka, Earl Cameron. w. Lawrence Roman, d. Sidney Poitier.

DRAMA: ROMANCE: Romantic Drama; Disease Stories; Tearjerkers; Black Men; Black People; England; Americans Abroad; Africans
(For Love of Ivy; Love Story; A Patch of Blue)

Warm Nights on a Slow Moving Train, 1987, 90m, ★★-/$, Prism/Prism, Par, R/ES-FN-MN. A teacher takes a train through Australia and meets a sexy fellow with a way to spend the ride time. Wendy Hughes, Colin Friels, Norman Kaye. w. Bob Ellis, Denny Lawrence, d. Bob Ellis.

MELODRAMA: Erotic Drama; Erotic Thriller; Trains; Sexy Men; Dangerous Men; Hidden Gems; Australian Films

Warning Sign, 1985, 100m, ★★/$, 20th/CBS-Fox. A lethal plague may be inadvertently unleashed by a group of scientists, and a lone cop is the only one who knows it. Sam Waterston, Kathleen Quinlan, Yaphet Kotto, Richard Dysart. w. Hal Barwood, Matthew Robbins, d. Hal Barwood.

SUSPENSE: THRILLER: SCI-FI: Message Films; Disaster Movies; Conspiracy; Unbelieved; Corporation as Enemy; Scientists; Plagues
(The Stand; Prophecy; The Cassandra Crossing; Acceptable Risks; Rage)

The Warriors, 1979, 94m, ★★/$$$, Par/Par, R/EV-P-S. New York street gangs have an all-out war for territory. Michael Beck, James Remar, Thomas Waites. w. David Shaber, Walter Hill, N-adap. Sol Yurick, d. Walter Hill.

ACTION: Teenagers; Teenage Movies; Gangs-Street; New York Life; Inner City Life
(The Lords of Flatbush; Five Corners; A Bronx Tale; The Wanderers; Paradise Alley; FIST)
(Ed: More exploitative action and violence than character; controversial in its initial release)

The Warrior's Husband, 1933, 75m, ★★1/2/$, 20th/NA. Greek warriors conquer the women of Amazonia and incur their wrath. Elissa Landi, Marjorie Rambeau, Ernest Treux, David Manners, Helen Ware. w. Sonya Levien, P-adap. Julian Thompson, d. Walter Lang.

COMEDY DRAMA: SATIRE: FARCE: Marriage Comedy; Marriage Drama; Battle of the Sexes; Ancient Times; Greeks; Female Protagonists; Ensembles-Female; Female Screenwriters
(The Trojan Women)

The War Room, 1993, 93m, ★★★/$$, Vidmark/Vidmark, PG. Story of President Clinton's rise from Arkansas governor to the White House from the point of view of his campaign staff. d. Chris Hegedus, D.A. Pennebaker. BDocumentary. Oscars: 1-0.

Documentaries; Presidents; Political Campaigns; Behind the Scenes; Politicians; Washington D.C.; Arkansas
(Power; State of the Union; The Candidate)

Washington Story, 1952, 82m, ★★/$$, MGM/NA. A female journalist goes to D.C. in search of corruption to expose, but ends up in love with an ethical congressman. Van Johnson, Patricia Neal, Louis Calhern, Sidney Blackmer, Philip Ober. w. d. Robert Pirosh.

DRAMA: MELODRAMA: ROMANCE: Ethics; Corruption; Patriotism; Traitors; Journalists; Congressmen; Washington D.C.; Female Protagonists; Writer-Directors
(The American President)

Watch It, 1993, 102m, ★★★/VR, Par/Par. Several thirtyish guys live in a house in Chicago where one wants to marry his old girl but his pal, who's a heel, has gotten engaged to her. Getting her to change her mind leads to a rift between them all. Peter Gallagher, John C. McGinley, Suzy Amis, Jon Tenney, Tom Sizemore, Lili Taylor, Cynthia Stevenson. w. d. Tom Flynn.

COMEDY DRAMA: Ensemble Films; Ensembles-Male; Men's Films; Men Fighting Over Women; Marriage-Impending; Engagements-Breaking; Yuppies; 20-Somethings; Mean Men; Romance-Choosing the Right Person; Battle of the Sexes; Young People; Young Men; Chicago; Hidden Gems; Writer-Directors
(The Men's Club; The Brothers McMullen)
(Ed: Some well-written and insightful dialogue, if not the most likable-but probably normal-characters)

Watch on the Rhine, 1943, 114m, ★★★1/2/$$$, WB/WB. A man who fled Germany to escape persecution during World War II finds Nazi agents pursuing him in Washington. Paul Lukas (**BActor**), Bette Davis, Lucile Watson (BSActress), George Coulo* Geraldine Fitzgerald, Beulah Bondi. w. Dashiell Hammett (BScr), P-adap. Lillian Hellman, d. Herman Shumlin. BPicture. Oscars: 4-1.

DRAMA: SUSPENSE: Spies; Nazi Stories; Impostors; Female Screenwriters; Washington D.C.; World War II Era; Secrets; Germans as Enemy; Stagelike Films
(The Stranger; The House on 92nd Street; The House on Carroll Street)

The Watcher in the Woods, 1980, 100m, ★★/$$, Disney/Disney. A teenage American girl has supernatural visions in the English countryside. Bette Davis, Carroll Baker, David McCallum, Kyle Richards. w. Brian Clemens, Harry Spaulding, Rosemary Anne Sisson, N-adap. Florence Engel Randall, d. John Hough, Vincent McEveety.

HORROR: SCI-FI: SUSPENSE: Psychics; Supernatural Danger; Curiosities; Gothic Style
(Wicked Stepmother; The Medusa Touch)
(Ed: A feeble attempt by the pre-Touchstone Disney crew to go mainstream)

Watchers, 1988, 91m, ★★1/2/$ (VR), Carolco/Live, PG-13/V-B&G. Two "experiments gone wrong"—a dog with superior intelligence, and an ape-like hybrid-escape from the lab and go on a killing spree. Corey Haim, Michael Ironside, Christopher Carey, Graeme Campbell. w. Bill Freed, Damian Lee, N-adap. w. Dean Koontz, d. Jon Hess

Watchers II, 1990, 101m, ★★/$, Carolco/Live, R/EV. The dog continues his adventures with his psychic skills and an animal shrink. Marc Singer, Tracy Scoggins. d. Thierry Notz.

HORROR: SCI-FI: Experiments; Scientists-Mad; Animals into Humans; Primates; Deaths-One by One

Water, 1985, 95m, ★★/$, Handmade/Par, PG. A poor Caribbean island is rumored to have mineral springs which brings in a flood of developers and schemers. Michael Caine, Valerie Perrine, Brenda Vaccaro, Billy Connolly, Fred Gwynne. w. Dick Clement, Ian La Frennais, Bill Bersky, d. Dick Clement.

COMEDY: Con Artists; Islands; Caribbean

Water Babies, 1979, 93m, ★★1/2/$, Ind/Sultan. A boy runs from the law after being accused of stealing silver and dives into a pond full of interesting animated characters. James Mason, Billie Whitelaw, David Tomlinson. d. Lionel Jeffries.

CHILDREN'S: FAMILY: Fantasy; Animation-Partial; Animals-Talking; Fugitives from the Law; Boys; Accused Unjustly; British Films

(Bedknobs & Broomsticks)

The Waterdance, 1991, 107m, ★★★/$, Goldwyn/Goldwyn, R/S-P. Three men confined to wheelchairs adjust to life in the world of the handicapped. Eric Stoltz, Wesley Snipes, William Forsythe, Helen Hunt, Elizabeth Pena, Grace Zabriskie. w. Neil Jimenez, d. Neil Jimenez, Michael Steinberg.

DRAMA: COMEDY DRAMA: Disabled People; Hospitals; Friendships-Male; Ensembles-Male

(Inside Moves; Born on the Fourth of July)

Waterland, 1991, 95m, ★★1/2/$, Col/Col, R/S-MN. A teacher originally from England in a Pittsburgh school tells his pupils of his childhood and its tragedy. Jeremy Irons, Sinead Cusack, Ethan Hawke. w. Peter Prince, N-adap. Graham Swift, d. Stephen Gyllenhaal.

DRAMA: Art Films; Coming of Age; Abused Children; Abused Women; Boyhood; Flashbacks; Memories; Autobiographical Stories; Teachers; Teachers & Students; Men and Boys; Teenagers; British Films

Waterloo, 1970, 132m, ★★/$, Col/Par, PG. The history leading up to Napoleon's famous 1815 defeat. Rod Steiger, Christopher Plummer, Orson Welles, Jack Hawkins, Virginia McKenna, Dan

O'Herlihy, Rupert Davies. w. H. A. L. Craig, Sergei Bondarchuk, d. Sergei Bondarchuk.

DRAMA: Epics; Biographies; Leaders-Tyrants; War Movies; War Battles; Napoleon; Flops-Major

(Desiree)

Waterloo Bridge, 1931, 72m, ★★1/2/$$$, MGM/NA. Mae Clarke, Kent Douglas, Doris Lloyd, Bette Davis. w. Tom Reed, Benn W. Levy, P-adap. Robert E. Sherwood, d. James Whale.

Waterloo Bridge, 1940, 103m, ★★★/$$$, MGM/MGM-UA. A military man marries a ballerina but when he becomes a casualty of war, she becomes despondent and eventually sinks into prostitution. Vivien Leigh, Robert Taylor, Lucile Watson, Virginia Field. w. S. N. Behrman, Hans Rameau, George Froeschel, P-adap. Robert E. Sherwood, d. Mervyn Le Roy.

ROMANCE: MELODRAMA: DRAMA: Romantic Drama; Tearjerkers; Romance-Doomed; Soldiers; Prostitutes-Low Class; Dancers; Ballet

(Fire Over London; Hanover Street; Romance)

Watermelonman, 1970, 100m, ★★★/$$, Col/Col. A white racist wakes up one morning to discover he's black. Godfrey Cambridge, Estelle Parsons, Howard Caine, Mantan Moreland. w. Herman Raucher, d. Melvin Van Peebles.

SATIRE: COMEDY: Black Comedy; Black People; Black vs. White; White as Black; Role Reversal; Body Switching; Coulda Been Great

(True Identity; Heart Condition; Black Like Me; Soul Man; Brother John; Putney Swope)

(Ed: A good premise not fully explored or made up; the makeup of *True Identity* pulls off turning a black man white, however)

Watership Down, 1978, 92m, ★★★/$$$, MGM-UA/MGM-UA. A community of rabbits foresees the destruction of its home then searches far and wide for a new one. Voices of: John Hurt, Richard Briers, Ralph Richardson, Zero Mostel, Roy Kinnear, Denholm Elliott, John Bennett, Simon Cadell. w. d. Martin Rosen, N-adap. Richard Adams.

CHILDREN'S: FAMILY: Cartoons; Animals-Smart; Fantasy; Mortgage Drama; Rabbits

(The Secret of NIMH)

Waterworld, 1995, 120m, ★★1/2/$$$$, U/MCA-U, PG-13/P-S-V. In a world after the polar ice caps have melted and the earth is covered with water, a man fights for his existence and his limes while everyone recycles their urine. Kevin Costner, Dennis Hopper, Jeanne Tripplehorn, Tina Majorino, Michael Jeter, Chaim Jeraffi, Ric Aviles, R. D. Call, Zitto Kazann, Leonardo Cimino. w. Peter Rader, David Twohy. d. Kevin Reynolds.

ACTION: SCI-FI: Futuristic Films; Apocalyptic Stories; Adventure at Sea; Environmental Dilemmas; Outstanding Production Design

(The Road Warrior; Robin Hood: Prince of Thieves)

(Ed: Actually not a flop, except in terms of the $80 million gross vs. the $170 million+ cost-and the overall quality. But it could have been worse)

Waxwork, 1988, 96m, ★★1/2/$$, Vestron/Vestron, R/V. A group of youths visit a wax museum where—surprise—they're attacked by the figures. w. d. Anthony Hickox.

HORROR: ACTION: Chase Movies; Horror Comedy; Black Comedy; Spoofs; Movies Within Movies; Trials; Fast-Paced Films; Accused Unjustly; Writer-Directors

(Murder in the Wax Museum)

Waxwork II: Lost in Time, 1992, 100m, ★★1/2/VR, Vestron-Ind/Live, R/P-V-B&G-S. A young couple (Zach Galligan, Monika Schnarre) break free of the wax museum of monsters from the first film, but find themselves in a time travel trap of horror movie scenarios from *Frankenstein* to *Alien* on their way to re-animating life to get out of a murder wrap. Patrick MacNee, Juliet Mills, Bruce Campbell, Martin Kemp, Alexander Gudonov. w. d. Anthony Hickox.

HORROR: ACTION: Chase Movies; Horror Comedy; Black Comedy; Spoofs; Movies Within Movies; Time Travel; Trials; Accused Unjustly

SEQUEL TO: Waxwork.

(Murder in the Wax Museum; Bill and Ted's Excellent Adventure; Bill and Ted's Bogus Journey)

(Ed: Actually better than the first, though very different, and only for fans of horror comedy)

The Way Ahead, see Immortal Battalion

Way Down East, 1920, 110m, ★★★/ $$$$$, Griffith/Nos. Lillian Gish, Richard Bethelmes, Lowell Sherman. w. Anthony Paul Kelly, Joseph R. Grismer, D. W. Griffith, P-adap. Lottie Blair Parker, d. D. W. Griffith.

Way Down East, 1935, 85m, ★★1/2/$$, 20th/NA. A small-town girl has a baby out of wedlock and tries to commit suicide, but a nice farmer intervenes. Rochelle Hudson, Henry Fonda, Slim Summerville, Edward Trevor, Margaret Hamilton. w. Howard Estabrook, William Hurlbut, P-adap, w. Lottie Blair Parker, d. Henry King.
ROMANCE: MELODRAMA: Tearjerkers; Suicidal Tendencies; Small-town Life; Small-town Scandals; Southerns; Mothers-Unwed; Farmers; Female Protagonists; Female Screenwriters
(Johnny Belinda; The Miracle of Morgan's Creek; Birth of a Nation)

The Way of All Flesh, 1928, 94m, ★★★/$$$$, Par/NA. Emil Jannings (BActor), Belle Bennett, Phyllis Haver. w. N-adap. Perley Sheehan, d. Victor Fleming.

The Way of All Flesh, 1940, 82m, ★★1/2/$$, Par/Par. Akim Tamiroff, Gladys George, Muriel Angelus. w. Leonore Coffee, Jules Furthman, Lajos Biro, N-adap. Perley Sheehan, d. Louis King.
A philandering man leaves his wife and when his luck runs dry, he's too ashamed to go back to her.
MELODRAMA: Tearjerkers; Cheating Men; Marriage on the Rocks; Nervous Breakdowns

Way Out West, 1937, 66m, ★★★1/2/ $$$, Hal Roach-UA/MGM-UA. Two boobs are entrusted with the task of delivering the deed to a goldmine out west in Brushwood Gulch. Stan Laurel, Oliver Hardy, James Finlayson, Sharon Lynne, Rosina Lawrence. w. Jack Jevne, Charles Rogers, James Parrott, Felix Adler, d. James Horne.
COMEDY: WESTERNS: Western Comedy; Gold Mining; Treasure Hunts; Fools-Bumbling
(Bonnie Scotland; The Piano)

The Way to the Stars, see **Johnny in the Clouds**

The Way We Were, 1973, 118m, ★★★1/2/$$$$, Columbia/RCA-Col, PG/S. A wallflower campus radical (Barbra Streisand, BActress) pursues the strong,

silent campus hero (Robert Redford) and soon they're married and living in Hollywood, but soon their differences take their toll as the McCarthy era rises. w. N-adap. Arthur Laurents (BAScr), d. George Roy. Hill. BCin, **BOScore, BOSong.** Oscars: 6-2.
ROMANCE: DRAMA: Romantic Drama; Marriage Drama; Opposites Attract; Feisty Females; Wallflowers; Wallflowers & Hunks; Sexy Men; Elusive Men; Writers; Hollywood Life; College Life; Harvard Settings; 1940s; McCarthy Era; Conformism; Episodic Stories; Female Protagonists
(Summer and Smoke; The Sterile Cuckoo; Up Close and Personal; Havana)

The Way West, 1967, 122m, ★★/$$, UA/MGM-UA. A wagon train in 1843 has a perilous journey from missouri to Oregon. Kirk Douglas, Robert Mitchum, Richard Widmark, Lola Albright, Sally Field. w. Ben Maddox, Mitch Lindemann, N-adap. A. B. Guthrie, Jr., d. Andrew V. McLaglen.
WESTERNS: Journeys; Wagon Trains; Old West

Wayne's World, 1992, 95m, ★★★/ $$$$$, Par/Par, PG-13/P-S. Two nerdy suburbanites are happy just to have their own cable access show in Aurora, Illinois, when a sleazy Hollywood promoter dangles cash offers in their faces, tempting them to "go commercial." Mike Myers, Dana Carvey, Rob Lowe, Tia Carrera, Lara Flynn Boyle, Brian Doyle-Murray. w. Mike Myers, Bonnie Turner, Terry Turner, d. Penelope Spheeris.
COMEDY: Comedy-Character; Comedy-Skits; Saturday Night Live Movies; Comedy-Slapstick; Corporation as Enemy; Greed; Musicians; Fame-Rise to; Female Screenwriters; Female Directors

Wayne's World 2, 1993, 98m, ★★/$$, Par/Par, PG-13/P-S. This time, more sleazy record promoters, concert dreams, and sing-alongs. Mike Myers, Dana Carvey, Tia Carrere, Christopher Walken, Kevin Pollack, Olivia D'Abo, Kim Basinger. w. Bonnie Turner, Terry Turner, Mike Myers, d. Stephen Surjik.
COMEDY: Comedy-Character; Comedy-Skits; Saturday Night Live Movies; Comedy-Slapstick; Corporation as Enemy; Greed; Musicians; Fame-Rise to; Female Screenwriters; Flops-Major
(So I Married an Axe Murderer; Opportunity Knocks)

We Are Not Alone, 1939, 112m, ★★★/$$, WB/WB. A man is having a meaningless affair until, one day, his wife turns up murdered and he's the prime suspect. Paul Muni, Jane Bryan, Flora Robson, Raymond Severn, Una O'Connor, Cecil Kellaway w. James Hilton, Milton Krims, N-adap. James Hilton, d. Edmund Golding.
DRAMA: SUSPENSE: MURDER: Framed?; Accused Unjustly; Defending Oneself; British Films; England

A Wedding, 1978, 125m, ★★★/$$, 20th/Fox, R/P-S-MRN. Two families come together for a wedding and their meticulous plans go comically awry. Carol Burnett, Paul Dooley, Amy Stryker, Mia Farrow, Lillian Gish, Vittorio Gassman, Desi Arnaz, Jr., Geraldine Chaplin, Lauren Hutton, John Cromwell. w. John Considine, Patricia Resnick, Allan Nichols, Robert Altman, d. Robert Altman.
SATIRE: Black Comedy; **COMEDY:** Tragi-Comedy; **FARCE:** Multiple Stories; Interwoven Stories; Weddings; Family Stories; Newlyweds; Ensemble Films; Art Films; Female Screenwriters; Female Protagonists
(Lovers and Other Strangers; Nashville; Health; Short Cuts; Betsy's Wedding; Passed Away)

The Wedding March, 1928, 196m, ★★★/$$$, Par/Par. A poor girl is in love with a prince who also loves her, but, unfortunately, he may not be able to get out of his arranged marriage plans. Erich Von Stroheim, Fay Wray, Zasu Pitts, Matthew Betz, Maude George, George Fawcett. w. Harry Carr, Erich Von Stroheim, d. Erich Von Stroheim.
DRAMA: MELODRAMA: ROMANCE: TRAGEDY: Romance-Doomed; Romance-Mismatched; Princes; Class Conflicts; Weddings

The Wedding Banquet, 1993, 111m, ★★★1/2/$$$, GoodMachine/Goldwyn, R/S-P. A gay Chinese-American man marries a Chinese woman to cover for his lifestyle, but his white lover doesn't like it much and complications arise when the new wife doesn't behave properly. Winston Chao, May Chin, Mitchell Lichtenstein. w. Ang Lee, Neil Peng, James Schamus, d. Ang Lee.
COMEDY: Comedy of Errors; Marriage Comedy; Romance-Triangles; Marriage of Convenience; Marriage for Citizenship;

Gay Men; Bisexuality; Homophobia; Chinese People; Asian-Americans; Sleeper Hits; Hidden Gems; Ind Films
(La Cage Aux Folles SERIES; Green Card; Beyond Therapy; The Birdcage)
(Ed: A fascinating cross-section of points of view from sexual to cultural which meld into a unique comic style. Also the most profitable film of the year in terms of cost and earnings)

The Wedding Night, 1935, 83m, ★★★/$$, Goldwyn-UA/Goldwyn. A writer living in Connecticut gets too involved with the local Polish immigrants, falling for one of their daughters, and must face the repercussions. Gary Cooper, Anna Sten, Sig Rumann, Ralph Bellamy. w. Edith Fitzgerald, d. King Vidor.
DRAMA: ROMANCE: Romantic Drama; TRAGEDY: Political Drama; Romance-Mismatched; Writers; Small-town Life

Wedding Present, 1936, 81m, ★★1/2/$$, Par/Par. Newspaper reporters flirting with love while covering stories. Cary Grant, Joan Bennett, George Bancroft, Conrad Nagel, Gene Lockhart, William Demarest. w. Joseph Anthony, Paul Gallico, d. Richard Wallace.
COMEDY: ROMANCE: Romantic Comedy; Screwball Comedy; Journalists
(His Girl Friday; Libeled Lady; After Office Hours)
(Ed: Sort of a prelude to *His Girl Friday*-perhaps the inspiration to reverse the sex roles in that remake)

Wedlock, 1991, 98m, ★★/$, Spectacor/Live, R/V. Two cons hooked together by an electronic collar have to make a getaway and survive, even though they'll explode if they're too far apart. Rutger Hauer, Mimi Rogers, Joan Chen, James Remar. w. Broderick Miller, d. Lewis Teague.
ACTION: SUSPENSE: Fugitives from the Law; Chase Movies; Romance-Bickering; Exploding Heads; Cuff to Cuff; Ind Films
(Scanners; D.O.A.; The Defiant Ones)

Wee Willie Winkie, 1937, 99m, ★★★/$$$, 20th/CBS-Fox. Twinkletoes Temple makes good with India royalty. Shirley Temple, Victor McLaglen, Cesar Romero. w. Ernest Pascal, Julien Josephson, SS-adap. Rudyard Kipling, d. John Ford.
CHILDREN'S: MUSICAL: ADVENTURE: Royalty; India; Child Protagonists; Female Protagonists
(Bright Eyes; A Little Princess)

(Ed: Most interesting is that Ford directed it)

Weeds, 1987, 115m, ★★1/2/$, DEG-MGM/HBO, R/EP. Prisoners are led by a fellow prisoner-playwright in putting on a production. Nick Nolte, Rita Taggart, William Forsythe, Lane Smith, Joe Mantegna, Ernie Hudson, Anne Ramsey. w. John Hancock, Dorothy Tristan, d. John Hancock.
MELODRAMA: Prison Drama; True Stories; Putting on a Show; Writers; Actors; Ensemble Films; Ensembles-Male
(The Jericho Mile; The Shawshank Redemption)

Weekend, 1968, 103m, ★★★1/2/$$, New Yorker/New Yorker, R/S. A wealthy couple from Paris go to the country for the weekend and run into tragic but blackly comical situations representing the hell of modern life. Mirielle Darc, Jean Yanne, Jean-Pierre Leaud. w. d. Jean Luc Godard.
SATIRE: Black Comedy; Tragi-Comedy; Comedy of Errors; Rich People; Art Films; Avant-Garde Films; French Films; French New Wave Films; Writer-Directors
(The Discreet Charm of the Bourgeoisie)

Weekend at Bernie's, 1989, 99m, ★★1/2/$$$, 20th/Fox, PG-13/P-S. Two junior execs (Jonathan Silverman, Andrew McCarthy) go for a weekend at boss Bernie's swanky beach house, only when they get there, they find his body and have several reasons to hide it or prop him up to pretend he's alive. Terry Kiser, Catherine Mary Stewart, Ted Kotcheff. w. Robert Klane, d. Ted Kotcheff.
COMEDY: Comedy of Errors; Hide the Dead Body; Vacations; Mob Comedy; Fugitives from the Mob; Framed?; Zombies; Sleeper Hits
(Over Her Dead Body; The Trouble with Harry)

Weekend at Bernie's 2, 1991, 100m, ★★/$, 20th/Fox, PG-13/P-S. The fun continues beyond reason or plausibility-but so what? Andrew McCarthy, Jonathan Silverman, Terry Kiser.
COMEDY: Comedy of Errors; Hide the Dead Body; Vacations; Mob Comedy; Fugitives from the Mob; Framed?

Weekend at the Waldorf, 1945, 130m, ★★★/$$$, MGM/MGM-UA. Veiled remake of *Grand Hotel* with more of a comic touch as several guests intermingle and play out their problems in the famous New York hotel. Ginger Rogers,

Walter Pidgeon, Can Johnson, Lana Turner, Edward Arnold, Constance Collier, Phyllis Thaxter, Keenan Wynn, Xavier Cugat. w. Sam and Bella Spewack, d. Robert Z. Leonard.
COMEDY DRAMA: DRAMA: MELO-DRAMA: Ensemble Films; Multiple Stories; Interwoven Stories; Hotels
REMAKE/RETREAD OF: Grand Hotel. (Grand Hotel; Plaza Suite; California Suite)

Weird Science, 1985, 94m, ★★/$$, U/MCA-U, PG-13/S. Two nerd scientist teens conjure up the perfect woman. Anthony Michael Hall, Ilan Mitchell Smith, Kelly LeBrock, w. d. John Hughes.
COMEDY: Fantasy; Teenagers; Teenage Movies; Computers; Magic; Dreams
(Bedazzled)

Welcome Home, 1989, 92m, ★★1/2/$, Col/RCA-Col, R/S-FN-MRN. A Vietnam vet returns after two decades of being presumed dead and finds his wife remarried. Kris Kristofferson, Jobeth Williams, Brian Keith, Sam Waterston, Trey Wilson. w. Maggie Kleinman, d. Franklin J. Schaffner.
DRAMA: MELODRAMA: ROMANCE: Romance-Reunited; Missing Persons; Dead-Back from the; Vietnam Veterans; Reunions; Old-Fashioned Recent Films; Female Screenwriters
(Coming Home; Return of the Soldier)
(Ed: What would have worked well forty years ago seems trite and superficial now)

Welcome Home, Roxy Carmichael, 1991, 96m, ★★★/$, Par/Par, PG-13/P-S. An adopted teen (Winona Ryder) dreams that maybe she's the long-lost daughter of a famous actress coming home for a visit. Jeff Daniels, Laila Robins, Thomas Wilson Brown, Frances Fisher. w. Karen Leigh Hopkins, d. Jim Abrahams.
DRAMA: COMEDY DRAMA: Feisty Females; Children-Adopted; Children-Long Lost; Small-town Life; Slice of Life; Reunions; Dreams; Actresses; Old-Fashioned Recent Films; Teenagers; Female Protagonists; Female Screenwriters; Coulda Been Great
(Square Dance; The Miracle [1990])
(Ed: A little more whimsy and little less cynicism would've helped)

Welcome to Hard Times, 1967, 103m, ★★1/2/$$, MGM/MGM-UA. A small western town readies for a mysterious badman rumored to be on the way for a showdown. Henry Fonda, Janice Rule, Keenan Wynn,

Janis Paige, John Anderson, Warren Oates, Edgar Buchanan, Aldo Ray. w. d. Burt Kennedy, N-adap. E. L. Doctorow.
WESTERNS: DRAMA: Paranoia; Rumors; Drifters; Men in Conflict; Allegorical Stories (Warlock)

Welcome to L.A., 1976, 106m, ★★½/$, UA/Fox, R/P-S. A musician in L.A. during the sexual revolution's peak has some rather odd experiences. Keith Carradine, Sally Kellerman, Geraldine Chaplin, Harvey Keitel, Lauren Hutton, Viveca Lindfors, Sissy Spacek. w. d. Alan Rudolph.
DRAMA: Ensemble Films; Multiple Stories; Interwoven Stories; Sexual Revolution; Los Angeles; 1970s; Musicians; Writer-Directors (Nashville; Tales of the City; Shampoo)

The Well, 1951, 85m, ★★½/$$, Ind/VCI. A black girl falls down a well and despite her color, her small town bands together to save her. Richard Rober, Henry Morgan. w. Russell Rouse, Clarence Green, d. Russell Rouse, Leo Popkin.
DRAMA: MELODRAMA: Tearjerkers; Rescue Drama; Small-town Life; Black People; Black vs. White; Race Relations; Trapped; Trapped in a Hole (Ace in the Hole; Baby Jessica)

Wells Fargo, 1937, 115m, ★★½/$$$, Par/Par. The beginnings and tribulations of the cross-country courier service in the wild west. Joel McCrea, Bob Burns, Frances Dee, Lloyd Nolan. w. Paul Scholfield, Gerald Geraghty, John Boland, Stuart Lake, d. Frank Lloyd.
WESTERNS: COMEDY DRAMA: ADVENTURES: Journies; Old West (San Antonio; Western Union; Union Pacific; Foreign Correspondent)

We of the Never Never, 1982, 134m, ★★½/$$, Col/Col, G. A city girl marries a cattle farmer in the outback of Australia and has to learn to adapt to the different ways there. Angela Punch-McGregor, Arthur Dignam, Tony Barry, Martin Vaughan. w. Peter Schreck, N-adap., Mrs. Aneas Gunn, d. Igor Auzins.
DRAMA: Family Drama; Sagas; Cattle Ranchers; City vs. Country; Newlyweds; Starting Over; Australian Films (The Piano; The Sundowners; Under Capricorn; The Thorn Birds; The Getting of Wisdom)

Went the Day Well? (Forty-eight Hours), 1942, 92m, ★★★/$$, Ealing/NA. German paratroopers invade an English

village and put up a bit of a fight, though some a bit of a problem. Leslie Banks, Elizabeth Allan, Frank Lawton. d. Alberto Cavalcenti.
COMEDY DRAMA: SATIRE: DRAMA: War Movies; World War II Era; What if . . . Stories; Small-town Life; Germans as Enemy; British Films; England (The Russians Are Coming . . .)

We're Back! A Dinosaur's Story, 1993, 78m, ★★½/$$, U/MCA-U, G. Animated dinosaurs appear in modern day and go back to their old home which is now New York. w. John Patrick Shanley, N-adap. Hudson Talbott, d. Dick Zondag, Ralph Zondag, Phil Nibbelink, Simon Wells.
CHILDREN'S: FAMILY: Dinosaurs; Time Travel; Dead-Back from the; Fish out of Water Stories (The Land Before Time) (Ed: From the writer of *Moonstruck* and *Alive*)

We're No Angels, 1954, 106m, ★★★/$$$, Par/Par. An unsuccessful store-keeper is aided in outwitting a scheming relative by three escaped convicts from Devil's Island. Humphrey Bogart, Peter Ustinov, Aldo Ray, Joan Bennett, Basil Rathbone. w. Ranald MacDougall, P-adap. Albert Husson, *La Cuisine des Anges*, d. Michael Curtiz.
REMAKE: 1989 version.

We're No Angels, 1989, 106m, ★★½/$$, Par/Par, PG-13/P-S. Escaped convicts disguise themselves as priests and hide out in a monastery. Robert De Niro, Sean Penn, Demi Moore, Bruno Kirby. w. David Mamet, P-adap. Albert Husson, *La Cuisine des Anges*, d. Neil Jordan. (Ed: The remake was substantially re-shaped and made more comical)
COMEDY DRAMA: Fugitives from the Law; Con Artists; Romance-Triangles; Hiding Out; Depression Era; Priests (Some Like It Hot; When in Rome)

We're Not Married, 1952, 85m, ★★★/$$, 20th/Fox. When a judge finds out he wasn't actually licensed when five couples were married, the couples debate whether to retie the knot or not. Ginger Rogers, Fred Allen, Marilyn Monroe, Paul Douglas, Victor Moore, James Gleason, Eve Arden, Louis Calhern, Jane Darwell, Mitzi Gaynor. w. Nunnally Johnson, Dwight Taylor, d. Edmund Goulding.
COMEDY: Marriage Comedy; Divorce; Comedy of Errors; Misunderstandings;

Married Couples; Ensemble Films; Hidden Gems

The Werewolf, 1956, 80m, ★★/$$, Col/NA. In a village in the mountains, a man exposed to radiation becomes a werewolf. The villagers hunt him down. Steven Ritch, Don McGowan, Joyce Holden. w. Robert E. Kent, James B. Gordon, d. Fred F. Sears.
HORROR: Werewolves; Radiation Poisoning; Humans into Animals (Wolf; An American Werewolf in London)

Werewolf of London, 1935, 75m, ★★★/$$, Universal/MCA-U. Werewolves fight over a rare Tibetan flower which could cure their condition. Henry Hull, Warner Oland, Valerie Hobson. w. Robert Harris, d. Stuart Walker.
HORROR: SUSPENSE: Werewolves; England; British Films (Wolf; An American Werewolf in London)

West Point Story, 1950, 107m, ★★½/$$$, WB/WB. A Broadway producer puts on a show at West Point. James Cagney, Virginia Mayo, Doris Day, Gordon McCrea, Alan Hale, Jr. w. John Monks, Jr., Charles Hoffman, Irving Wallace, d. Roy del Ruth.
MUSICAL: Military Academies; Reunions; Theater Life (Ed: Rather pointless, apparently to recapture *Yankee Doodle Dandy*)

West Side Story, 1961, 155m, ★★★★/$$$$$, UA/CBS-Fox. Romeo and Juliet as (pseudo)Puerto-Rican hoods in Spanish Harlem. Natalie Wood (sung by Marnie Nixon), Richard Beymer (sung by Jimmy Bryant), Russ Tamblyn, Rita Moreno (**BSActress**), George Chakiris (BSActor). w. Ernest Lehman (BAScr), P-adap, Arthur Laurents, based upon William Shakespeare, *Romeo & Juliet*, d. Robert Wise & Jerome Robbins (**BDirector**). **BPicture**, BCCin, BCArt, BCCost, BEdit, BSound, BMScore. Oscars: 11-10, second only to *Ben-Hur* in number of wins.
MUSICAL: ROMANCE: Musical Romance; **DRAMA:** Musical Drama; **TRAGEDY:** Romantic Drama; Romance-Doomed; Gangs-White; Gangs-Latin; New York Life; Revisionist Films; Production Design-Outstanding (Carousel; Romeo and Juliet)

Western Union, 1941, 94m, ★★★/$$$, 20th/CBS-Fox. The laying of the tele-graph cables is interrupted by political corruption. Randolph Scott, Robert

Young, Dean Jagger, Virginia Gilmore, Slim Summerville, John Carradine, Chill Wills. w. Robert Carson, N-adap. Zane Grey, d. Fritz Lang.

WESTERNS: Political Drama; Politicians; Corruption; Political Corruption
(Wells Fargo; Union Pacific)

The Westerner, 1940, 99m, ★★★1/2/ $$$$, Samuel Goldwyn-UA/Goldwyn. Judge Roy Bean suffers at the hands of his enemies, as well as his love, Lily Langtry, and tries to hang on-while hanging others, of course. Gary Cooper, Walter Brennan (**BSActor**), Doris Davenport, Fred Stone, Chill Wills, Forrest Tucker, Dana Andrews, Lilian Bond, Tom Tyler. w. Jo Swerling, Niven Busch, story Stuart N. Lake (BOStory), d. William Wyler. BB&WArt. Oscars: 3-1.

WESTERN: COMEDY DRAMA: Western Comedy; **ROMANCE: MELODRAMA:** Old West; Arkansas; Judges; Romance-Reunited; Dancers
(The Life and Times of Judge Roy Bean; Destry Rides Again)

Westworld, 1973, 89m, ★★★/$$$, MGM/MGM-UA, PG/V. At a fantasy high-tech resort, the robots which entertain the visitors run amok. Yul Brynner, Richard Benjamin, James Brolin, Alan Oppenheimer. w. d. Michael Crichton.

SCI-FI: SUSPENSE: MURDER: Chase Movies; Nightmares; Fantasy; Futuristic Films; Robots; Androids; Resorts; Writer-Directors

SEQUEL: Future World.
(Logan's Run; Bladerunner)
(Ed: Innovative for then and entertaining, but not for those looking for incredible special effects)

The Wet Parade, 1932, 122m, ★★★/$, MGM/NA. A politician fights prohibition because of the resulting corruption-posing a few questions germane to today's drug problems. Walter Huston, Myrna Loy, Neil Hamilton, Lewis Stone, Jimmy Durante, Robert Young. w. John Lee Mahin, N-adap. Upton Sinclair, d. Victor Fleming.

DRAMA: Social Drama; Political Drama; Politicians; Corruption; Political Corruption; Alcoholism; Prohibition Era; 1920s; Forgotten Films

Wetherby, 1985, 97m, ★★★/$, UAC/ MGM-UA, R/V-S-FN. A college student shoots himself after a particularly depressing party and the professor who he was staying with must face the

question of her culpability in letting him do it. Vanessa Redgrave, Ian Holm, Judi Dench, Stuart Wilson. w. d. David Hare.

DRAMA: TRAGEDY: Character Studies; Psychological Drama; Suicidal Tendencies; Ethics; Teachers and Students; Professors; Obsessions; Flashbacks; Nervous Breakdowns; Depression; British Films; England; Coulda Been Great; What if . . . Stories; Female Protagonists; Writer-Directors
(An Unsuitable Job for a Woman; Permanent Record; Ordinary People; Plenty)
(Ed: Haunting and moving once you get into it and poses a very original question, though not necessarily a terribly dramatic one)

We Think the World of You, 1988, 94m, ★★★/$, New Line/New Line, PG/S. After his lover dies, a gay man (Alan Bates) takes on his dog as his object of love. Max Wall, Liz Smith, Frances Barber, Gary Oldman, Sheila Ballantine. w. Hugh Stoddart, N-adap. J. R. Ackerley, d. Colin Gregg.

DRAMA: COMEDY DRAMA: Character Studies; Gay Men; Widowers; Dogs; Pet Stories; British Films
(Prick Up Your Ears; A Man of No Importance)

We Were Strangers, 1949, 105m, ★★1/2/$, Col/NA. In 1930s Cuba, insurgents plan to assassinate a high official of the government. Jennifer Jones, John Garfield, Pedro Armendariz, Gilbert Roland, Ramon Navarro. w. Peter Viertel, John Huston, N-adap, w. Robert Sylvester, *Rough Sketch*, d. John Huston.

DRAMA: SUSPENSE: Spies; Assassinations; Political Drama; Political Unrest; Coulda Been Great; Cuba
(Havana; Cuba; The Man Who Knew Too Much)

What? (Che?), 1972, 113m, ★★★/$$, Gala/NA, R/S-FN. A sexy American hitchhiker has an extended stay at the home of an Italian millionaire and his lecherous houseguests. Sydne Rome, Marcello Mastroianni, Hugh Griffith, Romolo Valli, Roman Polanski. w. Gerard Brach, Roman Polanski, d. Roman Polanski.

COMEDY DRAMA: SATIRE: Erotic Drama; Erotic Comedy; Americans Abroad; Sexy Women; Rich-Decadent; Beautiful People

(La Dolce Vita; The Fearless Vampire Killers; Repulsion; Do You Like Women?; The Comfort of Strangers)

What a Way to Go, 1964, 111m, ★★★/$$$, 20th/CBS-Fox, AMC. A rich woman tells her psychiatrist how all her previous husbands died in freak accidents. Shirley MacLaine, Bob Cummings, Dick Van Dyke, Robert Mitchum, Gene Kelly, Dean Martin, Paul Newman, Reginald Gardiner, Margaret Dumont. w. Betty Comden, Adolph Green, d. J. Lee-Thompson.

COMEDY: SATIRE: Black Comedy; Murders/Deaths-One by One; Accident Prone; Death-Accidental; Good Premise Unfulfilled; Coulda Been Great; Female Protagonists; Female Screenwriters
(Lady L; A Shock to the System)

What About Bob?, 1990, 1991, ★★★1/2/$$$$, Touchstone/Touchstone, PG/P. A psychiatrist (Richard Dreyfuss) wants to go on vacation to get away from his patients, but one named Bob (Bill Murray) follows him and endears himself to the shrink's family, much to the shrink's frustration. Julie Hagerty. w. Tom Schulman, Alvin Sargent, Laura Ziskin, d. Frank Oz.

COMEDY: SATIRE: Stalkers; Nuisances; Mental Illness; Psychiatrists; Roommates from Hell; Vacations; Old-Fashioned Recent Films; Female Screenwriters
(Housesitter)
(Ed: A commercial but thoughtful gem)

What Every Woman Knows, 1934, 90m, ★★★/$$, MGM/NA. The story of the "woman behind the man," as a housewife prods her husband into running for parliament. Helen Hayes, Brian Aherne, Madge Evans, Lucile Watson, Dudley Digges. w. Monckton Hoffe, John Meehan, James Kevin McGuinness, P-adap. J. M. Barrie, d. Gregory La Cava.

DRAMA: MELODRAMA: Woman Behind the Man; Politician; Politicians' Wives; England; Female Protagonists
(Harriet Craig; Ada; State of the Union)

Whatever Happened to Aunt Alice?, 1969, 101m, ★★★/$, Palomar-20th/NA, R/V-B&G. An elderly landlady murders her tenants and steals their money. Geraldine Page, Ruth Gordon, Rosemary Forsyth, Robert Fuller, Mildred Dunnock. w. Theodore Apstein, N-adap. Ursula Curtiss, *The Forbidden Garden*, d. Lee H. Katzin.

HORROR: Black Comedy; Horror Comedy; **MURDER:** Murders-One by One; Murderers-Female; Elderly Women; Murderers-Nice; Cult Films; Camp; Female Protagonists
REMAKE/RETREAD OF: Ladies in Retirement.
(Ladies in Retirement; Arsenic and Old Lace; Who Slew Auntie Roo?; Die, Die, My Darling!; Whatever Happened to Baby Jane?)

Whatever Happened to Baby Jane?, 1962, 132m, ★★★★/$$$$, 7-Arts-WB/WB, PG/V. A former child star Baby Jane (Bette Davis, BActress) wants to make a comeback but her actress sister (Joan Crawford) is still more famous and likable despite her career coming to an end when Baby Jane ran her down, so Jane sets out to destroy what's left of her. Victor Buono (BSActor), Anna Lee. w. Lukas Heller, N-adap. Henry Farrell, d. Robert Aldrich. BB&WCin. Oscars: 3-0.
HORROR: SUSPENSE: Black Comedy; Horror Comedy; Past-Haunted by the; Mental Illness; Jealousy; Rivalries; Women in Conflict; Comebacks; Hollywood Life; Vaudeville; Revenge; Hostage Situations; Elderly Women; Actresses; Sisters; Silent Film Era; Camp; Female Protagonists; Sleeper Hits; Cult Films
TV REMAKE: 1989, ABC (Lynn Redgrave & Vanessa Redgrave)
(Whatever Happened to Aunt Alice?; Who Slew Auntie Roo?; What's the Matter With Helen?; Hush, Hush, Sweet Charlotte)

What Price Hollywood?, 1932, 87m, ★★★/$$, RKO/Turner. An alcoholic director "discovers" a waitress, then has problems when she becomes a star. w. Ben Markson, Gene Fowler, Rowland Brown, SS-adap, w. Adela Rogers, d. George Cukor.
DRAMA: MELODRAMA: TRAGEDY: Fame-Rise to; Actresses; Directors; Hollywood Life; Suicidal Tendencies; Svengalis; Female Screenwriters; Female Protagonists; Hidden Gems
(A Star Is Born [1937])
(Ed: A little more dark and satirical than the A Star Is Born cycle; a great title)
What's Eating Gilbert Grape?, 1993, 123m, ★★★½/$, Par/Par, PG/S. Good Gilbert (Johnny Depp) is stuck in Iowa with an older mistress (Mary Steenburgen) and a visiting girl he likes (Juliette Lewis) as he tries to hold his family together with his retarded brother (Leonardo deCaprio, BSActor) and five-hundred-pound mother (Darlene Cates). w. N-adap. Peter Hedges, d. Lasse Hallestrom. Oscars: 1-0.
DRAMA: COMEDY DRAMA: TRAGEDY: ROMANCE: Black Comedy; Family Drama; Young Men; Coming of Age; Mothers-Troublesome; Mothers & Sons; Weight Problems; Mentally Disabled; Death-Dealing with; Romance-Older Women/Younger Men; Romance-Choosing Right Person; Small-town Life; Midwestern Life; Ordinary People Stories; Poor People; Old-Fashioned Recent Films; Overlooked at Release
(The Last Picture Show; Tex; Benny & Joon)

What's New Pussycat?, 1965, 108m, ★★★/$$$$, UA/CBS-Fox, PG/S. A fashion editor has trouble keeping his mind on his work, what with all the gorgeous models floating around and a retreat doesn't help matters. Peter O'Toole, Peter Sellers, Woody Allen, Ursula Andress, Romy Schneider, Capucine, Paula Prentiss. w. Woody Allen, d. Clive Donner. BOSong. Oscars: 1-0.
COMEDY: Erotic Comedy; **FARCE:** Fashion World; Sexy Women; 1960s; Beautiful People; Promiscuity; Playboys; Cult Films
(Casino Royale; There's a Girl in My Soup)

What's So Bad About Feeling Good?, 1965, 94m, ★★½/$$, Universal/MCA-U. A toucan carries a "happy virus" into New York and infects a bunch of pseudo-artist types. George Peppard, Mary Tyler Moore, Dom De Luise, John McMartin, Susan St. James, Don Stroud, Charles Lane. w. George Seaton, Robert Pirosh, d. George Seaton.
COMEDY: SATIRE: Fantasy; Artists; New York Life; Birds; What if . . . Stories; Epidemics; Good Premise Unfulfilled; Curiosities

What's the Matter with Helen?, 1971, 101m, ★★/$, Filmways-MGM/MGM-UA, R/V. Two women run a dance academy for child stars in 1934 Hollywood. Trouble is, one of them's a killer. Debbie Reynolds, Shelley Winters, Michael MacLiammoir, Dennis Weaver, Agnes Moorehead. w. Henry Farrell, d. Curtis Harrington.
HORROR: MURDER: Murderers-Female; Black Comedy; Hollywood Life; Dancers; Insane-Plot to Drive; Illusions/Hallucina-

tions; Mental Illness; Women in Conflict; Cult Films; Camp; Female Protagonists
(Whatever Happened to Aunt Alice?; Who Slew Auntie Roo?; Whatever Happened to Baby Jane?; The Mad Room)
(Ed: Not up to Baby Jane, but still interesting for those who like bitch fights and black humor, though there's not much of it)

What's Up, Doc?, 1972, 99m, ★★★★/$$$$$, WB/WB, PG. A nerdy professor (Ryan O'Neal) is in San Francisco for a grant interview when a free-spirited nuisance (Barbra Streisand) begins following him around, wreaking havoc and yet helping him get the grant, until the mob, secret agents, and stolen jewels get confused with her underwear. Madeline Kahn, Austin Pendleton, Kenneth Mars. w. Buck Henry, Robert Benton, David Newman, d. Peter Bogdanovich.
COMEDY: FARCE: Screwball Comedy; **ROMANCE:** Romantic Comedy; Action Comedy; Chase Movies; Romance-Girl Wants Boy; Con Artists; Identities-Mistaken; Misunderstandings; Feisty Females; Nerds; Extrovert vs. Introvert; Romance-Opposites Attract; Wives-Troublesome; Nuisances; Accident Prone; Escalating Plots; Complicated Plots; Clever Plots & Endings; San Francisco; San Francisco Chases; Old-Fashioned Recent Films
(Bringing Up Baby; For Pete's Sake; Sylvia Scarlett; Hotel Paradiso; Blame It on the Bellboy)

What's Up, Tiger Lily?, 1966, 80m, ★★★/$$, Ind/Vestron. A secret agent enters the fray in an all-out search for the world's greatest egg-salad sandwich recipe. Tatsua Mihashi, Mie Hama, Akiko Wakabayashi, Woody Allen, VOICES OF: Frank Buxton, Len Maxwell, Louise Lasser, Mickey Rose. w. Kazuo Yamada, Woody Allen. d. Senkichi Taniguchi, Woody Allen.
COMEDY: Spoofs; **SCI-FI:** Scientists-Mad; Japanese Films; Cult Films; Camp
(The Green Slime)

When a Man Loves a Woman, 1994, 124m, ★★★/$$$, Touchstone/Touchstone, R/S-P. An alcoholic woman has a man who stands by her. Meg Ryan, Andy Garcia, Lauren Tom, Tina Majorino, Ellen Burstyn, Eugene Roche. w. Ronald Bass, Al Franken, d. Luis Mandoki.
MELODRAMA: Marriage Drama; Alcoholics; Romantic Drama; Tearjerkers
(A Woman Under the Influence)

When a Stranger Calls, 1979, 97m, ★★½/$$$, Col/Col, R/V-B&G. A baby murderer is on the prowl. A lone cop is determined to hunt him down before he gets to a babysitter. Charles Durning, Tony Beckley, Carol Kane, Colleen Dewhurst, Rachel Roberts. w. Steve Feke, Fred Walton, d. Fred Walton.
THRILLERS: SUSPENSE: Women in Jeopardy; **MURDER:** Serial Killers; Trail of a Killer; Sleeper Hits; Babysitters; Babysitters in Jeopardy; Stalkers; Telephones
SEQUEL: When a Stranger Calls Back, 1993.
(Halloween; He Knows You're Alone)
When Dinosaurs Ruled the Earth, 1969, 100m, ★★/$, WB/WB. A dinosaur rescues and cares for a cavewoman who is lost at sea during a storm. Victoria Vetri, Patrick Allen, Robin Hawdon. w. d. Val Guest, story J. G. Ballard.
SCI-FI: Cave People; Prehistoric Times; Dinosaurs; Sexy Women; Cult Films; Camp
SEQUEL TO: One Million B.C.
(The Land That Time Forgot; Jurassic Park)
When Father Was Away on Business, 1985, 136m, ★★★/$$, Cannon/MGM-UA, PG-13. The political situation in Yugoslavia in the 1950s encroaches on the life of a young boy when his father is sent to the mines. Moreno de Bartoli, Miki Manojlovic, Mirjana Karanovic, Mustafa Nadarevic. w. Abdulah Sidran, d. Emir Kusturica (Palme d'Or, Best Film, Cannes, 1985). BFLFilm. Oscars: 1-0.
DRAMA: Boyhood; Political Drama; Family Drama; Oppression; Character Studies; Coming of Age; Fathers & Sons; Europeans-Eastern
When Harry Met Sally, 1989, 95m, ★★★/$$$$$, Col/Col, R/P-S. Over a period of a dozen years, a man and woman who meet as law graduates on a cross-country trip from Chicago to New York, debate whether men and women can be "just friends" and provide the answer by flirting and falling in love. Meg Ryan, Billy Crystal, Carrie Fisher, Bruno Kirby. w. Nora Ephron (BOScr), d. Rob Reiner. Oscars: 1-0.
COMEDY: ROMANCE: Romantic Comedy; Friends as Lovers; Romance-Opposites Attract; Battle of the Sexes; Sidekicks-Wisecracking; Episodic

Stories; Neurotic People; New York Life; Blockbusters; Female Screenwriters
REMAKE/RETREAD OF: Just You and Me; Annie Hall; Manhattan; Reds (the interviews).
(Sleepless in Seattle; Annie Hall; Just You and Me; Manhattan)
When Hell Was in Session, 1982, 98m, ★★★/$$$, CBS/Time-Life. A Vietnam War P.O.W. relives his torture there once finally free. Hal Holbrook, Eva Marie Saint, Ronny Cox. d. Paul Krasny.
DRAMA: True Stories; P.O.W.s; Vietnam War; Nightmares; Flashbacks; Torture; TV Movies
(The Deer Hunter; Cease Fire)
When in Rome, 1952, 78m, ★★½/$$, MGM/Turner. An American gangster in Rome adopts a priest's disguise to hide out, then is taken for the real thing. Van Johnson, Paul Douglas, Joseph Calleia, Carlo Rizzo. w. Charles Schnee, Dorothy Kingsley, Robert Buckner, d. Clarence Brown.
COMEDY: COMEDY DRAMA: Mob Stories; Hiding Out; Americans Abroad; Disguises; Disguised as Priest; Impostors; Priests; Italy
(We're No Angels)
When Ladies Meet, 1933, 73m, MGM/Turner. Ann Harding, Robert Montgomery, Myrna Loy, Alice Brady. w. John Meehan, Leon Gordon, P-adap. Rachel Crothers, d. Harry Beaumont.
When Ladies Meet, 1941, 108m, MGM/MGM-UA. Remake of above. Joan Crawford, Robert Taylor, Greer Garson, w. S. K. Lauren, Anita Loos, d. Robert Z. Leonard.
A popular female novelist falls in love with her publisher. Only problem is, he's married.
ROMANCE: MELODRAMA: Romance with Married Person; Writers; Publishing World; Female Screenwriters; Female Protagonists
(Hired Wife; The Best of Everything)
When My Baby Smiles at Me, 1948, 98m, ★★★/$$$, 20th/Fox. A vaudeville performer's career is in the dumps, but his faithful wife stands by him. Betty Grable, Dan Dailey, Jack Oakie, James Gleason. w. Lamar Trotti, P-adap. w. George Manker Walters, Arthur Hopkins, *Burlesque*, d. Walter Lang.
MUSICAL: ROMANCE: Musical Romance; Musical Drama; **COMEDY DRAMA:** Marriage Drama; Vaudeville;

Comebacks; Dancers; Comedians; Woman Behind the Man; Life; Transitions
(The Country Girl; The Comic; The Entertainer)
When Strangers Marry (Betrayed), 1944, 67m, ★★½/$, Monogram/NA. A young newlywed becomes suspicious that her wonderful husband may in fact be a murderer! Dean Jagger, Kim Hunter, Robert Mitchum, Dewey Robinson. w. Philip Yordan, Dennis Cooper, d. William Castle.
SUSPENSE: Film Noir; **MURDER:** Enemies-Sleeping with; Love-Questionable; Cult Films
(Undercurrent; Rebecca; Beyond the Secret Door; Deceived)
(Ed: Slight but effective)
When the Legends Die, 1972, 105m, ★★/$, 20th/Fox. A young American Indian boy looks up to a burnt-out old rodeo rider who shows him the ropes, literally. Richard Widmark, Frederic Forrest, Luana Anders, John War Eagle. w. Robert Dozier, N-adap. Hal Borland, d. Stuart Miller.
WESTERNS: Westerns-Modern; Teachers and Students; Cowboys; Indians-American; Coming of Age
(Bronco Billy; J. W. Coop; The Cowboys)
When the Whales Came, 1989, 100m, ★★½/$, 20th/Fox, PG. A young boy and an old recluse persuade fishermen in 1914 on the Sicily Isles to save a beached whale. When they do so, it brings luck to the village. Helen Mirren, Paul Scofield, David Suchet, Jeremy Kemp, Helen Pearce. w. Michael Morpurgo, N-adap, w. Michael Morpurgo, *Why the Whales Came*, d. Clive Rees.
FAMILY: MELODRAMA: CHILDREN'S: Animal Rights; 1900s; Italy; British Films; Whales
(Free Willy; Turtle Diary; The Whales of August)
(Ed: A good cast but too staid to appeal to the *Free Willy* crowd)
When Time Ran Out, 1980, 109m, ★/$, WB/WB, PG. A volcano on a South Sea island threatens to erupt. (The natives are clueless and the all-star cast of veterans barely outruns the lava-too bad.) Paul Newman, Jacqueline Bisset, William Holden, Eddie Albert, Burgess Meredith, Valentina Cortesa, Red Buttons, Alex Carras, Ernest Borgnine, James Franciscus. w. Carl Foreman, Stirling Silliphant, N-adap, w. Max Morgan Witts,

Gordon Thomas, t. *The Day the World Ended,* d. James Goldstone.
Disaster Movies; Flops-Major; Hawaii; Pacific Islands; Volcanos; Apocalyptic Stories
(The Swarm; Krakatoa, East of Java)
(Ed: Obviously money was the motive here. Unfortunately, they didn't intend to lose it)

When Tomorrow Comes, 1939, 82m, ★★½/$$$, Universal/NA. A concert pianist is torn between his sense of loyalty to his neurotic invalid wife and his stirring feelings for the beautiful waitress who loves him. Charles Boyer, Irene Dunne, Barbara O'Neil. w. Dwight Taylor, SS-adap. James M. Cain, d. John M. Stahl.
MELODRAMA: ROMANCE: Romance with Married Person; Romance-Triangles; Musicians; Waitresses; Mental Illness

When Worlds Collide, 1951, 82m, ★★★/$$$, Par/Par. A planet swings out of its orbit and heads toward Earth. Before the collision occurs, the few people with enough foresight to plan ahead for such things plan to escape on a space ship. Richard Derr, Barbara Rush, Larry Keating, Peter Hanson. w. Sidney Boehm, N-adap. Philip Wylie, Edwin Balmer, d. Rudolph Maté. BSFX, BCCin. Oscars: 2-1.
SCI-FI: Sci-Fi-1950s; Apocalytpic Stories; Outer Space Movies; Asteroids-Dangerous; Paranoia; Floods; Fires
(Meteor; War of the Worlds; Fire in the Sky [1978])

When You're in Love, 1937, 110m, ★★½/$$, Col/NA. A "marriage of convenience" between a European opera star wanting U.S. citizenship and a convenient American male, takes on greater significance as they get to know one another. Grace Moore, Cary Grant, Aline MacMahon, Emma Dunn. w. d. Robert Riskin.
COMEDY DRAMA: COMEDY: ROMANCE: MUSICAL: Musical Romance; Romantic Comedy; Marriage Comedy; Marriage for Citizenship; Opera Singers
(Green Card; One Night of Love)

Where Angels Fear to Tread, 1991, 112m, ★★★/$$, Fine Line/New Line, PG/S. A British woman married a sexy Italian man in Italy and died giving birth to his child. Now, her uptight relatives have come to claim the child and encounter problems. Judy Davis, Rupert Graves, Helena Bonham Carter, Giovanni Guidelli, Helen Mirren. w. Tim Sullivan, Derek Granger, Charles Sturridge, N-adap. E. M. Forster, d. Sturridge.
COMEDY DRAMA: Comedy of Manners; DRAMA: MELODRAMA: Family Drama; Babies-Having, Late in Life; Babies-Having Custody Battles; Lover Family Dislikes; Italy; British Films; 1900s; Edwardian Era
(Howards End; A Room with a View; A Passage to India; Maurice)
(Ed: Nearly as good as the Merchant Ivory Forster adaptations, but then, this novel is not regarded as one of Forster's best)

Where Angels Go, Trouble Follows, 1968, 95m, ★★/$, Col/RCA-Col, G. Catholic school students and the nuns who take them to a California youth rally have their eyes opened. Rosalind Russell, Stella Stevens, Binnie Barnes, Milton Berle, Arthur Godfrey, Susan St. James. w. Blanche Hanalis, d. James Neilson.
COMEDY: COMEDY DRAMA: Nuns; Girlhood; Teenagers; Women and Girls; Female Screenwriters; Female Protagonists
SEQUEL TO: The Trouble with Angels.

Where Are the Children?, 1985, 92m, ★★/$, Col/Col, R/V. A woman who was accused of murdering the children from her first marriage starts having her second marriage's children disappear. Jill Clayburgh, Barnard Hughes, Clifton James, Max Gail. N-adap Mary Higgins Clark, d. Bruce Malmuth.
SUSPENSE: MURDER: Kidnappings; Missing Persons; Missing Children; Accused Unjustly; Starting Over; Good Premise Unfulfilled
(Dolores Claiborne)

Where Do We Go from Here?, 1945, 77m, ★★½/$$, 20th/NA. A genie takes a modern-day writer on a guided tour of American history, starting with a stint on Columbus' ship. Fred MacMurray, June Haver, Joan Leslie, Gene Sheldon, Anthony Quinn, Otto Preminger. w. Morrie Ryskind, d. Gregory Ratoff.
COMEDY: Fantasy; MUSICAL: Musical Fantasy; Time Travel; Genies; Writers
(Bill and Ted's Excellent Adventure; Anthony Adverse)

Where Does It Hurt?, 1971, 88m, ★★/$, Ind/NA, R/S-FN. A hospital is run by a corrupt, bloodsucking huckster with a lecherous penchant for nurses. Peter Sellers, Jo Ann Pflug, Rick Lenz, Eve Druce. w. d. Rod Amateau, N-adap. Budd Robinson, *The Operator.*
COMEDY: Erotic Comedy; Corruption; Hospitals; Sexual Revolution; Playboys; Doctors; Nurses
(Brittania Hospital; The Hospital; Carry On Doctor SERIES; There's a Girl in My Soup; The Prisoner of Zenda [1974]; Alvin Purple; Young Doctors in Love)

Where Eagles Dare, 1969, 155m, ★★★/$$$$, MGM/MGM-UA, PG/V. Seven British pilots during World War II attempt to rescue a fellow officer from a guarded castle in the Bavarian Alps. Richard Burton, Clint Eastwood, Mary Ure, Patrick Wymark, Robert Beatty. w. Alistair MacLean, N-adap. Alistair MacLean, d. Brian G. Hutton.
ACTION: War Movies; Rescue Drama; World War II Movies; Kidnappings; Alps; Special Teams-Military
(Castle Keep; Breakout)

Where Love Has Gone, 1964, 114m, ★★½/$$, Par/Par. A teenage girl thinks her father will be pleased that she's planning to kill her mother's lover. Susan Hayward, Bette Davis, Mike Connors, Joey Heatherton, Jane Greer, George McReady. w. John Michael Hayes, N-adap. Harold Robbins, d. Edward Dmytryk.
SUSPENSE: MURDER: Romance-Triangles; Fathers & Daughters; Murder of Parents; Parents vs. Children; Cheating Women; Electra Complex; Lover Family Dislikes; Camp
(Madame X; Mildred Pierce)

Where the Boys Are, 1960, 99m, ★★½/$$$, MGM/MGM-UA. Four young women spend spring break near a Florida military base. Everything's hunky-dory. George Hamilton, Dolores Hart, Paula Prentiss, Yvette Mimieux, Connie Francis, Frank Gorshin, Chill Wills, Barbara Nichols. w. George Wells, N-adap. Glendon Swarthout, d. Henry Levin.
COMEDY: Beach Movies; Teenage Movies; Teenagers; Music Movies; Vacations; Resorts; Female Protagonists
REMAKE: Where the Boys Are '84.
(Shag; Beach Party; Beach Blanket Bingo; The Look of Love)

Where the Boys Are '84, 1984, 94m, ★/$, ITC-Tri Star/Col-Tri, PG. Remake of above as disjointed teenage sexploitation, with more hunk-sightings than babe-watching. Lisa Hartman, Lorna Luft,

Wendy Schaal, Russel Todd. w. Stu Krieger, Jeff Burkhart, N-adap. Glendon Swarthout, d. Hy Averback.

COMEDY: Beach Movies; Teenage Movies; Teenagers; Music Movies; Vacations; Resorts; Sexy Men; Sexy Women; Female Protagonists

REMAKE OF: Where the Boys Are '84. (Shag; Hardbodies; Spring Break)

Where the Buffalo Roam, 1980, 98m, ★★/$, Universal/MCA-U, R/EP. A strung out journalist, based on Hunter S. Thompson, takes us on a tour of Nixon-era politics and American culture. Bill Murray, Peter Boyle, Bruno Kirby, Rene Auberjonois, Leonard Frey. w. John Kaye, d. Art Linson.

COMEDY: COMEDY DRAMA: Writers; Drugs; 1970s; Road Movies
(Stripes; The Razor's Edge)

Where the Day Takes You, 1992, 105m, ★★1/2/$, Col/Col, R/P-S. Slice of life of runaways and homeless people on Hollywood Boulevard. Dermot Mulroney, Lara Flynn Boyle, Balthazar Getty, Sean Astin, Kyle MacLachlan, James LeGros, Ricki Lake, Will Smith, Nancy McKeon, Rachel Ticotin. w. Michael Hitchcock, Kurt Voss, Marc Rocco, d. Marc Rocco.

MELODRAMA: ROMANCE: Slice of Life Stories; Multiple Stories; Homeless People; Runaways; Los Angeles; Young People; One Day Stories; Teenagers; Coulda Been Good
(Twenty Bucks; The Saint of Fort Washington)

Where the Green Ants Dream, 1984, 100m, ★★/$, Ind/Media. A mining company threatens to destroy the home of some Aborigines. Bruce Spence, Wandjuk Marika, Roy Marika, Ray Barrett, Norman Kaye, Colleen Clifford. w. Werner Herzog, Bob Ellis, d. Werner Herzog.

DRAMA: Art Films; Corporation as Enemy; Mortgage Drama; Mining Towns; Australia; Aborigines; German Films
(Fitzcarraldo; The Last Wave; The Coca-Cola Kid)

Where the Heart Is, 1990, 94m, ★★★/$ (LR-VR), Touchstone/Touchstone, PG/FFN. A wrecking-company tycoon orders his mooching but rebellious kids to make it on their own, so they strike out in a condemned slum building, living out a 60s fantasy of body painting and freedom-until things fall apart-literally. Dabney Coleman, Uma Thurman, Crispin Glover,

Suzy Amis, Christopher Plummer. w. John Boorman, Telsche Boorman. d. John Boorman.

COMEDY: COMEDY DRAMA: MELO-DRAMA: Family Drama; Fantasy; Capra-esque; New York Life; Mortgage Drama; Fathers & Daughters; Rich People; Artists; Sisters; Rich vs. Poor; Homeless People; Riches to Rags; Old-Fashioned Recent Films; Hidden Gems
(For Richer or Poorer; Life Stinks)
(Ed: A bit out of touch, but enchanting)

Where the Lilies Bloom, 1974, 96m, ★★★/$$$, 20th/MGM-UA, G. Four poor children in the Appalachian mountains keep the death of their father a secret for fear of being taken by the state. Julie Gholson, Harry Dean Stanton, Jan Smithers, Helen Bragdon. w. Earl Hammer, Jr., N-adap. Vera and Bill Cleaver, d. William A. Graham.

MELODRAMA: DRAMA: Family Drama; Orphans; Mountain Life
(Where the Red Fern Grows; The Waltons SERIES; Christy SERIES; Tex)
(Ed: From the creator of *The Waltons*)

Where the Red Fern Grows, 1973, 97m, ★★1/2/$$$, Ind/Vestron, Live. A boy growing up in Depression era Oklahoma has two hounddogs which help he and his family through the rough times. James Whitmore, Jack Ging, Loni Chapman, Beverly Garland. d. Norman Tokar.

MELODRAMA: Coming of Age; Boy and His Dog; Dogs; Poor People; Farm Life; Depression Era; Sleeper Hits

SEQUEL: Where the Red Fern Grows, Part 2.
(Old Yeller; Savage Sam; The Homecoming/The Waltons TV Series; Where the Lilies Bloom)

Where the Spies Are, 1965, 113m, ★★1/2/$, MGM/MGM-UA. Interpol bribes a country doctor with an expensive car to become a spy. David Niven, Françoise Dorleac, Nigel Davenport, Cyril Cusak. w. Wolfmankowitz, Val Guest, N-adap. James Leasor, *Passport to Oblivion*, d. Val Guest.

COMEDY DRAMA: Spoofs-Spy; Spies; Spy Films; Farmers; City vs. Country; British Films; Bribes; Undercover
(The Billion Dollar Brain; Casino Royale)

Where Were You When the Lights Went Out?, 1968, 94m, ★★★/$$$, MGM/MGM-UA. Broadway singer's life is changed during the New York Blackout of 1965 when she winds up with a strange

man in her bed the next morning. Doris Day, Terry Thomas, Patrick O'Neal, Robert Morse, Jim Backus. w. Everett Freeman, Karl Turnberg, P-adap. Claude Magnier, d. Hy Averback.

COMEDY: FARCE: Blackouts; Romance-Triangles; Misunderstandings; Mistaken Identities; Marriage on the Rocks; Singers; Actresses; New York Life; Stagelike Films; Coulda Been Great
(Pillow Talk; Any Wednesday; Move Over, Darling)
(Ed: For Doris fans and those of farce, but not all it could be)

Where's Poppa?, 1970, 82m, ★★★1/2/ $$, UA/Key, R/S-MRN. The ultimate Jewish mother who's senile, always asking the title question, gives her lawyer son hell, particularly with his lovelife. He dreams of bumping her off to liberate himself and instead gets chaos. George Segal, Ruth Gordon, Trish Van Devere, Ron Leibman. w. Robert Klane, N-adap. Robert Klane, d. Carl Reiner.

COMEDY: FARCE: MURDER: Black Comedy; Murder Attempts-Comic; Mothers-Troublesome; Jewish People; Elderly Women; Single Men; Mama's Boys; Mothers & Sons; New York Life; Thieves; Cult Films; Forgotten Films; Coulda Been Great; Hidden Gems
(Throw Momma from the Train; Little Murders)

Which Way Is Up?, 1977, 94m, ★★-/$$, U/MCA-U, R/S-P. A migrant worker winds up a union leader and goes to the big city for a new life, becoming corrupt along the way. Richard Pryor, Lonette McKee, Margaret Avery, Morgan Woodward. w. Carl Gottlieb, d. Michael Schultz.

COMEDY: SATIRE: Social Satire; Ethics; Unions; Power-Rise to; Black Men; Working Class; Foreign Film Remakes

REMAKE OF: The Seduction of Mimi.
(Thunder and Lightning; Bustin' Loose; Blue Collar)

W.H.I.F.F.S., 1975, 92m, ★★/$, Avco/Media, R/S. An army veteran steals some mysterious gas from the base and discovers some interesting side effects. Elliott Gould, Eddie Albert, Harry Guardino, Godfrey Cambridge, Jennifer O'Neill. w. Malcolm Marmorstein, d. Ted Post.

COMEDY: ROMANCE: Promiscuity; Sexuality; Sexual Problems; Military Comedy; Good Premise Unfulfilled
(MASH; Catch 22; Who?)

While the City Sleeps, 1956, 100m, ★★½/$$, RKO/VCI. Three bigwigs at a New York newspaper battle for first coverage on a murder scoop. Dana Andrews, George Sanders, Ida Lupino, Sally Forrest, Vincent Price, John Barrymore, Jr. w. Casey Robinson, N-adap. Charles Einstein, d. Fritz Lang.

DRAMA: Newspapers; Journalists; MURDER: Men in Conflict; Competitions; Race Against Time; New York Life; 1950s; Forgotten Films; Could Have Been Great

(The Paper; Between the Lines; The Sweet Smell of Success; Five-Star Final; The Front Page)

(Ed: Okay, but the dated nature makes it hard to take. Could have been on the level of *Bachelor Party* [1957])

Whipsaw, 1935, 88m, ★★½/$$, MGM/NA. A detective goes undercover in the mob via a female member. Spencer Tracy, Myrna Loy, Harvey Stephens, Clay Clements. w. Howard Emmett Rogers, d. Sam Wood.

DRAMA: Crime Drama; Mob Stories; Mob Girls; Detective Stories; Detectives-Police; Love-Questionable; Female Among Males

Whirlpool, 1950, 98m, ★★½/$, 20th/Fox. A hypnotist uses his mental powers to restore his failing health, and then commits a murder, which one of his "patients" is subsequently accused of. Gene Tierney, José Ferrer, Richard Conte, Charles Bickford, Barbara O'Neill. w. Lester Barstow, Andrew Solt, N-adap. Guy Endore, d. Otto Preminger

SUSPENSE: MURDER: Psychological Drama; Hypnosis; Framed?; Accused Unjustly; Women in Jeopardy

(Laura; Dark Mirror; Bedlam)

Whiskey Galore (*Tight Little Island*), 1948, 82m, ★★★/$$, Ealing/Home Vision. A ship full of whiskey is wrecked on an island off the coast of Scotland during World War II, and the locals soon find it. Basil Radford, Joan Greenwood, Jean Cadell. w. Compton Mackenzie, Angus Macphail, N-adap. Compton Mackenzie, d. Alexander Mackendrick.

COMEDY: SATIRE: Comedy of Manners; FARCE: Shipwrecked; Alcoholism; Small-town Life; Scotland; England; British Films; What if . . . Stories; Forgotten Films; Hidden Gems

(Cold Turkey; Local Hero)

The Whisperers, 1967, 106m, ★★★/$$, UA/NA, PG. An elderly woman, besieged by her son and tormented by her often absent husband, begins to hear voices. Edith Evans (BActress), Eric Portman, Avis Bunnage. w. Bryan Forbes, N-adap. Robert Nicolson, d. Bryan Forbes. Oscars: 1-0.

DRAMA: MELODRAMA: SUSPENSE: Ghosts; Mental Illness; Elderly Women; Illusions/Hallucinations; Character Studies; British Films; Female Protagonists

(The Chalk Garden; Gaslight; Dream Child; Seance on a Wet Afternoon)

Whispers in the Dark, 1992, 103m, ★/$, Par/Par, R/EV-S-FN. A psychiatrist finds out two of her patients are actually seeing each other, but doesn't realize how personally she's soon going to be involved. Annabella Sciorra, Jamey Sheridan, Anthony LaPaglia, Jill Clayburgh, John Leguizamo, Alan Alda, Anthony Heald. w. d. Christopher Crowe.

SUSPENSE: Psychological Thriller; MURDER: MYSTERY: MURDER MYSTERY: Psychologists; Psychologist as Detective; Secrets-Keeping; Crazy Shrinks; Romance-Dangerous; Dangerous Men; Female Protagonists; Writer-Directors; Good Premise Unfulfilled; Unintentionally Funny

(Color of Night)

(Ed: Starts off interestingly enough, but becomes incredibly ridiculous)

Whistle Down the Wind, 1961, 99m, ★★★-/$, Rank/New Line. A murderer on the lam befriends three country children who think he's Jesus Christ. Hayley Mills, Alan Bates. w. Keith Waterhouse, Willis Hall, N-adap. Mary Hayley Bell, d. Bryan Forbes.

COMEDY DRAMA: MURDER: FAMILY: Fugitives from the Law; Hiding Out; Rural Life; England; Childhood; Impostors; Jesus Christ; British Films; Hidden Gems; Forgotten Films

(Tiger Bay; Russkies)

Whistling in the Dark, 1941, 77m, ★★★/$$$, MGM/MGM-UA. A criminal holds a radio detective hostage and forces him to devise a "perfect murder," which will in the end be pinned on him. Red Skelton, Conrad Veidt, Ann Rutherford, Virginia Grey, Eve Arden. w. Robert MacGunigle, Harry Clork, Albert Mannheimer, P-adap. Laurence Gross, Edward Childs Carpenter, d. S. Sylvan Simon.

COMEDY: SUSPENSE: Comic Thriller; MURDER: Spoofs-Detective; Radio Life; Actors; Criminals-Stupid; Perfect Crimes; Kidnappings

(I Dood It; The Big Broadcast SERIES)

White Banners, 1938, 88m, ★★★/$$, WB/WB. A social worker's case family includes her own son, whom she gave up for adoption. Fay Bainter, Claude Rains, Jackie Cooper. w. Lenore Coffee, Cameron Rogers, Abem Finkel, N-adap. Lloyd C. Douglas, d. Edmund Goulding.

DRAMA: MELODRAMA: Social Drama; Social Workers; Children-Adopted; Children-Long Lost; Reunions; Mothers & Sons; Mothers-Unwed; Forgotten Films; Hidden Gems; Coulda Been Great; Good Premise Unfulfilled

(Losing Isaiah; Stella Dallas)

(Ed: Daring in its time and adequate)

The White Buffalo, 1977, 97m, ★★½/$, UA/MGM-UA, PG/V. A western frontiersman searches for a mythical white buffalo, the last of the dying breed, which mirrors the man himself. Charles Bronson, Jack Warden, Will Sampson, Kim Novak, Stuart Whitman, Slim Pickens, John Carradine. d. J. Lee Thompson.

WESTERNS: Legends; Hunters; Searches; Allegorical Stories; Good Premise Unfulfilled

White Cargo, 1942, 90m, ★★-/$$$, UA/MGM-UA. A native girl in the tropics causes passion problems for a rubber plantation owner. Hedy Lamarr, Walter Pidgeon, Richard Carlson, Frank Morgan. w. P-adap. Leon Gordon, N-adap. Ida Simmons (*Hell's Playground*), d. Richard Thorpe.

MELODRAMA: ROMANCE: Cheating Men; Sexy Women; Africa; Plantation Owners; Novel and Play Adaptations

White Christmas, 1954, 120m, ★★★/$$$$$$, Par/Par. A failing winter resort is brought back to life by two entertainers who help their old army buddy by performing there. Bing Crosby, Danny Kaye, Rosemary Clooney. w. Norman Krasna, Norman Panama, Melvin Frank, d. Michael Curtiz. BOSong ("Count Your Blessings Instead of Sheep"). Oscars: 1-0.

MELODRAMA: Mortgage Drama; Resorts; Hotels; Snow Settings; Putting on a Show; Comebacks; Christmas; Song Title Movies; Blockbusters

SEQUEL TO: Holiday Inn (which included the original song).

(Holiday Inn; The Band Wagon)
(Ed: A blockbuster in its day based on a blockbuster song)

The White Cliffs of Dover, 1944, 126m, ★★/$$$, MGM/MGM-UA. An American woman marries into the British aristocracy. Tragedy ensues when her husband dies in World War I and her son in World War II. Irene Dunne, Alan Marshal, Frank Morgan, Roddy McDowell, Peter Lawford, Van Johnson. w. Claudine West, Jan Lustig, George Froeschel, Poem-adap. w. Alice Duermille, d. Clarence Brown.

MELODRAMA: DRAMA: TRAGEDY: Death-Dealing with; Death of a Child; Widows; World War I Era; World War II Era; England; Americans Abroad; Marrying Up; Social Climbing; Soldiers; Female Protagonists; Female Screenwriters
(East Lynne; Forever Amber; The Mudlark)

White Dog, 1982, 90m, ★★½/$, Par/Par, R/V. An actress buys a guard dog, not knowing that it was trained to attack blacks. Kristy McNichol, Paul Winfield, Burl Ives. w. Samuel Fuller, Curtis Hanson, N-adap. Romain Gary, d. Samuel Fuller.

DRAMA: SUSPENSE: Animal Monsters; Social Drama; Race Relations; Black vs. White; Dogs; Actresses; Bigots; Overlooked at Release; Underrated; Young Women; Female Protagonists
(Betrayed; Man's Best Friend)
(Ed: The racial misunderstandings about the film confused portrayal with advocacy and the studio chickened out)

White Fang, 1990, 109m, ★★★/$$$, Disney/Disney, G. A young adventurer and gold-seeker in the Klondikes befriends a dog that's half-wolf. Klaus Maria Brandauer, Ethan Hawke, Seymour Cassel, Susan Hogan. w. Jeanne Rosenberg, Nick Thiel, David Fallon, N-adap. Jack London, d. Randal Kleiser.

ADVENTURE: CHILDREN'S: FAMILY: Journies; Pet Stories; Dogs; Gold Mining; Treasure Hunts; Canada; Classic Literary Adaptations; Female Screenwriters
(Call of the Wild; The Journey of Natty Gann)

White Heat, 1949, 114m, ★★★½/$$$, WB/WB. A violent, powder keg of a gangster loves his mother and just wants to please her. Trouble is, she's the head of his gang. James Cagney, Edmund O'Brien, Margaret Wycherly. w. Ivan Goff, Ben Roberts, SS-adap. Virginia Kellogg, d. Raoul Walsh.

ACTION: Crime Drama; Mob Stories; Family Drama; Mothers & Sons; Mothers-Criminal; Mothers-Troublesome; Rebels; Young Men-Angry; Criminals-Female; Feisty Females; Movie Theaters
(Strangers on a Train; Manpower)

White Hunter, Black Heart, 1990, 112m, ★★★/$, WB/WB, R/V-S. A film director (based on John Huston) and his egotism drive his cast and crew to distraction. Their patience is tried as he abandons them in Africa to hunt an elephant he's obsessed with. Clint Eastwood, Jeff Fahey, Charlotte Cornwell, Norman Lumsden, George Dzundza. w. Peter Viertel, James Bridges, Burt Kennedy, N-adap. Peter Viertel, d. Clint Eastwood.

DRAMA: ADVENTURE: Character Studies; Hollywood Life; Directors; Moviemaking; Africa; Biographies; Biographies-Fictional; Obsessions; Elephants

White Lightning, 1973, 101m, ★★½/$$$, UA/MGM-UA, R/P-S-V. After a corrupt southern sheriff kills his brother, a convict escapes to seek his vengeance. Burt Reynolds, Jennifer Billingsley, Ned Beatty. w. William Norton, d. Joseph Sargent.

ACTION: MURDER: MURDER MYSTERY: Rednecks; Police Corruption; Arkansas
(Gator; Thunder and Lightning; Macon County Line; Return to Macon County)

White Mama, 1980, 96m, ★★★/$$$, CBS/Live. A poor white woman adopts a black street kid in order for him to help protect her from the crime in the area. Bette Davis, Ernest Harden, Eileen Heckart, Anne Ramsey, Virginia Capers. d. Jackie Cooper.

DRAMA: MELODRAMA: Black vs. White; Inner City Life; Children-Adopted; Protecting Someone; Elderly Women; TV Movies; Hidden Gems
(A Piano for Mrs. Cimino; Strangers: The Story of a Mother and Daughter)

White Man's Burden, 1995, 96m, ★★/$, Savoy/Savoy-HBO, PG-13/P. In a world where whites live in a ghetto and work mostly for wealthy black men, a young man tries to make his way despite the obstacles. John Travolta, Harry Belafonte, Kelly Lynch, Margaret Avery, Tom Bower, Andrew Lawrence, Carrie Snodgress, Willie C. Carpenter, Robert Gossett, Sheryl Lee Ralph, Bumper Robinson, Tom Wright. w. d. Desmond Nakano.

DRAMA: Allegorical Stories; Social Drama; What if . . . Stories; Racism; Working Class; Poor People; White Among Blacks; Writer-Directors
(Black Like Me; I Passed for White)
(Ed: Again, a great premise gone awry due to lack of story development and direction)

White Men Can't Jump, 1992, 112m, ★★★/$$$$, 20th/Fox, R/EP-S. A goofy-looking white guy comes up to a group of black playground-basketball players, plays ineptly, then challenges them to a game for money. Suddenly he can play. He wins hands down. One of the black players realizes it's the perfect scam, and they team up to con others. Wesley Snipes, Woody Harrelson, Rosie Perez, Tyra Ferrell. w. d. Ron Shelton.

COMEDY: COMEDY DRAMA: Con Artists; Race Relations; Black vs. White; White Among Blacks; Basketball; Sports Movies; Romance-Interracial; Dreams; Writer-Directors; Sleeper Hits
(Money Train; The Air Up There)

White Mile, 1994, 100m, ★★½/$$, HBO/HBO, NR/P-V. A corporate executive gathers together a group of mostly elderly friends and enemies under the macho guise of river rafting on a dangerous stretch of river. Alan Alda, Robert Loggia, Peter Gallagher.

DRAMA: TRAGEDY: River Trauma; Elderly Men; Men Proving Themselves; Business Life; Executives; Macho Men; Power Struggles; Fathers & Sons; True Stories; TV Movies
(Deliverance; The River Wild)

White Mischief, 1987, 107m, ★★★/$$, Ind/New Line, R/S-FN. The true story of the unsolved murder of Lord Erroll in Kenya among the sexually desperate aristocrats there. Charles Dance, Greta Scacchi, Joss Ackland, Sarah Miles, John Hurt, Trevor Howard. w. Michael Radford, Jonathan Gems, N-adap. James Fox, d. Michael Radford.

DRAMA: Erotic Drama; **MURDER: MURDER MYSTERY:** Crimes of Passion; Sexy Men; Playboys; Diplomats; Africa; British Films
(The Letter; East of Elephant Rock)
(Ed: A few titillating scenes had them lined up at the art houses for a while but nothing outrageous)

White Nights, 1957, 107m, ★★★/$, Ind/Facets. While a woman waits for her soldier boy to return, a nerdy fellow wants to change her mind. Maria Schell, Jean Marais, Marcello Mastroianni. SS-adap. Fyodor Dostoyevski. d. Luchino Visconti.

MELODRAMA: ROMANCE: Romantic Drama; Romance-Choosing the Right Person; Romance-Triangles; Cheating Women; Female Protagonists; Italian Films
(A Love in Germany; The Rose Tattoo)

White Nights, 1985, 135m, ★★★/$$$, Col/RCA-Col, PG-13/V. A Russian dancer who's now an American citizen is kidnapped by the KGB when his plane is forced to land in Siberia and it's up to a black American dancer working for the KGB (and his American manager stranded there) to get him back. Mikhail Baryshnikov, Geraldine Page, Isabella Rossellini, Gregory Hines, Jerzy Skolimowski, Helen Mirren. w. James Goldman, Eric Hughes, d. Taylor Hackford. **BOSong**, "Say You Say Me." BOSong, "Separate Lives." Oscars: 2-1.

DRAMA: ACTION: SUSPENSE: Fugitives from the Law; Russia; Russians as Enemy; Dancers; Spies; Race Relations; Cold War Era; KGB Agents; Kidnappings; Airplane Crashes
(Dancers; Company Business)

White Palace, 1990, 103m, ★★★/$$, Universal/MCA-U, R/S-FN-MRN. A yuppie Jewish advertising executive falls in love with an older, uncultured waitress in a diner in St. Louis and tries to decide if it's real love. Susan Sarandon, James Spader, Jason Alexander, Kathy Bates, Eileen Brennan. w. Ted Tally, Alvin Sargent, N-adap. Glenn Savan, d. Luis Mandoki.

ROMANCE: DRAMA: Romantic Drama; Romance-Mismatched; Romance-Class Conflicts; Romance-Older Women/Younger Man; Romance-Choosing the Right Person; Yuppies; Waitresses; Jewish People; Working Class; Advertising World; Class Conflicts; Coulda Been Great
(Of Human Bondage; sex, lies & video-tape)

The White Rose, 1983, 108m, ★★★/$, UA/MGM-UA, PG. The story of Hans and Sophie Scholl and the group they were with who tried to spread the truth of the concentration camps in wartime Germany. Unfortunately, their vocal protests were not unnoticed by the Nazis. Lana Stolze, Wulf Kessler, Oliver Siebert. d. Michael Verhoeven.

DRAMA: TRAGEDY: True Stories; World War II Stories; Concentration Camps; Jews-Saving; Nazi Stories; Brothers & Sisters; Rebels; Hidden Gems
(Schindler's List; The Diary of Anne Frank)

White Sands, 1992, 101m, ★ 1/2/$$, 20th/Fox, R/EV-P. A deputy sheriff in New Mexico begins a murder investigation which eventually leads to the FBI, CIA, and international arms dealers. Mickey Rourke, Mary Elizabeth Mastrantonio, Willem Dafoe, Mimi Rogers. w. Daniel Pyne, d. Roger Donaldson.

SUSPENSE: MYSTERY: Conspiracy; Romance-Triangles; Arms Dealers; Double Crossings; CIA Agents; FBI Agents; New Mexico; Dead-Back from the
(Against All Odds; Out of the Past; Off Limits)
(Ed: A dumb mess. Extremely confusing at points with a contrived ending)

The White Sister, 1933, 110m, ★★★/$$$, MGM/Horizon Entertainment. An Italian noblewoman mourns for her lover, reported killed in the war. Then he returns. Helen Hayes, Clark Gable, Lewis Stone. w. Donald Ogden Stewart, N-adap. F. Marion Crawford, Walter Hackett, d. Victor Fleming.

MELODRAMA: ROMANCE: Romance-Reunited; Widows; Dead-Back from the; Death-Dealing with; Italians; Italy
(Sommersby; The Return of Martin Guerre; Return of the Soldier; Welcome Home)

The White Tower, 1950, 98m, ★★/$$, RKO/Turner. Attempted allegory about a group of stereotypical characters and their various reasons for climbing a mountain. Glenn Ford, Claude Rains, Alida Valli, Oscar Homolka, Lloyd Bridges. w. Paul Jarrico, N-adap. James Ramsay Ullman, d. Ted Tetzlaff.

DRAMA: ADVENTURE: Mountain Climbing; Alps; Obsessions; Multiple Stories
(K2; The Snows of Kilimanjaro)

White Zombie, 1932, 74m, ★★★/$$, U/Nos, Prism. In Haiti, a white, sugar cane farmer employs black Haitian zombies to do the dirty work. Bela Lugosi, Madge Bellamy, John Harron, Joseph Cawthorn. w. Garnett Weston, d. Victor Halperin.

HORROR: SCI-FI: Race Relations; Black vs. White; Voodoo; Plantations; Caribbean; Islands; Forgotten Films; Cult Films; Hidden Gems
(Dracula; Night of the Living Dead; The Serpent and the Rainbow)

Who? (*The Final Option*), 1974, 93m, Ind/NA, ★★/NA. The Russians have captured a noted American scientist. When he is returned six months later, he's not quite himself. Elliott Gould, Trevor Howard, Joseph Bova. w. John Gould, N-adap. Algis Budrys, d. Jack Gold.

DRAMA: Character Studies; Impostors; Spies; Spy Films; Cold War Era; Russians As Enemy; Russia; Brainwashing; Scientists; Kidnappings
(Ed: Originally unreleased and for good reason, even with Gould just past his career peak)

Who Done It?, 1942, 77m, ★★1/2/$$, Universal/MCA-U. Soda jerks in New York catch a murderer despite themselves. Bud Abbott, Lou Costello, William Gargan, Louise Allbritton, William Bendix. w. Stanley Roberts, Edmund Joseph, John Grant, d. Erle C. Kenton.

COMEDY: MURDER: MYSTERY: MURDER MYSTERY: Comic Mystery; Fools-Bumbling; Abbott & Costello; Heroes-Unwitting
(Abbott & Costello SERIES)

Who Done It?, 1956, 103m, ★★1/2/$$, Ealing/NA. A janitor in an ice rink breaks a spy ring. Benny Hill, Belinda Lee, David Kossoff. w. T. E. B. Clarke, d. Basil Dearden.

COMEDY: Conspiracy; Spies; Spoofs-Spy; Heroes-Unwitting; Ordinary People vs. Criminals
(Fuller Brush Man; The Man from Diner's Club)
(Ed: A must for fans of Hill, otherwise, passable)

Who Framed Roger Rabbit?, 1988, 103m, ★★★1/2/$$$$$$, Touchstone/Touchstone, PG/P. A murder in Toon Town forces a human detective to enter the world of cartoons. Bob Hoskins, Christopher Lloyd, Joanna Cassidy, & the voices of Charles Fleischer, Kathleen Turner, Amy Irving. w. Jeffrey Price, Peter S. Seaman, N-adap, w. Gary K. Wold, *Who Censored Roger Rabbit?*, d. Robert Zemeckis.

COMEDY: MYSTERY: MURDER MYSTERY: Comic Mystery; FAMILY: SATIRE: Hollywood Life; Hollywood Satire; Cartoon; Fantasy; CHILDREN'S: Detective Stories-; Detectives-Private; Spoofs-Detective; Dangerous Women; Conspiracy; Corruption; Corporation as Enemy; Film Noir-Modern; Animation-Partial; Rabbits; 1940s; Production Design-Outstanding
(Anchors Aweigh; Bedknobs & Broomsticks; Song of the South)

Who Is Harry Kellerman and Why Is He Saying These Terrible Things About Me?, 1971, 108m, ★★★/$$, NG/WB, R/S. A New York musician/folk singer is pursued by himself, sort of. An art film from the early 70s. Dustin Hoffman, Barbara Harris (BSActress), Jack Warden, Dom De Luise. w. Herb Gardner, d. Ulu Grosbard. Oscars: 1-0.
DRAMA: Art Films; Avant-Garde; COMEDY DRAMA: Psychological Drama; 1970s; Singers; Musicians; New York Life; Narrated Films; Fantasies; Flashbacks; Mental Illness; Depression; Coulda Been Great; Forgotten Films; Hidden Gems
(Alice's Restaurant; Carnal Knowledge; I Love You, Alice B. Toklas; The Last Waltz)
(Ed: A fascinating, well-intentioned misfire)

Who Is Killing the Great Chefs of Europe?, 1978, 112m, ★★★/$$, Lorimar-WB/WB, PG/P-S. Chefs are being killed in manners befitting their culinary styles. A fast-food mogul in London finds himself "embroiled" in the plot with his chef girlfriend. George Segal, Jacqueline Bisset, Robert Morley, Jean-Pierre Cassel, Philippe Noiret, Jean Rochefort, Madge Ryan. w. Peter Stone, N-adap. Nan and Ivan Lyons, d. Ted Kotcheff.
COMEDY: Black Comedy; MURDER: MYSTERY: MURDER MYSTERY: Murders-One by One; Murder Comic Attempts; Restaurant Settings; Detective Stories; Detectives-Amateur; Detective Couples; England; Old-Fashioned Recent Films; Overlooked at Release; Underrated; Forgotten Films; Hidden Gems
(Theater of Blood; The Abominable Dr. Phibes; A Night to Remember [1946]; Manhattan Murder Mystery)
(Ed: A few rough edges, but if it were

from the 30s it would be better remembered)

Who Is the Black Dahlia?, 1975, 96m, ★★★/$$$, CBS/Worldvision. The still unsolved mystery of the hopeful actress who was murdered in post-war Hollywood. Efrem Zimbalist, Jr., Lucie Arnaz, Ronny Cox, Macdonald Carey. w. Robert Lenski, d. Joseph Pevney.
DRAMA: MYSTERY: MURDER: MURDER MYSTERY: Actresses; Hollywood Life; 1940s; True Stories; TV Movies
(True Confessions)

Who'll Stop the Rain?, 1978, 125m, UA/MGM-UA, R/V-P-S. A Vietnam vet destroys his life by getting his wife and friend involved in heroin smuggling. Nick Nolte, Tuesday Weld, Michael Moriarty, Anthony Zerbe, Richard Masur. w. Judith Roscoe, N-adap. w. Robert Stone, *Dog Soldiers*, d. Karel Reisz.
DRAMA: Drugs-Dealing; Veterans-Vietnam; Character Studies; Risking it All; Female Screenwriters; Curiosities; Song Title Movies
(Mike's Murder)

Wholly Moses, 1980, 109m, ★★/$$, Col/RCA-Col, PG/P-S. While God is talking to Moses, a shepherd in an adjoining field overhears and thinks God's talking to him. Dudley Moore, James Coco, Paul Sand, Jack Gilford, Dom De Luise, John Houseman, Madeline Kahn. w. Guy Thomas, d. Gary Weis.
COMEDY: Biblical Stories; Religious Comedy; Middle East; Jewish People; Ancient Times; Misunderstandings; Illusions/Hallucinations; God; Spoofs
(Monty Python's Life of Brian)

Whoopee, 1930, 94m, ★★-/$$$, Samuel Goldwyn/Sultan, HBO. A nervous and reticent young man has adventures thrust upon him and sings and dances his way out of them. Eddie Cantor, Eleanor Hunt, Paul Gregory. w. William Conselman, (Musical)-adap. w. William Anthony McGuire, P-adap, Owen Davis, *The Nervous Wreck.*, d. Thornton Freeland.
MUSICAL: Musical Comedy; Journies; Free Spirits; Nerds; Nerds & Babes; Comedians; Comedy-Slapstick
REMAKE: Up in Arms

Whoops! Apocalypse, 1983, 137m, ★★★/$$$, BBC/BBC. England winds up in nuclear war in this spoof of the Falkland Islands war. John Cleese, John Barron, Barry Morse. w. Andrew

Marshall, David Renwick, d. Tom Bussmann.
COMEDY: COMEDY DRAMA: Black Comedy; Apocalyptic Stories; Presidents; TV Movies; British Films; Cult Films; Monty Pythoners
(Dr. Strangelove)

Whoops! Apocalypse, 1986, 91m, ★★/$, ITC/Vidmark, PG. The first female president tries to avoid a nuclear war, despite her colleagues. Loretta Swit, Peter Cook, Rik Mayall, Ian Richardson. w. Andrew Marshall, David Renwick, d. Tom Bussmann.
COMEDY: COMEDY DRAMA: Black Comedy; Apocalyptic Stories; Presidents
(Dr. Strangelove)

Whore, 1991, 85m, ★★★/$, Vidmark/Vidmark, R/EP-S-FN-MRN. The title character often addresses the camera as she tells of her customers, past and present, and hides from her violent pimp. Theresa Russell, Benjamin Mouton, Antonio Fargas. w. Ken Russell, Deborah Dalton, P-adap. David Hines, *Bondage*, d. Ken Russell.
DRAMA: COMEDY DRAMA: Erotic Drama; Black Comedy; SATIRE: Prostitutes-Low Class; Narrated Films; Crossing the Line; Female Protagonists; Abused Women; Female Screenwriters
(Crimes of Passion; Hustling; Alfie; 21)
(Ed: An acquired taste. Pretentious to those expecting a porn film or those who want more in-depth info)

Who's Afraid of Virginia Woolf?, 1966, 127m, ★★★★/$$$$, WB/WB, R/P-S. A middle-aged couple (Elizabeth Taylor, BActress; Richard Burton, BActor) spend a confrontative, marathon evening with a younger couple (George Segal, BSActor) (Sandy Dennis, BSActress) who are much like they were years before, spilling forth many hidden demons. w. Ernest Lehman (BAScr), adap. Edward Albee, d. Mike Nichols (BDirector). BPicture, BB&WCin, BB&WArt, BB&WCostume, BOScore, BSound, BEdit. Oscars: 13-5; only film nominated in all top 7 categories, tie for 2nd most nominations ever.
DRAMA: TRAGEDY: Marriage Drama; Psychological Drama; Secrets-Consuming; Past-Haunted by the; One Day Stories; Mental Illness; Dinner Parties; College Life; Professors;

Escalating Plots; Camp; Midlife Crisis; Generation Gap; Stagelike Films
(Taming of the Shrew; Don's Party; Lips Together; Teeth Apart [play])
(Ed: A mesmerizing, powerful film everyone should see for many reasons. The fact that little is changed from the play helps the tension. Nichols' direction is every bit up to Albee's dialogue)

Who's Been Sleeping in My Bed?, 1963, 103m, ★★★/$$, Par/Par. A TV star discovers his sexual prowess in middle-age just as Miss Right has come along, and it's up to her goofy friend to prove it with a rouse. Dean Martin, Elizabeth Montgomery, Martin Balsam, Jill St. John, Carol Burnett. w. Jack Rose, d. Daniel Mann.
COMEDY: ROMANCE: Romantic Comedy; FARCE: Playboys; Sexy Men; Psychologists; TV Life; Artists; Sidekicks-Wisecracking; Forgotten Films
(Ed: Worth it for the Burnett role and Montgomery, too, used as set pieces at the time)

Whose Life Is It Anyway?, 1981, 118m, MGM/MGM-UA, R/S-P. A sculptor, totally paralyzed in a car accident, wishes to die, since he can no longer do what gives him pleasure. Richard Dreyfuss, John Cassavetes, Christine Lahti, Bob Balaban, Kenneth McMillan. w. Brian Clark, Reginald Rose, P-adap. Brian Clark, d. John Badham.
DRAMA: COMEDY DRAMA: Death-Dealing with; Euthanasia; Disabled People; Accidents; Hospitals; Nurses; Midlife Crisis; Suicidal Tendencies
(Right of Way)

Who's Harry Crumb?, 1989, 90m, ★★★/$$, Tri/Col-Tri, PG. A klutzy private eye is hired by a millionaire to find his kidnapped daughter. John Candy, Jeffrey Jones, Annie Potts, Barry Corbin. w. Robert Conte, Peter Martin Wortmann, d. Paul Flaherty.
COMEDY: MYSTERY: Kidnappings; Detective Stories; Spoofs-Detectives; Comic Mystery; Fools-Bumbling; Accident Prone; Cartoonlike Films; Underrated
COMEDY REMAKE OF: The Big Sleep.
(Ed: A few hilarious scenes)

Who Slew Auntie Roo?, 1972, 91m, ★★½/$, EMI-MGM/Vestron, PG/V. A crazy old woman harasses two orphan children, much like Hansel and Gretel.

Shelley Winters, Ralph Richardson, Mark Lester, Lionel Jeffries. w. Robert Blees, Jimmy Sangster, d. Curtis Harrington.
HORROR: MURDER: Black Comedy; Orphans; Mental Illness; Evil Women; Camp
(Whatever Happened to Baby Jane?; Whatever Happened to Aunt Alice?; What's the Matter with Helen?; The Mad Room)
(Ed: Not up to similar films, and strangely more appealing to children)

Who's Minding the Mint?, 1967, 97m, ★★½/$$, Col/Goodtimes, G. A bill printer at the U.S. mint sneaks in at night to print bills for himself and friends. Jim Hutton, Dorothy Provine, Milton Berle, Joey Bishop, Bob Denver, Walter Brennan, Victor Buono, Jack Gilford. w. R. S. Allen, Harvey Bullock, d. Howard Morris.
COMEDY: Capers; Heist Stories; Thieves; Bank Robberies; Ensemble Films; Female Among Males; Counterfeiters
(Mister 880)

Who's Minding the Store?, 1963, 90m, ★★★/$$$, Par/Par. A nerdy klutz gets a job in a department store, and since it's Jerry Lewis, guess what happens. Jerry Lewis, Jill St. John, Agnes Moorehead. w. Frank Tashlin, Harry Tugend, d. Frank Tashlin.
COMEDY: FARCE: Comedy-Slapstick; Character Comedy; Department Stores; Fools-Bumbling
(The Bellboy; The Big Store)

Who's That Girl?, 1987, 94m, ★★/$, WB/WB, PG-13/P-S. A romance ensues between a mild-mannered lawyer and his obnoxious jailbird/starlet client. Madonna, Griffin Dunne, Haviland Morris. w. Andrew Smith, Ken Finkleman, d. James Foley.
COMEDY: ROMANCE: Romantic Comedy; Screwball Comedy; Nerds & Babes; Free Spirits; Sexy Women; Comedy-Slapstick
REMAKE/RETREAD OF: Bringing Up Baby; What's Up Doc?.
(Ed: A pretty big mess with a few moments and Madonna trying to be an out-of-control ditz when she is neither and can play neither)

Who's That Knocking at My Door?, 1968, 90m, ★★★/$, WB/WB. An Italian teenage boy's life in New York, having to choose between the street life and col-

lege. Harvey Keitel, Zena Bethune. w. d. Martin Scorsese.
COMEDY DRAMA: Autobiographical Stories; Coming of Age; Young Men; Pre-Life Crisis; Italians; New York Life; Gangs-Street; Writer-Directors; Hidden Gems; Cult Films; Ind Films
(A Bronx Tale; Greetings; Hi, Mom)

Who Was That Lady?, 1960, 115m, ★★½/$$, Col/NA. In order to cover up for an indiscretion with a coed, a professor has a friend tell his wife that he and his student are actually FBI agents posing as a couple. Trouble is, foreign spies get wind of this and believe it. Tony Curtis, Dean Martin, Janet Leigh, James Whitmore. w. Norman Krasna, P-adap. Norman Krasna, d. George Sidney.
COMEDY: FARCE: College Life; Professors; Teachers and Students; Misunderstandings; Mistaken Identities; Liars; Impostors; FBI Agents; Spies; KGB Agents; Forgotten Films; Hidden Gems
(The Man from the Diner's Club; Caprice; Forty Pounds of Trouble)

Why Me?, 1989, 87m, ★★/$, Col/Col, R/S-P-V. Two inept jewel thieves get lucky and nab a famous ruby ring. Then they thwart authorities who demand its return. Christopher Lambert, Kim Greist, Christopher Lloyd. w. Donald E. Westlake, Leonard Maas Jr., N-adap. Westlake, d. Gene Quintano.
ACTION: Heist Stories; Action Comedy; Comic Thriller; Criminals-Stupid; Jewel Thieves
(The Hot Rock; The Real McCoy; Knight Moves)

Why Shoot the Teacher?, 1976, 99m, ★★★/$, Ind/Sultan, PG. A schoolteacher settles in a small town in Canada during the Depression and has trouble fitting in, especially with one particular young man. Samantha Eggar, Bud Cort, Chris Wiggins. w. James Defilice, N-adap. Max Braithwaite, d. Silvio Narizzano.
DRAMA: COMEDY DRAMA: Teachers; Teachers and Students; Fish out of Water Stories; Small-town Life; Depression Era; Canada; Canadian Films
(Sarah Plain and Tall; Up the Down Staircase; My Brilliant Career; The Brood)

Wichita, 1955, 81m, ★★½/$$, AA/NA. Wyatt Earp lays down the law in this Kansas cow town. Joel McCrea, Vera Miles, Lloyd Bridges, Wallace Ford, Edgar Buchanan, Peter Graves. w. Daniel Ullman, d. Jacques Tourneur.

WESTERNS: Westerns-City Titles; Men in Conflict

(Wyatt Earp; Tombstone)

Wicked As They Come, 1956, 94m, ★★/$, Col/NA. A poor girl from the slums rises to money and fame through a beauty pageant but doesn't exactly take the high road. She, of course, loses her soul in the process. Arlene Dahl, Herbert Marshall, Phil Carey. w. d. Ken Hughes.

MELODRAMA: Rags to Riches; Fame-Rise to; Beauty Pageants; Evil Women; Writer-Directors

(What Price Hollywood?; The Goddess)

The Wicked Lady, 1945, 104m, ★★★/$$$, Gainsborough/NA. During the reign of Charles II, Lady Skelton takes up with criminal types for highway robbery and whatnot. Margaret Lockwood, James Mason, Griffith Jones, Patricia Roc, Michael Rennie. w. d. Leslie Arliss, N-adap. Magdalen King-Hall (*The Life and Death of the Wicked Lady Skelton*).

DRAMA: ROMANCE: Costume Drama; Thieves; Criminals-Female; Ordinary People Turned Criminal; Female Protagonists; Restoration Period; 1600s

REMAKE: 1983.

The Wicked Lady, 1983, 99m, ★★★/$$, Cannon/MGM-UA, R/S-FFN-MRN. A remake of above, with punched-up sex and violence. Faye Dunaway, Alan Bates, John Gielgud, Denholm Elliot, Prunella Scales. w. Leslie Arlis, Michael Winner, N-adap. Magdalen King-Hall (*The Life and Death of the Wicked Lady Skelton*), d. Michael Winner.

DRAMA: ROMANCE: Costume Drama; Erotic Drama; Thieves; Female Criminals; Ordinary People Turned Criminal; Female Protagonists; Restoration Period; 1600s

REMAKE OF: The Wicked Lady, 1945.

(The Three Musketeers; The Gambler [1988])

The Wicker Man, 1973, 86m, ★★★/$, Ind/Media, R/V-S. A police detective investigating a murder on a desolate island off the coast of Scotland discovers a weird pagan cult cut off from the rest of the world. Edward Woodward, Britt Ekland, Christopher Lee, Ingrid Pitt, Diane Cilento. w. Anthony Shaffer, d. Robin Hardy.

SUSPENSE: MYSTERY: MURDER: MURDER MYSTERY: Detective Stories; Detectives-Police; Cults; Islands;

Overlooked at Release; Underrated; Cult Films

Widows' Peak, 1994, 101m, ★★★/$$, Fine Line-Rank/Fine Line, PG/S. A mysterious young woman enters an Irish village and infighting begins between her and another local woman while she tries to marry the town's richest young man-whose mother may not let him, especially if all of their secrets wreck everything. w. Hugh Leonard, d. John Irvin.

COMEDY: COMEDY DRAMA: FARCE: MYSTERY: MURDER: Strangers in Town; Women in Conflict; Prostitutes-High Class; Mothers & Sons; Spinsters; Sexy Women; Con Artists; Clever Plots & Endings; Ireland; Irish Films; Female Protagonists; Accused Unjustly; Death-Faked

(Enchanted April; Summer House)

Wife, Doctor and Nurse, 1937, 84m, ★★½/$$, 20th/NA. A doctor becomes involved with his nurse, much to the chagrin of his wife. Loretta Young, Warner Baxter, Virginia Bruce, Lon Chaney Jr., Jane Darwell. w. Kathryn Scola, Darrell Ware, Lamar Trotti, d. Walter Lang.

COMEDY: COMEDY DRAMA: ROMANCE: Romantic Comedy; Screwball Comedy; Romance-Triangles; Ménage à Trois; Doctors; Nurses; Romance with a Married Person; Marriage on the Rocks; Cheating Men; Female Screenwriters

(Wife versus Secretary)

Wife, Husband and Friend, 1939, 80m, ★★½/$$, 20th/NA. A singer's husband, jealous of her career, tries to sabotage it. Loretta Young, Warner Baxter, Binnie Barnes, Cesar Romero. w. Nunnally Johnson, SS-adap. James M. Cain, d. Gregory Ratoff.

COMEDY: ROMANCE: Romantic Comedy; Screwball Comedy; Marriage Comedy; Romance-Bickering; Jealousy; Singers; Sabotage

COMEDY VERSION OF: A Star Is Born.

Wife versus Secretary, 1936, 88m, ★★★/$$$, MGM/MGM-UA. A woman begins to suspect her husband is having an affair with none other than his secretary. Clark Gable, Myrna Loy, Jean Harlow, May Robson, James Stewart. w. Norman Krasna, Alice Duer Miller, John LeeMahin, N-adap. Faith Baldwin, d. Clarence Brown.

COMEDY: ROMANCE: Romantic Comedy; Screwball Comedy; Marriage Comedy; Misunderstandings; Romance

with a Married Person; Jealousy; Cheating Men; Secretaries; Faded Hits; Hidden Gems; Forgotten Films

(Wife, Doctor and Nurse; My Dear Secretary)

The Wilby Conspiracy, 1975, 105m, ★★★/$$, UA/MGM-UA. In South Africa, a white miner helps a black revolutionary in hiding get to safety in Johannesburg. Sidney Poitier, Michael Caine, Nicol Williamson, Persis Khambatta. w. Rod Amateau, Harold Nebenzal, N-adap. Peter Driscoll, d. Ralph Nelson.

ACTION: SUSPENSE: Escape Adventure; Chase Movies; Conspiracy; Fugitives from the Law; Fugitives-Harboring; Rebels; Political Drama; Race Relations; Apartheid; South Africa; Saving Someone; Black vs. White; Underrated; Overlooked at Release; Forgotten Films

(Cry Freedom; Bopha!; Mandela)

The Wild Angels, 1966, 85m, ★★½/$$$, AIP/Sultan, Vestron, R/V. A motorcycle gang becomes more like a cult for some of its members, leading to violence. Peter Fonda, Nancy Sinatra, Bruce Dern, Michael J. Pollard. w. Charles B. Griffith, d. Roger Corman.

ACTION: MELODRAMA: Chase Movies; Cults; Motorcycles; Gangs

(The Wild One; Hell's Angels; Spinout)

Wild at Heart, 1990, 127m, ★★★/$$, IRS/Media, R/S-EP-V-FFN-MRN. A violent, erratic criminal and his sexy girlfriend find that love conquers all as they drive through Texas seeking sanctuary. Nicolas Cage, Laura Dern, Diane Ladd (BSActress), Willem Dafoe, Isabella Rossellini, Harry Dean Stanton, Crispin Glover. w. d. David Lynch, N-adap. Barry Gifford. Oscars: 1-0.

DRAMA: Erotic Drama; Crime Drama; Art Films; Chase Movies; Road Movies; Outlaw Road Movies; Fugitives from the Law; Criminal Couples; Eccentric People; Film Noir-Modern

(True Romance; Kalifornia; Natural Born Killers; Gun Crazy)

The Wild Bunch, 1969, 145m, ★★★/$$$, WB/WB, R (X)/EV-S. A band of outlaws in Texas are ambushed and fight to the death defending one of their own in a landmark bloody showdown in the history of films. William Holden, Ernest Borgnine, Robert Ryan, Edmond O'Brien, Warren Oates, Strother Martin. w. Walon Green, Sam Peckinpah (BOScr), d. Sam Peckinpah. BOScore. Oscars: 2-0.

WESTERNS: ACTION: Men in Conflict; Good vs. Evil; Ensembles-Male; Violence-Sudden; Blood & Gore
(The Professionals; Bring Me the Head of Alfred Garcia; Straw Dogs; Chato's Land)
The Wild Child, 1969, 117m, ★★★¹/₂/ $$, UA/MGM-UA. The true story of a doctor in 1700s France who treats and tries to recivilize a boy who has been found growing up in the wilderness. w. d. François Truffaut.
DRAMA: Coming of Age; Medical Detectives; Raised by Animals; Boys; Fish out of Water Stories; Hidden Gems; Writer-Directors; True Stories; Incredible but Mostly True
(Nell; Greystoke: The Legend of Tarzan)
The Wild Duck, 1984, 96m, ★★/$, Vestron/Vestron, PG. A father turns against his daughter when he finds out she's not his, so the daughter goes to extreme measures. Jeremy Irons, Liv Ullman, Lucinda Jones. P-adap. Henrik Ibsen, d. Henry Safran.
DRAMA: TRAGEDY: Fathers & Daughters; Family Drama; Classic Literary Adaptations; Coulda Been Good
The Wild Geese, 1978, 134m, ★★¹/₂/ $$, UA/Fox, R/V. British mercenaries live by their wits in Africa while working special missions. Roger Moore, Richard Burton, Richard Harris, Kenneth Griffith, Jane Hylton. w. Reginald Rose, N-adap. Daniel Carney, d. Andrew V. McLaglen.
ACTION: Soldiers; Mercenaries; Spies; Africa; Old-Fashioned Recent Films; Special Teams; Hitmen
SEQUEL: The Wild Geese II.
(Force Ten from Navarone; Ffolkes; The Dogs of War)
The Wild Geese II, 1985, 125m, ★★/$, Thorn EMI-UA/MGM-UA, R/V-P. A television station pays a mercenary to extricate Rudolf Hess from prison. Scott Glenn, Barbara Carrera, Edward Fox, Laurence Olivier. w. Reginald Rose, N-adap. Daniel Carney (The Square Circle), d. Peter Hunt.
ACTION: Soldiers; Mercenaries; Hitmen; Kidnappings; Rescue Drama; Special Teams
(Ed: A sequel in name only)
Wild Hearts Can't Be Broken, 1991, 89m, ★★¹/₂/$, Disney/Disney, G. A poor girl joins the circus during the Depression and is blinded in a horse-diving accident but finds a honey, just the same. Gabrielle Anwar, Cliff Robertson,

Michael Schoeffling, Dylan Kussman. w. Oley Sassone, d. Steve Miner.
MELODRAMA: ROMANCE: True Stories; Biographies; Romantic Drama; Blind People; Horses; Circus Life; Depression Era; Female Protagonists; Young Women; Old-Fashioned Recent Films; Coulda Been Good
(National Velvet; Dark Victory)
Wild in the Country, 1961, 114m, ★★¹/₂/$$, UA/Fox. Elvis is a singer who wants to be a writer and a psychologist falls for it. Elvis Presley, Hope Lange, Tuesday Weld, Millie Perkins, John Ireland, Gary Lockwood. w. Clifford Odets, d. Philip Dunne.
MELODRAMA: ROMANCE: Romantic Drama; Music Movies; Singers; Writers; Psychologists; City vs. Country; College Life; Coulda Been Good; Southerns; Forgotten Films
Wild in the Streets, 1968, 97m, ★★★/ $$$, AIP/HBO, R/V-S. A futuristic yarn in which a teen-idol singer becomes president and spawns a teenage emancipation movement-in the streets. Shelley Winters, Christopher Jones, Diane Varsi, Hal Holbrook, Millie Perkins. w. Robert Thom, d. Barry Shear. BEdit. Oscars: 1-0.
DRAMA: ACTION: Action Drama; Teenagers; Teenage Movies; Generation Gap; Anti-Establishment Films; 1960s; Hippies; Rebels; Presidents; Power-Rise to; Heroes-Unlikely; Musicians; Mothers & Sons; Political Unrest; Futuristic Films; What if . . . Stories
(Medium Cool; The Looking Glass War)
Wild Is the Wind, 1957, 114m, ★★★/ $$$, Par/Par. A love triangle develops between a widower, his Italian wife's sister, and his adopted son. Anna Magnani (BActress), Anthony Quinn (BActor), Tony Franciosa. w. Arnold Schulman, d. George Cukor. BOSong. Oscars: 3-0.
MELODRAMA: DRAMA: Romance-Triangles; Romance with Relative's Lover; Romance with Relatives; Romance-Older Women/Younger Men; Family Drama; Rural Life; Romance-Doomed
(The Fugitive Kind; Orpheus Descending; The Rose Tattoo)
The Wild Life, 1984, 96m, ★★/$, U/MCA-U, R/S-EP. Life after Ridgemont High as the rowdy suburbanites move into their own digs, which they then proceed to tear apart. Christopher Penn, Eric Stoltz, Rick Moranis, Hart Bochner,

Randy Quaid, Jenny Wright. w. Cameron Crowe, d. Art Linson.
COMEDY: High School Life; Pre-Life Crisis; Teenagers; Teenage Movies; Bathroom Humor; Party Movies
SEQUEL TO: Fast Times at Ridgemont High.
(Foxes; Hollywood Boulevard; Fraternity Vacation)
The Wild One, 1954, 79m, ★★/$$$, Col/RCA-Col. A motorcycle gang terrorizes a small California town in the fifties by dancing in the streets and drinking beer. Marlon Brando, Lee Marvin, Mary Murphy, Robert Keith. w. John Paston, SS-adap. Frank Rooney, The Cyclists' Raid, d. Laslo Benedek.
DRAMA: ACTION: Action Drama; Rebels; Motorcycles; Gangs; Anti-Establishment Films; Teenagers
Wild Orchid, 1989, 111m, ★★/$$, Vision-Triumph/Col, R/ES-FFN-MN. A sleazy jet-setter plays mind-and-sexual-games with two female lawyers in a power play to gain control of a Brazilian hotel. Mickey Rourke, Jacqueline Bisset, Carre Otis, Assumpta Serna. w. Patricia Louisianna Knop, Zalman King, d. Zalman King.
MELODRAMA: Erotic Drama; Sexy Women; Sexy Men; Romance-Triangles; Ménage à Trois; Brazil; Female Screenwriters
SEQUEL: Wild Orchid 2.
(9½ Weeks; Two Moon Junction; Wild Orchid 2)
Wild Palms, 1993, 300m, ★★¹/₂/###, ABC/ABC, S-V. In the future of L.A., a virtual reality TV station is the center of mysterious goings-on that lead to death and a conspiracy. Jim Belushi, Robert Loggia, Angie Dickinson, Dana Delany, Kim Cattrall, Nick Mancuso, Brad Dourif, Charles Rocket, Bebe Neuwirth. w. Bruce Wagner, based on his comic, d. Phil Joanou, Kathryn Bigelow, Keith Gordon, Pete Hewitt.
SUSPENSE: SCI-FI: MYSTERY: Conspiracy; Virtual Reality; Political Corruption; Politicians; Detective Stories; Film Noir-Modern; Detectives-Amateur; TV Life; Futuristic Films; Los Angeles; Female Directors; TV Movies; Miniseries
(Twin Peaks; Virtuosity; Videodrome)
The Wild Party, 1974, 91m, ★★★/$$, AIP/Sultan, Vestron, R/S. A washed-up silent film star throws a depressing Hollywood party in 1929 in which a sexy

woman becomes the main party favor. James Coco, Raquel Welch, Perry King, Tiffany Bollin. w. Walter Marks, (Poem)-adap, w. Joseph Moncure March, d. James Ivory.

DRAMA: MELODRAMA: TRAGEDY: Party Movies; Hollywood Life; Silent Film Era; Actors; Actresses; Sexy Women; Sexy Men; Rape/Rapists; Hollywood Biographies; Biographies-Fictional
(Our Dancing Daughters; Inserts; The Great Gatsby)
(Ed: A fictionalization of Fatty Arbuckle's alleged murder of a starlet and the resulting scandal)

Wild River, 1960, 115m, ★★★/$$, 20th/Fox. In 1933, a tough old woman refuses to leave the Tennessee Valley, even though it is about to be flooded by the T.V.A. Montgomery Clift, Jo Van Fleet, Lee Remick, Albert Salmi, Bruce Dern. w. Paul Osborn, N-adap. Borden Deal, William Bradford Huie, d. Elia Kazan.

DRAMA: Depression Era; Life Transitions; Documentary Style; Government as Enemy
(The River [1951]; The River [1984]; A Face in the Crowd)

Wild Strawberries, 1959, 93m, ★★★★/$$, Svensk/Fox. An old college professor fears death and looks back over his long life. Victor Sjostrom, Ingrid Thulin, Gunnar Bjornstrand. w. d. Ingmar Bergman (BOScr). Oscars: 1-0.

DRAMA: Character Studies; Psychological Drama; Life Transitions; Memories; Flashbacks; Fantasies; Nightmares; Illusions/Hallucinations; Midlife Crisis; Elderly Men; Professors; Swedish Films; Writer-Directors; Film History
(Another Woman; Autumn Sonata; Persona; Cries and Whispers; Face to Face)

Wild West, 1992, 100m, ★★½/$ (LR), Ind/NA. Young Indian immigrants form a country band and seek out fame in London with quite a few mishaps and oddities along the way. Naveen Andrews, Sarita Choudhury, Ronny Jhutti, Ravi Kapoor. w. Harwant Bains, d. David Attwood.

COMEDY DRAMA: Musicians; Indian People; British Films; Fish out of Water Stories

Wildcats, 1986, 107m, ★★½/$$$, WB/WB, PG-13/P. A ghetto high school gets a daffy but plucky woman for a foot-ball coach. She surprises everyone and whips them into shape-of course. Goldie Hawn, Swoosie Kurtz, Robyn Lively, M. Emmett Walsh. w. Ezra Sacks, d. Michael Ritchie.

COMEDY: Fish out of Water Stories; Underdog Stories; Female Protagonists; Turning the Tables; Female Among Males (Coach; Private Benjamin; Renaissance Man)

Wilder Napalm, 1993, 109m, ★★/$, Col/Col, PG-13/S. Two brothers with the power to start fires telekinetically feud over the use of the power and one of their wives. Dennis Quaid, Debra Winger, Arliss Howard, Jim Varney. w. Vince Gilligan, d. Glenn Gordon Caron.

COMEDY: SCI-FI: Brothers; Psychics; Fires; Men Fighting Over Women; Flops-Major; Curiosities
(Firestarter)

Wildflower, 1991, 94m, ★★★/##, Lifetime/Worldvision. A deaf girl in Depression-era Georgia suffers abuse from her stepfather and seeks refuge on a neighboring farm with a brother and sister. Patricia Arquette, Beau Bridges, Susan Blakeley, William McNamara, Reese Witherspoon. w. N-adap. Sara Flanigan, d. Diane Keaton.

DRAMA: MELODRAMA: Girls; Deaf People; Abused Children; Stepfathers-Troublesome; Rape/Rapists; Rural Life; Poor People; Southerns; Female Protagonists; Female Directors; Female Screenwriters; Actor Directors; TV Movies; Hidden Gems
(Sudie and Simpson; Cold Sassy Tree; Johnny Belinda)

Will Penny, 1967, 109m, ★★★/$$, Par/Par. A gang of ruffians harrass a middle-aged cowboy who gets in their way, and he must decide whether to fight back. Charlton Heston, Joan Hackett, Donald Pleasence, Lee Majors, Bruce Dern. w. d. Tom Gries.

WESTERNS: DRAMA: Cowboys; Generation Gap; Men in Conflict; Men Proving Themselves; Revenge; Westerns-Revenge

Will Success Spoil Rock Hunter?, 1957, 95m, ★★★/$$$, 20th/NA, AMC. A shy, nerdy advertising executive is used in a publicity campaign as the model for the world's greatest lover. Jayne Mansfield, Tony Randall, Betsy Drake, Joan Blondell. w. Frank Tashlin, P-adap. George Axelrod, d. Frank Tashlin.

SATIRE: COMEDY: Fame-Rise to; Fish out of Water Stories; Advertising World; Nerds; Nerds & Babes; Sexy Women; Bimbos; Hidden Gems; Faded Hits; Forgotten Films
(The Love God; Oh, Men! Oh, Women!)

Willard, 1971, 95m, ★★★/$$$$, Cinerama/Par, R/V-B&G. A young antisocial nerd trains rats to kill his enemies. Bruce Davison, Elsa Lanchester, Ernest Borgnine, Sondra Locke. w. Gilbert Ralston, N-adap. Stephen Gilbert (*Ratman's Notebooks*), d. Daniel Mann. BOSong. Oscars: 1-1.

HORROR: Revenge; Monsters-Animal; Animal Stories; Nerds; Psycho-Killers; Rodents

SEQUEL: Ben.
(Ed: For horror and rodent fans)

Willie and Phil, 1980, 116m, ★★½/$, 20th/CBS-Fox, R/S. Two men and a woman cavort through 70s New York very intimately with each other, though not without spats. Michael Ontkean, Margot Kidder, Ray Sharkey. w. d. Paul Mazursky.

DRAMA: COMEDY DRAMA: ROMANCE: Erotic Drama; Romance-Triangles; Ménage à Trois; New York Life; 1970s; Alternative Lifestyles; Friendships-Male; Writer-Directors

GENRE GLUT (1980): Ménage à Trois: A Small Circle of Friends; Four Friends.
(A Small Circle of Friends; Four Friends; Jules and Jim)

Willow, 1988, 126m, ★★★/$$$$, MGM/MGM-UA, PG. A dwarf and assorted characters in a fantasy world must bring a baby to safety to fulfill an ancient prophecy. Val Kilmer, Joanne Whalley, Warwick Davies, Jean Marsh, Billy Barty, David Steinberg. w. Bob Dolman, SS-adap. George Lucas, d. Ron Howard.

ACTION: ADVENTURE: CHILDREN'S: FAMILY: SCI-FI: Fantasy; Journey; Saving Someone; Little People-Midgets
(Krull; Star Wars; Ladyhawke)

Willy Wonka and the Chocolate Factory, 1971, 100m, ★★★½/$$$, WB/WB, G. In a faraway land, poor boy wins a tour of a local chocolate factory and finds a bizarre world of magic and evil within. Gene Wilder, Jack Albertson, Peter Ostrum, Roy Kinnear, Aubrey Woods. w. Roald Dahl, N-adap. Roald Dahl, d. Mel Stuart. BSScore. Oscars: 1-0.

ADVENTURE: Fantasy; **CHILDREN'S: FAMILY: COMEDY DRAMA:** Black Comedy; Kingdoms; Contests; Lotteries;

Deaths-One by One; Old-Fashioned Recent Films
(Alice in Wonderland; Chitty Chitty Bang Bang)
(Ed: A classic among a generation of children, and though some of it is a bit disturbing [Willie Wonka can be a jerk], the fantasy aspect makes it all innocuous and funny)

Wilson, 1944, 154m, ★★★/$$$, 20th/Fox. A historically accurate telling of this president's life. Alexander Knox (BActor), Charles Coburn, Cedric Hardwicke, Geraldine Fitzgerald, Vincent Price, Sidney Blackmer, Thurston Hall. w. Lamar Trotti (BOScr), d. Henry King (BDirector). BPicture, BScore, **BEdit, BCCin, BCArt, BSound.** Oscars: 9-5.
DRAMA: Biographies; Presidents; Character Studies; Epics; Episodic Stories
(Sunrise at Campobello; Young Mr. Lincoln)

Wilt, 1989, 93m, ★★¹/₂/$, Ind/NA. A bumbling police detective mistakenly suspects that a professor has murdered his wife. Griff Rhys Joes, Mel Smith, Alison Steadman, Diana Quick. w. Andrew Marshall, David Renwick, N-adap. Tom Sharpe, d. Michael Tuchner.
DRAMA: COMEDY DRAMA: MURDER: MYSTERY: MURDER MYSTERY: Black Comedy; Detective Stories; Detectives-Police; Accused Unjustly; Eccentric People; British Films; Quiet Little Films

Winchester 73, 1950, 92m, ★★¹/₂/$$$, U-I/MCA-U. Two archenemies finally have it out in a gun battle. James Stewart, Shelley Winters, Dan Duryea, Rock Hudson, Tony Curtis. w. Robert L. Richards, Borden Chase, SS-adap. Stuart N. Lake, d. Anthony Mann.
WESTERNS: ACTION: Men in Conflict; Duels; Feuds; All-Star Casts
(High Noon; Gunfight at the OK Corral)

Wind, 1992, 125m, ★★/$, Col/Col, PG-13/S-P. After losing the America's Cup yacht race, a young sailor has a designer build an unstoppable yacht to try again. Matthew Modine, Jennifer Grey, Stellan Skarsgard, Cliff Robertson. w. Rudy Wurlitzer, Mac Gudgeon, SS-adap. Jeff Benjamin, Roger Vaughan, Kimball Livingston, d. Carroll Ballard.
ADVENTURE: DRAMA: Sailing; Adventure at Sea; Contest/Competitions; Flops-Major
(White Squall; Flight of Doves)

The Wind and the Lion, 1975, 119m, ★★★/$$$, MGM/MGM-UA, PG. An American woman (Candice Bergen) is kidnapped in turn-of-the-century Africa by a Moroccan (Sean Connery) whom she can't completely despise. Brian Keith, John Huston, Geoffrey Lewis. w. d. John Milius. BOScore, BSound. Oscars: 2-0.
DRAMA: ADVENTURE: Hostage Situations; Kidnappings; Kidnappers-Sympathizing with; Feisty Females; Romance-Bickering; Africa; True Stories; World War I Era; Presidents; Writer-Directors
(Masquerade [1965])
(Ed: If you don't take it too seriously, it's fun and nice to look at)

The Window, 1949, 73m, ★★★¹/₂/$$, RKO/Turner. In the slums of New York, a young boy witnesses a murder. No one believes him, however, because he's always telling stories. So he's left alone to flee from the murderer, who knows he was watched. Bobby Driscoll, Barbara Hale, Arthur Kennedy, Paul Stewart. w. Mel Dinelli, d. Ted Tetzlaff.
SUSPENSE: Film Noir; Witness to Murder; Witness to Murder-Child; Child Protagonists; Children in Jeopardy; Unbelieved; Forgotten Films; Hidden Gems
(Fallen Idol; Witness; Eyewitness [1970])
(Ed: Much-imitated, low-budget effort that hit on a classic premise and pulled it off effortlessly)

Window to Paris, 1995, 87m, ★★★/$, Ind/NA. A man in Russia rents out an apartment to an old lady who disappears. The owner soon finds a hole in the closet, which, if stepped into, brings one out under the Eiffel Tower in Paris. Soon everyone wants to travel to France, but not everyone has a good time, as dreams have a price. Agnes Soral, Serguej Dontsov, Viktor Michailov, Nina Oussatova, Kira Kreylis-Petrova, Natalja Ipatova, Viktor Gogolev, Tamara Timofeevad. w. Yuri Mamin, Arkadi Tigai, d. Yuri Mamin.
COMEDY DRAMA: Fantasy; Surrealism; Time Travel; Russia; Paris; Russian Films

Winged Victory, 1944, 130m, ★★¹/₂/$$$, 20th/NA. Young Air Force recruits during World War II are trained for dangerous missions, then sent out to seek their glory in victory or death. Lon McCallister, Jeanne Crain, Edmond O'Brien, Jane Ball, Lee J. Cobb, Judy Holliday, Red Buttons, Karl Malden, Martin Ritt. w. Moss Hart, P-adap. Moss Hart, d. George Cukor.
ACTION: MELODRAMA: War Movies; World War II Movies; Soldiers; Pilots-Airplane; Ensemble Films; Ensembles-Male

Wings, 1927, 136m, ★★★¹/₂/$$$$, Par/Par. During World War I, two young friends in the Air Force court tragedy when, in the heat of battle, one accidently shoots the other down. Clara Bow, Charles Buddy Rogers, Richard Arlen, Gary Cooper, Jobyna Ralston. w. Hope Loring, Harry D. Lighton, d. William Wellman.
ACTION: MELODRAMA: War Movies; World War I Stories; **TRAGEDY:** Friendships-Male; Accidents; Death-Accidental; Pilots-Airplane; Female Screenwriters

Wings in the Dark, 1935, 75m, ★★/$$, Par/Par. A young man who's been blinded helps his girlfriend out in time of need despite his setbacks. Cary Grant, Myrna Loy, Dean Jagger. w. Jack Kirkland, Frank Partos, d. James Flood.
MELODRAMA: Tearjerkers; **ROMANCE:** Romantic Drama; Blind People; Pilots-Airplane; Heroes-Unlikely; Forgotten Films
(Ed: Fairly preposterous and forgotten for a reason)

Wings of Desire, 1987, 127m, ★★★¹/₂/$$$, Orion/Orion, PG-13. A pair of angels read the minds of people they encounter in 80s Berlin. One of the angels falls in love with a trapeze artist and wants to become human. Bruno Ganz, Solveig Dommartin, Otto Sander, Peter Falk. w. Wim Wenders, Peter Handke, d. Wim Wenders.
DRAMA: COMEDY DRAMA: ROMANCE: Fantasy; Art Films; Avant Garde Films; Angels; Psychics; German Films; Berlin; Circus Life; Cult Films
SEQUEL: Far Away, So Close.
(Far Away, So Close; Until the End of the World)
(Ed: Chosen on several polls as one of the best of the 80s, but not for everyone)

The Wings of Eagles, 1957, 110m, ★★★/$$$, MGM/MGM-UA. A navy pilot is paralyzed after an accident and becomes a screenwriter. John Wayne, Ward Bond, Maureen O'Hara, Dan Daily, Ken Curtis. w. Frank Fenton, William Haines, d. John Ford.

DRAMA: MELODRAMA: Veterans; Disabled People; Comebacks; Pilot-Military; Writers; Hollywood Life; Biographies; Biographies-Fictional; True Stories
(Bright Victory; Waterdance)
(Ed: A rare legit drama for Wayne; based on the life of writer Frank Wead, including a character based on director Ford)
Wings of Fame, 1990, 109m, ★★1/2/$, Par/Par. A writer kills an actor and then winds up in a purgatory of sorts-a cruise ship for the undead famous where as long as they're worthy of fame, they can hang around. Colin Firth, Peter O'Toole. w. Otakar Votocek, Herman Koch, d. Votocek.
DRAMA: Fantasy; **MURDER:** Art Films; Dead-Back from the; Ships; Actors; Writers; Hell
(Bitter Moon; Voyage of the Damned)
Wings of the Morning, 1937, 89m, ★★1/2/$$, 20th/NA. The descendants of an Irish nobleman and a gypsy princess find their romantic adventures mirror those of their parents. Henry Fonda, Annabella, Stewart Rome, John McCormack, Helen Haye. w. Tom Geraghty, SS-adap. Donn Byrne, d. Harold Schuster.
ROMANCE: MELODRAMA: Romantic Drama; Ireland; Reincarnation; Royalty; Gypsies; Forgotten Films
Winning, 1969, 123m, ★★1/2/$$, Universal/MCA-U, PG/S. A race car driver's obsessive nature mars his relationship with his wife. Paul Newman, Joanne Woodward, Richard Thomas, Robert Wagner. w. Howard Rodman, d. James Goldstone.
ACTION: DRAMA: Action Drama; Character Studies; Marriage Drama; Marriage on the Rocks; Car Racing
(Days of Thunder; Grand Prix; Le Mans)
The Winslow Boy, 1948, 117m, ★★★/$$, BL-London/Horizon Entertainment. A young recruit is expelled from the navy for a crime that he swears he didn't commit. His father spares no expense to prove his innocence. Robert Donat, Cedric Hardwicke, Margaret Leighton, Frank Lawton. w. Terrence Rattigan, Anatole de Grunwald, P-adap. Terrence Rattigan, d. Anthony Asquith.
DRAMA: Courtroom Drama; Courts Martial; Trials; Accused Unjustly; Boarding Schools; Soldiers; Young Men; Class Conflicts; British Films
(Prisoner of Honor; Missing)

Winter Kills, 1979, 97m, Avco/Col, R/V-P-S-FFN-MRN. After the president is assassinated, his brother follows the trail of clues, leading him to a shocking revelation. Jeff Bridges, John Huston, Anthony Perkins, Elizabeth Taylor, Sterling Hayden, Eli Wallach, Dorothy Malone, Toshiro Mifune. w. d. William Richert, N-adap. Richard Condon.
MYSTERY: SUSPENSE: Conspiracy; Spies; Spy Films; Presidents; Assassination Plots; Government as Enemy; Brothers; Overlooked at Release; Underrated
(The Parallax View; Three Days of the Condor; The Manchurian Candidate; The President's Analyst)
(Ed: Somewhat confusing, but stylish and worth checking out for fans of the genre)
The Winter Light, 1962, 80m, ★★★/$$, Embassy/Sultan. A priest tries to find a reason to believe what he's supposed to be preaching. Gunnar Borgstrand, Ingrid Thulin, Max Von Sydow. w. d. Ingmar Bergman.
DRAMA: Character Studies; Art Films; Priests; Religion; Ethics; Swedish Films; Hidden Gems; Forgotten Films; Writer-Directors
SEQUEL TO: The Silence and Through a Glass Darkly.
(The Seventh Seal; Wild Strawberries)
Winter People, 1988, 111m, ★★1/2/$, Lorimar/WB. Two feuding backwoods families in the 1930s are helped by a wanderer who enters their woods. Kurt Russell, Kelly McGillis, Lloyd Bridges. w. Carol Sobieski, N-adap. John Ehle, d. Ted Kotcheff.
DRAMA: MELODRAMA: Feuds; Mountain People; Depression Era; Female Protagonists; Mothers-Struggling; Drifters
(Foxfire; The Lolly Madonna War)
Winterset, 1936, 78m, ★★1/2/$$, RKO/Turner. A wanderer on the New York waterfront tracks down the men who killed his father. Burgess Meredith, Eduardo Cianneli, John Carradine. w. Anthony Veiller, P-adap. Maxwell Anderson, d. Alfred Santell. BScore, BArt. Oscars: 2-0.
DRAMA: MELODRAMA: MURDER: Drifters; Revenge; Avenging Death of Someone; Pulitzer Prize Adaptations
Wired, 1989, 109m, ★★/$, Ind/Live, R/P-S. After he dies of a drug overdose, John Belushi (or his ghost) takes us on a

tour of his frenetic life. Michael Chiklist, Patti D'Arbanville, J. T. Walsh, Ray Sharkey. w. Earl Rauch, NF-adap. Bob Woodward (*Wired: The Short Life and Fast Times of John Belushi*), d. Larry Peerce.
DRAMA: COMEDY DRAMA: TRAGEDY: Biographies; Hollywood Biographies; Hollywood Life; Actors; Comedians
Wisdom, 1987, 109m, ★/$, WB/WB, R/S-V. An ordinary not-so-bright ne'er-do-well decides to rob a bank to impress his girl-and help farmers! Emilio Estevez, Demi Moore, Tom Skerritt, Veronica Cartwright. w. d. Estevez.
MELODRAMA: Crime Drama; Bank Robberies; Thieves; Save the Farm; Farm Life; Criminal Couples; Flops-Major; Unintentionally Funny; Writer-Directors; Actor Directors
(Miles from Home; Men at Work)
(Ed: The title certainly couldn't refer to anything but the name of the character)
Wise Blood, 1979, ★★★★/$$, New World/New World, PG. A young man (Brad Dourif) proselytizing the Church Without Christ meets up with an eccentric assortment of Georgians on his mission to get the word out before he self-destructs. Ned Beatty, Amy Wright. w. Benedict Fitzgerald, N-adap. Flannery O'Connor, d. John Huston.
COMEDY: SATIRE: TRAGEDY: Black Comedy; Tragicomedy; Religion; Southerns; Preachers; Georgia; Classic Literary Adaptations; Oedipal Stories; Overlooked at Release; Hidden Gems
(A Good Man Is Hard to Find [short]; Stars and Bars)
Wise Guys, 1986, 91m, ★★★/$$, MGM/MGM-UA, R/P-V. Two petty thieves unwittingly steal Mafia money, then have to run for their lives. Danny DeVito, Joe Piscopo, Harvey Keitel, Ray Sharkey, Patti LuPone. w. George Gallo, d. Brian de Palma.
COMEDY: Black Comedy; Mob Stories; Mob Comedy; Fools-Bumbling; Comedy of Errors; Fugitives from the Mob; Chase Stories
(Broadway Danny Rose; Money for Nothing)
(Ed: Derivative, but still some entertaining moments)
Wish You Were Here, 1987, 92m, ★★★/$$, Palace/Fries, PG-13/P-S. A rebellious girl grows up in a conservative British resort town, but may be pushing

her rebellion too far. Emily Lloyd, Tom Bell, Clare Clifford. w. d. David Leland.

COMEDY: COMEDY DRAMA: Coming of Age; Teenagers; Girlhood; Female Protagonists; Small-town Life; Free Spirits; Rebels; Hairdressers; British Films; Hidden Gems; Writer-Directors **SEQUEL:** Personal Services.
(Personal Services; Georgy Girl; Muriel's Wedding)
(Ed: Breakthrough part for Lloyd)

The Witches, 1966, see **The Devil's Own**

The Witches, 1990, 91m, ★★★/$, WB/WB, G. After a witch turns him into a mouse, a young orphan boy persuades his grandmother to help him stop a convention of witches from poisoning all the children in England. Anjelica Huston, Mai Zetterling, Jasen Fisher, Rowan Atkinson, Bill Patterson. w. Allan Scott, N-adap. Roald Dahl, d. Nicolas Roeg.
Fantasy; **COMEDY DRAMA: CHILDREN'S:** Horror Comedy; Witches; Black Comedy; Humans into Animals; Grandmothers-Fascinating; Child Protagonists; Boyhood; Rodents
(Ed: Barely released because of a marketing dilemma—perhaps too strong for children, too silly for adults, yet good for intelligent children)

The Witches of Eastwick, 1987, 118m, ★★★1/2/$$$$, WB/WB, R/P-S. Three women (Cher, Susan Sarandon, Michelle Pfeiffer) wish for the perfect man when suddenly a chubby, balding, lecherous but wealthy man (Jack Nicholson) shows up who might just be the devil himself. w. Michael Cristofer, N-adap. John Updike, d. George Kennedy, George Miller. BOScore. Oscars: 1-0.

COMEDY DRAMA: Fantasy; **SCI-FI:** Romantic Comedy; Romance-Triangles; Women Fighting Over Men; Women in Conflict; Satan; Witches; Battle of the Sexes; Ensembles-Female; Curses; Female Protagonists
(I Married a Witch; Bell, Book and Candle)

The Witches of Salem, 1957, 143m, ★★★/$$, Pathé/NA. The famous tale of the 1690s Massachusetts witch trials, drawing parallels to the 50s McCarthy trials in America. Simone Signoret, Yves Montand, Mylene Demongeot, Jean Debucourt. w. Jean-Paul Sartre, P-adap. Arthur Miller, *The Crucible*, d. Raymond Rouleau.

DRAMA: TRAGEDY: Allegorical Stories; Paranoia; Accused Unjustly; Witches; Trials; 1600s; Early America
(The Crucible; Maid of Salem)

Withnail and I, 1987, 108m, ★★1/2/$, HandMade/Media, R/EP. In 60s England, two down-and-out actors squat in a run-down old country house and bicker incomprehensibly. Richard E. Grant, Paul McGann, Richard Griffiths, Ralph Brown. w. d. Bruce Robinson.

COMEDY DRAMA: Actors; City vs. Country; Depression; Friendships-Male; Men in Conflict; Art Films; British Films; Cult Films; Writer-Directors
(How to Get Ahead in Advertising)
(Ed: If you can understand a word they say, you're ahead of the game)

Without a Clue, 1988, 107m, ★★★/$$, ITC-Orion/Orion, PG. In this spoof, Dr. Watson is revealed to be the master detective who must hire a bumbling actor to portray the fictitious character he created-Sherlock Holmes. Michael Caine, Ben Kingsley, Jeffrey Jones, Lysette Anthony, Peter Cook. w. Gary Murphy, Larry Strawther, d. Thom Eberhardt.

COMEDY: MYSTERY: Comic Mystery; Spoofs-Detective; Detective Stories; Fools-Bumbling; Revisionist Films; Sherlock Holmes; British Films
(The Adventures of Sherlock Holmes' Smarter Brother; They Might Be Giants)

Without a Trace, 1983, 120m, ★★1/2/$$, 20th/CBS-Fox, PG. When her child suddenly disappears, a mother must do her own detective work to find his whereabouts. Kate Nelligan, Judd Hirsch, David Dukes, Stockard Channing, Jacqueline Brooks. w. Beth Gutcheon, N-adap. Beth Gutcheon, *Still Missing*, d. Stanley R. Jaffe.

DRAMA: MELODRAMA: Detective Stories; Detectives-Police; Detectives-Amateur; Detectives-Female; Searches; Missing Persons; Missing Children; Happy Endings; True Stories; Female Screenwriters; Female Protagonists
(Adam; Into Thin Air; Missing)

Without Love, 1945, 111m, ★★★/$$$, MGM/MGM-UA. During the war, housing in Washington is limited, so a widow must share her house with a middle-aged scientist. Spencer Tracy, Katharine Hepburn, Lucille Ball, Keenan Wynn, Carl Esmond, Patricia Morison, Felix Bressart, Gloria Grahame. w. Donald

Ogden Stewart, P-adap. Philip Barry, d. Harold S. Bucquet.

COMEDY: ROMANCE: Romantic Comedy; Comedy-Light; Roommates; Situation Comedy; Professors; Forgotten Films; Hidden Gems; Tracy & Hepburn
(The More the Merrier; Adam's Rib; Woman of the Year)

Without Reservations, 1946, 101m, ★★1/2/$$, RKO/Turner. A female screenwriter meets her ideal leading man on a train ride to Los Angeles. Claudette Colbert, John Wayne, Don Defore, Phil Brown, Frank Puglia. w. Andrew Solt, d. Mervyn Le Roy.

COMEDY: ROMANCE: Romantic Comedy; Screwball Comedy; Forgotten Films; Female Protagonists; Female Screenwriters; Actors
(It Happened One Night; The Egg and I)

Without You I'm Nothing, 1990, 89m, ★★★/$, MCEG/Live, R/P-S. Sandra Bernhard performs her one-woman show, in part a pastiche of growing up in the 50s and the roles women were expected to fill. Sandra Bernhard, John Doe, Steve Antin. w. Sandra Bernhard, John Boscovich, d. John Boscovich.

COMEDY: SATIRE: Comedians; Stage Filmings; Female Protagonists; Female Screenwriters
(The Search for Signs of Intelligent Life in the Universe; The King of Comedy)

Witness, 1985, 112m, ★★★★/$$$$, Par/Par, R/S-V. A cop (Harrison Ford, BActor) investigating a murder and the little Amish boy (Lukas Haas) who witnessed it soon realizes cops did it and takes the boy and his mother (Kelly McGillis) on the run before what they know kills them. w. Earl Wallace, Pamela Wallace, William Kelley (**BScr**), d. Peter Weir (BDirector). BPicture, **BCinema, BEditing.** BOScore, BArt. Oscars: 8-3.

SUSPENSE: ROMANCE: MURDER: Conspiracy; Fugitives; Fugitives from the Law; Fugitives from a Murderer; Opposites Attract; Stern People; Murder Witness; Fish out of Water Stories; Police Stories; Police Corruption; Children in Jeopardy; Romance-Unprofessional; Hiding Out; Corruption; Drugs-Dealing; Female Screenwriters
(The Window; Eyewitness; Three Days of the Condor; The Fugitive [1993]; The Birch Interval)

(Ed: Almost flawless, and amazingly so, considering what Hollywood could have done with it)

Witness for the Prosecution, 1957, 114m, ★★★/$$$, UA/MGM-UA. A lawyer on sabbatical takes on a murder case only to find himself implicated in a web of deceit. Charles Laughton (BActor), Tyrone Power, Marlene Deitrich, John Williams, Elsa Lanchester (BSActress). w. Billy Wilder, Harry Kurnitz, P-adap. Agatha Christie, d. Billy Wilder (BDirector). BPicture, BEdit. Oscars: 5-0.
DRAMA: Courtroom Drama; SUSPENSE: MURDER: MYSTERY: MURDER MYS-TERY: Trials; Disguises; Clever Plots & Endings; Agatha Christie
(Stage Fright; Anatomy of a Murder; The Paradine Case; Presumed Innocent)

Witness to Murder, 1954, 81m, ★★½/$$, UA/NA. A woman witnesses a murder in a neighboring house, but the police don't believe her and the killer saw her watching. Barbara Stanwyck, George Sanders, Gary Merrill. w. Chester Erskine, d. Roy Rowland.
SUSPENSE: MURDER: Witness to Murder; Witness to Murder-Child; Unbelieved; Women in Jeopardy; Voyeurs; Good Premise Unfulfilled; Coulda Been Great
(Rear Window; Somebody's Watching Me; I Saw What You Did; Woman Screaming)

Wives and Lovers, 1963, 103m, ★★½/$$, Par/Par. A writer moves his family to the country in Connecticut where Shelley Winters awaits him. Van Johnson, Janet Leigh, Shelley Winters, Ray Walston, Martha Hyer, Jeremy Slate. w. Edward Anhalt, P-adap. Jay Presson Allen (The First Wife), d. John Rich.
COMEDY: ROMANCE: Romantic Comedy; FARCE: Suburban Life; City vs. Country; Romance-Triangles; Sexy Women
(Please Don't Eat the Daisies; The Egg and I)

The Wiz, 1978, 134m, ★★★/$$, Universal/MCA-U, PG/V. A black Dorothy in New York has a funky excursion into Oz via Harlem. Diana Ross, Michael Jackson, Nipsy Russell, Ted Ross, Lena Horne, Richard Pryor, Mabel King. w. Joel Schumacher, P-adap, w. Charlie Smalls, William Brown, d. Sidney Lumet.
MUSICAL: DRAMA: Musical Drama; Surrealism; Fantasy; Revisionist Films; Black Women; Black Casts; Female Protagonists; New York Life; Poor People; Teachers; Black Screenwriters; Flops-Major
(The Wizard of Oz; Mahogany)
(Ed: A fairly big flop, though mainly due to its big budget; too dark and brooding for its own good)

The Wizard, 1989, 97m, ★★/$, Universal/MCA, PG. Two video-game-playing brothers compete in a contest to become the fictional Wizard. Fred Savage, Luke Edwards, Christian Slater, Beau Bridges. w. David Chisholm, d. Todd Holland.
CHILDREN'S: Fantasy; Contests; Games; Child Protagonists; Boyhood; Brothers; Video Game Movies
(Little Monsters; Tron; Super Mario Brothers)

The Wizard of Oz, 1925, 70m, ★★★/$$$, Larry Semon/Nos, Voyager. An orphan girl in Kansas discovers, on her 18th birthday, that she is the Queen of Oz. She decides to stay there. Larry Semon, Oliver Hardy, Dorothy Dwan, Mary Carr. w. L. Frank Baum Jr., Leon Lee Larry Semon, N-adap. L. Frank Baum, d. Larry Semon.
(Ed: Deviates just a bit from the story we all know so well below)

The Wizard of Oz, 1939, 102m, ★★★★/$$$$$, MGM/MGM-UA, G. Young Dorothy becomes the savior of the munch-kins when her Kansas farmhouse, trans-ported to Oz by a tornado, lands on the Wicked Witch of the West. Now she must find the Wizard to help her get back to Kansas. Along the way, she picks up the Scarecrow, the Lion, and the Tinman, who also have their own reasons to see the Wiz. Judy Garland, Frank Morgan, Ray Bolger, Bert Lahr, Jack Haley, Margaret Hamilton, Billie Burke. w. Noel Langley, Florence Ryerson, Edgar Allan Wolfe, N-adap. L. Frank Baum, d. Victor Fleming (King Vidor did the B&W sequences). BPicture, BOSong. BArt. Oscars: 3-1.
Fantasy; CHILDREN'S: FAMILY: SCI-FI: ADVENTURE: Dreams; Journey; Girlhood; Surrealism; Female Protagonists; Female Screenwriters; Blockbusters; Production Design-Outstanding
SEQUEL: Journey Back to Oz; SEQUEL: Return to Oz.

Wolf, 1994, 125m, ★★½/$$$, Col/Col, R/V-S-B&G. A book editor is bitten by a wolf in the wild and comes back to New York with a new-found aggressive streak-and hairy side effects. But when the animal instincts starting taking over everything, only the love of a woman may save him. Jack Nicholson, Michelle Pfeiffer, James Spader, Kate Nelligan, Christopher Plummer, Richard Jenkins, David Hyde Pierce. w. Jim Harrison, Welsey Strick, d. Mike Nichols.
SUSPENSE: HORROR: ROMANCE: SATIRE: Romantic Drama; Black Comedy; Werewolves; Humans into Animals; Monsters-Human; Power Struggles; Publishing World; Murder of Spouse; Revisionist Films
(Werewolf of London; Wolfen; The Shining)
(Ed: Though it grossed very well, it's considered widely to be a flop. The erratic tone and ending could be the reason)

Wolfen, 1981, 115m, ★★½/$$, Orion-WB/WB, R/EV. A series of grisly murders in New York turns out to be the work of invisible wolves possessed by the spirits of ancient Indians. Albert Finney, Diane Venora, Edward James Olmos, Gregory Hines. w. David Eyre, Michael Wadleigh, N-adap. Whitley Strieber, d. Michael Wadleigh.
HORROR: MURDER: Murders-One by One; Animal Monsters; Possessions; Invisibility
(Predator; Predator 2; Wolf)
(Ed: Preposterous but quite a few scary moments)

The Wolfman, 1940, 70m, ★★★/$$$, Universal/MCA-U. A man, bitten by a werewolf, becomes one himself, grows hair, etc. Lon Chaney Jr., Claude Rains, Warren William, Ralph Bellamy, Bela Lugosi, Maria Ouspenskaya. w. Curt Siodmak, d. George Waggner.
HORROR: Humans into Animals; Human Monsters; Werewolves
(Werewolf of London; Wolf)

The Wolves of Willoughby Chase, 1988, 93m, ★★½/$, Ind/NA. An evil governess who's attempting to steal her employer's fortune is thwarted by the two girls in her care. Stephanie Beacham, Mel Smith, Geraldine James. w. William Akers, N-adap. Joan Aiken, d. Stuart Orme.
DRAMA: SUSPENSE: CHILDREN'S: FAMILY: Evil Women; Child Protagonists; Baby-sitters; Baby-sitters-Evil; Thieves; Inheritances at Stake; British Films
(Ladies in Retirement; The Nightcomers)

The Woman I Love, 1937, 85m, ★★¹/₂/ $$, RKO/Turner. A French pilot in World War I has a small problem: he's in love with the squadron commander's wife. Paul Muni, Miriam Hopkins, Louis Hayward, Colin Clive, Minor Watson. w. Mary Borden, N-adap. Joseph Kessel, *L'Equipage*, d. Anatole Litvak.

ROMANCE: MELODRAMA: Romance-Triangles; Cheating Women

Woman in the Dunes, 1964, 127m, ★★★¹/₂/$$, Teshigahara/Nos, Vidmark. An Japanese entomologist on a bug-gathering vacation discovers a community of people who live in caves under the sand when his supposed night's lodgings become more "permanent." Eiji Okada, Kyoko Kishoda. w. Kobo Abe, d. Hiroshi Teshigahara (BDirector). BFLFilm. Oscars: 2-0.

DRAMA: ADVENTURE: Psychological Drama; Art Films; Surrealism; Stranded; Kidnapped; Desert Setting; Trapped in a Hole; Japanese Films; Scientists (Zabriskie Point)

A Woman in Flames, 1984, 106m, ★★★/$, Ind/German Language Video. A housewife leaves home to become a hooker and finds a male hooker with bisexual tastes instead. Gudrun Langrebe, Robert Van Ackeren. d. Robert Van Ackeren.

DRAMA: ROMANCE: Character Studies; Prostitutes-Ordinary People Turned; Bisexuality; Prostitutes-Male; Alternative Lifestyles; Quiet Little Films; German Films

(A Man Like Eva; Veronika Voss)

The Woman in Red, 1984, 86m, ★★¹/₂/$$$, Orion/Orion, PG-13/P-S. The title character gets a married man hot under the collar, exacerbating his midlife crisis. Gene Wilder, Charles Grodin, Joseph Bologna, Gilda Radner, Kelly LeBrock. w. d. Gene Wilder, S-adap. Jean-Loup Dabadie, Yves Robert, *Un Eléphant Ça Trompe Enormément.* **BOSong**, "I Just Called to Say I Love You." Oscars: 1-1.

COMEDY: ROMANCE: Romantic Comedy; Elusive Women; Romance-Boy Wants Girl; Sexy Women; Nerds; Nerds & Babes; Midlife Crisis; Cheating Men; Marriage on the Rocks; Foreign Film Remakes

(10; The Man Who Loved Women; Funny About Love)

The Woman in the Window, 1944, 95m, ★★★¹/₂/$$, U-I/NA. A reticent, middle-aged professor meets a young woman who gets him involved in a mur-

der. Edward G. Robinson, Joan Bennett, Raymond Massey, Dan Duryea. w. Nunnally Johnson, N-adap. J. H. Wallis, *Once Off Guard*, d. Fritz Lang.

SUSPENSE: MYSTERY: MURDER: MURDER MYSTERY: Innocent Bystanders; Film Noir; Professors; Romance-Older Men/Younger Women; Dangerous Women; Infatuations; Dreams; Ordinary People Turned Criminal; Forgotten Films; Hidden Gems

The Woman in White, 1948, 109m, ★★¹/₂/$$, WB/NA. A wandering tutor comes to live in a strange household where he'd be able to teach if it weren't for the odd occupants and their mysterious, perhaps dangerous ways. Gig Young, Eleanor Parker, Sidney Greenstreet, Alexis Smith, Agnes Moorehead, John Abbott. w. Stephen Morehouse Avery, N-adap. Wilkie Collins, d. Peter Godfrey.

SUSPENSE: MYSTERY: Teachers; Eccentric People; 1870s; Victorian Era; Coulda Been Great

See also **Lady in White**.

A Woman Is a Woman, 1961, 85m, ★★★/$$, Ind/Interama. A stripper wants to have a baby. Her boyfriend isn't too keen on the idea. Jean-Paul Belmondo, Jean-Claude Brialy, Anna Karina, Jeanne Moreau. w. d. Jean-Luc Goddard.

DRAMA: COMEDY DRAMA: MUSICALS: Music Movies; Babies-Having; Abortion Dilemmas; Mothers-Unwed; Strippers; Dancers; Female Protagonists; Writer-Directors

(Breathless [1959])

(Ed: Not a Hollywood musical, but more of an homage to one)

The Woman Next Door, 1981, 106m, ★★★/$$, UAC/MGM-UA, R/S. A middle-aged man has his old paramour move next door. Their romance re-ignites, exploding their comfortable suburban lives. Gérard Depardieu, Fanny Ardant, Henri Garcin, Michele Baumgarner. w. François Truffaut, Suzanne Schiffman, Jean Aurel, d. François Truffaut.

DRAMA: ROMANCE: Romantic Drama; **TRAGEDY:** Neighbors; Romance-Reunited; Cheating Women; Cheating Men; Romance with Married Person; Romance-Middle Aged; Midlife Crisis; Female Screenwriters

(Confidentially Yours; Love on the Run)

Woman Obsessed, 1959, 102m, ★★/ $$, 20th/NA. A mountain woman in the Canadian Rockies remarries. Her son

proves a tough customer for her new husband. Susan Hayward, Stephen Boyd, Dennis Holmes, Theodore Bikel, Arthur Franz. w. Sidney Boehm, N-adap. John Mantley, d. Henry Hathaway.

DRAMA: WESTERNS: Marrying Again; Stepparents vs. Children; Obsessions; Mothers-Struggling; Female Protagonists (Firstborn)

A Woman of Paris, 1923, 85m (Silent), ★★★/$$$$, Chaplin-UA/Fox. A simple country girl gets corrupted by the big city. Edna Purviance, Adolphe Menjou, Carl Miller, Lydia Knott. w. d. Charles Chaplin.

COMEDY: MELODRAMA: City vs. Country; Coming of Age; Female Protagonists; Writer-Directors; Film History

Woman of the Year, 1942, 114m, ★★★★/$$$$, MGM/MGM-UA. A political writer (Katharine Hepburn, BActress) and a sports writer (Spencer Tracy) butt heads and share beds in this battle of the sexes that started their off-screen union. The only thing they can agree on is that they're in love. Fay Bainter, Reginald Owen, William Bendix. w. Ring Lardner Jr., Michael Kanin (**BOScr**), d. George Stevens. Oscars: 2-1.

COMEDY: ROMANCE: Romantic Comedy; Romance-Bickering; Romance-Opposites Attract; Politicians; Writers; Journalists; Macho Men; Feisty Females; Battle of the Sexes; Female Protagonists; Tracy & Hepburn

REMAKE: Musical on Broadway, 1981. (Pat and Mike; Adam's Rib; Desk Set; Without Love)

(Ed: A must-see; not as frenetic as some other screwball or sex comedies, but well worth it)

The Woman on the Beach, 1947, 71m, ★★¹/₂/$, RKO/Turner. A man who's suffering from mental problems meets a dangerous woman on the beach with an even more dangerous husband. Robert Ryan, Joan Bennett, Charles Bickford, Walter Sande, Irene Ryan. w. Frank Davis, Jean Renoir, N-adap. Mitchell Wilson, *None So Blind*, d. Renoir.

SUSPENSE: DRAMA: ROMANCE: Love-Dangerous; Romance-Triangles; Film Noir; Dangerous Women; Dangerous Men; Abused Women; Mental Illness; Beach Movies

(Autumn Leaves; Beware, My Lovely)

A Woman Rebels, 1936, 88m, ★★★/ $$, RKO/Turner. A Victorian suffragette fights back when she's victimized by society for having a child out of wedlock. Katharine Hepburn, Herbert Marshall, Elizabeth Allan, Donald Crisp, Lucile Watson. w. Anthony Veiller, Ernest Vajda, N-adap. Netta Syrett, *Portrait of a Rebel*, d. Mark Sandrich.

DRAMA: Biographies-Fictional; Rebels; Womens' Rights; Feisty Females; Mothers-Unwed; Babies-Having; Female Protagonists; Scandals; Ahead of Its Time; Hidden Gems

(Christopher Strong; The Scarlet Letter; Bad Girl)

Woman Screaming, 1971, 80m, ★★★/ ###, ABC/NA. When a wealthy and lonely elderly woman goes strolling on her estate near a new subdivision, she thinks she hears a woman screaming under the ground. But when she goes to get neighbors to help dig, she may just knock on the wrong door. Olivia DeHavilland. w. d. John Llewellyn Moxey.

SUSPENSE: Women in Jeopardy; Unbelieved; Elderly Women; Buried Alive; Murder of Spouse; TV Movies; Hidden Gems

Woman Times Seven, 1967, 99m, ★★¹/₂/$$, Col/Col. Seven separate vignettes, each illustrating a "truism" about women, circa 1967. Shirley MacLaine, Peter Sellers, Rosanno Brazzi, Vittorio Gassman, Lex Barker, Elsa Martinelli, Robert Morley, Adrienne Corri, Patrick Wymark, Alan Arkin, Michael Caine, Anita Eckberg, Philippe Noiret. w. Cesare Zavattini, d. Vittorio de Sica.

DRAMA: COMEDY DRAMA: Multiple Stories; Multiple Performances; Marriage Comedy; Feisty Females; Neurotic People; Eccentric People; Fantasies; Flashbacks; Women's Films; Female Protagonists

(What a Way to Go!; The Women)

Woman to Woman, 1923, 83m, ★★¹/₂/$$$, Ind/Nos, NA. A soldier recovering from the Great War marries into high society, but then his illegitimate son with a ballerina catches up with him and his new wife. w. Alfred Hitchcock, P-adap. Michael Morton, d. Graham Cutts.

MELODRAMA: DRAMA: Tearjerkers; Romance-Triangles; Marrying Up; Secrets-Haunted by; Children-Long-lost

A Woman Under the Influence, 1974, 155m, ★★★¹/₂/$$$, Faces/Touchstone, R/S-P. A housewife in 1970s Los Angeles feels alienated from herself, her husband, and her children. Her despair leads to

drinking and a breakdown. Gena Rowlands (BActress), Peter Falk, Matthew Cassel, Katherine Cassavetes. w. d. John Cassavetes (BDirector). Oscars: 2-0.

DRAMA: Character Studies; **TRAGEDY:** Alcoholics; Depression; Female Protagonists; Marriage on the Rocks; Writer-Directors; Hidden Gems; Quiet Little Films; Art Films; Cult Films

(Another Woman; Gloria; Opening Night; Minnie and Moskowitz; Dangerous; The Morning After; Leaving Las Vegas)

A Woman's Face, 1941, 105m, ★★★/ $$$, MGM/MGM-UA. A disfigured woman turns to a life of crime in this courtroom drama. Joan Crawford, Melvyn Douglas, Conrad Veidt, Osa Massen. w. Donald Ogden Stewart, P-adap. François de Croisset, *Il Etait une Fois*, d. George Cukor.

DRAMA: MELODRAMA: Crime Drama; Courtroom Drama; Trials; Criminals-Female; Ordinary People Turned Criminal; Disabled People; Accidents; Cosmetic Surgery; Sweden; Female Protagonists

(The Last of Mrs. Cheyney; Mildred Pierce)

A Woman's Tale, 1992, 94m, ★★★¹/₂/ $, Orion/Orion, PG. The story of a colorful elderly woman's life as she and her son bide time until her death. Sheilah Florence, Norman Kaye. w. d. Paul Cox.

DRAMA: Character Studies; Elderly Women; Death-Impending; Lonely People; Quiet Little Films; Australian Films; Hidden Gems; Underrated

(The Trip to Bountiful; The Shell Seekers; Rachel, Rachel; Strangers in Good Company; Travelling North)

(Ed: A great little film that has been overlooked in this age of action and hype)

A Woman's World, 1954, 94m, ★★★/ $$$, 20th/CBS-Fox. The wives are herded along as three salesmen go to New York to compete for the job of general manager of a large car manufacturer. Clifton Webb, Lauren Bacall, Van Heflin, June Allyson, Fred MacMurray, Arlene Dahl, Cornel Wilde. w. Claude Binyon, Mary Loos, Richard Sale, d. Jean Negulesco.

MELODRAMA: Business Life; Marriage Drama; Executives; Married Couples; Contests/Competitions; Woman Behind the Man; Ensemble Films; Car Racing; Female Screenwriters; Female Protagonists

(How to Marry a Millionaire)

The Women, 1939, 132m, ★★★★/$$$$, MGM/MGM-UA. An all-woman gossiping cast is either losing a cheating husband or is the one he's cheating with. Norma Shearer, Joan Crawford, Rosalind Russell, Joan Fontaine, Paulette Goddard, Mary Boland, Ruth Hussey. w. Anita Loos, Jane Murfin, P-adap. Lillian Hellman, d. George Cukor.

COMEDY: FARCE: Interwoven Stories; Multiple Stories; Cheating Men; Cheated Upon; Meet; Divorce; Starting Over; Women's Films; Women in Conflict; Women Fighting Over Men; Jealousy; Rumors; Friendships-Female; Ensemble Films; Ensembles-Female; Female Screenwriters; Female Protagonists

REMAKE: The Opposite Sex

(The Opposite Sex [1956]; His Girl Friday; Alice; Steel Magnolias)

Women in Love, 1970, 129m, ★★★¹/₂/ $$$, UA/Key, R/S-FFN-MFN. Two lovers die and two other relationships continue over the years in 1920s England. Glenda Jackson (**BActress**), Oliver Reed, Alan Bates, Eleanor Bron. w. Larry Kramer (BAScr), N-adap. D. H. Lawrence, d. Ken Russell (BDirector). BCin. Oscars: 4-1.

DRAMA: ROMANCE: Erotic Drama; Romantic Drama; Character Studies; Romance-Triangles; Friendships-Female; Coming of Age; Feisty Females; Sexuality; Men in Conflict; Ahead of Its Time; Female Protagonists

PREQUEL: The Rainbow.

(Priest of Love; Lady Chatterley's Lover; The Boy Friend)

(Ed: Shocking in its day and still a bit; still only for fans of British detail and manners)

Women on the Verge of a Nervous Breakdown, 1988, 88m, ★★★¹/₂/$$$$, Orion/Orion, R/S. The manic lives of several neurotic, hip Spanish women are detailed up to the point another woman who has a gun enters. Antonio Banderas, Carmen Maura, Julieta Serrano. w. d. Pedro Almodovar. BFLFilm. Oscars: 1-0.

COMEDY: Black Comedy; **SATIRE:** Tragicomedy; Neurotic People; Nervous Breakdowns; Actresses; Suicidal Tendencies; Female Protagonists; Women's Films; Spanish; Writer-Directors

(Crimes of the Heart; Kika; Tie Me Up! Tie Me Down!)

Wonder Bar, 1934, 84m, ★★¹/₂/$$, WB/WB. All the fireworks at a 30s Parisian nightclub aren't happening

onstage. Al Jolson, Kay Francis, Dolores del Rio, Ricardo Cortez, Dick Powell, Hugh Herbert. w. Earl Baldwin, P-adap. Geza Herczeg, Karl Farkas, Robert Katscher, d. Lloyd Bacon.
MUSICAL: Musical Drama; **DRAMA: MELODRAMA: ROMANCE:** Theater Life; Singers; Dancers; Paris; Behind the Scenes

Wonder Man, 1945, 97m, ★★★/$$$, Samuel Goldwyn-UA/HBO. A nerdy college student whose twin brother was killed by mobsters gets embroiled when his brother comes back from the dead to persuade him to avenge his murder. Danny Kaye, Vera-Ellen, Virginia Mayo, Steve Cochran, Natalie Schaefer. w. Don Hartman, Melville Shavelson, Philip Rapp, SS-adap. Arthur Sheekman, d. Bruce Humberstone. **BSFX,** BSound, BOScore, BOSong. Oscars: 4-1.
COMEDY: COMEDY DRAMA: Chase Stories; Mob Stories; Mob Comedy; Fugitives from the Mob; Revenge; Brothers; Twins; Multiple Performances
(Topper SERIES; Beetlejuice; The Secret Life of Walter Mitty)

The Wonderful World of the Brothers Grimm, 1962, 134m, ★★★/$$$, MGM/MGM-UA. The lives of the German storytellers are recounted, along with three of their famous stories. Laurence Harvey, Karl Boehm, Claire Bloom, Barbara Eden, Walter Slezak, Oscar Homolka, Martita Hunt, Russ Tamblyn, Yvette Mimieux, Jim Backus, Beulah Bondi, Buddy Hackett, Otto Kruger. w. David P. Harmon, Charles Beaumont, William Roberts, d. Henry Levin, George Pal. BCCin, BOScore. Oscars: 2-0.
MELODRAMA: COMEDY DRAMA: CHILDREN'S: FAMILY: Fairy Tales; Biographies; Multiple Stories; Dragons; Invisibility; Writers; Brothers; Germany

Won Ton Ton, the Dog Who Saved Hollywood, 1976, 92m, ★★/$, Par/Par, G. A dog becomes a film star in 20s Hollywood, then falls from fortune when his former owner arrives. Madeline Kahn, Art Carney, Bruce Dern, Ron Leibman. w. Arnold Schulman, Cy Howard, d. Michael Winner.
COMEDY: COMEDY DRAMA: FARCE: Chase Movies; Dogs; Pet Stories; Animals in Jeopardy; Hollywood Life; Silent Film Era; All-Star Casts; All-Star Cameos; Flops-Major

(Under the Rainbow; Nickelodeon)
(Ed: Cameos from every star from the old days still alive at the time)
The Wooden Horse, 1950, 101m, ★★¹/2/$$, British Lion/NA. British soldiers in World War II escape from a German prison by tunneling under a big horse. Leo Genn, David Tomlinson, Anthony Steele, David Greene, Michael Goodliffe. w. Eric Williams, N-adap. Eric Williams, d. Jack Lee.
DRAMA: War Movies; Escape Drama; World War II Movies; Germans as Enemy; POWs; British Films; Soldiers; Germany; Horses
(The Great Escape; Von Ryan's Express)
Woodstock, 1969, 120m, ★★★/$$$, WB/WB, R/P-S-FN-MN. Concert film of the legendary psychedelic and sexual revolution extravaganza.
BDocumentary Feature, BSound, BEditing. Oscars: 3-1.
Concert Films; Documentaries; Psychedelic Era; Hippies; Rock Stars; 1960s; Anti-Establishment Films; Cult Films
(Medium Cool; Alice's Restaurant)
The Woo Woo Kid, see **In the Mood**
Words and Music, 1948, 121m, ★★¹/2/$$$, MGM/MGM-UA. The lives and musical collaboration of Richard Rodgers and Lorenz Hart. Tom Drake, Mickey Rooney, Perry Como, Mel Tormé, June Allyson, Lena Horne, Ann Sothern, Gene Kelly, Vera-Ellen, Cyd Charisse, Janet Leigh. w. Fred Finklehoffe, d. Norman Taurog.
MUSICAL: Musical Drama; Biographies; True Stories; Writers; Music Composers; Musicians; Theater Life; All-Star Casts; Famous People When Young
(Night and Day; Three Little Words; Rhapsody in Blue)
Working Girl, 1988, 113m, ★★★¹/2/$$$$, 20th/Fox, R/P-S-FFN. A modern-day, female Horatio Alger pulls herself straight up the corporate ladder, from secretary to CEO, with sheer ingenuity, foiling her bitchy female boss in business *and* romance. Melanie Griffith (BActress), Harrison Ford, Sigourney Weaver (BSActress), Alec Baldwin, Joan Cusack (BSActress), Philip Bosco, Nora Dunn, Olympia Dukakis. w. Kevin Wade, d. Mike Nichols (BDirector). BPicture, **BOSong.** Oscars: 5-1.
COMEDY: COMEDY DRAMA: ROMANCE: Romantic Comedy; Romance-Triangles; Spies; Business Life; Executives; Secretaries; Women in

Conflict; Evil Women; Class Conflicts; Power-Rise to; Wall Street; Women-Working; Women Proving Themselves; Female Protagonists
(Solid Gold Cadillac; Bells Are Ringing; Milk Money)
Working Girls, 1986, 90m, ★★★/$$, New Line/Col, R/ES-EP-FFN. A prostitute wants out of her New York brothel in order to change her life but wonders if she can. Louise Smith, Ellen McElduff, Amanda Goodwin. w. Lizzie Borden, Sandra Kay, d. Lizzie Borden.
DRAMA: Character Studies; Documentary Style; Prostitutes-Low Class; Prostitutes-High Class; Prostitutes-Ordinary People Turned; New York Life; Poor People; Abused Women; Female Protagonists; Female Screenwriters; Female Directors
(Not a Love Story; Whore; Love Crimes)
The World According to Garp, 1982, 136m, ★★★¹/2/$$$, WB/WB, R/P-S-FFN-MRN. A young man with a very eccentric mother grows up wanting to become a writer, and with his mother's friends and his own sex life he has plenty of material. Robin Williams, Mary Beth Hurt, Glenn Close (BSActress), John Lithgow (BSActor), Hume Cronyn, Jessica Tandy, Swoosie Kurtz. w. Steve Tesich, N-adap. John Irving, d. George Roy Hill. Oscars: 2–0.

COMEDY: COMEDY DRAMA: TRAGEDY: Tragicomedy; Black Comedy; Eccentric People; Free Spirits; Writers; Nurses; Marriage on the Rocks; Mothers & Sons; Mothers-Unwed; Accidents; Transvestites; Transsexuals; Women's Rights; Rebels; Cult Films; Underrated
(The Hotel New Hampshire)
(Ed: Although it may not follow the enormous bestseller to the letter, it creates a world of its own you can't forget and wish for more of-unless you just don't get it)
A World Apart, 1987, 110m, ★★★/$$, Atlantic/Atlantic-Par, PG/V. In the 60s in South Africa, a 13-year-old girl grows up against the backdrop of apartheid, which invades her life when her mother is imprisoned for her pro-ANC activities. Barbara Hershey (BActress, Cannes), Johdi May, Jeroen Krabbé, Linda Mvusi, David Suchet. w. Shawn Slovo, d. Chris Menges.
DRAMA: Political Drama; Social Drama; Autobiographical Stories; True Stories; Character Studies; Girlhood; Coming of Age; Rebels; Mothers-Troublesome;

Mothers-Struggling; South Africa; Apartheid; Race Relations; Black vs. White; Female Protagonists
(Sarafina!; Bopha!; Cry Freedom)

The World Is Full of Married Men, 1979, 106m, ★★/$, 20th/Fox, R/S-FN. The wife of a philandering executive decides to engage in some escapades herself for the sake of revenge. Carroll Baker, Anthony Franciosa, Sherrie Cronn, Gareth Hunt, Anthony Steel. w. Jackie Collins, N-adap. Jackie Collins, d. Robert Young.

MELODRAMA: Erotic Drama; ROMANCE: Romance with Married Person; Revenge; Revenge on Cheaters; Cheating Women; Cheating Men; Promiscuity; Sexuality; Midlife Crisis; Female Protagonists; Female Screenwriters
(The Secret Life of an American Wife; The Bitch; The Stud)

The World of Apu, 1959, 106m, ★★★1/2/$, Satyajit Ray Prods. A poor young writer's wife dies, after which he rejects his son because of the painful memories he conjures up. Soumitra Chatterjee, Sarmila Tagore, Alok Chakravarti, Swapan Mukherjee. w. d. Satyajit Ray.

DRAMA: TRAGEDY: Death-Dealing with; Widowers; Writers; Fathers & Sons; Indian People; Indian Films; Writer-Directors; Art Films; Cult Films
(Distant Thunder; An Enemy of the People [1977])

The World of Henry Orient, 1964, 106m, ★★★/$, UA/MGM-UA. Two upper-class girls from New York fantasize about the supposedly mysterious life of an eccentric concert pianist. Tippy Walker, Meri Spaeth, Peter Sellers, Angela Lansbury, Paula Prentiss, Tom Bosley. w. Nora and Nunnally Johnson, N-adap. Nora Johnson, d. George Roy Hill.

COMEDY DRAMA: COMEDY: Fantasy; Fantasies; Musicians; Infatuations; Stalkers; Girls; Fans-Crazed; Teenagers; Forgotten Films; Hidden Gems; Cult Films; Female Screenwriters; Female Protagonists
(No Small Affair; The Bobo)

The World of Suzie Wong, 1960, 129m, ★★★/$$$$, Par/Par. A sweet but tenacious prostitute in Hong Kong comes onto a painter from America but their love is fleeting. William Holden, Nancy

Kwan, Sylvia Syms, Michael Wilding, Jackie Chan. w. John Patrick, P-adap. Paul Osborn, d. Richard Quine.

MELODRAMA: DRAMA: ROMANCE: Romantic Drama; Romance-Doomed; Romance-Opposites Attract; Romance-Reluctant; Painters; Prostitutes; Romance-Interracial; Romance with a Prostitute; Americans Abroad; Floods; Hong Kong; Asia
(Love Is a Many-Splendored Thing; A Girl Named Tamiko; Flower Drum Song; Sayonara)
(Ed: Not all there, but a big hit that year. Shades of *Love Is a Many . . .* but too dark to compete)

The World's Greatest Athlete, 1973, 92m, ★★/$$$, Disney/Disney, G. A high school gym teacher on a trip to Africa finds a young white boy raised by cheetahs who can run 100 mph and who looks just like a surfer dude. Tim Conway, Jan-Michael Vincent, John Amos, Roscoe Lee Browne. w. Gerald Gardiner, Dee Caruso, d. Robert Sheerer.

CHILDREN'S: FAMILY: COMEDY: ADVENTURE: Fantasy; Running; Africa; Raised by Animals; Fish out of Water Stories
(Tarzan SERIES; Gus)
(Ed: Dumb, but may have led to other, more believable fish out of water tales)

The World's Greatest Lover, 1977, 89m, ★★1/2/$$, 20th/CBS-Fox, PG. In the 20s, in order to compete with Valentino's films, a rival studio searches for their *own* Valentino and winds up with something less than what they had in mind. Gene Wilder, Carol Kane, Dom DeLuise, Fritz Feld. w. d. Gene Wilder.

COMEDY: Spoofs; Hollywood Life; Silent Film Era; Searches; Actors; Sexy Men; Fools-Bumbling
(Valentino; Inserts; Hollywood Babylon)

The Wrath of God, 1972, 111m, ★1/2/$, MGM/NA. In a banana republic in the twenties, a defrocked priest and a bootlegger join together to fight in the revolution. Robert Mitchum, Frank Langella, Rita Hayworth, Victor Buono. w. d. Ralph Nelson, N-adap. James Graham.

DRAMA: Political Unrest; Central America; Latin People; 1920s

The Wreck of the Mary Deare, 1959, 108m, ★★1/2/$$, MGM/MGM-UA. When a salvage boat is discovered adrift at sea, an insurance scam is slowly unraveled in

what becomes a courtroom drama. Charlton Heston, Gary Cooper, Michael Redgrave, Emlyn Williams, Virginia McKenna, Richard Harris. w. Eric Ambler, N-adap. Hammond Innes, d. Michael Anderson.

DRAMA: Rescue Drama; Conspiracy; Shipwrecked; Courtroom Drama; Con Artists; Insurance Scams; Death-Faked

The Wrecking Crew, 1968, 104m, ★★1/2/$$$, Col/RCA-Col. Matt Helm, a close cousin to James Bond, goes after some stolen gold-in between liaisons. Dean Martin, Elke Sommer, Sharon Tate, Nancy Kwan, Nigel Green, Tina Louise. w. William McGivern, N-adap. Donald Hamilton, d. Phil Karlson.

ACTION: COMEDY: Action Comedy; Spoofs; Spoofs-Spy; Spy Films; Spies; Heist Stories; Playboys; Camp; Faded Hits
SEQUEL TO: The Ambushers, Murderer's Row.

Written on the Wind, 1956, 99m, ★★★/$$$, U-I/MCA-U. An oil tycoon with what would now be described as a "dysfunctional family" marries his secretary, who becomes the calm at the center of the family's storms. Rock Hudson, Lauren Bacall, Robert Stack (BSActor), Dorothy Malone (**BSActress**), Robert Keith, Grant Williams. w. George Zuckerman, N-adap. Robert Wilder, d. Douglas Sirk. BOSong. Oscars: 3-1.

MELODRAMA: DRAMA: ROMANCE: Family Drama; Oil People; Rich People; Secretaries; Marrying Up
(Giant; Wild Is the Wind; The Carpetbaggers)

The Wrong Arm of the Law, 1962, 94m, ★★★/$$, Romulus-UA/Monarch. British mobsters decide to get revenge on some Australians and involve Scotland Yard in their convoluted plot. Peter Sellers, Lionel Jeffries, Bernard Cribbins, Nanette Newman. w. Ray Galton, Alan Simpson, John Antrobus, S-adap. Len Neath, John Warren, d. Cliff Owen.

COMEDY: FARCE: Criminals-Stupid; Australian People
(The Lavender Hill Mob; The Italian Job)

The Wrong Box, 1966, 110m, ★★★/$, Col/Col. Two brothers with a keen sense of rivalry are the last remaining competitors in an involved game in Victorian England, which if completed will leave one dead for the other to collect an inheritance. Ralph

Richardson, John Mills, Michael Caine, Wilfrid Lawson, Nanette Newman, Peter Cook, Dudley Moore, Peter Sellers. w. Larry Gelbart, Burt Shevelove, N-adap. Robert Louis Stevenson, Lloyd Osbourne, d. Bryan Forbes.

COMEDY: Black Comedy; **FARCE:** Comedy-Morbid; Brothers; Inheritances at Stake; Men in Conflict; Feuds; Lotteries; Games; Double Crossings; Elderly Men; All-Star Casts
(Sleuth)

Wrong Is Right, 1982, 117m, ★★½/$, Col/RCA-Col, R/P-S-V. A television anchorman discovers that the CIA is behind every evil on earth. Sean Connery, George Grizzard, Katharine Ross, Robert Conrad, Leslie Nielsen, Rosalind Cash, Dean Stockwell, Ron Moody. w. d. Richard Brooks., N-adap. Charles McCarry, *The Deadly Angels.*

SATIRE: Black Comedy; Political Satire; Political Drama; SUSPENSE: Conspiracy; Spies; CIA Agents; Americans Abroad; Journalists; TV Life

The Wrong Man, 1957, 105m, ★★★/$, WB/WB. The police and several witnesses suspect a musician in New York of being an armed robber through overwhelming circumstantial evidence. He must fight to prove his innocence and find the real culprit. Henry Fonda, Vera Miles, Anthony Quayle, Harold J. Stone, Esther Minciotti. w. Maxwell Anderson, Angus MacPhail, d. Alfred Hitchcock.

DRAMA: MYSTERY: True Stories; Docudrama; Saving Oneself; Thieves; Accused Unjustly; Innocent Bystanders; Musicians; Hitchcockian

(An Innocent Man; The Fugitive)
(Ed: Might be just a routine TV docudrama today if it weren't for the Hitch touch)

Wuthering Heights, 1939, 104m, ★★★½/$$$$, Goldwyn-UA/Goldwyn. Laurence Olivier, Merle Oberon, David Niven, Hugh Williams, Flora Robson, Geraldine Fitzgerald, Miles Mander. w. Ben Hecht, Charles MacArthur, N-adap. Emily Brontë, d. William Wyler.

Wuthering Heights, 1953, 90m, ★★½/$, Ind/Media. A loose Spanish arty adaptation. Irasema Dillian, Jorge Mistral. d. Luis Bunuel.
Art Films; Forgotten Films

Wuthering Heights, 1970, 105m, ★★½/$, AIP/Vestron, Karol Video, Par. A remake of the above, with an attempt at a more contemporary feel. Anna Calder-Marshall, Timothy Dalton, Harry Andrews, Pamela Brown, Judy Cornwell. w. Patrick Tilley, N-adap. Emily Brontë, d. Robert Fuest.

Wuthering Heights, 1992, 106m, ★★½/$ (LR), Par/Par. Yet another remake, this time with more emphasis on Heathcliff's humiliation and revenge. Juliette Binoche, Ralph Fiennes, Janet McTeer, Sophie Ward. w. Anne Devlin, N-adap. Emily Brontë, d. Peter Kosminsky. >The daughter of a landowner in the English moors falls passionately in love with the tempestuous gypsy her father brought home from London when she was a girl.

MELODRAMA: ROMANCE: DRAMA: Female Screenwriters; Romantic Drama; Love-First; Infatuations; Romance-

Reluctant; Romance-Doomed; Sexy Men; Gypsies; Orphans; England; Class Conflicts; Classic Literary Adaptations; Female Protagonists
(Jane Eyre; Sense and Sensibility; Pride and Prejudice)
(Ed: The best is still, of course, the first)

Wyatt Earp, 1994, 189m, ★★/$, WB/WB, PG-13/V. Biographical tale of the famous Wild West law enforcer and his pals, such as Doc Holliday, leading right through to his death. Kevin Costner, Dennis Quaid, Gene Hackman, Jeff Fahey, Mark Harmon, Michael Madsen, Mare Winningham, Betty Buckley, Isabella Rossellini, Bill Pullman, JoBeth Williams, Annabeth Gish. w. Dan Gordon, Lawrence Kasdan, d. Kasdan.

DRAMA: WESTERNS: Westerns-Neo; Westerns-Revisionist; Biographies; Police Stories; Marshals; Duels; Gunfighters; Episodic Stories; Flops-Major; Wyatt Earp
(Tombstone; Gunfight at the O.K. Corral)
(Ed: Bo-ring . . .)

Wyoming, 1940, 88m, ★★★/$$, MGM/NA. A rough-riding, straight-shooting cowboy is persuaded to reform his ways and settle down in . . . Wyoming. Wallace Beery, Marjorie Main, Leo Carrillo, Ann Rutherford, Joseph Calleia, Lee Bowman, Henry Travers. w. Jack Jevne, Hugo Butler, d. Richard Thorpe.

WESTERNS: Cowboys; Settling Down; ROMANCE: Romance-Bickering; Hidden Gems
(Min and Bill; Tugboat Annie)
(Ed: Worth watching even for non-western fans because of the actors)

X—The Man with X-Ray Eyes, 1963, 80m, ★★¹/₂/$, AIP/WB. A mad scientist invents X-ray vision for himself and becomes even madder. Ray Milland, Don Rickles. w. Robert Dillon, Ray Russell, d. Roger Corman.
HORROR: SCI-FI: Scientists-Mad; Inventors; Camp

X, Y, & Zee, 1971, 109m, ★★/$, Col/Goodtimes, R/EP. A British architect has an affair, driven away by his histrionic wife, Zee, who doesn't intend to let him or the other woman off the hook. Elizabeth Taylor, Michael Caine, Susannah York, Margaret Leighton, John Standing. w. Edna O'Brien, d. Brian Hutton.
DRAMA: Psychological Drama;
MELODRAMA: Marriage Drama; Cheating Men; Neurotic People; Evil Women; Romance-Triangles; Ménage à Trois; Revenge; Revenge on Cheaters; Female Protagonists; Female Screenwriters
(Sunday, Bloody Sunday; Hammersmith Is Out)

Xanadu, 1980, 93m, ★¹/₂/$$$, U/MCA-U, PG. A singing, roller-skating muse comes to help out a musician and roller-disco owner. Olivia Newton-John, Gene Kelly, Michael Beck. w. Richard Daus, Marc Rubel, d. Robert Greenwald.
MUSICAL: Musicals-Disco Era; Roller Skating; Fantasy; Angels; Musicians; Disco Era; Old-Fashioned Recent Films; Camp; Cult Films; Unintentionally Funny (Grease; Rollerboogie)
(Ed: Made some money and the sound-track was huge . . . but the movie itself was into the abyss and deeply so)

Xtro, 1982, 86m, ★★/$, New Line/New Line, R/B&G-V. An outer space visitor rapes a woman who then gives birth to a child/man who looks just like a man abducted by a UFO a few years before. Bernice Stegers, Philip Sayers, Maryam D'Abo. w. Ian Cassie, Robert Smith, Joann Kaplan, Michael Parry, Harry Davenport, d. Davenport.
HORROR: Aliens-Outer Space; Evil; Rape/Rapists; Lookalikes; Babies-Having; Camp; Unintentionally Funny

Y

The Yakuza, 1975, 112m, ★★¹/₂/$, WB/WB, R/P-V. The Japanese mob kidnaps the daughter of an American millionaire and Americans must infiltrate the mob to find her. Robert Mitchum, Brian Keith, Takakura Ken. w. Paul Schrader, Robert Towne, d. Sydney Pollack.
ACTION: Crime Drama; Mob Stories; Mob-Asian; Japanese People; Martial Arts; Kidnappings; Hitmen; Undercover
(The Killing of a Chinese Bookie; The Year of the Dragon; The Friends of Eddie Coyle)
A Yank at Eton, 1942, 88m, ★★¹/₂/$$, MGM/NA. An unruly American boy gets shipped off to a British boarding school. Mickey Rooney, Freddie Bartholemew, Ian Hunter, Edmund Gwenn, Alan Napier. w. George Oppenheimer, Lionel House, Thomas Phipps, d. Norman Taurog.
COMEDY: COMEDY DRAMA: Fish out of Water Stories; Americans Abroad; Boarding Schools; England; Boyhood
REMAKE/RETREAD OF: A Yank at Oxford
(A Yank at Oxford; Oxford Blues)
A Yank at Oxford, 1937, 105m, ★★★/$$$, MGM/NA. An American student goes to Oxford and gets into trouble, refusing to be reserved. Robert Taylor, Vivien Leigh, Maureen O'Sullivan, Lionel Barrymore, Robert Coote, Edmund Gwenn. w. Malcolm Boylan, Walter Ferris,

George Oppenheimer, Leon Gordon, Roland Pertwee, John Saunders, Sidney Gilliatt, Michael Hogan, d. Jack Conway.
COMEDY DRAMA: COMEDY: Fish out of Water Stories; College Life; Rebels; Free Spirits; Americans Abroad; Young Men; England; Faded Hits
REMAKE: Oxford Blues.
(Oxford Blues; A Yank at Eton)
(Ed: Apparently more than two dozen other writers took a shot at this script, though it doesn't seem so much worse for the wear)
Yankee Doodle Dandy, 1942, 126m, ★★★★/$$$$, WB/WB. Hoofer George M. Cohan, great vaudeville and Broadway star of the early days, rises to fame. James Cagney (**BActor**), Joan Leslie, Walter Huston (BSActor), Rosemary deCamp. w. Robert Buckner, Edmund Joseph, d. Michael Curtiz (BDirector). **BMScore,** BPicture, BOStory, BEdit. Oscars: 7-2.
MUSICAL: Fame-Rise to; Patriotic Films; Dancers; Singers; Vaudeville; Theater Life
(Three Little Words; Till the Clouds Roll By)
Yanks, 1979, 141m, ★★★/$, U/MCA-U, R/S-FFN. American soldiers in England during World War II fall in love and deal with whether to stay or return home. Richard Gere, Vanessa Redgrave, William Devane, Lisa Eichhorn, Rachel Roberts, Chick Venerra. w. Colin

Welland, Walter Bernstein, d. John Schlesinger.
DRAMA: MELODRAMA: ROMANCE: Romantic Drama; Americans Abroad; Soldiers; World War II Stories; Forgotten Films; Overlooked at Release
(Hanover Street; Hope and Glory)
(Ed: Overpaid, Oversexed, and Over Here, but two and a half hours may be too long of a visit for some)
The Year My Voice Broke, 1987, 105m, ★★★/$$, Ind/Live, PG-13/S. A teenage boy with a problematic girlfriend becomes intrigued with a supposedly haunted house in his Australian town. Noah Taylor, Leone Carmen, Ben Mendelsohn. w. d. John Duigan.
DRAMA: SUSPENSE: Character Studies; Secrets; Houses-Creepy; ROMANCE: Romance-Boy Wants Girl; Love-First; Writer-Directors; Australian Films; Hidden Gems
(Careful, Cal, He Might Hear You)
The Year of Living Dangerously, 1983, 114m, ★★★¹/₂/$$, MGM/MGM-UA, R/S. A journalist (Mel Gibson) sent to cover the 1965 coup of Jakarta gets inside information from a diplomat attaché (Sigourney Weaver) that may betray the romance they've developed. Linda Hunt (**BSActress**), Michael Murphy. w. David Williamson, Peter Weir, C. J. Koch, d. Weir. Oscars: 1-1.

DRAMA: Political Drama; Political Unrest; **ROMANCE:** Romantic Drama; Diplomats; Women as Men; Race Against Time; Betrayals; Decisions-Big (Burn!; The Ugly American; Gallipoli)

Year of the Comet, 1992, 93m, ★★★/ $$, Columbia/New Line, PG/S. This charming attempt at old-style romantic comedy has an uptight wine company heiress (Penelope Ann Miller) and a macho, handsome rake (Timothy Daly) both looking for the same rare bottle of wine, which may get them killed if they don't bicker each other to death before ever kissing. w. William Goldman, d. Peter Yates.

COMEDY: ROMANCE: Romantic Comedy; Action Comedy; Treasure Hunt; Capers; Reward at Stake; Fugitives; Chase Movie; Romance-Bickering; Opposites Attract; Wallflowers; Macho Men; Old-Fashioned Recent Films; Coulda Been Great
(Foul Play; Hanky Panky)
(Ed: There's something amiss with Miss Miller, though Daley's charm is apparent if a bit too believable. Aside from the silly third act, the script really has something going we haven't seen in a long time)

The Year of the Dragon, 1985, 136m, ★★★/$$, MGM-UA/MGM-UA, R/EP-EV-S-FFN. A renegade detective in New York cracks a heroin smuggling operation between the Chinese mob and the Italian mob but may lose everything in his pursuit. Mickey Rourke, John Lone, Ariane, Leonard Termo. w. Oliver Stone, Michael Cimino, N-adap. Robert Daley, d. Cimino.

ACTION: SUSPENSE: TRAGEDY: Crime Drama; Mob Stories; Mob-Asian; Asian-Americans; Gangs-Asian; Chase Movies; Detective Stories; Detectives-Police; Drugs-Dealing; Rebels; Journalists; New York Life
(The Yakuza; The Killing of a Chinese Bookie; Scarface)
(Ed: Some astounding moments, others over-the-top misfires, but most of all a clinker ending to a plot destined to be defined by its resolution; therefore, a major letdown)

Year of the Gun, 1991, 111m, ★★½/ $$, Col/Col, R/S-V. An American student in Italy gets too close to the Red Brigade terrorists and winds up in a conspiracy only resolved by guns. Andrew McCarthy, Sharon Stone, Valeria Golino, John

Pankow, George Murcell. w. David Ambrose, N-adap. Michael Mewshaw, d. John Frankenheimer.

ACTION: SUSPENSE: Chase Movies; Terrorists; Journalists; Detectives-Amateur; Journalists as Detectives; Americans Abroad; Innocent Bystanders; 1970s; Coulda Been Good
REMAKE/RETREAD: Marathon Man. (Marathon Man; The Conformist; The Salamander)
(Ed: Had it been made in the 70s as it's set, it might have been passable. It's simply not serious enough with the casting and/or writing to cut it)

The Yearling, 1946, 134m, ★★★★/ $$$$$, MGM/MGM-UA. A boy in the swamps of Florida becomes attached to a wild fawn, but his cantankerous father won't let him keep it. Gregory Peck (BActor), Jane Wyman (BActress), Claude Jarman (**BChild Actor**), Chill Wills, Margaret Wycherly, Forest Tucker. w. Paul Osborn, N-adap. Marjorie Kinnans Rawlings, d. Clarence Brown (BDirector). BPicture, **BCArt**, BEdit, **BCCin**. Oscars: 8-3.

DRAMA: MELODRAMA: CHILDREN'S: FAMILY: Family Drama; Pet Stories; Tearjerkers; Fathers-Troublesome; Child Protagonists; Swamps; Florida; Poor People; Blockbusters
RETOLD: Cross Creek, story of Marjorie Rawlings, author.
(Old Yeller; Cross Creek)

The Yellow Balloon, 1952, 80m, ★★/$, Ind/NA. A boy wonders if he didn't kill his friend, but the person who really did is soon after him to answer the question. Kenneth More, William Sylvester, Kathleen Ryan. w. Anne Burnaby, J-Lee Thompson, d. Thompson.

SUSPENSE: MURDER: Witness to Murder; Witness to Murder-Child; Boys; Child Protagonists; Children in Jeopardy; Fugitives from a Murderer; Balloons; Female Screenwriters
REMAKE/RETREAD: The Window. (The Window; Witness; Eyewitness; Fallen Idol)
(Ed: Just a twist of difference from *The Window*)

Yellow Canary, 1963, 93m, ★★½/$, 20th/NA. A singer's baby boy is kidnapped. Pat Boone, Barbara Eden, Steve Forrest, Jack Klugman. w. Rod Serling, N-adap. Whit Masterson (*Evil Come, Evil Go*), d. Buzz Kulik.

SUSPENSE: Psychological Drama; Kidnappings; Missing Children; Singers
(Ed: If it weren't for Serling's writing, there wouldn't be much at all, and even that can be too much; the novel's title would have been better)

The Yellow Rolls Royce, 1964, 122m, ★★★/$$$, MGM/MGM-UA. A fabulous yellow Rolls changes owners three times over the years between a wealthy man, a mobster, and then a very wealthy eccentric woman. Ingrid Bergman, Rex Harrison, Jeanne Moreau, Shirley MacLaine, George C. Scott, Alain Delon, Art Carney, Omar Sharif. w. Terence Rattigan, d. Anthony Asquith.

DRAMA: COMEDY DRAMA: Multiple Stories; Hand-Me-Down Stories; Episodic Stories; Interwoven Stories; Rich People; Mob Comedy; Royalty; 1930s; All-Star Casts

The Yellow Submarine, 1968, 87m, ★★★/$$$, King-Apple-UA/MGM-UA, G. The Beatles in Pepperland, a fantasy kingdom, are attacked by a band of Blue Meanies and must escape in the title vehicle. Voices of the Beatles. w. Lee Minoff, Al Brodax, Jack Mendlesohn, Erich Segal, d. George Duning.

ADVENTURE: Fantasy; Cartoons; Animated; Submarines; **MUSICALS:** Musicals-Animated; Singers; Drugs; Anti-Establishment Films; Hippies; Mod Era; 1960s; Cult Films
(The Phantom Telephone Booth; Help; Let it Be)
(Ed: But unfortunately beyond the Peter Max-style visuals, one needs to be high to enjoy this as more than a curiosity)

Yellowbeard, 1983, 96m, ★★/$, Orion/ Orion, PG-13/P. A goofy pirate roams the seas with vulgarians in tow. Graham Chapman, Peter Boyle, Cheech Marin, Tommy Chong, Peter Cook, Madeline Kahn, Marty Feldman, Eric Idle, James Mason, John Cleese, Kenneth Mars, Susannah York, Beryl Reid, Spike Milligan. w. Graham Chapman, Peter Cook, Bernard McKenna, d. Mel Damski.

COMEDY: FARCE: Spoofs; Pirates; Swashbucklers; Bathroom Humor; All-Star Casts; All-Star Cameos
(Erik the Viking; Blackbeard's Ghost)
(Ed: So much gone to waste with the bathroom humor)

Yentl, 1983, 132m, ★★★½/$$$$, UA/ MGM-UA, PG/S-MRN. A Jewish girl

(Barbra Streisand) in turn-of-the-century Czechoslovakia wants to study religion, but since women are forbidden to do so she dresses as a boy, then soon discovers she's in love with one of her male classmates. Mandy Patinkin, Amy Irving (BSActress). w. Jack Rose, Barbra Streisand, SS-adap. Isaac Bashevis Singer, d. Streisand. BArt, **BOSScore**, BOSong, BOSong. Oscars: 5-1.

DRAMA: ROMANCE: MUSICAL: Musical Drama; Romantic Drama; Dreams; Female in Male Domain; Jewish People; Religion; Impostors; Women as Men; Europeans-Eastern; 1900s; Female Protagonists; Female Screenwriters; Female Directors; Underrated
(Fiddler on the Roof; Tootsie; The Chosen)
(Ed: Though thoroughly original in its own niche, it was dubbed *Tootsie on the Roof* upon its much-awaited release)

Yes, Giorgio, 1982, 110m, ★★/$, MGM/ MGM-UA, PG. A weighty opera star falls in love with his throat doctor and goes on balloon rides which do not sink. Luciano Pavarotti, Kathryn Harrold, Eddie Albert. w. Norman Steinberg, N-adap. Anne Piper, d. Franklin J. Schaffner.

ROMANCE: MELODRAMA: Opera Singers; Romance with Doctor; Doctors; Old-Fashioned Recent Films; Flops-Major
(La Traviata; Carmen)
(Ed: The big budget for the big opera star could not be recouped, and for fairly good reason; however, for diehard fans of Pavarotti, it's passable)

Yesterday, Today and Tomorrow, 1963, 119m, ★★★/$$$, Avco/Hollywood Home. The wicked adventures of several couples coupling about Rome, centering around the ladies. Sophia Loren, Marcello Mastroianni. w. Eduardo de Filippo, Cesare Zavattini, d. Vittorio de Sica. **BFLFilm**. Oscars: 1-1.

COMEDY DRAMA: ROMANCE: FARCE: Multiple Stories; Multiple Performances; Erotic Drama; Erotic Comedy; Married Couples; Sexy Women; Sexy Men; Prostitutes; Italian Films
(Boccacio '70; La Dolce Vita; The Umbrellas of Cherbourg)

Yesterday's Hero, 1979, 95m, ★1/2/$, Col/Hollywood Home. A soccer hero's life falls apart after he retires. Ian McShane, Suzanne Somers, Adam Faith. w. Jackie Collins, d. Neil Leifer.

DRAMA: MELODRAMA: Character Studies; Redemption; Sports Movies; Soccer; Sexy Men; Rise and Fall Stories; Depression; Female Screenwriters

Yojimbo, 1961, 110m, ★★★1/2/$$$, Toho/Sultan, Hollywood Home. A samurai warrior exacts his revenge by driving two unwitting warring gangs against each other. Toshiro Mifune, Eijiro Tono. w. Ryuzo Kikushima, Akira Kurosawa, d. Kurosawa.

ACTION: Gangs; Revenge; Men in Conflict; Martial Arts; Japanese Films

REMAKE: A Fistful of Dollars.
(Throne of Blood; Samurai)

Yolanda and the Thief, 1945, 108m, ★★1/2/$$, MGM/MGM-UA. A con artist protects an heiress dancing down Mexico way. Fred Astaire, Lucile Bremer, Frank Morgan, Leon Ames, Mildred Natwick. w. Irving Brecher, Ludwig Bemelmas, Jacques Thery, d. Vincente Minnelli.

MUSICALS: COMEDY: Musical Comedy; **ROMANCE:** Con Artists; Heiresses; Thieves; Mexico; Great Art Direction
(Flying Down to Rio; Holiday in Mexico; Down Argentine Way)

You Belong to Me, 1941, 94m, ★★1/2/ $$, Col/NA. A freewheeling husband doesn't like some of the patients his doctor wife has in the examination room. Barbara Stanwyck, Henry Fonda, Edgar Buchanan, Ruth Donelly, Roger Clark. w. Claude Binyon, Dalton Trumbo, d. Wesley Ruggles.

COMEDY: ROMANCE: Romantic Comedy; Screwball Comedy; Marriage Comedy; Jealousy; Doctors; Playboys

You Belong to My Heart, 1951, 87m, ★★/$$, MGM/NA. A king visiting Hollywood runs across an old flame who's now a movie star. Lana Turner, Ezio Pinza, Marjorie Main, Barry Sullivan, Debbie Reynolds. w. Edwin Knopf, Don Hartman, d. Don Hartman.

ROMANCE: MELODRAMA: MUSICALS: Music Movies; Singers; Hollywood Life; Actresses; Romance-Reunited

You Can Never Tell, 1951, 78m, ★★★/$, U/NA. A pedigreed dog is killed and then reincarnated as a P.I. on the trail of the killer. Dick Powell, Peggy Dow, Charles Drake. w. Lou Breslow, David Chandler, d. Lou Breslow.

COMEDY: COMEDY DRAMA: Fantasy; **MURDER: MYSTERY: MURDER MYSTERY:** Detective Stories; Detectives-Private; Reincarnations; Pet Stories; Humans into Animals; Dogs; Good

Premise Unfulfilled; Coulda Been Great; Ahead of Its Time; Body Switching
(Here Comes Mr. Jordan; Heaven Can Wait; Look Who's Talking Now; Baxter)
(Ed: So whacked-out conceptually, you have to give it credit)

You Can't Cheat an Honest Man, 1939, 79m, ★★1/2/$$, U/Barr Video. A circus owner tries to keep the show together. W. C. Fields, Edgar Bergen, Constance Moore. w. George Marion, Richard Mack, Everett Freeman, W. C. Fields, d. George Marshall.

COMEDY: Comedy Slapstick; Circus Life; Comedy of Errors
(At the Circus; The Big Circus; My Little Chickadee; International House)

You Can't Get Away with Murder, 1939, 78m, ★★1/2/$$, WB/WB. A street punk takes up with a mobster and winds up in big trouble. Humphrey Bogart, Billy Halop, Henry Travers. w. Robert Bruckner, Don Ryan, Kenneth Gamet, P-adap. Lewis Lawes & Johnathan Finn, *Chalked Out*, d. Lewis Seiler.

ACTION: DRAMA: Crime Drama; Mob Stories; Juvenile Delinquents; Protégés; Framed?; Warner Gangster Era; Accused Unjustly

You Can't Run Away from It, 1956, 96m, ★★/$$, Col/NA. A madcap heiress runs away from her father and the fiancé he's found her and winds up sharing motel rooms with a reporter who wonders who she really is. Jack Lemmon, June Allyson, Charles Bickford, Jim Backus, Stubby Kaye. w. Claude Binyon, Robert Riskin, d. Dick Powell.

COMEDY: ROMANCE: Romantic Comedy; Screwball Comedy; Road Movies; Heiresses-Madcap; Hiding Out; Fugitives; Roommates; Journalists; Secrets; Fathers & Daughters; Forgotten Films

REMAKE OF: It Happened One Night.
(Ed: The directing was apparently askew here-how could you screw this up? But they did then and it still falls short now)

Young and Innocent, see **A Girl Was Young**

You Can't Take it with You, 1938, 127m, ★★★/$$$, Columbia/RCA-Col. An eccentric family and the many people who live in their big house want their daughter to marry a wealthy heir, but their own shenanigans may end the relationship with a big bang. Lionel Barrymore, Jean Arthur, Spring Byington

(BSActress), James Stewart, Mischa Auer, Ann Miller, Eddie Anderson, Charles Lane. w. Robert Riskin, adap. George Kaufman, M. Hart (BScr), d. Frank Capra (**BDirector**). BPicture, BCin, BSound, BEdit. Oscars: 7-2.

COMEDY: FARCE: ROMANCE: FAMILY: Romance-Class Conflict; Comedy of Errors; Screwball Comedy; Family Comedy; Eccentric People; Snobs vs. Slobs; Rich People; In-Laws-Troublesome; Social Climbing; Marrying Up; Stagelike Films
(The Male Animal; Cheaper by the Dozen; Life with Father; Merrily We Live)
(Ed: A 1986 stage version starring Jason Robards was much better)

You Light Up My Life, 1977, 90m, ★★/$$$, Col/RCA-Col, PG. A young woman who's grown up in show business with a comedian father tries to make it in the music arena. Didi Conn, Joe Silver, Melanie Mayron. w. d. (also song) Joseph Brooks. BOSong. Oscars: 1-1.

MELODRAMA: ROMANCE: Romantic Drama; Musicians; Hollywood Life; Young Women; Female Protagonists; Forgotten Films; 1970s; Faded Hits; Sleeper Hits; Writer-Directors
(Ed: Spawned one of the biggest hit songs in history, which is where Mr. Brooks should have stopped writing)

You'll Like My Mother, 1972, 92m, ★★1/2/$$, U/NA, R/V. A young widow who's pregnant has to stay with her deceased husband's mother, who rules the roost in a big house on a hill and plans to make life hell for the widow. Patty Duke, Rosemary Murphy, Richard Thomas, Sian Barbara Allen. w. Jo Heims, N-adap. Naomi Hintze, d. Lamont Johnson.

SUSPENSE: THRILLER: Psychological Thriller; Women in Jeopardy; Women in Conflict; Widows; Babies-Having; In-Laws-Troublesome; Mothers Alone; Houses-Creepy
(Die! Die! My Darling!; Fanatic; Sister, Sister)

You'll Never Get Rich, 1941, 88m, ★★★/$$$, Col/RCA-Col. A choreographer helps out his producer when a paramour the producer wants to move on from gets too clingy—the choreographer gets her to cling to him instead. Fred Astaire, Rita Hayworth, Robert Benchley. w. Michael Fessier, Ernest Pagano, d. Sidney Lanfield. BOScore, BOSong. Oscars: 2-0.

MUSICALS: ROMANCE: Musical Romance; Theater Life; Dancers; Directors; Romance-Older Men/Younger Women; Romance-Triangles; Playboys; Sexy Women
(You Were Never Lovelier; Cover Girl)

Young at Heart, 1954, 117m, ★★★/$$$, WB/WB. A small-town music teacher has daughters who all are having trouble dealing with men-but they do know how to sing. Doris Day, Frank Sinatra, Ethel Barrymore, Gig Young, Dorothy Malone, Alan Hale, Robert Keith, Elizabeth Fraser. w. Julius J. Epstein, Lenore Coffee, N-adap. Fannie Hurst, d. Gordon Douglas.

MUSICALS: ROMANCE: Musical Romance; Fathers & Daughters; Small-town Life; Female Screenwriters; Musicians

MUSICAL REMAKE OF: Four Daughters.
(Ed: Contains the clichéd but classic song "**Young at Heart**," by Sinatra)

Young Bess, 1953, 112m, ★★1/2/$$, MGM/MGM-UA. Queen Elizabeth's romance with Tom Seymour is chronicled without much truth. Jean Simmons, Deborah Kerr, Stewart Granger, Charles Laughton, Kay Walsh, Cecil Kellaway, Leo G. Carroll. w. Arthur Wimperis, Jan Lustig, N-adap. Margaret Irwin, d. George Sidney.

MELODRAMA: ROMANCE: Historical Drama; Costume Drama; Biographies-Fictional; Queens; Famous People When Young
(Elizabeth and Essex; Elizabeth R.)

Young Catherine, 1991, 150m, ★★★/$$$$, NBC/Turner. The rise of the great empress of Russia who reigned more powerfully than any other female but Elizabeth. Vanessa Redgrave, Julia Ormond, Marthe Keller, Christopher Plummer, Maximillian Schell, Franco Nero. w. Chris Bryant, d. Michael Anderson.

DRAMA: Biographies; Famous People When Young; Queen; Power-Rise to; Costume Drama; Catherine the Great; Historical Drama; Russia; 1700s; TV Movies
(Catherine the Great; Great Catherine; Rasputin and the Empress)

The Young Doctors, 1961, 102m, ★★1/2/$$, UA/NA. The rivalry between an older doctor and young resident almost results in tragedy. Frederic March, Ben Gazzara, Dick Clark, George Segal, Eddie Albert, Ina Balin, Aline MacMahon,

Arthur Hill, Rosemary Murphy. w. Joseph Hayes, N-adap. Arthur Haily (*The Final Diagnosis*), d. Phil Karlson.

DRAMA: MELODRAMA: Doctors; Medical Drama; Men in Conflict; Generation Gap; Medical School; Hospitals; Ensemble Films; Ensembles-Male
(Dr. Kildare SERIES; The Interns; The New Interns; Gross Anatomy; Vital Signs)

Young Doctors in Love, 1982, 95, ★★1/2/$$$, 20th/CBS-Fox, R/P-S. A whacked-out and silly hospital staff hardly has time for surgery with all of the other bodies they're touching. Michael McKean, Sean Young, Harry Dean Stanton, Dabney Coleman, Patrick MacNee, Hector Elizondo. w. Rich Eustis, Michael Elias, d. Garry Marshall.

COMEDY: FARCE: Spoofs; Doctors; Nurses; Hospitals
(Where Does It Hurt?; Serial; Carry on SERIES)

Young Einstein, 1989, 91m, ★★1/2/$, WB/WB, PG-13. Young Einstein discovers all those theories, then decides to invent the surfboard and the electric guitar and goes on tour. Yahoo Serious. w. Serious, David Roach, d. Serious.

COMEDY: Spoofs; Comedy-Slapstick; Musicians; Rock Stars; Revisionist Films; Eccentric People; Surfers; Australian Films
(Dogs in Space)
(Ed: An Aussie punk Jerry Lewis; a huge hit down under, went under real quick in America)

Young Frankenstein, 1974, 108m, ★★★1/2/$$$$$, 20th/CBS-Fox, R/P-S. The grandson of Dr. Frankenstein tries to recapture his experiments with the help of his faithful but inept assistant, Igor. Gene Wilder, Marty Feldman, Madeline Kahn, Teri Garr, Peter Boyle, Cloris Leachman, Kenneth Mars, Gene Hackman. w. Gene Wilder, Mel Brooks (BAScr), d. Brooks. Oscars: 1-0.

COMEDY: FARCE: Spoofs; Comedy of Errors; Horror Comedy; Monsters-Manmade; Hunchbacks
(Dracula: Dead and Loving It; Ed Wood; I Was a Teenage Frankenstein)

The Young Girls of Rochefort, 1968, 126m, ★★★/$$, Ind/NA. Two French girls from the country join a traveling song-and-dance troupe, meet Gene Kelly, and find love. Catherine Deneuve, François Dorléac, Gene Kelly, George

Chakiris, Danielle Darrieux. w. d. Jacques Demy. BOScore. Oscars: 1-0.

MUSICALS: ROMANCE: Musical Romance; Fantasy; Dancers; French Films; Writer-Directors; Curiosities (Lili, Therese and Isabelle; Jacques Brel . . .)

Young Guns, 1988, 107m, ★★½/$$$, 20th/Vestron, R/EV-S-MRN. The beginning of Billy the Kid and pals is revised and made more action-oriented. Emilio Estevez, Charlie Sheen, Kiefer Sutherland, Lou Diamond Phillips, Jack Palance, Dermot Mulroney, Casey Siezmasko, Terence Stamp. w. John Fusco, d. Christopher Cain. BOSong, "Blaze of Glory." Oscars: 1-0.

WESTERNS: ACTION: Criminal Biographies; Fugitives from the Law; Crime Sprees; Young Men; Bratpack Movies; Teenagers; Teenage Movies; Ensemble Films; Billy the Kid; Ensembles-Male; Westerns-Neo

SEQUEL: Young Guns II.

Young Guns II, 1990, 103m, ★★/$$, 20th/Fox, R/EV. The Billy the Kid gang rides again, only now there's more conflict within the gang while they're on the run. Emilio Estevez, Kiefer Sutherland, Lou Diamond Phillips, Christian Slater, William Peterson, Alan Ruck, James Coburn. w. John Fusco, d. Geoff Murphy.

WESTERNS: ACTION: Famous Criminals When Young; Fugitives from the Law; Crime Sprees; Young Men; Bratpack Movies; Teenagers; Teenage Movies; Ensemble Films; Ensembles-Male; Westerns-Neo

The Young in Heart, 1938, 91m, ★★★½/$$, Selznick-UA/Video Treasures. A family of con artists goes after a little old lady who's not so little or so old and who plans to tame them. Douglas Fairbanks Jr., Janet Gaynor, Roland Young, Billie Burke, Minnie Dupree, Paulette Goddard, Richard Carlson. w. Paul Osborn, Charles Bennett, N-adap. IAR Wylie (*The Gay Banditti*), d. Richard Wallace. BScore, BCin. Oscars: 2-0.

COMEDY: Screwball Comedy; Eccentric People; Family Stories; **FAMILY: ROMANCE:** Romantic Comedy; Con Artists; Turning the Tables; Elderly Women; Hidden Gems; Forgotten Films (You Can't Take It With You; The Ladykillers; Oliver Twist)

(Ed: Probably suffered from the nondescript title and being released at same time as *You Can't Take it With You*, though it's quite different)

The Young Lions, 1958, 167m, ★★★/$$$, 20th/CBS-Fox. Two Americans and a German cross paths during World War II in their war lives and social lives. Marlon Brando, Montgomery Clift, Dean Martin, Maximilian Schell, Hope Lange, Barbara Rush, May Britt, Lee Van Cleef. w. Edward Anhalt, N-adap. Irwin Shaw, d. Edward Dmytryk. BCin, BOScore. Oscars: 2-0.

DRAMA: War Stories; Epics; Character Studies; Young Men; Soldiers; Americans Abroad; Interwoven Stories (The Men)

Young Man with a Horn, 1950, 112m, ★★½/$$, WB/WB. The life of trumpet player Bix Beiderbecke, on and off the horn. Kirk Douglas, Lauren Bacall, Doris Day, Hoagy Carmichael. w. Carl Foreman, Edmund H. North, NFN-adap. Dorothy Baker, d. Michael Curtiz.

DRAMA: MELODRAMA: ROMANCE: Biographies; Biographies-Fictional; Musicians; Jazz Life; Big Band Era (All the Fine Young Cannibals; Too Late Blues)

Young Mr. Lincoln, 1939, 100m, ★★★★/$$$, 20th/CBS-Fox. Old Abraham, when young, saves a man about to be lynched for a murder he didn't commit. Henry Fonda, Alice Brady, Marjorie Wesver, Richard Cromwell. w. Lamar Trotti (BScr), d. John Ford. Oscars: 1-0.

DRAMA: MURDER: Courtroom Drama; Historical Drama; Trials; Biographies; Presidents; Famous People When Young; Accused Unjustly; Lawyers; Lincoln-Abraham; 1800s; Lynchings; Early America (Abraham Lincoln; Abe Lincoln in Illinois)

The Young Philadelphians, 1959, 136m, ★★★/$$$, WB/WB. A good-looking, brash young lawyer makes his way out of working-class beginnings into the Philadelphia political arena, but once there, blackmail attempts are made threatening to expose his illegitimate birth. Paul Newman, Robert Vaughan (BSActor), Barbara Rush, Alexis Smith, Brian Keith, Billie Burke, Otto Kruger. w. James Gunn, N-adap. Richard Powell (*The Philadelphian*), d. Vincent Sherman. BB&WCin, BB&WCostume. Oscars: 3-0.

DRAMA: MELODRAMA: Political Drama; Social Drama; Politicians; Lawyers; Power-Rise to; Class Conflicts; Secrets-Haunting; Blackmail; Evil Men; Philadelphia (From the Terrace; True Colors; The Best Man)

(Ed: Is the motto here that if you're good-looking enough, you can overcome anything?)

The Young Savages, 1961, 103m, ★★½/$$, UA/NA. An assistant DA in New York goes after three street toughs but then must wrestle with the fact that one or more may not be guilty at all. Burt Lancaster, Shelley Winters, John David Chandler, Dina Merrill, Telly Savalas.

DRAMA: Courtroom Drama; Accused Unjustly; Lawyers; Gangs; Inner-City Life; New York Life

Young Sherlock Holmes, 1985, 109m, ★★★/$$, Amblin-Par/Par, PG/V. Sherlock and Dr. Watson meet while still students and solve a series of murders involving a great deal of mysticism and special effects. Nicholas Rowe, Alan Cox, Sophie Ward, Freddie Jones. w. Chris Columbus, d. Barry Levinson. BSFX. Oscars: 1-0.

MYSTERY: Detective Stories; Young People; 1890s; Famous People When Young; Sherlock Holmes; Cults; Magic; England (Sherlock Holmes' Smarter Brother)

Young Tom Edison, 1940, 82m, ★★★/$$$, MGM/MGM-UA. Edison's education and the beginning of his experiments into adulthood. Mickey Rooney, Eugene Pallette, Fay Bainter, Virginia Weidler. w. Bradbury Foote, Dore Schary, Hugo Butler, d. Norman Taurog.

DRAMA: Biographies; Inventors; Experiments; Famous People When Young; Geniuses

SEQUEL: Edison, the Man.

Young Winston, 1972, 157, ★★★/$$, Col/RCA-Col, PG. The early life and rise of Winston Churchill on the road to becoming prime minister. Simon Ward, Robert Shaw, Anne Bancroft, Jack Hawkins, Ian Holm, Anthony Hopkins, John Mills, Patrick Magee, Edward Woodward. w. Carl Foreman (BAScr), NF-adap. Winston Churchill, *My Early Life*, d. Richard Attenborough. Oscars: 1-0.

DRAMA: Biographies; Autobiographical Stories; Power-Rise to; Famous People When Young; Boyhood; British Films; England; Leaders; All-Star Casts (Disraeli)

Youngblood, 1985, 109m, ★1/2/$, UA/MGM-UA, PG-13/S-MRN. A sexy hockey star fights off female fans while romancing other women. Rob Lowe, Cynthia Gibb, Patrick Swayze, Ed Lauter. w. Peter Markle, Patrick Wells, d. Markle.

COMEDY DRAMA: Sports Movies; Playboys; Young Men; ROMANCE: Romantic Comedy; Hockey; Bratpack Movies

(St. Elmo's Fire; About Last Night)

Youngblood Hawke, 1964, 137m, ★★/$, WB/WB. A truck driver from the hills of Kentucky somehow writes a brilliant novel, moves to New York, and is assigned a beautiful editor who introduces him to beautiful people who may ruin him. James Franciscus, Suzanne Pleshette, Eva Gabor, Genevieve Page, Mary Astor, Don Porter. w. d. Delmer Daves, N-adap. Herman Wouk.

DRAMA: MELODRAMA: Writers; Fame-Rise to; Rise and Fall Stories; City vs. Country; Fish out of Water Stories; Publishing World

You Only Live Twice, 1968, 117m, ★★★/$$$$, UA/MGM-UA, PG/S. Bond dies and comes back to life to take on a plot to knock out U.S. and Russian satellites. Sean Connery, Tetsuro Tamba, Bernard Lee, Lois Maxwell, Desmond Llewellyn, Charles Gray, Donald Pleasance. w. Roald Dahl, N-adap. Ian Fleming, d. Lewis Gilbert.

ACTION: ADVENTURE: Spies; Dead-Back from the; Undercover; Japan; James Bond; Volcanoes

(Thunderball; Goldfinger; The Man with the Golden Gun)

Your Witness, see Eye Witness.

You're a Big Boy Now, 1966, 96m, ★★★/$$, WB/WB, R/S. A nerdy librarian (Peter Kastner) comes out of his shell and finds real women to have relationships with. Elizabeth Hartman, Geraldine Page

(BSActress), Julie Harris, Rip Torn, Tony Bill, Karen Black, Michael Dunn. w. d. Francis Ford Coppola. Oscars: 1-0.

COMEDY: COMEDY DRAMA: ROMANCE: Romantic Comedy; Eccentric People; Nerds; Sexuality; Virgins; Coming of Age; Mothers & Sons; Writer-Directors (Marty; Hi, Mom; Greetings)

You're in the Army Now, 1941, 79m, ★★★/$$$, WB/WB. Two losers give up selling vacuum cleaners when they find they have somehow joined the army. Jimmy Durante, Phil Silvers, Donald MacBride, Jane Wyman, Regis Toomey. w. Paul Gerard Smith, George Beatty, d. Lewis Seiler.

COMEDY: Military Comedy; Fish out of Water Stories; Comedy-Slapstick; Forgotten Films; Hidden Gems; Comedians

(In the Army Now; Bonnie Scotland)

You're in the Navy Now, 1951, 93m, ★★1/2/$$, 20th/NA. Navy men have trouble with an experimental engine on a boat. Gary Cooper, Millard Mitchell, Jane Greer, Eddie Albert. w. Richard Murphy, d. Henry Hathaway.

COMEDY: Military Comedy; Comedy of Errors

You're Telling Me, 1934, 66m, ★★★/$$$, Par/NA. An inventor meets up with a princess, charms her, and tries to fit into high society-if he doesn't make too much of a mess with it all. W. C. Fields, Buster Crabbe, Joan Marsh. w. Walter de Leon, Paul Jones, d. Erle C. Kenton.

COMEDY: Comedy-Slapstick; Comedy of Errors; Fish out of Water Stories; Marrying Up; Social Climbing; Inventors; Princesses

(My Little Chickadee; Never Give a Sucker an Even Break)

Yours, Mine and Ours, 1968, 111m, ★★★/$$$$, UA/MGM-UA, G. A widower with nine children manages to find and

marry a widow with eight kids while the Vietnam War looms and battle calls for one of the sons. Lucille Ball, Henry Fonda, Van Johnson, Tim Matheson. w. Mel Shavelson, Mort Lachman, d. Shavelson.

MELODRAMA: COMEDY DRAMA: Family Comedy; Family Drama; Marriage Comedy; Starting Over; Vietnam War Era; Conservative Value Films; Widows; Widowers

(With Six You Get Eggroll; Cheaper by the Dozen; The Brady Bunch TV Series; The Brady Bunch Movie)

(Ed: Popular at the time, it's a dated, melodramatic, flag-waving, pro-Vietnam forerunner to *The Brady Bunch*)

You've Got to Live Dangerously, 1975, 100m, ★★1/2/$, 20th/NA, R/S-V-FN-MN. A detective following a woman stumbles onto a ring of diamond thieves, which leads to murder. Claude Braseur, Annie Girardot. w. Nelly Kaplan, d. Claude Makovsky.

SUSPENSE: MYSTERY MURDER: Detective Stories; Detectives in Deep; Conspiracy; Heist Stories; Jewel Thieves; Young Women; French Films; Female Screenwriters

You Were Never Lovelier, 1942, 97m, ★★1/2/$$$, Col/RCA-Col. A hotel owner gets a man to sweep his daughter off her feet in the hope she'll settle down. Instead, they dance! Fred Astaire, Rita Hayworth, Adolphe Menjou, Leslie Brookes, Xavier Cugat, Larry Parks. w. Michael Fessier, Ernest Pagano, Delmer Daves, d. William Seiter. BOScore, BOSong. Oscars: 2-0.

MUSICALS: ROMANCE: Musical Romance; Romance-Older Men/Younger Women; Matchmakers; Fathers & Daughters; Dancers; Settling Down; Sexy Women; Hotels

(You'll Never Get Rich; Cover Girl)

Z

Z, 1969, 125m, ★★★¹/₂/$$$, Col/Col, R/V. When a political official opposing the current government in Algeria is murdered at a rally, the police want to cover it up. Jean-Louis Trintignant, Yves Montand, Irene Papas. w. Costa-Gavras, Jorge Sempron (BAScr), N-adap. Vassili Vassilikos, d. Costa-Gavras (BDirector). BPicture, **BFLFilm**. Oscars: 4-1.
DRAMA: SUSPENSE: Political Drama; Political Thriller; Assassination Plots; Conspiracy; Political Unrest; Africa; French Films
(State of Siege; Missing)

Zabriskie Point, 1970, 112m, ★★/$$, MGM/MGM-UA, R/FN-MN. A young rebel decides to pick up and drop out of LA heading for the desert where other young people live a Dionysian existence in caves near Death Valley. Mark Frechette, Daria Halprin, Rod Taylor. w. Michelangelo Antonioni, Fred Gardner, Sam Shepard, Tonino Guerra, Clare Peploe, d. Antonioni.
DRAMA: Art Films; Avant Garde; Surrealism; Erotic Drama; Young Men-Angry; Young People; Rebels; Desert Life; Cult Films; 1970s; Art Films; Female Screenwriters
(Beyond the Valley of the Dolls; Red Desert)
(Ed: A big misfire, but another curiosity for the 70s time capsule)

Zandalee, 1991, 104m, ★¹/₂/$, Ind/Live, R/P-S-V-FN. An artist in New Orleans has an affair with his best friend's wife, leading to tragedy. Nicolas Cage, Judge Reinhold, Erika Anderson, Joe Pantoliano, Steve Buscemi, Aaron Neville. w. Mari Kornhauser, d. Sam Pillsbury.
DRAMA: TRAGEDY: MELODRAMA: ROMANCE: Erotic Drama; Romance-Triangles; Artists; Friendship-Male; Friends as Enemies; New Orleans
(Against All Odds; Leaving Las Vegas)
(Ed: Though a few moments are attractive with the New Orleans scenery, it's truly awful, a definite Z-picture.)

Zandy's Bride, 1974, 116m, ★★¹/₂/$, WB/WB, PG. A pioneer fellow gets a cantankerous Swedish bride and deals with running a family. Gene Hackman, Liv Ullman, Eileen Heckart, Harry Dean Stanton, Joe Santos. w. Marc Norma, N-adap. Lillian Bos Ross, *The Stranger*, d. Jan Troell.
COMEDY DRAMA: WESTERN: Western Comedy; **ROMANCE:** Marriage Comedy; Brides-Mail Order; Swedish People
(Goin' South; Mail Order Bride)

Zapped!, 1982, 98m, ★★/$$$, Ind/New World, PG/S. A teenager discovers he has special powers that allow him to flip girls' skirts up. Scott Baio, Willie Aames, Robert Mandan, Scatman Crothers.

w. Bruce Joel Rubin, Robert Rosenthal, d. Rosenthal.
Zapped Again. Same thing again.
COMEDY: Fantasy; Teenage Movies; Teenagers; Magic; Psychics; Romance-Boy Wants Girl
SEQUEL: Zapped Again!
(Ed: Lots of skirts flying up)

Zardoz, 1973, 105m, ★★/$, 20th/Fox, R/S. Bizarre neomedieval types with spaceships rule the future, which looks a lot like Scotland. Sean Connery, Charlotte Rampling, John Alderton. w. d. John Boorman.
SCI-FI: Fantasy; Futuristic Films; UFOs; Outer Space Movies; Apocalyptic Stories
(Ed: *Dune* it isn't . . . which is actually a compliment, but in a word—bizarre)

Zazie dans le Métro, 1960, 88m, ★★★-/$, New Yorker/New Yorker. A seemingly naive girl goes to Paris and has a lot of fun while causing calamities for others. Catherine Demongeot, Philippe Noiret, Vittorio Caprioli. w. d. Louis Malle.
COMEDY: FARCE: Free Spirits; Young Women; Comedy of Errors; Paris; French Films; French New Wave Films; Writer-Directors; Hidden Gems; Cult Films
(Sundays & Cybele)

Zebrahead, 1992, 102m, ★★★/$$, Col/Col, R/EP-EV-S. An interracial high-school romance causes sparks to fly in inner-city Detroit. Michael Rappaport, N'Bushe Wright, Ray Sharkey, Ron Johnson, Helen Shaver. w. d. Tony Drazan.

MELODRAMA: ROMANCE: Romance-Interracial; High School Life; Black vs. White; Black Women; Inner City Life; Writer-Directors
(South Central, A Bronx Tale; Juice)

A Zed and Two Noughts (ZOO), 1985, 111m, ★★★/$, Film Four/Playtime, Tape Worm Video, R/P-ES-FFN-MFN. Twin brothers' wives are killed in a car wreck, after which they become obsessed with a female amputee in between a lot of fascinating visuals and nude bodies, particularly the twins. Eric Deacon, Brian Deacon, Andrea Ferreol, Joss Ackland. w. d. Peter Greenaway.

DRAMA: Art Films; Avant Garde; Erotic Drama; Surrealism; Twins; Brothers; Romance-Triangles; Suicidal Tendencies; Death-Dealing with; Writer-Directors
(Drowning by Numbers; Prospero's Books)

Zelig, 1983, 83m, ★★★★/$$$, Orion/Orion, PG. A documentary spoof about a man (Woody Allen) who can change shape or form to conform to whatever environment he's in-the human chameleon. Mia Farrow. w. d. Woody Allen, BCin, BCostume. Oscars: 2-0.

COMEDY: Documentary-Style; Spoofs; Spoofs-Documentary; Fantasy; Psychologists; Biographies-Fictional; Surrealism; Romance with Psychologist
(All You Need Is Cash)

Zelly and Me, 1988, 87m, ★★★/$, Col/Col, G. A governess (Isabella Rosellini) tries to rescue a little girl from her stern and unfeeling grandmother (Glynis Johns), to the point of plotting to steal her. Alexandra Johnes, David Lynch. w. d. Tina Rathbone.

DRAMA: MELODRAMA: Tearjerkers; Baby-sitters; Rich People; Stern Women; Mothers-Surrogate; Girlhood; Women and Girls; Female Protagonists; Female Screenwriters; Female Directors; Writer-Directors

Zeppelin, 1971, 97m, ★★½/$$, WB/WB. During World War I, the British send spies to steal secrets about the

dreaded Germans' blimps. Michael York, Elke Sommer, Peter Carsten. w. Arthur Rowe, Donald Churchill, d. Etienne Périer.

DRAMA: ADVENTURE: War Stories; World War I Stories; Germans as Enemy; Pilots-Military; Balloons
(The Hindenburg)

Zero Population Growth (Z.P.G.), 1971, 96m, ★★/$, Par/Par, R. In the future, giving birth means death, but one couple risks it anyway. Oliver Reed, Geraldine Chaplin, Diane Cilento, Don Gordon. w. Max Ehrlich, Frank de Felita, d. Michael Campus.

SCI-FI: Futuristic Films; Babies-Having; Abortion Dilemmas; Oppressive Societies
(The Handmaid's Tale)

Ziegfeld Follies, 1945, 110m, ★★★/$$$, MGM/MGM-UA. From heaven, the Great Ziegfeld produces one last show. Fred Astaire, Lucille Ball, William Powell, Jimmy Durante, Fanny Brice, Edward Arnold, Lena Horne, Judy Garland, Gene Kelly, Red Skelton, Hume Cronyn. w. (various), d. Vincente Minnelli.

MUSICALS: Dancers; Theater Life; Heaven; All-Star Casts; All-Star Cameos
(The Great Ziegfeld)

Ziegfeld Girl, 1941, 131m, ★★★/$$$, MGM/MGM-UA. The backstage lives of the chorus girls in the Follies. Judy Garland, James Stewart, Hedy Lamarr, Lana Turner, Tony Martin, Jackie Cooper, Ian Hunter, Charles Winninger, Al Shean, Edward Everett Horton, Eve Arden. w. Marguerite Roberts, Sonya Levien, d. Robert Z. Leonard.

MUSICALS: DRAMA: Behind the Scenes; Dancers; Young Women; Multiple Stories; Interwoven Stories; Ensemble Films; Ensembles-Female; Female Protagonists; Female Screenwriters

Zigzag, 1970, 104m, ★★½/$, MGM/MGM-UA. A man who is dying takes the blame for a murder, turning himself in and giving the reward money to his wife. George Kennedy, Anne Jackson, Eli Wallach. w. John T. Kelley, d. Richard A. Colla.

DRAMA: SUSPENSE: Psychological Drama; **MURDER:** Framed?; Death-Impending; Insurance Scams

Zorba the Greek, 1964, 142m, ★★★½/$$$, 20th/CBS-Fox. A Greek with a huge sense of loving life meets up with a British writer and teaches him a few things. Anthony Quinn (BActor), Alan Bates, Lila Kedrova (**BSActress**), Irene Papas. w. d. Michael Cacoyannis (BAScr, Director), N-adap. Nikos Kazantzakis. BPicture, **BB&WCin**. Oscars: 6-2.

COMEDY DRAMA: Free Spirits; Greeks; Writers; Friendships-Interracial; Eccentric People

Zorro, the Gay Blade, 1981, 92m, ★★★/$$, 20th/CBS-Fox, PG. Zorro has a rather different twin brother who interferes with his love life and enemies in old Mexico. George Hamilton, Lauren Hutton, Brenda Vaccaro, Ron Leibman. w. Hal Dresner, d. Peter Medak.

COMEDY: FARCE: Spoofs; Western Comedy; Comedy-Slapstick; Swashbucklers; Gay Men; Twins; Brothers; Impostors; Mexico; 1800s; Hidden Gems
(Love at First Bite; The Frisco Kid)

Zulu, 1964, 135m, ★★½/$$, Par/Par. British soldiers battle African warriors in the famous standoff. Stanley Baker, Michael Caine, Jack Hawkins, Nigel Green. w. John Prebble, Cy Endfield, d. Endfield.

DRAMA: Epics; War Stories; War Battles; Africa; Imperialist Problems; British Films

REMAKE: Zulu Dawn

Zulu Dawn, 1979, 117m, ★★/$$, Ind/Trans-World, PG/V. Retelling of the great battle and massacre of British soldiers by African tribes in the late 1800s. Burt Lancaster, Denholm Elliott, Peter O'Toole, John Mills. Simon Ward, Christopher Cazenove. w. Cy Endfield, Anthony Story, d. Douglas Hickox.

DRAMA: Epics; War Stories; War Battles; British Films; Africa

REMAKE OF: Zulu.
(Zulu; Shaka Zulu [miniseries])

1500s
1600s
1700s
1800s
1860s
1890s
1900s
1910s
1920s
1930s
1940s
1950s
1960s
1970s
1980s
1990s

A

Abandoned People
Abortion Dilemmas
Abused Children
Abused Men
Abused Women
Accident Prone
Accidents
Accused Unjustly
ACTION
Action Comedy
Action Drama
Actor/Actress
    Directors
Actors
Actresses

Addicted but
    Nominated
ADVENTURE
Adventure at Sea
Advertising People
Affair Lairs
Africa
Africans
Agatha Christie
Aging
Aging-Reverse
Ahead of Its Time
AIDS Stories
Airlines/Airplanes
Airplane Crashes
Alamo Stories
Alaska
Al Capone
Alcatraz
Alcoholism
Alienation
Aliens-Outer
    Space-Evil
Aliens-Outer
    Space-Good
Allegorical Stories
Alligators
All-Star Cameos
All-Star Cast
Alps-Mountains
Alternative
    Lifestyles
Amazon River

American Dream
American Myth
Americans Abroad
Americans as
    Enemy
Amnesia
Anarchists
Ancient Times
Androids
Angels
Animal Rights
Animals in
    Jeopardy
Animals into
    Humans
Animals-Mutant
Animals-Talking/
    Smart
Animal Stories
Animation-Partial
Animation-Stop
Antarctica
Anti-Establishment
    Films
Anti-Semitism
Anti-War Stories
Apartheid
Apartment
    Buildings
Apocalyptic Stories
Arab People
Archaeologists/
    Paleontologists

Arctic
Argentina
Arkansas
Arms Dealers
Art Films
Artists
Artists-Famous
Art Thieves
Asia (General)
Asian-Americans
Assassination Plots
Astaire & Rogers
Astronauts
Asylums
Atlantic City
Australia
Australian Films
Austria/Vienna
Autobiographical
    Stories
Autobiographical
    Stars
Avant-Garde Films
Avenging Death of
    Someone

B

Babies
Babies-Finding/
    Inheriting
Babies-Having
Babies-Having,
    Late in Life

Babies-Men Having
Babies-Stealing/
    Selling
Baby-sitters
Baby-sitters-Evil
Baby-sitters in
    Jeopardy
Back to School
Ballet
Balloons
Baltimore
Bank Robberies
Baseball
Basketball
Bathroom Humor
Battle of the Bulge
Battle of the Sexes
Beach Movies
Beatnik Era
Beautiful People
Beauty Pageants
Behind the Scenes
Bergmanesque
Berlin
Betrayals
Bets
Beverly Hills
Biblical Stories
Bicycles
Bigamy
Big Band Era
Bigots
Billy the Kid

Bimbos
Bimboys
Biographies
Biographies-
    Fictional
Birds
Bisexuality
Black Among
    Whites
Black & White
    Together
Black as White
Black Casts/Films
Black Comedy
Black Cowboys
Black Directors
Blackmail
Black Men
Blackouts
Black
    Screenwriters
Black Soldiers
Black vs. White
Black Women
Blaxploitation Era
Blind People
Blockbusters
Boardinghouses
Boarding Schools
Boats/Boat Chases/
    Boat Racing
Body Building/
    Body Builders

Jim Thompsonesque
Journalists
Journalists/Writers
   as Detectives
Journey
Judges
Jungles/Jungle Life
Juries
Juvenile
   Delinquents

K
KGB Agents
Kidnappers-
   Sympathizing
   with
Kidnappings
Kill the Beast
Kingdoms
King Henry VIII
Kings
Kitchen Sink
   Drama
Korea
Korean War
Ku Klux Klan

L
L.A. 90s Indies
Las Vegas
Lassie Movies
Latin People/Films
Law School
Lawyers
Lawyers as
   Detectives
Lawyers vs.
   Clients
Leaders
Leaders-Female
Leaders-Tyrant
Legal Thrillers
Legends
Leprechauns
Lesbians
Letters
Liars
Libraries/
   Librarians
Life Transitions
Lincoln-Abraham
Little
   People/Midgets
London
Lonely People
Lookalikes
Looksism
Los Angeles

Losing it All
Lotteries
Louisiana
Love-First
Love-Forbidden
Love-Questionable
Love-Unrequited
Lover Family
   Dislikes
Lovers-Live-in
Lucky People
Lynchings/
   Lynch Mobs
Lyrical Films

M
Macho Men
Madams
Magic/Magicians
Magic Realism
Making a Living
Male Among
   Females
Malicious Menaces
Mama's Boys
Manhunts
Marriage Comedy
Marriage Drama
Marriage-
   Elopement
Marriage-Fake
Marriage-Forced
Marriage for
   Citizenship
Marriage-
   Impending
Marriage-
   Intergenerational
Marriage of
   Convenience
Marriage on the
   Rocks
Married Couples
Marrying Again
Marrying Up
Marshals
Martial Arts
Martians
Marx Brothers
Massacres
Matchmakers
McCarthy Era
Mean Men
Mean Women
Media Satire
Medical Detectives
Medical Drama
Medical School

Medical Thrillers
Medieval Times
Mediterranean
MELODRAMA
Memories
Ménage à Trois
Men and Babies
Men and Boys
Men and Girls
Men as Women
Men Fighting
   Over Women
Men in Conflict
Men in Jeopardy
Men Proving
   Themselves
Men's Films
Mental Illness
Mentally Disabled
   People
Mentors & Role
   Models
Men Who Leave
Mercenaries
Mermaids
Message Films
Meteors
Mexican/Central
   American Films
Mexico
Miami
Middle Ages
Middle East
Midlife Crisis
Midwestern Life
Military Comedy
Military Leaders
Military Schools
Military Stories
Mind-Games
Mining
   Towns/Miners
Miniseries
Miracles
Missing Children
Missing Persons
Missing Person
   Thriller
Missionaries
Mississippi
Mistresses
Misunderstandings
Mix-Ups
Mob-Asian
Mob Comedy
Mob Girls
Mob Stories
Mob Wars

Models
Mod Era
Molestation
Monks
Monologues-
   Interior
Monsters (General)
Monsters-Animal
Monsters-Machine
Monsters-Manmade
Monsters-Mutant
Monsters-
   Mythology
Monsters-
   Toys/Dolls as
Monsters-
   Underwater
Montana Cattle
   Problems
Monte Carlo
Monty Pythoners
Morgues
Morocco
Mortgage Drama
Mothers Alone
Mothers
   & Daughters
Mothers & Sons
Mothers-Struggling
Mothers-Surrogate/
   Adopted
Mothers-
   Troublesome
Mothers-Unwed
Motorcycles
Mountain Climbing
Mountain People
Movie Making
Movie Theaters
Movie within
   a Movie
Multiple
   Performances
Multiple
   Personalities
Multiple Stories
Mummies
Muppets
MURDER
Murder-Attempted
Murder-Clearing
   Oneself
Murder-Coerced/
   Persuaded
Murder-Comic
   Attempts
Murder-Debate
   to Confess

Murder-Discovering
Murderer-Debate
   to Reveal
Murderers-Black
   Widow
Murderers-Female
Murderers-
   Homosexual
Murderers-Nice
Murder in
   Self-Defense
Murder-
   Invitation to
Murder-Learning/
   Teaching to
MURDER
   MYSTERY
Murder of Spouse
Murder-Persuaded/
   Coerced to
Murder of Parents
Murders/
   Murderers-Mass
Murders of
   Children
Murders of
   Homosexuals
Murders of Police
Murders of
   Prostitutes
Murders of
   Teenagers
Murders of Women
Murders (Deaths)-
   One by One
Murphy's Law
   Stories
Muses
Museums
Musical Comedy
Musical Drama
Musical Fantasy
Musical Romance
MUSICALS
Musicals-Animated
Musicals-Disco Era
Musicals-Hippie
Musicals-Operettas
Musicals-
   Rock Opera
Musicals-Westerns
Music Composers/
   Biographies
Music Dies
Musicians
Music Movies
Music Video Style
Mute People

MYSTERY
Mystery-
   Whodunits
Mythology

N
Napoleon
Narrated Films
Native Americans
   (Modern)
Nature-Back to
Nazi Stories
Neighbors-
   Troublesome
Neorealistic Films
Nerds
Nerds & Babes
Nerds
   & Wallflowers
Nerds vs.
   Macho Men
Nervous
   Breakdowns
Neurotic People
New England
New in Town
Newlyweds
New Mexico
New Orleans
Newspapers
New Year's Day/
   Eve
New York Life
New York vs.
   Los Angeles
New Zealand/New
   Zealand Films
Nightclubs
Nightmare
   Journey
Nightmares
North Carolina
North vs. South
Nostalgia
Novel and Play
   Adaptations
Nuclear Energy
Nudism/Nudist
   Colonies
Nuisances
Nuns
Nurses

O
Objects with
   Personalities
Obsessions
Occult

PART 1
General Periods/Decades

see *Prehistoric Settings*
see *Ancient Times*
1500s: see also *Elizabethan Era: Middle Ages: Medieval Era:* The Affairs of Cellini; Aguirre, the Wrath of God; Cyrano de Bergerac; Ivan the Terrible; The Return of Martin Guerre
1600s: see also *1500s: Medieval Era:* Against All Flags; Beau Brummell (1924); Beau Brummell (1954); Blackbeard, The Pirate; Blood on Satan's Claw; Hudson's Bay; Lorna Doone; Maid of Salem; Monsieur Vincent; Rembrandt; The Adventures of Don Juan; The Black Robe; The House of Seven Gables; The Scarlet Letter (1926); The Scarlet Letter (1934); The Scarlet Letter (1980); Squanto; The Wicked Lady (1945); The Wicked Lady (1983); The Witches of Salem
1700s: see also *1600s: Early America: Colonial America:* Barry Lyndon; The Bawdy Adventures of Tom Jones; Botany Bay; Casanova (Fellini's Casanova); The Count of Monte Cristo (1934); The Count of Monte Cristo (1974); Dangerous Liaisons; Danton; Day of Wrath; The Doctor and the Devils; Dr. Syn Alias the Scarecrow; The Draughtsman's Contract; Dubarry Was a Lady; Fanny Hill; Forever Amber; The Four Musketeers; Immortal Beloved; John Paul Jones; Joseph Andrews; Lock Up Your Daughters; The Master of Ballantrae; Monsieur

Beaucaire; Revolution; The Rise of Louis XIV; Rob Roy; The Three Musketeers (1935); The Three Musketeers (1939); The Three Musketeers (1948); The Three Musketeers (1973); The Three Musketeers (1993); Valmont; Young Catherine
1800s: see also *1890s: Civil War Era:* Abe Lincoln in Illinois; The Adventures of Captain Fabian; The Adventures of Gerard; The Adventures of Huckleberry Finn (1960); The Adventures of Huckleberry Finn (1985); The Adventures of Tom Sawyer; The Age of Innocence (1934); The Age of Innocence (1993); All That Money Can Buy; All the Brothers Were Valiant; Angel and the Badman; Anthony Adverse; The Barbary Coast; The Barretts of Wimpole Street (1934); The Barretts of Wimpole Street (1956); Bartleby; Bedlam; Belizaire the Cajun; Bitter Sweet (1933); Bitter Sweet (1940); The Bostonians; Camille (1936); Captain Horatio Hornblower; The Castaway Cowboy; Centennial Summer; Children of Paradise; Come and Get It; The Curse of the Werewolf; David Copperfield; Davy Crockett; The Deceivers Desiree; Doctor Quinn, Medicine Woman; The Duellists; The Frisco Kid (1935); Gervaise; The House of Rothschild; Huckleberry Finn (1939); Huckleberry Finn (1960); Huckleberry

Finn (1974); I Dream of Jeannie; The Immortal Story; The Inheritance; In Old Chicago; Interview with the Vampire; Kitty; Lady Caroline Lamb; The Little Minister; Little Women (1933); Little Women (1949); Little Women (1978); Little Women (1994); Louisiana Purchase; Love and Death; Ludwig; The Man in the Attic; Man in the Wilderness; The Man Who Would Be King; The Mask of the Avenger; The Molly Maguires; Mountains of the Moon; Mrs. Soffel; Nate and Hayes; Nicholas Nickleby; The Old Curiosity Shop; Parnell; The Piano; The Pride and the Passion; Princess Caraboo; Prisoner of Honor; Pudd'nhead Wilson; The Royal Flash; The Sea Devils (1953); Smilin' Through (1932); Smilin' Through (1941); Souls at Sea; Swann in Love; Tai Pan; Tamango; The Toast of New York; 20,000 Leagues Under the Sea; Twins of Evil; The Woman in White; Young Mr. Lincoln; Zorro, the Gay Blade
1860s: see *Civil War Era: Reconstruction Era*
1890s: see also *1800s: 1900s:* The Belle of New York; Can Can; Conduct Unbecoming; Gentleman Jim; The Harvey Girls; Hello Dolly; Here Come the Girls; Hotel Paradiso; I Accuse; I Wonder Who's Kissing Her Now; The Importance of Being Earnest; Irish Eyes Are Smiling; McCabe and Mrs. Miller; A Message to

1960s: see also *Anti-Establishment Films: Anti-War Stories: Hippies: Mod Era: Vietnam Era:* April Fools; Bachelor in Paradise; Backbeat; Banning; Barefoot in the Park; Beyond the Valley of the Dolls; Les Biches; Blowup; Blue Sky; Bob&Carol&Ted&Alice; Born Losers; The Boys in the Band; The Bride Wore Black; A Bronx Tale; Cash McCall; The Chapman Report; Charlie Bubbles; The Cool Ones; Criss Cross (1992); Dirty Dancing; Divorce, American Style; Don't Look Back; The Doors; Easy Rider; The Endless Summer; Experience Preferred . . . ; Faces; Five Corners; The Five Heartbeats; Generation; Getting Straight; GoodFellas; The Graduate; Hair; Hairspray; Helter Skelter (1976); I Love You, Alice B. Toklas; I Wanna Hold Your Hand; The Idolmaker; I'll Never Forget Whatshisname; The Impossible Years; In Cold Blood; Indian Runner; JFK; John and Mary Katherine; Les Liaisons Dangereuses; Live for Life; Love Field; The Love God?; The Magic Christian; Matinee; Me, Natalie; Medium Cool; Mickey One; Midnight Cowboy; A New Kind of Love; Our Man Flint; The President's Analyst; Private Matter; Promise Her Anything; Psych-Out; Quadrophenia; Radio Flyer; Rude Awakening; Scandal; Shampoo; Skidoo; Small Circle of Friends; Some Kind of a Nut; Subject Was Roses; There's a Girl in My Soup; Trash; Trip; Used People; What's New Pussycat?; Wild in the Streets; Woodstock; Yellow Submarine

1970s: see also *Disco Era: Sexual Revolution:* The Adventurers; Alex in Wonderland; Apollo 13; Arousers; The Baby Maker; The Bad News Bears; Blume in Love; The Brady Bunch Movie; Bram Stoker's Count Dracula (1970); California Dreaming; Car Wash; Carlito's Way; Carnal Knowledge; Carrie (1976); The Choirboys; Convoy; Corvette Summer; Count Yorga, Vampire; Crooklyn; Cruising; Dazed and Confused; Driver's Seat; The End of the Road; The Fish that Saved Pittsburgh; FM; Foxes; Fritz the Cat; Fun with Dick and Jane; Gasses; Godspell; The Grass Is Always Greener Over the Septic Tank; Health; A Hero Ain't Nothin' but a Sandwich; Hooper; I Will . . . I Will . . . for Now; I'm Gonna Git You Sucka; Joe; Katherine; Klute; The Last Detail; The Last Married Couple in America; Lifeguard; Little Darlings; Little Murders; The Long Goodbye; Looking for Mr. Goodbar; The Love Machine; Lovers and Other Strangers; Maybe I'll Be Home in the Spring; Minnie and Moskowitz; Move; Nashville; O Lucky Man; One Is a Lonely Number; The Panic in Needle Park; Patty Hearst; Performance; Play It Again, Sam; Pulp Fiction; Return of the Secaucus Seven; The Ritz; River Niger; Rock n' Roll High School; Roller Boogie; RPM; The Scarecrow; Sergeant Pepper's Lonely Hearts Club Band; A Small Circle of Friends; Spirit of '76; Stand Up and Be Counted; The Stepford Wives; Taking Off; Thank God It's Friday; Ticket to Heaven; Turkish Delight; Two People; The War; Welcome to LA; Where the Buffalo Roam; Who Is Harry Kellerman . . . ; Willie and Phil; WUSA; Year of the Gun; You Light Up My Life; Zabriskie Point

1980s: see also *Yuppies: Greed:* Biggles; The Bonfire of the Vanities; Breaking Glass; Campus Man; Decline of Western Civilization; Decline of Western Civilization 2: The Metal Years; Down and Out in Beverly Hills; Fast Times at Ridgemont High; Key Exchange; Lost in America; Paris Is Burning; Perfect; Power; Scarface (1983); Texasville; This Is Spinal Tap; Times Square; To Live and Die in L.A.; Top Gun; Torch Song Trilogy; Wall Street

1990s: see also *1980s:* The Brady Bunch Movie; Higher Learning; PCU

Films by Category

A

Abandoned People: see also *Stranded: Trapped: Children Alone: Children-Finding: Lonely People: Divorce: Cheating Men: Cheating Women:* Aaron Slick from Punkin Crick; Bachelor Mother; Bagdad Café; A Bedtime Story (1933); Blame It on the Night; Dying Room Only; The Kid (1921); Killing Dad; Little Miss Marker (1934); Little Miss Marker (1980); Splitting Heirs; The State of Things; Vagabond

Abbott & Costello (their movies not containing their names in the title): see also *Vaudeville: Abbott & Costello . . . listings:* Africa Screams; Buck Privates; Hold That Ghost; In Society; It Ain't Hay; Jack and the Beanstalk; The Little Giant (1946); Mexican Hayride; Ride 'Em Cowboy; Who Done It? (1942)

Aborigines (Australian black native people): see also *Australia:* The Coca-Cola Kid; Walkabout; Where the Green Ants Dream

Abortion Dilemmas: see also *Mothers-Unwed: Babies-Having:* Agnes of God; Alfie; Blue Denim; Criminal Law; Detective Story; Hedda; Love With the Proper Stranger; Never Too Late; The Carey Treatment; The L-Shaped Room; A Private Matter; A Simple Story; The Unborn; A Woman Is a Woman; Zero Population Growth (Z.P.G.)

Abraham Lincoln: see *Lincoln-Abraham*

Abused Children: see also *Abused Women: Incest: Molestation-Child:* Carrie (1976); David Copperfield; Flowers in the Attic; The Great Santini; Mommie Dearest; Never Take Sweets from a Stranger; September; Small Change; Small Sacrifices; Sybil; This Boy's Life; Waterland; Wildflower

Abused Men: see also *Evil Men: Mean Men: Abused Women: Wives-Troublesome:* Black Angel; The Beguiled; The Rose of Washington Square

Abused Women: see also *Evil Women: Mean Women: Husbands-Troublesome:* Anne of the Thousand Days; Bitter Moon; Blue Velvet; Boxing Helena; The Burning Bed; Caught; Cobb; The Color Purple; Dangerous Game; Diabolique (1955); Dolores Claiborne; Extremities; The Firstborn; The Goddess; Grifters; Jinxed; Kings Row; Klute; Ladybird, Ladybird; The Last Seduction; Looking for Mr. Goodbar; The Match Factory Girl; Monsieur Hire; Mortal Thoughts; The Night Porter; Once Were Warriors; 9½ Weeks; Paris Trout; A Patch of Blue; Radio Flyer; Raging Bull; Sanctuary; Sleeping with the Enemy; Star 80; Sweet Dreams; The Taming of the Shrew; This Boy's Life; Turkish Delight; Under

Capricorn; Waterland; Whore Woman on the Beach; Working Girls

Accident Prone: see also *Accidents: Comedy of Errors: Murphy's Law Stories: Unlucky People:* The Beautiful Blonde from Bashful Bend; Bringing Up Baby; Calamity Jane; Deal of the Century; Delirious; The Disorderly Orderly; Her Alibi; La Chèvre; Legal Eagles; Man of the House; Pure Luck; Running Scared; Some Kind of a Nut; The Tall Blond Man with One Black Shoe; That Touch of Mink; What a Way to Go; What's Up, Doc?; Who's Harry Crumb?

Accidents: see also *Accident Prone: Comedy of Errors: Murphy's Law Stories: Unlucky People:* Blind Side; The Bonfire of the Vanities; The Bowery; The Bullfighter and the Lady; Children of the Corn; Class Action; Darkman; Dead Ahead, the Exxon Valdez Disaster; Dead in the Water; The Dead Zone; Disaster at Silo 7; Dr. Strangelove; The Enchanted Cottage; Erendira; The Fortune Cookie; The Freshman (1925); Friday the Thirteenth (1933); Golden Years; The Hand (1960); The Hand (1981); Ice Castles; In the Cool of the Day; An Italian Straw Hat; Laughter in the Dark; Mad Love; Magnificent Obsession (1935); Magnificent Obsession (1954); The Man Who Came to Dinner; The Man Who

Would Be King; Marooned; The Night Walker; The Promise; Resurrection; A Separate Peace; Shattered; Short Cuts; Smilin' Through (1932); Smilin' Through (1941); The Stunt Man; Whose Life Is It Anyway?; Wings; A Woman's Face; The World According to Garp

Accountants: see Bankers: Embezzlers

Accused Unjustly (of a crime or anything else): see also *Framed?: Murder-Clearing Oneself: Committed-Wrongly: Saving Oneself: Courtroom Drama: Death-Accidental:* Absence of Malice; The Accused (1948); Accused of Murder; An Act of Murder; Action Jackson; After Hours; Agnes of God; Alice's Restaurant; All-American Murder; Along Came Jones; Along the Great Divide; Apartment Zero; The Appaloosa; Assassin; Baby, Take a Bow; Bedroom Eyes; The Bedroom Window; Beyond a Reasonable Doubt; The Big Clock; The Big Steal; The Bigamist; The Bird with the Crystal Plumage; Blackmail (1939); Blood Alley; Blood Relatives; The Blue Dahlia; Body of Evidence; Boomerang (1947); Born in East L.A.; Born Losers; Botany Bay; Bramble Bush; Bread and Chocolate; Breaker Morant; Breakout; Bullitt; Business as Usual; Caged; Caged Heat; Calling Dr. Kildare; Calling Northside 777; The Candy Man; Captain Blood; A Case for Murder; Cause for Alarm; Clockers; Conduct Unbecoming; Confession; Confidentially Yours; The Count of Monte Cristo (1934); The Count of Monte Cristo (1974); A Cry in the Dark; A Dangerous Woman; Daniel; The Dark Half; Dark Passage; Dead in the Water; Death and the Maiden; Defenseless; The Devil's Disciple; Devlin; Dial M For Murder; Disappearance of Aimee; Dolores Claiborne; Doppelganger: The Evil Within; Dunera Boys; The Earl of Chicago; Eddie Macon's Run; Eight on the Lam; The Eyes of Laura Mars; A Few Good Men; The File on Thelma Jordon; A Fire in the Sky; The Fixer; Fly By Night; The Front Page (1931); The Front Page (1974); The Fugitive (1993); The Fugitive: The Final Episode; The Fuller Brush Girl; The Fuller Brush Man; Fury (1936); F/X; F/X 2: The Deadly Art of Illusion; Glass House; The Glass Key (1935); The Glass Key (1942); Good Day for a Hanging; The Grapes of Wrath; Guilty as Sin; The Gun in Betty Lou's Handbag; Hider in the House; House of Women; How to Murder

Your Wife; I Accuse; I Am a Fugitive from a Chain Gang; I Confess; I Want to Live!; I'm No Angel; Illegally Yours; In a Lonely Place; In the Name of the Father; Incident at Oglala; An Innocent Man; Interrogation; Intruder in the Dust; It's a Wonderful World; Jagged Edge; Jennifer 8; Just Cause; Killer McCoy; The Kiss (1929); Kiss the Blood Off My Hands; Knock on Any Door; The Lady from Shanghai; Legal Eagles; Les Misérables (1978); Les Misérables (1935); Les Misérables (1952); Let Him Have It; The Letter (1929); The Letter (1940); The Life of Emile Zola; Light Sleeper; Lightning Strikes Twice; The Lindbergh Kidnapping Case; Lock Up; London Belongs to Me; The Long Goodbye; The Lost Honor of Katharina Blum; Love Has Many Faces; The Lucky Stiff; Macao; Madame X (1929); Madame X (1937); Madame X (1965); Maid of Salem; The Man in the Middle; Mandela; Mary Burns, Fugitive; Meet Me after the Show; Midnight Express; Mildred Pierce; The Morning After; Murder in the First; The Murder Man; Murder of Mary Phagan; Murphy's Law; My Cousin Rachel; My Cousin Vinny; My Forbidden Past; My Learned Friend; Never Take Sweets from a Stranger; No Escape (1936); No Way Out (1987); North by Northwest; The Notorious Landlady; The October Man; Of Mice and Men (1939); Of Mice and Men (1993); The Offence; The Oklahoma Kid; Once Upon a Crime; The Onion Field; Ordeal by Innocence; The Ox-Bow Incident; Paid; The Paper; A Passage to India; Past Midnight; The People against O'Hara; Peter Ibbetson; Physical Evidence; Prisoner of Honor; The Railway Children; Razorback; The Reckless Moment; Remember My Name; Reversal of Fortune; Roxie Hart; The Runner Stumbles; Running on Empty; Saboteur; Sacco and Vanzetti; Salome, Where She Danced; Scarlet Street; See No Evil, Hear No Evil; Seems Like Old Times; Shakes the Clown; The Shawshank Redemption; Shocker; Silas Marner; Slamdance; Spellbound; Stir Crazy; Storyville; Strange Bargain; Strangers on a Train; A Tale of Two Cities (1935); A Tale of Two Cities (1958); A Tale of Two Cities (1982); The Talk of the Town; The Tall Blond Man with One Black Shoe; Tango & Cash; Tank; Term of Trial; Thelma & Louise; These Three; They Live by Night; They Made Me a Criminal; They Won't Believe Me; They Won't Forget; The

Thin Blue Line; The Thirty-Nine Steps (1935); The Thirty-Nine Steps (1959); The Thirty-Nine Steps (1978); Three Fugitives; Time Without Pity; To Catch a Thief; To Kill a Mockingbird; Tom Horn; Touch of Evil; Traces of Red; Trade Winds; Trial (1955); The Trial (1962); Trial (1993); Trial and Error; True Believer; True Confession; Under Suspicion; Unlawful Entry; Vicki; The Walking Dead; The Water Babies; Waxwork; Waxwork II: Lost in Time; We Are Not Alone; Where Are the Children?; Whirlpool; Widows' Peak; Wilt; The Winslow Boy; The Witches of Salem; The Wrong Man; You Can't Get Away with Murder; Young Mr. Lincoln; The Young Savages

Acting Teams: see *Astaire & Rogers: Tracy & Hepburn: Abbott & Costello*

ACTION: see also *ADVENTURE: Crime Drama: Action Comedy: Chase Movies: War Stories:* The Abductors; About Face; Above the Law; Above the Rim; Aces, Iron Eagle 3; Across 110th Street; Action in Arabia; Action in the North Atlantic; Action Jackson; The Adventures of Ford Fairlane; The Adventures of Tartu; Air America; Air Force; Aladdin; Aloha, Bobby and Rose; The Amateur; Amazing Stories; Amazon; The Ambushers; American Anthem; American Ninja; American Ninja 2, The Confrontation; American Ninja 3, Amsterdamned; Angel; Another 48 Hours; Any Which Way You Can; Appointment in Honduras; Arabesque; Armed Response; Army of Darkness; Assault on Precinct 13; Attack; The Atomic City; Avalanche Express; Back to the Future; Back to the Future II; Back to the Future III; Backdraft; Bad Boys (1994); Bad Man's River; Bandolero!; Batman; Batman Returns; Batman, the Movie; Battle for the Planet of the Apes; The Battle of Algiers; Battle of Britain; The Battle of the Bulge; The Battle of Neretva; Battleground; The Beastmaster; The Beastmaster 2; The Bedford Incident; Ben Hur (1959); Ben Hur: A Tale of the Christ (1925); Beneath the Twelve Mile Reef; Best of the Best; Beverly Hills Cop; Beverly Hills Cop 2; Beverly Hills Cop 3; Big Bad Mama; The Big Brawl; Big Foot; The Biggest Bundle of Them All; The Big House; The Big Red One; The Big Steal; Big Trouble in Little China; Billy Jack; Black Caesar; The Black Cauldron; The Black Hole; Black Moon Rising; The Black Pirate; Black Rain (1989); Black

Sunday (1977); Blade Runner; Blind Fury; Blood and Concrete; Bloodfist; Bloodfist II; Bloodfist III; Blood Hunt; Bloodsport; Bloody Mama; Blown Away; The Blue Max; The Blues Brothers; Blue Thunder; Body and Soul (1981); Body Slam; The Bold and the Brave; Bonnie and Clyde; Borderline; Born Losers; The Bounty Hunters; The Boys Next Door; Brain Smasher: A Love Story; Brainscan; Brannigan; Brass Target; Braveheart; Breakheart Pass; Breakout; Bring Me the Head of Alfredo Garcia; The Buccaneer (1938); The Buccaneer (1958); Buck and the Preacher; A Bullet for the General; The Bullfighter and the Lady; Bullitt; Bunny O'Hare; Butch Cassidy and the Sundance Kid; Caged Fear; Caged Heat; The Cannonball Run; The Cannonball Run 2; Capone; Captain America; Captain Blood; Captains of the Clouds; The Car; Casino Royale; Cast a Giant Shadow; The Challenge; Champion; The Charge of the Light Brigade (1936); The Charge of the Light Brigade (1968); Charley Varrick; The Chase (1947); The Chase (1994); Cherry 2000; China; China Girl (1987); China Seas; The Choirboys; The Cisco Kid; City Streets; Clash of the Titans; Class of 1999; Class of '84; Clear and Present Danger; Cleopatra Jones; Cleopatra Jones & The Casino of Gold; Cliffhanger; Cobra; Code of Silence; Cohen and Tate; Colors; The Comancheros; Comin' At Ya!; Command Decision; Commando; Conan, the Barbarian; Conan, the Destroyer; Confessions of a Hit Man; Conflict of Interest; Conquest of the Planet of the Apes; Convoy; Coogan's Bluff; Cop; The Corsican Brothers; Cotton Comes to Harlem; The Crow; Cyborg; The Dam Busters; Dangerous Curves; Dark of the Sun; Darkman; The Dawn Patrol; Days of Thunder; Dead Bang; Dead Boyz Can't Fly; Dead Heat; Dead Heat on a Merry Go Round; Deadlier Than the Male; Deadlock; The Dead Pool; Death Race 2000; Death Warrant; Death Wish; Death Wish 2; Death Wish 3; Death Wish 4; Death Wish 5; The Deep; The Defiant Ones; Delta Force; Delta Force 2; Delta Heat; Demolition Man; The Desert Fox; The Desert Rats; Desert Law; Desperate Journey; Destination Tokyo; Detonator; The Devil's Brigade; Diamonds Are Forever; Dick Tracy; Die Hard; Die Hard 2; The Dion Brothers; The Dirty Dozen; Dirty Harry; The Dogs of War; The

Domino Principle; The Double O Kid; Double Impact; The Driver; DROP Squad; Drop Zone; Dr. No; D2: The Mighty Ducks; Duel; The Eagle Has Landed; Eat My Dust; Eddie Macon's Run; The Eiger Sanction; 8 Million Ways to Die; Eighty-Four Charlie Mopic; El Cid; El Mariachi; Embassy; The Empire Strikes Back; The Enforcer (1950); The Enforcer (1976); Enter the Dragon; Escape from Alcatraz; Escape from New York; Evel Knievel; Every Which Way But Loose; The Evil That Men Do; Excalibur; Excessive Force; The Exterminator; The Exterminator 2; Extreme Justice; Extreme Prejudice; An Eye for an Eye; Fatal Beauty; Fathom; The FBI Story; Fifty/Fifty; 55 Days at Peking; The Fighting Seabees; The Final Countdown; Fire Over England; Firefox (1982); Firepower; First Blood; The Flame and the Arrow; Flaming Star; The Flash; Flash Gordon; Flashpoint; Flesh and Blood (1985); Flight of the Intruder; Flight of the Navigator; Flying Leathernecks; Flying Tigers; A Force of One; Force Ten from Navarone; For Your Eyes Only; Fort Apache, the Bronx; Fortress; 48 Hours; The Four Feathers (1929); The Four Feathers (1939); The Four Feathers (1977); The Four Musketeers; Freebie and the Bean; Freejack; The French Connection; The French Connection II; The Friends of Eddie Coyle; From Russia with Love; The Fugitive (1993); Funeral in Berlin; G Men; A Game of Death; A Gathering of Eagles; Gator; The Gauntlet; The Getaway (1972); The Getaway (1994); Get Carter; Ghostbusters; Ghostbusters II; The Gladiator; Gleaming the Cube; Gloria; Glory; The Godfather; The Godfather Part II; The Godfather Part III; God Is My Co-Pilot; Godzilla (1955); Godzilla versus Gigan; Godzilla versus Megalon; Gold; The Golden Voyage of Sinbad; Goldfinger; Good Guys Wear Black; Goodbye Pork Pie; The Goonies; Grand Prix; Grand Theft Auto; Greased Lightning; The Great Escape; The Great Escape 2: The Untold Story; The Great Race; The Great Smokey Roadblock; The Green Berets; Green Ice; Guadalcanal Diary; The Gumball Rally; Gun Crazy (1950); Gun Crazy (1992); Gunfight at the OK Corral; Gung Ho! (1943); Gunga Din; The Guns of Navarone; Guns of the Magnificent Seven; Gymkata; Hammerhead; Hanna's War; Hard Contract; Hard to Kill; The Hard Way (1991); Harlem Nights; Harley

Davidson and the Marlboro Man; Heartbreak Ridge; Heat; Hell and High Water; Hell's Angels; Hellcats of the Navy; Herbie Goes Bananas; Herbie Goes to Monte Carlo; Herbie Rides Again; Hercules (1957); Hercules in New York; Hercules Unchained; Hero at Large; The Heroes of Telemark; High Plains Drifter; High Risk; High Road to China; High Sierra; High-Ballin'; Highlander; Highlander II-The Quickening; Highlander III, The Sorcerer; Highpoint; Hit!; The Hit; Hit Man; Hombre; Honey, I Blew Up the Kid; Honey, I Shrunk the Kids; Hooper; Hornet's Nest; Hot Shots!; Hot Shots, Part Deux; Hudson Hawk; The Hunt for Red October; The Hunter; Hustle; I Died a Thousand Times; I the Jury (1953); I the Jury (1982); I Walk the Line; I'm Gonna Git You, Sucka; Ice Pirates; In Like Flint; In the Heat of the Night; Inchon; Indiana Jones and the Last Crusade; Indiana Jones and the Temple of Doom; Innerspace; Inside Out; The Internecine Project; Into the Sun; Iron Eagle; Iron Eagle II; The Iron Mask (1929); Iron Maze; The Island (1980); The Italian Job; It's a Mad Mad Mad Mad World; Ivanhoe; Jack of All Trades; Jackson County Jail; Jakarta; Jane and the Lost City; Jason and the Argonauts; Jaws; Jaws 2; Jaws 3-D; Jaws 4: The Revenge; Jewel of the Nile; Joe Panther; Josh and S.A.M.; Judgment Night; Jurassic Park; K-9; K9000; Kagemusha; Kansas City Bomber; Kansas City Confidential; The Karate Kid; The Karate Kid Part II; The Karate Kid III; Kelly's Heroes; Khartoum; Kickboxer; Kickboxer 2; Kidnapped (1938); Kidnapped (1959); Kidnapped (1971); The Kidnapping of the President; The Killer Elite; Killer Fish; The Killers (1964); Killing Zoe; Kindergarten Cop; King Kong (1933); King Kong (1976); King of New York; The King of the Hill (1965); Kinjite, Forbidden Subjects; Kiss Tomorrow Goodbye; The Klansman; Knightriders; Knute Rockne, All American; Krull; Kuffs; La Femme Nikita; Lady Killer (1933); The Land That Time Forgot; The Last Action Hero; The Last American Hero; The Last Boy Scout; Last House on the Left; The Last of the Mohicans (1936); The Last of the Mohicans (1992); The Last Starfighter; The Last Valley; The Lavender Hill Mob; The Legend of the Lone Ranger; Le Mans; Lethal Weapon; Lethal Weapon 2; Lethal

Weapon 3; License to Kill; The Lighthorsemen; Lion of the Desert; The Liquidator; Little Caesar; Live a Little, Steal a Lot; Live and Let Die; Live Wire; Lives of a Bengal Lancer; The Living Daylights; Lock Up; The Lolly Madonna War; Lone Wolf McQuade; The Lone Ranger (1955); The Lone Ranger and the Lost City of Gold; The Longest Yard; Love and Bullets; The Loveless; Low Down Dirty Shame; Machine Gun McCain; Macon County Line; Mad Max; Mad Max Beyond Thunderdome; Madigan; Magnum Force; The Magnificent Seven; Major Dundee; Malone; A Man Could Get Killed; The Man from Snowy River; Manhunter; Maniac Cop; Maniac Cop 2; The Man with the Golden Gun; Marked for Death; The Mark of Zorro (1920); The Mark of Zorro (1940); The Mask (1994); The Mask of Fu Manchu; Mask of the Avenger; Masquerade (1965); McBain; McQ; The Mechanic; The Menace; Men of the Fighting Lady; Men with Wings; The Meteor Man; Midnight Run; Midway; Mighty Joe Young; Millennium; Missing in Action; Missing in Action 2-The Beginning; The Mob; Modesty Blaise; Moonraker; The Most Dangerous Game; Mother, Jugs and Speed; Moving Violation; Mr. Billion; Mr. Nanny; Murder, Inc.; Murderer's Row; Murphy's Law; My Learned Friend; The Naked and the Dead; The Naked Prey; Navy SEALS; Never Say Never Again; Never So Few; The New Barbarians; New Jack City; Next of Kin (1989); Nighthawks (1981); 1941; 99 and 44/100 Per Cent Dead; Nitti, the Enforcer; No Escape (1994); No Escape, No Return; No Man's Land (1987); No Mercy; None But the Brave; North by Northwest; Northwest Mounted Police; Northwest Passage; O.S.S.; Objective Burma; The Octagon; Octopussy; On Deadly Ground; On Her Majesty's Secret Service; One Million BC (1940); One Million Years BC (1966); Operation Amsterdam; Operation CIA; Operation Crossbow; Orca-Killer Whale; Our Man Flint; Outbreak; The Outfit (1973); The Outfit (1993); Outland; Outlaw Blues; The Outside Man; The Outsiders; Over the Top; The Package; Passenger 57; Pat Garrett and Billy the Kid; Patriot Games; Pink Cadillac; Planet of the Apes; Point Break; Point of No Return; Pork Chop Hill; The Poseidon Adventure; Posse (1975); Predator; Predator 2; The Pride and the Passion;

Prime Cut; The Professional; Public Enemy; Pulp Fiction; Quick; The Quick and the Dead; Quicksilver; Raid on Rommel; Raiders of the Lost Ark; Rambo: First Blood Part Two; Rambo III; Ransom; Rapid Fire; Raw Deal; Real Men; Rebel Rousers; Red Dawn; Red Heat; Red Line 7000; Red Sonja; Remo Williams: The Adventure Begins; Renegades; The Rescue; Rescue Me; Reservoir Dogs; Return of Superfly; Return of the Jedi; Return to Macon County; The Return of the Musketeers; Richie Rich; Ricochet; Rififi; Ring of the Musketeers; The Rise and Fall of Legs Diamond; The River Wild; Road House; The Road Warrior; The Roaring Twenties; Robin Hood (1922); Robin Hood (1973); Robin Hood (1990); Robin Hood: Prince of Thieves (1991); Robocop; Robocop 2; Rob Roy; The Rocketeer; Rocky; Rocky II; Rocky III; Rocky IV; Rollerball; Rolling Thunder; Romper Stomper; The Rookie; Rosebud; Run for the Sun; Runaway; Runaway Train; The Running Man (1987); S*P*Y*S; Sabre Jet; The St. Valentine's Day Massacre; Samson and Delilah; The Sands of Iwo Jima; The Satan Bug; Scaramouche; Scarface (1932); Scarface (1983); The Scarface Mob/The Untouchables Pilot; The Scarlet Pimpernel; The Sea Wolves; The Second Best Secret Agent in the Whole Wide World; Seven Samurai; The Seventh Voyage of Sinbad; The Seven-Ups; The Shadow (1940); The Shadow (1994); Shaft; Shaft in Africa; Shaft's Big Score; Shakedown; Shaker Run; Shalako; Sharky's Machine; Sheena, Queen of the Jungle; Shogun Assassin; The Shooting; Shoot to Kill; The Sicilian; The Silencers; Silverado; Sitting Target; Sky Devils; Skyjacked; Slap Shot; Slipstream; A Small Town in Texas; Smokey and the Bandit; Smokey and the Bandit II; Smokey and the Bandit III; The Sniper; Sodom and Gomorrah; Solarbabies; Son of Kong; Son of Sinbad; Spartacus; The Specialist; Speed; Speedway; Spinout; Split Second; Spymaker, The Secret Life of Ian Fleming; The Spy Who Loved Me; Stakeout; Stargate; Star Trek: The Motion Picture; Star Trek II: The Wrath of Khan; Star Trek III: The Search for Spock; Star Trek IV: The Voyage Home; Star Trek V: The Final Frontier; Star Trek VI: The Undiscovered Country; Star Trek: Generations; Star Wars; State of Grace; Stick; Stone Cold;

Strategic Air Command; Street Fighter; Streets of Fire; Streets of Gold; Striking Distance; Stroker Ace; Suburban Commando; Subway; Sudden Impact; Sugar Hill; The Sugarland Express; Super Mario Brothers; Super Cops; Superfly; Supergirl; Superman; Superman 2; Superman 3; Superman 4; Swashbuckler; The Sword and the Sorcerer; The Sword in the Stone; Sword of the Valiant; The Taking of Beverly Hills; The Taking of Pelham 123; Tango & Cash; Tank; Tank Girl; Taps; Target; The Tarnished Angels; Teenage Mutant Ninja Turtles; Teenage Mutant Ninja Turtles 2; Teenage Mutant Ninja Turtles 3; Tequila Sunrise; Terminal Velocity; The Terminator; Terminator 2: Judgment Day; That Man from Rio; Thelma & Louise; They Call Me Mister Tibbs!; They Died with Their Boots On; They Live; They Only Kill Their Masters; The Thief of Bagdad (1924); The Thief of Baghdad (1940); 13 Rue Madeleine; Thirty Seconds Over Tokyo; This Gun for Hire; The 300 Spartans; The Three Musketeers (1935); The Three Musketeers (1939); The Three Musketeers (1948); The Three Musketeers (1973); The Three Musketeers (1993); Those Daring Young Men in Their Jaunty Jalopies; Those Magnificent Men in Their Flying Machines; Three Ninjas; Three Ninjas Kick Back; Thunder and Lightning; Thunder Bay; Thunder Road; Thunderball; Thunderbolt and Lightfoot; Time Cop; The Time Machine; Time Runner; Timebomb; Timerider; To Live and Die in L.A.; Tobruk; Too Late the Hero; Top Gun; Tora! Tora! Tora!; Total Recall; Tough Guys; The Towering Inferno; The Toxic Avenger; The Toxic Avenger, Part II; The Toxic Avenger Part III; Toy Soldiers; The Train; The Trap; Treasure Island (1934); Treasure Island (1971); Treasure Island (1990); Treasure Island (1991); Trespass; The Trojan War; Tron; True Lies; True Romance; Tuff Turf; Twenty Thousand Years in Sing Sing; Twins; Two Lane Blacktop; Two Minute Warning; Ulysses (1954); Uncommon Valor; Under Fire; Under Siege; Undercover Blues; Underworld, USA; Universal Soldier; Unlawful Entry; The Untouchables; Vanishing Point; The Victors; Victory; A View to a Kill; The Vikings; Viva Zapata; Von Ryan's Express; WW and the Dixie Dancekings; Wake Island; A Walk in the Sun; The Wanderers; Wanted Dead or Alive; Warlock (1989);

The Warriors; Waxwork II: Lost in Time; Wedlock; Where Eagles Dare; White Heat; White Lightning; Why Me?; The Wilby Conspiracy; The Wild Angels; The Wild Bunch; The Wild Geese; The Wild Geese II; The Wild One; Willow; Winchester 73; Winged Victory; Wings; Winning; The Wrecking Crew; The Yakuza; The Year of the Dragon; Year of the Gun; Yojimbo; You Can't Get Away with Murder; You Only Live Twice; Young Guns; Young Guns II

Action Comedy: see also *ACTION: Capers: Fugitives: Heist Stories: FARCE:* Adventures in Babysitting; After the Fox; Air America; All Through the Night; The Ambushers; Another 48 Hours; Any Which Way You Can; Arabesque; Back to the Future; Back to the Future 2; Back to the Future 3; Bad Boys (1994); Bad Man's River; Batman, the Movie; Behave Yourself!; Beverly Hills Cop; Beverly Hills Cop 2; Beverly Hills Cop 3; The Big Brawl; Biggest Bundle of Them All; Bird on a Wire; Blind Fury; Blood and Concrete; The Blues Brothers; Bonnie and Clyde; Brain Smasher: A Love Story; The Brinks Job; Broadway Danny Rose; Bunny O'Hare; Butch Cassidy and the Sundance Kid; Cannonball Run; Cannonball Run 2; Casino Royale; The Chase (1994); Cherry 2000; The Corsican Brothers; Cotton Comes to Harlem; D.C. Cab; D2: The Mighty Ducks; Dead Heat; Deadlier Than the Male; Diamonds Are Forever; Die Laughing; Dion Brothers; Double O Kid; DROP Squad; Eat My Dust; El Mariachi; Every Which Way But Loose; A Fish Called Wanda; The Flame and the Arrow; Flashback; Fletch; Fletch Lives; Flight of the Navigator; 48 Hours; Freebie and the Bean; Ghostbusters; Ghostbusters 2; The Goonies; Grand Theft Auto; Greased Lightning; The Great Race; The Great Smokey Roadblock; The Gumball Rally; Gunga Din; Hanky Panky; A Hard Day's Night; The Hard Way (1991); Harlem Nights; Harley Davidson and the Marlboro Man; Herbie Goes Bananas; Herbie Goes to Monte Carlo; Herbie Rides Again; Hero at Large; High Risk; High-Ballin'; High Road to China; Home Alone; Home Alone 2: Lost in New York; Hooper; Hot Shots!; Hot Shots, Part Deux; Hudson Hawk; I Love Trouble (1994); I'm Gonna Git You, Sucka; Ice Pirates; In Like Flint; Indiana Jones & The Last Crusade; Indiana Jones and the Temple of Doom; Innerspace; Into the Sun; The Italian Job; It's a Mad Mad

Mad Mad World!; Jewel of the Nile; Josh and S.A.M.; K-9; K9000; Kindergarten Cop; Kuffs; Last Action Hero; The Lavender Hill Mob; Lethal Weapon; Lethal Weapon 2; Lethal Weapon 3; The Liquidator; Low Down Dirty Shame; A Man Could Get Killed; The Man with the Golden Gun; The Mask (1994); Meteor Man; Midnight Run; Miracles; Money for Nothing; Moonraker; Mother, Jugs and Speed; Mr. Nanny; Never Say Never Again; 1941; No Deposit, No Return; North by Northwest; Octopussy; One, Two, Three; Our Man Flint; Outlaw Blues; Outrageous Fortune; Pee-wee's Big Adventure; Pink Cadillac; Pulp Fiction; Raiders of the Lost Ark; Raising Arizona; Real Men; Return to Macon County; Richie Rich; Ring of the Musketeers; S*P*Y*S; The Second Best Secret Agent in the Whole Wide World; Short Time; Slither; Smokey and the Bandit; Smokey and the Bandit II; Smokey and the Bandit III; The Spy Who Loved Me; Stakeout; Stroker Ace; Suburban Commando; Sugarland Express; Sullivan's Travels; The Super Cops; Superfly; Supergirl; Taking of Beverly Hills; Tango & Cash; Tank; Teen Wolf; Teen Wolf Too; Teenage Mutant Ninja Turtles; Teenage Mutant Ninja Turtles 2; Teenage Mutant Ninja Turtles 3; That Man from Rio; Thelma & Louise; Those Daring Young Men in Their Jaunty Jalopies; Those Magnificent Men in Their Flying Machines; The Three Musketeers (1973); The Three Musketeers (1993); Three Ninjas; Three Ninjas Kick Back; Three O'Clock High; Thunder and Lightning; Tough Guys; True Lies; Twins; Undercover Blues; View to a Kill; WW and the Dixie Dancekings; What's Up, Doc?; Why Me?; The Wrecking Crew; Year of the Comet

Action Drama (a story that is primarily a drama, but that has substantial action sequences): see also *ACTION: Action Comedy: Crime Drama:* Above the Rim; Across the Pacific; Action in Arabia; Action in the North Atlantic; Aloha, Bobby and Rose; The Amateur; Amazon; The Atomic City; Back to Bataan; Backdraft; Battle of the Bulge; The Battle of Neretva; Battleground; Big Bad Mama; The Big House; The Big Red One; Billy Jack; Black Rain (1989); Black Sunday (1977); Blown Away; Blue Thunder; The Bold and the Brave; Bonnie and Clyde; The Bounty Hunters; Caged Fear; Cast a

Giant Shadow; Ceiling Zero; Champion; The Charge of the Light Brigade (1936); The Charge of the Light Brigade (1968); The Chase (1947); China Seas; The Cisco Kid; City Streets; Colors; Command Decision; Coogan's Bluff; Days of Thunder; Dead Boyz Can't Fly; The Desert Fox; The Desert Rats; Desperate Journey; The Driver; Escape from Alcatraz; Evel Knievel; Fifty/Fifty; 55 Days at Peking; Firepower; The French Connection; French Connection II; A Gathering of Eagles; Glory; The Godfather; The Godfather Part II; The Godfather Part III; Good Guys Wear Black; Goodbye, Pork Pie; The Great Escape; Guadalcanal Diary; Guns of the Magnificent Seven; Hellcats of the Navy; High Sierra; Hit; Hornet's Nest; The Hunt for Red October; The Hunter; Hustle; Jack of All Trades; Jakarta; Joan of Paris; Kagemusha; The Kidnapping of the President; The Killers (1964); Killing Zoe; King of the Hill (1965); The Klansman; Les Valseuses; Lighthorsemen; Little Fauss and Big Halsey; The Long Good Friday; Men of the Fighting Lady; Men with Wings; Murder Inc.; None But the Brave; Objective Burma; One That Got Away; Orca-Killer Whale; The Outfit (1973); The Outfit (1993); The Outside Man; The Outsiders; Paths of Glory; Pork Chop Hill; Posse (1975); The Pride and the Passion; The Professional; The Public Enemy; Quick and the Dead; Rebel Rousers; Reservoir Dogs; Return of Superfly; The Roaring Twenties; Rocky; Rocky II; Rocky III; Rocky IV; Romper Stomper; Rookie; Runaway Train; The Shooting; State of Grace; Strategic Air Command; Sugar Hill; Taps; Target; Tequila Sunrise; Thelma & Louise; They Died with Their Boots On; They Only Kill Their Masters; 13 Rue Madeleine; Thirty Seconds Over Tokyo; Thunder Bay; Thunder Road; Thunderbolt and Lightfoot; Too Late the Hero; The Towering Inferno; True Romance; Twelve O'Clock High; Twenty Thousand Years in Sing Sing; Two Lane Blacktop; Wild in the Streets; The Wild One; Winning

Actor/Actress Directors: (Notable actors or actresses who are also directors of these particular films, but not necessarily starring in them): see also **Directors: Actors: Writer-Directors:** Adventures of Sherlock Holmes' Smarter Brother; Angelo, My Love; The Bellboy; Born in East L.A.; Born Losers;

Braveheart; A Bronx Tale; The Buccaneer (1938); The Buccaneer (1958); Buck and the Preacher; Cadence; A Chorus Line; Christmas in Connecticut (1992); The Conqueror; Cooperstown; Cop and a Half; Cotton Comes to Harlem; Cracking Up; Dr. Faustus; Drive, He Said; The Effect of Gamma Rays on Man-in-the-Moon Marigolds; Fatso; The Four Seasons; Gandhi; Gator; The Gauntlet; Grand Theft Auto; A Guide for the Married Man; Harlem Nights; Hide in Plain Sight; Husbands; Husbands and Wives; The Immortal Story; Indian Runner; J. W. Coop; Jo Jo Dancer, Your Life Is Calling; The Kentuckian; Kotch; Lady L.; Let's Do It Again (1975); Little Murders; Low Down Dirty Shame; The Man on the Eiffel Tower; Manhattan; Manhattan Murder Mystery; Masala; Midnight Clear; The Midnight Man; The Milagro Beanfield War; Miles from Home; Mr. Saturday Night; The Naked Prey; New Life; The Night of the Hunter; Of Mice and Men (1993); On Deadly Ground; One Eyed Jacks; Out of the Blue; Outrage (1956); Pedestrian; Play Misty for Me; Posse (1975); The Prince and the Showgirl; Psycho 3; Quiz Show; Rachel, Rachel; Reality Bites; Shadow Box; Shadowlands; Sometimes a Great Notion; Stick; Sword of Lancelot; The Three Sisters; The Two Jakes; The Unforgiven (1992); Wildflower; Wisdom

Actor Impostors: see Impostors-Actor

Actors: see also *Hollywood Life: Biographies: Biographies-Fictional:* An Actor's Revenge; After the Rehearsal; Amber Waves; Andy Warhol's Heat; Band Wagon; The Big Knife; Bottoms Up; Broadway Melody of 1936; Broadway Melody of 1938; Broadway Melody of 1940; Bullets Over Broadway; Callaway Went Thataway; Career; Casanova's Big Night; Caught in the Act; Caught in the Draft; Children of Paradise; A Chorus Line; The Country Girl; Cracking Up; Dancing in the Dark; A Double Life; The Dresser; Enter Laughing; Evil Under the Sun; F/X; F/X 2: The Deadly Art of Illusion; Fellow Traveller; Footlight Parade; Forever James Dean; The French Lieutenant's Woman; Gable and Lombard; General Della Rovere; The George Raft Story; Glamour Boy; Good Companions (1933); Good Companions (1956); The Goodbye Girl; The Great Garrick; The Guardsman; The Hard Way (1991); Heart

of the West; Hearts of Darkness: A Filmmaker's Apocalypse; Hell, Heaven, and Hoboken; Hollywood Boulevard (1936); Hollywood Canteen; Hollywood or Bust; Hollywood Shuffle; The Icicle Thief; I'll Do Anything; Inserts; Inside Daisy Clover; Into the Sun; Ishtar; It's a Great Feeling; It's Love I'm After; Jesus of Montreal; Jimmy Hollywood; Kiss Me Kate (1953); Lady Killer (1933); The Last Command; The Last Movie; Law of Desire; Life Begins at 8:30; Life with Mikey; Lily in Love; Living in Oblivion; Long Day's Journey into Night; The Love Lottery; Madhouse; Man in Love; A Man Like Eva; Man of a Thousand Faces; The Man with Two Faces; Mary, Mary; Men Are Not Gods; Mephisto; The Mirror Crack'd; Moon Over Parador; Movers and Shakers; Mrs. Doubtfire; My Favorite Year; Never a Dull Moment (1967); Nicholas Nickleby; Noises Off; On the Air; On the Avenue; On the Double; The One and Only; The Oscar; The Pirate; The Producers; The Purple Rose of Cairo; Rehearsal for Murder; Rendez-Vous; Rock Hudson's Home Movies; The Royal Family of Broadway; Scaramouche; The Secret Life of an American Wife; Shakespeare Wallah; Showboat (1936); Showboat (1951); Sing Baby Sing; Soapdish; S.O.B.; Speaking Parts; Stage Fright; A Star Is Born (1937); A Star Is Born (1954); A Star Is Born (1976); The Stunt Man; Sunset; Sweet Liberty Sweethearts; The Tall Guy; Targets; That's Adequate; Theatre of Blood; There's No Business like Show Business; This Happy Feeling; To Be or Not to Be (1942); To Be or Not to Be (1983); Tootsie; Torch Song Trilogy; 29th Street; Two Weeks in Another Town; Under the Rainbow; Valentino (1951); Valentino (1977); W. C. Fields and Me; Weeds; Whistling in the Dark; The Wild Party; Wings of Fame; Wired; Withnail and I; Without Reservations; The World's Greatest Lover

Actresses: see also *Hollywood Life: Biographies: Biographies-Fictional: Female Protagonists:* Actors and Sin; The Actress (1928); The Actress (1953); The Affairs of Annabel; After the Rehearsal; All About Eve; Anna; April in Paris; At Long Last Love; The Barefoot Contessa; The Barkleys of Broadway; Bedtime Story (1941); Bellisima; Best Foot Forward; Black Widow (1954); The Bodyguard; Bombshell; Boy, Did I Get a Wrong

Number; Broadway Melody of 1936; Broadway Melody of 1938; Broadway Melody of 1940; Bullets Over Broadway; Cabaret; Cairo (1942); Calendar Girl; California Suite; The Cameraman; Carrie (1952); Chapter Two; Chatterbox; Children of Paradise; A Chorus Line; Dangerous; A Dangerous Game; Darling; Darling Lili; Day for Night; Dead of Winter; Death Becomes Her; Diamond Jim; Dramatic School; Echo Park; Exorcist; The Fan; Fedora; Follies in Concert; Fools for Scandal; Footlight Parade; Forever Female; Frances; The French Lieutenant's Woman; The Fuzzy Pink Nightgown; Gable and Lombard; Garbo Talks; The Girl Can't Help It; Give the Girl a Break; Go West Young Man; The Goddess; The Good Companions (1933); The Good Companions (1956); The Hard Way (1943); Harlow; Harum Scarum; The Helen Morgan Story; Hollywood Boulevard (1977); Hollywood Canteen; Hollywood Hotel; Hollywood Shuffle; I Am a Camera; I Could Go on Singing; I Dood It!; I Found Stella Parish; I Ought to Be in Pictures; I'll Cry Tomorrow; I'll Do Anything; Imitation of Life (1934); Imitation of Life (1959); In Person; The Incredible Sarah; Indiscreet; Inside Daisy Clover; It's a Date; It's a Great Feeling; It's Love I'm After; The Killing of Sister George; Kiss Me Kate (1953); La Maschera; The Lady Is Willing; The Last Movie; Legend of Lylah Clare; A Little Night Music; The Lonely Lady; The Love Goddesses; La Lumière; A Man Like Eva; Mardi Gras; Marilyn, the Untold Story; A Matter of Time; Meet Me after the Show; Meet the People; The Miracle (1990); The Miracle of the Bells; The Mirror Crack'd; The Moon's Our Home; The Morning After; Morning Glory; Movers and Shakers; My Six Loves; My Wild Irish Rose; Noises Off; On the Air; Opening Night; The Oscar; Outrageous Fortune; Passion Fish; The Perfect Furlough; The Perils of Pauline; Please Don't Eat the Daisies; Poor Little Rich Girl; Postcards from the Edge; Power, Passion, and Murder; Presenting Lily Mars; The Prince and the Showgirl; The Prizefighter and the Lady; Rehearsal for Murder; Rendez-Vous; Rock a Bye Baby; Rollover; The Roman Spring of Mrs. Stone; Rose of Washington Square; The Royal Family of Broadway; Savage Intruder; Sayonara; Scenes from the Class

Struggle in Beverly Hills; Second Fiddle; September; Showboat (1936); Showboat (1951); Sidewalks of London; Singin' in the Rain; Soapdish; Somewhere in Time; Sophia Loren, Her Own Story; St. Martin's Lane; Stage Door; Stage Fright; Stage Struck; Star; A Star Is Born (1937); A Star Is Born (1954); Star of Midnight; The Stunt Man; Sunset Boulevard; Sweet Bird of Youth; Sweet Liberty; Sweethearts; The Tender Trap; There's No Business like Show Business; To Be or Not to Be (1942); To Be or Not to Be (1983); Torch Song; Twentieth Century; Two Weeks in Another Town; Under the Rainbow; Valley of the Dolls; The Velvet Touch; Veronika Voss; Welcome Home, Roxy Carmichael; What Price Hollywood?; Whatever Happened to Baby Jane?; Where Were You When the Lights Went Out?; White Dog; Who Is the Black Dahlia?; The Wild Party; Women on the Verge of a Nervous Breakdown

Addictions: see *Drug Addictions: Alcoholism: Sex Addicts: Eating Disorders: Obsessions*

Adolescence: see *Boyhood: Girlhood: Teenagers: Teenage Movies: Coming of Age: Love-First: Infatuations: Elementary School Life: High School Life*

Adoptions-Forced/Inherited: see *Babies-Inherited: Babies-Finding: Children-Inherited: Children-Adopted*

ADVENTURE (usually pertaining to an exciting journey): see also *Adventure Drama: Adventure at Sea: Escape Adventure: Treasure Hunts: Quests: Epics: Romantic Adventure: Comic Adventure:* The Abyss; Adventure Island; The Adventures of Baron Munchausen (1943); The Adventures of Baron Munchausen (1987); The Adventures of Captain Fabian; Adventures of Casanova; The Adventures of Don Juan; The Adventures of Hajji Baba; The Adventures of Huckleberry Finn (1960); The Adventures of Huckleberry Finn (1985); The Adventures of Marco Polo; The Adventures of Robin Hood; The Adventures of Robinson Crusoe; The Adventures of Tom Sawyer; Africa, Texas Style; The African Queen; Against a Crooked Sky; Against All Flags; Aguirre, the Wrath of God; Aladdin; Ali Baba and the Forty Thieves; Allan Quatermain and the Lost City of Gold; Amazing Stories; Anthony Adverse; Apocalypse Now; Appointment in Honduras; Around the

World in Eighty Days; Around the World under the Sea; Arrowsmith; Assisi Underground; At Play in the Fields of the Lord; At the Earth's Core; Avalanche Express; Baby-Secret of the Lost Legend; Bad Company; Bandolero!; Barabbas; Barbarella; Batman; Batman Returns; Battle for the Planet of the Apes; Bedknobs and Broomsticks; Ben Hur (1959); Ben Hur: A Tale of the Christ (1925); Beneath the Planet of the Apes; Benji; Benji the Hunted; Biggles; Bill and Ted's Bogus Journey; Bill and Ted's Excellent Adventure; Bird of Paradise (1932); Bird of Paradise (1951); Bite the Bullet; Black Arrow; The Black Cauldron; The Black Hole; The Black Pirate; Black Robe; The Black Rose; Blackbeard the Pirate; Bonnie Prince Charlie; Born Free; The Bounty; Braveheart; The Bridge on the River Kwai; Brigadoon; Brighty of the Grand Canyon; The Buccaneer (1938); The Buccaneer (1958); Burke and Wills; Butch Cassidy and the Sundance Kid; Call of the Wild (1935); Call of the Wild (1972); Candy; Candy Mountain; Captain America; Captain Blood; Captain Horatio Hornblower; Captain Kidd; Captains Courageous; The Caravans; The Care Bears' Adventure in Wonderland!; Casino Royale; The Castaway Cowboy; The Charge of the Light Brigade (1936); The Charge of the Light Brigade (1968); Chattanooga Choo Choo; China Clipper; Chitty Chitty Bang Bang; Christopher Columbus (1949); Christopher Columbus: The Discovery (1992); City Boy; City of Joy; Clan of the Cave Bear; Clash of the Titans; Cliffhanger; Cloak and Dagger (1946); Close Encounters of the Third Kind; Commando; The Corsican Brothers; The Count of Monte Cristo (1934); The Count of Monte Cristo (1974); Crocodile Dundee; Crusoe; Dances with Wolves; Dark of the Sun; Davy Crockett; Deceivers; The Deep; Deliverance; The Desert Fox; The Desert Rats; Dick Tracy; Distant Drums; Doctor Zhivago; Dr. Dolittle; Dr. No; Dr. Syn Alias Scarecrow; The Dove; Dragonslayer; Dreamscape; Drums Along the Mohawk; Dune; E.T.: The Extra-Terrestrial; Eagle's Wing; El Cid; Elephant Boy; The Elusive Pimpernel; The Emerald Forest; The Empire Strikes Back; Escape to Witch Mountain; Excalibur; Exodus; Fantastic Voyage; Farewell to the King; Far from

Home; The Fifth Musketeer; The Final Countdown; Fire Over England; Fitzcarraldo; Five Came Back; Five Graves to Cairo; The Flame and the Arrow; Flame Over India; Flatliners; The Flight of the Phoenix; 1492: Conquest of Paradise; For Your Eyes Only; The Four Feathers (1929); The Four Feathers (1939); The Four Musketeers; A Game of Death; The Garden of Allah; The General Died at Dawn; Genghis Khan; Gold; The Gold Rush; The Golden Child; The Golden Voyage of Sinbad; Goldfinger; The Goonies; Great Expectations; Green Dolphin Street; The Green Goddess; Green Mansions; Greystoke: The Legend of Tarzan; Gulliver's Travels (1939); Gulliver's Travels (1976); Gunga Din; Hatari!; Hawaii; Hell and High Water; Hemingway's Adventures of a Young Man; High Road to China; Highlander; Highlander II: The Quickening; Highlander III: The Sorcerer; His Majesty O'Keefe; Holy Matrimony; Honey, I Blew Up the Kid; Honey, I Shrunk the Kids; Hook; How the West Was Won; Huckleberry Finn (1939); Huckleberry Finn (1960); Huckleberry Finn (1974); Hudson's Bay; The Hurricane (1937); Hurricane (1979); Ice Station Zebra; In Search of the Castaways; Indiana Jones and the Last Crusade; Indiana Jones and the Temple of Doom; Innocents in Paris (1953); The Island at the Top of the World; Jack London; Jason and the Argonauts; Jaws; Jaws 2; Jaws 3-D; Jaws 4: The Revenge; Jeremiah Johnson; The Journey of Natty Gann; Journey to the Center of the Earth; The Jungle Book (1967); The Jungle Book (1994); K-2; Kagemusha; The Keys of the Kingdom; Kidnapped (1938); Kidnapped (1959); Kidnapped (1971); Kim; King Kong (1933); King Kong (1976); King Solomon's Mines (1937); King Solomon's Mines (1950); King Solomon's Mines (1985); Kings of the Sun; Knights of the Round Table; Krakatoa, East of Java; Krull; Ladyhawke; The Land That Time Forgot; The Last of the Mohicans (1936); The Last of the Mohicans (1992); The Last Outpost; The Last Remake of Beau Geste; The Last Valley; Lawrence of Arabia; Legend; Legend of the Lost; Legends of the Fall; License to Kill; The Light at the Edge of the World; The Light in the Forest; The Lighthorsemen; Lionheart; The Little Mermaid; Live and

Affair Lairs (places, usually apartments, where people rendezvous): see also *Cheating Men: Playboys: Bachelors-Confirmed:* Any Wednesday; The Apartment; Boeing-Boeing; Boys' Night Out; Come September; The Key (1958); The Pad, and How to Use It

Affairs: see *Romance-Clandestine: Romance: Romance with Married Person:* also *Romantic Comedy: Romantic Drama: Cheating Men: Cheating Women: Cheaters-Avenging*

Africa: see also *Africans: ADVENTURE: Jungles: South Africa:* Africa Screams; Africa, Texas Style; The African Queen; The Air Up There; Algiers; Allan Quatermain and the Lost City of Gold; Ashanti: Land of No Mercy; Babar: The Movie; Baby-Secret of the Lost Legend; The Battle of Algiers; Beat the Devil; Black and White in Color; The Black Stallion Returns; Born Free; Call Me Bwana; Chocolat; Clarence, the Cross-Eyed Lion; Coming to America; Coup de Torchon; Dark of the Sun; The Desert Fox; The Dogs of War; Five Came Back; Five Graves to Cairo; The Four Feathers (1929); The Four Feathers (1939); The Gods Must Be Crazy; The Gods Must Be Crazy II; A Good Man in Africa; Gorillas in the Mist; Greystoke: The Legend of Tarzan; Hatari!; The Heart of the Matter; Hell, Heaven, and Hoboken; The Hill; Immortal Sergeant; The Jewel in the Crown; Khartoum; King of the Hill (1965); King Solomon's Mines (1937); King Solomon's Mines (1950); King Solomon's Mines (1985); The Kiss (1988); The Kitchen Toto; Legend of the Lost; Lion of the Desert; Lost Command; The Man Who Knew Too Much (1956); The Mark of the Hawk; Mighty Joe Young; Mogambo; Mountains of the Moon; Mr. Johnson; The Naked Jungle; The Naked Prey; The Nun's Story; The Passenger; Road to Zanzibar; The Roots of Heaven; Rope of Sand; Sahara (1943); Sands of the Kalahari; Shaft in Africa; Sheena, Queen of the Jungle; The Sheltering Sky; Simba; The Sins of Rachel Cade; The Snows of Kilimanjaro; The Southern Star; Stanley and Livingstone; Sundown; Tarzan and His Mate; Tarzan Escapes; Tarzan the Ape Man (1932); Tarzan the Ape Man (1981); Tarzan's New York Adventure; Tobruk; Trader Horn; White Cargo; White Hunter, Black Heart; White Mischief; The Wild Geese; The Wind and the Lion; The World's Greatest Athlete; Z; Zulu; Zulu Dawn

African-American People/Films (not all people who are dark are of African descent): so see *Black Films: Black Men: Black Women: Latin People: Latin Films*

Africans: see also *Africa: Black Casts:* Blacula; Coming to America; The Gods Must Be Crazy; The Gods Must Be Crazy II; The Mark of the Hawk; A Warm December

Afterlife (as in after death): see *Ghosts: Heaven: Hell: Reincarnation: Soul-Selling One's: Immortality*

Agatha Christie (based upon books by the famous author): see also *Mystery-Whodunit?: Detectives-Female:* The Alphabet Murders; And Then There Were None; Appointment with Death; The Body in the Library; Death on the Nile; Evil Under the Sun; Love from a Stranger (1936); Love from a Stranger (1947); The Mirror Crack'd; Murder Ahoy; Murder at the Gallop; Murder Most Foul; Murder on the Orient Express; Murder She Said; Ordeal by Innocence; Ten Little Indians; Witness for the Prosecution

Aging (relating to problems of or the actual process dramatized over time): see also *Aging-Reverse: Body Switching: Elderly People: Death-Dealing with: Death-Impending: Cosmetic Surgery: Cures/Elixirs: Episodic Stories:* Age Isn't Everything; Death Becomes Her; A Delicate Balance; Fedora; Gassss; Golden Years; The Hunger; Monkey Business (1952); Monte Walsh; Monty Python's The Meaning of Life; The Picture of Dorian Gray; Prelude to a Kiss; The Roman Spring of Mrs. Stone

Aging-Reverse (growing younger, though not necessarily literally): see also *Rejuvenation: Aging: Cures/Elixirs:* Billy Madison; Cocoon; Cocoon: The Return; Death Becomes Her; 18 Again; Golden Years; Hook; The Hunger; Lost Horizon (1937); Lost Horizon (1973); Monkey Business; Monty Python's The Meaning of Life; Peter Pan; The Picture of Dorian Gray; Prelude to a Kiss; Orlando; She (1935); She (1965)

Ahead of Its Time (a film not really appreciated upon its initial release, or ahead in terms of subject matter or perspective): see also *Avant-Garde Films: Cult Films: Overlooked at Release: Forgotten Films:* The Accused (1948); Act of Murder; The Appaloosa; The Baby Maker; The Bachelor Party (1957); Behave Yourself!; The Big Bus; The Bingo Long Traveling All-Stars and Motor Kings; The Bitter Tears of Petra von Kant; Black Christmas; Black Legion; The Blackboard Jungle; Blonde Venus; Blue Denim; The Boston Strangler; The Boys in the Band; The Bride Walks Out; Bright Road; Bringing Up Baby; The Chapman Report; Cheyenne Autumn; The Children's Hour; Christopher Strong; A Clockwork Orange; Crossfire; Cruising; Daddy's Gone A-Hunting; Deadfall (1968); The Defiant Ones; Demon Seed; Designing Woman; The Detective (1968); The Diary of a Madman; A Different Story; A Doll's House; Dr. Cyclops; Dreams That Money Can Buy; The FBI Story; Finger of Guilt; Fog over Frisco; The Forbin Project; Fort Apache, the Bronx; Fortune and Men's Eyes; Fox; Go for Broke; The Great White Hope; Greed; Guest in the House; A Hatful of Rain; The High and the Mighty; I Am a Fugitive from a Chain Gang; I Passed for White; I Want What I Want; Intruder in the Dust; Kings Go Forth; A Kiss Before Dying (1956); Kisses for My President; The Last Command; The Last Hunt; Learning Tree; Leave Her to Heaven; Limbo; Lost Boundaries; Love with the Proper Stranger; Making Love; Man on Fire; The Man Upstairs; The Man Who Came to Dinner; The Man with Nine Lives; The Man with the Golden Arm; The Mark; The Mark of the Hawk; The Masquerader; The Mating of Willie; The Men (1950); Min and Bill; Moonrise; The Music Lovers; Myra Breckinridge; Never Take Sweets from a Stranger; No Way Out (1950); Norman, Is That You?; Oh, Dad, Poor Dad . . . ; One Million BC (1940); Outrage (1956); Petulia; The Rains Came; Rider on the Rain; Salt and Pepper; Saturday Night and Sunday Morning; Scarlet Street; The Sergeant; The Seventh Cross; The Seventh Victim; Shadows; The Slender Thread; The Snake Pit; The Sniper; Something for Everyone; Something Wild (1960); Stairway to Heaven; Start the Revolution Without Me; Storm Warning; Strange Interlude (1932); Strange Interlude (1990); The Super Cops; Sylvia Scarlett; Tea and Sympathy; Term of Trial; Terminal Man; Terror on a Train; They Drive by Night (1938); They Live by Night; They Won't Forget; Things to Come; This Thing Called Love; Tokyo Joe; Tommy; A Town like Alice (1956); A Town like Alice (1985); Town without Pity; Up the Sandbox; The Vampire Lovers; Victim; A Woman Rebels; Women in Love; You Can Never Tell

AIDS Stories: see also *Gay Men: Disease Stories: Epidemics:* André's Mother; Boys on the Side; Citizen Cohn; The Cure; Daybreak; Dying Young; Early Frost; Joey Breaker; Killing Zoe; The Living End; Longtime Companion; Parting Glances; Peter's Friends; Philadelphia

Air Daredevils: see *Pilots-Daredevil: Pilots-Military*

Airlines/Airplanes (usually set on airplane or in airport): see also *Airplane Crashes: Pilots-Airline: Military Stories: War Stories:* Ace Eli and Roger of the Skies; Air America; Airplane!; Airplane 2, the Sequel; Airport; Airport 1977; Airport '79, The Concorde; The Aviator; Delta Force; Men with Wings; Passenger 57; Skyjacked; Those Magnificent Men in Their Flying Machines

Airplane Crashes: see also *Disaster Movies: Airlines/Airplanes: Rescue Adventure/Dramas: Survival Dramas:* Airplane!; Airport 1975; Airport 1977; Alive; The Aviator; The Bride Came C.O.D.; The Buddy Holly Story; Cliffhanger; Drop Zone; Fate Is the Hunter; Fearless; Five Came Back; The Flight of the Phoenix; Foreign Correspondent; Gable and Lombard; The Glenn Miller Story; The Great Lie; Here Comes Mr. Jordan; The Hero; The High and the Mighty; The Hindenburg; La Bamba; The Last Flight of Noah's Ark; Lord of the Flies (1963); Lord of the Flies (1990); The Medusa Touch; Millennium; The Mountain; The Night My Number Came Up; No Highway in the Sky; None But the Brave; Sands of the Kalahari; September Affair; The Story of Will Rogers; Survive; Sweet Dreams; Twilight Zone: The Movie; White Nights (1985)

Alamo Stories (stories about the great Texas battle in San Antonio): see also *Westerns: Texas:* The Alamo; The Last Command; Lone Star of Gold

Alaska: see also *Snow Settings:* Abbott and Costello Lost in Alaska; Call of the Wild; Call of the Wild (1935); The Call of the Wild (1972); The Golden Seal; Hell and High Water; Ice Palace; Jack London; Map of the Human Heart; North to Alaska; On Deadly Ground; Salmonberries; Spawn of the North

Al Capone: see also *Mob Stories: Criminals-Famous:* Capone; Nitti, the Enforcer; Scarface (1932); Scarface Mob/The Untouchables Pilot; The Untouchables

Alcatraz (Prison): see also *Prison Drama: San Francisco:* Birdman of Alcatraz; Escape from Alcatraz; Murder in the First; The Scarface Mob

Alcoholism: see also *Drug Addictions: Obsessions: Bootlegging: Prohibition Era:* The African Queen; Arthur; Arthur 2, On the Rocks; Barfly; Beloved Infidel; Black Angel; The Bottom of the Bottle; Callaway Went Thataway; Career; Cat Ballou; Cat on a Hot Tin Roof (1958); Cat on a Hot Tin Roof (1984); Chu Chu and the Philly Flash; Clean and Sober; The Clown; Come Back, Little Sheba; The Country Girl; Dangerous; The Day of the Locust; Days of Wine and Roses (1958); Days of Wine and Roses (1962); Easy Virtue; Fat City; Fathers and Sons; A Fine Romance; Gervaise; Going Home; The Great Santini; The Green Man; The Helen Morgan Story; Hollywood Boulevard (1936); I'll Cry Tomorrow; Inside Moves; Jacknife; Legend of the Holy Drinker; Life Begins at 8:30; The Lost Weekend; Lover Come Back (1961); The Man Who Fell to Earth; The Moonshine War; The Morning After; Mouchette; Murphy's Law; My Favorite Year; My Sin; Naked Lunch; The Night of the Iguana; Papa's Delicate Condition; The People against O'Hara; Postcards from the Edge; Rancho De Luxe; Reuben, Reuben; Ryan's Daughter; Sing Baby Sing; Small Town Girl (1936); Small Town Girl (1953); Smash-up, the Story of a Woman; Strange Brew; Swing High, Swing Low; Tender Mercies; This Sporting Life; Time without Pity; A Tree Grows in Brooklyn; Tunes of Glory; The Tunnel of Love; Twin Beds; Under the Volcano; The Verdict; The Voice in the Mirror; The Wet Parade; When a Man Loves a Woman; Whiskey Galore; A Woman under the Influence

Alienation (the psychological condition of feeling separated from society): see also *Social Drama: Depression:* Alphaville; Ash Wednesday; The Bell Jar; Bodies, Rest & Motion; Bright Lights, Big City; Butterfield 8; Caged; The Conversation; Cries and Whispers; The Crowd; Death of a Salesman (1950); Death of a Salesman (1985); Despair; Desperate

Characters; Diary of a Mad Housewife; East of Eden (1955); East of Eden (1980); Easy Rider; Fearless; Five Easy Pieces; Good Father; Interiors; Joe versus the Volcano; Koyaanisqatsi; Last Tango in Paris; Less than Zero; Life Upside Down; Little Vera; Living End; The Long Goodbye; Lost Angels; Moonlighting (1982); Pink Floyd: The Wall; Plenty; Postcards from the Edge; Repo Man; Risk; The River's Edge; Slacker; Slaughterhouse Five; Smithereens; Stardust Memories; The Subject Was Roses; Suburbia; They Shoot Horses, Don't They?; Through a Glass Darkly; Two for the Road; Two Lane Blacktop; 2001: A Space Odyssey

Aliens-Outer Space, Evil (bad creatures on earth or in outer space): see also *UFOs: Outer Space Movies: Monsters-Alien: Monsters: Monsters-Mutant: Martians:* Alien; Alien 3; Aliens; The Andromeda Strain; Attack of the 50 ft. Woman (1958); The Attack of the Fifty Foot Woman (1993); Beware!; The Blob; Blue Monkey; The Body Snatchers; Borrower; Brain Damage; Children of the Damned; Communion; Dark Star; Enemy from Space; Forbidden Planet; Green Slime; Hidden; Hidden 2; I Married a Monster from Outer Space; Invaders from Mars (1953); Invaders from Mars (1986); Invasion; Invasion of the Body Snatchers (1956); Invasion of the Body Snatchers (1978); It Came from Outer Space; Life Force; Millennium; Monolith; Not of This Earth (1956); Predator; Predator 2; The Puppetmasters; The Quatermass Experiment; Solaris; Strange Invaders; They Live; The Thing (1951); The Thing (1982); This Island Earth; Time Runner; Tommyknockers; The War of the Worlds; Xtro

Aliens-Outer Space, Good (good creatures on earth or in outer space): see also *UFOs: Outer Space Movies: SCI-FI: Fish out of Water Stories:* Alien Nation; batteries not included; The Brother from Another Planet; Close Encounters of the Third Kind; Cocoon; Cocoon: The Return; Coneheads; The Day the Earth Stood Still; Earth Girls Are Easy; Escape to Witch Mountain; E.T.: The Extra-Terrestrial; Explorers; Flight of the Navigator; Hangar 18; The Man Who Fell to Earth; Moon Pilot; My Stepmother Is an Alien; Repo Man; Return from Witch Mountain; Spaced Invaders; Starman; Suburban Commando; Visit to a Small Planet

Last; Lonesome Cowboys; Loving Couples; Maitresse; Making Love; Menage; My Father Is Coming; My Own Private Idaho; Myra Breckinridge; Noir et Blanc; Norman, Is That You?; Pulp Fiction; Rapture; The Rocky Horror Picture Show; Salmonberries; Serial; Sunday, Bloody Sunday; Switch; A Taste of Honey; This Thing Called Love; Threesome; To Forget Venice; Torch Song Trilogy; Travels with My Aunt; Tropic of Cancer; Willie and Phil; Woman in Flames

Amazon River: see also *Brazil: Jungles: South America: Rainforests:* At Play in the Fields of the Lord; Burden of Dreams; The Creature of the Black Lagoon; The Emerald Forest; Fitzcarraldo; Green Mansions; Medicine Man; The Mission

Ambassadors: see *Diplomats*

Americana: see *American Myth: Capra-esque*

American Dream (stories about achieving it or living what is conventionally supposed to be it): see also *American Myth: Capra-esque: Dreams:* All the Right Moves; America, America; An American Romance; An American Tail; An American Tail 2; The Apartment; Avalon; The Heartbreak Kid; Hoop Dreams; The King of Marvin Gardens; A Kiss before Dying (1956); A Kiss before Dying (1991); Lost in America; Magic Town; The Magnificent Ambersons; The Man in the Gray Flannel Suit; Meet Me in St. Louis; Meet the Applegates; Pretty Woman; Roger & Me; Rosalie Goes Shopping; Tucker: The Man and His Dream

American Myth (stories about both the mythical places created that embody the country's historical mythology or that depict the "all-American dream" and/or its delusions and realities): see also *Capra-esque: Conservative Value Stories: Fantasy: Small-Town Life: Old-Fashioned Recent Films:* The Adventures of Huckleberry Finn (1960); The Adventures of Huckleberry Finn (1985); Blue Velvet; Come to the Stable; Dancing Co-Ed; A Family Affair; Field of Dreams; Follow Me, Boys!; Forrest Gump; Four Daughters; Gidget; Girl Crazy; Groundhog Day; Harper Valley P.T.A.; How the West Was Won; Huckleberry Finn (1939); Huckleberry Finn (1960); The Human Comedy; It Happened to

Jane; Leningrad Cowboys Go to America; Moscow on the Hudson; Mr. Deeds Goes to Town; Mr. Smith Goes to Washington; The Music Man; My Darling Clementine; Of Human Hearts; One Foot in Heaven; Our Vines Have Tender Grapes; Pollyanna; Rally Round the Flag, Boys; The Reflecting Skin; Riding High; The Russians Are Coming, The Russians Are Coming; Sergeant Pepper's Lonely Hearts Club Band; Shadow of a Doubt; Smile; The Stepfather; The Stepfather 2: Make Room for Daddy; The Stepfather 3: Father's Day; The Stepford Wives; Stroszek; Tom, Dick and Harry

Americans Abroad (Americans in other countries, not necessarily on vacation and not necessarily doing anything in particular that could be categorized, like spying): see also *Vacations: Vacation Romance: Vacations-European: Nightmares Abroad: Exchange Students:* Above Suspicion; Act of Love; The Air Up There; An Almost Perfect Affair; The Ambassador; The American Friend; The Americanization of Emily; Another Time, Another Place; Arise, My Love; Ash Wednesday; Avanti!; Barcelona; Baxter (1972); Before Sunrise; The Belly of an Architect; Beyond the Limit; The Big Blue; Black Rain (1989); Blind Husbands; The Bliss of Mrs. Blossom; Blood on the Sun; Bobby Deerfield; Boeing-Boeing; Bolero (1934); Bon Voyage!; Brannigan; Brigadoon; Bunny Lake Is Missing; Buona Sera, Mrs. Campbell; Burn!; The Bushido Blade; Café Metropole; Candleshoe; Caravans; The Challenge; Chicago Joe and the Showgirl; China; China Girl (1942); The Coca-Cola Kid; Come September; Comrades of Summer; Daisy Miller; A Damsel in Distress; Dangerous When Wet; Design for Living; Desire; Dollars; Don't Raise the Bridge, Lower the Water!; The Dressmaker; The End of the World . . . ; Every Time We Say Goodbye; 55 Days at Peking; Finian's Rainbow; For Whom the Bell Tolls; Four Weddings and a Funeral; Frantic (1988); French Postcards; GI Blues; The Gay Divorcee; The Girl from Petrovka; A Girl Named Tamiko; The Girl Who Couldn't Say No; Hard Contract; Hidden Agenda; Holiday in Mexico; House of Cards; Hysteria; I Am a Camera; I Could Go on Singing; I, Jane Doe; I Was a Male War Bride; If You Knew Susie; Indiscretion of an American Wife; In the Cool of the Day; In the French Style;

Interlude (1957); Interlude (1968); Ishtar; It Started in Naples; It Started with a Kiss; Jakarta; The Josephine Baker Story; Journey for Margaret; Kaleidoscope; The Killing Fields; Killing Zoe; King Ralph; Kings Go Forth; Lassiter; The Last Flight; Le Mans; The Light in the Piazza; Little Lord Fauntleroy (1936); Little Lord Fauntleroy (1980); The Little Princess; Live for Life; Local Hero; The Lost Moment; Love Affair (1939); Love and Pain and the Whole Damn Thing; The Luck of the Irish; Lured; Macaroni; The Mad Monkey; Madame Butterfly; A Man Could Get Killed; Man in Love; The Man in the Middle; Man Who Knew Too Much (1934); The Man Who Knew Too Much (1956); Midnight Express; Midnight Lace; The Miracle (1990); The Mirror Crack'd; My Own Private Idaho; Never Say Goodbye; Night and the City (1950); Nobody's Perfect; The Notorious Landlady; Object of Beauty; Once in a Blue Moon; Once in Paris; One, Two, Three; The Other Side of Midnight; Our Hearts Were Young and Gay; Oxford Blues; Pandora and the Flying Dutchman; Paris Blues; The Party's Over; Patriot Games; The Pink Panther; The Prize; The Rachel Papers; Reds; Round Midnight; Saint Jack; Shadowlands; Shanghai Surprise; Soldier of Fortune; Stormy Monday; Strange Bedfellows; Strapless; Straw Dogs; Summer Wishes, Winter Dreams; Summertime; The Tall Guy; Tears in the Rain; Three Comrades; Tokyo Joe; Tokyo Pop; Tom & Viv; Top Secret!; Trade Winds; Tropic of Cancer; A Warm December; What?; When in Rome; The White Cliffs of Dover; The World of Suzie Wong; Wrong Is Right; A Yank at Eton; A Yank at Oxford; Yanks; Year of the Gun; The Young Lions

Americans as Enemy: see also *American Dream: Political Drama:* Barcelona; Das Boot; The Field; The Ugly American

Americans & Russians: see *Russians & Americans*

Amnesia: see also *Disease Stories: Screwball Comedy: FARCE: Mentally Disabled:* Ali Baba Goes to Town; American Dreamer; Anastasia (1956); Anastasia (1984); Bourne Identity; The Chase (1947); Clean Slate; The Constant Husband; Dead Again; Delirious; Desperately Seeking Susan; Detour; The Disappearance of Nora; The Double; A Fire in the Sky; The First Time; The

Groundstar Conspiracy; Hallelujah, I'm a Bum; Hysteria; I Love You Again; Long Live Life; Love Letters (1945); Lover Come Back (1961); The Miracle of Morgan's Creek; Mirage; Mister Buddwing; The October Man; Overboard; Possessed (1947); Random Harvest; Remember?; The Return of the Soldier; Run a Crooked Mile; Shattered; Siesta; Spellbound; Sundays and Cybele; The Testament of Orpheus; They Might Be Giants; Total Recall; The Tunnel of Love

Anarchists: see also *Political Unrest: Terrorists: Political Drama:* Captain Blood; The Comancheros; Death of a Gunfighter; Hell and High Water; The Manchurian Candidate; Saboteur; The Salamander; The Secret People; Seven Days in May; Viva Maria!

Ancient Times (at least a thousand years ago): see also *Historical Drama: Prehistoric Settings: Biblical Stories: Epics:* The Agony and the Ecstasy; Alexander the Great; Androcles and the Lion; Barabbas; Ben Hur (1926); Ben Hur (1959); The Bible; The Big Fisherman; Caesar and Cleopatra; Clash of the Titans; Cleopatra (1934); Cleopatra (1963); Conan the Barbarian; Conan the Destroyer; The Conqueror; David and Bathsheba; The Fall of the Roman Empire; A Funny Thing Happened on the Way to the Forum; Genghis Khan; The Gospel According to St. Matthew; The Greatest Story Ever Told; Hercules (1957); Hercules in New York; Hercules Unchained; History of the World Part One; Jason and the Argonauts; Jesus of Nazareth; Julius Caesar; Jupiter's Darling; Kagemusha; King David; King of Kings (1927); King of Kings (1961); Kings of the Sun; The Last Days of Pompeii; The Leopard; Monty Python and the Holy Grail; Monty Python's Life of Brian; Oedipus Rex; Quo Vadis; Red Sonja; Roman Scandals; Samson and Delilah; Satyricon (Fellini's); The Seventh Voyage of Sinbad; The Sign of the Cross; The Silver Chalice; Sodom and Gomorrah; Son of Sinbad; Spartacus; The 300 Spartans; The Trojan War; The Trojan Women; Ulysses (1954); The Vikings; The Warrior's Husband; Wholly Moses

Androids (humanlike robots, usually in outer space): see also *Outer Space Movies: Robots: Futuristic Films:* Alien; Aliens; Bill and Ted's Bogus Journey; Blade Runner; Cherry 2000; Class of

1999; Cyborg; Cyborg 2067; D.A.R.Y.L.; Deadly Friend; Eve of Destruction; Futureworld; Hardware; Making Mr. Right; Metropolis; Robocop; Saturn 3; Spaceballs; The Stepford Wives; The Terminator; Terminator 2: Judgment Day; Toys; Westworld

Angels: see also *Heaven: Afterlife: Aliens-Good:* All Dogs Go to Heaven; All That Jazz; Almost an Angel; Always; Angel in My Pocket; Angels in the Outfield (1951); Angels in the Outfield (1994); Barbarella; The Bishop's Wife; Brewster McCloud; Brother John; Charley and the Angel; Date with an Angel; Defending Your Life; Down to Earth; Faraway, So Close!; Forever Darling; Green Pastures; Heart and Souls; Heaven Can Wait (1943); Heaven Can Wait (1978); Heavenly Kid; Heaven Only Knows; Here Comes Mr. Jordan; The Horn Blows at Midnight; I Married an Angel; It's a Wonderful Life; Made in Heaven; Mr. Destiny; One Magic Christmas; Two of a Kind; Waiting for the Light; Wings of Desire; Xanadu

Angry Young Men: see *Young Men-Angry: Rebels: Fighting the System*

Animal Monsters: see *Monsters-Animal:* also *Monsters: Human Eaters: Humans into Animals: Monsters-Mythological: Insects: Monsters-Mutants*

Animal Rights: see also *Animal Stories: Pet Stories: Animals in Jeopardy:* The Big Blue; Bless the Beasts and the Children; Born Free; Born to Be Wild; A Breed Apart; Clarence, the Cross-Eyed Lion; Escape from the Dark; Flipper; The Golden Seal; Hatari!; Iceman; Man's Best Friend; The Miracle of the White Stallions; A Private Function; The Roots of Heaven; Spawn of the North; Star Trek IV: The Voyage Home; Turtle Diary; When the Whales Came

Animals in Jeopardy (animals in dangerous circumstances): see also *Pet Stories: CHILDREN'S: FAMILY: Kidnappings:* Ace Ventura, Pet Detective; All Dogs Go to Heaven; Andy Warhol's Bad; The Black Marble; The Black Stallion; The Black Stallion Returns; Born Free; The Incredible Journey; The Late Show; Million Dollar Duck; Mr. Drake's Duck; The Muppet Movie; 101 Dalmatians; Pet Sematary; Pet Sematary 2; Won Ton Ton, the Dog Who Saved Hollywood

Animals into Humans (critters that change into humans): see also *Monsters-Animals: Humans into Animals:* Island of Dr. Moreau (1977); Island of Lost Souls (1932); Ladyhawke; Mysterious Island; The Swan Princess; Watchers; Watchers II

Animals-Mutant: see also *Monsters-Mutant: Insects: Monsters-Animal:* Digby, the Biggest Dog in the World; Dr. Dolittle; Island of Dr. Moreau; Mysterious Island; Night of the Lepus; Teenage Mutant Ninja Turtles SERIES; Them!

Animal Stories: see also *Talking Animals: Magic: Fantasy: CHILDREN'S: Dogs: Cats:* The Adventures of Milo and Otis; The Advocate; All Creatures Great and Small; All Dogs Go to Heaven; An Alligator Named Daisy; An American Tail; An American Tail 2; Animal Behavior; Animal Farm; Babar: The Movie; The Bear; The Bears and I; Benji; Benji the Hunted; Billy Rose's Jumbo; Born Free; Born to Be Wild; Brighty of the Grand Canyon; The Care Bears' Adventure in Wonderland; The Care Bears Movie; Cat's Eye; Charlotte's Web; Clarence, the Cross-Eyed Lion; Cujo; The Day of the Dolphin; A Dog of Flanders; Dumbo; Felix the Cat: The Movie; FernGully: The Last Rainforest; Flipper; Fluffy; The Fox and the Hound; Francis the Talking Mule; Free Willy; The Golden Seal; The Great Mouse Detective; The Great Muppet Caper; Grizzly; Gus; Harry and the Hendersons; Hatari!; The Hellstrom Chronicle; The Horse in the Grey Flannel Suit; Howard the Duck; Ichabod and Mr. Toad/The Legend of Sleepy Hollow; The Incredible Journey; Jungle Book (1967); Jungle Book (1994); Ladyhawke; The Last Flight of Noah's Ark; The Living Desert; Look Who's Talking Now; Matilda; Mr. Drake's Duck; Mr. Forbush and the Penguins; Never Cry Wolf; Old Yeller; Oliver and Company; 101 Dalmatians; Perri; Pet Sematary; Pet Sematary 2; The Red Pony (1949); The Red Pony (1976); The Rescuers; Rescuers Down Under; Rock-a Doodle; The Secret of NIMH; The Swan Princess; Teenage Mutant Ninja Turtles; Teenage Mutant Ninja Turtles 2; Teenage Mutant Ninja Turtles 3; That Darn Cat!; They Only Kill Their Masters; The Three Lives of Thomasina; Thunderhead, Son of Flicka; Turner & Hooch; Turtle Diary; Willard

Animals-Talking/Smart: see also *Animal Stories: Pet Stories: Objects with Personalities:* The Adventures of Milo and Otis; An American Tail; An American Tail 2; Anchors Aweigh; Androcles and the Lion; Animal Farm; Any Which Way You Can; Babar: The Movie; Bambi; The Barefoot Executive; Baxter (1990); The Bear; The Beastmaster; The Beastmaster 2; Bedknobs and Broomsticks; Bedtime for Bonzo; Beneath the Planet of the Apes; Big Top Pee Wee; A Boy and His Dog; Chronicles of Narnia; Dr. Dolittle; Dumbo; Francis the Talking Mule; High Spirits; Hot to Trot; The Little Prince; Look Who's Talking Now; Monkey Shines; The Neverending Story; The Neverending Story II: The Next Chapter; Planet of the Apes; Road to Morocco; Road to Utopia; The Water Babies; Watership Down

Animation-Computer: see *Computers: Virtual Reality: Video Game Movies*

Animation-Partial: see also *Cartoons: Animation-Stop: Cartoonlike Films: Special Effects:* Anchors Aweigh; Bedknobs and Broomsticks; Cool World; Gulliver's Travels (1939); Gulliver's Travels (1976); The Incredible Mr. Limpet; Mary Poppins; Pete's Dragon; Pink Floyd: The Wall; The Seventh Voyage of Sinbad; So Dear to My Heart; Song of the South; The Three Caballeros; Tron; Twilight Zone: The Movie; The Water Babies; Who Framed Roger Rabbitt?

Animation-Stop (live action or claymation animation that isn't a drawn cartoon): see also *Cartoons: Animation-Partial:* Clash of the Titans; Jason and the Argonauts; The Nightmare Before Christmas; Return to Oz; The Seventh Voyage of Sinbad

Antagonistic Couples: see *Romance-Bickering: Romance-Opposites Attract*

Antarctica: see also *Arctic: Snow Settings:* Mr. Forbush and the Penguins; Scott of the Antarctic; The Thing (1982)

Anthologies: see *Multiple Stories: Interwoven Stories: Trilogies: TV Series: Miniseries; Hand-Me-Down Stories*

Anti-Establishment Films: see also *Vietnam Era: 1960s: 1970s: Hippies: Anti-War Films: Sexual Revolution: Alternative Lifestyles: Rebels: Young Men-Angry: Women Against Male Establishment: Cult Films: Ahead of Its Time:* Alice's Restaurant; Article 99; Barbarella; Billy Jack; Bonnie and Clyde; Born Losers; Born on the Fourth of July;

The Boy Who Had Everything; The Bridges at Toko-Ri; Butterflies Are Free; Catch Me a Spy; Cisco Pike; A Clockwork Orange; Don't Look Back; Drive, He Said; Drugstore Cowboy; Easy Rider; The End of the Road; Five Easy Pieces; Getting Straight; The Graduate; Hair; I Love You, Alice B. Toklas; I'll Never Forget Whatshisname; The Idolmaker; The Legend of Billie Jean; MASH; The Magic Christian; Medium Cool; Missing; Morgan!; Network; The Panic in Needle Park; Shampoo; Slaughterhouse Five; Some Kind of a Nut; The Strawberry Statement; Suburbia; Tribes; Vanishing Point; Wild in the Streets; The Wild One; Woodstock; Yellow Submarine

Anti-Semitism (hatred/prejudice toward Jewish people): see also *Nazi Stories: Jewish People: Concentration Camps: Israel: Middle East:* Assisi Underground; Au Revoir, les Enfants; Betrayed (1989); Cast a Giant Shadow; Crossfire; The Diary of Anne Frank (1959); Fiddler on the Roof; The Fixer; Gentleman's Agreement; Hanna's War; Homicide; The Last Metro; Me and the Colonel; The Murder of Mary Phagan; Prisoner of Honor; Remains of the Day; Reunion; Schindler's List; School Ties; Ship of Fools; The Wandering Jew

Anti-War Stories: see also *Anti-Establishment Films: Vietnam Era: 1960s: 1970s: Vietnam War:* Drive, He Said; The Four Feathers (1929); The Four Feathers (1939); Gardens of Stone; Hair; Lost Horizon (1937); Lost Horizon (1973); MASH; Master of the World; Nous Sommes Tous les Assassins; Paths of Glory; Platoon; Slaughterhouse Five; A Small Circle of Friends; Streamers; Testament

Apartheid (South African segregation dividing whites and blacks): see also *South Africa: Race Relations: Civil Rights: Slavery-Black:* Bopha!; Cry Freedom; A Dry White Season; Mandela; Sarafina!; The Wilby Conspiracy; A World Apart

Apartment Buildings: see also *Boardinghouses: Neighbors-Troublesome: Roommates: Roommates from Hell:* The Apartment; Apartment Zero; Hi, Mom!; The Landlord; Love Nest; New Year's Day; The Night We Never Met; No Down Payment; Pacific Heights; Parlor, Bedroom and Bath; The Passing of the Third Floor Back; Penthouse;

Poltergeist III; Rear Window; Single White Female; Sliver; The Super; The Tenant; A Time for Loving; Under the Yum Yum Tree

Apes: see *Primates*

Apocalyptic Stories (the end of the world is nigh or already passed): see also *Futuristic Films: Nuclear Power: Bombs-Atomic: Oppression:* Battle for the Planet of the Apes; Beneath the Planet of the Apes; A Boy and His Dog; Cherry 2000; Cyborg; The Day After; The Day of the Triffids; The Day the Earth Caught Fire; The Day the Earth Stood Still; Daybreak; The Dead Zone; Dr. Strangelove; Escape from New York; Escape from the Planet of the Apes; Fail Safe; Fire Next Time; Fortress; The Fourth Protocol; Gassss; Hardware; Heart of Glass; Holocaust 2000; The Horn Blows at Midnight; J'Accuse; The Last Wave; Letters from a Dead Man; Light Years; Long Live Life; Mad Max; Mad Max Beyond Thunderdome; The Man Who Could Work Miracles; Memoirs of a Survivor; Meteor; Miracle Mile; The New Barbarians; Night of the Comet; Night of the Living Dead (1968); Night of the Living Dead (1990); The Omega Man; The Omen; The Omen IV: The Awakening; On the Beach; Panic in Year Zero; Planet of the Apes; Quintet (1979); Rapture; The Road Warrior; Rollerball; Sacrifice; The Seventh Sign; Silent Running; Slipstream; Sodom and Gomorrah; Solarbabies; Soylent Green; The Stand; Stargate; Steel Dawn; Tank Girl; Terminator 2: Judgment Day; Testament; Twilight's Last Gleaming; Until the End of the World; War Games; The War of the Worlds; Warlock (1989); When Time Ran Out; Whoops! Apocalypse (1983); Whoops! Apocalypse (1986); Zardoz; When Worlds Collide

Arab People: see also *Middle East: Muslim/Islamic People: Israel: Bible Stories:* Action in Arabia; The Adventures of Hajji Baba; Aladdin; Ali Baba and the Forty Thieves; The Ambassador; Arabesque; Beau Geste (1926); Beau Geste (1939); Beau Geste (1966); Beau Ideal; Desert Law; Dream Wife; Exodus; Frantic (1988); Lawrence of Arabia; Lion of the Desert; The Little Drummer Girl; March or Die; Masquerade (1965); Mohammed, Messenger of God; Navy SEALS; Not Without My Daughter; Road to Morocco;

The Sheik; Son of Sinbad; Things Are Tough All Over

Archaeologists/Paleontologists: see also *Dinosaurs: Treasure Hunts: Egypt:* The Awakening; Blood from the Mummy's Tomb; Boy on a Dolphin; Bringing Up Baby; Five Million Years to Earth; The Ghoul (1933); I Live My Life; Indiana Jones and the Last Crusade; Indiana Jones and the Temple of Doom; Journey to the Center of the Earth; Jurassic Park; The Mummy (1932); The Mummy (1959); The Mummy's Hand; The Mummy's Shroud; One of Our Dinosaurs Is Missing; One Woman or Two; Raiders of the Lost Ark; She (1935); She (1965); Skullduggery; Sphinx; Stargate; Valley of the Kings

Arctic: see also *Antarctica: Snow Settings:* The Bedford Incident; Iceman; Ice Station Zebra; The Island at the Top of the World; Never Cry Wolf; Santa Claus; She (1935); She (1965); Superman II; The Thing (1951); Voyage to the Bottom of the Sea

Argentina: see also *Brazil: South America:* Apartment Zero; Eversmile, New Jersey; The Four Horsemen of the Apocalypse; I Don't Want to Talk About It; Kiss of the Spider Woman; Naked Tango; Official Story

Arkansas: see also *Southerns: Mountain People: Hillbillies: Rednecks: Plantation Life:* Boxcar Bertha; Dangerous When Wet; The Devil Came from Arkansas; Disaster at Silo 7; End of the Line; Ernest Green Story; A Face in the Crowd; Gator; The Iron Mistress; The Legend of Boggy Creek; Li'l Abner; The Life and Times of Judge Roy Bean; 9/30/55; No Time for Sergeants; One False Move; Pass the Ammo; Rosalie Goes Shopping; Spitfire; The Story of Dr. Wassell; Thelma & Louise; Town That Dreaded Sundown; The Trail of the Lonesome Pine; True Grit; War Room; The Westerner; White Lightning

Armageddon: see *Apocalyptic Stories*

Arms Dealers (guns or munitions sellers): see also *Bombs: Spies: Mercenaries: Terrorists:* American Ninja; Best Defense; Blue Ice; China; The Comancheros; Confidential Agent; Deal of the Century; Gunrunner; Journey into Fear; Lethal Weapon 3; The Living Daylights; Major Barbara; Passenger; Remo Williams: The Adventure Begins; Superman 4; Three Ninjas; Three Ninjas Kick Back; Toys; Undercover Blues; White Sands

Art Direction-Great: see *Outstanding Production Design*

Art Films (independent, experimental, non-Hollywood type films that played primarily in exclusive art-house theaters): see also *Avant-Garde: Best Foreign-Language Film Nominees/Winners: Cult Films: Ahead of Its Time:* Accattone; The Accident; The Adjuster; Aguirre, the Wrath of God; All the Vermeers in New York; Alphaville; Alpine Fire; Amarcord; Bad Timing: A Sensual Obsession; Bagdad Cafe; The Balcony; Barcelona; Barton Fink; Beauty and the Beast (1946); Before Sunrise; The Moon in the Gutter; Moonlighting (1982); Muriel; The Music Lovers; Music of Chance; My American Uncle; My Dinner with André; My Father Is Coming; Mystery Train; Naked; Naked in New York; Naked Lunch; Naked Tango; Near Dark; The Night Is Young; Night of the Following Day; The Night Porter; The Ninth Configuration; Nouvelle Vague; Numero Deux; Oblomov; Once Were Warriors; One from the Heart; Orlando; Orphans; Paisan; Paris By Night; Paris, Texas; The Party and the Guests; The Passenger; Passion; Pedestrian; Performance; Persona; Phantom of Liberty; Point Blank; Poison; Powaqqatsi, Life in Transformation; The President's Analyst; Proof; Prospero's Books; Providence; Querelle; Raise the Red Lantern; Rashomon; Ready to Wear; The Red Balloon; The Red Desert; Repentance; Return to Oz; Reunion; Rhapsody in August; Risk; The River (1951); River Niger; Romeo Is Bleeding; Rosencrantz and Guildenstern Are Dead; Round Midnight; Salaam Bombay!; Salome's Last Dance; Samurai; Sandakan No. 8; Santa Sangre; Satyricon (Fellini's); Savages; Scenes from a Marriage; The Servant; The Seventh Seal; Shadows; Shadows and Fog; Shame (1968); The Sheltering Sky; Shoot the Piano Player; The Silence; Silent Tongue; Simple Men; Sirens; Six in Paris; Slacker; Smiles of a Summer Night; Smithereens; Soft Skin; Speaking Parts; The Spider's Stratagem; Stardust Memories; The State of Things; Stop Making Sense; Stranger Than Paradise; Strapless; Stromboli; Subterraneans Subway; Sugarbaby; Surviving Desire; The Swimmer; The Testament of Orpheus; That Obscure Object of Desire; 32 Short Films about

Glenn Gould; The Threepenny Opera; Through a Glass Darkly; Thunder Rock; Tie Me Up! Tie Me Down!; The Tin Drum; Tokyo Decadence; Track 29; The Tragedy of a Ridiculous Man; Trash; The Tree of Wooden Clogs; The Trial (1962); The Trial (1993); Tristana; Triumph of the Will; Trouble in Mind; Trust; Two or Three Things I Know About Her; 2001: A Space Odyssey; Un Chien Andalou; Unbelievable Truth; Until the End of the World; Valentino (1977); Variety; Veronika Voss; Vincent and Theo; Viridiana; Voyager; Walkabout; Walker; Waterland; A Wedding; Weekend; Where the Green Ants Dream; Who Is Harry Kellerman . . . ; Wild at Heart; Wings of Desire; Wings of Fame; Winter Light; Withnail and I; Woman in the Dunes; A Woman under the Influence; World of Apu; Wuthering Heights (1953); Zabriskie Point; Zed and Two Noughts

Artists: see also *Romance with Artist: Biographies: Writers:* Art Thieves: Ace of Aces; After Hours; Age of Consent; The Agony and the Ecstasy; All the Vermeers in New York; The Art of Love; Artists and Models (1937); Artists and Models (1955); Backtrack; The Belly of an Architect; Brideshead Revisited; Call Me Genius; Camille Claudel; Condorman; Cool World; Dante's Inferno; The Draughtsman's Contract; Ebony Tower; Ex-Lady; The Fountainhead; Girlfriends; The Good Mother; Hannah and Her Sisters; Holy Matrimony; The Horse's Mouth; House of Wax; I've Heard the Mermaids Singing; Islands in the Stream; Keep the Change; The L-Shaped Room; La Belle Noiseuse; La Vie de Boheme; Le Million; Legal Eagles; The Light that Failed; Linguini Incident; Little Noises; Live, Love and Learn; Lust for Life; Me, Natalie; The Moderns; Modigliani; The Moon and Sixpence; Morgan!; Moulin Rouge; My Left Foot; Mystery of the Wax Museum; Naked in New York; The Naked Maja; New York Stories; Paint It Black; Portrait of Jennie; Rashomon; Ready to Wear; The Red Balloon; The Red Desert; Repentance; Return to Oz; Reunion; Rhapsody in August; Risk; The River (1951); River Niger; Romeo Is Bleeding; Rosencrantz and Guildenstern Are Dead; Round Midnight; Salaam Bombay!; Salome's Last Dance; Samurai; Sandakan No. 8; The Sandpiper; Santa Sangre; Satyricon (Fellini's); Savages; Scenes from a

Marriage; The Servant; The Seventh Seal; Shadows; Shadows and Fog; Shame (1968); The Sheltering Sky; Shoot the Piano Player; The Silence; Silent Tongue; Simple Men; Sirens; Six Degrees of Separation; Raise the Red Lantern; Six in Paris; Slacker; Slaves of New York; Smiles of a Summer Night; Smithereens; So Big (1932); So Big (1953); Soft Skin; Speaking Parts; The Spider's Stratagem; Stardust Memories; The State of Things; The Statue; Stop Making Sense; Stranger than Paradise; Strapless; Stromboli; The Subterraneans Subway; Sugarbaby; The Sun Also Rises; Sunday, Bloody Sunday; Sunday in the Country; Superstar, The Life and Times of Andy Warhol; Surrender; The Surviving Desire; The Swimmer; The Testament of Orpheus; That Obscure Object of Desire; 32 Short Films about Glenn Gould; The Threepenny Opera; Through a Glass Darkly; Thunder Rock; Tie Me Up! Tie Me Down!; The Tin Drum; Tokyo Decadence; Track 29; The Tragedy of a Ridiculous Man; Trash; The Tree of Wooden Clogs; The Trial (1962); The Trial (1993); Tristana; Triumph of the Will; Trouble in Mind; Trust; Two or Three Things I Know About Her; 2001: A Space Odyssey; Un Chien Andalou; Unbelievable Truth; Until the End of the World; Valentino (1977); Variety; Veronika Voss; Vincent and Theo; Viridiana; Voyager; Walkabout; Walker; Waterland; A Wedding; Weekend; Where the Green Ants Dream; Who Is Harry Kellerman . . . ; Wild at Heart; Wings of Desire; Wings of Fame; Winter Light; Withnail and I; Woman in the Dunes; A Woman under the Influence; World of Apu; Wuthering Heights (1953); Zabriskie Point; Zed and Two Noughts

Artists-Famous: see also *Artists: Biographies:* The Agony and the Ecstasy; Camille Claudel; La Belle Noiseuse; Lust for Life; The Moderns; Modigliani; The Moon and Sixpence; Moulin Rouge; My Left Foot; The Naked Maja; Superstar, The Life and Times of Andy Warhol; Van Gogh; Vincent and Theo

Art Thieves: see also *Heist Stories: Thieves: Jewel Thieves: Bank Robberies:* Airport 1977; Animal Crackers; Arsène Lupin; Arsène Lupin Returns; Boy on a Dolphin; Deceived; F/X 2: The Deadly Art of Illusion; Gambit; How to Steal a Million; Hudson Hawk; Legal Eagles; Merry Andrew; Night Moves; Object of

Beauty; Topkapi; The Train; Utz; Valley of the Kings

Asia (General): see also *China: Chinese People: Japan: Japanese People: Vietnam War: Asian-Americans:* The Adventures of Marco Polo; Air America; Anna and the King of Siam; The Bridge on the River Kwai; The Charge of the Light Brigade (1936); The Charge of the Light Brigade (1968); China Seas; Cleopatra Jones & the Casino of Gold; Conqueror; Emmanuelle SERIES; Empire of the Sun; Farewell to the King; Fifty/Fifty; 55 Days at Peking; Gambit; Indiana Jones and the Temple of Doom; Indochine; Jakarta; The Killing Fields; The King and I; King Rat; Krakatoa, East of Java; Little Buddha; Lord Jim; Lost Command; Lost Horizon (1937); Lost Horizon (1973); Lover; Macao; Malaya; Never So Few; Objective Burma; An Outcast of the Islands; The Razor's Edge (1946); The Razor's Edge (1986); Red Dust; The River (1951); Road to Singapore; Saint Jack; The Sand Pebbles; The Seventh Dawn; Skullduggery; Soldier of Fortune; Somewhere I'll Find You; Three Came Home; Trade Winds; Traffik; Turtle Beach; The Ugly American; The World of Suzie Wong

Asian-Americans: see also *Ethnic-Minority Films: Japanese People: Chinese People:* Alamo Bay; Chan Is Missing; China Girl (1987); Combination Platter; Flower Drum Song; A Girl Named Tamiko; Go for Broke; Green Eyes; The Hatchet Man; The Joy Luck Club; The Karate Kid; The Karate Kid Part II; The Karate Kid Part III; Life Is Cheap, but Toilet Paper Is Expensive; Love Is a Many-Splendored Thing; Rhapsody in August; Romper Stomper; Surviving Desire; The Teahouse of the August Moon; True Believer; Wedding Banquet; The Year of the Dragon

Assassination Plots: see also *Spy Films: Hit Men: Diplomats: Rule the World-Plots to:* Assassin; Assassination; The Assassination Bureau; The Assassination of Trotsky; Behold a Pale Horse; Betrayed (1989); The Big Fisherman; Brass Target; A Bullet for the General; The Day of the Dolphin; The Day of the Jackal; Deadlier Than the Male; Deceivers; Domino Principle; Double McGuffin; The Eagle Has Landed; Embassy; Escape from the Planet of the Apes; The Evil That Men Do; Eyewitness (1970); F/X; Foreign

Correspondent; From Russia with Love; Futureworld; Gandhi; The Godfather; The Godfather Part II; The Godfather Part III; Gore Vidal's Lincoln; Half Moon Street; Hangmen Also Die; Hoffa; Illustrious Corpses; In the Line of Fire; The Internecine Project; JFK; Julius Caesar; The Killer Elite; King; La Femme Nikita; La Passante; Love Field; Man Hunt; The Man Who Knew Too Much (1934); The Man Who Knew Too Much (1956); The Man with the Golden Gun; The Manchurian Candidate; McBain; The Mechanic; Melancholia; Naked Gun; The Naked Runner; Nashville; Network; Nous Sommes Tous les Assassins; The Package; The Parallax View; The Pelican Brief; Point of No Return; Protocol; The Revolutionary; Ruby; The St. Valentine's Day Massacre; State of Siege; Talk Radio; The Tall Target; Taxi Driver; This Is My Affair; Timebomb; The Times of Harvey Milk; Topaz (1969); We Were Strangers; Winter Kills; Z

Astaire & Rogers: see also *Dance Movies: Dancers:* The Barkleys of Broadway; Carefree; Flying Down to Rio; Follow the Fleet; The Gay Divorcee; That's Dancin'!; Top Hat; Swing Time; Roberta; Shall We Dance; The Story of Vernon and Irene Castle

Asteroids: see *Meteors*

Astronauts: see also *Outer Space Movies:* Apollo 13; Beneath the Planet of the Apes; Call Me Bwana; Capricorn One; Countdown; Heavens Above; Journey to the Far Side of the Sun; Marooned; Moon Pilot; Planet of the Apes; The Quatermass Experiment; Queen of Outer Space; The Right Stuff; Robinson Crusoe on Mars; Solaris; Terms of Endearment

Asylums: see also *Mental Illness: Psychiatrists/Psychologists: Committed-Wrongly:* Alone in the Dark; Asylum; Awakenings; Bad Dreams; Beautiful Dreamers; Bedlam; A Bill of Divorcement (1932); A Bill of Divorcement (1940); The Cabinet of Dr. Caligari (1919); The Cabinet of Dr. Caligari (1962); Candyman; The Caretakers; Chattahoochee; Choose Me; Committed; Crazy People; Dialogues with Madwomen; The Disorderly Orderly; Disturbed; Dr. Giggles; The Dream Team; The End of the Road; Equus; A Fine Madness; Flesh of the Orchid; Frances; Halloween; Halloween 2; Halloween 4: The Return of Michael Myers; Halloween 5: The Revenge of Michael Myers;

Hammersmith Is Out; Harvey; Hellbound: Hellraiser II; High Anxiety; I Never Promised You a Rose Garden; Indecent Obsession; Killer Nun; King of Hearts; Lilith; Lizzie; Lost Angels; Marat/Sade; Murmur of the Heart; The Ninth Configuration; One Flew Over Cuckoo's Nest; Persona; The Pink Panther Strikes Again; Possessed (1947); The Raging Moon; Random Harvest; Rosie; Shock Corridor; Shock Treatment; The Snake Pit; The Strait Jacket; Suddenly Last Summer; Tommy

Athletes: see *Sports Movies: Biographies*

Atlantic City (set in the New Jersey city): see also *Gambling: Atlantic City;* The King of Marvin Gardens; The Lemon Sisters

Atomic Bombs: see *Bombs: Rule the World-Plots to*

Atomic Bombs: see *Bombs-Atomic: Nuclear Energy: Apocalyptic Stories*

Attorneys: see *Lawyers: Lawyers as Detectives: Law School: Courtroom Drama*

Aunts: see *Relatives-Troublesome*

Australia: see also *Australian Films: New Zealand:* Aborigines: Adventures of Eliza Frazer; Age of Consent; Australia; The Coca Cola Kid; Comrades; Crocodile Dundee; A Cry in the Dark; Dunera Boys; Efficiency Expert; Kangaroo; The Man from Snowy River; Million Dollar Mermaid; The Overlanders; Quigley Down Under; Rescuers Down Under; Rikky and Pete; Road Games; Romper Stomper; The Sea Chase; Shrimp on the Barbie; Silver City; Sister Kenny; Starstruck; Strangers in Good Company; The Sundowners; A Town Like Alice (1956); A Town Like Alice (1985); Under Capricorn; Where the Green Ants Dream; The Wrong Arm of the Law

Australian Films: see also *Australia: New Zealand:* Alvin Purple; Alvin Rides Again; Bliss; The Boy Who Had Everything; Breaker Morant; Burke and Wills; Cactus Caddie; Careful, He Might Hear You; The Cars That Ate Paris; Celia; Crocodile Dundee; Death in Brunswick; The Devil's Playground; Dogs in Space; Don's Party; Flirting; Gallipoli; The Getting of Wisdom; Ghosts . . . of the Civil Dead; Golden Braid; The Good Wife; Heatwave; Indecent Obsession; The Last Days of Chez Nous; The Last Wave; The Lighthorsemen; Lonely

Hearts; Mad Max; Mad Max Beyond Thunderdome; Malcolm; The Man from Snowy River; Muriel's Wedding; My Brilliant Career; Newsfront; Picnic at Hanging Rock; Proof; Puberty Blues; Rikky and Pete; The Road Warrior; Romper Stomper; Shame (1987); Sirens; Starstruck; Strangers in Good Company; Strictly Ballroom; The Sum of Us; Tim; Travelling North; Turtle Beach; Walkabout; Warm Nights on a Slow Moving Train; We of the Never Never; A Woman's Tale; The Year My Voice Broke; Young Einstein

Austria/Vienna: see also *Alps: Germany:* Amadeus; Bad Timing: A Sensual Obsession; Bitter Sweet (1933); Bitter Sweet (1940); Blind Husbands; Burning Secret; The Emperor Waltz; Freud; The Great Waltz (1938); The Great Waltz (1972); Letter from an Unknown Woman; Ten Little Indians; A Little Night Music; The Smiling Lieutenant; The Sound of Music; Twins of Evil

Autobiographical Stories: see also *Biographies: True Stories: Writers:* Act One; Alex in Wonderland; All That Jazz; All the Way Home; America, America; American Graffiti; Annie Hall; Aspen Extreme; Attic: The Hiding of Anne Frank; Au Revoir, les Enfants; The Autobiography of Miss Jane Pittman; Avalon; Becoming Colette; Beloved Infidel; Biloxi Blues; Blue; Born Again; Born on the Fourth of July; Bound for Glory; Brighton Beach Memoirs; Bring on the Night; Broadway Bound; A Bronx Tale; Caddie; The Caddy; Chaplin; Chapter Two; Cinema Paradiso; Cobb; Communion; Crooklyn; Cross Creek; Day for Night; Drifting; 8½; Empire of the Sun; Entre Nous; Fanny and Alexander; Four Friends; The Four Hundred Blows; Gaily, Gaily; Ghostwriter; The Grass Is Always Greener Over the Septic Tank; The Happy Hooker; Heartburn; Henry and June; Hope and Glory; I Am a Camera; I Know Why the Caged Bird Sings; I Vitelloni; I'm Dancing as Fast as I Can; Intervista; Islands in the Stream; Jo Jo Dancer, Your Life Is Calling; Julia; King of the Hill (1993); Lawrenceville Stories; The Learning Tree; Little Big Man; Long Day's Journey into Night; Malcolm X; Mommie Dearest; My Father's Glory; My Mother's Castle; Naked Lunch; Next Stop, Greenwich Village; One Trick Pony; Personal

Services; Platoon; Please Don't Eat the Daisies; Postcards from the Edge; A River Runs Through It; Romantic Comedy; The Sheltering Sky; Sister Kenny; Taxi zum Klo; This Boy's Life; To Hell and Back; Tom Horn; Tropic of Cancer; Truth or Dare; Under Milk Wood; Waterland; Who's That Knocking at My Door?; A World Apart; Young Winston

Autobiographical Stars (where the stars played themselves or relatives): see also *Autobiographical Stories:* Ballad in Blue; Bound for Glory; The Fabulous Dorseys (Jimmy Dorsey); Twins of Evil; The Jackie Robinson Story (Jackie Robinson); Out on a Limb (Shirley MacLaine); Spirit of Youth; Sophia Loren: Her Own Story (Sophia Loren)

Avant-Garde Films (stylistically experimental and therefore revolutionary at their time or simply so nonmainstream but not necessarily surreal that they defy genres): see also *Ahead of Its Time: Art Films: Cult Films: Filmumentaries:* Accident; Alphaville; And the Ship Sails On; Balcony; The Betrayal; The Blood of a Poet; Blowup; Blue; Boxing Helena; Breathless (1959); Candide; The Caretaker; City of Women; The Comfort of Strangers; The Day the Fish Came Out; The Devils; The Discreet Charm of the Bourgeoisie; The Double Life of Veronique; Dreams That Money Can Buy; Drowning by Numbers; Edward II; 8½; The Elephant Man; Eraserhead; Faces; First Name: Carmen; Flesh; Full Metal Jacket; The Garden; Gothic; Histoires Extraordinaires; The Homecoming (1973); Insignificance; Kings of the Road; Koyaanisqatsi; The Last of England; Last Year at Marienbad; L'Avventura; Law of Desire; Les Enfants Terribles; Life Is a Bed of Roses; Lisztomania; Little Shop of Horrors (1960); Lonesome Cowboys; The Magnificent Ambersons; The Maids; A Man Like Eva; The Man Who Fell to Earth; A Married Woman; Medium Cool; Merry Christmas, Mr. Lawrence; Metropolis; The Milky Way (1968); The Mind of Mr. Soames; Naked Lunch; Poison; Prospero's Books; Providence; Salome's Last Dance; Santa Sangre; Satyricon (Fellini's); Savages; The Seventh Seal; Shadows; The Silence; Stardust Memories; The Testament of Orpheus; Tommy; Track 29; The Trial (1962); The Trial (1993); Until the End of the World;

Viridiana; Weekend; Who Is Harry Kellerman . . . ; Wings of Desire; Zabriskie Point; Zed and Two Noughts

Avenging Death of Someone: see also *Revenge: Ordinary Person vs. Criminals: Vigilantes:* Affair in Trinidad; American Ninja 3; The Black Arrow; Bloodline; The Blue Lamp; Bounty Hunters; Breaking Point; Calcutta; The Cowboy Way; The Crow; The Deadly Affair; Death Wish; Death Wish 2; Death Wish 3; Death Wish 4; Death Wish 5; Delta Heat; Die! Die! My Darling; Double Impact; Dressed to Kill; Drop Zone; Fatal Vision; Fellow Traveller; 52 Pick-up; Fighting Back; Fighting Mad;

Firepower; Frenchie; G Men; Get Carter; Ghost; Gleaming the Cube; Good Guys Wear Black; The Goonies; Gordon's War; Hamlet (1948); Hamlet (1964); Hamlet (1969); Hamlet (1991); The Hand that Rocks the Cradle; Hard to Kill; Hidden Agenda; Hit!; Hit Man; I the Jury (1953); I the Jury (1982); Kid (1990); Kuffs; Last House on the Left; The Left Handed Gun; The Man from Laramie; Mask of the Avenger; McQ; Murphy's Law; Nevada Smith; Next of Kin (1989); On the Waterfront; The Onion Field; The Outlaw Josey Wales; Patriot Games; Pumpkinhead; Quick and the Dead; Rage; Razorback; Red Sonja; The Return

of the Musketeers; The Revengers; Ride the Pink Horse; Rolling Thunder; Scandalous!; Scaramouche; The Searchers; Shaft's Big Score; Shoot the Piano Player; The Specialist; Stick; The Sting; Striking Distance; Suddenly Last Summer; Tale of a Vampire; Tightrope; A Time of Destiny; To Live and Die in L.A.; Topper Returns; True Grit; Ulzana's Raid; Uncommon Valor; Underworld, USA; The Vanishing (1988); The Vanishing (1993); The Virgin Spring; Wanted Dead or Alive

Average Joes: see *Ordinary People Stories: Working Class: Kitchen Sink Drama*

Films by Category

B

B-Movies: see *Sexploitation: Cult Films Horror: Sci-Fi: Art Films*

Babes & Nerds: see *Nerds & Babes: Wallflowers and Hunks*

Babies: (in prominent roles): see also *Babies-Having: Children-Adopted: Child Protagonists:* Baby's Day Out; Honey, I Blew Up the Kid; Look Who's Talking Now; Look Who's Talking Too; The Mind of Mr. Soames; Promise Her Anything; Three Godfathers

Babies-Finding/Inheriting (getting stuck with an infant somehow): see also *Babies-Inheriting: Children-Adopted: Orphans: Men and Babies:* Baby Boom; Bachelor Mother; A Bedtime Story (1933); Bundle of Joy; Father Is a Bachelor; Jack and Sarah; The Lady Is Willing; Little Miss Marker (1934); Little Miss Marker (1980); Ragtime; Three Godfathers; Three Men and a Baby; Three Men and a Cradle

Babies-Having: see also *Mothers-Unwed: Fathers Who Leave: Children-Adopted/Unwanted:* Agnes of God; Almost Pregnant; Always Goodbye; The Americanization of Emily; Angie; The Baby Maker; Brink of Life; Bundle of Joy; Casanova Brown; Caught; Christopher Strong; Demon Seed; A Diary for Timothy; Doctor, You've Got to Be Kidding; Entertaining Mr. Sloane; Eraserhead; Escape from the Planet of the Apes; The Fly (1958); The Fly (1986); Fortress;

Frozen Assets; Funny About Love; Generation; Georgy Girl; The Hand that Rocks the Cradle; The Handmaid's Tale; Hawaii; Heartburn; Hold Your Man; House of Women; The Hunter; I Married a Dead Man; Immediate Family; It's Alive; It's Alive II; It's Alive III; Johnny Belinda; Journey for Margaret; Junior; Just Another Girl on the IRT; Just Between Friends; Kiss and Tell; Look Who's Talking; The Marquise of O; The Marriage Go Round; Micki and Maude; The Miracle (1948); The Miracle of Morgan's Creek; My Blue Heaven (1950); My Foolish Heart; My Life; Never Too Late; The Old Maid; Our Town; Paid in Full; Paternity; Popeye; Promises! Promises!; Rabbit Test; Raising Arizona; Rebel Rousers; Rich in Love; Rosemary's Baby; The Seventh Sign; She's Having a Baby; The Snapper; Strange Interlude (1932); Strange Interlude (1990); Switch; THX 1138; A Tiger's Tale; 'Tis a Pity She's a Whore; To Find a Man; Trust; The Umbrellas of Cherbourg; Unborn; Where Angels Fear to Tread; A Woman Is a Woman; The Woman Rebels; Xtro; You'll Like My Mother; Zero Population Growth (Z.P.G.)

Babies-Having, Late in Life: see also *Midlife Crisis: Mothers-Unwed: Fathers Who Leave: Children-Adopted/Unwanted:* And Baby Makes Six; Never Too Late; Prudence and the Pill; The

Tenth Month; Where Angels Fear to Tread

Babies-Inheriting: see *Babies-Finding/Inheriting*

Babies-Men Having: see also *Role Reversal: Men as Women:* Blue Monkey; Junior; Rabbit Test; A Slightly Pregnant Man; Switch

Babies-Stealing/Selling: see also *Babies-Having: Children-Adopted:* Aaron Slick from Punkin Crick; Abandoned; The Great Lie; Pudd'nhead Wilson

Babysitters (Nannies and Governesses as well): see also *Babysitters-Evil: Mothers: Mothers-Surrogate: Fathers-Surrogate: Servants:* Adam Had Four Sons; Adventures in Babysitting; All This and Heaven Too; Anna and the King of Siam; The Babysitter; The Chalk Garden; Clara's Heart; Devotion; Don't Bother to Knock; Don't Tell Mom the Babysitter's Dead; The Guardian; The Hand that Rocks the Cradle; Houseboat; Imitation of Life (1934); Imitation of Life (1959); The Innocents; Jack and Sarah; Jack and the Beanstalk; Jane Eyre (1934); Jane Eyre (1943); Jane Eyre (1971); The King and I; Mary Poppins; Miss Mary; Mr. Belvedere Goes to College; Mr. Nanny; The Nanny; Promise Her Anything; Rita, Sue and Bob Too; Rock a Bye Baby; Sitting Pretty; The Sound of Music; Uncle Buck; The Unseen; When a Stranger

Calls; The Wolves of Willoughby Chase; Zelly and Me

Babysitters-Evil: see also *Evil Women: Children in Jeopardy: Babysitters:* Babysitter; Don't Bother to Knock; The Guardian; The Hand that Rocks the Cradle; The Nanny; The Wolves of Willoughby Chase

Bachelor Pads: see *Affair Lairs: Playboys*

Bachelors-Confirmed (men set against marriage for whatever reason): see *Playboys: Marriage-Impending: Single Men: Young Men: Settling Down: Gay Men*

Backstory Exposition: see also *Flashbacks: Narrated Films*

Back to School (usually older people returning to finish): The Animal Kingdom; Back to School; Billy Madison; Mother Is a Freshman; Mr. Belvedere Goes to College; She's Working Her Way Through College

Bad Seeds: see *Evil Children*

Ballet: see also *Dancers: Theater Life: Opera:* An American in Paris; Dance, Girl, Dance; Dancers; Gaby; The Girl from Petrovka; Grand Hotel; Honeymoon; I Was an Adventuress; Invitation to the Dance; Limelight; Meet Me in Las Vegas; The Men in Her Life; The Night Is Young (1934); Nijinsky; Nutcracker (1993); Nutcracker-The Motion Picture (1986); On Your Toes; The Red Shoes; Slow Dancing in the Big City; The Tales of Hoffman; Top of the Town; The Turning Point; Waterloo Bridge (1931); Waterloo Bridge (1940)

Balloons/Blimps/Zeppelins: see also *World Travel: Airlines/Airplanes:* The Adventures of Baron Munchausen (1987); Around the World in 80 Days; Chitty Chitty Bang Bang; Charlie Bubbles; Flight of the Eagle; The Great Race; The Hindenburg; Master of the World; Mysterious Island; Night Crossing; Olly Olly Oxen Free; The Red Balloon; Those Magnificent Men in Their Flying Machines; The Yellow Balloon; Zeppelin

Baltimore: see also *Working Class: Ordinary People Stories:* The Accidental Tourist; Avalon; Cry Baby; Diner; Hairspray; Men Don't Leave; Miss Susie Slagle's; Sleepless in Seattle; Tin Men

Bank Robberies: see also *Heist Stories: Capers: Thieves:* The Apple Dumpling Gang; The Apple Dumpling Gang Rides Again; The Bank Dick; The Bank Shot; Belle of the Yukon; Big Bad Mama; Big Deal on Madonna Street; Blue Iguana; Bonnie and Clyde; Bunny O'Hare; Buster; Cahill, United States Marshal; Car 99; Charley Varrick; Colorado Territory; Criss Cross (1947); Dead Heat on a Merry Go Round; Dog Day Afternoon; Dollars; Eight on the Lam; Experiment in Terror; A Fistful of Dynamite; The Getaway (1972); The Getaway (1994); Go Chase Yourself; Going in Style; The Good Die Young; The Great Bank Hoax; The Great Northfield Minnesota Raid; Inspector Clouseau; The Italian Job; Killing Zoe; Larceny, Inc.; The Lavender Hill Mob; The League of Gentlemen; The Long Riders; Loophole; A Man, a Woman and a Bank; Miracles; A Nice Little Bank That Should Be Robbed; Nightfall; Penelope; Point Break; Quick Change; Real McCoy; The River Wild; The Rounders; Scotland Yard; Seems Like Old Times; The Silent Partner; Silver Bears; Take the Money and Run; Terminal Velocity; That Darn Cat!; The Thomas Crown Affair; Three Fugitives; Thunderbolt and Lightfoot; The Tin Star; Trapped in Paradise; Who's Minding the Mint?; Wisdom

Bankruptcy: see *Mortgage Drama: Losing It All: Risking It All: Unemployment: Making a Living*

Barbara Stanwyck Cattle Problems: see *Cattle Herded by Barbara Stanwyck: Cattle Ranchers*

Barren Women: see *Women-Childless: Children-Adopted*

Baseball: see also *Sports Movies:* Angels in the Outfield (1951); Angels in the Outfield (1994); The Babe; The Babe Ruth Story; The Bad News Bears; The Bad News Bears Go to Japan; The Bad News Bears in Breaking Training; Bang the Drum Slowly; The Bingo Long Traveling All-Stars and Motor Kings; Bull Durham; Cobb; Comrades of Summer; Cooperstown; Damn Yankees; Eight Men Out; Fear Strikes Out; Field of Dreams; It Happens Every Spring; Jackie Robinson Story; The Kid from Left Field; League of Their Own; Little Big League; Major League; Major League 2; Mr. Destiny; My Blue Heaven (1990); The Natural; The Naughty Nineties; The Pride of the Yankees; Sandlot; The Scout; Squeeze Play; Strategic Air Command; The Stratton Story; Take Me Out to the Ball Game; Talent for the Game

Basketball: see also *Sports Movies:* Above the Rim; The Absent-Minded Professor; The Air Up There; Amazing Grace and Chuck; Blue Chips; Coach; Drive, He Said; Fast Break; The Fish that Saved Pittsburgh; Hoop Dreams; Hoosiers; Inside Moves; Mixed Company; Tall Story; Teen Wolf; That Championship Season; White Men Can't Jump

Bastards: see *Mothers-Unwed: Evil Men: Mean Men*

Bathroom Humor (nasty, scatalogical humor, preoccupied with things coming out of the body mostly): see also *Party Movies: Teenage Movies: Fraternity Life: College Life: Comedy-Gag:* And Now for Something Completely Different; The Bachelor Party (1984); The Bad News Bears; The Bad News Bears Go to Japan; The Bad News Bears in Breaking Training; Blazing Saddles; Caddyshack; Caddyshack 2; Caveman; Cheech and Chong: Still Smokin'; Cheech and Chong's Next Movie; Cheech and Chong's Nice Dreams; Cheech and Chong's The Corsican Brothers; Gorp!; The Great Outdoors; Grumpy Old Men; History of the World Part One; Life Stinks!; The Magic Christian; Meatballs; Naked Gun; Naked Gun 2½; Naked Gun 33⅓; National Lampoon's Animal House; O.C. and Stiggs; Pink Flamingos; The Road to Wellville; Robin Hood, Men in Tights; Scenes from the Class Struggle in Beverly Hills; Shakes the Clown; Spaceballs; Stripes; Sweetie; Things Are Tough All Over; Tommy Boy; Uncle Buck; Up the Academy; Up the Creek (1984); Wild Life; Yellowbeard

Battle of the Bulge: see also *War Battles:* A Bridge Too Far; Battle of the Bulge; Battleground

Battle of the Sexes: see also *Sex Comedy: Romantic Comedy: Romance-Opposites Attract: Romance-Bickering: Screwball Comedy: Female Among Males: Women Against Male Establishment: Role Reversal:* Adam's Rib (1949); The African Queen; Another Stakeout; Bad Company (1995); The Bad News Bears; The Battle of the Sexes; Boomerang; Castaway; Casual Sex?; The Competition; Continental Divide; Disclosure; The Enforcer (1976); Fawlty Towers; A Fine Romance; First Monday in October; Gin Game; Guys and Dolls; Heaven Knows, Mr. Allison; Hedda; High Road to China; I Will . . . I Will . . . for Now; Improper Channels; June Bride; Kisses for My President; The Lady Eve; The Last Married Couple in

America; Little Rascals; The Main
Event; Major League; Making Mr. Right;
The Male Animal; McClintock!; Men . . .
(1985); Nine to Five; Ninotchka; No
More Ladies; Oklahoma Crude; Only
Angels Have Wings; Operation Petticoat;
The Opposite Sex and How to Live with
Them; Other People's Money; The
Paleface; The Paper; Pat and Mike; PCU;
The Pickwick Papers; Pillow Talk; Sex
and the Single Girl; She's Gotta Have It;
She's Working Her Way Through College;
Shoot the Moon; Speechless; The Sure
Thing; Sweethearts; Swept Away; Take a
Letter, Darling; Take Me Out to the Ball
Game; The Taming of the Shrew;
Threesome; The Thrill of It All; Variety;
The War between Men and Women; The
Warrior's Husband; Watch It; When
Harry Met Sally; The Witches of
Eastwick; Woman of the Year

Battles-Great: see *War Battles: War*
Stories: Military Stories
Beach Movies: see also *Surfers:*
Divers: California Life: L'Année des
Meduses; Back to the Beach; Beach
Blanket Bingo; Beach Party; Big
Wednesday; Bikini Beach; Blood Beach;
Breaking Up Is Hard to Do; Calendar
Girl; California Dreaming; Can
Hieronymus Merkin Ever Forget Mercy
Humppe and Find True Happiness?;
C'est la Vie; Clambake; Don't Make
Waves; Earth Girls Are Easy; The
Endless Summer; Female on the Beach;
The Ghost in the Invisible Bikini;
Gidget; Girls! Girls! Girls!; Jaws; Last
Summer; Lifeguard; Lord Love a Duck;
Love in a Goldfish Bowl; Moment by
Moment; Muscle Beach Party; Pauline at
the Beach; Ruby in Paradise; The
Sandpiper; Side Out; Summer of '42;
Tentacles; To Kill a Clown; Where the
Boys Are; Where the Boys Are '84;
Woman on the Beach

Beatnik Era (the hip, cool cats and
poets of the pre-Vietnam era): see also
Poets: Jazz Players: Musicians: 1950s:
1960s: Anti-Establishment Films:
Absolute Beginners; The Beat
Generation; Expresso Bongo; Funny
Face; The Gene Krupa Story; Heart Beat;
Next Stop, Greenwich Village; The
Subterraneans; The Testament of
Orpheus; Too Late Blues

Beautiful People (they may not be
perfect but they hang with the set who
are or want to be): see also *Fashion*

World: Models: Eurotrash: Sexy Men:
Sexy Women: Alternative Lifestyles: All
the Fine Young Cannibals; Another
Country; The April Fools; Bell, Book, and
Candle; Beyond the Valley of the Dolls;
Blow Up; Bob&Carol&Ted&Alice;
Breakfast at Tiffany's; Bright Lights, Big
City; Charade; The Comfort of Strangers;
Darling; Desperately Seeking Susan; 8½;
The Eyes of Laura Mars; Fathom; Female
on the Beach; First Name: Carmen;
Goodbye Gemini; The Great Gatsby
(1949); The Great Gatsby (1974); The
Group; Hearts of Fire; Johnny Suede;
L'Année des Meduses; La Dolce Vita;
Lady L.; The Last Run; Laughter in the
Dark; The Linguini Incident; Man of
Flowers; Montenegro; 9½ Weeks; The
Picture of Dorian Gray; Quartet (1981);
Shampoo; Siesta; Slaves of New York; The
Subterraneans; The Sun Also Rises;
Superstar, The Life and Times of Andy
Warhol; Tale of a Vampire; A Talent for
Loving; The Testament of Orpheus; The
VIPs; What?; What's New Pussycat?

Beauty Pageants: see also *Beautiful*
People: Models: Carrie (1976); The
Duchess of Idaho; Free and Easy; Miss
Firecracker; Old Dracula; Smile; Waikiki
Wedding; Wicked As They Come

Bedroom Farce: see *Farce-Bedroom*
Beginning Life Again: see *Starting*
Over: Life Transitions: Midlife Crisis
Behind the Scenes (things hidden
from the public in each of the stories,
primarily in theater, however): see also
Attic: The Hiding of Anne Frank; A
Chorus Line; Cobb; Command Decision;
Commitments; The Country Girl; Dancers;
Follies in Concert; Footlight Parade; 42nd
Street; George White's 1935 Scandals;
George White's Scandals (1934); George
White's Scandals 1945; Give the Girl a
Break; The Great Ziegfeld; The Hard Way
(1943); The Idolmaker; It's Love I'm
After; King's Row; Kiss Me Kate (1953);
Kiss the Boys Goodbye; Let's Dance;
Murder at the Vanities; Murders in the
Rue Morgue; Noises Off; On Your Toes;
Opening Night; The Private Life of
Sherlock Holmes; Rosencrantz and
Guildenstern Are Dead; Simon and Laura;
Smile; Truth or Dare; Twentieth Century;
Under the Rainbow; The War Room;
Wonder Bar; Ziegfeld Girl

Bergmanesque (films reminiscent of
the stark, somber style of Swedish
director Ingmar Bergman): see also

Swedish Films: Art Films: Avant-Garde
Films: Depression: Alienation: After the
Rehearsal; Another Woman; Autumn
Sonata; Brink of Life; The Devil's Eye;
The Devil's Wanton; Face to Face; Fanny
and Alexander; Interiors; A Lesson in
Love; September

Berlin: see also *Germany: Nazi Stories:*
World War II Era: Cold War Era:
Abschied von Gestern; Berlin
Alexanderplatz; Berlin Express; The Big
Lift; Cabaret; Despair; Faraway, So
Close!; A Foreign Affair; Funeral in
Berlin; Grand Hotel; I Am a Camera; The
Looking Glass War; Mephisto; Never Say
Goodbye; One, Two, Three!; Salon Kitty;
Shining Through; The Spy Who Came in
from the Cold; Wings of Desire

Betrayals (among friends as opposed
to Double Crossings, which refers more
to plot): see also *Double-Crossings:*
Traitors: Friends Turned Enemies:
Dangerous Lovers: Dangerous Spouses:
All the Way Up; Betrayal; Betrayed
(1954); Betrayed (1989); The Big Knife;
Blood on the Moon; The Blue Max;
Bodyguard; Bullets or Ballots; The
Bullfighter and the Lady; By Love
Possessed; Chimes at Midnight; The
Conformist; Dangerous Liaisons; Daniel;
Darling; Fahrenheit 451; Fox and His
Friends; Friends and Husbands;
Geronimo (1962); Geronimo (1993); Good
Fellas; Hamlet (1948); Hamlet (1964);
Hamlet (1969); Hamlet (1991); His
Brother's Wife; I Cover the Waterfront;
I Found Stella Parish; Illegal; The
Inheritance; Internal Affairs; Island in the
Sun; Kiss of the Spider Woman; The Last
Seduction; The Man in Grey; Mantrap;
New Jack City; Obsession; The Oscar;
Otello; Othello (1951); Othello (1965);
Out of the Past; The Quiet American;
Reunion; Scorpio; The Secret Partner; The
Sicilian; Strangers on a Train; Sweet Bird
of Youth; Tequila Sunrise; Valmont;
Verdict; Veronika Voss; The Walking
Stick; The Year of Living Dangerously

Bets: see also *Gambling: Risking It All:*
Losing It All: Billy Madison; The Bobo;
The Bowery; Brewster's Millions (1935);
Brewster's Millions (1945); Brewster's
Millions (1985); Broadway Bill; California
Split; Cold Turkey; Dangerous Liaisons;
Diggstown; Dirty Rotten Scoundrels;
Doctors' Wives; Dogfight; Easy Money
(1983); Eight Men Out; Guys and Dolls;
Honeymoon in Vegas; House of Games;

House of the Long Shadows; Indecent Proposal; Life Stinks!; Meet the People; No Man of Her Own; Nothing But the Truth; Rhinestone; The Set Up; The Seventh Seal; Tea for Two; Trading Places

Beverly Hills: see also *Los Angeles: Rich People: Snobs:* American Gigolo; Beverly Hillbillies; Beverly Hills Cop; Beverly Hills Cop 2; Beverly Hills Madam; California Suite; Death Becomes Her; Down and Out in Beverly Hills; Less Than Zero; Night on Earth; Pretty Woman; Scenes from the Class Struggle in Beverly Hills; Shampoo; Strangers When We Meet; The Taking of Beverly Hills; Troop Beverly Hills

Biblical Stories: see also *God: Jesus Christ: Religion: Ancient Times:* Barabbas; Ben Hur (1959); Ben Hur: A Tale of the Christ (1925); The Bible; The Big Fisherman; David and Bathsheba; Godspell; The Gospel According to St. Matthew; The Greatest Story Ever Told; Green Pastures; Intolerance; Jesus Christ Superstar; Jesus of Nazareth; King David; King of Kings (1927); King of Kings (1961); The Last Temptation of Christ; Monty Python and the Holy Grail; Monty Python's Life of Brian; The Prodigal; Raiders of the Lost Ark; Salome (1953); Samson and Delilah; The Seventh Sign; The Sign of the Cross; The Silver Chalice; Sodom and Gomorrah; Solomon and Sheba; Spartacus; The Ten Commandments; Wholly Moses

Bicycles: see also *Sports Movies: Motorcycles:* American Flyers; The Bicycle Thief; Breaking Away; The Gang That Couldn't Shoot Straight; Key Exchange; Pee-Wee's Big Adventure; Quicksilver

Bigamy: see also *Marriage: Cheating Men: Cheating Women: Alternative Lifestyles: Marrying Again:* Autumn Leaves; The Bigamist; The Constant Husband; Deceived; Enemies, a Love Story; Handle with Care; Henry VIII and His Six Wives; I, Jane Doe; Micki and Maude; Monsieur Verdoux; Move Over, Darling; My Favorite Wife; Paint Your Wagon; Piccadilly Incident; Raise the Red Lantern; Tomorrow Is Forever

Big Band Era: see also *1930s: 1940s: MUSICALS: Musicians: Music Composers:* Alexander's Ragtime Band; The Benny Goodman Story; The Clock; The Glenn Miller Story; Love and Hisses; Naughty But Nice; Orchestra Wives; Song

of the Thin Man; Swing Kids; Top of the Town; Young Man with a Horn

Big City Life: see *Urban Life: Inner City Life: Social Drama: Social Satire: Homeless People: New York Life*

Bigots: see also *Neo-Nazis: Race Relations: Homophobia: Hate Crimes: Black vs. White: Ku Klux Klan:* All the Young Men; Betrayed (1989); Black Legion; Cadence; Carbon Copy; Chocolat; Citizen Cohn; A Cry in the Dark; Dead Bang; Drifting; Early Frost; Go for Broke; Hairspray; Heart Condition; Higher Learning; Jim Thorpe, All American; Joe; The Josephine Baker Story; The Klansman; Mississippi Burning; The Murder of Mary Phagan; Native Son (1951); Native Son (1986); No Way Out (1950); Nothin' But a Man; Paris Trout; A Patch of Blue; Q & A; Romper Stomper; Sacco and Vanzetti; School Ties; Separate but Equal; Shame (1961); Silver City; South Pacific; Storm Warning; Talk Radio; Tell Them Willie Boy Is Here; Till Death Us Do Part; To Kill a Mockingbird; Trial (1955); The Unforgiven (1960); Valdez Is Coming; White Dog

Bikers: see *Motorcycles: Bicycles*

Billionaires: see *Moguls: Leaders: Rule the World-Plots to: Rich People*

Billy the Kid: see also *WESTERNS:* Gore Vidal's Billy the Kid; The Left Handed Gun; The Outlaw; Pat Garrett and Billy the Kid; Young Guns; Young Guns II

Bimbos (pretty and not-too-bright females): see also *Simple Minds: Sexy Women: Bimboys:* All Night Long (1981); Andy Warhol's Heat; Auntie Lee's Meat Pies; Barbarella; Behave Yourself!; Body Double; Body of Evidence; Bombshell; Born Yesterday (1950); Born Yesterday (1993); Candy; Cat Women of the Moon; A Change of Seasons; Confessions of a Window Cleaner; Cool World; Die Watching; Doctor Detroit; Faster Pussycat! Kill! Kill!; Flamingo Road; The Girl Can't Help It; Gold Diggers in Paris; Gold Diggers of 1933; Gold Diggers of 1935; Gold Diggers of 1937; Gold Diggers of Broadway; Goldfinger; Greedy; The Grifters; Guys and Dolls; Island of Love; Jinxed!; Las Vegas Hillbillies; The Love Goddesses; The Misfits; My Cousin Vinny; My Stepmother Is an Alien; Octopussy; Oh Men! Oh Women!; Old Dracula; Promises! Promises!; Queen of Outer Space; Radio Days; Rock a Bye Baby;

The Seven-Year Itch; Ski School; Some Like It Hot; Star 80; The Stripper; Stroker Ace; Tarzan and His Mate; Tarzan Escapes; Tarzan the Ape Man (1932); Tarzan the Ape Man (1981); There's a Girl in My Soup; They All Laughed; Thunderball; Twentieth Century; Used Cars; Victor/Victoria; Will Success Spoil Rock Hunter?

Bimbos & Bad Guys: see *Bimbos: Dangerous Men: Outlaw Road Movies: Criminal Couples: Tough Guys and Religious Women*

Bimboys (pretty and not-too-bright males): see *Simple Minds: Sexy Men: Macho Men: Body Builders*

Biographies: see also *Autobiographical Stories: True Stories: Leaders: Charismatic People: Fame-Rise to: Power-Rise to: Music Composers: Character Studies: Criminal Biographies:* Abe Lincoln in Illinois; Above and Beyond; Abraham Lincoln; Absolute Beginners; Act One; The Agony and the Ecstasy; Al Capone; Alexander the Great; All the Fine Young Cannibals; All You Need Is Cash; The Amazing Howard Hughes; The Assassination of Trotsky; The Babe; The Babe Ruth Story; Backbeat; Barfly; Battle Hymn; Beau James; Beautiful Dreamers; Becoming Colette; Beloved Infidel; The Benny Goodman Story; Bird; Birdman of Alcatraz; Blaze; Blind Ambition; Blossoms in the Dust; Blue; Bound for Glory; Brother Sun, Sister Moon; The Buddy Holly Story; Buffalo Bill; Buffalo Bill and the Indians, or Sitting Bull's History Lesson; Bugsy; Caesar and Cleopatra; Camille Claudel; Capone; Casanova (Fellini's Casanova); Catherine the Great; Chaplin; Che!; The Childhood of Maxim Gorky; Citizen Cohn; Citizen Kane; Coal Miner's Daughter; Cobb; The Conqueror; The Court Martial of Jackie Robinson; Cross Creek; Dance with a Stranger; Dante's Inferno; The Desert Fox; The Desert Rats; Desirée; Diamond Jim; Diana: Her True Story; Diary of Anne Frank (1959); Dillinger (1945); Dillinger (1973); Disappearance of Aimee; Disraeli; Dixie; Doc; Don't Look Back; Doors; Double Exposure; Dr. Ehrlich's Magic Bullet; The Eddie Cantor Story; The Eddy Duchin Story; Edison, the Man; Eleanor and Franklin; Eleni; The Elephant Man; Elvis: The Movie; The Executioner's Song; F. Scott Fitzgerald in Hollywood; Fat Man and Little Boy; The Five Pennies;

Forever James Dean; Frances; Francis, God's Jester; Freud; Funny Girl; Funny Lady; G.I. Joe; Gable and Lombard; Gaily, Gaily; Gandhi; The Gene Krupa Story; Gentleman Jim; The George Raft Story; The Glenn Miller Story; The Gorgeous Hussy; Gorillas in the Mist; The Gospel According to St. Matthew; Greased Lightning; Great Balls of Fire; The Great Caruso; The Great Garrick; The Great Impostor; The Great Moment; The Great Waltz (1938); The Great Waltz (1972); The Great Ziegfeld; The Greatest; The Greek Tycoon; Hail, Hail, Rock n Roll; Hans Christian Andersen; Harlow; Haunted Summer; Heart Beat; Heart Like a Wheel; The Helen Morgan Story; Henry and June; Henry: Portrait of a Serial Killer; The Hitler Gang; Hitler-The Last Ten Days; Hoffa; Hollywood Cavalcade; Houdini; Hour of the Gun; A House Is Not a Home; The House of Rothschild; The Hunter; The I Don't Care Girl; I Dream of Jeannie; I Want to Live; I'll Cry Tomorrow; I'll See You in My Dreams; I'm Dancing as Fast as I Can; Immortal Beloved; The Incredible Sarah; The Inn of the Sixth Happiness; The Interrupted Melody; Irish Eyes Are Smiling; Isadora; I Wonder Who's Kissing Her Now; Jack London; Jefferson in Paris; JFK; Jim Thorpe, All American; Joan of Arc; Jolson Sings Again; The Jolson Story; The Josephine Baker Story; Khartoum; King; King of Kings (1927); King of Kings (1961); Knute Rockne: All-American; The Krays; La Bamba; Lady Caroline Lamb; Lady in Red; Lady Sings the Blues; The Last Command; Lawrence of Arabia; LBJ: The Early Years; Leadbelly; Lenny; Let's Get Lost; Lightning Over Water; Listen Up: The Lives of Quincy Jones; Lisztomania; The Long Gray Line; Love Me or Leave Me; Lust for Life; Luther; MacArthur; Madame Curie; The Magic Box; Magnificent Doll; The Magnificent Yankee; Mahler; Malcolm X; A Man Like Eva; Man of a Thousand Faces; Mandela; Marie Antoinette; Marilyn, the Untold Story; Martin Luther; Mary of Scotland; Mary Queen of Scots; Mask (1985); McVicar; Million Dollar Mermaid; The Miracle Worker; Mishima; Mobsters; Modilgiani; Mommie Dearest; The Moon and Sixpence; Moulin Rouge; Mrs. Parker and the Vicious Circle; The Music Lovers; My Gal Sal; My Left Foot; My Wild Irish Rose; Naked Lunch; The Naked Maja; Napoleon; Nijinsky; Now I'll Tell; The Nun's Story;

Nurse Edith Cavell; Old Gringo; One Foot in Heaven; Oscar Wilde; The Other Side of the Mountain; The Other Side of the Mountain Part Two; Out of Africa; Patton; Patty Hearst; The Perils of Pauline; The Pride of the Yankees; Priest of Love; The Private Life of Henry VIII; Queen of Destiny; Raging Bull; Reckless (1935); Reds; Rembrandt; Reversal of Fortune; Rhapsody in Blue; The Rise and Fall of Legs Diamond; The Rise of Louis XIV; Romero; Rose of Washington Square; Round Midnight; Ruby; Rudy; St. Louis Blues; The St. Valentine's Day Massacre; Sakharov; Santa Fe Trail; The Scarlet Empress; Sergeant York; Serpico; The Seven Little Foys; Sinatra; The Singing Nun; Sister Kenny; Somebody Up There Likes Me; Song of Norway; A Song to Remember; Song without End; Sophia Loren, Her Own Story; The Spirit of St. Louis; Spymaker, the Secret Life of Ian Fleming; Stalin; Star!; Star 80; Stars and Stripes Forever; Stormy Weather; The Story of Adèle H.; The Story of Alexander Graham Bell; The Story of Dr. Wassell; The Story of Louis Pasteur; The Story of Vernon and Irene Castle; The Story of Will Rogers; Suez; Sunrise at Campobello; Superstar, the Life and Times of Andy Warhol; Sweet Dreams; 32 Short Films about Glenn Gould; This Boy's Life; Three Little Words; Till the Clouds Roll By; To Hell and Back; To Kill a Priest; The Toast of New York; Tom & Viv; Tom Horn; The Trials of Oscar Wilde; Truth or Dare; Tucker: The Man and His Dream; Under Milk Wood; The Unsinkable Molly Brown; Valentino (1951); Valentino (1977); Van Gogh; Vincent and Theo; The Virgin Queen; Viva Villa!; Voltaire; W. C. Fields and Me; Waterloo; White Hunter, Black Heart; Wild Hearts Can't Be Broken; Wilson; The Wings of Eagles; Wired; The Wonderful World of the Brothers Grimm; Words and Music; Wyatt Earp; Young Catherine; Young Man with a Horn; Young Mr. Lincoln; Young Tom Edison; Young Winston

Biographies-Fictional (biographical stories with veiled resemblances to real people or fictionalizations involving real people doing things they never necessarily did): see also _Biographies: Fame-Rise to: Power-Rise to: Incredible but Mostly True: True or Not:_ All the Fine Young Cannibals; All the King's Men; All the Way Home; All You

Need Is Cash; Angelo, My Love; The Arrangement; The Autobiography of Miss Jane Pittman; Bob Roberts; The Cardinal; The Caretakers; Carousel; Cheers for Miss Bishop; Christopher Strong; Citizen Kane; Colonel Redl; Come and Get It; The Comic; Daniel; Darling; David Copperfield; Diamond Jim; Diary of a Mad Housewife; Fat Man and Little Boy; Five Heartbeats; Ghostwriter; The Greek Tycoon; Hammett; Haunted Summer; Heart of Dixie; Heartburn; Henry: Portrait of a Serial Killer; Hollywood Cavalcade; In Cold Blood; Insignificance; Kafka; Katherine; La Nuit de Varennes; Lady Caroline Lamb; The Lady in Red; The Last Tycoon; Little Big Man; Little Caesar; Lloyd's of London; Main Street to Broadway; Man of Iron; Meet Danny Wilson; The Miracle Worker; The Moderns; Monty Python's Life of Brian; Mr. Saturday Night; Natural Ragtime; Red Line 7000; The Revolutionary; The Rose; Rose of Washington Square; The Royal Family of Broadway; Scarface (1932); Scarface (1983); The Shoes of the Fisherman; Sparkle; Spymaker, the Secret Life of Ian Fleming; Sunset; Tall Target; This Is Spinal Tap; Tommy; White Hunter, Black Heart; The Wild Party; The Wings of Eagles; Young Bess; Young Man with a Horn

Biographies-Fictional: The Boys from Brazil; A Face in the Crowd; The Goddess; One Trick Pony; Zelig

Birds: see also _Monsters-Animal:_ Birdman of Alcatraz; The Birds; The Birds II; Birdy; The Blue Bird (1940); The Blue Bird (1976); Champagne for Caesar; Howard the Duck; Johnathan Livingston Seagull; Ladyhawke; The Swan Princess; What's So Bad About Feeling Good?

Bisexuality: see also _Gay Men: Lesbians: Alternative Lifestyles: Ménage à Trois: Gay Awakenings:_ The Adjuster; Alexander, the Other Side of Dawn; Apartment Zero; Basic Instinct; Beyond Therapy; Les Biches; The Bitter Tears of Petra Von Kant; The Boys in the Band; Cabaret; Deadfall (1968); Deathtrap; A Different Story; England Made Me; Entertaining Mr. Sloane; Fortune and Men's Eyes; The Fourth Man; Girlfriends; Henry and June; Hunger; In a Shallow Grave; Interview with the Vampire; Joshua Then and Now; Kiss of the Spider Woman; The Lair of the White Worm; Lake Consequence; The Leather Boys; A Man Like Eva; The Music Lovers; Proof; The Rainbow; Ready to Wear; Satyricon (Fellini's); Something for Everyone; Speaking Parts; Sunday, Bloody Sunday; Three of Hearts; Threesome; The Vampire Lovers; Victor/Victoria; The Wedding Banquet; Woman in Flames

Bitches: see *Mean Women: Evil Women: Women in Conflict*

Black Among Whites (a black person surrounded by mostly white people in the story): see also *Black & Whites Together: Black vs. Whites: White Among Blacks:* All the Young Men; Blazing Saddles; Christmas Lilies of the Field; Cop and a Half; Greased Lightning; The L-Shaped Room; Lilies of the Field; Sister Act 2; Tick, Tick, Tick . . . ; To Sir with Love; Trading Places

Black & White Together (racially mixed partners, general): see also *Black Among White: Black vs. White/Black & White Together: Race Relations: Buddy Films: Romance-Interracial:* Another 48HRS.; Bad Company (1995); Crossroads (1986); 48 Hours; Just Cause; The Last Boy Scout; Lethal Weapon; Lethal Weapon 2; Lethal Weapon 3; Lightning Jack; Passion Fish; Pulp Fiction; Rising Sun; Running Scared; Saint of Fort Washington; The Shawshank Redemption

Black as White (black person posing as a white one): see also *White as Black:* Coming to America; I Passed for White; True Identity

Black Casts/Films (note: see also *Black Directors: Black Screenwriters:* **these categories are difficult to be completely accurate about as there were very few before 1970 and the race of filmmakers is not always noted in lesser known films): see also** *Blaxploitation: Black Men: Black Women: Race Relations: Black vs. White: Gangs-Black: Africans:* Aaron Loves Angela; Above the Rim; Almos' a Man; Bebe's Kids; The Bingo Long Traveling All-Stars and Motor Kings; Black Caesar; Black Orpheus; Blacula; Boomerang; Bopha!; Boyz N the Hood; Breakin'; Breakin' 2: Electric Boogaloo; Bright Road; Brother John; Buck and the Preacher; Bustin' Loose; Cabin in the Sky; Car Wash; Carmen Jones; CB4: The Movie; Claudine; The Color Purple; Come

Back Charleston Blue; Coming to America; Conrack; Cool Runnings; Crooklyn; Dead Boyz Can't Fly; Do the Right Thing; DROP Squad; Ernest Green Story; Fresh; Glory; The Goonies; Gordon's War; Graffiti Bridge; The Green Pastures; Hallelujah!; Hangin' with the Homeboys; Harlem Nights; A Hero Ain't Nothin' but a Sandwich; Hit!; Hit Man; Hollywood Shuffle; I Know Why the Caged Bird Sings; I Like It Like That; I Passed for White; I'm Gonna Git You, Sucka; The Inkwell; Jungle Fever; Just Another Girl on the IRT; King; Lady Sings the Blues; Laurel Avenue; Leadbelly; Lean on Me; Learning Tree; Let's Do It Again (1975); The Lost Man; Low Down Dirty Shame; Mandela; The Mark of the Hawk; Menace II Society; Meteor Man; Mo' Better Blues; New Jack City; New Orleans; Norman, Is That You?; Nothin' But a Man; Posse (1993); Rage in Harlem; A Raisin in the Sun; Return of Superfly; River Niger; Roots; Roots, the Gift; St. Louis Blues; Sarafina!; Say Amen, Somebody!; School Daze; Shadows; Shaft; Shaft in Africa; Shaft's Big Score; She's Gotta Have It; A Soldier's Story; Sophisticated Gents; Sounder; South Central; Sparkle; Stormy Weather; Straight out of Brooklyn; Strictly Business; Sugar Hill; Superfly; Tap; They Call Me Mr. Tibbs!; To Sleep with Anger; Uptown Saturday Night; The Wiz

Black Comedy: see also *Comedy-Morbid: SATIRE: COMEDY: Tragicomedy: Comedy & Violence:* Abel; The Abominable Dr. Phibes; Ace in the Hole; Actors and Sin; The Addams Family; Addams Family Values; The Adventures of Buckaroo Banzai Across the Eighth Dimension; The Advocate; After Hours; All the Way Up; Alligator; Alligator II: The Mutation; Ambulance; American Gothic; An American Werewolf in London; And Justice for All; And Then There Were None; Andy Warhol's Bad; The Anniversary; Arachnophobia; Army of Darkness; Arnold; Arsenic and Old Lace; The Assassination Bureau; Attack of the Killer Tomatoes; Auntie Lee's Meat Pies; Bagdad Cafe; The Battle of the Sexes; Baxter (1990); Beat the Devil; Being There; Better Off Dead; Beyond the Valley of the Dolls; Beyond Therapy; Black and White in Color; The Black Marble; Black Sunday (1960); Blind Fury; Blood and Concrete; Blood Simple; Blue Velvet; The Bonfire of the Vanities; Bonnie and Clyde;

Borrower; A Boy and His Dog; Brazil; Brewster McCloud; The Bride of Frankenstein; Brimstone and Treacle; Brittania Hospital; The Brother from Another Planet; Buddy Buddy; Buffet Froid; Bullseye!; Bunny O'Hare; The 'burbs; Cadillac Man; California Split; The Cars That Ate Paris; Catch Me a Spy; Checking Out; Child's Play (1988); Child's Play 2; Child's Play 3; Cold Feet; The Comedy of Terrors; Compromising Positions; Consuming Passions; The Cook, the Thief, His Wife & Her Lover; Crimes of Passion; Crimes of the Heart; Dark Star; Death Becomes Her; Death in Brunswick; Delicatessen; Demon Knight; Desperate Living; Dion Brothers; The Discreet Charm of the Bourgeoisie; Divorce, Italian Style; Do You Like Women?; Down By Law; Dr. Giggles; Dr. Phibes Rises Again; Dr. Strangelove; Dudes; Eating Raoul; Eleven Harrowhouse; The End; The End of the Road; The End of the World . . . ; Entertaining Mr. Sloane; The Exterminating Angel; Fatso; Fingers; A Fish Called Wanda; A Fistful of Dynamite; Folks!; The Fortune; The Fortune Cookie; 48 HRS.; Frankenhooker; Frenzy; The Freshman (1990); Full Metal Jacket; Fuzz; The Gang That Couldn't Shoot Straight; The Gazebo; The Girl Most Likely to . . . (1971); Grace Quigley; The Great Lover (1949); Greedy; Gremlins; Gremlins 2: The New Batch; The Gun in Betty Lou's Handbag; Hairspray; Hammersmith Is Out; Happy Birthday, Wanda June; Harold and Maude; The Haunted Palace; Hawks; Heathers; Homecoming (1973); The Honey Pot; The Honeymoon Killers; The Hospital; Housekeeping; How to Get Ahead in Advertising; How to Murder Your Wife; I Love You to Death; I Was a Teenage Frankenstein; I Was a Teenage Werewolf; Improper Channels; Inside Daisy Clover; Into the Night; The January Man; Joe Versus the Volcano; Kalifornia; The Kill-Off; Killing Dad; The Killing of Sister George; Kind Hearts and Coronets; King of Comedy; Ladies in Retirement; The Ladykillers; The Lair of the White Worm; The Last of Sheila; The Late Show; Laughter in the Dark; Law of Desire; Let's Kill Uncle; Life Force; Life Is Cheap, but Toilet Paper Is Expensive; Little Murders; Little Shop of Horrors (1960); Little Shop of Horrors (1986); Live Now, Pay Later; Loot; The Lost Boys; Love and Death; The Loved One; The Lovely Way to Die; Luv;

MASH; Mad Love; The Mad Room; Man Bites Dog; A Man Like Eva; The Man Who Came to Dinner; The Man with Two Brains; Manhattan Murder Mystery; Marat/Sade; The Marriage of Maria Braun; Married to the Mob; Martin; The Match Factory Girl; Melvin and Howard; Men of Respect; Ménage; Miami Blues; Mikey and Nicky; Miss Firecracker; Mixed Nuts; Mommie Dearest; Monsieur Verdoux; Mother, Jugs and Speed; Murders in the Rue Morgue; My New Gun; The Naked Truth; Nashville; Nasty Habits; Natural Born Killers; Neighbors; Network; A New Leaf; The Nightmare Before Christmas; Night Stalker/The Night Strangler; 99 and 44/100 Per Cent Dead; No Surrender; No Way to Treat a Lady; O Lucky Man; Oh, Dad, Poor Dad . . . ; Oh, What a Lovely War; 101 Dalmatians; On the Air; Orphans; Out Cold; Out of the Dark; Over Her Dead Body; Pain in the A . . . ; Parents; The Player; The Positively True Adventures of the Alleged Texas Cheerleader-Murdering Mom; Pretty Poison; Prizzi's Honor; Pulp Fiction; Quick; Rabbit Test; Rabid Grannies; Rancho De Luxe; Re-Animator; Re-Animator 2; The Red Inn; The Reflecting Skin; Remember Last Night?; Repentance; The Return of the Living Dead; The Return of the Living Dead Part II; The Revenge of Billy the Kid; Robocop; Robocop 2; Rubin & Ed; Saint Jack; Scandalous!; Schtonk!; Seconds; Serial Mom; The Servant; Seven Beauties; Shakes the Clown; A Shock to the System; A Shock Treatment; Short Time; Sitting Ducks; Situation Hopeless But Not Serious; Skin Deep; A Slight Case of Murder; Slither Society; Something for Everyone; Something Wild (1986); Stranger Than Paradise; Substitute; Such Good Friends; Sugarbaby; Superfly; The Survivors; Sweeney Todd, the Demon Barber of Fleet Street; Tatie Danielle; Taxing Woman; Teachers; Theater of Blood; They Might Be Giants; To Sleep with Anger; Tristana; Trouble for Two; The Trouble with Harry; Trust; The Tunnel of Love; Unfaithfully Yours (1948); Unfaithfully Yours (1984); Used Cars; Vampire's Kiss; Viridiana; The Visit; Volpone; The War of the Roses; Watermelon Man; Waxwork; Waxwork II: Lost in Time; A Wedding; Weekend; What a Way to Go; What's Eating Gilbert Grape?; What's the Matter with Helen?;

Whatever Happened to Aunt Alice?; Whatever Happened to Baby Jane?; Where's Poppa?; Who Is Killing the Great Chefs of Europe?; Who Slew Auntie Roo?; Whoops! Apocalypse (1983); Whoops! Apocalypse (1986); Whore; Willy Wonka and the Chocolate Factory; Wilt; Wise Blood; Wise Guys; The Witches; Wolf; Women on the Verge of a Nervous Breakdown; The World According to Garp; The Wrong Box; Wrong Is Right

Black Cowboys: see also *Black Casts: Black Men: Westerns-Revisionist:* Children of the Dust; Posse; The Scalphunters; Unforgiven (1992)

Black Directors: see also *Black Casts/Films: Black Screenwriters:* Aaron Loves Angela; Blacula; Boomerang; Boyz N the Hood; Buck and the Preacher; The Cemetery Club; Claudine; Clockers; Cotton Comes to Harlem; Deep Cover; Demon Knight; Do the Right Thing; DROP Squad; Five Heartbeats; Fresh; Graffiti Bridge; Harlem Nights; A Hero Ain't Nothin' but a Sandwich; Higher Learning; Hollywood Shuffle; House Party; House Party 2; I Like It Like That; I'm Gonna Git You, Sucka; The Inkwell; Juice; Jungle Fever; Leadbelly; Learning Tree; Let's Do It Again (1975); Low Down Dirty Shame; Menace II Society; Meteor Man; Mo' Better Blues; Mo' Money; New Jack City; Nothin' But a Man; Passenger 57; Posse (1993); A Rage in Harlem; A Raisin in the Sun; Return of Superfly; Roots, the Gift; Sarafina!; School Daze; Shaft; Shaft's Big Score; She's Gotta Have It; A Soldier's Story; South Central; Stir Crazy; Straight out of Brooklyn; Strictly Business; The Super Cops; Superfly; Swing Kids; They Call Me Mr. Tibbs!; To Sleep with Anger; Uptown Saturday Night

Blackmail: see also *Revenge: Double Crossing: Murder-Coerced to:* Absolution; Ada; The Anderson Tapes; The Big Knife; Black Sunday (1977); Blackmail (1929); Blackmail (1939); Blackmailed; Conan the Destroyer; Cop and a Half; Criss Cross (1947); Delicatessen; The Drowning Pool; 52 Pick-up; For Love of Ivy; Foreign Intrigue; The Gazebo; Getting Even with Dad; Harper; The Heart of the Matter; Hoffman; I Found Stella Parish; I Walk the Line; Joe; Kitten with a Whip; La Femme Nikita; Le Corbeau; The League of Gentlemen; The Letter (1929); The

Letter (1940); Libeled Lady; The Longest Yard; The Mackintosh Man; Mamma Rosa; Mantrap; The Naked Truth; Point of No Return; The Promise; The Real McCoy; The Reckless Moment; Rented Lips; The Secret Partner; The Shadow (1936); The Strange Loves of Martha Ivers; Strangers on a Train; Thief of Hearts; Throw Momma from the Train; Twilight's Last Gleaming; Victim; The Young Philadelphians

Black Men (in prominent, lead roles): see also *Black Casts: Black Women:* Above the Rim; Aces, Iron Eagle 3; Action Jackson; The Adventures of Huckleberry Finn (1960); The Adventures of Huckleberry Finn (1985); Almos' a Man; Amos and Andrew; Attica (1971); Attica (1991); Bad Boys; Bebe's Kids; Beverly Hills Cop; Beverly Hills Cop 2; Beverly Hills Cop 3; The Bingo Long Traveling All-Stars and Motor Kings; Bird; Black Caesar; Black Orpheus; Blacula; Blankman; Blazing Saddles; Blue Chips; Boomerang; Bopha!; Boyz N the Hood; The Brother from Another Planet; Brother John; Bustin' Loose; Cabin in the Sky; Cadence; California Suite; Candyman; Candyman: Farewell to the Flesh; Carmen Jones; CB4: The Movie; Christmas Lilies of the Field; Class Act; Claudine; Clockers; Coming to America; Cool Runnings; The Cotton Club; Cotton Comes to Harlem; Court Martial of Jackie Robinson; Critical Condition; Crooklyn; Cry Freedom; Deep Cover; Do the Right Thing; DROP Squad; Ernest Green Story; Fear of a Black Hat; Five Heartbeats; For Love of Ivy; 48HRS.; For Queer and Country; Fresh; Full Eclipse; Glory; The Golden Child; Graffiti Bridge; Greased Lightning; Green Eyes; Guess Who's Coming to Dinner; Hail, Hail, Rock n Roll; Hallelujah!; A Hero Ain't Nothin' but a Sandwich; Higher Learning; Hit!; Hit Man; Hollywood Shuffle; Hoop Dreams; House Party; House Party 2; Houseguest; Huckleberry Finn (1939); Huckleberry Finn (1960); Huckleberry Finn (1974); I'm Gonna Git You, Sucka; In the Heat of the Night; The Inkwell; Intruder in the Dust; Island in the Sun; Jo Jo Dancer, Your Life Is Calling; Juice; Jungle Fever; Just Cause; King; The Kitchen Toto; Laurel Avenue; Leadbelly; Lean on Me; Learning Tree; Let's Do It Again (1975); Lilies of the Field; Listen Up: The Lives of Quincy Jones; Live and

Let Die; The Lost Man; Low Down Dirty Shame; Major Payne; Malcolm X; Mandela; The Mark of the Hawk; The McMasters; Menace II Society; Meteor Man; The Mighty Quinn; Mississippi Masala; Mo' Better Blues; Mo' Money; Moving; New Jack City; Norman, Is That You?; Nothin' But a Man; An Officer and a Gentleman; Otello; Othello (1951); Othello (1965); Passenger 57; A Patch of Blue; Posse (1993); Predator 2; A Rage in Harlem; A Raisin in the Sun; Return of Superfly; River Niger; Roots; Roots, the Gift; Round Midnight; St. Louis Blues; Separate but Equal; Shaft; Shaft in Africa; Shaft's Big Score; The Shawshank Redemption; She's Gotta Have It; Shoot to Kill; Showboat (1936); Showboat (1951); Six Degrees of Separation; The Slender Thread; A Soldier's Story; Some Kind of Hero; Song of the South; Sophisticated Gents; Sounder; South Central; Stormy Weather; Straight out of Brooklyn; Strictly Business; Sudie and Simpson; Sugar Hill; Superfly; Tap; They Call Me Mr. Tibbs!; Tick, Tick, Tick . . . ; To Sleep with Anger; To Wong Foo, Thanks for Everything, Julie Newmar; Trading Places; Trespass; True Identity; Uncle Tom's Cabin (1914); Uncle Tom's Cabin (1969); Under the Cherry Moon; Uptown Saturday Night; A Warm December; Watermelon Man; The Well; Which Way is Up?

Blackouts (power outages): see also Crisis Situations: Trapped: Alone in the Dark; Any Wednesday; Critical Condition; The Day the Earth Stood Still; I Like It Like That; Mirage; Where Were You When the Lights Went Out?

Black Screenwriters: see also *Black Directors:* Aaron Loves Angela; Boomerang; Boyz N the Hood; Claudine; Crooklyn; Do the Right Thing; DROP Squad; Five Heartbeats; Fresh; Harlem Nights; A Hero Ain't Nothin' but a Sandwich; Higher Learning; Hollywood Shuffle; House Party; House Party 2; I Like It Like That; I'm Gonna Git You, Sucka; The Inkwell; Juice; Jungle Fever; Lady Sings the Blues; Leadbelly; The Learning Tree; Low Down Dirty Shame; Major Payne; Menace II Society; Meteor Man; Mo' Better Blues; Mo' Money; New Jack City; Nothin' But a Man; Posse (1993); A Raisin in the Sun; Return of Superfly; Sarafina!; School Daze; Shaft; Shaft's Big Score; She's Gotta Have It; A

Soldier's Story; Sophisticated Gents; Sounder; South Central; Straight out of Brooklyn; Strictly Business; Superfly; To Sleep with Anger; Uptown Saturday Night; The Wiz

Black Soldiers: see also *Black Men: Soldiers: Military Stories:* Court Martial of Jackie Robinson; For Queen and Country; Glory; The Goonies; Gordon's War; The McMasters; A Soldier's Story

Black vs. White: see also *Black & White Together: Bigots: White Supremacists: Race Relations: Civil Rights: Ku Klux Klan:* Across 110th Street; All the Young Men; Amos and Andrew; As Summers Die; Attica (1971); Attica (1991); The Bingo Long Traveling All-Stars and Motor Kings; The Biscuit Eater (1940); The Biscuit Eater (1972); Black and White in Color; Bronx Tale; Buck and the Preacher; Cadence; Chocolat; Come Back Charleston Blue; Cotton Comes to Harlem; The Defiant Ones; Do the Right Thing; DROP Squad; Drum; A Dry White Season; Edge of the City; Flirting; 48HRS.; The Gladiator; A Good Man in Africa; Grand Canyon; Greased Lightning; The Great White Hope; Green Eyes; Guess Who's Coming to Dinner; Heart Condition; Heart of Dixie; Higher Learning; Hurry Sundown; I Passed for White; Imitation of Life (1934); Imitation of Life (1959); In the Heat of the Night; The Intruder; Intruder in the Dust; Island in the Sun; Jungle Fever; Kings Go Forth; The Klansman; Losing Isaiah; Made in America; Malcolm X; Man Friday; Mandela; Mandingo; The McMasters; Native Son (1951); Native Son (1986); No Way Out (1950); Nothin' But a Man; Paris Trout; A Patch of Blue; The People Under the Stairs; Philadelphia; Pinky; Posse (1993); Power of One; A Raisin in the Sun; Ricochet; Roots; Sapphire; Separate but Equal; The Skin Game; Soul Man; Tamango; To Kill a Mockingbird; Trading Places; Trespass; Uncle Tom's Cabin (1914); Uncle Tom's Cabin (1969); The Watermelon Man; The Well; White Dog; White Mama; White Men Can't Jump; White Zombie; The Wilby Conspiracy; A World Apart; Zebrahead

Black Women (in prominent, lead roles): see also *Black Films: Black Men:* The Autobiography of Miss Jane Pittman; Bebe's Kids; Boomerang; Bopha!; Bustin' Loose; Cabin in the Sky; Candyman;

Carmen Jones; Clara's Heart; Claudine; Cleopatra Jones; Cleopatra Jones & the Casino of Gold; The Color Purple; Corrina, Corrina; The Cotton Club; Crooklyn; The Disappearance of Christina; Fatal Beauty; Father Hood; For Love of Ivy; Ghost; Gone With the Wind; A Hero Ain't Nothin' but a Sandwich; Hollywood Shuffle; I Know Why the Caged Bird Sings; I Passed for White; Island in the Sun; The Josephine Baker Story; Juice; Jumpin' Jack Flash; Just Another Girl on the IRT; Kings Go Forth; Kiss Shot; Ladybird, Ladybird; Lady Sings the Blues; The Landlord; Laurel Avenue; Made in America; Mahogany; Mandela; Menace II Society; Momma, There's a Man in Your Bed; Nothin' But a Man; The Omega Man; One False Move; Passion Fish; Pinky; Pudd'nhead Wilson; A Rage in Harlem; A Raisin in the Sun; River Niger; Roots; Sarafina!; Say Amen, Somebody!; She's Gotta Have It; Show Boat (1936); Show Boat (1951); Sister Act; Sister Act 2; Sounder; Sparkle; The Wiz; Zebrahead

Blaxploitation (somewhat derogatory nickname for black-cast action movies, usually but not necessarily from the early 70s): see also *Black Films: 1970s:* Action Jackson; Black Caesar; Blacula; Car Wash; Cleopatra Jones; Cleopatra Jones & the Casino of Gold; Cotton Comes to Harlem; Come Back Charleston Blue; Hit!; Hit Man; I'm Gonna Git You, Sucka; New Jack City; Return of Superfly; Shaft; Shaft in Africa; Shaft's Big Score; Superfly; Uptown Saturday Night

Blind Dates: see *Dating Scene: Matchmakers*

Blind People: see also *Disabled People: Disabled People in Jeopardy:* Afraid of the Dark; Amsterdamned; Amy; The Anniversary; Blink; Blind Fury; Body Bags; Bright Victory; Butterflies Are Free; Cactus; City for Conquest; City Lights; Dark Angel (1935); Dark Victory; Eyes in the Night; Ice Castles; Jennifer 8; Laughter in the Dark; The Light that Failed; Madness of the Heart; Magnificent Obsession (1935); Magnificent Obsession (1954); Midnight Crossing; The Miracle Worker; Mr. Skeffington; Night Gallery; On Dangerous Ground; A Patch of Blue; Proof; Safe Passage; Scent of a Woman; See No Evil; See No Evil, Hear No Evil; Seventh Heaven (1927); Seventh Heaven (1937);

Sneakers; Stolen Hours; They; Torch Song; Twenty-Three Paces to Baker Street; Until the End of the World; Wait Until Dark; Wild Hearts Can't Be Broken; Wings in the Dark

Blizzards: see *Snow Settings*

Blockbusters (movies reaching a massive audience; includes very big box-office hits or, in the case of TV movies, major ratings winners): see also *APPENDIX: Box Office Hits by Year: Sleeper Hits:* The Absent-Minded Professor; The Addams Family; Airport; All the President's Men; American Graffiti; The Amityville Horror; Arthur; The Bachelor and the Bobby-Soxer; Back to the Future; Batman; Batman Returns; Beauty and the Beast (1991); The Bells of St. Mary's; Ben Hur (1959); Ben Hur: A Tale of the Christ (1925); Benji; The Best Little Whorehouse in Texas; The Best Years of Our Lives; Beverly Hills Cop; Beverly Hills Cop 2; Billy Jack; The Birth of a Nation; The Black Pirate; Blazing Saddles; The Bodyguard; Bonnie and Clyde; Brian's Song; The Burning Bed; Butch Cassidy and the Sundance Kid; Carousel; Cleopatra (1963); Close Encounters of the Third Kind; The Color Purple; Coming to America; Crocodile Dundee; Dances with Wolves; Dark Victory; David and Bathsheba; The Day After; Dead Poets Society; Dick Tracy; Doctor Zhivago; Driving Miss Daisy; Duel; Duel in the Sun; Dumb and Dumber; E.T.: The Extra-Terrestrial; Earthquake; The Egg and I; Every Which Way But Loose; The Exorcist; Fatal Attraction; Fatal Vision; A Few Good Men; Fiddler on the Roof; Flashdance; The Flintstones; Forrest Gump; 42nd Street; Frankenstein (1931); From Here to Eternity; The Fugitive (1993); Ghost; Ghostbusters; Ghostbusters 2; Giant; Gigi (1958); Gilda; The Godfather; Going My Way; Goldfinger; Gone With the Wind; Good Morning, Vietnam; The Goodbye Girl; The Graduate; Grand Hotel; Grease; The Great Ziegfeld; The Greatest Show on Earth; Gremlins; Guess Who's Coming to Dinner; Gunga Din; Halloween; Heaven Can Wait (1978); Hell's Angels; Holiday Inn; Home Alone; Home Alone 2: Lost in New York; Honey, I Shrunk the Kids; How the West Was Won; The Hunt for Red October; In Search of the Castaways; Interview with the Vampire; It Happened One Night; Jaws; Jaws 2; The Jazz Singer (1927); Jurassic Park; The Karate Kid; Kramer vs. Kramer; Lawrence of Arabia; Like Water for Chocolate; Look Who's Talking; Love Story (1970); MASH; Mary Poppins; The Mask (1994); Mrs Doubtfire; Murder by Death; The Music Man; My Fair Lady; National Lampoon's Animal House; Nine to Five; The Odd Couple; Oh, God; Oliver!; On Golden Pond; One Flew Over Cuckoo's Nest; 101 Dalmatians; Operation Petticoat; Out of Africa; The Parent Trap; Parenthood; Peyton Place; Pillow Talk; Pinocchio; Planet of the Apes; Platoon; Poltergeist; Porky's; The Poseidon Adventure; Pretty Woman; Private Benjamin; The Public Enemy; Rain Man; Rambo: First Blood Part Two; Return of the Jedi; The Robe; Romeo and Juliet (1968); Roots; Samson and Delilah; The Santa Clause; Saturday Night Fever; Schindler's List; Shane; The Sheik; The Silence of the Lambs; Sister Act; Sleeping with the Enemy; Sleepless in Seattle; Smokey and the Bandit; Smokey and the Bandit II; Snow White and the Seven Dwarfs; Some Like It Hot; The Sound of Music; Spartacus; Speed; Stand Up and Cheer; A Star Is Born (1976); Star Trek: The Motion Picture; Star Wars; Steel Magnolias; Stir Crazy; The Swiss Family Robinson; Sybil; Ten; The Ten Commandments; Terminator 2: Judgment Day; Terms of Endearment; Three Men and a Baby; Thunderball; Tom Jones; Tootsie; Top Gun; Total Recall; The Towering Inferno; True Lies; Twins; 2001: A Space Odyssey; Valley of the Dolls; When Harry Met Sally; White Christmas; The Wizard of Oz (1939); The Yearling

Blood and Gore (not necessarily Horror): see individual film entries for 'B&G': *HORROR: Comedy-Morbid: Violence in Comedy: Experiments: Serial Killers: Body Parts*

Boardinghouses: see also *Apartment Buildings: Ensemble Films:* About Face; About Mrs. Leslie; According to Mrs. Hoyle; Gigot; It All Came True; A Kiss in the Dark; The L-Shaped Room; London Belongs to Me; The Man in the Attic; The Man Upstairs

Boarding Schools: see also *Boys' Schools: Girls' Schools: High School Life: College Life:* Absolution; Another Country; Brides of Dracula; The Browning Version; A Child Is Waiting; Child's Play (1972); Circle of Friends; David and Lisa; Dead Poets Society; The Devil's Playground; Diabolique (1955); Flirting; Follow Me, Boys!; The Getting of Wisdom; Goodbye Mr. Chips (1939); Goodbye Mr. Chips (1969); The Harrad Experiment; Harrad Summer; The Idolmaker; Jennifer 8; Ladies' Man (1961); Lawrenceville Stories; The Little Princess; The Lords of Discipline; Mad About Music; Scent of a Woman; School for Scoundrels; School Ties; A Separate Peace; The Strange One; Suspiria; Tea and Sympathy; Topaze (1933); Up the Academy; The Winslow Boy; A Yank at Eton

Boats/Boat Chases/Boat Racing: see also *Boat Racing: Car Chases: Sailing:* Amsterdamned; The Boatniks; Live and Let Die; The Man with the Golden Gun; Steamboat Bill Jr.; Thunder and Lightning

Body Building/Body Builders: see also *Sexy Men: Sports Movies:* Hercules (1957); Hercules in New York; Hercules Unchained; La Strada; Muscle Beach Party; Perfect; Pumping Iron; Pumping Iron 2; Raw Deal; Stay Hungry; Stone Cold; Suburban Commando; Trojan War; Twins

Bodyguards: see *Protecting People: Romance with Protector*

Body Parts (having in some way to do with): see also *HORROR: SCI-FI: Scientists-Mad: Experiments: Blood and Gore: Brain Transplants:* Ambulance; Andy Warhol's Frankenstein; Body Bags; Body Parts; The Body Snatcher; Brittania Hospital; Coma; The Doctor and the Devils; Fantastic Voyage; Fingers; Frankenhooker; Frankenstein (1931); Frankenstein '70; Frankenstein and the Monster from Hell; Frankenstein Created Woman; Frankenstein Unbound; The Hand (1960); The Hand (1981); Heart Condition; Innerspace; Mad Love; Re-Animator; Re-Animator 2; Roxanne; Santa Sangre; Scream and Scream Again!; Son of Frankenstein

Body Switching (either literally, or just identities are switched): see also *Role Reversals: Identities-Assumed: Reincarnation: Men as Women: Women as Men: Mix-Ups: Reincarnation:* Age Isn't Everything; Big; The Boys from Syracuse; Class Act; The Fifth Musketeer; Freaky Friday; Freejack; Goodbye, Charlie; The Grifters; Heaven Can Wait (1978); Here Comes Mr. Jordan; It Came from Outer Space; Lady in the

Iron Mask; Like Father, Like Son; The Parent Trap; Prelude to a Kiss; The Prince and the Pauper (1937); The Prisoner of Zenda (1937); The Prisoner of Zenda (1952); The Prisoner of Zenda (1979); Switch; Taking Care of Business; That Obscure Object of Desire; Trading Places; Vice Versa; The Watermelon Man; You Can Never Tell

Bombs (regular vs. atomic; devices that blow up or could blow up, but not movie flops): see also *Bombs-Atomic: Terrorists: Arms Dealers: Rule the World-Plot to: Disaster Movies: Crisis Situations:* Airport; The Big Heat; Blown Away; Brazil; The Dam Busters; Drop Zone; Hairspray; Juggernaut; Kamikaze 89; Lethal Weapon 3; Live Wire; The Long Good Friday; Nighthawks (1981); The Nude Bomb; Ragtime; Sabotage; Skyjacked; The Specialist; Speed; Stone Cold; Target; Terror on a Train; 13 Rue Madeleine; Touch of Evil; Twelve O'Clock High

Bombs-Atomic: see also *Bombs: Apocalyptic Stories: Terrorists: Rule the World-Plot to: Disaster Movies: Crisis Situations: Radiation Poisoning: Nuclear Energy: Arms Dealers:* Above and Beyond; Amazing Grace and Chuck; The Atomic City; The Atomic Kid; The Bedford Incident; Black Rain (1988); Blue Sky; Bullseye!; Children of Hiroshima; Day After; Day One; The Day the Earth Caught Fire; The Day the Fish Came Out; Desert Bloom; Detonator; Disaster at Silo 7; Dr. Strangelove; Fail Safe; Fat Man and Little Boy; The Fourth Protocol; The Fourth War; Frantic (1988); Hiroshima, Mon Amour; The House on 92nd Street; Iron Eagle II; Living It Up; The Manhattan Project; The Miracle Mile; The Mouse That Roared; The Omega Man; On the Beach; Panic in Year Zero; The Philadelphia Experiment; Rhapsody in August; Sakharov; Special Bulletin; Stand Stargate; Superman 4; Terminator 2: Judgment Day; Testament; Them!; The Thief (1952); True Lies; Twilight's Last Gleaming; Under Siege; Until the End of the World

Bootleggers/Bootlegging: see also *Prohibition Era: 1920s: Alcoholism: Mob Stories:* Gator; Greased Lightning; Gunrunner; I Walk the Line; The Last American Hero; Lucky Lady; Miller's Crossing; The Moonshine War; Murder, Inc.; Once Upon a Time in America;

Paper Moon; The Roaring Twenties; Sanctuary; Scarface (1932); The Scarface Mob/The Untouchables Pilot; Smokey and the Bandit; Smokey and the Bandit II; Smokey and the Bandit III; Thunder and Lightning; Thunder Road; The Untouchables

Bosses-Bad: see also *Evil Men: Evil Women: Office Comedy: Business Life: Marrying the Boss:* The Apartment; Barbary Coast; The Big Clock; Madison Avenue; The Man on the Flying Trapeze; Scrooged

Boston: see also *College Life: Harvard Settings:* Altered States; Between the Lines; Billy Galvin; The Bostonians; By Love Possessed; The Europeans; Fuzz; The Hospital; The Late George Apley; The Shocking Miss Pilgrim; The Verdict

Bothersome People: see *Malicious Menaces: Stalkers: Relatives-Bothersome: Husbands-Troublesome: Wives-Troublesome: Neighbors-Troublesome*

Bounty Hunters: see also *ACTION: Chase Movies: Manhunts: Trail of a Killer: WESTERNS:* Blackbeard, The Pirate; Blade Runner; Borderline; Bring Me the Head of Alfredo Garcia; The Brother from Another Planet; Buck and the Preacher; Chato's Land; For a Few Dollars More; Ghostbusters; Ghostbusters 2; The Hunter; The Last Sunset; Love and Bullets; Midnight Run; The Naked Spur; The Paleface; Pink Cadillac; Santa Fe Trail; The Sea Wolves; The Shooting; Slipstream; Soldier of Fortune; Suburban Commando; The Terminator; Terminator 2: Judgment Day; True Grit; The Unforgiven (1992); Wanted Dead or Alive; Warlock (1989)

Boxers/Boxing: see also *Sports Movies: Roman Wrestling:* After Dark, My Sweet; All-American Boy; Any Which Way Can; The Big Man; Body and Soul (1947); Body and Soul (1981); Broken Noses; Cain and Mabel; The Challenge; The Champ (1931); The Champ (1979); Champion; City for Conquest; Designing Woman; Diggstown; Every Which Way But Loose; Fat City; Gentleman Jim; The Gladiator; Golden Boy; The Great White Hope; The Greatest; Hard Promises; The Harder They Fall; Here Comes Mr. Jordan; Homeboy; Invitation to Happiness; Iron Man; The Kid from Brooklyn; Kid Galahad; Killer McCoy; The Killers (1946); Killer's Kiss;

The Leather Saint; Let's Do It Again (1975); The Main Event; Matilda; Movie Movie; Night after Night; Night and the City (1950); Night and the City (1992); On the Waterfront; The Prizefighter and the Lady; The Quiet Man; Raging Bull; Requiem for a Heavyweight (1956); Requiem for a Heavyweight (1962); Rocky; Rocky II; Rocky III; Rocky IV; Rocky V; Second Chance; The Set Up; Somebody Up There Likes Me; Streets of Gold; Teen Wolf; Teen Wolf Too; They Made Me a Criminal; Triumph of the Spirit

A Boy and His Dog (the classic setup, specific to boys and dogs): see also *Pet Stories: Animal Stories:* Big Red; The Biscuit Eater (1940); The Biscuit Eater (1972); A Boy and His Dog; A Dog of Flanders; Far from Home; Goodbye My Lady; Lassie Come Home; Old Yeller; Savage Sam; Where the Red Fern Grows

Boy Cries Wolf: see also *Unbelieved: Accused Unjustly: Witness to Murder-Child:* Eyewitness (1970); The Fallen Idol; Fright Night; The Window

Boyhood (more about growing up as a boy): see also *Boys: Coming of Age: Teenage Movies: Elementary School: Boys' Schools:* The Adventures of Huckleberry Finn (1960); The Adventures of Huckleberry Finn (1985); The Adventures of Tom Sawyer; Aladdin; Almost Angels; Anchors Aweigh; Au Revoir, les Enfants; Babar: The Movie; The Bad News Bears Go to Japan; Big Red; The Biscuit Eater (1940); The Biscuit Eater (1972); Blame It on the Night; Bless the Beasts and the Children; The Boy Who Could Fly; The Boy with Green Hair; Boys' Town; Bright Road; Brighton Beach Memoirs; Broken Noses; Careful, He Might Hear You; Cinema Paradiso; The Dark at the Top of the Stairs; D.A.R.Y.L.; David Copperfield; The Devil Is a Sissy; The Devil's Playground; A Diary for Timothy; A Dog of Flanders; E.T.: The Extra-Terrestrial; Empire of the Sun; Europa, Europa; Explorers; Fanny and Alexander; The 400 Blows; Hope and Glory; How Green Was My Valley; Huckleberry Finn (1939); Huckleberry Finn (1960); Huckleberry Finn (1974); Into the West; Kes; King of the Hill (1993); Lady in White; Lies My Father Told Me; Little Lord Fauntleroy (1936); Little Lord Fauntleroy (1980); The Long Day Closes; Lord of the Flies (1963); Lord of the Flies (1990);

Louisiana Story; Men of Boys' Town; My Friend Flicka; My Life as a Dog; The Other; Risky Business; The Sailor Who Fell from Grace with the Sea; The Savage; This Boy's Life; The War; Waterland; When Father Was Away on Business; The Witches; The Wizard; A Yank at Eton; Young Winston

Boys (having boys in prominent roles, though not necessarily about growing up): see also Boyhood: Child Protagonists: Alan and Naomi; Alsino and the Condor; And You Thought Your Parents Were Weird; Baxter (1972); Cameron's Closet; Captains Courageous; The Champ (1931); The Champ (1979); A Child Is Waiting; The Chocolate War; City Boy; The Client; Clockers; Cold Sassy Tree; Cop and a Half; The Courtship of Eddie's Father; The Cure; Dennis the Menace; Double O Kid; Elephant Boy; Fear Strikes Out; The Five Thousand Fingers of Doctor T.; Follow Me, Boys!; Forbidden Games; Fresh; Gate; Gate II; The Go-Between; The Golden Seal; The Good Son; Goodbye My Lady; Grand Highway; Grandview, USA; Great Expectations; The Green Years; Gunga Din; Harold and Maude; Home Alone; Home Alone 2: Lost in New York; The Horse in the Grey Flannel Suit; Invaders from Mars (1986); Ivan's Childhood; Jack and the Beanstalk; Jack the Giant Killer; Josh and S.A.M.; Juice; The Jungle Book (1967); The Jungle Book (1994); Kidnapped (1938); Kidnapped (1959); Kidnapped (1971); Ladyhawke; Let's Kill Uncle; Little Buddha; The Little Giants; Little Rascals; London Belongs to Me; Lost in Yonkers; The Lucky Star; The Man from Snowy River; The Man Without a Face; Melody; The Mighty Ducks; Milk Money; Misunderstood; Murmur of the Heart; My Father's Glory; My Mother's Castle; The Neverending Story; The Neverending Story II: The Next Chapter; Newsies; A Night in the Life of Jimmy Reardon; North; No Small Affair; O.C. and Stiggs; Oh God Book Two; Oh, What a Night; Oliver!; Oliver Twist (1948); Oliver Twist (1982); Olivier, Olivier; Once Upon a Time; Paperhouse; Paradise (1991); Pathfinder; Pelle the Conqueror; The People Under the Stairs; Pete's Dragon; Peter Pan; The Phantom Tollbooth; Pinocchio; Pixote; Radio Days; Radio Flyer; Rambling Rose; The Red Badge of Courage; The Red Balloon; Richie Rich;

Sandlot; Scalawag; Searching for Bobby Fischer; A Separate Peace; Seventeen; The Shaggy Dog; Shane; A Short Film About Killing; Silent Fall; Silver Bullet; Skippy; Smugglers; Stand by Me; Straight out of Brooklyn; The Sword in the Stone; Tabu; Tales from the Darkside: The Movie; Taps; Tea and Sympathy; Tex; The Thief of Bagdad (1924); The Thief of Baghdad (1940); This Boy's Life; Three Ninjas; Three Ninjas Kick Back; Thunderhead, Son of Flicka; Time Bandits; The Tin Drum; Tom Sawyer; Tommy; Toy Soldiers; Treasure Island (1934); Treasure Island (1971); Treasure Island (1990); Treasure Island (1991); Treasure of Matecumbe; Trial (1955); Vision Quest; The War; The Water Babies; Where the Red Fern Grows; The Yellow Balloon

Boys' Schools: see also Boarding Schools: Boyhood: Another Country; Best Foot Forward; Child's Play (1972); The Chocolate War; Dead Poets Society; The Devil's Playground; Dynasty of Fear; Follow Me, Boys!; The Happiest Days of Your Life; Heaven Help Us; The Idolmaker; Lawrenceville Stories; Taps; Tea and Sympathy; Topaze (1933); Toy Soldiers

Boy Scouts: see also Girl Scouts: Boyhood: Follow Me, Boys; The Great Lover; Rally Round the Flag Boys; This Boy's Life; The Wrong Guys

Brains/Brain Transplants: see also Scientists-Mad: HORROR: SCI-FI: Body Parts: Change of Mind; Donovan's Brain; The Man with Two Brains

Brainwashing: see also Occult: Cults: A Clockwork Orange; Fahrenheit 451; Hammersmith Is Out; The Ipcress File; La Femme Nikita; The Manchurian Candidate; 1984 (1955); 1984 (1984); Patty Hearst; Point of No Return; Simon; Split Image; They Live; Ticket to Heaven; Total Recall; Who?

Bratpack Movies (not necessarily starring the few actors interviewed in the infamous New York **magazine article that introduced the term; expanded to include the whole subgenre of largely innocuous [often an understatement] "date movies" of the 80s starring 20-year-olds in the type of big-budget films theretofore usually reserved for much more accomplished actors): see also** Teenage Movies: Young Men: Young Women: About Face; Bad Boys; Blue City; The Breakfast Club; Bright

Lights, Big City; Class; Footloose; Fresh Horses; Gotcha!; Heaven Help Us; The Hotel New Hampshire; Less Than Zero; Pretty in Pink: Quicksilver; Say Anything; Sixteen Candles; Some Girls; St. Elmo's Fire; Taps; The Three Musketeers (1993); Top Gun; Vision Quest; Young Guns; Young Guns II; Youngblood

Brazil/Brazilian Films: see also Argentina: South America: Amazon River: Amazon; At Play in the Fields of the Lord; Black Orpheus; Burning Season; Bye Bye Brazil; Flying Down to Rio; Gabriela; Pixote; That Man from Rio; Wild Orchid

Breakdowns-Nervous: see Nervous Breakdown: also Mental Illness: Depression: Asylums

Brides-Mail Order: see also Dating Scene: Marriage of Convenience: Mail Order Bride; The Piano; Zandy's Bride

British Directors of Southerns: see Southerns-British Directors of: also Foreign Directors of Southerns: British Films: Southerns

British Films: see also Irish Films: Australian Films: Canadian Films: England: Ireland: Canada: Australia: New Zealand: Scotland: Wales: Mod Era: Kitchen Sink Drama: Absolute Beginners; Accident; Aces High; Across the Bridge; Adventures of Casanova; The Adventures of Eliza Frazer; The Adventures of Robin Hood; The Adventures of Sherlock Holmes; The Adventures of Tartu; The Adventuress; Africa, Texas Style; Against the Wind; Agatha; Age of Consent; Alfie; Alive and Kicking; All Creatures Great and Small; All You Need Is Cash; An Alligator Named Daisy; The Amazing Mr. Blunden; American Friends; And Now for Something Completely Different; The Angry Silence; Another Country; Are You Being Served?; Aren't We All?; Asylum; The Baby and the Battleship; Barnacle Bill (1957); Bartleby; Battle of Britain; The Bawdy Adventures of Tom Jones; Baxter (1972); Bedazzled; Bedknobs and Broomsticks; The Belles of St. Trinian's; Bellman and True; Better Late Than Never; The Big Man; Billion Dollar Brain; Billy Liar; Black Beauty (1946); Black Beauty (1971); Black Beauty (1994); Blackmail (1929); Bleak Moments; Blithe Spirit; The Blood Beast Terror; Blood from the Mummy's Tomb; Bloodbath at the House of Death; Blow Up; Blue; Bombay

Talkie; Bonnie Prince Charlie; The Borrowers; The Brain; Bram Stoker's Dracula (1970); Breaking Glass; Breaking the Sound Barrier; Brideshead Revisited; The Bridge on the River Kwai; Brighton Rock; Brimstone and Treacle; The Brothers; Buddy's Song; Bullseye!; Bullshot; Business as Usual; Cage of Gold; Camelot; A Canterbury Tale; The Captive Heart; The Caretaker; Castaway; Champions; The Charge of the Light Brigade (1936); The Charge of the Light Brigade (1968); Chariots of Fire; Charlie Bubbles; Charmer; Children of the Damned; A Chorus of Disapproval; The Citadel; Class of Miss MacMichael; Clockwise; A Clockwork Orange; Close My Eyes; The Collector; The Company of Wolves; Comrades; The Constant Husband; The Cook, the Thief, His Wife & Her Lover; The Crash of Silence; Cromwell; The Crying Game; Damage; Darling; The Day the Earth Caught Fire; Deceivers; Desert Victory; The Detective (1954); Devotion; Disraeli; The Divorce of Lady X; Doctor in the House; Does This Mean We're Married?; Dr. Jekyll and Sister Hyde; The Dressmaker; Drowning by Numbers; Dunera Boys; Eagle in a Cage; East of Elephant Rock; Ebony Tower; Educating Rita; Efficiency Expert; Enchanted April; Encore; Endless Game; England Made Me; The Entertainer; Entertaining Mr. Sloane; Every Home Should Have One; Excalibur; Experience Preferred . . . ; Eye of the Needle; The Fallen Idol; Far from the Madding Crowd; The Favour, the Watch & the Very Big Fish; Fawlty Towers; Fear in the Night; Finger of Guilt; Fire Over England; The First of the Few; A Fish Called Wanda; Five Million Years to Earth; Flesh and Blood (1951); Flight of the Doves; Fool; Fortunes of War; Freddie as F.R.0.7.; Friday the Thirteenth (1933); Funeral in Berlin; The Garden; The Gentle Sex; Georgy Girl; Get Carter; Getting It Right; The Ghost Goes West; The Ghoul (1933); Girl with Green Eyes; Good Companions (1933); The Good Companions (1956); Good Father; Goodbye Gemini; Great Expectations; Green for Danger; Ground Zero; Gumshoe; Half a Sixpence; A Handful of Dust; A Hard Day's Night; The Hasty Heart; Hear My Song; Hearts of Fire; Heat and Dust; Heavenly Pursuits; Hedda; Helter Skelter (1949); Henry V (1944); Henry V (1989); Henry VIII and

His Six Wives; High Hopes; The Hireling; The Hit; The Holly and the Ivy; Holy Matrimony; Hope and Glory; The Horse's Mouth; The Hound of the Baskervilles (1939); The Hound of the Baskervilles (1959); The Hound of the Baskervilles (1977); The House that Dripped Blood; How to Get Ahead in Advertising; I Believe in You; I Know Where I'm Going; I Was a Teenage Frankenstein; The Idolmaker; If Winter Comes; I'll Never Forget Whatshisname; The Importance of Being Earnest; In Search of Gregory; The Innocents; Innocents in Paris (1953); An Inspector Calls; The Ipcress File; It Always Rains on Sunday; The Italian Job; Jack and Sarah; Jack of All Trades; Jack the Giant Killer; The Jewel in the Crown; Jigsaw Man; John Cleese on How to Irritate People; Jude the Obscure; Killing Dad; A Kind of Loving; Kipps; Kiss of Evil; The Knack; Knave of Hearts; The Krays; Ladybird, Ladybird; Lady Jane; The Lady Vanishes (1938); The Lady Vanishes (1979); The Ladykillers; The Lair of the White Worm; Lawrence of Arabia; The Leather Boys; Leon, the Pig Farmer; A Letter to Brezhnev; The Life and Death of Colonel Blimp; Life at the Top; Life Is Sweet; Lily in Love; The Liquidator; Live Now, Pay Later; Lives of a Bengal Lancer; Lock Up Your Daughters; London Kills Me; The Loneliness of the Long Distance Runner; The Long Day Closes; The Long Good Friday; Look Back in Anger (1959); Look Back in Anger (1980); Look Back in Anger (1989); Loophole; Loot; Lost; The Lost Language of Cranes; The Love Lottery; Love on the Dole; Love Story (1944); Madame Sousatzka; The Magic Box; Mahler; Make Me an Offer; A Man About the House; A Man of No Importance; The Man Upstairs; The Man Who Could Work Miracles; Maurice; McVicar; The Millionairess; The Mind Benders; Mine Own Executioner; Ministry of Fear; Miranda; The Missionary; Modesty Blaise; Mona Lisa; A Month in the Country; Monty Python and the Holy Grail; Monty Python's Life of Brian; Monty Python's The Meaning of Life; Moonlighting (1982); Mother Love; The Mouse that Roared; Murder Ahoy; Murder at the Gallop; My Beautiful Laundrette; My Learned Friend; Naked; The Nanny; Nasty Habits; The Nature of the Beast; Never Let Go; Next of Kin (1942); The

Night Has Eyes; Night Must Fall (1964); The Night My Number Came Up; No Escape (1936); No Surrender; Nothing But the Best; Number 17; Nuns on the Run; O Lucky Man; The October Man; Odd Man Out; The Offence; Oh, What a Lovely War; The Old Curiosity Shop; Old Mother Riley SERIES; Once Upon a Dream; Only Two Can Play; Only When I Larf; Operation Amsterdam; Operation Crossbow; Oscar Wilde; Our Man in Havana; The Overlanders; A Pair of Briefs; Paper Marriage; Paranoia; Paris By Night; Parsifal; A Passage to India; Passport to Pimlico; Paths of Glory; Payment Deferred; Peeping Tom; The Penthouse; Performance; Personal Services; Peter's Friends; Piccadilly Incident; The Pickwick Papers; Plenty; The Ploughman's Lunch; Prick Up Your Ears; Priest; The Prime of Miss Jean Brodie; Prime Suspect; The Prisoner (1955); Prisoner: Arrival; The Private Life of Henry VIII; The Promoter; Prospero's Books; Quadrophenia; Quartet (1948); Queen of Destiny; Queen of Hearts; Quiet Wedding; The Raging Moon; The Railway Children; Rebecca's Daughters; The Red Shoes; The Reflecting Skin; Remains of the Day; RentaDick; The Return of the Soldier; The Return of the Vampire; Riff-Raff (1991); The Rise and Rise of Michael Rimmer; Rita, Sue and Bob Too; Rome Express; Room at the Top; A Room with a View; A Run for Your Money; Sabotage; Salome's Last Dance; Sammy and Rosie Get Laid; Sapphire; Saturday Night and Sunday Morning; Say Hello to Yesterday; Scandal; School for Scoundrels; Sea Wife; Seance on a Wet Afternoon; The Secret Agent; The Secret Partner; The Secret People; The Secret Policeman's Ball; The Secret Policeman's Other Ball; The Secret Policeman's Private Parts; The Secret Policeman's Third Ball; The Servant; The Seventh Veil; The Shadow (1936); Shadowlands; Shakespeare Wallah; Shallow Grave; She'll Be Wearing Pink Pajamas; Shirley Valentine; The Shooting Party; Sidewalks of London; Simba; Simon and Laura; Sing as We Go; St. Martin's Lane; Staircase; Stairway to Heaven; Steaming; Stevie; Storm in a Teacup; Stormy Monday; The Story of Robin Hood and His Merrie Men; The Stud; A Summer Story; Sunday, Bloody Sunday; Sword of the Valiant; The Tall Guy; A Taste of Honey; Tears in the

Rain; Term of Trial; Terror by Night; That Hamilton Woman; They Drive by Night (1938); 30 Is a Dangerous Age, Cynthia; This Happy Breed; This Sporting Life; Those Magnificent Men in Their Flying Machines; Tiger Bay; Till Death Us Do Part; Time Bandits; Time without Pity; The Titfield Thunderbolt; To Paris with Love; To Sir with Love; Tom & Viv; Tom Jones; Tommy; A Touch of Class; Town; A Town like Alice (1956); A Town like Alice (1985); Traffik; Trial and Error; The Trials of Oscar Wilde; Tunes of Glory; Turtle Diary; 21; Two Way Stretch; The Unnamable; The Unnamable Returns; An Unsuitable Job for a Woman; Up the Creek (1958); Vacation from Marriage; The Virgin Soldiers; The W. Plan; The Walking Stick; The Water Babies; Waterland; We Are Not Alone; We Think the World of You; Went the Day Well?; Werewolf of London; Wetherby; When the Whales Came; Where Angels Fear to Tread; Where the Spies Are; Whiskey Galore; The Whisperers; Whistle Down the Wind; White Mischief; Whoops! Apocalypse (1983); Wild West; Wilt; The Winslow Boy; Wish You Were Here; Withnail and I; Without a Clue; The Wolves of Willoughby Chase; The Wooden Horse; You Only Live Twice; Young Winston; Zulu; Zulu Dawn

British Films Mod Era: see *Mod Era*

British People: see *England: British Films: Australians*

Broadway: see *Theater Life: Play Adaptations: Stagelike Films*

Brooklyn Life: see *New York Life*

Brothers (when the focus is only on male siblings): see also *Siblings: Sisters: Family Comedy: Family Drama: Ensembles-Female: Twins:* Affair in Trinidad; All Fall Down; All the Brothers Were Valiant; American Flyers; Beau Geste (1926); Beau Geste (1939); Beau Geste (1966); The Big Broadcast of 1938; The Black Room; Bloodbrothers; Blues Brothers; Bright Angel; Brotherhood; The Brothers; The Brothers Karamazov; The Caretaker; The Challenge; Cheech and Chong's The Corsican Brothers; City for Conquest; Come Blow Your Horn; The Corsican Brothers; Dead Ringers; Death of a Salesman; Devlin; Dion Brothers; Dominick and Eugene; Double Impact; Drop Zone; Duel in the Sun; Dunera Boys; Equinox; Eye of the Storm; The Fabulous Baker Boys; Force of Evil; Get

Carter; The Godfather; The Godfather Part II; The Godfather Part III; His Brother's Wife; A Hole in the Head; Hot Lead and Cold Feet; Indian Runner; The Irish in Us; Islands in the Stream; Jack's Back; Josh and S.A.M.; Jumpin at the Boneyard; Kickboxer; Kickboxer 2; The King of Marvin Gardens; The Krays; Kuffs; La Vie Continue; Legends of the Fall; Long Day's Journey Into Night; The Long Riders; Love Me Tender; Lust for Life; Mambo Kings; The Man from Laramie; The Master of Ballantrae; Men Don't Leave; The Mountain; Mr. Saturday Night; Murder by Television; My Gal Sal; My Life as a Dog; Nazi Agent; Next of Kin (1989); On the Waterfront; Orphans; Paradise Alley; Radio Flyer; Rain Man; Ran; A River Runs Through It; Sabrina; Santa Fe; The School for Scandal; Shadow Riders; Simple Men; Solomon and Sheba; Somewhere I'll Find You; The Sons of Katie Elder; Starstruck; Staying Together; Sugar Hill; Tex; Trapped in Paradise; True Confessions; Twins; Undercurrent; Van Gogh; The Vikings; Vincent and Theo; Wilder Napalm; Winter Kills; The Wizard; Wonder Man; The Wonderful World of the Brothers Grimm; The Wrong Box; Zed and Two Noughts; Zorro the Gay Blade

Brothers & Sisters: see *Siblings: Brothers: Sisters*

Buddy Cops/Detectives: see also *Police: Buddy Films: Detectives-Police: Friendships-Male:* Another 48HRS.; Another Stakeout; Bad Boys (1994); Cotton Comes to Harlem; 48HRS.; Freebie and the Bean; The Hard Way (1991); La Chèvre; Last Boy Scout; Les Compères; Lethal Weapon; Lethal Weapon 2; Lethal Weapon 3; Pure Luck; Red Heat; Rising Sun; Running Scared; The Super Cops

Buddy Films: see also *Buddy Cops: Friendships-Male: Buddy Films-Female:* All the President's Men; American Flyers; Another 48HRS.; Another You; Bad Boys; Barcelona; Boys Next Door; Buddy Buddy; Butch and Sundance: The Early Days; Butch Cassidy and the Sundance Kid; California Split; Cheech and Chong: Still Smokin'; Cheech and Chong's Next Movie; Cheech and Chong's Nice Dreams; Cheech and Chong's The Corsican Brothers; Les Comperes; Cotton Comes to Harlem; Dumb and Dumber; 48HRS.; The Hard Way (1991); Harry

and Walter Go to New York; Henry: Portrait of a 48HRS.; Serial Killer; House Party; House Party 2; K-2; The Last Boy Scout; Leaving Normal; The Legend of the Lone Ranger; Macaroni; Midnight Cowboy; Le Million; Missing Pieces; Nate and Hayes; A Nice Little Bank That Should Be Robbed; Outrageous Fortune; Patti Rocks; Planes, Trains, and Automobiles; Pulp Fiction; Pure Luck; Red Heat; Renegades; Road to Bali; Road to Hong Kong; Road to Morocco; Road to Rio; Road to Singapore; Road to Utopia; Road to Zanzibar; Roadside Prophets; Rubin & Ed; Running Scared; Sailor Beware; The Saint of Fort Washington; Salt and Pepper; The Scarecrow; See No Evil, Hear No Evil; Shoot to Kill; S*P*Y*S; The Sting; Stir Crazy; The Stooge; Sunset; Thunderbolt and Lightfoot; Tough Guys; Les Valseuses

Buddy Films-Female: see also *Ensembles-Female: Buddy Films: Buddy Cops: Friendships-Female: Law Officers:* Boys on the Side; Cagney & Lacey; Feds; Leaving Normal; Outrageous Fortune; Thelma & Louise

Bullfighters/Bullfighting: see also *Spanish Films: Spain:* Blood and Sand (1922); Blood and Sand (1941); The Bullfighter and the Lady; The Bullfighters; Cityslickers; Fiesta; The Kid from Spain; Kid Millions; Mexican Hayride

Buppies (black, upwardly mobile young people): see *Yuppies: Black Casts/Films*

Buried Alive: see also *Trapped: Kidnappings: HORROR:* Ace in the Hole; Blood Simple; Buried Alive; The Fall of the House of Usher (1928); Histoires Extraordinaires; House of Usher (1960); House of Usher (1990); Night Gallery; The Oblong Box; Tales from the Darkside: The Movie; Tales of Terror; The Tomb of Ligeia; Woman Screaming

Burglars: see *Thieves: Art Thieves: Jewel Thieves: Heist Stories: Bank Robberies*

Buses (set on a bus somehow): see also *Truck Drivers: Taxi Drivers: Working Class: Ordinary People Stories:* The Big Bus; Bus Stop; Dead of Night (1945); Friday the Thirteenth (1933); Fugitive Lovers; The Gauntlet; Kings of the Road; The Laughing Policeman; A Man of No Importance; Separate but

Equal; Shame (1961); Speed; Strangers in Good Company

Business Life: see also *Executives: Office Comedy: Wall Street: Corporation as Enemy: Marrying the Boss: Power Struggles: Yuppies: 1980s:* The Apartment; Ask Any Girl; Babbitt; The Bad Sleep Well; The Barefoot Executive; The Betsy; Big Business; Boomerang; Business as Usual; Carnal Knowledge; Cash McCall; The Crowd; The Desk Set; For Richer, for Poorer; The Garment Jungle; Glengarry Glen Ross; The Godfather Part III; Hired Wife; How to Succeed in Business without Really Trying; The Hucksters; The Hudsucker Proxy; Jack of All Trades; Network; Other People's Money; Patterns; The Promoter; Save the Tiger; Schindler's List; The Secret of My Success; The Solid Gold Cadillac; Stand In; Take a Letter, Darling; Thursday's Game; Wall Street; White Mile; Woman's World; Working Girl

C

Cajuns (Louisiana "Acadian" people of French-Canadian descent): see also *Swamp Life: Louisiana: New Orleans:* Belizaire the Cajun; Casey's Shadow; Louisiana Story; Shy People
Calamities: see *Comedy of Errors: FARCE: Unlucky People*
California Life: see also *Hollywood Life: Beverly Hills: San Francisco: Surfers: Beach Movies: Desert Life: Southwestern Life:* American Graffiti; Big Wednesday; Bill and Ted's Excellent Adventure; The Birds; The Birds II; The Candidate; Earth Girls Are Easy; Earthquake; East of Eden (1955); East of Eden (1980); Encino Man; The Endless Summer; The Graduate; The Grapes of Wrath; The Impossible Years; It's a Gift; Lifeguard; The Living End; Lord Love a Duck; The Mark of Zorro (1920); The Mark of Zorro (1940); Of Mice and Men (1939); Of Mice and Men (1993); The River's Edge; The Sandpiper; Serial; Things Are Tough All Over; Tortilla Flat
Callers-Prank: see *Telephone Terror*
Call Girls: see *Prostitutes-High Class*
Camelot Stories: see also *Medieval Times: England:* Army of Darkness; Camelot; A Connecticut Yankee; A Connecticut Yankee in King Arthur's Court; Excalibur; Gawain and the Green Knight; King Arthur Was a Gentleman; Knightriders; Knights of the Round Table; Monty Python and the Holy Grail; Parsifal; Prince Valiant; The Sword in the Stone; The Sword of Lancelot; Unidentified Flying Oddball
Camp (esoteric, tongue-in-cheek or unintentional humor): see also *Cult Films: COMEDY: Spoofs: Unintentionally Funny:* The Abominable Dr. Phibes; Alexander, the Other Side of Dawn; All the Fine Young Cannibals; American Anthem; Ants; Attack of the Killer Tomatoes; The Babysitter; Batman, the Movie; Beach Blanket Bingo; Beach Party; Berserk!; Beyond the Forest; Beyond the Valley of the Dolls; Big Bad Mama; Big Foot; Bittersweet Love; Blacula; Blood and Black Lace; Blood Beach; Blue Steel; Bolero (1984); The Borrower; Bunny O'Hare; Burning; Caged Heat; Campus Man; Can't Stop the Music; Candy; The Car; Car Wash; Cat Women of the Moon; Che!; The Cheap Detective; Claudelle Inglish; The Commies Are Coming, the Commies Are Coming; The Conqueror; Convoy; D.C. Cab; The Day of the Triffids; Dead Bang; The Dead Pool; Dead Ringer; Deadlier Than the Male; Desperate Living; Dick Tracy; Die! Die! My Darling!; Donovan's Brain; Double Impact; Double Threat; Dragnet (1954); Driver's Seat; Drum; Ed and His Dead Mother; Ed Wood; The Fan; Fathom; Female on the Beach; Female Trouble; The Fish That Saved Pittsburgh; Flamingo Road; Flash Gordon; Frankenhooker; Fresh Horses; Ghosts Can't Do It; The Girl Can't Help It; Glen or Glenda?; Gold Diggers in Paris; Gold Diggers of 1933; Gold Diggers of 1935; Gold Diggers of 1937; Gold Diggers of Broadway; The Gong Show Movie; Green Slime; The Guardian; Gymkata; The Hand (1960); The Hand (1981); Hannie Caulder; Harlow; Hellcats of the Navy; Hercules (1957); Hercules in New York; Hercules Unchained; House on Haunted Hill; I Thank a Fool; I Want What I Want; I Was a Communist for the FBI; The Invisible Woman; Johnny Guitar; The Killers (1964); Kitten with a Whip; Lady in a Cage; Las Vegas Hillbillies; Law of Desire; The Legend of Lylah Clare; A Life of Her Own; Little Shop of Horrors (1960); Little Shop of Horrors (1986); Lonesome Cowboys; Lust in the Dust; Mahogany; Mandingo; A Matter of Time; The Medusa Touch; Mommie Dearest; The Monster Club; Mothra; Mrs. Pollifax, Spy; Murder by Phone; Muscle Beach Party; The Music Lovers; My Blood Runs Cold; My Forbidden Past; A Night in Heaven; The Nightmare Before Christmas; Night of the Lepus; Norman, Is That You?; One Million BC (1940); One Million Years BC (1966); The Oscar; Paradise (1982); Pink Flamingos;

Piranha; Plan 9 from Outer Space; Priscilla, Queen of the Desert; Queen Bee; Queen of Outer Space; Reefer Madness; Rocky Horror Picture Show; Roustabout; Ruby Gentry; Scent of Mystery; Sergeant Pepper's Lonely Hearts Club Band; Sextette; Shock Treatment; Skidoo; Son of Dracula; Staircase; The Statue; Strait Jacket; Strange Cargo; Street Angel; The Stud; The Stuff; Tarzan and His Mate; Tarzan Escapes; Tarzan the Ape Man (1932); Tarzan the Ape Man (1981); The Temp; Third Sex; To Kill a Clown; To Wong Foo, Thanks for Everything, Julie Newmar; Troop Beverly Hills; 2000 Maniacs; Valley of the Dolls; Venom; Viva Las Vegas; What's the Matter with Helen?; What's Up, Tiger Lily?; Whatever Happened to Aunt Alice?; Whatever Happened to Baby Jane?; When Dinosaurs Ruled the Earth; Where Love Has Gone; Who Slew Auntie Roo?; Who's Afraid of Virginia Woolf?; The Wrecking Crew; X-The Man with X-Ray Eyes; Xanadu; Xtro

Camps/Camping/Summer Camps: see also *Coming of Age: Teenage Movies: Wilderness Life: Summer Camp:* Addams Family Values; Breaking the Rules; Burning; Cityslickers; Cityslickers 2; Ernest Goes to Camp; Friday the 13th (1980); Friday the 13th: The Final Chapter; Friday the 13th Part 3-D; Friday the 13th Part II; Friday the 13th Part V-A New Beginning; Friday the Thirteenth Part VI-Jason Lives; Friday the 13th Part VII-The New Blood; Friday the 13th Part VIII-Jason Takes Manhattan; Gorp!; Great Outdoors; Grizzly; Heavyweights; Little Darlings; Mask (1985); Meatballs; Panic in Year Zero; The Parent Trap; Picnic at Hanging Rock; Return of the Secaucus Seven; She'll Be Wearing Pink Pajamas; Ski School; Star Trek V: The Final Frontier; Stripes; Up the Creek (1984)

Campus Life: see *High School Life: College Life: Boarding Schools*

Canada (as a setting, or made in Canada): see also *Canadian Films:* Black Robe; Canadian Bacon; Finders Keepers; Flashpoint; Fortune and Men's Eyes; The Girl of the Golden West; The Gold Rush; The Grey Fox; The Happy Time; Oh, What a Night; Rose Marie (1936); Rose Marie (1954); Saskatchewan; The Scarlet Claw; Silence of the North; Some Girls; The Story of Adèle H.; Strange Brew; The Terry Fox Story; White Fang; Why Shoot the Teacher?

Canadian Films: see also *French-Canadian Films: Canada:* Act of the Heart; The Adjuster; The Bay Boy; The Bear; Beautiful Dreamers; Café Romeo; Candy Mountain; Circle of Two; Echoes of a Summer; Exotica; Fortune and Men's Eyes; The Grey Fox; Jesus of Montreal; Joshua Then and Now; Kings and Desperate Men; Lies My Father Told Me; The Lucky Star; A Man, a Woman and a Bank; Martin's Day; Masala; Oh, What a Night; The Silent Partner; Speaking Parts; 32 Short Films about Glenn Gould; Threshold; Why Shoot the Teacher?

Cannibalism (usually humans eating humans): see also *Human Eaters: Monsters: Horror:* Alive; Auntie Lee's Meat Pies; C.H.U.D.; C.H.U.D. 2; Consuming Passions; The Cook, the Thief, His Wife & Her Lover; Delicatessen; Do You Like Women?; Eating Raoul; Eat the Rich; Farewell to the King; The Fearless Vampire Killers; Five Came Back; Fried Green Tomatoes; The Hills Have Eyes; The Kindred; Motel Hell; Parents; The Return of the Living Dead; The Return of the Living Dead Part II; The Revenge of Billy the Kid; The Silence of the Lambs; Society; Soylent Green; Survive; Sweeney Todd, Demon Barber of Fleet Street; Tales from the Darkside: The Movie; The Texas Chainsaw Massacre; Trilogy of Terror

Cannibalism-Funny (where people eating people is funny, and usually from England): see also *Cannibalism: Black Comedy:* Auntie Lee's Meat Pies; Consuming Passions; The Cook, the Thief, His Wife & Her Lover; Delicatessen; Do You Like Women?; Eating Raoul; Eat the Rich; Fried Green Tomatoes; Sweeney Todd, the Demon Barber of Fleet Street

Capers (usually a heist that's also a Farce): see also *Heist Stories: Action Comedy: FARCE: Screwball Comedy:* The Adventures of Arsène Lupin; The Anderson Tapes; The Brain; The Brinks Job; Broadway Danny Rose; Cat and Mouse; The Doberman Gang; The Double McGuffin; Eleven Harrowhouse; Finders Keepers; A Fish Called Wanda; Fitzwilly; Fun with Dick and Jane; The Good Die Young; The Great Bank Robbery; The Great Muppet Caper; Hanky Panky;

Happy New Year (1973); Happy New Year (1987); Harry and Walter Go to New York; Harry in Your Pocket; Hopscotch; Hot Millions; Hot Rock; How to Steal a Million; The Italian Job; The Lavender Hill Mob; Law and Disorder (1958); The League of Gentlemen; Legal Eagles; Les Fugitifs; Live a Little, Steal a Lot; A Lovely Way to Die; Missing Pieces; The North Avenue Irregulars; Once Upon a Crime; Paris Holiday; The Pink Panther; Quick Change; Raffles; The Real McCoy; Shanghai Surprise; Silver Bears; Sneakers; Special Delivery; That Darn Cat!; Three Fugitives; Tough Guys; Two Way Stretch; The Year of the Comet; Who's Minding the Mint?

Capone: see *Al Capone*

Capra-esque (like the films of Frank Capra-feelgood celebrations of Americana): see also *American Myth: American Dream: Conservative Value Films: Small-Town Life: Magic Realism:* Come to the Stable; Dave; Doc Hollywood; End of the Line; Field of Dreams; Four Daughters; Good Sam; Groundhog Day; Hero; A Kid for Two Farthings; Leap of Faith; Magic Town; The Man Who Broke the Bank at Monte Carlo; Mother Carey's Chickens; Mr. Deeds Goes to Town; Mr. Smith Goes to Washington; Nothing Sacred; Our Vines Have Tender Grapes; Pocketful of Miracles; Riding High; She Couldn't Say No; The Solid Gold Cadillac; The Southerner; Storm in a Teacup; Where the Heart Is

Car Chases: see also *Chase Movies: San Francisco Chases: ACTION: Car Wrecks:* The Blues Brothers; Boys Next Door; Bullitt; The Car; The Chase (1994); Dangerous Curves; Duel; Eat My Dust; Freebie and the Bean; The French Connection; Goodbye, Pork Pie; Grand Theft Auto; The Great Race; Hooper; The Last Boy Scout; Macon County Line; Mad Max; Mad Max Beyond Thunderdome; The Man with the Golden Gun; Moving Violations (1985); Mr. Billion; No Man's Land (1987); Road Warrior; The Seven-Ups; Sex and the Single Girl; Shaker Run; Sharky's Machine; Short Time; Slither; Smokey and the Bandit; Smokey and the Bandit II; Smokey and the Bandit III; Thunder and Lightning

Car Crashes (containing a substantial amount): see also *Car Chases: Chase Stories:* Black Moon Rising; The Blues

Brothers; The Cars That Ate Paris; Death Race 2000; Dutch; Freebie and the Bean; Friday the Thirteenth (1933); Hideaway; Honky Tonk Freeway; Hooper; The Intersection; The Italian Job; It's a Small World; Lethal Weapon; Lethal Weapon 2; Lethal Weapon 3; The Love Bug; The Last Boy Scout; Moving Violations (1985); The Promise; Smokey and the Bandit; Smokey and the Bandit II; Smokey and the Bandit III; Speed

Cardinals: see *Popes/Cardinals*

Career Women: see *Women-Working: Business Life: Office Comedies: Women Proving Themselves: Women's Rights*

Career Ambitions: see *Career Women: Power-Rise to: Business Life: Dreams: Quests*

Caribbean: see also *Exotic Locales: Islands: Cuba: Vacations:* Arrowsmith; Black Sunday (1977); Blackbeard, the Pirate; Burn!; Captain Blood; Captain Ron; Cat Chaser; Christopher Columbus (1949); Christopher Columbus: The Discovery (1992); Cocktail; The Comedians; Cool Runnings; Cuba; Dr. No; 1492: Conquest of Paradise; The Ghost Breakers; Hot Pursuit; I Walked with a Zombie; The Island (1980); Island in the Sun; Islands in the Stream; Live and Let Die; Long John Silver; The Mighty Quinn; The Pirate; The Princess and the Pirate; Scared Stiff; The Serpent and the Rainbow; The Tamarind Seed; Water; White Zombie

Car Racing: see also *Sports Movies: Car Crashes:* Bobby Deerfield; Cannonball Run; Cannonball Run 2; Cherry 2000; Days of Thunder; Death Race 2000; Freejack; Genevieve; Grand Prix; Greased Lightning; Great Race; The Gumball Rally; Heart like a Wheel; Herbie Goes Bananas; Herbie Goes to Monte Carlo; Herbie Rides Again; The Last American Hero; Le Mans; A Man and a Woman; A Man and a Woman: Twenty Years Later; Red Line 7000; Six Pack; Speedway; Spinout; Stroker Ace; Those Daring Young Men in Their Jaunty Jalopies; Tucker: The Man and His Dream; Two Lane Blacktop; Viva Las Vegas; Winning; Woman's World

Cartoonlike Movies (movies that may have animation but definitely have the fantastic humor and visuals of cartoon tradition): see also *Animation-Partial: Animation-Stop: Musicals-Animated:* Ace Ventura, Pet Detective; The

Adventures of Buckaroo Banzai Across the Eighth Dimension; Batman, the Movie; Beetlejuice; Boris & Natasha; The Borrowers; The 'burbs; Casper; Coneheads; Death Becomes Her; Edward Scissorhands; The Flintstones; Goldengirl; The Great Race; Home Alone; Home Alone 2: Lost in New York; Honey, I Blew Up the Kid; Honey, I Shrunk the Kids; Hot Shots!; Hot Shots Part Deux; Leonard, Part 6; North; Oh, Dad, Poor Dad . . . ; The Pagemaster; Pee-Wee's Big Adventure; The Princess Bride; Pure Luck; The Santa Clause; Street Fighter; Super Mario Brothers; Tarzan the Ape Man (1981); Teenage Mutant Ninja Turtles; Teenage Mutant Ninja Turtles 2; Teenage Mutant Ninja Turtles 3; Twilight Zone: The Movie; Undercover Blues; The Villain; Who's Harry Crumb?

Cartoons: see also *Musicals-Animated: Superheroes: Animation-Stop:* The Adventures of Milo & Otis; Aladdin; Alice in Wonderland; All Dogs Go to Heaven; Allegro Non Troppo; An American Tail; An American Tail 2; Anchors Aweigh; Animal Farm; The Aristocats; Bambi; Babar: The Movie; Beauty and the Beast (1991); Bebe's Kids; Bedknobs and Broomsticks; The Black Cauldron; Bon Voyage, Charlie Brown; The Care Bears' Adventure in Wonderland; The Care Bears Movie; Charlotte's Web; Cinderella; Cool World; Dumbo; Fantasia; Felix the Cat: The Movie; FernGully: The Last Rainforest; The Flintstones; The Fox and the Hound; Freddie as F.R.O.7.; Fritz the Cat; Gay Purree; A Goofy Movie; The Great Mouse Detective; Gulliver's Travels (1939); Gulliver's Travels (1976); Heavy Metal; Hey, Good Lookin'; The Incredible Mr. Limpet; The Jetsons Movie; The Jungle Book (1967); Lady and the Tramp; The Land Before Time; Light Years; Lord of the Rings; Make Mine Music; The Nightmare Before Christmas; 101 Dalmatians; Oliver and Company; Peter Pan; The Phantom Tollbooth; Pinocchio; The Rescuers; The Rescuers Down Under; Rock-a Doodle; The Secret of NIMH; Sleeping Beauty; Snow White and the Seven Dwarfs; The Swan Princess; The Sword in the Stone; The Three Caballeros; Thumbelina; Watership Down; Who Framed Roger Rabbitt?; Yellow Submarine

Car Wrecks: see *Car Crashes: Car Chases: Car Racing: Chase Movies: Violence in Comedy*

Casinos: see *Gambling: Nightclubs: Las Vegas*

Castles: see also *Fairy Tales: Kings: Queens: Princes: Princesses: Royalty: Medieval Times: Middle Ages:* Beauty and the Beast (1991); The Black Cat; The Canterville Ghost; Castle Keep; Dementia 13; The Devil's Bride; Dubarry Was a Lady; The Dunwich Horror; Edward Scissorhands; Eye of the Devil; The Ghost Breakers; The Ghost Goes West; The Gorgon; Gothic; Hamlet (1948); Hamlet (1964); Hamlet (1969); Hamlet (1991); High Spirits; House of Dracula; Kafka; The Keep; The King's Whore; Ludwig; Old Dracula; Scared Stiff; Sylvia and the Ghost

Casts of Thousands: see also *Epics: ADVENTURE: All-Star Casts:* The Alamo; Alexander Nevsky; Barabbas; The Battle of Britain; Ben Hur: A Tale of the Christ (1925); Ben Hur (1959); Doctor Zhivago; Earthquake; El Cid; Exodus; The Fall of the Roman Empire; Gandhi; Genghis Khan; Gettysburg; The Greatest Story Ever Told; How the West Was Won; It's a Mad Mad Mad Mad World; Kagemusha; King of Kings (1927); King of Kings (1961); La Marseillaise; The Last Emperor; The Longest Day; The Music Man; Napoleon; The Sign of the Cross; Solomon and Sheba; Suez; The Ten Commandments; Union Pacific; War and Peace (1956); War and Peace (1967)

Cat and Mouse Stories: see also *Capers: Farce:* Black Widow (1987); Boiling Point; Cat and Mouse; Crime and Punishment; Death Trap; House of Games; How to Steal a Million; Live Wire; Nighthawks (1981); Pascali's Island; Sleuth; The Sniper; To Catch a Thief

Catherine the Great (famous empress of Russia): see also *Russia: Queens:* Great Catherine; The Scarlet Empress; Young Catherine

Catholicism: see *Monks: Nuns: Priests: Religion*

Cats: see also *Dogs: Pet Stories: Animal Monsters:* The Aristocats; The Black Cat; The Blue Bird (1940); The Blue Bird (1976); Cat Women of the Moon; Cat's Eye; The Curse of the Cat People; Eye of the Cat; Felix the Cat: The Movie; Gay Purree; Harry and Tonto; Homeward Bound; The Incredible Journey; The Incredible Shrinking Man; Lady and the Tramp; The Late Show; Oliver and

Company; Rubin & Ed; Tales from the Darkside: The Movie; That Darn Cat!; The Three Lives of Thomasina; The Tomb of Ligeia

Cattle Herded by Barbara Stanwyck: see also *WESTERNS: Female Among Males: Cattle People: Cattle Rustlers: Montana Cattle Problems:* Cattle Queen of Montana; Forty Guns; The Furies; The Maverick Queen; The Violent Men

Cattle People/Ranchers: see also *WESTERNS: Farm Life: Barbara Stanwyck Cattle Problems:* Alvarez Kelly; Broken Lance; Cattle Annie and Little Britches; Cattle Queen of Montana; Chisum; Cimarron (1930); Cimarron (1960); Cityslickers; Comes a Horseman; The Cowboys; Duel in the Sun; Forty Guns; The Four Horsemen of the Apocalypse; The Furies; Giant; Heaven's Gate; J. W. Coop; Junior Bonner; Kangaroo; The Man without a Star; The Maverick Queen; The Missouri Breaks; Monte Walsh; Never a Dull Moment (1950); The Overlanders; Painted Desert; The Rare Breed; Red River; Ruggles of Red Gap; Scandalous John; The Sea of Grass; Texas; The Unforgiven (1960); The Violent Men; We of the Never Never

Cattle Rustlers (thieves of cattle): see also *WESTERNS: Thieves:* Abilene Town; Blood on the Moon; Cattle Queen of Montana; Chisum; Cityslickers; Forty Guns; Heaven's Gate; Lone Wolf McQuade; The Maverick Queen; The Missouri Breaks; Rancho De Luxe

Cautionary Tales: see *Message Films: Ethics: TRAGEDY*

Cavalry/Cavalry vs. Indians: see also *WESTERNS: Indians-American: Conflict with:* Cheyenne Autumn; Dances with Wolves; Fort Apache; Geronimo (1962); Geronimo (1993); The Horse Soldiers; How the West Was Won; Little Big Horn; Major Dundee; Northwest Passage; Rio Grande; Santa Fe Trail; Seventh Cavalry; She Wore a Yellow Ribbon; They Died with Their Boots On

Cave People: see also *Prehistoric Settings: Dinosaurs:* Caveman; Clan of the Cave Bear; Encino Man; Iceman; Link; One Million BC (1940); One Million Years BC (1966); The People That Time Forgot; Quest for Fire; Skullduggery; Trog; When Dinosaurs Ruled the Earth

Censorship: see also *McCarthy Era: Oppression: Fascism:* Fahrenheit 451; Footloose; Inherit the Wind

Central America: see also *Mexico: South America: Latin People:* The Adventurers; Alsino and the Condor; The Amateur; Appointment in Honduras; Bananas; Blue Iguana; Christopher Columbus (1949); Christopher Columbus: The Discovery (1992); Commando; Deal of the Century; Double-Crossed; El Norte; The Evil that Men Do; The In-Laws; The Mosquito Coast; Romero; Salvador; The Sniper; Sorcerer; Under Fire; Viva Maria!; Wages of Fear; Walker; The Wrath of God

Chance Meetings: see *Romance-Brief*

Character Comedy: see *Comedy-Character: Comedy-Skit: Vaudeville*

Character Studies (stories dealing specifically with the psychological workings of a person, what makes them tick): see also *Monologues-Interior: Autobiographical Stories: Narrated Films: Comedy-Character:* About Face; The Adjuster; The Adventures of Reinette and Mirabelle; The Adventures of Robinson Crusoe; The Affairs of Susan; Alfie; Alice Adams; All-American Boy; Always Leave Them Laughing; The Amazing Dr. Clitterhouse; An Angel at My Table; Annie Hall; Another Woman; Ash Wednesday; Atlantic City; The Autobiography of Miss Jane Pittman; The Bachelor; The Bachelor Party (1957); The Beekeeper; Being Human; The Belly of an Architect; Best Intentions; The Best Little Girl in the World; Between Two Women; Billy Bathgate; Billy Galvin; Bird; Birdman of Alcatraz; Blessing; Blue Sky; The Bride Wore Black; The Bridge of San Luis Rey; Bright Lights, Big City; Bright Victory; Buffalo Bill and the Indians, or Sitting Bull's History Lesson; Caddie; Call Me Genius; Camilla (1994); Careful, He Might Hear You; Cat on a Hot Tin Roof (1958); Cat on a Hot Tin Roof (1984); Closer; The Collector; Colonel Redl; The Color of Money; The Color Purple; Come Back to the Five and Dime, Jimmy Dean, Jimmy Dean; Conversation Piece; The Corn is Green (1945); The Corn is Green (1979); The Country Girl; Cracking Up; Cries and Whispers; Crimes and Misdemeanors; Cross Creek; Da; Daddy Nostalgia; Dangerous; A Dangerous Woman; Darling; A Day in the Death of Joe Egg; The Day of the Locust; Death in Venice; A Delicate Balance; Dersu Uzala; Desert Bloom; Despair; Detective Story;

The Diary of a Country Priest; The Diary of a Mad Housewife; Diary of a Madman; Doc; Doctor Jekyll and Mr. Hyde (1931); Dr. Jekyll and Mr. Hyde (1941); Doctor's Dilemma; The Double Life of Veronique; Downhill Racer; Drifting; A Dry White Season; The Eclipse; The End of Innocence; England Made Me; The Entertainer; The Executioner's Song; Fat City; Fearless; Fever Pitch; Five Easy Pieces; The Five Pennies; The Fixer; For Queen and Country; The 400 Blows; Fourteen Hours; Foxes; Friends and Husbands; Gertrude; Glass House; Glengarry Glen Ross; Golden Braid; The Good Father; The Goodbye People; Gorillas in the Mist; The Grasshopper; The Great Santini; The Great Sinner; The Great Waldo Pepper; The Hairdresser's Husband; The Happy Ending; Hard Contract; Hardcore; Harry and Son; Heart Beat; The Heart Is a Lonely Hunter; Heart like a Wheel; Heartburn; Heartland; The Hustler; I Know Why the Caged Bird Sings; I Vitelloni; I Want What I Want; Images; The Immortal Sergeant; In a Year with 13 Moons; In Cold Blood; In Love and War; In Praise of Older Women; Indian Runner; The Innocents; Inserts; Interiors; Investigation of a Citizen above Suspicion; It's a Wonderful Life; Ivan the Terrible; Je Vous Aime; Jersey Girl; Joan of Arc; Joey Breaker; Joshua Then and Now; Juliet of the Spirits; Keep the Change; The Killer Inside Me; King of the Hill (1993); Kings of the Road; La Belle Noiseuse; La Lectrice; The Lacemaker; Last Summer; The Last Temptation of Christ; Lawrence of Arabia; Lianna; The Life and Death of Colonel Blimp; Life Is Sweet; Life Upside Down; Lifeguard; Living End; Lola (1982); London Kills Me; The Loneliness of the Long Distance Runner; Lonely Are the Brave; Lonely Guy; The Lonely Passion of Judith Hearne; The Long Day Closes; The Long Voyage Home; Looking for Mr. Goodbar; The Lost Weekend; Love Letters (1984); Love on the Run (1979); Love Streams; Ludwig; Lust for Life; Mala Noche; A Man Called Horse; A Man of No Importance; The Man with the Golden Arm; The Man Without a Face; The Mark; A Married Woman; Martin Luther; Marty; Mask (1985); Mean Streets; The Mechanic; Medium Cool; Meeting Venus; Men Don't Leave; The Men's Club; Mickey One; Middle of the

Night; Mignon Has Left; Minnie and Moskowitz; The Misfits; Mishima; Mister Buddwing; Mr. Forbush and the Penguins; Mr. Johnson; Mr. and Mrs. Bridge; The Money Trap; Montenegro; A Month in the Country; The Moon and Sixpence; Moonlighting (1982); Moonrise; Morgan!; Moscow Does Not Believe in Tears; Mouchette; Moulin Rouge; The Music Lovers; My American Uncle; My Brilliant Career; My Dinner with André; My Father's Glory; My Life; My Mother's Castle; Naked; Never Too Late; 'Night, Mother; Night on Earth; 9/30/55; 92 in the Shade; Nobody's Fool (1994); No Man's Land; Not as a Stranger; The Nun's Story; Nuts; The Old Man and the Sea; Olivier, Olivier; Once More with Feeling; One Is a Lonely Number; Opening Night; An Outcast of the Islands; Passion Fish; Patterns; Patti Rocks; The Pawnbroker; The Pearl; The People against O'Hara; Persona; Personal Best; Philadelphia; Plenty; Possessed (1947); Queen of the Stardust Ballroom; Rabbit, Run; Rachel, Rachel; A Rage to Live; Raging Bull; The Rain People; The Red Desert; Rendez-Vous; Repulsion; Requiem for a Heavyweight (1956); Requiem for a Heavyweight (1962); Resurrection; Reunion; Reversal of Fortune; Rhapsody in August; The Romantic Englishwoman; Ruby in Paradise; Safe Passage; Sandakan No. 8; Save the Tiger; Scarecrow; Secret Friends; Secret Honor; Secret Places; See How She Runs; Seize the Day; September; The Sergeant; Seven Thieves; Shadows and Fog; Shame (1961); Shoot the Moon; Sid and Nancy; Simple Story; The Slender Thread; Soft Skin; Sons and Lovers; Stagecoach (1939); Stagecoach (1966); The Star; Stardust Memories; Stevie; The Subject Was Roses; Summer of '42; Summer Wishes, Winter Dreams; Sunday, Bloody Sunday; Swann in Love; The Swimmer; A Talent for Loving; Tall Story; Taxi zum Klo; Tempest; The Tenant; Tex; Therese and Isabelle; 36 Fillette; Thousand Pieces of Gold; Thursday's Game; 21; Two or Three Things I Know About Her; Two People; Two Weeks in Another Town; Ulysses (1967); Umberto D.; The Unbearable Lightness of Being; Under Milk Wood; Under the Volcano; An Unmarried Woman; Up the Sandbox; Vagabond; Valentino (1977); Valmont; Van Gogh; The Verdict; Veronika Voss; La

Vie Continue; La Vie de Bohème; Vincent and Theo; Voyager; The War against Mrs. Hadley; We Think the World of You; Wetherby; When Father Was Away on Business; The Whisperers; White Hunter, Black Heart; Who?; Who'll Stop the Rain?; Wild Strawberries; Wilson; Winning; Winter Light; Woman in Flames; A Woman under the Influence; A Woman's Tale; Women in Love; Working Girls; A World Apart; The Year My Voice Broke; Yesterday's Hero; The Young Lions

Charismatic People (colorful and persuasive if not powerful people): see also *Leaders: Free Spirits: Eccentric People: Wild People: Feisty Women: Biographies: Biographies-Fictional:* Auntie Mame; Black God, White Devil; Charlotte's Web; Cheers for Miss Bishop; Conrack; Eleanor and Franklin; A Face in the Crowd; Gandhi; The Great Gatsby (1949); The Great Gatsby (1974); Guyana Tragedy, the Story of Jim Jones; King; The Last Hurrah; Lawrence of Arabia; Luther; Malcolm X; Monty Python's Life of Brian; Mr. North; Rebecca of Sunnybrook Farm (1925); Strange Cargo; Tucker: The Man and His Dream

Charlatans: see *Con Artists: Impostors*
Chase Stories: see also *Fugitives: Race Against Time: ACTION: Capers: FARCE: San Francisco Chases: Car Chases:* Ace Ventura, Pet Detective; Adventures in Babysitting; The Adventures of Milo and Otis; After Hours; Amsterdamned; Any Which Way You Can; Arabesque; The Aristocats; Baby's Day Out; Backtrack; Bandolero!; Bank Shot; The Bedford Incident; Behave Yourself!; Benji; Benji the Hunted; The Bicycle Thief; Big Bad Mama; The Big Steal; Billy the Kid; Bite the Bullet; The Black Marble; Black Moon Rising; The Black Windmill; Blackbeard the Pirate; Blade Runner; Blame It on the Bellboy; Blind Date (1987); Blown Away; Blue Iguana; Blue Thunder; The Blues Brothers; Boiling Point; Bonnie and Clyde; Bound and Gagged, a Love Story; The Bourne Identity; The Boys from Brazil; Boys Next Door; Brain Smasher: A Love Story; Brannigan; Broadway Danny Rose; Buck and the Preacher; Bullitt; Butch Cassidy and the Sundance Kid; Cannonball Run; Cannonball Run 2; Casanova's Big Night; Charley Varrick; The Chase (1947); The Chase (1966); The Chase (1994); Chato's

Land; Clan of the Cave Bear; Clear and Present Danger; The Client; Cloak and Dagger (1984); Cobra; Color Me Dead; Dangerous Curves; The Day of the Jackal; Dead Bang; Deadlock; The Defiant Ones; Demolition Man; Demon Knight; Detonator; Diamonds Are Forever; Die Laughing; Dirty Harry; Diva; D.O.A. (1949); D.O.A. (1988); Dollars; The Domino Principle; Double O Kid; Double-Crossed; Dressed to Kill; Drop Zone; The Duchess and the Dirtwater Fox; Duel; Dumb and Dumber; Eat My Dust; Eddie Macon's Run; Eight on the Lam; Eleven Harrowhouse; El Mariachi; The Empire Strikes Back; The Enforcer (1976); Escape to Witch Mountain; Europa, Europa; Eyewitness (1970); Family Plot; Fancy Pants; Fatal Beauty; Ferris Bueller's Day Off; Finders Keepers; A Fine Madness; Firepower; A Fish Called Wanda; Flashback; Flight of the Doves; The Flim Flam Man; Fly By Night; Fools Parade; For a Few Dollars More; Foreign Correspondent; For Pete's Sake; Forty Pounds of Trouble; For Your Eyes Only; The Fourth Man; The Fourth Protocol; Freaky Friday; Freebie and the Bean; The French Connection; The Fugitive (1947); The Fugitive (1993); Fugitive Lovers; Fugitive: The Final Episode; The Fury (1978); F/X; F/X 2: The Deadly Art of Illusion; A Game of Death; The Gauntlet; The General; The Getaway (1972); The Getaway (1994); Get Carter; Gleaming the Cube; Gloria; Gotcha!; Goldfinger; Good Guys Wear Black; Grand Theft Auto; The Great Locomotive Chase; The Great Muppet Caper; The Great Smokey Roadblock; Gun Crazy (1950); Gun Crazy (1992); Gun Fury; Hanky Panky; A Hard Day's Night; Harley Davidson and the Marlboro Man; Harvey; High-Ballin'; Highlander; Highlander II-The Quickening; Highlander III-The Sorcerer; The Hit; Honey, I Shrunk the Kids; Honeymoon in Vegas; Hopscotch; Hot Pursuit; The House on Carroll Street; Hudson Hawk; The Hunt for Red October; I Am a Fugitive from a Chain Gang; Illegally Yours; The In-Laws; Indiana Jones and the Last Crusade; Indiana Jones and the Temple of Doom; In the Line of Fire; Into the Night; Island of Love; It's a Mad Mad Mad Mad World; The Italian Job; Jewel of the Nile; Judgment Night; Jumpin' Jack Flash; Jurassic Park; Kelly's Heroes;

Chases-Boat or Car: see *Boat Chases: Car Chases: Chase Movies: Fugitives: ACTION: San Francisco Chases: Car Wrecks*

Cheated Upon Meet (spouses or lovers whose partners are having an affair together or who are sharing someone): see also *Cheating Men: Cheating Women: Romance-Triangles:*

Cheaters-Avenging: see *Revenge on Cheaters: Crimes of Passion: Cheating Men: Cheating Women: Jealous Spouses: Turning the Tables*

Cheating Men (at center of story, married or committed men who stray): see also *Crimes of Passion: Cheating Women: Jealous Spouses: Turning the Tables:*

Bedfellows; Strangers, the Story of a Mother and Daughter; Switch; A Talent for Loving; The Tender Trap; Terms of Endearment; That's Life!; These Three; They All Laughed; This Thing Called Love; Three Husbands; A Time for Loving; Tom Jones; Too Beautiful for You; Torrents of Spring; A Touch of Class; Twice in a Lifetime; An Unmarried Woman; Violets Are Blue; Wait until Spring, Bandini; The Way of All Flesh (1928); The Way of All Flesh (1940); White Cargo; Wife, Doctor and Nurse; Wife versus Secretary; The Woman in Red; The Woman Next Door; The Women; The World Is Full of Married Men; X, Y, & Zee

Cheating Women (at center of story, married or committed women who stray): see also *Crimes of Passion: Cheating Women: Jealous Spouses:* Against All Odds; All Night Long (1961); All Night Long (1981); The Ambassador; Aren't We All?; Baby Doll; Betrayal; Beyond the Limit; Beyond Therapy; The Bliss of Mrs. Blossom; Blonde Venus; Blood Simple; The Blue Dahlia; The Blue Max; Blue Sky; Bob&Carol& Ted&Alice; Bordertown; Buried Alive; C'est la Vie; Caught; Chained; Charming Sinners; China Moon; Come September; Coming Home; The Cook, the Thief, His Wife & Her Lover; Cousin, Cousine; Cousins; David and Bathsheba; Dead On; Deception (1946); The Deep Blue Sea; Desire and Hell at Sunset Motel; Devil and the Deep; Devil in the Flesh (1946); Devil in the Flesh (1987); Dial M For Murder; Diary of a Mad Housewife; The Disappearance of Aimee; The Divorcée; Double Indemnity; Dynasty of Fear; Elephant Walk; Falling in Love; A Fine Romance; Frantic (1958); Gertrude; The Girl Most Likely . . . (1958); The Good Wife; The Grass is Greener; Greed; The Guardsman; A Handful of Dust; The Hanging Tree; The Hireling; Hot Spot; Hotel Paradiso; Husbands and Wives; I Married a Woman; Impact; Inferno; The Key (1934); The Kiss (1929); La Bete Humaine; Lady Chatterley's Lover (1955); Lady Chatterley's Lover (1981); Lady with a Dog; Lake Consequence; The Letter (1929); The Letter (1940); Letter to Three Wives; Life at the Top; The Living Corpse; Lover Come Back (1946); The Macomber Affair; Madame Bovary; The Man Who Haunted Himself;

Married to It; A Married Woman; Melo; The Men (1985); Midnight (1939); Moonstruck; Mrs. Soffel; Murder by Natural Causes; My Foolish Heart; Next Time We Love; Niagara; Night Walker; Nightmare in the Sun; No Way Out (1987); Noises Off; Not with My Wife You Don't; Once Upon a Dream; One More River; Only Two Can Play; Orpheus Descending; Ossessione; The Other Side of Midnight; Out of Africa; Painted Veil; Pauline at the Beach; Peter Ibbetson; The Piano; Plaza Suite; Polyester; Private Lives; A Rage to Live; Red Sky at Morning; Regarding Henry; Return to Peyton Place; Romance; The Romantic Englishwoman; Room at the Top; Royal Scandal; Ryan's Daughter; Same Time, Next Year; The Scarlet Letter (1926); The Scarlet Letter (1934); The Scarlet Letter (1980); The Scarlet Letter (1995); The September Affair; Serial; The Severed Head; Shattered; Skylark; So Big (1932); So Big (1953); The Statue; Strange Bedfellows; Strange Interlude (1932); Strange Interlude (1990); Strangers, the Story of a Mother and Daughter; Street Scene; The Tempest; That Forsyte Woman; These Three; They All Laughed; Thief of Hearts; This Thing Called Love; Three Husbands; Time for Loving; 'Tis a Pity She's a Whore; 21 Days; Under the Volcano; Unfaithful; Unfaithfully Yours (1948); Unfaithfully Yours (1984); Violent Men; Where Love Has Gone; White Nights (1957); The Woman I Love; Woman Next Door; The World is Full of Married Men

Chefs: see *Restaurant Settings*
Chess: see also *Games: Geniuses:* Fresh; Knight Moves; Searching for Bobby Fisher; Dangerous Moves
Chicago: see also *Midwestern Life: Parents are Gone from Chicago: Mob Stories:* About Face; Al Capone; Baby's Day Out; Backdraft; Bad Boys; Big Town; The Blues Brothers; Calling Northside 777; Candyman; Capone; Carrie (1952); City Boy; Code of Silence; Compulsion; Deadly Matrimony; Dillinger (1945); Dillinger (1973); Earl of Chicago; Eight Men Out; Ferris Bueller's Day Off; Folks!; The Front Page (1931); The Front Page (1974); The Fugitive (1993); The Fugitive: The Final Episode; Gaily, Gaily; Go-Fish; Hoop Dreams; I Love Trouble (1994); In Old Chicago; A League of Their Own; Limit Up; Little Caesar; Mad

Dog and Glory; The Man with the Golden Arm; Medium Cool; My Bodyguard; Naked Face; Nitti, The Enforcer; Raisin in the Sun; Raw Deal; Red Heat; Risky Business; Robin and the Seven Hoods; Roxie Hart; Running Scared; St. Valentine's Day Massacre; Say Amen, Somebody!; Scarface (1932); The Scarface Mob/"The Untouchables" Pilot; Sons of the Desert; Straight Talk; Swoon; T. R. Baskin; Tall, Dark & Handsome; Things Change; Thunder Road; The Untouchables; Wabash Avenue; Watch It

Child Abuse: see *Abused Children: Molestation-Child: Social Drama*
Childhood Memories: see also *Memories: Boyhood: Girlhood: Elementary School Life: Flashbacks: Molestation-Child:* Drop Dead Fred; Ikiru; Kes; The Land Before Time; My Father's Glory; My Mother's Castle; Salaam Bombay!; To Kill a Mockingbird; Whistle Down the Wind
Child Molestation: see *Molestation-Child*
Child Protagonists: see also *Children-Little Adults: CHILDREN: Boys: Girls:* Afraid of the Dark; Aladdin; Alice, Sweet Alice; All I Want For Christmas; Amazing Mr. Blunden; Annie; Assault; Baby, Take A Bow; Black Beauty (1946); Black Beauty (1971); Black Beauty (1994); Black Hand; The Black Stallion; The Black Stallion Returns; Blood on Satan's Claw; The Blue Bird (1940); The Blue Bird (1976); Bright Eyes; Bugsy Malone; Cameron's Closet; Candleshoe; Careful, He Might Hear You; Celia; Client; Cloak and Dagger (1984); Crash of Silence; Double O Kid; E.T.: The Extra-Terrestrial; Echoes of a Summer; Empire of the Sun; Eyewitness (1970); Fallen Idol; Firestarter; Firstborn; The Five Thousand Fingers of Doctor T.; Flight of the Doves; Fresh; The 400 Blows
Children-Little Adults (intelligent, overly mature children, though not nec-essarily extremely educated): see also *Children-Gifted: Geniuses:* Bugsy Malone; The Champ (1931); The Champ (1979); Fresh; Glamour Boy; The Goodbye Girl; I'll Do Anything; Life With Mikey; Little Big League; Little Man Tate; Rich Kids; Searching for Bobby Fischer; Skippy; Village of the Damned
Children-Long-Lost: see also *Orphans: Men Who Leave: Women Who Leave:*

B. F.'s Daughter; The Bawdy Adventures of Tom Jones; Bittersweet Love; Born to Be Bad (1934); Bright Angel; Buona Sera, Mrs. Campbell; Carbon Copy; Chase a Crooked Shadow; Close My Eyes; Dancing in the Dark; Distant Thunder (1988); East of Eden (1955); East of Eden (1980); Green Eyes; High Tide; I Could Go on Singing; I Ought to Be in Pictures; The Importance of Being Earnest; Kangaroo; Leon, the Pig Farmer; Madame X (1929); Madame X (1937); Madame X (1965); Made in America; Man, Woman and Child; Min and Bill; My Girl 2; Olivier, Olivier; One False Move; Return of the Jedi; Rich, Young and Pretty; Right to Love; River Rat; Simple Men; Soapdish; Splitting Heirs; Tess; Three Men and a Little Lady; To Each His Own; Tom Jones; Track 29; Travels with My Aunt; Tribute; Twins; Welcome Home, Roxy Carmichael; White Banners; Woman to Woman

Children-Parting With/Losing: see also *Missing Persons: Parents vs. Children:* The Accidental Tourist; Adam; Au Revoir, les Enfants; The Champ (1931); The Champ (1979); The Goddess; The Good Mother; Ladybird, Ladybird; Losing Isaiah; Safe Passage; The Singing Fool; Six Weeks; Sophie's Choice; Sugarland Express; Tender Mercies; The White Cliffs of Dover

Children-Problem: see *Evil Children: Children-Little Adults:* CHILDREN

Children-Saving/Rescuing: see also *Children Saving Parents: Parents are Gone: Trapped in a Hole:* Baby Jessica; Lorenzo's Oil; Min and Bill; Three Fugitives; The Well

Children Saving Parents: The Foreign Correspondent; The Man Who Knew Too Much (1956); Music Box; North by Northwest; Railway Children; Target

Children-Search for: see *Missing Children: Children-Parting with: Family/Heritage-Search for*

Children-Suburban/Middle Class: see *Suburban Kids: Rich Kids: Poor Kids*

Children-Troublesome: see *Children-Brats: Children-Problem*

Children of Unwed Mothers: see *Mothers-Unwed: Orphans*

CHILDREN'S: see also *Poor Kids: Rich Kids: Suburban Kids: Suburban Life: FAMILY: Coming of Age: Teenage Movies: Comedy-Children's: Fantasy:*

The Absent-Minded Professor; Ace Eli and Rodger of the Skies; The Adventures of Baron Munchausen (1943); The Adventures of Baron Munchausen (1987); The Adventures of Milo and Otis; The Adventures of the Wilderness Family; Africa Screams; Against a Crooked Sky; Alice in Wonderland; All Dogs Go to Heaven; Almost Angels; Amazing Mr. Blunden; American Tail; American Tail 2: Fievel Goes West; And You Thought Your Parents Were Weird; Animal Farm; The Apple Dumpling Gang; The Apple Dumpling Gang Rides Again; The Aristocats; Babar: The Movie; Babes in Toyland (1934); Babes in Toyland (1961); Baby, Secret of the Lost Legend; The Bad News Bears; The Bad News Bears Go to Japan; The Bad News Bears in Breaking Training; Bambi; Barefoot Executive; batteries not included; The Bear; The Bears & I; Beauty and the Beast (1991); Bedknobs and Broomsticks; Beethoven; Beethoven's 2nd; Benji; Benji the Hunted; Big Red; Biscuit Eater (1940); Biscuit Eater (1972); Black Beauty (1946); Black Beauty (1971); Black Beauty (1994); The Black Cauldron; The Black Stallion; The Black Stallion Returns; Blackbeard's Ghost; Blank Check; Bless the Beasts and the Children; The Blue Bird (1940); The Blue Bird (1976); Boatniks; Bon Voyage, Charlie Brown; Born to be Wild; The Borrowers; The Boy Who Could Fly; Brighty of the Grand Canyon; Bugsy Malone; Cannonball Run; Cannonball Run 2; Captains Courageous; The Care Bears' Adventure in Wonderland; The Care Bears Movie; Career Opportunities; Casey's Shadow; Casper; The Castaway Cowboy; Chalk Garden; Charlotte's Web; Chitty Chitty Bang Bang; CHOMPS; Chronicles of Narnia; Clarence, the Cross-Eyed Lion; Cloak and Dagger (1984); The Cure; Curly Sue; D.A.R.Y.L.; D2: The Mighty Ducks; Darby O'Gill and the Little People; Dark Crystal; Dennis the Menace; The Devil is a Sissy; Digby, the Biggest Dog in the World; Dog of Flanders; Double McGuffin; The Double O Kid; Dr. Dolittle; Dreamchild; Driftwood; Drop Dead Fred; Dumbo; Dutch; E.T.: The Extra-Terrestrial; Enchanted Forest; Ernest Goes to Camp; Ernest Goes to Jail; Ernest Rides Again; Ernest Saves Christmas; Ernest Scared Stupid; Escape From the Dark; Escape to

Witch Mountain; Explorers; Fantasia; Far From Home; Felix the Cat: The Movie; FernGully: The Last Rainforest; Field of Dreams; Flash; Flight of the Navigator; Flintstones; Flipper; Fluffy; For the Love of Benji; The Fox and the Hound; Freaky Friday; Freddie as F.R.0.7.; Free Willy; French Postcards; Gay Purree; The Ghost and Mr. Chicken; Gleaming the Cube; Gnome Mobile; The Golden Seal; Goodbye My Lady; A Goofy Movie; Goonies; The Great Locomotive Chase; The Great Mouse Detective; The Great Muppet Caper; The Great Outdoors; The Green Years; Gremlins; Gremlins 2: The New Batch; Gulliver's Travels (1939); Gulliver's Travels (1976); Gus; Hangar 18; Harry and the Hendersons; Hatari!; Heavyweights; Heidi (1939); Hello Down There; Herbie Goes Bananas; Herbie Goes to Monte Carlo; Herbie Rides Again; Honey, I Blew Up the Kid; Honey, I Shrunk the Kids; Hook; The Horse in the Grey Flannel Suit; Hot Lead and Cold Feet; Howard the Duck; Ichabod and Mr. Toad/The Legend of Sleepy Hollow; Incredible Journey; The Incredible Mr. Limpet; The Innocents; In Search of the Castaways; International Velvet; Into the West; It Grows on Trees; Jack and the Beanstalk; Jack the Giant Killer; Jetsons Movie; Josh and S.A.M.; Journey of Natty Gann; Journey to the Center of the Earth; The Kid from Left Field; Labyrinth; Lady and the Tramp; Lady Bugs; The Land Before Time; The Last Flight of Noah's Ark; Let's Scare Jessica to Death; Lionheart; The Little Ark; Little Giants; The Little Mermaid; The Little Prince; The Little Rascals; Little Women (1933); Little Women (1949); Little Women (1978); Little Women (1994); Living Desert; The Lone Ranger (1955); The Lone Ranger and the Lost City of Gold; Long John Silver; Lord of the Rings; The Love Bug; Lucky Star; The Magic of Lassie; Make Mine Music; The Man from Snowy River; Man of the House; Mary Poppins; Melody; Million Dollar Duck; Miracle of the White Stallions; Miracle on 34th Street (1947); Mom and Dad Save the World; Monkey Trouble; Monster Squad; Moon Pilot; Moon Spinners; Mrs. Doubtfire; The Muppet Christmas Carol; Muppet Movie; Muppets Take Manhattan; My Bodyguard; My Father the Hero; My Friend Flicka; My Girl; My Girl 2; Napoleon and Samantha; National Velvet;

The Neverending Story; The Neverending Story II: The Next Chapter; Newsies; The Nightmare Before Christmas; No Deposit, No Return; North; The North Avenue Irregulars; Nothing but Trouble (1991); Now You See Him, Now You Don't; Nutcracker (1993); Nutcracker-The Motion Picture (1986); Old Yeller; Oliver and Company; One of Our Dinosaurs is Missing; The Pagemaster; The Parent Trap; Pee-Wee's Big Adventure; Perri; Peter Pan; The Phantom Tollbooth; Pinocchio; Pippi Longstocking; Planet of the Apes; Pollyanna; The Prince of Central Park; Radio Flyer; Railway Children; Ratboy; The Red Balloon; The Rescuers; The Rescuers Down Under; Return from Witch Mountain; Return to Oz; Richie Rich; Rock-a-doodle; Russkies; Samantha; Sandlot; Santa Claus, The Movie; Savage Sam; The Secret Garden (1984); The Secret Garden (1993); The Secret of NIMH; The Seven Faces of Dr. Lao; The Shakiest Gun in the West; Six Pack; Skippy; Sleeping Beauty; The Slipper and the Rose; Snow White & The Seven Dwarfs; So Dear to My Heart; Son of Lassie; Song of the South; Spaced Invaders; Squanto; Street Fighter; SuperDad; Supergirl; The Swan Princess; Swiss Family Robinson; The Sword in the Stone; Teenage Mutant Ninja Turtles; Teenage Mutant Ninja Turtles 2; Teenage Mutant Ninja Turtles 3; That Darn Cat!; The Three Lives of Thomasina; The Three Musketeers (1993); Three Ninjas; Three Ninjas Kick Back; Thumbelina; Thunderhead, Son of Flicka; Tiger Bay; To Kill a Mockingbird; Tom Sawyer; Tom Thumb; Treasure of Matecumbe; Troop Beverly Hills; The Trouble with Angels; The Ugly Dachshund; Uncle Buck; Water Babies; Watership Down; We're Back! A Dinosaur's Story; Wee Willie Winkie; When the Whales Came; White Fang; Who Framed Roger Rabbit?; Willow; Willy Wonka and the Chocolate Factory; Witches; Wizard; The Wizard of Oz (1925); The Wizard of Oz (1939); The Wolves of Willoughby Chase; The Wonderful World of the Brothers Grimm; The World's Greatest Athlete; Yearling

China: see also *Chinese People: Chinese Films: Asia: Asian-Americans: Asian-American Films: Japan:* The Adventures of Marco Polo; Blood Alley; The Chairman; China; China Girl (1942); The Conqueror; Dersu Uzala; Dragon Seed; Empire of the Sun; Farewell My Concubine; 55 Days at Peking; Flying Tigers; The General Died at Dawn; Genghis Khan; The Golden Child; The Good Earth; The Gunrunner; The Inn of the Sixth Happiness; International House; Joy Luck Club; Keys of the Kingdom; The Last Emperor; Lost Horizon (1937); Lost Horizon (1973); M. Butterfly; Painted Veil; Red Sorghum; Seven Women; Shanghai Express; Shanghai Gesture; Shanghai Surprise; Somewhere I'll Find You; Tai Pan; The Thousand Pieces of Gold

Chinese Films: see also *Taiwanese Films: Asian-American Films: Asian-Americans: China: Asian-Americans: Japanese Films:* Ju Dou; Raise the Red Lantern; Shangai Triad; To Live; The Wedding Banquet

Chinese People: see also *Chinese Films: China: Asian-American Films: Asian-Americans: Japanese People:* The Big Brawl; Broken Blossoms; Chan is Missing; China; China Girl (1942); China Girl (1987); Combination Platter; The Courtship of Eddie's Father; Dim Sum: a Little Bit of Heart; Flower Drum Song; The Good Earth; Hammett; The Hatchet Man; Hell and High Water; Joy Luck Club; The Killing of a Chinese Bookie; Kung Fu; Life is Cheap, but Toilet Paper is Expensive; M. Butterfly; Red Sorghum; Thoroughly Modern Millie; The Thousand Pieces of Gold; Wedding Banquet

Choosing Between Loves: see *Romance-Choosing the Right Person: Romance-Triangles: Swapping Partners*

Choosing the Right Person: see *Romance-Choosing the Right Person: Marriage Impending: Engagements-Breaking*

Christian Films: see *Biblical Films: Jesus Christ: Conservative Value Films: FAMILY: Monks: Priests: Nuns: Christmas*

Christmas: see also *Jesus Christ: Santa Claus: Reunions: New Years Eve & Day:* All I Want For Christmas; Babes in Toyland (1934); Babes in Toyland (1961); The Bishop's Wife; Black Christmas; A Christmas Carol (1938); A Christmas Carol (1951); Christmas Holiday; Christmas in Connecticut (1945); Christmas in Connecticut (1992); Christmas Lilies of the Field; Die Hard; Die Hard 2; Ernest Saves Christmas; The Gathering; Gremlins; Holiday Inn; The Holly and the Ivy; Home Alone; Home Alone 2; I'll Be Seeing You; It's a Wonderful Life; The Lemon Drop Kid; Life Begins at 8:30; Mame; Midnight Clear; Miracle on 34th Street (1947); The Muppet Christmas Carol; National Lampoon's Christmas Vacation; Nightmare Before Christmas; Nightmare on Elm Street; Nutcracker (1993); One Magic Christmas; Prancer; The Ref; Roots, the Gift; Santa Claus, The Movie; The Santa Clause; Scrooge (1935); Scrooge (1970); Silent Night, Deadly Night SERIES; White Christmas

CIA Agents: see also *Spy Films: Assassination Plots:* Above the Law; Air America; The Amateur; Bad Company (1995); The Bourne Identity; Clear and Present Danger; Cleopatra Jones; Cleopatra Jones & The Casino of Gold; Cloak and Dagger (1946); Deadly Currents; Desert Law; Eiger Sanction; Fifty/Fifty; Highpoint; Hopscotch; The Hunt for Red October; The Innocent; The Killer Elite; The Kremlin Letter; Malone; Memoirs of an Invisible Man; Mrs. Pollifax, Spy; North by Northwest; Operation CIA; The Osterman Weekend; The Package; Patriot Games; Predator; Real Men; Remo Williams: The Adventure Begins; Russia House; S*P*Y*S; Scorpio; Three Days of the Condor; Time Bomb; White Sands; Wrong is Right

Cinderella Stories: see also *Fairy Tales: Rags to Riches:* Cinderella; Cinderfella; Mahogany; Maid to Order; The Slipper and the Rose

Cinema Verite (a French term for a realistic, documentary style of filmmaking, though not necessarily a documentary): see *Documentary Style: Documentaries: Filmumentaries*

Circus Life: see also *CHILDREN: Fantasy:* At the Circus; Berserk!; Billy Rose's Jumbo; Carny; Clown; A Day at the Circus; Dumbo; Fox and His Friends; Freaks; Gorilla at Large; The Greatest Show on Earth; Heller in Pink Tights; Invitation to the Dance; The Jerk; Julia Misbehaves; La Strada; The Men in Her Life; Merry Andrew; Octopussy; Roustabout; Sally of the Sawdust; Sawdust and Tinsel; The Serpent's Egg; The Seven Faces of Dr. Lao; Shadows and Fog; Shakes the Clown; Something Wicked This Way Comes; Street Angel; Tarnished Angels; The Three Lives of Thomasina; Tin Drum; To Catch a Killer;

Trapeze; Wild Hearts Can't Be Broken; Wings of Desire; You Can't Cheat an Honest Man

City Life: see *Urban Life: Inner City Life*

City vs. Country: see also *Urban Life: Rural Life: Snobs vs. Slobs: Class Conflicts: New York vs. Los Angeles:* Aaron Slick from Punkin Crick; Act of the Heart; Adam at 6 A.M.; The Adventures of Reinette and Mirabelle; The Adventures of the Wilderness Family; Amber Waves; Baby Boom; The Beverly Hillbillies; Birch Interval; Boy, Did I Get a Wrong Number!; The Bride is Much Too Beautiful; The Butcher's Wife; Carrie (1952); The Citadel; City Boy; Cityslickers; Cityslickers 2; Come Blow Your Horn; Continental Divide; The Cowboy Way; Doc Hollywood; Dudes; The Egg and I; The Farmer Takes a Wife; Foolin' Around; Forest Rangers; Gay Purree; George Washington Slept Here; Greenwich Village; Greystoke: The Legend of Tarzan; I Take this Woman; In Person; In the Heat of the Night; Jude the Obscure; Koyaanisqatsi; Leon, the Pig Farmer; Lightnin'; Lilies of the Field; Local Hero; Ma and Pa Kettle; Mister Cory; Mosquito Coast; Mountain Eagle; Moving; Mr. Blandings Builds His Dream House; My Cousin Vinny; My Six Loves; My Sweet Little Village; Never a Dull Moment (1950); No Time for Sergeants; Not as a Stranger; Playtime; Please Don't Eat the Daisies; The Prince of Tides; Pure Country; Safety Last; Scent of Green Papaya; Second Fiddle; The Secret of My Success; The Seduction of Mimi; Sheepman; Shy People; Spirit Rider; Spitfire; Stars and Bars; Straight Talk; Susan Lenox, Her Fall and Rise; Tillie's Punctured Romance; Tokyo Story; We of the Never Never; Where the Spies Are; Wild in the Country; Withnail and I; Wives and Lovers; A Woman of Paris; Youngblood Hawke

Civil Rights: see *Race Relations: Apartheid: Black vs. White: Social Drama*

Civil War Era: see also *1860s: War Stories: World War I Era: World War II Era: Reconstruction Era:* Alvarez Kelly; Autobiography of Miss Jane Pittman; Bad Company; Band of Angels; The Beguiled; The Birth of a Nation; Dallas; Dark Command; Drum; Escape from Fort Bravo; The Execution of Private Slovik;

Flaming Star; The General; Gettysburg; Glory; Gone With the Wind; Gore Vidal's Lincoln; Gorgeous Hussy; Great Day in the Morning; The Great Locomotive Chase; The Horse Soldiers; Isn't it Romantic?; Jezebel; The Little Foxes; Little Women (1933); Little Women (1949); Little Women (1978); Little Women (1994); Love Me Tender; The Man from Colorado; Mandingo; The McMasters; Mourning Becomes Electra; The Old Maid; Our Hospitality; The Red Badge of Courage; Rio Lobo; The Searchers; The Shadow Riders; Shenandoah; Skin Game; Sommersby; Song of the South; So Red the Rose; A Southern Yankee; The Tall Men; The Tall Target; Texas; 2000 Maniacs; The Undefeated

Clairvoyants: see *Psychics: Mindreading: Future-Seeing the: Fortune Tellers*

Class Clash: see *Class Conflicts*

Class Conflicts: see also *Snobs vs Slobs: Social Drama: Comedy-Social: Smart vs. Dumb: Romance-Class Conflict: Race Relations: Civil Rights: Lover Family Dislikes:* An Actor's Revenge; Alamo Bay; Alice Adams; All That Heaven Allows; Angry Silence; Animal Farm; Baby, It's You; Beer; The Best Years of Our Lives; The Breakfast Club; Breaking Away; Bringing Up Baby; Carbon Copy; Charlie Bubbles; The Citadel; The Crowd; Death of a Salesman (1950); Death of a Salesman (1985); Dinner at Eight; The Discreet Charm of the Bourgeoisie; Down and Out in Beverly Hills; The Dressmaker; Dutch; Easy Living (1937); Easy Living (1949); Emma; The Europeans; Eyewitness (1981); Fools; For Queen and Country; The French Lieutenant's Woman; From the Terrace; Grand Canyon; The Hairy Ape; Half a Sixpence; Howards End; I Live My Life; I'm All Right, Jack; The Importance of Being Earnest; Irene; Jude the Obscure; Kipps; Kitty; Knock on Any Door; The Landlord; Letter to Brezhnev; Letter to Three Wives; Life at the Top; Lifeboat; Life of Riley; Life Stinks!; The Little Giant (1933); Little Man Tate; Local Hero; Loulou; Love Affair (1932); Lumiere d'Ete; Mademoiselle Fifi; The Man in Grey; Mating Season; Meet the People; Metropolitan (1990); Momma, There's a Man in Your Bed; My Little Girl; The Naked Kiss; Night on Earth;

Oblomov; Once Were Warriors; The Phantom of Liberty; Princess Caraboo; The Reluctant Debutante; Roberta; Rob Roy; Room at the Top; Room with a View; Rules of the Game; Scenes from the Class Struggle in Beverly Hills; Scent of Green Papaya; Six Degrees of Separation; Society; Steelyard Blues; Story of Robin Hood and his Merry Men; Swept Away; Take This Job and Shove It; Taste for Killing; The Wedding March; White Palace; Winslow Boy; Working Girl; Wuthering Heights (1939); Wuthering Heights (1953); Wuthering Heights (1970); Wuthering Heights (1992); The Young Philadelphians

Classic Greek Stories: see *Mythology: Ancient Times: Greece*

Classic Literary Adaptations: see also *Classic Play Adaptations: Novel Adaptations: Pulitzer Prize Adaptations:* The Adventures of Huckleberry Finn (1960); The Adventures of Huckleberry Finn (1985); The Adventures of Robin Hood; The Adventures of Tom Sawyer; Almost a Man; Babbitt; Bartleby; Becky Sharp; Black Sabbath; The Bostonians; Bounty; Bram Stoker's Count Dracula (1970); Bram Stoker's Dracula (1992); Brothers Karamazov; Call of the Wild (1935); Call of the Wild (1972); Candide; Cannery Row; The Corsican Brothers; Dangerous Liaisons; The Day of the Locust; Death in Venice; Doctor Jekyll and Mr. Hyde (1931); Dodsworth; A Doll's House; Dr. Jekyll and Mr. Hyde (1941); Dracula (1931); Dracula (1979); Dracula Has Risen from the Grave; Dracula (Horror of Dracula, 1958); Dracula, Prince of Darkness; Dracula's Daughter; The Duellists; The Elusive Pimpernel; Ethan Fromme; The Europeans; Fanny Hill; Far from the Madding Crowd; A Farewell to Arms (1932); A Farewell to Arms (1957); The Fixer; For Whom the Bell Tolls; The Grapes of Wrath; Great Catherine; Great Expectations; Gulliver's Travels (1939); Gulliver's Travels (1976); The Hairy Ape; The Heart is a Lonely Hunter; Hedda; Histoires Extraordinaires; The House of Usher (1960); The House of Usher (1990); Howards End; Huckleberry Finn (1939); Huckleberry Finn (1960); Huckleberry Finn (1974); The Hunchback of Notre Dame (1923); The Hunchback of Notre Dame (1939); The Hunchback of Notre Dame (1956);

The Hunchback of Notre Dame (1982); The Hunchback of Notre Dame (1996); The Innocents; Intruder in the Dust; Ivanhoe; Jane Eyre (1934); Jane Eyre (1943); Jane Eyre (1971); Jude the Obscure; Kidnapped (1938); Kidnapped (1959); Kidnapped (1971); Kim; King Lear (1971); Kiss Me Kate (1953); Lady Chatterley's Lover (1955); Lady Chatterley's Lover (1981); The Last Tycoon; Les Misérables (1935); Les Misérables (1952); Les Misérables (1978); Little Dorrit; Little Women (1933); Little Women (1949); Little Women (1978); Little Women (1994); Long Hot Summer (1958); Lord Jim; Love; Madame Bovary; Masque of the Red Death; A Midsummer Night's Dream; The Mill on the Floss; Moby Dick; Nicholas Nickleby; 1984 (1955); 1984 (1984); O Pioneers!; Of Human Bondage (1934); Of Human Bondage (1946); Of Human Bondage (1964); Of Mice and Men (1939); Of Mice and Men (1993); Old Man and the Sea; Oliver!; Oliver Twist (1948); Oliver Twist (1982); The Pearl; The Pickwick Papers; Picture of Dorian Gray; A Place in the Sun; The Plague; Pride and Prejudice; Prince and the Pauper (1937); Prisoner of Zenda (1937); Prisoner of Zenda (1952); Prisoner of Zenda (1979); Pudd'nhead Wilson; The Red Badge of Courage; The Red Pony (1949); Red Pony (1976); The Reivers; Return of the Musketeers; Return of the Scarlet Pimpernel; The Scarlet Letter (1926); The Scarlet Letter (1934); The Scarlet Letter (1980); The Scarlet Letter (1995); A Separate Peace; Silas Marner; A Simple Twist of Fate; Sons and Lovers; The Sound and the Fury; The Sun Also Rises; A Tale of Two Cities (1935); A Tale of Two Cities (1958); A Tale of Two Cities (1982); The Taming of the Shrew; Tender is the Night; Tess; The Three Musketeers (1935); The Three Musketeers (1939); The Three Musketeers (1948); The Three Sisters; The Three Worlds of Gulliver; To Have and Have Not; Tom Sawyer; Tortilla Flat; Treasure Island (1934); Treasure Island (1971); Treasure Island (1990); Treasure Island (1991); The Trial (1962); The Trial (1993); Tropic of Cancer; 20,000 Leagues Under the Sea; Ulysses (1967); Uncle Tom's Cabin (1914); Uncle Tom's Cabin (1969); Under the Volcano; Valmont; Vanity Fair; War and Peace (1956); War and Peace

(1967); White Fang; Wild Duck; Wise Blood; Wuthering Heights (1939); Wuthering Heights (1953); Wuthering Heights (1970); Wuthering Heights (1992)

Classic Play Adaptations (when the play version is the origin or more noted than other sources such as novels or legends, when applicable; does not include many originating in the last fifty years where classic status is debatable): see also *Pulitzer Prize Adaptations: Novel & Play Adaptations: Classic Literary Adaptations:* As You Like It (1936); As You Like It (1992); Boys from Syracuse; Cat on a Hot Tin Roof (1958); Cat on a Hot Tin Roof (1984); Cyrano de Bergerac (1950); Cyrano de Bergerac (1990); Dr. Faustus; Death of a Salesman (1950); Death of a Salesman (1985); Desire Under the Elms; A Flea in Her Ear; Glass Menagerie (1950); The Glass Menagerie (1973); The Glass Menagerie (1987); Hamlet (1948); Hamlet (1964); Hamlet (1969); Hamlet (1991); Henry V (1944); Henry V (1989); The Honey Pot; The Importance of Being Earnest; Inspector General; Julius Caesar; The Madwoman of Chaillot; Miss Julie; Mourning Becomes Electra; My Fair Lady; Oedipus Rex; Otello; Othello (1951); Othello (1965); Othello (1995); Prospero's Books; Pygmalion; Romeo and Juliet (1936); Romeo and Juliet (1954); Romeo and Juliet (1968); Saint Joan; School for Scandal; Sea Beast; The Sea Gull; Strange Interlude (1932); Strange Interlude (1990); A Streetcar Named Desire; Throne of Blood; 'Tis a Pity She's a Whore; Trojan Women; Volpone

Classic Tragedy: see also *TRAGEDY:* Anna Christie; Anna Karenina (1935); Anna Karenina (1985); Anne of the Thousand Days; Battleship Potemkin; Beau Geste (1926); Beau Geste (1939); Beau Geste (1966); Camille (1936); Dangerous Liaisons; Dr. Faustus; Hamlet (1948); Hamlet (1964); Hamlet (1969); Hamlet (1991); The Hunchback of Notre Dame (1923); The Hunchback of Notre Dame (1939); The Hunchback of Notre Dame (1956); The Hunchback of Notre Dame (1982); The Hunchback of Notre Dame (1996); King Lear (1971); La Traviata; Last of the Mohicans (1936); Last of the Mohicans (1992); Les Liaisons Dangereuses; Madame Bovary; Madame Butterfly; Miss Julie; Oedipus Rex;

Otello; Othello (1951); Othello (1965); Parsifal; The Phantom of the Opera (1925); The Phantom of the Opera (1941); The Phantom of the Opera (1962); The Phantom of the Opera (1989); Quo Vadis; Ran; Romeo and Juliet (1936); Romeo and Juliet (1954); Romeo and Juliet (1968); Saint Joan; The Scarlet Letter (1926); The Scarlet Letter (1934); The Scarlet Letter (1980); The Scarlet Letter (1995); A Tale of Two Cities (1935); A Tale of Two Cities (1958); A Tale of Two Cities (1982); Throne of Blood

Class Struggles: see *Class Conflicts*
Clever Murder Plot: see *Perfect Crimes: Clever Plots & Endings*
Clever Plots & Endings: see also *Perfect Crimes: Faked Death: Complicated Plots:* Absence of Malice; Absolution; Alice, Sweet Alice; The Alphabet Murders; Asylum; Based on an Untrue Story; Beyond a Reasonable Doubt; Body Heat; A Boy and His Dog; Breathless (1959); Breathless (1983); Charley Varrick; China Moon; The Crying Game; Dark Mirror; Deathtrap; Diabolique (1955); Dial M For Murder; Dirty Rotten Scoundrels; Dollars; Dressed to Kill; Eleven Harrowhouse; Experiment in Terror; Eyes of Laura Mars; F/X; F/X 2: The Deadly Art of Illusion; Fallen Angel; Family Plot; Frantic (1958); Getaway (1972); Getaway (1994); Going in Style; Green for Danger; The Grifters; Groundhog Day; Guilty as Sin; Guilty Conscience; The Honey Pot; Hot Millions; The Hot Rock; Impact; It's a Mad Mad Mad Mad World!; The January Man; Kansas City Confidential; Killjoy; Kill Me Again; Kiss Me Deadly; The Lady from Shanghai; Lady Killer (1992); The Lady Vanishes (1938); The Lady Vanishes (1979); The Last of Sheila; The Lavender Hill Mob; The Letter (1929); The Letter (1940); The List of Adrian Messenger; A Lovely Way to Die; Malice; The Man Who Never Was; Manhattan Murder Mystery; Mastergate; Max and Helen; Midnight Run; Mildred Pierce; Mirage; Mother Love; Mr. Klein; Murder by Natural Causes; No Escape (1936); No Way Out (1987); No Way to Treat a Lady; The Player; Presumed Innocent; Prizzi's Honor; Quick; Raising Cain; Red Rock West; Sapphire; The Scapegoat; Schindler's List; Shallow Grave; The Shawshank Redemption; Shock to the

System; The Shooting; The Shop Around the Corner; Sleuth; St. Ive's; The Sting; Stolen Life (1939); Stolen Life (1946); Strange Bargain; Talk of the Town; The Tenth Man; The Thomas Crown Affair; Throw Momma from the Train; Tom Jones; Vertigo; What's Up, Doc?; Widows' Peak; Witness for the Prosecution

Coaches (where coaches are the central character): see also Sports Movies: Baseball: Basketball: Football: Soccer: Skiing: Skating: Blue Chips; Comrades of Summer; Cool Runnings; D2: The Mighty Ducks; Hoosiers; The Long Gray Line; Mixed Company; Necessary Roughness; The Program; Slap Shot; The Terry Fox Story; Trouble Along the Way

Cold People: see Stern Men: Stern Women

Cold Spots: see Snow Settings: Arctic/Anarctica

Cold War Era: see also Cold War Error: Communists: Russians as Enemy: McCarthy Era: Russian Revolution: Spy Films: Spies: Traitors: Airport '79, The Concorde; The Chairman; The Commies are Coming, the Commies are Coming; Conspirator; A Dandy in Aspic; Dangerous Moves; Daniel; The Day After; The Day the Earth Stood Still; Dr. Strangelove; Embassy; The Experts; Fail Safe; Fellow Traveler; The Forbin Project; The Fourth War; Hell and High Water; The Hunt for Red October; I Was a Communist for the FBI; The Innocent; Invasion of the Body Snatchers (1956); The Kremlin Letter; The Manchurian Candidate; Night Crossing; Pickup on South Street; The Prisoner (1955); Red Dawn; Rocky IV; Romanoff and Juliet; The Russia House; The Russians Are Coming, the Russians Are Coming; S*P*Y*S; The Spy Who Came in from the Cold; The Spy Who Loved Me; Superman 4; Telefon; The Thief (1952); The Thing (1951); Topaz (1969); Torn Curtain; The Ugly American; The Unbearable Lightness of Being; War Games; White Nights (1985)

Cold War Error: see also Cold War Era: The Atomic Kid; The Bedford Incident; Crimson Tide; Dr. Strangelove; Fail Safe; The Hunt for Red October; The Russians Are Coming, the Russians Are Coming

College Life: see also Party Movies: Fraternity Life: Sorority Life: High School Life: Young Men: Young Women: Coming of Age: All-American Murder; Allnighter; Baby, It's You; Bachelor Party (1984); Back to School; The Bell Jar; The Big Chill; Big Man On Campus; The Boy Who Had Everything; Campus Man; Carnal Knowledge; Charley's Aunt; Children of a Lesser God; Class of '44; The Computer Wore Tennis Shoes; Doctor Detroit; Educating Rita; End of the Road; Fandango; Fraternity Row; The Freshman (1925); Fright Night Part 2; Getting Straight; Girl Crazy; Girl Most Likely to . . . (1971); Goodbye My Fancy; Good News; Gotcha!; The Graduate; Group; The Harrad Experiment; The Harrad Summer; Heart of Dixie; Here We Go Round the Mulberry Bush; Higher Learning; Horse Feathers; How I Got Into College; How to Be Very Very Popular; Johnny Be Good; Jude the Obscure; The Male Animal; Malice; Marathon Man; Million Dollar Legs; Mother is a Freshman; Mr. Belvedere Goes to College; National Lampoon's Animal House; Necessary Roughness; Now You See Him, Now You Don't; Oxford Blues; The Paper Chase; PCU; The Program; The Rachel Papers; A Rage to Live; Rapid Fire; Return of the Secaucus Seven; Reuben, Reuben; RPM; Rudy; School Daze; She Loves Me Not; She's Working Her Way Through College; Ski School; Small Circle of Friends; Sniper; St. Elmo's Fire; The Sterile Cuckoo; The Strawberry Statement; Sure Thing; Tall Story; Threesome; Trouble Along the Way; Unnamable; Unnamable Returns; Up the Sandbox; The Way We Were; Who Was That Lady?; Who's Afraid of Virginia Woolf?; Wild in the Country; Yank at Oxford

Colonial America: see Revolutionary War: 1700s: 1800s: War of 1812

Comas: see also Medical Drama: Amnesia: Bad Dreams; Brimstone & Treacle; Coma; The Dead Zone; The First Deadly Sin; Halloween 4: The Return of Michael Myers; Hard to Kill; The Mind of Mr. Soames; Reversal of Fortune

Comebacks: see also Underdog Stories: Redemption: Starting Over: Sports Movies: One Last Chance: Risking it All: Losing it All: Angels in the Outfield (1951); Angels in the Outfield (1994); Avalon; Band Wagon; The Barkleys of Broadway; Behold a Pale Horse; Breaking In; Bright Victory; Callaway Went Thataway; The Clown; The Color of Money; The Cool Ones; The Country Girl; Dancing in the Dark; Dangerous; Diggstown; The Entertainer; Fedora; Homeboy; The Hustler; If I Had My Way; Jolson Sings Again; The Jolson Story; The Kid from Left Field; Late Show; Let's Dance; Life With Mikey; Lightning Over Water; Limelight; Lusty Men; Madhouse; Major League 2; Matilda; Postcards from the Edge; Requiem for a Heavyweight (1956); Requiem for a Heavyweight (1962); Rocky II; Rocky III; Rocky IV; The Singing Fool; Star; Staying Alive; Stepping Out; Sunset Boulevard; The Sunshine Boys; Sweet Bird of Youth; Tap; Targets; Tender Mercies; Veronika Voss; Whatever Happened to Baby Jane?; When My Baby Smiles at Me; White Christmas; Wings of Eagles

Comedians: see also COMEDY: Comedy Performance: Comedy-Character Comedy-Skit: Vaudeville: Practical Jokers: Abbott & Costello Go to Mars; Abbott & Costello in Hollywood; Abbott & Costello in the Foreign Legion; Abbott & Costello Lost in Alaska; Abbott & Costello Meet Captain Kidd; Abbott & Costello Meet the Keystone Cops; The Adventures of Ford Fairlane; Always Leave Them Laughing; And Now For Something Completely Different; Arkansas Traveler; Artists and Models (1937); Artists and Models Abroad; Back to School; Born in East L.A.; The Caddy; Can Hieronymus Merkin Ever Forget Mercy Humppe and Find True Happiness?; Car Wash; Cheech and Chong: Still Smokin'; Cheech and Chong's Next Movie; Cheech and Chong's Nice Dreams; Cheech and Chong's The Corsican Brothers; The Comic; The Court Jester; Did You Hear the One About the Travelling Saleslady?; Divine Madness; Does This Mean We're Married?; The Eddie Cantor Story; The Entertainer; Errand Boy; Hellzapoppin; Hollywood or Bust; Hollywood Revue of 1929; The Horn Blows at Midnight; If I Had My Way; If You Knew Susie; Ishtar; Jo Jo Dancer, Your Life is Calling; The Kid From Spain; Kid Millions; The King of Comedy; Knock on Wood; Last of the Secret Agents; Lenny; Limelight; Love in Bloom; Love Thy Neighbor; Magic; The Man on the Flying Trapeze; Merton of the Movies; Mickey One; Mother Wore Tights; Mr. Saturday Night; Mrs. Parker

Burglar; Bustin' Loose; Butterflies Are Free; Bye Bye Birdie; Bye Bye Braverman; Bye Bye Love; Cabin Boy; Cactus Flower; The Caddy; Caddyshack; Caddyshack 2; Cafe Metropole; Cafe Society; Cain and Mabel; Cairo (1942); Calamity Jane; Calendar Girl; California Split; California Suite; Call Me Bwana; Call Me Madam; Callaway Went Thataway; The Cameraman; Can She Bake a Cherry Pie?; Can't Buy Me Love; Can-Can; Canadian Bacon; Cancel My Reservation; Candleshoe; Candy; Caprice; Captain Newman, M.D.; Captain Ron; Car 54, Where Are You?; Car Wash; Carbon Copy; Career Opportunities; Carefree; Casanova's Big Night; Casino Royale; Casper; Castaway Cowboy; Casual Sex?; The Cat and the Canary (1927); The Cat and the Canary (1939); The Cat and the Canary (1979); Cat Ballou; Caught in the Draft; Caveman; CB4: The Movie; The Cemetery Club; A Certain Smile; Champagne for Caesar; Chan is Missing; Chances Are; A Change of Seasons; Charley's Aunt; Charlie Chan and the Curse of the Dragon Queen; Chase (1994); Chastity Belt; Chattanooga Choo Choo; Chatterbox; The Cheap Detective; Cheaper by the Dozen; Cheaper to Keep Her; The Check is in the Mail; Checking Out; Cheech and Chong: Still Smokin'; Cheech and Chong's Next Movie; Cheech and Chong's Nice Dreams; Cheech and Chong's The Corsican Brothers; Cherry 2000; The Cheyenne Social Club; The Chicken Chronicles; Chitty Chitty Bang Bang; A Chorus of Disapproval; Christmas in Connecticut (1945); Christmas in Connecticut (1992); Christmas in July; Chu Chu and the Philly Flash; Cinderella Jones; Cinderfella; City Lights; Cityslickers 2; Class Act; Clean Slate; Clockwise; Club Paradise; Cocoanuts; Cold Feet; Cold Turkey; Come Blow Your Horn; Come September; Comfort and Joy; Coming to America; The Computer Wore Tennis Shoes; Condorman; Coneheads; Confessions of a Window Cleaner; A Connecticut Yankee; A Connecticut Yankee in King Arthur's Court; Constant Husband; Consuming Passions; Continental Divide; Cookie; The Cool Ones; Cool Runnings; Cop and a Half; Copacabana; Cops and Robbersons; Coquette; Cotton Comes to Harlem; The Couch Trip; A Countess from Hong Kong;

Court Jester; The Courtship of Eddie's Father; The Cowboy and the Lady; The Cowboy Way; Crackers; Critical Condition; Crocodile Dundee; Cross My Heart; Crossing Delancey; Cry Baby; Curly Sue; The Curse of the Pink Panther; The Cutting Edge; D.C. Cab; Damn Yankees; Dangerous When Wet; Darling Lili; Date with an Angel; A Date with Judy; Dave; A Day at the Races; Dazed and Confused; Dead Men Don't Wear Plaid; Deal of the Century; Dear Ruth; Death Becomes Her; Defending Your Life; Delicate Delinquent; Delirious; Dennis the Menace; Designing Woman; Desk Set; Desperate Living; Desperately Seeking Susan; The Devil and Max Devlin; The Devil and Miss Jones; Did You Hear the One About the Travelling Saleslady?; Die Laughing; Dirty Rotten Scoundrels; The Discreet Charm of Bourgeoisie; Disorderly Orderly; Disorganized Crime; Divine Madness; Divorce, American Style; Doc Hollywood; Doctor Detroit; Doctor Takes a Wife; Does This Mean We're Married?; Don't Just Stand There; Don't Make Waves; Don't Raise the Bridge, Lower the Water!; Don't Tell Her It's Me; Don't Tell Mom the Babysitter's Dead; Double Wedding; Doughgirls; Down and Out in Beverly Hills; Dr. Heckyl and Mr. Hype; Dr. Phibes Rises Again; Dr. Strangelove; Dragnet (1987); Dream Team; Dream Wife; Drop Dead Fred; Dubarry Was a Lady; Duchess of Idaho; Duck Soup; Dumb and Dumber; Earth Girls are Easy; Easy Living (1937); Easy Money (1983); Easy to Love; Easy to Wed; Eat the Rich; Eating Raoul; Ed and His Dead Mother; Ed Wood; Educating Rita; Edward Scissorhands; Egg & I; Eight on the Lam; Electric Dreams; The Elusive Pimpernel; Encino Man; The End; End of the Line; Ensign Pulver; Enter Laughing; Entertaining Mr. Sloane; Erik The Viking; Ernest Goes to Camp; Ernest Goes to Jail; Ernest Rides Again; Ernest Saves Christmas; Ernest Scared Stupid; Errand Boy; Eternally Yours; Every Day's A Holiday; Every Girl Should be Married; Every Home Should Have One; Every Thing You Always Wanted to Know About Sex . . . ; Every Which Way But Loose; Ex-Mrs. Bradford; The Experts; Exterminating Angel; The Facts of Life; A Family Affair; Fancy Pants; Fast Times at Ridgemont High; Faster Pussycat! Kill!

Kill!; Father Goose; Father of the Bride (1950); Father of the Bride (1991); Fatso; Favor; Favour, the Watch & the Very Big Fish; Fawlty Towers; Fear of a Black Hat; Female Trouble; Ferris Bueller's Day Off; Feud; Fiendish Plot of Dr. Fu Manchu; Finders Keepers; A Fine Madness; A Fine Mess; A Fine Romance; Fireman's Ball; First Nudie Musical; A Fish Called Wanda; The Fish that Saved Pittsburgh; Fitzwilly; Flashback; A Flea in Her Ear; Fletch Lives; Flintstones; Folies Bergere; Folks!; Foolin' Around; Fools for Scandal; Footlight Parade; For Love of Ivy; For Pete's Sake; For Richer, For Poorer; A Foreign Affair; Forever Darling; Forrest Gump; Fortune; Forty Pounds of Trouble; 42nd Street; Foul Play; Four Clowns; Four for Texas; Four Seasons; Four's a Crowd; Francis the Talking Mule; Freaky Friday; Free and Easy; Freebie and the Bean; The Freshman (1925); The Freshman (1990); Fried Green Tomatoes; The Frisco Kid (1979); The Front Page (1974); Frozen Assets; Full Moon in Blue Water; The Fuller Brush Girl; The Fuller Brush Man; Fun With Dick and Jane; Funny About Love; Funny Girl; A Funny Thing Happened on the Way to the Forum; Fuzz; Fuzzy Pink Nightgown; Gabriel over the White House; Gaily, Gaily; Garbo Talks; The General; Generation; Genevieve; Gentlemen Prefer Blondes; George Washington Slept Here; George White's 1935 Scandals; George White's Scandals (1934); George White's Scandals 1945; Getting Even with Dad; Getting It Right; Ghost and Mr. Chicken; Ghost Breakers; Ghost in the Invisible Bikini; Ghostbusters; Ghostbusters 2; Ghosts Can't Do It; Gidget; Gilda Live; Gin Game; The Girl Can't Help It; Girl Crazy; The Girl Most Likely (1958); The Girl Most Likely to . . . (1971); The Girl Who Couldn't Say No; Girls! Girls! Girls!; Give Me a Sailor; Give My Regards to Broadway; Glamour Boy; Glass Bottom Boat; Glen or Glenda?; Gnome Mobile; Go Chase Yourself; Go into Your Dance; Go West; Go West Young Man; The Gods Must Be Crazy; The Gods Must Be Crazy II; Goin' To Town; Gold Diggers in Paris; Gold Diggers of Broadway; Gold Diggers of 1933; Gold Diggers of 1935; Gold Diggers of 1937; The Gold Rush; The Golden Age of Comedy; The Golden Child; Goldwyn Follies; The Gong Show Movie; The Good Fairy; Good Morning,

Li'l Abner; Lily in Love; The Linguini Incident; The Liquidator; Little Big League; Little Big Man; Little Darlings; The Little Giant (1933); Little Giant (1946); Little Giants; The Little Minister; Little Miss Marker (1980); The Little Rascals; A Little Romance; A Little Sex; Little Shop of Horrors (1960); Little Shop of Horrors (1986); Little Treasure; Little Vegas; Living it Up; Lock up Your Daughters; The Lonely Guy; Lonesome Cowboys; The Long Long Trailer; Look Who's Talking; Look Who's Talking Now; Look Who's Talking Too; Lookin' to Get Out; Loose Ankles; Loot; Lord Love a Duck; Losin' It; Lost and Found; Lost in America; Louisiana Purchase; Love and Death; Love and Hisses; Love at First Bite; Love Before Breakfast; The Love Bug; Love Crazy; Love God?; Love in a Goldfish Bowl; Love in Bloom; Love is a Ball; The Love Lottery; Love Me Tonight; Love Nest; Love on the Run (1936); Love Parade; Love Potion #9; Love Thy Neighbor; The Loved One; Loverboy; Lover Come Back (1946); Lover Come Back (1961); Lovers and Other Strangers; Lovesick; Loving; Loving Couples; Luck of the Irish; Lucky Me; Lucky Night; Lucky Stiff; Lust in the Dust; Luv; MASH; Ma and Pa Kettle; Macaroni; Mad Miss Manton; Mad Wednesday; Made for Each Other; Made in America; Madhouse; The Magic Christian; The Magic Face; Magic Town; Maid to Order; The Main Event; The Major and the Minor; Major League; Major League 2; Major Payne; Make Me an Offer; Make Mine Mink; Making Mr. Right; Male Animal; Mame; Man Alive; A Man Could Get Killed; The Man from the Diners' Club; The Man in the White Suit; The Man on the Flying Trapeze; Man Trouble; The Man Who Broke the Bank at Monte Carlo; The Man Who Came to Dinner; The Man Who Lost Himself; The Man Who Loved Women (1977); The Man Who Loved Women (1983); The Man with the Golden Gun; Man with Two Brains; Man's Favorite Sport?; Manhattan; Manhattan Murder Mystery; Mannequin (1987); Mannequin 2: On the Move; Margie; Marriage Go Round; Marriage on the Rocks; Married to It; Married to the Mob; Marrying Kind; Marrying Man; Mary, Mary; Mary Poppins; Mask (1994); Masquerader; Mastergate; Matilda; Matinee; The Mating Game; Maverick;

Max Dugan Returns; Maxie; McClintock!; Me and Him; Me and My Gal; Me and the Colonel; Me, Natalie; Meatballs; Medicine Man; Meet Me After the Show; Meet the Applegates; Meet the People; Meet the Stewarts; Melvin and Howard; Men (1985); Men at Work; Menage; Merrily We Live; Merry Andrew; The Merry Wives of Reno; Merton of the Movies; Meteor Man; Metropolitan (1990); Mexican Hayride; Micki and Maude; Midnight (1939); Midnight (1989); Midnight Run; A Midsummer Night's Dream; A Midsummer Night's Sex Comedy; The Mighty Ducks; Mikey and Nicky; Milk Money; Milky Way (1936); Million Dollar Baby; Million Dollar Duck; Million Dollar Legs; The Millionaire; The Millionairess; Miracle (1990); Miracle of Morgan's Creek; Miracles; Miranda; Mischief; Miss Firecracker; Miss Grant Takes Richmond; Miss Robin Hood; Missing Pieces; The Missionary; Mister 880; Mister Cory; Mister Roberts; Mo' Money; The Model and the Marriage Broker; Modern Times; Mom and Dad Save the World; Money for Nothing; Money from Home; The Money Pit; Monkey Business (1931); Monkey Business (1952); Monkey Trouble; Monkeys Go Home; Monsieur Beaucaire; Monsieur Hulot's Holiday; Monsieur Verdoux; Monster in a Box; Monte Carlo; Monte Carlo Story; Monty Python and the Holy Grail; Monty Python's Life of Brian; Monty Python's The Meaning of Life; The Moon is Blue; Moon Over Parador; Moonlighting (1985); Moonstruck; More American Graffiti; More Than a Secretary; The More the Merrier; Morgan!; Morgan Stewart's Coming Home; Mother is a Freshman; Mother, Jugs & Speed; The Mouse That Roared; Move Over, Darling; Moving; Moving Violations (1985); Mr. and Mrs. North; Mr. Belvedere Goes to College; Mr. Belvedere Rings the Bell; Mr. Blandings Builds His Dream House; Mr. Deeds Goes to Town; Mr. Destiny; Mr. Mom; Mr. Music; Mr. Nanny; Mr. Peabody and the Mermaid; Mrs. Brown, You've Got a Lovely Daughter; Mrs Doubtfire; The Muppet Christmas Carol; Muppet Movie; Muppets Take Manhattan; Murder by Death; Murder, He Says; Muriel's Wedding; Muscle Beach Party; Music Box; My Blue Heaven (1990); My Cousin Vinny; My Dear Secretary; My Dinner With Andre;

My Fair Lady; My Father the Hero; My Favorite Blonde; My Favorite Brunette; My Favorite Spy; My Favorite Wife; My Favorite Year; My Friend Irma; My Friend Irma Goes West; My Little Chickadee; My Man Godfrey (1936); My Man Godfrey (1956); My Science Project; My Sister Eileen (1942); My Sister Eileen (1955); My Stepmother is an Alien; My Tutor; Myra Breckinridge; Nadine; Naked Gun; Naked Gun 2½; Naked Gun 33⅓; Naked in New York; The Naked Truth; Nasty Habits; National Lampoon's Animal House; National Lampoon's Christmas Vacation; National Lampoon's Class Reunion; National Lampoon's European Vacation; National Lampoon's Movie Madness; National Lampoon's Vacation; The Naughty Nineties; The Navigator; Necessary Roughness; Neighbors; Never a Dull Moment (1950); Never a Dull Moment (1967); Never Give a Sucker an Even Break; Never Say Die; New Kind of Love; New Leaf; New Year's Day; Newsies; Nickelodeon; Night in Casablanca; Night Shift; Night to Remember (1946); Night We Never Met; Nine to Five; 1941; Ninotchka; No Deposit, No Return; No More Ladies; No Room for the Groom; No Sex, Please, We're British; No Time for Comedy; No Time for Sergeants; Nobody's Perfect; Noises Off; Norman, Is That You?; North; North Avenue Irregulars; Not with My Wife You Don't; Nothing But the Best; Nothing But the Truth; Nothing but Trouble (1941); Nothing but Trouble (1991); Nothing Sacred; Now You See Him, Now You Don't; The Nude Bomb; Nudo di Donna; Nuns on the Run; The Nutty Professor (1963); O.C. and Stiggs; The Odd Couple; Off and Running; Oh, Dad, Poor Dad . . . ; Oh, God; Oh God Book Two; Oh God, You Devil; Oh Heavenly Dog; Oh Men! Oh Women!; Oh, Rosalinda!; On Approval; On the Air; On the Avenue; On the Double; On the Town; Once Bitten; Once in a Lifetime; Once Upon a Crime; Once Upon a Time; One and Only; One Body Too Many; 101 Dalmatians; One of Our Dinosaurs is Missing; One, Two, Three!; One Woman or Two; Only When I Larf; Only You; Operation Petticoat; Opportunity Knocks; The Opposite Sex; Oscar; Our Hospitality; Our Man Flint; Our Relations; Out Cold; Out of This World; Outoftowners; Outrageous Fortune;

Overboard; Over Her Dead Body; The Owl and the Pussycat; Oxford Blues; Pad, and How to Use It; Pain in the A . . . ; Pair of Briefs; The Pajama Game; Paleface; Palm Beach Story; Panama Hattie; Pandemonium; Papa's Delicate Condition; Paper Marriage; Paper Tiger; Pardners; The Parent Trap; Parenthood; Parents; Paris Holiday; Paris When it Sizzles; Parlor, Bedroom and Bath; The Party; Pass the Ammo; Passed Away; Passionate Plumber; Passport to Pimlico; Pat and Mike; Patsy; PCU; Pee-Wee's Big Adventure; Peggy Sue Got Married; Pepe; Perfect Furlough; Period of Adjustment; Pete 'n Tillie; Pete's Dragon; Peter's Friends; The Phantom President; Philadelphia Story; Pickup Artist; Pillow Talk; Pink Cadillac; Pink Flamingos; The Pink Panther; The Pink Panther Strikes Again; The Pirate; The Pirate Movie; Planes, Trains, and Automobiles; Platinum Blonde; Play it Again, Sam; Playtime; Please Don't Eat the Daisies; Pocketful of Miracles; Police Academy; Police Squad! Help Wanted!; Polyester; The Pope Must Die(t); Porky's; Porky's 2; Porky's Revenge; The Positively True Adventures of the Alleged Texas Cheerleader-Murdering Mom; Pretty Woman; The Princess and the Pirate; Princess Bride; Prisoner of Second Avenue; Prisoner of Zenda (1979); Private Benjamin; Private Function; Private Lives; Private School; Problem Child; Problem Child 2; The Producers; The Program; Promise Her Anything; Promises! Promises!; Promoter; Protocol; Pure Luck; The Purple Rose of Cairo; Quick Change; Rabbit Test; Radio Days; Rafferty and the Gold Dust Twins; The Radioland Murders; A Rage in Harlem; Raising Arizona; Rally Round the Flag, Boys; Rat Race; Ready to Wear; Real Men; Rebecca's Daughters; Ref; Remember Last Night?; Renaissance Man; Rent-a-Dick; Rented Lips; Reposessed; The Return of the Pink Panther; The Revenge of the Pink Panther; Rhinestone; Rhythm on the Range; The Richest Girl in the World; Ride 'Em Cowboy; Riding High; Rise and Rise of Michael Rimmer; Risky Business; Ritz; Road to Bali; Road to Hong Kong; Road to Morocco; Road to Rio; Road to Singapore; Road to Utopia; The Road to Wellville; Road to Zanzibar; Roberta; Robin and the Seven Hoods; Robin Hood,

Men in Tights; Rock a Bye Baby; Rock n' Roll High School; The Rocky Horror Picture Show; Roger & Me; Roman Scandals; Romance on the High Seas; Romancing the Stone; Romanoff and Juliet; Romantic Comedy; Room Service; Roxanne; The Royal Family of Broadway; Royal Flash; Royal Wedding; Rubin and Ed; Rude Awakening; Ruggles of Red Gap; Run for Your Money; Running Mates; Running Scared; The Russians Are Coming, The Russians Are Coming; Ruthless People; S*P*Y*S; Sad Sack; Safety Last; Sailor Beware; Same Time, Next Year; Sandlot; The Santa Clause; Saving Grace; Say Anything; Scared Stiff; Scavenger Hunt; Scenes from the Class Struggle in Beverly Hills; School for Husbands; School for Scandal; School for Scoundrels; Schtonk!; Scout; Scrooged; The Second Best Secret Agent in the Whole Wide World; Second Honeymoon; Second Sight; Secret Admirer; The Secret Life of Walter Mitty; The Secret of My Success; The Secret Policeman's Ball; The Secret Policeman's Other Ball; The Secret Policeman's Private Parts; The Secret Policeman's Third Ball; The Secret War of Harry Frigg; See No Evil, Hear No Evil; Seems Like Old Times; Semi-Tough; The Senator Was Indiscreet; Send Me No Flowers; Serial; Serial Mom; Seven Chances; Seven Days Leave; The Seven Faces of Dr. Lao; The Seven Little Foys; The Seven-Year Itch; Sex and the Single Girl; Sextette; S.F.W. Shag; The Shaggy D.A.; The Shaggy Dog; Shakes the Clown; The Shakiest Gun in the West; She Devil; She Done Him Wrong; She Loves Me Not; She'll Be Wearing Pink Pajamas; She's Gotta Have It; She's Having a Baby; She's Out of Control; She's Working Her Way Through College; Shirley Valentine; Shock to the System; Shock Treatment; Shocking Miss Pilgrim; Short Circuit; Short Circuit 2; Short Time; Shot in the Dark; Show Business; Shrimp on the Barbie; Sibling Rivalry; Silent Movie; Silver Bears; Silver Streak; Simon; Simon and Laura; Sing Baby Sing; Singing in the Rain; Sister Act; Sister Act 2; Sitting Ducks; Sitting Pretty; Six Degrees of Separation; Ski School; Skidoo; Skin Deep; Skin Game; The Sky's the Limit; Sleeper; Slight Case of Murder; Small Town Girl (1936); Smashing Time; Smile; Smiles of a Summer Night; Smiling Lieutenant; Smokey and the Bandit;

Smokey and the Bandit II; Smokey and the Bandit III; Snow White and the Three Stooges; So Fine; Soapdish; SOB; Solid Gold Cadillac; Some Kind of a Nut; Some Like it Hot; Something for Everyone; Son of Paleface; A Song is Born; Sons of the Desert; Sorrowful Jones; Soul Man; Soup for One; A Southern Yankee; Spaceballs; Speak Easily; Speechless; Spies Like Us; Spirit of '76; Splash!; Splitting Heirs; Spring Break; Squeeze; Stakeout; Stand In; Star of Midnight; Star Spangled Girl; Star Spangled Rhythm; Stars and Bars; Starstruck; Start the Revolution Without Me; Starting Over; Statue; Stay Tuned; Steamboat Bill Jr.; Steel Magnolias; Stepping Out; Sticky Fingers; The Sting; The Sting 2; Stir Crazy; Stooge; Stop! Or My Mom Will Shoot; Storm in a Teacup; Straight Talk; Strange Bedfellows; Strange Brew; Strictly Ballroom; Stripes; Stroker Ace; Suburban Commando; Sugarbaby; Sullivan's Travels; Sunday in New York; Sunset; The Sunshine Boys; The Super; Super Cops; SuperDad; Superfly; Support Your Local Gunfighter; Support Your Local Sheriff; Suppose They Gave a War and Nobody Came; Sure Thing; Survivors; Susan Slept Here; Sweet Liberty; Sweet Rosie O'Grady; Swept Away; Swimming to Cambodia; Switching Channels; Sylvia Scarlett; Take a Letter, Darling; Take Her, She's Mine; Take Me Out to the Ball Game; Take the Money and Run; Take This Job and Shove It; Taking Care of Business; Taking Off; Talk of the Town; The Tall Blond Man with One Red Shoe; The Tall Guy; The Taming of the Shrew; Tampopo; Tatie Danielle; Tea for Two; Teacher's Pet; Teachers; Teahouse of the August Moon; Teen Wolf; Teen Wolf Too; Teenage Mutant Ninja Turtles; Teenage Mutant Ninja Turtles 2; Teenage Mutant Ninja Turtles 3; Ten; Ten Thousand Bedrooms; Tender Trap; That Certain Age; That Certain Feeling; That Darn Cat!; That Lady in Ermine; That Man From Rio; That Night in Rio; That Touch of Mink; That Uncertain Feeling; That's Adequate; Theodora Goes Wild; There's a Girl in My Soup; They All Laughed; They Knew What They Wanted; The Thin Man; Things Are Tough All Over; 30 is a Dangerous Age, Cynthia; This Could Be the Night; This Is My Life; This is Spinal Tap; This Thing Called Love; Thoroughly Modern Millie; Those Daring Young Men in Their Jaunty

Jalopies; Those Magnificent Men in Their Flying Machines; Thousands Cheer; Three Amigos; Three Blind Mice; Three for the Road; Three Fugitives; Three Men and a Baby; Three Men and a Cradle; Three Men and a Little Lady; Three Ninjas; Three Ninjas Kick Back; Three O'Clock High; Three of Hearts; Three on a Couch; Three Smart Girls; Three Smart Girls Grow Up; Thrill of It All; Throw Momma from the Train; Thunder and Lightning; Tiger's Tale; Till Death Us Do Part; Tillie and Gus; Titfield Thunderbolt; To Be or Not to Be (1942); To Be or Not to Be (1983); Tobacco Road; Tom, Dick and Harry; Tom Jones; Tom Sawyer; Tommy Boy; Too Many Husbands; Tootsie; Top Secret!; Topper; Topper Returns; Topper Takes a Trip; Touch of Class; Tough Guys; Tovarich; Trading Places; The Trail of the Pink Panther; Trapped in Paradise; Travels with My Aunt; Troop Beverly Hills; Trouble in Paradise; Trouble with Angels; True Confession; True Identity; True Stories; Tugboat Annie; Tugboat Annie Sails Again; Tune in Tomorrow; Tunnel of Love; Turnabout; Turner & Hooch; Twelve Chairs; Twelve Plus One; Twentieth Century; Twin Beds; Twins; Two Girls and a Sailor; Two Way Stretch; Two-Faced Woman; The Ugly Dachshund; UHF; Uncle Buck; Under the Rainbow; Under the Yum Yum Tree; Undercover Blues; Unfaithfully Yours (1948); Unfaithfully Yours (1984); The Unsinkable Molly Brown; Up in Arms; Up in Smoke; Up the Academy; Up the Creek (1958); Up the Creek (1984); Uptown Saturday Night; Used Cars; Valley Girl; Vampire's Kiss; Vibes; Vice Versa; Victor/Victoria; Villain; Visit to a Small Planet; Vivacious Lady; Volpone; W.H.I.F.F.S.; Wackiest Ship in the Army; Waiting For the Light; Walk, Don't Run; Waltz Across Texas; The War Between Men and Women; Water; Watermelonman; Way Out West; Wayne's World; Wayne's World 2; We're Not Married; The Wedding; The Wedding Banquet; The Wedding Present; Weekend at Bernie's; Weekend at Bernie's 2; Weird Science; What a Way to Go; What About Bob?; What's New Pussycat?; What's So Bad About Feeling Good?; What's Up, Doc?; What's Up, Tiger Lily?; When Harry Met Sally; When in Rome; When You're in Love; Where Angels Go, Trouble Follows;

Where Do We Go from Here?; Where Does it Hurt?; Where the Boys Are; Where the Boys Are '84; Where the Buffalo Roam; Where the Heart Is; Where Were You When the Lights Went Out?; Where's Poppa?; Which Way is Up?; Whiskey Galore; Whistling in the Dark; White Men Can't Jump; Who Done It? (1942); Who Done It? (1957); Who Framed Roger Rabbitt?; Who is Killing the Great Chefs of Europe?; Who Was That Lady?; Who's Been Sleeping in My Bed?; Who's Harry Crumb?; Who's Minding the Mint?; Who's Minding the Store?; Who's That Girl?; Wholly Moses; Whoops! Apocalypse (1983); Whoops! Apocalypse (1986); Widows' Peak; Wife, Doctor and Nurse; Wife, Husband and Friend; Wife Versus Secretary; Wild Life; Wildcats; Wilder Napalm; Will Success Spoil Rock Hunter?; Wise Blood; Wise Guys; Wish You Were Here; Without a Clue; Without Love; Without Reservations; Without You I'm Nothing; Wives and Lovers; The Woman in Red; A Woman of Paris; Woman of the Year; Women; Women on the Verge of a Nervous Breakdown; Won Ton Ton, the Dog Who Saved Hollywood; Wonder Man; Working Girl; The World According to Garp; The World of Henry Orient; The World's Greatest Athlete; The World's Greatest Lover; The Wrecking Crew; The Wrong Arm of the Law; The Wrong Box; A Yank at Eton; A Yank at Oxford; Year of the Comet; Yellowbeard; Yolanda and the Thief; You Belong to Me; You Can Never Tell; You Can't Cheat an Honest Man; You Can't Run Away From It; You Can't Take it With You (1938); You Can't Take it With You (1986); You're a Big Boy Now; You're in the Army Now; You're in the Navy Now; You're Telling Me; Young Doctors in Love; Young Einstein; Young Frankenstein; The Young in Heart; Zapped!; Zapped Again; Zazie dans le Metro; Zelig; Zorro and the Gay Blade

Comedy & Violence (notable examples of major shifts from free-spirited comedy to serious violence): see also *Comedy-Morbid: Tragi-Comedy: Comic Thrillers:* An American Werewolf in London; Bonnie and Clyde; Bunny O'Hare; The 'burbs; 48 Hours; Foul Play; Full Metal Jacket; The Gun in Betty Lou's Handbag; I Love Trouble (1994); MASH; Natural Born Killers; True Romance

Comedy-Character (based on characters created by actors or comedians elsewhere, or built around a particularly unique, often very unreal performance): see also *Comedy-Skit: Comedians: Vaudeville:* Arkansas Traveler; The Bank Dick; The Bellboy; Billy Madison; Born in East L.A.; City Lights; Coneheads; The Delicate Delinquent; The Disorderly Orderly; The Fiendish Plot of Dr. Fu Manchu; Four Clowns; Gilda Live; The Gold Rush; The Golden Age of Comedy; In the Army Now; It's Pat; The Jerky Boys; Jour de Fete; Mr. Saturday Night; A Night at the Opera; The Nutty Professor (1963); Patsy; Pee-Wee's Big Adventure; Playtime; The Secret Policeman's Ball; The Secret Policeman's Other Ball; The Secret Policeman's Private Parts; The Secret Policeman's Third Ball; Trading Places; Twelve Chairs; Twelve Plus One; Wayne's World; Wayne's World 2; Who's Minding the Store?

Comedy-Children's: see *Disney Comedy: CHILDREN'S: Musicals-Animated*

Comedy-Disneyesque: see *Disney Comedy*

COMEDY DRAMA (Dramedy): see also *COMEDY: DRAMA: MELODRAMA: Comic Thrillers: Comic Adventure:* Abel; About Face; Above Suspicion; Accent on Love; The Accidental Tourist; According to Mrs. Hoyle; Actors and Sin; The Actress (1953); Adam and Evelyne; Adam at 6 A.M.; Adventure for Two; The Adventures of Gerard; The Adventures of Reinette and Mirabelle; The Adventures of the Wilderness Family; The Adventures of Tom Sawyer; The Affairs of Susan; Africa, Texas Style; The African Queen; The Agency; Ah, Wilderness; Alex and the Gypsy; Alex in Wonderland; Alfie; Alfredo, Alfredo; Ali Baba and the Forty Thieves; Alice Doesn't Live Here Anymore; Alice in the Cities; Alice's Restaurant; Alive and Kicking; All Creatures Great and Small; All I Want For Christmas; All Night Long (1981); All That Money Can Buy; All The Marbles; All the Way Up; All Through the Night; An Alligator Named Daisy; Almost You; Along Came Jones; Amateur Night at the Dixie Bar and Grill; American Graffiti; American Hotwax; And God Created Woman (1957); And Now, My Love; The Anderson Tapes; Androcles and the Lion;

Angel in My Pocket; Angel on My Shoulder; Angie; Animal Kingdom; Anna and the King of Siam; Annie Oakley; Anthony Adverse; Antonia and Jane; Apartment; April Fools; Are Husbands Necessary?; Aren't We All?; Arkansas Traveler; Arsene Lupin; Arsene Lupin Returns; Article 99; As You Like It (1936); As You Like It (1992); The Associate; Author! Author!; Avanti!; Aviator; Baby, It's You; Baby, Take A Bow; Babycakes; Bachelor Mother; Backbeat; Bagdad Cafe; The Ballad of Josie; Banjo on My Knee; Bank Shot; Barbary Coast; Barcelona; Battle of the Sexes; Baxter (1990); The Bears and I; Beat Street; Beat the Devil; Beau James; Beauty for the Asking; Becky Sharp; Becoming Colette; Bedtime for Bonzo; A Bedtime Story (1933); Before Sunrise; Being Human; Being There; Bell, Book, and Candle; Belle Epoque; Best Friends; Between Friends; The Big Chill; The Big Easy; The Big Fix; Big Girls Don't Cry . . . They Get Even; The Big Picture; The Bigamist; Bill; Bill: On His Own; Billie; Billy Liar; Biloxi Blues; The Bingo Long Traveling All-Stars and Motor Kings; Bishop's Wife; Black and White in Color; Black Marble; Black Sunday (1960); Blaze; Blessing; Bloodhounds of Broadway (1952); Bloodhounds of Broadway (1989); Blue Hawaii; Blume in Love; Bob&Carol&Ted&Alice; Bob Roberts; Bocaccio '70; Bon Voyage!; Bonnie and Clyde; Boom Town; Boomerang; Born Yesterday (1950); Born Yesterday (1993); Bottoms Up; Boudu Saved From Drowning; Boy Friend; Boy on a Dolphin; Boyfriends and Girlfriends; Boys from Syracuse; The Boys in the Band; Boys' Night Out; Boys on the Side; Brazil; Breakfast at Tiffany's; The Breakfast Club; Breaking Away; Breaking In; Breaking the Rules; Breaking Up is Hard to Do; Brenda Starr; Brewster McCloud; The Brinks Job; Broadcast News; Broadway Bill; Broadway Bound; The Brother From Another Planet; Brother John; Buck and the Preacher; Buddy System; Bunny O'Hare; Buona Sera, Mrs. Campbell; The Burglars; Bus Stop; Buster; Bustin' Loose; Butch Cassidy and the Sundance Kid; Butcher's Wife; Butterflies are Free; Bye Bye Braverman; Cactus Flower; Cadillac Man; Caesar and Cleopatra; Calendar Girl; California Dreaming; California Split;

California Suite; Call Me Bwana; Call Me Genius; Can Hieronymus Merkin Ever Forget Mercy Humppe and Find True Happiness?; The Candidate; Candy; Candy Mountain; Cannery Row; A Canterbury Tale; The Canterville Ghost; Captain Newman, M.D.; Captains Courageous; The Cars That Ate Paris; Casanova '70; Casanova (Fellini's Casanova); Casey's Shadow; Cash McCall; Cass Timberlane; Cat and Mouse; The Cat and the Canary (1927); The Cat and the Canary (1939); The Cat and the Canary (1979); Catch Me a Spy; The Cemetery Club; Centennial Summer; A Certain Smile; Chan is Missing; A Change of Habit; Chantilly Lace; The Chapman Report; Chapter Two; Charley and the Angel; Charlie Bubbles; Chatterbox; Cheaper by the Dozen; Children (1990); A Chorus of Disapproval; Christmas in Connecticut (1945); Christmas in Connecticut (1992); Christmas in July; The Cincinnati Kid; Circle of Friends; Cityslickers; Clara's Heart; Class; Class of '44; Claudia; Claudine; Closely Watched Trains; The Clown; Cluny Brown; The Coca-Cola Kid; Cocktail; Cocoon; Cocoon, The Return; The Color Purple; Combination Platter; Come and Get It; Come Back Charleston Blue; Come Back to the Five and Dime, Jimmy Dean, Jimmy Dean; Come Blow Your Horn; Come to the Stable; The Comedians; Comfort and Joy; Comic Commitments; The Comrades of Summer; The Cook, the Thief, His Wife & Her Lover; Cookie; Corrina, Corrina; Corvette Summer; Coupe de Ville; The Courtship of Eddie's Father; Cousin, Cousine; Cousins; Crackers; Crimes and Misdemeanors; Crimes of Passion; Crimes of the Heart; Crossroads (1986); Cyrano de Bergerac (1950); Cyrano de Bergerac (1990); D.A.R.Y.L.; Dad; Daddy Longlegs; Daddy's Dyin'; Daisy Miller; Dancing in the Dark; Dark Angel (1991); Day For Night; A Day in the Death of Joe Egg; The Day the Fish Came Out; Days of Wine and Roses (1958); Days of Wine and Roses (1962); Dazed and Confused; Dead; Dead Poet's Society; Death Takes a Holiday; The Decline of the American Empire; Desert Hearts; Design for Living; Desperately Seeking Susan; Destry Rides Again; Devil's Eye; Diamond Jim; Diamonds for Breakfast; A Different Story; Diggstown; Dim Sum: a Little Bit

of Heart; Diner; Dinner at Eight; Dion Brothers; Dirty Dozen; Divorce, Italian Style; The Divorce of Lady X; The Divorcée; Doc Hollywood; Doctor in the House; Doctor, You've Got to be Kidding; Does This Mean We're Married?; Dollars; Dominick and Eugene; Don Juan DeMarco; Don't Go Near the Water; Dona Flor and Her Two Husbands; Donovan's Reef; A Double Life; Down By Law; Dr. Jekyll and Sister Hyde; Dramatic School; Driving Miss Daisy; Dudes; Duffy's Tavern; Dutch; E.T.: The Extra-Terrestrial; Easy Living (1949); Eat the Peach; Echo Park; Educating Rita; Efficiency Expert; Electra Glide in Blue; Electric Dreams; Electric Horseman; Elena and Her Men; Eleven Harrowhouse; The Elusive Pimpernel; Emma; Emperor Waltz; Enchanted April; The End of Innocence; End of the Line; The End of the World . . . ; Ensign Pulver; Enter Laughing; Entertaining Mr. Sloane; Escape Artist; Evelyn Prentice; Even Cowgirls Get the Blues; Experience Preferred . . . ; The Experts; Expresso Bongo; Exterminating Angel; The Facts of Life; Fandango; Fanny; Fanny Hill; Faraway, So Close!; The Farmer Takes a Wife; Farmer's Daughter; Fast Company; Fast Times at Ridgemont High; Father Goose; Father Hood; Father is a Bachelor; Father of the Bride (1950); Father of the Bride (1991); The Feud; Field of Dreams; Fireman's Ball; First Monday in October; First Time; Fitzwilly; Five Corners; Five Heartbeats; The Flame of New Orleans; Flame of the Barbary Coast; Flamingo Kid; Fletch; Fletch Lives; Flim Flam Man; Flirting FM; Follow Me, Boys!; Follow That Dream; Fool for Love; Fools Parade; Footloose; For Keeps; For Love of Ivy; For Love or Money (1963); For Love or Money (1993); For Me and My Gal; For the Boys; A Foreign Affair; Forest Rangers; Forever Darling; Forever Female; Forrest Gump; Fortune Cookie; Forty Carats; Forty Pounds of Trouble; Four Daughters; Four Friends; Four Seasons; Four Weddings and a Funeral; Four-Poster; Frankie and Johnny; Fraternity Row; French Postcards; Fried Green Tomatoes; Frog Prince; From the Hip; The Front; The Front Page (1931); The Front Page (1974); Fugitive Lovers; Full Moon in Blue Water; Fun Down There; Funny About Love; Funny Girl;

Funny Lady; Fuzz; Gabriel over the White House; Gaily, Gaily; Gambit; Garbo Talks; Gas Food Lodging; Gassss; Generation; Genevieve; Gentleman Jim; Georgy Girl; Get Out Your Handkerchiefs; The Getting of Wisdom; Getting Straight; Ghost; Ghost and Mrs. Muir; Gidget; Gigi (1948); Gigi (1958); Gilded Lily; Gin Game; Ginger and Fred; Girlfriends; The Girl in the Watermelon; Glamour Boy; Glory! Glory!; Go-Fish; Go into Your Dance; Goin' South; Going in Style; Going My Way; The Golden Child; Good Companions (1933); Good Companions (1956); The Good Die Young; Good Morning, Vietnam; Good Sam; Goodbye Columbus; Goodbye, My Fancy; The Goodbye People; The Graduate; Grand Highway; The Grass is Greener; Great Balls of Fire; Great Expectations; The Great Garrick; The Great Impostor; The Great Lover (1931); The Greatest; Green Card; Green Pastures; The Green Years; Gregory's Girl; Groundhog Day; Guarding Tess; Guardsman; Gumshoe; Gung Ho (1986); A Guy Named Joe; Hail the Conquering Hero; Half a Sixpence; Handle with Care; Hannah and Her Sisters; The Happiest Millionaire; Happy Birthday, Wanda June; Happy Land; Happy Time; Hard Promises; Hard to Handle; Harry and Tonto; Harry in Your Pocket; Hawks; He Was Her Man; Hear My Song; Heartbreak Kid; Heartbreak Ridge; Heartburn; Heaven Can Wait (1943); Heaven Can Wait (1978); Heaven Help Us; Heaven Knows, Mr. Allison; Heaven Only Knows; Heavenly Pursuits; Heidi (1939); Here Comes Mr. Jordan; Here Comes the Groom; Here Comes the Navy; Hero; A Hero Ain't Nothin' but a Sandwich; Heroes; Hey, Good Lookin'; High Heels; High Hopes; High Season; Hobson's Choice; Hold Your Man; A Hole in the Head; Holiday; Home Alone; Home Alone 2: Lost in New York; Honeymoon; Honeymoon in Vegas; The Honeymoon Machine; Honeysuckle Rose; Honky Tonk; Hoosiers; The Horse in the Grey Flannel Suit; Horse's Mouth; The Hospital; The Hotel New Hampshire; Houdini; Household Saints; Housekeeping; The Hudsucker Proxy; Husbands; Husbands and Wives; I am a Camera; I Don't Buy Kisses Anymore; I Don't Want to Talk About it; I Know Where I'm Going; I Like it Like That; I Love My Wife; I Love Trouble (1994); I Love You, Alice B. Toklas; I Ought to Be in Pictures; I Remember Mama; I Take this Woman; I Wanna Hold Your Hand; I Was an Adventuress; I'll Give a Million; I'll Never Forget Whatshisname; I've Heard the Mermaids Singing; If I Had My Way; If I Were King; If It's Tuesday, This Must Be Belgium; Impatient Years; Impromptu; Improper Channels; In Old Kentucky; The Incredible Shrinking Woman; Indiscreet; Innocents in Paris (1953); Inside Daisy Clover; Inside Monkey Zetterland; Inside Moves; Insignificance; Into the Night; Into the Sun; The Irish in Us; Irma La Douce; Iron Petticoat; Irreconcilable Differences; It All Came True; It Always Rains on Sunday; It Could Happen to You; It Happened in Brooklyn; It Happened on Fifth Avenue; It Happened Tomorrow; It Started in Naples; It's a Wonderful Life; It's My Turn; The Italian Straw Hat; Jack and Sarah; Jack of Diamonds; Jackpot; Jo Jo Dancer, Your Life is Calling; Joe vs. the Volcano; Joey Breaker; Johnny Suede; Joke of Destiny; Julia Misbehaves; Juliet of the Spirits; Jungle Fever; Just Another Girl on the IRT; Kaos; Kentucky; Key Exchange; Key to the City; A Kid for Two Farthings; The Kid from Left Field; Kim; Kindergarten Cop; A King in New York; King Lear (1987); The King of Comedy; King of Hearts; King, Queen, Knave; Kipps; Kiss in the Dark; Kiss Me Goodbye; Kitty; Kitty Foyle; Knack; Knave of Hearts; Knickerbocker Holiday; Kotch; L'Invitation; The L-Shaped Room; La Nuit de Varennes; La Ronde (1950); La Ronde (1964); La Vie Continue; Ladies in Retirement; The Ladies They Talk About; Lady Caroline Lamb; Lady for a Day; Lady Godiva; Lady Killer (1933); Lady L.; Lady Takes a Flyer; The Landlord; Larceny, Inc.; The Last American Hero; The Last of Mrs. Cheyney; Late for Dinner; The Late George Apley; Late Show; The Lavender Hill Mob; Law and Disorder (1974); Law of Desire; Lawrenceville Stories; The League of Gentlemen; A League of Their Own; Leap of Faith; Leaving Normal; Les Visiteurs du Soir; A Lesson in Love; Let it Ride; Let's Hope it's a Girl; Let's Make it Legal; Letter to Brezhnev; Letter to Three Wives; Lies My Father Told Me; The Life and Death of Colonel Blimp; The Life and Times of Judge Roy Bean; Life is Cheap, but Toilet Paper is Expensive; Life is Sweet; The Life of Riley; Life Upside Down; Life With Father; Life With Mikey Lightnin'; Lilies of the Field; Lily in Love; Limit Up; Little Man Tate; Little Miss Marker (1934); Little Miss Marker (1980); Little Murders; Little Noises; The Little Princess; A Little Romance; The Little Thief; Little Women (1933); Little Women (1949); Little Women (1978); Little Women (1994); Live a Little, Steal a Lot; Live, Love and Learn; Living in a Big Way; Living in Oblivion; Local Hero; London Belongs to Me; London Kills Me; The Lonely Guy; Lonely Hearts; Lookin' to Get Out; Loophole; Loot; The Lords of Flatbush; Loser Takes All; Lost Angel; Lost Boys; Lost in America; Lost in Yonkers; Love Affair (1932); Love Among the Ruins; Love and Pain and the Whole Damn Thing; Love at Large; Love Hurts; Love in the Afternoon; Love Nest; Love Story (1970); Love With the Proper Stranger; The Loved One; Lovers and Other Strangers; Loves of a Blonde; Lovesick; Lovin' Molly; Lucky Lady; Lucky Star; Lunatics, A Love Story; Lunch on the Grass; Lured; M*A*S*H; Macaroni; Mad Dog and Glory; Madame Sousatzka; Made for Each Other; The Madwoman of Chaillot; Magic Town; Majority of One; Make Me an Offer; Malcolm; The Male Animal; Man of Flowers; The Man Who Broke the Bank at Monte Carlo; The Man Who Could Work Miracles; The Man Who Loved Women (1977); The Man Who Loved Women (1983); The Man Who Shot Liberty Valance; The Man Who Understood Women; The Man with Bogart's Face; Margie; Marquise of O; Marriage of a Young Stockbroker; Marriage on the Rocks; The Marrying Kind; Mary, Mary; Mask (1985); Mass Appeal; Mastergate; Match Factory Girl; Matchmaker; Mating Game; Mating of Willie; The Mating Season; A Matter of Time; Max Dugan Returns; May Fools; Me and Him; Me and My Gal; Me and the Colonel; Me, Natalie; Medicine Man; Mediterraneo; Meet John Doe; Meet the People; Meet the Stewarts; Meeting Venus; Melody; Melvin and Howard; Memoirs of an Invisible Man; Men Don't Leave; Men of Boys' Town; Mermaids; Metropolitan (1990); Middle Age Crazy; A Midsummer Night's Sex Comedy;

Mignon Has Left; The Milagro Beanfield War; The Millionaire; The Millionairess; Min and Bill; Minnie and Moskowitz; The Miracle (1990); The Miracle of the Bells; Miracle on 34th Street (1947); The Miracle Woman; Miranda; The Missionary; Mississippi Masala; Mister Cory; Mistress; Mixed Company; Mixed Nuts; The Model and the Marriage Broker; Moderns; Mogambo; Momma, There's a Man in Your Bed; The Moon is Blue; Moon Spinners; Morning Glory; Moscow on the Hudson; Mother Carey's Chickens; Mother Wore Tights; Mountain Eagle; Movers and Shakers; Movie Movie; Mr. and Mrs. Smith; Mr. Deeds Goes to Town; Mr. Drake's Duck; Mr. Hobbs Takes a Vacation; Mr. Jones; Mr. Lucky; Mr. North; Mr. Saturday Night; Mr. Smith Goes to Washington; Mr. Wonderful; Mr. and Mrs. Bridge; Mrs Doubtfire; Mrs. Parker and the Vicious Circle; Mrs. Pollifax, Spy; Mrs. Wiggs of the Cabbage Patch; Mudlark; Murder, Inc.; Murphy's Romance; The Music of Chance; The Music Teacher; My Beautiful Laundrette; My Best Friend's Girl; My Blue Heaven (1950); My Bodyguard; My Father is Coming; My Little Girl; My New Gun; My Six Loves; My Wife's Best Friend; Mystery Train; Mystic Pizza; Nashville; Natural Born Killers; Never Cry Wolf; Never on Sunday; New Life; New Year's Day; New York Stories; Next Stop, Greenwich Village; Nice Little Bank That Should Be Robbed; Night after Night; Night in Heaven; A Night in the Life of Jimmy Reardon; Night of the Comet; Night on Earth; The Night They Raided Minsky's; The Night We Never Met; Nights of Cabiria; 1969; 9/30/55; 92 in the Shade; No Down Payment; No Man of Her Own; No No Nanette (1930); No No Nanette (1940); No Small Affair; No Time for Love; No Way to Treat a Lady; Nobody's Fool (1986); Nobody's Fool (1994); Noir et Blanc; North Dallas Forty; Nothing in Common; Notorious Landlady; Now and Forever; O'Hara's Wife; Object of Beauty; Oh, Mr. Porter; Oh, Rosalinda!; Oh, What a Lovely War; Oh, What a Night; Oklahoma!; Old Acquaintance; The Oldest Profession; Oliver!; Olly Olly Oxen Free; On a Clear Day You Can See Forever; On Golden Pond; Once Around; Once in a Blue Moon; Once More with Feeling; Once Upon a

Honeymoon; One Hour with You; One Touch of Venus; Only Angels Have Wings; Only the Lonely; Only Two Can Play; Operation Mad Ball; The Opposite Sex and How to Live With Them; Orphans; Other People's Money; Our Man in Havana; Over the Brooklyn Bridge; P.K and the Kid; Pain in the A . . . ; Paint Your Wagon; Pal Joey; Papa's Delicate Condition; The Paper; Paper Lion; Paper Moon; Pardon Mon Affaire; Parenthood; Passed Away; Paternity; Patti Rocks; Pauline at the Beach; Peggy Sue Got Married; Penelope; Pennies from Heaven (1936); Pennies from Heaven (1981); People Will Talk; Peppermint Soda; Perfect; Perfect Couple; Perfect Marriage; Personal Services; Pete 'n Tillie; Phffft!; The Pickwick Papers; Plain Clothes; Plaza Suite; Pocketful of Miracles; Pollyanna; Popeye; Popi; Pornographers; The Portrait; The Positively True Adventures of the Alleged Texas Cheerleader-Murdering Mom; Postcards from the Edge; Prelude to a Kiss; Presenting Lily Mars; The President's Analyst; Pretty Poison; The Prince and the Showgirl; The Prince of Central Park; Princess Caraboo; Prisoner of Second Avenue; Prisoner of Zenda (1937); Prisoner of Zenda (1952); Prisoner of Zenda (1979); The Private Affairs of Bel Ami; The Private Life of Sherlock Holmes; The Prize; Prizzi's Honor; Puberty Blues; Pulp Fiction; Pump Up the Volume; Punchline; Quackser Fortune Has a Cousin in the Bronx; Quartet (1948); Queen of Hearts; Queens Logic; Quicksilver; Quiet Wedding; The Rachel Papers; Raffles; Rally Round the Flag, Boys; Rambling Rose; Rancho De Luxe; Rat Race; Reality Bites; Red Sky at Morning; The Reivers; The Reluctant Debutante; Renaissance Man; Repo Man; Return of the Secaucus Seven; Return to Macon County; Reuben, Reuben; Rich and Famous; Rich Kids; The Richest Girl in the World; Riff-Raff (1991); The Right Stuff; Rikky and Pete; Rio Bravo; Risky Business; Rita, Sue and Bob, Too; Roadside Prophets; Robert et Robert; Robin and Marian; Roman Holiday; Romanoff and Juliet; Romantic Comedy; Roommates; A Room with a View; Rosalie Goes Shopping; Rosencrantz and Guildenstern Are Dead; Rosie; Rough Cut; Roustabout; Rules of the Game; Ruling Class; Saint Benny, the Dip; Saint

Jack; Sally of the Sawdust; Salome's Last Dance; Salty O'Rourke; Samantha; Same Time, Next Year; Sammy and Rosie Get Laid; San Francisco Story; Saratoga; Satisfaction; Saving Grace; Say Anything; Scenes from a Mall; Scent of a Woman; School Daze; Scorchers; The Scout; Scrooged; Second Thoughts; The Secret Life of an American Wife; Secrets; The Seduction of Mimi; Sergeant York; Serial; The Servant; Seven Beauties; Seven Thieves; Seventeen; S.F.W.; Shag; Shakespeare Wallah; Shaking the Tree; Shanghai Surprise; She Couldn't Say No; She's Gotta Have It; She's Having a Baby; She's Working Her Way Through College; Sheepman; Shirley Valentine; Shocking Miss Pilgrim; Shop Around the Corner; Short Cuts; Show-Off; Sidewalks of London; Simple Men; Sing; Sing as We Go; Sing You Sinners; Singles; Sirens; Situation Hopeless But Not Serious; Six Degrees of Separation; Six in Paris; Skin Deep; Skin Game; Skippy; Slacker; Slap Shot; Slaughterhouse Five; Slaves of New York; Sleepless in Seattle; Sleuth; Slither; Small Change; Small Circle of Friends; Smart Woman; Smiles of a Summer Night; The Smiling Lieutenant; The Snapper; So Dear to My Heart; SOB; Soldier in the Rain; Solid Gold Cadillac; Some Girls; Some Kind of Hero; Some Kind of Wonderful; Somebody Up There Likes Me; Something for Everyone; Something Wild (1986); Song of the South; Sons of Katie Elder; Sorrowful Jones; The Sound of Music; Soup for One; Southern Star; Special Day; Special Delivery; Spencer's Mountain; Spetters; The Spirit of St. Louis; Spitfire; Square Dance; St. Elmo's Fire; St. Martin's Lane; Stacy's Knights; Stage Struck; Stagedoor; Staircase; Stalag 17; Stand and Deliver; Stand by Me; Stand Up and Be Counted; Starman; Starting Over; State Fair (1933); State Fair (1945); State Fair (1962); State of the Union; Stay Hungry; Steagle; Steaming; Steel Magnolias; Steelyard Blues; Stepping Out; The Sterile Cuckoo; The Sting; The Sting 2; Stolen Kisses; The Story of Dr. Wassell; The Story of Will Rogers; Stranger Than Paradise; Strangers in Good Company; Strawberry Blonde; Such Good Friends; Sugarbaby; Sugarland Express; Sullivan's Travels; The Sum of Us; Summer of '42; Sunburn; The Sunshine Boys; Surrender; Survivors; Susan and God; Suzy; The Swan;

Sweeney Todd, Demon Barber of Fleet Street; Sweet Charity; Sweet Liberty; Sweet Lorraine; Sweet November; Sweethearts Dance; Sweetie; Swing; Swing High, Swing Low; Swing Shift; Switch; Sylvia and the Ghost; Sylvia Scarlett; Taking Off; Tales of Manhattan; Talk of the Town; Tall, Dark and Handsome; Tall Story; The Taming of the Shrew; Tammy and the Bachelor; Tank; A Taste of Honey; Tatie Danielle; A Taxing Woman; Teachers; Teahouse of the August Moon; Tell Me a Riddle; Teresa; Terms of Endearment; Test Pilot; Texasville; That Darn Cat!; That Obscure Object of Desire; That Uncertain Feeling; That's Life!; Thelma & Louise; Theodora Goes Wild; There Was a Crooked Man; There's No Business Like Show Business; They Might be Giants; They Won't Believe Me; The Thief Who Came to Dinner; Thieves Like Us; Thing Called Love; Things Change; This Happy Feeling; This Is My Life; Those Were the Days; A Thousand Clowns; Three Coins in the Fountain; Three Cornered Moon; Three Godfathers; Three Men and a Baby; Three Men and a Cradle; Three Men and a Little Lady; Three of Hearts; Threesome; Thursday's Game; Tie Me Up! Tie Me Down!; Time for Loving; Time of Your Life; Tin Men; To Forget Venice; To Sleep with Anger; To Wong Foo, Thanks for Everything, Julie Newmar; Tobacco Road; Together Again; Tokyo Pop; Tokyo Story; Tom, Dick and Harry; Tom Sawyer; Top Secret Affair; Topkapi!; Tough Guys Don't Dance; Tovarich; Toys; Trade Winds; Travels with My Aunt; Trial and Error; Tribes; Trip to Bountiful; Trouble Along the Way; Trouble in Mind; Trouble in Paradise; The Trouble with Girls; The Trouble with Harry; True Love; Truly, Madly, Deeply; Trust; Tune in Tomorrow; Turtle Diary; Twenty Bucks; 21; 29th Street; Twice in a Lifetime; Two for the Seesaw; Two Mules for Sister Sara; Two of a Kind; UFOria; Umberto D.; Uncle Buck; Up the Creek (1958); Up the Sandbox; Urban Cowboy; Used People; Utz; Valentino Returns; VIPs; Virgin Soldiers; Viridiana; The Visit; Viva Maria!; Volpone; Voltaire; W.C. Fields and Me; W.W. & The Dixie Dancekings; Wait 'Til the Sun Shines, Nellie; Wait Until Spring, Bandini; Waiting For the Light; Walk, Don't Run; The War Between Men and Women; War of the Roses; Warrior's Husband; Watch It; Waterdance; We Think the World of You; We're No Angels (1955); We're No Angels (1989); Weekend at the Waldorf; Welcome Home, Roxy Carmichael; Wells Fargo; Went the Day Well?; The Westerner; What?; What's Eating Gilbert Grape?; When in Rome; When My Baby Smiles at Me; When You're in Love; Where Angels Fear to Tread; Where Angels Go, Trouble Follows; Where the Buffalo Roam; Where the Heart Is; Where the Spies Are; Whistle Down the Wind; White Men Can't Jump; Who is Harry Kellerman . . . ; Who's That Knocking at My Door?; Whoops! Apocalypse (1983); Whoops! Apocalypse (1986); Whore; Whose Life Is it Anyway?; Why Shoot the Teacher?; Widows' Peak; Wife, Doctor and Nurse; Wild West; Willie and Phil; Willy Wonka and the Chocolate Factory; Wilt; Window to Paris; Wings of Desire; Wired; Wish You Were Here; Witches; Witches of Eastwick; Withnail and I; A Woman is a Woman; Woman Times Seven; Won Ton Ton, the Dog Who Saved Hollywood; Wonder Man; The Wonderful World of the Brothers Grimm; Working Girl; The World According to Garp; The World of Henry Orient; A Yank at Eton; A Yank at Oxford; Yellow Rolls Royce; Yesterday, Today and Tomorrow; You Can Never Tell; You're a Big Boy Now; Youngblood; Yours, Mine and Ours; Zandy's Bride; Zorba, The Greek

Comedy-Gag (with sight gag jokes, not just slapstick or pratfalls): see also *Comedy-Slapstick: COMEDY: Spoofs: Comedy-Skit: Marx Brothers: Jerry Lewis Movies:* Airplane!; Airplane 2, the Sequel; Animal Crackers; At the Circus; The Brady Bunch Movie; The Disorderly Orderly; Hellzapoppin'; Naked Gun; Naked Gun 2½; Naked Gun 33⅓; The Nutty Professor; On the Air; Police Academy; Police Squad! Help Wanted!; Robin Hood, Men in Tights; The Secret Policeman's Ball; The Secret Policeman's Other Ball; The Secret Policeman's Private Parts; The Secret Policeman's Third Ball; Top Secret!

Comedy-Light (the laughs aren't big, but they should be there): see also *Comedy of Manners: Comic Mystery: Comic Thriller:* All Night Long (1981); Almost an Angel; Arsène Lupin; Arsene Lupin Returns; Bagdad Cafe; Barnacle Bill (1957); Better Late Than Never; Big Deal on Madonna Street; Breaking In; Brewster McCloud; A Chorus of Disapproval; Cluny Brown; Cops and Robbersons; Cross My Heart; Crossing Delancey; Desk Set; Divorce, Italian Style; Experience Preferred . . . ; Family Plot; The Fortune; The Frisco Kid (1979); Full Moon in Blue Water; Garbo Talks; Holiday; The Hotel New Hampshire; Little Treasure; Melvin and Howard; Monsieur Hulot's Holiday; Monsieur Verdoux; Movers and Shakers; My New Gun; Paris When it Sizzles; Playtime; Popeye; Ready to Wear; Rebecca's Daughters; Rikky and Pete; Roman Holiday; A Room with a View; Rubin and Ed; Simple Men; Somebody Killed Her Husband; They All Laughed; Trouble in Paradise; Truly, Madly, Deeply; UFOria; Without Love

Comedy-Morbid (having to do with death or grotesqueries somehow): see also *Black Comedy: Death-Dealing with: Tragi-Comedy: Violence in Comedy:* The Addams Family; Addams Family Values; Arsenic and Old Lace; Billy Liar; Black Sunday (1960); Blood Simple; Blue Velvet; Brimstone and Treacle; Bye Bye Braverman; Child's Play (1988); Child's Play 2; Child's Play 3; Comedy of Terrors; Compromising Positions; Consuming Passions; The Cook, the Thief, His Wife & Her Lover; Crimes of the Heart; Desperate Living; Dion Brothers; The Discreet Charm of Bourgeoisie; Do You Like Women?; Dr. Giggles; Dr. Heckyl and Mr. Hype; Eaten Alive; Eating Raoul; Ed Wood; The End; Entertaining Mr. Sloane; Folks!; Frankenhooker; Frenzy; Full Metal Jacket; Grace Quigley; Harold and Maude; Heathers; I Love You to Death; Joe vs. the Volcano; Kalifornia; Killing Dad; Kind Hearts and Coronets; Little Murders; Little Shop of Horrors (1960); Little Shop of Horrors (1986); Loot; Love and Death; The Loved One; Mad Love; Mad Room; Man Bites Dog; The Man with Two Brains; Match Factory Girl; Miami Blues; Monsieur Verdoux; Oh, Dad, Poor Dad . . . ; Out Cold; Rabid Grannies; Repentance; Robocop; Robocop 2; Santa Sangre; Scandalous!; Serial Mom; Short Time; Slight Case of Murder; Society; Sweeney Todd, Demon Barber of Fleet Street; The Trouble with Harry; Unfaithfully Yours (1948); Unfaithfully Yours (1984); The Wrong

Box; An American Werewolf in London; Beetlejuice; Brittania Hospital; Buddy Buddy; Death Becomes Her

Comedy of Errors (the humor comes out of the farcical mistakes inevitably leading to confusion, etc): see also *FARCE: Screwball: Comedy: Murphy's Law Stories: Unlucky People: Accident Prone: Misunderstandings: Mistaken Identities: Criminals-Stupid: House Havoc:* Adventures in Babysitting; The Adventures of Barry McKenzie; The Affairs of Annabel; An Alligator Named Daisy; Armed and Dangerous; Artists and Models (1955); Bananas; The Bank Dick; Barnacle Bill (1957); The Bellboy; Best Defense; The Big Bus; Big Deal on Madonna Street; The Big Store; Blind Date (1987); The Blues Brothers; Boys from Syracuse; Brazil; Bread and Chocolate; The Bride Came C.O.D.; The Brinks Job; Buck Privates; Caught in the Draft; Cheap Detective; Clockwise; Club Paradise; Cool Runnings; Did You Hear the One About the Travelling Saleslady?; The Disorderly Orderly; Disorganized Crime; Doughgirls; Dr. Strangelove; Erik The Viking; Errand Boy; Every Home Should Have One; Fawlty Towers; A Fish Called Wanda; Folks!; For Pete's Sake; The Freshman (1925); George Washington Slept Here; The Gold Rush; The Great Race; Greetings; Happening; The Happiest Days of Your Life; Harold Lloyd's World of Comedy; Her Alibi; Her Husband's Affairs; The Horn Blows at Midnight; The Hospital; The Hot Rock; Hot Stuff; I Love You to Death; In Society; In-Laws; Inspector Clouseau; Invisible Woman; Invitation to the Wedding; It Ain't Hay; It's a Gift; It's Only Money; Italian Job; The Italian Straw Hat; Johnny Stecchino; Jour de Fete; Kid Brother; The Kid from Brooklyn; The Lavender Hill Mob; The Lemon Drop Kid; Little Giant (1946); The Little Rascals; The Long Long Trailer; Loose Ankles; Loot; Love at First Bite; Ma and Pa Kettle; The Man with Bogart's Face; Me and Him; Miracles; Money from Home; The Money Pit; Monkey Business (1931); Monsieur Hulot's Holiday; The Mouse That Roared; Mr. Blandings Builds His Dream House; Music Box; My Favorite Year; National Lampoon's Christmas Vacation; National Lampoon's European Vacation; National Lampoon's Vacation; The Navigator; Necessary

Roughness; Never Give a Sucker an Even Break; A Night at the Opera; A Night in Casablanca; 1941; On the Air; Once Upon a Crime; Outoftowners; Over Her Dead Body; The Owl and the Pussycat; Pardon Mon Affaire; The Party; Patsy; The Pink Panther; The Pink Panther Strikes Again; Planes, Trains, and Automobiles; Police Academy; Police Squad! Help Wanted!; Problem Child; Problem Child 2; The Producers; Quick Change; Ritz; Rock a Bye Baby; Running Scared; The Russians Are Coming, The Russians Are Coming; Safety Last; Second Sight; See No Evil, Hear No Evil; The Shakiest Gun in the West; She'll Be Wearing Pink Pajamas; Short Circuit; Short Circuit 2; Silent Movie; Sons of the Desert; Spaceballs; Special Delivery; Spies Like Us; Stars and Bars; Steamboat Bill Jr.; Sticky Fingers; Stir Crazy; Three Fugitives; Turner & Hooch; Visit to a Small Planet; The Wackiest Ship in the Army; We're Not Married; The Wedding Banquet; Weekend; Weekend at Bernie's; Weekend at Bernie's 2; Wise Guys; You Can't Cheat an Honest Man; You Can't Take it With You (1938); You Can't Take it With You (1986); You're in the Navy Now; You're Telling Me; Young Frankenstein; Zazie dans le Metro

Comedy of Manners (the humor comes out of behavior in a more intellectual, subtle approach): see also *Comedy-Light: Romantic Comedy:* Animal Kingdom; Aren't We All?; Blithe Spirit; Boys from Syracuse; Cluny Brown; Daisy Miller; The Europeans; The Grass is Greener; The Great Catherine; The Great Garrick; The Importance of Being Earnest; Love Among the Ruins; Metropolitan (1990); Midnight (1939); The Millionairess; My Fair Lady; Phantom of Liberty; The Pickwick Papers; A Room with a View; School for Husbands; School for Scandal; Show-Off; The Taming of the Shrew; Where Angels Fear to Tread; Whiskey Galore

Comedy-Performance (from stand-up to one-person shows, usually taped): see also *Comedians: Comedy-Skit: Comedy-Character: One Performer Shows:* Divine Madness; Gilda Live; Good Morning, Vietnam; Monster in a Box

Comedy-Physical: see *Comedy-Slapstick*

Comedy-Situation (the humor comes out of the particular predicament the characters are together stuck in): see also *Trapped: Sharing a Home: Marriages-Fake:* Bachelor and the Bobby-Soxer; The Blessed Event; Brewster's Millions (1935); Brewster's Millions (1945); Brewster's Millions (1985); The Check is in the Mail; The Doctor Takes a Wife; Echo Park; Frozen Assets; The Goodbye Girl; Green Card; I Take this Woman; I'd Rather Be Rich; It Ain't Hay; It's a Small World; The Italian Straw Hat; Just You and Me; The Man Who Came to Dinner; Mediterraneo; The More the Merrier; My Friend Irma; No Room for the Groom; The Odd Couple; Overboard; Talk of the Town; Without Love

Comedy-Skit (based on skits or like skits in that the story or humor is possibly one-note): see also *Comedy Performance: Comedy-Character: Vaudeville: Comedy-Gag: Saturday Night Live Movies:* Amazon Women on the Moon; And Now For Something Completely Different; The Blues Brothers; The Caddy; Car Wash; Coneheads; A Day at the Races; Erik The Viking; Every Thing You Always Wanted to Know About Sex . . . ; Gilda Live; History of the World Part One; Hollywood Revue of 1929; Hollywood Shuffle; John Cleese on How to Irritate People; Kentucky Fried Movie; Kentucky Moonshine; The Magic Christian; The Man on the Flying Trapeze; Meatballs; Monty Python and the Holy Grail; Monty Python's Life of Brian; Monty Python's The Meaning of Life; Mother, Jugs and Speed; Moving Violations (1985); National Lampoon's Class Reunion; National Lampoon's Movie Madness; The Naughty Nineties; Rent a Dick; The Secret Policeman's Ball; The Secret Policeman's Other Ball; The Secret Policeman's Private Parts; The Secret Policeman's Third Ball; Stay Tuned; Stooge; Strange Brew; Stripes; Up in Smoke; Wayne's World; Wayne's World 2

Comedy-Slapstick (very physical and broad, pratfalls, etc.): see also *Comedy-Gag: Comedy-Character: Comedy-Skit: COMEDY: Screwball Comedy: FARCE: Comedy of Errors: Accident Prone:* Abbott & Costello Go to Mars; Abbott & Costello in Hollywood; Abbott & Costello in the Foreign Legion; Abbott & Costello Meet Captain Kidd; Abbott & Costello Meet Dr. Jekyll and Mr. Hyde; Abbott & Costello Meet Frankenstein; Abbott &

Costello Meet the Invisible Man; Abbott & Costello Meet the Keystone Cops; Abbott & Costello Meet the Killer: Boris Karloff; Abbott & Costello Meet the Mummy; Ace Ventura, Pet Detective; Adventures of Sherlock Holmes' Smarter Brother; Africa Screams; Ali Baba Goes to Town; Amazon Women on the Moon; American Dreamer; And Now For Something Completely Different; Artists and Models (1955); Assassination Bureau; The Bellboy; Big Mouth; The Big Store; Blind Date (1987); Bobo; Boeing-Boeing; Brain Donors; Caddyshack; Caddyshack 2; The Cameraman; Cat Ballou; Cinderfella; City Lights; Clean Slate; Comfort and Joy; Cops and Robbersons; A Day at the Races; Dirty Rotten Scoundrels; The Disorderly Orderly; Don't Raise the Bridge, Lower the Water!; Dragnet (1987); Erik The Viking; Ernest Goes to Camp; Ernest Goes to Jail; Ernest Rides Again; Ernest Saves Christmas; Ernest Scared Stupid; Errand Boy; Every Thing You Always Wanted to Know About Sex . . . ; The Fiendish Plot of Dr. Fu Manchu; A Fine Mess; Fletch Lives; Folks!; Four Clowns; Free and Easy; The Freshman (1925); The Fuller Brush Girl; The Fuller Brush Man; A Funny Thing Happened on the Way to the Forum; The General; The Girl Most Likely to . . . (1971); Go West; The Gold Rush; The Golden Age of Comedy; The Great Catherine; The Great Outdoors; The Great Race; Harold Lloyd's World of Comedy; Her Alibi; Herbie Goes Bananas; Herbie Goes to Monte Carlo; Herbie Rides Again; Hook, Line and Sinker; The Horn Blows at Midnight; Hot Shots!; Hot Shots, Part Deux; Hot Stuff; I Dood It!; In-Laws; In the Army Now; The Jerk; Johnny Stecchino; Jour de Fete; Jumpin' Jack Flash; The Kid (1921); Kid Brother; The Kid from Brooklyn; Ladies' Man (1961); Last of the Secret Agents; Life Stinks!; Living it Up; Long Long Trailer; Love and Death; Love at First Bite; Milky Way (1936); The Money Pit; Monkey Business (1952); Monsieur Hulot's Holiday; Monty Python and the Holy Grail; Monty Python's Life of Brian; Monty Python's The Meaning of Life; Moving Violations (1985); Mr. Mom; Mrs Doubtfire; Music Box (1932); My Favorite Blonde; My Favorite Year; Naked Gun; Naked Gun 2½; Naked Gun 33⅓; National Lampoon's

Christmas Vacation; National Lampoon's Vacation; The Navigator; Never Give a Sucker an Even Break; A Night at the Opera; No Time for Love; Nuns on the Run; The Nutty Professor (1963); O.C. and Stiggs; On the Air; Our Hospitality; Parlor, Bedroom and Bath; The Party; The Pink Panther; Police Academy; Problem Child; Problem Child 2; The Return of the Pink Panther; Robin Hood, Men in Tights; Roman Scandals; Room Service; Safety Last; Sailor Beware; Seven Chances; Shot in the Dark; Silent Movie; Silver Streak; Skin Deep; Snow White and the Three Stooges; SOB; Son of Paleface; Sons of the Desert; Speak Easily; Start the Revolution Without Me; Steamboat Bill Jr.; Stir Crazy; Tillie's Punctured Romance; Top Secret!; The Trail of the Pink Panther; Tugboat Annie; Turner & Hooch; Twelve Chairs; Twelve Plus One; Up in Arms; Up the Creek (1984); Used Cars; Vice Versa; Villain; Visit to a Small Planet; The Wackiest Ship in the Army; Wayne's World; Wayne's World 2; Who's Minding the Store?; Who's That Girl?; Whoopee; You Can't Cheat an Honest Man; Young Einstein; You're in the Army Now; You're Telling Me; Zorro and the Gay Blade

Comic Adventure: see also *Comic Thriller:* **ADVENTURE:** The Adventures of Robin Hood; Allan Quatermain and the Lost City of Gold; Around the World in 80 Days; Baby, Secret of the Lost Legend; Barbarella; Bill & Ted's Bogus Journey; Bill & Ted's Excellent Adventure; Butch Cassidy and the Sundance Kid; Call Me Bwana; Candy; Casper; Castaway Cowboy; Chattanooga Choo Choo; Crocodile Dundee; E.T.: The Extra-Terrestrial; The Elusive Pimpernel; Fanny Hill; The Gold Rush; The Golden Child; Goonies; Gunga Din; Hatari!; High Road to China; Honey, I Blew Up the Kid; Honey, I Shrunk the Kids; Ladyhawke; The Last Remake of Beau Geste; Monty Python and the Holy Grail; North; North to Alaska; The Prince and the Pauper (1937); The Princess Bride; Prisoner of Zenda (1937); Prisoner of Zenda (1952); Prisoner of Zenda (1979); Raiders of the Lost Ark; Road to Bali; Road to Hong Kong; Road to Morocco; Road to Rio; Road to Singapore; Road to Utopia; Road to Zanzibar; Romancing the Stone; Royal Flash; Southern Star; Spacehunter, Adventures in the

Forbidden Zone; Tarzan and His Mate; Tarzan Escapes; Tarzan, The Ape Man (1932); Tarzan, the Ape Man (1981); That Man From Rio; The Three Musketeers (1939); The Three Musketeers (1973); The Three Musketeers (1993); Tom Sawyer; Travels with My Aunt

Comic Heroes (based upon comic book characters): see also *Superheroes:* *Heroes-Classic: Cartoons:* The Adventures of Buckaroo Banzai Across the Eighth Dimension; Annie; Artists and Models (1955); Batman; Batman Forever; Batman Returns; Batman, The Movie; Blondie SERIES; Brenda Starr; Captain America; Casper; Condorman; The Crow; Flash; Flash Gordon; Flesh Gordon; Greystoke: The Legend of Tarzan; Hercules (1957); Hercules in New York; Hercules Unchained; How to Murder Your Wife; Howard the Duck; In Old Arizona; Jane and the Lost City; The Legend of the Lone Ranger; Li'l Abner; The Lone Ranger (1955); The Lone Ranger and the Lost City of Gold; Mark of Zorro (1920); The Mark of Zorro (1940); The Mask (1994); Meteor Man; Popeye; Richie Rich; The Shadow (1940); The Shadow (1994); Sheena, Queen of the Jungle; Shogun Assassin; Street Fighter; Suburban Commando; Subway; Supergirl; Superman; Superman 2; Superman 3; Superman 4; Swamp Thing; Tank Girl; Tarzan SERIES; Teenage Mutant Ninja Turtles; Teenage Mutant Ninja Turtles 2; Teenage Mutant Ninja Turtles 3

Comic Mystery: see also *Comic Thrillers: Tragi-Comedy: Action Comedy: Morbid Comedy:* Above Suspicion; According to Mrs. Hoyle; The Accused (1948); The Adventures of Sherlock Holmes' Smarter Brother; After Office Hours; The Alphabet Murders; And Then There Were None; Another Thin Man; The Big Fix; The Burglar; Cancel My Reservation; Charade; Charlie Chan and the Curse of the Dragon Queen; Club Paradise; Compromising Positions; Cotton Comes to Harlem; Dead Men Don't Wear Plaid; Dear Inspector; Detective (1954); Ex-Mrs. Bradford; Fast Company; Fog over Frisco; The Fuller Brush Girl; The Fuller Brush Man; The Great Lover (1949); Gumshoe; Her Alibi; Here Come the Girls; Hound of the Baskervilles (1977); It's a Wonderful World; January Man; Jumpin' Jack Flash; Lady of Burlesque; Lady on a Train; Late

Show; Legal Eagles; The Linguini Incident; Mad Miss Manton; Man Trouble; Manhattan Murder Mystery; Mark of the Vampire; Miss Grant Takes Richmond; Miss Robin Hood; Moonlighting (1985); Mr. and Mrs. North; Murder at the Vanities; Murder, He Says; Nadine; A Night to Remember (1946); The Notorious Landlady; Off and Running; Oh Heavenly Dog; Once Upon a Crime; One Body Too Many; The Prize; The Radioland Murders; Remember Last Night?; Salt and Pepper; Scandalous!; Shadow of the Thin Man; A Shot in the Dark; Somebody Killed Her Husband; Song of the Thin Man; Star of Midnight; Sunset; That Darn Cat!; They Won't Believe Me; The Thin Man; Trade Winds; True Confession; Who Done It? (1942); Who Framed Roger Rabbitt?; Who's Harry Crumb?; Without a Clue

Comic Thriller: see also *THRILLERS: Tragi-Comedy: Action Comedy: Comedy-Morbid; Comedy & Violence:* Abbott & Costello Meet Dr. Jekyll and Mr. Hyde; Abbott & Costello Meet Frankenstein; Abbott & Costello Meet the Invisible Man; Abbott & Costello Meet the Killer: Boris Karloff; Abbott & Costello Meet the Mummy; Another Stakeout; Arabesque; The Big Easy; Blue Velvet; Charade; Dear Inspector; Family Plot; Gotcha!; Jumpin' Jack Flash; Manhattan Murder Mystery; A Night to Remember (1946); Out of the Dark; The Prize; The Radioland Murders; Sneakers; Somebody Killed Her Husband; Whistling in the Dark; Why Me?

Coming of Age: see also *Teenage Movies: Life Transitions: Young Men: Young Women: Virgins: Bratpack Stories: Love-Infatuation:* The Actress (1953); The Affairs of Dobie Gillis; Alice Adams; Alice's Restaurant; All Fall Down; All Quiet on the Western Front; All the Right Moves; Almost a Man; Aloha Summer; Amarcord; American Graffiti; Amsterdamned; And God Created Woman (1957); Annie Get Your Gun!; Annie Oakley; Another Country; Baby, It's You; Bad Boys; Barbarosa; Baxter (1990); Bay Boy; The Bell Jar; Big Girls Don't Cry . . . They Get Even; Bilitis; Billie; Billy Bathgate; Billy Liar; Biloxi Blues; Blame it on Rio; Blue Lagoon (1948); The Blue Lagoon (1980); Bonjour, Tristesse; Book of Love; The Boy Who Could Fly; Breaking Away; Breaking

the Rules; Brighton Beach Memoirs; Broadway Bound; Broken Noses; A Bronx Tale; Buster and Billie; Cafe Romeo; California Dreaming; Captains Courageous; Carnal Knowledge; Carrie (1976); Celia; Charly; The Chicken Chronicles; The Chocolate War; The Chosen; Cinema Paradiso; Circle of Friends; City Boy; Clan of the Cave Bear; Class; Class of '44; Closely Watched Trains; Cold Sassy Tree; Consenting Adult; The Dark at the Top of the Stairs; David and Lisa; Dazed and Confused; Dead Poet's Society; Desert Bloom; Desire Under the Elms; Devil in the Flesh (1946); Devil in the Flesh (1987); Devil is a Sissy; Devil's Playground; Diner; Dirty Dancing; The Dove; East of Eden (1955); East of Eden (1980); Endless Love; Equus; Erendira; Europa, Europa; Experience Preferred . . . ; Fame; Father of the Bride (1950); Father of the Bride (1991); Fear Strikes Out; Firstborn; Flamingo Kid; Flirting; For Keeps; The Fox and the Hound; Foxes; The Frog Prince; Fun Down There; Gas Food Lodging; Georgy Girl; Getting It Right; The Getting of Wisdom; Gigi (1948); Gigi (1958); The Glass Menagerie (1950); The Glass Menagerie (1973); The Glass Menagerie (1987); Goodbye Columbus; The Graduate; Grandview, USA; Happy Time; The Heart is a Lonely Hunter; Heaven Help Us; Hemingway's Adventures of a Young Man; Hey, Good Lookin'; A Home of Our Own; Hope and Glory; The Hotel New Hampshire; How Green Was My Valley; I Never Promised You A Rose Garden; I Vitelloni; The Impossible Years; Impudent Girl; In Country; Inkwell; Joseph Andrews; Just Another Girl on the IRT; The Karate Kid; The Karate Kid, Part II; The Karate Kid, Part III; Kes; A Kind of Loving; King, Queen, Knave; La Vie Continue; The Last Picture Show; Lawrenceville Stories; The Learning Tree; Lies My Father Told Me; Little Darlings; Lola (1960); The Long Day Closes; The Lords of Discipline; Love in a Goldfish Bowl; Love on the Run (1979); Man in the Moon; Marty Masculine, Feminine Mask (1985); Me, Natalie; The Member of the Wedding; Men Don't Leave; Mermaids; Metropolitan (1990); Mignon Has Left; Mina Tannenbaum; Mischief; Monty Python's The Meaning of Life; The Moon is Blue; Moonrise; More American

Graffiti; Murmur of the Heart; My Bodyguard; My Life as a Dog; Mystic Pizza; A Night in the Life of Jimmy Reardon; 1969; Oh, What a Night; Once Is Not Enough; Ordinary People; Our Town; Our Vines Have Tender Grapes; The Pad, and How to Use It; Peggy Sue Got Married; Peppermint Soda; Peyton Place; Pink Floyd: The Wall; Power of One; Puberty Blues; Queen of Hearts; Rachel, Rachel; Racing with the Moon; Rainbow; Rambling Rose; Rebel Without a Cause; Reckless (1983); The Red Badge of Courage; Red Sky at Morning; Rich in Love; Risky Business; A River Runs Through It; A Room with a View; Ruby in Paradise; Rumble Fish; Running on Empty; Sabrina; Scent of a Woman; Scent of Green Papaya; School Ties; Secret Places; A Separate Peace; Seven Brides for Seven Brothers; Seventeen; Shadow of a Doubt; Shag; She's Out of Control; Sing as We Go; Sirens; Small Change; Smooth Talk; Sons and Lovers; Spanking the Monkey; Splendor in the Grass; Stand by Me; Staying Together; Step Down to Terror; Stolen Kisses; Straight out of Brooklyn; Summer of '42; Sweet Lorraine; A Taste of Honey; Tex; That Was Then . . . This Is Now; Therese and Isabelle; 36 Fillette; This Boy's Life; Three Smart Girls Grow Up; Threesome; Tiger's Tale; The Tin Drum; Tommy; A Tree Grows in Brooklyn; Valentino Returns; Vision Quest; The Wanderers; The War; Waterland; What's Eating Gilbert Grape?; When Father Was Away on Business; When the Legends Die; Where the Red Fern Grows; Who's That Knocking at My Door?; Wild Child; Wish You Were Here; Woman of Paris; Women in Love; World Apart; You're a Big Boy Now

Committed-Wrongly (to an asylum): see also *Accused-Unjustly: Asylums: Mental Illness: Insane-Plot to Drive:* Asylum; Bedlam; Blue Sky; Flesh of the Orchid; Frances; Rosie; Suddenly, Last Summer

Communication Problems: see *Misunderstandings: FARCE: Mistaken Identity: Screwball Comedy: Mix-Ups*

Communists: see also *Russians as Enemy: McCarthy Era: Cold War Era: Spy Films:* Abschied von Gestern; The Assassination of Trotsky; The Atomic Kid; The Chairman; The Confession; Conspirator; Cuba; Daniel; Earth; Eminent Domain; Fellow Traveler;

Snatchers (1956); Invasion of the Body Snatchers (1978); Last Summer; The Lords of Discipline; Ratboy; The Strange One; Tea and Sympathy; The Third Sex; The Way We Were

Congressmen/Senators (either or): see also *Politicians: Washington D.C.:* Adventure in Washington; Goodbye My Fancy; The Senator Was Indiscreet; Washington Story

Conservative Value Films/Stories (either very wholesome, religious, or patriotic): see also *Patriotic Films: FAMILY: Old-Fashioned Recent Films:* Air Force; Bon Voyage!; Born Again; Chariots of Fire; China Cry; Doctor Quinn, Medicine Woman; Follow Me, Boys!; Forrest Gump; The Green Berets; It's A Big Country; Joni; Lilies of the Field; My Son John; An Officer and a Gentleman; Red Dawn; Sands of Iwo Jima; Shadowlands; So Dear to My Heart; Top Gun; Yours, Mine and Ours

Conspiracy: see also *Spy Films: Political Drama: Corruption: Mindgames: Unbelieved:* The Advocate; Alien Nation; The Assassination; The Big Clock; Billion Dollar Brain; Blackmailed; Blood on the Sun; Blow Out; Blue Ice; Blue Sky; Body Double; The Bodyguard; The Bourne Identity; Brasher Doubloon; Brass Target; Caprice; Capricorn One; Caught in the Act; Cause for Alarm; Children of the Corn; The China Syndrome; Chinatown; Class Action; Clear and Present Danger; Coma; Darkman; Day of the Dolphin; Dead of Winter; Dead Reckoning; Deadly Affair; Defense of the Realm; The Detective (1968); Diabolique (1955); Die Laughing; Double McGuffin; Drowning Pool; Dying Room Only; The Eagle Has Landed; Endangered Species; Endless Game; Escape from the Planet of the Apes; Farewell, My Lovely (1944); Farewell, My Lovely (1975); Fear in the Night; Fear Inside; A Few Good Men; The Fifth Musketeer; Firepower; Fly By Night; The Foreign Correspondent; Foreign Intrigue; The Formula; The Fugitive (1993); The Fugitive: The Final Episode; Full Eclipse; F/X; F/X 2: The Deadly Art of Illusion; Gaslight (1939); Gaslight (1944); Ghost; Gold; Golden Earrings; Good Guys Wear Black; Gorky Park; Ground Zero; Groundstar Conspiracy; Hangar 18; Hanky Panky; Harper; Hidden Agenda; The Holcroft Covenant; The House on

Carroll Street; Hush, Hush, Sweet Charlotte; I Love Trouble (1994); Ice Pirates; Illustrious Corpses; Impulse (1984); In the Heat of the Night; Indiana Jones and The Last Crusade; Indiana Jones and The Temple of Doom; The Ipcress File; Iron Maze; Jarrapellejos; JFK; Jumpin' Jack Flash; Kafka; Kidnapping of the President; The Killer Elite; Killjoy; Kiss Me Deadly; Lady in Cement; Lady in the Iron Mask; The Lady Vanishes (1938); The Lady Vanishes (1979); The Last Boy Scout; Legal Eagles; Lethal Weapon; The Little Drummer Girl; The Lodger (1926); The Lodger (1932); The Lodger (1944); Logan's Run; Looker; Mackintosh Man; The Man I Married; The Man in the White Suit; The Man Who Knew Too Much (1934); The Man Who Knew Too Much (1956); The Manchurian Candidate; Marathon Man; Ministry of Fear; Mirage; Mississippi Burning; The Morning After; Mr. Arkadin; Naked Gun 2½; Naked Gun 33⅓; The Naked Runner; Night Nurse; No Way Out (1987); North by Northwest; Obsession; Otello; Othello (1951); Othello (1965); The Package; The Parallax View; The Passenger; The Pelican Brief; The Ploughman's Lunch; Primary Motive; Prime Cut; The Prize; Public Eye; Q & A; Rage; Rising Sun; River's Edge; Rollover; Rome Express; Rosemary's Baby; Ruby; Saboteur; Seven Days in May; Shaker Run; Shame (1987); Show of Force; Silkwood; St. Ive's; Star Chamber; State of Siege; The Stepford Wives; The Stunt Man; Suspect; They Only Kill Their Masters; The Third Man; The Thirty-Nine Steps (1935); The Thirty-Nine Steps (1959); The Thirty-Nine Steps (1978); This Gun for Hire; Three Days of the Condor; Thunderheart; Timebomb; Touch of Evil; Trouble for Two; Two Jakes; Under Suspicion; V.I. Warshawski; Vertigo; Virginia City; Warning Sign; White Sands; Who Done It? (1957); Who Framed Roger Rabbit?; Wilby Conspiracy; Wild Palms; Winter Kills; Witness; The Wreck of the Mary Deare; Wrong is Right; You've Got to Live Dangerously; Z

Consuming Secrets: see *Secrets-Haunting*

Contests/Competitions: see *Competitions/Contests: also Rags to Riches: Underdog Stories: Lucky People: Unlucky People*

Convicts-Escaped: see *Fugitive from the Law: Prison Escapes*

Convicts-Ex: see *Ex-Convicts: Dangerous Men: Evil Men*

Convict's Revenge: see *Criminal's Revenge/Criminal Pursues Good Guy's Family: Revenge: Dangerous Men: Evil Men: Dangerous Women: Evil Women*

Cop Killers: see *Murderer of Police*

Cops: see *Police: Crime Drama: ACTION: Buddy Cops: Partners*

Cops-Vigilante: see *Police-Vigilante*

Corporate Corruption: see also *Corporation as Enemy: Greed: Scandals: Business Life: Yuppies:* The China Syndrome; Class Action; The Hucksters; Other People's Money; Prime Cut; Quiz Show; Roger & Me; V.I. Warshawski; Wall Street

Corporation as Enemy: see also *Government as Enemy: Corporate Corruption:* Aliens; Bikini Beach; Black Fury; Champagne for Caesar; The Coca-Cola Kid; Disclosure; The Efficiency Expert; End of the Line; Executive Suite; The Field; Fighting Mad; Firepower; The Fountainhead; The Gay Sisters; Herbie Rides Again; The Hudsucker Proxy; Iron Maze; It Happened to Jane; Local Hero; Memoirs of an Invisible Man; The Milagro Beanfield War; Modern Times; Network; Nine to Five; Other People's Money; The Opposite Sex (Alec Guinness); Silkwood; Taffin; Toxic Avenger; Toxic Avenger, Part II; Toxic Avenger Part III; Wall Street; Warning Sign; Wayne's World; Wayne's World 2; Where the Green Ants Dream; Who Framed Roger Rabbitt?

Corruption: see also *Social Drama: Politicians: Political Films: Political Satire: Reformers:* Accused of Murder; Ace in the Hole; Advise and Consent; All My Sons (1949); All My Sons (1986); All the King's Men; All the President's Men; And Justice for All; Angel on My Shoulder; Ann Vickers; Apocalypse Now; Armed and Dangerous; Athena; Babbitt; Backdraft; The Bad and the Beautiful; Bad Day at Black Rock; Bad Lieutenant; The Bad Sleep Well; Beau James; The Best Little Whorehouse in Texas; The Big Fix; Billy Jack; Bitter Moon; Black Fury; Blaze; Blue Chips; Blue Velvet; Bonfire of the Vanities; Border Boss; Brubaker; A Canterbury Tale; The China Syndrome; City and the Dogs; City of Hope; Company Limited; Comrades; The

Conformist; Cop; Deep Cover; Diggstown; Everybody Wins; F.I.S.T.; A Face in the Crowd; The Falcon and the Snowman; A Few Good Men; Fortune Cookie; The Fountainhead; From the Hip; The Fugitive (1947); The Garment Jungle; Gladiator; The Glass Key (1935); The Glass Key (1942); Glengarry Glen Ross; The Great McGinty; The Harder They Fall; Harper Valley P.T.A.; The Hill; The Hucksters; Ice Pirates; Mark of Zorro (1920); Mark of Zorro (1940); Mastergate; Monsignor; Mr. Smith Goes to Washington; My Learned Friend; Network; Night and the City (1992); Pass the Ammo; Powwow Highway; Quick Millions; Rising Sun; Robocop; Robocop 2; Silkwood; Suspect; Sweet Smell of Success; The Taxing Woman; Thief of Bagdad (1924); Thief of Bagdad (1940); Three Days of the Condor; Top Secret Affair; Touch of Evil; Towering Inferno; Town Without Pity; Wall Street; Washington Story; Western Union; Wet Parade; Where Does it Hurt?; Who Framed Roger Rabbitt?; Witness

Cosmetic Surgery: see also *Aging: Beautiful People: Elderly Women: Disguises:* Ash Wednesday; Dark Passage; Death Becomes Her; Doc Hollywood; Girl Most Likely to . . . (1971); Groundstar Conspiracy; Jigsaw Man; Johnny Handsome; Looker; The Mirror Has Two Faces; The Promise; Raven; Seconds; Shattered; Woman's Face

Costume Drama: see also *Historical Drama:* The Abdication; The Adventures of Baron Munchausen (1987); The Adventures of Captain Fabian; The Adventures of Casanova; The Adventures of Don Juan; The Adventures of Gerard; The Adventures of Marco Polo; The Affairs of Cellini; Against All Flags; The Age of Innocence (1934); The Age of Innocence (1993); The Agony and the Ecstasy; Anne of the Thousand Days; The Barretts of Wimpole Street (1934); The Barretts of Wimpole Street (1956); Barry Lyndon; Beau Brummell (1924); Beau Brummell (1954); Becket; Becky Sharp; Black Arrow; Black Rose; Black Sunday (1977); Blackbeard, The Pirate; Bonnie Prince Charlie; The Bostonians; Braveheart; A Breath of Scandal; Brideshead Revisited; Brother Sun, Sister Moon; The Buccaneer (1938); The Buccaneer (1958); Burke and Wills;

Caesar and Cleopatra; Camille (1936); Camille Claudel; Cardinal Richelieu; Catherine the Great; Chariots of Fire; The Corsican Brothers; Cromwell; Dangerous Liaisons; The Dead; Desiree; Dragon Seed; The Elusive Pimpernel; The Europeans; Fanny and Alexander; Fanny Hill; Fire Over England; Firefly; The Flame and the Arrow; Forever Amber; Forever and a Day; 1492: Conquest of Paradise; The Four Musketeers; The Frenchman's Creek; Genevieve; Gigi (1958); The Go-Between; Gone With the Wind; Gorgeous Hussy; The Great Garrick; The Great Waltz (1938); The Great Waltz (1972); The Heiress; Henry VIII and His Six Wives; House of Rothschild; If I Were King; Immortal Beloved; Interview with the Vampire; Ivan the Terrible; Ivanhoe; Jefferson in Paris; John Paul Jones; The King's Whore; Knights of the Round Table; La Marseillaise; La Maschera; La Nuit de Varennes; Lady Caroline Lamb; Lady Jane; The Last Emperor; Little Dorrit; A Little Night Music; The Little Princess; Lloyd's of London; Lola Montes; Louisiana Purchase; Ludwig; Madame Dubarry; A Man for All Seasons; The Man in Grey; The Man Who Would Be King; Marie Antoinette; Mary of Scotland; Mary, Queen of Scots; Mayerling (1935); Mayerling (1968); Monsieur Beaucaire; Mourning Becomes Electra; My Cousin Rachel; The Naked Maja; Nicholas and Alexandra; On a Clear Day You Can See Forever; Orlando; Passion/Madame Dubarry (1919); Pollyanna; Pride and Prejudice; The Prince and the Pauper (1937); Prince Valiant; The Prisoner of Zenda (1937); The Prisoner of Zenda (1952); The Prisoner of Zenda (1979); The Private Affairs of Bel Ami; Private Lives of Elizabeth and Essex; Quality Street; Queen of Destiny; Ragtime; Raintree County; Rasputin and the Empress; Rembrandt; The Return of Martin Guerre; The Road to Wellville; A Royal Scandal; Royal Wedding; Salome (1953); Scandal in Paris; Scaramouche; The Scarlet Empress; The Scarlet Pimpernel; Shoes of the Fisherman; Smilin' Through (1932); Smilin' Through (1941); Sommersby; Song to Remember; Song Without End; Summer Story; Swann in Love; Swashbuckler; Sword of Lancelot; Tai Pan; A Tale of Two Cities (1935); A Tale of Two Cities (1958); A

Tale of Two Cities (1982); The Taming of the Shrew; Tess; That Forsyte Woman; The Three Musketeers (1973); The Three Musketeers (1993); Toast of New Orleans; Torrents of Spring; Under Capricorn; Valmont; War and Peace (1956); War Lord; Wicked Lady (1945); Wicked Lady (1983); Young Bess; Young Catherine

Coulda Been Good (potential, but missed the mark): see also *Good Premise Unfulfilled:* The Accused (1948); Act One; Almost an Angel; Almost Pregnant; Americana; Americathon; Amos and Andrew; Animal Behavior; Another Stakeout; The Applegates; Arriverderci, Baby!; Ash Wednesday; Audrey Rose; Aviator; Band of Angels; Barbarosa; Believers; Best Seller; Betrayed (1989); Betsy's Wedding; Blue Iguana; Boiling Point; Boxing Helena; The Boys in Company C; Brainscan; Brainstorm (1965); Brannigan; Brass Target; Breakheart Pass; Breezy; Buffy, The Vampire Slayer; Bullseye!; Busy Body; The Butcher's Wife; Cadillac Man; Candleshoe; Car 54, Where Are You?; Carbon Copy; Carny; Cass Timberlane; Cat Chaser; Cause for Alarm; The Chairman; Charlie Chan and the Curse of the Dragon Queen; Chastity Belt; China Girl (1987); China Moon; A Chorus of Disapproval; Claudelle Inglish; Cloak and Dagger (1946); Closer; Closet Land; Club Paradise; Cold Feet; Cool World; Conduct Unbecoming; Crackers; D.A.R.Y.L.; Dangerous Game; Dark of the Sun; Dark Wind; Deadfall (1968); Deadly Currents; Deadly Friend; The Deceivers; Desert Law; Desire and Hell at Sunset Motel; Desperate Hours (1990); The Devil and Max Devlin; Devil's Advocate; Diary of a Madman; Did You Hear the One About the Travelling Saleslady?; Die Laughing; Disorganized Crime; Doctor's Wives; Domino Principle; Don't Just Stand There; Don't Tell Mom the Babysitter's Dead; Dragonwyck; Dream Lover (1986); The Drowning Pool; Dudes; The Dunwich Horror; Dying Young; Everybody Wins; Everybody's All American; The Experts; Fallen Sparrow; Fathom; The Favour, the Watch & the Very Big Fish; The Feud; Fighting Back; A Fine Mess; Finger of Guilt; The First Deadly Sin; The First Time; A Fistful of Dynamite; Flare Up; Fletch; Fletch Lives; Flight of the Navigator; Flowers in the Attic; Fly By Night; Folks!; For Keeps;

For Love or Money (1993); Forever Darling; Formula; Forty Carats; Four Friends; From the Hip; The Gang That Couldn't Shoot Straight; Gigot; Give My Regards to Broad Street; Going Home; Golden Gate; Good Sam; Goodbye, New York; The Goodbye People; Gorky Park; Gotcha!; Gotham; Grandview, USA; Great Catherine; The Great Outdoors; Green Ice; Gross Anatomy; Gung Ho (1986); Half Moon Street; Hammerhead; Hammersmith is Out; Hanna's War; The Happy Hooker; Harlow; Haunted Honeymoon; The Haunted Palace; Haunted Summer; Havana; He Married His Wife; He Said, She Said; Heart of Dixie; Heat; Her Alibi; Hero; A Hero Ain't Nothin' but a Sandwich; Hide in Plain Sight; Hider in the House; High Season; The Holcroft Covenant; Holiday for Sinners; Honeymoon in Vegas; Hot Pursuit; Hot Spell; Hour of the Gun; House of Cards; The House of the Long Shadows; Hudson Hawk; Hustle; I Love Trouble (1994); Improper Channels; Impulse (1984); Impulse (1990); In Country; In Search of Gregory; In the Spirit; Inkwell Into the Sun; Iron Maze; Ivy; Jinxed; Johnny Dangerously; Justine; Kansas; The Key (1958); Key Exchange; The Kidnapping of the President; The Killer Elite; Killing Dad; King David; King Lear (1971); King of New York; King of the Gypsies; King Ralph; Kings and Desperate Men; The Kiss (1988); Kiss for Corliss; Kiss in the Dark; The Klansman; Knight Moves; Lady in Red; Last Action Hero; The Last Boy Scout; The Last Remake of Beau Geste; Last Sunset; Laughter in the Dark; Leap of Faith; Let No Man Write My Epitaph; Leviathan; Life Stinks!; Light at the Edge of the World; The Linguini Incident; Lipstick; Little Buddha; A Little Sex; Little Treasure; Little Vegas; Live Wire; Look in Any Window; Lookin' to Get Out; Love Hurts; Luna; M. Butterfly; Macaroni; Madhouse; Madison Avenue; Maid to Order; Malone; A Man Could Get Killed; Man on a Swing; Man on Fire; The Man Who Lost Himself; The Man with Bogart's Face; Man, Woman and Child; Man's Favorite Sport?; Marriage Go Round; Martin's Day; Masquerade (1988); Maxie; Me and Him; Me and Veronica; Meet the Applegates; Meeting Venus; Melancholia; Mikey and Nicky; Millennium; The Millionairess; The Mind

of Mr. Soames; The Miracle of the Bells; Miracles; The Missionary; Mississippi Masala; Mixed Company; Modesty Blaise; The Money Trap; More American Graffiti; Mother's Boys; Movers and Shakers; Moving Violations (1985); Mr. Nanny; Music of Chance; My Father the Hero; The Naked Face; New Life; Night of the Juggler; Night Watch; The Night We Never Met; 1969; Nomads; Off and Running; The Oldest Profession; Once Upon a Time; Operation Amsterdam; Ordeal by Innocence; Oscar; The Osterman Weekend; Other People's Money; Out Cold; Outfit (1973); Outlaw Blues; Outside Man; Over the Brooklyn Bridge; Passed Away; The Pelican Brief; Permanent Record; Physical Evidence; The Pickup Artist; Power; Primary Motive; Pure Luck; Quintet; Rabbit, Run; A Rage to Live; The Real McCoy; Reckless (1983); Revolution; Rising Sun; Roadside Prophets; Robin Hood, Men in Tights; Romeo is Bleeding; Rough Cut; Runner Stumbles; Saratoga Trunk; Satisfaction; Savages; Say One for Me; Scandal Sheet; Scarecrow; Scavenger Hunt; School Ties; Scorchers; Scorpio; Second Honeymoon; Second Sight; Second Thoughts; The Secret of My Success; See No Evil, Hear No Evil; Sender; The Seventh Sign; Severed Head; Shadow (1940); Shadow (1994); Shadows and Fog; Shakes the Clown; Show of Force; Sibling Rivalry; Silent Fall; Sing; Singles; Sky's the Limit; Slamdance; Small Circle of Friends; Smart Woman; Society; Solarbabies; Soldier in the Rain; Some Kind of a Nut; Some Kind of Wonderful; Something Wicked This Way Comes; Son of Kong; Song Without End; Sphinx; Spies Like Us; Spirit of '76; Stand Up and Be Counted; Star 80; State of Grace; Statue; Stay Tuned; Staying Together; Stepping Out; Sticky Fingers; Stop! Or My Mom Will Shoot; Storyville; Streets of Fire; Streets of Gold; Substitute; Sunburn; The Super; Surrender; Swing Shift; Tango & Cash; Target; Tattoo; Tell Me that You Love Me, Junie Moon; Tell Them Willie Boy is Here; Ten Thousand Bedrooms; Texasville; They All Laughed; They Live; They Only Kill Their Masters; Three for the Road; Three on a Couch; Tiger Bay; Time of Destiny; To Kill a Clown; Tunnel of Love; Under the Rainbow; The Unholy; The Unnamable; The Unnamable

Returns; V.I. Warshawski; Vibes; The Visit; Waiting For the Light; Where the Day Takes You; Wild Duck; Wild Hearts Can't Be Broken; Wild in the Country; Year of the Gun

Coulda Been Great (okay, but classic potential missed): see also *Good Premise Unfulfilled:* Across the Bridge; The Advocate; Alan and Naomi; All the Way Home; The Alphabet Murders; Angie; Annie; At Close Range; Attic; Baby, It's You; Bachelor; Back to the Beach; Bad Company (1995); Bank Shot; Barton Fink; batteries not included; Beau Pere; The Best Little Whorehouse in Texas; Betty Blue; Between the Lines; The Beverly Hillbillies; Beyond a Reasonable Doubt; Big Business; The Big Combo; The Big Picture; Black Angel; Blind Fury; Blood and Concrete; Blown Away; Blue Sky; Bonfire of the Vanities; Boost; Boy on a Dolphin; Brain Donors; Brighton Beach Memoirs; Buddy Buddy; Bunny Lake is Missing; The Burglars; Cabin Boy; Camelot; Cannery Row; The Cardinal; Carefree; Cash McCall; Caught; Caveman; Celia; Charley's Aunt; The Chase (1966); Chase a Crooked Shadow; Choice of Arms; Chu Chu and the Philly Flash; City of Hope; Clockwise; Cobb; Cohen and Tate; The Comic; Coneheads; Consenting Adults; Continental Divide; Cops and Robbersons; Cotton Club; A Countess from Hong Kong; Criminal Law; Criss Cross (1992); Cruising; The Cutting Edge; Darling Lili; Deadly Trap; Design for Living; Desire Under the Elms; Desperate Characters; Desperate Living; Desperately Seeking Susan; Devil Doll; The Devil's Disciple; Diamonds for Breakfast; Dominique; Don's Party; Doors; Down to Earth; Dragonslayer; Dream Wife; Duchess and the Dirtwater Fox; The Duellists; Eagle's Wing; End of the Line; End of the Road; Exposed; Eye of the Needle; Fallen Angel; Fame; Farewell to the King; Fedora; File on Thelma Jordon; Finders Keepers; A Fire in the Sky; Firstborn; First Monday in October; Five Heartbeats; Five Miles to Midnight; The Five Thousand Fingers of Doctor T.; The Fixer; A Flea in Her Ear; Flim Flam Man; Foolin' Around; The Fortune; Four's a Crowd; Fourth Protocol; Frankenhooker; Freebie and the Bean; The Freshman (1990); Full Moon in Blue Water; Fuzz; The Gambler; Gardens of

Stone; George Washington Slept Here; Ghosts . . . of the Civil Dead; Glory! Glory!; Go West Young Man; A Good Man in Africa; Good Morning, Babylon; The Goonies; Grand Canyon; The Grass is Greener; The Great Gatsby (1949); The Great Gatsby (1974); Greedy; Guarding Tess; Guest Wife; A Guide for the Married Man; The Gun in Betty Lou's Handbag; Hair; Handle with Care; The Handmaid's Tale; Happy New Year (1987); Hard Contract; Hard Promises; The Hard Way (1991); Harry and Walter Go to New York; Harry in Your Pocket; Health; Heartburn; Heaven's Gate; Hello Again; Hideaway; Hired Wife; Hitler-The Last Ten Days; Honky Tonk Freeway; Honkytonk Man; Hook; The Hotel New Hampshire; Hotel Paradiso; The House on Carroll Street; How to Succeed in Business without Really Trying; Hurry Sundown; Hysteria; I Saw What You Did; I Stole a Million; Impromptu; The Inquisitor; Inside Monkey Zetterland; Internal Affairs; It Could Happen to You; Jacob's Ladder; January Man; Johnny Stecchino; Juice; Jumpin' Jack Flash; Just Tell Me What You Want; Kafka; Kansas City Confidential; The Keep; Keeper of the Flame; Key to the City; A Kid for Two Farthings; The Kill-Off; Kim; Kindred; King Creole; King of Hearts; A Kiss Before Dying (1956); A Kiss Before Dying (1991); Kiss Me Goodbye; Kiss Them For Me; Lady in Question; The Lady is Willing; Lady of Burlesque; Lady on a Train; The Lady Vanishes (1979); The Last Married Couple in America; The Last Run; The Lawrenceville Stories; Legend; Let's Do it Again (1953); Letter to Three Wives; Life and Nothing But; Life With Mikey; Little Murders; A Little Night Music; Little Noises; Little Shop of Horrors (1986); Living End; Lock up Your Daughters; The Long Hot Summer (1958); Loot; Lord Jim; Lost and Found; Lost in America; Love and Pain and the Whole Damn Thing; Love at Large; Love Crimes; Love Potion #9; Lovesick; Luck of the Irish; Lunatics, A Love Story; Made in America; Magic Town; Malice; The Man Who Never Was; The Man with the Golden Arm; The Marrying Man; Matilda; The Mechanic; Medicine Man; The Men's Club; Milk Money; Miller's Crossing; Ministry of Fear; Miranda; The Mission; Mississippi Burning; Mississippi Mermaid; Mister Buddwing; Mistress;

Mixed Nuts; The Model and the Marriage Broker; The Money Pit; Monsignor; The Moon is Down; Moon Over Parador; Mosquito Coast; Move; Mr. Jones; Mrs. Parker and the Vicious Circle; Murphy's War; The Music Box; My Blue Heaven (1990); My Forbidden Past; My New Gun; Myra Breckinridge; Nadine; Nasty Habits; Nevada Smith; Never a Dull Moment (1967); New Kind of Love; Nickelodeon; 'Night, Mother; Night of the Generals; The Night They Raided Minsky's; Nightwing; Nijinsky; 92 in the Shade; Noises Off; None But the Brave; North; Not Without My Daughter; Oklahoma Crude; Old Gringo; Olly Olly Oxen Free; One Woman or Two; Only Angels Have Wings; Orphans; The Parallax View; PCU; The People Under the Stairs; Peter's Friends; Phobia; The Pope of Greenwich Village; Prelude to a Kiss; The Prince and the Showgirl; The Quiet American; The Radioland Murders; Raging Moon; Ragtime; Rat Race; The Return of Martin Guerre; Rhinestone; Riff-Raff (1947); The Road to Wellville; Rock a Bye Baby; Rock 'n' Roll High School; The Rocketeer; Rollover; Running Mates; Saving Grace; Scapegoat; Scar; Scenes from the Class Struggle in Beverly Hills; School Daze; School for Scandal; The Scout; Scrooged; Seance on a Wet Afternoon; The Second Best Secret Agent in the Whole Wide World; The Secret Admirer; Secret Life of an American Wife; Secret Partner; See You in the Morning; The Senator Was Indiscreet; Serial; Serial Mom; Seven Women; Sextette; Shattered; She Devil; The Shining; Sicilian Silverado; Slaughterhouse Five; Slaves of New York; Sleeping Car Murders; Sliver; Snakepit; Soapdish; SOB; Someone to Watch Over Me; Something Wild (1960); Sometimes a Great Notion; Sommersby; Sorcerer; The Sound and the Fury; Speechless; Stage Struck; Staircase; The Stand In; Star Chamber; Stargate; Stars and Bars; Start the Revolution Without Me; The Stepford Wives; Still of the Night; Stormy Monday; Straight out of Brooklyn; Strange Bedfellows; A Stranger is Watching; The Subterraneans; Sweet Liberty; Sylvia and the Ghost; Teachers; Tempest; Tender Trap; Tequila Sunrise; That Championship Season; They Won't Believe Me; Three of Hearts; Thunder Rock; Timebomb; Trade Winds; Tragedy

of a Ridiculous Man; Travels with My Aunt; Triumph of the Spirit; True Colors; True Confessions; Tune in Tomorrow; Twenty Bucks; Twin Beds; The Two Jakes; Two-Faced Woman; 2010; An Unsuitable Job For a Woman; The Unsuspected; Vampire's Kiss; The Vanishing (1993); Variety; Venom; Victory; View from the Bridge; Violent Men; The War Between Men and Women; The Watermelon Man; We Were Strangers; Welcome Home, Roxy Carmichael; Wetherby; What a Way to Go; Where Were You When the Lights Went Out?; Where's Poppa?; While the City Sleeps; White Banners; White Palace; Who is Harry Kellerman . . . ; Witness to Murder; The Woman in White; Year of the Comet; You Can Never Tell

Counterfeiters: see also *Embezzlers: Thieves: Bank Robberies:* Mister 880; Paris Holiday; To Live and Die in L.A.; Who's Minding the Mint?

Country Club Life: see also *Golf: Debutantes: Rich People: Suburban Life:* Banning; Caddyshack; The Flamingo Kid; Goodbye Columbus; The Landlord; Mister Cory; O.C. and Stiggs

Country Life: see *Rural Life: City vs. Country: Rednecks: Southerns: Southwestern Life: Midwesterns: Farm Life: Country Singers*

Country Music/Singers: see also *Nashville: Musicians: Country singers: Music Dies: Southerns:* All Night Long (1981); Amateur Night at the Dixie Bar and Grill; Baby, The Rain Must Fall; The Best Little Whorehouse in Texas; Bound For Glory; Coal Miner's Daughter; A Face in the Crowd; Honeysuckle Rose; Honkytonk Man; My New Gun; Nashville; Pure Country; Rhinestone; Six Pack; Songwriter; Sweet Dreams; Take This Job and Shove It; Tender Mercies; Thing Called Love; Urban Cowboy

Country People: see *Rural Life: Farm Life: Hillbillies: Rednecks: Midwesterns: Southerns: Southwestern Life*

Coups: see *Political Unrest*

Courtroom Drama: see also *Accused Unjustly: Lawyers: Lawyers as Detective: Trials: Judges:* The Accused (1988); Adam's Rib (1949); All That Money Can Buy; Anatomy of a Murder; And Justice for All; As Summers Die; Billy Budd; Body of Evidence; Boomerang (1947); Breaker Morant; Burning Bed; Business as Usual; The

Per Cent Dead; Nitti, The Enforcer; No Escape, No Return; No Mercy; No Orchids for Miss Blandish; Nocturne; On Dangerous Ground; Once Upon a Time in America; One False Move; The Onion Field; Outfit (1973); Outfit (1993); Party Girl; Pete Kelly's Blues; Petrified Forest; Point Blank; Point Break; The Pope of Greenwich Village; Pulp Fiction; Q & A; Quick; Quick Millions; Quicksand; Raffles; Raw Deal; Remember My Name; Report to the Commissioner; Reservoir Dogs; Return of Superfly; Ride the Pink Horse; Rififi; The Rise and Fall of Legs Diamond; The Roaring Twenties; Robocop; Robocop 2; Rolling Thunder; Romeo is Bleeding; Roxie Hart; Rush; Saint Benny, the Dip; Scarface (1932); Scarface (1983); Scarface Mob/The Untouchables Pilot; Serpico; Set-Up; Sexton Blake and the Hooded Terror; Shake Hands with the Devil; Shakedown; Sicilian; Sitting Target; Slaughter on Tenth Avenue; The Sniper; South Central; St. Valentine's Day Massacre; State of Grace; Stick; Stormy Monday; Straight out of Brooklyn; Straight Time; Street Smart; Sugar Hill; Taking of Pelham 123; Tango & Cash; Tequila Sunrise; That Certain Woman; Thelma & Louise; They Call Me Mr. Tibbs!; They Drive by Night (1940); Thieves Like Us; Thunder Road; True Romance; Twenty Thousand Years in Sing Sing; Underworld, USA; The Untouchables; The Valachi Papers; Whipsaw; White Heat; Wild at Heart; Wisdom; Woman's Face; Yakuza; Year of the Dragon; You Can't Get Away With Murder

Crime Pays (notable instances where they get away with it): see also *Perfect Crimes: Escapes-Clever: Endings-Happy: Clever Plots & Endings: MYSTERY-Murder: Heist Stories:* Dollars; A Fish Called Wanda; Fun With Dick and Jane; The Getaway (1972); The Getaway (1994); The Hot Rock; The Killer Elite; The Lavender Hill Mob; A Man, a Woman and a Bank; The Man with Two Faces; Scarlet Street; The Thomas Crown Affair

Crime Sprees: see also *Outlaw Road Movies:* Bloody Mama; Bonnie and Clyde; Boxcar Bertha; Butterfly; Dion Brothers; Macon County Line; Natural Born Killers; Young Guns; Young Guns II

Crimes of Passion (not necessarily vengeance or infidelity; more general than other specific murder categories):

see also *Cheating Men: Cheating Women: Revenge on Cheaters: Erotic Thrillers: Erotic Drama: Courtroom Drama: Mental Illness:* Adam's Rib (1949); All Fall Down; Dance with a Stranger; David and Bathsheba; East of Elephant Rock; Girl in the Red Velvet Swing; Goonies; Gordon's War; The Great Gatsby (1949); The Great Gatsby (1974); Greed; The Hanging Tree; Investigation of a Citizen Above Suspicion; Killing in a Small Town; King of the Gypsies; Ladykiller (1992); Long Night; Maytime; Min and Bill; Native Son (1951); Native Son (1986); Player; Prick Up Your Ears; Ragtime; Reckless Moment; A Short Film About Killing; Street Scene; Sunset Boulevard; Unfaithful; White Mischief

Crimes-Perfect: see *Perfect Crimes: also Clever Plots and Endings*

Crime-Urban: see *Inner City Life: Crime Drama*

Criminal Biographies: see also *Biographies: Crime Drama:* Al Capone; Billy Bathgate; Bloody Mama; Bonnie and Clyde; Bugsy; Butch Cassidy and the Sundance Kid; Capone; Dillinger; FBI Story; Machine Gun Kelly; Mobsters; Pretty Boy Floyd; The Rise and Fall of Legs Diamond; The Scarface Mob; Scarface (1932); Scarface (1983); The Valachi Papers; Young Guns; Young Guns 2

Criminal Couples: see also *Outlaw Road Movies:* Badlands; Bonnie and Clyde; Boxcar Bertha; Boys Next Door; Breathless (1959); Bunny O'Hare; Buster; Chicago Joe and the Showgirl; Dollars; Fun With Dick and Jane; The Getaway (1972); The Getaway (1994); Gun Crazy (1950); Gun Crazy (1992); Henry: Portrait of a Serial Killer; In Cold Blood; My Little Chickadee; Natural Born Killers; Now and Forever; Rafferty and the Gold Dust Twins; They Live by Night; True Romance; Wild at Heart; Wisdom

Criminal Mothers: see also *Criminals-Female:* Bloody Mama; Ed and His Dead Mother; White Heat

Criminals-Clever: see *Perfect Crimes: Clever Plots and Endings*

Criminals-Famous: see *Criminals-Famous: When Young: Hitwomen: Mob Girls: Murderers-Female*

Criminals-Famous, When Young: see *Famous People When Young: Criminal Biographies*

Criminals-Female: see also *Criminal Mothers: Hitwomen:* And God Created Woman (1988); Because of You; Born to Be Bad (1934); Cat Ballou; Class of 1999; Class of '84; Desire; Gambling Lady; The Getaway (1972); The Getaway (1994); Gun Crazy (1950); Gun Crazy (1992); Hannie Caulder; I Married a Dead Man; I'll Be Seeing You; The Last of Mrs. Cheyney; Law and the Lady; Marnie; Match Factory Girl; Me and Veronica; Miracle Woman; Mi Vida Loca; Montana Belle; Paid; Prison Stories: Women on the Inside; Psycho; Rafferty and the Gold Dust Twins; The Real McCoy; Remember My Name; Romeo is Bleeding; Son of Paleface; That Certain Woman; Thelma & Louise; The Unconquered; White Heat; Wicked Lady (1945); Wicked Lady (1983); Woman's Face

Criminal's Revenge/Pursues Good Guy's Family: see also *Revenge of Ex-Convict: Revenge: Ordinary People vs. Criminal:* Cape Fear (1962); Cape Fear (1991); Carlito's Way; Exorcist III; Five Card Stud; He Was Her Man; I Walk Alone; King of New York; Kiss Tomorrow Goodbye; Last Hard Men; Menace; My Learned Friend; No Way to Treat a Lady; Patriot Games; Rampage; Relentless; Relentless 2; Relentless 3; Ricochet; Scanner Cop; Shocker; Sitting Target; Small Town in Texas; Stick

Criminals-Stupid: see also *Simple Minds:* Another You; The Apple Dumpling Gang; The Apple Dumpling Gang Rides Again; Big Deal on Madonna Street; Big Mouth; The Boatniks; The Brinks Job; Crackers; Disorganized Crime; Dumb and Dumber; Family Plot; A Fish Called Wanda; Fuzz; The Gang That Couldn't Shoot Straight; Getting Even with Dad; The Great Bank Robbery; I Love You to Death; Lightning Jack; Mo' Money; Oh, Mr. Porter; Quick Change; Saint Benny, the Dip; Scavenger Hunt; Special Delivery; Take the Money and Run; Trapped in Paradise; Whistling in the Dark; Why Me?; Wrong Arm of the Law

Crippled People: see *Disabled People*

Crisis Situation: see also *Hostage Situation: Trapped: Disaster Movies: Stranded: Midlife Crisis:* Ace in the Hole; Airport; Airport 1975; Airport 1977; Apollo 13; Black Sunday (1977); Die Hard 2; Fail Safe; Fourteen Hours; Gray Lady Down; Marooned; Safe Passage; Taps; Test Pilot

Critics (film, TV, etc): see also *Theater Life: Hollywood Life:* Critic's Choice; Never a Dull Moment (1950); Please Don't Eat the Daisies; Rehearsal for Murder

Crossing the Border: see also *Fugitives from the Law: Fugitives:* Aloha, Bobby and Rose; Bandolero; The Big Steal; Border Borderline; Bordertown; Breathless (1983); Charley Varrick; Extreme Prejudice; The Getaway (1972); The Getaway (1994); Losin' It; Northwest Mounted Police; Rio Grande; Texas Across the River; Thelma & Louise; Touch of Evil; The Trap

Crossing the Line (breaking the fourth, invisible wall between the audience and the camera, known in film theory as reification): see also *Character Studies: Monologues-Interiors: Narrated Films:* After The Fox; Alfie; Annie Hall; Another Woman; A Chorus Line; A Double Life; Ferris Bueller's Day Off; Icicle Thief; Kuffs; Last Action Hero; Matchmaker; New Nightmare; A Night in the Life of Jimmy Reardon; The Opposite Sex and How to Live With Them; The Pickup Artist; Providence; The Purple Rose of Cairo; Slacker; Someone to Love; Stay Tuned; Stevie 21; Videodrome; Whore

Cruelty: see *Evil Men: Evil Women: Sexual Kinkiness: Abusive Men: Abusive Women*

Crushes: see *Love-Infatuation: Romance-Boy Wants Girl: Romance-Girl Wants Boy: Coming of Age*

Crying in Baseball or other Sports (tearjerkers and diseases in sports): see also *Baseball: Sports Movies: Tearjerkers:* Bang the Drum Slowly; Brian's Song; Pride of the Yankees; Stratton Story

Cuba: see also *Caribbean: Communists:* Che!; The Godfather II; Havana; Mambo Kings; Message to Garcia; We Were Strangers

Cuban Missile Crisis: Waiting For the Light; Matinee; The Steagle

Cuckolded (man whose wife is cheating): see *Cheating Women: Cheating Men: Romance: Infidelity: Triangles: Restoration Era*

Cult Films (films with a very loyal, if sometimes small, following): see also *Camp: Spoofs: Art Films: Unintentionally Funny: Underrated: Overlooked at Release: Ahead of its*

Time: Curiosities: Actors and Sin; The Adventures of Buckaroo Banzai Across the Eighth Dimension; All the Fine Young Cannibals; All You Need is Cash; Andy Warhol's Bad; Andy Warhol's Dracula; Andy Warhol's Heat; Apartment Zero; Arousers; Babette's Feast; Beach Party; The Beat Generation; Beat the Devil; Beauty and the Beast (1946); Bedazzled; Bedlam; Bedtime for Bonzo; Beneath the Planet of the Apes; Berserk!; Better Off Dead; Beyond the Valley of the Dolls; Big Knife; Big Trouble in Little China; Blood Simple; Blue Velvet; Born to Kill; A Boy and His Dog; Brazil; Breakfast at Tiffany's; Breaking Glass; Breathless (1959); Brewster McCloud; Brideshead Revisited; Brief Encounter (1946); Brimstone and Treacle; Bringing Up Baby; The Brood; Bugsy Malone; Caligula; Can She Bake a Cherry Pie?; Candy; Car Wash; Carmen Jones; Carnival of Souls; Carrie (1976); The Cars That Ate Paris; Cat Women of the Moon; Catch Me a Spy; Children of the Damned; Chilly Scenes of Winter; Chitty Chitty Bang Bang; Chloe in the Afternoon; Choose Me; Class of 1999; Class of '84; Cleopatra Jones; Cleopatra Jones and The Casino of Gold; Cutter and Bone; D.C. Cab; David and Lisa; Dawn of the Dead; Day of the Dead; Day of the Triffids; The Day the Earth Stood Still; Dazed and Confused; Dead Ringer; The Dead Zone; The Decline of Western Civilization; The Decline of Western Civilization 2: The Metal Years; Deliverance; Dementia 13; Desperate Living; Detour; The Devils; Digby, the Biggest Dog in the World; Diner; Diva; Don't Look Now; Donovan's Brain; Down By Law; Dr. Cyclops; Dr. Phibes Rises Again; Dr. Strangelove; Dragnet (1954); Dreamchild; Driver's Seat; Drop Dead Fred; Drugstore Cowboy; Drum; Duel; Dune; Eating Raoul; Ed Wood; End of the Road; Endless Summer; Even Cowgirls Get the Blues; Exorcist III; Exterminating Angel; Eye of the Devil; A Face in the Crowd; Fade to Black (1979); Fahrenheit 451; Fandango; Fanny Hill; Faster Pussycat! Kill! Kill!; Fawlty Towers; The Fearless Vampire Killers; Female Trouble; Fingers; First Nudie Musical; Five Came Back; The Five Thousand Fingers of Doctor T.; Flesh; Flesh Gordon; FM; Forbidden Planet; The Fountainhead; The Fourth Man; Foxes;

Freaks; Freddy's Dead: The Final Nightmare; Freud; Fritz the Cat; Frogs; Full Metal Jacket; Fury (1978); Garden; Georgy Girl; Gettysburg; Girl Most Likely to . . . (1971); Glen or Glenda?; Goddess; The Gods Must Be Crazy; Godzilla (1955); Godzilla versus Gigan; Godzilla versus Megalon; Gold Diggers in Paris; Gold Diggers of 1933; Gold Diggers of 1935; Gold Diggers of 1937; Gold Diggers of Broadway; Good Times; The Graduate; Grand Illusion; Green Slime; Greetings; Gun Crazy (1950); Gun Crazy (1992); Handle with Care; Happy Birthday, Wanda June; Harold and Maude; The Head; Heartland; Heavy Metal; Hellbound: Hellraiser II; Hellraiser; Hellraiser III: Hell on Earth; Hellzapoppin'; Hester Street; Hi, Mom!; High Heels; The Hills Have Eyes; Hold Me, Thrill Me, Kiss Me; The Honeymoon Killers; Hoop Dreams; House of Games; House of Wax; The House on Haunted Hill; How I Won the War; How to Get Ahead In Advertising; The Hunger; Husbands; Hush, Hush, Sweet Charlotte; I Love a Mystery; I Want What I Want; I Was a Communist for the FBI; I Was a Teenage Frankenstein; I Was a Teenage Werewolf; I'll Take Sweden; In Like Flint; In the Realm of the Senses; Interview with the Vampire; Invasion of the Body Snatchers (1956); Is There Sex After Death?; Jailhouse Rock; Jason and the Argonauts; Johnny Guitar; Jules and Jim; Kentucky Fried Movie; Kes; Killer's Kiss; The Killing; The Killing of Sister George; The Kindred; The Kingdom; Kiss Me Deadly; The Knack; Knightriders; Kwaidan; La Dolce Vita; Ladykillers; Las Vegas Hillbillies; Last of England; The Last Seduction; Last Tango in Paris; The Last Temptation of Christ; The Last Waltz; The Last Wave; Last Year at Marienbad; Laura; The Lavender Hill Mob; Lawnmower Man; Legend of Lylah Clare; Lenny; Les Biches; Lisztomania; Little Noises; Little Shop of Horrors (1960); Lolita; Lonesome Cowboys; Long, Good Friday; The Long Goodbye; Lord Love a Duck; Lord of the Rings; The Loved One; Loveless; The Magic Christian; Mandingo; Marat/Sade; Marius; McCabe and Mrs. Miller; Mean Streets; Medium Cool; Medusa Touch; Menace II Society; Menage; Misfits; Miss Firecracker; The Mole People; Mommie Dearest; Mondo Cane; Montenegro;

Morgan!; Mothra; Murmur of the Heart; Muscle Beach Party; My Dinner With Andre; My Favorite Year; Myra Breckinridge; Naked Lunch; Napoleon; Natural Born Killers; Night of the Living Dead (1968); Night of the Living Dead (1990); Night of the Shooting Stars; Night Porter; Nighthawks (1978); Nighthawks, 2: Strip Jack Naked (1991); The Nightmare Before Christmas; Nightmare on Elm Street; Nightmare on Elm Street Part Four; Nightmare on Elm Street Part Three; Nightmare on Elm Street Part Two; Nightmare on Elm Street: The Dream Child; 9½ Weeks; 9/30/55; Ninth Configuration; Nosferatu; Not of This Earth (1956); Nothin' But a Man; Oh, Dad, Poor Dad . . . ; Omega Man; On the Air; On the Beach; Once Upon a Time in America; One Eyed Jacks; Oscar; Ossessione; The Other; Out of the Past; Outoftowners; Paris is Burning; The Passenger; Pennies from Heaven (1981); Performance; Petulia; Phantasm; The Phantom of Liberty; The Phantom Tollbooth; Pink Flamingos; Pixote; Plan 9 From Outer Space; Play it Again, Sam; Play Misty for Me; Playtime; Point Blank; Police Squad! Help Wanted!; Portrait of Jennie; Powaqqatsi, Life in Transformation; The President's Analyst; Pretty Baby; Pretty Poison; Prime Suspect; The Prince of Central Park; The Prisoner: Arrival; The Producers; The Professionals; The Projectionist; Psych-Out; Psycho; Public Enemy; Pulp Fiction; Pumping Iron; Pumping Iron 2; Puppet Master; Quadrophenia; Querelle; Quintet; Rear Window; Rebel Rousers; Red Desert; The Red House; Reefer Madness; Reflections in a Golden Eye; Remember My Name; Repo Man; Repulsion; Reservoir Dogs; Return of the Fly; Return of the Living Dead; Return of the Living Dead Part II; Return of the Secaucus Seven; Return to Oz; The Rise and Rise of Michael Rimmer; The River's Edge; The Rocky Horror Picture Show; Rope; Rumble Fish; Salome, Where She Danced; Sergeant Pepper's Lonely Hearts Club Band; Serial Mom; The Seven Faces of Dr. Lao; Sextette; Shallow Grave; The Shooting; Short Eyes; Sisters; Sitting Ducks; Slaughterhouse Five; Slither; Smile; Smithereens; Son of Dracula; Spanking the Monkey; Staircase; Star Wars; Stop Making Sense; Strait Jacket; Superfly; Suspiria; Sylvia Scarlett; Take

the Money and Run; Taking Off; The Tall Blond Man with One Black Shoe; Tampopo; The Tenant; Testament of Orpheus; The Texas Chainsaw Massacre; Things to Come; The Third Man; The Thousand Eyes of Dr. Mabuse; Tie Me Up! Tie Me Down!; Time after Time; Tin Drum; Tommy; Touch of Evil; Track 29; Tremors; The Trial (1962); Tribes; The Trip; Triumph of the Will; Trog; Truth or Dare; Turkish Delight; Twin Peaks; Twin Peaks: Fire Walk with Me; Two For the Road; 2000 Maniacs; 2001: A Space Odyssey; Two Weeks in Another Town; Unfaithfully Yours (1948); Used Cars; Valley Obscured by the Clouds; Village of the Damned; What's New Pussycat?; What's the Matter with Helen?; What's Up, Tiger Lily?; Whatever Happened to Aunt Alice?; Whatever Happened to Baby Jane?; When Dinosaurs Ruled the Earth; When Strangers Marry; Where's Poppa?; White Zombie; Who's That Knocking at My Door?; Whoops! Apocalypse (1983); The Wicker Man; The Wild Bunch; Willy Wonka and the Chocolate Factory; Wings of Desire; Withnail and I; Woman Under the Influence; Woodstock; The World According to Garp; World of Apu; The World of Henry Orient; Xanadu; Yellow Submarine; Zabriskie Point; Zazie dans le Metro

Cults (religious sects): see also *Religious Zealots: Occult: Mental Illness: Religion: Brainwashing:* Bad Dreams; Believers; Birch Interval; Black God, White Devil; A Boy and His Dog; Children of the Corn; Guyana Tragedy, The Story of Jim Jones; I Love a Mystery; Necromancy; Rapture; Serial; Split Image; Ticket to Heaven; The War Lord; The Wicker Man; Wild Angels; Young Sherlock Holmes

Cures/Elixirs/Potions: see also *Cures-Search for: Magic: Witches:* The Absent-Minded Professor; The Alchemist; The Ape; Bride of the Gorilla; Death Becomes Her; Deep Cover; Dr. Heckyl and Mr. Hype; Doctor Jekyll and Mr. Hyde (1931); Dr. Jekyll and Mr. Hyde (1941); Dr. Phibes Rises Again; The Hunger; Medicine Man; Monkey Business (1952); The Night is Young (1946); Seconds; Something Wicked This Way Comes; Son of Sinbad; The Story of Louis Pasteur

Cures/Solutions-Search for: see also *Medical Drama: Scientists: Doctors: Quests: Aging:* Alice; Angel Baby;

Arrowsmith; Awakenings; Bell, Book, and Candle; Circle of Power; The Cure; Dr. Ehrlich's Magic Bullet; The Formula; Frankenstein Meets the Wolf Man; Lorenzo's Oil; Love Potion #9; The Story of Louis Pasteur; Potions

Curiosities (odd successes and failures alike, but not necessarily with a cult following or campy): see also *Cult Films: Coulda Been Good: Ahead of its Time:* The Adventurers; Alexander, the Other Side of Dawn; Angel Baby; Appaloosa; The Arousers; Baxter (1990); The Beat; Bebe's Kids; Bilitis; The Black Hand; Blind Fury; Body Slam; The Burning; C.H.U.D.; C.H.U.D. 2; Call Me Bwana; Can't Stop the Music; Candy Mountain; Carbon Copy; Carey Treatment; Carnival of Souls; Carny; Cars That Ate Paris; Casino Royale; Castle Keep; Central Park; The Check is in the Mail; The Chicken Chronicles; A Child is Waiting; Child's Play (1972); The Children (1980); Christmas Holiday; Christopher Strong; Circle of Power; Circle of Two; The Clairvoyant (1934); Cleopatra Jones; Cleopatra Jones and The Casino of Gold; The Comedians; Communion; The Company of Wolves; The Conqueror; Cool World; Countdown; The Day the Fish Came Out; Deadlier Than the Male; Delicatessen; Die! Die! My Darling!; Don't Bother to Knock; Dreams That Money Can Buy; DROP Squad; Duffy's Tavern; F for Fake; Fathom; The Fearless Vampire Killers; Fedora; Female on the Beach; Fingers; The First Nudie Musical; The Fish that Saved Pittsburgh; Flaming Star; Fog over Frisco; Footloose; For Love of Ivy; Forever Darling; The Fourth Man; Francis the Talking Mule; Franken-hooker; Frankenstein '70; Freaks; Freaky Friday; Fuzzy Pink Nightgown; From the Life of the Marionettes; Gassss; The Gene Krupa Story; The Gentle Sex; Ghost in the Invisible Bikini; Go for Broke; Godspell; The Gong Show Movie; The Good Son; Good Times; Goodbye, Pork Pie; Gorgeous Hussy; Gorilla at Large; The Gospel According to St. Matthew; The Grasshopper; Greased Lightning; The Great Impostor; The Great Lover (1949); The Great Manhunt; The Great Moment; The Great Scout and Cathouse Thursday; The Great Smokey Roadblock; The Greatest; The Green Goddess; Green Mansions; A Guest in the House; A

Gunfight; The Hairdresser's Husband; Hallelujah!; Hammersmith is Out; The Hand (1960); The Hand (1981); Handle with Care; Hannie Caulder; The Happening; Happy Birthday, Wanda June; The Happy Hooker; Harrad Experiment; Harrad Summer; The Hatchet Man; Health; Heart Beat; Heart of Glass; Heartbreakers; Heimat; Hell in the Pacific; Heller in Pink Tights; Hello Again; The Hellstrom Chronicle; Hellzapoppin'; Helter Skelter (1949); Hider in the House; High Road to China; Histoires Extraordinaires; Holiday for Sinners; Hollywood Boulevard (1936); Hollywood Boulevard (1977); Hollywood Canteen; Hollywood Revue of 1929; Honky Tonk Freeway; Honkytonk Man; Hornet's Nest; The Hotel New Hampshire; How to Beat the High Cost of Living; Howard the Duck; The Hunter; I, Mobster; Inside Monkey Zetterland; The January Man; Katherine; Kisses for My President; The Lady in the Car with Glasses and a Gun; Leather Saint; The Legend of the Holy Drinker; Light Years; The Linguini Incident; Look in Any Window; Losin' It; Love God?; Love Me Tender; Maitresse; Me and Him; Memoirs of a Survivor; Mr. Arkadin; My Dinner With Andre; My New Gun; Myra Breckinridge; Mystery Street; Naked Lunch; Necromancy; Negatives; New Barbarians; A Night in the Life of Jimmy Reardon; Night of the Comet; Night of the Following Day; Night of the Lepus; Night Porter; Night unto Night; Nightcomers; Ninth Configuration; No Orchids for Miss Blandish; No Small Affair; Nomads; Norman, Is That You?; O.C. and Stiggs; Oh, Dad, Poor Dad . . . ; On Her Majesty's Secret Service; Once Bitten; One That Got Away; Out of Order; Paint Your Wagon; Parents; Party and the Guests; Passing of the Third Floor Back;

Pepe; Perfect Furlough; Period of Adjustment; Perri; The Pirate Movie; Popeye; The Possession of Joel Delaney; The President's Analyst; The Private Life of Sherlock Holmes; Promise Her Anything; Quackser Fortune Has a Cousin in the Bronx; Quadrophenia; Queen Bee; Quest for Fire; Quintet; Rabbit Test; Rabid Grannies; A Rage to Live; Raging Moon; The Rain People; Ratboy; Return of the Vampire; Return to Oz; Revenge of Billy the Kid; The Revolutionary; Rhapsody in August; Ricochet; Rider on the Rain; Riff-Raff (1991); The Right Stuff; The Rise and Rise of Michael Rimmer; Roger & Me; Rolling Thunder; Romeo is Bleeding; Roustabout; The Royal Family of Broadway; Royal Flash; Rubin & Ed; Ruby Gentry; Ruling Class; Savage Sam; The Secret Ceremony; Shame (1961); The Shooting; Shout; Silent Tongue; Sophia Loren, Her Own Story; Soup for One; Sparkle; Steagle; The Suicide Club; T.R. Baskin; Tall Story; Tamango; Taps; Targets; Tarnished Angels; Tarzan and His Mate; Tarzan Escapes; Tarzan, The Ape Man (1932); Tarzan, the Ape Man (1981); Tattoo; Tea and Sympathy; Tell Me that You Love Me, Junie Moon; Ten Days Wonder; Terminal Man; Thank God It's Friday; The Young Girls of Rochefort; The Thief (1952); Thieves Like Us; Thin Ice; The Third Sex; 30 is a Dangerous Age, Cynthia; Three Comrades; Three O'Clock High; Through a Glass Darkly; Tick, Tick, Tick . . . ; Tickle Me; Tim; The Time of Your Life; Time Without Pity; Times Square; To Paris with Love; To Wong Foo, Thanks for Everything, Julie Newmar; Too Late Blues; The Trail of the Pink Panther; Tree of Wooden Clogs; Trog; Tropic of Cancer; Trouble Along the Way; The Trouble with Girls; Trust; Twenty Bucks; 21; Twisted; The

Two Mrs. Carrolls; Two of a Kind; Two-Faced Woman; Walker; Watcher in the Woods; What's So Bad About Feeling Good?; Who'll Stop the Rain?; Wilder Napalm

Curses: see also *Magic: Witchcraft: Fortune Tellers: Gypsies: Genies: Occult:* The Believers; Charlie Chan and the Curse of the Dragon Queen; The Curse of the Cat People; Day of Wrath; Five Million Years to Earth; I Walked with a Zombie; The Sphinx; Ulysses (1954); Valley of the Kings; The Witches of Eastwick

Custer's Last Stand (stories including the famous battle): see also *Cavalry: Cavalry vs. Indians: Massacres: WESTERNS:* Geronimo (1962); Geronimo (1993); Little Big Horn; Little Big Man; Seventh Cavalry; They Died With Their Boots On

Custody Battles: see also *Divorce: Courtroom Drama: Parents vs. Children: Step-Parents vs. Children:* The Awful Truth; Baby Maker; Bright Eyes; Careful, He Might Hear You; The Champ (1931); The Champ (1979); Cheaper to Keep Her; Fine Things; Forty Pounds of Trouble; The Good Father; The Good Mother; Irreconcilable Differences; Kramer vs. Kramer; Little Gloria, Happy At Last; Man on Fire; Mother's Boys; Move Over, Darling; Mrs Doubtfire; My Favorite Wife; My Heart Belongs to Daddy; Not Without My Daughter; One Potato, Two Potato; A Simple Twist of Fate; Trouble Along the Way; Where Angels Fear to Tread

Czech (Czechoslovakian) Films/Czech People: see also *Polish Films: Europeans-Eastern:* Anna; Closely Watched Trains; Fireman's Ball; Loves of a Blonde; My Sweet Little Village

D

Daddy's Girls: see also *Children-Problem: Tomboys: Mama's Boys:* Eat My Dust; Impossible Years; Oscar; She's Out of Control; Take Her, She's Mine

A Damsel in Distress: see *Women in Jeopardy*

Dance Movies: see also *Musicals: Dancers: Music Movies: Music Video Style:* All That Jazz; An American in Paris; Beat Street; The Big Broadcast; The Big Broadcast of 1936; Bolero (1934); Born to Dance; Breakin'; Breakin' 2: Electric Boogaloo; Call Me Mister; Can-Can; Carmen (1983); A Chorus Line; Cover Girl; Daddy Longlegs; A Damsel in Distress; Dancers; Dancing Co-Ed; Dirty Dancing; Fame; Flashdance; Flying Down to Rio; Follow the Fleet; Footlight Parade; Footloose; Forbidden Dance; The Gang's All Here; George White's 1935 Scandals; George White's Scandals (1934); George White's Scandals 1945; Ginger and Fred; Give the Girl a Break; Gold Diggers in Paris; Gold Diggers of Broadway; Gold Diggers of 1933; Gold Diggers of 1935; Gold Diggers of 1937; The Goldwyn Follies; Grease 2; The Great Waltz (1938); The Great Waltz (1972); The Great Ziegfeld; Hairspray; Invitation to the Dance; It's Always Fair Weather; The Kid From Spain; Kid Millions; The King of Jazz; Lambada; Let's Dance; Moon Over Miami; Movie; The Naked Tango; Newsies; Nutcracker (1993); Nutcracker-The Motion Picture (1986); Paris is Burning; Pennies from Heaven (1981); Queen of the Stardust Ballroom; Red Shoes; Roberta; Salsa; Saturday Night Fever; Shall We Dance?; Shout; Singing in the Rain; Small-town Girl (1953); Stand Up and Cheer; Staying Alive; Stepping Out; The Story of Vernon and Irene Castle; Strictly Ballroom; Swing Kids; Swing Time; Tales of Hoffman; Tap; That's Dancin'!; That's Entertainment; That's Entertainment Part Two; They Shoot Horses, Don't They?; Tin Pan Alley; Tonight and Every Night; Top Hat; Top of the Town; Turning Point

Dancers: see also *Musicals: Dance Movies:* The Accused (1948); Ain't Misbehavin'; An American in Paris; April in Paris; Artists and Models (1955); Band Wagon; The Barkleys of Broadway; Belle of the Yukon; Bert Rigby, You're a Fool!; The Big Broadcast; Bolero (1934); Born to Dance; Breakin'; Breakin' 2: Electric Boogaloo; The Bride Wore Red; Broadway Melody; Broadway Melody of 1936; Broadway Melody of 1938; Broadway Melody of 1940; Call Me Mister; Can-Can; Carlito's Way; A Chorus Line; A Damsel in Distress; Dancers; Dancing Lady; Diamond Horseshoe; Dirty Dancing; Dixie; Dolly Sisters; Fame; Flamingo Road; Flashdance; Folies Bergere; Follow the Fleet; Footlight Parade; Frenchie; G.I. Blues; Gaby; The Gang's All Here; The Gay Divorcee; Gentlemen Prefer Blondes; The George Raft Story; George White's 1935 Scandals; George White's Scandals (1934); George White's Scandals 1945; Gilda; Ginger and Fred; Give My Regards to Broadway; Give the Girl a Break; Gold Diggers in Paris; Gold Diggers of Broadway; Gold Diggers of 1933; Gold Diggers of 1935; Gold Diggers of 1937; Goldwyn Follies; The Great Waltz (1938); The Great Waltz (1972); The Great Ziegfeld; Gypsy; Hairspray; High, Wide and Handsome; How to Be Very Very Popular; I am a Camera; I Love Melvin; I Was an Adventuress; Idiot's Delight; In Old Chicago; Invitation to the Dance; Isadora; It's Always Fair Weather; The King of Jazz; Kiss the Boys Goodbye; Lady By Choice; The Lady of Burlesque; Laughter; Le Bal; Let's Dance; The Lights of New York; The Limelight; Lola (1960); Loves of Carmen; Lucky Me; Lured; Manpower; Mata Hari (1931); Mata Hari (1985); Mata Hari, Agent H21 (1964); Meet Me in Las Vegas; The Men in Her Life; Moon Over Miami; Morocco; Mother Wore Tights; Moulin Rouge; Murder at the Vanities; A Night in Heaven; The Night is Young (1934); Nijinsky; On Your Toes;

The Only Game in Town; Operation Mad Ball; Our Dancing Daughters; Party Girl; Pennies from Heaven (1981); Ragtime; Red Shoes; Salome (1953); Salome, Where She Danced; Salome's Last Dance; Salsa; Saturday Night Fever; Screaming Mimi; Shall We Dance?; Shining Hour; The Sidewalks of London; Singing in the Rain; Small-town Girl (1953); St. Martin's Lane; Staying Alive; Stepping Out; Strictly Ballroom; Sweet Charity; Sweet Rosie O'Grady; Swing Time; Tap; That's Dancin'!; The Young Girls of Rochefort; Tin Pan Alley; To Wong Foo, Thanks for Everything, Julie Newmar; Tonight and Every Night; Top Hat; Top of the Town; Turning Point; Two for the Seesaw; Two Girls and a Sailor; Vivacious Lady; Wabash Avenue; Waterloo Bridge (1931); Waterloo Bridge (1940); The Westerner; What's the Matter with Helen?; When My Baby Smiles at Me; White Nights (1985); A Woman is a Woman; Wonder Bar; Yankee Doodle Dandy; You Were Never Lovelier; You'll Never Get Rich; Ziegfeld Follies; The Ziegfeld Girl

Dangerous Lovers: see *Dangerous Spouses: Romance-Dangerous*

Dangerous Men (Hommes Fatales, usually in a romantic context): see also *Film Noir: Evil Men: Romance-Dangerous: Dangerous Spouses: Love-Questionable: Mean Men: Playboys: Dangerous Spouses:* Against All Odds; And Now the Screaming Starts; Autumn Leaves; Bad Company; Backtrack; Bad Day at Black Rock; Bad Influence; Betrayed (1989); Brimstone and Treacle; Cast a Dark Shadow; The Cat Chaser; Caught; Charade; Choose Me; Christmas Holiday; A Clockwork Orange; The Comfort of Strangers; The Conspirator; Dangerous Liaisons; Deceived; Desert Fury; Dragonwyck; Entertaining Mr. Sloane; Ever in My Heart; Exposed; Foolish Wives; Ghost; Good Fellas; Heathers; Johnny Eager; King and Four Queens; La Maschera; The Last Seduction; The Locket; Looking for Mr. Goodbar; Lost Honor of Katharina Blum; Love From a Stranger (1936); Love From a Stranger (1947); Mack the Knife; Malice; Montenegro; Mrs. Soffel; On Dangerous Ground; Past Midnight; Performance; The Postman Always Rings Twice (1945); The Postman Always Rings Twice (1981); Sliver; Smooth Talk; Something Wild (1986); Star 80; Stepfather; Stepfather 2:

Make Room for Daddy; Stepfather 3: Father's Day; Suspicion; Tamarind Seed; To Catch a Thief; Warm Nights on a Slow Moving Train; Whispers in the Dark; The Woman on the Beach

Dangerous Romance: see *Romance-Dangerous: Film Noir: Love-Questionable*

Dangerous Spouses: see also *Romance-Dangerous:* And Now the Screaming Starts; Autumn Leaves; Caught; Christmas Holiday; The Conspirator; Deceived; Desert Fury; Dragonwyck; Dream Lover (1994); Flare Up; Gaslight (1939); Gaslight (1944); Jet Pilot; The Naked Jungle; Niagara; Not Without My Daughter; Once Upon a Honeymoon; Rebecca; Sabotage; The Two Mrs. Carrolls

Dangerous Women (Femmes Fatales): see also *Film Noir: Evil Women: Love-Questionable: Mean Women: Dangerous Spouses:* Addams Family Values; Arabesque; Batman Returns; Body Heat; Body of Evidence; Born to Be Bad (1950); Casino; China Moon; Damn Yankees; Dance with a Stranger; Dangerous Liaisons; Dead Men Don't Wear Plaid; Dead Reckoning; The Devil is a Woman; Dick Tracy; Double Indemnity; Double Jeopardy; Dream Lover (1994); Fatal Attraction; Femme Fatale; File on Thelma Jordon; The Fourth Story; Gun Crazy (1950); Gun Crazy (1992); Havana; I Want to Live!; Johnny Guitar; Johnny Stecchino; A King and Four Queens; La Femme Nikita; The Lady in Question; The Lady in Red; Last Rites; The Last Seduction; The Locket; Loves of Carmen; Marathon Man; Marnie; Mata Hari (1931); Mata Hari (1985); Mata Hari, Agent H21 (1964); Mi Vida Loca; Montana Belle; Ossessione; Out of the Past; Point of No Return; The Postman Always Rings Twice (1945); The Postman Always Rings Twice (1981); Pulp Fiction; Rancho Notorious; Red Rock West; Red Sonja; Revenge; Romeo is Bleeding; Saratoga Trunk; Sea of Love; The Shooting; Something Wild (1986); The Stand; Still of the Night; Terminal Velocity; They Drive by Night (1940); Tristana; Who Framed Roger Rabbit?; Woman in the Window; The Woman on the Beach

Danish Films: see also *Swedish Films: Scandinavia:* Babette's Feast; The Kingdom; Pelle, the Conqueror; Zentropa

Darkside of Life: see *Underworld: Film Noir: THRILLERS: HORROR: MYS-*

TERY: Mental Illness: Murder: Spy Films: Mob Stories: Evil Men: Evil Women: Inner City Life: Gangs

Dates-Hired: see *Hired Dates: Prostitutes-Male: Prostitutes-High Class: Matchmakers: Brides-Mail Order*

Dating Scene: see also *Personal Ads: Romance-Choosing the Right Person: Brides-Mail Order:* Beyond Therapy; Blind Date (1987); Bound and Gagged, a Love Story; Bye Bye Love; The Cemetery Club; Chapter Two; The Courtship; The Courtship of Eddie's Father; Cross My Heart; Getting It Right; A Guide for the Married Man; It's Pat; The Lonely Guy; Milk Money; Mr. Wonderful; The Pad, and How to Use It; Perfect; The Perfect Couple; Robert et Robert; Three Smart Girls Grow Up; 21

Daughters: see *Mothers & Daughters: Fathers & Daughters: Daughters-in-Law*

Daughters-in-Law: see *Mothers & Daughters: Fathers & Daughters: Sisters*

David vs. Goliath Stories (Nerd vs. Macho Man): see *Underdog Stories: Man vs. Man*

D-Day Stories (stories of the great World War II battle on the shores of Normandy): see also *World War II Stories: War Stories: War Stories:* The Longest Day; Code Name: Emerald

Dead-Back from the: see also *Afterlife: Heaven: Hell: Deaths-Faked:* All Dogs Go to Heaven; Almost an Angel; Andy Warhol's Frankenstein; Angel on My Shoulder; Asphyx; Back From the Dead; Black Sunday (1960); Blacula; Blind Side; Blood Simple; Buried Alive; Carousel; Chances Are; Chase a Crooked Shadow; Child's Play (1988); Child's Play 2; Child's Play 3; Cold Heaven; Conan, the Destroyer; The Crow; Darkman; Dead Heat; Dead of Night (1977); Deadly Friend; Deathtrap; Desire Me; The Devil and Max Devlin; Divorce, Italian Style; Dominique; Dona Flor and Her Two Husbands; Dr. Phibes Rises Again; Ed and His Dead Mother; Enemies, A Love Story; Field of Dreams; Five Card Stud; Five Miles to Midnight; Flatliners; Flight of the Navigator; The Fog; Franken-hooker; Frankenstein (1931); Frankenstein '70; Frankenstein and the Monster from Hell; Frankenstein Created Woman; Frankenstein Unbound; Freejack; Friday the 13th (1980); Friday the 13th: Final Chapter; Friday the 13th, Part 3-D; Friday the 13th, Part II; Friday the 13th Part V-A New Beginning; Friday the 13th Part VI-Jason Lives; Friday the 13th Part VII-The New Blood; Friday the 13th Part VIII-Jason Takes Manhattan; The Fury (1936); Ghost in the Invisible Bikini; Ghosts Can't Do It; Goodbye, Charlie; Gotham; The Great Lie; Hang 'em High; Happy Birthday, Wanda June; Heart and Souls; Heaven Can Wait (1943); Heaven Can Wait (1978); Hello Again; Here Comes Mr. Jordan; Hideaway; Horror Hotel; I'd Rather Be Rich; Impact; It Started with Eve; J'Accuse; Kill Me Again; Kiss Me Goodbye; Laura; Lucky Stiff; Made in Heaven; Man Alive; The Man Who Haunted Himself; The Man with Nine Lives; Maniac Cop; Maniac Cop 2; Mephisto Waltz; Miracle in the Rain; The Mummy (1932); The Mummy (1959); The Mummy's Hand; The Mummy's Shroud; Night Gallery; Night of the Living Dead (1968); Night of the Living Dead (1990); The Oblong Box; Oh Heavenly Dog; Old Dracula; Pet Sematary; Pet Sematary 2; The Piccadilly Incident; The Return of Martin Guerre; Return of the Living Dead; Return of the Living Dead Part II; Scoundrel; Seconds; The Secret Ceremony; The September Affair; Shocker; Sisters; Sleeper; Snow White and The Seven Dwarfs; Some Kind of Hero; Sommersby; Starman; Star Trek III: The Search for Spock; Stolen Life (1939); Stolen Life (1946); Sullivan's Travels; Suzy; Taste the Blood of Dracula; Tell Them Willie Boy is Here; Tomb of Ligea; Tomorrow is Forever; Too Many Husbands; Topper; Topper Returns; Topper Takes a Trip; Truly, Madly, Deeply; Universal Soldier; Vertigo; The Walking Dead; We're Back! A Dinosaur's Story; Welcome Home; White Sands; Wings of Fame; You Only Live Twice; The White Sister

Dead Body, Hide the: see *Hide the Dead Body*

Dead-Left for: see *Abandoned People: Dead-Back from the*

Deaf People: see also *Mute People: Disabled People: Blind People: Disabled People in Jeopardy:* Alpine Fire; Amsterdamned; Amy; And Now, Tomorrow; Children of a Lesser God; The Crash of Silence; Gigot; Hear No Evil; The Heart is a Lonely Hunter; Johnny Belinda; The Linguini Incident; Little Noises; Looking for Mr. Goodbar; The Man of a Thousand Faces; Psych-Out; See No Evil, Hear No Evil; The Story of Alexander Graham Bell; Voices; Wildflower

Death-Accidental: see also *Deaths-Faked: Death-Dealing with: Tearjerkers: Violence-Unexpected: TRAGEDY: MELO-DRAMA: Accident Prone:* The Accident; Black Orpheus; Blind Side; Death in Brunswick; The Disappearance of Christina; A Few Good Men; Girl Most Likely to . . . (1971); Hallelujah!; It Ain't Hay; The McConnell Story; The Mechanic; Murder by Natural Causes; Naked Lunch; Native Son (1951); Native Son (1986); Out Cold; Over Her Dead Body; Razorback; The Reckless Moment; They Drive by Night (1940); They Live by Night; They Made Me a Criminal; 21 Days; War Party; What a Way to Go; Wings

Death-Dealing With: see also *Tearjerkers: Disease Stories: Death-Impending: Dying Young: Widows: Widowers: Children-Parting with/ Losing: Deaths-Faked: Reincarnation: MELODRAMA: MURDER: TRAGEDY:* The Accident; The Accidental Tourist; Act of Murder; All Quiet on the Western Front; All That Jazz; All the Way Home; Always American Flyers; Andre's Mother; The Bachelor; Beaches; Between Two Women; Bliss; Blue Lamp; Brimstone and Treacle; Celia; Charlotte's Web; Consenting Adult; Cries and Whispers; Da; Dark Waters; Death Takes a Holiday; The Devil's Advocate; Don't Look Now; Family Pictures; Fate is the Hunter; Fathers and Sons; Fearless; Fighting Back; Fine Things; Friendly Fire; Gardens of Stone; Gathering; Golden Braid; Ground Zero; Happy Land; The Human Comedy; I Never Sang for My Father; In Country; An Inspector Calls; Island (1961); Just Between Friends; Kes; L'Invitation; Last Tango in Paris; The Last Tycoon; The Loved One; Made for Each Other; May Fools; Medal for Benny; Mike's Murder; The Millionairess; The Miracle of the Bells; Mouchette; Muriel; My Cousin Rachel; My Girl; My Girl 2; Never Say Die; No Way Out (1950); None But the Lonely Heart; Old Yeller; Once Around; One Good Cop; The Onion Field; Ordinary People; Promised Land; River's Edge; Safe Passage; The Seventh Seal; Shadow Box; Shadowlands; Short Cuts; Singing Fool; Six Weeks; Slow Dancing in the Big City; Smilin' Through (1932); Smilin' Through (1941); SOB; Steel; The Story of Vernon and Irene Castle; Summer Wishes, Winter Dreams; Table for Five; They; Together Again; Trail of the Lonesome Pine; Travelling North; Tribute; Truly, Madly, Deeply; Twelve O'Clock High; The Uninvited; What's Eating Gilbert Grape?; White Sister; Whose Life Is It Anyway?; The World of Apu; A Zed and Two Noughts; The Cemetery Club; Death Wish; Grace Quigley; How I Won the War; Husbands; Tender Mercies; To Dance with the White Dog; The White Cliffs of Dover

Death-Impending: see also *Death-Impending, False: Tearjerkers: Disease Stories: Dying Young: Children-Parting with/Losing: Death-Dealing with: MELODRAMA:* Ace High; Aces High; All That Jazz; Always Together; American Flyers; Anne of the Thousand Days; Ballad of a Soldier; The Belly of an Architect; Being There; Best Man; Boom!; Checking Out; A Christmas Carol (1938); Color Me Dead; Conversation Piece; D.O.A. (1949); D.O.A. (1988); Dad; Daddy's Dyin'; Daisy Miller; Dark Victory; Dawn Patrol; Death in Venice; Death Watch; A Delicate Balance; The Devil's Advocate; The Devil's Disciple; The Diary of a Country Priest; Doc; Doctor; Dying Young; Dynamite; Early Frost; The Eddy Duchin Story; The End; Eric; Family Upside Down; The First Deadly Sin; The Gathering; Going in Style; Greedy; Gross Anatomy; Hasty Heart; Hawks; Hitler-The Last Ten Days; Hook, Line and Sinker; I Stand Condemned; I Want to Live!; I'd Rather Be Rich; Ikiru; In the Cool of the Day; The Invitation; It Started with Eve; Jesus of Nazareth; Joe vs. the Volcano; The Killers (1946); The Killers (1964); Lightning Over Water; Love and Death; Love and Pain and the Whole Damn Thing; Love Story (1944); Love Story (1970); Max Dugan Returns; Miracle Mile; The Muppet Christmas Carol; My Life; My Name is Nobody; Never Say Die; None But the Lonely Heart; Nothing Sacred; On Golden Pond; One Way Passage; Priest of Love; Providence; Right of Way; Send Me No Flowers; Sentimental Journey; Shadow Box; Shadowlands; The Shootist; Short Time; Six Weeks; Souls at Sea; Stolen Hours; Sweet November; Tears in the Rain; Terry Fox Story; That's Life!; Travelling North;

Tribute; Trip to Bountiful; Van Gogh; Volpone; Voyage of the Damned; Wake of the Red Witch; A Woman's Tale; Zigzag

Death-Impending, False (when death warnings are given, usually by doctors, which turn out to be wrong): see also American Friend; Hook, Line and Sinker; Living it Up; Nothing Sacred; Send Me No Flowers; Short Time

Death Personified (Death as a character): see also *Satan: HORROR:* The Adventures of Baron Munchausen; All That Jazz; Bill & Ted's Bogus Journey; Death Takes a Holiday; The Devil's Bride; The Masque of Red Death; Monty Python's The Meaning of Life; Orpheus (1949); The Seventh Seal

Deaths-Faked: see also *Dead-Back from the: Deaths-Accidental: Missing Persons: Accused Unjustly: Framed?: MURDER: Con Artists:* The Art of Love; The Deceived; Five Miles to Midnight; The Great Manhunt; Guilty Conscience; Holy Matrimony; Killjoy; The Lady from Shanghai; No Escape (1936); The Running Man (1963); Seconds; Sleeping With the Enemy; Tell Them Willie Boy is Here; Vertigo; Widows' Peak; The Wreck of the Mary Deare

Deaths of Celebrities: see *Biographies: Music Dies: Hollywood Life: Country Singers*

Deaths-One by One: see *Murders-One by One*

Debutantes: see *Social Climbing: Rich People*

Deceptions/Deceivers: see *Liars: Mindgames: Con Artists: Love-Questionable*

Decisions-Big: see also *Virgins: Coming of Age: Life Transitions: Power Struggles: Mindgames: Psychological Drama: Abortion Dilemmas: Political Drama: War Stories:* Above the Rim; Back Street (1932); Back Street (1941); Back Street (1961); Best Intentions; The Conversation; Cover Girl; Dr. Socrates; The Garment Jungle; Hook; It's My Turn; Lacombe, Lucien; The Man in the Grey Flannel Suit; Marius; Marjorie Morningstar; Mo' Better Blues; The Moon is Blue; Move; Music Box; Never Too Late; Private Function; The Private Lives of Elizabeth and Essex; Private Matter; Red Shoes; Souls at Sea; State of the Union; Strawberry Blonde; To Find a Man; To Have and Have Not; Tom, Dick and Harry; The Year of Living Dangerously

Defending Oneself: see *Saving Oneself: Murder-Clearing Oneself*

Delinquents: see *Juvenile Delinquents: Thieves: Gangs: Rebels*

Demons: see *Satanism: Occult: Monsters*

Dentists: see also *Doctors:* Bells Are Ringing; Cactus Flower; Compromising Positions; The Dentist; Eversmile New Jersey; The In-Laws; Little Shop of Horrors (1960); Little Shop of Horrors (1986); Marathon Man; One Sunday Afternoon; Paleface; Rocket to the Moon; The Strawberry Blonde

Department Stores (large or small): see also *Business Life:* Are You Being Served?; The Big Store; The Devil and Miss Jones; Mannequin (1987); Mannequin 2: On the Move; Miracle on 34th Street; Moscow on the Hudson; One Touch of Venus; The Shop Around the Corner; The Shop on Main Street; Somebody Killed Her Husband; Who's Minding the Store?

Depression (the mental condition): see also *Alienation: Mental Illness: Starting Over: Alcoholism: Addictions: Midlife Crisis:* Act of Love; Ash Wednesday; Autobus; Barfly; Bartleby; Bell Jar; The Blue Veil; Death of a Salesman (1950); Death of a Salesman (1985); Despair; Desperate Characters; Diary of a Country Priest; Diary of a Mad Housewife; Easy Virtue; The Effect of Gamma Rays on Man-in-the-Moon Marigolds; Electra Glide in Blue; The End; Fatso; Fearless; The Good Father; Gross Anatomy; Interiors; Ironweed; Joe vs. the Volcano; La Vie Continue; The Lacemaker; The Lady Takes a Flyer; Last Tango in Paris; Lenny; Life Upside Down; Little Vera; The Loneliness of the Long Distance Runner; Long Day's Journey Into Night; Look Back in Anger (1959); Look Back in Anger (1980); Look Back in Anger (1989); Lost Weekend; Love Letters (1984); Men Don't Leave; Miss Julie; Naked; Naked Lunch; No Man's Land; No Time for Comedy; Numero Deux; Of Human Bondage (1934); Of Human Bondage (1946); Of Human Bondage (1964); One Magic Christmas; Pain in the A . . . ; Plenty; Postcards from the Edge; Requiem for a Heavyweight (1956); Requiem for a Heavyweight (1962); Rocket to the Moon; Secret Honor; Seize the Day; Smash-Up, the Story of a Woman; Snakepit; So Big (1932); So Big (1953); SOB; Splendor in

the Grass; A Star is Born (1976); Stardust Memories; Swing High, Swing Low; Taxi zum Klo; They Shoot Horses, Don't They?; The Verdict; A View from the Bridge; Vincent and Theo; Walkabout; Wetherby; Who is Harry Kellerman . . . ; Withnail and I; A Woman Under the Influence; Yesterday's Hero

Depression Era (the time period of the 1930s): see also *1930s: Poor People:* Almost a Man; Always Goodbye; Annie; Bad Girl; Ballad of the Sad Cafe; The Bay Boy; Big Bad Mama; The Big Broadcast; Billy Bathgate; Bloody Mama; Bonnie and Clyde; Bound For Glory; Butterfly; Careful, He Might Hear You; Carousel; Charley and the Angel; Chinatown; The Day of the Locust; Dinner at Eight; Double Exposure; East of Eden (1955); East of Eden (1980); Enter Laughing; From This Day Forward; The Gilded Lily; The Grapes of Wrath; Hallelujah, I'm a Bum; Hard Promises; Honkytonk Man; I'll Give a Million; The Incredible Journey of Dr. Meg Laurel; Inside Daisy Clover; Ironweed; It's a Wonderful Life; The Journey of Natty Gann; King of the Hill (1993); Lady for a Day; Learning Tree; Lost Lady; Lovin' Molly; Mame; Man's Castle; Mary Burns, The Fugitive; The Millionaire; Mr. and Mrs. Bridge; Mrs. Wiggs of the Cabbage Patch; My Man Godfrey (1936); Nous La Liberte; Of Mice and Men (1939); Of Mice and Men (1993); Once Upon a Time in America; One More Spring; Outfit (1993); Paper Moon; Pennies from Heaven (1936); Pennies from Heaven (1981); Places in the Heart; Portrait of Jennie; The Purple Rose of Cairo; Rambling Rose; Riff-Raff (1935); Rocket to the Moon; The Shop Around the Corner; Skippy; Sounder; Spencer's Mountain; Splendor in the Grass; Stand Up and Cheer; The Sting; The Sting 2; Street Scene; Sullivan's Travels; They Shoot Horses, Don't They?; Thieves Like Us; This Property is Condemned; Three Cornered Moon; Thunder Rock; To Kill a Mockingbird; Tortilla Flat; Walk on the Wild Side; We're No Angels (1989); Where the Red Fern Grows; Why Shoot the Teacher?; Wild Hearts Can't Be Broken; Wild River; Winter People

Desert Settings: see also *Southwestern Life: WESTERNS: Stranded: Middle East:* The Andromeda Strain; Bad Day at Black Rock; Bagdad

Cafe; Bite the Bullet; The Bride Came C.O.D.; Brighty of the Grand Canyon; Butterfly; The Car; Caravans; Christmas Lilies of the Field; The Dark Wind; Desert Bloom; The Desert Fox; Desert Fury; Desert Rats; Desert Victory; Duel; Duel in the Sun; Dying Room Only; Eagle's Wing; Electra Glide in Blue; Five Graves to Cairo; Flight of the Phoenix; Fool for Love; Foxfire (1955); Gallipoli; Garden of Allah; Gas Food Lodging; Goodbye, New York; Greed; Harley Davidson and the Marlboro Man; Hell, Heaven, and Hoboken; The Hill; The Hills Have Eyes; Inferno; It Came From Outer Space; Khartoum; Kill Me Again; Kingdom of the Spiders; Kiss Me, Stupid!; The Last Temptation of Christ; Late for Dinner; Lawrence of Arabia; Legend of the Lost; Lion of the Desert; Little Fauss and Big Halsey; The Little Prince; Little Vegas; The Living Desert; March or Die; McLintock!; The Misfits; Night of the Lepus; Night Terror; Nightwing; Over Her Dead Body; Petrified Forest; The Professionals; Rapture; Rope of Sand; Rubin & Ed; Sahara (1943); Salome, Where She Danced; Sands of the Kalahari; Scalawag; The Sheltering Sky; The Shooting; Suez; Sundown; Them!; Thief of Bagdad (1924); Thief of Baghdad (1940); Three Godfathers; Thunderbirds; Tobruk; Tremors; Two Lane Blacktop; UFOria; Woman in the Dunes; Zabriskie Point

Detective Couples (partners in crime detection, usually married): see also *Partners-Married: Buddy Films: Detective Stories: Comic Mystery:*
Another Thin Man; The Big Easy; Dear Inspector; Fast Company; I Wake Up Screaming; Manhattan Murder Mystery; Moonlighting (1985); Mr. and Mrs. North; A Night to Remember (1946); Object of Beauty; Shadow of the Thin Man; Song of the Thin Man; The Thin Man; Undercover Blues; Who is Killing the Great Chefs of Europe?

Detective Stories: see also *Detective Couples: Police Stories: Detectives-Police: Journalists as Detectives: MYS-TERY: Film Noir: Detectives-Amateur: Medical Detectives: Scientist Detectives: Spoofs-Detective: Undercover: Disguises: Suspecting Oneself:*
Accused (1948); Ace Ventura, Pet Detective; Action Jackson; The Adventures of Ford Fairlane; The

Adventures of Sherlock Holmes; All the President's Men; The Alphabet Murders; The Amateur; Amsterdamned; Another Thin Man; Armed Response; Arsene Lupin Returns; Backdraft; Bad Lieutenant; Badge 373; Basic Instinct; Being at Home with Claude; The Big Easy; The Big Fix; The Big Sleep (1946); The Big Sleep (1977); Black Marble; Black Rain (1989); Black Widow (1987); Blackmail (1929); Blood on the Sun; Blue Iguana; Body in the Library; Boiling Point; Boomerang (1947); Boston Strangler; Brannigan; Brasher Doubloon; Brenda Starr; The Bride Wore Black; Bulldog Drummond (1929); Bulldog Drummond at Bay; Bulldog Drummond Strikes Back; Bullets or Ballots; Bullitt; Bullshot; Bunny Lake is Missing; The Burglars; Cahill: United States Marshal; Calling Bulldog Drummond; Calling Northside 777; Caprice; Carey Treatment; Cassandra Crossing; The Castle in the Desert; Chan is Missing; Chandler; Cheap Detective; Cheaper to Keep Her; The Chiefs; The China Syndrome; Chinatown; Class Action; Clean Slate; Clockers; Cobra; Coma; Come Back Charleston Blue; Compromising Positions; Confidentially Yours; Cop au Vin; Cruising; The Curse of the Pink Panther; Dark Corner; The Dark Wind; Day of the Jackal; Dead Bang; Dead Pool; Deadlier Than the Male; Deadly Affair; Deadly Currents; Dear Inspector; Death on the Nile; Death Warrant; Deep Cover; The Detective (1954); The Detective (1968); Detective (1985); Detective Story; Dial M For Murder; Dick Tracy; Dirty Harry; Don't Just Stand There; Dragnet (1954); Dragnet (1987); Dream Lover (1986); Dream Team; The Drowning Pool; The Enforcer (1950); The Enforcer (1976); Everybody Wins; Evil Under the Sun; Eyes in the Night; Farewell, My Lovely (1944); Farewell, My Lovely (1975); Fast Company; Fatal Beauty; Fate is the Hunter; Fear; A Fine Mess; The First Deadly Sin; First Power; Flare Up; Fletch; Fletch Lives; Fog over Frisco; The Forbidden; Foreign Correspondent; Foreign Intrigue; The Fourth Story; The French Connection; The French Connection II; Frenzy; From the Life of the Marionettes; The Front Page (1931); The Front Page (1974); F/X; F/X 2: The Deadly Art of Illusion; Gator; Gentleman's Agreement; Glass Bottom

Boat; Gleaming the Cube; Gorky Park; Gotham; The Great Mouse Detective; Green for Danger; The Groundstar Conspiracy; Gumshoe; Hammett; Harper; Hidden; Hidden 2; Hide in Plain Sight; Homicide; Hound of the Baskervilles (1939); Hound of the Baskervilles (1959); Hound of the Baskervilles (1977); The House on Carroll Street; Hudson Hawk; I Love Trouble (1947); I Love Trouble (1994); I, the Jury (1953); I, The Jury (1982); I Wake Up Screaming; The Inquisitor; An Inspector Calls; Inspector Clouseau; It's Only Money; Jack the Ripper (1958); Just Cause; Kamikaze 89; Kennel Murder Case; Kill Me Again; Kindergarten Cop; Kinjite, Forbidden Subjects; Kiss Me Deadly; Klute; Knight Moves; Kuffs; La Chevre; The Lady in Cement; Lady in the Lake; The Lady of Burlesque; Ladykiller (1992); Lassiter; The Last Boy Scout; The Late Show; The Laughing Policeman; Laura; Les Comperes; The Life of Emile Zola; The List of Adrian Messenger; The Long Goodbye; Lorenzo's Oil; Love at Large; Love Crimes; Low Down Dirty Shame; Mad Miss Manton; Madigan; Magnum Force; The Maltese Falcon (1931); The Maltese Falcon (1941); Man on a Swing; Man on the Eiffel Tower; The Man with Bogart's Face; Manhattan Murder Mystery; Manhunter; Marlowe; McQ; Mean Season; Men at Work; Miami Blues; Mighty Quinn; Miss Grant Takes Richmond; Mississippi Burning; The Mob; Molly Maguires; Monolith; Moonlighting (1985); Mr. Arkadin; Murder Ahoy; Murder at the Gallop; Murder by Death; Murder by Decree; Murder Most Foul; Murder of Mary Phagan; Murder on the Orient Express; Murder She Said; Mystery Street; Nadine; The Naked City; The Name of the Rose; Night Moves; Night Stalker/The Night Strangler; A Night to Remember (1946); No Way to Treat a Lady; Nocturne; Object of Beauty; Odessa File; Oh Heavenly Dog; The Omen; Omen IV: The Awakening; Ordeal by Innocence; Out of the Past; Outland; Outrage (1964); Panic in the Streets; The Parallax View; The Party's Over; Peeper; The Pink Panther Strikes Again; Plain Clothes; Point Break; Primary Motive; Prime Cut; Prime Suspect; The Private Life of Sherlock Holmes; Pure Luck; Q (The Winged Serpent); Raw Deal; Rent a Dick; The

Scarface Mob/The Untouchables Pilot; Sea of Love; Second Sight; Serpico; The Shadow (1936); Shakedown; She Done Him Wrong; Shot in the Dark; Slaughter on Tenth Avenue; Sniper; Someone to Watch Over Me; The Specialist; Stakeout; State of Grace; Strange Bargain; Sudden Impact; Tango & Cash; They Call Me Mr. Tibbs!; Tick, Tick, Tick . . . ; Tightrope; To Live and Die in L.A.; The Town; Traces of Red; Turner & Hooch; Twin Peaks; Twin Peaks: Fire Walk with Me; The Untouchables; Whipsaw; The Wicker Man; Year of the Dragon; Wilt

Detectives-Private: see also *Detective Couples: Detective Stories: Detective Partners: Detectives in Deep: Detectives-Amateur: Journalists as Detectives: Medical Detectives: Scientist Detectives:* The Big Fix; The Big Sleep (1946); The Big Sleep (1977); Blue Iguana; Brasher Doubloon; Bulldog Drummond (1929); Bulldog Drummond at Bay; Bulldog Drummond Strikes Back; Chandler; Clean Slate; Come Back Charleston Blue; The Driver; Everybody Wins; Evil Under the Sun; Farewell, My Lovely (1944); Farewell, My Lovely (1975); The Fourth Story; From the Life of the Marionettes; F/X; F/X 2: The Deadly Art of Illusion; Gotham; Gumshoe; How to Steal a Million; I Love Trouble (1947); I, the Jury (1953); I, The Jury (1982); I Wake Up Screaming; Kiss Me Deadly; Klute; Kuffs; Lady in Cement; Lady in the Lake; Lassiter; The Late Show; The Long Goodbye; The Maltese Falcon (1931); The Maltese Falcon (1941); The Man with Bogart's Face; Marlowe; Maverick Queen; Night Moves; The Private Life of Sherlock Holmes; Satan Met a Lady; The Seven Percent Solution; Shaft; Shaft in Africa; Shaft's Big Score; Shamus; Sherlock Holmes; Sherlock Holmes and the Secret Weapon; Sherlock Holmes and the Spider Woman; Sherlock Holmes and the Voice of Terror; Sherlock Holmes Faces Death; Sherlock Holmes in Washington; Sherlock Holmes: The Spider Woman Strikes Back; Terror By Night; They Might be Giants; Tony Rome; V.I. Warshawski; Vertigo; Who Framed Roger Rabbitt?; You Can Never Tell

Detectives as Suspects: see *Murder-Clearing Oneself: Suspecting Oneself: Detectives in Deep: Saving Oneself: Murder-Debate to Reveal Killer*

Devil's Island (stories set on the French-owned South American island prison): see also *Prison Escapes: Islands:* Devil Doll; Papillon; Strange Cargo

Devil Worship: see *Satanism*

Dictators: see *Leaders-Tyrants: Fascism: Oppression*

Die Hard Stories (stories similar to the vigilante cop who happens upon a terrorist hostage situation in the film *Die Hard***): see also** *ACTION: Hostage Situations: Crisis Situations: Terrorists:* Passenger 57; Die Hard; Die Hard 2; Speed; Under Siege

Diner Life: see *Restaurant Settings*

Dinner Parties: see also *Comedy of Manners: Ensemble Films: Party Movies: Restaurant Settings:* Babette's Feast; The Dead; Dinner at Eight; The Discreet Charm of Bourgeousie; Don's Party; The Exterminating Angel; Guess Who's Coming to Dinner; La Cage Aux Folles; L'Invitation; Married to It; Monty Python's The Meaning of Life; My Dinner With Andre; The Party; Someone to Love; Who's Afraid of Virginia Woolf?

Dinosaurs: see also *Archaeologists/ Paleontologists: Prehistoric Settings:* At the Earth's Core; Baby, Secret of the Lost Legend; Caveman; The Flintstones; Jurassic Park; King Kong (1933); The Land Before Time; The Land that Time Forgot; My Science Project; One Million BC (1940); One Million Years BC (1966); One Woman or Two; The People That Time Forgot; We're Back! A Dinosaur's Story; When Dinosaurs Ruled the Earth

Diplomats: see also *Assassination Plots: Spy Films: Political Drama: CIA Agents: Americans Abroad: Political Unrest:* The Ambassador; Barbarian and the Geisha; Battement de Coeur; Beyond the Limit; Burn!; Bushido Blade; A Countess from Hong Kong; Damage; Deadly Affair; The Final Conflict; Fools for Scandal; Half Moon Street; Holiday in Mexico; Indiscreet; Lethal Weapon 2; M. Butterfly; The Omen; Plenty; Ransom; Romanoff and Juliet; The Ugly American; White Mischief; The Year of Living Dangerously

Directed by Brothers: see also *Writer-Directors: Directors:* Menace II Society; Night of the Shooting Stars

Directors (characters who are movie or stage directors): see also *Actor Directors: Writers: Hollywood Life: Movie Making: Movies within Movies:* After the Rehearsal; Alex in Wonderland; The Barefoot Contessa; The Big Picture; Blue; Bombay Talkie; Carousel; Cinema Paradiso; Dangerous Game; Day For Night; The Devil's Wanton; 8½; Fathers and Sons; Finger of Guilt; Hearts of Darkness: A Filmmaker's Apocalypse; High Risk; Hollywood Cavalcade; I'm Dancing as Fast as I Can; The Icicle Thief; I'll Do Anything; Intervista; Irreconcilable Differences; It's a Great Feeling; Jesus of Montreal; Last Command; The Last Movie; Law of Desire; The Legend of Lylah Clare; Lightning Over Water; Living in Oblivion; The Magic Box; A Man Like Eva; The Man Who Understood Women; The Mistress; Movers and Shakers; My Geisha; New Nightmare; Nickelodeon; Noises Off; Once Is Not Enough; The Passion; The Producers; SOB; Stardust Memories; State of Things; The Stunt Man; Success is the Best Revenge; Sullivan's Travels; Sweet Liberty; That's Adequate; The Trip; Twentieth Century; Two Weeks in Another Town; What Price Hollywood?; White Hunter, Black Heart; You'll Never Get Rich

Disabled but Nominated (for an Oscar, performances of disabled characters): see also *Disabled People: Prostitute but Nominated:* Bright Victory; Charly; Coming Home; Interrupted Melody; Johnny Belinda; The Piano; Wait Until Dark; Children of a Lesser God; Rain Man; Nell; Passion Fish

Disabled People: see also *Blind People: Deaf People: Disabled People in Jeopardy:* An Affair to Remember; The Barretts of Wimpole Street (1934); The Barretts of Wimpole Street (1956); Basket Case; Basket Case 2; Basket Case 3; Baxter (1972); Beneath the Planet of the Apes; The Big Street; Bitter Moon; Born on the Fourth of July; Bright Victory; Brimstone and Treacle; Coming Home; Cutter and Bone; Daddy Nostalgia; Darkman; The Elephant Man; Eye of the Needle; Family Pictures; The Glass Menagerie (1950); The Glass Menagerie (1973); The Glass Menagerie (1987); The Hunchback of Notre Dame (1923); The Hunchback of Notre Dame (1939); The Hunchback of Notre Dame (1956); The Hunchback of Notre Dame (1982); The Hunchback of Notre Dame (1996); In a Shallow Grave; Inside Moves; Interrupted Melody; Joni; Knickerbocker Holiday; Lady in a Cage; Lorenzo's Oil; The Man Without a Face; Mask (1985); The Men

(1950); The Miracle Worker; Monkey Shines; Moulin Rouge; My Left Foot; The Other Side of the Mountain; The Other Side of the Mountain Part Two; Passion Fish; Rear Window; Richard III; Savage Intruder; Scalawag; Scent of a Woman; Sorry, Wrong Number; Stairway to Heaven; Tell Me that You Love Me, Junie Moon; Waterdance; Whose Life Is It Anyway?; Wings of Eagles; A Woman's Face

Disabled People in Jeopardy: see also *Disabled People: Deaf People: Blind People: Women in Jeopardy: Men in Jeopardy: SUSPENSE:* The Fear Inside; Hear No Evil; Jennifer 8; Johnny Belinda; Lady in a Cage; Monkey Shines; See No Evil; Sorry, Wrong Number; The Spiral Staircase (1946); The Spiral Staircase (1975); Twenty-Three Paces to Baker Street; Wait Until Dark

Disaster Movies: see also *Floods: Tornadoes: Earthquakes: Volcanoes: Hurricanes: Fires: Crisis Situations:* After the Shock; Airplane!; Airplane 2, the Sequel; Airport; Airport 1975; Airport 1977; Airport '79, The Concorde; Alive; Avalanche; Beyond the Poseidon Adventure; The Big Bus; The Big One, The Great Los Angeles; The Bridge of San Luis Rey; Cassandra Crossing; China Seas; China Syndrome; Earthquake; Fate is the Hunter; Fearless; Flood!; Friday the Thirteenth (1933); The Greatest Show on Earth; High and the Mighty; Hindenburg; Hurricane (1937); Hurricane (1979); In Old Chicago; Juggernaut; Krakatoa, East of Java; The Last Days of Pompeii; Lifeboat; The Medusa Touch; The Meteor; Miracle Mile; Nanook of the North; A Night to Remember (1958); No Highway in the Sky; No Man of Her Own (1949); The Poseidon Adventure; The Rains Came; Runaway Train; San Francisco; Survive; The Swarm; Titanic; The Towering Inferno; Warning Sign; When Time Ran Out

Disc Jockeys: see *Radio Life*

Disco Era: see also *Musicals-Disco Era: 1970s: Dance Movies: MUSICALS: Music Movies:* Can't Stop the Music; Car Wash; FM; Looking for Mr. Goodbar; Roller Boogie; Saturday Night Fever; Sergeant Pepper's Lonely Hearts Club Band; The Spirit of '76; Staying Alive; Thank God It's Friday; Xanadu

Disease Stories: see also *MELO-DRAMA: Tearjerkers: Epidemics: Cures/Solutions-Search for: Death-*

Dealing with: AIDS Stories: Medical Drama: Social Drama: American Flyers; An Angel at My Table; And Now, Tomorrow; The Andromeda Strain; Bang the Drum Slowly; Based on an Untrue Story; Beaches; Bobby Deerfield; Body and Soul (1981); Breaking the Rules; Brian's Song; Camille (1936); Cassandra Crossing; Champions; Constant Nymph (1933); Constant Nymph (1943); The Cure; Daisy Miller; Dark Angel (1935); Dark Victory; Diary of a Country Priest; The Doctor; Dying Young; Early Frost; Echoes of a Summer; The Eddy Duchin Story; The Elephant Man; Eric; Family Upside Down; Four Frightened People; Gaby, a True Story; The Good Fight; Griffin and Phoenix, A Love Story; Gross Anatomy; Hasty Heart; Hawks; House of Cards; Interrupted Melody; Joe vs. the Volcano; Lorenzo's Oil; Love and Pain and the Whole Damn Thing; Love Story (1944); Love Story (1970); Magnificent Obsession (1935); Magnificent Obsession (1954); The Man with the Golden Arm; Mask (1985); Miniver Story; The Miracle Worker; My Left Foot; 1918; None But the Lonely Heart; Nothing Sacred; The Nun's Story; The Other Side of the Mountain; Outbreak; Pete 'n Tillie; Philadelphia; The Plague; Pride of the Yankees; Priest of Love; Promises in the Dark; Red Pony (1949); Red Pony (1976); Sentimental Journey; Shadow Box; Shadowlands; Sister Kenny; Stairway to Heaven; Steel Magnolias; Stolen Hours; The Stratton Story; Sunrise at Campobello; Sweet November; Terms of Endearment; That's Life!; Three Comrades; The Three Faces of Eve; Unnatural Causes; Untamed Heart; Walking Stick; Warm December

Disguised as a Priest: see also *Disguises: Priests:* Cassandra Crossing; We're No Angels (1955); We're No Angels (1989); Left Hand of God

Disguises: see also *Impostors: Impostors-Actor: Identities-Assumed: Identities-Mistaken: Spy Films: Spies: Multiple Performances:* The Affairs of Annabel; After The Fox; The Applegates; The Barefoot Contessa; Black Widow (1987); Bottoms Up; Brubaker; Burglar; Call Me Bwana; Consenting Adults; Crimes of Passion; Darkman; Day of the Jackal; Devil Doll; Dick Tracy; Europa, Europa; Fancy Pants; Femme Fatale; The Fool; Gentleman's Agreement; The Great

Bank Robbery; The Great Impostor; The Great Train Robbery; The Guardsman; Happy New Year (1987); Has Anybody Seen My Gal?; Hold Me, Thrill Me, Kiss Me; The Left Hand of God; Lily in Love; The List of Adrian Messenger; M. Butterfly; The Major and the Minor; The Man with Two Faces; Mark of the Vampire; Meet the Applegates; Menace Mikado; Mrs Doubtfire; My Geisha; My Man Godfrey (1936); My Man Godfrey (1956); A New Kind of Love; No Way to Treat a Lady; Nuns on the Run; The Passage; The Pirate; Saint Benny, the Dip; Salome, Where She Danced; Saving Grace; Scaramouche; The Seven Faces of Dr. Lao; Shaggy Dog; Soul Man; Some Like it Hot; Sylvia Scarlett; Tootsie; Two Mules for Sister Sara; When in Rome; Witness for the Prosecution

Disney Comedy (a children's/family comedy made by Disney): see also *Comedy-Disneyesque: CHILDREN'S: FAMILY: Children's Comedy:* The Absent-Minded Professor; The Apple Dumpling Gang; The Apple Dumpling Gang Rides Again; Babe; Baby, Secret of the Lost Legend; Bambi; Blackbeard's Ghost; Boatniks; Bon Voyage!; Candleshoe; The Castaway Cowboy; The Computer Wore Tennis Shoes; Darby O'Gill and the Little People; The Devil and Max Devlin; Follow Me, Boys!; Freaky Friday; Gnome Mobile; A Goofy Movie; The Happiest Millionaire; The Horse in the Grey Flannel Suit; Hot Lead and Cold Feet; Love Bug; Monkeys Go Home; Moon Pilot; No Deposit, No Return; North Avenue Irregulars; Now You See Him, Now You Don't; One of Our Dinosaurs is Missing; The Parent Trap; The Shaggy D.A.; The Shaggy Dog; Superdad; Three Ninjas; Three Ninjas Kick Back; The Ugly Dachschund

Disneyesque Comedy: see also *Disney Comedy:* Charley and the Angel; Double McGuffin; Freddie as F.R.O.7.; The Ghost and Mr. Chicken; Matilda; Monkey Trouble; My Father the Hero; My Science Project; Never a Dull Moment (1967)

Disorders-Personality: see *Multiple Personalities: Mental Illness: Psychological Drama: Psychologists*

Divers: see *Swimming: Adventure at Sea: Underwater Adventure: Treasure Hunts: Sharks: Sailing*

Divorce: see also *Custody Battles: Marriage on the Rocks: Detectives-*

Matrimonial: The Age of Innocence (1934); The Age of Innocence (1993); All I Want For Christmas; Author! Author!; The Awful Truth; Between Friends; A Bill of Divorcement (1932); A Bill of Divorcement (1940); Blume in Love; Breaking Up is Hard to Do; Bright Eyes; C'est la Vie; Casanova Brown; The Champ (1931); The Champ (1979); Chapter Two; Cheaper to Keep Her; Desert Hearts; Divorce of Lady X; The Divorcee; The Dream Wife; East Lynne; Easy Virtue; Family Pictures; Firstborn; Forty Pounds of Trouble; The Gay Divorcee; The Good Father; Hilda Crane; Husbands and Wives; I Will . . . I Will . . . for Now; Irreconcilable Differences; Kramer vs. Kramer; The Last Married Couple in America; Let's Do it Again (1953); Let's Make it Legal; Living Corpse; Love Crazy; Love Hurts; Love Matters; Love Streams; A Man for All Seasons; Man on Fire; Marriage on the Rocks; Mary, Mary; The Merry Wives of Reno; Move Over, Darling; Mr. Wonderful; Mrs Doubtfire; My Favorite Wife; A New Life; Nothing in Common; One Is a Lonely Number; Opposite Sex; The Parent Trap; Paris, Texas; Payment on Demand; Penny Serenade; Perfect Marriage; Phffft!; The Philadelphia Story; Rich Kids; See You in the Morning; Shoot the Moon; Starting Over; Total Recall; Twice in a Lifetime; Two for the Seesaw; War of the Roses; We're Not Married; Women

Dizzy Blondes: see *Bimbos: Heiresses-Madcap: Simple Minds: Screwball Comedy*

Doctors: see also *Medical Drama: Medical Detectives: Disease Stories: Hospitals: Medical Students: Medical Thriller: Romance with Doctor: Veterinarians:* All Creatures Great and Small; Appointment for Love; Arrowsmith; Article 99; Awakenings; The Bachelor; Belle du Jour; Beyond the Limit; Boxing Helena; Bramble Bush; Calling Dr. Gillespie; Calling Dr. Kildare; Captain Blood; Carey Treatment; A Change of Habit; The Chapman Report; Christ Stopped at Eboli; Chronicle of a Death Foretold; Citadel; City of Joy; Coma; Come Back, Little Sheba; Crimes and Misdemeanors; Critical Condition; Dead Ringers; Disorderly Orderly; Doc Hollywood; The Doctor; Doctor in the House; Doctor Quinn, Medicine Woman;

The Doctor Takes a Wife; Doctor's Dilemma; Doctor's Wives; Dominick & Eugene; Dr. Dolittle; Dr. Ehrlich's Magic Bullet; Dr. Jekyll and Sister Hyde; Dr. Socrates; Driftwood; Ex-Mrs. Bradford; Fatal Vision; Finishing School; Flatliners; Frantic (1988); The Fugitive (1993); The Fugitive: The Final Episode; The Girl Who Couldn't Say No; The Great Moment; Green for Danger; Gross Anatomy; Hanging Tree; The Homecoming (1948); Hospital; House Calls; The Hunger; I Love My Wife; I, Monster; The Incredible Journey of Dr. Meg Laurel; Interns; Killjoy; The Lady is Willing; The Last Angry Man; Lesson in Love; Letters from a Dead Man; MASH; Magnificent Obsession (1935); Magnificent Obsession (1954); Making Love; Malice; The Man with Two Brains; Men in White; Mister Frost; Murder in Texas; Myra Breckinridge; Never Say Goodbye; New Interns; Night unto Night; No Way Out (1950); Not as a Stranger; Of Human Bondage (1934); Of Human Bondage (1946); Of Human Bondage (1964); One Hour with You; Outbreak; Painted Veil; People Will Talk; Petulia Plague; Promises in the Dark; Shake Hands with the Devil; The Story of Dr. Wassell; The Story of Louis Pasteur; Such Good Friends; Sunday, Bloody Sunday; Threshold; Where Does it Hurt?; Wife, Doctor and Nurse; Yes, Giorgio; You Belong to Me; Young Doctors; Young Doctors in Love

Doctors as Detectives: see *Medical Detectives: Medical Thriller: Detectives-Amateur: Detective Stories: MYSTERY*

Docudrama: see also *True Stories: True or Not?: Documentary Style: Incredible but Mostly True:* Al Capone; American Hotwax; Angelo, My Love; Awakenings; Based on an Untrue Story; Best Boy; Bleak Moments; Boomerang (1947); Children of Hiroshima; The Crash of Silence; Dead Ahead, the Exxon Valdez Disaster; Deliberate Stranger; Duffy's Tavern; Eight Men Out; Eighty-Four Charlie Mopic; Elephant Boy; Evel Knievel; Fourteen Hours; The Gospel According to St. Matthew; The Greatest; Guyana Tragedy, The Story of Jim Jones; Hide in Plain Sight; Hoop Dreams; I Was a Communist for the FBI; The Killing Fields; Lightning Over Water; The Lindbergh Kidnapping Case; Louisiana Story; Man of Aran; Man of Iron; Man of

Marble; McVicar; A Night to Remember (1958); The Rise of Louis XIV; Romero; Salaam Bombay!; Salvador; Shadows; Someone to Love; Split Image; Stage Door Canteen; Stand and Deliver; The Terry Fox Story; Three Came Home; The Three Faces of Eve; A Town Like Alice (1956); A Town Like Alice (1985); Voyage of the Damned; The Wrong Man

Documentaries: see also *True Stories: Interviews: Filmumentaries: Docudrama:* All This and World War II; Best Boy; Blue Water, White Death; A Brief History of Time; Broken Noses; Burden of Dreams; The Commies are Coming, the Commies are Coming; Dear America: Letters Home from Vietnam; The Decline of Western Civilization; Desert Victory; The Devil's Wanton; Dialogues with Madwomen; A Diary for Timothy; Don't Look Back; Endless Summer; The Epic That Never Was; F for Fake; Forever James Dean; The Gentle Sex; The Gong Show Movie; The Gospel According to St. Matthew; Hail, Hail, Rock 'n Roll; Harlan County, USA; Hearts of Darkness: A Filmmaker's Apocalypse; The Hellstrom Chronicle; Helter Skelter (1949); High Risk; Hoop Dreams; Incident at Oglala; Intervista; I Was a Communist for the FBI; Koyaanisqatsi; The Last of England; The Last Waltz; Let's Get Lost; Lightning Over Water; Listen Up: The Lives of Quincy Jones; The Living Desert; The Louisiana Story; Love Goddesses; Mein Kampf; Mondo Cane; Next of Kin (1942); Olympische Spiele; Paris is Burning; Perri Powaqqatsi, Life in Transformation; Pumping Iron; Pumping Iron 2; Real Life; Reefer Madness; Rented Lips; Rock Hudson's Home Movies; Roger & Me; Say Amen, Somebody!; Someone to Love; Stage Door Canteen; Superstar, The Life and Times of Andy Warhol; The Thin Blue Line; The Three Caballeros; The Times of Harvey Milk; Triumph of the Will; True Glory; Truth or Dare; Valley Obscured by the Clouds; The War Room; Woodstock

Documentary Style (all or partial "cinema verite," realistic, journalistic-style filmmaking): **see also** *Avant-Garde: Documentaries: True Stories: Interviews:* Andy Warhol's Heat; Bob Roberts; Central Park; Children of Hiroshima; The Crash of Silence; Day For Night; The Devil's Wanton; A Diary for Timothy; Flesh; Fourteen Hours; Ghosts . . . of the Civil Dead; The Gods Must Be Crazy; The Gods Must Be Crazy II; The Gong Show Movie; The Gospel According to St. Matthew; Hollywood Canteen; Husbands and Wives; I am a Fugitive from a Chain Gang; I Was a Communist for the FBI; Intervista; Is There Sex After Death?; JFK; Jud Suess; Leningrad Cowboys Go to America; The Louisiana Story; Man Bites Dog; Man of Aran; Man of Marble; Medium Cool; Men of the Fighting Lady; Mi Vida Loca; Naked City; New Orleans; New Year's Day; Newsfront; Nighthawks (1978); Nighthawks, 2: Strip Jack Naked (1991); Pixote; Real Life; Revolt of Job; Rise of Louis XIV; Salaam Bombay!; Shadows; The Sniper; Special Bulletin; Strike; Trash; Tree of Wooden Clogs; True Stories; Wild River; Working Girls; Zelig

Dogs: see also *Animals-Talking: Pet Stories: Boy and His Dog: Cats:* The Awful Truth; Baxter (1990); Beethoven; Beethoven's 2nd; Behave Yourself!; Benji; Benji the Hunted; Big Red; The Biscuit Eater (1940); The Biscuit Eater (1972); A Boy and His Dog; The Call of the Wild (1935); The Call of the Wild (1972); CHOMPS; Clean Slate; A Cry in the Dark; Cujo; Homeward Bound; Incredible Journey; Goodbye My Lady; A Goofy Movie; Kennel Murder Case; K-9; K-9000; Lady and the Tramp; Lassie; Lassie Come Home; Magic of Lassie; Man's Best Friend; Mask (1994); Mrs. Brown, You've Got a Lovely Daughter; Oh Heavenly Dog; Oliver and Company; Old Yeller; Once Upon a Crime; 101 Dalmatians; Pack; Sandlot; Savage Sam; The Shaggy D.A.; The Shaggy Dog; Son of Lassie; Sounder; They Only Kill Their Masters; The Thin Man; To Dance with the White Dog; Turner & Hooch; The Ugly Dachshund; Umberto D.; We Think the World of You; Where the Red Fern Grows; White Dog; White Fang; Won Ton Ton, the Dog Who Saved Hollywood; You Can Never Tell

Doing the Right Things: see *Ethics: Morality Plays: Justice-Search for* **Dolls:** see *Monsters-Toys/Dolls as: CHILDREN'S*

Dolphins: see also *Fish: Sea Creatures: Sharks:* Ace Ventura, Pet Detective; Big Blue; Boy on a Dolphin; Day of the Dolphin; Flipper

Domestic Life: see *Suburban Life: Housewives: Ordinary People Stories*
Dose of Own Medicine-Given: see *Turning the Tables: Revenge:* Blackmailed; Flesh and the Devil; Go into Your Dance; Goodbye, Charlie; Hedda; Hobson's Choice; Hollywood Boulevard (1936); Honky Tonk; Lipstick; Mr. Klein; Switch; The Tender Trap; Trading Places
Double Crossings (where there's usually a series of betrayals and counterbetrayals): see *Clever Plots & Endings: Betrayals: Mindgames: Con Artists: Sabotage: Traitors: Liars: Love-Questionable: Dangerous Men: Dangerous Women:* Absence of Malice; After Dark, My Sweet; Against All Odds; Arabesque; Bad Influence; The Ballad of Cable Hogue; Bedroom Window; Big Knife; Bitter Rice; Body Heat; Brainstorm (1965); Captain Kidd; Charley Varrick; Chimes at Midnight; China Moon; Clear and Present Danger; Cliffhanger; The Cook, the Thief, His Wife & Her Lover; Criss Cross (1947); Dangerous Liaisons; Dead in the Water; Dead On; Deathtrap; Double-Crossed; Easy to Wed; Everybody Wins; The Experts; Femme Fatale; Final Analysis; Five Fingers; F/X; F/X 2: The Deadly Art of Illusion; Geronimo (1962); Geronimo (1993); Happy New Year (1973); The Human Factor; The Informer; Innocent; Jet Pilot; La Balance; Last Rites; The Last Seduction; The Law and Jake Wade; Libeled Lady; The Little Drummer Girl; The Looking Glass War; Love at Large; Mackintosh Man; The Maltese Falcon (1931); The Maltese Falcon (1941); The Man in Grey; Manhattan Murder Mystery; Man-trap; Masquerade (1965); Midnight Crossing; Miller's Crossing; Murder by Natural Causes; Oscar; Prizzi's Honor; Quick; Red Rock West; Rome Express; Roxie Hart; Scorpio; The Secret Partner; The Sicilian; The Silent Partner; Ski School; Slither; Sneakers; The Sniper; The Specialist; The Spy in Black; Strangers on a Train; Strictly Business; Tequila Sunrise; Topaz (1969); The Trap; Valmont; White Sands; The Wrong Box
Doubles: see *Lookalikes: Twins: Identities-Mistaken: Identities-Assumed*
Dracula: see *Vampires: Monsters-Human: HORROR: Spoofs-Vampires*
Dragons: see also *Mythology: Monsters-Mythological: Medieval Times:* Dragonslayer; Erik the Viking;

Jabberwocky; Pete's Dragon; Q (The Winged Serpent); Siegfried; Sleeping Beauty; The Wonderful World of the Brothers Grimm

DRAMA: see also *COMEDY DRAMA: TRAGEDY: Medical Drama: Musical-Drama: Political Drama: Rescue Adventure/Drama: Romantic Drama:* Aaron Loves Angela; Abandoned; The Abdication; The Abductors; Abe Lincoln in Illinois; Abel; Abie's Irish Rose; Abilene Town; About Face; About Last Night; About Mrs. Leslie; Above and Beyond; Above the Rim; Above Us The Waves; Abraham Lincoln; Abschied von Gestern; Absence of Malice; Absolution; Accatone; The Accident; The Accidental Tourist; The Accused (1988); Ace Eli and Rodger of the Skies; Ace in the Hole; Ace of Aces; Aces High; Across the Pacific; Across the Wide Missouri; Act of Love; Act of Murder; Act of the Heart; Act of Violence; Act One; Action for Slander; Action in Arabia; Action in the North Atlantic; The Actor's Revenge; Actors and Sin; The Actress (1928); The Actress (1953); Ada; Adalen 31; Adam; Adam and Eva; Adam at 6 A.M.; Adam Had Four Sons; The Adjuster; Adventure for Two; Adventure in Washington; The Adventures of Arsène Lupin; The Adventures of Casanova; The Adventures of Reinette and Mirabelle; The Adventures of Robinson Crusoe; The Adventuress; Advise and Consent; An Affair to Remember; The Affairs of Susan; The African Queen; After Dark, My Sweet; After the Rehearsal; After the Shock; Against All Odds; Against the Wind; Agatha; Age of Consent; The Age of Innocence (1934); The Age of Innocence (1993); Agnes of God; Agony and the Ecstasy; Aguirre, the Wrath of God; Ah, Wilderness; Airport; Airport 1975; Airport 1977; Airport '79, The Concorde; Akira Kurosawa's Dreams; Al Capone; Alamo Bay; Alan and Naomi; Alex in Wonderland; Alexander Nevsky; Alexander the Great; Alexander, the Other Side of Dawn; Algiers; Alice Adams; Alice Doesn't Live Here Anymore; Alice in the Cities; Alien Nation; Alive; All About Eve; All Fall Down; All My Sons (1949); All My Sons (1986); All Night Long (1961); All Quiet on the Western Front; All That Jazz; All That Money Can Buy; All the Brothers Were Valiant; All the Fine Young

Boyz N the Hood; Brainstorm (1983); Brass Target; Break of Hearts; Breaker Morant; The Breakfast Club; Breaking Glass; Breaking Point; Breaking the Sound Barrier; Breaking Up is Hard to Do; A Breath of Scandal; Breathless (1959); Breathless (1983); A Breed Apart; Breezy; Brian's Song; The Bride; The Bride is Much Too Beautiful; The Bride Wore Black; The Bride Wore Red; Brideshead Revisited; The Bridge; The Bridge of San Luis Rey; Bridge on the River Kwai; Bridges at Toko-Ri; A Bridge Too Far; Brief Encounter (1946); Bright Angel; Bright Lights, Big City; Bright Road; Brighton Rock; Brimstone and Treacle; Bring Me the Head of Alfredo Garcia; The Brink of Life; Broadway Bound; Broken Blossoms; Broken Lance; A Bronx Tale; Brother Sun, Sister Moon; Brotherhood Brothers; The Brothers Karamazov; The Browning Version; Brubaker; The Buddy Holly Story; Buddy's Song; Buffalo Bill; Buffalo Bill and the Indians, or Sitting Bull's History Lesson; Buffet Froid; Bugsy; Bugsy Malone; A Bullet for the General; Bullets or Ballots; Bullfighter and the Lady; Bullitt; Bunny Lake is Missing; Bureau of Missing Persons; Burke and Wills; Burmese Harp; Burn!; Burning Bed; Burning Season; Burning Secret; Bus Stop; Bushido Blade; Business as Usual; Buster; Buster and Billie; Butch and Sundance, The Early Days; Butterfield 8; Bye Bye Brazil; C'est la Vie; Cabaret; Cactus Caddie; Cadence; Cafe Romeo; Caged; Cahill: United States Marshal; The Caine Mutiny (1954); The Caine Mutiny Court Martial (1988); Cairo (1963); Cal; Calcutta; Caligula; Call Me Genius; Call of the Wild (1935); Call of the Wild (1972); Calling Dr. Gillespie; Calling Dr. Kildare; Calling Northside 777; Camelot; Camilla (1994); Camille (1936); Camille Claudel; The Candidate; Candide; Capricorn One; Captain Carey, USA; The Captive Heart; Car 99; Cardinal; Cardinal Richelieu; The Career; Careful, He Might Hear You; The Caretaker; Caretakers; Carey Treatment; Carlito's Way; Carmen (1983); Carmen Jones; Carmen (Opera, 1984); Carnal Knowledge; Carny; Carousel; Carrie (1952); Casablanca; Casanova '70; Casino; Casque d'Or; Cast a Dark Shadow; Cast a Giant Shadow; Castaway; Casualties of War; Cat and Mouse; Cat on

a Hot Tin Roof (1958); Cat on a Hot Tin Roof (1984); Catch 22; The Catered Affair; Catherine the Great; Cattle Queen of Montana; Cavalcade; Ceiling Zero; Celia; Central Park; Chalk Garden; The Champ (1931); The Champ (1979); Champion; Chantilly Lace; Chaplin; The Chapman Report; Chapter Two; The Charge of the Light Brigade (1936); The Charge of the Light Brigade (1968); Chariots of Fire; Charlie Bubbles; Charly; The Chase (1966); Chase a Crooked Shadow; Chattahoochee; Che!; Cheyenne Autumn; Chicago Joe and the Showgirl; Chiefs; A Child is Waiting; The Childhood of Maxim Gorky; The Children (1990); Children of a Lesser God; Children of Hiroshima; Children of Paradise; Children's Hour; Chilly Scenes of Winter; Chimes at Midnight; China Beach; China Seas; The China Syndrome; Chinatown; Chloe in the Afternoon; Chocolat; The Chocolate War; Choice of Arms; Choirboys; Choose Me; A Chorus Line; Chosen; Christ Stopped at Eboli; Christiane F.; A Christmas Carol (1938); Christmas Holiday; Christopher Strong; Chronicle of a Death Foretold; Cimarron (1930); Cimarron (1960); The Cincinnati Kid; Cinderella Liberty; Cinema Paradiso; Circle of Power; The Cisco Kid; Cisco Pike; Citadel; Citizen Cohn; Citizen Kane; City and the Dogs; City Boy; City of Hope; City of Women; Claire's Knee; Clan of the Cave Bear; Clash by Night; Class Action; Class of Miss MacMichael; Claudine; Cleopatra (1934); Cleopatra (1963); Clockers; A Clockwork Orange; Close My Eyes; Close to Eden; Closer; Closet Land; Coach; Coal Miner's Daughter; Cobb; Cocktail; Cold Heaven; Cold Sassy Tree; The Collector; Colonel Redl; The Color of Money; The Color Purple; Colors; Come Back, Little Sheba; Come Back to the Five and Dime, Jimmy Dean, Jimmy Dean; Come See the Paradise; Comes a Horseman; The Comfort of Strangers; Comic; Coming Home; Communion; Company Limited; Compulsion; Comrades; Conduct Unbecoming; The Confession; Confessions of a Nazi Spy; Confidential Agent; The Conformist; The Conqueror; Conquest; Conrack; Consenting Adult; The Conversation; Conversation Piece; Convicts; Cool Hand Luke; Cooperstown; Cop au Vin; The Corn is Green (1945); The Corn is Green (1979); Cornered; The

Cotton Club; Countdown; Country; Country Girl; The Courtship; Cracking Up; The Crash of Silence; Cries and Whispers; Crime and Punishment; Crimes and Misdemeanors; Crimes of Passion; Criss Cross (1992); Cromwell; Crooklyn; Cross Creek; Crossfire; The Crowd; Cruising; Crusoe; Cry Freedom; A Cry in the Dark; The Crying Game; Cuba; Da; Daddy Nostalgia; Damage; The Damned; Dance with a Stranger; Dances With Wolves; Dangerous; Dangerous Game; Dangerous Liaisons; Dangerous Moves; A Dangerous Woman; Daniel; Dante's Inferno; Danton; Dark Angel (1991); The Dark at the Top of the Stairs; Dark Obsession; Dark Passage; Dark Waters; Darling; Das Boot; David and Bathsheba; David and Lisa; David Copperfield; The Day After; A Day in October; Day of the Locust; Day of Wrath; Day One; Daybreak; Days of Heaven; Days of Wine and Roses (1958); Days of Wine and Roses (1962); The Dead; Dead Ahead, the Exxon Valdez Disaster; Dead End; Dead Poet's Society; Dead Ringers; Deadfall (1968); Deadline USA; Deadly Affair; Dear Heart; Dear John; Death and the Maiden; Death in Venice; Death of a Salesman (1950); Death of a Salesman (1985); Death Watch; Death Wish; The Deceivers; Decline of the American Empire; Deep Cover; The Deer Hunter; Defense of the Realm; The Defiant Ones; Deliberate Stranger; A Delicate Balance; Deliverance; Dersu Uzala; Desert Bloom; Desert Fox; Desert Rats; Desire; Desire Me; Desire Under the Elms; Despair; Desperate Characters; Desperate Hours (1955); Desperate Hours (1990); Desperate Journey; Destiny of a Man; The Detective (1968); The Detective (1985); Detective Story; The Devil and the Deep; The Devil at Four O'Clock; Devil in the Flesh (1946); Devil in the Flesh (1987); The Devil's Advocate; The Devil's Disciple; The Devil's Eye; The Devil's Playground; The Devil's Wanton; Devils; Devlin; Diary for My Children; A Diary for Timothy; Diary of a Chambermaid (1946); Diary of a Chambermaid (1963); Diary of a Country Priest; Diary of a Mad Housewife; Diary of a Madman; Diary of Anne Frank (1959); Diggstown; Dillinger (1945); Dillinger (1973); Diner; Dinner at Eight; Dino; Dirty Little Billy; The Disappearance of Aimee; Disaster at Silo 7; Disclosure; Displaced Person; Disraeli;

Distant Drums; Distant Thunder (1973); Distant Thunder (1988); Diva; Doc; Doctor; Doctor Jekyll and Mr. Hyde (1931); Doctor Zhivago; Doctor's Dilemma; Dodsworth; Dog Day Afternoon; Dogfight; Dogs in Space; A Doll's House; Don's Party; Don't Look Now; Doors; Double Exposure; The Double Life of Veronique; The Downhill Racer; Dr. Ehrlich's Magic Bullet; Dr. Faustus; Dr. Jekyll and Mr. Hyde (1941); Dr. Socrates; Dr. Syn, the Alias Scarecrow; Dragnet (1954); Dragon Seed; The Draughtsman's Contract; Dreamchild; Dreams That Money Can Buy; The Dresser; The Dressmaker; Drifting; Drive, He Said; Driver's Seat; Driving Miss Daisy; Drowning By Numbers; Drugstore Cowboy; A Dry White Season; The Duellists; The Dunera Boys; Eagle in a Cage; Earl of Chicago; Early Frost; Early Summer; Earth; Earthquake; East Lynne; East of Eden (1955); East of Eden (1980); East of Elephant Rock; East Side, West Wide; Easy Living (1949); Easy Money (1948); Easy Rider; Easy Virtue; Ebb Tide; Ebony Tower; Echo Park; Echoes of a Summer; Eclipse; The Eddy Duchin Story; Edge of Doom; Edge of the City; Edison, the Man; Edward II; Edward, My Son; The Effect of Gamma Rays on Man-in-the-Moon Marigolds; 8½; Eight Men Out; 8 Seconds; Eighty-Four Charing Cross Road; Eighty-Four Charlie Mopic; El Cid; El Norte; Eleanor & Franklin; Electra Glide in Blue; Eleni; Elephant Boy; The Elephant Man; Elephant Walk; Elmer Gantry; Elvira Madigan; Elvis: The Movie; Emerald Forest; Emigrants; Eminent Domain; Emmanuelle SERIES; The Emperor Waltz; Empire of the Sun; Enchanted April; The Enchanted Cottage; Encore; The End of the Game; End of the Road; Enemies, A Love Story; Enemy Mine; Enemy of the People (1977); Enemy of the People (1989); Les Enfants Terribles; England Made Me; The Entertainer; Entre-Nous; Equinox; Equus Erendira; The Ernest Green Story; Escape; Escape Artist; Escape from Fort Bravo; Escape From the Dark; Escape from the Planet of the Apes; Ethan Fromme; Eureka; Europa, Europa; The Europeans; Ever in My Heart; Eversmile New Jersey; Every Man for Himself (and God Against All); Every Time We Say Goodbye; Everybody Wins; Everybody's Fine; Ex-Lady; The Execution of Private

Slovik; The Executioner's Song; Executive Suite; Exodus; Exotica; Exposed; Extremities; F.I.S.T.; F. Scott Fitzgerald in Hollywood; The Fabulous Baker Boys; A Face in the Crowd; Face to Face; Faces; Fahrenheit 451; Fail Safe; Falcon and the Snowman; The Fall of the Roman Empire; Fallen Idol; Fallen Sparrow; Falling in Love; Falling in Love Again; Fame; Family; Family Business; Family Pictures; Family Upside Down; Fanny and Alexander; Far from the Madding Crowd; Faraway, So Close!; Farewell My Concubine; Farewell to the King; Fat City; Fat Man and Little Boy; Fatal Attraction; Fate is the Hunter; Fathers and Sons; Faust; Fear Strikes Out; Fearless; Fedora; Fellow Traveler; Fever Pitch; A Few Good Men; Fiddler on the Roof; Field; 55 Days at Peking; Fighting Back; File on Thelma Jordon; The Final Conflict; Fingers; A Fire in the Sky; Fire Next Time; Fire Over England; The First Deadly Sin; First Name: Carmen; First of the Few; Firstborn; The Fisher King; Fitzcarraldo; Five Came Back; Five Corners; Five Days One Summer; Five Easy Pieces; Five Pennies; Five Star Final; The Fixer; Flame Over India; Flatliners; Flesh; Flesh and Blood (1951); Flesh and Bone; Flight of the Doves; Flight of the Phoenix; Fool for Love; For Queen and Country; For Whom the Bell Tolls; Forbidden Games; Forgotten Prisoners; 1492: Conquest of Paradise; Fortune and Men's Eyes; Fortunes of War; Forty Guns; The Fountainhead; Four Frightened People; Four Horsemen of the Apocalypse; The 400 Blows; Four Sons; Fourteen Hours; The Fox; Fox and His Friends; Foxes; Foxfire (1987); Frances; Francis, God's Jester; Fraternity Row; Freaks; The French Connection; The French Lieutenant's Woman; Fresh Freud; Friday the Thirteenth (1933); Friendly Fire; Friendly Persuasion; Friends and Husbands; Friends Forever; From Here to Eternity; From the Life of the Marionettes; From the Terrace; From This Day Forward; The Front; The Fugitive (1947); The Fugitive Kind; Full Metal Jacket; Full Moon in Paris; Fun Down There; Funny Lady; Furies; The Fury (1936); G.I. Joe; Gallant Hours; Gallipoli; The Gambler; The Game is Over; Gandhi; Garden; The Garden of the Finzi-Continis; Gardens of Stone; Garment

Jungle; Gas Food Lodging; Gaslight (1939); Gaslight (1944); Gate of Hell; The Gathering; A Gathering of Eagles; The Gene Krupa Story; General Della Rovere; Gentleman Jim; Gentleman's Agreement; Geronimo (1993); Gervaise; Getting of Wisdom; Gettysburg; Ghosts . . . of the Civil Dead; Ghostwriter; Giant; Ginger and Fred; Ginger in the Morning; The Girl From Petrovka; Girl in the Red Velvet Swing; The Girl with Green Eyes; Girlfriends; Glass House; The Glass Menagerie (1950); The Glass Menagerie (1973); The Glass Menagerie (1987); Glengarry Glen Ross; Gloria; Glory; Go for Broke; The Go-Between; The Goalie's Anxiety at the Penalty Kick; God Bless the Child; God's Little Acre; Goddess; The Godfather; The Godfather, Part II; The Godfather, Part III; Godspell; Going Home; The Golden Boy; Golden Braid; Golden Gate; The Golem; Gone With the Wind; The Good Earth; The Good Father; GoodFellas; The Good Fight; Good Morning, Babylon; The Good Mother; The Good Wife; Goodbye Mr. Chips (1939); Goodbye Mr. Chips (1969); The Goodbye People; Goodbye, Pork Pie; Gordon's War; Gore Vidal's Lincoln; Gorillas in the Mist; The Gospel According to St. Matthew; Grand Canyon; Grand Hotel; Grand Illusion; The Grapes of Wrath; Grasshopper; Gray Lady Down; Great Balls of Fire; The Great Escape; The Great Gatsby (1949); The Great Gatsby (1974); The Great Locomotive Chase; The Great Manhunt; The Great Moment; The Great Santini; The Great Sinner; The Great Waldo Pepper; The Great Waltz (1938); The Great Waltz (1972); The Great White Hope; The Greatest; The Greatest Story Ever Told; Green Eyes; Griffin and Phoenix, A Love Story; The Grifters; Gross Anatomy; Ground Zero; The Group; Guadalcanal Diary; Guess Who's Coming to Dinner; Guilty by Suspicion; The Gunrunner; Guyana Tragedy, The Story of Jim Jones; Gypsy Moths; Hair; The Hairdresser's Husband; The Hairy Ape; Hallelujah, I'm a Bum; Hamburger Hill; Hamlet (1948); Hamlet (1964); Hamlet (1969); Hamlet (1991); Hammersmith is Out; A Handful of Dust; A Handmaid's Tale; Hangmen Also Die; Hanussen; Happy Ending; Hard Country; Hard Times; The Hard Way (1943); Hardcore; The Harder They Fall; Hasty Heart; The Hatchet Man; A

Hatful of Rain; Haunted Summer; Havana; Hawaii; Hawaiians; Heart Beat; The Heart is a Lonely Hunter; Heart Like a Wheel; Heart of Glass; Heartbreakers; Heartland; Heat and Dust; Heatwave; Heaven and Earth; Heaven with a Gun; Heaven's Gate; Hedda; Heimat; The Heiress; The Helen Morgan Story; Hell in the Pacific; Helter Skelter (1976); Hemingway's Adventures of a Young Man; Henry and June; Henry: Portrait of a Serial Killer; Henry V (1944); Henry V (1989); Henry VIII and His Six Wives; Here Comes the Navy; Hero; A Hero Ain't Nothin' but a Sandwich; Hester Street; Hidden Agenda; Hide in Plain Sight; High and the Mighty; High Noon; High Sierra; High Tide; Higher Learning; The Hill; The Hindenburg; The Hireling; Hiroshima, Mon Amour; His Brother's Wife; The Hit; Hitler Gang; Hitler-The Last Ten Days; Hoffa; Holiday for Sinners; Home from the Hill; Homeboy; The Homecoming (1973); Homicide; Honkytonk Man; Hook; Hoosiers; Hope and Glory; Hornet's Nest; Hot Spell; Hot Spot; Hotel; Houdini; Hour of the Gun; A House Divided; A House is Not a Home; House of Cards; House of Games; The House of Rothschild; The House of Seven Gables; House of Strangers; House of the Spirits; House of Women; The House on 92nd Street; How Do I Love Thee; How I Won the War; How the West Was Won; Howards End; The Howards of Virginia; The Hucksters; Hud; Hudson's Bay; Hurry Sundown; Husbands; Husbands and Wives; The Hustler; I Accuse; I Am a Fugitive from a Chain Gang; I Am the Law; I Believe in You; I Confess; I Could Go on Singing; I Cover the Waterfront; I Dream of Jeannie; I Know Why the Caged Bird Sings; I Like it Like That; I Never Promised You A Rose Garden; I Never Sang for My Father; I Passed for White; I Sent a Letter to My Love; I Stole a Million; I Thank a Fool; I, the Worst of All; I Vitelloni; I Walk Alone; I Walk the Line; I Want to Live!; I Want What I Want; I Want You; I Was a Communist for the FBI; I Was a Spy; I'll Cry Tomorrow; I'm Dancing as Fast as I Can; I've Heard the Mermaids Singing; Ice Palace; Iceman; Idol; The Idolmaker; If Winter Comes; Ikiru; The Illustrated Man; Illustrious Corpses; Images; Imaginary Crimes; Imitation of Life (1934); Imitation of Life (1959); Immediate

Family; Immortal Beloved; Immortal Sergeant; The Immortal Story; Impudent Girl; In a Lonely Place; In a Shallow Grave; In a Year with 13 Moons; In Cold Blood; In Country; In Love and War; In Name Only; In Old Chicago; In Our Time; In Praise of Older Women; In Search of Gregory; In the Cool of the Day; In the French Style; In the Heat of the Night; In The Name of the Father; In the Realm of the Senses; Inchon; The Incredible Sarah; The Incredible Shrinking Man; Indecent Proposal; Indian Runner; Indiscretion of an American Wife; Indochine; Inferno; The Informer; Inherit the Wind; The Inheritance; Inn of the Sixth Happiness; Inner Circle; An Innocent Man; Innocents in Paris (1953); Inserts; Inside Daisy Clover; Inside Moves; Insignificance; Interiors; Internal Affairs; Interns; The Interrogation; Interrupted Melody; Interview with the Vampire; Into the West; Intolerance; The Intruder; Intruder in the Dust; Investigation of a Citizen Above Suspicion; Invitation; Iron Man; Ironweed; Is Paris Burning?; Isadora; Island (1961); Island in the Sun; Islands in the Stream; It Happened Here; It's A Big Country; It's a Wonderful Life; Ivan the Terrible; Ivan's Childhood; Ivanhoe; Ivy; J.W. Coop; J'Accuse; Jacknife; Jacob's Ladder; Jamaica Inn (1939); Jamaica Inn (1982); Jamaica Run; Jane Eyre (1934); Jane Eyre (1943); Jane Eyre (1971); Jarrapellejos; Je Vous Aime; Jean de Florette; Jefferson in Paris; Jeremiah Johnson; Jesus of Montreal; Jesus of Nazareth; Jewel in the Crown; JFK; The Jigsaw Man; Jim Thorpe, All American; Joan of Arc; Joan of Paris; Joe; John and Mary; John Paul Jones; Johnny Be Good; Johnny Belinda; Johnny Eager; Johnny Handsome; The Josephine Baker Story; Joshua Then and Now; Journey into Fear; Journey of Hope; The Journey of Natty Gann; The Joy Luck Club; Juarez; Jud Suess; Jude the Obscure; Judgment at Nuremburg; Juggernaut; Juice; Jules and Jim; Julia; Julia and Julia; Julius Caesar; Jumpin at the Boneyard; Jungle Fever; Junior Bonner; Justine; K-2; Kafka; Kagemusha; Kaleidoscope; Kalifornia; Kamikaze 89; Kangaroo; Kansas; Kansas City Bomber; Katherine; Keep the Change; Keeper of the Flame; Kes; The Key (1958); Key Largo; Keys of the Kingdom; Khartoum; Kidnapping of the

President; The Killer's Kiss; The Killers (1946); The Killers (1964); The Killing; The Killing Fields; A Killing in a Small Town; The Killing of a Chinese Bookie; The Killing of Sister George; Killing Zoe; A Kind of Loving King; King David; King Lear (1971); King of Kings (1927); King of Kings (1961); King of Marvin Gardens; King of the Gypsies; King of The Hill (1965); King of the Hill (1993); King Rat; Kings and Desperate Men; Kings Go Forth; Kings of the Road; Kings Row; A Kiss Before Dying (1956); A Kiss Before Dying (1991); Kiss of the Spider Woman; Kitchen Toto; Kitten with a Whip; The Klansman; Klute; Knock on Any Door; Kotch; Krakatoa, East of Java; Kramer vs. Kramer; The Krays; Kremlin Letter; Kung Fu; L'Avventura; La Bamba; La Belle Noiseuse; La Chienne; La Dolce Vita; La Lectrice; La Marseillaise; La Notte; La Passante; La Ronde (1950); La Ronde (1964); La Vie Continue; La Vie de Boheme; The Lacemaker; Lacombe, Lucien; Lady from Shanghai; The Lady Gambles; Lady in a Cage; Lady in Red; Lady Jane; Lady Killer (1933); Lady Sings the Blues; Ladybird, Ladybird; The Lamb; The Last Angry Man; Last Days of Pompeii; The Last Detail; The Last Emperor; Last Exit to Brooklyn; The Last Flight; The Last Hurrah; The Last Metro; The Last Movie; Last of His Tribe; The Last Picture Show; Last Summer; Last Tango in Paris; The Last Temptation of Christ; The Last Tycoon; The Last Voyage; Last Year at Marienbad; Late for Dinner; The Laughing Policeman; Laughter in the Dark; Laurel Avenue; Lawrence of Arabia; LBJ: The Early Years; Le Bal; Leadbelly; Lean on Me; Learning Tree; Leather Boys; Leave Her to Heaven; The Legend of Billie Jean; The Legend of Lylah Clare; Legends of the Fall; Lenny; Leopard; Less Than Zero; Let Him Have It; Let No Man Write My Epitaph; The Letter (1929); The Letter (1940); Letter From an Unknown Woman; Letter to Brezhnev; Letter to Three Wives; Letters from a Dead Man; Lianna Liebestraum; Les Liaisons Dangereuses; Lies My Father Told Me; Life and Death of Colonel Blimp; Life and Nothing But; Life at the Top; Life Begins at 8:30; Life is a Bed of Roses; Life is Cheap, but Toilet Paper is Expensive; The Life of Emile Zola; The Life of Riley; Life Upside Down; Life

(1986); The Natural; Nazi Agent; Negatives; Nell; Network; Never Let Go; Never Love a Stranger; Never Take Sweets from a Stranger; Never Too Late; New Life; Newsfront; Niagara; Nicholas and Alexandra; Nicholas Nickleby; Night and Day (1946); Night and the City (1950); Night and the City (1992); Night Crossing; Night Games; The Night is Young (1946); 'Night, Mother; The Night My Number Came Up; Night of the Hunter; Night of the Iguana; Night of the Shooting Stars; The Night Porter; A Night to Remember (1958); Night Train to Munich; Nighthawks (1978); Nighthawks 2: Strip Jack Naked (1991); Nijinsky; 1918; 1984 (1955); 1984 (1984); 1900; 1969; Nobody's Fool (1994); No Highway in the Sky; No Man's Land; No Way Out (1950); Nomads; None But the Brave; Norma Rae; Norwood; Nothin' But a Man; Nous La Liberte; Nous Sommes Tous les Assassins; Nouvelle Vague; Now I'll Tell; Numero Deux; The Nun's Story; The Nurse; Nuts; O Lucky Man; O Pioneers!; Oblomov; October; Odette; Oedipus Rex; Of Mice and Men (1939); Of Mice and Men (1993); The Offence; An Officer and a Gentleman; The Official Story; Oklahoma Crude; The Old Curiosity Shop; Old Gringo; Old Maid; Old Man and the Sea; Olivier, Olivier; On the Beach; On the Waterfront; Once Upon a Time in America; Once Were Warriors; One Deadly Summer; One Flew Over Cuckoo's Nest; One Is a Lonely Number; One Sings, the Other Doesn't; The One That Got Away; The Onion Field; Open City; Opening Night; Ordinary People; Orlando; Orpheus Descending; Oscar Wilde; Otello; Othello (1951); Othello (1965); Our Town; Out of Africa; Out of Order; Out of the Blue; Out of the Past; Outcast of the Islands; Outrage (1956); The Outsiders; The Overlanders; The Ox-Bow Incident; Paisan; Panic in Needle Park; Panic in the Streets; Panic in the Year Zero; The Paper; The Paper Chase; Paper Lion; Papillon; The Paradine Case; Paris Blues; Paris By Night; Paris, Texas; Paris Trout; The Party and the Guests; The Party's Over; The Passage; A Passage to India; The Passenger; Passion; Passion Fish; Passion/Madame Dubarry (1919); Patch of Blue; Pathfinder; Paths of Glory; Patterns; Patton; Patty Hearst; The Pawnbroker; The Pearl; The Pedestrian; Pelle the Conqueror; Penny Serenade;

People Against O'Hara; The People Next Door; The Performance; Permanent Record; Persona; Personal Best; The Petrified Forest; Petulia; Peyton Place; Phantom of Liberty; Phenix City Story; Philadelphia; The Piano; Picnic at Hanging Rock; The Picture of Dorian Gray; Pink Floyd: The Wall; Pinky; Pixote; A Place in the Sun; Places in the Heart; The Plague (1992); Platoon; Play Misty for Me; Playboys; Playing for Time; Plenty; The Ploughman's Lunch; Point Blank; The Pointsman; Poison; Poison Ivy (1992); The Pope of Greenwich Village; Pork Chop Hill; The Pornographers; Port of Call; Portrait of Jennie; The Possession of Joel Delaney; The Power; Power, Passion, and Murder; Powwow Highway; A Prayer for the Dying; The Preppie Murder; Pretty Baby; Prick Up Your Ears; Pride and Prejudice; The Priest; Priest of Love; Prime Cut; The Prime of Miss Jean Brodie; Prince of the City; The Prince of Tides; Prince Valiant; Prison Stories: Women on the Inside; The Prisoner (1955); The Prisoner: Arrival; Prisoner of Honor; The Private Life of Henry VIII; The Private Lives of Elizabeth and Essex; A Private Matter; The Professional; The Projectionist; The Promised Land; Proof; Prospero's Books; Providence; Psych-Out; Public Enemy; Public Eye; Pudd'nhead Wilson; Q & A; Quartet (1948); Quartet (1981); Queen Christina; Queen of Destiny; Queen of the Stardust Ballroom; Querelle; Quest for Fire; Quick Millions; The Quiet American; The Quiet Man; Quintet; Quiz Show; Quo Vadis; Rabbit, Run; Rachel, Rachel; Racing with the Moon; The Rack; Rage; A Rage to Live; The Raggedy Man; Raging Bull; Raging Moon; Ragtime; Railway Children; Rain Man; The Rain People; The Rainbow; The Rainmaker; Raise the Red Lantern; A Raisin in the Sun; Rambling Rose; Ran; Rapture; Rashomon; Ratboy; Razor's Edge (1946); Razor's Edge (1986); Razorback; Real Life; Rebecca; Rebel Without a Cause; The Red Badge of Courage; The Red Balloon; Red Desert; Red Kiss; The Red Pony (1949); Red Shoes; Red Sky at Morning; Red Sorghum; Reds; Reflections in a Golden Eye; Regarding Henry; Remains of the Day; Rembrandt; Remember My Name; Rendez-Vous; Repulsion; Requiem for a Heavyweight (1956); Requiem for a Heavyweight (1962); Reservoir Dogs;

Resurrection; Return of a Man Called Horse; The Return of Martin Guerre; The Return of the Secaucus Seven; Return of the Soldier; Reunion; Reversal of Fortune; Revolt of Job; Revolution; The Revolutionary; Rhapsody in August; Rich and Famous; Richard III; Rich in Love; Ride the Pink Horse; Rider on the Rain; Riff-Raff (1991); Right of Way; The Right Stuff; The Rise of Louis XIV; Risk; The River (1951); The River (1984); The River Niger; River of No Return; River Rat; A River Runs Through It; The River's Edge; The Road Back; Roanoak; The Robe; Rocket to the Moon; Rocky; Rocky II; Rocky III; Rocky IV; Rocky V; Rolling Thunder; Rollover; The Roman Spring of Mrs. Stone; The Romantic Englishwoman; Romeo and Juliet (1936); Romeo and Juliet (1954); Romeo and Juliet (1968); Romeo is Bleeding; Romero; Romper Stomper; Room at the Top; Roots; Roots of Heaven; The Rose; The Rose Tattoo; 'Round Midnight; Roxie Hart; Royal Scandal; RPM; Ruby; Ruby in Paradise; Rumble Fish; Run Silent Run Deep; Runaway Train; The Runner Stumbles; Running on Empty; Rush; The Russia House; Ryan's Daughter; Sacco and Vanzetti; Sacrifice; Sadie Thompson; Sahara (1943); The Sailor Who Fell From Grace with the Sea; Saint Jack; Saint Joan; The Saint of Fort Washington; Sakharov; Salaam Bombay!; Salamander; Sally of the Sawdust; Salmonberries; Salo: 120 Days of Sodom; Salome (1953); Salome, Where She Danced; Salon Kitty; Salty O'Rourke; Salvador; San Francisco; San Francisco Story; San Quentin; Sanctuary; Sand Pebbles; Sandakan No. 8; The Sandpiper; Sands of Iwo Jima; Sands of the Kalahari; Santa Sangre; Sarafina!; Sarah, Plain and Tall; Saratoga Trunk; Saskatchewan; Satan Met a Lady; Saturday Night and Sunday Morning; Saturday Night Fever; Saturn 3; Satyricon (Fellini's); Savage Sam; Savages; Save the Tiger; Sawdust and Tinsel; Say Hello to Yesterday; Say One for Me; Sayonara; Scandal; Scandal in Paris; Scandalous John; Scaramouche; Scarecrow; The Scarlet Empress; The Scarlet Letter (1926); The Scarlet Letter (1934); The Scarlet Letter (1980); Scarlet Street; Scene of the Crime; Scenes from a Marriage; The Scent of Green Papaya; Schindler's List; School Ties; Scotland Yard; Scott of the Antarctic; Scoundrel;

Twelve O'Clock High; 21; Twice in a Lifetime; Two For the Road; Two for the Seesaw; The Two Jakes; Two Lane Blacktop; Two or Three Things I Know About Her; Two People; Two Weeks in Another Town; Two Women; Ugetsu Monogatari; The Ugly American; Ulysses (1967); Umberto D.; Un Coeur en Hiver; The Unbearabale Lightness of Being; The Unbelievable Truth; Under Fire; Under Milk Wood; Under the Volcano; Undercurrent; Underworld, USA; The Unforgiven (1960); Unforgiven (1992); Union Pacific; An Unmarried Woman; Unnatural Causes; Until the End of the World; The Untouchables; Up the Down Staircase; Up the Sandbox; Uranus; Used People; Vagabond; The Valachi Papers; Valdez is Coming; Valentino (1977); Valley of the Kings; Valmont; Les Valseuses; Van Gogh; Variety; Vera Cruz; Verdict; Veronika Voss; Victim; Victory; A View from the Bridge; The Vikings; Vincent and Theo; Violette; The Virgin and the Gypsy; The Virgin Queen; The Virgin Spring; Vision Quest; Visit; Viva Zapata; Voyage of the Damned; Voyager; W.C. Fields and Me; W. Plan; Waco; Wages of Fear; Wake of the Red Witch; Walk in the Spring Rain; Walk on the Wild Side; Walkabout; Walker; Walking Stick; Wall Street; The Wanderers; The Wandering Jew; The War; The War Against Mrs. Hadley; War and Peace (1956); War and Peace (1967); War Games; The War Lover; War Party; Warm December; Washington Story; Watch on the Rhine; Waterdance; Waterland; Waterloo; Waterloo Bridge (1931); Waterloo Bridge (1940); The Way We Were; We Are Not Alone; We of the Never Never; We Think the World of You; We Were Strangers; The Wedding March; Wedding Night; Weekend at the Waldorf; Welcome Home; Welcome Home, Roxy Carmichael; Welcome to Hard Times; Welcome to L.A.; Well; Went the Day Well?; West Side Story; Wet Parade; Wetherby; What Every Woman Knows; What Price Hollywood?; What's Eating Gilbert Grape?; When Father Was Away on Business; When Hell Was in Session; Where Angels Fear to Tread; Where the Green Ants Dream; Where the Lilies Bloom; While the City Sleeps; Whipsaw; The Whisperers; White Banners; White Cliffs of Dover; White Dog; White Hunter, Black Heart; White Mama; White Mile; White Mischief; White Nights (1985); White Palace; White Rose; The White Tower; Who?; Who is Harry Kellerman . . . ; Who is the Black Dahlia?; Who'll Stop the Rain?; Who's Afraid of Virginia Woolf?; Whore; Whose Life Is It Anyway?; Why Shoot the Teacher?; The Wicked Lady (1945); The Wicked Lady (1983); Wild at Heart; Wild Child; Wild Duck; Wild in the Streets; Wild Is the Wind; The Wild One; The Wild Party; Wild River; Wild Strawberries; Wildflower; Will Penny; Willie and Phil; Wilson; Wilt; Wind; The Wind and the Lion; Wings of Desire; The Wings of Eagles; Wings of Fame; Winning; The Winslow Boy; Winter Light; Winter People; Winterset; Wired; Witches of Salem; Without a Trace; Witness for the Prosecution; The Wiz; The Wolves of Willoughby Chase; Woman in Flames; Woman in the Dunes; A Woman is a Woman; The Woman Next Door; Woman Obsessed; Woman on the Beach; Woman Rebels; Woman Times Seven; Woman to Woman; A Woman Under the Influence; A Woman's Face; A Woman's Tale; Women in Love; Wonder Bar; The Wooden Horse; Working Girls; A World Apart; The World of Apu; The World of Suzie Wong; The Wrath of God; The Wreck of the Mary Deare; Written on the Wind; The Wrong Man; WUSA; Wuthering Heights (1939); Wuthering Heights (1953); Wuthering Heights (1970); Wuthering Heights (1992); Wyatt Earp; X, Y, & Zee; Yanks; The Year My Voice Broke; The Year of Living Dangerously; The Yearling; Yellow Rolls Royce; Yentl; Yesterday's Hero; You Can't Get Away With Murder; Young Catherine; Young Doctors; The Young Lions; Young Man with a Horn; Young Mr. Lincoln; The Young Philadelphians; Young Savages; Young Tom Edison; Young Winston; Youngblood Hawke; Z; Zabriskie Point; Zandalee; A Zed and Two Noughts; Zelly and Me; Zeppelin; Ziegfeld Girl; Zigzag; Zulu; Zulu Dawn

Dramedy: see **COMEDY DRAMA**

Dreams (figurative, ambitions): see also *Underdog Stories: Quests: ADVENTURE: Treasure Hunts:* Above the Rim; Alice Doesn't Live Here Anymore; All the Right Moves; All-American Boy; Alsino and the Condor; Amateur Night at the Dixie Bar and Grill; America, America; An American Romance; Americana; And God Created Woman (1988); Anna; Baby, It's You; Baby, The Rain Must Fall; Babycakes; Blessing; Bound For Glory; The Boy Who Could Fly; Breakfast at Tiffany's; Breaking the Rules; Breaking the Sound Barrier; Brewster McCloud; The Bride is Much Too Beautiful; Bugsy; Bus Stop; Call Me Genius; Career; Celia; Chatterbox; China Clipper; Close Encounters of the Third Kind; Condorman; Dead Poet's Society; Edison, the Man; Educating Rita; El Norte; The Epic That Never Was; Field of Dreams; The Fountainhead; Freud; The Girl in the Watermelon; God's Little Acre; Goddess; Good Morning, Babylon; Gross Anatomy; Hard Country; High Tide; Hoop Dreams; I Wanted Wings; I Want to Live!; Jersey Girl; Johnny Suede; Lady in the Dark; Leningrad Cowboys Go to America; Let it Ride; Let No Man Write My Epitaph; The Little Mermaid; Little Noises; Lloyd's of London; Lost Horizon (1937); Lost Horizon (1973); Man of La Mancha; Mary Burns, Fugitive; Melvin and Howard; A Member of the Wedding; Midnight Cowboy; Miracle on 34th Street (1947); Miss Firecracker; Mosquito Coast; Mr. Destiny; Muriel's Wedding; Music in My Heart; My Brilliant Career; Nashville; New York Stories; Next Stop, Greenwich Village; Nicholas Nickleby; The Night My Number Came Up; Nights of Cabiria; Nous La Liberte; Once Upon a Dream; The Pearl; Popi; Pretty Woman; Promoter; Radio Flyer; Rocket Gibraltar; Rocky; Rocky II; Rocky III; Rocky IV; Rocky V; Roman Scandals; Rudy; The Secret Life of an American Wife; The Secret Life of Walter Mitty; The Secret of Roan Inish; The Seven Percent Solution; The Seven-Year Itch; Shampoo; Slipper and the Rose; Stagedoor; The Stratton Story; Suburbia; Sweet Bird of Youth; Sweet Charity; They Shoot Horses, Don't They?; Things to Come; 30 is a Dangerous Age, Cynthia; Three Sisters; Tokyo Pop; A Tree Grows in Brooklyn; The Trip to Bountiful; True Confession; Tucker: The Man and His Dream; Weird Science; Welcome Home, Roxy Carmichael; White Men Can't Jump; Yentl

Dream Sequences: see also *Fantasies:* The Advocate; Akira Kurosawa's Dreams; Bedazzled; City of Women; Dream Lover (1986); Dreams That Money Can Buy; Dreamscape; The Five Thousand Fingers of Doctor T.; The Fourth Man; Kiss of the Spider Woman; Portrait of Jennie;

Rosemary's Baby; Siesta; Somewhere in Time; Spellbound; The Wizard of Oz (1925); The Wizard of Oz (1939); Woman in the Window

Dreams-Broken: see *Underdog Stories: Illusions Destroyed*

Drifters: see also *Hitchhikers: New in Town:* All Fall Down; Back Roads; Barry Lyndon; Beware, My Lovely; Boom!; Brimstone and Treacle; The Call of the Wild (1935); The Call of the Wild (1972); Candide; Castaway Cowboy; A Dangerous Woman; Every Man for Himself (and God Against All); A Fistful of Dollars; For a Few Dollars More; The Fugitive Kind; Intruder; Jeremiah Johnson; Joe Kidd; Johnny Guitar; Kangaroo; Kansas; Kung Fu; Life Upside Down; Man from Laramie; Milky Way (1968); Nobody's Fool (1986); None But the Lonely Heart; Outcast of the Islands; Pale Rider; Paris, Texas; Picnic; Raggedy Man; The Rainmaker; Red Rock West; Saint Jack; San Francisco Story; Scarecrow; Shane; Shepherd of the Hills; Silver Lode; Something for Everyone; They Made Me a Criminal; This Property is Condemned; Thunderbolt and Lightfoot; Ticket to Heaven; The Unbelievable Truth; Vagabond; Welcome to Hard Times; Winter People; Winterset; WUSA

Drownings: see also *Shellepy Winters Drowns: Death-Dealing with:* The Disappearance of Christina; Drowning By Numbers; The Drowning Pool; Leave Her to Heaven; Night of the Hunter; A Place in the Sun; The Poseidon Adventure; The Reincarnation of Peter Proud; Thunder Rock; The Unsinkable Molly Brown

Drugs-Addictions/Use (where the focus of the story is more about a user): see also *Drugs-Dealing: Alcoholism: Psychedelic Era:* Above the Law; Altered States; Bad Lieutenant; Blind Spot; Boost; Brain Damage; Cheech and Chong: Still Smokin'; Cheech & Chong's Next Movie; Cheech & Chong's Nice Dreams; Cheech & Chong's The Corsican Brothers; Christiane F.; Clean and Sober; Coal Miner's Daughter; Cold Turkey; Cracking Up; Dazed and Confused; Diary of a Hitman; Drugstore Cowboy; Easy Rider; Ed Wood; Fathers and Sons; Firstborn; Fox and His Friends; The Gene Krupa Story; A Hatful of Rain; Haunted Summer; I'm Dancing as Fast as I Can; Jo Jo Dancer, Your Life is Calling; Jumpin' at the Boneyard;

Killing Zoe; Lady Sings the Blues; Last Exit to Brooklyn; Lenny; Less Than Zero; Let's Get Lost; Light Sleeper; Long Day's Journey Into Night; Losing Isaiah; Lost Angels; Mad Monkey; Man of Flowers; The Man with the Golden Arm; The Masquerader; My Own Private Idaho; The Mystery of Edwin Drood; Naked Lunch; Panic in Needle Park; People Next Door; Postcards from the Edge; Pulp Fiction; Reefer Madness; The Rose; Rush; The Serpent and the Rainbow; The Seven Percent Solution; Sid and Nancy; A Simple Twist of Fate; Stuff; Terminal Bliss; Things Are Tough All Over; THX 1138; Tiger Bay; Tokyo Decadence; Traffik; Transmutations; Trash; The Trip; Turkish Delight 21; Vagabond; Valley of the Dolls; Vanishing Point; Videodrome; Up in Smoke; Where the Buffalo Roam; Yellow Submarine

Drugs-Dealing (where the story has a focus which is more about the seller): see also *Drugs-Addictions: Crime Drama:* Above the Rim; Aces, Iron Eagle 3; Another 48 Hours; Atlantic City; Bad Boys (1994); Bad Lieutenant; Beverly Hills Cop 3; Carlito's Way; Cisco Pike; Clear and Present Danger; Cleopatra Jones; Cleopatra Jones and The Casino of Gold; Clockers; Code of Silence; Dark Wind; Deep Cover; Delta Heat; The Discreet Charm of Bourgeoisie; Double-Crossed; DROP Squad; Drop Zone; 8 Million Ways to Die; Excessive Force; Extreme Prejudice; Eye for an Eye; Fatal Beauty; Firepower; Fort Apache, The Bronx; The French Connection; The French Connection II; Fresh; High Risk; Hit!; Jakarta Joe; Jumpin at the Boneyard; King of New York; The Last Seduction; Less Than Zero; Lethal Weapon; Lethal Weapon 2; License to Kill; Light Sleeper; Living Daylights; London Kills Me; Low Down Dirty Shame; Marked for Death; McBain; Midnight Express; Mike's Murder; New Jack City; No Escape, No Return; One False Move; Panic in Needle Park; Quick; Rapid Fire; Red Heat; The Return of Superfly; The Revenge of the Pink Panther; Robocop; Robocop 2; Rush; Salaam Bombay!; Scarface (1983); Shaft; Sticky Fingers; Sugar Hill; Superfly; Tequila Sunrise; Terminal Bliss; Three Men and a Baby; Three Men and a Cradle; To Live and Die in L.A.; Touch of Evil; Toy Soldiers; Traffik; Wait Until

Dark; Who'll Stop the Rain?; Witness; Year of the Dragon

Dry Humor: see *COMEDY: French Comedy: British Films Comedy: Comedy-Light*

Dual Lives (a secret life): see also *Moonlighting: Multiple Personalities: Secrets: Cheating Men: Cheating Women:* Angel; Another Country; The Beautiful Blonde from Bashful Bend; Belle du Jour; Body Double; Bowery at Midnight; Boys in the Band; Consenting Adults; Crimes of Passion; Daniel; Darling Lili; Desperately Seeking Susan; Doctor Jekyll and Mr. Hyde (1931); Dr. Jekyll & Mr. Hyde (1941); Dr. Jekyll and Sister Hyde; Dr. Heckyl and Mr. Hype; Dr. Syn Alias Scarecrow; A Double Life; Dubarry Was a Lady; Exotica; Hero at Large; The Hustle; I Love You Again; I, Monster; Julia and Julia; Looking for Mr. Goodbar; Madame Rosa; Making Love; Mask (1994); Miami Blues; Miller's Crossing; Night in Heaven; The Nutty Professor (1963); Paris By Night; Penelope; Raffles; Scar; Sea Wolf; The Secret Life of Walter Mitty; Serial Mom; Sexton Blake and the Hooded Terror; The Shadow (1940); The Shadow (1994); Shadow of a Doubt; Sleeping With the Enemy; Step Down to Terror; A Stolen Life (1939); A Stolen Life (1946); Sullivan's Travels; Superman; Superman 2; Superman 3; Superman 4; Switch; True Lies; Two or Three Things I Know About Her; Two Worlds of Jenny Logan; Up the Sandbox

Duels: see also *WESTERNS: Men in Conflict: Women in Conflict: Man vs. Machine: Feuds:* Death of a Gunfighter; Dodge City; The Duel; Duellists; Gate of Hell; A Gunfight; A Gunfight at the O.K. Corral; Heaven with a Gun; High Noon; Maverick; The Missouri Breaks; Murphy's War; My Darling Clementine; My Name is Nobody; One Eyed Jacks; Outland; Pat Garrett and Billy the Kid; Quintet; Red Garters; Return of the Jedi; San Antonio; Scalphunters; Sword of the Valiant; Three O'Clock High; Undefeated; Winchester 73; Wyatt Earp

Dumb Jocks: see *Macho Men: Bimboys*

Dummies: see *Puppets:* also *Simple Minds*

Duos and Partner Films: see *Partners: Buddy Films: Buddy Cops*

Dutch Films: see also *Danish Films: Swedish Films:* The Fourth Man; Spetters; Turkish Delight

E

Early America: see also *Revolutionary War: 1600s: 1700s: 1800s:* Botany Bay; Come and Get It; Davy Crockett; Drums Along the Mohawk; Far and Away; The House of Seven Gables; Hudson's Bay; Knickerbocker Holiday; Last of the Mohicans (1936); Last of the Mohicans (1992); Light in the Forest; Little Women (1933); Little Women (1949); Little Women (1978); Little Women (1994); Lone Star of Gold; The Maid of Salem; Roanoak; The Scarlet Letter (1926); The Scarlet Letter (1934); The Scarlet Letter (1980); The Scarlet Letter (1995); 1776; Squanto; The Unconquered; The Witches of Salem; Young Mr. Lincoln

Earth-Center of the: see also *ADVENTURE: SCI-FI: Journeys:* At the Earth's Core; Crack in the World; Journey to the Center of the Earth; The Mole People

Earthquakes: see also *Disaster Movies: California Life: Volcanoes: Crisis Situations:* After the Shock; The Big One, The Great Los Angeles Earthquake; Bug; Crack in the World; Earthquake; Flame of the Barbary Coast; Grand Canyon; Green Dolphin Street; Impulse (1984); In Search of the Castaways; The Rains Came; San Francisco; Short Cuts; Skin Deep; Superman; Tremors; The Two Jakes; A View to a Kill

Eastern Europeans: see *Europeans-Eastern*

Eavesdropping: see also *Surveillance: Spy Films: Voyeurs: Detectives: Gossips:* Another Woman; Sorry, Wrong Number; Rear Window

Eccentric People: see also *Families-Eccentric: Charismatic People: Wild People: Fathers-Fascinating: Mothers-Fascinating: Grandmothers-Fascinating: Grandfathers-Fascinating:* The Absent-Minded Professor; The Accidental Tourist; Ace Ventura, Pet Detective; The Adventures of Baron Munchausen (1987); The Adventures of Buckaroo Banzai Across the Eighth Dimension; Alice Doesn't Live Here Anymore; The Amazing Howard Hughes; And the Ship Sails On; Angel; Animal Behavior; Barnacle Bill (1957); Barton Fink; Beat the Devil; Beetlejuice; Big Girls Don't Cry . . . They Get Even; Bill; Bill: On His Own; Blood and Concrete; Brewster McCloud; Brimstone and Treacle; Bugsy; Bull Durham; Bullets Over Broadway; The Butcher's Wife; Can Hieronymus Merkin Ever Forget Mercy Humppe and Find True Happiness?; Can She Bake a Cherry Pie?; Candy; Car Wash; Carny; The Cat and the Canary (1927); The Cat and the Canary (1939); The Cat and the Canary (1979); Cheaper by the Dozen; A Child is Waiting; Chilly Scenes of Winter; Chitty Chitty Bang Bang; A Chorus of Disapproval; Cold Feet; Coneheads;

David and Lisa; Dion Brothers; Dream Team; Driving Miss Daisy; Ed Wood; Edward Scissorhands; Eraserhead; Every Man for Himself (and God Against All); Every Which Way But Loose; Eyewitness (1981); The Fearless Vampire Killers; Ferris Bueller's Day Off; A Fine Madness; Fitzcarraldo; Full Moon in Blue Water; The Gong Show Movie; The Goodbye People; Gore Vidal's Lincoln; Great Catherine; The Great Smokey Roadblock; The Hairdresser's Husband; The Happiest Millionaire; Harley Davidson and the Marlboro Man; Harry and Tonto; Health; Hello Again; Helter Skelter (1949); Heroes; Hi, Mom!; High Anxiety; High Heels; High Hopes; Honky Tonk Freeway; The Horse's Mouth; Housekeeping; Housesitter; If I Had a Million; In the Spirit; Inside Monkey Zetterland; Isadora; It Should Happen to You; Just You and Me; Keep the Change; Kiss in the Dark; L-Shaped Room; The Last Run; The Late Show; The Life and Times of Judge Roy Bean; Life is Sweet; Life With Father; The Linguini Incident; Little Noises; Lost in Yonkers; Love Streams; Lovesick; Lunatics, A Love Story; Madame Sousatzka; Made for Each Other; Madwoman of Chaillot; The Mating Game; Mermaids; Merrily We Live; Mighty Quinn; Minnie & Moskowitz; Miss Firecracker; Mister

Buddwing; Mister 880; Mosquito Coast; Mr. Belvedere Goes to College; Mr. Belvedere Rings the Bell; My New Gun; Mystery Train; 92 in the Shade; Nothing but Trouble (1991); Oh, Dad, Poor Dad . . . ; Olly Olly Oxen Free; Palm Beach Story; Passed Away; Pee-Wee's Big Adventure; Pete 'n Tillie; Reuben, Reuben; Rikky and Pete; Rio Bravo; Roadside Prophets; Rubin & Ed; Ruling Class; Samantha; Scavenger Hunt; Scorchers; Silent Tongue; Simple Men; Situation Hopeless But Not Serious; Slither; Sound and the Fury; Stars and Bars; The Sterile Cuckoo; Stevie; Stranger Than Paradise; Subway; The Sum of Us; Sweetie; Tell Me that You Love Me, Junie Moon; That Uncertain Feeling; 32 Short Films about Glenn Gould; Tie Me Up! Tie Me Down!; Tillie and Gus; The Time of Your Life; Topkapi!; Travels with My Aunt; True Stories; Tune in Tomorrow; Turtle Diary; Two Lane Blacktop; Under the Rainbow; Until the End of the World; Used People; Waiting For the Light; Wild at Heart; Wilt; Woman in White; Woman Times Seven; The World According to Garp; You Can't Take it With You; You're a Big Boy Now; Young Einstein; Young in Heart; Zorba, The Greek

Education Clash: see *Smart vs. Dumb: Class Conflict: Romance-Class Conflict: Snobs vs. Slobs*

Edwardian Era (mostly British stories set between 1890 and World War I, around the time of King Edward): see also *Victorian Era: 1900s: British Films:* Brideshead Revisited; Half a Sixpence; Howards End; Ivy; Kipps; Love Among the Ruins; Mary Poppins; Maurice; My Fair Lady; The Picture of Dorian Gray; A Room with a View; Where Angels Fear to Tread

Efficiency Experts: see also *Corporate Life: Bankers:* Cheaper by the Dozen; The Efficiency Expert; The Stand In; Take This Job and Shove It

Egypt/Pyramids: see also *Arab People: Ancient Times: Middle East:* The Awakening; Blood from the Mummy's Tomb; Caesar and Cleopatra; Cairo (1942); Cleopatra (1934); Cleopatra (1963); Dr. Phibes Rises Again; King Solomon's Mines; Mountains on the Moon; The Mummy (1932); The Mummy (1959); The Mummy's Hand; The Mummy's Shroud; Sphinx; Stargate; Valley of the Kings

Elderly Men: see also *Elderly People: Death-Dealing with: Widowers: Retirement:* The Adventures of Baron Munchausen (1943); The Arrangement; Better Late Than Never; Brighty of the Grand Canyon; Come and Get It; Conversation Piece; Deadly Currents; Death in Venice; End of the Line; Family; The Field; Full Moon in Blue Water; Ghost Story; Going in Style; The Great Smokey Roadblock; The Grey Fox; Grumpy Old Men; Harry and Tonto; Home Alone; Home Alone 2: Lost in New York; Knickerbocker Holiday; Kotch; The Late Show; A Little Romance; May Fools; Middle of the Night; Mister 880; The Music Room; Never Take Sweets from a Stranger; Nobody's Fool (1994); Old Dracula; Old Gringo; Old Man and the Sea; On Golden Pond; Prelude to a Kiss; Scandalous John; Seven Thieves; Sunday in the Country; The Sunshine Boys; Targets; Tell Me a Riddle; Things Change; To Dance with the White Dog; Toto le Heros; Tough Guys; Trading Places; Travelling North; True Grit; Umberto D.; White Mile; Wild Strawberries; The Wrong Box

Elderly People (about people in general with characters of mixed genders): see also *Aging: Death-Dealing with: Death-Impending: Elderly Men: Elderly Women: Romance-Reunited: Lonely People:* Age Isn't Everything; batteries not included; Best Friends; Boardwalk; Bunny O'Hare; Cloak and Dagger (1984); Cocoon; Cocoon, The Return; Driving Miss Daisy; Family Upside Down; Folks!; Gin Game; Ginger and Fred; The Goodbye People; Grace Quigley; Green Pastures; Harry and Tonto; Love Among the Ruins; Mr. Belvedere Rings the Bell; Nobody's Fool (1994); On Golden Pond; Portrait; Right of Way; Rooster Cogburn; Shadow Box; Tell Me a Riddle; Tokyo Story; Twilight Zone: The Movie

Elderly Women: see also *Elderly People: Death-Dealing with: Widows: Retirement:* Airport; Alive and Kicking; Arsenic and Old Lace; The Autobiography of Miss Jane Pittman; Blackbeard's Ghost; Camilla (1994); The Cemetery Club; Cold Sassy Tree; Crossing Delancey; A Delicate Balance; Dreamchild; Driving Miss Daisy; Fitzwilly; Flight of the Doves; Foxfire (1987); Fried Green Tomatoes; Harold and Maude; Herbie Rides Again; Lady By Choice; Lady for a Day; Ladykillers; Lost

Moment; The Mad Room; Madame Rosa; Madwoman of Chaillot; Min and Bill; The Mirror Crack'd; Mrs. Doubtfire; Night of the Hunter; Olly Olly Oxen Free; On Golden Pond; Passage to India; Pocketful of Miracles; The Prince of Central Park; The Producers; Rabid Grannies; Rosemary's Baby; Savage Intruder; Shell Seekers; Stop! Or My Mom Will Shoot; Storm in a Teacup; Strangers in Good Company; Swing; Tatie Danielle; Tell Me a Riddle; Travels with My Aunt; The Trip to Bountiful; Tugboat Annie; Tugboat Annie Sails Again; VIPs; Whatever Happened to Aunt Alice?; Whatever Happened to Baby Jane?; Where's Poppa?; The Whisperers; White Mama; A Woman's Tale; Woman Screaming; The Young in Heart

Electra Stories (daughters in love with fathers): see also *Fathers & Daughters: Daddy's Girls: Oedipal Stories:* Furies; Soapdish; Where Love Has Gone

Elementary School Life: see *School Life: Boyhood: Girlhood: High School Life: CHILDREN'S*

Elephants: see also *Circus Life: Africa:* Babar: The Movie; Billy Rose's Jumbo; Dumbo; Elephant Walk; Hannibal; The Tall Guy; White Hunter, Black Heart

Elites: see *Rich People: Snobs vs. Slobs: Snobs*

Elixirs: see *Cures/Elixirs: Cures-Solutions-Search for: Fantasy*

Elizabethan Era: see also *Queen Elizabeth: Shakespeare: 1500s/1600s: Restoration Era: Royalty Stories: Kings: Queens: Princes: Princesses:* Anne of the Thousand Days; Elizabeth R.; Fire Over England; The Private Lives of Elizabeth & Essex; Sea Hawk; The Virgin Queen

Elusive Men: see also *Romance-Girl Wants Boy: Romance-Reluctant: Sexy Men: Wallflowers & Hunks: Dreams: Quests: Drifters: Loners:* Belle Epoque; Diary of a Mad Housewife; Give Me a Sailor; Gone With the Wind; The Great Gatsby (1949); The Great Gatsby (1974); Kaleidoscope; Out of Africa; Rachel, Rachel; Roman Spring of Mrs. Stone; Romance; Thoroughly Modern Millie; The Way We Were

Elusive Women: see *Romance-Boy Wants Girl: Romance-Reluctant: Sexy Women: Nerds & Babes: Dreams: Quests:* After Hours; The Apartment; Bedazzled; City of Women; Claire's Knee;

Four Weddings and a Funeral; Gilda;
Goodbye Columbus; Guys and Dolls; The
Heartbreak Kid; Kiss Me Kate (1953);
The Last Picture Show; Laura; The Man
Who Loved Women (1977); The Man
Who Loved Women (1983); Manpower;
Morocco; Queen Christina; The Rachel
Papers; Reckless (1935); Rhapsody; Soup
for One; Tales of Hoffman; The Taming of
the Shrew; Teacher's Pet; Ten; That Kind
of Woman; That Obscure Object of
Desire; 30 is a Dangerous Age, Cynthia;
This Property is Condemned; Tie Me Up!
Tie Me Down!; The Two Jakes; The
Woman in Red

Embezzlers: see *Bank Robberies:*
Thieves: Corporate Corruption

End of the World Stories: see
Apocalyptic Stories: also SCI-FI:
Futuristic Films: Disaster Movies:
Meteors: UFO Stories: Martians: Biblical
Stories: Death-Impending

Enemies: see *Rivalries: Revenge:*
Friendships on the Rocks: Germans as
Enemies: Russians as Enemies

Enemies-Friends Turned: see *Friends*
Turned Enemies

Enemies-Sleeping with: see also
Dangerous Spouses: Romance-
Dangerous: Love-Forbidden: Love-
Questionable: Dangerous Men:
Dangerous Women: Evil Men: Evil
Women: Film Noir: Abusive Men:
Abusive Women: Basic Instinct;
Blackmail (1929); Brighton Rock; The
Conspirator; Desert Fury; Ever in My
Heart; Exposed; Eye of the Needle; The
Eyes of Laura Mars; Jagged Edge; Lady
Eve; Ladykiller (1992); Lightning Strikes
Twice; A Kiss Before Dying (1956); A
Kiss Before Dying (1991); Love From a
Stranger (1936); Love From a Stranger
(1947); Man About the House; The Man I
Married; Midnight Lace; The Morning
After; No Orchids for Miss Blandish;
Sitting Ducks; Sleeping with the Enemy;
Sliver; The Stranger; Undercurrent; When
Strangers Marry

Enemies-Sympathizing with: see
Kidnappings: Kidnappers-Sympathizing
with: Mindgames: Double Crossings:
Friends as Enemies: Enemies Unite

Enemies Unite: see also *Teams-*
Mismatched: Partners-Mismatched:
Race Relations: Black vs. White:
Romance-Bickering: Opposites Attract:
The Buccaneer (1938); The Buccaneer
(1958); Comancheros; Enemy Mine; Kiss

of the Spider Woman; Outrageous
Fortune; Never Love a Stranger; Shadow
Riders; Swashbuckler; Terminator 2:
Judgment Day

Engagements: see *Marriage-*
Impending: Romance-Choosing the
Right Person

Engagements-Breaking: see also
Marriage-Impending: Romance-
Choosing the Right Person: The Age of
Innocence (1934); The Age of Innocence
(1993); Cafe Romeo; Carefree; Children
(1990); Date with an Angel; Deception
(1946); Early Summer; The French
Lieutenant's Woman; Girl Most Likely
(1958); High Society; His Girl Friday; Hit
Parade of 1941; Holiday; Housesitter; It
Had to Be You; It Started with Eve; Love
Among the Ruins; Marrying Man;
Moonstruck; Move Over, Darling; My
Favorite Wife; My Forbidden Past; On
Approval; Only You; The Philadelphia
Story; Ten; True Love; Watch It

**England (not necessarily British but set
in England):** see also *British Films:*
Ireland: Wales: Scotland: Mod Era:
Absolute Beginners; The Adventuress;
All Creatures Great and Small; The
Amazing Mr. Blunden; An American
Werewolf in London; The American-
ization of Emily; Another Time, Another
Place; Aren't We All?; Backbeat; Barry
Lyndon; The Battle of Britain; The Bawdy
Adventures of Tom Jones; Baxter (1972);
Beau Brummell (1924); Beau Brummell
(1954); Beau Geste (1926); Beau Geste
(1939); Beau Geste (1966); Beau Ideal;
Becky Sharp; Bedlam; Billy Liar; Bleak
Moments; Bliss of Mrs. Blossom; Blood
on Satan's Claw; Bloodbath at the House
of Death; Bram Stoker's Count Dracula
(1970); Bram Stoker's Dracula (1992);
Brannigan; Bunny Lake is Missing;
Camelot; A Canterbury Tale; The
Canterville Ghost; Cavalcade; Chalk
Garden; The Charge of the Light Brigade
(1936); The Charge of the Light Brigade
(1968); Charley's Aunt; Citadel; Cluny
Brown; Comrades; Confidential Agent;
The Corn is Green (1945); The Corn is
Green (1979); Cromwell; Dangerous
When Wet; Dark Angel (1991); Devotion;
Dial M For Murder; Diana: Her True
Story; A Diary for Timothy; Die! Die! My
Darling!; Disraeli; Dr. Syn Alias Scare-
crow; Dracula (1931); Dracula (1979);
Dracula Has Risen from the Grave;
Dracula (Horror of Dracula, 1958);

Dracula, Prince of Darkness; Dracula's
Daughter; The Draughtsman's Contract;
The Dressmaker; The Eagle Has Landed;
East Lynne; Edward II; Edward, My Son;
The Elephant Man; Escape From the
Dark; Excalibur; Far from the Madding
Crowd; The Fool; For Queen and
Country; Forever Amber; Forever and a
Day; Four Weddings and a Funeral; The
French Lieutenant's Woman; Frenzy;
Funeral in Berlin; Gambit; Get Carter;
The Ghost and Mrs. Muir; The Go-
Between; Goodbye Mr. Chips (1939);
Goodbye Mr. Chips (1969); The Grass is
Greener; Greystoke: The Legend of
Tarzan; Half a Sixpence; Half Moon
Street; Hanover Street; Hear My Song;
Hearts of Fire; Henry VIII and His Six
Wives; Here We Go Round the Mulberry
Bush; The Holly and the Ivy; Hope and
Glory; Hound of the Baskervilles (1939);
Hound of the Baskervilles (1959); Hound
of the Baskervilles (1977); How Green
Was My Valley; I Could Go on Singing;
I'll Never Forget Whatshisname; I'm All
Right, Jack; Idol; If Winter Comes; In
Our Time; Indiscreet; Inspector Clouseau;
Invasion; It Happened Here; Jack the
Giant Killer; Jamaica Inn (1939); Jamaica
Inn (1982); Joseph Andrews; Jude the
Obscure; A Kind of Loving; King Ralph;
Kipps; Kiss the Blood Off My Hands;
Kitty; Knights of the Round Table; Lady
Godiva; Lady Jane; Lassiter; Last of
England; Lionheart; The List of Adrian
Messenger; Love Letters (1945); Love on
the Dole; Love Story (1944); Lured;
Mackintosh Man; Madame Sousatzka; A
Man for All Seasons; Man in the Attic;
Mary Poppins; McVicar; The
Millionairess; Ministry of Fear; Miniver
Story; The Mirror Crack'd; The
Missionary; Moonlighting (1982); Mrs.
Miniver; Mudlark; Nicholas Nickleby;
The Night Has Eyes; Night Must Fall
(1937); Night Must Fall (1964); No
Surrender; None But the Lonely Heart; O
Lucky Man; Oh, What a Lovely War; On
the Double; Only Two Can Play; Orlando;
Oxford Blues; The Party's Over; Passport
to Pimlico; Princess Caraboo; The Private
Life of Henry VIII; Quadrophenia; Queen
of Destiny; The Rachel Papers; Railway
Children; The Reluctant Debutante;
Remains of the Day; Rough Cut; Salt and
Pepper; Sammy and Rosie Get Laid;
Scandal; Sea Hawk; Separate Tables; The
Shell Seekers; The Shooting Party;

Smilin' Through (1932); Smilin' Through (1941); Sons and Lovers; Star!; Straw Dogs; Success is the Best Revenge; The Sword in the Stone; Sword of the Valiant; The Tall Guy; A Taste of Honey; Term of Trial; Tess; They Drive by Night (1938); This Happy Breed; Titfield; Thunderbolt; To Each His Own; Tommy; Tonight and Every Night; Topaze (1933); Tower of London (1939); The Town; The Trials of Oscar Wilde; Trouble for Two; Tunes of Glory; Turtle Diary; Twenty-Three Paces to Baker Street; Under Milk Wood; Under Suspicion; Village of the Damned; War Lord; Warm December; We Are Not Alone; Went the Day Well?; Werewolf of London; Wetherby; What Every Woman Knows; Whiskey Galore; Whistle Down the Wind; The White Cliffs of Dover; Who is Killing the Great Chefs of Europe?; Wuthering Heights (1939); Wuthering Heights (1953); Wuthering Heights (1970); Wuthering Heights (1992); A Yank at Eton; A Yank at Oxford; Young Sherlock Holmes; Young Winston

Ensemble Films (mixed genders, focusing on a group of characters): see also *Reunions: All-Star Casts: Ensembles-Female: Ensembles-Male:*
Airport Alive; American Graffiti; Apollo 13; Babette's Feast; Bachelor Party (1957); The Bad News Bears; The Bad News Bears Go to Japan; The Bad News Bears in Breaking Training; The Balcony; Bar Girls; The Battle of the Bulge; Battleground; Beat the Devil; Betsy's Wedding; Between the Lines; The Big Broadcast; The Big Broadcast of 1936; The Big Broadcast of 1937; The Big Broadcast of 1938; The Big Chill; Big Deal on Madonna Street; Big Trail; The Biggest Bundle of Them All; The Bingo Long Traveling All-Stars and Motor Kings; Black and White in Color; Blue Collar; Blues in the Night; Boyfriends and Girlfriends; The Boys in the Band; The Brady Bunch Movie; The Breakfast Club; Breaking Away; The Bridge of San Luis Rey; A Bridge Too Far; The Brinks Job; Broadway Melody of 1936; Broadway Melody of 1938; Broadway Melody of 1940; Bullets Over Broadway; Bus Stop; By Love Possessed; Bye Bye Braverman; Cafe Romeo; Caged; The Caine Mutiny (1954); The Caine Mutiny Court Martial (1988); Captain Newman, M.D.; Casino Royale; Cassandra Crossing; The Cat and

the Canary (1927); The Cat and the Canary (1939); The Cat and the Canary (1979); Chantilly Lace; The Chase (1966); The Cheap Detective; China Beach; Choirboys; A Chorus Line; Club Paradise; Cocoanuts; The Color Purple; Come Back to the Five and Dime, Jimmy Dean, Jimmy Dean; The Comedians; The Commitments; Compromising Positions; Cool Hand Luke; Cotton Club; Crackers; Crimes of the Heart; Daddy's Dyin Day After; A Day at the Races; Death on the Nile; Decline of the American Empire; The Deer Hunter; A Delicate Balance; Desperate Characters; Desperate Journey; The Detective (1985); The Devil's Brigade; The Diary of Anne Frank (1959); Diner; Dinner at Eight; The Dirty Dozen; Disorganized Crime; Doctor in the House; Don's Party; Don't Go Near the Water; Double McGuffin; Dramatic School; Earthquake; Enchanted April; End of the Line; Ensign Pulver; Evil Under the Sun; Executive Suite; Experience Preferred . . . ; Faces; Fame; Fanny; Fanny and Alexander; Fat City; Five Corners; Flight of the Phoenix; Flying Tigers; Footlight Parade; Four Daughters; Four Friends; The Four Musketeers; Four Seasons; Foxes; From Here to Eternity; Garbo Talks; Ghost Story; Glengarry Glen Ross; Good Companions (1933); Good Companions (1956); The Good Die Young; A Good Man in Africa; Grand Illusion; The Great Bank Robbery; Great Escape; Great Northfield; Minnesota Raid; The Greatest Show on Earth; Group; Gumball Rally; Gunga Din; Guns of the Magnificent Seven; Hamburger Hill; The Harrad Experiment; The Harrad Summer; Health; Heart and Souls; Heaven Help Us; Heaven's Gate; Heller in Pink Tights; High Hopes; High Season; Hit Parade; Holiday for Sinners; Hollywood Shuffle; Honky Tonk Freeway; The Hot Rock; The Hotel New Hampshire; Hurry Sundown; If It's Tuesday, This Must Be Belgium; In Old Chicago; Innocents in Paris (1953); Inside Moves; Insignificance; Interiors; Interns; Irish in Us; Is Paris Burning?; Island in the Sun; Isn't it Romantic?; It; It Happened in Brooklyn; Jewel in the Crown; Journey to the Center of the Earth; Judgment at Nuremburg; Kelly's Heroes; The Killer Elite; The Kingdom; Kings Row; L-Shaped Room; The Last Picture Show; Last Run; Law and

Disorder (1958); Le Bal; A League of Their Own; Letter to Three Wives; The Life and Times of Judge Roy Bean; Lifeboat; The Linguini Incident; Little Women (1933); Little Women (1949); Little Women (1978); Little Women (1994); London Belongs to Me; London Kills Me; The Long Riders; Lord Love a Duck; Lord of the Flies (1963); Lord of the Flies (1990); Lords of Flatbush; Lost Horizon (1937); Lost Horizon (1973); Love Nest; MASH; The Magnificent Ambersons; The Magnificent Seven; Manhattan; Married to It; May Fools; Mean Streets; Memphis Belle; The Men's Club; Metropolitan (1990); A Midsummer Night's Sex Comedy; Mighty Quinn; Miss Susie Slagle's; Mixed Nuts; Mobsters; The Moderns; More American Graffiti; Mother Carey's Chickens; Mrs. Wiggs of the Cabbage Patch; Murder at the Vanities; Murder by Death; Murder, Inc.; Murder on the Orient Express; Mystic Pizza; Naked; New Interns; New Year's Day; A Night to Remember (1958); 9/30/55; No Down Payment; North Avenue Irregulars; North to Alaska; The Old Dark House (1932); The Old Dark House (1962); The Opposite Sex; Out of Order; Parenthood; Permanent Record; Peter's Friends; Police Academy; Pork Chop Hill; The Poseidon Adventure; Posse (1993); The Professionals; The Program; The Promised Land; Radio Days; Raise the Titanic!; Reality Bites; Rehearsal for Murder; Remember Last Night?; Return of the Secaucus Seven; Riff-Raff (1991); Rififi; The Right Stuff; Risk; The Road to Wellville; Romance on the High Seas; Rome Express; Room Service; A Room with a View; Ruthless People; Salaam Bombay!; Sammy and Rosie Get Laid; Scavenger Hunt; The Sea Gull; Separate Tables; September; Seven Brides for Seven Brothers; Seven Women; Shag; Shaking the Tree; Shallow Grave; Shepherd of the Hills; Ship of Fools; The Shooting Party; Show Business; Showboat (1936); Showboat (1951); Silver Bears; Silverado; Singles; The Skin Game; Small Change; Smiles of a Summer Night; Sneakers; Soapdish; SOB; A Soldier's Story; Some Came Running; Springtime in the Rockies; St. Elmo's Fire; Stagecoach (1939); Stagecoach (1966); Stagedoor; Stalag 17; Star Trek II: The Wrath of Khan; Star Trek III: The Search for Spock; Star Trek IV: The Voyage

Home; Star Trek: The Motion Picture; Star Trek V: The Final Frontier; Star Trek VI: The Undiscovered Country; State Fair (1933); State Fair (1945); State Fair (1962); Staying Together; Steaming; Steel Magnolias; Story of Boys and Girls; Streamers; The Subterraneans; Such Good Friends; The Sun Also Rises; Support Your Local Sheriff; Survive; Sweet Liberty; Sylvia Scarlett; Taps; Teahouse of the August Moon; Tell Me that You Love Me, Junie Moon; Ten Little Indians; Thank God It's Friday; That Championship Season; There's No Business Like Show Business; Thing Called Love; This Happy Breed; Three Blind Mice; The Three Godfathers; Three Men and a Baby; Three Men and a Cradle; Three Men and a Little Lady; The Three Musketeers (1935); The Three Musketeers (1939); The Three Musketeers (1948); The Three Musketeers (1973); The Three Musketeers (1993); Three Sisters; The Threepenny Opera; The Titfield Thunderbolt; To Wong Foo, Thanks for Everything, Julie Newmar; Topkapi!; The Towering Inferno; Toy Soldiers; A Tree Grows in Brooklyn; Tree of Wooden Clogs; Trojan Women; Twelve Angry Men; Twilight for the Gods; Union Pacific; Up the Creek (1984); Valley of the Dolls; Victors; Victory; VIPs; Voyage of the Damned; Watch It; We're Not Married; The Wedding; Weeds; Weekend at the Waldorf; Welcome to L.A.; Who's Minding the Mint?; Winged Victory; Woman's World; The Women; Young Doctors; Young Guns; Young Guns II; Ziegfeld Girl

Ensembles-Children/Teens: see also *Ensemble Films: High School Life: School Life: CHILDREN'S: Disney Comedy:* The Bad News Bears; The Bad News Bears Go to Japan; The Bad News Bears in Breaking Training; Double McGuffin; Little Giants; The Little Rascals; Lord of the Flies (1963); Lord of the Flies (1990); Sandlot; Small Change; Three Ninjas; Three Ninjas Kick Back

Ensembles-Female: see also *Ensemble Films: Women's Films: Girls' Schools:* Boys on the Side; Caged; Chantilly Lace; China Beach; The Color Purple; Come Back to the Five and Dime, Jimmy Dean, Jimmy Dean; Crimes of the Heart; Dramatic School; Enchanted April; Four Daughters; Foxes; The Group; How to Beat the High Cost of Living; How to

Marry a Millionaire; Isn't it Romantic?; The Joy Luck Club; A League of Their Own; Let's Hope it's a Girl; Letter to Three Wives; Little Women (1933); Little Women (1949); Little Women (1978); Little Women (1994); Lumiere; Mi Vida Loca; Miss Susie Slagle's; Mystic Pizza; Nasty Habits; New Year's Day; Nine to Five; North Avenue Irregulars; The Opposite Sex; Picnic at Hanging Rock; Seven Women; Shag; Sister Act 2; Sparkle; Stagedoor; Steaming; Steel Magnolias; Strangers in Good Company; Three Blind Mice; Trojan Women; Valley of the Dolls; Waiting to Exhale; Warrior's Husband; The Witches of Eastwick; The Women; Ziegfeld Girl

Ensembles-Male: see also *Ensemble Films: Men's Films: Boys' Schools: Brat Pack Stories:* Alive; Angels in the Outfield (1951); Angels in the Outfield (1994); Apollo 13; Bachelor Party (1957); Back to Bataan; The Bad News Bears; The Bad News Bears Go to Japan; The Bad News Bears in Breaking Training; The Battle of the Bulge; Battleground; The Best of Times; Biggest Bundle of Them All; The Bingo Long Traveling All-Stars and Motor Kings; The Boys in the Band; Breaking Away; Breaking Up is Hard to Do; Bye Bye Braverman; Bye Bye Love; The Caine Mutiny (1954); The Caine Mutiny Court Martial (1988); Captain Newman, M.D.; Choirboys; Cool Hand Luke; Coupe de Ville; Desperate Journey; The Devil's Brigade; Diner; The Dirty Dozen; Ensign Pulver; Five Heartbeats; Flight of the Phoenix; Flying Tigers; Four Feathers (1929); Four Feathers (1939); Ghost Story; Glengarry Glen Ross; The Great Escape; Gunga Din; Guns of the Magnificent Seven; Hamburger Hill; Heaven Help Us; Horse Soldiers; The Hot Rock; Husbands; I Vitelloni; Inside Moves; Interns; The Irish in Us; Judgment Night; Kelly's Heroes; The Killer Elite; Law and Disorder (1958); Little Giants; London Belongs to Me; The Long Riders; Long Voyage Home; Lord of the Flies (1963); Lord of the Flies (1990); The Lords of Flatbush; MASH; The Magnificent Seven; Major League; Major League 2; Manpower; Mean Streets; Memphis Belle; Men of the Fighting Lady; The Mens' Club; A Midnight Clear; The Mighty Ducks; Mobsters; The Naked and the Dead; New Interns; North to Alaska; Objective Burma; On the Town; Once Upon a Time in the

West; One Flew Over Cuckoo's Nest; Only When I Larf; The Pickwick Papers; Platoon; Pork Chop Hill; Posse (1993); The Professionals; The Program; Pulp Fiction; Reservoir Dogs; Rififi; The Right Stuff; Sahara (1943); Sandlot; The Secret Policeman's Ball; The Secret Policeman's Other Ball; The Secret Policeman's Private Parts; The Secret Policeman's Third Ball; Shepherd of the Hills; Short Eyes; Show Business; Sophisticated Gents; Stacy's Knights; Stalag 17; Staying Together; Streamers; Survive; Taps; Teahouse of the August Moon; That Championship Season; The Three Godfathers; Three Men and a Baby; Three Men and a Cradle; Three Men and a Little Lady; The Three Musketeers (1935); The Three Musketeers (1939); The Three Musketeers (1948); The Three Musketeers (1973); The Three Musketeers (1993); To Wong Foo, Thanks for Everything, Julie Newmar; Toy Soldiers; Twelve Angry Men; Up the Academy; Uptown Saturday Night; Usual Suspects; Victors; Victory; Watch It; Waterdance; Weeds; The Wild Bunch; Winged Victory; Young Doctors; Young Guns; Young Guns II

Ensembles-Young People: see also *20-Something Movies: Ensembles-Children:* Boyfriends and Girlfriends; The Breakfast Club; Diner; Reality Bites; Thing Called Love

Entertainment Business: see *Theater Life: Hollywood Life: Radio: Music: TV Life: Starring ShowBiz Offspring*

Environmental Dilemmas: see also *Scientists: Scientists as Detectives: Toxins:* Akira Kurosawa's Dreams; Amazon; Big Trees; Body Snatchers; A Breed Apart; Bye Bye Brazil; FernGully: The Last Rainforest; The Fire Next Time; Food of the Gods; Fortress; Impulse (1984); The Incredible Shrinking Man; Jetsons Movie; Louisiana Story; Nightwing; On Deadly Ground; The Prophecy; Superman 3; Toxic Avenger; Toxic Avenger, Part II; Toxic Avenger Part III

Epics: see also *ADVENTURE: Journeys: Costume Drama: Historical Drama: Quests: Cast of Thousands:* Alamo; Alexander Nevsky; America; America, America; Apocalypse Now; Around the World in 80 Days; Barabbas; Ben-Hur (1959); Ben-Hur: A Tale of Christ (1925); Bhowani Junction; The Bible; The Big Country; The Big Fisherman; The Birth of a Nation; The Black Rose; Bonnie Prince Charlie; The Bridge on the River Kwai; A

Shop Around the Corner; The Story of Adèle H.

Erotic Comedy (very sexual to soft core, as opposed to the more innocent, teasing Sex Comedy): see also *Erotic Drama: Erotic Thriller: Pornography World:* The Adventures of Eliza Frazer; The Advocate; Almost Pregnant; Alvin Purple; Alvin Rides Again; The Amorous Adventures of Moll Flanders; Andy Warhol's Dracula; Auntie Lee's Meat Pies; Belle Epoque; Beyond the Valley of the Dolls; Bilitis; Bound and Gagged, a Love Story; Bull Durham; Candy; A Canterbury Tale; Caveman; Class; Confessions of a Window Cleaner; Dona Flor and Her Two Husbands; Every Thing You Always Wanted to Know About Sex . . . ; Fanny Hill; Faster Pussycat! Kill! Kill!; The Favour, the Watch & the Very Big Fish; The First Nudie Musical; The First Time; Flesh Gordon; Fritz the Cat; Get Out Your Handkerchiefs; Ghosts Can't Do It; The Happy Hooker; Here We Go Round the Mulberry Bush; High Heels; Jane and the Lost City; Las Vegas Hillbillies; Le Cavaleur; Lock up Your Daughters; Losin' It; Loverboy; Lust in the Dust; My Tutor; Myra Breckinridge; Porky's; Porky's 2; Porky's Revenge; Private School; Ready to Wear; Rita, Sue and Bob, Too; The Rocky Horror Picture Show; Scenes from the Class Struggle in Beverly Hills; Spring Break; Tarzan and His Mate; Tarzan Escapes; Tarzan, The Ape Man (1932); Tarzan, the Ape Man (1981); Ten; Tie Me Up! Tie Me Down!; Tom Jones; Up the Academy; What?; What's New Pussycat?; Where Does it Hurt?; Yesterday, Today and Tomorrow

Erotic Drama (very sensual to soft core, as opposed to the more innocent Romantic Drama): see also *Erotic Comedy: Erotic Thriller: Pornography World:* The Adjuster; The Adventurers; Almost Perfect Affair; American Gigolo; And God Created Woman (1957); And God Created Woman (1988); And Now, My Love; Andy Warhol's Dracula; Andy Warhol's Heat; Anne and Muriel; Bad Timing: A Sensual Obsession; Beau Pere; Being at Home with Claude; Betsy; Betty Blue; Bitch (1979); Bolero (1984); Boxing Helena; Breathless (1959); Breathless (1983); Butterfly; Caligula; Casanova (Fellini's Casanova); Castaway; City of Women; Damage; Dante's Inferno; Dark Obsession; Devil in the Flesh (1946);

Devil in the Flesh (1987); Don't Look Now; Double Jeopardy; The Draughtsman's Contract; Dream Lover (1994); Drowning By Numbers; Drum; Ebony Tower; Emmanuelle SERIES; Endless Love; Exotica; Exposed; First Name: Carmen; Flesh; Flesh and Blood (1985); Forbidden Dance; The Fox; Full Moon in Paris; Gabriela; Get Out Your Handkerchiefs; Ghosts Can't Do It; Gothic; Grasshopper; The Hairdresser's Husband; The Harrad Experiment; The Harrad Summer; The Haunted Summer; Henry and June; Hireling; The Hot Spot; The Hunger; The Hustle; In Praise of Older Women; In the Realm of the Senses; Indecent Proposal; Interview with the Vampire; Jules and Jim; Julia and Julia; The King's Whore; L'Annee des Meduses; La Balance; La Maschera; Lady Chatterley's Lover (1955); Lady Chatterley's Lover (1981); Lake Consequence; Last Days of Chez Nous; Last Tango in Paris; Les Biches; Like Water For Chocolate; Lonely Lady; Love Machine; Love Matters; The Lover; Mad Monkey; Maitresse; A Man in Love; Man of Flowers; The Man Who Fell to Earth; Mandingo; Monsieur Hire; Montenegro; Moon in the Gutter; Naked Tango; Negatives; Night and Day; Night in Heaven; Night Porter; 9½ Weeks; Nouvelle Vague; The Other Side of Midnight; Paradise (1982); The Passion; Personal Best; The Piano; Poison Ivy (1992); The Pornographers; The Postman Always Ring Twice (1945); The Postman Always Rings Twice (1981); Pretty Baby; Prospero's Books; Quartet (1981); Querelle; Rainbow; Red Shoe Diaries; The Return to the Blue Lagoon; Risk; The Sailor Who Fell From Grace with the Sea; Salo: 120 Days of Sodom; Salon Kitty; Satyricon (Fellini's); Scandal; Shampoo; Siesta; Sirens; Smash Palace; Smooth Talk; Spanking the Monkey; Stealing Heaven; Stud; Tattoo; Thief of Hearts; Threesome; Tie Me Up! Tie Me Down!; Tokyo Decadence; Trash; Tropic of Cancer; Turkish Delight; Two Moon Junction; The Unbearable Lightness of Being; Valentino (1977); Valmont; The Virgin and the Gypsy; Warm Nights on a Slow Moving Train; What?; White Mischief; Whore; Wicked Lady (1983); Wild at Heart; Wild Orchid; Willie and Phil; Women in Love; The World is Full of Married Men; Yesterday, Today and Tomorrow; Zabriskie Point; Zandalee; A Zed and Two Noughts

Erotic Thrillers (very sensual to soft core, as opposed to the just plainly frightening suspense film): see also *Erotic Comedy: Erotic Drama: Pornography World:* After Dark, My Sweet; Bad Company (1995); Bedroom Eyes; Bedroom Eyes 2; Blindfold: Acts of Obsession; Body Heat; Body of Evidence; Call Me; Cold Sweat; Color of Night; Desire and Hell at Sunset Motel; Die Watching; Disturbed; Double Threat; Dream Lover (1994); Femme Fatale; The Hunger; Interview with the Vampire; Kill Me Again; La Balance; The Last Seduction; Lipstick; Paint it Black; Sliver; The Specialist; Tale of a Vampire; Tattoo; Warm Nights on a Slow Moving Train

Escape Adventures/Dramas: see also *Escapes-Clever: Prison Escapes: ADVENTURE: Tunnels: Crossing the Border: Prison Escapes:* Abschied von Gestern; Aces, Iron Eagle 3; Alive and Kicking; Appointment in Honduras; Bittere Ernte; Blood Alley; Born to be Wild; Breakout; Captain Blood; Casablanca; Charley Varrick; The Count of Monte Cristo (1934); The Count of Monte Cristo (1974); A Day in October; The Defiant Ones; Destiny of a Man; Devil at Four O'Clock; The Devil's Bride; Distant Drums; Dream Team; El Norte; Escape from Alcatraz; Escape from Fort Bravo; Fahrenheit 451; The Fire Next Time; Going in Style; The Great Escape; The Great Escape 2: The Untold Story; Ivan's Childhood; Journey of Hope; Knight Without Armor; Little Ark; Night Crossing; Night Train to Munich; Not Without My Daughter; Papillon; The Passage; The Poseidon Adventure; The Scarlet Pimpernel; The Secret War of Harry Frigg; The Serpent's Egg; The Seventh Cross; Shining Through; Son of Sinbad; The Sound of Music; Sugarland Express; Swing Kids; Three Came Home; Victory; Von Ryan's Express; Two Women; The Unbearable Lightness of Being; Victory Wilby Conspiracy; The Wooden Horse

Escape from Iron Curtain: see *Iron Curtain-Escape From-Iron Curtain-Behind the: Spy Films: Russians as Enemy: Germans as Enemy: Europeans-Eastern*

Espionage: see *Spy Films: Spies*

Ethics: see also *Corruption: Political Drama: Political Satire: Romance-Unprofessional: Conformism: Scandals:* Absence of Malice; Ace in the Hole; Action for Slander; Advise and Consent;

Alice's Restaurant; All My Sons (1949); All My Sons (1986); All Quiet on the Western Front; All the King's Men; All the President's Men; Angel on My Shoulder; The Apartment; Arrowsmith; At Close Range; The Big Picture; Big Trees; Black Legion; Blue Chips; Blue Sky; Boomerang (1947); The Bostonians; Breaking the Sound Barrier; Cahill: United States Marshal; The Caine Mutiny (1954); The Caine Mutiny Court Martial (1988); Campus Man; The Candidate; Cape Fear (1962); Cape Fear (1991); Chariots of Fire; Chocolate War; City and the Dogs; City of Hope; Company Limited; The Conformist; The Conversation; Coup de Torchon; Crazy People; Crimes and Misdemeanors; Cutter and Bone; Deadline USA; Deep Cover; Detective Story; The Devil's Disciple; Diary of a Hitman; Doctor's Dilemma; Dr. Socrates; Eight Men Out; Electric Horseman; F.I.S.T.; Family Business; A Few Good Men; Five Star Final; Fortune Cookie; The Fountainhead; Friendly Persuasion; The Front Page (1931); The Front Page (1974); Gardens of Stone; Garment Jungle; The Glass Key (1935); The Glass Key (1942); Glengarry Glen Ross; The Good Fight; A Good Man in Africa; The Good Mother; The Great Lie; Guilty by Suspicion; The Harder They Fall; Hero; Hit Parade of 1943; Homicide; Hook; The Hucksters; I'll Give a Million; I'll Never Forget Whatshisname; Iceman; Illegal; Immediate Family; Inherit the Wind; Intolerance; Invisible Man's Revenge; It Could Happen to You; It Happened Tomorrow; Johnny Be Good; La Vie Continue; The Lawman; Legend of the Holy Drinker; Major Barbara; The Man Who Shot Liberty Valance; Men Don't Leave; The Mikado; Miller's Crossing; Mortal Thoughts; The Mountain; Move; Mr. Klein; The Music Box; The Naked Truth; Natural Born Killers; Necessary Roughness; Night and the City (1992); No Way Out (1950); Nothing But the Truth; Nous Sommes Tous les Assassins; Now and Forever; Oh, God; Oh God Book Two; Oh God, You Devil; On the Waterfront; The Outsider; The Ox-Bow Incident; The Paradine Case; People Will Talk; Perfect; The Player; The Ploughman's Lunch; Pollyanna; The Posse (1975); Power; Primary Motive; Prodigal; Quiz Show;

Save the Tiger; Say One for Me; Schindler's List; A Separate Peace; Showdown; A Slight Case of Murder; Souls at Sea; Spellbound; State of the Union; Susan and God; Sweet Smell of Success; Talent for the Game; Tequila Sunrise; Town Without Pity; Trading Places; True Believer; True Colors; True Confessions; Twelve O'Clock High; Two Against the World; Unforgiven (1992); Vincent and Theo; Wall Street; Washington Story; Wetherby; Which Way is Up?; Winter Light

Ethnic/Minority Films (miscellaneous ethnicities): see *Asian-American Films: Black Casts/Films: Gay/Lesbian Films: Latin Films: Third World Films: various countries*

Europeans-Eastern: see also *Communism: Russians: Iron Curtain-Escape from: Iron Curtain-Behind the: Polish Films: Czech Films:* Anna; Ashes and Diamonds; The Battle of Neretva; Closely Watched Trains; Colonel Redl; Diary for My Children; Displaced Person; Elena and Her Men; Fiddler on the Roof; Four Sons; Hangmen Also Die; In Our Time; Interrogation; Kiss of Evil; Loves of a Blonde; Man of Iron; Meeting Venus; Moonlighting (1982); The Music Box; My Sweet Little Village; Revolt of Job; The Shop Around the Corner; The Shop on Main Street; A Short Film About Killing; Silver City; Stranger Than Paradise; Streets of Gold Stromboli; Success is the Best Revenge; The Swan; To Be or Not to Be (1942); To Be or Not to Be (1983); To Kill a Priest; The Unbearable Lightness of Being; When Father Was Away on Business; Yentl

Eurotrash: see *Rich People-Decadent: Riviera Life: Beautiful People: Vacations-European*

Euthanasia: see also *Death-Dealing With: Suicidal Tendencies:* An Act of Murder; Bramble Bush; Folks!; Grace Quigley; Right of Way; Whose Life Is It Anyway?

Everyman Stories: see *Ordinary People Stories: Working Class*

Everyman vs. Criminals: see *Ordinary Person vs. Criminals: Vigilantes: Avenging Death of Someone: Revenge: Turning the Tables*

Evil: see *Fighting Evil: Satan: Satanism: Satan-Children of: Possessions: Evil Men: Evil Women: Evil Children*

Evil Children: see also *Children-Brats: Satan-Children of: Evil Men: Evil Women: Twins-Evil:* The Bad Seed (1956); The Bad Seed (1986); The Children (1980); Children of the Damned; Doppelganger: The Evil Within; The Exorcist; The Exorcist II: The Heretic; The Little Girl Who Lives Down the Lane; Other Problem Child; Problem Child 2; Teenage Rebel

Evil Men: see also *Mean Men: Dangerous Men: Double Crossings: Liars: Con Artists: Twins-Evil:* The Abominable Dr. Phibes; Absolution; Albuquerque; Anne of the Thousand Days; Apocalypse Now; The Bad and the Beautiful; Bad Lieutenant; Behold a Pale Horse; Billy Budd; Bitter Moon; Black Hole; Black Room; Blue Max; The Boys from Brazil; The Boys in Company C; Bugsy Child's Play (1972); A Christmas Carol (1938); Citizen Cohn; Citizen Kane; Cobb; The Comfort of Strangers; The Count of Monte Cristo (1934); The Count of Monte Cristo (1974); The Dark Half; The Dead Zone; Dr. Faustus; Ebb Tide; Edward, My Son; The Empire Strikes Back; Eureka; Ever in My Heart; The Evil That Men Do; Experiment Perilous; Flight of the Doves; The Four Musketeers; Freddy's Dead: The Final Nightmare; Full Metal Jacket; Gaslight (1939); Gaslight (1944); Genghis Khan; The Godfather; The Godfather, Part II; The Godfather, Part III; GoodFellas; Hammersmith is Out; Henry VIII and His Six Wives; The Hitler Gang; Hitler—The Last Ten Days; House of the Spirits; The Hudsucker Proxy; In Cold Blood; Internal Affairs; Island (1980); Les Liaisons Dangereuses; Lock Up; Looking for Mr. Goodbar; Mask of Fu Manchu; Masque of the Red Death; Miller's Crossing; Mind Benders; The Muppet Christmas Carol; Murder in Texas; Murders in the Rue Morgue; Mutiny on the Bounty (1935); Mutiny on the Bounty (1962); Natural Born Killers; Needful Things; New Nightmare; Night of the Hunter; Nightmare on Elm Street; Nightmare on Elm Street Part Four; Nightmare on Elm Street Part Three; Nightmare on Elm Street Part Two; Nightmare on Elm Street: The Dream Child; On Deadly Ground; Once Upon a Time in the West; Paris Trout; Passenger 57; Payment Deferred; Peter Pan; Phantom of the Rue Morgue; The Private Life of Henry VIII; The Prowler; Pulp

Fiction; Raising Cain; Reservoir Dogs; The Rise and Fall of Legs Diamond; Rob Roy; Sabotage; Scarface (1932); Scarface (1983); Scrooged; Shock Corridor; Shogun Assassin; Sleeping With the Enemy; Something Wild (1986); St. Valentine's Day Massacre; Stargate; Star Trek: Generations; The Stepfather; Stepfather 2: Make Room for Daddy; Stepfather 3: Father's Day; Strange One; A Streetcar Named Desire; Thief of Bagdad (1924); Thief of Baghdad (1940); The Three Musketeers (1935); The Three Musketeers (1939); The Three Musketeers (1948); To Kill a Clown; Tower of London (1939); Tower of London (1962); Usual Suspects; Young Philadelphians

Evil Twins: see *Twins-Evil*

Evil Women: see also *Mean Women: Dangerous Women: Double Crossings: Liars: Con Artists: Twins-Evil:* All About Eve; Annie; Anniversary; The Beguiled; Born to Be Bad (1950); Bugsy; Cabin in the Cotton; Carrie (1976); Chicago Joe and the Showgirl; Cinderella; Conan, the Destroyer; Dance with a Stranger; Die! Die! My Darling!; Disclosure; Doppelganger: The Evil Within; East of Eden (1955); East of Eden (1980); Erendira; Final Analysis; Flowers in the Attic; The Four Musketeers; The Fourth Man; The Guardian; Gun Crazy (1950); Gun Crazy (1992); Inheritance; Kansas City Bomber; Kitten with a Whip; Last Summer; Leave Her to Heaven; Les Liaisons Dangereuses; The Letter (1929); The Letter (1940); The Little Foxes; The Little Girl Who Lives Down the Lane; The Locket; The Manchurian Candidate; The Match Factory Girl; Mommie Dearest; Mother's Boys; My Forbidden Past; Network; One Flew Over Cuckoo's Nest; 101 Dalmatians; Positively True Adventures of the Alleged Texas Cheerleader-Murdering Mom; Pretty Poison; Rasputin and the Empress; Romeo is Bleeding; Savage Intruder; Siegfried; Sleeping Beauty; The Slipper and the Rose; Small Sacrifices; Snow White & The Seven Dwarfs; Sybil; A Tale of Two Cities (1935); A Tale of Two Cities (1958); A Tale of Two Cities (1982); Teenage Rebel; Ulysses (1954); Valmont; The Virgin Queen; Who Slew Auntie Roo?; Wicked As They Come; The Wolves of Willoughby Chase; Working Girl; X, Y, & Zee

Exchange Students: see also *Americans Abroad: Teachers & Students:*

College Life: High School Life: Foreign Misfits: Grease; Grease 2; Higher Learning; Quackser Fortune Has a Cousin in the Bronx; The Rachel Papers

Ex-Convicts (having just recently gotten out of prison or relating to their trying to go straight): see also *Prison Drama: Crime Drama: Criminal's Revenge:* Always in My Heart; And God Created Woman (1988); The Anderson Tapes; Arsène Lupin Returns; The Asphalt Jungle; Baby, The Rain Must Fall; Battle of Algiers Bitch (La Garce) (1984); Blackmail (1939); Cat and Mouse; Charley Varrick; Dark Passage; Dead Heat on a Merry Go Round; Demolition Man; Father Hood; Fools Parade; Frankie and Johnny; Gator; Going Home; The Grey Fox; Happy New Year (1973); Happy New Year (1987); He Was Her Man; The Hot Rock; I'll Be Seeing You; J.W. Coop; Jailhouse Rock; Johnny Handsome; The Killing; King of New York; Larceny, Inc.; The Mackintosh Man; The Mark; Mayor of Hell; McVicar; Les Miserables (1978); Les Miserables (1935); Les Miserables (1952); The Naked Street; Only When I Larf; Out of the Blue; Outfit (1973); Outlaw Blues; The Real McCoy; River Rat; Scar; Slither; South Central; Steelyard Blues; Straight Time; Taking Care of Business; There Was a Crooked Man; Three Fugitives; Tough Guys

Executions: see also *Death-Impending: Prison Drama: Lynchings:* Cat and Mouse; Dance with a Stranger; Day of Wrath; The Devil's Disciple; Dynamite; The Execution of Private Slovik; The Executioner's Song; Female Trouble; The Front Page (1931); The Front Page (1974); Fury (1936); Goin' South; Good Day for a Hanging; Guilty as Charged; Hang 'em High; Henry VIII and His Six Wives; His Girl Friday; Hook; I Stand Condemned; Jesus of Nazareth; The Last Temptation of Christ; Lucky Stiff; Marie Antoinette; Mary of Scotland; Mary, Queen of Scots; The Mikado; Nicholas and Alexandra; The Ox-Bow Incident; The Private Life of Henry VIII; The Return of the Scarlet Pimpernel; The Revenge of Frankenstein; The Robe; Rollerball; Sacco and Vanzetti; Saint Joan; The Scarlet Pimpernel; Sebastiane; The Seventh Cross; Shocker; A Short Film About Killing; Switching Channels; A Tale of Two Cities (1935); A Tale of

Two Cities (1958); A Tale of Two Cities (1982); Tom Horn; Tom Jones; The Walking Dead

Executives (high-powered business types): see also *Business Life: Yuppies: Corporate Corruption: Moguls:* Any Wednesday; Ask Any Girl; The Associate; The Bad Sleep Well; Boomerang; Carnal Knowledge; The Coca Cola Kid; Executive Suite; Kramer vs. Kramer; Madison Avenue; The Man in the Gray Flannel Suit; Network; Patterns; Scrooged; The Secret of My Success; Solid Gold Cadillac; Take a Letter, Darling; Wall Street; White Mile; Woman's World; Working Girl

Exorcisms: see *Possessions: Satanism*

Exotic Locales: see *Vacations: Pacific Ocean/Islands: Islands: Caribbean: Riviera Life: Hawaii: South America*

Exotic Romance: see *Erotic Drama: Erotic Thriller: Romance-Exotic Locales*

Experimental Films: see *Avant-Garde Films: Art Films: Documentary-Style Films: Cult Films: Curiosities*

Experiments: see also *Brain Transplants: Monsters-Human: Monsters-Mutant: Body Switching: Mad Scientists: HORROR:* Altered States; The Andromeda Strain; Bedtime for Bonzo; Black Sleep; Blood Beast Terror; The Boys from Brazil; Boys' Night Out; Brainstorm (1983); Bride of the Gorilla; Bride of the Monster; The Brood; Cameron's Closet; Darkman; Day of the Dolphin; Demon Seed; The Doctor and the Devils; Doctor Jekyll and Mr. Hyde (1931); Donovan's Brain; Dr. Cyclops; Dr. Heckyl and Mr. Hype; Dr. Jekyll & Mr. Hyde (1941); Dreamscape; Entity; Escape from the Planet of the Apes; A Fine Madness; Flatliners; The Fly (1958); The Fly (1986); The Fly II; The Fury (1978); Goldengirl; Groundstar Conspiracy; The Harrad Experiment; The Harrad Summer; Hello Down There; I, Monster; Innerspace; Junior; Late for Dinner; The Lawnmower Man; Link; Mad Love; Man Made Monster; The Man with Nine Lives; Man's Best Friend; Memoirs of an Invisible Man; Mind Benders; Monkey Shines; My Fair Lady; Philadelphia Experiment; Prince of Darkness; Quatermass Experiment; The Raven (1935); Re-Animator; Re-Animator 2; Return of the Fly; Revenge of Frankenstein; The Rocketeer; The Rocky Horror Picture Show; Runaway;

Scream and Scream Again!; Sender; Silent Running; Simon; Splash!; Swamp Thing; Terminal Man; Them!; This Island Earth; The Thousand Eyes of Dr. Mabuse; Time Machine; Timerider; Total Recall; Transmutations; Trog Twins; Watchers; Watchers II; Young Tom Edison

Exploitation: see *Cult Films: Blaxploitation Era*

Explorers: see also *ADVENTURE: Adventure at Sea: Quests: Treasure Hunts: Mountain Climbing: Pirates:* The Adventures of Marco Polo; Baby, Secret of the Lost Legend; The Black Robe; Black Rose; Burke and Wills; China Clipper; Christopher Columbus

(1949); Christopher Columbus: The Discovery (1992); 1492: Conquest of Paradise; The Green Goddess; Happy Birthday, Wanda June; Hawaii; Hudson's Bay; Jeremiah Johnson; The Land that Time Forgot; The Mole People; Mountains on the Moon; Ordeal by Innocence; Scott of the Antarctic; The Snows of Kilimanjaro; Stanley and Livingstone; The Thing (1951); The Thing (1982); Walker

Ex-Spouse Trouble: see *Divorce: Custody Battles: Marriage Drama*

Extroverted vs. Introverted: see also *Smart vs. Dumb: Nerds & Babes: Wallflowers & Hunks:* Ball of Fire; Blue

Angel (1930); Blue Angel (1959); Bocaccio '70; Broadcast News; Captain Ron; Cass Timberlane; Come Blow Your Horn; Exotica; A Fine Romance; Georgy Girl; Impromptu; I.Q.; Joy of Living; Les Comperes; Love Potion #9; Macaroni; The Male Animal; Moonlighting (1985); Ninotchka; The Nutty Professor (1963); The Odd Couple; Outrageous Fortune; Owl and the Pussycat; The Pad, and How to Use It; Pillow Talk; Say Anything; She's Working Her Way Through College; A Song is Born; Strictly Business; Taking Off; Travels with My Aunt; Two-Faced Woman; What's Up, Doc?

F

Factory Life: see also *Corporation as Enemy: Fighting the System: Poor People: Unions: Working Class:* Angry Silence; Blue Collar; Cannery Row; Gung Ho (1986); Heart of Glass; The Match Factory Girl; Matewan; Norma Rae; The Pajama Game; The Passion; Roger & Me; The Strike; Swing Shift; Take This Job and Shove It; Tommy Boy; Toys

Faded Hits (big critical or commercial hits in their day, they've since faded into relative obscurity or aren't highly regarded): see also *Forgotten Films: Hidden Gems: Overrated:* The Affairs of Cellini; All That Money Can Buy; America, America; The Amityville Horror; Anthony Adverse; Bandolero; The Barefoot Executive; The Bellboy; Billy Jack; Blue Denim; Boom Town; Born Free; Bound For Glory; Brazil; Broken Lance; Career Carousel; Caught in the Draft; Cavalcade; Ceiling Zero; The Champion; The Changeling; Charlotte's Web; The Cincinnati Kid; Colors; Come to the Stable; A Connecticut Yankee; Constant Nymph (1933); Constant Nymph (1943); Cool Hand Luke; Coquette; The Corsican Brothers; Cotton Comes to Harlem; Court Jester; Crossfire; The Deer Hunter; Designing Woman; Detective Story; The End; Escape; Escape from Alcatraz; Every Which Way But Loose; Excalibur; Fanny; Father Goose; Fighting

Kentuckian; Five Fingers; The Five Pennies; Five Star Final; Flower Drum Song; Fort Apache; Four Daughters; Four Feathers (1929); The Four Feathers (1939); The Four Seasons; The Fox; A Free Soul; The French Connection; Fury (1936); Fuzz; Gaily, Gaily; Gandhi; The General Died at Dawn; Gentleman's Agreement; Get Carter; Get Out Your Handkerchiefs; Getting Straight; Ghost Breakers; The Girl Can't Help It; Girls! Girls! Girls!; Going My Way; Go into Your Dance; Goodbye, Columbus; Gorgeous Hussy; The Great Race; The Guardsman; A Gunfight at the O.K. Corral; The Guns of Navarone; Gus; Hard to Handle; The Hard Way (1943); The Heartbreak Kid; Heartbreak Ridge; Heaven Can Wait (1943); Hell and High Water; Hell's Angels; Hello Frisco Hello; Here Comes Mr. Jordan; Here Comes the Navy; Heroes; High Plains Drifter; High Road to China; High Sierra; Hold That Ghost; Hold Your Man; A Hole in the Head; Hollywood Cavalcade; Hollywood Revue of 1929; Hombre; Honky Tonk; Hook; Horse Soldiers; Hot Stuff; Hotel; House Calls; How to Succeed in Business without Really Trying; I Never Sang for My Father; In Old Arizona; In Search of the Castaways; Joe; John and Mary; Journey to the Center of the Earth; Joy of Living; Kitty Foyle; The Last Emperor; Lenny;

Les Biches; Letter to Three Wives; Little Darlings; Lives of a Bengal Lancer; Lloyd's of London; The Long, Good Friday; Love is a Many-Splendored Thing; M*A*S*H; A Man for All Seasons; Marty; McClintock!; Mrs. Miniver; My Love Came Back; Never on Sunday; The Oklahoma Kid; The Old Man and the Sea; Old Mother Riley SERIES; On Approval; On the Riviera; The One and Only; One Hour with You; One in a Million; One Way Passage; Only Angels Have Wings; Operation Petticoat; Our Man Flint; Our Relations; Our Town; Paid; The Pajama Game; Panic in the Streets; Papillon; Pardners; Passage to Marseilles; Patch of Blue; Patton; Pepe; Personal Property; Peter Ibbetson; Petrified Forest; Pickup on South Street; Pinky; Platinum Blonde; Pollyanna; The Poseidon Adventure; The Prime of Miss Jean Brodie; The Prize; The Prizefighter and the Lady; Public Enemy; Raffles; The Rains Came; Raintree County; A Raisin in the Sun; The Red Headed Woman; Rhapsody; Rhythm on the Range; The Right Stuff; Rio Bravo; Rock a Bye Baby; Rocky; Rocky III; Romance on the High Seas; Room at the Top; Rose Marie (1936); Rose Marie (1954); Rose of Washington Square; Royal Wedding; Ruggles of Red Gap; Ryan's Daughter; Scenes from a Marriage; The Shaggy Dog;

Smash-Up, the Story of a Woman; A Special Day; Spoilers; Stalag 17; Stand Up and Cheer; Stanley & Livingstone; A Star is Born (1937); Stir Crazy; Strangers, the Story of a Mother and Daughter; The Sundowners; Sweethearts; Take a Letter, Darling; Talk of the Town; The Tender Trap; Tequila Sunrise; Tess; Test Pilot; That Certain Age; That Darn Cat!; That Night in Rio; Theodora Goes Wild; There's a Girl in My Soup; They Died with Their Boots On; They Knew What They Wanted; Thief of Baghdad (1940); Thin Ice; This Above All; This Happy Breed; Thoroughly Modern Millie; A Thousand Clowns; Thousands Cheer; Three Coins in the Fountain; Through a Glass Darkly; Till the Clouds Roll By; Tillie's Punctured Romance; Time Machine; Tin Pan Alley; Tin Star; To Each His Own; Tobacco Road; Tom, Dick and Harry; Tom Sawyer; Tom Thumb; Top Gun; Topkapi!; Topper; Topper Returns; Topper Takes a Trip; Torch Song; Torn Curtain; A Touch of Class; Tovarich; The Towering Inferno; A Tree Grows in Brooklyn; Tristana; Tron; Tugboat Annie; Twelve Angry Men; Twelve O'Clock High; Twentieth Century; Twenty Thousand Years in Sing Sing; Twins; Two Girls and a Sailor; Two Women; Vacation from Marriage; VIPs; Viva Villa!; Wife Versus Secretary; Will Success Spoil Rock Hunter?; Wilson; The Wrecking Crew; A Yank at Oxford; You Light Up My Life

Fake Marriages: see *Marriages-Faked*
Faked Deaths: see *Deaths-Faked: also Clever Plots & Endings: Death-Dealing with: Double Crossings: Mindgames*
Failures: see *Coulda Been Good: Coulda Been Great: Dreams-Broken: Losing It All*
Fairy Tales: see also *Castles: Mythology: Princes: Princesses:* The Adventures of Hajji Baba; Alice in Wonderland; Babes in Toyland (1934); Babes in Toyland (1961); Beauty and the Beast (1991); Camelot; The Care Bears Adventure in Wonderland; Cinderella; Cinderfella; Coming to America; Darling; Dr. Dolittle; Edward Scissorhands; The Enchanted Cottage; The Enchanted Forest; Father of the Bride (1950); Father of the Bride (1991); Green Mansions; Hans Christian Andersen; Heidi (1939); Hook; Jack and the Beanstalk; Ladyhawke; Legend; The Legend of the Holy Drinker; Les Visiteurs du Soir; Lili;

The Little Mermaid; The Little Prince; Love Parade; Max Dugan Returns; Meet Me in St. Louis; A Midsummer Night's Dream; Nutcracker-The Motion Picture (1986); Peter Pan; The Princess Bride; Ratboy; Roman Holiday; The Secret of Roan Inish; Sleeping Beauty; The Slipper and the Rose; Snow White and the Three Stooges; Snow White and The Seven Dwarfs; The Swan; The Swan Princess; Sylvia Scarlett; Thumbelina; Tom Thumb; The Wonderful World of the Brothers Grimm

Fame-Rise to: see also *Biographies: Famous People When Young: Hollywood Biographies: Rags to Riches:* Act One; Actors and Sin; The Actress (1953); All-American Boy; April in Paris; B.F.'s Daughter; The Babe Ruth Story; The Barefoot Contessa; Being There; Body and Soul (1947); Bound For Glory; The Bride Is Much Too Beautiful; Broadway Melody; The Caddy; Can't Stop the Music; Career Champion; Chaplin; Chatterbox; The Childhood of Maxim Gorky; Coal Miner's Daughter; The Commitments; The Cotton Club; Dancing Co-Ed; Darling Diana: Her True Story; Doors; Eddie and the Cruisers; The Eddie Cantor Story; Edison, the Man; Elvis: The Movie; The Errand Boy; Expresso Bongo; A Face in the Crowd; The Five Heartbeats; The Five Pennies; 42nd Street; Frances; Funny Face; Funny Girl; The Gene Krupa Story; Gentleman Jim; The George Raft Story; Glamour Boy; Goddess; The Great Caruso; The Greatest; The Hard Way (1943); Harlow; The Helen Morgan Story; Hello Frisco Hello; Hollywood Hotel; Hollywood or Bust; The Hollywood Shuffle; Houdini; The Idolmaker; Imitation of Life (1934); Imitation of Life (1959); Inside Daisy Clover; Iron Man; It Happened in Brooklyn; It Happens Every Spring; It Should Happen to You; Jailhouse Rock; The Jazz Singer (1927); The Jazz Singer (1953); The Jazz Singer (1980); The Jerk; Jim Thorpe, All American; Jimmy Hollywood; Jolson Sings Again; The Jolson Story; The Josephine Baker Story; Lady Killer (1933); Lady Sings the Blues; Leadbelly; A Life of Her Own; Lili Marleen; Listen Up: The Lives of Quincy Jones; Little Noises; Lonely Lady; Love Me or Leave Me; The Mad Magician; Mahogany; The Man of a

Thousand Faces; Meet Danny Wilson; The Men in Her Life; Merton of the Movies; Morning Glory; Mr. Saturday Night; Music in My Heart; My Gal Sal; The Natural; Naughty But Nice; New York, New York; Nijinsky; Oscar; Out of This World; Pepe; Poor Little Rich Girl; Presenting Lily Mars; Raging Bull; Reckless (1935); Rock Around the Clock; Rocky; Rocky II; Rocky III; Rocky IV; Rocky V; Searching for Bobby Fischer; Second Chorus; Second Fiddle; Sinatra; Singing in the Rain; The Singing Nun; Smashing Time; Somebody Up There Likes Me; Sophia Loren, Her Own Story; Sparkle; St. Louis Blues; Stage Struck; Stagedoor; Star!; A Star is Born (1937); A Star is Born (1954); A Star is Born (1976); Starstruck; The Stooge; The Story of Vernon and Irene Castle; The Story of Will Rogers; Straight Talk; Sweet Dreams; This Is My Life; The Thrill of It All; Times Square; Toast of New Orleans; Tommy; Tootsie; Valley of the Dolls; W.C. Fields and Me; Wayne's World; Wayne's World 2; What Price Hollywood?; Wicked As They Come; Will Success Spoil Rock Hunter?; WUSA; Yankee Doodle Dandy; Youngblood Hawke

Families-Eccentric: see *Eccentric People: Family Comedy: Family Stories*
Families-Extended/Large: see also *Eccentric People: Ensemble Films: Family Stories:* Claudine; Drugstore Cowboy; The King and I; The L-Shaped Room; The Land Before Time; Law of Desire; Mixed Company; Places in the Heart; Spencer's Mountain; Tell Me that You Love Me, Junie Moon; Yours, Mine and Ours

FAMILY: see also *CHILDREN'S: Family Comedy: Family Drama: Families-Eccentric:* The Absent-Minded Professor; Ace Eli and Rodger of the Skies; The Adventures of Baron Munchausen (1943); The Adventures of Milo and Otis; The Adventures of the Wilderness Family; Against a Crooked Sky; Ah, Wilderness; Alice in Wonderland; All Creatures Great and Small; All Dogs Go to Heaven; Almost Angels; The Amazing Mr. Blunden; An American Tail; American Tail 2; Anchors Aweigh; And You Thought Your Parents Were Weird; Angel in My Pocket; The Aristocats; Avalon; Babar, The Movie; Babes in Toyland (1934); Babes in Toyland (1961);

batteries not included; The Bear; Bears & I; Beauty and the Beast (1991); Bebe's Kids; Beethoven; Beethoven's 2nd; Big Red; Billy Rose's Jumbo; The Biscuit Eater (1940); The Biscuit Eater (1972); Black Beauty (1946); Black Beauty (1971); Black Beauty (1994); The Black Cauldron; The Black Stallion; The Black Stallion Returns; Blackbeard's Ghost; Bless the Beasts and the Children; The Boatniks; Bon Voyage!; Bon Voyage, Charlie Brown; The Borrowers; The Boy Who Could Fly; Brigadoon; Brighton Beach Memoirs; Brighty of the Grand Canyon; Captains Courageous; The Care Bears Movie; Casey's Shadow; The Castaway Cowboy; The Chalk Garden; Charley and the Angel; Charlotte's Web; Chitty Chitty Bang Bang; CHOMPS; The Chosen; The Chronicles of Narnia; City Boy; Clara's Heart; Clarence, the Cross-Eyed Lion; Cloak and Dagger (1984); Close Encounters of the Third Kind; The Cure; Curly Sue; D.A.R.Y.L.; Darby O'Gill and the Little People; Dennis the Menace; The Devil Is a Sissy; Digby, the Biggest Dog in the World; Dog of Flanders; Driftwood; Dumbo; Dutch; E.T.: The Extra-Terrestrial; The Enchanted Forest; Ernest Saves Christmas; Escape From the Dark; The Explorers; Fantasia; Far From Home; Felix the Cat: The Movie; FernGully: The Last Rainforest; Field of Dreams; Flight of the Navigator; The Flintstones; Flipper; Fluffy; For the Love of Benji; The Fox and the Hound; Freaky Friday; Freddie as F.R.0.7.; Free Willy; French Postcards; Gay Purree; The Ghost and Mr. Chicken; The Gnome Mobile; The Golden Seal; Goodbye My Lady; The Great Locomotive Chase; The Great Muppet Caper; The Great Outdoors; The Greatest Show on Earth; The Green Years; Gulliver's Travels (1939); Gulliver's Travels (1976); Hangar 18; The Happiest Millionaire; Harry and the Hendersons; Hello Down There; Herbie Goes Bananas; Herbie Goes to Monte Carlo; Herbie Rides Again; A Hole in the Head; Honey, I Blew Up the Kid; Honey, I Shrunk the Kids; Hook; Hope and Glory; The Horse in the Grey Flannel Suit; Hot Lead and Cold Feet; I Remember Mama; Ichabod and Mr. Toad/Legend of Sleepy Hollow; If I Had My Way; If You Knew Susie; In Search of the Castaways; The Incredible Journey;

International Velvet; Into the West; It Grows on Trees; Jack the Giant Killer; Jetsons Movie; Joe Panther; The Journey of Natty Gann; Journey to the Center of the Earth; The Kid from Left Field; Kotch; Labyrinth; Lady and the Tramp; Last Flight of Noah's Ark; Late George Apley; Life With Father; Lionheart; The Little Ark; Little Dorrit; The Little Mermaid; The Little Rascals; Little Women (1933); Little Women (1949); Little Women (1978); Little Women (1994); The Living Desert; Long John Silver; The Love Bug; Lucky Star; The Magic of Lassie; Make Mine Music; The Man from Snowy River; Mary Poppins; A Matter of Time; Meet Me in St. Louis; Million Dollar Duck; Miracle of the White Stallions; Miracle on 34th Street (1947); Mixed Company; Mom and Dad Save the World; Monkey Trouble; Moon Pilot; The Moon Spinners; Mr. Hobbs Takes a Vacation; Mrs Doubtfire; Mrs. Miniver; The Muppet Christmas Carol; The Muppet Movie; The Muppets Take Manhattan; My Bodyguard; My Father the Hero; My Father's Glory; My Friend Flicka; My Girl; My Girl 2; My Mother's Castle; My Six Loves; Napoleon and Samantha; National Velvet; Newsies; Night Crossing; The Nightmare Before Christmas; No Deposit, No Return; North; North Avenue Irregulars; Now You See Him, Now You Don't; Nutcracker (1993); Nutcracker-The Motion Picture (1986); Old Yeller; Oliver and Company; One of Our Dinosaurs is Missing; Our Vines Have Tender Grapes; Paradise (1991); The Parent Trap; Parenthood; Pee-Wee's Big Adventure; Peter Pan; The Phantom Tollbooth; Pinocchio; Planet of the Apes; Please Don't Eat the Daisies; Pollyanna; The Prince of Central Park; The Radio Flyer; Railway Children; Ratboy; The Red Balloon; The Rocketeer; Samantha; Sandlot; Santa Claus, The Movie; Sarah, Plain and Tall; Savage Sam; The Secret Garden (1949); The Secret Garden (1984); The Secret Garden (1987); The Secret Garden (1993); The Secret of NIMH; The Seven Faces of Dr. Lao; The Shakiest Gun in the West; Shenandoah; Sitting Pretty; Six Pack; Skippy; Sleeping Beauty; The Slipper and the Rose; Snow White and The Seven Dwarfs; So Dear to My Heart; Son of Lassie; Song of the South; The Sound of Music; Spaced Invaders;

Squanto; State Fair (1933); State Fair (1945); State Fair (1962); SuperDad; Swing; Swiss Family Robinson; The Sword in the Stone; Table for Five; Take Her, She's Mine; Talent for the Game; That Darn Cat!; The Three Lives of Thomasina; The Three Musketeers (1993); Thunderhead, Son of Flicka; Tiger Bay; Tom Sawyer; Tom Thumb; The Treasure of Matecumbe; Troop Beverly Hills; The Trouble with Angels; The Ugly Dachshund; Uncle Buck; Water Babies; Watership Down; We're Back! A Dinosaur's Story; When the Whales Came; Whistle Down the Wind; White Fang; Who Framed Roger Rabbitt?; Willow; Willy Wonka and the Chocolate Factory; The Wizard of Oz (1925); The Wizard of Oz (1939); The Wolves of Willoughby Chase; The Wonderful World of the Brothers Grimm; The World's Greatest Athlete; The Yearling; You Can't Take It With You (1938); You Can't Take It With You (1986); The Young in Heart

Family Comedy: *see also* *CHILDREN'S: Family Comedy: Family Drama: Families-Eccentric: Disney Comedy: Comedy-Disneyesque:* The Adventures of the Wilderness Family; Angel in My Pocket; Angie; Baby Boom; Beethoven; Beethoven's 2nd; Betsy's Wedding; Big Girls Don't Cry . . . They Get Even; Bon Voyage!; The Brady Bunch Movie; Bye Bye Love; Captain Ron; The Cat and the Canary (1927); The Cat and the Canary (1939); The Cat and the Canary (1979); Centennial Summer; Charley and the Angel; Cheaper by the Dozen; Checking Out; Christmas in Connecticut (1945); Christmas in Connecticut (1992); Cops and Robbersons; Corrina, Corrina; The Courtship of Eddie's Father; Cousin, Cousine; Cousins; Daddy's Dyin; Dangerous When Wet; Eight on the Lam; A Family Affair; The Father Hood; The Feud; The Flintstones; Follow That Dream; For Richer, For Poorer; Four Daughters; Getting Even with Dad; Give My Regards to Broadway; The Gnome Mobile; The Grass Is Always Greener Over the Septic Tank; Greedy; Happy Anniversary; Happy Land; Happy Time; Harry and the Hendersons; Has Anybody Seen My Gal?; Hello Down There; Here Comes the Groom; High Hopes; A Hole in the Head; Honey, I Blew Up the Kid; Honey, I Shrunk the Kids; The Hotel New Hampshire; Houseboat; Housekeeping;

Inside Monkey Zetterland; It's a Gift; Jackpot; Jetsons Movie; Julia Misbehaves; Killing Dad; Life Is Sweet; Look Who's Talking Now; Lost in Yonkers; Love in a Goldfish Bowl; Ma and Pa Kettle; Made in America; Man of the House; Max Dugan Returns; McClintock!; Merrily We Live; Mixed Company; Mom and Dad Save the World; Monkey Trouble; Moonstruck; Morgan Stewart's Coming Home; Mother Wore Tights; Mr. Hobbs Takes a Vacation; Mrs Doubtfire; Mrs. Wiggs of the Cabbage Patch; National Lampoon's Christmas Vacation; National Lampoon's European Vacation; National Lampoon's Vacation; North; Nothing in Common; Now and Forever; Oh, Dad, Poor Dad . . . ; Our Hospitality; Parenthood; The Parents; Passed Away; The Perfect Couple; Pete 'n Tillie; Popi; Private Function; The Quiet Wedding; Radio Days; Rally Round the Flag, Boys; Rich, Young and Pretty; The Royal Family of Broadway; Ruggles of Red Gap; The Santa Clause; Serial Mom; Seven Little Foys; Sing You Sinners; Sitting Pretty; Six Pack; The Snapper; So Dear to My Heart; The Sound of Music; Spencer's Mountain; State Fair (1933); State Fair (1945); State Fair (1962); The Sum of Us; SuperDad; Sweetie; Swing; Take Her, She's Mine; Tatie Danielle; Tell Me a Riddle; The Three Cornered Moon; Till Death Us Do Part; Tillie and Gus; To Sleep with Anger; Tokyo Story; The Ugly Dachshund; Uncle Buck; You Can't Take It With You (1938); You Can't Take It With You (1986); Young at Heart; Yours, Mine and Ours

Family Drama: see also *CHILDREN'S: Family Comedy: Family Drama: Families-Eccentric: Families-Extended:*
Abel; Abie's Irish Rose; Adam Had Four Sons; Ah, Wilderness; All Fall Down; All My Sons (1949); All My Sons (1986); All the Way Home; Amber Waves; America, America; Angie; At Close Range; Australia; Avalon; Beau Pere; Best Little Girl in the World; Big Country; Black Rain (1988); The Blessing; Blind Spot; Bliss; Bloodbrothers; Bonnie Prince Charlie; Bon Voyage!; Boyz N the Hood; Brighton Beach Memoirs; Broadway Bound; Cafe Romeo; Captain Ron; Careful, He Might Hear You; The Caretaker; The Carousel; The Catered Affair; Cavalcade; Centennial Summer; C'est la Vie; Cimarron (1930); Cimarron

(1960); City of Hope; Countdown; Country; Crooklyn; Dad; The Damned; The Dark at the Top of the Stairs; A Day in the Death of Joe Egg; A Delicate Balance; Desert Bloom; Desire Under the Elms; Destiny of a Man; Diamond Head; Diary for My Children; Dominick & Eugene; The Dressmaker; Early Summer; Edward, My Son; Effect of Gamma Rays on Man-in-the-Moon; Marigolds; The Emerald Forest; Everybody's Fine; The Family; Family Business; Family Pictures; A Family Upside Down; Fanny and Alexander; Far and Away; Fiddler on the Roof; The Fire Next Time; The Firstborn; Flaming Star; Forever and a Day; Fort Apache; Forty Guns; Four Daughters; Friendly Persuasion; The Garden of the Finzi-Continis; Garment Jungle; Gas Food Lodging; The Gathering; The Gay Sisters; Giant; The Glass Menagerie (1950); The Glass Menagerie (1973); The Glass Menagerie (1987); God's Little Acre; The Godfather; The Godfather, Part II; The Godfather, Part III; Grand Highway; The Grapes of Wrath; The Great Santini; Guest in the House; Gypsy; Gypsy Moths; Hallelujah Trail; Hamlet (1948); Hamlet (1964); Hamlet (1969); Hamlet (1991); Happiest Millionaire; Happy Land; Happy Time; Harry and Son; Heartland; Heiress; Hemingway's Adventures of a Young Man; A Hero Ain't Nothin' but a Sandwich; Hider in the House; High Hopes; The Holly and the Ivy; Home from the Hill; The Homecoming (1973); A Home of Our Own; Honkytonk Man; Hope and Glory; Hot Spell; House of Rothschild; The House of Seven Gables; House of Strangers; House of the Spirits; Household Saints; How Green Was My Valley; Howards End; Howards of Virginia; Hud; I Never Sang for My Father; I Remember Mama; I Want You; Imaginary Crimes; Inkwell; Interiors; Into the West; Island (1961); Islands in the Stream; Jackpot; Jamaica Run; Journey of Hope; Kentucky; Kings Row; Kotch; Kramer vs. Kramer; La Vie Continue; Lassie; Late for Dinner; The Late George Apley; Laurel Avenue; The Leopard; Life With Father; Lion in Winter; Little Foxes; Long Day's Journey Into Night; The Long Hot Summer (1958); Lorenzo's Oil; The Lost Language of Cranes; The Magnificent Ambersons; Mame; Man, Woman and Child; May Fools; Maybe I'll

Be Home in the Spring; Meet Me in St. Louis; Men Don't Leave; The Millionairess; Misunderstood; Mosquito Coast; Mother Carey's Chickens; Mouchette; Mourning Becomes Electra; Mr. and Mrs. Bridge; Mrs. Miniver; Mrs. Wiggs of the Cabbage Patch; My Six Loves; My Son John; Nicholas and Alexandra; Night Crossing; 1900; Not Without My Daughter; Numero Deux; Once Upon a Time in America; On Golden Pond; Ordinary People; Our Vines Have Tender Grapes; Out of the Blue; Over the Brooklyn Bridge; Paid in Full; Panic in the Year Zero; Paradise (1991); The People Next Door; Portrait; Queen Bee; Queen of Hearts; The Radio Flyer; Raggedy Man; A Raisin in the Sun; Real Life; Red Sky at Morning; Rich in Love; The River (1984); River Niger; A River Runs Through It; The River Wild; Rocket Gibraltar; Romeo and Juliet (1954); Romeo and Juliet (1968); Romeo and Juliet (1936); Roots; Running on Empty; Safe Passage; Santa Fe; Sarah, Plain and Tall; The Sea Gull; Searching for Bobby Fischer; Secret of Santa Vittoria; See You in the Morning; September; Seven Little Foys; Shenandoah; Shy People; Silent Tongue; A Simple Twist of Fate; Since You Went Away; So Red the Rose; Sometimes a Great Notion; Sound and the Fury; Sounder; Spencer's Mountain; Stanley & Iris; Stepfather; Stepfather 2: Make Room for Daddy; Stepfather 3: Father's Day; Story of Boys and Girls; Strangers, the Story of a Mother and Daughter; The Subject Was Roses; Success Is the Best Revenge; Summer Wishes, Winter Dreams; Sunday in the Country; Sundowners; The Swiss Family Robinson; Table for Five; Taras Bulba; Tarnished Angels; Teresa; Terms of Endearment; That Forsyte Woman; There's No Business Like Show Business; This Happy Breed; The Three Cornered Moon; Three Sisters; To Sleep with Anger; Tokyo Story; Tortilla Flat; Toys in the Attic; Trail of the Lonesome Pine; A Tree Grows in Brooklyn; 29th Street; Twice in a Lifetime; Ugetsu Monogatari; Unfinished Piece for a Player; The Piano; Wait Until Spring, Bandini; War and Peace (1956); War and Peace (1967); The Wedding; We of the Never Never; What's Eating Gilbert Grape? When Father Was Away on Business; Where Angels Fear to Tread;

Where the Heart Is; Where the Lilies Bloom; White Heat; Wild Duck; Wild Is the Wind; Written on the Wind; The Yearling; The Young in Heart; Yours, Mine and Ours

Family/Heritage-Search for: see also *Children-Adopted: Children-Long Lost: Life Transitions:* Based on an Untrue Story; Heat and Dust; My Girl 2; Samantha; Shy People; To Sleep with Anger; Twins

Family Stories: see *Domestic Life: Family Comedy: Family Drama: Families-Eccentric: Farm Life: Feuds: Housewives: Mortgage Drama: Rural Life: Small-Town Life: Suburban Life*

Famous People: see *Biographies: Hollywood Life: Actors: Actresses: Musicians: Fashion World: Deaths of Celebrities*

Famous People When Young: see also *Biographies: Fame-Rise to: Rags to Riches: Underdog Stories:* Abe Lincoln in Illinois; Anthony Adverse; Backbeat; Butch and Sundance, The Early Days; Elvis: The Movie; Haunted Summer; Julia; LBJ: The Early Years; Mobsters; Sinatra; Sunrise at Campobello; Words and Music; Young Bess; Young Catherine; Young Mr. Lincoln; Young Sherlock Holmes; Young Tom Edison; Young Winston

Fanatics: see *Terrorists: Religious Zealots: Obsessions: Fatal Attractions: Mental Illness: Leaders-Tyrant*

Fans-Crazed: see also *Stalkers: Obsessions: Psychotics: Mental Illness: Actors: Actresses:* Calendar Girl; The Cameraman; Come Back to the Five and Dime, Jimmy Dean, Jimmy Dean, Diva; Fade to Black (1979); The Fan; Fuzzy Pink Nightgown; Garbo Talks; The King of Comedy; Last Action Hero; Misery; Mystery Train; 9/30/55; No Small Affair; Play it Again, Sam; The Secret Life of an American Wife; Smithereens; Tattoo; The World of Henry Orient

Fantasies: see also *Dream Sequences: Erotic Comedy: Erotic Drama: Fantasy: Flashbacks: Illusions/Hallucinations: Memories:* Alsino and the Condor; Billy Liar; Birdy; Blindfold: Acts of Obsession; The Cabinet of Caligari (1962); The Cabinet of Dr. Caligari (1919); Career Opportunities; Catch Me a Spy; Celia; Chloe in the Afternoon; City of Women; Condorman; Delirious; Despair; Don't Look Now; A Double

Life; Dreamchild; Dubarry Was a Lady; 8½; The Fourth Man; Golden Braid; Good Times; Grand Illusion; Grandview, USA; Gumshoe; The Immortal Story; Juliet of the Spirits; Lake Consequence; The Last Temptation of Christ; Like Water For Chocolate; Lovesick; Mary Poppins; Memoirs of a Survivor; Mr. Peabody and the Mermaid; My Wife's Best Friend; Naked Lunch; Negatives; New Leaf; On a Clear Day You Can See Forever; One Touch of Venus; Paris When it Sizzles; Petulia; Phantasm; Play it Again, Sam; The President's Analyst; Providence; Psycho 2; Psycho 3; Psycho 4; Rachel, Rachel; The Radio Flyer; Rainbow; Raising Cain; The Red Shoes; Roman Scandals; Romeo is Bleeding; The Sailor Who Fell From Grace with the Sea; Secret Friends; The Secret Garden (1949); The Secret Garden (1984); The Secret Garden (1987); The Secret Garden (1993); The Secret Life of an American Wife; The Secret Life of Walter Mitty; The Seven-Year Itch; Sisters; Slaughterhouse Five; Stairway to Heaven; Stand by Me; Stay Tuned; Steagle; They Might be Giants; Thief of Hearts; Track 29; Treasure Island (1991); The Trip; True Confession; Tune in Tomorrow; Unfaithfully Yours (1948); Unfaithfully Yours (1984); Up the Sandbox; Vampire's Kiss; Who is Harry Kellerman . . . ; Wild Strawberries; Woman Times Seven; The World of Henry Orient

Fantasy: see also *CHILDREN'S: SCI-FI: Musical-Fantasy: Magic: Surrealism: Supernatural: Illusions/Hallucinations: Dreams: Dream Sequences: Potions: What if . . . : Stories: Fantasies:* The Absent-Minded Professor; The Abyss; The Adventures of Baron Munchausen (1987); The Adventures of Buckaroo Banzai Across the 8th Dimension; Agnes of God; Akira Kurosawa's Dreams; The Alchemist; Alice; Allegro Non Troppo; Alphaville; Alsino and the Condor; Amazing Stories; An American in Paris; And the Ship Sails On; Angel on My Shoulder; Angels in the Outfield (1951); Angels in the Outfield (1994); The Applegates; Asphyx; At the Earth's Core; The Atomic Kid; Attack of the 50-Foot Woman (1958); Attack of the 50-Foot Woman (1993); Babar, The Movie; Babes in Toyland (1934); Babes in Toyland (1961); Back to the Future; Back to the

Future 2; Back to the Future 3; Barbarella; The Barefoot Executive; batteries not included; Beauty and the Beast (1991); Bedknobs and Broomsticks; Beetlejuice; Beneath the Planet of the Apes; Berkeley Square; Big; Big Blue; Big Trouble in Little China; Billy Liar; The Bishop's Wife; The Black Cauldron; The Black Hole; Blackbeard's Ghost; Blithe Spirit; Blue Bird (1940); Blue Bird (1976); The Borrowers; A Boy and His Dog; The Boy Who Could Fly; Brewster McCloud; Brigadoon; The Butcher's Wife; Bye Bye Brazil; Cabin Boy; Cabin in the Sky; Casper; Charley and the Angel; Children of Paradise; Chitty Chitty Bang Bang; A Christmas Carol (1938); The Chronicles of Narnia; Cinderella; City of Women; Close Encounters of the Third Kind; Cocoon; Cocoon, The Return; A Connecticut Yankee; A Connecticut Yankee in King Arthur's Court; Conquest of the Planet of the Apes; Cool World; Damn Yankees; Darby O'Gill and the Little People; Dark Crystal; Death Becomes Her; Death Takes a Holiday; The Devil Came from Arkansas; Devils; Dick Tracy; Digby, the Biggest Dog in the World; Don Juan DeMarco; Dr. Cyclops; Dr. Dolittle; Dragonslayer; Dreamchild; Dreams That Money Can Buy; Drop Dead Fred; Dubarry Was a Lady; Dune; E.T.: The Extra-Terrestrial; Edward Scissorhands; Electric Dreams; The Empire Strikes Back; The Enchanted Forest; Eraserhead; Erendira; Erik The Viking; Escape to Witch Mountain; Even Cowgirls Get the Blues; Every Thing You Always Wanted to Know About Sex . . . ; Excalibur; The Explorers; Fantastic Voyage; Faraway, So Close!; Field of Dreams; Finian's Rainbow; The Five Thousand Fingers of Doctor T.; Flesh Gordon; Flight of the Navigator; Futureworld; Ghost; The Ghost and Mrs. Muir; The Ghost Goes West; Give My Regards to Broad Street; The Gnome Mobile; Golden Braid; The Golden Child; The Golem; Goonies; Gothic; Great Expectations; The Great Race; Green Mansions; Harry and the Hendersons; Heart and Souls; Heart of Glass; Heaven Can Wait (1943); Here Comes Mr. Jordan; Honey, I Blew Up the Kid; Honey, I Shrunk the Kids; Hook; Howard the Duck; I Don't Want to Talk About it; Ichabod and Mr. Toad/Legend of Sleepy Hollow; The Illustrated Man; The

Immortal Story; In Search of the Castaways; In the Mouth of Madness; The Incredible Shrinking Man; Innerspace; The Innocents; Inside Daisy Clover; The Invisible Man Returns; The Invisible Man's Revenge; Invitation to the Dance; It Grows on Trees; It Happened Tomorrow; It Happens Every Spring; Jack and the Beanstalk; Jack the Giant Killer; Jason and the Argonauts; The Keep; A Kid for Two Farthings; King of Hearts; Kismet (1944); Kismet (1955); Kiss of the Spider Woman; Krull; Labyrinth; Last Action Hero; The Last Flight of Noah's Ark; Legend; Les Visiteurs du Soir; Life Is a Bed of Roses; Limit Up; Little Buddha; The Little Mermaid; The Little Prince; The Lord of the Rings; Lost Horizon (1937); Lost Horizon (1973); Made in Heaven; The Magus; Mahler; Maid to Order; The Man Who Fell to Earth; Mannequin (1987); Mannequin 2: On the Move; Mary Poppins; Mask (1994); Master of the World; Matter of Time; Max Dugan Returns; Maxie; Me and Him; Medusa Touch; Meet the Applegates; A Midnight Clear; A Midsummer Night's Dream; Millennium; The Miracle (1948); Miracle in the Rain; Miracle on 34th Street (1947); Mom and Dad Save the World; Mr. Destiny; The Muppet Christmas Carol; The Muppet Movie; The Muppets Take Manhattan; The Neverending Story; Neverending Story II: The Next Chapter; Nightbreed; The Nightmare Before Christmas; North; One Touch of Venus; The Pagemaster; Paperhouse; Pennies from Heaven (1981); Pete's Dragon; Peter Pan; The Phantom Tollbooth; The Picture of Dorian Gray; Pink Floyd: The Wall; Pinocchio; Pippi Longstocking; Portrait of Jennie; The Prince of Central Park; The Princess Bride; The Purple Rose of Cairo; The Radio Flyer; Rashomon; Ratboy; Return to Oz; Richie Rich; Rock-a Doodle; Santa Claus, The Movie; Scoundrel; Scrooge (1935); Scrooge (1970); Seconds; The Secret Garden (1949); The Secret Garden (1984); The Secret Garden (1987); The Secret Garden (1993); The Secret Life of Walter Mitty; The Secret of Roan Inish; The Seven Faces of Dr. Lao; She (1935); She (1965); Slaughterhouse Five; Song of Norway; Steagle; Supergirl; Superman; Superman 2; Superman 3; Superman 4; The Swan Princess; Sword in the Stone; Sword of the Valiant; Sword & the

Sorcerer; Sylvia and the Ghost; Tales of Hoffman; The Thief of Bagdad (1924); The Thief of Baghdad (1940); Things to Come; The Three Lives of Thomasina; The Three Worlds of Gulliver; Thumbelina; Time Bandits; Tom Thumb; Tomb of Ligea; Tommy; Topper; Topper Returns; Topper Takes a Trip; Toys; Tron; 20,000 Leagues Under the Sea; Twilight Zone: The Movie; Two of a Kind; The Wandering Jew; Warlock (1989); Water Babies; Watership Down; Weird Science; Westworld; What's So Bad About Feeling Good?; Where Do We Go from Here?; Where the Heart Is; Who Framed Roger Rabbitt?; Willow; Willy Wonka and the Chocolate Factory; Window to Paris; Wings of Desire; Wings of Fame; Witches; The Witches of Eastwick; The Wiz; Wizard; The Wizard of Oz (1925); The Wizard of Oz (1939); The World of Henry Orient; The World's Greatest Athlete; Xanadu; Yellow Submarine; You Can Never Tell; The Young Girls of Rochefort; Zapped!; Zapped Again; Zardoz; Zelig

FARCE (complicated, frenetic, and often bawdy comedy of errors): see also *Farce-Bedroom: COMEDY: Comedy of Errors: Screwball Comedy: Identities-Mistaken: Misunderstandings:* The Adventures of Eliza Frazer; The Adventures of Gerard; The Affairs of Cellini; All the Way Up; Alvin Purple; Alvin Rides Again; American Dreamer; The Amorous Adventures of Moll Flanders; Animal Crackers; Any Wednesday; Are You Being Served?; Arsenic and Old Lace; The Assassination Bureau; At the Circus; Babette Goes to War; Baby and the Battleship; Bachelor in Paradise; The Bank Dick; Bank Shot; Based on an Untrue Story; The Bawdy Adventures of Tom Jones; The Bellboy; Belles of St. Trinians; Bert Rigby, You're a Fool!; Best Defense; Beyond Therapy; The Big Bus; Big Business; Blame it on the Bellboy; Blind Date (1987); Blues Brothers; Bobo; Boeing-Boeing; Bombshell; Boys' Night Out; Brain Donors; Brazil; Bread and Chocolate; Breakfast for Two; Bringing Up Baby; Brittania Hospital; Bullets Over Broadway; Bullfighters; Cactus Flower; Caddyshack; California Suite; Canadian Bacon; Caprice; The Cat and the Canary (1927); The Cat and the Canary (1939); The Cat and the Canary (1979); Chances

Are; Charley's Aunt; Chastity Belt; Clockwise; Club Paradise; Cocoanuts; Cold Turkey; Come September; Comfort and Joy; Constant Husband; Copacabana; The Curse of the Pink Panther; Darling Lili; Desperately Seeking Susan; The Discreet Charm of the Bourgeoisie; The Doctor Takes a Wife; Doughgirls; Dr. Strangelove; Duck Soup; Dumb and Dumber; Easy Living (1937); Easy to Wed; Eleven Harrowhouse; Enter Laughing; Entertaining Mr. Sloane; Fanny Hill; The Favour, the Watch and the Very Big Fish; Fawlty Towers; Ferris Bueller's Day Off; Finders Keepers; A Fine Madness; Fireman's Ball; A Fish Called Wanda; A Flea in Her Ear; Foolish Wives; For Pete's Sake; The Four Musketeers; The Front Page (1931); The Front Page (1974); The Fuller Brush Girl; The Fuller Brush Man; A Funny Thing Happened on the Way to the Forum; Fuzz; Fuzzy Pink Nightgown; Gaily, Gaily; Gazebo; Good Neighbor Sam; The Guest Wife; The Gun in Betty Lou's Handbag; Hannah and Her Sisters; The Happiest Days of Your Life; Harvey; His Girl Friday; Hold Me, Thrill Me, Kiss Me; Honky Tonk Freeway; Horse Feathers; Hotel Paradiso; I Love You Again; I Was a Male War Bride; I'd Rather Be Rich; I'm All Right, Jack; The Importance of Being Earnest; In Society; In-Laws; Inspector Clouseau; The Inspector General; International House; It Happened to Jane; It Happens Every Thursday; It's a Great Feeling; It's a Mad Mad Mad Mad World!; It's a Wonderful World; Joseph Andrews; Jour de Fete; The Key to the City; Kind Hearts and Coronets; Kiss and Tell; The Knack; La Cage Aux Folles; La Cage Aux Folles 2; La Cage Aux Folles 3: The Wedding; La Chevre; La Ronde (1950); La Ronde (1964); The Lavender Hill Mob; Libeled Lady; The Lieutenant Wore Skirts; Little Vegas; Living it Up; Lock up Your Daughters; Love God?; Love Lottery; Love on the Run (1936); Lovely Way to Die; Lover Come Back (1961); Loverboy; Lovers and Other Strangers; Luv; MASH; Mad Wednesday; Madhouse; Make Mine Mink; The Man in the White Suit; The Man Who Came to Dinner; The Man Who Lost Himself; The Man Who Loved Women (1977); The Man Who Loved Women (1983); Man's Favorite Sport?; Manhattan Murder Mystery; The

Marrying Man; Mastergate; Micki and Maude; Midnight (1939); Mixed Nuts; Monty Python and the Holy Grail; Monty Python's Life of Brian; Monty Python's The Meaning of Life; Moonlighting (1985); Moonstruck; Move Over, Darling; Murder by Death; Murder, He Says; My Favorite Blonde; My Favorite Wife; My Man Godfrey (1936); My Man Godfrey (1956); The Naked Truth; Nashville; National Lampoon's Christmas Vacation; Night at the Opera; 1941; Nine to Five; No Sex, Please, We're British; Noises Off; Norman, Is That You?; Oh Men! Oh Women!; On Approval; On the Air; Once Upon a Crime; One, Two, Three!; One Woman or Two; The Opposite Sex; Oscar; Our Relations; Pain in the A . . . ; Passport to Pimlico; Peter's Friends; The Pink Panther; The Pink Panther Strikes Again; Planes, Trains, and Automobiles; The Pope Must Die(t); Pure Luck; Quiet Wedding; The Radioland Murders; Raising Arizona; Ready to Wear; Return of the Pink Panther; Revenge of the Pink Panther; Riding High; The Rise and Rise of Michael Rimmer; Ritz; The Road to Wellville; Room Service; Rules of the Game; Run for Your Money; Russians Are Coming, The Russians Are Coming; Ruthless People; Scavenger Hunt; Scenes from the Class Struggle in Beverly Hills; School for Scandal; School for Scoundrels; Schtonk!; Secret Admirer; The Secret of My Success; The Seduction of Mimi; Seems Like Old Times; Senator Was Indiscreet; Send Me No Flowers; Serial; A Shot in the Dark; Sibling Rivalry; Six Degrees of Separation; Skin Deep; A Slight Case of Murder; Soapdish; SOB; Some Like it Hot; Star Spangled Rhythm; Stars and Bars; Start the Revolution Without Me; Statue; Stir Crazy; Strange Bedfellows; Sullivan's Travels; Suppose They Gave a War and Nobody Came; Switching Channels; The Tall Blond Man with One Black Shoe; Ten Thousand Bedrooms; They All Laughed; Those Magnificent Men in Their Flying Machines; Three Fugitives; The Three Musketeers (1973); The Three Musketeers (1993); Titfield Thunderbolt; To Be or Not to Be (1942); To Be or Not to Be (1983); Tom Jones; Tootsie; Tune in Tomorrow; Twelve Chairs; Twelve Plus One; Twin Beds; Two Way Stretch; Under the Rainbow; Under the Yum Yum Tree; Victor/Victoria; The Wackiest Ship in the Army; Warrior's Husband; Wedding; What's New Pussycat?; What's Up, Doc?; Where Were You When the Lights Went Out?; Whiskey Galore; Who Was That Lady?; Who's Been Sleeping in My Bed?; Who's Minding the Store?; Widows' Peak; Wives and Lovers; The Women; Won Ton Ton, the Dog Who Saved Hollywood; The Wrong Arm of the Law; The Wrong Box; Yellowbeard; Yesterday, Today and Tomorrow; You Can't Take it With You (1938); You Can't Take it With You (1986); Young Doctors in Love; Young Frankenstein; Zazie dans le Metro; Zorro and the Gay Blade

Farce-Bedroom: see also *FARCE: Erotic Comedy: Romantic Comedy: Sex Comedy: Screwball Comedy:* Blame It on the Bellboy; The Bellboy; Doughgirls; A Flea in Her Ear; Hotel Paradiso; Lock Up Your Daughters; Noises Off; Peter's Friends; Rules of the Game; Scenes from the Class Struggle in Beverly Hills; Strange Bedfellows; Twin Beds; Victor/Victoria

Farm Life: see also *Rural Life: Small-Town Life: Mortgage Drama: Save the Farm:* Aaron Slick from Punkin Crick; All That Money Can Buy; Almost a Man; Amber Waves; Animal Farm; Ballad of Josie; The Betrayed (1989); Birch Interval; Bittere Ernte; The Blessing; Blockade; Carrie (1952); Castaway Cowboy; Charlotte's Web; Comrades; Country; Days of Heaven; Displaced Person; The Earth; East of Eden (1955); East of Eden (1980); The Egg and I; Emerald Forest; Endangered Species; The Farmer Takes a Wife; Field of Dreams; The Fox; Friendly Fire; The Go-Between; The Good Earth; The Good Wife; High, Wide and Handsome; Honkytonk Man; Jean de Florette; Leon, the Pig Farmer; Let's Hope It's a Girl; Love on the Dole; Man in the Moon; The Mating Game; Miles From Home; Monkeys Go Home; Mother Carey's Chickens; Night of the Hunter; O Pioneers!; Of Mice and Men (1939); Of Mice and Men (1993); Oklahoma!; Old Yeller; Our Vines Have Tender Grapes; Out of Africa; Pelle the Conqueror; Places in the Heart; Pumpkinhead; Rage; Rare Breed; Rebecca of Sunnybrook Farm (1925); The Red Pony (1949); The Red Pony (1976); The Revenge of Billy the Kid; The Revolt of Job; The River (1984); Rosalie Goes Shopping; Sea of Grass; Sheepman; So Big (1932); So Big (1953); So Dear to My Heart; The Southerner; The Sundowners; Tortilla Flat; Tree of Wooden Clogs; Wisdom; Way Down East (1920); Way Down East (1935); Where the Red Fern Grows; Where the Spies Are

Fascism: see *Communists: Oppression: Dictators: Leaders-Tyrants: Police Corruption: Evil Men: KGB Agents: Nazi Stories*

Fashion World: see also *Photographers: Beautiful People: Models: Sexy Women: Sexy Men:* The Adventurers; Bitter Tears of Petra Von Kant; Blood and Black Lace; Bloodline; The Bride Is Much Too Beautiful; Bright Lights, Big City; Daisy Kenyon; Darling; Designing Woman; A Different Story; Exposed; The Eyes of Laura Mars; Funny Face; Garment Jungle; I Can Get it For You Wholesale; Kiss (1988); Lady in the Dark; A Life of Her Own; Lipstick; Live for Life; Looker; Love Me Tonight; Lovely to Look At; Lucy Gallant; Mahogany; The Man in the White Suit; Man of Flowers; The Middle of the Night; New Kind of Love; Paris Model; Ready to Wear; Roberta; Save the Tiger; Single White Female; Six Weeks; Slaves of New York; So Fine; Strapless; Switch; Tattoo; Two People; What's New Pussycat?

Fatal Attractions (unwanted love that won't go away): see also *Obsessions: Stalkers: Infatuations: Fans-Crazed:* The Big Broadcast of 1936; Choose Me; The Crush; Daddy's Gone A-Hunting; Dance with a Stranger; Fatal Attraction; Finger of Guilt; Gate of Hell; The Girl in the Red Velvet Swing; The Graduate; The Hideaway; Hold Me, Thrill Me, Kiss Me; Housesitter; The Hunchback of Notre Dame (1923); The Hunchback of Notre Dame (1939); The Hunchback of Notre Dame (1956); The Hunchback of Notre Dame (1982); Leave Her to Heaven; Misery; My New Gun; Play Misty for Me; Reckless (1935); Star 80; Taxi Driver; That Cold Day in the Park

Fathers: see *Fathers-Alone: Family Stories: Parents-Overprotective: Parents vs. Children*

Fathers Alone/Struggling: see also *Fathers-Surrogate: Mothers Alone:* Annie; Author! Author!; Betsy's Wedding; Buddy System; Chitty Chitty Bang Bang; Corrina, Corrina; Death of a Salesman

(1950); Death of a Salesman (1985); Driftwood; Fine Things; Flipper; The Good Father; Hide in Plain Sight; A Hole in the Head; Houseboat; I'll Do Anything; Jack and Sarah; Kindergarten Cop; Kramer vs. Kramer; Life With Father; Love Hurts; Mrs Doubtfire; Paternity; Rich in Love; River of No Return; Sarah, Plain and Tall; See You in the Morning; She's Out of Control; A Simple Twist of Fate; Table for Five; Unforgiven (1992); Walkabout

Fathers & Daughters: see also *Electra Complex:* The Actress (1953); Adam and Evelyne; Always in My Heart; The Attic; The Awakening; Baby, Take A Bow; Beau Pere; Betsy's Wedding; Better Late Than Never; The Big Fisherman; The Black Orchid; The Black Rainbow; The Blessing; Bloodline; Bonjour, Tristesse; Broken Blossoms; Caravans; Cat Ballou; Cattle Queen of Montana; The Chase (1994); Class Action; Corrina, Corrina; Curly Sue; Daddy Nostalgia; Donovan's Reef; Dracula's Daughter; Everybody's Fine; Fatal Vision; The Father Hood; Father of the Bride (1950); Father of the Bride (1991); Fine Things; Fort Apache; Forty Pounds of Trouble; A Free Soul; Frenchie; Furies; Gambling Lady; The Girl in the Watermelon; The Girl Who Had Everything; Goldengirl; Hardcore; Hit!; Hospital; How to Steal a Million; I Cover the Waterfront; I Ought to Be in Pictures; I'll Do Anything; I'll Take Sweden; Imaginary Crimes; Impossible Years; Improper Channels; In Country; In Search of Gregory; In-Laws; Joe; King Lear (1971); King Lear (1987); Lady Eve; Late for Dinner; Life With Mikey; Little Miss Marker (1934); Little Miss Marker (1980); Little Treasure; Love Hurts; Major Barbara; Max Dugan Returns; Music Box; My Father the Hero; Night of the Juggler; Now and Forever; On Golden Pond; Once Is Not Enough; One in a Million; Oscar; Out of the Blue; Paper Moon; Parenthood; Party's Over; The People Next Door; The Professional; Regarding Henry; Rich, Young and Pretty; River Rat; She's Out of Control; A Simple Twist of Fate; SuperDad; Sylvia Scarlett; Table for Five; Take Her, She's Mine; Tea for Two; They; Three Sisters; To Kill a Mockingbird; Trouble Along the Way; Twice in a Lifetime; The Unforgiven (1960); Where Love Has Gone; Where the Heart Is; Wild Duck; You Can't Run Away From It; You Were Never Lovelier;

Young at Heart

Fathers & Sons: see also *Parents vs. Children: Stern Men: Men Proving Themselves:* Abel; Ace Eli and Rodger of the Skies; Adam Had Four Sons; All My Sons (1949); All My Sons (1986); All the Way Up; Amber Waves; Angelo, My Love; At Close Range; Atomic City; Back to School; The Big Fix; Big Jake; Billy Galvin; Billy Madison; Black Windmill; Blame it on the Night; Bopha!; Boys Town; Boyz N the Hood; Broken Lance; A Bronx Tale; The Brothers Karamazov; Buddy's Song; Cahill: United States Marshal; Carbon Copy; Careful, He Might Hear You; The Champ (1931); The Champ (1979); The Clown; The Courtship of Eddie's Father; Da; The Dad; Deadfall (1993); Death of a Salesman (1950); Death of a Salesman (1985); Desire Under the Elms; Distant Thunder (1988); Edward, My Son; Emerald Forest; Everybody's Fine; Family Business; Fathers and Sons; Fear Strikes Out; Fiesta; Flipper; Fly II; For Richer, For Poorer; Freud; Getting Even with Dad; Go Naked in the World; The Godfather; The Godfather, Part II; The Godfather, Part III; Going Home; The Good Father; A Goofy Movie; The Great Santini; Ground Zero; Harry and Son; Hide in Plain Sight; Holocaust 2000; Home from the Hill; The Homecoming (1973); Honkytonk Man; Hook; House of Strangers; How Do I Love Thee; Hud; I Never Sang for My Father; Indiana Jones and The Last Crusade; Into the West; Iron Eagle; Island (1980); Island at the Top of the World; Islands in the Stream; It Started with Eve; The Jazz Singer (1927); The Jazz Singer (1953); The Jazz Singer (1980); Johnny Angel; Kentuckian; The Kid from Left Field; King of the Hill (1993); Kissing Bandit; Kramer vs. Kramer; Lady in Question; Lies My Father Told Me; Light in the Piazza; Like Father, Like Son; Little Lord Fauntleroy (1936); Little Lord Fauntleroy (1980); The Lost Language of Cranes; Man on Fire; Marius; Men of Boys' Town; Missing in Action; Missing in Action 2-The Beginning; Misunderstood; Morgan Stewart's Coming Home; Mosquito Coast; Muriel; My Son, My Son; The Name of the Father; Nothing in Common; Of Human Hearts; Ordinary People; Over the Top; Parenthood; Pelle the Conqueror; Prodigal; Pulse;

Pumpkinhead; Quiz Show; Rage; Ran; Regarding Henry; The Red Pony (1949); The Red Pony (1976); The Return of the Fly; The Return of the Jedi; Revolution; River of No Return; A River Runs Through It; Rocket Gibraltar; Rocky V; Salem's Lot; The Santa Clause; Searching for Bobby Fischer; So Fine; Solomon and Sheba; Son of Frankenstein; Sons of Katie Elder; South Central; Spider's Stratagem; Success is the Best Revenge; The Sum of Us; Tank; Taras Bulba; A Thousand Clowns; Time Without Pity; To Paris with Love; Tommy Boy; Tribute; Uncommon Valor; Vice Versa; The War; When Father Was Away on Business; White Mile; World of Apu

Fathers Controlling Daughters: see *Daddy's Girls*

Fathers-Surrogate/Hired: see also *Mothers-Surrogate: Mothers Alone:* Almost Pregnant; Angelo, My Love; Boys Town; Captains Courageous; Driftwood; Dutch; Father Goose; Green Years; If I Had My Way; Interview with the Vampire; Kitchen Toto; Kotch; Lost Angel; Mad About Music; Made in America; Marriage Go Round; Men of Boys' Town; Scent of a Woman; Six Pack; Sorrowful Jones; Strange Interlude (1932); Strange Interlude (1990); A Thousand Clowns; The Three Godfathers; Three Men and a Baby; Three Men and a Cradle; Three Men and a Little Lady

Fathers-Troublesome: see also *Men Who Leave: Children Alone: Mothers Alone: Eccentric People:* Cheaper by the Dozen; Folks!; The Great Santini; Here Comes the Groom; The Hero; I Never Sang for My Father; Islands in the Stream; Killing Dad; King and I; Miracle of Morgan's Creek; Papa's Delicate Condition; The Red House; Simple Men; SuperDad; Till Death Us Do Part; Tribute; The Yearling

Fathers Who Leave: see *Men Who Leave: Mothers Who Leave: Mothers Alone*

Father-Who's the?: see also *Soul-Selling One's:* Better Late than Never; Buona Sera, Mrs. Campbell; The Girl in the Watermelon; Miracle (1948); Miracle of Morgan's Creek; Promises! Promises!

Fat People: see *Weight Problems*

Faustian Stories: see *Soul-Selling One's: Family Heritage-Search For: Satan*

Said; Heartbreak Kid; Hester Street; High Tide; Household Saints; I Don't Want to Talk About It; I Like It Like That; I Take this Woman; I'm Dancing as Fast as I Can; I've Heard the Mermaids Singing; Impulse (1990); In the Spirit; Is There Sex After Death?; It's My Turn; Jane Eyre (1934); Johnny Dangerously; Joke of Destiny; Jumpin' Jack Flash; Just Another Girl on the IRT; Just One of the Guys; Just You and Me; The Kill-Off; Killing Dad; LaMaschera; Last Days of Chez Nous; The Lemon Sisters; Listen Up: The Lives of Quincy Jones; Little Dorrit; Little Man Tate; Little Noises; Little Rascals; Little Women (1994); Look Who's Talking; Lost in Yonkers; Love Crimes; Love Letters (1984); Loveless; Loverboy; Lumiere; Making Mr. Right; A Man in Love; Me and Him; Mi Vida Loca; Mignon Has Left; Mikey and Nicky; Mina Tannenbaum; Mississippi Masala; Moment by Moment; Momma, There's a Man in Your Bed; Mrs. Soffel; Murder in New Hampshire; My Brilliant Career; My Father is Coming; My Little Girl; Near Dark; New Leaf; Night and Day; Night Games; Nobody's Fool (1986); One Sings, the Other Doesn't; Orlando; Outrage (1956); Paris is Burning; Peppermint Soda; Permanent Record; Pet Sematary; Pet Sematary 2; The Piano; Plain Clothes; Point Break; Poison Ivy (1992); Powwow Highway; The Priest; The Prince of Tides; Proof; Pure Luck; Rabbit Test; Rambling Rose; Ratboy; Red Kiss; Renaissance Man; Risk; Rush; Salaam Bombay!; The Secret Garden (1984); The Secret Garden (1993); The Secret Places; The Seven Beauties; Shag; The She Devil; Siesta; Silver City; Smithereens; Spellbinder; Starstuck; Staying Together; Sticky Fingers; Suburbia; Sudie and Simpson; Super Mario Brothers; Sweetie; Swept Away; Tank Girl; Tell Me a Riddle; Tentacles; Testament; 36 Fillette; This Is My Life; Thousand Pieces of Gold; Triumph of the Will; The Trouble with Angels; True Love; Twenty Bucks; Vagabond; Valley Girl; Variety; Wayne's World; Wild Palms; Wildflower; Working Girls; Yentl; Zelly and Me

Female in Male Domain (usually in competition with males, in a position usually held by males): see also *Female Among Males: Male in Female Domain: Role Reversal: Women as Men:* Disclosure; Fuller Brush Girl; Gloria;

Heart Like a Wheel; Kisses for My President; A League of Their Own; Major League; Montana Belle; Pat and Mike; Private Benjamin; The River Wild; Satisfaction; Sundown; Take a Letter, Darling; Tank Girl; Working Girl; Yentl

Female Law Officers: see also *Police Stories:* Another Stakeout; Betrayed; Black Widow (1987); Blue Steel; Internal Affairs; The Feds; The Enforcer

Female Leaders: see *Leaders-Female*

Female Protagonists (the story not only has a female lead, but is centered around and driven by a female): see also *Heroines-Classics: Women's Films: Ensembles-Female: Female Among Males:* The Abdication; About Face; Abschied von Gestern; Absence of Malice; The Accused (1988); Act of the Heart; Actors and Sin; The Actress (1953); Adventures in Babysitting; The Adventuress; Agnes of God; Airport 1975; Airport 1977; Alice Adams; Alice, Sweet Alice; Alien; Alien3; Aliens; All About Eve; All in a Night's Work; Allnighter; American Dreamer; Amsterdamned; Amy; An Angel at My Table; Anastasia (1956); Anastasia (1984); And Now, My Love; Angela; Angelina; Angie; Ann Vickers; Anna; Anna and the King of Siam; Anna Christie; Anna Karenina (1935); Anna Karenina (1948); Annie; Annie Get Your Gun!; Annie Oakley; Another Woman; Antonia and Jane; Ash Wednesday; The Assassination Bureau; Attack of the 50-Foot Woman (1958); Attack of the 50-Foot Woman (1993); The Attic: The Hiding of Anne Frank; Auntie Mame; The Autobiography of Miss Jane Pittman; B.F.'s Daughter; Babette's Feast; Baby Doll; Baby Maker; Bachelor Mother; The Bad Seed (1956); The Bad Seed (1986); Bagdad Cafe; Ballad of Josie; Bar Girls; Barbarella; The Barbary Coast; Barefoot in the Park; Barkleys of Broadway; Beaches; The Beautiful Blonde from Bashful Bend; Beauty for the Asking; Because of You; Becky Sharp; Becoming Colette; Beetlejuice; The Bell Jar; Beloved Infidel; Berserk!; The Best of Everything; Betrayed (1989); Beverly Hills Madam; Beware, My Lovely; Beyond the Forest; Bhowani Junction; Big Bad Mama; Big Business; The Big One, The Great Los Angeles Earthquake; Bitter Tears of Petra Von Kant; Bittere Ernte; Black Widow (1987); Blink; The

Bliss of Mrs. Blossom; Bloody Mama; Blossoms in the Dust; Blue Bird (1940); Blue Bird (1976); Blue Sky; Blue Steel; Blue Veil; Bob & Carol & Ted & Alice; Bodies, Rest & Motion; The Body Snatchers; Born Free; Born to Be Bad (1950); Born Yesterday (1950); Born Yesterday (1993); Boxcar Bertha; Boxing Helena; Boys' Night Out; Break of Hearts; Brenda Starr; Bride Walks Out; The Bride Wore Black; Brief Encounter (1946); Brief Encounter (1974); The Brink of Life; Broadcast News; Buddy System; Buffy, The Vampire Slayer; The Burglar; The Burning Bed; Business as Usual; Butterfield 8; C'est La Vie; Cabaret; Cafe Society; The Caged; Calamity Jane; Call Me Madam; Camilla (1994); Camille (1936); Camille Claudel; Candleshoe; Candy; The Candyman; Caprice; Carnival of Souls; Carrie (1976); Casual Sex?; Cat Ballou; Catherine the Great; Cattle Queen of Montana; Cause for Alarm; Celia; Cemetery Club; A Certain Smile; Chantilly Lace; Cheers for Miss Bishop; Children's Hour; China Beach; The China Syndrome; Christopher Strong; Circle of Friends; Class Action; Class of Miss MacMichael; Claudia; Claudine; Cleopatra Jones; Cleopatra Jones and the Casino of Gold; Coach; Coal Miner's Daughter; Coma; Come Back, Little Sheba; Confidentially Yours; Consenting Adult; The Conspirator; Constant Nymph (1943); Cookie; Corrina, Corrina; Country; Cousin, Cousine; Crimes of the Heart; Crossing Delancey; A Dangerous Woman; A Date with Judy; Dear Inspector; Death Becomes Her; Deceived; Deception (1992); The Deep Blue Sea; Defenseless; Desert Hearts; Desire; Desiree; Desk Set; Desperately Seeking Susan; Diabolique (1955); Diary of a Mad Housewife; Diary of Anne Frank (1959); Did You Hear the One About the Travelling Saleslady?; Dim Sum: a Little Bit of Heart; Dinner at Eight; Dirty Dancing; The Disappearance of Aimee; Disappearance of Christina; Dishonored; The Divorcée; Doctor Quinn, Medicine Woman; Does This Mean We're Married?; A Doll's House; Doppelganger: The Evil Within; Double Exposure; The Double Life of Veronique; Down Argentine Way; Dracula's Daughter; Dramatic School; Dressed to Kill; Dying Room Only; Early Summer; Earthquake; East Lynne; East of Elephant Rock; Easy Living (1937);

Eating Raoul; Echo Park; Echoes of a Summer; Eclipse; Educating Rita; Emma; Emmanuelle SERIES; Enchanted April; The End of Innocence; The Entity; Entre-Nous; Even Cowgirls Get the Blues; Every Day's A Holiday; Ex-Lady; Eyewitness (1981); The Fan; The Farmer's Daughter; Faster Pussycat! Kill! Kill!; Fatal Beauty; Fathom; The Favor; Fear; First Monday in October; Flare Up; Flashdance; Flesh of the Orchid; For the Boys; A Foreign Affair; Four Daughters; Foxes; Foxfire (1955); Frances; Frankenstein Unbound; Freddy's Dead: The Final Nightmare; Frenchie; The Frenchman's Creek; Fried Green Tomatoes; Friendly Fire; The Fuller Brush Girl; Funny Girl; Funny Lady; The Furies; Gentlemen Prefer Blondes; Gertrude; Getting of Wisdom; Gidget; Gigi (1948); The Girl Most Likely (1958); The Girl Most Likely to . . . (1971); Girl of the Golden West; Gloria; Go-Fish; Goldengirl; The Good Fight; The Good Mother; Goodbye My Fancy; Gorillas in the Mist; The Grass Is Always Greener Over the Septic Tank; Grease; Grease 2; Great Catherine; Group; Gun in Betty Lou's Handbag; Gypsy; Half Moon Street; The Hand that Rocks the Cradle; The Handmaid's Tale; Hannie Caulder; Happy Ending; The Happy Hooker; Harriet Craig; The Haunting; Hearse; Heart Like a Wheel; Heart of Dixie; Heartland; Heat and Dust; Heatwave; Heaven Knows, Mr. Allison; Hedda; The Helen Morgan Story; ·Hello Again; Hello Dolly; Hello Frisco Hello; Hester Street; High Season; High Tide; Hilda Crane; Hired Wife; A Home of Our Home; House is Not a Home; House of Women; The House on Carroll Street; Household Saints; Housekeeping; Howard the Duck; Howards End; The Hunger; Hurricane (1937); Hurricane (1979); Hush, Hush, Sweet Charlotte; I Believe in You; I Could Go on Singing; I Found Stella Parish; I Know Why the Caged Bird Sings; I Like it Like That; I Married a Dead Man; I Ought to Be in Pictures; I Passed for White; I Remember Mama; I Want to Live!; I Want You; I Was a Spy; I Was an Adventuress; I'll Be Seeing You; I'll Cry Tomorrow; I've Heard the Mermaids Singing; Idol; If a Man Answers; If It's Tuesday, This Must Be Belgium; Images; I'm Dancing as Fast as I Can; I'm No Angel; Imitation of Life (1934); Imitation of Life (1959); Impromptu; Impulse (1990); In Person; In

the French Style; In the Spirit; The Incredible Journey of Dr. Meg Laurel; Incredible Sarah; The Incredible Shrinking Woman; Indecent Proposal; The Indiscretion of an American Wife; Indochine; Inside Daisy Clover; Interiors; Interlude (1957); Interlude (1968); Intermezzo (1939); Invitation to Happiness; Is There Sex After Death?; Isn't it Romantic?; It Grows on Trees; It Had to Be You; It Happened on Fifth Avenue; It Happened to Jane; It's A Big Country; It's a Wonderful World; It's My Turn; It's Pat; Ivy; Jagged Edge; Je Vous Aime; Jersey Girl; Joan of Arc; Joan of Paris; Johnny Belinda; Johnny Guitar; Journey of Natty Gann; The Joy Luck Club; Julia; Julia and Julia; Jumpin' Jack Flash; Just Between Friends; Just One of the Guys; Just You and Me; Kansas City Bomber; The Killer Nun; Killing in a Small Town; The Killing of Sister George; Kiss and Tell; Kiss Me Goodbye; Kiss Shot; Kisses for My President; Kitty Foyle; The L-Shaped Room; La Femme Nikita; Ladies in Retirement; Lady Caroline Lamb; Lady Gambles; Lady in a Cage; Lady in the Car with Glasses and a Gun; Lady in the Iron Mask; Lady of Burlesque; Lady Sings the Blues; The Lady Vanishes (1938); The Lady Vanishes (1979); Ladybird, Ladybird; Ladykiller (1992); Last of Mrs. Cheyney; A League of Their Own; Leaving Normal; The Legend of Billie Jean; Let's Hope it's a Girl; The Letter (1929); The Letter (1940); Letter From an Unknown Woman; Letter to Brezhnev; Lianna Life of Her Own; Lifeguard; Like Water for Chocolate; Lili; Lili Marleen; Limbo; Little Darlings; Little Dorrit; Little Drummer Girl; The Little Girl Who Lives Down the Lane; Little Minister; A Little Romance; Little Thief; Little Vera; Little Women (1933); Little Women (1949); Little Women (1978); Lizzie; Locket Lola (1982); Look Who's Talking; Look Who's Talking Now; Look Who's Talking Too; Looking for Love; Looking for Mr. Goodbar; Losing Isaiah; Lost Honor of Katharina Blum; Loulou; Love Crimes; Love in Germany; Love Letters (1984); The Lover; Lucky Night; Lucky Stiff; Lumiere; Ma and Pa Kettle; Mad Miss Manton; Madame Bovary; Madame Butterfly; Madame Curie; Madame Rosa; Madame Sousatzka; Madame X (1929); Madame X (1937); Madame X (1965); The Madwoman of

Chaillot; Magnificent Doll; Mahogany; Main Event; Major Barbara; Making Mr. Right; The Man in Grey; The Man in the Moon; Man Trouble; Manhattan Murder Mystery; Mannequin (1937); Manon Margie Marie; Marked Woman; Marriage of Maria Braun; Married to It; A Married Woman; Mary Burns, Fugitive; Mary of Scotland; Mary Poppins; Mary, Queen of Scots; The Mask (1985); Mata Hari (1931); Mata Hari (1985); Mata Hari, Agent H21 (1964); The Match Factory Girl; Matchmaker; Mating of Willie; Mating Season; Maverick Queen; Me, Natalie; Me and Veronica; Meet John Doe; Meeting Venus; Meet the People; Memoirs of a Survivor; Mermaids; Mi Vida Loca; Midnight (1939); Mike's Murder; Million Dollar Mermaid; The Millionairess; Mina Tannenbaum; Miniver Story; The Miracle (1948); The Miracle of Morgan's Creek; Miracle Woman; The Miracle Worker; Miss Julie; Miss Rose White; Model and the Marriage Broker; Moment by Moment; Momma, There's a Man in Your Bed; Mommie Dearest; Montenegro; The Morning After; Morning Glory; Mountain Eagle; Mrs. Miniver; Mrs. Parker and the Vicious Circle; Mrs. Soffel; Murder; Muriel's Wedding; The Music Box; My Brilliant Career; My Father is Coming; My Foolish Heart; My Friend Irma; My Girl; My Girl 2; My Love Came Back; My New Gun; My Reputation; My Sister Eileen (1942); My Sister Eileen (1955); Mystic Pizza; Nadine; The Naked Kiss; Naked Tango; Nasty Habits; National Velvet; Never a Dull Moment (1950); Night and Day; Night Gallery; Night in Heaven; Night Terror; Night unto Night; Night Walker; 9 1/2 Weeks; Nine to Five; Nobody's Fool (1986); Norwood; Nothing Sacred; The Nun's Story; Nuts; O Pioneers!; Odette; Off and Running; The Official Story; Old Gringo; On a Clear Day You Can See Forever; Once Around; Once Is Not Enough; Only You; Opposite Sex; Orlando; The Other Side of Midnight; The Other Side of the Mountain; The Other Side of the Mountain Part Two; Outrage (1956); Outrageous Fortune; Over Twenty-One; Overboard; Pacific Heights; Pandora and the Flying Dutchman; Paper Marriage; Passion Fish; The Passion of Joan of Arc; Peeping Tom; Peggy Sue Got Married; The Pelican Brief; Penny Serenade; Peppermint Soda; Perfect Strangers; Perils of Pauline; Persona;

Personal Services; The Piano; Pinky; Pippi Longstocking; Places in the Heart; Playing for Time; Please Don't Eat the Daisies; Plenty; The Point of No Return; Poison Ivy (1992); The Possessed (1947); Presenting Lily Mars; Pride and Prejudice; Private Benjamin; Private Matter; Private School; Psycho; Queen of Outer Space; Queen of the Stardust Ballroom; Quick; Quick and the Dead; Raise the Red Lantern; Real McCoy; Reality Bites; The Red Shoes; Resurrection; Return to Peyton Place; Rhinestone; Rich and Famous; Rich Kids; Risk; The River Wild; Roberta; Romance; The Rose; Rosemary's Baby; Ruby Gentry; Ruby in Paradise; Rush; Safe Passage; Saint Joan; Sarafina!; Saratoga; Satisfaction; Scandal; Scarlet Empress; The Scarlet Letter (1926); The Scarlet Letter (1934); The Scarlet Letter (1980); Scent of Green Papaya; Seance on a Wet Afternoon; Second Chorus; Second Thoughts; Secret Beyond the Door; The Secret Garden (1949); The Secret Garden (1984); The Secret Garden (1987); The Secret Garden (1993); Secret Places; Seems Like Old Times; Sentinel; September; Serial Mom; Seven Women; Seventh Victim; Sex and the Single Girl; Shag; Shame (1987); She Devil; She Loves Me Not; Sheena, Queen of the Jungle; Shirley Valentine; Shocking Miss Pilgrim; Siesta; Silence; Silence of the Lambs; Silence of the North; Silkwood; Simple Story; Sin of Madelon Claudet; Since You Went Away; Sister Act 2; Sister Kenny; Six Degrees of Separation; Skylark; Slaves of New York; Small Town Girl (1936); Smashing Time; Smash-Up, the Story of a Woman; Smooth Talk; Snakepit; So Long at the Fair; So Proudly We Hail; Solid Gold Cadillac; Something Wild (1960); Sorry, Wrong Number; Spellbound; Spitfire; Splendor in the Grass; Stage Struck; Stanley & Iris; Star; A Star Is Born (1937); A Star Is Born (1954); A Star Is Born (1976); State Fair (1933); Steaming; Steel Stella (1990); Stella Dallas (1925); Stella Dallas (1937); Stevie; Sticky Fingers; Stolen Hours; Stolen Life (1939); Stolen Life (1946); The Story of Adele H.; Strange Bargain; Strange Loves of Martha Ivers; Strangers, the Story of a Mother and Daughter; Street Angel; A Streetcar Named Desire; Such Good Friends; Sudden Fear; Sudie and Simpson; Sugarland Express; Summer and

Smoke; Summer Wishes, Winter Dreams; Summertime; Sunday in New York; Supergirl; Susan and God; Suspect; Sweet Charity; Sweet Dreams; Sweethearts; Sweetie; Swing; Swing Shift; Sybil; Sylvia and the Ghost; Sylvia Scarlett; Take a Letter, Darling; Talk of the Town; Tamarind Seed; Tammy and the Bachelor; Tampopo; Tank Girl; Tears in the Rain; Tell Me a Riddle; Tell Me that You Love Me, Junie Moon; Tess; Testament; That Certain Woman; That Darn Cat!; That Lady in Ermine; Thelma & Louise; Theodora Goes Wild; There's No Business Like Show Business; These Three; This Is My Life; This Thing Called Love; A Thousand Pieces of Gold; Three Blind Mice; Three Came Home; The Three Faces of Eve; Three Smart Girls; Three Smart Girls Grow Up; Thunderbirds; Tiger Bay; To Each His Own; To Find a Man; To Kill a Mockingbird; Tokyo Decadence; Tokyo Pop; Tonight and Every Night; Top Secret Affair; A Town Like Alice (1956); A Town Like Alice (1985); Trade Winds; Trail of the Lonesome Pine; Trojan Women; Troop Beverly Hills; The Trouble with Angels; True Confession; True Love; Truth or Dare; Tugboat Annie; Tugboat Annie Sails Again; Tulsa; Turning Point; Turtle Beach; 21; Two Girls and a Sailor; Two Women; The Two Worlds of Jenny Logan; The Unbelievable Truth; The Unconquered; Under Capricorn; Undercurrent; The Uninvited; An Unmarried Woman; The Unsinkable Molly Brown; An Unsuitable Job For a Woman; Untamed Heart; Up the Down Staircase; Up the Sandbox; V. I. Warshawski; Vagabond; Valley Girl; Valley of the Dolls; Vampire Lovers; Variety; Velvet Touch; Veronika Voss; Vicki; Victor/Victoria; Violets are Blue; Violette; Visit; Wait Until Dark; Warrior's Husband; Washington Story; Way Down East (1920); Way Down East (1935); The Way We Were; Wee Willie Winkie; Welcome Home, Roxy Carmichael; Wetherby; What a Way to Go; What Every Woman Knows; What Price Hollywood?; What's the Matter with Helen?; Whatever Happened to Aunt Alice?; Whatever Happened to Baby Jane?; When Ladies Meet (1933); When Ladies Meet (1941); Where Angels Go, Trouble Follows; Where the Boys Are; Where the Boys Are '84; Whispers in the Dark; The White Cliffs of Dover; White Dog; White Nights (1957); Whore;

Wicked Lady (1945); Wicked Lady (1983); Widows' Peak; Wild Hearts Can't Be Broken; Wildcats; Wildflower; Winter People; Wish You Were Here; The Witches of Eastwick; Without a Trace; Without Reservations; Without You I'm Nothing; The Wiz; The Wizard of Oz (1925); The Wizard of Oz (1939); A Woman Is a Woman; Woman Obsessed; A Woman of Paris; Woman of the Year; Woman Rebels; Woman Times Seven; A Woman Under the Influence; A Woman's Face; Woman's World; Women; Women in Love; Women on the Verge of a Nervous Breakdown; Working Girl; Working Girls; A World Apart; The World Is Full of Married Men; Wuthering Heights (1939); Wuthering Heights (1953); Wuthering Heights (1970); Wuthering Heights (1992); X, Y, & Zee; Yentl; You Light Up My Life; Zelly and Me; Ziegfeld Girl

Female Screenwriters (films written at least in part by women): see also *Writers: Hollywood Life:* The Abdication; About Face; About Last Night; The Accused (1948); Ace Eli and Rodger of the Skies; The Actress (1953); Adam at 6 A.M.; Adam's Rib (1922); Adam's Rib (1949); The Addams Family; The Affairs of Cellini; The Age of Innocence (1934); Ah, Wilderness; Alamo Bay; Alexander's Ragtime Band; Alice Adams; All That Heaven Allows; Always; Always Goodbye; Always in My Heart; Always Together; An Angel at My Table; Anchors Aweigh; Angels in the Outfield (1951); Ann Vickers; Anna and the King of Siam; Anna Christie; Another Thin Man; Antonia and Jane; Appointment in Honduras; Arkansas Traveler; The Band Wagon; Bar Girls; Barkleys of Broadway; Bathing Beauty; Beaches; Beauty and the Beast (1991); Because of You; Becoming Colette; Beetlejuice; The Bell Jar; Ben-Hur: A Tale of Christ (1925); The Best of Everything; Beyond the Forest; Bhowani Junction; Big Bad Mama; Big Business; Big Trail; Billy the Kid; Birch Interval; Bitter Sweet (1933); Bittere Ernte; Blacula; Blink; Blood Feud; Bloodfist; Bloodfist II; Bloodfist III; Blood on the Moon; Blue Sky; Bolero (1934); Bombay Talkie; Born to Kill; Boxcar Bertha; Boxing Helena; Brasher Doubloon; Break of Hearts; The Bride Wore Red; Burning Bed; Business as Usual; C'est la Vie; Cafe Society; Caged Cairo (1963); Camila

Good Friends; Sudden Fear; Sudie and Simpson; Summer Story; The Sundowners; Susan Lenox, Her Fall and Rise; Suzy; Sweetie; The Swimmer; Swing High, Swing Low; Sylvia Scarlett; Tatie Danielle; Tattoo; Tell Me a Riddle; Tell Me that You Love Me, Junie Moon; Testament; That Night in Rio; Thelma & Louise; They; The Thing Called Love; This Is My Life; This Property Is Condemned; A Thousand Pieces of Gold; Three Blind Mice; Three Husbands; Three Men and a Cradle; Three Men and a Little Lady; Three Smart Girls; To Dance with the White Dog; Together Again; Town Without Pity; Trade Winds; Travels with My Aunt; Troop Beverly Hills; Tropic of Cancer; Trouble with Angels; True Grit; True Love; Two Girls and a Sailor; Undercurrent; The Uninvited; The Unsinkable Molly Brown; An Unsuitable Job For a Woman; Vagabond; Valley of the Dolls; Variety; Victim; Violets are Blue; Virgin Spring; Viva Las Vegas; Wait Until Dark; The War; Warrior's Husband; Watch on the Rhine; Way Down East (1920); Way Down East (1935); Wayne's World; Wayne's World 2; Welcome Home; Welcome Home, Roxy Carmichael; What a Way to Go; What About Bob?; What Price Hollywood?; When Ladies Meet (1933); When Ladies Meet (1941); Where Angels Go, Trouble Follows; White Cliffs of Dover; White Fang; Who'll Stop the Rain?; Whore; Wild Orchid; Wildflower; Wings; Without a Trace; Without Reservations; Without You I'm Nothing; Witness; The Wizard of Oz (1939); Woman Next Door; Woman's World; Women; Working Girls; The World Is Full of Married Men; The World of Henry Orient; Wuthering Heights (1992); X, Y, & Zee; Yellow Balloon; Yentl; Yesterday's Hero; Young at Heart; Zelly and Me; Ziegfeld Girl

Feminist Films/Stories (usually political for and from a female perspective): see also *Female in Male Domain: Women Fighting the System: Lesbians: Women's Films:* Dialogues with Madwomen; The Divorcée; A Doll's House; A Handmaid's Tale; Lianna; My Wife's Best Friend; Saint Joan; Stand Up and Be Counted; Up the Sandbox

Femmes Fatales: see *Dangerous Women: Evil Women: Film Noir: Love-Questionable: Mindgames*

Feuds: see also *Family Stories: Parents vs. Children: Friendships on the Rocks: War Stories:* All About Eve; Amadeus; Angels With Dirty Faces; Anna; Beaches; Ben-Hur (1959); Ben-Hur: A Tale of Christ (1925); Big Country; The Brotherhood; The Cat and the Canary (1927); The Cat and the Canary (1939); The Cat and the Canary (1979); The Challenge; The Chosen; Comfort and Joy; Dersu Uzala; Duellists; The Feud; Flaming Star; Fourth War; Friendly Persuasion; Genevieve; Give Me a Sailor; Gone With the Wind; Great Day in the Morning; Grumpy Old Men; Happy Anniversary; Harlem Nights; Here Comes the Navy; High Hopes; Highlander; Highlander II-The Quickening; Highlander III, The Sorcerer; Hot Lead and Cold Feet; In Old Kentucky; Jean de Florette; Joe Kidd; Johnny Guitar; Kentucky; Kentucky Moonshine; Lolly Madonna War; Love and Hisses; Love Thy Neighbor; Matewan; Metropolitan (1935); Mill on the Floss; Mirror Crack'd; The Missouri Breaks; National Lampoon's Christmas Vacation; Neighbors; One Eyed Jacks; Our Hospitality; Paid in Full; The Raven (1963); Rich and Famous; Romanoff and Juliet; Romeo and Juliet (1954); Romeo and Juliet (1968); Romeo and Juliet (1936); Scavenger Hunt; The Sea Gull; Shadow Riders; Stars and Bars; The Sunshine Boys; Thunder and Lightning; Thunder Road; Tin Men; Toto le Heros; Trail of the Lonesome Pine; Trapeze; The Turning Point; The Undefeated; Valley of the Dolls; Vikings; Whatever Happened to Baby Jane?; Winchester 73; Winter People; The Wrong Box

Fictionalizations: see *Biographies-Fictional: True Stories: True or Not?: Docudramas*

Fighting Evil: see *Good vs. Evil: Satanism: Supernatural Danger: Evil Men: Evil Women: Evil Children: Medieval Times*

Fighting Over Rewards: see *Rewards at Stake: Inheritances at Stake*

Fighting the System: see also *Women Fighting the System: Women's Rights: Underdog Stories: Feisty Females: Whistleblowers: Reformers: Social Drama: Ethics: Corruption: Civil Rights: Race Relations: Apartheid: Rebels:* The Accused (1988); The Adventures of Robin Hood; Alice's Restaurant; And Justice for All; Brubaker; Burning Season; Caged; Chattahoochee; China Syndrome; Dog Day Afternoon; Fahrenheit 451; The Field; Fighting Back; Fighting Mad; First Blood; FM; The Fountainhead; Frances; Friendly Fire; Ghosts . . . of the Civil Dead; Heart of Dixie; Heatwave; I Want to Live!; Ice Palace; It Happened to Jane; The Klansman; The Little Princess; Lorenzo's Oil; The Madwoman of Chaillot; A Man for All Seasons; Man of Iron; The Mask (1985); Miles From Home; The Moon Is Down; Mr. Smith Goes to Washington; Norma Rae; Not Without My Daughter; One Flew Over Cuckoo's Nest; Philadelphia; Quiet American; Rage; Rally Round the Flag, Boys; Saint Joan; The Secret of Santa Vittoria; Serpico; Solarbabies; Solid Gold Cadillac; Sometimes a Great Notion; Storm in a Teacup; Taffin; Take This Job and Shove It; Talk of the Town; Taps; THX 1138; Titfield Thunderbolt; Tobacco Road; Tribes; Tucker: The Man and His Dream; Twelve Angry Men; Unnatural Causes

Film History: see also *Filmumentaries:* Alexander Nevsky; The Battleship Potemkin; The Bicycle Thief; The Birth of a Nation; Children of Paradise; Citizen Kane; City Lights; The Crowd; Earth; Grand Illusion; Intolerance; The Kid (1921); La Dolce Vita; The Last Command; Metropolis; Napoleon; Rules of the Game; Stagecoach (1939); Strike; The Third Man; Un Chien Andalou; Wages of Fear; Wild Strawberries; Woman of Paris

Filmmaking: see *Movie Making: Movies within Movies: Film Students*

Film Noir (the style of the postwar era delving into the dark side of life and crime): see also *Underworld: Crime Drama: Dangerous Women: Dangerous Men:* Asphalt Jungle; The Bad and the Beautiful; Bedlam; The Big Clock; The Big Combo; The Big Heat; The Big Knife; The Big Sleep (1946); The Big Sleep (1977); The Big Steal; Black Angel; Black Hand; The Blue Dahlia; Body and Soul (1947); The Body Snatcher; Born to Kill; Casablanca; Cat People (1942); Cornered; Criss Cross (1947); Crossfire; D.O.A. (1949); Dark Corner; Dark Mirror; Dark Passage; Dead Men Don't Wear Plaid; Dead Reckoning; Detour; Double Indemnity; Fallen Angel; Fallen Sparrow; Farewell, My Lovely (1944); Farewell, My Lovely (1975); Forbidden; Force of Evil; Gilda; The Glass Key (1935); The Glass

Key (1942); Gun Crazy (1950); I, the Jury (1953); I, The Jury (1982); I Wake Up Screaming; I Walk Alone; I Want to Live!; Impact; In a Lonely Place; In Cold Blood; Intruder in the Dust; Johnny Angel; Johnny Eager; The Killers (1946); Kiss of Death (1947); La Bete Humaine; The Lady from Shanghai; Lady in the Lake; Laura; The Locket; The Long Night; M (1931); M (1951); Macao; The Maltese Falcon (1941); Mildred Pierce; Ministry of Fear; Ossessione; Out of the Past; The Postman Always Ring Twice (1945); Prowler; Rancho Notorious; Ride the Pink Horse; Riff-Raff (1947); Satan Met a Lady; Secret Beyond the Door; Sorry, Wrong Number; Sunset Boulevard; Sweet Smell of Success; They Drive by Night (1940); They Live by Night; This Gun for Hire; Touch of Evil; Underworld, USA; When Strangers Marry; The Window; Woman in the Window; Woman on the Beach

Film Noir-Modern (updated versions, mostly in color, whereas the originals were mostly in black and white): see also *Underworld: Crime Drama: Dangerous Women: Dangerous Men:* After Dark, My Sweet; Against All Odds; American Gigolo; American Me; Angel Heart; Bad Boys; Bad Company (1995); Batman; Blade Runner; Blood and Concrete; Blue Velvet; Body Heat; Boiling Point; Bugsy Malone; Butterfly; Casino Chandler; The Cheap Detective; Chinatown; Dead Again; Deep Cover; Dick Tracy; Down By Law; 8 Million Ways to Die; Everybody Wins; The Grifters; Gun Crazy (1992); Hammett; The Hot Spot; The Hustle; I Married a Dead Man; I, The Jury (1982); Johnny Handsome; The Killing of a Chinese Bookie; Kiss of Death; Klute; The Last Boy Scout; The Last Seduction; Light Sleeper; Low Down Dirty Shame; Mack the Knife; The Mechanic; Mona Lisa; Night Moves; One from the Heart; Pawnbroker; Peeper; Point Blank; The Postman Always Rings Twice (1981); Pulp Fiction; Quick; Red Rock West; Report to the Commissioner; Romeo is Bleeding; Rumble Fish; Samurai; The Shadow (1940); The Shadow (1994); Shamus; Shock Corridor; Shoot the Piano Player; Slamdance; Something Wild (1986); Stormy Monday; Streets of Fire; Taxi Driver; Tough Guys Don't Dance; The Two Jakes; Under Suspicion; Who

Framed Roger Rabbitt?; Wild at Heart; Wild Palms

Film Students: see also *Movie Making: Hollywood Life: Directors:* The Big Picture; The Freshman (1990); Man of Marble

Films Within Films: see *Movies within Movies: Crossing the Line: Movie Making: Hollywood Life*

Filmumentaries: see also *Documentaries: Avant-Garde Films: Art Films: Experimental Films: Movies within Movies:* All This and World War II; Burden of Dreams; The Epic That Never Was; Hearts of Darkness: A Filmmaker's Apocalypse; That's Dancin'!; That's Entertainment; That's Entertainment Part Two

Finding Money/Valuables: see also *Lucky People: Treasure Hunts: Murder-Discovering:* Boy on a Dolphin; Chu Chu and the Philly Flash; Finders Keepers; Finian's Rainbow; Flashpoint; If I Had a Million; The Last Seduction; Money for Nothing; Number 17; Shallow Grave; Taking Care of Business; True Romance; Twenty Bucks

Finding New Mate for Spouse: see also *Return of Spouse: Dating Scene:* Dark Angel (1935); Mr. Wonderful; Send Me No Flowers; Sentimental Journey; Move Over, Darling

Finding the Loot: see also *Treasure Hunts: Bank Robberies: Ex-convicts:* Cat and Mouse; The Cat and the Canary (1927); The Cat and the Canary (1939); The Cat and the Canary (1979); The Cat Chaser; The Count of Monte Cristo (1934); The Count of Monte Cristo (1974); Fools Parade; Gaslight (1939); Getting Even with Dad; King and Four Queens; Number 17; Slither; There Was a Crooked Man; Thunderbolt & Lightfoot

Fire Fighters: see *Fires*

Fires: see also *Disaster Movies: Fires-Arsonists:* Audrey Rose; Avalon; Backdraft; Barton Fink; Betty Blue; Burning Bed; The Children (1980); City of Hope; The Day the Earth Caught Fire; Do The Right Thing; Dumbo; Endless Love; Erendira; Fahrenheit 451; Firestarter; Gone With the Wind; Hero at Large; In Old Chicago; Picture Mommy Dead; Revenge; Roxanne; Save the Tiger; Towering Inferno; Trespass; Wilder Napalm

Fires-Arsonists: see also *Fires: Psycho Killers:* Backdraft; Betty Blue; Fahrenheit 451; Talk of the Town

First Love: see *Love-First: also Coming of Age: Virgins: Love-Forbidden: Infatuations*

Fish: see also *Fishermen: Sharks: Dolphins: Whales: Sea Creatures: Sea Adventure:* The Day the Fish Came Out; The Incredible Mr. Limpet; Killer Fish; The Little Mermaid; Piranha

Fishermen: see also *Adventure at Sea: Dolphins: Sharks:* All the Brothers Were Valiant; Barnacle Bill (1941); Brothers; Cannery Row; Captains Courageous; Flipper; Full Moon in Blue Water; Girls! Girls! Girls!; A House Divided; Ice Palace; Islands in the Stream; It Happened to Jane; Man of Aran; Man's Favorite Sport?; Moby Dick; 92 in the Shade; Old Man and the Sea; Orca-Killer Whale; Riff-Raff (1935); Sea Beast; Spawn of the North; Stromboli; Tabu; Under Milk Wood

Fish out of Water Stories: see also *Misfits-Foreign: Female Among Males: Male Among Females: COMEDY: Comedy of Manners: Comedy of Errors: City vs. Country:* Adam at 6 A.M.; Adventure for Two; The Adventures of Barry McKenzie; The Adventures of Bullwhip Griffin; Africa, Texas Style; The Air Up There; Alamo Bay; Alfredo, Alfredo; Alligator Named Daisy; American Tail 2; Annie Get Your Gun!; The Aviator; Back to the Future; Bagdad Cafe; Bananas; Being There; The Beverly Hillbillies; Beverly Hills Cop; Beverly Hills Cop 2; Big; Biloxi Blues; Blazing Saddles; Bonnie Scotland; Boy, Did I Get a Wrong Number!; The Brady Bunch Movie; Brannigan; The Brother From Another Planet; Buck Privates; Butcher's Wife; Call Me Madam; Casque d'Or; Cityslickers; Cityslickers 2; Class of 1999; Class of '84; Coach; Combination Platter; Come Blow Your Horn; Coming to America; Comrades of Summer; Coneheads; A Connecticut Yankee; A Connecticut Yankee in King Arthur's Court; Continental Divide; Coogan's Bluff; Cool Runnings; The Cowboy Way; Crocodile Dundee; Cross Creek; Dangerous When Wet; Dave; Despair; Displaced Person; Doc Hollywood; Down and Out in Beverly Hills; Down Argentine Way; Dudes; Elena and Her Men; Encino Man; Escape from the Planet of the Apes; Eversmile New Jersey; Experts; Fancy Pants; A Foreign Affair; Forest Rangers; Forever Young;

The Frisco Kid (1979); Gabriel over the White House; Gay Purree; George Washington Slept Here; The Glass House; Go West; Go West Young Man; The Gods Must Be Crazy II; Goin' To Town; Goodbye, New York; The Grass Is Always Greener Over the Septic Tank; The Great Outdoors; Green Years; Greenwich Village; Greystoke: The Legend of Tarzan; Harry and the Hendersons; Iceman; If You Knew Susie; I'm No Angel; In Person; In the Army Now; In the Heat of the Night; I Take This Woman; It's a Gift; The Jerk; The Kentuckian; Kindergarten Cop; King in New York; King Ralph; Ladies' Man (1947); Leon, the Pig Farmer; Life is Cheap, but Toilet Paper is Expensive; Life Stinks!; Light in the Forest; Lightnin'; Lilies of the Field; Little Big Man; Local Hero; Ma and Pa Kettle; A Man Called Horse; The Mating Game; Mediterraneo; Meet the People; Merton of the Movies; Milk Money; Miranda; Mister Cory; Monkeys Go Home; Moscow on the Hudson; Moving; Mr. Blandings Builds His Dream House; Mr. Nanny; Murder, He Says; My Beautiful Laundrette; My Blue Heaven (1990); My Cousin Vinny; My Sister Eileen (1942); My Sister Eileen (1955); Naked Jungle; Never a Dull Moment (1950); No Time for Sergeants; Nobody's Perfect; Not as a Stranger; The Outoftowners; Overboard; Paleface; Paper Lion; Pardners; Private Benjamin; The Purple Rose of Cairo; Red Headed Woman; Red Heat; Red Sky at Morning; Reluctant Debutante; Renaissance Man; Rented Lips; Return of a Man Called Horse; Ride 'Em Cowboy; The Ritz; Romancing the Stone; Rosalie Goes Shopping; The Rose Tattoo; Rude Awakening; Ruggles of Red Gap; Savage; Saving Grace; Say One for Me; Secret of My Success; She'll Be Wearing Pink Pajamas; The Sheepman; Shrimp on the Barbie; Shy People; Sister Act; Sitting Pretty; Speak Easily; Splash!; Star Trek IV: The Voyage Home; Starman; Stars and Bars; The Story of Dr. Wassell; Straight Talk; Stranger Among Us; Straw Dogs; Suburban Commando; The Super; Susan Lenox, Her Fall and Rise; Taking Off; Tarzan's New York Adventure; Teahouse of the August Moon; Tribes; Troop Beverly Hills; Trouble Along the Way; True Identity; Up in Arms; Virgin Soldiers; Visit to a Small Planet; Wait

Until Spring, Bandini; We're Back! A Dinosaur's Story; Why Shoot the Teacher?; Wild Child; Wild West; Wildcats; Will Success Spoil Rock Hunter?; Witness; The World's Greatest Athlete; A Yank at Eton; A Yank at Oxford; You're in the Army Now; You're Telling Me; Youngblood Hawke

Flashbacks (sequences of memories or previous scenes): see also *Memories: Dream Sequences: Narrated Films:* The Accident; The Affairs of Susan; All That Jazz; American Hotwax; Another Country; Backfire; The Bad and the Beautiful; Betrayal; Between Two Women; Birdy; The Bridge of San Luis Rey; Burning Bed; Caddy; Casualties of War; A Chorus Line; Cobb; Dear John; Dolores Claiborne; 8½; Eleni; The End of Innocence; The Escape Artist; Falling in Love Again; Family; FBI Story; Fearless; A Fire in the Sky; Flesh and Bone; For the Boys; Forrest Gump; Friday the Thirteenth (1933); From This Day Forward; Going Home; Groundhog Day; Happy Ending; Hiroshima, Mon Amour; Hunger; I Don't Care Girl; I Remember Mama; Images; Immortal Beloved; Indochine; Ironweed; Irreconcilable Differences; It's a Wonderful Life; Jacob's Ladder; The Killers (1946); The Killers (1964); La Passante; Lady L.; Laura; A League of Their Own; Letter to Three Wives; Little Big Man; Lola Montes; Loneliness of the Long Distance Runner; The Long Day Closes; Lost Moment; Lydia; Margie; The Marrying Kind; Mister Buddwing; Moscow Does Not Believe in Tears; Mother Wore Tights; Murder in the First; Natural Obsession; The Pawnbroker; Penny Serenade; Petulia Poison; Psycho 4; Screaming Mimi; Scrooge (1935); Scrooge (1970); The Search for Bridey Murphy; Siesta; Six Degrees of Separation; The Snows of Kilimanjaro; Stand by Me; Suddenly, Last Summer; Sunset Boulevard; Swing; Toto le Heros; Travels with My Aunt; 21; Two For the Road; Vagabond; The Valachi Papers; Valentino (1977); Voyager; A Walk in the Sun; Waterland; Wetherby; When Hell Was in Session; Who is Harry Kellerman . . .; Wild Strawberries; Woman Times Seven

Flings: see *Romance-Brief: Romance-On Again/Off Again*

Floods: see also *Disaster Movies: Drownings:* Flood!; Little Ark;

Metropolis; The Rains Came; The River (1984); When Worlds Collide; The World of Suzie Wong

Flops-Major (major financial catastrophes, sometimes with major stars who didn't bring audiences; sometimes, just extremely bad): see also *Curiosities: Unintentionally Funny:* The Abyss; Ace in the Hole; Act One; The Adventurers; The Adventures of Baron Munchausen (1987); The Adventures of Buckaroo Banzai, Across the 8th Dimension; Airheads; Airport '79, The Concorde; Alex and the Gypsy; Alphabet Murders; At Long Last Love; At Play in the Fields of the Lord; Baby's Day Out; The Barbarian and the Geisha; Beat the Devil; The Beautiful Blonde from Bashful Bend; Being Human; Best Defense; Beverly Hills Cop 3; Beyond the Limit; The Big Town; Billy Bathgate; Black Cauldron; Blankman; Blown Away; Bobby Deerfield; Bolero (1984); Bonfire of the Vanities; Boom!; Boxing Helena; A Breed Apart; Breezy; Brenda Starr; Bride; A Bridge Too Far; Buffalo Bill and the Indians, or Sitting Bull's History Lesson; Caligula; Can Hieronymus Merkin Ever Forget Mercy Humppe and Find True Happiness?; Can't Stop the Music; Cannery Row; Che!; A Chorus Line; Cimarron (1960); City of Joy; Cityslickers 2; Cobb; Comic; Communion; The Conqueror; Cool World; The Cotton Club; A Countess from Hong Kong; The Cowboy Way; Crackers; Death and the Maiden; Desire Me; Dune; Empire of the Sun; Enemy Mine; Even Cowgirls Get the Blues; Exorcist II: The Heretic; Eye of the Devil; Fall of the Roman Empire; Farewell to the King; Fat Man and Little Boy; Fedora; Fever Pitch; Fiendish Plot of Dr. Fu Manchu; A Fine Mess; The First Deadly Sin; A Fistful of Dynamite; Fitzcarraldo; Flash Gordon; Flesh and Bone; Flight of the Intruder; Fortune; 1492: Conquest of Paradise; The French Connection II; The Frenchman's Creek; The Fugitive (1947); Gable and Lombard; The Gambler; The Gang That Couldn't Shoot Straight; Genghis Khan; Geronimo (1993); The Getaway (1994); Getting Even with Dad; Gigot; Girl Who Couldn't Say No; Give My Regards to Broad Street; The Golden Child; The Good Mother; Grease 2; Great Balls of Fire; Great Catherine; Great Moment; Great Waldo Pepper; The Greatest; Greedy Greek

American; Johnny Be Good; Knute Rockne: All-American; Little Giants; Longest Yard; Necessary Roughness; North Dallas Forty; Paper Lion; Program; Rudy; School Ties; Semi-Tough; Trouble Along the Way; Two Minute Warning

Foreign Film Remakes: see also various country listings: Babycakes; Blame it on Rio; Buddy, Buddy; Cousins; Crackers; Happy New Year (1987); I Married a Dead Man; Intersection; Iron Maze; Kiss Me Goodbye; Lady in Question; The Long Night; M (1951); The Magnificent Seven; Men Don't Leave; Mixed Nuts; My Father the Hero; Once Upon a Crime; Oscar; Paradise (1991); Point of No Return; Pure Luck; Scarlet Street; Sommersby; Sorcerer; Three Fugitives; Three Men and a Baby; True Lies; The Vanishing (1993); Victor/Victoria; Which Way is Up?; Woman in Red

Foreign Legion: see also *Military Stories:* Abbott & Costello in the Foreign Legion; Beau Geste (1926); Beau Geste (1939); Beau Geste (1966); Morocco; Beau Ideal; The Last Remake of Beau Geste; March or Die; Ten Tall Men; Under Two Flags

Foreign Lovers: see *Romance on Vacation: Lovers-Foreign: Lovers-Mismatched: Romance-Doomed: Exotic Locales: Erotic Drama*

Foreign Misfits: see *Fish out of Water Stories*

Foreign Nightmares: see *Nightmare Vacations: Americans Abroad*

Forgotten Films (films that either once made a splash or could have, and that may deserve a second look—or a first): see also *Underrated: Overlooked at Release: Hidden Gems: Flops-Major: Faded Hits:* Aaron Slick from Punkin Crick; Ace in the Hole; Across the Bridge; Actors and Sin; Adventure for Two; The Adventurers; The Adventures of Barry McKenzie; The Affairs of Cellini; Age of Consent; Alfredo, Alfredo; Always Together; America, America; The Amorous Adventures of Moll Flanders; Angel Baby; April Fools; Arizona; Armored Command; The Assassination Bureau; At Close Range; Avanti!; Baby Face; Bad Company; Badge 373; The Balcony; Bandolero; The Beat Generation; The Beautiful Blonde from Bashful Bend; Because You're Mine; Bedlam; The Beguiled; The Bellboy; Between the

Lines; Beyond a Reasonable Doubt; Beyond the Forest; Beyond the Limit; The Big Knife; The Big Lift; Big Trees; The Bird With the Crystal Plumage; Bitter Tears of Petra Von Kant; Bittersweet Love; The Black Cat; The Black Hand; Blood and Black Lace; Blue Denim; Bombshell; Boomerang (1947); Bound For Glory; Boy on a Dolphin; Boys in Company C; Brainstorm (1965); Bramble Bush; Breakfast for Two; Breaking the Sound Barrier; Bright Road; Bright Victory; Brother Rat; Buddy System; Bureau of Missing Persons; The Burning; Butterfly; Bye Bye Braverman; Caesar and Cleopatra; Cafe Metropole; Cage of Gold; Call of the Wild (1935); Call of the Wild (1972); Captains of the Clouds; Cardinal; Carey Treatment; Casanova Brown; Cash McCall; Casque d'Or; Cavalcade; Ceiling Zero; Chained; Check Is in the Mail; China; A Chorus Line; Christopher Strong; The Cincinnati Kid; Cisco Pike; City for Conquest; Clairvoyant (1934); Clash by Night; Cloak and Dagger (1946); Come to the Stable; Comedy of Terrors; The Comic; Confessions of a Nazi Spy; Confidential Agent; The Conquest; The Conspirator; Continental Divide; Copacabana; Cornered; Countdown; Crackers; Crossfire; Cuba; Daddy's Gone A-Hunting; Dante's Inferno; Dark Corner; Dark Crystal; Dark Waters; A Day in the Death of Joe Egg; Day of the Dolphin; The Day the Earth Caught Fire; Dead Heat on a Merry Go Round; Deadfall (1968); The Deadly Affair; Dear Heart; Death of a Gunfighter; Desert Bloom; Desire; Detective Story; The Devil and the Deep; Devil at Four O'Clock; The Devil Came from Arkansas; Devil Doll; The Devil Is a Woman; Devil's Brigade; The Devil's Wanton; Diamond Head; Dino; Dirty Little Billy; Do You Like Women?; The Doctor Takes a Wife; Don't Just Stand There; Don't Make Waves; Double Wedding; Doughgirls; Down to Earth; Dr. Ehrlich's Magic Bullet; Dr. Socrates; Dragon Seed; Dramatic School; Dream Wife; Dreams That Money Can Buy; The Dresser; Driftwood; The Dunwich Horror; Dynamite; East Lynne; Electra Glide in Blue; Elena and Her Men; Eleven Harrowhouse; The End; The Epic That Never Was; Errand Boy; Escape; Eye of the Cat; Eye of the Devil; Eyes in the Night; Fall of the House of Usher (1928); Fallen Angel; Fallen Sparrow; A Family

Affair; The Farmer Takes a Wife; Father Is a Bachelor; Fiesta; Finishing School; Fire Over England; Firecreek; First Love; Five Came Back; Five Fingers; Five Graves to Cairo; Five Miles to Midnight; Five Star Final; The Fixer; The Flame and the Arrow; Flare Up; Flesh and Blood (1951); Flesh of the Orchid; Flower Drum Song; Fly By Night; FM; Folies Bergere; Follow Me, Boys!; Follow That Dream; Fools for Scandal; Fools Parade; Footlight Parade; The Forbidden; Forbin Project; Force of Evil; Forest Rangers; Forever Darling; Forever Female; Forty Pounds of Trouble; Four Sons; Four's a Crowd; Fourteen Hours; Foxfire (1955); Francis, God's Jester; Frantic (1958); Free and Easy; Frenchie; Friday the Thirteenth (1933); The Friends of Eddie Coyle; Frisco Kid (1935); From This Day Forward; The Fugitive (1947); Fugitive Lovers; Furies; Fury (1936); Fuzz; Gaily, Gaily; Gambling Lady; Garden of Evil; Gaslight (1939); The Gene Krupa Story; The General Died at Dawn; Ghost Breakers; The Ghost Goes West; Ghoul (1933); Ghoul (1975); Gigot; Ginger in the Morning; The Girl From Petrovka; The Girl Who Couldn't Say No; The Girl Who Had Everything; Give Me a Sailor; Glass House; Go Chase Yourself; Godspell; Go into Your Dance; Go West Young Man; Goin' To Town; Gold; The Golden Age of Comedy; Golden Earrings; The Golden Voyage of Sinbad; Golem; Gong Show Movie; Good Fairy; Good News; Good Sam; Goodbye Gemini; Goodbye My Lady; Goonies; Gordon's War; Gorgeous Hussy; Gorilla; Grasshopper; Great Garrick; Great Impostor; Great Locomotive Chase; Great Lover (1931); Great Manhunt; Great Sinner; Great Waltz (1938); Great White Hope; Greatest; Green Fire; Green Goddess; Greenwich Village; A Guest in the House; The Guest Wife; A Guide for the Married Man; Gun Fury; A Gunfight; A Gunfighter; Gunrunner; Gypsy Moths; Hallelujah, I'm a Bum; Hallelujah Trail; Hammerhead; Hammersmith is Out; Hands Across the Table; The Hanging Tree; Hangmen Also Die; Happiest Days of Your Life; The Happiest Millionaire; Happy Anniversary; Happy Ending; Happy Land; Happy Time; Hard to Handle; Harlow; Harry and Son; Harum Scarum; The Hatchet Man; The Haunted Palace; He Married His Wife; Heart of the West; Heavens Above;

The Helen Morgan Story; Hell's Angels; Heller in Pink Tights; Hemingway's Adventures of a Young Man; Her Husband's Affairs; Here Comes the Navy; Here We Go Round the Mulberry Bush; Hero at Large; Heroes; Hester Street; High Pressure; High, Wide and Handsome; Hill; The Hired Wife; Hireling; Hiroshima, Mon Amour; His Majesty O'Keefe; Histoires Extraordinaires; Hit!; Hitler Gang; Hitler-The Last Ten Days; Hoffman; The Holly and the Ivy; The Hollywood Revue of 1929; Holy Matrimony; The Honeymoon Machine; Horror Hotel; The Horse in the Grey Flannel Suit; Horse Soldiers; Hot Spell; A House Divided; House Is Not a Home; How Do I Love Thee; How I Won the War; How to Be Very Very Popular; Howards of Virginia; I Found Stella Parish; I Love My Wife; I, Mobster; I Never Sang for My Father; I Wake Up Screaming; I Want What I Want; I'll Be Seeing You; Ice Palace; If I Were King; Impulse (1984); Inside Moves; Interlude (1957); Interlude (1968); Intruder in the Dust; Invisible Woman; Invitation to Happiness; Invitation to the Dance; Iron Petticoat; Island in the Sun; Island of Love; Isle of the Dead; It All Came True; It Happened in Brooklyn; It Happened Tomorrow; It Happens Every Spring; It's a Great Feeling; It's Only Money; Ivy; Jack of All Trades; Joan of Paris; Joe; John and Mary; Johnny Angel; June Bride; Jupiter's Darling; Justine; The Keep; The Kennel Murder Case; Kes; The Key (1934); The Key (1958); Key Exchange; Key to the City; Killer McCoy; King; King and Four Queens; King, Queen, Knave; Kings Go Forth; Kings of the Sun; Kiss the Blood Off My Hands; Kiss Them For Me; Kiss Tomorrow Goodbye; The Kissing Bandit; Kitty; Knickerbocker Holiday; Knock on Any Door; Lady in Red; The Lady in the Dark; Lady of Burlesque; Lady Takes a Flyer; Lancer Spy; Last American Hero; The Last Angry Man; Last Hunt; Last of Mrs. Cheyney; Last of the Red Hot Lovers; Last of the Secret Agents; The Last Outpost; Last Sunset; Last Valley; Late George Apley; Laughter; Law and Disorder (1958); The Law and Jake Wade; The Law and the Lady; Le Million; Leadbelly; The Learning Tree; Leather Saint; Legend of the Lost; The Leopard; Let No Man Write My Epitaph; Let's Dance; Let's Do it Again (1953); Let's

Make it Legal; Let's Make Love; Lion is in the Streets; Little Big Horn; A Little Sex; Live for Life; Live, Love and Learn; Living in a Big Way; Lolly Madonna War; Lone Star of Gold; Long Gray Line; Long John Silver; Long Night; Look in Any Window; Lost Angel; Lost Boundaries; Lost Moment; Love Before Breakfast; Love Parade; Lover Come Back (1946); Lovin' Molly; Loving; Lucky Me; Lucky Stiff; Lucretia Borgia; Luna; Lusty Men; Luv; Mad Love; Mad Wednesday; The Magic Christian; Magic Face; Magic Town; The Magnificent Doll; Main Street to Broadway; Making Mr. Right; The Maltese Falcon (1931); Mamma Rosa; Man Could Get Killed; The Man in the Grey Flannel Suit; The Man in the White Suit; Man of a Thousand Faces; Man of Aran; Man on a Swing; Man on Fire; The Man Who Came to Dinner; The Man Who Could Work Miracles; The Man Who Never Was; The Man Who Understood Women; Man, Woman and Child; Man's Favorite Sport?; Marat/Sade; Marie; Marius; Mark; Mark of the Hawk; Marriage of a Young Stockbroker; Martin; Masquerader; Mechanic; Melody; Men (1950); Merrily We Live; The Merry Wives of Reno; Mickey One; Middle of the Night; Min and Bill; Ministry of Fear; Miracle in the Rain; Miracle of the Bells; Mirage; Miranda; Mischief; Mississippi Mermaid; Mister 880; Mister Buddwing; The Model and the Marriage Broker; Modesty Blaise; Modigliani; The Molly Maguires; The Money Trap; Monkey Business (1952); Monkeys Go Home; Monsignor; Monte Carlo; Moon's Our Home; More Than a Secretary; Mouchette; Mountain Move; Murder by Television; Murder Man; Murphy's War; My Bodyguard; My Sin; My Six Loves; My Son John; My Wife's Best Friend; Myra Breckinridge; Mystery Street; Naked Truth; Napoleon; Nate and Hayes; Negatives; Nevada Smith; Never Love a Stranger; Never So Few; Never Take Sweets from a Stranger; The New Interns; New Orleans; A Night in the Life of Jimmy Reardon; The Night is Young (1934); Night of the Generals; Night People; A Night to Remember (1946); No Down Payment; No Highway in the Sky; No Small Affair; No Time for Comedy; No Time for Love; Nocturne; Norman, Is That You?; Nothin' But a Man; Now and Forever; Now I'll Tell; Number 17; Nurse

Edith Cavell; Of Human Hearts; The Offence; Old Maid; Old Mother Riley SERIES; On the Avenue; Once in a Lifetime; Once More with Feeling; Once Upon a Honeymoon; One Foot in Heaven; One Is a Lonely Number; One More River; One More Spring; One Trick Pony; One Way Passage; Only Angels Have Wings; Only When I Larf; Opening Night; Operation CIA; Operation Mad Ball; Over Twenty-One; P.K and the Kid; Paid; Painted Veil; Pandora and the Flying Dutchman; Panic in the Year Zero; Paper Tiger; The Parallax View; Paris Blues; Parlor, Bedroom and Bath; Parnell Party; Party Girl; Passionate Plumber; Payment Deferred; Payment on Demand; Perfect Furlough; Perfect Marriage; Period of Adjustment; Pete Kelly's Blues; The Phantom President; Pinky; Pork Chop Hill; The Posse (1975); Possession of Joel Delaney; President's Analyst; Pretty Poison; Pride and the Passion; Prime Cut; The Prince and the Showgirl; The Private Affairs of Bel Ami; The Prize; Prodigal; Promises! Promises!; The Prophecy; Prowler; Quality Street; Quartet (1948); Quick Millions; Rack; Rafferty and the Gold Dust Twins; Raffles; Raging Moon; Raid on Rommel; Rain People; Rancho Notorious; Ransom; Rat Race; Reap the Wild Wind; Rebel Rousers; Red Garters; Red Headed Woman; Red Inn; The Reivers; The Reluctant Debutante; Remember Last Night?; Rent-a-Dick; Report to the Commissioner; Return of Dracula; Return of the Vampire; Return to Oz; Revolutionary; Rhapsody; Rich, Young and Pretty; Ride the High Country; Rider on the Rain; Riff-Raff (1935); Riff-Raff (1947); The Right Stuff; Right to Love; Rise and Rise of Michael Rimmer; The River Niger; The River of No Return; Road Back; Robin and Marian; Rock a Bye Baby; Rollerball; Rolling Thunder; Romantic Comedy; Rome Express; Roots of Heaven; Rope of Sand; Rose of Washington Square; Rough Cut; Royal Family of Broadway; Ruby Gentry; Run for the Sun; Runaway; The Samurai; Sapphire; Save the Tiger; Scandalous John; Scapegoat; Scar; Scarlet Street; Scent of Mystery; School for Scoundrels; The Sea Gull; Seance on a Wet Afternoon; Search; Second Best Secret Agent in the Whole Wide World; Second Fiddle; Second Honeymoon Seconds; The Secret Agent; Secret Beyond the Door; The

Stuntman; Talk of the Town; Tall Blond Man with One Black Shoe; Tango & Cash; Tank; The Temp; They Won't Believe Me; They Won't Forget; The Thirty-Nine Steps (1935); The Thirty-Nine Steps (1959); The Thirty-Nine Steps (1978); To Catch a Thief; To Kill a Mockingbird; Tom Horn; Touch of Evil; Traces of Red; Trial (1955); The Trial (1962); The Trial (1993); Trial and Error; Under Suspicion; Unlawful Entry; Vertigo; Walking Dead; We Are Not Alone; Weekend at Bernie's; Weekend at Bernie's 2; Whirlpool; You Can't Get Away With Murder; Zigzag

Frankenstein Stories (not necessarily Frankenstein itself, but those similar to it as well): see also *Monsters: Monsters-Manmade: Body Parts: HORROR:* Andy Warhol's Frankenstein; The Body Snatcher; The Bride of Frankenstein; The Doctor and the Devils; House of Dracula; House of Frankenstein; I Was a Teenage Frankenstein; Re-Animator; Re-Animator 2; Revenge of Frankenstein; Runaway; Son of Frankenstein

Fraternity Life: see also *College Life: Party Movies: Sorority Life: Young Men: Coming of Age: Men Proving Themselves:* Bachelor Party (1984); The Boy Who Had Everything; Dead Poet's Society; Fraternity Row; National Lampoon's Animal House; School Daze; Ski School; Tommy Boy

Freeloaders: see *Con Artists: Relatives-Unwanted: Nuisances: Malicious Menaces*

Free Spirits (free-wheeling people who are fun-loving more than wild): see also *Eccentric People: Charismatic People: Wild People:* Angelo, My Love; Arizona; The Baby Maker; Bachelor Party (1984); Ball of Fire; The Beautiful Blonde from Bashful Bend; Bebe's Kids; Breakfast at Tiffany's; Breezy; Bull Durham; Bus Stop; Butterflies are Free; Career Opportunities; Claudelle Inglish; Conrack; Cookie; Coquette; Desperately Seeking Susan; Elena and Her Men; Ferris Bueller's Day Off; The Fisher King; Flame and the Arrow; Flame of New Orleans; 48 Hours; Fried Green Tomatoes; The Fugitive Kind; Gabriela; Gentleman Jim; Georgy Girl; Gidget; Ginger in the Morning; Holiday; Housesitter; I Am a Camera; I Ought to Be in Pictures; Impromptu; Isadora; It

Should Happen to You; January Man; Lawrence of Arabia; The Little Minister; Little Women (1933); Little Women (1949); Little Women (1978); Little Women (1994); Macaroni; Mad Miss Manton; Mermaids; Moon's Our Home; Morgan!; Morning Glory; Mr. Jones; Night of the Iguana; On a Clear Day You Can See Forever; Once Around; Orpheus Descending; Petulia; Pippi Longstocking; Pretty Woman; The Prime of Miss Jean Brodie; Protocol; The Rose Tattoo; Ruling Class; Sabrina; The Sandpiper; Saratoga Trunk; Say Anything; Something Wild (1986); A Song is Born; The Sound of Music; Spitfire; Stage Struck; Star Spangled Girl; The Sterile Cuckoo; Sunday, Bloody Sunday; Sweet Charity; Take Her, She's Mine; This Property Is Condemned; A Thousand Clowns; Three Comrades; Thunderbolt and Lightfoot; Who's That Girl?; Whoopee; Wish You Were Here; The World According to Garp; A Yank at Oxford; Zazie dans le Metro; Zorba, The Greek

French Films: see also *French New Wave Films: French-Canadian Films: France: Paris: Riviera Life: Art Films: Avant-Garde Films:* The Adventures of Arsene Lupin; The Adventures of Reinette and Mirabelle; All the Mornings of the World; Alphaville; Alpine Fire; And God Created Woman (1957); And Now, My Love; Anne and Muriel; Army in the Shadows; The Associate; Au Revoir, les Enfants; Australia; Babette Goes to War; Baxter (1990); Beauty and the Beast (1946); Bed and Board; Being at Home with Claude; Belle du Jour; Betty Blue; Big Blue; Black and White in Color; Blood Relatives; Bob le Flambeur; Boudu Saved From Drowning; Boyfriends and Girlfriends; Breathless (1959); The Bride is Much Too Beautiful; The Bride Wore Black; Buffet Froid; C'est la Vie; Candide; Casque d'Or; Children of Paradise; Chloe in the Afternoon; Chocolat; Choice of Arms; Claire's Knee; Cop au Vin; Coup de Torchon; Cousin, Cousine; Cousins; Crime and Punishment (1935); Cyrano de Bergerac (1990); Daddy Nostalgia; Dangerous Moves; Danton; Day For Night; Death Watch; The Detective (1985); Diabolique (1955); The Discreet Charm of Bourgeousie; Diva; Do You Like Women?; The Double Life of Veronique; Elena and Her Men; Entre-

Nous; The Fearless Vampire Killers; First Name: Carmen; Flesh of the Orchid; Forbidden Games; The 400 Blows; Frantic (1958); Full Moon in Paris; The Game is Over; Gervaise; Get Out Your Handkerchiefs; The Hairdresser's Husband; Happy New Year (1973); Hiroshima, Mon Amour; Histoires Extraordinaires; I Married a Dead Man; I Sent a Letter to My Love; Indochine; The Inquisitor; Je Vous Aime; Jean de Florette; Jour de Fete; Jules and Jim; King Lear (1987); The King's Whore; L'Annee des Meduses; L'Invitation; La Balance; La Belle Noiseuse; La Boum; La Cage Aux Folles; La Cage Aux Folles 2; La Cage Aux Folles 3: The Wedding; La Chevre; La Chienne; La Femme Nikita; La Lectrice; La Marseillaise; La Nuit de Varennes; La Ronde (1950); La Ronde (1964); La Vie Continue; La Vie de Boheme; The Lacemaker; Lacombe, Lucien; The Last Metro; Last Tango in Paris; Last Year at Marienbad; Le Bal; Le Cavaleur; Le Corbeau; Le Million; Les Bas-Fonds; Les Biches; Les Comperes; Les Enfants Terribles; Les Liaisons Dangereuses; Les Valseuses; Les Visiteurs du Soir; Life and Nothing But; Life is a Bed of Roses; Life Upside Down; The Little Thief; Live for Life; Lola (1960); Loulou; Love on the Run (1979); The Lover; Lumiere; Lumiere d'Ete; Lunch on the Grass; Madame Rosa; Maitresse; A Man and A Woman; A Man and a Woman: Twenty Years Later; Man Bites Dog; The Man Who Watched Trains Go By; Manon; Manon des Sources (1952); Manon des Sources (1986); Marquise of O; Married Woman; Masculine, Feminine; May Fools; Menage; Mina Tannenbaum; Mississippi Mermaid; Modilgiani; Momma, There's a Man in Your Bed; Monsieur Hire; Monsieur Hulot's Holiday; Moon in the Gutter; Mouchette; Muriel; Murmur of the Heart; Music Teacher; My American Uncle; My Best Friend's Girl; My Father's Glory; My Mother's Castle; My Night at Maud's; Night and Day; No Man's Land; Noir et Blanc; Nous La Liberte; Nous Sommes Tous les Assassins; Nouvelle Vague; Olivier, Olivier; One Deadly Summer; One Sings, the Other Doesn't; Pain in the A . . .; Pardon Mon Affaire; The Passion; Pauline at the Beach; Phantom of Liberty; Playtime; Querelle; The Red

Balloon; Red Kiss; Rendez-Vous; Repulsion; The Return of Martin Guerre; The Rise of Louis XIV; Robert et Robert; 'Round Midnight; Rules of the Game; Samurai; Scent of Green Papaya; Shoot The Piano Player; Simple Story; Six in Paris; Sleeping Car Murders; Small Change; Soft Skin; Stolen Kisses; The Story of Adele H.; Subway; Summer; Sunday in the Country; Sundays and Cybele; Sylvia and the Ghost; The Tall Blond Man with One Black Shoe; Tatie Danielle; Ten Days Wonder; That Man From Rio; That Obscure Object of Desire; Therese and Isabelle; 36 Fillette; Three Men and a Cradle; Too Beautiful For You; Toto le Heros; Tristana; Two or Three Things I Know About Her; Umbrellas of Cherbourg; Un Chien Andalou; Un Coeur en Hiver; Uranus; Vanishing (1988); Violette; Viva Maria!; Volpone; Wages of Fear; Weekend; The Young Girls of Rochefort; You've Got to Live Dangerously; Z; Zazie dans le Metro

French New Wave Films (notable art films from the '50s and '60s of a particularly avant-garde style, some more representative than others): see also *French Films: Avant-Garde Films: Art Films: 1950s: 1960s:* Alphaville; Bob le Flambeur; Breathless (1959); Diabolique (1955); The 400 Blows; Hiroshima, Mon Amour; Last Year at Marienbad; Les Liaisons Dangereuses; Lola (1960); Masculine, Feminine; Mouchette; Six in Paris; Shoot the Piano Player; Sundays and Cybele; Two or Three Things I Know About Her; Weekend; Zazie dans le Metro

French Revolution: see also *1700s: Historical Drama:* Cheech & Chong's The Corsican Brothers; Danton; The Elusive Pimpernel; La Marseillaise; The Rise of Louis XIV; Scaramouche; The Scarlet Pimpernel; Start the Revolution Without Me; A Tale of Two Cities (1935); A Tale of Two Cities (1958); A Tale of Two Cities (1982)

Freud (about or including character based on the great psychoanalyst): see also *Psychologists: Psychological Drama:* The Seven Percent Solution; Freud; Lovesick

Friends-Deceptive: see *Friends as Enemies: Friendship on the Rocks: Double Crossings: Con Artists: Liars: Love-Questionable*

Friends as Enemies: see also *Feuds: Men in Conflict: Women in Conflict:*

Bad Influence; Blame it on Rio; Blood on the Moon; The Brotherhood; Bullets or Ballots; Chimes at Midnight; Consenting Adults; The Duellists; Ebony Tower; The End of the Game; Fortune Cookie; Ghost; The Hatchet Man; Hell in the Pacific; Here Comes the Navy; I Died a Thousand Times; Internal Affairs; Kansas; The Law and Jake Wade; Letter to Three Wives; Love and Hisses; Malice; Manhattan Melodrama; Mantrap; Marriage on the Rocks; My Best Friend's Girl; Never Love a Stranger; Not with My Wife You Don't; Obsession; The Odd Couple; Once Upon a Time in America; One Eyed Jacks; Ride the High Country; Rosemary's Baby; The Seventh Dawn; Showdown; A Slight Case of Murder; Sneakers; State of Grace; Toto le Heros; True Colors; Turning Point; Unlawful Entry; Valentino (1977); Viva Zapata; Zandalee

Friends in Love: see also *ROMANCE: Friendships-Between Sexes:* Best Friends; Broadcast News; The Drowning Pool; Harper; Minnie & Moskowitz; My Own Private Idaho; The Remains of the Day; Samantha; Same Time, Next Year; When Harry Met Sally

Friendships-Between Sexes: see also *Friends in Love: Buddy Films:* Alan and Naomi; The Big Chill; Four Friends; Guarding Tess; The Heart Is a Lonely Hunter; Mike's Murder; P.K. and the Kid; Peter's Friends; The Promised Land; Punchline; The Return of the Secaucus Seven; Sudie and Simpson; To Forget Venice; Trapeze

Friendships-Female: see also *Buddy Films-Female:* Antonia and Jane; Beaches; Between Friends; Between Two Women; Camilla (1994); The Cemetery Club; The Children's Hour; A Date with Judy; Death Becomes Her; Defenseless; Diabolique (1955); Entre-Nous; The Favor; The Foxes; Fried Green Tomatoes; Friends and Husbands; The Group; Housekeeping; How to Marry a Millionaire; Howards End; Imitation of Life (1934); Imitation of Life (1959); Julia; Just Between Friends; Kiss and Tell; Leaving Normal; Life of Her Own; Me and Veronica; Mina Tannenbaum; Mortal Thoughts; Old Acquaintance; On Approval; One Sings, the Other Doesn't; Our Hearts Were Young and Gay; Outrageous Fortune; Passion Fish; Personal Best; Personal Services; Pete 'n Tillie; Poison Ivy (1992); Prison Stories: Women on the Inside; Rich and

Famous; Sandakan No. 8; Secret Ceremony; Silkwood; St. Elmo's Fire; Swing Shift; Thelma & Louise; These Three; Three Blind Mice; Turning Point; The Women; Women in Love

Friendships-Great/Lifetime: The Angels with Dirty Faces; Antonia and Jane; Bang the Drum Slowly; Beaches; Beautiful Dreamers; Becket; Birdy; Brideshead Revisited; A Bronx Tale; Driving Miss Daisy; Fox and the Hound; Inside Moves; Julia; Kotch; Manhattan Melodrama; Mina Tannenbaum; Miracle Worker; My Own Private Idaho; Rich and Famous; A Separate Peace; Shaking the Tree; Song of Love; Sundays and Cybele; Sunshine Boys; Test Pilot; Vincent and Theo

Friendships-Interracial: see also *Black vs. White/Black & White Together: Race Relations:* The Adventures of Huckleberry Finn (1960); The Adventures of Huckleberry Finn (1985); batteries not included; The Biscuit Eater (1940); The Biscuit Eater (1972); Blue Collar; Driving Miss Daisy; Gladiator; Gone With the Wind; Grand Canyon; Huckleberry Finn (1939); Huckleberry Finn (1960); Huckleberry Finn (1974); A Member of the Wedding; Reivers; Running Scared; Salt and Pepper; The Shawshank Redemption; Stir Crazy; Sudie and Simpson; Unnatural Causes; Zorba, The Greek

Friendships-Intergenerational: see also *Men and Girls: Men and Boys: Women and Boys: Women and Girls: Romance-Older Men/Younger Women: Romance: Older Women/Younger Men:* The Adventures of Reinette and Mirabelle; Barbarosa; Between Two Women; Bill; Bill: On His Own; Camilla (1994); Convicts; Ebony Tower

Friendships-Lifetime: see *Friendships-Great/Lifetime*

Friendships-Male: see also *Men in Conflict: Men's Films: Buddy Films: Ensembles-Male:* The Adventures of Robinson Crusoe; Amadeus; American Flyers; Aspen Extreme; Bang the Drum Slowly; Barbarosa; Barcelona; Beau Brummell (1924); Beau Brummell (1954); Beau Geste (1926); Beau Geste (1939); Beau Geste (1966); Beautiful Dreamers; Becket; Ben-Hur (1959); Ben-Hur: A Tale of Christ (1925); Big Wednesday; Birdy; The Biscuit Eater (1940); The Biscuit Eater (1972); Blame it on Rio;

The Blue Lamp; Boom Town; The Boys in the Band; Breaking Away; Breaking Point; Brian's Song; Brideshead Revisited; Bridge on the River Kwai; A Bronx Tale; The Bullfighter and the Lady; Caddy; Calcutta; California Split; Campus Man; The Caretaker; Carnal Knowledge; Chimes at Midnight; Chronicle of a Death Foretold; Color of Money; Convicts; Cooperstown; Coupe de Ville; Danton; Dead Poet's Society; Dead Reckoning; The Deer Hunter; Deliverance; Dersu Uzala; Diner; Dominick & Eugene; The Dresser; The Duellists; The Fabulous Baker Boys; The Family Business; The Fisher King; Five Corners; G-Men; Gallipoli; Genevieve; Ghost Story; Going in Style; Grumpy Old Men; Harry and Walter Go to New York; Harry in Your Pocket; Harvey; The Hatchet Man; Heartbreakers; Hell's Angels; Henry: Portrait of a Serial Killer; Henry V (1944); Henry V (1989); Here Comes the Navy; Holiday for Sinners; How to Save a Marriage and Ruin Your Life; Husbands; The Illustrated Man; Jacknife; Joe; Jules and Jim; K-2; Kidnapped (1938); Kidnapped (1959); Kidnapped (1971); Kim; King of Marvin Gardens; Kings of the Road; The Last Detail; The Law and Jake Wade; Les Valseuses; Longtime Companion; Lovin' Molly; Macaroni; Mambo Kings; The Man Who Shot Liberty Valance; Manhattan Melodrama; Martin's Day; Melody Men (1985); Midnight Cowboy; Mikey and Nicky; Mister Roberts; A Month in the Country; My Best Friend's Girl; My Bodyguard; My Own Private Idaho; Never Love a Stranger; New Life; 1969; The Odd Couple; Of Mice and Men (1939); Of Mice and Men (1993); Once Upon a Time in America; One Flew Over Cuckoo's Nest; Papillon; Patti Rocks; Platoon; The Pope of Greenwich Village; The Promised Land; Queens Logic; Rain Man; Requiem for a Heavyweight (1956); Requiem for a Heavyweight (1962); Robert et Robert; Robinson Crusoe on Mars; Rosencrantz and Guildenstern Are Dead; Rounders; Salvador; San Francisco; Scarecrow; A Separate Peace; The Shawshank Redemption; Showdown; Song of Love; Songwriter; Spartacus; St. Elmo's Fire; The Sunshine Boys; Tequila Sunrise; Terry Fox Story; Test Pilot; Texas; That Was Then . . . This Is Now; Three Comrades; Three Godfathers;

Thunderbolt and Lightfoot; Tin Men; Toto le Heros; Trapeze; True Colors; Ulysses (1967); Un Coeur en Hiver; Viva Zapata; Waterdance; Willie and Phil; Wings; Withnail and I; Zandalee

Friendships on the Rocks: see also *Feuds: Friends as Enemies: Friends-Deceptive:* Holiday for Sinners; The Horse's Mouth; Johnny Be Good; Pete n Tillie; The Pope of Greenwich Village; Reunion; Rich and Famous; Toto le Heros; Turning Point (1977); True Colors

Friendships-Reunited: see *Reunions*

Friendships with Royalty: Becket; Beau Brummell; Chimes at Midnight; The Mudlark

Frozen in Time: see *Time Sleepers*

Frozen People: see also *Snow Settings: Time Sleepers:* Captain America; Demolition Man; Forever Young; Friday the 13th: Final Chapter; Iceman; Out Cold

Fugitives (general; not fleeing any of the category references below): see also *Fugitives from the Law: Fugitives from the Mob: Fugitive from a Murderer: Chase Movies: Accused Unjustly: Framed?:* The Adventures of Eliza Frazer; After Hours; After The Fox; Aloha, Bobby and Rose; The American Friend; An American Werewolf in London; Bad Company; Badlands; Bandolero; The Big Clock; Bird on a Wire; Blues Brothers; The Body Snatchers; Boy, Did I Get a Wrong Number!; Breathless (1959); Breathless (1983); Casanova's Big Night; Charley Varrick; Fancy Pants; The Fugitive (1947); The Fugitive (1993); Great Smokey Roadblock; His Brother's Wife; Hopscotch; Invasion of the Body Snatchers (1956); Invasion of the Body Snatchers (1978); Married to the Mob; Me and the Colonel; Midnight Run; Miles From Home; Mirage; Most Dangerous Game; The Naked Prey; The President's Analyst; The Puppetmasters; Roman Holiday; Romancing the Stone; Running on Empty; Saboteur; Scorpio; Seems Like Old Times; Shame (1968); She Loves Me Not; Sleeper; Sleeping With the Enemy; Some Like it Hot; They Live; Three Days of the Condor; Three Fugitives; Witness; Year of the Comet; You Can't Run Away From It

Fugitives from the Law: see also *Outlaw Road Movies: Fugitives from the Mob: Chase Movies:* Accatone;

Across the Bridge; After The Fox; Aloha, Bobby and Rose; Along Came Jones; Amazon; And God Created Woman (1988); Asphalt Jungle; Assassination; Bad Company; Badlands; Bandolero; The Beautiful Blonde from Bashful Bend; The Big Steal; Billy the Kid; Bird on a Wire; Bitter Rice; Black Angel; Black Moon Rising; The Blue Dahlia; Blues Brothers; Bonnie and Clyde; Breathless (1983); Breathless (1959); Butch Cassidy and the Sundance Kid; Captain Blood; The Cat Chaser; The Chase (1966); Chato's Land; Convicts; Convoy; Coogan's Bluff; Dark Passage; Day of the Jackal; Eddie Macon's Run; Eight on the Lam; The Enforcer (1950); Europa, Europa; The Flim Flam Man; Forty Pounds of Trouble; Frenzy; The Front Page (1931); The Front Page (1974); The Fugitive (1993); Fugitive Lovers; The Fugitive: The Final Episode; The Gauntlet; The Getaway (1972); The Getaway (1994); The Girl of the Golden West; Gloria; Gorilla at Large; The Great Locomotive Chase; The Great Smokey Roadblock; Grey Fox; Gun Crazy (1950); Gun Crazy (1992); Hanky Panky; Harley Davidson and the Marlboro Man; Her Alibi; Hider in the House; Highpoint; His Girl Friday; Hold Me, Thrill Me, Kiss Me; Hunted; I am a Fugitive from a Chain Gang; In-Laws; Into the Night; It's a Wonderful World; King and Four Queens; Kiss the Blood Off My Hands; The Lodger (1926); The Lodger (1932); The Lodger (1944); Logan's Run; Lolita; Lost Honor of Katharina Blum; The Lost Man; M (1931); M (1951); Macao; Mad Miss Manton; Martin's Day; Mary Burns, Fugitive; Memoirs of an Invisible Man; Midnight Run; Miles From Home; Mister 880; Money for Nothing; Moving Violation; Mrs. Soffel; Naked Spur; Narrow Margin (1952); Narrow Margin (1990); Never a Dull Moment (1967); Night of the Hunter; Night Train to Munich; Nightfall; No Escape (1994); North by Northwest; Northwest Mounted Police; Nuns on the Run; October Man; Odd Man Out; One False Move; Planet of the Apes; Raven (1935); Report to the Commissioner; River Rat; Road Games; Rose Marie (1936); Rose Marie (1954); Running Man (1963); Running on Empty; Russkies; Saboteur; Saint Benny, the Dip; Santa Fe Trail; Scene of the Crime; See No Evil, Hear No Evil; Seems Like Old

Times; Shaker Run; Shakes the Clown; Simple Men; Smokey and the Bandit; Smokey and the Bandit II; Smokey and the Bandit III; Sneakers; Speedway; Sugarland Express; Summer of My German Soldier; Swamp Water; Take the Money and Run; Talk of the Town; The Tall Blond Man with One Black Shoe; Tango & Cash; Texas Across the River; Thelma & Louise; There Was a Crooked Man; They Live; They Live by Night; The Thief (1952); Thieves Like Us; The Thirty-Nine Steps (1935); The Thirty-Nine Steps (1959); The Thirty-Nine Steps (1978); This Gun for Hire; Three Days of the Condor; Three Fugitives; Total Recall; Trade Winds; Trap; Water Babies; We're No Angels (1955); We're No Angels (1989); Wedlock; Whistle Down the Wind; White Nights (1985); Wilby Conspiracy; Wild at Heart; Witness; Young Guns; Young Guns II

Fugitives from a Murderer: see also *Trail of a Killer: Serial Killers: Women in Jeopardy: Men in Jeopardy:* Backtrack; Broadway Danny Rose; Clean Slate; Double O Kid; Dumb and Dumber; El Mariachi; Fools Parade; The Fugitive: The Final Episode; I Love Trouble (1994); In the Spirit; Judgment Night; Jumpin' Jack Flash; Most Dangerous Game; Moving Violation; My Favorite Blonde; Night of the Hunter; No Escape (1994); North by Northwest; Off and Running; Package; Pickup on South Street; Romancing the Stone; Running Man (1987); Shallow Grave; She Loves Me Not; Silhouette; Sister Act; Sleeping With the Enemy; Some Like it Hot; Three Days of the Condor; Witness; Yellow Balloon

Fugitives from the Mob: see also *Mob Stories: Fugitives from the Law: Fugitives from a Murderer: Mob Girls:* After the Fox; Against All Odds; All Through the Night; American Friend; Any Which Way You Can; Atlantic City; Ball of Fire; Behave Yourself!; Bird on a

Wire; Bitch (1979); Boy on a Dolphin; Brain Smasher: A Love Story; Broadway Danny Rose; Casanova's Big Night; Charley Varrick; Diva; Domino Principle; Double-Crossed; Dumb and Dumber; Eyewitness (1970); F/X; A Fine Mess; Flesh of the Orchid; Forbidden; Force of Evil; The Freshman (1990); The Friends of Eddie Coyle; The Gauntlet; The George Raft Story; The Getaway (1972); The Getaway (1994); Gloria; Heat; Highpoint; How to Be Very Very Popular; The In-Laws; Into the Night; Jinxed; Knock on Wood; Last Rites; The Lemon Drop Kid; M (1931); M (1951); The Man from the Diners' Club; Married to the Mob; The Marrying Man; Mary Burns, Fugitive; Midnight Run; Million Dollar Duck; Money for Nothing; My Blue Heaven (1990); My Favorite Brunette; The Naked Face; Narrow Margin (1952); Narrow Margin (1990); Never a Dull Moment (1967); Nightfall; No Mercy; Number 17; Opportunity Knocks; Outfit (1973); The Outside Man; Paper Moon; Party Girl; Pete Kelly's Blues; The Pope Must Die(t); The Princess and the Pirate; Rapid Fire; Run; Shaker Run; Sister Act; Some Like it Hot; A Song is Born; Sticky Fingers; Survivors; True Identity; True Romance; Weekend at Bernie's; Weekend at Bernie's 2; Wise Guys; Wonder Man

Fugitives-Hiding/Harboring: see also *Hiding Out: Fugitive Convicts:* The Attic: The Hiding of Anne Frank; Christmas Holiday; Diary of Anne Frank (1959); The Front Page (1931); The Front Page (1974); Fugitive Lovers; Girl of the Golden West; Her Alibi; Russkies; Scene of the Crime; Seems Like Old Times; Shakes the Clown; Summer of My German Soldier; Talk of the Town; Wilby Conspiracy

Funerals: see also *Comedy-Morbid: Death-Dealing with: Death-Impending: Widows: Widowers:* Avanti!; Babycakes; The Bad and the Beautiful; The Big Chill; Billy Liar; Busy Body; Bye Bye

Braverman; Comedy of Terrors; Da; Four Weddings and a Funeral; Funeral in Berlin; Gardens of Stone; Harold and Maude; It Started in Naples; Love Field; The Loved One; May Fools; Only the Lonely; Passed Away; Sons of Katie Elder; The Trail of the Lonesome Pine

Future-Seeing the (predicting the future, premonitions): see also *Psychics: Mindreading: Fortunetellers: Supernatural Danger:* The Clairvoyant (1934); The Dead Zone; Hanussen

Futuristic Films (set in the future): see also *SCI-FI: Oppression: Surrealism: Avant-Garde: Outer Space Movies:* The Absent-Minded Professor; Alien Nation; Alphaville; Americathon; Back to the Future 2; Balcony; Beneath the Planet of the Apes; Black Hole; Blade Runner; A Boy and His Dog; Brazil; Casanova '70; Cherry 2000; Class of 1999; A Clockwork Orange; Closet Land; Conquest of the Planet of the Apes; Day the Fish Came Out; Daybreak; Death Race 2000; Death Watch; Delicatessen; Demolition Man; Escape From New York; Escape from the Planet of the Apes; Fahrenheit 451; Fortress; Freejack; Futureworld; Gassss; A Handmaid's Tale; Hardware; The Illustrated Man; Knightriders; The Lodger (1926); The Lodger (1932); The Lodger (1944); Logan's Run; Mad Max; Mad Max Beyond Thunderdome; Memoirs of a Survivor; Metropolis; The New Barbarians; The Night is Young; Night of the Comet; 1984 (1955); 1984 (1984); No Escape (1994); Planet of the Apes; Prisoner: Arrival; Quintet; Revolutionary; Road Warrior; Robinson Crusoe on Mars; Robocop; Robocop 2; Rollerball; Running Man (1987); Sleeper; Solarbabies; Soylent Green; Split Second; Terminator; Terminator 2: Judgment Day; Things to Come; THX 1138; The Trial (1962); The Trial (1993); Trouble in Mind; Until the End of the World; Westworld; Wild in the Streets; Wild Palms; Zardoz; Zero Population Growth (Z.P.G.)

G

Gag Comedy: see *Comedy-Gag:* also *COMEDY: Slaptick Comedy: Spoofs/ Spoofs: Skit Comedy*

Gamblers/Gambling: see also *Bets: Horse Racing: Las Vegas: Games: Risking It All: Losing It All:* The Action for Slander; The Amazing Dr. Clitterhouse; Any Which Way You Can; Atlantic City; Banjo on My Knee; The Big Town; Bitter Sweet (1933); Bitter Sweet (1940); Bob le Flambeur; Bullets or Ballots; California Split; Casino; The Cincinnati Kid; Doctor Mabuse, the Gambler; Fever Pitch; Force of Evil; Freebie and the Bean; Funny Girl; Gambling Lady; Garden of Evil; Great Sinner; Guys and Dolls; Havana Heat; Honeymoon in Vegas; Honeymoon Machine; House of Games; In Old Chicago; Indecent Proposal; Jinxed; Kaleidoscope; Lady Eve; Lady Gambles; Last Boy Scout; Let it Ride; Let's Make it Legal; Little Miss Marker (1934); Little Miss Marker (1980); Lookin' to Get Out; Loser Takes All; Lost in America; The Man Who Broke the Bank at Monte Carlo; Man with the Golden Arm; Maverick; Max Dugan Returns; Meet Me in Las Vegas; Mister Cory; Money from Home; Monte Carlo; The Monte Carlo Story; Mr. Lucky; Mrs. Brown, You've Got a Lovely Daughter; Music of Chance; No Man of Her Own; North Avenue Irregulars; Now I'll Tell; The Only Game in Town; Queen of Hearts; Requiem for a Heavyweight (1956); Requiem for a Heavyweight (1962); Rose of Washington Square; San Francisco; Saratoga; The Set-Up; Seven Thieves; Silver Bears; Stacy's Knights

Games: see also *Power Struggles: Mindgames: Gambling:* The Cincinnati Kid; Dangerous Moves; Fresh Gin Game; The Hustler; Knight Moves; Music of Chance; Quiz Show; Running Man (1987); Searching for Bobby Fischer; Stacy's Knights; Suicide Club; Thursday's Game; The Wizard; The Wrong Box

Game Shows: see also *Contests/ Competitions: Games: Gamblers: TV Life:* Champagne for Caesar; The Gong Show Movie; The Lemon Sisters; Melvin and Howard; Running Man; Quiz Show; Stay Tuned

Gangs-Street or General: see *Gangs-Black: Gangs-Latin: Gangs-White: Mob Stories: Inner City Life: Urban Horrors:* Bad Boys; The Beat; The Bowery; Colors; Death Wish 3; Exterminator; Exterminator 2; Fort Apache, The Bronx; The Karate Kid; Last Exit to Brooklyn; Mad Max; Mad Max Beyond Thunderdome; Near Dark; Never Let Go; The New Barbarians; The Outsiders; Quadrophenia; Road Warrior; Rumble Fish; The Wanderers; Warriors; Wild Angels; The Wild One; Yojimbo; Young Savages; West Side Story; Who's That Knocking at My Door?

Gangs-Asian: see also *Martial Arts: Gangs-Black: Gangs-Latin: Gangs-White: Drugs: Inner City Life: Urban Horrors:* Black Rain (1989); China Girl; Rising Sun; Year of the Dragon

Gangs-Black: see also *Gangs-Asian: Gangs-Latin: Gangs-White: Drugs: Inner City Life: Urban Horrors:* Boyz N the Hood; CB4: The Movie; Colors; Fort Apache, The Bronx; Menace II Society; New Jack City; South Central; Trespass

Gangs-Latin: see also *Gangs-Asian: Gangs-Black: Gangs-White: Drugs: Inner City Life: Urban Horrors:* American Me; Colors; Mi Vida Loca; West Side Story

Gangs-White: see also *Mob Stories: Gangs-Asian: Gangs-Black: Drugs: Inner City Life: Urban Horrors:* The Lords of Flatbush; Mean Streets; The Wanderers; West Side Story

Gangsters (c. 1930s): see *Warner Gangster Era: Mob Stories: Fugitives from the Mob: Prohibition Era: Gangs*

Gay & Lesbian Films (notably made by gay and/or lesbian filmmakers): see also *Gay Men: Lesbians: Ethnic/Minority Films: Alternative Lifestyles: Anti-Establishment Films:* Bar Girls; Fox and His Friends; Fun Down There; Parting Glances; Poison; Rock Hudson's Home Movies; Swoon; Taxi zum Klo; The Life and Times of Harvey Milk

Gay Awakenings: see also *Gay Men:*
Lesbians: Gay/Lesbian Films: Coming of
Age: Desert Hearts; The Devil's
Playground; Fox and His Friends; Fun
Down There; Girlfriends; Joshua Then
and Now; Last Exit to Brooklyn; Leather
Boys; Lianna; The Lost Language of
Cranes; A Man of No Importance;
Norman, Is That You?; The Priest;
Reflections in a Golden Eye; Tea and
Sympathy; Therese and Isabelle; Third
Sex; Threesome

Gay Men: see also *Homoeroticism:*
Lesbians: Homosexual Suicides:
Murders of Homosexuals: Homosexual
Secrets: Homophobia: Alternative
Lifestyles: San Francisco: The Adjuster;
Alexander, the Other Side of Dawn;
Andre's Mother; Another Country;
Beautiful Dreamers; Being at Home with
Claude; Beyond Therapy; Big Business;
Blood and Concrete; The Boys in the
Band; Citizen Cohn; Compulsion;
Consenting Adult; Cruising; Deadfall
(1968); Death in Venice; Deathtrap; The
Detective (1968); The Devil's Playground;
A Different Story; Dog Day Afternoon;
The Dresser; Drifting; Early Frost;
Edward II; England Made Me;
Entertaining Mr. Sloane; Exotica;
Farewell My Concubine; The Fearless
Vampire Killers; Fortune and Men's Eyes;
The Fourth Man; Fox and His Friends;
Friends Forever; Fun Down There; The
Garden; Interview with the Vampire;
Joshua Then and Now; Kiss of the Spider
Woman; La Cage Aux Folles; La Cage
Aux Folles 2; La Cage Aux Folles 3: The
Wedding; Last Exit to Brooklyn; Law of
Desire; Leather Boys; Living End;
Lonesome Cowboys; Longtime
Companion; The Lost Language of
Cranes; Making Love; Mala Noche; Man
Like Eva; A Man of No Importance;
Maurice; Menage; Music Lovers; My
Beautiful Laundrette; My Own Private
Idaho; Myra Breckinridge; New
Barbarians; Nighthawks (1978);
Nighthawks, 2: Strip Jack Naked (1991);
Nijinsky; Norman, Is That You?; Oscar
Wilde; Paris is Burning; Parting Glances;
Peter's Friends; Philadelphia; Poison;
Prick Up Your Ears; The Priest; Querelle;
Ready to Wear; Reflections in a Golden
Eye; Ricochet; The Ritz; Rock Hudson's
Home Movies; The Rocky Horror Picture
Show; Rope; Satyricon (Fellini's);
Sebastiane; The Sergeant; Six Degrees of

Separation; Something for Everyone;
Speaking Parts; Special Day; The
Staircase; The Sum of Us; Sunday, Bloody
Sunday; Swoon; Taste of Honey; Taxi zum
Klo; Tea and Sympathy; The Third Sex;
Threesome; Tightrope; The Times of
Harvey Milk; To Catch a Killer; To Forget
Venice; Torch Song Trilogy; The Trials of
Oscar Wilde; Victim; Victor/Victoria; We
Think the World of You; Wedding
Banquet; Zorro and the Gay Blade

Generation Gap (old vs. young): see
also *Generation X: Parents vs. Children:*
Anti-Establishment Films: All the Way
Up; Atlantic City; Days of Thunder; Die!
Die! My Darling!; Early Summer; Ferris
Bueller's Day Off; The First Monday in
October; Forever Female; Gassss;
Generation; Going My Way; The
Happening; Hardcore; Harry and Son;
Harry in Your Pocket; How Sweet It Is;
Idol; Impossible Years; Kotch; Late for
Dinner; Life is Sweet; Married to It; Mass
Appeal; Nothing in Common; The
Reluctant Debutante; Rock n' Roll High
School; Roller Boogie; The Rookie;
Sandakan No. 8; Skidoo; Strangers, the
Story of a Mother and Daughter; The
Subject Was Roses; Suburbia; Take Her,
She's Mine; Taking Off; Tokyo Story;
Valley of the Dolls; Vice Versa; Who's
Afraid of Virginia Woolf?; Wild in the
Streets; Will Penny; The Young Doctors

Genetics (genetic engineering): see
Monsters-Mutant: Scientists: Scientist
Detectives: Experiments: Monsters-
Human: Humans into Animals: Disease
Stories

Genies (magic wish-givers): see also
Wishes: Magic: Witchcraft: Fantasy:
Aladdin; Where Do We Go from Here?

Geniuses: see also *Children-Gifted:*
Children-Little Adults: Inventors: The
Computer Wore Tennis Shoes; Deadly
Friend; Edison, the Man; Fantastic
Voyage; I.Q.; Little Man Tate; Man on the
Flying Trapeze; Rain Man; Searching for
Bobby Fischer; Sneakers; War Games;
Young Tom Edison

Georgia: see also *Southerns:* The Color
Purple; Deliverance; Gone With the Wind;
Love Crimes; Macon County Line; Return
to Macon County; Stars and Bars; Sudie
and Simpson; Tobacco Road; Wise Blood

German Films: see also *Germany:*
Nazi Stories: Germans as Enemy:
Abschied von Gestern; Aguirre, the
Wrath of God; Alice in the Cities; Berlin

Alexanderplatz; Bitter Tears of Petra Von
Kant; Bittere Emte; Christiane F.; Das
Boot; Day of Wrath; Despair; Every Man
for Himself (and God Against All);
Faraway, So Close!; Faust; Fox and His
Friends; Friends and Husbands; The
Goalie's Anxiety at the Penalty Kick;
Heart of Glass; Heimat; In a Year with 13
Moons; Jud Suess; Kamikaze 89;
Lightning Over Water; Lili Marleen; Lola
(1982); Lost Honor of Katharina Blum;
Love in Germany; M (1931); A Man Like
Eva; Melancholia; Mephisto; Nasty Girl;
Olympische Spiele; Out of Order;
Pedestrian; Schtonk!; Siegfried; The State
of Things; Stroszek; Sugarbaby; Swing;
Taxi zum Klo; Threepenny Opera; Tin
Drum; Triumph of the Will; Veronika
Voss; Voyager; Where the Green Ants
Dream; Wings of Desire; Woman in
Flames

Germans as Enemy: see also *Nazi*
Stories: Concentration Camps:
Germany: Berlin: Japanese as Enemy:
Russians as Enemies: Above Suspicion;
Above the Rim; Action in Arabia; Action
in the North Atlantic; Adventures of
Tartu; The Adventuress; Alexander
Nevsky; The Battle of Britian; The Battle
of the Bulge; The Battle of the Neretva;
The Big Lift; Bittere Ernte; Captive
Heart; Dam Busters; A Day in October;
Desperate Journey; Destiny of a Man; Die
Hard; The Eagle Has Landed; The
Escape; Europa, Europa; Ever in My
Heart; Eyes in the Night; Grand Illusion;
The Great Escape; Great Escape 2: The
Untold Story; Hell, Heaven, and
Hoboken; Hindenburg; Hitler Gang;
Hitler-The Last Ten Days; The House on
Carroll Street; The Incredible Mr. Limpet;
Inside Moves; It Happened Here; Lancer
Spy; Lassiter; Man Hunt; The Man I
Married; The Man Who Never Was; The
Moon is Down; Murphy's War; Night
Train to Munich; Odessa File; The One
That Got Away; Philadelphia Experiment;
Raid on Rommel; Raiders of the Lost
Ark; The Remains of the Day; Road
Back; Sahara (1943); Sea Wolves;
Sergeant York; Seventh Cross; Shining
Through; The Shop on Main Street;
Situation Hopeless But Not Serious; The
Sound of Music; Spy in Black; Stalag 17;
Summer of My German Soldier; Voyage of
the Damned; W. Plan; Watch on the
Rhine; Went the Day Well?; The Wooden
Horse; Zeppelin

Germany: see also *German Films: Germans as Enemy: Austria/Vienna:* Berlin Alexanderplatz; Berlin Express; Bittere Ernte; Captive Heart; Christiane F.; The Damned; The Dishonored; Dollars; A Foreign Affair; Fox and His Friends; G.I. Blues; The Goalie's Anxiety at the Penalty Kick; Gorgon; Grand Hotel; Grand Illusion; Hangmen Also Die; Heimat; Hindenburg; Hitler Gang; Hitler-The Last Ten Days; Lili Marleen; Lola (1982); Love in Germany; Ludwig; Magic Face; The Marriage of Maria Braun; Mein Kampf; Nasty Girl; Night Train to Munich; Reunion; Road Back; Schtonk!; Sugarbaby; Swing Kids; A Time to Love and A Time to Die; Tin Drum; Town Without Pity; Triumph of the Will; The Wonderful World of the Brothers Grimm; The Wooden Horse

Ghosts: see also *Afterlife: Haunted Houses: Supernatural Danger:* Always; The Amazing Mr. Blunden; The Amityville Horror; And Now the Screaming Starts; Back From the Dead; Beetlejuice; Blackbeard's Ghost; Blithe Spirit; Bloodbath at the House of Death; Candyman; Candyman: Farewell to the Flesh; The Canterville Ghost; Carousel; Casper; Castle Keep; The Changeling; A Christmas Carol (1938); Cold Heaven; Cold Sweat; Cooperstown; The Crow; The Curse of the Cat People; Dead of Night (1945); Dona Flor and Her Two Husbands; Down to Earth; Entity; Field of Dreams; The Fog; Foxfire (1987); Ghost; The Ghost and Mr. Chicken; The Ghost and Mrs. Muir; Ghost Breakers; The Ghost Goes West; Ghost Story; Ghostbusters; Ghostbusters 2; Green Man; A Guy Named Joe; Hamlet (1948); Hamlet (1964); Hamlet (1969); Hamlet (1991); Happy Land; Haunted Honeymoon; The Haunted Palace; The Haunting; Hearse; Hellbound: Hellraiser II; Hellraiser; Hellraiser III: Hell on Earth; High Spirits; Hold That Ghost; House of the Spirits; The Innocents; The Keep; Kiss Me Goodbye; Kwaidan; Lady in White; Legend of Hell House; Lovesick; Lucky Stiff; Man Alive; The Man Who Haunted Himself; Maxie; Miracle in the Rain; Muppet A Christmas Carol; Night unto Night; Night Walker; Night Watch; The Nightcomers; Nomads; O'Hara's Wife; Oh, Mr. Porter; Pandora and the Flying Dutchman; Poltergeist; Poltergeist 2; Poltergeist 3; Portrait of Jennie; Rashomon; Scared Stiff; The

Scoundrel; Scrooge (1935); Scrooge (1970); Scrooged; Shy People; Sylvia and the Ghost; Thunder Rock; Topper; Topper Returns; Topper Takes a Trip; Truly, Madly, Deeply; 2000 Maniacs; The Uninvited; Unseen Whisperers

Giants: see also *Fantasy: Shrinking People: SCI-FI:* Attack of the 50-Foot Woman (1958); Attack of the 50-Foot Woman (1993); The 30-Foot Bride of Candy Rock; Honey, I Blew Up the Kid; Jack and the Beanstalk; New York Stories; The Three Worlds of Gulliver; Village of Giants

Gifted Children: see *Children-Gifted: Children-Little Adults: Geniuses*

Gigolos: see *Prostitutes-Male*

Girlhood (about growing up as a girl): see also *Girls: Coming of Age: Teenage Movies: Girls' Schools:* Alan and Naomi; The Attic: The Hiding of Anne Frank; Beau Pere; The Best Little Girl in the World; Better Late Than Never; Bilitis; Birch Interval; Bunny Lake Is Missing; Cattle Annie and Little Britches; Celia; A Certain Smile; Chalk Garden; Corrina, Corrina; The Crash of Silence; Driftwood; Father Hood; Firestarter; First Love; Forbidden Games; Gaby, a True Story; Getting of Wisdom; Gidget; Gigi (1948); Gigi (1958); The Heart is a Lonely Hunter; Heidi (1939); The Honeymoon; I Saw What You Did; If I Had My Way; Jamaica Inn (1939); Jamaica Inn (1982); Jane Eyre (1934); Jane Eyre (1943); Jane Eyre (1971); The Journey of Natty Gann; Just Another Girl on the IRT; Kinjite, Forbidden Subjects; Kiss and Tell; Kiss for Corliss; The Little Rascals; The Little Thief; The Miracle Worker; Monkey Trouble; Moon Spinners; Mouchette; Music For Millions; Mystic Pizza; National Velvet; One in a Million; Our Vines Have Tender Grapes: Paperhouse; The Parent Trap; Peppermint Soda; Pippi Longstocking; Poison Ivy (1992); Pollyanna; Poor Little Rich Girl; The Positively True Adventures of the Alleged Texas Cheerleader-Murdering Mom; Puberty Blues; Rebecca of Sunnybrook Farm (1925); Rebecca of Sunnybrook Farm (1938); Red Kiss; Return to Oz; Scent of Mystery; The Secret Garden (1949); The Secret Garden (1984); The Secret Garden (1987); The Secret Garden (1993); She's Out of Control; Smile; Smooth Talk; Sorrowful Jones; Spitfire; Square Dance; Stand Up

and Cheer; Sudie and Simpson; Summer of My German Soldier; Sundays and Cybele; Sylvia and the Ghost; That Certain Age; Therese and Isabelle; 36 Fillette; Three Lives of Thomasina; Three Men and a Little Lady; Three Smart Girls; Three Smart Girls Grow Up; Thumbelina; To Kill a Mockingbird; Town Without Pity; A Tree Grows in Brooklyn; Troop Beverly Hills; The Trouble with Angels; Wildflower; The World of Henry Orient

Girls (girls as central characters): see also *Girlhood: Child Protagonists: Female Protagonists: Tomboys: Boys: Boyhood: Coming of Age:* Actors and Sin; Annie; Beaches; Belles of St. Trinians; Bellisima; Big Girls Don't Cry . . . They Get Even; Billie; The Blessing; Bright Eyes; Casper; Christiane F.; Circle of Friends; The Curse of the Cat People; Desert Bloom; Diary of Anne Frank (1959); Erendira; Fanny and Alexander; The Girl in the Watermelon; House of Cards; I Never Promised You A Rose Garden; Impudent Girl; In Country; International Velvet; Interview with the Vampire; Irreconcilable Differences; La Boum; Little Darlings; Little Dorrit; Little Miss Marker (1934); Little Miss Marker (1980); The Little Princess; Mad About Music; The Man in the Moon; A Member of the Wedding; Rich in Love; The Secret of Roan Inish; Where Angels Go, Trouble Follows; Wish You Were Here; The Wizard of Oz (1925); The Wizard of Oz (1939); A World Apart; Zelly and Me

Girls of Dreams: see *Elusive Women: Romance-Boy Wants Girl: Sexy Women: Bimbos: Beautiful People: Models*

Girl Scouts: see also *Girlhood: Camps/Camping: Boy Scouts:* Troop Beverly Hills

Girls' Schools: see also *Boarding Schools: Girlhood: Elementary School Life: Boys' Schools:* The Beguiled; The Children's Hour; Belles of St. Trinians; Bilitis; The Getting of Wisdom; The Happiest Days of Your Life; Jane Eyre (1934); Jane Eyre (1943); Jane Eyre (1971); The Little Princess; Picnic at Hanging Rock; The Prime of Miss Jean Brodie; Private School; St. Trinian's SERIES; These Three

Glamorous Men/Women: see *Beautiful People: Playboys: Bimbos: Bimboys: Sexy Men/Sexy Women: Fashion World: Models*

God (where God is either personified or His direct action plays a central role): see also *Biblical Stories: Jesus Christ: Religion:* Little Buddha; Oh, God; Oh God Book Two; Oh God, You Devil; Sacrifice; Stargate; The Ten Commandments; Wholly Moses

Gold Diggers: see also *Marrying Up:* Arrivederci, Baby!; Dynamite; Gentlemen Prefer Blondes; Give the Girl a Break; Gold Diggers in Paris; Gold Diggers of 1933; Gold Diggers of 1935; Gold Diggers of 1937; Gold Diggers of Broadway; Hands Across the Table; The Heiress; How to Marry a Millionaire; Moon Over Miami; The Richest Girl in the World; Three Blind Mice; Three Coins in the Fountain

Gold Mining: see also *Treasure Hunts: Jewel Thieves:* The Atomic Kid; The Ballad of Cable Hogue; Garden of Evil; Gold; Gold Rush; Kelly's Heroes; MacKenna's Gold; Million Dollar Duck; Mother Lode; North to Alaska; Paint Your Wagon; Painted Desert; Pale Rider; Ride the High Country; Rio Lobo; River of No Return; Road to Utopia; The Spoilers; Support Your Local Sheriff; Tall Men; Treasure of the Sierra Madre; Way Out West; White Fang

Going Home: see *Homecomings: Reunions*

Golf: see also *Country Club Life: Rich People: Suburban Life:* Banning; Caddy; Caddyshack; Caddyshack 2; Enter the Dragon; In Like Flint; Goldfinger; Once You Kiss a Stranger

Good Premise Unfulfilled (a good or great premise/idea behind the story which might be enough to interest you, but overall missed the mark): see also *Coulda Been Good: Coulda Been Great: Faded Hits: Forgotten Films:* The Accused (1948); Almost an Angel; Amos and Andrew; Another You; Avalanche Express; Backtrack; Baby's Day Out; Bank Shot; The Believers; Big Man On Campus; Black Caesar; Blind Fury; Blindfold: Acts of Obsession; Blink; The Bliss of Mrs. Blossom; Bound and Gagged, a Love Story; Brain Damage; Breakheart Pass; The Burglars; Cadillac Man; Cage of Gold; Calcutta; Callaway Went Thataway; Capricorn One; Carbon Copy; Carefree; A Case for Murder; Chase a Crooked Shadow; Cheaper to Keep Her; Checking Out; Chronicle of a Death Foretold; Closer; Cohen and Tate;

Color of Night; The Conspirator; Cookie; The Couch Trip; Crazy People; The Cutting Edge; A Dandy in Aspic; Dark of the Sun; Dead in the Water; Delirious; Demon Seed; Desire Me; Diamond Head; Diamonds for Breakfast; Die Laughing; A Different Story; Dirty Little Billy; Disorganized Crime; Doctor's Wives; Don't Just Stand There; Don't Tell Her It's Me; Dream Lover (1986); Dream Wife; Duchess and the Dirtwater Fox; Dudes; Dutch; Dying Room Only; Errand Boy; Experts; Fallen Angel; Fatso; Fear; Final Analysis; The Final Countdown; Firepower; The First Monday in October; First Power; First Time; Fitzwilly; Flashback; Flesh of the Orchid; Flight of the Navigator; Folks!; Foolin' Around; Forever Young; For Love of Ivy; Four's a Crowd; Freejack; Good Morning, Babylon; Gotham; Guarding Tess; Halloween 5: The Revenge of Michael Myers; The Hatchet Man; Heart Condition; Hell in the Pacific; Her Alibi; Hide in Plain Sight; High Risk; High Spirits; Honeymoon Machine; Hysteria; In the Mouth of Madness; Innerspace; Into the Sun; Island of Love; I Saw What You Did; I Stole a Million; It Ain't Hay; It Happens Every Thursday; Keep; The Key (1958); Key to the City; A Kid for Two Farthings; The Kill-Off; Killing Dad; King and Four Queens; Kiss Shot; Ladies' Man (1947); Lady on a Train; Ladyhawke; Lancer Spy; The Last Married Couple in America; Last Rites; The Last Run; Lightning Jack; Lily in Love; Living End; London Kills Me; Lost Man; Love at Large; Love Crimes; Love Potion #9; Lucky Night; Lucky Stiff; Mad Wednesday; Made in America; Madhouse; Madison Avenue; Magic Face; Magic Town; Maid to Order; The Main Event; Man on a Swing; The Man Without a Face; Marriage Go Round; Marrying Man; Meteor Man; Mikey and Nicky; Milk Money; Millennium; Miracles; Miranda; Miss Robin Hood; The Model and the Marriage Broker; Moon Over Parador; Mother, Jugs & Speed; The Move; Moving; Mr. Destiny; My Blue Heaven (1990); My Little Girl; My Wife's Best Friend; Mystery Train; The Naked Runner; The Name of the Rose; Necessary Roughness; Never a Dull Moment (1967); The Night Is Young; Night My Number Came Up; Night of the Generals; Night People; Night Terror;

Nightfall; No Time for Comedy; Norman, Is That You?; No Room for the Groom; Not with My Wife You Don't; Nous Sommes Tous les Assassins; Oh, Mr. Porter; Oh, Rosalinda!; Old Dracula; Once Upon a Honeymoon; Outrage (1964); Pass the Ammo; Paternity; Penelope; Perfect; Promises! Promises!; Rabbit Test; Reckless Moment; The Reincarnation of Peter Proud; Renaissance Man; Rented Lips; Repossessed; Rhinestone; Rollover; Royal Flash; Rude Awakening; Second Best Secret Agent in the Whole Wide World; Second Honeymoon; Second Sight; Secret Admirer; Secret Ceremony; The Secret Life of an American Wife; The Secret of My Success; See No Evil, Hear No Evil; Sender; Serial Mom; The Seventh Sign; Sextette; S.F.W.; Shanghai Surprise; Shrimp on the Barbie; Sibling Rivalry; Some Kind of a Nut; Speechless; Star Chamber; Stay Tuned; Sticky Fingers; Stop! Or My Mom Will Shoot; Straight out of Brooklyn; Strange Bedfellows; Stroker Ace; Super; Surrender; Sweet Liberty; Sweet November; Taking Care of Business; Tank; Timebomb; Toy Soldiers; Trapped in Paradise; True Identity; Twenty-Three Paces to Baker Street; Twilight's Last Gleaming; Under Suspicion; Under the Rainbow; Unsuitable Job For a Woman; The Unsuspected; Vampire's Kiss; W.H.I.F.F.S.; What a Way to Go; What's So Bad About Feeling Good?; Where Are the Children?; Whispers in the Dark; White Banners; White Buffalo; Witness to Murder; You Can Never Tell

Good vs. Evil: see also *Power Struggles:* Angel on My Shoulder; Angel Wore Red; Babes in Toyland (1934); Babes in Toyland (1961); Batman, The Movie; Beastmaster; Beastmaster 2; Behold a Pale Horse; Bend of the River; The Big Town; Cabin in the Sky; Captain America; The Care Bears Movie; Dark Crystal; Demon Knight; The Empire Strikes Back; Excalibur; The Exorcist; Exorcist II: Extreme Prejudice; Flash Gordon; The Heretic; Ice Pirates; In Old Arizona; Kismet (1944); Kismet (1955); Knights of the Round Table; The Mask of Fu Manchu; Never Love a Stranger; The Neverending Story; Neverending Story II: The Next Chapter; The Player; Return of the Jedi; The Rocketeer; Santa Claus, The Movie; Santa Fe; The Satan Bug; Scarface Mob/The

Untouchables Pilot; Sexton Blake and the Hooded Terror; Sleeping Beauty; Snow White and The Seven Dwarfs; The Stand; Star Trek II: The Wrath of Khan; Star Wars; Supergirl; Sword of the Valiant; Sword & the Sorcerer; The Unholy; The Wild Bunch

Gorillas: see *Primates*

Gossip/Gossips: see also *Journalists: Rumors: Scandal: Storytellers: Writers:* Bells Are Ringing; The Blessed Event; Cold Sassy Tree; A Fire in the Sky; French Lieutenant's Woman; The Grass is Always Greener Over the Septic Tank; Harper Valley P.T.A.; If Winter Comes; It Happens Every Thursday; Kill-Off; Ladies Should Listen; Love and Hisses; Love Thy Neighbor; The Naked Truth; SOB; Steel Magnolias

Gothic Style: see also *HORROR: Houses-Creepy: Southerns:* Ballad of the Sad Cafe; The Beguiled; Carnival of Souls; Die! Die! My Darling!; Doctor and the Devils; The Dunwich Horror; Evictors; Hound of the Baskervilles (1939); Hound of the Baskervilles (1959); Hound of the Baskervilles (1977); House of the Long Shadows; Hush, Hush, Sweet Charlotte; Jamaica Inn (1939); Jamaica Inn (1982); The Keep; Kwaidan; Lady in a Cage; The Little Foxes; Masque of the Red Death; The Night Has Eyes; Night of the Hunter; Obsession; See No Evil; Sister, Sister; Sleeping Beauty; Watcher in the Woods

Government as Enemy (where the government is the oppressor or villain): see also *Government Corruption: Conspiracy: CIA Agents: FBI Agents: Corporation as Enemy: Oppression: Futuristic Films: Nazi Stories:* Article 99; The Body Snatchers; Boss; Brainstorm (1983); Cheyenne Autumn; The China Syndrome; Deep Cover; Dreamscape; E.T.: The Extra-Terrestrial; Earth; Escape from the Planet of the Apes; A Few Good Men; The Fountainhead; Golden Years; The Groundstar Conspiracy; Hangar 18; Kissin' Cousins; The Lodger (1926); The Lodger (1932); The Lodger (1944); Logan's Run; Mastergate; The Mating Game; Million Dollar Duck; Missing; Mr. Drake's Duck; Murder in the First; 1984 (1955); 1984 (1984); Powwow Highway; The President's Analyst; Rage; The Rescue; Running on Empty; Scandalous John; The Shawshank Redemption; Soylent Green; Splash!; Star Chamber; Viva Villa!; Wild River; Winter Kills

Government Corruption (usually corruption within a government agency): see also *Government as Enemy: Corporate Corruption: Political Drama: Oppression:* Angel on My Shoulder; The Big Fix; Brainstorm (1983); Chattahoochee; Chinatown; City of Hope; The Detective (1968); Enemy of the People (1977); Enemy of the People (1989); The Falcon and the Snowman; Hurricane (1937); Hurricane (1979); Julius Caesar; Lion is in the Streets; Mr. Smith Goes to Washington; The Official Story; The Pelican Brief; Prince of the City; The Shawshank Redemption; Solarbabies; State of the Union; The Suspect; Time Cop

Governesses: see *Babysitters*

Graduate School: see *College Life: Law School: Professors*

Grandfathers-Fascinating: see also *Elderly Men: Eccentric People: Charismatic People:* The Adventures of Baron Munchausen (1987); Big Jake; Cold Sassy Tree; Dad; Dennis the Menace; The Family Business; Green Years; I'd Rather Be Rich; It Started with Eve; Kotch; Lies My Father Told Me; Little Lord Fauntleroy (1936); Little Lord Fauntleroy (1980); A Little Romance; The Magic of Lassie; Max Dugan Returns; Rocket Gibraltar; Roommates; Square Dance; Tokyo Story

Grandmothers-Fascinating: see also *Elderly Women: Eccentric People: Charismatic People:* Celia; A Christmas Memory; Flowers in the Attic; Inside Daisy Clover; The Other; Sweet Lorraine; Swing; Tokyo Story; Witches

Great Britain: see *British Films: Irish: England: Ireland: Wales: Scotland: Australia: Canada: New Zealand*

Great Scenery or Great Production Design: see *Production Design-Outstanding: Scenery-Outstanding*

Greece: see also *Mediterranean: Mythology:* The Beekeeper; Boy on a Dolphin; Clash of the Titans; The Day the Fish Came Out; Eleni; For the Love of Benji; For Your Eyes Only; Greek Tycoon; Hercules (1957); Hercules in New York; Hercules Unchained; High Season; Island of Love; The Magus; Never on Sunday; New York Stories; Oedipus Rex; Tempest; 300 Spartans; The Trojan War; Trojan Women; The Warrior's Husband; Zorba, The Greek

Greed: see also *Murder for Money: Corruption: Corporate Corruption: Government Corruption: Treasure Hunts: Ethics: Rich People:* Ace in the Hole; Arrowsmith; The Bad and the Beautiful; The Ballad of Cable Hogue; The Bonfire of the Vanities; The Border; Brewster's Millions (1935); Brewster's Millions (1945); Brewster's Millions (1985); Chinatown; Clean and Sober; Dr. Faustus; A Face in the Crowd; Five Star Final; Flesh of the Orchid; Gay Sisters; The Good Earth; A Good Man in Africa; Greed; Greedy; Inheritance; It Could Happen to You; Julius Caesar; Just Tell Me What You Want; King Lear (1971); Little Noises; Network; Night Gallery; Other People's Money; Painted Desert; Payment Deferred; Pearl; The Player; Power; The Prodigal; Quiz Show; Ready to Wear; S.F.W.; The Shawshank Redemption; Six Degrees of Separation; Strange Bargain; Sweet Smell of Success; A Taxing Woman; Tillie and Gus; Treasure of the Sierra Madre; True Colors; Volpone; Wall Street; Wayne's World; Wayne's World 2

Green Cards: see *Marriage for Citizenship*

Greenwich Village/Soho: see also *New York Life: Artists: Writers: Gay Men: Lesbians: Alternative Lifestyles:* Desperately Seeking Susan; Flesh; Fun Down There; Funny Face; Greenwich Village; Me, Natalie; My Sister Eileen (1942); My Sister Eileen (1955); Next Stop, Greenwich Village; A Night to Remember (1946); Reds; Slaves of New York

Groups: see *Ensemble Casts: Reunions: Family Stories: Families-Extended*

Guilty Conscience: see also *Murder-Debate to Confess: Murder-Debate to Reveal Killer: Ethics: Redemption: Psychological Drama:* American Dream; Avenging Conscience; Bitch (La Garce) (1984); Black Orpheus; Cal Carey Treatment; Crime and Punishment; Crimes and Misdemeanors; Edge of Doom; Fearless; The Fisher King; Ghost Story; Hallelujah!; The Hatchet Man; I Love My Wife; The Informer; The Inspector Calls; Investigation of a Citizen Above Suspicion; Joe; The Kiss (1929); Larceny, Inc.; Leap of Faith; Loving; Magnificent Obsession (1935); Magnificent Obsession (1954); Melo; Mourning Becomes Electra; Red House; They Made Me a Criminal; To Have and Have Not; The Velvet Touch

Hairdressers: see also *Ordinary People Stories: Working Class:* Business as Usual; The Crying Game; Earth Girls are Easy; Educating Rita; Getting It Right; The Great Dictator; The Hairdresser's Husband; Love Field; Monsieur Beaucaire; Nadine; Shampoo; The Staircase; Steel Magnolias; Sweeney Todd, Demon Barber of Fleet Street; Twice in a Lifetime; Wish You Were Here

Halloween: see also *HORROR: Serial Killers:* The Addams Family; Addams Family Values; Halloween SERIES; The Nightmare Before Christmas

Hallucinations: see *Illusions/ Hallucinations*

Handicapped People: see *Disabled People: Disabled People in Jeopardy: Blind People: Deaf People*

Hand-Me-Down Stories (stories in which things are passed along and the stories of their owners are told): see also *Multiple Stories: Episodic Stories:* Baxter (1990); Black Beauty (1946); Black Beauty (1971); Black Beauty (1994); Cat's Eye; La Ronde (1950); La Ronde (1964); Paris Model; Secret Admirer; Tales of Manhattan; Twenty Bucks; Yellow Rolls Royce

Hangings: see *Executions: Lynchings/Lynch Mobs: Posses: WESTERNS*

Happy Endings: see *Conservative Value Films: Old-Fashioned Recent Films: CHILDREN'S: FAMILY*

Hard to Get-Playing: see *Romance-Reluctant: Elusive Men: Elusive Women: Opposites Attract*

Harvard Settings: see also *Boston: College Life: Intellectuals:* Love Story (1970); Mystery Street; Small Circle of Friends; The Way We Were

Hate Crimes: see *Anti-Semitism: Homophobia: Bigots: Oppression: Gay Men: Lesbians: Murders of Homosexuals: Nazi Stories: Ku Klux Klan: Race Relations: Black vs. White: Civil Rights*

Haunted by the Past: see *Past-Haunted by the:* also *Secrets-Consuming: Secrets-Keeping*

Haunted Houses: see also *Houses-Creepy: Ghosts: Afterlife: Supernatural: Possessions:* Amityville 1992: It's About Time; Amityville 4; Amityville, a New Generation; The Amityville Curse; The Amityville Horror; Amityville Horror 2, The Possession; The Avenging Conscience; Beetlejuice; Bloodbath at the House of Death; Burnt Offerings; Casper; Cat People (1942); The Changeling; The Evictors; The Ghost and Mrs. Muir; Ghost Breakers; The Ghost Goes West; Ghost in the Invisible Bikini; Ghost Story; Haunted Honeymoon; The Haunted Palace; The Haunting; Hearse; High Spirits; Hold That Ghost; House; House II: The Second Story; House III; House IV; House of the Long Shadows; The House That Dripped Blood; Legend of Hell House; Mark of the Vampire; Night unto Night; Night Walker; Night Watch; The Nightcomers; Poltergeist; Poltergeist 2; Poltergeist 3; Scared Stiff; The Uninvited

Having a Baby: see *Babies-Having*

Hawaii: see also *Exotic Locales: Vacations: Islands:* Aloha Summer; Black Widow; Blue Hawaii; Castaway Cowboy; Diamond Head; From Here to Eternity; Hawaii; The Hawaiians; Love in a Goldfish Bowl; Tora! Tora! Tora!; Waikiki Wedding; When Time Ran Out

Heaven: see also *Afterlife: Angels: Hell: Biblical Stories:* All Dogs Go to Heaven; Almost an Angel; Altered States; Always; The Blue Bird (1940); The Blue Bird (1976); Cabin in the Sky; Defending Your Life; Down to Earth; Green Pastures; Heaven; Heaven Can Wait (1943); Heaven Can Wait (1978); The Heavenly Kid; Here Comes Mr. Jordan; The Horn Blows at Midnight; J'Accuse; Made in Heaven; Oh, God; Oh God Book Two; Oh God, You Devil; Peter Ibbetson; Resurrection; Stairway to Heaven; Two of a Kind; Ziegfeld Follies

Heiresses: see also *Heiresses-Madcap: Rich People: Inheritances at Stake:* Breakfast for Two; The Bride Came C.O.D.; Chase (1994); Dark Angel (1991); Death on the Nile; Easy to Wed; Eyes in the Night; Fog over Frisco; The Fortune; Goin' To Town; The Heiress; Helter Skelter (1949); High Road to China; I'd Rather Be Rich; Invitation; Katherine; Libeled Lady; Loose Ankles; Lorna Doone; Love Affair (1932); Lucky Night; Million Dollar Baby; The Millionairess; My Name is Julia Ross; New Leaf; On Approval; Overboard; Patty Hearst; The Philadelphia Story; Richest Girl in the World; She Couldn't Say No; Stolen Hours; Sudden Fear; Suspicion; Yolanda and the Thief

Heiresses-Madcap: see also *Screwball Comedy: Feisty Women: Wild People:* Bringing Up Baby; The Cowboy and the Lady; It Happened One Night; Libeled Lady; Love on the Run (1936); My Man Godfrey (1936); My Man Godfrey (1956); You Can't Run Away From It

Heirs: see also *Inheritances at Stake: Rich People:* Brewster's Millions (1935); Brewster's Millions (1945); Brewster's Millions (1985); Carousel; Cheyenne Social Club; Half a Sixpence; Kangaroo; King Ralph; Kipps; Little Big League; Monkeys Go Home; Mr. Billion; Mrs. Brown, You've Got a Lovely Daughter; Random Harvest; Speak Easily; Stay Hungry

Heist Stories: see also *Thieves: Bank Robberies: Art Thieves: Jewel Thieves: Con Artists:* The Adventures of Arsene Lupin; After The Fox; Airport 1977; The Anderson Tapes; Arsene Lupin; Arsene Lupin Returns; The Asphalt Jungle; Bad Man's River; Bank Shot; Belle of the Yukon; Bellman and True; Big Deal on Madonna Street; Big Mouth; Biggest Bundle of Them All; Blue Collar; Blue Ice; Bob le Flambeur; Boxcar Bertha; Brain; Brass Target; Breakheart Pass; The Brink's Job; The Burglars; Buster; Butch and Sundance, The Early Days; Butch Cassidy and the Sundance Kid; Cairo (1963); Charley Varrick; Cold Feet; Colorado Territory; Cliffhanger; Crackers; Criss Cross (1947); Dark of the Sun; Dead Heat on a Merry Go Round; Deadfall (1968); Diamonds for Breakfast; Disorganized Crime; Dollars; Duchess and the Dirtwater Fox; Eleven Harrowhouse; F/X 2: The Deadly Art of Illusion; The Family Business; Family Plot; The Fiendish Plot of Dr. Fu Manchu; A Fish Called Wanda; A Fistful of Dynamite; Flashpoint; Four for Texas; Fun With Dick and Jane; Gambit; The Getaway (1972); The Getaway (1994); Go Chase Yourself; Going in Style; The Good Die Young; The Great Bank Hoax; The Great Bank Robbery; The Great Muppet Caper; The Great Northfield Minnesota Raid; Green Ice; Grey Fox; The Grifters; Happy New Year (1973); Happy New Year (1987); Harley Davidson and the Marlboro Man; Harry and Walter Go to New York; The Honeymoon Machine; Hot Millions; The Hot Rock; How to Beat the High Cost of Living; How to Steal a Million; Hudson Hawk; I Died a Thousand Times; The Italian Job; Jack of Diamonds; Kansas City Confidential; Kelly's Heroes; Killer Fish; The Killing; Killing Zoe; Kiss Tomorrow Goodbye; Larceny, Inc.; The Lavender Hill Mob; Law and Disorder (1958); League of Gentlemen; Live a Little, Steal a Lot; Loophole; Mackintosh Man; Man, a Woman and a Bank; The Man Who Loved Cat Dancing; The Man Who Watched Trains Go By; Modesty Blaise; Montana Belle; Moon Spinners; Mountain; A Nice Little Bank That Should Be Robbed; Nightfall; Oh, Mr. Porter; Only When I Larf; Operation Amsterdam; Our Man Flint; The Pink Panther; Pulp Fiction; Quick Change; Rage in Harlem; Real McCoy; Reservoir Dogs; Ride the High Country; Rififi; Rio Lobo; Rough Cut; Rounders; Scotland Yard; Seven Thieves; Shanghai Surprise; Silent Partner; Silver Bears; Sneakers; Special Delivery; The Sting; Take the Money and Run; That Darn Cat!; That Man From Rio; They Drive by Night (1940); The Thief Who Came to Dinner; Thomas Crown Affair; Three Fugitives; Thunderbolt and Lightfoot; Topkapi!; Tough Guys; Two Way Stretch; Virginia City; Who's Minding the Mint?; Why Me?; Wrecking Crew; You've Got to Live Dangerously

Hell: see also *Satan: Afterlife: Heaven: Soul-Selling One's:* All That Money Can Buy; Altered States; Bill & Ted's Bogus Journey; The Devil and Max Devlin; The Gate; The Gate II; Heaven Can Wait (1943); Hellbound: Hellraiser II; Hellraiser; Hellraiser III: Hell on Earth; 976-Evil; Rawhead Rex; The Sentinel; Stay Tuned; Wings of Fame

Heritage-Finding Roots: see *Family/Heritage-Search for:* also *Family Drama: Sagas: Historical Drama*

Hermits: see *Lonely People*

Heroes-General/Classic: see *Heroes-Ordinary: Comic Heroes: Mythology*

Heroes-Ordinary/Unwitting: see also *Ordinary People Stories: Impostors:* Cobb; Die Hard; The Fixer; The Frisco Kid (1979); Geronimo (1962); Geronimo (1993); Hail the Conquering Hero; Kid from Brooklyn; Man of Marble; The Man Who Shot Liberty Valance; Milky Way (1936); Mr. Deeds Goes to Town; Norma Rae; Patriot Games; Shane; Silkwood; Spider's Stratagem; This Land Is Mine; To Hell and Back; Who Done It? (1942); Who Done It? (1957)

Heroes-Superhuman: see *Comic/Superhuman Heroes*

Heroes-Unlikely: see also *Heroes-False: Ordinary People Stories:* The Adventures of Bullwhip Griffin; The African Queen; Big Man On Campus; The Boatniks; D.C. Cab; Darkman; Dream Team; Four Feathers (1929); Four Feathers (1939); Gunga Din; Hail the Conquering Hero; Heavens Above; Hero; Hero at Large; Hombre; Hornet's Nest; I'm All Right, Jack; It All Came True; Jabberwocky; Jimmy Hollywood; The Legend of Billie Jean; Lucky Star; The Man Who Shot Liberty Valance; Meteor Man; Miles From Home; Nothing but Trouble (1941); Nothing Sacred; Protocol; Schindler's List; Sea Wolf; The Secret War of Harry Frigg; Sergeant York; Seventh Cavalry; The Shakiest Gun in the West; Shocking Miss Pilgrim; Sky Devils; Solid Gold Cadillac; Some Kind of a Nut; Son of Lassie; Spartacus; Storm in a Teacup; Straight Talk; Subway; Targets; The Thief of Bagdad (1924); The Thief of Baghdad (1940); Tom Thumb; Toxic Avenger; Toxic Avenger, Part II; Toxic Avenger Part III; Under Siege; The Unsinkable Molly Brown; Von Ryan's Express; Wild in the Streets; Wings in the Dark

Heroines (females doing battle as the males would): see also *ACTION: Female Protagonists: Female in Male Domain:* Alien; Aliens; Alien 3; Annie Get Your Gun; Belle Starr; Hannie Caulder; The River Wild; Silence of the Lambs

Hexes: see *Occult/Mysticism:* also
Witchcraft: Satanism

**Hidden Gems (hard-to-find films that
you may not be aware of, but that
are well worth checking into): see
also** *Forgotten Films: Film History:*
Aaron Slick from Punkin Crick; About
Face; Ace in the Hole; Adventure for Two;
The Adventures of Reinette and
Mirabelle; The Adventures of Sadie; The
Advocate; After Dark, My Sweet; After
Hours; Alan and Naomi; All Night Long
(1981); All That Money Can Buy;
Ambulance; Andre's Mother; The
Andromeda Strain; Angel on My
Shoulder; Anna; Another Woman;
Apartment Zero; April Fools; Arsenic and
Old Lace; The Assassination Bureau;
Atlantic City; Avanti!; The Awful Truth;
Babette's Feast; Baby Boom; Baby Doll;
Babysitter; The Bachelor; Bachelor and
the Bobby-Soxer; Bachelor Party (1957);
Bad Day at Black Rock; Based on an
Untrue Story; Battle of the Sexes; Beau
Pere; Bedlam; The Beguiled; Behave
Yourself!; Better Off Dead; Between Two
Women; Big Knife; Bitter Moon; Bitter
Tears of Petra Von Kant; Blame it on the
Bellboy; The Bliss of Mrs. Blossom; Blood
of a Poet; Blood Simple; Blow Up; Blue
Collar; Blue Sky; Bombshell; Boom!;
Boomerang (1947); Born to Kill; Boudu
Saved From Drowning; Bound For Glory;
Boy on a Dolphin; Breakfast for Two;
Breaking the Sound Barrier; The Bride of
Frankenstein; The Bridge of San Luis
Rey; A Brief History of Time; Brimstone
and Treacle; The Brink's Job; Broadway
Danny Rose; The Browning Version;
Cabin in the Sky; Call Me Genius;
Camilla (1994); Candy; Captive Heart;
Cardinal; Carefree; Careful, He Might
Hear You; Carmen Jones; Carousel; Carrie
(1952); Casanova (Fellini's Casanova);
Casque d'Or; Castaway Cowboy; Cat and
Mouse; Cat People (1942); Cattle Annie &
Little Britches; Cavalcade; Celia; Chalk
Garden; Champagne for Caesar;
Champion; Chan is Missing; Chapman
Report; Charley Varrick; Charley's Aunt;
Charlie Bubbles; Charlotte's Web; Cheers
for Miss Bishop; Cheyenne Social Club; A
Child is Waiting; Children of Paradise;
Chloe in the Afternoon; Choice of Arms;
Christ Stopped at Eboli; Christmas in
Connecticut (1945); Christmas in July;
Circle of Friends; City of Hope; City

Streets; Claudelle Inglish; Cloak and
Dagger (1984); Clockwise; Cluny Brown;
Cold Sassy Tree; The Collector; Come to
the Stable; The Comedians; Comedy of
Terrors; Compromising Positions; A
Connecticut Yankee; Conrack;
Continental Divide; The Conversation;
Convicts; The Corn is Green (1945); The
Corn is Green (1979); Cotton Comes to
Harlem; Court Jester; Courtship; Cousin,
Cousine; Cousins; Cover Girl; The
Cowboy and the Lady; Cries and
Whispers; Crimes of the Heart; Criss
Cross (1947); Crossfire; The Crowd;
D.O.A. (1949); Daddy Nostaglia; Daddy's
Dyin'; Daddy's Gone A-Hunting; Dark
Crystal; Darling; David and Lisa; A Day
in the Death of Joe Egg; Day of the
Locust; Deadly Affair; Dear America:
Letters Home from Vietnam; Dear Heart;
Dear Inspector; Dear Ruth; Death in
Brunswick; Death Watch; Deep Cover;
Designing Woman; Desperate Characters;
Desperate Living; Detective Story; Detour;
The Devil and Miss Jones; Devil Doll;
The Devils; Diabolique (1955); Diary for
My Children; Diary of a Mad Housewife;
Dion Brothers; Disorderly Orderly; Doc
Hollywood; Doctor Takes a Wife;
Dogfight; Don't Look Now; Dona Flor and
Her Two Husbands; Doughgirls; Dr.
Cyclops; Dr. Phibes Rises Again; Dr.
Socrates; Dreams That Money Can Buy;
The Dresser; Dynamite; Easy Living
(1937); Eating Raoul; The Effect of
Gamma Rays on Man-in-the-Moon
Marigolds; El Norte; Encore; End of the
Road; Experienced Preferred . . .; A Face
in the Crowd; Faces; Fahrenheit 451; Fail
Safe; Falling in Love Again; Family Plot;
The Farmer's Daughter; Fat City; Father
Goose; Fearless; Fedora; Finders Keepers;
A Fine Madness; Fingers; Finian's
Rainbow; The Fireman's Ball; Five Came
Back; Five Corners; The Five Fingers;
Five Graves to Cairo; Five Miles to
Midnight; Five Star Final; Five Thousand
Fingers of Doctor T.; Flame and the
Arrow; Flight of the Phoenix; The Flim
Flam Man; Flirting; Flower Drum Song;
Foolish Wives; Fools for Scandal; The
Fools' Parade; Footlight Parade;
Forbidden Planet; Force of Evil; A
Foreign Affair; Foreign Correspondent;
The Fortune; Fortune Cookie; The
Fountainhead; Four Daughters; The 400
Blows; The Four Seasons; Fourteen

Hours; The Fox; Foxfire (1987); Frances;
Francis, God's Jester; Frantic (1958);
Freaks; Frenzy; The Freshman (1925);
The Freshman (1990); Friendly
Persuasion; From This Day Forward; A
Funny Thing Happened on the Way to the
Forum; Fury (1936); Fuzz; Gabriel over
the White House; Gaily, Gaily; Gambling
Lady; Garbo Talks; Garden of the Finzi-
Continis; Gaslight (1939); The General;
The General Died at Dawn; George
Washington Slept Here; Georgy Girl; Get
Carter; Get Out Your Handkerchiefs; The
Getting of Wisdom; The Ghost and Mrs.
Muir; Ghost Breakers; The Ghost Goes
West; Gilda; Gilda Live; The Gin Game;
The Girl Most Likely to . . . (1971); Girl
with Green Eyes; Glamour Boy; Glass
Bottom Boat; Glass House; Gloria; Glory!
Glory!; Go for Broke; Go-Between; God's
Little Acre; Goddess; Goin' To Town;
Going in Style; Gold Rush; Golden Boy;
Golden Braid; Good Companions (1933);
Good Companions (1956); The Good Die
Young; The Good Fairy; The Good Father;
The Good Mother; Good Neighbor Sam;
Goodbye Again; Goodbye Mr. Chips
(1939); Goodbye Mr. Chips (1969); The
Gospel According to St. Matthew; Grace
Quigley; Grand Highway; Grand Illusion;
The Grass is Always Greener Over the
Septic Tank; The Great Dictator; Great
Expectations; The Great Garrick; The
Great Impostor; The Great Lie; The Great
Lover (1949); The Great McGinty; The
Great Race; The Great Waltz (1938); The
Great White Hope; Greed; Green Card;
Green Eyes; Green Fire; Green for
Danger; Green Pastures; Green Years;
Gremlins 2: The New Batch; The Grey
Fox; The Group; The Guardsman; The
Guest Wife; A Guide for the Married Man;
Guilty Conscience; Gun Crazy (1950);
Gun Crazy (1992); A Guy Named Joe;
Hail the Conquering Hero; The Hair-
dresser's Husband; Hallelujah!; Handle
with Care; A Handmaid's Tale; Hands
Across the Table; Happiest Days of Your
Life; Happy Ending; Happy New Year
(1973); Happy New Year (1987); Happy
Time; The Hard Way (1943); Harley
Davidson and the Marlboro Man; Harold
and Maude; Harold Lloyd's World of
Comedy; The Haunting; Health; Heart
Beat; The Heart is a Lonely Hunter;
Heartbreak Kid; Heartland; Heat and
Dust; Heaven Can Wait (1943); Heaven

Help Us; Heaven Knows, Mr. Allison; Hedda; The Heiress; Heller in Pink Tights; Hellzapoppin; Hemingway's Adventures of a Young Man; Henry: Portrait of a Serial Killer; Here Comes Mr. Jordan; Here We Go Round the Mulberry Bush; Hester Street; The Hidden; High Pressure; High Sierra; The Hired Wife; Hiroshima, Mon Amour; Hitler Gang; Hobson's Choice; Hold Me, Thrill Me, Kiss Me; Hold That Ghost; Hold Your Man; Hombre; Home from the Hill; Homicide; The Honeymoon Killers; Hope and Glory; Hopscotch; Horn Blows at Midnight; The Horse's Mouth; The Hospital; Hot Millions; The Hot Rock; Hotel Paradiso; House Calls; House of Games; The House of Seven Gables; Housekeeping; Housesitter; How to Succeed in Business without Really Trying; The Hucksters; Hud; The Hunger; I Found Stella Parish; I Love You to Death; I Never Sang for My Father; I Passed for White; I Vitelloni; I Wake Up Screaming; I Was a Male War Bride; If I Were King; Ikiru; In a Lonely Place; In Search of the Castaways; The Incredible Journey of Dr. Meg Laurel; The Inquisitor; Inside Moves; Intruder in the Dust; The Invisible Woman; Iron Petticoat; It All Came True; It Grows on Trees; It Happened in Brooklyn; It Happened Tomorrow; It Happens Every Spring; It Should Happen to You; It's a Great Feeling; J'Accuse; Jack's Back; Joan of Paris; John and Mary; Johnny Angel; Johnny Eager; Johnny Stecchino; Joshua Then and Now; Jour de Fete; Journey into Fear; The Journey of Natty Gann; Joy of Living; June Bride; Just Tell Me What You Want; Just You and Me; The Kennel Murder Case; Kes; The Killing of a Chinese Bookie; Killjoy; Kind Hearts and Coronets; The Kindred; The King; The King of Comedy; King of Hearts; The King of Jazz; King of the Hill (1993); King, Queen, Knave; Kipps; Kiss Me Deadly; Kiss of Death (1947); Kitty; Knock on Wood; La Chevre; La Chienne; La Lectrice; La Nuit de Varennes; La Ronde (1950); La Ronde (1964); La Strada; La Vie de Boheme; Ladies in Retirement; The Lady in Question; Lady in White; Lady of Burlesque; Lady on a Train; Ladykillers; The Landlord; The Last Angry Man; The Last Command; Last Exit to Brooklyn; The Last of Sheila; Last of the Red Hot Lovers; Last Valley; The

Last Wave; Late for Dinner; The Late Show; Laughter; Laurel Avenue; The Lavender Hill Mob; Law and Disorder (1958); Le Corbeau; Le Million; League of Gentlemen; Legend of Hell House; The Legend of Lylah Clare; Les Biches; Les Comperes; Les Enfants Terribles; Les Visiteurs du Soir; Let's Make it Legal; Let's Make Love; The Libeled Lady; Life and Nothing But; The Life of Emile Zola; Lili; Limbo; Limelight; The Little Girl Who Lives Down the Lane; Little Man Tate; Little Noises; The Little Princess; A Little Romance; Little Shop of Horrors (1986); Local Hero; London Belongs to Me; The Lonely Guy; The Long, Good Friday; Lord Love a Duck; Lorenzo's Oil; Lost in America; The Lost Language of Cranes; Lost Moment; The Louisiana Purchase; Love Among the Ruins; Love Crazy; Love Me Tonight; Love With the Proper Stranger; The Loved One; Lovin' Molly; The Luck of the Irish; Lust for Life; Mad Love; Mad Miss Manton; Magic Town; Mamma Rosa; The Man from Snowy River; The Man in the Grey Flannel Suit; Man in the White Suit; A Man of No Importance; The Man Who Came to Dinner; The Man Who Could Work Miracles; The Man with Two Brains; Marat/Sade; The Marriage of a Young Stockbroker; Marty; Masculine, Feminine; The Masquerader; Matewan; Matter of Time; Maybe I'll Be Home in the Spring; McClintock!; Mean Streets; Melvin and Howard; The Men (1950); Menace II Society; Menage; Merrily We Live; Miami Blues; Mickey One; Middle of the Night; Mike's Murder; Min and Bill; Miracle (1948); Mirage; Miranda; Miss Firecracker; Mississippi Mermaid; Mister 880; Mister Buddwing; Modern Times; The Moderns; Modigliani; Monkey Business (1952); Monsieur Hire; Monsieur Hulot's Holiday; Montenegro; The More the Merrier; Morgan!; The Most Dangerous Game; Mouchette; Mountains on the Moon; Mr. Klein; Mr. and Mrs. Bridge; Mrs. Parker and the Vicious Circle; Murder by Natural Causes; Murder, He Says; The Music Lovers; My Beautiful Laundrette; My Bodyguard; My Father's Glory; My Favorite Blonde; My Favorite Brunette; My Favorite Spy; My Favorite Wife; My Favorite Year; My Forbidden Past; My Mother's Castle; My Sister Eileen (1942); Myra Breckinridge; The Mystery of the Wax Museum; Mystery

Street; Nadine; Naked in New York; The Naked Prey; The Naked Spur; The Naked Truth; Nanny; Nashville; Nasty Girl; Nasty Habits; Network; Never Give a Sucker an Even Break; New York, New York; Niagara; The Night Has Eyes; Night of the Hunter; Night of the Shooting Stars; A Night to Remember (1946); 1918; 9/30/55; 92 in the Shade; No Down Payment; No Sex, Please, We're British; No Time for Comedy; No Time for Sergeants; No Way to Treat a Lady; Not of This Earth (1956); Nothin' But a Man; Nothing But the Best; Nothing Sacred; The Notorious Landlady; Nudo di Donna; The Nun's Story; O.C. and Stiggs; Oblomov; The October Man; Odd Man Out; Of Human Hearts; The Offence; The Official Story; Oh, Dad, Poor Dad . . .; Oh Men! Oh Women!; Old Acquaintance; Old Dark House (1932); Old Dark House (1962); Old Man and the Sea; Olly Olly Oxen Free; The Omega Man; On a Clear Day You Can See Forever; On Approval; On the Air; Once Upon a Crime; One False Move; One Magic Christmas; One, Two, Three!; The Onion Field; Only Angels Have Wings; Only Two Can Play; Open City; Opening Night; Orpheus Descending; Oscar Ossessione; Our Hospitality; Our Man in Havana; Our Relations; Our Town; Our Vines Have Tender Grapes; Out of the Past; Over Her Dead Body; The Owl and the Pussycat; The Ox-Bow Incident; Pain in the A . . .; The Pajama Game; Palm Beach Story; Paperhouse; Parents; Paris When it Sizzles; The Party; Party Girl; Patch of Blue; The Pathfinder; Paths of Glory; Patterns; The Pawnbroker; The Pedestrian; Peeping Tom; Pelle the Conqueror; Pennies from Heaven (1981); People Will Talk; The Performance; Period of Adjustment; Peter's Friends; The Petrified Forest; Petulia; The Phantom Tollbooth; Pickup on South Street; Pixote; Playing for Time; Plenty; The Ploughman's Lunch; Point Blank; Portrait of Jennie; The Positively True Adventures of the Alleged Texas Cheerleader-Murdering Mom; Power, Passion, and Murder; Presenting Lily Mars; Pretty Poison; Prick Up Your Ears; The Prince of Central Park; Prince of the City; Private Function; The Projectionist; Promise Her Anything; Public Eye; Quartet (1948); Quartet (1981); Queen Bee; The Quiet Wedding; Rachel, Rachel;

Frank (1959); E.T.: The Extra-Terrestrial; Fancy Pants; Flight of the Doves; The Flim Flam Man; Force of Evil; The Frenchman's Creek; Gun Crazy (1950); Gun Crazy (1992); Hider in the House; His Girl Friday; Hold Me, Thrill Me, Kiss Me; Hopscotch; How to Be Very Very Popular; The Hunted; Island of Love; Isle of the Dead; It All Came True; It Always Rains on Sunday; Just One of the Girls; Key Largo; Kiss the Blood Off My Hands; The Last Metro; Lightship; Lorna Doone; The Lost Man; Magic; Malone; Monster Squad; Night of the Hunter; Nuns on the Run; Odd Man Out; Opportunity Knocks; A Prayer for the Dying; Revolt of Job; Ritz; Saint Benny, the Dip; Salome, Where She Danced; Scene of the Crime; The Secret of Santa Vittoria; Seems Like Old Times; September Affair; Serpent's Egg; Shame (1987); She Loves Me Not; Shining Through; The Shop on Main Street; Sister Act; Sleeping With the Enemy; A Song is Born; The Stranger; Survivors; Swamp Water; Sweet Bird of Youth; We're No Angels (1955); We're No Angels (1989); When in Rome; Whistle Down the Wind; Witness; You Can't Run Away From It

Hiding-Keeping Someone in: see *FARCE: COMEDY: Hiding Out: Witnesses: Saving Someone*

High-Rise Settings: see also *Urban Life:* Die Hard; King Kong; The Towering Inferno; Poltergeist 3

High School Life: see also *Elementary School Life: College Life: Coming of Age: Teenagers: Teenage Movies:* The Affairs of Dobie Gillis; The Best Little Girl in the World; Better Off Dead; Breakfast Club; Can't Buy Me Love; Carrie (1976); The Chicken Chronicles; Class Act; Class of 1999; Class of '84; Dazed and Confused; Encino Man; The Ernest Green Story; Fame; Fast Times at Ridgemont High; Ferris Bueller's Day Off; Foxes; Friends Forever; Grease; Grease 2; Gregory's Girl; Happy Birthday to Me; Hoop Dreams; Hoosiers; How I Got Into College; Just One of the Girls; Just One of the Guys; Lean on Me; Listen to Me; Murder in New Hampshire; Peggy Sue Got Married; Permanent Record; Plain Clothes; Porky's; Porky's 2; Porky's Revenge; Prom Night SERIES; Pump Up the Volume; Rebel Without a Cause;

Rock n' Roll High School; Secret Admirer; Sing; Some Kind of Wonderful; Stand and Deliver; Strike Up the Band; Substitute; Teachers; Terminal Bliss; Three O'Clock High; To Sir with Love; Wild Life; Zebrahead

Hijackings (of planes, trains, etc.): see also *Heist Stories: Thieves:* Autobus; China Seas; Cliffhanger; Delta Force; Gun Fury; High-Ballin'; Mademoiselle Fifi; Mantrap; Rawhide; Skyjacked; Under Siege

Hillbillies (in keeping with the older moonshine stereotype): see also *Rednecks: Country Life: Mountain People: Mountain Settings: Southerns:* Annie Get Your Gun!; The Beverly Hillbillies; Boxcar Bertha; Deliverance; The Egg and I; I Walk the Line; Kentucky Moonshine; Kissin' Cousins; Li'l Abner; Lolly Madonna War; Ma and Pa Kettle; Moonshine War; Murder, He Says; No Time for Sergeants; Sergeant York; Shepherd of the Hills; Spitfire; Tammy and the Bachelor; Thunder Road

Himalayas: see also *Mountain Climbing: Asia: China:* The Abominable Snowman; Black Narcissus; High Road to China; K-2; Razor's Edge (1946); Razor's Edge (1986)

Hippies: see also *1960s: Anti-Establishment Films: Psychedelic Era: Vietnam Era: Alternative Lifestyles: Environmental Dilemmas:* Alice's Restaurant; Baby Maker; Born Losers; Breezy; Butterflies are Free; Daddy's Dyin'; Drugstore Cowboy; Easy Rider; Flashback; Gassss; Generation; Godspell; The Happening; Hospital; I Love You, Alice B. Toklas; Inside Monkey Zetterland; Joe; Knightriders; Mosquito Coast; Out of the Blue; Psych-Out; Rude Awakening; Running on Empty; Skidoo Tribes; True Believer; Two Lane Blacktop; Valley Obscured by the Clouds; Wild in the Streets; Woodstock; Yellow Submarine

Hired Dates: see also *Dating Scene: Prostitutes:* Can't Buy Me Love; Castaway; For Love of Ivy; Guest Wife; It Started with Eve; Milk Money; Passionate Plumber; Shrimp on the Barbie; Three of Hearts

Hispanic People: see *Latin People*

Historical Drama: see also *Ancient Times: Costume Drama: Epics:* The Abdication; Abe Lincoln in Illinois; Above and Beyond; Abraham Lincoln;

Adventures of Casanova; The Adventures of Marco Polo; The Advocate; The Agony and the Ecstasy; Alamo; Alexander Nevsky; Alexander the Great; All the Mornings of the World; Anastasia (1984); Anne of the Thousand Days; Anthony Adverse; Apollo 13; The Assassination of Trotsky; The Attic: The Hiding of Anne Frank; The Autobiography of Miss Jane Pittman; The Barbarian and the Geisha; The Barretts of Wimpole Street (1934); The Barretts of Wimpole Street (1956); Barry Lyndon; Beau Brummell (1924); Beau Brummell (1954); Becket; Being Human; Ben-Hur (1959); Ben-Hur: A Tale of Christ (1925); Big Fisherman; Billy Budd; The Birth of a Nation; Black Arrow; Black Rain (1988); Black Rain (1989); Black Robe; Black Rose; Bonnie Prince Charlie; Braveheart; A Breath of Scandal; The Bridge of San Luis Rey; A Brief History of Time; Brother Sun, Sister Moon; Buccaneer (1938); Buccaneer (1958); Buffalo Bill and the Indians, or Sitting Bull's History Lesson; Burke and Wills; Bushido Blade; Caesar and Cleopatra; Cardinal Richelieu; Catherine the Great; Chaplin; Chinatown; Christopher Columbus (1949); Christopher Columbus: The Discovery (1992); Comrades; Conqueror; Conquest; Cromwell; Danton; Day One; The Desert Fox; Desert Rats; Desiree Devils; Dr. Ehrlich's Magic Bullet; Eagle in a Cage; Edward II; The Elusive Pimpernel; Empire of the Sun; Ernest Green Story; Every Man for Himself (and God Against All); Fall of the Roman Empire; Fat Man and Little Boy; Fellow Traveler; 55 Days at Peking; Fire Over England; For Whom the Bell Tolls; Forever and a Day; 1492: Conquest of Paradise; Fortunes of War; Francis, God's Jester; Front; Gallipoli; Genghis Khan; Geronimo (1962); Geronimo (1993); Gervaise; Gone With the Wind; Gore Vidal's Lincoln; Gorgeous Hussy; Grapes of Wrath; Great Moment; Great White Hope; Hallelujah Trail; Hangmen Also Die; Hawaii; Hawaiians; Heimat; Henry V (1944); Henry V (1989); Henry VIII and His Six Wives; History of the World Part One; Hitler Gang; Hitler-The Last Ten Days; House of Rothschild; How the West Was Won; Howards of Virginia; Hudson's Bay; I Accuse; I, the Worst of All; If I Were King; Immortal Beloved; Inherit the Wind; It's A Big Country; Ivan the Terrible; Ivanhoe; Jefferson in Paris; John

Paul Jones; Juarez; Judgment at Nuremburg; Kagemusha; Khartoum; King La Marseillaise; La Nuit de Varennes; Lady Godiva; Lady Jane; Last Emperor; Lawrence of Arabia; Les Miserables (1935); Les Miserables (1952); Les Miserables (1978); Life of Emile Zola; Lion in Winter; Lionheart; Lloyd's of London; The Longest Day; Love and Death; Lucretia Borgia; Ludwig; Luther; Madame Dubarry; Magic Box; Magnificent Doll; Malcolm X; A Man Called Horse; A Man for All Seasons; The Man Who Would Be King; Mandela; Marie Antoinette; Marquise of O; Martin Luther; Mary of Scotland; Mary, Queen of Scots; Master of Ballantree; Matewan; Mayerling (1935); Mayerling (1968); Message to Garcia; Mississippi Burning; Moon and Sixpence; My Wife's Best Friend; Napoleon; Nasty Girl; Nicholas and Alexandra; A Night to Remember (1958); 1900; Orlando; Passion/Madame Dubarry (1919); The Passion of Joan of Arc; Pride and the Passion; The Private Life of Henry VIII; Private Lives of Elizabeth & Essex; Queen Christina; Queen of Destiny; Quo Vadis; Ragtime; Railway Children; Ran; Rasputin and the Empress; Red Sorghum; Reds; Rembrandt; Richard III; Right Stuff; Roanoak; Robe; Roots; Royal Flash; Royal Scandal; Salome (1953); Sand Pebbles; The Scarlet Empress; Secret Honor; Separate but Equal; 1776; Silas Marner; Song of Bernadette; Spirit of St. Louis; Stealing Heaven; Story of Alexander Graham Bell; Suez; Sunrise at Campobello; A Tale of Two Cities (1935); A Tale of Two Cities (1958); A Tale of Two Cities (1982); Tall Target; That Lady in Ermine; This is My Affair; Tower of London (1939); Tower of London (1962); Tree of Wooden Clogs; The Trials of Oscar Wilde; Trojan Women; Ugetsu Monogatari; Union Pacific; Uranus; Vikings; Virgin Queen; Viva Zapata; War and Peace (1956); War and Peace (1967); War Lord; Young Bess; Young Catherine; Young Mr. Lincoln

Hitchcockian (a style similar to and in many cases highly derivative of the great director's suspenseful and often comical style, but usually far inferior; however, includes films of Hitchcock's as well): see also *SUSPENSE: Comic Mystery: Dangerous Spouses:*
Apartment Zero; Arabesque; Bedroom Window; Birds; Blackmail (1929); The

Bride Wore Black; Caught; Charade; Chase a Crooked Shadow; Confidentially Yours; Dead Again; Diabolique (1955); Dial M For Murder; Dolores Claiborne; Dominique; Dressed to Kill; Family Plot; Final Analysis; Fly By Night; Frantic (1988); Frenzy; Fury (1978); Gaslight (1939); Gaslight (1944); High Anxiety; House of Games; The House on Carroll Street; I Confess; Jamaica Inn (1939); Jamaica Inn (1982); The Lady Vanishes; Liebestraum; Lifeboat; The Man Who Knew Too Much (1934); The Man Who Knew Too Much (1956); Marnie; Monsieur Hire; Murder (1929); Niagara; North by Northwest; Obsession; October Man; The Paradine Case; Phobia; The Prize; Psycho; Rear Window; Rebecca; Rope; Scapegoat; Shallow Grave; Shadow of a Doubt (1943); Silent Partner; Stage Fright; Step Down to Terror; Strangers on a Train; Stuntman; Suspicion; The Thirty-Nine Steps; Topaz (1969); To Catch a Thief; Torn Curtain; Under Capricorn; Vertigo; The Wrong Man

Hitchhikers: see also *Road Movies:*
Detour; Even Cowgirls Get the Blues; Ginger in the Morning; Great Smokey Roadblock; Harry and Tonto; The Hitcher; It Happened One Night; Jackson County Jail; Kalifornia; Knife in the Water; P.K. and the Kid; Rafferty and the Gold Dust Twins; Road Games; Scarecrow; Sure Thing

Hitler-Adolf: see also *Nazi Stories: Anti-Semitism: Fascism: Oppression: Leaders-Tyrant: World War II Era:* Boys From Brazil; The Bunker; Great Dictator; Hitler Gang; Hitler-The Last Ten Days; The Holcroft Covenant; Inside the Third Reich; The Magic Face; Man Hunt; Mein Kampf; The Producers; Rogue Male; Schtonk!; To Be or Not to Be; Triumph of the Will

Hitmen: see also *Mob Stories: Hitwomen: Fugitives from a Murderer:* All Dogs Go to Heaven; The American Friend; Assassination; Backtrack; Bad Company (1995); Best Seller; Bitch (1979); Blame it on the Bellboy; Bugsy; A Bullet for the General; Cat Ballou; Cohen and Tate; ColdSweat; Confessions of a Hit Man; Crimes and Misdemeanors; A Dandy in Aspic; The Deceivers; Desire and Hell at Sunset Motel; Diary of a Hitman; Divorce, Italian Style; Domino Principle; Driver; El Mariachi; The Enforcer (1950); Eureka; The Evil That

Men Do; Eye of the Needle; Flesh of the Orchid; F/X; The Godfather; The Godfather, Part II; The Godfather, Part III; Good Fellas; Grace Quigley; Hard Contract; Hardware; The Hatchet Man; The Hit; Hit Man; Johnny Stecchino; Killer Elite; The Killers (1946); The Killers (1964); The Killing of Chinese Bookie; Kiss of Death (1947); Kiss of Death (1995); Last Rites; Machine Gun McCain; The Magnificent Seven; Malone; Marked Woman; The Mechanic; Mikey and Nicky; Murder in New Hampshire; Murder, Inc.; 99 and 44/100 Per Cent Dead; Nitti, The Enforcer; No Mercy; Nous Sommes Tous les Assassins; Once Upon a Time in the West; Outside Man; Pain in the A . . . ; A Prayer for the Dying; Prizzi's Honor; The Professional; The Quick; Red Rock West; Running Man (1987); Samurai; Second Chance; Sitting Ducks; St. Valentine's Day Massacre; Star Chamber; Survivors; Terminator; This Gun for Hire; Three Days of the Condor; Timebomb; Tin Star; The Visit; Warlock (1958); Wild Geese; Wild Geese II; Yakuza

Hits that Faded: see *Faded Hits:* also *Forgotten Films*

Hitwomen: see also *Mob Girls: Hitmen: Evil Women:* Andy Warhol's Bad; Bad Company (1995); Gloria; La Femme Nikita; Point of No Return; Prizzi's Honor; Quick; The Quick and the Dead; Romeo Is Bleeding; Sitting Ducks; Terminator 2: Judgment Day

Hoaxes: see also *Practical Jokers: Con Artists:* April Fool's Day; Capricorn One; The Great Bank Hoax; Hail the Conquering Hero; Lady By Choice; Living It Up; Nancy Steele is Missing; No Escape (1936); Nothing Sacred; Schtonk!; Seance on a Wet Afternoon

Hockey: see also *Skating: Coaches: Snow Settings: Canada:* The Cutting Edge; Deadliest Season; D2: The Mighty Ducks 2; The Mighty Ducks; Slap Shot; Touch and Go; Youngblood

Hollywood Biographies: see *Hollywood Life: Actors: Actresses: Directors: Writers: Biographies: Autobiographical: Deaths of Celebrities: Music Dies: Silent Film Era:* The Amazing Howard Hughes; Beloved Infidel; Bugsy; Chaplin; Eddie Cantor Story; Forever James Dean; Frances; Funny Girl; Funny Lady; Gable and Lombard; The George Raft Story; Harlow; Jolson Sings Again;

Jolson Story; Last Tycoon; Lenny; Lightning Over Water; Man of a Thousand Faces; Marilyn, the Untold Story; Mommie Dearest; Mrs. Parker and the Vicious Circle; Rose of Washington Square; Sinatra; Sophia Loren, Her Own Story; Star!; Story of Will Rogers; To Hell and Back; Valentino (1951); Valentino (1977); W. C. Fields and Me; The Wild Party; Will There Really Be a Morning?; Wired

Hollywood Life (set in Hollywood or about movie people): see also *Hollywood Biographies: Movie Making: Movies within Movies: Silent Film Era: Actors: Actresses: Directors: Writers: Los Angeles: California Life:* Abbott & Costello in Hollywood; Actors and Sin; Adventures of Ford Fairlane; Affairs of Annabel; Alex in Wonderland; Alexander, the Other Side of Dawn; Ali Baba Goes to Town; An Almost Perfect Affair; The Amazing Howard Hughes; Andy Warhol's Heat; The Bad and the Beautiful; The Barefoot Contessa; The Barefoot Executive; Barfly; Barton Fink; Beloved Infidel; Bert Rigby, You're a Fool!; Best Friends; Beyond the Valley of the Dolls; Big Knife; The Big Picture; Bombshell; Bottoms Up; Boy, Did I Get a Wrong Number!; Boy Friend; Bugsy; Cameraman; Carousel; Chaplin; Comic; Dancing Co-Ed; Dancing in the Dark; Day of the Locust; Duffy's Tavern; Ed Wood; The Eddie Cantor Story; Errand Boy; F. Scott Fitzgerald in Hollywood; Fade to Black (1979); Fedora; Fellow Traveler; Fools for Scandal; Frances; The Front; Funny Lady; F/X; F/X 2: The Deadly Art of Illusion; Gable and Lombard; Gazebo; The George Raft Story; Glamour Boy; Go into Your Dance; Goddess; Goldwyn Follies; Good Morning, Babylon; Grand Canyon; Guilty by Suspicion; The Hard Way (1943); Harlow; Heart of the West; Hearts of Darkness: A Filmmaker's Apocalypse; Hellzapoppin; Hollywood Boulevard (1936); Hollywood Boulevard (1977); Hollywood Canteen; Hollywood Cavalcade; Hollywood Hotel; Hollywood or Bust; Hollywood Shuffle; Hooper; I Ought to Be in Pictures; I Wake Up Screaming; I'll Cry Tomorrow; I'll Do Anything; In a Lonely Place; In Person; Inserts; Inside Daisy Clover; Irreconcilable Differences; It's a Great Feeling; Jimmy Hollywood; King Kong (1933); King Kong (1976); Kiss Me Deadly; Lady Killer (1933); Last Action

Hero; Last of Sheila; Last Tycoon; Legend of Lylah Clare; Lenny; Less Than Zero; Life With Mikey; Love Goddesses; Love Me or Leave Me; Man of a Thousand Faces; The Man Who Understood Women; The Man with Bogart's Face; Mastergate; Merton of the Movies; The Mirror Crack'd; Mistress; Mommie Dearest; Morning After; Movers and Shakers; Mrs. Parker and the Vicious Circle; My Friend Irma Goes West; My Geisha; Myra Breckinridge; The Naked Truth; Network; Nickelodeon; Once in a Lifetime; Once Is Not Enough; Once Upon a Time; Oscar; Pepe; The Perils of Pauline; The Player; Point Blank; Postcards from the Edge; Power, Passion, and Murder; Savage Intruder; Scenes from a Mall; Second Fiddle; Silent Movie; Singing in the Rain; Skin Deep; SOB; The Stand In; Star; Star Spangled Rhythm; The Story of Will Rogers; The Stuntman; Sullivan's Travels; Sunset; Sunset Boulevard; Susan Slept Here; The Tender Trap; That's Life!; Trip; Two Weeks in Another Town; Under the Rainbow; Valentino (1951); Valley of the Dolls; Vicki; W. C. Fields and Me; The Way We Were; What Price Hollywood?; What's the Matter with Helen?; Whatever Happened to Baby Jane?; White Hunter, Black Heart; Who Framed Roger Rabbitt?; Who Is the Black Dahlia?; The Wild Party; Wings of Eagles; Wired; Won Ton Ton, the Dog Who Saved Hollywood; World's Greatest Lover; You Light Up My Life

Hollywood Satire (tales of corruption and debauchery in filmland): see also *Satire: Hollywood Life: Silent Film Era: Corruption: Greed: Actors: Actresses: Hollywood Biographies:* The Affairs of Annabel; Andy Warhol's Heat; Big Knife; The Big Picture; Boy Friend; The Cameraman; Chaplin; Ed Wood; F. Scott Fitzgerald in Hollywood; Free and Easy; Glamour Boy; Go into Your Dance; Goldwyn Follies; The Hard Way (1991); Heart of the West; Hellzapoppin; Hollywood Boulevard (1936); Hollywood Boulevard (1977); Hollywood or Bust; Hollywood Shuffle; I'll Do Anything; It's a Great Feeling; Joey Breaker; Last Action Hero; Last Command; Mistress; Movers and Shakers; Naked Gun 33 1/3; The Naked Truth; Nickelodeon; Once in a Lifetime; Once Upon a Time; Oscar; The Party; Pepe; The Player; Postcards from the Edge; Second Fiddle; The Stuntman; That's Adequate; Two

Weeks in Another Town; Valley of the Dolls; Who Framed Roger Rabbitt?

Homecomings: see *Reunions: Families/Heritage-Search for*

Homeless People: see also *Social Drama:* Ali Baba Goes to Town; Angel; Boudu Saved From Drowning; The Caretaker; Central Park; Dead End; Distant Thunder (1973); Down and Out in Beverly Hills; Exterminator; Exterminator 2; Fat City; Fisher King; God Bless the Child; Great McGinty; Hallelujah, I'm a Bum; Has Anybody Seen My Gal?; Hero; I'll Give a Million; Ironweed; It Happened on Fifth Avenue; Lady for a Day; Les Bas-Fonds; Life Stinks!; Little Noises; Man's Castle; Meet John Doe; Merrily We Live; Midnight Cowboy; Milky Way (1968); Monsieur Vincent; My Man Godfrey (1936); My Man Godfrey (1956); Nous La Liberte; Number 17; One Magic Christmas; One More Spring; Pennies from Heaven (1936); Pixote; Pocketful of Miracles; Quacker Fortune Has a Cousin in the Bronx; Saint of Fort Washington; Salaam Bombay!; Scarecrow; Sullivan's Travels; The Suspect; They Made Me a Criminal; Vagabond; Viridiana; Where the Day Takes You; Where the Heart Is

Hommes Fatales: **see** *Evil Men: Dangerous Men: Mindgames: Love-Questionable*

Homoeroticism (not necessarily openly gay or lesbian, but with over-tones): see also *Homosexual Secrets: Gay Men: Lesbians: Bisexuality: Alternative Lifestyles:* Another Country; Apartment Zero; Becket; Black Widow (1987); The Bostonians; Brideshead Revisited; Broken Noses; Cabaret; Dead Ringers; Death in Venice; Desert Hearts; The Devil's Playground; Entre-Nous; Fried Green Tomatoes; Hedda; The Hunger; In a Shallow Grave; Interview with the Vampire; Julia; Lamb; Lianna; Maurice; Merry Christmas, Mr. Lawrence; Midnight Express; My Own Private Idaho; Nijinsky; One Sings, the Other Doesn't; Proof; Querelle; Rebel Without a Cause; Robert et Robert; Sebastiane; A Separate Peace; Sergeant; Spartacus; Tea and Sympathy; The Testament of Orpheus

Homophobia: see also *Bigots: Oppression: Fascism: Gay Men: Lesbians:* Andre's Mother; Children's Hour; Citizen Cohn; Consenting Adult; Cruising; The Detective (1968); The Garden; Kiss of the Spider Woman; Mala

Noche; A Man of No Importance; Maurice; My Beautiful Laundrette; The New Barbarians; Oscar Wilde; Philadelphia; Reflections in a Golden Eye; The Ritz; Summer Wishes, Winter Dreams; Taxi zum Klo; Tea and Sympathy; The Third Sex; Tightrope; The Victim; The Wedding Banquet

Homosexuality: see *Gay Men: Lesbians: Homoeroticism: Gay/Lesbian Films: Homophobia: Bisexuality: Murders of Homosexuals*

Homosexual Murders: see *Murders of Homosexuals: Murderers-Homosexual: also Homophobia: Transvestite Killers*

Homosexual Secrets (gay people in the closet due to repression): see also *Bisexuality: Homophobia: Gay Men: Lesbians:* Deathtrap; The Detective (1968); Last Exit to Brooklyn; Last of Sheila; The Lost Language of Cranes; Music Lovers; Streetcar Named Desire; Suddenly, Last Summer; Summer Wishes, Winter Dreams

Homosexual Suicidal Tendencies: see *Suicidal Tendencies of Homosexuals: Homosexual Secrets: Homophobia: Suicidal Tendencies*

Honeymoons: see also *Newlyweds: Marriage-Impending: Marriage Comedy: Marriage Drama:* Doughgirls; Easy to Wed; Haunted Honeymoon; Heartbreak Kid; Kiss of Evil; Libeled Lady; My Favorite Spy; Prelude to a Kiss; Private Lives

Hong Kong: see also *China:* Blood Alley; Bloodsport; Cleopatra Jones and the Casino of Gold; Love is a Many-Splendored Thing; Revenge of the Pink Panther; Soldier of Fortune; Tai Pan; The World of Suzie Wong

Hookers with a Heart of Gold: see *Prostitutes with a Heart of Gold: also Prostitutes-Low Class: Prostitutes-High Class*

HORROR: see also *Blood & Gore: Monsters: THRILLERS: Experiments: Mad Scientists: Brain Transplants: Psychotics: Serial Killers: Stalkers: Human Eaters: Humans into Animals: Comedy-Morbid: Spoofs-Horror: Horror Comedy: Urban Horrors: Rural Horrors: Teenage Terrors: Body Parts: Teen Horror Flicks of the 80s:* Abbott & Costello Meet Dr. Jekyll & Mr. Hyde; Abbott & Costello Meet Frankenstein; Abbott & Costello Meet the Killer: Boris Karloff; Abbott & Costello Meet the Mummy; The Abominable Dr.

Phibes; The Abominable Snowman; The Addams Family; Addams Family Values; Adventure Island; Afraid of the Dark; The Alchemist; Alice, Sweet Alice; Alien; Alien3; Aliens; Alligator; Alligator II: The Mutation; Alligator People; Alone in the Dark; Ambulance; American Gothic; An American Werewolf in London; Amityville 1992: It's About Time; Amityville 4; Amityville, a New Generation; The Amityville Curse; The Amityville Horror; Amityville Horror 2, The Possession; And Now the Screaming Starts; Andy Warhol's Dracula; Andy Warhol's Frankenstein; Anniversary; Ants; Ape; April Fool's Day; Arachnophobia; Army of Darkness; Arnold; Arousers; Asphyx; Asylum; Attack of the Killer Tomatoes; Audrey Rose; Avenging Conscience; Awakening; Back From the Dead; Bad Dreams; Basket Case; Basket Case 2; Basket Case 3; Bat (1959); Bat Whispers; Beast Must Die; Beauty and the Beast (1946); Bedlam; The Beguiled; The Believers; Ben; Berserk!; Beware! The Blob!; Big Foot; Birds; Birds II; Black Cat; Black Christmas; Black God, White Devil; Black Room; Black Sabbath; Black Sleep; Black Sunday (1960); Blacula; The Blob (1958); The Blob (1988); Blood and Black Lace; Blood Beach; Blood Beast Terror; Blood from the Mummy's Tomb; Blood on Satan's Claw; Bloodbath at the House of Death; Body Bags; The Body Snatcher; Body Snatchers; The Borrower; The Bowery at Midnight; Brain Damage; The Brain Eaters; Bram Stoker's Count Dracula (1970); Bram Stoker's Dracula (1992); The Bride; The Bride of Frankenstein; Bride of the Gorilla; Bride of the Monster; Brides of Dracula; The Brood; Brotherhood of Satan; Buffy, The Vampire Slayer; The Bug; The 'Burbs; Burning; Burnt Offerings; Busy Body; C.H.U.D.; C.H.U.D.2; The Cabinet of Caligari (1962); The Cabinet of Dr. Caligari (1919); Cameron's Closet; Candyman; Candyman: Farewell to the Flesh; Car; Carnival of Souls; Carrie (1976); The Cars That Ate Paris; Castle Keep; Castle of Doom; Cat People (1942); Cat People (1983); Cat's Eye; The Changeling; Child's Play (1972); Child's Play (1988); Child's Play 2; Child's Play 3; Children (1980); Children of the Corn; Children of the Damned; Christine; Class of 1999; Class of '84; Comedy of Terrors; The Company of Wolves; Count Yorga, Vampire; The Creature of the Black

Lagoon; Cujo; The Curse of the Cat People; The Curse of the Werewolf; Dance Macabre; Dark Half; Darkman; Dawn of the Dead; Day of the Dead; Day of the Triffids; Dead Alive; Dead of Night (1945); Dead of Night (1977); Dead Ringers; DeadZone; Deadly Friend; Deepstar Six; Delicatessen; Deliverance; Dementia 13; Demon Knight; Demon Seed; The Devil Came from Arkansas; Devil Doll; The Devil's Bride; Diary of a Madman; Disturbed; Do You Like Women?; Doctor and the Devils; Doctor Jekyll and Mr. Hyde (1931); Doctor Mabuse, the Gambler; Don't Bother to Knock; Donovan's Brain; Dr. Cyclops; Dr. Giggles; Dr. Heckyl and Mr. Hype; Dr. Jekyll and Sister Hyde; Dr. Jekyll & Mr. Hyde (1941); Dr. M.; Dr. Phibes Rises Again; Dracula (1931); Dracula (1979); Dracula Has Risen from the Grave; Dracula (Horror of Dracula, 1958); Dracula, Prince of Darkness; Dracula's Daughter; Dune; Dunwich Horror; Eaten Alive; Ebb Tide; Ed and His Dead Mother; Empire of the Ants; Enemy from Space; The Entity; Eraserhead; Evictors; Evil Dead; The Exorcist; Exorcist II: The Heretic; Exorcist III; Eye of the Cat; Eye of the Devil; Fade to Black (1979); Fall of the House of Usher (1928); The Fan; Fear in the Night; The Fearless Vampire Killers; Final Conflict; Firestarter; Five Million Years to Earth; Flowers in the Attic; The Fly (1958); The Fly (1986); Fly II; The Fog; Food of the Gods; Frankenhooker; Frankenstein (1931); Frankenstein '70; Frankenstein and the Monster from Hell; Frankenstein Created Woman; Frankenstein Meets the Wolf Man; Frankenstein Unbound; Freaked; Freddy's Dead: The Final Nightmare; Friday the 13th (1980); Friday the 13th: Final Chapter; Friday the 13th, Part 3-D; Friday the 13th, Part II; Friday the 13th Part V-A New Beginning; Friday the 13th Part VI-Jason Lives; Friday the 13th Part VII-The New Blood; Friday the 13th Part VII-Jason Takes Manhattan; Fright Night; Fright Night Part 2; Frogs; Full Eclipse; The Fury (1978); The Gate; Gate II; Ghost in the Machine; Ghost Story; Ghoul (1933); Ghoul (1975); Godzilla (1955); Godzilla versus Gigan; Godzilla versus Megalon; Gorgon; Gorilla; Gothic; Graveyard Shift; Gremlins; Gremlins 2: The New Batch; Grizzly; Guardian; Guilty as Charged; Halloween; Halloween 2; Halloween 3:

Season of the Witch; Halloween 4: The Return of Michael Myers; Halloween 5: The Revenge of Michael Myers; Hammersmith Is Out; The Hand (1960); The Hand (1981); The Hand that Rocks the Cradle; Happy Birthday to Me; Hardware; The Haunted Palace; The Haunting; He Knows You're Alone; Hearse; Hellbound: Hellraiser II; Hellraiser; Hellraiser III: Hell on Earth; Henry: Portrait of a Serial Killer; The Hidden; Hidden 2; Hideaway; Hills Have Eyes; Histoires Extraordinaires; Hold That Ghost; Hollywood Boulevard (1977); Holocaust 2000; Horror Express; Horror Hotel; House; House II: The Second Story; House III; House IV; House of Dracula; House of Frankenstein; House of the Long Shadows; The House of Usher (1960); The House of Usher (1990); House of Wax; The House on Haunted Hill; The House That Dripped Blood; The Howling; Howling II; Howling III; Howling IV; Howling V; The Hunger; Hush, Hush, Sweet Charlotte; I Love a Mystery; I Married a Monster from Outer Space; I, Monster; I Saw What You Did; I Walked with a Zombie; I Was a Teenage Frankenstein; I Was a Teenage Werewolf; Ichabod and Mr. Toad/Legend of Sleepy Hollow; In the Mouth of Madness; The Incredible Shrinking Man; The Innocents; Invaders from Mars (1953); Invaders from Mars (1986); Invasion; Invasion of the Body Snatchers (1956); Invasion of the Body Snatchers (1978); Invisible Ray; Island of Dr. Moreau (1977); Island of Lost Souls (1932); Isle of the Dead; It; It Came From Outer Space; It's Alive; It's Alive II; It's Alive III; Jack's Back; Jaws; Jaws 2; Jaws 3-D; Jaws 4: The Revenge; Kafka; Kalifornia; Kaos; The Keep; Killer Fish; The Killer Nun; Kindred; The Kingdom; Kingdom of the Spiders; The Kiss (1988); Kiss of Evil; Kwaidan; Ladies in Retirement; Lady in a Cage; Lair of the White Worm; The Lawnmower Man; Legacy; Legend of Hell House; Leprechaun; Let's Kill Uncle; Let's Scare Jessica to Death; Leviathan; Life Force; Link; Little Girl Who Lives Down the Lane; Little Shop of Horrors (1960); Lost Boys; M (1931); M (1951); Mad Love; Mad Magician; Mad Room; Madhouse; Man Made Monster; The Man Who Reclaimed His Head; Man with Nine Lives; Man's Best Friend; Manitou; Mark of the Vampire; Martin; Masque of the Red Death; Maximum Overdrive; Mephisto

Waltz; Midnight (1989); Mind Benders; Misery; Mister Frost; Mole People; Monkey Shines; Monster Club; Monster Squad; Motel Hell; Mother's Boys; Mothra; The Mummy (1932); The Mummy (1959); The Mummy's Hand; The Mummy's Shroud; Murder by Phone; Murder by Television; Murders in the Rue Morgue; Mysterious Island; Mystery of the Wax Museum; Naked Lunch; Nanny; Nature of the Beast; Near Dark; Necromancy; Needful Things; New Nightmare; Night Gallery; Night of the Lepus; Night of the Living Dead (1968); Night of the Living Dead (1990); Night Stalker/The Night Strangler; Night Walker; Nightbreed; Nightcomers; Nightmare on Elm Street; Nightmare on Elm Street Part Four; Nightmare on Elm Street Part Three; Nightmare on Elm Street Part Two; Nightmare on Elm Street: The Dream Child; Nightwing; 976-Evil; Ninth Configuration; Nosferatu; Not of This Earth (1956); Oblong Box; Old Dark House (1932); Old Dark House (1962); Old Dracula; Omega Man; Omen; Omen IV: The Awakening; The Other; The Pack; Pandemonium; Paperhouse; Peeping Tom; People Under the Stairs; Pet Sematary; Pet Sematary 2; Phantasm; Phantasm II; Phantom of the Opera (1925); Phantom of the Opera (1941); Phantom of the Opera (1962); Phantom of the Opera (1989); Phantom of the Rue Morgue; Picture Mommy Dead; Piranha; Pit and the Pendulum (1961); Pit and the Pendulum (1991); Poltergeist; Poltergeist 2; Poltergeist 3; Predator; Prince of Darkness; Prom Night SERIES; The Prophecy; Psycho; Psycho 2; Psycho 3; Pulse; Pumpkinhead; Puppet Master; The Puppetmasters; Psycho 4; Q (The Winged Serpent); Rabid Grannies; Raising Cain; The Raven (1935); The Raven (1963); Rawhead Rex; Re-Animator; Re-Animator 2; Red Inn; Reflecting Skin; Reposessed; Return of Dracula; Return of the Fly; Return of the Living Dead; Return of the Living Dead Part II; Return of the Vampire; Revenge of Billy the Kid; Revenge of Frankenstein; Road Games; Rosemary's Baby; Salem's Lot; Saturn 3; Savage Intruder; Scanner Cop; Scanners; Scanners II, The New Order; Scream and Scream Again!; Sender; The Sentinel; Serpent and the Rainbow; The Shining; Shock Treatment; Shocker; Silver Bullet; Sister, Sister; Sisters; Sleepwalkers;

Society; Solaris; Something Wicked This Way Comes; Son of Dracula; Son of Frankenstein; Spellbinder; The Stepfather; Stepfather 2: Make Room for Daddy; Stepfather 3: Father's Day; Strait Jacket; Stuff; Substitute; Suspiria; Swamp Thing; Tale of a Vampire; Tales From the Crypt; Tales from the Darkside: The Movie; Tales of Terror; Taste the Blood of Dracula; Tentacles; Terminal Man; Terror Train; The Texas Chainsaw Massacre; The Texas Chainsaw Massacre, Part 2; Theater of Blood; Them!; The Thing (1951); The Thing (1982); The Thousand Eyes of Dr. Mabuse; To Kill a Clown; Tomb of Ligea; Tommyknockers; Tower of London (1939); Tower of London (1962); Toxic Avenger; Toxic Avenger, Part II; Toxic Avenger Part III; Transmutations; Tremors; Trilogy in Terror; Trog; Twilight Zone: The Movie; Twins of Evil; Twisted; Twisted Nerve; 2000 Maniacs; Un Chien Andalou; Unborn; The Unholy; The Uninvited; The Unnamable; Unnamable Returns; Vamp; Vampire Lovers; Venom; Videodrome; Village of the Damned; Walking Dead; War of the Worlds; Watcher in the Woods; Watchers; Watchers II; Waxwork; Waxwork II: Lost in Time; The Werewolf (1956); Werewolf of London; What's the Matter with Helen?; Whatever Happened to Aunt Alice?; Whatever Happened to Baby Jane?; White Zombie; The Who Slew Auntie Roo?; Willard; Wolf; Wolfen; The Wolfman; X-The Man with X-Ray Eyes; Xtro

Horror Comedy: see also *Spoofs-Horror: HORROR: Comic Thriller: Black Comedy: Comedy-Morbid: Comedy & Violence:* Abbott & Costello Meet Dr. Jekyll & Mr. Hyde; Abbott & Costello Meet Frankenstein; Abbott & Costello Meet the Killer: Boris Karloff; Abbott & Costello Meet the Mummy; The Abominable Dr. Phibes; The Addams Family; Addams Family Values; Alligator; Alligator II: The Mutation; An American Werewolf in London; Andy Warhol's Dracula; April Fool's Day; Arachnophobia; Army of Darkness; Blacula; Blood Beach; The Borrower; Buffy, The Vampire Slayer; Burbs; Cars That Ate Paris; Child's Play (1988); Child's Play 2; Child's Play 3; Delicatessen; Demon Knight; Dr. Giggles; Dr. Heckyl and Mr. Hype; Dr. Jekyll and Sister Hyde; Dr. Phibes Rises Again; Ed and His Dead Mother; Fearless Vampire Killers; Fright Night; Fright Night Part 2;

The Ghost and Mr. Chicken; Ghost Breakers; The Ghost Goes West; Ghost in the Invisible Bikini; Ghostbusters; Ghostbusters 2; Gremlins; Gremlins 2: The New Batch; Haunted Honeymoon; Hold That Ghost; I Was a Teenage Frankenstein; I Was a Teenage Werewolf; Ladies in Retirement; Lair of the White Worm; Little Shop of Horrors (1960); Lost Boys; Madhouse; Mark of the Vampire; Matinee; Midnight (1989); Monster Club; Monster Squad; National Lampoon's Class Reunion; Night Stalker/The Night Strangler; Old Dracula; Pandemonium; Rabid Grannies; Re-Animator; Re-Animator 2; Red Inn; Repossessed; Return of the Living Dead; Return of the Living Dead Part II; The Rocky Horror Picture Show; Scared Stiff; Shock Treatment; Targets; Teen Wolf; Teen Wolf Too; Theater of Blood; Tremors; Vamp; Waxwork; Waxwork II: Lost in Time; Whatever Happened to Aunt Alice?; Whatever Happened to Baby Jane?; Witches; Young Frankenstein

Horses/Horse Racing: see also *Gambling: Pet Stories:* Appaloosa; Ben-Hur (1959); Bite the Bullet; Black Beauty (1946); Black Beauty (1971); Black Beauty (1994); Black Stallion; Black Stallion Returns; Broadway Bill; Casey's Shadow; Champions; A Day at the Races; Down Argentine Way; Eagle's Wing; Electric Horseman; Equus; Escape From the Dark; Francis the Talking Mule; Fresh Horses; The Horse in the Grey Flannel Suit; Hot to Trot; In Old Kentucky; International Velvet; Into the West; It Ain't Hay; Kentucky; The Killing; Kim; The Lemon Drop Kid; Let it Ride; Little Miss Marker (1934); Little Miss Marker (1980); Man from Snowy River; Million Dollar Legs; Miracle of the White Stallions; Misfits; Money from Home; My Friend Flicka; National Velvet; Nice Little Bank That Should Be Robbed; Phar Lap; Red Pony (1949); Red Pony (1976); Riding High; Saratoga; Shadow of the Thin Man; Sing You Sinners; Sorrowful Jones; Sylvester; Thunderhead, Son of Flicka; Trojan War; Trojan Women; Wild Hearts Can't Be Broken; The Wooden Horse

Hospitals: see also *Doctors: Nurses: Disease Stories: Medical Thrillers: Medical Detectives:* Article 99; Bad Dreams; Brittania Hospital; The Calling Dr. Gillespie; Calling Dr. Kildare; Caretakers; City of Hope; Coma; Come to the Stable; Critical Condition;

Disorderly Orderly; Doctor; A Farewell to Arms (1932); A Farewell to Arms (1957); Finishing School; Garbo Talks; Green for Danger; Hospital; Improper Channels; Interns; Killjoy; The Kingdom; Mother, Jugs & Speed; My Little Girl; New Interns; Paper Mask; Shadow Box; Such Good Friends; Waterdance; Where Does it Hurt?; Whose Life Is It Anyway?; The Young Doctors; Young Doctors in Love

Hostage Situations: see also *Race Against Time: Kidnappings: Die-Hard Stories:* Airheads; Airport '79, The Concorde; Autobus; Bandolero; Cadillac Man; The Collector; Death and the Maiden; Die Hard; Die Hard 2; Dark Past; Delta Force; Desperate Hours (1955); Desperate Hours (1990); Dog Day Afternoon; Green Goddess; Hombre; Key Largo; Killing Zoe; Kings and Desperate Men; Lady in a Cage; Lightship; Man Upstairs; Miracles; Misery; Nighthawks (1981); Penthouse; Petrified Forest; Rescue; The River Wild; Seven Women; S.F.W.; Situation Hopeless But Not Serious; Skyjacked; Speed; Surrender; Taking of Beverly Hills; Taking of Pelham 123; That Cold Day in the Park; Three Days of the Condor; Three Worlds of Gulliver; Trouble in Paradise; View to a Kill; Whatever Happened to Baby Jane?; Wind and the Lion

Hotels/Motels: see also *Ensemble Films: FARCE:* Blackbeard's Ghost; Blame it on the Bellboy; California Suite; Cocoanuts; Come September; The Detective (1985); Doughgirls; Experience Preferred but not Essential; Fawlty Towers; A Flea in Her Ear; For Love or Money (1993); Grand Hotel; The Green Man; A Hole in the Head; Holiday Inn; Hollywood Hotel; Honeymoon Hotel; Horror Hotel; Hotel; The Hotel New Hampshire; Hotel Paradiso; Insignificance; International House; King of the Hill (1993); Ladies' Man (1961); Last Laugh; Last Year at Marienbad; Motel Hell; Plaza Suite; Private Lives; Private Resort; Room Service; Separate Tables; The Shining; Silence; Somewhere in Time; Sweet Lorraine; Ten Thousand Bedrooms; Weekend at the Waldorf; White Christmas; You Were Never Lovelier

House Havoc (trouble and chaos when moving in or remodeling): see also *Comedy of Errors:* Baby Boom; George Washington Slept Here; A Home of Our

Own; Money Pit; Moving; Mr. Blandings Builds His Dream House

Houses-Creepy (not necessarily haunted but not exactly safe): see also *Haunted Houses: Gothic Style: HOR-ROR:* The Addams Family; Addams Family Values; The Amazing Mr. Blunden; American Gothic; And Now the Screaming Starts; Back From the Dead; Bat (1959); Bat Whispers; Burnt Offerings; The Cabinet of Caligari (1962); The Cabinet of Dr. Caligari (1919); Castle in the Desert; Dark Angel (1991); Dementia 13; Die! Die! My Darling!; Dunwich Horror; Eye of the Cat; Eye of the Devil; The Fall of the House of Usher (1928); Flowers in the Attic; The Ghost and Mr. Chicken; The Ghost and Mrs. Muir; Ghost Breakers; The Ghost Goes West; Hold That Ghost; House; House II: The Second Story; House III; House IV; The House of Usher (1960); The House of Usher (1990); Hush, Hush, Sweet Charlotte; The Innocents; Legacy; Let's Scare Jessica to Death; Masque of the Red Death; Nightcomers; The Old Dark House (1932); Old Dark House (1962); Rebecca; Red House; Rosemary's Baby; Scared Stiff; The Secret Beyond the Door; See No Evil; Sister, Sister; Spiral Staircase (1946); Spiral Staircase (1975); The Uninvited; The Unseen; Year My Voice Broke; You'll Like My Mother

Housewives: see also *Domestic Life: Mothers: Suburban Life: Marriage Drama:* American Dreamer; Angelina; Barefoot in the Park; Belle du Jour; Blonde Venus; Christmas in Connecticut (1945); Christmas in Connecticut (1992); Compromising Positions; Desperate Living; Desperately Seeking Susan; Diary of a Mad Housewife; A Doll's House; Harriet Craig; How to Beat the High Cost of Living; Lady Takes a Flyer; Lake Consequence; Limbo; Marjorie Morningstar; Next Time We Love; Penelope; Please Don't Eat the Daisies; Polyester; The Positively True Adventures of the Alleged Texas Cheerleader-Murdering Mom; The Purple Rose of Cairo; Rain People; Red Desert; A Special Day; Thrill of It All; Twice in a Lifetime; Two or Three Things I Know About Her

Human Eaters: see also *Cannibalism: HORROR: Monsters:* Alien; Alien3; Aliens; Beware! The Blob!; Birds; Birds II; The Blob (1958); The Blob (1988); The Brain Eaters; Cat People (1942); A

Cry in the Dark; Eraserhead; Graveyard Shift; Jaws; Jaws 2; Jaws 3-D; Jaws 4: The Revenge; Kindred; Most Dangerous Game; Not of This Earth (1956); Parents; Q (The Winged Serpent); Sleepwalkers

Human Monsters: see also *Monsters: Human Eaters: Frankenstein Stories:* Basket Case; Basket Case 2; Basket Case 3; Black Sleep; Blue Monkey; Bram Stoker's Count Dracula (1970); Bride of the Gorilla; The Dunwich Horror; Horror Express; The Howling; Howling II; Howling III; Howling IV; Howling V; I, Monster; It's Alive; It's Alive II; It's Alive III; Kindred; The Lawnmower Man; Man Made Monster; The Mummy (1932); The Mummy (1959); The Mummy's Hand; The Mummy's Shroud; Phantom of the Opera (1925); Phantom of the Opera (1941); Phantom of the Opera (1962); Phantom of the Opera (1989); Scanners; Scanners II, The New Order; Scream and Scream Again!; Shocker; Sleepwalkers; Stuff; Terminal Man; Toxic Avenger; Toxic Avenger, Part II; Toxic Avenger Part III; Transmutations; Trog; The Unborn; Wolf; Wolfman

Humans into Animals: see also *Monsters: Monsters-Manmade: Werewolves: HORROR:* Alligator People; An American Werewolf in London; Ape; Beneath the Planet of the Apes; Black Sleep; Blood Beast Terror; Cat People (1942); Cat Women of the Moon; The Curse of the Werewolf; The Fly (1958); The Fly (1986); Fly II; The Incredible Mr. Limpet; Island of Lost Souls; Island of Dr. Moreau; Ladyhawke; Nightbreed; Oh Heavenly Dog; Ratboy; Return of the Fly; Revenge of Billy the Kid; Rock-a-Doodle; The Secret of Roan Inish; Seventh Voyage of Sinbad; The Shaggy D.A.; The Shaggy Dog; Sleepwalkers; Sssss . . . ; Swamp Thing; The Tomb of Ligeia; The Werewolf (1956); Witches; Wolf; The Wolfman

Hunchbacks (disfigured misfits): see also *Disabled People: Frankenstein Stories:* Five Corners; The Hunchback of Notre Dame; The Hunchback of Notre Dame; The Hunchback of Notre Dame; The Name of the Rose; Richard III; The Rocky Horror Picture Show; Ryan's Daughter; The Secret Garden (1949); The Secret Garden (1987); The Secret Garden (1993); Young Frankenstein

Hunks: see *Wallflowers & Hunks: Sexy Men*

Hunters: see also *Bounty Hunters: Safaris: Manhunts:* The Deer Hunter; Deliverance; Golden Seal; Hatari!; Jaws; Jaws 2; Jaws 3-D; Jaws 4: The Revenge; The Last Hunt; The Macomber Affair; Most Dangerous Game; The Naked Prey; Roots of Heaven; Shooting Party; Silence of the North; Spawn of the North; White Buffalo

Hurricanes: see also *Floods: Tornadoes:* Hurricane (1937); Hurricane (1979); Key Largo

Husbands-Troublesome: see also *Difficult Men: Abusive Men:* Compromising Positions; Diary of a Mad Housewife; Eternally Yours; Man Alive; Thrill of It All

Hypnosis: see also *Psychologists: Therapy: Psychological Drama:* Blindfold: Acts of Obsession; The Cabinet of Dr. Caligari (1919); The Cabinet of Dr. Caligari (1962); Carefree; Dr. Mabuse, the Gambler; Invaders from Mars (1953); Invaders from Mars (1986); I Was a Teenager Werewolf; Let's Do it Again (1975); On a Clear Day You Can See Forever; Road to Rio; The Search for Bridey Murphy; The Seven Percent Solution; Simon; Spellbound; Svengali (1931); Svengali (1983); Tales of Terror; Whirlpool

Hypochondriacs: Can She Bake a Cherry Pie?; Checking Out; Never Say Die; That Uncertain Feeling

Hypothetical Stories: see *What if . . . Stories: Good Premises Unfulfilled*

I

Identities-Assumed: see also *Impostors: Disguises: Identities-Mistaken: Body Switching: Lookalikes: Twins: Con Artists: Screwball Comedy: FARCE: Comedy of Errors:* Across the Bridge; The Associate; Backtrack; Caroline?; Class Act; The Couch Trip; Critical Condition; The Dark Half; Dark Passage; Dave; Dead Ringer; Detour; Don Juan DeMarco; Don't Tell Her It's Me; Great Impostor; Hero; Holy Matrimony; Houseguest; I Married a Dead Man; I Married a Monster from Outer Space; Inspector General; Kagemusha; Kiss and Tell; Kiss Before Dying; Libel!; Madame X (1929); Madame X (1937); Madame X (1965); Monte Carlo; Murder by Television; My Favorite Spy; Naked Tango; Ninth Configuration; No Man of Her Own (1949); Palm Beach Story; Paper Mask; Paper Tiger; Paranoia; The Parent Trap; The Passenger; The Prisoner of Zenda; Quality Street; Return of Dracula; The Return of Martin Guerre; Richest Girl in the World; Scarlet Angel; Shattered; Sleeping With the Enemy; Sommersby; Spellbound; Stolen Life (1939); Stolen Life (1946); Taking Care of Business; The Tenth Man; They Might be Giants; Tootsie; Trading Places; True Identity; Twisted Nerve; Two-Faced Woman; Victor/Victoria; White Sands

Identities-Mistaken: see also *Identities-Assumed: Body Switching: Lookalikes: Twins: Impostors: Misrepresentations: Con Artists: Screwball Comedy: FARCE: Comedy of Errors:* After Hours; Ali Baba Goes to Town; Along Came Jones; The Bawdy Adventures of Tom Jones; Big Business; Born in East L.A.; Bread and Chocolate; Bringing Up Baby; Broadway Danny Rose; Bullfighters; Cairo (1942); Desperately Seeking Susan; El Mariachi; Fancy Pants; First Time; Fury (1936); The Gay Divorcee; The Great Dictator; Gun in Betty Lou's Handbag; I Love You Again; The Inspector General; Johnny Stecchino; Kentucky Moonshine; The Kid from Spain; Kid Millions; Killjoy; Lock up Your Daughters; Lorna Doone; Love God?; A Man Could Get Killed; The Man Who Lost Himself; The Man Who Shot Liberty Valance; The Man Who Would Be King; The Mikado; Mr. Klein; My Favorite Brunette; Never a Dull Moment (1967); Once Upon a Crime; The Player; The Pope Must Die(t); Reckless Moment; Red Rock West; School for Scandal; Smokey and the Bandit II; Some Like it Hot; Spies Like Us; Statue; Straight Talk; Sullivan's Travels; Support Your Local Gunfighter; The Tall Blond Man with One Black Shoe; Tom Jones; Victor/Victoria; What's Up, Doc?; Where Were You When the Lights Went Out?; Who Was That Lady?

Idolization: see *Fans-Crazed: Obsessions*

Illinois: see *Midwestern Life: Chicago*

Illusions/Hallucinations: see also *Dream Sequences: Dreams: Fantasies: Fantasy: Insane-Plot to Drive: Mental Illness: Surrealism:* Amityville 1992: It's About Time; Amityville 4; Amityville, a New Generation; The Amityville Curse; Birdy; Blood of a Poet; Brainstorm (1983); Brigadoon; The Cabinet of Caligari (1962); The Cabinet of Dr. Caligari (1919); Candyman; Candyman: Farewell to the Flesh; Castle Keep; Castle of Doom; Celia; Cold Heaven; Diabolique (1955); Don Juan DeMarco; Don't Look Now; A Double Life; The Eyes of Laura Mars; Field of Dreams; Foxfire (1987); Gaslight (1939); Gaslight (1944); Gothic; Hamlet (1948); Hamlet (1964); Hamlet (1969); Hamlet (1991); Images; The Innocents; Jacob's Ladder; Joan of Arc; Julia and Julia; Kiss of the Spider Woman; Lady in the Car with Glasses and a Gun; Last of Sheila; Let's Scare Jessica to Death; Lost Weekend; The Magus; Medusa Touch; Men Are Not Gods; The Miracle of the Bells; Miracle on 34th Street (1947); Mr. Peabody and the Mermaid; Naked Lunch; Network; Night Walker; Night Watch; The Other; A

Passage to India; Petulia; Portrait of Jennie; The Purple Rose of Cairo; Raising Cain; Random Harvest; Rosemary's Baby; Siesta; Snakepit; Song of Bernadette; Streetcar Named Desire; The Stuntman; Sunset Boulevard; Taxi Driver; The Tenant; Testament of Orpheus; They Might be Giants; To Dance with the White Dog; Topper; Topper Returns; Topper Takes a Trip; The Trip; Twilight Zone: The Movie; Waiting For the Light; What's the Matter with Helen?; Whisperers; Wholly Moses; Wild Strawberries

Illusions Destroyed: see also *Dreams-Broken:* Abschied von Gestern; All Fall Down; Career; Chalk Garden; The Fountainhead; The Glass Menagerie (1950); The Glass Menagerie (1973); The Glass Menagerie (1987); Hardcore; High Tide; Hope and Glory; The King of Comedy; Landlord; Martin's Day; A Member of the Wedding; Miss Firecracker; Music Box; My Little Girl; Queen of Hearts; The Red Pony (1949); The Red Pony (1976); Rosemary's Baby; Shadow of a Doubt; Shane; Six Degrees of Separation; Smugglers; The Spider's Stratagem; Stagedoor; Step Down to Terror; The Stratton Story; Sunset Boulevard; Sweet Bird of Youth; Sweet Charity; Swimmer; They Shoot Horses, Don't They?; Toys; Tucker: The Man and His Dream; Turning Point (1952); Up the Down Staircase

Immigrants: see also *Historical Drama: Sagas: Epics: Third World Countries: Latin People:* Alamo Bay; America, America; American Romance; An American Tail; American Tail 2; Anna; Avalon; Born in East L.A.; Combination Platter; Despair; Displaced Person; Dolly Sisters; Dream Wife; Emigrants; Enemies, A Love Story; Far and Away; Flower Drum Song; Good Morning, Babylon; Green Card; Hester Street; I Remember Mama; I Was a Male War Bride; Miss Rose White; Moonlighting (1982); Moscow on the Hudson; Music in My Heart; My Girl Tisa; Orpheus Descending; Our Vines Have Tender Grapes; Pelle the Conqueror; Red Kiss; Romper Stomper; Sacco and Vanzetti; Silver City; Sophie's Choice; Stranger Than Paradise; Streets of Gold; Stroszek; Tell Me a Riddle; Tortilla Flat; A Tree Grows in Brooklyn; Wait Until Spring, Bandini

Immigrants-Marriage for Citizenship: see *Marriage for Citizenship:* also *Marriage of Convenience: Immigrants: Foreign Misfits*

Immortality: see *Soul-Selling One's: Aging: Aging-Reverse*

Imperialist Problems: see also *Third World Countries:* Black and White in Color; Burn!; Charge of the Light Brigade (1936); Charge of the Light Brigade (1968); Chocolat; Conduct Unbecoming; Coup de Torchon; A Good Man in Africa; Heart of the Matter; Jungle Book (1967); Jungle Book (1994); Kim; Rains Came; River (1951); Seventh Dawn; Simba; Ugly American; Zulu

Impostors: see also *Disguises: Pretending: Identities-Assumed: Lookalikes:* Anastasia (1956); The Addams Family; Anastasia (1984); The Applegates; The Associate; Based on an Untrue Story; Bedroom Window; Bottoms Up; Cactus Flower; Cafe Metropole; Call Me Bwana; Candleshoe; Casanova's Big Night; Charley's Aunt; Christmas in Connecticut (1945); Christmas in Connecticut (1992); City Lights; The Couch Trip; A Countess from Hong Kong; Cyrano de Bergerac (1950); Cyrano de Bergerac (1990); The Dark Half; Dave; Dear Ruth; Desperately Seeking Susan; Easy to Wed; Fancy Pants; Favour, the Watch & the Very Big Fish; Finger of Guilt; Folies Bergere; The Front; Futureworld; General Della Rovere; Good Neighbor Sam; Great Impostor; Guardsman; Hail the Conquering Hero; Hands Across the Table; Hear My Song; Hell, Heaven, and Hoboken; Hero; Houseguest; I Married a Dead Man; I'd Rather Be Rich; Idiot's Delight; The Importance of Being Earnest; Invasion of the Body Snatchers (1956); Invasion of the Body Snatchers (1978); Iron Mask (1929); It Started with Eve; Kangaroo; Killjoy; A Kiss Before Dying (1956); A Kiss Before Dying (1991); Libeled Lady; Magic Face; The Man Who Haunted Himself; The Man Who Lost Himself; Mark of the Vampire; Masquerader; Meet the Applegates; Miami Blues; Monsieur Beaucaire; Monte Carlo; Moon Over Parador; Mrs Doubtfire; My Man Godfrey (1936); My Man Godfrey (1956); My Name is Julia Ross; No Man of Her Own (1949); No Mercy; No Way to Treat a Lady; Nothing Sacred; On the Double; On the Riviera; Only You; Opportunity Knocks; Paranoia; Phantom President; Pillow Talk; Pirate; The Pope Must Die(t); The Prince and the Pauper (1937); Princess Caraboo; Prisoner of Zenda (1937); Prisoner of Zenda (1952); Prisoner of Zenda (1979); The Prize; Quality Street; The Return of Martin Guerre; Roxanne; Ruling Class; Saint Benny, the Dip; Saving Grace; Scar; Schtonk!; Scotland Yard; Sex and the Single Girl; Shining Through; Silver Lode; Six Degrees of Separation; Sommersby; Soul Man; Southern Yankee; Star Spangled Rhythm; Starman; Start the Revolution Without Me; Statue; Sunburn; The Tenth Man; That Certain Feeling; That Night in Rio; They Knew What They Wanted; They Live; Things Change; Tootsie; True Lies; Twisted Nerve; Two-Faced Woman; Victor/Victoria; Virginia City; Watch on the Rhine; When in Rome; Whistle Down the Wind; Who?; Who Was That Lady?; Yentl; Zorro and the Gay Blade

Impostors-Actor (actors who play parts of others, usually hired): see also *Impostors: Identities-Assumed:* Callaway Went Thataway; Fancy Pants; General Della Rovere; Moon Over Parador

Impressing People: see *Social Climbing*

Improvisational Films (films which are noted to have had substantial portions of the dialogue improvised by the actors either before or during production): see also *Art Films:* Chantilly Lace; Faces; Lumiere; Mi Vida Loca; Queens Logic; Shadows; Sleep With Me; Someone to Love; Time of Your Life; Trapped in Paradise

In a Jam: see *Situation Comedy: Trapped*

Incest: see also *Molestation: Sex Offenders:* All the Fine Young Cannibals; Alpine Fire; Angela; Beau Pere; Bittersweet Love; Butterfly; Chances Are; Chinatown; Close My Eyes; Defenseless; Dolores Claiborne; Flesh and Bone; Fool for Love; Freud; Goodbye Gemini; The Homecoming (1973); The Hotel New Hampshire; The House of Usher (1960); The House of Usher (1990); I Sent a Letter to My Love; Late for Dinner; Les Enfants Terribles; Luna; Mad Monkey; Mildred Pierce; Mother's Boys; Murmur of the Heart; Nuts;

Obsession; Oedipus Rex; Shy People; Soapdish; Spanking the Monkey; Ten Days Wonder; Track 29; Twin Peaks; Twin Peaks: Fire Walk with Me

Incognito: see *Disguises: Spy Films: Undercover*

Incredible but Mostly True: see also *True or Not?: True Stories:* Anastasia (1956); Anastasia (1984); It Could Happen to You; The Positively True Adventures of the Alleged Texas Cheerleader-Murdering Mom; I Love You to Death; Outbreak; Princess Caraboo; The Search for Bridey Murphy; Sergeant York; Wild Child

Independent Films: see *Curiosities: Avant-Garde: Art Films: Cult Films*

India: see also *Indian/Pakistani People:* Bhowani Junction; Bonnie Scotland; Calcutta; City of Joy; Company Limited; Conduct Unbecoming; Deceivers; Distant Thunder (1973); Elephant Boy; Elephant Walk; Flame Over India; Gandhi; Green Goddess; Gunga Din; Heat and Dust; Jungle Book (1967); Jungle Book (1994); Kim; Lives of a Bengal Lancer; Mahabharata; Man in the Middle; Music Room; A Passage to India; The Rains Came; River (1951); Salaam Bombay!; Shakespeare Wallah; Wee Willie Winkie

Indian Films (of India in Asia): see also *India: Indian/Pakistani People:* Company Limited; An Enemy of the People (1989); Music Room; The World of Apu

Indian/Pakistani People (not necessarily in Asia): see also *India: England: Immigrants:* Bombay Talkie; Kim; London Kills Me; Madame Sousatzka; Masala; The Millionairess; Mississippi Masala; My Beautiful Laundrette; River (1951); Shakespeare Wallah; Two Way Stretch; Wild West; The World of Apu

Indians-American: see also *Native Americans (Modern): Westerns: West-Old:* Across the Wide Missouri; The Adventures of Tom Sawyer; Against a Crooked Sky; The Big Sky; Black Robe; Broken Arrow; Buffalo Bill; Buffalo Bill and the Indians, or Sitting Bull's History Lesson; Casque d'Or; Chato's Land; Cheyenne Autumn; Dark Wind; Distant Drums; Duel in the Sun; Eagle's Wing; Flaming Star; Foxfire (1955); Geronimo (1962); Geronimo (1993); How the West Was Won; Hudson's Bay; Incident at Oglala; Indian Fighter; Jim Thorpe, All American; Joe Panther; Kings of the Sun;

Last of His Tribe; The Last of the Mohicans (1936); The Last of the Mohicans (1992); Legend of the Lone Ranger; Light in the Forest; Little Big Horn; Little Big Man; The Lone Ranger (1955); The Lone Ranger and the Lost City of Gold; MacKenna's Gold; Major Dundee; A Man Called Horse; The Milagro Beanfield War; Naughty Marietta; Nightwing; Northwest Passage; One Flew Over Cuckoo's Nest; Outlaw; The Outsider; Poltergeist 2; Powwow Highway; Renegades; Return of a Man Called Horse; The Revengers; Rio Grande; Roanoak; Savage Sam; Scalphunters; The Searchers; The Seventh Cavalry; Shalako; Silent Tongue; Soldier Blue; Spirit Rider; Squanto; Squaw Man; Stagecoach (1939); Stagecoach (1966); Stalking Moon; Tell Them Willie Boy is Here; Thunderheart; Triumphs of a Man Called Horse; The Unforgiven (1960); Union Pacific; War Party; When the Legends Die

Indians-American, Conflict with (most anyone against the Indians, the Indians usually as enemy): see also *Cavalry vs. Indians: Cavalry: Indians-American:* Apache Uprising; Billy Jack; Broken Arrow; Drums Along the Mohawk; Fort Apache; The Frisco Kid (1979); Garden of Evil; Geronimo (1962); Geronimo (1993); Hallelujah Trail; How the West Was Won; The Last of the Mohicans (1936); The Last of the Mohicans (1992); The Party; Red River; Return of a Man Called Horse; The Revengers; Rio Grande; Roanoak; Savage Sam; Tell Them Willie Boy is Here; They Died with Their Boots On

Indians-Raised by: see also *Indians-American:* Triumphs of a Man Called Horse; Dances with Wolves; Little Big Man

Industrial Life: see *Factory Workers: Working Class*

Infatuations: see also *Love-First: Fatal Attractions: Obsessions: Coming of Age:* Accent on Youth; The Bachelor and the Bobby-Soxer; Best Foot Forward; Calendar Girl; Cameraman; A Certain Smile; A Child is Waiting; Chloe in the Afternoon; The Collector; The Crush; Cyrano de Bergerac (1950); Cyrano de Bergerac (1990); Daddy Longlegs; Death in Venice; The Devil and Miss Jones; Devotion; Diamond Jim; Easy to Love; Everybody's All American; Forever

Female; Gidget; Hairdresser's Husband; Hired Wife; Hud; I Dood It!; I Love Melvin; It's a Date; La Lectrice; The Last Tycoon; Laura; Lolita; A Man of No Importance; Miss Firecracker; No Small Affair; Of Mice and Men (1939); Of Mice and Men (1993); Play Misty for Me; Poison Ivy (1992); The Pornographers; Public Eye; Rambling Rose; Roman Spring of Mrs. Stone; The Secret Life of an American Wife; The Seven-Year Itch; Shadow of a Doubt; Sidewalks of London; Somewhere in Time; Sophie's Choice; St. Martin's Lane; Step Down to Terror; Stripper; Summer and Smoke; Summer of '42; Svengali (1931); Svengali (1983); Swann in Love; Teacher's Pet; Ten; That Certain Age; Thoroughly Modern Millie; Threshold; To Sir with Love; Tootsie; Uncle Buck; An Unsuitable Job For a Woman; Woman in the Window; Wuthering Heights (1939); Wuthering Heights (1953); Wuthering Heights (1970); Wuthering Heights (1992); Kiss for Corliss; Mona Lisa; The World of Henry Orient

Infidelity: see *Cheating Men: Cheating Women: Romance with Married Person: Murder of Spouse: Crimes of Passion*

Infidelity Crimes: see *Crimes of Passion: Jealous Spouses: Cheating Men: Cheating Women*

Informers: see also *Crime Drama:* Big Mouth; Captain Carey, USA; Double-Crossed; The Friends of Eddie Coyle; 48 Hours; The Fugitive (1947); Gator; The Gauntlet; Good Fellas; He Was Her Man; Kiss of Death (1947); Kiss of Death (1995); Narrow Margin (1952); Narrow Margin (1990)

Ingenues: see *Young Women: Feisty Females: Theater Life*

Inheritances At Stake: see also *Heirs: Heiresses: Rewards at Stake: Death-Dealing with: Royalty-Sudden/Inherited:* About Face; The Addams Family; Addams Family Values; Always Together; Aristocats; Arnold; Arthur; B.F.'s Daughter; Baby Boom; Better Late Than Never; Beverly Hillbillies; Billy Madison; Body Heat; Bonnie Scotland; Brain Donors; Brewster's Millions (1935); Brewster's Millions (1945); Brewster's Millions (1985); Candleshoe; Cat and Mouse; The Cat and the Canary (1927); The Cat and the Canary (1939); The Cat and the Canary (1979); Chase a Crooked Shadow; Chattanooga Choo Choo;

Cheyenne Social Club; Cinderella Jones; Daddy's Dyin'; Dark Angel (1991); Dynamite; Easy Money (1983); Equinox; Executive Suite; Flesh of the Orchid; Flight of the Doves; The Fortune; The Girl in the Watermelon; Good Neighbor Sam; Greedy; Harvey; Has Anybody Seen My Gal?; Honey Pot; Howards End; Hush, Hush, Sweet Charlotte; I'd Rather Be Rich; The Inheritance; The Invitation; It Started with Eve; It's Only Money; Jamaica Run; Kind Hearts and Coronets; King Lear (1971); King Ralph; La Cage Aux Folles 3: The Wedding; Lady Jane; Legacy; Lion in Winter; Little Big League; Little Foxes; Little Lord Fauntleroy (1936); Little Lord Fauntleroy (1980); Little Vegas; Loose Ankles; Man About the House; Melvin and Howard; Million Dollar Baby; Mr. Billion; Murder, He Says; My Forbidden Past; Never Say Die; Nicholas Nickleby; Night of the Hunter; Pass the Ammo; Passed Away; Payment Deferred; Ran; Richie Rich; Rosie; Ruling Class; Ruthless People; Scavenger Hunt; Servant; Seven Chances; Seven Days Leave; Short Time; A Simple Twist of Fate; Speak Easily; Splitting Heirs; Stay Hungry; Strange Bargain; Tears in the Rain; That Forsyte Woman; Tillie and Gus; Twelve Chairs; Twelve Plus One; Violette; Volpone; The Wolves of Willoughby Chase; The Wrong Box

In-Laws-Troublesome: see also *Relatives-Troublesome:* Best Friends; Between Two Women; Cat on a Hot Tin Roof (1958); Cat on a Hot Tin Roof (1984); Die! Die! My Darling!; Heartbreak Kid; Kind of Loving; Lolita; No Room for the Groom; 'Tis a Pity She's a Whore; Vivacious Lady; You Can't Take It With You (1938); You Can't Take It With You (1986); You'll Like My Mother

Inner City Life: see also *Big City Life: Skid Row: Gangs: Poor People: Social Drama: New York Life:* Above the Rim; Accatone; Angel; Angelo, My Love; Angels With Dirty Faces; Assault on Precinct 13; The Beat; Blackboard Jungle; Blankman; Bloodhounds of Broadway (1952); Bloodhounds of Broadway (1989); Breakin'; Breakin' 2: Electric Boogaloo; Candyman; Carlito's Way; A Change of Habit; Choirboys; Christiane F.; Chu Chu and the Philly Flash; Cinderella Liberty; Class of 1999; Class of '84; Class of Miss MacMichael; Clockers; Come Back Charleston Blue;

Daybreak; Dead Boyz Can't Fly; Dead End; Death Wish 2; Death Wish 3; Death Wish 4; Death Wish 5; Desperate Characters; Devil is a Sissy; DROP Squad; Fighting Back; Five Corners; Fort Apache, The Bronx; Fresh; Gigot; Golden Boy; Guys and Dolls; Hangin' with the Homeboys; Harlem Nights; A Hero Ain't Nothin' but a Sandwich; Hoop Dreams; I Like it Like That; I, Mobster; I'm Gonna Git You Sucka; Jacob's Ladder; Juice; Jumpin at the Boneyard; Just Another Girl on the IRT; King of the Gypsies; Landlord; The Last Angry Man; Last Exit to Brooklyn; Last of England; Lean on Me; Let No Man Write My Epitaph; Listen Up: The Lives of Quincy Jones; London Belongs to Me; The Lords of Flatbush; Man with the Golden Arm; Manhattan Melodrama; Mean Streets; Menace II Society; Midnight Cowboy; Mi Vida Loca; Mo' Money; Mother, Jugs & Speed; My Bodyguard; The Naked Kiss; Oliver!; Oliver Twist (1948); Oliver Twist (1982); Panic in Needle Park; Pixote; Popi; The River Niger; Saint of Fort Washington; Salaam Bombay!; Sammy and Rosie Get Laid; Say Amen, Somebody!; Shadows; Shaft; Shaft's Big Score; She's Gotta Have It; Skippy; Slow Dancing in the Big City; Somebody Up There Likes Me; Soylent Green; Stand and Deliver; State of Grace; Straight out of Brooklyn; Street Scene; Street Smart; Streets of Gold; Sundays and Cybele; The Super; Superfly; Teachers; To Sir with Love; Trespass; Underworld, USA; Up the Down Staircase; Uptown Saturday Night; The Wanderers; Warriors; White Mama; Young Savages; Zebrahead

Innocence Lost: see *Virgins: Illusions Destroyed: Dreams-Broken*

Innocent Bystanders: see also *Witnesses:* The American Friend; Behave Yourself!; Big Mouth; Casanova's Big Night; The Client; House of Cards; Human Factor; I am a Fugitive from a Chain Gang; In-Laws; The Inspector General; Jumpin' Jack Flash; Legacy; Lost Honor of Katharina Blum; Lured; The Man Who Knew Too Much (1934); The Man Who Knew Too Much (1956); Marathon Man; Mary Burns, Fugitive; Mask of Dimitrios; Masters; Miracles; Miss Grant Takes Richmond; Our Man in Havana; The Passenger; Pepe; Pickup on South Street; Protocol; Run; The Seduction of Mimi; The Third Man;

Trouble for Two; Twenty-Three Paces to Baker Street; Woman in the Window; The Wrong Man; Year of the Gun

Insane-Plot to Drive: see also *Mindgames: Illusions: Committed Wrongly: Love-Questionable: Mental Illness: Asylums:* And Now the Screaming Starts; Asylum; Avenging Conscience; Dark Waters; Dead of Night (1945); Dominique; Dead of Winter; Fear in the Night; Gaslight (1939); Gaslight (1944); Hush, Hush, Sweet Charlotte; Lady in the Car with Glasses and a Gun; Let's Scare Jessica to Death; Night Walker; North by Northwest; The Pit and the Pendulum (1961); The Pit and the Pendulum (1991); Rosemary's Baby; Shock Corridor; Suspicion; The Tenant; What's the Matter with Helen?

Insanity: see *Mental Illness: Asylums: Serial Killers: Insane-Plot to Drive: Psycho Thrillers*

Mental Illness-Questionable: see *Mental Illness: Insane-Plot to Make*

Insects (as monsters or not): see also *Monsters-Mutants: Monsters-Animal:* Ants; The Applegates; Arachnophobia; The Bug; Charlotte's Web; Creepshow; Empire of the Ants; The Fly (1958); The Fly (1986); Fly II; The Hellstrom Chronicle; Honey, I Shrunk the Kids; Kingdom of the Spiders; Meet the Applegates; Mothra; Mysterious Island; Naked Lunch; Return of the Fly; Swarm; Them!; Wasp Woman

Inspirational: see *Underdog Stories: Disabled People: Tearjerkers: Disease Stories: Religion: Old-Fashioned Recent Films*

Insurance Scams: see also *Con Artists: Thieves: Embezzlers: Inheritances at Stake: Rewards at Stake:* The Adjuster; Consenting Adults; Double Indemnity; Five Miles to Midnight; Fortune Cookie; Malice; The Producers; Pursuit of D. B. Cooper; Running Man (1963); The Thomas Crown Affair; Wreck of the Mary Deare; Zigzag

Intellectuals: see also *Geniuses: College Life: Professors:* Barcelona; The Devil's Wanton; Half Moon Street; Metropolitan (1990); My Dinner With Andre; Reds; The Return of the Secaucus Seven; The Third Man; This Island Earth; The Time of Your Life

Intellectual vs. Uneducated: see *Smart vs. Dumb: Snobs vs. Slobs*

Intergenerational Love: see *Older*

Men with Younger Women: Older Women with Younger Men

International Cast: see also **All-Star Casts: Ensemble Films:** Around the World in 80 Days; Avalanche Express; Babette's Feast; Bitter Moon; Black Orpheus; Blame it on the Bellboy; Blood Relatives; AA; A Bridge Too Far; Cassandra Crossing; The Damned; Danton; Dersu Uzala; El Cid; Fanny; Five Graves to Cairo; Gaby, a True Story; Gandhi; Histoires Extraordinaires; International House; Is Paris Burning?; The Italian Job; Knave of Hearts; Kremlin Letter; Let's Hope it's a Girl; Lili Marleen; Little Drummer Girl; Ludwig; Marquise of O; Melancholia; Murder on the Orient Express; Oldest Profession; Serpent's Egg; Shalako; Tess; Torrents of Spring; Toto le Heros; Tristana; The Visit; Viva Maria!

Interracial Friendships: see **Friendships-Interracial: Race Relations**

Interracial Love: see **Romance-Interracial**

Interviews (included in a conventional, narrative film): see also **Documentaries: Docudrama: Documentary Style:** Annie Hall; The Autobiography of Miss Jane Pittman; The Chapman Report; Husbands and Wives; Intervista; Reds; Roger & Me; Stardust Memories; Superstar, The Life and Times of Andy Warhol; The Thin Blue Line; Trail of the Pink Panther

Interwoven Stories (stories in which the characters are linked eventually, though not necessarily directly): see also **Parallel Stories: Slice of Life Stories: Multiple Stories: FARCE:** Amarcord; Battle Cry; Battle of Britian; Berlin Alexanderplatz; California Suite; City of Hope; Dead of Night (1945); Earthquake; Exodus; The Four Seasons; Friday the Thirteenth (1933); Gettysburg; Grand Hotel; The Greatest Story Ever Told; Guyana Tragedy, The Story of Jim Jones; Hannah and Her Sisters; Heimat; Hotel; Hotel Paradiso; How the West Was Won; Howards End; If I Had a Million; Intolerance; Is Paris Burning?; Juice; Kaos; La Ronde (1950); La Ronde (1964); La Vie de Boheme; The Last Days of Pompeii; The Last Picture Show; Laurel Avenue; Lawrenceville Stories; Matinee; Midway; Mixed Nuts; Mystery Train; Nashville; A Night to Remember (1958); 92 in the Shade; No Down

Payment; Noises Off; Opposite Sex; Our Town; The Paper; Peyton Place; Places in the Heart; Ragtime; Ready to Wear; Run for Your Money; San Francisco; Scorchers; Separate Tables; Shampoo; Ship of Fools; Short Cuts; Slacker; Slaves of New York; Stand; The Story of Three Loves; Street Scene; Tales of Manhattan; They All Laughed; Time for Loving; Traffik; Twenty Bucks; VIPs; Voyage of the Damned; The Wedding; Weekend at the Waldorf; Welcome to L.A.; Women; Yellow Rolls Royce; The Young Lions; Ziegfeld Girl

Introverted vs. Extroverted: see **Extroverted vs. Introverted:** also **Smart vs. Dumb: Free Spirits: Nerds**

Inventors: see also **Scientists: Geniuses: Biographies: Eccentric People: Mad Scientists:** The Absent-Minded Professor; Beauty for the Asking; Chitty Chitty Bang Bang; Edison, the Man; The Great Moment; The Great Race; Hello Down There; Her Husband's Affairs; High Pressure; Honey, I Blew Up the Kid; Honey, I Shrunk the Kids; The Hudsucker Proxy; It Happens Every Spring; Madame Curie; Magic Box; The Man in the White Suit; Master of the World; Promoter; Rikky and Pete; The Road to Wellville; Story of Alexander Graham Bell; Tucker: The Man and His Dream; 20,000 Leagues Under the Sea; Until the End of the World; X-The Man with X-Ray Eyes; You're Telling Me; Young Tom Edison

Invisibility: see also **Fantasy: SCI-FI: Illusions:** Abbott & Costello Meet the Invisible Man; Alice; Drop Dead Fred; Forbidden Planet; Harvey; The Invisible Man Returns; The Invisible Man's Revenge; The Invisible Woman; Memoirs of an Invisible Man; The Neverending Story 2; Now You See Him, Now You Don't; Predator; Predator 2; Sleepwalkers; Wolfen; The Wonderful World of Brothers Grimm

Ireland: see also **Irish Films: IRA: Leprechauns: British Films: Scotland: Wales:** The Adventuress; Alive and Kicking; Cal; Circle of Friends; The Commitments; The Crying Game; Da; The Dead; Dementia 13; Eat the Peach; Finian's Rainbow; Flight of the Doves; The Girl with Green Eyes; Green Years; Hidden Agenda; High Spirits; The Informer; Into the West; Irish Eyes Are Smiling; Kes; The Key (1934); The Lamb;

Leprechaun; The Lonely Passion of Judith Hearne; Luck of the Irish; Man of Aran; A Man of No Importance; The Name of the Father; Odd Man Out; Parnell; Playboys; A Prayer for the Dying; Quackser Fortune Has a Cousin in the Bronx; The Quiet Man; Rawhead Rex; Ryan's Daughter; The Secret of Roan Inish; Shake Hands with the Devil; The Snapper; Taffin; Widows' Peak; Wings of the Morning

Irish Films (films made in Ireland and usually Irish-British-financed): see also **Ireland: Irish Land Battles: Leprechauns: British Films: Scotland: Wales:** Cal; Circle of Friends; The Commitments; Eat the Peach; Field; Into the West; Kes; Lamb; My Left Foot; The Name of the Father; Playboys; A Prayer for the Dying; The Snapper; Taffin; Widows' Peak

Irish Land Battles: see also **Ireland: Save the Farm/Land: Mortgage Drama:** The Field; Taffin; Local Hero

Irish People (not necessarily in Ireland): The Commitments; Da; Darby O'Gill and the Little People; Far and Away; Field; Finian's Rainbow; Fitzcarraldo; The Girl with Green Eyes; Green Years; Hear My Song; Hidden Agenda; Irish Eyes Are Smiling; Irish in Us; Miller's Crossing; My Left Foot; No Surrender; Only the Lonely; Quackser Fortune Has a Cousin in the Bronx; The Quiet Man; State of Grace; A Tree Grows in Brooklyn; Ulysses (1967)

Irish Republican Army (IRA): see also **Terrorists: Ireland:** The Adventuress; Blown Away; The Crying Game; Hidden Agenda; The Informer; The Name of the Father; Odd Man Out; Patriot Games; A Prayer for the Dying; Shake Hands with the Devil

Iron Curtain-Behind the (going across the line, during Communist rule): see also **Escape from Iron Curtain: Spy Films: Cold War Era: Berlin: Communists:** Cloak and Dagger (1946); Colonel Redl; The Confession; Eminent Domain; The Fourth War; A Funeral in Berlin; The Looking Glass War; Night Crossing; Night People; The Prisoner (1955); The Spy Who Came in from the Cold; Torn Curtain

Iron Curtain-Escape from: see also **Escape Adventure: Iron Curtain-Behind the:** Abschied von Gestern; A Funeral in Berlin; The Looking Glass War; Night Crossing; Torn Curtain

J

Jack the Ripper: see also *Serial Killers: HORROR: Victorian Era:* Jack the Ripper (1958); Jack the Ripper (1985); Jack's Back; The Lodger (1926); The Lodger (1932); The Lodger (1944); Man in the Attic; Murder by Decree; Pandora's Box; Time after Time

Jailed Children/Teens: see *Juvenile Delinquents: Teenage Terrors: Gangs*

Jailed People: see *Criminals: Prison Drama: Courtroom Drama: Trials*

Jails: see *Prison Drama*

James Bond: see also *Secret Agents: Spies: Spy Films: Playboys:* Casino Royale; Diamonds are Forever; Dr. No; For Your Eyes Only; From Russia with Love; Goldeneye; Goldfinger; License to Kill; Live and Let Die; Living Daylights; Man with the Golden Gun; Moonraker; Never Say Never Again; Octopussy; The Spy Who Loved Me; Spymaker, The Secret Life of Ian Fleming; Thunderball; A View to a Kill; You Only Live Twice

James Dean Fans: Forever James Dean; Come Back to the Five and Dime, Jimmy Dean, Jimmy Dean; 9-30-55

Japan (as a setting): see also *Japanese People: Japanese as Enemy: Japanese Mob: Japanese Films:* The Barbarian and the Geisha; Black Rain (1988); Black Rain (1989); Bushido Blade; The Challenge; Children of Hiroshima; Destination Tokyo; Early Summer; A Girl

Named Tamiko; Godzilla (1955); Godzilla versus Gigan; Godzilla versus Megalon; In the Realm of the Senses; Kagemusha; Kwaidan; Madame Butterfly; The Mikado; Mishima; My Geisha; Nobody's Perfect; Rhapsody in August; Sayonara; The Seven Samurai; Shogun Assassin; Tampopo; A Taxing Woman; Teahouse of the August Moon; Thirty Seconds Over Tokyo; Tokyo Pop; Ugetsu Monogatari; Walk, Don't Run; You Only Live Twice

Japanese as Enemy: see also *World War II Era: Pearl Harbor: Japanese People: Japan: Japanese Mob: Germans as Enemy:* Across the Pacific; Blood on the Sun; Bridge on the River Kwai; Come See the Paradise; Destination Tokyo; Farewell to the King; Fighting Seabees; The Flying Leathernecks; The Flying Tigers; Go for Broke; God Is My Co-Pilot; Guadalcanal Diary; Gung Ho! (1943); Gung Ho (1986); Hell in the Pacific; Hellcats of the Navy; Malaya; Merry Christmas, Mr. Lawrence; 1941; None But the Brave; Overlanders; Rising Sun; Thirty Seconds Over Tokyo; Three Came Home; Tokyo Joe; Tora! Tora! Tora!; A Town Like Alice (1956); A Town Like Alice (1985); The Wackiest Ship in the Army

Japanese Films: see also *Japan:* An Actor's Revenge; The Adventures of Milo and Otis; Akira Kurosawa's Dreams; The

Bad Sleep Well; Black Rain (1988); Burmese Harp; Children of Hiroshima; Dersu Uzala; Early Summer; Gate of Hell; Godzilla (1955); Godzilla versus Gigan; Godzilla versus Megalon; Green Slime; Ikiru; In the Realm of the Senses; Island (1961); Kagemusha; Kwaidan; Merry Christmas, Mr. Lawrence; The Pornographers; Ran; Rhapsody in August; Sandakan No. 8; The Seven Samurai; Shogun; The Assassin; Tampopo; A Taxing Woman; Throne of Blood; Tokyo Decadence; Tokyo Story; Ugetsu Monogatari; What's Up, Tiger Lily?; Woman in the Dunes; Yojimbo

Japanese Mob: see *Mob-Asian: Mob Stories: Martial Arts: Japanese Films*

Japanese People: see also *Japan: Japanese as Enemy: Japanese Mob:* Children of Hiroshima; Come See the Paradise; Die Hard; A Girl Named Tamiko; Go for Broke; Gung Ho (1986); Hell in the Pacific; Hiroshima, Mon Amour; Iron Maze; Madame Butterfly; Majority of One; The Mikado; Mystery Train; Rhapsody in August; Sayonara; Teahouse of the August Moon; Tokyo Joe; Tokyo Pop; Tokyo Story; Tora! Tora! Tora!; Yakuza

Jazz Life: see also *Musicians: New Orleans:* Bird; Birth of the Blues; Blues in the Night; Five Pennies; The Gene Krupa Story; Greenwich Village; King of

Damned; The Wandering Jew; Where's Poppa?; White Palace; Wholly Moses; Yentl

Jews-Saving/Hiding: see also *Jewish People: Concentration Camps: Nazi Stories: Saving Someone: Anti-Semitism:* Assisi Underground; Bittere Ernte; Diary of Anne Frank (1959); Escape; The Golem; Love in Germany; Me and the Colonel; Mr. Klein; The Revolt of Job; Schindler's List; Shining Through; The Shop on Main Street; White Rose

JFK (stories involving John Fitzgerald Kennedy and/or his assassination): see also *Assassination Plots: Kennedy Family: Presidents:* In the Line of Fire; JFK; Love Field; Ruby

Jim Thompson-esque Stories (suspense with film noir overtones, investigating the underworld of usually small-time con artists and killers, including this author's work): see also *Crime Drama: Film Noir: SUSPENSE:* After Dark, My Sweet; The Killer Inside Me; Coup de Torchon; Desire and Hell at Sunset Motel; The Getaway (1972); The Getaway (1994); The Grifters; Kill Me Again; The Kill-Off

Jobs-Second: see *Making a Living: Moonlighting: Mothers-Struggling: Unemployment*

Journalists: see also *Journalist Detectives: Writers: TV Life: Publishing World:* Aaron Slick from Punkin Crick; Absence of Malice; Ace in the Hole; Action in Arabia; After Office Hours; All the President's Men; Ambulance; Arise, My Love; Assassination Bureau; The Blessed Event; Blood on the Sun; Broadcast News; Cafe Society; Cairo (1942); Calling Northside 777; China Girl (1942); The China Syndrome; Christmas in Connecticut (1945); Christmas in Connecticut (1992); Continental Divide; Cry Freedom; Deadline USA; Defense of the Realm; Dolores Claiborne; Easy to Wed; Eleni; Eyewitness (1981); Fever Pitch; Five Star Final; Fletch; Fletch Lives; Foreign Intrigue; Front Page (1931); Front Page (1974); Funny Face; G.I. Joe; Gaily, Gaily; The Ghost and Mr. Chicken; Girl from Petrovka; The Great Race; The Harder They Fall; Here Comes the Groom; Hero; His Girl Friday; I Cover the Waterfront; I Love Trouble (1994); Island (1980); It Happened One

Night; It Happened Tomorrow; Journey for Margaret; Keeper of the Flame; The Killing Fields; La Dolce Vita; Libeled Lady; Living it Up; Lost Angel; Love and Hisses; Love Is a Many-Splendored Thing; Love Machine; Love on the Run (1936); Lover Come Back (1946); Luck of the Irish; Mad Miss Manton; Mean Season; Medium Cool; Meet John Doe; Murder Man; The Naked Truth; Natural Born Killers; Network; New Kind of Love; Newsfront; Newsies; Next Time We Love; No Time for Love; Nothing Sacred; The Odessa File; The Osterman Weekend; The Paper; Paper Lion; The Parallax View; The Passenger; Perfect; The Philadelphia Story; Platinum Blonde; Ploughman's Lunch; Quiet American; Rollover; Salvador; Sandakan No. 8; Scandal Sheet; Show of Force; Shy People; Sky's the Limit; Slow Dancing in the Big City; Somewhere I'll Find You; Special Bulletin; St. Ive's; Stand Up and Be Counted; Street Smart; The Sun Also Rises; Superman; Superman 2; Superman 3; Superman 4; Sweet Smell of Success; Switching Channels; Tarnished Angels; Teacher's Pet; Three O'Clock High; Top Secret Affair; Turtle Beach; Two Against the World; Ulysses (1967); Under Fire; Violets are Blue; Washington Story; The Wedding Present; While the City Sleeps; Woman of the Year; Wrong is Right; Year of the Dragon; Year of the Gun; You Can't Run Away From It

Journalists/Writers as Detectives: see also *Detective Stories: Detectives-Amateur: Writers:* Absence of Malice; All the President's Men; Brenda Starr; Calling Northside 777; China Syndrome; City in Fear; Compromising Positions; Deadline USA; Defense of the Realm; Fletch; Fletch Lives; The Foreign Correspondent; Foreign Intrigue; The Front Page (1931); The Front Page (1974); Gentleman's Agreement; I Love Trouble (1994); Les Comperes; Mean Season; Night Stalker/The Night Strangler; The Odessa File; The Osterman Weekend; The Parallax View; The Passenger; Quiz Show; Rollover; Scandal Sheet; Shock Corridor; Show of Force; Turtle Beach; Year of the Gun

Journeys: see also *ADVENTURE: Nightmare Journeys: Quests: Treasure Hunts: Vacations:* Action in the North Atlantic; The Adventures of Huckleberry Finn (1960); The Adventures of

Huckleberry Finn (1985); The Adventures of Marco Polo; The Adventures of Milo and Otis; Apache Uprising; Around the World in 80 Days; Beat the Devil; Bend of the River; Benji the Hunted; The Big Sky; Bill & Ted's Bogus Journey; Bill & Ted's Excellent Adventure; Black Rose; Blonde Venus; The Blue Bird (1940); The Blue Bird (1976); Burke and Wills; Caravans; Chattanooga Choo Choo; Cherry 2000; Cheyenne Autumn; Close Encounters of the Third Kind; Comancheros; Dark of the Sun; The Deer Hunter; Desperate Journey; Destiny of a Man; Doctor Zhivago; Dudes; El Norte; Emerald Forest; Erik The Viking; Everybody's Fine; Fitzcarraldo; Five Came Back; Flame Over India; Flight of the Phoenix; For a Few Dollars More; Forbidden Planet; Gallipoli; Goonies; The Grapes of Wrath; Great Expectations; Green Mansions; Hallelujah Trail; Hawaii; Heat and Dust; Heller in Pink Tights; Huckleberry Finn (1939); Huckleberry Finn (1960); Huckleberry Finn (1974); In Search of the Castaways; Incredible Journey; Indiana Jones and The Last Crusade; Indiana Jones and The Temple of Doom; Iron Mistress; Island at the Top of the World; Jack London; Jason and the Argonauts; Jeremiah Johnson; Journey into Fear; Journey of Hope; Journey of Natty Gann; King Solomon's Mines (1937); King Solomon's Mines (1950); King Solomon's Mines (1985); La Strada; Lady in the Car with Glasses and a Gun; Lassie Come Home; Legend; Legend of the Lost; Light at the Edge of the World; Light in the Forest; Lili; A Little Romance; Mister Buddwing; Mountains on the Moon; The Neverending Story; Neverending Story II: The Next Chapter; Night on Earth; North; Northwest Mounted Police; Outcast of the Islands; Passage to Marseilles; Pelle the Conqueror; The People That Time Forgot; Railway Children; Rain Man; Rambo: First Blood Part Two; Razor's Edge (1946); Razor's Edge (1986); Red River; Renegades; Return to Oz; Revolution; Rikky and Pete; Rio Lobo; Roadside Prophets; Rock-a Doodle; Rope of Sand; Royal Flash; Scott of the Antarctic; Sea Chase; The Searchers; The Secret of NIMH; Seventh Cavalry; The Sheltering Sky; Ship of Fools; Sitting Ducks; Soldier Blue; The Sorcerer; Stagecoach (1939);

Stagecoach (1966); Star Trek II: The Wrath of Khan; Star Trek III: The Search for Spock; Star Trek: The Motion Picture; Star Trek V: The Final Frontier; Star Trek VI: The Undiscovered Country; Strangers in Good Company; Sundowners; Tall Men; The Ten Commandments; The Time Machine; A Trip to Bountiful; Two Mules for Sister Sara; 2010; Two Women; Valley Obscured by the Clouds; Wagonmaster; Walkabout; The Way West; Wells Fargo; White Fang; Whoopee; Willow; The Wizard of Oz (1925); The Wizard of Oz (1939)

Judaism: see *Israel: Israeli Films: Jewish People: Nazi Stories: Religious Films*

Judges: see also *Courtroom Drama: Lawyers: Supreme Court: Trials:* Act of Murder; And Justice for All; Angel on My Shoulder; Ann Vickers; The Bachelor and the Bobby-Soxer; Cass Timberlane; A Family Affair; First Monday in October; The Life and Times of Judge Roy Bean; The Magnificent Yankee; Man from

Colorado; The Pelican Brief; Star Chamber; Talk of the Town; The Westerner

Judgment Day: see *Apocalyptic Stories: Biblical Stories: God: Heaven: Hell*

Jungles: see also *ADVENTURE: Africa: Amazon River: Primates: South America:* The African Queen; Africa Screams; Amazon; Apocalypse Now; Appointment in Honduras; Burmese Harp; Bye Bye Brazil; Call Me Bwana; FernGully: The Last Rainforest; Five Came Back; Green Mansions; Greystoke: The Legend of Tarzan; Hearts of Darkness: A Filmmaker's Apocalypse; Medicine Man; The Mission; Murphy's War; Predator; Run for the Sun; Sheena, Queen of the Jungle; Skullduggery; Sniper; Tarzan and His Mate; Tarzan Escapes; Tarzan, The Ape Man (1932); Tarzan, the Ape Man (1981); Tarzan's New York Adventure

Juries (behind the scenes of a courtroom): see also *Courtroom Drama:* Lady in Question; Twelve Angry Men

Justice-Search for: see *Accused Unjustly: Framed?: Ethics: Courtroom Drama: Lawyer Detectives: Lawyers: Judges*

Juvenile Deliquents: see also *Teenage Terrors: Teenage Movies: Rebels: Prison Drama: Children-Troublesome:* Bad Boys; Badlands; Blackboard Jungle; The Boys Next Door; Boys Town; Class of 1999; Class of '84; A Clockwork Orange; The Cowboys; Cry Baby; Delicate Delinquent; The Devil is a Sissy; Dino; The Drowning Pool; The 400 Blows; Goodbye, Pork Pie; Grease; Grease 2; I Believe in You; Kitten with a Whip; Last Summer; London Belongs to Me; Look in Any Window; Mayor of Hell; Men of Boys' Town; Murder in New Hampshire; O.C. and Stiggs; Oliver!; Oliver Twist (1948); Oliver Twist (1982); Olivier, Olivier; Once Upon a Time in America; Saint Benny, the Dip; Susan Slept Here; Take the Money and Run; That Was Then . . . This Is Now; Three for the Road; You Can't Get Away With Murder

K

KGB Agents: see also *CIA Agents: Cold War Era: Russians: Russians as Enemy: Secret Agents: Spy Films: Spies:*
Embassy; The Experts; Interrogation; Kremlin Letter; The Osterman Weekend; Outrageous Fortune; Russia House; S*P*Y*S; Telefon; White Nights (1985); Who Was That Lady?

Kidnappers-Sympathizing with: see also *Kidnappings:* Backtrack; The Chase (1994); Fuzzy Pink Nightgown; Flesh and Blood (1985); The Getaway (1972); The Getaway (1994); It's a Wonderful World; No Orchids for Miss Blandish; Patty Hearst; Quick; Rafferty and the Gold Dust Twins; Ruthless People; Three Days of the Condor; Tiger Bay; The Wind and the Lion

Kidnappings: see also *Hostage Drama:*
The Abductors; Ace Ventura, Pet Detective; Adam; After Dark, My Sweet; Against a Crooked Sky; Ambassador; American Ninja 2; Any Which Way You Can; Arabesque; Ashanti: Land of No Mercy; Atomic City; Autobus; Bandolero; Beach Blanket Bingo; Beethoven; Beethoven's 2nd; Benji; Beverly Hillbillies; The Big Broadcast of 1936; Big Foot; Big Jake; Black Marble; The Black Stallion Returns; Black Windmill; Born in East L.A.; Bound and Gagged, a Love Story; Bride Came C.O.D.; The Cabinet of Caligari (1962); Candleshoe;

Chitty Chitty Bang Bang; Cliffhanger; Cloak and Dagger (1946); Cohen and Tate; The Collector; Comin' At Ya!; Conflict of Interest; D.C. Cab; Deadly Trap; Desert Law; The Devil's Bride; Disappearance of Aimee; Don't Just Stand There; Dr. Cyclops; DROP Squad; Dumb and Dumber; Emerald Forest; Escape From New York; Experts; 52 Pick-up; Flesh and Blood (1985); Flight of the Navigator; The Foreign Correspondent; Frantic (1988); Fuzzy Pink Nightgown; The General; The Getaway (1972); The Getaway (1994); Green Goddess; Guarding Tess; Gun Fury; Happening; Harum Scarum; The Hunchback of Notre Dame (1923); The Hunchback of Notre Dame (1939); The Hunchback of Notre Dame (1956); The Hunchback of Notre Dame (1982); In Like Flint; Indiana Jones and the Last Crusade; The Ipcress File; Iron Mask (1929); Island (1980); It's a Wonderful World; Jack the Giant Killer; Kidnapped (1938); Kidnapped (1959); Kidnapped (1971); Kidnapping of the President; The King of Comedy; Labyrinth; Last Outpost; Lethal Weapon; Light in the Forest; The Lindbergh Kidnapping Case; Lorna Doone; The Lost; Love and Bullets; Love and Money; Mademoiselle Fifi; The Man Who Knew Too Much (1934); The Man Who Knew Too Much (1956); Masquerade (1965);

Miracles; Misery; Moon Over Parador; Mothra; Murderer's Row; My Name is Julia Ross; Nancy Steele is Missing; Never Say Never Again; Night of the Following Day; Night of the Juggler; Night People; Nine to Five; No Deposit, No Return; No Orchids for Miss Blandish; North by Northwest; Notorious; Obsession; Orphans; Pathfinder; Patty Hearst; Poltergeist; Prize; The Professionals; Rafferty and the Gold Dust Twins; Raising Arizona; Ransom Rawhide; The Real McCoy; Rescue Me; The Rescuers; Rescuers Down Under; Return from Witch Mountain; Return of the Seven; Rhythm on the Range; Ring of the Musketeers; Romancing the Stone; Rosebud; Ruthless People; Savage; Seance on a Wet Afternoon; Seems Like Old Times; Shadow Riders; Short Circuit; Short Circuit 2; Skyjacked; Spacehunter, Adventures in the Forbidden Zone; Star Wars; Street Fighter; Streets of Fire; Taking of Pelham 123; Target; Tattoo; That Cold Day in the Park; That Darn Cat!; Three Days of the Condor; The Three Musketeers (1935); The Three Musketeers (1939); The Three Musketeers (1948); Tiger Bay; Toy Soldiers; Tragedy of a Ridiculous Man; Union Station; Venom; Villain; Where Are the Children?; Where Eagles Dare; Whistling in the Dark; White Nights (1985); Who?; Who's

Harry Crumb?; Wild Geese II; Wind and the Lion; Woman in the Dunes; Yakuza; Yellow Canary

Killing Sprees: see *Murder Sprees: Mass Murderers: Serial Killers: Outlaw Road Movies: Criminal Couples*

Kill the Beast (a plot/theme in which the constant, nagging goal is the necessity to kill a monster-animal, human, or otherwise, not just run away from the menace or warn people about it): see also *Rogue Plots: THRILLERS: Malicious Menaces: Serial Killers: Trail of a Killer: Psycho Killers:* Alien; Aliens; Alligator; Alligator II: The Mutation; Blind Side; Car; Child's Play (1988); Child's Play 2; Child's Play 3; Criminal Law; Daddy's Gone A-Hunting; Duel; Exorcist III; Extremities; Fatal Attraction; Frankenstein (1931); Frankenstein '70; Frankenstein and the Monster from Hell; Frankenstein Created Woman; Frankenstein Unbound; Friday the 13th (1980); Friday the 13th: Final Chapter; Friday the 13th, Part II; Friday the 13th, Part 3-D; Friday the 13th Part V-A New Beginning; Friday the 13th Part VI-Jason Lives; Friday the 13th Part VII-The New Blood; Friday the 13th Part VIII-Jason Takes Manhattan; Gorgon; Graveyard Shift; Grizzly; Halloween; Halloween 2; Halloween 3: Season of the Witch; Halloween 4: The Return of Michael Myers; Halloween 5: The Revenge of Michael Myers; The Hand (1960); The Hand (1981); Hardware; Jaws; Jaws 2; Jaws 3-D; Jaws 4: The Revenge; Jurassic Park; Leviathan; Mother's Boys; Split Second; A Stranger Is Watching; Temp; Tentacles; Terminal Man; Unlawful Entry

King Arthur Legend: see *Camelot Stories: England: Medieval Times: Magic: Legends: Mythology:*

Kingdoms: see also *Castles: Fairy Tales: Camelot Stories: Legends: Mythology: Royalty:* Alice in Wonderland; Apocalypse Now; Beauty and the Beast (1991); Call Me Madam; Chitty Chitty Bang Bang; Coming to America; Court Jester; Duck Soup; Farewell to the King; Hook; King and I; The Mouse That Roared; Prisoner of Zenda; Romanoff and Juliet; Sword & the Sorcerer; The Thief of Bagdad (1924); The Thief of Baghdad (1940); Willy Wonka and the Chocolate Factory

King Henry VIII: see also *Kings: Queen Elizabeth:* Anne of a Thousand Days; Henry VIII and His Six Wives

Kings: see also *Royalty: Queens: Castles: Friendship with Royalty:* Alexander the Great; All the Mornings of the World; Anna and the King of Siam; As You Like It (1936); As You Like It (1992); Becket; Braveheart; Captain Kidd; Cardinal Richelieu; Chimes at Midnight; Christopher Columbus (1949); Christopher Columbus: The Discovery (1992); Coming to America; Court Jester; Cromwell; David and Bathsheba; Dubarry Was a Lady; Edward II; Farewell to the King; Henry V (1944); Henry V (1989); Henry VIII and His Six Wives; If I Were King; Ivan the Terrible; Julius Caesar; King and I; King David; King in New York; King Lear (1971); King of Hearts; King Ralph; King's Whore; La Nuit de Varennes; The Last Emperor; The Lion in Winter; Lola Montes; Ludwig; Madame Dubarry; A Man for All Seasons; The Man Who Would Be King; Merry Widow (1925); Merry Widow (1934); Merry Widow (1952); Monsieur Beaucaire; Nicholas and Alexandra; Nouvelle Vague; Parsifal Passion/Madame Dubarry (1919); The

Prince and the Pauper (1937); Prince Valiant; Prisoner of Zenda (1937); Prisoner of Zenda (1952); Prisoner of Zenda (1979); Private Life of Henry VIII; Richard III; Rise of Louis XIV; Sword of Lancelot; The Thief of Bagdad (1924); The Thief of Baghdad (1940); Tower of London (1939); Tower of London (1962)

Kitchen Sink Drama (the style of film-making in 1960s Britain that dealt with ordinary working people in realistic terms, but category includes films made later echoing era): see also *British Films: 1960s: Ordinary People Stories: Working Class:* Caretaker; Charlie Bubbles; The Girl with Green Eyes; A Kind of Loving; Leather Boys; Let Him Have It; Live Now, Pay Later; Room at the Top; Saturday Night and Sunday Morning; A Taste of Honey; Term of Trial; This Sporting Life

Klutzes: see *Accident Prone: Comedy of Errors: Fools-Bumbling:*

Korea/Korean War: see also *Japanese as Enemy: China: Japan:* All the Young Men; Battle Hymn; Best of the Best; The Bold and the Brave; Bridges at Toko-Ri; For the Boys; Hook; Inchon; I Want You; Love is a Many-Splendored Thing; MacArthur; The Manchurian Candidate; M*A*S*H; The McConnell Story; Men of the Fighting Lady; Pork Chop Hill; The Quiet American; Rack; Saber Jet; Strange Intruder; Torpedo Alley

Ku Klux Klan: see also *Bigots: White Supremacists: Race Relations: Black vs. White: Rednecks: Southerns:* As Summers Die; Betrayed; The Birth of a Nation; Black Legion; Dead Bang; FBI Story; Fried Green Tomatoes; The Fugitive Kind; Klansman; Mississippi Burning; Sommersby; Storm Warning

Kung Fu: see *Martial Arts*

L

L.A. 90s Indies (little independent movies made in the 1990s in Los Angeles with young stars and eccentric, offbeat plots): Blood and Concrete; Hold Me, Thrill Me, Kiss Me; Inside Monkey Zetterland; Quick; Sleep With Me

Labor Struggles: see *Worker vs. Boss: Unions: Risking it All: Unemployment*

Landlords: see *Apartment Buildings*

Last Chances: see *One Last Time/Chance: Redemption: Starting Over*

Las Vegas: see also *Gambling:* Breathless (1959); Breathless (1983); Bugsy; Casino; Desert Bloom; Diamonds Are Forever; Electric Horseman; Grasshopper; Heat; Honey, I Blew Up the Kid; Honey, I Shrunk the Kids; Honeymoon in Vegas; Honeymoon Machine; Indecent Proposal; Jinxed; Lookin' to Get Out; Lost in America; Machine Gun McCain; A Marrying Man; Meet Me in Las Vegas; One from the Heart; Only Game in Town; Roadside Prophets; Things Are Tough All Over; Viva Las Vegas

Lassie Movies: Lassie Come Home; Magic of Lassie

Last Wishes: see *Dying Wishes/Words*

Latin Films (films made by or about Latin American people): see *Latin People: Mexico: Mexican Films: Mexicans: South America: Spanish Films*

Latin People/Films (featuring people of Hispanic-Latin descent, Mexican, Central and South American): see also *Mexican/Central American Films: Immigrants: South America: Mexico: Central America: Argentina: Brazil: Spanish Films: Spain:* American Me; Beyond the Limit; Black Orpheus; Blood and Sand (1922); Blood and Sand (1941); Born in East L.A.; Burning Season; Carlito's Way; Che!; Cheech and Chong: Still Smokin'; Cheech & Chong's Next Movie; Cheech & Chong's Nice Dreams; Cheech & Chong's The Corsican Brothers; Cisco Kid; City and the Dogs; Commando; Down Argentine Way; El Mariachi; El Norte; The Exterminating Angel; Fiesta; Flying Down to Rio; For Whom the Bell Tolls; Forbidden Dance; Gabriela; Gaby, a True Story; Hangin' with the Homeboys; Hold Back the Dawn; Holiday in Mexico; I Like It Like That; I Don't Want to Talk About It; Kings of the Sun; La Bamba; Ladybird, Ladybird; Like Water For Chocolate; Mala Noche; Mambo Kings; Mark of Zorro (1920); Mark of Zorro (1940); Mi Vida Loca; The Milagro Beanfield War; Old Gringo; Pepe; Popi; Romero; Salsa; Show of Force; Stand and Deliver; Things Are Tough All Over; Three Amigos; Three Caballeros; To Wong Foo, Thanks for Everything, Julie Newmar; Topaz (1969); Tortilla Flat;

Touch of Evil; The Trial (1955); Up in Smoke; Valdez Is Coming; Vera Cruz; Viva Zapata; Walker; Wrath of God

Law Officers-Female: see *Female Law Officers*

Law School: see also *College Life: Lawyers: Lawyer Detectives: Professors:* Love Story (1970); The Paper Chase; Soul Man

Lawyers: see also *Courtroom Drama: Trials: Legal Thrillers: Judges:* Accused of Murder; Adam's Rib (1949); All That Money Can Buy; Anatomy of a Murder; And Justice for All; As Summers Die; Barefoot in the Park; Blume in Love; Body Heat; Bridges at Toko-Ri; Business as Usual; Cape Fear (1962); Cape Fear (1991); A Case for Murder; Class Action; The Client; Criminal Law; Curly Sue; Deliberate Stranger; Divorce of Lady X; Early Frost; A Few Good Men; A Fish Called Wanda; For Love or Money (1963); Fortune Cookie; A Free Soul; From the Hip; G-Men; Girl from Tenth Avenue; The Girl Who Had Everything; The Good Fight; Guilty Conscience; Helter Skelter (1976); Hurry Sundown; I Am the Law; I Love You, Alice B. Toklas; I Thank a Fool; Illegal; Inherit the Wind; The Inquisitor; Jagged Edge; Johnny Eager; Legal Eagles; Made for Each Other; Magnificent Yankee; Manhattan Melodrama; Mr. and Mrs. Bridge; Murder of Mary Phagan; Music

Box; My Cousin Vinny; The Name of the Father; Night and the City (1992); Oliver's Story; Other People's Money; Pair of Briefs; The Paper Chase; The Paradine Case; The Pelican Brief; People Against O'Hara; Perfect Strangers; Philadelphia; Physical Evidence; Pickwick Papers; Presumed Innocent; Rampage; Regarding Henry; Reversal of Fortune; Second Thoughts; Seems Like Old Times; Separate but Equal; The Shaggy D.A.; Shakedown; Smart Woman; Soul Man; Spellbinder; Star Chamber; Strictly Business; The Suspect; Take Her, She's Mine; Town Without Pity; The Trial (1955); Trial and Error; True Believer; Turning Point (1952); Two for the Seesaw; Verdict; Victim; Young Mr. Lincoln; Young Philadelphians; Young Savages

Lawyers as Detectives: see also *Legal Thrillers: Detective Stories: Courtroom Drama:* As Summers Die; Boomerang (1947); Class Action; Client; Criminal Law; The Enforcer (1950); Helter Skelter (1976); I Am the Law; Jagged Edge; Love Crimes; Murder of Mary Phagan; The Name of the Father; Presumed Innocent; Rampage; Shame (1987); A Soldier's Story; Suspect; Verdict

Lawyers in Love: see *Romance With Your Lawyer*

Lawyers vs. Clients: see also *Romance with Lawyer: Ethics: Courtroom Drama: Enemies-Sleeping with: Enemies-Sympathizing with:* Criminal Law; Guilty as Sin; Jagged Edge; The Trap; True Believer

Leaders (about leadership in general): see also *Leaders: Tyrants: Dictators: Military Leaders: Royalty: Kings: Queens: Presidents: War Stories: Biographies: Rule the World-Plots to: Hitler-Adolf: Political Unrest:* The Assassination of Trotsky; Beau James; Caesar and Cleopatra; The Eagle Has Landed; Hoffa; Immortal Sergeant; Kings of the Sun; Knute Rockne: All-American; The Lion in Winter; Man of Iron; The Ten Commandments; Young Winston

Leaders-Female: see also *Biographies: Female Among Males:* Catherine the Great; Faster Pussycat! Kill! Kill!; Great Catherine; Green Goddess; Joan of Arc; Queen of Outer Space

Leaders-Military: see *Military Leaders*

Leaders-Tyrant: see also *Military Leaders: Evil Men: Evil Women: Political Unrest: Kings: Queens: Third World*

Countries: *Napoleon:* Aguirre, the Wrath of God; The Big Red One; Billy Budd; Bounty; Caligula; The Comedians; Commando; Desiree; A Few Good Men; Genghis Khan; Great Catherine; The Great Dictator; The Great Manhunt; Hammersmith is Out; Hitler Gang; Hitler-The Last Ten Days; The In-Laws; Inner Circle; Ivan the Terrible; Julius Caesar; The Killing Fields; MacArthur; The Mark of Zorro (1920); The Mark of Zorro (1940); Octopussy; Patton; Stalin; Sword & the Sorcerer; Twilight's Last Gleaming; Walker; Waterloo

Legal Thrillers (not necessarily set in the courtroom, but lawyers are central characters): see also *Lawyers as Detectives: Lawyers: Courtroom Drama:* Class Action; The Client; Guilty as Sin; The Pelican Brief; Physical Evidence; Presumed Innocent

Legends: see also *Fairy Tales: Fantasy: Historical Drama: Mythology:* The Adventures of Casanova; The Adventures of Hajji Baba; Ali Baba and the Forty Thieves; Androcles and the Lion; Big Foot; Camelot; Candyman; Casanova (Fellini's Casanova); Dr. Faustus; Dr. Syn Alias Scarecrow; Faust; Golden Child; Golem; Greystoke: The Legend of Tarzan; Harry and the Hendersons; Ichabod and Mr. Toad/Legend of Sleepy Hollow; Immortal Story; In Old Arizona; Indiana Jones and the Last Crusade; Indiana Jones and the Temple of Doom; Into the West; Intolerance; Iron Mistress; Joan of Arc; King David; King Solomon's Mines (1937); King Solomon's Mines (1950); King Solomon's Mines (1985); Kings of the Sun; Kismet (1944); Kismet (1955); Knights of the Round Table; The Last Command; The Last of His Tribe; Last Wave; Legend of the Lost; The Prophecy; Q (The Winged Serpent); Raiders of the Lost Ark; The Robe; Robin Hood (1922); Robin Hood (1973); Robin Hood (1990); Robin Hood: Prince of Thieves (1991); The Secret of Roan Inish; Siegfried; Stealing Heaven; Sword of Lancelot; Trojan War; True Stories; Virgin Spring; White Buffalo

Leprechauns: see also *Ireland: Fantasy: Little People:* Darby O'Gill and the Little People; Finian's Rainbow; The Leprechaun; Luck of the Irish

Lesbians: see also *Homoeroticism: Gay/Lesbian Films: Homosexual Secrets: Bisexuality: Tomboys: Homophobia:*

Gay Men: Women's Films: Feminist Films: Bar Girls; Basic Instinct; Belle Epoque; Bitter Tears of Petra Von Kant; Black Widow (1987); The Bostonians; The Brady Bunch Movie; Children's Hour; Desert Hearts; Desperate Living; Dialogues with Madwomen; A Different Story; Entre-Nous; Even Cowgirls Get the Blues; The Fox; Fried Green Tomatoes; Girlfriends; Go-Fish; The Group; Henry and June; The Hunger; I've Heard the Mermaids Singing; Inside Monkey Zetterland; Internal Affairs; Julia; The Killing of Sister George; The L-Shaped Room; Lair of the White Worm; Lenny; Les Biches; Lianna; My Father Is Coming; Myra Breckinridge; Personal Best; Poison Ivy (1992); The Rainbow; The Rose; Salmonberries; Silkwood; Switch; Therese and Isabelle; Three of Hearts; To Forget Venice; Vampire Lovers

Letters (where the story is centered on a letter, though it is not necessarily told in it): see also *Epistolaries:* Address Unknown; Captive Heart; Cause for Alarm; Cyrano de Bergerac (1950); Cyrano de Bergerac (1990); Dear Brigitte; Ice Palace; Immortal Beloved; The Letter (1929); The Letter (1940); Love Letters (1945); Love Letters (1984); No Sex, Please, We're British; Secret Admirer; Touched by Love

Liars: see also *Con-Artists: Dangerous Men: Dangerous Women: Mean Men: Mean Women: Cheating Men: Cheating Women: Guilty Conscience:* Action for Slander; The Adventures of Tom Sawyer; All About Eve; Another You; Baby Blue Marine; Bedroom Window; Billy Liar; Body and Soul (1947); The Conformist; Crazy People; Cyrano de Bergerac (1950); Cyrano de Bergerac (1990); A Dangerous Woman; Disclosure; Divorce of Lady X; Dream Lover (1994); Fortune Cookie; Good Son; Guilty as Sin; Gun in Betty Lou's Handbag; Hail the Conquering Hero; Hands Across the Table; Hero; Hit Parade of 1943; Housesitter; I Want to Live!; The Linguini Incident; Marnie; Murder in New Hampshire; Mystic Pizza; Olivier, Olivier; Otello; Othello (1951); Othello (1965); Overboard; Pinocchio; Quiz Show; River's Edge; Roxie Hart; Sex, Lies, and Videotape; Six Degrees of Separation; Suspicion; These Three; To Kill a Mockingbird; Trapped in Paradise; Who Was That Lady?

Libraries/Librarians: see also *College Life: Shy People:* Adventure; Desk Set; Foul Play; Goodbye, Columbus; Gun in Betty Lou's Handbag; The Music Man; Off Beat; On a Clear Day You Can See Forever; Only Two Can Play; Salmonberries; The Seven Faces of Dr. Lao; The Shawshank Redemption; Something Wicked This Way Comes

Life Lessons: see *Coming of Age: Life Transitions: Teenage Movies*

Life Transitions (changes in the main character's life trigger changes in everything, focusing on the process of that change): see also *Coming of Age: Pre-Life Crisis: Mid-Life Crisis: Death-Dealing With: Family/Heritage-Search for: Decisions-Big:* Alice; American Graffiti; The Apartment; Baby, It's You; Bachelor; Back Street (1932); Back Street (1941); Back Street (1961); Bed and Board; Being Human; The Bell Jar; The Best Years of Our Lives; The Beverly Hills Madam; Beyond the Forest; The Bishop's Wife; Bliss; Bodies, Rest & Motion; Breaking Away; The Brothers Karamazov; Camille Claudel; Carnal Knowledge; Cash McCall; Christmas in July; Dad; Desert Hearts; Desire Under the Elms; Diary of a Mad Housewife; Early Frost; Easy Living (1949); Eclipse; 8 1/2; Electra Glide in Blue; End; Fathers and Sons; Fiddler on the Roof; For Richer, For Poorer; Georgy Girl; Girlfriends; The Godfather; The Godfather, Part II; The Godfather, Part III; The Good Mother; The Graduate; House of the Spirits; The Hustler; Joey Breaker; Knickerbocker Holiday; Kotch; Last of Mrs. Cheyney; The Last Picture Show; The Law and the Lady; Leap of Faith; Leaving Normal; Lifeguard; Light Sleeper; Lonely Are the Brave; The Lonely Guy; Male Animal; A Member of the Wedding; Miss Firecracker; The Moon and Sixpence; The Moon is Blue; Moscow on the Hudson; Moving; My Life; My Life as a Dog; Nicholas Nickleby; Nobody's Fool (1994); None But the Lonely Heart; Oblomov; Only the Lonely; Passing of the Third Floor Back; Plenty; Rachel, Rachel; The Scoundrel; She's Working Her Way Through College; Shirley Valentine; Smooth Talk; Sometimes a Great Notion; Stanley & Iris; Stardust Memories; Street Angel; The Subject Was Roses; Summer of '42; The Sundowners; Susan and God; Tall Story;

A Thousand Clowns; Toys in the Attic; Two for the Seesaw; An Unmarried Woman; When My Baby Smiles at Me; Wild River; Wild Strawberries

Lincoln-Abraham (stories involving): see also *Presidents: Civil War Era:* The Abductors; Abe Lincoln in Illinois; Abraham Lincoln; Anthony Adverse; Gore Vidal's Lincoln; The Tall Target; Young Mr. Lincoln

Little Adults: see *Children-Little Adults: Children-Gifted: Geniuses: Famous People When Young*

Little Old Ladies: see *Elderly Women*

Little People (dwarfs, midgets, very short or tiny people): see also *Circus Life:* Babes in Toyland (1934); Babes in Toyland (1961); The Borrowers; Darby O'Gill and the Little People; Devil Doll; Dr. Cyclops; Fantastic Voyage; Freaks; The Gnome Mobile; Gulliver's Travels (1939); Gulliver's Travels (1976); I Don't Want to Talk About It; Krull; The Leprechaun; Living in Oblivion; Luck of the Irish; The Mole People; Moulin Rouge; Revenge of Frankenstein; Snow White and The Seven Dwarfs; Spaced Invaders; The Three Worlds of Gulliver; Time Bandits; Tin Drum; Tom Thumb; Under the Rainbow; Willow

London: see also *British Films: England: Mod Era:* April Fools; Bitch (1979); Broken Blossoms; Damage; Don't Raise the Bridge, Lower the Water!; Give My Regards to Broad Street; Goodbye Gemini; The Horse's Mouth; Hysteria; A Kid for Two Farthings; The Knack; The L-Shaped Room; Life at the Top; Life Force; Light that Failed; Little Dorrit; Lloyd's of London; London Belongs to Me; The Long, Good Friday; Love Among the Ruins; Melancholia; Midnight Lace; Murders in the Rue Morgue; My Fair Lady; Naked; The Notorious Landlady; The Old Curiosity Shop; Oliver!; Oliver Twist (1948); Oliver Twist (1982); Phantom of the Rue Morgue; The Picture of Dorian Gray; Queen of Hearts; Return of the Vampire; Salt and Pepper; Sammy and Rosie Get Laid; Say Hello to Yesterday; Smashing Time; Split Second; Strange Bedfellows; Strapless; Tale of a Vampire; There's a Girl in My Soup; Time after Time; To Sir with Love; Top Hat; Turtle Diary; The Unseen; Venom

Lonely People: see also *Fathers Alone: Mothers Alone: Elderly People: Midlife Crisis:* The Adventures of

Robinson Crusoe; After Hours; The Amazing Howard Hughes; The Apartment; Apartment Zero; The Attic; Babette's Feast; Black Cat; The Collector; Come Back, Little Sheba; Conversation Piece; Cries and Whispers; Crusoe; Dark Victory; Darling; Dear Heart; Diary of a Mad Housewife; Driving Miss Daisy; Eighty-Four Charing Cross Road; The Enchanted Cottage; The Enchanted Forest; The Girl with Green Eyes; Grace Quigley; I Sent a Letter to My Love; Interiors; La Lectrice; Ladykiller (1992); Life Upside Down; Like Water for Chocolate; Loneliness of the Long Distance Runner; The Lonely Guy; Lonely Hearts; Lost in Yonkers; Love Letters (1984); Man Upstairs; Moment by Moment; Monsieur Hire; Mr. Belvedere Rings the Bell; Never Cry Wolf; Night, Mother; Old Man and the Sea; Only the Lonely; Over Twenty-One; Queen of the Stardust Ballroom; Rachel, Rachel; Silas Marner; Silent Running; Stevie; Summer Wishes, Winter Dreams; Summertime; T. R. Baskin; Tell Me that You Love Me, Junie Moon; Through a Glass Darkly; Thunder Rock; 2001: A Space Odyssey; A Woman's Tale

Lookalikes: see also *Twins: Identities-Mistaken: Clever Plots & Endings: Impostors: Multiple Performances:* Body Heat; Brain Eaters; Bullseye!; Cat Ballou; Dance Macabre; Dave; Dead of Winter; Doppelganger; The Double Life of Veronique; Double Threat; The Eagle Has Landed; Ernest Goes to Jail; Fahrenheit 451; Folies Bergere; Johnny Stecchino; Julia and Julia; Kagemusha; Kissin' Cousins; Lancer Spy; The Last Tycoon; The Legend of Lylah Clare; The Man Who Haunted Himself; The Man Who Lost Himself; The Man with Bogart's Face; Masquerader; Moon Over Parador; Murder by Television; My Favorite Spy; Never a Dull Moment (1967); Obsession; The Patsy; Phantom President; The Prince and the Pauper (1937); Prisoner of Zenda; The Prize; Scapegoat; The Scar; Scotland Yard; The Secret Ceremony; Shattered; Single White Female; Sisters; That Night in Rio; Things Change; Vertigo; Xtro

Looksism: see also *Beautiful People: Nerds & Babes: Wallflowers & Hunks:* Cyrano de Bergerac (1950); Cyrano de Bergerac (1990); Don't Tell Her It's Me; I Don't Buy Kisses Anymore; In a Shallow

Grave; The Man Without a Face; Momma, There's a Man in Bed; Perfect Prelude to a Kiss; They Knew What They Wanted; Too Beautiful For You

Los Angeles: see also *Beverly Hills: California Life: Hollywood Life: New York vs. Los Angeles:* Against All Odds; Aloha, Bobby and Rose; American Gigolo; Bar Girls; The Big One, The Great Los Angeles Earthquake; The Big Sleep (1946); The Big Sleep (1977); Blade Runner; Blood and Concrete; Blue Thunder; Blume in Love; Bob & Carol & Ted & Alice; Born in East L.A.; Boyz N the Hood; Chinatown; Colors; Count Yorga, Vampire; Dead Again; The Decline of Western Civilization; The Decline of Western Civilization 2: The Metal Years; Dragnet (1954); Dragnet (1987); Earthquake; Echo Park; Extreme Justice; Farewell, My Lovely (1944); Farewell, My Lovely (1975); Fast Times at Ridgemont High; Fun With Dick and Jane; Grand Canyon; The Grifters; Heartbreakers; The Karate Kid; The Killing of Chinese Bookie; The Last Boy Scout; The Last Married Couple in America; The Last Run; Life Stinks!; Lifeguard; The Long Goodbye; Lost Angels; Lunatics, A Love Story; Making Love; Marlowe; Minnie & Moskowitz; Mixed Nuts; Morning After; New Year's Day; 1941; Predator 2; Rapture; Rebel Without a Cause; Reservoir Dogs; Rising Sun; Short Cuts; Skin Deep; Surrender; Taking Care of Business; That's Life!; To Live and Die in L.A.; To Sleep with Anger; The Two Jakes; Up in Smoke; Valley Girl; Welcome to L.A.; Where the Day Takes You; Wild Palms

Losing it All: see also *Bets: Gambling: Making a Living: Risking it All: Unemployment:* The Bonfire of the Vanities; Cracking Up; Dinner at Eight; Fever Pitch; Folks!; The Great Sinner; High Pressure; Lost in America; Miss Firecracker; Music of Chance; New Leaf; Nicholas Nickleby; Rosalie Goes Shopping; Rosie; Seize the Day

Lotteries: see also *Contests/Competitions: Lucky People: Rags to Riches:* Christmas in July; Easy Money (1948); Fox and His Friends; It Could Happen to You; Jackpot; La Vie Continue; Le Million; Love Lottery; Men Don't Leave; Squeeze; Uptown Saturday Night; 29th Street; Willy Wonka and the Chocolate Factory; The Wrong Box

Louisiana: see also *Cajuns: New Orleans: Southerns: Swamp Settings:* All the King's Men; Louisiana Story; Southern Comfort; Steel Magnolias; Thunder Bay

LOVE: see also *Romance: Boy Wants Girl/Girl Wants Boy: First Love: Friends in Love*

Love at Last: see *Romance-Reluctant: Romance-Reunited*

Love-Boy Wants Girl/Girl Wants Boy: see *Romance-Boy Wants Girl/Girl Wants Boy: also First Love: Infatuations: Coming of Age: Obsessions*

Love-Deception: see *Love-Questionable*

Love-First: see also *Coming of Age: Infatuations:* Aladdin; Alan and Naomi; Alice Adams; All-American Boy; Aloha Summer; Baby, It's You; The Bell Jar; The Blue Lagoon (1948); The Blue Lagoon (1980); Bonjour, Tristesse; Buster and Billie; David and Lisa; The Dove; Edward Scissorhands; Endless Love; Ex-Lady; Falling in Love Again; First Love; First Time; Flirting; Gidget; Gregory's Girl; Happy Time; The Heart is a Lonely Hunter; Heaven Help Us; Here We Go Round the Mulberry Bush; Home from the Hill; The Karate Kid; Karate Kid, Part II; Karate Kid, Part III; The Last Picture Show; La Vie Continue; The Little Girl Who Lives Down the Lane; A Little Romance; Love in a Goldfish Bowl; The Lover; The Man in the Moon; Map of the Human Heart; Marty; Mask (1985); Meet Me in St. Louis; Melody; Men Don't Leave; Mermaids; Mignon Has Left; Miracle (1990); Mischief; Moulin Rouge; My Girl; My Girl 2; Nanou; Never Give a Sucker an Even Break; Oh, What a Night; Ordinary People; Paradise (1991); Peppermint Soda; Peter Ibbetson; Rachel, Rachel; Racing with the Moon; Rainbow; Rainmaker; Rambling Rose; Reckless (1983); Red Kiss; Return to the Blue Lagoon; Rich Kids; Romeo and Juliet (1936); Romeo and Juliet (1954); Romeo and Juliet (1968); Running on Empty; Small Change; Smooth Talk; Splendor in the Grass; Square Dance; State Fair (1933); State Fair (1945); State Fair (1962); Summer and Smoke; Summer of My German Soldier; Tea and Sympathy; Those Were the Days; Tim; Walk on the Wild Side; Wuthering Heights (1939); Wuthering Heights (1953); Wuthering Heights (1970); Wuthering Heights (1992); The Year My Voice Broke

Love-Forbidden: see also *Lover Family Dislikes: Romance-Unprofessional: Romance-Doomed: Romance-Reluctant:* The Age of Innocence (1934); The Age of Innocence (1993); All Night Long (1981); Alpine Fire; Angela; Anna Karenina (1935); Anna Karenina (1948); Beau Pere; Blue Velvet; Casino; Cousin, Cousine; Cousins; Daybreak; Duel in the Sun; Ethan Fromme; French Lieutenant's Woman; Goodbye Gemini; The Graduate; Great Balls of Fire; The Great White Hope; Jefferson in Paris; The Little Minister; A Little Romance; Ode to Billy Joe; Patch of Blue; Peg o' My Heart; Quo Vadis; Rain; Reckless (1983); Stealing Heaven; A Stranger Among Us; Tears in the Rain; Ten Days Wonder; That Forsyte Woman; These Three; Two Moon Junction

Love-Infatuations: see *Infatuations: also First Love: Love-Unrequited: Romance-Boy Wants Girl/Girl Wants Boy: Coming of Age: Wallflowers: Nerds: Wallflowers & Hunks: Nerds & Babes: Love-Reluctant*

Love-Obsessions: see *Fatal Attractions*

Love-Questionable: see also *Romance-Dangerous: Enemies-Sleeping with: Liars: Cheating Men: Cheating Women:* Absence of Malice; After Dark, My Sweet; Against All Odds; The Age of Innocence (1934); The Age of Innocence (1993); Arch of Triumph; The Barefoot Contessa; The Betrayed (1989); Body Heat; Born to Be Bad (1950); Brighton Rock; Bugsy; Charade; Chinatown; Cold Sassy Tree; Dangerous Liaisons; Darling; The Deceived; Diabolique (1955); Dirty Rotten Scoundrels; Double Indemnity; Dynamite; Eye of the Needle; Eyes in the Night; The Invitation; Kangaroo; Lady Eve; Lady in Question; The Man with Two Brains; Marathon Man; Masquerade (1988); The Merry Widow (1925); The Merry Widow (1934); The Merry Widow (1952); Mildred Pierce; Million Dollar Baby; Moment by Moment; Morning After; My Blood Runs Cold; San Quentin; Saratoga Trunk; Sea of Love; Second Thoughts; Secret Beyond the Door; Silent Partner; Star 80; Suspicion; Vertigo; When Strangers Marry; Whipsaw

Love-Reluctant: see also *Romance-Reluctant: Love-Unrequited:* The Big Street; Born to Be Bad (1950); The Collector; Elephant Man; A House Divided; I Am a Camera; Illegally Yours; Letter From an Unknown Woman; Love and Death; The Man in the Moon; Metropolitan (1990); A Midsummer Night's Sex Comedy; Misery; Reckless (1935); The Remains of the Day; The Seven-Year Itch; The Sidewalks of London; Smiles of a Summer Night; St. Martin's Lane; Sunset Boulevard; Svengali (1931); Svengali (1983); Taxi Driver; That Cold Day in the Park; The Threesome; Tootsie; A View from the Bridge

Love-Unlikely: see *Romance-Mismatched: Opposites Attract*

Love-Unrequited: see also *Romance-Doomed: Infatuations: First Love: Coming of Age:* Big Street; Born to Be Bad (1950); Butterfield 8; The Collector; Cyrano de Bergerac (1950); Cyrano de Bergerac (1990); Elephant Man; Georgy Girl; A House Divided; I am a Camera; Illegally Yours; It's a Date; It's a Wonderful World; Letter From an Unknown Woman; Love and Death; The Man in the Moon; Metropolitan (1990); A Midsummer Night's Sex Comedy; Misery; Reckless (1935); The Remains of the Day; The Seven-Year Itch; The Sidewalks of London; Smiles of a Summer Night; Summer and Smoke; Sunset Boulevard; Svengali (1931); Svengali (1983); Taxi Driver; That Cold Day in the Park; The Threesome; Tootsie; A View from the Bridge

Love-Unwanted: see *Romance-Reluctant: Romance-Boy Wants Girl/Girl Wants Boy*

Love with a Protector: see *Protecting People: Romance with Protector: Witnesses-Protecting*

Love with Wrong Person: see *Romance-Dangerous: Romance-Forbidden: Love-Questionable: Enemies-Sleeping with*

Lover Family Dislikes: see also *In-Laws-Troublesome: Marriage-Impending:* Aaron Loves Angela; Abie's Irish Rose; All That Heaven Allows; Andre's Mother; Arthur; Baby, It's You; Bachelor Party (1984); The Barretts of Wimpole Street (1934); The Barretts of Wimpole Street (1956); Best Intentions; Big Country; Bird of Paradise (1932); Bird of Paradise (1951); Black Orchid; Bonjour, Tristesse; A Breath of Scandal; Buster and Billie; Camila (1984); The Cowboy and the Lady; Cry Baby; Endless Love; Flower Drum Song; Foolin' Around; A Free Soul; Fresh Horses; The Girl Who Had Everything; The Graduate; The Grifters; Heartbreak Kid; Heiress; Holiday in Mexico; House of the Spirits; I'll Take Sweden; Joe; Johnny Eager; Little Vegas; Lolita; Loves of a Blonde; Mill on the Floss; Mississippi Masala; Norman, Is That You?; Ode to Billy Joe; Once Around; One, Two, Three!; Oscar; The Paper Chase; The Promise; Reckless (1983); Red Kiss; Reuben, Reuben; Romanoff and Juliet; Romeo and Juliet (1936); Romeo and Juliet (1954); Romeo and Juliet (1968); A Room with a View; Ryan's Daughter; Shining Hour; The Show-Off; Shrimp on the Barbie; Stealing Heaven; Storm Warning; Teresa; Thunder and Lightning; Turkish Delight; Valley of Decision; Vivacious Lady; Where Angels Fear to Tread; Where Love Has Gone

Lovers-Foreign: see *Vacation Romance: Americans Abroad: Romance-Doomed: Exotic Locales: Erotic Drama*

Lovers-Live-in: see *Friends in Love: Marriage-Impending: Newlyweds: Roommates*

Lovers-Unsatisfied: see *Sexual Problems: Cheating Men: Cheating Women*

Lucky People: see also *Unlucky People: Lotteries: Contests/Competitions: Rags to Riches:* Easy Living (1937); Easy Money (1948); Flashpoint; Lady Eve; Meet Me in Las Vegas

Lycanthropy: see *Humans into Animals: Monsters-Human: Werewolves*

Lynchings/Lynch Mobs: see also *Executions: Manhunts: Bounty Hunters: Ku Klux Klan: Fugitives from the Law: WESTERNS: Manhunts:* Five Card Stud; Fury (1936); Good Day for a Hanging; Hang 'em High; The Hanging Tree; Mississippi Burning; Ox-Bow Incident; Storm Warning; They Won't Forget; Young Mr. Lincoln

Lyrical Films (stylistically and rhythmically paced films, usually with beautiful sets or scenery and evocative music scores): see also *Scenery-Outstanding: Art Films: French Films: Italian Films: Bergmanesque Films:* Babette's Feast; Barry London; Birdy; The Black Stallion; The Black Stallion Returns; Blood and Sand (1922); Blood and Sand (1941); Body and Soul (1947); Dances With Wolves; Death in Venice; The Double Life of Veronique; Dreamchild; Eureka; Exposed; The Good, The Bad, & The Ugly; House of the Spirits; The Long Day Closes; Manon des Sources (1952); Manon des Sources (1986); Maurice; McCabe and Mrs. Miller; The Mission; Moulin Rouge; Napoleon; The Natural; Nijinsky; A River Runs Through It; The Searchers; Sirens; Tess; Testament of Orpheus; The Umbrellas of Cherbourg

M

Macho Men: see also *Abusive Men: Bodybuilding: Football: Mean Men: Sports Movies:* Any Which Way You Can; Beer; The Cutting Edge; Don't Tell Her It's Me; The Great Santini; Heartbreak Ridge; Heaven Knows, Mr. Allison; Islands in the Stream; Kiss of the Spider Woman; Les Comperes; The Macomber Affair; My Bodyguard; North Dallas Forty; Pat and Mike; Patti Rocks; Raging Bull; Semi-Tough; Sergeant; Seven Days in May; She's Gotta Have It; Swept Away; Tea and Sympathy; This Boy's Life; Trouble Along the Way; White Mile; Woman of the Year; Year of the Comet

Madams: see also *Prostitutes: Pimps:* Beverly Hills Madam; Cheyenne Social Club; A House is Not a Home; Mayflower Madam; Personal Services; The Roman Spring of Mrs. Stone

Mad Scientists: see *Scientists-Mad:* also *HORROR: Monsters-Manmade: Experiments: Scientists: SCI-FI: Frankenstein*

Magic/Magicians: see also *Curses: Witchcraft:* The Adventures of Baron Munchausen (1943); Alice; Beastmaster; Beastmaster 2; Bedknobs and Broomsticks; Bell, Book, and Candle; Berkeley Square; Black Cauldron; The Butcher's Wife; Camelot; Darby O'Gill and the Little People; Dark Crystal; Dragonslayer; Escape Artist; Eternally

Yours; Finian's Rainbow; Freaky Friday; Golden Voyage of Sinbad; Gremlins; Gremlins 2: The New Batch; Heart of Glass; Houdini; It Happens Every Spring; A Kid for Two Farthings; Kismet (1944); Kismet (1955); Knights of the Round Table; Leprechaun; Lili; Luck of the Irish; The Man Who Could Work Miracles; Mr. North; Nutcracker (1993); The Raven (1963); Repo Man; Return from Witch Mountain; Rock-a Doodle; The Seven Faces of Dr. Lao; The Shadow (1940); The Shadow (1994); Shadows and Fog; Something Wicked This Way Comes; Sword in the Stone; Sword & the Sorcerer; The Thief of Bagdad (1924); The Thief of Baghdad (1940); The Three Lives of Thomasina; Time Bandits; The Tomb of Ligeia; Weird Science; Young Sherlock Holmes; Zapped!; Zapped Again

Magic Realism (style combining mysticism and surrealism with a healthy dose of optimism): see also *Surrealism: Latin Films: Capra-esque: All-American Myth:* The Butcher's Wife; El Norte; Erendira; Field of Dreams; House of the Spirits; I Don't Want to Talk About it; Kiss of the Spider Woman; Like Water For Chocolate; Mr. North; Naked Tango; The Natural; Prelude to a Kiss; Waiting For the Light

Maids: see *Servants*

Making a Living: see also *Working Class: Mothers-Struggling: Fathers-Struggling: Parents-Struggling: Rags to Riches; Riches to Rags: Unemployment: Moonlighting:* Alice Doesn't Live Here Anymore; Barefoot in the Park; Betsy's Wedding; Bill; Bill: On His Own; Bottoms Up; The Bride Walks Out; The Crowd; Death of a Salesman (1950); Death of a Salesman (1985); Divorce, American Style; Don't Tell Mom the Babysitter's Dead; For Pete's Sake; Fun With Dick and Jane; Gas Food Lodging; Heartland; A Home of Our Own; How to Beat the High Cost of Living; I Like it Like That; I Stole a Million; Imaginary Crimes; Kiss Shot; Kitty Foyle; La Vie de Boheme; Life of Riley; Live Now, Pay Later; Love on the Dole; Made for Each Other; Mayflower Madam; Me and Veronica; Mr. Mom; My Beautiful Laundrette; Nothin' But a Man; The Promoter; Rat Race; Reality Bites; The River Wild; The Southerner; Stanley & Iris; Unforgiven (1992)

Male Among Females: see also *Fish out of Water Stories: Role Reversal: Female Among Males:* Belle Epoque; King and Four Queens; A League of Their Own; Mr. Mom; Sitting Pretty; Take a Letter, Darling

Male Bonding: see *Friendships-Male: Buddy Films*

Male Partners: see *Buddy Films: Buddy Cops: Partners in Crime: Friendships-Male*

Malicious Menaces: see also *Stalkers: Serial Killers: Psycho Killers: Kill the Beast: Roommates from Hell: THRILLERS:* Absolution; The Bat (1959); The Bat Whispers; Blind Side; Brimstone and Treacle; Child's Play (1972); A Conflict of Interest; Cop; Daddy's Gone A-Hunting; Dark Corner; Die! Die! My Darling!; A Guest in the House; Kitten with a Whip; Knife in the Water; Les Miserables (1978); Les Miserables (1935); Les Miserables (1952); Mister Frost; The Old Curiosity Shop; Pacific Heights; The Servant; Something for Everyone; Strangers on a Train; Teenage Rebel; The Temp; To Kill a Clown; Twisted; Unlawful Entry; Victim

Mama's Boys: see also *Children-Brats: Daddy's Girls: Mothers & Sons: Tomboys:* Anniversary; Ed and His Dead Mother; Mother's Boys; Murmur of the Heart; Only the Lonely; Throw Momma from the Train; Where's Poppa?

Manhunts: see also *Bounty Hunters: Lynchings/Lynch Mobs: Searches:* Billy the Kid; Blade Runner; Blown Away; City in Fear; Cornered; The Friends of Eddie Coyle; The Fugitive: G-Men; Game of Death; Gleaming the Cube; Gun Fury; The Hunted; Hunter; Madigan; Moon in the Gutter; The Most Dangerous Game; Murderer's Row; The Naked Prey; Nevada Smith; Northwest Mounted Police; The Outlaw Josey Wales; Santa Fe Trail; Savage Sam; Scalphunters; Sea Wolves; The Search; The Searchers; Shaft's Big Score; Shame (1987); Shoot to Kill; Slipstream; Split Second; Stick; They Won't Forget Tin Star; True Grit; Unforgiven (1992)

Man vs. Machine: see also *Computers: Inventors: Social Drama: Social Satire:* Christine; D.A.R.Y.L.; Demon Seed; Desk Set; Electric Dreams; The Forbin Project; Hardware; Lonely Are the Brave; Ma and Pa Kettle; Maximum Overdrive; Modern Times; Robocop; Robocop 2; Saturn 3; Silent Running; The Sorcerer; Terminal Man; 2001: A Space Odyssey; Universal Soldier; Videodrome; War Games

Man vs. Man: see *Men in Conflict: Women in Conflict: Feuds: WESTERNS: Duels*

Man vs. Nature: see *Nature-Back to: Disaster Stories*

Man vs. Society (or women): see *Anti-Establishment Films: Alienation: Fighting the System: Rebels: Reformers: Women Fighting the System*

Manic Characters: see *Eccentric People: Mental Illness: Wild People*

Maniacs: see *Psycho-Killers: Serial Killers: Rogue Plots: Stalkers: HORROR: Mental Illness: Murderers-Mass*

Manners: see *Comedy of Manners*

Mansions-Creepy: see *Houses-Creepy: Haunted Houses: Gothic Style: HORROR: Ghosts*

Marooned: see *Abandoned People: Ship Wrecks: Stranded*

Marriage Comedy: see also *Marriage-Newlyweds: Lovers-Live-in: Marriage-Impending: Engagements-Breaking: Marriage Drama:* Adam's Rib (1949); Alfredo, Alfredo; Almost Pregnant; Almost You; Arthur 2, On the Rocks; The Awful Truth; Beauty for the Asking; Bedtime Story (1941); Best Friends; The Bishop's Wife; Bob & Carol & Ted & Alice; Breakfast for Two; The Bride Walks Out; Cafe Society; California Suite; Carefree; Cass Timberlane; Chastity Belt; Constant Husband; Divorce, American Style; Does This Mean We're Married?; Down Argentine Way; Dream Wife; Farmer Takes a Wife; Fawlty Towers; A Fine Romance; A Flea in Her Ear; The Flintstones; For Keeps; Forever Darling; The Four Seasons; Four-Poster; Fun With Dick and Jane; Genevieve; George Washington Slept Here; Get Out Your Handkerchiefs; Goin' South; The Grass Is Always Greener Over the Septic Tank; The Guardsman; The Guest Wife; A Guide for the Married Man; Happy Anniversary; He Married His Wife; He Said, She Said; Hello Again; Her Husband's Affairs; Here Comes the Groom; Heroes; High Heels; How Sweet It Is; How to Murder Your Wife; How to Save a Marriage and Ruin Your Life; I Love My Wife; I Love You to Death; I Married a Woman; I Take this Woman; I Was a Male War Bride; I Will . . . I Will . . . for Now; If a Man Answers; If You Knew Susie; Invitation to Happiness; It Started with a Kiss; It's Love I'm After; Jack and Sarah; Julia Misbehaves; Kisses for My President; Knave of Hearts; La Cage Aux Folles; La Cage Aux Folles 2; La Cage Aux Folles 3: The Wedding; Lady Be Good; Lady Is Willing; The Last Married Couple in America; Let's Do it

Again (1953); Let's Make It Legal; The Lieutenant Wore Skirts; The Long Long Trailer; Love Crazy; Loving; Loving Couples; Made in America; Male Animal; Marriage on the Rocks; Married to It; The Marrying Kind; The Marrying Man; Meet the Stewarts; Melvin and Howard; The Merry Wives of Reno; A Midsummer Night's Sex Comedy; Mixed Company; The Money Pit; Moon's Our Home; Moonstruck; Move Over, Darling; Mr. and Mrs. Smith; Mr. Wonderful; My Blue Heaven (1950); My Favorite Wife; My Geisha; Nadine; Never a Dull Moment (1950); New Leaf; No Man of Her Own; No Room for the Groom; Nudo di Donna; Once Around; The One and Only; Our Hospitality; The Outoftowners; Palm Beach Story; Pardon Mon Affaire; Parenthood; Parlor, Bedroom and Bath; Peggy Sue Got Married; Perfect Marriage; Period of Adjustment; Pete 'n Tillie; Peter's Friends; Phffft!; Platinum Blonde; Please Don't Eat the Daisies; Rally Round the Flag, Boys; The Ref; Running Mates; Scenes from a Mall; Second Honeymoon; Send Me No Flowers; Seven Brides for Seven Brothers; Shadow of the Thin Man; She's Having a Baby; She's Working Her Way Through College; Simon and Laura; Smiles of a Summer Night; The Taming of the Shrew; This Thing Called Love; The Thrill of It All; Too Many Husbands; Topper; Topper Returns; Topper Takes a Trip; True Lies; Twin Beds; The Ugly Dachshund; Vivacious Lady; The War Between Men and Women; War of the Roses; Warrior's Husband; We're Not Married; The Wedding Banquet; When You're in Love; Wife, Husband and Friend; Wife Versus Secretary; Woman Times Seven; You Belong to Me; Yours, Mine and Ours; Zandy's Bride

Marriage Drama: see also *Marriage on the Rocks: Divorce: Custody Battles: Swapping Partners: Alternative Lifestyles:* Anne of the Thousand Days; Are Husbands Necessary?; Beauty for the Asking; Bed and Board; Between Two Women; Bitter Moon; Blind Ambition; Blonde Venus; Blue Sky; Blume in Love; Bob & Carol & Ted & Alice; Boost; Break of Hearts; Buster; Casanova Brown; Cat on a Hot Tin Roof (1958); Cat on a Hot Tin Roof (1984); The Chapman Report; Chapter Two; Claudia; Come See the Paradise; Consenting Adults; Country

Girl; Dangerous Game; Days of Wine and Roses (1958); Days of Wine and Roses (1962); Decline of the American Empire; Desire Me; Desperate Characters; Detective Story; The Devil and the Deep; Diana: Her True Story; The Divorcée; The Doctor; The Doctor's Dilemma; Dodsworth; Don Juan DeMarco; Don't Look Now; Dream Lover (1994); Eleanor & Franklin; Ethan Fromme; Evelyn Prentice; The Executioner's Song; Faces; Falling in Love; Family Pictures; Family Upside Down; Far from the Madding Crowd; Firstborn; For Keeps; For the Boys; Fortunes of War; The Four Seasons; Four-Poster; Friends and Husbands; From the Terrace; From This Day Forward; Funny Girl; Funny Lady; Ghost; Girl from Tenth Avenue; Gone With the Wind; The Good Earth; Good Fellas; Gore Vidal's Lincoln; Great Ziegfeld; Green Dolphin Street; Guess Who's Coming to Dinner; Happy Ending; Harriet Craig; Hawaii; Heartbreak Ridge; Heartburn; Heaven and Earth; The Helen Morgan Story; Henry VIII and His Six Wives; Hilda Crane; Hold Your Man; Howards End; The Hunter; Husbands; Husbands and Wives; I Love My Wife; I'll See You in My Dreams; Immediate Family; Impatient Years; In Name Only; Indecent Proposal; Intersection; Irreconcilable Differences; The Jazz Singer (1927); The Jazz Singer (1953); The Jazz Singer (1980); Journey for Margaret; Jude the Obscure; Just Between Friends; La Notte; Lady Takes a Flyer; LBJ: The Early Years; Leather Boys; Live, Love and Learn; Longtime Companion; Lorenzo's Oil; Love Matters; A Man and a Woman: Twenty Years Later; Man on Fire; The Man Who Understood Women; Man, Woman and Child; Marriage of a Young Stockbroker; The Marriage of Maria Braun; Mating Season; Men (1950); Men in White; Mo' Better Blues; Mr. and Mrs. Bridge; Mrs. Parkington; My Foolish Heart; My Life; Naked Jungle; Naked Lunch; Never Too Late; New Life; Once Around; Once More with Feeling; Once Were Warriors; One Trick Pony; Over the Brooklyn Bridge; The Paper; Paris By Night; Payment on Demand; Penny Serenade; Piccadilly Incident; Plaza Suite; Plenty; The Possessed (1947); Pride of the Yankees; Priest of Love; Prisoner of Second Avenue; The Private Life of Henry VIII;

Private Matter; Punchline; Quicksand; A Rage to Live; Raging Bull; Raintree County; Random Harvest; Rebecca; Red Headed Woman; Regarding Henry; Return of the Soldier; Right of Way; The River (1984); Rocky II; The Romantic Englishwoman; Rose of Washington Square; Saber Jet; Saturday Night and Sunday Morning; Scenes from a Marriage; Secrets; The Seduction of Joe Tynan; Severed Head; Shadow Box; Shame (1968); Shoot the Moon; Short Cuts; Sisters; Smash Palace; Staircase; A Star is Born (1937); A Star is Born (1954); A Star is Born (1976); State of the Union; Story of Three Loves; Strange Interlude (1932); Strange Interlude (1990); The Stratton Story; Stromboli; Summer Wishes, Winter Dreams; Suspicion; Sweet Dreams; Sweethearts Dance; Swing High, Swing Low; Tall Story; Teresa; Terms of Endearment; That's Life!; This Boy's Life; Those Were the Days; Thursday's Game; Time for Loving; To Forget Venice; Tokyo Joe; Tomorrow Is Forever; Twice in a Lifetime; Two For the Road; An Unmarried Woman; Up the Sandbox; Vacation from Marriage; War of the Roses; Warrior's Husband; The Way We Were; When a Man Loves a Woman; When My Baby Smiles at Me; Who's Afraid of Virginia Woolf?; Winning; A Woman's World; X, Y, & Zee

Marriage-Elopement: see also *Engagements-Breaking: Marriage-Impending: Marriage Forced: Runaways: Courtship:* Grand Theft Auto; Honeymoon; A Little Romance; No Room for the Groom; Valley of Decision

Marriage-Fake: see also *Marrying Up: Settling Down: Romance-Choosing the Right Person: Pretending: Marriage-Forced:* Appointment for Love; Cactus Flower; Cafe Society; Cinderella Jones; The Doctor Takes a Wife; Does This Mean We're Married?; Easy to Wed; A Girl Named Tamiko; Good Neighbor Sam; Green Card; The Guest Wife; I'd Rather Be Rich; Indiscreet; It Started with Eve; La Cage Aux Folles 3: The Wedding; Lady Eve; Libeled Lady; Mr. and Mrs. Smith; Something Wild (1986); Shall We Dance?

Marriage-Forced (by parents or society, or by becoming expectant parents): see also *Marriage-Impending: Marriage-Fake: Babies-Having:*

Mothers-Unwed: The Age of Innocence (1934); The Age of Innocence (1993); Blue Denim; Early Summer; A Kind of Loving; Love With the Proper Stranger; Lover Come Back (1961); Music Lovers; Small Town Girl (1936); Small Town Girl (1953); Susan Lenox, Her Fall and Rise

Marriage for Citizenship: see also *Marriage of Convenience: Marriage-Fake:* Does This Mean We're Married?; A Girl Named Tamiko; Green Card; Hold Back the Dawn; I Was a Male War Bride; Ladybird, Ladybird; Music in My Heart; Paper Marriage; Stromboli; The Wedding Banquet; When You're in Love

Marriage for Money: see *Marrying Up: Gold Diggers: Rich People*

Marriage-Impending: see also *Romance-Choosing the Right Person:* About Face; The Age of Innocence (1934); The Age of Innocence (1993); Angie; Best Friends; Best Intentions; The Best Years of Our Lives; Cafe Romeo; Carefree; The Catered Affair; The Children (1990); Clash of the Titans; The Devil's Eye; Dim Sum: a Little Bit of Heart; Every Girl Should be Married; Father of the Bride (1950); Father of the Bride (1991); Foolin' Around; The French Lieutenant's Woman; The Girl Most Likely (1958); The Graduate; Hard Promises; High Noon; High Society; His Girl Friday; Honeymoon; Hot Lead and Cold Feet; The House of Seven Gables; Housesitter; I'd Rather Be Rich; The Importance of Being Earnest; The In-Laws; It Had to Be You; La Cage Aux Folles; La Cage Aux Folles 2; La Cage Aux Folles 3: The Wedding; Libeled Lady; Love on the Run (1936); A Man and a Woman; The Marrying Man; The Mating Season; McClintock!; Min and Bill; Moonstruck; My Forbidden Past; Nothin' But a Man; The Passionate Plumber; The Philadelphia Story; Prelude to a Kiss; Pride and Prejudice; Private Benjamin; The Quiet Wedding; Royal Wedding; Seven Brides for Seven Brothers; Seven Chances; Seven Days Leave; Sisters; Skin Deep; The Swan; Switching Channels; That Forsyte Woman; Three on a Couch; Trouble for Two; True Love; Twenty Bucks; Two Moon Junction; A View from the Bridge; Watch It

Marriage-Intergenerational: see *Romance-Older Men/Younger Women: Romance-Older Women/Younger Men: Romance-Opposites Attract*

Marriage of Convenience: see also *Marriages-Fake: Marriage for Citizenship: Marrying Up: Brides-Mail Order: Settling Down: Romance-Choosing the Right Person:* Appointment for Love; Baby Doll; A Different Story; The Doctor Takes a Wife; Green Card; The Hired Wife; Hold Back the Dawn; Howards End; The Lady Is Willing; Mail Order Bride; The Mating of Willie; Naked Jungle; Out of Africa; The Paper Marriage; The Piano; They Knew What They Wanted; This Thing Called Love; The Thousand Pieces of Gold; To Find a Man; The Wedding Banquet

Marriage on the Rocks: see also *Marriage Drama: Divorce: Marriage Comedy: Custody Battles:* The Abyss; Adam's Rib (1949); Altered States; At Play in the Fields of the Lord; The Awful Truth; Babe; Baby Maker; Bachelor Party (1957); Banjo on My Knee; Because of You; The Belly of an Architect; A Bill of Divorcement (1932); A Bill of Divorcement (1940); Bitter Moon; Blind Ambition; Bliss; Blume in Love; Bob & Carol & Ted & Alice; Boost; The Border; Boyz N the Hood; Break of Hearts; Bride Walks Out; Buster; C'est la Vie; Cadillac Man; Caged Fear; California Suite; Cast a Dark Shadow; Cat on a Hot Tin Roof (1958); Cat on a Hot Tin Roof (1984); Caught; A Change of Seasons; Chapter Two; Checking Out; China Clipper; Christmas Holiday; Constant Nymph (1933); Constant Nymph (1943); Dark at the Top of the Stairs; Detective Story; Devil and the Deep; Diana: Her True Story; Divorce, American Style; The Divorcée; Dodsworth; Don't Look Now; Don't Raise the Bridge, Lower the Water!; Ethan Fromme; Evelyn Prentice; The Executioner's Song; Experiment Perilous; Faces; Falling in Love; Family Pictures; Forever Darling; The Four-Poster; Fried Green Tomatoes; Friends and Husbands; Funny Girl; Funny Lady; The Godfather; The Godfather, Part II; The Godfather, Part III; The Good Wife; Guilty Conscience; Happy Ending; Hard Promises; Harriet Craig; Heartbreak Ridge; Helen Morgan Story; Hilda Crane; Honeymoon in Vegas; I Like It Like That; Indecent Proposal; Irreconcilable Differences; It's Love I'm After; Jet Pilot; Joshua Then and Now; Knave of Hearts; Kramer vs. Kramer; La Chienne; La

Notte; The Lady Gambles; Lady Takes a Flyer; Laughter; Leather Boys; Lesson in Love; Let It Ride; Let's Do It Again (1953); A Little Night Music; The Little Sex; The Living Corpse; Look Who's Talking Too; Loser Takes All; Love Crazy; Love Hurts; Love Matters; Lovers and Other Strangers; Loving Couples; Making Love; Man on Fire; The Man Who Understood Women; Man, Woman and Child; Mannequin (1937); Marriage on the Rocks; The Marrying Kind; Meet the Stewarts; The Merry Wives of Reno; Middle Age Crazy; The Moon's Our Home; Morgan!; Mr. and Mrs. Smith; The Music Lovers; My Blue Heaven (1950); My Blue Heaven (1990); My Foolish Heart; Next Time We Love; Norman, Is That You?; Not Without My Daughter; Once Were Warriors; The One and Only; Parting Glances; Payment on Demand; Peggy Sue Got Married; Pennies from Heaven (1981); Penny Serenade; Period of Adjustment; Plaza Suite; The Prisoner of Second Avenue; The Private Life of Henry VIII; Q & A; Rabbit, Run; Raging Bull; Raintree County; The Ref; Reflections in a Golden Eye; Regarding Henry; The River (1984); The Road to Wellville; Romantic Englishwoman; Rose of Washington Square; Running Mates; Saber Jet; Safe Passage; Scenes from a Mall; Scenes from a Marriage; Second Honeymoon; Secrets; Severed Head; The Shining; Shoot the Moon; Short Cuts; Simon and Laura; Smash Palace; Smile; SOB; Soft Skin; A Star Is Born (1937); A Star Is Born (1954); A Star Is Born (1976); State of the Union; Story of Three Loves; Stromboli; Sweet Smell of Success; Sweethearts Dance; Sweetie; A Talent for Loving; Tales of Terror; The Tempest; That Forsyte Woman; That's Life!; The Three Faces of Eve; Three Husbands; Three Smart Girls; Thunder Bay; Tin Men; Twin Beds; Two For the Road; Two-Faced Woman; Violent Men; The War Lover; War of the Roses; The Way of All Flesh (1928); The Way of All Flesh (1940); Where Were You When the Lights Went Out?; Wife, Doctor and Nurse; Winning; The Woman in Red; Woman Under the Influence; The World According to Garp

Marriage Plans: see *Marriage-Impending: Engagements-Breaking: Romance-Choosing the Right Person: Settling Down: Marriage Comedy: Newlyweds: Lovers-Live-in*

Marriages-Unhappy: see *Marriage on the Rocks: Divorce: Marriage Drama*

Married Couples (usually more than one couple prominent in story, not necessarily a story about marriage, however): see also *Marriage Drama: Marriage Comedy: Ensemble Films:* Don's Party; The Grass Is Greener; The Last Married Couple in America; The Lieutenant Wore Skirts; Love Matters; Married to It; Menage; Sweethearts Dance; Undercover Blues; We're Not Married; Woman's World; Yesterday, Today and Tomorrow

Married Couples-Childless: see *Women-Childless*

Married-Pretending to be: see *Marriage-Fake: also Secrets-Keeping: Inheritances at Stake: Screwball Comedy: FARCE: Immigrants*

Marrying Again (married once before, not necessarily divorced, then doing it again): see also *Bigamy: Romance-On Again/Off Again:* He Married His Wife; Let's Make It Legal; The Marrying Man; Mr. Wonderful; Phffft!; A Woman Obsessed

Marrying the Boss: see *Romance with Boss: Romance with Boss' Lover: Marrying Up: Romance with Co-Worker: Romance-Unprofessional: Business Life: Office Comedy*

Marrying Up: see also *Social Climbing: Rich People: Rich People vs. Poor: Gold Diggers: Bimbos: Bimboys:* The Actress (1928); Ada; Addams Family Values; Ain't Misbehavin'; Ann Vickers; Carrie (1952); Caught; Claudelle Inglish; Darling; Dynamite; Gentlemen Prefer Blondes; Hands Across the Table; Heartbreak Kid; How to Marry a Millionaire; I Know Where I'm Going; In Our Time; Is There Sex After Death?; Kitty; Laughter; Life at the Top; Love Among the Ruins; Mannequin (1937); Masquerade (1988); The Merry Widow (1925); The Merry Widow (1934); The Merry Widow (1952); Moon Over Miami; More Than a Secretary; Mrs. Parkington; My Lucky Star; New Leaf; Nights of Cabiria; Pal Joey; Palm Beach Story; A Place in the Sun; Reckless (1935); Red Headed Woman; A Room at the Top; Sabrina; Sanctuary; Stella (1990); Stella Dallas (1925); Stella Dallas (1937); Three Blind Mice; Three Coins in the Fountain; White Cliffs of Dover; Woman to Woman; Written on the Wind; You Can't Take It

With You (1938); You Can't Take It With You (1986); You're Telling Me

Marshals: see also *WESTERNS: Police Stories:* Cahill: United States Marshal; Chato's Land; Death of a Gunfighter; A Good Day for a Hanging; High Noon; Kansan; The Law and Jake Wade; Lawman; Tin Star; Wyatt Earp

Martial Arts: see also *ACTION: Chinese Films: Japanese Films:* Above the Law; American Ninja; American Ninja 2; American Ninja 3; Armed Response; Beastmaster; Beastmaster 2; Best of the Best; Big Brawl; Big Trouble in Little China; Billy Jack; Blind Fury; Bloodfist; Bloodfist II; Bloodfist III; Bloodsport; Brain Smasher: A Love Story; Challenge; Death Warrant; Enter the Dragon; Excessive Force; Eye for an Eye; A Force of One; Gate of Hell; Good Guys Wear Black; Gymkata; Hard to Kill; The Karate Kid; The Karate Kid, Part II; The Karate Kid, Part III; Kickboxer; Kickboxer 2; Kung Fu; Lone Wolf McQuade; Marked for Death; Octagon; On Deadly Ground; Paper Tiger; Rapid Fire; Remo Williams: The Adventure Begins; Rescue Me; Rising Sun; Road House; Shogun Assassin; Teenage Mutant Ninja Turtles; Teenage Mutant Ninja Turtles 2; Teenage Mutant Ninja Turtles 3; Three Ninjas; Three Ninjas Kick Back; Throne of Blood; Yakuza; Yojimbo

Martians: see also *Aliens-Outer Space: Evil: UFOs:* Invaders from Mars (1953); Invaders from Mars (1986); War of the Worlds

Marx Brothers: see also *Comedy-Slapstick: Screwball Comedy:* At the Circus; The Big Store; Copacabana; Go West; A Night at the Opera; A Night in Casablanca; Room Service

Massacres: see also *Custer's Last Stand: Murders-Mass: War Battles:* Gassss; Major Dundee; Shalako

Mass Murders: see *Murders-Mass: Murderers-Mass:* also *Serial Killers: Psycho Killers: Snipers*

Matchmakers: see also *Blind Dates: Dating Scene: Dates-Hired:* The Bachelor and the Bobby-Soxer; The Bride of Frankenstein; Buddy System; Crossing Delancey; Dim Sum: a Little Bit of Heart; Don't Tell Her It's Me; For Love of Ivy; The Glass Menagerie (1950); The Glass Menagerie (1973); The Glass Menagerie (1987); Hello Dolly; I'd Rather Be Rich; I.Q.; Ladies Should Listen; Ladyhawke;

Love Is a Ball; Luck of the Irish; Mail Order Bride; The Matchmaker; The Model and the Marriage Broker; The More the Merrier; Short Circuit; Three Smart Girls; Three Smart Girls Grow Up; To Paris with Love; Walk, Don't Run; You Were Never Lovelier

Matrimonial Detectives: see *Detectives-Matrimonial:* also *Cheating Men: Cheating Women*

McCarthy Era: see also *Communists: 1950s: Cold War Era: Fascism: Oppression: Censorship: Courtroom Drama:* Citizen Cohn; The Commies are Coming, the Commies are Coming; The Conspirator; Daniel; Fellow Traveler; The Front; Golden Gate; Guilty by Suspicion; The House on Carroll Street; I Was a Communist for the FBI; Keeper of the Flame; My Son John; The Trial (1955); The Way We Were

Mean Men (not quite evil, but still nasty jerks): see also *Evil Men: Selfish People:* Anne of the Thousand Days; The Browning Version; Fawlty Towers; The Gathering; Glengarry Glen Ross; Go into Your Dance; The Great Santini; Hasty Heart; Heartbreak Ridge; Oscar; Otello; Othello (1951); Othello (1965); Other People's Money; Patti Rocks; Patton; The Player; Radio Flyer; Regarding Henry; Reversal of Fortune; Ruthless People; Sandlot; The Secret Garden (1949); The Secret Garden (1984); The Secret Garden (1987); The Secret Garden (1993); Shame (1961); The Taming of the Shrew; Watch It

Mean Women (not quite evil, but still nasty): see also *Evil Women: Selfish People:* All About Eve; The Cutting Edge; Death Becomes Her; Die! Die! My Darling!; Georgy Girl; Gone With the Wind; The Graduate; Guarding Tess; A Guest in the House; Hedda; The Little Foxes; Inside Monkey Zetterland; Miss Firecracker; Mommie Dearest; Night of the Iguana; Of Human Bondage (1934); Of Human Bondage (1946); Of Human Bondage (1964); One Deadly Summer; Ordinary People; Oscar; Overboard; The Paper; Passion Fish; Private Benjamin; Queen Bee; Raintree County; Ruthless People; Swept Away; Tatie Danielle; Total Recall; Turning Point; Valley of the Dolls

Media Satire: see also *Hollywood Satire: Satire: TV Life:* A Face in the Crowd; Jimmy Hollywood; Last

Command; Man Bites Dog; Natural Born Killers; The Purple Rose of Cairo; S.F.W.

Medical Detectives: see also *Medical Mystery: Medical Thrillers:* Awakenings; Carey Treatment; Coma; Dream Lover (1986); Green for Danger; The Hunger; Looker; Lorenzo's Oil; Mystery Street; Panic in the Streets; Wild Child

Medical Drama: see also *Disease Stories: Death-Dealing With: Doctors: Hospitals: Nurses:* Arrowsmith; Awakenings; Cactus; The Great Moment; Gross Anatomy; The Last Flight; Magnificent Obsession (1934); Magnificent Obsession (1954); The Men (1950); A Month in the Country; Nurse; The Painted Veil; People Will Talk; Regarding Henry; Resurrection; Spellbound; Stairway to Heaven; Threshold; Unnatural Causes; Young Doctors

Medical Mystery: see *Medical Detectives: Medical Thrillers*

Medical Recovery: see *Disease Stories:* also *Cures/Solutions-Search for*

Medical School: see also *Doctors: Hospitals: Scientists:* A Doctor in the House; Flatliners; Gross Anatomy; New Interns; Not as a Stranger; Of Human Bondage (1934); Of Human Bondage (1946); Of Human Bondage (1964); Punchline; Young Doctors

Medical Thrillers: see also *Medical Mystery: Medical Detectives:* Ambulance; The Andromeda Strain; Coma; Green for Danger; Outbreak

Medieval Times: see also *Castles: Fairy Tales: King Arthur Legend: Legends: Mythology:* The Adventures of Robin Hood; Beastmaster; Beastmaster 2; Becket; Black Arrow; Black Cauldron; Camelot; A Canterbury Tale; Dragonslayer; Edward II; El Cid; Erik The Viking; Excalibur; Flesh and Blood (1985); Ivanhoe; Knights of the Round Table; Krull; Lady Jane; Ladyhawke; The Last Valley; Legend; Lionheart; Prince Valiant; Robin and Marian; Robin Hood (1922); Robin Hood (1973); Robin Hood (1990); Robin Hood: Prince of Thieves (1991); Siegfried; The Story of Robin Hood and his Merry Men; The Sword in the Stone; Sword of the Valiant; Sword & the Sorcerer; Virgin Spring; War Lord

Mediterranean (set on that sea): see also *Riviera Life: French Films: Italian Films:* America, America; Boy on a

Dolphin; Eyewitness (1970); For Your Eyes Only; From Russia with Love; Girl Who Couldn't Say No; L'Avventura; Mackintosh Man; Mediterraneo; Moon Spinners; Pascali's Island; Shirley Valentine

MELODRAMA (dramas that could be set to music, literally, usually accompanied by the wringing of handkerchiefs): see also *Tearjerkers: Disease Stories: Underdog Stories: Family Stories:* Aaron Loves Angela; Abie's Irish Rose; About Face; Ace Eli and Rodger of the Skies; Act of Love; Act of Violence; Action for Slander; The Actress (1928); The Actress (1953); Ada; Adam and Eva; Adam Had Four Sons; Adam's Rib (1922); The Adventurers; The Adventures of Captain Fabian; The Adventures of Don Juan; The Adventures of the Wilderness Family; The Adventuress; An Affair to Remember; After the Rehearsal; The Age of Innocence (1934); The Age of Innocence (1993); The Agony and the Ecstasy; Ah, Wilderness; Alex and the Gypsy; Alexander's Ragtime Band; Alice Adams; All About Eve; All Creatures Great and Small; All I Want For Christmas; All That Heaven Allows; All the Brothers Were Valiant; All the Fine Young Cannibals; All the Way Home; All This and Heaven, Too; Always Goodbye; Always in My Heart; Always Leave Them Laughing; Amarcord; Amazing Grace and Chuck; American Flyers; American in Paris; The Americanization of Emily; Amsterdamned; Amy; And Now, Tomorrow; Angel and the Badman; Angel Baby; Angel in My Pocket; Angel Wore Red; Angelina; Angie; Ann Vickers; Anna; Anna Christie; Anna Karenina (1935); Anna Karenina (1948); Another Time, Another Place; Are Husbands Necessary?; Arise, My Love; The Arrangement; Ash Wednesday; Aspen Extreme; Assault; Audrey Rose; Australia; Author! Author!; The Autobiography of Miss Jane Pittman; Avalanche; Avalon; The Aviator; Awakenings; Baby Doll; Baby Face; Baby Maker; Baby, Take A Bow; Babycakes; Bachelor Mother; Back Street (1932); Back Street (1941); Back Street (1961); The Bad and the Beautiful; Bad Timing: A Sensual Obsession; The Balcony; Ballad of a Soldier; Ballad of the Sad Cafe; Bambi; Band of Angels; Bang the Drum Slowly; Barbary Coast; The Barretts

of Wimpole Street (1934); The Barretts of Wimpole Street (1956); Battle Cry; Baxter (1972); Bay Boy; Beaches; Beat Generation; Beau Brummell (1924); Beau Brummell (1954); Beau Geste (1926); Beau Geste (1939); Beau Geste (1966); Beau James; Beautiful Dreamers; Beauty for the Asking; Because of You; Bed and Board; A Bedtime Story (1933); Beekeeper; Bellisima; Bells of St. Mary's; Beloved Infidel; Beneath the 12 Mile Reef; Benji; Benny Goodman Story; Berkeley Square; Berlin Alexanderplatz; Best Boy; Best Intentions; Best of Everything; Best Years of Our Lives; Betrayed (1954); Betsy; Between Two Women; Beverly Hills Madam; Beware, My Lovely; Beyond the Forest; Beyond the Poseidon Adventure; Bhowani Junction; The Bicycle Thief; Big Blue; The Big Chill; The Big Fisherman; The Big Heat; Big Man; Big Red; The Big Street; The Big Town; Big Trees; Bill; A Bill of Divorcement (1932); A Bill of Divorcement (1940); Bill: On His Own; Billy Rose's Jumbo; The Birdman of Alcatraz; Birdy; Birth of the Blues; The Biscuit Eater (1940); The Biscuit Eater (1972); Bitch (1979); Bitter Sweet (1933); Bitter Sweet (1940); Bittersweet Love; Black Beauty (1946); Black Beauty (1971); Black Beauty (1994); Black Orchid; The Black Stallion; The Black Stallion Returns; Blame it on the Night; Bless the Beasts and the Children; Blonde Venus; Blood Alley; Blood and Sand (1922); Blood and Sand (1941); Blood Feud; Bloodhounds of Broadway (1952); Bloodhounds of Broadway (1989); Bloodline; Blossoms in the Dust; Blowing Wild; Blue Angel (1930); Blue Angel (1959); Blue Denim; Blue Veil; Blues in the Night; Bobby Deerfield; Body and Soul (1947); Body and Soul (1981); Bodyguard; Bolero (1934); Bolero (1984); Bombay Talkie; Bon Voyage, Charlie Brown; Bonjour, Tristesse; Boom!; Bordertown; Born Again; Born Free; Born Losers; Born to Be Bad (1934); Born to Be Bad (1950); Boss; Boy on a Dolphin; The Boy Who Could Fly; The Boy With Green Hair; Boys in the Band; Boys on the Side; Boys Town; Brainstorm (1965); Brainstorm (1983); Break of Hearts; Brian's Song; Bride Is Much Too Beautiful; The Bride Walks Out; Bright Eyes; Bright Victory; Brink of Life; Broadway Bound; Broken Blossoms; The

Browning Version; Bundle of Joy; Bus Stop; Butterfly; By Love Possessed; By the Light of the Silvery Moon; Cabin in the Cotton; Caddie; Caged; Cahill: United States Marshal; Call of the Wild (1935); Call of the Wild (1972); Calling Dr. Gillespie; Calling Dr. Kildare; Camila (1984); Camila (1994); Camille (1936); Campus Man; A Canterbury Tale; Canyon Passage; Cardinal Richelieu; The Carpetbaggers; Casablanca; Casanova Brown; Casey's Shadow; Casque d'Or; Cat on a Hot Tin Roof (1958); Cat on a Hot Tin Roof (1984); The Catered Affair; Cavalcade; The Champ (1931); The Champ (1979); Champions; A Change of Habit; Chapter Two; Chariots of Fire; Charming Sinners; The Chase (1966); Cheers for Miss Bishop; China Girl (1942); Chocolate Soldier; Christmas Lilies of the Field; Christopher Strong; Circle of Two; City for Conquest; City Lights; City of Joy; Clara's Heart; Clash by Night; Class of '44; Claudelle Inglish; Claudia; Clean and Sober; The Client; The Clock; Close My Eyes; Clown; Come Back, Little Sheba; Come See the Paradise; Coming Home; Competition; Conrack; The Conspirator; Constant Nymph (1933); Constant Nymph (1943); Cooperstown; The Cotton Club; Country; Coupe de Ville; Courtship; Cousins; Cover Girl; The Crash of Silence; Criss Cross (1992); The Cure; Cyrano de Bergerac (1950); Cyrano de Bergerac (1990); Dad; Daisy Kenyon; Daisy Miller; Dancers; Dancing in the Dark; Dancing Lady; Dangerous Liaisons; Dark Angel (1935); Dark at the Top of the Stairs; Dark Victory; David Copperfield; Dead End; Dear Heart; Deception (1946); The Deep Blue Sea; Desert Fury; Desire; Desire Me; Desiree; Detective Story; Devil and the Deep; The Devil Is a Sissy; The Devil Is a Woman; Devotion; Diamond Head; Diamond Horseshoe; Diana: Her True Story; A Diary for Timothy; Diary of Anne Frank (1959); Dino; Dirty Dancing; The Disappearance of Aimee; Dishonored; The Disturbed; Diving In; Doctor in the House; Doctor Quinn, Medicine Woman; The Dog of Flanders; Dominick & Eugene; Don't Bother to Knock; Dove; Dr. Socrates; Dramatic School; Driftwood; Drum; Drums Along the Mohawk; Duel in the Sun; Dumbo; Dutch; Dying Young; Dynamite; Eagle's Wing; East Lynne;

East of Eden (1955); East of Eden (1980); East Side, West Wide; Easy Virtue; Echoes of a Summer; Eddy Duchin Story; Edward, My Son; Effect of Gamma Rays on Man-in-the-Moon Marigolds; Eleni; Elephant Man; Elmer Gantry; Elvira Madigan; Emma; Encore; Endless Love; England Made Me; The Entertainer; Eric; Escape; E.T.; The Europeans; Evelyn Prentice; Ever in My Heart; Every Time We Say Goodbye; Everybody's All American; Executive Suite; Experiment in Terror; Experiment Perilous; Expresso Bongo; A Family Affair; Family Upside Down; Far and Away; Far From Home; A Farewell to Arms (1932); A Farewell to Arms (1957); Fate is the Hunter; Father Hood; Fedora; Female on the Beach; Field of Dreams; Fighting Kentuckian; Fine Things; Finishing School; Firefly; The First Deadly Sin; Firstborn; Five Star Final; Flame of New Orleans; Flame of the Barbary Coast; Flamingo Road; Flashdance; Flesh and Blood (1951); Flesh and the Devil; Flood!; Follow Me, Boys!; Follow That Dream; Foolish Wives; For Love or Money (1963); For the Boys; Forbidden Dance; Forest Rangers; Forever Amber; Forever and a Day; Forever Female; Forever Young; Forrest Gump; Forty Carats; Four Daughters; The Four Friends; The Four Horsemen of the Apocalypse; Foxfire (1955); Foxfire (1987); Freaks; A Free Soul; The Frenchman's Creek; Fresh Horses; From Here to Eternity; From This Day Forward; Furies; G.I. Blues; G.I. Joe; G-Men; Gable and Lombard; Gabriela; Gaby; Gaby, a True Story; Gambling Lady; Game is Over; Garden of Allah; Garden of the Finzi-Continis; Garment Jungle; Gay Sisters; The General Died at Dawn; The George Raft Story; Gertrude; Gervaise; Ghost; The Ghost and Mrs. Muir; Giant; Gigot; Gilda; Girl From Petrovka; Girl from Tenth Avenue; Girl in the Red Velvet Swing; A Girl Named Tamiko; Girl of the Golden West; The Girl Who Had Everything; The Glass Menagerie (1950); The Glass Menagerie (1973); The Glass Menagerie (1987); Glen or Glenda?; The Glenn Miller Story; Gloria; Go Naked in the World; The Go-Between; God's Little Acre; Godspell; Going My Way; Golden Boy; The Golem; Gone With the Wind; The Good Die Young; The Good Earth; Goodbye Again; Goodbye Gemini; Goodbye Mr. Chips

(1939); Goodbye Mr. Chips (1969); Goodbye My Fancy; Goodbye My Lady; Gorgeous Hussy; Grand Highway; Grand Hotel; Great Caruso; Great Lie; Great Moment; Great Sinner; The Great Waltz (1938); The Great Waltz (1972); Great Ziegfeld; The Greatest Show on Earth; The Greek Tycoon; Green Dolphin Street; Green Fire; Green Goddess; Green Mansions; Green Years; Greystoke: The Legend of Tarzan; Griffin and Phoenix, A Love Story; Guarding Tess; Guess Who's Coming to Dinner; Guest in the House; Gypsy; Hallelujah!; Hallelujah, I'm a Bum; Hanging Tree; Hanover Street; Happy Land; Hard Country; The Hard Way (1943); Harder They Fall; Harlow; Harrad Experiment; Harrad Summer; Harriet Craig; Harry and Son; Harry and Tonto; Hasty Heart; A Hatful of Rain; Hear My Song; Heart of Dixie; Heart of the Matter; Heartbreakers; Hearts of Fire; Heaven and Earth; Heidi (1939); The Heiress; The Helen Morgan Story; Hellcats of the Navy; Hide in Plain Sight; High and the Mighty; High Heels; High Tide; High, Wide and Handsome; Hilda Crane; His Brother's Wife; Hold Back the Dawn; Holiday for Sinners; Holiday Inn; Holly and the Ivy; Hollywood Boulevard (1936); Hollywood Boulevard (1977); Hollywood Cavalcade; Holy Matrimony; Home from the Hill; A Home of Our Own; The Homecoming (1948); Honky Tonk; Hot Spell; Hotel; A House Divided; A House Is Not a Home; Household Saints; How Green Was My Valley; The Howards of Virginia; Human Comedy; Humoresque; The Hunchback of Notre Dame (1923); The Hunchback of Notre Dame (1939); The Hunchback of Notre Dame (1956); The Hunchback of Notre Dame (1982); The Hunted; Hunter; Hurricane (1937); Hurricane (1979); Hurry Sundown; I Believe in You; I Can Get It For You Wholesale; I Could Go on Singing; I Cover the Waterfront; I Dream of Jeannie; I Dream Too Much; I Found Stella Parish; I, Jane Doe; I Know Where I'm Going; I Live My Life; I, Mobster; I Ought to Be in Pictures; I Remember Mama; I Sent a Letter to My Love; I Stand Condemned; I Take this Woman; I Want What I Want; I Wanted Wings; I'll Be Seeing You; I'll Cry Tomorrow; Ice Castles; If Winter Comes; Imitation of Life (1934); Imitation of Life (1959); Immediate Family; Impatient Years;

Impudent Girl; In a Shallow Grave. In Name Only; In Old Chicago; In Old Kentucky; In the Cool of the Day; In the Good Old Summertime; The Incredible Journey of Dr. Meg Laurel; Incredible Sarah; Indecent Obsession; Indecent Proposal; Inheritance; Inkwell; Inn of the Sixth Happiness; Innocent Man; Inserts; Inspiration; Interlude (1957); Interlude (1968); Intermezzo (1939); International Velvet; Interns; Interrupted Melody; Intersection; Invitation; Iron Man; Ironweed; Island in the Sun; Islands in the Stream; It Always Rains on Sunday; It's A Big Country; Jane Eyre (1934); Jane Eyre (1943); Jane Eyre (1971); The Jazz Singer (1927); The Jazz Singer (1953); The Jazz Singer (1980); Jersey Girl; Jet Pilot; Jezebel; Jo Jo Dancer, Your Life is Calling; Joan of Arc; Johnny Belinda; Joni; Journey for Margaret; Journey of Hope; The Joy Luck Club; Judgment at Nuremburg; Just Between Friends; Justine; Kansas City Bomber; The Karate Kid; The Karate Kid, Part II; The Karate Kid, Part III; Keeper of the Flame; The Kentuckian; Kentucky; The Key (1934); The Key (1958); Keys of the Kingdom; The Kid from Left Field; Kid Galahad; The Killer's Kiss; The Killing Fields; The King and Four Queens; King Creole; King of Kings (1927); King of Kings (1961); The King's Whore; Kings Row; Kismet (1944); Kismet (1955); The Kiss (1929); Kiss the Blood Off My Hands; Kitten with a Whip; Kitty Foyle; Knight Without Armor; Knute Rockne: All-American; Kotch; Kramer vs. Kramer; L'Annee des Meduses; La Bamba; La Boum; La Chienne; La Maschera; La Strada; La Traviata; Ladies Should Listen; Ladies They Talk About; Lady for a Day; Lady Gambles; Lady in the Dark; Lady in the Iron Mask; Lady with a Dog; Lake Consequence; Lambada; Lassie; Lassie Come Home; The Last Days of Chez Nous; The Last Emperor; The Last Flight; The Last Hurrah; The Last of Mrs. Cheyney; The Last Tycoon; Late for Dinner; Laughing Sinners; Laura; The Law and the Lady; A League of Their Own; Lean on Me; Leather Saint; Leaving Normal; Left Hand of God; The Legend of Billie Jean; The Legend of Lylah Clare; The Legend of the Holy Drinker; Les Liaisons Dangereuses; Less Than Zero; Let No Man Write My Epitaph; The Letter (1929); The Letter (1940); Letter

From an Unknown Woman; Letter to Three Wives; Life at the Top; Life Begins at 8:30; The Life of Emile Zola; A Life of Her Own; The Life of Riley; Life With Father; Light in the Piazza; Light that Failed; Lili Marleen; Limelight; Little Foxes; Little Gloria, Happy At Last; Little Lord Fauntleroy (1936); Little Lord Fauntleroy (1980); Little Man Tate; Little Miss Marker (1934); Little Miss Marker (1980); The Little Princess; Little Women (1933); Little Women (1949); Little Women (1978); Little Women (1994); Live for Life; Live, Love and Learn; Living in a Big Way; Lloyd's of London; Lonely Lady; Long Hot Summer (1958); Looking for Love; Lorenzo's Oil; Losing Isaiah; Lost Angel; Lost Boundaries; Lost Lady; Lost Moment; The Lost Weekend; Love; The Love Affair (1939); Love and Money; Love and Pain and the Whole Damn Thing; Love Field; Love Has Many Faces; Love Hurts; Love is a Many-Splendored Thing; Love Letters (1945); Love Machine; Love Matters; Love Me or Leave Me; Love Story (1944); Love Story (1970); Loves of Carmen; Lucy Gallant; Luna; Lust for Life; Lusty Men; Lydia; Macao; Macomber Affair; Madame Bovary; Madame Butterfly; Madame Dubarry; Madame Rosa; Madame Sousatzka; Madame X (1929); Madame X (1937); Madame X (1965); Made for Each Other; Made in Heaven; Mademoiselle Fifi; Madison Avenue; Madness of the Heart; Magnificent Obsession (1935); Magnificent Obsession (1954); Mahogany; Maid of Salem; Main Street to Broadway; Majority of One; Making Love; Mamma Rosa; A Man and A Woman; The Man I Married; Man in Grey; The Man in the Moon; Man with the Golden Arm; The Man with Two Faces; The Man Without a Face; Man, Woman and Child; Man's Castle; Mandingo; Manhattan Melodrama; Mannequin (1937); Manon des Sources (1952); Manon des Sources (1986); Map of the Human Heart; March or Die; Mardi Gras; Marie; Marie Antoinette; Marius; Marjorie Morningstar; Mark; Marked Woman; Marnie; The Marriage of Maria Braun; Martin's Day; Marty; Mary Burns, Fugitive; Masala; Mask (1985); Mata Hari (1931); Mata Hari (1985); Mata Hari, Agent H21 (1964); The Mating of Willie; Mating Season; A Matter of Time; Mayerling (1935); Mayerling (1968); Maytime; The McConnell Story; McVicar;

Mean Streets; Medal for Benny; Meet Danny Wilson; Melo; Member of the Wedding; Memphis Belle; Men Are Not Gods; Men in Her Life; Men in White; Men of Boys' Town; Men with Wings; The Merry Widow (1925); The Merry Widow (1934); The Merry Widow (1952); Metropolitan (1935); Midnight Cowboy; Midnight Lace; Mildred Pierce; Mill on the Floss; The Millionairess; Min and Bill; Miniver Story; Miracle in the Rain; Miracle Worker; Misfits; Miss Sadie Thompson; Miss Susie Slagle's; Missing; Mississippi; Mississippi Masala; Misunderstood; Moment by Moment; Monsieur Vincent; Morning Glory; Movie Movie; Mr. Lucky; Mrs. Miniver; Mrs. Parkington; Mudlark; Music For Millions; My Cousin Rachel; My Foolish Heart; My Forbidden Past; My Geisha; My Girl; My Girl 2; My Life; My Love Came Back; My Name is Julia Ross; My Reputation; My Six Loves; My Son John; My Son, My Son; My Sweet Little Village; My Wife's Best Friend; The Mystery of Edwin Drood; Naked Jungle; Nancy Steele is Missing; Nanou; National Velvet; Natural; Never Say Goodbye; Never Too Late; New Interns; New York, New York; Night is Young (1934); Night Nurse; Night of the Following Day; Night of the Iguana; Night Train to Munich; Night unto Night; Nights of Cabiria 1918; No Down Payment; No Man of Her Own (1949); No More Ladies; No Orchids for Miss Blandish; None But the Lonely Heart; North Star; Not as a Stranger; Not Without My Daughter; Now, Voyager; Nun's Story; Nurse Edith Cavell; O'Hara's Wife; Ode to Billy Joe; Odette; Of Human Bondage (1934); Of Human Bondage (1946); Of Human Bondage (1964); Of Human Hearts; Of Love and Desire; Old Acquaintance; Old Gringo; Old Maid; Old Yeller; Oliver Twist (1948); Oliver Twist (1982); Oliver's Story; On Dangerous Ground; On Golden Pond; On the Waterfront; On Your Toes; Once Around; Once in Paris; Once Is Not Enough; Once More with Feeling; Once Upon a Dream; One Flew Over Cuckoo's Nest; One Foot in Heaven; One from the Heart; One Good Cop; One Hour with You; One in a Million; One Magic Christmas; One More River; One More Spring; One Night of Love; One Sunday Afternoon; One Trick Pony; One Way Passage; Only Game in Town; Opening Night; Oscar; The Other Side of

Midnight; The Other Side of the Mountain; The Other Side of the Mountain Part Two; Our Dancing Daughters; Our Hearts Were Young and Gay; Our Town; Our Vines Have Tender Grapes; Over the Brooklyn Bridge; Over Twenty-One; Paid; Paid in Full; Painted Desert; Painted Veil; Pandora and the Flying Dutchman; Paradise (1982); Paradise (1991); Paradise Alley; Paranoia; Paris Model; Parnell; Parting Glances; Party Girl; Passing of the Third Floor Back; Passion/Madame Dubarry (1919); Passion of Joan of Arc; Payment Deferred; Payment on Demand; Peg o' My Heart; Pennies from Heaven (1936); Penny Serenade; Perfect Strangers; Personal Property; Pete Kelly's Blues; Peter Ibbetson; Peyton Place; Phar Lap; Piccadilly Incident; Picnic; The Picture of Dorian Gray; Pinky; Places in the Heart; Pollyanna; Poor Little Rich Girl; Port of Call; The Portrait; The Poseidon Adventure; The Possessed (1947); Power of One; Presenting Lily Mars; Pride and Prejudice; Pride of the Yankees; The Prince of Tides; The Prizefighter and the Lady; Prodigal; The Promise; Promises in the Dark; Pudd'nhead Wilson; Punchline; Pure Country; Quality Street; Quartet (1948); Queen Bee; Queen Christina; Queen of Hearts; Quicksand; Radio Flyer; Raggedy Man; Rain; Rain Man; Rainmaker; Rains Came; Raintree County; Rancho Notorious; Random Harvest; Rasputin and the Empress; Razorback; Reap the Wild Wind; Rebecca of Sunnybrook Farm (1925); Reckless (1935); Reckless (1983); Red Dust; Red Headed Woman; The Red Pony (1949); The Red Pony (1976); Reflections in a Golden Eye; Regarding Henry; The Remains of the Day; The Return of Martin Guerre; Return of the Soldier; Return to Peyton Place; Return to the Blue Lagoon; Revenge; Rhapsody; Rhapsody in Blue; Riff-Raff (1935); Right to Love; River (1984); RobRoy; Rocket Gibraltar; Roller Boogie; Roman Spring of Mrs. Stone; Romance; Romeo and Juliet (1936); Romeo and Juliet (1954); Romeo and Juliet (1968); Roommates; Roots, the Gift; Rose Marie (1936); Rose Marie (1954); Rose of Washington Square; Rose Tattoo; Royal Scandal; Ruby Gentry; Rudy; Runner Stumbles; Running on Empty; Saber Jet; Sadie McKee; Safe Passage; The Saint of

Fort Washington; Sally of the Sawdust; Salome, Where She Danced; Salsa; Samson and Delilah; San Francisco; Sanctuary; The Sandpiper; Sarafina!; Sarah, Plain and Tall; Saratoga Trunk; Saskatchewan; Satisfaction; Saturday Night Fever; Savage Sam; Say One for Me; Sayonara; The Scarlet Letter (1926); The Scarlet Letter (1934); The Scarlet Letter (1980); Scent of a Woman; Schindler's List; Scorchers; Scrooge (1935); Search; Searching for Bobby Fischer; Second Chorus; Secrets; See You in the Morning; Sentimental Journey; A Separate Peace; Separate Tables; September Affair; Seventh Heaven (1927); Seventh Heaven (1937); The Seventh Veil; Shadows of our Forgotten Ancestors; Shane; Shanghai Gesture; She Couldn't Say No; She Wore a Yellow Ribbon; Sheik; Shell Seekers; Shenandoah; Shepherd of the Hills; Shining Hour; Shining Through; The Shootist; Shop Around the Corner; Show Business; Showboat (1936); Showboat (1951); Shy People; Side Out; Sign of the Cross; A Simple Twist of Fate; Sin of Madelon Claudet; Since You Went Away; Singing Fool; Singing Nun; Sins of Rachel Cade; Sister Act 2; Sister Kenny; Sisters; Six Weeks; Skylark; Sleepless in Seattle; Slow Dancing in the Big City; Small Circle of Friends; Smash-Up, the Story of a Woman; Smilin' Through (1932); Smilin' Through (1941); Smugglers; Snakepit; So Big (1932); So Big (1953); So Dear to My Heart; So Proudly We Hail; So Red the Rose; Soft Skin; Soldier of Fortune; Some Came Running; Some Kind of Hero; Someone to Watch Over Me; Something Wild (1960); Somewhere I'll Find You; Somewhere in Time; Sommersby; Song of Bernadette; Song of Love; A Song to Remember; Song Without End; Songwriter; Sons and Lovers; Sophia Loren, Her Own Story; The Sound and the Fury; Sounder; The Southerner; Sparkle; Spawn of the North; Spencer's Mountain; Spetters; Spirit Rider; Splendor in the Grass; Square Dance; St. Elmo's Fire; Stagedoor; Staircase; Stairway to Heaven; Star; A Star Is Born (1937); A Star Is Born (1954); A Star Is Born (1976); Stars and Stripes Forever; State Fair (1933); State Fair (1945); State Fair (1962); State of the Union; Staying Alive; Staying Together; Stealing Heaven; Steel; Steel

Magnolias; Stella (1990); Stella Dallas (1925); Stella Dallas (1937); The Sterile Cuckoo; Stolen Hours; Stolen Kisses; Stormy Weather; The Story of Alexander Graham Bell; The Story of Boys and Girls; The Story of Dr. Wassell; The Story of Louis Pasteur; The Story of Three Loves; The Story of Vernon and Irene Castle; Straight out of Brooklyn; Strange Cargo; The Strange Loves of Martha Ivers; Strangers, the Story of a Mother and Daughter; The Stratton Story; Street Angel; Street Scene; A Streetcar Named Desire; Stripper; Stud; The Subterraneans; Subway; Success is the Best Revenge; Suddenly, Last Summer; Suez; Summer and Smoke; Summer of '42; Summer of My German Soldier; A Summer Place; Summer Story; Summertime; Sunday in the Country; Sundays and Cybele; Sundown; Sunflower; Susan Lenox, Her Fall and Rise; Suzy; Svengali (1931); Svengali (1983); Swamp Water; Swarm; Sweet Bird of Youth; Swing Kids; Switch; T. R. Baskin; Table for Five; Tai Pan; Talent for the Game; Tammy and the Bachelor; Targets; Tarnished Angels; Tarzan Escapes; Tarzan, The Ape Man (1932); Tarzan, the Ape Man (1981); A Taste of Honey; Tattoo; Tea and Sympathy; Tears in the Rain; Teenage Rebel; Tell Me that You Love Me, Junie Moon; Ten Commandments; Tender is the Night; Teresa; Terminal Bliss; Terms of Endearment; The Terry Fox Story; Tess; Test Pilot; Testament; That Certain Woman; That Forsyte Woman; That Hamilton Woman; That Was Then . . . This Is Now; That's Life!; These Three; They Made Me a Criminal; This Above All; This Happy Breed; This Land Is Mine; This Property Is Condemned; Those Were the Days; Three Coins in the Fountain; Three Comrades; Three Cornered Moon; Three Godfathers; Three Husbands; Threshold; Thunderbirds; Tiger Bay; Till the Clouds Roll By; Till the End of Time; Time of Destiny; A Time to Love and a Time to Die; Titanic; To Dance with the White Dog; To Each His Own; To Find a Man; To Paris with Love; To Sir with Love; Toast of New Orleans; Today We Live; Tokyo Joe; Tomorrow is Forever; Torch Song; Torrents of Spring; Toys in the Attic; Trapeze; Travelling North; A Tree Grows in Brooklyn; Tribute; Trouble Along the Way; Truly,

Madly, Deeply; Tulsa; 21 Days; Twenty Thousand Years in Sing Sing; Two Against the World; Two Moon Junction; Two Women; The Two Worlds of Jenny Logan; Umbrellas of Cherbourg; Uncle Tom's Cabin (1914); Uncle Tom's Cabin (1969); The Unconquered; Under Capricorn; Under the Cherry Moon; Under Two Flags; Unfaithful; Unfinished Piece for a Player The Piano; Union Station; Untamed Heart; Vacation from Marriage; Valentino (1951); Valley of Decision; Valley of the Dolls; Vanity Fair; A View from the Bridge; Violent Men; Violets are Blue; Voices; Wabash Avenue; Wait 'Til the Sun Shines, Nellie; Wait Until Spring, Bandini; Wake of the Red Witch; Walk in the Spring Rain; Walk on the Wild Side; Walking Stick; The War; War Against Mrs. Hadley; War and Peace (1956); Warm Nights on a Slow Moving Train; Washington Story; Waterloo Bridge (1931); Waterloo Bridge (1940); Way Down East (1920); Way Down East (1935); The Way of All Flesh (1928); The Way of All Flesh (1940); Wedding March; Weeds; Weekend at the Waldorf; Welcome Home; The Well; The Westerner; What Every Woman Knows; What Price Hollywood?; When a Man Loves a Woman; When Ladies Meet (1933); When Ladies Meet (1941); When the Whales Came; When Tomorrow Comes; Where Angels Fear to Tread; Where the Day Takes You; Where the Heart Is; Where the Lilies Bloom; Where the Red Fern Grows; Whisperers; White Banners; White Cargo; White Christmas; White Cliffs of Dover; White Mama; White Nights (1957); White Sister; Wicked As They Come; Wild Angels; Wild Hearts Can't Be Broken; Wild in the Country; Wild Is the Wind; Wild Orchid; Wild Party; Wildflower; Winged Victory; Wings; Wings in the Dark; Wings of Eagles; Wings of the Morning; Winter People; Winterset; Wisdom; Without a Trace; The Woman I Love; Woman of Paris; Woman to Woman; The Woman's Face; Woman's World; Wonder Bar; The Wonderful World of the Brothers Grimm; The World Is Full of Married Men; The World of Suzie Wong; Written on the Wind; Wuthering Heights (1939); Wuthering Heights (1953); Wuthering Heights (1970); Wuthering Heights (1992); X, Y, & Zee; Yanks; The Yearling; Yes, Giorgio; Yesterday's Hero; You Light

Up My Life; Young Bess; Young Doctors; Young Man with a Horn; Young Philadelphians; Youngblood Hawke; Yours, Mine and Ours; Zandalee; Zebrahead; Zelly and Me

Memories: see also *Childhood Memories: Boyhood: Girlhood: Flashbacks:* The Affairs of Susan; All the Mornings of the World; American Hotwax; Au Revoir, les Enfants; Becoming Colette; Book of Love; Caddy; Chocolat; Cinema Paradiso; Come Back to the Five and Dime, Jimmy Dean, Jimmy Dean; Cooperstown; The Dead; Diary for My Children; Dreamchild; The Entertainer; Falling in Love Again; Family; Fanny and Alexander; FBI Story; For the Boys; The 400 Blows; Fried Green Tomatoes; From This Day Forward; Gable and Lombard; Gin Game; Golden Braid; Happy Ending; Hiroshima, Mon Amour; Hollywood Boulevard (1936); How Do I Love Thee; How Green Was My Valley; I Don't Care Girl; I Know Why the Caged Bird Sings; I Remember Mama; Ikiru; Images; Intervista; Joshua Then and Now; King of the Hill (1993); Lady L.; Last Year at Marienbad; Let's Get Lost; Lydia; Margie; Matter of Time; Mister Buddwing; Moonrise; Moscow Does Not Believe in Tears; Mother Wore Tights; Muriel; My Father's Glory; My Life as a Dog; My Mother's Castle; Nous La Liberte; Now I'll Tell; Penny Serenade; Radio Days; Red Shoe Diaries; Reunion; Rhapsody in August; Shaking the Tree; Shell Seekers; Slaughterhouse Five; Snows of Kilimanjaro; Stand by Me; Strawberry Blonde; Summer of '42; Swimming to Cambodia; Swing; Tea and Sympathy; That Championship Season; Those Were the Days; To Kill a Mockingbird; Total Recall; Toto le Heros; Trail of the Pink Panther; Travels with My Aunt; 21; Two For the Road; The Valachi Papers; Valentino (1977); Voyager; Waterland; Wild Strawberries

Ménage à Trois (a single romance of three parties): see also *Alternative Lifestyles: Bisexuality: Romance-Triangles: Swapping Partners:* Design for Living; The Fortune; Heart Beat; Heartbreakers; Henry and June; Jules and Jim; Lucky Lady; Mad Monkey; Mediterraneo; Menage; Quartet (1981); The Sheltering Sky; Speaking Parts; Wife,

Doctor and Nurse; Wild Orchid; Willie and Phil; X, Y, & Zee

Men and Babies: see also *Babies-Finding: Babies-Inheriting: Fathers-Surrogate:* The Baby and the Battleship; A Bedtime Story (1933); Father Goose; Father Is a Bachelor; Three Godfathers; Three Men and a Baby; Three Men and a Cradle

Men and Boys: see also *Fathers & Sons: Women and Boys:* Absolution; Against a Crooked Sky; Amazing Grace and Chuck; Angelo, My Love; Angels in the Outfield (1951); Angels in the Outfield (1994); Billy Bathgate; Billy Madison; Boys Town; Broken Noses; A Bronx Tale; Captains Courageous; The Champ (1931); The Champ (1979); The Clown; Convicts; Cop and a Half; The Cowboys; Crossroads (1986); D2: The Mighty Ducks; Death in Venice; Dennis the Menace; The Devil Is a Sissy; The Enchanted Forest; Father Is a Bachelor; Follow Me, Boys!; Forever Young; Great Expectations; The Green Years; Gunga Din; Home Alone; Home Alone 2: Lost in New York; The Hornet's Nest; The Hunted; Kidnapped (1938); Kidnapped (1959); Kidnapped (1971); Kim; Lamb; The Last Starfighter; Like Father, Like Son; Little Big League; Long John Silver; Major Payne; The Man from Snowy River; The Man Without a Face; Martin's Day; Men of Boys' Town; The Mighty Ducks; Mr. Nanny; Once Upon a Time; The Princess Bride; Rocket Gibraltar; Roommates; Scalawag; Scene of the Crime; Scent of a Woman; Search; Shane; Silent Fall; Terminator 2: Judgment Day; Treasure Island (1934); Treasure Island (1971); Treasure Island (1990); Treasure Island (1991); Waterland

Men and Girls: see also *Romance-Older Men/Younger Women:* Alice in the Cities; Baby, Take A Bow; The Bachelor and the Bobby-Soxer; Beau Pere; The Beguiled; Blame it on Rio; Brighty of the Grand Canyon; Cape Fear (1962); Cape Fear (1991); Casey's Shadow; Cattle Annie & Little Britches; A Certain Smile; Circle of Two; Forty Pounds of Trouble; Gigot; Heidi (1939); Honeymoon; Life With Mikey; Little Miss Marker (1934); Little Miss Marker (1980); Lost Angel; Lover; Mad About Music; Monsieur Hire; Never Take Sweets from a Stranger; One Good Cop; P.K and the Kid; Paper Moon; Pennies

from Heaven (1936); Pretty Baby; The Professional; Sudie and Simpson; Sundays and Cybele; That Certain Age; Three Men and a Little Lady; Town Without Pity; Trouble Along the Way

Men as Women: see also *Transvestites: Transsexuals: Role Reversal: Women as Men:* Ace Ventura; Pet Detective; Charley's Aunt; Cinderfella; The Crying Game; Dog Day Afternoon; Dr. Jekyll and Sister Hyde; Ed Wood; Female Trouble; Glen or Glenda?; Goodbye, Charlie; Hairspray; I Want What I Want; I Was a Male War Bride; It's Pat; Junior; Just One of the Girls; Lady Bugs; Lust in the Dust; M. Butterfly; The Mouse That Roared; Mr. Mom; Myra Breckinridge; Nuns on the Run; Polyester; Rabbit Test; Rebecca's Daughters; Some Like it Hot; Switch; Thunderbolt and Lightfoot; Tootsie; To Wong Foo, Thanks for Everything, Julie Newmar

Men-Elderly: see *Elderly Men*

Men Fighting Over Women: see also *Women Fighting Over Men:* The Adventures of Sadie; Alexander's Ragtime Band; Backbeat; Boiling Point; Captain Horatio Hornblower; Clash by Night; Dead Ringers; Deception (1946); Design for Living; The Devil Is a Woman; Doctor, You've Got to be Kidding; Duel in the Sun; Ebony Tower; Fabulous Baker Boys; The First Time; Flesh and the Devil; For Love or Money (1993); Four Friends; Giant; The Girl Most Likely (1958); Good Fairy; The Great Race; Green Fire; Grumpy Old Men; High Society; Jules and Jim; Kings Go Forth; Lady in the Dark; Legends of the Fall; Love Before Breakfast; Lovin' Molly; Lusty Men; Manpower; Men with Wings; Mystery of Edwin Drood; North to Alaska; Oklahoma!; The Outlaw; Paint Your Wagon; The Princess Bride; Reap the Wild Wind; Rebel Rousers; Rhapsody; Riff-Raff (1935); Sabrina; Sadie McKee; Sayonara; Semi-Tough; Seventh Veil; She's Gotta Have It; Showdown; Something Wild (1986); Somewhere I'll Find You; Son of Paleface; Spetters; Stakeout; Star Spangled Girl; Tall Men; Terminal Bliss; This Could Be the Night; Three Comrades; Thunderbirds; Tin Men; Tom, Dick and Harry; Tomorrow Is Forever; Too Many Husbands; Top Gun; Trapeze; Un Coeur en Hiver; Watch It; Wilder Napalm

Men in Conflict: see also WESTERNS: Power Struggles: Abilene Town; Act of Violence; All the Brothers Were Valiant; All the Way Up; Amadeus; Angry Silence; Apocalypse Now; Ben-Hur (1959); Bend of the River; Billy Galvin; Billy the Kid; Black Room; Bloodfist; Bloodfist II; Bloodfist III; Botany Bay; Cadence; Dangerous Moves; Dark Command; Death of a Gunfighter; The Defiant Ones; Demolition Man; The Driver; Duellists; Ebony Tower; Eureka; Extreme Prejudice; Fifth Musketeer; Firecreek; Flying Leathernecks; Flying Tigers; Four for Texas; Fourth War; Ghosts . . . of the Civil Dead; God Is My Co-Pilot; The Godfather; The Godfather, Part II; The Godfather, Part III; Great Day in the Morning; A Gunfight at the O.K. Corral; The Hard Way (1991); Harlem Nights; Hawaiians; High Noon; Highlander; Highlander II-The Quickening; Highlander III, The Sorcerer; Hot Lead and Cold Feet; The Hustler; If I Were King; Inherit the Wind; Into the Sun; Jacknife; Jean de Florette; Joe Kidd; Juarez; Julius Caesar; The Last Hunt; The Last Valley; Lock Up; The Long, Good Friday; Lord of the Flies (1963); Lord of the Flies (1990); The Lords of Discipline; Love and Hisses; Love Me Tender; Love Thy Neighbor; Man from Laramie; The Man Who Would Be King; Mutiny on the Bounty (1935); Mutiny on the Bounty (1962); Man Without a Star; Manpower; Merry Christmas, Mr. Lawrence; The Missouri Breaks; Mobsters; Montana; Monte Walsh; Mother Lode; Mountain; Muscle Beach Party; My Darling Clementine; My Name is Nobody; Night of the Shooting Stars; No Escape (1994); No Man's Land (1987); No Surrender; The Old Curiosity Shop; On the Waterfront; Outland; Pat Garrett and Billy the Kid; Paths of Glory; Patterns; People Will Talk; Posse (1993); The Princess Bride; Querelle; Ran; The Raven (1963); Ricochet; Road House; Robin Hood (1922); Robin Hood (1973); Robin Hood (1990); Robin Hood: Prince of Thieves (1991); Run Silent Run Deep; San Antonio; Sands of the Kalahari; Santa Fe; Saturn 3; Scalphunters; Seven Samurai; Showdown; Skullduggery; Sleuth; A Slight Case of Murder; Somewhere I'll Find You; The Sons of Katie Elder; The Sorcerer; Southern Comfort; Spawn of the North; Speed; Spoilers; Staircase; Stone Cold; Stooge; Tall Men; Texas; Time of Destiny; Tombstone; Treasure of the Sierra Madre; True Confessions; 21 Days; Ulzana's Raid; Undefeated; The Unforgiven (1960); Up the Creek (1958); Used Cars; Valdez is Coming; Vikings; Wagonmaster; Wake of the Red Witch; War Party; Warlock (1958); Welcome to Hard Times; While the City Sleeps; Wichita; The Wild Bunch; Will Penny; Winchester 73; Withnail and I; Women in Love; The Wrong Box; Yojimbo; Young Doctors

Men in Jeopardy: see also Women in Jeopardy: Children in Jeopardy: THRILLERS: Film Noir: HORROR: Black Widow (1987); Cruising; Disclosure; Dracula (1931); Dracula (1979); Dracula Has Risen from the Grave; Dracula (Horror of Dracula, 1958); Dracula, Prince of Darkness; Dracula's Daughter; Extremities; Fade to Black (1993); Fatal Attraction; From Russia with Love; Game of Death; Illegal; Jaws; The Killer Nun; Kiss Me Deadly; The Lady in Question; Mean Season; Night Stalker/The Night Strangler; Omen; Play Misty for Me; The Prize; Rafferty and the Gold Dust Twins; Red Rock West; Second Chance; Short Eyes; The Still of the Night; Sudden Impact; The Towering Inferno; Twenty-Three Paces to Baker Street

Men Proving Themselves: see also Coming of Age: Life Transitions: Teenage Movies: Women Proving Themselves: Underdog Stories: The Best of Times; Billy Madison; Captains of the Clouds; Car 99; Carnal Knowledge; Cityslickers; Days of Thunder; Destry Rides Again; Dodge City; Don't Just Stand There; Downhill Racer; Fear Strikes Out; The Fighting Kentuckian; For Love or Money (1993); Four Feathers (1929); Four Feathers (1939); Four Horsemen of the Apocalypse; The Graduate; The Great Santini; Gross Anatomy; Heaven Can Wait (1943); High Noon; In the Line of Fire; The January Man; Kid Brother; The Kissing Bandit; Lusty Men; An Officer and a Gentleman; On the Waterfront; Over the Top; Rebel Without a Cause; The Red Badge of Courage; Rocky; Rocky II; Rocky III; Siegfried; Something Wild (1986); The Tall Target; This Above All; To Have and Have Not; Tommy Boy; Top Gun; Topaze (1933); Tuff Turf; White Mile; Will Penny

Men Settling Down: see Settling Down: Bachelors-Confirmed: Playboys: Marriage-Impending: Engagements-Breaking: Coming of Age: Life Transitions

Men-Sexy: see Sexy Men: Playboys: Gigolos: Beautiful People: Models

Men's Films: see also Ensembles-Male: ACTION: Women's Films: Closer; The Good Father; Heartbreakers; Husbands; Patterns; Patti Rocks; That Championship Season; Thursday's Game; Voyager; Watch It

Men Together: see Ensemble Films: Ensembles-Men: Buddy Films: Friendships-Male: Gay Men

Men-Young: see Young Men: College Life: Fraternity Life

Mental Illness/Insanity: see also Asylums: Depression: Mentally Disabled People: Nervous Breakdowns: Psycho Killers: Aguirre, the Wrath of God; Alone in the Dark; An Angel at My Table; Angel Face; Asylum; Autobus; Autumn Leaves; Awakenings; Bartleby; Beautiful Dreamers; Bedlam; The Bell Jar; Betty Blue; Beware, My Lovely; A Bill of Divorcement (1932); A Bill of Divorcement (1940); Birdy; Blowing Wild; Blue Sky; Blue Thunder; The Body Snatchers; Boston Strangler; Brainstorm (1965); Brewster McCloud; Bunny Lake is Missing; Burmese Harp; The Cabinet of Caligari (1962); The Cabinet of Dr. Caligari (1919); Caine Mutiny (1954); Caine Mutiny Court Martial (1988); The Caretakers; Cast a Dark Shadow; Catch Me a Spy; Catherine the Great; Chattahoochee; Chinatown; Choose Me; The Collector; Comfort of Strangers; The Couch Trip; Crazy People; Dark Mirror; David and Lisa; Dead of Night (1945); Despair; Dialogues with Madwomen; Diary of a Madman; Disorderly Orderly; Disturbed; Doctor Mabuse, the Gambler; Dominique; Don Juan DeMarco; Don't Bother to Knock; Dream Team; Dunwich Horror; Effect of Gamma Rays on Man-in-the-Moon Marigolds; End of the Road; Endless Love; Equus; Eraserhead; Exorcist III; Fear in the Night; A Fine Madness; The Fisher King; Fitzcarraldo; Flesh and Blood (1951); Flesh of the Orchid; Flowers in the Attic; Frances; Gaslight (1939); Gaslight (1944); Girl in the Red Velvet Swing; Good Fellas; Great Lie; Hamlet (1948); Hamlet (1964); Hamlet (1969); Hamlet (1991);

Hammersmith is Out; Harvey; Helter Skelter (1976); Henry: Portrait of a Serial Killer; House of Cards; House of Dracula; House of Wax; I Never Promised You A Rose Garden; Images; Impulse (1984); Interiors; Interlude (1957); Interlude (1968); Invasion of the Body Snatchers (1956); Invasion of the Body Snatchers (1978); Jacknife; The King of Comedy; King of Hearts; Kings Row; Ladies in Retirement; Lady in the Car with Glasses and a Gun; Let's Scare Jessica to Death; Lilith; Lizzie; Look in Any Window; Love at First Bite; Love Streams; Ludwig; Lunatics, A Love Story; M (1931); M (1951); Man Upstairs; Man with Nine Lives; Marat/Sade; Martin; Men Are Not Gods; Mine Own Executioner; Ministry of Fear; Misery; Miss Firecracker; Mommie Dearest; Montenegro; Morgan!; Mr. Jones; Music Lovers; Network; Night of the Generals; The Night Porter; Night unto Night; Nuts; One Flew Over Cuckoo's Nest; Orpheus Descending; Persona; Plenty; The Positively True Adventures of the Alleged Texas Cheerleader-Murdering Mom; The Possessed (1947); The Prince of Tides; Psycho 2; Psycho 3; Psycho 4; The Puppetmasters; Raging Moon; Reflections in a Golden Eye; Return of the Pink Panther; The Roman Spring of Mrs. Stone; Rope; Ruling Class; Saint of Fort Washington; Shining; Shock Corridor; Short Eyes; Situation Hopeless But Not Serious; Small Sacrifices; Snakepit; Sniper; Sophie's Choice; Sound and the Fury; Splendor in the Grass; Star 80; Step Down to Terror; Strait Jacket; Strange Brew; Strangers on a Train; A Streetcar Named Desire; Suddenly, Last Summer; Sunset Boulevard; Taxi Driver; Tenant; Tender is the Night; They Shoot Horses, Don't They?; The Three Faces of Eve; Ticket to Heaven; Tie Me Up! Tie Me Down!; Tin Drum; Tommy; Trust; Turkish Delight; Twilight's Last Gleaming; The Vampire's Kiss; Van Gogh; What About Bob?; What's the Matter with Helen?; Whatever Happened to Baby Jane?; When Tomorrow Comes; Whisperers; Who is Harry Kellerman . . . ; Who Slew Auntie Roo?; Who's Afraid of Virginia Woolf?; Woman on the Beach

Mentally Disabled People (retarded): see also *Mental Illness: Eccentric People: Misfits:* All That Heaven Allows; Baxter (1972); Best Boy; Bill; Bill: On

His Own; Charly; A Child is Waiting; A Dangerous Woman; David and Lisa; A Day in the Death of Joe Egg; Dirty Little Billy; Dominick & Eugene; Family Pictures; House of Cards; Jerk; The Lawnmower Man; Let Him Have It; Light in the Piazza; Mad Room; Malcolm; My Sweet Little Village; Nell; Of Mice and Men (1939); Of Mice and Men (1993); On Dangerous Ground; Rain Man; Rain People; Random Harvest; Regarding Henry; Rocky V; Silent Fall; Square Dance; Stanley & Iris; Sundays and Cybele; Tim; Twisted Nerve; What's Eating Gilbert Grape?

Mentors & Role Models: see also *Teachers: Teachers & Students: Children-Gifted: Men and Boys: Women and Girls:* The Blue Lamp; Calling Dr. Kildare; Clara's Heart; The Color of Money; Colors; Delicate Delinquent; Educating Rita; The Godfather, Part III; My Name is Nobody; Rookie; Tin Star; Twentieth Century

Mercenaries: see also *Terrorist: Soldiers: Arms Dealers: Political Unrest: Snipers:* Apartment Zero; A Bullet for the General; China; Dark of the Sun; Dogs of War; Fifty/Fifty; First Blood; For Whom the Bell Tolls; The General Died at Dawn; Gunga Din; Guns of the Magnificent Seven; The Magnificent Seven; Nous Sommes Tous les Assassins; Predator; Professionals; Sea Wolves; Seven Samurai; Wild Geese; Wild Geese II

Mermaids: see also *Fish out of Water Stories:* The Glass Bottom Boat; The Little Mermaid; Miranda; Mr. Peabody and the Mermaid; Splash!

Message Films: see also *Social Drama: Social Satire: Political Films: Ethics:* Accent on Love; Act of Murder; Amazing Grace and Chuck; Babbitt; Bad Girl; Big Trees; Boxing Helena; The Burning Season; The China Syndrome; A Christmas Carol (1938); Day After; The Day the Earth Stood Still; Days of Wine and Roses (1958); Days of Wine and Roses (1962); Do The Right Thing; Elmer Gantry; Enemy of the People (1977); Enemy of the People (1989); Extremities; FernGully: The Last Rainforest; The Fool; The Fountainhead; Front; Gentleman's Agreement; How I Won the War; J'Accuse; Jungle Fever; Lean on Me; Lion is in the Streets; Listen to Me; Living in a Big Way; Lord of the Flies (1963); Lord of the Flies (1990); Lost Weekend; Louisiana

Story; My Son John; Network; Never Take Sweets from a Stranger; Nous Sommes Tous les Assassins; The Pearl; The Phantom Tollbooth; The Plague; Rage; Reefer Madness; School Ties; Silkwood; Soylent Green; Special Bulletin; Split Image; Terminator 2: Judgment Day; Testament; Variety; Wall Street; War Games; Warning Sign

Meteors: see also *Disaster Movies: SCI-FI: Space Travel: UFOs: Apocalyptic Stories:* Day of the Triffids; A Fire in the Sky; Green Slime; Meteor; Night of the Comet; When Worlds Collide

Mexican/Central American Films: see also *Latin People: Brazil: Argentina: South America:* El Norte; I, the Worst of All; Like Water for Chocolate

Mexicans: see *Latin Films: Latin People*

Mexico: see also *Mexicans: Latin Films: Latin People: Central America: South America:* Across the Bridge; Against All Odds; The Assassination of Trotsky; Bad Man's River; Bandolero; Blind Side; Blowing Wild; Borderline; Bordertown; Born in East L.A.; Breakout; A Bullet for the General; The Bullfighter and the Lady; Bullfighters; Cisco Kid; El Mariachi; Exterminating Angel; Falcon and the Snowman; Fiesta; A Fistful of Dollars; A Fistful of Dynamite; The Fugitive (1947); Gaby, a True Story; Green Ice; Guns of the Magnificent Seven; Holiday in Mexico; Honeymoon; I, the Worst of All; Juarez; Kings of the Sun; La Chevre; Last Rites; License to Kill; Like Water for Chocolate; Little Treasure; Lucky Lady; The Magnificent Seven; Mark of Zorro (1920); Mark of Zorro (1940); Marriage on the Rocks; Mexican Hayride; Murderer's Row; Night of the Iguana; Old Gringo; Predator; The Professionals; Pure Luck; Revenge; Rio Grande; Run for the Sun; Second Chance; Sunburn; Three Amigos; Three Caballeros; Touch of Evil; Treasure of the Sierra Madre; Twilight for the Gods; Under the Volcano; Vera Cruz; Viridiana; Viva Villa!; Viva Zapata; Yolanda and the Thief; Zorro and the Gay Blade

Miami: see also *Florida: Florida Keys:* Ace Ventura; Pet Detective; Bad Boys (1994); Moon Over Miami; Scarface (1983); The Specialist; Stick

Middle-Aged Men: see *Young Men: Elderly Men: Mid-Life Crisis: Romance-Middle Aged*

Middle-Aged Romance: see *Romance-Middle Aged*

Middle-Aged Women: see *Young Women: Elderly Women: Mid-Life Crisis: Romance-Middle Aged*

Middle Ages: see also *Medieval Times:* The Advocate; As You Like It (1936); As You Like It (1992); Black Rose; Braveheart; Brother Sun, Sister Moon; Castle Keep; Chastity Belt; Conan, the Barbarian; Conan, the Destroyer; The Devils; Dr. Faustus; 1492: Conquest of Paradise; Henry V (1944); Henry V (1989); The Hunchback of Notre Dame (1923); The Hunchback of Notre Dame (1939); The Hunchback of Notre Dame (1956); The Hunchback of Notre Dame (1982); Jabberwocky; Joan of Arc; Last Valley; Les Visiteurs du Soir; Lion in Winter; Long Ships; Lucretia Borgia; Man of La Mancha; Masque of the Red Death; The Name of the Rose; Othello; Othello (1951); Othello (1965); The Return of Martin Guerre; Richard III; Rosencrantz and Guildenstem Are Dead; Saint Joan; The Seventh Seal; Stealing Heaven; The Taming of the Shrew; The Wandering Jew

Middle Class: see *Suburban Life: Domestic Life: Working Class: Ordinary People Stories*

Middle East: see also *Arab People: Jewish People: Israel: Israeli Films:* Action in Arabia; Aladdin; Alexander the Great; Ambassador; Appointment with Death; Beau Geste (1926); Beau Geste (1939); Beau Geste (1966); Beau Ideal; Best Defense; The Bible; The Big Fisherman; Caesar and Cleopatra; Caravans; Cast a Giant Shadow; Death on the Nile; Delta Force; Embassy; Exodus; Five Fingers; Five Graves to Cairo; Four Feathers (1929); Four Feathers (1939); Garden of Allah; The Greatest Story Ever Told; Harum Scarum; Iron Eagle; Iron Eagle II; Journey into Fear; Justine; King of Kings (1927); King of Kings (1961); Last Outpost; The Last Temptation of Christ; Lawrence of Arabia; Little Drummer Girl; The Man Who Would Be King; Mask of Dimitrios; Masquerade (1965); Midnight Express; Mohammed, Messenger of God; Monty Python's Life of Brian; Navy SEALS; Not Without My Daughter; Protocol; Raiders of the Lost Ark; Rambo III; Robe; Rosebud; Shark!; Silver Chalice; Sodom and Gomorrah; Son of Sinbad; Suez; The Ten Commandments; The Thief of Bagdad

(1924); The Thief of Baghdad (1940); Topkapi!; Wholly Moses

Midlife Crisis: see also *Middle-Aged Men: Middle-Aged Women: Romance-Middle Aged: Life Transitions: Starting Over:* The Accidental Tourist; Alex and the Gypsy; Alice; Alice Doesn't Live Here Anymore; All About Eve; Andy Warhol's Heat; April Fools; Arrangement; Ash Wednesday; Australia; Avanti!; Babbitt; Back to School; Belly of an Architect; Best of Times; Between Friends; The Big Chill; Bliss; Blonde Venus; Blue Chips; The Border; Breaking In; Breezy; Broadcast News; The Browning Version; Bull Durham; Cadillac Man; Call Me Genius; A Change of Seasons; Charlie Bubbles; Checking Out; Clean and Sober; Closer; Come Back, Little Sheba; The Conversation; Days of Wine and Roses (1958); Days of Wine and Roses (1962); Death of a Salesman (1950); Death of a Salesman (1985); Decline of the American Empire; Deep Blue Sea; A Delicate Balance; The Doctor; Face to Face; Fathers and Sons; Fried Green Tomatoes; Funny About Love; Ghostwriter; The Great Santini; Heartbreakers; High Season; High Tide; Holiday for Sinners; Honkytonk Man; The Hospital; Husbands; Husbands and Wives; I'm Dancing as Fast as I Can; Joshua Then and Now; Juliet of the Spirits; Keep the Change; L'Invitation; La Cage Aux Folles 2; Last of the Red Hot Lovers; Last Tango in Paris; Le Cavaleur; Leaving Normal; Let it Ride; Life is Sweet; Lifeguard; Limelight; The Lost Language of Cranes; Loving; Madame Bovary; Male Animal; Man in Love; A Man of No Importance; Man on Fire; The Men's Club; Middle Age Crazy; Montenegro; Mr. Destiny; Mr. Peabody and the Mermaid; New Life; Nurse; Once in Paris; One Trick Pony; Pardon Mon Affaire; Penny Serenade; The Perfect Couple; Petulia; Plaza Suite; Plenty; Postcards from the Edge; The Prince of Tides; The Prisoner of Second Avenue; Quiz Show; Rachel, Rachel; The Romantic Englishwoman; Rosie; Saint Jack; Save the Tiger; Scenes from a Mall; Scent of a Woman; Secret Friends; The Seduction of Joe Tynan; See How She Runs; Seize the Day; Sergeant; The Seven-Year Itch; She's Working Her Way Through College; Shirley Valentine; A Simple Story; Skin Deep; Skylark; The

Slender Thread; So Big (1932); So Big (1953); Soft Skin; Star; Starting Over; The Stripper; Summer Wishes, Winter Dreams; Sweet Bird of Youth; Swimmer; Ten; That's Life!; 30 is a Dangerous Age, Cynthia; This Happy Feeling; Twice in a Lifetime; Two For the Road; Under the Volcano; An Unmarried Woman; Who's Afraid of Virginia Woolf?; Whose Life Is It Anyway?; Wild Strawberries; Woman in Red; The Woman Next Door; The World is Full of Married Men

Midwestern Life: see also *Farm Life: Rural Life:* Abe Lincoln in Illinois; Ace Eli and Rodger of the Skies; Adam at 6 A.M.; All Fall Down; Babbitt; Badlands; Betrayed (1989); Breaking Away; Career Opportunities; Carnival of Souls; Carrie (1952); Cold Turkey; Come and Get It; Come Back, Little Sheba; Dark at the Top of the Stairs; Dark Command; Elmer Gantry; Farmer's Daughter; Field of Dreams; Four Friends; Friendly Fire; The Grapes of Wrath; Grumpy Old Men; Gypsy Moths; Hoosiers; In Cold Blood; Isn't it Romantic?; Kansas; Kings Row; Leap of Faith; The Magnificent Ambersons; Miles From Home; Mr. and Mrs. Bridge; The Music Man; Night of the Hunter; O Pioneers!; One Foot in Heaven; Other; Our Vines Have Tender Grapes; Paper Moon; Patti Rocks; Picnic; Rainmaker; Rumble Fish; Sarah, Plain and Tall; Seventeen; Silkwood; Some Came Running; Splendor in the Grass; The Stripper; Terms of Endearment; What's Eating Gilbert Grape?

Military Comedy: see also *Military Films: Spoofs: War Stories: Soldiers:* Abbott & Costello in the Foreign Legion; Babette Goes to War; Best Defense; Best Foot Forward; Biloxi Blues; Brother Rat; Buck Privates; Call Me Mister; Canadian Bacon; Captain Newman, M.D.; Caught in the Draft; Deal of the Century; Ensign Pulver; Good Morning, Vietnam; Goodbye, New York; Greetings; Hell, Heaven, and Hoboken; Here Comes the Navy; Honeymoon Machine; Hot Shots!; Hot Shots, Part Deux; In the Army Now; Lieutenant Wore Skirts; Major Payne; M*A*S*H; Me and the Colonel; Mister Roberts; 1941; No Time for Sergeants; Oh, What a Lovely War; On the Double; Operation Petticoat; Panama Hattie; Private Benjamin; Rally Round the Flag, Boys; Renaissance Man; Sad Sack; Sailor Beware; Secret War of Harry Frigg;

Stripes; Suppose They Gave a War and Nobody Came; Thank Your Lucky Stars; Tribes; Up in Arms; Up the Creek (1958); Virgin Soldiers; W.H.I.F.F.S.; Wackiest Ship in the Army; You're in the Army Now; You're in the Navy Now

Military Leaders: see also *Military Stories:* Captain Horatio Hornblower; Cleopatra (1934); Cleopatra (1963); Colonel Red!; Desert Fox; Desert Rats; Desiree; Distant Drums; Dr. Strangelove; Fat Man and Little Boy; Fourth War; Gardens of Stone; A Gathering of Eagles; A Handmaid's Tale; Khartoum; The Last Command; Patton; Mac Arthur; Twilight's Last Gleaming

Military Schools: see also *Military Stories: Boarding Schools: Soldiers:* Brother Rat; City and the Dogs; Long Gray Line; The Lords of Discipline; Strange One; Taps; Toy Soldiers; West Point Story

Military Stories (on the base or dealing with military personnel, usually not in battle): see also *War Stories: Courtroom Drama: Court Martials:* Bedford Incident; Biloxi Blues; Blue Sky; The Body Snatchers; Boys in Company C; Breaker Morant; Breaking the Sound Barrier; Bridges at Toko-Ri; Cadence; The Caine Mutiny (1954); The Caine Mutiny Court Martial (1988); Carmen Jones; Cast a Giant Shadow; Catch Me a Spy; Court Martial of Jackie Robinson; Das Boot; Don't Go Near the Water; Dr. Strangelove; Exodus; Fat Man and Little Boy; A Few Good Men; Final Countdown; Forbin Project; From Here to Eternity; Gardens of Stone; A Gathering of Eagles; Good Guys Wear Black; Gray Lady Down; Great Manhunt; Hasty Heart; Heartbreak Ridge; Hell and High Water; Here Comes the Navy; Hill; Homecoming (1948); The Hunt for Red October; Iron Eagle; Iron Eagle II; Jet Pilot; The Last Detail; Lieutenant Wore Skirts; The Life and Death of Colonel Blimp; The Lords of Discipline; Man in the Middle; M*A*S*H; Mister Roberts; Navy SEALS; Never So Few; Next of Kin (1942); Night People; The Ninth Configuration; No Time for Sergeants; No Way Out (1987); An Officer and a Gentleman; On the Beach; Package; Patton; Platoon; Rack; The Red Sky at Morning; Reflections in a Golden Eye; Sayonara; Sea Devils (1937); The Secret War of Harry Frigg; Seven Days in May; She Wore a Yellow Ribbon;

A Soldier's Story; Strange One; Stripes; Taps; Teahouse of the August Moon; Top Gun; Top Secret Affair; Toy Soldiers; Tribes; Tunes of Glory; Twilight's Last Gleaming; Virgin Soldiers

Mindgames: see also *Liars: Con Artists: Clever Plots & Endings: Perfect Crimes: Practical Jokers: Power Struggles: Framed?: Evil Women: Evil Men:* The Adventures of Sherlock Holmes; All the Way Up; Arabesque; Arrivederci, Baby!; The Bad and the Beautiful; Bad Influence; Bathing Beauty; Battle of the Sexes; Bears & I; Bedroom Window; Bitter Rice; Black Widow (1987); Body Heat; Brimstone and Treacle; Charade; Dangerous Liaisons; Dangerous Moves; Dark Mirror; Dead of Winter; Dead Ringers; Deathtrap; Defense of the Realm; Diabolique (1955); Divorce of Lady X; Double Indemnity; The Driver; End of the Game; Entertaining Mr. Sloane; The Experts; Fear; Femme Fatale; Final Analysis; Hobson's Choice; House of Games; The House of Seven Gables; If I Were King; In the Line of Fire; Kafka; Knight Moves; Kremlin Letter; Labyrinth; Last of Sheila; Last Rites; Last Sunset; Lord Love a Duck; Lucretia Borgia; Marat/Sade; Midnight (1939); Midnight Lace; Mistress; Mr. Arkadin; Nevada Smith; 9 1/2 Weeks; Obsession; Pascali's Island; Patterns; Prize; Prizzi's Honor; Querelle; Quintet; Rebecca; Reversal of Fortune; Running Man (1987); The Russia House; Secret Ceremony; Servant; The Seventh Seal; Sex, Lies, and Videotape; The Shooting; Silence of the Lambs; Silent Partner; Sleuth; Spy in Black; The Spy Who Came in from the Cold; The Sting; The Sting 2; Stolen Life (1939); Stolen Life (1946); The Stuntman; Suicide Club; A Taxing Woman; Three Days of the Condor; Valmont

Mindreading: see *Psychics: Supernatural: Future-Seeing the: Fortunetellers*

Mining Towns/Miners: see also *Factory Workers: Working Class:* All the Right Moves; Big Man; Black Fury; Citadel; The Corn is Green (1945); The Corn is Green (1979); The Deer Hunter; Foxfire (1955); Green Fire; The Hanging Tree; How Green Was My Valley; Iron Maze; Lady Chatterley's Lover (1955); Lady Chatterley's Lover (1981); Matewan; McCabe and Mrs. Miller; The Molly Maguires; Mother Lode; Outland;

Reckless (1983); School Ties; Silver Lode; Sons and Lovers; This Sporting Life; Where the Green Ants Dream

Miniseries (multi-part TV movies): see also *TV Movies: Anthologies: TV Series: Multiple Stories:* Anastasia (1984); Berlin Alexanderplatz; Body Bags; Bourne Identity; Brideshead Revisited; Chiefs; Deliberate Stranger; East of Eden (1980); Family Pictures; Guyana Tragedy, The Story of Jim Jones; Heimat; Jewel in the Crown; King; The Kingdom; Laurel Avenue; LBJ: The Early Years; Little Gloria, Happy At Last; Lonesome Dove; Mother Love; Murder in Texas; Power, Passion, and Murder; Prime Suspect; Red Shoe Diaries; Roots; Roots: The Next Generations; Salem's Lot; Separate but Equal; Sinatra; Sybil; Tommyknockers; Town Like Alice (1985); Wild Palms

Miracles: see also *Illusions: Dreams: Nuns: Priests: Religion: Cures/Solutions-Search for: Disease Stories: Happy Endings:* Heavenly Pursuits; Leap of Faith; The Man Who Could Work Miracles; Masala; Miracle (1948); Miracle of the Bells; Resurrection; Song of Bernadette; Waiting For the Light

Mirages: see *Illusions: Desert Life: Middle East*

Mischief: see *Practical Jokers: Wild People: Free Spirits: Juvenile Delinquents*

Misfits: see *Foreign Misfits: Fish out of Water Stories: Ostracism: Eccentric People: Nerds: Wallflowers*

Mismatched Love: see *Romance-Opposites Attract*

Mismatched Teams: see *Teams-Mismatched:*

Misrepresentations: see *Con Artists: Liars: Impostors: Identities-Assumed: Marriage-Fake*

Missing Children: see also *Missing Persons: Children-Parting With/Losing:* Adam; Bunny Lake is Missing; A Cry in the Dark; Deadly Trap; Dog of Flanders; Emerald Forest; Flight of the Navigator; A Little Romance; Lost; Peeper; The Search; Where Are the Children?; Without a Trace; Yellow Canary

Missing in Action: see *POWs/MIAs: War Stories*

Missing Persons: see also *Searches: Bounty Hunters: Detective Stories:* Adam; Against a Crooked Sky; Agatha; Allan Quatermain and the Lost City of Gold; Alphaville; Ambulance; Anastasia

(1956); The Baby and the Battleship; The Big Sleep (1946); The Big Sleep (1977); Blue Ice; Boy, Did I Get a Wrong Number!; Bunny Lake is Missing; Bureau of Missing Persons; Cage of Gold; Caravans; Chan is Missing; A Cry in the Dark; Dangerous Crossing; Dead Reckoning; Deception (1992); The Deer Hunter; The Disappearance of Aimee; Dying Room Only; Eagle's Wing; Emerald Forest; The Enchanted Forest; Farewell, My Lovely (1944); Farewell, My Lovely (1975); A Fire in the Sky; Fog over Frisco; The Forbidden; Forbidden Planet; Fourth Story; Frantic (1988); The French Lieutenant's Woman; Hallelujah, I'm a Bum; Happy Birthday, Wanda June; Hardcore; Hide in Plain Sight; Hot Pursuit; How to Murder Your Wife; Impulse (1990); Into Thin Air; Island (1980); Island at the Top of the World; Killjoy; L'Avventura; La Chevre; Lady in the Lake; The Lady Vanishes (1938); The Lady Vanishes (1979); Last Outpost; Les Comperes; Letters from a Dead Man; Life and Nothing But; A Little Romance; Little Treasure; Long Live Life; Lost; Madame X (1929); Madame X (1937); Madame X (1965); Marlowe; Missing; Missing in Action; Missing in Action 2-The Beginning; Monolith; Move Over, Darling; Mr. Arkadin; Murderer's Row; My Favorite Wife; Nancy Steele is Missing; The Night Has Eyes; Night Moves; The Official Story; Olivier, Olivier; One More River; Peeper; Picnic at Hanging Rock; Pure Luck; Roanoak; Rome Express; The Search; The Searchers; The Sentinel; The Seventh Victim; So Long at the Fair; Soldier of Fortune; Stanley & Livingstone; Star of Midnight; Star Trek III: The Search for Spock; State of Siege; Taking Off; The Third Man; Thoroughly Modern Millie; Tommyknockers; Trail of the Pink Panther; Uncommon Valor; Undercurrent; The Vanishing (1988); The Vanishing (1993); Welcome Home; Where Are the Children?; Without a Trace

Missing Person Thriller: see also *Missing Persons: Missing Children: Searches:* Dangerous Crossing; The Deadly Trap; Dying Room Only; Frantic (1988); L'Avventura; The Lady Vanishes (1938); The Lady Vanishes (1979); Missing; The Night Has Eyes; So Long at the Fair; The Vanishing (1988); The Vanishing (1993)

Missionaries: see also *Religion: Priests: Catholicism: Explorers:* African Queen; At Play in the Fields of the Lord; Battle Hymn; Crimes of Passion; The Devil at Four O'Clock; Inn of the Sixth Happiness; Keys of the Kingdom; The Mission; The Missionary; Monsieur Vincent; Mrs. Soffel; Nate and Hayes; The Nun's Story; The Right to Love; Rooster Cogburn; Seven Women; The Sins of Rachel Cade

Mississippi: see also *Southerns: Plantation Life:* Baby Doll; Banjo on My Knee; Crimes of the Heart; The Defiant Ones; The Fugitive Kind; The Heart is a Lonely Hunter; Hot Spell; Hurry Sundown; In the Heat of the Night; Mississippi; Mississippi Burning; Mississippi Masala; Reivers; The Rose Tattoo; Sanctuary; The Sound and the Fury; Summer and Smoke; The War

Mistaken Identity: see *Identities-Mistaken:* also *Body Switching: Screwball Comedy: FARCE: Comedy of Errors: Lookalikes: Twins*

Mistresses: see also *Romance: Cheating Men: Romance with Married People: Mob Girls:* Abel; Accused of Murder; Animal Kingdom; Any Wednesday; The Apartment; Back Street (1932); Back Street (1941); Back Street (1961); Bedroom Window; Being There; Blue Ice; Born Yesterday (1950); Born Yesterday (1993); Breakfast at Tiffany's; Come September; Crimes and Misdemeanors; Dark at the Top of the Stairs; East Side, West Wide; The Finger of Guilt; Folies Bergere; For Love or Money (1993); Guilty Conscience; How to Save a Marriage and Ruin Your Life; In Name Only; Intersection; Investigation of a Citizen Above Suspicion; It Always Rains on Sunday; Just Tell Me What You Want; The King's Whore; Lady in Red; A Life of Her Own; Love Matters; Loving; Micki and Maude; Mistress; Penthouse; Romance; Ruthless People; The Seduction of Joe Tynan; Shampoo; Summertime; A Touch of Class

Misunderstandings: see also *FARCE: Identities-Mistaken: Pretending: Screwball Comedy: Mix-Ups:* Ali Baba Goes to Town; All in a Night's Work; Bananas; The Bawdy Adventures of Tom Jones; Beyond Therapy; Big Business; Bittersweet Love; Blame it on the Bellboy; Bobo; Boeing-Boeing; Born in East L.A.; Boy, Did I Get a Wrong

Number!; Boys from Syracuse; Boys' Night Out; Bread and Chocolate; A A Bridge Too Far; Bringing Up Baby; Brittania Hospital; Buck Privates; Bullfighters; Bundle of Joy; Burmese Harp; Cairo (1942); California Suite; Canadian Bacon; Carefree; Children of a Lesser God; Copacabana; Darling Lili; A Date with Judy; Dear Ruth; The Doctor Takes a Wife; Dr. Strangelove; Duck Soup; Easy Living (1937); El Mariachi; The Experts; Fail Safe; Fancy Pants; Fawlty Towers; The Fifth Musketeer; A Fish Called Wanda; A Flea in Her Ear; The Fuller Brush Girl; The Fuller Brush Man; A Funny Thing Happened on the Way to the Forum; The Gay Divorcee; Glass Bottom Boat; Green Dolphin Street; Guest Wife; Happiest Days of Your Life; Hell, Heaven, and Hoboken; I Love You Again; I Sent a Letter to My Love; I'd Rather Be Rich; If a Man Answers; International House; Invitation to the Wedding; Kiss and Tell; The Kremlin Letter; Lady in the Iron Mask; Last of Sheila; The Last Remake of Beau Geste; Living it Up; Lock up Your Daughters; Love at Large; Love God?; Love Lottery; Lover Come Back (1946); Loverboy; Man from the Diners' Club; Miracle of Morgan's Creek; My Father the Hero; No Sex, Please, We're British; Nobody's Perfect; Not with My Wife You Don't; On the Air; Once Upon a Crime; Pain in the A . . . ; Passport to Pimlico; Real Men; Return of the Pink Panther; Rock a Bye Baby; Romance on the High Seas; School for Husbands; The Seduction of Mimi; Send Me No Flowers; September Affair; Some Like it Hot; Start the Revolution Without Me; Sundays and Cybele; That Obscure Object of Desire; They Knew What They Wanted; Throw Momma from the Train; Tom, Dick and Harry; Tom Jones; Too Many Husbands; Tootsie; Tune in Tomorrow; Tunnel of Love; Victor/Victoria; We're Not Married; What's Up, Doc?; Where Were You When the Lights Went Out?; Who Was That Lady?; Wholly Moses; Wife Versus Secretary

Mix-Ups: see also *Identities-Mistaken: Screwball Comedy: Misunderstandings:* Blame it on the Bellboy; The Boys from Syracuse; Bringing Up Baby; Brittania Hospital; Copacabana; Dead in the Water; Fawlty Towers; The Fifth Musketeer; A Flea in Her Ear; Goodbye,

New York; Green Dolphin Street; The Happiest Days of Your Life; How to Steal a Million; Innerspace; Invitation to the Wedding; It's in the Bag; Lady in the Iron Mask; Love Potion #9; Man from the Diners' Club; Mr. and Mrs. Smith; No Sex, Please, We're British; Private Benjamin; Pudd'nhead Wilson; School for Scandal; Secret Admirer; Send Me No Flowers; Start the Revolution Without Me; They Knew What They Wanted; Three Fugitives; Tom Jones

Mob-Asian: see also *Mob Stories: Japanese People: Asia: Martial Arts:* Armed Response; Black Rain (1989); The Hatchet Man; The Killing of a Chinese Bookie; Rising Sun; Yakuza; Year of the Dragon

Mob Comedy: see also *Mob Stories: Capers: Heist Movies:* Ball of Fire; Blame it on the Bellboy; Blank Check; Broadway Danny Rose; Bullets Over Broadway; Chu Chu and the Philly Flash; Cookie; Cool World; Doctor Detroit; Dumb and Dumber; A Fine Mess; Fitzwilly; For Pete's Sake; Freebie and the Bean; The Freshman (1990); Gabriel over the White House; The Gang That Couldn't Shoot Straight; The Girl Can't Help It; Go Chase Yourself; Goodbye, Charlie; Gun in Betty Lou's Handbag; Guys and Dolls; The Happening; Harlem Nights; The In-Laws; Island of Love; Johnny Dangerously; Johnny Stecchino; The Kid from Brooklyn; Lady for a Day; The Lemon Drop Kid; Little Giant (1933); Mad Dog and Glory; The Man from the Diners' Club; Married to the Mob; Marrying Man; Mask (1994); Midnight Run; Mikey and Nicky; Milky Way (1936); Money from Home; My Blue Heaven (1990); My Favorite Brunette; Never a Dull Moment (1967); Now You See Him, Now You Don't; Oscar; Pal Joey; Pocketful of Miracles; The Pope Must Die(t); Prizzi's Honor; A Rage in Harlem; The Ritz; Robin and the Seven Hoods; The Seduction of Mimi; Sitting Ducks; So Fine; Some Like it Hot; A Song is Born; Sorrowful Jones; Squeeze; Sticky Fingers; Tall, Dark & Handsome; Things Change; This Could Be the Night; True Identity; Victor/Victoria; Weekend at Bernie's; Weekend at Bernie's 2; Wise Guys; Wonder Man; Yellow Rolls Royce

Mob-Fugitives from the: see *Fugitives from the Mob*

Mob Girls: see also *Mob Stories: Bimbos:* Ball of Fire; Big Combo; Bitch (1979); Broadway Danny Rose; City Streets; Cookie; Cool World; The Cotton Club; Forbidden; Gilda; The Girl Can't Help It; Gloria; The Grifters; Island of Love; Johnny Dangerously; Lights of New York; Love and Bullets; Love Me or Leave Me; Mad Dog and Glory; Marked Woman; Married to the Mob; The Marrying Man; Mary Burns, Fugitive; Mask (1994); No Mercy; Public Enemy; Roxie Hart; Second Chance; A Song Is Born; That Certain Woman; They Drive by Night (1940); Twenty Thousand Years in Sing Sing; Whipsaw

Mob Stories: see also *Mob Comedy: Fugitives from the Mob: Gangs: Hitmen: Hitwomen: Mob Girls: Prohibition Era: Japanese Mob:* About Face; Above the Law; Across 110th Street; Affair in Trinidad; Al Capone; All Dogs Go to Heaven; All Through the Night; The Amazing Dr. Clitterhouse; American Dream; The American Friend; Angel on My Shoulder; Angels With Dirty Faces; Another Stakeout; Armed Response; The Asphalt Jungle; Beast of the City; Big Brawl; The Big Combo; Biggest Bundle of Them All; Billy Bathgate; Bitch (1979); Black Caesar; The Black Hand; Black Orchid; Black Rain (1989); Blank Check; Bloodhounds of Broadway (1952); Bloodhounds of Broadway (1989); Boiling Point; Bowery; Brighton Rock; A Bronx Tale; Brotherhood; Bugsy; Bugsy Malone; Bullets or Ballots; Capone; Carlito's Way; Casino; The Champion; China Girl (1987); Choice of Arms; Chu Chu and the Philly Flash; City of Joy; City Streets; The Client; Code of Silence; Cohen and Tate; Cold Sweat; Confessions of a Hit Man; Cookie; The Cotton Club; Dead End; Deadline USA; Deadly Matrimony; Dillinger (1945); Dillinger (1973); Diva; Domino Principle; Dr. Socrates; The Driver; Earl of Chicago; The Enforcer (1950); Eureka; F.I.S.T.; F/X; Fingers; Fitzwilly; Flesh of the Orchid; Forbidden; Force of Evil; A Free Soul; The French Connection; The French Connection II; Fresh; The Freshman (1990); The Friends of Eddie Coyle; G-Men; Gabriel over the White House; The Gang That Couldn't Shoot Straight; Garment Jungle; The Gauntlet; The George Raft Story; Get Carter; Gilda; The Girl Can't Help It;

Gloria; Go Chase Yourself; The Godfather; The Godfather, Part II; The Godfather, Part III; Good Fellas; Goodbye, Charlie; The Gun in Betty Lou's Handbag; The Gunrunner; Guys and Dolls; Hard Contract; Harlem Nights; The Hatchet Man; High Risk; High Sierra; Highpoint; The Hit; Hit Man; Hoffa; House of Strangers; I Am the Law; I, Mobster; Illegal; Island of Love; It All Came True; Key Largo; The Kid from Brooklyn; The Killer's Kiss; The Killers (1946); The Killers (1964); The Killing of Chinese Bookie; King Creole; King of New York; Kiss of Death (1947); Kiss of Death (1995); Lady for a Day; Lady in Red; Lady Killer (1933); The Last Boy Scout; Last Exit to Brooklyn; Last Rites; Last Run; The Lemon Drop Kid; Let No Man Write My Epitaph; Lights of New York; Lightship; Little Caesar; Little Giant (1933); The Long, Good Friday; Love and Bullets; Love and Money; Love Me or Leave Me; Machine Gun McCain; Mad Dog and Glory; Man from the Diners' Club; Manhattan Melodrama; Marked Woman; Married to the Mob; Marrying Man; Mary Burns, Fugitive; Masters; Mayor of Hell; Mean Streets; Meet Danny Wilson; Men of Respect; Midnight Run; Mikey and Nicky; The Milky Way (1936); Miller's Crossing; Mister Cory; Mob; Mobsters; Money for Nothing; Money from Home; Murder, Inc.; My Blue Heaven (1990); The Naked Face; The Naked Street; Naked Tango; Narrow Margin (1952); Narrow Margin (1990); Never a Dull Moment (1967); Never Let Go; New Jack City; Night and the City (1950); Night and the City (1992); 99 and 44/100 Per Cent Dead; Nitti, The Enforcer; No Escape, No Return; No Mercy; No Orchids for Miss Blandish; Now I'll Tell; Now You See Him, Now You Don't; On the Waterfront; Once Upon a Time in America; Orphans; Out of the Past; The Outfit (1973); The Outfit (1993); The Outside Man; Party Girl; Performance; Point Blank; The Pope of Greenwich Village; Prime Cut; Prizzi's Honor; The Professional; Public Enemy; Public Eye; Quick Millions; A Rage in Harlem; Rapid Fire; Raw Deal; The Rise and Fall of Legs Diamond; Rising Sun; Road House; Roaring Twenties; Robin and the Seven Hoods; Roxie Hart; Ruby; Run; Samurai; Scarface (1932); Scarface (1983); Second Chance; Secret Partner;

The Seduction of Mimi; The Set-Up; The Seven-Ups; Shaft; Shaft in Africa; Shaft's Big Score; The Sicilian; Sitting Ducks; Skidoo; Slaughter on Tenth Avenue; Slither; So Fine; Some Like it Hot; Sorry, Wrong Number; The Specialist; St. Valentine's Day Massacre; State of Grace; Stick; Stormy Monday; Tall, Dark & Handsome; That Certain Woman; They Drive by Night (1940); Things Change; This Gun for Hire; Thunder Road; Trouble in Mind; True Identity; Turning Point (1952); Twenty Thousand Years in Sing Sing; Underworld, USA; The Untouchables; The Valachi Papers; When in Rome; Whipsaw; White Heat; Wise Guys; Wonder Man; Yakuza; Year of the Dragon; You Can't Get Away With Murder

Mob Wars: see also *Police vs. Mob: Mob Stories:* Al Capone; All Through the Night; Billy Bathgate; Bowery; Bugsy; Carlito's Way; Casino; City Streets; Code of Silence; Colors; The Cotton Club; Dillinger (1945); Dillinger (1973); The Godfather; The Godfather, Part II; The Godfather, Part III; Hoffa; King of New York; The Long, Good Friday; Miller's Crossing; Murder, Inc.; New Jack City; 99 and 44/100 Per Cent Dead; No Escape, No Return; The Outfit (1993); Public Enemy; Scarface (1932); Scarface (1983); Scarface Mob/The Untouchables Pilot; The Sicilian; St. Valentine's Day Massacre; Stormy Monday; Trespass; The Untouchables; The Valachi Papers

Models: see also *Beautiful People: Fashion World: Photographers:* Amber Waves; Artists and Models (1937); Artists and Models (1955); Artists and Models Abroad; Cover Girl; Darling; Ebony Tower; Exposed; Funny Face; Her Alibi; Inspiration; Invisible Woman; It Should Happen to You; The Kiss (1988); La Belle Noiseuse; Life of Her Own; The Looker; Lovely to Look At; Mahogany; The Model and the Marriage Broker; Moonlighting (1985); Paris Model; Puzzle of a Downfall Child; The Sentinel; Sirens; Tattoo

Mod Era (that swinging, hip period in the '60s, mostly inspired by British music and movies): see also *British Films: 1960s:* Alfie; April Fools; Backbeat; Beyond the Valley of the Dolls; Blow Up; Bob & Carol & Ted & Alice; Bunny Lake is Missing; The Collector; The Cool Ones; Darling; Day the Fish

Came Out; Don't Raise the Bridge, Lower the Water!; Georgy Girl; Goodbye Gemini; A Hard Day's Night; Head; Here We Go Round the Mulberry Bush; Hysteria; I'll Never Forget Whatshisname; Idol; Kaleidoscope; The Knack; The L-Shaped Room; Laughter in the Dark; Life at the Top; Lonesome Cowboys; A Man and A Woman; Masculine, Feminine; Me, Natalie; Mickey One; Monsieur Hulot's Holiday; Morgan!; Mrs. Brown, You've Got a Lovely Daughter; The Party's Over; Performance; Quadrophenia; Salt and Pepper; Say Hello to Yesterday; Scandal; Smashing Time; Superstar, The Life and Times of Andy Warhol; There's a Girl in My Soup; Yellow Submarine

Moguls: see also *Leaders-Tyrant: Power-Rise to: Hollywood Life: Rich People*

Molestation (not necessarily of children): see also *Child Abuse: Social Drama: Rape/Rapists: Incest:* Adam Appaloosa; Get Out Your Handkerchiefs; The Good Mother; It; Just Cause; The Little Girl Who Lives Down the Lane; Separate Tables; The Mark; Never Take Sweets from a Stranger; The Nightcomers; The Offence; Short Eyes

Monaco/Monte Carlo: see *Monte Carlo: Gambling: Riviera Life: France*

Monarchs: see *Kings: Queens: Leaders-Tyrant: Dictators*

Money-Finding: see *Finding Money/Valuables: Treasure Hunts: Lucky People*

Monkeys: see *Primates*

Monks: see also *Priests: Nuns: Religion: Medieval Times:* The Assisi Underground; The Black Rose; Francis, God's Jester; Garden of Allah; The Name of the Rose; Tales From the Crypt

Monologues-Interior: see also *Crossing the Line: Narrated Films: Character Studies:* Another Woman; A Chorus Line; Dark Passage; Equus; Patton; Rachel, Rachel

Monsters (general): see also *HORROR: Aliens-Outer Space: Evil: Monsters-Animal: Rogue Plots: Stalkers: Kill the Beast: Frankenstein: Mummies: Vampires: Parasites:* The Abominable Snowman; Alien; Alien 3; Aliens; Attack of the Killer Tomatoes; Beware! The Blob!; C.H.U.D.; C.H.U.D. 2; Cameron's Closet; Forbidden Planet; Frankenstein (1931); Frankenstein '70; Frankenstein

and the Monster from Hell; Frankenstein Created Woman; Frankenstein Meets the Wolf Man; Frankenstein Unbound; Godzilla (1955); Godzilla versus Gigan; Godzilla versus Megalon; Goonies; Gorgon; Graveyard Shift; House of Dracula; Lair of the White Worm; Mighty Joe Young; Monster Club; Monster Squad; Nature of the Beast; Nightbreed; Predator; Q (The Winged Serpent); Rawhead Rex; Revenge of Frankenstein; Split Second; The Thing (1951); The Thing (1982); Twilight Zone: The Movie

Monsters-Alien: see *Aliens-Outer Space: Evil: UFOs: Outer Space Movies*

Monsters-Animal: see also *Monsters-Mutant: Monsters-Mythology:* The Abominable Snowman; Alligator; Alligator II: The Mutation; Alligator People; Ants; Arachnophobia; Ben; Big Foot; Birds; Birds II; Blood Beast Terror; Blue Water, White Death; Cat's Eye; Clash of the Titans; The Company of Wolves; The Creature of the Black Lagoon; Cujo; Dead Alive; Dune; Empire of the Ants; The Fearless Vampire Killers; Food of the Gods; Frogs; Gremlins; Gremlins 2: The New Batch; Grizzly; Harry and the Hendersons; Horror Express; Hound of the Baskervilles (1939); Hound of the Baskervilles (1959); Hound of the Baskervilles (1977); Island of Dr. Moreau (1977); Island of Lost Souls (1932); Jaws; Jaws 2; Jaws 3-D; Jaws 4: The Revenge; Jurassic Park; Killer Fish; King Kong (1933); King Kong (1976); Kingdom of the Spiders; The Kiss (1988); Link; Man's Best Friend; Mighty Joe Young; Moby Dick; The Mole People; Monkey Shines; Mothra; Murders in the Rue Morgue; Mysterious Island; Night of the Lepus; Nightwing; Orca-Killer Whale; The Pack; The Phantom of the Rue Morgue; Piranha; Razorback; Revenge of Billy the Kid; Shark!; Son of Kong; Swarm; Tentacles; Them!; They Only Kill Their Masters; Venom; White Dog; Willard; Wolfen

Monsters-Dolls: See *Monsters-Toys/Dolls*

Monsters-Human: see *Human Monsters: Body Parts: Monsters-Manmade: Cannibals: Human Eaters*

Monsters-Inanimate Objects: see *Monsters-Machine: Monsters-General: Possessions: Monsters-Toys/Dolls*

Monsters-Machine: see also
Monsters-Manmade: Man vs. Machine:
Christine; Ghost in the Machine;
Maximum Overdrive

Monsters-Manmade: see also *Robots:*
Androids: Man vs. Machine: Bride of
Frankenstein; Frankenhooker; Frank-
enstein (1931); Frankenstein '70;
Frankenstein and the Monster from Hell;
Frankenstein Created Woman; Frank-
enstein Meets the Wolf Man; Franken-
stein Unbound; Hardware; I Was a
Teenage Frankenstein; I Was a Teenage
Werewolf; The Lawnmower Man; Man
Made Monster; Revenge of Frankenstein;
Son of Frankenstein; Young Frankenstein

Monsters-Mutant: see also
Experiments: Scientists-Mad: Insects:
The Applegates; Attack of the 50-Foot
Woman (1958); Attack of the 50-Foot
Woman (1993); Attack of the Killer
Tomatoes; Bride of the Monster; The Bug;
The Children (1980); Day of the Triffids;
Digby, the Biggest Dog in the World;
Food of the Gods; Island of Dr. Moreau
(1977); Island of Lost Souls (1932); It's
Alive; It's Alive II; It's Alive III; Meet the
Applegates; Mothra; Mysterious Island;
Night of the Lepus; The Prophecy;
Swamp Thing; Them!; Toxic Avenger;
Toxic Avenger, Part II; Toxic Avenger
Part III; Tremors

Monsters-Mythology: see also
Mythology: Legends: Ancient Times:
Clash of the Titans; The Golden Voyage
of Sinbad; Gorgon; Labyrinth

Monsters-Toys/Dolls: see also
Toys/Toymakers: Monsters-General: Evil
Children: Child's Play (1988); Child's
Play 2; Child's Play 3; Halloween 3:
Season of the Witch; Trilogy in Terror

Monsters-Underwater: see also
Underwater Adventure: Sharks: The
Abyss; Deepstar Six; Leviathan

Montana Cattle Problems: see also
Cattle People: Cattle Herded by Barbara
Stanwyck: WESTERNS: Cattle Queen of
Montana; Comes a Horseman; Heaven's
Gate

Monte Carlo: see also *Gambling:*
Riviera Life: Foolish Wives; Herbie Goes
to Monte Carlo; Loser Takes All; The
Man Who Broke the Bank at Monte
Carlo; Monte Carlo; Monte Carlo Story;
Once Upon a Crime; Seven Thieves;
Silver Bears; Those Daring Young Men in
Their Jaunty Jalopies; Top Hat; Under the
Cherry Moon

**Monty Pythoners (starring members
of the Monty Python British comedy
troupe):** see also *Comedy-Skit:* All You
Need Is Cash; Clockwise; A Fish Called
Wanda; John Cleese on How to Irritate
People; The Missionary; Monty Python
and the Holy Grail; Monty Python's Life
of Brian; Monty Python's The Meaning of
Life; Rent-a-Dick; The Secret
Policeman's Ball; The Secret Policeman's
Other Ball; The Secret Policeman's
Private Parts; The Secret Policeman's
Third Ball; Splitting Heirs; Time Bandits;
Whoops! Apocalypse (1983)

Moochers: see *Con Artists*

Moonshiners: see *Bootleggers:*
Prohibition Era: Mountain People:
Hillbillies

Morality Play: see *Ethics: Message*
Films

Morbid Comedy: see *Comedy-Morbid:*
also *Death: Tragi-Comedy: Black*
Comedy

Morgues: see also *Funerals: Medical*
Detectives: Comedy of Terrors; Night Shift

Morocco: see also *Africa: Desert*
Settings: Casablanca; Ishtar; The Man
Who Knew Too Much (1956); Morocco

Mortgage Drama: see also *Save the*
Farm: Making a Living: Working Class:
Race Against Time: MELODRAMA: Poor
People: Farm Life: Albuquerque;
Arkansas Traveler; At the Circus;
batteries not included; The Bells of St.
Mary's; Between the Lines; Big
Broadcast; Bikini Beach; The Brady
Bunch Movie; Comes a Horseman;
Country; Duffy's Tavern; Field; Full Moon
in Blue Water; Gay Sisters; Harley
Davidson and the Marlboro Man; Hear
My Song; Heatwave; Heavyweights;
Herbie Rides Again; A Hole in the Head;
I Stole a Million; Li'l Abner; The Milagro
Beanfield War; Miles From Home; The
Old Curiosity Shop; Out of Africa;
Painted Desert; Places in the Heart;
Return of a Man Called Horse; The River
(1984); Roller Boogie; Scandalous John;
The Secret of NIMH; Shy People; Simba;
Sing; Starstruck; Steel; Taps; Titfield
Thunderbolt; Tobacco Road; Tugboat
Annie Sails Again; Watership Down;
Where the Green Ants Dream; Where the
Heart Is; White Christmas

Mother Love: see *Mothers-General*

Mothers (general): see *Mothers*
Alone: Mothers-Struggling: Mothers &
Daughters: Mothers & Sons:

Housewives: Stagemothers: Domestic
Life: FAMILY: Family Comedy: Family
Drama: Fathers

Mothers-Adopted: see *Children-*
Adopted: Mothers Alone: Mothers-
Surrogate

Mothers Alone: see also *Women*
Alone: Making a Living: Mothers-
Struggling: Fathers-Struggling:
Mothers-Unwed: Mothers-Surrogate:
Alice Doesn't Live Here Anymore; Angie;
Are Husbands Necessary?; Baby Boom;
Bachelor Mother; The Bad Seed (1956);
The Bad Seed (1986); The Ballad of
Josie; The Big Chill; Buddy System;
Bundle of Joy; Bunny Lake is Missing;
Caddie; Echo Park; The Effect of Gamma
Rays on Man-in-the-Moon Marigolds; The
Exorcist; Firstborn; Gas Food Lodging;
The Glass Menagerie (1950); The Glass
Menagerie (1973); The Glass Menagerie
(1987); God Bless the Child; The Good
Mother; Goodbye Girl; High Tide; Hold
Your Man; A Home of Our Own;
Intolerance; Kotch; La Vie Continue;
Little Man Tate; Made in America; Marie
Marquise of O; Marriage Go Round;
Marriage of Maria Braun; Married to the
Mob; Max Dugan Returns; Men Don't
Leave; Mildred Pierce; Murphy's
Romance; Parenthood; Promise Her
Anything; Shy People; Sin of Madelon
Claudet; Sins of Rachel Cade; The
Snapper; Stella (1990); Stella Dallas
(1925); Stella Dallas (1937); To Each His
Own; You'll Like My Mother

Mothers & Daughters: see also
Mothers & Sons: Fathers & Daughters:
Fathers & Sons: Parents vs. Children:
Women Proving Themselves: Adam's
Rib (1922); Angie; Audrey Rose; Autumn
Sonata; Bellisima; Blind Spot; Blue Sky;
C'est la Vie; The Coca-Cola Kid; The
Disappearance of Aimee; Dolores
Claiborne; The Effect of Gamma Rays on
Man-in-the-Moon Marigolds; Freaky
Friday; Gas Food Lodging; The Glass
Menagerie (1950); The Glass Menagerie
(1973); The Glass Menagerie (1987);
Gypsy; Hairspray; High Tide; A Home of
Our Own; House of Cards; Julia
Misbehaves; Light in the Piazza; Little
Foxes; Little Gloria, Happy At Last;
Margie; McClintock!; Mermaids; Mildred
Pierce; Min and Bill; Mourning Becomes
Electra; Nancy Goes to Rio; New York
Stories; Night, Mother; Not Without My
Daughter; Old Mother Riley SERIES;

Once Around; Parenthood; Peppermint Soda; Peyton Place; The Piano; A Pocketful of Miracles; The Portrait; The Positively True Adventures of the Alleged Texas Cheerleader-Murdering Mom; Postcards from the Edge; Pretty Baby; Rachel, Rachel; Reckless Moment; Right to Love; Rosie; The Secret Ceremony; September; Shanghai Gesture; Shy People; Six Weeks; Sophia Loren, Her Own Story; Steel Magnolias; Stella (1990); Stella Dallas (1925); Stella Dallas (1937); Stevie; Strangers, the Story of a Mother and Daughter; Summer Wishes, Winter Dreams; Sweet Lorraine; Tales of Terror; Teenage Rebel; Terms of Endearment; This Is My Life; Tiger's Tale; Turning Point; Two Women; Used People

Mothers & Sons: see also *Mothers & Daughters: Fathers & Sons:* Afraid of the Dark; Angela; The Birdman of Alcatraz; Bloody Mama; Broadway Bound; Buddy System; Burning Secret; Butterflies are Free; Careful, He Might Hear You; Consenting Adult; Criss Cross (1992); Cujo; Desert Law; Early Frost; Elvis: The Movie; Eric; Escape; Firstborn; Forrest Gump; Foxfire (1987); Freud; Friendly Fire; Garbo Talks; Gloria; Grace Quigley; Grapes of Wrath; The Grifters; Hamlet (1948); Hamlet (1964); Hamlet (1969); Hamlet (1991); Idol; Indochine; Killjoy; La Vie Continue; Liebestraum; Long Day Closes; Luna; Madame X (1929); Madame X (1937); Madame X (1965); Mamma Rosa; The Manchurian Candidate; The Mask (1985); The Mating Season; Max Dugan Returns; Men Don't Leave; Mother Love; Mother's Boys; Murmur of the Heart; Murphy's Romance; My Left Foot; New York Stories; None But the Lonely Heart; Oedipus Rex; Only the Lonely; Ordinary People; Parenthood; Paris, Texas; Psycho 2; Psycho 3; Psycho 4; The River Wild; Safe Passage; The Sailor Who Fell From Grace with the Sea; The Sandpiper; Santa Sangre; Scene of the Crime; Shy People; Sleepwalkers; Something for Everyone; Spanking the Monkey; Stop! Or My Mom Will Shoot; Suddenly, Last Summer; Summer Wishes, Winter Dreams; Teresa; Terms of Endearment; To Each His Own; Tommy; Torch Song Trilogy; Track 29; The Trip to Bountiful; Used People; What's Eating Gilbert Grape?; Where's Poppa?; White Banners; White Heat; Widows' Peak;

Wild in the Streets; The World According to Garp; You're a Big Boy Now

Mothers-Beleaguered: see *Mothers-Struggling: Fathers-Struggling: Parents-Struggling*

Mothers-Nagging: see *Mothers-Troublesome*

Mothers-Struggling: see also *Mothers Alone: Making a Living: Fathers-Struggling: Working Class: Unemployment: Parents-Struggling:* All the Way Home; Broadway Bound; Caddie; Child's Play (1988); Child's Play 2; Child's Play 3; Claudine; Country; Criss Cross (1992); Crooklyn; Diary for My Children; The Effect of Gamma Rays on Man-in-the-Moon Marigolds; Gas Food Lodging; God Bless the Child; Heartland; Hold Your Man; A Home of Our Own; I Remember Mama; It Grows on Trees; It Happened to Jane; Kid (1921); Kiss Shot; La Vie Continue; The Lady is Willing; Little Gloria, Happy At Last; Little Man Tate; Long Day's Journey Into Night; Marie; Max Dugan Returns; Men Don't Leave; Mildred Pierce; Min and Bill; Momma, There's a Man in Your Bed; My Left Foot; One Magic Christmas; Overboard; Playboys; Punchline; Raggedy Man; Right to Love; Rosemary's Baby; Safe Passage; Stella (1990); Stella Dallas (1925); Stella Dallas (1937); This Boy's Life; This Is My Life; Three Men and a Little Lady; Two or Three Things I Know About Her; Two Women; Up the Sandbox; Waiting For the Light; Winter People; Woman Obsessed; A World Apart

Mothers-Surrogate: see also *Children-Adopted: Fathers-Surrogate:* Adam Had Four Sons; Auntie Mame; Baby Maker; Bachelor Mother; Bundle of Joy; A Child is Waiting; Client; Gloria; Grace Quigley; A Handmaid's Tale; Mame; Mary Poppins; Min and Bill; Paternity; Sarah, Plain and Tall; Zelly and Me

Mothers-Troublesome: see also *Mothers-General: Parents vs. Children: Stagemothers:* Bellisima; Between Two Women; Big Bad Mama; Broadway Bound; Dim Sum: a Little Bit of Heart; East of Eden (1955); East of Eden (1980); Ed and His Dead Mother; The Effect of Gamma Rays on Man-in-the-Moon Marigolds; It's a Date; Kindred Krays; Little Gloria, Happy At Last; The Lost Language of Cranes; Mating Season; Mommie Dearest; Mother's Boys; My Life

as a Dog; New York Stories; Night Games; Patch of Blue; Small Sacrifices; Smooth Talk; Splitting Heirs; Square Dance; Stop! Or My Mom Will Shoot; Throw Momma from the Train; Torch Song Trilogy; What's Eating Gilbert Grape?; Where's Poppa?; White Heat; A World Apart

Mothers-Unwed: see also *Mothers Alone: Surrogate Mothers: Abortion Dilemmas:* Always Goodbye; Bad Girl; Born to Be Bad (1934); Bundle of Joy; Buona Sera, Mrs. Campbell; Christopher Strong; Dear John; Doctor, You've Got to be Kidding; For Keeps; If Winter Comes; Johnny Belinda; Kid (1921); Kotch; Look Who's Talking; Love With the Proper Stranger; Mating of Willie; Miracle (1948); Music For Millions; My Foolish Heart; No Man of Her Own (1949); Norma Rae; Old Maid; People Will Talk; Peyton Place; Right to Love; The Sandpiper; The Scarlet Letter (1926); The Scarlet Letter (1934); The Scarlet Letter (1980); Sin of Madelon Claudet; The Sins of Rachel Cade; Squaw Man; Stella (1990); Stella Dallas (1925); Stella Dallas (1937); Sweet Bird of Youth; Tess; To Each His Own; To Find a Man; Trust; The Umbrellas of Cherbourg; Way Down East (1920); Way Down East (1935); White Banners; A Woman Is a Woman; Woman Rebels; The World According to Garp

Mothers/Wives Who Leave: see *Women Who Leave: Fathers Who Leave: Fathers Alone*

Motorcycles/Motorcyclists: see also *Bicycles: Rebels: Wild People: Rednecks:* Born Losers; Death Race 2000; Easy Rider; Eat the Peach; Electra Glide in Blue; Evel Knievel; Faster Pussycat! Kill! Kill!; Ghost in the Invisible Bikini; The Great Escape; Harley Davidson and the Marlboro Man; Knightriders; Leather Boys; Little Fauss and Big Halsey; Loveless; Mad Max; Mad Max Beyond Thunderdome; Mask (1985); Rebel Rousers; Road Warrior; Roadside Prophets; Spetters; Stone Cold; Timerider; Viva Las Vegas; Wild Angels; The Wild One

Mountain Climbing: see also *Mountains: Wilderness Life: Explorers: Alps: Himalayas:* The Abominable Snowman; Alive; Breakout; A Breed Apart; Cliffhanger; The Eiger Sanction; Five Days One Summer; For Your Eyes

Only; Guns of Naravone; K-2; Mountain; Shoot to Kill; The Snows of Kilimanjaro; White Tower

Mountain People: see also *Mountain Settings: Hillbillies: Rednecks:* Continental Divide; The Devil Came from Arkansas; Foxfire (1987); Greased Lightning; Great Day in the Morning; The Incredible Journey of Dr. Meg Laurel; The Kentuckian; Kissin' Cousins; Lolly Madonna War; Matewan; Moonshine War; Murder, He Says; Nell; Pass the Ammo; Shenandoah; Shepherd of the Hills; Silence of the North; Sometimes a Great Notion; Spencer's Mountain; Springtime in the Rockies; The Story of Dr. Wassell; The Trail of the Lonesome Pine; True Grit; The Unsinkable Molly Brown

Mourning: see *Death-Dealing with*

Movie Making: see also *Hollywood Life: Directors: Writers:*

Actors/Actresses: After The Fox; Alex in Wonderland; The Barefoot Contessa; Bellisima; The Big Picture; Bombay Talkie; Burden of Dreams; Carousel; Dangerous Game; Day For Night; The Devil's Wanton; Ed Wood; 8 1/2; The Epic That Never Was; F/X; F/X 2: The Deadly Art of Illusion; Fathers and Sons; Good Morning, Babylon; Heart of the West; Hearts of Darkness: A Filmmaker's Apocalypse; Hellzapoppin; High Risk; Hollywood Cavalcade; Hooper; The Icicle Thief; I'll Do Anything; I'm Dancing as Fast as I Can; Inserts; Island of Love; It's a Great Feeling; The Last Action Hero; The Last Command; The Last Movie; Living in Oblivion; Magic Box; Man Bites Dog; Man in Love; Man Like Eva; Man of Marble; The Man Who Understood Women; Matinee; The Mirror Crack'd; Mistress; Movers and Shakers; My Geisha; National Lampoon's Movie Madness; New Nightmare; Nickelodeon; Paris Holiday; Paris When it Sizzles; The Player; Power, Passion, and Murder; Real Life; Rented Lips; Stardust Memories; State of Things; The Stuntman; Sweet Liberty; That's Adequate; Two Weeks in Another Town; Under the Rainbow; White Hunter, Black Heart

Movies within Movies: see also *Movie Making: Hollywood Life: Soliloquies:* After The Fox; Day For Night; Frankenstein '70; French Lieutenant's Woman; Hollywood Canteen; Inserts; It's a Great Feeling; The Last Movie; Man Bites Dog; A Man Like Eva;

Man of Marble; Mirror Crack'd; Real Life; Rosencrantz and Guildenstern Are Dead; Stuntman; Sweet Liberty; Under the Rainbow; Waxwork; Waxwork II: Lost in Time

Movie Theaters (as settings): see also *Theater Life:* Apartment Zero; The Blob (1958); Cinema Paradiso; Desperately Seeking Susan; The Good Fairy; Gremlins 2; Inner Circle; The Last Action Hero; The Last Picture Show; Manhattan Murder Mystery; Matinee; The Projectionist; The Purple Rose of Cairo; Targets; Variety; White Heat

Multiple Performances: see also *Multiple Stories: Multiple Personalities:* After The Fox; Being Human; Coming to America; Crimes of Passion; Dead of Winter; Dead Ringer; Double Impact; Dr. Strangelove; Fahrenheit 451; The Family Jewels; Gas Food Lodging; Gilda Live; Happy New Year (1987); Joe vs. the Volcano; Kind Hearts and Coronets; La Passante; Life of Brian; The Man Who Haunted Himself; The Mouse That Roared; No Way to Treat a Lady; Nothing but Trouble (1991); The Nutty Professor (1963); O Lucky Man; Plaza Suite; The Seven Faces of Dr. Lao; Sophia Loren, Her Own Story; That Obscure Object of Desire; Three on a Couch; Trilogy in Terror; Woman Times Seven; Wonder Man; Yesterday, Today and Tomorrow

Multiple Personalities: see also *Mental Illness: Multiple Performances: Nervous Breakdowns:* All of Me; The Boston Strangler; Crimes of Passion; Dance Macabre; Dark Mirror; A Double Life; Innerspace; Lizzie; Loose Cannons; Magic; Psycho; Raising Cain; Sybil; The Three Faces of Eve

Multiple Stories (containing several subplots which aren't necessarily interwoven or even related): see also *Interwoven Stories: Parallel Stories: Multiple Performances: Hand-Me-Down Stories:* Actors and Sin; The Adjuster; The Adventures of Baron Munchausen (1943); The Affairs of Susan; After the Shock; Airport; Amarcord; Amazing Stories; America; Aria; Asylum; Bachelor in Paradise; Barry Lyndon; Battle Cry; Battle of Britain; The Best Years of Our Lives; The Bible; The Big One, The Great Los Angeles Earthquake; Black Sabbath; Bleak Moments; Bloodhounds of Broadway (1952); Bloodhounds of Broadway (1989); Bocaccio '70; Body

Bags; California Suite; A Canterbury Tale; The Caretakers; Cat's Eye; Centennial Summer; Central Park; The Chapman Report; Charade; A Chorus Line; City of Hope; The Comedians; Dead End; Dead Men Don't Wear Plaid; Dead of Night (1945); Dead of Night (1977); Earthquake; Easy Money (1948); Encore; Every Thing You Always Wanted to Know About Sex . . . ; Exodus; Faces; Fanny; Fanny and Alexander; FBI Story; Forever and a Day; Fort Apache, The Bronx; The Four Seasons; Freud; Friday the Thirteenth (1933); Gettysburg; Good Die Young; Grand Hotel; Grand Prix; The Greatest Story Ever Told; Green Pastures; Guyana Tragedy, The Story of Jim Jones; Hannah and Her Sisters; Heimat; Higher Learning; Hotel; Hotel Paradiso; The House That Dripped Blood; How the West Was Won; Howards End; I Vitelloni; If I Had a Million; If It's Tuesday, This Must Be Belgium; The Illustrated Man; In Old Chicago; Isn't it Romantic?; Is Paris Burning?; It's A Big Country; Juice; Kaos; Kiss Them For Me; La Ronde (1950); La Ronde (1964); La Vie de Boheme; Lady L.; The Last Days of Pompeii; The Last Picture Show; Laurel Avenue; The Lawrenceville Stories; Make Mine Music; Manhattan; Matinee; Midway; Mister Buddwing; Mixed Nuts; Movie Movie; Mystery Train; Nashville; New York Stories; Night on Earth; A Night to Remember (1958); The Night We Never Met; 92 in the Shade; No Down Payment; No Highway in the Sky; No No Nanette (1930); No No Nanette (1940); Noises Off; Oh Men! Oh Women!; The Oldest Profession; On a Clear Day You Can See Forever; The Opposite Sex; Our Town; Paisan; Paper; Paris Model; Pauline at the Beach; Peyton Place; Places in the Heart; Plaza Suite; Poison; Power, Passion, and Murder; Prison Stories: Women on the Inside; Quartet (1948); Ragtime; Rashomon; Ready to Wear; Rich Kids; Run for Your Money; San Francisco; Scorchers; Shadow Box; Short Cuts; Singles; Six in Paris; Slaves of New York; Sophisticated Gents; Stand; State Fair (1933); State Fair (1945); State Fair (1962); The Story of Three Loves; Street Scene; Tales From the Crypt; Tales from the Darkside: The Movie; Tales of Manhattan; Tales of Terror; Tampopo; They All Laughed; This Happy Breed; A Time for Loving; Titanic; Tora! Tora!

Tora!; The Towering Inferno; Traffik; Tree of Wooden Clogs; Trilogy in Terror; Twenty Bucks; Twilight Zone: The Movie; Unfinished Piece for a Player The Piano; VIPs; Voyage of the Damned; War and Peace (1956); War and Peace (1967); The Wedding; Weekend at the Waldorf; Welcome to L.A.; Where the Day Takes You; White Tower; Woman Times Seven; The Women; The Wonderful World of the Brothers Grimm; Yellow Rolls Royce; Yesterday, Today and Tomorrow; Ziegfeld Girl

Mummies: see also *Zombies: Monsters: Egypt/Pyramids:* Abbott & Costello Meet the Mummy; The Awakening; Blood from the Mummy's Tomb; Ghoul (1933); The Mummy (1932); The Mummy (1959); The Mummy's Hand; The Mummy's Shroud; Sphinx; Tales of Terror

Muppets: see also *Puppets: CHIL-DREN'S: FAMILY:* The Dark Crystal; The Great Muppet Caper; The Muppet Christmas Carol; The Muppet Movie; The Muppets Take Manhattan

MURDER: see also *MURDER MYSTERY: MYSTERY: THRILLERS: Crime Drama: Courtroom Drama: Perfect Crimes: Framed?: Death-Accidental: Scared to Death: Trail of a Killer: Serial Killers: Psycho Killers:* Absolute Quiet; Absolution; The Accused (1948); Accused of Murder; Act of Murder; The Adventures of Ford Fairlane; The Adventures of Tom Sawyer; The Advocate; Affair in Trinidad; After Office Hours; All Fall Down; All This and Heaven, Too; All-American Murder; Aloha, Bobby and Rose; Along Came Jones; Along the Great Divide; The Alphabet Murders; The Amateur; The American Friend; Amsterdamned; And Then There Were None; Andy Warhol's Frankenstein; Angel; Angel Face; Angel Heart; Appointment with Death; Arriverderci, Baby!; Arousers; Ashes and Diamonds; The Assassin; At Close Range; Auntie Lee's Meat Pies; Avenging Conscience; Backfire; Bad Lieutenant; The Bad Seed (1956); The Bad Seed (1986); Basic Instinct; Bears & I; Bedroom Eyes; Bedroom Eyes 2; Bedroom Window; Being at Home with Claude; Beyond a Reasonable Doubt; Beyond the Forest; The Big Clock; The Big Sleep (1946); The Big Sleep (1977); Billy Budd; Bird With the Crystal Plumage; Black Angel; Black Marble;

Black Orpheus; Black Rainbow; Black Sunday (1960); Black Widow (1954); Black Widow (1987); Blackmail (1929); Blackmailed; Blindfold: Acts of Obsession; Blink; Blood and Black Lace; Blood from the Mummy's Tomb; Blood Relatives; Blood Simple; Bloodline; The Blue Dahlia; Blue Ice; Blue Lamp; Blue Steel; Body in the Library; Body of Evidence; The Body Snatcher; Boiling Point; Boomerang (1947); Born to Kill; The Bowery at Midnight; Boys from Brazil; Brainscan; Brainstorm (1965); Bram Stoker's Count Dracula (1970); Bram Stoker's Dracula (1992); Bramble Bush; Brass Target; Breakheart Pass; Breaking Point; Brighton Rock; Broken Blossoms; The Brood; Brubaker; Buffet Froid; Bugsy; Buried Alive; Burning; Butterfly; The Cabinet of Dr. Caligari (1919); The Cage of Gold; Cal; Calcutta; Call Me; Calling Dr. Kildare; Calling Northside 777; Cancel My Reservation; Candyman; Caprice; Carousel; A Case for Murder; Cast a Dark Shadow; Castle in the Desert; Caught in the Act; Cause for Alarm; Charade; Charmer; Chato's Land; Chicago Joe and the Showgirl; China Moon; Chinatown; Christmas Holiday; Chronicle of a Death Foretold; Clean Slate; Clockers; Club Paradise; Color Me Dead; Color of Night; Coma; Comedy of Terrors; Comfort of Strangers; Compulsion; Conan, the Barbarian; Confidentially Yours; Conflict of Interest; Cop au Vin; Coup de Torchon; Crime and Punishment; Crimes and Misdemeanors; Crossfire; Cruising; Cutter and Bone; D.O.A. (1949); D.O.A. (1988); Dance Macabre; Dance with a Stranger; Dark Corner; The Dark Half; Dark Passage; Dark Wind; Dead Heat; Dead in the Water; Dead of Night (1945); Dead of Winter; Dead On; Dead Pool; Dead Ringer; Deadfall (1993); Deadly Affair; Deadly Matrimony; Dear Inspector; Death in Brunswick; Death on the Nile; Death Warrant; Deathtrap; Defenseless; Desert Fury; Desire and Hell at Sunset Motel; Desperate Living; The Detective (1968); The Detective (1985); Devil Doll; The Devil's Disciple; Devlin; Diabolique (1955); Diary of a Hitman; Diary of a Madman; Dick Tracy; Die Laughing; Die Watching; Disappearance of Christina; Divorce, Italian Style; Do You Like Women?; Doctor's Wives; Dolores Claiborne; Don't Just Stand There;

Doppelganger: The Evil Within; Double Indemnity; A Double Life; Dracula (1931); Dracula (1979); Dracula Has Risen from the Grave; Dracula (Horror of Dracula, 1958); Dracula, Prince of Darkness; Dracula's Daughter; Dream Lover (1986); Dream Team; Drowning By Numbers; The Drowning Pool; Dying Room Only; Dynasty of Fear; Earl of Chicago; East of Elephant Rock; Edge of Doom; Endangered Species; Endless Game; Equus; The Evictors; The Evil Dead; The Executioner's Song; Eye of the Storm; Eyewitness (1970); Eyewitness (1981); F/X; Fade to Black (1979); Fade to Black (1993); Fallen Angel; Fallen Idol; Farewell, My Lovely (1944); Farewell, My Lovely (1975); Fast Company; Fatal Vision; Fear; Female Trouble; A Few Good Men; File on Thelma Jordon; Final Analysis; Five Million Years to Earth; Flare Up; Flesh and Bone; Flight of the Doves; Fly By Night; Fog over Frisco; Foreign Intrigue; Formula; Fourth Story; Frantic (1958); From the Hip; From the Life of the Marionettes; The Fuller Brush Girl; The Fuller Brush Man; Fury (1936); Gazebo; Ghost; The Ghoul (1933); The Ghoul (1975); Girl in the Red Velvet Swing; The Glass Key (1935); The Glass Key (1942); The Goalie's Anxiety at the Penalty Kick; The Godfather; The Godfather, Part II; The Godfather, Part III; Going Home; Good Fellas; Gorilla; Gorilla at Large; Gorillas in the Mist; Gorky Park; The Great Gatsby (1949); The Great Gatsby (1974); The Great Lover (1949); Greed; Green for Danger; The Green Man; The Grifters; Guilty as Sin; Guilty Conscience; Gun Crazy (1950); Gun Crazy (1992); Gun in Betty Lou's Handbag; Hairy Ape; Hallelujah!; Halloween 3: Season of the Witch; Hamlet (1948); Hamlet (1964); Hamlet (1969); Hamlet (1991); Hammersmith is Out; Hammett; The Hand (1960); The Hand (1981); The Hand that Rocks the Cradle; The Hanging Tree; Happy Birthday to Me; Harper; The Hatchet Man; Heathers; Heaven Can Wait (1978); Henry: Portrait of a Serial Killer; Her Alibi; Here Come the Girls; Hidden; Hidden 2; Hoffa; Homicide; Honey Pot; The Honeymoon Killers; Hound of the Baskervilles (1939); Hound of the Baskervilles (1959); Hound of the Baskervilles (1977); The House; House

II: The Second Story; House III; House IV; The House on Haunted Hill; How to Murder Your Wife; The Hunger; Hush, Hush, Sweet Charlotte; Hysteria; I Confess; I Love You to Death; I Saw What You Did; I Stand Condemned; I Thank a Fool; I, the Jury (1953); I, The Jury (1982); I Wake Up Screaming; I Want to Live!; I'm No Angel; Impact; Impulse (1990); In a Lonely Place; In Cold Blood; In the Heat of the Night; Incident at Oglala; The Inquisitor; Inspector Calls; Internal Affairs; Internecine Project; Intruder in the Dust; Investigation of a Citizen Above Suspicion; The Invisible Man's Revenge; Iron Maze; Island (1980); Isle of the Dead; It; It's a Wonderful World; Ivy; Jack the Ripper (1958); Jacob's Ladder; Jagged Edge; The January Man; Jennifer 8; Joe; Johnny Angel; Just Cause; The Kennel Murder Case; The Kill-Off; The Killer Inside Me; Killer McCoy; Killer Nun; Killing Dad; Killing in a Small Town; Killjoy; King of the Gypsies; The Kiss (1929); A Kiss Before Dying (1956); A Kiss Before Dying (1991); Kiss Me Deadly; Kiss the Blood Off My Hands; Kitchen Toto; Klute; Knife in the Water; Knight Moves; Knock on Any Door; Krays; La Bete Humaine; Ladies in Retirement; Lady from Shanghai; Lady in Cement; Lady in Question; Lady in White; Lady of Burlesque; Lady on a Train; Ladykiller (1992); Last Rites; Last Sunset; Late Show; Laura; Lawman; Leave Her to Heaven; Legacy; Legend of Hell House; Let Him Have It; Let's Kill Uncle; Letter (1929); Letter (1940); Liebestraum; Lightning Strikes Twice; The Lindbergh Kidnapping Case; The List of Adrian Messenger; The Little Girl Who Lives Down the Lane; Lizzie; London Belongs to Me; The Long Goodbye; The Long Night; Looker; Love Has Many Faces; Lovely Way to Die; Lucky Stiff; Lured; M (1931); M (1951); Mad Magician; Mad Miss Manton; Mad Room; Madame X (1929); Madame X (1937); Madame X (1965); Madhouse; Magic; Magnum Force; Malice; The Maltese Falcon (1931); The Maltese Falcon (1941); The Man in the Attic; The Man in the Middle; Man on a Swing; Man on the Eiffel Tower; Man Trouble; Man Who Reclaimed His Head; Man Who Watched Trains Go By; Manhunter; Maniac Cop; Maniac Cop 2; Mark of the Vampire; Married to the Mob;

Martin; Masque of the Red Death; Masquerade (1988); Maytime; Mean Season; Men Are Not Gods; Men at Work; Midnight (1989); Midnight Man; Mighty Quinn; Mike's Murder; Mildred Pierce; Mill on the Floss; Miller's Crossing; Mine Own Executioner; The Mirror Crack'd; Mississippi Burning; Mississippi Mermaid; Moment to Moment; Monkey Shines; Monolith; Monsieur Verdoux; Montenegro; Moonrise; Morning After; Mortal Thoughts; Most Dangerous Game; Motel Hell; Mother Love; Mother's Boys; Mourning Becomes Electra; Moving Violation; Mr. and Mrs. North; Mr. Arkadin; The Mummy (1959); The Mummy's Hand; The Mummy's Shroud; Murder; Murder Ahoy; Murder at the Gallop; Murder at the Vanities; Murder by Death; Murder by Decree; Murder by Natural Causes; Murder by Television; Murder in New Hampshire; Murder in Texas; Murder in the First; Murder Man; Murder Most Foul; Murder of Mary Phagan; Murder on the Orient Express; Murder She Said; Murders in the Rue Morgue; Murphy's Law; My Cousin Vinny; My Forbidden Past; Mystery of the Wax Museum; Mystery Street; Nadine; The Naked Street; The Name of the Rose; Native Son (1951); Native Son (1986); Natural; The New Barbarians; New Leaf; Niagara; Night Angel; Night Must Fall (1937); Night Must Fall (1964); Night of the Generals; Night of the Hunter; Night Terror; Nighthawks (1981); No Escape (1936); No Way Out (1987); No Way to Treat a Lady; Nocturne; North by Northwest; Notorious Landlady; Nous Sommes Tous les Assassins; Nuts; October Man; Off and Running; The Official Story; Oh Heavenly Dog; On Dangerous Ground; On the Waterfront; Once Upon a Time in the West; One Body Too Many; Onion Field; Ordeal by Innocence; Otello; Othello (1951); Othello (1965); Other; Out Cold; Out of the Dark; Outland; Outrage (1964); Over Her Dead Body; The Ox-Bow Incident; Pandora's Box; The Paradine Case; Past Midnight; Payment Deferred; The Pelican Brief; Perfect Strangers; Pet Sematary; Pet Sematary 2; Peter Ibbetson; Phantom of Paradise; Phantom of the Opera (1925); Phantom of the Opera (1941); Phantom of the Opera (1962); Phantom of the Opera (1989); Phantom of the Rue Morgue; Phobia; Physical Evidence; The

Pit and the Pendulum (1961); The Pit and the Pendulum (1991); A Place in the Sun; Plain Clothes; The Player; The Postman Always Ring Twice (1945); The Postman Always Rings Twice (1981); Power, Passion, and Murder; A Prayer for the Dying; Preppie Murder; Presumed Innocent; Prick Up Your Ears; Prime Cut; Prime Suspect; Prowler; Psycho; Q & A; Rabid Grannies; The Radioland Murders; Raising Cain; Rapid Fire; Rapture; Razorback; Reckless Moment; Red House; Red Inn; Red Rock West; Reflecting Skin; Rehearsal for Murder; The Reincarnation of Peter Proud; Relentless; Relentless 2; Relentless 3; Remember Last Night?; Report to the Commissioner; Revenge of Billy the Kid; Revengers; Reversal of Fortune; Rider on the Rain; Road Games; Rollover; Rope; Rosary Murders; Roxie Hart; Ruby; Runner Stumbles; Running Man (1963); Sacco and Vanzetti; Salt and Pepper; Samurai; Sapphire; Scalphunters; Scandal Sheet; Scandalous!; Scapegoat; Scar; Scaramouche; Scarlet Claw; Scarlet Street; Scream and Scream Again!; Screaming Mimi; Secret Agent; Secret Beyond the Door; Secret Friends; See No Evil; See No Evil, Hear No Evil; The Shadow (1936); Shadow of a Doubt; Shadow of the Thin Man; Shadows and Fog; Shakes the Clown; Shallow Grave; Shattered; The Shawshank Redemption; Shock Corridor; Shock to the System; Shock Treatment; Shocker; Shogun Assassin; Shoot to Kill; A Short Film About Killing; Shot in the Dark; Show of Force; Siesta; Silent Fall; Silhouette; Silver Streak; Single White Female; Slamdance; Slaughter on Tenth Avenue; Sleeping Car Murders; Sleuth; Slight Case of Murder; Sliver; Sniper; Somebody Killed Her Husband; Song of the Thin Man; Soylent Green; Spellbound; Spiral Staircase (1946); Spiral Staircase (1975); St. Ive's; Stage Fright; Stand by Me; Star Chamber; Star Trek VI: The Undiscovered Country; Step Down to Terror; Still of the Night; Storm Warning; Storyville; Strait Jacket; Strange Bargain; Strange Loves of Martha Ivers; Stranger; Stranger Among Us; Stranger is Watching; Strangers on a Train; Striking Distance; The Stuntman; The Substitute; Sunburn; Sunset; Sunset Boulevard; Suspect; Suspiria; Sweeney Todd, Demon Barber of Fleet Street; Swoon; Talk

Radio; Tango & Cash; A Taste for Killing; Tattoo; The Temp; Ten Days Wonder; Ten Little Indians; Terminal Man; Terminator; Terror By Night; Terror Train; The Texas Chainsaw Massacre; The Texas Chainsaw Massacre, Part 2; Theater of Blood; Thelma & Louise; They Call Me Mr. Tibbs!; They Drive by Night (1938); They Drive by Night (1940); They Live by Night; They Made Me a Criminal; They Only Kill Their Masters; They Won't Believe Me; They Won't Forget; The Thin Blue Line; The Thin Man; The Thirty-Nine Steps (1935); The Thirty-Nine Steps (1959); The Thirty-Nine Steps (1978); This Gun for Hire; Three Days of the Condor; Throne of Blood; Throw Momma from the Train; Thunderheart; Tick, Tick, Tick . . . ; Tiger Bay; Tightrope; Time Without Pity; To Catch a Killer; Tom Horn; Tony Rome; Topaz (1969); Toto le Heros; Tower of London (1939); Tower of London (1962); The Town; The Town That Dreaded Sundown; Traces of Red; Trade Winds; Trial and Error; Trouble for Two; Trouble with Girls; Trouble with Harry; True Confession; True Confessions; True Grit; Turner & Hooch; Twelve Angry Men; 21 Days; Twenty-Three Paces to Baker Street; Twin Peaks; Twin Peaks: Fire Walk with Me; Twisted Nerve; The Two Jakes; The Two Mrs. Carrolls; The Unbelievable Truth; Under Suspicion; Unfaithful; The Unnamable; The Unnamable Returns; The Unseen; Unsuspected; Vampire Lovers; Velvet Touch; Vertigo; Vicki; Violette; V. I. Warshawski; We Are Not Alone; Westworld; What's the Matter with Helen?; Whatever Happened to Aunt Alice?; When a Stranger Calls; When Strangers Marry; Where Are the Children?; Where Love Has Gone; Where's Poppa?; While the City Sleeps; Whirlpool; Whispers in the Dark; Whistle Down the Wind; Whistling in the Dark; White Lightning; White Mischief; Who Done It? (1942); Who Is Killing the Great Chefs of Europe?; Who Is the Black Dahlia?; Who Slew Auntie Roo?; The Wicker Man; Widows' Peak; Wilt; Wings of Fame; Winterset; Witness; Witness for the Prosecution; Witness to Murder; Wolfen; Woman in the Window; Yellow Balloon; You Can Never Tell; You've Got to Live Dangerously; Young Mr. Lincoln; Zigzag

Murder-Attempted: see also *Murder-Comic Attempts: Murder-Failed Attempts:* Autumn Leaves; Blackmailed; Bloodline; Bodyguard; Honey Pot; Ladykillers; Maids; Man About the House; Man Hunt; Men Are Not Gods; Midnight (1989); Nothing but Trouble (1941); The Positively True Adventures of the Alleged Texas Cheerleader-Murdering Mom; Throne of Blood; Twisted Nerve; Unfaithfully Yours (1948); Unfaithfully Yours (1984)

Murder-Clearing Oneself: see also *Saving Oneself: Framed?: Accused-Unjustly:* Bedroom Eyes 2; Bedroom Window; Bramble Bush; Caught in the Act; Cause for Alarm; Conduct Unbecoming; Conflict of Interest; Devlin; Fly By Night; The Fugitive (1993); The Fugitive: The Final Episode; The Fuller Brush Girl; The Fuller Brush Man; The Fury (1936); Jennifer 8; Mad Miss Manton; Murder; October Man; Ordeal by Innocence; Out Cold; Presumed Innocent; Strangers on a Train; Tango & Cash; They Drive by Night (1938); They Live by Night; The Thirty-Nine Steps (1935); The Thirty-Nine Steps (1959); The Thirty-Nine Steps (1978); Three Days of the Condor; Time Without Pity

Murder-Coerced/Persuaded to: see also *Murder of Spouse:* Absolution; The American Friend; Angel Face; Chicago Joe and the Showgirl; Fear in the Night; Gun Crazy (1950); Gun Crazy (1992); Killing of Chinese Bookie; La Femme Nikita; Loves of Carmen; Point of No Return; The Postman Always Ring Twice (1945); The Postman Always Rings Twice (1981); Pretty Poison; Secret Agent; Secret Partner

Murder-Comic Attempts: see also *Criminals-Stupid:* Andy Warhol's Bad; Arriverderci, Baby!; Better Off Dead; Buried Alive; Dirty Rotten Scoundrels; Divorce, Italian Style; Eating Raoul; A Fish Called Wanda; The Fortune; Heaven Can Wait (1978); Honey Pot; How to Murder Your Wife; I Love You to Death; Killing Dad; Kind Hearts and Coronets; Ladykillers; Monsieur Verdoux; New Leaf; Nothing but Trouble (1941); War of the Roses; Where's Poppa?; Who is Killing the Great Chefs of Europe?

Murder-Debate to Confess to: see also *Guilty Conscience: MURDER: Ethics: Saving Oneself: Suspecting Oneself:* All My Sons (1949); All My Sons (1986); American Dream; Cal; The Conversation; Cop and a Half; Crimes and Misdemeanors; Criminal Law; The Devil's Disciple; Double Indemnity; Edge of Doom; I Confess; Investigation of a Citizen Above Suspicion; Jack's Back; Lady in White; Mortal Thoughts; The Music Box; The Ox-Bow Incident; The Player; Samurai; Spellbound; Unsuspected; Velvet Touch

Murder-Discovering: see also *MURDER: Innocent Bystanders: Detectives-Amateur: Conspiracy:* Blow Out; Blow Up; Blue Velvet; Chinatown; Coma; The Conversation; Dream Team; The Eyes of Laura Mars; Fly By Night; Foreign Intrigue; Lady in Cement; Lady of Burlesque; Lured; Mad Miss Manton; Men at Work; Midnight Man; Moment to Moment; Mr. and Mrs. North; Nadine; One Body Too Many; Rear Window; Rebecca; River's Edge; Silver Streak; Stand by Me; Tony Rome; Twenty-Three Paces to Baker Street

Murderer-Debate to Reveal: see also *MURDER: Ethics: Guilty Conscience:* Blackmail (1929); Detour; Fallen Idol; Guilty as Sin; Joe; Sabotage; Serial Mom; Tiger Bay; Storm Warning

Murderers-Black Widow (women who kill a series of husbands or lovers): see also *Murderers-Merry Widow: Murderers-Female: Criminals-Female: Evil Women: Serial Killers:* Arrivederci, Baby!; Bride Wore Black; The Honeymoon Killers; The Man with Two Brains; Monsieur Verdoux

Murderers-Child (children who murder): see also *Evil Children: Children-Brats: Murderers of Children:* Alice, Sweet Alice; Blood Relatives; The Brood; The Drowning Pool; The Good Son; Let's Kill Uncle; The Little Girl Who Lives Down the Lane

Murderers-Female: see also *Murderers-Black Widow: Serial Killers: Murderers-Mass: Evil Women: Dangerous Women:* The Accused (1948); Angel Face; The Babysitter; Basic Instinct; Black Widow (1987); Blood from the Mummy's Tomb; The Bride Wore Black; Butterfly; China Moon; Crush; Dance with a Stranger; Defenseless; Dolores Claiborne; Don't Bother to Knock; Doppelganger: The Evil Within; Dracula's Daughter; The Drowning Pool; East of Elephant Rock; Ed and His Dead Mother; Female Trouble; File on Thelma Jordon; Final Analysis; The Fourth Man; Fried Green Tomatoes; The Hand that Rocks the Cradle; Happy Birthday to Me; Her Alibi; I Thank a Fool; I Want to

Christian Andersen; The Harvey Girls; Hello Dolly; The Hit Parade of 1943; The Hit Parade of 1947; Holiday Inn; Hollywood Hotel; How to Succeed in Business without Really Trying; Innocents of Paris (1929); The Joy of Living; Jupiter's Darling; The Kid From Spain; Kid Millions; Le Million; Let's Do it Again (1953); Let's Face It; Let's Make Love; Li'l Abner; The Little Shop of Horrors (1986); Louisiana Purchase; Love Me Tonight; Love Parade; Lovely to Look At; Lucky Me; Mame; Mary Poppins; Meet Me After the Show; The Muppet Christmas Carol; The Muppet Movie; The Muppets Take Manhattan; Muscle Beach Party; My Fair Lady; My Sister Eileen (1955); Newsies; The Nightmare Before Christmas; Oh, What a Lovely War; Oklahoma!; Oliver!; On a Clear Day You Can See Forever; On the Town; Paint Your Wagon; Pajama Game; Panama Hattie; Pardners; Pepe; Pete's Dragon; Rhythm on the Range; Roberta; The Rocky Horror Picture Show; Romance on the High Seas; Roman Scandals; The Royal Wedding; Sing You Sinners; Singing in the Rain; A Song is Born; Sweet Rosie O'Grady; Take Me Out to the Ball Game; Tea for Two; That Certain Age; That Lady in Ermine; That Night in Rio; This Could Be the Night; Thoroughly Modern Millie; Thousands Cheer; Tom Sawyer; Two Girls and a Sailor; The Unsinkable Molly Brown; Whoopee; Yolanda and the Thief

Musical Drama: see also *MUSICALS: Music Movies:* Bright Eyes; All That Jazz; An American in Paris; Boy Friend; Bugsy Malone; Bundle of Joy; By the Light of the Silvery Moon; Cabaret; Camelot; Carmen (Opera, 1984); Carousel; A Chorus Line; Fiddler on the Roof; Funny Girl; Funny Lady; Gigi (1958); Godspell; Goodbye Mr. Chips (1939); Goodbye Mr. Chips (1969); Great Caruso; Great Ziegfeld; Gypsy; Hair; Irma La Douce; Jesus Christ, Superstar; A Little Night Music; The Little Prince; Lost Horizon (1973); Mack the Knife; Man of La Mancha; On Your Toes; Pal Joey; Party Girl; Pennies from Heaven (1936); Rose Marie (1936); Rose Marie (1954); Sarafina!; School Daze; Scrooge (1970); 1776; Showboat (1936); Showboat (1951); South Pacific; Star!; Story of Vernon and Irene Castle; Tales of Hoffman; West Side Story; When My

Baby Smiles at Me; The Wiz; Wonder Bar; Words and Music; Yentl

Musical Fantasy: see also *Musicals-Animated: Fantasy: CHILDREN'S: FAMILY:* Beauty and the Beast (1991); Bedknobs and Broomsticks; Brigadoon; Cabin in the Sky; A Connecticut Yankee in King Arthur's Court; Finian's Rainbow; Give My Regards to Broad Street; Kismet (1955); The Little Prince; The Nightmare Before Christmas; Pennies from Heaven (1981); Pete's Dragon; Scrooge (1970); Tales of Hoffman; Where Do We Go from Here?

Musical-Operettas: see *Musicals-Operettas*

Musical-Romance: see also *MUSICALS: Musical Drama: Musical Comedy: Romantic Comedy:* Aaron Slick from Punkin Crick; Alexander's Ragtime Band; An American in Paris; At Long Last Love; Bathing Beauty; Belle of New York; Bitter Sweet (1933); Bitter Sweet (1940); Calamity Jane; Call Me Mister; Carmen Jones; Chocolate Soldier; Clambake; Cover Girl; Daddy Longlegs; A Damsel in Distress; Down Argentine Way; The Farmer Takes a Wife; Fiesta; Firefly; First Love; Flower Drum Song; Flying Down to Rio; Follow the Fleet; For Me and My Gal; Funny Face; The Gang's All Here; The Gay Divorcee; Gigi (1958); Girl of the Golden West; The Great Caruso; Hans Christian Andersen; The Harvey Girls; Hello Dolly; High Society; Hit the Deck; Holiday in Mexico; Holiday Inn; I Love Melvin; Isn't it Romantic?; The King and I; Kismet (1955); Kiss Me Kate (1953); Kiss the Boys Goodbye; Let's Dance; Lili; Live a Little, Love a Lot; Mardi Gras; Meet Me in Las Vegas; The Merry Widow (1934); The Merry Widow (1952); My Fair Lady; My Wild Irish Rose; Naughty Marietta; Neptune's Daughter; The Night Is Young (1934); On the Riviera; One from the Heart; One Night of Love; Paint Your Wagon; Party Girl; Pirate; Pirates of Penzance; Romance on the High Seas; Rose Marie (1936); Rose Marie (1954); The Royal Wedding; Second Fiddle; Seven Brides for Seven Brothers; The Slipper and the Rose; Small Town Girl (1953); A Song is Born; Song of the Islands; The Sound of Music; South Pacific; Springtime in the Rockies; Stars and Stripes Forever; State Fair (1945); State Fair (1962); The Stork Club; Story of Vernon and Irene Castle;

Sweethearts; Swing Time; Tales of Hoffman; Tammy and the Bachelor; That Certain Age; The Young Girls of Rochefort; Thin Ice; This Could Be the Night; Three Little Words; The Thrill of a Romance; Tickle Me; Tin Pan Alley; Two Girls and a Sailor; West Side Story; When My Baby Smiles at Me; When You're in Love; You Were Never Lovelier; You'll Never Get Rich; Young at Heart

MUSICALS: see also *Musical Drama: Music Movies: Music Videos: Music Video Style: Spoofs-Musical: Musicals-Animated:* Aaron Slick from Punkin Crick; Absolute Beginners; Aladdin; Alexander's Ragtime Band; Ali Baba Goes to Town; All That Jazz; American in Paris; Anchors Aweigh; Annie; Annie Get Your Gun!; April in Paris; Aristocats; At Long Last Love; Babes in Arms; Babes in Toyland (1934); Babes in Toyland (1961); Babes on Broadway; Back to the Beach; Balalaika; The Band Wagon; Barkleys of Broadway; Bathing Beauty; The Bawdy Adventures of Tom Jones; Beach Blanket Bingo; Beauty and the Beast (1991); Because You're Mine; Bedknobs and Broomsticks; Belle of New York; Belle of the Yukon; Bells Are Ringing; Best Foot Forward; The Best Little Whorehouse in Texas; The Big Broadcast; The Big Broadcast of 1936; The Big Broadcast of 1937; The Big Broadcast of 1938; Billy Rose's Jumbo; Bitter Sweet (1933); Bitter Sweet (1940); Born to Dance; Bottoms Up; The Boy Friend; The Boys from Syracuse; Brigadoon; Bright Eyes; Broadway Melody; Broadway Melody of 1936; Broadway Melody of 1938; Broadway Melody of 1940; Bugsy Malone; Bundle of Joy; By the Light of the Silvery Moon; Bye Bye Birdie; Cabaret; Cabin in the Sky; Calamity Jane; Call Me Madam; Call Me Mister; Camelot; Can't Stop the Music; Can-Can; Carmen Jones; Carousel; Chitty Chitty Bang Bang; Chocolate Soldier; A Chorus Line; Cinderella Jones; Cinderfella; Clambake; A Connecticut Yankee in King Arthur's Court; The Cotton Club; Court Jester; Cover Girl; Cry Baby; Daddy Longlegs; Damn Yankees; A Damsel in Distress; Dancing Co-Ed; Dangerous When Wet; Darling Lili; A Date with Judy; Diamond Horseshoe; Dirty Dancing; Dixie; Dolly Sisters; Down Argentine Way; Down to Earth; Dr. Dolittle; Earth Girls are Easy; Easter

Parade; Easy to Love; Fame; Fanny; Fantasia; The Farmer Takes a Wife; Fiddler on the Roof; Fiesta; Finian's Rainbow; Firefly; First Love; The First Nudie Musical; Flower Drum Song; Flying Down to Rio; Follies in Concert; Follow the Fleet; Footlight Parade; Footloose; For Me and My Gal; 42nd Street; Funny Face; Funny Girl; Funny Lady; Gang's All Here; The Gay Divorcee; Gay Purree; Gentlemen Prefer Blondes; George White's 1935 Scandals; George White's Scandals (1934); George White's Scandals 1945; G.I. Blues; Gigi (1958); Girl Crazy; Girl Most Likely (1958); Girl of the Golden West; Girls! Girls! Girls!; Give My Regards to Broad Street; Give My Regards to Broadway; Give the Girl a Break; Go into Your Dance; Godspell; Gold Diggers in Paris; Gold Diggers of 1933; Gold Diggers of 1935; Gold Diggers of 1937; Gold Diggers of Broadway; Goldwyn Follies; Good News; Goodbye Mr. Chips (1939); Goodbye Mr. Chips (1969); Graffiti Bridge; Grease; Grease 2; The Great Caruso; The Great Mouse Detective; The Great Waltz (1938); The Great Waltz (1972); The Great Ziegfeld; Greenwich Village; Guys and Dolls; Gypsy; Hair; Hairspray; Half a Sixpence; Hans Christian Andersen; Harum Scarum; The Harvey Girls; Head; Hello Dolly; Hello Frisco Hello; High Society; The Hit Parade of 1943; The Hit Parade of 1947; Hit the Deck; Holiday in Mexico; Holiday Inn; Hollywood Hotel; How to Succeed in Business without Really Trying; I Don't Care Girl; I Dood It!; I Love Melvin; I'll See You in My Dreams; In the Good Old Summertime; The Innocents of Paris (1929); Invitation to the Dance; Irene; Irish Eyes Are Smiling; Irma La Douce; It Happened in Brooklyn; It's a Date; It's Always Fair Weather; I Wonder Who's Kissing Her Now; Jailhouse Rock; Jesus Christ, Superstar; Jolson Sings Again; The Jolson Story; The Joy of Living; Jupiter's Darling; The Kid from Spain; Kid Millions; The King and I; King of Jazz; Kismet (1955); Kiss Me Kate (1953); Kiss the Boys Goodbye; The Kissing Bandit; Knickerbocker Holiday; La Traviata; Lady Be Good; Le Million; Let's Dance; Let's Do It Again (1953); Let's Face It; Let's Make Love; Li'l Abner; Lili; Lisztomania; A Little Night Music; The Little Prince; The Little Shop of Horrors (1986); Live a Little, Love a Lot; Looking for Love; Lost Horizon (1973); Louisiana Purchase; Love Me or Leave Me; Love Me Tonight; Love Parade; Lovely to Look At; Loves of Carmen; Lucky Me; Mack the Knife; Mad About Music; Mame; Man of La Mancha; Mardi Gras; Mary Poppins; Meet Me After the Show; Meet Me in Las Vegas; Meet Me in St. Louis; The Merry Widow (1934); The Merry Widow (1952); Metropolitan (1935); The Mikado; Million Dollar Mermaid; Miss Sadie Thompson; Mississippi; Moon Over Miami; Movie Movie; Mr. Music; The Muppet Christmas Carol; The Muppet Movie; The Muppets Take Manhattan; Murder at the Vanities; Muscle Beach Party; Music For Millions; Music in My Heart; The Music Man; My Gal Sal; My Fair Lady; My Sister Eileen (1955); My Wild Irish Rose; Nancy Goes to Rio; Naughty But Nice; Naughty Marietta; Neptune's Daughter; New Orleans; Newsies; Night and Day (1946); The Night Is Young; No No Nanette (1930); No No Nanette (1940); Nutcracker (1993); Nutcracker-The Motion Picture (1986); Oh, What a Lovely War; Oklahoma!; Oliver!; Oliver and Company; On a Clear Day You Can See Forever; On the Riviera; On the Town; On Your Toes; One from the Heart; One Night of Love; Orchestra Wives; Otello; Out of This World; Paint Your Wagon; Pajama Game; Pal Joey; Panama Hattie; Pardners; Parsifal Party Girl; Pennies from Heaven (1936); Pennies from Heaven (1981); Pepe; Perils of Pauline; Pete's Dragon; Peter Pan; Pinocchio; Pirate; Pirates of Penzance; Poor Little Rich Girl; Popeye; Red Garters; Red Shoes; Rhythm on the Range; Rich, Young and Pretty; Roberta; Rock Around the Clock; Rock-a Doodle; The Rocky Horror Picture Show; Roman Scandals; Romance on the High Seas; Rose Marie (1936); Rose Marie (1954); The Royal Wedding; Sarafina!; Saturday Night Fever; School Daze; Scrooge (1970); Second Chorus; Second Fiddle; Sergeant Pepper's Lonely Hearts Club Band; Seven Brides for Seven Brothers; 1776; Shall We Dance?; Shock Treatment; Shout; Showboat (1936); Showboat (1951); Silk Stockings; Sing; Sing You Sinners; Singing in the Rain; Slipper and the Rose; Small Town Girl (1953); Smiling Lieutenant; A Song Is Born; The Sound of Music; Song of Norway; Song of the Islands; Song of the South; South Pacific; Speedway; Spinout; Springtime in the Rockies; Stage Door Canteen; Stand Up and Cheer; Star!; A Star Is Born (1954); Stars and Stripes Forever; Starstruck; State Fair (1945); State Fair (1962); Stork Club; Stormy Weather; Story of Vernon and Irene Castle; Strike Up the Band; Sweet Charity; Sweet Rosie O'Grady; Sweethearts; Swing Time; Take Me Out to the Ball Game; Tales of Hoffman; The Tall Guy; Tammy and the Bachelor; Tap; Tea for Two; Thank God It's Friday; Thank Your Lucky Stars; That Certain Age; That Lady in Ermine; That Night in Rio; That's Dancin'!; That's Entertainment; That's Entertainment Part Two; The Young Girls of Rochefort; There's No Business Like Show Business; Thin Ice; This Could Be the Night; This Is the Army; Thoroughly Modern Millie; Thousands Cheer; Three Little Words; The Three Musketeers (1939); The Threepenny Opera; The Thrill of a Romance; Thumbelina; Tickle Me; Till the Clouds Roll By; Times Square; Tin Pan Alley; Tom Sawyer; Tommy; Tonight and Every Night; Top Hat; Top of the Town; Two Girls and a Sailor; The Unsinkable Molly Brown; Viva Las Vegas; Waikiki Wedding; Wee Willie Winkie; West Point Story; West Side Story; When My Baby Smiles at Me; When You're in Love; Where Do We Go from Here?; Whoopee; The Wiz; A Woman Is a Woman; Wonder Bar; Words and Music; Xanadu; Yankee Doodle Dandy; Yentl; Yellow Submarine; Yolanda and the Thief; You Were Never Lovelier; You'll Never Get Rich; Young at Heart; Ziegfeld Follies; The Ziegfeld Girl

Musicals-Animated: see also *Musical-Fantasy: Cartoons: CHILDREN'S: Animation-Partial:* An American Tail; American Tail 2; Aristocats; Fantasia; Gay Purree; The Great Mouse Detective; Heavy Metal; Oliver and Company; Peter Pan; Pinocchio; Rock-a Doodle; Song of the South; Thumbelina; Yellow Submarine

Musicals-Contemporary: see *Music Movies*

Musicals-Disco Era: see also *Disco Era: 1970s: Dance Movies:* Can't Stop the Music; Car Wash; FM; Roller Boogie; Saturday Night Fever; Sergeant Pepper's

Lonely Hearts Club Band; Thank God It's Friday; Xanadu

Musicals-Hippie: Godspell; Hair; Jesus Christ Superstar

Musicals-Operettas: see also *Opera:* *Opera Singers:* Balalaika; Chocolate Soldier; Firefly; Maytime; The Mikado; Naughty Marietta; Pirates of Penzance; Rose Marie (1936); Rose Marie (1954)

Musicals-Rock Opera: Jesus Christ Superstar; Tommy; Lisztomania; Pink Floyd's The Wall; Quadrophenia

Musical Spoofs: see *Spoofs-Musical*

Musicals-Westerns: see also *WESTERNS:* The Kissing Bandit; Paint Your Wagon

Music Composer Biographies: see also *Music Dies: Musicians: Biographies:* All the Mornings of the World; Amadeus; Bound For Glory; City for Conquest; Competition; Constant Nymph (1933); Constant Nymph (1943); The Great Waltz (1938); The Great Waltz (1972); I Dream of Jeannie; Immortal Beloved; Impromptu; Irish Eyes Are Smiling; Lisztomania; Mahler; The Music Lovers; My Gal Sal; Night and Day (1946); Nocturne; Rhapsody in Blue; Silk Stockings; Song of Love; Song of Norway; A Song to Remember; Song Without End; St. Louis Blues; Stars and Stripes Forever; Stormy Weather; Swanee River; 32 Short Films about Glenn Gould; Three Little Words; Till the Clouds Roll By; Tin Pan Alley; Words and Music

Music Dies (biographies of musicians or singers involving their deaths): see also *Deaths of Celebrities: Biographies:* *Singers: Musicians: TRAGEDY:* Bird; The Buddy Holly Story; Doors; The Glenn Miller Story; The Josephine Baker Story; LaBamba; Lady Sings the Blues; Love Me or Leave Me; Sid and Nancy; Singing Fool; Sweet Dreams

Musicians: see also *Biographies: Music Dies: Music Composer Biographies:* *Entertainment: Pianists: Jazz Players:* *MUSICALS: Music Movies:* Absolute Beginners; Airheads; Alexander's Ragtime Band; Alice Doesn't Live Here Anymore; All Night Long (1961); All the Fine Young Cannibals; All You Need is Cash; Allegro Non Troppo; Amadeus; American Hotwax; Backbeat; The Benny Goodman Story; Beyond the Valley of the Dolls; Bird; Birth of the Blues; Bitter Sweet (1933); Bitter Sweet (1940); Blame it on the Night; The Blues Brothers;

Blues in the Night; Bound For Glory; Break of Hearts; Breaking Glass; Buddy Holly Story; Buddy's Song; Bye Bye Birdie; Can't Stop the Music; Candy Mountain; The Commitments; The Cotton Club; Crossroads (1986); Deception (1946); The Decline of Western Civilization; The Decline of Western Civilization 2: The Metal Years; Dogs in Space; Don't Look Back; Easter Parade; Eddy Duchin Story; El Mariachi; The Five Heartbeats; Five Pennies; The Gene Krupa Story; The Getting of Wisdom; The Glenn Miller Story; Good Times; Graffiti Bridge; Great Balls of Fire; Greenwich Village; A Hard Day's Night; Head; Hearts of Fire; High Tide; The Hit Parade of 1943; The Hit Parade of 1947; Honeysuckle Rose; Humoresque; I Dream of Jeannie; I Dream Too Much; I Wanna Hold Your Hand; I Wonder Who's Kissing Her Now; Idiot's Delight; Idolmaker; Impromptu; Interlude (1957); Interlude (1968); Intermezzo (1939); It Happened in Brooklyn; A Kiss in the Dark; Lady Sings the Blues; The Last Waltz; Laughter; Let's Get Lost; Letter From an Unknown Woman; Listen Up; The Lives of Quincy Jones; Lisztomania; The Lonely Passion of Judith Hearne; Love and Hisses; Love Story (1944); Love With the Proper Stranger; Loves of a Blonde; Mad Love; Madame Sousatzka; Mahler; Mambo Kings; Mephisto Waltz; Missing Pieces; Mo' Better Blues; Mr. Music; The Music Room; The Music Teacher; My Love Came Back; Nashville; Naughty But Nice; New Orleans; New York, New York; Once More with Feeling; One Trick Pony; Orchestra Wives; Pal Joey; Paris Blues; Pete Kelly's Blues; Pillow Talk; Playing for Time; Quadrophenia; Rat Race; Return of Spinal Tap; Rhapsody; Rhapsody in Blue; Running on Empty; Samantha; Satisfaction; Second Chorus; The Seventh Veil; Shame (1968); Sid and Nancy; Silk Stockings; Singles; Smithereens; Some Kind of Wonderful; Song of Love; A Song to Remember; Song Without End; The Songwriter; St. Louis Blues; Sticky Fingers; Stop Making Sense; Stormy Weather; Strike Up the Band; That Uncertain Feeling; This is Spinal Tap; Too Late Blues; Un Coeur en Hiver; Unfaithfully Yours (1948); Unfaithfully Yours (1984); Up in Smoke; W.W. & The Dixie Dancekings; Wayne's World;

Wayne's World 2; Welcome to L.A.; When Tomorrow Comes; Who Is Harry Kellerman . . . ; Wild in the Streets; Wild West; Words and Music; The World of Henry Orient; The Wrong Man; Xanadu; You Light Up My Life; Young at Heart; Young Man with a Horn

Music Movies (with music and/or songs, a notable soundtrack, though not necessarily a real musical): see also *Musical Drama: MUSICALS: Musicians:* *Music Video Style:* Absolute Beginners; An American Tail; American Tail 2; Aria; Artists and Models (1955); Beach Party; Beat Street; Bird; Bitter Sweet (1933); Blue Hawaii; Body Slam; Bodyguard; Bottoms Up; The Boys from Syracuse; Breakin'; Breakin' 2: Electric Boogaloo; Breaking Glass; The Bride Wore Red; The Buddy Holly Story; Buddy's Song; Cabaret; Can't Stop the Music; Car Wash; Carmen (1983); A Chorus Line; The Commitments; The Cotton Club; Dancing in the Dark; Darling Lili; Diamond Horseshoe; Dirty Dancing; Dixie; Doors; Earth Girls are Easy; Expresso Bongo; Fame; Fanny; First Love; The Five Heartbeats; Flashdance; FM; Follow That Dream; Forbidden Dance; G.I. Blues; Girls! Girls! Girls!; Give My Regards to Broad Street; Good Companions (1933); Good Companions (1956); Good Times; Goodbye Mr. Chips (1939); Goodbye Mr. Chips (1969); Graffiti Bridge; Great Balls of Fire; The Great Waltz (1938); The Great Waltz (1972); Hairspray; Hallelujah!; A Hard Day's Night; Harum Scarum; The Head; Heavy Metal; I Could Go on Singing; I Don't Care Girl; I Dood It!; I Dream Too Much; I Wonder Who's Kissing Her Now; Inside Daisy Clover; It Happened in Brooklyn; King Creole; The Knack; Knickerbocker Holiday; Lambada; Leadbelly; The Little Princess; Living in a Big Way; Looking for Love; Love Me or Leave Me; Love Me Tender; Make Mine Music; Mardi Gras; Metropolitan (1935); Miss Sadie Thompson; Mississippi; Moon Over Miami; Music Room; My Gal Sal; Naughty But Nice; New Orleans; New York, New York; Night and Day (1946); Pardners; Quadrophenia; Rhapsody in Blue; Rock Around the Clock; Rock-a Doodle; Roller Boogie; Rose; Roustabout; Sarafina!; Saturday Night Fever; Sergeant Pepper's Lonely Hearts Club Band; Shock Treatment; Shout; Sing; Sister Act; The Smiling Lieutenant; Sparkle; Speedway;

Spinout; St. Louis Blues; A Star Is Born (1954); A Star Is Born (1976); Starstruck; Staying Alive; Story of Vernon and Irene Castle; Streets of Fire; Suburbia; Swing Kids; The Tall Guy; Tammy and the Bachelor; Tap; Thank God It's Friday; That's Entertainment; That's Entertainment Part Two; Till the Clouds Roll By; Times Square; Tommy; The Trouble with Girls; Under the Cherry Moon; Urban Cowboy; Viva Las Vegas; Where the Boys Are; Where the Boys Are '84; Wild in the Country; A Woman Is a Woman

Music Video Style (having visual style used in videos, or containing video sequences within film): see also *Rockumentaries: MUSICALS: Dance Movies: Music Movies:* Absolute Beginners; Allegro Non Troppo; Aria; Bring on the Night; Earth Girls are Easy; Fantasia; Footloose; Give My Regards to Broad Street; Grandview, USA; A Hard Day's Night; Head; Koyaanisqatsi; Pink Floyd: The Wall; Powaqqatsi, Life in Transformation; Streets of Fire; Strictly Ballroom; Tommy

Muslim/Islamic People: see *Arab People: Middle East*

Mute People: see also *Deaf People: Blind People: Disabled People: Disabled People in Jeopardy:* Angel Baby; Baxter (1972); Children of a Lesser God; Every Man for Himself (and God Against All); Gigot; The Heart Is a Lonely Hunter; Lightning Jack; Object of Beauty; Paisan; The Piano; Planet of the Apes; Quest for Fire; Spiral Staircase (1946); Spiral Staircase (1975); Suspect

MYSTERY: see also *MURDER MYSTERY: Mystery-Whodunits: MURDER: THRILLERS: Medical Mystery: Cures/Solutions-Search for: (italics denotes non-murder mystery)* The Accused (1948); Accused of Murder; The Adventures of Ford Fairlane; The Adventures of Sherlock Holmes; The Adventures of Sherlock Holmes' Smarter Brother; The Advocate; After Office Hours; *Agnes of God;* Alice, Sweet Alice; *All the President's Men;* All-American Murder; The Alphabet Murders; Alphaville; The Amateur; Ambulance; American Gigolo; *Anastasia (1956); Anastasia (1984);* Anatomy of a Murder; And Then There Were None; Angel Heart; Another Thin Man; Apartment Zero; Appointment with Death; Backfire; Bad

Day at Black Rock; Basic Instinct; Bears & I; Being at Home with Claude; Betrayed (1989); The Big Easy; The Big Fix; The Big Sleep (1946); The Big Sleep (1977); The Big Steal; Black Angel; Black Marble; Black Rain (1989); Black Widow (1954); Black Widow (1987); *Blade Runner;* Blink; Blood Relatives; Bloodline; Blow Out; Blow Up; The Blue Dahlia; Blue Velvet; Body Double; Body Heat; Body in the Library; Body of Evidence; Boomerang (1947); The Boston Strangler; The Bourne Identity; The Boys from Brazil; Brasher Doubloon; Breakheart Pass; The Bride Wore Black; Brubaker; Bulldog Drummond (1929); Bulldog Drummond at Bay; Bulldog Drummond Strikes Back; Bullitt; Bunny Lake is Missing; The Burglar; Cage of Gold; Cahill: United States Marshal; Calling Bulldog Drummond; Cancel My Reservation; A Case for Murder; Castle in the Desert; Cat Chaser; Caught in the Act; Cause for Alarm; Chandler; Charade; Charlie Chan and the Curse of the Dragon Queen; Chinatown; Chronicle of a Death Foretold; Clash by Night; Cloak and Dagger (1984); Clockers; Club Paradise; Cold Heaven; Color Me Dead; Coma; Come Back Charleston Blue; Compromising Positions; Confidentially Yours; Consenting Adults; The Conversation; Cop au Vin; Cotton Comes to Harlem; Criminal Law; Crossfire; A Cry in the Dark; Cutter and Bone; D. O. A. (1949); D. O. A. (1988); Dark Corner; Dark Mirror; Dark Wind; Day of the Dolphin; Dead Again; Dead Men Don't Wear Plaid; Dead Pool; Dead Reckoning; Deadly Affair; Deadly Trap; Dear Inspector; Death on the Nile; Death Warrant; Deceived; Deception (1992); Defenseless; Desert Fury; The Detective (1954); The Detective (1968); The Detective (1985); Detour; *Diabolique (1955);* Dial M For Murder; Dick Tracy; The Disappearance of Christina; Dolores Claiborne; Dominique; Dragonwyck; Dressed to Kill; The Drowning Pool; Dying Room Only; Endangered Species; Endless Game; *Equus;* Every Man for Himself (and God Against All); Everybody Wins; Evil Under the Sun; Ex-Mrs. Bradford; Experiment Perilous; Eye of the Storm; Eyes in the Night; The Eyes of Laura Mars; Eyewitness (1981); Fallen Idol; Farewell, My Lovely (1944); Farewell, My Lovely (1975); Fast

Company; Fatal Vision; The File on Thelma Jordon; Final Analysis; Finger of Guilt; A Fire in the Sky; Flesh and Bone; Fog over Frisco; The Foreign Correspondent; Foreign Intrigue; Formula; The Fourth Man; The Fourth Story; Fried Green Tomatoes; From the Life of the Marionettes; The Fuller Brush Girl; The Fuller Brush Man; Ghost; The Glenn Miller Story; Gorillas in the Mist; Gorky Park; Gotham; The Great Lover (1949); Green for Danger; The Green Man; Ground Zero; The Groundstar Conspiracy; Guilty as Sin; Gumshoe; Hammerhead; Hammett; Hangar 18; Harper; Her Alibi; Here Come the Girls; The Hidden; Hidden 2; Hidden Agenda; Homicide; Hound of the Baskervilles (1939); Hound of the Baskervilles (1959); Hound of the Baskervilles (1977); Hysteria; I Love a Mystery; I Love Trouble (1947); I, the Jury (1953); I, The Jury (1982); I Wake Up Screaming; Immortal Beloved; Impulse (1984); In a Lonely Place; In the Heat of the Night; The Inquisitor; The Inspector Calls; Internal Affairs; Internecine Project; Intruder in the Dust; Investigation of a Citizen Above Suspicion; The Ipcress File; Iron Maze; Island (1980); It's a Wonderful World; It's in the Bag; Jack the Ripper (1958); Jagged Edge; January Man; Jennifer 8; JFK; Johnny Angel; Just Cause; The Kennel Murder Case; Kill Me Again; Killer McCoy; Killjoy; Kiss Me Deadly; Lady from Shanghai; Lady in Cement; Lady in Question; Lady in the Car with Glasses and a Gun; Lady in the Lake; Lady in White; Lady of Burlesque; Lady on a Train; The Lady Vanishes (1938); The Lady Vanishes (1979); Ladykiller (1992); The Last Boy Scout; Last of Sheila; Last Wave; The Late Show; Laura; Legal Eagles; Legend of Lylah Clare; Letter to Three Wives; Liebestraum; The Life of Emile Zola; The List of Adrian Messenger; London Belongs to Me; The Long Goodbye; Long Live Life; Looker; Lovely Way to Die; Mad Miss Manton; Madhouse; Magus; The Maltese Falcon (1931); The Maltese Falcon (1941); The Man in the Attic; Man on a Swing; Man on the Eiffel Tower; Man Trouble; The Man Who Haunted Himself; *The Man Who Knew Too Much (1934); The Man Who Knew Too Much (1956);* The Man Who Watched Trains Go By; The Manchurian Candidate; Manhattan Murder Mystery; Manhunter; Mark of the

N

Nannies/Governesses: see *Babysitters*
Napoleon: see also *Military Leaders:*
France: Leaders-Tyrant: The Adventures
of Gerard; Conquest; Desiree; Eagle in a
Cage; House of Rothschild; Napoleon;
Sea Devils (1953); Waterloo
Narrated Films: see also *Character*
Studies: Soliloquies: Subjective Camera:
Across the Wide Missouri; The Affairs of
Dobie Gillis; The Age of Innocence
(1993); Alfie; All the Mornings of the
World; Angie; Annie Hall; Another
Woman; Au Revoir, les Enfants; The
Autobiography of Miss Jane Pittman; The
Bad and the Beautiful; Between Two
Women; Bitter Moon; The Body
Snatchers; Brief Encounter (1946); A
Brief History of Time; Bright Lights, Big
City; A Bronx Tale; Burning Bed; Carlito's
Way; Cold Sassy Tree; Criss Cross (1992);
A Dangerous Woman; Day For Night;
Days of Heaven; Deep Cover; The Devil's
Eye; A Diary for Timothy; Edward, My
Son; Eleni; The Escape Artist; Father of
the Bride (1991); Ferris Bueller's Day
Off; Forrest Gump; Frances; Fried Green
Tomatoes; The Gentle Sex; The Glass
Menagerie (1950); The Glass Menagerie
(1973); The Glass Menagerie (1987);
Glen or Glenda?; Good Fellas; The Great
Gatsby (1949); The Great Gatsby (1974);
The Hellstrom Chronicle; Husbands and
Wives; I Don't Care Girl; I Know Why the
Caged Bird Sings; I Ought to Be in
Pictures; I Remember Mama; The
Incredible Journey; Indecent Proposal;
Intervista; The Killer Inside Me; Kuffs;
LaRonde (1950); La Ronde (1964); Letter
to Three Wives; Little Big Man; Lola
Montes; Look Who's Talking; Look Who's
Talking Now; Look Who's Talking Too;
Lost in Yonkers; Louisiana Story; Lover;
Lydia; The Magnificent Ambersons;
Mahabharata; Making Love; The
Marrying Kind; Mary Poppins; The
Matchmaker; A Matter of Time; Memoirs
of an Invisible Man; Mina Tannenbaum;
Mosquito Coast; My Favorite Brunette;
My Favorite Year; My Life; A Night in the
Life of Jimmy Reardon; Now I'll Tell; The
Opposite Sex and How to Live With
Them; Our Town; Patton; The Pickup
Artist; Platoon; Poison Ivy (1992); The
Princess Bride; Prospero's Books; Psycho
4; Rachel, Rachel; Radio Days; Rambling
Rose; Rashomon; Red Shoe Diaries;
Risky Business; Romeo is Bleeding;
Secret Beyond the Door; The Shawshank
Redemption; Sophie's Choice; Stand by
Me; Stevie; Sunset Boulevard; Tales from
the Darkside: The Movie; Tea and
Sympathy; This Happy Breed;
Threesome; To Kill a Mockingbird;
Topkapi!; 21; Valley of the Dolls;
Voyager; Who is Harry Kellerman . . .;
Whore

Nashville: see *Country Music: Country*
Singers
Native Americans-Modern (modern
day Indians): see also *Indians-*
Americans: Cheyenne Autumn; Powwow
Highway; Renegades; Spirit Rider;
Thunderheart; War Party
Naturalistic Films: see *Quiet Little*
Films: Art Films: Ordinary People
Stories: Southerns: Midwestern Life:
1970s: Neo-Realistic Films
Nature-Back to: see also *City vs.*
Country: Rural Life: Adam at 6 A.M.; The
Adventures of Robinson Crusoe; The
Adventures of the Wilderness Family; At
Play in the Fields of the Lord; Baby
Boom; Bear; Bears & I; The Birds; The
Birds II; Continental Divide; Cross Creek;
Deliverance; Distant Thunder (1988); The
Egg and I; Electric Horseman; Elephant
Boy; Elvira Madigan; The Fire Next Time;
Forest Rangers; Free Willy; The Great
Outdoors; The Hellstrom Chronicle;
Hemingway's Adventures of a Young Man;
Honkytonk Man; Iceman; Ice Palace;
Islands in the Stream; Jungle Book (1967);
Jungle Book (1994); Koyaanisqatsi; Lake
Consequence; Louisiana Story; Lunch on
the Grass; Mosquito Coast; Never Cry
Wolf; Quest for Fire; A River Runs
Through It; Roots of Heaven; Tarzan's
New York Adventure; The Tempest; Valley
Obscured by the Clouds

Nazi Stories: see also *Anti-Semitism: Concentration Camps: World War II Era: Hate Crimes: White Supremacists: Germany:* Above Suspicion; Action in Arabia; Adventures of Tartu; The African Queen; All Through the Night; Armored Command; Assault; Assisi Underground; The Attic: The Hiding of Anne Frank; Au Revoir, les Enfants; Berlin Express; Bittere Emte; The Boys from Brazil; Cabaret; Candide; Captive Heart; Cloak and Dagger (1946); Confessions of a Nazi Spy; The Conformist; The Damned; A Day in October; Diary of Anne Frank (1959); Dunera Boys; Enemies, A Love Story; Escape; Europa, Europa; Eyes in the Night; Fallen Sparrow; FBI Story; Five Fingers; Fly By Night; Force Ten from Navarone; The Foreign Correspondent; Four Sons; Garden of the Finzi-Continis; Golden Earrings; The Great Dictator; The Great Escape; The Great Escape 2: The Untold Story; Guns of Navarone; Hangmen Also Die; Hanussen; Heimat; Hitler Gang; Hitler—The Last Ten Days; The Holcroft Covenant; The House on 92nd Street; The House on Carroll Street; In Our Time; Indiana Jones and The Last Crusade; Indiana Jones and The Temple of Doom; Inside Moves; Ivan's Childhood; Joan of Paris; Jud Suess; Judgment at Nuremburg; The Keep; Kelly's Heroes; Lacombe, Lucien; The Lady Vanishes (1938); The Lady Vanishes (1979); Lassiter; Lisa (1961); Love in Germany; Lucky Star; Magic Face; The Man I Married; Marathon Man; Max and Helen; Mein Kampf; Mephisto; Miracle of the White Stallions; The Moon Is Down; Mr. Klein; The Music Box; Nazi Agent; Night in Casablanca; Night of the Generals; The Night Porter; Night Train to Munich; North Star; Notorious; The Odessa File; Olympische Spiele; Once Upon a Honeymoon; Open City; Operation Amsterdam; Operation Crossbow; Panama Hattie; The Passage; The Pedestrian; Playing for Time; Raid on Rommel; Raiders of the Lost Ark; Reunion; Revolt of Job; The Rocketeer; RomperStomper; Run for the Sun; Sahara (1943); Salo: 120 Days of Sodom; Salon Kitty; Schindler's List; Scotland Yard; Sea Wolves; The Secret of Santa Vittoria; The Serpent's Egg; The Seventh Cross; Shining Through; Shoeshine; Shop on Main Street; Son of Lassie; Sophie's Choice; The Sound of Music; The Stranger; Swing Kids; The Tenth Man; 13 Rue Madeleine; This Land Is Mine; Time to Love and a Time to Die; Tin Drum; To Be or Not to Be (1942); To Be or Not to Be (1983); To Have and Have Not; Tobruk; Top Secret!; Train; Triumph of the Spirit; Triumph of the Will; Victory; Watch on the Rhine; White Rose

Nazis-Neo: see also *Nazi Stories: Hate Crimes: Anti-Semitism: White Supremacists: Germany: World War II Era*

Neighbors-Troublesome: see also *Nuisances: Malicious Menaces: Roommates from Hell:* The Apartment; Apartment Zero; Barton Fink; The 'burbs; Consenting Adults; Cops and Robbersons; Fade to Black (1993); Flare Up; Fright Night; Good Neighbor Sam; The Little Girl Who Lives Down the Lane; Love Nest; Madness of the Heart; My Reputation; Neighbors; The Seven-Year Itch; Star Spangled Girl; Strangers, the Story of a Mother and Daughter; Twin Beds; The Woman Next Door; Under the Yum Yum Tree

Neo-Realistic Films (art films, mostly from Italy in the postwar years, noted for a new frankness and for not having clear-cut endings): see also *Art Films: Film History: Avant-Garde Films: Italian Films: World War II-Post Era: 1940s: 1950s:* Bitter Rice; Francis, God's Jester; The Last Picture Show; L'Avventura; Ossessione; Paisan; Stromboli

Nerds (shy, awkward men): see also *Nerds & Babes: Misfits: Wallflowers: Scientists:* The Affairs of Dobie Gillis; Alfredo, Alfredo; American Friends; An Angel at My Table; Annie Hall; Artists and Models (1955); Ball of Fire; Barnacle Bill (1957); Ben; Big Man On Campus; Bocaccio '70; Bringing Up Baby; Can't Buy Me Love; Champagne for Caesar; Cinderella Jones; Cityslickers; Class Act; The Conformist; Don't Just Stand There; Don't Tell Her It's Me; Electric Dreams; The Enchanted Cottage; Ernest Saves Christmas; Falcon and the Snowman; The Freshman (1925); The Freshman (1990); Fright Night; The Ghost and Mr. Chicken; Goodbye Columbus; Goodbye Mr. Chips (1939); Goodbye Mr. Chips (1969); The Great Lover (1949); Hoffman; Impromptu; The Incredible Mr. Limpet; Irma La Douce; Jetsons Movie; Johnny Stecchino; The Kid from Brooklyn; A Kiss in the Dark; The Knack; L'Invitation; Ladies' Man (1947); Ladies' Man (1961); Lady Eve; The Lavender Hill Mob; Little Fauss and Big Halsey; Little Shop of Horrors (1960); Little Shop of Horrors (1986); The Lonely Guy; Love and Death; Love God?; Love Potion #9; Mad Wednesday; Male Animal; Marty; Mask (1994); The Mating Game; Merry Andrew; Meteor Man; Metropolitan (1990); My Bodyguard; Never on Sunday; New Leaf; Night Games; The Nutty Professor (1963); The Owl and the Pussycat; The Pad, and How to Use It; Pardon Mon Affaire; Play It Again, Sam; A Rage in Harlem; The Rain; Robert et Robert; Rock a Bye Baby; Rubin & Ed; The Scapegoat; Seven Chances; The Seven-Year Itch; The Shakiest Gun in the West; She's Working Her Way Through College; Sleeper; Son of Paleface; A Song Is Born; Soup for One; The Stand In; Steamboat Bill Jr.; The Sterile Cuckoo; Stolen Kisses; Strange Bargain; Strictly Business; Take the Money and Run; Tell Me that You Love Me, Junie Moon; Ten; The Thief Who Came to Dinner; Topaze (1933); Toxic Avenger; Toxic Avenger, Part II; Toxic Avenger Part III; Travels with My Aunt; Trust; Twisted; UHF; Up in Arms; Valentino Returns; The War Between Men and Women; What's Up, Doc?; Whoopee; Will Success Spoil Rock Hunter?; Willard; Woman in Red; You're a Big Boy Now

Nerds & Babes (shy, awkward men with beautiful women): see also *Nerds: Coming of Age: Wallflowers & Hunks: Romance-Opposites Attract:* Annie Hall; Artists and Models (1955); Big Man On Campus; Can't Buy Me Love; Cinderella Jones; Don't Tell Her It's Me; Electric Dreams; The Girl Can't Help It; Goodbye Columbus; Goodbye Mr. Chips (1939); Goodbye Mr. Chips (1969); The Great Lover (1949); Hoffman; Into the Night; Irma La Douce; Ladies' Man (1947); Ladies' Man (1961); Lady Eve; Love and Death; Love God?; Mask (1994); Never on Sunday; Owl and the Pussycat; Pad, and How to Use It; Play it Again, Sam; Public Eye; A Rage in Harlem; The Rain; Rock a Bye Baby; Roxanne; The Seven-Year Itch; So Fine; Soup for One; The Stand In; Steamboat Bill Jr.; Take the Money and Run; Ten; Tin Men; Valentino Returns; Vivacious Lady; Who's That Girl?; Whoopee; Will Success Spoil Rock Hunter?; Woman in Red

Nerds & Wallflowers: see also *Nerds: Wallflowers: Shy People:* Metropolitan (1990); New Leaf; The Sterile Cuckoo

Nerds vs. Macho Men: see also *Extroverted vs. Introverted: Men in Conflict:* The Adventures of Bullwhip Griffin; Cityslickers; Paper Lion; Revenge of the Nerds; Three O'Clock High

Nervous Breakdowns: see also *Mental Illness: Neurotic People: Asylums: Therapy: Psychologists:* Andy Warhol's Heat; Belly of an Architect; Birdy; Blue Thunder; Breaking Glass; Bright Lights, Big City; Can Hieronymus Merkin Ever Forget Mercy Humppe and Find True Happiness?; Cat on a Hot Tin Roof (1958); Cat on a Hot Tin Roof (1984); Chattahoochee; Coal Miner's Daughter; The Conversation; Cop; The Countdown; Crazy People; Dangerous; Dark Obsession; Dark Waters; Day of the Locust; The End of Innocence; Face to Face; The Fisher King; The Goalie's Anxiety at the Penalty Kick; Hamlet (1948); Hamlet (1964); Hamlet (1969); Hamlet (1991); A Hatful of Rain; How I Won the War; I'm Dancing as Fast as I Can; Images; Ironweed; Jacob's Ladder; Jo Jo Dancer, Your Life is Calling; The Killer Inside Me; Killing of Sister George; La Chienne; La Notte; Lady in the Dark; Last Command; Let's Scare Jessica to Death; Long Day's Journey Into Night; The Lost Language of Cranes; Lovesick; Mad Wednesday; Magic; Montenegro; A Month in the Country; Mr. Jones; Naked Lunch; No Man's Land; Numero Deux; Of Human Bondage (1934); Of Human Bondage (1946); Of Human Bondage (1964); Opening Night; Outrage (1956); Paris By Night; The Pawnbroker; Persona; Plenty; Postcards from the Edge; The Prisoner of Second Avenue; Rain People; Red Desert; Reflections in a Golden Eye; Repulsion; The Roman Spring of Mrs. Stone; Rosie; Secret Friends; Sergeant; A Shock to the System; Silence; Snakepit; The Sniper; Splendor in the Grass; A Streetcar Named Desire; Summer Wishes, Winter Dreams; Sweet Bird of Youth; The Tenant; Tender Is the Night; They Shoot Horses, Don't They?; Tin Drum; Twelve O'Clock High; Twilight's Last Gleaming; Under the Volcano; Valley of the Dolls; Vampire's Kiss; The Way of All Flesh (1928); The Way of All Flesh (1940); Wetherby;

Women on the Verge of a Nervous Breakdown

Neurotic People: see also *Therapy: Pyschologists: Depression: Alienation: Mental Illness:* Annie Hall; Apartment Zero; Broadcast News; Can She Bake a Cherry Pie?; Desperate Living; The Dresser; The Effect of Gamma Rays on Man-in-the-Moon Marigolds; The Fisher King; Heartbreak Kid; High Heels; Hilda Crane; Inside Monkey Zetterland; Made for Each Other; Manhattan; Naked in New York; On a Clear Day You Can See Forever; Opening Night; Petulia; Plenty; Scenes from a Mall; Semi-Tough; Send Me No Flowers; Separate Tables; Soapdish; Soup for One; Tell Me that You Love Me, Junie Moon; When Harry Met Sally; Woman Times Seven; Women on the Verge of a Nervous Breakdown; X, Y, & Zee

New England: see also *Boston: New York Life:* By Love Possessed; Ethan Fromme; Little Women (1933); Little Women (1949); Little Women (1978); Little Women (1994); Metropolitan (1990); Our Town; Salem's Lot; The Scarlet Letter (1926); The Scarlet Letter (1934); The Scarlet Letter (1980); Scent of a Woman; The Sterile Cuckoo; The Stranger; Sweet Liberty; Sweethearts Dance

New in Town (the story is centered around a person who's just come into town): see also *Drifters: Foreign Misfits: Fish out of Water Stories:* Angel in My Pocket; Bad Day at Black Rock; The Butcher's Wife; A Chorus of Disapproval; The Farmer Takes a Wife; A Fistful of Dollars; Flamingo Road; The Flim Flam Man; Follow That Dream; The Frisco Kind (1979); The Fugitive Kind; The Fury (1936); A Handful of Dust; Heathers; The Inspector Calls; Intruder; The Karate Kid; The Kentuckian; Lost Boys; Montana; Not of This Earth (1956); Pet Sematary; Pet Sematary 2; Raggedy Man; Rainmaker; Ride the Pink Horse; Silver Lode; Sleepwalkers; Tuff Turf; Three O'Clock High; The Unbelievable Truth; Widows' Peak

Newlyweds: see also *Lovers-Live-in: Marriage Comedy: Marriage Drama: Situation Comedy:* About Face; Alfredo, Alfredo; And Now the Screaming Starts; Back From the Dead; Bad Girl; Banjo on My Knee; Barefoot in the Park; Bed and Board; Beetlejuice; Behave Yourself!;

Best Intentions; Caged Fear; Cat on a Hot Tin Roof (1958); Cat on a Hot Tin Roof (1984); Claudia; The Conspirator; Diana: Her True Story; The Doctor Takes a Wife; Doughgirls; Elephant Walk; Emma; The Farmer Takes a Wife; Femme Fatale; Gaslight (1939); Gaslight (1944); Ghost; Goin' South; Good Fellas; Guess Who's Coming to Dinner; Haunted Honeymoon; Heartbreak Kid; High Heels; Honeymoon in Vegas; I Married a Monster from Outer Space; I Was a Male War Bride; Impatient Years; Kiss of Evil; Look Who's Talking Too; Love From a Stranger (1936); Love From a Stranger (1947); Love Story (1970); Lovers and Other Strangers; Made for Each Other; Madness of the Heart; The Marriage of Maria Braun; The Marrying Man; Mating Season; Miami Blues; The Millionairess; My Favorite Spy; Never a Dull Moment (1950); No Man of Her Own; Once Around; Once Upon a Honeymoon; Rebecca; Rosemary's Baby; Scorchers; The Secret Beyond the Door; Seven Brides for Seven Brothers; Sextette; She's Having a Baby; Show-Off; Somebody Killed Her Husband; The Stranger; Suzy; Time to Love and a Time to Die; Under the Yum Yum Tree; We of the Never Never; The Wedding

New Mexico: see also *Southwestern Life: WESTERNS:* Ace in the Hole; Fat Man and Little Boy; Living it Up; The Milagro Beanfield War; Red Sky at Morning; Ride the Pink Horse; Sea of Grass; White Sands

New Orleans: see also *Southerns: Louisiana: Swamp Settings: Cajuns:* The Adventures of Captain Fabian; Angel Heart; The Big Easy; Birth of the Blues; Candyman: Farewell to the Flesh; The Cincinnati Kid; D.O.A. (1988); Delta Heat; Down By Law; The Drowning Pool; Easy Rider; Flame of New Orleans; Hard Promises; Holiday for Sinners; Hotel; Interview with the Vampire; JFK; Johnny Handsome; King Creole; Mardi Gras; My Forbidden Past; New Orleans; No Mercy; Obsession; Panic in the Streets; The Pelican Brief; Pretty Baby; Rafferty and the Gold Dust Twins; Saratoga Trunk; Storyville; A Streetcar Named Desire; Suddenly, Last Summer; This Property is Condemned; Tightrope; Toast of New Orleans; Toys in the Attic; Tune in Tomorrow; Undercover Blues; Walk on the Wild Side; Zandalee

943

Newspapers: see also *Journalists:
Journalists as Detectives:* Arkansas
Traveler; Between the Lines; Deadline
USA; Five Star Final; The Front Page
(1931); The Front Page (1974); Gaily,
Gaily; It Happens Every Thursday; Meet
John Doe; Newsies; Nothing Sacred;
Paper; Platinum Blonde; Schtonk!; Slow
Dancing in the Big City; Superman;
Superman 2; Superman 3; Superman 4;
Sweet Rosie O'Grady; Teacher's Pet; Two
Against the World; While the City Sleeps

New Wave Films: see *French New
Wave Films*

New Year's Day/Eve: see also
Christmas: Bloodhounds of Broadway
(1952); Bloodhounds of Broadway (1989);
Happy New Year (1973); Happy New
Year (1987); The Inquisitor; Out of
Africa; The Poseidon Adventure;
Sleepless in Seattle

New York Life: see also *Urban Life:
Inner City Life: New York vs. LA:* After
Hours; The Age of Innocence (1934); The
Age of Innocence (1993); Alan and
Naomi; Alice; All the Vermeers in New
York; Almost You; Angie; Annie Hall;
The Apartment; Bachelor Party (1957);
Barefoot in the Park; Batteries Not
Included; Bell, Book, and Candle; The
Best of Everything; Billy Bathgate; The
Blessed Event; Bloodbrothers;
Bloodhounds of Broadway (1952);
Bloodhounds of Broadway (1989);
Boardwalk; The Bonfire of the Vanities;
The Bowery; Breakfast at Tiffany's; Bright
Lights, Big City; Brighton Beach
Memoirs; Broadway Danny Rose; A
Bronx Tale; The Brother From Another
Planet; The Butcher's Wife; Can She
Bake a Cherry Pie?; Central Park; The
Clock; Combination Platter; Come Back
Charleston Blue; Come Blow Your Horn;
Coogan's Bluff; The Cowboy Way;
Cracking Up; Crocodile Dundee; Crossing
Delancey; Daybreak; Death Wish;
Desperate Characters; Diary of a Mad
Housewife; Do The Right Thing; East
Side, West Wide; Enter Laughing; Escape
From New York; F.I.S.T.; Falling in Love;
Fame; A Fine Madness; The Fisher King;
Five Corners; The Flamingo Kid; For
Pete's Sake; Fort Apache, The Bronx;
Frankie and Johnny; Friday the 13th Part
VIII-Jason Takes Manhattan; From This
Day Forward; Funny Face; Funny Girl;
The Garment Jungle; Gay Sisters;
Girlfriends; Gloria; Good Fellas; Goodbye

Columbus; Goodbye Girl; Goodbye
People; Grace Quigley; Green Card; The
Group; Guys and Dolls; Hallelujah, I'm a
Bum; Hangin' with the Homeboys;
Hannah and Her Sisters; Heaven Help
Us; Hester Street; Hey, Good Lookin';
Home Alone 2: Lost in New York; How to
Succeed in Business without Really
Trying; The Hucksters; Husbands and
Wives; I Like it Like That; I've Heard the
Mermaids Singing; Irene; The Irish in Us;
It Happened in Brooklyn; It's Always Fair
Weather; The January Man; John and
Mary; Juice; Jumpin at the Boneyard;
Jungle Fever; Key Exchange; King in
New York; Knickerbocker Holiday;
Kramer vs. Kramer; The Last Angry Man;
Last Exit to Brooklyn; Law and Disorder
(1974); Legal Eagles; Light Sleeper;
Little Murders; Looking for Mr. Goodbar;
Lost Weekend; Made for Each Other;
Mambo Kings; Man's Castle; Manhattan;
Manhattan Murder Mystery; The Man in
the Grey Flannel Suit; Marjorie
Morningstar; Married to It; Mean Streets;
Metropolitan (1990); Midnight Cowboy;
Mister Buddwing; Moonstruck; Mortal
Thoughts; Moscow on the Hudson; Mr.
Blandings Builds His Dream House; My
Man Godfrey (1936); My Man Godfrey
(1956); Naked in New York; Next Stop,
Greenwich Village; 9½ Weeks; Nuts; On
the Town; The Outoftowners; Over the
Brooklyn Bridge; The Owl and the
Pussycat; Panic in Needle Park; Paris Is
Burning; Please Don't Eat the Daisies;
Prince of Central Park; The Prince of
Tides; The Prisoner of Second Avenue;
Q (The Winged Serpent); Queens Logic;
Quick Change; Radio Days; Rat Race;
Rear Window; Rich Kids; Ritz; Saturday
Night Fever; Scent of a Woman; The
Secret of My Success; Serpico; Shadows;
Single White Female; Six Degrees of
Separation; Slaves of New York; Soup for
One; Soylent Green; Straight out of
Brooklyn; Street Scene; Such Good
Friends; Sunday in New York; Superstar,
The Life and Times of Andy Warhol;
Sweet Charity; Taking of Pelham 123;
Tales of Manhattan; Taxi Driver;
A Thousand Clowns; Times Square; Toast
of New York; Tootsie; A Tree Grows in
Brooklyn; True Love; 29th Street; Used
People; The Wanderers; Warriors; West
Side Story; What's So Bad About Feeling
Good?; When Harry Met Sally; Where the
Heart Is; Where Were You When the

Lights Went Out?; Where's Poppa?;
While the City Sleeps; Who is Harry
Kellerman . . .; Who's That Knocking at
My Door?; Willie and Phil; Wiz; Working
Girls; Year of the Dragon; Young Savages

New York vs. Los Angeles: see also
*New York Life: Los Angeles: City vs.
Country: Hollywood Life: Theater Life:*
Annie Hall; California Suite; Prizzi's
Honor

New Zealand/New Zealand Films:
see also *Australian Films: British Films:*
An Angel at My Table; Dead Alive;
Goodbye, Pork Pie; Green Dolphin Street;
Once Were Warriors; The Piano; Smash
Palace; Sweetie

Nice Old Ladies: see *Elderly Women*

Nightclubs: see also *Gambling: Disco
Era: Dating Scene: Dancers: Party
Movies: Beautiful People:* Bar Girls;
Bolero (1934); Carlito's Way;
Copacabana; The Cotton Club; Don't
Raise the Bridge, Lower the Water!;
Forbidden Dance; Graffiti Bridge; Harlem
Nights; Hear My Song; Hello Frisco
Hello; Meet Danny Wilson; Mickey One;
Moulin Rouge; New Nightmare; Night
after Night; Pal Joey; Paris is Burning;
Rat Race; Seven Sinners; Shanghai
Gesture; Silent Fall; Stork Club; Strictly
Business; Stud; Thank God It's Friday;
This Could Be the Night; Top of the
Town; Urban Cowboy; Vamp

Nightmare Journeys: see also
*Nightmares: Murphy's Law Stories:
Stranded:* After Hours; Apache Uprising;
Detour; Dudes; Fitzcarraldo; Five Came
Back; Flight of the Phoenix; Full Metal
Jacket; Quick Change; The Sorcerer;
Southern Comfort

Nightmares: see also *HORROR:
Dreams: Dream Sequences: Illusions:
Surrealism:* After Hours; Audrey Rose;
Backfire; Bad Dreams; Bedlam; The
Beguiled; Birdy; Blindfold: Acts of
Obsession; The Cabinet of Caligari
(1962); The Cabinet of Dr. Caligari
(1919); Candyman; Castle of Doom; A
Christmas Carol (1938); Cold Sweat; The
Company of Wolves; Dead of Night
(1945); Despair; Detour; Don't Look Now;
Dream Lover (1986); Dreamscape;
Dressed to Kill; Eraserhead; The Five
Thousand Fingers of Doctor T.; Flesh and
Bone; The Fourth Man; Freddy's Dead:
The Final Nightmare; Full Metal Jacket;
Gothic; Groundhog Day; I Never
Promised You A Rose Garden; Jacob's

Ladder; Kitten with a Whip; Labyrinth; Lady in the Dark; Lady in White; The Last Wave; Long Day Closes; Lost Weekend; Maximum Overdrive; Medusa Touch; Midnight Crossing; Midnight Express; Mirage; Missing; Moonrise; The Most Dangerous Game; Motel Hell; Mr. Blandings Builds His Dream House; The Muppet Christmas Carol; Night Gallery; The Night My Number Came Up; Night Walker; Nightbreed; Nightmare on Elm Street; Nightmare on Elm Street Part Four; Nightmare on Elm Street Part Three; Nightmare on Elm Street Part Two; Nightmare on Elm Street: The Dream Child (1991); Nomads; Nothing but Trouble (1991); The Official Story; Paperhouse; The Pawnbroker; Phantasm; Phantasm II; Red Inn; The Reincarnation of Peter Proud; Rhapsody in August; Rosemary's Baby; Screaming Mimi; Scrooge (1935); Scrooge (1970); The Search for Bridey Murphy; Secret Friends; Sender; The Serpent and the Rainbow; The Seven Percent Solution; Shattered; Siesta; Sisters; Sleepwalkers; Solaris; The Sorcerer; Southern Comfort; Spellbound; Stay Tuned; Straw Dogs; Suddenly, Last Summer; They; They Shoot Horses, Don't They?; The Trial (1962); The Trial (1993); The Trip; The Vanishing (1988); The Vanishing (1993); Westworld; When Hell Was in Session; Wild Strawberries

Nightmare Vacations: see *Vacation Nightmares: also Americans Abroad: Nightmares: Nightmare Journeys: Murphy's Law Stories*

Ninjas: see *Martial Arts*

Noble Savages: see *Fish out of Water Stories: Foreign Misfits: City vs. Country: Missionaries*

Non-Fiction Adaptations: see *True Stories: True or Not: Biographies: Autobiographical Stories: Incredible but Mostly True*

Non-Fiction Films: see *Biographies: Documentaries: Filmumentaries: True Stories: Docudrama: Disease Stories: Historical Drama: War Stories*

North Carolina: see also *Southerns:* Cape Fear (1962); Cape Fear (1991); Nell; Norma Rae; Staying Together

North vs. South: see also *Southerns: Civil War Era: City vs. Country:* Biloxi Blues; Doc Hollywood; Dudes; Escape from Fort Bravo; Foolin' Around; Friendly Persuasion; Goin' To Town; My Cousin Vinny; Norma Rae; The Prince of Tides;

Rio Lobo; The Seduction of Joe Tynan; Southern Yankee; Stars and Bars; 2000 Maniacs; The Undefeated; Virginia City

Nostalgia (films where the central focus is on a nostalgic time): see also *Memories:* All This and World War II; American Graffiti; American Hotwax; At Long Last Love; Back to the Beach; Blue Sky; Calendar Girl; Centennial Summer; Class of '44; Dixie; Dolly Sisters; Falling in Love Again; Fanny and Alexander; The Five Heartbeats; Five Pennies; The Flamingo Kid; For the Boys; Fraternity Row; Gable and Lombard; Gaily, Gaily; Girl Crazy; Give My Regards to Broadway; Good News; Grease; Grease 2; Great Balls of Fire; Great Waldo Pepper; Hail, Hail, Rock n Roll; Hairspray; Happy Time; The Harvey Girls; Has Anybody Seen My Gal?; Heart Beat; Heart of the West; Hello Frisco Hello; Hey, Good Lookin'; I Wonder Who's Kissing Her Now; The Lords of Flatbush; The Man with Bogart's Face; March or Die; Mischief; More American Graffiti; Mother Wore Tights; Movie Movie; My Favorite Year; My Gal Sal; My Wild Irish Rose; Naughty Nineties; The Night They Raided Minsky's; Peggy Sue Got Married; Racing with the Moon; Radio Days; A River Runs Through It; Rock Around the Clock; Rose; Sandlot; Shout; So Dear to My Heart; Stars and Stripes Forever; Strawberry Blonde; That's Dancin'!; That's Entertainment; That's Entertainment Part Two; Those Daring Young Men in Their Jaunty Jalopies; Those Magnificent Men in Their Flying Machines; Those Were the Days; Wait 'Til the Sun Shines, Nellie

Nosy Neighbors: see *Neighbors-Troublesome*

Nouvelle Vague Films: see *French New Wave Films*

Novel and Play Adaptations (films associated with plays and novels either before or after the film version): see also *Pulitzer Prize Adaptations: Non-Fiction Adaptations: Stage Adaptations: Stage Tapings:* Auntie Mame; Billy Liar; The Caine Mutiny (1954); The Caine Mutiny Court Martial (1988); Dangerous Liaisons; Desperate Hours (1955); Desperate Hours (1990); The Devils; Diary of Anne Frank (1959); Dracula (1931); Dracula (1979); Dracula Has Risen from the Grave; Dracula (Horror of Dracula, 1958); Dracula, Prince of

Darkness; Lock up Your Daughters; Mame; Man About the House; Masquerader; A Member of the Wedding; Mister Roberts; Old Maid; Oliver!; One Flew Over Cuckoo's Nest; Pajama Game; White Cargo; Talk Radio

Novelists: see *Writers: Romance Novelists: Journalists: WRITERS' FILMOGRAPHIES*

Nuclear Energy: see also *Apocalyptic Stories: Bombs-Atomic: Monsters-Mutants: Radiation Poisoning: Message Films:* Amazing Grace and Chuck; Blue Sky; Bullseye!; The Children (1980); The China Syndrome; The Day the Fish Came Out; Holocaust 2000; Kiss Me Deadly; Li'l Abner; Living It Up; Madame Curie; Mr. Drake's Duck; Murder, He Says; Sacrifice; Silkwood; The Thief (1952)

Nudism/Nudist Colonies: see also *Alternative Lifestyles: Pornography World:* Calendar Girl; The First Nudie Musical; The Harrad Experiment; The Harrad Summer; I'm All Right, Jack; L'Annee des Meduses; Lady Godiva; The Prize; Shot in the Dark; The Statue; Surrender

Nuisances (fairly innocuous but persistent trouble-makers): see also *Relatives-Unwanted: Children-Brats: Stalkers: Malicious Menaces:* Beethoven; Beethoven's 2nd; Bringing Up Baby; Brothers; Cafe Society; Captain Ron; Dennis the Menace; Drop Dead Fred; The Favor; Ghost Goes West; A Guy Named Joe; Harry and the Hendersons; The Houseguest; It Started with a Kiss; Kitten with a Whip; Ladies Should Listen; Luv; Madhouse; The Man Who Came to Dinner; The Matchmaker; Monkey Trouble; Morgan Stewart's Coming Home; O.C. and Stiggs; Opportunity Knocks; The Show-Off; Sing Baby Sing; Singing in the Rain; Sitting Pretty; Something for Everyone; That Darn Cat!; These Three; Tom Sawyer; Topper; Topper Returns; Topper Takes a Trip; Trouble with Angels; Turner & Hooch; What About Bob?; What's Up, Doc?

Nuns: see also *Monks: Priests: Religion:* Agnes of God; Alvin Purple; Bad Lieutenant; Bells of St. Mary's; Canterville Ghost; A Change of Habit; Christmas Lilies of the Field; Come to the Stable; The Devils; Green Dolphin Street; Heaven Knows, Mr. Allison; Household Saints; I, the Worst of All; The Killer Nun; Lilies of the Field; Luck of the

Irish; Nasty Habits; The Nun's Story; Nuns on the Run; Runner Stumbles; Sea Wife; Second Sight; Singing Nun; Sister Act; Sister Act 2; Song of Bernadette; The Sound of Music; The Stand In; The Trouble with Angels; Two Mules for Sister Sara; Under the Yum Yum Tree; Viridiana; Where Angels Go, Trouble Follows

Nurses: see also *Doctors: Hospitals: Disease Stories:* Blue Veil; China Beach; Daddy Nostaglia; Dying Young; Ethan Frome; A Farewell to Arms (1932); A Farewell to Arms (1957); Hanover Street; The Homecoming (1948); The Honeymoon Killers; The Hospital; I Walked with a Zombie; I Was a Spy; Indecent Obsession; Kiss the Blood Off My Hands; Miss Susie Slagle's; Mother, Jugs & Speed; My Little Girl; Myra Breckinridge; Night Nurse; The Nun's Story; Nurse; Nurse Edith Cavell; One Flew Over Cuckoo's Nest; Operation Mad Ball; Operation Petticoat; Persona; The Possessed (1947); Savage Intruder; The Sins of Rachel Cade; Sister Kenny; So Proudly We Hail; This Above All; Unnatural Causes; Where Does It Hurt?; Whose Life Is It Anyway?; Wife, Doctor and Nurse; The World According to Garp; Young Doctors in Love

Nymphomaniacs: see *Promiscuity: Prostitutes: Bimbos: Pornography World: Sexy Women: Wild People: Sex Addicts*

Objects with Personalities (things, usually cars, that act like humans in some way): see also *Monsters-Manmade: Fantasy: SCI-FI: Magic:* Attack of the Killer Tomatoes; Car; Christine; Herbie Goes Bananas; Herbie Goes to Monte Carlo; Herbie Rides Again; Love Bug; Mannequin; Mannequin 2; One Touch of Venus; Pinocchio; Return to Oz

Obsessions: see also *Fatal Attractions: Addictions: Quests: Treasure Hunts: Stalkers: Romance-Boy Wants Girl: Romance-Girl Wants Boy:* Aguirre, the Wrath of God; Ashes and Diamonds; At Play in the Fields of the Lord; Babysitter; Bad Lieutenant; Betsy; Blue Angel (1930); Blue Angel (1959); Boost; Burden of Dreams; Chloe in the Afternoon; Claire's Knee; The Collector; Come Back to the Five and Dime, Jimmy Dean, Jimmy Dean; Cop; The Crush; Damage; Dance Macabre; Death in Venice; Die Watching; A Double Life; The Fan; Fatal Attraction; Fatso; Fever Pitch; Fitzcarraldo; Gambler; Garbo Talks; God's Little Acre; Golden Braid; Gorillas in the Mist; The Graduate; Great Sinner; The Hairdresser's Husband; Handle with Care; A Kiss for Corliss; The Lady Gambles; Leave Her to Heaven; Legend of Lylah Clare; Let it Ride; Light that Failed; Living in Oblivion; Lolita; Looking for Mr. Goodbar; Magic;

Magnificent Obsession (1935); Magnificent Obsession (1954); Make Me an Offer; Man with the Golden Arm; Mike's Murder; Moby Dick; Moulin Rouge; Music Room; 9/30/55; No Small Affair; Nudo di Donna; Of Human Bondage (1934); Of Human Bondage (1946); Of Human Bondage (1964); Promises in the Dark; Rosalie Goes Shopping; Sacrifice; Sea Beast; Sea of Grass; Somewhere in Time; Star 80; Swann in Love; Taps; Tattoo; Ten; An Unsuitable Job For a Woman; Videodrome; A View from the Bridge; The War Lover; Wetherby; White Hunter, Black Heart; White Tower; Woman Obsessed

Occult: see also *Satan/Satanism: Cults:* The Amityville Horror; Angel Heart; Believers; Bell, Book, and Candle; Black Cat; Black Sabbath; Christine; The Devil Came from Arkansas; Devil Doll; The Devil's Bride; The Evil Dead; Eye of the Devil; First Power; Gate; Gate II; Guardian; Legacy; Live and Let Die; Murder by Decree; Necromancy; Rampage; Rosemary's Baby; The Sentinel; The Serpent and the Rainbow; The Shadow (1940); The Shadow (1994); Tales From the Crypt; Ticket to Heaven; The Unnamable; The Unnamable Returns

Octopi-Angry (vengeful octopuses or ink-squirting squids that have been dis-

turbed): see also *Underwater Adventures: Underwater Creatures:* Beneath the 12 Mile Reef; Bride of the Monster; High Spirits; It Came from beneath the Sea; The Little Mermaid; Mysterious Island; Octopussy; Reap the Wild Wind; Road to Bali; Tentacles; 20,000 Leagues Under the Sea; Voyage to the Bottom of the Sea; Warlords of Atlantis

Oedipal Stories: see also *Mythology: Mothers & Sons: Incest: Classic Greek Stories:* Angela; Back to the Future; The Grifters; Luna; The Miracle (1990); Oedipus Rex; Spanking the Monkey; Tommy; Voyager; Wise Blood

Office Stories: see *Business Life: Office Comedy: Romance with Boss: Romance with Co-Workers: Marrying the Boss*

Office Comedy: see also *Business Life: Romance with the Boss: Marrying the Boss: Situation Comedy:* All in a Night's Work; The Apartment; The Associate; The Hired Wife; More Than a Secretary; Nine to Five; Promoter; Solid Gold Cadillac; Take a Letter, Darling

Oil People/Business: see also *Texas: Rich People:* Artists and Models Abroad; Blowing Wild; Boom Town; Breakfast for Two; Clambake; Dead Ahead, the Exxon Valdez Disaster; Five Easy Pieces; Formula; Giant; Goin' To Town; Hawaiians; Hellfighters; I'll Take

Sweden; Local Hero; Louisiana Story; Naked Gun 2½; Of Love and Desire; Oklahoma Crude; On Deadly Ground; Riff-Raff (1947); The Sorcerer; A Taste for Killing; Texasville; Thunder Bay; Tulsa; Wages of Fear; Waltz Across Texas; Written on the Wind

Older Men with Younger Women: see *Romance-Reunited: Older Women/Younger Men: also Love-Forbidden*

Older Women Seducers: see *Romance-Older Women/Younger Men: Sexy Women*

Older Women with Younger Men: see also *Romance-Reunited: Older Men/Younger Women: also Love-Forbidden*

Old-Fashioned Recent Films (films with that old-fashioned sense, beyond just being wholesome): see also *Nostalgia: Conservative Value Films:* All Creatures Great and Small; All of Me; Amsterdamned; Amy; Arthur; Baby Boom; Back Roads; The Boy Who Could Fly; Career Opportunities; Chances Are; Chaplin; Chariots of Fire; Charley and the Angel; The Color Purple; Continental Divide; Cookie; Curly Sue; Date with an Angel; Dead of Winter; Defending Your Life; Diggstown; Doctor Quinn, Medicine Woman; Eighty-Four Charing Cross Road; Electric Horseman; The Europeans; Falling in Love; Falling in Love Again; Father of the Bride (1991); A Fine Romance; Foolin' Around; Forever Young; Forrest Gump; Getting It Right; Goin' South; Griffin and Phoenix, A Love Story; Hanover Street; Hear My Song; Heart and Souls; Hero; High Road to China; A Home of Our Own; Honey, I Blew Up the Kid; Honey, I Shrunk the Kids; House Calls; Housesitter; The Incredible Journey of Dr. Meg Laurel; Incredible Sarah; I.Q.; It Could Happen to You; Legends of the Fall; Little Romance; Love at First Bite; The Man from Snowy River; The Man in the Moon; The Marrying Man; Matilda; A Matter of Time; Max Dugan Returns; Memphis Belle; Murphy's Romance; My Bodyguard; Nadine; Nate and Hayes; Newsies; The Nightmare Before Christmas; One Good Cop; Sarah, Plain and Tall; Scent of a Woman; Shadowlands; Sing; Sister Act; Sleepless in Seattle; Stanley & Iris; Stepping Out; The Sterile Cuckoo; Straight Talk;

Swashbuckler; Sweethearts Dance; Swept Away; Switching Channels; Tap; Tough Guys; Trading Places; Travels with My Aunt; Welcome Home; Welcome Home, Roxy Carmichael; What About Bob?; What's Eating Gilbert Grape?; What's Up, Doc?; Where the Heart Is; Who is Killing the Great Chefs of Europe?; Wild Geese; Wild Hearts Can't Be Broken; Willy Wonka and the Chocolate Factory; Xanadu; Year of the Comet; Yes, Giorgio

Old vs. Young: see *Generation Gap: Anti-Establishment Films*

Olympics (as a setting or centered on Olympic athletes): see also *Sports Movies:* American Anthem; Cool Runnings; The Cutting Edge; Diving In; Downhill Racer; Goldengirl; Gymkata; Jim Thorpe, All-American; The Loneliest Runner; Million Dollar Legs; Olympische Spiele; One in a Million; Other Side of the Mountain; Personal Best; Walk, Don't Run

One-by-One Deaths: see *Murders-One by One: Rogue Plots*

One-by-One Eliminations: see *Murders-One by One*

One Day Stories (stories notable for entirely or almost entirely taking place in a day): see also *Non-Stop Stories: Real Time Stories:* Adventures in Babysitting; After Hours; All-American Murder; Blind Date (1987); Bringing Up Baby; Car Wash; Dazed and Confused; Desperate Hours (1955); Desperate Hours (1990); The Dresser; Dying Room Only; Guess Who's Coming to Dinner; John and Mary; Key Largo; Lost Weekend; Lumiere; My Dinner With Andre; Night Terror; On the Town; Petrified Forest; Rope; Scenes from a Mall; Soldier in the Rain; Special Day; Tea for Two; Ulysses (1967); Where the Day Takes You; Who's Afraid of Virginia Woolf?

One Last Chance/Time (characters doing something once more before quitting or being unable to continue): see also *Retirement: Redemption: Starting Over: Men Proving Themselves: Women Proving Themselves:* The Asphalt Jungle; Biggest Bundle of Them All; Cairo (1963); Carlito's Way; Charley Varrick; Chattanooga Choo Choo; Colorado Territory; Cooperstown; Diary of a Hitman; Doc; Domino Principle; Going in Style; The Grey Fox; A Gunfighter;

Hawks; High Sierra; Hooper; I Died a Thousand Times; Johnny Dangerously; The Killing; Larceny, Inc.; The Last Detail; The Last Hurrah; The Last Run; Light Sleeper; The Living End; Lookin' to Get Out; Malone; A Prayer for the Dying; The Real McCoy; Requiem for a Heavyweight (1956); Requiem for a Heavyweight (1962); Rooster Cogburn; Rounders; Seven Thieves; Sugar Hill; That Certain Woman

One Performer/Person Shows: see also *Comedy-Performance:* Divine Madness; F for Fake; Gilda Live; Monster in a Box; Secret Honor; Swimming to Cambodia

One Woman Among Men: see *Female Among Males: Male in Female Domain: Fish out of Water Stories*

On the Run: see *Fugitives: Escalating Plots: Non-Stop Stories: Road Movies: Crossing the Border*

Opera: see also *MUSICALS: Ballet: Musicals-Operettas:* Amadeus; Because You're Mine; Carmen Jones; Carmen (Opera, 1984); Chocolate Soldier; Diva; Farewell My Concubine; Fitzcarraldo; The Great Caruso; The Great Lover (1931); Interrupted Melody; La Traviata; Love Parade; Luna; M. Butterfly; Maytime; Meeting Venus; Metropolitan (1935); A Night at the Opera; One Night of Love; Otello; Parsifal; Phantom of Paradise; Phantom of the Opera (1925); Phantom of the Opera (1941); Phantom of the Opera (1962); Phantom of the Opera (1989); Romance; Svengali (1931); Svengali (1983); Tales of Hoffman; The Toast of New Orleans; Yes, Giorgio

Opera Singers: see also *Singers: Opera:* Because You're Mine; Carmen (Opera, 1984); Farewell My Concubine; The Great Caruso; The Great Lover (1931); M. Butterfly; One Night of Love; Phantom of the Opera (1925); Phantom of the Opera (1941); Phantom of the Opera (1962); Phantom of the Opera (1989); Romance; The Toast of New Orleans; When You're in Love

Operettas: see *Musicals-Operettas*

Opposites Attract: see *Romance-Opposites Attract: also Romance-Reluctant: Nerds & Babes, Wallflowers & Hunks: Romance-Bickering*

Oppression/Oppressive Societies: see also *Fascism: Futuristic Films: McCarthy Era: Cold War Era: Social Drama: SCI-FI:* Alphaville; Brazil; Christ Stopped at

Eboli; Closet Land; The Conformist; The Court Martial of Jackie Robinson; Cromwell; Daniel; Death and the Maiden; Death Watch; The Devils; Diary for My Children; Diary of Anne Frank (1959); A Doll's House; The Dresser; El Norte; Fahrenheit 451; Fellow Traveler; The Five Thousand Fingers of Doctor T.; The Fixer; Footloose; The Garden of the Finzi-Continis; Golden Years; A Handmaid's Tale; I, the Worst of All; In the Realm of the Senses; Inner Circle; Intolerance; Journey of Hope; Kafka; Kiss of the Spider Woman; The Lodger (1926); The Lodger (1932); The Lodger (1944); Logan's Run; The Lords of Discipline; Man Friday; Man of Iron; Man of La Mancha; Metropolis; Missing 1984 (1955); 1984 (1984); The Official Story; Operation Mad Ball; The Plague; Poison; The Prisoner; Rock n' Roll High School; Rollerball; Shame (1968); Shoeshine; Sleeper; Stalin; Storm Warning; Strike; Swing Kids; THX1138; To Kill a Priest; The Trial (1955); The Trial (1962); The Trial (1993); The Trials of Oscar Wilde; Triumph of the Will; The Unbearable Lightness of Being; Village of the Damned; When Father Was Away on Business; Zero Population Growth (Z.P.G.)

Ordinary People in Extraordinary Situations: see also *Ordinary People Stories: Ordinary People Turned Criminal: Hitchcock FILMOGRAPHY:* American Dreamer; The American Friend; Brazil; The Man Who Knew Too Much; Mike's Murder; Our Man in Havana; Rapture; Tragedy of a Ridiculous Man

Ordinary People Stories: see also *Working Class: Poor People: Middle Class: Naturalistic Films: Ordinary People in Extraordinary Situations: Quiet Little Films:* The Accused (1988); Alamo Bay; Alex and the Gypsy; All Night Long (1981); All the Way Home; Aloha, Bobby and Rose; Amateur Night at the Dixie Bar and Grill; Angry Silence; Babbitt; Babette's Feast; Baby Face; Baby, The Rain Must Fall; Bachelor Party (1957); Bad Girl; Barnacle Bill (1941); Berlin Alexanderplatz; The Bicycle Thief; Billy Galvin; Black Fury; Bleak Moments; Bloodhounds of Broadway (1952); Bloodhounds of Broadway (1989); Blue Collar; Bodies, Rest & Motion; Bus Stop; Cactus; Caddie; California Split; Cannery

Row; A Chorus of Disapproval; Claire's Knee; Claudine; Closer; Compromising Positions; Country; Courtship; Criss Cross (1992); A Cry in the Dark; Days of Heaven; Dazed and Confused; The Dead; Death of a Salesman (1950); Death of a Salesman (1985); Death Wish; The Deer Hunter; Do The Right Thing; Eat the Peach; Electra Glide in Blue; End of the Line; Everybody's All American; A Face in the Crowd; Falling in Love; A Fire in the Sky; Firstborn; The Flim Flam Man; The Fool; For Pete's Sake; Foxfire (1987); Frankie and Johnny; Friendly Fire; Full Moon in Blue Water; Fun Down There; Fun With Dick and Jane; Georgy Girl; Gervaise; Gilded Lily; Girl with Green Eyes; Glengarry Glen Ross; God's Little Acre; Going Home; The Gun in Betty Lou's Handbag; Gung Ho (1986); Gypsy Moths; Handle with Care; Hands Across the Table; Hard Country; Hard Promises; Heart Like a Wheel; Heartbreakers; Hide in Plain Sight; Housekeeping; In Country; Inner Circle; Innocents of Paris (1929); Irene; Ironweed; Jackpot; Jean de Florette; Jersey Girl; Just Another Girl on the IRT; Keep the Change; The Last Picture Show; The Life of Riley; Lion Is in the Streets; Little Vera; Love Field; Love With the Proper Stranger; Magic Town; Make Me an Offer; Man of Aran; Mannequin (1937); The Marrying Kind; Marty; Me & Veronica; Meet John Doe; Melvin and Howard; Mi Vida Loca; Middle Age Crazy; Millionaire; Modern Times; Mr. Johnson; Mrs. and Mrs. Bridge; Mudlark; My New Gun; My Night at Maud's; 1918; 9/30/55; Norwood; Nothing But the Best; Old Mother Riley SERIES; On the Waterfront; One Magic Christmas; The Pawnbroker; Pelle the Conqueror; Popi; Queen of the Stardust Ballroom; Rat Race; Real Life; Red Headed Woman; Resurrection; The Return of the Secaucus Seven; Rudy; Salmonberries; Saturday Night and Sunday Morning; Saturday Night Fever; Saving Grace; Scenes from a Marriage; The Search for Bridey Murphy; Sing as We Go; Song of Bernadette; Southerner; Stanley & Iris; Star Spangled Rhythm; Steel Magnolias; Steelyard Blues; Stepping Out; Sugarland Express; Swamp Water; Terms of Endearment; Testament; Texasville; The Three Cornered Moon; Time of Your Life; To Kill a

Mockingbird; Tobacco Road; A Tree Grows in Brooklyn; The Trip to Bountiful; True Love; True Stories; Twenty Bucks; Twice in a Lifetime; UFOria; Under Milk Wood; Untamed Heart; Urban Cowboy; Used Cars; Vagabond; Wait 'Til the Sun Shines, Nellie; Waiting For the Light; What's Eating Gilbert Grape?

Ordinary People Turned Criminal: see also *Murder-Learning/Teaching to:* Aloha, Bobby and Rose; The Amazing Dr. Clitterhouse; Boss; Brotherhood of Satan; Buffet Froid; Cat Ballou; The Chase (1947); Closely Watched Trains; Dion Brothers; House of Strangers; I Stole a Million; An Innocent Man; Kansas City Confidential; Kidnapped (1938); Kidnapped (1959); Kidnapped (1971); Killing in a Small Town; Malaya; Mayflower Madam; Money Trap; Murder in New Hampshire; Penelope; Quick Millions; Quicksand; Sexton Blake and the Hooded Terror; Shake Hands with the Devil; Shoeshine; Silent Partner; Straw Dogs; They Live by Night; The Thief Who Came to Dinner; Wicked Lady (1945); Wicked Lady (1983); Woman in the Window; A Woman's Face

Ordinary People Turned Prostitutes: see *Prostitutes-Ordinary People Turned: Prostitutes-Housewife*

Ordinary People vs. Criminals: see also *Criminal Pursues Good Guy's Family:* Aloha, Bobby and Rose; The Big Brawl; Boardwalk; City of Joy; Dark Past; Desperate Hours (1955); Desperate Hours (1990); Fighting Back; The Gun in Betty Lou's Handbag; Jimmy Hollywood; Key Largo; Law and Disorder (1974); Miss Grant Takes Richmond; Miss Robin Hood; Never Let Go; Now You See Him, Now You Don't; Quick Millions; Thunder Road; Who Done It? (1957)

Organ Donors (often also Organ Donor Murders): see also *Medical Drama: Disease Stories: Body Parts: Brain Transplants:* Blink; Coma; Heart Condition

Organized Crime: see *Mob Stories: Corruption: Embezzlers*

Orgies: see also *Alternative Lifestyles: Sexual Kinkiness: Party Movies: Promiscuity: Sexual Revolution:* Beyond the Valley of the Dolls; Caligula; City of Women; Emmanuelle SERIES; La Dolce Vita; Mickey One; Satyricon (Fellini's); Scandal

Oriental People: see *Asian-Americans: Chinese People: Japanese People: Asia: Taiwanese Films: Hong Kong: Martial Arts*

Orphans: see also *Babies-Finding: Men and Babies: Family/Heritage-Search for: Children Alone: Abandoned People:* Annie; The Apple Dumpling Gang; The Apple Dumpling Gang Rides Again; Bachelor Mother; Bambi; Battle Hymn; The Bells of St. Mary's; Blame it on the Night; Blossoms in the Dust; The Boy With Green Hair; Boys Town; Bright Angel; Brothers; Captains Courageous; Christmas Lilies of the Field; Conan, the Barbarian; Daddy Longlegs; David Copperfield; Diary for My Children; Driftwood; Escape to Witch Mountain; Father is a Bachelor; First Love; The Good Son; Green Eyes; Heidi (1939); Here Comes the Groom; Housekeeping; If I Had My Way; Ivan's Childhood; Jane Eyre (1934); Jane Eyre (1943); Jane Eyre (1971); Kidnapped (1938); Kidnapped (1959); Kidnapped (1971); King of the Hill (1993); Kitchen Toto; Lady is Willing; The Land Before Time; Little Ark; Little Dorrit; The Little Girl Who Lives Down the Lane; Lost in Yonkers; Mad About Music; Men of Boys' Town; Min and Bill; My Life as a Dog; My Six Loves; Napoleon and Samantha; Nevada Smith; Oliver!; Oliver and Company; Oliver Twist (1948); Oliver Twist (1982); One Good Cop; Orphans; Pixote; Pollyanna; The Prince of Central Park; Salaam Bombay!; Sally of the Sawdust; Sentimental Journey; Sin of Madelon Claudet; Six Pack; Smugglers; Sorrowful Jones; Spirit Rider; Tex; A Thousand Clowns; Three Godfathers; Three Men and a Baby; Three Men and a Cradle; Three Men and a Little Lady; To Each His Own; Tom Jones; Tunnel of Love; The Unsinkable Molly Brown; Where the Lilies Bloom; Who Slew Auntie Roo? Wuthering Heights (1939); Wuthering Heights (1953); Wuthering Heights (1970); Wuthering Heights (1992)

Oscars (with scenes taking place during the Academy Awards festivities): see also *Hollywood Life:* California Suite; Naked Gun 33⅓; The Oscar; A Star is Born (1954)

Ostracism: see also *Conformism: Oppression: Snobs vs. Slobs: Snobs: Homophobia:* Absence of Malice; Apartment Zero; The Boy With Green Hair; Bright Road; Carrie (1976); The Children's Hour; Cold Sassy Tree; Easy Virtue; Emma; Fellow Traveler; Friends Forever; Guilty by Suspicion; The Heart Is a Lonely Hunter; The Match Factory Girl; Miss Firecracker; Ninth Configuration; Outcast of the Islands; Party and the Guests; Ratboy; School Ties; Sebastiane; Squaw Man; The Strange One; To Find a Man; Twisted

Outer Space Movies: see also *Astronauts: Star Wars: SCI-FI: Aliens-Outer Space: Good: Aliens-Outer Space: Evil:* Abbott & Costello Go to Mars; Alien; Alien3; Aliens; Alphaville; Apollo 13; Barbarella; Black Hole; Cat Women of the Moon; Dark Crystal; Dark Star; Dune; The Empire Strikes Back; Enemy Mine; The Explorers; Flash Gordon; Forbidden Planet; Ice Pirates; Jetsons Movie; Journey to the Far Side of the Sun; Krull; The Last Starfighter; Life Force; Light Years; Marooned; Millennium; Mom and Dad Save the World; Moon Pilot; Moonraker; The Neverending Story; The Neverending Story II: The Next Chapter; Outland; Queen of Outer Space; Return of the Jedi; Robinson Crusoe on Mars; Saturn 3; Silent Running; Slaughterhouse Five; Solaris; Spaceballs; Spaced Invaders; Spacehunter, Adventures in the Forbidden Zone; Stargate; Star Trek: Generations; Star Trek II: The Wrath of Khan; Star Trek III: The Search for Spock; Star Trek IV: The Voyage Home; Star Trek: The Motion Picture; Star Trek V: The Final Frontier; Star Trek VI: The Undiscovered Country; Star Wars; Total Recall; 2001: A Space Odyssey; 2010; When Worlds Collide; Zardoz

Outlaw Road Movies: see also *Law-Fugitive from the: Chase Movies: Road Movies: Criminal Couples:* Aloha, Bobby and Rose; Bad Company; Badlands; Bonnie and Clyde; The Boys Next Door; Breathless (1959); Butch Cassidy and the Sundance Kid; The Dion Brothers; Fugitive Lovers; The Good, The Bad, & The Ugly; Goodbye, Pork Pie; Great Smokey Roadblock; Gun Crazy (1950); Gun Crazy (1992); Henry: Portrait of a Serial Killer; Into the Night; Iron Mistress; Kalifornia; The Kissing Bandit; Les Valseuses; Living End; The Long Riders; Macon County Line; The Man Who Watched Trains Go By; Miles From Home; Rawhide; Return to Macon County; Road Games; Smokey and the Bandit; Smokey and the Bandit II; Smokey and the Bandit III; Sugarland Express; Thelma & Louise; They Live by Night; Thieves Like Us; W.W. & The Dixie Dancekings; Wild at Heart

Outstanding Production Design: see *Production Design-Outstanding*

Overlooked at Release (films that have gained stature or should gain a stature they didn't win when first released): see also *Ahead of Its Time: Underrated: Forgotten Films: Hidden Gems: Cult Films: Quiet Little Films:* Ace in the Hole; Age of Consent; Always Together; The Assassination Bureau; Avalanche Express; Back Roads; Bad Company (1995); Badge 373; Barbarosa; Based on an Untrue Story; The Beekeeper; Between the Lines; Beyond the Valley of the Dolls; The Big Bus; The Big Town; Blaze; Blind Fury; The Bliss of Mrs. Blossom; Blood and Concrete; Blood from the Mummy's Tomb; Blue Collar; Blue Sky; Born to Kill; Business as Usual; Cannery Row; Charley Varrick; The Children (1990); A Chorus of Disapproval; Class of '84; Cobb; Death in Brunswick; The Deceivers; Desert Bloom; The Dion Brothers; The Doctor and the Devils; Dogfight; Dreamchild; The Dresser; Drop Dead Fred; A Dry White Season; The Effect of Gamma Rays on Man-in-the-Moon Marigolds; The Efficiency Expert; Eleven Harrowhouse; Eyes in the Night; Fat City; Fearless; Fedora; Felix the Cat: The Movie; A Fine Romance; Fingers; Flirting; Fools Parade; For Queen and Country; 1492: Conquest of Paradise; Four Friends; Foxes; Frankenhooker; Frankenstein Unbound; Fraternity Row; Freddie as F.R.O.7.; The Frog Prince; Fun Down There; Gaby, a True Story; Garbo Talks; Glory! Glory!; Godspell; Golden Braid; The Gong Show Movie; The Good Father; A Good Man in Africa; The Good Mother; Goodbye Gemini; Goodbye People; Goonies; Gordon's War; Gorky Park; Grace Quigley; Great Balls of Fire; Greetings; Gremlins 2: The New Batch; Hair; Hammett; Happy Anniversary; Happy New Year (1987); Hard Promises; The Hard Way (1991); Harley Davidson and the Marlboro Man; Hearts of Fire; Higher Learning; The Human Factor; The Journey of Natty Gann; Jumpin at the Boneyard; The Kill-Off; Killing Dad; The

Killing of a Chinese Bookie; Kindred; The King of Comedy; King of New York; King of the Hill (1993); The King's Whore; Kings Go Forth; Kiss Me Goodbye; Kiss Shot; Krull; La Vie de Boheme; Labyrinth; Lady in White; Lamb; Last Exit to Brooklyn; The Last Hard Men; Late for Dinner; The Legend of Billie Jean; The Legend of the Holy Drinker; Let's Hope It's a Girl; Life and Nothing But; Limit Up; Lion Is in the Streets; Little Noises; London Kills Me; The Lonely Guy; Long Day Closes; Loophole; Loot; Lorenzo's Oil; Lost in Yonkers; Love Letters (1984); Making Mr. Right; A Man of No Importance; The Man Without a Face; Matewan; Me and Veronica; Menage; The Men's Club; Miracle Mile; Monolith; Monsieur Hire; Monster Squad; Month in the Country; Mountains on the Moon; Move; Mr. Johnson; Mr. and Mrs. Bridge; Mrs. Parker and the Vicious Circle; Music of Chance; My Favorite Year; My Little Girl; My New Gun; Naked in New York; No Surrender; The Old Curiosity Shop; Olly Olly Oxen Free; One Magic Christmas; Paperhouse; Paris By Night; The Party; Past Midnight; Patterns; Pennies from Heaven (1981); The Perfect Couple; Peter's Friends; Petulia; The Posse (1975); Prince of the City; The Private Life of Sherlock Holmes; Promised Land; Promises in the Dark; Public Eye; Quality Street; The Rachel Papers; Raggedy Man; Rancho De Luxe; Ransom; Rapture; Ratboy; Red Kiss; The Ref; Rendez-Vous; Repo Man; Rescue Me; Rich Kids; The River Niger; The Road to Wellville; Samurai; Sapphire; Scout; Searching for Bobby Fischer; Secret Friends; The Secret of Roan Inish; September; Shock to the System; Shock Treatment; A Short Film About Killing; Shy People; Silent Tongue; Slaves of New York; Slither; Smile; Solaris; Southern Comfort; Speaking Parts; Stanley & Iris; Stepping Out; Still of the Night; Story of Boys and Girls; Straight Time; Streets of Gold; Supergirl; Sweet Smell of Success; Sweethearts Dance; Sylvia Scarlett; T.R. Baskin; A Talent for Loving; Talent for the Game; Tell Me a Riddle; The Tenant; Tender Mercies; Term of Trial; Tex; That's Adequate; That's Life!; Threesome; Time of Destiny; Timebomb; Times Square; To Kill a Priest; The Torrents of Spring; Tragedy of a Ridiculous Man; Triumph of the Spirit; True Colors; Turtle Diary; Two For the Road; The Unbelievable Truth; Under Suspicion; The Unnamable; The Unnamable Returns; Until the End of the World; Used Cars; Utz; Vampire's Kiss; Vice Versa; Voyager; Walk in the Spring Rain; What's Eating Gilbert Grape?; White Dog; Who Is Killing the Great Chefs of Europe?; The Wicker Man; The Wilby Conspiracy; Winter Kills; Wise Blood; WUSA; Yanks

Films by Category

P

Pacific Islands/Ocean: see also *Adventure at Sea: Islands:* Back to Bataan; Bird of Paradise (1932); Bird of Paradise (1951); The Blue Lagoon (1948); The Blue Lagoon (1980); Castaway Cowboy; China Seas; Don't Go Near the Water; Donovan's Reef; Farewell to the King; Father Goose; The Fighting Seabees; The Flying Leathernecks; Gung Ho! (1943); Heaven Knows, Mr. Allison; Hellcats of the Navy; Hell in the Pacific; Hurricane (1937); Hurricane (1979); Immortal Story; Island of Dr. Moreau (1977); Macao; Malaya; Miss Sadie Thompson; The Moon and Sixpence; Mutiny on the Bounty (1935); Mutiny on the Bounty (1962); Mysterious Island; Nate and Hayes; None But the Brave; The Rain; Sadie Thompson; Seven Sinners; Song of the Islands; South Pacific; Tabu; Too Late the Hero; Twilight for the Gods; Wake Island; Wake of the Red Witch; When Time Ran Out

Pacificism: see *Peaceful People: Anti-War Films*

Painters: see *Artists: Artists-Famous*

Parallel Stories (usually only two stories that are alternately told before converging): see also *Multiple Stories: Interwoven Stories: Episodic Stories:* Crimes and Misdemeanors; Dead Again; Doctor Zhivago; The Double Life of Veronique; Eye of the Needle; The French Lieutenant's Woman; Frenzy; Fried Green Tomatoes; Guess Who's Coming to Dinner; He Said, She Said; She Devil; Sleepless in Seattle; Terms of Endearment

Paranoia: see also *THRILLER: HORROR: SCI-FI: SCI-FI-1950s: Cold War Era: Mental Illness: Women in Jeopardy: Men in Jeopardy: Children in Jeopardy:* After Hours; Amos and Andrew; The Andromeda Strain; The Blob (1958); The Blob (1988); Body Bags; The Body Snatchers; The Brain Eaters; Checking Out; Dark Star; Day of the Triffids; Dr. Strangelove; The Fourth Man; The Front; High Anxiety; I Married a Monster from Outer Space; Invasion; Invasion of the Body Snatchers (1956); Invasion of the Body Snatchers (1978); Matinee; Meet Me After the Show; My Wife's Best Friend; Never Say Die; 1941; 1984 (1955); 1984 (1984); Pulse; The Puppetmasters; Reflecting Skin; Shadows and Fog; Strange Invaders; Survivors; The Tenant; Them!; They Live; The Thing (1951); The Thing (1982); Unfaithfully Yours (1948); Unfaithfully Yours (1984); War of the Worlds; Welcome to Hard Times; When Worlds Collide; Witches of Salem

Parasites: see also *Monsters: Aliens-Outer Space: Evil:* Blue Monkey; The Body Snatchers; Brain Damage; The Dark Half; Green Slime; The Hidden; Hidden 2; Invasion of the Body Snatchers (1956); Invasion of the Body Snatchers (1978); It Came From Outer Space; The Puppetmasters; The Thing (1982)

Parents/Couples-Adoptive: see *Orphans: Babies-Findings: Children-Adopted: Fathers-Adopted: Mothers-Adopted: Mothers-Surrogate: Fathers-Surrogate: Women-Childless*

Parents Are Gone (when the parents are away, the children play): see also *Parents are Gone from Chicago: Party Movies: Crisis Situations:* Adventures in Babysitting; Don't Tell Mom the Babysitter's Dead; Ferris Bueller's Day Off; Home Alone; Home Alone 2: Lost in New York; Risky Business; Uncle Buck

Parents Are Gone from Chicago: see also *Parents Are Gone: Chicago:* Adventures in Babysitting; Ferris Bueller's Day Off; Home Alone; Risky Business; Uncle Buck

Parents-Overprotective: see *Daddy's Girls: Mama's Boys*

Parents-Struggling: see *Making a Living: Poor People: Mothers Alone: Fathers Alone: Unemployment*

Parents vs. Children: see also *Step-Parents vs. Children: Family Drama: Inheritances at Stake: Step-Fathers: Step-Mothers: Mothers Alone: Fathers*

Obsession; Ordinary People; The Pawnbroker; Plenty; Rachel, Rachel; The Reincarnation of Peter Proud; Shattered; Shy People; Sister, Sister; The Strange Loves of Martha Ivers; A Streetcar Named Desire; Summer Wishes, Winter Dreams; Sweet Bird of Youth; Sweet Rosie O'Grady; They Shoot Horses, Don't They?; This Property is Condemned; Tiger Bay; Walk on the Wild Side; Whatever Happened to Baby Jane?; Who's Afraid of Virginia Woolf?

Past-Living in the: see *Depression:*
Past-Haunted by the: Secrets-
Consuming

Pastorals: see *Nature-Back to: Rural*
Life: City vs. Country: Fish out of Water
Stories

Patriotic Films: see also *Conservative*
Value Films: War Stories: Military
Comedy: Military Stories: Political
Drama: Anti-War Films: Anti-
Establishment Films: The Bridges at Toko-Ri; China; Ever in My Heart; Follow Me, Boys!; God Is My Co-Pilot; The Green Berets; Hellcats of the Navy; The House on 92nd Street; The Hunt for Red October; I Wanted Wings; I Was a Communist for the FBI; It's A Big Country; Keeper of the Flame; The Man I Married; Mr. Lucky; Next of Kin (1942); North Star; An Officer and a Gentleman; The Russians Are Coming, The Russians Are Coming; Since You Went Away; So Proudly We Hail; Stars and Stripes Forever; Strategic Air Command; This Above All; This Land Is Mine; To Have and Have Not; Vacation from Marriage; Washington Story; Yankee Doodle Dandy

Peaceful People: see also *Anti-War*
Films: Blockade; The Bridges at Toko-Ri; Friendly Persuasion; How I Won the War; J'Accuse; La Passante; Nurse Edith Cavell; The Outsider; This Above All; Tribes; Two People; The War

Pearl Harbor: see also *World War II*
Stories: Japanese as Enemy: Hawaii:
Across the Pacific; Air Force; Come See the Paradise; Final Countdown; From Here to Eternity; Tora! Tora! Tora!

Peeping Toms: see *Voyeurism*

Peer Pressure: see *Conformism:*
Ostracism: Teenage Movies: Teenagers:
Coming of Age

Pentagon: see also *War Stories:*
Military Stories: Spy Films: CIA Agents:
Dr. Strangelove; Fail Safe; Forbin Project; No Way Out; Seven Days in May

People Who Aren't Who They Seem:
see *Love-Questionable: Liars*

Perfect Crimes: see also *Heist Stories:*
Clever Plots & Endings: Crime Pays:
Compulsion; Dial M For Murder; The Getaway (1972); The Getaway (1994); Guilty as Sin; Kansas City Confidential; The Lavender Hill Mob; Mother Love; Running Man (1963); Whistling in the Dark

Period Piece: see *Decade Categories:*
Historical Drama: Costume Drama:
Elizabethan Era: Edwardian Era:
Victorian Era

Persecution: see *Accused-Unjustly:*
Ostracism: Oppression: Religion:
Insane-Plot to Drive: Committed-
Wrongly: Nazi Stories

Personal Ads: see also *Romance-*
Chance Meetings: Dating Scene: Blind
Dates: Brides-Mail Order: Beyond Therapy; Castaway; Desperately Seeking Susan; I Sent a Letter to My Love; Ladykiller (1992); Mississippi Mermaid; Sea of Love; They Knew What They Wanted

Pet Stories: see also *Dogs: Cats:*
Talking Animals: Animals in Jeopardy:
Ace Ventura: Pet Detective; An Alligator Named Daisy; Baxter (1990); Bears & I; Beethoven; Beethoven's 2nd; Big Red; The Biscuit Eater (1940); The Biscuit Eater (1972); Black Beauty (1946); Black Beauty (1971); Black Beauty (1994); The Black Stallion; The Black Stallion Returns; A Boy and His Dog; Call of the Wild (1935); Call of the Wild (1972); Cat's Eye; CHOMPS; Clarence, the Cross-Eyed Lion; Digby, the Biggest Dog in the World; Dog of Flanders; E.T.: The Extra-Terrestrial; Far From Home; Flipper; Fluffy; For the Love of Benji; The Golden Seal; Goodbye My Lady; Gremlins; Gremlins 2: The New Batch; Harry and the Hendersons; Harry and Tonto; Horse in the Grey Flannel Suit; Incredible Journey; The Journey of Natty Gann; K-9; K-9000; Kes; A Kid for Two Farthings; Lady and the Tramp; Lassie; Lassie Come Home; Late Show; Look Who's Talking Now; The Magic of Lassie; Mighty Joe Young; Million Dollar Duck; Money from Home; Monkey Trouble; Mrs. Brown, You've Got a Lovely Daughter; My Friend Flicka; Napoleon and Samantha; National Velvet; Old Yeller; 101 Dalmatians; The Red Pony (1949); The Red Pony (1976); Rubin & Ed; Savage

Sam; Short Circuit; Sing You Sinners; Son of Lassie; Sounder; Three Lives of Thomasina; Thunderhead, Son of Flicka; Ugly Dachshund; Umberto D.; We Think the World of You; White Fang; Won Ton Ton, the Dog Who Saved Hollywood; The Yearling; You Can Never Tell

Philadelphia: see also *Inner City Life:*
Birdy; From the Terrace; Philadelphia; The Philadelphia Story; Rocky SERIES; Trading Places; Young Philadelphians

Philanderers-Avenging/Dumping:
see *Cheating Men: Cheating Women:*
Playboys: Engagements-Breaking

Phobias: see also *Psychological Drama:*
Psychological Thriller: Paranoia:
Arachnaphobia; Body Double; Diving In; Eye of the Cat; Phobia; Vertigo

Photographers: see also *Journalists:*
Fashion World: Artists: Pornography
World: Entertainment: Hollywood Life:
Blow Up; The Cameraman; China Girl (1942); Die Watching; Double Exposure; Eighty-Four Charlie Mopic; The Eyes of Laura Mars; Family Pictures; Funny Face; A Girl Named Tamiko; Girlfriends; Ground Zero; High Season; I Love Melvin; Little Murders; Live a Little, Love a Lot; Love Crimes; Lover Come Back (1946); My Favorite Brunette; Nadine; Naked in New York; No Small Affair; Peeping Tom; Promise Her Anything; Proof; Public Eye; Rear Window; The Sky's the Limit; Soldier of Fortune; Under Fire

Pianists: see also *Musicians: Jazz Life:*
Biographies: Music Composer
Biographies: Autumn Sonata; Competition; Constant Nymph (1933); Constant Nymph (1943); The Fabulous Baker Boys; Fingers; Five Easy Pieces; The Five Thousand Fingers of Doctor T.; The Getting of Wisdom; The Great Lie; A Kiss in the Dark; Le Cavaleur; Let No Man Write My Epitaph; Madame Sousatzka; Mephisto Waltz; The Music Teacher; Never Say Goodbye; The Only Game in Town; The Piano; Running on Empty; Seventh Veil; Shoot the Piano Player; That Uncertain Feeling; 30 Is a Dangerous Age, Cynthia; 32 Short Films about Glenn Gould; Torch Song

Pickpockets: see also *Con Artists:*
Thieves: Arthur; Battement de Coeur; Harry in Your Pocket; Life with Mikey; The Little Thief; Monkey Trouble; Oliver! Oliver Twist (1948); Oliver Twist (1982); The Passionate Thief; Pickpocket; Pickup on South Street

Pilots-Airline/General: see also
Airplanes: Airplane Crashes: Always;
Biggles; Blue Thunder; Boeing-Boeing;
The Bride Came C.O.D.; Carousel;
Ceiling Zero; China Clipper; Christopher
Strong; Fate is the Hunter; The High and
the Mighty; Lady Takes a Flyer; The
Lindbergh Kidnapping Case; Men with
Wings; Millennium; No Highway in the
Sky; Only Angels Have Wings; Running
Man (1963); Spirit of St. Louis; Sunday in
New York; Tammy and the Bachelor; Test
Pilot; Winged Victory; Wings; Wings in
the Dark

Pilots-Daredevil: see also *Airplanes:*
Biggles; Firefox (1982); The Great Waldo
Pepper; Gypsy Moths; High Road to
China; Tarnished Angels

Pilots-Military: see also *War Stories:
Military Stories:* Aces, Iron Eagle 3; Air
America; Air Force; The Aviator; Battle
of Britain; Blue Max; Bombers B-52; The
Bridges at Toko-Ri; Calcutta; Captains of
the Clouds; China Clipper; Cornered;
Dawn Patrol; Dive Bomber; The Fighting
Seabees; Firefox (1982); First of the Few;
Flight Angels; Flight of the Intruder;
Flying Tigers; God Is My Co-Pilot;
A Guy Named Joe; Hanover Street;
Hell's Angels; Hot Shots!; Hot Shots,
Part Deux; I Wanted Wings; Innerspace;
Into the Sun; Iron Eagle; Iron Eagle II;
Iron Petticoat; Joan of Paris; The Last
Flight; The McConnell Story; Memphis
Belle; Murphy's War; Saber Jet; Sayonara;
Sky Devils; The Sky's the Limit;
Stairway to Heaven; Strategic Air
Command; Sundays and Cybele; Suzy;
Thirty Seconds Over Tokyo; Thunder-
birds; Top Gun; Twelve O'Clock High;
The War Lover; Wings of Eagles;
Zeppelin

Pimps: see also *Madams: Prostitutes-
Low Class: Prostitutes-Male:* Accatone;
The Cheyenne Social Club; Coup de
Torchon; Doctor Detroit; Mamma Rosa;
McCabe and Mrs. Miller; Night Shift;
Saint Jack; Scarlet Street; Street Smart

Pioneers: see also *WESTERNS: Indians-
American, Conflict with:* Bend of the
River; Broken Arrow; Call of the Wild
(1935); Call of the Wild (1972); Canyon
Passage; Davy Crockett; Drums Along the
Mohawk; Emerald Forest; Exodus; Far
and Away; Forty Guns; Goin' South;
Gorillas in the Mist; Green Dolphin
Street; Hawaii; Heartland; Jeremiah
Johnson; O Pioneers; Red River; Silence

of the North; Silverado; Stalking Moon;
The Sundowners

Pirates: see also *Swashbucklers:
Adventure at Sea: ADVENTURE:
Treasure Hunts: Caribbean:* Abbott &
Costello Meet Captain Kidd; Against All
Flags; Black Pirate; Black Sunday
(1977); Black Swan; Blackbeard, The
Pirate; Blackbeard's Ghost; Buccaneer
(1938); Buccaneer (1958); Captain Blood;
Captain Horatio Hornblower; Captain
Kidd; China Seas; Dennis the Menace;
Fog; His Majesty O'Keefe; Hook; Ice
Pirates; Island (1980); Long John Silver;
Nate and Hayes; Peter Pan; The Pirate;
Pirates (1986); The Pirate Movie; The
Pirates of Penzance; The Princess Bride;
The Princess and the Pirate;
Shipwrecked; Swashbuckler; Treasure
Island (1934); Treasure Island (1971);
Treasure Island (1990); Treasure Island
(1991); Yellowbeard

Plagues: see *Epidemics: Disease
Stories: AIDS Stories*

Planets: see *Outer Space Movies:
Space Travel: SCI-FI*

Plantation Life: see also *Southerns:
Farm Life: Rural Life: Civil War Era:*
Baby Doll; Cabin in the Cotton; Cat on a
Hot Tin Roof (1958); Cat on a Hot Tin
Roof (1984); Diamond Head; Drum;
Elephant Walk; Fletch Lives; Gone With
the Wind; The Letter (1929); The Letter
(1940); Long Hot Summer (1958);
Mandingo; Naked Jungle; Out of Africa;
Queen Bee; Reap the Wild Wind; Red
Dust; Roots; Seventh Dawn; Simba; Son
of Dracula; Song of the South; So Red the
Rose; The Sound and the Fury; White
Cargo; White Zombie

Plastic Surgery: see *Cosmetic Surgery:
Disguises: Identities-Assumed: Deaths-
Faked: Doctors*

Play Adaptations: see *Classic Play
Adaptations: Stagelike Films: Stage
Tapings: Pulitzer Prize Adaptations:
Novel Adaptations*

Play and Novel Adaptations: see
Novel and Play Adaptations

Playboys: see also *Single Men: Sexy
Men: Evil Men: Settling Down: Bimboys:
Cheating Men: Bachelors-Confirmed:
Free Spirits: Wild People:* The
Adventures of Barry McKenzie; The
Affairs of Cellini; Alfie; Algiers; Anna
and the King of Siam; Arsenic and Old
Lace; The Bachelor and the Bobby-Soxer;
Banning; Beau Brummell (1924); Beau

Brummell (1954); A Bedtime Story
(1933); Bedtime Story (1964); Belle of
New York; The Bells Are Ringing; Better
Late Than Never; Bob le Flambeur;
Boeing-Boeing; Bolero (1934); Breakfast
for Two; Bulldog Drummond (1929);
Bulldog Drummond at Bay; Bulldog
Drummond Strikes Back; Casanova '70;
Casanova (Fellini's Casanova); Cash
McCall; The Charmer; The Cincinnati
Kid; Come Blow Your Horn; Confessions
of a Window Cleaner; Cracking Up;
Dancing Lady; Dead Heat on a Merry Go
Round; Deliberate Stranger; Diamond
Jim; Diamonds are Forever; Diamonds for
Breakfast; Dirty Rotten Scoundrels;
Double Wedding; Dr. No; England Made
Me; A Fine Madness; Foolish Wives; For
Your Eyes Only; From Russia with Love;
Goldfinger; Goodbye, Charlie; The Great
Gatsby (1949); The Great Gatsby (1974);
The Great Lover (1931); A Guide for the
Married Man; Guys and Dolls;
Hammerhead; Heartbreakers; Heaven
Can Wait (1943); Heiress; Hollywood or
Bust; Home from the Hill; Hud; The
Hustler; Jack of Diamonds; Joy of Living;
Kaleidoscope; Knack; Knave of Hearts;
La Dolce Vita; LeCavaleur; Live a Little,
Steal a Lot; Live, Love and Learn; Lock
up Your Daughters; Love Streams; The
Man Who Loved Women (1977); The Man
Who Loved Women (1983); My Blue
Heaven (1990); A Night in the Life of
Jimmy Reardon; Ninotchka; No More
Ladies; The Nutty Professor (1963); Oh,
Rosalinda!; On the Riviera; Once Is Not
Enough; One Hour with You; Only Two
Can Play; The Pad, and How to Use It;
Paris By Night; Pickup Artist; Picnic;
Pillow Talk; The Private Affairs of Bel
Ami; The Prize; Raffles; Red Line 7000;
Scandal in Paris; Second Thoughts;
Shampoo; Silencers; Star 80; Stay Hungry;
Staying Alive; Summer and Smoke;
Sunday in New York; Switch; A Talent for
Loving; Ten Thousand Bedrooms; The
Tender Trap; Terms of Endearment;
There's a Girl in My Soup; They Won't
Believe Me; The Thomas Crown Affair;
Three Men and a Baby; Three Men and a
Cradle; Three Men and a Little Lady;
Three on a Couch; Tom Jones; Toys in the
Attic; Tropic of Cancer; What's New
Pussycat?; Where Does it Hurt?; White
Mischief; Who's Been Sleeping in My
Bed?; Wrecking Crew; You Belong to Me;
You'll Never Get Rich; Youngblood

Playgirls: see also *Sexy Women: Bimbos: Prostitutes-High Class:* Breakfast at Tiffany's; Desperately Seeking Susan; Doctor's Wives; I Want to Live!; La Dolce Vita

Plot to Make Insane: see *Insane-Plot to Drive: Committed-Wrongly: Accused-Unjustly*

Plots to Rule the World: see *Rule the World-Plots to:* also *Leaders-Tyrant: Nazi Stories: Hitler: Corruption*

Poets: see also *Writers: Romance with Writers:* An Angel at My Table; The Barretts of Wimpole Street (1934); The Barretts of Wimpole Street (1956); Beat; Beautiful Dreamers; Blood of a Poet; Boom!; Doctor Zhivago; A Fine Madness; If I Were King; Lost Moment; Mr. Deeds Goes to Town; Next Stop, Greenwich Village; Reuben, Reuben; Stevie; The Subterraneans; Testament of Orpheus; Ulysses (1967); Under Milk Wood

Poisons: see also *MURDER: Crimes-Perfect: Clever Plots & Endings:* Bride of the Gorilla; Buried Alive; Color Me Dead; D.O.A. (1949); D.O.A. (1988); Dr. M.; Freaked; Ivy; Man About the House; The Mirror Crack'd; Nothing but Trouble (1941); Notorious; Rosemary's Baby; Snow White and The Seven Dwarfs; Stuff; The Two Mrs. Carrolls; Violette

Polemics: see *Message Films: Political Films*

Poles-North/South: see *Arctic/Antarctica*

Police Brutality: see also *Police-Corruption: Police Stories:* Cop; Extreme Justice; Fuzz; The Killer Inside Me; No Escape, No Return; Offence; The Official Story; Panic in Needle Park; Q&A; To Kill a Priest

Police Comedy: see also *Police Stories: Criminals-Stupid:* Abbott & Costello Meet the Keystone Cops; Another Stakeout; Armed and Dangerous; Baby's Day Out; Bad Boys (1994); Beverly Hills Cop 3; Car 54, Where Are You?; Convoy Cop and a Half; Cops and Robbersons; Cotton Comes to Harlem; Dead Heat; Delicate Delinquent; Dragnet (1987); Freebie and the Bean; Fuzz; The Hard Way (1991); Heart Condition; Hot Stuff; It Could Happen to You; K-9; Law and Disorder (1958); Law and Disorder (1974); Moving; Moving Violations (1985); Naked Gun; Naked Gun 2½; Naked Gun 33⅓; Police Academy; Police Squad!

Help Wanted!; Running Scared; Stop! Or My Mom Will Shoot

Police Corruption: see also *Police Brutality: Police Stories: Corruption:* Alien Nation; Armed and Dangerous; Bad Lieutenant; The Big Easy; Bullitt; Charley Varrick; Cop; Coup de Torchon; Deep Cover; Flashpoint; Fuzz; I Walk the Line; Innocent Man; Internal Affairs; Interrogation; Investigation of a Citizen Above Suspicion; Jackson County Jail; La Balance; Lethal Weapon 3; Macon County Line; Magnum Force; The Money Trap; Moving Violation; No Escape, No Return; Panic in Needle Park; Posse (1975); Prince of the City; The Prowler; Q & A; Rough Cut; Serpico; Shakedown; Smokey and the Bandit; Smokey and the Bandit II; Smokey and the Bandit III; Speed; Super Cops; Tango & Cash; The Thin Blue Line; To Kill a Priest; Touch of Evil; The Trial (1962); The Trial (1993); Unforgiven (1992); Unlawful Entry; White Lightning; Witness

Police-Former: see also *Police Stories: Detective Stories: Retirement:* FBI Story; Midnight Man; Tequila Sunrise; Vertigo

Police-Corruption: see also *Corruption: Underworld: Cops-Vigilante: Fascism: Oppression:* The Border; Burglars; Detective Story; Internal Affairs; Prince of the City; Serpico

Police Detectives: see *Detectives-Police*

Police Murderers: see *Murderers of Police*

Police Stories: see also *Crime Drama: Police Comedy: Buddy Cops: Cops-Vigilante: Police-Corruption: Detective Stories: Romance with Law Officers: Law Officers-Female: Canadian Mounties:* Abilene Town; Across 110th Street; Another Stakeout; Assault on Precinct 13; Bad Boys (1994); Badge 373; Big Heat; Bitch (La Garce) (1984); Black Rain (1989); Blue Lamp; Blue Thunder; Borderline; Brannigan; Buffet Froid; Bullets or Ballots; Bullitt; Bureau of Missing Persons; Burglars; Calling Northside 777; Car 99; Chato's Land; China Moon; Choirboys; Cisco Pike; Cobra; Code of Silence; Colors; Comancheros; Come Back Charleston Blue; Coogan's Bluff; Cop; Cotton Comes to Harlem; Coup de Torchon; Crime and Punishment; Dallas; Dark Wind; Dead Pool; Deadly Matrimony; Death of a Gunfighter; Deep Cover; Delicate

Delinquent; Delta Heat; Demolition Man; Destry Rides Again; Detective Story; Devlin; Dirty Harry; Dodge City; Dragnet (1954); Dragnet (1987); Drop Zone; 8 Million Ways to Die; Electra Glide in Blue; The Enforcer (1976); Excessive Force; Extreme Justice; Fatal Beauty; FBI Story; The First Deadly Sin; First Power; Flashpoint; Fort Apache, The Bronx; 48 Hours; Freebie and the Bean; The French Connection; The French Connection II; Full Eclipse; Fuzz; G-Men; Gator; The Gauntlet; Golden Gate; Good Day for a Hanging; Hard to Kill; The Hard Way (1991); Heart Condition; High Noon; Homicide; Hot Stuff; Hustle; I Walk the Line; The Indian Runner; Internal Affairs; Investigation of a Citizen Above Suspicion; K-9; Kansan; The Killer Inside Me; Kinjite, Forbidden Subjects; The Klansman; Last Hard Men; The Laughing Policeman; Law and Disorder (1958); Law and Disorder (1974); The Law and Jake Wade; Lawman; Lethal Weapon; Lethal Weapon 3; Live Wire; Lost; Love and Bullets; Madigan; Magnum Force; Maniac Cop; Maniac Cop 2; Maverick; McQ; Me and My Gal; The Money Trap; Monolith; Moving; Murphy's Law; My Darling Clementine; Naked City; Naked Gun; Naked Gun 2½; Naked Gun 33⅓; Narrow Margin (1952); Narrow Margin (1990); Needful Things; New Jack City; Nightfall; Nighthawks (1981); No Escape, No Return; No Man's Land (1987); No Mercy; Northwest Mounted Police; The Offence; On Dangerous Ground; One False Move; One Good Cop; The Onion Field; Only the Lonely; Out of the Dark; Physical Evidence; The Player; The Posse (1975); Predator 2; Prince of the City; The Prowler; Q & A; Red Heat; Relentless; Relentless 2; Relentless 3; Renegades; Report to the Commissioner; Return of the Pink Panther; The Rookie; Rose Marie (1936); Rose Marie (1954); Running Scared; Rush; Sapphire; Scandal in Paris; Scanner Cop; Scarface Mob/The Untouchables Pilot; Sea Devils (1937); Sea of Love; Serpico; Seven-Ups; Shakedown; Sharky's Machine; Shoot to Kill; Short Time; Showdown; Silver Lode; Slaughter on Tenth Avenue; The Sniper; Someone to Watch Over Me; Speed; Split Second; Stakeout; Stop! Or My Mom Will Shoot; A Stranger Among Us; Striking Distance; Sudden Impact; Super Cops; The Taking of Beverly Hills; The Taking of Pelham 123; The Tall Target; Tango & Cash; They Call Me Mr. Tibbs!; Tick, Tick, Tick . . .; Tightrope; Time Cop; Tin Star; To Live and Die in L.A.; Tombstone; The Town; Traces of Red; Trouble in Mind; True Confessions; Turner & Hooch; Witness; Wyatt Earp

Police-Vigilante: see also *Police-Corruption:* Badge 373; Beast of the City; Beverly Hills Cop; Beverly Hills Cop 2; Bullitt; Dead Bang; Die Hard; Die Hard 2; Dirty Harry; The Enforcer (1976); Excessive Force; Extreme Justice; Eye for an Eye; The Gauntlet; Hit!; The Klansman; Law and Disorder (1974); Magnum Force; Passenger 57; Sharky's Machine; Super Cops; Taking of Beverly Hills; To Live and Die in L.A.

Police vs. Mob: see also *Mob Wars:* Assault on Precinct 13; Beast of the City; Black Rain (1989); Boiling Point; Code of Silence; Cops and Robbersons; Excessive Force; G-Men; Good Fellas; Johnny Eager; One False Move; Scarface Mob/The Untouchables Pilot; The Seven-Ups

Policewomen: see *Female Law Officers*

Polish Films: see also *Europeans-Eastern: Czech People/Films:* Ashes and Diamonds; Danton; The Interrogation; Man of Iron; Man of Marble; A Short Film About Killing; To Kill a Priest; The Torrents of Spring

Polish People (not necessarily in Poland): see also *Europeans-Eastern:* Miss Rose White; Moonlighting (1982); Paper Marriage; The Passion; Red Kiss; Silver City; Success Is the Best Revenge

Political Activists: see also *Political Drama: Terrorists:* Daniel; Dark Command; Getting Straight; Heavens Above; Molly Maguires; Nanou; Reds; Stand Up and Be Counted; Viva Maria!

Political Campaigns: see also *Politicians: Political Films:* The Candidate; The Cowboy and the Lady; The Farmer's Daughter; Gabriel over the White House; The Great McGinty; The Last Hurrah; Meet John Doe; Power; Primary Motive; Running Mates; The Senator Was Indiscreet; Speechless; State of the Union; Storyville; Tanner '88; True Colors; The War Room

Political Comedy: see *Political Satire*

Political Corruption: see also *Government Corruption:* Beau James; A Canterbury Tale; Capricorn One; Diggstown; Flamingo Road; The Great

McGinty; The Last Hurrah; Louisiana Purchase; Lucretia Borgia; Miller's Crossing; Western Union; Wet Parade; Wild Palms

Political Drama: see also *Political Satire: Politicians: Message Films: Social Drama: Civil Rights: Ethics: Corruption: Government Corruption:* Adalen 31; Advise and Consent; All the King's Men; All the President's Men; Angelina; Best Man; Betrayed (1989); Beyond the Limit; Black Fury; Born Again; Boss; Brubaker; A Bullet for the General; Burn!; Bushido Blade; The Candidate; A Canterbury Tale; Capricorn One; The China Syndrome; Citizen Kane; City of Hope; The Comedians; The Confession; Daniel; Danton; Disraeli; Do The Right Thing; Dragon Seed; A Dry White Season; El Norte; Elmer Gantry; Enemy of the People (1977); Enemy of the People (1989); Eminent Domain; A Face in the Crowd; Falcon and the Snowman; The Fountainhead; The Glass Key (1935); The Glass Key (1942); Hanussen; Havana; Hidden Agenda; The Holcroft Covenant; I Am the Law; Illustrious Corpses; JFK; Jud Suess; Justine; Katherine; Keeper of the Flame; Kings and Desperate Men; Kiss of the Spider Woman; La Passante; The Last Emperor; The Last Hurrah; Lion is in the Streets; Lost Honor of Katharina Blum; Lucretia Borgia; Malcolm X; Manon; Mark of the Hawk; Matewan; Meet John Doe; Missing; Mr. Smith Goes to Washington; Nashville; Network; Night of the Shooting Stars; 1900; North Star; Oblomov; Odd Man Out; The Odessa File; Olympische Spiele; Open City; The Parallax View; Paris Trout; Party and the Guests; The Passenger; Power; Primary Motive; The Prisoner (1955); The Quiet American; Red Kiss; Red Sorghum; Romero; RPM; Sacrifice; Saint Joan; Sakharov; Salamander; Salvador; San Francisco Story; Scandal; Secret Honor; Secret People; 1776; Shame (1961); Shame (1968); Show of Force; State of Siege; Taxi Driver; This is My Affair; This Land is Mine; Timebomb; To Have and Have Not; Tragedy of a Ridiculous Man; Turtle Beach; Twilight's Last Gleaming; The Ugly American; The Unbearable Lightness of Being; Uranus; Walker; We Were Strangers; Wedding Night; Western Union; Wet Parade; When Father Was Away on Business; The Wilby Conspiracy; World Apart; Wrong Is Right;

The Year of Living Dangerously; Young Philadelphians; Z

Political Satire/Comedy: see also *SATIRE: Washington D.C.: Politicians:* Bananas; Bob Roberts; Call Me Madam; The Comedians; First Monday in October; Gabriel over the White House; The Great Dictator; The Great McGinty; Joke of Destiny; No Surrender; Phantom President; The President's Analyst; Running Mates; Secret Honor; The Seduction of Mimi; The Senator Was Indiscreet; Speechless; Tanner '88; Wrong is Right; WUSA

Political Thriller: see also *Political Drama: Spy Films:* All the President's Men; Clear and Present Danger; Forbin Project; Futureworld; The Holcroft Covenant; The Hunt for Red October; The Manchurian Candidate; The Parallax View; Taxi Driver; Twilight's Last Gleaming; War Games; Z

Political Unrest: see also *Third World Countries: Diplomats: Riots: Leaders-Tyrant: Dictators: South America: Africa:* Appointment in Honduras; Arise, My Love; Attica (1971); Attica (1991); Bananas; Battle of Algiers; The Battleship Potemkin; Black and White in Color; A Bullet for the General; Burn!; Bushido Blade; Candide; Che!; Christ Stopped at Eboli; Cisco Kid; The Comedians; The Confession; Conquest of the Planet of the Apes; Danton; Dark Command; Dogs of War; El Norte; The Fall of the Roman Empire; Fortunes of War; Gunga Din; Gunrunner; Havana; Heartbreak Ridge; House of the Spirits; Idolmaker; If I Were King; Illustrious Corpses; Island in the Sun Juarez; The Killing Fields; Knight Without Armor; La Marseillaise; The Last Emperor; Mademoiselle Fifi; Malaya; Malcolm X; Man of Marble; Mandela; Marie Antoinette; Mark of the Hawk; Mark of Zorro (1920); Mark of Zorro (1940); Marquise of O; Master of Ballantree; Mayerling (1935); Mayerling (1968); McBain; Medium Cool; Message to Garcia; Metropolis; Missing; The Molly Maguires; Moon Over Parador; Moonlighting (1982); Nicholas and Alexandra; The Official Story; Old Gringo; Rebecca's Daughters; Red Dawn; Red Sorghum; Reds; The Revolutionary; Romero; RPM; Sakharov; Salamander; Salvador; Seven Days in May; Seventh Dawn; Shake Hands with the Devil;

Shame (1968); The Sniper; Spartacus; The Strawberry Statement; Strike; A Tale of Two Cities (1935); A Tale of Two Cities (1958); A Tale of Two Cities (1982); That Lady in Ermine; Trader Horn; The Ugly American; The Unbearabale Lightness of Being; Uranus; Vera Cruz; Viva Maria!; Viva Zapata; We Were Strangers; Wild in the Streets; Wrath of God; The Year of Living Dangerously; Z

Politicians: see also *Political Campaigns: Washington D.C.: Presidents: Congressmen/Senators: Political Films: Corruption: Rags to Riches:* Abe Lincoln in Illinois; Accent on Love; Ada; Adventure in Washington; Advise and Consent; All the King's Men; Beau James; Being There; The Best Little Whorehouse in Texas; The Best Man; Black Sunday (1977); Blaze; Blow Out; Bob Roberts; Born Yesterday (1950); Born Yesterday (1993); Boss; The Candidate; A Canterbury Tale; Chinatown; Citizen Kane; City of Hope; The Detective (1968); Disraeli; A Face in the Crowd; The Farmer's Daughter; The Final Conflict; Flamingo Road; Futureworld; The Glass Key (1935); The Glass Key (1942); Goodbye My Fancy; The Great McGinty; Heavens Above; I Am the Law; I Love Trouble (1947); Internecine Project; Joke of Destiny; Key to the City; King; Kisses for My President; Kitten with a Whip; The Last Hurrah; LBJ: The Early Years; Lion is in the Streets; Louisiana Purchase; Magnificent Yankee; Malcolm X; Mark of the Hawk; The Masquerader; Mastergate; Morgan Stewart's Coming Home; Mr. Smith Goes to Washington; My Girl Tisa; Paris By Night; Parnell; Phantom President; Power; Primary Motive; Rising Sun; Running Mates; San Francisco Story; Sanctuary; Scandal; The Seduction of Joe Tynan; The Senator Was Indiscreet; 1776; The Shaggy D.A.; The Shaggy Dog; State of the Union; Storyville; Sweet Bird of Youth; Tanner '88; Three for the Road; Time Cop; The Times of Harvey Milk; Walker; The War Room; Western Union; Wet Parade; What Every Woman Knows; Wild Palms; Woman of the Year; Young Philadelphians

Politicians-Female: see also *Congressmen/Senators: Politicians:* Angelina; Call Me Madam; A Foreign Affair; Goodbye My Fancy; Kisses for My President

Politicians' Wives (where the story has a significant focus on them): Dave; Running Mates; The Seduction of Joe Tynan; State of the Union; What Every Woman Knows

Pool (the billiards game): see also *Games:* Baltimore Bullet; The Color of Money; The Hustler; Kiss Shot

Poor People: see also *Depression Era: Inner City Life: Rednecks: Working Class: Rags to Riches:* All the Right Moves; Always Goodbye; Arthur 2, On the Rocks; Barfly; Barnacle Bill (1941); batteries not included; The Bicycle Thief; Big Man; Christmas in July; Cinderella Liberty; Daybreak; Distant Thunder (1973); The Effect of Gamma Rays on Man-in-the-Moon Marigolds; Fat City; For Queen and Country; Gilded Lily; The Glass Menagerie (1950); The Glass Menagerie (1973); The Glass Menagerie (1987); God's Little Acre; Going My Way; The Good Earth; The Grapes of Wrath; Has Anybody Seen My Gal?; A Hero Ain't Nothin' but a Sandwich; Hoop Dreams; Jude the Obscure; Knock on Any Door; La Vie de Boheme; Ladybird, Ladybird; London Kills Me; Lunatics, A Love Story; Man's Castle; Max Dugan Returns; Min and Bill; Monsieur Vincent; Mrs. Wiggs of the Cabbage Patch; Object of Beauty; Once Were Warriors; One Magic Christmas; One More Spring; Pearl; Pixote; Popi; Private Function; The Purple Rose of Cairo; Rob Roy; Riff-Raff (1935); Salaam Bombay!; Sounder; The Southerner; Soylent Green; Tobacco Road; Tortilla Flat; Tovarich; A Tree Grows in Brooklyn; Tree of Wooden Clogs; Tropic of Cancer; The Wanderers; What's Eating Gilbert Grape?; Where the Red Fern Grows; Wildflower; The Wiz; Working Girls; The Yearling

Poor White Trash: see *Rednecks: Southerns*

Popes/Cardinals: see also *Priests: Nuns: Religion:* Abdication; The Agony and the Ecstasy; Becket; Cardinal; The Devils; Foul Play; The Godfather, Part III; Monsignor; Pope Joan; The Pope Must Die(t); Saving Grace; Shoes of the Fisherman; Sister Act; The Three Musketeers (1935); The Three Musketeers (1948); The Three Musketeers (1973); The Three Musketeers (1993)

Pornography World: see also *Photographers: Underworld: Erotic*

Drama: Erotic Thriller: Bloodline; Body Double; Defenseless; Die Watching; The Favour, the Watch & the Very Big Fish; 52 Pick-up; Hardcore; Hi, Mom!; Hold Me, Thrill Me, Kiss Me; Inserts; Is There Sex After Death?; Kinjite, Forbidden Subjects; Love Crimes; Love God?; Move; My Father is Coming; Nadine; No Sex, Please, We're British; The Pornographers; Promise Her Anything; Rented Lips; Tie Me Up! Tie Me Down!; Variety; Videodrome

Posses: see *Manhunts: Bounty Hunters: WESTERNS: Lynchings/Lynch Mobs: Fugitives from the Law*

Possessions: see also *Satan/Satanism: Supernatural: Hauntings: SCI-FI: Fantasy:* Amityville 1992: It's About Time; Amityville 4; Amityville, a New Generation; The Amityville Curse; The Amityville Horror; Amityville Horror 2, The Possession; Audrey Rose; The Awakening; Back From the Dead; Blood from the Mummy's Tomb; Blood on Satan's Claw; Burnt Offerings; Cameron's Closet; Carrie (1976); The Changeling; Child's Play (1988); Child's Play 2; Child's Play 3; Christine; Cujo; The Curse of the Cat People; Devil Doll; Devils; The Exorcist; Exorcist II: The Heretic; Exorcist III; Halloween 3: Season of the Witch; Heart Condition; The House; House II: The Second Story; House III; House IV; The Innocents; Legend of Hell House; Mad Love; Magic; Manitou; Mannequin 2: On the Move; Maxie; Medusa Touch; Needful Things; 976-Evil; Nomads; Poltergeist; Poltergeist 2; Poltergeist 3; Possession of Joel Delaney; Repossessed; The Stand; To Dance with the White Dog; Tommyknockers; Unholy; The Uninvited; The Unnamable; The Unnamable Returns; Wolfen

Post-War Eras: see *World War II-Post Era: Vietnam Era: Korean War: Civil War Era*

Potions: see *Cures/Elixirs: Magic: Fantasy: Cures/Solutions-Search for: Witchcraft*

POWs/MIAs: see also *Vietnam Era: Missing Persons:* Act of Violence; Blood Alley; Bridge on the River Kwai; Captive Heart; Code Name: Emerald; The Deer Hunter; Desperate Journey; Destiny of a Man; Distant Drums; Empire of the Sun; Grand Illusion; The Great Escape; Great Escape 2: The Untold Story; Hanoi

Hilton; Hook; Hot Shots, Part Deux; Indochine; In Love and War; King of The Hill (1965); King Rat; Merry Christmas, Mr. Lawrence; Missing in Action; Missing in Action 2-The Beginning; The One That Got Away; Raid on Rommel; Rambo: First Blood Part Two; Rambo III; Rolling Thunder; Shadow Riders; Situation Hopeless But Not Serious; Some Kind of Hero; Stalag 17; Summer of My German Soldier; The Tenth Man; Three Came Home; A Town Like Alice (1956); A Town Like Alice (1985); Uncommon Valor; Von Ryan's Express; When Hell Was in Session; Wooden Horse

Power-Fall from: see *Rise and Fall Stories: Political Films: Biographies: Riches to Rags: Political Unrest*

Power Outages: see *Blackouts*

Power-Rise to: see also *Political Drama: Biographies: Rags to Riches: Rise and Fall: American Dream:* Abe Lincoln in Illinois; About Face; Abraham Lincoln; Ada; All the King's Men; American Romance; The Bad and the Beautiful; The Barefoot Executive; Being There; The Big Town; Bob Roberts; Born to Be Bad (1950); The Candidate; Cardinal; Carousel; Citizen Kane; Come and Get It; Doctor Detroit; F.I.S.T.; A Face in the Crowd; Farmer's Daughter; The Final Conflict; Giant; Good Fellas; The Great McGinty; Hard to Handle; Hawaiians; Heavens Above; Hitler Gang; Hitler-The Last Ten Days; Hoffa; Hollywood Cavalcade; How to Succeed in Business without Really Trying; The Hudsucker Proxy; I Can Get It For You Wholesale; I, Mobster; Jack of All Trades; King David; King of New York; LBJ: The Early Years; Limit Up; Lion is in the Streets; Little Caesar; Lloyd's of London; Lucy Gallant; Malcolm X; The Man in the Grey Flannel Suit; Manhattan Melodrama; Mildred Pierce; Mobsters; Monsignor; Murder, Inc.; My Son, My Son; Nothing But the Best; The Ploughman's Lunch; Power; Public Enemy; The Rise and Rise of Michael Rimmer; Roaring Twenties; Roberta; Ruby Gentry; Scarface (1932); Scarface (1983); The Secret of My Success; Shoes of the Fisherman; Toast of New York; Tower of London (1939); Tower of London (1962); Tulsa; Which Way is Up?; Wild in the Streets; Working Girl; Young Catherine; Young Philadelphians; Young Winston

Power-Rise to: of Idiot: see also *Simple Minds:* The Barefoot Executive; Being There; CB4: The Movie; Doctor Detroit; Duck Soup; The Errand Boy; A Face in the Crowd; The Flintstones; How to Succeed in Business without Really Trying; The Hudsucker Proxy; The Jerk; The Rise and Rise of Michael Rimmer; Sad Sack; Up the Creek (1958)

Power Struggles: see also *Political Films: Mindgames: Power-Rise to:* Advise and Consent; Bad Company (1995); Becket; Behold a Pale Horse; Betsy; Big Country; Black Hole; Black Room; Bounty; Braveheart; Breaker Morant; Buccaneer (1938); Buccaneer (1958); Caesar and Cleopatra; The Caine Mutiny (1954); The Caine Mutiny; Court Martial (1988); Camelot; Casino; The Charge of the Light Brigade (1936); The Charge of the Light Brigade (1968); City Streets; Command Decision; The Commitments; Cromwell; Dangerous Liaisons; Demon Knight; Diamond Head; Eminent Domain; Executive Suite; The Fall of the Roman Empire; Flight of the Phoenix; From Here to Eternity; A Gathering of Eagles; The Godfather; The Godfather, Part II; The Godfather, Part III; Gung Ho (1986); Hedda; The Hudsucker Proxy; King Lear (1971); Lion in Winter; The Mouse That Roared; Murder, Inc.; Mutiny on the Bounty (1935); Mutiny on the Bounty (1962); Nasty Habits; Network; Oscar; The Paper; Paths of Glory; Patterns; Prince Valiant; Queen Bee; Ran; Romanoff and Juliet; Run Silent Run Deep; Sand Pebbles; Sands of the Kalahari; Scarface (1932); Scarface (1983); Skullduggery; Slight Case of Murder; Sodom and Gomorrah; State of Things; Treasure of the Sierra Madre; Wall Street; White Mile; Wolf

Powers-Fantasy: see *Magic: Psychics: Fairy Tales: SCI-FI*

Practical Jokers: see also *Mindgames: Wild People: Coming of Age: Teenage Movies: Juvenile Delinquents: Rebels:* Beverly Hills Cop; Beverly Hills Cop 2; The Big Broadcast of 1938; Brother Rat; Carrie (1976); The Great Garrick; The Great Santini; Grumpy Old Men; If I Were King; The Jerky Boys; The Lawrenceville Stories; Man of the House; M*A*S*H; Morgan Stewart's Coming Home; The Ninth Configuration; No Escape (1936); O.C. and Stiggs; Oh, Rosalinda!; The Program

Preachers/Ministers: see also *Priests: Religion: Conservative Value Films: Jewish People:* Angel Baby; Angel in My Pocket; Battle Hymn; Belizaire the Cajun; The Bishop's Wife; The Confession; Cotton Comes to Harlem; The Devil's Disciple; The Disappearance of Aimee; Distant Thunder (1973); Elmer Gantry; Fletch Lives; Footloose; The Ghoul (1975); Glory! Glory!; Hallelujah!; A Handmaid's Tale; Heaven with a Gun; Invitation to the Wedding; King; Leap of Faith; License to Kill; The Little Minister; Luther; Miracle Woman; Night of the Hunter; Night of the Iguana; Of Human Hearts; One Foot in Heaven; Pass the Ammo; The Rain; Rapture; Repossessed; Resurrection; The Sandpiper; Say Amen, Somebody!; Wise Blood

Predicaments: see *Trapped: Situation Comedy*

Pregnancies: see *Babies-Having: Mothers-Unwed: Mothers Alone*

Prehistoric Settings/Times (not necessarily including dinosaurs) see also *Cave People: Ancient Times: Dinosaurs:* Caveman; Clan of the Cave Bear; The Flintstones; One Million BC (1940); One Million Years BC (1966); Quest for Fire; When Dinosaurs Ruled the Earth

Pre-Life Crisis: see also *20-Somethings: Life Transitions: Coming of Age: Teenagers: Suicidal Tendencies of Young People: Mid-Life Crisis:* Bachelor Party (1957); Bed and Board; The Bell Jar; The Boy Who Had Everything; Bright Lights, Big City; Broadway Bound; Career Opportunities; Claudia; Diner; Fandango; For Keeps; The Graduate; Impatient Years; Jersey Girl; Life Is Sweet; Life of Her Own; Mickey One; The Paper Chase; The Rain People; Razor's Edge (1946); Razor's Edge (1986); Rocket to the Moon; Saturday Night and Sunday Morning; Shaking the Tree; She's Having a Baby; Singles; Slacker; Some Came Running; St. Elmo's Fire; Stolen Kisses; T.R. Baskin; Tall Story; 21; Up the Sandbox; Who's That Knocking at My Door?; Wild Life

Premonitions: see *Psychics: Future-Seeing the*

Presidents (American president characters, real or fictitious, in prominent roles) see also *Political Films: Political Campaigns: Congressmen/Senators: Washington D.C.:* Abe Lincoln in Illinois; Abraham Lincoln; Advise and Consent; The Assassination; The Best Man; Blind Ambition; Buccaneer (1938); Buccaneer (1958); The Cowboy and the Lady; Dave; Day of the Dolphin; The Dead Zone; Disraeli; Duck Soup; Eleanor & Franklin; Escape From New York; Fail Safe; First Family; Gabriel over the White House; Gore Vidal's Lincoln; Gorgeous Hussy; Guarding Tess; Hot Shots, Part Deux; In the Line of Fire; Intemecine Project; Jefferson in Paris; JFK; The Kidnapping of the President; Kisses for My President; LBJ: The Early Years; MacArthur; Magnificent Doll; My Girl Tisa; The Pelican Brief; The President's Analyst; Running Mates; Secret Honor; The Senator Was Indiscreet; Seven Days in May; 1776; Sunrise at Campobello; The Tall Target; This Is My Affair; Twilight's Last Gleaming; The War Room; Whoops! Apocalypse (1983); Whoops! Apocalypse (1986); Wild in the Streets; Wilson; The Wind and the Lion; Winter Kills; Young Mr. Lincoln

Pretending: see *Marriages-Fake: Death-Faked: Liars: Con Artists: Disguises: Impostors: Screwball Comedy: FARCE*

Priests: see also *Disguised as Priests: Religion: Popes: Nuns: Monks: Preachers/Ministers:* The Abdication; Absolution; Act of the Heart; The Angel Wore Red; Assisi Underground; Bay Boy; The Bells of St. Mary's; Best Intentions; Boys Town; Camila (1984); Cardinal; Cardinal Richelieu; The Detective (1954); The Devil's Advocate; The Devils; Diary of a Country Priest; Edge of Doom; The Exorcist; Exorcist II: The Heretic; Francis, God's Jester; The Fugitive (1947); Going My Way; Heaven Help Us; I Confess; Kitchen Toto; Lamb; Last Rites; Leather Saint; The Left Hand of God; Legend of the Holy Drinker; Mass Appeal; Men of Boys' Town; The Mission; Monsignor; The Priest; The Prisoner (1955); Romance; Romero; The Rosary Murders; Runner Stumbles; Saint Benny, the Dip; San Francisco; Say One for Me; Song of Bernadette; To Kill a Priest; True Confessions; Unholy; We're No Angels (1955); We're No Angels (1989); When in Rome; Winter Light

Primal Fears: see *Phobias: MURDER: THRILLERS*

Primates (non-human, gorillas to mon-keys, vague since there are so many varieties that are difficult to distin-guish): see also *Africa: Jungle Life:* Any Which Way You Can; Ape; The Barefoot Executive; Battle for the Planet of the Apes; Bedtime for Bonzo; Beneath the Planet of the Apes; Bonzo Goes to College; Born to be Wild; Conquest of the Planet of the Apes; Dead Alive; Escape from the Planet of the Apes; Every Which Way But Loose; Gorilla; Gorilla at Large; Gorillas in the Mist; Greystoke: The Legend of Tarzan; Horror Express; Island of Lost Souls; King Kong (1933); King Kong (1976); The Link; Mighty Joe Young; Monkey Business (1952); Monkey Shines; Monkey Trouble; Monkeys Go Home; Murders in the Rue Morgue; Outbreak; Phantom of the Rue Morgue; Planet of the Apes; Project X; Son of Kong; Tarzan and His Mate; Tarzan Escapes; Tarzan, The Ape Man (1932); Tarzan, the Ape Man (1981); Tarzan's New York Adventure; Trog; The Watchers; Watchers II

Princes: see also *Princesses: Fairy Tales: Royalty: Queens: Kings: Castles: Medieval Times:* Alexander Nevsky; Alice in Wonderland; Beau Brummell (1924); Beau Brummell (1954); Cinderella; Diana: Her True Story; The Fifth Musketeer; Flame Over India; Hamlet (1948); Hamlet (1964); Hamlet (1969); Hamlet (1991); Iron Mask (1929); Krull; The Little Prince; Love Parade; Masquerade (1965); Nothing but Trouble (1941); The Prince and the Showgirl; Prince Valiant; The Princess Bride; Rosencrantz and Guildenstern Are Dead; The Royal Wedding; Sleeping Beauty; The Slipper and the Rose; Snow White and the Seven Dwarfs; The Swan; The Swan Princess; Sword in the Stone; Sword and the Sorcerer; Thin Ice; Trouble for Two; The Wedding March

Princesses: see also *Princes: Fairy Tales: Royalty: Queens: Kings: Castles: Medieval Times:* Anastasia (1956); Anastasia (1984); Darling; Diana: Her True Story; Elena and Her Men; Felix the Cat: The Movie; Krull; Lady in the Iron Mask; Mothra; Naughty Marietta; The Princess Bride; Princess Caraboo; Roman Holiday; Siegfried; Sleeping Beauty; The Smiling Lieutenant; The Swan; The Swan Princess; You're Telling Me

Prison Drama (or comedy, as the case may be): see also *Prison Escapes:*

Women in Prison: Convicts: Escapes Drama: Social Drama: Juvenile Delinquents: Alien 3; American Me; Attica (1971); Attica (1991); Bad Boys; Big House; The Birdman of Alcatraz; Blood Alley; Born in East L.A.; Brubaker; Caged; Caged Fear; Caged Heat; Captive Heart; CB4: The Movie; Chattahoochee; Come See the Paradise; Comrades; Cool Hand Luke; The Count of Monte Cristo (1934); The Count of Monte Cristo (1974); Daybreak; Death Warrant; Desperate Journey; Devil Doll; The Dirty Dozen; Down By Law; Dunera Boys; Dynamite; Escape from Alcatraz; Escape From New York; The Executioner's Song; Forgotten Prisoners; Fortune and Men's Eyes; Ghosts . . . of the Civil Dead; Glass House; The Great Escape; Hill; Hold Your Man; House of Women; I Am a Fugitive from a Chain Gang; I Believe in You; I Never Promised You A Rose Garden; I Stand Condemned; An Innocent Man; The Interrogation; J.W. Coop; Jackson County Jail; Jailhouse Rock; King of The Hill (1965); King Rat; Kiss of the Spider Woman; Ladies They Talk About; Les Miserables (1935); Les Miserables (1952); Les Miserables (1978); Lock Up; Longest Yard; Love Child; Mackintosh Man; Mandela; The Mark; Mary Burns, Fugitive; McVicar; Merry Christmas, Mr. Lawrence; Midnight Express; Murder in the First; Naked Street; The Name of the Father; No Escape (1994); One Flew Over Cuckoo's Nest; The Onion Field; Paid; Papillon; Passage to Marseilles; Past Midnight; Poison; Prison Stories: Women on the Inside; The Prisoner: Arrival; Remember My Name; San Quentin; The Shawshank Redemption; Short Eyes; Silas Marner; Sitting Target; Situation Hopeless But Not Serious; Stalag 17; Stir Crazy; Straight Time; Strange Cargo; Tango & Cash; A Town Like Alice (1956); A Town Like Alice (1985); Twenty Thousand Years in Sing Song; The Unconquered; Victory; Weeds

Prison Escapes: see also *Escapes: Prison Drama:* After The Fox; Alone in the Dark; The Big House; Blood Alley; Breakout; Bright Angel; Caged Fear; Chase (1966); Colorado Territory; Cool Hand Luke; Dark Passage; Deadlock; Defiant Ones; Desperate Hours (1955); Desperate Hours (1990); Desperate Journey; Dr. Giggles; Drop Zone; Eddie

Macon's Run; Escape from Alcatraz; Escape from Fort Bravo; Fugitive (1993); The Fugitive Lovers; The Fugitive: The Final Episode; The Great Escape; Great Escape 2: The Untold Story; Halloween; Halloween 2; Halloween 4: The Return of Michael Myers; Halloween 5: The Revenge of Michael Myers; I am a Fugitive from a Chain Gang; It Always Rains on Sunday; King of The Hill (1965); Kiss Tomorrow Goodbye; The Last Hard Men; The Last House on the Left; Mad Max Beyond Thunderdome; Martin's Day; Mary Burns, Fugitive; McVicar; Menace; Mrs. Soffel; Papillon; Passage to Marseilles; Raid on Rommel; Rawhide; Runaway Train; Seventh Cross; Shocker; Stalag 17; Stir Crazy; Strange Cargo; Tango & Cash; Tank; They Live by Night; Twenty Thousand Years in Sing Sing; Two Way Stretch; Victory; Von Ryan's Express

Prisoners of War/Missing in Action: see *POWs/MIAs*

Problem Child: see *Children-Problem: Children-Brats*

Prodigies (child): see *Children-Gifted: also Children-Little Adults: Geniuses: Understudies*

Production Design-Outstanding (either outstanding in scope or in detail): see also *Scenery-Outstanding: Academy Awards Listings for Best Art Direction:* The Adventures of Baron Munchausen (1987); Amadeus; An American in Paris; Barry Lyndon; Beau Geste (1939); Ben-Hur (1926); Ben-Hur (1959); Big Town; Black Narcissus; Blade Runner; The Boy Friend; Brazil; Cleopatra (1934); Cleopatra (1963); The Cotton Club; Dangerous Liaisons; The Devils; Doctor Dolittle; Doctor Zhivago; Dune; Earthquake; Edward Scissorhands; Fall of Roman Empire; The Frenchman's Creek; Gigi; The Good Earth; Great Expectations; Hello, Dolly!; Honey, I Blew Up the Kid; Honey, I Shrunk the Kids; The Hudsucker Proxy; Joe vs. the Volcano; The King and I; Lost Horizon; Mary Poppins; Moulin Rouge; My Fair Lady; One From the Heart; Popeye; The Poseidon Adventure; Public Eye; Red Shoes; The Robe; The Shadow; Sign of the Cross; Spartacus; Star Wars; The Ten Commandments; The Thief of Bagdad; 20,000 Leagues Under the Sea; Vertigo; West Side Story; Who Framed Roger Rabbitt?; The Wizard of Oz; Yolanda and the Thief

Professors: see also *College Life: Teachers: Law School: Medical School:* The Accused (1948); Adam at 6 A.M.; Altered States; The Amazing Dr. Clitterhouse; American Friends; Animal Behavior; Another Woman; B.F.'s Daughter; Ball of Fire; Bedtime for Bonzo; Conversation Piece; Doctor Detroit; End of the Road; Fade to Black (1993); The Fearless Vampire Killers; From the Hip; Getting Straight; Glass House; Horse Feathers; How Do I Love Thee; Husbands and Wives; Impossible Years; Internecine Project; It Happens Every Spring; Journey to the Center of the Earth; Male Animal; Mother is a Freshman; Murder by Phone; Naughty But Nice; Never on Sunday; Night in Heaven; The Nutty Professor (1963); The Paper Chase; Quiz Show; Raiders of the Lost Ark; Reuben, Reuben; RPM; She's Working Her Way Through College; So Fine; A Song Is Born; Speak Easily; Surviving Desire; Vivacious Lady; Wetherby; Who Was That Lady?; Who's Afraid of Virginia Woolf?; Wild Strawberries; Without Love; Woman in the Window

Prohibition Era: see also *Bootlegging: 1920s: Mob Stories: Drugs:* Dillinger (1945); Dillinger (1973); Little Giant (1933); Miller's Crossing; Moonshine War; Murder, Inc.; Now I'll Tell; Roaring Twenties; Some Like it Hot; The Untouchables; Wet Parade

Promiscuity: see also *Sexy Women: Sexy Men: Prostitutes: Bimbos: Bimboys: Sexual Revolution: Sexual Kinkiness: Pornography World: Alternative Lifestyles:* Alvin Purple; Alvin Rides Again; The Amorous Adventures of Moll Flanders; And God Created Woman (1957); Baby Face; Bad Lieutenant; Banning; The Bawdy Adventures of Tom Jones; Blood and Concrete; Butterfly; Casanova '70; Casanova (Fellini's Casanova); Casual Sex?; Chapman Report; Claudelle Inglish; Dark Obsession; The Doctor's Wives; Emmanuelle SERIES; Fanny Hill; Forever Amber; A Guide for the Married Man; I Love My Wife; Is There Sex After Death?; Je Vous Aime; Little Vera; Lock up Your Daughters; Lola (1982); Lonely Lady; Looking for Mr. Goodbar; Love Machine; Love With the Proper Stranger; The Man Who Loved Women (1977); The Man Who Loved Women (1983); Night

and Day; A Night in the Life of Jimmy Reardon; Pickup Artist; A Rage to Live; Rambling Rose; Rapture; Royal Scandal; Sammy and Rosie Get Laid; Satyricon (Fellini's); Seven Sinners; Shanghai Gesture; Sin of Madelon Claudet; Sweet November; This Property Is Condemned; W.H.I.F.F.S.; What's New Pussycat?; The World Is Full of Married Men

Prostitutes-Child: see also *Children-Little Adults: Inner City Life: Molestation: Child Abuse: Pornography World:* Angel; Christiane F.; Erendira; Kinjite, Forbidden Subjects; Pretty Baby; Taxi Driver

Prostitutes-High Class (call girls, courtesans): see also *Hooking but Nominated: Prostitutes with a Heart of Gold: Prostitutes-Low Class: Bimbos: Madams: Pimps: Romance with Prostitute:* Ada; The Angel Wore Red; Anna Christie; Belle du Jour; The Best Little Whorehouse in Texas; Beverly Hills Madam; Black Rain (1989); Breakfast at Tiffany's; Butterfield 8; Camille (1936); Cardinal Richelieu; Doctor Detroit; Dubarry Was a Lady; 8 Million Ways to Die; Forever Amber; From the Life of the Marionettes; Gigi (1948); Gigi (1958); Go Naked in the World; Grasshopper; Half Moon Street; The Happy Hooker; A House is Not a Home; Hustle; Justine; The King's Whore; Killing Zoe; Klute; Lola Montes; Madame Dubarry; Madame Rosa; Mademoiselle Fifi; Mayflower Madam; Mona Lisa; Moulin Rouge; Night Angel; No Way Out (1987); Nuts; The Oldest Profession; Passion/Madame Dubarry (1919); Personal Services; Raise the Red Lantern; Risky Business; Scandal; Tokyo Decadence; Two or Three Things I Know About Her; Walk on the Wild Side; Widows' Peak; Working Girls

Prostitutes-Low Class/General: see also *Hooking but Nominated: Prostitutes with a Heart of Gold: Prostitutes-Child: Inner City Life: Madams: Pimps: Romance with Prostitute:* Accatone; Amsterdamned; Angel; Back Roads; Balcony; Bocaccio '70; California Split; The Cheyenne Social Club; Christiane F.; Cinderella Liberty; Crimes of Passion; Dishonored; Dr. Jekyll and Sister Hyde; The Drum; East of Eden (1955); East of Eden (1980); Elmer Gantry; Everybody Wins; First Time; Flesh; Frankenhooker; The

French Lieutenant's Woman; From Here to Eternity; The Gauntlet; Gigot; I Walk the Line; Irma La Douce; Jumpin at the Boneyard; La Balance; Last Exit to Brooklyn; Lust in the Dust; The Man Who Loved Cat Dancing; McCabe and Mrs. Miller; Miami Blues; Milk Money; The Missionary; Naked Kiss; Night Shift; Nights of Cabiria; The Oldest Profession; The Owl and the Pussycat; Paper Moon; Paris, Texas; Pretty Baby; Pretty Woman; Sadie Thompson; Salaam Bombay!; Salon Kitty; Scarlet Street; Scorchers; Sharky's Machine; Sin of Madelon Claudet; Street Smart; Stroszek; Sweet Charity; This Property is Condemned; Traces of Red; True Romance; Two Mules for Sister Sara; Unforgiven (1992); Waterloo Bridge (1931); Waterloo Bridge (1940); Whore; Working Girls; The World of Suzie Wong; Yesterday, Today and Tomorrow

Prostitutes-Male: see also *Sexy Men: Playboys: Bimboys: Madams: Pimps:* Alexander, the Other Side of Dawn; American Gigolo; Ash Wednesday; Aspen Extreme; Being at Home with Claude; Breakfast at Tiffany's; Dirty Rotten Scoundrels; Female on the Beach; Flesh; The Honeymoon Killers; Just a Gigolo; L'Annee des Meduses; Little Vegas; Love Has Many Faces; Love is a Ball; Loverboy; Masquerade (1988); Midnight (1939); Midnight Cowboy; Moment by Moment; My Own Private Idaho; Night in Heaven; Roman Spring of Mrs. Stone; Shampoo; Stud; Sunset Boulevard; Sweet Bird of Youth; Three of Hearts; Woman in Flames

Prostitutes-Ordinary People Turned: see also *Prostitues-High Class/Low Class: Ordinary People Turned Criminal: Madams: Pimps:* Castaway; Doctor Detroit; Grasshopper; The Homecoming (1973); Honeymoon in Vegas; 'Tis a Pity She's a Whore; Two or Three Things I Know About Her; Woman in Flames; Working Girls

Prostitutes-Romance with: see *Romance with Prostitute*

Prostitutes with a Heart of Gold: see also *Romance with Prostitute: Prostitutes-High Class/Low Class: Prostitutes-Housewife: Free Spirits: Madams: Pimps:* California Split; Great Scout and Cathouse Thursday; Heaven's Gate; Killing Zoe; Miami Blues; Norma Rae; Steelyard Blues; Street Angel; Sweet

Charity; The Thousand Pieces of Gold; Trading Places

Protagonists: see *Heroes/Heroines-Classic: Child Protagonists: Female Protagonists*

Protagonist Is Killed (the first lead character that we meet is suddenly killed off): see also *Female Protagonists: Child Protagonists:* Alien; Dressed to Kill; Psycho; Triumphs of a Man Called Horse

Protecting Someone: see also *Bodyguards: Witnesses-Protecting: Police: Romance with Protector:* The Big Sleep (1946); The Big Sleep (1977); Blackmail (1929); Bodyguard; Cape Fear (1962); Cape Fear (1991); Cat Ballou; Crocodile Dundee; Cyborg; 8 Million Ways to Die; Experiment in Terror; The Gauntlet; Ghost; Indian Fighter; The Killer's Kiss; Kiss and Tell; Kung Fu; The Last Metro; The Last of the Mohicans (1936); The Last of the Mohicans (1992); The Legend of Billie Jean; The Magnificent Seven; The Man Who Shot Liberty Valance; Mona Lisa; My Beautiful Laundrette; My Best Friend's Girl; My Bodyguard; Octagon; Pale Rider; Patriot Games; Raggedy Man; Rain People; Return of the Seven; Ride the High Country; Rio Bravo; Saskatchewan; Seven Samurai; Smugglers; Someone to Watch Over Me; Stakeout; Stalking Moon; Sunday in New York; Two Women; The Unforgiven (1960); White Mama

Proteges (unofficial students, apprentices): see also *Mentors: Understudies:* Billy Bathgate; The Bostonians; A Bronx Tale; Bull Durham; Jack of Diamonds; The Mechanic; Searching for Bobby Fischer; Talent for the Game; You Can't Get Away With Murder

Psychedelic Era/Films: see also *Vietnam Era: 1960s: Hippies:* Barbarella; Don't Look Back; Doors; Easy Rider; Forrest Gump; Fritz the Cat; Gassss; Hair; Helter Skelter (1976); I Love You, Alice B. Toklas; Is There Sex After Death?; The Magic Christian; Maybe I'll Be Home in the Spring; Medium Cool; Midnight Cowboy; Panic in Needle Park; Patty Hearst; The President's Analyst; Psych-Out; Rebel Rousers; Skidoo; Superstar, The Life and Times of Andy Warhol; Taking Off; There's a Girl in My Soup; Trash Trip; Two Lane Blacktop; Woodstock

Psychiatrists: see *Psychologists/ Psychiatrists*

Psychics: see also *Fortune Tellers: Future-Seeing the: Supernatural: SCI-FI:* Black Rainbow; A Boy and His Dog; Brainstorm (1983); The Brood; The Butcher's Wife; Carrie (1976); The Clairvoyant (1934); The Dead Zone; Deathtrap; Escape to Witch Mountain; Exorcist III; The Eyes of Laura Mars; Fear; Firestarter; First Power; Friday the 13th Part VII-The New Blood; The Fury (1978); Ghost; Ghostbusters; Ghostbusters 2; Halloween 5: The Revenge of Michael Myers; Hanussen; The Haunting; Hello Again; Hideaway; House of the Spirits; It Happened Tomorrow; Last Wave; The Legend of Hell House; Man on a Swing; The Man Who Could Work Miracles; Medusa Touch; The Night Has a Thousand Eyes; Puppet Master; Scanners; Scanners II, The New Order; Seance on a Wet Afternoon; The Search for Bridey Murphy; Second Sight; The Seven Faces of Dr. Lao; Sheena, Queen of the Jungle; They; Vibes; Watcher in the Woods; Wilder Napalm; Wings of Desire; Zapped!; Zapped Again

Psycho-Killers: see also *Serial Killers: Mental Illness:* Airport; Alone in the Dark; Autumn Leaves; Babysitter; Ben; Blue Steel; Cadillac Man; Cape Fear (1962); Cape Fear (1991); Cobra; Compulsion; Conflict of Interest; Criminal Law; Daddy's Gone A-Hunting; Dance Macabre; Desperate Living; Dirty Harry; Dressed to Kill; Dr. Giggles; Doppelganger: The Evil Within; Don't Bother to Knock; Do You Like Women?; Ed and His Dead Mother; Fade to Black (1979); The Fan; Fatal Attraction; The First Deadly Sin; Frenzy; Friday the 13th (1980); Friday the 13th: Final Chapter; Friday the 13th, Part 3-D; Friday the 13th, Part II; Friday the 13th Part V-A New Beginning; Friday the 13th Part VI-Jason Lives; Friday the 13th Part VII-The New Blood; Friday the 13th Part VIII-Jason Takes Manhattan; The Ghoul (1975); Good Fellas; Guilty as Charged; Halloween; Halloween 2; Halloween 3: Season of the Witch; Halloween 4: The Return of Michael Myers; Halloween 5: The Revenge of Michael Myers; Hammersmith is Out; Hand that Rocks the Cradle; Happy Birthday to Me; Helter Skelter (1976);

Henry: Portrait of a Serial Killer; How I Won the War; In the Line of Fire; Judgment Night; Kalifornia; The Killer Inside Me; The Killer Nun; Killing Zoe; Kiss of Death (1947); Kiss of Death (1995); Knife in the Water; Ladies in Retirement; Ladykiller (1992); Leave Her to Heaven; Magic; Man with Nine Lives; The Man with Two Brains; Martin; Misery; Mother's Boys; My New Gun; Nanny; National Lampoon's Class Reunion; Nighthawks (1981); Night of the Generals; Night of the Hunter; The Onion Field; Pacific Heights; Peeping Tom; Picture Mommy Dead; Psycho; Psycho 2; Psycho 3; Psycho 4; Raising Cain; Revenge of Frankenstein; Ricochet; Scanner Cop; See No Evil; The Shining; Shock Treatment; Single White Female; The Sniper; Speed; The Stepfather; Stepfather 2: Make Room for Daddy; Stepfather 3: Father's Day; Strangers on a Train; A Taste for Killing; Taxi Driver; The Temp; Terminal Man; Terror Train; The Texas Chainsaw Massacre; The Texas Chainsaw Massacre: Part 2; To Catch a Killer; Twisted; Twisted Nerve; Two Minute Warning; W; Willard

Psychological Drama: see also THRILLERS: Mindgames: Insane-Plot to Drive: The Adjuster; Altered States; The Attic; The Belly of an Architect; Betrayal; Bitter Moon; Brimstone and Treacle; Bunny Lake Is Missing; Circle of Power; The Clairvoyant (1934); A Clockwork Orange; Cold Heaven; The Company of Wolves; Compulsion; The Conformist; The Conversation; Crime and Punishment; Daddy's Gone A-Hunting; A Dandy in Aspic; Dangerous Game; Dark Mirror; Dark Obsession; Dark Waters; Das Boot; Dead Ringers; Death and the Maiden; Doctor Jekyll and Mr. Hyde (1931); Dolores Claiborne; Don't Look Now; Dr. Jekyll and Mr. Hyde (1941); Dream Lover (1986); Driver's Seat; Entity; Equinox; Equus; Face to Face; Flatliners; Flesh and Blood (1951); Forbidden Games; Fourteen Hours; Freaks; Freud; Friends and Husbands; The Gambler; Gaslight (1939); Gaslight (1944); Gertrude; Glass House; House of Cards; House of Games; Hysteria; I Never Promised You A Rose Garden; Jacob's Ladder; Journey to the Far Side of the Sun; Julia and Julia; Kafka; Kalifornia; Kamikaze 89; The Killer Inside Me; The Krays; L'Avventura;

La Bete Humaine; La Chienne; Lady in the Car with Glasses and a Gun; Lady in the Dark; Last Wave; Le Corbeau; Liebestraum; Look in Any Window; Looking for Mr. Goodbar; The Manchurian Candidate; Marat/Sade; Marnie; Mike's Murder; Mine Own Executioner; Misery; Mississippi Mermaid; Mister Buddwing; Monsieur Hire; Moonrise; Mortal Thoughts; Mother Love; Mr. Arkadin Negatives; Night Games; The Night of the Following Day; Night Walker; The Ninth Configuration; Nomads; Now, Voyager; Ordinary People; Paris By Night; Performance; Persona; Picnic at Hanging Rock; The Player; Pointsman; The Prisoner: Arrival; Proof; Rebecca; Reflections in a Golden Eye; Repulsion; Reversal of Fortune; Salo: 120 Days of Sodom; Salon Kitty; Scenes from a Marriage; Screaming Mimi; The Search for Bridey Murphy; The Secret Ceremony; Secret Places; Seven Days in May; The Seven Percent Solution; Sex, Lies, and Videotape; Silent Fall; Slender Thread; So Long at the Fair; Spanking the Monkey; Spellbound; Stolen Life (1939); Stolen Life (1946); The Stuntman; Suddenly, Last Summer; The Suicide Club; Surviving Desire; Suspicion; Swimmer; Sybil; Taxing Woman; The Tenant; That Cold Day in the Park; Thomas Crown Affair; Tin Drum; Turkish Delight; Under Capricorn; Undercurrent; Unlawful Entry; Up the Sandbox; Wages of Fear; Wetherby; Whirlpool; Who is Harry Kellerman . . .; Who's Afraid of Virginia Woolf?; Wild Strawberries; Woman in the Dunes; X, Y, & Zee; Yellow Canary; Zigzag

Psychological Thriller: see also THRILLERS: Mindgames: Insane-Plot to Drive: The Birds; The Birds II; Black Rainbow; Black Widow (1987); Blink; Blood Relatives; Cape Fear (1962); Cape Fear (1991); The Color of Night; The Company of Wolves; Consenting Adults; Criminal Law; The Crush; Dark Waters; Dead of Night (1945); Dead Ringers; The Dead Zone; Death and the Maiden; Disclosure; Dolores Claiborne; Dream Lover (1986); Dreamscape; Experiment in Terror; Eye of the Cat; The Eyes of Laura Mars; The Fall of the House of Usher (1928); Fatal Attraction; Flatliners; Flesh of the Orchid; The Fourth Man; Guilty as Sin; The Hand (1960); The Hand (1981); The

Hand that Rocks the Cradle; The Haunting; High Anxiety; House of Games; Hush, Hush, Sweet Charlotte; In the Line of Fire; Kalifornia; The Kingdom; Klute; Looking for Mr. Goodbar; Malice; Misery; Mother Love; Mother's Boys; Murder by Natural Causes; No Way to Treat a Lady; The Other; Pacific Heights; The Parallax View; Peeping Tom; Phobia; Psycho; Quintet; Raising Cain; Rampage; Rebecca; Repulsion; Rosemary's Baby; See No Evil; Sender; The Sentinel; Silence of the Lambs; Shadow of a Doubt; Silent Fall; Sister, Sister; The Sniper; Step Down to Terror; Still of the Night; Strangers on a Train; Sudden Fear; Tenant; Village of the Damned; Whispers in the Dark; You'll Like My Mother

Psychologists/Psychiatrists: see also Therapy: Mental Illness: Romance with Psychologist: Mental Illness: Asylums: Social Drama: The Accused (1948); Agnes of God; Another Woman; Baxter (1972); Bedtime for Bonzo; Beyond Therapy; Blindfold: Acts of Obsession; Captain Newman, M.D.; Carefree; The Caretakers; The Chapman Report; Choose Me; Circle of Power; The Color of Night; The Couch; The Couch Trip; Dark Mirror; Dark Past; David and Lisa; Don Juan DeMarco; Dressed to Kill; Equus; Face to Face; Final Analysis; A Fine Madness; Freud; Grace Quigley; Hammersmith is Out; Harvey; Hellbound: Hellraiser II; High Anxiety; House of Games; I Don't Buy Kisses Anymore; Impossible Years; Jacob's Ladder; Jack's Back; Klute; Lady in the Dark; Lilith; Lizzie; Lovesick; Mark; Mine Own Executioner; Mr. Jones; Naked Face; Negatives; The Ninth Configuration; Now, Voyager; Oh Men! Oh Women!; On a Clear Day You Can See Forever; Ordinary People; Phobia; The President's Analyst; The Prince of Tides; Raising Cain; Scar; The Sender; The Seven Percent Solution; Sex and the Single Girl; Simon; Snakepit; Starting Over; Still of the Night; Straight Talk; Suddenly, Last Summer; Sybil; Tender is the Night; They Might be Giants; The Three Faces of Eve; Three on a Couch; Veronika Voss; What About Bob?; Whispers in the Dark; Who's Been Sleeping in My Bed?; Wild in the Country; Zelig

Psychologists as Detective: see also Detective Stories: Mental Illness: MYS-

TERY: Psychologists: Agnes of God; The Color of Night; Don Juan DeMarco; Dream Lover (1986); Equus; Silent Fall; Spellbound; Still of the Night; Sybil; They Might Be Giants; Whispers in the Dark

Psychotics: see *Mental Illness: Psycho Killers: Asylums: Serial Killers: HORROR*

Publishing World: see also *Writers: Journalists: Advertising World:* The Best of Everything; The Man Who Reclaimed His Head; Mary, Mary; When Ladies Meet (1933); When Ladies Meet (1941); Wolf; Youngblood Hawke

Pulitzer Prize Adaptations: see also *Novel Adaptations (Major): Play Adaptations: Non-Fiction Adaptations: Stage Tapings:* All the King's Men; All the Way Home; The Caine Mutiny (1954); The Caine Mutiny Court Martial (1988); Cat on a Hot Tin Roof (1958); Cat on a Hot Tin Roof (1984); A Chorus Line; The Color Purple; Crimes of the Heart; Death of a Salesman (1950); Death of a Salesman (1985); A Delicate Balance; Driving Miss Daisy; The Effect of Gamma Rays on Man-in-the-Moon Marigolds; The Executioner's Song; Gettysburg; Glengarry Glen Ross; Gone With the Wind; The Grapes of Wrath; Harvey; How to Succeed in Business without Really Trying; The Human Comedy; Long Day's Journey Into Night; Lost in Yonkers; Mambo Kings; A Member of the Wedding; 'Night, Mother; Our Town; The River Niger; Shadow Box; A Soldier's Story; South Pacific; State of the Union; The Subject Was Roses; That Championship Season; To Kill a Mockingbird; Winterset

Puppets/Dummies: see also *Muppets: CHILDREN'S: Ventriloquists: Monsters-Toys/Dolls as:* Dark Crystal; The Muppet Christmas Carol; The Muppet Movie; The Muppets Take Manhattan; Pinocchio; Puppet Master

Pursuits: see *Chase Movies: Quests: Romance-Boy Wants Girl: Romance-Girl Wants Boy*

Putting on a Show: see also *Theater Life: Actors: Actresses: Directors:*

Writers: Addams Family Values; Breakin' 2; Broadway Melody of 1936; Broadway Melody of 1938; Broadway Melody of 1940; Bullets Over Broadway; Copacabana; The First Nudie Musical; Footlight Parade; 42nd Street; Hellzapoppin; Hit Parade; Hollywood Canteen; Hollywood Hotel; Jesus of Montreal; Lady Be Good; Lucky Me; The Muppets Take Manhattan; The Music Room; Noises Off; Please Don't Eat the Daisies; The Producers; Room Service; Sing; Stage Door Canteen; Stand Up and Cheer; Starstruck; Stepping Out; Tea for Two; This is the Army; Thousands Cheer; To Be or Not to Be (1942); To Be or Not to Be (1983); Weeds; White Christmas

Puzzles to Solve: see *Clever Plots & Endings: Mindgames: Double Crossing: Treasure Hunts: MYSTERY: Mystery-Whodunits*

Pyramids: see *Egypt/Pyramids*

Pyromaniacs: see *Fires-Arsonists: Juvenile Delinquents*

Q

Queen Elizabeth: see also *Elizabethan Era: Queens: British Films:* Elizabeth R.; Fire Over England; The Private Lives of Elizabeth and Essex; Virgin Queen
Queens: see also *Kings: Royalty: Leaders-Female: Biographies:* The Abdication; The Adventures of Don Juan; Caesar and Cleopatra; Catherine the Great; Christopher Columbus (1949); Christopher Columbus: The Discovery (1992); Cleopatra (1934); Cleopatra (1963); Coming to America; Conan, the Destroyer; Great Catherine; La Nuit de Varennes; Lady Jane; Lion in Winter; Marie Antoinette; Mary of Scotland; Mary, Queen of Scots; Mouse That Roared; Mudlark; Naked Gun; Nicholas and Alexandra; Prisoner of Zenda (1937); Prisoner of Zenda (1952); Prisoner of Zenda (1979); Private Lives of Elizabeth and Essex; Queen Christina; Queen of Destiny; Rasputin and the Empress; Royal Scandal; Scarlet Empress; Sea Hawk; Siegfried; Sleeping Beauty; Snow White and the Seven Dwarfs; Virgin Queen; Young Bess; Young Catherine
Questionable Lovers: see *Love-Questionable*
Quests: see also *ADVENTURE: Obsessions: Journeys: Treasure Hunts: Epics: Dreams: Cures/Solutions-Search for:* Adam; Allan Quatermain and the Lost City of Gold; Beat the Devil; Breaking the Sound Barrier; Canyon Passage; Clash of the Titans; Close Encounters of the Third Kind; The Devil Came from Arkansas; Eagle's Wing; Green Mansions; Heat and Dust; King Solomon's Mines (1937); King Solomon's Mines (1950); King Solomon's Mines (1985); Krull; Legend of the Lost; Moby Dick; Monty Python and the Holy Grail; Mosquito Coast; North; Raiders of the Lost Ark; Razor's Edge (1946); Razor's Edge (1986); Renegades; Rope of Sand; The Sorcerer; Treasure of the Sierra Madre; Twins; Wages of Fear

Quiet Little Films: see also *Overlooked: Ordinary People Stories:* About Face; Alamo Bay; All the Way Home; Atlantic City; Babette's Feast; Back Roads; Barcelona; Barfly; Before Sunrise; The Bicycle Thief; Bird; Bliss; Bodies, Rest & Motion; Bound For Glory; Boy on a Dolphin; C'est la Vie; Chariots of Fire; Chattahoochee; Choose Me; Country; Daddy Nostalgia; Day of the Locust; Days of Heaven; Dazed and Confused; Dear John; Decline of the American Empire; Desert Bloom; Diary of a Mad Housewife; Dogfight; Down By Law; The Dressmaker; A Dry White Season; Earth; Eclipse; Eight Men Out; Electra Glide in Blue; Enchanted April; Escape Artist; The Europeans; Everybody Wins; The Fabulous Baker Boys; Fearless; Five Easy Pieces; The Flim Flam Man; The 400 Blows; Fun Down There; Garbo Talks; Gas Food Lodging; The Getting of Wisdom; The Girl with Green Eyes; A Good Man in Africa; Grand Highway; Green Card; Gross Anatomy; A Handful of Dust; Heart Beat; The Heart Is a Lonely Hunter; Heartland; Heat and Dust; Heavenly Pursuits; High Season; Honkytonk Man; House of Cards; Jack and Sarah; J.W. Coop; La Lectrice; The Last Metro; The Last of His Tribe; The Last Picture Show; Le Bal; Little Noises; Local Hero; Lonely Hearts; The Long Day Closes; Loulou; The Man in the Moon; Mike's Murder; Miss Firecracker; A Month in the Country; Mr. Johnson; Mr. and Mrs. Bridge; My Brilliant Career; My Life as a Dog; Naked; Naked in New York; 1918; 9/30/55; Old Man and the Sea; One Sings, the Other Doesn't; Pascali's Island; A Patch of Blue; The Piano; Playboys; Rachel, Rachel; Raggedy Man; Rain Man; The Rain People; Resurrection; The Return of the Secaucus Seven; Rich in Love; Rich Kids; Risk; The Romantic Englishwoman; 'Round Midnight; Running on Empty; Seize the Day; Shoot the Moon; Shy People; Simple Story; Stanley & Iris;

R

Race Against Time: see also *Chase Movies: Mortgage Drama: Cures/Solutions-Search for:* Adventures in Babysitting; Alice in Wonderland; All-American Murder; American Ninja 3; The Andromeda Strain; Around the World in 80 Days; Atomic City; The Big Clock; The Big Lift; Black Sunday (1977); Bobo; The Bourne Identity; The Boys from Brazil; Breaking the Sound Barrier; Brewster's Millions (1935); Brewster's Millions (1945); Brewster's Millions (1985); Bringing up Baby; Busy Body; Cannonball Run; Cannonball Run 2; Carlito's Way; Cassandra Crossing; Christmas in Connecticut (1945); Christmas in Connecticut (1992); The Client; Clockwise; Cold Turkey; Color Me Dead; D.O.A. (1949); D.O.A. (1988); Day of the Jackal; Day One; Dead Heat on a Merry Go Round; Deadlock; Desperate Hours (1955); Desperate Hours (1990); Destination Tokyo; Detonator; Disaster at Silo 7; Dr. Strangelove; Easy Money (1983); Escape; Escape from New York; Escape to Witch Mountain; Footlight Parade; The Forbin Project; Fourth Protocol; Frantic (1988); The Front Page (1931); The Front Page (1974); The Gang That Couldn't Shoot Straight; Genevieve; Glengarry Glen Ross; The Great Race; The Green Man; A Hard Day's Night; His Girl Friday; I Confess; Ice Station Zebra;

In the Line of Fire; In the Mouth of Madness; It's a Mad Mad Mad Mad World!; It's in the Bag; The Italian Straw Hat; January Man; Joke of Destiny; Juggernaut; Key Largo; The Killing; Krakatoa, East of Java; Le Million; Li'l Abner; The Light that Failed; Live Wire; Lover Come Back (1961); The Maltese Falcon (1931); The Maltese Falcon (1941); Marooned; Meteor; Miracle Mile; Miracle of Morgan's Creek; Money for Nothing; My Life; New Leaf; No Escape (1994); Nothing But the Truth; October Man; Omen; Omen IV: The Awakening; One, Two, Three!; Outbreak; The Outoftowners; Outrageous Fortune; The Ox-Bow Incident; Patriot Games; Planes, Trains, and Automobiles; The Radioland Murders; Risky Business; The River Wild; Runaway; Runaway Train; Running Man (1987); Santa Claus, The Movie; The Satan Bug; Satan Met a Lady; Schindler's List; The Scout; Sea Chase; Seven Chances; Seven Days Leave; Short Time; The Slender Thread; The Slipper and the Rose; Sorry, Wrong Number; Speed; Spellbound; Spirit of St. Louis; Steel; Strangers on a Train; Switching Channels; The Taking of Pelham 123; Tall Target; Terminator; Terminator 2: Judgment Day; Terror on a Train; They Shoot Horses, Don't They?; 30 Is a Dangerous Age, Cynthia; Three Days of the Condor; Time

after Time; Timebomb; Tom Jones; Train; Troop Beverly Hills; Twilight's Last Gleaming; Two Minute Warning; Union Station; War Games; While the City Sleeps; The Year of Living Dangerously

Race Relations: see also *Friendships-Interracial: Romance-Interracial: Civil Rights: Social Drama:* Across 110th Street; Across the Wide Missouri; Alamo Bay; Alien Nation; All the Young Men; Amos and Andrew; As Summers Die; The Autobiography of Miss Jane Pittman; Band of Angels; The Bingo Long Travelling All-Stars and Motor Kings; The Birth of a Nation; The Biscuit Eater (1940); The Biscuit Eater (1972); Black and White in Color; Black Legion; Blackboard Jungle; Blazing Saddles; A Bronx Tale; Brother John; Buck and the Preacher; Cadence; Carbon Copy; Chocolat; Conrack; The Court Martial of Jackie Robinson; Cry Freedom; The Defiant Ones; Dixie; Do The Right Thing; Driving Miss Daisy; A Dry White Season; Edge of the City; Enemy Mine; Ernest Green Story; Flaming Star; Flirting; For Queen and Country; Glory; Go for Broke; A Good Man in Africa; Grand Canyon; The Great White Hope; Guess Who's Coming to Dinner; Hairspray; Heart Condition; Heart of Dixie; Heat and Dust; Hell in the Pacific; Higher Learning; Hollywood Shuffle; Hook; Hurry

Sundown; I Passed for White; Imitation of Life (1934); Imitation of Life (1959); In the Heat of the Night; Intruder; Intruder in the Dust; Just Cause; King; Kings Go Forth; The Klansman; The Landlord; Lost Boundaries; The Lost Man; Man Friday; Mandela; Map of the Human Heart; McMasters; Mississippi Burning; Mixed Company; Native Son (1951); Native Son (1986); No Way Out (1950); Nothin' But a Man; Paris Trout; Pinky; Posse (1993); Power of One; Pudd'nhead Wilson; Q & A; A Raisin in the Sun; Romper Stomper; Sapphire; Sarafina!; School Daze; Separate but Equal; Shame (1961); Showboat (1936); Showboat (1951); Six Degrees of Separation; The Skin Game; Sophisticated Gents; Soul Man; South Pacific; Storm Warning; Tick, Tick, Tick . . .; Till Death Us Do Part; To Kill a Mockingbird; Tortilla Flat; Trial (1955); True Believer; Uncle Tom's Cabin (1914); Uncle Tom's Cabin (1969); The Unforgiven (1960); Up the Down Staircase; Valdez is Coming; The Well; White Dog; White Men Can't Jump; White Nights (1985); White Zombie; The Wilby Conspiracy; A World Apart

Races-Long Distance: see *Car Racing: Race Against Time: Horses/Horse Racing: Competitions/Contests*

Radiation Poisoning: see *Nuclear Energy: Poisons:* The Atomic Kid; Black Rain (1988); Kiss Me Deadly; Teenage Mutant Ninja Turtles; Teenage Mutant Ninja Turtles 2; Teenage Mutant Ninja Turtles 3; Werewolf (1956)

Radio Life (set in a background of radio broadcasting): see also *Journalists: Hollywood Life: 1920s: 1930s: 1940s:* The Adventures of Ford Fairlane; Airheads; American Hotwax; The Big Broadcast; The Big Broadcast of 1936; The Big Broadcast of 1937; Choose Me; Comfort and Joy; The Couch Trip; The Fisher King; FM; Fog; Funny Lady; Good Morning, Vietnam; Handle with Care; Helter Skelter (1949); Hit Parade; Hit Parade of 1941; Hit Parade of 1943; Hit Parade of 1947; Hollywood Hotel; House of Games; Kentucky Moonshine; King of Marvin Gardens; Kings and Desperate Men; Love Thy Neighbor; Martin (1978); Play Misty for Me; Psycho 4; Pump Up the Volume; Radio Days; The Radioland Murders; Rebecca of Sunnybrook Farm (1938); Straight Talk; Talk Radio; Thank God It's Friday; Tune

in Tomorrow; The Unsuspected; Whistling in the Dark; WUSA

Rags to Riches: see also *Riches to Rags: Power-Rise to: Fame-Rise to: Famous People When Young:* American Romance; The Beverly Hillbillies; Broadway Bill; Christmas in July; Cinderella; Coal Miner's Daughter; Easy Money (1983); A Face in the Crowd; Fox and His Friends; Frances; Funny Girl; Giant; Gold Rush; Golden Boy; Gone With the Wind; The Good Earth; Great Expectations; Half a Sixpence; Hard to Handle; I'm No Angel; If I Had a Million; It Could Happen to You; Jackpot; Kid Galahad; Kipps; Kitty; Ladies' Man (1947); Lady Killer (1933); Lucy Gallant; The Man Who Broke the Bank at Monte Carlo; Max Dugan Returns; Melvin and Howard; The Men in Her Life; Mildred Pierce; Million Dollar Baby; Money for Nothing; Silent Partner; Sophia Loren, Her Own Story; Star!; To Sleep with Anger; Toast of New Orleans; Trading Places; Tulsa; 29th Street; The Unsinkable Molly Brown; Wicked As They Come

Rainforests: see also *Environmental Dilemmas: South America:* Amazon; At Play in the Fields of the Lord; Burning Season; Fern Gully; The Mission; Medicine Man

Raised by Animals: see also *Orphans: Humans into Animals:* Greystoke: The Legend of Tarzan; Jungle Book (1942); Jungle Book (1967); Jungle Book (1994); Nell; Sheena, Queen of the Jungle; Tarzan and His Mate; Tarzan Escapes; Tarzan, The Ape Man (1932); Tarzan, the Ape Man (1981); Tarzan's New York Adventure; Walk Like a Man; Wild Child; The World's Greatest Athlete

Raised by Indians (American): see also *Orphans: WESTERNS: Indians-American: Native Americans-Modern:* Dances With Wolves; The Last of the Mohicans (1936); The Last of the Mohicans (1992); Light in the Forest; Little Big Man; Return of a Man Called Horse; Savage

Rape/Rapists: see also *Abusive Men: Molestation: Incest: Evil Men:* The Accused (1948); The Accused (1988); The Adventurers; Alien3; Anatomy of a Murder; And Justice for All; Bad Lieutenant; Bandolero; The Beat Generation; Bedroom Window; Bitch (La Garce) (1984); Blind Side; Born Losers; Boston Strangler; Cape Fear (1962);

Cape Fear (1991); Casualties of War; Conduct Unbecoming; Criminal Law; Deadly Friend; Death and the Maiden; Death Wish; Death Wish 2; Death Wish 3; Death Wish 4; Death Wish 5; Deliverance; Demon Seed; Entity; Extremities; Five Corners; Flesh and Blood (1985); Hannie Caulder; Higher Learning; House of the Spirits; The House of Usher (1960); The House of Usher (1990); Jackson County Jail; Jagged Edge; Jarrapellejos; Johnny Belinda; Just Cause; Last Exit to Brooklyn; Last House on the Left; Last Summer; Lipstick; Lizzie; Lock up Your Daughters; Love Crimes; Mademoiselle Fifi; Mahogany; Mark; Max and Helen; Moon in the Gutter; New Interns; Of Mice and Men (1939); Of Mice and Men (1993); One Deadly Summer; Outrage (1956); Passage to India; Peeping Tom; The Prince of Tides; Rashomon; Rider on the Rain; River's Edge; Rosemary's Baby; Screaming Mimi; Shame (1987); The Shawshank Redemption; Something Wild (1960); Spellbinder; Stranger is Watching; Straw Dogs; A Streetcar Named Desire; Sudden Impact; Tattoo; Term of Trial; Thelma & Louise; They Won't Forget; Tie Me Up! Tie Me Down!; To Kill a Mockingbird; Town Without Pity; The Trial (1955); Twin Peaks; Twin Peaks: Fire Walk with Me; Two Mules for Sister Sara; Two Women; Virgin Spring; The Wild Party; Wildflower; Xtro

Rape-Male: see also *Rape/Rapists: Men in Jeopardy:* Brubaker; Deliverance; Fortune and Men's Eyes; The Prince of Tides; The Shawshank Redemption; Short Eyes

Rat Pack Movies (starring together, among others, Frank Sinatra, Sammy Davis, Jr., Dean Martin, Shirley MacLaine, Peter Lawford): Cannonball Run; Cannonball Run 2; Four for Texas; Career; Robin and the Seven Hoods; Salt and Pepper; Some Came Running

Real Time Stories: see *One Day Stories: Non-Stop Stories: Escalating Plots*

Rebels: see also *Wild People: Free Spirits: Juvenile Delinquents: Underdog Stories; Social Drama:* Absolute Beginners; Accent on Love; The Adventures of Tom Sawyer; Albuquerque; And Justice for All; Bachelor Party (1984); Behold a Pale Horse; Big Bounce;

Blackboard Jungle; Born Losers; The Boy Who Had Everything; The Boys Next Door; Boys Town; Burning Season; Captain Blood; Chalk Garden; Christ Stopped at Eboli; Clambake; Class of 1999; Class of '84; A Clockwork Orange; Conrack; Cool Hand Luke; The Court Martial of Jackie Robinson; Dead Bang; Dogs in Space; Earth; Edge of the City; Ex-Lady; Exodus; Fahrenheit 451; Flame and the Arrow; FM; Footloose; For Whom the Bell Tolls; Frances; Freud; From the Hip; The George Raft Story; Getting Straight; Good Morning, Vietnam; Grease; Grease 2; Great Balls of Fire; Hair; Heart of Dixie; The Hill; Hud; Idolmaker; Jailhouse Rock; Lady Godiva; The Landlord; The Last Command; Lost Angels; Major Barbara; A Man for All Seasons; Mandela; Men of Boys' Seasons; The Moon and Sixpence; Moon Is Down; Mutiny on the Bounty (1935); Mutiny on the Bounty (1962); My Left Foot; The Prime of Miss Jean Brodie; Pump Up the Volume; Rebel Without a Cause; Reckless (1983); Reds; Rock n' Roll High School; RPM; Ruby Gentry; Sakharov; Secret People; Spartacus; The Strange One; Suburbia; Susan Slept Here; Talk Radio; Teachers; Teenage Rebel; That Was Then . . . This Is Now; THX 1138; To Kill a Priest; Tom Sawyer; Twelve Angry Men; Vanishing Point; Viva Villa!; White Heat; White Rose; The Wilby Conspiracy; Wild in the Streets; The Wild One; Wish You Were Here; Woman Rebels; The World According to Garp; A World Apart; WUSA; A Yank at Oxford; Year of the Dragon; Zabriskie Point

Reconstruction Era (the period following the Civil War destruction): see also *Civil War Era: 1870s:* Gone With the Wind; Little Foxes; McMasters; Texas

Recovery-Medical: see *Disease Stories: Doctors: Cures/Solutions-Search for*

Redemption: see also *Starting Over: Life Transitions: Guilty Conscience:* The Accidental Tourist; Ace High; Airplane 2, the Sequel; Amazon; Angel Baby; Atlantic City; Band Wagon; Bliss; Born Again; The Browning Version; Bull Durham; Carlito's Way; A Christmas Carol (1938); Clean and Sober; Cliffhanger; Cocoon; Cocoon, The Return; The Color of Money; Crimes and Misdemeanors; Dallas; Dangerous; Days of Wine and Roses (1958); Days of Wine

and Roses (1962); Defending Your Life; The Doctor; Falling in Love Again; Fearless; The Fisher King; Hallelujah!; Heaven Only Knows; Hombre; Hospital; Ikiru; Imaginary Crimes; In the Line of Fire; Intersection; The January Man; Knave of Hearts; Laughing Sinners; Leap of Faith; Mayor of Hell; McVicar; Middle of the Night; The Muppet Christmas Carol; My Sin; The Naked Kiss; Night of the Iguana; Parsifal; The Prince of Tides; Salty O'Rourke; Scrooge (1935); Scrooge (1970); The Secret Garden (1949); The Secret Garden (1984); The Secret Garden (1987); The Secret Garden (1993); Straight Time; Tender Mercies; The Unconquered; Vacation from Marriage; Verdict; Vertigo; Yesterday's Hero

Rednecks (modern hillbillies, or particularly uncouth country people): see also *Rural Life: Southerns: Simple Minds: Bigots: White Supremacists:* Any Which Way You Can; At Close Range; Baby, The Rain Must Fall; Cape Fear (1962); Cape Fear (1991); Carny; Daddy's Dyin'; Deliverance; Dudes; Dying Room Only; Eddie Macon's Run; End of the Line; Ernest Saves Christmas; Every Which Way But Loose; A Fire in the Sky; Foolin' Around Gator; Going Home; Greased Lightning; The Gun in Betty Lou's Handbag; Handle with Care; Heart Like a Wheel; Hold Me, Thrill Me, Kiss Me; I Walk the Line; Last American Hero; Lolly Madonna War; Loveless; Macon County Line; The Mask (1985); Miami Blues; Moving Violation; Natural Born Killers; Next of Kin (1989); Night of the Hunter; One False Move; Overboard; The Positively True Adventures of the Alleged Texas Cheerleader-Murdering Mom; Raising Arizona; Return to Macon County; Road House; Rush; Shame (1961); Shy People; Small Town in Texas; Smokey and the Bandit; Smokey and the Bandit II; Smokey and the Bandit III; Smooth Talk; Southern Comfort; Stars and Bars; Straw Dogs; Sugarland Express; Thunder and Lightning; Tobacco Road; Trespass; Used Cars; White Lightning

Reformers: see also *Fighting the System: Women Against the System: Unions: Worker vs. Boss: Rebels:* Boys Town; Brubaker; The Caretaker; Charly; City of Joy; Day of the Dead; The Devil Is a Sissy; Efficiency Expert; Forgotten Prisoners; Fortune and Men's Eyes; Friendly Fire; Ghosts . . . of the Civil

Dead; Hoffa; Lean on Me; Men of Boys' Town; The Mission; The Missionary; Never on Sunday; No More Ladies; Scandal in Paris; Teachers; Tunes of Glory; The Unconquered

Reification: see *Crossing the Line: Soliloquies*

Reincarnation: see also *Afterlife: Heaven: Hell: Redemption: Starting Over: Death-Dealing With:* All of Me; Angel on My Shoulder; Asphyx; Audrey Rose; Berkeley Square; Chances Are; Dead Again; Dead of Night (1977); Defending Your Life; Faraway, So Close!; Goodbye, Charlie; Heat and Dust; Heaven Can Wait (1978); Here Comes Mr. Jordan; Little Buddha; The Mind of Mr. Soames; My Blood Runs Cold; Obsession; Oh, Heavenly Dog; On a Clear Day You Can See Forever; The Reincarnation of Peter Proud; Resurrection; The Search for Bridey Murphy; She (1935); She (1965); Somewhere in Time; Star Trek III: The Search for Spock; Switch; Three Lives of Thomasina; Wings of the Morning; You Can Never Tell

Rejuvenation (feeling younger, though not necessarily growing younger literally, as with reverse aging): see also *Aging: Aging-Reverse: Body Switching: Redemption:* Atlantic City; Cocoon; Cocoon, The Return; Death Becomes Her; Don Juan DeMarco; Falling in Love Again; Lady Chatterley's Lover (1955); Lady Chatterly's Lover (1981); Middle Age Crazy; Middle of the Night; Nobody's Fool (1994); Skylark

Relationships Over Time: see *Romance-Lifetime: Romance-Reunited: Friendships-Great: Episodic Stories*

Relatives-Troublesome: see also *In-Laws: Siblings: Brothers: Sisters: Lover Family Dislikes:* Arsenic and Old Lace; Good Neighbor Sam; Harvey; Haunted Palace; The House of Seven Gables; Let's Kill Uncle; Lost in Yonkers; Monsieur Hulot's Holiday; My American Uncle; National Lampoon's Vacation; A Simple Twist of Fate; Suddenly, Last Summer; Tatie Danielle; Tell Me a Riddle; Travels with My Aunt; Uncle Buck

Religion: see also *Jesus Christ: Biblical Stories: Preachers/Ministers: Priests: Nuns: Popes: Jewish People: Miracles: Missionaries:* The Abdication; Agnes of God; Angel and the Badman; Angel Baby; At Play in the Fields of the Lord;

Belizaire the Cajun; Big Trees; The Bishop's Wife; Born Again; Camila (1984); Cardinal; Chariots of Fire; The Chosen; A Cry in the Dark; Defending Your Life; Devils; Diary of a Country Priest; Distant Thunder (1973); Elmer Gantry; Francis, God's Jester; Friendly Persuasion; The Fugitive (1947); Gandhi; The Garden; Glory! Glory!; God's Little Acre; Going My Way; Guyana Tragedy, The Story of Jim Jones; A Handmaid's Tale; Hannah and Her Sisters; Heaven Can Wait (1978); Heaven Help Us; Heavenly Pursuits; Homicide; Household Saints; How Do I Love Thee; I, the Worst of All; Joan of Arc; Joni; Keys of the Kingdom; Lamb; Leap of Faith; Lilies of the Field; Little Buddha; Luther; Martin Luther; Masala; Mass Appeal; Miracle (1948); The Mission; The Missionary; Mohammed, Messenger of God; Monsignor; Monty Python's Life of Brian; Night of the Hunter; No No Nanette (1930); No No Nanette (1940); The Nun's Story; Of Human Hearts; Oh, God; Oh God Book Two; Oh God, You Devil; Pass the Ammo; Passion of Joan of Arc; The Pope Must Die(t); The Prisoner (1955); Quo Vadis; Rapture; Razor's Edge (1946); Razor's Edge (1986); Rebecca of Sunnybrook Farm (1925); Repossessed; Resurrection; Robe; Romance; Romero; The Rosary Murders; Sacrifice; Saint Joan; Say Amen, Somebody!; Shadowlands; Shoes of the Fisherman; Silver Chalice; The Singing Nun; Song of Bernadette; Spitfire; Split Image; The Stand; Susan and God; Tender Mercies; To Kill a Priest; Unholy; Viridiana; Winter Light; Wise Blood; Yentl

Religious Comedy/Satire: see also *Religion: SATIRE:* Heavenly Pursuits; Wholly Moses

Religious Zealots: see also *Religion: Cults:* Black God, White Devil; Carrie (1976); A Handmaid's Tale

Remakes of Foreign Films: see *Foreign Film Remakes:* also films listed by countries

Repentance: see *Murder-Debate to Confess: Redemption: Starting Over*

Reporter as Detective: see *Journalist Detectives*

Repression: see *Sexual Problems: Virgins: Stern Men: Stern Women: Oppression*

Reptiles: see also *Monsters-Animal: Alligators*

Rescue Adventure/Drama: see also *Children-Saving: Mothers Protecting Children: Fathers Protecting Children: Disaster Movies: Survival Drama: Trapped in a Hole:* Ace in the Hole; The Adventures of Milo and Otis; Alive; American Ninja 2; Avalanche; Backdraft; Benji; Benji the Hunted; Beyond the Poseidon Adventure; The Big Lift; Breakout; Captains Courageous; Cliffhanger; Close to Eden; Day in October; Distant Drums; Escape; Far From Home; Father Goose; Flood!; Forest Rangers; Garden of Evil; Guarding Tess; Gun Fury; Guns of the Magnificent Seven; Ice Station Zebra; Inn of the Sixth Happiness; Iron Eagle; Krakatoa, East of Java; Last Outpost; Lisa (1961); Mothra; Mountain; Nanook of the North; Night Crossing; Night Train to Munich; Not Without My Daughter; 101 Dalmatians; The Professionals; Raise the Titanic!; Rambo: First Blood Part Two; Rambo III; Rescue Rescue Me; Return of the Seven; The Rescuers; The Rescuers Down Under; Rhythm on the Range; Ring of the Musketeers; Sea Wolf; Shadow Riders; Spacehunter, Adventures in the Forbidden Zone; Speed; Star Trek: Generations; Survive; Three Came Home; Tom Sawyer; The Towering Inferno; Turtle Diary; Walkabout; The Well; Where Eagles Dare; Wild Geese II; The Wreck of the Mary Deare

Resorts: see also *Vacations:* Barnacle Bill (1957); The Bride Wore Red; Club Paradise; Futureworld; Inkwell; Lumiere d'Ete; Mighty Quinn; Mr. North; The Road to Wellville; Westworld; Where the Boys Are; Where the Boys Are '84; White Christmas

Restaurant Settings: see also *Chefs: Waiters/Waitresses: Ordinary People Stories:* Bagdad Cafe; Cafe Romeo; Come Back to the Five and Dime, Jimmy Dean, Jimmy Dean; Diner; For Richer, For Poorer; Frankie and Johnny; The Linguini Incident; Mystic Pizza; Petrified Forest; Tampopo; Untamed Heart; Who Is Killing the Great Chefs of Europe?

Restoration Period: see also *British Films: 1600s: 1700s: FARCE:* Joseph Andrews; The Frenchman's Creek; Lock Up Your Daughters; Tom Jones; Wicked Lady (1945); Wicked Lady (1983)

Retarded People: see *Mentally Disabled People: Mental Illness: Simple Minds*

Retirement: see also *Elderly Men: Elderly Women:* The Browning Version; Cocoon; Cocoon, The Return; Easy Living (1949); End of the Game; End of the Line; Folks!; The Friends of Eddie Coyle; A Gunfighter; High Sierra; Hooper; I'll Never Forget Whatshisname; The Last Hurrah; The Last Run; The Late Show; My Name Is Nobody; Portrait; Rounders; Seven Thieves; She Wore a Yellow Ribbon; The Shootist; Sugar Hill; Tough Guys; Travelling North

Return of Spouse (usually after a long period away): see also *Murder of Spouse: Marrying Again:* The Great Lie; Happy Birthday, Wanda June; Hard Promises; Hellbound: Hellraiser II; Hello Again; Hellraiser; Hellraiser III: Hell on Earth; Julia Misbehaves; Lover Come Back (1946); Move Over, Darling; My Favorite Wife; No Room for the Groom; The Piccadilly Incident; Quality Street; The Return of Martin Guerre; Return of the Soldier; Sommersby; Suzy; Too Many Husbands; Truly, Madly, Deeply

Reunions: see also *Reunions-Class: Romance-Reunited: Ensemble Films: FAMILY: Families-Extended: Friends-Old: Thanksgiving: Christmas:* All I Want For Christmas; Always in My Heart; The Asphalt Jungle; Autumn Sonata; The Best of Times; The Big Chill; Big Wednesday; Biggest Bundle of Them All; A Bill of Divorcement (1932); A Bill of Divorcement (1940); Blame It on the Night; Buona Sera, Mrs. Campbell; By the Light of the Silvery Moon; Bye Bye Braverman; Cairo (1963); Cheyenne Autumn; Children of Hiroshima; Clash by Night; Close My Eyes; Come Back to the Five and Dime . . . ; Daddy Nostaglia; Defenseless; A Delicate Balance; Destiny of a Man; East of Eden (1955); East of Eden (1980); Everybody's Fine; Falling in Love Again; Family; Five Corners; Fool for Love; The Gathering; Ghost Story; Ginger and Fred; Goodbye My Fancy; Group; Happy New Year (1973); Happy New Year (1987); Hard Promises; High Tide; Holly and the Ivy; Homecoming (1973); House of the Spirits; The Housekeeper; I Could Go on Singing; Indian Summer; In Love and War; Interiors; Islands in the Stream; Its' Always Fair Weather; Keep the Change; Killing Dad; Lassie Come Home; A League of Their Own; Let's Dance; Liebestraum; Love Hurts; Macaroni; The

Magic of Lassie; Max Dugan Returns; May Fools; National Lampoon's Class Reunion; Nazi Agent; The Night Porter; Nobody's Perfect; On Golden Pond; One Eyed Jacks; Peggy Sue Got Married; Peter's Friends; Promised Land; Queens Logic; The Quiet Man; The Return of the Secaucus Seven; Shaking the Tree; She Couldn't Say No; Shy People; Something Wild (1986); The Sons of Katie Elder; Sophisticated Gents; Spirit Rider; Story of Boys and Girls; Strange Loves of Martha Ivers; Strangers, the Story of a Mother and Daughter; The Subject Was Roses; The Sunshine Boys; Tell Them Willie Boy is Here; Texasville; That Championship Season; Tiger Bay; Tough Guys; Toys in the Attic; Trail of the Lonesome Pine; The Trip to Bountiful; Turning Point; Unfinished Piece for a Player The Piano; Violets are Blue; Welcome Home; Welcome Home, Roxy Carmichael; West Point Story; White Banners; Windy City

Reunions-Class: see also *Reunions: High School Life: College Life:* The Best of Times; The Big Chill; Indian Summer; National Lampoon's Class Reunion; Peggy Sue Got Married; The Return of the Secaucus Seven; Something Wild (1986); Windy City

Revenge: see also *Avenging Death of Someone: Vigilantes: Convict's Revenge: Turning the Tables:* The Accused (1988); Across 110th Street; Act of Violence; Actor's Revenge; The Adventurers; The Adventures of Captain Fabian; All About Eve; All Dogs Go to Heaven; Assault on Precinct 13; Awful Truth; The Bad and the Beautiful; Badge 373; The Ballad of Cable Hogue; Ballad of the Sad Cafe; Basket Case; Basket Case 2; Basket Case 3; Batman; Battle of the Sexes; Beast of the City; Better Off Dead; Beyond the Forest; The Big Heat; Black Arrow; Black Cat; Black Sunday (1960); Blind Side; Blue City; Blue Collar; Blue Max; Boardwalk; Bounty Hunters; Bring Me the Head of Alfredo Garcia; Burning; Cabin in the Cotton; Calling Dr. Gillespie; Cape Fear (1962); Cape Fear (1991); Captain Carey, USA; Carrie (1976); Champagne for Caesar; A Change of Seasons; Charming Sinners; Children's Hour; Chisum; Christine; Comin' At Ya!; Conan, the Barbarian; The Count of Monte Cristo (1934); The Count of Monte Cristo (1974); The Crow; Dangerous Liaisons; The Dark Half; Day

of Wrath; Dead Boyz Can't Fly; Dead Ringer; Deadly Friend; Death Becomes Her; Death Wish; Death Wish 2; Death Wish 3; Death Wish 4; Death Wish 5; Dial M For Murder; Diamonds for Breakfast; Double Impact; End of the Game; Endless Love; Exterminator; Exterminator 2; Extremities; Eye for an Eye; Fatal Attraction; 52 Pick-up; Fighting Back; Fighting Mad; Finian's Rainbow; First Blood; Five Card Stud; Flare Up; Flowers in the Attic; Fourth War; Freaks; Frenchie; A Funny Thing Happened on the Way to the Forum; Fury (1936); The General; Ghost; Girl Most Likely to . . . (1971); Gleaming the Cube; Great Scout and Cathouse Thursday; Guilty as Charged; Guilty Conscience; Guns of the Magnificent Seven; A Guy Named Joe; Hairy Ape; The Hand (1960); The Hand (1981); The Hand that Rocks the Cradle; Hang'em High; Hannie Caulder; Happy Birthday to Me; Hard to Kill; Harper Valley P.T.A.; He Was Her Man; Heat; Hedda; Hello Again; Henry: Portrait of a Serial Killer; Henry V (1944); Henry V (1989); High Plains Drifter; Hour of the Gun; House of Wax; I, Jane Doe; I Married a Witch; I Walk Alone; An Innocent Man; The Invisible Man's Revenge; Ivan's Childhood; Jaws 4: The Revenge; Johnny Handsome; Kickboxer; Kickboxer 2; Kid (1990); Kidnapped (1938); Kidnapped (1959); Kidnapped (1971); A Kiss Before Dying (1956); A Kiss Before Dying (1991); Kiss of Death (1947); Kiss of Death (1995); Knights of the Round Table; Lady Eve; Last House on the Left; The Last Hunt; The Last Laugh; The Left-Handed Gun; Legend of the Lone Ranger; Leprechaun; Les Liaisons Dangereuses; Les Miserables (1935); Les Miserables (1952); Les Miserables (1978); Let's Kill Uncle; Let's Make Love; Lethal Weapon; Lethal Weapon 2; The Letter (1929); The Letter (1940); Lipstick; The Locket; Love and Bullets; Machine Gun McCain; The Mad Magician; Madison Avenue Maids; The Man from Laramie; Man in the Wilderness; The Man Who Reclaimed His Head; Man with Two Faces; Maniac Cop; Maniac Cop 2; Manon des Sources (1952); Manon des Sources (1986); Mask of the Avenger; Match Factory Girl; The Mechanic; Menace; Moon in the Gutter; The Mummy's Hand; Murphy's War; My Forbidden Past; My Learned Friend;

Myra Breckinridge; Mystery of the Wax Museum; Nevada Smith; Next of Kin (1989); Night of the Juggler; Night Walker; No Way Out (1950); The Oblong Box; Oklahoma Kid; One Deadly Summer; Orca-Killer Whale; Ossessione; Outlaw Blues; The Outlaw Josey Wales; Paid; Patriot Games; The Pit and the Pendulum (1961); The Pit and the Pendulum (1991); Point Blank; Presumed Innocent; Pumpkinhead; Quick and the Dead; Quigley Down Under; Remember My Name; Return of Superfly; Return of the Pink Panther; Revenge; Ricochet; Rider on the Rain; Robin Hood (1922); Robin Hood (1973); Robin Hood (1990); Robin Hood: Prince of Thieves (1991); Rolling Thunder; Rosary Murders; Roxie Hart; Ruby Gentry; Samson and Delilah; San Antonio; Scanner Cop; Scaramouche; Searchers; Sebastiane; The Servant; Severed Head; Shock to the System; Silent Partner; Sitting Target; Skin Deep; A Small Town in Texas; Solomon and Sheba; Spoilers; Spy Who Came in from the Cold; Stick; The Sting; The Sting 2; Straw Dogs; Sudden Impact; Taffin; Tango & Cash; Tell Them Willie Boy is Here; Theater of Blood; Time of Destiny; 'Tis a Pity She's a Whore; To Live and Die in L.A.; Total Recall; Toto le Heros; Toxic Avenger; Toxic Avenger, Part II; Toxic Avenger Part III; Twisted; Twisted Nerve; Two Mules for Sister Sara; 2000 Maniacs; Ulzana's Raid; Underworld, USA; Unforgiven (1992); Virgin Spring; Viridiana; The Visit; W; Waco; Walking Dead; Whatever Happened to Baby Jane?; Will Penny; Willard; Winterset; Wonder Man; The World is Full of Married Men; X, Y, & Zee; Yojimbo

Revenge on Cheaters: see also *Cheating Men: Cheating Women: Cheated Upon Meet:* Alice; A Change of Seasons; Charming Sinners; Dial M For Murder; 'Tis a Pity She's a Whore; The World Is Full of Married Men; X, Y, & Zee

Revenge on Doctors: see also *Doctors: Revenge:* Basket Case; Basket Case 2; Basket Case 3; Calling Dr. Gillespie; The Hand that Rocks the Cradle; The Invisible Man's Revenge

Revenge on Rapists: see also *Rape/Rapists: Revenge: Avenging Death of Someone:* The Accused (1948); The Accused (1988); Death and the Maiden; Death Wish; Extremities; Hannie

Caulder; Last House on the Left; Lipstick; Two Mules for Sister Sara; Virgin Spring

Revisionist Films (films updating an old story with a modern perspective, usually making major changes): see also *Remakes of Foreign Films:* Aaron Loves Angela; All Night Long (1961); Aria; The Attic: The Hiding of Anne Frank; Big Man On Campus; Big Town; Black Caesar; Black Robe; Blacula; Body Snatchers; Bounty; The Boys from Syracuse; Brain Donors; Bram Stoker's Count Dracula (1970); Bram Stoker's Dracula (1992); Bride; Brideshead Revisited; Brother John; Buck and the Preacher; Buffalo Bill and the Indians, or Sitting Bull's History Lesson; The Cabinet of Caligari (1962); Candide; The Care Bears Adventure in Wonderland; Carmen Jones; Casanova '70; Chandler; Chastity Belt; Chimes at Midnight; Cinderfella; Cisco Kid; Count Yorga, Vampire; Crusoe; The Curse of the Werewolf; Dances With Wolves; Dirty Little Billy; Dr. Jekyll and Sister Hyde; Dracula's Daughter; Edward II; The Elusive Pimpernel; Empire of the Ants; 1492: Conquest of Paradise; Frankenstein '70; Frankenstein Created Woman; Frankenstein Unbound; Gore Vidal's Lincoln; The Gospel According to St. Matthew; Gothic; The Great Mouse Detective; Green Pastures; Hammett; Histoires Extraordinaires; Honey Pot; The Hunger; The Incredible Shrinking Woman; Jefferson in Paris; Jesus Christ, Superstar; Kaos; King Lear (1987); Kiss Me Kate (1953); Lady in the Iron Mask; Lair of the White Worm; Les Liaisons Dangereuses; Lisztomania; Little Ark; The Long Goodbye; The Madwoman of Chaillot; A Man Called Horse; Man Friday; Mandingo; Marlowe; Mary, Queen of Scots; Memoirs of an Invisible Man; Miss Robin Hood; The Muppet Christmas Carol; Murder by Death; Nightcomers; Phantom of Paradise; Pirate Movie; The Private Life of Sherlock Holmes; Prospero's Books; Ran; Richie Rich; Ring of the Musketeers; Robin and the Seven Hoods; Robinson Crusoe on Mars; Romanoff and Juliet; Rosencrantz and Guildenstern Are Dead; Roxanne; Scrooged; The Seven Percent Solution; Shamus; Silver Bullet; A Simple Twist of Fate; Snow White and the Three Stooges; Son of Dracula; Switching Channels; Swoon; The Taming of the Shrew; Taste the Blood of Dracula; The Tempest; The Three Musketeers (1973); The Three Musketeers (1993); Throne of Blood; Time after Time; Tombstone; Treasure Island (1991); Unforgiven (1992); Walker; West Side Story; Without a Clue; Wiz; Wolf; Young Einstein; Young Sherlock Holmes

Revolutionary War: see also *Early America: 1700s:* America; The Howards of Virginia; John Paul Jones; Revolution

Rewards at Stake: see also *Race Against Time: Inheritances at Stake: Lotteries: Contest/Competitions:* Bring Me the Head of Alfredo Garcia; Busy Body; Executive Suite; Good Neighbor Sam; Goodbye My Lady; It's a Mad Mad Mad Mad World!; It's in the Bag; Mad Dog and Glory; Once Upon a Crime; The Sorcerer; The Visit; Year of the Comet

Rich Bitches: see *Mean Women:* also *Heiresses: Rich People: Evil Women: Dangerous Women*

Rich Jerks: see *Mean Men:* also *Heirs: Rich People: Playboys: Evil Men: Dangerous Men*

Rich Kids: see also *Snobs: Snobs vs. Slobs: Rich People-Decadent: Children-Brats: Children-Little Adults: Rich People: CHILDREN'S: Heirs & Heiresses: Beautiful People:* Captains Courageous; Rich Kids; Six Weeks; A Taste for Killing; Terminal Bliss

Rich People: see also *Snobs: Snobs vs. Slobs: Rich People-Decadent: Rich Kids: Suburban Life: New York Life: Rich vs. Poor; Heirs & Heiresses: Inheritances At Stake: Oil People: Beautiful People:* Adam and Eva; The Adventurers; Alice; All This and Heaven, Too; The Amazing Howard Hughes; And Now, My Love; Animal Crackers; Annie; Aren't We All?; Arthur; At Long Last Love; Auntie Mame; Bachelor in Paradise; Bad Influence; Banning; Being There; Betsy; Beverly Hillbillies; Blind Husbands; Boom!; Boudu Saved From Drowning; Breakfast at Tiffany's; Brewster's Millions (1935); Brewster's Millions (1945); Brewster's Millions (1985); Bringing Up Baby; By Love Possessed; Caddyshack; Caddyshack 2; Cafe Society; Candleshoe; Castle in the Desert; The Cat and the Canary (1927); The Cat and the Canary (1939); The Cat and the Canary (1979); Caught; Citizen Kane; City Lights; Come and Get It; Come September; Compulsion; Daddy Longlegs; Dark Victory; Damage; The Damned; Death Takes a Holiday; Diamond Head; Diary of a Mad Housewife; Dinner at Eight; Dirty Rotten Scoundrels; The Discreet Charm of the Bourgeoisie; Donovan's Brain; Down and Out in Beverly Hills; Edward, My Son; Experiment Perilous; Exterminating Angel; Finishing School; From the Terrace; Gay Sisters; Go Naked in the World; Gold; Good Sam; The Graduate; The Grass Is Greener; The Great Gatsby (1949); The Great Gatsby (1974); Greedy; Greek Tycoon; The Group; Guilty as Charged; Half a Sixpence; Half Moon Street; The Happiest Millionaire; Has Anybody Seen My Gal?; High Pressure; High Society; The Hireling; Holiday; Home from the Hill; House of the Spirits; Humoresque; I Take this Woman; I'd Rather Be Rich; If I Had a Million; I'll Give a Million; Indiscreet; Indochine; Invitation; Invitation to the Wedding; Irene; It Started with Eve; Julia; Just Tell Me What You Want; Kipps; La Dolce Vita; The Last of Sheila; Late George Apley; Laughter in the Dark; The Lawrenceville Stories; The Leopard; Les Biches; Less Than Zero; Let's Make Love; Little Gloria, Happy At Last; Look in Any Window; The Magnificent Ambersons; Make Mine Mink; Masquerade (1988); Men in White; Metropolitan (1990); The Millionairess; Moment by Moment; Mr. North; Mrs. Parkington; Murder in Texas; Murder on the Orient Express; My Love Came Back; My Man Godfrey (1936); My Man Godfrey (1956); New Leaf; 9½ Weeks; Oblomov; On the Avenue; Paint it Black; Palm Beach Story; Philadelphia Story; Pretty Woman; Private Benjamin; Remember Last Night?; Reversal of Fortune; Rosebud; Rosie; Ruthless People; Sabrina; The Scarlet Pimpernel; Scenes from the Class Struggle in Beverly Hills; The Sea Gull; Serial; The Servant; The Shadow (1940); The Shadow (1994); Shining Hour; Shoot the Moon; Shooting Party; Six Degrees of Separation; Six Weeks; Someone to Watch Over Me; Splitting Heirs; Stork Club; Strangers, the Story of a Mother and Daughter; Such Good Friends; Suddenly, Last Summer; The Sun Also Rises; Susan and God; Swann in Love; Taking of Beverly Hills; Ten Thousand Bedrooms; Texasville; That Forsyte Woman; That Touch of Mink; The

Thin Man; Three Blind Mice; To Catch a Thief; To Find a Man; Tovarich; Tristana; Troop Beverly Hills; Tulsa; Undercurrent; Valley of Decision; Wall Street; War Against Mrs. Hadley; Weekend; Where the Heart Is; Written on the Wind; Yellow Rolls Royce; You Can't Take it With You (1938); You Can't Take it With You (1986); Zelly and Me

Rich People-Decadent: see also *Rich People: Snobs: Beautiful People: Fashion World: New York Life: Evil Men: Evil Women:* The Adventures of Captain Fabian; All This and Heaven, Too; The Comfort of Strangers; Compulsion; The Crush; Eureka; Evil Under the Sun; Exterminating Angel; Eye of the Devil; The Fall of the House of Usher (1928); The Hunger; Les Biches; Less Than Zero; Little Gloria, Happy At Last; Lumiere d'Ete; Rules of the Game; What?

Rich vs. Poor: see also *Snobs vs. Slobs: Class Conflicts: Romance-Class Conflicts: Lover Family Dislikes: Rich People: Poor People:* The Adventures of Captain Fabian; The Adventures of Robin Hood; Arthur; Boudu Saved From Drowning; Brideshead Revisited; Butterfield 8; Cabin in the Cotton; Camila (1984); Captains Courageous; Charlie Bubbles; Daddy Longlegs; Dead End; Down and Out in Beverly Hills; Dutch; The Flamingo Kid; Half a Sixpence; A Handful of Dust; Hands Across the Table; Has Anybody Seen My Gal?; Holiday; Howards End; I Live My Life; I Take this Woman; I'm No Angel; If I Had a Million; If You Could Only Cook; Immediate Family; Invitation to Happiness; It Happened on Fifth Avenue; It Started with Eve; Joe; Jude the Obscure; Kipps; Kitty; Landlord; Last Laugh; Life Stinks!; Mad Miss Manton; Maids; Make Mine Mink; Man in Grey; Man of Flowers; Meet the People; Meet the Stewarts; Melvin and Howard; Metropolis; Metropolitan (1990); The Millionaire; Mrs. Parkington; Mudlark; The Music Room; My Fair Lady; My Little Girl; The Outsiders; Oxford Blues; Platinum Blonde; The Prince and the Pauper (1937); Rebecca's Daughters; Red Headed Woman; The Reluctant Debutante; Richest Girl in the World; Roger & Me; Room at the Top; A Room with a View; Sabrina; She Devil; Society; Solid Gold Cadillac; The Story of Robin Hood and his Merry Men; Swept Away;

Taking Care of Business; Tovarich; The Ugly American; The Unsinkable Molly Brown; Valley of Decision; Where the Heart Is

Riches to Rags: see also *Power-Fall from: Fame-Fall from: Rags to Riches:*

Rise and Fall Stories: Adam and Eva; Andy Warhol's Heat; Arthur 2, On the Rocks; Auntie Mame; Blue Veil; Charlie Bubbles; Dishonored; Fitzwilly; Folks!; For Richer, For Poorer; Glamour Boy; Holy Matrimony; I'll Give a Million; It Could Happen to You; Katherine; Landlord; The Magnificent Ambersons; Maid to Order; The Main Event; The Millionaire; Monsieur Vincent; Overboard; Saratoga; Sullivan's Travels; The Three Cornered Moon; To Find a Man; Tovarich; Trading Places; Where the Heart Is

Rights-Fighting for: see *Civil Rights: Social Drama: Underdog Stories: Unions: Reformers: Fighting the System*

Riots: see also *Political Unrest: Inner City Life:* Attica (1971); Attica (1991); Do The Right Thing; Dog Day Afternoon; The Ernest Green Story; Medium Cool; RPM; The Strawberry Statement

Rise and Fall Stories: see also *Power-Rise to: Fame-Rise to: Biographies:* Al Capone; Doors; A Face in the Crowd; Fat City; Frances; The Gene Krupa Story; It Could Happen to You; The Josephine Baker Story; The Last Emperor; Lenny; Life at the Top; Life Begins at 8:30; Little Caesar; Ludwig; The Man Who Broke the Bank at Monte Carlo; Music Lovers; The Natural; Nijinsky; Raging Bull; Requiem for a Heavyweight (1956); Requiem for a Heavyweight (1962); Richard III; Rise and Fall of Legs Diamond; Singing Fool; Yesterday's Hero; Youngblood Hawke

Risking it All: see also *Bets: Gambling: Losing it All: Race Against Time:* All Night Long (1981); Carrie (1952); The Champion; Fever Pitch; Good Sam; The Great Sinner; High Pressure; Houdini; Killing Zoe; Lost in America; Music of Chance; Pacific Heights; Suicide Club; Tea for Two; Thunder Bay; Tristana; Who'll Stop the Rain?

Rivalries: see *Feuds: Men in Conflict: Women in Conflict: Enemies Unite: Friends as Enemies: Friendships on the Rocks: Jealousy*

River Trauma (shooting the rapids, et al.): The African Queen; Deliverance; Fitzcarraldo; Mississippi; Mountains on

the Moon; River of No Return; River Rat; The River Wild; Rooster Cogburn; Shoot to Kill; Up the Creek (1984); White Mile

Riviera Life: see also *France: Vacations-European: Monaco/Monte Carlo: Mediterranean: Beautiful People: Rich People: Rich People-Decadent: Exotic Locales:* An Almost Perfect Affair; And God Created Woman (1957); Bedtime Story (1964); Better Late Than Never; Bonjour, Tristesse; Boom!; Caprice; Deadlier Than the Male; Dirty Rotten Scoundrels; Evil Under the Sun; For Your Eyes Only; L'Annee des Meduses; Laughter in the Dark; Les Biches; Love Is a Ball; Marius; Moment to Moment; On the Riviera; Once Upon a Crime; Quartet (1981); Scapegoat; Silver Bears; To Catch a Thief

Road Movies: see also *Outlaw Road Movies: Fugitives: Journeys: Vacations: Fugitives from the Law: Fugitives from the Mob: Crossing the Border:* Aloha, Bobby and Rose; American Flyers; Anthony Adverse; Any Which Way You Can; Back Roads; Bad Company; Badlands; Bandolero; Barry Lyndon; Big Bus; The Bingo Long Travelling All-Stars and Motor Kings; Bite the Bullet; Blues in the Night; Bonnie and Clyde; Bound For Glory; Boxcar Bertha; Boys Next Door; Boys on the Side; Breaking the Rules; Bring Me the Head of Alfredo Garcia; Bustin' Loose; Butch and Sundance, The Early Days; Butch Cassidy and the Sundance Kid; Calendar Girl; Camilla (1994); Candy Mountain; Cannonball Run; Cannonball Run 2; Chase (1994); Cherry 2000; Convoy; Coupe de Ville; Crossroads (1986); Dangerous Curves; Detour; Dion Brothers; Dudes; Dutch; Easy Rider; Even Cowgirls Get the Blues; Fandango; Five Easy Pieces; Fugitive Lovers; The Gauntlet; Ginger in the Morning; Good Companions (1933); Good Companions (1956); Goodbye, Pork Pie; Grand Prix; Grand Theft Auto; Great Smokey Roadblock; Gumball Rally; Gun Crazy (1950); Gun Crazy (1992); Handle with Care; Harry and Tonto; Henry: Portrait of a Serial Killer; Honeysuckle Rose; Into the Night; It Happened One Night; Josh and S.A.M.; Just You and Me; Kalifornia; Kings of the Road; Leaving Normal; Les Valseuses; Living End; Long Long Trailer; The Long Riders; Losin' It; Lost in

America; Love Field; Midnight Run; Milky Way (1968); Mr. Billion; Muppet Movie; My Own Private Idaho; Mystery Train; North by Northwest; Paper Moon; Patti Rocks; Pink Cadillac; Rafferty and the Gold Dust Twins; Rain Man; The Rain People; The Reivers; Return to Macon County; Road Games; Road to Bali; Road to Hong Kong; Road to Morocco; Road to Rio; Road to Singapore; Road to Utopia; Road to Zanzibar; Roadside Prophets; Romancing the Stone; Scarecrow; Silver Streak; Sitting Ducks; Smokey and the Bandit; Smokey and the Bandit II; Smokey and the Bandit III; Something Wild (1986); Stranger Than Paradise; Sugarland Express; Sullivan's Travels; Sure Thing; The Terry Fox Story; Thelma & Louise; They Live by Night; Thieves Like Us; Things Are Tough All Over; Three for the Road; To Wong Foo, Thanks for Everything, Julie Newmar; Tom Jones; True Romance; Two For the Road; W.W. & The Dixie Dancekings; Where the Buffalo Roam; Wild at Heart; You Can't Run Away From It

Road Movies-Guys in Cars/ Convertibles: Breaking the Rules; Calendar Girl; Coupe de Ville; Fandango; Losin' It; To Wong Foo, Thanks for Everything, Julie Newmar

Road Movies-Transporting Girls: The Chase (1994); Dangerous Curves; Three for the Road

Road to California (road trips to the "Golden State"): see also *Road Movies: Outlaw Road Movies:* Boys on the Side; Calendar Girl; The Grapes of Wrath; Gumball Rally; Hollywood or Bust; Kalifornia; The Muppet Movie; Sure Thing; True Romance

Roaring 20s: see also *1920s: Prohibition Era: Mob Stories: Bootleggers:* Auntie Mame; Good News; The Great Gatsby; The Gunrunner; Has Anybody Seen My Gal?; Henry and June; The Hireling; The Josephine Baker Story; Margie; Maxie; Now I'll Tell; Our Dancing Daughters; Our Hearts Were Young and Gay; Pete Kelly's Blues; The Rise and Fall of Legs Diamond; The Roaring Twenties; Robin and the Seven Hoods; Roxie Hart; Tall, Dark & Handsome; Thoroughly Modern Millie; Three Comrades; Tropic of Cancer

Robin Hood Stories (stealing from rich, giving to poor, named Robin usu- ally)**: see also** *Riches to Rags:* The Adventures of Robin Hood; Flame and the Arrow; Guns of the Magnificent Seven; Harley Davidson and the Marlboro Man; Make Mine Mink; Miss Robin Hood; Robin and Marian; Robin and the Seven Hoods; Robin Hood (1922); Robin Hood (1973); Robin Hood (1990); Robin Hood, Men in Tights; Robin Hood: Prince of Thieves (1991); Rob Roy; The Sicilian; The Story of Robin Hood and His Merry Men; Viva Villa!

Robots (not necessarily human-looking or acting): see also *Androids: SCI-FI: Scientists-Mad: Monsters-Manmade: Experiments:* And You Thought Your Parents Were Weird; Black Hole; Boy and His Dog; Cherry 2000; CHOMPS; Class of 1999; The Day the Earth Stood Still; Deadly Friend; Forbidden Planet; Futureworld; Hardware; Heartbeeps; Josh and S.A.M.; K-9000; Man Made Monster; Robocop; Robocop 2; Runaway; Short Circuit; Short Circuit 2; Silent Running; Star Wars; The Stepford Wives; Westworld

Rock Stars/Bands: see also *Musicians: Singers: Concert Films: Rockumentaries:* Airheads; Backbeat; Breaking Glass; Bring on the Night; Can't Stop the Music; Cisco Pike; Clambake; The Commitments; Cool Ones; Cry Baby; The Decline of Western Civilization; The Decline of Western Civilization 2: The Metal Years; Don't Look Back; Doors; Elvis: The Movie; Fear of a Black Hat; The Five Heartbeats; Great Balls of Fire; Hail, Hail, Rock n Roll; A Hard Day's Night; Head; Hearts of Fire; Heavy Metal; High Heels; Howard the Duck; I Wanna Hold Your Hand; Jailhouse Rock; The Last Waltz; Leningrad Cowboys Go to America; Lisztomania; Mrs. Brown, You've Got a Lovely Daughter; No Small Affair; Oh God, You Devil; The Performance; Phantom of Paradise; Quadrophenia; Return of Spinal Tap; Rock Around the Clock; The Rose; Satisfaction; Sergeant Pepper's Lonely Hearts Club Band; Shout; Sid and Nancy; Smashing Time; Smithereens; Stop Making Sense; Streets of Fire; Suburbia; This is Spinal Tap; Times Square; Tokyo Pop; Tommy; Top Secret!; Truth or Dare; Woodstock; Young Einstein

Rockumentaries (documentaries or documentary-style films about rock musicians): see also *Documentaries:* *Music Videos: Music Video Style: Filmumentaries: Music Composer Biographies: Rock Stars:* All You Need is Cash; American Hotwax; Bring on the Night; The Decline of Western Civilization; The Decline of Western Civilization 2: The Metal Years; Hail, Hail, Rock n Roll; Hearts of Fire; The Last Waltz; Leningrad Cowboys Go to America; This is Spinal Tap; Truth or Dare

Rodents (usually rats or mice, but also rabbits and others): see also *Animal Stories: Animals-Mutant:* An American Tail; An American Tail 2; Anchors Aweigh; Ben; Cinderella (1950); The Great Mouse Detective; Night of the Lepus; Ratboy; The Rescuers; The Rescuers Down Under; Secret of NIMH; Willard; Witches

Rodeos: see also *Cowboys: WESTERNS: Rural Life: Southwestern Life:* Annie Get Your Gun!; Annie Oakley; Buffalo Bill; Buffalo Bill and the Indians, or Sitting Bull's History Lesson; Cattle Annie & Little Britches; 8 Seconds; J.W. Coop; Junior Bonner; Lusty Men; Tickle Me

Rogue Plots: see also *Kill the Beast: Murders-One-by-One: Monsters: Stalkers: Malicious Menaces: THRILLERS: HORROR: Psychotics: Philanderers: Roommates from Hell:* Alien; Aliens; Alien 3; The Andromeda Strain; Apartment Zero; The Birds; The Birds II; The Blob (1958); The Blob (1988); Cape Fear (1962); Cape Fear (1991); Car; Child's Play (1988); Child's Play 2; Child's Play 3; Christine; The Creature of the Black Lagoon; Day of the Jackal; Fatal Attraction; Frankenstein (1931); Frankenstein '70; Frankenstein and the Monster from Hell; Frankenstein Created Woman; Frankenstein Unbound; Friday the 13th (1980); Friday the 13th: Final Chapter; Friday the 13th, Part 3-D; Friday the 13th, Part II; Friday the 13th Part V-A New Beginning; Friday the 13th Part VI-Jason Lives; Friday the 13th Part VII-The New Blood; Friday the 13th Part VIII-Jason Takes Manhattan; Graveyard Shift; Grizzly; Halloween; Halloween 2; Halloween 3: Season of the Witch; Halloween 4: The Return of Michael Myers; Halloween 5: The Revenge of Michael Myers; The Hand (1960); The Hand (1981); Hardware; Horror Express; Mother's Boys;

Conagher; Confidential Agent; Conquest; Consenting Adult; Constant Nymph (1933); Constant Nymph (1943); Continental Divide; Conversation Piece; Coquette; Corrina, Corrina; Corvette Summer; Cotton Club; A Countess from Hong Kong; Courtship; The Courtship of Eddie's Father; Cousin, Cousine; Cousins; Cover Girl; The Cowboy and the Lady; Crocodile Dundee; Cross My Heart; Crossing Delancey; The Crying Game; Cuba; The Cutting Edge; Cyrano de Bergerac (1950); Cyrano de Bergerac (1990); Daddy Longlegs; Daisy Kenyon; Daisy Miller; A Damsel in Distress; Dance with a Stranger; Dancers; Dancing Lady; A Dangerous Woman; Dark Angel (1935); Dark Victory; Darling Lili; Date with an Angel; A Date with Judy; Dave; David and Bathsheba; David and Lisa; David Copperfield; Days of Heaven; Dead Again; Deadfall (1968); Dear Heart; Dear John; Dear Ruth; Deception (1946); Deception (1992); Deep Blue Sea; Defending Your Life; Desert Hearts; Design for Living; Designing Woman; Desire; Desire Under the Elms; Desiree; Desk Set; Destry Rides Again; The Devil and Miss Jones; The Devil Is a Woman; Devotion; Diamond Head; Diamond Horseshoe; Diamond Jim; Diamonds for Breakfast; Diary of a Chambermaid (1946); Diary of a Chambermaid (1963); A Different Story; Dim Sum: a Little Bit of Heart; Dirty Dancing; Diving In; Divorce of Lady X; Divorcee; Doc Hollywood; Doctor in the House; Doctor Jekyll and Mr. Hyde (1931); The Doctor Takes a Wife; Doctor, You've Got to be Kidding; Doctor Zhivago; Doctor's Dilemma; Dodsworth; Dogfight; Don Juan DeMarco; Don't Go Near the Water; Don't Make Waves; Don't Tell Her It's Me; Dona Flor and Her Two Husbands; Double Exposure; Double Indemnity; The Double Life of Veronique; Double Wedding; Dove; Down Argentine Way; Down to Earth; Dr. Jekyll and Mr. Hyde (1941); Dracula (1931); Dracula (1979); Dracula Has Risen from the Grave; Dracula (Horror of Dracula, 1958); Dracula, Prince of Darkness; Dracula's Daughter; The Draughtman's Contract; Dream Wife; The Dressmaker; Drum; Dubarry Was a Lady; Duchess and the Dirtwater Fox; Duel in the Sun; Dying Young; Dynamite; Earth Girls are Easy; East Lynne; East of Eden (1955); East of

Eden (1980); Easter Parade; Easy Living (1937); Echo Park; Eclipse; Educating Rita; Edward Scissorhands; 8 Seconds; Eighty-Four Charing Cross Road; Electric Dreams; Electric Horseman; Elena and Her Men; Elvira Madigan; The Emperor Waltz; The Enchanted Cottage; Encore; End of the World . . . ; Endless Love; Enemies, A Love Story; Escape from Fort Bravo; Eternally Yours; Ethan Fromme; The Europeans; Evelyn Prentice; Evermile New Jersey; Every Day's A Holiday; Every Girl Should be Married; Every Time We Say Goodbye; Everybody Wins; Everybody's All American; Ex-Lady; Experiment Perilous; The Experts; Exposed; Eye of the Needle; Eyewitness (1981); The Fabulous Baker Boys; Facts of Life; Fahrenheit 451; The Fall of the Roman Empire; Falling in Love; Falling in Love Again; Fanny; Far and Away; Far from the Madding Crowd; Farewell My Concubine; A Farewell to Arms (1932); A Farewell to Arms (1957); The Farmer Takes a Wife; The Farmer's Daughter; Father Goose; Favor; Fedora; Female on the Beach; Fiesta; Fighting Kentuckian; A Fine Romance; Finishing School; Firefly; First Love; First Name: Carmen; Flame of New Orleans; Flame of the Barbary Coast; The Flamingo Kid; Flamingo Road; Flashdance; Flesh and Blood (1985); Flesh and Bone; Flesh and the Devil; Flirting; Flower Drum Song; The Fly (1958); The Fly (1986); The Fly II; Flying Down to Rio; Folies Bergere; Follow the Fleet; Fool for Love; Foolin' Around; Foolish Wives; Fools for Scandal; For Keeps; For Love of Ivy; For Love or Money (1963); For Love or Money (1993); For Me and My Gal; For Whom the Bell Tolls; Forbidden Dance; A Foreign Affair; Forest Rangers; Forever Amber; Forever Female; Forever Young; Forrest Gump; Forty Carats; The Fountainhead; Four Daughters; Four Weddings and a Funeral; Four's a Crowd; Foxfire (1955); Frankie and Johnny; Free and Easy; The French Lieutenant's Woman; French Postcards; Frenchman's Creek; Fresh Horses; The Frisco Kid (1935); The Frog Prince; From Here to Eternity; From the Terrace; The Fugitive Kind; Fugitive Lovers; Full Moon in Blue Water; Full Moon in Paris; Funny About Love; Funny Face; Fuzzy Pink Nightgown; G.I. Blues; Gable and Lombard; Gabriela; Gaby; Gambit; The

Game Is Over; Gang's All Here; Garden of Allah; The Gay Divorcee; The General Died at Dawn; Genevieve; Gentlemen Prefer Blondes; Georgy Girl; Gertrude; Gervaise; The Getaway (1972); The Getaway (1994); Getting It Right; Ghost; The Ghost and Mrs. Muir; Ghost Breakers; Giant; Gigi (1948); Gigi (1958); Gilda; Gilded Lily; Ginger in the Morning; The Girl Can't Help It; Girl Crazy; Girl From Petrovka; A Girl Named Tamiko; Girl of the Golden West; The Girl Who Couldn't Say No; The Girl Who Had Everything; The Girl with Green Eyes; Girlfriends; Give Me a Sailor; Glass Bottom Boat; The Glass Menagerie (1950); The Glass Menagerie (1973); The Glass Menagerie (1987); Go Naked in the World; Go West Young Man; The Go-Between; Go-Fish; Goin' South; Goin' To Town; Gold; Golden Boy; Golden Gate; Gone With the Wind; The Good Earth; The Good Fairy; The Good Mother; The Good Wife; Goodbye Again; Goodbye Columbus; The Goodbye Girl; Goodbye Mr. Chips (1939); Goodbye Mr. Chips (1969); Goodbye My Fancy; Gorgeous Hussy; The Graduate; Grand Hotel; Grand Prix; Grandview, USA; Grass Is Greener; Grease; Grease 2; The Great Caruso; The Great Gatsby (1949); The Great Gatsby (1974); The Great Lover (1931); Great Scout and Cathouse Thursday; The Great White Hope; The Great Ziegfeld; Greek Tycoon; Green Card; Green Dolphin Street; Green Fire; Green Ice; Green Mansions; Gregory's Girl; Griffin and Phoenix, A Love Story; Groundhog Day; Grumpy Old Men; Guest Wife; A Guy Named Joe; Gypsy Moths; Hallelujah, I'm a Bum; A Handful of Dust; Hands Across the Table; Hannah and Her Sisters; Hanover Street; Hans Christian Andersen; Hard Promises; Harvey Girls; Haunted Summer; Havana; He Married His Wife; He Said, She Said; Heart of Dixie; Heartbreak Kid; Heaven Can Wait (1978); Heaven Knows, Mr. Allison; Heiress; The Helen Morgan Story; Hello Dolly; Henry and June; Henry V (1944); Henry V (1989); Her Alibi; Her Husband's Affairs; Here We Go Round the Mulberry Bush; Hero at Large; Heroes; High Heels; High Road to China; High Society; High, Wide and Handsome; The Hired Wife; The Hireling; Hiroshima, Mon Amour; His Brother's Wife; His Girl Friday; Hit

Parade of 1941; Hit the Deck; Hold Back the Dawn; Hold Me, Thrill Me, Kiss Me; Hold Your Man; Holiday; Holiday in Mexico; Holiday Inn; The Homecoming (1948); Honeymoon; Honeymoon in Vegas; Honeymoon Machine; Honeysuckle Rose; Honky Tonk; Hopscotch; Hospital; Hot Pursuit; Hot Spot; House Calls; A House Divided; Houseboat; Housesitter; How to Marry a Millionaire; How to Save a Marriage and Ruin Your Life; The Hudsucker Proxy; Humoresque; The Hunchback of Notre Dame (1923); The Hunchback of Notre Dame (1939); The Hunchback of Notre Dame (1956); The Hunchback of Notre Dame (1982); Hurricane (1937); Hurricane (1979); I Am a Camera; I Cover the Waterfront; I Don't Buy Kisses Anymore; I Don't Care Girl; I Don't Want to Talk About it; I Dood It!; I Dream Too Much; I Know Where I'm Going; I Live My Life; I Love Melvin; I Married a Witch; I Married a Woman; I.Q.; I Sent a Letter to My Love; I Stand Condemned; I Take this Woman; I Will . . . I Will . . . for Now; I'd Rather Be Rich; I'll Be Seeing You; I'll See You in My Dreams; I've Heard the Mermaids Singing; Ice Castles; Idiot's Delight; Idol; If a Man Answers; If You Could Only Cook; Illegally Yours; Immortal Beloved; Impromptu; Improper Channels; In a Lonely Place; In Name Only; In Old Chicago; In Praise of Older Women; In the Cool of the Day; In the French Style; In the Good Old Summertime; Indecent Obsession; Indecent Proposal; Indiscreet; Indiscretion of an American Wife; Innocents in Paris (1953); Innocents of Paris (1929); Inspiration; Interlude (1957); The Interlude (1968); Intermezzo (1939); Invitation to Happiness; Irene; Irma La Douce; Iron Petticoat; Is There Sex After Death?; It Could Happen to You; It Had to Be You; It Happened One Night; It Happens Every Spring; It Started in Naples; It Started with Eve; It's a Date; It's a Small World; It's a Wonderful World; It's Love I'm After; It's My Turn; Ivanhoe; Jacknife; Jamaica Inn (1939); Jamaica Inn (1982); Jefferson in Paris; Jennifer 8; Jersey Girl; Jewel of the Nile; Jezebel; John and Mary; Johnny Belinda; Johnny Eager; Johnny Handsome; Joseph Andrews; Joy of Living; Jude the Obscure; Jules and Jim; June Bride; Jungle Fever; Just Tell Me

What You Want; Just You and Me; Kaleidoscope; Kangaroo; Kansas; The Karate Kid; The Karate Kid, Part II; The Karate Kid, Part III; Kentucky; The Key (1934); The Key (1958); Key Exchange; Key to the City; Kid (1921); Kill Me Again; Killer's Kiss; Kind of Loving; Kindergarten Cop; The King and I; King of the Gypsies; King, Queen, Knave; The King's Whore; Kings Go Forth; Kismet (1955); A Kiss for Corliss; A Kiss in the Dark; Kiss Me Goodbye; Kiss Me Kate (1953); Kiss Me, Stupid!; Kiss of the Spider Woman; Kiss the Blood Off My Hands; Kiss the Boys Goodbye; Kiss Them For Me; Kitty; Kitty Foyle; Knack; Knave of Hearts; Knight Without Armor; Knights of the Round Table; L'Annee des Meduses; La Belle Noiseuse; La Chienne; La Dolce Vita; La Maschera; La Ronde (1950); La Ronde (1964); La Strada; La Traviata; La Vie Continue; La Vie de Boheme; Ladies Should Listen; Lady and the Tramp; Lady Chatterley's Lover (1955); Lady Chatterly's Lover (1981); Lady Eve; Lady in the Dark; The Lady Is Willing; Lady L.; Lady Takes a Chance; Lady with a Dog; Ladyhawke; The Last Flight of Noah's Ark; The Last Metro; The Last of Mrs. Cheyney; The Last of the Mohicans (1936); The Last of the Mohicans (1992); Last of the Red Hot Lovers; The Last Picture Show; The Last Run; Last Tango in Paris; The Last Tycoon; Last Year at Marienbad; Laughing Sinners; Laughter; Law and the Lady; Le Cavaleur; Legends of the Fall; Les Biches; Les Enfants Terribles; Les Visiteurs du Soir; Let's Dance; Let's Do it Again (1953); Let's Make Love; Lethal Weapon 3; Letter From an Unknown Woman; Lieutenant Wore Skirts; Life and Death of Colonel Blimp; Life of Her Own; Light in the Piazza; Light that Failed; Lili; Lili Marleen; Lilith; Limelight; Listen to Me; Little Minister; Little Murders; A Little Night Music; A Little Romance; A Little Sex; Little Shop of Horrors (1986); Live a Little, Love a Lot; Live for Life; Live, Love and Learn; Lola (1960); Lola Montes; Lolita; Lonely Guy; The Lonely Passion of Judith Hearne; Long Hot Summer (1958); Long Long Trailer; Looking for Love; Lorna Doone; Lost and Found; Lost Lady; Lost Moment; Loulou; Love; Love Affair (1932); Love Affair (1939); Love Among the Ruins; Love and Pain and the Whole Damn

Thing; Love Before Breakfast; Love Crazy; Love in a Goldfish Bowl; Love in Bloom; Love in Germany; Love in the Afternoon; Love is a Ball; Love is a Many-Splendored Thing; Love Letters (1945); Love Letters (1984); Love on the Dole; Love on the Run (1979); Love Potion #9; Love Story (1944); Love Story (1970); Love With the Proper Stranger; Lovely to Look At; Lover Come Back (1946); Lover Come Back (1961); Loves of a Blonde; Lovesick; Lovin' Molly; Loving; Loving Couples; Luck of the Irish; Lucky Lady; Lucky Night; Lucy Gallant; Lumiere d'Ete; Luna; Lunatics, A Love Story; Lunch on the Grass; Lusty Men; Lydia M. Butterfly; Macao; The Macomber Affair; Mad Dog and Glory; Mad Miss Manton; Madame Bovary; Madame Butterfly; Madame Dubarry; Made for Each Other; Made in America; Made in Heaven; Madness of the Heart; Magic; Magnificent Obsession (1935); Magnificent Obsession (1954); The Magus; Mahogany; Maid of Salem; Mail Order Bride; Main Event; Major and the Minor; Majority of One; Making Love; Making Mr. Right; Mala Noche; The Male Animal; Mambo Kings; A Man and A Woman; A Man and a Woman: Twenty Years Later; A Man in Love; Man of La Mancha; Man Trouble; The Man Who Fell to Earth; The Man Who Loved Cat Dancing; The Man Who Loved Women (1977); The Man Who Loved Women (1983); Man with the Golden Arm; The Man with Two Brains; Man's Castle; Man's Favorite Sport?; Manhattan; Mannequin (1937); Mannequin (1987); Mannequin 2: On the Move; March or Die; Mardi Gras; Margie; Marius; Marnie; Marriage Go Round; Married to the Mob; A Married Woman; The Marrying Man; Marty; Mary, Mary; Masculine, Feminine; The Mask (1985); Masquerade (1988); The Matchmaker; The Mating Game; Mating of Willie; Mating Season; Maurice; Maverick Queen; Max and Helen; Maytime; McCabe and Mrs. Miller; McClintock!; Me and My Gal; Medicine Man; Meet Me in Las Vegas; Meet the Stewarts; Meeting Venus; Melo; Melody; The Men (1950); Men Don't Leave; Men in Her Life; Men in White; Men with Wings; Mermaids; The Merry Widow (1925); The Merry Widow (1934); The Merry Widow (1952); Message to Garcia; Middle of the Night; Midnight

(1939); A Midsummer Night's Dream; A Midsummer Night's Sex Comedy; Mignon Has Left; Mill on the Floss; Million Dollar Legs; Million Dollar Mermaid; The Millionairess; Minnie & Moskowitz; The Miracle (1990); Miracle in the Rain; Mischief; Miss Sadie Thompson; Miss Susie Slagle's; Mississippi Masala; Mississippi Mermaid; Mo' Better Blues; The Model and the Marriage Broker; Modern Times; Mogambo; Moment by Moment; Momma, There's a Man in Your Bed; Mona Lisa; Monsieur Beaucaire; Monsignor; Monte Carlo; The Monte Carlo Story; Montenegro; Moon in the Gutter; The Moon Is Blue; The Moon's Our Home; More Than a Secretary; The More the Merrier; Morocco; Moscow Does Not Believe in Tears; Mother is a Freshman; Mountain Eagle; Mourning Becomes Electra; Move Over, Darling; Mr. and Mrs. Smith; Mr. Jones; Mr. Lucky; Mr. Music; Mr. Peabody and the Mermaid; Mrs. Parker and the Vicious Circle; Mrs. Soffel; Muriel's Wedding; Murmur of the Heart; Murphy's Romance; Music in My Heart; The Music Man; My Beautiful Laundrette; My Best Friend's Girl; My Blood Runs Cold; My Cousin Rachel; My Dear Secretary; My Fair Lady; My Favorite Wife; My Gal Sal; My Geisha; My Girl; My Girl 2; My Love Came Back; My Lucky Star; My Man Godfrey (1936); My Man Godfrey (1956); My Night at Maud's; My Own Private Idaho; My Sin; My Sister Eileen (1942); My Sister Eileen (1955); My Wild Irish Rose; The Mystery of Edwin Drood; Mystic Pizza; Naked in New York; The Naked Jungle; Naked Maja; Nanou; Naughty Marietta; Nell; Neptune's Daughter; Never a Dull Moment (1950); Never Give a Sucker an Even Break; Never on Sunday; Never Say Goodbye; New Kind of Love; New York, New York; Next Stop, Greenwich Village; Next Time We Love; Night Angel; The Night Is Young (1934); The Night Porter; Night unto Night; The Night We Never Met; Nights of Cabiria; Ninotchka; 9½ Weeks; No Man of Her Own; No More Ladies; No No Nanette (1930); No No Nanette (1940); No Small Affair; No Time for Love; No Way Out (1987); Nobody's Fool (1986); Noir et Blanc; Not with My Wife You Don't; Nothin' But a Man; Notorious; Notorious Landlady; Nouvelle Vague; Now, Voyager; Nudo di Donna; O

Pioneers!; Ode to Billy Joe; Of Human Bondage (1934); Of Human Bondage (1946); Of Human Bondage (1964); Of Love and Desire; Of Mice and Men (1939); Of Mice and Men (1993); An Officer and a Gentleman; Oh, What a Night; Oklahoma!; Oklahoma Crude; Old Gringo; Oliver's Story; On Approval; On Dangerous Ground; On Golden Pond; On the Avenue; On the Riviera; On the Town; Once Around; Once in Paris; Once Upon a Dream; Once Upon a Honeymoon; One from the Heart; One Hour with You; One Night of Love; One Sunday Afternoon; One Touch of Venus; One Way Passage; One Woman or Two; Only Game in Town; Only the Lonely; Only Two Can Play; Only You; Operation Mad Ball; The Opposite Sex and How to Live With Them; Orchestra Wives; Orpheus Descending; Ossessione; Other People's Money; The Other Side of Midnight; The Other Side of the Mountain; The Other Side of the Mountain Part Two; Our Hearts Were Young and Gay; Out of Africa; Out of the Past; Oxford Blues; Paint Your Wagon; Painted Desert; A Pair of Briefs; Paisan; Pal Joey; Pandora and the Flying Dutchman; The Paper Chase; Paper Marriage; The Paradine Case; Paradise (1982); Paradise (1991); Paris Blues; Paris When it Sizzles; Party Girl; Passion; Passion/Madame Dubarry (1919); Pat and Mike; Patch of Blue; Pauline at the Beach; Peg o' My Heart; Peggy Sue Got Married; Perfect; Perfect Furlough; Perfect Strangers; Period of Adjustment; Personal Property; Peter Ibbetson; Petulia; Pickup Artist; Picnic; Pirate; The Pirates of Penzance; Play it Again, Sam; Playboys; Pointsman; Popeye; Port of Call; Portrait of Jennie; The Postman Always Ring Twice (1945); The Postman Always Rings Twice (1981); Power, Passion, and Murder; Prelude to a Kiss; Pretty Baby; Pretty Woman; Pride and Prejudice; Pride of the Yankees; The Prince and the Showgirl; The Prince of Tides; The Princess and the Pirate; Prisoner of Zenda (1937); Prisoner of Zenda (1952); Prisoner of Zenda (1979); Private Lives; The Private Lives of Elizabeth and Essex; The Prizefighter and the Lady; The Promise; Promise Her Anything; The Purple Rose of Cairo; Quality Street; Quartet (1948); Quartet (1981); Queen Christina; Queen of the Stardust Ballroom; The Quiet Man; Quo

Vadis; The Rachel Papers; Rachel, Rachel; Racing with the Moon; Raging Moon; Rain; Rainbow; The Rainmaker; Raintree County; Rancho Notorious; Rare Breed; Rat Race; Razor's Edge (1946); Razor's Edge (1986); Reality Bites; Reap the Wild Wind; Reckless (1935); Reckless (1983); Red Dust; The Red Headed Woman; Red Kiss; The Red Shoe Diaries; Red Shoes; Red Sky at Morning; Red Sorghum; Reds; Rendez-Vous; The Return of Martin Guerre; Return of the Scarlet Pimpernel; Return of the Soldier; Return to Macon County; Return to the Blue Lagoon; Reuben, Reuben; Revenge; Rhapsody; Rhinestone; Rich Kids; Richest Girl in the World; Riding High; Riff-Raff (1935); Risky Business; River of No Return; A River Runs Through It; Road to Bali; Road to Hong Kong; Road to Morocco; Road to Rio; Road to Singapore; Road to Utopia; Road to Zanzibar; Robin and Marian; Robin Hood (1922); Robin Hood (1973); Robin Hood (1990); Robin Hood: Prince of Thieves (1991); Rob Roy; Rocky; Roman Holiday; Roman Spring of Mrs. Stone; Romance; Romance on the High Seas; Romancing the Stone; Romanoff and Juliet; Romantic Comedy; Romeo and Juliet (1936); Romeo and Juliet (1954); Romeo and Juliet (1968); Room at the Top; Room with a View; Rooster Cogburn; Rope of Sand; Rose Marie (1936); Rose Marie (1954); Rose of Washington Square; The Rose Tattoo; Rough Cut; Roxanne; The Royal Wedding; Russia House; Ryan's Daughter; Sabrina; Sadie McKee; Safety Last; The Sailor Who Fell From Grace with the Sea; Salmonberries; Salsa; Salty O'Rourke; Samantha; Same Time, Next Year; Sammy and Rosie Get Laid; Samson and Delilah; San Francisco; San Francisco Story; San Quentin; Sanctuary; Sand Pebbles; The Sandpiper; Sarah, Plain and Tall; Saratoga; Saratoga Trunk; Saskatchewan; Sawdust and Tinsel; Say Anything; Say Hello to Yesterday; Sayonara; Scared Stiff; Sea of Grass; Sea Wife; Second Chance; Second Fiddle; Second Honeymoon; Second Thoughts; The Secret of My Success; Secret Places; Secrets; The Seduction of Joe Tynan; See You in the Morning; Semi-Tough; Send Me No Flowers; Sentimental Journey; September Affair; Seven Brides for Seven Brothers; Seven Days Leave; Seven Sinners; The Seven-Year Itch; Seventh

Heaven (1927); Seventh Heaven (1937); Seventh Veil; Severed Head; Sex and the Single Girl; Sex, Lies, and Videotape; Shadowlands; Shadows of our Forgotten Ancestors; Shag; Shakespeare Wallah; Shall We Dance?; Shanghai Express; She (1935); She (1965); She Couldn't Say No; She Done Him Wrong; She's Gotta Have It; She's Working Her Way Through College; The Sheik; The Sheltering Sky; Shining Hour; Shining Through; The Shootist; The Shop Around the Corner; Showboat (1936); Showboat (1951); Sidewalks of London; Silence of the North; Silk Stockings; Simple Men; Sing Baby Sing; The Sins of Rachel Cade; Sisters; The Sky's the Limit; Skylark; Sleeper; Sleeping Beauty; Sleepless in Seattle; The Slipper and the Rose; Slow Dancing in the Big City; Small Circle of Friends; Small Town Girl (1936); Small Town Girl (1953); Smart Woman; Smiles of a Summer Night; Smiling Lieutenant; Smooth Talk; Snow White and the Seven Dwarfs; So Big (1932); So Big (1953); Some Came Running; Some Girls; Some Kind of Wonderful; Somebody Killed Her Husband; Someone to Love; Someone to Watch Over Me; Something Wild (1960); Something Wild (1986); Somewhere I'll Find You; Somewhere in Time; Sommersby; Son of Paleface; A Song Is Born; Song of the Islands; A Song to Remember; Song Without End; Sophie's Choice; The Sound of Music; South Pacific; Speaking Parts; Special Day; Speechless; Speedway; Spellbound; Spetters; Spinout; Spitfire; Springtime in the Rockies; St. Martin's Lane; Staircase; Stanley & Iris; A Star Is Born (1937); A Star Is Born (1954); A Star Is Born (1976); Star Spangled Girl; Star Trek IV: The Voyage Home; Starman; Stars and Stripes Forever; Starting Over; State Fair (1933); State Fair (1945); State Fair (1962); Stay Hungry; Staying Together; Stealing Heaven; Steamboat Bill Jr.; The Sterile Cuckoo; Stolen Hours; The Stork Club; The Story of Adele H.; The Story of Alexander Graham Bell; Story of Three Loves; The Story of Vernon and Irene Castle; Straight Talk; Strangers When We Meet; The Stratton Story; Strawberry Blonde; Streets of Fire; Strictly Ballroom; Strictly Business; The Stripper; Subway; Sugarbaby; Summer; Summer of '42; Summer of My German Soldier; A Summer Place; Summer Story;

Summertime; Sunday, Bloody Sunday; Sunday in New York; Sunflower; Sunrise at Campobello; Surrender; Surviving Desire; Susan Lenox, Her Fall and Rise; Suzy; Svengali (1931); Svengali (1983); The Swan; The Swan Princess; Swann in Love; Sweet Charity; Sweet November; Sweethearts; Sweethearts Dance; Swept Away; Swing High, Swing Low; Swing Shift; Swing Time; Switch; Switching Channels; Sword of Lancelot; Sylvia and the Ghost; T.R. Baskin; TaiPan; Take a Letter, Darling; Tales of Hoffman; Talk of the Town; Tall Guy; Tamarind Seed; Tammy and the Bachelor; Tarnished Angels; Taste of Honey; Teacher's Pet; Teahouse of the August Moon; Tell Me that You Love Me, Junie Moon; The Tempest; Ten Thousand Bedrooms; Tender is the Night; Tender Mercies; The Tender Trap; Tequila Sunrise; Teresa; Tess; Test Pilot; That Certain Age; That Certain Feeling; That Forsyte Woman; That Hamilton Woman; That Kind of Woman; That Obscure Object of Desire; That Touch of Mink; That Uncertain Feeling; The Young Girls of Rochefort; There's a Girl in My Soup; They All Laughed; They Knew What They Wanted; They Shoot Horses, Don't They?; Thief of Hearts; Thief Who Came to Dinner; Thieves Like Us; Thin Ice; Thing Called Love; 36 Fillette; This Above All; This Could Be the Night; This Happy Feeling; This is My Affair; This Property is Condemned; This Sporting Life; This Thing Called Love; Thomas Crown Affair; Those Magnificent Men in Their Flying Machines; Those Were the Days; A Thousand Clowns; Three Blind Mice; Three Coins in the Fountain; Three Comrades; Three Little Words; Three of Hearts; Three on a Couch; Three Smart Girls; Three Smart Girls Grow Up; The Threepenny Opera; Threesome; Thrill of a Romance; The Thrill of It All; Thunderbirds; Tickle Me; Tie Me Up! Tie Me Down!; Tiger's Tale; Tim; Time after Time; Time for Loving; A Time to Love & A Time to Die; Tin Pan Alley; To Catch a Thief; To Each His Own; To Find a Man; To Have and Have Not; To Paris with Love; To Sir with Love; Toast of New Orleans; Today We Live; Together Again; Tokyo Joe; Tokyo Pop; Tom & Viv; Tom, Dick and Harry; Tom Jones; Tomorrow is Forever; Too Beautiful For You; Too Late Blues; Too Many Husbands; Tootsie; Top

Gun; Top Hat; Top Secret Affair; Torch Song; Torch Song Trilogy; Torn Curtain; The Torrents of Spring; Trade Winds; Trapeze; Tristana; Trouble in Mind; Trouble in Paradise; Trouble with Girls; True Love; Truly, Madly, Deeply; Trust; Tuff Turf; Tugboat Annie; Tune in Tomorrow; Turning Point; Turtle Diary; 21 Days; Twenty Thousand Years in Sing Sing; Twice in a Lifetime; Twin Beds; Two For the Road; Two for the Seesaw; Two Girls and a Sailor; Two Moon Junction; Two of a Kind; Two People; Two Worlds of Jenny Logan; Two-Faced Woman; The Umbrellas of Cherbourg; Un Coeur en Hiver; The Unbearable Lightness of Being; Unbelievable Truth; The Unconquered; Under Milk Wood; Under the Yum Yum Tree; Under Two Flags; Unfinished Piece for a Player Piano; An Unmarried Woman; Untamed Heart; Urban Cowboy; Used People; Vacation from Marriage; Valentino Returns; Valley Girl; Valley of Decision; Vanity Fair; Vertigo; Vibes; Victor/Victoria; Violets are Blue; VIPs; The Virgin and the Gypsy; Virgin Queen; Visit to a Small Planet; Viva Las Vegas; Vivacious Lady; Voices; W.H.I.F.F.S.; Wabash Avenue; Waikiki Wedding; Wait Until Spring, Bandini; Wake of the Red Witch; Walk, Don't Run; Walk in the Spring Rain; Walk on the Wild Side; Walking Stick; Waltz Across Texas; War Between Men and Women; Warm December; Washington Story; Waterloo Bridge (1931); Waterloo Bridge (1940); Way Down East (1920); Way Down East (1935); The Way We Were; Wedding March; Wedding Night; Wedding Present; Welcome Home; West Side Story; The Westerner; What's Eating Gilbert Grape?; What's Up, Doc?; When Harry Met Sally; When Ladies Meet (1941); When My Baby Smiles at Me; When Tomorrow Comes; When You're in Love; Where the Day Takes You; White Cargo; White Nights (1957); White Palace; White Sister; Who's Been Sleeping in My Bed?; Who's That Girl?; Wicked Lady (1945); Wicked Lady (1983); Wife, Doctor and Nurse; Wife, Husband and Friend; Wife Versus Secretary; Wild Hearts Can't Be Broken; Wild in the Country; Willie and Phil; Wings in the Dark; Wings of Desire; Wings of the Morning; Without Love; Without Reservations; Witness; Wives and Lovers; Wolf; The Woman I Love;

Woman in Flames; Woman in Red; The Woman Next Door; Woman of the Year; Woman on the Beach; Women in Love; Wonder Bar; Working Girl; The World Is Full of Married Men; The World of Suzie Wong; Written on the Wind; Wuthering Heights (1939); Wuthering Heights (1953); Wuthering Heights (1970); Wuthering Heights (1992); Wyoming; Yanks; Year My Voice Broke; The Year of Living Dangerously; Year of the Comet; Yentl; Yes, Giorgio; Yesterday, Today and Tomorrow; Yolanda and the Thief; You Belong to Me; You Can't Run Away From It; You Can't Take it With You (1938); You Can't Take it With You (1986); You Light Up My Life; You Were Never Lovelier; You'll Never Get Rich; You're a Big Boy Now; Young at Heart; Young Bess; The Young in Heart; Young Man with a Horn; Youngblood; Zandalee; Zandy's Bride; Zebrahead

Romance-Affairs: see *Romance with Married Person*

Romance-Bickering: see also *Screwball Comedy: FARCE: Romantic Comedy: Romance-Opposites Attract:* Adam's Rib (1949); Athena; Aviator; The Barkleys of Broadway; The Big Easy; The Bodyguard; The Bride Came C.O.D.; Bye Bye Love; Cass Timberlane; Cocktail; Continental Divide; The Cutting Edge; Designing Woman; Divorce, American Style; The Doctor Takes a Wife; Dream Wife; The Duchess and the Dirtwater Fox; Electric Horseman; Gin Game; Goodbye Girl; He Married His Wife; He Said, She Said; High Road to China; His Girl Friday; Hopscotch; House Calls; I Love Trouble (1994); It Happened One Night; It's Love I'm After; Jinxed; Just Tell Me What You Want; Kiss Me Kate (1953); The Little Treasure; Lost and Found; Love Among the Ruins; Lover Come Back (1961); The Main Event; McClintock!; Medicine Man; Minnie & Moskowitz; The Moon's Our Home; Moonlighting (1985); The More the Merrier; Move Over, Darling; My Favorite Wife; New Kind of Love; Overboard; The Owl and the Pussycat; A Pair of Briefs; Pat and Mike; Perfect Marriage; Pillow Talk; Private Lives; The Ref; Romantic Comedy; Romancing the Stone; Rooster Cogburn; Scenes from a Mall; The Shop Around the Corner; Simon and Laura; A Smart Woman; Speechless; State of the Union; The Sure Thing; Sweethearts; Swept Away; Teacher's Pet; Touch of

Class; Tugboat Annie; Two For the Road; Walk, Don't Run; Waltz Across Texas; War of the Roses; Wedlock; Wife, Husband and Friend; Wind and the Lion; Woman of the Year; Wyoming; Year of the Comet

Romance-Boy Wants Girl (where the focus of the story is the pursuit): see also *Elusive Women: Romance-Reluctant: Nerds & Babes: Wallflowers & Hunks: First Love: Coming of Age: Obsessions: Fatal Attractions:* Blue Angel (1930); Blue Angel (1959); Blume in Love; Bobo; Book of Love; Bus Stop; The Butcher's Wife; Career Opportunities; Christine; Claire's Knee; Cocktail; Crossing Delancey; Cyrano de Bergerac (1950); Cyrano de Bergerac (1990); Defending Your Life; Disorderly Orderly; Divorce, Italian Style; The Double Wedding; Easy Living (1937); Echo Park; The Graduate; Groundhog Day; Heartbreak Kid; Hot Pursuit; How I Got Into College; I Love Melvin; Joy of Living; Mannequin (1987); Mannequin 2: On the Move; Mask (1994); The Miracle (1990); Mischief; The Mummy (1932); Next Stop, Greenwich Village; Night after Night; Ninotchka; No Small Affair; Oklahoma!; Orchestra Wives; Oxford Blues; Queen Christina; The Rachel Papers; Road to Bali; Road to Hong Kong; Road to Morocco; Road to Rio; Road to Singapore; Road to Utopia; Road to Zanzibar; Robin Hood (1922); Robin Hood (1973); Robin Hood (1990); Robin Hood: Prince of Thieves (1991); Rocky; A Room with a View; Rose Marie (1936); Rose Marie (1954); Roxanne; The Royal Wedding; Say Anything; Second Honeymoon; The Secret of My Success; Semi-Tough; The Sky's the Limit; Some Girls; Some Like it Hot; Somewhere in Time; Soup for One; Strictly Business; The Sure Thing; Tuff Turf; Voices; The Woman in Red; Year My Voice Broke; Zapped!; Zapped Again

Romance-Brief: see also *Romance-Doomed: Romance-Clandestine: Romance with Married Person:* April Fools; Every Time We Say Goodbye; Fatal Attraction; Girl from Tenth Avenue; John and Mary; Perfect Furlough; The Prince of Tides; Ready to Wear; Two People

Romance-Chance Meetings: see *Romance-Brief: One Night Stands*

Romance-Choosing the Right Person: see also *Marriage-Impending: Engagements-Breaking: Dating Scene:*

Matchmakers: About Face; The Adventures of Don Juan; The Age of Innocence (1934); The Age of Innocence (1993); Anne and Muriel; Arthur; Bodies, Rest & Motion; Broadcast News; Buster and Billie; Casual Sex?; Claudelle Inglish; Crossing Delancey; Daisy Kenyon; Dancing Lady; Date with an Angel; For Me and My Gal; Four Weddings and a Funeral; The Frenchman's Creek; Girl Most Likely (1958); The Graduate; Green Dolphin Street; Holiday; Holy Matrimony; I Live My Life; Indecent Proposal; Intersection; Jersey Girl; Lola (1960); Love; Love Before Breakfast; The Millionairess; Once Around; One Sunday Afternoon; Only You; Paternity; The Philadelphia Story; Pride and Prejudice; Rainbow; Reality Bites; Room at the Top; Sleepless in Seattle; Some Kind of Wonderful; The Strawberry Blonde; The Two Worlds of Jenny Logan; Watch It; What's Eating Gilbert Grape?; White Nights (1957); White Palace

Romance-Clandestine (secret romances and rendezvous): see also *Romance with Boss: Romance with Married Persons:* Alice; Any Wednesday; Bedroom Window; Blaze; The Bonfire of the Vanities; Born to Kill; Class; Coming Home; Defenseless; Facts of Life; From Here to Eternity; The Fugitive Kind; Gertrude; Hannah and Her Sisters; Key (1934); Key to the City; King, Queen, Knave; Lady with a Dog; Monsignor; My New Gun; 1984 (1955); 1984 (1984); Presumed Innocent; Red Shoe Diaries; Room at the Top; The Runner Stumbles; The Seduction of Joe Tynan; September Affair; A Severed Head; That Forsyte Woman; That Hamilton Woman; That Kind of Woman; These Three; A Touch of Class

Romance-Class Conflicts: see also *Class Conflicts: Lover Family Dislikes:* Arthur; Aviator; Baby, It's You; Barry Lyndon; A Breath of Scandal; Cabin in the Cotton; Cafe Society; Carmen Jones; Carrie (1952); Cass Timberlane; The Catered Affair; Chloe in the Afternoon; The Cowboy and the Lady; A Damsel in Distress; Emperor Waltz; Finishing School; The Flamingo Kid; Foolin' Around; Forest Rangers; Fresh Horses; From the Terrace; The Gang's All Here; Goodbye Columbus; A Handful of Dust; Holiday; Invitation to Happiness; I.Q.;

Jude the Obscure; Loves of a Blonde; Lucky Night; Lunch on the Grass; Mad Miss Manton; Man Trouble; Maurice; Meet the Stewarts; Mill on the Floss; Millionairess; Miss Julie; My Fair Lady; Night after Night; A Night in the Life of Jimmy Reardon; No More Ladies; No Time for Love; Nouvelle Vague; Of Human Bondage (1934); Of Human Bondage (1946); Of Human Bondage (1964); Peg o'My Heart; The Philadelphia Story; Platinum Blonde; The Rachel Papers; Reckless (1983); Rhinestone; Sabrina; Say Anything; School Ties; Shadows of our Forgotten Ancestors; The Sheik; Shining Hour; The Smiling Lieutenant; Someone to Watch Over Me; Splendor in the Grass; Summer Story; Twenty Bucks; Two Moon Junction; Valley Girl; Valley of Decision; Vivacious Lady; White Palace; You Can't Take it With You (1938); You Can't Take It With You (1986)

Romance-Dangerous: see also *Dangerous Men: Dangerous Women: Enemies-Sleeping with:* Betrayed (1989); Beyond the Limit; Bitch (1979); Black Widow (1987); Blue Velvet; Brighton Rock; Cast a Dark Shadow; China Girl (1987); China Moon; Choose Me; Coma; Dance with a Stranger; Death Watch; Desert Fury; Desire Me; Dragonwyck; The Dunwich Horror; Five Miles to Midnight; A Free Soul; Gilda; The Girl Who Had Everything; Gun Crazy (1950); Gun Crazy (1992); Havana; Heathers; Innocent; Johnny Eager; Johnny Handsome; A Kiss Before Dying (1956); A Kiss Before Dying (1991); Lady in Question; Ladykiller (1992); Lightning Strikes Twice; Looking for Mr. Goodbar; Lost Honor of Katharina Blum; Love From a Stranger (1936); Love From a Stranger (1947); Macao; Mrs. Soffel; My Blood Runs Cold; Night Eyes; No Way Out (1987); Notorious; Out of the Past; Past Midnight; Pulp Fiction; Sabotage; Scene of the Crime; Sea of Love; Second Chance; The Secret Beyond the Door; Secret Places; Smooth Talk; Something Wild (1986); The Stranger; Suspicion; Tamarind Seed; Tears in the Rain; They Drive by Night (1940); Tristana; The Unbelievable Truth; Verdict; Vertigo; Whispers in the Dark; Woman on the Beach

Romance-Doomed: see also *Romance-Clandestine: Romance-Brief: Lover*

Family Dislikes: TRAGEDY: Act of Love; Act of the Heart; All the Mornings of the World; Anna Karenina (1935); Anna Karenina (1948); Beloved Infidel; Best Intentions; Bitter Sweet (1933); Bitter Sweet (1940); Bittersweet Love; Boom!; Buster and Billie; Butterfield 8; Casablanca; Chilly Scenes of Winter; China Girl (1987); Close My Eyes; Daisy Miller; A Dangerous Woman; The Deep Blue Sea; Diary of a Mad Housewife; Double Indemnity; East Lynne; 8 Seconds; Elvira Madigan; Endless Love; Facts of Life; The Fly (1958); The Fly (1986); Fool for Love; Girl From Petrovka; The Glass Menagerie (1950); The Glass Menagerie (1973); The Glass Menagerie (1987); The Good Earth; Green Dolphin Street; Heathers; The Heiress; Hold Back the Dawn; The Homecoming (1948); Hot Spot; The Hunchback of Notre Dame (1923); The Hunchback of Notre Dame (1939); The Hunchback of Notre Dame (1956); The Hunchback of Notre Dame (1982); Inspiration; The Interlude (1957); The Interlude (1968); Intermezzo (1939); Jude the Obscure; King of the Gypsies; King, Queen, Knave; Kings Go Forth; La Traviata; La Vie de Boheme; Lacemaker; Lady with a Dog; Les Enfants Terribles; Love Affair (1939); Love Is a Many-Splendored Thing; Love Story (1970); M. Butterfly; Madame Bovary; Madame Butterfly; Mala Noche; Manhattan; Max and Helen; Melo; Mill on the Floss; Miracle in the Rain; Miss Julie; My Night at Maud's; Never Say Goodbye; New York, New York; The Night Porter; Now, Voyager; Ode to Billy Joe; Of Human Bondage (1934); Of Human Bondage (1946); Of Human Bondage (1964); Of Mice and Men (1939); Of Mice and Men (1993); One Way Passage; Orpheus Descending; Port of Call; Power, Passion, and Murder; The Purple Rose of Cairo; Quo Vadis; Romeo and Juliet (1936); Romeo and Juliet (1954); Romeo and Juliet (1968); Room at the Top; Rose; Samson and Delilah; Sayonara; Sea Wife; Shadowlands; Shadows of our Forgotten Ancestors; Sidewalks of London; The Sins of Rachel Cade; Sophie's Choice; Special Day; Splendor in the Grass; St. Martin's Lane; The Stripper; Sunflower; Taxi Driver; They Shoot Horses, Don't They?; A Time to Love & A Time to Die; Today We Live; Tokyo Joe; Toto le Heros;

Tristana; Turkish Delight; 21 Days; Untamed Heart; Walking Stick; Waterloo Bridge (1931); Waterloo Bridge (1940); Wedding March; West Side Story; Wild Is the Wind; The World of Suzie Wong; Wuthering Heights (1939); Wuthering Heights (1953); Wuthering Heights (1970); Wuthering Heights (1992)

Romance-Elderly: see also *Romance-Reunited:* Cocoon; Cocoon, The Return; Gin Game; Grumpy Old Men; Harold and Maude; Love Among the Ruins; Old Gringo; Only the Lonely; Right of Way; Rooster Cogburn; Tell Me a Riddle; To Dance with the White Dog; Used People

Romance-First Love: see *First Love: also Coming of Age: Romance-Boy Wants Girl: Romance-Girl Wants Boy*

Romance-Forbidden: see *Love-Forbidden: Romance-Unprofessional: Romance with Relative's Lover: Incest*

Romance-Getting Dumped/Ignored: see *Love-Unrequited: Romance-Doomed: Elusive Men: Elusive Women*

Romance-Girl Wants Boy: see also *Elusive Men: Romance-Reluctant: Wallflowers & Hunks: Nerds & Babes: First Love: Coming of Age: Obsessions: Fatal Attractions:* Bringing Up Baby; Camille (1936); Great Catherine; Hello Dolly; The Hired Wife; Impromptu; Lucky Night; Metropolitan (1990); My Father the Hero; My Man Godfrey (1936); My Man Godfrey (1956); New Kind of Love; Private School; Reality Bites; Small Town Girl (1936); Small Town Girl (1953); Song of the Islands; Sugarbaby; Two-Faced Woman; What's Up, Doc?

Romance-Infatuations: see *Infatuation*

Romance-Intergenerational: see *Romance-Reunited: Older Men/Younger Women: Romance-Reunited: Older Women/Younger Men:*

Romance-Interracial: see also *Race Relations: Love-Forbidden:* Across the Wide Missouri; Angel Heart; Bad Company (1995); The Barbarian and the Geisha; Bhowani Junction; Bird of Paradise (1932); Bird of Paradise (1951); The Border; Carbon Copy; Casque d'Or; China Girl (1942); China Girl (1987); Chocolat; Come See the Paradise; Corrina, Corrina; Daybreak; Drum; Duel in the Sun; The Eiger Sanction; Father Hood; Flirting; Foxfire (1955); A Girl Named Tamiko; The Great White Hope; Green Eyes; Guess Who's Coming to

Dinner; Heaven and Earth; Hiroshima, Mon Amour; Hurricane (1937); Hurricane (1979); I Passed for White; Jefferson in Paris; Joey Breaker; The Josephine Baker Story; Jungle Fever; Landlord; Little Big Man; Little Mermaid; Lost Boundaries; Lost Man; Love Field; Love is a Many Splendored Thing; The Lover; Madame Butterfly; Made in America; A Majority of One; Map of the Human Heart; Marriage of Maria Braun; Mississippi Masala; Momma, There's a Man in Your Bed; Mona Lisa; Naughty Marietta; Noir et Blanc; Norman, Is That You?; Omega Man; One False Move; Patch of Blue; Q & A; Sayonara; Showboat (1936); Showboat (1951); Silent Tongue; South Pacific; Squaw Man; Surviving Desire; Tamango; A Taste of Honey; Teahouse of the August Moon; Tokyo Joe; Tokyo Pop; Travels with My Aunt; Under the Cherry Moon; Unnatural Causes; Valdez Is Coming; A View to a Kill; White Men Can't Jump; The World of Suzie Wong; Zebrahead

Romance-Married Couples: see *Marriage Drama: Marriage Comedy*

Romance-Middle Aged: see also *Romance-Old: Romance-Reunited:* Barnacle Bill (1941); Black Orchid; Cemetery Club; Conagher; Dear Heart; Desk Set; Eighty-Four Charing Cross Road; Facts of Life; A Fine Romance; Goodbye My Fancy; Goodbye People; Guess Who's Coming to Dinner; Gypsy Moths; Happy Ending; House Calls; I Never Sang for My Father; I Ought to Be in Pictures; I Sent a Letter to My Love; Last of the Red Hot Lovers; Light in the Piazza; Lonely Hearts; The Lonely Passion of Judith Hearne; Love Among the Ruins; A Man and a Woman, Twenty Years Later; Middle of the Night; Mr. Belvedere Goes to College; Pete 'n Tillie; Queen of the Stardust Ballroom; Shadow Box; Shirley Valentine; Stanley & Iris; Terms of Endearment; That's Life!; Those Were the Days; Used People; Walk in the Spring Rain; The War Between Men and Women; Woman Next Door

Romance-Mismatched (primarily clashing personalities, not class or easily definable differences): see also *Romance-Opposites Attract:* Aaron Loves Angela; Abie's Irish Rose; Accidental Tourist; All That Heaven Allows; And Now, My Love; The Angel Wore Red; Anna and the King of Siam;

Annie Hall; April Fools; Babycakes; Baby, It's You; Bells Are Ringing; Bocaccio '70; Broadcast News; Broadway Danny Rose; Dirty Dancing; Dogfight; Echo Park; Eyewitness (1981); Frankie and Johnny; Garden of Allah; Girl with Green Eyes; Goodbye Columbus; Goodbye Mr. Chips (1939); Goodbye Mr. Chips (1969); Great Catherine; Hands Across the Table; Harold and Maude; High, Wide and Handsome; I Don't Buy Kisses Anymore; Moonlighting (1985); Muriel's Wedding; Overboard; The Passionate Plumber; People Will Talk; Pretty Woman; The Private Lives of Elizabeth and Essex; The Prizefighter and the Lady; Romantic Comedy; Shining Hour; Special Day; Splash! Too Beautiful For You; Voices; The Wedding March; The Wedding Night; White Palace

Romance Novelists: see also *Writers: Women Artists/Writers:* American Dreamer; Don't Tell Her It's Me; Jewel of the Nile; Old Acquaintance; Romancing the Stone; School for Husbands; She Devil

Romance-Old: see *Romance Reunited*

Romance-Older Men/Younger Women: see also *ROMANCE: Playgirls: Prostitutes:* Adam and Evelyne; Adam Had Four Sons; Age of Consent; Ain't Misbehavin'; Alex and the Gypsy; All Night Long (1981); American Friends; And Now, My Love; Angela; April Fools; The Arrangement; Atlantic City; Avanti!; Baby Doll; The Bachelor and the Bobby-Soxer; Back to School; The Beekeeper; The Belle of New York; Blame it on Rio; Blind Ambition; Blue Ice; Break of Hearts; Breezy; Cactus Flower; Camila (1984); Carlito's Way; Casablanca; A Certain Smile; Circle of Two; Claudia; Cold Sassy Tree; The Crush; Daddy Longlegs; Damage; Delirious; The Devil and Miss Jones; Divorce, Italian Style; Funny About Love; Game is Over; Great Balls of Fire; Great Scout and Cathouse Thursday; Grumpy Old Men; Hello Dolly; Honeymoon; The Hospital; Hot Spell; A House Divided; Husbands and Wives; I Don't Want to Talk About it; I Know Where I'm Going; I Love Trouble (1994); In the Cool of the Day; In the French Style; It's a Date; Kiss for Corliss; Kotch; La Belle Noiseuse; Last Tango in Paris; Legal Eagles; Let's Make Love; Lifeguard; Lolita; Lost Lady; Love in the Afternoon; The Lover; Lovesick; Loving

Couples; Man Trouble; Manhattan; Memoirs of an Invisible Man; Middle of the Night; The Moon is Blue; Mr. Music; Murphy's Romance; My Fair Lady; Nanou; Network; New York Stories; Night of the Iguana; Nobody's Fool (1994); Oklahoma Crude; Old Gringo; People Will Talk; Petulia; Poison Ivy (1992); Pretty Baby; Rambling Rose; Red Kiss; Reuben, Reuben; Rita, Sue and Bob, Too; Roman Holiday; Roxanne; Russia House; Sabrina; The Seduction of Joe Tynan; The Seven-Year Itch; The Sidewalks of London; Smooth Talk; Soapdish; Soft Skin; St. Martin's Lane; Teacher's Pet; That Certain Age; That Obscure Object of Desire; That Touch of Mink; There's a Girl in My Soup; 36 Fillette; This Happy Feeling; To Have and Have Not; Tristana; Violent Men; White Palace; Woman in the Window; You Were Never Lovelier; You'll Never Get Rich

Romance-Older Women/Younger Men: see also *Older Women Seducers: Playboys: Prostitutes-Male: ROMANCE:* Alfie; All Fall Down; All That Heaven Allows; Autumn Leaves; Billy Bathgate; Blue Velvet; The Bridge; Class; Coach; Come Back, Little Sheba; Devotion; Double Threat; Female on the Beach; Forty Carats; Foxfire (1955); The Fugitive Kind; Gertrude; Get Out Your Handkerchiefs; Getting It Right; Goodbye Again; Go West Young Man; The Graduate; Grandview, USA; A Handful of Dust; Harold and Maude; The Idol; In Praise of Older Women; In the French Style; Indiscretion of an American Wife; Joseph Andrews; King, Queen, Knave; La Vie Continue; The Last Picture Show; Letter From an Unknown Woman; Little Big Man; Losin' It; Love Among the Ruins; Love and Pain and the Whole Damn Thing; Love Has Many Faces; Love in Germany; Loverboy; Loving Couples; Men Don't Leave; Miracle (1990); Moment by Moment; My Tutor; Night in Heaven; A Night in the Life of Jimmy Reardon; The Only Game in Town; Orpheus Descending; Paint it Black; Roman Spring of Mrs. Stone; Say Hello to Yesterday; Sextette; Somewhere in Time; The Stripper; Sugarbaby; Summer of '42; Surrender; Sunday, Bloody Sunday; Tea and Sympathy; That Cold Day in the Park; That Forsyte Woman; Tiger's Tale; Tim; Tune in Tomorrow; What's Eating Gilbert Grape?; Wild Is the Wind

Romance-On Again/Off Again:
see also *Marrying Again: Love-Questionable: Engagements-Breaking:*
Casanova Brown; Falling in Love; Farewell My Concubine; Four Weddings and a Funeral; Gone With the Wind; Hannah and Her Sisters; Hard Country; Hard Promises; He Married His Wife; Heartburn; Come September; Fool for Love; Let's Make it Legal; My Wild Irish Rose; The Opposite Sex and How to Live With Them; Phffft!; The Philadelphia Story; Tom & Viv

Romance on Vacation: see also *Vacations: Romance-Brief: Americans Abroad:* An Affair to Remember; Almost Perfect Affair; Before Sunrise; Blame it on Rio; Bonjour, Tristesse; The Bridge; Cafe Metropole; C'est la Vie; Cactus; Chained; Cocktail; Desire; End of the World . . . ; Forty Carats; Foxfire (1955); The Gay Divorcee; Haunted Summer; Heartbreak Kid; High Season; Hot Pursuit; If It's Tuesday, This Must Be Belgium; In the Cool of the Day; Indiscretion of an American Wife; Innocents in Paris (1953); It Started in Naples; Joey Breaker; The Lady Takes a Chance; Light in the Piazza; Love Affair (1939); Love and Pain and the Whole Damn Thing; Love in a Goldfish Bowl; Majority of One; Nanou; Never on Sunday; Night of the Iguana; Once in Paris; One Way Passage; Only You; Our Hearts Were Young and Gay; Pandora and the Flying Dutchman; Pauline at the Beach; Perfect Furlough; The Romantic Englishwoman; Same Time, Next Year; Say Hello to Yesterday; The Sheltering Sky; Shirley Valentine; Sirens; Springtime in the Rockies; Story of Three Loves; Summer; A Summer Place; Summer Story; Summertime; There's a Girl in My Soup; Three Coins in the Fountain; Touch of Class

Romance-Opposites Attract: see also *Romance-Bickering: Nerds & Babes: Wallflowers & Hunks: Romantic Comedy: Romantic Drama:* The African Queen; Angel and the Badman; The Angel Wore Red; Athena; Ball of Fire; Battement de Coeur; Bringing Up Baby; The Cutting Edge; Designing Woman; Desk Set; The Doctor Takes a Wife; Heaven Knows, Mr. Allison; How I Got Into College; The Hunchback of Notre Dame (1923); The Hunchback of Notre Dame (1939); The Hunchback of Notre

Dame (1956); The Hunchback of Notre Dame (1982); I Don't Buy Kisses Anymore; I Take this Woman; I'll Be Seeing You; In the Good Old Summertime; Invitation to Happiness; It Happened One Night; Lady Takes a Chance; Legal Eagles; The Lonely Passion of Judith Hearne; Lost and Found; Love Affair (1932); Momma, There's a Man in Your Bed; Moon's Our Home; New Kind of Love; The Owl and the Pussycat; Pillow Talk; The Prince of Tides; The Prize; Rain; Rooster Cogburn; A Song Is Born; Swept Away; This Above All; A Touch of Class; Waltz Across Texas; The Way We Were; What's Up, Doc?; When Harry Met Sally; Witness; Woman of the Year; The World of Suzie Wong; Year of the Comet

Romance-Questionable: see *Love-Questionable:* also *Enemies-Sleeping with: Romance-Dangerous: Dangerous Men: Dangerous Women: Film Noir*

Romance-Reluctant: see also *Elusive Men: Elusive Women: Romance-Boy Wants Girl: Romance-Girl Wants Boy: Romance-Bickering: Romance-Opposites Attract:* Age of Consent; Algiers; All-American Boy; American Friends; Angel and the Badman; Anna and the King of Siam; Appointment for Love; Barfly; The Big Easy; The Bodyguard; Breakfast at Tiffany's; The Bride Came C.O.D.; Bringing Up Baby; Broadway Danny Rose; Buddy System; Burning Secret; Buster and Billie; Cactus Flower; Cafe Society; Cain and Mabel; Call of the Wild (1935); Call of the Wild (1972); Camille (1936); Camille Claudel; Cinderella Liberty; Claudelle Inglish; Cluny Brown; Continental Divide; Cross Creek; Cross My Heart; Desk Set; Divorce of Lady X; The Doctor Takes a Wife; Dying Young; A Fine Romance; The Fisher King; Flame of the Barbary Coast; Flesh and Blood (1985); Forrest Gump; Frankie and Johnny; The Freshman (1990); The Ghost and Mrs. Muir; The Glass Bottom Boat; The Glass Menagerie (1950); The Glass Menagerie (1973); The Glass Menagerie (1987); Goin' South; Gone With the Wind; Goodbye Girl; The Great Gatsby (1949); The Great Gatsby (1974); Green Card; Green Fire; Groundhog Day; Hands Across the Table; Hannah and Her Sisters; Hard Country; Heroes; Hired Wife; House Calls; Hud; I am a Camera; I

Live My Life; I Married a Witch; I.Q.; If You Could Only Cook; In the Good Old Summertime; Indiscreet; Irma La Douce; It Started with Eve; Jezebel; Kiss Me Kate (1953); Love Among the Ruins; Love at Large; Love Potion #9; Major and the Minor; Mala Noche; Mating of Willie; Maurice; Miss Sadie Thompson; Mrs. Parker and the Vicious Circle; Next Stop, Greenwich Village; Ninotchka; No Time for Love; Oliver's Story; Other People's Money; Out of Africa; Peter's Friends; The Philadelphia Story; Pickup Artist; Pirate; The Princess and the Pirate; Private Lives; The Private Lives of Elizabeth and Essex; The Prize; The Prizefighter and the Lady; Promise Her Anything; Public Eye; Queen Christina; The Quiet Man; Rain People; Reckless (1983); The Remains of the Day; Reuben, Reuben; Rhinestone; Robin Hood (1922); Robin Hood (1973); Robin Hood (1990); Robin Hood: Prince of Thieves (1991); Romance; A Room with a View; Rose Tattoo; Roxanne; Ryan's Daughter; Samantha; Sea of Grass; Sea Wife; She Done Him Wrong; Shop Around the Corner; Silk Stockings; Sing Baby Sing; A Song to Remember; Soup for One; A Stranger Among Us; The Sure Thing; Surrender; Sweet November; Swept Away; Swing Time; Take a Letter, Darling; Talk of the Town; Tarnished Angels; Teacher's Pet; Ten; Terms of Endearment; That Touch of Mink; They Knew What They Wanted; 36 Fillette; This Property is Condemned; Tootsie; Top Gun; Top Hat; Top Secret Affair; Trapeze; Untamed Heart; Victor/Victoria; Violets are Blue; Virgin Queen; The World of Suzie Wong; Wuthering Heights (1939); Wuthering Heights (1953); Wuthering Heights (1970); Wuthering Heights (1992)

Romance-Reunited: see also *Reunions:* Bird on a Wire; Blume in Love; Chances Are; Charming Sinners; Chloe in the Afternoon; Daddy's Gone A-Hunting; Dead Again; Desire Me; Doctor Zhivago; Double Jeopardy; The Drowning Pool; Ex-Mrs. Bradford; Falling in Love Again; The French Lieutenant's Woman; The Front Page (1931); The Front Page (1974); Gilda; Ginger and Fred; Goodbye My Fancy; Harper; Hedda; His Girl Friday; Home from the Hill; Idiot's Delight; Keep the Change; Laughter; Let's Make it Legal; A Little Night Music; Love Among the Ruins; Love Crazy; Love

Hurts; Lucy Gallant; Made in Heaven; Magnificent Obsession (1935); Magnificent Obsession (1954); A Man and a Woman: Twenty Years Later; Map of the Human Heart; The Marrying Kind; The Marrying Man; Mary, Mary; The Merry Wives of Reno; A Midsummer Night's Sex Comedy; Miracle in the Rain; Moulin Rouge; Move Over, Darling; My Favorite Wife; Never Say Goodbye; One False Move; One Sunday Afternoon; Peter Ibbetson; Ready to Wear; Rescue Me; Seems Like Old Times; Shanghai Express; She Couldn't Say No; Smiles of a Summer Night; Soapdish; Sunflower; Talk of the Town; Texasville; That Certain Feeling; Three Smart Girls; The Umbrellas of Cherbourg; Violets are Blue; Walk on the Wild Side; Welcome Home; The Westerner; White Sister; The Woman Next Door

Romance-Secret: see *Romance-Clandestine*

Romance-Triangles: see also *Romance-Choosing the Right Person*:
Ménage à Trois: Abel; The Adventures of Sadie; After Dark, My Sweet; Against All Odds; The Age of Innocence (1934); The Age of Innocence (1993); Alexander's Ragtime Band; All the Fine Young Cannibals; All This and Heaven, Too; Almost Perfect Affair; The Ambassador; Animal Behavior; Animal Kingdom; Anna Karenina (1935); Anna Karenina (1948); Anne and Muriel; Any Wednesday; Baby Doll; Baby Maker; Back Street (1932); Back Street (1941); Back Street (1961); Backbeat; Barfly; Beau Brummell (1924); Beau Brummell (1954); Beauty for the Asking; Bedroom Window; Betrayal; Beyond the Forest; Beyond the Limit; Beyond Therapy; Big Blue; The Big Town; Billy Bathgate; Bitter Tears of Petra Von Kant; Blind Date (1987); Blind Husbands; Bliss of Mrs. Blossom; Blithe Spirit; Blood Feud; Blood Simple; Blowing Wild; Blue Max; Blue Velvet; Blume in Love; Body Heat; Bombay Talkie; The Bonfire of the Vanities; Boom Town; Bordertown; Born to Kill; Botany Bay; Boyfriends and Girlfriends; Brainstorm (1965); The Bride Wore Red; Broadcast News; Bull Durham; Butch Cassidy and the Sundance Kid; By Love Possessed; Cabaret; Carny; Casablanca; Caught; Charming Sinners; China Moon; Chinatown; Come September; Circle of Friends; Coming Home; The Cook, the

Thief, His Wife & Her Lover; Daisy Kenyon; Damage; Dancing Lady; Dangerous Liaisons; Days of Heaven; Dead Ringers; Deadfall (1968); Death Becomes Her; Deception (1946); Defenseless; Design for Living; Desiree; Desk Set; Diabolique (1955); Dial M For Murder; A Different Story; Dirty Rotten Scoundrels; Divorce, Italian Style; The Doctor Takes a Wife; Dona Flor and Her Two Husbands; Double Threat; Down and Out in Beverly Hills; Duel in the Sun; East Lynne; East Side, West Wide; Easy to Love; Eclipse; Elephant Walk; End of the Game; End of the Road; Enemies, A Love Story; England Made Me; Ethan Fromme; Everybody's All American; Eye of the Needle; The Eyes of Laura Mars; The Fabulous Baker Boys; The Favor; Final Analysis; First Time; A Fish Called Wanda; Flame of the Barbary Coast; Flesh and the Devil; Foolish Wives; For Me and My Gal; A Foreign Affair; The Fortune; The Frenchman's Creek; The Front Page (1931); The Front Page (1974); The Fugitive Kind; Full Moon in Paris; The Game Is Over; The Gang's All Here; Garden of Evil; Gate of Hell; Georgy Girl; Gertrude; Get Out Your Handkerchiefs; Giant; Gilda; Gilded Lily; The Girl Most Likely (1958); Go Naked in the World; The Go-Between; God's Little Acre; The Good Fairy; The Good Wife; The Graduate; The Grass Is Greener; The Great Lie; Green Card; Green Fire; The Grifters; Guilty Conscience; A Guy Named Joe; Hands Across the Table; Hannah and Her Sisters; Happy Birthday, Wanda June; Harry and Walter Go to New York; Heart Beat; Heartbreakers; Henry and June; High Sierra; High Society; His Brother's Wife; His Girl Friday; Holiday; Holiday Inn; Honeymoon in Vegas; Honeysuckle Rose; Hot Spot; A House Divided; The House of Seven Gables; I Don't Care Girl; I, Jane Doe; I Love You Again; Immortal Beloved; Impact; In a Shallow Grave; In Name Only; In the French Style; Indecent Proposal; Inferno; Interlude (1957); Interlude (1968); Intermezzo (1939); Intersection; Irma La Douce; It Could Happen to You; It Had to Be You; It's My Turn; Jacknife; Jersey Girl; Jules and Jim; Just Between Friends; Just Tell Me What You Want; King and Four Queens; Kings Go Forth; Kiss Me Goodbye; Kiss Me, Stupid!; La Bete Humaine; La

Maschera; Lady in the Dark; Lake Consequence; Laughter; Laura; Les Biches; Les Comperes; Les Liaisons Dangereuses; Les Valseuses; Let's Do it Again (1953); Let's Make it Legal; Liebestraum; Lola (1960); Long Hot Summer (1958); The Long Night; Loser Takes All; Love; Love and Money; Love at Large; Love Before Breakfast; Love Has Many Faces; Lover Come Back (1946); Lovin' Molly; Loving; Lucky Lady; Lusty Men; Luv; Macomber Affair; Mad Dog and Glory; Mad Love; Making Love; Malice; Man in the Moon; Man of Flowers; Manhattan; Marriage Go Round; Married Woman; Mary, Mary; The Matchmaker; Maytime; Meeting Venus; Men (1985); Men with Wings; Midnight (1939); Mogambo; The Money Pit; Moon is Blue; Moonstruck; Mother is a Freshman; Mourning Becomes Electra; Move Over, Darling; Murder by Natural Causes; My Best Friend's Girl; My Night at Maud's; The Mystery of Edwin Drood; A Night in the Life of Jimmy Reardon; Night of the Iguana; Nightmare in the Sun; No Man's Land (1987); Noises Off; Norma Rae; Not with My Wife You Don't; Oh Men! Oh Women!; One from the Heart; One More River; One Sunday Afternoon; Only Two Can Play; Ossessione; Otello; Othello (1951); Othello (1965); The Other Side of Midnight; Out of Africa; Out of the Past; Paint Your Wagon; Palm Beach Story; Peter Ibbetson; The Philadelphia Story; Play Misty for Me; Playboys; Presumed Innocent; Prizzi's Honor; Proof; The Prowler; Quartet (1981); Rafferty and the Gold Dust Twins; Reap the Wild Wind; Red Dust; The Return of Martin Guerre; Return of the Soldier; Return to Macon County; Revenge; Rhapsody; Rich in Love; A River Runs Through It; Romance; Romance on the High Seas; Room at the Top; Ryan's Daughter; Sabrina; Sadie McKee; Sammy and Rosie Get Laid; San Francisco; Semi-Tough; Send Me No Flowers; Seventh Veil; Shampoo; The Sheltering Sky; Small Circle of Friends; The Smiling Lieutenant; Smokey and the Bandit; So Big (1932); So Big (1953); Some Kind of Wonderful; Someone to Watch Over Me; Something for Everyone; Something Wild (1986); Somewhere I'll Find You; Sommersby; Sophie's Choice; Speaking Parts; Spetters; Starting Over; Stork Club;

Strawberry Blonde; A Streetcar Named Desire; Summer Story; Sunday, Bloody Sunday; Surrender; Suzy; Swing Shift; Swing Time; Talk of the Town; Tequila Sunrise; Test Pilot; That Certain Feeling; That Uncertain Feeling; These Three; Three Comrades; Three Husbands; Three of Hearts; Threesome; Thunderbirds; Tiger's Tale; Today We Live; Tom, Dick and Harry; Tomorrow is Forever; Too Many Husbands; Tootsie; Trapeze; Two Girls and a Sailor; Un Coeur en Hiver; The Unbearable Lightness of Being; Unfaithful; Violent Men; Wabash Avenue; Wake of the Red Witch; The War Between Men and Women; The Wedding Banquet; We're No Angels (1955); We're No Angels (1989); When Tomorrow Comes; Where Love Has Gone; Where Were You When the Lights Went Out?; White Nights (1957); White Sands; Wife, Doctor and Nurse; Wild Is the Wind; Wild Orchid; Willie and Phil; The Witches of Eastwick; Wives and Lovers; Woman I Love; Woman on the Beach; Woman to Woman; Women in Love; Working Girl; X, Y, & Zee; You'll Never Get Rich; Zandalee; A Zed and Two Noughts

Romance-Troubled: see *Romance-On Again/Off Again*

Romance-Unlikely: see *Romance-Opposites Attract*

Romance-Unprofessional: see also *Ethics: Romance with Boss: Romance with Co-Worker: Love-Forbidden: Romance with Psychologist: Romance with Suspect:* Absence of Malice; Artists and Models (1937); Bedroom Window; Black Widow (1987); Blink; Body of Evidence; Camila (1984); Children of a Lesser God; The File on Thelma Jordon; Final Analysis; For Love or Money (1963); Jagged Edge; Lethal Weapon 3; Love Crimes; Murder in New Hampshire; No Man's Land (1987); One Hour with You; Other People's Money; Pajama Game; The Paradine Case; People Will Talk; Perfect Strangers; Spellbound; Tender Is the Night; The Thomas Crown Affair; Top Secret Affair; Under Suspicion; Witness

Romance-Unrequited: see *Love-Unrequited: Infatuations: Love-Questionable: Obsessions: Fatal Attractions: Lonely People*

Romance with Boss: see also *Romance with Boss' Lover: Marrying*

Up: Double Crossing: Romance-Clandestine: Accent on Youth; Accused of Murder; All in a Night's Work; The Devil and Miss Jones; Easy to Love; The Hired Wife; Kiss the Boys Goodbye; Is There Sex After Death?; More Than a Secretary; The Pajama Game; Promise Her Anything; Too Beautiful For You

Romance with Boss' Child: see also *Romance with Boss' Lover: Romance-Unprofessional: Marrying Up:* Four's a Crowd; The Freshman (1990); The Paper Chase; Used Cars

Romance with Boss' Lover: see also *Romance with Boss: Marrying Up: Double Crossing: Romance-Clandestine:* Bedroom Window; For Love or Money (1993); Forbidden; Frantic (1958); Night Eyes

Romance with Boxer: see also *Boxing: Sports Movies:* Cain and Mabel; Gentleman Jim; Main Event; Rocky

Romance with Clergy: see also *Preachers/Ministers: Clergy:* Act of the Heart; The Angel Wore Red; Camila (1984); Last Rites; The Priest; The Runner Stumbles; Sea Wife

Romance with Co-Worker: see *Romance-Unprofessional: Romance with Boss: Romance with Boss' Lover*

Romance with Doctor: see also *Doctors: Nurses: Hospitals: Medical School:* And Now, Tomorrow; Dark Victory; Yes, Giorgio

Romance with Friend's Lover: see also *Romance with Relative: Romance with Boss' Lover:* Betrayal; Beyond the Limit; Blowing Wild; Defenseless; Georgy Girl; Liebestraum; Look Back in Anger (1959); Look Back in Anger (1980); Look Back in Anger (1989); Manhattan; My Best Friend's Girl; Out of the Past; Play it Again, Sam; Sex, Lies, and Videotape; Toto le Heros

Romance with Friend's Relative: Blame it on Rio; Class; Jacknife; Poison Ivy (1992)

Romance with Lawyer: see also *Courtroom Drama:* Body of Evidence; Bordertown; The File on Thelma Jordon; For Love or Money (1963); The Girl from Tenth Avenue; Love Among the Ruins; My Sin

Romance with Lover's Friend: see also *Cheating Men: Cheating Women:* The Good Wife; In the Cool of the Day; Marriage on the Rocks; Once Upon a Dream; 'Tis a Pity She's a Whore

Romance with Lover's Relative: see also *Romance with Relative's Lover:* High Heels; Holiday; A House Divided; Moonstruck

Romance with Married Person (the protagonist is not necessarily married, but the love interest of the affair is): see also *Romance-Clandestine: Romance with Boss' Lover:*

Romance with Relative: Adam's Rib (1922); Another Time, Another Place; Ask Any Girl; Australia; Back Street (1932); Back Street (1941); Back Street (1961); Bed and Board; Belizaire the Cajun; Beyond the Forest; Beyond the Limit; Blaze; Blood Simple; Blume in Love; Bob & Carol & Ted & Alice; Body Heat; The Bonfire of the Vanities; Bordertown; The Bridge; Chained; Charming Sinners; Chilly Scenes of Winter; Chloe in the Afternoon; Christopher Strong; Confessions of a Window Cleaner; Dark at the Top of the Stairs; David and Bathsheba; The Deep Blue Sea; Devil in the Flesh (1946); Devil in the Flesh (1987); The Disappearance of Aimee; The Divorcée; Double Jeopardy; East of Elephant Rock; Evelyn Prentice; Facts of Life; Falling in Love; Fatal Attraction; A Fine Romance; From Here to Eternity; The Fugitive Kind; Gate of Hell; Gertrude; God's Little Acre; The Good Wife; The Grass Is Greener; The Great Gatsby (1949); The Great Gatsby (1974); Griffin and Phoenix, A Love Story; A Handful of Dust; Hannah and Her Sisters; Heart of the Matter; The Hireling; I Love My Wife; Indiscreet; Indiscretion of an American Wife; Interlude (1957); Interlude (1968); Intermezzo (1939); The Key (1934); Key to the City; Killing in a Small Town; Lady Chatterley's Lover (1955); Lady Chatterley's Lover (1981); Ladykiller (1992); Last of the Red Hot Lovers; Lesson in Love; Life at the Top; Life of Her Own; Live for Life; Look Who's Talking; Love Letters (1984); The Macomber Affair; Madame Bovary; Marriage Go Round; Melo; One More River; Only Two Can Play; Orpheus Descending; Ossessione; The Other Side of Midnight; Parnell; Play it Again, Sam; Plaza Suite; Power, Passion, and Murder; Private Lives; Same Time, Next Year; Saturday Night and Sunday Morning; Scandal; The Scarlet Letter (1926); The Scarlet Letter (1934); The Scarlet Letter

(1980); The Seduction of Joe Tynan; September Affair; Sibling Rivalry; Silver City; Skylark; Strangers, the Story of a Mother and Daughter; Summertime; These Three; A Touch of Class; Twice in a Lifetime; Two for the Seesaw; Wait Until Spring, Bandini; When Ladies Meet (1933); When Ladies Meet (1941); When Strangers Meet; When Tomorrow Comes; Wife, Doctor and Nurse; Wife Versus Secretary; Woman Next Door; The World Is Full of Married Men

Romance with Prostitute: see also *Prostitutes with a Heart of Gold:* Ada; The Angel Wore Red; Back Roads; Blaze; Breakfast at Tiffany's; Cinderella Liberty; Exotica; Forever Amber; Go Naked in the World; Great Scout and Cathouse Thursday; Hustle; Irma La Douce; Killing Zoe; La Chienne; La Ronde (1950); La Ronde (1964); Miami Blues; Miss Sadie Thompson; The Missionary; Mona Lisa; Never on Sunday; Night Angel; No Way Out (1987); Nouvelle Vague; Pretty Woman; Rabbit, Run; Rain; Red Dust; Sadie Thompson; True Romance; The World of Suzie Wong

Romance with Psychologist: see also *Psychologists/Psychiatrists: Therapy: Love-Forbidden:* Bad Timing; The Butcher's Wife; Dark Mirror; Final Analysis; Lilith; Mr. Jones; The Prince of Tides; A Sensual Obsession; Spellbound; Tender Is the Night; They Might be Giants; Zelig

Romance with Relatives (not in immediate family or necessarily blood relatives so as to be incest): see also *Love-Forbidden: Incest: Romance with Relative's Lover:* A Certain Smile; Chances Are; Cousin, Cousine; Cousins; Ethan Frome; Great Balls of Fire; It's My Turn; King, Queen, Knave; My Cousin Rachel; The Secret of My Success; A View from the Bridge; Wild Is the Wind

Romance with Relative's Lover: see also *Romance-Triangles: Love-Forbidden:* Adam's Rib (1922); All Night Long (1981); Avanti!; Damage; A Dangerous Woman; Game is Over; His Brother's Wife; The Idol; It Started in Naples; King and Four Queens; Last Days of Chez Nous; Legends of the Fall; Man in the Moon; Of Love and Desire; Over Her Dead Body; Prisoner of Zenda (1937); Prisoner of Zenda (1952); Prisoner of Zenda (1979); Rich in Love;

Sex, Lies, and Videotape; Sibling Rivalry; Wild Is the Wind

Romance with Servant: see also *Servants: Romance with Boss:* Corrina, Corrina; Diary of a Chambermaid (1946); Diary of a Chambermaid (1963); Down and Out in Beverly Hills; Dying Young; The Farmer's Daughter; For Love of Ivy; The Hireling; Houseboat; Hud; Jane Eyre (1934); Jane Eyre (1943); Jane Eyre (1971); Mr. Music; My Man Godfrey (1936); My Man Godfrey (1956); The Remains of the Day; Valley of Decision

Romance with Suspect: see also *Romance with Law Officer: Romance-Unprofessional:* The Accused (1948); Basic Instinct; Desperate Hours (1990); The File on Thelma Jordon; Jagged Edge; Romeo Is Bleeding; Stakeout

Romance with Teacher: see also *Teachers and Students: Mentors and Proteges:* Born Yesterday (1950); Born Yesterday (1993); Coach; Constant Nymph (1933); Constant Nymph (1943); Devil in the Flesh (1946); Devil in the Flesh (1987); Get Out Your Handkerchiefs; The Girl Can't Help It; Goodbye Mr. Chips (1939); Goodbye Mr. Chips (1969); Husbands and Wives; Murder in New Hampshire; Night in Heaven; Old Gringo; Stanley & Iris; The Substitute; Surviving Desire; Svengali (1931); Svengali (1983); Tea and Sympathy; Teacher's Pet; Term of Trial; To Sir with Love; Top Gun; Trilogy in Terror

Romans: see also *Ancient Times: Italy: Mythology:* The Abdication; The Agony and the Ecstasy; Androcles and the Lion; The Belly of an Architect; Cleopatra (1934); Cleopatra (1963); A Funny Thing Happened on the Way to the Forum; The History of the World Part One; Julius Caesar; Jupiter's Darling; La Dolce Vita; Mamma Rosa; Mignon Has Left; My Own Private Idaho; Nights of Cabiria; Quo Vadis; Roman Holiday; Roman Scandals; The Roman Spring of Mrs. Stone; Rome Express; Satyricon (Fellini's); Ten Thousand Bedrooms; Two Weeks in Another Town

Romantic Adventure: see also *Vacation Romance: ADVENTURE: Exotic Locales:* The African Queen; Garden of Allah; Gold; Green Dolphin Street; Holy Matrimony; Map of the Human Heart; Razor's Edge (1946); Razor's Edge

(1986); Return of the Scarlet Pimpernel; The River of No Return; Romancing the Stone; Tai Pan

Romantic Comedy: see also *Erotic Comedy: Screwball Comedy: FARCE:* Aaron Slick from Punkin Crick; About Face; Abroad with Two Yanks; Accent on Youth; Adam and Evelyne; Adam's Rib (1949); The Adventures of Gerard; The Adventures of Sadie; The Affairs of Cellini; The Affairs of Dobie Gillis; Ain't Misbehavin'; Airplane!; Airplane 2, the Sequel; All in a Night's Work; All Night Long (1981); Almost You; Always Together; American Friends; The Amorous Adventures of Moll Flanders; Animal Kingdom; Annie Get Your Gun!; Annie Hall; Annie Oakley; Another Thin Man; Any Wednesday; April Fools; Arizona; The Art of Love; Arthur; Arthur 2, On the Rocks; Artists and Models (1937); Artists and Models Abroad; Ask Any Girl; The Assassination Bureau; Athena; Avanti!; The Aviator; The Awful Truth; Babes in Arms; Babes on Broadway; Baby, It's You; Babycakes; The Bachelor and the Bobby-Soxer; Back to the Future; Back to the Future 3; Ball of Fire; Barefoot in the Park; Barkleys of Broadway; Barnacle Bill (1941); Battement de Coeur; Bedtime Story (1941); Bedtime Story (1964); Bell, Book, and Candle; Belle Epoque; Bells Are Ringing; Best Foot Forward; Best Friends; Beyond Therapy; Big; Bird on a Wire; Blame it on Rio; Blind Date (1987); Bliss of Mrs. Blossom; Blithe Spirit; Bobo; Boomerang; Born to Dance; Born Yesterday (1950); Born Yesterday (1993); Boys' Night Out; Breakfast at Tiffany's; Broadcast News; Buddy System; Bull Durham; Butterflies are Free; Bye Bye Love; Cactus Flower; Cafe Metropole; Cafe Society; Cain and Mabel; Cairo (1942); Can She Bake a Cherry Pie?; Career Opportunities; Carefree; Cash McCall; A Certain Smile; Chances Are; Chapter Two; Charade; Cherry 2000; City Lights; Class; Cluny Brown; Cocoon; Cocoon, The Return; Cold Feet; Come September; Continental Divide; Coquette; Corvette Summer; A Countess from Hong Kong; Courtship; The Courtship of Eddie's Father; Cousin, Cousine; Cousins; The Cowboy and the Lady; Crocodile Dundee; Cross My Heart; Crossing Delancey; Cry Baby; The Cutting Edge;

Darling Lili; Date with an Angel; Dave; Dear Inspector; Dear Ruth; Death Takes a Holiday; Defending Your Life; Design for Living; Designing Woman; Desk Set; The Devil and Miss Jones; Diamonds for Breakfast; A Different Story; Dim Sum: a Little Bit of Heart; Divorce of Lady X; Doc Hollywood; The Doctor Takes a Wife; Doctor, You've Got to be Kidding; Don Juan DeMarco; Don't Make Waves; Don't Tell Her It's Me; Double Wedding; Dream Wife; Dubarry Was a Lady; The Duchess and the Dirtwater Fox; Dumb and Dumber; Earth Girls are Easy; Easy Living (1937); Easy to Wed; Educating Rita; Edward Scissorhands; Egg & I; Electric Horseman; End of the World . . . ; Enter Laughing; Eternally Yours; Every Day's A Holiday; Every Girl Should be Married; Facts of Life; Father Goose; Favor; A Fine Romance; First Love; The Flamingo Kid; Folies Bergere; Foolin' Around; Fools for Scandal; For Love of Ivy; For Love or Money (1963); For Love or Money (1993); A Foreign Affair; Forty Carats; Four's a Crowd; Frankie and Johnny; Free and Easy; The Frisco Kid (1935); The Frog Prince; The Fugitive Lovers; Full Moon in Blue Water; Funny About Love; Fuzzy Pink Nightgown; Gambit; The Gang's All Here; The Gay Divorcee; Genevieve; Gentlemen Prefer Blondes; Georgy Girl; Ghost Breakers; Gidget; Gigi (1948); Gigi (1958); Gilded Lily; The Girl Can't Help It; Girl Crazy; Girl Who Couldn't Say No; Girls! Girls! Girls!; Give Me a Sailor; Glass Bottom Boat; Go West Young Man; Goin' South; Goin' To Town; Good Fairy; Goodbye Girl; The Grass Is Greener; Grease; Grease 2; The Great Lover (1931); Great Scout and Cathouse Thursday; Green Card; Gregory's Girl; Groundhog Day; Grumpy Old Men; The Guest Wife; A Guy Named Joe; Hands Across the Table; Hard Promises; The Harvey Girls; He Married His Wife; He Said, She Said; Heartbreak Kid; Heaven Knows, Mr. Allison; Her Alibi; Her Husband's Affairs; Here We Go Round the Mulberry Bush; Hero at Large; Heroes; High Heels; High Road to China; High Society; The Hired Wife; His Girl Friday; Hit the Deck; Hoffman; Hold Me, Thrill Me, Kiss Me; Holiday; Holiday Inn; Holy Matrimony; Honeymoon; Honeymoon in Vegas; Honeymoon

Machine; Honeysuckle Rose; Honky Tonk; Hopscotch; Hot Pursuit; House Calls; Houseboat; Housesitter; How to Marry a Millionaire; How to Save a Marriage and Ruin Your Life; The Hudsucker Proxy; I Don't Buy Kisses Anymore; I Married a Witch; I Married a Woman; I.Q.; I Will . . . I Will . . . for Now; I'd Rather Be Rich; Idiot's Delight; If You Could Only Cook; Illegally Yours; Impromptu; Indiscreet; Invitation to Happiness; Iron Petticoat; Is There Sex After Death?; It Could Happen to You; It Had to Be You; It Happened One Night; It Happens Every Spring; It Should Happen to You; It Started in Naples; It Started with Eve; It's a Date; It's a Small World; It's a Wonderful World; It's Love I'm After; Jack and Sarah; The January Man; Jerk; Jersey Girl; Jewel of the Nile; Joseph Andrews; Joy of Living; June Bride; Just Tell Me What You Want; Just You and Me; Key Exchange; Key to the City; The Kid (1921); Kindergarten Cop; Kiss for Corliss; Kiss in the Dark; Kiss Me Goodbye; Kiss Me, Stupid!; Kiss Them For Me; Knack; Knave of Hearts; Ladies Should Listen; Lady and the Tramp; Lady Eve; The Lady Is Willing; Lady L.; Lady Takes a Chance; Ladyhawke; Last of the Red Hot Lovers; Last Run; Laughter; LeCavaleur; Legal Eagles; Let's Make Love; Libeled Lady; The Lieutenant Wore Skirts; The Life and Death of Colonel Blimp; The Little Minister; Little Murders; Little Night Music; A Little Romance; A Little Sex; Little Shop of Horrors (1986); Live a Little, Love a Lot; Live, Love and Learn; The Lonely Guy; The Long Long Trailer; Lost and Found; Love Affair (1932); Love Among the Ruins; Love Before Breakfast; Love Crazy; Love in Bloom; Love in the Afternoon; Love is a Ball; Love Potion #9; Love With the Proper Stranger; Lovely to Look At; Lover Come Back (1946); Lover Come Back (1961); Loverboy; Lovesick; Loving; Loving Couples; Luck of the Irish; Lucky Night; Lunatics, A Love Story; Mad Dog and Glory; Mad Miss Manton; Made for Each Other; Made in America; The Main Event; Major and the Minor; Making Mr. Right; Man Trouble; The Man Who Loved Women (1977); The Man Who Loved Women (1983); The Man with Two Brains; Man's Favorite Sport?;

Manhattan; Mannequin (1987); Mannequin 2: On the Move; Margie; Marriage Go Round; Married to the Mob; The Marrying Man; Mary, Mary; The Matchmaker; The Mating Game; Maverick; McClintock!; Me and My Gal; Medicine Man; Meet the Stewarts; Metropolitan (1990); Midnight (1939); A Midsummer Night's Dream; A Midsummer Night's Sex Comedy; Miracle of Morgan's Creek; Mischief; Model and the Marriage Broker; Modern Times; Momma, There's a Man in Your Bed; Monsieur Beaucaire; Monte Carlo; Monte Carlo Story; The Moon is Blue; Moon Pilot; Moon's Our Home; More Than a Secretary; More the Merrier; Mother is a Freshman; Move Over, Darling; Mr. and Mrs. Smith; Mr. Lucky; Mr. Music; Mr. Peabody and the Mermaid; Muriel's Wedding; Murphy's Romance; My Best Friend's Girl; My Dear Secretary; My Fair Lady; My Favorite Wife; My Lucky Star; My Man Godfrey (1956); My Sister Eileen (1942); My Sister Eileen (1955); Naked in New York; Never a Dull Moment (1950); Never Give a Sucker an Even Break; Never on Sunday; A New Kind of Love; A Night to Remember (1946); The Night We Never Met; Ninotchka; No Man of Her Own; No More Ladies; No No Nanette (1930); No No Nanette (1940); No Time for Love; Nobody's Fool (1986); Not with My Wife You Don't; Notorious Landlady; Nudo di Donna; Oh, Rosalinda!; Oh, What a Night; Oklahoma!; On Approval; On the Avenue; On the Town; Once Upon a Dream; Once Upon a Honeymoon; One Touch of Venus; One Woman or Two; Only Angels Have Wings; Only the Lonely; Only Two Can Play; Only You; Operation Mad Ball; The Opposite Sex and How to Live With Them; The Owl and the Pussycat; Oxford Blues; A Pair of Briefs; Pal Joey; Palm Beach Story; Paper Marriage; Paris When it Sizzles; Pat and Mike; Pauline at the Beach; Perfect Furlough; Period of Adjustment; The Philadelphia Story; Pickup Artist; Pillow Talk; Pirate; Prelude to a Kiss; Pretty Woman; The Prince and the Showgirl; The Princess and the Pirate; Private Lives; Promise Her Anything; The Purple Rose of Cairo; The Rachel Papers; Rare Breed; Rat Race; Rhinestone; Richest Girl in the World; Riding High; Road to Bali; Road to Hong Kong; Road to Morocco; Road to Rio; Road to Singapore; Road to Utopia; Road to Zanzibar; Robin and Marian; Roman Holiday; Romance on the High Seas; Romancing the Stone; Romanoff and Juliet; Romantic Comedy; The Rose Tattoo; Rough Cut; Roxanne; Royal Wedding; Sabrina; Same Time, Next Year; Saratoga; Say Anything; Scared Stiff; Second Honeymoon; The Secret of My Success; Semi-Tough; Send Me No Flowers; Seven Days Leave; Sex and the Single Girl; Shall We Dance?; She Done Him Wrong; She's Gotta Have It; Shirley Valentine; Simple Men; Sing Baby Sing; The Sky's the Limit; Sleeper; Small Town Girl (1936); Smart Woman; Smiles of a Summer Night; The Smiling Lieutenant; Some Girls; Some Like it Hot; Son of Paleface; A Song Is Born; Special Day; Star Spangled Girl; The Sterile Cuckoo; Straight Talk; Strictly Ballroom; Sugarbaby; Sunday in New York; The Sure Thing; Surrender; Swept Away; Swing Shift; Switching Channels; Take a Letter, Darling; Talk of the Town; The Tall Guy; Tammy and the Bachelor; Teacher's Pet; Teahouse of the August Moon; Ten; Ten Thousand Bedrooms; The Tender Trap; That Certain Age; That Certain Feeling; That Obscure Object of Desire; That Touch of Mink; That Uncertain Feeling; There's a Girl in My Soup; They All Laughed; They Knew What They Wanted; The Thief Who Came to Dinner; This Could Be the Night; This Happy Feeling; This Thing Called Love; Those Magnificent Men in Their Flying Machines; A Thousand Clowns; Three Blind Mice; Three of Hearts; Three on a Couch; Three Smart Girls; Three Smart Girls Grow Up; The Thrill of It All; Tiger's Tale; A Time for Loving; To Paris with Love; Together Again; Tokyo Pop; Tom, Dick and Harry; Tom Jones; Too Many Husbands; Tootsie; Top Hat; Top Secret Affair; Touch of Class; Trade Winds; Trouble in Paradise; Trouble with Girls; True Love; Truly, Madly, Deeply; Trust; Tugboat Annie; Tune in Tomorrow; Twin Beds; Two of a Kind; Two-Faced Woman; Under the Yum Yum Tree; Used People; Valley Girl; Vibes; Visit to a Small Planet; Vivacious Lady; Waikiki Wedding; Walk, Don't Run; Waltz Across Texas; War Between Men and Women; Wedding Present; What's Up, Doc?; When Harry Met Sally; When You're in

Love; Who's Been Sleeping in My Bed?; Who's That Girl?; Wife, Doctor and Nurse; Wife, Husband and Friend; Wife Versus Secretary; The Witches of Eastwick; Without Love; Without Reservations; Wives and Lovers; Woman in Red; Woman of the Year; Working Girl; Year of the Comet; You Belong to Me; You Can't Run Away From It; You're a Big Boy Now; The Young in Heart; Youngblood

Romantic Drama: see also *Romantic Comedy: Erotic Drama: ROMANCE:* The Abdication; About Face; The Accidental Tourist; Act of the Heart; The Age of Innocence (1934); The Age of Innocence (1993); Algiers; All the Mornings of the World; All the Vermeers in New York; Almost Perfect Affair; Always; American in Paris; And Now, My Love; Animal Behavior; Anne and Muriel; Arch of Triumph; Arise, My Love; Ash Wednesday; Aspen Extreme; B.F.'s Daughter; Banning; The Barbarian and the Geisha; Beau Brummell (1924); Beau Brummell (1954); Belizaire the Cajun; Beloved Infidel; Betty Blue; Beyond the Limit; Bird of Paradise (1932); Bird of Paradise (1951); Bitter Sweet (1933); Bitter Sweet (1940); Bitter Tears of Petra Von Kant; Blind Husbands; Blonde Venus; Blood and Sand (1922); Blood and Sand (1941); Blue Angel (1930); Blue Angel (1959); Bobby Deerfield; Bodies, Rest & Motion; Boyfriends and Girlfriends; Bram Stoker's Dracula (1992); A Breath of Scandal; Breezy; Brideshead Revisited; Bridge; Brief Encounter (1946); Brief Encounter (1974); C'est la Vie; Camille (1936); Camille Claudel; Cardinal Richelieu; Carousel; Carrie (1952); Casablanca; Casanova (Fellini's Casanova); Casque d'Or; Castaway; Chapter Two; Children of a Lesser God; Children of Paradise; Chilly Scenes of Winter; Chloe in the Afternoon; Choose Me; Cinderella Liberty; Circle of Friends; Cleopatra (1934); Cleopatra (1963); The Clock; Cold Sassy Tree; Coming Home; Confidential Agent; Conquest; Constant Nymph (1933); Constant Nymph (1943); Conversation Piece; The Cotton Club; Cousin, Cousine; Cousins; Cuba; Cyrano de Bergerac (1950); Cyrano de Bergerac (1990); Damage; David and Lisa; Deadfall (1968); Dear John; Deception (1992); Devil in the Flesh (1946); Devil in the

Flesh (1987); Diamond Jim; Doctor Zhivago; The Double Life of Veronique; Dracula (1931); Dracula (1979); Dracula Has Risen from the Grave; Dracula (Horror of Dracula, 1958); Dracula, Prince of Darkness; Dracula's Daughter; Draughtman's Contract; Duel in the Sun; East Lynne; Eclipse; Eighty-Four Charing Cross Road; Elena and Her Men; Elephant Walk; Elvira Madigan; Enchanted Cottage; Encore; Endless Love; Enemies, A Love Story; Ethan Frome; The Europeans; Everybody's All American; Ex-Lady; Falling in Love; Falling in Love Again; Far and Away; Far from the Madding Crowd; Farewell My Concubine; A Farewell to Arms (1932); A Farewell to Arms (1957); Fearless; Fedora; Female on the Beach; Firefly; Flamingo Road; Flesh and the Devil; Fool for Love; For Whom the Bell Tolls; Forever Amber; Forty Carats; The Fountainhead; Four Weddings and a Funeral; Frankie and Johnny; The French Lieutenant's Woman; Fresh Horses; The Frog Prince; From Here to Eternity; From the Terrace; Gabriela; Game is Over; The General Died at Dawn; Ghost; The Ghost and Mrs. Muir; Gilda; Girl From Petrovka; A Girl Named Tamiko; The Girl with Green Eyes; The Go-Between; Go-Fish; Golden Gate; Gone With the Wind; Good Mother; The Good Wife; Goodbye Again; The Great White Hope; Greek Tycoon; Gypsy Moths; The Hairdresser's Husband; A Handful of Dust; Havana; Heaven Can Wait (1978); Heaven Knows, Mr. Allison; The Heiress; The Helen Morgan Story; Henry and June; Henry V (1944); Henry V (1989); High, Wide and Handsome; The Hireling; Hiroshima, Mon Amour; His Brother's Wife; Hold Back the Dawn; Hold Your Man; The Homecoming (1948); The Hospital; Humoresque; The Hunchback of Notre Dame (1923); The Hunchback of Notre Dame (1939); The Hunchback of Notre Dame (1956); The Hunchback of Notre Dame (1982); Hurricane (1937); Hurricane (1979); I Sent a Letter to My Love; Idol; Immortal Beloved; In Name Only; In Praise of Older Women; In the Cool of the Day; In the French Style; Indecent Obsession; Indecent Proposal; Indiscretion of an American Wife; Jacknife; Jamaica Inn (1939); Jamaica Inn (1982); Jezebel; Jude the Obscure; Jules and Jim; Jungle Fever; The King's

Whore; La Belle Noiseuse; La Ronde (1950); La Ronde (1964); Lady Chatterley's Lover (1955); Lady Chatterley's Lover (1981); Lady L.; Lady with a Dog; Last Tango in Paris; Last Year at Marienbad; Legends of the Fall; Lilith; Live for Life; Lola Montes; The Lonely Passion of Judith Hearne; Long Hot Summer (1958); Lost Lady; Lost Moment; Loulou; Love; Love Affair (1939); Love and Pain and the Whole Damn Thing; Love in Germany; Love in the Afternoon; Love is a Many-Splendored Thing; Love Letters (1945); Love on the Dole; Love on the Run (1979); Love Story (1970); The Lover; Lovin' Molly; M. Butterfly; Macomber Affair; Madame Bovary; Made in Heaven; Madness of the Heart; Magnificent Obsession (1935); Magnificent Obsession (1954); A Man and A Woman; A Man and a Woman: Twenty Years Later; A Man in Love; The Man in the Moon; Man of La Mancha; The Man Who Fell to Earth; Map of the Human Heart; Masculine, Feminine; Masquerade (1988); Maurice; Meeting Venus; Men in White; Middle of the Night; Mill on the Floss; Miss Sadie Thompson; Mississippi Masala; Moment by Moment; Moscow Does Not Believe in Tears; Mr. Jones; Mrs. Soffel; Murmur of the Heart; My Night at Maud's; The Naked Jungle; Naked Maja; Nell; New York, New York; Night and the City (1992); Night Angel; The Night is Young (1934); Nothin' But a Man; O Pioneers!; Of Human Bondage (1934); Of Human Bondage (1946); Of Human Bondage (1964); An Officer and a Gentleman; Oklahoma Crude; Old Gringo; On Dangerous Ground; Once Around; Once in Paris; Once Upon a Dream; One Sunday Afternoon; One Way Passage; The Only Game in Town; The Other Side of Midnight; The Other Side of the Mountain; Our Hearts Were Young and Gay; Out of Africa; Paris Blues; Party Girl; A Patch of Blue; Personal Property; Petulia; Picnic; The Private Lives of Elizabeth and Essex; The Promise; Quartet (1981); Queen Christina; Queen of the Stardust Ballroom; Quiet Man; Raging Moon; Rain; Rainbow; Rainmaker; Rancho Notorious; Red Kiss; Red Shoe Diaries; Reds; The Return of Martin Guerre; Revenge; Rhapsody; Rich in Love; RobRoy; Rocky; Romance; Romeo and Juliet (1936); Romeo and

Juliet (1954); Romeo and Juliet (1968); Room at the Top; Rope of Sand; Ryan's Daughter; The Sailor Who Fell From Grace with the Sea; Salmonberries; The Sandpiper; Sawdust and Tinsel; Say Hello to Yesterday; Sayonara; September Affair; The Severed Head; Shadowlands; Showboat (1936); Showboat (1951); Someone to Watch Over Me; Somewhere in Time; Sommersby; Splendor in the Grass; Stanley & Iris; A Star Is Born (1937); A Star Is Born (1954); A Star Is Born (1976); Stealing Heaven; The Sterile Cuckoo; Stolen Hours; Strangers, the Story of a Mother and Daughter; Summertime; Sunflower; Surviving Desire; Swann in Love; Sword of Lancelot; T.R. Baskin; Tales of Hoffman; A Taste of Honey; The Tempest; Tender Mercies; Tequila Sunrise; Teresa; Tess; That Forsyte Woman; That Hamilton Woman; That Kind of Woman; That Obscure Object of Desire; Thief of Hearts; Thieves Like Us; Thing Called Love; This is My Affair; This Property is Condemned; This Sporting Life; Thomas Crown Affair; Those Were the Days; Three Coins in the Fountain; Three Comrades; The Threepenny Opera; Threesome; Tie Me Up! Tie Me Down!; Tim; Time after Time; Time for Loving; To Catch a Thief; To Each His Own; To Find a Man; To Paris with Love; Today We Live; Tokyo Joe; Tom & Viv; Too Beautiful For You; Too Late Blues; Torch Song; The Torrents of Spring; Turning Point; Turtle Diary; 21; Twice in a Lifetime; Two for the Seesaw; Two Moon Junction; Two People; The Two Worlds of Jenny Logan; The Umbrellas of Cherbourg; Un Coeur en Hiver; The Unbearable Lightness of Being; Untamed Heart; Violets are Blue; Voices; Wait Until Spring, Bandini; Walk in the Spring Rain; Walk on the Wild Side; Warm December; Waterloo Bridge (1931); Waterloo Bridge (1940); The Way We Were; Wedding Night; West Side Story; When a Man Loves a Woman; White Nights (1957); White Palace; Wild Hearts Can't Be Broken; Wild in the Country; Wings in the Dark; Wings of the Morning; Wolf; The Woman Next Door; Women in Love; The World of Suzie Wong; Wuthering Heights (1939); Wuthering Heights (1953); Wuthering Heights (1970); Wuthering Heights (1992); Yanks; The Year of Living Dangerously; Yentl; You Light Up My Life

Romantic Thrillers: see *Erotic Thrillers: THRILLERS: Film Noir*
Rome: see *Romans/Rome*
Roommates: see also *Roommates from Hell: Apartment Buildings: Neighbors-Troublesome: Friendships: College Life: Situation Comedy:* Any Wednesday; Apartment Zero; A Different Story; The Duchess and the Dirtwater Fox; Echo Park; The Goodbye Girl; Green Card; Harry and the Hendersons; The Heart Is a Lonely Hunter; Heaven Knows, Mr. Allison; Knack; Lost in Yonkers; Loulou; More the Merrier; My Friend Irma; The Night We Never Met; The Odd Couple; The Performance; Rat Race; Reality Bites; Roommates; Star Spangled Girl; Talk of the Town; Tatie Danielle; Tell Me that You Love Me, Junie Moon; Under the Yum Yum Tree; Walk, Don't Run; Without Love; You Can't Run Away From It
Roommates from Hell: see also *Malicious Menaces: Neighbors-Troublesome: THRILLERS: HORROR: Rogue Plots: Stalkers: Psycho Killers:* Apartment Zero; Blithe Spirit; Buddy Buddy; Doppelganger: The Evil Within; Entertaining Mr. Sloane; The Goodbye Girl; Guest in the House; Hider in the House; The Housequest; I Thank a Fool; Ladykillers; Madhouse; Malice; The Man Who Came to Dinner; Pacific Heights; Shallow Grave; Single White Female; Tatie Danielle; Tenant; What About Bob?
Roots: see *Family/Heritage-Search for:* also *Children-Adopted*
Royalty (in general): see also *Queens: Kings: Princes: Princesses: Castles: Fairy Tales: Monaco/Monte Carlo: Queen Elizabeth:* Alexander the Great; All the Mornings of the World; Anastasia (1984); As You Like It (1936); As You Like It (1992); Beau Brummell (1924); Beau Brummell (1954); The Big Broadcast of 1936; Bonnie Prince Charlie; Braveheart; A Breath of Scandal; Caesar and Cleopatra; Catherine the Great; Coming to America; The Count of Monte Cristo (1934); The Count of Monte Cristo (1974); A Countess from Hong Kong; The Devil's Bride; Diana: Her True Story; Dubarry Was a Lady; The Fall of the Roman Empire; The Fifth Musketeer; Forever Amber; Genghis Khan; The Great Catherine; Henry V (1944); Henry V (1989); Holy Matrimony; Ivan the Terrible; King and I; King Lear (1971); The King's Whore; La Nuit de Varennes;

Lady Caroline Lamb; Lady in the Iron Mask; Lady Jane; The Last Emperor; The Leopard; Lion in Winter; Little Lord Fauntleroy (1936); Little Lord Fauntleroy (1980); Man in Grey; Marie Antoinette; Mary of Scotland; Mary, Queen of Scots; Mask of the Avenger; Mayerling (1935); Mayerling (1968); The Merry Widow (1925); The Merry Widow (1934); The Merry Widow (1952); Mudlark; Nicholas and Alexandra; Night is Young (1934); Peg o' My Heart; Prisoner of Zenda (1937); Prisoner of Zenda (1952); Prisoner of Zenda (1979); Queen Christina; Raise the Red Lantern; Ran; Rasputin and the Empress; Richard III; Rise of Louis XIV; Roman Holiday; Romanoff and Juliet; Royal Scandal; Royal Wedding; Ruling Class; The Scarlet Empress; The Scarlet Pimpernel; The Slipper and the Rose; Something for Everyone; Splitting Heirs; The Swan; Sword of Lancelot; That Hamilton Woman; That Night in Rio; The Thief of Bagdad (1924); The Thief of Baghdad (1940); The Three Musketeers (1935); The Three Musketeers (1939); The Three Musketeers (1948); Tovarich; Tower of London (1939); Tower of London (1962); Two Way Stretch; War and Peace (1956); War and Peace (1967); Wee Willie Winkie; Wings of the Morning; Yellow Rolls Royce

Royalty-Sudden/Inherited (catapulted to the throne): see also *Royalty: Heirs: Heiresses: Rags to Riches:* Dave; Earl of Chicago; Farewell to the King; Greystoke: The Legend of Tarzan; King Ralph; Little Lord Fauntleroy (1936); Little Lord Fauntleroy (1980); Prisoner of Zenda; Splitting Heirs

Rule the World-Plots to: see also *Anarchists: Corruption: Tyrant Leaders: Dictators: Nazi Stories: Hitler-Adolf:* Batman; Batman Returns; Billion Dollar Brain; Blood on the Sun; Boys from Brazil; Brenda Starr; Captain America; Diamonds are Forever; Doctor Mabuse, the Gambler; Dr. No; Enemy from Space; The Final Conflict; For Your Eyes Only; Highlander II-The Quickening; Highlander III, The Sorcerer; Goldfinger; Leonard, Part 6; License to Kill; Moonraker; Murderer's Row; Never Say Never Again; Nude Bomb; Octopussy; The Omen; Omen IV: The Awakening; Our Man Flint; The Pink Panther Strikes

Again; The Satan Bug; Silencers; Spaced Invaders; The Spy Who Loved Me; Superman; Superman 2; Superman 3; Superman 4; Swamp Thing; Thunderball; A View to a Kill

Rumors: see also *Gossip/Rumors:* Absence of Malice; The Children's Hour; A Cry in the Dark; Love and Hisses; Manon des Sources (1952); Manon des Sources (1986); Naked Truth; Notorious Landlady; The Opposite Sex; Steel Magnolias; Theodora Goes Wild; These Three; Twin Peaks; Twin Peaks: Fire Walk with Me; Welcome to Hard Times; The Women

Runaways: see also *Orphans: Fugitives from the Law: Children Alone: Prostitutes-Child: Inner City Life:* Angel; Blonde Venus; Captains Courageous; Days of Heaven; Dog of Flanders; Flight of the Doves; Griffin and Phoenix, A Love Story; Harry and Tonto; Home Alone; Home Alone 2: Lost in New York; The Honeymoon; The Hunted; It Happened One Night; Les Comperes; Maybe I'll Be Home in the Spring; Mountain Eagle; Napoleon and Samantha; Naughty Marietta; Night of the Hunter; P.K. and the Kid; Pixote; Psych-Out; The Rain People; Susan Lenox, Her Fall and Rise; Tom Sawyer; Where the Day Takes You

Running: see also *Sports Movies: Track and Field:* Billie; Chariots of Fire; Jim Thorpe, All American; The Loneliness of the Long Distance Runner; The Long Gray Line; Marathon Man; Personal Best; Running; See How She Runs; The Terry Fox Story

Running from the Law: see *Fugitives from the Law*

Running from the Mob: see *Fugitives from the Mob: also Mob Stories: Disguises: Deaths-Faked*

Rural Horrors (usually involves being trapped in a small town): see also *Rednecks: Ku Klux Klan: Gothic Style: HORROR:* The Fury (1936); Graveyard Shift; Halloween; Halloween 2; Halloween 4: The Return of Michael Myers; Halloween 5: The Revenge of Michael Myers; Jackson County Jail; The Texas Chainsaw Massacre; The Texas Chainsaw Massacre, Part 2

Rural Life: see also *Farm Life: Small-Town Life: Save the Farm: City vs. Country: Southerns: Midwestern Life: Southwestern Life: Urban Life:*

Rednecks: Hillbillies: Adam at 6 A.M.; All Creatures Great and Small; Amber Waves; Billy Liar; Birch Interval; Cityslickers; Diary of a Chambermaid (1946); Diary of a Chambermaid (1963); Far from the Madding Crowd; A Fire in the Sky; Fox; Go-Between; God's Little Acre; Going Home; Goodbye My Lady; Heart Like a Wheel; High, Wide and Handsome; The Holly and the Ivy; I Walk the Line; If You Knew Susie; In Country; Invaders from Mars (1986); Invasion; Love on the Dole; Love Story (1944); Lunch on the Grass; The Man in the Moon; Manon des Sources (1952); Manon des Sources (1986); Mississippi Masala; Monte Walsh; Mr. Blandings Builds His Dream House; Mrs. Wiggs of the Cabbage Patch; Raising Arizona; Ruggles of Red Gap; Shenandoah; Shepherd of the Hills; Shy People; Sometimes a Great Notion; Square Dance; Stand by Me; Starman; Straw Dogs; Sunday in the Country; Tammy and the Bachelor; Tender Mercies; Tex; Tobacco Road; Whistle Down the Wind; Wild Is the Wind; Wildflower

Russia: see also *KGB: Russian Revolution: Russian Films: Leaders-Tyrant: Communists: McCarthy Era: Europeans-Eastern: Cold War Era: Spy Films:* Action in the North Atlantic; Alexander Nevsky; Brothers Karamazov; Catherine the Great; Childhood of Maxim Gorky; Comrades of Summer; Crime and Punishment; Dersu Uzala; Doctor Zhivago; The Earth; The Fixer; The Girl from Petrovka; Gorky Park; The Great Catherine; The Great Race; Inner Circle; The Inspector General; Ivan the Terrible; Knight Without Armor; Kremlin Letter; Little Vera; Living Corpse; Moscow Does Not Believe in Tears; Night People; Once in a Blue Moon; Reds; Repentance; The Russia House; Stalin; Twelve Chairs; Unfinished Piece for a Player Piano; War and Peace (1956); War and Peace (1967); White Nights (1985); Who?; Window to Paris; Young Catherine

Russian Films: see also *Russians: Cold War Era: Oppression:* Alexander Nevsky; Arsenal; The Battleship Potemkin; The Childhood of Maxim Gorky; Close to Eden; Ivan the Terrible; Ivan's Childhood; Lady with a Dog; Letters from a Dead Man; Little Vera; Living Corpse; Moscow Does Not Believe in Tears; Oblomov;

Films by Category

S

Sabotage: see also *Spies: Spy Films: Traitors: Double Crossing: Corruption:* Against the Wind; All My Sons (1949); All My Sons (1986); Bridge on the River Kwai; The Deep; Five Graves to Cairo; Force Ten from Navarone; The Guns of Navarone; High Spirits; The Hindenburg; The Hornet's Nest; The Horse Soldiers; 13 Rue Madeleine; Tobruk; Wife, Husband and Friend

Sadism/S&M: see *Sexual Kinkiness: Abusive Men: Abusive Women*

Safaris: see also *Africa: Hunters:* Africa Screams; Africa, Texas Style; Born Free; Hatari!; The Macomber Affair; Mogambo; Road to Zanzibar; The Roots of Heaven

Sagas (family and/or immigrant stories over time): see also *Immigrants: Historical Dramas Epics: Episodic Stories: Family Drama:* America, America; Cavalcade; Early Summer; The Emerald Forest; Emigrants; Far and Away; Fiddler on the Roof; Forever and a Day; Giant; The Grapes of Wrath; Happy Time; How Green Was My Valley; The Howards of Virginia; Jewel in the Crown; The Leopard; The New Land; 1900; Once Upon a Time in America; Roots; Ryan's Daughter; Taras Bulba; We of the Never Never

Sailing: see also *Adventures at Sea: Boat Racing: Ships: Swimming: Beach Movies: Sports Movies:* Captain Ron; The Dove; Lady from Shanghai; The Wind

Sailors (usually military): see also *Soldiers: Sailing: Military Stories: Adventure at Sea:* Abroad with Two Yanks; Anchors Aweigh; The Baby and the Battleship; Barcelona; Billy Budd; Bird of Paradise (1932); Bird of Paradise (1951); Blood Alley; Born to Dance; Breaking Point; The Caine Mutiny (1954); The Caine Mutiny Court Martial (1988); Castaway Cowboy; Cinderella Liberty; Don't Go Near the Water; The Dove; Fanny; Follow the Fleet; The Fox; The Frisco Kid (1935); The Ghost and Mrs. Muir; Give Me a Sailor; His Majesty O'Keefe; Hit the Deck; Honeymoon Machine; I Know Where I'm Going; Johnny Angel; The Key (1958); Kiss Them For Me; Mister Roberts; On the Town; Operation Petticoat; Querelle; Reap the Wild Wind; The Sailor Who Fell From Grace with the Sea; Souls at Sea; 20,000 Leagues Under the Sea; Two Girls and a Sailor

Saintly People: see also *Religion:* City of Joy; Close to Eden; Cry Freedom; Devil's Advocate; Good Sam; I'll Give a Million; Joan of Arc; Joan of Paris; The King; The Last Angry Man; The Leather Saint; Monsieur Vincent; Mrs. Miniver; My Little Girl; No No Nanette (1930); No No Nanette (1940); The Nun's Story; O Lucky Man; One Foot in Heaven; Passing of the Third Floor Back; Rob Roy; Sister

Kenny; Song of Bernadette; Stand and Deliver; Stella (1990); Stella Dallas (1925); Stella Dallas (1937); The Story of Dr. Wassell; The Story of Louis Pasteur

Salesmen: see also *Con Artists: Working Class: Ordinary People Stories:* The Bigamist; The Closer; Company Limited; Deal of the Century; Desire and Hell at Sunset Motel; Did You Hear the One About the Travelling Saleslady?; The Fuller Brush Girl; The Fuller Brush Man; Glengarry Glen Ross; Imaginary Crimes; Little Giant (1946); Live Now, Pay Later; Made in America; Man's Favorite Sport?; O Lucky Man; Our Man in Havana; Pennies from Heaven (1981); Poltergeist; The Red Shoe Diaries; Tin Men; Toast of New York; Tommy Boy; Too Beautiful for You; The Trouble with Girls; Used Cars

Sally Field Goes Southern (she is one of three actresses whose most popular parts are those of southern women, though they are not southern themselves): see also *Jessica Lange Goes Southern, Susan Sarandon Goes Southern, Southerns:* Back Roads; Norma Rae; Places in the Heart; Stay Hungry; Steel Magnolias; A Woman of Independent Means

S&M: see *Sexual Kinkiness*

San Francisco: see also *California: San Francisco Chases: Alcatraz:* Barbary Coast; Basic Instinct; Big Trouble in

Dame (1982); I Stand Condemned; Indiana Jones and the Last Crusade; Indiana Jones and the Temple of Doom; The Innocents of Paris (1929); It's a Wonderful Life; Joan of Paris; Killer's Kiss; The Killing Fields; Knight Without Armor; Kotch; Lady from Shanghai; Lassie; The Last of the Mohicans (1936); The Last of the Mohicans (1992); Laughter in the Dark; The Legend of Billie Jean; The Life of Emile Zola; Lionheart; Love in Germany; Luv; Mad Dog and Glory; Maid of Salem; The Man with Two Faces; Marnie; Marooned; Miracle of the White Stallions; My Favorite Blonde; The Neverending Story; The Neverending Story II: The Next Chapter; Night Nurse; No No Nanette (1930); No No Nanette (1940); Only Angels Have Wings; The Ox-Bow Incident; Pain in the A . . .; The Prince of Tides; The Princess Bride; Promises in the Dark; The Quiet American; The Remains of the Day; The Rescue; Return of the Scarlet Pimpernel; Robin Hood (1922); Robin Hood (1973); Robin Hood (1990); Robin Hood: Prince of Thieves (1991); Roots, the Gift; Russkies; Salome (1953); San Francisco; San Quentin; Saskatchewan; The Scarlet Pimpernel; Schindler's List; The Secret War of Harry Frigg; The Seventh Seal; Sister Kenny; Slender Thread; Someone to Watch Over Me; Spellbinder; Stalking Moon; The Stork Club; Straw Dogs; Such Good Friends; The Swan Princess; A Tale of Two Cities (1935); A Tale of Two Cities (1958); A Tale of Two Cities (1982); Target; The Ten Commandments; Terminator 2: Judgment Day; Test Pilot; The Three Musketeers (1935); The Three Musketeers (1939); The Three Musketeers (1948); Ticket to Heaven; Time after Time; Time Without Pity; Timebomb; Twenty Thousand Years in Sing Sing; Two Mules for Sister Sara; Uncle Tom's Cabin (1914); Uncle Tom's Cabin (1969); Union Station; Untamed Heart; Vincent and Theo; The Wilby Conspiracy; Willow

Scams: see Insurance Scams: Con Artists

Scandals: see also Corruption: Videotape Scandals: Small-Town Scandals: Aces High; Ada; Adventure in Washington; Blaze; Blind Ambition; The Bonfire of the Vanities; A Breath of Scandal; Bundle of Joy; Business as Usual; Camila (1984); A Canterbury Tale;

Chinatown; Compulsion; Courtship; Diana: Her True Story; The Disappearance of Aimee; Donovan's Reef; Eight Men Out; Falcon and the Snowman; Flamingo Road; The Fountainhead; The French Lieutenant's Woman; Harper Valley P.T.A.; Hollywood Boulevard (1936); Hot Spell; If Winter Comes; Inspiration; Jarrapellejos; Johnny Belinda; Joshua Then and Now; Kiss and Tell; Lady Caroline Lamb; Lady Chatterly's Lover (1955); Lady Chatterly's Lover (1981); The Lindbergh Kidnapping Case; Loose Ankles; The Lover; Mastergate; Momma, There's a Man in Your Bed; My Reputation; National Lampoon's European Vacation; Necessary Roughness; The Night They Raided Minsky's; No Sex, Please, We're British; Parnell; Peyton Place; Playboys; The Positively True Adventures of the Alleged Texas Cheerleader-Murdering Mom; Quiz Show; Ricochet; The Right to Love; Rising Sun; Romance; Running Mates; Ryan's Daughter Scandal; Scandal Sheet; Schtonk!; Sitting Pretty; Small Sacrifices; Storyville; Strange Interlude (1932); Strange Interlude (1990); Term of Trial; Tess; That Forsyte Woman; That Hamilton Woman; Theodora Goes Wild; These Three; They Won't Forget; The Trials of Oscar Wilde; True Colors; Twin Peaks; Twin Peaks: Fire Walk with Me; Two Against the World; Woman Rebels

Scandinavia (Denmark, Finland, Norway, Sweden, Holland/The Netherlands) see also Swedish Films: Danish Films: Babette's Feast; A Doll's House; From the Life of the Marionettes; Gertrude; Hamlet (1948); Hamlet (1964); Hamlet (1969); Hamlet (1991); Hans Christian Andersen; Hedda; Heroes of Telemark; I Remember Mama; Leningrad Cowboys Go to America; The Long Ships; The Match Factory Girl; Montenegro; The Moon Is Down; Night on Earth; Pathfinder; Pelle the Conqueror; Pippi Longstocking; Queen Christina; Ransom; Son of Lassie; Song of Norway; Turkish Delight; The Vikings

Scenery-Outstanding (the setting; not to be confused with cinematography): see also Production Design-Outstanding: Epics: Mountain Settings: Islands: Lyrical Films: Around the World in 80 Days; Another Country; Days of Heaven; Doctor Zhivago; Hawaii; Koyanniquatsi; Legends of the Fall;

The Mission; Mountains on the Moon; Nell; A Passage to India; Powaqqatsi, Life in Transformation; Quiet Man; A River Runs Through It; The River Wild; Ryan's Daughter; The Sandpiper; Sirens; Song of Norway; The Sound of Music; Summertime

Schemes: see Insurance Scams: Con Artists: Thieves: Embezzlers: Heist Stories: Clever Plots & Endings

School Life (primarily primary or elementary school): see High School Life: Boarding Schools: College Life: Coming of Age: Boys' Schools: Girls' Schools: Billy Madison; Bon Voyage, Charlie Brown; Kindergarten Cop; Melody; Milk Money; Up the Down Staircase

SCI-FI/Science Fiction: see also SCI-FI-1950s: Futuristic Films: Outer Space Movies: Virtual Reality: HORROR: Fantasy: Abbott & Costello Go to Mars; The Absent-Minded Professor; The Abyss; Adventure Island; The Adventures of Baron Munchausen (1987); The Adventures of Buckaroo Banzai Across the 8th Dimension; Alien; Alien Nation; Alien3; Aliens; The Alligator People; Alphaville; Amazing Stories; Amazon Women on the Moon; And You Thought Your Parents Were Weird; Applegates; Asphyx; At the Earth's Core; Attack of the 50-Foot Woman (1958); Attack of the 50-Foot Woman (1993); Attack of the Killer Tomatoes; The Awakening; Back to the Future; Back to the Future 2; Back to the Future 3; batteries not included; Battle for the Planet of the Apes; Beneath the Planet of the Apes; Berkeley Square; Beware!; The Blob!; Biggles; Black Hole; Blade Runner; Blue Monkey; Body Bags; The Body Snatchers; The Borrower; A Boy and His Dog; The Boys from Brazil; Brain Eaters; Brainstorm (1983); The Brood; Bug; Carrie (1976); Castle Keep; Cat Women of the Moon; Chairman; Child's Play (1972); Children of the Damned; A Clockwork Orange; Close Encounters of the Third Kind; Closet Land; Cocoon; Cocoon, The Return; Communion; Conquest of the Planet of the Apes; Cool World; D.A.R.Y.L.; Dark Crystal; Dark Star; Darkman; Day of the Triffids; The Day the Earth Caught Fire; The Day the Earth Stood Still; Daybreak; Dead Alive; Dead of Night (1977); Deadlock; Death Becomes Her; Death Race 2000; Death Watch; Demolition Man; Demon Seed; The Devil Came from

Arkansas; Devil Doll; Digby, the Biggest Dog in the World; Donovan's Brain; Dr. Cyclops; Dr. Dolittle; Dragonslayer; Dreamscape; Dune; Ebb Tide; Edward Scissorhands; Electric Dreams; Empire of the Ants; The Empire Strikes Back; Endangered Species; Enemy from Space; Enemy Mine; Entity; Escape From New York; Escape from the Planet of the Apes; Escape to Witch Mountain; The Explorers; Fahrenheit 451; Fantastic Voyage; Final Countdown; The Five Thousand Fingers of Doctor T.; Flash; Flash Gordon; Flatliners; Flesh Gordon; Flight of the Navigator; The Fly (1958); The Fly (1986); The Fly II; Food of the Gods; Forbidden Planet; Forever Young; The Fortress; Freaked; Freddy's Dead: The Final Nightmare; Freejack; Full Eclipse; Futureworld; Ghost in the Machine; Godzilla (1955); Godzilla versus Gigan; Godzilla versus Megalon; The Golden Child; Golden Year; Goonies; Green Slime; The Groundstar Conspiracy; A Handmaid's Tale; Hangar 18; Hardware; Hellbound: Hellraiser II; Hellraiser; Hellraiser III: Hell on Earth; Hidden; Hidden 2; Hideaway; Honey, I Blew Up the Kid; Honey, I Shrunk the Kids; Howard the Duck; Ice Pirates; Ice Station Zebra; The Illustrated Man; Impulse (1984); The Incredible Shrinking Man; The Incredible Shrinking Woman; Innerspace; In Search of the Castaways; Invaders from Mars (1953); Invaders from Mars (1986); The Invasion; Invasion of the Body Snatchers (1956); Invasion of the Body Snatchers (1978); The Invisible Man's Revenge; The Invisible Ray; The Invisible Woman; Island of Lost Souls (1932); It Came From Outer Space; J'Accuse; Journey to the Center of the Earth; Journey to the Far Side of the Sun; The Keep; King Kong (1933); King Kong (1976); The Kingdom; Kingdom of the Spiders; Kismet (1944); Kismet (1955); The Kiss (1988); Knightriders; Krull; Labyrinth; The Land that Time Forgot; The Last Starfighter; Late for Dinner; The Lawnmower Man; Legend; Leviathan; Light Years; Link; The Little Prince; The Lodger (1926); The Lodger (1932); The Lodger (1944); Logan's Run; Looker; The Lord of the Rings; Mad Max; Mad Max Beyond Thunderdome; Man Made Monster; The Man Who Fell to Earth; The Man Who Reclaimed His Head; The Man with Nine Lives; The Man with Two Brains; Man's Best Friend; Manitou; Marooned; Master of the World; Maximum Overdrive; The Medusa Touch; Meet the Applegates; Memoirs of an Invisible Man; Mephisto Waltz; Meteor; Mighty Joe Young; Millennium; Mind Benders; The Mind of Mr. Soames; Miracle Mile; The Mole People; Mom and Dad Save the World; Monolith; Mothra; Murder by Television; Murder, He Says; My Stepmother Is an Alien; Mysterious Island; Nature of the Beast; The Neverending Story; The Neverending Story II: The Next Chapter; The New Barbarians; New Nightmare; The Night Has a Thousand Eyes; Night of the Comet; The Night Stalker/The Night Strangler; Nightmare on Elm Street Four; Nightmare on Elm Street Part Three; Nightmare on Elm Street Part Two; Nightmare on Elm Street: The Dream Child; 1984 (1955); 1984 (1984); The Ninth Configuration; Nomads; Not of This Earth (1956); The Omega Man; The Omen; Omen IV: The Awakening; On the Beach; Outland; Panic in the Year Zero; The People That Time Forgot; Phantasm; Phantasm II; Philadelphia Experiment; Plan 9 From Outer Space; Planet of the Apes; Poltergeist; Poltergeist 2; Poltergeist 3; The Possession of Joel Delaney; The Prisoner: Arrival; Pulse; The Puppetmasters; The Quatermass Experiment; Queen of Outer Space; Quintet; The Raven (1963); Re-Animator; Re-Animator 2; Repo Man; Return of the Fly; Return to Oz; Revenge of Frankenstein; Road Warrior; Robinson Crusoe on Mars; Robocop; Robocop 2; Rock-a Doodle; The Rocketeer; The Rocky Horror Picture Show; Runaway; Running Man (1987); Salem's Lot; Saturn 3; Scanner Cop; Scanners; Scanners II, The New Order; Seconds; The Seven Faces of Dr. Lao; The Seventh Sign; The Shadow (1940); The Shadow (1994); She (1935); She (1965); Sheena, Queen of the Jungle; Silent Running; Slaughterhouse Five; Sleeper; Slipstream; Solarbabies; Solaris; Something Wicked This Way Comes; Soylent Green; Spacehunter, Adventures in the Forbidden Zone; Sphinx; Spirit of '76; The Stand; Stargate; Star Trek: Generations; Star Wars; The Stepford Wives; Strange Invaders; Superman; Superman 2; Superman 3; Superman 4; Swamp Thing; Sword & the Sorcerer; Tank Girl; Terminal Man; Terminator; Terminator 2: Judgment Day; Them!; They Live; The Thing (1951); The Thing (1982); Things to Come; This Island Earth; THX1138; Time after Time; TimeCop; Time Machine; The Time Runner; Timerider; Tommyknockers; Total Recall; Toxic Avenger; Toxic Avenger, Part II; Toxic Avenger Part III; Trog; Tron; 20,000 Leagues Under the Sea; 2001: A Space Odyssey; 2010; Twilight Zone: The Movie; Twisted; The Unholy; Universal Soldier; The Unnamable Returns; Until the End of the World; Videodrome; Village of the Damned; War of the Worlds; Warlock (1989); Warning Sign; Watcher in the Woods; Watchers; Watchers II; Westworld; What's Up, Tiger Lily?; When Dinosaurs Ruled the Earth; When Worlds Collide; White Zombie; Wild Palms; Wilder Napalm; Willow; The Witches of Eastwick; The Wizard of Oz (1925); The Wizard of Oz (1939); X-The Man with X-Ray Eyes; Zardoz; Zero Population Growth (Z.P.G.)

SCI-FI/Science Fiction-1950s: see also *Paranoia: Camp: HORROR: Cold War Era:* Attack of the 50-Foot Woman (1958); Attack of the 50-Foot Woman (1993); Brain Eaters; Enemy from Space; Forbidden Planet; Invaders from Mars (1953); Invasion of the Body Snatchers (1956); It Came From Outer Space; Plan 9 From Outer Space; Them!; The Thing (1951); This Island Earth; War of the Worlds; When Worlds Collide

Scientists: see also *Scientists-Mad: Scientists as Detectives: Archaeologists: Inventors: Geniuses: Biographies: SCI-FI: Experiments:* Altered States; The Andromeda Strain; Arabesque; Atomic City; Awakenings; Baby, Secret of the Lost Legend; Back to the Future; Back to the Future 2; Back to the Future 3; Bloodbath at the House of Death; Brainstorm (1983); A Brief History of Time; Bullseye!; Cameron's Closet; Cloak and Dagger (1946); Darkman; Day of the Dead; Day of the Dolphin; Day One; Demon Seed; Die Laughing; Dr. Ehrlich's Magic Bullet; Dreamscape; Fantastic Voyage; Flatliners; Fluffy; The Fly (1958); The Fly (1986); The Fly II; Fury (1978); Goldengirl; Gorillas in the Mist; The Great Moment; The Groundstar Conspiracy; Hello Down There; His Brother's Wife; Horror Express; I,

Monster; I.Q.; Iceman; Invisible Ray; Ipcress File; Junior; Jurassic Park; Last of His Tribe; The Lawnmower Man; Link; Love Potion #9; Lover Come Back (1961); Lunch on the Grass; Madame Curie; Man in the White Suit; Man Made Monster; Medicine Man; Meteor; Mind Benders; Monkey Business (1952); Monkey Shines; Mr. Forbush & The Penguins; Murderer's Row; Never Cry Wolf; Nightwing; The Nutty Professor (1963); Operation Crossbow; Outbreak; The Passage; The Prize; Return of the Fly; Rikky and Pete; Sakharov; Scott of the Antarctic; The Serpent and the Rainbow; Silent Running; Simon; Skullduggery; Story of Louis Pasteur; Swamp Thing; Terminal Man; This Island Earth; Time Machine; Trog; Warning Sign; Who?; Woman in the Dunes

Scientists as Detectives: see also *Medical Detectives: Detectives-Amateur: Archaeologists*

Scientists-Mad: *Monsters: Monsters-Manmade: Experiments:* Adventure Island; The Adventures of Buckaroo Banzai Across the 8th Dimension; The Ape; Black Sleep; Blood Beast Terror; The Body Snatcher; The Boys from Brazil; The Bride; Bride of the Gorilla; Bride of the Monster; The Brood; The Cabinet of Caligari (1962); The Cabinet of Dr. Caligari (1919); The Doctor and the Devils; Doctor Jekyll and Mr. Hyde (1931); Donovan's Brain; Dr. Cyclops; Dr. Heckyl and Mr. Hype; Dr. Jekyll and Mr. Hyde (1941); Dr. Jekyll and Sister Hyde; Dr. M.; Ebb Tide; Frankenhooker; Frankenstein (1931); Frankenstein '70; Frankenstein and the Monster from Hell; Frankenstein Created Woman; Frankenstein Unbound; Freaked; House of Frankenstein; I, Monster; Island of Dr. Moreau (1977); Island of Lost Souls (1932); I Was a Teenage Frankenstein; I Was a Teenage Werewolf; Invisible Ray; The Invisible Woman; Kindred; Mad Love; The Man with Nine Lives; Master of the World; Mind Benders; Mysterious Island; North by Northwest; Our Man Flint; Philadelphia Experiment; The Raven (1935); The Raven (1963); Re-Animator; Re-Animator 2; Revenge of Frankenstein; Scanner Cop; Scream and Scream Again!; The Seven Faces of Dr. Lao; Splash!; Steagle; The Thousand Eyes of Dr. Mabuse; Transmutations; 20,000 Leagues Under the Sea; Watchers;

Watchers II; What's Up, Tiger Lily?; X-The Man with X-Ray Eyes

Scotland/Scottish People: see also *British Films: England: Ireland: Irish Films: Wales:* Battle of the Sexes; Bonnie Prince Charlie; Bonnie Scotland; Braveheart; Brigadoon; Comfort and Joy; A Fine Madness; Flesh and Blood (1951); Gregory's Girl; Hasty Heart; Heavenly Pursuits; Highlander; Highlander II-The Quickening; Highlander III, The Sorcerer; I Know Where I'm Going; The Little Minister; Local Hero; Lorna Doone; Mary of Scotland; Mary, Queen of Scots; Rob Roy; Shallow Grave; The Three Lives of Thomasina; Whiskey Galore

Screwball Comedy (usually made during the 1930s, it features madcap antics, often involving the wealthy, and is more intelligent and urbane than average comedy, particularly capers or action comedies of recent years): see also *Comedy of Errors: FARCE: Farce-Bedroom: Eccentric People: Heiresses-Madcap: Identities-Mistaken: Misunderstandings: Mix-Ups:* The Affairs of Cellini; After Office Hours; Alice; All of Me; Always Together; American Dreamer; Animal Crackers; Animal Kingdom; Are You Being Served?; Arthur; At the Circus; The Awful Truth; Baby Boom; The Beautiful Blonde from Bashful Bend; Bedtime Story (1941); The Belles of St. Trinians; Beyond Therapy; Blame It on the Bellboy; The Blessed Event; Blithe Spirit; Blondie; Bombshell; Breakfast for Two; Bringing Up Baby; Bullets Over Broadway; Carefree; Chances Are; The Cowboy and the Lady; Desperately Seeking Susan; The Discreet Charm of Bourgeoisie; The Doctor Takes a Wife; Duck Soup; Easy Living (1937); Easy to Wed; Eternally Yours; The Ex-Mrs. Bradford; A Fish Called Wanda; Fools for Scandal; Footlight Parade; For Pete's Sake; The Fortune; Fool's a Crowd; Go Chase Yourself; Grace Quigley; The Guest Wife; Harvey; He Married His Wife; Heaven Can Wait (1978); His Girl Friday; Hold Me, Thrill Me, Kiss Me; Horse Feathers; Housesitter; I'll Take Sweden; Illegally Yours; The Invisible Woman; Invitation to Happiness; It Happened One Night; Joy of Living; LaChevre; Libeled Lady; Life Stinks!; Loose Ankles; Love Before Breakfast; Love Crazy; Love in Bloom; Love on the

Run (1936); Lust in the Dust; Mad Miss Manton; The Man Who Came to Dinner; The Man with Two Brains; Man's Favorite Sport?; The Masquerader; The Merry Wives of Reno; Midnight (1939); Monkey Business (1952); Moonlighting (1985); My Favorite Wife; My Man Godfrey (1936); One Woman or Two; Over Her Dead Body; Overboard; The Owl and the Pussycat; Palm Beach Story; Platinum Blonde; Pure Luck; The Ref; The Road to Wellville; Scavenger Hunt; Sleeper; Soapdish; Some Like it Hot; Something Wild (1986); Star of Midnight; Sullivan's Travels; Swept Away; Switching Channels; Sylvia Scarlett; Ten; That Uncertain Feeling; Theodora Goes Wild; They Knew What They Wanted; The Thin Man; Three Fugitives; Tom, Dick and Harry; Too Many Husbands; Topper; Topper Returns; Topper Takes a Trip; Trading Places; Travels with My Aunt; Trouble in Paradise; True Confession; Twentieth Century; The Two-Faced Woman; Wedding Present; What's Up, Doc?; Who's That Girl?; Wife, Doctor and Nurse; Wife, Husband and Friend; Wife Versus Secretary; Without Reservations; You Belong to Me; You Can't Run Away From It; You Can't Take It With You (1938); You Can't Take It With You (1986); The Young in Heart

Scuba: see *Divers: Swimming: Underwater Adventure*

Sea Adventure: see *Adventure at Sea: also Pirates: Treasure Hunts: Journeys: Sailing: Islands*

Sea Creatures: see *Monsters-Underwater: Monsters-Animal: Adventure at Sea*

Search for Cure: see *Cure/Solutions-Search for*

Searches: see also *Missing Persons: Missing Person Thriller: Rescue Adventure/Drama: Bounty Hunters: Quests: Treasure Hunts: Chase Movies:* Atomic City; Big Jake; The Black Stallion Returns; The Black Windmill; Bushido Blade; Candy Mountain; Dangerous Crossing; Dark Crystal; Deadly Trap; Emerald Forest; F/X 2: The Deadly Art of Illusion; Farewell, My Lovely (1944); Farewell, My Lovely (1975); The French Lieutenant's Woman; The Fugitive (1993); Give My Regards to Broad Street; Goldwyn Follies; The Good, The Bad, & The Ugly; Hallelujah, I'm a Bum; Hardcore; Hide in Plain Sight; Indiana

Nervous Breakdowns: Mental Illness: Drugs-Addictions: Alcoholism

Selling One's Soul: see *Soul-Selling One's*

Senators: see *Congressmen/Senators: Politicians: Washington D.C.*

Senior Citizens: see *Elderly Men: Elderly Women*

Serial Killers: see also *Psycho Killers: MURDER: HORROR: Trail of a Killer: Murderers-Nice: Fugitive from a Murderer:* The Abominable Dr. Phibes; Afraid of the Dark; Alice, Sweet Alice; Alone in the Dark; American Gothic; Apartment Zero; The Arousers; Ashes and Diamonds; The Bad Seed (1956); The Bad Seed (1986); Basic Instinct; Bird With the Crystal Plumage; Black Christmas; Black Widow (1987); Blink; Blood and Black Lace; Blood from the Mummy's Tomb; Blue Steel; The Body Snatcher; The Boston Strangler; Chiefs; City in Fear; Cobra; Cop; Cop au Vin; Criminal Law; Cruising; Day of the Jackal; The Dead Pool; Deliberate Stranger; Dementia 13; Do You Like Women?; The Evictors; Exorcist III; Fade to Black (1979); First Power; Frankenhooker; Frenzy; Friday the 13th (1980); Friday the 13th: Final Chapter; Friday the 13th, Part 3-D; Friday the 13th, Part II; Friday the 13th Part V-A New Beginning; Friday the 13th Part VI-Jason Lives; Friday the 13th Part VII-The New Blood; Friday the 13th Part VIII-Jason Takes Manhattan; Ghost in the Machine; Ghoul (1975); The Good Son; Gorilla; The Great Lover (1949); Halloween 3: Season of the Witch; The Hand (1960); The Hand (1981); Happy Birthday to Me; He Knows You're Alone; Heathers; Helter Skelter (1976); Henry: Portrait of a Serial Killer; Hideaway; The Honeymoon Killers; It; Jack the Ripper (1958); Jack's Back; The January Man; Jennifer 8; Kalifornia; The Killer Inside Me; The Killer Nun; A Kiss Before Dying (1956); A Kiss Before Dying (1991); Knight Moves; The List of Adrian Messenger; The Little Girl Who Lives Down the Lane; M (1931); M (1951); Malice; Man Bites Dog; The Man in the Attic; Manhunter; Maniac Cop; Maniac Cop 2; Mean Season; Monsieur Verdoux; Mummy (1959); Murder by Decree; Murders in the Rue Morgue; Naked City; Natural Born Killers; Night Must Fall (1937); Night Must Fall (1964); Night of

the Generals; The Night Stalker/The Night Strangler; No Way to Treat a Lady; Pandemonium; Pandora's Box; Peeping Tom; Phantom of the Rue Morgue; Phobia; Prime Suspect; Prom Night SERIES; Psycho; Psycho 2; Psycho 3; Psycho 4; Raising Cain; Rampage; Relentless; Relentless 2; Relentless 3; Road Games; The Scarlet Claw; Scream and Scream Again!; Sea of Love; Serial Mom; Shadow of a Doubt; Shadows and Fog; The Shining; Shock to the System; Shock Treatment; Shocker; Shogun Assassin; Silence of the Lambs; Single White Female; The Sniper; Spiral Staircase (1946); Spiral Staircase (1975); Split Second; Step Down to Terror; Still of the Night; Strait Jacket; Striking Distance; Substitute; Sudden Impact; Sweeney Todd, Demon Barber of Fleet Street; Theater of Blood; They Drive by Night (1938); They Only Kill Their Masters; Tightrope; Time after Time; To Catch a Killer; Tower of London (1939); Tower of London (1962); The Town That Dreaded Sundown; The Vanishing (1988); The Vanishing (1993); When a Stranger Calls

Series-TV: see *TV Series:* also *Miniseries: TV Series Movies*

Serio-Comic: see *Tragi-Comedy: COMEDY DRAMA: Black Comedy*

Servants: see also *Romance with a Servant: Babysitters: Rich People: Slavery:* The Adventures of Bullwhip Griffin; Ali Baba and the Forty Thieves; Beware, My Lovely; The Courtship of Eddie's Father; Diary of a Chambermaid (1946); Diary of a Chambermaid (1963); Down and Out in Beverly Hills; The Dresser; Dying Young; Emma; Fancy Pants; The Farmer's Daughter; Fitzwilly; For Love of Ivy; Gone With the Wind; Hud; The Hireling; If You Could Only Cook; Imitation of Life (1934); Imitation of Life (1959); Jane Eyre (1934); Jane Eyre (1943); Jane Eyre (1971); Maid to Order; Maids; Man About the House; A Matter of Time; Merrily We Live; Momma, There's a Man in Your Bed; Mr. Music; Mrs. Parkington; My Man Godfrey (1936); My Man Godfrey (1956); Nothing but Trouble (1941); Princess Caraboo; The Remains of the Day; Ruggles of Red Gap; Rules of the Game; Sabrina; Sadie McKee; Santa Claus, The Movie; Scenes from the Class Struggle in Beverly Hills; Scent of Green Papaya; The Servant; That

Obscure Object of Desire; Tovarich; Valley of Decision; Venom

Settling Down (deciding to get married or at least stop drifting around and live a "normal" life): see also *Marriage-Impending: Engagements-Breaking: Marriage Comedy: Marriage Drama: Life Transitions: Playboys: Bachelors-Confirmed:* About Face; Alfie; Algiers; American Friends; A Bedtime Story (1933); Breakfast at Tiffany's; Breakfast for Two; Cash McCall; Diner; Every Girl Should be Married; Guys and Dolls; House Calls; The Hustler; If You Knew Susie; Je Vous Aime; Lifeguard; Live, Love and Learn; Mail Order Bride; Wyoming; You Were Never Lovelier

Sex Addicts: see *Promiscuity: Sexy Men: Sexy Women: Bimbos: Bimboys: Playboys*

Sex Changes: see *Transsexuals: Men as Women: Women as Men: Role Reversals*

Sex Comedy (the battle of the sexes romantic comedy popular in the '50s and '60s, which had no real sex displayed as is the case today, particularly in "erotic" comedies or "sexploitation"): see also *Romantic Comedy: Screwball Comedy: FARCE: Farce-Bedroom: Erotic Comedy: Romance-Opposites Attract: Battle of the Sexes: Teenage Movies:* Almost Pregnant; Ask Any Girl; Bilitis; Boeing-Boeing; Boys' Night Out; Casual Sex?; The Caveman; Chastity Belt; Come September; Facts of Life; Faster Pussycat! Kill! Kill!; Funny About Love; The Grass Is Greener; Here We Go Round the Mulberry Bush; High Heels; Hoffman; House Calls; I Married a Woman; I'm No Angel; If a Man Answers; Las Vegas Hillbillies; The Last Married Couple in America; Last of the Red Hot Lovers; Little Darlings; Losin' It; Loverboy; No Sex, Please, We're British; Oh Men! Oh Women!; Peter's Friends; Pillow Talk; Promises! Promises!; Send Me No Flowers; Sex and the Single Girl; Sextette; Sibling Rivalry; Strange Bedfellows; Such Good Friends; Sunday in New York; Surrender; That Touch of Mink; Three on a Couch; The Thrill of It All

Sex Crimes/Offenders: see *Incest: Rape/Rapists: Molestation: Serial Killers: Sexual Harassment*

Sexism: see *Sexual Harassment: Bigots: Women Against Male Establishment*

Sexploitation (B-movies bordering on pornography, usually humorous): see *Erotic Comedy: Bimbos: Bimboys: Pornography World*

Sexual Assault: see *Rape/Rapists: Molestation-Child: Incest*

Sexual Harassment: see also *Rape/Rapists: Sexual Assault: Sexism:* Barbary Coast; Business as Usual; Candy; Disclosure; Hand that Rocks the Cradle; The Homecoming (1973); Nine to Five; Rita, Sue and Bob, Too; Sebastiane; Term of Trial

Sexuality (in general): see also *Sexual Problems: Coming of Age: Virgins: Lovers-Unsatisfied: Sexual Kinkiness: Swapping Partners:* Blue Lagoon (1948); Blue Lagoon (1980); Carnal Knowledge; Casual Sex?; The Chapman Report; The Chicken Chronicles; Consenting Adult; The Devil's Playground; A Different Story; Dr. Ehrlich's Magic Bullet; Emmanuelle SERIES; Equus; Every Thing You Always Wanted to Know About Sex . . .; Ex-Lady; Freud; Fun Down There; The Harrad Experiment; The Harrad Summer; Heaven Help Us; The Homecoming (1973); I Love My Wife; Lady Chatterly's Lover (1955); Lady Chatterly's Lover (1981); Last Tango in Paris; Lola (1982); Looking for Mr. Goodbar; Love Goddesses; Lovers and Other Strangers; Luna; Making Love; The Man Who Loved Women (1977); The Man Who Loved Women (1983); Me and Him; Monty Python's The Meaning of Life; The Moon Is Blue; Move; Negatives; Night and Day; Night Games; The Night is Young; Noir et Blanc; A Rage to Live; The Rainbow; Rapture; Rita, Sue and Bob, Too; Room at the Top; Satyricon (Fellini's); The Scarlet Letter (1926); The Scarlet Letter (1934); The Scarlet Letter (1980); Sex and the Single Girl; Statue; Ten; Tie Me Up! Tie Me Down!; The Trials of Oscar Wilde; W.H.I.F.F.S.; Women in Love; The World Is Full of Married Men; You're a Big Boy Now

Sexual Kinkiness: see also *Sexuality: Sexual Problems: Alternative Lifestyles: Sexy Men: Sexy Women: Erotic Thrillers: Erotic Drama: Pornography World: Swapping Partners:* Baby Doll; Dark Obsession; The Hairdresser's Husband; Look in Any Window; Maitresse; Menage; The Night Porter; Noir et Blanc; Preppie Murder; Pretty Baby; Salo: 120 Days of Sodom; Tie Me Up! Tie Me Down!; Tightrope; Tokyo Decadence

Sexual Problems (impotence, frigidity, etc.): see also *Sexuality: Sexual Kinkiness: Promiscuity: Spinsters: Bachelors-Confirmed: Gay Awakenings:* Almost Pregnant; Blindfold: Acts of Obsession; Bolero (1984); Cat on a Hot Tin Roof (1958); Cat on a Hot Tin Roof (1984); The Chapman Report; Freud; Fun Down There; Get Out Your Handkerchiefs; Getting It Right; Ghostwriter; Hard Contract; The Harrad Experiment; The Harrad Summer; The Homecoming (1973); It's Pat; Joshua Then and Now; Look in Any Window; Maitresse; The Offence; A Period of Adjustment; The Priest; A Rage to Live; Reflections in a Golden Eye; Repulsion; Rita, Sue and Bob, Too; The Road to Wellville; Ruling Class; Separate Tables; Sirens; Spanking the Monkey; Tea and Sympathy; Three on a Couch; THX 1138; Trash; The Trials of Oscar Wilde; W.H.I.F.F.S.

Sexual Revolution (the late '60s and '70s when experimentation became fashionable): see also *1970s: Disco Era: Hippies: Anti-Establishment Films: Orgies: Alternative Lifestyles: Swapping Partners: Promiscuity: Pornography World:* Bob & Carol & Ted & Alice; Gassss; The Harrad Experiment; The Harrad Summer; I Will . . . I Will . . . for Now; Is There Sex After Death?; John and Mary; The Last Married Couple in America; Looking for Mr. Goodbar; Love Machine; Loving Couples; The Marriage of a Young Stockbroker; Move; Ritz; Stud; Taking Off; Turkish Delight; Welcome to L.A.; Where Does It Hurt?

Sexy Men (particularly so, as a point of the story): see also *Playboys: Bimboys: Prostitutes-Male: Erotic Thrillers: Erotic Drama: Promiscuity: Wild People: Evil Men: Sexploitation:* The Adventurers; The Adventures of Don Juan; Alvin Purple; Alvin Rides Again; American Gigolo; Andy Warhol's Dracula; Apartment Zero; The Arousers; Ash Wednesday; Aspen Extreme; Banning; Barbarella; The Bawdy Adventures of Tom Jones; Beau Brummell (1924); Beau Brummell (1954); Bitch (1979); Blood and Concrete; Breathless (1959); Breathless (1983); Bull Durham; Butch Cassidy and the Sundance Kid; Bye Bye Birdie; Campus Man; Captain Ron; Carousel; Casanova '70; Casanova (Fellini's Casanova); The Charmer; A Chorus of Disapproval; Dark Obsession; Doctor Quinn, Medicine Woman; Entertaining Mr. Sloane; Female on the Beach; A Fine Madness; Flash Gordon; Foolish Wives; The Frog Prince; The Great Gatsby (1949); The Great Gatsby (1974); Hold Your Man; In Praise of Older Women; Interview with the Vampire; Jailhouse Rock; Johnny Suede; La Dolce Vita; La Maschera; Let's Get Lost; Letter From an Unknown Woman; Lifeguard; Little Fauss and Big Halsey; Love God?; Love Has Many Faces; Love Machine; The Man Who Loved Women (1977); The Man Who Loved Women (1983); Mask of the Avenger; My Tutor; Night in Heaven; Personal Property; Picnic; The Picture of Dorian Gray; The Preppie Murder; The Private Affairs of Bel Ami; Risk; The Roman Spring of Mrs. Stone; Scene of the Crime; The School for Husbands; Sextette; Shampoo; Sheik; Sliver; Smooth Talk; Thief of Hearts; Thoroughly Modern Millie; To Catch a Thief; Tom Jones; Top Gun; Two Moon Junction; Valentino (1951); Valentino (1977); The Virgin and the Gypsy; Warm Nights on a Slow Moving Train; The Way We Were; Where the Boys Are '84; White Mischief; Who's Been Sleeping in My Bed?; Wild Orchid; The Wild Party; The World's Greatest Lover; Wuthering Heights (1939); Wuthering Heights (1953); Wuthering Heights (1970); Wuthering Heights (1992); Yesterday, Today and Tomorrow; Yesterday's Hero

Sexy Women (particularly so, as a point of the story): see also *Playgirls: Bimbos: Prostitutes: Erotic Thrillers: Erotic Drama: Promiscuity: Older Women Seducers: Wild People: Evil Women: Sexploitation:* The Adventurers; The Adventures of Sadie; Algiers; Alvin Purple; Alvin Rides Again; The Amorous Adventures of Moll Flanders; And God Created Woman (1957); And God Created Woman (1988); April Fools; Auntie Lee's Meat Pies; Babette Goes to War; Baby Doll; Baby Face; Bachelor Party (1957); Bad Timing: A Sensual Obsession; Barbarella; Becoming Colette; Biggest Bundle of Them All; Bitch (1979); Blood and Concrete; Blue Sky; Bocaccio '70; Body of Evidence; Bombshell; Bound and Gagged, a Love Story; Boy, Did I Get a Wrong Number!; Boy on a Dolphin; Boys on the Side; Breathless (1959); Breathless (1983); Bull Durham; Bus Stop; Butterfly; Candy; Casanova '70; Casanova (Fellini's Casanova); Cat Women of the Moon; A Change of Seasons; Clan of the Cave Bear; Claudelle Inglish; Cocoon; Cocoon, The Return; Color of Night; Cool World; Cover Girl; Damn Yankees; Dark Obsession; The Deep; Desire Under the Elms; Desperately Seeking Susan; The Devil is a Woman; Diary of a Chambermaid (1946); Diary of a Chambermaid (1963); Disturbed; Doctor Detroit; Doctor's Wives; Don't Bother to Knock; Don't Make Waves; Double Threat; Emmanuelle SERIES; Every Day's A Holiday; Experiment Perilous; The Fabulous Baker Boys; Fanny Hill; Faster Pussycat! Kill! Kill!; Fathom; The Final Analysis; First Time; Flame of New Orleans; Flamingo Road; Flare Up; Flash Gordon; Flashdance; Flesh and the Devil; Forever Amber; Frenchie; Gabriela; Gentlemen Prefer Blondes; George White's 1935 Scandals; George White's Scandals (1934); George White's Scandals 1945; Ghost in the Invisible Bikini; Gilda; Girl Can't Help It; Girls! Girls! Girls!; Go West Young Man; Goddess; Goin' To Town; Goldfinger; Good Neighbor Sam; The Gorgeous Hussy; Grasshopper; Heartbreak Kid; Heller in Pink Tights; Her Alibi; Hold Your Man; Houseboat; How to Marry a Millionaire; How to Murder Your Wife; I Don't Buy Kisses Anymore; I Take this Woman; In Praise of Older Women; The Josephine Baker Story; Kiss Them For Me; Klute; La Dolce Vita; La Lectrice; Lady Chatterly's Lover (1955); Lady Chatterly's Lover (1981); Lady in Red; Lady L.; Last Summer; Lipstick; Love God?; Love Goddesses; The Lover; Loves of Carmen; Lovin' Molly; Man of Flowers; The Man Who Loved Women (1977); The Man Who Loved Women (1983); Mannequin (1987); Mannequin 2: On the Move; Manpower; Marilyn, the Untold Story; Marriage Go Round; Mata Hari (1931); Mata Hari (1985); Mata Hari, Agent H21 (1964); Million Dollar Legs; Miss Sadie Thompson; Morocco; Mother, Jugs & Speed; My Little Chickadee; My Stepmother Is an Alien; My Tutor; Niagara; Night and Day; The Night They

Raided Minsky's; Nudo di Donna; Octopussy; Oh Men! Oh Women!; On Her Majesty's Secret Service; Once Is Not Enough; One Touch of Venus; The Outlaw; Pauline at the Beach; Personal Property; Poison Ivy (1992); The Prince and the Showgirl; Promises! Promises!; Public Eye; A Rage in Harlem; A Rage to Live; The Rain; Rally Round the Flag, Boys; Rambling Rose; Repulsion; Romeo Is Bleeding; Ruby Gentry; Saratoga; Seven Sinners; The Seven-Year Itch; Sextette; Shampoo; She Done Him Wrong; She's Gotta Have It; Sliver; Some Like it Hot; Spetters; Splash!; Stakeout; Star 80; Tales of Hoffman; Ten; That Kind of Woman; There's a Girl in My Soup; They All Laughed; To Catch a Thief; Top Gun; Travels with My Aunt; Tristana; Two Moon Junction; What?; What's New Pussycat?; When Dinosaurs Ruled the Earth; Where the Boys Are '84; White Cargo; Who's That Girl?; Widows' Peak; Wild Orchid; The Wild Party; Will Success Spoil Rock Hunter?; Wives and Lovers; Woman in Red; Yesterday, Today and Tomorrow; You Were Never Lovelier; You'll Never Get Rich

Sidekicks-Wisecracking: see *Wisecracking Sidekicks: Friendships*

Shakespeare (adaptations of the Master): see also *Elizabethan Era: WRITERS' FILMOGRAPHIES:* Aaron Loves Angela; As You Like It (1936); As You Like It (1992); Chimes at Midnight; Henry V (1944); Henry V (1989); Men of Respect; Otello; Othello (1951); Othello (1965); Ran; Richard III; Romeo and Juliet (1936); Romeo and Juliet (1954); Romeo and Juliet (1968); Throne of Blood

Sharing a Home: see *Roommates: Roommates from Hell: Comedy-Situation: Boarding Schools: Affair Lairs*

Sharks: see also *Animal Monsters: Fish: Sea Adventures:* Ace Ventura, Pet Detective; Blue Water, White Death; Islands in the Stream; Jaws SERIES; Shark!

Shelley Winters Drowns: see also *Drownings:* Night of the Hunter; A Place in the Sun; The Poseidon Adventure

Sherlock Holmes: see also *Detective Stories: Detectives-Private:* The Adventures of Sherlock Holmes; The Adventures of Sherlock Holmes' Smarter Brother; Crucifer of Blood; The Great Mouse Detective; Hound of the Basker-

villes (1939); Hound of the Baskervilles (1959); Hound of the Baskervilles (1977); Murder by Decree; The Private Life of Sherlock Holmes; The Scarlet Claw; The Seven Percent Solution; Sherlock Holmes; Sherlock Holmes and the Secret Weapon; Sherlock Holmes and the Spider Woman; Sherlock Holmes and the Voice of Terror; Sherlock Holmes Faces Death; Sherlock Holmes in Washington; Sherlock Holmes: The Spider Woman Strikes Back; Terror By Night; They Might be Giants; Without a Clue; Young Sherlock Holmes

Ships-Cruise or General types: see also *Ship Wrecks: Vacations: Sailing: Islands:* An Affair to Remember; All the Brothers Were Valiant; And the Ship Sails On; The Baby and the Battleship; Barnacle Bill (1957); Beat the Devil; The Bedford Incident; Beyond the Poseidon Adventure; Billy Budd; Bitter Moon; Blackbeard, The Pirate; Botany Bay; The Caine Mutiny (1954); The Caine Mutiny Court Martial (1988); Captain Kidd; Chained; China Seas; A Countess from Hong Kong; Dangerous Crossing; Death on the Nile; Fitzcarraldo; The Fog; Four Frightened People; The Girl Who Couldn't Say No; The Great Lover (1949); Greek Tycoon; The Hairy Ape; Johnny Angel; Juggernaut; Krakatoa, East of Java; Lady Eve; Last Voyage; Light at the Edge of the World; Lightship; The Long Voyage Home; Love Affair (1939); Majority of One; Midnight Crossing; Mister Roberts; Moby Dick; Monkey Business (1931); Mutiny on the Bounty (1935); Mutiny on the Bounty (1962); Nancy Goes to Rio; Navigator; A Night to Remember (1958); One Way Passage; The Poseidon Adventure; Promises! Promises!; Querelle; Raise the Titanic!; Romance on the High Seas; Scared Stiff; Sea Beast; The Sea Chase; Ship of Fools; Showboat (1936); Showboat (1951); Souls at Sea; The Story of Three Loves; Table for Five; Tamango; Titanic; Twilight for the Gods; Under Siege; Voyage of the Damned; Wings of Fame

Shipwrecked: see also *Disaster Movies: Sailing: Stranded: Islands:* The Adventures of Eliza Frazer; The Adventures of Robinson Crusoe; The Adventures of Sadie; Benji the Hunted; Beyond the Poseidon Adventure; Crusoe; Far From Home; Gulliver's Travels (1939); Gulliver's Travels (1976); Island of Dr. Moreau (1977); Island of Lost Souls (1932); The Land that Time Forgot; The Last Voyage; Lifeboat; Man Friday; Mysterious Island; A Night to Remember (1958); Raise the Titanic!; Return to the Blue Lagoon; The Sea Wife; Sea Wolf; Souls at Sea; The Swiss Family Robinson; Titanic; Too Many Husbands; 20,000 Leagues Under the Sea; The Unsinkable Molly Brown; Whiskey Galore; The Wreck of the Mary Deare

Shore Leave (usually involving sailors; the story taking place during their shore leave): see also *Sailors:* Abroad with Two Yanks; Born to Dance; Cinderella Liberty; Follow the Fleet; Hit the Deck; Kiss Them For Me; On the Town; Two Girls and a Sailor

Shrinking People: see also *SCI-FI: Magic: Giant People: Miniature People: Experiments: Scientists-Mad:* The Borrowers; Dr. Cyclops; Fantastic Voyage; Honey, I Shrunk the Kids; The Incredible Shrinking Man; Innerspace; The Seventh Voyage of Sinbad

Shy People: see also *Wallflowers: Nerds: Extroverted vs. Introverted: Lonely People: Spinsters: Life Transitions:* Alice; An Angel at My Table; Ball of Fire; Four Weddings and a Funeral; Marty; Metropolitan (1990); The Pad, and How to Use It; Seven Chances; The Seventh Cavalry; A Song Is Born; The Sterile Cuckoo

Siblings (when the focus is on male and female siblings together): see also *Brothers: Sisters: Family Comedy: Family Drama: Twins: Feuds:* All the Brothers Were Valiant; All the Fine Young Cannibals; Alpine Fire; Blood Relatives; The Brady Bunch Movie; Bunny Lake is Missing; Chase a Crooked Shadow; Close My Eyes; Crooklyn; Daddy's Dyin'; Dark at the Top of the Stairs; Days of Heaven; El Norte; Escape to Witch Mountain; Fool for Love; Forty Guns; Fury (1978); Goodbye Gemini; A Home of Our Own; The House of Seven Gables; The House of Usher (1960); The House of Usher (1990); I Sent a Letter to My Love; Kings Row; Labyrinth; The Legend of Billie Jean; Les Enfants Terribles; Love Streams; Lucretia Borgia; Mad Monkey; The Man with Two Faces; Marlowe; No Deposit, No Return; Paranoia; Passed Away; The Pit and the Pendulum (1961); The Pit and the Pendulum (1991); The Possession of Joel

Delaney; The Prince of Tides; Return from Witch Mountain; Rikky and Pete; So Long at the Fair; Steelyard Blues; Sunday in New York; Sweet Smell of Success; Tillie and Gus; To Kill a Mockingbird; Toys in the Attic; Trail of the Lonesome Pine; The Uninvited; White Rose

Silent Film Era (set during, but not necessarily silent): see also *Silent Films: Hollywood Life: 1920s: Roaring '20s:* The Cameraman; Chaplin; Comic; Four Clowns; Good Morning, Babylon; Heart of the West; Inserts; Man of a Thousand Faces; A Matter of Time; Maxie; Perils of Pauline; Silent Movie; Singing in the Rain; Sunset; Valentino (1951); Valentino (1977); Whatever Happened to Baby Jane?; The Wild Party; Won Ton Ton, the Dog Who Saved Hollywood; The World's Greatest Lover

Silent Films: see also *Silent Film Era: Film History:* America (1924); Arsenal; The Birth of a Nation; Blind Husbands; The Crowd; Intolerance; Mark of Zorro (1920); The Merry Widow (1925); Modern Times; Nanook of the North; Napoleon; Pandora's Box; Passion/Madame Dubarry (1919); Silent Movie; Strike; The Thief of Bagdad (1924); Tillie's Punctured Romance; Uncle Tom's Cabin (1914); Way Down East (1920); Way of All Flesh (1928); Wedding March; The Wizard of Oz (1925)

Simple Minds: see also *Childlike People: Fools-Bumbling: Criminals-Stupid: Bimbos: Bimboys: Rednecks:* Aaron Slick from Punkin Crick; After Dark, My Sweet; Airheads; All Night Long (1981); All That Heaven Allows; Awakenings; Being There; Big; Bill & Ted's Bogus Journey; Bill & Ted's Excellent Adventure; Blondie; Born Yesterday (1950); Born Yesterday (1993); Candy; Charly; Dumb and Dumber; Encino Man; A Fish Called Wanda; Forrest Gump; The Gods Must Be Crazy; The Gods Must Be Crazy II; Harvey; I Love You to Death; The Jerk; The Killers (1946); Lady Eve; The Lawnmower Man; Let Him Have It; Light in the Piazza; Little Big Man; Midnight Cowboy; Miss Grant Takes Richmond; Nell; New Leaf; The Pink Panther; Private Benjamin; Protocol; Radio Days; Rain Man; Rocky; Rocky II; Rocky III; Rocky IV; Rocky V; The Saint of Fort Washington; The Scout; Sergeant York; The Seven-Year Itch;

Simon; Singles; Splash!; Star 80; Starman; Strange Brew; This is Spinal Tap; Thoroughly Modern Millie; Tim; Valley Girl

Singers: see also *Musicians: MUSICALS: Music Dies: Country Singers: Opera Singers: Teen Idols: Dance Movies: Biographies: Theater Life: Music Video Style:* About Face; Absolute Beginners; The Adventures of Ford Fairlane; Almost Angels; American Hotwax; And God Created Woman (1988); Baby, The Rain Must Fall; Barbary Coast; Bathing Beauty; Beaches; Beyond the Valley of the Dolls; The Big Street; Birth of the Blues; Blame it on the Night; Blonde Venus; Blue Angel (1930); Blue Angel (1959); Blue Hawaii; The Blues Brothers; Bobo; The Bodyguard; Bound for Glory; Boys on the Side; Breaking Glass; Broadway Melody; Broadway Melody of 1936; Broadway Melody of 1938; Broadway Melody of 1940; The Buddy Holly Story; Bus Stop; Bye Bye Birdie; Cabaret; Christmas Holiday; Clock; Coal Miner's Daughter; The Cool Ones; Darling Lili; Diamond Horseshoe; Diva; Divine Madness; Dixie; Dolly Sisters; Don't Look Back; Doors; Easy to Love; Elvis: The Movie; Expresso Bongo; The Fabulous Baker Boys; A Face in the Crowd; Fame; Fear of a Black Hat; The Five Heartbeats; The Flame of the Barbary Coast; Footlight Parade; For the Boys; Funny Lady; The Gang's All Here; Gentlemen Prefer Blondes; Girls! Girls! Girls!; Give My Regards to Broad Street; Give My Regards to Broadway; Good Times; Graffiti Bridge; Great Balls of Fire; The Great Caruso; The Great Lover (1931); Hail, Hail, Rock n Roll; Harum Scarum; The Harvey Girls; Hear My Song; The Helen Morgan Story; Hello Frisco Hello; High Heels; The Hit Parade of 1941; The Hit Parade of 1947; Holiday in Mexico; Honeysuckle Rose; Honkytonk Man; I Could Go on Singing; I Don't Care Girl; I Dream Too Much; I'll Cry Tomorrow; I'll See You in My Dreams; Idolmaker; Inside Daisy Clover; Interrogation; Interrupted Melody; Ironweed; It Happened in Brooklyn; The Jazz Singer (1927); The Jazz Singer (1953); The Jazz Singer (1980); Jinxed; Johnny Suede; Jolson Sings Again; The Jolson Story; The Josephine Baker Story; Joy of Living; King Creole; King of Jazz; Kiss Me Kate (1953); Kiss Me, Stupid!;

La Bamba; Lady Sings the Blues; Lili Marleen; Lisztomania; Live a Little, Love a Lot; Lola (1982); Looking for Love; Love Me or Leave Me; Lucky Me; Luna; Masculine, Feminine; Meet Danny Wilson; Meeting Venus; Metropolitan (1935); Mississippi; Music For Millions; Music in My Heart; My Wild Irish Rose; Nancy Goes to Rio; Nashville; Naughty Marietta; New York, New York; No Small Affair; Norwood; One Trick Pony; Out of This World; Panama Hattie; The Perfect Couple; Presenting Lily Mars; Pure Country; Rancho Notorious; Random Harvest; Rebecca of Sunnybrook Farm (1938); Reckless (1935); Red Garters; Rhinestone; Rhythm on the Range; River of No Return; Romance on the High Seas; The Rose; The Roustabout; San Francisco; Say Amen, Somebody!; Seven Sinners; Showboat (1936); Showboat (1951); Sinatra; Sing Baby Sing; Singing Fool; The Singing Nun; Sister Act; Sister Act 2; Six Pack; Smashing Time; Sparkle; Speedway; Spinout; St. Louis Blues; Star!; A Star Is Born (1954); A Star Is Born (1976); Starstruck; Starting Over; The Stooge; Streets of Fire; Svengali (1931); Svengali (1983); Sweet Dreams; Tender Mercies; Thank God It's Friday; Thing Called Love; Three Little Words; Tickle Me; Tin Pan Alley; Tokyo Pop; Truth or Dare; Under the Cherry Moon; Valley of the Dolls; Victor/Victoria; Viva Las Vegas; Voices; Wait 'Til the Sun Shines, Nellie; Where Were You When the Lights Went Out?; Who Is Harry Kellerman . . .; Wife, Husband and Friend; Wild in the Country; Wonder Bar; Yankee Doodle Dandy; Yellow Canary; Yellow Submarine; Yes, Giorgio

Singer Dies: see *Music Dies*

Single Men (where being unmarried has its problems, with or without kids): see also *Fathers Alone: Playboys: Lonely People: Settling Down: Bachelors-Confirmed:* Alfie; The Bachelor; Breaking Up is Hard to Do; Can She Bake a Cherry Pie?; Crossing Delancey; Driftwood; Every Girl Should be Married; Getting It Right; I Will . . . I Will . . . for Now; John and Mary; Live, Love and Learn; The Lonely Guy; Lonely Hearts; The Odd Couple; Oliver's Story; Paternity; Sleepless in Seattle; Taxi zum Klo; Where's Poppa?

Single Parents: see *Fathers Alone: Mothers Alone*

Single Women (where being unmarried has its problems, with or without kids): see also *Mothers Alone: Spinsters: Lonely People: Settling Down:* Angie; Back Street (1932); Back Street (1941); Back Street (1961); Bells Are Ringing; Bodies, Rest & Motion; Broadcast News; Bull Durham; Can She Bake a Cherry Pie?; Casual Sex?; The Color Purple; A Dangerous Woman; Echo Park; Every Girl Should be Married; Ex-Lady; Good Mother; I Will . . . I Will . . . for Now; Je Vous Aime; John and Mary; Kitty Foyle; Ladykiller (1992); A Life of Her Own; Looking for Mr. Goodbar; Lost Lady; Mating of Willie; Mayflower Madam; Nurse; O Pioneers!; One Is a Lonely Number; Pillow Talk; Playboys; Rapture; Slaves of New York; Sleepless in Seattle; T.R. Baskin; Unmarried Woman; Waiting For the Light

Sisters (when the focus is only on female siblings): see also *Siblings: Family Stories: Ensembles-Female: Brothers: Twins:* Anne and Muriel; Athena; Big Business; Body and Soul (1981); The Bodyguard; C'est la Vie; Cabin in the Cotton; Crimes of the Heart; The Dead; Dead Ringer; Dear Ruth; Dolly Sisters; Double Wedding; Experiment in Terror; The Final Analysis; For Love or Money (1963); Gas Food Lodging; Gay Sisters; Give Me a Sailor; Gone With the Wind; Green Dolphin Street; The Hard Way (1943); Hello Again; I Remember Mama; Interiors; Isn't it Romantic?; Like Water for Chocolate; Lipstick; Man About the House; Man in the Moon; Me & Veronica; Miss Firecracker; Music For Millions; My Forbidden Past; Night of the Comet; Our Dancing Daughters; Paid in Full; The Parent Trap; Peppermint Soda; The Seventh Victim; Sex, Lies, and Videotape; Sibling Rivalry; Sister, Sister; Sisters; Slipper and the Rose; A Stolen Life (1939); A Stolen Life (1946); Strapless; Sweetie; Three Sisters; Toys in the Attic; Whatever Happened to Baby Jane?; Where the Heart Is

Situation Comedy: see *Comedy-Situation:* also *COMEDY: FARCE: Roommates: Play Adaptations: TV Series*

Skating (ice skating): see also *Roller Skating: Hockey: Sports Movies: Party Movies: Skiing:* The Cutting Edge; D2: The Mighty Ducks; Ice Castles; The Mighty Ducks; My Lucky Star; One in a Million; Second Fiddle; Slap Shot; Snow White and the Three Stooges; Thin Ice

Skid Row: see *Inner City Life: Homeless People*

Skiing: see also *Sports Movies: Party Movies: Skating:* Aspen Extreme; Avalanche; Cliffhanger; Downhill Racer; Lost and Found; The Other Side of the Mountain; Ski School; Spellbound; The Two-Faced Woman

Skit Comedy: see *Comedy-Skit:* also *Character Comedy: Vaudeville: Saturday Night Live Movies*

Skydiving: see also *Air Daredevils: Airplanes:* Drop Zone; Gypsy Moths; Honeymoon in Vegas; Point Break; Terminal Velocity

Slapstick: see *Comedy-Slapstick: Comedy-Gag:* also *COMEDY: Screwball Comedy: FARCE: Comedy of Errors*

Slasher Movies: see *Serial Killers: Psycho Killers: HORROR: Crime Drama*

Slave to Love: see *Romance-Dangerous: Dangerous-Spouse: Love-Questionable: Obsessions: Fatal Attraction: Abusive Men: Abusive Women: Sexy Men: Sexy Women: Erotic Thrillers: Erotic Drama*

Slavery (black, white, otherwise): see also *Historical Drama: Early America: Civil War Era: Enemies-Sleeping with: Civil Rights: Race Relations: Black People: Black Films:* Ashanti: Land of No Mercy; The Autobiography of Miss Jane Pittman; Band of Angels; Black Rain (1989); Buck and the Preacher; Conquest of the Planet of the Apes; Cromwell; A Funny Thing Happened on the Way to the Forum; Hallelujah!; A Handmaid's Tale; Jefferson in Paris; Kidnapped (1938); Kidnapped (1959); Kidnapped (1971); La Strada; Lightning Jack; Lionheart; A Man Called Horse; Man Friday; Mandingo; Music of Chance; Nate and Hayes; Planet of the Apes; Pudd'nhead Wilson; Roots; Roots, the Gift; Skin Game; Spartacus; Tamango; Thoroughly Modern Millie; The Thousand Pieces of Gold; Uncle Tom's Cabin (1914); Uncle Tom's Cabin (1969)

Sleeper Hits (films that were hits, though they were not expected to be): see also *Hidden Gems: Overlooked at Release:* Ace Ventura, Pet Detective; The Adventures of the Wilderness Family; The Amityville Horror; Arthur; Back to School; Beauty and the Beast (1991); Benji; Bill & Ted's Excellent Adventure;

Small Countries: see *Kingdoms: Third World Countries*

Small-Town Life: see also *Ordinary People Stories: Small-Town Scandals: Rural Life: Working Class:* Aaron Slick from Punkin Crick; Ah, Wilderness; All Fall Down; All the Right Moves; Amarcord; American Graffiti; Americana; Amos and Andrew; Angel in My Pocket; Babbitt; Babes in Arms; Babes on Broadway; Baby Blue Marine; Bad Day at Black Rock; Bagdad Cafe; Barnacle Bill (1957); Bay Boy; Billy Liar; The Blob (1958); The Blob (1988); Blue City; Blue Velvet; The Body Snatchers; Brotherhood of Satan; Brothers; Calling Bulldog Drummond; Cheers for Miss Bishop; Choice of Arms; A Chorus of Disapproval; Cinema Paradiso; Cold Sassy Tree; Cold Turkey; Come Back, Little Sheba; Come to the Stable; Coup de Torchon; The Courtship; Dark at the Top of the Stairs; A Date with Judy; Dazed and Confused; The Deer Hunter; Diggstown; Doc Hollywood; Electra Glide in Blue; Endangered Species; End of the Line; Everybody Wins; The Experts; A Family Affair; Fat City; The Feud; Fiddler on the Roof; A Fire in the Sky; Firecreek; The Fireman's Ball; Flamingo Road; The Flim Flam Man; Follow Me, Boys!; Footloose; Four Daughters; Full Moon in Blue Water; The Ghost and Mr. Chicken; The Goddess; Good Sam; Grandview, USA; Gremlins; Groundhog Day; Grumpy Old Men; The Gun in Betty Lou's Handbag; A Gunfighter; Gypsy Moths; Hail the Conquering Hero; Halloween; Halloween 2; Halloween 4: The Return of Michael Myers; Halloween 5: The Revenge of Michael Myers; Handle with Care; Hard Country; Harper Valley P.T.A.; Heaven with a Gun; Heaven's Gate; Heimat; The Holly and the Ivy; A Home of Our Own; Honky Tonk Freeway; Hoosiers; Hot Spot; Hud; The Human Comedy; I Vitelloni; I Want You; Impulse (1984); In the Heat of the Night; The Indian Runner; The Inspector General; Invasion of the Body Snatchers (1956); It; It Happened to Jane; It Happens Every Thursday; It's a Small World; It's a Wonderful Life; J.W. Coop; Jersey Girl; The Kill-Off; The Killer Inside Me; Killing in a Small Town; King of Hearts; Kings Row; Kiss Me, Stupid!; The Last Picture Show; The Lawman; Le Corbeau; Liebestraum; Little Giants; Local Hero; The Lost Boys; Love Hurts; Loveless; Love Letters (1945); Lovin' Molly; Magic Town; Manon des Sources (1952); Manon des Sources (1986); Matinee; Maximum Overdrive; McClintock!; Medal for Benny; Mermaids; Ministry of Fear; Miracle of Morgan's Creek; The Miracle of the Bells; Miss Firecracker; Mississippi Masala; The Moon Is Down; More American Graffiti; Mother Carey's Chickens; The Music Man; My Reputation; Nature of the Beast; Necromancy; Never Take Sweets from a Stranger; Night of the Shooting Stars; 1918; 1969; 92 in the Shade; Nobody's Fool (1986); North Star; Norwood; Of Human Hearts; One Foot in Heaven; Only Two Can Play; Orchestra Wives; Our Town; Outrage (1964); Over Her Dead Body; Papa's Delicate Condition; Picnic; Places in the Heart; Playboys; Pollyanna; The Positively True Adventures of the Alleged Texas Cheerleader-Murdering Mom; The Promised Land; The Puppetmasters; Quest for Fire; The Quiet Man; Racing with the Moon; Raggedy Man; Rainmaker; Rambling Rose; Rancho De Luxe; Rebecca's Daughters; The Red Sky at Morning; Reflecting Skin; The Reivers; Return of Dracula; Return to Peyton Place; Rio Bravo; A River Runs Through It; Rosalie Goes Shopping; Roxanne; The Russians Are Coming, The Russians Are Coming; Ryan's Daughter; Scene of the Crime; Scorchers; Secret of Santa Vittoria; Sergeant Pepper's Lonely Hearts Club Band; Seventeen; Shadow of a Doubt; Shame (1987); She Couldn't Say No; Shout; Silkwood; Sisters; Small Town Girl (1936); Small Town Girl (1953); A Small Town in Texas; Some Came Running; Song of Norway; Sons and Lovers; Splendor in the Grass; Stand by Me; Staying Together; Steel Magnolias; Step Down to Terror; Storm Warning; Strange Invaders; Strike Up the Band; The Stripper; Sudie and Simpson; Tank; A Taste of Honey; Texasville; Theodora Goes Wild; They Won't Forget; This Land Is Mine; Tiger's Tale; Till the End of Time; Titfield Thunderbolt; Tom, Dick and Harry; Tommyknockers; The Town; Trapped in Paradise; The Trip to Bountiful; The Trouble with Girls; The Trouble with Harry; True Stories; Twin Peaks; Twin Peaks: Fire Walk with Me; UFOria; Under Milk Wood; Uranus; Used Cars; Valentino Returns; Village of the Damned; Wait 'Til the Sun Shines, Nellie; Waiting For the Light; Way Down East (1920); Way Down East (1935); The Wedding Night; Welcome Home, Roxy Carmichael; Well; Went the Day Well?; What's Eating Gilbert Grape?; Whiskey Galore; Why Shoot the Teacher?; Wish You Were Here; Young at Heart

Small-Town Scandals: see also *Small-Town Life: Gossips/Rumors:* Anatomy of a Murder; Appaloosa; Camila (1984); The Chase (1966); Elmer Gantry; Flamingo Road; The Gun in Betty Lou's Handbag; Harper Valley P.T.A.; Heaven with a Gun; Hot Spell; If Winter Comes; It Happens Every Thursday; Jarrapellejos; Johnny Belinda; Le Corbeau; Lost Boundaries; Marquise of O; Miracle of Morgan's Creek; Nadine; Nasty Girl; Never Take Sweets from a Stranger; Orpheus Descending; Peyton Place; Playboys; The Positively True Adventures of the Alleged Texas Cheerleader-Murdering Mom; Return to Peyton Place; Sitting Pretty; Small Sacrifices; Sudie and Simpson; Tess; Theodora Goes Wild; Tiger's Tale; Twin Peaks; Twin Peaks: Fire Walk with Me; Valdez is Coming; Way Down East (1920); Way Down East (1935)

Smart Alecks: see *Wisecracking Sidekicks: Children-Brats: Children-Little Adults*

Smart vs. Dumb: see also *Simple Minds: Class Conflicts: Snobs vs. Slobs: Extrovert vs. Introvert: Bimbos: Bimboys: Intellectuals:* Annie Hall; Ball of Fire; Born Yesterday (1950); Born Yesterday (1993); Broadcast News; Dominick & Eugene; Dumb and Dumber; A Fish Called Wanda; The Girl Can't Help It; The Girl with Green Eyes; How I Got Into College; I.Q.; Jude the Obscure; Little Man Tate; Outrageous Fortune; The Owl and the Pussycat; A Song Is Born

Snakes: see also *Alligators: Monsters-Animal:* The Kiss (1988); Lair of the White Worm; Tremors; Venom

Snipers: see also *Murderers-Mass: Terrorists: Serial Killers:* Black Sunday (1977); Game of Death; The Sniper; Targets; Two Minute Warning

Snobs: see also *Rich People: Snobs vs. Slobs: Class Conflicts: Jetsetters: Debutantes:* Alice Adams; Animal Crackers; Auntie Mame; The Hairy Ape; The Landlord; The Last Run; Meet the

People; Metropolitan (1990); Naughty But Nice; New Leaf; Six Degrees of Separation

Snobs vs. Slobs (more comical, bathroom-humor oriented Rich vs. Poor): see also *Rich vs. Poor: Class Conflicts: Snobs:* Addams Family Values; The Adventures of Bullwhip Griffin; Ain't Misbehavin'; Animal Crackers; Beverly Hills Cop; Beverly Hills Cop 2; Big Business; Breaking Away; Caddyshack; Caddyshack 2; Easy Money (1983); Foolin' Around; Hairspray; I'm No Angel; In Society; Joe; King Ralph; Life Stinks!; Oxford Blues; PCU; Ruggles of Red Gap; Ski School; The Super; Taking Care of Business; Trading Places; Uncle Buck; The Unsinkable Molly Brown; You Can't Take It With You (1938); You Can't Take It With You (1986)

Snow Settings: see also *Mountain Settings: Arctic/Antarctica: Snowmen-The Abominable:* Abbott & Costello, Lost in Alaska; The Abominable Snowman; Avalanche; Call of the Wild (1935); Call of the Wild (1972); Cliffhanger; Cool Runnings; Dead of Winter; Doctor Zhivago; A Doll's House; Downhill Racer; Empire Strikes Back; The Gold Rush; The Great Race; Grumpy Old Men; Hell and High Water; Ice Palace; Ice Pirates; Ice Station Zebra; Iceman; Jack London; Jennifer 8; K-2; Map of the Human Heart; A Midnight Clear; Misery; Murder on the Orient Express; Nanook of the North; National Lampoon's Christmas Vacation; On Her Majesty's Secret Service; One in a Million; Orca-Killer Whale; The Pathfinder; Quintet; Runaway Train; She (1935); She (1965); The Shining; Ski School; The Snows of Kilimanjaro; Springtime in the Rockies; Sweethearts Dance; The Thing (1951); The Thing (1982); White Christmas

Soap Operas (usually ensemble melodramas with outlandish aspects): see *MELODRAMA: Tearjerkers: Ensemble Films: Interwoven Stories: Multiple Stories:* Adam's Rib (1922); Ada; The Best of Everything; By Love Possessed; The Carpetbaggers; East Side, West Wide; Flamingo Road; The Gorgeous Hussy; Hotel; I Can Get it For You Wholesale; I Found Stella Parish; L'Annee des Meduses; Madame X; The Last Days of Chez Nous; A Life of Her Own; Love Machine; My Forbidden Past;

Once Is Not Enough; The Oscar; The Other Side of Midnight; Return to Peyton Place; Peyton Place; Queen Bee; Valley of the Dolls; Written on the Wind

Soap Opera Shows (plot is connected with a show or with characters from one): The Butcher's Wife; Delirious; The Killing of Sister George; Naked in New York; Passion Fish; Phfft!; Soapdish; Tootsie; Tune in Tomorrow

Soccer: see also *Sports Movies:* The Goalie's Anxiety at the Penalty Kick; Gregory's Girl; Lady Bugs; Victory; Yesterday's Hero

Social Climbing: see also *Marrying Up: Beautiful People: Rich vs. Poor: Rich People: Romance-Choosing the Right Person: Life Transitions: Class Conflicts: Snobs:* Above the Rim; The Actress (1928); Ada; The Age of Innocence (1934); The Age of Innocence (1993); Ain't Misbehavin'; Alice Adams; All the Way Up; Ann Vickers; The Apartment; Becky Sharp; The Best of Everything; Breakfast at Tiffany's; The Bride Wore Red; Diary of a Mad Housewife; Easy Living (1937); Easy Money (1948); Easy Virtue; Emma; The Europeans; The Gang's All Here; Give the Girl a Break; Goin' To Town; Golden Boy; Half a Sixpence; I Know Where I'm Going; Irene; Kipps; Kitty; Little Giant (1933); Little Lord Fauntleroy (1936); Little Lord Fauntleroy (1980); Lloyd's of London; Love Me Tonight; The Man in Grey; Metropolitan (1990); Mildred Pierce; Min and Bill; Moon Over Miami; Mrs. Parkington; Night after Night; A Nous La Liberte; A Place in the Sun; The Private Affairs of Bel Ami; Puberty Blues; A Raisin in the Sun; The Reluctant Debutante; Roberta; Room at the Top; Stella (1990); Stella Dallas (1925); Stella Dallas (1937); Tall, Dark & Handsome; Wall Street; The War Against Mrs. Hadley; White Cliffs of Dover; You Can't Take It With You (1938); You Can't Take It With You (1986); You're Telling Me

Social Comedy: see *Social Satire*

Social Drama: see also *Political Drama: Message Films: Inner City Life: Civil Rights: Urban Horrors:* Aaron Slick from Punkin Crick; The Accused (1948); Act of Murder; Adam; The Age of Innocence (1934); The Age of Innocence (1993); Alamo Bay; All My Sons (1949); All My Sons (1986); All the Way Up; All the Young Men; Alsino and the Condor;

Always Goodbye; Amazing Grace and Chuck; An American Romance; And Justice for All; Animal Farm; Ann Vickers; Appaloosa; Arrowsmith; Article 99; At Close Range; At Play in the Fields of the Lord; Au Revoir, les Enfants; The Autobiography of Miss Jane Pittman; Babbitt; Bachelor Party (1957); Bad Girl; Bad Lieutenant; The Bad Sleep Well; Becky Sharp; Bedlam; Being There; The Best Years of Our Lives; The Bicycle Thief; Billy Jack; Black Fury; Black Legion; Blackboard Jungle; Blossoms in the Dust; Blue Collar; Bopha!; Born on the Fourth of July; The Bostonians; Brubaker; The Burning Bed; The Burning Season; Business as Usual; The Caretaker; Carey Treatment; Carrie (1952); Chattahoochee; Children of Paradise; The China Syndrome; Christiane F.; Citizen Kane; City of Hope; The Class of Miss MacMichael; Clean and Sober; Closer; Cool Hand Luke; Country; The Crowd; Cry Freedom; Days of Wine and Roses (1958); Days of Wine and Roses (1962); Death of a Salesman (1950); Death of a Salesman (1985); Death Wish; Deep Cover; Dialogues with Madwomen; Dinner at Eight; Distant Thunder (1973); Do The Right Thing; A Doll's House; The Dressmaker; Drugstore Cowboy; Earth; Easy Virtue; Edge of the City; El Norte; The Ernest Green Story; The Europeans; Extremities; The Fisher King; Five Easy Pieces; The Fixer; Forgotten Prisoners; Friendly Fire; Friends Forever; From the Terrace; From This Day Forward; The Front; Gentleman's Agreement; Gervaise; Ghosts . . . of the Civil Dead; God Bless the Child; The Golden Boy; The Good Earth; A Good Man in Africa; Grand Canyon; The Grapes of Wrath; The Great Gatsby (1949); The Great Gatsby (1974); Guess Who's Coming to Dinner; Guilty by Suspicion; Hair; The Hairy Ape; Hallelujah, I'm a Bum; Heart of Glass; Higher Learning; House of Women; Howards End; Hurry Sundown; I am a Fugitive from a Chain Gang; I Believe in You; I Never Promised You A Rose Garden; I Passed for White; I Was a Communist for the FBI; Iceman; In the Heat of the Night; In the Realm of the Senses; The Informer; Inherit the Wind; The Intruder; Juice; Jungle Fever; Knock on Any Door; Koyaanisqatsi; Lacemaker; The Last Angry Man; Last Exit to

Brooklyn; Lean on Me; Les Bas-Fonds; Let Him Have It; Life at the Top; Little Vera; London Kills Me; Longtime Companion; Look Back in Anger (1959); Look Back in Anger (1980); Look Back in Anger (1989); Look in Any Window; Lord of the Flies (1963); Lord of the Flies (1990); The Lords of Discipline; Lost Angels; Lost Man; Love on the Dole; Lumiere d'Ete; Mademoiselle Fifi; Major Barbara; The Man in the Grey Flannel Suit; Man of Iron; Man of Marble; A Man of No Importance; The Mark; The Marriage of a Young Stockbroker; Matewan; Meet John Doe; Mephisto; The Milagro Beanfield War; Mississippi Burning; The Molly Maguires; My Little Girl; Naked Kiss; Nasty Girl; Native Son (1951); Native Son (1986); Nature of the Beast; Never Take Sweets from a Stranger; No Way Out (1950); Norma Rae; Nothin' But a Man; Nuts; O Lucky Man; Oblomov; The Offence; The Official Story; Orphans; Outrage (1956); The Ox-Bow Incident; Patterns; The Pedestrian; The People Next Door; Permanent Record; The Phantom of Liberty; Philadelphia; Pinky; The Plague; Playing for Time; Prince of the City; A Private Matter; Q & A; A Raisin in the Sun; The Remains of the Day; Riff-Raff (1991); River's Edge; Road Back; Rollover; Romper Stomper; Room at the Top; Saint of Fort Washington; Save the Tiger; Scandal; School Ties; Separate Tables; Shame (1961); Ship of Fools; Short Eyes; Silkwood; Sin of Madelon Claudet; Smash-Up, the Story of a Woman; Snakepit; Something Wild (1960); Soylent Green; Split Image; Storm Warning; Suburbia; Sullivan's Travels; Talk Radio; Taxi Driver; Term of Trial; Thelma & Louise; To Sleep with Anger; Tokyo Joe; Tokyo Story; Tortilla Flat; Traffik; Trial (1955); Twelve Angry Men; The Ugly American; Up the Down Staircase; Uranus; Variety; Wall Street; The Wet Parade; White Banners; White Dog; A World Apart; The Young Philadelphians

Social Satire: see also SATIRE: *Black Comedy: Political Satire: Social Drama: Message Films: Hollywood Satire:* Adventure for Two; All the Way Up; Aren't We All?; Article 99; Brazil; The Caretaker; Christmas in July; City of Hope; A Clockwork Orange; Dave; Dinner at Eight; Dr. Strangelove; The Fool; Fortune Cookie; Fun With Dick and Jane; Goodbye Columbus; Grace Quigley; Grand Canyon; Heavens Above; The Hospital; Killing Dad; The Last Angry Man; The Little Murders; Magic Town; The Man Who Could Work Miracles; Modern Times; My Little Girl; Naked; Natural Born Killers; O Lucky Man; The Outoftowners; PCU; The Prisoner of Second Avenue; Rita, Sue and Bob, Too; River's Edge; Roger & Me; Savages; Six Degrees of Separation; Society; Soylent Green; Stand Up and Be Counted; Star Chamber; Storm in a Teacup; The Super; Talk Radio; Teachers; Titfield Thunderbolt; To Sleep with Anger; Tokyo Story; Tovarich; Trading Places; True Stories; Which Way is Up?

Social Workers: see also *Sociologists: Inner City Life: Homeless People:* A Change of Habit; The Devil Is a Sissy; Dino; God Bless the Child; Going My Way; The Golden Child; I Believe in You; The Last Angry Man; Living in a Big Way; Losing Isaiah; Past Midnight; Sin of Madelon Claudet; Skippy; Slender Thread; A Thousand Clowns; White Banners

Sociologists/Social Workers: see also *Psychologists: Inner City Life: Social Drama:* The Amazing Dr. Clitterhouse; Boys' Night Out; Candyman; The Chapman Report; Last of His Tribe; Nell

Soft Core Pornography: see *Erotic Drama: Erotic Thriller: Pornography World*

Soldiers: see also *Military Stories: War Stories: Homecomings: Black Soldiers:* Aces High; Act of Love; Aliens; All the Young Men; The Americanization of Emily; Ashes and Diamonds; Baby Blue Marine; Bad Company; Ballad of a Soldier; Bataan; Battle Cry; Because You're Mine; The Beguiled; Belle Epoque; The Best Years of Our Lives; Big Bounce; The Big Red One; The Big Steal; Biloxi Blues; Birdy; Blockade; The Blue Dahlia; Blue Hawaii; Bold and the Brave; The Boys in Company C; Breaker Morant; Bright Victory; Buck Privates; By the Light of the Silvery Moon; Cadence; Call Me Mister; The Canterville Ghost; Captain Newman, M.D.; Captive Heart; Carmen Jones; Castle Keep; Catch Me a Spy; Caught in the Draft; The Charge of the Light Brigade (1936); The Charge of the Light Brigade (1968); Chicago Joe and the Showgirl; City and the Dogs; Clock; The Court Martial of Jackie Robinson; Crossfire; Darling Lili; Dear America: Letters Home from Vietnam; Dear Ruth; Desert Victory; Destiny of a Man; Dogfight; The Dogs of War; Donovan's Reef; Every Time We Say Goodbye; A Farewell to Arms (1932); A Farewell to Arms (1957); The Fighting Kentuckian; The Flim Flam Man; Francis the Talking Mule; From Here to Eternity; Full Metal Jacket; G.I. Blues; G.I. Joe; Gaby; Gallipoli; The Gang's All Here; The General Died at Dawn; Good Guys Wear Black; Goonies; Gordon's War; The Great Escape; The Great Manhunt; The Great Santini; Guadalcanal Diary; Gunga Din; Hail the Conquering Hero; Heaven and Earth; Heaven Knows, Mr. Allison; Hell in the Pacific; Hook; How I Won the War; I, Jane Doe; I Wanted Wings; I'll Be Seeing You; Ice Palace; Immortal Sergeant; The Impatient Years; Indecent Obsession; It's Always Fair Weather; Kelly's Heroes; The Key (1934); King of Hearts; King Rat; Kings Go Forth; La Ronde (1950); La Ronde (1964); Lacombe, Lucien; The Last Command; The Last Detail; League of Gentlemen; The Life and Death of Colonel Blimp; Limbo; The Longest Day; Love Me Tender; Love Story (1944); Mademoiselle Fifi; The Major and the Minor; March or Die; Mardi Gras; Masculine, Feminine; Mediterraneo; A Midnight Clear; A Month in the Country; Murphy's War; The Naked and the Dead; The New Barbarians; No Room for the Groom; No Time for Sergeants; None But the Brave; Operation Mad Ball; The Outsider; Paisan; Panama Hattie; Perfect Furlough; Period of Adjustment; Pork Chop Hill; Private Benjamin; Return of the Soldier; The Road Back; Sad Sack; Safe Passage; Sands of Iwo Jima; The Search; Sebastiane; The Secret War of Harry Frigg; Sergeant York; Seven Sinners; She Wore a Yellow Ribbon; Since You Went Away; The Smiling Lieutenant; Soldier in the Rain; A Soldier's Story; South Pacific; The Stork Club; The Story of Vernon and Irene Castle; Streamers; Stripes; The Subject Was Roses; Sundown; Suppose They Gave a War and Nobody Came; Teahouse of the August Moon; Teresa; That Kind of Woman; Thousands Cheer; The Thrill of a Romance; A Time of Destiny; To Hell and Back; Tomorrow is Forever; Town Without Pity; Tunes of Glory; Twelve O'Clock High; 2000 Maniacs; Two People; The Umbrellas of

of Tides; Queen Bee; Raintree County; Rambling Rose; Reap the Wild Wind; The Reivers; Resurrection; Return to Macon County; Rich in Love; The River (1984); River Rat; Road House; Rolling Thunder; Roots; The Rose Tattoo; Ruby Gentry; Ruby in Paradise; Sanctuary; The Scorchers; Shag; Shenandoah; Showboat (1936); Showboat (1951); Shy People; Sister, Sister; Six Pack; Smokey and the Bandit; Smokey and the Bandit II; Smokey and the Bandit III; So Red the Rose; A Soldier's Story; Sommersby; Son of Dracula; Song of the South; The Sound and the Fury; Sounder; Southern Comfort; Southern Yankee; The Southerner; Spencer's Mountain; St. Louis Blues; Stars and Bars; Stay Hungry; Steel Magnolias; Storm Warning; Storyville; The Strange One; A Streetcar Named Desire; Suddenly, Last Summer; Sudie and Simpson; Summer and Smoke; Swamp Water; Sweet Dreams; Tammy and the Bachelor; Terms of Endearment; Texasville; Thelma & Louise; They; They Won't Forget; Thieves Like Us; This Property is Condemned; Thunder and Lightning; Thunder Road; Tick, Tick, Tick . . .; To Kill a Mockingbird; Tobacco Road; The Town That Dreaded Sundown; Traces of Red; Track 29; The Trip to Bountiful; True Stories; 2000 Maniacs; Two Moon Junction; Uncle Tom's Cabin (1914); Uncle Tom's Cabin (1969); W.W. & The Dixie Dancekings; The War; Way Down East (1920); Way Down East (1935); Wild in the Country; Wildflower; Wise Blood; WUSA

Southerns-British & Foreign Directors of (representing the fascination, particularly in recent years, of Europeans with Southern life and themes): see also *Southerns:* Angel Heart; Coal Miner's Daughter; Crimes of the Heart; Driving Miss Daisy; Marie; Mississippi Burning; Rich in Love; The Southerner; Swamp Water; Sweet Dreams; Tender Mercies; Thelma & Louise

South Pacific: see *Pacific Island/Ocean: Islands*

Southwestern Life: see also *Desert Life: Rednecks: Small-Town Life: WESTERNS: various southwestern states:* Alice Doesn't Live Here Anymore; Bodies, Rest & Motion; Casey's Shadow; Charley Varrick; Cimarron (1930); Cimarron (1960); Coogan's Bluff; 8 Seconds; A Fire in the Sky; Flesh and

Bone; Footloose; The Getaway (1972); The Getaway (1994); Hard Country; The Last Picture Show; Late for Dinner; The Milagro Beanfield War; Murphy's Romance; Near Dark; O.C. and Stiggs; Oklahoma!; Over Her Dead Body; Pardners; Powwow Highway; The Promised Land; Raising Arizona; Ride the Pink Horse; Tex; That Was Then . . . This Is Now; Tulsa; Two Lane Blacktop; UForia

Space Travel: see *Outer Space Movies: SCI-FI: Futuristic Films: Astronauts*

Spaghetti Westerns: see *Westerns-Spaghetti*

Spain: see also *Spanish Films: Spanish Revolution: Mediterranean:* Adventures of Don Juan; The Angel Wore Red; Barcelona; Before Sunrise; Behold a Pale Horse; Belle Epoque; Blockade; Blood and Sand (1922); Blood and Sand (1941); Bobo; Captain Horatio Hornblower; Carmen (Opera, 1984); Confidential Agent; Desire; The Devil Is a Woman; El Cid; Erendira; For Whom the Bell Tolls; 1492: Conquest of Paradise; History of the World Part One; The Hit; It Started with a Kiss; Jarrapellejos; Law of Desire; Love and Pain and the Whole Damn Thing; Loves of Carmen; Man of La Mancha; Mr. Arkadin; The Naked Maja; Running Man (1963); Scent of Mystery

Spanish Films: see also *Spain: Latin Films:* Belle Epoque; Carmen (1983); City and the Dogs; El Norte; Erendira; Exterminating Angel; High Heels; Jarrapellejos; Law of Desire; Tie Me Up! Tie Me Down!; Viridiana; Women on the Verge of a Nervous Breakdown

Spanish Revolution/Civil War: see also *Spain: Oppression: Political Unrest:* The Angel Wore Red; Arise, My Love; Behold a Pale Horse; Belle Epoque; Blockade; For Whom the Bell Tolls

Special Effects: see *Outer Space Movies: Spectacles: SCI-FI: Fantasy: Futuristic Films: Virtual Reality: Animation-Computer*

Special Teams (military or S.W.A.T.-type teams for special missions): see also *Military Stories: Mercenaries: Terrorists:* Bridge on the River Kwai; Commando; Delta Force; Delta Force 2; Devil's Brigade; Dirty Dozen; Force Ten from Navarone; Ghostbusters; Ghostbusters 2; Guns of Navarone; Hell and High Water; Heroes of Telemark; The Killer Elite; The Lives of a Bengal

Lancer; Navy SEALS; Never So Few; O.S.S.; Objective Burma; Operation Crossbow; Stargate; Teenage Mutant Ninja Turtles; Teenage Mutant Ninja Turtles 2; Teenage Mutant Ninja Turtles 3; Wild Geese; Wild Geese II; Rescue; Where Eagles Dare

Spectacles (not necessarily ACTION): see also *Cast of Thousands: Epics: ADVENTURE: Biblical Stories:* The Abyss; The Adventures of Baron Munchausen (1987); Around the World in 80 Days; Ben-Hur: A Tale of Christ (1925); The Conqueror; Sodom and Gomorrah; Solomon and Sheba; Spartacus; The Ten Commandments

Spiders: see also *Insects: Monsters-Animal:* Arachnophobia; Charlotte's Web; Kingdom of Spiders

Spies (about spies, but not necessarily in an espionage story): see also *Spy Films: Spoofs-Spy: Sabotage: Traitors: Rule the World-Plots to:* Above Suspicion; Across the Pacific; Adventure in Washington; The Adventures of Gerard; The Adventures of Tartu; The Adventuress; Against the Wind; All Through the Night; The Ambassador; Another Country; Arabesque; Armored Command; Army in the Shadows; The Assassination; The Assassination of Trotsky; Atomic Kid; Avalanche Express; Babette Goes to War; Berlin Express; Betrayed (1954); Billion Dollar Brain; Black Moon Rising; Black Windmill; Boris & Natasha; The Bourne Identity; Bullets or Ballots; Cairo (1942); The Chairman; Clear and Present Danger; Cloak and Dagger (1946); Cloak and Dagger (1984); Closely Watched Trains; Code Name: Emerald; Colonel Redl; Confessions of a Nazi Spy; Confidential Agent; A Dandy in Aspic; Daniel; Darling Lili; Day of the Jackal; Deadlier Than the Male; Deadly Affair; Dishonored; Double McGuffin; Double O Kid; The Dunera Boys; The Eagle Has Landed; The Eiger Sanction; Embassy; Endless Game; Enter the Dragon; Ever in My Heart; Exodus; The Experts; Exposed; Eye of the Needle; Eyes in the Night; Falcon and the Snowman; Fantastic Voyage; Fathom; Firefox (1982); Five Fingers; Five Graves to Cairo; Foreign Correspondent; Formula; The Fourth Protocol; From Russia with Love; Funeral in Berlin; The General Died at Dawn; Glass Bottom Boat; Golden Earrings;

Dance; Tremors; Troop Beverly Hills; True Stories; UHF; The Villain; Waxwork; Waxwork II: Lost in Time; What's Up, Tiger Lily?; Wholly Moses; The World's Greatest Lover; The Wrecking Crew; Yellowbeard; Young Doctors in Love; Young Einstein; Young Frankenstein; Zelig; Zorro and the Gay Blade

Spoofs-Detective: see also *Film Noir-Modern: Detective Stories: Comic Mystery:* Ace Ventura, Pet Detective; Blue Iguana; Bullshot; Caprice; The Cheap Detective; Don't Just Stand There; Fear of a Black Hat; Fletch; Fletch Lives; The Late Show; Mr. and Mrs. North; Murder by Death; My Favorite Brunette; Naked Gun; Naked Gun 2½; Naked Gun 33⅓; A Night to Remember (1946); The Pink Panther; Rent-a-Dick; Revenge of the Pink Panther; Tough Guys Don't Dance; Whistling in the Dark; Who Framed Roger Rabbit?; Who's Harry Crumb?; Without a Clue

Spoofs-Documentary: see also *Documentary Style: Documentaries:* All You Need Is Cash; Fear of a Black Hat; This is Spinal Tap; Zelig

Spoofs-Horror: see also *Horror Comedy: Comic Thriller: HORROR:* Andy Warhol's Frankenstein; Arousers; Attack of the Killer Tomatoes; Beware!; The Blob!; The Ghost and Mr. Chicken; Ghostbusters; Ghostbusters 2; Ghost in the Invisible Bikini; House of Dracula; House of Frankenstein; I Was a Teenage Frankenstein; I Was a Teenage Werewolf; The Man with Two Brains; Midnight (1989); The Monster Club; Mothra; National Lampoon's Class Reunion; Pandemonium; Piranha; Repossessed; The Rocky Horror Picture Show; Serial Mom; Shock Treatment; Teen Wolf; Teen Wolf Too; Tremors

Spoofs-Musical: see also *Musicals: Musical Comedy:* Cry Baby; The First Nudie Musical; SOB

Spoofs-Sci-Fi: see also *SCI-FI:* Flesh Gordon; The Man with Two Brains; Mom and Dad Save the World; Plan 9 From Outer Space; Spirit of '76

Spoofs-Spy: see also *Spies: Spy Films:* Above Suspicion; The Adventures of Gerard; The Ambushers; Babette Goes to War; Boris & Natasha; Caprice; Casino Royale; Double O Kid; Freddie as F.R.O.7.; The Glass Bottom Boat; Gotcha!; Hopscotch; Hudson Hawk; In Like Flint; Jane and the Lost City; La Cage Aux

Folles 2; Last of the Secret Agents; Leonard, Part 6; Liquidator; A Man Could Get Killed; Murderer's Row; My Favorite Spy; The Nude Bomb; Our Man Flint; Our Man in Havana; Outrageous Fortune; Queen of Outer Space; S*P*Y*S; The Second Best Secret Agent in the Whole Wide World; Silencers; Southern Yankee; Spies Like Us; Undercover Blues; Where the Spies Are; Who Done It? (1957); The Wrecking Crew

Spoofs-TV: see also *TV Series: TV Series Movies: TV Life: Hollywood Life:* The Explorers; On the Air; Stay Tuned; UHF

Spoofs-Vampire: see also *Vampires: Dracula:* Andy Warhol's Dracula; Billy the Kid vs. Dracula; Blacula; Buffy, The Vampire Slayer; The Fearless Vampire Killers; Fright Night; Fright Night Part 2; Love at First Bite; Mark of the Vampire; Old Dracula; Once Bitten; Vamp; The Vampire's Kiss

Spoofs-Western: see also *Western Comedy: WESTERNS:* The Adventures of Bullwhip Griffin; Blazing Saddles; Little Big Man; Tampopo; Three Amigos

Spooky Comedy: see *Comic Thriller: Horror Comedy: Spoofs-Horror: HORROR*

Sports Movies: see also *Underdog Stories: Olympics: Baseball: Basketball: Football: Running: Tennis: Track & Field: Romance with Boxer:* Above the Rim; The Air Up There; All The Marbles; All the Right Moves; All-American Boy; American Anthem; Angels in the Outfield (1951); Angels in the Outfield (1994); Aspen Extreme; Babe; The Babe Ruth Story; The Bad News Bears; The Bad News Bears Go to Japan; The Bad News Bears in Breaking Training; Bang the Drum Slowly; Best of the Best; Best of Times; Big Man; Big Wednesday; Billie; Billy the Kid vs. Dracula; The Bingo Long Travelling All-Stars and Motor Kings; Bloodfist; Bloodfist II; Bloodfist III; Bloodsport; Blue Chips; Body and Soul (1947); Body and Soul (1981); Body Slam; Breaking Away; Brian's Song; Broken Noses; Bull Durham; Cain and Mabel; Cat Ballou; The Challenge; The Champ (1931); The Champ (1979); The Champion; Champions; Chariots of Fire; Comrades of Summer; The Cutting Edge; D2: The Mighty Ducks; Damn Yankees; Days of Thunder; Designing Woman;

Diggstown; Diving In; Downhill Racer; Eight Men Out; 8 Seconds; Endless Summer; Eric; Fat City; Fear Strikes Out; Field of Dreams; The Fish that Saved Pittsburgh; The Frisco Kid (1979); Gentleman Jim; The Gladiator; Gleaming the Cube; The Goalie's Anxiety at the Penalty Kick; Golden Boy; Goldengirl; Go West; The Great White Hope; The Greatest; Gus; Gymkata; Hard Promises; Hoop Dreams; Hoosiers; Iron Man; Jim Thorpe, All American; Johnny Be Good; The Karate Kid; The Karate Kid, Part II; The Karate Kid, Part III; Kickboxer; Kickboxer 2; The Kid from Brooklyn; The Kid from Left Field; Kid Galahad; Killer McCoy; Knute Rockne: All-American; Lady Bugs; Le Mans; A League of Their Own; The Leather Saint; Let's Do It Again (1975); Little Big League; The Longest Yard; The Main Event; Major League; Major League 2; Matilda; The Mighty Ducks; Milky Way (1936); Million Dollar Mermaid; Movie Movie; Mr. Destiny; The Natural; Necessary Roughness; North Dallas Forty; Paper Lion; Paradise Alley; Pat and Mike; Pride of the Yankees; The Prizefighter and the Lady; The Program; Pumping Iron; Pumping Iron 2; Raging Bull; Requiem for a Heavyweight (1956); Requiem for a Heavyweight (1962); Rocky; Rocky II; Rocky III; Rocky IV; Rocky V; Rollerball; Rudy; Run for Your Money; Scout; See How She Runs; Side Out; Ski School; Slap Shot; Somebody Up There Likes Me; Streets of Gold; Take Me Out to the Ball Game; Talent for the Game; Tall Story; Teen Wolf; Teen Wolf Too; The Terry Fox Story; They Made Me a Criminal; This Sporting Life; Three Amigos; Victory; White Men Can't Jump; Yesterday's Hero; Youngblood

Spousal Abuse: see *Abusive Men: Abusive Women: Marriage on the Rocks: Divorce*

Spy Films: see also *Spies: Spoofs-Spy: Traitors: THRILLER: Cold War Era: Sabotage: CIA: FBI: KGB: Disguises: Spies-Female:* Above Suspicion; Across the Pacific; The Adventures of Tartu; The Adventuress; Arabesque; Armored Command; Army in the Shadows; The Assassination; Avalanche Express; Babette Goes to War; Berlin Express; Billion Dollar Brain; Black Moon Rising; The Bourne Identity; Casino Royale; The Chairman; Clear and Present Danger; Cleopatra Jones; Cleopatra Jones & The

Conflict: Lover Family Dislikes: Love-Forbidden

Starting Over: see also *Life Transitions: Widows: Widowers: Midlife Crisis: Divorce: Dating Scene:* Abel; About Face; The Accidental Tourist; Ace High; Alex and the Gypsy; Alice Doesn't Live Here Anymore; American Me; And Now, Tomorrow; April Fools; Atlantic City; Author! Author!; Baby, The Rain Must Fall; Back to School; Bagdad Cafe; Ballad of Josie; Because of You; The Big Bounce; Bliss; Bombshell; The Browning Version; The Buddy System; Bye Bye Love; Call Me Genius; Call of the Wild (1935); Call of the Wild (1972); Can She Bake a Cherry Pie?; The Cemetery Club; Chapter Two; Clean and Sober; Clown; Cold Sweat; The Courtship of Eddie's Father; Dallas; Dangerous; Dona Flor and Her Two Husbands; The Dream Wife; Fearless; Fire Next Time; The Fisher King; Follow That Dream; Frankie and Johnny; Fried Green Tomatoes; The Gay Divorcee; The Ghost and Mrs. Muir; Girlfriends; Going Home; The Good Mother; The Goodbye Girl; Greek Tycoon; A Gunfighter; Hallelujah!; Heartburn; The Hit Parade of 1943; Homeboy; House Calls; I Love You Again; I Never Sang for My Father; I Thank a Fool; I Want to Live!; Intersection; Jo Jo Dancer, Your Life is Calling; Johnny Handsome; Just Between Friends; Kansan; The Kentuckian; Knave of Hearts; L'Invitation; La Vie Continue; Leaving Normal; The Lonely Guy; Lonely Hearts; Lost and Found; Love Hurts; Love Streams; Madame Rosa; Making Love; Malone; Mamma Rosa; A Man and A Woman; Marie; The Mark; Mary Burns, Fugitive; Mayor of Hell; Me & Veronica; Men Don't Leave; Miami Blues; Middle of the Night; Midnight Man; Mister Cory; Moonshine War; Moonstruck; Mr. Wonderful; My Reputation; The Naked Kiss; The Naked Street; The Naked Tango; A New Life; Nicholas Nickleby; Night of the Iguana; The Night We Never Met; Nights of Cabiria; Now, Voyager; The Nurse; Obsession; Oliver's Story; Once Around; One Is a Lonely Number; The Opposite Sex; Oscar; The Other Side of the Mountain Part Two; Passing of the Third Floor Back; Passion Fish; The Perfect Couple; The Possessed (1947); Queen of the Stardust Ballroom; Rapture; Real McCoy; Regarding Henry; Return of Superfly; Rio Bravo; Rose Tattoo; Salome, Where She Danced; Salty O'Rourke; Secret of NIMH; See How She Runs; See You in the Morning; She Devil; Shirley Valentine; A Simple Story; Sleeping With the Enemy; A Slight Case of Murder; Something Wild (1960); Starting Over; Straight Time; Susan Lenox, Her Fall and Rise; Tall, Dark & Handsome; The Tempest; Tender Mercies; That Certain Woman; They Made Me a Criminal; Three Fugitives; Tiger Bay; Twice in a Lifetime; Two for the Seesaw; The Unconquered; An Unmarried Woman; The Verdict; Vertigo; We of the Never Never; Where Are the Children?; The Women; Yours, Mine and Ours

Step-Fathers: see also *Step-Mothers: Fathers:* Beau Pere; Dutch; Fallen Idol; Firstborn; Flight of the Doves; Man of the House; Night of the Hunter; Oedipus Rex; The Sailor Who Fell From Grace with the Sea; The Stepfather; Stepfather 2: Make Room for Daddy; Stepfather 3: Father's Day; Tender Mercies; This Boy's Life; Wildflower

Step-Mothers: see also *Step-Fathers: Mothers:* Alice in Wonderland; Bonjour, Tristesse; Desire Under the Elms; My Cousin Rachel; My Stepmother is an Alien; Picture Mommy Dead; See You in the Morning; The Slipper and the Rose

Step-Parents vs. Children: see also *Step-Mothers: Step-Fathers: Parents vs. Children:* Hamlet (1948); Hamlet (1964); Hamlet (1969); Hamlet (1991); Picture Mommy Dead; Radio Flyer; The Stepfather; This Boy's Life; Twisted Nerve; A Woman Obsessed

Stephen King: see also *HORROR:* Carrie; Christine; Cujo; The Dark Half; The Dead Zone; Dolores Claiborne; Golden Years; Graveyard Shift; It; Maximum Overdrive; Misery; The Shawshank Redemption; The Shining; Silver Bullet; The Stand; Stand By Me; Tales from the Darkside: The Movie; Tommyknockers

Stern Men (rather closed-up, unemotional types): see also *Fathers: Midwestern Life: Abusive Men: Mean Men: Leaders-Tyrant:* The Attic; Babbitt; Beverly Hills Madam; The Big Red One; The Big Street; Biloxi Blues; The Boys in Company C; Broken Lance; The Browning Version; Cahill: United States Marshal; The Caine Mutiny (1954); The Caine Mutiny Court Martial (1988); Cass Timberlane; The Chase (1994); Cheaper by the Dozen; A Christmas Carol (1938); Citizen Cohn; Citizen Kane; Cityslickers; Cityslickers 2; A Delicate Balance; Diamond Head; Dresser; Fat Man and Little Boy; The Gathering; Heartbreak Ridge; House of Strangers; Howards End; The Hudsucker Proxy; I Never Sang for My Father; The Inheritance; The King and I; King Lear (1971); Kings Row; The Last Angry Man; The Last Hurrah; The Last Tycoon; The Late George Apley; Lean on Me; The Life and Times of Judge Roy Bean; The Little Princess; MacArthur; Major Payne; Mr. and Mrs. Bridge; The Muppet Christmas Carol; Mutiny on the Bounty (1935); Mutiny on the Bounty (1962); Nobody's Fool (1994); An Officer and a Gentleman; One Night of Love; The Paper Chase; Patton; The Remains of the Day; The Road to Wellville; Sands of Iwo Jima; Scent of a Woman; Scrooge (1935); Scrooge (1970); Scrooged; Sea of Grass; The Sergeant; Sitting Pretty; Sleeping With the Enemy; This Boy's Life; Tunes of Glory; Un Coeur en Hiver

Stern Women (rather closed-up, unemotional types): see also *Mothers: Midwesterns: Abusive Women: Mean Women:* Andre's Mother; Another Woman; Autumn Sonata; Between Two Women; The Big Street; Country Girl; Cry Baby; Daddy's Dyin'; A Delicate Balance; Dolores Claiborne; Driving Miss Daisy; Early Frost; Guarding Tess; Interiors; Jezebel; Madame Sousatzka; Mary Poppins; Ninotchka; One Flew Over Cuckoo's Nest; Only the Lonely; Ordinary People; Plenty; The Pope of Greenwich Village; The Prime of Miss Jean Brodie; The Private Lives of Elizabeth and Essex; The Road to Wellville; Samson and Delilah; Silk Stockings; The Trouble with Angels; Tugboat Annie Sails Again; Used People; The Virgin Queen; Witness; Zelly and Me

Stock Brokers: see also *Business Life:* Cash McCall; Diary of a Hitman; Folks!; Limit Up; Nothing But the Truth; Quicksilver; Rollover; Toast of New York; Trading Places; Wall Street

Stores: see *Department Stores*

Storytellers: see also *Legends: Gossip/Rumors: Narrated Films: Soliloquies:* The Adventures of Baron Munchausen (1943); The Adventures of

Baron Munchausen (1987); Diary for My Children; Foxfire (1987); Fried Green Tomatoes; Ghost Story; Green Pastures; The Illustrated Man; The Immortal Story; Jack and the Beanstalk; Kwaidan; Monster in a Box; The Princess Bride; Song of the South; Stand by Me; The Story of Will Rogers; Swimming to Cambodia; Swing; Tales From the Crypt; Tales from the Darkside: The Movie

Stranded: see also *Stranded on an Island: Trapped: Trapped in a Hole: Situation Comedy: Abandoned People: Disaster Movies: Prison Dramas: Islands: Nightmare Journeys:* Alive; Artists and Models Abroad; Aviator; The Cabinet of Caligari (1962); Cassandra Crossing; Dead of Winter; Doc Hollywood; Dying Room Only; The Ghoul (1975); Go West Young Man; Goodbye, New York; Hold That Ghost; International House; It's a Small World; Kiss Me, Stupid!; Leap of Faith; Lifeboat; Lucky Me; The Man Who Came to Dinner; Marooned; Midnight (1939); Never Cry Wolf; None But the Brave; Nothing but Trouble (1991); Only Angels Have Wings; The Pointsman; Robinson Crusoe on Mars; The Sands of the Kalahari; The Shining; The State of Things; Survive; Tammy and the Bachelor; Tarzan and His Mate; Tarzan Escapes; Tarzan, The Ape Man (1932); Tarzan, the Ape Man (1981); Tarzan's New York Adventure; Through a Glass Darkly; VIPs; Woman in the Dunes

Stranded on an Island: see also *Stranded: Islands:* The Adventures of Robinson Crusoe; The Adventures of Sadie; Blue Lagoon (1948); Blue Lagoon (1980); The Bride Came C.O.D.; Castaway; Ebb Tide; Eye of the Needle; Far From Home; Gulliver's Travels (1939); Gulliver's Travels (1976); Heaven Knows, Mr. Allison; Hell in the Pacific; Island (1980); Island of Dr. Moreau (1977); Island of Lost Souls (1932); Isle of the Dead; The Last Flight of Noah's Ark; Lord of the Flies (1963); Lord of the Flies (1990); Man Friday; Mediterraneo; Mysterious Island; Rain; Return to the Blue Lagoon; Swept Away; The Swiss Family Robinson

Strangers in Town: see *New in Town: Drifters*

Streetgangs: see *Gangs-Street:* also *Inner City Life: Social Drama: Crime Drama: Mob Stories: Juvenile Delinquents*

Street Life: see *Inner City Life: Prostitutes-Low Class: Runaways*

Streetwalkers: see *Prostitutes-Low Class*

Strikes: see also *Unions: Workers vs. Boss: Reformers:* Adalen 31; Angry Silence; Arsenal; Blue Collar; Brittania Hospital; Comrades; The Garment Jungle; Harlan County USA; Hoffa; I'm All Right, Jack; Last Exit to Brooklyn; Man of Iron; Matewan; Newsies; Norma Rae; Nothin' But a Man; The Pajama Game; Rebecca's Daughters; Riff-Raff (1991); The Strike

Strippers (mostly female, but sometimes male): see also *Sexy Women: Dancers: Bimbos:* Ball of Fire; Between the Lines; Blaze; Criss Cross (1992); Exotica; Fear City; Flashdance; George White's 1935 Scandals; George White's Scandals (1934); George White's Scandals 1945; Gypsy; Ladies' Night Out; Lady of Burlesque; Lenny; Little Treasure; A Night in Heaven; The Night They Raided Minsky's; Ruby; Screaming Mimi; A Song Is Born; The Stripper; A Woman Is a Woman

Stuck in a Rut: see *Starting Over: Life Transitions: Trapped: Depression*

Studs: see *Prostitutes-Male: Sexy Men: Muscleheads: Body Builders*

Stuntmen: see also *Movie Making: Hollywood Life:* Evel Knievel; F/X; F/X 2: The Deadly Art of Illusion; Hooper; Night Moves; The Stuntman

Stupid People: see *Simple Minds: Criminals-Stupid: Bimbos: Bimboys: Muscleheads: Jocks-Dumb*

Submarines: see also *Underwater Adventure: Adventure at Sea: War Stories:* Above the Rim; Above Us the Waves; The Abyss; Around the World Under the Sea; The Bedford Incident; Das Boot; Destination Tokyo; The Devil and the Deep; Gray Lady Down; Hellcats of the Navy; The Hunt for Red October; Leviathan; Mysterious Island; On the Beach; Operation Petticoat; Run Silent Run Deep; The Russians Are Coming, The Russians Are Coming; The Spy in Black; 20,000 Leagues Under the Sea; Voyage to the Bottom of the Sea; Yellow Submarine

Suburban Kids: see *Children-Suburban*

Suburban Life: see also *Domestic Life: Housewives: Children-Suburban: Rich People: Rich Kids:* Adventures in Babysitting; Amityville 1992: It's About

Time; Amityville 4; Amityville, a New Generation; The Amityville Curse; Applegates; Bachelor in Paradise; Bill & Ted's Bogus Journey; Bill & Ted's Excellent Adventure; Billie; Bleak Moments; Blondie; Boyfriends and Girlfriends; The Brady Bunch Movie; The Breakfast Club; Brief Encounter (1974); The 'burbs; Bye Bye Birdie; Cadillac Man; The Chapman Report; Compromising Positions; Coneheads; Consenting Adults; Cops and Robbersons; Corrina, Corrina; Crimes of Passion; Dazed and Confused; Desperate Characters; Desperate Hours (1955); Desperate Hours (1990); Desperate Living; Divorce, American Style; Doctor's Wives; Don't Tell Mom the Babysitter's Dead; E.T.: The Extra-Terrestrial; Earth Girls are Easy; Edward Scissorhands; Encino Man; Faces; Facts of Life; Falling in Love; Fast Times at Ridgemont High; Father of the Bride (1950); Father of the Bride (1991); Ferris Bueller's Day Off; Firstborn; The Flamingo Kid; Foxes; Full Moon in Paris; Fun With Dick and Jane; The Gate; Gate II; Gidget; Gleaming the Cube; Good Neighbor Sam; The Graduate; The Grass Is Always Greener Over the Septic Tank; The Hand that Rocks the Cradle; Happy Anniversary; Harriet Craig; Hider in the House; How to Beat the High Cost of Living; I Married a Monster from Outer Space; The Incredible Shrinking Woman; The Karate Kid; Law and Disorder (1974); Letter to Three Wives; The Lord Love a Duck; The Man in the Grey Flannel Suit; The Man Who Came to Dinner; Married to the Mob; Meet the Applegates; Mister Cory; Mixed Nuts; The Money Pit; Mr. Mom; Mr. Nanny; My Blue Heaven (1990); Neighbors; O.C. and Stiggs; Oh, God; Oh God Book Two; Oh God, You Devil; Opportunity Knocks; Parenthood; Parents; The People Next Door; Please Don't Eat the Daisies; Poltergeist; Poltergeist 2; Polyester; A Raisin in the Sun; Rally Round the Flag, Boys; Real Life; Rebel Without a Cause; Repo Man; River's Edge; Say Anything; Secret Admirer; The Secret Life of an American Wife; Serial; Serial Mom; She's Having a Baby; Short Cuts; Sitting Pretty; Slacker; The Stepfather; Stepfather 2: Make Room for Daddy; Stepfather 3: Father's Day; The Stepford Wives; Suburban Commando; The Swimmer; Testament; Track 29; The Ugly

Dachshund; Uncle Buck; Valley Girl; Visit to a Small Planet; Wives and Lovers; Pulse

Subways: see also *Trains-Commuter: New York Life:* Eve of Destruction; The Last Metro; Speed; Subway; Taking of Pelham 123; Short Walk to Daylight; A Stranger is Watching

Suicidal Tendencies: see also *Euthanasia: Suicidal Tendencies of Homosexuals: Secrets-Consuming: Death-Dealing with: Depression: Mental Illness: DRAMA: TRAGEDY:* Absence of Malice; Act of Love; Angel Face; The Apartment; The Art of Love; Bad Dreams; The Bad Seed (1956); The Bad Seed (1986); Bedazzled; The Bell Jar; The Belly of an Architect; Better Off Dead; Betty Blue; Beyond the Forest; The Big Chill; Broken Blossoms; Buddy Buddy; Butterfield 8; Catch Me a Spy; The Chairman; The Children's Hour; Christopher Strong; Colonel Redl; Coming Home; Crimes of the Heart; Dead Poet's Society; Deadly Affair; The Deep Blue Sea; The Deer Hunter; Dirty Dozen; Dr. M.; The Drowning Pool; Easy Virtue; Elvira Madigan; The End; Fatal Attraction; Folks!; Fourteen Hours; Fox and His Friends; Frantic (1958); The Gambling Lady; Grace Quigley; Guyana Tragedy, The Story of Jim Jones; Harold and Maude; Heart of the Matter; Heathers; Hedda; The Hospital; I Never Promised You A Rose Garden; Inside Daisy Clover; Inside Moves; Interiors; It's a Wonderful Life; Keeper of the Flame; The Kennel Murder Case; La Dolce Vita; Ladykiller (1992); Leave Her to Heaven; Lenny; Les Comperes; Life Upside Down; Living Corpse; Luv; Madame Bovary; Madame Butterfly; Mayerling (1935); Mayerling (1968); Melo; The Mill on the Floss; Mishima; Miss Julie; Monsieur Hire; Mouchette; My Own Private Idaho; Network; 'Night, Mother; Ode to Billy Joe; One Flew Over Cuckoo's Nest; Ordinary People; Pain in the A . . .; Paranoia; Permanent Record; Petulia; The Red Shoe Diaries; The Right of Way; Romeo and Juliet (1936); Romeo and Juliet (1954); Romeo and Juliet (1968); The Rose; Sayonara; Scent of a Woman; Short Cuts; Short Time; Sid and Nancy; Six Degrees of Separation; Slender Thread; SOB; Squaw Man; Stagedoor; A Star Is Born (1937); A Star Is Born (1954); A Star Is Born (1976); Strange

Bargain; The Suicide Club; Swing High, Swing Low; They Shoot Horses, Don't They?; Tin Drum; Town Without Pity; Tragedy/Surviving; Two Against the World; An Unsuitable Job for a Woman; A View from the Bridge; Voyage of the Damned; Walkabout; Way Down East (1920); Way Down East (1935); Wetherby; What Price Hollywood?; Whose Life Is It Anyway?; Women on the Verge of a Nervous Breakdown; A Zed and Two Noughts

Suicidal Tendencies of Homosexuals: see also *Suicidal Tendencies: Murders of Homosexuals: Homophobia: Gay Men: Lesbians:* The Children's Hour; Fox and His Friends; My Own Private Idaho; No Way Out (1987); Six Degrees of Separation

Suicidal Tendencies of Young People: see also *Young People: Young Men-Angry: Depression: Mental Illness:* The Bell Jar; Dead Poet's Society; Harold and Maude; Heathers; I Never Promised You A Rose Garden; Life Upside Down; Ode to Billy Joe; Romeo and Juliet (1936); Romeo and Juliet (1954); Romeo and Juliet (1968)

Summer Camps: see *Camps/Camping*

Summer Vacations: see *Vacations-Summer*

Superhuman: see *Superheroes: Comic Hero Stories*

Supernatural Danger: see also *SCI-FI: Ghosts: Satan: Occult: Fantasy: Magic: Fortunetellers: Psychics: Mindreading:* The Amityville Horror; The Believers; Bloodbath at the House of Death; Cameron's Closet; Carrie (1976); The Changeling; Child's Play (1972); The Exorcist; Exorcist II: The Heretic; The Eyes of Laura Mars; The Final Conflict; First Power; The Fog; Fury (1978); The Gate; Gate II; Ghost; The Ghost and Mr. Chicken; Ghostbusters; Ghostbusters 2; The Haunting; The Legend of Hell House; Necromancy; Needful Things; Night Gallery; 976-Evil; Pet Sematary; Pet Sematary 2; Poltergeist; Poltergeist 2; Poltergeist 3; The Possession of Joel Delaney; Pumpkinhead; Puppet Master; Q (The Winged Serpent); Rawhead Rex; The Unholy; The Unnamable; The Unnamable Returns; Vibes; Watcher in the Woods

Supreme Court: see also *Judges: Lawyers: Washington D.C.: Courtroom Drama: Trials:* First Monday in October;

Listen to Me; Magnificent Yankee; Separate but Equal; Talk of the Town

Surfers: see also *Beach Movies: California Life: Swimming:* Big Wednesday; Bill & Ted's Bogus Journey; Bill & Ted's Excellent Adventure; Endless Summer; Gidget; Live a Little, Steal a Lot; Muscle Beach Party; Point Break; Puberty Blues; Young Einstein

Surrealism: see also *Fantasy: SCI-FI: Art Films: Avant-Garde:* After Hours; An American in Paris; And the Ship Sails On; Bad Timing: A Sensual Obsession; Bartleby; Barton Fink; Blood of a Poet; Bocaccio '70; Carrie (1976); Closet Land; The Comfort of Strangers; The Company of Wolves; Delicatessen; The Devils; The Discreet Charm of Bourgeoisie; Disorderly Orderly; Doctor Mabuse, the Gambler; Dreams That Money Can Buy; Eraserhead; Erendira; Eureka; Even Cowgirls Get the Blues; Eversmile New Jersey; The Five Thousand Fingers of Doctor T.; Freaks; Freud; Full Metal Jacket; Grand Illusion; Heathers; Hotel New Hampshire; How to Get Ahead in Advertising; J'Accuse; Joe vs. the Volcano; Johnny Suede; Juliet of the Spirits; Kafka; Kismet (1944); Kismet (1955); Kiss of the Spider Woman; La Strada; Lili; Memoirs of a Survivor; A Midnight Clear; Milky Way (1968); My American Uncle; Naked Lunch; New York Stories; The Ninth Configuration; Numero Deux; On the Air; The Other; The Phantom of Liberty; Pink Floyd: The Wall; Portrait of Jennie; Return to Oz; Santa Sangre; Scanners; Scanners II, The New Order; Shame (1968); Silent Tongue; Switch; Tales of Hoffman; Testament of Orpheus; Through a Glass Darkly; Tin Drum; Tommy; Track 29; Un Chien Andalou; Viridiana; Walker; The Wandering Jew; Window to Paris; The Wiz; The Wizard of Oz (1925); The Wizard of Oz (1939); Woman in the Dunes; Zabriskie Point; A Zed and Two Noughts; Zelig

Surrogate Mothers: see *Mothers-Surrogate: also Mothers Alone: Mothers-Unwed*

Surveillance: see also *Spies: Spy Films: Voyeurism: Eavesdropping:* The Amateur; The Anderson Tapes; Blow Out; The Conversation; Klute; Night Eyes; Rear Window; Sneakers

Survival Drama: see also *Disaster Movies: Rescue Adventure/Drama:*

Trapped: Stranded: The Adventures of Robinson Crusoe; Alive; Apollo 13; Bad Company (1995); The Big One, The Great Los Angeles Earthquake; Black Rain (1988); The Bride Came C.O.D.; The Crying Game; The Curse of the Cat People; Death and the Maiden; Desperate Journey; Disclosure; Dolores Claiborne; Five Came Back; Flight of the Phoenix; Four Frightened People; Gray Lady Down; Greed; Hideaway; In the Mouth of Madness; The Incredible Shrinking Man; Interview with the Vampire; Just Cause; K-2; The Killing Fields; The Kingdom; Kiss of Death (1947); Kiss of Death (1995); The Last Seduction; Lifeboat; Man Friday; Man in the Wilderness; Marooned; Mountain; No Man of Her Own (1949); None But the Brave; Outbreak; The Poseidon Adventure; The Professional; The River Wild; San Francisco; Sands of the Kalahari; Second Chance; September Affair; Seven Beauties; The Seventh Cross; Shallow Grave; Shop on Main Street; Silent Fall; The Snows of Kilimanjaro; Soldier Blue; Souls at Sea; Southern Comfort; Soylent Green; The Specialist; Stagecoach (1939); Stagecoach (1966); Stalag 17; Survive; The Swiss Family Robinson; Terminator 2: Judgment Day; The Towering Inferno
Susan Sarandon Goes Southern (she is one of three actresses whose most popular parts are those of southern women, though they are not southern themselves): see also *Sally Field Goes Southern: Jessica Lange Goes Southern: Southerns:* Bull Durham; The Client; Pretty Baby; Thelma & Louise; White Palace
Suspecting Oneself: see also *Murder-Debate to Confess: Murder-Debate to Reveal Killer:* Angel Heart; Bedroom Eyes 2; Black Angel; The Blue Dahlia; Cahill: United States Marshal; A Double Life; Detective Story; Detour; Investigation of a Citizen Above Suspicion; Shattered; Siesta; Spellbound; Tightrope; Traces of Red; True Confessions
SUSPENSE: see also *Erotic Thriller: Romantic Thriller: Comic Thrillers: Legal Thriller: Medical Thriller: Rogue Plots: HORROR: Monsters: Serial Killers: Stalkers: Malicious Menaces: Kill the Beast: Film Noir: Race Against Time: Conspiracy: Unbelieved: Animals in Jeopardy: Men in Jeopardy: Disabled People in Jeopardy: Women in*

Jeopardy: Rural Horrors: Urban Horrors: Abbott & Costello Meet Dr. Jekyll & Mr. Hyde; Abbott & Costello Meet Frankenstein; Abbott & Costello Meet the Invisible Man; Abbott & Costello Meet the Killer: Boris Karloff; Abbott & Costello Meet the Mummy; The Abominable Snowman; Absolution; The Accused (1948); Across the Bridge; Affair in Trinidad; Afraid of the Dark; After Dark, My Sweet; Airport; Airport 1975; Airport 1977; Airport '79, The Concorde; Alice, Sweet Alice; Alien; Alien3; Aliens; All This and Heaven, Too; All-American Murder; The Amateur; The Ambassador; Ambulance; An American Friend; Amityville 1992: It's About Time; Amityville 4; Amityville, a New Generation; Amityville Curse; The Amityville Horror; Amityville Horror 2, The Possession; Amsterdamned; And Now the Screaming Starts; The Andromeda Strain; Angel Heart; Anniversary; Apartment Zero; The Ape; Arabesque; The Arousers; Ashanti: Land of No Mercy; The Assassination; Atomic City; The Attic; Audrey Rose; Autumn Leaves; The Awakening; Babysitter; Back From the Dead; Backfire; Backtrack; Bad Day at Black Rock; Bad Dreams; Bad Influence; The Bad Seed (1956); The Bad Seed (1986); Basic Instinct; The Bat (1959); Bat Whispers; Bears & I; The Bedford Incident; Bedroom Eyes; Bedroom Eyes 2; Bedroom Window; The Beguiled; The Believers; Berlin Express; Berserk!; Best Seller; Betrayed; Beware, My Lovely; Beyond a Reasonable Doubt; The Big Clock; The Big Combo; The Big Easy; The Big Heat; The Big Knife; The Big Steal; The Bird With the Crystal Plumage; The Birds; The Birds II; The Black Hand; Black Sunday (1977); Black Widow (1987); The Black Windmill; Blackmail (1929); Blackmailed; Blind Side; Blindfold: Acts of Obsession; Blink; The Blob (1958); The Blob (1988); Blood and Black Lace; Blood on the Sun; Blood Relatives; Blood Simple; Blow Out; Blown Away; The Blue Dahlia; Blue Ice; Blue Steel; Blue Thunder; Body Double; Body Heat; Body of Evidence; The Body Snatcher; The Bodyguard; Boomerang (1947); Born to Kill; The Boston Strangler; The Bourne Identity; The Boys from Brazil; Brainscan; Brainstorm (1965); Bram Stoker's Count Dracula

(1970); Bram Stoker's Dracula (1992); Bramble Bush; The Bride Wore Black; Brighton Rock; The Brood; Buffet Froid; Bunny Lake is Missing; Buried Alive; Burnt Offerings; Butterfly; The Cabinet of Caligari (1962); The Cabinet of Dr. Caligari (1919); Cage of Gold; Call Me; Calling Northside 777; Cameron's Closet; Candyman; Cape Fear (1962); Cape Fear (1991); Capricorn One; Car; Carrie (1976); A Case for Murder; Cassandra Crossing; Castle Keep; Cat Chaser; Cat People (1942); Cat's Eye; Catch Me a Spy; Caught; Caught in the Act; Cause for Alarm; The Chairman; Chandler; The Changeling; Charade; The Charmer; The Chase (1947); Chase a Crooked Shadow; Child's Play (1988); Child's Play 2; Child's Play 3; Children of the Damned; China Moon; The China Syndrome; Chinatown; Choice of Arms; Christine; City in Fear; The Clairvoyant (1934); Class Action; Clear and Present Danger; The Client; Cloak and Dagger (1984); Closely Watched Trains; Code Name: Emerald; Cohen and Tate; Cold Sweat; Color Me Dead; Coma; The Company of Wolves; Confessions of a Hit Man; Confidentially Yours; Conflict of Interest; Consenting Adults; The Conspirator; Coup de Torchon; Criminal Law; Criss Cross (1947); The Crush; D.O.A. (1949); D.O.A. (1988); Daddy's Gone A-Hunting; Dance Macabre; A Dandy in Aspic; Dangerous Crossing; Dangerous Curves; The Dark Half; Dark Mirror; The Dark Past; Dark Waters; Day of the Dolphin; Day of the Jackal; Dead Again; Dead in the Water; Dead of Night (1945); Dead of Winter; Dead On; Dead Ringer; Dead Ringers; The Dead Zone; Deadfall (1993); Deadly Currents; Deadly Friend; Deadly Matrimony; Deadly Trap; Deathtrap; Deceived; Deception (1992); Deepstar Six; Defenseless; Deliverance; Desert Fury; Desire and Hell at Sunset Motel; Desperate Hours (1955); Desperate Hours (1990); Destination Tokyo; Detonator; Detour; Diabolique (1955); Dial M For Murder; Diary of a Hitman; Die! Die! My Darling!; Die Hard; Die Hard 2; Die Watching; The Disappearance of Christina; Diva; Dollars; Dominique; Domino Principle; The Doppelganger: The Evil Within; Double Indemnity; Double Jeopardy; A Double Life; Double Threat; Double-Crossed; Dracula (1931); Dracula (1979);

Dracula Has Risen from the Grave; Dracula (Horror of Dracula, 1958); Dracula, Prince of Darkness; Dracula's Daughter; Dragonwyck; The Dream Lover (1986); The Dream Lover (1994); Dressed to Kill; Duel; Dying Room Only; Dynasty of Fear; Ebb Tide; The Eiger Sanction; The Embassy; Endangered Species; The Enforcer (1950); Eureka; Europa, Europa; Ever in My Heart; The Evictors; The Exorcist; Exorcist II: The Heretic; Exorcist III; Experiment in Terror; Exposed; Eye of the Cat; Eye of the Devil; Eye of the Needle; Eye of the Storm; Eyes in the Night; Eyewitness (1970); Eyewitness (1981); F/X; F/X 2: The Deadly Art of Illusion; Fade to Black (1979); Fade to Black (1993); Fail Safe; The Fall of the House of Usher (1928); Fallen Angel; Fallen Sparrow; Family Plot; Fan; Farewell, My Lovely (1944); Farewell, My Lovely (1975); Fatal Attraction; Fear; Fear in the Night; Fear Inside; Femme Fatale; 52 Pick-up; The File on Thelma Jordon; Final Analysis; The Final Conflict; Finger of Guilt; Firepower; First Power; Five Fingers; Five Graves to Cairo; Five Miles to Midnight; Five Million Years to Earth; The Flare Up; Flesh of the Orchid; Flight of the Doves; Flowers in the Attic; Fly By Night; The Fog; Fools Parade; The Forbidden; Forbidden Planet; The Forbin Project; Force of Evil; The Foreign Correspondent; Formula; The Fourth Man; The Fourth Protocol; The Fourth Story; The Fourth War; Frantic (1958); Frantic (1988); Frenzy; The Friends of Eddie Coyle; The Fugitive (1993); Fugitive Lovers; The Fugitive: The Final Episode; Funeral in Berlin; Fury (1978); Gaslight (1939); Gaslight (1944); Get Carter; The Getaway (1972); The Getaway (1994); Ghost; Ghost Story; The Ghoul (1933); The Glass Key (1935); The Glass Key (1942); Golden Earrings; Goldengirl; The Good Son; Gorilla at Large; Gorky Park; Gotcha!; Gotham; Greed; Green for Danger; The Green Man; The Grifters; Grizzly; The Groundstar Conspiracy; Guardian; Guest in the House; Guilty as Sin; Guilty Conscience; Gun Crazy (1950); Gun Crazy (1992); Half Moon Street; Hand that Rocks the Cradle; The Haunting; The Hearse; The Heart of the Matter; The Hidden; Hidden 2; Hider in the House; High and the Mighty; High Anxiety; Highpoint; The Holcroft

Covenant; Holocaust 2000; The Honeymoon Killers; House of Cards; House of Games; The House on Carroll Street; The Human Factor; The Hunger; The Hunt for Red October; Hunted; Hush, Hush, Sweet Charlotte; Hysteria; I Confess; I Love a Mystery; I Love Trouble (1947); I Married a Dead Man; I Married a Monster from Outer Space; I Saw What You Did; I Thank a Fool; I Wake Up Screaming; I Walked with a Zombie; Illegal; Illustrious Corpses; Impact; Impulse (1984); Impulse (1990); In a Lonely Place; In Cold Blood; In the Line of Fire; The Incredible Shrinking Man; Inferno; Innocent; The Innocents; The Inquisitor; Inspector Calls; Internal Affairs; The Internecine Project; Intruder in the Dust; Investigation of a Citizen Above Suspicion; Ipcress File; Iron Maze; Ivy; Jack the Ripper (1958); Jack's Back; Jagged Edge; Jamaica Inn (1939); Jamaica Inn (1982); Jamaica Run; Jaws; Jaws 2; Jaws 3-D; Jaws 4: The Revenge; Jennifer 8; Johnny Angel; Journey into Fear; Judgment Night; Juggernaut; Julia; Jurassic Park; Kansas; Kaos; The Keep; Key Largo; Kidnapping of the President; Kill Me Again; The Kill-Off; The Killer Inside Me; Killer McCoy; The Killers (1946); The Killers (1964); The Killing; Killjoy; A Kiss Before Dying (1956); A Kiss Before Dying (1991); Kiss Me Deadly; Kiss of Death (1947); Klute; Knife in the Water; Knight Moves; Kwaidan; La Balance; La Bete Humaine; Lady from Shanghai; Lady in a Cage; The Lady in Question; Lady in the Car with Glasses and a Gun; Lady in the Lake; Lady in White; The Lady Vanishes (1979); Ladykiller (1992); Lancer Spy; Lassiter; Last House on the Left; Last Rites; The Last Run; The Last Wave; Laughter in the Dark; Le Corbeau; Leave Her to Heaven; Legacy; Let's Scare Jessica to Death; The Letter (1929); The Letter (1940); Leviathan; Life is Cheap, but Toilet Paper is Expensive; Light Sleeper; Lightning Strikes Twice; Lightship; The Little Drummer Girl; The Little Girl Who Lives Down the Lane; Live Wire; Living Corpse; The Locket; The Lodger (1926); The Lodger (1932); The Lodger (1944); Logan's Run; The Long Night; The Looker; Looking for Mr. Goodbar; The Looking Glass War; Lost Man; Love Crimes; Love From a Stranger (1936); Love From a Stranger (1947);

Love Has Many Faces; A Lovely Way to Die; M (1931); M (1951); Mackintosh Man; Madness of the Heart; Magic; Malaya; Malice; The Maltese Falcon (1931); The Maltese Falcon (1941); Man About the House; Man Hunt; Man in the Attic; Man on a Swing; The Man Who Haunted Himself; The Man Who Knew Too Much (1934); The Man Who Knew Too Much (1956); The Man Who Watched Trains Go By; Man's Best Friend; The Manchurian Candidate; Manhattan Murder Mystery; Manhunter; Mantrap; Marathon Man; Mask of Dimitrios; Mask of Fu Manchu; Masquerade (1965); Masquerade (1988); Masters; Mata Hari (1931); Mata Hari (1985); Mata Hari, Agent H21 (1964); Mean Season; The Mechanic; Melancholia; Memoirs of an Invisible Man; Men of Respect; Mephisto Waltz; Midnight Crossing; Midnight Lace; Midnight Man; Mike's Murder; Miller's Crossing; Mine Own Executioner; Ministry of Fear; Miracle Mile; Mirage; Misery; Mississippi Mermaid; Mister Frost; Mona Lisa; Monolith; Monsieur Hire; Morning After; Mortal Thoughts; The Most Dangerous Game; Mother Love; Mother's Boys; Murder; Murder by Natural Causes; Murder by Phone; My Blood Runs Cold; Naked City; The Naked Face; The Naked Prey; The Naked Runner; The Naked Street; Nancy Steele Is Missing; Nanny; Narrow Margin (1952); Narrow Margin (1990); Niagara; Night Eyes; Night Gallery; The Night Has Eyes; Night Moves; The Night Must Fall (1937); The Night Must Fall (1964); The Night My Number Came Up; Night of the Following Day; The Night of the Generals; Night of the Hunter; Night of the Juggler; Night of the Lepus; Night of the Living Dead (1968); Night of the Living Dead (1990); Night People; Night Terror; Night Train to Munich; Night Walker; Night Watch; Nightfall; Nightmare in the Sun; 976-Evil; No Escape (1936); No Highway in the Sky; No Man's Land (1987); No Way Out (1987); No Way to Treat a Lady; Nocturne; Notorious; Number 17; Obsession; October Man; Odd Man Out; The Odessa File; Old Dark House (1932); Old Dark House (1962); The Omen; Omen IV: The Awakening; One False Move; Orca-Killer Whale; Ossessione; The Osterman Weekend; The Other; Our Man in Havana; Out of Order; Out of the

Dark; Pacific Heights; The Package; Paint it Black; Pandora's Box; The Paradine Case; The Parallax View; Pascali's Island; Past Midnight; Patriot Games; The Peeper; Peeping Tom; The Pelican Brief; Penthouse; Phantom of Paradise; Phantom of the Opera (1941); Phantom of the Opera (1962); Phantom of the Opera (1989); Phobia; Physical Evidence; Pickup on South Street; Picture Mommy Dead; The Pit and the Pendulum (1961); The Pit and the Pendulum (1991); Play Misty for Me; The Player; Poltergeist; Poltergeist 2; Poltergeist 3; The Poseidon Adventure; The Postman Always Rings Twice (1945); The Postman Always Rings Twice (1981); Predator; Presumed Innocent; Primary Motive; The Prowler; Psycho; Psycho 2; Psycho 3; Psycho 4; Public Eye; Pulse; Raising Cain; Rampage; Rancho Notorious; Ransom; The Real McCoy; Rear Window; Rebecca; Reckless Moment; Red House; Red Inn; Red Rock West; The Reincarnation of Peter Proud; Relentless; Relentless 2; Relentless 3; Report to the Commissioner; Return of Dracula; Return of the Vampire; Ride the Pink Horse; Rider on the Rain; Riff-Raff (1947); Rising Sun; Road Games; Rollover; Rome Express; Romeo is Bleeding; Rope; Rosary Murders; Rosebud; Rosemary's Baby; Run; Running Man (1963); Sabotage; Saboteur; Salem's Lot; Samurai; Sapphire; Satan Bug; Scapegoat; Scar; Scent of Mystery; Scorpio; Scotland Yard; Sea of Love; The Sea Wolf; Seance on a Wet Afternoon; Second Chance; Seconds; Secret Agent; The Secret Beyond the Door; Secret Friends; Secret Partner; See No Evil; The Sender; The Sentinel; The Serpent and the Rainbow; The Seventh Sign; The Seventh Victim; The Shadow (1936); Shadow of a Doubt; Shaker Run; Shanghai Express; Shattered; The Shining; Shock Corridor; Shoot the Piano Player; Silence of the Lambs; Silent Partner; Silhouette; Silkwood; Single White Female; Sister, Sister; Sisters; Skyjacked; Slamdance; Sleeping Beauty; Sleeping With the Enemy; The Slender Thread; Sleuth; Sliver; Sneakers; The Sniper; Snow White and the Seven Dwarfs; So Long at the Fair; Somebody Killed Her Husband; Something Wicked This Way Comes; The Sorcerer; Sorry, Wrong Number; Spellbinder; The Sphinx;

Spiral Staircase (1946); Spiral Staircase (1975); The Spy in Black; St. Ive's; Stage Fright; Stalking Moon; The Stand; Star Chamber; Step Down to Terror; The Stepfather; Stepfather 2: Make Room for Daddy; Stepfather 3: Father's Day; The Stepford Wives; Still of the Night; Stolen Life (1946); Storm Warning; Storyville; Strange Bargain; The Stranger; A Stranger Among Us; A Stranger is Watching; Strangers on a Train; The Stuntman; Sudden Fear; The Suicide Club; Suspect; Suspicion; Suspiria; Taffin; The Taking of Pelham 123; Tall Target; The Tamarind Seed; Target; Targets; A Taste for Killing; Tattoo; Taxi Driver; Tears in the Rain; Teenage Rebel; Telefon; The Temp; Ten Days Wonder; Ten Little Indians; The Tenant; The Tenth Man; Tequila Sunrise; Terminator; Terminator 2: Judgment Day; Terror on a Train; They Drive by Night (1938); They Drive by Night (1940); They Live by Night; They Only Kill Their Masters; They Won't Believe Me; Thief (1952); Thief of Hearts; The Third Man; 13 Rue Madeleine; The Thirty-Nine Steps (1935); The Thirty-Nine Steps (1959); The Thirty-Nine Steps (1978); This Gun for Hire; The Thousand Eyes of Dr. Mabuse; Three Days of the Condor; Thunder Rock; Thunderheart; Tick, Tick, Tick . . .; Tiger Bay; Tightrope; Time after Time; Timebomb; To Catch a Thief; To Kill a Clown; Tony Rome; Topaz (1969); Torn Curtain; Toto le Heros; Tower of London (1939); Tower of London (1962); The Town That Dreaded Sundown; Traces of Red; The Train; The Trap; Tremors; Trilogy in Terror; Trouble for Two; Twenty-Three Paces to Baker Street; Twilight's Last Gleaming; Twin Peaks; Twin Peaks: Fire Walk with Me; Twisted Nerve; Two Minute Warning; The Two Mrs. Carrolls; Under Suspicion; Undercurrent; Unfaithful; The Uninvited; Union Station; Unlawful Entry; Unseen; The Unsuspected; Valley of the Kings; The Vanishing (1988); The Vanishing (1993); Velvet Touch; Venom; Vertigo; Vicki; Village of the Damned; Von Ryan's Express; W; Wages of Fear; Wait Until Dark; War Games; War of the Worlds; Warning Sign; Watch on the Rhine; Watcher in the Woods; We Are Not Alone; We Were Strangers; Wedlock; Werewolf of London; Westworld; Whatever Happened to Baby Jane?;

When a Stranger Calls; When Strangers Marry; Where Are the Children?; Where Love Has Gone; Whirlpool; Whisperers; Whispers in the Dark; Whistling in the Dark; White Dog; White Nights (1985); White Sands; The Wicker Man; The Wilby Conspiracy; Wild Palms; The Window; Winter Kills; Witness; Witness for the Prosecution; Witness to Murder; Wolf; The Wolves of Willoughby Chase; Woman in the Window; Woman in White; Woman on the Beach; Woman Screaming; Wrong is Right; The Year My Voice Broke; Year of the Dragon; Year of the Gun; The Yellow Balloon; The Yellow Canary; You'll Like My Mother; You've Got to Live Dangerously; Z; Zigzag

Svengalis (someone who supervises the complete personality or career makeover of someone else): see also *Teachers: Teachers & Students: Mentors/Proteges:* Ain't Misbehavin'; Cardinal Richelieu; Educating Rita; Expresso Bongo; Funny Face; The Girl Can't Help It; Hammersmith Is Out; The Hard Way (1943); Harlow; The Idolmaker; Kid Galahad; Kitty; Meet John Doe; My Fair Lady; Rasputin and the Empress; Rhinestone; Salty O'Rourke; Twentieth Century; What Price Hollywood?

Swamp Life/Settings: see also *Florida: Louisiana: Southerns: Cajuns:* Belizaire the Cajun; Conrack; Cross Creek; Distant Drums; Eaten Alive; Frogs; Gator; Joe Panther; Louisiana Story; Moonrise; No Mercy; Passion Fish; The Rescuers; Shy People; Sister, Sister; Southern Comfort; Swamp Thing; Swamp Water; Thunder Bay; The Yearling

Swapping Partners: see also *Sexual Kinkiness: Romance-Triangles: Ménage à Trois: Alternative Lifestyles: Marriage Comedy: Marriage Drama:* Bitter Moon; Bob & Carol & Ted & Alice; Boyfriends and Girlfriends; Consenting Adults; Don's Party; Drugstore Cowboy; A Fine Romance; The Guest Wife; The Haunted Summer; Husbands and Wives; Loving Couples; Manhattan Murder Mystery; Marriage on the Rocks; A Midsummer Night's Sex Comedy; On Approval; Palm Beach Story; Private Lives; Promises! Promises!; Serial; Sibling Rivalry

Swashbucklers: see also *Pirates: Historical Drama: ACTION: Adventure at Sea: 1700s: War of 1812:* The Adventures of Don Juan; Against All

Flags; Black Pirate; Black Sunday (1977); The Buccaneer (1938); The Buccaneer (1958); Captain Blood; Captain Kidd; The Corsican Brothers; Court Jester; Dr. Syn, Alias the Scarecrow; The Fifth Musketeer; Fire Over England; Flame and the Arrow; The Four Musketeers; The Frenchman's Creek; Iron Mask (1929); Krull; The Master of Ballantree; My Favorite Year; Nate and Hayes; Pirates of Penzance; The Prince and the Pauper (1937); Prince Valiant; Return of the Musketeers; Ring of the Musketeers; Robin Hood (1922); Robin Hood (1973); Robin Hood (1990); Robin Hood: Prince of Thieves (1991); Royal Flash; Scaramouche; The Scarlet Pimpernel; The Sea Devils (1953); Sea Hawk; Swashbuckler; The Three Musketeers (1935); The Three Musketeers (1939); The Three Musketeers (1948); The Three Musketeers (1973); The Three Musketeers (1993); Treasure Island (1934); Treasure Island (1971); Treasure Island (1990); Treasure Island (1991); Yellowbeard; Zorro and the Gay Blade

Sweden/Swedish People: see also *Scandinavia:* The Abdication; I'll Take Sweden; Marriage Go Round; The Prize; The Second Best Secret Agent in the Whole Wide World; A Woman's Face; Zandy's Bride

Swedish Films: see also *Scandinavia: Bergmanesque:* Adalen 31; After the Rehearsal; Autumn Sonata; Best Intentions; Brink of Life; Dear John; The Devil's Wanton; Elvira Madigan; The Emerald Forest; Face to Face; Fanny and Alexander; From the Life of the Marionettes; A Lesson in Love; The Match Factory Girl; Miss Julie; My Life as a Dog; Persona; Pippi Longstocking; Port of Call; Sacrifice; Sawdust and Tinsel; Scenes from a Marriage; Shame (1968); The Silence; Smiles of a Summer Night; Through a Glass Darkly; The Virgin Spring; Wild Strawberries; Winter Light

Swimming: see also *Musicals-Aquatic: Divers: Beach Movies: Sailing: Surfers:* Bathing Beauty; Dangerous When Wet; Diving In; Drowning By Numbers; The Duchess and the Dirtwater Fox; Easy to Love; Million Dollar Mermaid; Neptune's Daughter; The Swimmer; The Thrill of a Romance

Switch-ups: see *Mix-ups:* also *Misunderstandings: Identities-Mistaken: Screwball Comedy*

Sword & Sorcery: see also *King Arthur Legend: Medieval Times:* Beastmaster; Beastmaster 2; Black Cauldron; Conan, the Barbarian; Conan, the Destroyer; Flesh and Blood (1985); Highlander; Highlander II-The Quickening; Highlander III, The Sorcerer; Krull; Ladyhawke; Legend; Lord of the Rings; Red Sonja; Sword of the Valiant; Sword & the Sorcerer; The War Lord

Sympathizing with the Enemy: see *Enemies-Sympathizing with*

Films by Category

T

Taiwanese Films: see also *Chinese Films:* Eat Drink Man Woman; Farewell My Concubine; Raise the Red Lantern

Talking Animals: see *Animals-Talking: also Objects with Personalities*

Talking Babies: see *Babies-Talking*

Talking Objects: see *Objects with Personalities*

Talk Shows/Hosts: see also *Television: Radio:* Cancel My Reservation; Choose Me; He Said, She Said; The King of Comedy

Taxi Drivers: see also *Ordinary People Stories: New York Life:* The Catered Affair; Chan is Missing; D.C. Cab; Die Laughing; For Pete's Sake; Graveyard Shift; I Stole a Million; Look Who's Talking; The Man Who Broke the Bank at Monte Carlo; Mona Lisa; Night on Earth; Rhinestone; Taxi; Taxi Driver; Total Recall

Teachers: see also *Teachers & Students: Svengalis: High School Life: College Life: Elementary School Life:* According to Mrs. Hoyle; Amsterdamned; Amy; Anna and the King of Siam; The Beekeeper; Blackboard Jungle; The Browning Version; Charly; Cheers for Miss Bishop; A Child is Waiting; Child's Play (1972); Children of a Lesser God; Children of Hiroshima; Class of 1999; Class of '84; The Class of Miss MacMichael; Clockwise; The Color of Money; Conrack; The Corn is Green (1945); The Corn is Green (1979); A Day in the Death of Joe

Egg; Dead Poet's Society; Devil in the Flesh (1946); Devil in the Flesh (1987); The Eiger Sanction; Father Goose; Follow Me, Boys!; The Fortunes of War; Get Out Your Handkerchiefs; Going My Way; Goodbye Mr. Chips (1939); Goodbye Mr. Chips (1969); Gross Anatomy; Heavenly Pursuits; Hold Back the Dawn; House of Cards; Jack of Diamonds; Kindergarten Cop; The King and I; Knack; Lean on Me; Looking for Mr. Goodbar; The Man Without a Face; Masters; Meteor Man; The Miracle Worker; The Music Teacher; My Fair Lady; Nicholas Nickleby; Nighthawks (1978); Nighthawks, 2: Strip Jack Naked (1991); The Old Gringo; One Night of Love; The Other Side of the Mountain Part Two; The Prime of Miss Jean Brodie; Renaissance Man; Romantic Comedy; Ryan's Daughter; Sing; So Big (1932); So Big (1953); Stand and Deliver; Stanley & Iris; Starting Over; Stepping Out; Tea and Sympathy; Teacher's Pet; Teachers; Term of Trial; To Sir with Love; Top Gun; Topaze (1933); Up the Down Staircase; Waterland; Why Shoot the Teacher?; The Wiz; Woman in White

Teachers & Students: see also *Teachers: Svengalis: High School Life: College Life: Elementary School Life: Exchange Students: Film Students:* The Accused (1948); Bellman and True; The Best Man; Blackboard Jungle; Born

Yesterday (1950); Born Yesterday (1993); The Bostonians; Breaking In; Charly; A Child is Waiting; Child's Play (1972); Children of a Lesser God; The Chocolate War; Class of 1999; Class of '84; The Class of Miss MacMichael; The Color of Money; The Competition; Conrack; The Corn is Green (1945); The Corn is Green (1979); Dead Poet's Society; Father Goose; The Five Thousand Fingers of Doctor T.; Follow Me, Boys!; French Postcards; Going My Way; Goodbye Mr. Chips (1939); Goodbye Mr. Chips (1969); Gross Anatomy; International Velvet; Iron Eagle; The Karate Kid; The Karate Kid, Part II; The Karate Kid, Part III; Kid Galahad; Kitty; Lambada; The Long Gray Line; Madame Sousatzka; The Man Without a Face; The Mechanic; The Miracle Worker; Mother is a Freshman; Murder in New Hampshire; The Music Teacher; My Fair Lady; My Tutor; One Night of Love; Paper Tiger; The Prime of Miss Jean Brodie; Renaissance Man; The Rookie; Salty O'Rourke; Sarafina!; Sing; Sister Act; Stand and Deliver; Stanley & Iris; Stepping Out; The Substitute; Surviving Desire; Tea and Sympathy; Teacher's Pet; Teachers; Term of Trial; Thin Ice; To Sir with Love; Top Gun; Topaze (1933); Waterland; Wetherby; When the Legends Die; Who Was That Lady?; Why Shoot the Teacher?

The Warriors; Weird Science; Where the Boys Are; Where the Boys Are '84; Wild in the Streets; Wild Life; Young Guns; Young Guns II; Zapped!; Zapped Again

Teenagers: see also *Coming of Age: Young Men: Young Women: Sex Comedy: High School Life: Boarding Schools: Teenage Terrors:* Adventures in Babysitting; The Affairs of Dobie Gillis; Aloha Summer; Angel; April Fool's Day; Babes in Arms; Babes on Broadway; Baby, It's You; Back to the Future; Back to the Future 2; Bad Boys; Bad Girl; Bay Boy; Beach Blanket Bingo; Beach Party; Beat Street; Belles of St. Trinians; Better Off Dead; Big Girls Don't Cry . . . They Get Even; Bikini Beach; Bilitis; Bill & Ted's Bogus Journey; Bill & Ted's Excellent Adventure; Blame it on the Night; Bless the Beasts and the Children; The Blob (1958); The Blob (1988); Blue Denim; Blue Hawaii; Book of Love; Born Losers; Brain Damage; Brainscan; Breaking Away; Breaking the Rules; Buffy, The Vampire Slayer; Bye Bye Birdie; Caddyshack; Calendar Girl; California Dreaming; Can't Buy Me Love; Carrie (1976); The Chocolate War; Christiane F.; Class of '44; Cool Ones; Corvette Summer; Dangerous Curves; Dazed and Confused; Deadly Friend; Desert Bloom; Dogs in Space; Don't Tell Mom the Babysitter's Dead; Double O Kid; Dove; Dr. Giggles; Eat My Dust; Edward Scissorhands; The Evil Dead; Fame; Fast Times at Ridgemont High; Ferris Bueller's Day Off; The First Time; Firstborn; The Flamingo Kid; Flirting; Footloose; For Keeps; Foxes; Freddy's Dead: The Final Nightmare; French Postcards; Friday the 13th (1980); Friday the 13th: Final Chapter; Friday the 13th, Part 3-D; Friday the 13th, Part II; Friday the 13th Part V-A New Beginning; Friday the 13th Part VI-Jason Lives; Friday the 13th Part VII-The New Blood; Friday the 13th Part VIII-Jason Takes Manhattan; Friends Forever; Get Out Your Handkerchiefs; The Ghost in the Invisible Bikini; Gidget; Girls! Girls! Girls!; Gleaming the Cube; Gorp!; Grandview, USA; Grease; Grease 2; Hangin' with the Homeboys; Happy Birthday to Me; The Heart is a Lonely Hunter; Hemingway's Adventures of a Young Man; Hoop Dreams; The Hotel New Hampshire; How Sweet It Is; I Never Promised You A Rose Garden; I Saw What You Did; I Wanna Hold Your Hand; I Was a Teenage Frankenstein; I Was a Teenage Werewolf; Impossible Years; The Impudent Girl; In the French Style; Johnny Be Good; Just Another Girl on the IRT; Just One of the Guys; King, Queen, Knave; Kiss and Tell; A Kiss for Corliss; La Boum; Lady Bugs; Lady in a Cage; Ladyhawke; The Last Picture Show; The Last Starfighter; The Last Summer; Leather Boys; Listen to Me; Little Darlings; The Little Girl Who Lives Down the Lane; Look in Any Window; Looking for Love; Lord Love a Duck; The Lords of Discipline; Losin' It; Lost Angels; The Lost Boys; Love in a Goldfish Bowl; Major Payne; Man in the Moon; Matinee; Meatballs; Melody; Menace II Society; Mermaids; Mignon Has Left; Miracle (1990); Mischief; More American Graffiti; Mouchette; Mr. Hobbs Takes a Vacation; Murder in New Hampshire; My Science Project; My Tutor; Mystic Pizza; Newsies; A Night in the Life of Jimmy Reardon; Night Moves; Nightmare on Elm Street; Nightmare on Elm Street Part Four; Nightmare on Elm Street Part Three; Nightmare on Elm Street Part Two; Nightmare on Elm Street: The Dream Child; Now You See Him, Now You Don't; O.C. and Stiggs; Oh, What a Night; Once Bitten; The Outsiders; The Pad, and How to Use It; Pandemonium; Paradise (1982); Peppermint Soda; Permanent Record; Phantasm; Phantasm II; Pirate Movie; Porky's; Porky's 2; Porky's Revenge; Pretty Poison; Private School; Puberty Blues; Pump Up the Volume; Rambling Rose; Reckless (1983); Rescue; Rich Kids; Risky Business; River's Edge; Rock Around the Clock; Rock n' Roll High School; Roller Boogie; Rumble Fish; Say Anything; Scent of a Woman; School Ties; Secret Admirer; A Separate Peace; Seventeen; The Shaggy Dog; She's Out of Control; Shocker; A Short Film About Killing; Ski School; Small Change; Smile; Smooth Talk; Some Kind of Wonderful; Spirit Rider; Splendor in the Grass; Spanking the Monkey; Spring Break; Square Dance; Staying Together; The Strange One; The Substitute; Suburbia; The Sure Thing; Swing Kids; Take Her, She's Mine; Taps; Teen Wolf; Teen Wolf Too; Teenage Rebel; That Darn Cat!; That Was Then . . . This Is Now; This Boy's Life; Three O'Clock High; Tiger's Tale; Toy Soldiers; The Trial (1955); Tuff Turf; Twin Peaks; Twin Peaks: Fire Walk with Me; Uncle Buck; Up the Academy; Valentino Returns; Vision Quest; The Wanderers; War Games; The Warriors; Waterland; Weird Science; Welcome Home, Roxy Carmichael; Where Angels Go, Trouble Follows; Where the Boys Are; Where the Boys Are '84; Where the Day Takes You; Wild in the Streets; Wild Life; The Wild One; Wish You Were Here; The World of Henry Orient; Young Guns; Young Guns II; Zapped!; Zapped Again

Teen Horror Flicks of the '80s: see also *Murders of Teenagers: HORROR: Serial Killers:* April Fool's Day; Freddy's Dead: The Final Nightmare; The Fog; Friday the 13th (1980); Friday the 13th: Final Chapter; Friday the 13th, Part 3-D; Friday the 13th, Part II; Friday the 13th Part V-A New Beginning; Friday the 13th Part VI-Jason Lives; Friday the 13th Part VII-The New Blood; Friday the 13th Part VIII-Jason Takes Manhattan; Halloween series; Happy Birthday to Me; He Knows You're Alone; Lair of the White Worm; Nightbreed; Nightmare on Elm Street; Nightmare on Elm Street Part Four; Nightmare on Elm Street Part Three; Nightmare on Elm Street Part Two; Prom Night series; Pandemonium; Silent Scream; Terror Train

Teen Idols: see also *Singers: Fans-Crazed:* Bye Bye Birdie; Cool Ones; Expresso Bongo; The Gene Krupa Story; Girls! Girls! Girls!; Hairspray; The Head; La Bamba; Top Secret!

Telekinesis/Telepathy: see *Psychics: Mindreading: Future-Seeing the: Fortunetellers: Supernatural Danger*

Telephone Terror (from prank phone calls to explosions in one's ear): see also *HORROR: Practical Jokers:* Call Me; Experiment in Terror; Ghost in the Machine; I Saw What You Did; The Jerky Boys; Klute; Midnight Lace; Murder by Phone; Nighthawks; 976-Evil; Out of the Dark; Pillow Talk; Sorry, Wrong Number; Telefon; When a Stranger Calls

Tennessee Williams-esque (with works by the author in *italics***): see also** *Southerns: Baby Doll; Boom!;* Cat on a Hot Tin Roof; Claudelle Inglish; Come Back, Little Sheba; Dark at the Top of the Stairs; *The Fugitive Kind; The Glass Menagerie;* Home from the Hill; Hot Spell; *Last of the. . . .; Night of the Iguana; Orpheus Descending;* Picnic; *The Roman Spring of Mrs. Stone; The Rose*

and Punishment; Crossroads (1986); A Dangerous Woman; Dark Past; Dead Boyz Can't Fly; Desire; The Detective (1954); Disorganized Crime; Dr. Syn, Alias the Scarecrow; Drugstore Cowboy; Eight on the Lam; The Fiendish Plot of Dr. Fu Manchu; Firefox (1982); Four for Texas; Good Die Young; The Great Bank Hoax; The Great McGinty; The Grey Fox; Gun Crazy (1950); Gun Crazy (1992); Harry in Your Pocket; High Risk; High-Ballin'; The Hit Parade of 1943; Hombre; Home Alone; Home Alone 2: Lost in New York; Hot Stuff; I Died a Thousand Times; I Stole a Million; Ikiru; Indiana Jones and the Last Crusade; Jamaica Inn (1939); Jamaica Inn (1982); Kidnapped (1938); Kidnapped (1959); Kidnapped (1971); Ladykillers; The Last Detail; The Lavender Hill Mob; Law and Disorder (1958); Les Miserables (1978); Les Miserables (1935); Les Miserables (1952); Lightning Jack; A Little Romance; The Little Thief; Loot; Lost Man; Mack the Knife; Make Mine Mink; Malaya; A Man, a Woman and a Bank; The Man Who Loved Cat Dancing; The Man Who Watched Trains Go By; The Man Who Would Be King; Marnie; Menage; Miss Grant Takes Richmond; Mo' Money; Monkey Business (1931); Mountain; Never Let Go; A Nice Little Bank That Should Be Robbed; The Night is Young; No Deposit, No Return; No Man's Land; No Man's Land (1987); Nobody's Perfect; Object of Beauty; Oliver!; Oliver and Company; Oliver Twist (1948); Oliver Twist (1982); One of Our Dinosaurs is Missing; Pale Rider; Paleface; Papillon; Passage to Marseilles; The Pathfinder; Penelope; Pickup on South Street; The Pink Panther; The Prowler; Psycho; Quicksand; Raffles; Rashomon; The Real McCoy; The Ref; Robin and the Seven Hoods; Robin Hood (1922); Robin Hood (1973); Robin Hood (1990); Robin Hood: Prince of Thieves (1991); Scandal in Paris; Secret Partner; The Servant; Seven Women; Shanghai Express; Showdown; Smugglers; Stroszek; That Man From Rio; They Live by Night; Thief of Hearts; The Thief Who Came to Dinner; Thunderbolt and Lightfoot; Tin Star; To Catch a Thief; Tom Thumb; Trapped in Paradise; Trouble in Paradise; Uptown Saturday Night; Utz; W.W. & The Dixie Dancekings; Where's Poppa?; Who's Minding the Mint?; The Wicked Lady (1945); The Wicked Lady

(1983); Wisdom; The Wolves of Willoughby Chase; The Wrong Man; Yolanda and the Thief

3-D Movies: see also *1950s: Cult Films:* Andy Warhol's Frankenstein; Bwana Devil; Comin' At Ya!; The Creature of the Black Lagoon; Dial M For Murder; Friday the 13th Part 3; Gorilla at Large; Gun Fury; Hondo; House of Wax; Inferno; Invaders from Mars; I, the Jury (1953); It Came from Outer Space; Jaws 3-D; Kiss Me Kate; The Mad Magician; Miss Sadie Thompson; Money from Home; Phantom of the Rue Morgue; Second Chance; Spacehunter

Threesomes: see *Ménage à Trois: Romance-Triangles: Alternative Lifestyles: Swapping Partners*

Third World Countries: see *Political Unrest: Latin Films: Kingdoms*

THRILLERS: see *SUSPENSE: also Erotic Thriller: Romantic Thriller: Comic Thriller: Legal Thriller: Medical Thriller: Rogue Plots: HORROR: Monsters: Serial Killers: Stalkers: Malicious Menaces: Kill the Beast: Film Noir: Race Against Time: Conspiracy: Unbelieved: Animals in Jeopardy: Men in Jeopardy: Disabled People in Jeopardy: Women in Jeopardy: Rural Horrors: Urban Horrors*

Time Capsules (films which particularly represent a time period, either shot during the period or recreated in the film): see also year categories (1930s: 1940s: etc.): April Fools; Beyond the Valley of the Dolls; The Blessed Event; Bob & Carol & Ted & Alice; The Boy With Green Hair; The Brady Bunch Movie; The Breakfast Club; Breaking Glass; The Bride Wore Black; Bunny Lake is Missing; Calling Northside 777; Campus Man; Carrie (1976); Centennial Summer; Central Park; The Chapman Report; Cheers for Miss Bishop; Choirboys; Clock; A Clockwork Orange; Convoy; Cool Ones; Criss Cross (1992); The Crowd; A Date with Judy; Deadly Trap; The Defiant Ones; Desert Victory; Desperate Characters; A Diary for Timothy; Don't Make Waves; Driving Miss Daisy; Faces; Fail Safe; FBI Story; A Fine Madness; Five Corners; FM; The Fool; Fort Apache, The Bronx; Four Sons; Foxes; From the Terrace; From This Day Forward; Fun With Dick and Jane; Gassss; The Gene Krupa Story; Getting Straight; Gilded Lily; Give My Regards to Broad Street; Good Companions (1933); Good Companions (1956); Goodbye

Gemini; The Graduate; The Great McGinty; A Guide for the Married Man; Hair; Hallelujah, I'm a Bum; The Harrad Experiment; The Harrad Summer; Harriet Craig; Here We Go Round the Mulberry Bush; Hi, Mom!; Hitler Gang; Hitler-The Last Ten Days; Hollywood Canteen; The Hospital; The Hucksters; I Believe in You; I Love You, Alice B. Toklas; I Passed for White; I Wanna Hold Your Hand; I Want You; I Was a Communist for the FBI; It's a Great Feeling; Jolson Sings Again; The Jolson Story; Keeper of the Flame; A Kind of Loving; Kitty Foyle; Kramer vs. Kramer; The Landlord; The Last Angry Man; Letter to Three Wives; Life of Her Own; Lifeguard; Little Darlings; The Living End; Lonely Lady; The Long Goodbye; Looking for Mr. Goodbar; Lord Love a Duck; The Lords of Flatbush; Love Machine; The Man in the Grey Flannel Suit; Marjorie Morningstar; Maybe I'll Be Home in the Spring; Me, Natalie; Medium Cool; Mephisto; Mister Buddwing; Morgan!; Move; Mrs. Brown, You've Got a Lovely Daughter; My Sister Eileen (1942); Myra Breckinridge; Naked City; Nashville; Night in Heaven; Norman, Is That You?; One More Spring; Patterns; Pepe; Perfect; Promise Her Anything; Psych-Out; Quadrophenia; The Return of the Secaucus Seven; Rich Kids; Saturday Night Fever; Sergeant Pepper's Lonely Hearts Club Band; Shadows; Since You Went Away; Smashing Time; Stage Door Canteen; Stand Up and Be Counted; The Stepford Wives; The Strawberry Statement; Street Scene; The Subterraneans; Superstar, The Life and Times of Andy Warhol; Tea and Sympathy; Thank God It's Friday; Thursday's Game; Titfield Thunderbolt; To Find a Man; Toast of New York; Tokyo Story; Tortilla Flat; Trash; The Trial (1955); The Trip; The Trip to Bountiful; Triumph of the Will; Two for the Seesaw; Two or Three Things I Know About Her; Up the Down Staircase; Valley of the Dolls; Vicki; Viva Las Vegas; The Wanderers; WUSA

Time Sleepers (frozen in time somehow, then waking up): see also *Fish Out of Water Stories: Time Travel Stories: SCI-FI: Frozen People:* Anastasia (1956); Anastasia (1984); Awakenings; A Bill of Divorcement (1932); A Bill of Divorcement (1940); Captain America; Demolition Man; Fedora; Flashback; Forever Young; Friday the 13th: Final Chapter; Iceman;

The Land that Time Forgot; Late for Dinner; Mind of Mr. Soames; Rude Awakening; Sleeper; Sleeping Beauty; Some Kind of Hero

Time Travel/Machines: see also *Time Sleepers: SCI-FI:* The Amazing Mr. Blunden; Amityville 1992: It's About Time; Amityville 4; Amityville, a New Generation; The Amityville Curse; Army of Darkness; At the Earth's Core; Back to the Future; Back to the Future 2; Back to the Future 3; Beastmaster 2; Being Human; Berkeley Square; Big; Biggles; Bill & Ted's Bogus Journey; Bill & Ted's Excellent Adventure; Brigadoon; A Connecticut Yankee; A Connecticut Yankee in King Arthur's Court; Dubarry Was a Lady; Final Countdown; Frankenstein Unbound; Freejack; Highlander; Highlander II-The Quickening; Highlander III, The Sorcerer; Hook; I Married a Witch; In Search of the Castaways; Island (1980); It Happened Tomorrow; Millennium; My Science Project; Peggy Sue Got Married; Philadelphia Experiment; Planet of the Apes; Roman Scandals; Somewhere in Time; Spirit of '76; Star Trek IV; Star Trek: Generations; Terminator; Terminator 2: Judgment Day; Testament of Orpheus; 30-Foot Bride of Candy Rock; Time after Time; Time Bandits; Time Cop; Time Machine; Time Runner; Timerider; Total Recall; Two Worlds of Jenny Logan; Unidentified Flying Oddballs; Warlock (1989); Waxwork II: Lost in Time; We're Back! A Dinosaur's Story; Where Do We Go from Here?; Window to Paris

Titanic Stories: see also *Ship Wrecks:* A Night to Remember (1958); Raise the Titanic; Titanic; The Unsinkable Molly Brown

Tokyo: see *Japan*

Tomboys: see also *Girls: Girlhood: Feisty Females: Women as Men:* Ballad of the Sad Cafe; Billie; Calamity Jane; Days of Heaven; Gregory's Girl; Impromptu; Inside Daisy Clover; Queen Christina; Some Kind of Wonderful; A Song to Remember; Sylvia Scarlett; Tammy and the Bachelor

Tornadoes: see also *Disaster Movies: Hurricanes: Midwestern Life:* Country; Places in the Heart; Poltergeist

Torn Between Two Lovers: see *Romance-Triangles: Ménage à Trois*

Torture: see also *War Crimes: POWs/MIAs: Concentration Camps: Nazi Stories: Experiments: Rape/Rapists:* The Big Combo; Closet Land; Cool Hand Luke; Death and the Maiden; The Deer Hunter; Forgotten Prisoners; The Fortress; The Interrogation; Maitresse; Marat/Sade; Marathon Man; The Mask of Fu Manchu; Murder in the First; Music Box; Odette; The Pit and the Pendulum (1961); The Pit and the Pendulum (1991); The Rack; The Raven (1935); Return to Oz; Salo: 120 Days of Sodom; Salon Kitty; The Thousand Eyes of Dr. Mabuse; When Hell Was in Session

Tough Guys & Religious Women: see also *Wallflowers & Hunks: WESTERNS:* The African Queen; Angel and the Badman; Guys and Dolls; Heaven Knows, Mr. Allison; This Could Be the Night; Two Mules for Sister Sara

Tourists: see *Vacations: Vacations-European: World Travel: Vacation Romances: Exotic Locales: Ordinary People in Extraordinary Situations*

Toxins/Toxic Waste: see also *Environmental Dilemmas: Radiation Poisoning: Nuclear Energy:* Body Snatchers; The Day the Fish Came Out; Food of the Gods; Impulse (1984); Murder, He Says; The Prophecy; Rage; Toxic Avenger; Toxic Avenger, Part II; Toxic Avenger Part III

Toys/Toymakers: see also *CHILDREN'S: Fantasy: Monsters-Toys/Dolls:* Pinocchio; Toys; Santa Claus, The Movie

Track and Field: see *Running: Sports Movies: Olympics*

Tracy & Hepburn: see also *Romance-Bickering: Romantic Comedy:* Adam's Rib (1949); Desk Set; Guess Who's Coming to Dinner; Keeper of the Flame; Pat and Mike; Sea of Grass; State of the Union; Without Love; Woman of the Year

TRAGEDY (where everything comes apart in the end, meaning most of the cast usually dies): see also *DRAMA: MELODRAMA: Disease Stories: Mythology: Tragi-Comedy: Classic Greek Stories: Music Dies: Romance-Doomed:* The Abominable Snowman; The Actor's Revenge; Alive; All Fall Down; All My Sons (1949); All My Sons (1986); All Night Long (1961); All the Way Home; American Dream; American Me; And Now, Tomorrow; Angel Face; Angela;

Apache Uprising; The Asphalt Jungle; The Assault; Attica (1971); Attica (1991); Autobus; Avalon; The Bachelor; The Bad Seed (1956); The Bad Seed (1986); Ballad of the Sad Cafe; Band of Angels; Baxter (1972); Betty Blue; Beyond the Forest; Beyond the Valley of the Dolls; The Bicycle Thief; Billy Budd; Bitter Sweet (1933); Bitter Sweet (1940); Bittersweet Love; Black Orpheus; Black Rain (1988); Bloody Mama; Bonnie and Clyde; Bopha!; Botany Bay; The Boys in Company C; Boyz N the Hood; The Bridge of San Luis Rey; Broken Blossoms; A Bronx Tale; The Brothers Karamazov; The Buddy Holly Story; The Bullfighter and the Lady; Butterfield 8; Captive Heart; Casque d'Or; Champion; The Children's Hour; Chimes at Midnight; Christopher Strong; The Collector; Colonel Redl; Colorado Territory; The Comfort of Strangers; The Comic; Coming Home; Daisy Miller; Damage; The Damned; A Dangerous Woman; Dark Victory; Das Boot; Day of the Locust; Days of Wine and Roses (1958); Days of Wine and Roses (1962); Dead End; Dead Poet's Society; Dead Ringers; Death of a Salesman (1950); Death of a Salesman (1985); Despair; Destiny of a Man; The Devil's Playground; Diary of Anne Frank (1959); Dishonored; Do The Right Thing; Dog Day Afternoon; Double Indemnity; Dumbo; East Lynne; Easy Rider; Easy Virtue; Echoes of a Summer; 8 Seconds; End of the Game; Endless Love; Erendira; Escape from the Planet of the Apes; Fatal Vision; Five Star Final; Force of Evil; Fourteen Hours; Fox and His Friends; Frances; Fresh; Friday the Thirteenth (1933); Friends and Husbands; The Fugitive Kind; Full Metal Jacket; The Fury (1936); Gable and Lombard; Gallipoli; The Garden of the Finzi-Continis; Gate of Hell; The Gene Krupa Story; General Della Rovere; Get Carter; Ghosts . . . of the Civil Dead; Girl in the Red Velvet Swing; The Glass Menagerie (1950); The Glass Menagerie (1973); The Glass Menagerie (1987); The Glenn Miller Story; Good Fellas; The Good Mother; Gorillas in the Mist; Grand Illusion; The Great Gatsby (1949); The Great Gatsby (1974); The Great Lie; The Great Waldo Pepper; The Greatest Show on Earth; Griffin and Phoenix, A Love Story; The Grifters; Hamburger Hill; Hanna's War; Hawks; The Hindenburg; A House is Not a Home; Howards End; I am a Fugitive from a Chain Gang; I Want to Live!; Imitation of Life (1934); Imitation of Life (1959); Immortal Sergeant; In the Cool of the Day; The Informer; Inside Moves; Interiors; The Interrogation; Ironweed; Isadora; Judgment at Nuremburg; Jules and Jim; Julius Caesar; Kalifornia; Killing Zoe; The King of Marvin Gardens; King of the Gypsies; Kitchen Toto; La Bamba; Ladies in Retirement; Lady Sings the Blues; The Lamb; Last Exit to Brooklyn; The Last Summer; Leave Her to Heaven; Les Enfants Terribles; The Letter (1929); The Letter (1940); Letters from a Dead Man; Life and Nothing But; Life is Cheap, but Toilet Paper is Expensive; Lifeboat; Light Sleeper; Little Foxes; Living Corpse; Lizzie; Long Day's Journey Into Night; Long Night; Longest Day; Looking for Mr. Goodbar; Lord of the Flies (1963); Lord of the Flies (1990); Love; The Love Affair (1939); Love is a Many Splendored Thing; The Loves of Carmen; Luna; Mad Love; Madigan; The Magnificent Ambersons; Mamma Rosa; Man Upstairs; Manon; Marie Antoinette; The Marriage of Maria Braun; Mary of Scotland; Mary, Queen of Scots; Masque of the Red Death; Matewan; Mayerling (1935); Mayerling (1968); Maytime; The McConnell Story; Meet John Doe; Melo; Men Are Not Gods; Mildred Pierce; The Mill on the Floss; Min and Bill; Mishima; Monsieur Hire; Mouchette; Mourning Becomes Electra; My Girl; My Sin; Native Son (1951); Native Son (1986); The Natural; Network; Nicholas and Alexandra; Night and the City (1950); Night Angel; 'Night, Mother; A Night to Remember (1958); None But the Lonely Heart; Of Mice and Men (1939); Of Mice and Men (1993); The Official Story; One Flew Over Cuckoo's Nest; One Way Passage; Ordinary People; Orpheus Descending; The Other Side of the Mountain; Pandora's Box; A Place in the Sun; The Plague; Playing for Time; Prick Up Your Ears; Ragtime; Rapture; Reservoir Dogs; Rififi; Right of Way; San Francisco; Sayonara; Schindler's List; Sebastiane; A Separate Peace; Sergeant; Serpent's Egg; Shadows of our Forgotten Ancestors; Shoeshine; Shy People; The Sin of Madelon Claudet; Small Sacrifices; Smilin' Through (1932); Smilin' Through (1941); The Sniper; Soldier in the Rain; Sometimes a Great Notion; Sophie's

Choice; Southern Comfort; Spartacus; Special Bulletin; Squaw Man; Stagedoor; Star 80; A Star is Born (1937); A Star is Born (1954); Stealing Heaven; Steel Magnolias; The Story of Vernon and Irene Castle; The Story of Will Rogers; The Stratton Story; Straw Dogs; Street Scene; A Streetcar Named Desire; The Strike; Suddenly, Last Summer; Sugarland Express; Sundays and Cybele; Sunset Boulevard; Survive; The Swarm; Sweet Bird of Youth; Talk Radio; Taps; Tell Me that You Love Me, Junie Moon; They Died with Their Boots On; They Shoot Horses, Don't They?; They Won't Forget; 'Tis a Pity She's a Whore; Titanic; Today We Live; Tom Horn; Torch Song Trilogy; Touch of Evil; Town Without Pity; Treasure of the Sierra Madre; Tristana; Two Women; Ugetsu Monogatari; Under the Volcano; Unfaithful; Vagabond; Victors; A View from the Bridge; The Virgin Spring; Voyage of the Damned; Voyager; War of the Roses; The Wedding March; The Wedding Night; West Side Story; Wetherby; What Price Hollywood?; What's Eating Gilbert Grape?; White Cliffs of Dover; White Mile; White Rose; Who's Afraid of Virginia Woolf?; Wild Duck; The Wild Party; Wings; Wired; Wise Blood; Witches of Salem; The Woman Next Door; Woman Under the Influence; The World According to Garp; The World of Apu; Year of the Dragon; Zandalee

Tragi-Comedy: see also *SATIRE: Black Comedy: Comedy-Morbid:* Cadillac Man; Crimes of the Heart; The Discreet Charm of Bourgeoisie; Dog Day Afternoon; A Double Life; Hawks; Honey Pot; The Honeymoon Killers; Inside Moves; Mastergate; Miss Firecracker; Mommie Dearest; Mother, Jugs & Speed; Prick Up Your Ears; Scrooged; Situation Hopeless But Not Serious; SOB; Soldier in the Rain; Something Wild (1986); Sugarland Express; Tatie Danielle; War of the Roses; The Wedding; The Weekend; Wise Blood; Women on the Verge of a Nervous Breakdown; The World According to Garp

Trail of a Killer: see also *MURDER: Serial Killers: Detective Stories: Police Stories: Detectives-Police: Fugitive from a Murderer:* The Adventures of Tom Sawyer; Affair in Trinidad; Amsterdamned; Angel; Backdraft; Basic Instinct; Bird With the Crystal Plumage; Black Angel; Black Widow (1987); Blood

and Black Lace; Blue Lamp; Blue Steel; The Boston Strangler; Bounty Hunters; The Boys from Brazil; Breakheart Pass; The Bride Wore Black; Bullitt; Calcutta; City in Fear; Cobra; Coogan's Bluff; Cop; Cornered; Dead Heat; The Dead Pool; Deadly Matrimony; Dear Inspector; Deliberate Stranger; Exorcist III; Fear; Firepower; First Deadly Sin; First Power; Frenzy; He Knows You're Alone; Hidden; Hidden 2; Hit!; Hunter; I Wake Up Screaming; January Man; Kalifornia; Kindergarten Cop; Knight Moves; Last Sunset; The Laughing Policeman; Lawman; The List of Adrian Messenger; Lured; Madigan; Man from Laramie; Maniac Cop; McQ; Miami Blues; Murder by Decree; Murphy's Law; Naked City; Navy SEALS; The New Barbarians; Night of the Generals; Nighthawks (1981); No Way to Treat a Lady; Prime Suspect; Rampage; Rancho Notorious; Relentless; Relentless 2; Relentless 3; Report to the Commissioner; Shoot to Kill; Silence of the Lambs; The Sniper; Split Second; The Stranger; Stranger is Watching; Sunburn; Time after Time; The Town That Dreaded Sundown; Traces of Red; Wanted Dead or Alive; When a Stranger Calls

Trains: see also *Trains-Commuter: Subways: Tunnels: Orient Express:* Back to the Future 3; Berlin Express; Boxcar Bertha; Breakheart Pass; Brief Encounter (1946); Brief Encounter (1974); Canyon Passage; Cassandra Crossing; Chattanooga Choo Choo; Closely Watched Trains; End of the Line; Finders Keepers; Flame Over India; The General; The Great Locomotive Chase; The Greatest Show on Earth; The Harvey Girls; Horror Express; Horse Soldiers; Inspector Clouseau; It Happened to Jane; Lady on a Train; The Lady Vanishes (1938); The Lady Vanishes (1979); Love Letters (1945); The Major and the Minor; The Man Who Loved Cat Dancing; Murder on the Orient Express; Murder She Said; My Favorite Blonde; My Friend Irma Goes West; Mystery Train; Narrow Margin (1952); Narrow Margin (1990); Night Train to Munich; No Man of Her Own (1949); Oh, Mr. Porter; Once Upon a Time in the West; The Pointsman; Railway Children; Rome Express; Runaway Train; Shanghai Express; Silver Streak; Sleeping Car Murders; Strangers on a Train; The Tall

Target; Terror By Night; Terror on a Train; Terror Train; Throw Momma from the Train; Titfield Thunderbolt; Tough Guys; The Train; Travels with My Aunt; Twentieth Century; Union Pacific; Union Station; Von Ryan's Express; Warm Nights on a Slow Moving Train

Traitors: see also *Spies: Betrayals: Political Drama: Double-Crossings: Sabotage:* Across the Pacific; Against the Wind; All Through the Night; Another Country; Arch of Triumph; Army in the Shadows; Betrayed (1954); Blue Max; Captain Blood; Captain Carey, USA; The Conspirator; Cornered; The Dunera Boys; The Execution of Private Slovik; Falcon and the Snowman; Fantastic Voyage; Five Fingers; Geronimo (1962); Geronimo (1993); The Great Locomotive Chase; I Accuse; The Informer; Keeper of the Flame; Lacombe, Lucien; Manon; Mask of the Avenger; Masquerade (1965); Midnight Run; Prisoner of Honor; The Rack; Railway Children; Rio Lobo; Silas Marner; Sneakers; The Spider's Stratagem; The Thief (1952); Washington Story

Transsexuals (result of sex change): see also *Transvestites: Men as Women: Women as Men: Role Reversals:* Ace Ventura, Pet Detective; Come Back to the Five and Dime, Jimmy Dean, Jimmy Dean; Dog Day Afternoon; Dr. Jekyll and Sister Hyde; Glen or Glenda?; I Like it Like That; I Want What I Want; In a Year with 13 Moons; Law of Desire; A Man Like Eva; Myra Breckinridge; The Rocky Horror Picture Show; Second Serve; Soapdish; Switch; Tootsie; The World According to Garp

Transvestite Killers: see also *Murders of Homosexuals: Psycho Killers:* Dirty Harry; Freebie and the Bean; Dressed to Kill; Psycho SERIES

Transvestites (only dressed as opposite sex habitually, not necessarily homosexual): see also *Men as Women: Women as Men: Role Reversals: Disguises: Transsexuals:* The Crying Game; Ed Wood; Fade to Black (1979); Female Trouble; Glen or Glenda?; Kiss of the Spider Woman; La Cage Aux Folles; La Cage Aux Folles 2; La Cage Aux Folles 3: The Wedding; Last Exit to Brooklyn; Lonesome Cowboys; M. Butterfly; Paris is Burning; Pink Flamingos; Priscilla, Queen of the Desert; Psycho SERIES; The Rocky Horror Picture Show; Some Like it Hot; To

Wong Foo, Thanks for Everything, Julie Newmar; Torch Song Trilogy; Vamp; The World According to Garp

Tranvestites-Killers of: see *Murderers-Transvestite*

Trapped: see also *Trapped in a Hole: Disaster Stories: Rescue Adventure/ Drama: Stranded: Situation Comedy: Life Transitions: Depression:* The Beguiled; Lady in a Cage; Lifeboat; Out of Order; That Cold Day in the Park; Well

Trapped in a Hole: see also *Disaster Stories: Rescue Drama: Stranded:* Ace in the Hole; Garden of Evil; Well; Woman in the Dunes

Treasure Hunts (where there's a run for the money or valuables, either buried or hidden somehow): see also *ADVENTURE: Quests: Journeys: Adventures at Sea: Bounty Hunters: Finding Valuables/Money:* Ali Baba and the Forty Thieves; The Bat (1959); Bat Whispers; Beyond the Poseidon Adventure; Bringing Up Baby; Busy Body; Cat and Mouse; The Cat Chaser; Charade; Cityslickers 2; Cliffhanger; The Count of Monte Cristo (1934); The Count of Monte Cristo (1974); Dark Crystal; The Deep; Finders Keepers; Fools Parade; God's Little Acre; The Golden Voyage of Sinbad; The Good, The Bad, & The Ugly; Goonies; Indiana Jones and the Last Crusade; Indiana Jones and the Temple of Doom; Inside Moves; It's a Mad Mad Mad Mad World!; It's in the Bag; Jewel of the Nile; Jinxed; King and Four Queens; King Solomon's Mines (1937); King Solomon's Mines (1950); King Solomon's Mines (1985); Krull; Legend of the Lost; Leprechaun; Little Treasure; The Lone Ranger (1955); The Lone Ranger and the Lost City of Gold; Long John Silver; The Long Ships; MacKenna's Gold; The Maltese Falcon (1931); The Maltese Falcon (1941); The Man Who Would Be King; Mask of Dimitrios; Merry Andrew; Midnight Crossing; Million Dollar Duck; Missing Pieces; Night of the Hunter; Raiders of the Lost Ark; Raise the Titanic!; Renegades; Riff-Raff (1947); Romancing the Stone; Rope of Sand; Satan Met a Lady; Scalawag; Scavenger Hunt; Shark!; Slither; Soldier Blue; Southern Star; Stars and Bars; There Was a Crooked Man; Travels with My Aunt; Treasure Island (1934); Treasure Island (1971); Treasure Island (1990); Treasure Island (1991); Treasure of Matecumbe; Treasure

of the Sierra Madre; Trespass; Utz; Vibes; Wake of the Red Witch; Way Out West; White Fang; Year of the Comet

Trials (not necessarily the focal point of the story as in Courtroom Dramas): see also *Courtroom Drama: Court Martials:* Adam's Rib (1949); The Bigamist; Billy Budd; Boys on the Side; Business as Usual; The Caine Mutiny (1954); The Caine Mutiny Court Martial (1988); Can-Can; Class Action; Divorce, Italian Style; Earl of Chicago; A Few Good Men; From the Hip; Hidden Agenda; I Accuse; I'm No Angel; Illegal; Illegally Yours; The Informer; Inherit the Wind; It Happened to Jane; The Lady in Question; Ladybird, Ladybird; The Letter (1929); The Letter (1940); The Life of Emile Zola; Love Among the Ruins; Madame X (1929); Madame X (1937); Madame X (1965); A Man for All Seasons; Murder in the First; Native Son (1951); Native Son (1986); Oscar Wilde; Outbreak; A Pair of Briefs; The Paradine Case; Perfect Strangers; Repentance; The Trials of Oscar Wilde; Turning Point (1952); Twelve Angry Men; 21 Days; Waxwork; Waxwork II: Lost in Time; The Winslow Boy; Witches of Salem; Witness for the Prosecution; A Woman's Face; Young Mr. Lincoln

Triangles: see *Romance-Triangles: Ménage à Trois:* **also** *Alternative Lifestyles: Swapping Partners*

Trilogies: see *Multiple Stories: Mini-Series*

Truck Drivers: see also *Road Movies: Ordinary People Stories: Taxi Drivers:* Big Trouble in Little China; Close to Eden; Coast to Coast; Convoy; Duel; The Great Smokey Roadblock; Handle with Care; High-Ballin'; Jackson County Jail; Quick Millions; Road Games; The Sorcerer; They Drive by Night (1938); They Drive by Night (1940); Wages of Fear

True or Not? (not necessarily true, but likely to be a mystery): see also *Incredible but Mostly True: Mystery-Unsolved: True Stories: Docudrama: Unbelieved:* Agatha; The Amityville Horror; Amityville Horror 2, The Possession; Anastasia (1984); Brass Target; Bridge of San Luis Rey; Buster; Communion; The Disappearance of Aimee; Fatal Vision; A Fire in the Sky; The Glenn Miller Story; Hangar 18; The Magnificent Doll; The Miracle Woman; Olivier, Olivier; Return to Peyton Place;

Roanoak; Ruby; Sing Baby Sing; Small Sacrifices; State of Siege; To Kill a Priest; Tom Horn; Tower of London (1939); The Tower of London (1962)

True Stories: see also *Incredible but Mostly True: Docudramas: Biographies: Autobiographical: Documentaries: Interviews:* Adam; After the Shock; Agatha; The Agony and the Ecstasy; Al Capone; Alamo; Alive; The Amazing Howard Hughes; The Amityville Horror; Amityville Horror 2, The Possession; Anastasia (1984); The Assassination of Trotsky; At Close Range; The Attic: The Hiding of Anne Frank; Attica (1971); Attica (1991); Awakenings; Badlands; The Barretts of Wimpole Street (1934); The Barretts of Wimpole Street (1956); Battle Hymn; Beautiful Dreamers; Beloved Infidel; The Birdman of Alcatraz; Blaze; Blind Ambition; Blossoms in the Dust; Bonnie and Clyde; Boomerang (1947); Born Again; Born on the Fourth of July; Brian's Song; The Brink's Job; Brubaker; The Buddy Holly Story; Bugsy; The Burning Bed; Buster; Casualties of War; Champions; Chicago Joe and the Showgirl; Chiefs; Christiane F.; Compulsion; Cool Runnings; The Court Martial of Jackie Robinson; Cross Creek; A Cry in the Dark; Dance with a Stranger; Dark Obsession; Day One; Dead Ahead, the Exxon Valdez Disaster; Dear America: Letters Home from Vietnam; Deliberate Stranger; Diary of Anne Frank (1959); The Disappearance of Aimee; Disaster at Silo 7; Distant Drums; Dog Day Afternoon; Double Exposure; Eight Men Out; 8 Seconds; Eleni; The Elephant Man; Entre-Nous; Eric; The Ernest Green Story; Escape from Alcatraz; Evel Knievel; The Execution of Private Slovik; The Executioner's Song; F. Scott Fitzgerald in Hollywood; Falcon and the Snowman; Fatal Vision; A Fire in the Sky; Five Fingers; Fourteen Hours; 1492: Conquest of Paradise; G.I. Joe; Girl in the Red Velvet Swing; Glory; Gorillas in the Mist; Greased Lightning; The Great Escape 2: The Untold Story; The Great Impostor; The Grey Fox; Guadalcanal Diary; A Gunfight at the O.K. Corral; Hanna's War; Henry: Portrait of a Serial Killer; Hide in Plain Sight; A House is Not a Home; Hunter; I Love You to Death; In Cold Blood; The Name of the Father; Incident at Oglala; Inherit the Wind; Inn of the

Sixth Happiness; It Could Happen to You; JFK; Judgment at Nuremburg; The Killing Fields; A Killing in a Small Town; King of the Hill (1993); The Krays; Lean on Me; The Life of Emile Zola; Lightning Over Water; The Lindbergh Kidnapping Case; Listen Up: The Lives of Quincy Jones; Little Gloria, Happy At Last; Live a Little, Steal a Lot; Lorenzo's Oil; Love Thy Neighbor; M. Butterfly; Madame Curie; A Man Called Horse; Marie; Matewan; Mayflower Madam; McVicar; The Miracle Worker; Money for Nothing; Montana Belle; Mrs. Soffel; Murder in New Hampshire; Murder in Texas; Murder Inc.; The Murder of Mary Phagan; Mutiny on the Bounty (1935); Mutiny on the Bounty (1962); My Left Foot; The Night They Raided Minsky's; Old Gringo; One Foot in Heaven; The One That Got Away; The Onion Field; The Other Side of the Mountain; The Other Side of the Mountain Part Two; Patty Hearst; Personal Services; Picnic at Hanging Rock; The Positively True Adventures of the Alleged Texas Cheerleader-Murdering Mom; The Preppie Murder; Prick Up Your Ears; Pride of the Yankees; Prince of the City; Prisoner of Honor; A Private Matter; Queen Christina; Quiz Show; Rampage; Reckless (1935); Red Sorghum; Reds; Reversal of Fortune; Revolt of Job; Romero; Rope; Rose of Washington Square; Rudy; The Runner Stumbles; Sacco and Vanzetti; Santa Fe Trail; Scandal; Sergeant York; Serpico; The Shawshank Redemption; The Singing Nun; Small Sacrifices; The Sniper; Stand and Deliver; The Story of Adele H.; The Story of Alexander Graham Bell; The Story of Dr. Wassell; Sugarland Express; Survive; Swoon; Sybil; The Terry Fox Story; That Hamilton Woman; The Thin Blue Line; This is My Affair; Three Came Home; The Three Faces of Eve; The Times of Harvey Milk; Titanic; To Catch a Killer; To Hell and Back; To Kill a Priest; Tom Horn; Tower of London (1939); Tower of London (1962); A Town Like Alice (1956); A Town Like Alice (1985); The Town That Dreaded Sundown; The Trials of Oscar Wilde; Triumph of the Spirit; True Confessions; Tucker: The Man and His Dream; 29th Street; Unnatural Causes; Violette; Viva Villa!; Voyage of the Damned; Weeds; When Hell Was in Session; White Mile;

White Rose; Who is the Black Dahlia?; Wild Child; Wild Hearts Can't Be Broken; The Wind and the Lion; Wings of Eagles; Without a Trace; Words and Music; A World Apart; The Wrong Man

Turning the Tables (revenge, but with competition rather than just destruction): see also *Dose of Own Medicine-Given: Revenge: Ordinary Person vs. Criminal: Double Crossing: Mindgames:* Aaron Slick from Punkin Crick; The Adventures of Casanova; Arriverderci, Baby!; Bad Influence; Bedtime Story (1964); Bitch (La Garce) (1984); Bitter Rice; Black Sleep; Blackmailed; Boardwalk; Boomerang; Born Yesterday (1950); Born Yesterday (1993); Cafe Society; Champagne for Caesar; A Change of Seasons; Charming Sinners; Chisum; A Christmas Carol (1938); Crazy People; Dark Past; Death and the Maiden; Dial M For Murder; Dirty Rotten Scoundrels; Disclosure; Extremities; Fallen Angel; A Funny Thing Happened on the Way to the Forum; F/X; F/X 2: The Deadly Art of Illusion; Guilty Conscience; Harper Valley P.T.A.; Hobson's Choice; Home Alone; Home Alone 2: Lost in New York; Honky Tonk; Hot Stuff; I Stole a Million; An Innocent Man; Ivy; Kansan; Lady Eve; The Last Laugh; Let's Make Love; Lily in Love; Lipstick; The Men (1985); Mr. Klein; Mrs. Parkington; The Muppet Christmas Carol; My Little Chickadee; Niagara; Night of the Following Day; Nothing But the Best; Pass the Ammo; Platinum Blonde; The Ref; Remember My Name; Rider on the Rain; Rio Bravo; Scalphunters; Scar; Secret Partner; Send Me No Flowers; The Servant; The Shakiest Gun in the West; Silent Partner; Sleuth; Sneakers; Sting 2; Strangers on a Train; The Super; Susan Slept Here; Sweet Rosie O'Grady; Switch; Tattoo; The Tender Trap; There's a Girl in My Soup; Toy Soldiers; Trading Places; The Unsuspected; Uptown Saturday Night; Victim; Wait Until Dark; Wildcats; The Young in Heart

TV Life (stars and shows of the boob tube): see also *Spoofs-TV: Media Satire: Hollywood Life: TV Movies: TV Pilot Movies:* American Dream; Americathon; Andy Warhol's Heat; Avalon; The Barefoot Executive; Broadcast News; Cancel My Reservation; Champagne for Caesar; Delirious; Every Home Should

Have One; The Explorers; A Face in the Crowd; Frankenstein '70; Gazebo; Glory! Glory!; Hairspray; Happy Anniversary; A Hard Day's Night; He Said, She Said; Helter Skelter (1949); Hero; Kentucky Fried Movie; The Killing of Sister George; The King of Comedy; Love Machine; Medium Cool; Micki and Maude; Midnight (1989); Murder by Television; My Favorite Year; Network; Newsfront; On the Air; Pass the Ammo; Quiz Show; Running Man (1987); Scrooged; Simon and Laura; Soapdish; Stay Tuned; The Sunshine Boys; Switching Channels; There's a Girl in My Soup; The Thrill of it All; Tootsie; Trip; UHF; Videodrome; Who's Been Sleeping in My Bed?; Wild Palms; Wrong is Right

TV Movies (produced for or first shown on cable or network television; includes mini-series): see also *TV Pilot Movies: Mini-Series:* Adam; The Adventures of Huckleberry Finn (1985); After the Shock; All My Sons (1949); All My Sons (1986); Almos a Man; Almost Pregnant; Amateur Night at the Dixie Bar and Grill; The Amazing Howard Hughes; Amazing Stories; Amber Waves; Amityville 1992: It's About Time; Amityville 4; Amityville, a New Generation; The Amityville Curse; Andre's Mother; Anastasia (1984); Ants; As Summers Die; Attic: The Hiding of Anne Frank; Attica (1971); Attica (1991); The Autobiography of Miss Jane Pittman; Babycakes; The Babysitter; Based on an Untrue Story; The Best Little Girl in the World; Between Friends; Between Two Women; Beverly Hills Madam; The Big One, The Great Los Angeles Earthquake; Bill; Bill: On His Own; Billy Galvin; Blind Ambition; Blind Side; Blind Spot; Bloodhounds of Broadway (1989); Body Bags; Body in the Library; Bopha!; The Borrowers; The Bourne Identity; Breaking Up is Hard to Do; Brian's Song; Broadway Bound; Buried Alive; Burning Season; The Caine Mutiny Court Martial (1988); Chantilly Lace; Charmer; Chiefs; China Beach; Christmas Lilies of the Field; The Chronicles of Narnia; The Cisco Kid; Citizen Cohn; Comrades; Comrades of Summer; Conagher; Cooperstown; The Courtship; Dark Angel (1991); Day After; Day One; Dead of Night (1977); Deadlock; Deadly Matrimony; Deliberate Stranger; Diana: Her True Story; Diary of a Hitman; The Disappearance of Aimee;

Disaster at Silo 7; Displaced Person; Doctor Quinn, Medicine Woman; Double Exposure; Double Jeopardy; Dying Room Only; Early Frost; East of Eden (1980); Eleanor & Franklin; Elvis: The Movie; Eric; The Ernest Green Story; The Execution of Private Slovik; The Executioner's Song; F. Scott Fitzgerald in Hollywood; Family Pictures; Family Upside Down; Fatal Vision; Fear Inside; Fellow Traveler; The Feud; Fine Things; The Fire Next Time; Flash; Flood!; Forgotten Prisoners; Fortunes of War; The Fourth Story; Foxfire (1987); Full Eclipse; Girl Most Likely to . . . (1971); The Glass House; God Bless the Child; The Good Father; The Good Fight; Gore Vidal's Lincoln; The Grass is Always Greener Over the Septic Tank; The Great Escape 2: The Untold Story; Green Eyes; The Green Man; Griffin and Phoenix, A Love Story; Guilty Conscience; Gun Crazy (1992); Guyana Tragedy, The Story of Jim Jones; Hawks; Helter Skelter (1976); The Hunchback of Notre Dame (1982); I Know Why the Caged Bird Sings; The Incredible Journey of Dr. Meg Laurel; It; Jesus of Nazareth; Jewel in the Crown; The Josephine Baker Story; Katherine; Keep the Change; A Killing in a Small Town; Killjoy; The King; Ladykiller (1992); The Last Seduction; Laurel Avenue; LBJ: The Early Years; The Lindbergh Kidnapping Case; Little Gloria, Happy At Last; Live Wire; The Lost Language of Cranes; Marilyn, the Untold Story; Maybe I'll Be Home in the Spring; Miss Rose White; Moonlighting (1985); Murder by Natural Causes; Murder in Texas; Murder of Mary Phagan; Night Gallery; The Nurse; O Pioneers!; O'Hara's Wife; Oliver Twist (1982); Ordeal by Innocence; Paris Trout; The People Next Door; Playing for Time; Portrait; The Positively True Adventures of the Alleged Texas Cheerleader-Murdering Mom; Power, Passion, and Murder; The Preppie Murder; Prime Suspect; The Prince of Central Park; Prisoner of Honor; A Private Matter; Pudd'nhead Wilson; Queen of the Stardust Ballroom; The Red Pony (1976); Red Rock West; The Red Shoes Diaries; Rehearsal for Murder; Right of Way; Roanoak; Roots; Roots, the Gift; Running Mates; Sakharov; See How She Runs; Seize the Day; Separate but Equal; Shadow Riders; The Shell Seekers;

Silhouette; Sinatra; Small Sacrifices; The Sniper; Sophia Loren, Her Own Story; Sophisticated Gents; Special Bulletin; Stalin; Strangers, the Story of a Mother and Daughter; Sudie and Simpson; Summer of My German Soldier; Sybil; Tanner '88; The Tenth Man; The Terry Fox Story; They; The Thousand Pieces of Gold; Thursday's Game; To Catch a Killer; To Dance with the White Dog; Tommyknockers; A Town Like Alice (1985); Traffik; Tribes; Trilogy in Terror; The Two Worlds of Jenny Logan; Uncle Tom's Cabin (1969); Unnatural Causes; An Unsuitable Job For a Woman; When Hell Was in Session; White Mama; White Mile; Who is the Black Dahlia? Whoops! Apocalypse (1983); Wild Palms; Wildflower; Woman Screaming; Young Catherine

TV Series/TV Pilot Movies (series on tape and/or movies which were intended as or became series): see also *Mini-Series: TV Series:* The Addams Family; Addams Family Values; Batman, The Movie; The Brady Bunch Movie; China Beach; Clarence, the Cross-Eyed Lion; Dragnet (1987); Fawlty Towers; The Fugitive: The Final Episode; Golden Years; A Goofy Movie; John Cleese on How to Irritate People; Moonlighting (1985); The Nude Bomb; Nurse; On the Air; Police Squad! Help Wanted!; The Prisoner: Arrival; Scarface Mob/The Untouchables Pilot; Star Trek: The Motion Picture; Star Trek II: The Wrath of Khan; Star Trek III: The Search for Spock; Star Trek IV: The Voyage Home; Star Trek V: The Final Frontier; Star Trek VI: The Undiscovered Country; Star Trek: The Motion Picture; Twin Peaks; Star Trek: Generations; The Untouchables

TV Series Movies (based upon existing TV Series): see also *TV Series: TV Pilot Movies: Saturday Night Live Movies:* Are You Being Served?; Car 54, Where Are You?; The Flintstones; The Fugitive (1993); The Head; Jetsons Movie; The Little Rascals; Maverick; Till Death Us Do Part; Twilight Zone: The Movie

20-Somethings: see also *Coming of Age: Generation X: Pre-Life Crisis: Bratpack Stories:* Bodies, Rest & Motion; Boyfriends and Girlfriends; Clerks; Diner; Less Than Zero; Little Noises; Reality Bites; Rendez-Vous; Shaking the Tree; Singles; Slacker; St. Elmo's Fire;

U

UFOs: see also *Aliens-Outer Space: Good: Aliens-Outer Space: Evil: SCI-FI: Outer Space Movies: Martians: Mystery-Unsolved: True or Not?* The Ambushers; Batteries Not Included; Children of the Damned; Close Encounters of the Third Kind; The Day the Earth Stood Still; E.T.: The Extra-Terrestrial; A Fire in the Sky; Flight of the Navigator; Hangar 18; My Science Project; Spaced Invaders; Tommy-knockers; UFOria; Zardoz

Unattainable Men: see *Elusive Men: Sexy Men: Romance-Girl Wants Boy: Wallflowers & Hunks: Dreams: Quests*

Unattainable Women: see *Elusive Women: Sexy Women: Romance-Boy Wants Girl: Nerds & Babes: Dreams: Quests*

Unbelieved: see also *Accused Unjustly: Framed?: Liars: Paranoia: Women in Jeopardy:* The Adventures of Tom Sawyer; Alien 3; Aliens; Bunny Lake is Missing; Cameron's Closet; Cloak and Dagger (1984); Coma; Dangerous Crossing; Dream Team; Dying Room Only; The Entity; Escape from the Planet of the Apes; Ex-Mrs. Bradford; Eyewitness (1970); Fallen Idol; The Foreign Correspondent; Fright Night; Fright Night Part 2; I Saw What You Did; I Want to Live!; In a Lonely Place; Jackson County Jail; Jaws; Lady in White; Lady on a Train; The Lady Vanishes (1938); The Lady Vanishes (1979); Ladykiller (1992); Love at First Bite; Mad Miss Manton; Mannequin (1987); Mannequin 2: On the Move; Melvin and Howard; Midnight Lace; Mirage; Murder; Nanny; The Night Stalker/The Night Strangler; North by Northwest; Oh, God; Oh God Book Two; Oh God, You Devil; Omen; Omen IV: The Awakening; Primary Motive; The Prize; Rear Window; Reflecting Skin; Rosemary's Baby; Scarlet Street; The Secret Beyond the Door; The Sentinel; Shock Corridor; Silver Bullet; So Long at the Fair; Splash!; Striking Distance; Sylvia and the Ghost; UFOria; Warning Sign; Window; Witness to Murder; Woman Screaming

Uncles: see *Relatives-Troublesome*

Undercover: see also *Detective Stories: Disguises: Spy Films: Fugitives from the Law: Identities-Assumed: FBI: CIA:* Against the Wind; Air America; Another Stakeout; The Assassination Bureau; Betrayed (1989); Beverly Hills Cop 3; Big Combo; Black Widow (1987); Brubaker; Bullets or Ballots; Charade; Cleopatra Jones; Cleopatra Jones & The Casino of Gold; Coma; Death Warrant; The Deceivers; The Devil and Miss Jones; Diamonds are Forever; Europa, Europa; Fletch; Fletch Lives; For Your Eyes Only; The French Connection II; Gator; Gentleman's Agreement; Goldfinger; The Great Race; Gymkata; I Was a Communist for the FBI; I Was a Male War Bride; Jakarta; Journey into Fear; Just One of the Girls; Lancer Spy; Let's Face It; License to Kill; The Little Drummer Girl; The Looking Glass War; Lost Command; Love Crimes; Mackintosh Man; Mark of the Vampire; The Mob; Molly Maguires; Never Say Never Again; New Jack City; No Escape, No Return; No Man's Land (1987); No Mercy; North Avenue Irregulars; The Odessa File; Paleface; Paper Lion; Plain Clothes; Point Break; Raw Deal; Real Men; Red Heat; Revenge of the Pink Panther; Richest Girl in the World; Roxanne; Rush; The Russia House; Serpico; She Done Him Wrong; Shining Through; Shock Corridor; Southern Yankee; Stage Fright; Stakeout; State of Grace; A Stranger Among Us; Sullivan's Travels; Sunburn; The Tamarind Seed; Under Fire; Where the Spies Are; Yakuza; You Only Live Twice

Underdog Stories: see also *Rags to Riches: Sports Movies: Fighting the System: Social Drama: Civil Rights: Reformers: Rebels: Feisty Females:* The African Queen; All The Marbles; All the Right Moves; Best of the Best; The Best of Times; Born Yesterday (1950); Born Yesterday (1993); Breaking Away;

Broadway Bill; The Challenge; Charly; Coach; Cool Runnings; D2: The Mighty Ducks; Damn Yankees; Days of Thunder; 8 Seconds; The Fountainhead; Funny Girl; The Gladiator; Hoosiers; The Karate Kid; The Karate Kid, Part II; The Karate Kid, Part III; The Kid from Brooklyn; The Kid from Left Field; Little Giants; The Longest Yard; Major League; Major Payne; Matilda; The Mighty Ducks; Milky Way (1936); The Miracle Worker; Miss Firecracker; The Mouse That Roared; Norma Rae; Places in the Heart; The Power of One; Rocky; Rocky II; Rocky III; Rocky IV; Rocky V; Rudy; Satisfaction; Sing You Sinners; Sister Act 2; Slap Shot; Streets of Gold; Strictly Business; UHF; Victory; The Wackiest Ship in the Army; Wildcats

Underrated (movies which generally deserved more attention upon release and/or still do): see also *Overlooked at Release: Forgotten Films: Hidden Gems: Sleeper Hits: Cult Films:* Ace in the Hole; The Adventures of Barry McKenzie; All Night Long (1981); Always Together; Ambulance; The Amorous Adventures of Moll Flanders; Another Woman; Apartment Zero; Baby Boom; Bad Company; Better Off Dead; Beyond a Reasonable Doubt; Beyond the Valley of the Dolls; Bitter Moon; Black Widow (1987); Blame it on the Bellboy; Blood and Concrete; Blood from the Mummy's Tomb; Boomerang; The Breakfast Club; Brimstone and Treacle; Bunny Lake is Missing; Bye Bye Braverman; Candy; Cannery Row; Charley Varrick; City of Hope; Cloak and Dagger (1984); Cold Sassy Tree; The Comic; Compromising Positions; Continental Divide; Cops and Robbersons; D.O.A. (1949); Daddy's Gone A-Hunting; Day of the Dolphin; Dead of Winter; Death in Brunswick; Deep Cover; Defending Your Life; The Devils; Diary of a Mad Housewife; Disorderly Orderly; Dogfight; Dr. Phibes Rises Again; Drop Dead Fred; Eleven Harrowhouse; Exposed; Extremities; Eye of the Cat; Eyes in the Night; Falling in Love; Fearless; A Fine Madness; For Pete's Sake; Fortune; Guilty as Sin; Housesitter; I Love You to Death; I Wake Up Screaming; In a Lonely Place; Intruder in the Dust; Iron Petticoat; It Grows on Trees; The Jerk; Just Tell Me What You Want; The Killing of Chinese Bookie; Killing Zoe; The King of Comedy; A Kiss

Before Dying (1956); A Kiss Before Dying (1991); Krull; The Lamb; The Last Hunt; Last of the Red Hot Lovers; The Last Tycoon; The Legend of Lylah Clare; The Little Girl Who Lives Down the Lane; The Lonely Guy; The Long Day Closes; Lorenzo's Oil; Love at First Bite; Love Letters (1984); Lovesick; Mahogany; The Man with Two Brains; Marriage of a Young Stockbroker; Married to the Mob; The Mechanic; The Medusa Touch; Mickey One; Mike's Murder; Min and Bill; The Miracle (1990); Mirage; Momma, There's a Man in Your Bed; Mommie Dearest; Murder, He Says; My Bodyguard; My Cousin Vinny; My Favorite Year; New York, New York; 92 in the Shade; Notorious Landlady; The Nutty Professor (1963); Once Upon a Crime; The Outoftowners; The Owl and the Pussycat; Ready to Wear; Samurai; Say Anything; Scarlet Street; Scenes from the Class Struggle in Beverly Hills; Secret Partner; Semi-Tough; The Sentinel; Serial; The Set-Up; She Devil; Shock to the System; Shoot the Moon; Silent Partner; Situation Hopeless But Not Serious; Slaves of New York; Sleepless in Seattle; Slither; Smile; So Fine; Soapdish; SOB; Something Wild (1986); Splendor in the Grass; Stanley & Iris; Stars and Bars; Still of the Night; Straight Time; Sugarland Express; Supergirl; Suspiria; Sweet Dreams; Swept Away; Threesome; Uncle Buck; Under Milk Wood; Under the Yum Yum Tree; The Unsinkable Molly Brown; Up the Sandbox; Used Cars; Valentino (1977); Vanishing Point; Visit to a Small Planet; Walk in the Spring Rain; White Dog; Who is Killing the Great Chefs of Europe?; Who's Harry Crumb?; The Wicker Man; The Wilby Conspiracy; Winter Kills; A Woman's Tale; The World According to Garp; Yentl

Understudies: see also *Theater Life: Actors: Actresses: Mentors/Proteges: Svengalis:* All About Eve; Amadeus; Anna; Barbarosa; Breaking In; Broadway Melody; The Competition; 42nd Street; Singing in the Rain; The Stooge; Twentieth Century

Underwater Adventure: see also *Monsters-Underwater: Adventure at Sea: Submarines:* Above the Rim; Abyss; Airport 1977; Around the World Under the Sea; Beneath the 12 Mile Reef; Big Blue; The Deep; Deepstar Six; Gray Lady Down; Hello Down There; Leviathan; Shark!; The

Spy Who Loved Me; Thunderball; 20,000 Leagues Under the Sea

Unemployment: see also *Poor People: Making a Living: Ordinary People Stories: Working Class: Social Drama: Depression Era:* Bottoms Up; Career Opportunities; Chandler; Folks!; Fun With Dick and Jane; I'll Do Anything; Lost in America; Love on the Dole; Mad Wednesday; Mr. Mom; The Prisoner of Second Avenue; Reality Bites; Roger & Me; The Scout; Strange Bargain; They Shoot Horses, Don't They?; The Thousand Clowns; The Three Cornered Moon

Unintentionally Funny (films including funny things that weren't really supposed to be humorous-bad acting, bad direction, bad dialogue, etc.): see also *Flops-Major: Camp: Cult Films:* The Adventurers; The Agency; Airport '79, The Concorde; Alligator People; American Anthem; Ants; Attack of the 50-Foot Woman (1958); Attack of the 50-Foot Woman (1993); Bedtime for Bonzo; Bittersweet Love; Blood and Black Lace; Blue City; Blue Ice; Blue Steel; Body of Evidence; Bolero (1984); The Borrower; Bride of the Gorilla; Bride of the Monster; Butterfly; Campus Man; Car; Cat Women of the Moon; Circle of Two; The Commies are Coming, the Commies are Coming; Conflict of Interest; The Conqueror; D.O.A. (1988); Dead Bang; The Dead Pool; Desperate Hours (1990); The Domino Principle; Double Impact; Driver's Seat; Empire of the Ants; Endless Love; Evel Knievel; Eye of the Devil; The Eyes of Laura Mars; The Fan; Female on the Beach; Final Analysis; Flash Gordon; Forever Amber; Foxfire (1955); Fresh Horses; Glen or Glenda?; Golden Earrings; Goldengirl; The Greatest; Grizzly; The Guardian; Gymkata; Hannie Caulder; The Happy Hooker; Hellcats of the Navy; The Holcroft Covenant; I Thank a Fool; I Want What I Want; I Was a Communist for the FBI; Ice Castles; Inchon; The Invisible Woman; Ishtar; Jet Pilot; Johnny Guitar; Kalifornia; Killer Fish; The Killers (1964); King David; Lambada; Leviathan; Life Force; Like Father, Like Son; Lipstick; Listen to Me; Live a Little, Love a Lot; Lonely Lady; Look in Any Window; Losin' It; Lost Horizon (1973); Love Has Many Faces; Love is a Many Splendored Thing; Love Machine; Mahogany; Man with the Golden Arm; Manitou; A Matter of Time; Medusa

Touch; Midnight Crossing; Mississippi Burning; The Mole People; Mrs. Pollifax, Spy; Murder by Phone; My Blood Runs Cold; My Son John; My Stepmother is an Alien; On Deadly Ground; One Million BC (1940); One Million Years BC (1966); Orca-Killer Whale; Oscar; Over the Top; The Pelican Brief; Perfect; Plan 9 From Outer Space; Reefer Madness; The Reincarnation of Peter Proud; Run; Salome, Where She Danced; Saturn 3; Sentimental Journey; Shanghai Gesture; Shanghai Surprise; Side Out; Silver Chalice; Single White Female; Skidoo; The Statue; Stone Cold; Strait Jacket; Strange Cargo; Street Angel; The Swarm; Swing Kids; The Target; Tarzan and His Mate; Tarzan Escapes; Tarzan, the Ape Man (1932); Tarzan, the Ape Man (1981); The Temp; Tentacles; To Kill a Clown; Torch Song Trilogy; Toy Soldiers; Trog; The Trouble with Girls; Under the Cherry Moon; Valley of the Dolls; The Vanishing

(1993); Venom; Whispers in the Dark; Wisdom; Xanadu; Xtro

Unions: see also *Strikes: Reformers: Social Drama: Working Class: Underdog Stories:* Action Jackson; Adalen 31; Angry Silence; Blue Collar; Brother John; F.I.S.T.; Garment Jungle; Hoffa; I'm All Right, Jack; Last Exit to Brooklyn; Man of Iron; Matewan; The Molly Maguires; Norma Rae; The Pajama Game; Silkwood; The Strike; Which Way is Up?

Unjustly Accused: see *Accused-Unjustly*

Unlucky People: see also *Accident Prone: Comedy of Errors: Murphy's Law Stories: Lucky People:* La Chevre; Live Now, Pay Later; The Outoftowners; Pure Luck

Unsolved Mystery: see *Mystery-Unsolved: also True or Not?: Docudrama: Missing Persons: True Stories: Perfect Crimes: Clever Plots & Endings*

Unwed Mothers: see *Mothers-Unwed*

Upper Class: see *Rich People: Children-Rich: Snobs: Jetsetters: Eurotrash: Country Club Life: Debutantes: Moguls*

Urban Life: see *Inner City Life: Urban Horrors: Social Drama: Homeless People: New York Life:* Desperate Characters; Grand Canyon; Playtime

Urban Horrors (horrific happenings peculiar to big-city living): see also *Rural Horrors: HORROR: Inner City Life:* Grand Canyon; Judgment Night; Lady in a Cage; The Outoftowners; Quick Change; The Taking of Pelham 123

Urban vs. Rural: see *City vs. Country*

Users: see *Mindgames: Freeloaders: Con Artists: Liars*

Utopia (stories about supposedly perfect societies): see also *Resorts:* Demolition Man; Fahrenheit 451; Lost Horizon (1937); Lost Horizon (1973); Road to Utopia

V

Vacation Romance: see *Romance on Vacation:* also *Americans Abroad: ROMANCE: Vacations*

Vacations: see also *Romance on Vacation: Vacations-European: Americans Abroad: Islands: Exotic Locales:* Bagdad Cafe; Big Girls Don't Cry . . . They Get Even; Bon Voyage!; Bonjour, Tristesse; The Bridge; Brigadoon; Cactus; Captain Ron; C'est la Vie; Cancel My Reservation; Centennial Summer; C'est la Vie; Chained; Chantilly Lace; Club Paradise; Cocktail; Deliverance; Desire; Desire and Hell at Sunset Motel; Dodsworth; Dr. M.; Enchanted April; For the Love of Benji; The Four Seasons; Foxfire (1955); The Grand Highway; The Great Outdoors; Haunted Summer; Heartbreak Kid; High Season; High Spirits; The Hills Have Eyes; Honky Tonk Freeway; Hot Pursuit; If It's Tuesday, This Must Be Belgium; In the Cool of the Day; Innocents in Paris (1953); It Started in Naples; Joe vs. the Volcano; Joey Breaker; Knife in the Water; L'Avventura; Lady in the Car with Glasses and a Gun; The Lady Takes a Chance; Last of Sheila; Last Summer; Last Year at Marienbad; Light in the Piazza; The Long Long Trailer; Lost in America; Lumiere d'Ete; Magic; The Magus; Majority of One; The Man I Married; A Midsummer Night's Sex Comedy; Monsieur Hulot's Holiday; The Moon Spinners; Mr. Hobbs Takes a Vacation; My Father the Hero; My Six Loves; Nancy Goes to Rio; Nanou; National Lampoon's European Vacation; National Lampoon's Vacation; Never on Sunday; Night of the Iguana; Oh, Dad, Poor Dad . . .; On Golden Pond; Once in a Blue Moon; Only You; A Passage to India; Perfect Furlough; Piranha; The Return of the Secaucus Seven; The Romantic Englishwoman; Scapegoat; Scent of a Woman; Scent of Mystery; The Sheltering Sky; Ship of Fools; Smiles of a Summer Night; Sons of the Desert; Spring Break; Springtime in the Rockies; The Story of Three Loves; Strangers in Good Company; Summer; A Summer Place; Summertime; Sunday in the Country; Tender is the Night; To Forget Venice; Travels with My Aunt; Two For the Road; 2000 Maniacs; Weekend at Bernie's; Weekend at Bernie's 2; What About Bob?; Where the Boys Are; Where the Boys Are '84

Vacations-European: see also *Vacation Romance:* Bon Voyage!; Bon Voyage, Charlie Brown; Dodsworth; Driver's Seat; Hard Contract; How Sweet It Is; If It's Tuesday, This Must Be Belgium; The Love Affair (1939); The Man I Married; Montenegro; National Lampoon's European Vacation; Once in Paris; Pandora and the Flying Dutchman; Rich, Young and Pretty; Table for Five; Tender is the Night; Two For the Road

Vacations-Nightmares: see also *Nightmare Journeys: Murphy's Law Stories:* Deliverance; Dr. M.; The Great Outdoors; The Hills Have Eyes; Knife in the Water; The Long Long Trailer; Motel Hell; Nothing but Trouble (1991); Old Dark House (1932); Old Dark House (1962); The Pack; Piranha; Planes, Trains, and Automobiles; Rawhead Rex; The River Wild; Strangers in Good Company; To Kill a Clown; A Touch of Class

Vacations-Summer: see also *Camps/Camping: Vacations:* Aloha Summer; Grand Highway; Last Summer; Meatballs; Mr. Hobbs Takes a Vacation; Sing as We Go; A Summer Place; Summer Story; SuperDad; Sweet Lorraine

Vampires: see also *Dracula: Spoofs-Vampire: HORROR:* Andy Warhol's Dracula; Blacula; Bram Stoker's Count Dracula (1970); Bram Stoker's Dracula (1992); Brides of Dracula; Castle of Doom; Count Yorga, Vampire; Dead of Night (1977); Dracula (1931); Dracula (1979); Dracula Has Risen from the Grave; Dracula (Horror of Dracula, 1958); Dracula, Prince of Darkness; Dracula's Daughter; Ed Wood; The Fearless Vampire Killers; Fright Night;

Death Wish 4; Death Wish 5; Exterminator; Exterminator 2; Eye for an Eye; Fighting Back; Firecreek; First Blood; A Fistful of Dollars; Flash; For a Few Dollars More; A Force of One; Guilty as Charged; Hang 'em High; Hannie Caulder; High Plains Drifter; Hit!; Jimmy Hollywood; The Klansman; Law and Disorder (1974); The Lawman; The Legend of Billie Jean; Magnum Force; The Outlaw Josey Wales; Return of the Musketeers; Return of the Seven; Star Chamber; Super Cops; Tank; Two Mules for Sister Sara; Warlock (1958)

Vikings: see also *Scandinavia, Middle Ages:* Erik the Viking; Island at the Top of the World; The Last Valley; The Long Ships; Prince Valiant; Vikings

Violence in Comedy: see *Comedy & Violence:* also *Tragi-Comedy: Black Comedy: Comedy-Morbid: Violence-Unexpected*

**Violence-Sudden/Unexpected (where what is otherwise a stable story, something violent suddenly alters everything): see also *TRAGEDY: Comedy & Violence:* Barcelona; Before Sunrise; Billy Budd; Bring Me the Head of Alfredo Garcia; The Comfort of Strangers; Damage; Equus; Fingers; The Gun in Betty Lou's Handbag; Henry: Portrait of a Serial Killer; Howards End; Isadora; The King of Marvin Gardens; Little Murders; Looking for Mr. Goodbar;

Man of Flowers; The Man Upstairs; A Passage to India; Regarding Henry; A Room with a View; The Sailor Who Fell From Grace with the Sea; Straw Dogs; Sweet Dreams; Tattoo; Torch Song Trilogy

Virgins: see also *Coming of Age: Teenage Movies: Life Transitions: Decisions-Big: Wallflowers:* Abel; Agnes of God; The Americanization of Emily; Athena; Baby, It's You; Ballad of the Sad Cafe; The Bell Jar; Bilitis; Blame it on Rio; The Chicken Chronicles; Class; Closely Watched Trains; A Dangerous Woman; The Devil's Eye; Every Girl Should be Married; Experience Preferred . . .; First Time; The Frog Prince; Getting It Right; Goin' South; Guys and Dolls; Here We Go Round the Mulberry Bush; The Knack; Lair of the White Worm; The Last Picture Show; Little Darlings; The Little Girl Who Lives Down the Lane; A Little Night Music; Lolita; Losin' It; Marty; Me, Natalie; The Moon is Blue; Mystic Pizza; My Tutor; Never Give a Sucker an Even Break; Once Bitten; Romance; Scorchers; Sex and the Single Girl; Smooth Talk; Sophie's Choice; The Sterile Cuckoo; Summer and Smoke; Summer of '42; Sunday in New York; Three on a Couch; Valmont; The Virgin and the Gypsy; The Virgin Queen; Virgin Soldiers; You're a Big Boy Now

Virtual Reality: see also *Video Game Movies: Futuristic Films: Animation-Computer: SCI-FI:* Brainscan; Brainstorm (1983); Cool World; Disclosure; The Lawnmower Man; Total Recall; Wild Palms

Visionaries: see *Geniuses: Future-Seeing the: Psychics*

Volcanoes: see also *Disaster Movies: Earthquakes:* Around the World Under the Sea; Boom!; The Devil at Four O'Clock; Joe vs. Volcano; Krakatoa, East of Java; The Land That Time Forgot; The Last Days of Pompeii (1935, 1960); One Million Years B.C. (1940, 1966); Under the Volcano; When Time Ran Out; You Only Live Twice

Voodoo: see also *Caribbean: Magic: Witchcraft:* The Devil Doll; I Walked with a Zombie; Live and Let Die; White Zombie

Voyeurism: see also *Surveillance: Pornography World: Photographers: Videotape Scandals: Neighbors-Troublesome:* Bedroom Eyes; Blue Thunder; Body Double; Call Me; Confessions of a Window Cleaner; The Conversation; Death Watch; Die Watching; Exotica; Fade to Black (1993); Look in Any Window; Monsieur Hire; Night Eyes; 1984 (1955); 1984 (1984); Peeping Tom; Radio Days; Real Life; Rear Window; Sliver; Smile; Variety; Videodrome; Witness to Murder

Wacky Comedy: see *Comedy-Slapstick: FARCE: Action Comedy: COMEDY*

Wagon Trains: see also *Pioneers: Indians-American: Conflict with:* Apache Uprising; Arizona; Bend of the River; The Big Trail; Hallelujah Trail; The Indian Fighter; Red River; Stagecoach (1939); Stagecoach (1966); Wagonmaster; The Way West

Waiters/Waitresses: see also *Restaurant Settings: Working Class: Ordinary People Stories: Actors: Actresses:* Bread and Chocolate; Come Back to the Five and Dime, Jimmy Dean, Jimmy Dean; Dogfight; Frankie and Johnny; The Harvey Girls; It Could Happen to You; It Started with Eve; Of Human Bondage (1934); Of Human Bondage (1946); Of Human Bondage (1964); The Petrified Forest; Protocol; Under Two Flags; Untamed Heart; When Tomorrow Comes; White Palace

Wales: see also *England: British Films:* The Corn is Green; The Mill on the Floss

Wallflowers: see also *Wallflowers & Hunks: Spinsters: Women Alone: Nerds: Virgins:* Alice in Wonderland; Cabaret; Carrie (1976); Circle of Friends; Dirty Dancing; Dogfight; The Enchanted Cottage; Experience Preferred . . .; Funny Face; Georgy Girl; Give Me a Sailor; The Glass Menagerie (1950); The Glass Menagerie (1973); The Glass Menagerie (1987); The Gun in Betty Lou's Handbag; Guys and Dolls; The Heiress; The Last Summer; Little Shop of Horrors (1960); Little Shop of Horrors (1986); Love Potion #9; Me, Natalie; Metropolitan (1990); Muriel's Wedding; New Leaf; Now, Voyager; The Rainmaker; Smashing Time; Stacy's Knights; The Sterile Cuckoo; Summer and Smoke; Tell Me that You Love Me, Junie Moon; The Way We Were; Year of the Comet

Wallflowers & Hunks: see also *Romance-Girl Wants Boy: Nerds & Babes: Coming of Age:* Alice Adams; Alice in Wonderland; Babycakes; Buster and Billie; Cabaret; Circle of Friends; Dirty Dancing; Dogfight; Georgy Girl; Guys and Dolls; The Heiress; Masquerade (1988); Me, Natalie; Muriel's Wedding; Pillow Talk; Polyester; The Private Lives of Elizabeth & Essex; The Rainmaker; Sugarbaby; Tim; The Way We Were

Wall Street: see also *Business Life: Stock Brokers: New York Life: Power Struggles: Executives: Yuppies: Corruption:* Adventure in Washington; The Bonfire of the Vanities; How to Succeed in Business without Really Trying; Other People's Money; The Toast of New York; Working Girl

War at Home (life back home while the boys were at battle): see also *Veterans: World War II Era: Vietnam Era:* Au Revoir, les Enfants; Cavalcade; Coming Home; Gaby; Hope and Glory; Impatient Years; Limbo; The Millionairess; Mrs. Miniver; Over Twenty-One; Since You Went Away; Stage Door Canteen; Swing Shift; Till the End of Time; Today We Live; Trojan Women; Two Women

War at Sea: see also *Adventure at Sea: Pirates: World War II Stories: Japanese as Enemy:* Abroad with Two Yanks; Action in the North Atlantic; Air Force; Captain Horatio Hornblower; Captain Kidd; The Fighting Seabees; Flight of the Intruder; The Flying Leathernecks; God Is My Co-Pilot; Hellcats of the Navy; Midway; Too Late the Hero; Tora! Tora! Tora!

War Battles (where the battle's historical importance is usually the story's primary focus, not necessarily the individual lives of soldiers; most often true stories): see also *War Stories: World War I Stories: World War II Stories: Battle of the Bulge:* Air Force; The Alamo; Alexander Nevsky; All Quiet on the Western Front; America (1924); Back to Bataan; Ballad of a Soldier; Bataan; Battle Cry; Battle for the Planet of the Apes; Battle of Algiers; The Battle of Britain; Battle of Neretva; Battle of the

Bulge; Battleground; Beau Geste; Beau Ideal; The Big Red One; The Birth of a Nation; The Buccaneer (1936, 1958); Charge of the Light Brigade; The Commancheros; The Dam Busters; The Fighting Kentuckians; Gettysburg; Henry V (1944, 1989); Holy Matrimony; Inchon; Kagemusha; Khartoum; The Last Command (1955); The Last Valley; The Lion in the Desert; Little Big Horn; The Lives of a Bengal Lancer; Lone Star; The Longest Day; MacArthur; Midway; The Naked and the Dead; Northwest Passage; October; The Seventh Cavalry; Shenandoah; Strategic Air Command; To Hell and Back; Too Late the Hero; Tora! Tora! Tora!; The Trojan War; True Glory; Twelve O'Clock High; Ulzana's Raid; Vera Cruz; War and Peace (1967); Waterloo; Zulu; Zulu Dawn

War Crimes/Horrors: see *Torture: Concentration Camps: Nazi Stories: Hitler: World War II Stories*

Warlocks: see *Witches/Witchcraft: Satanism: Supernatural Danger: Evil Men: Magic: Occult*

Warner Gangster Era (Warner Bros. studio mob movies made mostly in the 1930s): Angels With Dirty Faces; Bullets or Ballots; G-Men; The Hatchet Man; He Was Her Man; Little Caesar; Little Giant (1933); Mayor of Hell; Public Enemy; The Roaring Twenties; They Drive by Night (1940); Twenty Thousand Years in Sing Sing; You Can't Get Away With Murder

War of 1812 Era: see also *1800s: Early America:* The Buccaneer (1938); The Buccaneer (1958); The Fighting Kentuckian

War Stories/Battles (generally centered around battles): see also *Military Stories: World War I Stories: World War II Stories: Korean War: Vietnam War: Nazi Stories:* Apocalypse Now; Above and Beyond; Above the Rim; Ace of Aces; Aces High; Action in Arabia; Action in the North Atlantic; Against the Wind; Air Force; The Alamo; Alexander Nevsky; All Quiet on the Western Front; All the Young Men; Alsino and the Condor; America; The Angel Wore Red; Arsenal; Assisi Underground; Atomic City; Babette Goes to War; Back to Bataan; Ballad of a Soldier; Bataan; Battle Cry; Battle for the Planet of the Apes; Battle of Algiers; The Battle of Britian; Battle of the Bulge; Battle of the

Neretva; Battleground; Beau Geste (1926); Beau Geste (1939); Beau Geste (1966); Beau Ideal; Because You're Mine; The Bedford Incident; Big Lift; The Big Red One; Birdy; The Birth of a Nation; Black and White in Color; Blockade; Blue Max; Bold and the Brave; Breaker Morant; Bridge on the River Kwai; A Bridge Too Far; Bridges at Toko-Ri; The Buccaneer (1938); The Buccaneer (1958); Bushido Blade; Captain Carey, USA; Captain Kidd; Captains of the Clouds; Cast a Giant Shadow; Casualties of War; Catch Me a Spy; The Charge of the Light Brigade (1936); The Charge of the Light Brigade (1968); China; Closely Watched Trains; Command Decision; Conquest of the Planet of the Apes; Cuba; Dam Busters; Dawn Patrol; The Deer Hunter; Desert Fox; Desert Rats; Destination Tokyo; The Devil's Brigade; The Dirty Dozen; Doctor Zhivago; Dogs of War; Duck Soup; Dune; Eighty-Four Charlie Mopic; Empire of the Sun; Exodus; Farewell My Concubine; Farewell to the King; Fifty/Fifty; 55 Days at Peking; The Fighting Kentuckian; The Fighting Seabees; Fire Over England; Five Graves to Cairo; Flaming Star; Flight of the Intruder; The Flying Leathernecks; Flying Tigers; For the Boys; For Whom the Bell Tolls; Forbidden Games; Force Ten from Navarone; The Fortunes of War; Four Feathers (1929); Four Feathers (1939); Four Horsemen of the Apocalypse; Four Sons; Friendly Persuasion; From Here to Eternity; G.I. Joe; Gallipoli; Gardens of Stone; Gate of Hell; A Gathering of Eagles; The General Died at Dawn; Genghis Khan; Glory; Go for Broke; Gone With the Wind; Grand Illusion; Gray Lady Down; The Great Locomotive Chase; The Great Manhunt; The Green Berets; Guadalcanal Diary; Gung Ho! (1943); Gunga Din; Guns of Navarone; Hamburger Hill; Hangmen Also Die; Hanussen; Happy Land; Heartbreak Ridge; Heaven Knows, Mr. Allison; Heimat; Hell and High Water; Hell, Heaven, and Hoboken; Hell in the Pacific; Hell's Angels; Hellcats of the Navy; Henry V (1944); Henry V (1989); Heroes of Telemark; The Hill; Hiroshima, Mon Amour; Hitler Gang; Hitler-The Last Ten Days; Holy Matrimony; Homecoming (1948); Hook; Hope and Glory; The Hornet's Nest; Horse Soldiers; How I Won the War; The Howards of

Virginia; Hudson's Bay; Inchon; I Want You; I Wanted Wings; I Was a Spy; Immortal Sergeant; Is Paris Burning? Juarez; Kagemusha; Kelly's Heroes; Khartoum; King Rat; La Marseillaise; Lacombe, Lucien; The Last Command; The Last of the Mohicans (1936); The Last of the Mohicans (1992); The Last Valley; Left Hand of God; The Lighthorsemen; Lion of the Desert; Lives of a Bengal Lancer; Lone Star of Gold; The Longest Day; Lost Command; MacArthur; Magic Face; Mahabharata; Malaya; March or Die; Master of Ballantree; Master of the World; Mayerling (1935); Mayerling (1968); The McConnell Story; Me and the Colonel; Memphis Belle; Men of the Fighting Lady; Message to Garcia; Midway; Murphy's War; The Naked and the Dead; Nazi Agent; Never Say Goodbye; Never So Few; None But the Brave; North Star; Northwest Passage; Objective Burma; Odette; Oh, What a Lovely War; The One That Got Away; Open City; Operation Crossbow; The Outsider; The Overlanders; Paisan; Paths of Glory; Patton; Platoon; Pork Chop Hill; Pride and the Passion; The Quiet American; Raid on Rommel; Ran; The Red Badge of Courage; Red Dawn; Return of the Vampire; The Road Back; Run Silent Run Deep; Saber Jet; Sahara (1943); Salvador; Sand Pebbles; Sands of Iwo Jima; The Sea Chase; Sea Devils (1953); Sea Hawk; Sea Wolves; The Secret War of Harry Frigg; Sergeant York; The Serpent's Egg; Seventh Heaven (1927); Seventh Heaven (1937); Shame (1968); So Proudly We Hail; So Red the Rose; Strategic Air Command; Taras Bulba; Thirty Seconds Over Tokyo; 300 Spartans; This Above All; This Is the Army; Three Came Home; A Time to Love and a Time to Die; To Hell and Back; Tobruk; Tonight and Every Night; Too Late the Hero; Tora! Tora! Tora!; A Town Like Alice (1956); A Town Like Alice (1985); The Trojan War; Trojan Women; Twelve O'Clock High; Two Women; Uncommon Valor; Under Fire; Under Two Flags; Vacation from Marriage; Vera Cruz; The Victors; The Vikings; Viva Zapata; Wake Island; A Walk in the Sun; War and Peace (1956); The War Lover; Waterloo; Went the Day Well?; Where Eagles Dare; Winged Victory; Wings; The Wooden Horse; The Young Lions; Zeppelin; Zulu; Zulu Dawn

Washington D.C.: see also *Political Drama: Political Satire: Politicians: Congressmen/Senators: Diplomats: Pentagon: CIA: FBI: Spy Films:* Adventure in Washington; Advise and Consent; All the President's Men; Being There; Best Man; Blind Ambition; Broadcast News; Call Me Madam; Dave; The Day the Earth Stood Still; Dead Reckoning; Dr. Strangelove; Fail Safe; First Monday in October; Gabriel over the White House; The Gorgeous Hussy; Heartburn; Kisses for My President; Listen to Me; Live Wire; Mastergate; The More the Merrier; Mr. Smith Goes to Washington; No Way Out (1987); Seven Days in May; St. Elmo's Fire; State of the Union; The War Against Mrs. Hadley; The War Room; Washington Story; Watch on the Rhine

Weddings: see also *Marriages-Impending: Marriage Drama: Marriage Comedy: Newlyweds: Engagements-Breaking:* Ballad of the Sad Cafe; Betsy's Wedding; The Catered Affair; The Deer Hunter; Double Wedding; Father of the Bride (1950); Father of the Bride (1991); Four Weddings and a Funeral; The Graduate; He Knows You're Alone; Heartbreak Kid; Heartburn; High Noon; High Society; In Search of Gregory; The In-Laws; Invitation to the Wedding; The Italian Straw Hat; Julia Misbehaves; The June Bride; Love Parade; Lovers and Other Strangers; The Member of the Wedding; Muriel's Wedding; My New Gun; New Jack City; New Leaf; On Approval; On Her Majesty's Secret Service; The Party and the Guests; The Philadelphia Story; Plaza Suite; Prizzi's Honor; The Quiet Wedding; The Royal Wedding; Story of Boys and Girls; Twenty Bucks; Twice in a Lifetime; The Wedding; Wedding March

Weight Problems: see also *Starting Over: Depression:* Babycakes; The Best Little Girl in the World; Fatso; Fried Green Tomatoes; Full Metal Jacket; Girl Most Likely to . . . (1971); Hairspray; Heavyweights; I Don't Buy Kisses Anymore; The Road to Wellville; They Knew What They Wanted; What's Eating Gilbert Grape?

Werewolves: see also *HORROR: Humans into Animals:* An American Werewolf in London; The Curse of the Werewolf; Frankenstein Meets the Wolf Man; Full Eclipse; Haunted Honeymoon; House of Dracula; House of Frankenstein; The Howling; Howling II; Howling III; Howling IV; Howling V; I Was a Teenage Werewolf; Silver Bullet; Sleepwalkers; Teen Wolf; Teen Wolf Too; Werewolf (1956); Werewolf of London; Wolf; The Wolfman

WESTERNS: see also *West-Old: Western Comedy: Westerns-Spaghetti: Spoofs-Western: Musicals-Western: Indians-American: Raised by Indians: Indians-American: Conflict with: Cattle Ranchers: Cattle Rustlers: Cavalry: Cavalry vs. Indians: Pioneers: Explorers: Alamo Stories:* Abilene Town; Ace High; Across the Wide Missouri; The Adventures of Bullwhip Griffin; Against a Crooked Sky; Alamo; Albuquerque; Along Came Jones; Along the Great Divide; Alvarez Kelly; American Tail 2; Angel and the Badman; Annie Get Your Gun!; Annie Oakley; Apache Uprising; Appaloosa; The Apple Dumpling Gang; The Apple Dumpling Gang Rides Again; Arizona; Back to the Future 3; Bad Company; Bad Day at Black Rock; Bad Man's River; Ballad of Cable Hogue; Ballad of Josie; Bandolero; Barbarosa; The Beautiful Blonde from Bashful Bend; Behold a Pale Horse; Belle of the Yukon; Bend of the River; Big Country; Big Jake; The Big Sky; The Big Trail; Billy the Kid; Billy the Kid vs. Dracula; Bite the Bullet; Black Robe; Blazing Saddles; Blood on the Moon; Breakheart Pass; Bring Me the Head of Alfredo Garcia; Broken Arrow; Broken Lance; Buck and the Preacher; Buffalo Bill; Buffalo Bill and the Indians, or Sitting Bull's History Lesson; Butch Cassidy and the Sundance Kid; Butch and Sundance, The Early Days; Cahill: United States Marshal; Call of the Wild (1935); Call of the Wild (1972); Callaway Went Thataway; Canyon Passage; Cat Ballou; Cattle Annie & Little Britches; Cattle Queen of Montana; Chato's Land; Cheyenne Autumn; Cheyenne Social Club; Chisum; The Cisco Kid; Colorado Territory; Comancheros; Comes a Horseman; Comin' At Ya!; Conagher; The Cowboys; Dallas; Dances With Wolves; Dark Command; Davy Crockett; Destry Rides Again; The Devil's Disciple; Dirty Little Billy; Doc; Doctor Quinn, Medicine Woman; Dodge City; Drums Along the Mohawk; The Duchess and the Dirtwater Fox; Duel in the Sun; Eagle's Wing; Escape from Fort Bravo; Extreme

Prejudice; Fancy Pants; Father is a Bachelor; Fighting Mad; Firecreek; A Fistful of Dollars; A Fistful of Dynamite; Five Card Stud; Flaming Star; For a Few Dollars More; Fort Apache; Forty Guns; Four for Texas; Frenchie; The Frisco Kid (1935); The Frisco Kid (1979); The Furies; The Garden of Evil; Geronimo (1962); Geronimo (1993); Go West; Goin' South; Good Day for a Hanging; The Good, the Bad, and the Ugly; The Great Bank Robbery; Great Day in the Morning; The Great Northfield Minnesota Raid; Great Scout and Cathouse Thursday; The Grey Fox; Gun Fury; A Gunfight; A Gunfight at the O.K. Corral; A Gunfighter; Guns of the Magnificent Seven; Hallelujah Trail; Hang 'em High; The Hanging Tree; Hannie Caulder; The Harvey Girls; Heart of the West; Heartland; Heaven Only Knows; Heaven with a Gun; Heaven's Gate; Heller in Pink Tights; High Noon; High Plains Drifter; Hombre; Honky Tonk; Horse Soldiers; Hot Lead and Cold Feet; Hour of the Gun; How the West Was Won; Hud; In Old Arizona; The Indian Fighter; Iron Mistress; Jeremiah Johnson; Joe Kidd; Johnny Guitar; Junior Bonner; The Kansan; The Kentuckian; The Kid (1990); The Kissing Bandit; Kung Fu; The Lady Takes a Chance; The Last Command; Last Hard Men; The Last Hunt; Last of His Tribe; The Last of the Mohicans (1936); The Last of the Mohicans (1992); Last Sunset; The Law and Jake Wade; The Lawman; The Left-Handed Gun; Legend of the Lone Ranger; Legends of the Fall; The Life and Times of Judge Roy Bean; Light in the Forest; Lightning Jack; Little Big Horn; Little Big Man; The Lone Ranger (1955); The Lone Ranger and the Lost City of Gold; Lone Star; Lone Wolf McQuade; Lonely Are the Brave; The Long Riders; Love Me Tender; Lust in the Dust; MacKenna's Gold; The Magnificent Seven; Mail Order Bride; Major Dundee; A Man Called Horse; The Man from Colorado; The Man from Laramie; Man from Snowy River; Man in the Wilderness; The Man Who Loved Cat Dancing; The Man Who Shot Liberty Valance; Man Without a Star; Maverick; Maverick Queen; McCabe and Mrs. Miller; McLintock!; The Missouri Breaks; Montana; Montana Belle; Monte Walsh; Mother Lode; My Darling Clementine; My Name is Nobody; The

Naked Spur; Nevada Smith; North to Alaska; Northwest Passage; The Oklahoma Kid; Once Upon a Time in the West; One Eyed Jacks; Out of This World; The Outlaw; The Outlaw Josey Wales; Outrage (1964); The Outsider; The Ox-Bow Incident; Paint Your Wagon; Pale Rider; Paleface; Pardners; Pat Garrett and Billy the Kid; The Posse (1975); Posse (1993); The Professionals; The Quick and the Dead; Quigley Down Under; Rancho De Luxe; The Rare Breed; Rawhide; Red Garters; Red River; Return of a Man Called Horse; Return of the Seven; The Revengers; Rhythm on the Range; Ride 'Em Cowboy; Ride the High Country; Rio Bravo; Rio Grande; Rio Lobo; Rooster Cogburn; Rounders; Ruggles of Red Gap; San Antonio; Santa Fe; The Santa Fe Trail; Saskatchewan; The Savage; The Scalawag; Scalphunters; Sea of Grass; The Searchers; The Seven Faces of Dr. Lao; The Seventh Cavalry; The Shadow Riders; The Shakiest Gun in the West; Shalako; Shane; She Wore a Yellow Ribbon; The Shootist; The Squaw Man; Showdown; Silence of the North; Silent Tongue; Silver Lode; Silverado; The Skin Game; Soldier Blue; Son of Paleface; The Sons of Katie Elder; Spoilers; Stagecoach (1939); Stagecoach (1966); The Stalking Moon; Sunset; Support Your Local Gunfighter; Support Your Local Sheriff; Tall Men; Tell Them Willie Boy is Here; Texas; Texas Across the River; There Was a Crooked Man; They Died with Their Boots On; The Thousand Pieces of Gold; Three Amigos; Three Godfathers; Timerider; Tin Star; Tom Horn; Tombstone; Treasure of the Sierra Madre; Triumphs of a Man Called Horse; True Grit; Two Mules for Sister Sara; Ulzana's Raid; The Undefeated; The Unforgiven (1960); Unforgiven (1992); The Union Pacific; The Unsinkable Molly Brown; Valdez is Coming; Vera Cruz; The Villain; Violent Men; Virginia City; Waco; Wagonmaster; Warlock (1958); Way Out West; The Way West; Welcome to Hard Times; Wells Fargo; The Westerner; Western Union; When the Legends Die; White Buffalo; Wichita; The Wild Bunch; Will Penny; Winchester 73; Woman Obsessed; Wyatt Earp; Wyoming; Young Guns; Young Guns II; Zandy's Bride

Westerns-City Titles: see also *WESTERNS:* Albuquerque; San Antonio; Santa Fe; Virginia City; Waco; Wichita

Westerns-Comedy: see also *WESTERNS: West-Old:* The Adventures of Bullwhip Griffin; American Tail 2; Annie Get Your Gun!; Annie Oakley; The Apple Dumpling Gang; The Apple Dumpling Gang Rides Again; Arizona; Back to the Future 3; Bad Man's River; Ballad of Josie; The Beautiful Blonde from Bashful Bend; Belle of the Yukon; Billy the Kid vs. Dracula; Blazing Saddles; Butch Cassidy and the Sundance Kid; Callaway Went Thataway; Cat Ballou; Cheyenne Social Club; Cityslickers; Cityslickers 2; The Cowboy Way; The Cowboys; Destry Rides Again; Duchess and the Dirtwater Fox; Fancy Pants; Father is a Bachelor; Four for Texas; The Frisco Kid (1979); Go West; Goin' South; The Great Bank Robbery; Great Scout and Cathouse Thursday; The Harvey Girls; Heart of the West; Heaven Only Knows; Heller in Pink Tights; Hot Lead and Cold Feet; The Lady Takes a Chance; The Life and Times of Judge Roy Bean; Lightning Jack; Little Big Man; Lust in the Dust; Mail Order Bride; Maverick; McLintock!; Out of This World; Paint Your Wagon; Paleface; Pardners; Rancho De Luxe; The Rare Breed; Rhythm on the Range; Ride 'Em Cowboy; Ruggles of Red Gap; The Seven Faces of Dr. Lao; The Shakiest Gun in the West; The Sheepman; The Skin Game; Son of Paleface; Support Your Local Gunfighter; Support Your Local Sheriff; Tampopo; Texas Across the River; Three Amigos; Three Godfathers; Two Mules for Sister Sara; The Unsinkable Molly Brown; The Villain; Way Out West; The Westerner; Zandy's Bride; Zorro and the Gay Blade

Westerns-Modern (set in modern times but harkening back to the style of old westerns): see also *Westerns-Neo/Revisionist:* Bad Day at Black Rock; Cityslickers; Fighting Mad; Junior Bonner; Legends of the Fall; Lone Wolf McQuade; Lonely Are the Brave; When the Legends Die; Rancho De Luxe

Westerns-Neo/Revisionist (primarily anti-violence stories or correcting history, made recently but set in the old west most often): see also *Westerns-Modern: WESTERNS: Revisionist Films:* Appaloosa; Black Robe; Cattle Annie & Little Britches; Cheyenne Autumn; Dances With Wolves; Dirty Little Billy; Doc; A Fistful of Dollars; For a Few Dollars More; Geronimo (1993); The Great Northfield Minnesota Raid; A Gunfight; Heartland; Hour of the Gun; Hud; Jeremiah Johnson; Johnny Guitar; Kung Fu; The Last Hunt; The Left-Handed Gun; Lonesome Cowboys; The Long Riders; A Man Called Horse; The Missouri Breaks; Once Upon a Time in the West; One Eyed Jacks; Outrage (1964); Pale Rider; Pat Garrett and Billy the Kid; Posse (1993); The Quick and the Dead; Silent Tongue; The Thousand Pieces of Gold; Tombstone; Unforgiven (1992); Wyatt Earp; Young Guns; Young Guns II

Westerns-Revenge (centering around a revenge story): see also *Revenge: Duels: WESTERNS:* Ballad of Cable Hogue; Comin' At Ya!; Fighting Mad; Five Card Stud; Frenchie; Gun Fury; Guns of the Magnificent Seven; Hang 'em High; Hannie Caulder; High Plains Drifter; Hour of the Gun; The Left-Handed Gun; Legend of the Lone Ranger; The Man from Laramie; Nevada Smith; The Oklahoma Kid; One Eyed Jacks; The Outlaw Josey Wales; The Quick and the Dead; Quigley Down Under; Tell Them Willie Boy is Here; Two Mules for Sister Sara; Ulzana's Raid; Unforgiven (1992); Waco; Will Penny

Westerns-Revisionist (correcting or re-telling history or changing the portrayals of certain *stock characters, i.e., Indians*): see also *Westerns-Neo: Revisionist Films:* Extreme Prejudice; Geronimo (1993); Heartland; Johnny Guitar; Posse (1993); The Quick and the Dead; Quigley Down Under; Wyatt Earp

Westerns-Spaghetti (westerns shot in Europe or by Europeans, usually by Italians): see also *WESTERNS:* Ace High; Bad Man's River; Behold a Pale Horse; A Fistful of Dollars; For a Few Dollars More; The Good, the Bad, and the Ugly; Hang 'em High; High Plains Drifter; Joe Kidd; Once Upon a Time in the West; My Name is Nobody; Triumphs of a Man Called Horse

West-Old (not necessarily a western): see also *WESTERNS: Western Comedy: Western-Spaghetti: 1800s: Early America:* Barbary Coast; The Big Sky; The Big Trail; Black Robe; Call of the Wild (1935); Call of the Wild (1972); Canyon Passage; Chisum; The Frisco Kid (1935); Iron Mistress; The Last Command; The Life and Times of Judge Roy Bean; Mark of Zorro (1920); Mark of Zorro (1940);

Northwest Passage; Paint Your Wagon; Rio Grande; Shalako; True Grit; The Way West; Wells Fargo; The Westerner

Whales: see also *Sharks: Fishermen: Adventure at Sea: Animal Rights:* Free Willy; Island at the Top of the World; Moby Dick (1930, 1956); Orca-Killer Whale; Pinocchio; When the Whales Came; Whales of August

What if . . . Stories (stories which ask questions about real happenings or what if . . . something unusual, unbelievable, or magical happened): see also *Fantasy: True or Not?:* Agatha; Agnes of God; Ali Baba Goes to Town; Altered States; Big; Blank Check; Blithe Spirit; Boys from Brazil; Capricorn One; Cocoon; Cocoon, The Return; The Commies are Coming, the Commies are Coming; Dreams That Money Can Buy; Fail Safe; Field of Dreams; Francis the Talking Mule; Gabriel over the White House; How to Get Ahead in Advertising; Iceman; The Icicle Thief; In the Mouth of Madness; The Incredible Journey; It Grows on Trees; It Happened Here; Journey to the Far Side of the Sun; Little Big League; Little Buddha; Magic Face; The Man Who Could Work Miracles; Marooned; Me and Him; The Miracle (1948); Miracle on 34th Street (1947); Mudlark; The Night My Number Came Up; Oh, God; Oh God Book Two; Oh God, You Devil; Private Benjamin; The Purple Rose of Cairo; Red Dawn; The Russians Are Coming, the Russians Are Coming; Salome's Last Dance; Somewhere in Time; Soul Man; The Sum of Us; Went the Day Well? Wetherby; What's So Bad About Feeling Good?; Whiskey Galore; Wild in the Streets

While the Parents are Away: see *Parents are Gone*

Whistleblowers: see also *Reformers: Fighting the System: Corruption: Government-Corruption: Corporate-Corruption Worker's Rights:* Black Fury; Black Legion; Enemy of the People (1977); Enemy of the People (1989); Falcon and the Snowman; The Harder They Fall; Mr. Smith Goes to Washington; Norma Rae; Prince of the City; Q & A; Serpico; Silkwood

White Among Blacks: see also *Black vs. White: Race Relations: Fish out of Water Stories:* The Air Up There; Blue Chips; Call Me Bwana; Candyman; Conrack; Cool Runnings; Glory; The Jerk; The Landlord; White Men Can't Jump

White as Black: see also *White Among Blacks:* Black Like Me; Call Me Bwana; The Watermelonman; Soul Man

White Man Among Indians-American: see *Raised by Indians: WESTERNS: White Man Among Indians:* A Man Called Horse

White Supremacists: see *Ku Klux Klan: Bigots: Neo-Nazis: Nazi Stories: Race Relations: Civil Rights: Black vs. White*

White vs. Black: see *Black vs. White: also Race Relations: Civil Rights*

Whodunit: see *Mystery-Whodunit*

Wholesome Movies: see *Old Fashioned Recent Films: Conservative Value Films*

Widowers: see also *Death-Dealing with: Starting Over: Men Alone:* The Accidental Tourist; Adam Had Four Sons; Chitty Chitty Bang Bang; Cold Sassy Tree; Corrina, Corrina; The Courtship of Eddie's Father; Fathers and Sons; Fine Things; Hello Again; House Calls; A House Divided; Houseboat; I Never Sang for My Father; The Last Tycoon; Lost and Found; A Man and A Woman; Misunderstood; O'Hara's Wife; Obsession; Oliver's Story; Silent Tongue; Sleepless in Seattle; Table for Five; To Dance with the White Dog; We Think the World of You; The World of Apu; Yours, Mine and Ours

Widows: see also *Death-Dealing with: Starting Over: Women Alone:* Alice Doesn't Live Here Anymore; All the Way Home; Arkansas Traveler; Ballad of Josie; Big Bad Mama; The Bride Wore Black; Call of the Wild (1935); Call of the Wild (1972); The Cemetery Club; Conagher; Die! Die! My Darling!; Dona Flor and Her Two Husbands; The Effect of Gamma Rays on Man-in-the-Moon Marigolds; Firepower; Foxfire (1987); Ghost; The Ghost and Mrs. Muir; The Glass Bottom Boat; Greek Tycoon; A Guy Named Joe; Hellbound: Hellraiser II; Hellraiser; Hellraiser III: Hell on Earth; House Calls; Just Between Friends; Keeper of the Flame; Kiss Me Goodbye; La Vie Continue; A Man and A Woman; Men Don't Leave; The Merry Widow (1925); The Merry Widow (1934); The Merry Widow (1952); Mr. Belvedere Goes to College; Muriel; My Cousin Rachel; My Reputation; Night Walker; Night Watch; The Nurse; The Old Maid; Once Around; Personal Property; Providence;

The Roman Spring of Mrs. Stone; The Rose Tattoo; Scene of the Crime; Send Me No Flowers; The Shell Seekers; Strangers, the Story of a Mother and Daughter; Terms of Endearment; That Certain Woman; Tim; Together Again; Truly, Madly, Deeply; Used People; White Cliffs of Dover; White Sister; You'll Like My Mother; Yours, Mine and Ours

Wife Abuse/Beating: see *Abusive Men: also Evil Men*

Wild People: see also *Free Spirits: Sexy Men: Sexy Women: Party Movies: Sexual Revolution: Sexual Kinkiness:* Bachelor Party (1984); Ball of Fire; Brimstone and Treacle; A Clockwork Orange; Fandango; Ferris Bueller's Day Off; A Fine Madness; Georgy Girl; Good Morning, Vietnam; Grandview, USA; Henry and June; I Want to Live! Lady Caroline Lamb; Mad Wednesday; Mail Order Bride; Masculine, Feminine; Moonlighting (1985); Morgan!; National Lampoon's Animal House; Neighbors; The Nutty Professor (1963); Our Dancing Daughters; Pulp Fiction; Rapture; The Rose Tattoo; Ruling Class; Saratoga Trunk; Something Wild (1986); A Song is Born; That Was Then . . . This Is Now; Theodora Goes Wild; This Property is Condemned; This Sporting Life; The Thousand Clowns; Tie Me Up! Tie Me Down!; Track 29

Wilderness Life: see *Nature-Back to: also City vs. Country: Rural Life: Mountain Settings: Explorers: Vacations: Exotic Locales*

Wiretapping: see *Surveillance: Spies: Spy Films: Voyeurism: Detective Stories*

Wisecracking Sidekicks: see also *Practical Jokers: Feisty Females: Wild People:* About Last Night; Chapter Two; Falling in Love; Frankie and Johnny; Goodbye My Fancy; Plenty; I Want to Live!; Sleepless in Seattle; Spacehunter, Adventures in the Forbidden Zone; Teacher's Pet; Thunderbolt and Lightfoot; When Harry Met Sally; Who's Been Sleeping in My Bed?

Wishes: see also *Dying Wishes: Genies:* Dreams That Money Can Buy; Maid to Order; Three Coins in the Fountain

Witches/Witchcraft: see also *Witches: Warlocks: Supernatural: Danger: Satan/Satanism: Magic:* Bedknobs and Broomsticks; Bell, Book, and Candle; Black Cauldron; Black Sunday (1960); Day of Wrath; Ed and His Dead Mother;

Halloween 3: Season of the Witch; Hocus Pocus; Horror Hotel; The House of Seven Gables; I Married a Witch; I Walked with a Zombie; Maid of Salem; Return from Witch Mountain; Sleeping Beauty; Spellbinder; Supergirl; Throne of Blood; Warlock (1989); Witches; The Witches of Eastwick; Witches of Salem

Witness Protection Program: see *Witnesses-Protecting*

Witness to Murder: see also *Witness to Murder-Child: Witnesses-Protecting: Courtroom Drama: MURDER:* Backtrack; Bird on a Wire; Black Hand; Blink; Blow Out; Call Me; Clean Slate; Client; Cohen and Tate; Cop and a Half; Double O Kid; Dressed to Kill; Eyewitness (1970); I Saw What You Did; Impulse (1990); Lady in White; Lady on a Train; Moving Violation; Night of the Hunter; Night Terror; A Prayer for the Dying; Rapid Fire; She Loves Me Not; Silhouette; Some Like it Hot; Storm Warning; Tiger Bay; Turtle Beach; Window; Witness; Witness to Murder; The Yellow Balloon

Witness to Murder-Child: see also *Witness to Murder: Children in Jeopardy:* Black Hand; Cohen and Tate; Window; Witness; The Yellow Balloon

Witnesses-Protecting: see also *Witness to Murder: MURDER:* Behave Yourself!; Chandler; The Gauntlet; Good Fellas; Hide in Plain Sight; My Blue Heaven (1990); Narrow Margin (1952); Narrow Margin (1990); Rapid Fire; Someone to Watch Over Me

Wives-Troublesome/Nagging: see also *Husbands-Troublesome: Cheating Women: Mean Woman:* Blithe Spirit; Blondie; The Catered Affair; Easy Living (1949); Ex-Mrs. Bradford; Fahrenheit 451; It Started with a Kiss; Lightnin' Movers and Shakers; My Geisha; Naked Lunch; No Room for the Groom; The Trip to Bountiful; What's Up, Doc?

Woman Behind the Man (stories of women who were instrumental in their men's success but not necessarily given credit): see also *Behind the Scenes: Politicians' Wives:* B.F.'s Daughter; Breakfast for Two; The Career; Country Girl; Desiree; Golden Boy; Harriet Craig; Iron Man; Limbo; The Men (1950); Men of Respect; Painted Veil; Second Chorus; Song of Love; State of the Union; Swing High, Swing Low; Twenty Thousand Years in Sing Sing; What Every Woman

Knows; When My Baby Smiles at Me; Woman's World

Woman vs. Woman: see *Women in Conflict*

Women Artists: see *Female Artists*

Women and Boys: see also *Mothers & Sons: Men & Boys:* Baxter (1972); A Child is Waiting; Clara's Heart; The Client; Harold and Maude; La Lectrice; Lost in Yonkers; Milk Money; Oh, What a Night; Olly Olly Oxen Free; Once Bitten; Prince of Central Park; Tea and Sympathy

Women and Girls: see also *Mothers & Daughters: Men & Girls:* Candleshoe; Chalk Garden; Curly Sue; The Member of the Wedding; National Velvet; Pollyanna; Promises in the Dark; Sarafina!; Where Angels Go, Trouble Follows; Zelly and Me

Women as Men: see also *Transvestites: Transsexuals: Role Reversals: Men as Women:* Impromptu; It's Pat; Just One of the Guys; A Man Like Eva; Orlando; Queen Christina; Sylvia Scarlett; Victor/Victoria; The Year of Living Dangerously; Yentl

Women at War: see also *War Stories: Female in Male Domain:* China Beach; Nurse Edith Cavell; So Proudly We Hail

Women-Childless (where the fact the woman is barren is causing problems): see also *Mothers-Surrogate:* Cat on a Hot Tin Roof (1958); Cat on a Hot Tin Roof (1984); Funny About Love; Grand Highway; The Lady is Willing; My Blue Heaven (1950); The Old Maid; Paradise (1991); Promises! Promises!; Raising Arizona; Strange Interlude (1932); Strange Interlude (1990)

Women-Elderly: see *Elderly Women: Elderly Men*

Women Ensembles: see *Ensembles-Women: also Ensemble Films: Women's Films: Sisters*

Women-Feisty: see *Feisty Females: also Women Fighting Back: Women's Rights: Underdog Stories: Heiresses-Madcap: Free Spirits: Reformers*

Women Fighting Over Men: see also *Men Fighting Over Women:* A Chorus of Disapproval; Circle of Friends; Death Becomes Her; Double Threat; The Duchess and the Dirtwater Fox; The Favor; Folies Bergere; For Love or Money (1963); Forever Female; Girls! Girls! Girls!; Give the Girl a Break; Green Dolphin Street; Hannah and Her Sisters; Honey Pot; Lust in the Dust; Man in the Moon; The Man Who Loved Women

(1977); The Man Who Loved Women (1983); Mogambo; Mother is a Freshman; Mother's Boys; Night of the Iguana; The Opposite Sex; Outrageous Fortune; Picnic; Raise the Red Lantern; Rally Round the Flag, Boys; Red Dust; Return of the Soldier; She Devil; Tin Pan Alley; Twice in a Lifetime; The Witches of Eastwick; The Women

Women Fighting the System (not necessarily the male establishment, but likely): see also *Women's Rights: Women Proving Themselves: Social Drama: Fighting the System: Underdog Stories: Feminist Films: Anti-Establishment Films: Female Among Males:* Born Yesterday (1950); Born Yesterday (1993); Business as Usual; The Color Purple; It Happened to Jane; The Madwoman of Chaillot; Out of Africa; Places in the Heart; Screaming Mimi; Silkwood; Skin Deep; Solid Gold Cadillac; Sudden Impact

Women in Conflict: see also *Women Proving Themselves: Mean Women: Duels: Feuds: Men in Conflict:* All About Eve; Antonia and Jane; Carrie (1976); Cinderella; Death Becomes Her; The Egg and I; Flamingo Road; Follies in Concert; Forever Female; Gentlemen Prefer Blondes; Gone With the Wind; The Great Lie; Hand that Rocks the Cradle; The Hard Way (1943); Johnny Guitar; Kansas City Bomber; A League of Their Own; Lust in the Dust; Mogambo; Mrs. Parkington; Old Acquaintance; The Opposite Sex; Pete 'n Tillie; The Positively True Adventures of the Alleged Texas Cheerleader-Murdering Mom; Prison Stories: Women on the Inside; Raise the Red Lantern; Rich and Famous; She Devil; Smile; Troop Beverly Hills; Turning Point; Valley of the Dolls; What's the Matter with Helen?; Whatever Happened to Baby Jane?; Widow's Peak; The Witches of Eastwick; The Women; Working Girl; You'll Like My Mother

Women in Jeopardy: see also *THRILLERS: HORROR: Slasher Stories: Rape/Rapists: Men in Jeopardy:* The Accused (1948); Afraid of the Dark; And Now the Screaming Starts; Autumn Leaves; Backtrack; Bad Dreams; Bandolero; Batman; Beware, My Lovely; The Big Combo; Big Man On Campus; The Birds; The Birds II; Blink; Bloodline; Blue Steel; Body Bags; The Boston Strangler; Brighton Rock; The Cabinet of

Caligari (1962); Cage of Gold; Cat People (1942); Child's Play (1988); Child's Play 2; Child's Play 3; City Streets; Clan of the Cave Bear; Clash of the Titans; Coma; Dangerous Crossing; Dark Waters; The Deceived; Demon Seed; The Domino Principle; Don't Just Stand There; Dracula (1931); Dracula (1979); Dracula Has Risen from the Grave; Dracula (Horror of Dracula, 1958); Dracula, Prince of Darkness; Dressed to Kill; 8 Million Ways to Die; The Entity; Ever in My Heart; Experiment in Terror; Extremities; Eye of the Needle; Eyes in the Night; The Eyes of Laura Mars; The Fan; Fatal Attraction; The Fear Inside; Five Corners; The Fog; The Four Musketeers; Frankenhooker; Frantic (1988); Garden of Evil; Goldengirl; Guilty as Sin; Gun Fury; Half Moon Street; Halloween; Halloween 2; Halloween 4: The Return of Michael Myers; Halloween 5: The Revenge of Michael Myers; The Hearse; The Hideaway; Hush, Hush, Sweet Charlotte; Jack's Back; Jackson County Jail; Jagged Edge; Jennifer 8; Johnny Belinda; King Kong (1933); King Kong (1976); Kiss Me Deadly; Klute; Krull; Lady in a Cage; Ladykiller (1992); Last Rites; Lethal Weapon; Lethal Weapon 2; Lisa (1961); Love Crimes; Love From a Stranger (1936); Love From a Stranger (1947); Man About the House; Man Trouble; Mantrap; Marked Woman; Masters; Mean Season; Midnight (1989); Midnight Crossing; Midnight Lace; Mike's Murder; The Morning After; Night Must Fall (1937); Night Must Fall (1964); Night of the Living Dead (1968); Night of the Living Dead (1990); The Night Stalker/ The Night Strangler; Night Terror; Nosferatu; Once Upon a Time in the West; Out of the Dark; Peeping Tom; The Pelican Brief; Phantom of Paradise; Phantom of the Opera (1925); Phantom of the Opera (1941); Phantom of the Opera (1962); Phantom of the Opera (1989); Play Misty for Me; Private Life of Henry VIII; Prom Night SERIES; The Prowler; Rashomon; Rear Window; Rosebud; Rosemary's Baby; Scent of Mystery; Second Chance; The Secret Beyond the Door; See No Evil; Seven Women; Shadow of a Doubt; Shadow Riders; Shoot to Kill; Silence of the Lambs; Silhouette; Single White Female; Sister, Sister; Sleeping With the Enemy; The Slender Thread; Someone to Watch Over Me; Sorry, Wrong

Number; The Sphinx; Spiral Staircase (1946); Spiral Staircase (1975); Stalking Moon; Star of Midnight; Star Wars; Step Down to Terror; The Stranger; A Stranger is Watching; Sudden Fear; Suspicion; Suspiria; Swashbuckler; The Tamarind Seed; The Target; Terminator; Thoroughly Modern Millie; Those Magnificent Men in Their Flying Machines; The Three Musketeers (1935); The Three Musketeers (1939); The Three Musketeers (1948); The Three Musketeers (1973); The Three Musketeers (1993); Tiger Bay; Time after Time; The Towering Inferno; Traces of Red; Trilogy in Terror; The Two Mrs. Carrolls; Undercurrent; The Villain; W; Wait Until Dark; Warlock (1989); When a Stranger Calls; Whirlpool; Witness to Murder; Woman Screaming; You'll Like My Mother

Women in Prison: see also *Prison Drama: Murderers-Female:* Caged; Caged Fear; Caged Heat; Dialogues with Madwomen; Female Trouble; House of Women; I Want to Live!; Jackson County Jail; The Ladies They Talk About; Mary Burns, Fugitive; Paid; Prison Stories: Women on the Inside; A Town Like Alice (1956); A Town Like Alice (1985)

Women Killers: see *Murderers-Female: Hitwomen: Evil Women*

Women Law Officers: see *Female Law Officers: Female Among Males: Police: FBI: CIA*

Women Leads: see *Female Protagonists*

Women Proving Themselves: see also *Female Among Males: Coming of Age: Underdog Stories: Women-Working: Virgins:* Flashdance; The Gun in Betty Lou's Handbag; Kramer vs. Kramer; Norma Rae; Places in the Heart; Roberta; True Confession; Working Girl

Women-Young: see *Young Women*

Women's Films (films primarily appealing to women and/or concerned with women's issues, though not necessarily 'feminists'): see also *Ensembles-Women: Female Protagonists: Heroines (Classic): Women-Working: Women's Rights: MELODRAMA: Tearjerkers:* Alice Doesn't Live Here Anymore; B.F.'s Daughter; Baby Face; Ballad of Josie; Beaches; The Best of Everything; Boys on the Side; Brink of Life; Caged; Chantilly Lace; Claudia; Crossing Delancey; Daisy Kenyon; The Deep Blue Sea; Diary of a

Mad Housewife; The Divorcée; Enchanted April; The End of Innocence; Entre-Nous; Ex-Lady; Fried Green Tomatoes; The Frenchman's Creek; Girl from Tenth Avenue; The Good Mother; Harriet Craig; Hilda Crane; Hold Back the Dawn; Je Vous Aime; The Joy Luck Club; A League of Their Own; The Letter (1929); The Letter (1940); Letter From an Unknown Woman; Letter to Three Wives; Lianna; Love Letters (1984); Magnificent Obsession (1935); Magnificent Obsession (1954); Mannequin (1937); Marjorie Morningstar; The Men in Her Life; Norma Rae; One Sings, the Other Doesn't; Opposite Sex; The Other Side of the Mountain; The Other Side of the Mountain Part Two; Paid in Full; The Piano; Smash-Up, the Story of a Woman; Steel Magnolias; Turning Point; An Unmarried Woman; Variety; Woman Times Seven; The Women; Women on the Verge of a Nervous Breakdown; Roberta; So Proudly We Hail; Steaming; Strangers, the Story of a Mother and Daughter; To Each His Own

Women's Rights: see also *Women Fighting System: Civil Rights:* The Accused (1988); Ann Vickers; Baby Boom; The Color Purple; Dialogues with Madwomen; Dream Wife; First Monday in October; A Handmaid's Tale; Harry and Walter Go to New York; Heart Like a Wheel; I, the Worst of All; Rambling Rose; Shocking Miss Pilgrim; Stand Up and Be Counted; Woman Rebels; The World According to Garp

Women Who Leave: see also *Runaways: Men Who Leave: Fathers Alone: Cheating Women:* Author! Author!; Autumn Sonata; Back Roads; Blonde Venus; Kramer vs. Kramer; The Man Who Loved Cat Dancing; Rich in Love; So Big (1932); So Big (1953)

Women-Working: see also *Business Life: Office Comedies: Women Proving Themselves: Women's Rights:* Baby Boom; Beverly Hills Madam; Broadcast News; Chantilly Lace; Christmas in Connecticut (1945); Christmas in Connecticut (1992); Coal Miner's Daughter; Daisy Kenyon; The Doctor Takes a Wife; Don't Tell Mom the Babysitter's Dead; I Can Get it For You Wholesale; Kitty Foyle; Lady in the Dark; Looking for Love; Loulou; Mannequin (1937); Marie; Marjorie Morningstar; Mr. Mom; Network; No Time for Love;

les Enfants; Babette Goes to War; Bataan; Battle Cry; The Battle of Britain; Battle of the Bulge; Battle of the Neretva; Battleground; Betrayed (1954); Betrayed (1954); The Big Lift; The Big Red One; Bittere Ernte; The Bold and the Brave; Bridge on the River Kwai; Cairo (1942); Calcutta; A Canterbury Tale; Canterbury Ghost; Captain Carey, USA; Captains of the Clouds; Casablanca; Caught in the Draft; Chicago Joe and the Showgirl; Class of '44; Cloak and Dagger (1946); Clock; Closely Watched Trains; Cluny Brown; Code Name: Emerald; Come See the Paradise; Command Decision; Confessions of a Nazi Spy; Confidential Agent; The Conformist; Cornered; Dam Busters; The Damned; Das Boot; A Day in October; Day One; The Desert Fox; Desert Rats; Desert Victory; Desire Me; Desperate Journey; Destiny of a Man; Devil in the Flesh (1946); Devil in the Flesh (1987); The Devil's Brigade; Diary of Anne Frank (1959); The Dirty Dozen; The Dressmaker; The Dunera Boys; The Eagle Has Landed; Eleni; Empire of the Sun; Escape; Europa, Europa; Exodus; Eye of the Needle; Fallen Sparrow; Farewell to the King; Fat Man and Little Boy; Father Goose; The Fighting Seabees; Final Countdown; First of the Few; Five Fingers; Five Graves to Cairo; The Flying Leathernecks; Flying Tigers; Force Ten from Navarone; The Foreign Correspondent; For the Boys; Four Horsemen of the Apocalypse; Four Sons; From Here to Eternity; Gaby; The Garden of the Finzi-Continis; Gentle Sex; G.I. Joe; The Glenn Miller Story; Go for Broke; God Is My Co-Pilot; Golden Earrings; The Great Dictator; The Great Escape; The Great Escape 2: The Untold Story; Green for Danger; Guadalcanal Diary; Gung Ho! (1943); Guns of Navarone; A Guy Named Joe; Hangmen Also Die; Hanna's War; Hanover Street; Hanussen; Happy Land; Heaven Knows, Mr. Allison; Heimat; Hell, Heaven, and Hoboken; Hell in the Pacific; Hellcats of the Navy; Heroes of Telemark; Hill; Hollywood Canteen; Homecoming (1948); Hope and Glory; Hornet's Nest; The House on 92nd Street; Human Comedy; Idiot's Delight; I Know Where I'm Going; I'll Be Seeing You; The Immortal Sergeant; The Impatient Years; Indecent Obsession; Indochine; In Our Time; The Incredible Mr. Limpet; Is Paris Burning?;

Ivan's Childhood; I Wanted Wings; Joan of Paris; Journey for Margaret; Journey into Fear; Keeper of the Flame; Kelly's Heroes; The Key (1958); King of Hearts; King of The Hill (1965); King Rat; Lacombe, Lucien; The Lady Vanishes (1938); The Lady Vanishes (1979); The Last Metro; A League of Their Own; The Left Hand of God; Lili Marleen; Love in Germany; Love is a Many Splendored Thing; Love on the Dole; Love Story (1944); Lover Come Back (1946); Lucky Star; MacArthur; Magic Face; Malaya; The Man I Married; The Man Who Never Was; Map of the Human Heart; Max and Helen; Me and the Colonel; Mein Kampf; Mephisto; Merry Christmas, Mr. Lawrence; Midway; The Millionairess; Mine Own Executioner; Ministry of Fear; Miracle of the White Stallions; The Moon is Down; The More the Merrier; Mr. Klein; Mr. Lucky; Mrs. Miniver; The Naked and the Dead; Nazi Agent; Never Say Goodbye; Never So Few; Next of Kin (1942); Night of the Generals; Night of the Shooting Stars; Night Train to Munich; 1941; 1900; None But the Brave; North Star; Objective Burma; Odette; Oh, What a Lovely War; Olympische Spiele; On the Double; Once Upon a Honeymoon; The One That Got Away; Open City; Operation Amsterdam; Operation Crossbow; Operation Mad Ball; Operation Petticoat; O.S.S.; The Other Side of Midnight; The Overlanders; Over Twenty-One; Paisan; Panama Hattie; The Passage; Patton; The Philadelphia Experiment; The Piccadilly Incident; Plenty; The Prisoner (1955); Private Function; Racing with the Moon; Radio Days; Raid on Rommel; The Reunion; The Rocketeer; Run Silent Run Deep; Sahara (1943); Salo: 120 Days of Sodom; Salon Kitty; Sands of Iwo Jima; Sayonara; Schindler's List; Scotland Yard; Sea Chase; Sea Wolves; The Secret of Santa Vittoria; The Secret War of Harry Frigg; The Serpent's Egg; Seven Sinners; Shining Through; Shoeshine; The Shop on Main Street; Since You Went Away; Situation Hopeless But Not Serious; A Soldier's Story; Somewhere I'll Find You; Son of Lassie; So Proudly We Hail; The Sound of Music; South Pacific; Special Day; The Spider's Stratagem; Spy in Black; Stage Door Canteen; Stalag 17; The Story of Dr. Wassell; Strategic Air Command; Sundown; Sunflower; Swing

Shift; Teahouse of the August Moon; The Tenth Man; Thank Your Lucky Stars; That Kind of Woman; 13 Rue Madeleine; This Happy Breed; This Is the Army; Thousands Cheer; Three Came Home; The Thrill of a Romance; Thunderbirds; Time of Destiny; A Time to Love and a Time to Die; Tin Drum; To Be or Not to Be (1942); To Be or Not to Be (1983); To Each His Own; To Hell and Back; Tobruk; Tommy; Tonight and Every Night; Too Late the Hero; Tora! Tora! Tora!; A Town Like Alice (1956); A Town Like Alice (1985); The Train; True Glory; Twelve O'Clock High; Two Women; Up in Arms; Vacation from Marriage; The Victors; Victory; Von Ryan's Express; Wake Island; A Walk in the Sun; The War Lover; Where Eagles Dare; The Wackiest Ship in the Army; White Cliffs of Dover; White Rose; Winged Victory; The Wooden Horse; Yanks

Wrestlers/Wrestling (male or female): see also *Sports Movies: Macho Men: Boxing:* All The Marbles; Body Slam; Joe Panther; Mr. Nanny; Night and the City (1950); The One and Only; Over the Top; Paradise Alley; Take Down; Tough Enough; Vision Quest

Writer-Directors (where the film was both written and directed by the same person): see also *Female Screenwriters: Writers: Directors: Writer-Directors:* Abel; Abschied von Gestern; The Abyss; Accatone; Ace High; Act of the Heart; Actors and Sin; Adalen 31; The Adjuster; The Adventures of Buckaroo Banzai Across the 8th Dimension; The Adventures of Reinette and Mirabelle; The Adventures of Sherlock Holmes' Smarter Brother; The Adventures of the Wilderness Family; Afraid of the Dark; After the Rehearsal; After the Shock; Age Isn't Everything; The Agency; Aguirre, the Wrath of God; Akira Kurosawa's Dreams; Aliens; All About Eve; All the Vermeers in New York; All the Young Men; All-American Boy; Aloha, Bobby and Rose; Alone in the Dark; Alphaville; Alpine Fire; Amarcord; Amateur Night at the Dixie Bar and Grill; The Amazing Mr. Blunden; The Ambulance; America, America; American Gigolo; An American Werewolf in London; Amos and Andrew; Amsterdamned; And Now, My Love; Andy Warhol's Dracula; Andy Warhol's Frankenstein; The Angel Wore Red; Angelo, My Love; Another Woman;

Arsenal; Ashes and Diamonds; Aspen Extreme; Assault on Precinct 13; Au Revoir, les Enfants; Autobus; Autumn Sonata; The Baby Maker; Baby it's You; Badlands; Bagdad Cafe; Bananas; Barcelona; The Battleship Potemkin; Bay Boy; Beat; Beau Pere; The Beautiful Blonde from Bashful Bend; Beautiful Dreamers; Beauty and the Beast (1946); The Bedroom Window; Before Sunrise; The Bellboy; The Belly of an Architect; Benji; The Benny Goodman Story; Best Boy; Betsy's Wedding; Better Late Than Never; Better Off Dead; The Big Lift; The Big Red One; Billy Galvin; Billy Jack; The Bird With the Crystal Plumage; Bite the Bullet; Bitter Tears of Petra Von Kant; Black Caesar; Black Rainbow; Blind Date (1987); Blind Husbands; Blindfold: Acts of Obsession; Blood Feud; Blood of a Poet; Blue; Blue Velvet; Blume in Love; Bob le Flambeur; Body Heat; Boiling Point; Bolero (1984); Born in East L.A.; Born Losers; Bound and Gagged, a Love Story; Boxing Helena; The Boy Who Could Fly; The Boy Who Had Everything; Boyfriends and Girlfriends; Boyz N the Hood; Brain Damage; The Breakfast Club; Breaking Glass; Bride of the Gorilla; The Brink of Life; The Brood; The Brother From Another Planet; Brother Sun, Sister Moon; Buffet Froid; Bugsy Malone; Bullets Over Broadway; Business as Usual; Cabin Boy; Caged Heat; Can She Bake a Cherry Pie?; Canadian Bacon; A Canterbury Tale; Capricorn One; Celia; The Chase (1994); Chimes at Midnight; Chloe in the Afternoon; Christmas in July; Cinema Paradiso; Circle of Power; Cisco Pike; City Lights; City of Hope; Claire's Knee; Close My Eyes; Closet Land; Club Paradise; Coach; Cohen and Tate; Cold Sassy Tree; Come See the Paradise; The Competition; The Conformist; The Cook, the Thief, His Wife & Her Lover; Corrina, Corrina; Court Jester; Cracking Up; Cries and Whispers; Crimes and Misdemeanors; Cromwell; Cruising; Cry Baby; Curly Sue; The Curse of the Pink Panther; D.C. Cab; Dance Macabre; Dangerous Curves; Dante's Inferno; Dawn of the Dead; Day After; Daybreak; Days of Heaven; Dazed and Confused; Dead Alive; Dead Heat on a Merry Go Round; Deadfall (1968); Deadline USA; Defending Your Life; Delicate Delinquent; Desert Bloom; Desire and

Hell at Sunset Motel; Desperate Living; Devil's Eye; The Devil's Playground; The Devil's Wanton; Diner; Distant Thunder (1973); Dollars; Don Juan DeMarco; Doppelganger: The Evil Within; The Double Life of Veronique; Double McGuffin; Down By Law; Dr. Heckyl and Mr. Hype; Dragonwyck; The Draughtman's Contract; Dream Lover (1994); Dressed to Kill; The Driver; Drowning By Numbers; Dynasty of Fear; Earth; Easy Living (1937); Eclipse; Eight Men Out; Eighty-Four Charlie Mopic; Elvira Madigan; Emperor Waltz; Eraserhead; Erik The Viking; Europa, Europa; The Evil Dead; Exposed; The Exterminating Angel; Exterminator; The Fabulous Baker Boys; Face to Face; Faces; Fandango; Far From Home; Farewell to the King; Fathers and Sons; Fatso; Fear; Fear of a Black Hat; Female Trouble; Fever Pitch; Fingers; First Name: Carmen; First Power; A Fistful of Dynamite; Fitzcarraldo; Flesh; Flesh and Bone; Flirting; Foolish Wives; For a Few Dollars More; Foreign Intrigue; Forty Guns; The 400 Blows; Four Seasons; Frantic (1958); Fresh; Friends and Husbands; Fright Night; From the Life of the Marionettes; Full Moon in Paris; Game is Over; Garden; Gate of Hell; Get Out Your Handkerchiefs; The Girl in the Watermelon; Go Naked in the World; Going in Style; Good Morning, Babylon; Goodbye People; The Gospel According to St. Matthew; Gotham; Grand Theft Auto; The Great Moment; The Great Northfield Minnesota Raid; Guilty by Suspicion; The Hand (1981); Hanover Street; Happy Ending; Happy New Year (1973); Hard Contract; Hardcore; Hardware; Heaven's Gate; Heavenly Pursuits; Hester Street; Hi, Mom!; Hidden 2; High Heels; High Hopes; High Risk; Higher Learning; History of the World Part One; Hold Me, Thrill Me, Kiss Me; Honeymoon in Vegas; The Honeymoon Killers; House of Cards; House of Games; How to Be Very Very Popular; How to Get Ahead in Advertising; Husbands; Husbands and Wives; I Like it Like That; I Passed for White; I've Heard the Mermaids Singing; Immortal Beloved; The Immortal Story; In a Year with 13 Moons; In Cold Blood; The Indian Runner; Inserts; Interiors; The Interrogation; Intolerance; Invitation to the Dance; Island (1961); It's Alive; It's

Alive II; It's Alive III; Ivan the Terrible; J'Accuse; Jamaica Run; Jennifer 8; Jesus of Montreal; Joe vs. the Volcano; John Cleese on How to Irritate People; Johnny Suede; Journey of Hope; Jungle Fever; Just Another Girl on the IRT; Just Between Friends; Kafka; The Keep; The Kid (1921); The Killer's Kiss; The Killing of Chinese Bookie; Killing Zoe; King and Four Queens; King of the Hill (1993); Kings of the Road; Kitchen Toto; La Bamba; La Chevre; La Femme Nikita; La Marseillaise; Lacombe, Lucien; Lady in White; Lady L.; Lair of the White Worm; Last House on the Left; The Last of England; Last Rites; Last Voyage; Law of Desire; Learning Tree; Leprechaun; Les Biches; Les Comperes; Les Valseuses; Lesson in Love; Letter to Three Wives; Letters from a Dead Man; Lianna; Liebestraum; The Life and Death of Colonel Blimp; Life and Nothing But; The Life of Riley; Life Upside Down; Light Sleeper; Limelight; Listen to Me; Lisztomania; Little Big Horn; Little Noises; Little Treasure; Little Vegas; Living in Oblivion; Local Hero; Lola (1960); The Long Day Closes; Long Live Life; Look Who's Talking; The Looker; Lost Man; Love and Death; Love and Money; Love at Large; Love in a Goldfish Bowl; Love Matters; Love Potion #9; Loveless; Lunatics, A Love Story; Lunch on the Grass; Macaroni; Mahler; Mamma Rosa; Man in Love; Manhattan; Manhattan Murder Mystery; Manon des Sources (1952); Man's Best Friend; Married Woman; Martin; Masala; Matewan; Maximum Overdrive; Men of Respect; Meteor Man; Mi Vida Loca; Mike's Murder; Mikey and Nicky; The Millionairess; Minnie & Moskowitz; Miracle Mile; The Miracle of Morgan's Creek; Mishima; Missing Pieces; Mississippi Mermaid; Mister Cory; Mo' Better Blues; Modern Times; Moment by Moment; Momma, There's a Man in Your Bed; Monkey Shines; Montenegro; Moonlighting (1985); Mr. Arkadin; The Mummy's Shroud; Murmur of the Heart; My Life; My Little Girl; My New Gun; My Night at Maud's; My Own Private Idaho; Mystery Train; Nadine; Naked; The Naked Kiss; Napoleon; Nasty Girl; Necromancy; New Life; New Nightmare; Next Stop, Greenwich Village; Night and Day; Night Angel; Night Games; The Night is Young; Night of the Comet; Night

Writers: see also *Female Writers: Journalists: Journalist Detectives: Publishing World: Romance with Writer: Poets: Biographies: Hollywood Life: Artists: Novel Adaptations: Plays Adaptations: Pulitzer Prize Adaptations:*

Acquaintance; Once in a Lifetime; Oscar Wilde; Out of Africa; The Owl and the Pussycat; Paris Holiday; Paris When it Sizzles; The Player; Prick Up Your Ears; Priest of Love; The Prize; Providence; Reds; Return to Peyton Place; Reuben, Reuben; Rich and Famous; Romancing the Stone; Romantic Comedy; The Romantic Englishwoman; Sacrifice; School for Husbands; Scoundrel; Shadow Box; Shoot the Moon; Shy People; Sitting Pretty; Skin Deep; Slamdance; Sleuth; Some Came Running; Somewhere in Time; A Song to Remember; Sophie's Choice; Speaking Parts; Speechless; Spymaker, The Secret Life of Ian Fleming;

Stand by Me; Star Spangled Girl; Stevie; Straw Dogs; The Subterraneans; Sudden Fear; The Sun Also Rises; Sunset Boulevard; Surrender; Susan Slept Here; Swann in Love; Swing; That Certain Feeling; Theodora Goes Wild; The Third Man; Three Came Home; Throw Momma from the Train; Tom & Viv; Tommyknockers; The Trials of Oscar Wilde; Tropic of Cancer; Tune in Tomorrow; Under Milk Wood; The Unsuspected; Voltaire; The War Between Men and Women; The Way We Were; Wedding Night; Weeds; When Ladies Meet (1933); When Ladies Meet (1941); Where Do We Go from Here?; Where the

Buffalo Roam; Wild in the Country; The Wings of Eagles; Wings of Fame; Woman of the Year; The Wonderful World of the Brothers Grimm; Words and Music; The World According to Garp; The World of Apu; Youngblood Hawke; Zorba, The Greek

Wrong Man Stories/Thrillers: see *Accused Unjustly: Framed?*

Wrong Side of the Tracks: see *Romance-Class Conflict: Class Conflicts: Snobs vs. Slobs*

Wyatt Earp: see also *WESTERNS:* Doc; A Gunfight at the O.K. Corral; Hour of the Gun; My Darling Clementine; Tombstone; Wyatt Earp

Y

Young Men: see also *Young Men-Angry: Famous People Young: Ensemble Films: Coming of Age: Teenage Movies: Pre-Life Crises: 20-Somethings:* Abel; Adam at 6 A.M.; Age Isn't Everything; Airheads; Alfredo, Alfredo; All Quiet on the Western Front; All-American Boy; The Apartment; Aspen Extreme; Autobus; Bachelor Party (1957); Bachelor Party (1984); The Bawdy Adventures of Tom Jones; Bay Boy; Belle Epoque; Better Off Dead; Big Bounce; The Big Picture; The Big Red One; Big Wednesday; Billy Budd; Billy Liar; Biloxi Blues; Birdy; Blondie; Blue Max; Botany Bay; A Boy and His Dog; The Boy Who Had Everything; Boyz N the Hood; Breaking Away; Breaking Rules; Bridge; Bright Lights, Big City; Brimstone and Treacle; Brother Sun, Sister Moon; Buster and Billie; Bye Bye Love; Calendar Girl; California Dreaming; The Candidate; The Cardinal; Career Opportunities; Cash McCall; Catch Me a Spy; Charlie Bubbles; The Chicken Chronicles; A Chorus Line; The Chosen; Christine; Class of '44; A Clockwork Orange; Closely Watched Trains; Cocktail; Come and Get It; Conrack; Cool Hand Luke; Days of Thunder; Destiny of a Man; Diner; Dino; Diva; Dogfight; Don Juan DeMarco; Dying Young; East of Eden (1955); East

of Eden (1980); Easy Rider; Edge of Doom; 8 Seconds; Eric; Falcon and the Snowman; Fandango; The Fear Inside; Fear Strikes Out; Firstborn; Five Easy Pieces; The Flamingo Kid; Flirting; Fraternity Row; Fun Down There; Gaily, Gaily; The Gene Krupa Story; The Glass Menagerie (1950); The Glass Menagerie (1973); The Glass Menagerie (1987); Golden Boy; Goodbye Columbus; Gotcha!; The Graduate; Hamburger Hill; Happy Time; Hemingway's Adventures of a Young Man; Henry V (1944); Henry V (1989); Here We Go Round the Mulberry Bush; I, Mobster; I Vitelloni; I'll Never Forget Whatshisname; The Illustrated Man; Impatient Years; Inkwell; Interns; The Intruder; The Irish in Us; Iron Eagle; Joseph Andrews; The Kid (1990); A Kind of Loving; The Landlord; The Last Detail; The Last Starfighter; Lawrence of Arabia; Life Upside Down; Lifeguard; Lilith; Little Big Man; Little Buddha; London Belongs to Me; The Loneliness of the Long Distance Runner; Look Back in Anger (1959); Look Back in Anger (1980); Look Back in Anger (1989); Look in Any Window; The Lords of Discipline; Lost Angels; Love and Pain and the Whole Damn Thing; Love on the Run (1979); Loverboy; Made in Heaven; The Magnificent Ambersons; Malcolm; The Man in the Grey Flannel Suit; Marius;

Martin; Mask of the Avenger; Me and Him; Medium Cool; Memphis Belle; Mickey One; A Midnight Clear; Mo' Better Blues; Mr. North; Mr. Smith Goes to Washington; Naked in New York; New Interns; Next Stop, Greenwich Village; A Night in the Life of Jimmy Reardon; The Night We Never Met; O Lucky Man; Oblomov; An Officer and a Gentleman; The Paper Chase; Patti Rocks; Pickup Artist; The Picture of Dorian Gray; Pink Floyd: The Wall; Quicksilver; Razor's Edge (1946); Razor's Edge (1986); Reckless (1983); The Red Badge of Courage; Rocket to the Moon; The Rookie; Rumble Fish; Running on Empty; Saturday Night and Sunday Morning; Say Anything; Scent of a Woman; School Ties; The Secret of My Success; Shallow Grave; She's Having a Baby; A Short Film About Killing; The Show-Off; Ski School; Sons and Lovers; Spanking the Monkey; Spetters; Split Image; Stay Hungry; Staying Together; Stolen Kisses; The Strange One; Streamers; The Subject Was Roses; The Sure Thing; Sweet Bird of Youth; Tall Story; Taps; The Terry Fox Story; Tex; 30 is a Dangerous Age, Cynthia; This Sporting Life; Ticket to Heaven; Tiger Bay; Tom Jones; Too Late Blues; Turkish Delight; Two Lane Blacktop; Underworld, USA; An Unsuitable Job For a Woman;

Urban Cowboy; Valentino Returns; The Virgin Soldiers; Voyager; The War Lover; Watch It; What's Eating Gilbert Grape?; Who's That Knocking at My Door?; The Winslow Boy; A Yank at Oxford; Young Guns; Young Guns II; The Young Lions; Youngblood

Young Men-Angry: see also *Rebels: Coming of Age: Men Proving Themselves:* All Fall Down; Autobus; The Big Bounce; Class of 1999; Class of '84; Dino; Do The Right Thing; Dog Day Afternoon; Dogs in Space; East of Eden (1955); East of Eden (1980); Five Easy Pieces; Henry V (1944); Henry V (1989); The Last Detail; The Left-Handed Gun; Lenny; Look Back in Anger (1959); Look Back in Anger (1980); Look Back in Anger (1989); Lost Angels; Moonrise; Naked; O Lucky Man; Pink Floyd: The Wall; Pump Up the Volume; Rebel Without a Cause; Reckless (1983); The Revolutionary; The Strange One; The Strawberry Statement; Streamers; Talk Radio; This Sporting Life; Turkish Delight; Twisted Nerve; Underworld, USA; White Heat; Zabriskie Point

Young People: see *Coming of Age: Teenage Movies: Pre-Life Crises: 20-Somethings: Famous People Young: Ensemble Films: Bratpack Stories: Dating Scene:* Aaron Loves Angela; Bad Girl; The Blessing; Blue Lagoon (1948); Blue Lagoon (1980); Boyfriends and Girlfriends; The Decline of Western Civilization; The Decline of Western Civilization 2: The Metal Years; Doctor in the House; First Name: Carmen; For Keeps; Gassss; The Girl in the Watermelon; The Harrad Experiment; The Harrad Summer; The Hotel New Hampshire; I Like it Like That; Indecent Proposal; John and Mary; Journey for Margaret; A Kind of Loving; The Knack; Knife in the Water; Less Than Zero; A Little Sex; Lord Love a Duck; Love With the Proper Stranger; Lovers and Other Strangers; Made for Each Other; Medium Cool; Metropolitan (1990); Morgan!; Nell; Perfect; The Preppie Murder; The Rachel Papers; The Rat Race; Rendez-Vous; The Return of the Secaucus Seven; River's Edge; Romeo and Juliet (1954); Romeo

and Juliet (1968); Romeo and Juliet (1936); Sammy and Rosie Get Laid; Secret People; Seven Brides for Seven Brothers; Shaking the Tree; She's Having a Baby; Singles; Ski School; Slacker; Smashing Time; Smithereens; Some Kind of Wonderful; St. Elmo's Fire; Under the Yum Yum Tree; Untamed Heart; Watch It; Where the Day Takes You; Young Sherlock Holmes; Zabriskie Point

Young Women: see also *Famous Young People: Ensemble Films: Bratpack Stories: Coming of Age: Teenage Movies: Pre-Life Crises:* Abschied von Gestern; Act of the Heart; Adam and Eva; Adam and Evelyne; Adventures in Babysitting; The Affairs of Susan; Alice Adams; Allnighter; The Americanization of Emily; Amsterdamned; Amy; Angie; Baby Doll; Becky Sharp; The Bell Jar; Belle Epoque; The Best Little Girl in the World; The Best of Everything; Bhowani Junction; Bilitis; The Body Snatchers; Bonjour, Tristesse; Cage of Gold; Camilla (1994); Candy; Casual Sex?; Cattle Annie & Little Britches; A Chorus Line; Claudia; Daisy Miller; Die! Die! My Darling!; Doctor, You've Got to be Kidding; Eclipse; Educating Rita; Experience Preferred . . .; Face to Face; Fanny; The Frog Prince; The Getting of Wisdom; Gidget; Gigi (1948); Gigi (1958); Girlfriends; The Good Fairy; The Grasshopper; The Group; The Gun in Betty Lou's Handbag; Happy Time; Hester Street; Hilda Crane; House of Women; I am a Camera; I Know Where I'm Going; I Never Promised You A Rose Garden; If a Man Answers; Interns; Jersey Girl; Joni; Katherine; Kiss and Tell; Kitty Foyle; Kotch; The L-Shaped Room; The Lacemaker; Lady L.; Letter to Brezhnev; A Life of Her Own; Lili; Limbo; Looking for Love; Love Letters (1984); Madame Bovary; The Major and the Minor; Major Barbara; Manon; Marjorie Morningstar; Maybe I'll Be Home in the Spring; Me, Natalie; Meet Me in St. Louis; Mermaids; Mike's Murder; Million Dollar Baby; The Miracle of Morgan's Creek; Miss Firecracker; Miss Susie Slagle's; Mountain Eagle; Music for Millions; My Fair Lady; My Little Girl; My New Gun; My Sister

Eileen (1942); My Sister Eileen (1955); Mystic Pizza; Naked in New York; The Night We Never Met; Nobody's Fool (1986); Once Is Not Enough; One Deadly Summer; A Passage to India; Presenting Lily Mars; The Rain People; Rebecca of Sunnybrook Farm (1925); Red Kiss; Repulsion; Return to Peyton Place; Rich in Love; Rosemary's Baby; Ruby in Paradise; Sabrina; Samantha; The Scent of Green Papaya; Scent of Mystery; Secret Places; Shag; Sing as We Go; Slaves of New York; Smile; Smooth Talk; Snakepit; Spitfire; Splendor in the Grass; Stage Struck; Stagedoor; The Story of Adele H.; The Suicide Club; Sunday in New York; The Sure Thing; Susan Lenox, Her Fall and Rise; Suspiria; T.R. Baskin; A Taste of Honey; Therese and Isabelle; Thoroughly Modern Millie; Three Blind Mice; Three on a Couch; Three Sisters; To Find a Man; 21; The Unbelievable Truth; The Unforgiven (1960); Up the Sandbox; Valley of the Dolls; Vanity Fair; Variety; White Dog; Wild Hearts Can't Be Broken; You Light Up My Life; You've Got to Live Dangerously; Zazie dans le Metro; Ziegfeld Girl

Younger Men with Older Women: see *Romance-Older Women/ Younger Men*

Younger Women with Older Men: see *Romance-Older Men/Younger Women*

Yuppies: see also *1980s: Business Life: Office Comedy: Wall Street: Young People: Snobs:* About Face; Almost You; Bad Influence; Barcelona; Bedroom Eyes; Before Sunrise; The Big Chill; Biggles; Blind Side; The Bonfire of the Vanities; Boys on the Side; Bright Lights, Big City; Clean and Sober; Ghost; Goodbye, New York; Immediate Family; Key Exchange; Letter to Three Wives; A Little Sex; Lost in America; Love Matters; Malice; The Marriage of a Young Stockbroker; Married to It; The Money Pit; My Life; The Night We Never Met; Oliver's Story; The Opposite Sex and How to Live With Them; Pacific Heights; Quicksilver; Strictly Business; They Live; Up the Creek (1984); Wall Street; Watch It; White Palace

Z

Zombies: see also *Mummies: HORROR: Monsters: Simple Minds:* American Ninja 2; Army of Darkness; Bad Dreams; Black Sleep; Dawn of the Dead; Day of the Dead; Dead Heat; Hellbound: Hellraiser II; Hellraiser; Hellraiser III: Hell on Earth; I Married a Monster from Outer Space; I Walked with a Zombie; My Boyfriend's Back; Night of the Comet; Night of the Living Dead (1968); Night of the Living Dead (1990); The Omega Man; The Puppetmasters; Return of the Living Dead; Return of the Living Dead Part II; The Serpent and the Rainbow; The Stuff; Transmutations; Weekend at Bernie's 2

Appendix A

BOX OFFICE HITS BY YEAR

Sources: *Variety, The Hollywood Reporter, The Book of Reel Facts.*

Figures for films before the 1950s are very difficult to come by and are often inaccurate.

The figures in sources were compared, and in some cases an average between disparate figures is listed.

You may notice how many films that were big hits in their initial release, such as 1947's Forever Amber, 1957's The Pride and the Passion, 1967's To Sir with Love, or 1980's Stir Crazy, have been long forgotten or disregarded. Very often the films that have won major awards turn up more often than the hits on television and on lists as perennial favorites. This is refreshing, considering the rising vapidity of Hollywood "hits" these days.

It should also be realized that some films, like A Few Good Men or Legal Eagles, made much higher than the 50% rental average return, making them seem like much bigger hits than they were. This is because of the deals the studios cut with the theaters, whereby they take much larger than normal percentages of the gross sales in the first weeks of release. This is common practice but usually evens out if the film plays a long time. It has unfortunately led to the situation of needing "high concept" films that can be easily described and marketed with "known/pre-promotable elements," such as cartoon characters or best-seller book title adaptations; or, particularly, stars who can "open" a movie "big" on the first weekend or two, thereby returning a much bigger amount to the studio in a shorter period of time, which offsets the chance of and cost of a "flop."

See also Flops-Major, Faded Hits, and Forgotten Films.
‡ denotes a major Oscar winner; * denotes multiple releases; the dollar amount given in parentheses after a year is the average price all tickets sold, including half-price children's.

Title	Studio	$$$	Later$

(please note that only films with rentals over $5.0 million are listed before 1947)

1915
Birth of a Nation (a legendary example of untraceable complete grosses)	Mutual	10.2	

1937 ($.23)
Snow White and the Seven Dwarfs‡	Disney	37.0	77.2

1939 ($.25)
Gone With the Wind‡	MGM	26.2	79.2
The Wizard of Oz‡	MGM	5.5	30.0

1940 ($.25)
Fantasia*	Disney	2.5	41.7
Pinocchio*	RKO-Dis	4.5	40.4

1942 ($.27)
Bambi*	RKO-Dis	5.0	47.3

1946 ($.40)
The Best Years of Our Lives‡	RKO	11.5	
The Jolson Story	Col	8.0	

Title	Studio	$$$	Later$	Title	Studio	$$$	Later$
The Yearling‡	MGM	7.0		6 The Snake Pit	20th	4.1	
The Razor's Edge	20th	6.6		7 Joan of Arc	RKO	4.1	
Margie	20th	5.0		8 The Stratton Story	MGM	3.7	
				9 Mr. Belvedere Goes to College	20th	3.7	
1947 ($.40)				10 Little Women	MGM	3.6	
1 Duel in the Sun	Selznick	10.8		11 Words and Music	MGM	3.5	
2 Forever Amber	Par	8.0		12 In the Good Old Summertime	MGM	3.4	
3 Unconquered	Par	7.5		13 Neptune's Daughter	MGM	3.4	
4 Bachelor & Bobbysoxer	RKO	7.0		14 Sorrowful Jones	Par	3.4	
5 Life with Father‡	WB	6.3		15 Take Me Out to the Ballgame	Par	3.4	
6 Welcome Stranger (NA)	NA	6.1		16 Come to the Stable	20th	3.3	
7 The Egg and I	U	5.8		17 The Barkleys of Broadway	MGM	3.2	
8 The Hucksters	MGM	5.6		18 A Connecticut Yankee in . . .	Par	3.0	
9 Green Dolphin Street	MGM	5.0					
10 Gentleman's Agreement‡	20th	5.0		**1950 ($.53)**			
11 Song of the South*	Disney	4.7	28.9	1 Samson and Delilah		11.0	
The Farmer's Daughter‡	RKO	4.7		2 Cinderella*	RKO-Dis	6.0	41.1
12 Till the Clouds Roll By	MGM	4.5		3 Adam's Rib	MGM	5.8	
13 Mother Wore Tights	20th	4.1		4 King Solomon's Mines	MGM	4.4	
14 California	WB	4.0		5 Cheaper by the Dozen	20th	4.3	
15 The Sea of Grass	MGM	4.0		6 Born Yesterday	Col	4.2	
16 Dear Ruth	Par	4.0		7 Annie Get Your Gun	MGM	4.2	
17 The Perils of Pauline	20th	3.9		8 Father of the Bride	MGM	4.1	
18 This Time for Keeps	NA	3.6		9 Sands of Iwo Jima	Republic	3.9	
				10 Broken Arrow	20th	3.6	
1948 ($.40)				11 Twelve O'Clock High	20th	3.3	
1 The Road to Rio	Par	4.5		12 All About Eve	20th	3.3	
2 Easter Parade	MGM	4.2		13 The Flame and the Arrow	WB	3.0	
3 Red River	Republic	4.2		14 On the Town	MGM	2.9	
4 The Three Musketeers	MGM	4.1		15 Three Little Words	MGM	2.8	
5 Johnny Belinda‡	WB	4.1		16 The Black Rose	20th	2.7	
6 Cass Timberlane	MGM	4.1		17 The Duchess of Idaho	MGM	2.6	
7 The Emperor Waltz	MGM	4.0		18 Fancy Pants	Par	2.6	
8 Date with Judy	MGM	3.7					
9 Sitting Pretty	20th	3.7		**1951 ($.53)**			
10 Paleface	Par	3.6		1 Quo Vadis	MGM	11.9	
11 State of the Union	MGM	3.5		2 David and Bathsheba	Par	7.0	
12 My Wild Irish Rose	20th	3.4		3 The African Queen	UA	6.0	
13 Captain from Castile	NA	3.4		4 Showboat	MGM	5.2	
14 Homecoming	MGM	3.4		5 An American in Paris	MGM	4.5	
15 Hamlet	U	3.3		6 The Great Caruso	MGM	4.5	
16 When My Baby Smiles at Me	20th	3.3		7 A Streetcar Named Desire	WB	4.4	
17 Key Largo	WB	3.3		8 That's My Boy	NA	3.8	
18 The Fuller Brush Man	Col	3.1		9 A Place in the Sun	Par	3.5	
19 On an Island with You		3.1		10 At War with the Army	WB	3.4	
				11 Father's Little Dividend	MGM	3.1	
1949 ($.46)				12 Detective Story	Par	2.8	
				13 Kim	MGM	2.8	
1 The Great Lover	MGM	5.9		14 Across the Wide Missouri	MGM	2.8	
2 Jolson Sings Again	Col	5.5		15 Captain Horatio Hornblower	MGM	2.7	
3 Battleground	MGM	4.6		16 Halls of Montezuma	U	2.6	
4 Pinky	20th	4.2		17 Flying Leathernecks	RKO	2.6	
5 I Was a Male War Bride	20th	4.1		18 Harvey	U	2.6	

Title	Studio	$$$	Later$		Title	Studio	$$$	Later$
19 Royal Wedding	MGM	2.6			16 Dragnet	WB	4.3	
20 On the Riviera	20th	2.5			17 Demetrius and the Gladiators	Col	4.2	
					18 Living It Up	Par	4.2	
1952 ($.60)					19 On the Waterfront	Col	4.2	
1 This Is Cinerama	Cin	15.4			20 Hondo	Par	4.1	
2 The Greatest Show on Earth	Par	12.0			21 River of No Return	20th	3.8	
3 Ivanhoe	MGM	7.0			22 Broken Lance	20th	3.8	
4 The Snows of Kilimanjaro	20th	6.5						
5 Moulin Rouge	UA	5.0			**1955 ($.50)**			
6 Sailor Beware	RKO	4.3			1 Cinerama Holiday	CRC	12.0	
7 Jumping Jacks	U	4.0			2 Mister Roberts	WB	8.5	
8 Singing in the Rain	MGM	3.6			3 Battle Cry	WB	8.0	
9 High Noon	UA	3.4			4 20,000 Leagues Under the Sea	Disney	8.0	20.5
10 With a Song in My Heart	20th	3.3			5 Not as a Stranger	RKO	7.1	
11 The Quiet Man	Republic	3.1			6 I'll Cry Tomorrow	MGM	6.5	
12 Plymouth Adventure	MGM	3.0			7 The Lady and the Tramp	Disney	6.5	40.3
13 The Bend of the River	U	3.0			8 Strategic Air Command	Par	6.5	
					9 Picnic	Col	6.3	
1953 ($.44)					10 Rebel Without a Cause	WB	6.0	
1 The Robe	20th	25.0			11 To Hell and Back	U	6.0	
2 From Here to Eternity	Col	12.2			12 Sea Chase	WB	6.0	
3 Shane	Par	9.0			13 The Rose Tattoo	Par	5.2	
4 How to Marry a Millionaire	20th	7.5			14 The Blackboard Jungle	MGM	5.2	
5 Peter Pan	Disney	7.0	37.5		15 East of Eden	WB	5.0	
6 Hans Christian Andersen	Goldwyn	6.0			16 Pete Kelly's Blues	Col	5.0	
7 House of Wax	WB	5.5			17 The Seven Year Itch	20th	5.0	
8 Mogambo	MGM	5.2			18 The Bridges at Toko-Ri	Par	4.7	
9 Gentlemen Prefer Blondes	20th	5.1			19 A Man Called Peter	RKO	4.5	
10 Salome	Col	4.8			20 There's No Business Like			
11 Charge at Feather River	RKO	3.7			Show Business	20th	4.5	
12 Stalag 17	Par	3.7			21 To Catch a Thief	Par	4.5	
13 Scared Stiff	Par	3.6			22 Vera Cruz	Par	4.5	
14 Roman Holiday	Par	3.5			23 The Man with the Golden Arm	Col	4.4	
15 The Stooge	Par	3.4						
16 Road to Bali	Par	3.0			**1956 ($.50)**			
					1 The Ten Commandments	Par	18.5	
1954 ($.45)					2 Around the World in 80 Days	UA	16.2	
1 White Christmas	Par	12.0			3 Giant	WB	14.0	
2 The Caine Mutiny	Par	8.7			4 Seven Wonders of the World	CRC	12.5	
3 The Glenn Miller Story	U	7.0			5 Guys and Dolls	MGM	9.1	
4 The Country Girl	Par	6.9			6 The King and I	20th	8.5	
5 The Egyptian	U	6.0			7 Trapeze	UA	7.5	
6 A Star Is Born	WB	6.0			8 High Society	MGM	6.5	
7 Rear Window	RKO	5.3			9 War and Peace	Par	6.3	
8 The High and the Mighty	20th	5.2			10 The Eddy Duchin Story	Col	5.3	
9 Sabrina	Par	5.1			11 Moby Dick	UA	5.2	
10 Magnificent Obsession	U	5.1			12 Anastasia	20th	5.0	
11 The Long Long Trailer	MGM	5.1			13 An Affair to Remember	U	5.0	
12 Three Coins in the Fountain	20th	5.0			14 The Searchers	WB	4.8	
13 Seven Brides for Seven Bros.	MGM	5.0			15 The Conquerer	Hughes-U	4.5	
14 Desirée	WB	4.5			16 The Man in the Gray			
15 Knights of the Round Table	MGM	4.4			Flannel Suit	UA	4.4	
					17 Bus Stop	20th	4.3	

Title	Studio	$$$	Later$
18 The Bad Seed	20th	4.1	
19 The Man Who Knew Too Much	Par	4.1	
20 Friendly Persuasion	AA	4.0	
21 The Proud and the Profane	Par	3.9	

1957 ($.51)

Title	Studio	$$$	Later$
1 Peyton Place	20th	12.0	
2 Pal Joey	Col	6.7	
3 Seven Wonders of the World	CRC	6.5	
4 The Teahouse of the August Moon	MGM	5.6	
5 The Pride and the Passion	Par	5.5	
6 Island in the Sun	20th	5.0	
7 Love Me Tender	MGM	4.5	
8 Written on the Wind	U	4.4	
9 Gunfight at the OK Corral	Par	4.3	
10 Heaven Knows, Mr. Allison	20th	4.2	
11 April Love	RKO	4.0	
12 Jailhouse Rock	MGM	4.0	
13 Battle Hymn	MGM	3.9	
14 Witness for the Prosecution	UA	3.8	
15 Bernardine	20th	3.7	
16 Loving You	NA	3.7	
17 The Sun Also Rises	Par	3.5	

1958 ($.51)

Title	Studio	$$$	Later$
1 The Bridge on the River Kwai	Col	18.0	
2 Sayonara	WB	10.5	
3 Cat on a Hot Tin Roof	MGM	9.5	
4 Auntie Mame	WB	8.8	
5 No Time for Sergeants	WB	7.2	
6 The Vikings	Col	7.0	
7 Search for Paradise	Ind.	6.5	
8 South Pacific	UA	6.4	
9 Raintree County	MGM	6.1	
10 Old Yeller	Disney	5.9	
11 A Farewell to Arms	20th	5.0	
12 The Young Lions	20th	5.0	
13 Don't Go Near the Water	MGM	4.5	
14 Some Came Running	MGM	4.2	
15 Separate Tables‡	UA	3.7	
16 Indiscreet	U	3.6	
17 Inn of the Sixth Happiness	20th	3.6	
18 God's Little Acre	UA	3.5	
19 I Want to Live	UA	3.5	
20 Houseboat	Par	3.5	
21 The Long Hot Summer	UA	3.5	
22 The Sad Sack	U	3.5	

1959 ($.51)

Title	Studio	$$$	Later$
1 Ben Hur‡	MGM	17.3	40.5
2 Pillow Talk	U	8.0	

Title	Studio	$$$	Later$
3 The Shaggy Dog	Disney	7.8	
4 Some Like It Hot	UA	7.0	
5 Operation Petticoat	UA	6.8	
6 Imitation of Life	U	6.2	
7 The Nun's Story‡	WB	6.1	
8 Suddenly Last Summer	Col	5.5	
9 Anatomy of a Murder‡	Col	5.3	
10 North by Northwest	MGM	5.3	
11 Rio Bravo	WB	5.2	
12 Sleeping Beauty*	Disney	4.3	22.0
13 A Hole in the Head	UA	4.0	
14 Hercules	Ind	4.0	
15 The Horse Soldiers	UA	3.3	
16 Don't Give Up the Ship	Col	3.2	
17 The 7 Voyages of Sinbad	Col	3.1	
18 The Buccaneer	Par	3.0	
19 The Geisha Boy	Par	3.0	
20 The Big Circus	U	2.7	

1960 ($.69)

Title	Studio	$$$	Later$
1 Psycho	U	8.5	11.2
2 Swiss Family Robinson	Disney	7.5	20.2
3 The Alamo‡	WB	7.3	
4 On the Beach	U	5.3	
5 Solomon and Sheba	UA	5.3	
6 The Apartment‡	UA	5.1	
7 From the Terrace	20th	5.0	
8 Please Don't Eat the Daisies	MGM	5.0	
9 Oceans 11	WB	4.9	
10 Journey to the Center of the Earth	20th	4.7	
11 Elmer Gantry‡	UA	4.5	
12 The Bellboy	Par	3.6	
13 Can Can	20th	3.5	
14 The Rat Race	Par	3.4	
15 The Wackiest Ship in Army	WB	3.3	
16 Portrait in Black	U	3.2	
17 Li'l Abner	Par	3.2	
18 Visit to a Small Planet	UA	3.2	
19 Home from the Hill	MGM	3.2	

1961 ($.70)

Title	Studio	$$$	Later$
1 West Side Story‡	UA	13.5	19.7
2 Spartacus	U	13.5	
3 The Guns of Navarone‡	Col	13.1	
4 Splendor in the Grass	WB	9.2	
5 The Absent-Minded Professor	Disney	8.2	13.5
6 The Parent Trap	Disney	8.0	11.4
7 El Cid	AA	8.0	12.0
8 Breakfast at Tiffany's	Par	7.5	
9 Exodus	UA	7.4	
10 The World of Suzie Wong	Par	7.3	

Title	Studio	$$$	Later$
11 101 Dalmatians*	Disney	5.8	68.6
12 La Dolce Vita	Astor	6.0	
13 Come September	U	4.5	
14 North to Alaska	20th	4.5	
15 Fanny‡	20th	4.5	
16 Pepe	Col	4.3	
17 One Eyed Jacks	WB	4.3	
18 Parrish	WB	4.2	
19 The Misfits	UA	3.9	
20 The Sundowners‡	WB	3.8	
21 Judgment at Nuremburg	UA	3.8	
22 Midnight Lace	U	3.7	
23 Never on a Sunday	MGM	3.4	
24 Where the Boys Are	MGM	3.3	

1962 ($.70)

Title	Studio	$$$	Later$
1 The Longest Day‡	20th	12.8	17.6
2 Lawrence of Arabia‡	Col	9.1	20.3
3 Lover Come Back	U	8.5	
4 That Touch of Mink	U	8.5	
5 The Music Man	WB	8.0	
6 Mutiny on the Bounty‡	MGM	7.7	
7 King of Kings	MGM	7.5	
8 To Kill a Mockingbird‡	U	6.7	
9 Hatari!	Par	6.0	
10 Dr. No	UA	6.0	
11 Gypsy	WB	5.4	
12 Flower Drum Song	Par	5.0	
13 The Interns	Col	5.0	
14 Whatever Happened to Baby Jane?	WB	4.9	
15 Blue Hawaii	MGM	4.7	
16 Lolita	MGM	4.5	
17 Babes in Toyland	Disney	4.4	
18 Bon Voyage	Disney	4.1	
19 Sergeants Three	U	3.9	
20 Man Who Shot Liberty Valance	Par	3.9	

1963 ($.85)

Title	Studio	$$$	Later$
1 Tom Jones‡	UA	17.1	20.3
2 Cleopatra‡	20th	15.7	26.0
3 It's a Mad Mad Mad Mad World	UA	10.5	20.9
4 Irma La Douce	UA	9.3	11.9
5 How the West Was Won	MGM	8.5	21.0
6 Son of Flubber	Disney	6.9	
7 Charade	U	6.2	
8 Bye Bye Birdie	U	5.6	
9 Come Blow Your Horn	Col	5.5	
10 The Castaways	Disney	4.7	
11 The Birds	U	4.7	
12 The Great Escape	UA	4.6	
13 The Brothers Grimm	MGM	4.5	

Title	Studio	$$$	Later$
14 Diamond Head	UA	4.3	
15 The Thrill of It All	U	4.3	
16 Spencer's Mountain	MGM	4.0	
17 55 Days at Peking	Par	3.9	
18 Hud‡	Par	3.9	
19 Love with the Proper Stranger	Par	3.9	
20 The Prize	UA	3.4	

1964 ($.93)

Title	Studio	$$$	Later$
1 Mary Poppins*	Disney	30.1	47.9
2 My Fair Lady*	WB	24.1	30.9
3 Goldfinger	UA	17.6	23.0
4 The Carpetbaggers	Par	15.5	
5 The Unsinkable Molly Brown	MGM	7.7	
6 Father Goose	U	6.0	
7 Move Over Darling	U	6.0	
8 Send Me No Flowers	U	5.4	
9 The Cardinal	UA	5.3	
10 What a Way to Go	Par	5.0	
11 Good Neighbor Sam	Col	5.0	
12 The Pink Panther	UA	4.9	
13 The Night of the Iguana	MGM	4.9	
14 Viva Las Vegas	MGM	4.7	
15 The Sword in the Stone	Disney	4.5	
16 A Hard Day's Night	UA	4.5	
17 Dr. Strangelove	Col	4.3	
18 Sex and the Single Girl	WB	4.0	
19 Misadventures of Merlin Jones	Disney	4.0	
20 From Russia with Love	UA	4.0	
21 Becket	Par	3.7	
22 Seven Days in May	MGM	3.4	

1965 ($1.01)

Title	Studio	$$$	Later$
1 The Sound of Music	20th	56.0	80.0
2 Doctor Zhivago	MGM	46.0	60.9
3 Thunderball	UA	28.6	
4 Those Magnificent Men in . . .	20th	14.4	
5 The Great Race	WB	11.4	
6 That Darn Cat	Disney	9.2	12.7
7 What's New Pussycat?	UA	7.1	
8 Shenandoah	U	7.0	
9 The Sandpiper	MGM	6.4	
10 A Patch of Blue	MGM	6.3	
11 Von Ryan's Express	20th	5.6	
12 The Yellow Rolls Royce	MGM	5.4	
13 How to Murder Your Wife	UA	5.4	
14 Cat Ballou	Col	5.2	9.3
15 The Sons of Katie Elder	Par	5.0	
16 Help	UA	4.2	
17 In Harm's Way	20th	4.0	
18 The Americanization of Emily	MGM	4.0	
19 Monkey's Uncle	Disney	3.5	

Title	Studio	$$$	Later$
20 The Train	UA	3.5	
21 Goodbye Charlie	Col	3.4	

1966 ($1.09)

Title	Studio	$$$	Later$
1 Hawaii	UA	15.6	
2 The Bible	20th	15.1	
3 Who's Afraid of Virginia Woolf?‡	WB	14.5	
4 The Sand Pebbles‡	20th	13.5	
5 A Man for All Seasons‡	Col	12.8	
6 The Professionals	Col	8.8	
7 The Russians Are Coming . . .‡	UA	7.8	
8 Lt. Robin Crusoe, USN	Disney	7.5	
9 Georgy Girl	Col	7.3	
10 Grand Prix	MGM	7.0	
11 The Silencers	Col	7.0	
12 Torn Curtain	U	7.0	
13 Blow Up	MGM	6.9	
14 Our Man Flint	20th	6.5	
15 The Ugly Dachshund	Disney	6.0	
16 Wild Angels	AP	5.5	
17 Harper	WB	5.3	
18 The Blue Max	20th	5.0	
19 Nevada Smith	Avco-Par	5.0	
20 The Battle of the Bulge	WB	4.5	
21 Fantastic Voyage	20th	4.5	

1967 ($1.20)

Title	Studio	$$$	Later$
1 The Graduate	Emb	44.1	
2 Guess Who's Coming to Dinner	Col	25.5	
3 Bonnie and Clyde	WB	22.8	
4 The Dirty Dozen	MGM	20.4	
5 Valley of the Dolls	20th	20.0	
6 To Sir with Love	Col	19.1	
7 Thoroughly Modern Millie	U	15.5	
8 Born Losers	AIP	14.7	
9 Jungle Book*	Disney	11.5	60.9
10 Barefoot in the Park	Par	8.3	
11 Camelot	WB	6.6	14.2
12 Hombre	20th	6.5	
13 Murderer's Row	Col	6.3	
14 In Cold Blood	Col	6.0	
15 El Dorado	WB	6.0	
16 War Wagon	U	5.5	
17 Follow Me, Boys	Disney	5.4	
18 Divorce American Style	Col	5.2	
19 In Like Flint	20th	5.0	
20 A Guide for the Married Man	20th	5.0	
21 Up the Down Staircase	WB	5.0	

1968 ($1.31)

Title	Studio	$$$	Later$
1 Funny Girl‡	Col	26.4	
2 The Odd Couple	Par	20.0	

Title	Studio	$$$	Later$
3 Bullitt	WB	19.0	
4 Romeo and Juliet‡	Par	17.5	
5 2001: A Space Odyssey*	MGM	17.0	25.5
6 Planet of the Apes	20th	15.5	
7 Rosemary's Baby	Par	15.5	
8 Oliver‡	Col	16.8	
9 Yours, Mine and Ours	Col	11.5	
10 Blackbeard's Ghost	Disney	9.7	
11 Chitty Chitty Bang Bang	UA	8.9	
12 The Green Berets	WB	8.7	
13 The Fox	Claridge	8.3	
14 Wait Until Dark	WB	8.0	
15 The Lion in Winter‡	Emb	8.0	
16 Rachel, Rachel‡	WB	7.0	
17 The Thomas Crown Affair	UA	7.0	
18 The Detective	WB	6.5	
19 The Impossible Years	MGM	6.0	
20 Bandolero	20th	5.5	
21 Finian's Rainbow	WB	5.1	
22 For the Love of Ivy	ABC-Cin	5.0	
23 Hang 'em High	WB	5.0	
24 The Happiest Millionaire	Disney	5.0	

1969 ($1.41)

Title	Studio	$$$	Later$
1 Butch Cassidy & Sundance Kid‡	20th	21.0	45.9
2 Love Bug*	Disney	17.0	23.1
3 Midnight Cowboy‡	UA	20.5	
4 Easy Rider	Col	19.2	
5 Hello Dolly	20th	15.2	
6 Bob & Carol & Ted & Alice	Col	14.6	
7 Paint Your Wagon	Par	14.5	
8 True Grit	Par	14.2	
9 Cactus Flower	Col	11.9	
10 Goodbye Columbus	Par	10.5	
11 On Her Majesty's Secret Service	UA	9.1	
12 The Reivers	UA	8.0	
13 Z‡	Col?	6.8	
14 They Shoot Horses, Don't They?	ABC	6.6	
15 I Am Curious Yellow	Svensk	6.6	
16 Where Eagles Dare	U	6.6	
17 Anne of the Thousand Days‡	U	6.5	
18 Winning	U	6.2	
19 A Boy Named Charlie Brown	NGP	6.0	
20 Support Your Local Sheriff	UA	5.0	

1970 ($1.55)

Title	Studio	$$$	Later$
1 Love Story	Par	48.7	
2 Airport	U	45.2	
3 M*A*S*H	20th	36.7	
4 Patton	20th	28.1	
5 In Search of Noah's Ark	Sunn	23.8	
6 Woodstock	WB	16.4	
7 Ryan's Daughter	MGM	14.6	

Title	Studio	$$$	Later$
8 Tora! Tora! Tora!	20th	14.5	
9 The Aristocats*	Disney	11.5	
10 Joe	Can-MGM	9.5	
11 Catch 22	Par	9.3	
12 The Boatniks	Disney	9.2	
13 Five Easy Pieces	Col	8.9	
14 The Adventurers	Par	7.8	
15 The Out of Towners	Par	7.4	
16 Beneath the Planet of the Apes	20th	7.3	
17 Chisum	WB	6.0	
18 A Man Called Horse	Cinerama	6.0	
19 Diary of a Mad Housewife	U	5.9	
20 On a Clear Day	Par	5.7	
21 Three in the Attic	Par	5.2	
The Landlord	UA	5.2	

1971 ($1.65)

Title	Studio	$$$	Later$
1 Fiddler on the Roof‡	UA	38.2	
2 Billy Jack	WB	32.5	
3 The French Connection‡	20th	26.3	
4 Summer of '42	WB	20.5	
5 Deep Throat	Damiano	20.0	
6 Diamonds Are Forever	UA	19.8	
7 Dirty Harry	WB	18.1	
8 A Clockwork Orange‡	WB	17.5	
9 Little Big Man	NG	17.0	
10 The Last Picture Show	Col	14.1	
11 The Owl and the Pussycat	Col	12.2	
12 Carnal Knowledge	Emb	12.1	
13 The Hospital	UA	9.5	
14 Willard	AIP	9.3	
15 The Andromeda Strain	U	8.0	
16 Big Jake	Cin Center	7.5	
17 The Stewardesses	Coons	7.0	
18 Klute	WB	7.0	
19 Nicholas and Alexandra‡	Col	6.9	
20 Shaft	MGM	6.1	
21 Cold Turkey	U	6.0	
22 LeMans	20th	5.7	
23 The Anderson Tapes	Col	5.5	
24 A New Leaf	Par	5.5	
25 There's a Girl in My Soup	Col	5.02	
26 The Million Dollar Duck	Disney	5.0	

1972 ($1.70)

Title	Studio	$$$	Later$
1 The Godfather‡	Par	86.3	
2 The Poseidon Adventure	20th	42.1	
3 What's Up, Doc?	WB	28.5	
4 Deliverance‡	WB	22.6	
5 Jeremiah Johnson*	WB	21.9	
6 Cabaret‡	AA-ABC	20.2	
7 The Getaway	NG-WB	18.4	
8 Lady Sings the Blues	Par	11.0	

Title	Studio	$$$	Later$
9 Sounder‡	20th	9.5	
10 Pete 'n Tillie	U	8.7	
11 Everything You Always . . . Sex	UA	8.5	
12 Bedknobs and Broomsticks	Disney	8.3	
13 The Cowboys	WB	7.0	
14 Frenzy	U	6.3	
15 Skyjacked	MGM	6.1	
16 Escape from the Planet of Apes	20th	5.5	
17 Butterflies Are Free	Col	5.5	
18 The New Centurions	Col	5.5	

1973 ($1.77)

Title	Studio	$$$	Later$
1 The Exorcist‡	WB	89.3	
2 The Sting‡	U	78.2	
3 American Graffiti‡*	U	55.2	
4 The Way We Were	Col	25.8	
5 Papillon	AA	22.5	
6 Magnum Force	WB	20.1	
7 Robin Hood*	Disney	17.2	
8 Last Tango in Paris	UA	16.7	
9 Paper Moon	Par	16.6	
10 Live and Let Die	UA	16.0	
11 Serpico	Par	14.6	
12 Jesus Christ Superstar	U	13.1	
13 Chariots of the Gods	Sunn	12.4	
14 Enter the Dragon	WB	11.5	
15 The World's Greatest Athlete	Disney	10.5	
16 The Day of the Jackal	U	8.7	
17 Walking Tall	Ind	8.5	
18 High Plains Drifter	WB	7.3	

1974 ($1.89)

Title	Studio	$$$	Later$
1 The Towering Inferno‡	20th-WB	55.8	
2 Blazing Saddles	WB	47.8	
3 Earthquake	U	35.9	
4 The Trial of Billy Jack	WB	31.1	
5 Benji	Mulberry	30.8	
6 The Godfather Part II‡	Par	30.7	
7 Young Frankenstein	20th	30.1	
8 Airport 1975	U	25.3	
9 The Longest Yard	Par	23.0	
10 That's Entertainment	MGM	19.1	
11 Murder on the Orient Express	Par	19.1	
12 Herbie Rides Again	Disney	17.1	
13 The Three Musketeers	20th	15.4	
14 Dirty Mary, Crazy Larry	20th	15.2	
15 For Pete's Sake	Col	14.5	
16 The Texas Chainsaw Massacre	New Line	14.4	
17 The Great Gatsy	Par	14.2	
18 Lenny‡	UA	11.5	
19 Freebie and the Bean	WB	12.5	
20 Thunderbolt and Lightfoot	UA	9.3	
21 The Groove Tube	L-P	9.3	

Title	Studio	$$$	Later$
22 Macon County Line	AIP	9.2	
23 Death Wish	U	8.8	

1975 ($2.05)

Title	Studio	$$$	Later$
1 Jaws	U	129.5	
2 One Flew over the Cuckoo's Nest	UA	60.0	
Rocky Horror Picture Show*	20th	3.5	40.0
3 Shampoo	Col	24.5	
4 Dog Day Afternoon	WB	22.5	
5 Return of the Pink Panther	UA	20.1	
6 Grizzly Adams	Sunn	21.9	
7 Three Days of the Condor	Par	21.5	
8 Funny Lady	Col	19.3	
9 The Other Side of the Mountain	U	18.0	
10 Tommy	Col	17.8	
11 Apple Dumpling Gang	Disney	16.6	
12 The Hindenburg	U	14.5	
13 Lucky Lady	U	12.1	
14 Let's Do It Again	WB	11.8	
15 Island at the Top of the World	Disney	10.5	
16 No Deposit, No Return	Disney	10.5	
17 Hustle	Par	10.4	
18 The Man with the Golden Gun	UA	10.0	
19 Barry Lyndon‡	WB	9.9	
20 Walking Tall	FW-CRC	9.4	
21 The Great Waldo Pepper	U	9.4	
22 Adv. of Sher. Holmes' Smarter Bro.	20th	9.4	
23 Nashville	Par	9.3	
24 Rollerball	UA	9.1	
25 Once Is Not Enough	Par	8.8	
26 Mandingo	Par	8.7	
27 Escape to Witch Mountain	Disney	8.7	

1976 ($2.12)

Title	Studio	$$$	Later$
1 Rocky‡	UA	56.5	
2 A Star Is Born	WB	37.1	
3 King Kong	Par	35.8	
4 All the President's Men‡	WB	31.0	
5 Silver Streak	20th	30.0	
6 The Omen	20th	28.5	
7 The Bad News Bears	Par	24.3	
8 The Enforcer	WB	24.1	
9 Midway	U	21.6	
10 Silent Movie	20th	21.2	
11 To Fly	IMAX	20.3	
12 The Pink Panther Strikes Again	UA	19.9	
13 Murder by Death	Col	19.1	
14 Network‡	MGM	15.1	
15 Marathon Man	Par	16.6	
16 Carrie	UA	15.2	
17 Taxi Driver	Col	11.7	
18 Freaky Friday	Disney	11.7	

Title	Studio	$$$	Later$
19 Ode to Billy Joe	WB	11.6	
20 The Outlaw Josey Wales	WB	10.6	
21 No Deposit, No Return	Disney	10.5	
22 The Shaggy D.A.	Disney	10.4	
23 Logan's Run	MGM	9.5	
24 Gus	Disney	9.0	

1977 ($2.23)

Title	Studio	$$$	Later$
1 Star Wars	20th	193.8	
2 Close Encounters of . . .	Col	82.8	
3 Saturday Night Fever	Par	74.1	
4 Smokey and the Bandit	U	59.0	
5 The Goodbye Girl	MGM-WB	41.9	
6 Oh, God	WB	31.5	
7 The Deep	Col	31.2	
8 The Rescuers*	Disney	30.1	
9 The Spy Who Loved Me	UA	24.3	
10 Semi-Tough	UA	22.9	
11 A Bridge Too Far	UA	20.4	
12 High Anxiety	20th	19.2	
13 Annie Hall	UA	19.0	
14 The Other Side of Midnight	20th	18.4	
15 Pete's Dragon	Disney	18.4	
16 The Gauntlet	WB	17.7	
17 The Turning Point	20th	17.1	
18 Looking for Mr. Goodbar	Par	16.9	
19 Airport '77	U	15.1	
20 The Bad News Bears II	Par	15.1	
21 Heroes	U	15.0	
22 Black Sunday	Par	14.2	
23 Exorcist II: The Heretic	WB	14.0	
24 Fun with Dick and Jane	Col	13.6	
25 Slapshot	U	13.6	
26 One on One	WB	13.0	
27 Julia	20th	13.0	
28 The World's Greatest Lover	20th	10.6	

1978 ($2.34)

Title	Studio	$$$	Later$
1 Grease	Par	96.3	
2 Superman	WB	82.8	
3 Animal House	U	70.9	
4 Every Which Way But Loose	WB	51.9	
5 Jaws II	U	50.4	
6 Heaven Can Wait	Par	49.4	
7 Hooper	WB	34.9	
8 California Suite	Col	29.2	
9 The Deer Hunter	EMI-U	28.0	
10 Foul Play	Par	27.5	
11 Up in Smoke	Par	26.3	
12 Revenge of the Pink Panther	UA	25.4	
13 The End	UA	20.7	
14 The Cheap Detective	Col	19.2	
15 Halloween	Compass	18.6	

Title	Studio	$$$	Later$
16 Midnight Express	Col	15.0	
17 House Calls	U	15.0	
18 Coma	MGM	14.8	
19 Coming Home	UA	13.5	
20 The Omen II	20th	12.1	
21 Lord of the Rings	UA	14.2	
22 Magic	20th	13.4	
23 The Wiz	U	12.3	
24 The One and Only	Par	12.1	
25 Capricorn One	WB	12.0	
26 An Unmarried Woman	20th	12.0	
27 Beyond and Back	Sunn	11.6	
28 Sergeant Peppers	U	11.4	
29 Same Time, Next Year	U	11.4	
30 Invasion of the Body Snatchers	UA	11.1	

1979 ($2.51)

Title	Studio	$$$	Later$
1 Kramer versus Kramer	Col	59.9	
2 Star Trek	Par	56.0	
3 The Jerk	U	43.0	
4 Rocky II	UA	42.1	
5 Alien	20th	40.3	
6 Apocalypse Now	UA	37.9	
7 10	Orion-WB	37.4	
8 The Amityville Horror	AIP	35.4	
9 Moonraker	UA	34.0	
10 The Muppet Movie	ITC-AFD	32.8	
11 The Electric Horseman	Col-U	30.2	
12 The Main Event	WB	26.4	
13 The China Syndrome	Col	25.8	
14 The Black Hole	Disney	25.4	
15 1941	U	23.2	
16 Escape from Alcatraz	Par	21.5	
17 Meatballs	Par	21.2	
18 All That Jazz	20th-Col	20.0	
19 Starting Over	Par	19.1	
20 The Rose	20th	19.1	
21 The In-Laws	WB	19.1	
22 Love at First Bite	AIP	18.7	
23 Manhattan	UA	17.6	
24 The Black Stallion	UA	17.3	
25 Little Darlings	Par	17.0	
26 North Dallas 40	Par	16.1	
27 And Justice for All	Col	14.5	
28 The Warriors	Par	14.5	
29 Going in Style	WB	14.1	
30 The Champ	MGM	12.5	
31 Norma Rae	20th	12.5	

1980 ($2.69)

Title	Studio	$$$	Later$
1 The Empire Strikes Back	20th	141.7	
2 Nine to Five	20th	59.1	
3 Stir Crazy	Col	58.3	

Title	Studio	$$$	Later$
4 Airplane	Par	40.6	
5 Any Which Way You Can	WB	40.5	
6 Smokey and the Bandit II	U	39.0	
7 Coal Miner's Daughter	U	35.5	
8 Private Benjamin	WB	34.4	
9 The Blues Brothers	U	32.1	
10 The Shining	WB	30.9	
11 The Blue Lagoon	Col	28.8	
12 Popeye	Par	24.5	
13 Urban Cowboy	Par	23.8	
14 Ordinary People	Par	23.1	
15 Seems Like Old Times	Col	21.6	
16 Cheech & Chong's Next Movie	U	21.5	
17 Caddyshack	Orion	20.0	
18 Brubaker	20th	19.0	
19 Friday the Thirteenth	Par	16.5	
20 Dressed to Kill	AIP-Orion	15.9	
21 Bronco Billy	WB	15.0	
22 Chapter Two	Col	14.9	
23 Flash Gordon	U	14.9	
24 The Jazz Singer	AFD	13.0	
25 Altered States	WB	12.5	
26 The Elephant Man	Par	12.5	
27 American Gigolo	Par	11.5	
28 Xanadu	U	11.0	
29 My Bodyguard	20th	10.7	

1981 ($2.80)

Title	Studio	$$$	Later$
1 Raiders of the Lost Ark	Par	115.6	
2 Superman II	WB	65.1	
3 On Golden Pond	ITC-U	61.2	
4 Arthur	Orion-WB	42.3	
5 Stripes	Col	40.8	
6 The Cannonball Run	20th	36.8	
7 Chariots of Fire	Ladd-WB	30.6	
8 The Fox and the Hound*	Disney	29.8	
9 The Four Seasons	U	27.1	
10 For Your Eyes Only	UA	26.6	
11 Reds	Par	21.0	
12 Cheech & Chong's Nice Dreams	Col	18.4	
13 Sharky's Machine	Orion-Wb	18.4	
14 Clash of the Titans	MGM	17.5	
15 Porky's 2	20th	17.2	
16 Neighbors	Col	17.1	
17 Excalibur	Orion	17.1	
18 The Great Muppet Caper	U/AFD	16.6	
19 Endless Love	U	16.5	
20 Tarzan the Ape Man	MGM	15.8	
21 Bustin' Loose	U	15.4	
22 French Lieutenant's Woman	MGM-UA	14.9	
23 Modern Problems	20th	14.8	
24 History of the World Part I	20th	14.4	
25 American Werewolf in London	U	13.8	

Title	Studio	$$$	Later$
26 Fort Apache the Bronx	20th	13.6	
27 Only When I Laugh	Col	12.5	
28 Private Lessons	JPF	12.5	
29 Eye of the Needle	UA	12.2	
30 Halloween II	U	11.9	
31 Ghost Story	U	11.9	
32 Escape from New York	Avco	11.9	
33 Body Heat	WB	11.4	

1982 ($3.05)

Title	Studio	$$$	Later$
1 E.T.	U	228.4	
2 Tootsie	Col	94.9	
3 Rocky III	MGM-UA	66.2	
4 Porky's	20th	55.6	
5 An Officer and Gentleman	Par	55.3	
6 The Best Little Whorehouse	U	47.3	
7 Star Trek II	Par	40.0	
8 Poltergeist	MGM	38.4	
9 Annie	Col	37.5	
10 48 Hours	Par	30.3	
11 The Verdict	20th	26.7	
12 Gandhi	Col	25.0	
13 The Toy	Col	24.4	
14 The Dark Crystal	U-AFD	23.9	
15 First Blood	Orion	22.9	
16 Conan the Barbarian	U	21.8	
17 Richard Pryor Live on Sunset Strip	Col	18.3	
18 Tron	Disney	16.7	
19 Friday the 13th Part III	Par	16.5	
20 Fast Times at Ridgemont High	U	15.8	
21 Young Doctors in Love	20th	15.2	
22 The World According to Garp	WB	14.9	
23 Sophie's Choice	ITC-U	14.9	
24 The World According to Garp	WB	14.9	
25 Bladerunner	WB	14.8	
26 Bladerunner	WB	14.8	
27 Never Cry Wolf	Disney	14.7	
28 Never Cry Wolf	Disney	14.7	
29 Quest for Fire	20th	12.2	
30 Dead Men Don't Wear Plaid	WB	11.5	
31 Deathtrap	WB	11.5	
32 Airplane II	Par	11.3	
33 Road Warrior	WB	11.3	
34 Victor/Victoria	MGM	10.5	

1983 ($3.25)

Title	Studio	$$$	Later$
1 Return of the Jedi	20th	169.2	
2 Terms of Endearment	Par	50.2	
3 Trading Places	Par	40.6	
4 War Games	MGM-UA	38.6	
5 Superman III	WB	37.2	

Title	Studio	$$$	Later$
6 Flashdance	Par	36.2	
7 Sudden Impact	EB	34.8	
8 Octopussy	MGM-UA	34.1	
9 Staying Alive	Par	33.3	
10 Mr. Mom	20th	32.1	
11 Risky Business	WB	30.4	
12 Vacation (Nat'l Lampoon's)	WB	30.4	
13 Never Say Never Again	WB	28.2	
14 Jaws 3-D	U	27.0	
15 The Big Chill*	Col	24.1	
16 Scarface	U	23.3	
17 Blue Thunder	Col	21.9	
18 Twilight Zone	WB	16.0	
19 Psycho II	U	15.9	
20 High Road to China	WB	15.5	
21 Easy Money	Orion	14.4	
22 Uncommon Valor	Par	13.0	
23 The Outsiders	Z-WB	12.3	
24 Spring Break	Col	11.3	

1984 ($3.40)

Title	Studio	$$$	Later$
1 Ghostbusters	Col	132.7	
2 Indiana Jones & Temple of Doom	Par	109.0	
3 Beverly Hills Cop	Par	108.0	
4 Gremlins	WB	79.5	
5 The Karate Kid	Col	43.2	
6 Star Trek III	Par	39.0	
7 Police Academy	WB	38.5	
8 Romancing the Stone	20th	36.6	
9 Splash	Touch	34.1	
10 Footloose	Par	34.0	
11 Purple Rain	WB	31.7	
12 The Natural	Tri	25.5	
13 Firefox	WB	25.4	
14 Greystoke	WB	23.2	
15 Amadeus	Orion	23.0	
16 Tightrope	WB	22.5	
17 City Heat	WB	21.0	
18 Terminator	Orion	16.9	
19 Dune	U	16.5	
20 Friday the 13th: Final Chapter	Par	16.0	
21 Places in the Heart	Tri	16.2	
22 Breakin'	MGM-UA	15.7	
23 All of Me	U	15.2	
24 Cannonball Run II	20th	14.3	
25 The Killing Fields	WB	14.3	
26 Conan the Destroyer	U	14.3	
27 Protocol	WB	14.2	
28 Starman	Col	13.6	
29 A Passage to India	Col	13.5	
30 The Last Starfighter	U	13.1	
31 The Gods Must Be Crazy	20th	13.0	

Title	Studio	$$$	Later$
32 The Muppets Take			
Manhattan	Tri	12.9	
33 Rhinestone	20th	12.2	
34 The Cotton Club	Orion	12.1	
35 Micki and Maude	Col	12.0	
36 Moscow on the Hudson	Col	12.0	
37 The Woman in Red	Orion	12.0	
38 Teachers	MGM	11.7	
39 The Flamingo Kid	20th	11.5	
40 A Nightmare on Elm Street	NL	11.0	

1985 ($3.51)

Title	Studio	$$$	Later$
1 Back to the Future	U	105.5	
2 Rambo: First Blood II	Tri	78.9	
3 Rocky IV	MGM-UA	76.1	
4 The Color Purple	WB	49.8	
5 Out of Africa	U	48.4	
6 Cocoon	20th	40.0	
7 The Jewel of the Nile	20th	36.5	
8 Spies Like Us	WB	30.5	
9 The Goonies	WB	29.9	
10 Witness	Par	28.5	
11 Police Academy 2	WB	27.2	
12 European Vacation	WB	25.6	
13 A View to a Kill	MGM-UA	25.3	
14 Fletch	U	24.9	
15 White Nights	Col	21.1	
16 Pale Rider	WB	20.8	
17 Pee Wee's Big	WB	18.1	
18 Mad Max Beyond	WB	18.1	
19 The Breakfast Club	U	17.7	
20 Commando	20th	17.0	
21 Jagged Edge	Col	16.8	
22 Silverado	Col	16.7	
23 St. Elmo's Fire	Col	16.7	
24 Prizzi's Honor	20th	13.5	
25 Murphy's Romance	Col	13.5	
26 Santa Claus	Tri	13.0	
27 Teen Wolf	Atlantic	12.9	
28 Agnes of God	Col	12.2	

1986 ($3.79)

Title	Studio	$$$	Later$
1 Top Gun	Par	79.4	
2 Crocodile Dundee	Par	70.2	
3 Platoon	Orion	69.9	
4 The Karate Kid 2	Col	58.3	
5 Star Trek IV	Par	56.8	
6 Aliens	20th	43.8	
7 Back to School	Orion	42.0	
8 The Golden Child	Par	39.7	
9 Ruthless People	Touch	31.7	
10 Cobra	Can-WB	28.8	
11 Ferris Bueller's Day Off	Par	28.6	

Title	Studio	$$$	Later$
12 Down & Out in Beverly Hills	Disney	28.3	
13 Legal Eagles	U	27.2	
14 The Color of Money	Disney	24.4	
15 An American Tail	U	22.9	
16 Stand by Me	Col	22.0	
17 Heartbreak Ridge	WB	21.6	
18 Police Academy 3	WB	21.0	
19 Hannah and Her Sisters	Orion	18.2	
20 The Fly	20th	17.5	
21 Short Circuit	Tri	17.0	
22 Peggy Sue Got Married	Tri	16.8	
23 The Money Pit	U	16.7	
24 Pretty in Pink	Par	16.6	
25 Running Scared	MGM-UA	16.4	
26 About Last Last Night	Tri	16.1	
27 Gung Ho	Par	15.5	
28 Nothing in Common	Tri	13.5	
29 Soul Man	New World	13.5	
30 Wild Cats	Wb	13.3	
31 The Morning After	20th	12.0	
32 Heartburn	Par	11.8	

1987 ($4.20)

Title	Studio	$$$	Later$
1 Three Men and a Baby	Touch	81.3	
2 Beverly Hills Cop 2	Par	80.9	
3 Fatal Attraction	Par	70.1	
4 Good Morning, Vietnam	Disney	58.0	
5 The Untouchables	Par	36.9	
6 Moonstruck	MGM-UA	34.8	
7 The Witches of Eastwick	WB	31.8	
8 Predator	20th	31.0	
9 Dragnet	U	30.2	
10 Lethal Weapon	WB	29.5	
11 Dirty Dancing	Vestron	29.0	
12 The Secret of My Success	U	28.4	
13 Stakeout	Touch	28.2	
14 The Living Daylights	MGM-UA	28.0	
15 Throw Momma from the Train	Orion	27.7	
16 Broadcast News	20th	26.5	
17 Raw	Par	24.8	
18 La Bamba	Col	24.3	
19 Robocop	Orion	24.6	
20 Outrageous Fortune	Touch	22.7	
21 Full Metal Jacket	WB	22.7	
22 Planes Trains & Automobiles	Par	22.1	
23 A Nightmare on Elm Street 3	NL	21.4	
24 Spaceballs	MGM	18.8	
25 Mannequin	20th	18.0	
26 Roxanne	WB	17.6	
27 Red Dawn	MGM	17.3	
28 Harry and the Hendersons	Amblin-U	17.0	
29 The Running Man	Tri	16.0	
30 No Way Out	Orion	15.9	

Title	Studio	$$$	Later$
31 Summer School	Par	15.8	
32 Blind Date	Tri	15.0	
33 Like Father, Like Son	Tri	15.0	
34 Nuts	WB	14.9	
35 Adventures in Babysitting	Touch	14.3	
36 Revenge of the Nerds II	20th	14.2	
37 Police Academy IV	WB	14.0	
38 The Lost Boys	WB	14.0	
39 Can't Buy Me Love	Touch	13.7	
40 Innerspace	WB	13.7	
41 The Princess Bride	CR-20th	12.9	
42 Wall Street	20th	12.9	
43 Tin Men	Touch	11.3	

1988 ($4.51)

Title	Studio	$$$	Later$
1 Rain Man	MGM-UA	86.8	
2 Who Framed Roger Rabbitt?	Touch	81.3	
3 Coming to America	Par	65.1	
4 Twins	U	57.7	
5 Crocodile Dundee II	Par	57.3	
6 Big	20th	53.7	
7 Cocktail	Touch	36.5	
8 Die Hard	20th	36.0	
9 The Naked Gun	Par	34.4	
10 Beetlejuice	WB	33.2	
11 Scrooged	Par	31.5	
12 A Fish Called Wanda	MGM	30.0	
13 Working Girl	20th	28.6	
14 Rambo III	Tri	28.5	
15 Willow	MGM-UA	27.8	
16 Oliver & Company	Disney	25.2	
17 Beaches	Touch	24.9	
18 The Land Before Time	U	23.0	
19 A Nightmare on Elm Street 4	NL	22.2	
20 Bull Durham	Orion	21.9	
21 Colors	Orion	21.1	
22 Young Guns	20th	20.8	

1989 ($4.70)

Title	Studio	$$$	Later$
1 Batman	WB	150.1	
2 Indiana Jones & Last Crusade	Par	115.5	
3 Lethal Weapon 2	WB	79.5	
4 Back to the Future II	U	72.3	
5 Honey, I Shrunk the Kids	Disney	72.0	
6 Look Who's Talking	Tri	68.9	
7 Ghostbusters 2	Col	60.5	
8 Driving Miss Daisy	WB	52.5	
9 Parenthood	U	50.0	
10 Dead Poets Society	Touch	48.4	
11 Steel Magnolias	Tri	42.4	
12 When Harry Met Sally	Col	41.8	
13 The War of the Roses	20th	41.4	
14 The Little Mermaid	Disney	40.2	

Title	Studio	$$$	Later$
15 Born on the Fourth of July	U	36.8	
16 Turner & Hooch	Touch	35.2	
17 Christmas Vacation	WB	34.8	
18 Harlem Nights	Par	33.0	
19 Field of Dreams	U	30.5	
20 Uncle Buck	U	30.3	
21 Tango & Cash	WB	30.1	
22 The Abyss	20th	28.8	
23 Sea of Love	U	28.6	
24 Star Trek V	Par	27.0	
25 Pet Sematary	Par	26.4	
26 Black Rain	Par	25.5	
27 Always	U	23.2	
28 Major League	Par	21.5	
29 Bill & Ted's Excellent Adventure	Orion	17.5	
30 The Karate Kid 3	Col	16.0	

1990 ($4.80)

Title	Studio	$$$	Later$
1 Home Alone	20th	140.1	
2 Ghost	Par	98.2	
3 Pretty Woman	Touch	81.9	
4 Dances with Wolves	Orion	81.5	
5 Teenage Mutant Ninja Turtles	NL	67.7	
6 Die Hard 2	20th	67.5	
7 Total Recall	Tri	63.5	
8 Dick Tracy	Touch	60.6	
9 The Hunt for Red October	Par	58.5	
10 Back to the Future III	U	49.1	
11 Kindergarten Cop	U	47.3	
12 Presumed Innocent	WB	43.8	
13 Another 48 Hours	Par	40.1	
14 Bird on a Wire	U	38.4	
15 The Godfather Part III	Par	38.1	
16 Days of Thunder	Par	37.9	
17 Three Men and a Little Lady	Touch	37.7	
18 Arachnophobia	Hollywood	31.4	
19 Hard to Kill	WB	30.2	
20 Flatliners	Col	28.8	
21 Edward Scissorhands	20th	27.5	
22 Misery	Col	26.9	
23 Problem Child	U	25.1	
24 Awakenings	Col	23.3	
25 Robocop 2	Orion	22.5	
26 Look Who's Talking Too	Tri	21.6	
27 Gremlins 2	WB	20.8	
28 GoodFellas	WB	20.5	
29 Marked for Death	20th	20.3	
30 Young Guns II	20th	19.7	
31 Rocky V	MGM-UA	19.3	
32 Joe Versus the Volcano	WB	18.9	
33 Postcards from the Edge	Col	17.3	
34 Darkman	U	16.2	
35 Predator 2	20th	15.7	

Title	Studio	$$$	Later$	Title	Studio	$$$	Later$
36 Mermaids	Orion	15.1		35 The Doors	Tri	16.5	
37 Pacific Heights	20th	14.5		36 Soapdish	Par	15.7	
38 Child's Play 2	U	14.0		37 Jungle Fever	U	15.7	
39 Green Card	Touch	13.8		38 King Ralph	U	15.3	
40 The Rescuers Down Under	Disney	13.6		39 White Fang	Disney	15.2	
41 Air America	Tri	13.5		40 Grand Canyon	20th	15.0	
42 The Hard Way	U	13.2		41 Curly Sue	WB	14.0	
43 Cadillac Man	Orion	12.6		42 Cop and a Half	WB	13.7	
44 House Party	NL	12.1		43 Class Action	20th	13.2	
45 Memphis Belle	WB	11.7		44 Necessary Roughness	Par	12.5	
46 Jacob's Ladders	Tri	11.6		45 LA Story	Tri	12.4	
47 Ernest Goes to Jail	Disney	11.5		46 Other People's Money	WB	12.3	
48 The Exorcist III	20th	11.5		47 Deceived	Disney	12.3	
49 The Adventures of Ford	20th	11.5		48 Double Impact	Col	12.1	
50 Ghost Dad	U	11.4		49 Only the Lonely	20th	11.8	
51 Navy Seals	Orion	11.3		50 Problem Child 2	U	11.7	
52 Internal Affairs	Par	11.0		51 Shining Through	20th	11.5	
				52 Frankie and Johnny	Par	11.0	

1991 ($4.90)

Title	Studio	$$$	Later$
1 Terminator 2	Tri	115.0	
2 Robin Hood Prince of Thieves	20th	86.1	
3 Beauty and the Beast	Disney	69.4	
4 The Silence of the Lambs	Orion	66.0	
5 Hook	Tri	65.0	
6 City Slickers	Col	60.7	
7 The Addams Family	Orion-Par	56.2	
8 Sleeping with the Enemy	20th	46.7	
9 Naked Gun 2½	Par	44.2	
10 Father of the Bride	Disney	43.8	
11 Teenage Mutant Ninja Turtles II	NL	41.9	
12 Backdraft	U	40.2	
13 Cape Fear	U	39.5	
14 Fried Green Tomatoes	U	37.8	
15 Star Trek VI	Par	36.1	
16 The Prince of Tides	Col	36.1	
17 JFK	WB	34.5	
18 Hot Shots!	20th	33.8	
19 My Girl	Col	27.7	
20 The Last Boy Scout	WB	27.6	
21 Boyz n the Hood	Col	26.7	
22 Doc Hollywood	WB	24.5	
23 The Rocketeer	Disney	23.1	
24 New Jack City	WB	22.3	
25 Regarding Henry	Par	20.4	
26 Bugsy	Tri	20.1	
27 Point Break	20th	19.8	
28 What About Bob?	Touch	19.2	
29 Dying Young	20th	19.2	
30 The Fisher King	Tri	18.3	
31 Freddy's Dead: The Final Night	NL	17.7	
32 Dead Again	Par	17.5	
33 The Doctor	Disney	17.5	
34 Ted and Bill's Bogus Journey	Orion	17.2	

1992 ($5.01)

Title	Studio	$$$	Later$
1 Home Alone 2	20th	103.4	
2 Batman Returns	WB	100.1	
3 Aladdin	Disney	82.5	
4 Lethal Weapon 3	WB	80.0	
5 A Few Good Men	Col	71.0	
6 Sister Act	Touch	62.4	
7 Basic Instinct	Tri	61.4	
8 The Bodyguard	WB	56.3	
9 Wayne's World	Par	54.4	
10 A League of Their Own	Col	53.5	
11 Bram Stoker's Dracula	Col	47.2	
12 Unforgiven	WB	44.4	
13 The Hand That Rocks the Cradle	Hwd	39.5	
14 Patriot Games	Par	37.5	
15 Under Siege	WB	37.1	
16 The Last of the Mohicans	20th	35.1	
17 Death Becomes Her	U	34.5	
18 White Men Can't Jump	20th	34.1	
19 Boomerang	Par	34.0	
20 Alien 3	20th	31.8	
21 Far and Away	20th	28.9	
22 Scent of a Woman	U	28.5	
23 Honey, I Blew Up the Kid	Disney	27.4	
24 The Crying Game	Miramax	26.6	
25 Beethoven	U	26.5	
26 Thelma & Louise	MGM-UA	26.5	
27 Unlawful Entry	20th	26.3	
28 My Cousin Vinny	20th	25.5	
29 Sneakers	U	24.3	
30 The Distinguished Gentleman	Disney	22.0	
31 Single White Female	Col	21.5	
32 Medicine Man	Touch	21.0	

Title	Studio	$$$	Later$
33 The Mighty Ducks	Disney	20.5	
34 Malcolm X	WB	19.4	
35 A River Runs Through It	Col	19.2	
36 Passenger 57	WB	18.3	
37 Housesitter	U	16.5	
38 Honeymoon in Vegas	Col	16.1	
39 Universal Soldier	Tri	16.0	
40 Encino Man	Disney	15.5	
41 Mo' Money	Col	15.2	
42 Howards End	Sony	14.5	
43 Hoffa	20th	14.5	
44 Forever Young	WB	14.4	
45 The Lawnmowerman	NL	13.6	
46 Sleepwalkers	Col	13.2	
47 Final Analysis	WB	12.7	
48 A Muppet Christmas Carol	Disney	12.5	
49 Menace II Society	NL	12.4	
50 Toys	20th	12.3	
51 Three Ninjas	Disney	11.9	
52 Stop or My Mom Will Shoot!	U	10.6	

1993 ($5.30)

Title	Studio	$$$	Later$
1 Jurassic Park	U	208.4	
2 Mrs. Doubtfire	20th	109.9	
3 The Fugitive	WB	92.6	
4 The Firm	Par	77.1	
5 Sleepless in Seattle	Tri	65.0	
6 Indecent Proposal	Par	50.9	
7 In the Line of Fire	Col	49.3	
8 Schindler's List	U	47.3	
9 Cliffhanger	Tri	43.3	
10 The Pelican Brief	WB	43.9	
11 Free Willy	WB	36.5	
12 Grumpy Old Men	WB	36.1	
13 Rising Sun	20th	33.3	
14 Groundhog Day	Col	32.5	
15 Philadelphia	Tri	31.7	
16 Cool Runnings	Disney	30.6	
17 Dave	WB	30.1	
18 The Last Action Hero	Col	26.8	
19 Demolition Man	WB	25.5	

Title	Studio	$$$	Later$
20 Beethoven's 2nd	U	25.4	
21 Rookie of the Year	20th	25.0	
22 Tombstone	Hollywood	24.4	
23 Dennis the Menace	WB	24.2	
24 Sister Act 2	Touch	24.0	
25 Addams Family Values	Par	23.4	
26 Wayne's World 2	Par	22.1	
27 Sommersby	WB	21.8	
28 Malice	Col	21.3	
29 The Good Son	20th	21.2	
30 Made in America	WB	20.7	
31 The Three Musketeers	Disney	20.3	
32 Carlito's Way	U	20.1	
33 Teenage Mutant Ninja Turtles 3	NL	19.9	
34 The Beverly Hillbillies	20th	19.4	
35 Hot Shots, Part Deux	20th	19.2	
36 Nightmare Before Christmas	Disney	18.9	
37 Falling Down	WB	18.1	
38 Sliver	Par	17.7	
39 The Piano	Miramax	17.2	
40 What's Love Got to Do with It?	Touch	16.8	
41 Dragon: The Bruce Lee Story	U	16.7	
42 Homeward Bound	Disney	16.0	
43 Hocus Pocus	Disney	15.9	
44 Robin Hood: Men in Tights	20th	15.0	
45 The Sandlot	20th	15.0	
46 Hard Target	U	14.7	
47 The Age of Innocence	Col	14.5	
48 Alive	Disney	14.5	
49 Son-in-Law	Touch	13.9	
50 A Perfect World	WB	13.9	
51 Poetic Justice	Col	13.8	
52 Point of No Return	WB	13.6	
53 The Secret Garden	WB	13.5	
54 My Girl 2	Col	13.5	
55 The Joy Luck Club	U	12.9	
56 My Life	Col	12.1	
57 Striking Distance	Col	11.5	
58 Remains of the Day	Col	11.3	
59 Shadowlands	Savoy	11.2	
60 In the Name of the Father	Gram-U	10.5	

Appendix B

STAR RATINGS BY YEAR (THE ALL-TIME TOP MOVIES WORTH SEEING)

Pre-1920

★★★½

Intolerance (1916)
Broken Blossoms (1919)

★★★

The Avenging Conscience
(1914)
The Birth of a Nation (1915)
Blind Husbands (1919)
Passion/Madame DuBarry
(1919)

1920s

1920
★★★

The Golem
The Mark of Zorro
Way Down East

1921
★★★

Foolish Wives
Nanook of the North
The Shiek

1922
★★★

Adam's Rib

Dr. Mabuse the Gambler
Robin Hood

1923
★★★½

Our Hospitality
Safety Last

★★★

A Woman of Paris

1924
★★★½

Greed
The Last Laugh
The Navigator
The Thief of Bagdad

★★★

America

1925
★★★½

Ben Hur, a Tale of Christ
The Freshman
The Gold Rush

★★★

The Merry Widow
Seven Chances
The Wizard of Oz

1926
★★★★

Metropolis

★★★½

Faust

★★★

Beau Geste
The Black Pirate
Flesh and the Devil
The Scarlet Letter
The Sea Beast

1927
★★★½

The General
Napoleon
Wings

★★★

The Cat and the Canary
An Italian Straw Hat
It
King of Kings
Love
Seventh Heaven

1928
★★★½

Sadie Thompson
The Cameraman

★★★

The Fall of the House of
Usher
The Last Command
The Living Corpse
The Singing Fool
Steamboat Bill
Junior
Street Angel
The Wedding March

1929
★★★

Arsenal
Blackmail
Broadway Melody
The Cocoanuts
Disraeli
Dynamite
The Four Feathers
Gold Diggers of
Broadway
Hallelujah!
Hollywood Revue
In Old Arizona
The Iron Mask
The Letter
The Love Parade
Madame X

1930s

1930
★★★★
All Quiet on the Western Front
Animal Crackers
Anna Christie
The Blue Angel
Doctor Jekyll and Mr. Hyde
Hell's Angels

★★★½
Earth
Laughter

★★★
The Bat Whispers
The Big House
The Dawn Patrol
The Divorcee
King of Jazz
Lightnin'
Loose Ankles
Monte Carlo
Morroco
Murder
Romance
The Royal Family of Broadway

1931
★★★★
Frankenstein
M

★★★½
The Champ
Dracula
Little Caesar
Marius
Le Million
Monkey Business
The Public Enemy

★★★
Bad Girl
The Blood of a Poet
Dishonored
Five Star Final
The Front Page
The Guardsman
A House Divided
The Iron Man
The Last Flight
The Maltese Falcon
Marius
Mata Hari
The Millionaire
The Sin of Madeleine Claudet
Skippy

Street Scene
Susan Lenox, Her Fall and
    Rise
Svengali
Tabu

1932
★★★★
Horse Feathers
I Am a Fugitive from a Chain
    Gang
Min and Bill
The Music Box

★★★½
Boudu Saved from Drowning
Grand Hotel
Love Me Tonight
The Most Dangerous Game
Red Dust
Rome Express
Triumph of the Will
20,000 Years at Sing-Sing

★★★
The Animal Kingdom
Arsène Lupin
Aren't We All?
Back Street
The Big Broadcast
A Bill of Divorcement
Bird of Paradise
Blessed Event
Blonde Venus
Cavalcade
Central Park
Emma
A Farewell to Arms
Five Fingers
Freaks
High Pressure
If I Had a Million
The Kid from Spain
Ladies They Talk About
Love Affair
Madame Butterfly
The Mask of Fu Manchu
Me and My Gal
Million Dollar Legs
The Miracle Woman
The Mummy
The Mystery of Edwin Drood
Night after Night
No Man of Her Own
Rain
Rasputin and the Empress
Shanghai Express

Smilin' Through
So Big
Tarzan the Ape Man
The Wet Parade
What Price Hollywood?
White Zombie

1933
★★★★
Duck Soup
King Kong
Lady for a Day
Little Women

★★★½
Bombshell
Dinner at Eight
42nd Street
Friday the Thirteenth
Golddiggers of 1933
I'm No Angel
The Invisible Man
Lady Killer
Morning Glory
Mystery of the Wax Museum
The Private Life of Henry VIII
Queen Christina
Tugboat Annie

★★★
Ann Vickers
Baby Face
A Bedtime Story
Berkeley Square
Dancing Lady
Ex-Lady
Footlight Parade
Flying Down to Rio
Gabriel over the White
    House
The Ghoul
The Good Companions
Hallelujah, I'm a Bum!
Hold Your Man
I Cover the Waterfront
It's a Gift
The Kennel Murder Case
Man's Castle
The Masquerader
Roman Scandals
State Fair
Voltaire
The Wandering Jew

1934
★★★★
It Happened One Night

★★★½
The Count of Monte Cristo
Manhattan Melodrama
Of Human Bondage
The Thin Man

★★★
The Affairs of Cellini
Babes in Toyland
Baby, Take a Bow
The Barretts of Wimpole
    Street
The Black Cat
Bolero
Bright Eyes
Catherine the Great
Cleopatra
Death Takes a Holiday
Gambling Lady
The Gay Divorcee
George White's Scandals
Imitation of Life
Lady By Choice
Little Miss Marker
Lives of a Bengal Lancer
Madame DuBarry
Man of Aran
The Man Who Knew Too Much
The Merry Widow
The Merry Wives of Reno
Mrs. Wiggs of the Cabbage
    Patch
Murder at the Vanities
The Richest Girl in the World
She Loves Me Not
The Show-Off
Spitfire
The Story of Vernon and Irene
    Castle
Tarzan and His Mate
Treasure Island
Twentieth Century
What Every Woman Knows

1935
★★★★
Alice Adams
Anna Karenina
David Copperfield
Mutiny on the Bounty
A Night at the Opera

★★★½
The Bride of Frankenstein
The Ghost Goes West
The Informer
The Ruggles of Red Gap

Sylvia Scarlett
A Tale of Two Cities

★★★
Accent on Youth
After Office Hours
Ah, Wilderness
Annie Oakley
Barbary Coast
Becky Sharp
Black Fury
Bonnie Scotland
Break of Hearts
Brewster's Millions
Captain Blood
China Seas
Dangerous
The Dark Angel
The Devil Is a Woman
Dr. Socrates
George White's Scandals
The Glass Key
G Men
Go Into Your Dance
Goin' to Town
Gold Diggers of 1935
The Good Fairy
Hands Across the Table
I Found Stella Parrish
In Old Kentucky
Kid Millions
The Last Days of Pompeii
The Last Outpost
Mad Love
Magnificent Obsession
The Man Who Broke the Bank
   at Monte Carlo
Mark of the Vampire
Mayerling
Naughty Marietta
The Raven
Roberta
The Ruggles of Red Gap
She
The Scoundrel
Scrooge
Star of Midnight
Sylvia Scarlett
The Three Musketeers
The Wedding Night
Werewolf of London

1936
★★★★
The Awful Truth
Libeled Lady

My Man Godfrey
Nothing Sacred
San Francisco
Things to Come

★★★¹/₂
Anthony Adverse
Camille
The Charge of the Light
   Brigade
Dodsworth
Fury
The Great Ziegfeld
The Green Pastures
Mr. Deeds Goes to Town
Our Relations
Rembrandt
Swing Time

★★★
Born to Dance
Banjo on My Knee
The Big Broadcast of 1936
Broadway Melody of 1936
Bullets or Ballets
Cain and Mabel
Come and Get It
The Devil Doll
Desire
Dracula's Daughter
The Ex-Mrs. Bradford
Follow the Fleet
The Garden of Allah
The General Died at Dawn
Go West, Young Man
The Gorgeous Hussy
The Last of the Mohicans
Little Lord Fauntleroy
Love on the Run
Lloyds of London
Love from a Stranger
The Man Who Could Work
   Miracles
Mary of Scotland
The Milky Way
No Escape
Remember Last Night?
Rhythm on the Range
Romeo and Juliet
The Secret Agent
Sing Baby Sing
Small Town Girl
Susie
Sweeney Todd, the Demon
   Barber of Fleet Street
Tarzan Escapes
Theodora Goes Wild

Three Smart Girls
The Trail of the Lonesome Pine
Trouble for Two
Wife versus Secretary
A Woman Rebels

1937
★★★★
Bringing Up Baby
A Day at the Races
Lost Horizon
Snow White and the Seven
   Dwarfs
Top Hat
The Shop Around the Corner

★★★¹/₂
Dead End
Easy Living
The Good Earth
The Life of Emile Zola
The Mad Miss Manton
Night Must Fall
The Prisoner of Zenda
They Won't Forget Me
Topper
Way Out West

★★★
Artists and Models
Black Legion
Breakfast for Two
The Bride Wore Red
Café Metropole
A Damsel in Distress
Double Wedding
Ebb Tide
Elephant Boy
A Family Affair
Fire over England
The Firefly
Gold Diggers of 1937
The Great Garrick
Heidi
In Old Chicago
It's Love I'm After
Kid Galahad
Knight without Armour
King Solomon's Mines
Maytime
Marked Woman
The Mill on the Floss
Quality Street
The Road Back
The Return of the Scarlet
   Pimpernel
Souls at Sea

Stand In
Storm in a Teacup
That Certain Woman
The Toast of New York
Tovarich
True Confession
Waikiki Wedding
Wee Willie Winky
A Yank at Oxford

1938
★★★★
Alexander Nevsky
The Adventures of Robin Hood
The Adventures of Tom Sawyer
Captains Courageous
Grand Illusion
Holiday
The Lady Vanishes
Stage Door

★★★¹/₂
Room Service
A Christmas Carol
Angels with Dirty Faces
Boys' Town
Four Daughters
The Great Waltz
Pygmalion
You Can't Take It with You
The Young in Heart

★★★
Alexander's Ragtime Band
Algiers
The Arkansas Traveler
The Buccaneer
Carefree
Fast Company
Fools for Scandal
The Girl of the Golden West
Gold Diggers in Paris
The Goldwyn Follies
Hollywood Hotel
If I Were King
Mad about Music
Made for Each Other
Marie Antoinette
La Marseillaise
Merrily We Live
Mother Carey's Chickens
Kentucky
Kentucky Moonshine
Kidnapped
St. Martin's Lane
Sidewalks of London
Sing You Sinners

Suez
Sweethearts
Test Pilot
That Certain Age
They Drive by Night
Three Blind Mice
White Banners

1939
★★★★

Destry Rides Again
The Four Feathers
Gone With the Wind
Goodbye Mr. Chips
Mr. Smith Goes to Washington
Ninotchka
Stagecoach
The Thirty-Nine Steps
The Wizard of Oz
The Women
Young Mr. Lincoln

★★★½

Abe Lincoln in Illinois
The Adventures of Sherlock
   Holmes
The Amazing Dr. Clitterhouse
The Cat and the Canary
Dark Victory
Gunga Din
Intermezzo
Love Affair
Only Angels Have Wings
The Roaring Twenties
Tower of London
What About Bob?
Wuthering Heights

★★★

Another Thin Man
Arrowsmith
At the Circus
Babes in Arms
Bachelor Mother
Balalaika
Beau Geste
The Divorce of Lady X
Dodge City
Drums Along the Mohawk
First Love
Five Came Back
Golden Boy
Gulliver's Travels
The Hound of the Baskervilles
Idiot's Delight
It's a Wonderful World
The Light That Failed

The Little Princess
The Mikado
My Little Chickadee
Raffles
The Rains Came
The Rose of Washington
   Square
Son of Frankenstein
The Spy in Black
The Story of Alexander
   Graham Bell
They Made Me a Criminal
The Three Musketeers
Three Smart Girls Grow Up
Trade Winds
Union Pacific
We Are Not Alone

1940s
1940
★★★★

Fantasia
Foreign Correspondent
The Grapes of Wrath
Modern Times
The Philadelphia Story

★★★½

The Bank Dick
Christmas in July
The Doctor Takes a Wife
The Ghost Breakers
The Great Dictator
The Great McGinty
Letter from an Unknown
   Woman
The Mark of Zorro
My Favorite Wife
Our Town
Quiet Wedding
Rebecca
Tai Pan
They Knew What They Wanted
The Westerner

★★★

All This and Heaven Too
The Biscuit Eater
Bitter Sweet
The Blue Bird
Dr. Cyclops
Dr. Ehrlich's Magic Bullet
The Doughgirls
Down Argentine Way
Edison the Man
Escape

Four Sons
Go West
Hired Wife
If I Had My Way
I Love You Again
The Invisible Man Returns
It All Came True
It's a Date
Kitty Foyle
Knute Rockne, All-American
The Lady in Question
The Mummy's Hand
Night Train to Munich
Northwest Mounted Police
Northwest Passage
No Time for Comedy
Santa Fe Trail
The Secret Life of Walter Mitty
Seventeen
Strange Cargo
Strike Up the Band
Susan and God
They Drive by Night
Turnabout
Waterloo Bridge
Western Union
Wildman
The Wolfman
Virginia City

1941
★★★★

All That Money Can Buy
His Girl Friday
King's Row
The Lady Eve
The Letter
The Little Foxes
The Maltese Falcon
The Man Who Came to Dinner
Suspicion

★★★½

Ball of Fire
The Great Lie
Here Comes Mr. Jordan
Kipps
Love Crazy
Major Barbara
That Uncertain Feeling
Tobacco Road

★★★

Bedtime Story
The Big Store
Billy the Kid
Blossoms in the Dust

The Bride Came C.O.D.
Caught in the Draft
Charley's Aunt
Cheers for Miss Bishop
The Devil and Miss Jones
Dillinger
Dr. Jekyll and Mr. Hyde
For Me and My Gal
Glamour Boys
High Sierra
Hold Back the Dawn
Hold That Ghost
Honky Tonk
It Started with Eve
I Wake Up Screaming
Kiss the Boys Goodbye
Ladies in Retirement
Love Crazy
Love on the Dole
Louisiana Purchase
The Maltese Falcon
The Man Who Came to
   Dinner
Manhunt
Meet John Doe
Men of Boys' Town
Mr. and Mrs. Smith
Moon over Miami
Rebecca's Daughters
Road to Zanzibar
Shepherd of the Hills
The Strawberry Blonde
Swamp Water
Take Me Out to the Ball
   Game
That Hamilton Woman
That Night in Rio
They Died with Their Boots On
This Thing Called Love
Tom, Dick and Harry
Topper Returns
Two-Faced Woman
Whistling in the Dark
A Woman's Face
You'll Never Get Rich
You're in the Army Now
Ziegfeld Girl

1942
★★★★

Bambi
Saboteur
Sullivan's Travels
To Be or Not to Be
Woman of the Year
Yankee Doodle Dandy

★★★½

Cat People
Hellzapoppin
I Married a Witch
Mrs. Miniver
My Favorite Blonde
Now Voyager
Ossessione
The Pride of the Yankees
Random Harvest
The Talk of the Town
The Thief of Bagdad

★★★

All Through the Night
Always in My Heart
The Black Swan
Cairo
Castle in the Desert
Desperate Journey
Eyes of the Night
The Gay Sisters
George Washington Slept
    Here
The Glass Key
The Hard Way
Holiday Inn
Keeper of the Flame
Life Begins at 8:30
The Major and the Minor
The Male Animal
My Gal Sal
My Sister Eileen
The Night Has Eyes
Reap the Wild Wind
Road to Morroco
Sherlock Holmes and the
    Secret Weapon
Sherlock Holmes and the Voice
    of Terror
Star Spangled Rhythm
Take a Letter, Darling
Tales of Manhattan
Tarzan's New York
    Adventure
This Above All
This Gun for Hire
Thunder Rock
Tortilla Flat
Went the Day Well

1943

★★★★

Casablanca
The More the Merrier
A Night to Remember

Shadow of a Doubt
Sorry, Wrong Number

★★★½

Cabin in the Sky
Day of Wrath
Five Graves to Cairo
For Whom the Bell Tolls
Heaven Can Wait
Lassie Come Home
The Moon and Sixpence
On Approval
Watch on the Rhine

★★★

Above Suspicion
The Adventures of Baron
    Munchausen
Claudia
Edward My Son
The Gang's All Here
Girl Crazy
Guadalcanal Diary
A Guy Named Joe
Happy Land
Hello Frisco, Hello
Hit Parade of 1943
Holy Matrimony
I Dood It
International House
I Walked with a Zombie
The Kid from Left Field
Lady of Burlesque
The Life and Death of Colonel
    Blimp
Lost Angel
Lumière D'Eté
Madame Curie
The Man in Grey
Millions Like Us
The Moon is Down
Mr. Lucky
My Friend Flika
My Learned Friend
Never Give a Sucker an Even
    Break
North Star
The Return of the Vampire
Sahara
The Seventh Victim
Sherlock Holmes Faces
    Death
So Proudly We Hail
Son of Dracula
The Song of Bernadette
Stagedoor Canteen
Sweet Rosie O'Grady

Tilly and Gus
This Is the Army
This Land Is Mine
Thousands Cheer
Too Many Husbands
Young Tom Edison

1944

★★★★

Arsenic and Old Lace
Lifeboat
The Miracle of Morgan's
    Creek

★★★½

The Bridge of San Luis
    Rey
Going My Way
Hail the Conquering Hero
None But the Lonely Heart
The Uninvited
The Woman in the Window

★★★

Bathing Beauty
The Canterville Ghost
Buffalo Bill
Farewell My Lovely
The Fighting Seabees
Frenchman's Creek
Gaslight
The Hitler Gang
Hollywood Canteen
I'll Be Seeing You
It Happened Tomorrow
Knickerbocker Holiday
Lady in the Dark
The Lodger
Mademoiselle Fifi
The Mask of Dimitrios
Mr. Drake's Duck
Mrs. Parkington
Music for Millions
The Scarlet Claw
The Seventh Cross
Sherlock Holmes and the
    Spider Woman
Show Business
A Song to Remember
The Story of Dr. Wassell
Sylvia and the Ghost
Thirty Seconds over Tokyo
Two Girls and a Sailor
Up in Arms
Wilson
The White Cliffs of Dover
You're Telling Me

1945

★★★★

Double Indemnity
It's a Wonderful Life
The Lost Weekend
The Magnificent Ambersons
Meet Me in St. Louis
Mildred Pierce
National Velvet

★★★½

And Then There Were None
The Body Snatcher
The Clock
Dead of Night
A Diary for Timothy
Murder, He Says
The Razor's Edge
The Three Caballeros
To Have and Have Not
A Tree Grows in Brooklyn
True Glory

★★★

Anchors Aweigh!
The Bells of St. Mary's
Blood on the Sun
The Bullfighters
Diamond Horseshoe
The Dolly Sisters
Easy to Wed
The Enchanted Cottage
Fallen Angel
Flame of the Barbary Coast
Guest Wife
The Horn Blows at Midnight
Isle of the Dead
It's in the Bag
The Keys of the Kingdom
A Kid for Two Farthings
Kiss and Tell
Kitty
Lady on a Train
Leave Her to Heaven
Love Letters
Ministry of Fear
My Name Is Julia Ross
The Naughty Nineties
Rhapsody in Blue
Road to Utopia
Scarlet Street
The Seventh Veil
That Forsyte Woman
The Two Mrs. Carrolls
The Wicked Lady
Without Love
Undercurrent

Weekend at the Waldorf
Wonder Man
Ziegfeld Follies
State Fair

1946
★★★★
The Best Years of Our Lives
The Big Sleep
Blithe Spirit
Brief Encounter
Laura
Notorious
The Yearling

★★★½
Gilda
The Harvey Girls
Ivan the Terrible
The Killers
My Darling Clementine
Odd Man Out
Paisan

★★★
Abie's Irish Rose
Angel on My Shoulder
Anna and the King of Siam
Beauty and the Beast
Bedlam
The Blue Dahlia
Caesar and Cleopatra
The Captive Heart
Centennial Summer
Cluny Brown
The Dark Corner
Deception
The Diary of a Chambermaid
Duel in the Sun
From This Day Forward
The Green Years
Holiday in Mexico
Hollywood Boulevard
The Kid from Brooklyn
The Late George Apley
Make Mine Music
Margie
Monsieur Beaucaire
A Night in Casablanca
Nocturne
Sister Kenny
The Strange Love of Martha
  Ivers
The Stranger
Terror by Night
Till the Clouds Roll By

1947
★★★★
Black Narcissus
The Egg and I
Great Expectations
Miracle on 34th Street

★★★½
The Bachelor and the
  Bobbysoxer
Boomerang
Born to Kill
Crossfire
The Dark Mirror
Dark Passage
Detour
A Double Life
The Farmer's Daughter
Gentleman's Agreement
The Lady from Shanghai
Monsieur Verdoux
Mourning Becomes
  Electra
Out of the Past

★★★
The Bishop's Wife
Body and Soul
Brighton Rock
Cass Timerlaine
Dear Ruth
Down to Earth
Forever Amber
The Ghost and Mrs. Muir
Green Dolphin Street
It Always Rains on Sunday
It Happened in Brooklyn
Kiss of Death
Life with Father
The Lost Moment
Mine Own Executioner
Miranda
Monsieur Vincent
Mother Wore Tights
My Favorite Brunette
Nicholas Nickleby
Road to Rio
Sea of Grass
The Senator Was Indiscreet
Song of Love
They Won't Believe Me

1948
★★★★
Hamlet
Key Largo

Naked City
The Red Shoes

★★★½
The Big Clock
Force of Evil
I Remember Mama
Mr. Blandings Builds His
  Dream House
Oliver Twist
Portrait of Jennie
Red River
The Search
The Treasure of the Sierra
  Madre
Unfaithfully Yours

★★★
Abbott and Costello Meet
  Frankenstein
The Adventures of Don Juan
Against the Wind
Always Together
Arch of Triumph
The Blue Lagoon
Bonny Prince Charlie
The Boy with Green Hair
Calling Northside
The Dark Past
Easter Parade
The Emperor Waltz
Every Girl Should Be Married
A Foreign Affair
Fort Apache
The Fuller Brush Man
Gigi
Give My Regards to Broadway
The Life of Riley
London Belongs to Me
Louisiana Story
The Luck of the Irish
The Miracle
Moonrise
My Girl Tisa
Quartet
Red River
Romance on the High Seas
Rope
The Scar
Scott of the Antarctic
The Secret Beyond the Door
The Snakepit
So Dear to My Heart
The Southern Yankee
They Live by Night
Three Godfathers

The Three Musketeers
The Time of Your Life
Wake of the Red Witch
When My Baby Smiles at
  Me
Whisky Galore
The Winslow Boy

1949
★★★★
All the King's Men
The Bicycle Thief
Fallen Idol
Intruder in the Dust
Kind Hearts and Coronets

★★★½
All My Sons
The Fountainhead
The Heiress
A Letter to Three Wives
On the Town
The Third Man
The Window
White Heat

★★★
Abbott and Costello Meet the
  Killer, Boris Karloff
Act of Violence
Battleground
Bitter Rice
The Blue Lamp
Caught
Champion
Come to the Stable
The File on Thelma Jordon
Flamingo Road
The Great Lover
Hasty Heart
Hollywood Cavalcade
The Inspector General
It's a Great Feeling
Knock on Any Door
Little Women
Ma and Pa Kettle
Malaya
Mr. Belvedere Goes to
  College
My Foolish Heart
My Friend Irma
Neptune's Daughter
The Sands of Iwo Jima
The Set-up
She Wore a Yellow Ribbon
Sorrowful Jones

Strange Bargain
Tokyo Joe

1950s
1950
★★★★
Adam's Rib
All About Eve
The Asphalt Jungle
Born Yesterday
Harvey
Sunset Boulevard

★★★¹/₂
DOA
The Enforcer
Father of the Bride
The Glass Menagerie
Gun Crazy
In a Lonely Place
King Solomon's Mines
The Men
Miss Julie

★★★
Annie Get Your Gun
The Black Rose
Caged
Champagne for Caesar
Cheaper by the Dozen
The Diary of a Country
  Priest
The Elusive Pimpernel
Fancy Pants
The Flame and the Arrow
Francis, God's Jester
The Fuller Brush Girl
The Gunfighter
Harriet Craig
Kim
Mr. 880
The Mudlark
Mystery Street
Never a Dull Moment
Night and the City
Rawhide
Riding High
La Ronde
So Long at the Fair
Stage Fright
Storm Warning
Tea for Two
Three Came Home
Three Little Words
Treasure Island

Twelve O'Clock High
Union Station

1951
★★★★
The African Queen
Alice in Wonderland
An American in Paris
Death of a Salesman
Strangers on a Train
A Streetcar Named Desire

★★★¹/₂
The Day the Earth Stood Still
Fourteen Hours
Man in White
People Will Talk
Rashomon
The River
The Thing

★★★
Behave Yourself
Bellisma
Bright Victory
The Browning Version
Calloway Went Thataway
The Desert Fox
Destination Tokyo
Detective Story
Early Summer
Go for Broke
The Great Caruso
The Magic Box
The Magic Face
The Mating Season
My Favorite Spy
My Forbidden Past
No Highway in the Sky
Quo Vadis
The Red Badge of Courage
The Red Inn
The River
Royal Wedding
Showboat
The Tales of Hoffman
A Tall Target
Teresa
When Worlds Collide
You Can Never Tell

1952
★★★★
High Noon
The Lavender Hill Mob

The Member of the
  Wedding
Moulin Rouge
The Quiet Man
Singing in the Rain

★★★¹/₂
The Adventures of Robinson
  Crusoe
The Bad and the Beautiful
Breaking the Sound Barrier
Casque D'Or
Come Back Little Sheba
The Greatest Show on Earth
Ikiru
The Importance of Being
  Earnest
Limelight
The Narrow Margin
Pat and Mike

★★★
Aaron Slick from Punkin
  Crick
The Atomic City
Bloodhounds of Broadway
Carrie
Children of Hiroshima
Don't Bother to Knock
Hans Christian Andersen
The Happy Time
Has Anybody Seen My Gal?
I Believe in You
Island of Lost Souls
It Grows on Trees
Ivanhoe
The Marrying Kind
Monkey Business
Niagara
Nous Sommes Tous Les
  Assassins
Ruby Gentry
Scaramouche
The Sniper
The Snows of Kilimanjaro
Son of Paleface
The Titfield Thunderbolt
Umberto D

1953
★★★★
Ace in the Hole
Lili
Monsieur Hulot's Holiday
Roman Holiday
The Wages of Fear

★★★¹/₂
The Band Wagon
Call Me Madam
From Here to Eternity
Gentlemen Prefer Blondes
Hobson's Choice
Kiss Me Kate
Mogambo
The Moon is Blue
Tokyo
The War of the Worlds

★★★
The Actress
Calamity Jane
Dangerous Crossing
Dangerous When Wet
Escape from Fort Bravo
The Five Thousand Fingers of
  Doctor T
Gate of Hell
The Heart of the Matter
House of Wax
I Confess
I Could Go on Singing
Inferno
Innocents in Paris
The Lion Is in the Streets
The Living Desert
The Love Lottery
Miss Sadie Thompson
My Cousin Rachel
The Naked Spur
The Robe
Sawdust and Tinsel
Titanic
Torch Song
Ugetsu Monogatari
Vera Cruz

1954
★★★★
Dial M for Murder
Genevieve
On the Waterfront
Rear Window
The Seven Samurai

★★★¹/₂
Brigadoon
The Caine Mutiny
Carmen Jones
The Country Girl
It Should Happen to You
Magnificent Obsession

Sabrina
20,000 Leagues Under the
Sea

★★★
About Mrs. Leslie
The Barefoot Contessa
Beat the Devil
Beau Brummell
Broken Lance
The Dam Busters
Doctor in the House
Elephant Walk
Executive Suite
The Good Die Young
Green Fire
Hell and High Water
The High and the Mighty
Indiscretion of an American
Wife
An Inspector Calls
Invitation to the Dance
Knave of Hearts
Knights of the Round Table
Knock on Wood
A Lesson in Love
Living It Up
The Long Long Trailer
Miracle in the Rain
Red Garters
Romeo and Juliet
Seven Brides for Seven
Brothers
The Silver Chalice
Them!
There's No Business Like Show
Business
Three Coins in the Fountain
To Paris with Love
We're No Angels
White Christmas
The Wild One
A Woman's World
Young at Heart

1955
★★★★
Bad Day at Black Rock
Diabolique
East of Eden
Marty
Night of the Hunter
Rebel Without a Cause
Richard III
Summertime
Wild Strawberries

★★★½
The Big Knife
The Blackboard Jungle
Bob le Flambeur
The Court Jester
Guys and Dolls
The Ladykillers
Oklahoma
The Rose Tattoo
To Catch a Thief

★★★
Androcles and the Lion
Animal Farm
Artists and Models
The Belles of St. Trinian's
The Bridges at Toko-Ri
Daddy Longlegs
Davy Crockett
Desperate Hours
Godzilla
I Am a Camera
Illegal
Interrupted Melody
It's Always Fair Weather
Killer's Kiss
Kismet
The Lieutenant Wore Skirts
Lola Montes
Love Is a Many Splendored
Thing
Love Me or Leave Me
The Man from Laramie
The Man Who Never Was
Marty
My Sister Eileen
1984
Not as a Stranger
The Quatermass Experiment
Queen Bee
Rififi
Simon and Laura
The Tender Trap
This Island Earth
Trial
The Trouble with Harry
The Virgin Queen

1956
★★★★
Invasion of the Body Snatchers
Lady and the Tramp
The Red Balloon

★★★½
Anastasia
Around the World in Days

Baby Doll
The Burmese Harp
Bus Stop
Forbidden Planet
Friendly Persuasion
Hollywood or Bust
The Killing
The King and I
Lust for Life
The Man Who Knew Too
Much
Patterns
Requiem for a Heavyweight
The Ten Commandments

★★★
The Adventures of Arsène
Lupin
An Affair to Remember
The Baby and the Battleship
Beyond a Reasonable Doubt
Big Deal on Madonna Street
The Bold and the Brave
The Boss
Bundle of Joy
The Catered Affair
The Glenn Miller Story
Gervaise
Goodbye My Lady
The Harder They Fall
High Society
The Iron Petticoat
A Kiss Before Dying
The Last Hunt
The Man in the Gray Flannel
Suit
Moby Dick
The Mountain
Not of This Earth
The Rainmaker
Rock around the Clock
Somebody Up There Likes
Me
The Swan
Tea and Sympathy
The Teahouse of the August
Moon
That Certain Feeling
These Three
This Property Is Condemned
To Each His Own
Town
Trapeze
Twenty-Three Paces to Baker
Street
Written on the Wind

1957
★★★★
The Bachelor Party
The Bridge on the River
Kwai
Funny Face
The Golden Age of Comedy
Twelve Angry Men

★★★½
The Desk Set
Heaven Knows, Mr. Allison
Nights of Cabria
Old Yeller
The Pajama Game
Pal Joey
Paths of Glory
The Sweet Smell of Suc-
cess
The Three Faces of Eve

★★★
And God Created Woman
Boy on a Dolphin
Carousel
Designing Woman
Edge of the City
Enemy from Space
A Farewell to Arms
The Garment Jungle
Gunfight at the O.K. Corral
A Hatful of Rain
The Incredible Shrinking
Man
I Was a Teenage Franken-
stein
I Was a Teenage Werewolf
Island in the Sun
It Came from Outer Space
Love in the Afternoon
Man of a Thousand Faces
The Naked Truth
The Quiet American
Raintree County
The Red House
Silk Stockings
Stage Struck
The Sun also Rises
Tammy and the Bachelor
Throne of Blood
Time Without Pity
Wild Is the Wind
Will Success Spoil Rock
Hunter?
The Wings of Eagles
The Witches of Salem
The Wrong Man

1958

★★★★

Auntie Mame
Cat on a Hot Tin Roof
A Face in the Crowd
God's Little Acre
I Want to Live
The Seventh Seal
Vertigo

★★★ 1/2

The Big Country
The Blob
Gigi
The Goddess
The Horse's Mouth
The Last Hurrah
The Mouse that Roared
A Night to Remember
The Old Man and the Sea

★★★

Ashes and Diamonds
Bell, Book and Candle
The Black Orchid
Black Orpheus
Bonjour Tristesse
The Bride Is Much too
   Beautiful
Brink of Life
The Buccaneer
Cat and Mouse
A Certain Smile
Chase a Crooked Shadow
Damn Yankees
The Defiant Ones
The Doctor's Dilemma
Dracula
The Fly
Hell, Heaven and Hoboken
I Accuse
I Am the Law
I Married a Monster from
   Outer Space
Indiscreet
The Inn of the Sixth
   Happiness
Law and Disorder
The Light in the Forest
The Long Hot Summer
The Music Room
A Night to Remember
No Time for Sergeants
Return of Dracula
Rockabye Baby
Rally Round the Flag Boys
St. Louis Blues

Scapegoat
Separate Tables
The Seventh Voyage of
   Sinbad
The Sheepman
Some Came Running
South Pacific
A Tale of Two Cities
Teacher's Pet
Touch of Evil
Tom Thumb
The Vikings
The Young Lions

1959

★★★★

Anatomy of a Murder
Breathless
The Blows
North by Northwest
The Nutty Professor
Room at the Top
Some Like It Hot
Suddenly Last Summer

★★★ 1/2

Ben Hur
Compulsion
The Diary of Anne Frank
The Fugitive Kind
Imitation of Life
The Last Angry Man
Look Back in Anger
Middle of the Night
The Nun's Story
Operation Petticoat
Rio Bravo
The World of Apu

★★★

Al Capone
Ask Any Girl
Ballad of a Soldier
The Beat Generation
Beloved Infidel
Blue Denim
The Brothers Karamazov
Career
Darby O'Gill and the Little
   People
Destiny of a Man
A Dog of Flanders
The Gazebo
Gidget
Green Mansions
Happy Anniversary

Hiroshima, Mon Amour
A Hole in the Head
Home from the Hill
It Happened to Jane
Kidnapped
Les Liaisons Dangereuses
Lil' Abner
Lunch on the Grass
The Mummy
The Red Pony
Shadows
The Testament of Orpheus
Tiger Bay
The Young Philadelphians

1960s

1960

★★★★

The Apartment

★★★ 1/2

L'Avventura
The Bad Sleep Well
Becket
Elmer Gantry
The Entertainer
A Fine Madness
Inherit the Wind
The Magnificent Seven
Mouchette
Peeping Tom
Pollyanna
The Swiss Family Robinson
The Virgin Spring

★★★

The Alamo
All the Fine Young Cannibals
The Battle of the Sexes
The Bellboy
Bells Are Ringing
Black Sunday
Brides of Dracula
Butterfield Eight
Call Me Genius
Can Can
Exodus
The Facts of Life
From the Terrace
The Grass Is Greener
Heller in Pink Tights
House of Usher
The League of Gentlemen
Let's Make Love
Little Shop of Horrors
Lola

Make Mine Mink
Midnight Lace
Murder Inc.
Never on Sunday
The Rat Race
Strangers When We Meet
The Subterraneans
The Sundowners
Sunrise at Campobello
Three Comrades
The Time Machine
The Trials of Oscar Wilde
Tunes of Glory
Two-Way Stretch
Underworld U.S.A.
Village of the Damned
Visit to a Small Planet
The Wackiest Ship in the Army
The World of Suzy Wong
Zazie dans le Métro

1961

★★★★

Breakfast at Tiffany's
Splendor in the Grass
West Side Story

★★★ 1/2

The Absent-Minded Professor
The Children's Hour
La Dolce Vita
In Search of the Castaways
Lover Come Back
One Eyed Jacks
101 Dalmations
One, Two, Three
The Parent Trap
The Roman Spring of Mrs.
   Stone
A Taste of Honey
The Victim
Two Women
Yojimbo

★★★

Accattone
Adalen
All in a Night's Work
El Cid
The Day the Earth Caught Fire
Divorce Italian Style
Fanny
Flower Drum Song
Forty Pounds of Trouble
The Four Horsemen of the
   Apocalypse

General Della Rovere
Goodbye Again
The Great Impostor
The Guns of Navarone
The Innocents
The Island
King of Kings
The Mark
Mein Kampf
The Misfits
Murder She Said
A Raisin in the Sun
The Secret Partner
Summer and Smoke
Tender Is the Night
Through a Glass Darkly
Town without Pity
Trial and Error
Viridiana
Whistle Down the Wind
A Woman Is a Woman

1962
★★★★
David and Lisa
Lawrence of Arabia
Long Day's Journey into Night
The Manchurian Candidate
To Kill a Mockingbird
Whatever Happened to Baby
  Jane?

★★★¹/₂
The Dark at the Top of the
  Stairs
Days of Wine and Roses
Dr. No
The Exterminating Angel
Gypsy
Harold Lloyd's World of
  Comedy
Last Year at Marienbad
Lolita
Mamma Rosa
The Miracle Worker
The Music Man
Sundays and Cybèle
Sweet Bird of Youth
That Touch of Mink

★★★
Advise and Consent
All Fall Down
Almost Angels
The Big Red
Billy Liar
The Birdman of Alcatraz

Boys' Night Out
Carnival of Souls
Cape Fear
The Chapman Report
The Eclipse
Experiment in Terror
The Exterminating Angel
Five Miles to Midnight
Freud
Gay Purree
Gypsy
Hatari!
Hemingway's Adventures of a
  Young Man
In the French Style
Ivan's Childhood
Knife in the Water
The Light in the Piazza
Live Now, Pay Later
The Loneliness of the Long
  Distance Runner
The Longest Day
Mr. Hobbes Takes a Vacation
Mutiny on the Bounty
The Notorious Landlady
Requiem for a Heavyweight
The Scarface Mob
Untouchables Pilot
Shoot the Piano Player
Tales of Terror
Term of Trial
The Trial
Two Weeks in Another Town
Walk on the Wild Side
The Wonderful World of the
  Brothers Grimm
The Wrong Arm of the Law

1963
★★★★
8½
It's a Mad Mad Mad Mad World
Lilies of the Field
Tom Jones

★★★¹/₂
All the Way Home
The Birds
The Incredible Journey
The L-Shaped Room
McLintock
Move Over, Darling
This Sporting Life

★★★
The Balcony
Beach Party

Billy Budd
Bye Bye Birdie
Captain Newman, M.D.
The Cardinal
The Caretakers
Charade
A Child Is Waiting
Come Blow Your Horn
The Comedy of Terrors
Cleopatra
55 Days at Peking
Flipper
From Russia with Love
Girl with Green Eyes
The Great Escape
The Haunting
Irma La Douce
It Happened Here
The Leather Boys
The Leopard
The List of Adrian Messenger
Lord of the Flies
Love with the Proper Stranger
The Mind Benders
Murder at the Gallop
Muriel
A New Kind of Love
North to Alaska
Shock Corridor
Spencer's Mountain
The Stripper
The Sword and the Stone
Take Her, She's Mine
The Three Lives of Thomasina
The Thrill of It All
Toys in the Attic
Two for the Seasaw
Under the Yum Yum Tree
The V.I.P.s
Who's Been Sleeping in My
  Bed?
Who's Minding the Store?
Wild in the Street
Yesterday, Today and
  Tomorrow

1964
★★★★
Mary Poppins
My Fair Lady
Night of the Iguana
A Shot in the Dark

★★★¹/₂
The Americanization of Emily
The Best Man

Fail Safe
Goldfinger
Lilith
That Man from Rio
The Train
The Unsinkable Molly Brown
Zorba the Greek

★★★
Bedtime Story
Black God, White Devil
The Caretaker
The Carpetbaggers
Cheyenne Autumn
The Chalk Garden
Dead Ringer
Dear Heart
Dear John
Father Goose
Fate Is the Hunter
A Fistful of Dollars
Goodbye Charlie
Good Neighbor Sam
I'd Rather Be Rich
Is Paris Burning?
Kwaidan
Lady in a Cage
Life Upside Down
Lord Jim
Marnie
A Married Woman
Mary Poppins
The Masque of the Red Death
The Moon Spinners
Murder Ahoy
Nothing But the Best
Robinson Crusoe on Mars
Seance on a Wet Afternoon
Seven Days in May
The Seven Faces of Dr. Lao
The Soft Skin
Sunday in New York
The Tomb of Ligeia
Topkapi
What a Way to Go
What's New Pussycat?
Woman of the Dunes
The World of Henry Orient
The Yellow Rolls Royce

1965
★★★★
Darling
Doctor Zhivago
A Hard Day's Night
The Sound of Music

★★★¹/₂
Cat Ballou
The Collector
The Knack
The Loved One
Mickey One
Othello
A Patch of Blue
The Pawnbroker
Repulsion
A Thousand Clowns
Thunderball

★★★
The Agony and the Ecstasy
Alphaville
America, America
The Amorous Adventures of
    Moll Flanders
The Angry Silence
Baby, the Rain Must Fall
Battle of the Bulge
The Bedford Incident
Bocaccio '70
Bunny Lake Is Missing
Casanova
Clarence the Cross-Eyed Lion
The Flight of the Phoenix
For a Few Dollars More
The Ghost and Mister Chicken
The Great Race
The Greatest Story Ever Told
The Hill
Inside Daisy Clover
The Ipcress File
King Rat
Life at the Top
The Liquidator
Loves of a Blonde
The Love Goddesses
Mirage
The Nanny
None But the Brave
Repulsion
The Sandpiper
Shenandoah
Shakespeare Wallah
The Shop on Main Street
Situation Hopeless But Not
    Serious
The Slender Thread
The Spy Who Came in from
    the Cold
That Darn Cat
Those Magnificent Men in
    Their Flying Machines

The Ugly Daschund
The Umbrellas of Cherbourg
Von Ryan's Express
The War Lord

1966
★★★★
Alfie
Blow Up
Fahrenheit 451
Georgy Girl
Who's Afraid of Virginia
    Woolf?

★★★¹/₂
After the Fox
Closely Watched Trains
A Fine Madness
The Fortune Cookie
A Funny Thing Happened on
    the Way to the Forum
The Group
Hotel Paradiso
Lord Love a Duck
A Man and a Woman
A Man for All Seasons
Masculin, Feminine
Morgan!
The Professionals
The Russians Are Coming, the
    Russians Are Coming

★★★
Any Wednesday
Batman, the Movie
The Battle of Algiers
The Bible
The Blue Max
Born Free
The Chase
Chimes at Midnight
Deadlier Than the Male
The Deadly Affair
Fantastic Voyage
Gambit
The Glass Bottom Boat
The Good, the Bad and the
    Ugly
The Gospel According to St.
    Matthew
Grand Prix
Harper
Hawaii
The Honey Pot
Kaleidoscope
Marat/Sade
Mister Buddwing

The Naked Prey
Night Games
The Rise of Louis XIV
The Sand Pebbles
Seconds
Seven Women
Ten Little Indians
Torn Curtain
What's Up Tiger Lily
The Wrong Box
You're a Big Boy Now

1967
★★★★
Bonnie and Clyde
The Graduate

★★★¹/₂
Barefoot in the Park
Belle du Jour
Camelot
Cool Hand Luke
Guess Who's Coming to Dinner
In Cold Blood
In the Heat of the Night
No Way to Treat a Lady
Two for the Road
Up the Down Staircase
Wait Until Dark

★★★
The Adventures of Bullwhip
    Griffin
Accident
Bedazzled
The Big Mouth
Casino Royale
The Comedians
The Dirty Dozen
Divorce American Style
Dr. Dolittle
Enter Laughing
Far from the Madding Crowd
The Fearless Vampire
    Killers . . .
The Fireman's Ball
Five Million Years to Earth
The Flim-Flam Man
Funeral in Beriln
A Guide for the Married Man
The Gnome Mobile
Half a Sixpence
Hang 'em High
The Happening
Here We Go 'Round the
    Mulberry Bush
Hombre

Hotel
Luv
Live for Life
Never a Dull Moment
The Night of the Generals
The Night of the Living Dead
Reflections in a Golden Eye
St. Valentine's Day Massacre
The Samurai
Smashing Time
The Taming of the Shrew
Targets
Thoroughly Modern Millie
Tony Rome
To Sir With Love
The Trip
Two or Three Things I Know
    About Her
Ulysses
Valley of the Dolls
The Whisperer

1968
★★★★
Funny Girl
The Lion in Winter
Rachel, Rachel
Romeo and Juliet
2001: A Space Odyssey

★★★¹/₂
Bullitt
Charlie Bubbles
Chitty Chitty Bang Bang
The Heart Is a Lonely Hunter
Isadora
Oliver!
Petulia
Planet of the Apes
Pretty Poison
Rosemary's Baby
Take the Money and Run
The Thomas Crown Affair
Weekend

★★★
Barbarella
The Big Fisherman
The Bliss of Mrs. Blossom
The Boston Strangler
The Bride Wore Black
Charly
The Devil's Bride
Faces
Finian's Rainbow
The Fixer
A Flea in Her Ear

The Fox
Head
Histoires Extraordinaires
Hot Millions
Ice Station Zebra
I Love You, Alice B. Toklas
The Impossible Years
The Killing of Sister George
King of Hearts
The Legend of Lylah Clare
Madigan
The Milky Way
The Night They Raided
  Minsky's
The Sea Gull
The Sergeant
The Shoes of the Fisherman
Star!
Support Your Local Sheriff
The Swimmer
Till Death Do Us Part
Where Were You When the
  Lights Went Out?
The Yellow Submarine
The Young Girls of Rochefort
You Only Live Twice
Yours, Mine and Ours

1969
★★★★
Last Summer
Midnight Cowboy
They Shoot Horses, Don't
  They?

★★★½
Anne of the Thousand Days
Bob and Carol and Ted and
  Alice
Butch Cassidy and the
  Sundance Kid
Death in Venice
Easy Rider
Kes
The Love Bug
Night Gallery
Once Upon a Time in the West
The Prime of Miss Jean Brodie
The Sterile Cuckoo
The Wild Child
Z

★★★
Age of Consent
The April Fools
The Assassination Bureau
Battle of Britain

Buona Sera, Mrs. Campbell
Burn
Cactus Flower
Candy
Daddy's Gone A-Hunting
The Damned
Elvira Madigan
Eye of the Cat
The Forbin Project
Gaily, Gaily
Goodbye Columbus
The Gypsy Moths
Hamlet
The Happy Ending
Hell in the Pacific
Hello Dolly
Hi, Mom!
The Honeymoon Killers
If . . .
If It's Tuesday, This Must Be
  Belgium
The Italian Job
Kes
The Madwoman of Chaillot
Me, Natalie
Medium Cool
The Mississippi Mermaid
The Reivers
The Secret of Santa Victoria
The Southern Star
Staircase
Start the Revolution without
  Me
True Grit
The Virgin Soldier
Whatever Happened to Aunt
  Alice?
Where Eagles Dare
The Wild Bunch

1970s
1970
★★★★
The Aristocats
Diary of a Mad Housewife
Five Easy Pieces

1970
★★★½
Beyond the Valley of the Dolls
The Four Clowns
Hoffman
I Never Sang for My Father
The Landlord
Loot

Love Story
M*A*S*H
Patton
Three Sisters
Tristana
Where's Poppa?
Women in Love

★★★
Airport
All the Way Up
The Baby Maker
Bartleby
Bed and Board
Beneath the Planet of the
  Apes
Bloody Mama
The Boatniks
The Boys in the Band
Brewster McCloud
Brian's Song
Catch-22
The Cheyenne Social Club
Darling Lili
End of the Road
Entertaining Mr. Sloan
The Great White Hope
I Walk the Line
The Last Valley
Lovers and Other Strangers
Loving
A Man Called Horse
Medea
Move
The Music Lovers
The Raging Moon
The Railway Children
Red Sky at Morning
Ryan's Daughter
Scrooge
There's a Girl in My Soup
THX 1138
'Tis a Pity She's a Whore
The Twelve Chairs
Watermelon Man
W.U.S.A.

1971
★★★★
A Clockwork Orange
Fiddler on the Roof
The Hospital
Klute
The Last Picture Show
Little Big Man
A New Leaf

★★★½
Alex in Wonderland
The Andromeda Strain
The Beguiled
Carnal Knowledge
The Devils
Diamonds Are Forever
Dollars
The French Connection
The Garden of the Finzi-
  Continis
The Girl Most Likely to . . .
The Go-Between
Kotch
McCabe and Mrs. Miller
Murmur of the Heart
Nicholas and Alexandra
Sunday, Bloody Sunday
The Summer of 42
Willie Wonka and the
  Chocolate Factory

★★★
The Abominable Dr. Phibes
The Adventures of Barry
  McKenzie
Bananas
The Battle of the Neretva
Bedknobs and Broomsticks
Bleak Moments
Blood from the Mummy's Tomb
The Boy Friend
Brother John
Buck and the Preacher
The Canterbury Tales
Cold Turkey
A Day in the Death of Joe Egg
Dirty Harry
Doc
Dying Room Only
Escape from the Planet of the
  Apes
Get Carter
Happy Birthday, Wanda June
The Hellstrom Chronicle
Investigation of a Citizen
  Above Suspicion
Kelly's Heroes
Let's Scare Jessica to Death
Little Murders
The Man in the Wilderness
The Marriage of a Young
  Stockbroker
Mary, Queen of Scots
Minnie and Moskowitz
The Nightcomers

Shaft
Silent Running
Sometimes a Great Notion
Such Good Friends
Taking Off
The Trojan Women
Under Milk Wood
Who Is Harry Kellerman . . .
Willard

1972
★★★★
Cabaret
The Candidate
The Discreet Charm of the
   Bourgeoisie
Duel
The Godfather
Harold and Maude
The Heartbreak Kid
Sleuth
Sounder
What's Up, Doc?

★★★¹/₂
Butterflies Are Free
Chloe in the Afternoon
Deliverance
The Effect of Gamma Rays . . .
The Emigrants
Everything You've Always
   Wanted to Know About Sex
Frenzy
The Hot Rock
Kung Fu
The Nightstalker
The Other
Pete 'n Tillie
Play It Again Sam
Up the Sandbox

★★★
Aguirre, the Wrath of God
The Amazing Mr. Blunden
Bad Company
Ben
Boxcar Bertha
Child's Play
Desperate Characters
Dr. Phibes Rises Again
England Made Me
Frogs
Fuzz
Gumshoe
The Getaway
High Plains Drifter
The King of Marvin Gardens

King, Queen, Knave
Lady Sings the Blues
The Last of the Red Hot
   Lovers
The Life and Times of Judge
   Roy Bean
Limbo
Love and Pain and the Whole
   Damned Thing
Man of La Mancha
The Mechanic
The Ruling Class
1776
Solaris
Superfly
Theatre of Blood
They Might Be Giants
Travels with My Aunt
The War Between Men and
   Women
What?
Young Winston

1973
★★★★
American Graffiti
Day for Night
The Glass Menagerie
Save the Tiger

★★★¹/₂
Blume in Love
Charley Varrick
Charlotte's Web
Cries and Whispers
The Day of the Jackal
The Exorcist
The Homecoming
The Last Detail
Mean Streets
A Pain in the A . . .
The Return of the Pink
   Panther
Summer Wishes, Winter
   Dreams
The Three Musketeers
The Way We Were
A Woman Under the Influence

★★★
Bang the Drum Slowly
The Bitter Tears of Petra Von
   Kant
Bread and Chocolate
Brother Sun, Sister Moon
Class of '44
The Day of the Dolphin

A Delicate Balance
Dillinger
Distant Thunder
A Doll's House (Claire Bloom)
A Doll's House (Jane Fonda)
Fritz the Cat
Godspell
Happy New Year
The Last of Sheila
Last Tango in Paris
The Laughing Policeman
The Legend of Hell House
Live and Let Die
The Long Goodbye
Lovin' Molly
Magnum Force
Mean Streets
No Sex Please, We're British
Robin Hood
The Rocky Horror Picture
   Show
Sisters
Soylent Green
The Taking of Pelham 1-2-3
The Tall Blond Man with One
   Black Shoe
Tom Sawyer
Turkish Delight
Westworld
The Wicker Man

1974
★★★★
Alice Doesn't Live Here
   Anymore
Chinatown
The Conversation
The Godfather Part II
Lenny
Murder on the Orient Express
The Sugarland Express

★★★¹/₂
Amarcord
The Autobiography of Miss
   Jane Pittman
Conrack
For Pete's Sake
The Great Gatsby
Harry and Tonto
Lacombe, Lucien
Phantom of Liberty
The Prisoner of Second Avenue
That's Entertainment
Thunderbolt and Lightfoot
Young Frankenstein

★★★
All Creatures Great and Small
The Bears and I
Benji
Blazing Saddles
Bring Me the Head of Alfredo
   Garcia
Buster and Billie
California Split
Claudine
The Castaway Cowboy
Daisy Miller
Dark Star
Deathwish
The Dion Brothers
Earthquake
Eleven Harrow House
Fortune and Men's Eyes
The Four Musketeers
Freebie and the Bean
The Front Page
Herbie Rides Again
The Island at the Top of the
   World
The Land That Time Forgot
The Longest Yard
The Little Prince
The Lords of Flatbush
The Maids
The Man Who Would Be King
The Man with the Golden Gun
Rancho De Luxe
Thieves Like Us
The Towering Inferno
Where the Lillies Bloom
The Wild Party

1975
★★★★
Dog Day Afternoon
Love Among the Ruins
Nashville
Shampoo
Three Days of the Condor

★★★¹/₂
Funny Lady
Hedda
Hester Street
Monty Python and the Holy
   Grail
The Sunshine Boys
Tommy

★★★
Against a Crooked Sky
Airport '75

And Now, My Love
The Apple Dumpling Gang
Barry Lyndon
Bite the Bullet
Blue Water, White Death
The Day of the Locust
Dersu Uzala
The Eiger Sanction
The Fortune
Fox and His Friends
Hard Times
The Hindenburg
Next Stop, Greenwich Village
Night Moves
92 in the Shade
The Romantic Englishwoman
Rooster Cogburn
The Stepford Wives
The Story of Adele H.
The Wilby Conspiracy
The Wind and the Lion

1976
★★★★
All the President's Men
Love and Death
Murder by Death
Network
Swept Away
Taxi Driver

★★★½
Bound for Glory
Carrie
Cousin, Cousine
The Disappearance of Aimee
The Displaced Person
Eleanor and Franklin
Face to Face
Marathon Man
The Omen
The Pink Panther Strikes
   Again
Rocky

★★★
Allegro Non Troppo
The Bad News Bears
The Big Bus
Black and White in Color
A Boy and His Dog
Buffalo Bill and the
   Indians . . .
Bugsy Malone
Car Wash
Casanova
The Cassandra Crossing

The Devil's Playground
Dona Flor and Her Two
   Husbands
Don's Party
The Enforcer
Eraserhead
Freaky Friday
The Front
Fun with Dick and Jane
Heart of Glass
The Incredible Sarah
The Killing of a Chinese
   Bookie
King Kong
The Last Tycoon
Lies My Father Told Me
Lifeguard
The Little Girl Who Lives
   Down the Lane
Logan's Run
The Man Who Fell to Earth
Nasty Habits
1900
No Deposit, No Return
Norman, Is That You?
The Ritz
Robin and Marian
The Sentinel
The Shaggy D.A.
Silver Bears
The Silver Streak
Small Change
A Star Is Born
Suspiria
The Tenant
That's Entertainment Part Two
A Town Like Alice
The Town That Dreaded
   Sundown
Voyage of the Damned
Why Shoot the Teacher?

1977
★★★★
Annie Hall
Close Encounters of the Third
   Kind
The Goodbye Girl
Looking for Mr. Goodbar
The Turning Point

★★★½
Don't Look Now
Equus
High Anxiety
The Late Show

Star Wars
That Obscure Object of Desire

★★★
Airport '77
The Amazing Howard Hughes
The American Friend
Are You Being Served?
Between the Lines
Black Sunday
Dear Inspector
Fingers
Fraternity Row
The Gauntlet
The Getting of Wisdom
Handle with Care
I Never Promised You a Rose
   Garden
Islands in the Stream
Kentucky Fried Movie
The Lacemaker
The Last Wave
A Little Night Music
Madame Rosa
The Man Who Loved Women
New York, New York
9/30/55
Opening Night
The Rescuers
Saturday Night Fever
Semi-Tough
The Shootist
Slap Shot
The Slipper and the Rose
Smokey and the Bandit
The Spy Who Loved Me
Stroszek
Telefon

1978
★★★★
Coming Home
The Deer Hunter
Interiors
An Unmarried Woman

★★★½
Autumn Sonata
Blue Collar
The Buddy Holly Story
California Suite
Coma
Days of Heaven
Halloween
Heaven Can Wait
House Calls
The Marriage of Maria Braun

Midnight Express
Pretty Baby
Return of the Secaucus
   Seven
Revenge of the Pink
   Panther

★★★
All You Need Is Cash
The Bell Jar
Bloodbrothers
The Boys from Brazil
The Brinks Job
The Cheap Detective
Comes a Horseman
Despair
Desperate Living
Death on the Nile
The End
Family Plot
Fat City
Eyes of Laura Mars
Fedora
Foul Play
The Fury
Girlfriends
Goin' South
Grease
The Grey Fox
Hardcore
Harper Valley P.T.A.
Invasion of the Body
   Snatchers
King of the Gypsies
The Last Waltz
Lord of the Rings
Magic
Man of Marble
Murder by Decree
National Lampoon's Animal
   House
Straight Time
Superman
The Tree of Wooden Clogs
Watership Down
A Wedding
Who's Killing the Great Chefs
   of Europe?
The Wiz

1979
★★★★
Alien
Being There
La Cage aux Folles
The China Syndrome

Kramer versus Kramer
Manhattan
Norma Rae
Raging Bull
Wise Blood

★★★¹/₂
A Little Romance
All That Jazz
Apocalypse Now
Best Boy
Breaking Away
Christ Stopped at Eboli
The Corn Is Green
Going in Style
The In-Laws
The Muppet Movie
Murder by Natural Causes
The Rose
Time After Time
The Tin Drum

★★★
Agatha
Amateur Night at the Dixie Bar
    and Grill
And Baby Makes Six
And Justice for All
The Black Stallion
The Brood
Cattle Annie and Little
    Britches
The Champ
Chapter Two
Dawn of the Dead
Dracula
The Electric Horseman
The Europeans
Every Day's a Holiday
The Fog
Hair
Heart Beat
Heartland
Love at First Bite
Love on the Run
Mad Max
Monty Python's Life of Brian
Moonraker
North Dallas Forty
Real Life
Rich Kids
Salem's Lot
The Seduction of Joe Tynan
Silent Partner
Ten
The Wanderers
Yanks

1980s
1980
★★★★
Airplane
Coal Miner's Daughter
The Elephant Man
Gloria
Melvin and Howard

★★★¹/₂
American Gigolo
Dressed to Kill
Gilda Live
The Great Santini
Kagemusha
The Last Metro
My Bodyguard
My Brilliant Career
Nine to Five
Playing for Time
Private Benjamin
Resurrection
Tess

★★★
Alligator
Altered States
An American Werewolf in
    London
Attack of the Killer Tomatoes
The Big Red One
The Black Marble
The Blues Brothers
Boardwalk
Bon Voyage, Charlie Brown
Brubaker
Caddyshack
The Changeling
Chilly Scenes of Winter
Divine Madness
The Empire Strikes Back
Falling in Love Again
Fame
Fort Apache, the Bronx
Foxes
Friday the Thirteenth
From the Life of the
    Marionettes
Hopscotch
Inside Moves
Lightning over Water
Lili Marleen
Little Lord Fauntleroy
Little Miss Marker
The Long Riders
The Mirror Crack'd

Moscow Does Not Believe in
    Tears
My American Uncle
Nijinsky
Serial
The Shining
Somewhere in Time
Stardust Memories
The Stuntman
Superman II
Tell Me a Riddle
Tribute
Used Cars

1981
★★★★
Atlantic City
Arthur
Chariots of Fire
The French Lieutenant's
    Woman
Raiders of the Lost Ark
Reds

★★★¹/₂
Absence of Malice
All Night Long
Body Heat
Christiane F.
Gallipoli
My Dinner with André
Pixote
Ragtime

★★★
Back Roads
Buddy Buddy
La Cage aux Folles II
The Chosen
City of Women
Clash of the Titans
Class of 1984
Continental Divide
Excalibur
Eye of the Needle
The Final Conflict
First Monday in October
For Your Eyes Only
The Four Seasons
The Fox and the Hound
Ghost Story
The Gods Must Be Crazy
The Great Muppet Caper
Gregory's Girl
The Hand
History of the World Part One
I Sent a Letter to My Love

Killjoy
The Lemon Drop Kid
Lonely Hearts
Man of Iron
Mephisto
Mommie Dearest
Montenegro
Neighbors
Quartet
Quest for Fire
Quick Millions
Rich and Famous
Road Warrior
Sharkey's Machine
Silence of the North
S.O.B.
So Fine
Southern Comfort
Taps
Time Bandits
True Confessions
Victory
The Woman Next Door

1982
★★★★
Diva
E.T.
Missing
Sophie's Choice
Tootsie
The Verdict
Victor/Victoria

★★★¹/₂
A Tale of Two Cities
Blade Runner
Das Boot
Deathtrap
Diner
The Executioner's Song
My Favorite Year
Night of the Shooting Stars
Poltergeist
The World According toGarp

★★★
Airplane II: The Sequel
La Balance
Le Bal
Best Friends
Burden of Dreams
Cannery Row
Chan Is Missing
Come Back to the Five and
    Dime, Jimmy Dean, Jimmy
    Dean

The Dark Crystal
Dead Men Don't Wear Plaid
Diary for My Children
Evil Under the Sun
Fast Times at Ridgemont High
Firefox
First Blood
Fitzcarraldo
Frances
Gandhi
Hammett
Heat and Dust
Hours
Making Love
The Man from Snowy River
A Midsummer Night's Sex
    Comedy
Moonlighting (Jeremy Irons)
Night Shift
Rocky III
The Secret of NIMH
Still of the Night
That Championship Season
The Thing
An Unsuitable Job for a
    Woman
Veronica Voss
Zorro the Gay Blade

1983
★★★★
Cross Creek
The King of Comedy
Risky Business
Silkwood
Tender Mercies
Terms of Endearment
Zelig

★★★¹/₂
Betrayal
The Big Chill
Brimstone and Treacle
The Dresser
Fanny and Alexander
The Hunger
Local Hero
The Man with Two Brains
Never Say Never Again
El Norte
The Return of Martin Guerre
Trading Places
War Games
The Year of Living
    Dangerously
Yentl

★★★
Baby It's You
Bad Boys
Berlin Alexanderplatz
Blue Thunder
Brainstorm
Can She Bake a Cherry Pie?
Carmen
Cat People
Daniel
D.C. Cab
The Dead Zone
The Draughtsman's Contract
Educating Rita
Erendira
Exposed
Flashdance
I Married a Dead Man
Koyaanisqatsi
Lianna
Life Is a Bed of Roses
A Love in Germany
Lovesick
A Man Like Eva
Man of Flowers
Max Dugan Returns
Mr. Mom
Monty Python's the Meaning of
    Life
National Lampoon's Vacation
Never Cry Wolf
Return of the Jedi
Reuben, Reuben
The Revolt of Job
The Right Stuff
Rumble Fish
Say Amen, Somebody
Streamers
Suburbia
The Swing
Testament
Twilight Zone: The Movie
Under Fire
The Wicked Lady

1984
★★★★
All of Me
Amadeus
Broadway Danny Rose

★★★¹/₂
Birdy
Blood Simple
The Burning Bed
Carmen

Falling in Love
Love Letters
The Natural
Romancing the Stone
The Terminator

★★★
Adam
The Adventures of Buckaroo
    Banzai . . . Across the
    Eighth Dimension
Against All Odds
American Dreamer
Angelo, My Love
Another Country
Beverly Hills Cop
The Bitch
The Bostonians
The Bounty
The Brother from Another
    Planet
Cal
Camila
Carmen
Choose Me
Cloak and Dagger
Crimes of Passion
Finders Keepers
The Flamingo Kid
The Fourth Man
The Frog Prince
Full Moon in Paris
Ghostbusters
Gremlins
Greystoke
Heart Breakers
Heimat
The Hotel New Hampshire
Iceman
Indiana Jones and the Temple
    of Doom
Irreconcilable Differences
Kaos
The Karate Kid
The Killing Fields
The Last Starfighter
The Lonely Guy
Long Live Life
Love Streams
Mass Appeal
Micki and Maude
Moscow on the Hudson
The Neverending Story
Night of the Comet
A Nightmare on Elm Street
Repo Man

A Short Film about Killing
A Soldier's Story
Sugarbaby
Sunday in the Country
Swann in Love
Teachers
This Is Spinal Tap
Tightrope
Top Secret!
Under the Volcano

1985
★★★★
Back to the Future
Death of a Salesman
Kiss of the Spider Woman
Out of Africa
Ran
The Trip to Bountiful
Witness

★★★¹/₂
After Hours
Brazil
The Breakfast Club
Careful, He Might Hear You
The Color Purple
Compromising Positions
Guilty Conscience
Mask
The Official Story
Plenty
Vagabond

★★★
After the Rehearsal
Agnes of God
Brighton Beach Memoirs
Cocoon
Colonel Redl
Consenting Adult
Dance with a Stranger
Desert Hearts
Desperately Seeking Susan
Dim Sum
Dreamchild
Eleni
The Emerald Forrest
The Falcon and the Snowman
Firstborn
Fool for Love
Fright Night
Grace Quigley
Heaven Help Us
Insignificance
The Left Hand of God
A Letter to Breshnev

Letters from a Dead Man
Lost in America
Mad Max Beyond Thunderdome
Men
Mishima
Murphy's Romance
National Lampoon's European
  Vacation
Rendez-Vous
The Return of the Soldier
Runaway Train
Steaming
Stop Making Sense
The Sure Thing
Sweet Dreams
That's Dancin'
Three Men and a Cradle
To Live and Die in L.A.
Turtle Diary
Twice in a Lifetime
Wetherby
When Father Was Away on
  Business
White Nights
The Year of the Dragon
Young Sherlock Holmes
A Zed and Two Noughts

1986
★★★★
Crimes of the Heart
Down and Out in Beverly Hills
Hannah and Her Sisters
A Room with a View

★★★¹/₂
About Last Night
Aliens
Between Two Women
Blue Velvet
Children of a Lesser God
Crocodile Dundee
Ferris Bueller's Day Off
Little Shop of Horrors
Menage
Mona Lisa
The Mosquito Coast
My Beautiful Laundrette
Otello
Peggy Sue Got Married
River's Edge
Ruthless People

★★★
Absolute Beginners
All My Sons
An American Tale

At Close Range
The Bad Seed
Back to School
Betty Blue
The Boy Who Could Fly
Burke and Wills
Cactus
The Color of Money
Desert Bloom
Down by Law
84 Charing Cross Road
Extremities
The Fly
F/X
Ginger and Fred
The Great Mouse Detective
Heartburn
Hoosiers
House
Lady Jane
Lamb
Legal Eagles
Manon of the Spring
Mélo
The Mission
The Morning After
Native Son
Night, Mother
9½ Weeks
Nobody's Fool
Nothing in Common
Nutcracker—The Motion
  Picture
Round Midnight
Running Scared
Shy People
Sid and Nancy
Square Dance
Star Trek IV: The Voyage Home
Tampopo
That's Life
Top Gun
Tough Guys
Traveling North
True Stories
Wiseguys
Working Girls

1987
★★★★
Moonstruck
Raising Arizona

★★★¹/₂
The Assault
Au Revoir les Enfants

Babette's Feast
Baby Boom
The Big Easy
Black Widow
Broadcast News
Courtship
A Cry in the Dark
Fatal Attraction
Full Metal Jacket
Good Morning, Vietnam
Hope and Glory
Ironweed
The Murder of Mary Phagan
My Life as a Dog
The Naked Gun
No Way Out
Outrageous Fortune
Pathfinder
Pelle the Conqueror
Radio Days
Roxanne
Talk Radio
Wings of Desire
The Witches of Eastwick

★★★
The Adventures of Baron
  Munchausen
Amazon Women on the Moon
Barfly
Batteries Not Included
Belly of an Architect
The Big Town
Born in East L.A.
The Burglar
The Dead
Dangerous Moves
Dead of Winter
Decline of the American
  Empire
Empire of the Sun
Gaby, a True Story
The Glass Menagerie
The Good Father
Gothic
The Grand Highway
Happy New Year
Hollywood Shuffle
House of Games
Intervista
The Kitchen Toto
The Last Emperor
The Last of England
Law of Desire
Lethal Weapon
Little Dorritt

The Living Daylights
The Lonely Passion of Judith
  Hearne
The Lost Boys
Making Mr. Right
Matewan
Maurice
A Month in the Country
Nadine
No Down Payment
Nuts
Red Sorghum
Rita, Sue and Bob Too
Robocop
The Running Man
Shame
The Sicilian
Siesta
Someone to Love
Stakeout
Street Smart
Sweet Lorraine
Swimming to Cambodia
A Taxing Woman
Three Men and a Baby
Throw Momma from the
  Train
A Tiger's Tale
Tin Men
The Tin Star
Wall Street
White Mischief
Wish You Were Here
A World Apart
The Year My Voice Broke

1988
★★★★
Another Woman
Dangerous Liaisons
A Fish Called Wanda
Monsieur Hire

★★★¹/₂
The Accidental Tourist
Bagdad Cafe
Big
Bird
Bull Durham
Dear America
Die Hard
Five Corners
Hairspray
Heathers
La Lectrice
Married to the Mob

Midnight Run
Running on Empty
Who Framed Roger Rabbit?
Women on the Verge of a
    Nervous Breakdown
Working Girl

★★★
The Accused
Appointment with Death
Anna
Aria
The Bear
Beetlejuice
Bellman and True
Big Business
Biloxi Blues
Black Rain
The Boost
Boyfriends and Girlfriends
Burning Secret
Business as Usual
Buster
Camille Claudel
Celia
Chocolat
Clean and Sober
Coming to America
Criminal Law
Da
Dead Ringers
Dirty Rotten Scoundrels
The Dressmaker
Drowning by Numbers
Eight Men Out
Frantic
Ghosts . . . of the Civil Dead
The Good Mother
Gorillas in the Mist
Hanussen
The Hidden
The House on Carroll Street
I'm Gonna Git You, Sucka
Lady in White
Lair of the White Worm
The Land Before Time
The Last Temptation of Christ
Legend of the Holy Drinker
Let's Get Lost
Little Vera
Madame Sousatzka
Mala Noche
Mignon Has Left
The Milagro Beanfield War
Mr. North

Mystic Pizza
Rain Man
The Rainbow
Salaam Bombay!
Salome's Last Dance
Scandal
School Daze
Scrooged
Stand and Deliver
Stars and Bars
Things Change
Torch Song Trilogy
Tucker
The Unbearable Lightness of
    Being
Up In Smoke
The Vanishing
Vice Versa
Warlock
We Think the World of You
Willow
Without a Clue
Zelly and Me

1989
★★★★
Born on the Fourth of July
Driving Miss Daisy
The Little Mermaid

★★★½
After Dark, My Sweet
Apartment Zero
Cinema Paradiso
Cold Sassy Tree
Dead Poets Society
The Fabulous Baker Boys
Field of Dreams
Henry V
Last Exit to Brooklyn
Miss Firecracker
My Left Foot
Three Fugitives
Uncle Buck

★★★
All Dogs Go to Heaven
Always
Babar: The Movie
Batman
Betrayed
Bill and Ted's Excellent
    Adventure
Blaze
Blind Fury
Breaking In

Chances Are
Chattahoochee
Do the Right Thing
Enemies, a Love Story
Fellow Traveller
Fletch Lives
Flirting
Getting It Right
Glory
Gremlins
A Handful of Dust
Honey, I Shrunk the Kids
The Icicle Thief
Indiana Jones and the Last
    Crusade
Kill Me Again
Lean on Me
Leningrad Cowboys Go to
    America
Lethal Weapon 2
Licence to Kill
Life and Nothing But
Look Who's Talking
Lost Angels
A Midsummer Night's Dream
Music Box
Mystery Train
National Lampoon's Christmas
    Vacation
Q & A
Queen of Hearts
The Rachel Papers
Roger & Me
Rosalie Goes Shopping
Sammy and Rosie Get Laid
Scenes from the Class Struggle
    in Beverly Hills
Sea of Love
See You in the Morning
Shag
She-Devil
Shirley Valentine
Slaves of New York
Speaking Parts
Stanley & Iris
Sweetie
The Tall Guy
Tie Me Up! Tie Me Down!
Tremors
True Love
Twin Peaks
The War of the Roses
The Waterdance
When Harry Met Sally
Who's Harry Crumb?

1990s
1990
★★★★
Good Fellas
The Grifters
Reversal of Fortune

★★★½
Alice
La Femme Nikita
Ghost
Henry, Portrait of a Serial
    Killer
Home Alone
I Love You to Death
A Killing in a Small Town
Men Don't Leave
Metropolitan
Misery
Mr. and Mrs. Bridge
Momma, There's a Man in Your
    Bed
The Nasty Girl
Postcards from the Edge
Presumed Innocent

★★★
An Angel at My Table
Avalon
Awakenings
Back to the Future III
Barton Fink
The Black Robe
C'est La Vie
Daddy Nostalgia
Dances with Wolves
Darkman
Dick Tracy
Drugstore Cowboy
The Exorcist III
The Field
Flatliners
The Fool
Frankenstein Unbound
The Freshman
Green Card
The Godfather Part Three
Golden Braid
Guilty by Suspicion
The Hairdresser's Husband
The Handmaid's Tale
Hardware
Henry and June
Hidden Agenda
Impromptu
Internal Affairs

Interrogation
The King's Whore
The Krays
Life Is Cheap, but Toilet Paper
    Is Expensive
Life Is Sweet
Listen Up: The Lives of
    Quincy Jones
Love at Large
The Memphis Belle
Mermaids
Miami Blues
Mr. Johnson
Naked Tango
Narrow Margin
Quick Change
The Rescuers Down Under
Rhapsody in August
A Shock to the System
Tatie Danielle
To Sleep With Anger
Total Recall
Treasure Island
Truly, Madly, Deeply
Tune in Tomorrow
Uranus
Vincent and Theo
Welcome Home, Roxy
    Carmichael
White Fang
White Hunter, Black Heart
White Palace
Wild at Heart
The Witches
Without You I'm Nothing

1991
★★★★

Beauty and the Beast
Fried Green Tomatoes
The Silence of the Lambs

★★★ 1/2

Boyz n the Hood
Bugsy
Dead Again
Deep Cover
Defending Your Life
Delicatessen
Doc Hollywood
Europa, Europa
The Fisher King
Hearts of Darkness
Homicide
JFK

Little Man Tate
Little Noises
Mother Love
My Mother's Castle
Orpheus Descending
Paris Trout
Reservoir Dogs
Thelma & Louise

★★★

An American Tail 2
Autobus
Broadway Bound
Cape Fear
City Slickers
The Comfort of Strangers
Defenseless
The Doctor
Dogfight
The Double Life of Veronique
Father of the Bride
For the Boys
Frankie and Johnny
Grand Canyon
Hamlet
Hard Promises
The Hard Way
Harley Davidson & the
    Marlboro Man
Hear My Song
High Heels
Hot Shots
A Kiss Before Dying
L.A. Story
Late for Dinner
Let Him Have It
Light Sleeper
London Kills Me
The Man in the Moon
Mastergate
The Match Factory Girl
Monster in a Box
Mortal Thoughts
My Own Private Idaho
The Naked Gun 2½
Naked Lunch
Night and Day
A Rage in Harlem
Raise the Red Lantern
Soapdish
Star Trek VI: The
    Undiscovered Country
Straight Out of Brooklyn
Terminator II
Toto le Hero

Truth or Dare
Until the End of the World
Waterland
Where Angels Fear to Tread
Whore

1992
★★★★
Lorenzo's Oil
Rambling Rose
The Rapture

★★★ 1/2
Aladdin
Blame It on the Bellboy
A Brief History of Time
The Crying Game
Damage
Death Becomes Her
Doc Hollywood
Glengarry Glen Ross
The Hand That Rocks the
    Cradle
Lethal Weapon
The Long Day Closes
My Cousin Vinny
On the Air
Once Upon a Crime
One False Move
Patriot Games
Prime Suspect
The Public Eye
A River Runs Through It
Unforgiven
A Woman's Tale

★★★
Afraid of the Dark
American Me
As You Like It
The Bad Lieutenant
Batman Returns
Basic Instinct
The Best Intentions
Bob Roberts
Boomerang
Bram Stoker's Dracula
Candyman
Chaplin
Class Action
Criss Cross
Enchanted April
Fern Gully
A Few Good Men
The Gun in Betty Lou's
    Handbag

Honey, I Blew Up the Kids
Honeymoon in Vegas
Indochine
Into the West
Kiss Me Goodbye
K-2
Ladykiller
The Last Days of Chez Nous
The Last of His Tribe
The Last of the Mohicans
The Lawnmower Man
Love Field
Malcolm X
The Mambo Kings
Man Bites Dog
Mediterraneo
Night on Earth
Romper Stomper
Rush
Schtonk
Slacker
Sneakers
Straight Talk
Strictly Business
Swoon
This Is My Life
Under Siege
Unlawful Entry
Utz
Wayne's World
White Men Can't Jump
The Year of the Comet

1993
★★★★
Short Cuts
Six Degrees of Separation

★★★ 1/2
The Age of Innocence
Belle Epoque
A Bronx Tale
Dave
Fearless
The Fugitive
Gypsy
Hold Me, Thrill Me, Kiss Me
In the Line of Fire
Like Water for Chocolate
Manhattan Murder Mystery
Menace II Society
The Nightmare Before
    Christmas
The Piano
Remains of the Day

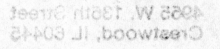

This Boy's Life
The Wedding Banquet
What's Eating Gilbert
  Grape?

★★★
Addams Family Values
Alive
All the Mornings of the
  World
The Bachelor
Based on an Untrue Story
Body Snatchers
Bopha!
The Borrowers
Brain Donors
Captain Ron
Carlito's Way
The Cemetery Club
City Boy
Cliffhanger
Un Coeur en Hiver
A Dangerous Woman
The Dark Half
Daybreak
Dazed and Confused
Dennis the Menace
The Ernest Green Story
Family Pictures
Farewell, My Concubine
A Fire in the Sky
Flirting
Gettysburg
Groundhog Day
Guilty as Sin
In the Name of the Father
Indecent Proposal
Into the West
Joey Breaker

Jurassic Park
King of the Hill
Laurel Avenue
Lost in Yonkers
Mad Dog & Glory
Malice
Map of the Human Heart
El Mariachi
Mrs. Doubtfire
Money for Nothing
My New Gun
Naked
Of Mice and Men
Philadelphia
Point of No Return
The Portrait
Quick
Ready to Wear
Red Rock West
Ruby in Paradise
The Sandlot
Searching for Bobby Fischer
Scent of Green Papaya
The Secret Garden
Sniper
Sommersby
The Spirit Rider
They
32 Short Films About Glenn
  Gould
Three of Hearts
Tombstone
La Vie de Bohème
The War Room
Watch It

1994
★★★★
Forrest Gump

★★★½
A Man of No Importance
Bitter Moon
The Burning Season
Ed Wood
Hoop Dreams
The Last Seduction
Little Women
Nobody's Fool
Once Were Warriors
Pulp Fiction
Quiz Show
The Ref
The Shadow
Spanking the Monkey

★★★
Ace Ventura, Pet Detective
The Advocate
Attica
Backbeat
Barcelona
Black Beauty
Blink
Blue
Blue (Jarman)
Blue Sky
Clear and Present Danger
The Client
Cobb
Corrina, Corrina
Crooklyn
Dialogues with Madwomen
Dumb & Dumber
Exotica
Four Weddings and a
  Funeral
Fresh
A Home of Our Own

The House of the Spirits
The Hudsucker Proxy
Interview with a Vampire
Immortal Beloved
IQ
The Jungle Book
Killing Zoe
Legends of the Fall
Little Giants
Little Rascals
Love Affair
The Mask
Maverick
Nell
No Escape
Only You
Princess Caraboo
The Professional
The Puppetmasters
Risk
The River Wild
The Road to Wellville
Safe Passage
The Santa Clause
Sirens
Speed
The Stand
Stargate
The Swan Princess
Threesome
To Dance with the White
  Dog
Tom & Viv
True Lies
When a Man Loves a
  Woman
Widow's Peak